53rd Annual Meeting of the Association for Computational Linguistics and 7th International Joint Conference on Natural Language Processing of the Asian Federation of Natural Language Processing

(ACL-IJCNLP 2015)

Long Papers

Beijing, China
26 – 31 July 2015

Volume 1 of 2

ISBN: 978-1-5108-0842-3

Printed from e-media with permission by:

Curran Associates, Inc.
57 Morehouse Lane
Red Hook, NY 12571

Some format issues inherent in the e-media version may also appear in this print version.

Printed by Curran Associates, Inc. (2015)

For permission requests, please contact the Association for Computational Linguistics
at the address below.

Association for Computational Linguistics
209 N. Eighth Street
Stroudsburg, Pennsylvania 18360

Phone: 1-570-476-8006
Fax: 1-570-476-0860

acl@aclweb.org

Additional copies of this publication are available from:

Curran Associates, Inc.
57 Morehouse Lane
Red Hook, NY 12571 USA
Phone: 845-758-0400
Fax: 845-758-2634
Email: curran@proceedings.com
Web: www.proceedings.com

ACL-IJCNLP July 26-31 2015

The 53rd Annual Meeting of the Association for Computational Linguistics and the 7th International Joint Conference on Natural Language Processing of the Asian Federation of Natural Language Processing

Proceedings of the Conference

Long Papers

ACL 2015
July 26-31
Beijing, China

Platinum Sponsors:

Gold Sponsors:

Silver Sponsors:

Bronze Sponsor:

Best Paper Sponsor:

Preface: General Chair

It was fifteen years ago when ACL first came to Asia in 2000. The conference in Hong Kong was a very excited one and attracted lots of people. It was a great opportunity for a number of Asian NLP researchers to meet face-to-face in such a large scale meeting. Establishment of AFNLP (Asian Federation of Natural Language Processing) was discussed soon after this wonderful event, and then AFNLP started IJCNLP (the International Joint Conference of Natural Language Processing) as a biennial flagship conference of AFNLP. ACL's three year regional rotation and IJCNLP's two year cycle meet every six years, and this is the second joint ACL-IJCNLP conference following the first held in Singapore in 2009. ACL meetings in Asia and IJNCLPs are now a propelling force of NLP research in Asian regions, and provide valuable experiences especially to young researchers and students who first attend this size of a big conference.

The success of ACL-IJCNLP owes a great deal to the hard work and dedication of many people. I would like to thank all of them for their time and contribution to this joint ACL-AFNLP conference.

Priscilla Rasmussen (the ACL Business Manager), Gertjan van Noord (ACL Past President), Chris Manning (ACL President), Graeme Hirst (ACL Treasurer), Dragomir Radev (ACL Secretary), Keh-Yih Su (AFNLP Past President), Fam-Fai Wong (AFNLP President), all other ACL and AFNLP Executive Committee members and ACL-AFNLP Conference Coordinating Committee members (forgive me for not listing all their names) have always been very helpful and guided me anytime I missed something or was behind the schedule, and given me appropriate advice. Without their help, I could not fulfill even half my duty.

I was very lucky to have a wonderful team of chairs, who have done a fantastic job for leading this conference to an invaluable one. I would like to express my deepest gratitude to Michael Strube and Chengqing Zong (Program Committee Co-Chairs), Le Sun and Yang Liu (Local Arrangement Co-Chairs), Hang Li and Sebastian Riedel (Workshop Co-Chairs), Kevin Duh and Eneko Agirre (Tutorial Co-Chairs), Hsin-His Chen and Katja Markert (System Demonstration Co-Chairs), Wanxiang Che and Guodong Zhou (Publications Co-Chairs), Stephan Oepen, Chin-Yew Lin and Emily Bender (Student Research Workshop Faculty Advisors), Kuan-Yu Chen, Angelina Ivanova and Ellie Pavlick (Student Research Workshop Co-Chairs), Francis Bond (Mentoring Chair), Xianpei Han and Kang Liu (Publicity Co-Chairs), Zhiyuan Liu (Webmaster), and all the team members of the Local Organizing Committee. Thanks to their dedicated efforts, we now have a great conference consisting of the Presidential Address (by Chris Manning), two Keynote Addresses (by Marti Hearst and Jiawei Han), 173 long and 145 short papers, 12 TACL papers, 7 Student Research Workshop papers, 25 system demonstrations, 8 tutorials, 15 workshops, one collocated conference (CoNLL-2015), and a not yet known Lifetime Achievement Awardee's speech.

I am also grateful to our sponsors for their generous contributions. ACL-IJCNLP-2015 is supported by six Platinum Sponsors (CreditEase, Baidu, Tencent, Alibaba Group, SAMSUNG, and Microsoft), four Gold Sponsors (Google, Facebook, SinoVoice, and Huawei), three Silver Sponsors (Nuance, Amazon, and Sogou), one Bronze Sponsor (Yandex), one Oversea Student Fellowship Sponsor (Baobab), and one Best Paper Sponsor (IBM). I would express special thanks to Yiqun Liu (Local Sponsorship Chair) and all members of the International Sponsorship Committee (Ting Liu, Hideto Kazawa, Asli Celikyilmaz, Julia Hochenmaier, and Alessandro Moschitti).

Finally, I would like to thank two keynote speakers, the area chairs of the main conference, the workshop organizers, the tutorial presenters, the authors of main conference and demo papers, the reviewers for their contribution, and all the attendees for participation. I hope everyone have a great time and enjoy this conference.

ACL-IJCNLP 2015 General Chair
Yuji Matsumoto
Nara Institute of Science and Technology

Preface: Program Committee Co-Chairs

Welcome to the 53rd Annual Meeting of the Association for Computational Linguistics and the 7th International Joint Conference on Natural Language Processing of the Asian Federation of Natural Language Processing (ACL-IJCNLP)! This year ACL-IJCNLP received 692 long paper submissions and 648 short paper submissions which sets a new record for ACL for both long and short papers! We are pleased to observe that our community continues to grow. Of the long papers, 173 were accepted for presentation at ACL-IJCNLP – 105 as oral and 68 as poster presentations. 145 short papers were accepted – 50 as oral and 95 as poster presentations. In addition, ACL-IJCNLP also features 12 presentations of papers accepted in the Transactions of the Association for Computational Linguistics (TACL).

The submissions were reviewed under different categories and using different review forms for empirical/data-driven, theoretical, applications/tools, resources/evaluation, and survey papers. This year we introduced the item "MENTORING" to the review form to indicate whether a paper needs the help of a mentor in its writing, organization or presentation. For short papers, following up on last year's successful experiences, we also welcomed submissions describing negative results. We are glad to see that the community is becoming more open towards negative results so that such papers have the chance to be published, so that other researchers do not fall in the same trap.

We view posters as an integral part of ACL-IJCNLP. Half of the papers have been accepted as posters. Hence, we spent a great deal of time to ensure that the poster session will be a good experience for poster presenters and their audience. Following last year's exciting poster session, we also organized the posters in two large poster sessions to accommodate the high-quality submissions accepted in poster presentation format. We hope attendees and authors will benefit from this additional time to present and have more time to discuss with each other.

ACL-IJCNLP 2015 will have two distinguished invited speakers. Marti Hearst (professor at UC Berkeley in the School of Information and EECS) and Jiawei Han (Abel Bliss Professor at University of Illinois at Urbana-Champaign). We are grateful that they accepted our invitation.

There are many individuals to thank for their contributions to ACL-IJCNLP 2015. We would like to thank the 37 area chairs for their hard work on recruiting reviewers, leading the discussion process, and carefully ranking the submissions. We would also like to thank the 749 primary and the 137 secondary reviewers on whose efforts we depended to select high-quality and timely scientific work. This year we specifically acknowledge around 18.2% of the reviewers who went the extra mile and provided extremely helpful reviews (their names are marked with a * in the organization section of the proceedings). The ACL coordinating committee members, including Dragomir Radev, Graeme Hirst, Jian Su, and Gertjan van Noord were invaluable on various issues relating to the organization. We would like to thank the prior conference chairs Kristina Toutanova and Hua Wu and their predecessors for their advice. We are very grateful for the guidance and support of the general chair Yuji Matsumoto, to the ACL Business Manager Priscilla Rasmussen who knew practically everything, to the local chairs Le Sun and Yang Liu, the publication chairs Wanxiang Che and Guodong Zhou, and webmaster Zhiyuan Liu. We would also like to thank Jiajun Zhang who helped with reviewer assignment and numerous other tasks. Rich Gerber and Paolo Gai from Softconf were extremely responsive to all of our requests, and we are grateful for that.

We are indebted to the best paper award committee which consisted of Eneko Agirre, Tim Baldwin, Philipp Koehn, Joakim Nivre, and Yue Zhang. They read the candidate papers, ranked them and provided comments on a very short notice.

We hope you will enjoy ACL-IJCNLP 2015 in Beijing!

ACL-IJCNLP 2015 Program Co-Chairs
Chengqing Zong, Chinese Academy of Sciences
Michael Strube, Heidelberg Institute for Theoretical Studies

Organizing Committee

General Chair

Yuji Matsumoto, Nara Institute of Science and Technology

Program Committee Co-Chairs

Chengqing Zong, Institute of Automation, Chinese Academy of Sciences
Michael Strube, Heidelberg Institute for Theoretical Studies

Local Co-Chairs

Le Sun, Institute of Software, Chinese Academy of Sciences
Yang Liu, Tsinghua University

Workshop Co-Chairs

Hang Li, Huawei
Sebastian Riedel, University College London

Tutorial Co-Chairs

Kevin Duh, Nara Institute of Science and Technology
Eneko Agirre, University of the Basque Country

Publications Chairs

Wanxiang Che, Harbin Institute of Technology
Guodong Zhou, Suzhou University

Demonstration Co-Chairs

Hsin-Hsi Chen, National Taiwan University
Katja Markert, University of Leeds

Sponsorship Chair

Yiqun Liu, Tsinghua University

Publicity Co-Chairs

Xianpei Han, Institute of Software, Chinese Academy of Sciences
Kang Liu, Institute of Automation, Chinese Academy of Sciences

Student Research Workshop Faculty Advisors

Stephan Oepen, University of Oslo
Chin-Yew Lin, Microsoft Research Asia
Emily Bender, University of Washington

Student Co-Chairs (Student Research Workshop)

Kuan-Yu Chen, National Taiwan University
Angelina Ivanova, University of Oslo
Ellie Pavlick, University of Pennsylvania

Mentoring Chair

Francis Bond, Nanyang Technological University

Student Volunteer Co-Chairs

Erhong Yang, Beijing Language and Culture University
Dong Yu, Beijing Language and Culture University

Webmasters

Zhiyuan Liu, Tsinghua University
Qi Zhang, Fudan University

Entertainment Chair

Binyang Li, University of International Relations

Space Management Co-Chairs

Jiajun Zhang, Institute of Automation, Chinese Academy of Sciences
Wenbin Jiang, Institute of Computing Technology, Chinese Academy of Sciences
Qiuye Zhao, Institute of Computing Technology, Chinese Academy of Sciences

Graphic Design

Yi Han, Tsinghua University
Ying Lin, Beijing University of Posts and Telecommunications

Program Committee

Program Committee Co-Chairs

Chengqing Zong, Institute of Automation, Chinese Academy of Sciences
Michael Strube, Heidelberg Institute for Theoretical Studies

Area Chairs

Srinivas Bangalore, Interactions
Regina Barzilay, MIT
Steven Bethard, University of Alabama at Birmingham
Chris Biemann, TU Darmstadt
Razvan Bunescu, Ohio University
Pascal Denis, INRIA Lille
Mark Dras, Macquarie University
James Fan
Raquel Fernandez, University of Amsterdam
Jianfeng Gao, Microsoft Research
Julia Hirschberg, Columbia University
Fei Huang, Facebook
Mausam, IIT Dehli
Jing Jiang, Singapore Management University
John Kelleher, Dublin Institute of Technology
Jin-Dong Kim, Research Organization of Information and Systems
Greg Kondrak, University of Alberta
Zornitsa Kozareva, Yahoo! Labs
Lun-Wei Ku, Academia Sinica
Tom Kwiatkowski, Google Research
Mirella Lapata, University of Edinburgh
Shou-De Lin, National Taiwan University
Qin Lu, The Hong Kong Polytechnic University
Yusuke Miyao, National Institute of Informatics
Daichi Mochihashi, The Institute of Statistical Mathematics
Jian-Yun Nie, Université de Montréal
Alice Oh, KAIST
Rashmi Prasad, University of Wisconsin-Milwaukee
Marta Recasens, Google Research
David Schlangen, University of Bielefeld
Anders Søgaard, University of Copenhagen
Suzanne Stevenson, University of Toronto
Joel Tetreault, Yahoo! Labs
Xiaojun Wan, Peking University
Taro Watanabe, Google
Eric Xing, Carnegie Mellon University
Min Zhang, Soochow University

Primary Reviewers

Reviewers who are acknowledged by the program committee for providing one or more outstanding reviews are marked with "*".

Ahmed Abbasi, Omri Abend*, Stergos Afantenos, Eneko Agirre*, Željko Agić*, Cem Akkaya, Jan

Alexandersson, Enrique Alfonseca*, Afra Alishahi, Yiannis Aloimonos, David Alvarez-Melis*, Richard Andersson, Ion Androutsopoulos*, Gabor Angeli*, Yuki Arase*, Cedric Archambeau, Yasuo Ariki, Ron Artstein*, Yoav Artzi*, Nicholas Asher, Giuseppe Attardi, Michael Auli, AiTi Aw, Necip Fazil Ayan

Olga Babko-Malaya, JinYeong Bak, Niranjan Balasubramanian, Timothy Baldwin*, Miguel Ballesteros, David Bamman, Carmen Banea, Srinivas Bangalore, Mohit Bansal, Ken Barker, Marco Baroni, Loïc Barrault, Regina Barzilay, Roberto Basili, Timo Baumann, Frederic Bechet, Barend Beekhuizen*, Núria Bel, Anja Belz, Jose Miguel Benedi, Jonathan Berant, Taylor Berg-Kirkpatrick, Steven Bethard, Suma Bhat*, Archna Bhatia*, Klinton Bicknell, Chris Biemann, Anders Björkelund*, Alan W Black, Nate Blaylock, John Blitzer, Bernd Bohnet, Dan Bohus*, Ondrej Bojar, Gemma Boleda*, Kalina Bontcheva, Antoine Bordes, Mihaela Bornea, Johan Bos, Alexandre Bouchard, Johan Boye, Kristy Boyer, S.R.K. Branavan, António Branco, Chris Brew, Ted Briscoe, Chris Brockett*, Julian Brooke, Eric Brown, Elia Bruni, Paul Buitelaar, Razvan Bunescu, Harry Bunt, Jill Burstein, Miriam Butt

Elena Cabrio, Aoife Cahill*, Nicoletta Calzolari, Erik Cambria, Marie Candito, Yunbo Cao, Xavier Carreras*, Tommaso Caselli, Taylor Cassidy, Vittorio Castelli, Asli Celikyilmaz, Daniel Cer, Christophe Cerisara, Nathanael Chambers*, Yee Seng Chan, Yi Chang, Wanxiang Che, Boxing Chen, Chen Chen, Wenliang Chen, Colin Cherry*, David Chiang, Christian Chiarcos, Laura Chiticariu*, Eunsol Choi, Jinho D. Choi, Key-Sun Choi, Yejin Choi, Monojit Choudhury, Munmun De Choudhury, Grzegorz Chrupała, Jennifer Chu-Carroll, Cindy Chung, Alexander Clark, Stephen Clark, Ann Clifton, Moreno Coco*, Shay B. Cohen, Trevor Cohn, Nigel Collier, Gao Cong, Miriam Connor, John Conroy, Paul Cook*, Bonaventura Coppola, Anna Corazza, Mark Core, Marta R. Costa-jussà, Danilo Croce, Paul Crook, Tim Van De Cruys, Xiaodong Cui

Robert Daland*, Bharath Dandala, Kareem Darwish, Dipanjan Das, Thierry Declerck, Estelle Delpech, Vera Demberg, John DeNero, Pascal Denis, Leon Derczynski, David DeVault*, Jacob Devlin, Mona Diab, Marco Dinarelli, Georgiana Dinu, Stefanie Dipper, Dmitriy Dligach, Simon Dobnik*, Bill Dolan, Mathew Magimai Doss, Doug Downey, Mark Dras, Mark Dredze*, Markus Dreyer, Gregory Druck*, Lan Du, Xiangyu Duan, Ewan Dunbar*, Benjamin Van Durme*, Greg Durrett*, Chris Dyer

Matthias Eck, Jens Edlund, Koji Eguchi, Yo Ehara*, Patrick Ehlen, Vladimir Eidelman, Jacob Eisenstein, Michael Elhadad*, Desmond Elliott, Klaus-Peter Engelbrecht, Erkut Erdem*, Katrin Erk*, Maxine Eskenazi

Giuseppe Di Fabbrizio, Anthony Fader*, James Fan, Benoit Favre*, Anna Feldman, Naomi Feldman, Raquel Fernandez, Katja Filippova, Nicholas FitzGerald, Darja Fišer, Margaret Fleck, Radu Florian, Antske Fokkens*, David Forsyth, Karën Fort, George Foster, Jennifer Foster, James Foulds*, Stella Frank, Alexander Fraser, Dayne Freitag*, Guohong Fu

Michel Galley, Michael Gamon*, Kuzman Ganchev, Juri Ganitkevitch, Jianfeng Gao, Qin Gao, Wei Gao, Yue Gao, Claire Gardent, Albert Gatt*, Maria Gavrilidou, Kallirroi Georgila*, Daniel Gildea, Alastair Gill, Jennifer Gillenwater*, Kevin Gimpel*, Filip Ginter, Roxana Girju, Adrià De Gispert, Alfio Gliozzo, Amir Globerson, Yoav Goldberg, Dan Goldwasser, Matthew R. Gormley, Cyril Goutte, Amit Goyal, Joao Graca, Brigitte Grau, Agustin Gravano, Edouard Grave*, Spence Green, Edward Grefenstette, Gregory Grefenstette, Ralph Grishman, Marco Guerini, Curry Guinn*, Weiwei Guo, Yuhong Guo, Rahul Gupta*, Sonal Gupta, Carlos Gómez-Rodríguez*

Ben Hachey, Barry Haddow, Gholamreza Haffari, Hannaneh Hajishirzi, Dilek Hakkani-Tur, John Hale, David Hall, Keith Hall, Bo Han, Xianpei Han, Mark Hasegawa-Johnson*, Hany Hassan, Kenneth Heafield*, Peter Heeman, Ulrich Heid, James Henderson, John Henderson, Karl Moritz Hermann, Tsutomu Hirao, Keikichi Hirose, Julia Hirschberg, Graeme Hirst, Anna Hjalmarsson, Hieu Hoang, Julia Hockenmaier, Johannes Hoffart, Veronique Hoste, Dirk Hovy*, Yuening Hu, Fei Huang (Facebook), Fei Huang (Temple University), Liang Huang, Ruihong Huang, Xuanjing

Huang, Zhongqiang Huang, Mans Hulden, Gerhard Van Huyssteen, Rebecca Hwa*, Young-Sook Hwang

Nancy Ide, Ryu Iida, Hal Daumé III*, Shajith Ikbal, Iustina Ilisei, Diana Inkpen, Kentaro Inui, Hitoshi Isahara, Abe Ittycheriah, Mohit Iyyer

Jagadeesh Jagarlamudi, Yacine Jernite, Rahul Jha, Heng Ji, Yangfeng Ji, Jing Jiang, Richard Johansson*, Mark Johnson, Michael Johnston, Kristiina Jokinen, Arne Jonsson, Shafiq Joty

Kyo Kageura, Min-Yen Kan*, Pallika Kanani, Daisuke Kawahara, Tatsuya Kawahara, Hideto Kazawa, Simon Keizer, John Kelleher, Frank Keller*, Emre Kiciman, Bernd Kiefer, Dongwoo Kim, Jin-Dong Kim, Seungyeon Kim, Su Nam Kim, Suin Kim, Tracy Holloway King, Brian Kingsbury, Kevin Knight, Alistair Knott, Philipp Koehn, Oleksandr Kolomiyets, Mamoru Komachi, Kazunori Komatani, Grzegorz Kondrak, Stefan Kopp, Parisa Kordjamshidi, Valia Kordoni, Anna Korhonen, Milen Kouylekov*, Zornitsa Kozareva, Emiel Krahmer, Jayant Krishnamurthy, Lun-Wei Ku*, Marco Kuhlmann, Roland Kuhn*, Tsung-Ting Kuo, Nate Kushman*, Polina Kuznetsova, Tom Kwiatkowski, Sandra Kübler

Wai Lam, Patrik Lambert, Guy Lapalme, Mirella Lapata, Shalom Lappin, Dominique Laurent, Alan Lee, Kenton Lee, Sungjin Lee, Yoong Keok Lee, Young-Suk Lee, Els Lefever, Fabrice Lefevre, Tao Lei, Alessandro Lenci, James Lester, Rivka Levitan, Gina-Anne Levow, Omer Levy*, Mike Lewis, Cheng-Te Li, Haibo Li, Hang Li, Jiwei Li, Lishuang Li, Mu Li, Qi Li*, Shoushan Li, Tao Li, Wenjie Li, Zhenghua Li, Chin-Yew Lin*, Shou-de Lin, Keith Vander Linden, Bing Liu, Fei Liu, Jing Liu, Kang Liu, Lemao Liu, Qun Liu, Ting Liu, Xiaohua Liu, Yang Liu (University Of Texas At Dallas), Yang Liu (Tsinghua University), Yiqun Liu, Zhanyi Liu, Zhiyuan Liu, Annie Louis, Wei Lu, Marco Lui, Xiaoqiang Luo, Franco M. Luque, Yajuan Lv

Klaus Macherey, Wolfgang Macherey, Nitin Madnani*, Daniel Marcu*, Marco Marelli, Anna Margolis, Joseph Mariani, Marie-Catherine De Marneffe, Erwin Marsi, Toni Marti, James H. Martin, Scott Martin*, André F. T. Martins, Vivien Mast*, Yuji Matsumoto, Takuya Matsuzaki, Mausam, Arne Mauser, Jonathan May*, David McClosky, Kathy McCoy*, Ryan McDonald, Tara McIntosh, Kathy McKeown, Susan McRoy, Alexander Mehler, Edgar Meij, Yelena Mejova, Gerard De Melo, Arul Menezes, Helen Meng, Florian Metze, Christian M. Meyer*, Adam Meyers, Haitao Mi, Rada Mihalcea, Timothy Miller*, Tristan Miller*, Bonan Min, Wolfgang Minker, Margaret Mitchell, Yusuke Miyao, Daichi Mochihashi, Marie-Francine Moens, Saif Mohammad, Karo Moilanen, Christian Monson, Manuel Montes, Christof Monz, Robert Moore, Roser Morante, Andrea Moro, Alessandro Moschitti, Arjun Mukherjee*, Philippe Muller*, Yugo Murawaki*, Smaranda Muresan

Seiichi Nakagawa, Mikio Nakano, Ndapandula Nakashole, Preslav Nakov, Jason Naradowsky*, Karthik Narasimhan, Shashi Narayan, Tahira Naseem, Vivi Nastase, Borja Navarro, Roberto Navigli, Mark-Jan Nederhof, Matteo Negri, Aida Nematzadeh, Ani Nenkova*, Graham Neubig*, Hwee Tou Ng, Vincent Ng, Dong Nguyen, Truc-Vien T. Nguyen, Viet-An Nguyen, Jian-Yun NIE, Joakim Nivre, Scott Nowson

Douglas O'Shaughnessy, Douglas Oard*, Stephan Oepen, Kemal Oflazer, Alice Oh, Jong-Hoon Oh, Naoaki Okazaki, Manabu Okumura, Constantin Orasan, Miles Osborne, Petya Osenova, Mari Ostendorf, Ekaterina Ovchinnikova

Ulrike Pado, John Paisley, Alexis Palmer, Martha Palmer*, Patrick Pantel, Aasish Pappu, Ankur P. Parikh, Cecile Paris, Souneil Park, Patrick Paroubek, Kristen Parton, Marius Pasca, Katerina Pastra*, Siddharth Patwardhan, Michael J. Paul, Adam Pauls, Bolette Pedersen, Edgar Gonzàlez Pellicer, Marco Pennacchiotti, Wim Peters, Slav Petrov, Anselmo Peñas, Maciej Piasecki, Olivier Pietquin, Juan Pino, Yuval Pinter*, Emily Pitler, Paul Piwek, Barbara Plank, Massimo Poesio, Simone Paolo Ponzetto, Hoifung Poon, Fred Popowich*, Christopher Potts*, Sameer Pradhan, Rashmi Prasad, Daniel Preoţiuc-Pietro, Emily Prud'hommeaux, Adam Przepiórkowski, Laurent Prévot, Stephen Pulman, Matthew Purver*, Sampo Pyysalo*, Verónica Pérez-Rosas

Guojun Qi, Xian Qian, Lu Qin, Xipeng Qiu, Ariadna Quattoni

Stephan Raaijmakers, Altaf Rahman, Jonathan Raiman, Ganesh Ramakrishnan, Owen Rambow, Ari Rappoport, Antoine Raux*, Sujith Ravi*, Marta Recasens, Siva Reddy, Sravana Reddy*, Roi Reichart, Joseph Reisinger, Ehud Reiter, Norbert Reithinger, David Reitter, Steffen Remus, Matthew Richardson, Sebastian Riedel, Martin Riedl*, German Rigau, Laura Rimell*, Alan Ritter, Brian Roark*, Andrew Rosenberg, Robert Ross, Paolo Rosso, Michael Roth, Joseph Le Roux, Alla Rozovskaya*, Frank Rudzicz, Alexander M. Rush, Christopher Ré

Mrinmaya Sachan, Markus Saers*, Kenji Sagae, Saurav Sahay, Patrick Saint-dizier, Murat Saraclar, Felix Sasaki, Roser Saurí, David Schlangen, Helmut Schmid, Nathan Schneider*, William Schuler*, Lane Schwartz*, Roy Schwartz*, Holger Schwenk, Djamé Seddah*, Frederique Segond, Satoshi Sekine, Pavel Serdyukov, Violeta Seretan*, Hendra Setiawan*, Serge Sharoff, Shuming Shi, Xiaodong Shi, Hiroyuki Shindo, Szymon Sidor, Avirup Sil, Fabrizio Silvestri, Yanchuan Sim, Khalil Sima'an, Sameer Singh, Gabriel Skantze, Ielka Van Der Sluis, Kevin Small*, Alan Smeaton, Noah A. Smith*, Richard Socher, Stephen Soderland, Eduardo Lleida Solano, Thamar Solorio*, Sa-kwang Song, Lucia Specia, Caroline Sporleder*, Rachele Sprugnoli, Vivek Srikumar, Edward Stabler, Maria Staudte, Georg Stemmer, Suzanne Stevenson, Svetlana Stoyanchev*, Veselin Stoyanov, Keh-Yih Su*, L V Subramaniam, Ke SUN, Le Sun, Weiwei Sun, Xu Sun, Mihai Surdeanu, Jun Suzuki*, Marc Swerts*, Stan Szpakowicz, Idan Szpektor, Diarmuid Ó Séaghdha, Anders Søgaard

Marko Tadić, Hiroya Takamura, Partha P. Talukdar, Akihiro Tamura, Kumiko Tanaka-Ishii, Joel Tetreault, Kapil Thadani, Ran Tian, Jörg Tiedemann, Christoph Tillmann, Ivan Titov, Takenobu Tokunaga*, Sara Tonelli, Kentaro Torisawa*, Kristina Toutanova, Isabel Trancoso, David Traum*, Richard Tzong-Han Tsai, Reut Tsarfaty, Masashi Tsubaki, Oren Tsur, Yoshimasa Tsuruoka, Oscar Täckström

Olga Uryupina, Masao Utiyama

Lucy Vanderwende*, Ashish Vaswani, Eva Maria Vecchi, Paola Velardi, Marc Verhagen, Yannick Versley*, Renata Vieira, Laure Vieu, David Vilar, Aline Villavicencio*, Andreas Vlachos, Svitlana Volkova, Piek Vossen

Michael Walsh, Stephen Wan, Xiaojun Wan, Bin Wang, Chong Wang, Haifeng Wang, Hongning Wang, Hsin-Min Wang, Jun Wang, Lu Wang, Leo Wanner, Nigel Ward, Taro Watanabe, Bonnie Webber, Ingmar Weber, Furu Wei, Gerhard Weikum, Michael White*, Janyce Wiebe*, Jason D Williams*, Theresa Wilson, Shuly Wintner, Derek F. Wong, Kristian Woodsend, Hua Wu, Joern Wuebker*

Fei Xia, Bing Xiang, Tong Xiao, Pengtao Xie, Eric Xing, Deyi Xiong, Ruifeng Xu*, Wei Xu, Ying Xu

Bishan Yang, Charles Yang, Muyun Yang, Yi Yang*, Xuchen Yao, Mark Yatskar, Xing Yi, Wentau Yih, Anssi Yli-Jyrä, Dani Yogatama, Steve Young, Bei Yu, Liang-Chih Yu, Nicholas Yuan, François Yvon

David Zajic*, Alessandra Zarcone, Xiaodong Zeng, Torsten Zesch, Luke Zettlemoyer, Deniz Zeyrek, Congle Zhang*, Dongdong Zhang, Hao Zhang, Jiajun Zhang*, Joy Ying Zhang, Min Zhang, Qi Zhang, Yu Zhang, Yuan Zhang, Yue Zhang, Zhe Zhang, Dongyan Zhao, Jun Zhao, Shiqi Zhao, Tiejun Zhao, Yanyan Zhao, Bowen Zhou, Guangyou Zhou, Ming Zhou, Yu Zhou, Jingbo Zhu, Jun Zhu

Secondary Reviewers

Nitish Aggarwal, Zejlko Agic, Henry Anaya-Sanchez, Héctor Martínez Alonso, Shunsuke Aoki, Kartik Asooja, Isabelle Augenstein, Wilker Aziz

Gianni Barlacchi, Lisa Beinborn, Adrian Benton, Georgeta Bordea, Fethi Bougares, Tim vor der Brück

Ming-Lun Cai, Hailong Cao, Houwei Cao, Giuseppe Castellucci, Kehai Chen, Xiao Chen, Edgar Chávez, James Cross, Lei Cui

Dezhong Deng, Aliya Deri, Anton Dil, Xiao Ding, Li Dong, Qing Dou, Avinava Dubey

Bradley Ellert, Aykut Erdem

Yang Feng, Francis Ferraro, Tiziano Flati, Marc Franco-Salvador

Michael Glass, Martin Gleize, Genevieve Gorrell, James Gung, Jiang Guo, Parth Gupta

Patrick Haffner, Wei He, Zhongjun He, Daniel Hershcovich, Cong Duy Vu Hoang, Hao Hu

Ruben Izquierdo

Anders Johannsen

Savvas Karagiannidis, Ghazaleh Kazeminejad, Daniel Khashabi, Jooyeon Kim, Wu Kui, Mikael Kågebäck

Oier Lopez de Lacalle, Gianluca Lebani, Chen Li, Jing Li, Peng Li, Rui Li, Sujian Li, Jianxun Lian, Anne-Laure Ligozat, Chen Lin, Xiao Ling, Alessandro Lopopolo, Michal Lukasik, Andy Lücking

Wei-Yun Ma, Todor Milanov

Steven Neale, Massimo Nicosia, Hiroshi Noji

Tim O'Gorman, Lydia Odilinye, Alexander Ororbia

Umashanthi Pavalanathan, Benjamin Piwowarski

Preethi Raghavan, Balamurali ANDIYAKKAL RAJENDRAN, Pushpendre Rastogi, Alex Ratner, Paul Reisert, Marco Tulio Ribeiro

Benoit Sagot, Christer Samuelsson, Fernando Sanchez Vega, Maarten Sap, Daniele Sartiano, Aliaksei Severyn, Lifeng Shang, Huaxing Shi, Parinaz Sobhani, Sanja Stajner, Jinsong Su, Elior Sulem

Kaveh Taghipour, Zhixing Tan, Irina Temnikova, Milan Tofiloski, Marco Del Tredici, William Trimble, Marco del Tredici

Jorrig Vogels, Greg Vorsanger, Hoang Cong Duy Vu

Baoxun Wang, Longyue Wang, Quan Wang, Xuancong Wang, Yingzi Wang, Zhongyu Wei, Travis Wolfe, Shumin Wu

Rui Xia, Xinyan Xiao, Wang Xuancong

Mo Yu

Jia Zeng, Ke Zhai, Ce Zhang, Chunyue Zhang, Meng Zhang, Muyu Zhang, Renxian Zhang, Xi Zhang, Xiaojun Zhang, Kai Zhao, Kaiqi Zhao, Zhou Zhao, Junguo Zhu, Xiaoning Zhu

Invited Talk: Can Natural Language Processing Become Natural LanguageCoaching?

Marti A. Hearst

School of Information and EECS, UC Berkeley

Abstract

How we teach and learn is undergoing a revolution, due to changes in technology and connectivity. Education may be one of the best application areas for advanced NLP techniques, and NLP researchers have much to contribute to this problem, especially in the areas of learning to write, mastery learning, and peer learning. In this talk I consider what happens when we convert natural language processors into natural language coaches.

Biography

Marti Hearst is a Professor at UC Berkeley in the School of Information and EECS. She received her PhD in CS from UC Berkeley in 1994 and was a member of the research staff at Xerox PARC form 1994-1997. Her research is in computational linguistics, search user interfaces, information visualization, and improving learning at scale. Her NLP work includes automatic acquisition of hypernym relations ("Hearst Patterns"), TextTiling discourse segmentation, abbreviation recognition, and multiword semantic relations. She wrote the book "Search User Interfaces" (Cambridge) in 2009, co-founded the ACM Conference on Learning at Scale in 2014, and was named an ACM Fellow in 2013. She has received four student-initiated Excellence in Teaching Awards, including in 2014 and 2015.

Invited Talk: Construction and Mining of Heterogeneous Information Networks from Text Data

Jiawei Han

Department of Computer Science, University of Illinois at Urbana-Champaign

Abstract

The real-world data are unstructured but interconnected. The majority of such data is in the form of natural language text. One of the grand challenges is to turn such massive data into actionable knowledge. In this talk, we present our vision on how to turn massive unstructured, text-rich, but interconnected data into knowledge. We propose a data-to-network-to-knowledge (i.e., D2N2K) paradigm, which is to first turn data into relatively structured heterogeneous information networks, and then mine such text-rich and structure-rich heterogeneous networks to generate useful knowledge. We show why such a paradigm represents a promising direction and present some recent progress on the development of effective methods for construction and mining of structured heterogeneous information networks from text data.

Biography

Jiawei Han is Abel Bliss Professor in the Department of Computer Science, University of Illinois at Urbana-Champaign. He has been researching into data mining, information network analysis, database systems, and data warehousing, with over 600 journal and conference publications. He has chaired or served on many program committees of international conferences, including PC co-chair for KDD, SDM, and ICDM conferences, and Americas Coordinator for VLDB conferences. He also served as the founding Editor-In-Chief of ACM Transactions on Knowledge Discovery from Data and is serving as the Director of Information Network Academic Research Center supported by U.S. Army Research Lab, and Director of KnowEnG, an NIH funded Center of Excellence in Big Data Computing. He is a Fellow of ACM and Fellow of IEEE, and received 2004 ACM SIGKDD Innovations Award, 2005 IEEE Computer Society Technical Achievement Award, 2009 IEEE Computer Society Wallace McDowell Award, and 2011 Daniel C. Drucker Eminent Faculty Award at UIUC. His co-authored book "Data Mining: Concepts and Techniques" has been adopted as a textbook popularly worldwide.

Table of Contents

On Using Very Large Target Vocabulary for Neural Machine Translation
Sébastien Jean, Kyunghyun Cho, Roland Memisevic and Yoshua Bengio 1

Addressing the Rare Word Problem in Neural Machine Translation
Thang Luong, Ilya Sutskever, Quoc Le, Oriol Vinyals and Wojciech Zaremba 11

Encoding Source Language with Convolutional Neural Network for Machine Translation
Fandong Meng, Zhengdong Lu, Mingxuan Wang, Hang Li, Wenbin Jiang and Qun Liu 20

Statistical Machine Translation Features with Multitask Tensor Networks
Hendra Setiawan, Zhongqiang Huang, Jacob Devlin, Thomas Lamar, Rabih Zbib, Richard Schwartz and John Makhoul 31

Describing Images using Inferred Visual Dependency Representations
Desmond Elliott and Arjen de Vries 42

Text to 3D Scene Generation with Rich Lexical Grounding
Angel Chang, Will Monroe, Manolis Savva, Christopher Potts and Christopher D. Manning 53

MultiGranCNN: An Architecture for General Matching of Text Chunks on Multiple Levels of Granularity
Wenpeng Yin and Hinrich Schütze 63

Weakly Supervised Models of Aspect-Sentiment for Online Course Discussion Forums
Arti Ramesh, Shachi H. Kumar, James Foulds and Lise Getoor 74

Semantically Smooth Knowledge Graph Embedding
Shu Guo, Quan Wang, Bin Wang, Lihong Wang and Li Guo 84

SensEmbed: Learning Sense Embeddings for Word and Relational Similarity
Ignacio Iacobacci, Mohammad Taher Pilehvar and Roberto Navigli 95

Revisiting Word Embedding for Contrasting Meaning
Zhigang Chen, Wei Lin, Qian Chen, Xiaoping Chen, Si Wei, Hui Jiang and Xiaodan Zhu 106

Joint Models of Disagreement and Stance in Online Debate
Dhanya Sridhar, James Foulds, Bert Huang, Lise Getoor and Marilyn Walker 116

Low-Rank Regularization for Sparse Conjunctive Feature Spaces: An Application to Named Entity Classification
Audi Primadhanty, Xavier Carreras and Ariadna Quattoni 126

Learning Word Representations by Jointly Modeling Syntagmatic and Paradigmatic Relations
Fei Sun, Jiafeng Guo, Yanyan Lan, Jun Xu and Xueqi Cheng 136

Learning Dynamic Feature Selection for Fast Sequential Prediction
Emma Strubell, Luke Vilnis, Kate Silverstein and Andrew McCallum 146

Compositional Vector Space Models for Knowledge Base Completion
Arvind Neelakantan, Benjamin Roth and Andrew McCallum 156

Event Extraction via Dynamic Multi-Pooling Convolutional Neural Networks
Yubo Chen, Liheng Xu, Kang Liu, Daojian Zeng and Jun Zhao 167

Stacked Ensembles of Information Extractors for Knowledge-Base Population
Vidhoon Viswanathan, Nazneen Fatema Rajani, Yinon Bentor and Raymond Mooney 177

Generative Event Schema Induction with Entity Disambiguation
Kiem-Hieu Nguyen, Xavier Tannier, Olivier Ferret and Romaric Besançon 188

Syntax-based Simultaneous Translation through Prediction of Unseen Syntactic Constituents
Yusuke Oda, Graham Neubig, Sakriani Sakti, Tomoki Toda and Satoshi Nakamura 198

Efficient Top-Down BTG Parsing for Machine Translation Preordering
Tetsuji Nakagawa 208

Online Multitask Learning for Machine Translation Quality Estimation
José G. C. de Souza, Matteo Negri, Elisa Ricci and Marco Turchi 219

A Context-Aware Topic Model for Statistical Machine Translation
Jinsong Su, Deyi Xiong, Yang Liu, Xianpei Han, Hongyu Lin, Junfeng Yao and Min Zhang ... 229

Learning Answer-Entailing Structures for Machine Comprehension
Mrinmaya Sachan, Kumar Dubey, Eric Xing and Matthew Richardson 239

Learning Continuous Word Embedding with Metadata for Question Retrieval in Community Question Answering
Guangyou Zhou, Tingting He, Jun Zhao and Po Hu 250

Question Answering over Freebase with Multi-Column Convolutional Neural Networks
Li Dong, Furu Wei, Ming Zhou and Ke Xu 260

Hubness and Pollution: Delving into Cross-Space Mapping for Zero-Shot Learning
Angeliki Lazaridou, Georgiana Dinu and Marco Baroni 270

A Generalisation of Lexical Functions for Composition in Distributional Semantics
Antoine Bride, Tim Van de Cruys and Nicholas Asher 281

Simple Learning and Compositional Application of Perceptually Grounded Word Meanings for Incremental Reference Resolution
Casey Kennington and David Schlangen 292

Neural CRF Parsing
Greg Durrett and Dan Klein 302

An Effective Neural Network Model for Graph-based Dependency Parsing
Wenzhe Pei, Tao Ge and Baobao Chang 313

Structured Training for Neural Network Transition-Based Parsing
David Weiss, Chris Alberti, Michael Collins and Slav Petrov 323

Transition-Based Dependency Parsing with Stack Long Short-Term Memory
Chris Dyer, Miguel Ballesteros, Wang Ling, Austin Matthews and Noah A. Smith 334

Leveraging Linguistic Structure For Open Domain Information Extraction
Gabor Angeli, Melvin Jose Johnson Premkumar and Christopher D. Manning 344

Joint Information Extraction and Reasoning: A Scalable Statistical Relational Learning Approach
William Yang Wang and William W Cohen 355

A Knowledge-Intensive Model for Prepositional Phrase Attachment
Ndapandula Nakashole and Tom M. Mitchell 365

A Convolution Kernel Approach to Identifying Comparisons in Text
Maksim Tkachenko and Hady Lauw 376

It Depends: Dependency Parser Comparison Using A Web-based Evaluation Tool
Jinho D. Choi, Joel Tetreault and Amanda Stent 387

Generating High Quality Proposition Banks for Multilingual Semantic Role Labeling
Alan Akbik, laura chiticariu, Marina Danilevsky, Yunyao Li, Shivakumar Vaithyanathan and Huaiyu Zhu 397

Aligning Opinions: Cross-Lingual Opinion Mining with Dependencies
Mariana S. C. Almeida, Claudia Pinto, Helena Figueira, Pedro Mendes and André F. T. Martins 408

Learning to Adapt Credible Knowledge in Cross-lingual Sentiment Analysis
Qiang Chen, Wenjie Li, Yu Lei, Xule Liu and Yanxiang He 419

Learning Bilingual Sentiment Word Embeddings for Cross-language Sentiment Classification
HuiWei Zhou, Long Chen, Fulin Shi and Degen Huang 430

Content Models for Survey Generation: A Factoid-Based Evaluation
Rahul Jha, Catherine Finegan-Dollak, Ben King, Reed Coke and Dragomir Radev 441

Training a Natural Language Generator From Unaligned Data
Ondřej Dušek and Filip Jurcicek 451

Event-Driven Headline Generation
Rui Sun, Yue Zhang, Meishan Zhang and Donghong Ji 462

New Transfer Learning Techniques for Disparate Label Sets
Young-Bum Kim, Karl Stratos, Ruhi Sarikaya and Minwoo Jeong 473

Matrix Factorization with Knowledge Graph Propagation for Unsupervised Spoken Language Understanding
Yun-Nung Chen, William Yang Wang, Anatole Gershman and Alexander Rudnicky 483

Efficient Disfluency Detection with Transition-based Parsing
Shuangzhi Wu, Dongdong Zhang, Ming Zhou and Tiejun Zhao 495

S-MART: Novel Tree-based Structured Learning Algorithms Applied to Tweet Entity Linking
Yi Yang and Ming-Wei Chang 504

Entity Retrieval via Entity Factoid Hierarchy
Chunliang Lu, Wai Lam and Yi Liao 514

Encoding Distributional Semantics into Triple-Based Knowledge Ranking for Document Enrichment
Muyu Zhang, Bing Qin, Mao Zheng, Graeme Hirst and Ting Liu 524

A Strategic Reasoning Model for Generating Alternative Answers
Jon Stevens, Anton Benz, Sebastian Reuße and Ralf Klabunde 534

Modeling Argument Strength in Student Essays
Isaac Persing and Vincent Ng 543

Summarization of Multi-Document Topic Hierarchies using Submodular Mixtures
Ramakrishna Bairi, Rishabh Iyer, Ganesh Ramakrishnan and Jeff Bilmes 553

Learning to Explain Entity Relationships in Knowledge Graphs
Nikos Voskarides, Edgar Meij, Manos Tsagkias, Maarten de Rijke and Wouter Weerkamp 564

Bring you to the past: Automatic Generation of Topically Relevant Event Chronicles
Tao Ge, Wenzhe Pei, Heng Ji, Sujian Li, Baobao Chang and Zhifang Sui 575

Context-aware Entity Morph Decoding
Boliang Zhang, Hongzhao Huang, Xiaoman Pan, Sujian Li, Chin-Yew Lin, Heng Ji, Kevin Knight, Zhen Wen, Yizhou Sun, Jiawei Han and Bulent Yener 586

Multi-Objective Optimization for the Joint Disambiguation of Nouns and Named Entities
Dirk Weissenborn, Leonhard Hennig, Feiyu Xu and Hans Uszkoreit 596

Building a Scientific Concept Hierarchy Database (SCHBase)
Eytan Adar and Srayan Datta 606

Sentiment-Aspect Extraction based on Restricted Boltzmann Machines
Linlin Wang, Kang Liu, Zhu Cao, Jun Zhao and Gerard de Melo 616

Classifying Relations by Ranking with Convolutional Neural Networks
Cicero dos Santos, Bing Xiang and Bowen Zhou 626

Semantic Representations for Domain Adaptation: A Case Study on the Tree Kernel-based Method for Relation Extraction
Thien Huu Nguyen, Barbara Plank and Ralph Grishman 635

Omnia Mutantur, Nihil Interit: Connecting Past with Present by Finding Corresponding Terms across Time
Yating Zhang, Adam Jatowt, Sourav Bhowmick and Katsumi Tanaka 645

Negation and Speculation Identification in Chinese Language
Bowei Zou, Qiaoming Zhu and Guodong Zhou 656

Learning Relational Features with Backward Random Walks
Ni Lao, Einat Minkov and William Cohen 666

Learning the Semantics of Manipulation Action
Yezhou Yang, Yiannis Aloimonos, Cornelia Fermuller and Eren Erdal Aksoy 676

Knowledge Graph Embedding via Dynamic Mapping Matrix
Guoliang Ji, Shizhu He, Liheng Xu, Kang Liu and Jun Zhao 687

How Far are We from Fully Automatic High Quality Grammatical Error Correction?
Christopher Bryant and Hwee Tou Ng 697

Knowledge Portability with Semantic Expansion of Ontology Labels
Mihael Arcan, Marco Turchi and Paul Buitelaar 708

Automatic disambiguation of English puns
Tristan Miller and Iryna Gurevych 719

Unsupervised Cross-Domain Word Representation Learning
Danushka Bollegala, Takanori Maehara and Ken-ichi Kawarabayashi 730

A Unified Multilingual Semantic Representation of Concepts
José Camacho-Collados, Mohammad Taher Pilehvar and Roberto Navigli 741

Demographic Factors Improve Classification Performance
Dirk Hovy 752

Vector-space calculation of semantic surprisal for predicting word pronunciation duration
Asad Sayeed, Stefan Fischer and Vera Demberg 763

Efficient Methods for Inferring Large Sparse Topic Hierarchies
Doug Downey, Chandra Bhagavatula and Yi Yang 774

Trans-dimensional Random Fields for Language Modeling
Bin Wang, Zhijian Ou and Zhiqiang Tan 785

Gaussian LDA for Topic Models with Word Embeddings
Rajarshi Das, Manzil Zaheer and Chris Dyer 795

Pairwise Neural Machine Translation Evaluation
Francisco Guzmán, Shafiq Joty, Lluís Màrquez and Preslav Nakov 805

String-to-Tree Multi Bottom-up Tree Transducers
Nina Seemann, Fabienne Braune and Andreas Maletti 815

Non-linear Learning for Statistical Machine Translation
Shujian Huang, Huadong Chen, Xin-Yu Dai and Jiajun Chen 825

Unifying Bayesian Inference and Vector Space Models for Improved Decipherment
Qing Dou, Ashish Vaswani, Kevin Knight and Chris Dyer 836

Non-projective Dependency-based Pre-Reordering with Recurrent Neural Network for Machine Translation
Antonio Valerio Miceli Barone and Giuseppe Attardi 846

Detecting Deceptive Groups Using Conversations and Network Analysis
Dian Yu, Yulia Tyshchuk, Heng Ji and William Wallace 857

WikiKreator: Improving Wikipedia Stubs Automatically
Siddhartha Banerjee and Prasenjit Mitra 867

Language to Code: Learning Semantic Parsers for If-This-Then-That Recipes
Chris Quirk, Raymond Mooney and Michel Galley 878

Deep Questions without Deep Understanding
Igor Labutov, Sumit Basu and Lucy Vanderwende 889

The NL2KR Platform for building Natural Language Translation Systems
Nguyen Vo, Arindam Mitra and Chitta Baral 899

Multiple Many-to-Many Sequence Alignment for Combining String-Valued Variables: A G2P Experiment
Steffen Eger 909

Tweet Normalization with Syllables
Ke Xu, Yunqing Xia and Chin-Hui Lee 920

Improving Named Entity Recognition in Tweets via Detecting Non-Standard Words
Chen Li and Yang Liu 929

A Unified Kernel Approach for Learning Typed Sentence Rewritings
Martin Gleize and Brigitte Grau 939

Perceptually Grounded Selectional Preferences
Ekaterina Shutova, Niket Tandon and Gerard de Melo 950

Joint Case Argument Identification for Japanese Predicate Argument Structure Analysis
Hiroki Ouchi, Hiroyuki Shindo, Kevin Duh and Yuji Matsumoto 961

Jointly optimizing word representations for lexical and sentential tasks with the C-PHRASE model
Nghia The Pham, Germán Kruszewski, Angeliki Lazaridou and Marco Baroni 971

Robust Subgraph Generation Improves Abstract Meaning Representation Parsing
Keenon Werling, Gabor Angeli and Christopher D. Manning 982

Environment-Driven Lexicon Induction for High-Level Instructions
Dipendra Kumar Misra, Kejia Tao, Percy Liang and Ashutosh Saxena 992

Structural Representations for Learning Relations between Pairs of Texts
Simone Filice, Giovanni Da San Martino and Alessandro Moschitti 1003

Learning Semantic Representations of Users and Products for Document Level Sentiment Classification
Duyu Tang, Bing Qin and Ting Liu 1014

Towards Debugging Sentiment Lexicons
Andrew Schneider and Eduard Dragut 1024

Sparse, Contextually Informed Models for Irony Detection: Exploiting User Communities, Entities and Sentiment
Byron C. Wallace, Do Kook Choe and Eugene Charniak 1035

Sentence-level Emotion Classification with Label and Context Dependence
Shoushan Li, Lei Huang, Rong Wang and Guodong Zhou 1045

Co-training for Semi-supervised Sentiment Classification Based on Dual-view Bags-of-words Representation
Rui Xia, Cheng Wang, Xin-Yu Dai and Tao Li 1054

Improving social relationships in face-to-face human-agent interactions: when the agent wants to know user's likes and dislikes
Caroline Langlet and Chloé Clavel 1064

Learning Word Representations from Scarce and Noisy Data with Embedding Subspaces
Ramón Astudillo, Silvio Amir, Wang Ling, Mario Silva and Isabel Trancoso 1074

Automatic Spontaneous Speech Grading: A Novel Feature Derivation Technique using the Crowd
Vinay Shashidhar, Nishant Pandey and Varun Aggarwal 1085

Driving ROVER with Segment-based ASR Quality Estimation
Shahab Jalalvand, Matteo Negri, Falavigna Daniele and Marco Turchi 1095

A Hierarchical Neural Autoencoder for Paragraphs and Documents
Jiwei Li, Thang Luong and Dan Jurafsky 1106

Joint Dependency Parsing and Multiword Expression Tokenization
Alexis Nasr, Carlos Ramisch, José Deulofeu and André Valli 1116

End-to-end learning of semantic role labeling using recurrent neural networks
Jie Zhou and Wei Xu 1127

Feature Optimization for Constituent Parsing via Neural Networks
Zhiguo Wang, Haitao Mi and Nianwen Xue 1138

Identifying Cascading Errors using Constraints in Dependency Parsing
Dominick Ng and James R. Curran 1148

A Re-ranking Model for Dependency Parser with Recursive Convolutional Neural Network
Chenxi Zhu, Xipeng Qiu, Xinchi Chen and Xuanjing Huang 1159

Transition-based Neural Constituent Parsing
Taro Watanabe and Eiichiro Sumita 1169

Feature Selection in Kernel Space: A Case Study on Dependency Parsing
Xian Qian and Yang Liu 1180

Semantic Role Labeling Improves Incremental Parsing
Ioannis Konstas and Frank Keller 1191

Discontinuous Incremental Shift-reduce Parsing
Wolfgang Maier 1202

A Neural Probabilistic Structured-Prediction Model for Transition-Based Dependency Parsing
Hao Zhou, Yue Zhang, Shujian Huang and Jiajun Chen 1213

Parsing Paraphrases with Joint Inference
Do Kook Choe and David McClosky 1223

Cross-lingual Dependency Parsing Based on Distributed Representations
Jiang Guo, Wanxiang Che, David Yarowsky, Haifeng Wang and Ting Liu 1234

Can Natural Language Processing Become Natural Language Coaching?
Marti A. Hearst 1245

Machine Comprehension with Discourse Relations
Karthik Narasimhan and Regina Barzilay 1253

Implicit Role Linking on Chinese Discourse: Exploiting Explicit Roles and Frame-to-Frame Relations
Ru Li, Juan Wu, Zhiqiang Wang and Qinghua Chai 1263

Discourse-sensitive Automatic Identification of Generic Expressions
Annemarie Friedrich and Manfred Pinkal 1272

Model-based Word Embeddings from Decompositions of Count Matrices
Karl Stratos, Michael Collins and Daniel Hsu 1282

Entity Hierarchy Embedding
Zhiting Hu, Poyao Huang, Yuntian Deng, Yingkai Gao and Eric Xing 1292

Orthogonality of Syntax and Semantics within Distributional Spaces
Jeff Mitchell and Mark Steedman 1301

Scalable Semantic Parsing with Partial Ontologies
Eunsol Choi, Tom Kwiatkowski and Luke Zettlemoyer 1311

Semantic Parsing via Staged Query Graph Generation: Question Answering with Knowledge Base
Wen-tau Yih, Ming-Wei Chang, Xiaodong He and Jianfeng Gao 1321

Building a Semantic Parser Overnight
Yushi Wang, Jonathan Berant and Percy Liang 1332

Predicting Polarities of Tweets by Composing Word Embeddings with Long Short-Term Memory
Xin Wang, Yuanchao Liu, Chengjie SUN, Baoxun Wang and Xiaolong Wang 1343

Topic Modeling based Sentiment Analysis on Social Media for Stock Market Prediction
Thien Hai Nguyen and Kiyoaki Shirai 1354

Learning Tag Embeddings and Tag-specific Composition Functions in Recursive Neural Network
Qiao Qian, Bo Tian, Minlie Huang, Yang Liu, Xuan Zhu and Xiaoyan Zhu 1365

A convex and feature-rich discriminative approach to dependency grammar induction
Edouard Grave and Noémie Elhadad 1375

Parse Imputation for Dependency Annotations
Jason Mielens, Liang Sun and Jason Baldridge 1385

Probing the Linguistic Strengths and Limitations of Unsupervised Grammar Induction
Yonatan Bisk and Julia Hockenmaier 1395

Entity-Centric Coreference Resolution with Model Stacking
Kevin Clark and Christopher D. Manning 1405

Learning Anaphoricity and Antecedent Ranking Features for Coreference Resolution
Sam Wiseman, Alexander M. Rush, Stuart Shieber and Jason Weston 1416

Transferring Coreference Resolvers with Posterior Regularization
André F. T. Martins 1427

Tea Party in the House: A Hierarchical Ideal Point Topic Model and Its Application to Republican Legislators in the 112th Congress
Viet-An Nguyen, Jordan Boyd-Graber, Philip Resnik and Kristina Miler 1438

KB-LDA: Jointly Learning a Knowledge Base of Hierarchy, Relations, and Facts
Dana Movshovitz-Attias and William W. Cohen 1449

A Computationally Efficient Algorithm for Learning Topical Collocation Models
Zhendong Zhao, Lan Du, Benjamin Börschinger, John K Pate, Massimiliano Ciaramita, Mark Steedman and Mark Johnson 1460

Compositional Semantic Parsing on Semi-Structured Tables
Panupong Pasupat and Percy Liang 1470

Graph parsing with s-graph grammars
Jonas Groschwitz, Alexander Koller and Christoph Teichmann 1481

Sparse Overcomplete Word Vector Representations
Manaal Faruqui, Yulia Tsvetkov, Dani Yogatama, Chris Dyer and Noah A. Smith 1491

Learning Semantic Word Embeddings based on Ordinal Knowledge Constraints
Quan Liu, Hui Jiang, Si Wei, Zhen-Hua Ling and Yu Hu 1501

Adding Semantics to Data-Driven Paraphrasing
Ellie Pavlick, Johan Bos, Malvina Nissim, Charley Beller, Benjamin Van Durme and Chris Callison-Burch 1512

Parsing as Reduction
Daniel Fernández-González and André F. T. Martins 1523

Optimal Shift-Reduce Constituent Parsing with Structured Perceptron
Le Quang Thang, Hiroshi Noji and Yusuke Miyao 1534

A Data-Driven, Factorization Parser for CCG Dependency Structures
Yantao Du, Weiwei Sun and Xiaojun Wan 1545

Improved Semantic Representations From Tree-Structured Long Short-Term Memory Networks
Kai Sheng Tai, Richard Socher and Christopher D. Manning 1556

genCNN: A Convolutional Architecture for Word Sequence Prediction
Mingxuan Wang, Zhengdong Lu, Hang Li, Wenbin Jiang and Qun Liu 1567

Neural Responding Machine for Short-Text Conversation
Lifeng Shang, Zhengdong Lu and Hang Li 1577

Abstractive Multi-Document Summarization via Phrase Selection and Merging
Lidong Bing, Piji Li, Yi Liao, Wai Lam, Weiwei Guo and Rebecca Passonneau 1587

Joint Graphical Models for Date Selection in Timeline Summarization
Giang Tran, Eelco Herder and Katja Markert 1598

Predicting Salient Updates for Disaster Summarization
Chris Kedzie, Kathleen McKeown and Fernando Diaz 1608

Unsupervised Prediction of Acceptability Judgements
Jey Han Lau, Alexander Clark and Shalom Lappin 1618

A Frame of Mind: Using Statistical Models for Detection of Framing and Agenda Setting Campaigns
Oren Tsur, Dan Calacci and David Lazer 1629

Why discourse affects speakers' choice of referring expressions
Naho Orita, Eliana Vornov, Naomi Feldman and Hal Daumé III 1639

Linguistic Harbingers of Betrayal: A Case Study on an Online Strategy Game
Vlad Niculae, Srijan Kumar, Jordan Boyd-Graber and Cristian Danescu-Niculescu-Mizil 1650

Who caught a cold ? - Identifying the subject of a symptom
Shin Kanouchi, Mamoru Komachi, Naoaki Okazaki, Eiji ARAMAKI and Hiroshi Ishikawa . . 1660

Weakly Supervised Role Identification in Teamwork Interactions
Diyi Yang, Miaomiao Wen and Carolyn Rose 1671

Deep Unordered Composition Rivals Syntactic Methods for Text Classification
Mohit Iyyer, Varun Manjunatha, Jordan Boyd-Graber and Hal Daumé III 1681

SOLAR: Scalable Online Learning Algorithms for Ranking
Jialei Wang, Ji Wan, Yongdong Zhang and Steven Hoi 1692

Text Categorization as a Graph Classification Problem
Francois Rousseau, Emmanouil Kiagias and Michalis Vazirgiannis 1702

Inverted indexing for cross-lingual NLP
Anders Søgaard, Željko Agić, Héctor Martínez Alonso, Barbara Plank, Bernd Bohnet and Anders Johannsen 1713

Multi-Task Learning for Multiple Language Translation
Daxiang Dong, Hua Wu, Wei He, Dianhai Yu and Haifeng Wang 1723

Accurate Linear-Time Chinese Word Segmentation via Embedding Matching
Jianqiang Ma and Erhard Hinrichs 1733

Gated Recursive Neural Network for Chinese Word Segmentation
Xinchi Chen, Xipeng Qiu, Chenxi Zhu and Xuanjing Huang 1744

An analysis of the user occupational class through Twitter content
Daniel Preoţiuc-Pietro, Vasileios Lampos and Nikolaos Aletras 1754

Tracking unbounded Topic Streams
Dominik Wurzer, Victor Lavrenko and Miles Osborne 1765

Inducing Word and Part-of-Speech with Pitman-Yor Hidden Semi-Markov Models
Kei Uchiumi, Hiroshi Tsukahara and Daichi Mochihashi 1774

Coupled Sequence Labeling on Heterogeneous Annotations: POS Tagging as a Case Study
Zhenghua Li, Jiayuan Chao, Min Zhang and Wenliang Chen 1783

AutoExtend: Extending Word Embeddings to Embeddings for Synsets and Lexemes
Sascha Rothe and Hinrich Schütze 1793

Improving Evaluation of Machine Translation Quality Estimation
Yvette Graham 1804

Conference Program

Sunday, July 26

18:00–21:00 Welcome Reception

Monday, July 27

07:30–18:00 Registration

08:45–09:00 Welcome to ACL-IJCNLP 2015

09:00–09:40 Presidential Address: Christopher D. Manning

09:40–10:10 Coffee Break

10:10–11:50 Session 1: TACL and Long Papers

Session 1A: 10:10–11:50 Machine Translation: Neural Networks

On Using Very Large Target Vocabulary for Neural Machine Translation
Sébastien Jean, Kyunghyun Cho, Roland Memisevic and Yoshua Bengio

Addressing the Rare Word Problem in Neural Machine Translation
Thang Luong, Ilya Sutskever, Quoc Le, Oriol Vinyals and Wojciech Zaremba

Encoding Source Language with Convolutional Neural Network for Machine Translation
Fandong Meng, Zhengdong Lu, Mingxuan Wang, Hang Li, Wenbin Jiang and Qun Liu

Statistical Machine Translation Features with Multitask Tensor Networks
Hendra Setiawan, Zhongqiang Huang, Jacob Devlin, Thomas Lamar, Rabih Zbib, Richard Schwartz and John Makhoul

Session 1B: 10:10–11:50 Language and Vision/NLP Applications

Describing Images using Inferred Visual Dependency Representations
Desmond Elliott and Arjen de Vries

Text to 3D Scene Generation with Rich Lexical Grounding
Angel Chang, Will Monroe, Manolis Savva, Christopher Potts and Christopher D. Manning

MultiGranCNN: An Architecture for General Matching of Text Chunks on Multiple Levels of Granularity
Wenpeng Yin and Hinrich Schütze

Weakly Supervised Models of Aspect-Sentiment for Online Course Discussion Forums
Arti Ramesh, Shachi H. Kumar, James Foulds and Lise Getoor

Session 1C: 10:10–11:50 Semantics: Embeddings

[TACL] Improving Distributional Similarity with Lessons Learned from Word Embeddings
Omer Levy, Yoav Goldberg, Ido Dagan

Semantically Smooth Knowledge Graph Embedding
Shu Guo, Quan Wang, Bin Wang, Lihong Wang and Li Guo

SensEmbed: Learning Sense Embeddings for Word and Relational Similarity
Ignacio Iacobacci, Mohammad Taher Pilehvar and Roberto Navigli

Revisiting Word Embedding for Contrasting Meaning
Zhigang Chen, Wei Lin, Qian Chen, Xiaoping Chen, Si Wei, Hui Jiang and Xiaodan Zhu

Session 1D: 10:10–11:50 Machine Learning

Joint Models of Disagreement and Stance in Online Debate
Dhanya Sridhar, James Foulds, Bert Huang, Lise Getoor and Marilyn Walker

Low-Rank Regularization for Sparse Conjunctive Feature Spaces: An Application to Named Entity Classification
Audi Primadhanty, Xavier Carreras and Ariadna Quattoni

Learning Word Representations by Jointly Modeling Syntagmatic and Paradigmatic Relations
Fei Sun, Jiafeng Guo, Yanyan Lan, Jun Xu and Xueqi Cheng

Learning Dynamic Feature Selection for Fast Sequential Prediction
Emma Strubell, Luke Vilnis, Kate Silverstein and Andrew McCallum

Session 1E: 10:10–11:50 Information Extraction 1

Compositional Vector Space Models for Knowledge Base Completion
Arvind Neelakantan, Benjamin Roth and Andrew McCallum

Event Extraction via Dynamic Multi-Pooling Convolutional Neural Networks
Yubo Chen, Liheng Xu, Kang Liu, Daojian Zeng and Jun Zhao

Stacked Ensembles of Information Extractors for Knowledge-Base Population
Vidhoon Viswanathan, Nazneen Fatema Rajani, Yinon Bentor and Raymond Mooney

Generative Event Schema Induction with Entity Disambiguation
Kiem-Hieu Nguyen, Xavier Tannier, Olivier Ferret and Romaric Besançon

Monday, July 27 (continued)

11:50–13:20 Lunch Break; Student Lunch

13:20–15:00 Session 2: TACL and Long Papers

Session 2A: 13:20–15:00 Machine Translation

Syntax-based Simultaneous Translation through Prediction of Unseen Syntactic Constituents
Yusuke Oda, Graham Neubig, Sakriani Sakti, Tomoki Toda and Satoshi Nakamura

Efficient Top-Down BTG Parsing for Machine Translation Preordering
Tetsuji Nakagawa

Online Multitask Learning for Machine Translation Quality Estimation
José G. C. de Souza, Matteo Negri, Elisa Ricci and Marco Turchi

A Context-Aware Topic Model for Statistical Machine Translation
Jinsong Su, Deyi Xiong, Yang Liu, Xianpei Han, Hongyu Lin, Junfeng Yao and Min Zhang

Session 2B: 13:20–15:00 Question Answering

Learning Answer-Entailing Structures for Machine Comprehension
Mrinmaya Sachan, Kumar Dubey, Eric Xing and Matthew Richardson

Learning Continuous Word Embedding with Metadata for Question Retrieval in Community Question Answering
Guangyou Zhou, Tingting He, Jun Zhao and Po Hu

Question Answering over Freebase with Multi-Column Convolutional Neural Networks
Li Dong, Furu Wei, Ming Zhou and Ke Xu

[TACL] Higher-order Lexical Semantic Models for Non-factoid Answer Reranking
Daniel Fried, Peter Jansen, Gustave Hahn-Powell, Mihai Surdeanu, Peter Clark

Session 2C: 13:20–15:00 Semantics: Distributional Approaches

Hubness and Pollution: Delving into Cross-Space Mapping for Zero-Shot Learning
Angeliki Lazaridou, Georgiana Dinu and Marco Baroni

[TACL] Learning a Compositional Semantics for Freebase with an Open Predicate Vocabulary
Jayant Krishnamurthy and Tom M. Mitchell

A Generalisation of Lexical Functions for Composition in Distributional Semantics
Antoine Bride, Tim Van de Cruys and Nicholas Asher

Simple Learning and Compositional Application of Perceptually Grounded Word Meanings for Incremental Reference Resolution
Casey Kennington and David Schlangen

Session 2D: 13:20–15:00 Parsing: Neural Networks

Neural CRF Parsing
Greg Durrett and Dan Klein

An Effective Neural Network Model for Graph-based Dependency Parsing
Wenzhe Pei, Tao Ge and Baobao Chang

Structured Training for Neural Network Transition-Based Parsing
David Weiss, Chris Alberti, Michael Collins and Slav Petrov

Transition-Based Dependency Parsing with Stack Long Short-Term Memory
Chris Dyer, Miguel Ballesteros, Wang Ling, Austin Matthews and Noah A. Smith

Monday, July 27 (continued)

Session 2E: 13:20–15:00 Information Extraction 2

Leveraging Linguistic Structure For Open Domain Information Extraction
Gabor Angeli, Melvin Jose Johnson Premkumar and Christopher D. Manning

Joint Information Extraction and Reasoning: A Scalable Statistical Relational Learning Approach
William Yang Wang and William W Cohen

A Knowledge-Intensive Model for Prepositional Phrase Attachment
Ndapandula Nakashole and Tom M. Mitchell

A Convolution Kernel Approach to Identifying Comparisons in Text
Maksim Tkachenko and Hady Lauw

15:00–15:30 Coffee Break

15:30–16:45 Session 3: TACL and Long Papers

Session 3A: 15:30–16:45 Language Resources

[TACL] A New Corpus and Imitation Learning Framework for Context-Dependent Semantic Parsing
Andreas Vlachos and Stephen Clark

It Depends: Dependency Parser Comparison Using A Web-based Evaluation Tool
Jinho D. Choi, Joel Tetreault and Amanda Stent

Generating High Quality Proposition Banks for Multilingual Semantic Role Labeling
Alan Akbik, laura chiticariu, Marina Danilevsky, Yunyao Li, Shivakumar Vaithyanathan and Huaiyu Zhu

Session 3B: 15:30–16:45 Sentiment Analysis: Cross-/Multi Lingual

Aligning Opinions: Cross-Lingual Opinion Mining with Dependencies
Mariana S. C. Almeida, Claudia Pinto, Helena Figueira, Pedro Mendes and André F. T. Martins

Learning to Adapt Credible Knowledge in Cross-lingual Sentiment Analysis
Qiang Chen, Wenjie Li, Yu Lei, Xule Liu and Yanxiang He

Learning Bilingual Sentiment Word Embeddings for Cross-language Sentiment Classification
HuiWei Zhou, Long Chen, Fulin Shi and Degen Huang

Session 3C: 15:30–16:45 Natural Language Generation

Content Models for Survey Generation: A Factoid-Based Evaluation
Rahul Jha, Catherine Finegan-Dollak, Ben King, Reed Coke and Dragomir Radev

Training a Natural Language Generator From Unaligned Data
Ondřej Dušek and Filip Jurcicek

Event-Driven Headline Generation
Rui Sun, Yue Zhang, Meishan Zhang and Donghong Ji

Session 3D: 15:30–16:45 Spoken Language Processing and Understanding

New Transfer Learning Techniques for Disparate Label Sets
Young-Bum Kim, Karl Stratos, Ruhi Sarikaya and Minwoo Jeong

Matrix Factorization with Knowledge Graph Propagation for Unsupervised Spoken Language Understanding
Yun-Nung Chen, William Yang Wang, Anatole Gershman and Alexander Rudnicky

Efficient Disfluency Detection with Transition-based Parsing
Shuangzhi Wu, Dongdong Zhang, Ming Zhou and Tiejun Zhao

Session 3E: 15:30–16:45 Information Extraction 3/Information Retrieval

S-MART: Novel Tree-based Structured Learning Algorithms Applied to Tweet Entity Linking
Yi Yang and Ming-Wei Chang

[TACL] Design Challenges for Entity Linking
Xiao Ling, Sameer Singh, Daniel S. Weld

Entity Retrieval via Entity Factoid Hierarchy
Chunliang Lu, Wai Lam and Yi Liao

16:45–17:00 **Short Break**

17:00–18:00 **Session 4: Short Papers**

18:00–21:00 **Poster and Dinner Session 1: TACL Papers, Long Papers, System Demonstrations**

Session P1.01: 18:00–21:00 Poster: Pragmatics

Encoding Distributional Semantics into Triple-Based Knowledge Ranking for Document Enrichment
Muyu Zhang, Bing Qin, Mao Zheng, Graeme Hirst and Ting Liu

A Strategic Reasoning Model for Generating Alternative Answers
Jon Stevens, Anton Benz, Sebastian Reuße and Ralf Klabunde

Modeling Argument Strength in Student Essays
Isaac Persing and Vincent Ng

Monday, July 27 (continued)

Session P1.02: 18:00–21:00 Poster: Information Retrieval

Summarization of Multi-Document Topic Hierarchies using Submodular Mixtures
Ramakrishna Bairi, Rishabh Iyer, Ganesh Ramakrishnan and Jeff Bilmes

Learning to Explain Entity Relationships in Knowledge Graphs
Nikos Voskarides, Edgar Meij, Manos Tsagkias, Maarten de Rijke and Wouter Weerkamp

Session P1.03: 18:00–21:00 Poster: Information Extraction

[TACL] Exploiting Parallel News Streams for Unsupervised Event Extraction
Congle Zhang, Stephen Soderland, Daniel Weld

Bring you to the past: Automatic Generation of Topically Relevant Event Chronicles
Tao Ge, Wenzhe Pei, Heng Ji, Sujian Li, Baobao Chang and Zhifang Sui

Context-aware Entity Morph Decoding
Boliang Zhang, Hongzhao Huang, Xiaoman Pan, Sujian Li, Chin-Yew Lin, Heng Ji, Kevin Knight, Zhen Wen, Yizhou Sun, Jiawei Han and Bulent Yener

Multi-Objective Optimization for the Joint Disambiguation of Nouns and Named Entities
Dirk Weissenborn, Leonhard Hennig, Feiyu Xu and Hans Uszkoreit

Building a Scientific Concept Hierarchy Database (SCHBase)
Eytan Adar and Srayan Datta

Sentiment-Aspect Extraction based on Restricted Boltzmann Machines
Linlin Wang, Kang Liu, Zhu Cao, Jun Zhao and Gerard de Melo

Classifying Relations by Ranking with Convolutional Neural Networks
Cicero dos Santos, Bing Xiang and Bowen Zhou

Semantic Representations for Domain Adaptation: A Case Study on the Tree Kernel-based Method for Relation Extraction
Thien Huu Nguyen, Barbara Plank and Ralph Grishman

Omnia Mutantur, Nihil Interit: Connecting Past with Present by Finding Corresponding Terms across Time
Yating Zhang, Adam Jatowt, Sourav Bhowmick and Katsumi Tanaka

Negation and Speculation Identification in Chinese Language
Bowei Zou, Qiaoming Zhu and Guodong Zhou

Learning Relational Features with Backward Random Walks
Ni Lao, Einat Minkov and William Cohen

Session P1.04: 18:00–21:00 Poster: Language and Vision

Learning the Semantics of Manipulation Action
Yezhou Yang, Yiannis Aloimonos, Cornelia Fermuller and Eren Erdal Aksoy

Session P1.05: 18:00–21:00 Poster: Language Resources

Knowledge Graph Embedding via Dynamic Mapping Matrix
Guoliang Ji, Shizhu He, Liheng Xu, Kang Liu and Jun Zhao

How Far are We from Fully Automatic High Quality Grammatical Error Correction?
Christopher Bryant and Hwee Tou Ng

Session P1.06: 18:00–21:00 Poster: Lexical Semantics and Ontology

Knowledge Portability with Semantic Expansion of Ontology Labels
Mihael Arcan, Marco Turchi and Paul Buitelaar

Automatic disambiguation of English puns
Tristan Miller and Iryna Gurevych

Unsupervised Cross-Domain Word Representation Learning
Danushka Bollegala, Takanori Maehara and Ken-ichi Kawarabayashi

A Unified Multilingual Semantic Representation of Concepts
José Camacho-Collados, Mohammad Taher Pilehvar and Roberto Navigli

Session P1.07: 18:00–21:00 Poster: Linguistic and Psycholinguistic Aspects of CL

Demographic Factors Improve Classification Performance
Dirk Hovy

Vector-space calculation of semantic surprisal for predicting word pronunciation duration
Asad Sayeed, Stefan Fischer and Vera Demberg

Session P1.08: 18:00–21:00 Poster: Machine Learning and Topic Modeling

Efficient Methods for Inferring Large Sparse Topic Hierarchies
Doug Downey, Chandra Bhagavatula and Yi Yang

Trans-dimensional Random Fields for Language Modeling
Bin Wang, Zhijian Ou and Zhiqiang Tan

Gaussian LDA for Topic Models with Word Embeddings
Rajarshi Das, Manzil Zaheer and Chris Dyer

Session P1.09: 18:00–21:00 Poster: Machine Translation

Pairwise Neural Machine Translation Evaluation
Francisco Guzmán, Shafiq Joty, Lluís Màrquez and Preslav Nakov

String-to-Tree Multi Bottom-up Tree Transducers
Nina Seemann, Fabienne Braune and Andreas Maletti

Non-linear Learning for Statistical Machine Translation
Shujian Huang, Huadong Chen, Xin-Yu Dai and Jiajun Chen

Unifying Bayesian Inference and Vector Space Models for Improved Decipherment
Qing Dou, Ashish Vaswani, Kevin Knight and Chris Dyer

Non-projective Dependency-based Pre-Reordering with Recurrent Neural Network for Machine Translation
Antonio Valerio Miceli Barone and Giuseppe Attardi

Monday, July 27 (continued)

Session P1.10: 18:00–21:00 Poster: NLP Applications

Detecting Deceptive Groups Using Conversations and Network Analysis
Dian Yu, Yulia Tyshchuk, Heng Ji and William Wallace

WikiKreator: Improving Wikipedia Stubs Automatically
Siddhartha Banerjee and Prasenjit Mitra

Language to Code: Learning Semantic Parsers for If-This-Then-That Recipes
Chris Quirk, Raymond Mooney and Michel Galley

Deep Questions without Deep Understanding
Igor Labutov, Sumit Basu and Lucy Vanderwende

The NL2KR Platform for building Natural Language Translation Systems
Nguyen Vo, Arindam Mitra and Chitta Baral

Session P1.12: 18:00–21:00 Poster: Morphology

Multiple Many-to-Many Sequence Alignment for Combining String-Valued Variables: A G2P Experiment
Steffen Eger

Session P1.11: 18:00–21:00 Poster: NLP for the Web and Social Media

Tweet Normalization with Syllables
Ke Xu, Yunqing Xia and Chin-Hui Lee

Improving Named Entity Recognition in Tweets via Detecting Non-Standard Words
Chen Li and Yang Liu

Monday, July 27 (continued)

Session P1.13: 18:00–21:00 Poster: Question Answering

A Unified Kernel Approach for Learning Typed Sentence Rewritings
Martin Gleize and Brigitte Grau

Session P1.14: 18:00–21:00 Poster: Semantics

[TACL] From Visual Attributes to Adjectives through Decompositional Distributional Semantics
Angeliki Lazaridou, Georgiana Dinu, Adam Liska, Marco Baroni

Perceptually Grounded Selectional Preferences
Ekaterina Shutova, Niket Tandon and Gerard de Melo

Joint Case Argument Identification for Japanese Predicate Argument Structure Analysis
Hiroki Ouchi, Hiroyuki Shindo, Kevin Duh and Yuji Matsumoto

Jointly optimizing word representations for lexical and sentential tasks with the C-PHRASE model
Nghia The Pham, Germán Kruszewski, Angeliki Lazaridou and Marco Baroni

Robust Subgraph Generation Improves Abstract Meaning Representation Parsing
Keenon Werling, Gabor Angeli and Christopher D. Manning

Environment-Driven Lexicon Induction for High-Level Instructions
Dipendra Kumar Misra, Kejia Tao, Percy Liang and Ashutosh Saxena

Structural Representations for Learning Relations between Pairs of Texts
Simone Filice, Giovanni Da San Martino and Alessandro Moschitti

Session P1.15: 18:00–21:00 Poster: Sentiment Analysis

[TACL] Joint Modeling of Opinion Expression Extraction and Attribute Classification
Bishan Yang and Claire Cardie

Learning Semantic Representations of Users and Products for Document Level Sentiment Classification
Duyu Tang, Bing Qin and Ting Liu

Towards Debugging Sentiment Lexicons
Andrew Schneider and Eduard Dragut

Sparse, Contextually Informed Models for Irony Detection: Exploiting User Communities, Entities and Sentiment
Byron C. Wallace, Do Kook Choe and Eugene Charniak

Sentence-level Emotion Classification with Label and Context Dependence
Shoushan Li, Lei Huang, Rong Wang and Guodong Zhou

Co-training for Semi-supervised Sentiment Classification Based on Dual-view Bags-of-words Representation
Rui Xia, Cheng Wang, Xin-Yu Dai and Tao Li

Improving social relationships in face-to-face human-agent interactions: when the agent wants to know user's likes and dislikes
Caroline Langlet and Chloé Clavel

Learning Word Representations from Scarce and Noisy Data with Embedding Subspaces
Ramón Astudillo, Silvio Amir, Wang Ling, Mario Silva and Isabel Trancoso

Monday, July 27 (continued)

Session P1.16: 18:00–21:00 Poster: Spoken Language Processing

Automatic Spontaneous Speech Grading: A Novel Feature Derivation Technique using the Crowd
Vinay Shashidhar, Nishant Pandey and Varun Aggarwal

Driving ROVER with Segment-based ASR Quality Estimation
Shahab Jalalvand, Matteo Negri, Falavigna Daniele and Marco Turchi

Session P1.17: 18:00–21:00 Poster: Natural Language Generation

A Hierarchical Neural Autoencoder for Paragraphs and Documents
Jiwei Li, Thang Luong and Dan Jurafsky

Session P1.18: 18:00–21:00 Poster: Tagging, Chunking, Parsing

[TACL]Domain Adaptation for Syntactic and Semantic Dependency Parsing Using Deep Belief Networks
Haitong Yang, Tao Zhuang, Chengqing Zong

Joint Dependency Parsing and Multiword Expression Tokenization
Alexis Nasr, Carlos Ramisch, José Deulofeu and André Valli

End-to-end learning of semantic role labeling using recurrent neural networks
Jie Zhou and Wei Xu

Feature Optimization for Constituent Parsing via Neural Networks
Zhiguo Wang, Haitao Mi and Nianwen Xue

Identifying Cascading Errors using Constraints in Dependency Parsing
Dominick Ng and James R. Curran

A Re-ranking Model for Dependency Parser with Recursive Convolutional Neural Network
Chenxi Zhu, Xipeng Qiu, Xinchi Chen and Xuanjing Huang

Transition-based Neural Constituent Parsing
Taro Watanabe and Eiichiro Sumita

Monday, July 27 (continued)

Feature Selection in Kernel Space: A Case Study on Dependency Parsing
Xian Qian and Yang Liu

Semantic Role Labeling Improves Incremental Parsing
Ioannis Konstas and Frank Keller

Discontinuous Incremental Shift-reduce Parsing
Wolfgang Maier

A Neural Probabilistic Structured-Prediction Model for Transition-Based Dependency Parsing
Hao Zhou, Yue Zhang, Shujian Huang and Jiajun Chen

Parsing Paraphrases with Joint Inference
Do Kook Choe and David McClosky

Cross-lingual Dependency Parsing Based on Distributed Representations
Jiang Guo, Wanxiang Che, David Yarowsky, Haifeng Wang and Ting Liu

Tuesday, July 28

07:30–18:00 **Registration**

09:00–10:00 **Keynote Address: "Can Natural Language Processing Become Natural Language Coaching?" - Marti A. Hearst**

Can Natural Language Processing Become Natural Language Coaching?
Marti A. Hearst

Tuesday, July 28 (continued)

10:00–10:30 Coffee Break

10:30–12:00 Session 5: Short Papers

12:00–13:30 Lunch Break

13:30–14:45 Session 6: Long Papers

Session 6A: 13:30–14:45 Discourse, Pragmatics

Machine Comprehension with Discourse Relations
Karthik Narasimhan and Regina Barzilay

Implicit Role Linking on Chinese Discourse: Exploiting Explicit Roles and Frame-to-Frame Relations
Ru Li, Juan Wu, Zhiqiang Wang and Qinghua Chai

Discourse-sensitive Automatic Identification of Generic Expressions
Annemarie Friedrich and Manfred Pinkal

Session 6B: 13:30–14:45 Machine Learning: Embeddings

Model-based Word Embeddings from Decompositions of Count Matrices
Karl Stratos, Michael Collins and Daniel Hsu

Entity Hierarchy Embedding
Zhiting Hu, Poyao Huang, Yuntian Deng, Yingkai Gao and Eric Xing

Orthogonality of Syntax and Semantics within Distributional Spaces
Jeff Mitchell and Mark Steedman

Session 6C: 13:30–14:45 Semantics: Semantic Parsing

Scalable Semantic Parsing with Partial Ontologies
Eunsol Choi, Tom Kwiatkowski and Luke Zettlemoyer

Semantic Parsing via Staged Query Graph Generation: Question Answering with Knowledge Base
Wen-tau Yih, Ming-Wei Chang, Xiaodong He and Jianfeng Gao

Building a Semantic Parser Overnight
Yushi Wang, Jonathan Berant and Percy Liang

Session 6D: 13:30–14:45 Sentiment Analysis: Learning

Predicting Polarities of Tweets by Composing Word Embeddings with Long Short-Term Memory
Xin Wang, Yuanchao Liu, Chengjie SUN, Baoxun Wang and Xiaolong Wang

Topic Modeling based Sentiment Analysis on Social Media for Stock Market Prediction
Thien Hai Nguyen and Kiyoaki Shirai

Learning Tag Embeddings and Tag-specific Composition Functions in Recursive Neural Network
Qiao Qian, Bo Tian, Minlie Huang, Yang Liu, Xuan Zhu and Xiaoyan Zhu

Session 6E: 13:30–14:45 Grammar Induction and Annotation

A convex and feature-rich discriminative approach to dependency grammar induction
Edouard Grave and Noémie Elhadad

Parse Imputation for Dependency Annotations
Jason Mielens, Liang Sun and Jason Baldridge

Probing the Linguistic Strengths and Limitations of Unsupervised Grammar Induction
Yonatan Bisk and Julia Hockenmaier

Tuesday, July 28 (continued)

14:45–15:15 Coffee Break

15:15–16:30 Session 7: TACL and Long Papers

Session 7A: 15:15–16:30 Discourse, Coreference

Entity-Centric Coreference Resolution with Model Stacking
Kevin Clark and Christopher D. Manning

Learning Anaphoricity and Antecedent Ranking Features for Coreference Resolution
Sam Wiseman, Alexander M. Rush, Stuart Shieber and Jason Weston

Transferring Coreference Resolvers with Posterior Regularization
André F. T. Martins

Session 7B: 15:15–16:30 Topic Modeling

Tea Party in the House: A Hierarchical Ideal Point Topic Model and Its Application to Republican Legislators in the 112th Congress
Viet-An Nguyen, Jordan Boyd-Graber, Philip Resnik and Kristina Miler

KB-LDA: Jointly Learning a Knowledge Base of Hierarchy, Relations, and Facts
Dana Movshovitz-Attias and William W. Cohen

A Computationally Efficient Algorithm for Learning Topical Collocation Models
Zhendong Zhao, Lan Du, Benjamin Börschinger, John K Pate, Massimiliano Ciaramita, Mark Steedman and Mark Johnson

Session 7C: 15:15–16:30 Semantics: Semantic Parsing

[TACL] Efficient Inference and Structured Learning for Semantic Role Labeling
Oscar Täckström, Kuzman Ganchev, Dipanjan Das

Compositional Semantic Parsing on Semi-Structured Tables
Panupong Pasupat and Percy Liang

Graph parsing with s-graph grammars
Jonas Groschwitz, Alexander Koller and Christoph Teichmann

Session 7D: 15:15–16:30 Lexical Semantics

Sparse Overcomplete Word Vector Representations
Manaal Faruqui, Yulia Tsvetkov, Dani Yogatama, Chris Dyer and Noah A. Smith

Learning Semantic Word Embeddings based on Ordinal Knowledge Constraints
Quan Liu, Hui Jiang, Si Wei, Zhen-Hua Ling and Yu Hu

Adding Semantics to Data-Driven Paraphrasing
Ellie Pavlick, Johan Bos, Malvina Nissim, Charley Beller, Benjamin Van Durme and Chris Callison-Burch

Session 7E: 15:15–16:30 Parsing

Parsing as Reduction
Daniel Fernández-González and André F. T. Martins

Optimal Shift-Reduce Constituent Parsing with Structured Perceptron
Le Quang Thang, Hiroshi Noji and Yusuke Miyao

A Data-Driven, Factorization Parser for CCG Dependency Structures
Yantao Du, Weiwei Sun and Xiaojun Wan

Tuesday, July 28 (continued)

16:30–19:30 Poster and Dinner Session 2: Short Papers, Student Research Workshop Papers

19:45–22:00 Social Event

Wednesday, July 29

07:30–18:00 Registration

09:00–10:00 Keynote Address: "Construction and Mining of Heterogenous Information Networks from Data" - Jiawei Han

10:00–10:30 Coffee Break

10:30–11:45 Session 8: Long Papers

Session 8A: 10:30–11:45 Machine Learning: Neural Networks

Improved Semantic Representations From Tree-Structured Long Short-Term Memory Networks
Kai Sheng Tai, Richard Socher and Christopher D. Manning

genCNN: A Convolutional Architecture for Word Sequence Prediction
Mingxuan Wang, Zhengdong Lu, Hang Li, Wenbin Jiang and Qun Liu

Neural Responding Machine for Short-Text Conversation
Lifeng Shang, Zhengdong Lu and Hang Li

Session 8B: 10:30–11:45 Automatic Summarization

Abstractive Multi-Document Summarization via Phrase Selection and Merging
Lidong Bing, Piji Li, Yi Liao, Wai Lam, Weiwei Guo and Rebecca Passonneau

Joint Graphical Models for Date Selection in Timeline Summarization
Giang Tran, Eelco Herder and Katja Markert

Predicting Salient Updates for Disaster Summarization
Chris Kedzie, Kathleen McKeown and Fernando Diaz

Session 8C: 10:30–11:45 Linguistic and Psycholinguistic Aspects of NLP

Unsupervised Prediction of Acceptability Judgements
Jey Han Lau, Alexander Clark and Shalom Lappin

A Frame of Mind: Using Statistical Models for Detection of Framing and Agenda Setting Campaigns
Oren Tsur, Dan Calacci and David Lazer

Why discourse affects speakers' choice of referring expressions
Naho Orita, Eliana Vornov, Naomi Feldman and Hal Daumé III

Session 8D: 10:30–11:45 NLP for the Web: Social Media

Linguistic Harbingers of Betrayal: A Case Study on an Online Strategy Game
Vlad Niculae, Srijan Kumar, Jordan Boyd-Graber and Cristian Danescu-Niculescu-Mizil

Who caught a cold ? - Identifying the subject of a symptom
Shin Kanouchi, Mamoru Komachi, Naoaki Okazaki, Eiji ARAMAKI and Hiroshi Ishikawa

Weakly Supervised Role Identification in Teamwork Interactions
Diyi Yang, Miaomiao Wen and Carolyn Rose

Wednesday, July 29 (continued)

Session 8E: 10:30–11:45 Text Categorization/Information Retrieval

Deep Unordered Composition Rivals Syntactic Methods for Text Classification
Mohit Iyyer, Varun Manjunatha, Jordan Boyd-Graber and Hal Daumé III

SOLAR: Scalable Online Learning Algorithms for Ranking
Jialei Wang, Ji Wan, Yongdong Zhang and Steven Hoi

Text Categorization as a Graph Classification Problem
Francois Rousseau, Emmanouil Kiagias and Michalis Vazirgiannis

11:45–13:00 Lunch Break

13:00–14:30 ACL Business Meeting

14:35–15:25 Session 9: TACL and Long papers

Session 9A: 14:35–15:25 Multilinguality

Inverted indexing for cross-lingual NLP
Anders Søgaard, Željko Agić, Héctor Martínez Alonso, Barbara Plank, Bernd Bohnet and Anders Johannsen

Multi-Task Learning for Multiple Language Translation
Daxiang Dong, Hua Wu, Wei He, Dianhai Yu and Haifeng Wang

Session 9B: 14:35–15:25 Word Segmentation

Accurate Linear-Time Chinese Word Segmentation via Embedding Matching
Jianqiang Ma and Erhard Hinrichs

Gated Recursive Neural Network for Chinese Word Segmentation
Xinchi Chen, Xipeng Qiu, Chenxi Zhu and Xuanjing Huang

Session 9C: 14:35–15:25 Morphology, Phonology

[TACL] An Unsupervised Method for Uncovering Morphological Chains
Karthik Narasimhan, Regina Barzilay, Tommi Jaakkola

[TACL] Modeling Word Forms Using Latent Underlying Morphs and Phonology
Ryan Cotterell, Nanyun Peng, Jason Eisner

Session 9D: 14:35–15:25 NLP for the Web: Twitter

An analysis of the user occupational class through Twitter content
Daniel Preoţiuc-Pietro, Vasileios Lampos and Nikolaos Aletras

Tracking unbounded Topic Streams
Dominik Wurzer, Victor Lavrenko and Miles Osborne

Session 9E: 14:35–15:25 POS Tagging

Inducing Word and Part-of-Speech with Pitman-Yor Hidden Semi-Markov Models
Kei Uchiumi, Hiroshi Tsukahara and Daichi Mochihashi

Coupled Sequence Labeling on Heterogeneous Annotations: POS Tagging as a Case Study
Zhenghua Li, Jiayuan Chao, Min Zhang and Wenliang Chen

15:25–15:55 Coffee Break

Session BP: 15:55–17:10 Best Paper Session

AutoExtend: Extending Word Embeddings to Embeddings for Synsets and Lexemes
Sascha Rothe and Hinrich Schütze

Improving Evaluation of Machine Translation Quality Estimation
Yvette Graham

17:10–18:30 Lifetime Achievement Award

18:30–19:00 Closing Session

Day Date

Session Ses Code: Ses Time–Ses End Time Ses Title

Gen *Time–Gen End Time Gen Title*
Gen Presenter

On Using Very Large Target Vocabulary for Neural Machine Translation

Sébastien Jean Kyunghyun Cho
Roland Memisevic
Université de Montréal

Yoshua Bengio
Université de Montréal
CIFAR Senior Fellow

Abstract

Neural machine translation, a recently proposed approach to machine translation based purely on neural networks, has shown promising results compared to the existing approaches such as phrase-based statistical machine translation. Despite its recent success, neural machine translation has its limitation in handling a larger vocabulary, as training complexity as well as decoding complexity increase proportionally to the number of target words. In this paper, we propose a method based on importance sampling that allows us to use a very large target vocabulary without increasing training complexity. We show that decoding can be efficiently done even with the model having a very large target vocabulary by selecting only a small subset of the whole target vocabulary. The models trained by the proposed approach are empirically found to match, and in some cases outperform, the baseline models with a small vocabulary as well as the LSTM-based neural machine translation models. Furthermore, when we use an ensemble of a few models with very large target vocabularies, we achieve performance comparable to the state of the art (measured by BLEU) on both the English→German and English→French translation tasks of WMT'14.

1 Introduction

Neural machine translation (NMT) is a recently introduced approach to solving machine translation (Kalchbrenner and Blunsom, 2013; Bahdanau et al., 2015; Sutskever et al., 2014). In neural machine translation, one builds a single neural network that reads a source sentence and generates its translation. The whole neural network is jointly trained to maximize the conditional probability of a correct translation given a source sentence, using the bilingual corpus. The NMT models have shown to perform as well as the most widely used conventional translation systems (Sutskever et al., 2014; Bahdanau et al., 2015).

Neural machine translation has a number of advantages over the existing statistical machine translation system, specifically, the phrase-based system (Koehn et al., 2003). First, NMT requires a minimal set of domain knowledge. For instance, all of the models proposed in (Sutskever et al., 2014), (Bahdanau et al., 2015) or (Kalchbrenner and Blunsom, 2013) do not assume any linguistic property in both source and target sentences except that they are sequences of words. Second, the whole system is jointly trained to maximize the translation performance, unlike the existing phrase-based system which consists of many separately trained features whose weights are then tuned jointly. Lastly, the memory footprint of the NMT model is often much smaller than the existing system which relies on maintaining large tables of phrase pairs.

Despite these advantages and promising results, there is a major limitation in NMT compared to the existing phrase-based approach. That is, the number of target words must be limited. This is mainly because the complexity of training and using an NMT model increases as the number of target words increases.

A usual practice is to construct a target vocabulary of the K most frequent words (a so-called shortlist), where K is often in the range of $30k$ (Bahdanau et al., 2015) to $80k$ (Sutskever et al., 2014). Any word not included in this vocabulary is mapped to a special token representing an *unknown* word [UNK]. This approach works well when there are only a few unknown words in the target sentence, but it has been observed

Proceedings of the 53rd Annual Meeting of the Association for Computational Linguistics and the 7th International Joint Conference on Natural Language Processing, pages 1–10,
Beijing, China, July 26-31, 2015.

that the translation performance degrades rapidly as the number of unknown words increases (Cho et al., 2014a; Bahdanau et al., 2015).

In this paper, we propose an approximate training algorithm based on (biased) importance sampling that allows us to train an NMT model with a much larger target vocabulary. The proposed algorithm effectively keeps the computational complexity during training at the level of using only a small subset of the full vocabulary. Once the model with a very large target vocabulary is trained, one can choose to use either all the target words or only a subset of them.

We compare the proposed algorithm against the baseline shortlist-based approach in the tasks of English→French and English→German translation using the NMT model introduced in (Bahdanau et al., 2015). The empirical results demonstrate that we can potentially achieve better translation performance using larger vocabularies, and that our approach does not sacrifice too much speed for both training and decoding. Furthermore, we show that the model trained with this algorithm gets the best translation performance yet achieved by single NMT models on the WMT'14 English→French translation task.

2 Neural Machine Translation and Limited Vocabulary Problem

In this section, we briefly describe an approach to neural machine translation proposed recently in (Bahdanau et al., 2015). Based on this description we explain the issue of limited vocabularies in neural machine translation.

2.1 Neural Machine Translation

Neural machine translation is a recently proposed approach to machine translation, which uses a single neural network trained jointly to maximize the translation performance (Forcada and Ñeco, 1997; Kalchbrenner and Blunsom, 2013; Cho et al., 2014b; Sutskever et al., 2014; Bahdanau et al., 2015).

Neural machine translation is often implemented as the encoder–decoder network. The encoder reads the source sentence $x = (x_1, \ldots, x_T)$ and encodes it into a sequence of hidden states $h = (h_1, \cdots, h_T)$:

$$h_t = f\left(x_t, h_{t-1}\right). \qquad (1)$$

Then, the decoder, another recurrent neural network, generates a corresponding translation $y = (y_1, \cdots, y_{T'})$ based on the encoded sequence of hidden states h:

$$p(y_t \mid y_{<t}, x) \propto \exp\left\{q\left(y_{t-1}, z_t, c_t\right)\right\}, \qquad (2)$$

where

$$z_t = g\left(y_{t-1}, z_{t-1}, c_t\right), \qquad (3)$$

$$c_t = r\left(z_{t-1}, h_1, \ldots, h_T\right), \qquad (4)$$

and $y_{<t} = (y_1, \ldots, y_{t-1})$.

The whole model is jointly trained to maximize the conditional log-probability of the correct translation given a source sentence with respect to the parameters $\boldsymbol{\theta}$ of the model:

$$\boldsymbol{\theta}^* = \arg\max_{\boldsymbol{\theta}} \sum_{n=1}^{N} \sum_{t=1}^{T_n} \log p(y_t^n \mid y_{<t}^n, x^n),$$

where (x^n, y^n) is the n-th training pair of sentences, and T_n is the length of the n-th target sentence (y^n).

2.1.1 Detailed Description

In this paper, we use a specific implementation of neural machine translation that uses an attention mechanism, as recently proposed in (Bahdanau et al., 2015).

In (Bahdanau et al., 2015), the encoder in Eq. (1) is implemented by a bi-directional recurrent neural network such that

$$h_t = \left[\overleftarrow{h}_t; \overrightarrow{h}_t\right],$$

where

$$\overleftarrow{h}_t = f\left(x_t, \overleftarrow{h}_{t+1}\right), \overrightarrow{h}_t = f\left(x_t, \overrightarrow{h}_{t-1}\right).$$

They used a gated recurrent unit for f (see, e.g., (Cho et al., 2014b)).

The decoder, at each time, computes the context vector c_t as a convex sum of the hidden states $(h_1, \ldots, h_T)$ with the coefficients $\alpha_1, \ldots, \alpha_T$ computed by

$$\alpha_t = \frac{\exp\left\{a\left(h_t, z_{t-1}\right)\right\}}{\sum_k \exp\left\{a\left(h_k, z_{t-1}\right)\right\}}, \qquad (5)$$

where a is a feedforward neural network with a single hidden layer.

A new hidden state z_t of the decoder in Eq. (3) is computed based on the previous hidden state z_{t-1}, previous generated symbol y_{t-1} and the computed context vector c_t. The decoder also uses the gated recurrent unit, as the encoder does.

The probability of the next target word in Eq. (2) is then computed by

$$p(y_t \mid y_{<t}, x) = \frac{1}{Z} \exp\left\{ \mathbf{w}_t^\top \phi\left(y_{t-1}, z_t, c_t\right) + b_t \right\}, \tag{6}$$

where ϕ is an affine transformation followed by a nonlinear activation, and $\mathbf{w}_t$ and b_t are respectively the *target word vector* and the target word bias. Z is the normalization constant computed by

$$Z = \sum_{k:y_k \in V} \exp\left\{ \mathbf{w}_k^\top \phi\left(y_{t-1}, z_t, c_t\right) + b_k \right\}, \tag{7}$$

where V is the set of all the target words.

For the detailed description of the implementation, we refer the reader to the appendix of (Bahdanau et al., 2015).

2.2 Limited Vocabulary Issue and Conventional Solutions

One of the main difficulties in training this neural machine translation model is the computational complexity involved in computing the target word probability (Eq. (6)). More specifically, we need to compute the dot product between the feature $\phi\left(y_{t-1}, z_t, c_t\right)$ and the word vector w_t as many times as there are words in a target vocabulary in order to compute the normalization constant (the denominator in Eq. (6)). This has to be done for, on average, 20–30 words per sentence, which easily becomes prohibitively expensive even with a moderate number of possible target words. Furthermore, the memory requirement grows linearly with respect to the number of target words. This has been a major hurdle for neural machine translation, compared to the existing non-parametric approaches such as phrase-based translation systems.

Recently proposed neural machine translation models, hence, use a shortlist of 30k to 80k most frequent words (Bahdanau et al., 2015; Sutskever et al., 2014). This makes training more feasible, but comes with a number of problems. First of all, the performance of the model degrades heavily if the translation of a source sentence requires many words that are not included in the shortlist (Cho et al., 2014a). This also affects the performance evaluation of the system which is often measured by BLEU. Second, the first issue becomes more problematic with languages that have a rich set of words such as German or other highly inflected languages.

There are two *model-specific* approaches to this issue of large target vocabulary. The first approach is to stochastically approximate the target word probability. This has been proposed recently in (Mnih and Kavukcuoglu, 2013; Mikolov et al., 2013) based on noise-contrastive estimation (Gutmann and Hyvarinen, 2010). In the second approach, the target words are clustered into multiple classes, or hierarchical classes, and the target probability $p(y_t|y_{<t}, x)$ is factorized as a product of the class probability $p(c_t|y_{<t}, x)$ and the intra-class word probability $p(y_t|c_t, y_{<t}, x)$. This reduces the number of required dot-products into the sum of the number of classes and the words in a class. These approaches mainly aim at reducing the computational complexity during training, but do not often result in speed-up when decoding a translation during test time.[1]

Other than these model-specific approaches, there exist *translation-specific* approaches. A translation-specific approach exploits the properties of the rare target words. For instance, Luong et al. proposed such an approach for neural machine translation (Luong et al., 2015). They replace rare words (the words that are not included in the shortlist) in both source and target sentences into corresponding $\langle \text{OOV}_n \rangle$ tokens using the word alignment model. Once a source sentence is translated, each $\langle \text{OOV}_n \rangle$ in the translation will be replaced based on the source word marked by the corresponding $\langle \text{OOV}_n \rangle$.

It is important to note that the model-specific approaches and the translation-specific approaches are often complementary and can be used together to further improve the translation performance and reduce the computational complexity.

3 Approximate Learning Approach to Very Large Target Vocabulary

3.1 Description

In this paper, we propose a *model-specific* approach that allows us to train a neural machine translation model with a very large target vocabulary. With the proposed approach, the compu-

[1] This is due to the fact that the beam search requires the conditional probability of *every* target word at each time step regardless of the parametrization of the output probability.

tational complexity of training becomes constant with respect to the size of the target vocabulary. Furthermore, the proposed approach allows us to efficiently use a fast computing device with limited memory, such as a GPU, to train a neural machine translation model with a much larger target vocabulary.

As mentioned earlier, the computational inefficiency of training a neural machine translation model arises from the normalization constant in Eq. (6). In order to avoid the growing complexity of computing the normalization constant, we propose here to use only a small subset V' of the target vocabulary at each update. The proposed approach is based on the earlier work of (Bengio and Sénécal, 2008).

Let us consider the gradient of the log-probability of the output in Eq. (6). The gradient is composed of a positive and negative part:

$$\nabla \log p(y_t \mid y_{<t}, x) \qquad (8)$$
$$= \nabla \mathcal{E}(y_t) - \sum_{k: y_k \in V} p(y_k \mid y_{<t}, x) \nabla \mathcal{E}(y_k),$$

where we define the energy $\mathcal{E}$ as

$$\mathcal{E}(y_j) = \mathbf{w}_j^\top \phi(y_{j-1}, z_j, c_j) + b_j.$$

The second, or negative, term of the gradient is in essence the expected gradient of the energy:

$$\mathbb{E}_P \left[\nabla \mathcal{E}(y) \right], \qquad (9)$$

where P denotes $p(y \mid y_{<t}, x)$.

The main idea of the proposed approach is to approximate this expectation, or the negative term of the gradient, by importance sampling with a small number of samples. Given a predefined proposal distribution Q and a set V' of samples from Q, we approximate the expectation in Eq. (9) with

$$\mathbb{E}_P \left[\nabla \mathcal{E}(y) \right] \approx \sum_{k: y_k \in V'} \frac{\omega_k}{\sum_{k': y_{k'} \in V'} \omega_{k'}} \nabla \mathcal{E}(y_k), \qquad (10)$$

where

$$\omega_k = \exp \left\{ \mathcal{E}(y_k) - \log Q(y_k) \right\}. \qquad (11)$$

This approach allows us to compute the normalization constant during training using only a small subset of the target vocabulary, resulting in much lower computational complexity for each parameter update. Intuitively, at each parameter update, we update only the vectors associated with the correct word $\mathbf{w}_t$ and with the sampled words in V'. Once training is over, we can use the full target vocabulary to compute the output probability of each target word.

Although the proposed approach naturally addresses the computational complexity, using this approach naively does not guarantee that the number of parameters being updated for each sentence pair, which includes multiple target words, is bounded nor can be controlled. This becomes problematic when training is done, for instance, on a GPU with limited memory.

In practice, hence, we partition the training corpus and define a subset V' of the target vocabulary for each partition prior to training. Before training begins, we sequentially examine each target sentence in the training corpus and accumulate unique target words until the number of unique target words reaches the predefined threshold τ. The accumulated vocabulary will be used for this partition of the corpus during training. We repeat this until the end of the training set is reached. Let us refer to the subset of target words used for the i-th partition by V'_i.

This may be understood as having a separate proposal distribution Q_i for each partition of the training corpus. The distribution Q_i assigns equal probability mass to all the target words included in the subset V'_i, and zero probability mass to all the other words, i.e.,

$$Q_i(y_k) = \begin{cases} \frac{1}{|V'_i|} & \text{if } y_t \in V'_i \\ 0 & \text{otherwise.} \end{cases}$$

This choice of proposal distribution cancels out the correction term $-\log Q(y_k)$ from the importance weight in Eqs. (10)–(11), which makes the proposed approach equivalent to approximating the exact output probability in Eq. (6) with

$$p(y_t \mid y_{<t}, x) = \frac{\exp \left\{ \mathbf{w}_t^\top \phi(y_{t-1}, z_t, c_t) + b_t \right\}}{\sum_{k: y_k \in V'} \exp \left\{ \mathbf{w}_k^\top \phi(y_{t-1}, z_t, c_t) + b_k \right\}}.$$

It should be noted that this choice of Q makes the estimator biased.

The proposed procedure results in speed up against usual importance sampling, as it exploits the advantage of modern computers in doing matrix-matrix vs matrix-vector multiplications.

3.1.1 Informal Discussion on Consequence

The parametrization of the output probability in Eq. (6) can be understood as arranging the vectors associated with the target words such that the dot product between the most likely, or correct, target word's vector and the current hidden state is maximized. The exponentiation followed by normalization is simply a process in which the dot products are converted into proper probabilities.

As learning continues, therefore, the vectors of all the likely target words tend to align with each other but not with the others. This is achieved exactly by moving the vector of the correct word in the direction of $\phi(y_{t-1}, z_t, c_t)$, while pushing all the other vectors away, which happens when the gradient of the logarithm of the exact output probability in Eq. (6) is maximized. Our approximate approach, instead, moves the word vectors of the correct words and of only a subset of sampled target words (those included in V').

3.2 Decoding

Once the model is trained using the proposed approximation, we can use the full target vocabulary when decoding a translation given a new source sentence. Although this is advantageous as it allows the trained model to utilize the whole vocabulary when generating a translation, doing so may be too computationally expensive, e.g., for real-time applications.

Since training puts the target word vectors in the space so that they align well with the hidden state of the decoder only when they are likely to be a correct word, we can use only a subset of candidate target words during decoding. This is similar to what we do during training, except that at test time, we do not have access to a set of correct target words.

The most naïve way to select a subset of candidate target words is to take only the top-K most frequent target words, where K can be adjusted to meet the computational requirement. This, however, effectively cancels out the whole purpose of training a model with a very large target vocabulary. Instead, we can use an existing word alignment model to align the source and target words in the training corpus and build a dictionary. With the dictionary, for each source sentence, we construct a target word set consisting of the K-most frequent words (according to the estimated unigram probability) and, using the dictionary, at most K' likely target words for each source word. K and K' may be chosen either to meet the computational requirement or to maximize the translation performance on the development set. We call a subset constructed in either of these ways a *candidate list*.

3.3 Source Words for Unknown Words

In the experiments, we evaluate the proposed approach with the neural machine translation model called RNNsearch (Bahdanau et al., 2015) (see Sec. 2.1.1). In this model, as a part of decoding process, we obtain the alignments between the target words and source locations via the alignment model in Eq. (5).

We can use this feature to infer the source word to which each target word was most aligned (indicated by the largest α_t in Eq. (5)). This is especially useful when the model generated an [UNK] token. Once a translation is generated given a source sentence, each [UNK] may be replaced using a translation-specific technique based on the aligned source word. For instance, in the experiment, we try replacing each [UNK] token with the aligned source word or its most likely translation determined by another word alignment model. Other techniques such as transliteration may also be used to further improve the performance (Koehn, 2010).

4 Experiments

We evaluate the proposed approach in English→French and English→German translation tasks. We trained the neural machine translation models using only the bilingual, parallel corpora made available as a part of WMT'14. For each pair, the datasets we used are:

- English→French:[2]
  - Common Crawl
  - News Commentary
  - Gigaword
  - Europarl v7
  - UN
- English→German:
  - Common Crawl
  - News Commentary
  - Europarl v7

[2]The preprocessed data can be found and downloaded from `http://www-lium.univ-lemans.fr/~schwenk/nnmt-shared-task/README`.

	English-French		English-German	
	Train	Test	Train	Test
15k	93.5	90.8	88.5	83.8
30k	96.0	94.6	91.8	87.9
50k	97.3	96.3	93.7	90.4
500k	99.5	99.3	98.4	96.1
All	100.0	99.6	100.0	97.3

Table 1: Data coverage (in %) on target-side corpora for different vocabulary sizes. "All" refers to all the tokens in the training set.

To ensure fair comparison, the English→French corpus, which comprises approximately 12 million sentences, is identical to the one used in (Kalchbrenner and Blunsom, 2013; Bahdanau et al., 2015; Sutskever et al., 2014). As for English→German, the corpus was preprocessed, in a manner similar to (Peitz et al., 2014; Li et al., 2014), in order to remove many poorly translated sentences.

We evaluate the models on the WMT'14 test set (news-test 2014),[3] while the concatenation of news-test-2012 and news-test-2013 is used for model selection (development set). Table 1 presents data coverage w.r.t. the vocabulary size, on the target side.

Unless mentioned otherwise, all reported BLEU scores (Papineni et al., 2002) are computed with the multi-bleu.perl script[4] on the cased tokenized translations.

4.1 Settings

As a baseline for English→French translation, we use the **RNNsearch** model proposed by (Bahdanau et al., 2015), with 30k source and target words.[5] Another RNNsearch model is trained for English→German translation with 50k source and target words.

For each language pair, we train another set of RNNsearch models with much larger vocabularies of 500k source and target words, using the proposed approach. We call these models **RNNsearch-LV**. We vary the size of the shortlist used during training (τ in Sec. 3.1). We tried 15k and 30k for English→French, and 15k and 50k for English→German. We later report the results for the best performance on the development set, with models generally evaluated every twelve hours. The training speed is approximately the same as for RNNsearch. Using a 780 Ti or Titan Black GPU, we could process 100k mini-batches of 80 sentences in about 29 and 39 hours respectively for $\tau = 15k$ and $\tau = 50k$.

For both language pairs, we also trained new models, with $\tau = 15k$ and $\tau = 50k$, by reshuffling the dataset at the beginning of each epoch. While this causes a non-negligible amount of overhead, such a change allows words to be contrasted with different sets of other words each epoch.

To stabilize parameters other than the word embeddings, at the end of the training stage, we freeze the word embeddings and tune only the other parameters for approximately two more days after the peak performance on the development set is observed. This helped increase BLEU scores on the development set.

We use beam search to generate a translation given a source. During beam search, we keep a set of 12 hypotheses and normalize probabilities by the length of the candidate sentences, as in (Cho et al., 2014a).[6] The candidate list is chosen to maximize the performance on the development set, for $K \in \{15k, 30k, 50k\}$ and $K' \in \{10, 20\}$. As explained in Sec. 3.2, we test using a bilingual dictionary to accelerate decoding and to replace unknown words in translations. The bilingual dictionary is built using *fast_align* (Dyer et al., 2013). We use the dictionary only if a word starts with a lowercase letter, and otherwise, we copy the source word directly. This led to better performance on the development sets.

Note on ensembles For each language pair, we began training four models from each of which two points corresponding to the best and second-best performance on the development set were collected. We continued training from each point, while keeping the word embeddings fixed, until the best development performance was reached, and took the model at this point as a single model in an ensemble. This procedure resulted in a total of eight models from which we averaged the length-normalized log-probabilities. Since much of training had been shared, the composition of

[3] To compare with previous submissions, we use the filtered test sets.

[4] `https://github.com/moses-smt/mosesdecoder/blob/master/scripts/generic/multi-bleu.perl`

[5] The authors of (Bahdanau et al., 2015) gave us access to their trained models. We chose the best one on the validation set and resumed training.

[6] These experimental details differ from (Bahdanau et al., 2015).

	RNNsearch	RNNsearch-LV	Google	Phrase-based SMT	
Basic NMT	29.97 (26.58)	32.68 (28.76)	30.6⋆	33.3*	37.03•
+Candidate List	–	33.36 (29.32)	–		
+UNK Replace	33.08 (29.08)	34.11 (29.98)	33.1°		
+Reshuffle (τ=50k)	–	34.60 (30.53)	–		
+Ensemble	–	37.19 (31.98)	37.5°		

(a) English→French

	RNNsearch	RNNsearch-LV	Phrase-based SMT
Basic NMT	16.46 (17.13)	16.95 (17.85)	20.67◇
+Candidate List	–	17.46 (18.00)	
+UNK Replace	18.97 (19.16)	18.89 (19.03)	
+Reshuffle	–	19.40 (19.37)	
+Ensemble	–	21.59 (21.06)	

(b) English→German

Table 2: The translation performances in BLEU obtained by different models on (a) English→French and (b) English→German translation tasks. RNNsearch is the model proposed in (Bahdanau et al., 2015), RNNsearch-LV is the RNNsearch trained with the approach proposed in this paper, and Google is the LSTM-based model proposed in (Sutskever et al., 2014). Unless mentioned otherwise, we report single-model RNNsearch-LV scores using $\tau = 30k$ (English→French) and $\tau = 50k$ (English→German). For the experiments we have run ourselves, we show the scores on the development set as well in the brackets. (⋆) (Sutskever et al., 2014), (∘) (Luong et al., 2015), (•) (Durrani et al., 2014), (∗) Standard Moses Setting (Cho et al., 2014b), (◇) (Buck et al., 2014).

such ensembles may be sub-optimal. This is supported by the fact that higher cross-model BLEU scores (Freitag et al., 2014) are observed for models that were partially trained together.

4.2 Translation Performance

In Table 2, we present the results obtained by the trained models with very large target vocabularies, and alongside them, the previous results reported in (Sutskever et al., 2014), (Luong et al., 2015), (Buck et al., 2014) and (Durrani et al., 2014). Without translation-specific strategies, we can clearly see that the RNNsearch-LV outperforms the baseline RNNsearch.

In the case of the English→French task, RNNsearch-LV approached the performance level of the previous best single neural machine translation (NMT) model, even without any translation-specific techniques (Sec. 3.2–3.3). With these, however, the RNNsearch-LV outperformed it. The performance of the RNNsearch-LV is also better than that of a standard phrase-based translation system (Cho et al., 2014b). Furthermore, by combining 8 models, we were able to achieve a translation performance comparable to the state of the art, measured in BLEU.

For English→German, the RNNsearch-LV outperformed the baseline before unknown word replacement, but after doing so, the two systems performed similarly. We could reach higher large-vocabulary single-model performance by reshuffling the dataset, but this step could potentially also help the baseline. In this case, we were able to surpass the previously reported best translation result on this task by building an ensemble of 8 models.

With $\tau = 15k$, the RNNsearch-LV performance worsened a little, with best BLEU scores, without reshuffling, of 33.76 and 18.59 respectively for English→French and English→German.

The English→German ensemble described in this paper has also been used for the shared translation task of the 10th Workshop on Statistical Machine Translation (WMT'15), where it was ranked first in terms of BLEU score. The translations by this ensemble can be found online.[7]

4.3 Analysis

4.3.1 Decoding Speed

In Table 3, we present the timing information of decoding for different models. Clearly, decoding from RNNsearch-LV with the full target vocab-

[7]`http://matrix.statmt.org/matrix/output/1774?run_id=4079`

	CPU*	GPU$^\circ$
RNNsearch	0.09 s	0.02 s
RNNsearch-LV	0.80 s	0.25 s
RNNsearch-LV +Candidate list	0.12 s	0.05 s

Table 3: The average per-word decoding time. Decoding here does not include parameter loading and unknown word replacement. The baseline uses 30k words. The candidate list is built with $K = 30k$ and $K' = 10$. ($\star$) i7-4820K (single thread), ($\circ$) GTX TITAN Black

ulary is slowest. If we use a candidate list for decoding each translation, the speed of decoding substantially improves and becomes close to the baseline RNNsearch.

A potential issue with using a candidate list is that for each source sentence, we must re-build a target vocabulary and subsequently replace a part of the parameters, which may easily become time-consuming. We can address this issue, for instance, by building a common candidate list for multiple source sentences. By doing so, we were able to match the decoding speed of the baseline RNNsearch model.

4.3.2 Decoding Target Vocabulary

For English→French ($\tau = 30k$), we evaluate the influence of the target vocabulary when translating the test sentences by using the union of a fixed set of $30k$ common words and (at most) K' likely candidates for each source word according to the dictionary. Results are presented in Figure 1. With $K' = 0$ (not shown), the performance of the system is comparable to the baseline when not replacing the unknown words (30.12), but there is not as much improvement when doing so (31.14). As the large vocabulary model does not predict [UNK] as much during training, it is less likely to generate it when decoding, limiting the effectiveness of the post-processing step in this case. With $K' = 1$, which limits the diversity of allowed uncommon words, BLEU is not as good as with moderately larger K', which indicates that our models can, to some degree, correctly choose between rare alternatives. If we rather use $K = 50k$, as we did for testing based on validation performance, the improvement over $K' = 1$ is approximately 0.2 BLEU.

When validating the choice of K, we found it to be correlated with the value of τ used during

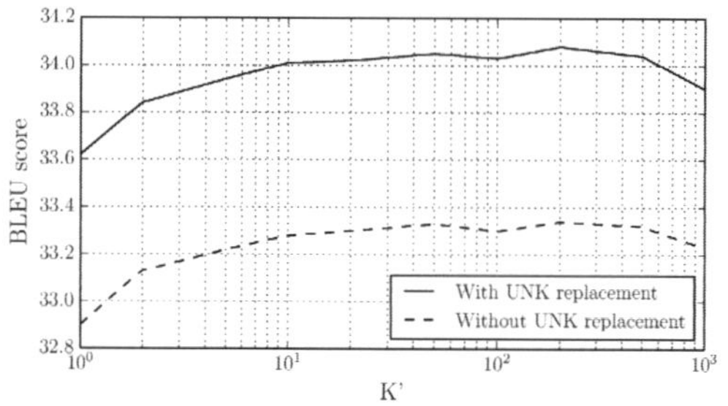

Figure 1: Single-model test BLEU scores (English→French) with respect to the number of dictionary entries K' allowed for each source word.

training. For example, on the English→French validation set, with $\tau = 15k$ (and $K' = 10$), the BLEU score is 29.44 with $K = 15k$, but drops to 29.19 and 28.84 respectively for $K = 30k$ and $50k$. For $\tau = 30k$, the score increases moderately from $K = 15k$ to $K = 50k$. A similar effect was observed for English→German and on the test sets. As our implementation of importance sampling does not apply the usual correction to the gradient, it seems beneficial for the test vocabularies to resemble those used during training.

5 Conclusion

In this paper, we proposed a way to extend the size of the target vocabulary for neural machine translation. The proposed approach allows us to train a model with much larger target vocabulary without any substantial increase in computational complexity. It is based on the earlier work in (Bengio and Sénécal, 2008) which used importance sampling to reduce the complexity of computing the normalization constant of the output word probability in neural language models.

On English→French and English→German translation tasks, we observed that the neural machine translation models trained using the proposed method performed as well as, or better than, those using only limited sets of target words, even when replacing unknown words. As performance of the RNNsearch-LV models increased when only a selected subset of the target vocabulary was used during decoding, this makes the proposed learning algorithm more practical.

When measured by BLEU, our models showed translation performance comparable to the state-of-the-art translation systems on both the English→French task and English→German task. On the English→French task, a model trained with the proposed approach outperformed the best single neural machine translation (NMT) model from (Luong et al., 2015) by approximately 1 BLEU point. The performance of the ensemble of multiple models, despite its relatively less diverse composition, is approximately 0.3 BLEU points away from the best system (Luong et al., 2015). On the English→German task, the best performance of 21.59 BLEU by our model is higher than that of the previous state of the art (20.67) reported in (Buck et al., 2014).

Finally, we release the source code used in our experiments to encourage progress in neural machine translation.[8]

Acknowledgments

The authors would like to thank the developers of Theano (Bergstra et al., 2010; Bastien et al., 2012). We acknowledge the support of the following agencies for research funding and computing support: NSERC, Calcul Québec, Compute Canada, the Canada Research Chairs, CIFAR and Samsung.

References

Dzmitry Bahdanau, Kyunghyun Cho, and Yoshua Bengio. 2015. Neural machine translation by jointly learning to align and translate. In *ICLR'2015, arXiv:1409.0473*.

Frédéric Bastien, Pascal Lamblin, Razvan Pascanu, James Bergstra, Ian J. Goodfellow, Arnaud Bergeron, Nicolas Bouchard, and Yoshua Bengio. 2012. Theano: new features and speed improvements. Deep Learning and Unsupervised Feature Learning NIPS 2012 Workshop.

Yoshua Bengio and Jean-Sébastien Sénécal. 2008. Adaptive importance sampling to accelerate training of a neural probabilistic language model. *IEEE Trans. Neural Networks*, 19(4):713–722.

James Bergstra, Olivier Breuleux, Frédéric Bastien, Pascal Lamblin, Razvan Pascanu, Guillaume Desjardins, Joseph Turian, David Warde-Farley, and Yoshua Bengio. 2010. Theano: a CPU and GPU math expression compiler. In *Proceedings of the Python for Scientific Computing Conference (SciPy)*, June. Oral Presentation.

[8] https://github.com/sebastien-j/LV_groundhog

Christian Buck, Kenneth Heafield, and Bas van Ooyen. 2014. N-gram counts and language models from the common crawl. In *Proceedings of the Language Resources and Evaluation Conference*, Reykjavík, Iceland, May.

Kyunghyun Cho, Bart van Merriënboer, Dzmitry Bahdanau, and Yoshua Bengio. 2014a. On the properties of neural machine translation: Encoder–Decoder approaches. In *Eighth Workshop on Syntax, Semantics and Structure in Statistical Translation*, October.

Kyunghyun Cho, Bart van Merrienboer, Caglar Gulcehre, Fethi Bougares, Holger Schwenk, and Yoshua Bengio. 2014b. Learning phrase representations using RNN encoder-decoder for statistical machine translation. In *Proceedings of the Empiricial Methods in Natural Language Processing (EMNLP 2014)*, October.

Nadir Durrani, Barry Haddow, Philipp Koehn, and Kenneth Heafield. 2014. Edinburgh's phrase-based machine translation systems for WMT-14. In *Proceedings of the Ninth Workshop on Statistical Machine Translation*, pages 97–104. Association for Computational Linguistics Baltimore, MD, USA.

Chris Dyer, Victor Chahuneau, and Noah A. Smith. 2013. A simple, fast, and effective reparameterization of IBM Model 2. In *Proceedings of the 2013 Conference of the North American Chapter of the Association for Computational Linguistics: Human Language Technologies*, pages 644–648, Atlanta, Georgia, June. Association for Computational Linguistics.

Mikel L. Forcada and Ramón P. Ñeco. 1997. Recursive hetero-associative memories for translation. In José Mira, Roberto Moreno-Díaz, and Joan Cabestany, editors, *Biological and Artificial Computation: From Neuroscience to Technology*, volume 1240 of *Lecture Notes in Computer Science*, pages 453–462. Springer Berlin Heidelberg.

Markus Freitag, Stephan Peitz, Joern Wuebker, Hermann Ney, Matthias Huck, Rico Sennrich, Nadir Durrani, Maria Nadejde, Philip Williams, Philipp Koehn, et al. 2014. Eu-bridge MT: Combined machine translation. In *Proc. of the Workshop on Statistical Machine Translation*, pages 105–113.

M. Gutmann and A. Hyvarinen. 2010. Noise-contrastive estimation: A new estimation principle for unnormalized statistical models. In *Proceedings of The Thirteenth International Conference on Artificial Intelligence and Statistics (AISTATS'10)*.

Nal Kalchbrenner and Phil Blunsom. 2013. Recurrent continuous translation models. In *Proceedings of the ACL Conference on Empirical Methods in Natural Language Processing (EMNLP)*, pages 1700–1709. Association for Computational Linguistics.

Philipp Koehn, Franz Josef Och, and Daniel Marcu. 2003. Statistical phrase-based translation. In *Proceedings of the 2003 Conference of the North American Chapter of the Association for Computational Linguistics on Human Language Technology - Volume 1*, NAACL '03, pages 48–54.

Philipp Koehn. 2010. *Statistical Machine Translation*. Cambridge University Press, New York, NY, USA, 1st edition.

Liangyou Li, Xiaofeng Wu, Santiago Cortes Vaillo, Jun Xie, Andy Way, and Qun Liu. 2014. The DCU-ICTCAS MT system at WMT 2014 on German-English translation task. In *Proceedings of the Ninth Workshop on Statistical Machine Translation*, pages 136–141, Baltimore, Maryland, USA, June. Association for Computational Linguistics.

Minh-Thang Luong, Ilya Sutskever, Quoc V. Le, Oriol Vinyals, and Wojciech Zaremba. 2015. Addressing the rare word problem in neural machine translation. In *Proceedings of ACL*.

Tomas Mikolov, Kai Chen, Greg Corrado, and Jeffrey Dean. 2013. Efficient estimation of word representations in vector space. In *International Conference on Learning Representations: Workshops Track*.

Andriy Mnih and Koray Kavukcuoglu. 2013. Learning word embeddings efficiently with noise-contrastive estimation. In C.J.C. Burges, L. Bottou, M. Welling, Z. Ghahramani, and K.Q. Weinberger, editors, *Advances in Neural Information Processing Systems 26*, pages 2265–2273. Curran Associates, Inc.

Kishore Papineni, Salim Roukos, Todd Ward, and Wei-Jing Zhu. 2002. BLEU: A method for automatic evaluation of machine translation. In *Proceedings of the 40th Annual Meeting on Association for Computational Linguistics*, ACL '02, pages 311–318, Stroudsburg, PA, USA. Association for Computational Linguistics.

Stephan Peitz, Joern Wuebker, Markus Freitag, and Hermann Ney. 2014. The RWTH Aachen German-English machine translation system for WMT 2014. In *Proceedings of the Ninth Workshop on Statistical Machine Translation*, pages 157–162, Baltimore, Maryland, USA, June. Association for Computational Linguistics.

Ilya Sutskever, Oriol Vinyals, and Quoc V. Le. 2014. Sequence to sequence learning with neural networks. In *NIPS'2014*.

Addressing the Rare Word Problem in Neural Machine Translation

Minh-Thang Luong[†] [*]
Stanford
lmthang@stanford.edu

Ilya Sutskever[†] Google
Quoc V. Le[†] Google
Oriol Vinyals Google
{ilyasu,qvl,vinyals}@google.com

Wojciech Zaremba[*] New York University
woj.zaremba@gmail.com

Abstract

Neural Machine Translation (NMT) is a new approach to machine translation that has shown promising results that are comparable to traditional approaches. A significant weakness in conventional NMT systems is their inability to correctly translate very rare words: end-to-end NMTs tend to have relatively small vocabularies with a single *unk* symbol that represents every possible out-of-vocabulary (OOV) word. In this paper, we propose and implement an effective technique to address this problem. We train an NMT system on data that is augmented by the output of a word alignment algorithm, allowing the NMT system to emit, for each OOV word in the target sentence, the position of its corresponding word in the source sentence. This information is later utilized in a post-processing step that translates every OOV word using a dictionary. Our experiments on the WMT'14 English to French translation task show that this method provides a substantial improvement of up to 2.8 BLEU points over an equivalent NMT system that does not use this technique. With 37.5 BLEU points, our NMT system is the first to surpass the best result achieved on a WMT'14 contest task.

1 Introduction

Neural Machine Translation (NMT) is a novel approach to MT that has achieved promising results (Kalchbrenner and Blunsom, 2013; Sutskever et al., 2014; Cho et al., 2014; Bahdanau et al., 2015; Jean et al., 2015). An NMT system is a conceptually simple large neural network that reads the entire source sentence and produces an output translation one word at a time. NMT systems are appealing because they use minimal domain knowledge which makes them well-suited to any problem that can be formulated as mapping an input sequence to an output sequence (Sutskever et al., 2014). In addition, the natural ability of neural networks to generalize implies that NMT systems will also generalize to novel word phrases and sentences that do not occur in the training set. In addition, NMT systems potentially remove the need to store explicit phrase tables and language models which are used in conventional systems. Finally, the decoder of an NMT system is easy to implement, unlike the highly intricate decoders used by phrase-based systems (Koehn et al., 2003).

Despite these advantages, conventional NMT systems are incapable of translating rare words because they have a fixed modest-sized vocabulary[1] which forces them to use the *unk* symbol to represent the large number of out-of-vocabulary (OOV) words, as illustrated in Figure 1. Unsurprisingly, both Sutskever et al. (2014) and Bahdanau et al. (2015) have observed that sentences with many rare words tend to be translated much more poorly than sentences containing mainly frequent words. Standard phrase-based systems (Koehn et al., 2007; Chiang, 2007; Cer et al., 2010; Dyer et al., 2010), on the other hand, do not suffer from the rare word problem to the same extent because they can support a much larger vocabulary, and because their use of explicit alignments and phrase tables allows them to memorize the translations of even extremely rare words.

Motivated by the strengths of standard phrase-

*Work done while the authors were in Google. † indicates equal contribution.

[1]Due to the computationally intensive nature of the softmax, NMT systems often limit their vocabularies to be the top 30K-80K most frequent words in each language. However, Jean et al. (2015) has very recently proposed an efficient approximation to the softmax that allows for training NTMs with very large vocabularies. As discussed in Section 2, this technique is complementary to ours.

Proceedings of the 53rd Annual Meeting of the Association for Computational Linguistics and the 7th International Joint Conference on Natural Language Processing, pages 11–19,
Beijing, China, July 26-31, 2015.

en: The *ecotax* portico in *Pont-de-Buis* , . . . [truncated] . . . , was taken down on Thursday morning

fr: Le *portique* *écotaxe* de *Pont-de-Buis* , . . . [truncated] . . . , a été *démonté* jeudi matin

nn: Le `unk` de `unk` à `unk` , . . . [truncated] . . . , a été pris le jeudi matin

Figure 1: **Example of the rare word problem** – An English source sentence (*en*), a human translation to French (*fr*), and a translation produced by one of our neural network systems (*nn*) before handling OOV words. We highlight *words* that are unknown to our model. The token `unk` indicates an OOV word. We also show a few important alignments between the pair of sentences.

based system, we propose and implement a novel approach to address the rare word problem of NMTs. Our approach annotates the training corpus with explicit alignment information that enables the NMT system to emit, for each OOV word, a "pointer" to its corresponding word in the source sentence. This information is later utilized in a post-processing step that translates the OOV words using a dictionary or with the identity translation, if no translation is found.

Our experiments confirm that this approach is effective. On the English to French WMT'14 translation task, this approach provides an improvement of up to 2.8 (if the vocabulary is relatively small) BLEU points over an equivalent NMT system that does not use this technique. Moreover, our system is the first NMT that outperforms the winner of a WMT'14 task.

2 Neural Machine Translation

A neural machine translation system is any neural network that maps a source sentence, $s_1, \ldots, s_n$, to a target sentence, $t_1, \ldots, t_m$, where all sentences are assumed to terminate with a special "end-of-sentence" token <eos>. More concretely, an NMT system uses a neural network to parameterize the conditional distributions

$$p(t_j | t_{<j}, s_{\leq n}) \quad (1)$$

for $1 \leq j \leq m$. By doing so, it becomes possible to compute and therefore maximize the log probability of the target sentence given the source sentence

$$\log p(t|s) = \sum_{j=1}^{m} \log p\left(t_j | t_{<j}, s_{\leq n}\right) \quad (2)$$

There are many ways to parameterize these conditional distributions. For example, Kalchbrenner and Blunsom (2013) used a combination of a convolutional neural network and a recurrent neural network, Sutskever et al. (2014) used a deep Long Short-Term Memory (LSTM) model, Cho et al. (2014) used an architecture similar to the LSTM, and Bahdanau et al. (2015) used a more elaborate neural network architecture that uses an attentional mechanism over the input sequence, similar to Graves (2013) and Graves et al. (2014).

In this work, we use the model of Sutskever et al. (2014), which uses a deep LSTM to encode the input sequence and a separate deep LSTM to output the translation. The encoder reads the source sentence, one word at a time, and produces a large vector that represents the entire source sentence. The decoder is initialized with this vector and generates a translation, one word at a time, until it emits the end-of-sentence symbol <eos>.

None the early work in neural machine translation systems has addressed the rare word problem, but the recent work of Jean et al. (2015) has tackled it with an efficient approximation to the softmax to accommodate for a very large vocabulary (500K words). However, even with a large vocabulary, the problem with rare words, e.g., names, numbers, etc., still persists, and Jean et al. (2015) found that using techniques similar to ours are beneficial and complementary to their approach.

3 Rare Word Models

Despite the relatively large amount of work done on pure neural machine translation systems, there has been no work addressing the OOV problem in NMT systems, with the notable exception of Jean et al. (2015)'s work mentioned earlier.

We propose to address the rare word problem by training the NMT system to track the origins of the unknown words in the target sentences. If we knew the source word responsible for each un-en: The $\underline{unk_1}$ portico in $\underline{unk_2}$ ...

fr: Le $\underline{unk_\emptyset}$ $\underline{unk_1}$ de $\underline{unk_2}$ ...

Figure 2: **Copyable Model** – an annotated example with two types of unknown tokens: "copyable" $\underline{unk_n}$ and null $\underline{unk_\emptyset}$.

en: The $\underline{unk}$ portico in $\underline{unk}$ ...

fr: Le p_0 $\underline{unk}$ p_{-1} $\underline{unk}$ p_1 de $p_\emptyset$ $\underline{unk}$ p_{-1} ...

Figure 3: **Positional All Model** – an example of the PosAll model. Each word is followed by the relative positional tokens p_d or the null token $p_\emptyset$.

known target word, we could introduce a post-processing step that would replace each $\underline{unk}$ in the system's output with a translation of its source word, using either a dictionary or the identity translation. For example, in Figure 1, if the model knows that the second unknown token in the NMT (line *nn*) originates from the source word `ecotax`, it can perform a word dictionary lookup to replace that unknown token by `écotaxe`. Similarly, an identity translation of the source word `Pont-de-Buis` can be applied to the third unknown token.

We present three annotation strategies that can easily be applied to any NMT system (Kalchbrenner and Blunsom, 2013; Sutskever et al., 2014; Cho et al., 2014). We treat the NMT system as a black box and train it on a corpus annotated by one of the models below. First, the alignments are produced with an unsupervised aligner. Next, we use the alignment links to construct a word dictionary that will be used for the word translations in the post-processing step.[2] If a word does not appear in our dictionary, then we apply the identity translation.

The first few words of the sentence pair in Figure 1 (lines *en* and *fr*) illustrate our models.

3.1 Copyable Model

In this approach, we introduce multiple tokens to represent the various unknown words in the source and in the target language, as opposed to using only one $\underline{unk}$ token. We annotate the OOV words in the source sentence with $\underline{unk_1}$, $\underline{unk_2}$, $\underline{unk_3}$, in that order, while assigning repeating unknown words identical tokens. The annotation of the unknown words in the target language is slightly more elaborate: (a) each unknown target word that is aligned to an unknown source word is assigned the same unknown token (hence, the "copy" model) and (b) an unknown target word that has no alignment or that is aligned with a known word uses the special null token $\underline{unk_\emptyset}$. See Figure 2 for an example. This annotation enables us to translate every non-null unknown token.

3.2 Positional All Model (PosAll)

The copyable model is limited by its inability to translate unknown target words that are aligned to *known* words in the source sentence, such as the pair of words, "portico" and "portique", in our running example. The former word is known on the source sentence; whereas latter is not, so it is labelled with $\underline{unk_\emptyset}$. This happens often since the source vocabularies of our models tend to be much larger than the target vocabulary since a large source vocabulary is cheap. This limitation motivated us to develop an annotation model that includes the complete alignments between the source and the target sentences, which is straightforward to obtain since the complete alignments are available at training time.

Specifically, we return to using only a single universal $\underline{unk}$ token. However, on the target side, we insert a positional token p_d after every word. Here, d indicates a relative position ($d = -7, \ldots, -1, 0, 1, \ldots, 7$) to denote that a target word at position j is aligned to a source word at position $i = j - d$. Aligned words that are too far apart are considered unaligned, and unaligned words rae annotated with a null token p_n. Our annotation is illustrated in Figure 3.

3.3 Positional Unknown Model (PosUnk)

The main weakness of the PosAll model is that it doubles the length of the target sentence. This makes learning more difficult and slows the speed of parameter updates by a factor of two. However, given that our post-processing step is concerned only with the alignments of the unknown words, so it is more sensible to only annotate the unknown words. This motivates our *positional unknown* model which uses $\mathtt{unkpos}_d$ tokens (for d in $-7, \ldots, 7$ or $\emptyset$) to simultaneously denote (a)

[2]When a source word has multiple translations, we use the translation with the highest probability. These translation probabilities are estimated from the unsupervised alignment links. When constructing the dictionary from these alignment links, we add a word pair to the dictionary only if its alignment count exceeds 100.

the fact that a word is unknown and (b) its relative position d with respect to its aligned source word. Like the PosAll model, we use the symbol $\underline{\texttt{unkpos}_\emptyset}$ for unknown target words that do not have an alignment. We use the universal $\underline{\texttt{unk}}$ for all unknown tokens in the source language. See Figure 4 for an annotated example.

en: The $\underline{\texttt{unk}}$ portico in $\underline{\texttt{unk}}$ ...

fr: Le $\underline{\texttt{unkpos}_1}$ $\underline{\texttt{unkpos}_{-1}}$ de $\underline{\texttt{unkpos}_1}$ ...

Figure 4: **Positional Unknown Model** – an example of the PosUnk model: only aligned unknown words are annotated with the $\texttt{unkpos}_d$ tokens.

It is possible that despite its slower speed, the PosAll model will learn better alignments because it is trained on many more examples of words and their alignments. However, we show that this is not the case (see §5.2).

4 Experiments

We evaluate the effectiveness of our OOV models on the WMT'14 English-to-French translation task. Translation quality is measured with the BLEU metric (Papineni et al., 2002) on the newstest2014 test set (which has 3003 sentences).

4.1 Training Data

To be comparable with the results reported by previous work on neural machine translation systems (Sutskever et al., 2014; Cho et al., 2014; Bahdanau et al., 2015), we train our models on the same training data of 12M parallel sentences (348M French and 304M English words), obtained from (Schwenk, 2014). The 12M subset was selected from the full WMT'14 parallel corpora using the method proposed in Axelrod et al. (2011).

Due to the computationally intensive nature of the naive softmax, we limit the French vocabulary (the *target* language) to the either the 40K or the 80K most frequent French words. On the *source* side, we can afford a much larger vocabulary, so we use the 200K most frequent English words. The model treats all other words as unknowns.[3]

We annotate our training data using the three schemes described in the previous section. The alignment is computed with the Berkeley aligner (Liang et al., 2006) using its default settings. We discard sentence pairs in which the source or the target sentence exceed 100 tokens.

4.2 Training Details

Our training procedure and hyperparameter choices are similar to those used by Sutskever et al. (2014). In more details, we train multi-layer deep LSTMs, each of which has 1000 cells, with 1000 dimensional embeddings. Like Sutskever et al. (2014), we reverse the words in the source sentences which has been shown to improve LSTM memory utilization and results in better translations of long sentences. Our hyperparameters can be summarized as follows: (a) the parameters are initialized uniformly in [-0.08, 0.08] for 4-layer models and [-0.06, 0.06] for 6-layer models, (b) SGD has a fixed learning rate of 0.7, (c) we train for 8 epochs (after 5 epochs, we begin to halve the learning rate every 0.5 epoch), (d) the size of the mini-batch is 128, and (e) we rescale the normalized gradient to ensure that its norm does not exceed 5 (Pascanu et al., 2012).

We also follow the GPU parallelization scheme proposed in (Sutskever et al., 2014), allowing us to reach a training speed of 5.4K words per second to train a depth-6 model with 200K source and 80K target vocabularies ; whereas Sutskever et al. (2014) achieved 6.3K words per second for a depth-4 models with 80K source and target vocabularies. Training takes about 10-14 days on an 8-GPU machine.

4.3 A note on BLEU scores

We report BLEU scores based on both: (a) *detokenized* translations, i.e., WMT'14 style, to be comparable with results reported on the WMT website[4] and (b) *tokenized translations*, so as to be consistent with previous work (Cho et al., 2014; Bahdanau et al., 2015; Schwenk, 2014; Sutskever et al., 2014; Jean et al., 2015).[5]

The existing WMT'14 state-of-the-art system (Durrani et al., 2014) achieves a detokenized BLEU score of 35.8 on the newstest2014 test set for English to French language pair (see Table 2). In terms of the tokenized BLEU, its performance is 37.0 points (see Table 1).

[3]When the French vocabulary has 40K words, there are on average 1.33 unknown words per sentence on the target side of the test set.

[4]`http://matrix.statmt.org/matrix`

[5]The `tokenizer.perl` and `multi-bleu.pl` scripts are used to tokenize and score translations.

System	Vocab	Corpus	BLEU
State of the art in WMT'14 (Durrani et al., 2014)	All	36M	**37.0**
Standard MT + neural components			
Schwenk (2014) – neural language model	All	12M	33.3
Cho et al. (2014)– phrase table neural features	All	12M	34.5
Sutskever et al. (2014) – 5 LSTMs, reranking 1000-best lists	All	12M	36.5
Existing end-to-end NMT systems			
Bahdanau et al. (2015) – single gated RNN with search	30K	12M	28.5
Sutskever et al. (2014) – 5 LSTMs	80K	12M	34.8
Jean et al. (2015) – 8 gated RNNs with search + UNK replacement	500K	12M	37.2
Our end-to-end NMT systems			
Single LSTM with 4 layers	40K	12M	29.5
Single LSTM with 4 layers + PosUnk	40K	12M	31.8 (+2.3)
Single LSTM with 6 layers	40K	12M	30.4
Single LSTM with 6 layers + PosUnk	40K	12M	32.7 (+2.3)
Ensemble of 8 LSTMs	40K	12M	34.1
Ensemble of 8 LSTMs + PosUnk	40K	12M	36.9 (+2.8)
Single LSTM with 6 layers	80K	36M	31.5
Single LSTM with 6 layers + PosUnk	80K	36M	33.1 (+1.6)
Ensemble of 8 LSTMs	80K	36M	35.6
Ensemble of 8 LSTMs + PosUnk	80K	36M	**37.5 (+1.9)**

Table 1: **Tokenized BLEU on newstest2014** – Translation results of various systems which differ in terms of: (a) the architecture, (b) the size of the vocabulary used, and (c) the training corpus, either using the full WMT'14 corpus of 36M sentence pairs or a subset of it with 12M pairs. We highlight the performance of our best system in bolded text and state the improvements obtained by our technique of handling rare words (namely, the PosUnk model). Notice that, for a given vocabulary size, the more accurate systems achieve a greater improvement from the post-processing step. This is the case because the more accurate models are able to pin-point the origin of an unknown word with greater accuracy, making the post-processing more useful.

System	BLEU
Existing SOTA (Durrani et al., 2014)	35.8
Ensemble of 8 LSTMs + PosUnk	**36.6**

Table 2: **Detokenized BLEU on newstest2014** – translation results of the existing state-of-the-art system and our best system.

4.4 Main Results

We compare our systems to others, including the current state-of-the-art MT system (Durrani et al., 2014), recent end-to-end neural systems, as well as phrase-based baselines with neural components.

The results shown in Table 1 demonstrate that our unknown word translation technique (in particular, the PosUnk model) significantly improves the translation quality for both the individual (non-ensemble) LSTM models and the ensemble models.[6] For 40K-word vocabularies, the performance gains are in the range of 2.3-2.8 BLEU points. With larger vocabularies (80K), the performance gains are diminished, but our technique can still provide a nontrivial gains of 1.6-1.9 BLEU points.

It is interesting to observe that our approach is more useful for ensemble models as compared to the individual ones. This is because the usefulness of the PosUnk model directly depends on the ability of the NMT to correctly locate, for a given OOV target word, its corresponding word in the source sentence. An ensemble of large models identifies these source words with greater accuracy. This is why for the same vocabulary size, better models obtain a greater performance gain

[6]For the 40K-vocabulary ensemble, we combine 5 models with 4 layers and 3 models with 6 layers. For the 80K-vocabulary ensemble, we combine 3 models with 4 layers and 5 models with 6 layers. Two of the depth-6 models are regularized with dropout, similar to Zaremba et al. (2015) with the dropout probability set to 0.2.

our post-processing step. e Except for the very recent work of Jean et al. (2015) that employs a similar unknown treatment strategy[7] as ours, our best result of 37.5 BLEU outperforms all other NMT systems by a arge margin, and more importanly, our system has established a new record on the WMT'14 English to French translation.

5 Analysis

We analyze and quantify the improvement obtained by our rare word translation approach and provide a detailed comparison of the different rare word techniques proposed in Section 3. We also examine the effect of depth on the LSTM architectures and demonstrate a strong correlation between perplexities and BLEU scores. We also highlight a few translation examples where our models succeed in correctly translating OOV words, and present several failures.

5.1 Rare Word Analysis

To analyze the effect of rare words on translation quality, we follow Sutskever et al. (Sutskever et al., 2014) and sort sentences in newstest2014 by the average inverse frequency of their words. We split the test sentences into groups where the sentences within each group have a comparable number of rare words and evaluate each group independently. We evaluate our systems before and after translating the OOV words and compare with the standard MT systems – we use the best system from the WMT'14 contest (Durrani et al., 2014), and neural MT systems – we use the ensemble systems described in (Sutskever et al., 2014) and Section 4.

Rare word translation is challenging for neural machine translation systems as shown in Figure 5. Specifically, the translation quality of our model before applying the postprocessing step is shown by the green curve, and the current best NMT system (Sutskever et al., 2014) is the purple curve. While (Sutskever et al., 2014) produces better translations for sentences with frequent words (the left part of the graph), they are worse than best

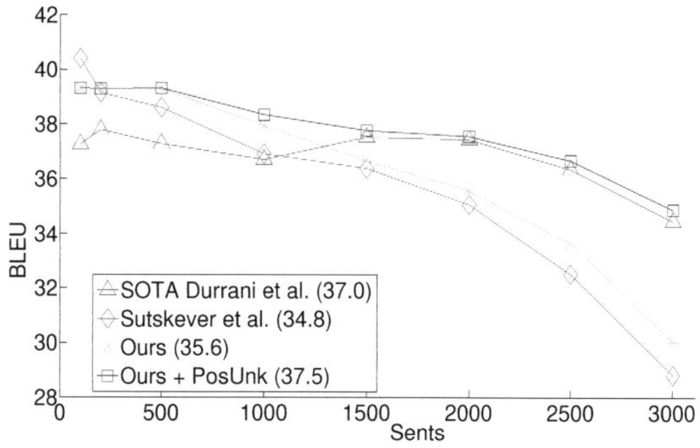

Figure 5: **Rare word translation** – On the x-axis, we order newstest2014 sentences by their *average frequency rank* and divide the sentences into groups of sentences with a comparable prevalence of rare words. We compute the BLEU score of each group independently.

system (red curve) on sentences with many rare words (the right side of the graph). When applying our unknown word translation technique (purple curve), we significantly improve the translation quality of our NMT: for the last group of 500 sentences which have the greatest proportion of OOV words in the test set, we increase the BLEU score of our system by 4.8 BLEU points. Overall, our rare word translation model interpolates between the SOTA system and the system of Sutskever et al. (2014), which allows us to outperform the winning entry of WMT'14 on sentences that consist predominantly of frequent words and approach its performance on sentences with many OOV words.

5.2 Rare Word Models

We examine the effect of the different rare word models presented in Section 3, namely: (a) *Copyable* – which aligns the unknown words on both the input and the target side by learning to copy indices, (b) the Positional All (*PosAll*) – which predicts the aligned source positions for every target word, and (c) the Positional Unknown (*PosUnk*) – which predicts the aligned source positions for only the unknown target words.[8] It is also interest-

[7]Their unknown replacement method and ours both track the locations of target unknown words and use a word dictionary to post-process the translation. However, the mechanism used to achieve the "tracking" behavior is different. Jean et al. (2015)'s uses the attentional mechanism to track the origins of all target words, not just the unknown ones. In contrast, we only focus on tracking unknown words using unsupervised alignments. Our method can be easily applied to any sequence-to-sequence models since we treat any model as a blackbox and manipulate only at the input and output levels.

[8]In this section and in section 5.3, all models are trained on the unreversed sentences, and we use the following hyperparameters: we initialize the parameters uniformly in [-0.1, 0.1], the learning rate is 1, the maximal gradient norm is 1, with a source vocabulary of 90k words, and a target vocabulary of 40k (see Section 4.2 for more details). While these LSTMs do not achieve the best possible performance, it is still useful to analyze them.

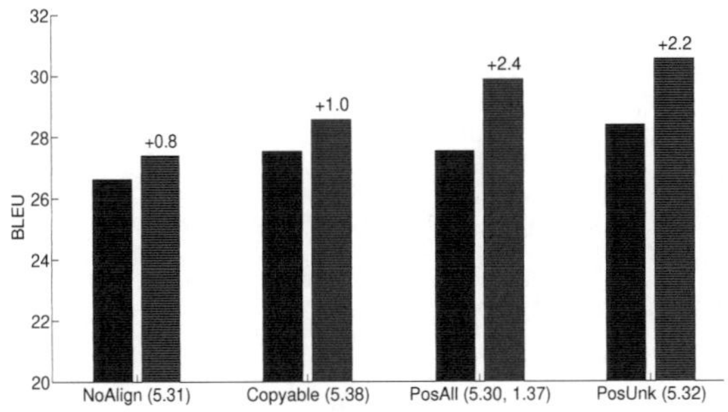

Figure 6: **Rare word models** – translation performance of 6-layer LSTMs: a model that uses no alignment (*NoAlign*) and the other rare word models (*Copyable, PosAll, PosUnk*). For each model, we show results before (*left*) and after (*right*) the rare word translation as well as the perplexity (in parentheses). For *PosAll*, we report the perplexities of predicting the words and the positions.

ing to measure the improvement obtained when no alignment information is used during training. As such, we include a baseline model with no alignment knowledge (*NoAlign*) in which we simply assume that the ith unknown word on the target sentence is aligned to the ith unknown word in the source sentence.

From the results in Figure 6, a simple monotone alignment assumption for the *NoAlign* model yields a modest gain of 0.8 BLEU points. If we train the model to predict the alignment, then the *Copyable* model offers a slightly better gain of 1.0 BLEU. Note, however, that English and French have similar word order structure, so it would be interesting to experiment with other language pairs, such as English and Chinese, in which the word order is not as monotonic. These harder language pairs potentially imply a smaller gain for the NoAlign model and a larger gain for the Copyable model. We leave it for future work.

The positional models (*PosAll* and *PosUnk*) improve translation performance by more than 2 BLEU points. This proves that the limitation of the copyable model, which forces it to align each unknown output word with an unknown input word, is considerable. In contrast, the positional models can align the unknown target words with any source word, and as a result, post-processing has a much stronger effect. The PosUnk model achieves better translation results than the PosAll model which suggests that it is easier to train the LSTM on shorter sequences.

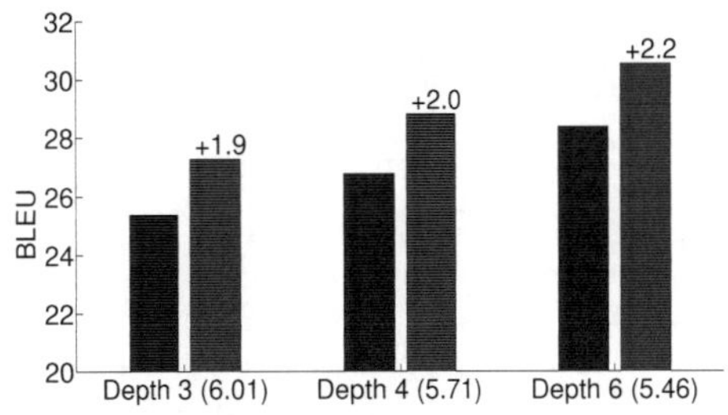

Figure 7: **Effect of depths** – BLEU scores achieved by *PosUnk* models of various depths (3, 4, and 6) before and after the rare word translation. Notice that the PosUnk model is more useful on more accurate models.

5.3 Other Effects

Deep LSTM architecture – We compare PosUnk models trained with different number of layers (3, 4, and 6). We observe that the gain obtained by the PosUnk model increases in tandem with the overall accuracy of the model, which is consistent with the idea that larger models can point to the appropriate source word more accurately. Additionally, we observe that on average, each extra LSTM layer provides roughly 1.0 BLEU point improvement as demonstrated in Figure 7.

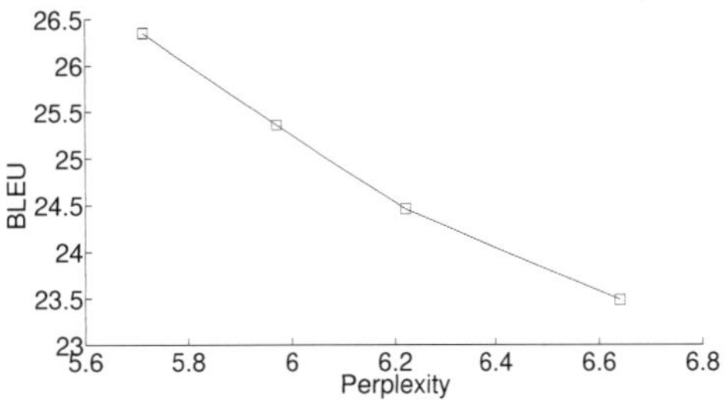

Figure 8: **Perplexity vs. BLEU** – we show the correlation by evaluating an LSTM model with 4 layers at various stages of training.

Perplexity and BLEU – Lastly, we find it interesting to observe a strong correlation between the perplexity (our training objective) and the translation quality as measured by BLEU. Figure 8 shows the performance of a 4-layer LSTM, in which we compute both perplexity and BLEU scores at different points during training. We find that on average, a reduction of 0.5 perplexity gives us roughly 1.0 BLEU point improvement.

	Sentences
src	An additional *2600* operations including *orthopedic* and *cataract* surgery will help clear a backlog .
trans	En outre , $\underline{\texttt{unkpos}_1}$ opérations supplémentaires , dont la chirurgie $\underline{\texttt{unkpos}_5}$ et la $\underline{\texttt{unkpos}_6}$, permettront de résorber l' arriéré .
+unk	En outre , *2600* opérations supplémentaires , dont la chirurgie *orthopédiques* et la *cataracte* , permettront de résorber l' arriéré .
tgt	2600 opérations supplémentaires , notamment dans le domaine de la chirurgie orthopédique et de la cataracte , aideront à rattraper le retard .
src	This *trader* , Richard *Usher* , left RBS in *2010* and is understand to have be given leave from his current position as European head of forex spot trading at *JPMorgan* .
trans	Ce $\underline{\texttt{unkpos}_0}$, Richard $\underline{\texttt{unkpos}_0}$, a quitté $\underline{\texttt{unkpos}_1}$ en 2010 et a compris qu' il est autorisé à quitter son poste actuel en tant que leader européen du marché des points de vente au $\underline{\texttt{unkpos}_5}$.
+unk	Ce *négociateur* , Richard *Usher* , a quitté RBS en *2010* et a compris qu' il est autorisé à quitter son poste actuel en tant que leader européen du marché des points de vente au *JPMorgan* .
tgt	Ce trader , Richard Usher , a quitté RBS en 2010 et aurait été mis suspendu de son poste de responsable européen du trading au comptant pour les devises chez JPMorgan
src	But concerns have grown after Mr *Mazanga* was quoted as saying *Renamo was* abandoning the 1992 peace accord .
trans	Mais les inquiétudes se sont accrues après que M. $\underline{\texttt{unkpos}_3}$ a déclaré que la $\underline{\texttt{unkpos}_3}$ $\underline{\texttt{unkpos}_3}$ l' accord de paix de 1992 .
+unk	Mais les inquiétudes se sont accrues après que M. *Mazanga* a déclaré que la *Renamo était* l' accord de paix de 1992 .
tgt	Mais l' inquiétude a grandi après que M. Mazanga a déclaré que la Renamo abandonnait l' accord de paix de 1992 .

Table 3: **Sample translations** – the table shows the source (*src*) and the translations of our best model before (*trans*) and after (*+unk*) unknown word translations. We also show the human translations (*tgt*) and italicize words that are involved in the unknown word translation process.

5.4 Sample Translations

We present three sample translations of our best system (with 37.5 BLEU) in Table 3. In our first example, the model translates all the unknown words correctly: *2600*, *orthopédiques*, and *cataracte*. It is interesting to observe that the model can accurately predict an alignment of distances of 5 and 6 words. The second example highlights the fact that our model can translate long sentences reasonably well and that it was able to correctly translate the unknown word for *JPMorgan* at the very far end of the source sentence. Lastly, our examples also reveal several penalties incurred by our model: (a) incorrect entries in the word dictionary, as with *négociateur* vs. *trader* in the second example, and (b) incorrect alignment prediction, such as when $\texttt{unkpos}_3$ is incorrectly aligned with the source word *was* and not with *abandoning*, which resulted in an incorrect translation in the third sentence.

6 Conclusion

We have shown that a simple alignment-based technique can mitigate and even overcome one of the main weaknesses of current NMT systems, which is their inability to translate words that are not in their vocabulary. A key advantage of our technique is the fact that it is applicable to any NMT system and not only to the deep LSTM model of Sutskever et al. (2014). A technique like ours is likely necessary if an NMT system is to achieve state-of-the-art performance on machine translation.

We have demonstrated empirically that on the

WMT'14 English-French translation task, our technique yields a consistent and substantial improvement of up to 2.8 BLEU points over various NMT systems of different architectures. Most importantly, with 37.5 BLEU points, we have established the first NMT system that outperformed the best MT system on a WMT'14 contest dataset.

Acknowledgments

We thank members of the Google Brain team for thoughtful discussions and insights. The first author especially thanks Chris Manning and the Stanford NLP group for helpful comments on the early drafts of the paper. Lastly, we thank the annonymous reviewers for their valuable feedback.

References

Amittai Axelrod, Xiaodong He, and Jianfeng Gao. 2011. Domain adaptation via pseudo in-domain data selection. In *EMNLP*.

D. Bahdanau, K. Cho, and Y. Bengio. 2015. Neural machine translation by jointly learning to align and translate. In *ICLR*.

D. Cer, M. Galley, D. Jurafsky, and C. D. Manning. 2010. Phrasal: A statistical machine translation toolkit for exploring new model features. In *ACL, Demonstration Session*.

David Chiang. 2007. Hierarchical phrase-based translation. *Computational Linguistics*, 33(2):201–228.

Kyunghyun Cho, Bart van Merrienboer, Caglar Gulcehre, Fethi Bougares, Holger Schwenk, and Yoshua Bengio. 2014. Learning phrase representations using rnn encoder-decoder for statistical machine translation. In *EMNLP*.

Nadir Durrani, Barry Haddow, Philipp Koehn, and Kenneth Heafield. 2014. Edinburgh's phrase-based machine translation systems for WMT-14. In *WMT*.

Chris Dyer, Jonathan Weese, Hendra Setiawan, Adam Lopez, Ferhan Ture, Vladimir Eidelman, Juri Ganitkevitch, Phil Blunsom, and Philip Resnik. 2010. cdec: A decoder, alignment, and learning framework for finite-state and context-free translation models. In *ACL, Demonstration Session*.

A. Graves, G. Wayne, and I. Danihelka. 2014. Neural turing machines. *arXiv preprint arXiv:1410.5401*.

A. Graves. 2013. Generating sequences with recurrent neural networks. In *Arxiv preprint arXiv:1308.0850*.

Sébastien Jean, Kyunghyun Cho, Roland Memisevic, and Yoshua Bengio. 2015. On using very large target vocabulary for neural machine translation. In *ACL*.

N. Kalchbrenner and P. Blunsom. 2013. Recurrent continuous translation models. In *EMNLP*.

Philipp Koehn, Franz Josef Och, and Daniel Marcu. 2003. Statistical phrase-based translation. In *NAACL*.

Philipp Koehn, Hieu Hoang, Alexandra Birch, Chris Callison-Burch, Marcello Federico, Nicola Bertoldi, Brooke Cowan, Wade Shen, Christine Moran, Richard Zens, et al. 2007. Moses: Open source toolkit for statistical machine translation. In *ACL, Demonstration Session*.

P. Liang, B. Taskar, and D. Klein. 2006. Alignment by agreement. In *NAACL*.

Kishore Papineni, Salim Roukos, Todd Ward, and Wei jing Zhu. 2002. BLEU: a method for automatic evaluation of machine translation. In *ACL*.

R. Pascanu, T. Mikolov, and Y. Bengio. 2012. On the difficulty of training recurrent neural networks. *arXiv preprint arXiv:1211.5063*.

H. Schwenk. 2014. University le mans. `http://www-lium.univ-lemans.fr/~schwenk/cslm_joint_paper/`. [Online; accessed 03-September-2014].

I. Sutskever, O. Vinyals, and Q. V. Le. 2014. Sequence to sequence learning with neural networks. In *NIPS*.

Wojciech Zaremba, Ilya Sutskever, and Oriol Vinyals. 2015. Recurrent neural network regularization. In *ICLR*.

Encoding Source Language with Convolutional Neural Network for Machine Translation

Fandong Meng[1] **Zhengdong Lu**[2] **Mingxuan Wang**[1] **Hang Li**[2] **Wenbin Jiang**[1] **Qun Liu**[3,1]
[1]Key Laboratory of Intelligent Information Processing,
Institute of Computing Technology, Chinese Academy of Sciences
{mengfandong,wangmingxuan,jiangwenbin,liuqun}@ict.ac.cn
[2]Noah's Ark Lab, Huawei Technologies
{Lu.Zhengdong,HangLi.HL}@huawei.com
[3]ADAPT Centre, School of Computing, Dublin City University

Abstract

The recently proposed neural network joint model (NNJM) (Devlin et al., 2014) augments the n-gram target language model with a heuristically chosen source context window, achieving state-of-the-art performance in SMT. In this paper, we give a more systematic treatment by summarizing the relevant source information through a convolutional architecture guided by the target information. With different guiding signals during decoding, our specifically designed convolution+gating architectures can pinpoint the parts of a source sentence that are relevant to predicting a target word, and fuse them with the context of entire source sentence to form a unified representation. This representation, together with target language words, are fed to a deep neural network (DNN) to form a stronger NNJM. Experiments on two NIST Chinese-English translation tasks show that the proposed model can achieve significant improvements over the previous NNJM by up to +1.08 BLEU points on average.

1 Introduction

Learning of continuous space representation for source language has attracted much attention in both traditional statistical machine translation (SMT) and neural machine translation (NMT). Various models, mostly neural network-based, have been proposed for representing the source sentence, mainly as the encoder part in an encoder-decoder framework (Bengio et al., 2003; Auli et al., 2013; Kalchbrenner and Blunsom, 2013; Cho et al., 2014; Sutskever et al., 2014). There has been some quite recent work on encoding only "relevant" part of source sentence during the decoding process, most notably neural network joint model (NNJM) in (Devlin et al., 2014), which extends the n-grams target language model by additionally taking a fixed-length window of source sentence, achieving state-of-the-art performance in statistical machine translation.

In this paper, we propose novel convolutional architectures to dynamically encode the relevant information in the source language. Our model covers the entire source sentence, but can effectively find and properly summarize the relevant parts, guided by the information from the target language. With the guiding signals during decoding, our specifically designed convolution architectures can pinpoint the parts of a source sentence that are relevant to predicting a target word, and fuse them with the context of entire source sentence to form a unified representation. This representation, together with target words, are fed to a deep neural network (DNN) to form a stronger NNJM. Since our proposed joint model is purely lexicalized, it can be integrated into any SMT decoder as a feature.

Two variants of the joint model are also proposed, with coined name tagCNN and inCNN, with different guiding signals used from the decoding process. We integrate the proposed joint models into a state-of-the-art dependency-to-string translation system (Xie et al., 2011) to evaluate their effectiveness. Experiments on NIST Chinese-English translation tasks show that our model is able to achieve significant improvements of +2.0 BLEU points on average over the baseline. Our model also outperforms Devlin et al. (2014)'s NNJM by up to +1.08 BLEU points.

Proceedings of the 53rd Annual Meeting of the Association for Computational Linguistics and the 7th International Joint Conference on Natural Language Processing, pages 20–30,
Beijing, China, July 26-31, 2015.

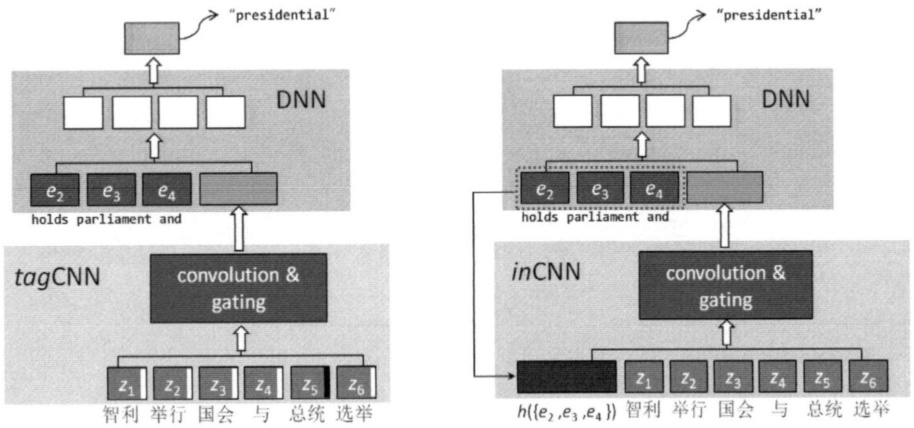

(a) tagCNN (b) inCNN

Figure 1: Illustration for joint LM based on CNN encoder.

RoadMap: In the remainder of this paper, we start with a brief overview of joint language model in Section 2, while the convolutional encoders, as the key component of which, will be described in detail in Section 3. Then in Section 4 we discuss the decoding algorithm with the proposed models. The experiment results are reported in Section 5, followed by Section 6 and 7 for related work and conclusion.

2 Joint Language Model

Our joint model with CNN encoders can be illustrated in Figure 1 (a) & (b), which consists 1) a CNN encoder, namely tagCNN or inCNN, to represent the information in the source sentences, and 2) an NN-based model for predicting the next words, with representations from CNN encoders and the history words in target sentence as inputs.

In the joint language model, the probability of the target word $\mathbf{e}_n$, given previous k target words $\{\mathbf{e}_{n-k}, \cdots, \mathbf{e}_{n-1}\}$ and the representations from CNN-encoders for source sentence S are

$$tag\text{CNN:} \quad p(\mathbf{e}_n | \phi_1(S, \{a(\mathbf{e}_n)\}), \{\mathbf{e}\}_{n-k}^{n-1})$$

$$in\text{CNN:} \quad p(\mathbf{e}_n | \phi_2(S, h(\{\mathbf{e}\}_{n-k}^{n-1})), \{\mathbf{e}\}_{n-k}^{n-1}),$$

where $\phi_1(S, \{a(\mathbf{e}_n)\})$ stands for the representation given by tagCNN with the set of indexes $\{a(\mathbf{e}_n)\}$ of source words aligned to the target word $\mathbf{e}_n$, and $\phi_2(S, h(\{\mathbf{e}\}_{n-k}^{n-1}))$ stands for the representation from inCNN with the attention signal $h(\{\mathbf{e}\}_{n-k}^{n-1})$.

Let us use the example in Figure 1, where the task is to translate the Chinese sentence

Chinese: 智利 举行 国会 与 总统 选举
Pinyin: Zhìlì Jǔxíng Guóhuì Yǔ Zǒngtǒng Xuǎnjǔ

into English. In evaluating a target language sequence "`holds parliament and presidential`", with "`holds parliament and`" as the proceeding words (assume 4-gram LM), and the affiliated source word[1] of "`presidential`" being "`Zǒngtǒng`" (determined by word alignment), tagCNN generates $\phi_1(S, \{4\})$ (the index of "`Zǒngtǒng`" is 4), and inCNN generates $\phi_2(S, h(\texttt{holds parliament and}))$. The DNN component then takes `"holds parliament and"` and (ϕ_1 or ϕ_2) as input to give the conditional probability for next word, e.g., $p(\texttt{"presidential"}|\phi_{1|2}, \{\texttt{holds, parliament, and}\})$.

3 Convolutional Models

We start with the generic architecture for convolutional encoder, and then proceed to tagCNN and inCNN as two extensions.

[1] For an aligned target word, we take its aligned source words as its affiliated source words. And for an unaligned word, we inherit its affiliation from the closest aligned word, with preference given to the right (Devlin et al., 2014). Since the word alignment is of many-to-many, one target word may has multi affiliated source words.

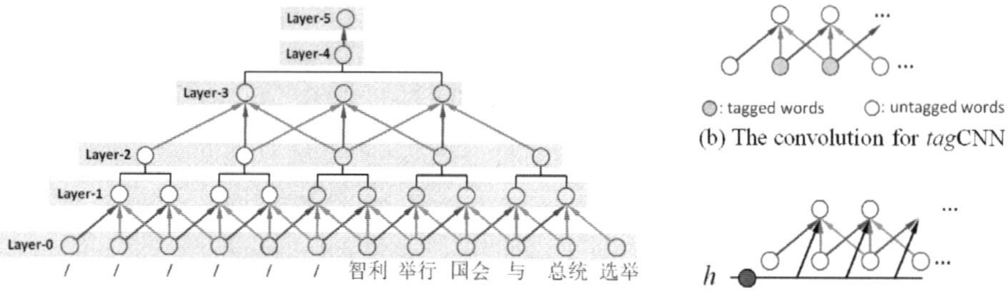

(a) The generic architecture for CNN encoder

(b) The convolution for *tag*CNN

(c) The convolution for *in*CNN

Figure 2: Illustration for the CNN encoders.

3.1 Generic CNN Encoder

The basic architecture is of a generic CNN encoder is illustrated in Figure 2 (a), which has a fixed architecture consisting of six layers:

Layer-0: the input layer, which takes words in the form of embedding vectors. In our work, we set the maximum length of sentences to 40 words. For sentences shorter than that, we put zero padding at the beginning of sentences.

Layer-1: a convolution layer after Layer-0, with window size = 3. As will be discussed in Section 3.2 and 3.3, the guiding signal are injected into this layer for "guided version".

Layer-2: a local gating layer after Layer-1, which simply takes a weighted sum over feature-maps in non-adjacent window with size = 2.

Layer-3: a convolution layer after Layer-2, we perform another convolution with window size = 3.

Layer-4: we perform a global gating over feature-maps on Layer-3.

Layer-5: fully connected weights that maps the output of Layer-4 to this layer as the final representation.

3.1.1 Convolution

As shown in Figure 2 (a), the convolution in Layer-1 operates on sliding windows of words (width k_1), and the similar definition of windows carries over to higher layers. Formally, for source sentence input $\mathbf{x} = \{\mathbf{x}_1, \cdots, \mathbf{x}_N\}$, the convolution unit for feature map of type-f (among F_ℓ of them) on Layer-ℓ is

$$z_i^{(\ell,f)}(\mathbf{x}) = \sigma(\mathbf{w}^{(\ell,f)}\hat{\mathbf{z}}_i^{(\ell-1)} + b^{(\ell,f)}),$$
$$\ell = 1, 3, \qquad f = 1, 2, \cdots, F_\ell \quad (1)$$

where

- $z_i^{(\ell,f)}(\mathbf{x})$ gives the output of feature map of type-f for location i in Layer-ℓ;
- $\mathbf{w}^{(\ell,f)}$ is the parameters for f on Layer-ℓ;
- $\sigma(\cdot)$ is the Sigmoid activation function;
- $\hat{\mathbf{z}}_i^{(\ell-1)}$ denotes the segment of Layer-$\ell-1$ for the convolution at location i , while

  $$\hat{\mathbf{z}}_i^{(0)} \stackrel{\text{def}}{=} [\mathbf{x}_i^\top,\ \mathbf{x}_{i+1}^\top,\ \mathbf{x}_{i+2}^\top]^\top$$

  concatenates the vectors for 3 words from sentence input $\mathbf{x}$.

3.1.2 Gating

Previous CNNs, including those for NLP tasks (Hu et al., 2014; Kalchbrenner et al., 2014), take a straightforward convolution-pooling strategy, in which the "fusion" decisions (e.g., selecting the largest one in max-pooling) are based on the values of feature-maps. This is essentially a soft template matching, which works for tasks like classification, but harmful for keeping the composition functionality of convolution, which is critical for modeling sentences. In this paper, we propose to use separate gating unit to release the score function duty from the convolution, and let it focus on composition.

We take two types of gating: 1) for Layer-2, we take a local gating with non-overlapping windows (size = 2) on the feature-maps of convolutional Layer-1 for representation of segments, and 2) for Layer-4, we take a global gating to fuse all the segments for a global representation. We found that this gating strategy can considerably improve the performance of both tagCNN and inCNN over pooling.

- **Local Gating:** On Layer-1, for every gating window, we first find its original input (before convolution) on Layer-0, and merge them for the input of the gating network. For example, for the two windows: word (3,4,5) and word (4,5,6) on Layer-0, we use concatenated vector consisting of embedding for word (3,4,5,6) as the input of the local gating network (a logistic regression model) to determine the weight for the convolution result of the two windows (on Layer-1), and the weighted sum are the output of Layer-2.

- **Global Gating:** On Layer-3, for feature-maps at each location i, denoted $\mathbf{z}_i^{(3)}$, the global gating network (essentially soft-max, parameterized $\mathbf{w}_g$), assigns a normalized weight

$$\omega(\mathbf{z}_i^{(3)}) = e^{\mathbf{w}_g^\top \mathbf{z}_i^{(3)}} / \sum_j e^{\mathbf{w}_g^\top \mathbf{z}_j^{(3)}},$$

  and the gated representation on Layer-4 is given by the weighted sum $\sum_i \omega(\mathbf{z}_i^{(3)})\mathbf{z}_i^{(3)}$.

3.1.3 Training of CNN encoders

The CNN encoders, including tagCNN and inCNN that will be discussed right below, are trained in a joint language model described in Section 2, along with the following parameters

- the embedding of the words on source and the proceeding words on target;

- the parameters for the DNN of joint language model, include the parameters of soft-max for word probability.

The training procedure is identical to that of neural network language model, except that the parallel corpus is used instead of a monolingual corpus. We seek to maximize the log-likelihood of training samples, with one sample for every target word in the parallel corpus. Optimization is performed with the conventional back-propagation, implemented as stochastic gradient descent (LeCun et al., 1998) with mini-batches.

3.2 tagCNN

tagCNN inherits the convolution and gating from generic CNN (as described in Section 3.1), with the only modification in the input layer. As shown in Figure 2 (b), in tagCNN, we append an extra tagging bit (0 or 1) to the embedding of words in the input layer to indicate whether it is one of affiliated words

$$\mathbf{x}_i^{(\text{AFF})} = [\mathbf{x}_i^\top \; 1]^\top, \quad \mathbf{x}_j^{(\text{NON-AFF})} = [\mathbf{x}_j^\top \; 0]^\top.$$

Those extended word embedding will then be treated as regular word-embedding in the convolutional neural network. This particular encoding strategy can be extended to embed more complicated dependency relation in source language, as will be described in Section 5.4.

This particular "tag" will be activated in a parameterized way during the training for predicting the target words. In other words, the supervised signal from the words to predict will find, through layers of back-propagation, the importance of the tag bit in the "affiliated words" in the source language, and learn to put proper weight on it to make tagged words stand out and adjust other parameters in tagCNN accordingly for the optimal predictive performance. In doing so, the joint model can pinpoint the parts of a source sentence that are relevant to predicting a target word through the already learned word alignment.

3.3 inCNN

Unlike tagCNN, which directly tells the location of affiliated words to the CNN encoder, inCNN sends the information about the proceeding words in target side to the convolutional encoder to help retrieve the information relevant for predicting the next word. This is essentially a particular case of attention model, analogous to the automatic alignment mechanism in (Bahdanau et al., 2014), where the at-

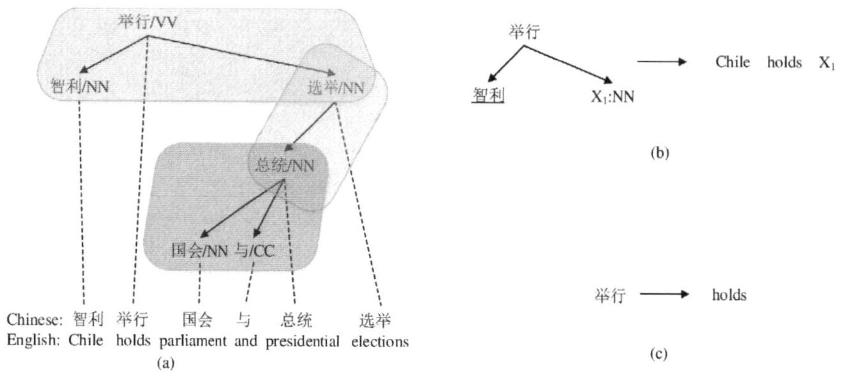

Figure 3: Illustration for a dependency tree (a) with three head-dependents relations in shadow, an example of head-dependents relation rule (b) for the top level of (a), and an example of head rule (c). "X_1:NN" indicates a substitution site that can be replaced by a subtree whose root has part-of-speech "NN". The underline denotes a leaf node.

tention signal is from the state of a generative recurrent neural network (RNN) as decoder.

Basically, the information from proceeding words, denoted as $h(\{\mathbf{e}\}_{n-k}^{n-1})$, is injected into every convolution window in the source language sentence, as illustrated in Figure 2 (c). More specifically, for the window indexed by t, the input to convolution is given by the concatenated vector

$$\hat{\mathbf{z}}_t = [h(\{\mathbf{e}\}_{n-k}^{n-1}),\ \mathbf{x}_t^\top,\ \mathbf{x}_{t+1}^\top,\ \mathbf{x}_{t+2}^\top]^\top.$$

In this work, we use a DNN to transform the vector concatenated from word-embedding for words $\{\mathbf{e}_{n-k}\cdots,\mathbf{e}_{n-k}\}$ into $h(\{\mathbf{e}\}_{n-k}^{n-1})$, with sigmoid activation function. Through layers of convolution and gating, *in*CNN can 1) retrieve the relevant segments of source sentences, and 2) compose and transform the retrieved segments into representation recognizable by the DNN in predicting the words in target language. Different from that of *tag*CNN, *in*CNN uses information from proceeding words, hence provides complementary information in the augmented joint language model of *tag*CNN. This has been empirically verified when using feature based on *tag*CNN and that based on *in*CNN in decoding with greater improvement.

4 Decoding with the Joint Model

Our joint model is purely lexicalized, and therefore can be integrated into *any* SMT decoders as a feature. For a hierarchical SMT decoder, we adopt the integrating method proposed by Devlin et al. (2014). As inherited from the n-gram language model for performing hierarchical decoding, the leftmost and rightmost $n-1$ words from each constituent should be stored in the state space. We extend the state space to also include the indexes of the affiliated source words for each of these edge words. For an aligned target word, we take its aligned source words as its affiliated source words. And for an unaligned word, we use the affiliation heuristic adopted by Devlin et al. (2014). In this paper, we integrate the joint model into the state-of-the-art dependency-to-string machine translation decoder as a case study to test the efficacy of our proposed approaches. We will briefly describe the dependency-to-string translation model and then the description of MT system.

4.1 Dependency-to-String Translation

In this paper, we use a state-of-the-art dependency-to-string (Xie et al., 2011) decoder (Dep2Str), which is also a hierarchical decoder. This dependency-to-string model employs rules that represent the source side as head-dependents relations and the target side as strings. A head-dependents relation (HDR) is composed of a head and all its dependents in dependency trees. Figure 3 shows a dependency tree (a) with three HDRs (in shadow), an example of HDR rule (b) for the top level of (a), and an example of head rule (c). HDR rules are constructed from head-dependents relations. HDR rules can act as both translation rules and reordering rules. And head rules are used for translating source words.

We adopt the decoder proposed by Meng et al. (2013) as a variant of Dep2Str translation that is easier to implement with comparable performance. Basically they extract the HDR rules with GHKM (Galley et al., 2004) algorithm. For the decoding procedure, given a source dependency tree T, the decoder transverses T in post-order. The bottom-up chart-based decoding algorithm with cube pruning (Chiang, 2007; Huang and Chiang, 2007) is used to find the k-best items for each node.

4.2 MT Decoder

Following Och and Ney (2002), we use a general loglinear framework. Let d be a derivation that convert a source dependency tree into a target string e. The probability of d is defined as:

$$P(d) \propto \prod_i \phi_i(d)^{\lambda_i} \tag{2}$$

where ϕ_i are features defined on derivations and λ_i are the corresponding weights. Our decoder contains the following features:

Baseline Features:

- translation probabilities $P(t|s)$ and $P(s|t)$ of HDR rules;
- lexical translation probabilities $P_{\text{LEX}}(t|s)$ and $P_{\text{LEX}}(s|t)$ of HDR rules;
- rule penalty $\exp(-1)$;
- pseudo translation rule penalty $\exp(-1)$;
- target word penalty $\exp(|e|)$;
- n-gram language model $P_{\text{LM}}(e)$;

Proposed Features:

- n-gram tagCNN joint language model $P_{\text{TLM}}(e)$;
- n-gram inCNN joint language model $P_{\text{ILM}}(e)$.

Our baseline decoder contains the first eight features. The pseudo translation rule (constructed according to the word order of a HDR) is to ensure the complete translation when no matched rules is found during decoding. The weights of all these features are tuned via minimum error rate training (MERT) (Och, 2003). For the dependency-to-string decoder, we set rule-threshold and stack-threshold to 10^{-3}, rule-limit to 100, stack-limit to 200.

5 Experiments

The experiments in this Section are designed to answer the following questions:

1. Are our tagCNN and inCNN joint language models able to improve translation quality, and are they complementary to each other?
2. Do inCNN and tagCNN benefit from their guiding signal, compared to a generic CNN?
3. For tagCNN, is it helpful to embed more dependency structure, e.g., dependency head of each affiliated word, as additional information?
4. Can our gating strategy improve the performance over max-pooling?

5.1 Setup

Data: Our training data are extracted from LDC data[2]. We only keep the sentence pairs that the length of source part no longer than 40 words, which covers over 90% of the sentence. The bilingual training data consist of 221K sentence pairs, containing 5.0 million Chinese words and 6.8 million English words. The development set is NIST MT03 (795 sentences) and test sets are MT04 (1499 sentences) and MT05 (917 sentences) after filtering with length limit.

Preprocessing: The word alignments are obtained with GIZA++ (Och and Ney, 2003) on the corpora in both directions, using the "grow-diag-final-and" balance strategy (Koehn et al., 2003). We adopt SRI Language Modeling

[2]The corpora include LDC2002E18, LDC2003E07, LDC2003E14, LDC2004T07, LDC2005T06.

Systems	MT04	MT05	Average
Moses	34.33	31.75	33.04
Dep2Str	34.89	32.24	33.57
+ BBN-JM (Devlin et al., 2014)	36.11	32.86	34.49
+ CNN (generic)	36.12*	33.07*	34.60
+ *tag*CNN	36.33*	**33.37***	34.85
+ *in*CNN	**36.92***	**33.72***	35.32
+ *tag*CNN + *in*CNN	**36.94***	**34.20***	35.57

Table 1: BLEU-4 scores (%) on NIST MT04-test and MT05-test, of Moses (default settings), dependency-to-string baseline system (Dep2Str), and different features on top of Dep2Str: neural network joint model (BBN-JM), generic CNN, *tag*CNN, *in*CNN and the combination of *tag*CNN and *in*CNN. The boldface numbers and superscript * indicate that the results are significantly better (p<0.01) than those of the BBN-JM and the Dep2Str baseline respectively. "+" stands for adding the corresponding feature to Dep2Str.

Toolkit (Stolcke and others, 2002) to train a 4-gram language model with modified Kneser-Ney smoothing on the Xinhua portion of the English Gigaword corpus (306 million words). We parse the Chinese sentences with Stanford Parser into projective dependency trees.

Optimization of NN: In training the neural network, we limit the source and target vocabulary to the most frequent 20K words for both Chinese and English, covering approximately 97% and 99% of two corpus respectively. All the out-of-vocabulary words are mapped to a special token UNK. We used stochastic gradient descent to train the joint model, setting the size of minibatch to 500. All joint models used a 3-word target history (i.e., 4-gram LM). The dimension of word embedding and the attention signal $h(\{\mathbf{e}\}_{n-k}^{n-1})$ for *in*CNN are 100. For the convolution layers (Layer 1 and Layer 3), we apply 100 filters. And the final representation of CNN encoders is a vector with dimension 100. The final DNN layer of our joint model is the standard multi-layer perceptron with softmax at the top layer.

Metric: We use the case-insensitive 4-gram NIST BLEU[3] as our evaluation metric, with statistical significance test with *sign-test* (Collins et al., 2005) between the proposed models and two baselines.

[3]ftp://jaguar.ncsl.nist.gov/mt/resources/mteval-v11b.pl

5.2 Setting for Model Comparisons

We use the *tag*CNN and *in*CNN joint language models as additional decoding features to a dependency-to-string baseline system (Dep2Str), and compare them to the neural network joint model with 11 source context words (Devlin et al., 2014). We use the implementation of an open source toolkit[4] with default configuration except the global settings described in Section 5.1. Since our *tag*CNN and *in*CNN models are source-to-target and left-to-right (on target side), we only take the source-to-target and left-to-right type NNJM in (Devlin et al., 2014) in comparison. We call this type NNJM as BBN-JM hereafter. Although the BBN-JM in (Devlin et al., 2014) is originally tested in the hierarchical phrase-based (Chiang, 2007) SMT and string-to-dependency (Shen et al., 2008) SMT, it is fairly versatile and can be readily integrated into Dep2Str.

5.3 The Main Results

The main results of different models are given in Table 1. Before proceeding to more detailed comparison, we first observe that

- the baseline Dep2Str system gives BLEU 0.5+ higher than the open-source phrase-based system Moses (Koehn et al., 2007);
- BBN-JM can give about +0.92 BLEU score over Dep2Str, a result similar as reported in (Devlin et al., 2014).

[4]http://nlg.isi.edu/software/nplm/

Systems	MT04	MT05	Average
Dep2str	34.89	32.24	33.57
+*tag*CNN	36.33	33.37	34.85
+*tag*CNN_dep	36.54	33.61	35.08

Table 2: BLEU-4 scores (%) of *tag*CNN model with dependency head words as additional tags (*tag*CNN_dep).

Clearly from Table 1, *tag*CNN and *in*CNN improve upon the Dep2Str baseline by +1.28 and +1.75 BLEU, outperforming BBN-JM in the same setting by respectively +0.36 and +0.83 BLEU, averaged on NIST MT04 and MT05. These indicate that *tag*CNN and *in*CNN can individually provide discriminative information in decoding. It is worth noting that *in*CNN appears to be more informative than the affiliated words suggested by the word alignment (GIZA++). We conjecture that this is due to the following two facts

- *in*CNN avoids the propagation of mistakes and artifacts in the already learned word alignment;
- the guiding signal in *in*CNN provides complementary information to evaluate the translation.

Moreover, when *tag*CNN and *in*CNN are both used in decoding, it can further increase its winning margin over BBN-JM to +1.08 BLEU points (in the last row of Table 1), indicating that the two models with different guiding signals are complementary to each other.

The Role of Guiding Signal It is slight surprising that the generic CNN can also achieve the gain on BLEU similar to that of BBN-JM, since intuitively generic CNN encodes the entire sentence and the representations should in general far from optimal representation for joint language model. The reason, as we conjecture, is CNN yields fairly informative summarization of the sentence (thanks to its sophisticated convolution and gating architecture), which makes up some of its loss on resolution and relevant parts of the source senescence. That said, the guiding signal in both *tag*CNN and *in*CNN are crucial to the

Systems	MT04	MT05	Average
Dep2Str	34.89	32.24	33.57
+*in*CNN	36.92	33.72	35.32
+*in*CNN-2-pooling	36.33	32.88	34.61
+*in*CNN-4-pooling	36.46	33.01	34.74
+*in*CNN-8-pooling	36.57	33.39	34.98

Table 3: BLEU-4 scores (%) of *in*CNN models implemented with gating strategy and k max-pooling, where k is of $\{2, 4, 8\}$.

power of CNN-based encoder, as can be easily seen from the difference between the BLEU scores achieved by generic CNN, *tag*CNN, and *in*CNN. Indeed, with the signal from the already learned word alignment, *tag*CNN can gain +0.25 BLEU over its generic counterpart, while for *in*CNN with the guiding signal from the proceeding words in target, the gain is more saliently +0.72 BLEU.

5.4 Dependency Head in *tag*CNN

In this section, we study whether *tag*CNN can further benefit from encoding richer dependency structure in source language in the input. More specifically, the dependency head words can be used to further improve *tag*CNN model. As described in Section 3.2, in *tag*CNN, we append a tagging bit (0 or 1) to the embedding of words in the input layer as tags on whether they are affiliated source words. To incorporate dependency head information, we extend the tagging rule in Section 3.2 to add another tagging bit (0 or 1) to the word-embedding for original *tag*CNN to indicate whether it is part of dependency heads of the affiliated words. For example, if $\mathbf{x}_i$ is the embedding of an affiliated source word and $\mathbf{x}_j$ the dependency head of word $\mathbf{x}_i$, the extended input of tagCNN would contain

$$\mathbf{x}_i^{(\text{AFF, NON-HEAD})} = [\mathbf{x}_i^\top \ 1 \ 0]^\top$$
$$\mathbf{x}_j^{(\text{NON-AFF, HEAD})} = [\mathbf{x}_j^\top \ 0 \ 1]^\top$$

If the affiliated source word is the root of a sentence, we only append 0 as the second tagging bit since the root has no dependency head. From Table 2, with the help of dependency head information, we can improve *tag*CNN by +0.23 BLEU points averagely on two test sets.

5.5 Gating Vs. Max-pooling

In this section, we investigate to what extent that our gating strategy can improve the translation performance over max pooling, with the comparisons on inCNN model as a case study. For implementation of inCNN with max-pooling, we replace the local-gating (Layer-2) with max-pooling with size 2 (2-pooling for short), and global gating (Layer-4) with k max-pooling ("k-pooling"), where k is of $\{2, 4, 8\}$. Then, we use the mean of the outputs of k-pooling as the final input of Layer-5. In doing so, we can guarantee the input dimension of Layer-5 is the same as the architecture with gating. From Table 3, we can clearly see that our gating strategy can improve translation performance over max-pooling by 0.34~0.71 BLEU points. Moreover, we find 8-pooling yields performance better than 2-pooling. We conjecture that this is because the useful relevant parts for translation are mainly concentrated on a few words of the source sentence, which can be better extracted with a larger pool size.

6 Related Work

The seminal work of neural network language model (NNLM) can be traced to Bengio et al. (2003) on monolingual text. It is recently extended by Devlin et al. (2014) to include additional source context (11 source words) in modeling the target sentence, which is clearly most related to our work, with however two important differences: 1) instead of the ad hoc way of selecting a context window in (Devlin et al., 2014), our model covers the entire source sentence and automatically distill the context relevant for target modeling; 2) our convolutional architecture can effectively leverage guiding signals of vastly different forms and nature from the target.

Prior to our model there is also work on representing source sentences with neural networks, including RNN (Cho et al., 2014; Sutskever et al., 2014) and CNN (Kalchbrenner and Blunsom, 2013). These work typically aim to map the entire sentence to a vector, which will be used later by RNN/LSTM-based decoder to generate the target sentence. As demonstrated in Section 5, the representation learnt this way cannot pinpoint the relevant parts of the source sentences (e.g., words or phrases level) and therefore is inferior to be directly integrated into traditional SMT decoders.

Our model, especially inCNN, is inspired by is the automatic alignment model proposed in (Bahdanau et al., 2014). As the first effort to apply attention model to machine translation, it sends the state of a decoding RNN as attentional signal to the source end to obtain a weighted sum of embedding of source words as the summary of relevant context. In contrast, inCNN uses 1) a different attention signal extracted from proceeding words in partial translations, and 2) more importantly, a convolutional architecture and therefore a highly nonlinear way to retrieve and summarize the relevant information in source.

7 Conclusion and Future Work

We proposed convolutional architectures for obtaining a guided representation of the entire source sentence, which can be used to augment the n-gram target language model. With different guiding signals from target side, we devise tagCNN and inCNN, both of which are tested in enhancing a dependency-to-string SMT with +2.0 BLEU points over baseline and +1.08 BLEU points over the state-of-the-art in (Devlin et al., 2014). For future work, we will consider encoding more complex linguistic structures to further enhance the joint model.

Acknowledgments

Meng, Wang, Jiang and Liu are supported by National Natural Science Foundation of China (Contract 61202216). Liu is partially supported by the Science Foundation Ireland (Grant 12/CE/I2267 and 13/RC/2106) as part of the ADAPT Centre at Dublin City University. We sincerely thank the anonymous reviewers for their thorough reviewing and valuable suggestions.

References

[Auli et al.2013] Michael Auli, Michel Galley, Chris Quirk, and Geoffrey Zweig. 2013. Joint language and translation modeling with recurrent neural networks. In *Proceedings of the*

2013 Conference on Empirical Methods in Natural Language Processing, pages 1044–1054, Seattle, Washington, USA, October.

[Bahdanau et al.2014] Dzmitry Bahdanau, Kyunghyun Cho, and Yoshua Bengio. 2014. Neural machine translation by jointly learning to align and translate. *arXiv preprint arXiv:1409.0473*.

[Bengio et al.2003] Yoshua Bengio, Rjean Ducharme, Pascal Vincent, and Christian Jauvin. 2003. A neural probabilistic language model. *Journal OF Machine Learning Research*, 3:1137–1155.

[Chiang2007] David Chiang. 2007. Hierarchical phrase-based translation. *Computational Linguistics*, 33(2):201–228.

[Cho et al.2014] Kyunghyun Cho, Bart van Merrienboer, Caglar Gulcehre, Dzmitry Bahdanau, Fethi Bougares, Holger Schwenk, and Yoshua Bengio. 2014. Learning phrase representations using rnn encoder–decoder for statistical machine translation. In *Proceedings of the 2014 Conference on Empirical Methods in Natural Language Processing (EMNLP)*, pages 1724–1734, Doha, Qatar, October.

[Collins et al.2005] Michael Collins, Philipp Koehn, and Ivona Kučerová. 2005. Clause restructuring for statistical machine translation. In *Proceedings of the 43rd Annual Meeting on Association for Computational Linguistics*, pages 531–540.

[Devlin et al.2014] Jacob Devlin, Rabih Zbib, Zhongqiang Huang, Thomas Lamar, Richard Schwartz, and John Makhoul. 2014. Fast and robust neural network joint models for statistical machine translation. In *Proceedings of the 52nd Annual Meeting of the Association for Computational Linguistics (Volume 1: Long Papers)*, pages 1370–1380, Baltimore, Maryland, June.

[Galley et al.2004] Michel Galley, Mark Hopkins, Kevin Knight, and Daniel Marcu. 2004. What's in a translation rule. In *Proceedings of HLT/NAACL*, volume 4, pages 273–280. Boston.

[Hu et al.2014] Baotian Hu, Zhengdong Lu, Hang Li, and Qingcai Chen. 2014. Convolutional neural network architectures for matching natural language sentences. In *NIPS*.

[Huang and Chiang2007] Liang Huang and David Chiang. 2007. Forest rescoring: Faster decoding with integrated language models. In *Annual Meeting-Association For Computational Linguistics*, volume 45, pages 144–151.

[Kalchbrenner and Blunsom2013] Nal Kalchbrenner and Phil Blunsom. 2013. Recurrent continuous translation models. In *Proceedings of the 2013 Conference on Empirical Methods in Natural Language Processing*, pages 1700–1709, Seattle, Washington, USA, October.

[Kalchbrenner et al.2014] Nal Kalchbrenner, Edward Grefenstette, and Phil Blunsom. 2014. A convolutional neural network for modelling sentences. *ACL*.

[Klein and Manning2002] Dan Klein and Christopher D Manning. 2002. Fast exact inference with a factored model for natural language parsing. In *Advances in neural information processing systems*, volume 15, pages 3–10.

[Koehn et al.2003] Philipp Koehn, Franz Josef Och, and Daniel Marcu. 2003. Statistical phrase-based translation. In *Proceedings of the 2003 Conference of the North American Chapter of the Association for Computational Linguistics on Human Language Technology-Volume 1*, pages 48–54.

[Koehn et al.2007] Philipp Koehn, Hieu Hoang, Alexandra Birch, Chris Callison-Burch, Marcello Federico, Nicola Bertoldi, Brooke Cowan, Wade Shen, Christine Moran, Richard Zens, Chris Dyer, Ondrej Bojar, Alexandra Constantin, and Evan Herbst. 2007. Moses: Open source toolkit for statistical machine translation. In *Proceedings of the 45th Annual Meeting of the Association for Computational Linguistics Companion Volume Proceedings of the Demo and Poster Sessions*, pages 177–180, Prague, Czech Republic, June.

[LeCun et al.1998] Y. LeCun, L. Bottou, G. Orr, and K. Muller. 1998. Efficient backprop. In *Neural Networks: Tricks of the trade*. Springer.

[Meng et al.2013] Fandong Meng, Jun Xie, Linfeng Song, Yajuan Lü, and Qun Liu. 2013. Translation with source constituency and dependency trees. In *Proceedings of the 2013 Conference on Empirical Methods in Natural Language Processing*, pages 1066–1076, Seattle, Washington, USA, October.

[Och and Ney2002] Franz Josef Och and Hermann Ney. 2002. Discriminative training and maximum entropy models for statistical machine translation. In *Proceedings of the 40th Annual Meeting on Association for Computational Linguistics*, pages 295–302.

[Och and Ney2003] Franz Josef Och and Hermann Ney. 2003. A systematic comparison of various statistical alignment models. *Computational linguistics*, 29(1):19–51.

[Och2003] Franz Josef Och. 2003. Minimum error rate training in statistical machine translation. In *Proceedings of the 41st Annual Meeting on Association for Computational Linguistics-Volume 1*, pages 160–167.

[Shen et al.2008] Libin Shen, Jinxi Xu, and Ralph Weischedel. 2008. A new string-to-dependency machine translation algorithm with a target dependency language model. In *Proceedings of ACL-08: HLT*, pages 577–585.

[Stolcke and others2002] Andreas Stolcke et al. 2002. Srilm-an extensible language modeling toolkit. In *Proceedings of the international conference on spoken language processing*, volume 2, pages 901–904.

[Sutskever et al.2014] Ilya Sutskever, Oriol Vinyals, and Quoc V. Le. 2014. Sequence to sequence learning with neural networks. *CoRR*, abs/1409.3215.

[Xie et al.2011] Jun Xie, Haitao Mi, and Qun Liu. 2011. A novel dependency-to-string model for statistical machine translation. In *Proceedings of the Conference on Empirical Methods in Natural Language Processing*, pages 216–226.

Statistical Machine Translation Features with Multitask Tensor Networks

Hendra Setiawan, Zhongqiang Huang, Jacob Devlin[†*], Thomas Lamar,
Rabih Zbib, Richard Schwartz and John Makhoul
Raytheon BBN Technologies, 10 Moulton St, Cambridge, MA 02138, USA
[†]Microsoft Research, One Microsoft Way, Redmond, WA 98052, USA
{hsetiawa,zhuang,tlamar,rzbib,schwartz,makhoul}@bbn.com
jdevlin@microsoft.com

Abstract

We present a three-pronged approach to improving Statistical Machine Translation (SMT), building on recent success in the application of neural networks to SMT. First, we propose new *features* based on neural networks to model various non-local translation phenomena. Second, we augment the *architecture* of the neural network with tensor layers that capture important higher-order interaction among the network units. Third, we apply multitask *learning* to estimate the neural network parameters jointly. Each of our proposed methods results in significant improvements that are complementary. The overall improvement is +2.7 and +1.8 BLEU points for Arabic-English and Chinese-English translation over a state-of-the-art system that already includes neural network features.

1 Introduction

Recent advances in applying Neural Networks to Statistical Machine Translation (SMT) have generally taken one of two approaches. They either develop neural network-based features that are used to score hypotheses generated from traditional translation grammars (Sundermeyer et al., 2014; Devlin et al., 2014; Auli et al., 2013; Le et al., 2012; Schwenk, 2012), or they implement the whole translation process as a single neural network (Bahdanau et al., 2014; Sutskever et al., 2014). The latter approach, sometimes referred to as *Neural Machine Translation*, attempts to overhaul SMT, while the former capitalizes on the strength of the current SMT paradigm and leverages the modeling power of neural networks to improve the scoring of hypotheses generated by phrase-based or hierarchical translation rules. This paper adopts the former approach, as n-best scores from state-of-the-art SMT systems often suggest that these systems can still be significantly improved with better features.

We build on (Devlin et al., 2014) who proposed a simple yet powerful feedforward neural network model that estimates the translation probability conditioned on the target history and a large window of source word context. We take advantage of neural networks' ability to handle sparsity, and to infer useful abstract representations automatically. At the same time, we address the challenge of learning the large set of neural network parameters. In particular,

- We develop new *Neural Network Features* to model non-local translation phenomena related to word reordering. Large fully-lexicalized contexts are used to model these phenomena effectively, making the use of neural networks essential. All of the features are useful individually, and their combination results in significant improvements (Section 2).
- We use a *Tensor Neural Network Architecture* (Yu et al., 2012) to automatically learn complex pairwise interactions between the network nodes. The introduction of the tensor hidden layer results in more powerful features with lower model perplexity and significantly improved MT performance for all of neural network features (Section 3).
- We apply *Multitask Learning* (MTL) (Caruana, 1997) to jointly train related neural network features by sharing parameters. This allows parameters learned for one feature to benefit the learning of the other features. This results in better trained models and achieves additional MT improvements (Section 4).

We apply the resulting *Multitask Tensor Networks* to the new features and to existing ones,

[*] Research conducted when the author was at BBN.

Proceedings of the 53rd Annual Meeting of the Association for Computational Linguistics and the 7th International Joint Conference on Natural Language Processing, pages 31–41,
Beijing, China, July 26-31, 2015.

obtaining strong experimental results over the strongest previous results of (Devlin et al., 2014). We obtain improvements of +2.5 BLEU points for Arabic-English and +1.8 BLEU points for Chinese-English on the DARPA BOLT Web Forum condition. We also obtain improvements of +2.7 BLEU point for Arabic-English and +1.9 BLEU points for Chinese-English on the NIST Open12 test sets over the best previously published results in (Devlin et al., 2014). Both the tensor architecture and multitask learning are general techniques that are likely to benefit other neural network features.

2 New Non-Local SMT Features

Existing SMT features typically focus on local information in the source sentence, in the target hypothesis, or both. For example, the n-gram language model (LM) predicts the next target word by using previously generated target words as context (local on target), while the lexical translation model (LTM) predicts the translation of a source word by taking into account surrounding source words as context (local on source).

In this work, we focus on non-local translation phenomena that result from non-monotone reordering, where *local* context becomes *non-local* on the other side. We propose a new set of powerful MT features that are motivated by this simple idea. To facilitate the discussion, we categorize the features into *hypothesis-enumerating* features that estimates a probability for each generated target word (e.g., n-gram language model), and *source-enumerating* features that estimates a probability for each source word (e.g., lexical translation).

More concretely, we introduce a) *Joint Model with Offset Source Context* (JMO), a hypothesis enumerating feature that predicts the next target word the source context affiliated to the previous target words; and b) *Translation Context Model* (TCM), a source-enumerating feature that predicts the context of the translation of a source word rather than the translation itself. These two models extend pre-existing features: the Joint (language and translation) Model (JM) of (Devlin et al., 2014) and the LTM respectively respectively. We use a large lexicalized context for there features, making the choice of implementing them as neural networks essential. We also present neural-network implementations of pre-existing source-enumerating features: lexical translation, orientation and fertility models. We obtain additional gains from using tensor networks and multitask learning in the modeling and training of all the features.

2.1 Hypothesis-Enumerating Features

As mentioned, hypothesis-enumerating features score each word in the hypothesis, typically by conditioning it on a context of n-1 previous target words as in the n-gram language model. One recent such model, the joint model of Devlin et al. (2014) achieves large improvements to the state-of-the-art SMT by using a large context window of 11 source words and 3 target words. The Joint Model with Offset Source Context (JMO) is an extension of the JM that uses the source words affiliated with the n-gram target history as context. The source contexts of JM and JMO overlap highly when the translation is monotone, but are complementary when the translation requires word reordering.

2.1.1 Joint Model with Offset Source Context

Formally, JMO estimates the probability of the target hypothesis E conditioned on the source sentence F and a target-to-source *affiliation* $\boldsymbol{A}$:

$$P(E|F,\boldsymbol{A}) \approx \prod_{i=1}^{|E|} P(e_i|e_{i-1}^{i-n+1}, \mathcal{C}_{a_{i-k}} = f_{a_{i-k}-m}^{a_{i-k}+m})$$

where e_i is the word being predicted; e_{i-1}^{i-n+1} is the string of $n-1$ previously generated words; $\mathcal{C}_{a_{i-k}}$ to the source context of m source words around $f_{a_{i-k}}$, the source word affiliated with e_{i-k}. We refer to k as the offset parameter. We use the definition of *word affiliation* introduced in Devlin et al. (2014). When no source context is used, the model is equivalent to an n-gram language model, while an offset parameter of $k = 0$ reduces the model to the JM of Devlin et al. (2014).

When $k > 0$, the JMO captures non-local context in the prediction of the next target word. More specifically, e_{i-k} and e_i, which are local on the target side, are affiliated to $f_{a_{i-k}}$ and f_{a_i} which may be distant from each other on the source side due to non-monotone translation, even for $k = 1$. The offset model captures reordering constraints by encouraging the predicted target word e_i to fit well with the previous affiliated source word $f_{a_{i-k}}$ and its surrounding words. We implement a separate feature for each value of k, and later train them jointly via multitask learning. As our experiments in Section 5.2.1 confirm, the history-affiliated source context results in stronger SMT improvement than just increasing the number of surrounding words in JM.

Fig. 1 illustrates the difference between JMO and JM. Assuming $n = 3$ and $m = 1$, then JM estimates $P(e_5|e_4, e_3, \mathcal{C}_{a_5} = \{f_6, f_7, f_8\})$. On the other hand, for $k = 1$, $\text{JMO}_{k=1}$ estimates $P(e_5|e_4, e_3, \mathcal{C}_{a_4} = \{f_8, f_9, f_{10}\})$.

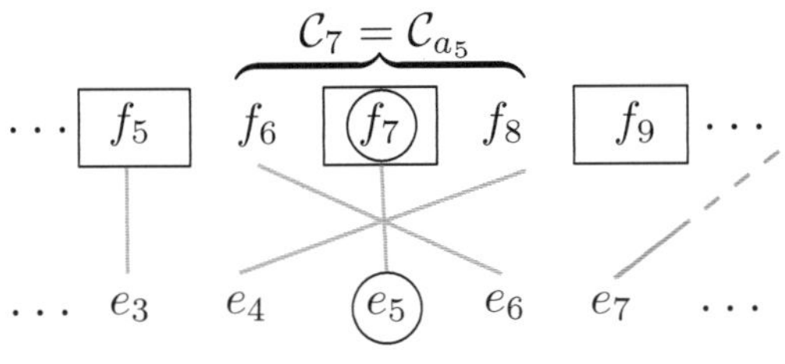

Figure 1: Example to illustrate features. f_5^9 is the source segment, e_3^7 is the corresponding translation and lines refer to the alignment. We show hypothesis-enumerating features that look at f_7 and source-enumerating features that look at e_5. We surround the source words affiliated with e_5 and its n-gram history with a bracket, and surround the source words affiliated with the history of e_5 with squares.

2.2 Source-Enumerating Features

Source-Enumerating Features iterate over words in the source sentence, including unaligned words, and assign it a score depending on what aspect of translation they are modeling. A source-enumerating feature can be formulated as follows:

$$P(E|F, \boldsymbol{A}) \approx \prod_{j=1}^{|F|} P(Y_j|\mathcal{C}_j = f_{j-m}^{j+m})$$

where $\mathcal{C}_{a_j}$ is the source context (similar to the hypothesis-enumerating features above) and Y_j is the label being predicted by the feature. We first describe pre-existing source-enumerating features: the lexical translation model, the orientation model and the fertility model, and then discuss a new feature: Translation Context Model (TCM), which is an extension of the lexical translation model.

2.2.1 Pre-existing Features

Lexical Translation model (LTM) estimates the probability of translating a source word f_j to a target word $l(f_j) = e_{b_j}$ given a source context $\mathcal{C}_j$, $b_j \in \boldsymbol{B}$ is the source-to-target word affiliation as defined in (Devlin et al., 2014). When f_j is translated to more than one word, we arbitrarily keep the left-most one. The target word vocabulary V is extended with a $NULL$ token to accommodate unaligned source words.

Orientation model (ORI) describes the probability of orientation of the translation of phrases surrounding a source word f_j relative to its own translation. We follow (Setiawan et al., 2013) in modeling the orientation of the left and right phrases of f_j with maximal orientation span (the longest neighboring phrase consistent with alignment), which we denote by L_j and R_j respectively. Thus, $o(f_j) = \langle o_{L_j}(f_j), o_{R_j}(f_j)\rangle$, where o_{L_j} and o_{R_j} refer to the orientation of L_j and R_j respectively. For unaligned f_j, we set $o(f_j) = o_{L_j}(R_j)$, the orientation of R_j with respect to L_j.

Fertility model (FM) models the probability that a source word f_j generates $\phi(f_j)$ words in the hypothesis. Our implemented model only distinguishes between aligned and unaligned source words (i.e., $\phi(f_j) \in \{0, 1\}$). The generalization of the model to account for multiple values of $\phi(f_i)$ is straightforward.

2.2.2 Translation Context Model

As with JMO in Section 2.1.1, we aim to capture translation phenomena that appear local on the target hypothesis but non-local on the source side. Here, we do so by extending the LTM feature to predict not only the translated word e_{b_j}, but also its surrounding context. Formally, we model $P(l(f_j)|\mathcal{C}_j)$, where $l(f_j) = e_{b_j-d}, \cdots, e_{b_j}, \cdots e_{b_j+d}$ is the hypothesis word window around e_{b_j}. In practice, we decompose TCM further into $\prod_{d'=-d}^{+d} P(e_{b_j+d'}|\mathcal{C}_j)$ and implemented each as a separate neural network-based feature. Note that TCM is equivalent to the LTM when $d = 0$. Because of word reordering, a given hypothesis word in $l(f_j)$ might not be affiliated with f_j or even to the words in $\mathcal{C}_j$. TCM can model non-local information in this way.

2.2.3 Combined Model

Since the feature label is undefined for unaligned source words, we make the model hierarchical, based on whether the source word is aligned or not, and thus arrive at the following formulation:

$$P(l(f_j)) \cdot P(ori(f_j)) \cdot P(\phi(f_j)) = \begin{cases} P(\phi_p(f_j) = 0) \cdot P(o_{L_j}(R_j)) \\ P(\phi_p(f_j) \geq 1) \cdot \prod_{d'=-d}^{+d} P(e_{b_j+d'}) \\ \cdot P(o_{L_j}(f_j), o_{R_j}(f_j)) \end{cases}$$

We dropped the common context ($\mathcal{C}_j$) for readability.

We reuse Fig. 1 to illustrate the source-enumerating features. Assuming $d = 1$, the scores associated with f_7 are $P(\phi(f_7) \geq 1|\mathcal{C}_7)$ for the FM; $P(e_4|\mathcal{C}_7) \cdot P(e_5|\mathcal{C}_7) \cdot P(e_6)|\mathcal{C}_7)$ for the TCM; and $P(o(f_7) = \langle o_{L_7}(f_7) = RA, o_{R_7}(f_7) = RA \rangle)$ for the ORI(RA refers to *Reverse Adjacent*). L_7 and R_7 (i.e. f_6 and f_8^9 respectively), the longest neighboring phrase of f_7, are translated in reverse order and adjacent to e_5.

3 Tensor Neural Networks

The second part of this work improves SMT by improving the neural network architecture. Neural Networks derive their strength from their ability to learn a high-level representation of the input automatically from data. This high-level representation is typically constructed layer by layer through a weighted sum linear operation and a non-linear activation function. With sufficient training data, neural networks often achieve state-of-the-art performance on many tasks. This stands in sharp contrast to other algorithms that require tedious manual feature engineering. For the features presented in this paper, the context words are fed to the network network with minimal engineering.

We further strengthen the network's ability to learn rich interactions between its units by introducing tensors in the hidden layers. The multiplicative property of the tensor bares a close resemblance to collocation of context words which are useful in many natural language processing tasks.

In conventional feedforward neural networks, the output of hidden layer l is produced by multiplying the output vector from the previous layer with a weight matrix (W_l) and then applying the activation function σ to the product. Tensor Neural Networks generalize this formulation by using a tensor U_l of order 3 for the weights. The output of node k in layer l is computed as follows:

$$h_l[k] = \sigma\left(h_{l-1} \cdot U_l[k] \cdot h_{l-1}^T\right)$$

where $U_l[k]$, the k-th slice of U_l, is a square matrix.

In our implementation, we follow (Yu et al., 2012; Hutchinson et al., 2013) and use a low-rank approximation of $U_l[k] = Q_l[k] \cdot R_l[k]^T$, where $Q_l[k], R_l[k] \in \mathbb{R}^{n \times r}$. The output of node k becomes:

$$h_l[k] = \sigma\left(h_{l-1} \cdot Q_l[k] \cdot R_l[k]^T \cdot h_{l-1}^T\right)$$

In our experiments, we choose $r = 1$, and also apply the non-linear activation function σ distributively. We arrive at the following three equations for computing the hidden layer outputs ($0 < l < L$):

$$\begin{aligned} v_l &= \sigma\left(h_{l-1} \cdot Q_l\right) \\ v_l' &= \sigma\left(h_{l-1} \cdot R_l\right) \\ h_l &= v_l \otimes v_l' \end{aligned}$$

where h_{l-1} is double-projected to v_l and v_l', and the two projections are merged using the Hadamard element-wise product operator $\otimes$.

This formulation allows us to use the same infrastructure of the conventional neural networks by projecting the previous layer to two different spaces of the same dimensions, then multiplying them element-wise. The only component that is different from conventional feedforward neural networks is the multiplicative function, which is trivially differentiable with respect to the learnable parameters. Figure 3(b) illustrates the tensor architecture for two hidden layers.

The tensor network can learn collocation features more easily. For example, it can learn a collocation feature that is activated only if $h_{l-1}[i]$ collocates with $h_{l-1}[j]$ by setting $U_l[k][i][j]$ to some positive number. This results in SMT improvements as we describe in Section 5.

4 Multitask Learning

The third part of this paper addresses the challenge of effectively learning a large number of neural network parameters without overfitting. The challenge is even larger for tensor network since they practically doubles the number of parameters. In this section, we propose to apply Multitask Learning (MTL) to partially address this issue. We implement MTL as parameter sharing among the networks. This effectively reduces the number of parameters, and more importantly, it takes advantage of parameters learned for one feature to better

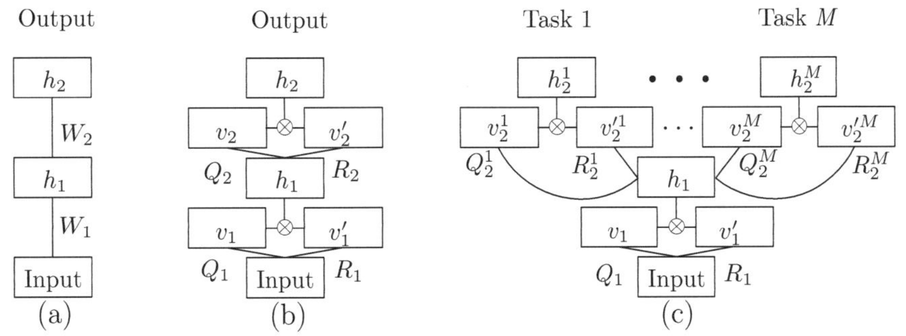

Figure 2: The network architecture for (a) a conventional feedforward neural network, (b) tensor hidden layers, and (c) multitask learning with M features that share the embedding and first hidden layers ($t = 1$).

learn the parameters of the other features. Another way of looking at this is that MTL facilitates regularization through learning the other tasks.

MTL is suitable for SMT features as they model different but closely related aspects of the same translation process. MTL has long been used by the wider machine learning community (Caruana, 1997) and more recently for natural language processing (Collobert and Weston, 2008; Collobert et al., 2011). The application of MTL to machine translation, however, has been much less restricted, which is rather surprising since SMT features arise from the same translation task and are naturally related.

We apply MTL for the features described in Section 2. We design all the features to also share the same neural network architecture (in this case, the tensor architecture described in Section 3) and the same input, thus resulting in two large neural networks: one for the hypothesis-enumerating features and another for the source-enumerating ones. This simplifies the implementation of MTL. Using this setup, it is possible to vary the number of shared hidden layers t from 0 (only sharing the embedding layer) to $L - 1$ (sharing all the layers except the output). Note that in principle MTL is applicable to other set of networks that have different architecture or even different input set. With MTL, the training procedure is the same as that of standard neural networks.

We use the back propagation algorithm, and use as the loss function the product of likelihood of each feature[1]:

[1]In this and in the other parts of the paper, we add the normalization regularization term described in (Devlin et al., 2014) to the loss function to avoid computing the normalization constant at model query/decoding time.

$$Loss = \sum_i \sum_j^M \log \left(P \left(Y_j(X_i) \right) \right)$$

where X_i is the training sample and Y_j is one of the M models trained. We use the sum of log likelihoods since we assume that the features are independent.

Fig. 3(c) illustrates MTL between M models sharing the input embedding layer and the first hidden layer ($t = 1$) compared to the separately-trained conventional feedforward neural network and tensor neural network.

5 Experiments

We demonstrate the impact of our work with extensive MT experiments on Arabic-English and Chinese-English translation for the DARPA BOLT Web Forum and the NIST OpenMT12 conditions.

5.1 Baseline MT System

We run our experiments using a state-of-the-art string-to-dependency hierarchical decoder (Shen et al., 2010). The baseline we use includes a set of powerful features as follow:

- Forward and backward rule probabilities
- Contextual lexical smoothing (Devlin, 2009)
- 5-gram Kneser-Ney LM
- Dependency LM (Shen et al., 2010)
- Length distribution (Shen et al., 2010)
- Trait features (Devlin and Matsoukas, 2012)
- Factored source syntax (Huang et al., 2013)
- Discriminative sparse feature, totaling 50k features (Chiang et al., 2009)
- Neural Network Joint Model (NNJM) and Neural Network Lexical Translation Model

(NNLTM) (Devlin et al., 2014)

As shown, our baseline system already includes neural network-based features. NNJM, NNLTM and use two hidden layers with 500 units and use embedding of size 200 for each input.

We use the MADA-ARZ tokenizer (Habash et al., 2013) for Arabic word tokenization. For Chinese tokenization, we use a simple longest-match-first lexicon-based approach. We align the training data using GIZA++ (Och and Ney, 2003). For tuning the weights of MT features including the new features, we use iterative k-best optimization with an ExpectedBLEU objective function (Rosti et al., 2010), and decode the test sets after 5 tuning iteration. We report the lower-cased BLEU and TER scores.

5.2 BOLT Discussion Forum

The bulk of our experiments is on the BOLT Web Discussion Forum domain, which uses data collected by the LDC. The parallel training data consists of all of the high-quality NIST training corpora, plus an additional 3 million words of translated forum data. The tuning and test sets consist of roughly 5000 segments each, with 2 independent references for Arabic and 3 for Chinese.

5.2.1 Effects of New Features

We first look at the effects of the proposed features compared to the baseline system. Table 1 summarizes the primary results of the Arabic-English and Chinese-English experiments for the BOLT condition. We show the experimental results related to hypothesis-enumerating features (HypEn) in rows S_2-S_5, those related to source-enumerating features (SrcEn) in rows S_6-S_9, and the combination of the two in row S_{10}. For all the features, we set the source context length to $m = 5$ (11-word window). For JM and JMO, we set the target context length to $n = 4$. For the offset parameter k of JMO, we use values 1 to 3. For TCM, we model one word around the translation ($d = 1$). Larger values of d did not result in further gains. The baseline is comparable to the best results of (Devlin et al., 2014).

In rows S_3 to S_5, we incrementally add a model with different offset source context, from $k = 1$ to $k = 3$. For AR-EN, adding JMOs with different offset source context consistently yields positive effects in BLEU score, while in ZH-EN, it yields positive effects in TER score. Utilizing all offset source contexts "+JMO$_{k\leq3}$" (row S_5) yields around 0.9 BLEU point improvement in AR-EN and around 0.3 BLEU in ZH-EN compared to the baseline. The JMO consistently provides better improvement compared to a larger JM context (row S_2), validating our hypothesis that using offset source context captures important non-local context.

Rows S_6 to S_9 present the improvements that result from implementing pre-existing source-enumerating SMT features as neural networks, and highlight the contribution of our translation context model (TCM). This set of experiments is orthogonal to the HypEn experiments (rows S_2-S_5). Each pre-existing model has a modest positive cumulative effect on both BLEU and TER. We see this result as further confirming the current trend of casting existing SMT features as neural network since our baseline already contains such features. The next row present the results of adding the translation context model, with one word surrounding the translation ($d = 1$). As shown, TCM yields a positive effect of around 0.5 BLEU and TER improvements in AR-EN and around 0.2 BLEU and TER improvements in ZH-EN.

Separately, the set of source-enumerating features and the set of target-enumerating features produce around 1.1 to 1.2 points BLEU gain in AR-EN and 0.3 to 0.5 points BLEU gain in ZH-EN. The combination of the two sets produces a complementary gain in addition to the gains of the individual models as Row (S_{10}) shows. The combined gain improves to 1.5 BLEU points in AR-EN and 0.7 BLEU points in ZH-EN.

System	AR-EN		ZH-EN	
	BL	TER	BL	TER
S_1: Baseline	43.2	45.0	30.2	58.3
S_2: S_1+JM$_{LC_8}$	43.5	45.0	30.2	58.5
S_3: S_1+JMO$_{k=1}$	43.9	44.7	30.8	57.8
S_4: S_3+JMO$_{k=2}$	43.9	44.7	30.7	57.8
S_5: S_4+JMO$_{k=3}$	44.4	44.5	30.5	57.5
S_6: S_1+LTM	43.5	44.7	30.3	58.0
S_7: S_6+ORI	43.7	44.6	30.4	57.8
S_8: S_7+FERT	43.8	44.7	30.5	57.8
S_9: S_8+TCM	44.3	44.2	30.7	57.5
S_{10}: S_9+JMO$_{k\leq3}$	44.7	44.1	30.9	57.3

Table 1: MT results of various model combination in BLEU and in TER.

5.2.2 Effects of Tensor Network and Multitask Learning

We first analyze the impact of tensor architecture and MTL intrinsically by reporting the models' average log-likelihood on the validation sets (a subset of the test set) in Table 2. As mentioned, we group the models to HypEn (JM and $\text{JMO}_{k\leq3}$) and SrcEn (LTM, ORI,FERT and TCM) as we perform MTL on these two groups. Likelihood of these two groups in the previous subsection are in column "NN" (for Neural Network), which serves as a baseline. The application of the tensor architecture improves their likelihood as shown in column "Tensor" for both languages and models.

	Feat.	Independent		MTL	
		NN	Tensor	$t=0$ $L=2$	$t=1$ $L=3$
AR	HypEn	-8.85	-8.54	-8.35	-
AR	SrcEn	-8.47	-8.32	-8.10	-8.09
ZH	HypEn	-11.48	-11.06	-10.87	-
ZH	SrcEn	-10.77	-10.66	-10.54	-10.49

Table 2: Sum of the average log-likelihood of the models in HypEn and SrcEn. $t=0$ refers to MTL that shares only the embedding layer, while $t=1$ shares the first hidden layer as well. L refers to the network's depth. Higher value is better.

The likelihoods of the MTL-related experiments are in columns with "MTL" header. We present two set of results. In the first set (column "MTL,t=0,L=2"), we run MTL for features from column "Tensor" by sharing the embedding layer only ($t=0$). This allows us to isolate the impact of MTL in the presence of Tensors. Column "MTL,t=1,l=3" corresponds to the experiment that produces the best intrinsic result, where each model uses Tensors with three hidden layers (500x500x500, $l=3$) and the models share the embedding and the first hidden layers ($t=1$). MTL consistently gives further intrinsic gain compared to tensors. More sharing provides an extra gain for SrcEn as shown in the last column. Note that we only experiment with different l and t for SrcEn and not for HypEn because the models in HypEn have different input sets. In our experiments, further sharing and more hidden layers resulted in no further gain. In total, we see a consistent positive effect in intrinsic evaluation from the tensor networks and multitask learning.

Moving on to MT evaluation, we summarize the experiments showing the impact of Tensors and MTL in Table 3. For MTL, we use $L=3, t=2$ since it gives the best intrinsic score. Employing tensors instead of regular neural networks gives a significant and consistent positive impact for all models and language pairs. For the system with the baseline features, we use the tensor architecture for both the joint model and the lexical translation model of Devlin et al. resulting in an improvement of around 0.7 BLEU points, and showing the wide applicability of the tensor architecture. On top of this improved baseline, we also observe an improvement of the same scale for other models (column "Tensor"), except for HypEn features in AR-EN experiment. Moving to MTL experiments, we see improvements, especially from SrcEn features. MTL gives around 0.5 BLEU point improvement for AR-EN and around 0.4 BLEU point for ZH-EN. When we employ both HypEn and SrcEn together, MTL gives around 0.4 BLEU point in AR-EN and 0.2 BLEU point in ZH-EN. In total, our work results in an improvement of 2.5 BLEU point for AR-EN and 1.8 for BLEU point in ZH-EN on top of the best results in (Devlin et al., 2014).

5.3 NIST OpenMT12

Our NIST system is compatible with the OpenMT12 constrained track, which consists of 10M words of high-quality parallel training for Arabic, and 25M words for Chinese. The n-gram LM is trained on 5B words of data from the English GigaWord. For test, we use the "Arabic-To-English Original Progress Test" (1378 segments) and "Chinese-to-English Original Progress Test + OpenMT12 Current Test" (2190 segments), which consists of a mix of newswire and web data. All test segments have 4 references. Our tuning set contains 5000 segments, and is a mix of the MT02-05 eval set as well as additional held-out parallel data from the training corpora.

We report the experiments for the NIST condition in Table 4. In particular, we investigate the impact of deploying our new features (column "Feat") and demonstrate the effects of the tensor architecture (column "Tensor") and multitask learning (column "MTL"). As shown the results are inline with the BOLT condition where we observe additive improvements from adding our new features, applying tensor network and multitask learning. On Arabic-English, we see a gain of 2.7

Feature set	AR-EN			ZH-EN		
	NN	Tensor	MTL	NN	Tensor	MTL
R_1: Baseline Features	*43.2*	43.9	-	*30.2*	30.8	-
R_2: R_1 + HypEn	44.4	44.4	44.5	30.5	31.5	31.3
R_3: R_1 + SrcEn	44.3	44.9	45.5	30.7	31.5	31.9
R_4: R_1 + HypEn + SrcEn	44.7	45.3	**45.7**	30.9	31.8	**32.0**

Table 3: Experimental results to investigate the effects of the new features, DTN and MTL. The top part shows the BOLT results, while the bottom part shows the NIST results. The best results for each conditions and each language-pair are in **bold**. The baselines are in *italics*. .

	Base.	Feat	Tensor	MTL
AR-EN	*53.7*	55.4	55.9	56.4
mixed-case	*51.8*	53.1	53.7	54.1
ZH-EN	*36.6*	37.8	38.2	38.5
mixed-case	*34.4*	35.5	35.9	36.1

Table 4: Experimental results for the NIST condition. Mixed-case scores are also reported. Baselines are in *italics*.

BLEU point and on Chinese-English, we see a 1.9 BLEU point gain. We also report the mixed-cased BLEU scores for comparison with previous best published results, i.e. Devlin et al. (2014) report 52.8 BLEU for Arabic-English and 34.7 BLEU for Chinese-English. Thus, our results are around 1.3-1.4 BLEU point better. Note that they use additional rescoring features but we do not.

6 Related Work

Our work is most closely related to Devlin et al. (2014). They use a simple feedforward neural network to model two important MT features: A joint language and translation model, and a lexical translation model. They show very large improvements on Arabic-English and Chinese-English web forum and newswire baselines. We improve on their work in 3 aspects. First, we model more features using neural networks, including two novel ones: a joint model with offset source context and a translation context model. Second, we enhance the neural network architecture by using tensor layers, which allows us to model richer interactions. Lastly, we improve the performance of the individual features by training them using multitask learning. In the remainder of this section, we describe previous work relating to the three aspect of our work, namely MT modeling, neural network architecture and model learning.

The features we propose in this paper address the major aspects of SMT modeling that have informed much of the research since the original IBM models (Brown et al., 1993): lexical translation, reordering, word fertility, and language models. Of particular relevance to our work are approaches that incorporate context-sensitivity into the models (Carpuat and Wu, 2007), formulate reordering as orientation prediction task (Tillman, 2004) and that use neural network language models (Bengio et al., 2003; Schwenk, 2010; Schwenk, 2012), and incorporate source-side context into them (Devlin et al., 2014; Auli et al., 2013; Le et al., 2012; Schwenk, 2012).

Approaches to incorporating source context into a neural network model differ mainly in how they represent the source sentence and in how long is the history they keep. In terms of representation of the source sentence, we follow (Devlin et al., 2014) in using a window around the *affiliated* source word. To name some other approaches, Auli et al. (2013) uses latent semantic analysis and source sentence embeddings learned from the recurrent neural network; Sundermeyer et al. (2014) take the representation from a bidirectional LSTM recurrent neural network; and Kalchbrenner and Blunsom (2013) employ a convolutional sentence model. For target context, recent work has tried to look beyond the classical n-gram history. (Auli et al., 2013; Sundermeyer et al., 2014) consider an unbounded history, at the expense of making their model only applicable for N-best rescoring. Another recent line of research (Bahdanau et al., 2014; Sutskever et al., 2014) departs more radically from conventional feature-based SMT and implements the MT system as a single neural network. These models use a representation of the whole input sentence.

We use a feedforward neural network in this work. Besides feedforward and recurrent networks, other network architectures that have been applied to SMT include convolutional networks (Kalchbrenner et al., 2014) and recursive networks (Socher et al., 2011). The simplicity of feedforward networks works to our advantage. More specifically, due to the absence of a feedback loop, the feedforward architecture allows us to treat individual decisions independently, which makes parallelization of the training easy and the querying the network at decoding time straightforward. The use of tensors in the hidden layers strengthens the neural network model, allowing us to model more complex feature interactions like collocation, which has been long recognized as important information for many NLP tasks (e.g. word sense disambiguation (Lee and Ng, 2002)). The tensor formulation we use is similar to that of (Yu et al., 2012; Hutchinson et al., 2013). Tensor Neural Networks have a wide application in other field, but have only been recently applied in NLP (Socher et al., 2013; Pei et al., 2014). To our knowledge, our work is the first to use tensor networks in SMT.

Our approach to multitask learning is related to work that is often labeled joint training or transfer learning. To name a few of these works, Finkel and Manning (2009) successfully train name entity recognizers and syntactic parsers jointly, and Singh et al. (2013) train models for coreference resolution, named entity recognition and relation extraction jointly. Both efforts are motivated by the minimization of cascading errors. Our work is most closely related to Collobert and Weston (2008; Collobert et al. (2011), who apply multitask learning to train neural networks for multiple NLP models: part-of-speech tagging, semantic role labeling, named-entity recognition and language model variations.

7 Conclusion

This paper argues that a relatively simple feedforward neural network can still provides significant improvement to Statistical Machine Translation (SMT). We support this argument by presenting a multi-pronged approach that addresses modeling, architectural and learning aspects of pre-existing neural network-based SMT features. More concretely, we paper present a new set of neural network-based SMT features to capture important translation phenomena, extend feedforward neural network with tensor layers, and apply multitask learning to integrate the SMT features more tightly. Empirically, all our proposals successfully produce an improvement over state-of-the-art machine translation system for Arabic-to-English and Chinese-to-English and for both BOLT web forum and NIST conditions. Building on the success of this paper, we plan to develop other neural-network-based features, and to also relax the limiteation of current rule extraction heuristics by generating translations word-by-word.

Acknowledgement

This work was supported by DARPA/I2O Contract No. HR0011-12-C-0014 under the BOLT Program. The views, opinions, and/or findings contained in this article are those of the author and should not be interpreted as representing the official views or policies, either expressed or implied, of the Defense Advanced Research Projects Agency or the Department of Defense.

References

Michael Auli, Michel Galley, Chris Quirk, and Geoffrey Zweig. 2013. Joint language and translation modeling with recurrent neural networks. In *Proceedings of the 2013 Conference on Empirical Methods in Natural Language Processing*, pages 1044–1054, Seattle, Washington, USA, October. Association for Computational Linguistics.

Dzmitry Bahdanau, Kyunghyun Cho, and Yoshua Bengio. 2014. Neural machine translation by jointly learning to align and translate. Technical Report 1409.0473, arXiv.

Yoshua Bengio, Réjean Ducharme, Pascal Vincent, and Christian Jauvin. 2003. A neural probabilistic language model. *Journal of Machine Learning Research*, 3:1137–1155.

Peter F. Brown, Vincent J. Della Pietra, Stephen A. Della Pietra, and Robert L. Mercer. 1993. The mathematics of statistical machine translation: Parameter estimation. *Comput. Linguist.*, 19(2):263–311, June.

Marine Carpuat and Dekai Wu. 2007. Improving statistical machine translation using word sense disambiguation. In *Proceedings of the 2007 Joint Conference on Empirical Methods in Natural Language Processing and Computational Natural Language Learning (EMNLP-CoNLL)*, pages 61–72, Prague, Czech Republic, June. Association for Computational Linguistics.

Rich Caruana. 1997. Multitask learning. *Machine Learning*, 28(1):41–75.

David Chiang, Kevin Knight, and Wei Wang. 2009. 11,001 new features for statistical machine translation. In *HLT-NAACL*, pages 218–226.

Ronan Collobert and Jason Weston. 2008. A unified architecture for natural language processing: Deep neural networks with multitask learning. In *Proceedings of the 25th International Conference on Machine Learning*, ICML '08, pages 160–167, New York, NY, USA. ACM.

Ronan Collobert, Jason Weston, Léon Bottou, Michael Karlen, Koray Kavukcuoglu, and Pavel Kuksa. 2011. Natural language processing (almost) from scratch. *J. Mach. Learn. Res.*, 12:2493–2537, November.

Jacob Devlin and Spyros Matsoukas. 2012. Trait-based hypothesis selection for machine translation. In *Proceedings of the 2012 Conference of the North American Chapter of the Association for Computational Linguistics: Human Language Technologies*, NAACL HLT '12, pages 528–532, Stroudsburg, PA, USA. Association for Computational Linguistics.

Jacob Devlin, Rabih Zbib, Zhongqiang Huang, Thomas Lamar, Richard Schwartz, and John Makhoul. 2014. Fast and robust neural network joint models for statistical machine translation. In *Proceedings of the 52nd Annual Meeting of the Association for Computational Linguistics (Volume 1: Long Papers)*, pages 1370–1380, Baltimore, Maryland, June. Association for Computational Linguistics.

Jacob Devlin. 2009. Lexical features for statistical machine translation. Master's thesis, University of Maryland.

Jenny Rose Finkel and Christopher D. Manning. 2009. Joint parsing and named entity recognition. In *Proceedings of Human Language Technologies: The 2009 Annual Conference of the North American Chapter of the Association for Computational Linguistics*, pages 326–334, Boulder, Colorado, June. Association for Computational Linguistics.

Nizar Habash, Ryan Roth, Owen Rambow, Ramy Eskander, and Nadi Tomeh. 2013. Morphological analysis and disambiguation for dialectal arabic. In *HLT-NAACL*, pages 426–432.

Zhongqiang Huang, Jacob Devlin, and Rabih Zbib. 2013. Factored soft source syntactic constraints for hierarchical machine translation. In *EMNLP*, pages 556–566.

Brian Hutchinson, Li Deng, and Dong Yu. 2013. Tensor deep stacking networks. *IEEE Trans. Pattern Anal. Mach. Intell.*, 35(8):1944–1957, August.

Nal Kalchbrenner and Phil Blunsom. 2013. Recurrent continuous translation models. In *Proceedings of the 2013 Conference on Empirical Methods in Natural Language Processing*, pages 1700–1709, Seattle, Washington, USA, October. Association for Computational Linguistics.

Nal Kalchbrenner, Edward Grefenstette, and Phil Blunsom. 2014. A convolutional neural network for modelling sentences. In *Proceedings of the 52nd Annual Meeting of the Association for Computational Linguistics (Volume 1: Long Papers)*, pages 655–665, Baltimore, Maryland, June. Association for Computational Linguistics.

Hai-Son Le, Alexandre Allauzen, and François Yvon. 2012. Continuous space translation models with neural networks. In *Proceedings of the 2012 Conference of the North American Chapter of the Association for Computational Linguistics: Human Language Technologies*, NAACL HLT '12, pages 39–48, Stroudsburg, PA, USA. Association for Computational Linguistics.

Yoong Keok Lee and Hwee Tou Ng. 2002. An empirical evaluation of knowledge sources and learning algorithms for word sense disambiguation. In *Proceedings of the ACL-02 Conference on Empirical Methods in Natural Language Processing - Volume 10*, EMNLP '02, pages 41–48, Stroudsburg, PA, USA. Association for Computational Linguistics.

Franz Josef Och and Hermann Ney. 2003. A systematic comparison of various statistical alignment models. *Computational Linguistics*, 29(1):19–51.

Wenzhe Pei, Tao Ge, and Baobao Chang. 2014. Max-margin tensor neural network for chinese word segmentation. In *Proceedings of the 52nd Annual Meeting of the Association for Computational Linguistics (Volume 1: Long Papers)*, pages 293–303, Baltimore, Maryland, June. Association for Computational Linguistics.

Antti Rosti, Bing Zhang, Spyros Matsoukas, and Rich Schwartz. 2010. BBN system description for WMT10 system combination task. In *WMT/MetricsMATR*, pages 321–326.

Holger Schwenk. 2010. Continuous-space language models for statistical machine translation. *Prague Bull. Math. Linguistics*, 93:137–146.

Holger Schwenk. 2012. Continuous space translation models for phrase-based statistical machine translation. In *COLING (Posters)*, pages 1071–1080.

Hendra Setiawan, Bowen Zhou, Bing Xiang, and Libin Shen. 2013. Two-neighbor orientation model with cross-boundary global contexts. In *Proceedings of the 51st Annual Meeting of the Association for Computational Linguistics (Volume 1: Long Papers)*, pages 1264–1274, Sofia, Bulgaria, August. Association for Computational Linguistics.

Libin Shen, Jinxi Xu, and Ralph Weischedel. 2010. String-to-dependency statistical machine translation. *Computational Linguistics*, 36(4):649–671, December.

Sameer Singh, Sebastian Riedel, Brian Martin, Jiaping Zheng, and Andrew McCallum. 2013. Joint inference of entities, relations, and coreference. In *Proceedings of the 2013 Workshop on Automated Knowledge Base Construction*, AKBC '13, pages 1–6, New York, NY, USA. ACM.

Matthew Snover, Bonnie Dorr, and Richard Schwartz. 2008. Language and translation model adaptation using comparable corpora. In *Proceedings of the Conference on Empirical Methods in Natural Language Processing*, EMNLP '08, pages 857–866, Stroudsburg, PA, USA. Association for Computational Linguistics.

Richard Socher, Cliff C. Lin, Andrew Y. Ng, and Christopher D. Manning. 2011. Parsing Natural Scenes and Natural Language with Recursive Neural Networks. In *Proceedings of the 26th International Conference on Machine Learning (ICML)*.

Richard Socher, Danqi Chen, Christopher D Manning, and Andrew Ng. 2013. Reasoning with neural tensor networks for knowledge base completion. In C.J.C. Burges, L. Bottou, M. Welling, Z. Ghahramani, and K.Q. Weinberger, editors, *Advances in Neural Information Processing Systems 26*, pages 926–934. Curran Associates, Inc.

Martin Sundermeyer, Tamer Alkhouli, Joern Wuebker, and Hermann Ney. 2014. Translation modeling with bidirectional recurrent neural networks. In *Proceedings of the 2014 Conference on Empirical Methods in Natural Language Processing (EMNLP)*, pages 14–25, Doha, Qatar, October. Association for Computational Linguistics.

Ilya Sutskever, Oriol Vinyals, and Quoc V. V Le. 2014. Sequence to sequence learning with neural networks. In Z. Ghahramani, M. Welling, C. Cortes, N.D. Lawrence, and K.Q. Weinberger, editors, *Advances in Neural Information Processing Systems 27*, pages 3104–3112. Curran Associates, Inc.

Christoph Tillman. 2004. A unigram orientation model for statistical machine translation. In Daniel Marcu Susan Dumais and Salim Roukos, editors, *HLT-NAACL 2004: Short Papers*, pages 101–104, Boston, Massachusetts, USA, May 2 - May 7. Association for Computational Linguistics.

Dong Yu, Li Deng, and Frank Seide. 2012. Large vocabulary speech recognition using deep tensor neural networks. In *INTERSPEECH*. ISCA.

Describing Images using Inferred Visual Dependency Representations

Desmond Elliott and **Arjen P. de Vries**
Information Access Group
Centrum Wiskunde & Informatica
Amsterdam, The Netherlands
elliott@cwi.nl, arjen@acm.org

Abstract

The Visual Dependency Representation (VDR) is an explicit model of the spatial relationships between objects in an image. In this paper we present an approach to training a VDR Parsing Model without the extensive human supervision used in previous work. Our approach is to find the objects mentioned in a given description using a state-of-the-art object detector, and to use successful detections to produce training data. The description of an unseen image is produced by first predicting its VDR over automatically detected objects, and then generating the text with a template-based generation model using the predicted VDR. The performance of our approach is comparable to a state-of-the-art multimodal deep neural network in images depicting actions.

1 Introduction

Humans typically write the text accompanying an image, which is a time-consuming and expensive activity. There are many circumstances in which people are well-suited to this task, such as captioning news articles (Feng and Lapata, 2008) where there are complex relationships between the modalities (Marsh and White, 2003). In this paper we focus on generating *literal* descriptions, which are rarely found alongside images because they describe what can easily be seen by others (Panofsky, 1939; Shatford, 1986; Hodosh et al., 2013). A computer that can automatically generate these literal descriptions, filling the gap left by humans, may improve access to existing image collections or increase information access for visually impaired users.

There has been an upsurge of research in this area, including models that rely on spatial relationships (Farhadi et al., 2010), corpus-based relationships (Yang et al., 2011), spatial and visual attributes (Kulkarni et al., 2011), n-gram phrase fusion from Web-scale corpora (Li et al., 2011), tree-substitution grammars (Mitchell et al., 2012), selecting and combining phrases from large image-description collections (Kuznetsova et al., 2012), using Visual Dependency Representations to capture spatial and corpus-based relationships (Elliott and Keller, 2013), and in a generative framework over densely-labelled data (Yatskar et al., 2014). The most recent developments have focused on deep learning the relationships between visual feature vectors and word-embeddings with language generation models based on recurrent neural networks or long-short term memory networks (Karpathy and Fei-Fei, 2015; Vinyals et al., 2015; Mao et al., 2015; Fang et al., 2015; Donahue et al., 2015; Lebret et al., 2015). An alternative thread of research has focused on directly pairing images with text, based on kCCA (Hodosh et al., 2013) or multimodal deep neural networks (Socher et al., 2014; Karpathy et al., 2014).

We revisit the Visual Dependency Representation (Elliott and Keller, 2013, VDR), an intermediate structure that captures the spatial relationships between objects in an image. Spatial context has been shown to be useful in object recognition and naming tasks because humans benefit from the visual world conforming to their expectations (Biederman et al., 1982; Bar and Ullman, 1996). The spatial relationships defined in VDR are closely, but independently, related to cognitively plausible spatial templates (Logan and Sadler, 1996) and region connection calculus (Randell et al., 1992). In the image description task, explicitly modelling the spatial relationships between observed objects constrains how an image should be described. An example can be seen in Figure 1, where the training VDR identifies the defining relationship between the man and the laptop, which may be re-

Proceedings of the 53rd Annual Meeting of the Association for Computational Linguistics and the 7th International Joint Conference on Natural Language Processing, pages 42–52,
Beijing, China, July 26-31, 2015.

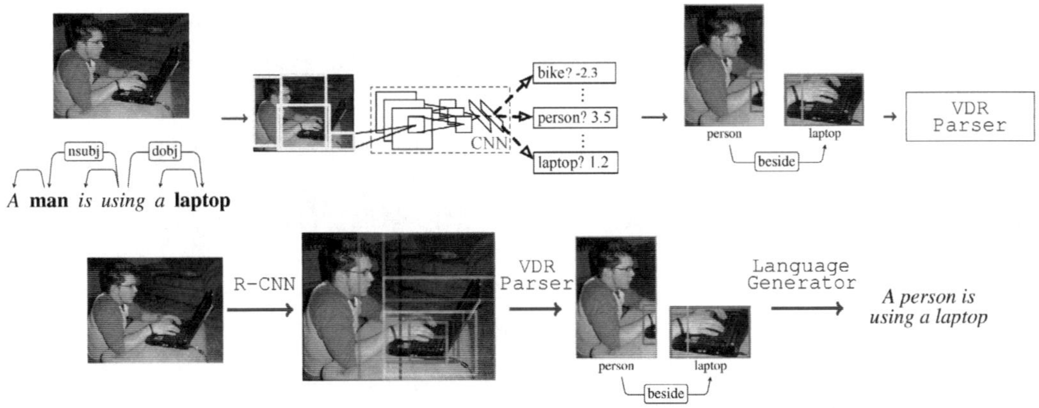

Figure 1: We present an approach to inferring VDR training data from images paired with descriptions (top), and for generating descriptions from VDR (bottom). Candidates for the subject and object in the image are extracted from the description. An object detector[1] searches for the objects and deterministically produces a training instance, which is used to train a VDR Parser to predict the relationships between objects in unseen images. When an unseen image is presented to the model, we first extract N-candidate objects for the image. The detected objects are then parsed into a VDR structure, which is passed into a template-based language generator to produce a description of the image.

alised as a "using", "typing", or "working" relationship between the objects.

The main limitation of previous research on VDR has been the reliance on gold-standard training annotations, which requires trained annotators. We present the first approach to automatically inferring VDR training examples from natural scenes using only an object detector and an image description. Ortiz et al. (2015) have recently presented an alternative treatment of VDR within the context of abstract scenes and phrase-based machine translation. Figure 1 shows a detailed overview of our approach. At training time, we learn a VDR Parsing model from representations that are constructed by searching for the subject and object in the image. The description of an unseen image is generated using a template-based generation model that leverages the VDR predicted over the top-N objects extracted from an object detector.

We evaluate our method for inferring VDRs in an image description experiment on the Pascal1K (Rashtchian et al., 2010) and VL2K data sets (Elliott and Keller, 2013) against two models: the bi-directional recurrent neural network (Karpathy and Fei-Fei, 2015, BRNN) and MIDGE (Mitchell et al., 2012). The main finding is that the quality of the descriptions generated by our method depends on whether the images depict an action. In the VLT2K data set of people performing actions, the performance of our approach is comparable to the BRNN; in the more diverse Pascal1K dataset, the BRNN is substantially better than our method. In a second experiment, we transfer the VDR-based model from the VLT2K data set to the Pascal1K data set without re-training, which improves the descriptions generated in the Pascal1K data set. This suggests that refining how we extract training data may yield further improvements to VDR-based image description.

The code and generated descriptions are available at `http://github.com/elliottd/vdr/`.

2 Automatically Inferring VDRs

The Visual Dependency Representation is a structured representation of an image that explicitly models the spatial relationships between objects. In this representation, the spatial relationship between a pair of objects is encoded with one of the following eight options: above, below, beside, opposite, on, surrounds, infront, and behind. Previous work on VDR-based image description has relied on training data from expert human annotators, which is expensive and difficult to scale to other data sets. In this paper, we describe an approach to automatically inferring VDRs using only an object detector and the description of an image. Our aim is to define an automated version

[1]The image of the R-CNN object detector was modified with permission from Girshick et al. (2014).

Relation	Definition
Beside	The angle between the subject and the object is either between 315° and 45° or 135° and 225°.
Above	The angle between the subject and object is between 225° and 315°.
Below	The angle between the subject and object is between 45° and 135°.
On	More than 50% of the subject overlaps with the object.
Surrounds	More than 90% of the subject overlaps with the object.

Table 1: The cascade of spatial relationships between objects in VDR. We always use the last relationship that matches. These definitions are mostly taken from (Elliott and Keller, 2013), except that we remove the 3D relationships. Angles are defined with respect to the unit circle, which has 0° on the right. All relations are specific with respect to the centroid of the bounding boxes.

Figure 2: An example of the most confident object detections from the R-CNN object detector.

of the human process used to create gold-standard data (Elliott and Keller, 2013).

An inferred VDR is constructed by searching for the subject and object referred to in the description of an image using an object detector. If both the subject and object can be found in the image, a VDR is created by attaching the detected subject to the detected object, given the spatial relationship between the object bounding boxes. The spatial relationships that can be applied between subjects and objects are defined in the cascade defined in Table 1. The set of relationships was reduced from eight to six due to the difficulty in predicting the 3D relationships in 2D images (Eigen et al., 2014). The spatial relation selected for a pair of objects is determined by applying each template defined in Table 1 to the object pair. We use only the final matching relationship, although future work may consider applying multiple matching relationships between objects.

Given a set of inferred VDR training examples, we train a VDR Parsing Model with the VDR+IMG feature set using only the inferred examples (Elliott et al., 2014). We tried training a model by combining the inferred and gold-standard VDRs but this lead to an erratic parsing model that would regularly predict flat structures instead of object–object relationships. One possibility for this behaviour is the mismatch caused by removing the infront and behind relationships in the inferred training data. Another possible explanation is the gold-standard data contains deeper and more complex structures than the simple object–object structures we infer.

2.1 Linguistic Processing

The description of an image is processed to extract candidates for the mentioned objects. We extract candidates from the `nsubj` and `dobj` tokens in the dependency parsed description[2]. If the parsed description does not contain both a subject and an object, as defined here, the example is discarded.

2.2 Visual Processing

If the dependency parsed description contains candidates for the subject and object of an image, we attempt to find these objects in the image. We use the Regions with Convolutional Neural Network features object detector (Girshick et al., 2014, R-CNN) with the pre-trained `bvlc_reference_ilsvrc13` detection model implemented in Caffe (Jia et al., 2014). This object detection model is able to detect 200 different types of objects, with a mean average precision of 31.4% in the ImageNet Large-Scale Visual Recognition Challenge[3] (Russakovsky et al., 2014). The output of the object detector is a bounding box with real-valued confidence scores, as shown in

[2]The descriptions are Part-of-Speech tagged using the Stanford POS Tagger v3.1.0 (Toutanova et al., 2003) with the `english-bidirectional-distsim` pre-trained model. The tagged descriptions are then Dependency Parsed using Malt Parser v 1.7.2 (Nivre et al., 2007) with the `engmalt.poly-1.7` pre-trained model.

[3]The state-of-the-art result for this task is 37.2% using a Network in Network architecture (Lin et al., 2014a); a pre-trained detection model was not available in the Caffe Model Zoo at the time of writing.

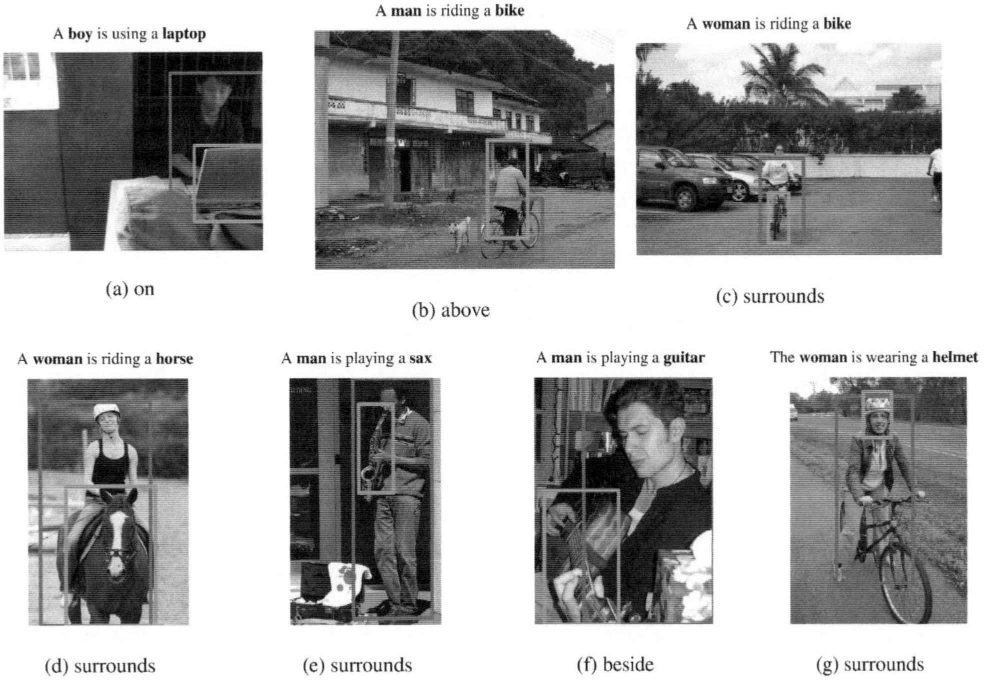

Figure 3: Examples of the object detections and automatically inferred VDR. In each example, the object detector candidates were extracted from the description and the VDR relationships were determined by the cascade in Table 1. Automatically inferring VDR allows us to learn differences in spatial relationships from different camera viewpoints, such as people riding bicycles.

Figure 2. The confidence scores are not probabilities and can vary widely across images.

The words in a description that refer to objects in an image are not always within the constrained vocabulary of the object labels in the object detection model. We increase the chance of finding objects with two simple back-offs: by lemmatising the token, and transforming the token into its WordNet hypernym parent. If the subject and the object can be found in the image, we create an inferred VDR from the detections, otherwise we discard this training example.

Figure 3 shows a collection of automatically inferred VDRs. One of the immediate benefits of VDR, as a representation, is that we can easily interpret the structures extracted from images. An example of helpful object orientation invariance can be seen in 3 (b) and (c), where VDR captures the two different types of spatial relationships between people and bicycles that are grounded in the verb "riding". This type of invariance is useful and it suggests VDR can model interacting objects from various viewpoints. We note here the similarities between automatically inferred VDR and Visual Phrases (Sadeghi and Farhadi, 2011). The main difference between these models is that VDR is primarily concerned with object–object interactions for generation and retrieval tasks, whereas Visual Phrases were intended to model person–object interactions for *activity recognition*.

2.3 Building a Language Model

We build a language model using the subjects, verbs, objects, and spatial relationships from the successfully constructed training examples. The subjects and objects take the form of the object detector labels to reduce the effects of sparsity. The verbs are found as the direct common verb parent of the subject and object in the dependency parsed sentence. We stem the verbs using *morpha*, to reduce sparsity, and inflect them in a generated description with +ing using *morphg* (Minnen et al., 2001). The spatial relationship between the subject and object region is used to help constrain language generation to produce descriptions, given observed spatial contexts in a VDR.

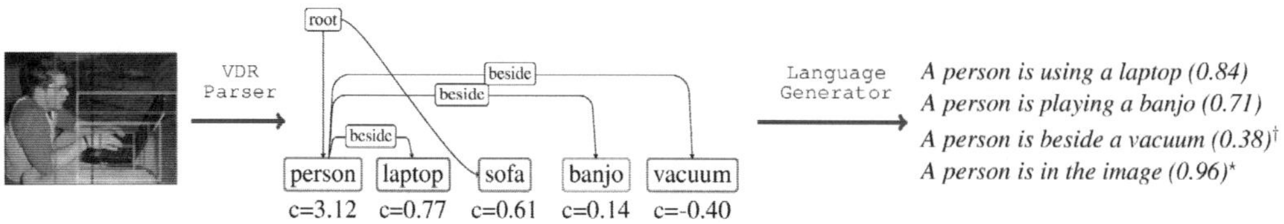

Figure 4: An overview of VDR-constrained language generation. We extract the top-N objects from an image using an object detector and predict the spatial relationships between the objects using a VDR Parser trained over the inferred training data. Descriptions are generated for all parent–child subtrees in the VDR, and the final text has the highest combined corpus and visual confidence. †: only generated is there are no verbs between the objects in the language model; ⋆: only generated if there are no verbs between any pairs of objects in the image.

3 Generating Descriptions

The description of an image is generated using a template-based language generation model designed to exploit the structure encoded in VDR. The language generation model extends Elliott and Keller (2013) with the visual confidence scores from the object detector. Figure 4 shows an overview of the generation process.

The top-N objects are extracted from an image using the pre-trained R-CNN object detector (see Section 2.2 for more details). We remove non-maximal detections with the same class label that overlap by more than 30%. The objects are then parsed into a VDR structure using the VDR Parser trained on the automatically inferred training data. Given the VDR over the set of detected objects, we generate all possible descriptions of the image that can be produced in a depth-first traversal of the VDR. A description is assigned a score that combines the corpus-based evidence and visual confidence of the objects selected for the description. The descriptions are generated using the following template:

DT **head** is V DT **child**.

In this template, **head** and **child** are the labels of the objects that appear in the head and child positions of a specific VDR subtree. V is a verb determined from a subject-verb-object-spatial relation model derived from the training data descriptions. This model captures statistics about nouns that appear as subjects and objects, the verbs between them, and spatial relationships observed in the inferred training VDRs. The verb v that satisfies the V field is determined as follows:

$$v = \arg\max_{v} p(v|head, child, spatial) \quad (1)$$

$$\begin{aligned} p(v|head,child, spatial) = \\ p(v|head) \cdot p(child|v, head) \cdot \\ p(spatial|child, v, head) \end{aligned} \quad (2)$$

If no verbs were observed between a particular object–object pair in the training corpus, V is filled using a back-off that uses the spatial relationship label between the objects in the VDR.

The object detection confidence values, which are not probabilities and can vary substantially between images, are transformed into the range [0,1] using $sgm(conf) = \frac{1}{1+e^{-conf}}$. The final score assigned to a description is then used to rank all of the candidate descriptions, and the highest-scoring description is assigned to an image:

$$\begin{aligned} score(head, v,child, spatial) = \\ p(v|head, child, spatial) \cdot \\ sgm(head) \cdot sgm(child) \end{aligned} \quad (3)$$

If the VDR Parser does not predict any relationships between objects in an image, which may happen if all of the objects have never been observed in the training data, we use a back-off template to generate the description. In this case, the most confidently detected object in the image is used with the following template:

A/An **object** is in the image.

The number of objects N objects extracted from an unseen image is optimised by maximising the sentence-level Meteor score of the generated descriptions in the development data.

4 Experiments

We evaluate our approach to automatically inferring VDR training data in an automatic image description experiment. The aim in this task is to generate a natural language description of an image, which is evaluated directly against multiple reference descriptions.

4.1 Models

We compare our approach against two state-of-the-art image description models. MIDGE generates text based on tree-substitution grammar and relies on discrete object detections (Mitchell et al., 2012) for visual input. We make a small modification to MIDGE so it uses all of the top-N detected objects, regardless of the confidence of the detections[4]. BRNN is a multimodal deep neural network that generates descriptions directly from vector representations of the image and the description (Karpathy and Fei-Fei, 2015). The images are represented by the visual feature vector extracted from the FC_7 layer of the VGG 16-layer convolutional neural network (Simonyan and Zisserman, 2015) and the descriptions are represented as a word-embedding vector.

4.2 Evaluation Measures

We evaluate the generated descriptions using sentence-level Meteor (Denkowski and Lavie, 2011) and BLEU4 (Papineni et al., 2002), which have been shown to have moderate correlation with humans (Elliott and Keller, 2014). We adopt a jack-knifing evaluation methodology, which enables us to report human–human results (Lin and Och, 2004), using MultEval (Clark et al., 2011).

4.3 Data Sets

We perform our experiments on two data sets: Pascal1K and VLT2K. The Pascal1K data set contains 1,000 images sampled from the PASCAL Object Detection Challenge data set (Everingham et al., 2010); each image is paired with five reference descriptions collected from Mechanical Turk. It contains a wide variety of subject matter drawn from the original 20 PASCAL Detection classes. The VLT2K data set contains 2,424 images taken from the trainval 2011 portion of the PASCAL Action Recognition Challenge; each image is paired with three reference descriptions, also collected from Mechanical Turk. We randomly split the images into 80% training, 10% validation, and 10% test.

[4]In personal communication with Margaret Mitchell, she explained that the object confidence thresholds for MIDGE were determined by visual inspection on held-out data, which we decided was not feasible for 200 new detectors.

	VLT2K		Pascal1K	
	Meteor	BLEU	Meteor	BLEU
VDR	16.0	14.8	7.4	9.0
BRNN	18.6	23.7	12.6	16.0
-genders	16.6	17.4	12.1	15.1
MIDGE	5.5	8.2	3.6	9.1
Human	26.4	23.3	21.7	20.6

Table 2: Sentence-level evaluation of the generated descriptions. VDR is comparable to BRNN when the images exclusively depict actions (VLT2K). In a more diverse data set, BRNN generates better descriptions (Pascal1K).

4.4 Results

Table 2 shows the results of the image description experiment. The main finding of our experiments is that the performance of our proposed approach VDR depends on the type of images. We found that VDR is comparable to the deep neural network BRNN on the VLT2K data set of people performing actions. This is consistent with the hypothesis underlying VDR: it is useful to encode the spatial relationships between objects in images. The difference between the models is increased by the inability of the object detector used by VDR to predict bounding boxes for three objects (cameras, books, and phones) crucial to describing 30% of the images in this data set. In the more diverse Pascal1K data set, which does not necessarily depict people performing actions, the deep neural network generates substantially better descriptions than VDR and MIDGE. The tree-substitution grammar approach to generating descriptions used by MIDGE does not perform well on either data set.

There is an obvious discrepancy between the BLEU4 and Meteor scores for the models. BLEU4 relies on lexical matching between sentences and thus penalises semantically equivalent descriptions. For example, identifying the gender of a person is important for generating a good description. However, object recognizers are not (yet) able to reliably achieve this distinction, and we only have a single recogniser for "persons". The BRNN generates descriptions with "man" and "woman", which leads to higher BLEU scores than our VDR model, but this is based on corpus statistics than the observed visual information. Me-

Figure 5: Examples of descriptions generated using VDR and the BRNN in the VLT2K data set. Keen readers are encouraged to inspect the second image with a magnifying glass or an object detector.

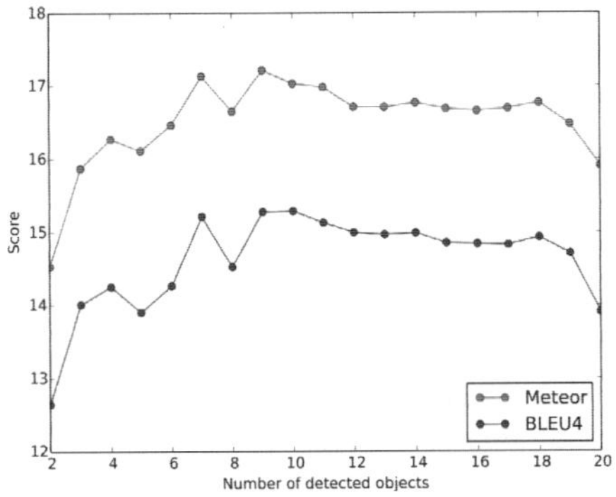

Figure 6: Optimising the number of detected objects against generated description Meteor scores for our model. Improvements are seen until eight objects, which suggests good descriptions do not always need the most confident detections.

teor is able to back-off from "man" or "woman" to "person" and still give partial credit to the description. If we replace the gendered referents in the descriptions generated by the BRNN, its performance on the VLT2K data set drops by 2.0 Meteor points and 6.3 BLEU points.

Figure 6 shows the effect of optimising the number of objects extracted from an image against the eventual Meteor score of a generated description in the validation data. It can be seen that the most confidently predicted objects are not always the most useful objects for generating descriptions. Interestingly, the quality of the descriptions does not significantly decrease with an increased number of detected objects, suggesting our model formulation is appropriately discarding unsuitable detections.

Figure 5 shows examples of the descriptions generated by VDR and BRNN on the VLT2K validation set. The examples where VDR generates better descriptions than BRNN are because the VDR Parser makes good decisions about which objects are interacting in an image. In the examples where the BRNN is better than VDR, we see that the multimodal RNN language model succeeds at describing intransitive verbs, group events, and objects not present in the R-CNN object detector. Both models generate bad descriptions when the visual input pushes them in the wrong direction, seen at the bottom of the figure.

	VLT → Pascal	
	Meteor	BLEU
VDR	7.4 → 8.2	9.1 → 9.2
BRNN	12.6 → 8.1	16.0 → 10.2

Table 3: Sentence-level scores when transferring models directly between data sets with no retraining. The VDR-based approach generates better descriptions in the Pascal1K data set if we transfer the model from the VLT2K data set.

4.5 Transferring Models

The main reason for the low performance of VDR on the Pascal1K data set is that the linguistic and visual processing steps (Section 2) discard too many training examples. We found that only 190 of the 4,000 description in the training data were used to infer VDRs. This was because most of the descriptions did not contain both a subject and an object, as required by our method. This observation led us to perform a second experiment where we transferred the VDR Parsing and Language Generation models between data sets. The aim of this experiment was to determine whether VDR simply cannot work on more widely diverse data sets, or whether the process we defined to replicate human VDR annotation was too strict.

Table 3 shows the results of the model transfer experiment. In general, neither model is particularly good at transferring between data sets. This could be attributed to the shift in the types of scenes depicted in each data set. However, transferring VDR from the VLT2K to the Pascal1K data set *improves* the generated descriptions from 7.4 → 8.2 Meteor points. The performance of BRNN substantially decreases when transferring between data sets, suggesting that the model may be overfitting its training domain.

4.6 Discussion

Notwithstanding the conceptual differences between multi-modal deep learning and learning an explicit spatial model of object–object relationships, two key differences between the BRNN and our approach are the nature visual input and the language generation models.

The neural network model can readily use the pre-softmax visual feature vector from any of the pre-trained models available in the Caffe Model

Zoo, whereas VDR is currently restricted to discrete object detector outputs from those models. The implication of this is that the VDR-based approach is unable to describe 30% of the data in the VLT2K data set. This is due to the object detection model not recognising crucial objects for three of the action classes: cameras, books, and telephones. We considered using the VGG-16 pretrained model from the ImageNet Recognition and Localization task in the RCNN object detector, thus mirroring the detection model used by the neural network. Frustratingly, this does not seem possible because none of the 1,000 types of objects in the recognition task correspond to a person-type of entity. One approach to alleviating this problem could be to use weakly-supervised object localisation (Oquab et al., 2014).

The template-based language generation model used by VDR lacks the flexibility to describe interesting prepositional phrases or variety within its current template. An n-gram language generator, such as the phrase-based approaches of (Ortiz et al., 2015; Lebret et al., 2015), that works within the constraints imposed by VDR structure may generate better descriptions of images than the current template.

5 Conclusions

In this paper we showed how to infer useful and reliable Visual Dependency Representations of images without expensive human supervision. Our approach was based on searching for objects in images, given a collection of co-occurring descriptions. We evaluated the utility of the representations on a downstream automatic image description task on two data sets, where the quality of the generated text largely depended on the data set. In a large data set of people performing actions, the descriptions generated by our model were comparable to a state-of-the-art multimodal deep neural network. In a smaller and more diverse data set, our approach produced poor descriptions because it was unable to extract enough useful training examples for the model. In a follow-up experiment that transferred the VDR Parsing and Language Generation model between data, we found improvements in the diverse data set. Our experiments demonstrated that explicitly encoding the spatial relationships between objects is a useful way of learning how to describe actions.

There are several fruitful opportunities for future work. The most immediate improvement may be found with broader coverage object detectors. It would be useful to search for objects using multiple pre-trained visual detection models, such as a 200-class ImageNet Detection model and a 1,000-class ImageNet Recognition and Localisation model. A second strand of further work would be to relax the strict mirroring of human annotator behaviour when searching for subjects and objects in an image. It may be possible to learn good representations using only the nouns in the POS tagged description. Our current approach strictly limits the inferred VDRs to transitive verbs; images with descriptions such as "A large cow in a field" or "A man is walking" are also a focus for future relaxations of the process for creating training data. Another direction for future work would be to use a n-gram based language model constrained by the structured predicted in VDR. The current template based method is limiting the generation of objects that are being correctly realised in images.

Tackling the aforementioned future work opens up opportunities to working with larger and more diverse data sets such as the Flickr8K (Hodosh et al., 2013), Flickr30K (Young et al., 2014), and MS COCO (Lin et al., 2014b) or larger action recognition data sets such as TUHOI (Le et al., 2014) or MPII Human Poses (Andriluka et al., 2014).

Acknowledgements

We thank the anonymous reviewers for their comments, and members of LaCo at ILLC and WILLOW at INRIA for comments on an earlier version of the work. We thank the Database Architectures Group and the Life Sciences Group at CWI for access to their NVIDIA Tesla K20 GPUs. D. Elliott is funded by an Alain Bensoussain Career Development Fellowship, A. P. de Vries is partially funded by COMMIT/.

References

Mykhaylo Andriluka, Leonid Pishchulin, Peter Gehler, and Bernt Schiele. 2014. 2D Human Pose Estimation: New Benchmark and State of the Art Analysis. In *CVPR '14*, pages 3686–3693, Columbus, OH, US.

Moshe Bar and Shimon Ullman. 1996. Spatial Context in Recognition. *Perception*, 25(3):343–52.

Irving Biederman, Robert J Mezzanotte, and Jan C Rabinowitz. 1982. Scene perception: Detecting and judging objects undergoing relational violations. *Cognitive Psychology*, 14(2):143–177.

JH Clark, Chris Dyer, Alon Lavie, and NA Smith. 2011. Better hypothesis testing for statistical machine translation: Controlling for optimizer instability. In *ACL-HTL '11*, pages 176–181, Portland, OR, U.S.A.

Michael Denkowski and Alon Lavie. 2011. Meteor 1.3: Automatic metric for reliable optimization and evaluation of machine translation systems. In *SMT at EMNLP '11*, Edinburgh, Scotland, U.K.

Jeff Donahue, Lisa Anne Hendricks, Sergio Guadarrama, Marcus Rohrbach, Subhashini Venugopalan, Kate Saenko, and Trevor Darrell. 2015. Long-term Recurrent Convolutional Networks for Visual Recognition and Description. In *CVPR '15*, Boston, MA, U.S.A.

David Eigen, Christian Puhrsch, and Rob Fergus. 2014. Depth Map Prediction from a Single Image using a Multi-Scale Deep Network. In *NIPS 27*, Lake Tahoe, CA, U.S.A, June.

Desmond Elliott and Frank Keller. 2013. Image Description using Visual Dependency Representations. In *EMNLP '13*, pages 1292–1302, Seattle, WA, U.S.A.

Desmond Elliott and Frank Keller. 2014. Comparing Automatic Evaluation Measures for Image Description. In *ACL '14*, pages 452–457, Baltimore, MD, U.S.A.

Desmond Elliott, Victor Lavrenko, and Frank Keller. 2014. Query-by-Example Image Retrieval using Visual Dependency Representations. In *COLING '14*, pages 109–120, Dublin, Ireland.

Mark Everingham, Luc Van Gool, Christopher Williams, John Winn, and Andrew Zisserman. 2010. The PASCAL Visual Object Classes Challenge. *IJCV*, 88(2):303–338.

Hao Fang, Saurabh Gupta, Forrest Iandola, Rupesh Srivastava, Li Deng, Piotr Dollár, Jianfeng Gao, Xiaodong He, Margaret Mitchell, John C. Platt, C. Lawrence Zitnick, and Geoffrey Zweig. 2015. From Captions to Visual Concepts and Back. In *CVPR '15*, Boston, MA, U.S.A.

Ali Farhadi, Mohsen Hejrati, Mohammad Amin Sadeghi, Peter Young, Cyrus Rashtchian, Julia Hockenmaier, and David Forsyth. 2010. Every picture tells a story: generating sentences from images. In *ECCV '10*, pages 15–29, Heraklion, Crete, Greece.

Yansong Feng and Mirella Lapata. 2008. Automatic Image Annotation Using Auxiliary Text Information. In *ACL '08*, pages 272–280, Colombus, Ohio.

Ross Girshick, Jeff Donahue, Trevor Darrell, and Jitendra Malik. 2014. Rich feature hierarchies for accurate object detection and semantic segmentation. *CoRR*, abs/1311.2.

Micah Hodosh, Peter Young, and Julia Hockenmaier. 2013. Framing Image Description as a Ranking Task: Data, Models and Evaluation Metrics. *JAIR*, 47:853–899.

Yangqing Jia, Evan Shelhamer, Jeff Donahue, Sergey Karayev, Jonathan Long, Ross B. Girshick, Sergio Guadarrama, and Trevor Darrell. 2014. Caffe: Convolutional Architecture for Fast Feature Embedding. In *MM '14*, pages 675–678, Orlando, FL, U.S.A.

Andrej Karpathy and Li Fei-Fei. 2015. Deep Visual-Semantic Alignments for Generating Image Descriptions. In *CVPR '15*, Boston, MA, U.S.A.

Andrej Karpathy, Armand Joulin, and Li Fei-Fei. 2014. Deep Fragment Embeddings for Bidirectional Image Sentence Mapping. In *NIPS 28*, Montreal, Quebec, Canada.

Girish Kulkarni, Visruth Premraj, Sagnik Dhar, Siming Li, Yejin Choi, Alexander C. Berg, and Tamara L. Berg. 2011. Baby talk: Understanding and generating simple image descriptions. In *CVPR '11*, pages 1601–1608, Colorado Springs, CO, U.S.A.

Polina Kuznetsova, Vicente Ordonez, Alexander C. Berg, Tamara L. Berg, and Yejin Choi. 2012. Collective Generation of Natural Image Descriptions. In *ACL '12*, pages 359–368, Jeju Island, South Korea.

Dieu-thu Le, Jasper Uijlings, and Raffaella Bernardi. 2014. TUHOI : Trento Universal Human Object Interaction Dataset. In *WVL at COLING '14*, pages 17–24, Dublin, Ireland.

Remi Lebret, Pedro O. Pinheiro, and Ronan Collobert. 2015. Phrase-based Image Captioning. In *ICML '15*, Lille, France, February.

Siming Li, Girish Kulkarni, Tamara L. Berg, Alexander C. Berg, and Yejin Choi. 2011. Composing simple image descriptions using web-scale n-grams. In *CoNLL '11*, pages 220–228, Portland, OR, U.S.A.

Chin-Yew Lin and Franz Josef Och. 2004. Automatic evaluation of machine translation quality using longest common subsequence and skip-bigram statistics. In *ACL '04*, pages 605–612, Barcelona, Spain.

Min Lin, Qiang Chen, and Shuicheng Yan. 2014a. Network In Network. In *ICLR '14*, volume abs/1312.4, Banff, Canada.

Tsung-Yi Lin, Michael Maire, Serge Belongie, Lubomir Bourdev, Ross Girshick, James Hays, Pietro Perona, Deva Ramanan, C. Lawrence Zitnick, and Piotr Dollár. 2014b. Microsoft COCO: Common Objects in Context. In *ECCV '14*, pages 740–755, Zurich, Switzerland.

GD Logan and DD Sadler. 1996. A computational analysis of the apprehension of spatial relations. In Paul Bloom, Mary A. Peterson, Lynn Nadel, and Merrill F. Garrett, editors, *Language and Space*, pages 492–592. MIT Press.

Junhua Mao, Wei Xu, Yi Yang, Yiang Wang, and Alan L. Yuille. 2015. Deep captioning with multimodal recurrent neural networks (m-rnn). In *ICLR '15*, volume abs/1412.6632, San Diego, CA, U.S.A.

Emily E. Marsh and Marilyn Domas White. 2003. A taxonomy of relationships between images and text. *Journal of Documentation*, 59(6):647–672.

Guido Minnen, John Carroll, and Darren Pearce. 2001. Applied morphological processing of English. *Natural Language Engineering*, 7(3):207–223.

Margaret Mitchell, Jesse Dodge, Amit Goyal, Kota Yamaguchi, Karl Stratos, Alyssa Mensch, Alex Berg, Tamara Berg, and Hal Daum. 2012. Midge : Generating Image Descriptions From Computer Vision Detections. In *EACL '12*, pages 747–756, Avignon, France.

Joakim Nivre, Johan Hall, Jens Nilsson, Atanas Chanev, Gülsen Eryigit, Sandra Kübler, Svetoslav Marinov, and Erwin Marsi. 2007. MaltParser: A language-independent system for data-driven dependency parsing. *Natural Language Engineering*, 13(2):1.

Maxime Oquab, Leon Bottou, Ivan Laptev, and Josef Sivic. 2014. Learning and Transferring Mid-level Image Representations Using Convolutional Neural Networks. In *CVPR '14*, pages 1717–1724, Columbus, OH, US.

Luis M. G. Ortiz, Clemens Wolff, and Mirella Lapata. 2015. Learning to Interpret and Describe Abstract Scenes. In *NAACL '15*, Denver, CO, U.S.A.

Erwin Panofsky. 1939. *Studies in Iconology*. Oxford University Press.

Kishore Papineni, Salim Roukos, Todd Ward, and WJ Zhu. 2002. BLEU: a method for automatic evaluation of machine translation. In *ACL '02*, pages 311–318, Philadelphia, PA, U.S.A.

DA Randell, Z Cui, and AG Cohn. 1992. A spatial logic based on regions and connection. In *Principles of Knowledge Representation and Reasoning*, pages 165–176.

Cyrus Rashtchian, Peter Young, Micah Hodosh, and Julia Hockenmaier. 2010. Collecting image annotations using Amazon's Mechanical Turk. In *AMT at NAACL '10*, pages 139–147, Los Angeles, CA, U.S.A.

Olga Russakovsky, Jia Deng, Hao Su, Jonathan Krause, Sanjeev Satheesh, Sean Ma, Zhiheng Huang, Andrej Karpathy, Aditya Khosla, Michael Bernstein, Alexander C Berg, and Li Fei-Fei. 2014. ImageNet Large Scale Visual Recognition Challenge.

Mohammad A Sadeghi and Ali Farhadi. 2011. Recognition Using Visual Phrases. In *CVPR '11*, pages 1745–1752, Colorado Springs, CO, U.S.A.

Sara Shatford. 1986. Analysing the Subject of a Picture: A Theoretical Approach. *Cataloging & Classification Quarterly*, 6(3):39–62.

Karen Simonyan and Andrew Zisserman. 2015. Very Deep Convolutional Networks for Large-Scale Image Recognition. In *ICLR '15*, volume abs/1409.1, San Diego, CA, U.S.A.

Richard Socher, Andrej Karpathy, Q Le, C Manning, and A Ng. 2014. Grounded Compositional Semantics for Finding and Describing Images with Sentences. *TACL*, 2:207–218.

Kristina Toutanova, Dan Klein, and Christopher D Manning. 2003. Feature-Rich Part-of-Speech Tagging with a Cyclic Dependency Network. In *HLT-NAACL '03*, pages 173–180, Edmonton, Canada.

Oriol Vinyals, Alexander Toshev, Samy Bengio, and Dumitru Erhan. 2015. Show and tell: A neural image caption generator. In *CVPR '15*, Boston, MA, U.S.A.

Yezhou Yang, Ching Lik Teo, Hal Daumé III, and Yiannis Aloimonos. 2011. Corpus-Guided Sentence Generation of Natural Images. In *EMNLP '11*, pages 444–454, Edinburgh, Scotland, UK.

Mark Yatskar, Michel Galley, L Vanderwende, and L Zettlemoyer. 2014. See No Evil, Say No Evil: Description Generation from Densely Labeled Images. In **SEM*, pages 110–120, Dublin, Ireland.

Peter Young, Alice Lai, Micah Hodosh, and Julia Hockenmaier. 2014. From image descriptions to visual denotations: New similarity metrics for semantic inference over event descriptions. *TACL*, 2:67–78.

Text to 3D Scene Generation with Rich Lexical Grounding

Angel Chang*, **Will Monroe***, **Manolis Savva,**
Christopher Potts and **Christopher D. Manning**
Stanford University, Stanford, CA 94305
{angelx,wmonroe4,msavva}@cs.stanford.edu,
{cgpotts,manning}@stanford.edu

Abstract

The ability to map descriptions of scenes to 3D geometric representations has many applications in areas such as art, education, and robotics. However, prior work on the *text to 3D scene generation* task has used manually specified object categories and language that identifies them. We introduce a dataset of 3D scenes annotated with natural language descriptions and learn from this data how to ground textual descriptions to physical objects. Our method successfully grounds a variety of lexical terms to concrete referents, and we show quantitatively that our method improves 3D scene generation over previous work using purely rule-based methods. We evaluate the fidelity and plausibility of 3D scenes generated with our grounding approach through human judgments. To ease evaluation on this task, we also introduce an automated metric that strongly correlates with human judgments.

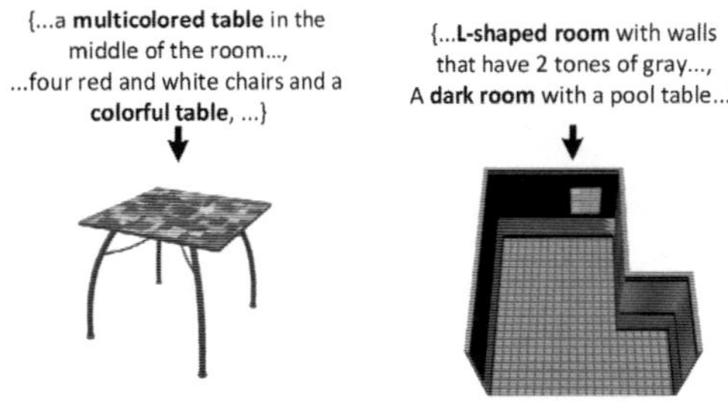

Figure 1: We learn how to ground references such as "L-shaped room" to 3D models in a paired corpus of 3D scenes and natural language descriptions. Sentence fragments in bold were identified as high-weighted references to the shown objects.

1 Introduction

We examine the task of *text to 3D scene generation*. The ability to map descriptions of scenes to 3D geometric representations has a wide variety of applications; many creative industries use 3D scenes. Robotics applications need to interpret commands referring to real-world environments, and the ability to visualize scenarios given high-level descriptions is of great practical use in educational tools. Unfortunately, 3D scene design user interfaces are prohibitively complex for novice users. Prior work has shown the task remains challenging and time intensive for non-experts, even with simplified interfaces (Savva et al., 2014).

Language offers a convenient way for designers to express their creative goals. Systems that can interpret natural descriptions to build a visual representation allow non-experts to visually express their thoughts with language, as was demonstrated by WordsEye, a pioneering work in text to 3D scene generation (Coyne and Sproat, 2001).

WordsEye and other prior work in this area (Seversky and Yin, 2006; Chang et al., 2014) used manually chosen mappings between language and objects in scenes. To our knowledge, we present the first 3D scene generation approach that learns from data how to map textual terms to objects. First, we collect a dataset of 3D scenes along with textual descriptions by people, which we contribute to the community. We then train a classifier on a scene discrimination task and extract high-weight features that ground lexical terms to 3D models. We integrate our learned lexical groundings with a rule-based scene generation approach, and we show through a human-judgment evaluation that the combination outperforms both approaches in isolation. Finally, we introduce a scene similarity metric that correlates with human judgments.

*The first two authors are listed in alphabetical order.

Proceedings of the 53rd Annual Meeting of the Association for Computational Linguistics and the 7th International Joint Conference on Natural Language Processing, pages 53–62,
Beijing, China, July 26-31, 2015.

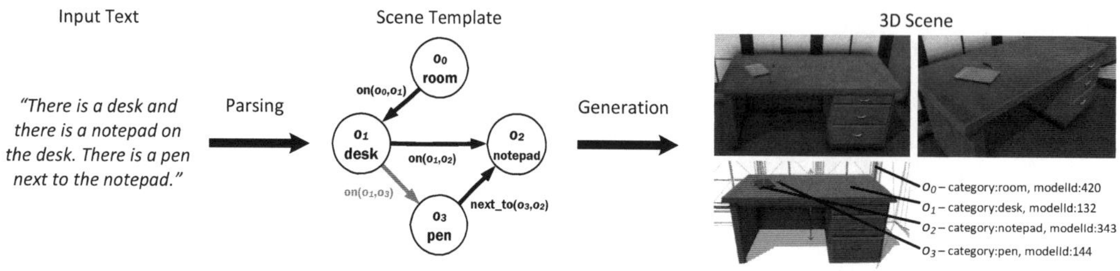

Figure 2: Illustration of the text to 3D scene generation pipeline. The input is text describing a scene (left), which we parse into an abstract scene template representation capturing objects and relations (middle). The scene template is then used to generate a concrete 3D scene visualizing the input description (right). The 3D scene is constructed by retrieving and arranging appropriate 3D models.

2 Task Description

In the text to 3D scene generation task, the input is a natural language description, and the output is a 3D representation of a plausible scene that fits the description and can be viewed and rendered from multiple perspectives. More precisely, given an utterance x as input, the output is a scene y: an arrangement of 3D models representing objects at specified positions and orientations in space.

In this paper, we focus on the subproblem of lexical grounding of textual terms to 3D model referents (i.e., choosing 3D models that represent objects referred to by terms in the input utterance x). We employ an intermediate *scene template* representation parsed from the input text to capture the physical objects present in a scene and constraints between them. This representation is then used to generate a 3D scene (Figure 2).

A naïve approach to scene generation might use keyword search to retrieve 3D models. However, such an approach is unlikely to generalize well in that it fails to capture important object attributes and spatial relations. In order for the generated scene to accurately reflect the input description, a deep understanding of language describing environments is necessary. Many challenging subproblems need to be tackled: physical object mention detection, estimation of object attributes such as size, extraction of spatial constraints, and placement of objects at appropriate relative positions and orientations. The subproblem of lexical grounding to 3D models has a larged impact on the quality of generated scenes, as later stages of scene generation rely on having a correctly chosen set of objects to arrange.

Another challenge is that much common knowledge about the physical properties of objects and the structure of environments is rarely mentioned in natural language (e.g., that most tables are supported on the floor and in an upright orientation). Unfortunately, common 3D representations of objects and scenes used in computer graphics specify only geometry and appearance, and rarely include such information. Prior work in text to 3D scene generation focused on collecting manual annotations of object properties and relations (Rouhizadeh et al., 2011; Coyne et al., 2012), which are used to drive rule-based generation systems. Regrettably, the task of scene generation has not yet benefited from recent related work in NLP.

3 Related Work

There is much prior work in image retrieval given textual queries; a recent overview is provided by Siddiquie et al. (2011). The image retrieval task bears some similarity to our task insofar as 3D scene retrieval is an approach that can approximate 3D scene generation.

However, there are fundamental differences between 2D images and 3D scenes. Generation in image space has predominantly focused on composition of simple 2D clip art elements, as exemplified recently by Zitnick et al. (2013). The task of composing 3D scenes presents a much higher-dimensional search space of scene configurations where finding plausible and desirable configurations is difficult. Unlike prior work in clip art generation which uses a small pre-specified set of objects, we ground to a large database of objects that can occur in various indoor environments: 12490 3D models from roughly 270 categories.

There is a bed and there is a nightstand next to the bed.

There is a chair and a table.

There is a table and there are four chairs. There are four plates and there are four sandwiches.

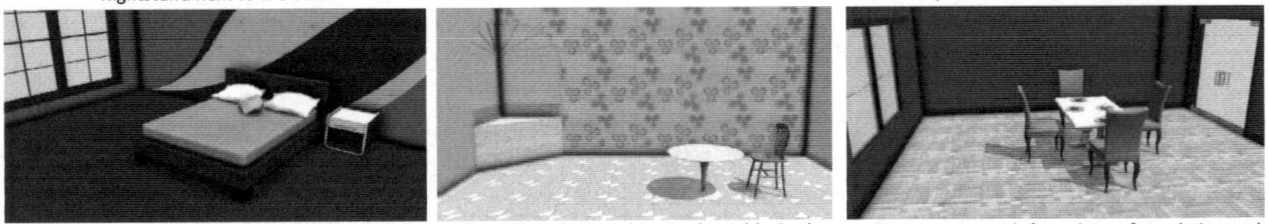

- There is a bed with three pillows and a bedside table next to it.
- The room appears to be a bedroom. A blue bed and white nightstand are pushed against the furthest wall. A window is on the left side.
- A dark bedroom with a queen bed with blue comforter and three pillows. There is a night stand. One wall is decorated with a large design and another wall has three large windows.

- There is a chair and a circular table in the middle of a floral print room.
- a corner widow room with a a table and chair sitting to the east side.
- There's a dresser in the corner of the room, and a yellow table with a brown wooden chair.

- dinning room with four plates, four chairs, and four sandwiches
- dark room with two small windows. A rectangular table seating four is in the middle of the room with plates set. There is a set of two gray double doors on another wall.
- i see a rectangular table in the center of the room. There are 4 chairs around the table and 4 plates on the table

Figure 3: Scenes created by participants from seed description sentences (**top**). Additional descriptions provided by other participants from the created scene (**bottom**). Our dataset contains around 19 scenes per seed sentence, for a total of 1129 scenes. Scenes exhibit variation in the specific objects chosen and their placement. Each scene is described by 3 or 4 other people, for a total of 4358 descriptions.

3.1 Text to Scene Systems

Pioneering work on the SHRDLU system (Winograd, 1972) demonstrated linguistic manipulation of objects in 3D scenes. However, the discourse domain was restricted to a micro-world with simple geometric shapes to simplify parsing and grounding of natural language input. More recently, prototype text to 3D scene generation systems have been built for broader domains, most notably the WordsEye system (Coyne and Sproat, 2001) and later work by Seversky and Yin (2006). Chang et al. (2014) showed it is possible to learn spatial priors for objects and relations directly from 3D scene data.

These systems use manually defined mappings between language and their representation of the physical world. This prevents generalization to more complex object descriptions, variations in word choice and spelling, and other languages. It also forces users to use unnatural language to express their intent (e.g., *the table is two feet to the south of the window*).

We propose reducing reliance on manual lexicons by learning to map descriptions to objects from a corpus of 3D scenes and associated textual descriptions. While we find that lexical knowledge alone is not sufficient to generate high-quality scenes, a learned approach to lexical grounding can be used in combination with a rule-based system for handling compositional knowledge, resulting in better scenes than either component alone.

3.2 Related Tasks

Prior work has generated sentences that describe 2D images (Farhadi et al., 2010; Kulkarni et al., 2011; Karpathy et al., 2014) and referring expressions for specific objects in images (FitzGerald et al., 2013; Kazemzadeh et al., 2014). However, generating scenes is currently out of reach for purely image-based approaches. 3D scene representations serve as an intermediate level of structure between raw image pixels and simpler microcosms (e.g., grid and block worlds). This level of structure is amenable to the generation task but still realistic enough to present a variety of challenges associated with natural scenes.

A related line of work focuses on grounding referring expressions to referents in 3D worlds with simple colored geometric shapes (Gorniak and Roy, 2004; Gorniak and Roy, 2005). More recent work grounds text to object attributes such as color and shape in images (Matuszek et al., 2012; Krishnamurthy and Kollar, 2013). Golland et al. (2010) ground spatial relationship language in 3D scenes (e.g., *to the left of*, *behind*) by learning from pairwise object relations provided by crowdworkers. In contrast, we ground general descriptions to a wide variety of possible objects. The objects in our scenes represent a broader space of possible referents than the first two lines of work. Unlike the latter work, our descriptions are provided as unrestricted free-form text, rather than filling in specific templates of object references and fixed spatial relationships.

4 Dataset

We introduce a new dataset of 1128 scenes and 4284 free-form natural language descriptions of these scenes.[1] To create this training set, we used a simple online scene design interface that allows users to assemble scenes using available 3D models of common household objects (each model is annotated with a category label and has a unique ID). We used a set of 60 seed sentences describing simple configurations of interior scenes as prompts and asked workers on the Amazon Mechanical Turk crowdsourcing platform to create scenes corresponding to these seed descriptions. To obtain more varied descriptions for each scene, we asked other workers to describe each scene. Figure 3 shows examples of seed description sentences, 3D scenes created by people given those descriptions, and new descriptions provided by others viewing the created scenes.

We manually examined a random subset of the descriptions (approximately 10%) to eliminate spam and unacceptably poor descriptions. When we identified an unacceptable description, we also examined all other descriptions by the same worker, as most poor descriptions came from a small number of workers. From our sample, we estimate that less than 3% of descriptions were spam or unacceptably incoherent. To reflect natural use, we retained minor typographical and grammatical errors.

Despite the small set of seed sentences, the Turker-provided scenes exhibit much variety in the specific objects used and their placements within the scene. Over 600 distinct 3D models appear in at least one scene, and more than 40% of non-room objects are rotated from their default orientation, despite the fact that this requires an extra manipulation in the scene-building interface. The descriptions collected for these scenes are similarly diverse and usually differ substantially in length and content from the seed sentences.[2]

5 Model

To create a model for generating scene templates from text, we train a classifier to learn lexical groundings. We then combine our learned lexical groundings with a rule-based scene generation model. The learned groundings allow us to select better models, while the rule-based model offers simple compositionality for handling coreference and relationships between objects.

5.1 Learning lexical groundings

To learn lexical mappings from examples, we train a classifier on a related grounding task and extract the weights of lexical features for use in scene generation. This classifier learns from a "discrimination" version of our scene dataset, in which the scene in each scene–description pair is hidden among four other distractor scenes sampled uniformly at random. The training objective is to maximize the L_2-regularized log likelihood of this scene discrimination dataset under a one-vs.-all logistic regression model, using each true scene and each distractor scene as one example (with *true*/*distractor* as the output label).

The learned model uses binary-valued features indicating the co-occurrence of a unigram or bigram and an object category or model ID. For example, features extracted from the scene-description pair shown in Figure 2 would include the tuples (*desk*, `modelId:132`) and (*the notepad*, `category:notepad`).

To evaluate our learned model's performance at discriminating scenes, independently of its use in scene generation, we split our scene and description corpus (augmented with distractor scenes) randomly into train, development, and test portions 70%-15%-15% by scene. Using only model ID features, the classifier achieves a discrimination accuracy of 0.715 on the test set; adding features that use object categories as well as model IDs improves accuracy to 0.833.

5.2 Rule-based Model

We use the rule-based parsing component described in Chang et al. (2014). This system incorporates knowledge that is important for scene generation and not addressed by our learned model (e.g., spatial relationships and coreference). In Section 5.3, we describe how we use our learned model to augment this model.

This rule-based approach is a three-stage process using established NLP systems: 1) The input text is split into multiple sentences and parsed using the Stanford CoreNLP pipeline (Manning et

[1] Available at `http://nlp.stanford.edu/data/text2scene.shtml`.

[2] Mean 26.2 words, SD 17.4; versus mean 16.6, SD 7.2 for the seed sentences. If one considers seed sentences to be the "reference," the macro-averaged BLEU score (Papineni et al., 2002) of the Turker descriptions is 12.0.

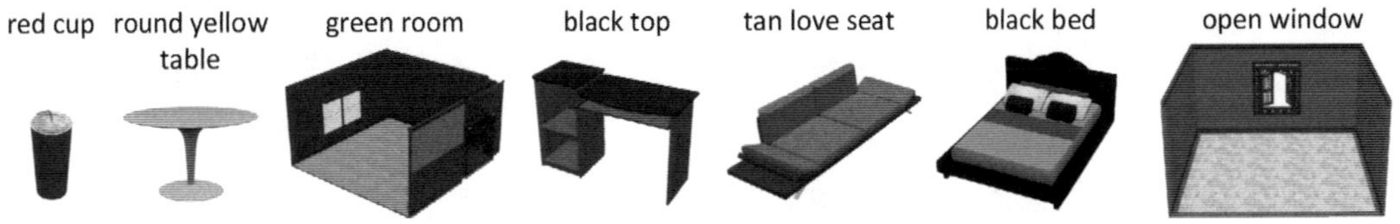

Figure 4: Some examples extracted from the top 20 highest-weight features in our learned model: lexical terms from the descriptions in our scene corpus are grounded to 3D models within the scene corpus.

al., 2014). Head words of noun phrases are identified as candidate object categories, filtered using WordNet (Miller, 1995) to only include physical objects. 2) References to the same object are collapsed using the Stanford coreference system. 3) Properties are attached to each object by extracting other adjectives and nouns in the noun phrase. These properties are later used to query the 3D model database.

We use the same model database as Chang et al. (2014) and also extract spatial relations between objects using the same set of dependency patterns.

5.3 Combined Model

The rule-based parsing model is limited in its ability to choose appropriate 3D models. We integrate our learned lexical groundings with this model to build an improved scene generation system.

Identifying object categories Using the rule-based model, we extract all noun phrases as potential objects. For each noun phrase p, we extract features $\{\phi_i\}$ and compute the score of a category c being described by the noun phrase as the sum of the feature weights from the learned model in Section 5.1:

$$\text{Score}(c \mid p) = \sum_{\phi_i \in \phi(p)} \theta_{(i,c)},$$

where $\theta_{(i,c)}$ is the weight for associating feature ϕ_i with category c. From categories with a score higher than $T_c = 0.5$, we select the best-scoring category as the representative for the noun phrase. If no category's score exceeds T_c, we use the head of the noun phrase for the object category.

3D model selection For each object mention detected in the description, we use the feature weights from the learned model to select a specific object to add to the scene. After using dependency rules to extract spatial relationships and descriptive terms associated with the object, we compute the score of a 3D model m given the category c and a set of descriptive terms d using a similar sum of feature weights. As the rule-based system may not accurately identify the correct set of terms d, we augment the score with a sum of feature weights over the entire input description x:

$$m = \arg\max_{m \in \{c\}} \lambda_d \sum_{\phi_i \in \phi(d)} \theta_{(i,m)} + \lambda_x \sum_{\phi_i \in \phi(x)} \theta_{(i,m)}$$

For the results shown here, $\lambda_d = 0.75$ and $\lambda_x = 0.25$. We select the best-scoring 3D model with positive score. If no model has positive score, we assume the object mention was spurious and omit the object.

text	category	text	category
chair	`Chair`	round	`RoundTable`
lamp	`Lamp`	laptop	`Laptop`
couch	`Couch`	fruit	`Bowl`
vase	`Vase`	round table	`RoundTable`
sofa	`Couch`	laptop	`Computer`
bed	`Bed`	bookshelf	`Bookcase`

Table 1: Top groundings of lexical terms in our dataset to categories of 3D models in the scenes.

6 Learned lexical groundings

By extracting high-weight features from our learned model, we can visualize specific models to which lexical terms are grounded (see Figure 4). These features correspond to high frequency text–3D model pairs within the scene corpus. Table 1 shows some of the top learned lexical groundings to model database categories. We are able to recover many simple identity mappings without using lexical similarity features, and we capture several lexical variants (e.g., *sofa* for `Couch`). A few erroneous mappings reflect common co-occurrences; for example, *fruit* is mapped to `Bowl` due to fruit typically being observed in bowls in our dataset.

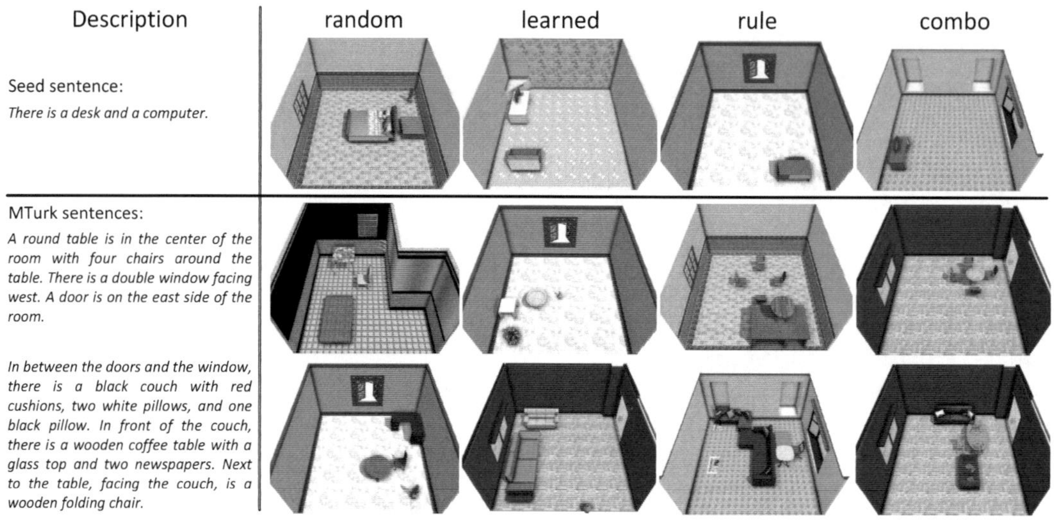

Figure 5: Qualitative comparison of generated scenes for three input descriptions (one *Seed* and two *MTurk*), using the four different methods: *random*, *learned*, *rule*, *combo*.

7 Experimental Results

We conduct a human judgment experiment to compare the quality of generated scenes using the approaches we presented and baseline methods. To evaluate whether lexical grounding improves scene generation, we need a method to arrange the chosen models into 3D scenes. Since 3D scene layout is not a focus of our work, we use an approach based on prior work in 3D scene synthesis and text to scene generation (Fisher et al., 2012; Chang et al., 2014), simplified by using sampling rather than a hill climbing strategy.

Conditions We compare five conditions: {*random, learned, rule, combo, human*}. The *random* condition represents a baseline which synthesizes a scene with randomly-selected models, while *human* represents scenes created by people. The *learned* condition takes our learned lexical groundings, picks the four[3] most likely objects, and generates a scene based on them. The *rule* and *combo* conditions use scenes generated by the rule-based approach and the combined model, respectively.

Descriptions We consider two sets of input descriptions: {*Seeds, MTurk*}. The *Seeds* descriptions are 50 of the initial seed sentences from which workers were asked to create scenes. These seed sentences were simple (e.g., *There is a desk and a chair*, *There is a plate on a table*) and did not have modifiers describing the objects. The *MTurk* descriptions are much more descriptive and exhibit a wider variety in language (including misspellings and ungrammatical constructs). Our hypothesis was that the rule-based system would perform well on the simple *Seeds* descriptions, but it would be insufficient for handling the complexities of the more varied *MTurk* descriptions. For these more natural descriptions, we expected our combination model to perform better. Our experimental results confirm this hypothesis.

7.1 Qualitative Evaluation

Figure 5 shows a qualitative comparison of 3D scenes generated from example input descriptions using each of the four methods. In the top row, the *rule-based* approach selects a CPU chassis for *computer*, while *combo* and *learned* select a more iconic monitor. In the bottom row, the rule-based approach selects two newspapers and places them on the floor, while the combined approach correctly selects a coffee table with two newspapers on it. The learned model is limited to four objects and does not have a notion of object identity, so it often duplicates objects.

7.2 Human Evaluation

We performed an experiment in which people rated the degree to which scenes match the textual descriptions from which they were generated.

[3] The average number of objects in a scene in our human-built dataset was 3.9.

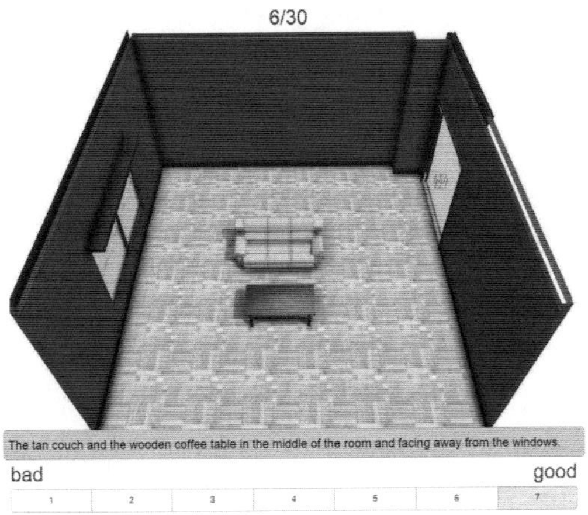

Figure 6: Screenshot of the UI for rating scene-description match.

Such ratings are a natural way to evaluate how well our approach can generate scenes from text: in practical use, a person would provide an input description and then judge the suitability of the resulting scenes. For the *MTurk* descriptions, we randomly sampled 100 descriptions from the development split of our dataset.

Procedure During the experiment, each participant was shown 30 pairs of scene descriptions and generated 3D scenes drawn randomly from all five conditions. All participants provided 30 responses each for a total of 5040 scene-description ratings. Participants were asked to rate how well the generated scene matched the input description on a 7-point Likert scale, with 1 indicating a poor match and 7 a very good one (see Figure 6). In a separate task with the same experimental procedure, we asked other participants to rate the overall plausibility of each generated scene without a reference description. This plausibility rating measures whether a method can generate plausible scenes irrespective of the degree to which the input description is matched. We used Amazon Mechanical Turk to recruit 168 participants for rating the match of scenes to descriptions and 63 participants for rating scene plausibility.

Design The experiment followed a within-subjects factorial design. The dependent measure was the Likert rating. Since per-participant and per-scene variance on the rating is not accounted for by a standard ANOVA, we use a mixed effects model which can account for both fixed effects and random effects to determine the statistical significance of our results.[4] We treat the participant and the specific scene as random effects of varying intercept, and the method condition as the fixed effect.

method	Seeds	MTurk
random	2.03 (1.88 – 2.18)	1.68 (1.57 – 1.79)
learned	3.51 (3.23 – 3.77)	2.61 (2.40 – 2.84)
rule	**5.44** (5.26 – 5.61)	3.15 (2.91 – 3.40)
combo	5.23 (4.96 – 5.44)	**3.73** (3.48 – 3.95)
human	6.06 (5.90 – 6.19)	5.87 (5.74 – 6.00)

Table 2: Average scene-description match ratings across sentence types and methods (95% C.I.).

Results There was a significant effect of the method condition on the scene-description match rating: $\chi^2(4, N = 5040) = 1378.2, p < 0.001$. Table 2 summarizes the average scene-description match ratings and 95% confidence intervals for all sentence type–condition pairs. All pairwise differences between ratings were significant under Wilcoxon rank-sum tests with the Bonferroni-Holm correction ($p < 0.05$). The scene plausibility ratings, which were obtained independent of descriptions, indicated that the only significant difference in plausibility was between scenes created by people (*human*) and all the other conditions. We see that for the simple seed sentences both the rule-based and combined model approach the quality of human-created scenes. However, all methods have significantly lower ratings for the more complex *MTurk* sentences. In this more challenging scenario, the combined model is closest to the manually created scenes and significantly outperforms both rule-based and learned models in isolation.

7.3 Error Analysis

Figure 7 shows some common error cases in our system. The top left scene was generated with the rule-based method, the top right with the learned method, and the bottom two with the combined approach. At the top left, there is an erroneous selection of concrete object category (wood logs) for the *four wood chairs* reference in the input description, due to an incorrect head identification. At top right, the learned model identifies the

[4] We used the `lme4` R package and optimized fit with maximum log-likelihood (Baayen et al., 2008). We report significance results using the likelihood-ratio (LR) test.

Figure 7: Common scene generation errors. From top left clockwise: *Wood table and four wood chairs in the center of the room*; *There is a black and brown desk with a table lamp and flowers*; *There is a white desk, a black chair, and a lamp in the corner of the room*; *There in the middle is a table, on the table is a cup.*

presence of brown desk and lamp but erroneously picks two desks and two lamps (since we always pick the top four objects). The scene on the bottom right does not obey the expressed spatial constraints (*in the corner of the room*) since our system does not understand the grounding of room corner and that the top right side is not a good fit due to the door. In the bottom left, incorrect coreference resolution results in two tables for *There in the middle is a table, on the table is a cup.*

7.4 Scene Similarity Metric

We introduce an automated metric for scoring scenes given a scene template representation, the *aligned scene template similarity* (ASTS). Given a one-to-one alignment A between the nodes of a scene template and the objects in a scene, let the alignment penalty $J(A)$ be the sum of the number of unaligned nodes in the scene template and the number of unaligned objects in the scene. For the aligned nodes, we compute a similarity score S per node pair (n, n') where $S(n, n') = 1$ if the model ID matches, $S(n, n') = 0.5$ if only the category matches and 0 otherwise.

We define the ASTS of a scene with respect to a scene template to be the maximum alignment score over all such alignments:

method	Human	ASTS
random	1.68	0.08
learned	2.61	0.23
rule	3.15	0.32
combo	**3.73**	**0.44**

Table 3: Average human ratings (out of 7) and aligned scene template similarity scores.

$$\text{ASTS}(s, z) = \max_A \frac{\sum_{(n,n')\in A} S(n, n')}{J(A) + |A|}.$$

With this definition, we compare average ASTS scores for each method against average human ratings (Table 3). We test the correlation of the ASTS metric against human ratings using Pearson's r and Kendall's rank correlation coefficient r_τ. We find that ASTS and human ratings are strongly correlated ($r = 0.70$, $r_\tau = 0.49$, $p < 0.001$). This suggests ASTS scores could be used to train and algorithmically evaluate scene generation systems that map descriptions to scene templates.

8 Future Work

Many error cases in our generated scenes resulted from not interpreting spatial relations. An obvious improvement would be to expand our learned lexical grounding approach to include spatial relations. This would help with spatial language that is not handled by the rule-based system's dependency patterns (e.g., *around*, *between*, *on the east side*). One approach would be to add spatial constraints to the definition of our scene similarity score and use this improved metric in training a semantic parser to generate scene templates.

To choose objects, our current system uses information obtained from language–object co-occurrences and sparse manually-annotated category labels; another promising avenue for achieving better lexical grounding is to propagate category labels using geometric and image features to learn the categories of unlabeled objects. Novel categories can also be extracted from Turker descriptions. These new labels could be used to improve the annotations in our 3D model database, enabling a wider range of object types to be used in scene generation.

Our approach learns object references without using lexical similarity features or a manually-assembled lexicon. Thus, we expect that our method for lexical grounding can facilitate development of text-to-scene systems in other languages. However, additional data collection and experiments are necessary to confirm this and identify challenges specific to other languages.

The necessity of handling omitted information suggests that a model incorporating a more sophisticated theory of pragmatic inference could be beneficial. Another important problem not addressed here is the role of context and discourse in interpreting scene descriptions. For example, several of our collected descriptions include language imagining embodied presence in the scene (e.g., *The wooden table is to your right, if you're entering the room from the doors*).

9 Conclusion

Prior work in 3D scene generation relies on purely rule-based methods to map object references to concrete 3D objects. We introduce a dataset of 3D scenes annotated with natural language descriptions which we believe will be of great interest to the research community. Using this corpus of scenes and descriptions, we present an approach that learns from data how to ground textual descriptions to objects.

To evaluate how our grounding approach impacts generated scene quality, we collect human judgments of generated scenes. In addition, we present a metric for automatically comparing generated scene templates to scenes, and we show that it correlates strongly with human judgments.

We demonstrate that rich lexical grounding can be learned directly from an unaligned corpus of 3D scenes and natural language descriptions, and that our model can successfully ground lexical terms to concrete referents, improving scene generation over baselines adapted from prior work.

Acknowledgments

We thank Katherine Breeden for valuable feedback. The authors gratefully acknowledge the support of the Defense Advanced Research Projects Agency (DARPA) Deep Exploration and Filtering of Text (DEFT) Program under Air Force Research Laboratory (AFRL) contract no. FA8750-13-2-0040, the National Science Foundation under grant no. IIS 1159679, the Department of the Navy, Office of Naval Research, under grant no. N00014-10-1-0109, and the Stanford Graduate Fellowship fund. Any opinions, findings, and conclusions or recommendations expressed in this material are those of the authors and do not necessarily reflect the views of the National Science Foundation, the Office of Naval Research, DARPA, AFRL, or the US government.

References

R.H. Baayen, D.J. Davidson, and D.M. Bates. 2008. Mixed-effects modeling with crossed random effects for subjects and items. *Journal of Memory and Language*, 59(4):390–412.

Angel X. Chang, Manolis Savva, and Christopher D. Manning. 2014. Learning spatial knowledge for text to 3D scene generation. In *Proceedings of Empirical Methods in Natural Language Processing (EMNLP)*.

Bob Coyne and Richard Sproat. 2001. WordsEye: an automatic text-to-scene conversion system. In *Proceedings of the 28th Annual Conference on Computer Graphics and Interactive Techniques*.

Bob Coyne, Alexander Klapheke, Masoud Rouhizadeh, Richard Sproat, and Daniel Bauer. 2012. Annotation tools and knowledge representation for a text-to-scene system. *Proceedings of COLING 2012: Technical Papers*.

Ali Farhadi, Mohsen Hejrati, Mohammad Amin Sadeghi, Peter Young, Cyrus Rashtchian, Julia Hockenmaier, and David Forsyth. 2010. Every picture tells a story: Generating sentences from images. In *Computer Vision–ECCV 2010*.

Matthew Fisher, Daniel Ritchie, Manolis Savva, Thomas Funkhouser, and Pat Hanrahan. 2012. Example-based synthesis of 3D object arrangements. *ACM Transactions on Graphics (TOG)*, 31(6):135.

Nicholas FitzGerald, Yoav Artzi, and Luke Zettlemoyer. 2013. Learning distributions over logical forms for referring expression generation. In *Proceedings of Empirical Methods in Natural Language Processing (EMNLP)*.

Dave Golland, Percy Liang, and Dan Klein. 2010. A game-theoretic approach to generating spatial descriptions. In *Proceedings of Empirical Methods in Natural Language Processing (EMNLP)*.

Peter Gorniak and Deb Roy. 2004. Grounded semantic composition for visual scenes. *Journal of Artificial Intelligence Research (JAIR)*, 21(1):429–470.

Peter Gorniak and Deb Roy. 2005. Probabilistic grounding of situated speech using plan recognition and reference resolution. In *Proceedings of the 7th International Conference on Multimodal Interfaces*.

Andrej Karpathy, Armand Joulin, and Li Fei-Fei. 2014. Deep fragment embeddings for bidirectional image sentence mapping. In *Advances in Neural Information Processing Systems*.

Sahar Kazemzadeh, Vicente Ordonez, Mark Matten, and Tamara L. Berg. 2014. ReferItGame: Referring to objects in photographs of natural scenes. In *Proceedings of Empirical Methods in Natural Language Processing (EMNLP)*.

Jayant Krishnamurthy and Thomas Kollar. 2013. Jointly learning to parse and perceive: Connecting natural language to the physical world. *Transactions of the Association for Computational Linguistics*, 1:193–206.

Girish Kulkarni, Visruth Premraj, Sagnik Dhar, Siming Li, Yejin Choi, Alexander C. Berg, and Tamara L. Berg. 2011. Baby talk: Understanding and generating simple image descriptions. In *IEEE Conference on Computer Vision and Pattern Recognition (CVPR)*.

Christopher D. Manning, Mihai Surdeanu, John Bauer, Jenny Finkel, Steven J. Bethard, and David McClosky. 2014. The Stanford CoreNLP natural language processing toolkit. In *Proceedings of the 52nd Annual Meeting of the Association for Computational Linguistics: System Demonstrations*.

Cynthia Matuszek, Nicholas FitzGerald, Luke Zettlemoyer, Liefeng Bo, and Dieter Fox. 2012. A joint model of language and perception for grounded attribute learning. In *International Conference on Machine Learning (ICML)*.

George A. Miller. 1995. WordNet: A lexical database for English. *Communications of the ACM*, 38(11):39–41.

Kishore Papineni, Salim Roukos, Todd Ward, and Wei-Jing Zhu. 2002. BLEU: A method for automatic evaluation of machine translation. In *Proceedings of the 40th Annual Meeting of the Association for Computational Linguistics*.

Masoud Rouhizadeh, Margit Bowler, Richard Sproat, and Bob Coyne. 2011. Collecting semantic data by Mechanical Turk for the lexical knowledge resource of a text-to-picture generating system. In *Proceedings of the Ninth International Conference on Computational Semantics*.

Manolis Savva, Angel X. Chang, Gilbert Bernstein, Christopher D. Manning, and Pat Hanrahan. 2014. On being the right scale: Sizing large collections of 3D models. In *SIGGRAPH Asia 2014 Workshop on Indoor Scene Understanding: Where Graphics meets Vision*.

Lee M. Seversky and Lijun Yin. 2006. Real-time automatic 3D scene generation from natural language voice and text descriptions. In *Proceedings of the 14th Annual ACM International Conference on Multimedia*.

Behjat Siddiquie, Rogério Schmidt Feris, and Larry S. Davis. 2011. Image ranking and retrieval based on multi-attribute queries. In *IEEE Conference on Computer Vision and Pattern Recognition (CVPR)*.

Terry Winograd. 1972. Understanding natural language. *Cognitive Psychology*, 3(1):1–191.

C. Lawrence Zitnick, Devi Parikh, and Lucy Vanderwende. 2013. Learning the visual interpretation of sentences. In *IEEE International Conference on Computer Vision (ICCV)*.

MultiGranCNN: An Architecture for General Matching of Text Chunks on Multiple Levels of Granularity

Wenpeng Yin and **Hinrich Schütze**
Center for Information and Language Processing
University of Munich, Germany
wenpeng@cis.uni-muenchen.de

Abstract

We present MultiGranCNN, a general deep learning architecture for matching text chunks. MultiGranCNN supports *multigranular comparability* of representations: shorter sequences in one chunk can be directly compared to longer sequences in the other chunk. MultiGranCNN also contains a *flexible and modularized match feature component* that is easily adaptable to different types of chunk matching. We demonstrate state-of-the-art performance of MultiGranCNN on clause coherence and paraphrase identification tasks.

1 Introduction

Many natural language processing (NLP) tasks can be posed as classifying the relationship between two TEXTCHUNKS (cf. Li et al. (2012), Bordes et al. (2014b)) where a TEXTCHUNK can be a sentence, a clause, a paragraph or any other sequence of words that forms a unit.

Paraphrasing (Figure 1, top) is one task that we address in this paper and that can be formalized as classifying a TEXTCHUNK relation. The two classes correspond to the sentences being (e.g., the pair <$\mathbf{p}$, $\mathbf{q}^+$>) or not being (e.g., the pair <$\mathbf{p}$, $\mathbf{q}^-$>) paraphrases of each other. Another task we look at is clause coherence (Figure 1, bottom). Here the two TEXTCHUNK relation classes correspond to the second clause being (e.g., the pair <$\mathbf{x}$, $\mathbf{y}^+$>) or not being (e.g., the pair <$\mathbf{x}$, $\mathbf{y}^-$>) a discourse-coherent continuation of the first clause. Other tasks that can be formalized as TEXTCHUNK relations are question answering (QA) (is the second chunk an answer to the first?), textual inference (does the first chunk imply the second?) and machine translation (are the two chunks translations of each other?).

$\mathbf{p}$	PDC will also almost certainly *fan the flames of* speculation about *Longhorn's release*.
$\mathbf{q}^+$	PDC will also almost certainly *reignite* speculation about *release dates of Microsoft 's new products*.
$\mathbf{q}^-$	PDC is indifferent to the release of Longhorn.
$\mathbf{x}$	The dollar suffered its worst one-day loss in a month,
$\mathbf{y}^+$	falling to 1.7717 marks ... from 1.7925 marks yesterday.
$\mathbf{y}^-$	up from 112.78 yen in late New York trading yesterday.

Figure 1: Examples for paraphrasing and clause coherence tasks

In this paper, we present MultiGranCNN, a general architecture for TEXTCHUNK relation classification. MultiGranCNN can be applied to a broad range of different TEXTCHUNK relations. This is a challenge because natural language has a complex structure – both sequential and hierarchical – and because this structure is usually not parallel in the two chunks that must be matched, further increasing the difficulty of the task. A successful detection algorithm therefore needs to capture not only the internal structure of TEXTCHUNKS, but also the rich pattern of their interactions.

MultiGranCNN is based on two innovations that are critical for successful TEXTCHUNK relation classification. First, the architecture is designed to ensure *multigranular comparability*. For general matching, we need the ability to match short sequences in one chunk with long sequences in the other chunk. For example, what is expressed by a single word in one chunk ("reignite" in $\mathbf{q}^+$ in the figure) may be expressed by a sequence of several words in its paraphrase ("fan the flames of" in $\mathbf{p}$). To meet this objective, we learn representations for words, phrases and the entire sentence that are all mutually comparable; in particular, these representations all have the same dimensionality and live in the same space.

Most prior work (e.g., Blacoe and Lapata (2012; Hu et al. (2014)) has neglected the need for multigranular comparability and performed matching within fixed levels only, e.g., only words were

Proceedings of the 53rd Annual Meeting of the Association for Computational Linguistics and the 7th International Joint Conference on Natural Language Processing, pages 63–73,
Beijing, China, July 26-31, 2015.

matched with words or only sentences with sentences. For a general solution to the problem of matching, we instead need the ability to match a unit on a lower level of granularity in one chunk with a unit on a higher level of granularity in the other chunk. Unlike (Socher et al., 2011), our model does not rely on parsing and it can more exhaustively search the hypothesis space of possible matchings, including matchings that correspond to conflicting segmentations of the input chunks (see Section 5).

Our second contribution is that MultiGranCNN contains a *flexible and modularized match feature component*. This component computes the basic features that measure how well phrases of the two chunks match. We investigate three different *match feature models* that demonstrate that a wide variety of different match feature models can be implemented. The match feature models can be swapped in and out of MultiGranCNN, depending on the characteristics of the task to be solved.

Prior work that has addressed matching tasks has usually focused on a single task like QA (Bordes et al., 2014a; Yu et al., 2014) or paraphrasing (Socher et al., 2011; Madnani et al., 2012; Ji and Eisenstein, 2013). The ARC architectures proposed by Hu et al. (2014) are intended to be more general, but seem to be somewhat limited in their flexibility to model different matching relations; e.g., they do not perform well for paraphrasing.

Different match feature models may also be required by factors other than the characteristics of the task. If the amount of labeled training data is small, then we may prefer a match feature model with few parameters that is robust against overfitting. If there is lots of training data, then a richer match feature model may be the right choice. This motivates the need for an architecture like MultiGranCNN that allows selection of the task-appropriate match feature model from a range of different models and its seamless integration into the architecture.

In remaining parts, Section 2 introduces some related work; Section 3 gives an overview of the proposed MultiGranCNN; Section 4 shows how to learn representations for generalized phrases (g-phrases); Section 5 describes the three matching models: DIRECTSIM, INDIRECTSIM and CONCAT; Section 6 describes the two 2D pooling methods: grid-based pooling and phrase-based pooling; Section 7 describes the match feature CNN; Section 8 summarizes the architecture of MultiGran CNN; and Section 9 presents experiments; finally, Section 10 concludes.

2 Related Work

Paraphrase identification (PI) is a typical task of sentence matching and it has been frequently studied (Qiu et al., 2006; Blacoe and Lapata, 2012; Madnani et al., 2012; Ji and Eisenstein, 2013). Socher et al. (2011) utilized parsing to model the hierarchical structure of sentences and uses unfolding recursive autoencoders to learn representations for single words and phrases acting as nonleaf nodes in the tree. The main difference to MultiGranCNN is that we stack multiple convolution layers to model flexible phrases and learn representations for them, and aim to address more general sentence correspondence. Bach et al. (2014) claimed that elementary discourse units obtained by segmenting sentences play an important role in paraphrasing. Their conclusion also endorses (Socher et al., 2011)'s and our work, for both take interactions between component phrases into account.

QA is another representative sentence matching problem. Yu et al. (2014) modeled sentence representations in a simplified CNN, finally finding the match score by projecting question and answer candidates into the same space. Other relevant QA work includes (Bordes et al., 2014c; Bordes et al., 2014a; Yang et al., 2014; Iyyer et al., 2014)

For more general matching, Chopra et al. (2005) and Liu (2013) used a Siamese architecture of shared-weight neural networks (NNs) to model two objects simultaneously, matching their representations and then learning a specific type of sentence relation. We adopt parts of their architecture, but we model phrase representations as well as sentence representations.

Li and Xu (2012) gave a comprehensive introduction to query-document matching and argued that query and document match at different levels: term, phrase, word sense, topic, structure etc. This also applies to sentence matching.

Lu and Li (2013) addressed matching of short texts. Interactions between the two texts were obtained via LDA (Blei et al., 2003) and were then the basis for computing a matching score. Compared to MultiGranCNN, drawbacks of this approach are that LDA parameters are not optimized for the specific task and that the interactions are formed on the level of single words only.

Gao et al. (2014) modeled interestingness between two documents with deep NNs. They mapped source-target document pairs to feature vectors in a latent space in such a way that the distance between the source document and its corresponding interesting target in that space was minimized. Interestingness is more like topic relevance, based mainly on the aggregated meaning of keywords, as opposed to more structural relationships as is the case for paraphrasing and clause coherence.

We briefly discussed (Hu et al., 2014)'s ARC in Section 1. MultiGranCNN is partially inspired by ARC, but introduces multigranular comparability (thus enabling crosslevel matching) and supports a wider range of match feature models.

Our unsupervised learning component (Section 4, last paragraph) resembles word2vec CBOW (Mikolov et al., 2013), but learns representations of TEXTCHUNKS as well as words. It also resembles PV-DM (Le and Mikolov, 2014), but our TEXTCHUNK representation is derived using a *hierarchical* architecture based on *convolution and pooling*.

3 Overview of MultiGranCNN

We use convolution-plus-pooling in two different components of MultiGranCNN. The first component, the *generalized phrase CNN* (gpCNN), will be introduced in Section 4. This component learns representations for *generalized phrases* (g-phrases) where a generalized phrase is a general term for subsequences of all granularities: words, short phrases, long phrases and the sentence itself. The gpCNN architecture has L layers of convolution, corresponding (for $L = 2$) to words, short phrases, long phrases and the sentence. We test different values of L in our experiments. We train gpCNN on large data in an unsupervised manner and then fine-tune it on labeled training data.

Using a *Siamese configuration*, two copies of gpCNN, one for each of the two input TEXTCHUNKS, are the input to the *match feature model*, presented in Section 5. This model produces $s_1 \times s_2$ matching features, one for each pair of g-phrases in the two chunks, where s_1, s_2 are the number of g-phrases in the two chunks, respectively.

The $s_1 \times s_2$ match feature matrix is first reduced to a fixed size by *dynamic 2D pooling*. The resulting fixed size matrix is then the input to the second convolution-plus-pooling component, the *match feature CNN* (mfCNN) whose output is fed to a *multilayer perceptron* (MLP) that produces the final match score. Section 6 will give details.

We use convolution-plus-pooling for both word sequences and match features because we want to compute increasingly abstract features at multiple levels of granularity. To ensure that g-phrases are mutually comparable when computing the $s_1 \times s_2$ match feature matrix, we impose the constraint that *all g-phrase representations live in the same space and have the same dimensionality.*

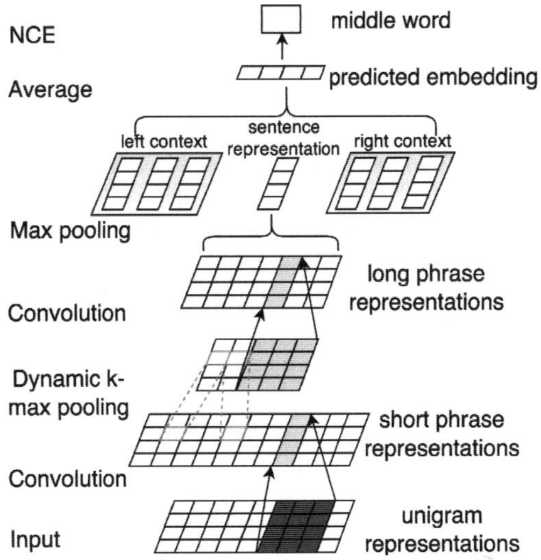

Figure 2: gpCNN: learning g-phrase representations. This figure only shows two convolution layers (i.e., $L = 2$) for saving space.

4 gpCNN: Learning Representations for g-Phrases

We use several stacked *blocks*, i.e., convolution-plus-pooling layers, to extract increasingly abstract features of the TEXTCHUNK. The input to the first block are the words of the TEXTCHUNK, represented by CW (Collobert and Weston, 2008) embeddings. Given a TEXTCHUNK of length $|S|$, let vector $\mathbf{c}_i \in \mathbb{R}^{wd}$ be the concatenated embeddings of words $v_{i-w+1}, \ldots, v_i$ where $w = 5$ is the filter width, $d = 50$ is the dimensionality of CW embeddings and $0 < i < |S| + w$. Embeddings for words v_i, $i < 1$ and $i > |S|$, are set to zero. We then generate the representation $\mathbf{p}_i \in \mathbb{R}^d$ of the g-phrase $v_{i-w+1}, \ldots, v_i$ using the convolution matrix $\mathbf{W}_l \in \mathbb{R}^{d \times wd}$:

$$\mathbf{p}_i = \tanh(\mathbf{W}_l \mathbf{c}_i + \mathbf{b}_l) \quad (1)$$

where block index $l = 1$, bias $\mathbf{b}_l \in \mathbb{R}^d$. We use *wide convolution* (i.e., we apply the convolution matrix $\mathbf{W}_l$ to words v_i, $i < 1$ and $i > |S|$) because this makes sure that each word v_i, $1 \leq i \leq |S|$, can be detected by all weights of $\mathbf{W}_l$ – as opposed to only the rightmost (resp. leftmost) weights for initial (resp. final) words in narrow convolution.

The configuration of convolution layers in following blocks ($l > 1$) is exactly the same except that the input vectors $\mathbf{c}_i$ are not words, but the output of pooling from the previous layer of convolution – as we will explain presently. The configuration is the same (e.g., all $\mathbf{W}_l \in \mathbb{R}^{d \times wd}$) because, by design, all g-phrase representations have the same dimensionality d. This also ensures that each g-phrase representation can be directly compared with each other g-phrase representation.

We use *dynamic k-max pooling* to extract the k_l top values from each dimension after convolution in the lth block and the k_L top values in the final block. We set

$$k_l = \max(\alpha, \lceil \frac{L-l}{L} |S| \rceil) \quad (2)$$

where $l = 1, \cdots, L$ is the block index, and $\alpha = 4$ is a constant (cf. Kalchbrenner et al. (2014)) that makes sure a reasonable minimum number of values is passed on to the next layer. We set $k_L = 1$ (not 4, cf. Kalchbrenner et al. (2014)) because our design dictates that all g-phrase representations, including the representation of the TEXTCHUNK itself, have the same dimensionality. Example: for $L = 4, |S| = 20$, the k_i are $[15, 10, 5, 1]$.

Dynamic k-max pooling keeps the most important features and allows us to stack multiple blocks to extract hiearchical features: units on consecutive layers correspond to larger and larger parts of the TEXTCHUNK thanks to the subset selection property of pooling.

For many tasks, labeled data for training gpCNN is limited. We therefore employ *unsupervised training* to initialize gpCNN as shown in Figure 2. Similar to CBOW (Mikolov et al., 2013), we predict a sampled middle word v_i from the average of seven vectors: the TEXTCHUNK representation (the final output of gpCNN) and the three words to the left and to the right of v_i. We use noise-contrastive estimation (Mnih and Teh, 2012) for training: 10 noise words are sampled for each true example.

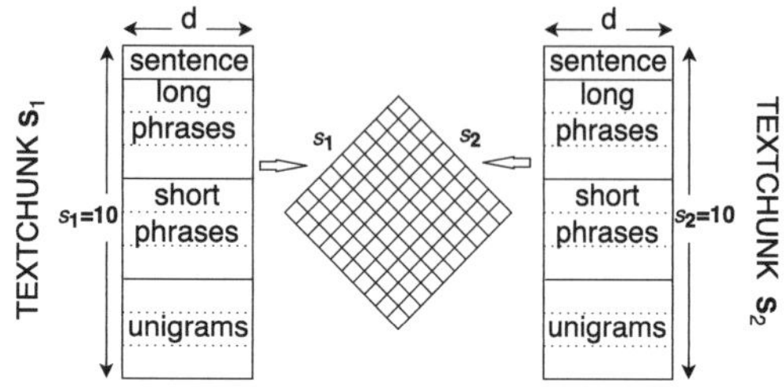

Figure 3: General illustration of match feature model. In this example, both S_1 and S_2 have 10 g-phrases, so the match feature matrix $\hat{\mathbf{F}} \in \mathbb{R}^{s_1 \times s_2}$ has size 10×10.

5 Match Feature Models

Let $g_1, \ldots, g_{s_k}$ be an enumeration of the s_k g-phrases of TEXTCHUNK S_k. Let $\mathbf{S}_k \in \mathbb{R}^{s_k \times d}$ be the matrix, constructed by concatenating the four matrices of unigram, short phrase, long phrase and sentence representations shown in Figure 2 that contain the learned representations from Section 4 for these s_k g-phrases; i.e., row $\mathbf{S}_{ki}$ is the learned representation of g_i.

The basic design of a match feature model is that we produce an $s_1 \times s_2$ matrix $\hat{\mathbf{F}}$ for a pair of TEXTCHUNKS S_1 and S_2, shown in Figure 3. $\hat{\mathbf{F}}_{i,j}$ is a score that assesses the relationship between g-phrase g_i of S_1 and g-phrase g_j of S_2 *with respect to the* TEXTCHUNK *relation of interest* (paraphrasing, clause coherence etc). This score $\hat{\mathbf{F}}_{i,j}$ is computed based on the vector representations $\mathbf{S}_{1i}$ and $\mathbf{S}_{2j}$ of the two g-phrases.[1]

We experiment with three different feature models to compute the match score $\hat{\mathbf{F}}_{i,j}$ because we would like our architecture to address a wide variety of different TEXTCHUNK relations. We can model a TEXTCHUNK relation like paraphrasing as "for each meaning element in one sentence, there must be a similar meaning element in the other sentence"; thus, a good candidate for the match score $\hat{\mathbf{F}}_{i,j}$ is simply vector similarity. In contrast, similarity is a less promising match score for clause coherence; for clause coherence, we want a score that models how good a continuation one g-phrase is for the other. These considerations motivate us to define three different match feature models that we will introduce now.

The first match feature model is DIRECTSIM.

[1]In response to a reviewer question, recall that s_i is the total number of g-phrases of S_i, so there is only one $s_1 \times s_2$ matrix, not several on different levels of granularity.

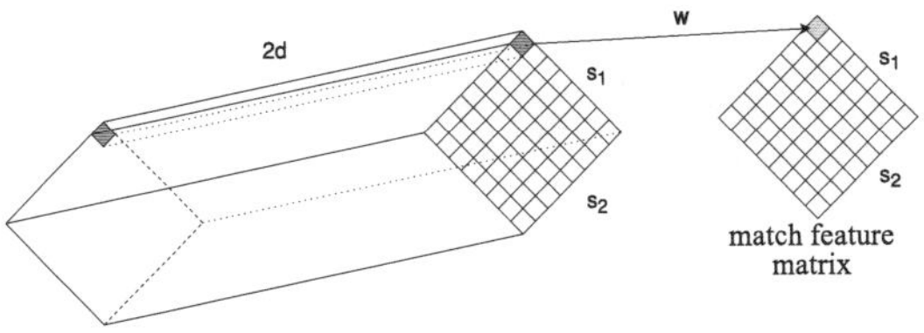

Figure 4: CONCAT match feature model

This model computes the match score of two g-phrases as their similarity using a radial basis function kernel:

$$\hat{\mathbf{F}}_{i,j} = \exp(\frac{-||\mathbf{S}_{1i} - \mathbf{S}_{2j}||^2}{2\beta}) \quad (3)$$

where we set $\beta = 2$ (cf. Wu et al. (2013)). DIRECTSIM is an appropriate feature model for TEXTCHUNK relations like paraphrasing because in that case direct similarity features are helpful in assessing meaning equivalence.

The second match feature model is INDIRECTSIM. Instead of computing the similarity directly as we do for DIRECTSIM, we first transform the representation of the g-phrase in one TEXTCHUNK using a transformation matrix $\mathbf{M} \in \mathbb{R}^{d \times d}$, then compute the match score by inner product and sigmoid activation:

$$\hat{\mathbf{F}}_{i,j} = \sigma(\mathbf{S}_{1i}\mathbf{M}\mathbf{S}_{2j}^{\mathrm{T}} + b), \quad (4)$$

Our motivation is that for a TEXTCHUNK relation like clause coherence, the two TEXTCHUNKS need not have any direct similarity. However, if we map the representations of TEXTCHUNK S_1 into an appropriate space then we can hope that similarity between these transformed representations of S_1 and the representations of TEXTCHUNK S_2 do yield useful features. We will see that this hope is borne out by our experiments.

The third match feature model is CONCAT. This is a general model that can learn any weighted combination of the values of the two vectors:

$$\hat{\mathbf{F}}_{i,j} = \sigma(\mathbf{w}^{\mathrm{T}}\mathbf{e}_{i,j} + b) \quad (5)$$

where $\mathbf{e}_{i,j} \in \mathbb{R}^{2d}$ is the concatenation of $\mathbf{S}_{1i}$ and $\mathbf{S}_{2j}$. We can learn different combination weights $\mathbf{w}$ to solve different types of TEXTCHUNK matching.

We call this match feature model CONCAT because we implement it by concatenating g-phrase vectors to form a tensor as shown in Figure 4.

The match feature models implement multi-granular comparability: they match all units in one TEXTCHUNK with all units in the other TEXTCHUNK. This is necessary because a general solution to matching must match a low-level unit like "reignite" to a higher-level unit like "fan the flames of" (Figure 1). Unlike (Socher et al., 2011), our model does not rely on parsing; therefore, it can more exhaustively search the hypothesis space of possible matchings: mfCNN covers a wide variety of different, possibly overlapping units, not just those of a single parse tree.

6 Dynamic 2D Pooling

The match feature models generate an $s_1 \times s_2$ matrix. Since it has variable size, we apply two different dynamic 2D pooling methods, *grid-based pooling* and *phrase-focused pooling*, to transform it to a fixed size matrix.

6.1 Grid-based pooling

We need to map $\hat{\mathbf{F}} \in \mathbb{R}^{s_1 \times s_2}$ into a matrix $\mathbf{F}$ of fixed size $s^* \times s^*$ where s^* is a parameter. Grid-based pooling divides $\hat{\mathbf{F}}$ into $s^* \times s^*$ nonoverlapping *(dynamic) pools* and copies the maximum value in each dynamic pool to $\mathbf{F}$. This method is similar to (Socher et al., 2011), but preserves locality better.

$\hat{\mathbf{F}}$ can be split into equal regions only if both s_1 and s_2 are divisible by s^*. Otherwise, for $s_1 > s^*$ and if $s_1 \bmod s^* = b$, the dynamic pools in the first $s^* - b$ splits each have $\lfloor \frac{s_1}{s^*} \rfloor$ rows while the remaining b splits each have $\lfloor \frac{s_1}{s^*} \rfloor + 1$ rows. In Figure 5, a $s_1 \times s_2 = 4 \times 5$ matrix (left) is split into $s^* \times s^* = 3 \times 3$ dynamic pools (middle): each row is split into [1, 1, 2] and each column is split into [1, 2, 2].

If $s_1 < s^*$, we first repeat all rows in batch style with size s_1 until no fewer than s^* rows remain. Then the first s^* rows are kept and split into s^* dynamic pools. The same principle applies to the partitioning of columns. In Figure 5 (right), the areas with dashed lines and dotted lines are repeated parts for rows and columns, respectively; each cell is its own dynamic pool.

6.2 Phrase-focused pooling

In the match feature matrix $\hat{\mathbf{F}} \in \mathbb{R}^{s_1 \times s_2}$, row i (resp. column j) contains all feature values for g-phrase g_i of S_1 (resp. g_j of S_2). Phrase-focused pooling attempts to pick the largest match features

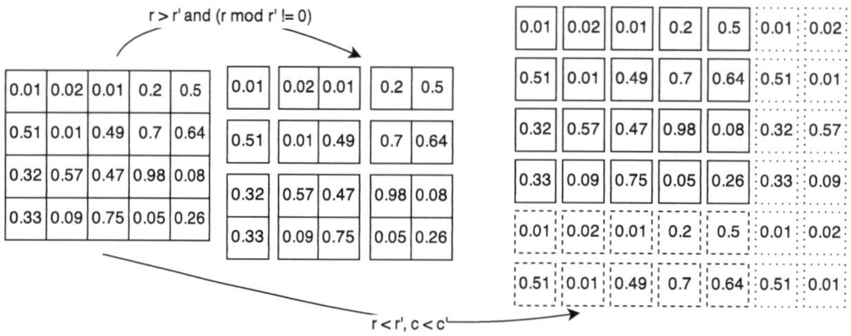

Figure 5: Partition methods in grid-based pooling. Original matrix with size 4×5 is mapped into matrix with size 3×3 and matrix with size 6×7, respectively. Each dynamic pool is distinguished by a border of empty white space around it.

for a g-phrase g on the assumption that they are the best basis for assessing the relation of g with other g-phrases. To implement this, we sort the values of each row i (resp. each column j) in decreasing order giving us a matrix $\hat{\mathbf{F}}_r \in \mathbb{R}^{s_1 \times s_2}$ with sorted rows (resp. $\hat{\mathbf{F}}_c \in \mathbb{R}^{s_1 \times s_2}$ with sorted columns). Then we concatenate the columns of $\hat{\mathbf{F}}_r$ (resp. the rows of $\hat{\mathbf{F}}_c$) resulting in list $F_r = \{f_1^r, \dots, f_{s_1 s_2}^r\}$ (resp. $F_c = \{f_1^c, \dots, f_{s_1 s_2}^c\}$) where each f^r (f^c) is an element of $\hat{\mathbf{F}}_r$ ($\hat{\mathbf{F}}_c$). These two lists are merged into a list F by interleaving them so that members from F_r and F_c alternate. F is then used to fill the rows of $\mathbf{F}$ from top to bottom with each row being filled from left to right.[2]

7 mfCNN: Match feature CNN

The output of dynamic 2D pooling is further processed by the match feature CNN (mfCNN) as depicted in Figure 6. mfCNN extracts increasingly abstract interaction features from lower-level interaction features, using several layers of 2D wide convolution and fixed-size 2D pooling.

We call the combination of a 2D wide convolution layer and a fixed-size 2D pooling layer a *block*, denoted by index b ($b = 1, 2 \dots$). In general, let tensor $\mathbf{T}^b \in \mathbb{R}^{c_b \times s_b \times s_b}$ denote the feature maps in block b; block b has c_b feature maps, each of size $s_b \times s_b$ ($\mathbf{T}^1 = \mathbf{F} \in \mathbb{R}^{1 \times s^* \times s^*}$). Let $\mathbf{W}^b \in \mathbb{R}^{c_{b+1} \times c_b \times f_b \times f_b}$ be the filter weights of 2D wide convolution in block b, $f_b \times f_b$ is then the size of sliding convolution regions. Then the convolution is performed as element-wise multiplication between $\mathbf{W}^b$ and $\mathbf{T}^b$ as follows:

$$\hat{\mathbf{T}}^{b+1}_{m,i-1,j-1} = \sigma\left(\sum \mathbf{W}^b_{m,:,:,:} \mathbf{T}^b_{:,i-f_b:i,j-f_b:j} + \mathbf{b}^b_m\right) \quad (6)$$

where $0 \leq m < c_{b+1}$, $1 \leq i,j < s_b + f_b$, $\mathbf{b}^b \in \mathbb{R}^{c_{b+1}}$.

Subsequently, fixed-size 2D pooling selects dominant features from $k_b \times k_b$ non-overlapping windows of $\hat{\mathbf{T}}^{b+1}$ to form a tensor as input of block $b+1$:

$$\mathbf{T}^{b+1}_{m,i,j} = \max(\hat{\mathbf{T}}^{b+1}_{m,ik_b:(i+1)k_b,jk_b:(j+1)k_b}) \quad (7)$$

where $0 \leq i,j < \lfloor \frac{s_b + f_b - 1}{k_b} \rfloor$.

Hu et al. (2014) used narrow convolution which would limit the number of blocks. 2D wide convolution in this work enables to stack multiple blocks of convolution and pooling to extract higher-level interaction features. We will study the influence of the number of blocks on performance below.

For the experiments, we set $s^* = 40$, $c_b = 50$, $f_b = 5$, $k_b = 2$ ($b = 1, 2, \cdots$).

8 MultiGranCNN

We can now describe the overall architecture of MultiGranCNN. First, using a Siamese configuration, two copies of gpCNN, one for each of the two input TEXTCHUNKS, produce g-phrase representations on different levels of abstraction (Figure 2). Then one of the three match feature models (DIRECTSIM, CONCAT or INDIRECTSIM) produces an $s_1 \times s_2$ match feature matrix, each cell of which assesses the match of a pair of g-phrases from the two chunks. This match feature matrix is reduced to a fixed size matrix by dynamic 2D pooling (Section 6). As shown in Figure 6, the resulting fixed size matrix is the input for mfCNN, which extracts interaction features of

[2]If $\hat{\mathbf{F}}$ has fewer cells than $\mathbf{F}$, then we simply repeat the filling procedure to fill all cells.

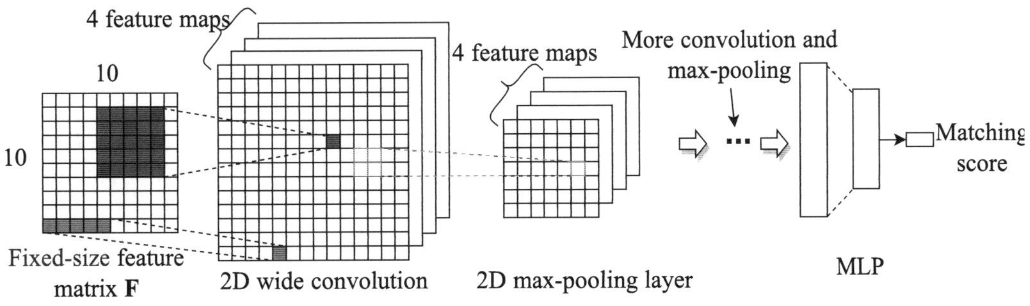

Figure 6: mfCNN & MLP for matching score learning. $s^* = 10$, $f_b = 5$, $k_b = 2$, $c_b = 4$ in this example.

increasing complexity from the basic interaction features computed by the match feature model. Finally, the output of the last block of mfCNN is the input to an MLP that computes the match score.

MultiGranCNN bears resemblance to previous work on clause and sentence matching (e.g., Hu et al. (2014), Socher et al. (2011)), but it is more general and more flexible. It learns representations of g-phrases, i.e., representations of parts of the TEXTCHUNK at multiple granularities, not just for a single level such as the sentence as ARC-I does (Hu et al., 2014). MultiGranCNN explores the space of interactions between the two chunks more exhaustively by considering interactions between every unit in one chunk with every other unit in the other chunk, at all levels of granularity. Finally, MultiGranCNN supports a number of different match feature models; the corresponding module can be instantiated in a way that ensures that match features are best suited to support accurate decisions on the TEXTCHUNK relation task that needs to be addressed.

9 Experimental Setup and Results

9.1 Training

Suppose the triple $(\mathbf{x}, \mathbf{y}^+, \mathbf{y}^-)$ is given and $\mathbf{x}$ matches $\mathbf{y}^+$ better than $\mathbf{y}^-$. Then our objective is the minimization of the following ranking loss:

$$l(\mathbf{x}, \mathbf{y}^+, \mathbf{y}^-) = \max(0, 1 + s(\mathbf{x}, \mathbf{y}^-) - s(\mathbf{x}, \mathbf{y}^+))$$

where $s(\mathbf{x}, \mathbf{y})$ is the predicted match score for $(\mathbf{x}, \mathbf{y})$. We use stochastic gradient descent with Adagrad (Duchi et al., 2011), L_2 regularization and minibatch training.

We set initial learning rate to 0.05, batch size to 70, L_2 weight to $5 \cdot 10^{-4}$.

Recall that we employ unsupervised pretraining of representations for g-phrases. We can either *freeze* these representations in subsequent supervised training; or we can *fine-tune* them. We study the performance of both regimes.

9.2 Clause Coherence Task

As introduced by Hu et al. (2014), the *clause coherence* task determines for a pair $(\mathbf{x}, \mathbf{y})$ of clauses if the sentence "$\mathbf{xy}$" is a coherent sentence. We construct a clause coherence dataset as follows (the set used by Hu et al. (2014) is not yet available). We consider all sentences from English Gigaword (Parker et al., 2009) that consist of two comma-separated clauses $\mathbf{x}$ and $\mathbf{y}$, with each clause having between five and 30 words. For each $\mathbf{y}$, we choose four clauses $\mathbf{y}' \ldots \mathbf{y}''''$ randomly from the 1000 second clauses that have the highest similarity to $\mathbf{y}$, where similarity is cosine similarity of TF-IDF vectors of the clauses; restricting the alternatives to similar clauses ensures that the task is hard. The clause coherence task then is to select $\mathbf{y}$ from the set $\mathbf{y}, \mathbf{y}', \ldots, \mathbf{y}''''$ as the correct continuation of $\mathbf{x}$. We create 21 million examples, each consisting of a first clause $\mathbf{x}$ and five second clauses. This set is divided into a training set of 19 million and development and test sets of one million each. An example from the training set is given in Figure 1.

Then, we study the performance variance of different MultiGranCNN setups from three perspectives: a) layers of CNN in both unsupervised (gpCNN) and supervised (mfCNN) training phases; b) different approaches for clause relation feature modeling; c) dynamic pooling methods for generating same-sized feature matrices.

Figure 7 (top table) shows that (Hu et al., 2014)'s parameters are good choices for our setup as well. We get best result when both gpCNN and mfCNN have three blocks of convolution and pooling. This suggests that multiple layers of convolution succeed in extracting high-level features that are beneficial for clause coherence.

Figure 7 (2nd table) shows that INDIRECTSIM and CONCAT have comparable performance and both outperform DIRECTSIM. DIRECTSIM is expected to perform poorly because the contents in the two clauses usually have little or no overlapping meaning. In contrast, we can imagine that INDIRECTSIM first transforms the first clause $\mathbf{x}$ into a counterpart and then matches this counterpart with the second clause $\mathbf{y}$. In CONCAT, each of $s_1 \times s_2$ pairs of g-phrases is concatentated and supervised training can then learn an unrestricted function to assess the importance of this pair for clause coherence (cf. Eq. 5). Again, this is clearly a more promising TEXTCHUNK relation model for clause coherence than one that relies on DIRECTSIM.

acc		mfCNN 0	mfCNN 1	mfCNN 2	mfCNN 3
gpCNN	0	38.02	44.08	47.81	48.43
gpCNN	1	40.91	45.31	51.73	52.13
gpCNN	2	43.10	48.06	54.14	54.86
gpCNN	3	45.62	51.77	55.97	**56.31**

match feature model	acc
DIRECTSIM	25.40
INDIRECTSIM	**56.31**
CONCAT	56.12

freeze g-phrase represenations or not	acc
MultiGranCNN (freeze)	55.79
MultiGranCNN (fine-tune)	**56.31**

pooling method	acc
dynamic (Socher et al., 2011)	55.91
grid-based	56.07
phrase-focused	**56.31**

Figure 7: Effect on dev acc (clause coherence) of different factors: # convolution blocks, match feature model, freeze vs. fine-tune, pooling method.

Figure 7 (3rd table) demonstrates that fine-tuning g-phrase representations gives better performance than freezing them. Also, grid-based and phrase-focused pooling outperform dynamic pooling (Socher et al., 2011) (4th table). Phrase-focused pooling performs best.

Table 1 compares MultiGranCNN to ARC-I and ARC-II, the architectures proposed by Hu et al. (2014). We also test the five baseline systems from their paper: DeepMatch, WordEmbed, SENMLP, SENNA+MLP, URAE+MLP. For MultiGranCNN, we use the best dev set settings: number of convolution layers in gpCNN and mfCNN is 3; INDIRECTSIM; phrase-focused pooling. Table 1 shows that MultiGranCNN outperforms all other approaches on clause coherence test set.

9.3 Paraphrase Identification Task

We evaluate paraphrase identification (PI) on the PAN corpus (http://bit.ly/mt-para, (Madnani et al., 2012)), consisting of training and test sets of 10,000 and 3000 sentence pairs, respectively. Sentences are about 40 words long on average.

Since PI is a binary classification task, we replace the MLP with a logistic regression layer. As phrase-focused pooling was proven to be optimal, we directly use phrase-focused pooling in PI task without comparison, assuming that the choice of dynamic pooling is task independent.

For parameter selection, we split the PAN training set into a core training set (core) of size 9000 and a development set (dev) of size 1000. We then train models on core and select parameters based on best performance on dev. The best results on dev are obtained for the following parameters: freezing g-phrase representations, DIRECTSIM, two convolution layers in gpCNN, no convolution layers in mfCNN. We use these parameter settings to train a model on the entire training set and report performance in Table 2.

We compare MultiGranCNN to ARC-I/II (Hu et al., 2014), and two previous papers reporting performance on PAN. Madnani et al. (2012) used a combination of three *basic MT metrics* (BLEU, NIST and TER) and five complex MT metrics (TERp, METEOR, BADGER, MAXISIM,

model	acc
Random Guess	20.00
DeepMatch	34.17
WordEmbed	38.28
SENMLP	34.57
SENNA+MLP	42.09
URAE+MLP	27.41
ARC-I	45.04
ARC-II	50.18
MultiGranCNN	**56.27**

Table 1: Performance on clause coherence test set.

SEPIA), computed on entire sentences. Bach et al. (2014) applied MT metrics to elementary discourse units. We integrate these eight MT metrics from prior work.

method	acc	F_1
ARC-I	61.4	60.3
ARC-II	64.9	63.5
basic MT metrics	88.6	87.8
+ TERp	91.5	91.2
+ METEOR	92.0	91.8
+ Others	92.3	92.1
(Bach et al., 2014)	93.4	93.3
8MT+MultiGranCNN (fine-tune)	94.1	94.0
8MT+MultiGranCNN (freeze)	**94.9**	**94.7**

Table 2: Results on PAN. "8MT" = 8 MT metrics

Table 2 shows that MultiGranCNN in combination with MT metrics obtains state-of-the-art performance on PAN. *Freezing* weights learned in unsupervised training (Figure 2) performs better than *fine-tuning* them; also, Table 3 shows that the best result is achieved if *no convolution* is used in mfCNN. Thus, the best configuration for paraphrase identification is to "forward" fixed-size interaction matrices as input to the logistic regression, without any intermediate convolution layers.

Freezing weights learned in unsupervised training and no convolution layers in mfCNN both protect against overfitting. Complex deep neural networks are in particular danger of overfitting when training sets are small as in the case of PAN (cf. Hu et al. (2014)). In contrast, fine-tuning weights and several convolution layers were the optimal setup for clause coherence. For clause coherence, we have a much larger training set and therefore can successfully train a much larger number of parameters.

Table 3 shows that CONCAT performs badly for PI while DIRECTSIM and INDIRECTSIM perform well. We can conceptualize PI as the task of determining if each meaning element in S_1 has a similar meaning element in S_2. The $s_1 \times s_2$ DIRECTSIM feature model directly models this task and the $s_1 \times s_2$ INDIRECTSIM feature model also models it, but learning a transformation of g-phrase representations before applying similarity. In contrast, CONCAT can learn arbitrary relations between parts of the two sentences, a model that seems to be too unconstrained for PI if insufficient training resources are available.

In contrast, for the clause coherence task, concatentation worked well and DIRECTSIM worked poorly and we provided an explanation based on the specific properties of clause coherence (see discussion of Figure 7). We conclude from these results that it is dependent on the task what the best feature model is for matching two linguistic objects. Interestingly, INDIRECTSIM performs well on both tasks. This suggests that INDIRECTSIM is a general feature model for matching, applicable to tasks with very different properties.

10 Conclusion

In this paper, we present MultiGranCNN, a general deep learning architecture for classifying the relation between two TEXTCHUNKS. MultiGranCNN supports *multigranular comparability* of representations: shorter sequences in one TEXTCHUNK can be directly compared to longer sequences in the other TEXTCHUNK. MultiGranCNN also contains a *flexible and modularized match feature component* that is easily adaptable to different TEXTCHUNK relations. We demonstrated state-of-the-art performance of MultiGranCNN on paraphrase identification and clause coherence tasks.

Acknowledgments

Thanks to CIS members and anonymous reviewers for constructive comments. This work was supported by Baidu (through a Baidu scholarship awarded to Wenpeng Yin) and by Deutsche Forschungsgemeinschaft (grant DFG SCHU 2246/8-2, SPP 1335).

F_1		mfCNN 0	mfCNN 1	mfCNN 2	mfCNN 3
gpCNN	0	92.7	92.9	92.9	93.9
gpCNN	1	93.2	93.5	93.9	93.5
gpCNN	2	**94.7**	94.2	93.7	93.3
gpCNN	3	94.5	94.0	93.6	92.9

match feature model	acc	F_1
DIRECTSIM	**94.9**	**94.7**
INDIRECTSIM	94.7	94.5
CONCAT	93.0	92.9

Table 3: Effect on dev F_1 (PI) of different factors: # convolution blocks, match feature model.

References

Ngo Xuan Bach, Nguyen Le Minh, and Akira Shimazu. 2014. Exploiting discourse information to identify paraphrases. *Expert Systems with Applications*, 41(6):2832–2841.

William Blacoe and Mirella Lapata. 2012. A comparison of vector-based representations for semantic composition. In *Proceedings of the 2012 Joint Conference on Empirical Methods in Natural Language Processing and Computational Natural Language Learning*, pages 546–556. Association for Computational Linguistics.

David M Blei, Andrew Y Ng, and Michael I Jordan. 2003. Latent dirichlet allocation. *the Journal of machine Learning research*, 3:993–1022.

Antoine Bordes, Sumit Chopra, and Jason Weston. 2014a. Question answering with subgraph embeddings. *Proceedings of the 2014 Conference on Empirical Methods in Natural Language Processing*.

Antoine Bordes, Xavier Glorot, Jason Weston, and Yoshua Bengio. 2014b. A semantic matching energy function for learning with multi-relational data. *Machine Learning*, 94(2):233–259.

Antoine Bordes, Jason Weston, and Nicolas Usunier. 2014c. Open question answering with weakly supervised embedding models. *Proceedings of 2014 European Conference on Machine Learning and Principles and Practice of Knowledge Discovery in Databases*.

Sumit Chopra, Raia Hadsell, and Yann LeCun. 2005. Learning a similarity metric discriminatively, with application to face verification. In *Computer Vision and Pattern Recognition, 2005. CVPR 2005. IEEE Computer Society Conference on*, volume 1, pages 539–546. IEEE.

Ronan Collobert and Jason Weston. 2008. A unified architecture for natural language processing: Deep neural networks with multitask learning. In *Proceedings of the 25th international conference on Machine learning*, pages 160–167. ACM.

John Duchi, Elad Hazan, and Yoram Singer. 2011. Adaptive subgradient methods for online learning and stochastic optimization. *The Journal of Machine Learning Research*, 12:2121–2159.

Jianfeng Gao, Patrick Pantel, Michael Gamon, Xiaodong He, Li Deng, and Yelong Shen. 2014. Modeling interestingness with deep neural networks. In *Proceedings of the 2014 Conference on Empirical Methods in Natural Language Processing*.

Baotian Hu, Zhengdong Lu, Hang Li, and Qingcai Chen. 2014. Convolutional neural network architectures for matching natural language sentences. In *Advances in Neural Information Processing Systems*, pages 2042–2050.

Mohit Iyyer, Jordan Boyd-Graber, Leonardo Claudino, Richard Socher, and Hal Daumé III. 2014. A neural network for factoid question answering over paragraphs. In *Proceedings of the 2014 Conference on Empirical Methods in Natural Language Processing*, pages 633–644.

Yangfeng Ji and Jacob Eisenstein. 2013. Discriminative improvements to distributional sentence similarity. In *Proceedings of the 2013 Conference on Empirical Methods in Natural Language Processing*, pages 891–896.

Nal Kalchbrenner, Edward Grefenstette, and Phil Blunsom. 2014. A convolutional neural network for modelling sentences. In *Proceedings of the 52nd Annual Meeting of the Association for Computational Linguistics*. Association for Computational Linguistics.

Quoc V Le and Tomas Mikolov. 2014. Distributed representations of sentences and documents. *Proceedings of The 31st International Conference on Machine Learning*, pages 1188–1196.

Hang Li and Jun Xu. 2012. Beyond bag-of-words: machine learning for query-document matching in web search. In *Proceedings of the 35th international ACM SIGIR conference on Research and development in information retrieval*, pages 1177–1177. ACM.

Xutao Li, Michael K Ng, and Yunming Ye. 2012. Har: Hub, authority and relevance scores in multirelational data for query search. In *Proceedings of the 12th SIAM International Conference on Data Mining*, pages 141–152. SIAM.

Chen Liu. 2013. *Probabilistic Siamese Network for Learning Representations*. Ph.D. thesis, University of Toronto.

Zhengdong Lu and Hang Li. 2013. A deep architecture for matching short texts. In *Advances in Neural Information Processing Systems*, pages 1367–1375.

Nitin Madnani, Joel Tetreault, and Martin Chodorow. 2012. Re-examining machine translation metrics for paraphrase identification. In *Proceedings of the 2012 Conference of the North American Chapter of the Association for Computational Linguistics: Human Language Technologies*, pages 182–190. Association for Computational Linguistics.

Tomas Mikolov, Ilya Sutskever, Kai Chen, Greg S Corrado, and Jeff Dean. 2013. Distributed representations of words and phrases and their compositionality. In *Advances in Neural Information Processing Systems*, pages 3111–3119.

Andriy Mnih and Yee Whye Teh. 2012. A fast and simple algorithm for training neural probabilistic language models. In *Proceedings of the 29th International Conference on Machine Learning*, pages 1751–1758.

Robert Parker, Linguistic Data Consortium, et al. 2009. *English gigaword fourth edition*. Linguistic Data Consortium.

Long Qiu, Min-Yen Kan, and Tat-Seng Chua. 2006. Paraphrase recognition via dissimilarity significance classification. In *Proceedings of the 2006 Conference on Empirical Methods in Natural Language Processing*, pages 18–26. Association for Computational Linguistics.

Richard Socher, Eric H Huang, Jeffrey Pennin, Christopher D Manning, and Andrew Y Ng. 2011. Dynamic pooling and unfolding recursive autoencoders for paraphrase detection. In *Advances in Neural Information Processing Systems*, pages 801–809.

Pengcheng Wu, Steven CH Hoi, Hao Xia, Peilin Zhao, Dayong Wang, and Chunyan Miao. 2013. Online multimodal deep similarity learning with application to image retrieval. In *Proceedings of the 21st ACM international conference on Multimedia*, pages 153–162. ACM.

Min-Chul Yang, Nan Duan, Ming Zhou, and Hae-Chang Rim. 2014. Joint relational embeddings for knowledge-based question answering. In *Proceedings of the 2014 Conference on Empirical Methods in Natural Language Processing*, pages 645–650.

Lei Yu, Karl Moritz Hermann, Phil Blunsom, and Stephen Pulman. 2014. Deep learning for answer sentence selection. *NIPS deep learning workshop*.

Weakly Supervised Models of Aspect-Sentiment for Online Course Discussion Forums

Arti Ramesh,[1] Shachi H. Kumar,[2] James Foulds,[2] Lise Getoor[2]
[1]University of Maryland, College Park [2]University of California, Santa Cruz
artir@cs.umd.edu, {shulluma, jfoulds, getoor}@ucsc.edu

Abstract

Massive open online courses (MOOCs) are redefining the education system and transcending boundaries posed by traditional courses. With the increase in popularity of online courses, there is a corresponding increase in the need to understand and interpret the communications of the course participants. Identifying topics or *aspects* of conversation and inferring sentiment in online course forum posts can enable instructor interventions to meet the needs of the students, rapidly address course-related issues, and increase student retention. Labeled aspect-sentiment data for MOOCs are expensive to obtain and may not be transferable between courses, suggesting the need for approaches that do not require labeled data. We develop a weakly supervised joint model for aspect-sentiment in online courses, modeling the dependencies between various aspects and sentiment using a recently developed scalable class of statistical relational models called hinge-loss Markov random fields. We validate our models on posts sampled from twelve online courses, each containing an average of 10,000 posts, and demonstrate that jointly modeling aspect with sentiment improves the prediction accuracy for both aspect and sentiment.

1 Introduction

Massive Open Online Courses (MOOCs) have emerged as a powerful medium for imparting education to a wide geographical population. Discussion forums are the primary means of communication between MOOC participants (students, TAs, and instructors). Due to the open nature of these courses, they attract people from all over the world leading to large numbers of participants and hence, large numbers of posts in the discussion forums. In the courses we worked with, we found that over the course of the class there were typically over 10,000 posts.

Within this slew of posts, there are valuable *problem-reporting* posts that identify issues such as broken links, audio-visual glitches, and inaccuracies in the course materials. Automatically identifying these reported problems is important for several reasons: *i*) it is time-consuming for instructors to manually screen through all of the posts due to the highly skewed instructor-to-student ratio in MOOCs, *ii*) promptly addressing issues could help improve student retention, and *iii*) future iterations of the course could benefit from identifying technical and logistical issues currently faced by students. In this paper, we investigate the problem of determining the fine-grained topics of posts (which we refer to as "MOOC aspects") and the sentiment toward them, which can potentially be used to improve the course.

While aspect-sentiment has been widely studied, the MOOC discussion forum scenario presents a unique set of challenges. Labeled data are expensive to obtain, and posts containing fine-grained aspects occur infrequently in courses and differ across courses, thereby making it expensive to get sufficient coverage of all labels. Few distinct aspects occur per course, and only 5-10% of posts in a course are relevant. Hence, getting labels for fine-grained labels involves mining and annotating posts from a large number of courses. Further, creating and sharing labeled data is difficult as data from online courses is governed by IRB regula-

Proceedings of the 53rd Annual Meeting of the Association for Computational Linguistics and the 7th International Joint Conference on Natural Language Processing, pages 74–83,
Beijing, China, July 26-31, 2015.

tions. Privacy restrictions are another reason why unsupervised/weakly-supervised methods can be helpful. Lastly, to design a system capable of identifying all possible MOOC aspects across courses, we need to develop a system that is not fine-tuned to any particular course, but can adapt seamlessly across courses.

To this end, we develop a weakly supervised system for detecting aspect and sentiment in MOOC forum posts and validate its effectiveness on posts sampled from twelve MOOC courses. Our system can be applied to any MOOC discussion forum with no or minimal modifications.

Our contributions in this paper are as follows:

- We show how to encode weak supervision in the form of seed words to extract extract course-specific features in MOOCs using SeededLDA, a seeded variation of topic modeling (Jagarlamudi et al., 2012).

- Building upon our SeededLDA approach, we develop a joint model for aspects and sentiment using the *hinge-loss Markov random field (HL-MRF)* probabilistic modeling framework. This framework is especially well-suited for this problem because of its ability to combine information from multiple features and jointly reason about aspect and sentiment.

- To validate the effectiveness of our system, we construct a labeled evaluation dataset by sampling posts from twelve MOOC courses, and annotating these posts with fine-grained MOOC aspects and sentiment via *crowdsourcing*. The annotation captures fine-grained aspects of the course such as content, grading, deadlines, audio and video of lectures and sentiment (i.e., *positive, negative, and neutral*) toward the aspect in the post.

- We demonstrate that the proposed HL-MRF model can predict fine-grained aspects and sentiment and outperforms the model based only on SeededLDA.

2 Related Work

To the best of our knowledge, the problem of predicting aspect and sentiment in MOOC forums has not yet been addressed in the literature. We review prior work in related areas here.

Aspect-Sentiment in Online Reviews It is valuable to identify the sentiment of online reviews towards aspects such as hotel cleanliness and cellphone screen brightness, and sentiment analysis at the aspect-level has been studied extensively in this context (Liu and Zhang, 2012). Several of these methods use latent Dirichlet allocation topic models (Blei et al., 2003) and variants of it for detecting aspect and sentiment (Lu et al., 2011; Lin and He, 2009). Liu and Zhang (2012) provide a comprehensive survey of techniques for aspect and sentiment analysis. Here, we discuss works that are closely related to ours.

Titov and McDonald (2008) emphasize the importance of an unsupervised approach for aspect detection. However, the authors also indicate that standard LDA (Blei et al., 2003) methods capture global topics and not necessarily pertinent aspects — a challenge that we address in this work. Brody and Elhadad (2010), Titov and McDonald (2008), and Jo and Oh (2011) apply variations of LDA at the sentence level for online reviews. We find that around 90% of MOOC posts have only one aspect, which makes sentence-level aspect modeling inappropriate for our domain.

Most previous approaches for sentiment rely on manually constructed lexicons of strongly positive and negative words (Fahrni and Klenner, 2008; Brody and Elhadad, 2010). These methods are effective in an online review context, however sentiment in MOOC forum posts is often implicit, and not necessarily indicated by standard lexicons. For example, the post "Where is my certificate? Waiting over a month for it." expresses negative sentiment toward the *certificate* aspect, but does not include any typical negative sentiment words. In our work, we use a data-driven model-based approach to discover domain-specific lexicon information guided by small sets of seed words.

There has also been substantial work on joint models for aspect and sentiment (Kim et al., 2013; Diao et al., 2014; Zhao et al., 2010; Lin et al., 2012), and we adopt such an approach in this paper. Kim et al. (2013) use a hierarchical aspect-sentiment model and evaluate it for online reviews. Mukherjee and Liu (2012) use seed words for discovering aspect-based sentiment topics. Drawing on the ideas of Mukherjee and Liu (2012) and Kim et al. (2013), we propose a statistical relational learning approach that combines the advantages of seed words, aspect hierarchy, and flat

Post 1: I have not received the **midterm**.
Post 2: No **lecture subtitles** week, will they be uploaded?
Post 3: I am ... and I am looking forward to learn more ...

Table 1: Example posts from MOOC forums. Aspect words are highlighted in **bold**.

aspect-sentiment relationships. It is important to note that a broad majority of the previous work on aspect sentiment focuses on the specific challenges of online review data. As discussed in detail above, MOOC forum data have substantially different properties, and our approach is the first to be designed particularly for this domain.

Learning Analytics In another line of research, there is a growing body of work on the analysis of online courses. Regarding MOOC forum data, Stump et al. (2013) propose a framework for taxonomically categorizing forum posts, leveraging manual annotations. We differ from their approach in that we develop an automatic system to predict MOOC forum categories without using labeled training data. Ramesh et al. (2014b) categorize forum posts into three broad categories in order to predict student engagement. Unlike this method, our system is capable of fine-grained categorization and of identifying aspects in MOOCS. Chaturvedi et al. (2014) focus on predicting instructor intervention using lexicon features and thread features. In contrast, our system is capable of predicting fine MOOC aspects and sentiment of discussion forum posts and thus provides a more informed analysis of MOOC posts.

3 Problem Setting and Data

MOOC participants primarily communicate through discussion forums, consisting of posts, which are short pieces of text. Table 1 provides examples of posts in MOOC forums. Posts *1* and *2* report issues and feedback for the course, while post *3* is a social interaction message. Our goal is to distinguish *problem-reporting* posts such as *1* and *2* from *social* posts such as *3*, and to *identify the issues* that are being discussed.

We formalize this task as an *aspect-sentiment* prediction problem (Liu and Zhang, 2012). The issues reported in MOOC forums can be related to the different elements of the course such as *lectures* and *quizzes*, which are referred to as *aspects*. The aspects are selected based on MOOC domain expertise and inspiration from Stump et al. (2013), aiming to cover common concerns that could benefit from intervention. The task is to predict these

COARSE-ASPECT	FINE-ASPECT	Description	# of posts
LECTURE	LECTURE-CONTENT	Content of lectures.	559
	LECTURE-VIDEO	Video of lectures.	215
	LECTURE-SUBTITLES	Subtitles of lecture.	149
	LECTURE-AUDIO	Audio of lecture.	136
	LECTURE-LECTURER	Delivery of instructor.	69
QUIZ	QUIZ-CONTENT	Content in quizzes.	439
	QUIZ-GRADING	Grading of quizzes.	360
	QUIZ-SUBMISSION	Quiz submission.	329
	QUIZ-DEADLINE	Deadline of quizzes.	142
CERTIFICATE		Course certificates.	194
SOCIAL		Social interaction posts.	1187

Table 2: Descriptions of *coarse* and *fine* aspects.

aspects for each post, along with the *sentiment* polarity toward the aspect, which we code as *positive*, *negative*, or *neutral*. The negative-sentiment posts, along with their aspects, allow us to identify potentially correctable issues in the course. As labels are expensive in this scenario, we formulate the task as a *weakly supervised* prediction problem. In our work, we assume that a post has at most one fine-grained aspect, as we found that this was true for 90% of the posts in our data. This property is due in part to the brevity of forum posts, which are much shorter documents than those considered in other aspect-sentiment scenarios such as product reviews.

3.1 Aspect Hierarchy

While we do not require labeled data, our approaches allow the analyst to instead relatively easily encode a small amount of domain knowledge by seeding the models with a few words relating to each aspect of interest. Hence, we refer to our approach as *weakly supervised*. Our models can further make use of hierarchical structure between the aspects. The proposed approach is flexible, allowing the aspect seeds and hierarchy to be selected for a given MOOC domain.

For the purposes of this study, we represent the MOOC aspects with a two-level hierarchy. We identify a list of *nine* fine-grained aspects, which are grouped into *four* coarse topics. The *coarse* aspects consist of LECTURE, QUIZ, CERTIFICATE, and SOCIAL topics. Table 2 provides a description of each of the aspects and also gives the number of posts in each aspect category after annotation.

As both LECTURE and QUIZ are key coarse-level aspects in online courses, and more nuanced aspect information for these is important to facilitate instructor interventions, we identify fine-grained aspects for these coarse aspects.

For LECTURE we identify LECTURE-CONTENT, LECTURE-VIDEO, LECTURE-AUDIO, LECTURE-SUBTITLES, and LECTURE-LECTURER as fine aspects. For QUIZ, we identify the fine aspects QUIZ-CONTENT, QUIZ-GRADING, QUIZ-DEADLINES, and QUIZ-SUBMISSION. We use the label SOCIAL to refer to social interaction posts that do not mention a problem-related aspect.

3.2 Dataset

We construct a dataset by sampling posts from MOOC courses to capture the variety of aspects discussed in online courses. We include courses from different disciplines (business, technology, history, and the sciences) to ensure broad coverage of aspects. Although we adopt an approach that does not require labeled data for training, which is important for most practical MOOC scenarios, in order to validate our methods we obtain labels for the sampled posts using *Crowdflower*,[1] an online crowd-sourcing annotation platform. Each post was annotated by at least 3 annotators. Crowdflower calculates *confidence* in labels by computing trust scores for annotators using test questions. Kolhatkar et al. (2013) provide a detailed analysis of Crowdflower trust calculations and the relationship to inter-annotator agreement. We follow their recommendations and retain only labels with *confidence* > 0.5.

4 Aspect-Sentiment Prediction Models

In this section, we develop models and feature-extraction techniques to address the challenges of aspect-sentiment prediction for MOOC forums. We present two weakly-supervised methods—first, using a seeded topic modeling approach (Jagarlamudi et al., 2012) to identify aspects and sentiment. Second, building upon this method, we then introduce a more powerful statistical relational model which reasons over the seeded LDA predictions as well as sentiment side-information to encode hierarchy information and correlations between sentiment and aspect.

4.1 Seeded LDA Model

Topic models (Blei et al., 2003), which identify latent semantic themes from text corpora, have previously been successfully used to discover aspects for sentiment analysis (Diao et al., 2014). By equating the topics, i.e. discrete distributions over words, with aspects and/or sentiment polarities, topic models can recover aspect-sentiment predictions. In the MOOC context we are specifically interested in problems with the courses, rather than general topics which may be identified by a topic model, such as the topics of the course material. To guide the topic model to identify aspects of interest, we use *SeededLDA* (Jagarlamudi et al., 2012), a variant of LDA which allows an analyst to "seed" topics by providing key words that should belong to the topics.

We construct SeededLDA models by providing a set of seed words for each of the coarse and fine aspects in the aspect hierarchy of Table 2. We also seed topics for *positive*, *negative* and *neutral* sentiment polarities. The seed words for coarse topics are provided in Table 3, and fine aspects in Table 4. For the sentiment topics (Table 5), the seed words for the topic *positive* are positive words often found in online courses such as *thank*, *congratulations*, *learn*, and *interest*. Similarly, the seed words for the *negative* topic are negative in the context of online courses, such as *difficult*, *error*, *issue*, *problem*, and *misunderstand*.

Additionally, we also use SeededLDA for isolating some common problems in online courses that are associated with sentiment, such as *difficulty*, *availability*, *correctness*, and course-specific seed words from the syllabus as described in Table 6. Finally, having inferred the SeededLDA model from the data set, for each post p we predict the most likely aspect and the most likely sentiment polarity according to the post's inferred distribution over topics $\theta^{(p)}$.

In our experiments, we tokenize and stem the posts using NLTK toolkit (Loper and Bird, 2002), and use a stop word list tuned to online course discussion forums. The topic model Dirichlet hyperparameters are set to $\alpha = 0.01$, $\beta = 0.01$ in our experiments. For SeededLDA models corresponding to the seed sets in Tables 3, 4, and 5, the number of topics is equal to the number of seeded topics. For SeededLDA models corresponding to the seed words in Tables 6 and 3, we use 10 topics, allowing for some *unseeded* topics that are not captured by the seed words.

4.2 Hinge-loss Markov Random Fields

The approach described in the previous section automatically identifies user-seeded aspects and sentiment, but it does not make further use of struc-

[1] http://www.crowdflower.com/

LECTURE: lectur, video, download, volum, low, headphon, sound, audio, transcript, subtitl, slide, note	
QUIZ: quiz, assignment, question, midterm,exam, submiss, answer, grade, score, grad, midterm, due, deadlin	
CERTIFICATE: certif, score, signatur, statement, final, course, pass, receiv, coursera, accomplish, fail	
SOCIAL: name, course, introduction, stud, group, everyon, student	

Table 3: Seed words for *coarse* aspects

LECTURE-VIDEO: video, problem, download, play, player, watch, speed, length, long, fast, slow, render, qualiti	
LECTURE-AUDIO: volum, low, headphon, sound, audio, hear, maximum, troubl, qualiti, high, loud, heard	
LECTURE-LECTURER: professor, fast, speak, pace, follow, speed, slow, accent, absorb, quick, slowli	
LECTURE-SUBTITLES: transcript, subtitl, slide, note, lectur, difficult, pdf	
LECTURE-CONTENT: typo, error, mistak, wrong, right, incorrect, mistaken	
QUIZ-CONTENT: question, challeng, difficult, understand, typo, error, mistak, quiz, assignment	
QUIZ-SUBMISSION: submiss, submit, quiz, error, unabl, resubmit	
QUIZ-GRADING: answer, question, answer, grade, assignment, quiz, respons ,mark, wrong, score	
QUIZ-DEADLINE: due, deadlin, miss, extend, late	

Table 4: Seed words for *fine* aspects

POSITIVE: interest, excit, thank, great, happi, glad, enjoy, forward, insight, opportun, clear, fantast, fascin, learn, hope, congratul	
NEGATIVE: problem, difficult, error, issu, unabl, misunderstand, terribl, bother, hate, bad, wrong, mistak, fear, troubl	
NEUTRAL: coursera, class, hello, everyon, greet, nam, meet, group, studi, request, join, introduct, question, thank	

Table 5: Seed words for *sentiment*

DIFFICULTY: difficult, understand, ambigu, disappoint, hard, follow, mislead, difficulti, challeng, clear	
CONTENT: typo, error, mistak, wrong, right, incorrect, mistaken, score	
AVAILABILITY: avail, nowher, find, access, miss, view, download, broken, link, bad, access, deni, miss, permiss	
COURSE-1: develop, eclips, sdk, softwar, hardware, accuser, html, platform, environ, lab, ide, java,	
COURSE-2: protein, food, gene, vitamin, evolut, sequenc, chromosom, genet, speci, peopl, popul, evolv, mutat, ancestri	
COURSE-3: compani, product, industri, strategi, decision, disrupt, technolog, market	

Table 6: Seed words for sentiment specific to online courses

ture or dependencies between these values, or any additional side-information. To address this, we propose a more powerful approach using hinge-loss Markov random fields (HL-MRFs), a scalable class of continuous, conditional graphical models (Bach et al., 2013). HL-MRFs have achieved state-of-the-art performance in many domains including knowledge graph identification (Pujara et al., 2013), understanding engagements in MOOCs (Ramesh et al., 2014a), biomedicine and multi-relational link prediction (Fakhraei et al., 2014), and modelling social trust (Huang et al., 2013). These models can be specified using *Probabilistic Soft Logic (PSL)* (Bach et al., 2015), a weighted first order logical templating language. An example of a PSL rule is

$$\lambda : P(a) \wedge Q(a,b) \rightarrow R(b),$$

where P, Q, and R are predicates, a and b are *variables*, and λ is the weight associated with the rule. The weight of the rule indicates its importance in the HL-MRF probabilistic model, which defines a probability density function of the form

$$P(\mathbf{Y}|\mathbf{X}) \propto \exp\Big(-\sum_{r=1}^{M}\lambda_r\phi_r(\mathbf{Y},\mathbf{X})\Big)$$
$$\phi_r(\mathbf{Y},\mathbf{X}) = (\max\{l_r(\mathbf{Y},\mathbf{X}),0\})^{\rho_r}\ , \qquad (1)$$

where $\phi_r(\mathbf{Y},\mathbf{X})$ is a *hinge-loss potential* corresponding to an instantiation of a rule, and is specified by a linear function l_r and optional exponent $\rho_r \in \{1,2\}$. For example, in our MOOC aspect-sentiment model, if P and F denote *post P* and *fine aspect F*, then we have predicates SEEDLDA-FINE(P, F) to denote the value corresponding to topic F in SeededLDA, and FINE-ASPECT(P, F) is the target variable denoting the fine aspect of the post P. A PSL rule to encode that the SeededLDA topic F suggests that aspect F is present is

$$\lambda : \text{SEEDLDA-FINE}(P,F) \rightarrow \text{FINE-ASPECT}(P,F).$$

We can generate more complex rules connecting the different features and target variables, e.g.

$$\lambda : \text{SEEDLDA-FINE}(P,F) \wedge \text{SENTIMENT}(P,S) \rightarrow \text{FINE-ASPECT}(P,F).$$

This rule encodes a dependency between SENTIMENT and FINE-ASPECT, namely that the SeededLDA topic and a strong sentiment score increase the probability of the fine aspect. The HL-MRF model uses these rules to encode domain knowledge about dependencies among the predicates. The continuous value representation further helps in understanding the confidence of predictions.

4.3 Joint Aspect-Sentiment Prediction using Probabilistic Soft Logic (PSL-Joint)

In this section, we describe our joint approach to predicting aspect and sentiment in online discussion forums, leveraging the strong dependence between aspect and sentiment. We present a system designed using HL-MRFs which combines different features, accounting for their respective uncertainty, and encodes the dependencies between aspect and sentiment in the MOOC context.

Table 7 provides some representative rules from our model.[2] The rules can be classified into two broad categories—1) rules that combine multiple features, and 2) rules that encode the dependencies between aspect and sentiment.

4.3.1 Combining Features

The first set of rules in Table 7 combine different features extracted from the post. SEEDLDA-FINE, SEEDLDA-COARSE and SEEDLDA-SENTIMENT-COURSE predicates in rules refer to SeededLDA posterior distributions using *coarse*, *fine*, and course-specific *sentiment* seed words respectively. The strength of our model comes from its ability to encode different combinations of features and weight them according to their importance. The first rule in Table 7 combines the SeededLDA features from both SEEDLDA-FINE and SEEDLDA-COARSE to predict the fine aspect. Interpreting the rule, the fine aspect of the post is more likely to be LECTURE-LECTURER if the coarse SeededLDA score for the post is LECTURE, *and* the fine SeededLDA score for the post is LECTURE-LECTURER. Similarly, the second rule provides combinations of some of the other features used by the model—two different SeededLDA scores for sentiment, as indicated by seed words in Tables 5 and 6. The third rule states that certain fine aspects occur together with certain values of sentiment more than others. In online courses, posts that discuss grading usually talk about grievances and issues. The rule captures that QUIZ-GRADING occurs with negative sentiment in most cases.

[2]Full model available at https://github.com/artir/ramesh-acl15

4.3.2 Encoding Dependencies Between Aspect and Sentiment

In addition to combining features, we also encode rules to capture the taxonomic dependence between coarse and fine aspects, and the dependence between aspect and sentiment (Table 7, bottom). Rules 4 and 5 encode pair-wise dependency between FINE-ASPECT and SENTIMENT, and COARSE-ASPECT and FINE-ASPECT respectively. Rule 4 uses the SeededLDA value for QUIZ-DEADLINES to predict both SENTIMENT, and FINE-ASPECT jointly. This together with other rules for predicting SENTIMENT and FINE-ASPECT individually creates a constrained satisfaction problem, forcing aspect and sentiment to agree with each other. Rule 5 is similar to rule 4, capturing the taxonomic relationship between target variables COARSE-ASPECT and FINE-ASPECT.

Thus, by using conjunctions to combine features and appropriately weighting these rules, we account for the uncertainties in the underlying features and make them more robust. The combination of these two different types of weighted rules, referred to below as *PSL-Joint*, is able to reason collectively about aspect and sentiment.

5 Empirical Evaluation

In this section, we present the quantitative and qualitative results of our models on the annotated MOOC dataset. Our models do not require labeled data for training; we use the label annotations only for evaluation. Tables 8 – 11 show the results for the SeededLDA and PSL-Joint models. Statistically significant differences, evaluated using a paired t-test with a rejection threshold of *0.01*, are typed in bold.

5.1 SeededLDA for Aspect-Sentiment

For SeededLDA, we use the seed words for *coarse*, *fine*, and *sentiment* given in Tables 3 – 5. After training the model, we use the SeededLDA multinomial posterior distribution to predict the target variables. We use the maximum value in the posterior for the distribution over topics for each post to obtain predictions for coarse aspect, fine aspect, and sentiment. We then calculate precision, recall and F1 values comparing with our ground truth labels.

PSL-JOINT RULES
Rules combining features
SEEDLDA-FINE(POST, LECTURE-LECTURER) ∧ SEEDLDA-COARSE(POST, LECTURE) → FINE-ASPECT(POST, LECTURE-LECTURER)
SEEDLDA-SENTIMENT-COURSE(POST, NEGATIVE) ∧ SEEDLDA-SENTIMENT(POST, NEGATIVE) → SENTIMENT(POST, NEGATIVE)
SEEDLDA-SENTIMENT-COURSE(POST, NEGATIVE) ∧ SEEDLDA-FINE(POST, QUIZ-GRADING) → FINE-ASPECT(POST, QUIZ-GRADING)
Encoding dependencies between aspect and sentiment
SEEDLDA-FINE(POST, QUIZ-DEADLINES) ∧ SENTIMENT(POST, NEGATIVE) → FINE-ASPECT(POST, QUIZ-DEADLINES)
SEEDLDA-FINE(POST, QUIZ-SUBMISSION) ∧ FINE-ASPECT(POST, QUIZ-SUBMISSION) → COARSE-ASPECT(POST, QUIZ)

Table 7: Representative rules from PSL-Joint model

Model	LECTURE-CONTENT			LECTURE-VIDEO			LECTURE-AUDIO			LECTURE-LECTURER			LECTURE-SUBTITLES		
	Prec.	Rec.	F1	Prec.	Rec.	F1	Prec.	Rec.	F1	Prec.	Rec.	F1	Prec.	Rec.	F1
SEEDEDLDA	0.137	0.057	0.08	0.156	0.256	0.240	0.684	0.684	0.684	0.037	0.159	0.06	0.289	0.631	0.397
PSL-JOINT	**0.407**	**0.413**	**0.410**	**0.411**	**0.591**	**0.485**	0.635	0.537	0.582	**0.218**	**0.623**	**0.323**	**0.407**	0.53	**0.461**

Table 8: Precision, recall and F1 scores for LECTURE fine aspects

Model	QUIZ-CONTENT			QUIZ-SUBMISSION			QUIZ-DEADLINES			QUIZ-GRADING		
	Prec	Rec.	F1	Prec	Rec.	F1	Prec.	Rec.	F1	Prec.	Rec.	F1
SEEDEDLDA	0.042	0.006	0.011	0.485	0.398	0.437	0.444	0.141	0.214	0.524	0.508	0.514
PSL-JOINT	**0.324**	**0.405**	**0.36**	**0.521**	0.347	0.416	**0.667**	**0.563**	**0.611**	**0.572**	**0.531**	**0.550**

Table 9: Precision, recall and F1 scores for QUIZ fine aspects

Model	LECTURE			QUIZ			CERTIFICATE			SOCIAL		
	Prec	Rec.	F1	Prec.	Rec.	F1	Prec.	Rec.	F1	Prec.	Rec.	F1
SEEDEDLDA	0.597	0.673	0.632	0.752	0.583	0.657	0.315	0.845	0.459	0.902	0.513	0.654
PSL-JOINT	0.563	**0.715**	0.630	0.724	**0.688**	**0.706**	**0.552**	0.711	**0.621**	0.871	**0.530**	**0.659**

Table 10: Precision, recall and F1 scores for coarse aspects

Model	POSITIVE			NEGATIVE			NEUTRAL		
	Prec	Rec.	F1	Prec.	Rec.	F1	Prec.	Rec.	F1
SEEDEDLDA	0.104	0.721	0.182	0.650	0.429	0.517	0.483	0.282	0.356
PSL-JOINT	**0.114**	0.544	**0.189**	0.571	**0.666**	**0.615**	**0.664**	**0.322**	**0.434**

Table 11: Precision, recall and F1 scores for sentiment

5.2 PSL for Joint Aspect-Sentiment (PSL-Joint)

Tables 8 and 9 give the results for the fine aspects under LECTURE and QUIZ. PSL-JOINT performs better than SEEDEDLDA in most cases, without suffering any statistically significant losses. Notable cases include the increase in scores for LECTURE-LECTURER, LECTURE-SUBTITLES, LECTURE-CONTENT, QUIZ-CONTENT, QUIZ-GRADING, and QUIZ-DEADLINES, for which the scores increase by a large margin over SeededLDA. We observe that for LECTURE-CONTENT and QUIZ-CONTENT, the increase in scores is more significant than others with SeededLDA performing very poorly. Since both lecture and quiz content have the same kind of words related to the course material, SeededLDA is not able to distinguish between these two aspects. We found that in 63% of these missed predictions, SeededLDA predicts LECTURE-CONTENT, instead of QUIZ-CONTENT, and vice versa. In contrast, PSL-Joint uses both coarse and fine SeededLDA scores and captures the dependency between a coarse aspect and its corresponding fine aspect. Therefore, PSL-Joint is able to distinguish between LECTURE-CONTENT and QUIZ-CONTENT. In the next section, we present some examples of posts that SEEDEDLDA misclassified but were predicted correctly by PSL-Joint.

Table 10 presents results for the *coarse-aspects*. We observe that PSL-Joint performs better than SeededLDA for all classes. In particular for CERTIFICATE and QUIZ, PSL-Joint exhibits a marked increase in scores when compared to SeededLDA. This is also true for sentiment, for which the scores for NEUTRAL and NEGATIVE sentiment show significant improvement (Table 11).

Correct Label	PSL	SeededLDA	Post
QUIZ-CONTENT	QUIZ-CONTENT	LECTURE-CONTENT	There is a typo or other mistake in the assignment instructions (e.g. essential information omitted) Type ID: programming-content Problem ID: programming-mistake Browser: Chrome 32 OS: Windows 7
QUIZ-CONTENT	QUIZ-CONTENT	LECTURE-CONTENT	There is a typo or other mistake on the page (e.g. factual error information omitted) Week 4 Quiz Question 6: Question 6 When a user clicks on a View that has registered to show a Context Menu which one of the following methods will be called?
LECTURE-AUDIO	LECTURE-AUDIO	LECTURE-SUBTITLES	Thanks for the suggestion about downloading the video and referring to the subtitles. I will give that a try but I would also like to point out that what the others are saying is true for me too: The audio is just barely audible even when the volume on my computer is set to 100%.
SOCIAL	SOCIAL	LECTURE-VIDEO	Let's start a group for discussing the lecture videos.

Table 12: Example posts that PSL-Joint predicted correctly, but were misclassified by SeededLDA

Correct Label	Predicted Label	Second Prediction	Post
LECTURE-CONTENT	QUIZ-CONTENT	LECTURE-CONTENT	I have a difference of opinion to the answer for Question 6 too. It differs from what is presented in lecture 1.
SOCIAL	LECTURE-SUBTITLES	SOCIAL	Hello guys!!! I am ... The course materials are extraordinary. The subtitles are really helpful! Thanks to instructors for giving us all a wonderful opportunity.
LECTURE-CONTENT	QUIZ-CONTENT	LECTURE-CONTENT	As the second lecture video told me I started windows telnet and connected to the virtual device. Then I typed the same command for sending an sms that the lecture video told me to. The phone received a message all right and I was able to open it but the message itself seems to be written with some strange characters.

Table 13: Example posts whose second-best prediction is correct

5.3 Interpreting PSL-Joint Predictions

Table 12 presents some examples of posts that PSL-Joint predicted correctly, and which SeededLDA misclassified. The first two examples illustrate that PSL can predict the subtle difference between LECTURE-CONTENT and QUIZ-CONTENT. Particularly notable is the third example, which contains mention of both *subtitles* and *audio*, but the negative sentiment is associated with *audio* rather than *subtitles*. PSL-Joint predicts the fine aspect as LECTURE-AUDIO, even though the underlying SeededLDA feature has a high score for LECTURE-SUBTITLES. This example illustrates the strength of the joint reasoning approach in PSL-Joint. Finally, in the last example, the post mentions starting a *group* to discuss videos. This is an ambiguous post containing the keyword *video*, while it is in reality a social post about starting a group. PSL-Joint is able to predict this because it uses both the sentiment scores associated with the post and the SeededLDA scores for fine aspect, and infers that social posts are generally positive. So, combining the feature values for social aspect and positive sentiment, it is able to predict the fine aspect as SOCIAL correctly.

The continuous valued output predictions produced by PSL-Joint allow us to rank the predicted variables by output prediction value. Analyzing the predictions for posts that PSL-Joint misclassified, we observe that for *four* out of *nine* fine aspects, more than 70% of the time the correct label is in the top three predictions. And, for all fine aspects, the correct label is found in the top 3 predictions around 40% of the time. Thus, using the top three predictions made by PSL-Joint, we can understand the fine aspect of the post to a great extent. Table 13 gives some examples of posts for which the second best prediction by PSL-Joint is the correct label. For these examples, we found that PSL-Joint misses the correct prediction by a small margin(< 0.2). Since our evaluation scheme only considers the maximum value to determine the scores, these examples were treated as misclassified.

5.4 Understanding Instructor Intervention using PSL-Joint Predictions

In our 3275 annotated posts, the instructor replied to 787 posts. Of these, 699 posts contain a mention of some MOOC aspect. PSL-Joint predicts 97.8% from those as having an aspect and 46.9% as the correct aspect. This indicates that PSL-Joint is capable of identifying the most important posts, i.e. those that the instructor replied to, with high accuracy. PSL-Joint's MOOC aspect predictions can potentially be used by the instructor to select a subset of posts to address in order to cover the main reported issues. We found in our data that some fine aspects, such as CERTIFICATE, have a higher percentage of instructor replies than others, such as QUIZ-GRADING. Using our system, instructors can sample from multiple aspect categories, thereby making sure that all categories of problems receive attention.

6 Conclusion

In this paper, we developed a weakly supervised joint probabilistic model (PSL-Joint) for predicting aspect-sentiment in online courses. Our model provides the ability to conveniently encode domain information in the form of seed words, and weighted logical rules capturing the dependencies between aspects and sentiment. We validated our approach on an annotated dataset of MOOC posts sampled from twelve courses. We compared our PSL-Joint probabilistic model to a simpler SeededLDA approach, and demonstrated that PSL-Joint produced statistically significantly better results, exhibiting a 3–5 times improvement in F1 score in most cases over a system using only SeededLDA. As further shown by our qualitative results and instructor reply information, our system can potentially be used for understanding student requirements and issues, identifying posts for instructor intervention, increasing student retention, and improving future iterations of the course.

Acknowledgements This work was supported by NSF grant IIS1218488, and IARPA via DoI/NBC contract number D12PC00337. The U.S. Government is authorized to reproduce and distribute reprints for governmental purposes notwithstanding any copyright annotation thereon. Disclaimer: The views and conclusions contained herein are those of the authors and should not be interpreted as necessarily representing the official policies or endorsements, either expressed or implied, of IARPA, DoI/NBC, or the U.S. Government.

References

Stephen H. Bach, Bert Huang, Ben London, and Lise Getoor. 2013. Hinge-loss Markov random fields: Convex inference for structured prediction. In *Proceedings of the Conference on Uncertainty in Artificial Intelligence (UAI)*.

S. H. Bach, M. Broecheler, B. Huang, and L. Getoor. 2015. Hinge-loss Markov random fields and probabilistic soft logic. arXiv:1505.04406 [cs.LG].

David M. Blei, Andrew Y. Ng, and Michael I. Jordan. 2003. Latent Dirichlet allocation. *Journal of Machine Learning Research (JMLR)*.

Samuel Brody and Noemie Elhadad. 2010. An unsupervised aspect-sentiment model for online reviews. In *Proceedings of Human Language Technologies: Conference of the North American Chapter of the Association for Computational Linguistics (HLT)*.

Snigdha Chaturvedi, Dan Goldwasser, and Hal Daumé III. 2014. Predicting instructor's intervention in mooc forums. In *Proceedings of the Annual Meeting of the Association for Computational Linguistics (ACL)*.

Qiming Diao, Minghui Qiu, Chao-Yuan Wu, Alexander J. Smola, Jing Jiang, and Chong Wang. 2014. Jointly modeling aspects, ratings and sentiments for movie recommendation (JMARS). In *Proceedings of the SIGKDD International Conference on Knowledge Discovery and Data Mining (KDD)*.

Angela Fahrni and Manfred Klenner. 2008. Old wine or warm beer: Target-specific sentiment analysis of adjectives. In *Proceedings of the Symposium on Affective Language in Human and Machine (AISB)*.

Shobeir Fakhraei, Bert Huang, Louiqa Raschid, and Lise Getoor. 2014. Network-based drug-target interaction prediction with probabilistic soft logic. *IEEE/ACM Transactions on Computational Biology and Bioinformatics (TCBB)*.

Bert Huang, Angelika Kimmig, Lise Getoor, and Jennifer Golbeck. 2013. A flexible framework for probabilistic models of social trust. In *Proceedings of the International Conference on Social Computing, Behavioral-Cultural Modeling, & Prediction (SBP)*.

Jagadeesh Jagarlamudi, Hal Daumé, III, and Raghavendra Udupa. 2012. Incorporating lexical priors into topic models. In *Proceedings of the European Chapter of the Association for Computational Linguistics (EACL)*.

Y. Jo and A.H. Oh. 2011. Aspect and sentiment unification model for online review analysis. In *Proceedings of the International Conference on Web Search and Data Mining (WSDM)*.

Suin Kim, Jianwen Zhang, Zheng Chen, Alice Oh, and Shixia Liu. 2013. A hierarchical aspect-sentiment model for online reviews. In *Proceedings of the AAAI Conference on Artificial Intelligence (AAAI)*.

Varada Kolhatkar, Heike Zinsmeister, and Graeme Hirst. 2013. Annotating anaphoric shell nouns with their antecedents. In *Linguistic Annotation Workshop and Interoperability with Discourse*.

Chenghua Lin and Yulan He. 2009. Joint sentiment/topic model for sentiment analysis. In *Proceedings of the Conference on Information and Knowledge Management (CIKM)*.

Chenghua Lin, Yulan He, R. Everson, and S. Ruger. 2012. Weakly supervised joint sentiment-topic detection from text. *IEEE Transactions on Knowledge and Data Engineering*.

Bing Liu and Lei Zhang. 2012. A survey of opinion mining and sentiment analysis. In *Mining Text Data*.

Edward Loper and Steven Bird. 2002. NLTK: The natural language toolkit. In *Proceedings of the ACL Workshop on Effective Tools and Methodologies for Teaching Natural Language Processing and Computational Linguistics (ETMTNLP)*.

Bin Lu, Myle Ott, Claire Cardie, and Benjamin K. Tsou. 2011. Multi-aspect sentiment analysis with topic models. In *Proceedings of the International Conference on Data Mining Workshops (ICDMW)*.

Arjun Mukherjee and Bing Liu. 2012. Aspect extraction through semi-supervised modeling. In *Proceedings of the Annual Meeting of the Association for Computational Linguistics (ACL)*.

Jay Pujara, Hui Miao, Lise Getoor, and William Cohen. 2013. Knowledge graph identification. In *International Semantic Web Conference (ISWC)*.

Arti Ramesh, Dan Goldwasser, Bert Huang, Hal Daume III, and Lise Getoor. 2014a. Learning latent engagement patterns of students in online courses. In *Proceedings of the AAAI Conference on Artificial Intelligence (AAAI)*.

Arti Ramesh, Dan Goldwasser, Bert Huang, Hal Daumé III, and Lise Getoor. 2014b. Understanding MOOC discussion forums using seeded lda. In *ACL Workshop on Innovative Use of NLP for Building Educational Applications (BEA)*.

Glenda S. Stump, Jennifer DeBoer, Jonathan Whittinghill, and Lori Breslow. 2013. Development of a framework to classify MOOC discussion forum posts: Methodology and challenges. In *NIPS Workshop on Data Driven Education*.

Ivan Titov and Ryan McDonald. 2008. Modeling online reviews with multi-grain topic models. In *Proceedings of the International Conference on World Wide Web (WWW)*.

Wayne Xin Zhao, Jing Jiang, Hongfei Yan, and Xiaoming Li. 2010. Jointly modeling aspects and opinions with a maxEnt-LDA hybrid. In *Proceedings of the Conference on Empirical Methods in Natural Language Processing (EMNLP)*.

Semantically Smooth Knowledge Graph Embedding

Shu Guo[†], **Quan Wang**[†*], **Bin Wang**[†], **Lihong Wang**[‡], **Li Guo**[†]
[†]Institute of Information Engineering, Chinese Academy of Sciences, Beijing 100093, China
{guoshu,wangquan,wangbin,guoli}@iie.ac.cn
[‡]National Computer Network Emergency Response Technical Team
Coordination Center of China, Beijing 100029, China
wlh@isc.org.cn

Abstract

This paper considers the problem of embedding Knowledge Graphs (KGs) consisting of entities and relations into low-dimensional vector spaces. Most of the existing methods perform this task based solely on observed facts. The only requirement is that the learned embeddings should be compatible within each individual fact. In this paper, aiming at further discovering the intrinsic geometric structure of the embedding space, we propose *Semantically Smooth Embedding* (SSE). The key idea of SSE is to take full advantage of additional semantic information and enforce the embedding space to be semantically smooth, i.e., entities belonging to the same semantic category will lie close to each other in the embedding space. Two manifold learning algorithms Laplacian Eigenmaps and Locally Linear Embedding are used to model the smoothness assumption. Both are formulated as geometrically based regularization terms to constrain the embedding task. We empirically evaluate SSE in two benchmark tasks of link prediction and triple classification, and achieve significant and consistent improvements over state-of-the-art methods. Furthermore, SSE is a general framework. The smoothness assumption can be imposed to a wide variety of embedding models, and it can also be constructed using other information besides entities' semantic categories.

1 Introduction

Knowledge Graphs (KGs) like WordNet (Miller, 1995), Freebase (Bollacker et al., 2008), and DBpedia (Lehmann et al., 2014) have become extremely useful resources for many NLP related applications, such as word sense disambiguation (Agirre et al., 2014), named entity recognition (Magnini et al., 2002), and information extraction (Hoffmann et al., 2011). A KG is a multi-relational directed graph composed of entities as nodes and relations as edges. Each edge is represented as a triple of fact $\langle e_i, r_k, e_j \rangle$, indicating that head entity e_i and tail entity e_j are connected by relation r_k. Although powerful in representing structured data, the underlying symbolic nature makes KGs hard to manipulate.

Recently a new research direction called knowledge graph embedding has attracted much attention (Socher et al., 2013; Bordes et al., 2013; Bordes et al., 2014; Lin et al., 2015). It attempts to embed components of a KG into continuous vector spaces, so as to simplify the manipulation while preserving the inherent structure of the original graph. Specifically, given a KG, entities and relations are first represented in a low-dimensional vector space, and for each triple, a scoring function is defined to measure its plausibility in that space. Then the representations of entities and relations (i.e. embeddings) are learned by maximizing the total plausibility of observed triples. The learned embeddings can further be used to benefit all kinds of tasks, such as KG completion (Socher et al., 2013; Bordes et al., 2013), relation extraction (Riedel et al., 2013; Weston et al., 2013), and entity resolution (Bordes et al., 2014).

To our knowledge, most of existing KG embedding methods perform the embedding task based solely on observed facts. The only requirement is that the learned embeddings should be compatible within each individual fact. In this paper we propose *Semantically Smooth Embedding* (SSE), a new approach which further imposes constraints on the geometric structure of the embedding space. The key idea of SSE is to make ful-

* Corresponding author: Quan Wang.

Proceedings of the 53rd Annual Meeting of the Association for Computational Linguistics and the 7th International Joint Conference on Natural Language Processing, pages 84–94,
Beijing, China, July 26-31, 2015.

l use of additional semantic information (i.e. semantic categories of entities) and enforce the embedding space to be semantically smooth—entities belonging to the same semantic category should lie close to each other in the embedding space. This smoothness assumption is closely related to the local invariance assumption exploited in manifold learning theory, which requires nearby points to have similar embeddings or labels (Belkin and Niyogi, 2001). Thus we employ two manifold learning algorithms Laplacian Eigenmaps (Belkin and Niyogi, 2001) and Locally Linear Embedding (Roweis and Saul, 2000) to model the smoothness assumption. The former requires an entity to lie close to every other entity in the same category, while the latter represents that entity as a linear combination of its nearest neighbors (i.e. entities within the same category). Both are formulated as manifold regularization terms to constrain the KG embedding objective function. As such, SSE obtains an embedding space which is semantically smooth and at the same time compatible with observed facts.

The advantages of SSE are two-fold: 1) By imposing the smoothness assumption, SSE successfully captures the semantic correlation between entities, which exists intrinsically but is overlooked in previous work on KG embedding. 2) KGs are typically very sparse, containing a relatively small number of facts compared to the large number of entities and relations. SSE can effectively deal with data sparsity by leveraging additional semantic information. Both aspects lead to more accurate embeddings in SSE. Moreover, our approach is quite general. The smoothness assumption can actually be imposed to a wide variety of KG embedding models. Besides semantic categories, other information (e.g. entity similarities specified by users or derived from auxiliary data sources) can also be used to construct the manifold regularization terms. And besides KG embedding, similar smoothness assumptions can also be applied in other embedding tasks (e.g. word embedding and sentence embedding).

Our main contributions can be summarized as follows. First, we devise a novel KG embedding framework that naturally requires the embedding space to be semantically smooth. As far as we know, it is the first work that imposes constraints on the geometric structure of the embedding space during KG embedding. By leveraging additional semantic information, our approach can also deal with the data sparsity issue that commonly exists in typical KGs. Second, we evaluate our approach in two benchmark tasks of link prediction and triple classification, and achieve significant and consistent improvements over state-of-the-art models.

In the remainder of this paper, we first provide a brief review of existing KG embedding models in Section 2, and then detail the proposed SSE framework in Section 3. Experiments and results are reported in Section 4. Then in Section 5 we discuss related work, followed by the conclusion and future work in Section 6.

2 A Brief Review of KG Embedding

KG embedding aims to embed entities and relations into a continuous vector space and model the plausibility of each fact in that space. In general, it consists of three steps: 1) representing entities and relations, 2) specifying a scoring function, and 3) learning the latent representations. In the first step, given a KG, entities are represented as points (i.e. vectors) in a continuous vector space, and relations as operators in that space, which can be characterized by vectors (Bordes et al., 2013; Bordes et al., 2014; Wang et al., 2014b), matrices (Bordes et al., 2011; Jenatton et al., 2012), or tensors (Socher et al., 2013). In the second step, for each candidate fact $\langle e_i, r_k, e_j\rangle$, an energy function $f(e_i, r_k, e_j)$ is further defined to measure its plausibility, with the corresponding entity and relation representations as variables. Plausible triples are assumed to have low energies. Then in the third step, to obtain the entity and relation representations, a margin-based ranking loss, i.e.,

$$\mathcal{L}=\sum_{t^+\in\mathcal{O}}\sum_{t^-\in\mathcal{N}_{t^+}}\left[\gamma+f(e_i,r_k,e_j)-f(e'_i,r_k,e'_j)\right]_+, \quad (1)$$

is minimized. Here, $\mathcal{O}$ is the set of observed (i.e. positive) triples, and $t^+ = \langle e_i, r_k, e_j\rangle \in \mathcal{O}$; $\mathcal{N}_{t^+}$ denotes the set of negative triples constructed by replacing entities in t^+, and $t^- = \langle e'_i, r_k, e'_j\rangle \in \mathcal{N}_{t^+}$; $\gamma > 0$ is a margin separating positive and negative triples; and $[x]_+ = \max(0, x)$. The ranking loss favors lower energies for positive triples than for negative ones. Stochastic gradient descent (in mini-batch mode) is adopted to solve the minimization problem. For details please refer to (Bordes et al., 2013) and references therein.

Different embedding models differ in the first two steps: entity/relation representation and energy

Method	Entity/Relation embeddings	Energy function
TransE (Bordes et al., 2013)	$\mathbf{e}, \mathbf{r} \in \mathbb{R}^d$	$f(e_i, r_k, e_j) = \|\mathbf{e}_i + \mathbf{r}_k - \mathbf{e}_j\|_{\ell_1/\ell_2}$
SME (lin) (Bordes et al., 2014)	$\mathbf{e}, \mathbf{r} \in \mathbb{R}^d$	$f(e_i, r_k, e_j) = (\mathbf{W}_{u1}\mathbf{r}_k + \mathbf{W}_{u2}\mathbf{e}_i + \mathbf{b}_u)^T \left(\mathbf{W}_{v1}\mathbf{r}_k + \mathbf{W}_{v2}\mathbf{e}_j + \mathbf{b}_v\right)$
SME (bilin) (Bordes et al., 2014)	$\mathbf{e}, \mathbf{r} \in \mathbb{R}^d$	$f(e_i, r_k, e_j) = \left(\left(\underline{\mathbf{W}}_u \bar{\times}_3 \mathbf{r}_k\right)\mathbf{e}_i + \mathbf{b}_u\right)^T \left(\left(\underline{\mathbf{W}}_v \bar{\times}_3 \mathbf{r}_k\right)\mathbf{e}_j + \mathbf{b}_v\right)$
SE (Bordes et al., 2011)	$\mathbf{e} \in \mathbb{R}^d, \mathbf{R}^u, \mathbf{R}^v \in \mathbb{R}^{d\times d}$	$f(e_i, r_k, e_j) = \|\mathbf{R}_k^u\mathbf{e}_i - \mathbf{R}_k^v\mathbf{e}_j\|_{\ell_1}$

Table 1: Existing KG embedding models.

function definition. Three state-of-the-art embedding models, namely TransE (Bordes et al., 2013), SME (Bordes et al., 2014), and SE (Bordes et al., 2011), are detailed below. Please refer to (Jenatton et al., 2012; Socher et al., 2013; Wang et al., 2014b; Lin et al., 2015) for other methods.

TransE (Bordes et al., 2013) represents both entities and relations as vectors in the embedding space. For a given triple $\langle e_i, r_k, e_j \rangle$, the relation is interpreted as a translation vector $\mathbf{r}_k$ so that the embedded entities $\mathbf{e}_i$ and $\mathbf{e}_j$ can be connected by $\mathbf{r}_k$ with low error. The energy function is defined as $f(e_i, r_k, e_j) = \|\mathbf{e}_i + \mathbf{r}_k - \mathbf{e}_j\|_{\ell_1/\ell_2}$, where $\|\cdot\|_{\ell_1/\ell_2}$ denotes the ℓ_1-norm or ℓ_2-norm.

SME (Bordes et al., 2014) also represents entities and relations as vectors, but models triples in a more expressive way. Given a triple $\langle e_i, r_k, e_j \rangle$, it first employs a function $g_u(\cdot, \cdot)$ to combine $\mathbf{r}_k$ and $\mathbf{e}_i$, and $g_v(\cdot, \cdot)$ to combine $\mathbf{r}_k$ and $\mathbf{e}_j$. Then, the energy function is defined as matching $g_u(\cdot, \cdot)$ and $g_v(\cdot, \cdot)$ by their dot product, i.e., $f(e_i, r_k, e_j) = g_u(\mathbf{r}_k, \mathbf{e}_i)^T g_v(\mathbf{r}_k, \mathbf{e}_j)$. There are two versions of SME, linear and bilinear (denoted as SME (lin) and SME (bilin) respectively), obtained by defining different $g_u(\cdot, \cdot)$ and $g_v(\cdot, \cdot)$.

SE (Bordes et al., 2011) represents entities as vectors but relations as matrices. Each relation is modeled by a left matrix $\mathbf{R}_k^u$ and a right matrix $\mathbf{R}_k^v$, acting as independent projections to head and tail entities respectively. If a triple $\langle e_i, r_k, e_j \rangle$ holds, $\mathbf{R}_k^u\mathbf{e}_i$ and $\mathbf{R}_k^v\mathbf{e}_j$ should be close to each other. The energy function is $f(e_i, r_k, e_j) = \|\mathbf{R}_k^u\mathbf{e}_i - \mathbf{R}_k^v\mathbf{e}_j\|_{\ell_1}$. Table 1 summarizes the entity/relation representations and energy functions used in these models.

3 Semantically Smooth Embedding

The methods introduced above perform the embedding task based solely on observed facts. The only requirement is that the learned embeddings should be compatible within each individual fact. However, they fail to discover the intrinsic geometric structure of the embedding space. To deal with this limitation, we introduce *Semantically Smooth Embedding* (SSE) which constrains the embedding task by incorporating geometrically based regularization terms, constructed by using additional semantic categories of entities.

3.1 Problem Formulation

Suppose we are given a KG consisting of n entities and m relations. The facts observed are stored as a set of triples $O = \left\{\langle e_i, r_k, e_j \rangle\right\}$. A triple $\langle e_i, r_k, e_j \rangle$ indicates that entity e_i and entity e_j are connected by relation r_k. In addition, the entities are classified into multiple semantic categories. Each entity e is associated with a label c_e indicating the category to which it belongs. SSE aims to embed the entities and relations into a continuous vector space which is compatible with the observed facts, and at the same time semantically smooth.

To make the embedding space compatible with the observed facts, we make use of the triple set O and follow the same strategy adopted in previous methods. That is, we define an energy function on each candidate triple (e.g. the energy functions listed in Table 1), and require observed triples to have lower energies than unobserved ones (i.e. the margin-based ranking loss defined in Eq. (1)).

To make the embedding space semantically smooth, we further leverage the entity category information $\{c_e\}$, and assume that entities within the same semantic category should lie close to each other in the embedding space. This smoothness assumption is similar to the local invariance assumption exploited in manifold learning theory (i.e. nearby points are likely to have similar embeddings or labels). So we employ two manifold learning algorithms Laplacian Eigenmaps (Belkin and Niyogi, 2001) and Locally Linear Embedding (Roweis and Saul, 2000) to model such semantic smoothness, termed as LE and LLE for short respectively.

3.2 Modeling Semantic Smoothness by LE

Laplacian Eigenmaps (LE) is a manifold learning algorithm that preserves local invariance between each two data points (Belkin and Niyogi, 2001). We borrow the idea of LE and enforce semantic smoothness by assuming:

Smoothness Assumption 1 *If two entities e_i and e_j belong to the same semantic category, they will have embeddings $\mathbf{e}_i$ and $\mathbf{e}_j$ close to each other.*

To encode the semantic information, we construct an adjacency matrix $\mathbf{W}_1 \in \mathbb{R}^{n \times n}$ among the entities, with the ij-th entry defined as:

$$w_{ij}^{(1)} = \begin{cases} 1, & \text{if } c_{e_i} = c_{e_j}, \\ 0, & \text{otherwise}, \end{cases}$$

where c_{e_i}/c_{e_j} is the category label of entity e_i/e_j. Then, we use the following term to measure the smoothness of the embedding space:

$$\mathcal{R}_1 = \frac{1}{2} \sum_{i=1}^{n} \sum_{j=1}^{n} \|\mathbf{e}_i - \mathbf{e}_j\|_2^2 w_{ij}^{(1)},$$

where $\mathbf{e}_i$ and $\mathbf{e}_j$ are the embeddings of entities e_i and e_j respectively. By minimizing $\mathcal{R}_1$, we expect Smoothness Assumption 1: if two entities e_i and e_j belong to the same semantic category (i.e. $w_{ij}^{(1)} = 1$), the distance between $\mathbf{e}_i$ and $\mathbf{e}_j$ (i.e. $\|\mathbf{e}_i - \mathbf{e}_j\|_2^2$) should be small.

We further incorporate $\mathcal{R}_1$ as a regularization term into the margin-based ranking loss (i.e. Eq. (1)) adopted in previous KG embedding methods, and propose our first SSE model. The new model performs the embedding task by minimizing the following objective function:

$$\mathcal{L}_1 = \frac{1}{N} \sum_{t^+ \in \mathbb{O}} \sum_{t^- \in \mathbb{N}_{t^+}} \ell(t^+, t^-) + \frac{\lambda_1}{2} \sum_{i=1}^{n} \sum_{j=1}^{n} \|\mathbf{e}_i - \mathbf{e}_j\|_2^2 w_{ij}^{(1)},$$

where $\ell(t^+, t^-) = \left[\gamma + f(e_i, r_k, e_j) - f(e'_i, r_k, e'_j)\right]_+$ is the ranking loss on the positive-negative triple pair (t^+, t^-), and N is the total number of such triple pairs. The first term in $\mathcal{L}_1$ enforces the resultant embedding space compatible with all the observed triples, and the second term further requires that space to be semantically smooth. Hyperparameter λ_1 makes a trade-off between the two cases.

The minimization is carried out by stochastic gradient descent. Given a randomly sampled positive triple $t^+ = \langle e_i, r_k, e_j \rangle$ and the associated negative triple $t^- = \langle e'_i, r_k, e'_j \rangle$,[1] the stochastic gradient w.r.t. $\mathbf{e}_s$ ($s \in \{i, j, i', j'\}$) can be calculated as:

$$\nabla_{\mathbf{e}_s} \mathcal{L}_1 = \nabla_{\mathbf{e}_s} \ell(t^+, t^-) + 2\lambda_1 \mathbf{E}(\mathbf{D} - \mathbf{W}_1)\mathbf{1}_s,$$

[1]The negative triple is constructed by replacing one of the entities in the positive triple.

where $\mathbf{E} = [\mathbf{e}_1, \mathbf{e}_2, \cdots, \mathbf{e}_n] \in \mathbb{R}^{d \times n}$ is a matrix consisting of entity embeddings; $\mathbf{D} \in \mathbb{R}^{n \times n}$ is a diagonal matrix with the i-th entry on the diagonal being $d_{ii} = \sum_{j=1}^{n} w_{ij}^{(1)}$; and $\mathbf{1}_s \in \mathbb{R}^n$ is a column vector where the s-th entry is 1 and the others are 0. Other parameters are not included in $\mathcal{R}_1$, and their gradients remain the same as defined in previous work.

3.3 Modeling Semantic Smoothness by LLE

As opposed to LE which preserves local invariance within data pairs, Locally Linear Embedding (LLE) expects each data point to be roughly reconstructed by a linear combination of its nearest neighbors (Roweis and Saul, 2000). We borrow the idea of LLE and enforce semantic smoothness by assuming:

Smoothness Assumption 2 *Each entity e_i can be roughly reconstructed by a linear combination of its nearest neighbors in the embedding space, i.e., $\mathbf{e}_i \approx \sum_{e_j \in \mathcal{N}(e_i)} \alpha_j \mathbf{e}_j$. Here nearest neighbors refer to entities belonging to the same semantic category with e_i.*

To model this assumption, for each entity e_i, we randomly sample K entities uniformly from the category to which e_i belongs, denoted as the nearest neighbor set $\mathcal{N}(e_i)$. We construct a weight matrix $\mathbf{W}_2 \in \mathbb{R}^{n \times n}$ by defining:

$$w_{ij}^{(2)} = \begin{cases} 1, & \text{if } e_j \in \mathcal{N}(e_i), \\ 0, & \text{otherwise}, \end{cases}$$

and normalize the rows so that $\sum_{j=1}^{n} w_{ij}^{(2)} = 1$ for each row i. Note that $\mathbf{W}_2$ is no longer a symmetric matrix. The smoothness of the embedding space can be measured by the reconstruction error:

$$\mathcal{R}_2 = \sum_{i=1}^{n} \left\| \mathbf{e}_i - \sum_{e_j \in \mathcal{N}(e_i)} w_{ij}^{(2)} \mathbf{e}_j \right\|_2^2.$$

Minimizing $\mathcal{R}_2$ results in Smoothness Assumption 2: each entity can be linearly reconstructed from its nearest neighbors with low error.

By incorporating $\mathcal{R}_2$ as a regularization term into the margin-based ranking loss defined in Eq. (1), we obtain our second SSE model, which performs the embedding task by minimizing:

$$\mathcal{L}_2 = \frac{1}{N} \sum_{t^+ \in \mathbb{O}} \sum_{t^- \in \mathbb{N}_{t^+}} \ell(t^+, t^-) + \lambda_2 \sum_{i=1}^{n} \left\| \mathbf{e}_i - \sum_{e_j \in \mathcal{N}(e_i)} w_{ij}^{(2)} \mathbf{e}_j \right\|_2^2.$$

The resultant embedding space is also semantically smooth and compatible with the observed triples. Hyperparameter λ_2 makes a trade-off between the two cases.

Similar to the first model, stochastic gradient descent is used to solve the minimization problem. Given a positive triple $t^+ = \langle e_i, r_k, e_j \rangle$ and the associated negative triple $t^- = \langle e'_i, r_k, e'_j \rangle$, the gradient w.r.t. $\mathbf{e}_s$ ($s \in \{i, j, i', j'\}$) is calculated as:

$$\nabla_{\mathbf{e}_s} \mathcal{L}_2 = \nabla_{\mathbf{e}_s} \ell(t^+, t^-) + 2\lambda_2 \mathbf{E} (\mathbf{I} - \mathbf{W}_2)^T (\mathbf{I} - \mathbf{W}_2) \mathbf{1}_s,$$

where $\mathbf{I} \in \mathbb{R}^{n \times n}$ is the identity matrix. Other parameters are not included in $\mathcal{R}_2$, and their gradients remain the same as defined in previous work. To better capture the cohesion within each category, during each stochastic step we resample the nearest neighbors for each entity, uniformly from the category to which it belongs.

3.4 Advantages and Extensions

The advantages of our approach can be summarized as follows: 1) By incorporating geometrically based regularization terms, the SSE models are able to capture the semantic correlation between entities, which exists intrinsically but is overlooked in previous work. 2) By leveraging additional entity category information, the SSE models can deal with the data sparsity issue that commonly exists in most KGs. Both aspects lead to more accurate embeddings.

Entity category information has also been investigated in (Nickel et al., 2012; Chang et al., 2014; Wang et al., 2015), but in different manners. Nickel et al. (2012) take categories as pseudo entities and introduce a specific relation to link entities to categories. Chang et al. (2014) and Wang et al. (2015) use entity categories to specify relations' argument expectations, removing invalid triples during training and reasoning respectively. None of them considers the intrinsic geometric structure of the embedding space.

Actually, our approach is quite general. 1) The smoothness assumptions can be imposed to a wide variety of KG embedding models, not only the ones introduced in Section 2, but also those based on matrix/tensor factorization (Nickel et al., 2011; Chang et al., 2013). 2) Besides semantic categories, other information (e.g. entity similarities specified by users or derived from auxiliary data sources) can also be used to construct the manifold regularization terms. 3) Besides KG embedding, similar smoothness assumptions can also be applied in other embedding tasks (e.g. word embedding and sentence embedding).

L	S
CityCapitalOfCountry	AthleteLedSportTeam
CityLocatedInCountry	AthletePlaysForTeam
CityLocatedInGeopoliticallocation	AthletePlaysInLeague
CityLocatedInState	AthletePlaysSport
CountryLocatedInGeopoliticallocation	CoachesInLeague
StateHasCapital	CoachesTeam
StateLocatedInCountry	TeamPlaysInLeague
StateLocatedInGeopoliticallocation	TeamPlaysSport

Table 2: Relations in L and S .

4 Experiments

We empirically evaluate the proposed SSE models in two tasks: link prediction (Bordes et al., 2013) and triple classification (Socher et al., 2013).

4.1 Data Sets

We create three data sets with different sizes using NELL (Carlson et al., 2010): L , S , and N 186. L and S are two small-scale data sets, both containing 8 relations on the topics of "location" and "sport" respectively. The corresponding relations are listed in Table 2. N 186 is a larger data set containing the most frequent 186 relations. On all the data sets, entities appearing only once are removed. We extract the entity category information from a specific relation called `Generalization`, and keep non-overlapping categories.[2] Categories containing less than 5 entities on L and S as well as categories containing less than 50 entities on N 186 are further removed. Table 3 gives some statistics of the three data sets, where # Rel./# Ent./# Trip./# Cat. denotes the number of relations/entities/observed triples/categories respectively, and # c-Ent. denotes the number of entities that have category labels. Note that our SSE models do not require every entity to have a category label. From the statistics, we can see that all the three data sets suffer from the data sparsity issue, containing a relatively small number of observed triples compared to the number of entities.

On the two small-scale data sets L and S , triples are split into training/validation/test sets, with the ratio of 3:1:1. The first set is used for modeling training, the second for hyperparameter tuning, and the third for evaluation. All experiments are repeated 5 times by drawing new

[2] If two categories overlap, the smaller one is discarded.

	# Rel.	# Ent.	# Trip.	# Cat.	# c-Ent.
L	8	380	718	5	358
S	8	1,520	3,826	4	1,506
N 186	186	14,463	41,134	35	8,590

Table 3: Statistics of data sets.

training/validation/test splits, and results averaged over the 5 rounds are reported. On N 186 experiments are conducted only once, using a training/validation/test split with 31,134/5,000/5,000 triples respectively. We will release the data upon request.

4.2 Link Prediction

This task is to complete a triple $\langle e_i, r_k, e_j \rangle$ with e_i or e_j missing, i.e., predict e_i given (r_k, e_j) or predict e_j given (e_i, r_k).

Baseline methods. We take TransE, SME (lin), SME (bilin), and SE as our baselines. We then incorporate manifold regularization terms into these methods to obtain the SSE models. A model with the LE/LLE regularization term is denoted as TransE-LE/TransE-LLE for example. We further compare our SSE models with the setting proposed by Nickel et al. (2012), which also takes into account the entity category information, but in a more direct manner. That is, given an entity e with its category label c_e, we create a new triple $\langle e, \texttt{Generalization}, c_e \rangle$ and add it into the training set. Such a method is denoted as TransE-Cat for example.

Evaluation protocol. For evaluation, we adopt the same ranking procedure proposed by Bordes et al. (2013). For each test triple $\langle e_i, r_k, e_j \rangle$, the head entity e_i is replaced by every entity e'_i in the KG, and the energy is calculated for the corrupted triple $\langle e'_i, r_k, e_j \rangle$. Ranking the energies in ascending order, we get the rank of the correct entity e_i. Similarly, we can get another rank by corrupting the tail entity e_j. Aggregated over all test triples, we report three metrics: 1) the averaged rank, denoted as Mean (the smaller, the better); 2) the median of the ranks, denoted as Median (the smaller, the better); and 3) the proportion of ranks no larger than 10, denoted as Hits@10 (the higher, the better).

Implementation details. We implement the methods based on the code provided by Bordes et al. (2013)[3]. For all the methods, we create 100 mini-batches on each data set. On L and S , the dimension of the embedding space d is set in the range of $\{10, 20, 50, 100\}$, the margin γ is set in the range of $\{1, 2, 5, 10\}$, and the learning rate is fixed to 0.1. On N 186, the hyperparameters d and γ are fixed to 50 and 1 respectively, and the learning rate is fixed to 10. In LE and LLE, the regularization hyperparameters λ_1 and λ_2 are tuned in $\{10^{-4}, 10^{-5}, 10^{-6}, 10^{-7}, 10^{-8}\}$. And the number of nearest neighbors K in LLE is tuned in $\{5, 10, 15, 20\}$. The best model is selected by early stopping on the validation sets (by monitoring Mean), with a total of at most 1000 iterations over the training sets.

[3]https://github.com/glorotxa/SME

Results. Table 4 reports the results on the test sets of L , S , and N 186. From the results, we can see that: 1) SSE (regularized via either LE or LLE) outperforms all the baselines on all the data sets and with all the metrics. The improvements are usually quite significant. The metric Mean drops by about 10% to 65%, Median drops by about 5% to 75%, and Hits@10 rises by about 5% to 190%. This observation demonstrates the superiority and generality of our approach. 2) Even if encoded in a direct way (e.g. TransE-Cat), the entity category information can still help the baseline methods in the link prediction task. This observation indicates that leveraging additional information is indeed useful in dealing with the data sparsity issue and hence leads to better performance. 3) Compared to the strategy which incorporates the entity category information directly, formulating such information as manifold regularization terms results in better and more stable results. The *-Cat models sometimes perform even worse than the baselines (e.g. TransE-Cat on S data), while the SSE models consistently achieve better results. This observation further demonstrates the superiority of constraining the geometric structure of the embedding space.

We further visualize and compare the geometric structures of the embedding spaces learned by traditional embedding and semantically smooth embedding. We select the 10 largest semantic categories in N 186 (specified in Figure 1) and the 5,740 entities therein. We take the embeddings of these entities learned by TransE, TransE-Cat, TransE-LE, and TransE-LLE, with the optimal hyperparameter settings determined in the link prediction task. Then we create 2D plots using t-SNE (Van der Maaten and Hinton, 2008)[4]. The results are shown in Figure 1, where a different

[4]http://lvdmaaten.github.io/tsne/

	L			S			N 186		
	Mean	Median	Hits@10 (%)	Mean	Median	Hits@10 (%)	Mean	Median	Hits@10 (%)
TransE	30.94	10.70	50.56	362.66	62.90	43.86	924.37	94.00	16.95
TransE-Cat	28.48	**8.90**	52.43	320.30	86.40	37.46	657.53	80.50	19.14
TransE-LE	28.59	**8.90**	**53.06**	**183.10**	**23.20**	**45.83**	573.55	**79.00**	**20.26**
TransE-LLE	**28.03**	9.20	52.36	231.67	52.40	43.18	**535.32**	95.00	20.02
SME (lin)	63.01	24.10	40.90	266.50	87.10	32.34	427.86	26.00	35.97
SME (lin)-Cat	41.12	18.30	42.43	263.88	70.80	35.03	309.60	**25.00**	36.22
SME (lin)-LE	**36.19**	16.10	43.75	**237.38**	**50.80**	**38.35**	276.94	**25.00**	**37.14**
SME (lin)-LLE	38.22	**15.60**	**43.96**	241.70	63.70	36.54	**252.87**	**25.00**	**37.14**
SME (bilin)	47.66	20.90	37.85	314.49	124.00	33.83	848.39	28.00	35.71
SME (bilin)-Cat	40.75	16.20	42.71	298.09	**103.80**	35.86	560.76	**24.00**	**37.83**
SME (bilin)-LE	33.41	14.00	44.24	297.90	116.10	**38.95**	**448.31**	**24.00**	**37.80**
SME (bilin)-LLE	**32.84**	**13.60**	**46.25**	**286.63**	110.10	35.67	452.43	28.00	36.51
SE	108.15	69.90	14.72	426.70	242.60	24.72	904.84	44.00	27.81
SE-Cat	88.36	48.20	20.76	435.44	231.00	35.39	529.38	40.00	28.68
SE-LE	**36.43**	**16.00**	**42.92**	252.30	**90.50**	37.19	456.20	43.00	30.89
SE-LLE	38.47	17.50	42.08	**235.44**	105.40	**37.83**	**447.05**	**37.00**	**31.55**

Table 4: Link prediction results on the test sets of L, S, and N 186.

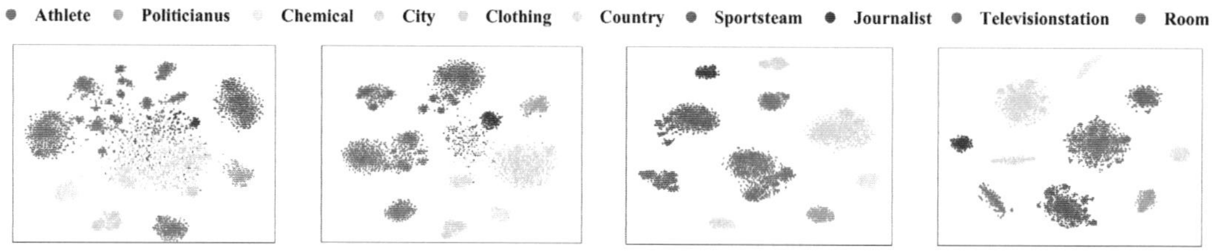

(a) TransE. (b) TransE-Cat. (c) TransE-LE. (d) TransE-LLE.

Figure 1: Embeddings of entities belonging to the 10 largest categories in N 186 (best viewed in color).

color is used for each category. It is easy to see that imposing the semantic smoothness assumptions helps in capturing the semantic correlation between entities in the embedding space. Entities within the same category lie closer to each other, while entities belonging to different categories are easily distinguished (see Figure 1(c) and Figure 1(d)). Incorporating the entity category information directly could also helps. But it fails on some "hard" entities (i.e., those belonging to different categories but mixed together in the center of Figure 1(b)). We have conducted the same experiments with the other methods and observed similar phenomena.

4.3 Triple Classification

This task is to verify whether a given triple $\langle e_i, r_k, e_j \rangle$ is correct or not. We test our SSE models in this task, with the same comparison settings as used in the link prediction task.

Evaluation protocol. We follow the same evaluation protocol used in (Socher et al., 2013; Wang et al., 2014b). To create labeled data for classification, for each triple in the test and validation sets, we construct a negative triple for it by randomly corrupting the entities. To corrupt a position (head or tail), only entities that have appeared in that position are allowed. During triple classification, a triple is predicted as positive if the energy is below a relation-specific threshold δ_r; otherwise as negative. We report two metrics on the test sets: micro-averaged accuracy and macro-averaged accuracy, denoted as Micro-ACC and Macro-ACC respectively. The former is a per-triple average, while the latter is a per-relation average.

Implementation details. We use the same hyperparameter settings as in the link prediction task. The relation-specific threshold δ_r is determined by maximizing Micro-ACC on the validation sets. Again, training is limited to at most 1000 iterations, and the best model is selected by early stopping on the validation sets (by monitoring Micro-ACC).

Results. Table 5 reports the results on the test sets of L, S, and N 186. The results indicate that: 1) SSE (regularized via either LE or LLE) performs consistently better than the base-

	L		S		N 186	
	Micro-ACC	Macro-ACC	Micro-ACC	Macro-ACC	Micro-ACC	Macro-ACC
TransE	86.11	81.66	72.52	73.78	84.21	77.86
TransE-Cat	82.50	77.81	75.09	74.23	87.34	81.27
TransE-LE	86.39	81.50	79.88	77.34	**90.32**	**84.61**
TransE-LLE	**87.01**	**83.03**	**80.29**	**77.71**	90.08	84.50
SME (lin)	75.90	71.82	72.61	71.24	88.54	84.17
SME (lin)-Cat	83.33	**80.90**	73.52	72.28	91.00	86.20
SME (lin)-LE	**84.65**	79.33	79.25	74.95	92.44	88.07
SME (lin)-LLE	84.58	79.60	**79.45**	**75.61**	**92.99**	**88.68**
SME (bilin)	73.06	67.26	71.33	67.78	88.78	84.79
SME (bilin)-Cat	79.38	74.35	75.12	72.41	91.67	86.48
SME (bilin)-LE	**83.75**	79.66	79.23	**76.18**	93.37	89.29
SME (bilin)-LLE	83.54	**80.36**	**79.33**	75.35	**93.64**	**89.39**
SE	65.14	60.01	68.61	63.71	90.18	83.93
SE-Cat	68.61	62.82	67.62	62.17	92.87	87.72
SE-LE	81.67	**77.52**	**81.46**	74.72	93.94	**88.62**
SE-LLE	**82.01**	77.45	80.25	**76.07**	**93.95**	88.54

Table 5: Triple classification results (%) on the test sets of L , S , and N 186.

line methods on all the data sets in both metrics. The improvements are usually quite substantial. The metric Micro-ACC rises by about 1% to 25%, and Macro-ACC by about 2% to 30%. 2) Incorporating the entity category information directly can also improve the baselines in the triple classification task, again demonstrating the effectiveness of leveraging additional information to deal with the data sparsity issue. 3) It is a better choice to incorporate the entity category information as manifold regularization terms as opposed to encoding it directly. The *-Cat models sometimes perform even worse than the baselines (e.g. TransE-Cat on L data and SE-Cat on S data), while the SSE models consistently achieve better results. The observations are similar to those observed during the link prediction task, and further demonstrate the superiority and generality of our approach.

5 Related Work

This section reviews two lines of related work: KG embedding and manifold learning.

KG embedding aims to embed a KG composed of entities and relations into a low-dimensional vector space, and model the plausibility of each fact in that space. Yang et al. (2014) categorized the literature into three major groups: 1) methods based on neural networks, 2) methods based on matrix/tensor factorization, and 3) methods based on Bayesian clustering. The first group performs the embedding task using neural network architectures (Bordes et al., 2013; Bordes et al., 2014; Socher et al., 2013). Several state-of-the-art neural network-based embedding models have been introduced in Section 2. For other work please refer to (Jenatton et al., 2012; Wang et al., 2014b; Lin et al., 2015). In the second group, KGs are represented as tensors, and embedding is performed via tensor factorization or collective matrix factorization techniques (Singh and Gordon, 2008; Nickel et al., 2011; Chang et al., 2014). The third group embeds factorized representations of entities and relations into a nonparametric Bayesian clustering framework, so as to obtain more interpretable embeddings (Kemp et al., 2006; Sutskever et al., 2009). Our work falls into the first group, but differs in that it further imposes constraints on the geometric structure of the embedding space, which exists intrinsically but is overlooked in previous work. Although this paper focuses on incorporating geometrically based regularization terms into neural network architectures, it can be easily extended to matrix/tensor factorization techniques.

Manifold learning is a geometrically motivated framework for machine learning, enforcing the learning model to be smooth w.r.t. the geometric structure of data (Belkin et al., 2006). Within this framework, various manifold learning algorithms have been proposed, such as ISOMAP (Tenenbaum et al., 2000), Laplacian Eigenmaps (Belkin and Niyogi, 2001), and Locally Linear Embedding (Roweis and Saul, 2000). All these algorithms are based on the so-called local invariance assumption, i.e., nearby points are likely to have similar embeddings or labels. Manifold learning has been widely applied in many different areas, from dimensionality reduction (Belkin and Niyogi, 2001; Cai et al., 2008) and semi-supervised learning (Zhou et al., 2004; Zhu and Niyogi, 2005) to recommender systems (Ma et al., 2011) and community question answering (Wang et al., 2014a). This paper employs manifold learning algorithms to model the semantic smoothness assumptions in KG embedding.

6 Conclusion and Future Work

In this paper, we have proposed a novel approach to KG embedding, referred to as *Semantically Smooth Embedding* (SSE). The key idea of SSE is to impose constraints on the geometric structure of the embedding space and enforce it to be semantically smooth. The semantic smoothness assumptions are constructed by using entities' category information, and then formulated as geometrically based regularization terms to constrain the embedding task. The embeddings learned in this way are capable of capturing the semantic correlation between entities. By leveraging additional information besides observed triples, SSE can also deal with the data sparsity issue that commonly exists in most KGs. We empirically evaluate SSE in two benchmark tasks of link prediction and triple classification. Experimental results show that by incorporating the semantic smoothness assumptions, SSE significantly and consistently outperforms state-of-the-art embedding methods, demonstrating the superiority of our approach. In addition, our approach is quite general. The smoothness assumptions can actually be imposed to a wide variety of embedding models, and it can also be constructed using other information besides entities' semantic categories.

As future work, we would like to: 1) Construct the manifold regularization terms using other data sources. The only information required to construct the manifold regularization terms is the similarity between entities (used to define the adjacency matrix in LE and to select nearest neighbors for each entity in LLE). We would try entity similarities derived in different ways, e.g., specified by users or calculated from entities' textual descriptions. 2) Enhance the efficiency and scalability of SSE. Processing the manifold regularization terms can be time- and space-consuming (especially the one induced by the LE algorithm). We would investigate how to address this problem, e.g., via the efficient iterative algorithms introduced in (Saul and Roweis, 2003) or via parallel/distributed computing. 3) Impose the semantic smoothness assumptions on other KG embedding methods (e.g. those based on matrix/tensor factorization or Bayesian clustering), and even on other embedding tasks (e.g. word embedding or sentence embedding).

Acknowledgments

We would like to thank the anonymous reviewers for their valuable comments and suggestions. This work is supported by the National Natural Science Foundation of China (grant No. 61402465), the Strategic Priority Research Program of the Chinese Academy of Sciences (grant No. XDA06030200), and the National Key Technology R&D Program (grant No. 2012BAH46B03).

References

Eneko Agirre, Oier Lopez de Lacalle, and Aitor Soroa. 2014. Random walks for knowledge-based word sense disambiguation. *Computational Linguistics*, 40(1):57–84.

Mikhail Belkin and Partha Niyogi. 2001. Laplacian eigenmaps and spectral techniques for embedding and clustering. In *Advances in Neural Information Processing Systems*, pages 585–591.

Mikhail Belkin, Partha Niyogi, and Vikas Sindhwani. 2006. Manifold regularization: A geometric framework for learning from labeled and unlabeled examples. *Journal of Machine Learning Research*, 7:2399–2434.

Kurt Bollacker, Colin Evans, Praveen Paritosh, Tim Sturge, and Jamie Taylor. 2008. Freebase: A collaboratively created graph database for structuring human knowledge. In *Proceedings of the 2008 ACM SIGMOD International Conference on Management of Data*, pages 1247–1250.

Antoine Bordes, Jason Weston, Ronan Collobert, and Yoshua Bengio. 2011. Learning structured embeddings of knowledge bases. In *Proceedings of the 25th AAAI Conference on Artificial Intelligence*, pages 301–306.

Antoine Bordes, Nicolas Usunier, Alberto Garcia-Durán, Jason Weston, and Oksana Yakhnenko. 2013. Translating embeddings for modeling multi-relational data. In *Advances in Neural Information Processing Systems*, pages 2787–2795.

Antoine Bordes, Xavier Glorot, Jason Weston, and Yoshua Bengio. 2014. A semantic matching energy function for learning with multi-relational data. *Machine Learning*, 94(2):233–259.

Deng Cai, Xiaofei He, Xiaoyun Wu, and Jiawei Han. 2008. Non-negative matrix factorization on manifold. In *Proceedings of the 8th IEEE International Conference on Data Mining*, pages 63–72.

Andrew Carlson, Justin Betteridge, Bryan Kisiel, Burr Settles, Estevam R. Hruschka Jr, and Tom M. Mitchell. 2010. Toward an architecture for never-ending language learning. In *Proceedings of the 24th AAAI Conference on Artificial Intelligence*, pages 1306–1313.

Kai-Wei Chang, Wen-tau Yih, and Christopher Meek. 2013. Multi-relational latent semantic analysis. In *Proceedings of the 2013 Conference on Empirical Methods in Natural Language Processing*, pages 1602–1612.

Kai-Wei Chang, Wen-tau Yih, Bishan Yang, and Christopher Meek. 2014. Typed tensor decomposition of knowledge bases for relation extraction. In *Proceedings of the 2014 Conference on Empirical Methods in Natural Language Processing*, pages 1568–1579.

Raphael Hoffmann, Congle Zhang, Xiao Ling, Luke Zettlemoyer, and Daniel S. Weld. 2011. Knowledge-based weak supervision for information extraction of overlapping relations. In *Proceedings of the 49th Annual Meeting of the Association for Computational Linguistics: Human Language Technologies*, pages 541–550.

Rodolphe Jenatton, Nicolas L. Roux, Antoine Bordes, and Guillaume R. Obozinski. 2012. A latent factor model for highly multi-relational data. In *Advances in Neural Information Processing Systems*, pages 3167–3175.

Charles Kemp, Joshua B. Tenenbaum, Thomas L. Griffiths, Takeshi Yamada, and Naonori Ueda. 2006. Learning systems of concepts with an infinite relational model. In *Proceedings of the 21st AAAI Conference on Artificial Intelligence*, pages 381–388.

Jens Lehmann, Robert Isele, Max Jakob, Anja Jentzsch, Dimitris Kontokostas, Pablo N. Mendes, Sebastian Hellmann, Mohamed Morsey, Patrick van Kleef, Sören Auer, et al. 2014. Dbpedia: A large-scale, multilingual knowledge base extracted from wikipedia. *Semantic Web Journal*.

Yankai Lin, Zhiyuan Liu, Maosong Sun, Yang Liu, and Xuan Zhu. 2015. Learning entity and relation embeddings for knowledge graph completion. In *Proceedings of the 29th AAAI Conference on Artificial Intelligence*, pages 2181–2187.

Hao Ma, Dengyong Zhou, Chao Liu, Michael R. Lyu, and Irwin King. 2011. Recommender systems with social regularization. In *Proceedings of the 4th ACM International Conference on Web Search and Data Mining*, pages 287–296.

Bernardo Magnini, Matteo Negri, Roberto Prevete, and Hristo Tanev. 2002. A wordnet-based approach to named entities recognition. In *Proceedings of the 2002 Workshop on Building and Using Semantic Networks*, pages 1–7.

George A. Miller. 1995. Wordnet: A lexical database for english. *Communications of the ACM*, 38(11):39–41.

Maximilian Nickel, Volker Tresp, and Hans-Peter Kriegel. 2011. A three-way model for collective learning on multi-relational data. In *Proceedings of the 28th International Conference on Machine Learning*, pages 809–816.

Maximilian Nickel, Volker Tresp, and Hans-Peter Kriegel. 2012. Factorizing yago: Scalable machine learning for linked data. In *Proceedings of the 21st International Conference on World Wide Web*, pages 271–280.

Sebastian Riedel, Limin Yao, Andrew McCallum, and Benjamin M. Marlin. 2013. Relation extraction with matrix factorization and universal schemas. In *Proceedings of the 2013 Conference on North American Chapter of the Association for Computational Linguistics: Human Language Technologies*, pages 74–84.

Sam T. Roweis and Lawrence K. Saul. 2000. Nonlinear dimensionality reduction by locally linear embedding. *Science*, 290(5500):2323–2326.

Lawrence K. Saul and Sam T. Roweis. 2003. Think globally, fit locally: Unsupervised learning of low dimensional manifolds. *Journal of Machine Learning Research*, 4:119–155.

Geoffrey J. Singh and Ajit P. Gordon. 2008. Relational learning via collective matrix factorization. In *Proceedings of the 14th ACM SIGKDD International Conference on Knowledge Discovery and Data Mining*, pages 650–658.

Richard Socher, Danqi Chen, Christopher D. Manning, and Andrew Y. Ng. 2013. Reasoning with neural tensor networks for knowledge base completion. In *Advances in Neural Information Processing Systems*, pages 926–934.

Ilya Sutskever, Joshua B. Tenenbaum, and Ruslan R. Salakhutdinov. 2009. Modelling relational data using bayesian clustered tensor factorization. In *Advances in Neural Information Processing Systems*, pages 1821–1828.

Joshua B. Tenenbaum, Vin De Silva, and John C. Langford. 2000. A global geometric framework for nonlinear dimensionality reduction. *Science*, 290(5500):2319–2323.

Laurens Van der Maaten and Geoffrey Hinton. 2008. Visualizing data using t-sne. *Journal of Machine Learning Research*, 9(85):2579–2605.

Quan Wang, Jing Liu, Bin Wang, and Li Guo. 2014a. A regularized competition model for question difficulty estimation in community question answering services. In *Proceedings of the 2014 Conference on Empirical Methods in Natural Language Processing*, pages 1115–1126.

Zhen Wang, Jianwen Zhang, Jianlin Feng, and Zheng Chen. 2014b. Knowledge graph embedding by translating on hyperplanes. In *Proceedings of the 28th AAAI Conference on Artificial Intelligence*, pages 1112–1119.

Quan Wang, Bin Wang, and Li Guo. 2015. Knowledge base completion using embeddings and rules. In *Proceedings of the 24th International Joint Conference on Artificial Intelligence*.

Jason Weston, Antoine Bordes, Oksana Yakhnenko, and Nicolas Usunier. 2013. Connecting language and knowledge bases with embedding models for relation extraction. In *Proceedings of the 2013 Conference on Empirical Methods in Natural Language Processing*, pages 1366–1371.

Bishan Yang, Wen-tau Yih, Xiaodong He, Jianfeng Gao, and Li Deng. 2014. Learning multi-relational semantics using neural-embedding models. *arXiv preprint arXiv:1411.4072*.

Dengyong Zhou, Olivier Bousquet, Thomas Navin Lal, Jason Weston, and Bernhard Schölkopf. 2004. Learning with local and global consistency. In *Advances in Neural Information Processing Systems*, pages 321–328.

Xiaojin Zhu and Partha Niyogi. 2005. Harmonic mixtures: combining mixture models and graph-based methods for inductive and scalable semi-supervised learning. In *Proceedings of the 22nd International Conference on Machine Learning*, pages 1052–1059.

SENSEMBED: Learning Sense Embeddings for Word and Relational Similarity

Ignacio Iacobacci, Mohammad Taher Pilehvar and **Roberto Navigli**
Department of Computer Science
Sapienza University of Rome
{iacobacci,pilehvar,navigli}@di.uniroma1.it

Abstract

Word embeddings have recently gained considerable popularity for modeling words in different Natural Language Processing (NLP) tasks including semantic similarity measurement. However, notwithstanding their success, word embeddings are by their very nature unable to capture polysemy, as different meanings of a word are conflated into a single representation. In addition, their learning process usually relies on massive corpora only, preventing them from taking advantage of structured knowledge. We address both issues by proposing a multi-faceted approach that transforms word embeddings to the sense level and leverages knowledge from a large semantic network for effective semantic similarity measurement. We evaluate our approach on word similarity and relational similarity frameworks, reporting state-of-the-art performance on multiple datasets.

1 Introduction

The much celebrated word embeddings represent a new branch of corpus-based distributional semantic model which leverages neural networks to model the context in which a word is expected to appear. Thanks to their high coverage and their ability to capture both syntactic and semantic information, word embeddings have been successfully applied to a variety of NLP tasks, such as Word Sense Disambiguation (Chen et al., 2014), Machine Translation (Mikolov et al., 2013b), Relational Similarity (Mikolov et al., 2013c), Semantic Relatedness (Baroni et al., 2014) and Knowledge Representation (Bordes et al., 2013).

However, word embeddings inherit two important limitations from their antecedent corpus-based distributional models: (1) they are unable to model distinct meanings of a word as they conflate the contextual evidence of different meanings of a word into a single vector; and (2) they base their representations solely on the distributional statistics obtained from corpora, ignoring the wealth of information provided by existing semantic resources.

Several research works have tried to address these problems. For instance, basing their work on the original sense discrimination approach of Reisinger and Mooney (2010), Huang et al. (2012) applied K-means clustering to decompose word embeddings into multiple prototypes, each denoting a distinct meaning of the target word. However, the sense representations obtained are not linked to any sense inventory, a mapping that consequently has to be carried out either manually, or with the help of sense-annotated data. Another line of research investigates the possibility of taking advantage of existing semantic resources in word embeddings. A good example is the Relation Constrained Model (Yu and Dredze, 2014). When computing word embeddings, this model replaces the original co-occurrence clues from text corpora with the relationship information derived from the Paraphrase Database[1] (Ganitkevitch et al., 2013, PPDB), an automatically extracted dataset of paraphrase pairs.

However, none of these techniques have simultaneously solved both above-mentioned issues, i.e., inability to model polysemy and reliance on text corpora as the only source of knowledge. We propose a novel approach, called SENSEMBED, which addresses both drawbacks by exploiting semantic knowledge for modeling arbitrary word senses in a large sense inventory. We evaluate our representation on multiple datasets in two standard tasks: word-level semantic similarity and relational similarity. Experimental results show that moving from words to senses, while making use

[1] http://paraphrase.org/#/download

Proceedings of the 53rd Annual Meeting of the Association for Computational Linguistics and the 7th International Joint Conference on Natural Language Processing, pages 95–105,
Beijing, China, July 26-31, 2015.

of lexical-semantic knowledge bases, makes embeddings significantly more powerful, resulting in consistent performance improvement across tasks.

Our contributions are twofold: (1) we propose a knowledge-based approach for obtaining continuous representations for individual word senses; and (2) by leveraging these representations and lexical-semantic knowledge, we put forward a semantic similarity measure with state-of-the-art performance on multiple datasets.

2 Sense Embeddings

Word embeddings are vector space models (VSM) that represent words as real-valued vectors in a low-dimensional (relative to the size of the vocabulary) semantic space, usually referred to as the continuous space language model. The conventional way to obtain such representations is to compute a term-document occurrence matrix on large corpora and then reduce the dimensionality of the matrix using techniques such as singular value decomposition (Deerwester et al., 1990; Bullinaria and Levy, 2012, SVD). Recent predictive techniques (Bengio et al., 2003; Collobert and Weston, 2008; Mnih and Hinton, 2007; Turian et al., 2010; Mikolov et al., 2013a) replace the conventional two-phase approach with a single supervised process, usually based on neural networks.

In contrast to word embeddings, which obtain a single model for potentially ambiguous words, sense embeddings are continuous representations of individual word senses. In order to be able to apply word embeddings techniques to obtain representations for individual word senses, large sense-annotated corpora have to be available. However, manual sense annotation is a difficult and time-consuming process, i.e., the so-called knowledge acquisition bottleneck. In fact, the largest existing manually sense annotated dataset is the SemCor corpus (Miller et al., 1993), whose creation dates back to more than two decades ago. In order to alleviate this issue, we leveraged a state-of-the-art Word Sense Disambiguation (WSD) algorithm to automatically generate large amounts of sense-annotated corpora.

In the rest of Section 2, first, in Section 2.1, we describe the sense inventory used for SENSEMBED. Section 2.2 introduces the corpus and the disambiguation procedure used to sense annotate this corpus. Finally in Section 2.3 we discuss how we leverage the automatically sense-tagged dataset for the training of sense embeddings.

2.1 Underlying sense inventory

We selected BabelNet[2] (Navigli and Ponzetto, 2012) as our underlying sense inventory. The resource is a merger of WordNet with multiple other lexical resources, the most prominent of which is Wikipedia. As a result, the manually-curated information in WordNet is augmented with the complementary knowledge from collaboratively-constructed resources, providing a high coverage of domain-specific terms and named entities and a rich set of relations. The usage of BabelNet as our underlying sense inventory provides us with the advantage of having our sense embeddings readily applicable to multiple sense inventories.

2.2 Generating a sense-annotated corpus

As our corpus we used the September-2014 dump of the English Wikipedia.[3] This corpus comprises texts from various domains and topics and provides a suitable word coverage. The unprocessed text of the corpus includes approximately three billion tokens and more than three million unique words. We only consider tokens with at least five occurrences.

As our WSD system, we opted for Babelfy[4] (Moro et al., 2014), a state-of-the-art WSD and Entity Linking algorithm based on BabelNet's semantic network. Babelfy first models each concept in the network through its corresponding "semantic signature" by leveraging a graph random walk algorithm. Given an input text, the algorithm uses the generated semantic signatures to construct a subgraph of the semantic network representing the input text. Babelfy then searches this subgraph for the intended sense of each content word using an iterative process and a dense subgraph heuristic. Thanks to its use of BabelNet, Babelfy inherently features multilinguality; hence, our representation approach is equally applicable to languages other than English. In order to guarantee high accuracy and to avoid bias towards more frequent senses, we do not consider those judgements made by Babelfy while backing off to the most frequent sense, a case that happens when a certain confidence threshold is not met by the algorithm. The disambiguated items with high confidence correspond to more than 50% of all the

[2] http://www.babelnet.org/
[3] http://dumps.wikimedia.org/enwiki/
[4] http://www.babelfy.org/

bank$^n_1$ (geographical)	***bank***$^n_2$ (financial)	***number***$^n_4$ (phone)	***number***$^n_3$ (acting)	***hood***$^n_1$ (gang)	***hood***$^n_{12}$ (convertible car)
upstream$^r_1$	commercial_bank$^n_1$	calls$^n_1$	appearing$^v_6$	tortures$^n_5$	taillights$^n_1$
downstream$^r_1$	financial_institution$^n_1$	dialled$^v_1$	minor_roles$^n_1$	vengeance$^n_1$	grille$^n_2$
runs$^v_6$	national_bank$^n_1$	operator$^n_{20}$	stage_production$^n_1$	badguy$^n_1$	bumper$^n_2$
confluence$^n_1$	trust_company$^n_1$	telephone_network$^n_1$	supporting_roles$^n_1$	brutal$^a_1$	fascia$^n_2$
river$^n_1$	savings_bank$^n_1$	telephony$^n_1$	leading_roles$^n_1$	execution$^n_1$	rear_window$^n_1$
stream$^n_1$	banking$^n_1$	subscriber$^n_2$	stage_shows$^n_1$	murders$^n_1$	headlights$^n_1$

Table 1: Closest senses to two senses of three ambiguous nouns: *bank*, *number*, and *hood*

content words. As a result of the disambiguation step, we obtain sense-annotated data comprising around one billion tagged words with at least five occurrences and 2.5 million unique word senses.

2.3 Learning sense embeddings

The disambiguated text is processed with the Word2vec (Mikolov et al., 2013a) toolkit[5]. We applied Word2vec to produce continuous representations of word senses based on the distributional information obtained from the annotated corpus. For each target word sense, a representation is computed by maximizing the log likelihood of the word sense with respect to its context. We opted for the Continuous Bag of Words (CBOW) architecture, the objective of which is to predict a single word (word sense in our case) given its context. The context is defined by a window, typically with the size of five words on each side with the paragraph ending barrier. We used hierarchical softmax as our training algorithm. The dimensionality of the vectors were set to 400 and the subsampling of frequent words to 10^{-3}.

As a result of the learning process, we obtain vector-based semantic representations for each of the word senses in the automatically-annotated corpus. We show in Table 1 some of the closest senses to six sample word senses: the geographical and financial senses of *river*, the performance and phone number senses of *number*, and the gang and car senses of *hood*.[6] As can be seen, sense embeddings can capture effectively the clear distinctions between different senses of a word. Additionally, the closest senses are not necessarily constrained to the same part of speech. For instance, the river sense of *bank* has the adverbs *upstream* and *downstream* and the "move along, of liquid" sense of the verb *run* among its closest senses.

[5] `http://code.google.com/p/word2vec/`

[6] We follow Navigli (2009) and show the nth sense of the *word* with part of speech x as $word^x_n$.

	Synset Description	Synonymous senses
hood$^n_1$	rough or violent youth	hoodlum$^n_1$, goon$^n_2$, thug$^n_1$
hood$^n_4$	photography equipment	lens_hood$^n_1$
hood$^n_9$	automotive body parts	bonnet$^n_2$, cowl$^n_1$, cowling$^n_1$
hood$^n_{12}$	car with retractable top	convertible$^n_1$

Table 2: Sample initial senses of the noun *hood* (leftmost column) and their synonym expansion (rightmost column).

3 Similarity Measurement

This Section describes how we leverage the generated sense embeddings for the computation of word similarity and relational similarity. We start the Section by explaining how we associate a word with its set of corresponding senses and how we compare pairs of senses in Sections 3.1 and 3.2, respectively. We then illustrate our approach for measuring word similarity, together with its knowledge-based enhancement, in Section 3.3, and relational similarity in Section 3.4. Hereafter, we refer to our similarity measurement approach as SENSEMBED.

3.1 Associating senses with words

In order to be able to utilize our sense embeddings for a word-level task such as word similarity measurement, we need to associate each word with its set of relevant senses, each modeled by its corresponding vector. Let $\mathcal{S}_w$ be the set of senses associated with the word w. Our objective is to cover as many senses as can be associated with the word w. To this end we first initialize the set $\mathcal{S}_w$ by the word senses of the word w and all its synonymous word senses, as defined in the BabelNet sense inventory. We show in Table 2 some of the senses of the noun *hood* and the synonym expansion for these senses. We further expand the set $\mathcal{S}_w$ by repeating the same process for the lemma of word w (if not already in lemma form).

3.2 Vector comparison

For comparing vectors, we use the *Tanimoto* distance. The measure is a generalization of Jaccard similarity for real-valued vectors in [-1, 1]:

$$\mathcal{T}(\vec{w_1}, \vec{w_2}) = \frac{\vec{w_1} \cdot \vec{w_2}}{\|\vec{w_1}\|^2 + \|\vec{w_2}\|^2 - \vec{w_1} \cdot \vec{w_2}} \quad (1)$$

where $\vec{w_1} \cdot \vec{w_2}$ is the dot product of the vectors $\vec{w_1}$ and $\vec{w_2}$ and $\|\vec{w_1}\|$ is the Euclidean norm of $\vec{w_1}$. Rink and Harabagiu (2013) reported consistent improvements when using vector space metrics, in particular the Tanimoto distance, on the SemEval-2012 task on relational similarity (Jurgens et al., 2012) in comparison to several other measures that are designed for probability distributions, such as Jensen-Shannon divergence and Hellinger distance.

3.3 Word similarity

We show in Algorithm 1 our procedure for measuring the semantic similarity of a pair of input words w_1 and w_2. The algorithm also takes as its inputs the similarity strategy and the *weighted* similarity parameter α (Section 3.3.1) along with a *graph vicinity factor* flag (Section 3.3.2).

Algorithm 1 Word Similarity

Input: Two words w_1 and w_2
Str, the similarity strategy
Vic, the *graph vicinity factor* flag
α parameter for the *weighted* strategy
Output: The similarity between w_1 and w_2

$\mathcal{S}_{w_1} \leftarrow$ *getSenses*(w_1), $\mathcal{S}_{w_2} \leftarrow$ *getSenses*(w_2)
if *Str* **is** *closest* **then**
  sim $\leftarrow$ -1
else
  sim $\leftarrow$ 0
end if
for each $s_1 \in \mathcal{S}_{w_1}$ **and** $s_2 \in \mathcal{S}_{w_2}$ **do**
  if *Vic* **is** *true* **then**
    tmp $\leftarrow \mathcal{T}^*(\vec{s_1},\vec{s_2})$
  else
    tmp $\leftarrow \mathcal{T}(\vec{s_1},\vec{s_2})$
  end if
  if *Str* **is** *closest* **then**
    sim $\leftarrow$ max (*sim*, *tmp*)
  else
    sim $\leftarrow$ *sim* + *tmp*$^{\alpha} \times d(s_1) \times d(s_2)$
  end if
end for

3.3.1 Similarity measurement strategy

We take two strategies for calculating the similarity of the given words w_1 and w_2. Let $\mathcal{S}_{w_1}$ and $\mathcal{S}_{w_2}$ be the sets of senses associated with the two respective input words w_1 and w_2, and let $\vec{s_i}$ be the sense embedding vector of the sense s_i. In the first strategy, which we refer to as *closest*, we follow the conventional approach (Budanitsky and Hirst, 2006) and measure the similarity of the two words as the similarity of their closest senses, i.e.:

$$Sim_{closest}(w_1, w_2) = \max_{\substack{s_1 \in \mathcal{S}_{w_1} \\ s_2 \in \mathcal{S}_{w_2}}} \mathcal{T}(\vec{s_1}, \vec{s_2}) \quad (2)$$

However, taking the similarity of the closest senses of two words as their overall similarity ignores the fact that the other senses can also contribute to the process of similarity judgement. In fact, psychological studies suggest that humans, while judging semantic similarity of a pair of words, consider different meanings of the two words and not only the closest ones (Tversky, 1977; Markman and Gentner, 1993). For instance, the WordSim-353 dataset (Finkelstein et al., 2002) contains the word pair *brother-monk*. Despite having the religious devotee sense in common, the two words are assigned the similarity judgement of 6.27, which is slightly above the middle point in the similarity scale [0,10] of the dataset. This clearly indicates that other non-synonymous, yet still related, senses of the two words have also played a role in the similarity judgement. Additionally, the relatively low score reflects the fact that the religious devotee sense is not a dominant meaning of the word *brother*.

We therefore put forward another similarity measurement strategy, called *weighted*, in which different senses of the two words contribute to their similarity computation, but the contributions are scaled according to their relative importance. To this end, we first leverage sense occurrence frequencies in order to estimate the dominance of each specific word sense. For each word w, we first compute the dominance of its sense $s \in \mathcal{S}_w$ by dividing the frequency of s by the overall frequency of all senses associated with w, i.e., $\mathcal{S}_w$:

$$d(s) = \frac{freq(s)}{\sum_{s' \in \mathcal{S}_w} freq(s')} \quad (3)$$

We further recognize that the importance of a specific sense of a word can also be triggered by the word it is being compared with. We model this by biasing the similarity computation towards closer senses, by increasing the contribution of closer senses through a power function with parameter α. The similarity of a pair of words w_1 and w_2 according to the *weighted* strategy is computed as:

$$Sim_{weighted}(w_1, w_2) = \sum_{s_1 \in \mathcal{S}_{w_1}} \sum_{s_2 \in \mathcal{S}_{w_2}} d(s_1)\, d(s_2)\, \mathcal{T}(\vec{s_1}, \vec{s_2})^{\alpha} \quad (4)$$

where the α parameter is a real-valued constant greater than one. We show in Section 4.1.3 how we tune the value of this parameter.

3.3.2 Enhancing similarity accuracy

Our similarity measurement approach takes advantage of lexical knowledge at two different levels. First, as we described in Sections 2.2 and 2.3, we use a knowledge-based disambiguation approach, i.e., Babelfy, which exploits BabelNet's semantic network. Second, we put forward a methodology that leverages the relations in BabelNet's graph for enhancing the accuracy of similarity judgements, to be discussed next.

As a distributional vector representation technique, our sense embeddings can potentially suffer from inaccurate modeling of less frequent word senses. In contrast, our underlying sense inventory provides a full coverage of all its concepts, with relations that are taken from WordNet and Wikipedia. In order to make use of the complementary information provided by our lexical knowledge base and to obtain more accurate similarity judgements, we introduce a *graph vicinity factor*, that combines the structural knowledge from BabelNet's semantic network and the distributional representation of sense embeddings. To this end, for a given sense pair, we scale the similarity judgement obtained by comparing their corresponding sense embeddings, based on their placement in the network. Let E be the set of all sense-to-sense relations provided by BabelNet's semantic network, i.e., $E = \{(s_i, s_j) : s_i - s_j\}$. Then, the similarity of a pair of words with the *graph vicinity factor* in formulas 2 and 4 is computed by replacing $\mathcal{T}$ with $\mathcal{T}^*$, defined as:

$$\mathcal{T}^*(\vec{s_1}, \vec{s_2}) = \begin{cases} \mathcal{T}(\vec{s_1}, \vec{s_2}) \times \beta, & \text{if } (s_1, s_2) \in E \\ \mathcal{T}(\vec{s_1}, \vec{s_2}) \times \beta^{-1}, & \text{otherwise} \end{cases} \quad (5)$$

We show in Section 4.1.3 how we tune the parameter β. This procedure is particularly helpful for the case of less frequent word senses that do not have enough contextual information to allow an effective representation. For instance, the SimLex-999 dataset (Hill et al., 2014), which we use as our tuning dataset (see Section 4.1.3), contains the highly-related pair *orthodontist-dentist*. We observed that the intended sense of the noun *orthodontist* occurs only 70 times in our annotated corpus. As a result, the obtained representation was not accurate, resulting in a low similarity score for the pair. The two respective senses are, however, directly connected in the BabelNet graph. Hence, the *graph vicinity factor* scales up the computed similarity value for the word pair.

3.4 Relational similarity

Relational similarity evaluates the correspondence between relations (Medin et al., 1990). The task can be viewed as an analogy problem in which, given two pairs of words (w_a, w_b) and (w_c, w_d), the goal is to compute the extent to which the relations of w_a to w_b and w_c to w_d are similar. Sense embeddings are suitable candidates for measuring this type of similarity, as they represent relations between senses as linear transformations. Given this property, the relation between a pair of words can be obtained by subtracting their corresponding normalized embeddings. Following Zhila et al. (2013), the relational similarity between two pairs of word (w_a, w_b) and (w_c, w_d) is accordingly calculated as:

$$\text{ANALOGY}(\vec{w_a}, \vec{w_b}, \vec{w_c}, \vec{w_d}) = \mathcal{T}(\vec{w_b} - \vec{w_a}, \vec{w_d} - \vec{w_c}) \quad (6)$$

We show the procedure for measuring the relational similarity in Algorithm 2. The algorithm first finds the closest senses across the two word pairs: s_a^* and s_b^* for the first pair and s_c^* and s_d^* for the second. The analogy vector representations are accordingly computed as the difference between the sense embeddings of the corresponding closest senses. Finally, the relational similarity is computed as the similarity of the analogy vectors of the two pairs.

4 Experiments

We evaluate our sense-enhanced semantic representation on multiple word similarity and relatedness datasets (Section 4.1), as well the relational similarity framework (Section 4.2).

Algorithm 2 Relational Similarity

Input: Two pairs of words w_a, w_b and w_c, w_d

Output: The degree of analogy between the two pairs

1: $\mathcal{S}_{w_a} \leftarrow getSenses(w_a)$, $\mathcal{S}_{w_b} \leftarrow getSenses(w_b)$

2: $(s_a^*, s_b^*) \leftarrow argmax_{\substack{s_a \in \mathcal{S}_{w_a} \\ s_b \in \mathcal{S}_{w_b}}} \mathcal{T}(\vec{s_a}, \vec{s_b})$

3: $\mathcal{S}_{w_c} \leftarrow getSenses(w_c)$, $\mathcal{S}_{w_d} \leftarrow getSenses(w_d)$

4: $(s_c^*, s_d^*) \leftarrow argmax_{\substack{s_c \in \mathcal{S}_{w_c} \\ s_d \in \mathcal{S}_{w_d}}} \mathcal{T}(\vec{s_c}, \vec{s_d})$

5: **return:** $\mathcal{T}(\vec{s_b}^* - \vec{s_a}^*, \vec{s_d}^* - \vec{s_c}^*)$

4.1 Word similarity experiment

Word similarity measurement is one of the most popular evaluation methods in lexical semantics, and semantic similarity in particular, with numerous evaluation benchmarks and datasets. Given a set of word pairs, a system's task is to provide similarity judgments for each pair, and these judgements should ideally be as close as possible to those given by humans.

4.1.1 Datasets

We evaluate SENSEMBED on standard word similarity and relatedness datasets: the RG-65 (Rubenstein and Goodenough, 1965) and the WordSim-353 (Finkelstein et al., 2002, WS-353) datasets. Agirre et al. (2009) suggested that the original WS-353 dataset conflates similarity and relatedness and divided the dataset into two subsets, each containing pairs for just one type of association measure: similarity (the WS-Sim dataset) and relatedness (the WS-Rel dataset).

We also evaluate our approach on the YP-130 dataset, which was created by Yang and Powers (2005) specifically for measuring verb similarity, and also on the Stanford's Contextual Word Similarities (SCWS), a dataset for measuring word-in-context similarity (Huang et al., 2012). In the SCWS dataset each word is provided with the sentence containing it, which helps in pointing out the intended sense of the corresponding target word.

Finally, we also report results on the MEN dataset which was recently introduced by Bruni et al. (2014). MEN contains two sets of English word pairs, together with human-assigned similarity judgments, obtained by crowdsourcing using Amazon Mechanical Turk.

4.1.2 Comparison systems

We compare the performance of our similarity measure against twelve other approaches. As regards traditional distributional models, we report the best results computed by Baroni et al. (2014) for PMI-SVD, a system based on Pointwise Mutual Information (PMI) and SVD-based dimensionality reduction. For word embeddings, we report the results of Pennington et al. (2014, GloVe) and Collobert and Weston (2008). GloVe is an alternative way for learning embeddings, in which vector dimensions are made explicit, as opposed to the opaque meaning of the vector dimensions in Word2vec. The approach of Collobert and Weston (2008) is an embeddings model with a deeper architecture, designed to preserve more complex knowledge as distant relations. We also show results for the word embeddings trained by Baroni et al. (2014). The authors first constructed a massive corpus by combining several large corpora. Then, they trained dozens of different Word2vec models by varying the system's training parameters and reported the best performance obtained on each dataset.

As representatives for graph-based similarity techniques, we report results for the state-of-the-art approach of Pilehvar et al. (2013) which is based on random walks on WordNet's semantic network. Moreover, we present results for the graph-based approach of Zesch et al. (2008), which compares a pair of words based on the path lengths on Wiktionary's semantic network.

We also compare our word similarity measure against the multi-prototype models of Reisinger and Mooney (2010) and Huang et al. (2012), and against the approaches of Yu and Dredze (2014) and Chen et al. (2014), which enhance word embeddings with semantic knowledge derived from PPDB and WordNet, respectively. Finally, we report results for word embeddings, as our baseline, obtained using the Word2vec toolkit on the same corpus that was annotated and used for learning our sense embeddings (cf. Section 2.3).

4.1.3 Parameter tuning

Recall from Sections 3.3.1 and 3.3.2 that our algorithm has two parameters: the α parameter for the *weighted* strategy and the β parameter for the *graph vicinity factor*. We tuned these two parameters on the SimLex-999 dataset (Hill et al., 2014). We picked SimLex-999 since there are not many comparison systems in the literature that report re-

Measure	Dataset					
	RG-65	WS-Sim	WS-Rel	YP-130	MEN	Average
Pilehvar et al. (2013)	0.868	0.677	0.457	0.710	0.690	0.677
Zesch et al. (2008)	0.820	—	—	0.710	—	—
Collobert and Weston (2008)	0.480	0.610	0.380	—	0.570	—
Word2vec (Baroni et al., 2014)	0.840	0.800	0.700	—	0.800	—
GloVe	0.769	0.666	0.559	0.577	0.763	0.737
ESA	0.749	—	—	—	—	—
PMI-SVD	0.738	0.659	0.523	0.337	0.726	0.695
Word2vec	0.732	0.707	0.476	0.343	0.665	0.644
SENSEMBED$_{closest}$	**0.894**	0.756	0.645	**0.734**	0.779	0.769
SENSEMBED$_{weighted}$	0.871	**0.812**	**0.703**	0.639	**0.805**	**0.794**

Table 3: Spearman correlation performance on five word similarity and relatedness datasets.

sults on the dataset. We found the optimal values for α and β to be 8 and 1.6, respectively.

4.1.4 Results

Table 3 shows the experimental results on five different word similarity and relatedness datasets. We report the Spearman correlation performance for the two strategies of our approach as well as eight other comparison systems. SENSEMBED proves to be highly reliable on both similarity and relatedness measurement tasks, obtaining the best performance on most datasets. In addition, our approach shows itself to be equally suitable for verb similarity, as indicated by the results on YP-130.

The rightmost column in the Table shows the average performance weighted by dataset size. Between the two similarity measurement strategies, *weighted* proves to be the more suitable, achieving the best overall performance on three datasets and the best mean performance of 0.794 across the two strategies. This indicates that our assumption of considering all senses of a word in similarity computation was beneficial.

We report in Table 4 the Spearman correlation performance of four approaches that are similar to SENSEMBED: the multi-prototype models of Reisinger and Mooney (2010) and Huang et al. (2012), and the semantically enhanced models of Yu and Dredze (2014) and Chen et al. (2014). We provide results only on WS-353 and SCWS, since the above-mentioned approaches do not report their performance on other datasets. As we can see from the Table, SENSEMBED outperforms the other approaches on the WS-353 dataset. However, our approach lags behind on SCWS, highlighting the negative impact of taking the closest senses as the intended meanings. In fact, on this dataset, SENSEMBED$_{weighted}$ provides better performance owing to its taking into account other senses as well. The better performance of the multi-prototype systems can be attributed to their coarse-grained sense inventories which are automatically constructed by means of Word Sense Induction.

Measure	WS-353	SCWS
Huang et al. (2012)	0.713	0.628
Reisinger and Mooney (2010)	0.770	–
Chen et al. (2014)	–	**0.662**
Yu and Dredze (2014)	0.537	–
Word2vec	0.694	0.642
SENSEMBED$_{closest}$	0.714	0.589
SENSEMBED$_{weighted}$	**0.779**	0.624

Table 4: Spearman correlation performance of the multi-prototype and semantically-enhanced approaches on the WordSim-353 and the Stanford's Contextual Word Similarities datasets.

4.2 Relational similarity experiment

Dataset and evaluation. We take as our benchmark the SemEval-2012 task on Measuring Degrees of Relational Similarity (Jurgens et al., 2012). The task provides a dataset comprising 79 graded word relations, 10 of which are used for training and the rest for test. The task evaluated the participating systems in terms of the Spearman correlation and the MaxDiff score (Louviere, 1991).

Model	Setting			Dataset					
	Strategy	Vicinity	Expansion	RG-65	WS-Sim	WS-Rel	YP-130	MEN	Average
Word2vec	–	–		0.732	0.707	0.476	0.343	0.665	0.644
Word2vec$_{exp}$	–	–	✓	0.700	0.665	0.326	0.621	0.655	0.632
SENSEMBED	closest			0.825	0.693	0.488	0.492	0.712	0.690
	closest		✓	0.844	0.714	0.562	0.681	0.743	0.728
	closest	✓	✓	**0.894**	0.756	0.645	**0.734**	0.779	0.769
	weighted			0.877	0.776	0.639	0.446	0.783	0.762
	weighted		✓	0.864	0.783	0.665	0.591	0.773	0.761
	weighted	✓	✓	0.871	**0.812**	**0.703**	0.639	**0.805**	**0.794**

Table 6: Spearman correlation performance of word embeddings (Word2vec) and SENSEMBED on different semantic similarity and relatedness datasets.

Measure	MaxDiff	Spearman
Com	45.2	0.353
PairDirection	45.2	—
RNN-1600	41.8	0.275
UTD-LDA	—	0.334
UTD-NB	39.4	0.229
UTD-SVM	34.7	0.116
PMI baseline	33.9	0.112
Word2vec	43.2	0.288
SENSEMBED$_{closest}$	**45.9**	**0.358**

Table 5: Spearman correlation performance of different systems on the SemEval-2012 Task on Relational Similarity.

Comparison systems. We compare our results against six other systems and the PMI baseline provided by the task organizers. As for systems that use word embeddings for measuring relational similarity, we report results for RNN-1600 (Mikolov et al., 2013c) and PairDirection (Levy and Goldberg, 2014). We also report results for UTD-NB and UTD-SVM (Rink and Harabagiu, 2012), which rely on lexical pattern classification based on Naïve Bayes and Support Vector Machine classifiers, respectively. UTD-LDA (Rink and Harabagiu, 2013) is another system presented by the same authors that casts the task as a selectional preferences one. Finally, we show the performance of Com (Zhila et al., 2013), a system that combines Word2vec, lexical patterns, and knowledge base information. Similarly to the word similarity experiments, we also report a baseline based on word embeddings (Word2vec) trained on the same corpus and with the same settings as SENSEMBED.

Results. Table 5 shows the performance of different systems in the task of relational similarity in terms of the Spearman correlation and MaxDiff score. A comparison of the results for Word2vec and SENSEMBED shows the advantage gained by moving from the word to the sense level. Among the comparison systems, Com attains the closest performance. However, we note that the system is a combination of several methods, whereas SENSEMBED is based on a single approach.

4.3 Analysis

In order to analyze the impact of the different components of our similarity measure, we carried out a series of experiments on our word similarity datasets. We show in Table 6 the experimental results in terms of Spearman correlation. Performance is reported for the two similarity measurement strategies, i.e., *closest* and *weighted*, and for different system settings with and without the expansion procedure (cf. Section 3.1) and *graph vicinity factor* (cf. Section 3.3.2). As our comparison baseline, we also report results for word embeddings, obtained using the Word2vec toolkit on the same corpus and with the same configuration (cf. Section 2.3) used for learning the sense embeddings (Word2vec in the Table). The rightmost column in the Table reports the mean performance weighted by dataset size. Word2vec$_{exp}$ is the word embeddings system in which the similarity of the two words is determined in terms of the closest word embeddings among all the corresponding synonyms obtained with the expansion procedure (cf. Section 3.1).

A comparison of word and sense embeddings in the vanilla setting (with neither the expansion procedure nor *graph vicinity factor*) indicates the consistent advantage gained by moving from word to sense level, irrespective of the dataset and the similarity measurement strategy. The consistent improvement shows that the semantic information provided more than compensates for the inherently imperfect disambiguation. Moreover, the results indicate the consistent benefit gained by introducing the *graph vicinity factor*, highlighting the fact that our combination of the complementary knowledge from sense embeddings and information derived from a semantic network is beneficial. Finally, note that the expansion procedure leads to performance improvement in most cases for sense embeddings. In direct contrast, the step proves harmful in the case of word embeddings, mainly due to their inability to distinguish individual word senses.

5 Related Work

Word embeddings were first introduced by Bengio et al. (2003) with the goal of statistical language modeling, i.e., learning the joint probability function of a sequence of words. The initial model was a Multilayer Perceptron (MLP) with two hidden layers: a shared non-linear and a regular hidden hyperbolic tangent one. Collobert and Weston (2008) deepened the original neural model by adding a convolutional layer and an extra layer for modeling long-distance dependencies. A significant contribution was later made by Mikolov et al. (2013a), who simplified the original model by removing the hyperbolic tangent layer and hence significantly speeding up the training process. Other related work includes GloVe (Pennington et al., 2014), which is an effort to make the vector dimensions in word embeddings explicit, and the approach of Bordes et al. (2013), which trains word embeddings on the basis of relationship information derived from WordNet.

Several techniques have been proposed for transforming word embeddings to the sense level. Chen et al. (2014) leveraged word embeddings in Word Sense Disambiguation and investigated the possibility of retrofitting embeddings with the resulting disambiguated words. Guo et al. (2014) exploited parallel data to automatically generate sense-annotated data, based on the fact that different senses of a word are usually translated to different words in another language (Chan and Ng, 2005). The automatically-generated sense-annotated data was later used for training sense-specific word embeddings. Huang et al. (2012) adopted a similar strategy by decomposing each word's single-prototype representation into multiple prototypes, denoting different senses of that word. To this end, they first gathered the context for all occurrences of a word and then used spherical K-means to cluster the contexts. Each cluster was taken as the context for a specific meaning of the word and hence used to train embeddings for that specific meaning (i.e., word sense). However, these techniques either suffer from low coverage as they can only model word senses that occur in the parallel data, or require manual intervention for linking the obtained representations to an existing sense inventory. In contrast, our approach enables high coverage and is readily applicable for the representation of word senses in widely-used lexical resources, such as WordNet, Wikipedia and Wiktionary, without needing to resort to additional manual effort.

6 Conclusions and Future Work

We proposed an approach for obtaining continuous representations of individual word senses, referred to as sense embeddings. Based on the proposed sense embeddings and the knowledge obtained from a large-scale lexical resource, i.e., BabelNet, we put forward an effective technique, called SENSEMBED, for measuring semantic similarity. We evaluated our approach on multiple datasets in the tasks of word and relational similarity. Two conclusions can be drawn on the basis of the experimental results: (1) moving from word to sense embeddings can significantly improve the effectiveness and accuracy of the representations; and (2) a meaningful combination of sense embeddings and knowledge from a semantic network can further enhance the similarity judgements. As future work, we intend to utilize our sense embeddings to perform WSD, as was proposed in Chen et al. (2014), in order to speed up the process and train sense embeddings on larger amounts of sense-annotated data.

Acknowledgments

The authors gratefully acknowledge the support of the ERC Starting Grant MultiJEDI No. 259234.

References

Eneko Agirre, Enrique Alfonseca, Keith Hall, Jana Kravalova, Marius Paşca, and Aitor Soroa. 2009. A Study on Similarity and Relatedness Using Distributional and WordNet-based Approaches. In *Proceedings of Human Language Technologies: The 2009 Annual Conference of the North American Chapter of the Association for Computational Linguistics*, pages 19–27, Boulder, Colorado.

Marco Baroni, Georgiana Dinu, and Germán Kruszewski. 2014. Don't count, predict! A systematic comparison of context-counting vs. context-predicting semantic vectors. In *Proceedings of the 52nd Annual Meeting of the Association for Computational Linguistics*, volume 1, pages 238–247, Baltimore, Maryland.

Yoshua Bengio, Réjean Ducharme, Pascal Vincent, and Christian Janvin. 2003. A Neural Probabilistic Language Model. *The Journal of Machine Learning Research*, 3:1137–1155.

Antoine Bordes, Nicolas Usunier, Alberto Garcia-Duran, Jason Weston, and Oksana Yakhnenko. 2013. Translating Embeddings for Modeling Multi-relational Data. In *Advances in Neural Information Processing Systems*, volume 26, pages 2787–2795.

Elia Bruni, Nam Khanh Tran, and Marco Baroni. 2014. Multimodal Distributional Semantics. *Journal of Artificial Intelligence Research*, 49(1):1–47.

Alexander Budanitsky and Graeme Hirst. 2006. Evaluating WordNet-based measures of Lexical Semantic Relatedness. *Computational Linguistics*, 32(1):13–47.

John A. Bullinaria and Joseph P. Levy. 2012. Extracting Semantic Representations from Word Co-occurrence Statistics: Stop-lists, Stemming and SVD. *Behavior Research Methods*, 44:890–907.

Yee Seng Chan and Hwee Tou Ng. 2005. Scaling Up Word Sense Disambiguation via Parallel Texts. In *Proceedings of the 20th National Conference on Artificial Intelligence - Volume 3*, pages 1037–1042, Pittsburgh, Pennsylvania.

Xinxiong Chen, Zhiyuan Liu, and Maosong Sun. 2014. A unified model for word sense representation and disambiguation. In *Proceedings of the 2014 Conference on Empirical Methods in Natural Language Processing (EMNLP)*, pages 1025–1035, Doha, Qatar.

Ronan Collobert and Jason Weston. 2008. A unified architecture for natural language processing: Deep neural networks with multitask learning. In *Proceedings of the 25th International Conference on Machine Learning*, pages 160–167, Helsinki, Finland.

Scott C. Deerwester, Susan T. Dumais, Thomas K. Landauer, George W. Furnas, and Richard A. Harshman. 1990. Indexing by latent semantic analysis. *Journal of American Society for Information Science*, 41(6):391–407.

Lev Finkelstein, Gabrilovich Evgeniy, Matias Yossi, Rivlin Ehud, Solan Zach, Wolfman Gadi, and Ruppin Eytan. 2002. Placing Search in Context: The Concept Revisited. *ACM Transactions on Information Systems*, 20(1):116–131.

Juri Ganitkevitch, Benjamin Van Durme, and Chris Callison-Burch. 2013. PPDB: The Paraphrase Database. In *Proceedings of Human Language Technologies: The 2013 Annual Conference of the North American Chapter of the Association for Computational Linguistics*, pages 758–764, Atlanta, Georgia.

Jiang Guo, Wanxiang Che, Haifeng Wang, and Ting Liu. 2014. Learning Sense-specific Word Embeddings By Exploiting Bilingual Resources. In *Proceedings of COLING 2014, the 25th International Conference on Computational Linguistics: Technical Papers*, pages 497–507, Dublin, Ireland.

Felix Hill, Roi Reichart, and Anna Korhonen. 2014. SimLex-999: Evaluating semantic models with (genuine) similarity estimation. *arXiv preprint arXiv:1408.3456*.

Eric H. Huang, Richard Socher, Christopher D. Manning, and Andrew Y. Ng. 2012. Improving Word Representations Via Global Context And Multiple Word Prototypes. In *Proceedings of 50th Annual Meeting of the Association for Computational Linguistics*, volume 1, pages 873–882, Jeju Island, South Korea.

David A. Jurgens, Peter D. Turney, Saif M. Mohammad, and Keith J. Holyoak. 2012. Semeval-2012 task 2: Measuring degrees of relational similarity. In *Proceedings of the First Joint Conference on Lexical and Computational Semantics - Volume 1: Proceedings of the Main Conference and the Shared Task, and Volume 2: Proceedings of the Sixth International Workshop on Semantic Evaluation*, pages 356–364, Montreal, Canada.

Omer Levy and Yoav Goldberg. 2014. Linguistic regularities in sparse and explicit word representations. In *Proceedings of the Eighteenth Conference on Computational Natural Language Learning*, pages 171–180, Ann Arbor, Michigan.

Jordan Louviere. 1991. Best-Worst Scaling: A Model for the Largest Difference Judgments. Working paper, University of Alberta.

Arthur B. Markman and Dedre Gentner. 1993. Structural alignment during similarity comparisons. *Cognitive Psychology*, 25(4):431 – 467.

Douglas L. Medin, Robert L. Goldstone, and Dedre Gentner. 1990. Similarity involving attributes and relations: Judgments of similarity and difference are not inverses. *Psychological Science*, 1(1):64–69.

Tomas Mikolov, Kai Chen, Greg Corrado, and Jeffrey Dean. 2013a. Efficient Estimation of Word Representations in Vector Space. *CoRR*, abs/1301.3781.

Tomas Mikolov, Quoc V. Le, and Ilya Sutskever. 2013b. Exploiting Similarities among Languages for Machine Translation. *arXiv preprint arXiv:1309.4168*.

Tomas Mikolov, Wen-tau Yih, and Geoffrey Zweig. 2013c. Linguistic Regularities in Continuous Space Word Representations. In *Proceedings of Human Language Technologies: The 2013 Annual Conference of the North American Chapter of the Association for Computational Linguistics*, pages 746–751, Atlanta, Georgia.

George A. Miller, Claudia Leacock, Randee Tengi, and Ross T. Bunker. 1993. A Semantic Concordance. In *Proceedings of the Workshop on Human Language Technology*, pages 303–308, Princeton, New Jersey.

Andriy Mnih and Geoffrey Hinton. 2007. Three New Graphical Models for Statistical Language Modelling. In *Proceedings of the 24th International Conference on Machine Learning*, pages 641–648, Corvallis, Oregon.

Andrea Moro, Alessandro Raganato, and Roberto Navigli. 2014. Entity Linking meets Word Sense Disambiguation: a Unified Approach. *Transactions of the Association for Computational Linguistics (TACL)*, 2:231–244.

Roberto Navigli and Simone Paolo Ponzetto. 2012. BabelNet: The Automatic Construction, Evaluation and Application of a Wide-Coverage Multilingual Semantic Network. *Artificial Intelligence*, 193:217–250.

Roberto Navigli. 2009. Word Sense Disambiguation: A survey. *ACM Computing Surveys*, 41(2):1–69.

Jeffrey Pennington, Richard Socher, and Christopher D Manning. 2014. GloVe: Global Vectors for Word Representation. In *Proceedings of the Empirical Methods in Natural Language Processing (EMNLP)*, volume 12, pages 1532–1543, Doha, Qatar.

Mohammad Taher Pilehvar, David A. Jurgens, and Roberto Navigli. 2013. Align, Disambiguate and Walk: a Unified Approach for Measuring Semantic Similarity. In *Proceedings of the 51st Annual Meeting of the Association for Computational Linguistics*, pages 1341–1351, Sofia, Bulgaria.

Joseph Reisinger and Raymond J. Mooney. 2010. Multi-Prototype Vector-Space Models of Word Meaning. In *Proceedings of Human Language Technologies: The 2010 Annual Conference of the North American Chapter of the Association for Computational Linguistics*, pages 109–117, Los Angeles, California.

Bryan Rink and Sanda Harabagiu. 2012. UTD: Determining relational similarity using lexical patterns. In **SEM 2012: The First Joint Conference on Lexical and Computational Semantics – Volume 1: Proceedings of the main conference and the shared task, and Volume 2: Proceedings of the Sixth International Workshop on Semantic Evaluation (SemEval 2012)*, pages 413–418, Montreal, Canada.

Bryan Rink and Sanda Harabagiu. 2013. The Impact of Selectional Preference Agreement on Semantic Relational Similarity. In *Proceedings of the 10th International Conference on Computational Semantics (IWCS) – Long Papers*, pages 204–215, Potsdam, Germany.

Herbert Rubenstein and John B. Goodenough. 1965. Contextual Correlates of Synonymy. *Communications of the ACM*, 8(10):627–633.

Joseph Turian, Lev Ratinov, and Yoshua Bengio. 2010. Word Representations: A Simple and General Method for Semi-supervised Learning. In *Proceedings of the 48th Annual Meeting of the Association for Computational Linguistics*, pages 384–394, Uppsala, Sweden.

Amos Tversky. 1977. Features of similarity. *Psychological Review*, 84:327–352.

Dongqiang Yang and David M. W. Powers. 2005. Measuring semantic similarity in the taxonomy of wordnet. In *Proceedings of the Twenty-eighth Australasian Conference on Computer Science*, volume 38, pages 315–322, Darlinghurst, Australia.

Mo Yu and Mark Dredze. 2014. Improving Lexical Embeddings with Semantic Knowledge. In *Proceedings of the 52nd Annual Meeting of the Association for Computational Linguistics*, volume 2, pages 545–550, Baltimore, Maryland.

Torsten Zesch, Christof Müller, and Iryna Gurevych. 2008. Using Wiktionary for Computing Semantic Relatedness. In *Proceedings of the 23rd National Conference on Artificial Intelligence*, volume 2, pages 861–866, Chicago, Illinois.

Alisa Zhila, Wen-tau Yih, Christopher Meek, Geoffrey Zweig, and Tomas Mikolov. 2013. Combining Heterogeneous Models for Measuring Relational Similarity. In *Proceedings of Human Language Technologies: The 2013 Annual Conference of the North American Chapter of the Association for Computational Linguistics*, pages 1000–1009, Atlanta, Georgia.

Revisiting Word Embedding for Contrasting Meaning

Zhigang Chen†, Wei Lin‡, Qian Chen*,
Xiaoping Chen†, Si Wei‡, Hui Jiang§ and Xiaodan Zhu§
†School of Computer Science and Technology, *NELSLIP,
University of Science and Technology of China, Hefei, China
‡ iFLYTEK Research, Hefei, China
§Department of EECS, York University, Toronto, Canada
emails: zgchen9517017@gmail.com, weilin2@iflytek.com, cq1231@mail.ustc.edu.cn,
xpchen@ustc.edu.cn, siwei@iflytek.com, hj@cse.yorku.ca, zhu2048@gmail.com

Abstract

Contrasting meaning is a basic aspect of semantics. Recent word-embedding models based on *distributional semantics hypothesis* are known to be weak for modeling lexical contrast. We present in this paper the embedding models that achieve an F-score of 92% on the widely-used, publicly available dataset, the GRE "most contrasting word" questions (Mohammad et al., 2008). This is the highest performance seen so far on this dataset. Surprisingly at the first glance, unlike what was suggested in most previous work, where relatedness statistics learned from corpora is claimed to yield extra gains over lexicon-based models, we obtained our best result relying solely on lexical resources (Roget's and WordNet)—corpora statistics did not lead to further improvement. However, this should not be simply taken as that distributional statistics is not useful. We examine several basic concerns in modeling contrasting meaning to provide detailed analysis, with the aim to shed some light on the future directions for this basic semantics modeling problem.

1 Introduction

Learning good representations of meaning for different granularities of texts is core to human language understanding, where a basic problem is representing the meanings of words. Distributed representations learned with neural networks have recently showed to result in significant improvement of performance on a number of language understanding problems (e.g., speech recognition and automatic machine translation) and on many non-language problems (e.g., image recognition). Distributed representations have been leveraged to represent words as in (Collobert et al., 2011; Mikolov et al., 2013).

Contrasting meaning is a basic aspect of semantics, but it is widely known that word embedding models based on *distributional semantics hypothesis* are weak in modeling this—contrasting meaning is often lost in the low-dimensional spaces based on such a hypothesis, and better models would be desirable.

Lexical contrast has been modeled in (Lin and Zhao, 2003; Mohammad et al., 2008; Mohammad et al., 2013). The recent literature has also included research efforts of modeling contrasting meaning in embedding spaces, leading to state-of-the-art performances. For example, Yih et al. (2012) proposed to use polarity-primed latent semantic analysis (LSA), called PILSA, to capture contrast, which was further used to initialize a neural network and achieved an F-score of 81% on the same GRE "most contrasting word" questions (Mohammad et al., 2008). More recently, Zhang et al. (2014) proposed a tensor factorization approach to solving the problem, resulting in a 82% F-score.

In this paper, we present embedding models that achieve an F-score of 92% on the GRE dataset, which outperforms the previous best result (82%) by a large margin. Unlike what was suggested in previous work, where relatedness statistics learned from corpora is often claimed to yield extra gains over lexicon-based models, we obtained this new state-of-the-art result relying solely on lexical resources (Roget's and WordNet), and corpus statistics does not seem to bring further improvement. To provide a comprehensive understanding, we constructed our study in a framework that examines a number of basic concerns in modeling contrasting meaning. We hope our efforts would help shed some light on future directions for this basic semantic modeling problem.

Proceedings of the 53rd Annual Meeting of the Association for Computational Linguistics and the 7th International Joint Conference on Natural Language Processing, pages 106–115,
Beijing, China, July 26-31, 2015.

2 Related Work

The terms *contrasting*, *opposite*, and *antonym* have different definitions in the literature, while sometimes they are used interchangeably. Following (Mohammad et al., 2013), in this paper we refer to *opposites* as word pairs that "have a strong binary incompatibility relation with each other or that are saliently different across a dimension of meaning", e.g., *day* and *night*. *Antonyms* are a subset of opposites that are also gradable adjectives, with same definition as in (Cruse, 1986) as well. *Contrasting* word pairs have the broadest meaning among them, referring to word pairs having "some non-zero degree of binary incompatibility and/or have some non-zero difference across a dimension of meaning." Therefore by definition, opposites are a subset of contrasting word pairs (refer to (Mohammad et al., 2013) for detailed discussions).

Word Embedding Word embedding models learn continuous representations for words in a low dimensional space (Turney and Pantel, 2010; Hinton and Roweis, 2002; Collobert et al., 2011; Mikolov et al., 2013; Liu et al., 2015), which is not new. Linear dimension reduction such as Latent Semantic Analysis (LSA) has been extensively used in lexical semantics (see (Turney and Pantel, 2010) for good discussions in vector space models.) Non-linear models such as those described in (Roweis and Saul, 2000) and (Tenenbaum et al., 2000), among many others, can also be applied to learn word embeddings. A particularly interesting model is stochastic neighbor embedding (SNE) (Hinton and Roweis, 2002), which explicitly enforces that in the embedding space, the distribution of neighbors of a given word to be similar to that in the original, uncompressed space. SNE can learn multiple senses of a word with a mixture component. Recently, neural-network based model such as those proposed by (Collobert et al., 2011) and (Mikolov et al., 2013) have attracted extensive attention; particularly the latter, which can scale up to handle large corpora efficiently.

Although word embeddings have recently showed to be superior in some NLP tasks, they are very weak in distinguishing contrasting meaning, as the models are often based on the well-known *distributional semantics hypothesis*— words in similar context have similar meanings. Contrasting words have similar context too, so contrasting meaning is not distinguished well in such representations. Better models for contrasting meaning is fundamentally interesting.

Modeling Contrasting Meaning Automatically detecting contrasting meaning has been studied in earlier work such as (Lin and Zhao, 2003; Mohammad et al., 2008; Mohammad et al., 2013). Specifically, as far as the embedding-based methods are concerned, PILSA (Yih et al., 2012) made a progress in achieving one of the best results, by priming LSA to encode contrasting meaning. In addition, PILSA was also used to initialize a neural network to get a further improvement on the GRE benchmark, where an F-score of 81% was obtained. Another recent method was proposed by (Zhang et al., 2014), called Bayesian probabilistic tensor factorization. It considered multi-dimensional semantic information, relations, unsupervised data structure information in tensor factorization, and achieved an F-score of 82% on the GRE questions. These methods employed both lexical resources and corpora statistics to achieve their best results. In this paper, we show that using only lexical resources to construct embedding systems can achieve significantly better results (an F-score of 92%). To provide a more comprehensive understanding, we constructed our study in a framework that examines a number of basic concerns in modeling contrasting meaning within embedding.

Note that sentiment contrast may be viewed as a specific case of more general semantic contrast or semantic differentials (Osgood et al., 1957). Tang et al. (2014) learned sentiment-specific embedding and applied it to sentiment analysis of tweets, which was often solved with more conventional methods (Zhu et al., 2014b; Kiritchenko et al., 2014a; Kiritchenko et al., 2014b).

3 The Models

We described in this section the framework in which we study word embedding for contrasting meaning. The general aim of the models is to enforce that in the embedding space, the word pairs with higher degrees of contrast will be put farther from each other than those of less contrast. How to learn this is critical. Figure 1 describes a very high-level view of the framework.

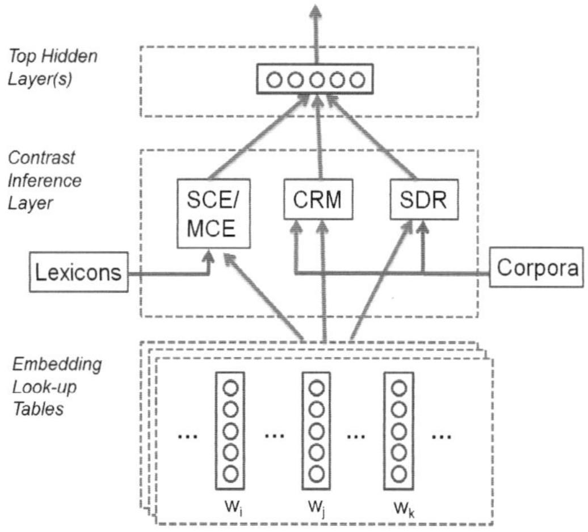

Figure 1: A high-level view of the contrasting embedding framework.

3.1 Top Hidden Layer(s)

It is widely recognized that contrasting words, e.g., *good* and *bad*, also intend to appear in similar context or co-occur with each other. For example, opposite pairs, special cases of contrasting words, tend to co-occur more often than chance (Charles and Miller, 1989; Fellbaum, 1995; Murphy and Andrew, 1993). Mohammad et al. (2013), in addition, proposed a *degree of contrast hypothesis*, stating that "if a pair of words, A and B, are contrasting, then their degree of contrast is proportional to their tendency to co-occur in a large corpus."

These suggest some non-linear interaction between distributional relatedness and the degree of contrast: the increase of relatedness correspond to the increase of both semantic contrast and semantic closeness; for example, they can form a U-shaped curve if one plots the word pairs on a two dimensional plane with y-axis denoting relatedness scores, while the most contrasting and (semantically) close pairs lie on the two side of the x-axis, respectively. In this paper, when combining word-pair distances learned by different components of the contrasting inference layer, we use some top hidden layer(s) to provide a non-linear combination. Specifically, we use two hidden layers, which is able to express complicated functions (Bishop, 2006). We use ten hidden units in each hidden layer.

3.2 Stochastic Contrast Embedding (SCE)

Hinton and Roweis (2002) proposed a stochastic neighbor embedding (SNE) framework. Informally, the objective is to explicitly enforce that in the learned embedding space, the distribution of neighbors of a given word w to be similar to the distribution of its neighbors in the original, uncompressed space.

In our study, we instead use the concept of "neighbors" to encode the contrasting pairs, and we call the model stochastic contrasting embedding (SCE), depicted by the left component of the *contrast inference layer* in Figure 1. The model is different from SNE in three respects. First, as mentioned above, "neighbors" here are actually contrasting pairs—we enforce that in the embedding space, the distribution of the contrasting "neighbors" to be close to the distribution of the "neighbors" in the original, higher-dimensional space. The probability of word w_k being contrasting neighbor of the given word w_i can be computed as:

$$p_1(w_k|w_i) = \frac{\exp(-d_{i,k}^2)}{\sum_{m\neq i}^{v} \exp(-d_{i,m}^2)} \quad (1)$$

where d is some distance metric between w_i and w_k, and v is the size of a vocabulary.

Second, we train SCE using only lexical resources but not corpus statistics, so as to explore the behavior of lexical resources separately (we will use the relatedness modeling component below to model distributional semantics). Specifically, we use antonym pairs in lexical resources to learn *contrasting neighbors*. Hence in the original high-dimensional space, all antonyms of a given word w_i have the same probability to be its contrasting neighbors. That is, d in Equation (1) takes a binary score, with value *1* indicating an antonym pair and *0* not. In the embedding space, the corresponding probability of w_k to be the contrasting neighbor of w_i , denoted as $q_1(w_k|w_i)$, can be computed similarly with Equation (1). But since the embedding is in a continuous space, d is not binary but can be computed with regular distance metric such as euclidean and cosine. The objective is minimizing the KL divergence between $p(.)$ and $q(.)$.

Third, semantic closeness or contrast are not independent. For example, if a pair of words, A and B, are synonyms, and if the pair of words, A and C, are contrasting, then A and C is likely to be contrasting than a random chance. SCE considers both semantic contrast and closeness. That is, for a given word w_i, we jointly force that in the embedding space, its contrasting neighbors and semantically close neighbors to be similar to those in the original uncompressed space. These two objective functions are linearly combined with a parameter λ and are jointly optimized to learn one embedding. The value of λ is determined on the development questions of the GRE data. Later in Section 4, we will discuss how the training pairs of semantic contrast and closeness are obtained from lexical resources.

3.3 Marginal Contrast Embedding (MCE) [1]

In this paper, we use also another training criteria, motivated by the *pairwise ranking* approach (Cohen et al., 1998). The motivation is to explicitly enforce the distances between contrasting pairs to be larger than distances between unrelated word pairs by a margin, and enforce the distances between semantically close pairs to be smaller than unrelated word pairs by another margin. More specifically, we minimize the following objective functions:

$$Obj^{s}_{(mce)} = \sum_{(w_i,w_j)\in \mathbf{S}} \max\{0, \alpha - d_{i,r} + d_{i,j}\} \quad (2)$$

$$Obj^{a}_{(mce)} = \sum_{(w_i,w_k)\in \mathbf{A}} \max\{0, \beta - d_{i,k} + d_{i,r}\} \quad (3)$$

where $\mathbf{A}$ and $\mathbf{S}$ are the set of contrasting pairs and semantically close pairs in lexicons respectively; d denotes distance function between two words in the embedding space. The subscript r indicates a randomly sampled unrelated word. We call this model Marginal Contrasting Embedding (MCE).

Intuitively, if two words w_i and w_j are semantically close, the model maximizes Equation (2), which attempts to force the $d_{i,j}$ (distance between w_i and w_j) in the embedding space to be different from that of two unrelated words $d_{i,r}$ by a margin α. For each given word pair, we sample 100 random words during training. Similarly, if two words w_i and w_k are contrasting, the model maximizes Equation (3), which attempts to force the distance between w_i and w_k to be different from that of two unrelated words $d_{i,r}$ by a margin β. Same as in SCE, these two objective functions are linearly combined with a parameter λ and are jointly optimized to learn one embedding for each word. This joint objective function attempts to force the values of $d_{i,r}$ (distances of unrelated pairs) to be in between $d_{i,k}$ (distances of contrasting pairs) and $d_{i,j}$ (distances of semantically close pairs) by two margins.

[1]We made the code of MCE available at https://github.com/lukecq1231/mce, as MCE achieved the best performance according to the experimental results described later in this paper.

3.4 Corpus Relatedness Modeling (CRM)

As discussed in previous work and above as well, relatedness obtained with corpora based on distributional hypothesis interplays with semantic closeness and contrast. Mohammad et al. (2013) proposed a *degree of contrast hypothesis*, stating that "if a pair of words, A and B, are contrasting, then their degree of contrast is proportional to their tendency to co-occur in a large corpus." In embedding, such dependency can be used to help measure the degree of contrast. Specifically, we use the skip-gram model (Mikolov et al., 2013) to learn the relatedness embedding.

As discussed above, through the top hidden layers, the word embedding and distances learned in SCE/MCE and CRM, together with that learned with SDR below, can be used to predict the GRE "most contrasting word"' questions. With enough GRE data, the prediction error may be backpropagated to directly adjust or learn embedding in the look-up tables. However, given the limited size of the GRE data, we only employed the top hidden layers to non-linearly merge the distances between a word pair that are obtained within each of the modules in the Contrast Inference Layer. We did not backpropagate the errors to fine-tune already learned word embeddings.

Note that embeddings in the look-up tables were learned independently in different modules in the contrast inference layer, e.g., in SCE, MCE and CRM, respectively. And in each module, given the corresponding objective functions, unconstrained optimization (e.g., in the paper SGD) was used to find embeddings that optimize the corresponding objectives. The embeddings were then used out-of-box and not further fine-tuned. Depending on experiment settings, embeddings learned in each module are either used separately or jointly (through the top hidden lay) to predict test cases.

More details will be discussed in the experiment section below.

3.5 Semantic Differential Reconstruction (SDR)

Using factor analysis, Osgood et al. (1957) identified three dimensions of semantics that account for most of the variation in the connotative meaning of adjectives. These three dimensions are *evaluative* (good-bad), *potency* (strong-weak), and *activity*(active-passive). We hypothesize that such information should help reconstruct contrasting meaning.

The General Inquirer lexicon (Stone1966) represents these three factors but has a limited coverage. We used the algorithm of (Turney and Littman, 2003) to extend the labels to more words with Google one billion words corpus (refer to Section 4 for details). For example, to obtain the *evaluative* score for a candidate word w, the pointwise mutual information (PMI) between w and a set of seed words *eval*$^+$ and *eval*$^-$ are computed respectively, and the *evaluative* value for w is calculated with:

$$eval(w) = PMI(w, eval^+) - PMI(w, eval^-) \quad (4)$$

where *eval*$^+$ contains predefined positive *evaluative* words, e.g., *good, positive, fortunate*, and *superior*, while *eval*$^-$ includes negative *evaluative* words like *passive, slow, treble,* and *old.* The seed words were selected as described in (Turney and Littman, 2003) to have a good coverage and to avoid redundancy at the same time. Similarly, the *potency* and *activity* scores of a word can be obtained. The distances of a word pair on these three dimensions can therefore be obtained.

4 Experiment Set-Up

Data Our experiment uses the "most contrasting word" questions collected by Mohammad et al. (2008) from Graduate Record Examination (GRE), which was originally created by Educational Testing Service (ETS). Each GRE question has a target word and five candidate choices; the task is to identify among the choices the most contrasting word with regard to the given target word. The dataset consists of a development set and a test set, with 162 and 950 questions, respectively.

As an example from (Mohammad et al., 2013), one of the questions has the target word *adulterate* and the five candidate choices: (A) *renounce*, (B) *forbid*, (C) *purify*, (D) *criticize*, and (E) *correct*. While in this example the choice *correct* has a meaning that is contrasting with that of *adulterate*, the word *purify* is the gold answer as it has the greatest degree of contrast with *adulterate*.

Lexical Resources In our work, we use two publicly available lexical resources, *WordNet* (Miller, 1995) (version 3.0) and the *Roget's Thesaurus* (Kipfer, 2009). We utilized the labeled antonym relations to obtain more contrasting pairs under the contrast hypothesis (Mohammad et al., 2013), by assuming a contrasting pair is related to a pair of opposites (antonyms here). Specifically in WordNet, we consider the word pairs with relations other than antonym as semantically close. In this way, we obtained a thesaurus containing 83,118 words, 494,579 contrasting pairs, and 368,209 close pairs. Note that we did not only use synonyms to expand the contrasting pairs. We will discuss how this affects the performance in the experiment section.

In the Roget's Thesaurus, every word or entry has its synonyms and/or antonyms. We obtained 35,717 antonym pairs and 346,619 synonym pairs, which consist of 43,409 word types. The antonym and synonym pairs in Roget's were combined with contrasting pairs and semantically close pairs in WordNet, respectively. And in total, we have 92,339 word types, 520,734 antonym pairs, and 646,433 close pairs.

Google Billion-Word Corpus The corpus used in our experiment for modeling lexical relatedness in the CRM component was Google one billion word corpus (Chelba et al., 2013). Normalization and tokenization were performed using the scripts distributed from https://code.google.com/p/1-billion-word-language-modeling-benchmark/, and sentences were shuffled randomly. We computed embedding for a word if its count in the corpus is equal to or larger than five, with the method described in Section 3.4. Words with counts lower than five were discarded.

Evaluation Metric Same as in previous work, the evaluation metric is F-score, where *precision* is the percentage of the questions answered correctly over the questions the models attempt to answer, and *recall* is the percentage of the questions that are answered correctly among all questions.

5 Experiment Results

In training, we used stochastic gradient descent (SGD) to optimize the objective function, and the dimension of embedding was set to be 200. In MCE (Equation 2 and 3) the margins α and β are both set to be 0.4. During testing, when using SCE or MCE embedding to answer the GRE questions, we directly calculated distances for a pair between a question word and a candidate choice in these two corresponding embedding spaces to report their performances. We also combined SCE/MCE with other components in the contrast inference layer, for which we used ten-fold cross validation to tune the weights of the top hidden layers on nine fold and test on the rest and repeated this for ten times to report the results. As discussed above, errors were not backpropagated to modify word embedding.

5.1 General Performance of the Models

The performance of the models are showed in Table 1. For comparison, we list the results reported in (Yih et al., 2012) and (Zhang et al., 2014). The table shows that on the GRE dataset, both SCE (a 90% F-score) and MCE (92%) significantly outperform the previous best results reported in (Yih et al., 2012) (81%) and (Zhang et al., 2014) (82%). The F-score of MCE outperforms that of SCE by 2%, which suggests the ranking criterion fits the dataset better. In our experiment, we found that the MCE model achieved robust performances on different distance metrics, e.g., the cosine similarity and Euclidean distance. In the paper, we present the results with cosine similarity. SCE is slightly more sensitive to distance metrics, and the best performing metric on the development set is inner product, so we chose that for testing.

Unlike what was suggested in the previous work, where semantics learned from corpus is claimed to yield extra gains in performance, we obtained this result by using solely lexical resources (Roget's and WordNet) with SCE and MCE. Using corpus statistics that model *distributional hypothesis* (MCE+CRM) and utilize semantic differential categories (MCE+CRM+SDR) does not bring further improvement here (they are useful in the experiments discussed below in Section 5.3).

5.2 Roles of Lexical Resources

To provide a more detailed comparison, we also present lexicon lookup results, together with those reported in (Zhang et al., 2014) and (Yih et al., 2012). For our lookup results and those copied here from (Zhang et al., 2014), the methods do not randomly guess an answer if the target word is in the vocabulary but none of the choices are, while the results of (Yih et al., 2012) randomly guess an answer in this situation. The Encarta thesaurus used in (Yih et al., 2012) is not publicly available, so we did not use it in our experiments. We due the differences among the lookup results on WordNet (WordNet lookup) to the differences in preprocessing as well as the way we expanded indirect contrasting word pairs. As described in Section 4, we utilized all relations other than antonym pairs to expand our indirect antonym pairs. These also have impact on the W&R lookup results (WordNet and Roget's pairs are combined). For both settings, our expansion resulted in much better performances.

Whether the differences between the F-scores of MCE/SCE and that reported in (Zhang et al., 2014) and (Yih et al., 2012) are also due to the differences in expanding indirect pairs? To answer this, we downloaded the word pairs that Zhang et al. (2014) used to train their models,[2] but we used them to train our MCE. The result are presented in Table 1 and the F-score on test set is 91%, which is only slightly lower than MCE using our lexicon. So the extension is very helpful for lookup methods, but the MCE appears to be able to cover such information by itself.

SCE and MCE learn contrasting meaning that is not explicitly encoded in lexical resources. The experiment results show that such implicit contrast can be recovered by jointly learning the embedding by using contrasting words and other semantically close words.

To help better understand why corpus statistics does not further help SCE and MCE, we further demonstrate that most of the target-gold-answer pairs in the GRE test set are connected by short paths (with length between 1 to 3). More specifically, based on breadth-first search, we found the nearest paths that connect target-gold-answer pairs, in the graph formed by WordNet and Roget's—each word is a vertex, and contrasting words and semantically close words are

[2]https://github.com/iceboal/word-representations-bptf

	Development Set			Test Set		
	Prec.	Rec.	F_1	Prec.	Rec.	F_1
WordNet PILSA (Yih et al., 2012)	0.63	0.62	0.62	0.60	0.60	0.60
WordNet MRLSA (Yih et al., 2012)	0.66	0.65	0.65	0.61	0.59	0.60
Encarta lookup (Yih et al., 2012)	0.65	0.61	0.63	0.61	0.56	0.59
Encarta PILSA (Yih et al., 2012)	0.86	0.81	0.84	0.81	0.74	0.77
Encarta MRLSA (Yih et al., 2012)	0.87	0.82	0.84	0.82	0.74	0.78
WordNet lookup (Yih et al., 2012)	0.40	0.40	0.40	0.42	0.41	0.42
WordNet lookup (Zhang et al., 2014)	0.93	0.32	0.48	0.95	0.33	0.49
WordNet lookup	0.97	0.37	0.54	0.97	0.41	0.58
Roget lookup (Zhang et al., 2014)	1.00	0.35	0.52	0.99	0.31	0.47
Roget lookup	1.00	0.32	0.49	0.97	0.29	0.44
W&R lookup (Zhang et al., 2014)	1.00	0.48	0.64	0.98	0.45	0.62
W&R lookup	0.98	0.52	0.68	0.97	0.52	0.68
(Mohammad et al., 2008) Best	0.76	0.66	0.70	**0.76**	**0.64**	**0.70**
(Yih et al., 2012) Best	0.88	0.87	0.87	**0.81**	**0.80**	**0.81**
(Zhang et al., 2014) Best	0.88	0.88	0.88	**0.82**	**0.82**	**0.82**
SCE	0.94	0.93	0.93	0.90	0.90	0.90
MCE (using zhang et al. lex.)	0.94	0.93	0.94	0.92	0.91	0.91
MCE	0.96	0.94	0.95	**0.92**	**0.92**	**0.92**
MCE+CRM	0.94	0.93	0.93	0.90	0.90	0.90
MCE+CRM+SDR	0.04	0.94	0.94	0.90	0.90	0.90

Table 1: Results on the GRE "most contrasting words" questions.

connected with these two types of edges respectively. Then we require the shortest path must have one and only one contrasting edge. Word pairs that cannot be connected by such paths are regarded to have an infinite length of distance.

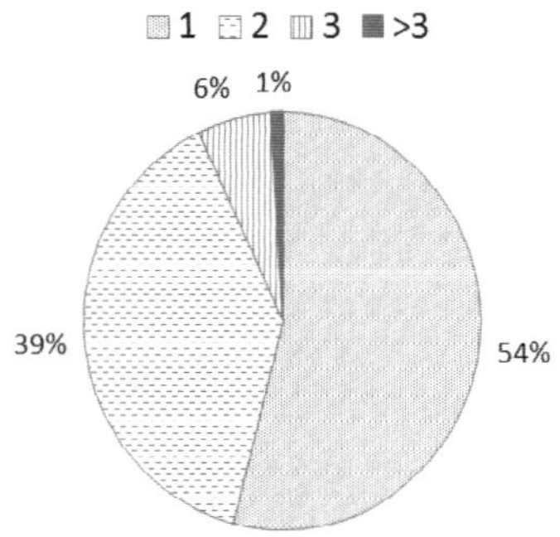

Figure 2: Percentages of target-gold-answer word pairs, categorized by the shortest lengths of paths connecting them.

The pie graph in Figure 2 shows the percentages of target-gold-answer word pairs, categorized by the lengths of shortest paths defined above. We can see that in the GRE data, the percentage of paths with a length larger than three is very small (1%). It seems that SCE and MCE can learn this very well. Again, they force semantically close pairs to be close in the embedding spaces which "share" similar contrasting pairs.

Figure 3 draws the envelope of histogram of cosine distance between all target-choice word pairs in the GRE test set, calculated in the embedding space learned with MCE. The figure intuitively shows how the target-gold-answer pairs (most contrasting pairs) are discriminated from the other target-choice pairs. We also plot the MCE results without using the random sampling depicted in Equation (2) and Equation (3), showing that discriminative power dramatically dropped. Without the sampling, the F-score achieved on the test data is 83%.

5.3 Roles of Corpus-based Embedding

However, the findings presented above should not be simply taken as that distributional hypothesis is not useful for learning lexical contrast. Our results and detailed analysis has showed it is due to the good coverage of the manually created lexical resources and the capability of the SCE and

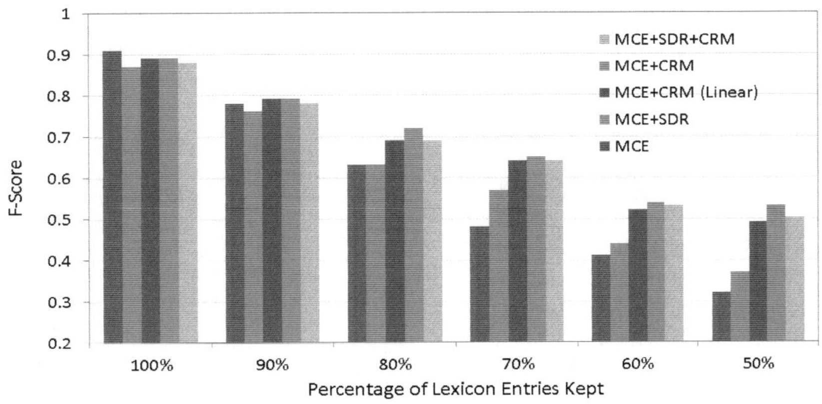

Figure 4: The effect of removing lexicon items.

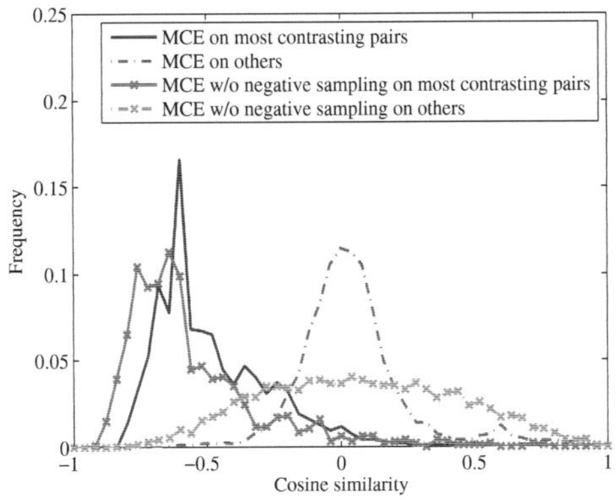

Figure 3: The envelope of histogram of cosine distance between word pair embeddings in GRE test set.

MCE models in capturing indirect semantic relations. There may exist circumstances where the coverage is be lower, e.g., for resource-poor languages or social media text where (indirect) out-of-vocabulary pairs may be frequent.

To simulate the situations, we randomly removed different percentages of words from the combined thesaurus used above in our experiments, and removed all the corresponding word pairs. The performances of different models are showed in Figure 4. It is observed that as the out of vocabulary (OOV) becomes more serious, the MCE suffered the most. Using the semantic differential (MCE+SDR) showed to be helpful as 50% to 70% lexicon entries are kept. Considering relatedness learned from corpus together with MCE (MCE+CRM), i.e., combining MCE distances with CRM distances for target-choice pairs, yielded robust performance—the F-score of MCE+CRM drops significantly slower than that of MCE, as we removed lexical entries. We also combined MCE distances and CRM distances linearly (MCE+CRM (linear)), with a coefficient determined with the development set. It showed a performance worse than that of MCE+CRM when 50%–80% entries kept, while as discussed above, MCE+CRM combines the two parts with the non-linear top layers. In general, using corpora statistics make the models more robust as OOV becomes more serious. It deserves to note that the use of corpora here is rather straightforward; more patterns may be learned from corpora to capture contrasting expressions as discussed in (Mohammad et al., 2013). Also, context such as negation may change contrasting meaning, e.g., sentiment contrast (Kiritchenko et al., 2014b; Zhu et al., 2014a), in a dramatic and complicated manner, which has been considered in learning sentiment contrast (Kiritchenko et al., 2014b).

6 Conclusions

Contrasting meaning is a basic aspect of semantics. In this paper, we present a new state-of-the-art result, a 92% F-score, on the GRE dataset created by (Mohammad et al., 2008), which is widely used as the benchmark for modeling lexical contrast. The result reported here outperforms the best reported in previous work (82%) by a large margin. Unlike what was suggested in most previous work, we show that this performance can be achieved without relying on corpora statistics. To provide a more comprehensive understanding, we constructed our study in a framework that examines a number of concerns in modeling contrasting meaning. We hope our work could help shed some light on future directions on this basic semantic problem.

From our own viewpoints, creating more evaluation data for measuring further progress in contrasting-meaning modeling, e.g., handling real OOV issues, is interesting to us. Also, the degree of contrast may be better formulated as a regression problem rather than a classification problem, in which finer or even real-valued annotation would be desirable.

References

Christopher M. Bishop. 2006. *Pattern Recognition and Machine Learning*. Springer-Verlag New York, Inc., Secaucus, NJ, USA.

Walter G. Charles and George A. Miller. 1989. Contexts of antonymous adjectives. *Applied Psychology*, 10:357–375.

Ciprian Chelba, Tomas Mikolov, Mike Schuster, Qi Ge, Thorsten Brants, Phillipp Koehn, and Tony Robinson. 2013. One billion word benchmark for measuring progress in statistical language modeling. *arXiv:1312.3005*.

William W. Cohen, Robert E. Schapire, and Yoram Singer. 1998. Learning to order things. *Journal of Articial Intelligence Research (JAIR)*, 10:243–270.

Ronan Collobert, Jason Weston, Léon Bottou, Michael Karlen, Koray Kavukcuoglu, and Pavel Kuksa. 2011. Natural language processing (almost) from scratch. *The Journal of Machine Learning Research*, 12:2493–2537.

David A. Cruse. 1986. *Lexical semantics*. Cambridge University Press.

Christiane Fellbaum. 1995. Co-occurrence and antonymy. *International Journal of Lexicography*, 8:281–303.

Geoffrey Hinton and Sam Roweis. 2002. Stochastic neighbor embedding. In *Advances in Neural Information Processing Systems 15*, pages 833–840. MIT Press.

Barbara Ann Kipfer. 2009. *Rogets 21st Century Thesaurus*. Philip Lief Group, third edition edition edition.

Svetlana Kiritchenko, Xiaodan Zhu, and Saif Mohammad. 2014a. Nrc-canada-2014: Detecting aspects and sentiment in customer reviews. In *Proceedings of International Workshop on Semantic Evaluation*, Dublin, Ireland.

Svetlana Kiritchenko, Xiaodan Zhu, and Saif Mohammad. 2014b. Sentiment analysis of short informal texts. *Journal of Artificial Intelligence Research*, 50:723–762.

Dekang Lin and Shaojun Zhao. 2003. Identifying synonyms among distributionally similar words. In *In Proceedings of IJCAI-03*, pages 1492–1493.

Quan Liu, Hui Jiang, Si Wei, Zhen-Hua Ling, and Yu Hu. 2015. Learning semantic word embeddings based on ordinal knowledge constraints. In *Proceedings of ACL*, Beijing, China.

Tomas Mikolov, Ilya Sutskever, Kai Chen, Greg S Corrado, and Jeff Dean. 2013. Distributed representations of words and phrases and their compositionality. In *Advances in Neural Information Processing Systems*, pages 3111–3119.

George A Miller. 1995. WordNet: a lexical database for English. *Communications of the ACM*, 38(11):39–41.

Saif Mohammad, Bonnie Dorr, and Graeme Hirst. 2008. Computing word-pair antonymy. In *Proceedings of the Conference on Empirical Methods in Natural Language Processing*, pages 982–991. Association for Computational Linguistics.

Saif M. Mohammad, Bonnie J. Dorr, Graeme Hirst, and Peter D. Turney. 2013. Computing lexical contrast. *Computational Linguistics*, 39(3):555–590.

Gregory L. Murphy and Jane M. Andrew. 1993. The conceptual basis of antonymy and synonymy in adjectives. *Journal of Memory and Language*, 32(3):1–19.

Charles E Osgood, George J Suci, and Percy Tannenbaum. 1957. *The measurement of meaning*. University of Illinois Press.

Sam T. Roweis and Lawrence K. Saul. 2000. Nonlinear dimensionality reduction by locally linear embedding. *Science*, 290:2323–2326.

Duyu Tang, Furu Wei, Nan Yang, Ming Zhou, Ting Liu, and Bing Qin. 2014. Learning sentiment-specific word embedding for twitter sentiment classification. In *Proceedings of ACL*, Baltimore, Maryland, USA, June.

Joshua B. Tenenbaum, Vin de Silva, and John C. Langford. 2000. A global geometric framework for nonlinear dimensionality reduction. *Science*, 290(5500):2319.

Peter Turney and Michael Littman. 2003. Measuring praise and criticism: Inference of semantic orientation from association. *ACM Transactions on Information Systems (TOIS)*, 21(4):315–346.

Peter D. Turney and Patrick Pantel. 2010. From frequency to meaning: Vector space models of semantics. *J. Artif. Int. Res.*, 37(1):141–188, January.

Wen-tau Yih, Geoffrey Zweig, and John C Platt. 2012. Polarity inducing latent semantic analysis. In *Proceedings of the 2012 Joint Conference on Empirical Methods in Natural Language Processing and Computational Natural Language Learning*, pages 1212–1222. Association for Computational Linguistics.

Jingwei Zhang, Jeremy Salwen, Michael Glass, and Alfio Gliozzo. 2014. Word semantic representations using bayesian probabilistic tensor factorization. In *Proceedings of the 2014 Conference on Empirical Methods in Natural Language Processing (EMNLP)*, pages 1522–1531, Doha, Qatar, October. Association for Computational Linguistics.

Xiaodan Zhu, Hongyu Guo, Saif Mohammad, and Svetlana Kiritchenko. 2014a. An empirical study on the effect of negation words on sentiment. In *Proceedings of ACL*, Baltimore, Maryland, USA, June.

Xiaodan Zhu, Svetlana Kiritchenko, and Saif Mohammad. 2014b. Nrc-canada-2014: Recent improvements in the sentiment analysis of tweets. In *Proceedings of International Workshop on Semantic Evaluation*, Dublin, Ireland.

Joint Models of Disagreement and Stance in Online Debate

Dhanya Sridhar,[1] James Foulds,[1] Bert Huang,[2] Lise Getoor,[1] Marilyn Walker[1]
[1]Department of Computer Science, University of California Santa Cruz
{dsridhar, jfoulds, getoor, mawalker}@ucsc.edu
[2]Department of Computer Science, Virginia Tech
bhuang@vt.edu

Abstract

Online debate forums present a valuable opportunity for the understanding and modeling of dialogue. To understand these debates, a key challenge is inferring the stances of the participants, all of which are interrelated and dependent. While collectively modeling users' stances has been shown to be effective (Walker et al., 2012c; Hasan and Ng, 2013), there are many modeling decisions whose ramifications are not well understood. To investigate these choices and their effects, we introduce a scalable unified probabilistic modeling framework for stance classification models that 1) are collective, 2) reason about disagreement, and 3) can model stance at either the author level or at the post level. We comprehensively evaluate the possible modeling choices on eight topics across two online debate corpora, finding accuracy improvements of up to 11.5 percentage points over a local classifier. Our results highlight the importance of making the correct modeling choices for online dialogues, and having a unified probabilistic modeling framework that makes this possible.

1 Introduction

Understanding stance and opinion in dialogues can provide critical insight into the theoretical underpinnings of discourse, argumentation, and sentiment. Systems for predicting the stances of individuals can potentially have positive social impact and are of practical interest to non-profits, governmental organizations, and companies. For example, stance predictions may be used to target public awareness and advocacy campaigns, direct political fundraising and get-out-the vote efforts, and improve personalized recommendations.

Dialogue Turns	Stance
User 1: 18. That's the smoking age thats the shooting age. Why do you think they call it ATF?	ANTI
User 2: Shooting age? I know 7 year old shooters. 18 should be the gun purchasing age, but there is really no "shooting" age.	ANTI
User 1: I know. I was just pointing out that the logic used to propose a 21 year "shooting age" was inconsistent.	ANTI
User 2: I see. I dont think its really fair that you can join the army at 18 and use handguns and military weapons, but you cant purchase a handgun until 21.	ANTI

Figure 1: Example of a debate dialogue turn between two users on the *gun control* topic, from 4FORUMS.COM.

Online debate websites are a particularly rich source of argumentative dialogic data (Fig. 1). On these websites, users debate and share their opinions on a variety of social and political issues. Previous work (Somasundaran and Wiebe, 2010; Walker et al., 2012c) has shown that stance classification in online debates is a challenging problem. While collective approaches that jointly predict user stance seem promising (Walker et al., 2012c; Hasan and Ng, 2013), the rich structure of online debate forums necessitates many modeling choices. For example, users publish opinions and reply and respond to each others' posts. In so doing, they may agree or disagree with either all or a portion of another user's post, suggesting that collective classifiers for stance may benefit from text-based disagreement modeling. Furthermore, one can model stance either at the author level—assuming that an author's stance is based on all of their posts on a topic (Burfoot et al., 2011)—or at

Proceedings of the 53rd Annual Meeting of the Association for Computational Linguistics and the 7th International Joint Conference on Natural Language Processing, pages 116–125,
Beijing, China, July 26-31, 2015.

the post level—assuming that an author's stance is post-specific and may vary across posts (Hasan and Ng, 2013). These decisions can drastically change the nature of stance models, so understanding their implications is critical.

In this paper, we develop a flexible modeling framework for stance classification using probabilistic soft logic (PSL) (Bach et al., 2013; Bach et al., 2015), a recently introduced probabilistic modeling framework.[1] PSL is a probabilistic programming system that allows models to be specified using a declarative, rule-like language. The resulting models are a special form of conditional random field, called a hinge-loss Markov random field, which admits highly scalable exact inference (Bach et al., 2013). Modeling stance in large, richly connected online debate forums requires a careful exploration of many modeling choices. This complex domain especially benefits from PSL's flexibility and scalability. PSL makes it easy to develop model variations and extensions, as one can readily incorporate new factors capturing additional intuitions about dependencies in a domain.

We evaluate our models on data from two debate sites, 4FORUMS and CREATEDEBATE (Walker et al., 2012b; Hasan and Ng, 2013), which we describe in detail in Section 2. Our experimental results show that there are important ramifications of several modeling decisions, including whether to use collective or non-collective models, to represent stance at the post level or the author level, and how to model disagreement. We find that with appropriate modeling choices, our approach leads to improvements of up to 11.5 percentage points of accuracy over simple classification approaches.

Our contributions include (1) a flexible, unified framework for modeling online debates, (2) extensive experimental study of many possible models on eight forum datasets, collected across two different debate websites, and (3) general modeling recommendations resulting from our empirical studies.

2 Online Debate Forums

Online debate forums represent richly structured argumentative dialogues. On these forums, users debate with each other in discussion threads on a variety of topics or issues, such as *gun control*, *gay marriage*, and *marijuana legalization*. Each discussion consists of a number of posts, which are short text documents authored by users of the forum. A post is either a reply to a previous post, or it is the start (root) of a thread. As users engage with each other, a thread branches out into a tree of argumentative interactions between the users. Forum users often post numerous times and across multiple discussions and topics, which creates a richly structured interaction graph. Online debates present different challenges than more controlled dialogic settings such as congressional debates. Posts are short and informal, there is limited external information about authors, and debate topics admit many modes of argumentation ranging from serious, to tangential, to sarcastic. The reply graph in online debates also has substantially different semantics to networks in other debate settings, such as the graph of speaker mentions in congressional debates. To illustrate this setting, Fig. 1 shows an example dialogue between two users who are debating their opinions on the topic of gun control.

In the context of online debate forums, *stance classification* (Thomas et al., 2006; Somasundaran and Wiebe, 2009) is the task of assigning stance labels with respect to a discussion topic, either at the level of the user or the level of the post. Stance is typically treated as a binary classification problem, with labels PRO and ANTI. In Fig. 1, both users' stances toward gun control are ANTI.

Previous work on stance in online debates has shown that contextual information given by reply links is important for stance classification (Walker et al., 2012a), and that collective classification often outperforms methods which treat each post independently. Hasan and Ng (2013) use conditional random fields (CRFs) to encourage opposite stances between sequences of posts, and Walker et al. (2012c) use MaxCut over explicitly given rebuttal links between posts to separate them into PRO and ANTI clusters. Sridhar et al. (2014) use hinge-loss Markov random fields (HL-MRFs) to encourage consistency between post level stance labels and observed post-level textual agreements and disagreements.

While the first two approaches leverage rebuttal or reply links, they model reply links as being indicative of opposite stances. However, as shown in Fig. 1, responses—even rebuttals—can occur be-

[1]PSL is an open-source Java toolkit, available here: http://psl.cs.umd.edu.

tween users with the same stance, which suggests the benefit of a more nuanced treatment of reply links. The approach of Sridhar et al. (2014) considers text-based agreement annotations between posts, though it requires that reply links are labeled. Accurate reply polarity labels are likely to be as expensive to obtain as the stance labels that we aim to predict. Noisy or sparse reply labels are cheaper, though likely to reduce performance. In this work, we show how to reason over uncertain reply label predictions to improve stance classification.

Also in the online debate setting, Hasan and Ng (2014) show the benefits of joint modeling to classify post-level stance and the authors' reasons for their stances. In contrast, in this work we focus on the dependencies between stance and polarity of replies.

In the context of opinion subgroup discovery, Abu-Jbara and Radev (2013) demonstrate the effectiveness of clustering users by opinion-target similarity. In contrast, Murakami and Raymond (2010) use simple recurring patterns such as "*that's a good idea*" to categorize reply links as *agree*, *disagree* or *neutral*, prior to using MaxCut for subgroup clustering of comment streams on government websites. This approach improves over a MaxCut approach that casts all reply links as disagreements. Building on this work, Lu et al. (2012) model unsupervised discovery of supporting and opposing groups of users for topics in online military forums. They improve upon a MaxCut baseline by formulating a linear program (LP) to combine multiple textual and reply-link signals, suggesting the benefits of jointly modeling textual and reply-link features.

In a different line of work, while Somasundaran and Wiebe (2010) do not use relational information between users or posts, their approach shows the benefit of modeling opinions and their targets at a fine-grained level using relational sentiment analysis techniques. Similarly, Wang and Cardie (2014) demonstrate the effectiveness of using sentiment analysis to identify disputes on Wikipedia Talk pages. Boltužić and Šnajder (2014) and Ghosh et al. (2014) study various linguistic features to model stance and agreement interactions respectively.

In the congressional debate setting, approaches using CRFs and similar collective techniques such as minimum-cut have also leveraged reply link

	4FORUMS	CREATEDEBATE
Users per topic	336	311
Posts per user, per topic	19	4
Words per user, per topic	2511	476
Words per post	134	124
Distinct reply links per user, per topic	6	3
Stance labels given for	Users	Posts
%Post-level reply links have opposite-stance users	71.6	73.9
%Author-level reply links have opposite-stance users	52.0	68.9

Table 1: Structural statistics averages for 4FORUMS and CREATEDEBATE.

polarity for improvements in stance classification (Thomas et al., 2006; Bansal et al., 2008; Balahur et al., 2009; Burfoot et al., 2011). However, these methods rely heavily on features specific to the congressional setting in order to predict link polarity, and make little use of textual features. In contrast, Abbott et al. (2011) use a range of linguistic features from the text of posts and their parents to classify agreement or disagreement between posts on the online debate website 4FORUMS.COM, without the goal of classifying stance.

In this work, we study datasets from two online debate websites: 4FORUMS.COM, from the Internet Argument Corpus (Walker et al., 2012b), and CREATEDEBATE.COM (Hasan and Ng, 2013). Table 1 shows statistics about these datasets including the average number of users per discussion topic and average number of posts authored. The best stance classification accuracy to date for online debate forums ranges from 70.1% on CONVINCEME.NET to 75.4% on CREATEDEBATE.COM (Walker et al., 2012c; Hasan and Ng, 2013). The web interface for CONVINCEME.NET enforces opposite stances for reply posts, making this dataset inapplicable for text-based disagreement modeling, and so we do not consider it in our experiments. In the more typical online debate forum corpora that we study, the presence of a reply, or even a textual disagreement between posts, does not necessarily indicate opposite stance (e.g. in gun control debates on 4Forums, 23% of disagreements correspond with same stance).

For our unified framework, we specify a hinge-loss Markov random field to reason jointly about stance and reply-link polarity labels. A closely related line of work focuses on improving structured prediction with domain knowledge modeled as constraints in the objective function (Chang et al., 2012; Ganchev et al., 2010; Mann and McCallum, 2010). Though more often used in semi-supervised settings, constraint-based learning can be especially appropriate for supervised learning when commonly used feature functions for linear models do not capture the richness of the data. Our HL-MRF formulation admits highly expressive features while maintaining a convex objective, thereby enjoying both tractability and a fully probabilistic interpretation.

3 Modeling Choices

We face multiple modeling decisions that may impact predictive performance when classifying stance in online debates. A key contribution of this work is the exploration of the ramifications of these choices. We consider the following variations on modeling: collective (**C**) versus local (**L**) classifiers, whether to explicitly model disagreement (**D**), and author-level (**A**) versus post-level (**P**) models.

Collective versus Local. Both collective and non-collective methods for stance prediction require a strong local text classifier. The methods proposed in this paper build upon the state-of-the-art local classification approach of Walker et al. (2012a), which trains a supervised classifier using features including n-grams, lexical category counts, and text lengths. We use logistic regression for the local classifier. These models will be referred to as *local* (**L**). In *collective* (**C**) classification approaches for stance prediction, the stance labels are all predicted jointly, leveraging relationships along the graph of replies. The simplest way to make use of reply links is to encode that the stance of posts (or authors) that reply to each other is likely to be opposite (Walker et al., 2012c; Hasan and Ng, 2013). Collective approaches attempt to find the most likely joint stance labeling that is consistent with both the local classifier's predictions and the alternation of stance along response threads. The alternating stance assumption is not necessarily a hard constraint, and may potentially be overridden by the local predictions. **C** and **L** models can be constructed with **A** or **P**-level granularity as described below, resulting in four modeling combinations.

Modeling Disagreement. As seen in Fig. 1 and Table 1, the assumption that reply links correspond to opposite stance is not always correct. This suggests the potential benefit of more nuanced models of agreement and disagreement. A natural disagreement modeling approach is to predict the polarity of reply links jointly with stance.

There are two variants of reply link polarity to consider. In *textual disagreement*, replying posts are coded as expressing agreement or disagreement with the text of the parent post. This may not correspond to a disagreement in stance *relative to the thread topic*. Some forum interfaces support user self-labeling of post reply links as rebuttals or agreements, thereby explicitly providing textual disagreement labels for posts. Alternatively, in the *stance disagreement* variant, reply links denote either same or opposite *stance* between users (posts). In Fig. 1, User 1 and User 2 disagree in text but have the same stance. For collective modeling of stance and disagreement, it is useful to consider the stance disagreement variant which identifies opposite and same-stance reply links, and jointly encourage stance predictions to be consistent with the disagreement predictions.

As with the local classification of stance, we can construct local classifiers for stance disagreement. In this work, for each reply link instance, we use a copy of the local stance classification features for each author/post at the ends of the reply link. The linguistic features further include discourse markers such as "actually" and "because" from the disagreement classifier of Abbott et al. (2011). Additionally, we use textual disagreement as a feature for stance disagreementwhen available. When reply links are not explicitly labeled as rebuttals or agreements, or only rebuttals are known, we instead predict textual disagreement using the features given above, trained on a separate data set with textual-disagreement labels.

Finally, with a stance disagreement classifier in hand, we can build collective models that predict stance based on predicted stance disagreement polarity. We denote these models as *disagreement* (**D**). When applied at one of **A** or **P**-level modeling, this yields two more possible modeling configurations. These models are certainly more complex than others we consider, but their design is consistent with intuition about the nature of discourse, so the added complexity may yield better accuracy.

All models:		Collective models only:		Disagreement models only:	
localPro(X1)	→ *pro*(X1)	*disagree*(X1, X2) ∧ *pro*(X1)	→ ¬ *pro*(X2)	*localDisagree*(X1, X2)	→ *disagree*(X1, X2)
¬ *localPro*(X1)	→ ¬ *pro*(X1)	*disagree*(X1, X2) ∧ ¬ *pro*(X1)	→ *pro*(X2)	¬ *localDisagree*(X1, X2)	→ ¬ *disagree*(X1, X2)
		¬ *disagree*(X1, X2) ∧ *pro*(X1)	→ *pro*(X2)	*pro*(X1) ∧ ¬ *pro*(X2)	→ *disagree*(X1, X2)
		¬ *disagree*(X1, X2) ∧ ¬ *pro*(X1)	→ ¬ *pro*(X2)	*pro*(X1) ∧ *pro*(X2)	→ ¬ *disagree*(X1, X2)
		disagree(X1, X2)	= 1	¬ *pro*(X1) ∧ ¬ *pro*(X2)	→ ¬ *disagree*(X1, X2)

Figure 2: PSL rules to define the collective classification models, both for post-level and author-level models. Each X is an author or a post, depending on the level of granularity that the model is applied at. The *disagree*(X_1, X_2) predicates apply to post reply links, and to pairs of authors connected by reply links.

Author-Level versus Post-Level. When modeling debates, stance classifiers can predict either the stance of a debate participant (i.e. an *author* (**A**)) (Burfoot et al., 2011), or the stance expressed by a specific dialogue act (i.e. a *post* (**P**)) (Hasan and Ng, 2013). The choice of prediction target may depend on the downstream goal, such as user modeling or the study of the dialogic expression of disagreement. From a philosophical perspective, authors are individuals who hold opinions, while posts are not. A post is simply a piece of text which may or may not express the opinions of its author.

Nevertheless, given a prediction target, either author or post, it may be beneficial to consider modeling at a different level of granularity. For example, Hasan and Ng (2013) find that post-level prediction accuracy can be improved by "clamping" all posts by a given author to the same stance in order to smooth their labels. Alternatively, author-level predictions may potentially be improved by first treating each post separately, thereby effectively giving a classifier more training examples, i.e. the number of *posts* instead of the number of *authors*. With this procedure, a final author-level prediction can be obtained by averaging the predictions over the posts for the author, trading the noisiness of post-level instances against the smoothing afforded by the final aggregation. When designing a stance classifier, the modeler must decide the level of granularity for the prediction target and find the best model therein.

4 A Collective Classification Framework

To study these choices, we build a flexible stance classification framework that implements the above variations using probabilistic soft logic (PSL) (Bach et al., 2015; Bach et al., 2013), a recently introduced probabilistic programming system. Like other probabilistic modeling frameworks, notably Markov logic (Richardson and Domingos, 2006), PSL uses a logic-like language for defining the potential functions for a conditional random field. However, unlike Markov logic, PSL makes inference tractable, even in the loopy author-level networks and the very large post-level networks of online debates.

PSL's tractability arises from the use of a special class of conditional random field models referred to as hinge-loss MRFs (HL-MRFs), which admit efficient, scalable and exact maximum a posteriori (MAP) inference (Bach et al., 2013). These models are defined over continuous random variables, and MAP inference is a convex optimization problem over these variables. Formally, a hinge-loss MRF defines a probability density function of the form

$$P(\mathbf{Y}|\mathbf{X}) = \frac{1}{\mathcal{Z}} \exp\Big(- \sum_{r=1}^{M} \lambda_r \phi_r(\mathbf{Y}, \mathbf{X})\Big), \quad (1)$$

where the entries of $\mathbf{Y}$ and $\mathbf{X}$ are in $[0, 1]$, λ is a vector of weight parameters, $\mathcal{Z}$ is a normalization constant, and

$$\phi_r(\mathbf{Y}, \mathbf{X}) = (\max\{l_r(\mathbf{Y}, \mathbf{X}), 0\})^{\rho_r} \quad (2)$$

is a *hinge-loss potential* specified by a linear function l_r and optional exponent $\rho_r \in \{1, 2\}$. Given a collection of first-order PSL rules, each instantiation of the rules maps to a hinge-loss potential function as in Equation 2, and the potential functions define an HL-MRF model. For example, $a \Rightarrow b \triangleq \max(a - b, 0)$, where a and b are ground variables, and $\max(a - b, 0)$ is a convex relaxation of logical implication, and which can be understood as its *distance to satisfaction*. For a full description of PSL, see (Bach et al., 2015).

The models we introduce are specified by the PSL rules in Fig. 2, with both post-level and author-level models following the same design. We denote the different modeling choices with the letters defined in Section 3. First, local logistic regression classifiers output stance probabilities based on textual features of posts or authors. All of the models begin with these real-valued stance predictions, encoded by the observed predicate *localPro*(X_i). The rules listed for all models encourage the inferred global predictions *pro*(X_i) to match these local predictions.

This defines the *local classification* models **L**, which are HL-MRFs with node potentials and no edge potentials, and which are equivalent to the local classifiers. The collective models extend the **L** models by adding edge potentials which encourage the stance labels to respect disagreement relationships along reply links. Specifically, every reply link between authors (for author-level models) or between posts (for post-level models) x_1 and x_2 is associated with a latent variable *disagree*(x_1, x_2). The rules encourage the global stance variables to respect the polarity of the disagreement variables (same stance, or opposite stance) and while also trying to match the stance classifiers. For the models that do not explicitly model disagreement, it is assumed that every reply edge constitutes a disagreement, i.e. *disagree*$(x_1, x_2) = 1$. These models are denoted **C**.

Otherwise, the disagreement variables are encouraged to match binary-valued predictions from the local disagreement classifiers. We binarize the predictions of the disagreement classifiers to encourage propagation. The disagreement variables are modeled jointly with the stance variables, and label information propagates in both directions between stance and disagreement variables. The full joint stance/disagreement collective models are denoted **D**. In the following, the models are denoted by pairs of letters according to their collectivity level and modeling granularity. For example, **AC** denotes collective classification performed at the author level, without joint modeling of disagreement. To train these models and use them for prediction, weight learning and MAP inference are performed using the structured perceptron algorithm and ADMM algorithm of Bach et al. (2013).

5 Experimental Evaluation

The goals of our experiments were to validate the proposed collective modeling framework, and to make substantive conclusions about the merits of the different possible modeling options described in Section 3. To this end, we evaluated the models on eight topics from 4FORUMS.COM (Walker et al., 2012b) and CREATEDEBATE.COM (Hasan and Ng, 2013), for classification tasks at both the author level and the post level. With comparison to Hasan and Ng (2013), our collective models (**C**) are essentially equivalent to their CRF, up to the form of the CRF potential function, which is not explicitly specified in the paper. A further goal of our experiments was to determine whether the modeling options in our more general CRF could improve performance over models with this structure.

On average, each topic-wise data set contains hundreds of authors and thousands of posts. The 4FORUMS data sets are annotated for stance at the author level, while CREATEDEBATE has stance labels at the post level. To perform post-level evaluations on 4FORUMS we apply author labels to the posts of each author, and on CREATEDEBATE we computed author labels by selecting the majority label of their posts. For 4FORUMS, since post-level stance labels correspond directly to author-level stance labels, we use averages of post-level predictions as the local classifier output for authors. Section 2 includes an overview of these debate forum data sets.

In the experiments, classification accuracy was estimated via five repeats of 5-fold cross-validation. In each fold, we ran logistic regression using the scikit-learn software package,[2] using the default settings, except for the L1 regularization trade-off parameter C which was tuned on a within-fold hold-out set consisting of 20% of the discussions within the fold. For the collective models, weight learning was performed on the same in-fold tuning sets. We trained via 700 iterations of structured perceptron, and ran the ADMM MAP inference algorithm to convergence at test time. On average, weight learning and inference took around 1 minute per fold.

The full results for author-level and post-level predictions are given in Table 2 and Table 3, respectively. In the tables, entries in bold identify statistically significant differences from the local classifier baseline under a paired t-test with significance level $\alpha = 0.05$. These results are summarized in Fig. 3, which shows box plots for the six possible models, computed over the final cross-validated accuracy scores of each of the four data

[2] Available at `http://scikit-learn.org/`.

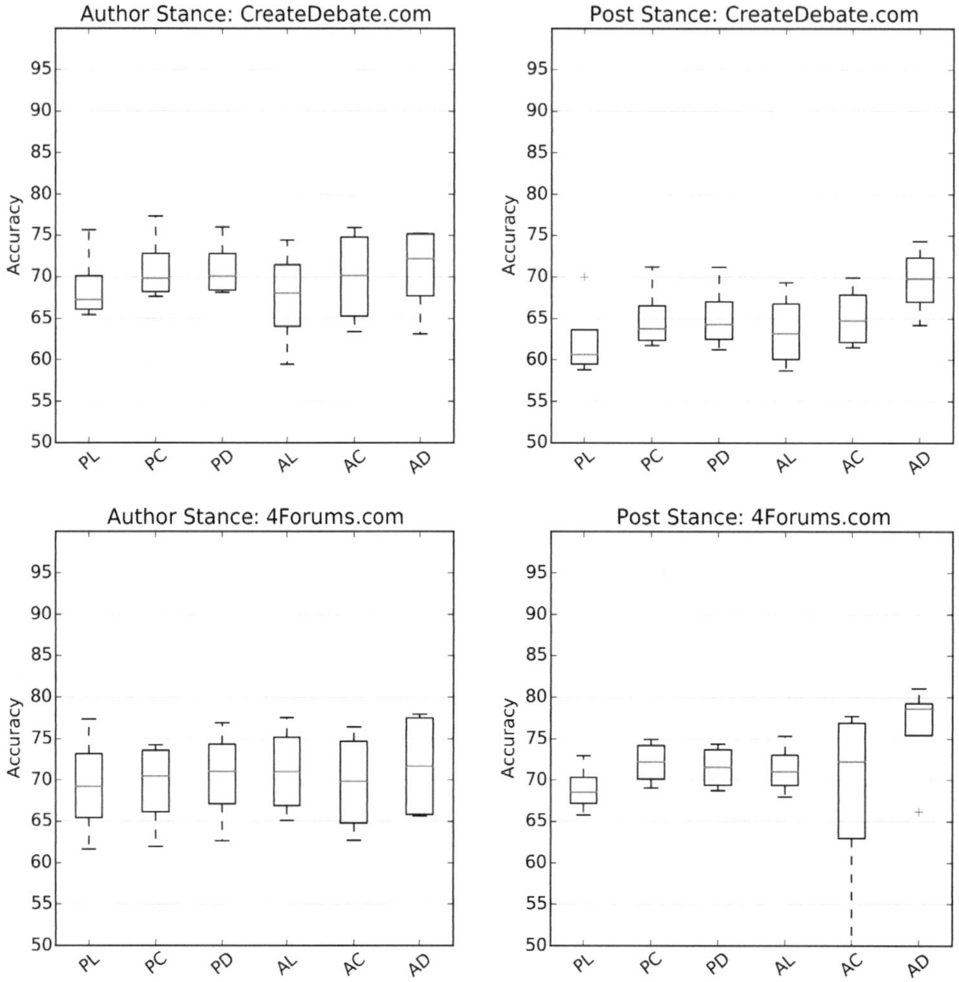

Figure 3: Overall accuracies per model for the author stance prediction task, computed over the final results for each of the four data sets per forum. Note that we expect significant variation in these plots, as the data sets are of varying degrees of difficulty.

sets from each forum. The overall trends can be seen by reading the box plots in each figure from left to right. In general, collective models outperform local models, and modeling disagreement further improves accuracy. Author-level modeling is typically better than post-level, even for the post-level prediction task. The improvements shown by collective models and author-level models are consistent with Hasan and Ng (2013)'s conclusion about the benefits of user-level constraints. This may suggest that posts only provide relatively noisy observations of the underlying author-level stance. Modeling at the author level results in more stable predictions, as noisy posts are pooled together. But here we also show that the full joint disagreement model at the author level, **AD**, performs the best overall, for both prediction tasks and for both forums, gaining up to 11.5 percentage points of post-level accuracy over the local post-level classifier.

A closer analysis reveals some subtleties. When comparing **D** models with **C** models in Fig. 3, disagreement modeling makes a much bigger difference at the author level than at the post level. This is likely impacted by the level of class imbalance for *disagreement* classification in the different levels of modeling. Disagreement, rather than agreement, between authors prompts many responses. Thus, reply links are more likely disagreements when measured at the post level, as seen in Ta-

	4FORUMS				CREATEDEBATE			
Models	Abortion	Evolution	Gay Marriage	Gun Control	Abortion	Gay Rights	Marijuana	Obama
PL	61.9 ± 4.3	76.6 ± 3.9	72.0 ± 3.6	66.4 ± 4.6	66.4 ± 5.2	70.2 ± 5.0	74.1 ± 6.5	**63.8 ± 8.7**
PC	63.4 ± 5.9	74.6 ± 4.1	73.7 ± 4.3	68.3 ± 5.5	**68.7 ± 5.7**	**72.6 ± 5.6**	75.4 ± 7.4	**66.1 ± 8.5**
PD	63.0 ± 5.4	76.7 ± 4.2	73.7 ± 4.6	67.9 ± 5.0	**69.5 ± 5.7**	**73.2 ± 5.9**	74.7 ± 7.0	**66.1 ± 8.5**
AL	64.9 ± 4.2	77.3 ± 2.9	74.5 ± 2.9	67.1 ± 4.5	65.2 ± 6.5	69.5 ± 4.4	74.0 ± 6.6	59.0 ± 7.5
AC	**66.0 ± 5.0**	74.4 ± 4.2	75.7 ± 5.1	61.5 ± 5.6	65.8 ± 7.0	**73.6 ± 3.5**	73.9 ± 7.6	**62.5 ± 8.3**
AD	**65.8 ± 4.4**	**78.7 ± 3.3**	**77.1 ± 4.4**	67.1 ± 5.4	**67.4 ± 7.5**	**74.0 ± 5.3**	74.8 ± 7.5	**63.0 ± 8.3**

Table 2: Author stance classification accuracy and standard deviation for 4FORUMS (*left*) and CREATEDEBATE (*right*), estimated via 5 repeats of 5-fold cross-validation. Bolded figures indicate statistically significant ($\alpha = 0.05$) improvement over AL, the baseline model for the author stance classification task.

	4FORUMS				CREATEDEBATE			
Models	Abortion	Evolution	Gay Marriage	Gun Control	Abortion	Gay Rights	Marijuana	Obama
PL	66.1 ± 2.5	72.4 ± 4.2	69.0 ± 2.7	67.8 ± 3.5	60.2 ± 3.2	62.7 ± 4.4	68.1 ± 6.1	59.4 ± 6.0
PC	**70.5 ± 2.5**	**74.1 ± 3.8**	**73.2 ± 3.1**	**69.1 ± 3.0**	**62.8 ± 3.8**	**66.1 ± 4.9**	68.7 ± 7.9	**61.1 ± 6.6**
PD	**69.7 ± 2.5**	**73.9 ± 4.0**	**72.5 ± 3.0**	**68.8 ± 3.0**	**62.6 ± 4.1**	**66.2 ± 5.4**	69.1 ± 7.4	**61.0 ± 6.6**
AL	**74.7 ± 7.1**	73.0 ± 5.7	70.3 ± 6.0	68.7 ± 5.3	61.6 ± 9.8	63.7 ± 5.3	66.7 ± 6.7	59.7 ± 13.6
AC	**76.8 ± 8.1**	68.3 ± 5.3	72.7 ± 11.1	46.9 ± 8.0	63.4 ± 12.4	**71.2 ± 8.4**	66.9 ± 9.0	63.7 ± 15.6
AD	**77.0 ± 8.9**	**80.3 ± 5.5**	**80.5 ± 8.5**	65.4 ± 8.3	**66.8 ± 12.2**	**72.7 ± 8.9**	69.0 ± 8.3	63.5 ± 16.3

Table 3: Post stance classification accuracy and standard deviations for 4FORUMS (*left*) and CREATEDEBATE (*right*), estimated via 5 repeats of 5-fold cross-validation. Bolded figures indicate statistically significant ($\alpha = 0.05$) improvement over PL, the baseline model for the post stance classification task.

ble 1. Therefore, enforcing disagreement may be a better assumption at the post level, and the nuanced disagreement model is not necessary in this case. The overall improvements in accuracy from disagreement modeling for post-level models were small.

On the other hand, the assumption that reply edges constitute disagreement is less accurate when modeling at the author level (see Table 1). In this case, the full joint disagreement model is necessary to obtain good performance. In an extreme example, the two datasets with the lowest disagreement rates at the author level are evolution (44.4%) and gun control (50.7%) from 4FORUMS. The **AC** classifier performed very poorly for these data sets, dropping to 46.9% accuracy in one instance, as the "opposite stance" assumption did not hold (Tables 2 and 3). The full joint disagreement model **AD** performed much better, in fact achieving an outstanding accuracy rates of 80.3% and 80.5% for posts on evolution and gay marriage respectively. To illustrate the benefits of author-level disagreement modeling, Fig. 4 shows a post for an author whose stance towards gun control is correctly predicted by **AD** but not the **AC** model,

Text	Stance
Post: I agree with everything except the last part. Safe gun storage is very important, and sensible storage requirements have two important factors.	ANTI
Reply: I can agree with this. And in case it seemed otherwise, I know full well how to store guns safely, and why it's necessary. My point was that I don't like the idea of such a law, especially when you consider the problem of enforcement.	ANTI

Figure 4: A post-reply pair by 4FORUMS.COM authors whose gun control stance is correctly predicted by **AD**, but not by **AC**.

along with a subsequent reply. The authors largely agree with each other's views, which the joint disagreement model leverages, while the simpler collective model encourages opposite stance due to the presence of reply links between them.

To summarize our conclusions from these experiments, the results suggest that author-level modeling is the preferred strategy, regardless of the prediction task. In this scenario, it is essential to explicitly model disagreement in the collective classifier. Our top performing **AD** model statistically significantly outperforms the respective prediction task baseline on 6 out of 8 topics for both tasks with p-values less than 0.001. Based on our experimental results, we recommend the full author-disagreement model **AD** as the classifier of choice.

6 Discussion and Future Work

The prediction of user stance in online debate forums is a valuable task, and modeling debate dialogue is complex and requires many decisions such collective or non-collective reasoning, nuanced or naive use of disagreement information, and post versus author-level modeling granularity. We systematically explore each choice, and in doing so build a unified joint framework that incorporates each salient decision. Our method uses a hinge-loss Markov random field to encourage consistency between local classifier predictions for stance and disagreement information. We find that modeling at the author level gives better predictive performance regardless of the granularity of the prediction task, and that nuanced disagreement modeling is of particular importance for author-level collective modeling. The resulting collective classifier gives improved predictive performance over both the simple non-collective and standard collective approaches, with a running time overhead of only a few minutes, thanks to the efficient nature of hinge-loss MRFs.

There are many directions for future work. Our results have found that collective reasoning can also be beneficial at the post level, as previously reported by Hasan and Ng (2013). It is likely that a multi-level model for a combination of post- and author-level collective modeling of both stance and disagreement could bring further improvements in performance. It would also be informative to explore dynamic models which elucidate trends of opinions over time. Another direction is to model influence between users in online debate forums, and to identify the most influential users who are able to convince other users to change their opinions. Finally, we note that stance and disagreement classification are both challenging and important problems, and going forward, there is likely to be much room for improvement in these prediction tasks.

Acknowledgments

This work was supported by NSF grant IIS1218488, and IARPA via DoI/NBC contract number D12PC00337. The U.S. Government is authorized to reproduce and distribute reprints for governmental purposes notwithstanding any copyright annotation thereon. Disclaimer: The views and conclusions contained herein are those of the authors and should not be interpreted as necessarily representing the official policies or endorsements, either expressed or implied, of IARPA, DoI/NBC, or the U.S. Government.

References

Rob Abbott, Marilyn Walker, Jean E. Fox Tree, Pranav Anand, Robeson Bowmani, and Joseph King. 2011. How can you say such things?!?: Recognizing disagreement in informal political argument. In *ACL Workshop on Language and Social Media*.

Amjad Abu-Jbara and Dragomir R Radev. 2013. Identifying opinion subgroups in Arabic online discussions. In *ACL*.

Stephen H. Bach, Bert Huang, Ben London, and Lise Getoor. 2013. Hinge-loss Markov random fields: Convex inference for structured prediction. In *Uncertainty in Artificial Intelligence (UAI)*.

S. H. Bach, M. Broecheler, B. Huang, and L. Getoor. 2015. Hinge-loss Markov random fields and probabilistic soft logic. arXiv:1505.04406 [cs.LG].

Alexandra Balahur, Zornitsa Kozareva, and Andres Montoyo. 2009. Determining the polarity and source of opinions expressed in political debates. *Computational Linguistics and Intelligent Text Processing*.

Mohit Bansal, Claire Cardie, and Lillian Lee. 2008. The power of negative thinking: Exploiting label disagreement in the min-cut classification framework. *COLING*.

Filip Boltužić and Jan Šnajder. 2014. Back up your stance: recognizing arguments in online discussions. In *ACL Workshop on Argumentation Mining*.

Clinton Burfoot, Steven Bird, and Timothy Baldwin. 2011. Collective classification of congressional floor-debate transcripts. In *ACL*.

Ming-Wei Chang, Lev Ratinov, and Dan Roth. 2012. Structured learning with constrained conditional models. *Machine learning*, 88(3):399–431.

Kuzman Ganchev, Joao Graça, Jennifer Gillenwater, and Ben Taskar. 2010. Posterior regularization for structured latent variable models. *Machine Learning*, 11:2001–2049.

Debanjan Ghosh, Smaranda Muresan, Nina Wacholder, Mark Aakhus, and Matthew Mitsui. 2014. Analyzing argumentative discourse units in online interactions. In *ACL Workshop on Argumentation Mining*.

Kazi Saidul Hasan and Vincent Ng. 2013. Stance classification of ideological debates: Data, models, features, and constraints. *International Joint Conference on Natural Language Processing*.

Kazi Saidul Hasan and Vincent Ng. 2014. Why are you taking this stance? Identifying and classifying reasons in ideological debates. In *EMNLP*.

Y. Lu, H. Wang, C. Zhai, and D. Roth. 2012. Unsupervised discovery of opposing opinion networks from forum discussions. In *CIKM*.

Gideon S Mann and Andrew McCallum. 2010. Generalized expectation criteria for semi-supervised learning with weakly labeled data. *Machine Learning*, 11:955–984.

Akiko Murakami and Rudy Raymond. 2010. Support or Oppose? Classifying positions in online debates from reply activities and opinion expressions. In *ACL*.

Matthew Richardson and Pedro Domingos. 2006. Markov logic networks. *Machine learning*, 62(1-2).

Swapna Somasundaran and Janyce Wiebe. 2009. Recognizing stances in online debates. In *ACL and AFNLP*.

Swapna Somasundaran and Janyce Wiebe. 2010. Recognizing stances in ideological on-line debates. In *NAACL HLT 2010 Workshop on Computational Approaches to Analysis and Generation of Emotion in Text*.

Dhanya Sridhar, Lise Getoor, and Marilyn Walker. 2014. Collective stance classification of posts in online debate forums. In *ACL Joint Workshop on Social Dynamics and Personal Attributes in Social Media*.

Matt Thomas, Bo Pang, and Lillian Lee. 2006. Get out the vote: Determining support or opposition from Congressional floor-debate transcripts. In *EMNLP*.

Marilyn Walker, Pranav Anand, Rob Abbott, Jean E. Fox Tree, Craig Martell, and Joseph King. 2012a. That's your evidence?: Classifying stance in online political debate. *Decision Support Sciences*.

Marilyn Walker, Pranav Anand, Robert Abbott, and Jean E. Fox Tree. 2012b. A corpus for research on deliberation and debate. In *LREC*.

Marilyn Walker, Pranav Anand, Robert Abbott, and Richard Grant. 2012c. Stance classification using dialogic properties of persuasion. In *NAACL*.

Lu Wang and Claire Cardie. 2014. A piece of my mind: A sentiment analysis approach for online dispute detection. In *ACL*.

Low-Rank Regularization for Sparse Conjunctive Feature Spaces: An Application to Named Entity Classification

Audi Primadhanty
Universitat Politècnica de Catalunya
primadhanty@cs.upc.edu

Xavier Carreras **Ariadna Quattoni**
Xerox Research Centre Europe
xavier.carreras@xrce.xerox.com
ariadna.quattoni@xrce.xerox.com

Abstract

Entity classification, like many other important problems in NLP, involves learning classifiers over sparse high-dimensional feature spaces that result from the conjunction of elementary features of the entity mention and its context. In this paper we develop a low-rank regularization framework for training max-entropy models in such sparse conjunctive feature spaces. Our approach handles conjunctive feature spaces using matrices and induces an implicit low-dimensional representation via low-rank constraints. We show that when learning entity classifiers under minimal supervision, using a seed set, our approach is more effective in controlling model capacity than standard techniques for linear classifiers.

1 Introduction

Many important problems in NLP involve learning classifiers over sparse high-dimensional feature spaces that result from the conjunction of elementary features. For example, to classify an entity in a document, it is standard to exploit features of the left and right context in which the entity occurs as well as spelling features of the entity mention itself. These sets of features can be grouped into vectors which we call elementary feature vectors. In our example, there will be one elementary feature vector for the left context, one for the right context and one for the features of the mention. Observe that, when the elementary vectors consist of binary indicator features, the outer product of any pair of vectors represents all conjunctions of the corresponding elementary features.

Ideally, we would like to train a classifier that can leverage all conjunctions of elementary features, since among them there might be some that are discriminative for the classification task at hand. However, allowing for such expressive high dimensional feature space comes at a cost: data sparsity becomes a key challenge and controlling the capacity of the model is crucial to avoid overfitting the training data.

The problem of data sparsity is even more severe when the goal is to train classifiers with minimal supervision, i.e. small training sets. For example, in the entity classification setting we might be interested in training a classifier using only a small set of examples of each entity class. This is a typical scenario in an industrial setting, where developers are interested in classifying entities according to their own classification schema and can only provide a handful of examples of each class.

A standard approach to control the capacity of a linear classifier is to use ℓ_1 or ℓ_2 regularization on the parameter vector. However, this type of regularization does not seem to be effective when dealing with sparse conjunctive feature spaces. The main limitation is that ℓ_1 and ℓ_2 regularization can not let the model give weight to conjunctions that have not been observed at training. Without such ability it is unlikely that the model will generalize to novel examples, where most of the conjunctions will be unseen in the training set.

Of course, one could impose a strong prior on the weight vector so that it assigns weight to unseen conjunctions, but how can we build such a prior? What kind of reasonable constraints can we put on unseen conjunctions?

Another common approach to handle high dimensional conjunctive feature spaces is to manually design the feature function so that it includes

Proceedings of the 53rd Annual Meeting of the Association for Computational Linguistics and the 7th International Joint Conference on Natural Language Processing, pages 126–135,
Beijing, China, July 26-31, 2015.

only a subset of "relevant" conjunctions. But designing such a feature function can be time consuming and one might need to design a new feature function for each classification task. Ideally, we would have a learning algorithm that does not require such feature engineering and that it can automatically leverage rich conjunctive feature spaces.

In this paper we present a solution to this problem by developing a regularization framework specifically designed for sparse conjunctive feature spaces. Our approach results in a more effective way of controlling model capacity and it does not require feature engineering.

Our strategy is based on:

- Employing tensors to define the scoring function of a max-entropy model as a multilinear form that computes weighted inner products between elementary vectors.
- Forcing the model to induce low-dimensional embeddings of elementary vectors via low-rank regularization on the tensor parameters.

The proposed regularization framework is based on a simple conceptual trick. The standard approach to handle conjunctive feature spaces in NLP is to regard the parameters of the linear model as long vectors computing an inner product with a high dimensional feature representation that lists explicitly all possible conjunctions. Instead, the parameters of our the model will be tensors and the compatibility score between an input pattern and a class will be defined as the sum of multilinear functions over elementary vectors.

We then show that the rank[1] of the tensor has a very natural interpretation. It can be seen as the intrinsic dimensionality of a latent embedding of the elementary feature vectors. Thus by imposing a low-rank penalty on the tensor parameters we are encouraging the model to induce a low-dimensional projection of the elementary feature vectors . Using the rank itself as a regularization constraint in the learning algorithm would result in a non-convex optimization. Instead, we follow a standard approach which is to use the nuclear norm as a convex relaxation of the rank.

In summary the main contributions of this paper are:

- We develop a new regularization framework for training max-entropy models in high-dimensional sparse conjunctive feature spaces. Since the proposed regularization implicitly induces a low dimensional embedding of feature vectors, our algorithm can also be seen as a way of implicitly learning a latent variable model.
- We present a simple convex learning algorithm for training the parameters of the model.
- We conduct experiments on learning entity classifiers with minimal supervision. Our results show that the proposed regularization framework is better for sparse conjunctive feature spaces than standard ℓ_2 and ℓ_1 regularization. These results make us conclude that encouraging the max-entropy model to operate on a low-dimensional space is an effective way of controlling the capacity of the model an ensure good generalization.

2 Entity Classification with Log-linear Models

The formulation we develop in this paper applies to any prediction task whose inputs are some form of tuple. We focus on classification of entity mentions, or entities in the context of a sentence. Formally, our input objects are tuples $x = \langle l, e, r \rangle$ consisting of an entity e, a left context l and a right context r. The goal is to classify x into one entity class in the set $\mathcal{Y}$.

We will use log-linear models of the form:

$$\Pr(y \mid x; \theta) = \frac{\exp\{s_\theta(x, y)\}}{\sum_{y'} \exp\{s_\theta(x, y')\}} \quad (1)$$

where $s_\theta : \mathcal{X} \times \mathcal{Y} \to \mathbb{R}$ is a scoring function of entity tuples with a candidate class, and θ are the parameters of this function, to be specified below.

In the literature it is common to employ a feature-based linear model. That is, one defines a feature function $\phi : \mathcal{X} \to \{0, 1\}^n$ that represents entity tuples in an n-dimensional binary feature space[2], and the model has a weight vector for each class, $\theta = \{\mathbf{w}_y\}_{y \in \mathcal{Y}}$. Then $s_\theta(x, y) = \phi(x) \cdot \mathbf{w}_y$.

[1]There are many ways of defining the rank of a tensor. In this paper we *matricize* tensors into matrices and use the rank of the resulting matrix. Matricization is also referred to as unfolding.

[2]In general, all models in this paper accept real-valued feature functions. But we focus on binary *indicator* features because in practice these are the standard type of features in NLP classifiers, and the ones we use here. In fact, in this paper we develop feature spaces based on *products* of elementary feature functions, in which case the resulting representations correspond to conjunctions of the elementary features.

3 Low-rank Entity Classification Models

In this section we propose a specific family of models for classifying entity tuples.

3.1 A Low-rank Model of Left-Right Contexts

We start from the observation that when representing tuple objects such as $x = \langle l, e, r\rangle$ with features, we often depart from a feature representation of each element of the tuple. Hence, let ϕ_{l} and ϕ_{r} be two feature functions representing left and right contexts, with binary dimensions d_1 and d_2 respectively. For now, we will define a model that ignores the entity mention e and makes predictions using context features. It is natural to define conjunctions of left and right features. Hence, in its most general form, one can define a matrix $\mathbf{W}_y \in \mathbb{R}^{d_1 \times d_2}$ for each class, such that $\theta = \{\mathbf{W}_y\}_{y \in \mathcal{Y}}$ and the score is:

$$s_\theta(\langle l, e, r\rangle, y) = \phi_{\mathrm{l}}(l)^\top \mathbf{W}_y \phi_{\mathrm{r}}(r) \quad . \quad (2)$$

Note that this corresponds to a feature-based linear model operating in the product space of ϕ_{l} and ϕ_{r}, that is, the score has one term for each pair of features: $\sum_{i,j} \phi_{\mathrm{l}}(l)[i]\ \phi_{\mathrm{r}}(r)[j]\ \mathbf{W}_y[i,j]$. Note also that it is trivial to include elementary features of ϕ_{l} and ϕ_{r}, in addition to conjunctions, by having a constant dimension in each of the two representations set to 1.

In all, the model in Eq. (2) is very expressive, with the caveat that it can easily overfit the data, specially when we work only with a handful of labeled examples. The standard way to control the capacity of a linear model is via ℓ_1 or ℓ_2 regularization.

Regarding our parameters as matrices allows us to control the capacity of the model via regularizers that favor parameter matrices with low rank. To see the effect of these regularizers, consider that $\mathbf{W}_y$ has rank k, and let $\mathbf{W}_y = \mathbf{U}_y \mathbf{\Sigma}_y \mathbf{V}_y^\top$ be the singular value decomposition, where $\mathbf{U}_y \in \mathbb{R}^{d_1 \times k}$ and $\mathbf{V}_y \in \mathbb{R}^{d_2 \times k}$ are orthonormal projections and $\mathbf{\Sigma}_y \in \mathbb{R}^{k \times k}$ is a diagonal matrix of singular values. We can rewrite the score function as

$$s_\theta(\langle l, e, r\rangle, y) = (\phi_{\mathrm{l}}(l)^\top \mathbf{U}_y)\ \mathbf{\Sigma}_y\ (\mathbf{V}_y^\top \phi_{\mathrm{r}}(r)) \quad . \quad (3)$$

In words, the rank k is the *intrinsic dimensionality* of the inner product behind the score function. A low-rank regularizer will favor parameter matrices that have low intrinsic dimensionality. Below we describe a convex optimization for low-rank models using *nuclear norm* regularization.

3.2 Adding Entity Features

The model above classifies entities based only on the context. Here we propose an extension to make use of features of the entity. Let $\mathcal{T}$ be a set of possible entity feature tags, i.e. tags that describe an entity, such as IsCapitalized, ContainsDigits, SingleToken, ... Let ϕ_{e} be a feature function representing entities. For this case, to simplify our expression, we will use a set notation and denote by $\phi_{\mathrm{e}}(e) \subseteq \mathcal{T}$ the set of feature tags that describe e. Our model will be defined with one parameter matrix per feature tag and class label, i.e. $\theta = \{\mathbf{W}_{t,y}\}_{t \in \mathcal{T}, y \in \mathcal{Y}}$. The model form is:

$$s_\theta(\langle l, e, r\rangle, y) = \sum_{t \in \phi_{\mathrm{e}}(e)} \phi_{\mathrm{l}}(l)^\top \mathbf{W}_{t,y} \ .\phi_{\mathrm{r}}(r). \quad (4)$$

3.3 Learning with Low-rank Constraints

In this section we describe a convex procedure to learn models of the above form that have low rank. We will define an objective that combines a loss and a regularization term.

Our first observation is that our parameters are a tensor with up to four axes, namely left and right context representations, entity features, and entity classes. While a matrix has a clear definition of rank, it is not the case for general tensors, and there exist various definitions in the literature. The technique that we use is based on *matricization* of the tensor, that is, turning the tensor into a matrix that has the same parameters as the tensor but organized in two axes. This is done by partitioning the tensor axes into two sets, one for matrix rows and another for columns. Once the tensor has been turned into a matrix, we can use the standard definition of matrix rank. A main advantage of this approach is that we can make use of standard routines like singular value decomposition (SVD) to decompose the matricized tensor. This is the main reason behind our choice.

In general, different ways of partitioning the tensor axes will lead to different notions of intrinsic dimensions. In our case we choose the left context axes as the row dimension, and the rest of axes as the column dimension.[3] In this section, we will

[3] In preliminary experiments we tried variations, such as having right prefixes in the columns, and left prefixes, entity tags and classes in the rows. We only observer minor, non-significant variations in the results.

denote as $\mathbf{W}$ the matricized version of the parameters θ of our models.

The second observation is that minimizing the rank of a matrix is a non-convex problem. We make use of a convex relaxation based on the nuclear norm (Srebro and Shraibman, 2005). The *nuclear norm*[4] of a matrix $\mathbf{W}$, denoted $\|\mathbf{W}\|_\star$, is the sum of its singular values: $\|\mathbf{W}\|_\star = \sum_i \mathbf{\Sigma}_{i,i}$ where $\mathbf{W} = \mathbf{U}\mathbf{\Sigma}\mathbf{V}^\top$ is the singular value decomposition of $\mathbf{W}$. This norm has been used in several applications in machine learning as a convex surrogate for imposing low rank, e.g. (Srebro et al., 2004).

Thus, the nuclear norm is used as a regularizer. With this, we define our objective as follows:

$$\operatorname*{argmin}_{\mathbf{W}} L(\mathbf{W}) + \tau R(\mathbf{W}) \quad , \tag{5}$$

where $L(\mathbf{W})$ is a convex loss function, $R(\mathbf{W})$ is a regularizer, and τ is a constant that trades off error and capacity. In experiments we will compare nuclear norm regularization with ℓ_1 and ℓ_2 regularizers. In all cases we use the negative log-likelihood as loss function, denoting the training data as $\mathcal{D}$:

$$L(\mathbf{W}) = \sum_{(\langle l,e,r\rangle,y)\in\mathcal{D}} -\log \Pr(y \mid \langle l,e,r\rangle;\mathbf{W}) \quad . \tag{6}$$

To solve the objective in Eq. (5) we use a simple optimization scheme known as *forward-backward splitting (FOBOS)* (Duchi and Singer, 2009). In a series of iterations, this algorithm performs a gradient update followed by a proximal projection of the parameters. Such projection depends on the regularizer used: for ℓ_1 it thresholds the parameters; for ℓ_2 it scales them; and for nuclear-norm regularization it thresholds the singular values. This means that, for nuclear norm regularization, each iteration requires to decompose $\mathbf{W}$ using SVD. See (Madhyastha et al., 2014) for details about this optimization for a related application.

4 Related Work

The main aspect of our approach is the use of a spectral penalty (i.e., the rank) to control the capacity of multilinear functions parameterized by matrices or tensors. Quattoni et al. (2014) used nuclear-norm regularization to learn latent-variable max-margin sequence taggers. Madhyastha et al. (2014) defined bilexical distributions parameterized by matrices which result lexical embeddings tailored for a particular linguistic relation. Like in our case, the low-dimensional latent projections in these papers are learned implicitly by imposing low-rank constraints on the predictions of the model.

Lei et al. (2014) also use low-rank tensor learning in the context of dependency parsing, where like in our case dependencies are represented by conjunctive feature spaces. While the motivation is similar, their technical solution is different. We use the technique of matricization of a tensor combined with a nuclear-norm relaxation to obtain a convex learning procedure. In their case they explicitly look for a low-dimensional factorization of the tensor using a greedy alternating optimization.

Also recently, Yao et al. (2013) have framed entity classification as a low-rank matrix completion problem. The idea is based on the fact that if two entities (in rows) have similar descriptions (in columns) they should have similar classes. The low-rank structure of the matrix defines intrinsic representations of entities and feature descriptions. The same idea was applied to relation extraction (Riedel et al., 2013), using a matrix of entity pairs times descriptions that corresponds to a matricization of an entity-entity-description tensor. Very recently Singh et al. (2015) explored alternative ways of applying low-rank constraints to tensor-based relation extraction.

Another aspect of this paper is training entity classification models using minimal supervision, which has been addressed by multiple works in the literature. A classical successful approach for this problem is to use co-training (Blum and Mitchell, 1998): learn two classifiers that use different views of the data by using each other's predictions. In the same line, Collins and Singer (1999) trained entity classifiers by bootstraping from an initial set of seeds, using a boosting version of co-training. Seed sets have also been exploited by graphical model approaches. Haghighi and Klein (2006) define a graphical model that is soft-constrained such that the prediction for an unlabeled example agrees with the labels of seeds that are distributionally similar. Li et al. (2010) present a Bayesian approach to expand an initial seed set, with the goal of creating a gazetteer.

Another approach to entity recognition that, like in our case, learns projections of contextual features is the method by Ando and Zhang (2005).

[4] Also known as the trace norm.

Class	10-30 Seed	Nb Mentions 10-30	40-120	640-1920	All
PER	clinton, dole, arafat, yeltsin, wasim akram, lebed, dutroux, waqar younis, mushtaq ahmed, croft	334	747	3,133	6,516
LOC	u.s., england, germany, britain, australia, france, spain, pakistan, italy, china	1,384	2,885	5,812	6,159
ORG	reuters, u.n., oakland, puk, osce, cincinnati, eu, nato, ajax, honda	295	699	3,435	5,271
MISC	russian, german, british, french, dutch, english, israeli, european, iraqi, australian	611	1326	3,085	3,205
O	year, percent, thursday, government, police, results, tuesday, soccer, president, monday, friday, people, minister, sunday, division, week, time, state, market, years, officials, group, company, saturday, match, at, world, home, august, standings	5,326	11,595	31,071	36,673

Table 1: For each entity class, the seed of entities for the **10-30** set, together with the number of mentions in the training data that involve entities in the seed for various sizes of the seeds.

They define a set of auxiliary tasks, which can be supervised using unlabeled data, and find a projection of the data that works well as input representation for the auxiliary tasks. This representation is then used for the target task.

More recently Neelakantan and Collins (2014) presented another approach to gazetteer expansion using an initial seed. A novel aspect is the use of Canonical Correlation Analysis (CCA) to compute embeddings of entity contexts, that are used by the named entity classifier. Like in our case, their method learns a compressed representation of contexts that helps prediction.

5 Experiments

In this section we evaluate our regularization framework for training models in high-dimensional sparse conjunctive feature spaces. We run experiments on learning entity classifiers with minimal supervision. We focus on classification of unseen entities to highlight the ability of the regularizer to generalize over conjunctions that are not observed at training. We simulate minimal supervision using the CoNLL-2003 Shared Task data (Tjong Kim Sang and De Meulder, 2003), and compare the performance to ℓ_1 and ℓ_2 regularizers.

5.1 Minimal Supervision Task

We use a minimal supervision setting where we provide the algorithm a seed of entities for each class, that is, a list of entities that is representative for that class. The assumption is that any mention of an entity in the seed is a positive example for the corresponding class. Given unlabeled data and a seed of entities for each class, the goal is to learn a model that correctly classifies mentions of entities that are not in the seed. In addition to standard entity classes, we also consider a special non-entity class, which is part of the classification but is excluded from evaluation.

Note that named entity classification for *unseen* entities is a challenging problem. Even in the standard fully-supervised scenario, when we measure the performance of state-of-the-art methods on unseen entities, the F1 values are in the range of 60%. This represents a significant drop with respect to the standard metrics for named entity recognition, which consider all entity mentions of the test set irrespective of whether they appear in the training data or not, and where F1 values at 90% levels are obtained (e.g. (Ratinov and Roth, 2009)). This suggests that part of the success of state-of-the-art models is in storing known entities together with their type (in the form of gazetteers or directly in lexicalized parameters of the model).

5.2 Setting

We use the CoNLL-2003 English data, which is annotated with four types: person (PER), location (LOC), organization (ORG), and miscellaneous (MISC). In addition, the data is tagged with parts-of-speech (PoS), and we compute word clusters running the Brown clustering algorithm (Brown et al., 1992) on the words in the training set.

We consider annotated entity phrases as candidate entities, and all single nouns that are not part of an entity as candidate non-entities (O). Both candidate entities and non-entities will be referred to as candidates in the remaining of this section. We lowercase all candidates and remove the am-

Features	Window	Bag-of-words		N-grams	
		Lexical	Cluster	Lexical	Cluster
Elementary features of left and right contexts	1	13.63	**14.59**	13.63	**14.59**
	2	**15.49**	13.86	13.08	**13.54**
	3	12.18	**14.45**	12.14	**13.28**
Only full conjunctions of left and right contexts	1	12.90	**13.75**	12.90	**13.75**
	2	8.59	**8.85**	12.31	**12.43**
	3	8.57	**10.59**	10.15	**10.49**
Elementary features and all conjunctions of left and right contexts	1	15.30	**16.98**	15.30	**16.98**
	2	**13.26**	12.89	14.28	**15.33**
	3	**11.87**	11.54	**13.94**	**13.15**

Table 2: Average-F1 of classification of unseen entity candidates on development data, using the **10-30** training seed and ℓ_2 regularization, for different conjunctive spaces (elementary only, full conjunctions, all). **Bag-of-words** elementary features contain all clusters/PoS in separate windows to the left and to the right of the candidate. **N-grams** elementary features contain all n-grams of clusters/PoS in separate left and right windows (e.g. for size 3 it includes unigrams, bigrams and trigrams on each side).

biguous ones (i.e., those with more than one label in different mentions).[5]

To simulate a minimal supervision, we create supervision seeds by picking the n most frequent training candidates for entity types, and the m most frequent candidate non-entities. We create seeds of various sizes n-m, namely **10-30**, **40-120**, **640-1920**, as well as **all** of the candidates. For each seed, the training set consists of all training mentions that involve entities in the seed. Table 1 shows the smaller seed, as well as the number of mentions for each seed size.

For evaluation we use the development and test sections of the data, but we remove the instances of candidates in the training data (i.e., that are in the **all** seed). We do not remove instances that are ambiguous in the tests. [6] As evaluation metric we use the average F1 score computed over all entity types, excluding the non-entity type.

[5]In the CoNLL-2003 English training set, only 235 candidates are ambiguous out of 13,441 candidates, i.e. less than 2%. This suggests that in this data the difficulty behind the task is in recognizing and classifying unseen entities, and not in disambiguating known entities in a certain context.

[6]After removing the ambiguous candidates from the training data, and removing candidates seen in the training from the development and test sets, this is the number of mentions (and number of unique candidates in parenthesis) in the data used in our experiments:

	training	dev.	test
PER	6,516 (3,489)	1,040 (762)	1,342 (925)
LOC	6,159 (987)	176 (128)	246 (160)
ORG	5,271 (2,149)	400 (273)	638 (358)
MISC	3,205 (760)	177 (142)	213 (152)
O	36,673 (5,821)	951 (671)	995 (675)

5.3 Context Representations

We refer to context as the sequence of tokens before (left context) and after (right context) a candidate mention in a sentence. Different classifiers can be built using different representations of the contexts. For example we can change the window size of the context sequence (i.e., for a window size of 1 we only use the last token before the mention and the first token after the mention). We can treat the left and right contexts independently of each other, we can treat them as a unique combination, or we can use both. We can also choose to use the word form of a token, its PoS tag, a word cluster, or a combination of these.

Table 2 compares different context representations and their performance in classifying unseen candidates using maximum-entropy classifiers trained with Mallet (McCallum, 2002) with ℓ_2 regularization, using the **10-30** seed. We use the lexical representation (the word itself) and a word cluster representation of the context tokens and use a window size of one to three. We use two types of features: bag-of-words features (1-grams of tokens in the specified window) and n-gram features (with n smaller or equal to the window size). The performance of using word clusters is comparable, and sometimes better, to using lexical representations. Moreover, using a longer window, in this case, does not necessarily result in better performance. [7] In the rest of the experiments

[7]Our learner and feature configuration, using ℓ_2 regularization, obtains state-of-the-art results on the standard evalu-

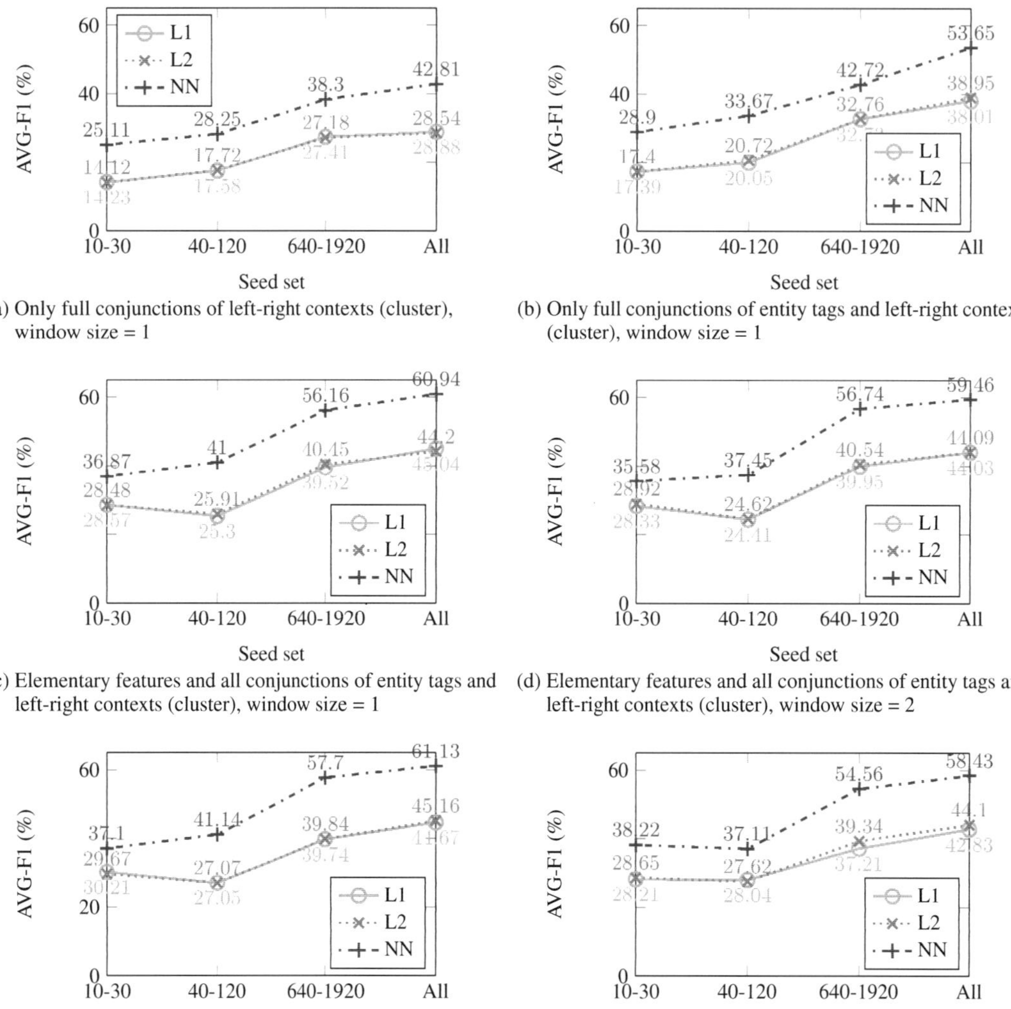

(a) Only full conjunctions of left-right contexts (cluster), window size = 1

(b) Only full conjunctions of entity tags and left-right contexts (cluster), window size = 1

(c) Elementary features and all conjunctions of entity tags and left-right contexts (cluster), window size = 1

(d) Elementary features and all conjunctions of entity tags and left-right contexts (cluster), window size = 2

(e) Elementary features and all conjunctions of entity tags and left-right contexts (cluster & PoS), window size = 1

(f) Elementary features and all conjunctions of entity tags and left-right contexts (cluster & PoS), window size = 2

Figure 1: Average F1 of classification of unseen entity candidates on development data, with respect to the size of the seed. NN refers to models with nuclear norm regularization, L1 and L2 refer to ℓ_1 and ℓ_2 regularization. Each plot corresponds to a different conjunctive feature space with respect to window size (1 or 2), context representation (cluster with/out PoS), using entity features or not, and combining or not full conjunctions with lower-order conjunctions and elementary features.

- **cap=1**, **cap=0**: whether the first letter of the entity candidate is uppercase, or not
- **all-low=1**, **all-low=0**: whether all letters of the candidate are lowercase letters, or not
- **all-cap1=1**, **all-cap1=0**: whether all letters of the candidate are uppercase letters, or not
- **all-cap2=1**, **all-cap2=0**: whether all letters of the candidate are uppercase letters and periods, or not
- **num-tokens=1**, **num-tokens=2**, **num-tok>2**: whether the candidate consists of one token, two or more
- **dummy**: a tag that holds for any entity candidate, used to capture context features alone

Table 3: The 12 entity tags used to represent entity candidates. The tags **all-cap1** and **all-cap2** are from (Neelakantan and Collins, 2014).

		PER			LOC			ORG			MISC			AVG F1
		PREC	REC	F1	PREC	REC	F1	PREC	REC	F1	PREC	REC	F1	
10-30	ℓ_1	65.69	65.40	65.55	**15.38**	**23.58**	**18.62**	59.33	19.44	**29.28**	23.36	30.05	26.28	34.93
	ℓ_1	65.54	64.80	65.17	15.12	23.17	18.30	**60.82**	18.50	28.37	23.30	30.52	26.42	34.56
	NN	**72.41**	**74.52**	**73.45**	14.89	21.55	17.61	49.09	**21.16**	17.61	**31.40**	**38.03**	**34.40**	**38.76**
40-120	ℓ_1	72.16	44.07	54.72	13.38	40.24	20.08	48.89	31.19	38.09	22.03	35.68	27.24	35.03
	ℓ_2	71.75	44.89	55.23	**13.61**	**41.87**	**20.54**	**49.39**	31.50	38.47	21.64	30.99	25.48	34.93
	NN	**75.16**	**61.33**	**67.54**	13.08	20.73	16.04	49.03	**35.74**	**41.34**	**29.97**	**47.42**	**36.73**	**40.41**
640-1920	ℓ_1	79.52	62.27	69.85	23.59	**44.31**	30.79	55.78	47.65	51.39	19.81	30.05	23.88	43.98
	ℓ_2	78.62	65.55	71.49	26.55	43.50	32.97	**60.19**	49.06	**54.06**	21.73	31.92	25.86	46.10
	NN	**80.73**	**80.55**	**80.64**	**51.91**	**44.31**	**47.81**	53.82	**54.08**	53.95	**29.14**	**51.17**	**37.14**	**54.88**
All	ℓ_1	75.58	72.48	74.00	32.84	36.18	34.43	57.28	46.24	51.17	27.93	29.11	28.51	47.03
	ℓ_2	**76.59**	70.77	73.57	34.21	**36.99**	35.55	57.79	**50.00**	53.61	28.93	32.86	30.77	48.37
	NN	73.83	**90.84**	**81.46**	**64.96**	36.18	**46.48**	**72.11**	44.98	**55.41**	**37.20**	**43.66**	**40.17**	**55.88**

Table 4: Results on the test for models trained with different sizes of the seed, using the parameters and features that obtain the best evaluation results the development set. NN refers to nuclear norm regularization, L1 and L2 refer to ℓ_1 and ℓ_2 regularization. Only test entities unseen at training are considered. Avg. F1 is over PER, LOC, ORG and MISC, excluding O.

we will use the elementary features that are more predictive and compact: clusters and PoS tags in windows of size at most 2.

5.4 Comparing Regularizers

We compare the performance of models trained using the nuclear norm regularizer with models trained using ℓ_1 and ℓ_2 regularizers. To train each model, we validate the regularization parameter and the number of iterations on development data, trying a wide range of values. The best performing configuration is then used for the comparison.

Figure 1 shows results on the development set for different feature sets. We started representing context using cluster labels, as it is the most compact representation obtaining good results in preliminary experiments. We tried several conjunctions: a conjunction of the left and right context, as well as conjunctions of left and right contexts and features of the candidate entity. We also tried all different conjunction combinations of the contexts and the candidate entity features, as well as adding PoS tags to represent contexts. To represent an entity candidate we use standard traits of the spelling of the mention, such as capitalization, the existence of symbols, as well as the number of tokens in the candidate. See Table 3 for the definition of the features describing entity candidates.

ation. Using our richest feature set, the model obtains 76.76 of accuracy in the development, for the task of classifing entities with correct boundaries. If we add features capturing the full entity and its tokens, then the accuracy is 87.63, which is similar to state-of-the-art performance (the best results in literature typically exploit additional gazetteers). Since our evaluation focuses on unknown entities, our features do not include information about the word tokens of entites.

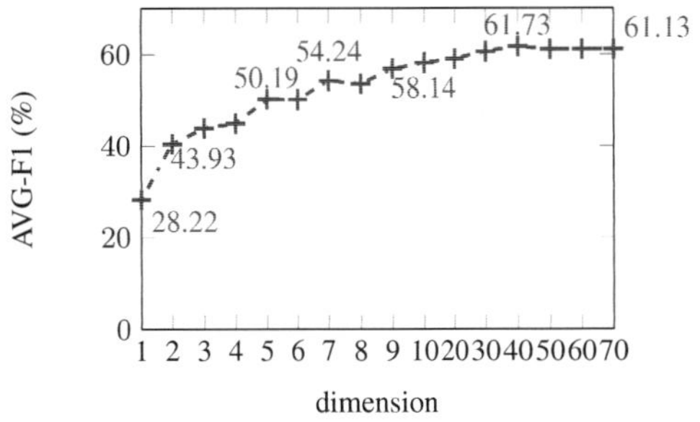

Figure 2: Avg. F1 on development for increasing dimensions, using the low-rank model in Figure 1e trained with **all** seeds.

We observe that for most conjunction settings our regularizer performs better than the ℓ_1 and ℓ_2 regularizers. Using the best model from each regularizer, we evaluated on the test set. Table 4 shows the test results. For all seed sets, the nuclear norm regularizer obtains the best average F1 performance. This shows that encouraging the max-entropy model to operate on a low-dimensional space is effective. Moreover, Figure 2 shows model performance as a function of the number of dimensions of the intrinsic projection. The model obtains a good performance even if only a few intrinsic dimensions are used.

Figure 3 shows the parameter matrix of the low-

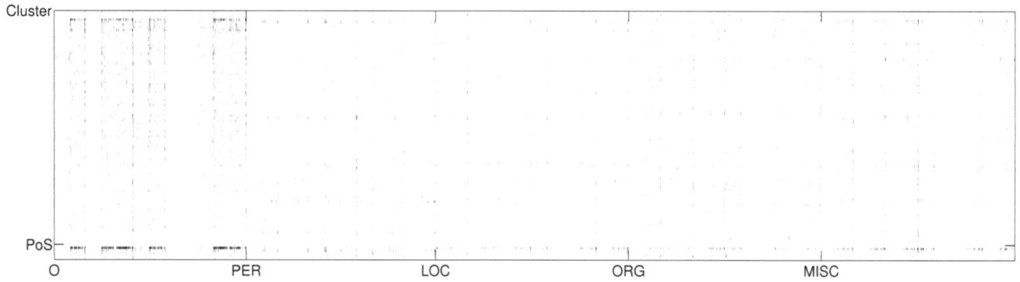

(a) Full parameter matrix of the low-rank model. The ticks in x-axis indicate the space for different entity types, while the ticks in y-axis indicate the space for different prefix context representations.

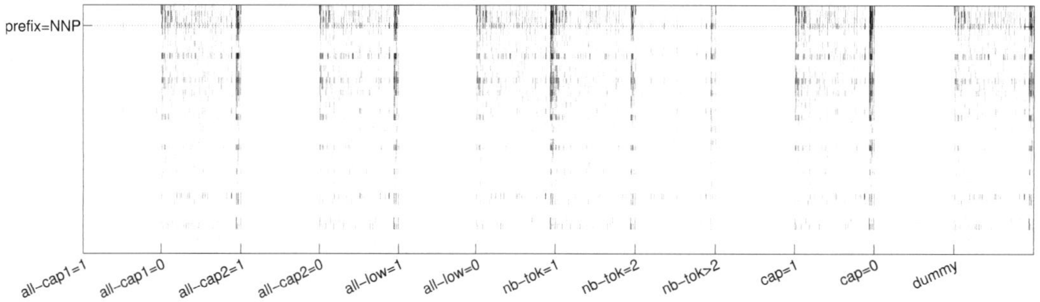

(b) The subblock for PER entity type and PoS representation of the prefixes. The ticks in x-axis indicate the space of the entity features used, while the tick in y-axis indicates an example of a frequently observed prefix for this entity type.

Figure 3: Parameter matrix of the low-rank model in Figure 1f trained with the **10-30** seed, with respect to observations of the associated features in training and development. Non-white conjunctions correspond to non-zero weights: black is for conjunctions seen in both the training and development sets; blue is for those seen in training but not in the development; red indicates that the conjunctions were observed only in the development; yellow is for those not observed in training nor development.

rank model in Figure 1f trained with the **10-30** seed, with respect to observed features in training and development data. Many of the conjunctions of the development set were never observed in the training set. Our regularizer framework is able to propagate weights from the conjunctive features seen in training to unseen conjunctive features that are close to each other in the projected space (these are the yellow and red cells in the matrix). In contrast, ℓ_1 and ℓ_2 regularization techniques can not put weight on unseen conjunctions.

6 Conclusion

We have developed a low-rank regularization framework for training max-entropy models in sparse conjunctive feature spaces. Our formulation is based on using tensors to parameterize classifiers. We control the capacity of the model using the nuclear-norm of a matricization of the tensor. Overall, our formulation results in a convex procedure for training model parameters.

We have experimented with these techniques in the context of learning entity classifiers. Compared to ℓ_1 and ℓ_2 penalties, the low-rank model obtains better performance, without the need to manually specify feature conjunctions. In our analysis, we have illustrated how the low-rank approach can assign non-zero weights to conjunctions that were unobserved at training, but are similar to observed conjunctions with respect to the low-dimensional projection of their elements.

We have used matricization of a tensor to define its rank, using a fixed transformation of the tensor into a matrix. Future work should explore how to combine efficiently different transformations.

Acknowledgements

We thank Gabriele Musillo and the anonymous reviewers for their helpful comments and suggestions. This work has been partially funded by the Spanish Government through the SKATER project (TIN2012-38584-C06-01) and an FPI predoctoral grant for Audi Primadhanty.

References

Rie Kubota Ando and Tong Zhang. 2005. A framework for learning predictive structures from multiple tasks and unlabeled data. *J. Mach. Learn. Res.*, 6:1817–1853, December.

Avrim Blum and Tom Mitchell. 1998. Combining labeled and unlabeled data with co-training. In *Proceedings of the Eleventh Annual Conference on Computational Learning Theory*, COLT' 98, pages 92–100, New York, NY, USA. ACM.

Peter F. Brown, Peter V. deSouza, Robert L. Mercer, Vincent J. Della Pietra, and Jenifer C. Lai. 1992. Class-based n-gram models of natural language. *Computational Linguistics*, 18:467–479.

Michael Collins and Yoram Singer. 1999. Unsupervised models for named entity classification. In *Joint SIGDAT Conference on Empirical Methods in Natural Language Processing and Very Large Corpora.*

John Duchi and Yoram Singer. 2009. Efficient online and batch learning using forward backward splitting. *Journal of Machine Learning Research*, 10:2899–2934.

Aria Haghighi and Dan Klein. 2006. Prototype-driven learning for sequence models. In *Proceedings of the Main Conference on Human Language Technology Conference of the North American Chapter of the Association of Computational Linguistics*, HLT-NAACL '06, pages 320–327, Stroudsburg, PA, USA. Association for Computational Linguistics.

Tao Lei, Yu Xin, Yuan Zhang, Regina Barzilay, and Tommi Jaakkola. 2014. Low-rank tensors for scoring dependency structures. In *Proceedings of the 52nd Annual Meeting of the Association for Computational Linguistics (Volume 1: Long Papers)*, pages 1381–1391, Baltimore, Maryland, June. Association for Computational Linguistics.

Xiao-Li Li, Lei Zhang, Bing Liu, and See-Kiong Ng. 2010. Distributional similarity vs. pu learning for entity set expansion. In *Proceedings of the ACL 2010 Conference Short Papers*, ACLShort '10, pages 359–364, Stroudsburg, PA, USA. Association for Computational Linguistics.

Pranava Swaroop Madhyastha, Xavier Carreras, and Ariadna Quattoni. 2014. Learning Task-specific Bilexical Embeddings. In *Proceedings of COLING 2014, the 25th International Conference on Computational Linguistics: Technical Papers*, pages 161–171, Dublin, Ireland, August. Dublin City University and Association for Computational Linguistics.

Andrew K. McCallum. 2002. Mallet: A machine learning for language toolkit.

Arvind Neelakantan and Michael Collins. 2014. Learning dictionaries for named entity recognition using minimal supervision. In *Proceedings of the 14th Conference of the European Chapter of the Association for Computational Linguistics*, pages 452–461, Gothenburg, Sweden, April. Association for Computational Linguistics.

Ariadna Quattoni, Borja Balle, Xavier Carreras, and Amir Globerson. 2014. Spectral regularization for max-margin sequence tagging. In Tony Jebara and Eric P. Xing, editors, *Proceedings of the 31st International Conference on Machine Learning (ICML-14)*, pages 1710–1718. JMLR Workshop and Conference Proceedings.

Lev Ratinov and Dan Roth. 2009. Design challenges and misconceptions in named entity recognition. In *Proceedings of the Thirteenth Conference on Computational Natural Language Learning (CoNLL-2009)*, pages 147–155, Boulder, Colorado, June. Association for Computational Linguistics.

Sebastian Riedel, Limin Yao, Andrew McCallum, and Benjamin M. Marlin. 2013. Relation extraction with matrix factorization and universal schemas. In *Proceedings of the 2013 Conference of the North American Chapter of the Association for Computational Linguistics: Human Language Technologies*, pages 74–84, Atlanta, Georgia, June. Association for Computational Linguistics.

Sameer Singh, Tim Rocktäschel, and Sebastian Riedel. 2015. Towards Combined Matrix and Tensor Factorization for Universal Schema Relation Extraction. In *NAACL Workshop on Vector Space Modeling for NLP (VSM)*.

Nathan Srebro and Adi Shraibman. 2005. Rank, trace-norm and max-norm. In *Learning Theory*, pages 545–560. Springer Berlin Heidelberg.

Nathan Srebro, Jason Rennie, and Tommi S Jaakkola. 2004. Maximum-margin matrix factorization. In *Advances in neural information processing systems*, pages 1329–1336.

Erik F. Tjong Kim Sang and Fien De Meulder. 2003. Introduction to the CoNLL-2003 Shared Task: Language-Independent Named Entity Recognition. In *Proceedings of the Seventh Conference on Natural Language Learning at HLT-NAACL 2003*, pages 142–147.

Limin Yao, Sebastian Riedel, and Andrew McCallum. 2013. Universal schema for entity type prediction. In *Proceedings of the 2013 Workshop on Automated Knowledge Base Construction*, AKBC '13, pages 79–84, New York, NY, USA. ACM.

Learning Word Representations by Jointly Modeling Syntagmatic and Paradigmatic Relations

Fei Sun, Jiafeng Guo, Yanyan Lan, Jun Xu, and **Xueqi Cheng**
CAS Key Lab of Network Data Science and Technology
Institute of Computing Technology
Chinese Academy of Sciences, China
ofey.sunfei@gmail.com
{guojiafeng, lanyanyan, junxu, cxq}@ict.ac.cn

Abstract

Vector space representation of words has been widely used to capture fine-grained linguistic regularities, and proven to be successful in various natural language processing tasks in recent years. However, existing models for learning word representations focus on either syntagmatic or paradigmatic relations alone. In this paper, we argue that it is beneficial to jointly modeling both relations so that we can not only encode different types of linguistic properties in a unified way, but also boost the representation learning due to the mutual enhancement between these two types of relations. We propose two novel distributional models for word representation using both syntagmatic and paradigmatic relations via a joint training objective. The proposed models are trained on a public Wikipedia corpus, and the learned representations are evaluated on word analogy and word similarity tasks. The results demonstrate that the proposed models can perform significantly better than all the state-of-the-art baseline methods on both tasks.

1 Introduction

Vector space models of language represent each word with a real-valued vector that captures both semantic and syntactic information of the word. The representations can be used as basic features in a variety of applications, such as information retrieval (Manning et al., 2008), named entity recognition (Collobert et al., 2011), question answering (Tellex et al., 2003), disambiguation (Schütze, 1998), and parsing (Socher et al., 2011).

A common paradigm for acquiring such representations is based on the *distributional hypothesis* (Harris, 1954; Firth, 1957), which states that words occurring in similar contexts tend to have similar meanings. Based on this hypothesis, various models on learning word representations have been proposed during the last two decades.

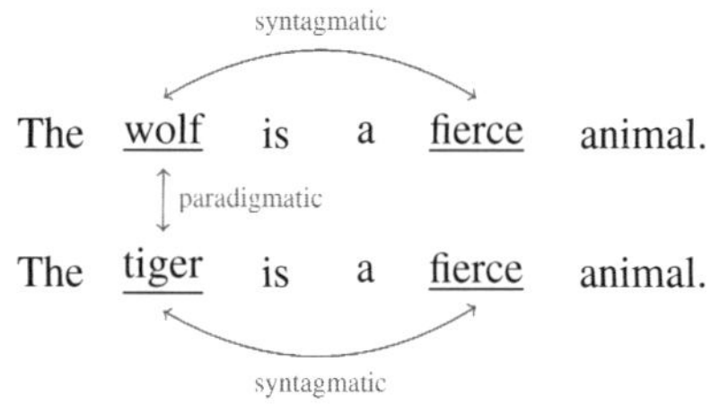

Figure 1: Example for syntagmatic and paradigmatic relations.

According to the leveraged distributional information, existing models can be grouped into two categories (Sahlgren, 2008). The first category mainly concerns the *syntagmatic relations* among the words, which relate the words that co-occur in the same text region. For example, "wolf" is close to "fierce" since they often co-occur in a sentence, as shown in Figure 1. This type of models learn the distributional representations of words based on the text region that the words occur in, as exemplified by Latent Semantic Analysis (LSA) model (Deerwester et al., 1990) and Non-negative Matrix Factorization (NMF) model (Lee and Seung, 1999). The second category mainly captures *paradigmatic relations*, which relate words that occur with similar contexts but may *not* co-occur in the text. For example, "wolf" is close to "tiger" since they often have similar context words. This type of models learn the word representations based on the surrounding words, as exemplified by the Hyperspace Analogue to Language (HAL) model (Lund et al., 1995), Continuous Bag-of-Words (CBOW) model and Skip-Gram (SG) model (Mikolov et al., 2013a).

In this work, we argue that it is important to

Proceedings of the 53rd Annual Meeting of the Association for Computational Linguistics and the 7th International Joint Conference on Natural Language Processing, pages 136–145,
Beijing, China, July 26-31, 2015.

take both syntagmatic and paradigmatic relations into account to build a good distributional model. Firstly, in distributional meaning acquisition, it is expected that a good representation should be able to encode a bunch of linguistic properties. For example, it can put semantically related words close (*e.g.*, "microsoft" and "office"), and also be able to capture syntactic regularities like "big is to bigger as deep is to deeper". Obviously, these linguistic properties are related to both syntagmatic and paradigmatic relations, and cannot be well modeled by either alone. Secondly, syntagmatic and paradigmatic relations are complimentary rather than conflicted in representation learning. That is relating the words that co-occur within the same text region (*e.g.*, "wolf" and "fierce" as well as "tiger" and "fierce") can better relate words that occur with similar contexts (*e.g.*, "wolf" and "tiger"), and vice versa.

Based on the above analysis, we propose two new distributional models for word representation using both syntagmatic and paradigmatic relations. Specifically, we learn the distributional representations of words based on the text region (*i.e.*, the document) that the words occur in as well as the surrounding words (*i.e.*, word sequences within some window size). By combining these two types of relations either in a parallel or a hierarchical way, we obtain two different joint training objectives for word representation learning. We evaluate our new models in two tasks, *i.e.*, word analogy and word similarity. The experimental results demonstrate that the proposed models can perform significantly better than all of the state-of-the-art baseline methods in both of the tasks.

2 Related Work

The distributional hypothesis has provided the foundation for a class of statistical methods for word representation learning. According to the leveraged distributional information, existing models can be grouped into two categories, *i.e.*, syntagmatic models and paradigmatic models.

Syntagmatic models concern combinatorial relations between words (*i.e.*, syntagmatic relations), which relate words that co-occur within the same text region (*e.g.*, sentence, paragraph or document).

For example, sentences have been used as the text region to acquire co-occurrence information by (Rubenstein and Goodenough, 1965; Miller and Charles, 1991). However, as pointed our by Picard (1999), the smaller the context regions are that we use to collect syntagmatic information, the worse the sparse-data problem will be for the resulting representation. Therefore, syntagmatic models tend to favor the use of larger text regions as context. Specifically, a document is often taken as a natural context of a word following the literature of information retrieval. In these methods, a words-by-documents co-occurrence matrix is built to collect the distributional information, where the entry indicates the (normalized) frequency of a word in a document. A low-rank decomposition is then conducted to learn the distributional word representations. For example, LSA (Deerwester et al., 1990) employs singular value decomposition by assuming the decomposed matrices to be orthogonal. In (Lee and Seung, 1999), non-negative matrix factorization is conducted over the words-by-documents matrix to learn the word representations.

Paradigmatic models concern substitutional relations between words (*i.e.*, paradigmatic relations), which relate words that occur in the same context but may not at the same time. Unlike syntagmatic model, paradigmatic models typically collect distributional information in a words-by-words co-occurrence matrix, where entries indicate how many times words occur together within a context window of some size.

For example, the Hyperspace Analogue to Language (HAL) model (Lund et al., 1995) constructed a high-dimensional vector for words based on the word co-occurrence matrix from a large corpus of text. However, a major problem with HAL is that the similarity measure will be dominated by the most frequent words due to its weight scheme. Various methods have been proposed to address the drawback of HAL. For example, the Correlated Occurrence Analogue to Lexical Semantic (COALS) (Rohde et al., 2006) transformed the co-occurrence matrix by an entropy or correlation based normalization. Bullinaria and Levy (2007), and Levy and Goldberg (2014b) suggested that positive pointwise mutual information (PPMI) is a good transformation. More recently, Lebret and Collobert (2014) obtained the word representations through a Hellinger PCA (HPCA) of the words-by-words co-occurrence matrix. Pennington et al. (2014) explicitly factorizes the words-by-words co-occurrence matrix to obtain the Global Vectors (GloVe) for word representation.

Alternatively, neural probabilistic language models (NPLMs) (Bengio et al., 2003) learn word representations by predicting the next word given previously seen words. Unfortunately, the training of NPLMs is quite time consuming, since computing probabilities in such model requires normalizing over the entire vocabulary. Recently, Mnih and Teh (2012) applied Noise Contrastive Estimation (NCE) to approximately maximize the probability of the softmax in NPLM. Mikolov et al. (2013a) further proposed continuous bag-of-words (CBOW) and skip-gram (SG) models, which use a simple single-layer architecture based on inner product between two word vectors. Both models can be learned efficiently via a simple variant of Noise Contrastive Estimation, *i.e.*, Negative sampling (NS) (Mikolov et al., 2013b).

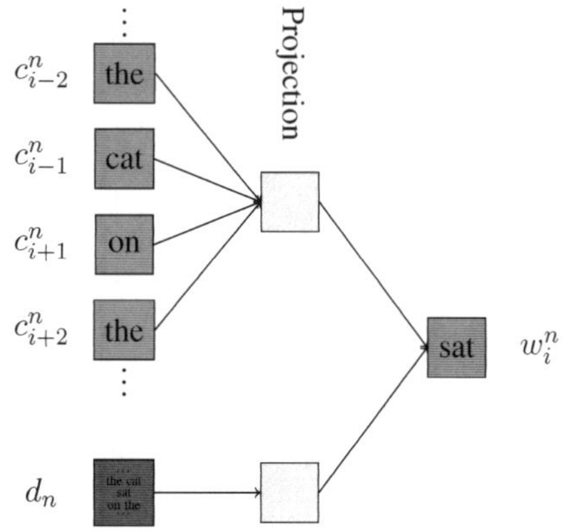

Figure 2: The framework for PDC model. Four words ("the", "cat", "on" and "the") are used to predict the center word ("sat"). Besides, the document in which the word sequence occurs is also used to predict the center word ("sat").

3 Our Models

In this paper, we argue that it is important to jointly model both syntagmatic and paradigmatic relations to learn good word representations. In this way, we not only encode different types of linguistic properties in a unified way, but also boost the representation learning due to the mutual enhancement between these two types of relations.

We propose two joint models that learn the distributional representations of words based on both the text region that the words occur in (*i.e.*, syntagmatic relations) and the surrounding words (*i.e.*, paradigmatic relations). To model syntagmatic relations, we follow the previous work (Deerwester et al., 1990; Lee and Seung, 1999) to take document as a nature text region of a word. To model paradigmatic relations, we are inspired by the recent work from Mikolov et al. (Mikolov et al., 2013a; Mikolov et al., 2013b), where simple models over word sequences are introduced for efficient and effective word representation learning.

In the following, we introduce the notations used in this paper, followed by detailed model descriptions, ending with some discussions of the proposed models.

3.1 Notation

Before presenting our models, we first list the notations used in this paper. Let $D=\{d_1,\ldots,d_N\}$ denote a corpus of N documents over the word vocabulary W. The contexts for word $w^n_i \in W$ (*i.e.* i-th word in document d_n) are the words surrounding it in an L-sized window $(c^n_{i-L},\ldots,c^n_{i-1},c^n_{i+1},\ldots,c^n_{i+L}) \in H$, where $c^n_j \in W, j\in\{i-L,\ldots,i-1,i+1,\ldots,i+L\}$. Each document $d \in D$, each word $w \in W$ and each context $c \in W$ is associated with a vector $\vec{d} \in \mathbb{R}^K$, $\vec{w} \in \mathbb{R}^K$ and $\vec{c} \in \mathbb{R}^K$, respectively, where K is the embedding dimensionality. The entries in the vectors are treated as parameters to be learned.

3.2 Parallel Document Context Model

The first proposed model architecture is shown in Figure 2. In this model, a target word is predicted by its surrounding context, as well as the document it occurs in. The former prediction task captures the paradigmatic relations, since words with similar context will tend to have similar representations. While the latter prediction task models the syntagmatic relations, since words co-occur in the same document will tend to have similar representations. More detailed analysis on this will be presented in Section 3.4. The model can be viewed as an extension of CBOW model (Mikolov et al., 2013a), by adding an extra document branch. Since both the context and document are parallel in predicting the target word, we call this model the Parallel Document Context (PDC) model.

More formally, the objective function of PDC

model is the log likelihood of all words

$$\ell = \sum_{n=1}^{N} \sum_{w_i^n \in d_n} \left(\log p(w_i^n|h_i^n) + \log p(w_i^n|d_n)\right)$$

where h_i^n denotes the projection of w_i^n's contexts, defined as

$$h_i^n = f(c_{i-L}^n, \dots, c_{i-1}^n, c_{i+1}^n, \dots, c_{i+L}^n)$$

where $f(\cdot)$ can be sum, average, concatenate or max pooling of context vectors[1]. In this paper, we use average, as that of `word2vec` tool.

We use softmax function to define the probabilities $p(w_i^n|h_i^n)$ and $p(w_i^n|d_n)$ as follows:

$$p(w_i^n|h_i^n) = \frac{\exp(\vec{w_i^n} \cdot \vec{h_i^n})}{\sum_{w \in W} \exp(\vec{w} \cdot \vec{h_i^n})} \quad (1)$$

$$p(w_i^n|d_n) = \frac{\exp(\vec{w_i^n} \cdot \vec{d_n})}{\sum_{w \in W} \exp(\vec{w} \cdot \vec{d_n})} \quad (2)$$

where $\vec{h_i^n}$ denotes projected vector of w_i^n's contexts.

To learn the model, we adopt the negative sampling technique (Mikolov et al., 2013b) for efficient learning since the original objective is intractable for direct optimization. The negative sampling actually defines an alternate training objective function as follows

$$\begin{aligned}\ell = \sum_{n=1}^{N} \sum_{w_i^n \in d_n} \Big(&\log \sigma(\vec{w_i^n} \cdot \vec{h_i^n}) + \log \sigma(\vec{w_i^n} \cdot \vec{d_n}) \\ &+ k \cdot \mathbb{E}_{w' \sim P_{\text{nw}}} \log \sigma(\vec{w'} \cdot \vec{h_i^n}) \\ &+ k \cdot \mathbb{E}_{w' \sim P_{\text{nw}}} \log \sigma(\vec{w'} \cdot \vec{d_n})\Big)\end{aligned} \quad (3)$$

where $\sigma(x) = 1/(1 + \exp(-x))$, k is the number of "negative" samples, w' denotes the sampled word, and P_{nw} denotes the distribution of negative word samples. We use stochastic gradient descent (SGD) for optimization, and the gradient is calculated via back-propagation algorithm.

3.3 Hierarchical Document Context Model

Since the above PDC model can be viewed as an extension of CBOW model, it is natural to introduce the same document-word prediction layer into the SG model. This becomes our second

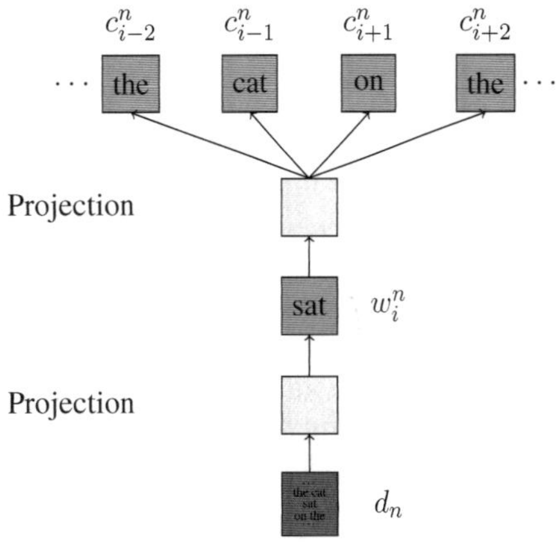

Figure 3: The framework for HDC model. The document is used to predict the target word ("sat"). Then, the word ("sat") is used to predict the surrounding words ("the", "cat", "on" and "the").

model architecture as shown in Figure 3. Specifically, the document is used to predict a target word, and the target word is further used to predict its surrounding context words. Since the prediction is conducted in a hierarchical manner, we name this model the Hierarchical Document Context (HDC) model. Similar as the PDC model, the syntagmatic relation in HDC is modeled by the document-word prediction layer and the word-context prediction layer models the paradigmatic relation.

Formally, the objective function of HDC model is the log likelihood of all words:

$$\ell = \sum_{n=1}^{N} \sum_{w_i^n \in d_n} \left(\sum_{\substack{j=i-L \\ j \neq i}}^{i+L} \log p(c_j^n|w_i^n) + \log p(w_i^n|d_n) \right)$$

where $p(w_i^n|d_n)$ is defined the same as in Equation (2), and $p(c_j^n|w_i^n)$ is also defined by a softmax function as follows:

$$p(c_j^n|w_i^n) = \frac{\exp(\vec{c_j^n} \cdot \vec{w_i^n})}{\sum_{c \in W} \exp(\vec{c} \cdot \vec{w_i^n})}$$

Similarly, we adopt the negative sampling technique for learning, which defines the following

[1] Note that the context window size L can be a function of the target word w_i^n. In this paper, we use the same strategy as `word2vec` tools which uniformly samples from the set $\{1, 2, \cdots, L\}$.

training objective function

$$\ell = \sum_{n=1}^{N} \sum_{w_i^n \in d_n} \Bigg(\sum_{\substack{j=i-L \\ j \neq i}}^{i+L} \Big(\log \sigma(\vec{c_j^n} \cdot \vec{w_i^n}) + k \cdot \mathbb{E}_{c' \sim P_{\text{nc}}} \log \sigma(\vec{c'} \cdot \vec{w_i^n}) \Big) + \log \sigma(\vec{w_i^n} \cdot \vec{d_n}) + k \cdot \mathbb{E}_{w' \sim P_{\text{nw}}} \log \sigma(\vec{w'} \cdot \vec{d_n}) \Bigg)$$

where k is the number of the negative samples, c' and w' denotes the sampled context and word respectively, and P_{nc} and P_{nw} denotes the distribution of negative context and word samples respectively[2]. We also employ SGD for optimization, and calculate the gradient via back-propagation algorithm.

3.4 Discussions

In this section we first show how PDC and HDC models capture the syntagmatic and paradigmatic relations from the viewpoint of matrix factorization. We then talk about the relationship of our models with previous work.

As pointed out in (Sahlgren, 2008), to capture syntagmatic relations, the implementational basis is to collect text data in a words-by-documents co-occurrence matrix in which the entry indicates the (normalized) frequency of occurrence of a word in a document (or, some other type of text region, *e.g.*, a sentence). While the implementational basis for paradigmatic relations is to collect text data in a words-by-words co-occurrence matrix that is populated by counting how many times words occur together within the context window. We now take the proposed PDC model as an example to show how it achieves these goals, and similar results can be shown for HDC model.

The objective function of PDC with negative sampling in Equation (3) can be decomposed into the following two parts:

$$\ell_1 = \sum_{w \in W} \sum_{h \in H} \big(\#(w,h) \cdot \log \sigma(\vec{w} \cdot \vec{h}) + k \cdot \#(h) \cdot p_{\text{nw}}(w) \log \sigma(-\vec{w} \cdot \vec{h}) \big) \tag{4}$$

$$\ell_2 = \sum_{d \in D} \sum_{w \in W} \big(\#(w,d) \cdot \log \sigma(\vec{w} \cdot \vec{d}) + k \cdot |d| \cdot p_{\text{nw}}(w) \log \sigma(-\vec{w} \cdot \vec{d}) \big) \tag{5}$$

where $\#(\cdot,\cdot)$ denotes the number of times the pair $(\cdot,\cdot)$ appears in D, $\#(h) = \sum_{w \in W} \#(w,h)$, $|d|$ denotes the length of document d, the objective function ℓ_1 corresponds to the context-word prediction task and ℓ_2 corresponds to the document-word prediction task.

Following the idea introduced by (Levy and Goldberg, 2014a), it is easy to show that the solution of the objective function ℓ_1 follows that

$$\vec{w} \cdot \vec{h} = \log\Big(\frac{\#(w,h)}{\#(h) \cdot p_{\text{nw}}(w)}\Big) - \log k$$

and the solution of the objective function ℓ_2 follows that

$$\vec{w} \cdot \vec{d} = \log\Big(\frac{\#(w,d)}{|d| \cdot p_{\text{nw}}(w)}\Big) - \log k$$

It reveals that the PDC model with negative sampling is actually factorizing both a words-by-contexts co-occurrence matrix and a words-by-documents co-occurrence matrix simultaneously. In this way, we can see that the implementational basis of the PDC model is consistent with that of syntagmatic and paradigmatic models. In other words, PDC can indeed capture both syntagmatic and paradigmatic relations by processing the right distributional information. Please notice that the PDC model is not equivalent to direct combination of existing matrix factorization methods, due to the fact that the matrix entries defined in PDC model are more complicated than the simple co-occurrence frequency (Lee and Seung, 1999).

When considering existing models, one may connect our models to the Distributed Memory model of Paragraph Vectors (PV-DM) and the Distributed Bag of Words version of Paragraph Vectors (PV-DBOW) (Le and Mikolov, 2014). However, both of them are quite different from our models. In PV-DM, the paragraph vector and context vectors are averaged or concatenated to predict the next word. Therefore, the objective function of PV-DM can no longer decomposed as the PDC model as shown in Equation (4) and (5). In other words, although PV-DM leverages both paragraph and context information, it is unclear how these information is collected and used in this model. As for PV-DBOW, it simply leverages paragraph vector to predict words in the paragraph. It is easy to show that it only uses the words-by-documents co-occurrence matrix, and thus only captures syntagmatic relations.

Another close work is the Global Context-Aware Neural Language Model (GCANLM for

[2] P_{nc} is not necessary to be the same as P_{nw}.

short) (Huang et al., 2012). The model defines two scoring components that contribute to the final score of a (word sequence, document) pair. The architecture of GCANLM seems similar to our PDC model, but exhibits lots of differences as follows: (1) GCANLM employs neural networks as components while PDC resorts to simple model structure without non-linear hidden layers; (2) GCANLM uses weighted average of all word vectors to represent the document, which turns out to model words-by-words co-occurrence (*i.e.*, paradigmatic relations) again rather than words-by-documents co-occurrence (*i.e.*, syntagmatic relations); (3) GCANLM is a language model which predicts the next word given the preceding words, while PDC model leverages both preceding and succeeding contexts for prediction.

4 Experiments

In this section, we first describe our experimental settings including the corpus, hyper-parameter selections, and baseline methods. Then we compare our models with baseline methods on two tasks, *i.e.*, word analogy and word similarity. After that, we conduct some case studies to show that our model can better capture both syntagmatic and paradigmatic relations and how it improves the performances on semantic tasks.

4.1 Experimental Settings

We select Wikipedia, the largest online knowledge base, to train our models. We adopt the publicly available April 2010 dump[3] (Shaoul and Westbury, 2010), which is also used by (Huang et al., 2012; Luong et al., 2013; Neelakantan et al., 2014). The corpus in total has $3,035,070$ articles and about 1 billion tokens. In preprocessing, we lowercase the corpus, remove pure digit words and non-English characters[4].

Following the practice in (Pennington et al., 2014), we set context window size as 10 and use 10 negative samples. The noise distributions for context and words are set as the same as used in (Mikolov et al., 2013a), $p_{\text{nw}}(w) \propto \#(w)^{0.75}$. We also adopt the same linear learning rate strategy described in (Mikolov et al., 2013a), where the initial learning rate of PDC model is 0.05, and HDC is 0.025. No additional regularization is used in our models[5].

Table 1: Corpora used in baseline models.

model	corpus	size
C&W	Wikipedia 2007 + Reuters RCV1	0.85B
HPCA	Wikipedia 2012	1.6B
GloVe	Wikipedia 2014+ Gigaword5	6B
GCANLM, CBOW, SG PV-DBOW, PV-DM	Wikipedia 2010	1B

We compare our models with various state-of-the-art models including C&W (Collobert et al., 2011), GCANLM (Huang et al., 2012), CBOW, SG (Mikolov et al., 2013a), GloVe (Pennington et al., 2014), PV-DM, PV-DBOW (Le and Mikolov, 2014) and HPCA (Lebret and Collobert, 2014). For C&W, GCANLM[6], GloVe and HPCA, we use the word embeddings they provided. For CBOW and SG model, we reimplement these two models since the original `word2vec` tool uses SGD but *cannot* shuffle the data. Besides, we also implement PV-DM and PV-DBOW models due to (Le and Mikolov, 2014) has not released source codes. We train these four models on the same dataset with the same hyper-parameter settings as our models for fair comparison. The statistics of the corpora used in baseline models are shown in Table 1. Moreover, since different papers report different dimensionality, to be fair, we conduct evaluations on three dimensions (*i.e.*, 50, 100, 300) to cover the publicly available results[7].

4.2 Word Analogy

The word analogy task is introduced by Mikolov et al. (2013a) to quantitatively evaluate the linguistic regularities between pairs of word representations. The task consists of questions like "*a* is to *b* as *c* is to __", where __ is missing and must be guessed from the entire vocabulary. To answer such questions, we need to find a word vector $\vec{x}$, which is the closest to $\vec{b} - \vec{a} + \vec{c}$ according to the cosine similarity:

$$\arg \max_{\substack{x \in W, x \neq a \\ x \neq b,\, x \neq c}} (\vec{b} + \vec{c} - \vec{a}) \cdot \vec{x}$$

The question is judged as correctly answered only if x is exactly the answer word in the evaluation

[3] http://www.psych.ualberta.ca/~westburylab/downloads/westburylab.wikicorp.download.html

[4] We ignore the words less than 20 occurrences during training.

[5] Codes avaiable at http://www.bigdatalab.ac.cn/benchmark/bm/bd?code=PDC, http://www.bigdatalab.ac.cn/benchmark/bm/bd?code=HDC.

[6] Here, we use GCANLM's single-prototype embedding.

[7] C&W and GCANLM only released the vectors with 50 dimensions, and HPCA released vectors with 50 and 100 dimensions.

Table 2: Results on the word analogy task. Underlined scores are the best within groups of the same dimensionality, while bold scores are the best overall.

model	size	dim	semantic	syntactic	total
C&W	0.85B	50	9.33	11.33	10.98
GCANLM	1B	50	2.6	10.7	7.34
HPCA	1.6B	50	3.36	9.89	7.2
GloVe	6B	50	48.46	45.24	46.22
CBOW	1B	50	54.38	49.64	52.01
SG	1B	50	53.73	46.12	49.04
PV-DBOW	1B	50	55.02	44.17	49.34
PV-DM	1B	50	45.08	43.22	44.25
PDC	1B	50	61.21	54.55	57.88
HDC	1B	50	57.8	49.74	53.41
HPCA	1.6B	100	4.16	15.73	10.79
GloVe	6B	100	65.34	61.51	63.11
CBOW	1B	100	70.73	63.01	66.87
SG	1B	100	67.66	59.72	63.45
PV-DBOW	1B	100	67.49	56.29	61.51
PV-DM	1B	100	57.72	58.81	58.45
PDC	1B	100	72.77	67.68	70.35
HDC	1B	100	69.57	63.75	66.67
GloVe	6B	300	77.44	67.75	71.7
CBOW	1B	300	76.2	68.44	72.39
SG	1B	300	78.9	65.72	71.88
PV-DBOW	1B	300	66.85	58.5	62.08
PV-DM	1B	300	56.88	68.35	63.39
PDC	1B	300	79.55	**69.71**	**74.76**
HDC	1B	300	**79.67**	67.1	73.13

set. The evaluation metric for this task is the percentage of questions answered correctly.

The dataset contains 5 types of semantic analogies and 9 types of syntactic analogies[8]. The semantic analogy contains $8,869$ questions, typically about people and place like "Beijing is to China as Paris is to France", while the syntactic analogy contains $10,675$ questions, mostly on forms of adjectives or verb tense, such as "good is to better as bad to worse".

Result Table 2 shows the results on word analogy task. As we can see that CBOW, SG and GloVe are much stronger baselines as compare with C&W, GCANLM and HPCA. Even so, our PDC model still performs significantly better than these state-of-the-art methods (p-value < 0.01), especially with smaller vector dimensionality. More interestingly, by only training on 1 billion words, our models can outperform the GloVe model which is trained on 6 billion words. The results demonstrate that by modeling both syntagmatic and paradigmatic relations, we can learn better word representations capturing linguistic regularities.

Besides, CBOW, SG and PV-DBOW can be viewed as sub-models of our proposed models, since they use either context (*i.e.*, paradigmatic relations) or document (*i.e.*, syntagmatic relations) alone to predict the target word. By comparing with these sub-models, we can see that the PDC and HDC models can perform significantly better on both syntactic and semantic subtasks. It shows that by jointly modeling the two relations, one can boost the representation learning and better capture both semantic and syntactic regularities.

4.3 Word Similarity

Besides the word analogy task, we also evaluate our models on three different word similarity tasks, including WordSim-353 (Finkelstein et al., 2002), Stanford's Contextual Word Similarities (SCWS) (Huang et al., 2012) and rare word (RW) (Luong et al., 2013). These datasets contain word paris together with human assigned similarity scores. We compute the Spearman rank correlation between similarity scores based on learned word representations and the human judgements. In all experiments, we removed the word pairs that cannot be found in the vocabulary.

Results Figure 4 shows results on three different word similarity datasets. First of all, our proposed PDC model always achieves the best performances on the three tasks. Besides, if we compare the PDC and HDC models with their corresponding sub-models (*i.e.*, CBOW and SG) respectively, we can see performance gain by adding syntagmatic information via document. This gain becomes even larger for rare words with low dimensionality as shown on RW dataset. Moreover, on the SCWS dataset, our PDC model using the single-prototype representations under dimensionality 50 can achieve a comparable result (65.63) to the state-of-the-art GCANLM (65.7 as the best performance reported in (Huang et al., 2012)) which uses multi-prototype vectors[9].

4.4 Case Study

Here we conduct some case studies to (1) gain some intuition on how these two relations affect

[8] http://code.google.com/p/word2vec/source/browse/trunk/questions-words.txt

[9] Note, in Figure 4, the performance of GCANLM is computed based on their released single-prototype vectors.

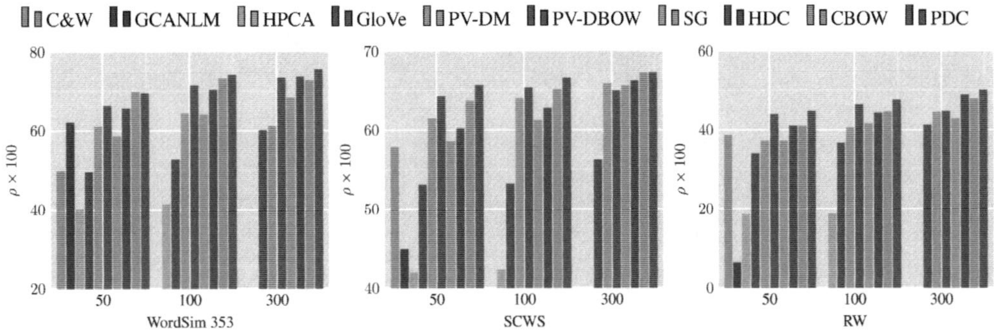

Figure 4: Spearman rank correlation on three datasets. Results are grouped by dimensionality.

Table 3: Target words and their 5 most similar words under different representations. Words in italic often co-occur with the target words, while words in bold are substitutable to the target words.

feynman	
CBOW	**einstein**, **schwinger**, **bohm**, **bethe** *relativity*
SG	**schwinger**, *quantum*, **bethe**, **einstein** *semiclassical*
PDC	*geometrodynamics*, **bethe**, *semiclassical* **schwinger**, *perturbative*
HDC	**schwinger**, *electrodynamics*, **bethe** *semiclassical*, *quantum*
PV-DBOW	*physicists*, *spacetime*, *geometrodynamics* *tachyons*, **einstein**
moon	
CBOW	**earth**, **moons**, **pluto**, **sun**, **nebula**
SG	**earth**, **sun**, **mars**, **planet**, **aquarius**
PDC	**sun**, **moons**, *lunar*, *heavens*, **earth**
HDC	**earth**, **sun**, **mars**, **planet**, *heavens*
PV-DBOW	*lunar*, **moons**, *celestial*, **sun**, *ecliptic*

the representation learning, and (2) analyze why the joint model can perform better.

To show how syntagmatic and paradigmatic relations affect the learned representations, we present the 5 most similar words (by cosine similarity with 50-dimensional vectors) to a given target word under the PDC and HDC models, as well as three sub-models, *i.e.*, CBOW, SG, and PV-DBOW. The results are shown in table 3, where words in italic are those often co-occurred with the target word (*i.e.*, syntagmatic relations), while words in bold are whose substitutable to the target word (*i.e.*, paradigmatic relation).

Clearly, top words from CBOW and SG models are more under paradigmatic relations, while those from PV-DBOW model are more under syntagmatic relations, which is quite consistent with the model design. By modeling both relations, the top words from PDC and HDC models become more diverse, *i.e.*, more syntagmatic relations than CBOW and SG models, and more paradigmatic relations than PV-DBOW model. The results reveal that the word representations learned by PDC and HDC models are more balanced with respect to the two relations as compared with sub-models.

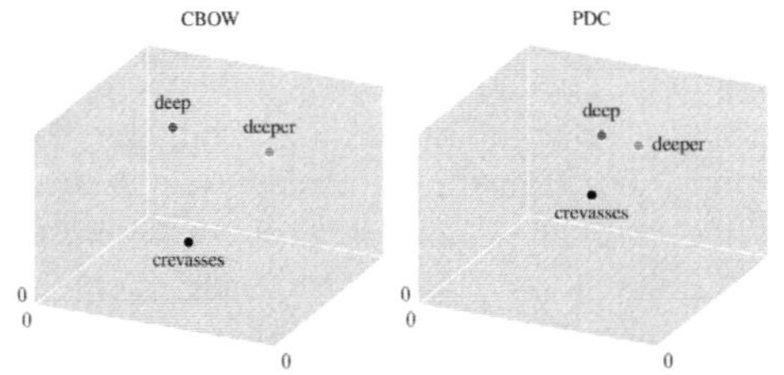

Figure 5: The 3-D embedding of learned word vectors of "deep", "deeper" and "crevasses" under CBOW and PDC models.

The next question is why learning a joint model can work better on previous tasks? We first take one example from the word analogy task, which is the question "*big* is to *bigger* as *deep* is to __" with the correct answer as "deeper". Our PDC model produce the right answer but the CBOW model fails with the answer "shallower". We thus embedding the learned word vectors from the two models into a 3-D space to illustrate and analyze the reason.

As shown in Figure 5, we can see that by jointly modeling two relations, PDC model not only requires that "deep" to be close to "deeper" (in cosine similarity), but also requires that "deep" and "deeper" to be close to "crevasses". The additional requirements further drag these three words closer as compared with those from the CBOW model, and this make our model outperform the CBOW model on this question. As for the word similarity tasks, we find that the word pairs are either syntagmatic (*e.g.*, "bank" and "money") or paradigmatic (*e.g.*, "left" and "abandon"). It is, therefore, not surprising to see that a more balanced representation can achieve much better performance than a biased representation.

5 Conclusion

Existing work on word representations models either syntagmatic or paradigmatic relations. In this paper, we propose two novel distributional models for word representation, using both syntagmatic and paradigmatic relations via a joint training objective. The experimental results on both word analogy and word similarity tasks show that the proposed joint models can learn much better word representations than the state-of-the-art methods.

Several directions remain to be explored. In this paper, the syntagmatic and paradigmatic relations are equivalently important in both PDC and HDC models. An interesting question would then be whether and how we can add different weights for syntagmatic and paradigmatic relations. Besides, we may also try to learn the multi-prototype word representations for polysemous words based on our proposed models.

Acknowledgments

This work was funded by 973 Program of China under Grants No. 2014CB340401 and 2012CB316303, and the National Natural Science Foundation of China (NSFC) under Grants No. 61232010, 61433014, 61425016, 61472401 and 61203298. We thank Ronan Collobert, Eric H. Huang, Rémi Lebret, Jeffrey Pennington and Tomas Mikolov for their kindness in sharing codes and word vectors. We also thank the anonymous reviewers for their helpful comments.

References

Yoshua Bengio, Réjean Ducharme, Pascal Vincent, and Christian Janvin. 2003. A neural probabilistic language model. *J. Mach. Learn. Res.*, 3:1137–1155, March.

John A. Bullinaria and Joseph P. Levy. 2007. Extracting semantic representations from word co-occurrence statistics: A computational study. *Behavior Research Methods*, 39(3):510–526.

Ronan Collobert, Jason Weston, Léon Bottou, Michael Karlen, Koray Kavukcuoglu, and Pavel Kuksa. 2011. Natural language processing (almost) from scratch. *J. Mach. Learn. Res.*, 12:2493–2537, November.

Scott Deerwester, Susan T. Dumais, George W. Furnas, Thomas K. Landauer, and Richard Harshman. 1990. Indexing by latent semantic analysis. *Journal of the American Society for Information Science*, 41(6):391–407.

Lev Finkelstein, Evgeniy Gabrilovich, Yossi Matias, Ehud Rivlin, Zach Solan andGadi Wolfman, and Eytan Ruppin. 2002. Placing search in context: The concept revisited. *ACM Trans. Inf. Syst.*, 20(1):116–131, January.

J. R. Firth. 1957. A synopsis of linguistic theory 1930-55. *Studies in Linguistic Analysis (special volume of the Philological Society)*, 1952-59:1–32.

Zellig Harris. 1954. Distributional structure. *Word*, 10(23):146–162.

Eric H. Huang, Richard Socher, Christopher D. Manning, and Andrew Y. Ng. 2012. Improving word representations via global context and multiple word prototypes. In *Proceedings of the 50th Annual Meeting of the Association for Computational Linguistics: Long Papers - Volume 1*, ACL '12, pages 873–882, Stroudsburg, PA, USA. Association for Computational Linguistics.

Quoc Le and Tomas Mikolov. 2014. Distributed representations of sentences and documents. In Tony Jebara and Eric P. Xing, editors, *Proceedings of the 31st International Conference on Machine Learning (ICML-14)*, pages 1188–1196. JMLR Workshop and Conference Proceedings.

Rémi Lebret and Ronan Collobert. 2014. Word embeddings through hellinger pca. In *Proceedings of the 14th Conference of the European Chapter of the Association for Computational Linguistics*, pages 482–490. Association for Computational Linguistics.

Daniel D. Lee and H. Sebastian Seung. 1999. Learning the parts of objects by non-negative matrix factorization. *Nature*, 401(6755):788–791, october.

Omer Levy and Yoav Goldberg. 2014a. Neural word embedding as implicit matrix factorization. In *Advances in Neural Information Processing Systems 27*, pages 2177–2185. Curran Associates, Inc., Montreal, Quebec, Canada.

Omer Levy and Yoav Goldberg, 2014b. *Proceedings of the Eighteenth Conference on Computational Natural Language Learning*, chapter Linguistic Regularities in Sparse and Explicit Word Representations, pages 171–180. Association for Computational Linguistics.

Kevin Lund, Curt Burgess, and Ruth Ann Atchley. 1995. Semantic and associative priming in a high-dimensional semantic space. In *Proceedings of the 17th Annual Conference of the Cognitive Science Society*, pages 660–665.

Minh-Thang Luong, Richard Socher, and Christopher D. Manning. 2013. Better word representations with recursive neural networks for morphology. In *Proceedings of the Seventeenth Conference on Computational Natural Language Learning*, pages 104–113. Association for Computational Linguistics.

Christopher D. Manning, Prabhakar Raghavan, and Hinrich Schütze. 2008. *Introduction to Information Retrieval*. Cambridge University Press, New York, NY, USA.

Tomas Mikolov, Kai Chen, Greg Corrado, and Jeffrey Dean. 2013a. Efficient estimation of word representations in vector space. In *Proceedings of Workshop of ICLR*.

Tomas Mikolov, Ilya Sutskever, Kai Chen, Greg S Corrado, and Jeff Dean. 2013b. Distributed representations of words and phrases and their compositionality. In C.J.C. Burges, L. Bottou, M. Welling, Z. Ghahramani, and K.Q. Weinberger, editors, *Advances in Neural Information Processing Systems 26*, pages 3111–3119. Curran Associates, Inc.

George A Miller and Walter G Charles. 1991. Contextual correlates of semantic similarity. *Language & Cognitive Processes*, 6(1):1–28.

Andriy Mnih and Yee Whye Teh. 2012. A fast and simple algorithm for training neural probabilistic language models. In *Proceedings of the 29th International Conference on Machine Learning*, pages 1751–1758.

Arvind Neelakantan, Jeevan Shankar, Alexandre Passos, and Andrew McCallum. 2014. Efficient non-parametric estimation of multiple embeddings per word in vector space. In *Proceedings of the 2014 Conference on Empirical Methods in Natural Language Processing (EMNLP)*, pages 1059–1069, Doha, Qatar, October. Association for Computational Linguistics.

Jeffrey Pennington, Richard Socher, and Christopher D. Manning. 2014. Glove: Global vectors for word representation. In *Proceedings of the 2014 Conference on Empirical Methods in Natural Language Processing, EMNLP 2014, October 25-29, 2014, Doha, Qatar, A meeting of SIGDAT, a Special Interest Group of the ACL*, pages 1532–1543.

Justin Picard. 1999. Finding content-bearing terms using term similarities. In *Proceedings of the Ninth Conference on European Chapter of the Association for Computational Linguistics*, EACL '99, pages 241–244, Stroudsburg, PA, USA. Association for Computational Linguistics.

Douglas L. T. Rohde, Laura M. Gonnerman, and David C. Plaut. 2006. An improved model of semantic similarity based on lexical co-occurence. *Communications of the ACM*, 8:627–633.

Herbert Rubenstein and John B. Goodenough. 1965. Contextual correlates of synonymy. *Commun. ACM*, 8(10):627–633, October.

Magnus Sahlgren. 2008. The distributional hypothesis. *Italian Journal of Linguistics*, 20(1):33–54.

Hinrich Schütze. 1998. Automatic word sense discrimination. *Comput. Linguist.*, 24(1):97–123, March.

Cyrus Shaoul and Chris Westbury. 2010. The westbury lab wikipedia corpus. *Edmonton, AB: University of Alberta*.

Richard Socher, Cliff C. Lin, Chris Manning, and Andrew Y. Ng. 2011. Parsing natural scenes and natural language with recursive neural networks. In Lise Getoor and Tobias Scheffer, editors, *Proceedings of the 28th International Conference on Machine Learning (ICML-11)*, pages 129–136, New York, NY, USA. ACM.

Stefanie Tellex, Boris Katz, Jimmy Lin, Aaron Fernandes, and Gregory Marton. 2003. Quantitative evaluation of passage retrieval algorithms for question answering. In *Proceedings of the 26th Annual International ACM SIGIR Conference on Research and Development in Informaion Retrieval*, SIGIR '03, pages 41–47, New York, NY, USA. ACM.

Learning Dynamic Feature Selection for Fast Sequential Prediction

Emma Strubell **Luke Vilnis** **Kate Silverstein** **Andrew McCallum**
College of Information and Computer Sciences
University of Massachusetts Amherst
Amherst, MA, 01003, USA
{strubell, luke, ksilvers, mccallum}@cs.umass.edu

Abstract

We present paired learning and inference algorithms for significantly reducing computation and increasing speed of the vector dot products in the classifiers that are at the heart of many NLP components. This is accomplished by partitioning the features into a sequence of templates which are ordered such that high confidence can often be reached using only a small fraction of all features. Parameter estimation is arranged to maximize accuracy and early confidence in this sequence. Our approach is simpler and better suited to NLP than other related cascade methods. We present experiments in left-to-right part-of-speech tagging, named entity recognition, and transition-based dependency parsing. On the typical benchmarking datasets we can preserve POS tagging accuracy above 97% and parsing LAS above 88.5% both with over a five-fold reduction in run-time, and NER F1 above 88 with more than 2x increase in speed.

1 Introduction

Many NLP tasks such as part-of-speech tagging, parsing and named entity recognition have become sufficiently accurate that they are no longer solely an object of research, but are also widely deployed in production systems. These systems can be run on billions of documents, making the efficiency of inference a significant concern—impacting not only wall-clock running time but also computer hardware budgets and the carbon footprint of data centers.

This paper describes a paired learning and inference approach for significantly reducing computation and increasing speed while preserving accuracy in the linear classifiers typically used in many NLP tasks. The heart of the prediction computation in these models is a dot-product between a dense parameter vector and a sparse feature vector. The bottleneck in these models is then often a combination of feature extraction and numerical operations, each of which scale linearly in the size of the feature vector. Feature extraction can be even more expensive than the dot products, involving, for example, walking sub-graphs, lexicon lookup, string concatenation and string hashing. We note, however, that in many cases not all of these features are necessary for accurate prediction. For example, in part-of-speech tagging if we see the word "the," there is no need to perform a large dot product or many string operations; we can accurately label the word a DETERMINER using the word identity feature alone. In other cases two features are sufficient: when we see the word "hits" preceded by a CARDINAL (e.g. "two hits") we can be confident that it is a NOUN.

We present a simple yet novel approach to improve processing speed by dynamically determining on a per-instance basis how many features are necessary for a high-confidence prediction. Our features are divided into a set of *feature templates*, such as current-token or previous-tag in the case of POS tagging. At training time, we determine an ordering on the templates such that we can approximate model scores at test time by incrementally calculating the dot product in template ordering. We then use a running confidence estimate for the label prediction to determine how many terms of the sum to compute for a given instance, and predict once confidence reaches a certain threshold.

In similar work, cascades of increasingly complex and high-recall models have been used for both structured and unstructured prediction. Viola and Jones (2001) use a cascade of boosted models to perform face detection. Weiss and Taskar (2010) add increasingly higher-order dependencies to a graphical model while filtering the out-

Proceedings of the 53rd Annual Meeting of the Association for Computational Linguistics and the 7th International Joint Conference on Natural Language Processing, pages 146–155,
Beijing, China, July 26-31, 2015.

put domain to maintain tractable inference. While most traditional cascades pass instances down to layers with increasingly higher recall, we use a single model and accumulate the scores from each additional template until a label is predicted with sufficient confidence, in a stagewise approximation of the full model score. Our technique applies to any linear classifier-based model over feature templates without changing the model structure or decreasing prediction speed.

Most similarly to our work, Weiss and Taskar (2013) improve performance for several structured vision tasks by dynamically selecting features at runtime. However, they use a reinforcement learning approach whose computational tradeoffs are better suited to vision problems with expensive features. Obtaining a speedup on tasks with comparatively cheap features, such as part-of-speech tagging or transition-based parsing, requires an approach with less overhead. In fact, the most attractive aspect of our approach is that it speeds up methods that are already among the fastest in NLP.

We apply our method to left-to-right part-of-speech tagging in which we achieve accuracy above 97% on the Penn Treebank WSJ corpus while running more than five times faster than our 97.2% baseline. We also achieve a five-fold increase in transition-based dependency parsing on the WSJ corpus while achieving an LAS just 1.5% lower than our 90.3% baseline. Named entity recognition also shows significant speed increases. We further demonstrate that our method can be tuned for $2.5 - 3.5$x multiplicative speedups with nearly no loss in accuracy.

2 Classification and Structured Prediction

Our algorithm speeds up prediction for multiclass classification problems where the label set can be tractably enumerated and scored, and the per-class scores of input features decompose as a sum over multiple feature templates. Frequently, classification problems in NLP are solved through the use of linear classifiers, which compute scores for input-label pairs using a dot product. These meet our additive scoring criteria, and our acceleration methods are directly applicable.

However, in this work we are interested in speeding up *structured prediction* problems, specifically part-of-speech (POS) tagging and dependency parsing. We apply our classification algorithms to these problems by reducing them to *sequential prediction* (Daumé III et al., 2009). For POS tagging, we describe a sentence's part of speech annotation by the left-to-right sequence of tagging decisions for individual tokens (Giménez and Màrquez, 2004). Similarly, we implement our parser with a classifier that generates a sequence of shift-reduce parsing transitions (Nivre, 2009).

The use of sequential prediction to solve these problems and others has a long history in practice as well as theory. Searn (Daumé III et al., 2009) and DAgger (Ross et al., 2011) are two popular principled frameworks for reducing sequential prediction to classification by learning a classifier on additional synthetic training data. However, as we do in our experiments, practitioners often see good results by training on the gold standard labels with an off-the-shelf classification algorithm, as though classifying IID data (Bengtson and Roth, 2008; Choi and Palmer, 2012).

Classifier-based approaches to structured prediction are faster than dynamic programming since they consider only a subset of candidate output structures in a greedy manner. For example, the Stanford CoreNLP classifier-based part-of-speech tagger provides a 6.5x speed advantage over their dynamic programming-based model, with little reduction in accuracy. Because our methods are designed for the greedy sequential prediction regime, we can provide further speed increases to the fastest inference methods in NLP.

3 Linear models

Our base classifier for sequential prediction tasks will be a *linear model*. Given an input $x \in \mathcal{X}$, a set of labels $\mathcal{Y}$, a feature map $\Phi(x, y)$, and a weight vector $\mathbf{w}$, a linear model predicts the highest-scoring label

$$y^* = \arg\max_{y \in \mathcal{Y}} \mathbf{w} \cdot \Phi(x, y). \quad (1)$$

The parameter $\mathbf{w}$ is usually learned by minimizing a regularized (R) sum of loss functions (ℓ) over the training examples indexed by i

$$\mathbf{w}^* = \arg\min_{\mathbf{w}} \sum_i \ell(x_i, y_i, \mathbf{w}) + R(\mathbf{w}).$$

In this paper, we partition the features into a set of *feature templates*, so that the weights, feature function, and dot product factor as

$$\mathbf{w} \cdot \Phi(x, y) = \sum_j \mathbf{w}_j \cdot \Phi_j(x, y) \quad (2)$$

for some set of *feature templates* $\{\Phi_j(x, y)\}$.

Our goal is to approximate the dot products in (1) sufficiently for purposes of prediction, while using as few terms of the sum in (2) as possible.

4 Method

We accomplish this goal by developing paired learning and inference procedures for feature-templated classifiers that optimize both accuracy and inference speed, using a process of *dynamic feature selection*. Since many decisions are easy to make in the presence of strongly predictive features, we would like our model to use fewer templates when it is more confident. For a fixed, learned ordering of feature templates, we build up a vector of class scores incrementally over each prefix of the sequence of templates, which we call the *prefix scores*. Once we reach a stopping criterion based on class confidence (margin), we stop computing prefix scores, and predict the current highest scoring class. Our aim is to train each prefix to be as good a classifier as possible without the following templates, minimizing the number of templates needed for accurate predictions.

Given this method for performing fast inference on an ordered set of feature templates, it remains to choose the ordering. In Section 4.5, we develop several methods for picking template orderings, based on ideas from group sparsity (Yuan and Lin, 2006; Swirszcz et al., 2009), and other techniques for feature subset-selection (Kohavi and John, 1997).

4.1 Definitions

Given a model that computes scores additively over template-specific scoring functions as in (2), parameters $\mathbf{w}$, and an observation $x \in X$, we can define the i'th *prefix score* for label $y \in \mathcal{Y}$ as:

$$P_{i,y}(x, \mathbf{w}) = \sum_{j=1}^{i} \mathbf{w}_j \cdot \Phi_j(x, y),$$

or $P_{i,y}$ when the choice of observations and weights is clear from context. Abusing notation we also refer to the vector containing all i'th prefix scores for observation x associated to each label in $\mathcal{Y}$ as $P_i(x, \mathbf{w})$, or P_i when this is unambiguous.

Given a parameter $m > 0$, called the *margin*, we define a function h on prefix scores:

$$h(P_i, y) = \max\{0, \max_{y' \neq y} P_{i,y'} - P_{i,y} + m\}$$

Algorithm 1 Inference

Input: template parameters $\{\mathbf{w}_i\}_{i=1}^{k}$, margin m and optional (for train time) true label y
Initialize: $i = 1$
while $l > 0 \wedge i \leq k$ **do**
  $l = \max_{y'} h(P_i, y')$ (test) or $h(P_i, y)$ (train)
  $i \leftarrow i + 1$
end while
return $\{P_j\}_{j=1}^{i}$ (train) or $\max_{y'} P_{i,y'}$ (test)

Algorithm 2 Parameter Learning

Input: examples $\{(x_i, y_i)\}_i^N$, margin m
Initialize: parameters $\mathbf{w}_0 = 0$, $i = 1$
while $i \leq N$ **do**
  prefixes $\leftarrow$ Infer$(x_i, y_i, \mathbf{w}_i, m)$
  $g_i \leftarrow$ ComputeGradient(prefixes)
  $\mathbf{w}_{i+1} \leftarrow$ UpdateParameters$(\mathbf{w}_i, g_i)$
  $i \leftarrow i + 1$
end while
return $\mathbf{w}_N$

This is the familiar structured hinge loss function as in structured support vector machines (Tsochantaridis et al., 2004), which has a minimum at 0 if and only if class y is ranked ahead of all other classes by at least m.

Using this notation, the condition that some label y be ranked first by a margin can be written as $h(P_i, y) = 0$, and the condition that any class be ranked first by a margin can be written as $\max_{y'} h(P_i, y') = 0$.

4.2 Inference

As described in Algorithm 1, at test time we compute prefixes until some label is ranked ahead of all other labels with a margin m, then predict with that label. At train time, we predict until the correct label is ranked ahead with margin m, and return the whole set of prefixes for use by the learning algorithm. If no prefix scores have a margin, then we predict with the final prefix score involving all the feature templates.

4.3 Learning

We split learning into two subproblems: first, given an ordered sequence of feature templates and our inference procedure, we wish to learn parameters that optimize accuracy while using as few of those templates as possible. Second, given a method for training feature templated classifiers, we want to learn an ordering of templates that optimizes accuracy.

We wish to optimize several different objectives during learning: template parameters should have strong predictive power on their own, but also work well when combined with the scores from later templates. Additionally, we want to encourage well-calibrated confidence scores that allow us to stop prediction early without significant reduction in generalization ability.

4.4 Learning the parameters

To learn parameters that encourage the use of few feature templates, we look at the model as outputting not a single prediction but a sequence of prefix predictions $\{P_i\}$. For each training example, each feature template receives a number of hinge-loss gradients equal to its distance from the index where the margin requirement is finally reached. This is equivalent to treating each prefix as its own model for which we have a hinge loss function, and learning all models simultaneously. Our high-level approach is described in Algorithm 2.

Concretely, for k feature templates we optimize the following structured max-margin objective (with the dependence of P's on $\mathbf{w}$ written explicitly where helpful):

$$\mathbf{w}^* = \arg\min_{\mathbf{w}} \sum_{(x,y)} \ell(x, y, \mathbf{w})$$

$$\ell(x, y, \mathbf{w}) = \sum_{i=1}^{i_y^*} h(P_i(x, \mathbf{w}), y)$$

$$i_y^* = \min_{i \in \{1..k\}} i \quad \text{s.t.} \quad h(P_i, y) = 0$$

The per-example gradient of this objective for weights $\mathbf{w}_j$ corresponding to feature template Φ_j then corresponds to

$$\frac{\partial \ell}{\partial \mathbf{w}_j} = \sum_{i=j}^{i_y^*} \Phi_j(x, y_{\text{loss}}(P_i, y)) - \Phi_j(x, y).$$

where we define

$$y_{\text{loss}}(P_i, y) = \arg\max_{y'} P_{i,y'} - m \cdot I(y' = y),$$

where I is an indicator function of the label y, used to define loss-augmented inference.

We add an ℓ_2 regularization term to the objective, and tune the margin m and the regularization strength to tradeoff between speed and accuracy. In our experiments, we used a development set to choose a regularizer and margin that reduced test-time speed as much as possible without decreasing accuracy. We then varied the margin for that same model at test time to achieve larger speed gains at the cost of accuracy. In all experiments, the margin with which the model was trained corresponds to the largest margin reported, i.e. that with the highest accuracy.

4.5 Learning the template ordering

We examine three approaches to learning the template ordering.

4.5.1 Group Lasso and Group Orthogonal Matching Pursuit

The Group Lasso regularizer (Yuan and Lin, 2006) penalizes the sum of ℓ_2-norms of weights of feature templates (different from what is commonly called "ℓ_2" regularization, penalizing squared ℓ_2 norms), $\sum_i c_i \|w_i\|_2$, where c_i is a weight for each template. This regularizer encourages entire groups of weights to be set to 0, whose templates can then be discarded from the model. By varying the strength of the regularizer, we can learn an ordering of the importance of each template for a given model. The included groups for a given regularization strength are nearly always subsets of one another (technical conditions for this to be true are given in Hastie et al. (2007)). The sequence of solutions for varied regularization strength is called the *regularization path*, and by slight abuse of terminology we use this to refer to the induced template ordering.

An alternative and related approach to learning template orderings is based on the Group Orthogonal Matching Pursuit (GOMP) algorithm for generalized linear models (Swirszcz et al., 2009; Lozano et al., 2011), with a few modifications for the setting of high-dimensional, sparse NLP data (described in Appendix B). Orthogonal matching pursuit algorithms are a set of stagewise feature selection techniques similar to forward stagewise regression (Hastie et al., 2007) and LARS (Efron et al., 2004). At each stage, GOMP effectively uses each feature template to perform a linear regression to fit the gradient of the loss function. This attempts to find the correlation of each feature subset with the residual of the model. It then adds the feature template that best fits this gradient, and retrains the model. The main weakness of this method is that it fits the gradient of the training error which can rapidly overfit for sparse, high-dimensional data. Ultimately, we would prefer to use a development set for feature selection.

4.5.2 Wrapper Method

The *wrapper method* (Kohavi and John, 1997) is a meta-algorithm for feature selection, usually based on a validation set. We employ it in a stage-wise approach to learning a sequence of templates. Given an ordering of the initial sub-sequence and a learning procedure, we add each remaining template to our ordering and estimate parameters, selecting as the next template the one that gives the highest increase in development set performance. We begin the procedure with no templates, and repeat the procedure until we have a total ordering over the set of feature templates. When learning the ordering we use the same hyperparameters as will be used during final training.

While simpler than the Lasso and Matching Pursuit approaches, we empirically found this approach to outperform the others, due to the necessity of using a development set to select features for our high-dimensional application areas.

5 Related Work

Our work is primarily inspired by previous research on cascades of classifiers; however, it differs significantly by approximating the score of a single linear model—scoring as few of its features as possible to obtain sufficient confidence.

We pose and address the question of whether a single, interacting set of parameters can be learned such that they efficiently both (1) provide high accuracy and (2) good confidence estimates throughout their use in the lengthening prefixes of the feature template sequence. (These two requirements are both incorporated into our novel parameter estimation algorithm.) In contrast, other work (Weiss and Taskar, 2013; He et al., 2013) learns a separate classifier to determine when to add features. Such heavier-weight approaches are unsuitable for our setting, where the core classifier's features and scoring are already so cheap that adding complex decision-making would cause too much computational overhead.

Other previous work on cascades uses a series of increasingly complex models, such as the Viola-Jones face detection cascade of classifiers (2001), which applies boosted trees trained on subsets of features in increasing order of complexity as needed, aiming to reject many sub-image windows early in processing. We allow scores from each layer to directly affect the final prediction, avoiding duplicate incorporation of evidence.

Our work is also related to the field of learning and inference under test-time budget constraints (Grubb and Bagnell, 2012; Trapeznikov and Saligrama, 2013). However, common approaches to this problem also employ auxiliary models to rank which feature to add next, and are generally suited for problems where features are expensive to compute (*e.g* vision) and the extra computation of an auxiliary pruning-decision model is offset by substantial reduction in feature computations (Weiss and Taskar, 2013). Our method uses confidence scores directly from the model, and so requires no additional computation, making it suitable for speeding up classifier-based NLP methods that are already very fast and have relatively cheap features.

Some cascaded approaches strive at each stage to prune the number of possible output structures under consideration, whereas in our case we focus on pruning the input features. For example, Xu et al. (2013) learn a tree of classifiers that subdivides the set of classes to minimize average test-time cost. Chen et al. (2012) similarly use a linear cascade instead of a tree. Weiss and Taskar (2010) prune output labels in the context of structured prediction through a cascade of increasingly complex models, and Rush and Petrov (2012) successfully apply these structured prediction cascades to the task of graph-based dependency parsing.

In the context of NLP, He et al. (2013) describe a method for dynamic feature template selection at test time in graph-based dependency parsing. Their technique is particular to the parsing task—making a binary decision about whether to lock in edges in the dependency graph at each stage, and enforcing parsing-specific, hard-coded constraints on valid subsequent edges. Furthermore, as described above, they employ an auxiliary model to select features.

He and Eisner (2012) share our goal to speed test time prediction by dynamically selecting features, but they also learn an additional model on top of a fixed base model, rather than using the training objective of the model itself.

While our comparisons above focus on other methods of *dynamic* feature selection, there also exists related work in the field of general (static) feature selection. The most relevant results come from the applications of *group sparsity*, such as the work of Martins et al. (2011) in *Group Lasso* for NLP problems. The Group Lasso regularizer (Yuan and Lin, 2006) sparsifies groups of feature weights (e.g. feature templates), and has been used to speed up test-time prediction by removing entire templates from the model. The key difference between this work and ours is that we select our templates based on the test-time difficulty of the inference problem, while the Group Lasso must do so at train time. In Appendix A, we compare against Group Lasso and show improvements in accuracy and speed.

Note that non-grouped approaches to selecting sparse feature subsets, such as boosting and ℓ_1 regularization, do not achieve our goal of fast test-time prediction in NLP models, as they would not zero-out entire templates, and still require the computation of a feature for every template for every test instance.

6 Experimental Results

We present experiments on three NLP tasks for which greedy sequence labeling has been a successful solution: part-of-speech tagging, transition-based dependency parsing and named entity recognition. In all cases our method achieves multiplicative speedups at test time with little loss in accuracy.

6.1 Part-of-speech tagging

We conduct our experiments on classifier-based greedy part-of-speech tagging. Our baseline tagger uses the same features described in Choi and Palmer (2012). We evaluate our models on the Penn Treebank WSJ corpus (Marcus et al., 1993), employing the typical split of sections used for part-of-speech tagging: 0-18 train, 19-21 development, 22-24 test. The parameters of our models are learned using AdaGrad (Duchi et al., 2011) with ℓ_2 regularization via regularized dual averaging (Xiao, 2009), and we used random search on the development set to select hyperparameters.

This baseline model (**baseline**) tags at a rate of approximately 23,000 tokens per second on a 2010 2.1GHz AMD Opteron machine with accuracy comparable to similar taggers (Giménez and Màrquez, 2004; Choi and Palmer, 2012; Toutanova et al., 2003). On the same machine the greedy Stanford CoreNLP left3words part-of-speech tagger also tags at approximately 23,000 tokens per second. Significantly higher absolute speeds for all methods can be attained on more modern machines.

Model/m	**Tok.**	**Unk.**	**Feat.**	**Speed**
Baseline	97.22	88.63	46	1x
Stagewise	96.54	83.63	9.50	2.74
Fixed	89.88	56.25	1	16.16x
Fixed	94.66	60.59	3	9.54x
Fixed	96.16	87.09	5	7.02x
Fixed	96.88	88.81	10	3.82x
Dynamic/15	96.09	83.12	1.92	**10.36x**
Dynamic/35	97.02	88.26	4.33	**5.22x**
Dynamic/45	97.16	88.84	5.87	3.97x
Dynamic/50	**97.21**	88.95	6.89	3.41x

Table 1: Comparison of our models using different margins m, with speeds measured relative to the baseline. We train a model as accurate as the baseline while tagging 3.4x tokens/sec, and in another model maintain $> 97\%$ accuracy while tagging 5.2x, and $> 96\%$ accuracy with a speedup of 10.3x.

We include additional baselines that divide the features into templates, but train the templates' parameters more simply than our algorithm. The **stagewise** baseline learns the model parameters for each of the templates in order, starting with only one template—once each template has been trained for a fixed number of iterations, that template's parameters are fixed and we add the next one. We also create a separately-trained baseline model for each fixed prefix of the feature templates (**fixed**). This shows that our speedups are not simply due to superfluous features in the later templates.

Our main results are shown in Table 1. We increase the speed of our baseline POS tagger by a factor of 5.2x without falling below 97% test accuracy. By tuning our training method to more aggressively prune templates, we achieve speedups of over 10x while providing accuracy higher than 96%. It is worth noting that the results for our method (**dynamic**) are all obtained from a single trained model (with hyperparameters optimized for $m = 50$, which we observed gave a good speedup with nearly no lossin accuracy on the development set), the only difference being

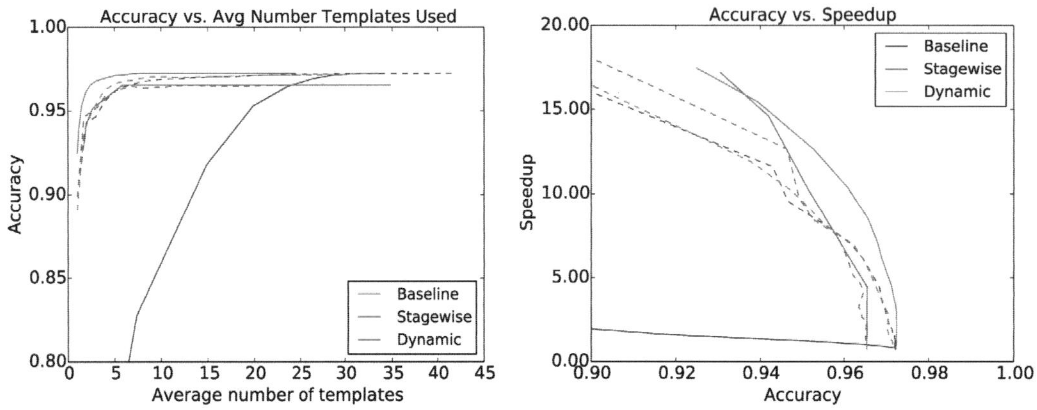

Figure 1: Left-hand plot depicts test accuracy as a function of the average number of templates used to predict. Right-hand plot shows speedup as a function of accuracy. Our model consistently achieves higher accuracy while using fewer templates resulting in the best ratio of speed to accuracy.

that we varied the margin at test time. Superior results for $m \neq 50$ could likely be obtained by optimizing hyperparameters for the desired margin.

Results show our method (**dynamic**) learns to dynamically select the number of templates, often using only a small fraction. The majority of test tokens can be tagged using only the first few templates: just over 40% use one template, and 75% require at most four templates, while maintaining 97.17% accuracy. On average 6.71 out of 46 templates are used, though a small set of complicated instances never surpass the margin and use all 46 templates. The right hand plot of Figure 1 shows speedup vs. accuracy for various settings of the confidence margin m.

The left plot in Figure 1 depicts accuracy as a function of the number of templates used at test time. We present results for both varying the number of templates directly (dashed) and margin (solid). The baseline model trained on all templates performs very poorly when using margin-based inference, since its training objective does not learn to predict with only prefixes. When predicting using a fixed subset of templates, we use a different baseline model for each one of the 46 total template prefixes, learned with only those features; we then compare the test accuracy of our dynamic model using template prefix i to the baseline model trained on the fixed prefix i. Our model performs just as well as these separately trained models, demonstrating that our objective learns weights that allow each prefix to act as its own high-quality classifier.

6.1.1 Learning the template ordering

As described in Section 4.5, we experimented on part-of-speech tagging with three different algorithms for learning an ordering of feature templates: Group Lasso, Group Orthogonal Matching Pursuit (GOMP), and the wrapper method. For the case of Group Lasso, this corresponds to the experimental setup used when evaluating Group Lasso for NLP in Martins et al. (2011). As detailed in the part-of-speech tagging experiments of Appendix A, we found the wrapper method to work best in our dynamic prediction setting. Therefore, we use it in our remaining experiments in parsing and named entity recognition. Essentially, the Group Lasso picks small templates too early in the ordering by penalizing template norms, and GOMP picks large templates too early by overfitting the train error.

6.2 Transition-based dependency parsing

We base our parsing experiments on the greedy, non-projective transition-based dependency parser described in Choi and Palmer (2011). Our model uses a total of 60 feature templates based mainly on the word form, POS tag, lemma and assigned head label of current and previous input and stack tokens, and parses about 300 sentences/second on a modest 2.1GHz AMD Opteron machine.

We train our parser on the English Penn TreeBank, learning the parameters using AdaGrad and the parsing split, training on sections 2–21, testing on section 23 and using section 22 for development and the Stanford dependency framework (de

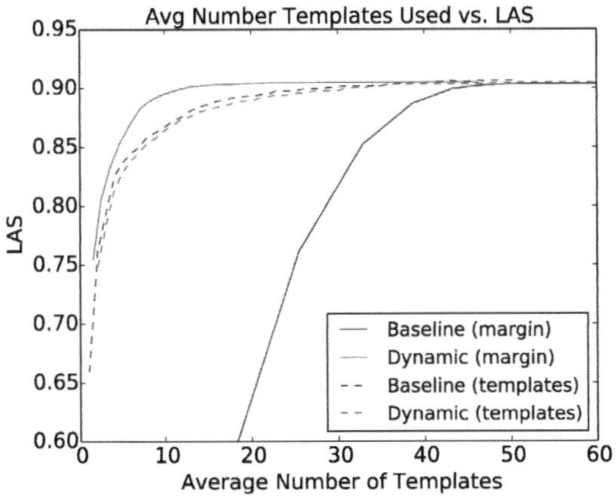

Figure 2: Parsing speedup as a function of accuracy. Our model achieves the highest accuracy while using the fewest feature templates.

Marneffe and Manning, 2008). POS tags were automatically generated via 10-way jackknifing using the baseline POS model described in the previous section, trained with AdaGrad using ℓ_2 regularization, with parameters tuned on the development set to achieve 97.22 accuracy on WSJ sections 22-24. Lemmas were automatically generated using the ClearNLP morphological analyzer. We measure accuracy using labeled and unlabeled attachment scores excluding punctuation, achieving a labeled score of 90.31 and unlabeled score of 91.83, which are comparable to similar greedy parsers (Choi and Palmer, 2011; Honnibal and Goldberg, 2013).

Our experimental setup is the same as for part-of-speech tagging. We compare our model (**dynamic**) to both a single **baseline** model trained on all features, and a set of 60 models each trained on a prefix of feature templates. Our experiments vary the margin used during prediction (solid) as well as the number of templates used (dashed).

As in part-of-speech tagging, we observe significant test-time speedups when applying our method of dynamic feature selection to dependency parsing. With a loss of only 0.04 labeled attachment score (LAS), our model produces parses 2.7 times faster than the baseline. As listed in Table 2, with a more aggressive margin our model can parse more than 3 times faster while remaining above 90% LAS, and more than 5 times faster while maintaining accuracy above 88.5%.

In Figure 2 we see not only that our **dynamic** model consistently achieves higher accuracy while using fewer templates, but also that our model (**dynamic**, dashed) performs exactly as well as separate models trained on each prefix of templates (**baseline**, dashed), demonstrating again that our training objective is successful in learning a single model that can predict as well as possible using any prefix of feature templates while successfully selecting which of these prefixes to use on a per-example basis.

Model/m	LAS	UAS	Feat.	Speed
Baseline	90.31	91.83	60	1x
Fixed	65.99	70.78	1	27.5x
Fixed	86.87	88.81	10	5.51x
Fixed	88.76	90.51	20	2.83x
Fixed	89.04	90.71	30	1.87x
Dynamic/6.5	88.63	90.36	7.81	5.16x
Dynamic/7.1	89.07	90.73	8.57	4.66x
Dynamic/10	90.16	91.70	13.27	3.17x
Dynamic/11	90.27	91.80	15.83	2.71x

Table 2: Comparison of our baseline and templated models using varying margins m and numbers of templates.

6.3 Named entity recognition

We implement a greedy left-to-right named entity recognizer based on Ratinov and Roth (2009) using a total of 46 feature templates, including surface features such as lemma and capitalization, gazetteer look-ups, and each token's *extended prediction history*, as described in (Ratinov and Roth, 2009). Training, tuning, and evaluation are performed on the CoNLL 2003 English data set with the BILOU encoding to denote label spans.

Our baseline model achieves F1 scores of 88.35 and 93.37 on the test and development sets, respectively, and tags at a rate of approximately 5300 tokens per second on the hardware described in the experiments above. We achieve a 2.3x speedup while maintaining F1 score above 88 on the test set.

7 Conclusions and Future Work

By learning to dynamically select the most predictive features at test time, our algorithm provides significant speed improvements to classifier-based structured prediction algorithms, which themselves already comprise the fastest methods in NLP. Further, these speed gains come at very lit-

Model/m	Test F1	Feat.	Speed
Baseline	88.35	46	1x
Fixed	65.05	1	19.08x
Fixed	85.00	10	2.14x
Fixed	85.81	13	1.87x
Dynamic/3.0	87.62	7.23	2.59x
Dynamic/4.0	88.20	9.45	2.32x
Dynamic/5.0	88.23	12.96	1.96x

Table 3: Comparison of our baseline and templated NER models using varying margin m and number of templates.

tle extra implementation cost and can easily be combined with existing state-of-the-art systems. Future work will remove the fixed ordering for feature templates, and dynamically add additional features based on the current scores of different labels.

8 Acknowledgements

This work was supported in part by the Center for Intelligent Information Retrieval, in part by DARPA under agreement number FA8750-13-2-0020, and in part by NSF grant #CNS-0958392. The U.S. Government is authorized to reproduce and distribute reprint for Governmental purposes notwithstanding any copyright annotation thereon. Any opinions, findings and conclusions or recommendations expressed in this material are those of the authors and do not necessarily reflect those of the sponsor.

References

Eric Bengtson and Dan Roth. 2008. Understanding the value of features for coreference resolution. In *Proceedings of the Conference on Empirical Methods in Natural Language Processing*, pages 294–303. Association for Computational Linguistics.

Minmin Chen, Zhixiang "Eddie" Xu, Kilian Q Weinberger, Olivier Chappele, and Dor Kedem. 2012. Classifier cascade for minimizing feature evaluation cost. In *AISTATS*.

Jinho Choi and Martha Palmer. 2011. Getting the Most out of Transition-based Dependency Parsing. *Association for Computational Linguistics*, pages 687–692.

Jinho Choi and Martha Palmer. 2012. Fast and robust part-of-speech tagging using dynamic model selection. In *Association for Computational Linguistics*.

Hal Daumé III, John Langford, and Daniel Marcu. 2009. Search-based structured prediction. *Machine Learning*, 75(3):297–325.

Marie-Catherine de Marneffe and Christopher D. Manning. 2008. The stanford typed dependencies representation. In *COLING 2008 Workshop on Cross-framework and Cross-domain Parser Evaluation*.

John Duchi, Elad Hazan, and Yoram Singer. 2011. Adaptive Subgradient Methods for Online Learning and Stochastic Optimization. *JMLR*, 12:2121–2159.

Bradley Efron, Trevor Hastie, Iain Johnstone, Robert Tibshirani, et al. 2004. Least angle regression. *The Annals of Statistics*, 32(2):407–499.

Jesús Giménez and Lluís Màrquez. 2004. Svmtool: A general pos tagger generator based on support vector machines. In *Proceedings of the 4th LREC*, Lisbon, Portugal.

Alexander Grubb and J. Andrew Bagnell. 2012. SpeedBoost: Anytime Prediction with Uniform Near-Optimality. In *AISTATS*.

Trevor Hastie, Jonathan Taylor, Robert Tibshirani, and Guenther Walther. 2007. Forward stagewise regression and the monotone lasso. *Electronic Journal of Statistics*, 1:1–29.

He He and Jason Eisner. 2012. Cost-sensitive dynamic feature selection. In *ICML Workshop on Inferning: Interactions between Inference and Learning*.

He He, Hal Daumé III, and Jason Eisner. 2013. Dynamic feature selection for dependency parsing. In *EMNLP*.

M Honnibal and Y Goldberg. 2013. A Non-Monotonic Arc-Eager Transition System for Dependency Parsing. *CoNLL*.

Ron Kohavi and George H John. 1997. Wrappers for feature subset selection. *Artificial Intelligence*, 97(1):273–324.

Aurélie C Lozano, Grzegorz Swirszcz, and Naoki Abe. 2011. Group orthogonal matching pursuit for logistic regression. In *International Conference on Artificial Intelligence and Statistics*, pages 452–460.

Mitchell P. Marcus, Beatrice Santorini, and Mary Ann Marcinkiewicz. 1993. Building a Large Annotated Corpus of English: The Penn Treebank. *Computational Linguistics*, 19(2):313–330.

André Martins, Noah Smith, Pedro Aguiar, and Mário Figueiredo. 2011. Structured sparsity in structured prediction. In *Proceedings of the Conference on Empirical Methods in Natural Language Processing*, pages 1500–1511. Association for Computational Linguistics.

Joakim Nivre. 2009. Non-projective dependency parsing in expected linear time. In *Proceedings of the Joint Conference of the 47th Annual Meeting of the ACL and the 4th International Joint Conference on Natural Language Processing of the AFNLP*, volume 1, pages 351–359. Association for Computational Linguistics.

Lev Ratinov and Dan Roth. 2009. Design challenges and misconceptions in named entity recognition. In *Proceedings of the Thirteenth Conference on Computational Natural Language Learning*, pages 147–155. Association for Computational Linguistics.

Stéphane Ross, Geoffrey J. Gordon, and Drew Bagnell. 2011. A reduction of imitation learning and structured prediction to no-regret online learning. In Geoffrey J. Gordon, David B. Dunson, and Miroslav Dudík, editors, *AISTATS*, volume 15 of *JMLR Proceedings*, pages 627–635.

Alexander M Rush and Slav Petrov. 2012. Vine pruning for efficient multi-pass dependency parsing. In *Proceedings of the 2012 Conference of the North American Chapter of the Association for Computational Linguistics: Human Language Technologies*, pages 498–507. Association for Computational Linguistics.

Grzegorz Swirszcz, Naoki Abe, and Aurelie C Lozano. 2009. Grouped orthogonal matching pursuit for variable selection and prediction. In *Advances in Neural Information Processing Systems*, pages 1150–1158.

Kristina Toutanova, Dan Klein, Christopher D Manning, and Yoram Singer. 2003. Feature-rich part-of-speech tagging with a cyclic dependency network. In *HLT-NAACL*.

Kirill Trapeznikov and Venkatesh Saligrama. 2013. Supervised sequential classification under budget constraints. In *AISTATS*.

Ioannis Tsochantaridis, Thomas Hofmann, Thorsten Joachims, and Yasemin Altun. 2004. Support vector machine learning for interdependent and structured output spaces. In *Proceedings of the Twenty-first International Conference on Machine Learning*, page 104.

Paul Viola and Michael Jones. 2001. Rapid object detection using a boosted cascade of simple features. In *Proceedings of the 2001 IEEE Computer Society Conference on Computer Vision and Pattern Recognition*, volume 1, pages I–511. IEEE.

David Weiss and Ben Taskar. 2010. Structured prediction cascades. In *AISTATS*.

David Weiss and Ben Taskar. 2013. Learning adaptive value of information for structured prediction. In *NIPS*.

Lin Xiao. 2009. Dual Averaging Method for Regularized Stochastic Learning and Online Optimization. In *NIPS*.

Zhixiang "Eddie" Xu, Matt J Kusner, Kilian Q Weinberger, and Minmin Chen. 2013. Cost-sensitive tree of classifiers. In *ICML*.

Ming Yuan and Yi Lin. 2006. Model selection and estimation in regression with grouped variables. *Journal of the Royal Statistical Society: Series B (Statistical Methodology)*, 68(1):49–67.

Compositional Vector Space Models for Knowledge Base Completion

Arvind Neelakantan, Benjamin Roth, Andrew McCallum
Department of Computer Science
University of Massachusetts, Amherst
Amherst, MA, 01003
{arvind,beroth,mccallum}@cs.umass.edu

Abstract

Knowledge base (KB) completion adds new facts to a KB by making inferences from existing facts, for example by inferring with high likelihood *nationality(X,Y)* from *bornIn(X,Y)*. Most previous methods infer simple one-hop relational synonyms like this, or use as evidence a multi-hop relational path treated as an atomic feature, like *bornIn(X,Z)* $\rightarrow$ *containedIn(Z,Y)*. This paper presents an approach that reasons about conjunctions of multi-hop relations *non-atomically*, composing the implications of a path using a recurrent neural network (RNN) that takes as inputs vector embeddings of the binary relation in the path. Not only does this allow us to generalize to paths unseen at training time, but also, with a single high-capacity RNN, to predict new relation types not seen when the compositional model was trained (zero-shot learning). We assemble a new dataset of over 52M relational triples, and show that our method improves over a traditional classifier by 11%, and a method leveraging pre-trained embeddings by 7%.

1 Introduction

Constructing large knowledge bases (KBs) supports downstream reasoning about resolved entities and their relations, rather than the noisy textual evidence surrounding their natural language mentions. For this reason KBs have been of increasing interest in both industry and academia (Bollacker et al., 2008; Suchanek et al., 2007; Carlson et al., 2010). Such KBs typically contain many millions of facts, most of them (entity1,relation,entity2) "triples" (also known as binary relations) such as *(Barack Obama, presidentOf, USA)* and *(Brad Pitt, marriedTo, Angelina Jolie)*.

However, even the largest KBs are woefully incomplete (Min et al., 2013), missing many important facts, and therefore damaging their usefulness in downstream tasks. Ironically, these missing facts can frequently be inferred from other facts already in the KB, thus representing a sort of inconsistency that can be repaired by the application of an automated process. The addition of new triples by leveraging existing triples is typically known as *KB completion*.

Early work on this problem focused on learning symbolic rules. For example, Schoenmackers et al. (2010) learns Horn clauses predictive of new binary relations by exhaustively exploring relational paths of increasing length, and selecting those surpassing an accuracy threshold. (A "path" is a sequence of triples in which the second entity of each triple matches the first entity of the next triple.) Lao et al. (2011) introduced the Path Ranking Algorithm (PRA), which greatly improves efficiency and robustness by replacing exhaustive search with random walks, and using unique paths as features in a per-target-relation binary classifier. A typical predictive feature learned by PRA is that *CountryOfHeadquarters(X, Y)* is implied by *IsBasedIn(X,A)* and *StateLocatedIn(A, B)* and *CountryLocatedIn(B, Y)*. Given *IsBasedIn(Microsoft, Seattle)*, *StateLocatedIn(Seattle, Washington)* and *CountryLocatedIn(Washington, USA)*, we can infer the fact *CountryOfHeadquarters(Microsoft, USA)* using the predictive feature. In later work, Lao et al. (2012) greatly increase available raw material for paths by augmenting KB-schema relations with relations defined by the text connecting mentions of entities in a large corpus (also known as OpenIE relations (Banko et al., 2007)).

However, these symbolic methods can produce many millions of distinct paths, each of which is categorically distinct, treated by PRA as a dis-

Proceedings of the 53rd Annual Meeting of the Association for Computational Linguistics and the 7th International Joint Conference on Natural Language Processing, pages 156–166,
Beijing, China, July 26-31, 2015.

tinct feature. (See Figure 1.) Even putting aside the OpenIE relations, this limits the applicability of these methods to modern KBs that have thousands of relation types, since the number of distinct paths increases rapidly with the number of relation types. If textually-defined OpenIE relations are included, the problem is obviously far more severe.

Better generalization can be gained by operating on embedded vector representations of relations, in which vector similarity can be interpreted as semantic similarity. For example, Bordes et al. (2013) learn low-dimensional vector representations of entities and KB relations, such that vector differences between two entities should be close to the vectors associated with their relations. This approach can find relation synonyms, and thus perform a kind of one-to-one, non-path-based relation prediction for KB completion. Similarly Nickel et al. (2011) and Socher et al. (2013a) perform KB completion by learning embeddings of relations, but based on matrices or tensors. Universal schema (Riedel et al., 2013) learns to perform relation prediction cast as matrix completion (likewise using vector embeddings), but predicts textually-defined OpenIE relations as well as KB relations, and embeds entity-pairs in addition to individual entities. Like all of the above, it also reasons about individual relations, not the evidence of a connected path of relations.

This paper proposes an approach combining the advantages of (a) reasoning about conjunctions of relations connected in a path, and (b) generalization through vector embeddings, and (c) reasoning non-atomically and compositionally about the elements of the path, for further generalization.

Our method uses recurrent neural networks (RNNs) (Werbos, 1990) to compose the semantics of relations in an arbitrary-length path. At each path-step it consumes both the vector embedding of the next relation, and the vector representing the path-so-far, then outputs a composed vector (representing the extended path-so-far), which will be the input to the next step. After consuming a path, the RNN should output a vector in the semantic neighborhood of the relation between the first and last entity of the path. For example, after consuming the relation vectors along the path *Melinda Gates* → *Bill Gates* → *Microsoft* → *Seattle*, our method produces a vector very close to the relation *livesIn*.

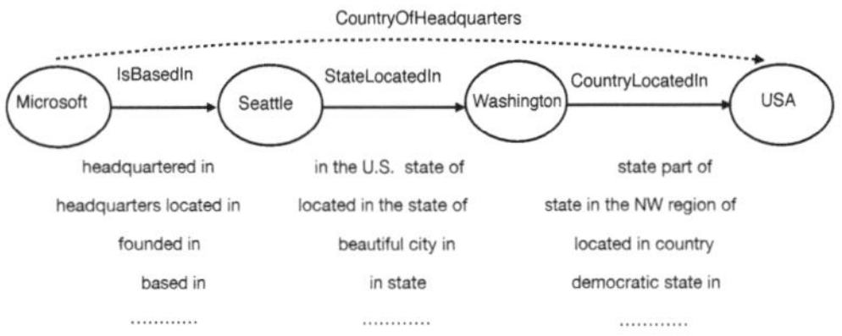

Figure 1: Semantically similar paths connecting entity pair (Microsoft, USA).

Our compositional approach allow us at test time to make predictions from paths that were unseen during training, because of the generalization provided by vector neighborhoods, and because they are composed in non-atomic fashion. This allows our model to seamlessly perform inference on many millions of paths in the KB graph. In most of our experiments, we learn a separate RNN for predicting each relation type, but alternatively, by learning a single high-capacity composition function for all relation types, our method can perform zero-shot learning—predicting new relation types for which the composition function was never explicitly trained.

Related to our work, new versions of PRA (Gardner et al., 2013; Gardner et al., 2014) use pre-trained vector representations of relations to alleviate its feature explosion problem—but the core mechanism continues to be a classifier based on atomic-path features. In the 2013 work many paths are collapsed by clustering paths according to their relations' embeddings, and substituting cluster ids for the original relation types. In the 2014 work unseen paths are mapped to nearby paths seen at training time, where nearness is measured using the embeddings. Neither is able to perform zero-shot learning since there must be a classifer for each predicted relation type. Furthermore their pre-trained vectors do not have the opportunity to be tuned to the KB completion task because the two sub-tasks are completely disentangled.

An additional contribution of our work is a new large-scale data set of over 52 million triples, and its preprocessing for purposes of path-based KB completion (can be downloaded from `http://iesl.cs.umass.edu/downloads/inferencerules/release.tar.gz`). The dataset is build from the combination of Freebase (Bollacker et al., 2008) and Google's entity linking in ClueWeb (Orr et al., 2013). Rather than Gardner's 1000 distinct paths per relation type, we have over 2 million. Rather than Gardner's 200

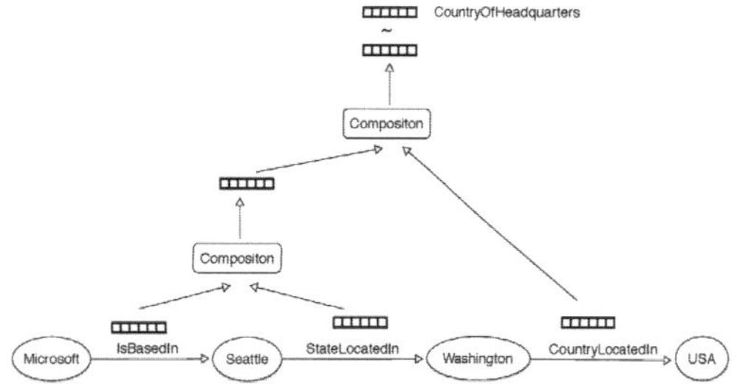

Figure 2: Vector Representations of the paths are computed by applying the composition function recursively.

entity pairs, we use over 10k. All experimental comparisons below are performed on this new data set.

On this challenging large-scale dataset our compositional method outperforms PRA (Lao et al., 2012), and Cluster PRA (Gardner et al., 2013) by 11% and 7% respectively. A further contribution of our work is a new, surprisingly strong baseline method using classifiers of path bigram features, which beats PRA and Cluster PRA, and statistically ties our compositional method. Our analysis shows that our method has substantially different strengths than the new baseline, and the combination of the two yields a 15% improvement over Gardner et al. (2013). We also show that our zero-shot model is indeed capable of predicting new unseen relation types.

2 Background

We give background on PRA which we use to obtain a set of paths connecting the entity pairs and the RNN model which we employ to model the composition function.

2.1 Path Ranking Algorithm

Since it is impractical to exhaustively obtain the set of all paths connecting an entity pair in the large KB graph, we use PRA (Lao et al., 2011) to obtain a set of paths connecting the entity pairs. Given a training set of entity pairs for a relation, PRA heuristically finds a set of paths by performing random walks from the source and target nodes keeping the most common paths. We use PRA to find millions of distinct paths per relation type. We do not use the random walk probabilities given by PRA since using it did not yield improvements in our experiments.

2.2 Recurrent Neural Networks

Recurrent neural network (RNN) (Werbos, 1990) is a neural network that constructs vector representation for sequences (of any length). For example, a RNN model can be used to construct vector representations for phrases or sentences (of any length) in natural language by applying a composition function (Mikolov et al., 2010; Sutskever et al., 2014; Vinyals et al., 2014). The vector representation of a phrase (w_1, w_2) consisting of words w_1 and w_2 is given by $f(W[v(w_1); v(w_2)])$ where $v(w) \in \mathbb{R}^d$ is the vector representation of w, f is an element-wise non linearity function, $[a; b]$ represents the concatenation two vectors a and b along with a bias term, and $W \in \mathbb{R}^{d \times 2*d+1}$ is the composition matrix. This operation can be repeated to construct vector representations of longer phrases.

3 Recurrent Neural Networks for KB Completion

This paper proposes a RNN model for KB completion that reasons on the paths connecting an entity pair to predict missing relation types. The vector representations of the paths (of any length) in the KB graph are computed by applying the composition function recursively as shown in Figure 2. To compute the vector representations for the higher nodes in the tree, the composition function consumes the vector representation of the node's two children nodes and outputs a new vector of the same dimension. Predictions about missing relation types are made by comparing the vector representation of the path with the vector representation of the relation using the sigmoid function.

We represent each binary relation using a d-dimensional real valued vector. We model composition using recurrent neural networks (Werbos, 1990). We learn a separate composition matrix for every relation that is predicted.

Let $v_r(\delta) \in \mathbb{R}^d$ be the vector representation of relation δ and $v_p(\pi) \in \mathbb{R}^d$ be the vector representation of path π. $v_p(\pi)$ denotes the relation vector if path π is of length one. To predict relation δ = *CountryOfHeadquarters*, the vector representation of the path π = *IsBasedIn* $\rightarrow$ *StateLocatedIn* containing two relations *IsBasedIn* and *StateLocatedIn* is computed by (Figure 2),

$$v_p(\pi) = f(W_\delta[v_r(\mathit{IsBasedIn}); v_r(\mathit{StateLocatedIn})])$$

where $f = sigmoid$ is the element-wise non-linearity function, $W_\delta \in \mathbb{R}^{d*2d+1}$ is the composition matrix for $\delta =$ *CountryOfHeadquarters* and $[a; b]$ represents the concatenation of two vectors $a \in \mathbb{R}^d, b \in \mathbb{R}^d$ along with a bias feature to get a new vector $[a; b] \in \mathbb{R}^{2d+1}$.

The vector representation of the path $\Pi =$ *IsBasedIn* $\rightarrow$ *StateLocatedIn* $\rightarrow$ *CountryLocatedIn* in Figure 2 is computed similarly by,

$$v_p(\Pi) = f(W_\delta[v_p(\pi); v_r(\textit{CountryLocatedIn})])$$

where $v_p(\pi)$ is the vector representation of path *IsBasedIn* $\rightarrow$ *StateLocatedIn*. While computing the vector representation of a path we always traverse left to right, composing the relation vector in the right with the accumulated path vector in the left[1]. This makes our model a recurrent neural network (Werbos, 1990).

Finally, we make a prediction regarding *CountryOfHeadquarters(Microsoft, USA)* using the path $\Pi =$ *IsBasedIn* $\rightarrow$ *StateLocatedIn* $\rightarrow$ *CountryLocatedIn* by comparing the vector representation of the path ($v_p(\Pi)$) with the vector representation of the relation *CountryOfHeadquarters* (v_r(*CountryOfHeadquarters*)) using the sigmoid function.

3.1 Model Training

We train the model with the existing facts in a KB using them as positive examples and negative examples are obtained by treating the unobserved instances as negative examples (Mintz et al., 2009; Lao et al., 2011; Riedel et al., 2013; Bordes et al., 2013). Unlike in previous work that use RNNs(Socher et al., 2011; Iyyer et al., 2014; Irsoy and Cardie, 2014), a challenge with using them for our task is that among the set of paths connecting an entity pair, we do not observe which of the path(s) is predictive of a relation. We select the path that is closest to the relation type to be predicted in the vector space. This not only allows for faster training (compared to marginalization) but also gives improved performance. This technique has been successfully used in models other than RNNs previously (Weston et al., 2013; Neelakantan et al., 2014).

[1]we did not get significant improvements when we tried more sophisticated ordering schemes for computing the path representations.

Algorithm 1 Training Algorithm of RNN model for relation δ

Input: $\Lambda_\delta = \Lambda_\delta^+ \cup \Lambda_\delta^-$, Φ_δ, number of iterations T, mini-batch size B
Initialize v_r, W_δ randomly
for $t = 1, 2, \ldots, T$ **do**
  $\nabla v_r = 0$, $\nabla W_\delta = 0$ and $b = 0$
  for $\lambda = (\gamma, \delta) \in \Lambda_\delta$ **do**
    $\mu_\lambda = \arg\max_{\pi \in \Phi_\delta(\gamma)} v_p(\pi).v_r(\delta)$
    Accumulate gradients to ∇v_r, ∇W_δ
  using path μ_λ.
    $b = b + 1$
    if $b = B$ **then**
      Gradient Update for v_r, W_δ
      $\nabla v_r = 0$, $\nabla W_\delta = 0$ and $b = 0$
    end if
  end for
  if $b > 0$ **then**
    Gradient Update for v_r, W_δ
  end if
end for
Output: v_r, W_δ

We assume that we are given a KB (for example, Freebase enriched with SVO triples) containing a set of entity pairs Γ, set of relations Δ and a set of observed facts Λ^+ where $\forall \lambda = (\gamma, \delta) \in \Lambda^+ (\gamma \in \Gamma, \delta \in \Delta)$ indicates a positive fact that entity pair γ is in relation δ. Let $\Phi_\delta(\gamma)$ denote the set of paths connecting entity pair γ given by PRA for predicting relation δ.

In our task, we only observe the set of paths connecting an entity pair but we do not observe which of the path(s) is predictive of the fact. We treat this as a latent variable (μ_λ for the fact λ) and we assign μ_λ the path whose vector representation has maximum dot product with the vector representation of the relation to be predicted. For example, μ_λ for the fact $\lambda = (\gamma, \delta) \in \Lambda^+$ is given by,

$$\mu_\lambda = \arg\max_{\pi \in \Phi_\delta(\gamma)} v_p(\pi).v_r(\delta)$$

During training, we assign μ_λ using the current parameter estimates. We use the same procedure to assign μ_λ for unobserved facts that are used as negative examples during training.

We train a separate RNN model for predicting each relation and the parameters of the model for predicting relation $\delta \in \Delta$ are $\Theta = \{v_r(\omega) \forall \omega \in \Delta,\ W_\delta\}$. Given a training set consisting of positive (Λ_δ^+) and negative (Λ_δ^-) instances[2] for relation δ, the parameters are trained to maximize the log likelihood of the training set with L-2 regularization.

$$\Theta^* = \arg\max_{\Theta} \sum_{\lambda=(\gamma,\delta)\in\Lambda_\delta^+} P(y_\lambda = 1;\Theta) + \sum_{\lambda=(\gamma,\delta)\in\Lambda_\delta^-} P(y_\lambda = 0;\Theta) - \rho\|\Theta\|^2$$

where y_λ is a binary random variable which takes the value 1 if the fact λ is true and 0 otherwise, and the probability of a fact $P(y_\lambda = 1;\Theta)$ is given by,

$$P(y_\lambda = 1;\Theta) = sigmoid(v_p(\mu_\lambda).v_r(\delta))$$
$$where \;\; \mu_\lambda = \arg\max_{\pi\in\Phi_\delta(\gamma)} v_p(\pi).v_r(\delta)$$

and $P(y_\lambda = 0;\Theta) = 1 - P(y_\lambda = 1;\Theta)$. The relation vectors and the composition matrix are initialized randomly. We train the network using backpropagation through structure (Goller and Küchler, 1996).

4 Zero-shot KB Completion

The KB completion task involves predicting facts on thousands of relations types and it is highly desirable that a method can infer facts about relation types without directly training for them. Given the vector representation of the relations, we show that our model described in the previous section is capable of predicting relational facts without explicitly training for the target (or test) relation types (zero-shot learning).

In zero-shot or zero-data learning (Larochelle et al., 2008; Palatucci et al., 2009), some labels or classes are not available during training the model and only a description of those classes are given at prediction time. We make two modifications to the model described in the previous section, (1) learn a general composition matrix, and (2) fix relation vectors with pre-trained vectors, so that we can predict relations that are unseen during training. This ability of the model to generalize to unseen relations is beyond the capabilities of all previous methods for KB inference (Schoenmackers et al., 2010; Lao et al., 2011; Gardner et al., 2013; Gardner et al., 2014).

We learn a general composition matrix for all relations instead of learning a separate composition matrix for every relation to be predicted. So, for example, the vector representation of the path π = *IsBasedIn* $\rightarrow$ *StateLocatedIn* containing two relations *IsBasedIn* and *StateLocatedIn* is computed by (Figure 2),

$$v_p(\pi) = f(W[v_r(\textit{IsBasedIn}); v_r(\textit{StateLocatedIn})])$$

where $W \in \mathbb{R}^{d*2d+1}$ is the general composition matrix.

We initialize the vector representations of the binary relations (v_r) using the representations learned in Riedel et al. (2013) and do not update them during training. The relation vectors are not updated because at prediction time we would be predicting relation types which are never seen during training and hence their vectors would never get updated. We learn only the general composition matrix in this model. We train a single model for a set of relation types by replacing the sigmoid function with a softmax function while computing probabilities and the parameters of the composition matrix are learned using the available training data containing instances of few relations. The other aspects of the model remain unchanged.

To predict facts whose relation types are unseen during training, we compute the vector representation of the path using the general composition matrix and compute the probability of the fact using the pre-trained relation vector. For example, using the vector representation of the path Π = *IsBasedIn* $\rightarrow$ *StateLocatedIn* $\rightarrow$ *CountryLocatedIn* in Figure 2, we can predict any relation irrespective of whether they are seen at training by comparing it with the pre-trained relation vectors.

5 Experiments

The hyperparameters of all the models were tuned on the same held-out development data. All the neural network models are trained for 150 iterations using 50 dimensional relation vectors, and we set the L2-regularizer and learning rate to 0.0001 and 0.1 respectively. We halved the learning rate after every 60 iterations and use minibatches of size 20. The neural networks and the classifiers were optimized using AdaGrad (Duchi et al., 2011).

5.1 Data

We ran experiments on Freebase (Bollacker et al., 2008) enriched with information from ClueWeb.

[2]we sub-sample a portion of the set of all unobserved instances.

Entities	18M
Freebase triples	40M
ClueWeb triples	12M
Relations	25,994
Relation types tested	46
Avg. paths/relation	2.3M
Avg. training facts/relation	6638
Avg. positive test instances/relation	3492
Avg. negative test instances/relation	43,160

Table 1: Statistics of our dataset.

We use the publicly available entity links to Freebase in the ClueWeb dataset (Orr et al., 2013). Hence, we create nodes only for Freebase entities in our KB graph. We remove facts containing /type/object/type as they do not give useful predictive information for our task. We get triples from ClueWeb by considering sentences that contain two entities linked to Freebase. We extract the phrase between the two entities and treat them as the relation types. For phrases that are of length greater than four we keep only the first and last two words. This helps us to avoid the time consuming step of dependency parsing the sentence to get the relation type. These triples are similar to facts obtained by OpenIE (Banko et al., 2007). To reduce noise, we select relation types that occur at least 50 times. We evaluate on 46 relation types in Freebase that have the most number of instances. The methods are evaluated on a subset of facts in Freebase that were hidden during training. Table 1 shows important statistics of our dataset.

5.2 Predictive Paths

Table 2 shows predictive paths for 4 relations learned by the RNN model. The high quality of unseen paths is indicative of the fact that the RNN model is able to generalize to paths that are never seen during training.

5.3 Results

Using our dataset, we compare the performance of the following methods:

PRA Classifier is the method in Lao et al. (2012) which trains a logistic regression classifier by creating a feature for every path type.

Cluster PRA Classifier is the method in Gardner et al. (2013) which replaces relation types from ClueWeb triples with their cluster membership in the KB graph before the path finding step. After this step, their method proceeds in exactly the same manner as Lao et al. (2012) training a logistic regression classifier by creating a feature for every path type. We use pre-trained relation vectors from Riedel et al. (2013) and use k-means clustering to cluster the relation types to 25 clusters as done in Gardner et al. (2013).

Composition-Add uses a simple element-wise addition followed by sigmoid non-linearity as the composition function similar to Yang et al. (2014).

RNN-random is the supervised RNN model described in section 3 with the relation vectors initialized randomly.

RNN is the supervised RNN model described in section 3 with the relation vectors initialized using the method in Riedel et al. (2013).

PRA Classifier-b is our simple extension to the method in Lao et al. (2012) which additionally uses bigrams in the path as features. We add a special *start* and *stop* symbol to the path before computing the bigram features.

Cluster PRA Classifier-b is our simple extension to the method in Gardner et al. (2013) which additionally uses bigram features computed as previously described.

RNN + PRA Classifier combines the predictions of *RNN* and *PRA Classifier*. We combine the predictions by assigning the score of a fact as the sum of their rank in the two models after sorting them in ascending order.

RNN + PRA Classifier-b combines the predictions of *RNN* and *PRA Classifier-b* using the technique described previously.

Table 3 shows the results of our experiments. The method described in Gardner et al. (2014) is not included in the table since the publicly available implementation does not scale to our large dataset. First, we show that it is better to train the models using all the path types instead of using only the top $1,000$ path types as done in previous work (Gardner et al., 2013; Gardner et al., 2014). We can see that the RNN model performs significantly better than the baseline methods of Lao et al. (2012) and Gardner et al. (2013). The performance of the RNN model is not affected by initialization since using random vectors and pre-trained vectors results in similar performance.

A surprising result is the impressive performance of our simple extension to the classifier approach. After the addition of bigram features, the naive PRA method is as effective as the Clus-

Relation: /book/written_work/original_language/ *(book "x" written in language "y")*
Seen paths:
/book/written_work/previous_in_series → /book/written_work/author → /people/person/nationality → /people/person/nationality^{-1} → /people/person/languages
/book/written_work/author → /people/ethnicity/people^{-1} → /people/ethnicity/languages_spoken
Unseen paths:
"in"$^{-1}$ - "writer"$^{-1}$ → /people/person/nationality^{-1} → /people/person/languages
/book/written_work/author → addresses → /people/person/nationality^{-1} → /people/person/languages

Relation: /people/person/place_of_birth/ *(person "x" born in place "y")*
Seen paths:
"was,born,in" → /location/mailing_address/citytown^{-1} → /location/mailing_address/state_province_region
"from" → /location/location/contains^{-1}
Unseen paths:
"born,in" → /location/location/contains → "near"$^{-1}$
"was,born,in" → commonly,known,as^{-1}

Relation: /geography/river/cities/ *(river "x" flows through or borders "y")*
Seen paths:
"at" → /location/location/contains^{-1}
"meets,the" → /transportation/bridge/body_of_water_spanned^{-1} → /location/location/contains^{-1} → "in"
Unseen paths:
/geography/lake/outflow^{-1} → /location/location/contains^{-1}
/geography/lake/outflow^{-1} → /location/location/contains^{-1} → "near"

Relation: /people/family/members/ *(person "y" part of family "x")*
Seen paths:
/royalty/monarch/royal_line^{-1} → /people/person/children → /royalty/monarch/royal_line → /royalty/royal_line/monarchs_from_this_line
/royalty/royal_line/monarchs_from_this_line → /people/person/parents^{-1} → /people/person/parents^{-1} → /people/person/parents^{-1}
Unseen paths:
/royalty/monarch/royal_line^{-1} → "leader"$^{-1}$ → "king" → "was,married,to"$^{-1}$
"of,the"$^{-1}$ → "but,also,of" → "married" → "defended"$^{-1}$

Table 2: Predictive paths, according to the *RNN* model, for 4 target relations. Two examples of seen and unseen paths are shown for each target relation. Inverse relations are marked by $^{-1}$, i.e, $r(x, y) \implies r^{-1}(y, x), \forall (x, y) \in r$. Relations within quotes are OpenIE (textual) relation types.

	train with top 1000 paths	train with all paths
Method	MAP	MAP
PRA Classifier	43.46	51.31
Cluster PRA Classifier	46.26	53.23
Composition-Add	40.23	45.37
RNN-random	45.52	56.91
RNN	46.61	56.95
PRA Classifier-b	48.09	58.13
Cluster PRA Classifier-b	48.72	58.02
RNN + PRA Classifier	49.92	58.42
RNN + PRA Classifier-b	51.94	**61.17**

Table 3: Results comparing different methods on 46 types. All the methods perform better when trained using all the paths than training using the top $1,000$ paths. When training with all the paths, *RNN* performs significantly ($p < 0.005$) better than *PRA Classifier* and *Cluster PRA Classifier*. The small difference in performance between *RNN* and both *PRA Classifier-b* and *Cluster PRA Classifier-b* is not statistically significant. The best results are obtained by combining the predictions of *RNN* with *PRA Classifier-b* which performs significantly ($p < 10^{-5}$) better than both *PRA Classifier-b* and *Cluster PRA Classifier-b*.

ter PRA method. The small difference in performance between *RNN* and both *PRA Classifier-b* and *Cluster PRA Classifier-b* is not statistically significant. We conjecture that our method has substantially different strengths than the new baseline. While the classifier with bigram features has an ability to accurately memorize important local structure, the RNN model generalizes better to un-

	train with top 1000 paths	train with all paths
Method	MAP	MAP
RNN	43.82	50.10
zero-shot	19.28	20.61
Random	7.59	

Table 4: Results comparing the zero-shot model with supervised RNN and a random baseline on 10 types. RNN is the fully supervised model described in section 3 while zero-shot is the model described in section 4. The zero-shot model without explicitly training for the target relation types achieves impressive results by performing significantly ($p < 0.05$) better than a random baseline.

seen paths that are very different from the paths seen is training. Empirically, combining the predictions of *RNN* and *PRA Classifier-b* achieves a statistically significant gain over *PRA Classifier-b*.

5.3.1 Zero-shot

Table 4 shows the results of the zero-shot model described in section 4 compared with the fully supervised RNN model (section 3) and a baseline that produces a random ordering of the test facts. We evaluate on randomly selected 10 (out of 46) relation types, hence for the fully supervised version we train 10 RNNs, one for each relation type. For evaluating the zero-shot model, we randomly split the relations into two sets of equal size and train a zero-shot model on one set and test on the other set. So, in this case we have two RNNs making predictions on relation types that they have never seen during training. As expected, the fully supervised RNN outperforms the zero-shot model by a large margin but the zero-shot model without using any direct supervision clearly performs much better than a random baseline.

5.3.2 Discussion

To investigate whether the performance of the RNNs were affected by multiple local optima issues, we combined the predictions of five different RNNs trained using all the paths. Apart from *RNN* and *RNN-random*, we trained three more RNNs with different random initialization and the performance of the three RNNs individually are 57.09, 57.11 and 56.91. The performance of the ensemble is 59.16 and their performance stopped improving after using three RNNs. So, this indicates that even though multiple local optima affects the performance, it is likely not the only issue since the performance of the ensemble is still less than the performance of *RNN + PRA Classifier-b*.

We suspect the RNN model does not capture some of the important local structure as well as the classifier using bigram features. To overcome this drawback, in future work, we plan to explore compositional models that have a longer memory (Hochreiter and Schmidhuber, 1997; Cho et al., 2014; Mikolov et al., 2014). We also plan to include vector representations for the entities and develop models that address the issue of polysemy in verb phrases (Cheng et al., 2014).

6 Related Work

KB Completion includes methods such as Lin and Pantel (2001), Yates and Etzioni (2007) and Berant et al. (2011) that learn inference rules of length one. Schoenmackers et al. (2010) learn general inference rules by considering the set of all paths in the KB and selecting paths that satisfy a certain precision threshold. Their method does not scale well to modern KBs and also depends on carefully tuned thresholds. Lao et al. (2011) train a simple logistic regression classifier with NELL KB paths as features to perform KB completion while Gardner et al. (2013) and Gardner et al. (2014) extend it by using pre-trained relation vectors to overcome feature sparsity. Recently, Yang et al. (2014) learn inference rules using simple element-wise addition or multiplication as the composition function.

Compositional Vector Space Models have been developed to represent phrases and sentences in natural language as vectors (Mitchell and Lapata, 2008; Baroni and Zamparelli, 2010; Yessenalina and Cardie, 2011). Neural networks have been successfully used to learn vector representations of phrases using the vector representations of the words in that phrase. Recurrent neural networks have been used for many tasks such as language modeling (Mikolov et al., 2010), machine translation (Sutskever et al., 2014) and parsing (Vinyals et al., 2014). Recursive neural networks, a more general version of the recurrent neural networks have been used for many tasks like parsing (Socher et al., 2011), sentiment classification (Socher et al., 2012; Socher et al., 2013c; Irsoy and Cardie, 2014), question answering (Iyyer et al., 2014) and natural language logical semantics (Bowman et al., 2014). Our overall approach is similar to RNNs with attention (Bahdanau et al., 2014; Graves, 2013) since we select a path among the set of paths connecting the entity pair to make the final prediction.

Zero-shot or zero-data learning was introduced in Larochelle et al. (2008) for character recognition and drug discovery. Palatucci et al. (2009) perform zero-shot learning for neural decoding while there has been plenty of work in this direction for image recognition (Socher et al., 2013b; Frome et al., 2013; Norouzi et al., 2014).

7 Conclusion

We develop a compositional vector space model for knowledge base completion using recurrent neural networks. In our challenging large-scale dataset available at `http://iesl.cs.umass.edu/downloads/inferencerules/release.tar.gz`, our method outperforms two baseline methods and performs competitively with a modified stronger baseline. The best results are obtained by combining the predictions of our model with the predictions of the modified baseline which achieves a 15% improvement over Gardner et al. (2013). We also show that our model has the ability to perform zero-shot inference.

Acknowledgments

We thank Matt Gardner for releasing the PRA code, and for answering numerous question about the code and data. We also thank the Stanford NLP group for releasing the neural networks code. This work was supported in part by the Center for Intelligent Information Retrieval, in part by DARPA under agreement number FA8750-13-2-0020, in part by an award from Google, and in part by NSF grant #CNS-0958392. The U.S. Government is authorized to reproduce and distribute reprints for Governmental purposes notwithstanding any copyright notation thereon. Any opinions, findings and conclusions or recommendations expressed in this material are those of the authors and do not necessarily reflect those of the sponsor.

References

Dzmitry Bahdanau, Kyunghyun Cho, and Yoshua Bengio. 2014. Neural machine translation by jointly learning to align and translate. In *ArXiv*.

Michele Banko, Michael J Cafarella, Stephen Soderland, Matt Broadhead, and Oren Etzioni. 2007. Open information extraction from the web. In *International Joint Conference on Artificial Intelligence.*

Marco Baroni and Roberto Zamparelli. 2010. Nouns are vectors, adjectives are matrices: Representing adjective-noun constructions in semantic space. In *Empirical Methods in Natural Language Processing*.

Jonathan Berant, Ido Dagan, and Jacob Goldberger. 2011. Global learning of typed entailment rules. In *Association for Computational Linguistics*.

Kurt Bollacker, Colin Evans, Praveen Paritosh, Tim Sturge, and Jamie Taylor. 2008. Freebase: a collaboratively created graph database for structuring human knowledge. In *Proceedings of the ACM SIGMOD International Conference on Management of Data*.

Antoine Bordes, Nicolas Usunier, Alberto García-Durán, Jason Weston, and Oksana Yakhnenko. 2013. Translating embeddings for modeling multi-relational data. In *Advances in Neural Information Processing Systems.*

Samuel R. Bowman, Christopher Potts, and Christopher D Manning. 2014. Recursive neural networks for learning logical semantics. In *CoRR*.

Andrew Carlson, Justin Betteridge, Bryan Kisiel, Burr Settles, Estevam R. Hruschka, and A. 2010. Toward an architecture for never-ending language learning. In *In AAAI*.

Cheng, Jianpeng Kartsaklis, and Edward Grefenstette. 2014. Investigating the role of prior disambiguation in deep-learning compositional models of meaning. In *In Learning Semantics workshop NIPS*.

Kyunghyun Cho, Bart van Merrienboer, Dzmitry Bahdanau, and Yoshua Bengio. 2014. On the properties of neural machine translation: Encoder–decoder approaches. In *Workshop on Syntax, Semantics and Structure in Statistical Translation*.

John Duchi, Elad Hazan, and Yoram Singer. 2011. Adaptive subgradient methods for online learning and stochastic optimization. In *Journal of Machine Learning Research*.

Andrea Frome, Gregory S. Corrado, Jonathon Shlens, Samy Bengio, Jeffrey Dean, Marc'Aurelio Ranzato, and Tomas Mikolov. 2013. Devise: A deep visual-semantic embedding model. In *Neural Information Processing Systems*.

Matt Gardner, Partha Pratim Talukdar, Bryan Kisiel, and Tom M. Mitchell. 2013. Improving learning and inference in a large knowledge-base using latent syntactic cues. In *Empirical Methods in Natural Language Processing*.

Matt Gardner, Partha Talukdar, Jayant Krishnamurthy, and Tom Mitchell. 2014. Incorporating vector space similarity in random walk inference over knowledge bases. In *Empirical Methods in Natural Language Processing*.

Christoph Goller and Andreas Küchler. 1996. Learning task-dependent distributed representations by backpropagation through structure. In *IEEE Transactions on Neural Networks*.

Alex Graves. 2013. Generating sequences with recurrent neural networks. In *ArXiv*.

Sepp Hochreiter and Jürgen Schmidhuber. 1997. Long short-term memory. In *Neural Computation*.

Ozan Irsoy and Claire Cardie. 2014. Deep recursive neural networks for compositionality in language. In *Neural Information Processing Systems*.

Mohit Iyyer, Jordan Boyd-Graber, Leonardo Claudino, Richard Socher, and Hal Daumé III. 2014. A neural network for factoid question answering over paragraphs. In *Empirical Methods in Natural Language Processing*.

Ni Lao, Tom Mitchell, and William W. Cohen. 2011. Random walk inference and learning in a large scale knowledge base. In *Conference on Empirical Methods in Natural Language Processing*.

Ni Lao, Amarnag Subramanya, Fernando Pereira, and William W. Cohen. 2012. Reading the web with learned syntactic-semantic inference rules. In *Joint Conference on Empirical Methods in Natural Language Processing and Computational Natural Language Learning*.

Hugo Larochelle, Dumitru Erhan, and Yoshua Bengio. 2008. Zero-data learning of new tasks. In *National Conference on Artificial Intelligence*.

Dekang Lin and Patrick Pantel. 2001. Dirt - discovery of inference rules from text. In *International Conference on Knowledge Discovery and Data Mining*.

Tomas Mikolov, Martin Karafiát, Lukas Burget, Jan Cernocký, and Sanjeev Khudanpur. 2010. Recurrent neural network based language model. In *Annual Conference of the International Speech Communication Association*.

Tomas Mikolov, Armand Joulin, Sumit Chopra, Michaël Mathieu, and Marc'Aurelio Ranzato. 2014. Learning longer memory in recurrent neural networks. In *CoRR*.

Bonan Min, Ralph Grishman, Li Wan, Chang Wang, and David Gondek. 2013. Distant supervision for relation extraction with an incomplete knowledge base. In *HLT-NAACL*, pages 777–782.

Mike Mintz, Steven Bills, Rion Snow, and Dan Jurafsky. 2009. Distant supervision for relation extraction without labeled data. In *Association for Computational Linguistics and International Joint Conference on Natural Language Processing*.

Jeff Mitchell and Mirella Lapata. 2008. Vector-based models of semantic composition. In *Association for Computational Linguistics*.

Arvind Neelakantan, Jeevan Shankar, Alexandre Passos, and Andrew McCallum. 2014. Efficient non-parametric estimation of multiple embeddings per word in vector space. In *Empirical Methods in Natural Language Processing*.

Maximilian Nickel, Volker Tresp, and Hans-Peter Kriegel. 2011. A three-way model for collective learning on multi-relational data. In *International Conference on Machine Learning*.

Mohammad Norouzi, Tomas Mikolov, Samy Bengio, Yoram Singer, Jonathon Shlens, Andrea Frome, Greg Corrado, and Jeffrey Dean. 2014. Zero-shot learning by convex combination of semantic embeddings. In *International Conference on Learning Representations*.

Dave Orr, Amarnag Subramanya, Evgeniy Gabrilovich, and Michael Ringgaard. 2013. 11 billion clues in 800 million documents: A web research corpus annotated with freebase concepts. http://googleresearch.blogspot.com/2013/07/11-billion-clues-in-800-million.html.

Mark Palatucci, Dean Pomerleau, Geoffrey Hinton, and Tom Mitchell. 2009. Zero-shot learning with semantic output codes. In *Neural Information Processing Systems*.

Sebastian Riedel, Limin Yao, Andrew McCallum, and Benjamin M. Marlin. 2013. Relation extraction with matrix factorization and universal schemas. In *HLT-NAACL*.

Stefan Schoenmackers, Oren Etzioni, Daniel S. Weld, and Jesse Davis. 2010. Learning first-order horn clauses from web text. In *Empirical Methods in Natural Language Processing*.

Richard Socher, Cliff Chiung-Yu Lin, Christopher D. Manning, and Andrew Y. Ng. 2011. Parsing natural scenes and natural language with recursive neural networks. In *Proceedings of the 26th International Conference on Machine Learning (ICML)*.

Richard Socher, Brody Huval, Christopher D. Manning, and Andrew Y. Ng. 2012. Semantic compositionality through recursive matrix-vector spaces. In *Joint Conference on Empirical Methods in Natural Language Processing and Computational Natural Language Learning*.

Richard Socher, Danqi Chen, Christopher D Manning, and Andrew Ng. 2013a. Reasoning with neural tensor networks for knowledge base completion. In *Advances in Neural Information Processing Systems*.

Richard Socher, Milind Ganjoo, Christopher D Manning, and Andrew Ng. 2013b. Zero-shot learning through cross-modal transfer. In *Neural Information Processing Systems*.

Richard Socher, Alex Perelygin, Jean Wu, Jason Chuang, Christopher D. Manning, Andrew Y. Ng, and Christopher Potts. 2013c. Recursive deep models for semantic compositionality over a sentiment treebank. In *Conference on Empirical Methods in Natural Language Processing*.

Fabian M. Suchanek, Gjergji Kasneci, and Gerhard Weikum. 2007. Yago: A core of semantic knowledge. In *Proceedings of the 16th International Conference on World Wide Web*.

Ilya Sutskever, Oriol Vinyals, and Quoc V. V Le. 2014. Sequence to sequence learning with neural networks. In *Advances in Neural Information Processing Systems*.

Oriol Vinyals, Lukasz Kaiser, Terry Koo, Slav Petrov, Ilya Sutskever, and Geoffrey Hinton. 2014. Grammar as a foreign language. In *CoRR*.

Paul Werbos. 1990. Backpropagation through time: what it does and how to do it. In *IEEE*.

Jason Weston, Ron Weiss, and Hector Yee. 2013. Nonlinear latent factorization by embedding multiple user interests. In *ACM International Conference on Recommender Systems*.

Bishan Yang, Wen-tau Yih, Xiaodong He, Jianfeng Gao, and Li Deng. 2014. Embedding entities and relations for learning and inference in knowledge bases. In *CoRR*.

Alexander Yates and Oren Etzioni. 2007. Unsupervised resolution of objects and relations on the web. In *North American Chapter of the Association for Computational Linguistics*.

Ainur Yessenalina and Claire Cardie. 2011. Compositional matrix-space models for sentiment analysis. In *Empirical Methods in Natural Language Processing*.

Event Extraction via Dynamic Multi-Pooling Convolutional Neural Networks

Yubo Chen, Liheng Xu, Kang Liu, Daojian Zeng and Jun Zhao
National Laboratory of Pattern Recognition
Institute of Automation, Chinese Academy of Sciences, Beijing, 100190, China
{yubo.chen, lhxu, kliu, djzeng, jzhao}@nlpr.ia.ac.cn

Abstract

Traditional approaches to the task of ACE event extraction primarily rely on elaborately designed features and complicated natural language processing (NLP) tools. These traditional approaches lack generalization, take a large amount of human effort and are prone to error propagation and data sparsity problems. This paper proposes a novel event-extraction method, which aims to automatically extract lexical-level and sentence-level features without using complicated NLP tools. We introduce a word-representation model to capture meaningful semantic regularities for words and adopt a framework based on a convolutional neural network (CNN) to capture sentence-level clues. However, CNN can only capture the most important information in a sentence and may miss valuable facts when considering multiple-event sentences. We propose a dynamic multi-pooling convolutional neural network (DMCNN), which uses a dynamic multi-pooling layer according to event triggers and arguments, to reserve more crucial information. The experimental results show that our approach significantly outperforms other state-of-the-art methods.

1 Introduction

Event extraction is an important and challenging task in Information Extraction (IE), which aims to discover event triggers with specific types and their arguments. Current state-of-the-art methods (Li et al., 2014; Li et al., 2013; Hong et al., 2011; Liao and Grishman, 2010; Ji and Grishman, 2008) often use a set of elaborately designed features that are extracted by textual analysis and linguistic knowledge. In general, we can divide the features into two categories: lexical features and contextual features.

Lexical features contain part-of-speech tags (POS), entity information, and morphology features (e.g., token, lemma, etc.), which aim to capture semantics or the background knowledge of words. For example, consider the following sentence with an ambiguous word *beats*:

S1: *Obama* ***beats*** *McCain.*

S2: *Tyson* ***beats*** *his opponent* .

In S1, *beats* is a trigger of type *Elect*. However, in S2, *beats* is a trigger of type *Attack*, which is more common than type *Elect*. Because of the ambiguity, a traditional approach may mislabel *beats* in S1 as a trigger of *Attack*. However, if we have the priori knowledge that *Obama* and *McCain* are presidential contenders, we have ample evidence to predict that *beats* is a trigger of type *Elect*. We call these knowledge **lexical-level clues**. To represent such features, the existing methods (Hong et al., 2011) often rely on human ingenuity, which is a time-consuming process and lacks generalization. Furthermore, traditional lexical features in previous methods are a one-hot representation, which may suffer from the data sparsity problem and may not be able to adequately capture the semantics of the words (Turian et al., 2010).

To identify events and arguments more precisely, previous methods often captured contextual features, such as syntactic features, which aim to understand how facts are tied together from a larger field of view. For example, in S3, there are two events that share three arguments as shown in Figure 1. From the dependency relation of *nsubj* between the argument *cameraman* and trigger *died*, we can induce a *Victim* role to *cameraman* in the *Die* event. We call such information **sentence-level clues**. However, the argument word *cameraman* and its trigger word *fired* are in different clauses, and there is no direct de-

Proceedings of the 53rd Annual Meeting of the Association for Computational Linguistics and the 7th International Joint Conference on Natural Language Processing, pages 167–176,
Beijing, China, July 26-31, 2015.

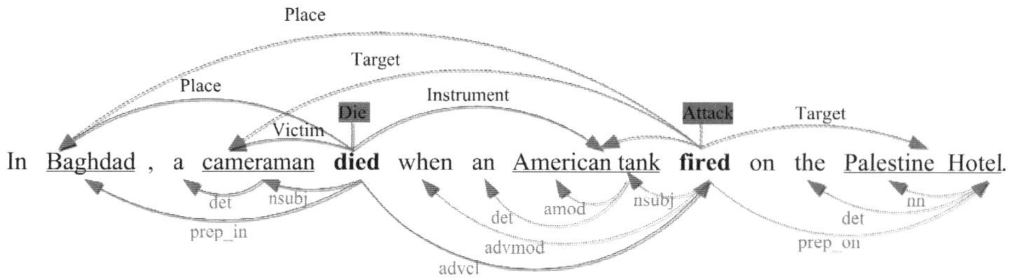

Figure 1: Event mentions and syntactic parser results of S3. The upper side shows two event mentions that share three arguments: the *Die* event mention, triggered by "died", and the *Attack* event mention, triggered by "fired". The lower side shows the collapsed dependency results.

pendency path between them. Thus it is difficult to find the *Target* role between them using traditional dependency features. In addition, extracting such features depends heavily on the performance of pre-existing NLP systems, which could suffer from error propagation.

S3: *In Baghdad, a cameraman* ***died*** *when an American tank* ***fired*** *on the Palestine Hotel.*

To correctly attach *cameraman* to *fired* as a *Target* argument, we must exploit internal semantics over the entire sentence such that the *Attack* event results in *Die* event. Recent improvements of convolutional neural networks (CNNs) have been proven to be efficient for capturing syntactic and semantics between words within a sentence (Collobert et al., 2011; Kalchbrenner and Blunsom, 2013; Zeng et al., 2014) for NLP tasks. CNNs typically use a max-pooling layer, which applies a max operation over the representation of an entire sentence to capture the most useful information. However, in event extraction, one sentence may contain two or more events, and these events may share the argument with different roles. For example, there are two events in S3, namely, the *Die* event and *Attack* event. If we use a traditional max-pooling layer and only keep the most important information to represent the sentence, we may obtain the information that depicts "a cameraman died" but miss the information about "American tank fired on the Palestine Hotel", which is important for predicting the *Attack* event and valuable for attaching *cameraman* to *fired* as an *Target* argument. In our experiments, we found that such multiple-event sentences comprise 27.3% of our dataset, which is a phenomenon we cannot ignore.

In this paper, we propose a dynamic multi-pooling convolutional neural network (**DMCNN**) to address the problems stated above. To capture lexical-level clues and reduce human effort, we introduce a word-representation model (Mikolov et al., 2013b), which has been shown to be able to capture the meaningful semantic regularities of words (Bengio et al., 2003; Erhan et al., 2010; Mikolov et al., 2013a). To capture sentence-level clues without using complicated NLP tools, and to reserve information more comprehensively, we devise a dynamic multi-pooling layer for CNN, which returns the maximum value in each part of the sentence according to event triggers and arguments. In summary, the contributions of this paper are as follows:

- We present a novel framework for event extraction, which can automatically induce lexical-level and sentence-level features from plain texts without complicated NLP preprocessing.
- We devise a dynamic multi-pooling convolutional neural network (DMCNN), which aims to capture more valuable information within a sentence for event extraction.
- We conduct experiments on a widely used ACE2005 event extraction dataset, and the experimental results show that our approach outperforms other state-of-the-art methods.

2 Event Extraction Task

In this paper, we focus on the event extraction task defined in Automatic Content Extraction[1] (ACE) evaluation, where an event is defined as a specific occurrence involving participants. First, we introduce some ACE terminology to understand this task more easily:

[1] http://projects.ldc.upenn.edu/ace/

- **Event mention**: a phrase or sentence within which an event is described, including a trigger and arguments.
- **Event trigger**: the main word that most clearly expresses the occurrence of an event (An ACE event trigger is typically a verb or a noun).
- **Event argument**: an entity mention, temporal expression or value (e.g. Job-Title) that is involved in an event (viz., participants).
- **Argument role**: the relationship between an argument to the event in which it participates.

Given an English text document, an event extraction system should predict event triggers with specific subtypes and their arguments for each sentence. The upper side of figure 1 depicts the event triggers and their arguments for S3 in Section 1. ACE defines 8 event types and 33 subtypes, such as *Attack* or *Elect*.

Although event extraction depends on name identification and entity mention co-reference, it is another difficult task in ACE evaluation and not the focus in the event extraction task. Thus, in this paper, we directly leverage the entity label provided by the ACE, following most previous works (Hong et al., 2011; Liao and Grishman, 2010; Ji and Grishman, 2008).

3 Methodology

In this paper, event extraction is formulated as a two-stage, multi-class classification via dynamic multi-pooling convolutional neural networks with the automatically learned features. The first stage is called *trigger classification*, in which we use a DMCNN to classify each word in a sentence to identify trigger words. If one sentence has triggers, the second stage is conducted, which applies a similar DMCNN to assign arguments to triggers and align the roles of the arguments. We call this *argument classification*. Because the second stage is more complicated, we first describe the methodology of argument classification in Section 3.1~3.4 and then illustrate the difference between the DMCNNs that are used for trigger classification and those used for argument classification in Section 3.5.

Figure 2 describes the architecture of argument classification, which primarily involves the following four components: (i) word-embedding learning, which reveals the embedding vectors of words in an unsupervised manner; (ii) lexical-level feature representation, which directly uses embedding vectors of words to capture lexical clues; (iii) sentence-level feature extraction, which proposes a DMCNN to learn the compositional semantic features of sentences; and (iv) argument classifier output, which calculates a confidence score for each argument role candidate.

3.1 Word Embedding Learning and Lexical-Level Feature Representation

Lexical-level features serve as important clues for event extraction (Hong et al., 2011; Li et al., 2013). Traditional lexical-level features primarily include *lemma, synonyms* and *POS tag of the candidate words*. The quality of such features depends strongly on the results of existing NLP tools and human ingenuity. Additionally, the traditional features remain unsatisfactory for capturing the semantics of words, which are important in event extraction, as showed in S1 and S2. As Erhan et al. (2010) reported, word embeddings learned from a significant amount of unlabeled data are more powerful for capturing the meaningful semantic regularities of words. This paper uses unsupervised pre-trained word embedding as the source of base features. We select the word embeddings of candidate words (candidate trigger, candidate argument) and the context tokens (left and right tokens of the candidate words). Then, all of these word embeddings are concatenated into the lexical-level features vector L to represent the lexical-level features in argument classification.

In this work, we use the Skip-gram model to pre-train the word embedding. This model is the state-of-the-art model in many NLP tasks (Baroni et al., 2014). The Skip-gram model trains the embeddings of words $w_1, w_2...w_m$ by maximizing the average log probability,

$$\frac{1}{m}\sum_{t=1}^{m}\sum_{-c\leq j\leq c, j\neq 0}\log p(w_{t+j}|w_t) \quad (1)$$

where c is the size of the training window. Basically, $p(w_{t+j}|w_t)$ is defined as,

$$p(w_{t+j}|w_t) = \frac{\exp(e_{t+j}^{'T} e_t)}{\sum_{w=1}^{m}\exp(e_w^{'T} e_t)} \quad (2)$$

where m is the vocabulary of the unlabeled text. $e_i^{'}$ is another embedding for e_i, see Morin and Bengio (2005) for details.

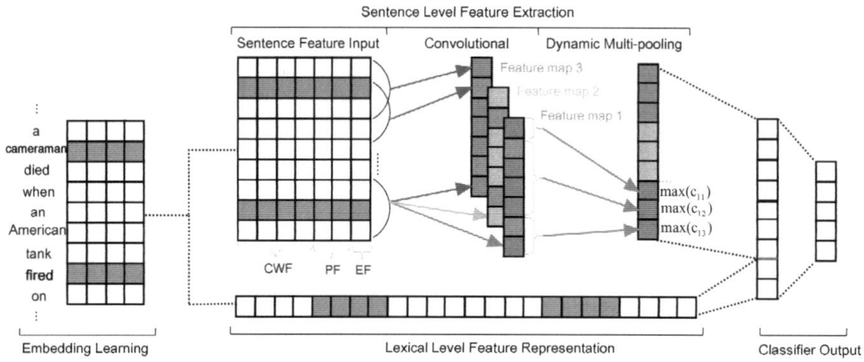

Figure 2: The architecture for the stage of argument classification in the event extraction. It illustrates the processing of one instance with the predict trigger *fired* and the candidate argument *cameraman*.

3.2 Extracting Sentence-Level Features Using a DMCNN

The CNN, with max-pooling layers, is a good choice to capture the semantics of long-distance words within a sentence (Collobert et al., 2011). However, as noted in the section 1, traditional CNN is incapable of addressing the event extraction problem. Because a sentence may contain more than one event, using only the most important information to represent a sentence, as in the traditional CNN, will miss valuable clues. To resolve this problem, we propose a DMCNN to extract the sentence-level features. The DMCNN uses a dynamic multi-pooling layer to obtain a maximum value for each part of a sentence, which is split by event triggers and event arguments. Thus, the DMCNN is expected to capture more valuable clues compared to traditional CNN methods.

3.2.1 Input

This subsection illustrates the input needed for a DMCNN to extract sentence-level features. The semantic interactions between the predicted trigger words and argument candidates are crucial for argument classification. Therefore, we propose three types of input that the DMCNN uses to capture these important clues:

- Context-word feature (CWF): Similar to Kalchbrenner et al. (2014) and Collobert et al. (2011), we take all the words of the whole sentence as the context. CWF is the vector of each word token transformed by looking up word embeddings.

- Position feature (PF): It is necessary to specify which words are the predicted trigger or candidate argument in the argument classification. Thus, we proposed the PF, which is defined as the relative distance of the current word to the predicted trigger or candidate argument. For example, in S3, the relative distances of *tank* to the candidate argument *cameraman* is 5. To encode the position feature, each distance value is also represented by an embedding vector. Similar to word embedding, Distance Values are randomly initialized and optimized through back propagation.

- Event-type feature (EF): The event type of a current trigger is valuable for argument classification (Ahn, 2006; Hong et al., 2011; Liao and Grishman, 2010; Li et al., 2013), so we encode event type predicted in the trigger classification stage as an important clue for the DMCNN, as in the PF.

Figure 2 assumes that word embedding has size $d_w = 4$, position embedding has size $d_p = 1$ and event-type embedding has size $d_e = 1$. Let $x_i \in \mathbb{R}^d$ be the d-dimensional vector representation corresponding to the i-th word in the sentence, where $d = d_w + d_p * 2 + d_e$. A sentence of length n is represented as follows:

$$x_{1:n} = x_1 \oplus x_2 \oplus ... \oplus x_n \tag{3}$$

where $\oplus$ is the concatenation operator. Thus, combined word embedding, position embedding and event-type embedding transform an instance as a matrix $X \in \mathbb{R}^{n \times d}$. Then, X is fed into the convolution part.

3.2.2 Convolution

The convolution layer aims to capture the compositional semantics of a entire sentence and compress these valuable semantics into feature maps. In general, let $x_{i:i+j}$ refer to the concatenation of words $x_i, x_{i+1}, ..., x_{i+j}$. A convolution operation involves a filter $w \in \mathbb{R}^{h \times d}$, which is applied to a window of h words to produce a new feature. For example, a feature c_i is generated from a window of words $x_{i:i+h-1}$ by the following operator,

$$c_i = f(w \cdot x_{i:i+h-1} + b) \tag{4}$$

where $b \in R$ is a bias term and f is a non-linear function such as the hyperbolic tangent. This filter is applied to each possible window of words in the sentence $x_{1:h}, x_{2:h+1}, ..., x_{n-h+1:n}$ to produce a feature map c_i where the index i ranges from 1 to $n - h + 1$.

We have described the process of how one feature map is extracted from one filter. To capture different features, it usually use multiple filters in the convolution. Assuming that we use m filters $W = w_1, w_2, ..., w_m$, the convolution operation can be expressed as:

$$c_{ji} = f(w_j \cdot x_{i:i+h-1} + b_j) \tag{5}$$

where j ranges from 1 to m. The convolution result is a matrix $C \in \mathbb{R}^{m \times (n-h+1)}$.

3.2.3 Dynamic Multi-Pooling

To extract the most important features (max value) within each feature map, traditional CNNs (Collobert et al., 2011; Kim, 2014; Zeng et al., 2014) take one feature map as a pool and only get one max value for each feature map. However, single max-pooling is not sufficient for event extraction. Because in the task of this paper, one sentence may contain two or more events, and one argument candidate may play a different role with a different trigger. To make an accurate prediction, it is necessary to capture the most valuable information with regard to the change of the candidate words. Thus, we split each feature map into three parts according to the candidate argument and predicted trigger in the argument classification stage. Instead of using one max value for an entire feature map to represent the sentence, we keep the max value of each split part and call it dynamic multi-pooling. Compared to traditional max-pooling, dynamic multi-pooling can reserve more valuable information without missing the max-pooling value.

As shown in Figure 2, the feature map output c_j is divided into three sections c_{j1}, c_{j2}, c_{j3} by "cameraman" and "fired". The dynamic multi-pooling can be expressed as formula 6,where $1 \leq j \leq m$ and $1 \leq i \leq 3$.

$$p_{ji} = \max(c_{ji}) \tag{6}$$

Through the dynamic multi-pooling layer, we obtain the p_{ji} for each feature map. Then, we concatenate all p_{ji} to form a vector $P \in \mathbb{R}^{3m}$, which can be considered as higher-level features (sentence-level features).

3.3 Output

The automatically learned lexical and sentence-level features mentioned above are concatenated into a single vector $F = [L, P]$. To compute the confidence of each argument role, the feature vector $F \in \mathbb{R}^{3m+d_l}$, where m is the number of the feature map and d_l is the dimension of the lexical-level features, is fed into a classifier.

$$O = W_s F + b_s \tag{7}$$

$W_s \in \mathbb{R}^{n_1 \times (3m+d_l)}$ is the transformation matrix and $O \in \mathbb{R}^{n_1}$ is the final output of the network, where n_1 is equal to the number of the argument role including the "None role" label for the candidate argument which don't play any role in the event. For regularization, we also employ dropout(Hinton et al., 2012) on the penultimate layer, which can prevent the co-adaptation of hidden units by randomly dropping out a proportion p of the hidden units during forward and backpropagation.

3.4 Training

We define all of the parameters for the stage of argument classification to be trained as $\theta = (E, PF_1, PF_2, EF, W, b, W_S, b_s)$. Specifically, E is the word embedding, PF_1 and PF_2 are the position embedding, EF is the embedding of the event type, W and b are the parameter of the filter, W_s and b_s are all of the parameters of the output layer.

Given an input example s, the network with parameter θ outputs the vector O, where the i-th component O_i contains the score for argument role i. To obtain the conditional probability $p(i|x, \theta)$, we apply a softmax operation over all argument role types:

$$p(i|x,\theta) = \frac{e^{o_i}}{\sum_{k=1}^{n_1} e^{o_k}} \tag{8}$$

Given all of our (suppose T) training examples $(x_i; y_i)$, we can then define the objective function as follows:

$$J(\theta) = \sum_{i=1}^{T} \log p(y^{(i)}|x^{(i)}, \theta) \tag{9}$$

To compute the network parameter θ, we maximize the log likelihood $J(\theta)$ through stochastic gradient descent over shuffled mini-batches with the Adadelta (Zeiler, 2012) update rule.

3.5 Model for Trigger Classification

In the above sections, we presented our model and features for argument classification. The method proposed above is also suitable for trigger classification, but the task only need to find triggers in the sentence, which is less complicated than argument classification. Thus we can used a simplified version of DMCNN.

In the trigger classification, we only use the candidate trigger and its left and right tokens in the lexical-level feature representation. In the feature representation of the sentence level, we use the same CWF as does in argument classification, but we only use the position of the candidate trigger to embed the position feature. Furthermore, instead of splitting the sentence into three parts, the sentence is split into two parts by a candidate trigger. Except for the above change in the features and model, we classify a trigger as the classification of an argument. Both stages form the framework of the event extraction.

4 Experiments

4.1 Dataset and Evaluation Metric

We utilized the ACE 2005 corpus as our dataset. For comparison, as the same as Li et al. (2013), Hong et al. (2011) and Liao and Grishman (2010), we used the same test set with 40 newswire articles and the same development set with 30 other documents randomly selected from different genres and the rest 529 documents are used for training. Similar to previous work (Li et al., 2013; Hong et al., 2011; Liao and Grishman, 2010; Ji and Grishman, 2008), we use the following criteria to judge the correctness of each predicted event mention:

- A trigger is correct if its event subtype and offsets match those of a reference trigger.
- An argument is correctly identified if its event subtype and offsets match those of any of the reference argument mentions.
- An argument is correctly classified if its event subtype, offsets and argument role match those of any of the reference argument mentions.

Finally we use *Precision (P)*, *Recall (R)* and *F measure (F_1)* as the evaluation metrics.

4.2 Our Method vs. State-of-the-art Methods

We select the following state-of-the-art methods for comparison.

1) **Li's baseline** is the feature-based system proposed by Li et al. (2013), which only employs human-designed lexical features, basic features and syntactic features.

2) **Liao's cross-event** is the method proposed by Liao and Grishman (2010), which uses document-level information to improve the performance of ACE event extraction.

3) **Hong's cross-entity** is the method proposed by Hong et al. (2011), which extracts event by using cross-entity inference. To the best of our knowledge, it is the best-reported feature-based system in the literature based on gold standards argument candidates.

4) **Li's structure** is the method proposed by Li et al. (2013), which extracts events based on structure prediction. It is the best-reported structure-based system.

Following Li et al. (2013), we tuned the model parameters on the development through grid search. Moreover, in different stages of event extraction, we adopted different parameters in the DMCNN. Specifically, in the trigger classification, we set the window size as 3, the number of the feature map as 200, the batch size as 170 and the dimension of the PF as 5. In the argument classification, we set the window size as 3, the number of the feature map as 300, the batch size as 20 and the dimension of the PF and EF as 5. Stochastic gradient descent over shuffled mini-batches with the Adadelta update rule(Zeiler, 2012) is used for training and testing processes. It mainly contains two parameters p and ε. We set $p = 0.95$ and $\varepsilon = 1e^{-6}$. For the dropout operation, we set the

Methods	Trigger Identification(%)			Trigger Identification + Classification(%)			Argument Identification(%)			Argument Role(%)		
	P	R	F	P	R	F	P	R	F	P	R	F
Li's baseline	76.2	60.5	67.4	74.5	59.1	65.9	74.1	37.4	49.7	65.4	33.1	43.9
Liao's cross-event	N/A			68.7	68.9	68.8	50.9	49.7	50.3	45.1	44.1	44.6
Hong's cross-entity	N/A			72.9	64.3	68.3	53.4	52.9	53.1	51.6	45.5	48.3
Li's structure	76.9	65.0	70.4	73.7	62.3	67.5	69.8	47.9	56.8	64.7	44.4	52.7
DMCNN model	80.4	67.7	**73.5**	75.6	63.6	**69.1**	68.8	51.9	**59.1**	62.2	46.9	**53.5**

Table 1: Overall performance on blind test data

$rate = 0.5$. We train the word embedding using the Skip-gram algorithm [2] on the NYT corpus [3].

Table 1 shows the overall performance on the blind test dataset. From the results, we can see that the DMCNN model we proposed with the automatically learned features achieves the best performance among all of the compared methods. DMCNN can improve the best F_1 (Li et al., 2013) in the state-of-the-arts for trigger classification by 1.6% and argument role classification by 0.8%. This demonstrates the effectiveness of the proposed method. Moreover, a comparison of *Liao's cross-event* with *Li's baseline* illustrates that *Liao's cross-event* achieves a better performance. We can also make the same observation when comparing *Hong's cross-entity* with *Liao's cross-event* and comparing *Li's structure* with *Hong's cross-entity*. It proves that richer feature sets lead to better performance when using traditional human-designed features. However, our method could obtain further better results on the condition of only using automatically learned features from original words. Specifically, compared to *Hong's cross-entity*, it gains 0.8% improvement on trigger classification F_1 and 5.2% improvement on argument classification F_1. We believe the reason is that the features we automatically learned can capture more meaningful semantic regularities of words. Remarkably, compared to *Li's structure*, our approach with sentence and lexical features achieves comparable performance even though we do not use complicated NLP tools.

4.3 Effect of The DMCNN on Extracting Sentence-Level Features

In this subsection, we prove the effectiveness of the proposed DMCNN for sentence-level feature extraction. We specifically select two methods as baselines for comparison with our DMCNN: Embeddings+T and CNN. Embeddings+T uses word embeddings as lexical-level features and traditional sentence-level features based on human design (Li et al., 2013). A CNN is similar to a DMCNN, except that it uses a standard convolutional neural network with max-pooling to capture sentence-level features. By contrast, a DMCNN uses the dynamic multi-pooling layer in the network instead of the max-pooling layer in a CNN. Moreover, to prove that a DMCNN could capture more precise sentence-level features, especially for those sentences with multiple events, we divide the testing data into two parts according the event number in a sentence (single event and multiple events) and perform evaluations separately. Table 2 shows the proportion of sentences with multiple events or a single event and the proportion of arguments that attend one event or more events within one sentence in our dataset. Table 3 shows the results.

Stage	1/1 (%)	1/N (%)
Trigger	72.7	**27.3**
Argument	76.8	**23.2**

Table 2: The proportion of multiple events within one sentence. 1/1 means that one sentence only has one trigger or one argument plays a role in one sentence; otherwise, 1/N is used.

Table 3 illustrates that the methods based on convolutional neural networks (CNN and DMCNN) outperform Embeddings+T. It proves that convolutional neural networks could be more effective than traditional human-design strategies for sentence-level feature extraction. In table 3, for all sentences, our method achieves improvements of approximately 2.8% and 4.6% over the CNN. The results prove the effectiveness of the dynamic multi-pooling layer. Interestingly, the DMCNN yields a 7.8% improvement for trigger classification on the sentences with multiple events. This improvement is larger than in sentences with a single event. Similar observations can be made for

[2]https://code.google.com/p/word2vec/

[3]https://catalog.ldc.upenn.edu/LDC2008T19

the argument classification results. This demonstrates that the proposed DMCNN can effectively capture more valuable clues than the CNN with max-pooling, especially when one sentence contains more than one event.

Stage	Method	1/1	1/N	all
		F_1	F_1	F_1
Trigger	Embedding+T	68.1	25.5	59.8
	CNN	72.5	43.1	66.3
	DMCNN	**74.3**	**50.9**	**69.1**
Argument	Embedding+T	37.4	15.5	32.6
	CNN	51.6	36.6	48.9
	DMCNN	**54.6**	**48.7**	**53.5**

Table 3: Comparison of the event extraction scores obtained for the Traditional, CNN and DMCNN models

4.4 Effect of Word Embedding on Extracting Lexical-Level Features

This subsection studies the effectiveness of our word embedding for lexical features. For comparison purposes, we select the baseline described by Li et al. (2013) as the traditional method, which uses traditional lexical features, such as n-grams, POS tags and some entity information. In contrast, we only use word embedding as our lexical feature. Moreover, to prove that word embedding could capture more valuable semantics, especially for those words in the test data that never appear to be the same event type or argument role in the training data, we divide the triggers and arguments in the testing data into two parts (1: appearing in testing data only, or 2: appearing in both testing and training data with the same event type or argument role) and perform evaluations separately. For triggers, 34.9% of the trigger words in the test data never appear to be the same event type in the training data. This proportion is 83.1% for arguments. The experimental results are shown in Table 4.

Table 4 illustrates that for all situations, our method makes significant improvements compared with the traditional lexical features in the classification of both the trigger and argument. For situation B, the lexical-level features extracted from word embedding yield a 18.8% improvement for trigger classification and an 8.5% improvement for argument classification. This occurs because the baseline only uses discrete features, so they suffer from data sparsity and could not adequately handle a situation in which a trigger or argument does not appear in the training data.

Stage	Method	A	B	All
		F_1	F_1	F_1
Trigger	Traditional	68.8	14.3	61.2
	Ours	**70.7**	**33.1**	**64.9**
Argument	Traditional	58.5	22.2	34.6
	Ours	**59.5**	**30.7**	**40.2**

Table 4: Comparison of the results for the traditional lexical feature and our lexical feature. A denotes the triggers or arguments appearing in both training and test datasets, and B indicates all other cases.

4.5 Lexical features vs. Sentence Features

To compare the effectiveness of different levels of features, we extract events by using lexical features and sentence features separately. The results obtained using the DMCNN are shown in table 5. Interestingly, in the trigger-classification stage, the lexical features play an effective role, whereas the sentence features play a more important role in the argument-classification stage. The best results are achieved when we combine lexical-level and sentence-level features. This observation demonstrates that both of the two-level features are important for event extraction.

Feature	Trigger	Argument
	F_1	F_1
Lexical	**64.9**	40.2
Sentence	63.8	**50.7**
Combine	**69.1**	**53.5**

Table 5: Comparison of the trigger-classification score and argument-classification score obtained by lexical-level features, sentence-level features and a combination of both

5 Related Work

Event extraction is one of important topics in NLP. Many approaches have been explored for event extraction. Nearly all of the ACE event extraction use supervised paradigm. We further divide supervised approaches into feature-based methods and structure-based methods.

In feature-based methods, a diverse set of strategies has been exploited to convert classification clues (such as sequences and parse trees) into feature vectors. Ahn (2006) uses the lexical features(e.g., full word, pos tag), syntactic features (e.g., dependency features) and external-knowledge features(WordNet) to extract the event. Inspired by the hypothesis of "One Sense Per Discourse"(Yarowsky, 1995), Ji and Grishman (2008) combined global evidence from related documents with local decisions for the event extraction. To capture more clues from the texts, Gupta and Ji (2009), Liao and Grishman (2010) and Hong et al. (2011) proposed the cross-event and cross-entity inference for the ACE event task. Although these approaches achieve high performance, feature-based methods suffer from the problem of selecting a suitable feature set when converting the classification clues into feature vectors.

In structure-based methods, researchers treat event extraction as the task of predicting the structure of the event in a sentence. McClosky et al. (2011) casted the problem of biomedical event extraction as a dependency parsing problem. Li et al. (2013) presented a joint framework for ACE event extraction based on structured perceptron with beam search. To use more information from the sentence, Li et al. (2014) proposed to extract entity mentions, relations and events in ACE task based on the unified structure. These methods yield relatively high performance. However, the performance of these methods depend strongly on the quality of the designed features and endure the errors in the existing NLP tools.

6 Conclusion

This paper proposes a novel event extraction method, which can automatically extract lexical-level and sentence-level features from plain texts without complicated NLP preprocessing. A word-representation model is introduced to capture lexical semantic clues and a dynamic multi-pooling convolutional neural network (DMCNN) is devised to encode sentence semantic clues. The experimental results prove the effectiveness of the proposed method.

Acknowledgments

This work was supported by the National Basic Research Program of China (No. 2014CB340503) and the National Natural Science Foundation of China (No. 61272332 and No. 61202329)

References

David Ahn. 2006. The stages of event extraction. In *Proceedings of ACL*, pages 1–8.

Marco Baroni, Georgiana Dinu, and Germán Kruszewski. 2014. Dont count, predict! a systematic comparison of context-counting vs. context-predicting semantic vectors. In *Proceedings of ACL*, pages 238–247.

Yoshua Bengio, Réjean Ducharme, Pascal Vincent, and Christian Jauvin. 2003. A neural probabilistic language model. *The Journal of Machine Learning Research*, 3:1137–1155.

Chen Chen and V Incent NG. 2012. Joint modeling for chinese event extraction with rich linguistic features. In *Proceedings of COLING*, pages 529–544.

Ronan Collobert, Jason Weston, Léon Bottou, Michael Karlen, Koray Kavukcuoglu, and Pavel Kuksa. 2011. Natural language processing (almost) from scratch. *The Journal of Machine Learning Research*, 12:2493–2537.

Dumitru Erhan, Yoshua Bengio, Aaron Courville, Pierre-Antoine Manzagol, Pascal Vincent, and Samy Bengio. 2010. Why does unsupervised pre-training help deep learning? *The Journal of Machine Learning Research*, 11:625–660.

Prashant Gupta and Heng Ji. 2009. Predicting unknown time arguments based on cross-event propagation. In *Proceedings of ACL-IJCNLP*, pages 369–372.

Geoffrey E Hinton, Nitish Srivastava, Alex Krizhevsky, Ilya Sutskever, and Ruslan R Salakhutdinov. 2012. Improving neural networks by preventing co-adaptation of feature detectors. *arXiv preprint arXiv:1207.0580*.

Yu Hong, Jianfeng Zhang, Bin Ma, Jianmin Yao, Guodong Zhou, and Qiaoming Zhu. 2011. Using cross-entity inference to improve event extraction. In *Proceedings of ACL-HLT*, pages 1127–1136.

Heng Ji and Ralph Grishman. 2008. Refining event extraction through cross-document inference. In *Proceedings of ACL*, pages 254–262.

Nal Kalchbrenner and Phil Blunsom. 2013. Recurrent convolutional neural networks for discourse compositionality. *arXiv preprint arXiv:1306.3584*.

Nal Kalchbrenner, Edward Grefenstette, and Phil Blunsom. 2014. A convolutional neural network for modelling sentences. *arXiv preprint arXiv:1404.2188*.

Yoon Kim. 2014. Convolutional neural networks for sentence classification. *arXiv preprint arXiv:1408.5882*.

Siwei Lai, Liheng Xu, Kang Liu, and Jun Zhao. 2015. Recurrent convolutional neural networks for text classification. In *Proceedings of AAAI*.

Qi Li, Heng Ji, and Liang Huang. 2013. Joint event extraction via structured prediction with global features. In *Proceedings of ACL*, pages 73–82.

Qi Li, Heng Ji, Yu Hong, and Sujian Li. 2014. Constructing information networks using one single model. In *Proceedings of EMNLP*, pages 1846–1851.

Shasha Liao and Ralph Grishman. 2010. Using document level cross-event inference to improve event extraction. In *Proceedings of ACL*, pages 789–797.

David McClosky, Mihai Surdeanu, and Christopher D Manning. 2011. Event extraction as dependency parsing. In *Proceedings of ACL-HLT*, pages 1626–1635.

Tomas Mikolov, Kai Chen, Greg Corrado, and Jeffrey Dean. 2013a. Efficient estimation of word representations in vector space. *arXiv preprint arXiv:1301.3781*.

Tomas Mikolov, Ilya Sutskever, Kai Chen, Greg S Corrado, and Jeff Dean. 2013b. Distributed representations of words and phrases and their compositionality. In *Proceedings of NIPS*, pages 3111–3119.

Frederic Morin and Yoshua Bengio. 2005. Hierarchical probabilistic neural network language model. In *Proceedings of AISTATS*, pages 246–252.

Joseph Turian, Lev Ratinov, and Yoshua Bengio. 2010. Word representations: a simple and general method for semi-supervised learning. In *Proceedings of ACL*, pages 384–394.

David Yarowsky. 1995. Unsupervised word sense disambiguation rivaling supervised methods. In *Proceedings of ACL*, pages 189–196.

Matthew D Zeiler. 2012. Adadelta: An adaptive learning rate method. *arXiv preprint arXiv:1212.5701*.

Daojian Zeng, Kang Liu, Siwei Lai, Guangyou Zhou, and Jun Zhao. 2014. Relation classification via convolutional deep neural network. In *Proceedings of COLING*, pages 2335–2344.

Stacked Ensembles of Information Extractors for Knowledge-Base Population

Nazneen Fatema Rajani* **Vidhoon Viswanathan*** **Yinon Bentor** **Raymond J. Mooney**
Department of Computer Science
University of Texas at Austin
Austin, TX 78712, USA
{nrajani,vidhoon,yinon,mooney}@cs.utexas.edu

Abstract

We present results on using stacking to ensemble multiple systems for the Knowledge Base Population English Slot Filling (KBP-ESF) task. In addition to using the output and confidence of each system as input to the stacked classifier, we also use features capturing how well the systems agree about the provenance of the information they extract. We demonstrate that our stacking approach outperforms the best system from the 2014 KBP-ESF competition as well as alternative ensembling methods employed in the 2014 KBP Slot Filler Validation task and several other ensembling baselines. Additionally, we demonstrate that including provenance information further increases the performance of stacking.

1 Introduction

Using *ensembles* of multiple systems is a standard approach to improving accuracy in machine learning (Dietterich, 2000). Ensembles have been applied to a wide variety of problems in natural language processing, including parsing (Henderson and Brill, 1999), word sense disambiguation (Pedersen, 2000), and sentiment analysis (Whitehead and Yaeger, 2010). This paper presents a detailed study of ensembling methods for the TAC *Knowledge Base Population* (KBP) *English Slot Filling* (ESF) task (Surdeanu, 2013; Surdeanu and Ji, 2014).

We demonstrate new state-of-the-art results on this KBP task using *stacking* (Wolpert, 1992), which trains a final classifier to optimally combine the results of multiple systems. We present results for stacking all systems that competed in both the 2013 and 2014 KBP-ESF tracks, training on 2013 data and testing on 2014 data. The resulting stacked ensemble outperforms all systems in the 2014 competition, obtaining an F1 of 48.6% compared to 39.5% for the best performing system in the most recent competition.

Although the associated KBP Slot Filler Validation (SFV) Track (Wang et al., 2013; Yu et al., 2014; Sammons et al., 2014) is officially focused on improving the precision of individual existing systems by filtering their results, frequently participants in this track also combine the results of multiple systems and also report increased recall through this use of ensembling. However, SFV participants have not employed stacking, and we demonstrate that our stacking approach outperforms existing published SFV ensembling systems.

KBP ESF systems must also provide *provenance* information, i.e. each extracted slot-filler must include a pointer to a document passage that supports it (Surdeanu and Ji, 2014). Some SFV systems have used this provenance information to help filter and combine extractions (Sammons et al., 2014). Therefore, we also explored enhancing our stacking approach by including additional input features that capture provenance information. By including features that quantify how much the ensembled systems agree on provenance, we further improved our F1 score for the 2014 ESF task to 50.1%.

The remainder of the paper is organized as follows. Section 2 provides background information on existing KBP-ESF systems and stacking. Section 3 provides general background on the KBP-ESF task. Section 4 describes our stacking approach, including how provenance information is used. Section 5 presents comprehensive experiments comparing this approach to existing results and several additional baselines, demonstrating new state-of-the-art results on KBP-ESF. Section 6 reviews prior related work on ensembling

* These authors contributed equally

Proceedings of the 53rd Annual Meeting of the Association for Computational Linguistics and the 7th International Joint Conference on Natural Language Processing, pages 177–187,
Beijing, China, July 26-31, 2015.

for information extraction. Section 7 presents our final conclusions and proposed directions for future research.

2 Background

For the past few years, NIST has been conducting the English Slot Filling (ESF) Task in the Knowledge Base Population (KBP) track among various other tasks as a part of the Text Analysis Conference(TAC)(Surdeanu, 2013; Surdeanu and Ji, 2014). In the ESF task, the goal is to fill specific slots of information for a given set of query entities (people or organizations) based on a supplied text corpus. The participating systems employ a variety of techniques in different stages of the slot filling pipeline, such as entity search, relevant document extraction, relation modeling and inference. In 2014, the top performing system, *DeepDive with Expert Advice* from Stanford University (Wazalwar et al., 2014), employed distant supervision (Mintz et al., 2009) and Markov Logic Networks (Domingos et al., 2008) in their learning and inferencing system. Another system, *RPI_BLENDER* (Hong et al., 2014), used a restricted fuzzy matching technique in a framework that learned event triggers and employed them to extract relations from documents.

Given the diverse set of slot-filling systems available, it is interesting to explore methods for ensembling these systems. In this regard, TAC also conducts a Slot Filler Validation (SFV) task who goal is to improve the slot-filling performance using the output of existing systems. The input for this task is the set of outputs from all slot-filling systems and the expected output is a filtered set of slot fills. As with the ESF task, participating systems employ a variety of techniques to perform validation. For instance, *RPI_BLENDER* used a Multi-dimensional Truth Finding model (Yu et al., 2014) which is an unsupervised validation approach based on computing multidimensional credibility scores. The *UI_CCG* system (Sammons et al., 2014) developed two different validation systems using entailment and majority voting.

However, *stacking* (Sigletos et al., 2005; Wolpert, 1992) has not previously been employed for ensembling KBP-ESF systems. In stacking, a meta-classifier is learned from the output of multiple underlying systems. In our work, we translate this to the context of ensembling slot filling systems and build a *stacked meta-classifier* that learns to combine the results from individual slot filling systems. We detail our stacking approach for ensembling existing slot filling systems in Section 4.

3 Overview of KBP Slot Filling Task

The goal of the TAC KBP-ESF task (Surdeanu, 2013; Surdeanu and Ji, 2014) is to collect information (fills) about specific attributes (slots) for a set of entities (queries) from a given corpus. The queries vary in each year of the task and can be either a person (PER) or an organization (ORG) entity. The slots are fixed and are listed in Table 1 by entity type. Some slots (like per:age) are *single-valued* while others (like per:children) are *list-valued* i.e., they can take multiple slot fillers.

3.1 Input and Output

The input for the task is a set of queries and the corpus in which to look for information. The queries are provided in an XML format containing basic information including an ID for the query, the name of the entity, and the type of entity (PER or ORG). The corpus consists of documents format from discussion forums, newswire and the Internet. Each document is identified by a unique document ID.

The output for the task is a set of slot fills for each input query. Depending on the type, each query should have a *NIL* or one or more lines of output for each of the corresponding slots. The output line for each slot fill contains the fields shown in Table 2. The query ID in Column 1 should match the ID of the query given as input. The slot name (Column 2) is one of the slots listed in Table 1 based on entity type. Run ID (Column 3) is a unique identifier for each system. Column 4 contains a *NIL* filler if the system could not find any relevant slot filler. Otherwise, it contains the *relation provenance*. Provenance is of the form *docid:startoffset-endoffset*, where *docid* specifies a source document from the corpus and the offsets demarcate the text in this document supporting the relation. The offsets correspond to the spans of the candidate document that describe the relation between the query entity and the extracted slot filler. Column 5 contains the extracted slot filler. Column 6 is a filler provenance that is similar in format to relation provenance but in this case the offset corresponds to the portion of the document containing the extracted filler. Column 7 is a confi-

Person		Organization	
per:alternate_names	per:cause_of_death	org:country_of_headquarters	org:founded_by
per:date_of_birth	per:countries_of_residence	org:stateorprovince_of_headquarters	org:date_dissolved
per:age	per:statesorprovinces_of_residence	org:city_of_headquarters	org:website
per:parents	per:cities_of_residence	org:shareholders	org:date_founded
per:spouse	per:schools_attended	org:top_members_employees	org:members
per:city_of_birth	per:city_of_death	org:political_religious_affiliation	org:member_of
per:origin	per:stateorprovince_of_death	org:number_of_employees_members	org:subsidiaries
per:other_family	per:country_of_death	org:alternate_names	org:parents
per:title	per:employee_or_member_of		
per:religion	per:stateorprovince_of_birth		
per:children	per:country_of_birth		
per:siblings	per:date_of_death		
per:charges			

Table 1: Slots for PER and ORG queries

dence score which systems can provide to indicate their certainty in the extracted information.

3.2 Scoring

The scoring for the ESF task is carried out as follows. The responses from all slot-filling systems are pooled and a *key file* is generated by having human assessors judge the correctness of these responses. In addition, LDC includes a manual key of fillers that were determined by human judges. Using the union of these keys as the gold standard, precision, recall, and F1 scores are computed.

Column	Field Description
Column 1	Query ID
Column 2	Slot name
Column 3	Run ID
Column 4	NIL or Relation Provenance
Column 5	Slot filler
Column 6	Filler Provenance
Column 7	Confidence score

Table 2: SF Output line fields

4 Ensembling Slot-Filling Systems

Given a set of query entities and a fixed set of slots, the goal of ensembling is to effectively combine the output of different slot-filling systems. The input to the ensembling system is the output of individual systems (in the format described in previous section) containing slot fillers and additional information such as provenance and confidence scores. The output of the ensembling system is similar to the output of an individual system, but it productively aggregates the slot fillers from different systems.

4.1 Algorithm

This section describes our ensembling approach which trains a final binary classifier using features that help judge the reliability and thus correctness of individual slot fills. In a final *post-processing* step, the slot fills that get classified as "correct" by the classifier are kept while the others are set to NIL.

4.1.1 Stacking

Stacking is a popular ensembling method in machine learning (Wolpert, 1992) and has been successfully used in many applications including the top performing systems in the Netflix competition (Sill et al., 2009). The idea is to employ multiple learners and combine their predictions by training a "meta-classifier" to weight and combine multiple models using their confidence scores as features. By training on a set of supervised data that is disjoint from that used to train the individual models, it learns how to combine their results into an improved ensemble model. We employ a single classifier to train and test on all slot types using an L1-regularized SVM with a linear kernel (Fan et al., 2008).

4.1.2 Using Provenance

As discussed above, each system provides provenance information for every non-NIL slot filler. There are two kinds of provenance provided: the relation provenance and the filler provenance. In our algorithm, we only use the filler provenance for a given slot fill. This is because of the changes in the output formats for the ESF task from 2013 to 2014. Specifically, the 2013 specification requires separate entity and justification provenance fields, but the 2014 collapses these into a single relation provenance field. An additional filler provenance field is common to both specifications. Hence, we use the filler provenance that is common between 2013 and 2014 formats. As described earlier, every provenance has a *docid* and *startoffset-endoffset* that gives information about the document and offset in the document from where the slot fill has been extracted. The UI-CCG SFV system Sammons et al. (2014) effectively used this provenance information to help validate and filter slot fillers. This motivated us to use provenance in our stacking approach as additional features as input to the meta-classifier.

We use provenance in two ways, first using the *docid* information, and second using the *offset* information. We use the *docids* to define a document-based provenance score in the following way: for a given query and slot, if N systems provide answers and a maximum of n of those systems give the same *docid* in their filler provenance, then the document provenance score for those n slot fills is n/N. Similarly, other slot fills are given lower scores based on the fraction of systems whose provenance document agree with theirs. Since this provenance score is weighted by the number of systems that refer to the same provenance, it measures the reliability of a slot fill based on the document from where it was extracted.

Our second provenance measure uses *offsets*. The degree of overlap among the various systems' offsets can also be a good indicator of the reliability of the slot fill. The Jaccard similarity coefficient is a statistical measure of similarity between sets and is thus useful in measuring the degree of overlap among the offsets of systems. Slot fills have variable lengths and thus the provenance offset ranges are variable too. A metric such as the Jaccard coefficient captures the overlapping offsets along with normalizing based on the union and thus resolving the problem with variable offset ranges. For a given query and slot, if N systems that attempt to fill it have the same *docid* in their document provenance, then the offset provenance (OP) score for a slot fill by a system x is calculated as follows:

$$OP(x) = \frac{1}{|N|} \times \sum_{i \in N, i \neq x} \frac{|\text{offsets(i)} \cap \text{offsets(x)}|}{|\text{offsets(i)} \cup \text{offsets(x)}|}$$

Per our definition, systems that extract slot fills from *different* documents for the same query slot have zero overlap among offsets. We note that the offset provenance is always used along with the document provenance and thus useful in discriminating slot fills extracted from a different document for the same query slot. Like the document provenance score, the offset provenance score is also a weighted feature and is a measure of reliability of a slot fill based on the offsets in the document from where it is extracted. Unlike past SFV systems that use provenance for validation, our approach does not need access to the large corpus of documents from where the slot fills are extracted and is thus very computationally inexpensive.

4.2 Eliminating Slot-Filler Aliases

When combining the output of different ESF systems, it is possible that some slot-filler entities might overlap with each other. An ESF system could extract a filler F_1 for a slot *S* while another ESF system extracts another filler F_2 for the same slot *S*. If the extracted fillers F_1 and F_2 are *aliases* (i.e. different names for the same entity), the scoring system for the TAC KBP SF task considers them redundant and penalizes the precision of the system.

In order to eliminate aliases from the output of ensembled system, we employ a technique derived by inverting the scheme used by the LSV ESF system (Roth et al., 2013) for query expansion. LSV ESF uses a Wikipedia anchor-text model (Roth and Klakow, 2010) to generate aliases for given query entities. By including aliases for query names, the ESF system increase the number of candidate sentences fetched for the query.

To eliminate filler aliases, we apply the same technique to generate aliases for all slot fillers of a given query and slot type. Given a slot filler, we obtain the Wikipedia page that is most likely linked to the filler text. Then, we obtain the anchor texts and their respective counts from all other Wikipedia pages that link to this page. Using these counts, we choose top N (we use N=10 as in LSV) and pick the corresponding anchor texts as aliases for the given slot filler. Using the generated aliases, we then verify if any of the slot fillers are redundant with respect to these aliases. This scheme is not applicable to slot types whose fillers are not entities (like date or age). Therefore, simpler matching schemes are used to eliminate redundancies for these slot types.

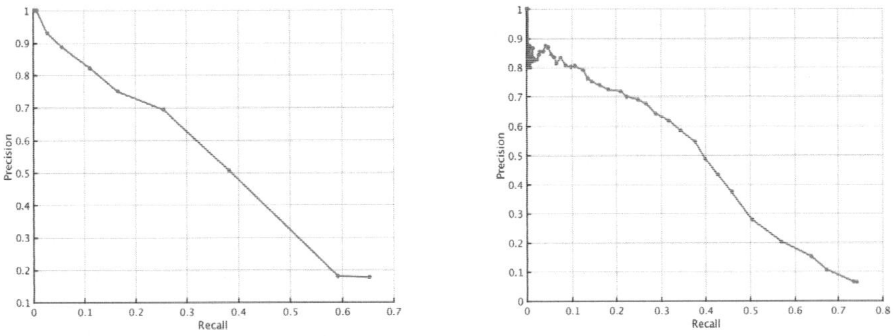

Common systems dataset   All 2014 SFV systems dataset

Figure 1: Precision-Recall curves for identifying the best voting performance on the two datasets

5 Experimental Evaluation

This section describes a comprehensive set of experiments evaluating ensembling for the KBP ESF task. Our experiments are divided into two subsets based on the datasets they employ. Since our stacking approach relies on 2013 SFV data for training, we build a dataset of one run for every team that participated in *both* the 2013 and 2014 competitions and call it the *common systems dataset*. There are 10 common teams of the 17 teams that participated in ESF 2014. The other dataset comprises of all 2014 SFV systems (including all runs of all 17 teams that participated in 2014). There are 10 systems in the common systems dataset, while there are 65 systems in the all 2014 SFV dataset. Table 3 gives a list of the common systems for 2013 and 2014 ESF task. ESF systems do change from year to year and it's not a perfect comparison, but systems generally get better every year and thus we are probably only underperforming.

Common Systems
LSV
IIRG
UMass_IESL
Stanford
BUPT_PRIS
RPI_BLENDER
CMUML
NYU
Compreno
UWashington

Table 3: Common teams for 2013 and 2014 ESF

5.1 Methodology and Results

For our unsupervised ensembling baselines, we evaluate on both the common systems dataset as well as the entire 2014 SFV dataset. We compare our stacking approach to three unsupervised baselines. The first is *Union* which takes the combination of values for all systems to maximize recall. If the slot type is list-valued, it classifies all slot fillers as correct and always includes them. If the slot type is single-valued, if only one systems attempts to answer it, then it includes that system's slot fill. Otherwise if multiple systems produce a response, it only includes the slot fill with the highest confidence value as correct and discards the rest.

The second baseline is *Voting*. For this approach, we vary the threshold on the number of systems that must agree on a slot fill from one to all. This gradually changes the system from the union to intersection of the slot fills, and we identify the threshold that results in the highest F1 score. We learn a threshold on the 2013 SFV dataset (containing 52 systems) that results in the best F1 score. We use this threshold for the voting baseline on 2014 SFV dataset. As we did for the 2013 common systems dataset, we learn a threshold on the 2013 common systems that results in the best F1 score and use this threshold for the voting baseline on 2014 common systems.

The third baseline is an "oracle threshold" version of *Voting*. Since the best threshold for 2013 may not necessarily be the best threshold for 2014, we identify the best threshold for 2014 by plotting a Precision-Recall curve and finding the best F1 score for the voting baseline on both the SFV and common systems datasets. Figure 1 shows the

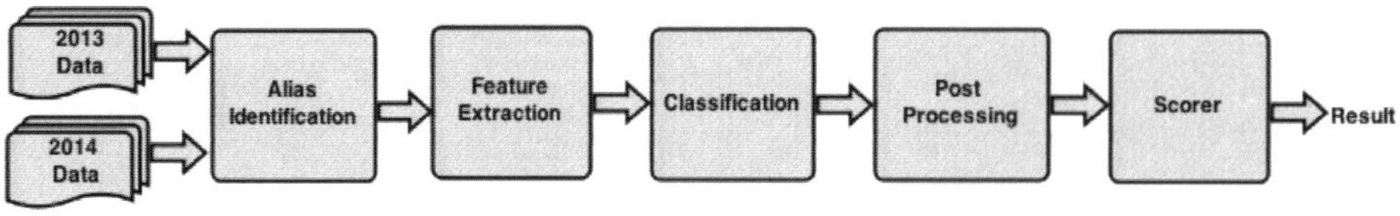

Figure 2: Our system pipeline for evaluating supervised ensembling approaches

Baseline	Precision	Recall	F1
Union	0.067	**0.762**	0.122
Voting (threshold learned on 2013 data)	**0.641**	0.288	0.397
Voting (optimal threshold for 2014 data)	0.547	0.376	**0.445**

Table 4: Performance of baselines on all 2014 SFV dataset (65 systems)

Approach	Precision	Recall	F1
Union	0.176	**0.647**	0.277
Voting (threshold learned on 2013 data)	**0.694**	0.256	0.374
Best ESF system in 2014 (Stanford)	0.585	0.298	0.395
Voting (optimal threshold for 2014 data)	0.507	0.383	0.436
Stacking	0.606	0.402	0.483
Stacking + Relation	0.607	0.406	0.486
Stacking + Provenance (document)	0.499	0.486	0.492
Stacking + Provenance (document) + Relation	0.653	0.400	0.496
Stacking + Provenance (document and offset) + Relation	0.541	0.466	**0.501**

Table 5: Performance on the common systems dataset (10 systems) for various configurations. All approaches except the Stanford system are our implementations.

Precision-Recall curve for two datasets for finding the best possible F1 score using the voting baseline. We find that for the common systems dataset, a threshold of 3 (of 10) systems gives the best F1 score, while for the entire 2014 SFV dataset, a threshold of 10 (of 65) systems gives the highest F1. Note that this gives an upper bound on the best results that can be achieved with voting, assuming an optimal threshold is chosen. Since the upper bound can not be predicted without using the 2014 dataset, this baseline has an unfair advantage. Table 4 shows the performance of all 3 baselines on the all 2014 SFV systems dataset.

For all our supervised ensembling approaches, we train on the 2013 SFV data and test on the 2014 data for the common systems. We have 5 different supervised approaches. Our first approach is stacking the common systems using their confidence scores to learn a classifier. As discussed earlier, in stacking we train a meta-classifier that combines the systems using their confidence scores as features. Since the common systems dataset has 10 systems, this classifier uses 10 features. The second approach also provides stacking with a nominal feature giving the relation name (as listed in Table 1) for the given slot instance. This allows the system to learn different evidence-combining functions for different slot types if the classifier finds this useful. For our third approach, we also provide the document provenance feature described in Section 4.1. Altogether this approach has 11 features (10 confidence score + 1 document provenance score). The fourth approach uses confidences, the document provenance feature, and a one-hot encoding of the relation name for the slot instance. Our final approach also includes the offset provenance (OP) feature discussed in Section 4.1. There are altogether 13 features in this approach. All our supervised approaches use the Weka package (Hall et al., 2009) for training the meta-classifier, using an L1-regularized SVM with a linear kernel (other classifiers gave similar results). Figure 2 shows our system pipeline for evaluating supervised ensembling approaches. Table 5 gives the performance of all our supervised approaches as well as our unsupervised baselines for the common systems dataset.

Analysis by Surdeanu and Ji (2014) suggests that 2014 ESF queries are more difficult than those for 2013. They compare two systems by running both on 2013 and 2014 data and find there is a considerable drop in the performance of both the systems. We note that they run the same exact system on 2013 and 2014 data. Thus, in order to have a better understanding of our results, we plot a learning curve by training on different sizes of the 2013 SFV data and using the scorer to measure the F1 score on the 2014 SFV data for the 10 common systems. Figure 3 shows the learning curve thus obtained. Although there are certain parts of the dataset when the F1 score drops which we suspect is due to overfitting the 2013 data, there is still a strong correlation between the 2013 training data size and F1 score on the 2014 dataset. Thus we can infer that training on 2013 data is useful even though the 2013 and 2014 data are fairly different. Although the queries change, the common systems remain more-or-less the same and stacking enables a meta-classifier to weigh those common systems based on their 2013 performance.

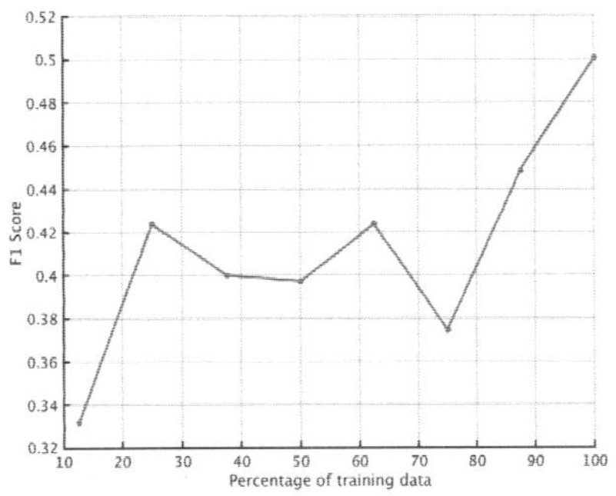

Figure 3: Learning curve for training on 2013 and testing on 2014 common systems dataset

To further validate our approach, we divide the 2013 SFV data based on the systems that extracted those slot fills. Then we sort the systems, from higher to lower, based on the number of false positives produced by them in the ensembling approach. Next we train a classifier in an incremental fashion adding one system's slot fills for training at each step and analyzing the performance on 2014 data. This allows us to analyze the results at the system level. Figure 4 shows the plot of F1 score vs. the number of systems at each step. The figure shows huge improvement in F1 score at steps 6 and 7. At step 6 the Stanford system is added to the pool of systems which is the best performing ESF system in 2014 and fourth best in 2013. At step 7, the UMass system is added to the pool and, although the system on it own is weak, it boosts the performance of our ensembling approach. This is because the UMass system alone contributes approximately 24% of the 2013 training data (Singh et al., 2013). Thus adding this one system significantly improves the training step leading to better performance. We also notice that our system becomes less conservative at this step and has higher recall. The reason for this is that the systems from 1 to 5 had very high precision and low recall whereas from system 6 onwards the systems have high recall. Thus adding the UMass system enables our meta-classifier to have a higher recall for small decrease in precision and thus boosting the overall F1 measure. Without it, the classifier produces high precision but low recall and decreases the overall F1 score by approximately 6 points.

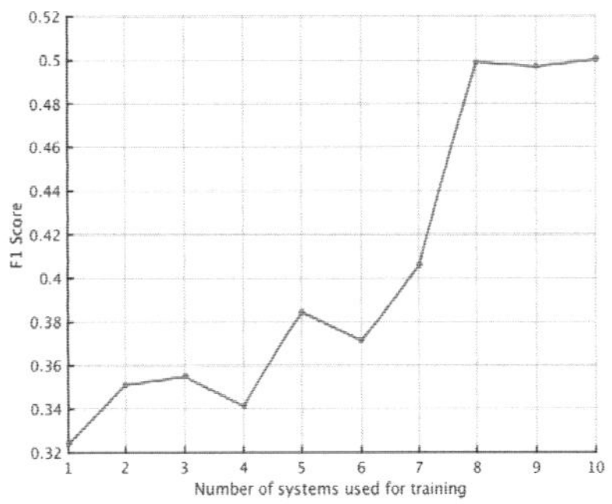

Figure 4: Incrementally training on 2013 by adding a system at each step and testing on 2014 common systems dataset

We also experimented with cross validation within the 2014 dataset. Since we used only 2014 data for this experiment, we also included the relation provenance as discussed in Section 4.1.2. Table 6 shows the results on 10-fold cross-validation on 2014 data with only the filler provenance and with both the filler and relation provenance. The performance of using only the filler provenance is slightly worse than training on 2013 because the 2014 SFV data has many fewer instances but uses more systems for learning compared to the 2013

Approach	Precision	Recall	F1
Stacking + Filler provenance + Relation	0.606	0.415	0.493
Stacking + Filler and Relation provenance + Relation	**0.609**	**0.434**	**0.506**

Table 6: 10-fold Cross-Validation on 2014 SFV dataset (65 systems)

Baseline	Precision	Recall	F1
Union	0.054	**0.877**	0.101
Voting (threshold learned on 2013 data)	**0.637**	0.406	0.496
Voting (optimal threshold for 2014 data)	0.539	0.526	**0.533**

Table 7: Baseline performance on all 2014 SFV dataset (65 systems) using unofficial scorer

Approach	Precision	Recall	F1
Union	0.177	**0.922**	0.296
Voting (threshold learned on 2013 data)	**0.694**	0.256	0.374
Best published SFV result in 2014 (UIUC)	0.457	0.507	0.481
Voting (optimal threshold for 2014 data)	0.507	0.543	0.525
Stacking + Provenance(document)	0.498	0.688	0.578
Stacking	0.613	0.562	0.586
Stacking + Relation	0.613	0.567	0.589
Stacking + Provenance (document and offset) + Relation	0.541	0.661	0.595
Stacking + Provenance (document) + Relation	0.659	0.56	**0.606**

Table 8: Performance on the common systems dataset (10 systems) for various configurations using the unofficial scorer. All approaches except the UIUC system are our implementations.

SFV data.

The TAC KBP official scoring key for the ESF task includes human annotated slot fills along with the pooled slot fills obtained by all participating systems. However, Sammons et al. (2014) use an unofficial scoring key in their paper that does not include human annotated slot fills. In order to compare to their results, we also present results using the same unofficial key. Table 7 gives the performance of our baseline systems on the 2014 SFV dataset using the unofficial key for scoring. We note that our *Union* does not produce a recall of 1.0 on the unofficial scorer due to our single-valued slot selection strategy for multiple systems. As discussed earlier for the single-valued slot, we include the slot fill with highest confidence (which may not necessarily be correct) and thus may not match the unofficial scorer.

Table 8 gives the performance of all our supervised approaches along with the baselines on the common systems dataset using the unofficial key for scoring. UIUC is one of the two teams participating in the SFV 2014 task and the only team to report results, but they report 6 different system configurations and we show their best performance.

5.2 Discussion

Our results indicate that stacking with provenance information and relation type gives the best performance using both the official ESF scorer as well as the unofficial scorer that excludes the human-generated slot fills. Our stacking approach that uses the 10 systems common between 2013 and 2014 also outperforms the ensembling baselines that have the advantage of using *all 65* of the 2014 systems. Our stacking approach would presumably perform even better if we had access to 2013 training data for all 2014 systems.

Of course, the best-performing ESF system for 2014 did not have access to the pooled slot fills of all participating systems. Although pooling the results has an advantage, naive pooling methods such as the ensembling baselines, in particular the voting approach, do not perform as well as our stacked ensembles. Our best approach outperforms the best baseline for both the datasets by at least 6 F1 points using both the official and unofficial scorer.

As expected the *Union* baseline has the highest recall. Among the supervised approaches, stacking with document provenance produces the highest precision and is significantly higher (approximately 5%) than the approach that produces the second highest precision. As discussed earlier, we also scored our approaches on the unofficial scorer so that we can compare our results to the UIUC system that was the best performer in the 2014 SFV task. Our best approach beats their best system configuration by a F1 score of 12 points. Our stacking approach also outperforms them on precision and recall by a large margin.

6 Related Work

Our system is part of a body of work on increasing the performance of relation extraction through ensemble methods.

The use of *stacked generalization* for information extraction has been demonstrated to outperform both majority voting and weighted voting methods (Sigletos et al., 2005). In relation extraction, a stacked classifier effectively combines a supervised, closed-domain Conditional Random Field-based relation extractor with an open-domain CRF Open IE system, yielding a 10% increase in precision without harming recall (Banko et al., 2008). To our knowledge, we are the first to apply stacking to KBP and the first to use provenance as a feature in a stacking approach.

Many KBP SFV systems cast validation as a single-document problem and apply a variety of techniques, such as rule-based consistency checks (Angeli et al., 2013), and techniques from the well-known Recognizing Textual Entailment (RTE) task (Cheng et al., 2013; Sammons et al., 2014). In contrast, the 2013 *JHUAPL* system aggregates the results of many different extractors using a constraint optimization framework, exploiting confidence values reported by each input system (Wang et al., 2013). A second approach in the *UI_CCG* system (Sammons et al., 2014) aggregates results of multiple systems by using majority voting.

In the database, web-search, and data-mining communities, a line of research into "truth-finding" or "truth-discovery" methods addresses the related problem of combining evidence for facts from multiple sources, each with a latent credibility (Yin et al., 2008). The *RPI_BLENDER* KBP system (Yu et al., 2014) casts SFV in this framework, using a graph propagation method that modeled the credibility of systems, sources, and response values. However they only report scores on the 2013 SFV data which contain less complicated and easier queries compared to the 2014 data. Therefore, we cannot directly compare our system's performance to theirs.

Google's Knowledge Vault system (Dong et al., 2014) combines the output of four diverse extraction methods by building a boosted decision stump classifier (Reyzin and Schapire, 2006). For each proposed fact, the classifier considers both the confidence value of each extractor and the number of responsive documents found by the extractor. A separate classifier is trained for each predicate, and Platt Scaling (Platt, 1999) is used to calibrate confidence scores.

7 Conclusion

This paper has presented experimental results showing that *stacking* is a very promising approach to ensembling KBP systems. From our literature survey, we observe that we are the first to employ stacking and combine it with provenance information to ensemble KBP systems. Our stacked meta-classifier provides an F1 score of 50.1% on 2014 KBP ESF, outperforming the best ESF and SFV systems from the 2014 competition, and thereby achieving a new state-of-the-art for this task. We found that provenance features increased accuracy, highlighting the importance of provenance information (even without accessing the source corpus) in addition to confidence scores for ensembling information extraction systems.

8 Acknowledgements

We thank the anonymous reviewers for their valuable feedback. This research was supported by the DARPA DEFT program under AFRL grant FA8750-13-2-0026.

References

Gabor Angeli, Arun Chaganty, Angel Chang, Kevin Reschke, Julie Tibshirani, Jean Y Wu, Osbert Bastani, Keith Siilats, and Christopher D Manning. 2013. Stanford's 2013 KBP system. In *Proceedings of the Sixth Text Analysis Conference (TAC2013)*.

Michele Banko, Oren Etzioni, and Turing Center. 2008. The tradeoffs between open and traditional relation extraction. In *ACL08*, volume 8, pages 28–36.

Xiao Cheng, Bingling Chen, Rajhans Samdani, Kai-Wei Chang, Zhiye Fei, Mark Sammons, John Wieting, Subhro Roy, Chizheng Wang, and Dan Roth. 2013. Illinois cognitive computation group UI-CCG TAC 2013 entity linking and slot filler validation systems. In *Proceedings of the Sixth Text Analysis Conference (TAC2013)*.

T. Dietterich. 2000. Ensemble methods in machine learning. In J. Kittler and F. Roli, editors, *First International Workshop on Multiple Classifier Systems, Lecture Notes in Computer Science*, pages 1–15. Springer-Verlag.

Pedro Domingos, Stanley Kok, Daniel Lowd, Hoifung Poon, Matthew Richardson, and Parag Singla. 2008. Markov logic. In Luc De Raedt, Paolo Frasconi, Kristian Kersting, and Stephen Muggleton, editors, *Probabilistic Inductive Logic Programming*, volume 4911 of *Lecture Notes in Computer Science*, pages 92–117. Springer.

Xin Dong, Evgeniy Gabrilovich, Geremy Heitz, Wilko Horn, Ni Lao, Kevin Murphy, Thomas Strohmann, Shaohua Sun, and Wei Zhang. 2014. Knowledge vault: A web-scale approach to probabilistic knowledge fusion. In *Proceedings of the 20th ACM SIGKDD International Conference on Knowledge Discovery and Data Mining*, pages 601–610. ACM.

Rong-En Fan, Kai-Wei Chang, Cho-Jui Hsieh, Xiang-Rui Wang, and Chih-Jen Lin. 2008. LIBLINEAR: A library for large linear classification. *Journal of Machine Learning Research*, 9:1871–1874.

Mark Hall, Eibe Frank, Geoffrey Holmes, Bernhard Pfahringer, Peter Reutemann, and Ian H Witten. 2009. The WEKA data mining software: an update. *ACM SIGKDD explorations newsletter*, 11(1):10–18.

John C. Henderson and Eric Brill. 1999. Exploiting diversity in natural language processing: Combining parsers. In *Proceedings of the Conference on Empirical Methods in Natural Language Processing and Very Large Corpora (EMNLP/VLC-99)*, pages 187–194, College Park, MD.

Yu Hong, Xiaobin Wang, Yadong Chen, Jian Wang, Tongtao Zhang, Jin Zheng, Dian Yu, Qi Li, Boliang Zhang, Han Wang, et al. 2014. RPI BLENDER TAC-KBP2014 knowledge base population system. *Proceedings of the Seventh Text Analysis Conference (TAC2014)*.

Mike Mintz, Steven Bills, Rion Snow, and Dan Jurafsky. 2009. Distant supervision for relation extraction without labeled data. In *Proceedings of the Joint Conference of the 47th Annual Meeting of the ACL and the 4th International Joint Conference on Natural Language Processing of the AFNLP: Volume 2-Volume 2*, pages 1003–1011. Association for Computational Linguistics.

Ted Pedersen. 2000. A simple approach to building ensembles of naive Bayesian classifiers for word sense disambiguation. In *Proceedings of the Meeting of the North American Association for Computational Linguistics*, pages 63–69.

John C. Platt. 1999. Probabilistic outputs for support vector machines and comparisons to regularized likelihood methods. In Peter J. Bartlett, Bernhard Schölkopf, Dale Schuurmans, and Alex J. Smola, editors, *Advances in Large Margin Classifiers*, pages 61–74. MIT Press, Boston.

Lev Reyzin and Robert E Schapire. 2006. How boosting the margin can also boost classifier complexity. In *Proceedings of the 23rd International Conference on Machine Learning*, pages 753–760. ACM.

Benjamin Roth and Dietrich Klakow. 2010. Cross-language retrieval using link-based language models. In *Proceedings of the 33rd International ACM SIGIR Conference on Research and Development in Information Retrieval*, pages 773–774. ACM.

Benjamin Roth, Tassilo Barth, Michael Wiegand, et al. 2013. Effective slot filling based on shallow distant supervision methods. *Proceedings of the Seventh Text Analysis Conference (TAC2013)*.

Mark Sammons, Yangqiu Song, Ruichen Wang, Gourab Kundu, et al. 2014. Overview of UI-CCG systems for event argument extraction, entity discovery and linking, and slot filler validation. *Proceedings of the Seventh Text Analysis Conference (TAC2014)*.

Georgios Sigletos, Georgios Paliouras, Constantine D Spyropoulos, and Michalis Hatzopoulos. 2005. Combining information extraction systems using voting and stacked generalization. *The Journal of Machine Learning Research*, 6:1751–1782.

Joseph Sill, Gábor Takács, Lester Mackey, and David Lin. 2009. Feature-weighted linear stacking. *arXiv preprint arXiv:0911.0460*.

Sameer Singh, Limin Yao, David Belanger, Ariel Kobren, Sam Anzaroot, Michael Wick, Alexandre Passos, Harshal Pandya, Jinho Choi, Brian Martin, and Andrew McCallum. 2013. Universal schema for slot filling and cold start: UMass IESL.

Mihai Surdeanu and Heng Ji. 2014. Overview of the English slot filling track at the TAC2014 Knowledge Base Population Evaluation. In *Proceedings of the Seventh Text Analysis Conference (TAC2014)*.

Mihai Surdeanu. 2013. Overview of the TAC2013 knowledge base population evaluation: English slot filling and temporal slot filling. In *Proceedings of the Sixth Text Analysis Conference (TAC 2013)*.

I-Jeng Wang, Edwina Liu, Cash Costello, and Christine Piatko. 2013. JHUAPL TAC-KBP2013 slot filler validation system. In *Proceedings of the Sixth Text Analysis Conference (TAC2013)*.

Anurag Wazalwar, Tushar Khot, Ce Zhang, Chris Re, Jude Shavlik, and Sriraam Natarajan. 2014. TAC KBP 2014 : English slot filling track DeepDive with expert advice. In *Proceedings of the Seventh Text Analysis Conference (TAC2014)*.

Matthew Whitehead and Larry Yaeger. 2010. Sentiment mining using ensemble classification models. In Tarek Sobh, editor, *Innovations and Advances in Computer Sciences and Engineering*. Springer Verlag, Berlin.

David H. Wolpert. 1992. Stacked generalization. *Neural Networks*, 5:241–259.

Xiaoxin Yin, Jiawei Han, and Philip S Yu. 2008. Truth discovery with multiple conflicting information providers on the web. *Knowledge and Data Engineering, IEEE Transactions on*, 20(6):796–808.

Dian Yu, Hongzhao Huang, Taylor Cassidy, Heng Ji, Chi Wang, Shi Zhi, Jiawei Han, Clare Voss, and Malik Magdon-Ismail. 2014. The wisdom of minority: Unsupervised slot filling validation based on multi-dimensional truth-finding. In *Proc. The 25th International Conference on Computational Linguistics (COLING2014)*.

Generative Event Schema Induction with Entity Disambiguation

Kiem-Hieu Nguyen[1, 2] **Xavier Tannier**[3, 1] **Olivier Ferret**[2] **Romaric Besançon**[2]
(1) LIMSI-CNRS
(2) CEA, LIST, Laboratoire Vision et Ingnierie des Contenus, F-91191, Gif-sur-Yvette
(3) Univ. Paris-Sud
{nguyen,xtannier}@limsi.fr, {olivier.ferret,romaric.besancon}@cea.fr

Abstract

This paper presents a generative model to event schema induction. Previous methods in the literature only use head words to represent entities. However, elements other than head words contain useful information. For instance, *an armed man* is more discriminative than *man*. Our model takes into account this information and precisely represents it using probabilistic topic distributions. We illustrate that such information plays an important role in parameter estimation. Mostly, it makes topic distributions more coherent and more discriminative. Experimental results on benchmark dataset empirically confirm this enhancement.

1 Introduction

Information Extraction was initially defined (and is still defined) by the MUC evaluations (Grishman and Sundheim, 1996) and more specifically by the task of template filling. The objective of this task is to assign event roles to individual textual mentions. A template defines a specific type of events (*e.g.* earthquakes), associated with semantic roles (or slots) hold by entities (for earthquakes, their location, date, magnitude and the damages they caused (Jean-Louis et al., 2011)).

Schema induction is the task of learning these templates with no supervision from unlabeled text. We focus here on *event* schema induction and continue the trend of generative models proposed earlier for this task. The idea is to group together entities corresponding to the same role in an event template based on the similarity of the relations that these entities hold with predicates. For example, in a corpus about terrorist attacks, entities that are objects of verbs *to kill*, *to attack* can be grouped together and characterized by a role named VICTIM. The output of this identification operation is a set of clusters of which members are both words and relations, associated with their probability (see an example later in Figure 4). These clusters are not labeled but each of them represents an event slot.

Our approach here is to improve this initial idea by entity disambiguation. Some ambiguous entities, such as *man* or *soldier*, can match two different slots (victim or perpetrator). An entity such as *terrorist* can be mixed up with victims when articles relate that a terrorist has been killed by police (and thus is object of *to kill*). Our hypothesis is that the immediate context of entities is helpful for disambiguating them. For example, the fact that *man* is associated with *armed*, *dangerous*, *heroic* or *innocent* can lead to a better attribution and definition of roles. We then introduce relations between entities and their attributes in the model by means of syntactic relations.

The document level, which is generally a center notion in topic modeling, is not used in our generative model. This results in a simpler, more intuitive model, where observations are generated from slots, that are defined by probabilistic distributions on entities, predicates and syntactic attributes. This model offers room for further extensions since multiple observations on an entity can be represented in the same manner.

Model parameters are estimated by Gibbs sampling. We evaluate the performance of this approach by an automatic and empiric mapping between slots from the system and slots from the reference in a way similar to previous work in the domain.

The rest of this paper is organized as follows: Section 2 briefly presents previous work; in Section 3, we detail our entity and relation representation; we describe our generative model in Section 4, before presenting our experiments and evaluations in Section 5.

Proceedings of the 53rd Annual Meeting of the Association for Computational Linguistics and the 7th International Joint Conference on Natural Language Processing, pages 188–197,
Beijing, China, July 26-31, 2015.

2 Related Work

Despite efforts made for making template filling as generic as possible, it still depends heavily on the type of events. Mixing generic processes with a restrictive number of domain-specific rules (Freedman et al., 2011) or examples (Grishman and He, 2014) is a way to reduce the amount of effort needed for adapting a system to another domain. The approaches of *On-demand information extraction* (Hasegawa et al., 2004; Sekine, 2006) and *Preemptive Information Extraction* (Shinyama and Sekine, 2006) tried to overcome this difficulty in another way by exploiting templates induced from representative documents selected by queries.

Event schema induction takes root in work on the acquisition from text of knowledge structures, such as the Memory Organization Packets (Schank, 1980), used by early text understanding systems (DeJong, 1982) and more recently by Ferret and Grau (1997). First attempts for applying such processes to schema induction have been made in the fields of Information Extraction (Collier, 1998), Automatic Summarization (Harabagiu, 2004) and event Question-Answering (Filatova et al., 2006; Filatova, 2008).

More recently, work after (Hasegawa et al., 2004) has developed weakly supervised forms of Information Extraction including schema induction in their objectives. However, they have been mainly applied to binary relation extraction in practice (Eichler et al., 2008; Rosenfeld and Feldman, 2007; Min et al., 2012). In parallel, several approaches were proposed for performing specifically schema induction in already existing frameworks: clause graph clustering (Qiu et al., 2008), event sequence alignment (Regneri et al., 2010) or LDA-based approach relying on FrameNet-like semantic frames (Bejan, 2008). More event-specific generative models were proposed by Chambers (2013) and Cheung et al. (2013). Finally, Chambers and Jurafsky (2008), Chambers and Jurafsky (2009), Chambers and Jurafsky (2011), improved by Balasubramanian et al. (2013), and Chambers (2013) focused specifically on the induction of event roles and the identification of chains of events for building representations from texts by exploiting coreference resolution or the temporal ordering of events. All this work is also linked to work about the induction of scripts from texts, more or less closely linked to

	Attributes	Head	Triggers
#1	[armed:amod]	man	[attack:nsubj, kill:nsubj]
#2	[police:nn]	station	[attack:dobj]
#3	[]	policeman	[kill:dobj]
#4	[innocent:amod, young:amod]	man	[wound:dobj]

Figure 1: Entity representation as tuples of ([attributes], head, [triggers]).

events, such as (Fremann et al., 2014), (Pichotta and Mooney, 2014) or (Modi and Titov, 2014).

The work we present in this article is in line with Chambers (2013), which will be described in more details in Section 5, together with a quantitative and qualitative comparison.

3 Entity Representation

An entity is represented as a triple containing: a head word h, a list A of attribute relations and a list T of trigger relations. Consider the following example:

(1) Two armed men attacked the police station and killed a policeman. An innocent young man was also wounded.

As illustrated in Figure 1, four entities, equivalent to four separated triples, are generated from the text above. Head words are extracted from noun phrases. A trigger relation is composed of a predicate (*attack*, *kill*, *wound*) and a dependency type (subject, object). An attribute relation is composed of an argument (*armed*, *police*, *young*) and a dependency type (adjectival, nominal or verbal modifier). In the relationship to triggers, a head word is argument, but in the relationship to attributes, it is predicate. We use Stanford NLP toolkit (Manning et al., 2014) for parsing and coreference resolution.

A head word is extracted if it is a nominal or proper noun and it is related to at least one trigger; pronouns are omitted. A trigger of an head word is extracted if it is a verb or an eventive noun and the head word serves as its subject, object, or preposition. We use the categories *noun.EVENT* and *noun.ACT* in WordNet as a list of eventive nouns. A head word can have more than one trigger. These multiple relations can come from a syntactic coordination inside a single sentence, as it is the case in the first sentence of the illustrating example. They can also represent a coreference

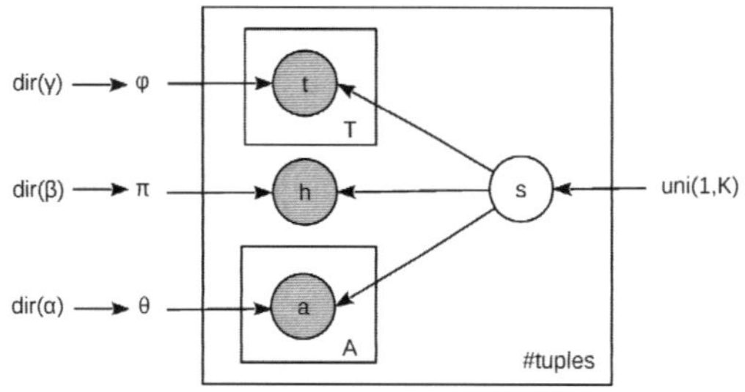

Figure 2: Generative model for event induction.

chain across sentences, as we use coreference resolution to merge the triggers of mentions corefering to the same entity in a document. Coreferences are useful sources for event induction (Chambers and Jurafsky, 2011; Chambers, 2013). Finally, an attribute is extracted if it is an adjective, a noun or a verb and serves as an adjective, verbal or nominal modifier of a head word. If there are several modifiers, only the closest to the head word is selected. This "best selection" heuristic allows to omit non-discriminative attributes for the entity.

4 Generative Model

4.1 Model Description

Figure 2 shows the plate notation of our model. For each triple representing an entity e, the model first assigns a slot s for the entity from an uniform distribution $uni(1, K)$. Its head word h is then generated from a multinominal distribution π_s. Each t_i of event trigger relations T_e is generated from a multinominal distribution ϕ_s. Each a_j of attribute relations A_e is similarly generated from a multinominal distribution θ_s. The distributions θ, π, and ϕ are generated from Dirichlet priors $dir(\alpha)$, $dir(\beta)$ and $dir(\gamma)$ respectively.

Given a set of entities E, our model (π, ϕ, θ) is defined by

$$P_{\pi,\phi,\theta}(E) = \prod_{e \in E} P_{\pi,\phi,\theta}(e) \tag{2}$$

where the probability of each entity e is defined by

$$\begin{aligned} P_{\pi,\phi,\theta}(e) &= P(s) \\ &\times P(h|s) \\ &\times \prod_{t \in T_e} P(t|s) \\ &\times \prod_{a \in A_e} P(a|s) \end{aligned} \tag{3}$$

The generative story is as follows:

for *slot* $s \leftarrow 1$ **to** K **do**
  Generate an attribute distribution θ_s from a Dirichlet prior $dir(\alpha)$;
  Generate a head distribution π_s from a Dirichlet prior $dir(\beta)$;
  Generate a trigger distribution ϕ_s from a Dirichlet prior $dir(\gamma)$;
end
for *entity* $e \in E$ **do**
  Generate a slot s from a uniform distribution $uni(1, K)$;
  Generate a head h from a multinominal distribution π_s;
  for $i \leftarrow 1$ **to** $|T_e|$ **do**
    Generate a trigger t_i from a multinominal distribution ϕ_s;
  end
  for $j \leftarrow 1$ **to** $|A_e|$ **do**
    Generate an attribute a_j from a multinominal distribution ϕ_s;
  end
end

4.2 Parameter Estimation

For parameter estimation, we use the Gibbs sampling method (Griffiths, 2002). The slot variable s is sampled by integrating out all the other variables.

Previous models (Cheung et al., 2013; Chambers, 2013) are based on document-level topic modeling, which originated from models such as Latent Dirichlet Allocation (Blei et al., 2003). Our model is, instead, independent from document contexts. Its input is a sequence of entity triples. Document boundary is only used in a post-processing step of filtering (see Section 5.3 for more details). There is a universal slot distribution instead of each slot distribution for one document. Furthermore, slot prior is ignored by using a uniform distribution as a particular case of categorical probability. Sampling-based slot assignment could depend on initial states and random seeds. In our implementation of Gibbs sampling, we use 2,000 *burn-in* of overall 10,000 iterations. The purpose of *burn-in* is to assure that parameters converge to a stable state before estimating the probability distributions. Moreover, an interval step of 100 is applied between consecutive samples in order to avoid too strong coherence.

Particularly, for tracking changes in probabilities resulting from attribute relations, we ran in the first stage a specific burn-in with only heads and trigger relations. This stable state was then used as initialization for the second burn-in in

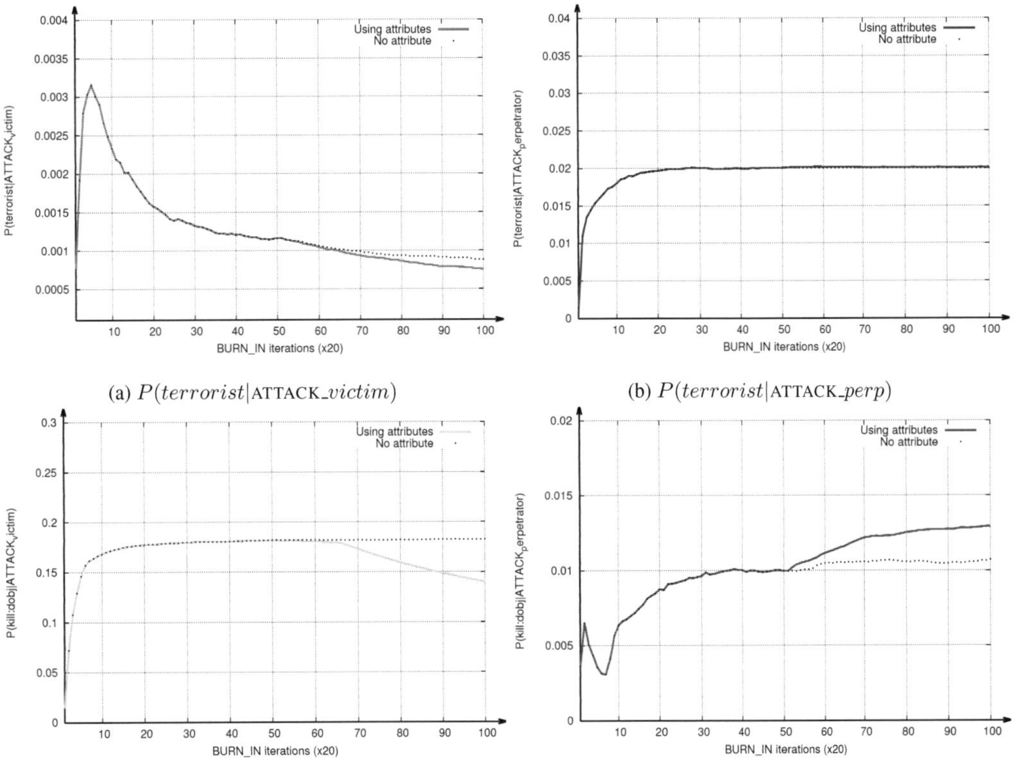

(a) $P(terrorist|\text{ATTACK\_}victim)$ (b) $P(terrorist|\text{ATTACK\_}perp)$

(c) $P(kill : dobj|\text{ATTACK\_}victim)$ (d) $P(kill : dobj|\text{ATTACK\_}perp)$

Figure 3: Probability convergence when using attributes in sampling. The use of attributes is started at point 50 (*i.e.*, 50% of burn-in phase). The dotted line shows convergence without attributes; the continuous line shows convergence with attributes.

which attributes, heads, and triggers were used altogether. This specific experimental setting made us understand how the attributes modified distributions. We observed that non-ambiguous words or relations (*i.e. explode*, *murder:nsubj*) were only slightly modified whereas probabilities of ambiguous words such as *man*, *soldier* or triggers such as *kill:dobj* or *attack:nsubj* converged smoothly to a different stable state that was semantically more coherent. For instance, the model interestingly realized that even if a *terrorist* was killed (*e.g.* by police), he was not actually a real victim of an attack. Figure 3 shows probability convergences of *terrorist* and *kill:dobj* given ATTACK_victim and ATTACK_perpetrator.

5 Evaluations

In order to compare with related work, we evaluated our method on the Message Understanding Conference (MUC-4) corpus (Sundheim, 1991) using precision, recall and F-score as conventional metrics for template extraction.

In what follows, we first introduce the MUC-4 corpus (Section 5.1.1), we detail the mapping technique between learned slots and reference slots (5.1.2) as well as the hyper-parameters of our model (5.1.3). Next, we present a first experiment (Section 5.2) showing how using attribute relations improves overall results. The second experiment (Section 5.3) studies the impact of document classification. We then compare our results with previous approaches, more particularly with Chambers (2013), from both quantitative and qualitative points of view (Section 5.4). Finally, Section 5.5 is dedicated to error analysis, with a special emphasis on sources of false positives.

5.1 Experimental Setups

5.1.1 Datasets

The MUC-4 corpus contains 1,700 news articles about terrorist incidents happening in Latin America. The corpus is divided into 1,300 documents for the development set and four test sets, each containing 100 documents.

We follow the rules in the literature to guarantee comparable results (Patwardhan and Riloff, 2007; Chambers and Jurafsky, 2011). The evaluation focuses on four template types – ARSON, ATTACK, BOMBING, KIDNAPPING – and four slots – Perpetrator, Instrument, Target, and Victim. Perpetrator is merged from Perpetrator_Individual and Perpetrator_Organization. The matching between system answers and references is based on head word matching. A head word is defined as the right-most word of the phrase or as the right-most word of the first 'of' if the phrase contains any. Optional templates and slots are ignored when calculating recall. Template types are ignored in evaluation: this means that a perpetrator of BOMBING in the answers could be compared to a perpetrator of ARSON, ATTACK, BOMBING or KIDNAPPING in the reference.

5.1.2 Slot Mapping

The model learns K slots and assigns each entity in a document to one of the learned slots. Slot mapping consists in matching each reference slot to an equivalent learned slot.

Note that among the K learned slots, some are irrelevant while others, sometimes of high quality, contain entities that are not part of the reference (spatio-temporal information, protagonist context, etc.). For this reason, it makes sense to have much more learned slots than expected event slots.

Similarly to previous work in the literature, we implemented an automatic empirical-driven slot mapping. Each reference slot was mapped to the learned slot that performed the best on the task of template extraction according to the F-score metric. Here, two identical slots of two different templates, such as ATTACK_victim and KIDNAPPING_victim, must to be mapped separately. Figure 4 shows the most common words of two learned slots which were mapped to BOMBING_instrument and KIDNAPPING_victim. This mapping is then kept for testing.

5.1.3 Parameter Tuning

We first tuned hyper-parameters of the models on the development set. The number of slots was set to $K = 35$. Dirichlet priors were set to $\alpha = 0.1$, $\beta = 1$ and $\gamma = 0.1$. The model was learned from the whole dataset. Slot mapping was done on tst1 and tst2. Outputs from tst3 and tst4 were evaluated using references and were averaged across ten runs.

	BOMBING_instrument	
Attributes	**Heads**	**Triggers**
car:nn	bomb	explode:nsubj
powerful:amod	fire	hear:dobj
explosive:amod	explosion	place:dobj
dynamite:nn	blow	cause:nsubj
heavy:amod	charge	set:dobj
	KIDNAPPING_victim	
Attributes	**Heads**	**Triggers**
several:amod	people	arrest:dobj
other:amod	person	kidnap:dobj
responsible:amod	man	release:dobj
military:amod	member	kill:dobj
young:amod	leader	identify:prep_as

Figure 4: Attribute, head and trigger distributions learned by the model *HT+A* for learned slots that were mapped to BOMBING_instrument and KIDNAPPING_victim.

5.2 Experiment 1: Using Entity Attributes

In this experiment, two versions of our model are compared: *HT+A* uses entity heads, event trigger relations and entity attribute relations. *HT* uses only entity heads and event triggers and omits attributes.

We studied the gain brought by attribute relations with a focus on their effect when coreference information was available or was missing. The variations on the model input are named *single*, *multi* and *coref*. *Single* input has only one event trigger for each entity. A text like *an armed man attacked the police station and killed a policeman* results in two triples for the entity *man*: *(armed:amod, man, attack:nsubj)* and *(armed:amod, man, kill:nsubj)*. In *multi* input, one entity can have several event triggers, leading for the text above to the triple *(armed:amod, man, [attack:nsubj, kill:nsubj])*. The *coref* input is richer than *multi* in that, in addition to triggers from the same sentence, triggers linked to the same corefered entity are merged together. For instance, if *man* in the above example corefers with *he* in *He was arrested three hours later*, the merged triple becomes *(armed:amod, man, [attack:nsubj, kill:nsubj, arrest:dobj])*. The plate notations of these model+data combinations are given in Figure 5.

Table 1 shows a consistent improvement when using attributes, both with and without coreferences. The best performance of 40.62 F-score is obtained by the full model on inputs with coref-

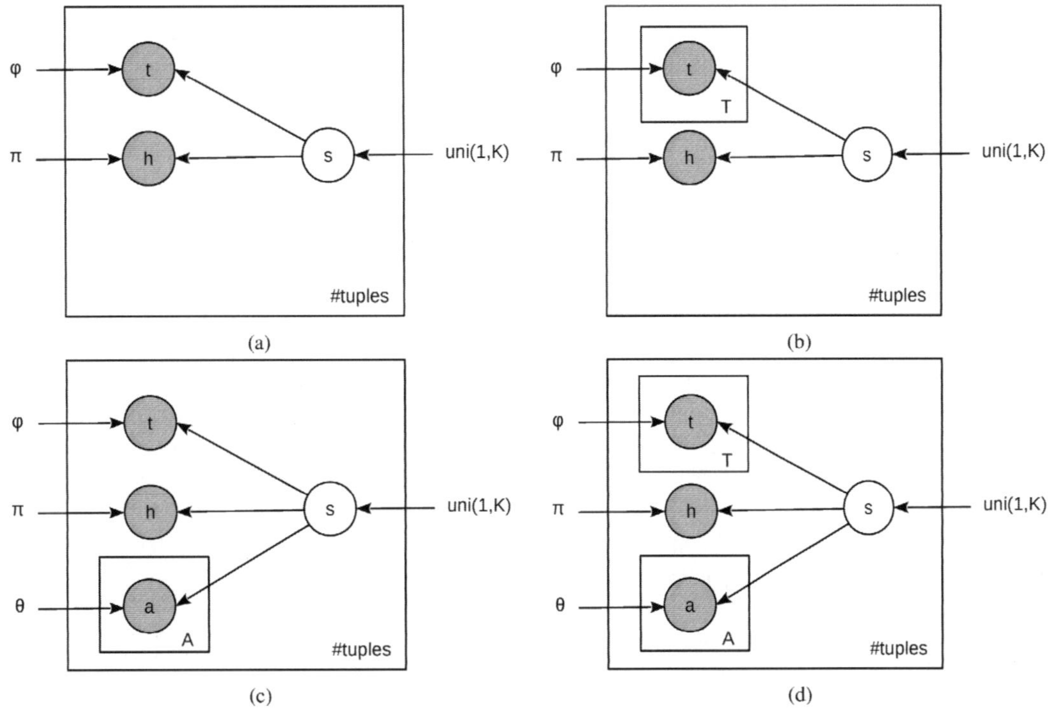

Figure 5: Model variants (Dirichlet priors are omitted for simplicity): 5a) HT model ran on single data. This model is equivalent to 5b) with T=1; 5b) HT model ran on multi data; 5c) HT+A model ran on single data; 5d) HT+A model ran on multi data.

Data	HT			HT+A		
	P	R	F	P	R	F
Single	29.59	51.17	37.48	30.22	52.41	38.33
Multi	29.32	52.21	37.52	30.82	51.68	38.55
Coref	39.99	53.53	40.01	32.42	54.59	40.62

Table 1: Improvement from using attributes.

erences. Using both attributes in the model and coreference to generate input data results in a gain of 3 F-score points.

5.3 Experiment 2: Document Classification

In the second experiment, we evaluated our model with a post-processing step of document classification.

The MUC-4 corpus contains many "irrelevant" documents. A document is irrelevant if it contains no template. Among 1,300 documents in the development set, 567 are irrelevant. The most challenging part is that there are many terrorist entities, *e.g. bomb, force, guerrilla*, occurring in irrelevant documents. That makes filtering out those documents important, but difficult. As document classification is not explicitly performed by our model, a post-processing step is needed. Document classification is expected to reduce false positives in irrelevant documents while not dramatically reducing recall.

Given a document d with slot-assigned entities and a set of mapped slots S_m resulting from slot mapping, we have to decide whether this document is relevant or not. We define the relevance score of a document as:

$$relevance(d) = \frac{\sum_{e \in d: s_e \in S_m} \sum_{t \in T_e} P(t|s_e)}{\sum_{e \in d} \sum_{t \in T_e} P(t|s_e)} \quad (4)$$

where e is an entity in the document d; s_e is the slot value assigned to e; and t is an event trigger in the list of triggers T_e.

The equation (4) defines the score of an entity as the sum of the conditional probabilities of triggers given a slot. The relevance score of the document is proportional to the score of the entities assigned to mapped slots. If this relevance score is higher than a threshold λ, then the document is considered as relevant. The value of $\lambda = 0.02$ was tuned

System	P	R	F
HT+A	32.42	54.59	40.62
HT+A + doc. classification	35.57	53.89	42.79
HT+A + oracle classification	44.58	54.59	49.08

Table 2: Improvement from document classification as post-processing.

System	P	R	F
Cheung et al. (2013)	32	37	34
Chambers and Jurafsky (2011)	**48**	25	33
Chambers (2013) (paper values)	41	41	41
HT+A + doc. classification	36	**54**	**43**

Table 3: Comparison to state-of-the-art unsupervised systems.

on the development set by maximizing the F-score of document classification.

Table 2 shows the improvement when applying document classification. The precision increases as false positives from irrelevant documents are filtered out. The loss of recall comes from relevant documents that are mistakenly filtered out. However, this loss is not significant and the overall F-score finally increases by 5%. We also compare our results to an "oracle" classifier that would remove all irrelevant documents while preserving all relevant ones. The performance of this oracle classification shows that there are some room for further improvement from document classification.

Irrelevant document filtering is a technique applied by most supervised and unsupervised approaches. Supervised methods prefer relevance detection at sentence or phrase-level (Patwardhan and Riloff, 2009; Patwardhan and Riloff, 2007). As for several unsupervised methods, Chambers (2013) includes document classification in his topic model. Chambers and Jurafsky (2011) and Cheung et al. (2013) use the learned clusters to classify documents by estimating the relevance of a document with respect to a template from *post-hoc* statistics about event triggers.

5.4 Comparison to State-of-the-Art

For comparing in more depth our results to the state-of-the-art in the literature. we reimplemented the method proposed in Chambers (2013) and integrated our attribute distributions into his model (as shown in Figure 6).

The main differences between this model and ours are the following:

1. The *full template model* of Chambers (2013) adds a distribution ψ linking events to documents. This makes the model more complex and maybe less intuitive since there is no reason to connect documents and slots (a document may contain references to several templates and slot mapping does not depend on document level). A benefit of this document distribution is that it leads to a free classification of irrelevant documents, thus avoiding a pre- or post-processing for classification. However, this issue of document relevance is very specific to the MUC corpus and the evaluation method; In a more general use case, there would be no "irrelevant" documents, only documents on various topics.

2. Each entity is linked to an event variable e. This event generates a predicate for each entity mention (recall that mentions of an entity are all occurrences of this entity in the documents, for example in a coreference chain). Our work instead focus on the fact that a probabilistic model could have multiple observations at the same position. Multiple triggers and multiple attributes are treated equally. The sources of multiple attributes and multiple triggers are not only from document-level coreferences but also from dependency relations (or even from domain-level entity coreferences if available). Hence, our model arguably generalizes better in terms of both modeling and input data.

3. Chambers (2013) applies a heuristic constraint during the sampling process, imposing that subject and object of the same predicate (*e.g. kill:nsubj* and *kill:dobj*) are not distributed into the same slot. Our model does not require this heuristic.

Some details concerning data preprocessing and model parameters are not fully specified by Chambers (2013); for this reason, our implementation of the model (applied on the same data) leads to slightly different results than those published. That is why we present the two results here (paper values in Table 3, reimplementation values in Table 4).

Table 3 shows that our model outperforms the others on recall by a large margin. It achieves the

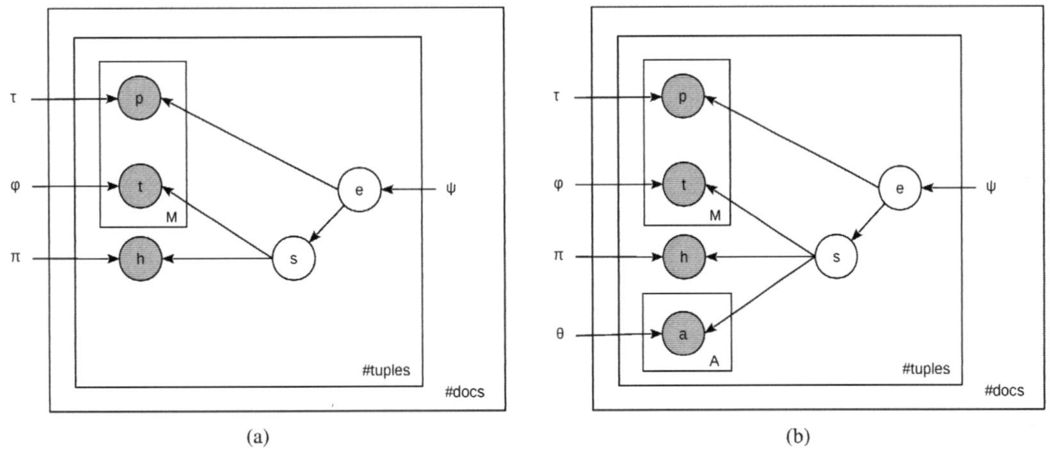

Figure 6: Variation of Chambers (2013) model: 6a) Original model; 6b) Original model + attribute distributions.

Chambers (2013)	P	R	F
Original reimpl.	38.65	42.68	40.56
Original reimpl. + Attribute	39.25	43.68	41.31

Table 4: Performance on reimplementation of Chambers (2013).

best overall F-score. In addition, as stated by our experiments, precision could be further improved by more sophisticated document classification. Interestingly, using attributes also proves to be useful in the model proposed by Chambers (2013) (as shown in Table 4).

5.5 Error Analysis

We performed an error analysis on the output of *HT+A + doc. classification* to detect the origin of false positives (FPs). 38% of FPs are mentions that never occur in the reference. Within this 38%, *attacker* and *killer* are among the most frequent errors. These words could refer to a perpetrator of an attack. These mentions, however, do not occur in the reference, possibly because human annotators consider them as too generic terms. Apart from such generic terms, other assignments are obvious errors of the system, *e.g. window*, *door* or *wall* as physical target; *action* or *massacre* as perpetrator; *explosion* or *shooting* as instrument. These kinds of errors are due to the fact that in our model, as in the one of Chambers (2013), the number of slots is fixed and is not equivalent to the real number of reference slots.

On the other hand, 62% of FPs are mentions of entities that occur at least once in the reference. On top of the list are perpetrators such as *guerrilla*, *group* and *rebel*. The model is capable of assigning *guerrilla* to *attribution* slot if it is accompanied by a trigger like *announce:nsubj*. However, triggers that describe quasi-terrorism events (*e.g.* menace, threatening, military conflict) are also grouped into *perpetrator* slots. Similarly, mentions of frequent words such as *bomb* (*instrument*), *building*, *house*, *office* (*targets*) tend to be systematically grouped into these slots, regardless of their relations. Increasing the number of slots (to sharpen their content) does not help overall. This is due to the fact that the MUC corpus is very small and is biased towards terrorism events. Adding a higher level of template type as in Chambers (2013) partially solves the problem but makes recall decrease (as shown in Table 3).

6 Conclusions and Perspectives

We presented a generative model for representing the roles played by the entities in an event template. We focused on using immediate contexts of entities and proposed a simpler and more effective model than those proposed in previous work. We evaluated this model on the MUC-4 corpus.

Even if our results outperform other unsupervised approaches, we are still far from results obtained by supervised systems. Improvements can be obtained by several ways. First, the characteristics of the MUC-4 corpus are a limiting factor. The corpus is small and roles are similar from a template to another, which does not reflect reality.

A bigger corpus, even partially annotated but presenting a better variety of templates, could lead to very different approaches.

As we showed, our model comes with a unified representation of all types of relations. This opens the way to the use of multiple types of relations (syntactic, semantic, thematic, etc.) to refine the clusters.

Last but not least, the evaluation protocol, that became a kind of *de facto* standard, is very much imperfect. Most notably, the way of finally mapping with reference slots can have a great influence on the results.

Acknowledgment

This work was partially financed by the Foundation for Scientific Cooperation "Campus Paris-Saclay" (FSC) under the project Digiteo ASTRE No. 2013-0774D.

References

Niranjan Balasubramanian, Stephen Soderland, Mausam, and Oren Etzioni. 2013. Generating Coherent Event Schemas at Scale. In *2013 Conference on Empirical Methods in Natural Language Processing (EMNLP 2013)*, pages 1721–1731, Seattle, Washington, USA, October.

Cosmin Adrian Bejan. 2008. Unsupervised Discovery of Event Scenarios from Texts. In *Twenty-First International Florida Artificial Intelligence Research Society Conference (FLAIRS 2008)*, pages 124–129, Coconut Grove, Florida.

David M. Blei, Andrew Y. Ng, and Michael I. Jordan. 2003. Latent Dirichlet Allocation. *Journal of Machine Learning Research*, 3:993–1022, March.

Nathanael Chambers and Dan Jurafsky. 2008. Unsupervised Learning of Narrative Event Chains. In *ACL-08: HLT*, pages 789–797, Columbus, Ohio, June.

Nathanael Chambers and Dan Jurafsky. 2009. Unsupervised Learning of Narrative Schemas and their Participants. In *Joint Conference of the 47th Annual Meeting of the ACL and the 4th International Joint Conference on Natural Language Processing of the AFNLP (ACL-IJCNLP'09)*, pages 602–610, Suntec, Singapore, August.

Nathanael Chambers and Dan Jurafsky. 2011. Template-Based Information Extraction without the Templates. In *49th Annual Meeting of the Association for Computational Linguistics: Human Language Technologies (ACL 2011)*, pages 976–986, Portland, Oregon, USA, June.

Nathanael Chambers. 2013. Event Schema Induction with a Probabilistic Entity-Driven Model. In *Proceedings of the 2013 Conference on Empirical Methods in Natural Language Processing*, pages 1797–1807, Seattle, Washington, USA, October.

Kit Jackie Chi Cheung, Hoifung Poon, and Lucy Vanderwende. 2013. Probabilistic Frame Induction. In *Proceedings of the 2013 Conference of the North American Chapter of the Association for Computational Linguistics: Human Language Technologies*, pages 837–846.

R. Collier. 1998. *Automatic Template Creation for Information Extraction*. Ph.D. thesis, University of Sheffield.

Gerald DeJong. 1982. An overview of the FRUMP system. In W. Lehnert and M. Ringle, editors, *Strategies for natural language processing*, pages 149–176. Lawrence Erlbaum Associates.

Kathrin Eichler, Holmer Hemsen, and Günter Neumann. 2008. Unsupervised Relation Extraction From Web Documents. In *6th Conference on Language Resources and Evaluation (LREC'08)*, Marrakech, Morocco.

Olivier Ferret and Brigitte Grau. 1997. An Aggregation Procedure for Building Episodic Memory. In *15th International Joint Conference on Artificial Intelligence (IJCAI-97)*, pages 280–285, Nagoya, Japan.

Elena Filatova, Vasileios Hatzivassiloglou, and Kathleen McKeown. 2006. Automatic Creation of Domain Templates. In *21st International Conference on Computational Linguistics and 44th Annual Meeting of the Association for Computational Linguistics (COLING-ACL 2006)*, pages 207–214, Sydney, Australia.

Elena Filatova. 2008. *Unsupervised Relation Learning for Event-Focused Question-Answering and Domain Modelling*. Ph.D. thesis, Columbia University.

Marjorie Freedman, Lance Ramshaw, Elizabeth Boschee, Ryan Gabbard, Gary Kratkiewicz, Nicolas Ward, and Ralph Weischedel. 2011. Extreme Extraction – Machine Reading in a Week. In *2011 Conference on Empirical Methods in Natural Language Processing (EMNLP 2011)*, pages 1437–1446, Edinburgh, Scotland, UK., July.

Lea Frermann, Ivan Titov, and Manfred Pinkal. 2014. A Hierarchical Bayesian Model for Unsupervised Induction of Script Knowledge. In *14th Conference of the European Chapter of the Association for Computational Linguistics (EACL 2014)*, pages 49–57, Gothenburg, Sweden, April.

Tom Griffiths. 2002. Gibbs sampling in the generative model of Latent Dirichlet Allocation. Technical report, Stanford University.

Ralph Grishman and Yifan He. 2014. An Information Extraction Customizer. In Petr Sojka, Ale Hork, Ivan Kopeek, and Karel Pala, editors, *17th International Conference on Text, Speech and Dialogue (TSD 2014)*, volume 8655 of *Lecture Notes in Computer Science*, pages 3–10. Springer International Publishing.

Ralph Grishman and Beth Sundheim. 1996. Message Understanding Conference-6: A Brief History. In *16th International Conference on Computational linguistics (COLING'96)*, pages 466–471, Copenhagen, Denmark.

Sanda Harabagiu. 2004. Incremental Topic Representation. In *Proceedings of the 20th International Conference on Computational Linguistics (COLING'04)*, Geneva, Switzerland, August.

Takaaki Hasegawa, Satoshi Sekine, and Ralph Grishman. 2004. Discovering Relations among Named Entities from Large Corpora. In *42nd Meeting of the Association for Computational Linguistics (ACL'04)*, pages 415–422, Barcelona, Spain.

Ludovic Jean-Louis, Romaric Besanon, and Olivier Ferret. 2011. Text Segmentation and Graph-based Method for Template Filling in Information Extraction. In *5th International Joint Conference on Natural Language Processing (IJCNLP 2011)*, pages 723–731, Chiang Mai, Thailand.

Christopher D. Manning, Mihai Surdeanu, John Bauer, Jenny Finkel, Steven J. Bethard, and David McClosky. 2014. The Stanford CoreNLP Natural Language Processing Toolkit. In *Proceedings of 52nd Annual Meeting of the Association for Computational Linguistics: System Demonstrations*, pages 55–60, Baltimore, USA, jun.

Bonan Min, Shuming Shi, Ralph Grishman, and Chin-Yew Lin. 2012. Ensemble Semantics for Large-scale Unsupervised Relation Extraction. In *2012 Joint Conference on Empirical Methods in Natural Language Processing and Computational Natural Language Learning (EMNLP-CoNLL 2012*, pages 1027–1037, Jeju Island, Korea.

Ashutosh Modi and Ivan Titov. 2014. Inducing neural models of script knowledge. In *Eighteenth Conference on Computational Natural Language Learning (CoNLL 2014)*, pages 49–57, Ann Arbor, Michigan.

Siddharth Patwardhan and Ellen Riloff. 2007. Effective Information Extraction with Semantic Affinity Patterns and Relevant Regions. In *Proceedings of the 2007 Joint Conference on Empirical Methods in Natural Language Processing and Computational Natural Language Learning (EMNLP-CoNLL 2007)*, pages 717–727, Prague, Czech Republic, June.

Siddharth Patwardhan and Ellen Riloff. 2009. A Unified Model of Phrasal and Sentential Evidence for Information Extraction. In *Proceedings of the 2009 Conference on Empirical Methods in Natural Language Processing (EMNLP 2009)*, pages 151–160.

Karl Pichotta and Raymond Mooney. 2014. Statistical script learning with multi-argument events. In *14th Conference of the European Chapter of the Association for Computational Linguistics (EACL 2014)*, pages 220–229, Gothenburg, Sweden.

Long Qiu, Min-Yen Kan, and Tat-Seng Chua. 2008. Modeling Context in Scenario Template Creation. In *Third International Joint Conference on Natural Language Processing (IJCNLP 2008)*, pages 157–164, Hyderabad, India.

Michaela Regneri, Alexander Koller, and Manfred Pinkal. 2010. Learning Script Knowledge with Web Experiments. In *48th Annual Meeting of the Association for Computational Linguistics (ACL 2010)*, pages 979–988, Uppsala, Sweden, July.

Benjamin Rosenfeld and Ronen Feldman. 2007. Clustering for unsupervised relation identification. In *Sixteenth ACM conference on Conference on information and knowledge management (CIKM'07)*, pages 411–418, Lisbon, Portugal.

Roger C. Schank. 1980. Language and memory. *Cognitive Science*, 4:243–284.

Satoshi Sekine. 2006. On-demand information extraction. In *21st International Conference on Computational Linguistics and 44th Annual Meeting of the Association for Computational Linguistics (COLING-ACL 2006)*, pages 731–738, Sydney, Australia.

Yusuke Shinyama and Satoshi Sekine. 2006. Preemptive Information Extraction using Unrestricted Relation Discovery. In *HLT-NAACL 2006*, pages 304–311, New York City, USA.

Beth M. Sundheim. 1991. Third Message Understanding Evaluation and Conference (MUC-3): Phase 1 Status Report. In *Proceedings of the Workshop on Speech and Natural Language*, HLT '91, pages 301–305.

Syntax-based Simultaneous Translation through Prediction of Unseen Syntactic Constituents

Yusuke Oda **Graham Neubig** **Sakriani Sakti** **Tomoki Toda** **Satoshi Nakamura**
Graduate School of Information Science
Nara Institute of Science and Technology
Takayamacho, Ikoma, Nara 630-0192, Japan
{oda.yusuke.on9, neubig, ssakti, tomoki, s-nakamura}@is.naist.jp

Abstract

Simultaneous translation is a method to reduce the latency of communication through machine translation (MT) by dividing the input into short segments before performing translation. However, short segments pose problems for syntax-based translation methods, as it is difficult to generate accurate parse trees for sub-sentential segments. In this paper, we perform the first experiments applying syntax-based SMT to simultaneous translation, and propose two methods to prevent degradations in accuracy: a method to predict unseen syntactic constituents that help generate complete parse trees, and a method that waits for more input when the current utterance is not enough to generate a fluent translation. Experiments on English-Japanese translation show that the proposed methods allow for improvements in accuracy, particularly with regards to word order of the target sentences.

1 Introduction

Speech translation is an application of machine translation (MT) that converts utterances from the speaker's language into the listener's language. One of the most identifying features of speech translation is the fact that it must be performed in real time while the speaker is speaking, and thus it is necessary to split a constant stream of words into translatable segments before starting the translation process. Traditionally, speech translation assumes that each segment corresponds to a sentence, and thus performs sentence boundary detection before translation (Matusov et al., 2006). However, full sentences can be long, particularly in formal speech such as lectures, and if translation does not start until explicit ends of sentences, listeners may be forced to wait a considerable time until receiving the result of translation. For example, when the speaker continues to talk for 10 seconds, listeners must wait at least 10 seconds to obtain the result of translation. This is the major factor limiting simultaneity in traditional speech translation systems.

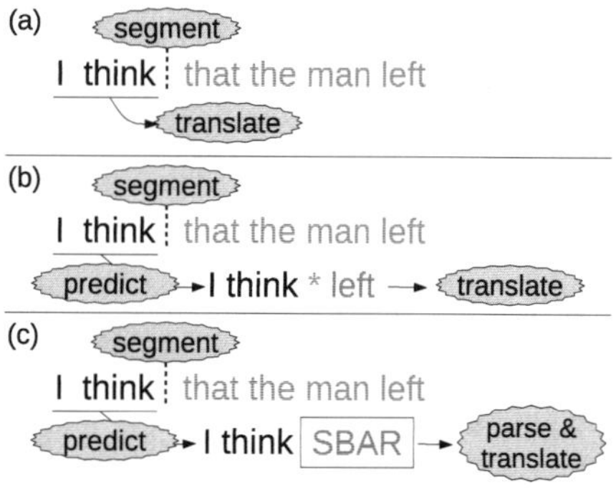

Figure 1: Simultaneous translation where the source sentence is segmented after "I think" and translated according to (a) the standard method, (b) Grissom II et al. (2014)'s method of final verb prediction, and (c) our method of predicting syntactic constituents.

Simultaneous translation (Section 2) avoids this problem by starting to translate before observing the whole sentence, as shown in Figure 1 (a). However, as translation starts before the whole sentence is observed, translation units are often not syntactically or semantically complete, and the performance may suffer accordingly. The deleterious effect of this missing information is less worrying in largely monotonic language pairs (e.g. English-French), but cannot be discounted in syntactically distant language pairs (e.g. English-Japanese) that often require long-distance reordering beyond translation units.

One way to avoid this problem of missing information is to explicitly predict information needed

Proceedings of the 53rd Annual Meeting of the Association for Computational Linguistics and the 7th International Joint Conference on Natural Language Processing, pages 198–207,
Beijing, China, July 26-31, 2015.

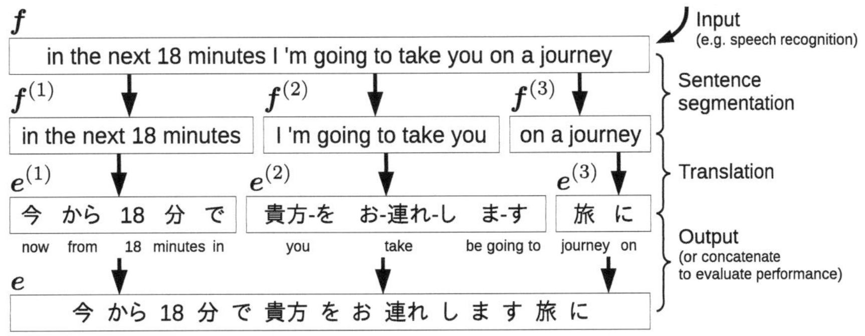

Figure 2: Process of English-Japanese simultaneous translation with sentence segmentation.

to translate the content accurately. An ambitious first step in this direction was recently proposed by Grissom II et al. (2014), who describe a method that predicts sentence-final verbs using reinforcement learning (e.g. Figure 1 (b)). This approach has the potential to greatly decrease the delay in translation from verb-final languages to verb-initial languages (such as German-English), but is also limited to only this particular case.

In this paper, we propose a more general method that focuses on a different variety of information: *unseen syntactic constituents*. This method is motivated by our desire to apply translation models that use source-side parsing, such as tree-to-string (T2S) translation (Huang et al., 2006) or syntactic pre-ordering (Xia and McCord, 2004), which have been shown to greatly improve translation accuracy over syntactically divergent language pairs. However, conventional methods for parsing are not directly applicable to the partial sentences that arise in simultaneous MT. The reason for this, as explained in detail in Section 3, is that parsing methods generally assume that they are given input that forms a complete syntactic phrase. Looking at the example in Figure 1, after the speaker has spoken the words "I think" we have a partial sentence that will only be complete once we observe the following SBAR. Our method attempts to predict exactly this information, as shown in Figure 1 (c), guessing the remaining syntactic constituents that will allow us to acquire a proper parse tree.

Specifically the method consists of two parts: First, we propose a method that trains a statistical model to predict future syntactic constituents based on features of the input segment (Section 4). Second, we demonstrate how to apply this syntactic prediction to MT, including the proposal of a heuristic method that examines whether a future constituent has the potential to cause a reordering problem during translation, and wait for more input in these cases (Section 5).

Based on the proposed method, we perform experiments in simultaneous translation of English-Japanese talks (Section 6). As this is the first work applying T2S translation to simultaneous MT, we first compare T2S to more traditional phrase-based techniques. We find that T2S translation is effective with longer segments, but drops off quickly with shorter segments, justifying the need for techniques to handle translation when full context is not available. We then compare the proposed method of predicting syntactic constituents, and find that it improves translation results, particularly with respect to word ordering in the output sentences.

2 Simultaneous Translation

In simultaneous translation, we assume that we are given an incoming stream of words $\boldsymbol{f}$, which we are expected to translate. As the $\boldsymbol{f}$ is long, we would like to begin translating before we reach the end of the stream. Previous methods to do so can generally be categorized into *incremental decoding* methods, and *sentence segmentation* methods.

In incremental decoding, each incoming word is fed into the decoder one-by-one, and the decoder updates the search graph with the new words and decides whether it should begin translation. Incremental decoding methods have been proposed for phrase-based (Sankaran et al., 2010; Yarmohammadi et al., 2013; Finch et al., 2014) and hierarchical phrase-based (Siahbani et al., 2014) SMT models.[1] Incremental decoding has the advantage of using information about the decoding graph in the choice of translation timing, but also requires significant changes to the internal workings of the decoder, precluding the use of standard decoding tools or techniques.

Sentence segmentation methods (Figure 2) provide a simpler alternative by first dividing $\boldsymbol{f}$ into subsequences of 1 or more words $[\boldsymbol{f}^{(1)}, \ldots, \boldsymbol{f}^{(N)}]$. These segments are then translated with a traditional decoder into output sequences $[\boldsymbol{e}^{(1)}, \ldots, \boldsymbol{e}^{(N)}]$, which each are output as soon as translation finishes. Many methods have been proposed to perform segmentation, including the use of prosodic boundaries (Fügen et al., 2007; Bangalore et al., 2012), predicting punctuation marks (Rangarajan Sridhar et al., 2013), reordering probabilities of phrases (Fujita et al., 2013), or models to explicitly optimize translation accuracy (Oda et al., 2014). Previous work often assumes that $\boldsymbol{f}$ is a single sentence, and focus on sub-sentential segmentation, an approach we follow in this work.

Sentence segmentation methods have the obvious advantage of allowing for translation as soon as a segment is decided. However, the use of the shorter segments also makes it necessary to translate while part of the utterance is still unknown. As a result, segmenting sentences more aggressively often results in a decrease translation accuracy. This is a problem in phrase-based MT, the framework used in the majority of previous research on simultaneous translation. However, it is an even larger problem when performing translation that relies on parsing the input sentence. We describe the problems caused by parsing a segment $\boldsymbol{f}^{(n)}$, and solutions, in the following section.

3 Parsing Incomplete Sentences

3.1 Difficulties in Incomplete Parsing

In standard phrase structure parsing, the parser assumes that each input string is a complete sentence, or at least a complete phrase. For example, Figure 3 (a) shows the phrase structure of the complete sentence "this is a pen." However, in the case of simultaneous translation, each translation unit

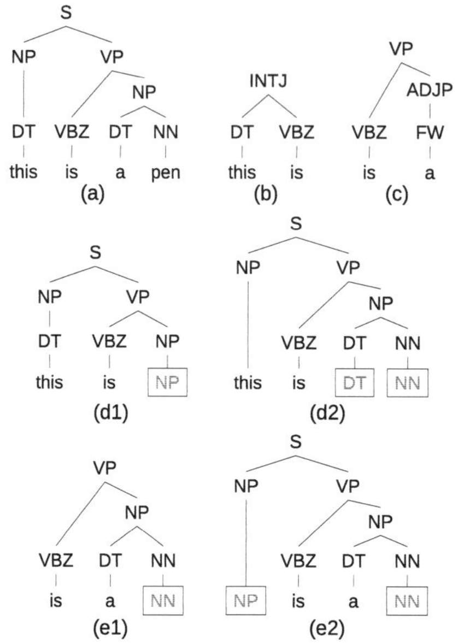

Figure 3: Phrase structures with surrounding syntactic constituents.

is not necessarily segmented in a way that guarantees that the translation unit is a complete sentence, so each translation unit should be treated not as a whole, but as a part of a spoken sentence. As a result, the parser input may be an incomplete sequence of words (e.g. "this is," "is a"), and a standard parser will generate an incorrect parse as shown in Figures 3(b) and 3(c).

The proposed method solves this problem by supplementing unseen syntactic constituents before and after the translation unit. For example, considering parse trees for the complete sentence in Figure 3(a), we see that a noun phrase (NP) can be placed after the translation unit "this is." If we append the syntactic constituent $\boxed{\text{NP}}$ as a "black box" before parsing, we can create a syntactically desirable parse tree as shown in Figure 3(d1) We also can construct another tree as shown in Figure 3(d2) by appending two constituents $\boxed{\text{DT}}$ and $\boxed{\text{NN}}$. For the other example "is a," we can create the parse tree in Figure 3(e1) by appending $\boxed{\text{NP}}$ before the unit and $\boxed{\text{NN}}$ after the unit, or can create the tree in Figure 3(e2) by appending only $\boxed{\text{NN}}$ after the unit.

3.2 Formulation of Incomplete Parsing

A typical model for phrase structure parsing is the probabilistic context-free grammar (PCFG). Parsing is performed by finding the parse tree T that

[1] There is also one previous rule-based system that uses syntax in incremental translation, but it is language specific and limited domain (Ryu et al., 2006), and thus difficult to compare with our SMT-based system. It also does not predict unseen constituents, relying only on the observed segment.

maximizes the PCFG probability given a sequence of words $\boldsymbol{w} \equiv [w_1, w_2, \cdots, w_n]$ as shown by Eq. (2):

$$T^* \equiv \arg\max_T \Pr(T|\boldsymbol{w}) \quad (1)$$

$$\simeq \arg\max_T [\sum_{(X\to[Y,\cdots])\in T} \log \Pr(X \to [Y,\cdots]) + \sum_{(X\to w_i)\in T} \log \Pr(X \to w_i)], \quad (2)$$

where $\Pr(X \to [Y,\cdots])$ represents the generative probabilities of the sequence of constituents $[Y,\cdots]$ given a parent constituent X, and $\Pr(X \to w_i)$ represents the generative probabilities of each word w_i $(1 \le i \le n)$ given a parent constituent X.

To consider parsing of incomplete sentences with appended syntactic constituents, We define $\boldsymbol{L} \equiv [L_{|\boldsymbol{L}|}, \cdots, L_2, L_1]$ as the sequence of preceding syntactic constituents of the translation unit and $\boldsymbol{R} \equiv [R_1, R_2, \cdots, R_{|\boldsymbol{R}|}]$ as the sequence of following syntactic constituents of the translation unit. For the example Figure 3(d1), we assume that $\boldsymbol{L} = [\,]$ and $\boldsymbol{R} = [\,\boxed{\text{NP}}\,]$.

We assume that both sequences of syntactic constituents $\boldsymbol{L}$ and $\boldsymbol{R}$ are predicted based on the sequence of words $\boldsymbol{w}$ before the main parsing step. Thus, the whole process of parsing incomplete sentences can be described as the combination of predicting both sequences of syntactic constituents represented by Eq. (3) and (4) and parsing with predicted syntactic constituents represented by Eq. (5):

$$\boldsymbol{L}^* \equiv \arg\max_{\boldsymbol{L}} \Pr(\boldsymbol{L}|\boldsymbol{w}), \quad (3)$$

$$\boldsymbol{R}^* \equiv \arg\max_{\boldsymbol{R}} \Pr(\boldsymbol{R}|\boldsymbol{w}), \quad (4)$$

$$T^* \equiv \arg\max_T \Pr(T|\boldsymbol{L}^*, \boldsymbol{w}, \boldsymbol{R}^*). \quad (5)$$

Algorithmically, parsing with predicted syntactic constituents can be achieved by simply treating each syntactic constituent as another word in the input sequence and using a standard parsing algorithm such as the CKY algorithm. In this process, the only difference between syntactic constituents and normal words is the probability, which we define as follows:

$$\Pr(X \to \boxed{Y}) \equiv \begin{cases} 1, & \text{if } Y = X \\ 0, & \text{otherwise.} \end{cases} \quad (6)$$

It should be noted that here $\boldsymbol{L}$ refers to syntactic constituents that have already been seen in the past. Thus, it is theoretically possible to store past parse trees as history and generate $\boldsymbol{L}$ based on this history, or condition Eq. 3 based on this information. However, deciding which part of trees to use as $\boldsymbol{L}$ is not trivial, and applying this approach requires that we predict $\boldsymbol{L}$ and $\boldsymbol{R}$ using different methods. Thus, in this study, we use the same method to predict both sequences of constituents for simplicity.

In the next section, we describe the actual method used to create a predictive model for these strings of syntactic constituents.

4 Predicting Syntactic Constituents

In order to define which syntactic constituents should be predicted by our model, we assume that each final parse tree generated by $\boldsymbol{w}$, $\boldsymbol{L}$ and $\boldsymbol{R}$ must satisfy the following conditions:

1. The parse tree generated by $\boldsymbol{w}$, $\boldsymbol{L}$ and $\boldsymbol{R}$ must be "complete." Defining this formally, this means that the root node of the parse tree for the segment must correspond to a node in the parse tree for the original complete sentence.
2. Each parse tree contains only $\boldsymbol{L}$, $\boldsymbol{w}$ and $\boldsymbol{R}$ as terminal symbols.
3. The number of nodes is the minimum necessary to satisfy these conditions.

As shown in the Figure 3, there is ambiguity regarding syntactic constituents to be predicted (e.g. we can choose either $[\,\boxed{\text{NP}}\,]$ or $[\,\boxed{\text{DT}}, \boxed{\text{NN}}\,]$ as $\boldsymbol{R}$ for $\boldsymbol{w} = [$ "this", "is" $]$). These conditions avoid ambiguity of which syntactic constituents should predicted for partial sentences in the training data. Looking at the example, Figures 3(d1) and 3(e1) satisfy these conditions, but 3(d2) and 3(e2) do not.

Figure 4 shows the statistics of the lengths of $\boldsymbol{L}$ and $\boldsymbol{R}$ sequences extracted according to these criteria for all substrings of the WSJ datasets 2 to 23 of the Penn Treebank (Marcus et al., 1993), a standard training set for English syntactic parsers. From the figure we can see that lengths of up to 2 constituents cover the majority of cases for both $\boldsymbol{L}$ and $\boldsymbol{R}$, but a significant number of cases require longer strings. Thus methods that predict a fixed number of constituents are not appropriate here. In Algorithm 1, we show the method we propose to

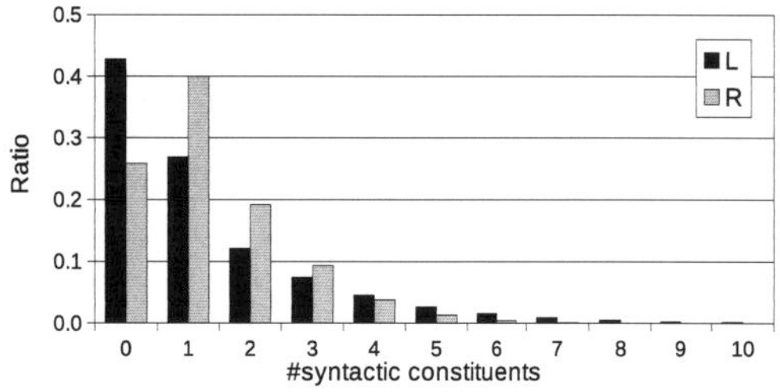

Figure 4: Statistics of numbers of syntactic constituents to be predicted.

predict $\boldsymbol{R}$ for constituent sequences of an arbitrary length. Here $+\!\!+$ represents the concatenation of two sequences.

First, our method forcibly parses the input sequence $\boldsymbol{w}$ and retrieves a potentially incorrect parse tree T', which is used to calculate features for the prediction model. The next syntactic constituent R^+ is then predicted using features extracted from $\boldsymbol{w}$, T', and the predicted sequence history $\boldsymbol{R}^*$. This prediction is repeated recurrently until the end-of-sentence symbol ("nil" in Algorithm 1) is predicted as the next symbol.

In this study, we use a multi-label classifier based on linear SVMs (Fan et al., 2008) to predict new syntactic constituents with features shown in Table 1. We treat the input sequence $\boldsymbol{w}$ and predicted syntactic constituents $\boldsymbol{R}^*$ as a concatenated sequence $\boldsymbol{w} +\!\!+ \boldsymbol{R}^*$. For example, if we have $\boldsymbol{w} = [\text{ this, is, a }]$ and $\boldsymbol{R}^* = [\ \boxed{\text{NN}}\ ]$, then the word features "3 rightmost 1-grams" will take the values "is," "a," and $\boxed{\text{NN}}$. Tags of semi-terminal nodes in T' are used as part-of-speech (POS) tags for corresponding words and the POS of each predicted syntactic constituent is simply its tag. "nil" is used when some information is not available. For example, if we have $\boldsymbol{w} = [\text{ this, is }]$ and $\boldsymbol{R}^* = [\,]$ then "3 rightmost 1-grams" will take the values "nil," "this," and "is." Algorithm 1 and Table 1 shows the method used to predict $\boldsymbol{R}^*$ but $\boldsymbol{L}^*$ can be predicted by performing the prediction process in the reverse order.

Algorithm 1 Prediction algorithm for following constituents $\boldsymbol{R}^*$

$T' \leftarrow \arg\max_T \Pr(T|\boldsymbol{w})$
$\boldsymbol{R}^* \leftarrow [\,]$
loop
  $R^+ \leftarrow \arg\max_R \Pr(R|T', \boldsymbol{R}^*)$
  if $R^+ = \text{nil}$ **then**
    return $\boldsymbol{R}^*$
  end if
  $\boldsymbol{R}^* \leftarrow \boldsymbol{R}^* +\!\!+ [R^+]$
end loop

Table 1: Features used in predicting syntactic constituents.

Type	Feature
Words	3 leftmost 1,2-grams in $\boldsymbol{w} +\!\!+ \boldsymbol{R}^*$
	3 rightmost 1,2-grams in $\boldsymbol{w} +\!\!+ \boldsymbol{R}^*$
	Left/rightmost pair in $\boldsymbol{w} +\!\!+ \boldsymbol{R}^*$
POS	Same as "Words"
Parse	Tag of the root node
	Tags of children of the root node
	Pairs of root and children nodes
Length	$\lvert\boldsymbol{w}\rvert$
	$\lvert\boldsymbol{R}^*\rvert$

5 Tree-to-string SMT with Syntactic Constituents

Once we have created a tree from the sequence $\boldsymbol{L}^* +\!\!+ \boldsymbol{w} +\!\!+ \boldsymbol{R}^*$ by performing PCFG parsing with predicted syntactic constituents according to Eqs. (2), (5), and (6), the next step is to use this tree in translation. In this section, we focus specifically on T2S translation, which we use in our experiments, but it is likely that similar methods are applicable to other uses of source-side syntax such as pre-ordering as well.

It should be noted that using these trees in T2S translation models is not trivial because each estimated syntactic constituent should be treated as an aggregated entity representing all possibilities of subtrees rooted in such a constituent. Specifically, there are two problems: the possibility of *reordering* an as-of-yet unseen syntactic constituent into the middle of the translated sentence, and the calculation of *language model probabilities* considering syntactic constituent tags.

With regards to the first problem of reordering, consider the example of English-Japanese translation in Figure 5(b), where a syntactic constituent $\boxed{\text{PP}}$ is placed at the end of the English sequence ($\boldsymbol{R}^*$), but the corresponding entity in the Japanese translation result should be placed in the middle of the sentence. In this case, if we attempt to translate immediately, we will have to omit the as-of-yet unknown $\boxed{\text{PP}}$ from our translation and translate it later, resulting in an unnatural word ordering in the

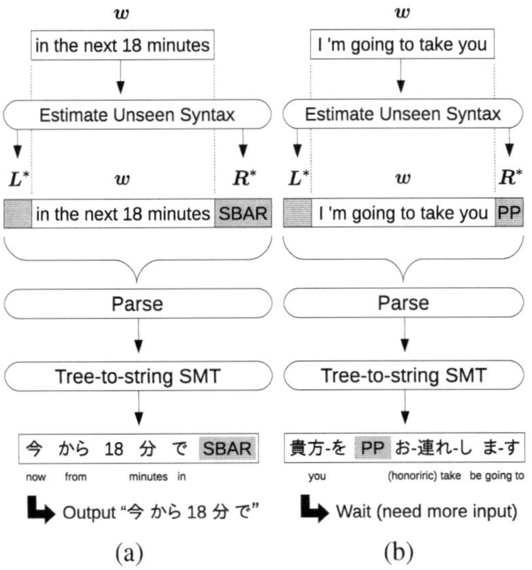

Figure 5: Waiting for the next translation unit.

target sentence.[2]

Thus, if any of the syntactic constituents in $\boldsymbol{R}$ are placed anywhere other than the end of the translation result, we can assume that this is a hint that the current segmentation boundary is not appropriate. Based on this intuition, we propose a heuristic method that ignores segmentation boundaries that result in a translation of this type, and instead wait for the next translation unit, helping to avoid problems due to inappropriate segmentation boundaries. Algorithm 2 formally describes this *waiting* method.

The second problem of language model probabilities arises because we are attempting to generate a string of words, some of which are not actual words but tags representing syntactic constituents. Creating a language model that contains probabilities for these tags in the appropriate places is not trivial, so for simplicity, we simply assume that every syntactic constituent tag is an unknown word, and that the output of translation consists of both translated normal words and non-translated tags as shown in Figure 5. We relegate a more complete handling of these tags to future work.

[2]It is also potentially possible to create a predictive model for the actual content of the PP as done for sentence-final verbs by Grissom II et al. (2014), but the space of potential prepositional phrases is huge, and we leave this non-trivial task for future work.

Algorithm 2 Waiting algorithm for T2S SMT

$\boldsymbol{w} \leftarrow [\,]$
loop
  $\boldsymbol{w} \leftarrow \boldsymbol{w} + \!\!\!+ \, \mathrm{NextSegment}()$
  $\boldsymbol{L}^* \leftarrow \arg\max_{\boldsymbol{L}} \Pr(\boldsymbol{L}|\boldsymbol{w})$
  $\boldsymbol{R}^* \leftarrow \arg\max_{\boldsymbol{R}} \Pr(\boldsymbol{R}|\boldsymbol{w})$
  $T^* \leftarrow \arg\max_{T} \Pr(T|\boldsymbol{L}^*, \boldsymbol{w}, \boldsymbol{R}^*)$
  $\boldsymbol{e}^* \leftarrow \arg\max_{\boldsymbol{e}} \Pr(\boldsymbol{e}|T^*)$
  if elements of $\boldsymbol{R}^*$ are rightmost in e^* **then**
    $\mathrm{Output}(\boldsymbol{e}^*)$
    $\boldsymbol{w} \leftarrow [\,]$
  end if
end loop

6 Experiments

6.1 Experiment Settings

We perform 2 types of experiments to evaluate the effectiveness of the proposed methods.

6.1.1 Predicting Syntactic Constituents

In the first experiment, we evaluate prediction accuracies of unseen syntactic constituents $\boldsymbol{L}$ and $\boldsymbol{R}$. To do so, we train a predictive model as described in Section 4 using an English treebank and evaluate its performance. To create training and testing data, we extract all substrings $\boldsymbol{w}$ s.t. $|\boldsymbol{w}| \geq 2$ in the Penn Treebank and calculate the corresponding syntactic constituents $\boldsymbol{L}$ and $\boldsymbol{R}$ by according to the original trees and substring $\boldsymbol{w}$. We use the 90% of the extracted data for training a classifier and the remaining 10% for testing estimation recall, precision and F-measure. We use the Ckylark parser(Oda et al., 2015) to generate T' from $\boldsymbol{w}$.

6.1.2 Simultaneous Translation

Next, we evaluate the performance of T2S simultaneous translation adopting the two proposed methods. We use data of TED talks from the English-Japanese section of WIT3 (Cettolo et al., 2012), and also append dictionary entries and examples in Eijiro[3] to the training data to increase the vocabulary of the translation model. The total number of sentences/entries is 2.49M (WIT3, Eijiro), 998 (WIT3), and 468 (WIT3) sentences for training, development, and testing respectively.

We use the Stanford Tokenizer[4] for English tokenization, KyTea (Neubig et al., 2011) for

[3]http://eijiro.jp/

[4]http://nlp.stanford.edu/software/tokenizer.shtml

Japanese tokenization, GIZA++ (Och and Ney, 2003) to construct word alignment, and KenLM (Heafield et al., 2013) to generate a 5-gram target language model. We use the Ckylark parser, which we modified to implement the parsing method of Section 3.2, to generate T^* from $\boldsymbol{L}^*$, $\boldsymbol{w}$ and $\boldsymbol{R}^*$.

We use Travatar (Neubig, 2013) to train the T2S translation model used in the proposed method, and also Moses (Koehn et al., 2007) to train phrase-based translation models that serve as a baseline. Each translation model is tuned using MERT (Och, 2003) to maximize BLEU (Papineni et al., 2002). We evaluate translation accuracies by BLEU and also RIBES (Isozaki et al., 2010), a reordering-focused metric which has achieved high correlation with human evaluation on English-Japanese translation tasks.

We perform tests using two different sentence segmentation methods. The first is n-words segmentation (Rangarajan Sridhar et al., 2013), a simple heuristic that simply segments the input every n words. This method disregards syntactic and semantic units in the original sentence, allowing us to evaluate the robustness of translation against poor segmentation boundaries. The second method is the state-of-the-art segmentation strategy proposed by Oda et al. (2014), which finds segmentation boundaries that optimize the accuracy of the translation output. We use BLEU+1 (Lin and Och, 2004) as the objective of this segmentation strategy.

We evaluate the following baseline and proposed methods:

PBMT is a baseline using phrase-based SMT.

T2S uses T2S SMT with parse trees generated from only $\boldsymbol{w}$.

T2S-Tag further predicts unseen syntactic constituents according to Section 4. Before evaluation, all constituent tags are simply deleted from the output.

T2S-Wait uses *T2S-Tag* and adds the waiting strategy described in Section 5.

We also show *PBMT-Sent* and *T2S-Sent* which are full sentence-based *PBMT* and *T2S* systems.

6.2 Results

6.2.1 Predicting Syntactic Constituents

Table 2 shows the recall, precision, and F-measure of the estimated $\boldsymbol{L}$ and $\boldsymbol{R}$ sequences. The table

Table 2: Performance of syntactic constituent prediction.

Target		P %	R %	F %
$\boldsymbol{L}$	(ordered)	31.93	7.27	11.85
	(unordered)	51.21	11.66	19.00
$\boldsymbol{R}$	(ordered)	51.12	33.78	40.68
	(unordered)	52.77	34.87	42.00

shows results of two evaluation settings, where the order of generated constituents is considered or not.

We can see that in each case recall is lower than the corresponding precision and the performance of $\boldsymbol{L}$ differs between ordered and unordered results. These trends result from the fact that the model generates fewer constituents than exist in the test data. However, this trend is not entirely unexpected because it is not possible to completely accurately guess syntactic constituents from every substring $\boldsymbol{w}$. For example, parts of the sentence "in the next 18 minutes" can generate the sequence "in the next $\boxed{\text{CD}}$ $\boxed{\text{NN}}$" and "$\boxed{\text{IN}}$ $\boxed{\text{DT}}$ $\boxed{\text{JJ}}$ 18 minutes," but the constituents $\boxed{\text{CD}}$ in the former case and $\boxed{\text{DT}}$ and $\boxed{\text{JJ}}$ in the latter case are not necessary in all situations. In contrast, $\boxed{\text{NN}}$ and $\boxed{\text{IN}}$ will probably be inserted most cases. As a result, the appearance of such ambiguous constituents in the training data is less consistent than that of necessary syntactic constituents, and thus the prediction model avoids generating such ambiguous constituents.

6.2.2 Simultaneous Translation

Next, we evaluate the translation results achieved by the proposed method. Figures 6 and 7 show the relationship between the mean number of words in the translation segments and translation accuracy of BLEU and RIBES respectively. Each horizontal axis of these graphs indicates the mean number of words in translation units that are used to generate the actual translation output, and these can be assumed to be proportional to the mean waiting time for listeners. In cases except *T2S-Wait*, these values are equal to the mean length of translation unit generated by the segmentation strategies, and in the case of *T2S-Wait*, this value shows the length of the translation units concatenated by the waiting strategy. First looking at the full sentence results (rightmost points in each graph), we can see that *T2S* greatly outperforms *PBMT* on full sentences,

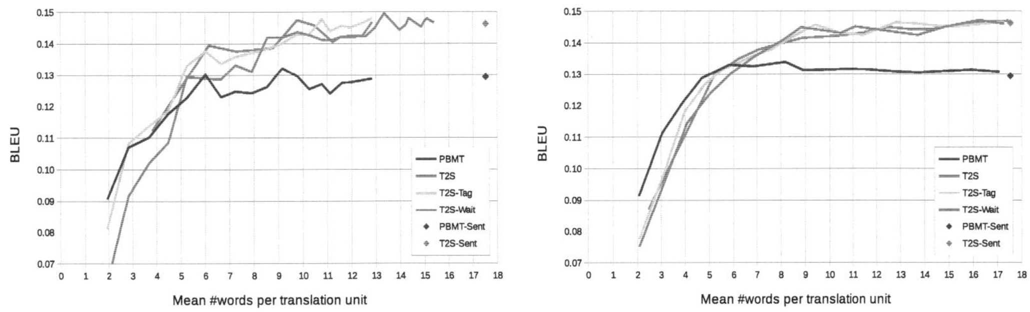

(a) n-words segmentation (b) optimized segmentation

Figure 6: Mean #words and BLEU scores of each method.

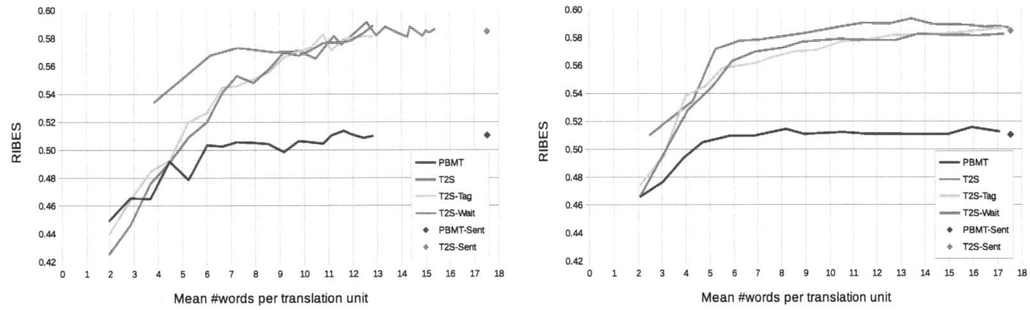

(a) n-words segmentation (b) optimized segmentation

Figure 7: Mean #words and RIBES scores of each method.

underlining the importance of considering syntax for this language pair.

Turning to simultaneous translation, we first consider the case of n-words segmentation, which will demonstrate robustness of each method to poorly formed translation segments. When we compare *PBMT* and *T2S*, we can see that *T2S* is superior for longer segments, but on shorter segments performance is greatly reduced, dropping below that of *PBMT* in BLEU at an average of 6 words, and RIBES at an average of 4 words. This trend is reasonable, considering that shorter translation units will result in syntactically inconsistent units and thus incorrect parse trees. Next looking at the results for *T2S-Tag*, we can see that in the case of the n-words segmentation, it is able to maintain the same translation performance of *PBMT*, even at the shorter settings. Furthermore, *T2S-Wait* also maintains the same performance of *T2S-Tag* in BLEU and achieves much higher performance than any of the other methods in RIBES, particularly with regards to shorter translation units. This result shows that the method of waiting for more input in the face of potential reordering problems is highly effective in maintaining the correct ordering of the output.

In the case of the optimized segmentation, all three T2S methods maintain approximately the same performance, consistently outperforming *PBMT* in RIBES, and crossing in BLEU around 5-6 words. From this, we can hypothesize that the optimized segmentation strategy learns features that maintain some syntactic consistency, which plays a similar role to the proposed method. However, RIBES scores for *T2S-Wait* is still generally higher than the other methods, demonstrating that waiting maintains its reordering advantage even in the optimized segmentation case.

7 Conclusion and Future Work

In this paper, we proposed the first method to apply SMT using source syntax to simultaneous translation. Especially, we proposed methods to maintain the syntactic consistency of translation units by predicting unseen syntactic constituents, and waiting until more input is available when it is necessary to achieve good translation results. Experiments on an English-Japanese TED talk translation task demonstrate that our methods are more robust to short, inconsistent translation segments.

As future work, we are planning to devise more sophisticated methods for language modeling using constituent tags, and ways to incorporate previously translated segments into the estimation process for left-hand constituents. Next, our method to predict additional constituents does not target the grammatically correct translation units for which $\boldsymbol{L} = [\,]$ and $\boldsymbol{R} = [\,]$, although there is still room for improvement in this assumption. In addition, we hope to expand the methods proposed here to a more incremental setting, where both parsing and decoding are performed incrementally, and the information from these processes can be reflected in the decision of segmentation boundaries.

Acknowledgement

Part of this work was supported by JSPS KAKENHI Grant Number 24240032, and Grant-in-Aid for JSPS Fellows Grant Number 15J10649.

References

Srinivas Bangalore, Vivek Kumar Rangarajan Sridhar, Prakash Kolan, Ladan Golipour, and Aura Jimenez. 2012. Real-time incremental speech-to-speech translation of dialogs. In *Proc. NAACL*.

Mauro Cettolo, Christian Girardi, and Marcello Federico. 2012. WIT^3: Web inventory of transcribed and translated talks. In *Proc. EAMT*.

Rong-En Fan, Kai-Wei Chang, Cho-Jui Hsieh, Xiang-Rui Wang, and Chih-Jen Lin. 2008. LIBLINEAR: A library for large linear classification. *The Journal of Machine Learning Research*.

Andrew Finch, Xiaolin Wang, and Eiichiro Sumita. 2014. An exploration of segmentation strategies in stream decoding. In *Proc. IWSLT*.

Christian Fügen, Alex Waibel, and Muntsin Kolss. 2007. Simultaneous translation of lectures and speeches. *Machine Translation*, 21.

Tomoki Fujita, Graham Neubig, Sakriani Sakti, Tomoki Toda, and Satoshi Nakamura. 2013. Simple, lexicalized choice of translation timing for simultaneous speech translation. In *Proc. Interspeech*.

Alvin Grissom II, He He, Jordan Boyd-Graber, John Morgan, and Hal Daumé III. 2014. Dont until the final verb wait: Reinforcement learning for simultaneous machine translation. In *Proc. EMNLP*.

Kenneth Heafield, Ivan Pouzyrevsky, Jonathan H. Clark, and Philipp Koehn. 2013. Scalable modified Kneser-Ney language model estimation. In *Proc. ACL*.

Liang Huang, Kevin Knight, and Aravind Joshi. 2006. Statistical syntax-directed translation with extended domain of locality. In *Proc. AMTA*.

Hideki Isozaki, Tsutomu Hirao, Kevin Duh, Katsuhito Sudoh, and Hajime Tsukada. 2010. Automatic evaluation of translation quality for distant language pairs. In *Proc. EMNLP*.

Philipp Koehn, Hieu Hoang, Alexandra Birch, Chris Callison-Burch, Marcello Federico, Nicola Bertoldi, Brooke Cowan, Wade Shen, Christine Moran, Richard Zens, Chris Dyer, Ondřej Bojar, Alexandra Constantin, and Evan Herbst. 2007. Moses: Open source toolkit for statistical machine translation. In *Proc. ACL*.

Chin-Yew Lin and Franz Josef Och. 2004. ORANGE: a method for evaluating automatic evaluation metrics for machine translation. In *Proc. COLING*.

Mitchell P Marcus, Mary Ann Marcinkiewicz, and Beatrice Santorini. 1993. Building a large annotated corpus of english: The Penn treebank. *Computational linguistics*, 19(2).

Evgeny Matusov, Arne Mauser, and Hermann Ney. 2006. Automatic sentence segmentation and punctuation prediction for spoken language translation. In *Proc. IWSLT*.

Graham Neubig, Yosuke Nakata, and Shinsuke Mori. 2011. Pointwise prediction for robust, adaptable japanese morphological analysis. In *Proc. ACL-HLT*.

Graham Neubig. 2013. Travatar: A forest-to-string machine translation engine based on tree transducers. In *Proc. ACL*.

Franz Josef Och and Hermann Ney. 2003. A systematic comparison of various statistical alignment models. *Computational linguistics*.

Franz Josef Och. 2003. Minimum error rate training in statistical machine translation. In *Proc. ACL*.

Yusuke Oda, Graham Neubig, Sakriani Sakti, Tomoki Toda, and Satoshi Nakamura. 2014. Optimizing segmentation strategies for simultaneous speech translation. In *Proc. ACL*.

Yusuke Oda, Graham Neubig, Sakriani Sakti, Tomoki Toda, and Satoshi Nakamura. 2015. Ckylark: A more robust PCFG-LA parser. In *Proc. NAACL-HLT*.

Kishore Papineni, Salim Roukos, Todd Ward, and Wei-Jing Zhu. 2002. Bleu: A method for automatic evaluation of machine translation. In *Proc. ACL*.

Vivek Kumar Rangarajan Sridhar, John Chen, Srinivas Bangalore, Andrej Ljolje, and Rathinavelu Chengalvarayan. 2013. Segmentation strategies for streaming speech translation. In *Proc. NAACL-HLT.*

Koichiro Ryu, Shigeki Matsubara, and Yasuyoshi Inagaki. 2006. Simultaneous english-japanese spoken language translation based on incremental dependency parsing and transfer. In *Proc. COLING.*

Baskaran Sankaran, Ajeet Grewal, and Anoop Sarkar. 2010. Incremental decoding for phrase-based statistical machine translation. In *Proc. WMT.*

Maryam Siahbani, Ramtin Mehdizadeh Seraj, Baskaran Sankaran, and Anoop Sarkar. 2014. Incremental translation using hierarchical phrase-based translation system. In *Proc. SLT.*

Fei Xia and Michael McCord. 2004. Improving a statistical MT system with automatically learned rewrite patterns. In *Proc. COLING.*

Mahsa Yarmohammadi, Vivek Kumar Rangarajan Sridhar, Srinivas Bangalore, and Baskaran Sankaran. 2013. Incremental segmentation and decoding strategies for simultaneous translation. In *Proc. IJCNLP.*

Efficient Top-Down BTG Parsing for Machine Translation Preordering

Tetsuji Nakagawa
Google Japan Inc.
tnaka@google.com

Abstract

We present an efficient incremental top-down parsing method for preordering based on Bracketing Transduction Grammar (BTG). The BTG-based preordering framework (Neubig et al., 2012) can be applied to any language using only parallel text, but has the problem of computational efficiency. Our top-down parsing algorithm allows us to use the early update technique easily for the latent variable structured Perceptron algorithm with beam search, and solves the problem.

Experimental results showed that the top-down method is more than 10 times faster than a method using the CYK algorithm. A phrase-based machine translation system with the top-down method had statistically significantly higher BLEU scores for 7 language pairs without relying on supervised syntactic parsers, compared to baseline systems using existing preordering methods.

1 Introduction

The difference of the word order between source and target languages is one of major problems in phrase-based statistical machine translation. In order to cope with the issue, many approaches have been studied. Distortion models consider word reordering in decoding time using such as distance (Koehn et al., 2003) and lexical information (Tillman, 2004). Another direction is to use more complex translation models such as hierarchical models (Chiang, 2007). However, these approaches suffer from the long-distance reordering issue and computational complexity.

Preordering (reordering-as-preprocessing) (Xia and McCord, 2004; Collins et al., 2005) is another approach for tackling the problem, which modifies the word order of an input sentence in a source language to have the word order in a target language (Figure 1(a)).

Various methods for preordering have been studied, and a method based on Bracketing Transduction Grammar (BTG) was proposed by Neubig et al. (2012). It reorders source sentences by handling sentence structures as latent variables. The method can be applied to any language using only parallel text. However, the method has the problem of computational efficiency.

In this paper, we propose an efficient incremental top-down BTG parsing method which can be applied to preordering. Model parameters can be learned using latent variable Perceptron with the early update technique (Collins and Roark, 2004), since the parsing method provides an easy way for checking the reachability of each parser state to valid final states. We also try to use forced-decoding instead of word alignment based on Expectation Maximization (EM) algorithms in order to create better training data for preordering. In experiments, preordering using the top-down parsing algorithm was faster and gave higher BLEU scores than BTG-based preordering using the CYK algorithm. Compared to existing preordering methods, our method had better or comparable BLEU scores without using supervised parsers.

2 Previous Work

2.1 Preordering for Machine Translation

Many preordering methods which use syntactic parse trees have been proposed, because syntactic information is useful for determining the word order in a target language, and it can be used to restrict the search space against all the possible permutations. Preordering methods using manually created rules on parse trees have been studied (Collins et al., 2005; Xu et al., 2009), but

Proceedings of the 53rd Annual Meeting of the Association for Computational Linguistics and the 7th International Joint Conference on Natural Language Processing, pages 208–218,
Beijing, China, July 26-31, 2015. ©2015 Association for Computational Linguistics

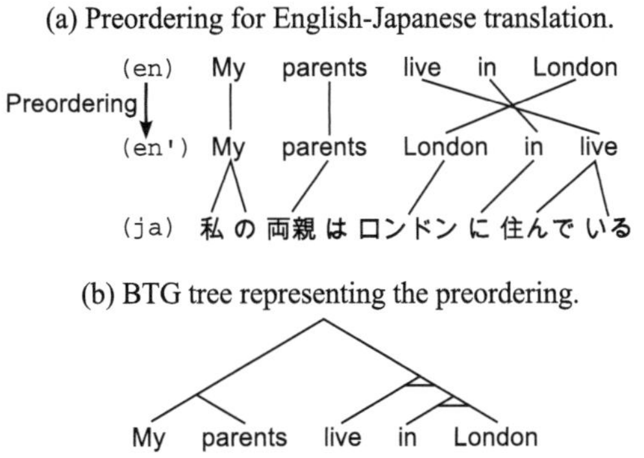

Figure 1: An example of preordering.

linguistic knowledge for a language pair is necessary to create such rules. Preordering methods which automatically create reordering rules or utilize statistical classifiers have also been studied (Xia and McCord, 2004; Li et al., 2007; Genzel, 2010; Visweswariah et al., 2010; Yang et al., 2012; Miceli Barone and Attardi, 2013; Lerner and Petrov, 2013; Jehl et al., 2014). These methods rely on source-side parse trees and cannot be applied to languages where no syntactic parsers are available.

There are preordering methods that do not need parse trees. They are usually trained only on automatically word-aligned parallel text. It is possible to mine parallel text from the Web (Uszkoreit et al., 2010; Antonova and Misyurev, 2011), and the preordering systems can be trained without manually annotated language resources. Tromble and Eisner (2009) studied preordering based on a Linear Ordering Problem by defining a pairwise preference matrix. Khalilov and Sima'an (2010) proposed a method which swaps adjacent two words using a maximum entropy model. Visweswariah et al. (2011) regarded the preordering problem as a Traveling Salesman Problem (TSP) and applied TSP solvers for obtaining reordered words. These methods do not consider sentence structures.

DeNero and Uszkoreit (2011) presented a preordering method which builds a monolingual parsing model and a tree reordering model from parallel text. Neubig et al. (2012) proposed to train a discriminative BTG parser for preordering directly from word-aligned parallel text by handling underlying parse trees with latent variables. This method is explained in detail in the next subsection. These two methods can use sentence structures for designing feature functions to score permutations.

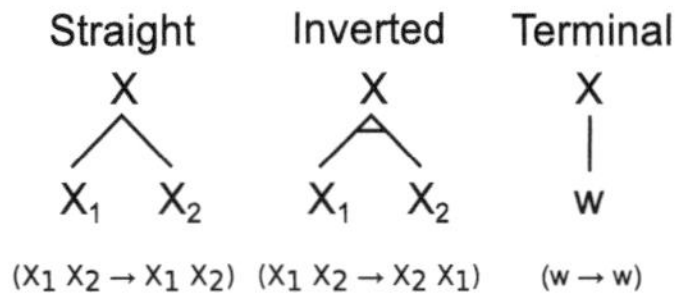

Figure 2: Bracketing transduction grammar.

2.2 BTG-based Preordering

Neubig et al. (2012) proposed a BTG-based preordering method. Bracketing Transduction Grammar (BTG) (Wu, 1997) is a binary synchronous context-free grammar with only one non-terminal symbol, and has three types of rules (Figure 2): *Straight* which keeps the order of child nodes, *Inverted* which reverses the order, and *Terminal* which generates a terminal symbol.[1]

BTG can express word reordering. For example, the word reordering in Figure 1(a) can be represented with the BTG parse tree in Figure 1(b).[2] Therefore, the task to reorder an input source sentence can be solved as a BTG parsing task to find an appropriate BTG tree.

In order to find the best BTG tree among all the possible ones, a score function is defined. Let $\Phi(m)$ denote the vector of feature functions for the BTG tree node m, and Λ denote the vector of feature weights. Then, for a given source sentence x, the best BTG tree $\hat{z}$ and the reordered sentence x' can be obtained as follows:

$$\hat{z} = \operatorname*{argmax}_{z \in Z(x)} \sum_{m \in Nodes(z)} \Lambda \cdot \Phi(m), \quad (1)$$

$$x' = Proj(\hat{z}), \quad (2)$$

where $Z(x)$ is the set of all the possible BTG trees for x, $Nodes(z)$ is the set of all the nodes in the tree z, and $Proj(z)$ is the function which generates a reordered sentence from the BTG tree z.

The method was shown to improve translation performance. However, it has a problem of processing speed. The CYK algorithm, whose computational complexity is $O(n^3)$ for a sen-

[1] Although *Terminal* produces a pair of source and target words in the original BTG (Wu, 1997), the target-side words are ignored here because both the input and the output of preordering systems are in the source language. In (Wu, 1997), (DeNero and Uszkoreit, 2011) and (Neubig et al., 2012), *Terminal* can produce multiple words. Here, we produce only one word.

[2] There may be more than one BTG tree which represents the same word reordering (e.g., the word reordering $C_3B_2A_1$ to $A_1B_2C_3$ has two possible BTG trees), and there are permutations which cannot be represented with BTG (e.g., $B_2D_4A_1C_3$ to $A_1B_2C_3D_4$, which is called the 2413 pattern).

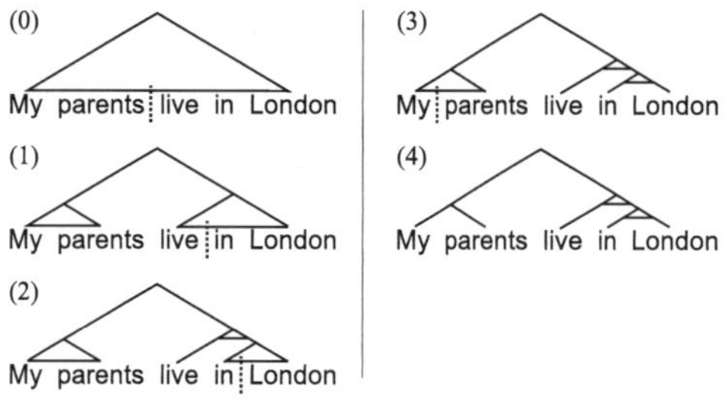

Figure 3: Top-down BTG parsing.

(0)	$\langle[[0,5)],[],0\rangle$
(1)	$\langle[[0,2),[2,5)],[(2,S)],v_1\rangle$
(2)	$\langle[[0,2),[3,5)],[(2,S),(3,I)],v_2\rangle$
(3)	$\langle[[0,2)],[(2,S),(3,I),(4,I)],v_3\rangle$
(4)	$\langle[],[(2,S),(3,I),(4,I),(1,S)],v_4\rangle$

Table 1: Parser states in top-down parsing.

tence of length n, is used to find the best parse tree. Furthermore, due to the use of a complex loss function, the complexity at training time is $O(n^5)$ (Neubig et al., 2012). Since the computational cost is prohibitive, some techniques like cube pruning and cube growing have been applied (Neubig et al., 2012; Na and Lee, 2013). In this study, we propose a top-down parsing algorithm in order to achieve fast BTG-based preordering.

3 Preordering with Incremental Top-Down BTG Parsing

3.1 Parsing Algorithm

We explain an incremental top-down BTG parsing algorithm using Figure 3, which illustrates how a parse tree is built for the example sentence in Figure 1. At the beginning, a tree (span) which covers all the words in the sentence is considered. Then, a span which covers more than one word is split in each step, and the node type (*Straight* or *Inverted*) for the splitting point is determined. The algorithm terminates after $(n-1)$ iterations for a sentence with n words, because there are $(n-1)$ positions which can be split.

We consider that the incremental parser has a *parser state* in each step, and define the state as a triple $\langle P, C, v\rangle$. P is a stack of unresolved spans. A span denoted by $[p, q)$ covers the words $x_p \cdots x_{q-1}$ for an input word sequence $x = x_0 \cdots x_{|x|-1}$. C is a list of past parser actions. A parser action denoted by (r, o) represents the action to split a span at the position between x_{r-1} and x_r with the node type $o \in \{\mathrm{S}, \mathrm{I}\}$, where S and I indicate *Straight* and *Inverted* respectively. v is the score of the state, which is the sum of the

```
Input: Sentence x, feature weights Λ, beam width k.
Output: BTG parse tree.
S_0 ← {⟨[[0,|x|)], [], 0⟩ }                         // Initial state.
for i := 1, ··· , |x| − 1 do
    S ← {}                                          // Set of the next states.
    foreach s ∈ S_{i−1} do
        S ← S ∪ τ_{x,Λ}(s)                          // Generate next states.
    S_i ← Top_k(S)                                  // Select k-best states.
ŝ = argmax_{s∈S_{|x|−1}} Score(s)
return Tree(ŝ)

function τ_{x,Λ}(⟨P, C, v⟩)
    [p, q) ← P.pop()
    S ← {}
    for r := p + 1, ··· , q do
        P′ ← P
        if r − p > 1 then
            P′.push([p, r))
        if q − r > 1 then
            P′.push([r, q))
        v^S ← v + Λ · Φ(x, C, p, q, r, S)
        v^I ← v + Λ · Φ(x, C, p, q, r, I)
        C^S ← C; C^S.append((r, S))
        C^I ← C; C^I.append((r, I))
        S ← S ∪ {⟨P′, C^S, v^S⟩, ⟨P′, C^I, v^I⟩}
    return S
```

Figure 4: Top-down BTG parsing with beam search.

scores for the nodes constructed so far. Parsing starts with the initial state $\langle[[0,|x|)],[],0\rangle$, because there is one span covering all the words at the beginning. In each step, a span is popped from the top of the stack, and a splitting point in the span and its node type are determined. The new spans generated by the split are pushed onto the stack if their lengths are greater than 1, and the action is added to the list. On termination, the parser has the final state $\langle[],[c_0,\cdots,c_{|x|-2}],v\rangle$, because the stack is empty and there are $(|x|-1)$ actions in total. The parse tree can be obtained from the list of actions. Table 1 shows the parser state for each step in Figure 3.

The top-down parsing method can be used with beam search as shown in Figure 4. $\tau_{x,\Lambda}(s)$ is a function which returns the set of all the possible next states for the state s. $Top_k(S)$ returns the top k states from S in terms of their scores, $Score(s)$ returns the score of the state s, and $Tree(s)$ returns the BTG parse tree constructed from s. $\Phi(x, C, p, q, r, o)$ is the feature vector for the node created by splitting the span $[p, q)$ at r with the node type o, and is explained in Section 3.3.

3.2 Learning Algorithm

Model parameters Λ are estimated from training examples. We assume that each training example consists of a sentence x and its word order in a target language $y = y_0 \cdots y_{|x|-1}$, where y_i is the position of x_i in the target language. For example, the example sentence in Figure 1(a) will have $y = 0, 1, 4, 3, 2$. y can have ambiguities. Multiple words can be reordered to the same position on the target side. The words whose target positions are unknown are indicated by position -1, and we consider such words can appear at any position.[3] For example, the word alignment in Figure 5 gives the target side word positions $y = -1, 2, 1, 0, 0$.

Statistical syntactic parsers are usually trained on tree-annotated corpora. However, corpora annotated with BTG parse trees are unavailable, and only the gold standard permutation y is available. Neubig et al. (2012) proposed to train BTG parsers for preordering by regarding BTG trees behind word reordering as latent variables, and we use latent variable Perceptron (Sun et al., 2009) together with beam search. In latent variable Perceptron, among the examples whose latent variables are compatible with a gold standard label, the one with the highest score is picked up as a positive example. Such an approach was used for parsing with multiple correct actions (Goldberg and Elhadad, 2010; Sartorio et al., 2013).

Figure 6 describes the training algorithm.[4] $\Phi(x, s)$ is the feature vector for all the nodes in the partial parse tree at the state s, and $\tau_{x,\Lambda,y}(s)$ is the set of all the next states for the state s. The algorithm adopts the early update technique (Collins and Roark, 2004) which terminates incremental parsing if a correct state falls off the beam, and there is no possibility to obtain a correct output. Huang et al. (2012) proposed the violation-fixing Perceptron framework which is guaranteed to converge even if inexact search is used, and also showed that early update is a special case of the framework. We define that a parser state is *valid* if the state can reach a final state whose BTG parse tree is compatible with y. Since this is a latent variable setting in which multiple states can reach correct final states, early update occurs when all the valid states fall off the beam (Ma et al., 2013; Yu et al., 2013). In order to use early update, we need to check the validity of each parser state. We extend the parser state to the four tuple $\langle P, A, v, w\rangle$, where $w \in \{\text{true}, \text{false}\}$ is the validity of the state. We remove training examples which cannot be represented with BTG beforehand and set w of the initial state to true. The function $Valid(s)$ in Figure 6 returns the validity of state s. One advantage of the top-down parsing algorithm is that it is easy to track the validity of each state. The validity of a state can be calculated using the following property, and we can implement the function $\tau_{x,\Lambda,y}(s)$ by modifying the function $\tau_{x,\Lambda}(s)$ in Figure 4.

Lemma 1. *When a valid state s, which has $[p, q)$ in the top of the stack, transitions to a state s' by the action (r, o), s' is also valid if and only if the following condition holds:*

$$\begin{aligned} &\forall i \in \{p, \cdots, r-1\}\, y_i = -1 \quad \vee \\ &\forall i \in \{r, \cdots, q-1\}\, y_i = -1 \quad \vee \\ &\Big(o = \mathrm{S} \wedge \max_{\substack{i=p,\cdots,r-1\\ y_i \neq -1}} y_i \leq \min_{\substack{i=r,\cdots,q-1\\ y_i \neq -1}} y_i\Big) \quad \vee \\ &\Big(o = \mathrm{I} \wedge \max_{\substack{i=r,\cdots,q-1\\ y_i \neq -1}} y_i \leq \min_{\substack{i=p,\cdots,r-1\\ y_i \neq -1}} y_i\Big). \end{aligned} \tag{3}$$

Proof. Let π_i denote the position of x_i after reordering by BTG parsing. If Condition (3) does not hold, there are i and j which satisfy $\pi_i < \pi_j \wedge y_i > y_j \wedge y_i \neq -1 \wedge y_j \neq -1$, and π_i and π_j are not compatible with y. Therefore, s' is valid only if Condition (3) holds.

When Condition (3) holds, a valid permutation can be obtained if the spans $[p, r)$ and $[r, q)$ are BTG-parsable. They are BTG-parsable as shown below. Let us assume that y does not have ambiguities. The class of the permutations which can be represented by BTG is known as *separable permutations* in combinatorics. It can be proven (Bose et al., 1998) that a permutation is a separable permutation if and only if it contains neither the 2413 nor the 3142 patterns. Since s is valid, y is a separable permutation. y does not contain the 2413 nor the 3142 patterns, and any subsequence of y also does not contain the patterns. Thus, $[p, r)$ and $[r, q)$ are separable permutations. The above argument holds even if y has ambiguities (duplicated positions or unaligned words). In such a case, we can always make a word order y' which specializes y and has no ambiguities (e.g., $y' = 2, 1.0, 0.0, 0.1, 1.1$ for $y = -1, 1, 0, 0, 1$), because s is valid, and there is at least one BTG parse tree which licenses y. Any subsequence in

[3] In (Neubig et al., 2012), the positions of such words were fixed by heuristics. In this study, the positions are not fixed, and all the possibilities are considered by latent variables.

[4] Although the simple Perceptron algorithm is used for explanation, we actually used the Passive Aggressive algorithm (Crammer et al., 2006) with the parameter averaging technique (Freund and Schapire, 1999).

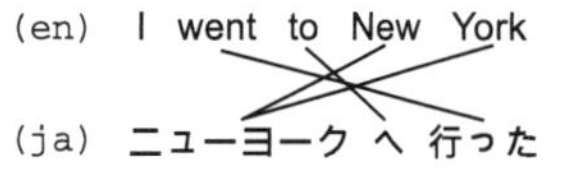

Figure 5: An example of word reordering with ambiguities.

y' is a separable permutation, and $[p, r)$ and $[r, q)$ are separable permutations. Therefore, s' is valid if Condition (3) holds. □

For dependency parsing and constituent parsing, incremental bottom-up parsing methods have been studied (Yamada and Matsumoto, 2003; Nivre, 2004; Goldberg and Elhadad, 2010; Sagae and Lavie, 2005). Our top-down approach is contrastive to the bottom-up approaches. In the bottom-up approaches, spans which cover individual words are considered at the beginning, then they are merged into larger spans in each step, and a span which covers all the words is obtained at the end. In the top-down approach, a span which covers all the words is considered at the beginning, then spans are split into smaller spans in each step, and spans which cover individual words are obtained at the end. The top-down BTG parsing method has the advantage that the validity of parser states can be easily tracked.

The computational complexity of the top-down parsing algorithm is $O(kn^2)$ for sentence length n and beam width k, because in Line 5 of Figure 4, which is repeated at most $k(n-1)$ times, at most $2(n-1)$ parser states are generated, and their scores are calculated. The learning algorithm uses the same decoding algorithm as in the parsing phase, and has the same time complexity. Note that the validity of a parser state can be calculated in $O(1)$ by pre-calculating $\min_{i=p,\cdots,r \wedge y_i \neq -1} y_i$, $\max_{i=p,\cdots,r \wedge y_i \neq -1} y_i$, $\min_{i=r,\cdots,q-1 \wedge y_i \neq -1} y_i$, and $\max_{i=r,\cdots,q-1 \wedge y_i \neq -1} y_i$ for all r for the span $[p, q)$ when it is popped from the stack.

3.3 Features

We assume that each word x_i in a sentence has three attributes: word surface form x_i^{w}, part-of-speech (POS) tag x_i^{p} and word class x_i^{c} (Section 4.1 explains how x_i^{p} and x_i^{c} are obtained).

Table 2 lists the features generated for the node which is created by splitting the span $[p, q)$ with the action (r, o). o' is the node type of the parent node, $d \in \{\text{left}, \text{right}\}$ indicates whether this node is the left-hand-side or the right-hand-side child of the parent node, and $Balance(p, q, r)$ returns a value among {'<', '=', '>'} according to the relation of the lengths of $[p, r)$ and $[r, q)$. The baseline feature templates are those used by Neubig et al. (2012), and the additional feature templates are extended features that we introduce in this study. The top-down parser is fast, and allows us to use a larger number of features.

```
Input: Training data {⟨x^l, y^l⟩}_{l=0}^{L-1},
       number of iterations T, beam width k.
Output: Feature weights Λ.
Λ ← 0
for t := 0, ··· , T − 1 do
  for l := 0, ··· , L − 1 do
    S_0 ← {⟨[[0, |x^l|)], [], 0, true⟩}
    for i := 1, ··· , |x^l| − 1 do
      S ← {}
      foreach s ∈ S_{i−1} do
        S ← S ∪ τ_{x^l,Λ,y^l}(s)
      S_i ← Top_k(S)
      ŝ ← argmax_{s∈S} Score(s)
      s* ← argmax_{s∈S∧Valid(s)} Score(s)
      if s* ∉ S_i then
        break                                // Early update.
    if ŝ ≠ s* then
      Λ ← Λ + Φ(x^l, s*) − Φ(x^l, ŝ)
return Λ
```

Figure 6: A training algorithm for latent variable Perceptron with beam search.

In order to make the feature generation efficient, the attributes of all the words are converted to their 64-bit hash values beforehand, and concatenating the attributes is executed not as string manipulation but as faster integer calculation to generate a hash value by merging two hash values. The hash values are used as feature names. Therefore, when accessing feature weights stored in a hash table using the feature names as keys, the keys can be used as their hash values. This technique is different from the hashing trick (Ganchev and Dredze, 2008) which directly uses hash values as indices, and no noticeable differences in accuracy were observed by using this technique.

3.4 Training Data for Preordering

As described in Section 3.2, each training example has y which represents correct word positions after reordering. However, only word alignment data is generally available, and we need to convert it to y. Let A_i denote the set of indices of the target-side words which are aligned to the source-side word x_i. We define an order relation between two words:

$$x_i \leq x_j \quad \Leftrightarrow \quad \forall a \in A_i \setminus A_j, \forall b \in A_j \; a \leq b \wedge \\ \forall a \in A_i, \forall b \in A_j \setminus A_i \; a \leq b. \quad (4)$$

Baseline Feature Template
$o(q-p), oBalance(p,q,r),$
$ox^{\mathrm{w}}_{p-1}, ox^{\mathrm{w}}_{p}, ox^{\mathrm{w}}_{r-1}, ox^{\mathrm{w}}_{r}, ox^{\mathrm{w}}_{q-1}, ox^{\mathrm{w}}_{q}, ox^{\mathrm{w}}_{p}x^{\mathrm{w}}_{q-1}, ox^{\mathrm{w}}_{r-1}x^{\mathrm{w}}_{r},$
$ox^{\mathrm{p}}_{p-1}, ox^{\mathrm{p}}_{p}, ox^{\mathrm{p}}_{r-1}, ox^{\mathrm{p}}_{r}, ox^{\mathrm{p}}_{q-1}, ox^{\mathrm{p}}_{q}, ox^{\mathrm{p}}_{p}x^{\mathrm{p}}_{q-1}, ox^{\mathrm{p}}_{r-1}x^{\mathrm{p}}_{r},$
$ox^{\mathrm{c}}_{p-1}, ox^{\mathrm{c}}_{p}, ox^{\mathrm{c}}_{r-1}, ox^{\mathrm{c}}_{r}, ox^{\mathrm{c}}_{q-1}, ox^{\mathrm{c}}_{q}, ox^{\mathrm{c}}_{p}x^{\mathrm{c}}_{q-1}, ox^{\mathrm{c}}_{r-1}x^{\mathrm{c}}_{r}.$

Additional Feature Template
$o\min(r-p,5)\min(q-r,5), oo', oo'd,$
$ox^{\mathrm{w}}_{p-1}x^{\mathrm{w}}_{p}, ox^{\mathrm{w}}_{p}x^{\mathrm{w}}_{r-1}, ox^{\mathrm{w}}_{p}x^{\mathrm{w}}_{r}, ox^{\mathrm{w}}_{r-1}x^{\mathrm{w}}_{q-1}, ox^{\mathrm{w}}_{r}x^{\mathrm{w}}_{q-1}, ox^{\mathrm{w}}_{q-1}x^{\mathrm{w}}_{q},$
$ox^{\mathrm{w}}_{r-2}x^{\mathrm{w}}_{r-1}x^{\mathrm{w}}_{r}, ox^{\mathrm{w}}_{p}x^{\mathrm{w}}_{r-1}x^{\mathrm{w}}_{r}, ox^{\mathrm{w}}_{r-1}x^{\mathrm{w}}_{r}x^{\mathrm{w}}_{q-1}, ox^{\mathrm{w}}_{r-1}x^{\mathrm{w}}_{r}x^{\mathrm{w}}_{r+1},$
$ox^{\mathrm{w}}_{p}x^{\mathrm{w}}_{r-1}x^{\mathrm{w}}_{r}x^{\mathrm{w}}_{q-1},$
$oo'dx^{\mathrm{w}}_{p}, oo'dx^{\mathrm{w}}_{r-1}, oo'dx^{\mathrm{w}}_{r}, oo'dx^{\mathrm{w}}_{q-1}, oo'dx^{\mathrm{w}}_{p}x^{\mathrm{w}}_{q-1},$
$ox^{\mathrm{p}}_{p-1}x^{\mathrm{p}}_{p}, ox^{\mathrm{p}}_{p}x^{\mathrm{p}}_{r-1}, ox^{\mathrm{p}}_{p}x^{\mathrm{p}}_{r}, ox^{\mathrm{p}}_{r-1}x^{\mathrm{p}}_{q-1}, ox^{\mathrm{p}}_{r}x^{\mathrm{p}}_{q-1}, ox^{\mathrm{p}}_{q-1}x^{\mathrm{p}}_{q},$
$ox^{\mathrm{p}}_{r-2}x^{\mathrm{p}}_{r-1}x^{\mathrm{p}}_{r}, ox^{\mathrm{p}}_{p}x^{\mathrm{p}}_{r-1}x^{\mathrm{p}}_{r}, ox^{\mathrm{p}}_{r-1}x^{\mathrm{p}}_{r}x^{\mathrm{p}}_{q-1}, ox^{\mathrm{p}}_{r-1}x^{\mathrm{p}}_{r}x^{\mathrm{p}}_{r+1},$
$ox^{\mathrm{p}}_{p}x^{\mathrm{p}}_{r-1}x^{\mathrm{p}}_{r}x^{\mathrm{p}}_{q-1},$
$oo'dx^{\mathrm{p}}_{p}, oo'dx^{\mathrm{p}}_{r-1}, oo'dx^{\mathrm{p}}_{r}, oo'dx^{\mathrm{p}}_{q-1}, oo'dx^{\mathrm{p}}_{p}x^{\mathrm{p}}_{q-1},$
$ox^{\mathrm{c}}_{p-1}x^{\mathrm{c}}_{p}, ox^{\mathrm{c}}_{p}x^{\mathrm{c}}_{r-1}, ox^{\mathrm{c}}_{p}x^{\mathrm{c}}_{r}, ox^{\mathrm{c}}_{r-1}x^{\mathrm{c}}_{q-1}, ox^{\mathrm{c}}_{r}x^{\mathrm{c}}_{q-1}, ox^{\mathrm{c}}_{q-1}x^{\mathrm{c}}_{q},$
$ox^{\mathrm{c}}_{r-2}x^{\mathrm{c}}_{r-1}x^{\mathrm{c}}_{r}, ox^{\mathrm{c}}_{p}x^{\mathrm{c}}_{r-1}x^{\mathrm{c}}_{r}, ox^{\mathrm{c}}_{r-1}x^{\mathrm{c}}_{r}x^{\mathrm{c}}_{q-1}, ox^{\mathrm{c}}_{r-1}x^{\mathrm{c}}_{r}x^{\mathrm{c}}_{r+1},$
$ox^{\mathrm{c}}_{p}x^{\mathrm{c}}_{r-1}x^{\mathrm{c}}_{r}x^{\mathrm{c}}_{q-1},$
$oo'dx^{\mathrm{c}}_{p}, oo'dx^{\mathrm{c}}_{r-1}, oo'dx^{\mathrm{c}}_{r}, oo'dx^{\mathrm{c}}_{q-1}, oo'dx^{\mathrm{c}}_{p}x^{\mathrm{c}}_{q-1}.$

Table 2: Feature templates.

Then, we sort x using the order relation and assign the position of x_i in the sorted result to y_i. If there are two words x_i and x_j in x which satisfy neither $x_i \leq x_j$ nor $x_j \leq x_i$ (that is, x does not make a totally ordered set with the order relation), then x cannot be sorted, and the example is removed from the training data. -1 is assigned to the words which do not have aligned target words. Two words x_i and x_j are regarded to have the same position if $x_i \leq x_j$ and $x_j \leq x_i$.

The quality of training data is important to make accurate preordering systems, but automatically word-aligned data by EM algorithms tend to have many wrong alignments. We use forced-decoding in order to make training data for preordering. Given a parallel sentence pair and a phrase table, forced-decoding tries to translate the source sentence to the target sentence, and produces phrase alignments. We train the parameters for forced-decoding using the same parallel data used for training the final translation system. Infrequent phrase translations are pruned when the phrase table is created, and forced-decoding does not always succeed for the parallel sentences in the training data. Forced-decoding tends to succeed for shorter sentences, and the phrase-alignment data obtained by forced-decoding is biased to contain more shorter sentences. Therefore, we apply the following processing for the output of forced-decoding to make training data for preordering:

1. Remove sentences which contain less than 3 or more than 50 words.
2. Remove sentences which contain less than 3 phrase alignments.
3. Remove sentences if they contain word 5-grams which appear in other sentences in order to drop boilerplates.
4. Lastly, randomly resample sentences from the pool of filtered sentences to make the distribution of the sentence lengths follow a normal distribution with the mean of 20 and the standard deviation of 8. The parameters were determined from randomly sampled sentences from the Web.

4 Experiments

4.1 Experimental Settings

We conduct experiments for 12 language pairs: Dutch (nl)-English (en), en-nl, en-French (fr), en-Japanese (ja), en-Spanish (es), fr-en, Hindi (hi)-en, ja-en, Korean (ko)-en, Turkish (tr)-en, Urdu (ur)-en and Welsh (cy)-en.

We use a phrase-based statistical machine translation system which is similar to (Och and Ney, 2004). The decoder adopts the regular distance distortion model, and also incorporates a maximum entropy based lexicalized phrase reordering model (Zens and Ney, 2006). The distortion limit is set to 5 words. Word alignments are learned using 3 iterations of IBM Model-1 (Brown et al., 1993) and 3 iterations of the HMM alignment model (Vogel et al., 1996). Lattice-based minimum error rate training (MERT) (Macherey et al., 2008) is applied to optimize feature weights. 5-gram language models trained on sentences collected from various sources are used.

The translation system is trained with parallel sentences automatically collected from the Web. The parallel data for each language pair consists of around 400 million source and target words. In order to make the development data for MERT and test data (3,000 and 5,000 sentences respectively for each language), we created parallel sentences by randomly collecting English sentences from the Web, and translating them by humans into each language.

As an evaluation metric for translation quality, BLEU (Papineni et al., 2002) is used. As intrinsic evaluation metrics for preordering, Fuzzy Reordering Score (FRS) (Talbot et al., 2011) and Kendall's τ (Kendall, 1938; Birch et al., 2010; Isozaki et al., 2010) are used. Let ρ_i denote the position in the input sentence of the $(i+1)$-th token in a preordered word sequence excluding unaligned words in the gold-standard evaluation data. For

	en-ja				ja-en			
	Training (min.)	Preordering (sent./sec.)	FRS	τ	Training (min.)	Preordering (sent./sec.)	FRS	τ
Top-Down (EM-100k)	63	87.8	77.83	87.78	81	178.4	74.60	83.78
Top-Down (Basic Feat.) (EM-100k)	9	475.1	75.25	87.26	9	939.0	73.56	83.66
Lader (EM-100k)	1562	4.3	75.41	86.85	2087	12.3	74.89	82.15

Table 3: Speed and accuracy of preordering.

		en-ja			ja-en		
		FRS	τ	BLEU	FRS	τ	BLEU
Top-Down	(Manual-8k)	81.57	90.44	18.13	79.26	86.47	14.26
	(EM-10k)	74.79	85.87	17.07	72.51	82.65	14.55
	(EM-100k)	77.83	87.78	17.66	74.60	83.78	14.84
	(Forced-10k)	76.10	87.45	16.98	75.36	83.96	14.78
	(Forced-100k)	78.76	89.22	17.88	76.58	85.25	**15.54**
Lader	(EM-100k)	75.41	86.85	17.40	74.89	82.15	14.59
No-Preordering		46.17	65.07	13.80	59.35	65.30	10.31
Manual-Rules		80.59	90.30	**18.68**	73.65	81.72	14.02
Auto-Rules		64.13	84.17	16.80	60.60	75.49	12.59
Classifier		80.89	90.61	**18.53**	74.24	82.83	13.90

Table 4: Performance of preordering for various training data. Bold BLEU scores indicate no statistically significant difference at $p < 0.05$ from the best system (Koehn, 2004).

example, the preordering result "New York I to went" for the gold-standard data in Figure 5 has $\rho = 3, 4, 2, 1$. Then FRS and τ are calculated as follows:

$$FRS = \frac{B}{|\rho| + 1}, \quad (5)$$

$$B = \sum_{i=0}^{|\rho|-2} \delta(y_{\rho_i}{=}y_{\rho_{i+1}} \vee y_{\rho_i}{+}1{=}y_{\rho_{i+1}}) + \delta(y_{\rho_0}{=}0) + \delta(y_{\rho_{|\rho|-1}}{=}\max_i y_i), \quad (6)$$

$$\tau = \frac{\sum_{i=0}^{|\rho|-2}\sum_{j=i+1}^{|\rho|-1} \delta(y_{\rho_i} \le y_{\rho_j})}{\frac{1}{2}|\rho|(|\rho|-1)}, \quad (7)$$

where $\delta(X)$ is the Kronecker's delta function which returns 1 if X is true or 0 otherwise. These scores are calculated for each sentence, and are averaged over all sentences in test data. As above, FRS can be calculated as the precision of word bigrams (B is the number of the word bigrams which exist both in the system output and the gold standard data). This formulation is equivalent to the original formulation based on chunk fragmentation by Talbot et al. (2011). Equation (6) takes into account the positions of the beginning and the ending words (Neubig et al., 2012). Kendall's τ is equivalent to the (normalized) crossing alignment link score used by Genzel (2010).

We prepared three types of training data for learning model parameters of BTG-based preordering:

Manual-8k Manually word-aligned 8,000 sentence pairs.

EM-10k, EM-100k These are the data obtained with the EM-based word alignment learning. From the word alignment result for phrase translation extraction described above, 10,000 and 100,000 sentence pairs were randomly sampled. Before the sampling, the data filtering procedure 1 and 3 in Section 3.4 were applied, and also sentences were removed if more than half of source words do not have aligned target words. Word alignment was obtained by symmetrizing source-to-target and target-to-source word alignment with the INTERSECTION heuristic.[5]

Forced-10k, Forced-100k These are 10,000 and 100,000 word-aligned sentence pairs obtained with forced-decoding as described in Section 3.4.

As test data for intrinsic evaluation of preordering, we manually word-aligned 2,000 sentence pairs for en-ja and ja-en.

Several preordering systems were prepared in order to compare the following six systems:

No-Preordering This is a system without preordering.

Manual-Rules This system uses the preordering method based on manually created rules (Xu

[5]In our preliminary experiments, the UNION and GROW-DIAG-FINAL heuristics were also applied to generate the training data for preordering, but INTERSECTION performed the best.

	No-Preordering	Manual-Rules	Auto-Rules	Classifier	Lader (EM-100k)	Top-Down (EM-100k)	Top-Down (Forced-100k)
nl-en	34.01	-	34.24	**35.42**	33.83	**35.49**	**35.51**
en-nl	25.33	-	25.59	**25.99**	25.30	**25.82**	25.66
en-fr	25.86	-	26.39	26.35	26.50	**26.75**	**26.81**
en-ja	13.80	**18.68**	16.80	**18.53**	17.40	17.66	17.88
en-es	29.50	-	29.63	**30.09**	29.70	**30.26**	**30.24**
fr-en	32.33	-	32.09	32.28	32.43	**33.00**	**32.99**
hi-en	19.86	-	-	-	24.24	**24.98**	**24.97**
ja-en	10.31	14.02	12.59	13.90	14.59	14.84	**15.54**
ko-en	14.13	-	15.86	19.46	18.65	**19.67**	**19.88**
tr-en	18.26	-	-	-	22.80	**23.91**	**24.18**
ur-en	14.48	-	-	-	16.62	17.65	**18.32**
cy-en	**41.68**	-	-	-	**41.79**	**41.95**	**41.86**

Table 5: BLEU score comparison.

	Distortion Limit	No-Preordering	Manual-Rules	Auto-Rules	Classifier	Lader (EM-100k)	Top-Down (EM-100k)	Top-Down (Forced-100k)
en-ja	5	13.80	**18.68**	16.80	**18.53**	17.40	17.66	17.88
en-ja	0	11.99	**18.34**	16.87	**18.31**	16.95	17.36	17.88
ja-en	5	10.31	14.02	12.59	13.90	14.59	14.84	**15.54**
ja-en	0	10.03	12.43	11.33	13.09	14.38	14.72	**15.34**

Table 6: BLEU scores for different distortion limits.

et al., 2009). We made 43 precedence rules for en-ja, and 24 for ja-en.

Auto-Rules This system uses the rule-based preordering method which automatically learns the rules from word-aligned data using the Variant 1 learning algorithm described in (Genzel, 2010). 27 to 36 rules were automatically learned for each language pair.

Classifier This system uses the preordering method based on statistical classifiers (Lerner and Petrov, 2013), and the 2-step algorithm was implemented.

Lader This system uses Latent Derivation Reorderer (Neubig et al., 2012), which is a BTG-based preordering system using the CYK algorithm.[6] The basic feature templates in Table 2 are used as features.

Top-Down This system uses the preordering system described in Section 3.

Among the six systems, Manual-Rules, Auto-Rules and Classifier need dependency parsers for source languages. A dependency parser based on the shift-reduce algorithm with beam search (Zhang and Nivre, 2011) is used. The dependency parser and all the preordering systems need POS taggers. A supervised POS tagger based on conditional random fields (Lafferty et al., 2001) trained with manually POS annotated data is used for nl, en, fr, ja and ko. For other languages, we use a POS tagger based on POS projection (Täckström et al., 2013) which does not need POS annotated data. Word classes in Table 2 are obtained by using Brown clusters (Koo et al., 2008) (the number of classes is set to 256). For both Lader and Top-Down, the beam width is set to 20, and the number of training iterations of online learning is set to 20.

The CPU time shown in this paper is measured using Intel Xeon 3.20GHz with 32GB RAM.

4.2 Results

4.2.1 Training and Preordering Speed

Table 3 shows the training time and preordering speed together with the intrinsic evaluation metrics. In this experiment, both Top-Down and Lader were trained using the EM-100k data. Compared to Lader, Top-Down was faster: more than 20 times in training, and more than 10 times in preordering. Top-down had higher preordering accuracy in FRS and τ for en-ja. Although Lader uses sophisticated loss functions, Top-Down uses a larger number of features.

Top-Down (Basic feats.) is the top-down method using only the basic feature templates in Table 2. It was much faster but less accurate than Top-Down using the additional features. Top-Down (Basic feats.) and Lader use exactly the same features. However, there are differences in the two systems, and they had different accuracies. Top-Down uses the beam search-based top-down method for parsing and the Passive-Aggressive algorithm for parameter estimation, and Lader uses the CYK algorithm with cube pruning and an on-

[6] lader 0.1.4. http://www.phontron.com/lader/

line SVM algorithm. Especially, Lader optimizes FRS in the default setting, and it may be the reason that Lader had higher FRS.

4.2.2 Performance of Preordering for Various Training Data

Table 4 shows the preordering accuracy and BLEU scores when Top-Down was trained with various data. The best BLEU score for Top-Down was obtained by using manually annotated data for en-ja and 100k forced-decoding data for ja-en. The performance was improved by increasing the data size.

4.2.3 End-to-End Evaluation for Various Language Pairs

Table 5 shows the BLEU score of each system for 12 language pairs. Some blank fields mean that the results are unavailable due to the lack of rules or dependency parsers. For all the language pairs, Top-Down had higher BLEU scores than Lader. For ja-en and ur-en, using Forced-100k instead of EM-100k for Top-Down improved the BLEU scores by more than 0.6, but it did not always improved.

Manual-Rules performed the best for en-ja, but it needs manually created rules and is difficult to be applied to many language pairs. Auto-Rules and Classifier had higher scores than No-Preordering except for fr-en, but cannot be applied to the languages with no available dependency parsers. Top-Down (Forced-100k) can be applied to any language, and had statistically significantly better BLEU scores than No-Preordering, Manual-Rules, Auto-Rules, Classifier and Lader for 7 language pairs (en-fr, fr-en, hi-en, ja-en, ko-en, tr-en and ur-en), and similar performance for other language pairs except for en-ja, without dependency parsers trained with manually annotated data.

In all the experiments so far, the decoder was allowed to reorder even after preordering was carried out. In order to see the performance without reordering after preordering, we conducted experiments by setting the distortion limit to 0. Table 6 shows the results. The effect of the distortion limits varies for language pairs and preordering methods. The BLEU scores of Top-Down were not affected largely even when relying only on preordering.

5 Conclusion

In this paper, we proposed a top-down BTG parsing method for preordering. The method incrementally builds parse trees by splitting larger spans into smaller ones. The method provides an easy way to check the validity of each parser state, which allows us to use early update for latent variable Perceptron with beam search. In the experiments, it was shown that the top-down parsing method is more than 10 times faster than a CYK-based method. The top-down method had better BLEU scores for 7 language pairs without relying on supervised syntactic parsers compared to other preordering methods. Future work includes developing a bottom-up BTG parser with latent variables, and comparing the results to the top-down parser.

References

Alexandra Antonova and Alexey Misyurev. 2011. Building a Web-Based Parallel Corpus and Filtering Out Machine-Translated Text. In *Proceedings of the 4th Workshop on Building and Using Comparable Corpora: Comparable Corpora and the Web*, pages 136–144.

Alexandra Birch, Miles Osborne, and Phil Blunsom. 2010. Metrics for MT Evaluation: Evaluating Reordering. *Machine Translation*, 24(1):15–26.

Prosenjit Bose, Jonathan F. Buss, and Anna Lubiw. 1998. Pattern matching for permutations. *Information Processing Letters*, 65(5):277–283.

Peter F. Brown, Vincent J. Della Pietra, Stephen A. Della Pietra, and Robert L. Mercer. 1993. The Mathematics of Statistical Machine Translation: Parameter Estimation. *Computational Linguistics*, 19(2):263–311.

David Chiang. 2007. Hierarchical Phrase-Based Translation. *Computational Linguistics*, 33(2):201–228.

Michael Collins and Brian Roark. 2004. Incremental Parsing with the Perceptron Algorithm. In *Proceedings of the 42nd Annual Meeting of the Association for Computational Linguistics*, pages 111–118.

Michael Collins, Philipp Koehn, and Ivona Kucerova. 2005. Clause Restructuring for Statistical Machine Translation. In *Proceedings of the 43rd Annual Meeting of the Association for Computational Linguistics*, pages 531–540.

Koby Crammer, Ofer Dekel, Joseph Keshet, Shai Shalev-Shwartz, and Yoram Singer. 2006. Online Passive-Aggressive Algorithms. *Journal of Machine Learning Research*, 7:551–585.

John DeNero and Jakob Uszkoreit. 2011. Inducing Sentence Structure from Parallel Corpora for Reordering. In *Proceedings of the 2011 Conference on*

Empirical Methods in Natural Language Processing, pages 193–203.

Yoav Freund and Robert E. Schapire. 1999. Large Margin Classification Using the Perceptron Algorithm. *Machine Learning*, 37(3):277–296.

Kuzman Ganchev and Mark Dredze. 2008. Small Statistical Models by Random Feature Mixing. In *Proceedings of the ACL-08: HLT Workshop on Mobile Language Processing*, pages 19–20.

Dmitriy Genzel. 2010. Automatically Learning Source-side Reordering Rules for Large Scale Machine Translation. In *Proceedings of the 23rd International Conference on Computational Linguistics*, pages 376–384.

Yoav Goldberg and Michael Elhadad. 2010. An Efficient Algorithm for Easy-first Non-directional Dependency Parsing. In *Human Language Technologies: The 2010 Annual Conference of the North American Chapter of the Association for Computational Linguistics*, pages 742–750.

Liang Huang, Suphan Fayong, and Yang Guo. 2012. Structured Perceptron with Inexact Search. In *Proceedings of the 2012 Conference of the North American Chapter of the Association for Computational Linguistics: Human Language Technologies*, pages 142–151.

Hideki Isozaki, Tsutomu Hirao, Kevin Duh, Katsuhito Sudoh, and Hajime Tsukada. 2010. Automatic Evaluation of Translation Quality for Distant Language Pairs. In *Proceedings of the 2010 Conference on Empirical Methods in Natural Language Processing*, pages 944–952.

Laura Jehl, Adrià de Gispert, Mark Hopkins, and Bill Byrne. 2014. Source-side Preordering for Translation using Logistic Regression and Depth-first Branch-and-Bound Search. In *Proceedings of the 14th Conference of the European Chapter of the Association for Computational Linguistics*, pages 239–248.

Maurice G. Kendall. 1938. A New Measure of Rank Correlation. *Biometrika*, 30(1/2):81–93.

Maxim Khalilov and Khalil Sima'an. 2010. Source reordering using MaxEnt classifiers and supertags. In *Proceedings of the 14th Annual Conference of the European Association for Machine Translation*.

Philipp Koehn, Franz Josef Och, and Daniel Marcu. 2003. Statistical Phrase-Based Translation. In *Proceedings of the 2003 Human Language Technology Conference of the North American Chapter of the Association for Computational Linguistics*, pages 48–54.

Philipp Koehn. 2004. Statistical Significance Tests for Machine Translation Evaluation. In *Proceedings of the 2004 Conference on Empirical Methods in Natural Language Processing*, pages 388–395.

Terry Koo, Xavier Carreras, and Michael Collins. 2008. Simple Semi-supervised Dependency Parsing. In *Proceedings of the 46th Annual Meeting of the Association for Computational Linguistics: Human Language Technologies*, pages 595–603.

John Lafferty, Andrew McCallum, and Fernando Pereira. 2001. Conditional Random Fields: Probabilistic Models for Segmenting and Labeling Sequence Data. In *Proceedings of the 18th International Conference on Machine Learning*, pages 282–289.

Uri Lerner and Slav Petrov. 2013. Source-Side Classifier Preordering for Machine Translation. In *Proceedings of the 2013 Conference on Empirical Methods in Natural Language Processing*, pages 513–523.

Chi-Ho Li, Minghui Li, Dongdong Zhang, Mu Li, Ming Zhou, and Yi Guan. 2007. A Probabilistic Approach to Syntax-based Reordering for Statistical Machine Translation. In *Proceedings of the 45th Annual Meeting of the Association of Computational Linguistics*, pages 720–727.

Ji Ma, Jingbo Zhu, Tong Xiao, and Nan Yang. 2013. Easy-First POS Tagging and Dependency Parsing with Beam Search. In *Proceedings of the 51st Annual Meeting of the Association for Computational Linguistics (Volume 2: Short Papers)*, pages 110–114.

Wolfgang Macherey, Franz Och, Ignacio Thayer, and Jakob Uszkoreit. 2008. Lattice-based Minimum Error Rate Training for Statistical Machine Translation. In *Proceedings of the 2008 Conference on Empirical Methods in Natural Language Processing*, pages 725–734.

Valerio Antonio Miceli Barone and Giuseppe Attardi. 2013. Pre-Reordering for Machine Translation Using Transition-Based Walks on Dependency Parse Trees. In *Proceedings of the 8th Workshop on Statistical Machine Translation*, pages 164–169.

Hwidong Na and Jong-Hyeok Lee. 2013. A Discriminative Reordering Parser for IWSLT 2013. In *Proceedings of the 10th International Workshop for Spoken Language Translation*, pages 83–86.

Graham Neubig, Taro Watanabe, and Shinsuke Mori. 2012. Inducing a Discriminative Parser to Optimize Machine Translation Reordering. In *Proceedings of the 2012 Joint Conference on Empirical Methods in Natural Language Processing and Computational Natural Language Learning*, pages 843–853.

Joakim Nivre. 2004. Incrementality in Deterministic Dependency Parsing. In *Proceedings of the Workshop on Incremental Parsing: Bringing Engineering and Cognition Together*, pages 50–57.

Franz Josef Och and Hermann Ney. 2004. The Alignment Template Approach to Statistical Machine Translation. *Computational Linguistics*, 30(4):417–449.

Kishore Papineni, Salim Roukos, Todd Ward, and Wei-Jing Zhu. 2002. BLEU: A Method for Automatic Evaluation of Machine Translation. In *Proceedings of the 40th Annual Meeting on Association for Computational Linguistics*, pages 311–318.

Kenji Sagae and Alon Lavie. 2005. A Classifier-Based Parser with Linear Run-Time Complexity. In *Proceedings of the 9th International Workshop on Parsing Technology*, pages 125–132.

Francesco Sartorio, Giorgio Satta, and Joakim Nivre. 2013. A Transition-Based Dependency Parser Using a Dynamic Parsing Strategy. In *Proceedings of the 51st Annual Meeting of the Association for Computational Linguistics*, pages 135–144.

Xu Sun, Takuya Matsuzaki, Daisuke Okanohara, and Jun'ichi Tsujii. 2009. Latent Variable Perceptron Algorithm for Structured Classification. In *Proceedings of the 21st International Joint Conference on Artificial Intelligence*, pages 1236–1242.

Oscar Täckström, Dipanjan Das, Slav Petrov, Ryan McDonald, and Joakim Nivre. 2013. Token and Type Constraints for Cross-Lingual Part-of-Speech Tagging. *Transactions of the Association of Computational Linguistics*, 1:1–12.

David Talbot, Hideto Kazawa, Hiroshi Ichikawa, Jason Katz-Brown, Masakazu Seno, and Franz J. Och. 2011. A Lightweight Evaluation Framework for Machine Translation Reordering. In *Proceedings of the 6th Workshop on Statistical Machine Translation*, pages 12–21.

Christoph Tillman. 2004. A Unigram Orientation Model for Statistical Machine Translation. In *Proceedings of the 2004 Human Language Technology Conference of the North American Chapter of the Association for Computational Linguistics (Short Papers)*, pages 101–104.

Roy Tromble and Jason Eisner. 2009. Learning Linear Ordering Problems for Better Translation. In *Proceedings of the 2009 Conference on Empirical Methods in Natural Language Processing*, pages 1007–1016.

Jakob Uszkoreit, Jay M. Ponte, Ashok C. Popat, and Moshe Dubiner. 2010. Large Scale Parallel Document Mining for Machine Translation. In *Proceedings of the 23rd International Conference on Computational Linguistics*, pages 1101–1109.

Karthik Visweswariah, Jiri Navratil, Jeffrey Sorensen, Vijil Chenthamarakshan, and Nandakishore Kambhatla. 2010. Syntax Based Reordering with Automatically Derived Rules for Improved Statistical Machine Translation. In *Proceedings of the 23rd International Conference on Computational Linguistics*, pages 1119–1127.

Karthik Visweswariah, Rajakrishnan Rajkumar, Ankur Gandhe, Ananthakrishnan Ramanathan, and Jiri Navratil. 2011. A Word Reordering Model for Improved Machine Translation. In *Proceedings of the 2011 Conference on Empirical Methods in Natural Language Processing*, pages 486–496.

Stephan Vogel, Hermann Ney, and Christoph Tillmann. 1996. HMM-based Word Alignment in Statistical Translation. In *Proceedings of the 16th Conference on Computational Linguistics*, pages 836–841.

Dekai Wu. 1997. Stochastic Inversion Transduction Grammars and Bilingual Parsing of Parallel Corpora. *Computational Linguistics*, 23(3):377–403.

Fei Xia and Michael McCord. 2004. Improving a Statistical MT System with Automatically Learned Rewrite Patterns. In *Proceedings of the 20th International Conference on Computational Linguistics*, pages 508–514.

Peng Xu, Jaeho Kang, Michael Ringgaard, and Franz Och. 2009. Using a Dependency Parser to Improve SMT for Subject-Object-Verb Languages. In *Proceedings of Human Language Technologies: The 2009 Annual Conference of the North American Chapter of the Association for Computational Linguistics*, pages 245–253.

Hiroyasu Yamada and Yuji Matsumoto. 2003. Statistical Dependency Analysis with Support Vector Machines. In *Proceedings of the 8th International Workshop on Parsing Technologies*, pages 195–206.

Nan Yang, Mu Li, Dongdong Zhang, and Nenghai Yu. 2012. A Ranking-based Approach to Word Reordering for Statistical Machine Translation. In *Proceedings of the 50th Annual Meeting of the Association for Computational Linguistics*, pages 912–920.

Heng Yu, Liang Huang, Haitao Mi, and Kai Zhao. 2013. Max-Violation Perceptron and Forced Decoding for Scalable MT Training. In *Proceedings of the 2013 Conference on Empirical Methods in Natural Language Processing*, pages 1112–1123.

Richard Zens and Hermann Ney. 2006. Discriminative Reordering Models for Statistical Machine Translation. In *Proceedings on the Workshop on Statistical Machine Translation*, pages 55–63.

Yue Zhang and Joakim Nivre. 2011. Transition-based Dependency Parsing with Rich Non-local Features. In *Proceedings of the 49th Annual Meeting of the Association for Computational Linguistics: Short Papers*, pages 188–193.

Online Multitask Learning for Machine Translation Quality Estimation

José G. C. de Souza[(1,2)], **Matteo Negri**[(1)], **Elisa Ricci**[(1)], **Marco Turchi**[(1)]
[(1)] FBK - Fondazione Bruno Kessler, Via Sommarive 18, 38123 Trento, Italy
[(2)] University of Trento, Italy
{desouza,negri,eliricci,turchi}@fbk.eu

Abstract

We present a method for predicting machine translation output quality geared to the needs of computer-assisted translation. These include the capability to: *i)* continuously learn and self-adapt to a stream of data coming from multiple translation jobs, *ii)* react to data diversity by exploiting human feedback, and *iii)* leverage data similarity by learning and transferring knowledge across domains. To achieve these goals, we combine two supervised machine learning paradigms, online and multitask learning, adapting and unifying them in a single framework. We show the effectiveness of our approach in a regression task (HTER prediction), in which online multitask learning outperforms the competitive online single-task and pooling methods used for comparison. This indicates the feasibility of integrating in a CAT tool a single QE component capable to simultaneously serve (and continuously learn from) multiple translation jobs involving different domains and users.

1 Introduction

Even if not perfect, machine translation (MT) is now getting reliable enough to support and speed-up human translation. Thanks to this progress, the work of professional translators is gradually shifting from full translation from scratch to MT post-editing. Advanced computer-assisted translation (CAT) tools[1] provide a natural framework for this activity by proposing, for each segment in a source document, one or more suggestions obtained either from a translation memory (TM) or from an MT engine. In both cases, accurate mechanisms to indicate the reliability of a suggestion are extremely useful to let the user decide whether to post-edit a given suggestion or ignore it and translate the source segment from scratch. However, while scoring TM matches relies on standard methods based on fuzzy matching, predicting the quality of MT suggestions at run-time and without references is still an open issue.

This is the goal of MT quality estimation (QE), which aims to predict the quality of an automatic translation as a function of the estimated number of editing operations or the time required for manual correction (Specia et al., 2009; Soricut and Echihabi, 2010; Bach et al., 2011; Mehdad et al., 2012). So far, QE has been mainly approached in controlled settings where homogeneous training and test data is used to learn and evaluate static predictors. Cast in this way, however, it does not fully reflect (nor exploit) the working conditions posed by the CAT framework, in which:

1. The QE module is exposed to a continuous stream of data. The amount of such data and the tight schedule of multiple, simultaneous translation jobs prevents from (theoretically feasible but impractical) complete re-training procedures in a batch fashion and advocate for continuous learning methods.

2. The input data can be diverse in nature. Continuous learning should be sensitive to such differences, in a way that each translation job and user is supported by a reactive model that is robust to variable working conditions.

3. The input data can show similarities with previous observations. Continuous learning should leverage such similarities, so that QE can capitalize from all the previously processed segments even if they come from different domains, genres or users.

While previous QE research disregarded these challenges or addressed them in isolation, our

[1] See for instance the open source MateCat tool (Federico et al., 2014).

Proceedings of the 53rd Annual Meeting of the Association for Computational Linguistics and the 7th International Joint Conference on Natural Language Processing, pages 219–228,
Beijing, China, July 26-31, 2015.

work tackles them in a single unifying framework based on the combination of two paradigms: *online* and *multitask* learning. The former provides continuous learning capabilities that allow the QE model to be robust and self-adapt to a stream of potentially diverse data. The latter provides the model with the capability to exploit the similarities between data coming from different sources. Along this direction our contributions are:

- The first application of online multitask learning to QE, geared to the challenges posed by CAT technology. In this framework, our models are trained to predict MT quality in terms of HTER (Snover et al., 2006).[2]
- The extension of current online multitask learning methods to regression. Prior works in the machine learning field applied this paradigm to classification problems, but its use for HTER estimation requires real-valued predictions. To this aim, we propose a new regression algorithm that, at the same time, handles positive and negative transfer and performs online weight updates.
- A comparison between online multitask and alternative, state-of-the-art online learning strategies. Our experiments, carried out in a realistic scenario involving a stream of data from four domains, lead to consistent results that prove the effectiveness of our approach.

2 Related Work

In recent years, sentence-level QE has been mainly investigated in controlled evaluation scenarios such as those proposed by the shared tasks organized within the WMT workshop on SMT (Callison-Burch et al., 2012; Bojar et al., 2013; Bojar et al., 2014). In this framework, systems trained from a collection of (*source*, *target*, *label*) instances are evaluated based on their capability to predict the correct label[3] for new, unseen test items. Compared to our application scenario, the shared tasks setting differs in two main aspects. First, the data used are substantially homogeneous (usually they come from the same domain, and target translations are produced by the same MT system). Second, training and test are carried out as distinct, sequential phases. Instead, in the CAT environment, a QE component should ideally serve, adapt to and continuously learn from simultaneous translation jobs involving different MT engines, domains, genres and users (Turchi et al., 2013).

These challenges have been separately addressed from different perspectives in few recent works. Huang et al. (2014) proposed a method to adaptively train a QE model for document-specific MT post-editing. Adaptability, however, is achieved in a batch fashion, by re-training an *ad hoc* QE component for each document to be translated. The adaptive approach proposed by Turchi et al. (2014) overcomes the limitations of batch methods by applying an online learning protocol to continuously learn from a stream of (potentially heterogeneous) data. Experimental results suggest the effectiveness of online learning as a way to exploit user feedback to tailor QE predictions to their quality standards and to cope with the heterogeneity of data coming from different domains. However, though robust to user and domain changes, the method is solely driven by the distance computed between predicted and true labels, and it does not exploit any notion of similarity between tasks (*e.g.* domains, users, MT engines).

On the other way round, task relatedness is successfully exploited by Cohn and Specia (2013), who apply multitask learning to jointly learn from data obtained from several annotators with different levels of expertise and reliability. A similar approach is adopted by de Souza et al. (2014a), who apply multitask learning to cope with situations in which a QE model has to be trained with scarce data from multiple domains/genres, different from the actual test domain. The two methods significantly outperform both individual single-task (in-domain) models and single pooled models. However, operating in batch learning mode, none of them provides the continuous learning capabilities desirable in the CAT framework.

The idea that online and multitask learning can complement each other if combined is suggested by (de Souza et al., 2014b), who compared the two learning paradigms in the same experimental setting. So far, however, empirical evidence of this complementarity is still lacking.

[2]The HTER is the minimum edit distance between a translation suggestion and its manually post-edited version in the [0,1] interval. Edit distance is calculated as the number of edits (word insertions, deletions, substitutions, and shifts) divided by the number of words in the reference.

[3]Possible label types include *post-editing effort* scores (*e.g.* 1-5 Likert scores indicating the estimated percentage of MT output that has to be corrected), *HTER* values, and post-editing *time* (*e.g.* seconds per word).

3 Online Multitask Learning for QE

Online learning takes place in a stepwise fashion. At each step, the learner processes an instance (in our case a feature vector extracted from source and target sentences) and predicts a label for it (in our case an HTER value). After the prediction, the learner receives the "true" label (in our case the actual HTER computed from a human post-edition) and computes a *loss* that indicates the distance between the predicted and the true label. Before going to the next step, the weights are updated according to the suffered loss.

Multitask learning (MTL) aims to simultaneously learn models for a set of possibly related tasks by exploiting their relationships. By doing this, improved generalization capabilities are obtained over models trained on the different tasks in isolation (single-task learning – STL). The relationships among tasks are provided by a shared structure, which can encode three types of relationships based on their correlation (Zhang and Yeung, 2010). Positive correlation indicates that the tasks are related and knowledge transfer should lead to similar model parameters. Negative correlation indicates that the tasks are likely to be unrelated and knowledge transfer should force an increase in the distance between model parameters. No correlation indicates that the tasks are independent and no knowledge transfer should take place. In our case, a task is a set of (instance, label) pairs obtained from source sentences coming from different translation jobs, together with their translations produced by several MT systems and the relative post-editions from various translators. In this paper the terms task and domain are used interchangeably.

Early MTL methods model only positive correlation (Caruana, 1997; Argyriou et al., 2008), which results in a positive knowledge transfer between all the tasks, with the risk of impairing each other's performance when they are unrelated or negatively correlated. Other methods (Jacob et al., 2009; Zhong and Kwok, 2012; Yan et al., 2014) cluster tasks into different groups and share knowledge only among those in the same cluster, thus implicitly identifying outlier tasks. A third class of algorithms considers all the three types of relationships by learning task interaction via the covariance of task-specific weights (Bonilla et al., 2008; Zhang and Yeung, 2010). All these methods, however, learn the task relationships in batch mode. To overcome this limitation, recent works propose the "lifelong learning" paradigm (Eaton and Ruvolo, 2013; Ruvolo and Eaton, 2014), in which all the instances of a task are given to the learner sequentially and the previously learned tasks are leveraged to improve generalization for future tasks. This approach, however, is not applicable to our scenario as it assumes that all the instances of each task are processed as separate blocks.

In this paper we propose a novel MTL algorithm for QE that learns the structure shared by different tasks in an online fashion and from an input stream of instances from all the tasks. To this aim, we extend the online passive aggressive (PA) algorithm (Crammer et al., 2006) to the multitask scenario, learning a set of task-specific regression models. The multitask component of our method is given by an "interaction matrix" that defines to which extent each encoded task can "borrow" and "lend" knowledge from and to the other tasks. Opposite to previous methods (Cavallanti et al., 2010) that assume fixed dependencies among tasks, we propose to learn the interaction matrix instance-by-instance from the data. To this aim we follow the recent work of Saha et al. (2011), extending it to a regression setting. The choice of PA is motivated by practical reasons. Indeed, by providing the best trade-off between accuracy and computational time (He and Wang, 2012) compared to other algorithms such as OnlineSVR (Parrella, 2007), it represents a good solution to meet the demand of efficiency posed by the CAT framework.

3.1 Passive Aggressive Algorithm

PA follows the typical online learning protocol. At each round t the learner receives an instance, $\mathbf{x}_t \in \mathbb{R}^d$ (d is the number of features), and predicts the label $\hat{y}_t$ according to a function parametrized by a set weights $\mathbf{w}_t \in \mathbb{R}^d$. Next, the learner receives the true label y_t, computes the ϵ-insensitive loss, ℓ_ϵ, measuring the deviation between the prediction $\hat{y}_t$ and the true label y_t and updates the weights. The weights are updated by solving the optimization problem:

$$\begin{aligned} \mathbf{w}_t = \arg\min_{\mathbf{w}} \quad & \mathcal{C}_{PA}(\mathbf{w}) + C\xi \\ \text{s.t.} \quad & \ell_\epsilon(\mathbf{w}, (\mathbf{x}_t, y_t)) \leq \xi \text{ and } \xi \geq 0 \end{aligned} \tag{1}$$

where $\mathcal{C}_{PA}(\mathbf{w}) = \frac{1}{2}||\mathbf{w} - \mathbf{w}_{t-1}||^2$ and ℓ_ϵ is the ϵ-insensitive hinge loss defined as:

$$\ell_\epsilon(\mathbf{w},(\mathbf{x},y)) = \begin{cases} 0, & \text{if } |y - \mathbf{w}\cdot\mathbf{x}| \le \epsilon \\ |y - \mathbf{w}\cdot\mathbf{x}| - \epsilon, & \text{otherwise} \end{cases} \quad (2)$$

The loss is zero when the absolute difference between the prediction and the true label is smaller or equal to ϵ, and grows linearly with this difference otherwise. The ϵ parameter is given as input and regulates the sensitivity to mistakes. The slack variable ξ acts as an upper-bound to the loss, while the C parameter is introduced to control the aggressiveness of the weights update. High C values lead to more aggressive weight updates. However, when the labels present some degree of noise (a common situation in MT QE), they might cause the learner to drastically change the weight vector in a wrong direction. In these situations, setting C to small values is desirable. As shown in (Crammer et al., 2006), a closed form solution for the weights update in Eq.1 can be derived as:

$$\mathbf{w}_t = \mathbf{w}_{t-1} + \text{sgn}(y_t - \hat{y}_t)\tau_t\mathbf{x}_t \quad (3)$$

with $\tau_t = \min(C, \frac{\ell_t}{||\mathbf{x}_t||^2})$ and $\ell_t = \ell_\epsilon(\mathbf{w},(\mathbf{x}_t, y_t))$.

3.2 Passive Aggressive MTL Algorithm

Our Passive Aggressive Multitask Learning (PAMTL) algorithm extends the traditional PA for regression to multitask learning. Our approach is inspired by the Online Task Relationship Learning algorithm proposed by Saha et al. (2011) which, however, is only defined for classification.

The learning process considers one instance at each round t. The random sequence of instances belongs to a fixed set of K tasks and the goal of the algorithm is to learn K linear models, one for each task, parametrized by weight vectors $\widetilde{\mathbf{w}}_{t,k}$, $k \in \{1, \ldots, K\}$. Moreover, the algorithm also learns a positive semidefinite matrix $\mathbf{\Omega} \in \mathbb{R}^{K\times K}$, modeling the relationship among tasks. Algorithm 1 summarizes our approach. At each round t, the learner receives a pair $(\mathbf{x}_t, i_t)$ where $\mathbf{x}_t \in \mathbb{R}^d$ is an instance and $i_t \in \{1, \ldots, K\}$ is the task identifier. Each incoming instance is transformed to a compound vector $\boldsymbol{\phi}_t = [0, \ldots, 0, \mathbf{x}_t, 0, \ldots, 0] \in \mathbb{R}^{Kd}$. Then, the algorithm predicts the HTER score corresponding to the label $\hat{y}$ by using the weight vector $\widetilde{\mathbf{w}}_t$. The weight vector is a compound vector $\widetilde{\mathbf{w}}_t = [\widetilde{\mathbf{w}}_{t,1}, \ldots, \widetilde{\mathbf{w}}_{t,K}] \in \mathbb{R}^{Kd}$, where $\widetilde{\mathbf{w}}_{t,k} \in \mathbb{R}^d$, $k \in \{1, \ldots, K\}$. Next, the learner receives the true HTER label y and computes the loss ℓ_ϵ (Eq. 2) for round t.

Algorithm 1 PA Multitask Learning (PAMTL)

Input: instances from K tasks, number of rounds $R > 0$, $\epsilon > 0, C > 0$
Output: $\mathbf{w}$ and $\mathbf{\Omega}$, learned after T rounds

Initialization: $\mathbf{\Omega} = \frac{1}{K} \times \mathbf{I}_k$, $\mathbf{w} = \mathbf{0}$
for t = 1 to T **do**
  receive instance $(\mathbf{x}_t, i_t)$
  compute $\boldsymbol{\phi}_t$ from $\mathbf{x}_t$
  predict HTER $\hat{y}_t = (\widetilde{\mathbf{w}}_t^T \cdot \boldsymbol{\phi}_t)$
  receive true HTER label y_t
  compute ℓ_t (Eq. 2)
  compute $\tau_t = \min(C, \frac{\ell_t}{||\boldsymbol{\phi}_t||^2})$
  `/* update weights */`
  $\widetilde{\mathbf{w}}_t = \widetilde{\mathbf{w}}_{t-1} + \text{sgn}(y_t - \hat{y}_t)\tau_t(\mathbf{\Omega}_{t-1} \otimes \mathbf{I}_d)^{-1}\boldsymbol{\phi}_t$
  `/* update task matrix */`
  if $t > R$ **then**
    update $\mathbf{\Omega}_t$ with Eq. 6 or Eq. 7
  end if
end for

We propose to update the weights by solving:

$$\widetilde{\mathbf{w}}_t, \mathbf{\Omega}_t = \underset{\mathbf{w},\mathbf{\Omega}\succ 0}{\text{argmin}} \quad \mathcal{C}_{MTL}(\mathbf{w},\mathbf{\Omega}) + C\xi + \mathcal{D}(\mathbf{\Omega}, \mathbf{\Omega}_{t-1})$$
$$\text{s.t.} \quad \ell_\epsilon(\mathbf{w},(\mathbf{x}_t, y_t)) \le \xi, \xi \ge 0 \quad (4)$$

The first term models the joint dependencies between the task weights and the interaction matrix and it is defined as $\mathcal{C}_{MTL}(\mathbf{w},\mathbf{\Omega}) = \frac{1}{2}(\mathbf{w} - \widetilde{\mathbf{w}}_t)^T\mathbf{\Omega}_\otimes(\mathbf{w} - \widetilde{\mathbf{w}}_t)$, where $\mathbf{\Omega}_\otimes = \mathbf{\Omega} \otimes \mathbf{I}_d$. The function $\mathcal{D}(\cdot)$ represents the divergence between a pair of positive definite matrices. Similar to (Saha et al., 2011), to define $\mathcal{D}(\cdot)$ we also consider the family of Bregman divergences and specifically the LogDet and the Von Neumann divergences. Given two matrices $\mathbf{X}, \mathbf{Y} \in \mathbb{R}^{n\times n}$, the LogDet divergence is $\mathcal{D}_{LD}(\mathbf{X},\mathbf{Y}) = \text{tr}(\mathbf{X}\mathbf{Y}^{-1}) - \log|\mathbf{X}\mathbf{Y}^{-1}| - n$, while the Von Neumann divergence is computed as $\mathcal{D}_{VN}(\mathbf{X},\mathbf{Y}) = \text{tr}(\mathbf{X}\log\mathbf{X} - \mathbf{Y}\log\mathbf{Y} - \mathbf{X} + \mathbf{Y})$.

The optimization process to solve Eq.4 is performed with an alternate scheme: first, with a fixed $\mathbf{\Omega}$, we compute $\mathbf{w}$; then, given $\mathbf{w}$ we optimize for $\mathbf{\Omega}$. The closed-form solution for updating $\mathbf{w}$, which we derived similarly to the PA update (Crammer et al., 2006), becomes:

$$\widetilde{\mathbf{w}}_t = \widetilde{\mathbf{w}}_{t-1} + \text{sgn}(y_t - \hat{y}_t)\tau_t(\mathbf{\Omega}_{t-1} \otimes \mathbf{I}_d)^{-1}\boldsymbol{\phi}_t \quad (5)$$

In practice, the interaction matrix works as a learning rate when updating the weights of each task. Similarly, following previous works (Tsuda et al., 2005), the update steps for the interaction matrix $\mathbf{\Omega}$ can be easily derived. For the Log-Det divergence we have:

$$\mathbf{\Omega}_t = (\mathbf{\Omega}_{t-1} + \eta\, \text{sym}(\widetilde{\mathbf{W}}_{t-1}^T\widetilde{\mathbf{W}}_{t-1}))^{-1} \quad (6)$$

while for the Von Neumann we obtain:

$$\Omega_t = \exp(\log \Omega_{t-1} - \eta \, \mathrm{sym}(\widetilde{\mathbf{W}}_{t-1}^T \widetilde{\mathbf{W}}_{t-1})) \quad (7)$$

where $\widetilde{\mathbf{W}}_t \in \mathbb{R}^{d \times K}$ is a matrix obtained by column-wise reshaping the weight vector $\widetilde{\mathbf{w}}_t$, $\mathrm{sym}(\mathbf{X}) = (\mathbf{X} + \mathbf{X}^T)/2$ and η is the learning rate parameter. The sequence of steps to compute Ω_t and $\widetilde{\mathbf{w}}_t$ is summarized in Algorithm 1. Importantly, the weight vector is updated at each round t, while Ω_t is initialized to a diagonal matrix and it is only computed after R iterations. In this way, at the beginning, the tasks are assumed to be independent and the task-specific regression models are learned in isolation. Then, after R rounds, the interaction matrix is updated and the weights are refined considering tasks dependencies. This leads to a progressive increase in the correlation of weight vectors of related tasks. In the following, PAMTL_{vn} refers to PAMTL with the Von Neumann updates and PAMTL_{ld} to PAMTL with LogDet updates.

4 Experimental Setting

In this section, we describe the data used in our experiments, the features extracted from the source and target sentences, the evaluation metric and the baselines used for comparison.

Data. We experiment with English-French datasets coming from Technology Entertainment Design talks (TED), Information Technology manuals (IT) and Education Material (EM). All datasets provide a set of tuples composed by (source, translation and post-edited translation).

The TED dataset is distributed in the Trace corpus[4] and includes, as source sentences, the subtitles of several talks spanning a range of topics presented in the TED conferences. Translations were generated by two different MT systems: a phrase-based statistical MT system and a commercial rule-based system. Post-editions were collected from four different translators, as described by Wisniewski et al. (2013).

The IT manuals data come from two language service providers, henceforth $LSP1$ and $LSP2$. The IT_{LSP1} tuples belong to a software manual translated by an SMT system trained using the Moses toolkit (Koehn et al., 2007). The post-editions were produced by one professional translator. The IT_{LSP2} data includes a software manual from the automotive industry; its source sentences are translated with an adaptive proprietary MT system and post-edited by several professional translators. The EM corpus is also provided by $LSP2$ and regards educational material (*e.g.* courseware and assessments) of various text styles. The translations and post-editions are produced in the same way as for IT_{LSP2}. The IT_{LSP2} and the EM datasets are derived from the Autodesk Post-Editing Data corpus.[5]

In total, we end up with four domains (TED, IT_{LSP1}, EM and IT_{LSP2}), which allows us to evaluate the PAMTL algorithm in realistic conditions where the QE component is exposed to a continuous stream of heterogeneous data. Each domain is composed by 1,000 tuples formed by: *i)* the English source sentence, *ii)* its automatic translation in French, and *iii)* a real-valued quality label obtained by computing the HTER between the translation and the post-edition with the TERCpp open source tool.[6]

Domain	**No. tokens**	**Vocab. Size**	**Avg. Snt. Length**
TED src	20,048	3,452	20
TED tgt	21,565	3,940	22
IT_{LSP1} src	12,791	2,013	13
IT_{LSP1} tgt	13,626	2,321	13
EM src	15,327	3,200	15
EM tgt	17,857	3,149	17
IT_{LSP2} src	15,128	2,105	13
IT_{LSP2} tgt	17,109	2,104	14

Table 1: Data statistics for each domain.

Table 1 reports some macro-indicators (number of tokens, vocabulary size, average sentence length) that give an idea about the similarities and differences between domains. Although they contain data from different software manuals, similar vocabulary size and sentence lengths for the two IT domains seem to reflect some commonalities in their technical style and jargon. Larger values for TED and EM evidence a higher lexical variability in the topics that compose these domains and the expected stylistic differences featured by speech transcriptions and non-technical writing. Overall, these numbers suggest a possible dissimilar-

[4] http://anrtrace.limsi.fr/trace_postedit.tar.bz2

[5] https://autodesk.app.box.com/Autodesk-PostEditing

[6] http://sourceforge.net/projects/tercpp/

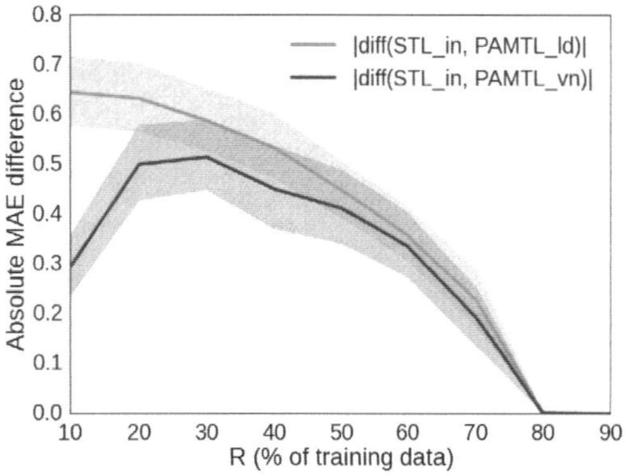

Figure 1: Validation curves for the R parameter.

ity between IT_{LSP1} and IT_{LSP2} and the other two domains, which might make knowledge transfer across them more difficult and QE model reactivity to domain changes particularly important.

Features. Our models are trained using the 17 baseline features proposed in (Specia et al., 2009), extracted with the online version of the QuEst feature extractor (Shah et al., 2014). These features take into account the complexity of the source sentence (*e.g.* number of tokens, number of translations per source word) and the fluency of the translation (*e.g.* language model probabilities). Their description is available in (Callison-Burch et al., 2012). The results of previous WMT QE shared tasks have shown that these features are particularly competitive in the HTER prediction task.

Baselines. We compare the performance of PAMTL against three baselines: *i)* pooling mean, *ii)* pooling online single task learning (STL_{pool}) and *iii)* in-domain online single task learning (STL_{in}). The pooling mean is obtained by assigning a fixed prediction value to each test point. This value is the average HTER computed on the entire pool of training data. Although assigning the same prediction to each test instance would be useless in real applications, we compare against the mean baseline since it is often hard to beat in regression tasks, especially when dealing with heterogeneous data distributions (Rubino et al., 2013).

The two online single task baselines implement the PA algorithm described in Section 3.1. The choice of PA is to make them comparable to our method, so that we can isolate more precisely the contribution of multitask learning. STL_{pool} results are obtained by a single model trained on the entire

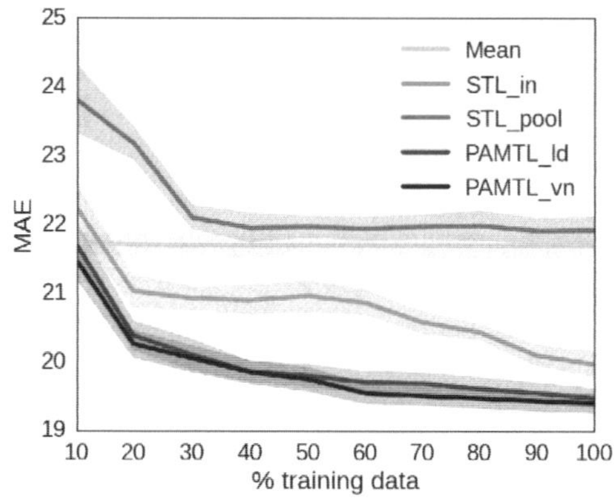

Figure 2: Learning curves for all the domains, computed by calculating the mean MAE (↓) of the four domains.

pool of available training data presented in random order. STL_{in} results are obtained by separately training one model for each domain. These represent two alternative strategies for the integration of QE in the CAT framework. The former would allow a single model to simultaneously support multiple translation jobs in different domains, without any notion about their relations. The latter would lead to a more complex architecture, organized as a pool of independent, specialized QE modules.

Evaluation metric. The performance of our regression models is evaluated in terms of mean absolute error (MAE), a standard error measure for regression problems commonly used also for QE (Callison-Burch et al., 2012). The MAE is the average of the absolute errors $e_i = |\hat{y}_i - y_i|$, where $\hat{y}_i$ is the prediction of the model and y_i is the true value for the ith instance. As it is an error measure, lower values indicate better performance (↓).

5 Results and Discussion

In this Section we evaluate the proposed PAMTL algorithm. First, by analyzing how the number of rounds R impacts on the performance of our approach, we empirically find the value that will be used to train the model. Then, the learned model is run on test data and compared against the baselines. Performance is analyzed both by averaging the MAE results computed on all the domains, and by separately discussing in-domain behavior. Finally, the capability of the algorithm to learn task correlations and, in turn, transfer knowledge across them, is analysed by presenting the correla-

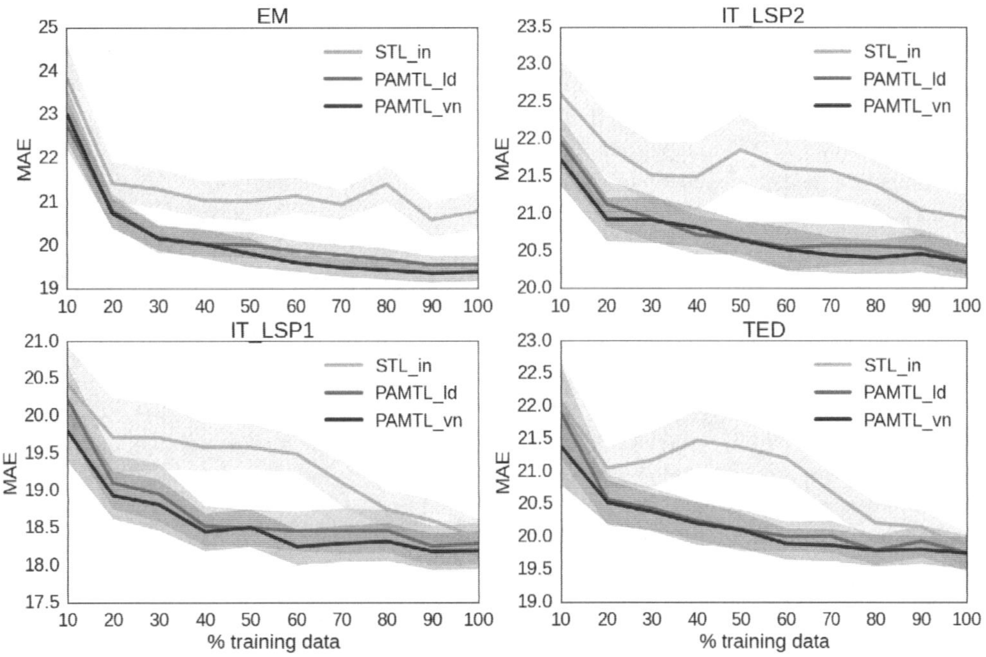

Figure 3: Learning curves showing MAE (↓) variations for each domain.

tion matrix of the task weights.

For the evaluation, we uniformly sample 700 instances from each domain for training, leaving the remaining 300 instances for test. The training sets of all the domains are concatenated and shuffled to create a random sequence of points. To investigate the impact of different amounts of data on the learning process, we create ten subsets of 10 to 100% of the training data. We optimize the parameters of all the models with a grid search procedure using 5-fold cross-validation. This process is repeated for 30 different train/test splits over the whole data. Results are presented with 95% confidence bands.[7]

Analysis of the R parameter. We empirically study the influence of the number of instances required to start updating the interaction matrix (the R parameter in Algorithm 1). For that, we perform a set of experiments where R is initialized with nine different values (expressed as percentage of training data). Figure 1 shows the validation curves obtained in cross-validation over the training data using the LogDet and Von Neumann updates. The curves report the performance (MAE) difference between STL_{in} and PAMTL_{ld} (black curve) and STL_{in} and PAMTL_{vn} (grey curve). The higher the difference, the better. The PAMTL_{vn} curve differs from PAMTL_{ld} one only for small values of R (< 20), showing that the two divergences are substantially equivalent. It is interesting to note that with only 20% of the training data ($R = 20$), PAMTL is able to find a stable set of weights and to effectively update the interaction matrix. Larger values of R harm the performance, indicating that the interaction matrix updates require a reasonable amount of points to reliably transfer knowledge across tasks. We use this observation to set R for our final experiment, in which we evaluate the methods over the test data.

Evaluation on test data. Global evaluation results are summarized in Figure 2, which shows five curves: one for each baseline (Mean, STL_{in}, STL_{pool}) and two for the proposed online multitask method (PAMTL_{vn} and PAMTL_{ld}). The curves are computed by calculating the average MAE achieved with different amounts of data on each domain's test set.

The results show that PAMTL_{ld} and PAMTL_{vn} have similar trends (confirming the substantial equivalence previously observed), and that both outperform all the baselines in a statistically significant manner. This holds for all the training set

[7] Confidence bands are used to show whether performance differences between the models are statistically significant.

sizes we experimented with. The maximum improvement over the baselines (+1.3 MAE) is observed with 60% of the training data when comparing PAMTL$_{vn}$ with STL$_{in}$. Even if this is the best baseline, also with 100% of the data its results are not competitive and of limited interest with respect to our application scenario (the integration of effective QE models in the CAT framework). Indeed, despite the STL$_{in}$ downward error trend, it's worth remarking that an increased competitiveness would come at the cost of: *i)* collecting large amounts of annotated data and *ii)* integrating the model in a complex CAT architecture organized as a pool of independent QE components. Under the tested conditions, it is also evident that the alternative strategy of using a single QE component to simultaneously serve multiple translation jobs is not viable. Indeed, STL$_{pool}$ is the worst performing baseline, with a constant distance of around 2 MAE points from the best PAMTL model for almost all the training set sizes. The fact that, with increasing amounts of data, the STL$_{pool}$ predictions get close to those of the simple mean baseline indicates its limitations to cope with the noise introduced by a continuous stream of diverse data. The capability to handle such stream by exploiting task relationships makes PAMTL a much better solution for our purposes.

Per-domain analysis. Figure 3 shows the MAE results achieved on each target domain by the most competitive baseline (STL$_{in}$) and the proposed online multitask method (PAMTL$_{vn}$, PAMTL$_{ld}$).

For all the domains, the behavior of PAMTL$_{ld}$ and PAMTL$_{vn}$ is consistent and almost identical. With both divergences, the improvement of PAMTL over online single task learning becomes statistically significant when using more than 30% of the training data (210 instances). Interestingly, in all the plots, with 20% of the training data (140 instances for each domain, *i.e.* a total of 560 instances adding data from all the domains), PATML results are comparable to those achieved by STL$_{in}$ with 80% of the training data (*i.e.* 560 in-domain instances). This confirms that PATML can effectively leverage data heterogeneity, and that a limited amount of in-domain data is sufficient to make it competitive. Nevertheless, for all domains except EM, the PATML and STL$_{in}$ curves converge to comparable performance when trained with 100% of the data. This is not surprising if we consider that EM has a varied vocabulary

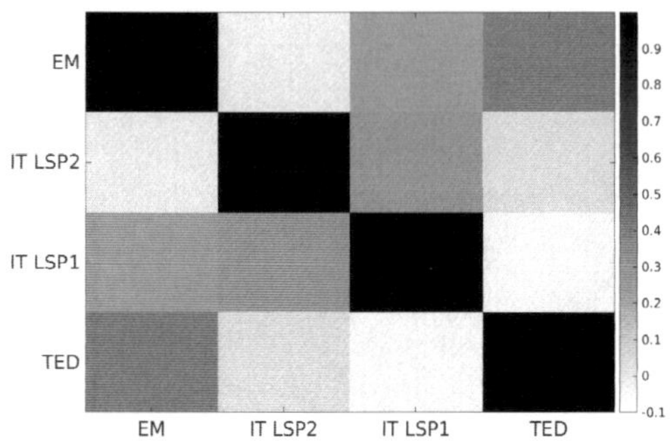

Figure 4: Correlation among the weights predicted by PATML$_{vn}$ using all the training data.

(see Table 1), which may be evidence of the presence of different topics, increasing its similarity with other domains. The same assumption should also hold for TED, given that its source sentences belong to talks about different topics. The results for the TED domain, however, do not present the same degree of improvement as for EM.

To better understand the relationships learned by the PAMTL models, we compute the correlation between the weights inferred for each domain (as performed by Saha et al. (2011)). Figure 4 shows the correlations computed on the task weights learned by PATML$_{vn}$ with all the training data. In the matrix, EM is the domain that presents the highest correlation with all the others. Instead, TED and IT$_{LSP2}$ are the less correlated with the other domains (even though, being close to the other IT domain, IT$_{LSP2}$ can share knowledge with it). This explains why the improvement measured on TED is smaller compared to EM. Although there is no canonical way to measure correlation among domains, the weights correlation matrix and the improvements achieved by PAMTL show the capability of the method to identify task relationships and exploit them to improve the generalization properties of the model.

6 Conclusion

We addressed the problem of developing quality estimation models suitable for integration in computer-assisted translation technology. In this framework, on-the-fly MT quality prediction for a stream of heterogeneous data coming from different domains/users/MT systems represents a major challenge. On one side, processing such stream calls for supervised solutions that avoid the bottleneck of periodically retraining the QE models in a batch fashion. On the other side, handling data heterogeneity requires the capability to leverage data similarities and dissimilarities. While previous works addressed these two problems in isolation, by proposing approaches respectively based on online and multitask learning, our solution unifies the two paradigms in a single online multitask approach. To this aim, we developed a novel regression algorithm, filling a gap left by current online multitask learning methods that only operate in classification mode. Our approach, which is based on the passive aggressive algorithm, has been successfully evaluated against strong online single-task competitors in a scenario involving four domains. Our future objective is to extend our evaluation to streams of data coming from a larger number of domains. Finding reasonably-sized datasets for this purpose is currently difficult. However, we are confident that the gradual shift of the translation industry towards human MT post-editing will not only push for further research on these problems, but also provide data for larger scale evaluations in a short time.

To allow for replicability of our results and promote further research on QE, the features extracted from our data, the computed labels and the source code of the method are available at `https://github.com/jsouza/pamtl`.

Acknowledgements

This work has been partially supported by the EC-funded H2020 project QT21 (grant agreement no. 645452). The authors would like to thank Dr. Ventsislav Zhechev for his support with the Autodesk Post-Editing Data corpus.

References

Andreas Argyriou, Theodoros Evgeniou, and Massimiliano Massimo Pontil. 2008. Convex multi-task feature learning. *Machine Learning*, 73(3):243–272, January.

Nguyen Bach, F. Huang, and Y. Al-Onaizan. 2011. Goodness: A method for measuring machine translation confidence. In *49th Annual Meeting of the Association for Computational Linguistics*.

Ondřej Bojar, Christian Buck, Chris Callison-Burch, Christian Federmann, Barry Haddow, Philipp Koehn, Christof Monz, Matt Post, Radu Soricut, and Lucia Specia. 2013. Findings of the 2013 Workshop on Statistical Machine Translation. In *Eighth Workshop on Statistical Machine Translation*, pages 1–44, Sofia, Bulgaria, August.

Ondrej Bojar, Christian Buck, Christian Federmann, Barry Haddow, Philipp Koehn, Johannes Leveling, Christof Monz, Pavel Pecina, Matt Post, Herve Saint-Amand, Radu Soricut, Lucia Specia, and Aleš Tamchyna. 2014. Findings of the 2014 Workshop on Statistical Machine Translation. In *Proceedings of the Ninth Workshop on Statistical Machine Translation*, pages 12–58, Baltimore, USA, June.

Edwin Bonilla, Kian Ming Chai, and Christopher Williams. 2008. Multi-task Gaussian Process Prediction. In *Advances in Neural Information Processing Systems 20: NIPS'08*.

Chris Callison-Burch, Philipp Koehn, Christof Monz, Matt Post, Radu Soricut, and Lucia Specia. 2012. Findings of the 2012 Workshop on Statistical Machine Translation. In *Proceedings of the 7th Workshop on Statistical Machine Translation*, pages 10–51, Montréal, Canada, June.

Rich Caruana. 1997. Multitask learning. In *Machine Learning*, pages 41–75.

Giovanni Cavallanti, N Cesa-Bianchi, and C Gentile. 2010. Linear algorithms for online multitask classification. *The Journal of Machine Learning Research*, 11:2901–2934.

Trevor Cohn and Lucia Specia. 2013. Modelling Annotator Bias with Multi-task Gaussian Processes: An application to Machine Translation Quality Estimation. In *Proceedings of the 51st Annual Meeting of the Association for Computational Linguistics*, pages 32–42, Sofia, Bulgaria, August.

Koby Crammer, Ofer Dekel, Joseph Keshet, Shai Shalev-Shwartz, and Yoram Singer. 2006. Online Passive-Aggressive Algorithms. *The Journal of Machine Learning Research*, 7:551–585.

José G. C. de Souza, Marco Turchi, and Matteo Negri. 2014a. Machine Translation Quality Estimation Across Domains. In *Proceedings of COLING 2014, the 25th International Conference on Computational Linguistics: Technical Papers*, pages 409–420, Dublin, Ireland, August.

José G. C. de Souza, Marco Turchi, and Matteo Negri. 2014b. Towards a Combination of Online and Multitask Learning for MT Quality Estimation: a Preliminary Study. In *Proceedings of Workshop on Interactive and Adaptive Machine Translation in 2014 (IAMT 2014)*, Vancouver, BC, Canada, October.

Eric Eaton and PL Ruvolo. 2013. ELLA: An efficient lifelong learning algorithm. In *Proceedings of the 30th International Conference on Machine Learning*, pages 507–515, Atlanta, Georgia, USA, June.

Marcello Federico, Nicola Bertoldi, Mauro Cettolo, Matteo Negri, Marco Turchi, Marco Trombetti, Alessandro Cattelan, Antonio Farina, Domenico

Lupinetti, Andrea Martines, Alberto Massidda, Holger Schwenk, Loïc Barrault, Frederic Blain, Philipp Koehn, Christian Buck, and Ulrich Germann. 2014. THE MATECAT TOOL. In *Proceedings of COLING 2014, the 25th International Conference on Computational Linguistics: System Demonstrations*, pages 129–132, Dublin, Ireland, August.

Fei Huang, Jian-Ming Xu, Abraham Ittycheriah, and Salim Roukos. 2014. Adaptive HTER Estimation for Document-Specific MT Post-Editing. In *Proceedings of the 52nd Annual Meeting of the Association for Computational Linguistics (Volume 1: Long Papers)*, pages 861–870, Baltimore, Maryland, June.

Laurent Jacob, Jean-philippe Vert, Francis R Bach, and Jean-philippe Vert. 2009. Clustered Multi-Task Learning: A Convex Formulation. In D Koller, D Schuurmans, Y Bengio, and L Bottou, editors, *Advances in Neural Information Processing Systems 21*, pages 745–752. Curran Associates, Inc.

Philipp Koehn, Hieu Hoang, Alexandra Birch, Chris Callison-Burch, Marcello Federico, Nicola Bertoldi, Brooke Cowan, Wade Shen, Christine Moran, Richard Zenz, Chris Dyer, Ondřej Bojar, Alexandra Constantin, and Evan Herbst. 2007. Moses: Open source toolkit for statistical machine translation. In *ACL 2007 Demo and Poster Sessions*, pages 177–180, Prague, Czech Republic, June.

Yashar Mehdad, Matteo Negri, and Marcello Federico. 2012. Match without a Referee: Evaluating MT Adequacy without Reference Translations. In *Proceedings of the Machine Translation Workshop (WMT2012)*, pages 171–180, Montréal, Canada, June.

Francesco Parrella. 2007. Online support vector regression. *Master's Thesis, Department of Information Science, University of Genoa, Italy.*

Raphael Rubino, José G. C. de Souza, and Lucia Specia. 2013. Topic Models for Translation Quality Estimation for Gisting Purposes. In *Machine Translation Summit XIV*, pages 295–302.

Paul Ruvolo and Eric Eaton. 2014. Online Multi-Task Learning via Sparse Dictionary Optimization. In *Proceedings of the 28th AAAI Conference on Artificial Intelligence (AAAI-14)*, Québec City, Québec, Canada, July.

Avishek Saha, Piyush Rai, Hal Daumé, and Suresh Venkatasubramanian. 2011. Online Learning of Multiple Tasks and their Relationships. In *Proceedings of the 14th International Conference on Artificial Intelligence and Statistics (AISTATS)*, Fort Lauderdale, FL, USA, April.

Kashif Shah, Marco Turchi, and Lucia Specia. 2014. An Efficient and User-friendly Tool for Machine Translation Quality Estimation. In *Proceedings of the Ninth International Conference on Language Resources and Evaluation*, Reykjavik, Iceland, May.

Matthew Snover, Bonnie Dorr, Richard Schwartz, Linnea Micciulla, and John Makhoul. 2006. A Study of Translation Edit Rate with Targeted Human Annotation. In *Association for Machine Translation in the Americas*, Cambridge, MA, USA, August.

Radu Soricut and A Echihabi. 2010. Trustrank: Inducing trust in automatic translations via ranking. In *Proceedings of the 48th Annual Meeting of the Association for Computational Linguistics*, number July, pages 612–621.

Lucia Specia, Nicola Cancedda, Marc Dymetman, Marco Turchi, and Nello Cristianini. 2009. Estimating the Sentence-Level Quality of Machine Translation Systems. In *Proceedings of the 13th Annual Conference of the EAMT*, pages 28–35, Barcelona, Spain, May.

Koji Tsuda, Gunnar Rätsch, and Manfred K Warmuth. 2005. Matrix exponentiated gradient updates for online learning and bregman projection. In *Journal of Machine Learning Research*, pages 995–1018.

Marco Turchi, Matteo Negri, and Marcello Federico. 2013. Coping with the Subjectivity of Human Judgements in MT Quality Estimation. In *Proceedings of the Eighth Workshop on Statistical Machine Translation (WMT)*, pages 240–251, Sofia, Bulgaria, August.

Marco Turchi, Antonios Anastasopoulos, José G. C. de Souza, and Matteo Negri. 2014. Adaptive Quality Estimation for Machine Translation. In *Proceedings of the 52nd Annual Meeting of the Association for Computational Linguistics (Volume 1: Long Papers)*, pages 710–720, Baltimore, Maryland, USA, June.

Guillaume Wisniewski, Anil Kumar Singh, Natalia Segal, and François Yvon. 2013. Design and Analysis of a Large Corpus of Post-Edited Translations: Quality Estimation, Failure Analysis and the Variability of Post-Edition. In *Machine Translation Summit XIV*, pages 117–124.

Yan Yan, Elisa Ricci, Ramanathan Subramanian, Gaowen Liu, and Nicu Sebe. 2014. Multitask linear discriminant analysis for view invariant action recognition. *IEEE Transactions on Image Processing*, 23(12):5599–5611.

Yu Zhang and Dit-yan Yeung. 2010. A Convex Formulation for Learning Task Relationships in Multi-Task Learning. In *Proceedings of the Twenty-Sixth Conference Annual Conference on Uncertainty in Artificial Intelligence (UAI-10)*, pages 733–742, Catalina Island, CA, USA, July.

Leon Wenliang Zhong and James T. Kwok. 2012. Convex multitask learning with flexible task clusters. In *Proceedings of the 29 th International Conference on Machine Learning*, Edinburgh, Scotland, June.

A Context-Aware Topic Model for Statistical Machine Translation

Jinsong Su[1], **Deyi Xiong**[2]*, **Yang Liu**[3], **Xianpei Han**[4], **Hongyu Lin**[1], **Junfeng Yao**[1], **Min Zhang**[2]
Xiamen University, Xiamen, China[1]
Soochow University, Suzhou, China[2]
Tsinghua University, Beijing, China[3]
Institute of Software, Chinese Academy of Sciences, Beijing, China[4]
{jssu, hylin, yao0010}@xmu.edu.cn
{dyxiong, minzhang}@suda.edu.cn
liuyang2011@tsinghua.edu.cn
xianpei@nfs.iscas.ac.cn

Abstract

Lexical selection is crucial for statistical machine translation. Previous studies separately exploit sentence-level contexts and document-level topics for lexical selection, neglecting their correlations. In this paper, we propose a context-aware topic model for lexical selection, which not only models local contexts and global topics but also captures their correlations. The model uses target-side translations as hidden variables to connect document topics and source-side local contextual words. In order to learn hidden variables and distributions from data, we introduce a Gibbs sampling algorithm for statistical estimation and inference. A new translation probability based on distributions learned by the model is integrated into a translation system for lexical selection. Experiment results on NIST Chinese-English test sets demonstrate that 1) our model significantly outperforms previous lexical selection methods and 2) modeling correlations between local words and global topics can further improve translation quality.

1 Introduction

Lexical selection is a very important task in statistical machine translation (SMT). Given a sentence in the source language, lexical selection statistically predicts translations for source words, based on various translation knowledge. Most conventional SMT systems (Koehn et al., 2003; Galley et al., 2006; Chiang, 2007) exploit very limited context information contained in bilingual rules for lexical selection.

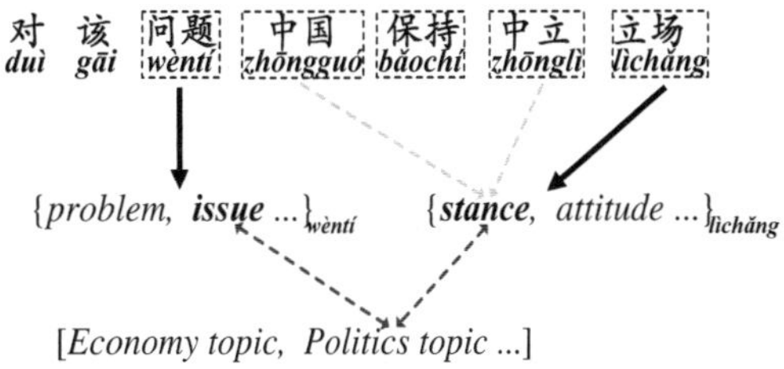

Figure 1: A Chinese-English translation example to illustrate the effect of local contexts and global topics as well as their correlations on lexical selection. Each black line indicates a set of translation candidates for a Chinese content word (within a dotted box). Green lines point to translations that are favored by local contexts while blue lines show bidirectional associations between global topics and their consistent target-side translations.

Previous studies that explore richer information for lexical selection can be divided into two categories: 1) incorporating sentence-level contexts (Chan et al., 2007; Carpuat and Wu, 2007; Hasan et al., 2008; Mauser et al., 2009; He et al., 2008; Shen et al., 2009) or 2) integrating document-level topics (Xiao et al., 2011; Ture et al., 2012; Xiao et al., 2012; Eidelman et al., 2012; Hewavitharana et al., 2013; Xiong et al., 2013; Hasler et al., 2014a; Hasler et al., 2014b) into SMT. The methods in these two strands have shown their effectiveness on lexical selection.

However, correlations between sentence- and document-level contexts have never been explored before. It is clear that local contexts and global topics are often highly correlated. Consider a Chinese-English translation example presented in Figure 1. On the one hand, if local contexts suggest that the source word "立场/*lìchǎng*" should be translated in-

*Corresponding author.

Proceedings of the 53rd Annual Meeting of the Association for Computational Linguistics and the 7th International Joint Conference on Natural Language Processing, pages 229–238,
Beijing, China, July 26-31, 2015.

to "*stance*", they will also indicate that the topic of the document where the example sentence occurs is about *politics*. The *politics* topic can be further used to enable the decoder to select a correct translation "*issue*" for another source word "问题/*wènti*", which is consistent with this topic. On the other hand, if we know that this document mainly focuses on the *politics* topic, the candiate translation "*stance*" will be more compatible with the context of "立场/*lìchǎng*" than the candiate translation "*attitude*". This is because neighboring source-side words "中国/*zhōnguó*" and "中立/*zhōnglì*" often occur in documents that are about international politics. We believe that such correlations between local contextual words and global topics can be used to further improve lexical selection.

In this paper, we propose a unified framework to jointly model local contexts, global topics as well as their correlations for lexical selection. Specifically,

- First, we present a context-aware topic model (CATM) to exploit the features mentioned above for lexical selection in SMT. To the best of our knowledge, this is the first work to jointly model both local and global contexts for lexical selection in a topic model.
- Second, we present a Gibbs sampling algorithm to learn various distributions that are related to topics and translations from data. The translation probabilities derived from our model are integrated into SMT to allow collective lexical selection with both local and global informtion.

We validate the effectiveness of our model on a state-of-the-art phrase-based translation system. Experiment results on the NIST Chinese-English translation task show that our model significantly outperforms previous lexical selection methods.

2 Context-Aware Topic Model

In this section, we describe basic assumptions and elaborate the proposed context-aware topic model.

2.1 Basic Assumptions

In CATM, we assume that each source document d consists of two types of words: *topical words* which are related to topics of the document and *contextual words* which affect translation selections of topical words.

As topics of a document are usually represented by content words in it, we choose source-side *nouns*, *verbs*, *adjectives* and *adverbs* as topical words. For contextual words, we use all words in a source sentence as contextual words. We assume that they are generated by target-side translations of other words than themselves. Note that a source word may be both topical and contextual. For each topical word, we identify its candidate translations from training corpus according to word alignments between the source and target language. We allow a target translation to be a phrase of length no more than 3 words. We refer to these translations of source topical words as *target-side topical items*, which can be either words or phrases. In the example shown in Figure 1, all source words within dotted boxes are topical words. Topical word "立场/*lìchǎng*" is supposed to be translated into a target-side topical item "*stance*", which is collectively suggested by neighboring contextual words "中国/*zhōngguó*", "中立/*zhōnglì*" and the topic of the corresponding document.

In our model, all target-side topical items in a document are generated according to the following two assumptions:

- *Topic consistency assumption*: All target-side topical items in a document should be consistent with the topic distribution of the document. For example, the translations "*issue*", "*stance*" tend to occur in documents about *politics* topic.
- *Context compatibility assumption*: For a topical word, its translation (i.e., the counterpart target-side topical item) should be compatible with its neighboring contextual words. For instance, the translation "*stance*" of "立场/*lìchǎng*" is closely related to contextual words "中国/*zhōnguó*" and "中立/*zhōnglì*".

2.2 Model

The graphical representation of CATM, which visualizes the generative process of training data $\boldsymbol{D}$, is shown in Figure 2. Notations of CATM are presented in Table 1. In CATM, each document d can be generated in the following three steps[1]:

[1]In the following description, $Dir(.)$, $Mult(.)$ and $Unif(.)$ denote *Dirichlet*, *Multinomial* and *Uniform* distributions, re-

Symbol	Meaning
α	hyperparameter for θ
β	hyperparameter for ϕ
γ	hyperparameter for ψ
δ	hyperparameter for ξ
f	topical word
c	contextual word
$\tilde{e}$	target-side topical item
$\tilde{e}'$	a sampled target-side topical item used to generate a source-side contextual word
θ	the topic distribution of document
ϕ	the distribution of a topic over target-side topical items
ψ	the translation probability distribution of a target-side topical item over source-side topical words
ξ	the generation probability distribution of a target-side topical item over source-side contextual words
N_z	topic number
N_d	document number
N_f	the number of topical words
N_c	the number of contextual words
$N_{\tilde{e}}$	the number of target-side topical items
$N_{f,d}$	the number of topical words in d
$N_{c,d}$	the number of contextual words in d

Table 1: Notations in CATM.

1. Sample a topic distribution $\theta_d \sim Dir(\alpha)$.

2. For each position i that corresponds to a topical word f_i in the document:

- **(a)** Sample a topic $z_i \sim Mult(\theta_d)$.
- **(b)** Conditioned on the topic z_i, sample a target-side topical item $\tilde{e}_i \sim Mult(\phi_{z_i})$.
- **(c)** Conditioned on the target-side topical item $\tilde{e}_i$, sample the topical word $f_i \sim Mult(\psi_{\tilde{e}_i})$.

3. For each position j that corresponds to a contextual word c_j in the document:

- **(a)** Collect all target-side topical items $\tilde{\boldsymbol{e}}_s$ that are translations of neighboring topical words within a window centered at c_j (window size w_s).
- **(b)** Randomly sample an item from $\tilde{\boldsymbol{e}}_s$, $\tilde{e}'_j \sim Unif(\tilde{\boldsymbol{e}}_s)$.
- **(c)** Conditioned on the sampled target-side topical item $\tilde{e}'_j$, sample the contextual word $c_j \sim Mult(\xi_{\tilde{e}'_j})$.

To better illustrate CATM, let us revisit the example in Figure 1. We describe how CATM generates top-

spectively.

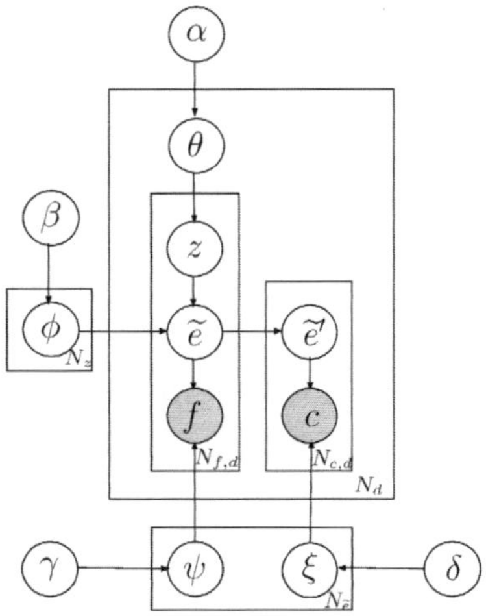

Figure 2: Graphical representation of our model.

ical words "问题/*wèntí*", "立场/*lìchǎng*", and contextual word "中立/*zhōnglì*" in the following steps:

Step 1: The model generates a topic distribution for the corresponding document as $\{economy^{0.25}, politics^{0.75}\}$.

Step 2: Based on the topic distribution, we choose "*economy*" and "*politics*" as topic assignments for "问题/*wèntí*" and "立场/*lìchǎng*" respectively; Then, according to the distributions of the two topics over target-side topical items, we generate target-side topical items "*issue*" and "*stance*"; Finally, according to the translation probability distributions of these two topical items over source-side topical words, we generate source-side topical words "问题/*wèntí*" and "立场/*lìchǎng*" for them respectively.

Step 3: For the contextual word "中立/*zhōnglì*", we first collect target-side topical items of its neighboring topical words such as "问题/*wèntí*", "保持/*bǎochí*" and "立场/*lìchǎng*" to form a target-side topical item set {"*issue*","*keep*", "*stance*"}, from which we randomly sample one item "*stance*". Next, according to the generation probability distribution of "*stance*" over source contextual words, we finally generate the source contextual word "中立/*zhōnglì*".

In the above generative process, all target-side topical items are generated from the underlying topics of a source document, which guarantees that selected target translations are topic-consistent. Additionally, each source contextual word is derived from a target-side topical item given its generation probability distribution. This makes selected target translations also compatible with source-side local contextual words. In this way, global topics, topical words, local contextual words and target-side topical items are highly correlated in CATM that exactly captures such correlations for lexical selection.

3 Parameter Estimation and Inference

We propose a Gibbs sampling algorithm to learn various distributions described in the previous section. Details of the learning and inference process are presented in this section.

3.1 The Probability of Training Corpus

According to CATM, the total probability of training data $\boldsymbol{D}$ given hyperparameters α, β, γ and δ is computed as follows:

$$\begin{aligned} P(\boldsymbol{D};\alpha,\beta,\gamma,\delta) &= \prod_d P(\boldsymbol{f}_d,\boldsymbol{c}_d;\alpha,\beta,\gamma,\delta) \\ &= \prod_d \sum_{\tilde{\boldsymbol{e}}_d} P(\tilde{\boldsymbol{e}}_d|\alpha,\beta)P(\boldsymbol{f}_d|\tilde{\boldsymbol{e}}_d,\gamma)P(\boldsymbol{c}_d|\tilde{\boldsymbol{e}}_d,\delta) \\ &= \int_\phi P(\phi|\beta)\int_\psi P(\psi|\gamma)\prod_d \sum_{\tilde{\boldsymbol{e}}_d} P(\boldsymbol{f}_d|\tilde{\boldsymbol{e}}_d,\psi) \\ &\times \int_\xi P(\xi|\delta)\sum_{\tilde{\boldsymbol{e}}'_d} P(\tilde{\boldsymbol{e}}'_d|\tilde{\boldsymbol{e}}_d)p(\boldsymbol{c}_d|\tilde{\boldsymbol{e}}'_d,\xi) \\ &\times \int_\theta P(\theta|\alpha)P(\tilde{\boldsymbol{e}}_d|\theta,\phi)d\theta d\xi d\psi d\phi \end{aligned} \quad (1)$$

where $\boldsymbol{f}_d$ and $\tilde{\boldsymbol{e}}_d$ denote the sets of topical words and their target-side topical item assignments in document d, $\boldsymbol{c}_d$ and $\tilde{\boldsymbol{e}}'_d$ are the sets of contextual words and their target-side topical item assignments in document d.

3.2 Parameter Estimation via Gibbs Sampling

The joint distribution in Eq. (1) is intractable to compute because of coupled hyperparameters and hidden variables. Following Han et al, (2012), we adapt the well-known Gibbs sampling algorithm (Griffiths and Steyvers, 2004) to our model. We compute the joint posterior distribution of hidden variables, denoted by $P(\boldsymbol{z},\tilde{\boldsymbol{e}},\tilde{\boldsymbol{e}}'|\boldsymbol{D})$, and then use this distribution to 1) estimate θ, ϕ, ψ and ξ, and 2) predict translations and topics of all documents in $\boldsymbol{D}$.

Specifically, we derive the joint posterior distribution from Eq. (1) as:

$$P(\boldsymbol{z},\tilde{\boldsymbol{e}},\tilde{\boldsymbol{e}}'|\boldsymbol{D}) \propto P(\boldsymbol{z})P(\tilde{\boldsymbol{e}}|\boldsymbol{z})P(\boldsymbol{f}|\tilde{\boldsymbol{e}})P(\tilde{\boldsymbol{e}}'|\tilde{\boldsymbol{e}})P(\boldsymbol{c}|\tilde{\boldsymbol{e}}') \quad (2)$$

Based on the equation above, we construct a Markov chain that converges to $P(\boldsymbol{z},\tilde{\boldsymbol{e}},\tilde{\boldsymbol{e}}'|\boldsymbol{D})$, where each state is an assignment of a hidden variable (including topic assignment to a topical word, target-side topical item assignment to a source topical or contextual word.). Then, we sequentially sample each assignment according to the following three conditional assignment distributions:

1. $P(z_i = z|\boldsymbol{z}_{-i},\tilde{\boldsymbol{e}},\tilde{\boldsymbol{e}}',\boldsymbol{D})$: topic assignment distribution of a topical word given $\boldsymbol{z}_{-i}$ that denotes all topic assignments but z_i, $\tilde{\boldsymbol{e}}$ and $\tilde{\boldsymbol{e}}'$ that are target-side topical item assignments. It is updated as follows:

$$P(z_i = z|\boldsymbol{z}_{-i},\tilde{\boldsymbol{e}},\tilde{\boldsymbol{e}}',\boldsymbol{D}) \propto \frac{C^{DZ}_{(-i)dz}+\alpha}{C^{DZ}_{(-i)d*}+N_z\alpha} \times \frac{C^{Z\tilde{E}}_{(-i)z\tilde{e}}+\beta}{C^{Z\tilde{E}}_{(-i)z*}+N_{\tilde{e}}\beta} \quad (3)$$

where the topic assignment to a topical word is determined by the probability that this topic appears in document d (the 1st term) and the probability that the selected item $\tilde{e}$ occurs in this topic (the 2nd term).

2. $P(\tilde{e}_i = \tilde{e}|\boldsymbol{z},\tilde{\boldsymbol{e}}_{-i},\tilde{\boldsymbol{e}}',\boldsymbol{D})$: target-side topical item assignment distribution of a source topical word given the current topic assignments $\boldsymbol{z}$, the current item assignments of all other topical words $\tilde{\boldsymbol{e}}_{-i}$, and the current item assignments of contextual words $\tilde{\boldsymbol{e}}'$. It is updated as follows:

$$\begin{aligned} P(\tilde{e}_i = \tilde{e}|\boldsymbol{z},\tilde{\boldsymbol{e}}_{-i},\tilde{\boldsymbol{e}}',\boldsymbol{D}) &\propto \frac{C^{Z\tilde{E}}_{(-i)z\tilde{e}}+\beta}{C^{Z\tilde{E}}_{(-i)z*}+N_{\tilde{e}}\beta} \\ \times \frac{C^{\tilde{E}F}_{(-i)\tilde{e}f}+\gamma}{C^{\tilde{E}F}_{(-i)\tilde{e}*}+N_f\gamma} &\times \left(\frac{C^{W\tilde{E}}_{(-i)w\tilde{e}}+1}{C^{W\tilde{E}}_{(-i)w\tilde{e}}}\right)^{C^{W\tilde{E}'}_{w\tilde{e}}} \end{aligned} \quad (4)$$

where the target-side topical item assignment to a topical word is determined by the probability that this item is from the topic z (the 1st term), the probability that this item is translated into the topical word f (the 2nd term) and the probability of contextual words within a w_s word window centered at the topical word f, which influence the selection of the target-side topical item $\tilde{e}$ (the 3rd term). It is very important to note that we use a parallel corpus to train the model. Therefore we directly identify target-side topical items for source topical words via word alignments rather than sampling.

3. $P(\tilde{e}'_i = \tilde{e}|\boldsymbol{z}, \tilde{\boldsymbol{e}}, \tilde{\boldsymbol{e}}'_{-i}, \boldsymbol{D})$: target-side topical item assignment distribution for a contextual word given the current topic assignments $\boldsymbol{z}$, the current item assignments of topical words $\tilde{\boldsymbol{e}}$, and the current item assignments of all other contextual words $\tilde{\boldsymbol{e}}'_{-i}$. It is updated as follows:

$$P(\tilde{e}'_i = \tilde{e}|\boldsymbol{z}, \tilde{\boldsymbol{e}}, \tilde{\boldsymbol{e}}'_{-i}, \boldsymbol{D}) \propto \frac{C^{W\tilde{E}}_{w\tilde{e}}}{C^{W\tilde{E}}_{w*}} \times \frac{C^{\tilde{E}C}_{(-i)\tilde{e}c} + \delta}{C^{\tilde{E}C}_{(-i)\tilde{e}*} + N_c\,\delta} \quad (5)$$

where the target-side topical item assignment used to generate a contextual word is determined by the probability of this item being assigned to generate contextual words within a surface window of size w_s (the 1st term) and the probability that contextual words occur in the context of this item (the 2nd term).

In all above formulas, C^{DZ}_{dz} is the number of times that topic z has been assigned for all topical words in document d, $C^{DZ}_{d*}=\sum_z C^{DZ}_{dz}$ is the topic number in document d, and $C^{Z\tilde{E}}_{z\tilde{e}}$, $C^{\tilde{E}F}_{\tilde{e}f}$, $C^{W\tilde{E}}_{w\tilde{e}}$, $C^{W\tilde{E}'}_{w\tilde{e}}$ and $C^{\tilde{E}C}_{\tilde{e}c}$ have similar explanations. Based on the above marginal distributions, we iteratively update all assignments of corpus $\boldsymbol{D}$ until the constructed Markov chain converges. Model parameters are estimated using these final assignments.

3.3 Inference on Unseen Documents

For a new document, we first predict its topics and target-side topical items using the incremental Gibbs sampling algorithm described in (Kataria et al., 2011). In this algorithm, we iteratively update topic assignments and translation assignments of an unseen document following the same process described in Section 3.2, but with estimated model parameters.

Once we obtain these assignments, we estimate lexical translation probabilities based on the sampled counts of target-side topical items. Formally, for the position i in the document corresponding to the content word f, we collect the sampled count that translation $\tilde{e}$ generates f, denoted by $C_{sam}(\tilde{e}, f)$. This count can be normalized to form a new translation probability in the following way:

$$p(\tilde{e}|f) = \frac{C_{sam}(\tilde{e}, f) + k}{C_{sam} + k \cdot N_{\tilde{e},f}} \quad (6)$$

where C_{sam} is the total number of samples during inference and $N_{\tilde{e},f}$ is the number of candidate translations of f. Here we apply *add-k* smoothing to refine this translation probability, where k is a tunable global smoothing constant. Under the framework of log-linear model (Och and Ney, 2002), we use this translation probability as a new feature to improve lexical selection in SMT.

4 Experiments

In order to examine the effectiveness of our model, we carried out several groups of experiments on Chinese-to-English translation.

4.1 Setup

Our bilingual training corpus is from the FBIS corpus and the Hansards part of LDC2004T07 corpus ($1M$ parallel sentences, $54.6K$ documents, with $25.2M$ Chinese words and $29M$ English words). We first used *ZPar* toolkit[2] and Stanford toolkit[3] to preprocess (i.e., word segmenting, PoS tagging) the Chinese and English parts of training corpus, and then word-aligned them using *GIZA++* (Och and Ney, 2003) with the option "*grow-diag-final-and*". We chose the NIST evaluation set of MT05 as the development set, and the sets of MT06/MT08 as test sets. On average, these three sets contain 17.2, 13.9 and 14.1 content words per sentence, respectively. We trained a 5-gram language model on the Xinhua portion of Gigaword corpus using the *SRILM* Toolkit (Stolcke, 2002).

Our baseline system is a state-of-the-art SMT system, which adapts bracketing transduction grammars (Wu, 1997) to phrasal translation and equips itself with a maximum entropy based reordering model (MEBTG) (Xiong et al., 2006). We used the toolkit[4] developed by Zhang (2004) to train the reordering model with the following parameters: iteration number $iter$=200 and Gaussian prior g=1.0. During decoding, we set the *ttable-limit* as 20, the *stack-size* as 100. The translation quality is evaluated by case-insensitive BLEU-4 (Papineni et al., 2002) metric. Finally, we conducted *paired bootstrap sampling* (Koehn, 2004) to test the significance in BLEU score differences.

[2] http://people.sutd.edu.sg/~yue_zhang/doc/index.html
[3] http://nlp.stanford.edu/software
[4] http://homepages.inf.ed.ac.uk/lzhang10/maxenttoolkit.html

Model	MT05
CATM (± 6w)	33.35
CATM (± 8w)	33.43
CATM (± 10w)	33.42
CATM (± 12w)	33.49
CATM (± 14w)	33.30

Table 2: Experiment results on the development set using different window sizes w_s.

To train CATM, we set the topic number N_z as 25.[5] For hyperparameters α and β, we empirically set α=$50/N_z$ and β=0.1, as implemented in (Griffiths and Steyvers, 2004). Following Han et al. (2012), we set γ and δ as $1.0/N_f$ and $2000/N_c$, respectively. During the training process, we ran 400 iterations of the Gibbs sampling algorithm. For documents to be translated, we first ran 300 rounds in a *burn-in* step to let the probability distributions converge, and then ran 1500 rounds where we collected independent samples every 5 rounds. The longest training time of CATM is less than four days on our server using 4GB RAM and one core of 3.2GHz CPU. As for the smoothing constant k in Eq. (6), we set its values to 0.5 according to the performance on the development set in additional experiments.

4.2 Impact of Window Size w_s

Our first group of experiments were conducted on the development set to investigate the impact of the window size w_s. We gradually varied window size from 6 to 14 with an increment of 2.

Experiment results are shown in Table 2. We achieve the best performance when w_s=12. This suggests that a ±12-word window context is sufficient for predicting target-side translations for ambiguous source-side topical words. We therefore set w_s=12 for all experiments thereafter.

4.3 Overall Performance

In the second group of experiments, in addition to the conventional MEBTG system, we also compared CATM with the following two models:

Word Sense Disambiguation Model (**WSDM**) (Chan et al., 2007). This model improves lexical selection in SMT by exploiting local contexts. For each content word, we construct a MaxEnt-based classifier incorporating local collocation and surrounding word features, which are also adopted by Chan et al. (2007). For each candidate translation $\tilde{e}$ of topical word f, we use WSDM to estimate the context-specific translation probability $P(\tilde{e}|f)$, which is used as a new feature in SMT system.

Topic-specific Lexicon Translation Model (**TLTM**) (Zhao and Xing, 2007). This model focuses on the utilization of document-level context. We adapted it to estimate a lexicon translation probability as follows:

$$\begin{aligned} p(f|\tilde{e},d) &\propto p(\tilde{e}|f,d)\cdot p(f|d) \\ &= \sum_z p(\tilde{e}|f,z)\cdot p(f|z)\cdot p(z|d) \end{aligned} \quad (7)$$

where $p(\tilde{e}|f,z)$ is the lexical translation probability conditioned on topic z, which can be calculated according to the principle of maximal likelihood, $p(f|z)$ is the generation probability of word f from topic z, and $p(z|d)$ denotes the posterior topic distribution of document d.

Note that our CATM is proposed for lexical selection on content words. To show the strong effectiveness of our model, we also compared it against the full-fledged variants of the above-mentioned two models that are built for all source words. We refer to them as **WSDM (All)** and **TLTM (All)**, respectively.

Table 3 displays BLEU scores of different lexical selection models. All models outperform the baseline. Although we only use CATM to predict translations for content words, CATM achieves an average BLEU score of **26.77** on the two test sets, which is higher than that of the baseline by **1.18** BLEU points. This improvement is statistically significant at p<0.01. Furthermore, we also find that our model performs better than WSDM and TLTM with significant improvements. Finally, even if WSDM (All) and TLTM (all) are built for all source words, they are still no better than than CATM that selects desirable translations for content words. These experiment results strongly demonstrate the advantage of CATM over previous lexical selection models.

5 Analysis

In order to investigate why CATM is able to outperform previous models that explore only local contex-

[5]We try different topic numbers from 25 to 100 with an increment of 25 each time. We find that N_z=25 produces a slightly better performance than other values on the development set.

Model	Local Context	Global Topic	MT06	MT08	Avg
Baseline	×	×	$29.66^{\downarrow\downarrow}$	$21.52^{\downarrow\downarrow}$	25.59
WSDM	√	×	$30.62^{\downarrow}$	$22.05^{\downarrow\downarrow}$	26.34
WSDM (All)	√	×	30.92	22.27	26.60
TLTM	×	√	$30.27^{\downarrow\downarrow}$	$21.70^{\downarrow\downarrow}$	25.99
TLTM (All)	×	√	$30.33^{\downarrow\downarrow}$	$21.58^{\downarrow\downarrow}$	25.96
CATM	√	√	**30.97**	**22.56**	**26.77**

Table 3: Experiment results on the test sets. **Avg** = average BLEU scores. **WSDM (All)** and **TLTM (All)** are models built for all source words. ↓: significantly worse than CATM (p<0.05), ↓↓: significantly worse than CATM (p<0.01)

.

tual words or global topics, we take a deep look into topics, topical items and contextual words learned by CATM and empirically analyze the effect of modeling correlations between local contextual words and global topics on lexical selection.

5.1 Outputs of CATM

We present some examples of topics learned by CATM in Table 4. We also list five target-side topical items with the highest probabilities for each topic, and the most probable five contextual words for each target-side topical item. These examples clearly show that target-side topical items tightly connect global topics and local contextual words by capturing their correlations.

5.2 Effect of Correlation Modeling

Compared to previous lexical selection models, CATM jointly models both local contextual words and global topics. Such a joint modeling also enables CATM to capture their inner correlations at the model level. In order to examine the effect of correlation modeling on lexical selection, we compared CATM with its three variants: ① **CATM (Context)** that only uses local context information. We determined target-side topical items for content words in this variant by setting the probability distribution that a topic generates a target-side topical item to be uniform; ② **CATM (Topic)** that explores only global topic information. We identified target-side topical items for content words in the model by setting w_s as 0, i.e., no local contextual words being used at all. ③ **CATM (Log-linear)** is the combination of the above-mentioned two variants (① and ②) in a log-linear manner, which does not capture correlations between local contextual words and global topics at the model level.

Model	MT06	MT08	Avg
CATM (Context)	$30.46^{\downarrow\downarrow}$	$22.02^{\downarrow\downarrow}$	26.24
CATM (Topic)	$30.20^{\downarrow\downarrow}$	$21.90^{\downarrow\downarrow}$	26.05
CATM (Log-linear)	$30.59^{\downarrow}$	$22.24^{\downarrow}$	26.42
CATM	**30.97**	**22.56**	**26.77**

Table 5: Experiment results on the test sets. CATM (Log-linear) is the combination of CATM (Context) and CATM (Topic) in a log-linear manner.

Results in Table 5 show that CATM performs significantlly better than both CATM (Topic) and CATM (Context). Even compared with CATM (Log-linear), CATM still achieves a significant improvement of 0.35 BLEU points (p<0.05). This validates the effectiveness of capturing correlations for lexical selection at the model level.

6 Related Work

Our work is partially inspired by (Han and Sun, 2012), where an entity-topic model is presented for entity linking. We successfully adapt this work to lexical selection in SMT. The related work mainly includes the following two strands.

(1) *Lexical Selection in SMT*. In order to explore rich context information for lexical selection, some researchers propose *trigger-based lexicon models* to capture long-distance dependencies (Hasan et al., 2008; Mauser et al., 2009), and many more researchers build classifiers to select desirable translations during decoding (Chan et al., 2007; Carpuat and Wu, 2007; He et al., 2008; Liu et al., 2008). Along this line, Shen et al. (2009) introduce four new linguistic and contextual features for translation selection in SMT. Recently, we have witnessed an increasing efforts in exploiting document-level context information to improve lexical selection. Xiao et al. (2011) impose a hard constraint to guarantee

Topic	***Target-side Topical Items***	***Source-side Contextual Words***
refugee	*UNHCR*	难民(refugee) 办事处(office) 专员(commissioner) 事务(affair) 高级(high-level)
	republic	联盟(union) 民主(democracy) 政府(government) 伊斯兰(Islam) 中非(Central Africa)
	refugee	难民(refugee) 返回(return) 流离失所(displaced) 遣返(repatriate) 保护(protect)
	Kosovo	梅托希亚(Metohija) 境内(territory) 危机(crisis) 局势(situation) 塞尔维亚(Serbia)
	federal	共和国(republic) 南斯拉夫(Yugoslavia) 科索沃(Kosovo) 政府(government) 当局(authority)
military	*military*	观察员(observer) 行动(action) 美国(USA) 人员(personnel) 部队(army)
	missile	防御(defense) 系统(system) 美国(USA) 发射(launch) 枚(*)
	United States	中国(China) 日本(Japan) 台湾(Taiwan) 军事(military) NMD(National Missile Defense)
	system	联合国(United Nations) 建立(build) 国(country) 国家(country) 信息(information)
	war	战争(war) 场(∗) 世界(world) 发动(wage) 海湾(gulf)
economy	*country*	发展中(developing) 发达(developed) 非洲(Africa) 发展(development) 中(China)
	development	可持续(sustainable) 经济(economy) 促进(promote) 社会(society) 事态(situation)
	international	社会(society) 组织(organization) 合作(coorporation) 国家(country) 联合国(United Nations)
	economic	社会(society) 发展(development) 增长(growth) 国家(country) 全球化(globalization)
	trade	发展(development) 国际(international) 世界(world) 投资(investment) 点(point)
cross-strait relation	*Taiwan*	中国(China) 大陆(mainland) 当局(authority) 美国(USA) 同胞(compatriot)
	China	说(say) 美国(USA) 台湾(Taiwan) 原则(principle) 两(*)
	relation	发展(development) 岸(*) 中(China) 两(*) 国(country)
	cross-strait	两(*) 关系(relation) 台湾(Taiwan) 岸(*) 交流(exchange)
	issue	解决(settlement) 讨论(discuss) 问题(issue) 重要(important) 台湾(Taiwan)

Table 4: Examples of topics, topical items and contextual words learned by CATM with N_z=25 and W_s=12. Chinese words that do not have direct English translations are denoted with "*". Here "枚" and "场" are Chinese quantifiers for *missile* and *war*, respectively; "两" and "岸" together means *cross-starit*.

the document-level translation consistency. Ture et al. (2012) soften this consistency constraint by integrating three counting features into decoder. Also relevant is the work of Xiong et al.(2013), who use three different models to capture lexical cohesion for document-level SMT.

(2) *SMT with Topic Models*. In this strand, Zhao and Xing (2006, 2007) first present a bilingual topical admixture formalism for word alignment in SMT. Tam et al. (2007) and Ruiz et al. (2012) apply topic model into language model adaptation. Su et al. (2012) conduct translation model adaptation with monolingual topic information. Gong et al. (2010) and Xiao et al. (2012) introduce topic-based similarity models to improve SMT system. Axelrod et al. (2012) build topic-specific translation models from the TED corpus and select topic-relevant data from the UN corpus to improve coverage. Eidelman et al. (2012) incorporate topic-specific lexical weights into translation model. Hewavitharana et al. (2013) propose an incremental topic based translation model adaptation approach that satisfies the causality constraint imposed by spoken conversations. Hasler et al. (2014) present a new bilingual variant of LDA to compute topic-adapted, probabilistic phrase translation features. They also use a topic model to learn latent distributional representations of different context levels of a phrase pair (Hasler et al., 2014b).

In the studies mentioned above, those by Zhao and Xing (2006), Zhao and Xing (2007), Hasler et al. (2014a), and Hasler et al. (2014b) are most related to our work. However, they all perform dynamic translation model adaptation with topic models. Significantly different from them, we propose a new topic model that exploits both local contextual words and global topics for lexical selection. To the best of our knowledge, this is first attempt to capture correlations between local words and global topics for better lexical selection at the model level.

7 Conclusion and Future Work

This paper has presented a novel context-aware topic model for lexical selection in SMT. Jointly modeling local contexts, global topics and their correlations in a unified framework, our model provides an effective way to capture context information at different levels for better lexical selection in SMT. Experiment results not only demonstrate the effectiveness of the proposed topic model, but also show that lexical selection benefits from correlation modeling.

In the future, we want to extend our model from the word level to the phrase level. We also plan to improve our model with monolingual corpora.

Acknowledgments

The authors were supported by National Natural Science Foundation of China (Grant Nos 61303082 and 61403269), Natural Science Foundation of Jiangsu Province (Grant No. BK20140355), National 863 program of China (No. 2015AA011808), Research Fund for the Doctoral Program of Higher Education of China (No. 20120121120046), the Special and Major Subject Project of the Industrial Science and Technology in Fujian Province 2013 (Grant No. 2013HZ0004-1), and 2014 Key Project of Anhui Science and Technology Bureau (Grant No. 1301021018). We also thank the anonymous reviewers for their insightful comments.

References

Amittai Axelrod, Xiaodong He, Li Deng, Alex Acero, and Mei-Yuh Hwang. 2012. New methods and evaluation experiments on translating TED talks in the I-WSLT benchmark. In *Proc. of ICASSP 2012*, pages 4945-4648.

Rafael E. Banchs and Marta R. Costa-jussà. 2011. A Semantic Feature for Statistical Machine Translation. In *Proc. of SSSST-5 2011*, pages 126-134.

David M. Blei. 2003. Latent Dirichlet Allocation. *Journal of Machine Learning*, pages 993-1022.

Marine Carpuat and Dekai Wu. 2007. Improving Statistical Machine Translation Using Word Sense Disambiguation. In *Proc. of EMNLP 2007*, pages 61-72.

Yee Seng Chan, Hwee Tou Ng, and David Chiang. 2007. Word Sense Disambiguation Improves Statistical Machine Translation. In *Proc. of ACL 2007*, pages 33-40.

David Chiang. 2007. Hierarchical Phrase-Based Translation. *Computational Linguistics*, pages 201-228.

Jonathan H. Clark, Chris Dyer, Alon Lavie, and Noah A. Smith. 2011. Better Hypothesis Testing for Statistical Machine Translation: Controlling for Optimizer Instability. In *Proc. of ACL 2011, short papers*, pages 176-181.

George Doddington. 2002. Translation Quality Using N-gram Cooccurrence Statistics. In *Proc. of HLT 2002*, 138-145.

Vladimir Eidelman, Jordan Boyd-Graber, and Philip Resnik. 2012. Topic Models for Dynamic Translation Model Adaptation. In *Proc. of ACL 2012, Short Papers*, pages 115-119.

Michel Galley, Jonathan Graehl, Kevin Knight, Daniel Marcu, Steve DeNeefe, Wei Wang, and Ignacio Thayer. 2006. Scalable Inference and Training of Context-Rich Syntactic Translation Models. In *Proc. of ACL 2006*, pages 961-968.

Zhengxian Gong and Guodong Zhou. 2010. Improve SMT with Source-side Topic-Document Distributions. In *Proc. of SUMMIT 2010*.

Thomas L. Griffiths and Mark Steyvers. 2004. Finding Scientific Topics. In *Proc. of the National Academy of Sciences 2004*.

Xianpei Han and Le Sun. 2012. An Entity-Topic Model for Entity Linking. In *Proc. of EMNLP 2012*, pages 105-115.

Saša Hasan, Juri Ganitkevitch, Hermann Ney, and Jesús Andrés-Ferrer 2008. Triplet Lexicon Models for Statistical Machine Translation. In *Proc. of EMNLP 2008*, pages 372-381.

Eva Hasler, Phil Blunsom, Philipp Koehn, and Barry Haddow. 2014. Dynamic Topic Adaptation for Phrase-based MT. In *Proc. of EACL 2014*, pages 328-337.

Eva Hasler, Phil Blunsom, Philipp Koehn, and Barry Haddow. 2014. Dynamic Topic Adaptation for SMT using Distributional Profiles. In *Proc. of WMT 2014*, pages 445-456.

Zhongjun He, Qun Liu, and Shouxun Lin. 2008. Improving Statistical Machine Translation using Lexicalized Rule Selection. In *Proc. of COLING 2008*, pages 321-328.

Sanjika Hewavitharana, Dennis Mehay, Sankaranarayanan Ananthakrishnan, and Prem Natarajan. 2013. Incremental Topic-based TM Adaptation for Conversational SLT. In *Proc. of ACL 2013, Short Papers*, pages 697-701.

Saurabh S. Kataria, Krishnan S. Kumar, and Rajeev Rastogi. 2011. Entity Disambiguation with Hierarchical Topic Models. In *Proc. of KDD 2011*, pages 1037-1045.

Philipp Koehn, Franz Josef Och, and Daniel Marcu. 2003. Statistical Phrase-based Translation. In *Proc. of NAACL-HLT 2003*, pages 127-133.

Philipp Koehn. 2004. Statistical Significance Tests for Machine Translation Evaluation. In *Proc. of EMNLP 2004*, pages 388-395.

Qun Liu, Zhongjun He, Yang Liu, and Shouxun Lin. 2008. Maximum Entropy based Rule Selection Model for Syntax-based Statistical Machine Translation. In *Proc. of EMNLP 2008*, pages 89-97.

Arne Mauser, Saša Hasan, and Hermann Ney. 2009. Extending Statistical Machine Translation with Discriminative and Trigger-based Lexicon Models. In *Proc. of EMNLP 2009*, pages 210-218.

Franz Joseph Och and Hermann Ney. 2002. Discriminative Training and Maximum Entropy Models for Statistical Machine Translation. In *Proc. of ACL 2002*, pages 295-302.

Franz Joseph Och and Hermann Ney. 2003. A Systematic Comparison of Various Statistical Alignment Models. *Computational Linguistics*, 2003(29), pages 19-51.

Franz Josef Och. 2003. Minimum Error Rate Training in Statistical Machine Translation. In *Proc. of ACL 2003*, pages 160-167.

Franz Joseph Och and Hermann Ney. 2004. The Alignment Template Approach to Statistical Machine Translation. *Computational Linguistics*, 2004(30), pages 417-449.

Kishore Papineni, Salim Roukos, Todd Ward, and Wei-Jing Zhu. 2007. BLEU: A Method for Automatic Evaluation of Machine Translation. In *Proc. of ACL 2002*, pages 311-318.

Nick Ruiz and Marcello Federico. 2012. Topic Adaptation for Lecture Translation through Bilingual Latent Semantic Models. In *Proc. of the Sixth Workshop on Statistical Machine Translation*, pages 294-302.

Libin Shen, Jinxi Xu, Bing Zhang, Spyros Matsoukas, and Ralph Weischedel. 2009. Effective Use of Linguistic and Contextual Information for Statistical Machine Translation. In *Proc. of EMNLP 2009*, pages 72-80.

Andreas Stolcke. 2002. Srilm - An Extensible Language Modeling Toolkit. In *Proc. of ICSLP 2002*, pages 901-904.

Jinsong Su, Hua Wu, Haifeng Wang, Yidong Chen, Xiaodong Shi, Huailin Dong, and Qun Liu. 2012. Translation Model Adaptation for Statistical Machine Translation with Monolingual Topic Information. In *Proc. of ACL 2012*, pages 459-468.

Yik-Cheung Tam, Ian R. Lane, and Tanja Schultz. 2007. Bilingual LSA-based adaptation for statistical machine translation. *Machine Translation*, 21(4), pages 187-207.

Ferhan Ture, DouglasW. Oard, and Philip Resnik. 2012. Encouraging Consistent Translation Choices. In *Proc. of NAACL-HLT 2012*, pages 417-426.

Dekai Wu. 1997. Stochastic inversion transduction grammars and bilingual parsing of parallel corpora. *Computational Linguistics*, 23(3):377-403.

Tong Xiao, Jingbo Zhu, Shujie Yao, and Hao Zhang. 2011. Document-level Consistency Verification in Machine Translation. In *Proc. of MT SUMMIT 2011*, pages 131-138.

Xinyan Xiao, Deyi Xiong, Min Zhang, Qun Liu, and Shouxun Lin. 2012. A Topic Similarity Model for Hierarchical Phrase-based Translation. In *Proc. of ACL 2012*, pages 750-758.

Deyi Xiong, Qun Liu, and Shouxun Lin. 2006. Maximum Entropy Based Phrase Reordering Model for Statistical Machine Translation. In *Proc. of ACL 2006*, pages 521-528.

Deyi Xiong, Guosheng Ben, Min Zhang, Yajuan Lü, and Qun Liu. 2013. Modeling Lexical Cohesion for Document-Level Machine Translation. In *Proc. of IJCAI 2013*, pages 2183-2189.

Deyi Xiong and Min Zhang. 2014. A Sense-Based Translation Model for Statistical Machine Translation. In *Proc. of ACL 2014*, pages 1459-1469.

Bing Zhao and Eric P.Xing. 2006. BiTAM: Bilingual Topic AdMixture Models for Word Alignment. In *Proc. of ACL/COLING 2006*, pages 969-976.

Bing Zhao and Eric P.Xing. 2007. HM-BiTAM: Bilingual Topic Exploration, Word Alignment, and Translation. In *Proc. of NIPS 2007*, pages 1-8.

Learning Answer-Entailing Structures for Machine Comprehension

Mrinmaya Sachan[1*] **Avinava Dubey**[1*] **Eric P. Xing**[1]
[1]Carnegie Mellon University
[1]{mrinmays, akdubey, epxing}@cs.cmu.edu

Matthew Richardson[2]
[2]Microsoft Research
[2]mattri@microsoft.com

Abstract

Understanding open-domain text is one of the primary challenges in NLP. Machine comprehension evaluates the system's ability to understand text through a series of question-answering tasks on short pieces of text such that the correct answer can be found only in the given text. For this task, we posit that there is a hidden (latent) structure that explains the relation between the question, correct answer, and text. We call this the *answer-entailing structure*; given the structure, the correctness of the answer is evident. Since the structure is latent, it must be inferred. We present a unified max-margin framework that learns to find these hidden structures (given a corpus of question-answer pairs), and uses what it learns to answer machine comprehension questions on novel texts. We extend this framework to incorporate multi-task learning on the different subtasks that are required to perform machine comprehension. Evaluation on a publicly available dataset shows that our framework outperforms various IR and neural-network baselines, achieving an overall accuracy of 67.8% (vs. 59.9%, the best previously-published result.)

1 Introduction

Developing an ability to understand natural language is a long-standing goal in NLP and holds the promise of revolutionizing the way in which people interact with machines and retrieve information (e.g., for scientific endeavor). To evaluate this ability, Richardson et al. (2013) proposed the task of machine comprehension (MCTest), along with a dataset for evaluation. Machine comprehension evaluates a machine's understanding by posing a series of reading comprehension questions and associated texts, where the answer to each question can be found only in its associated text. Solutions typically focus on some semantic interpretation of the text, possibly with some form of probabilistic or logical inference, in order to answer the questions. Despite significant recent interest (Burges, 2013; Weston et al., 2014; Weston et al., 2015), the problem remains unsolved.

In this paper, we propose an approach for machine comprehension. Our approach learns latent *answer-entailing structures* that can help us answer questions about a text. The answer-entailing structures in our model are closely related to the inference procedure often used in various models for MT (Blunsom and Cohn, 2006), RTE (MacCartney et al., 2008), paraphrase (Yao et al., 2013b), QA (Yih et al., 2013), etc. and correspond to the best (latent) alignment between a hypothesis (formed from the question and a candidate answer) with appropriate snippets in the text that are required to answer the question. An example of such an answer-entailing structure is given in Figure 1. The key difference between the answer-entailing structures considered here and the alignment structures considered in previous works is that we can align multiple sentences in the text to the hypothesis. The sentences in the text considered for alignment are not restricted to occur contiguously in the text. To allow such a discontiguous alignment, we make use of the document structure; in particular, we take help from rhetorical structure theory (Mann and Thompson, 1988) and event and entity coreference links across sentences. Modelling the inference procedure via answer-entailing structures is a crude yet effective and computationally inexpensive proxy to model the semantics needed for the problem. Learning these latent structures can also be bene-

*Work started while the first two authors were interns at Microsoft Research, Redmond.

Proceedings of the 53rd Annual Meeting of the Association for Computational Linguistics and the 7th International Joint Conference on Natural Language Processing, pages 239–249,
Beijing, China, July 26-31, 2015.

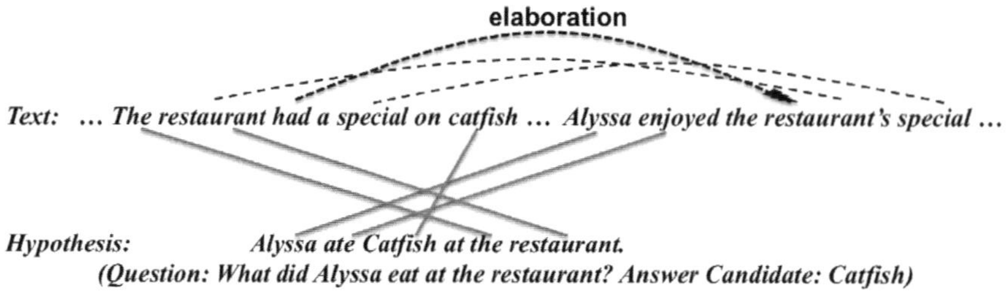

Figure 1: The *answer-entailing structure* for an example from MCTest500 dataset. The question and answer candidate are combined to generate a hypothesis sentence. Then latent alignments are found between the hypothesis and the appropriate snippets in the text. The solid red lines show the word alignments from the hypothesis words to the passage words, the dashed black lines show auxiliary co-reference links in the text and the labelled dotted black arrows show the RST relation (elaboration) between the two sentences. Note that the two sentences do not have to be contiguous sentences in the text. We provide some more examples of *answer-entailing structures* in the supplementary.

ficial as they can assist a human in verifying the correctness of the answer, eliminating the need to read a lengthy document.

The overall model is trained in a max-margin fashion using a latent structural SVM (LSSVM) where the answer-entailing structures are latent. We also extend our LSSVM to multi-task settings using a top-level question-type classification. Many QA systems include a question classification component (Li and Roth, 2002; Zhang and Lee, 2003), which typically divides the questions into semantic categories based on the type of the question or answers expected. This helps the system impose some constraints on the plausible answers. Machine comprehension can benefit from such a pre-classification step, not only to constrain plausible answers, but also to allow the system to use different processing strategies for each category. Recently, Weston et al. (2015) defined a set of 20 sub-tasks in the machine comprehension setting, each referring to a specific aspect of language understanding and reasoning required to build a machine comprehension system. They include fact chaining, negation, temporal and spatial reasoning, simple induction, deduction and many more. We use this set to learn to classify questions into the various machine comprehension subtasks, and show that this task classification further improves our performance on MCTest. By using the multi-task setting, our learner is able to exploit the commonality among tasks where possible, while having the flexibility to learn task-specific parameters where needed. To the best of our knowledge, this is the first use of multi-task learning in a structured prediction model for QA.

We provide experimental validation for our model on a real-world dataset (Richardson et al., 2013) and achieve superior performance vs. a number of IR and neural network baselines.

2 The Problem

Machine comprehension requires us to answer questions based on unstructured text. We treat this as selecting the best answer from a set of candidate answers. The candidate answers may be pre-defined, as is the case in multiple-choice question answering, or may be undefined but restricted (e.g., to yes, no, or any noun phrase in the text).

Machine Comprehension as Textual Entailment: Let for each question $q_i \in Q$, $\mathbf{t}_i$ be the unstructured text and $A_i = \{a_{i1}, \ldots, a_{im}\}$ be the set of candidate answers to the question. We cast the machine comprehension task as a textual entailment task by converting each question-answer candidate pair $(q_i, a_{i,j})$ into a hypothesis statement h_{ij}. For example, the question "What did Alyssa eat at the restaurant?" and answer candidate "Catfish" in Figure 1 can be combined to achieve a hypothesis "Alyssa ate Catfish at the restaurant". We use the question matching/rewriting rules described in Cucerzan and Agichtein (2005) to achieve this transformation. For each question q_i, the machine comprehension task reduces to picking the hypothesis $\hat{h}_i$ that has the highest likelihood of being entailed by the text among the set of hypotheses $\mathbf{h}_i = \{h_{i1}, \ldots, h_{im}\}$ generated for that question. Let $h_i^* \in \mathbf{h}_i$ be the correct hypothesis. Now let us define the latent answer-entailing structures.

3 Latent Answer-Entailing Structures

The latent answer-entailing structures help the model in providing evidence for the correct hypothesis. We consider the quality of a one-to-one word alignment from a hypothesis to snippets in the text as a proxy for the evidence. Hypothesis words are aligned to a unique text word in the text or an empty word. For example, in Figure 1, all words but "at" are aligned to a word in the text. The word "at" can be assumed to be aligned to an empty word and it has no effect on the model. Learning these alignment edges typically helps a model decompose the input and output structures into semantic constituents and determine which constituents should be compared to each other. These alignments can then be used to generate more effective features.

The alignment depends on two things: (a) snippets in the text to be aligned to the hypothesis and (b) word alignment from the hypothesis to the snippets. We explore three variants of the snippets in the text to be aligned to the hypothesis. The choice of these snippets composed with the word alignment is the resulting hidden structure called an answer-entailing structure.

1. Sentence Alignment: The simplest variant is to find a single sentence in the text that best aligns to the hypothesis. This is the structure considered in a majority of previous works in RTE (MacCartney et al., 2008) and QA (Yih et al., 2013) as they only reason on single sentence length texts.

2. Subset Alignment: Here we find a subset of sentences from the text (instead of just one sentence) that best aligns with the hypothesis.

3. Subset+ Alignment: This is the same as above except that the best subset is an ordered set.

4 Method

A natural solution is to treat MCTest as a structured prediction problem of ranking the hypotheses $\mathbf{h}_i$ such that the correct hypothesis is at the top of this ranking. This induces a constraint on the ranking structure that the correct hypothesis is ranked above the other competing hypotheses. For each text $\mathbf{t}_i$ and hypotheses set $\mathbf{h}_i$, let $\mathcal{Y}_i$ be the set of possible orderings of the hypotheses. Let $\mathbf{y}_i^* \in \mathcal{Y}_i$ be a correct ranking (such that the correct hypothesis is at the top of this ranking). Let the set of possible answer-entailing structures for each text hypothesis pair $(\mathbf{t}_i, \mathbf{h}_i)$ be denoted by $\mathcal{Z}_i$. For each text $\mathbf{t}_i$, with hypotheses set $\mathbf{h}_i$, an ordering of the hypotheses $\mathbf{y} \in \mathcal{Y}_i$, and hidden structure $\mathbf{z} \in \mathcal{Z}_i$, we define a scoring function $Score_{\mathbf{w}}(\mathbf{t}_i, \mathbf{h}_i, \mathbf{z}, \mathbf{y})$ parameterized by a weight vector $\mathbf{w}$ such that we have the prediction rule: $(\widehat{\mathbf{y}}_i, \widehat{\mathbf{z}}_i) = \arg\max_{\mathbf{y}\in\mathcal{Y}_i, \mathbf{z}\in\mathcal{Z}_i} Score_{\mathbf{w}}(\mathbf{t}_i, \mathbf{h}_i, \mathbf{z}, \mathbf{y})$. The learning task is to find $\mathbf{w}$ such that the predicted ordering $\widehat{\mathbf{y}}_i$ is close to the optimal ordering $\mathbf{y}_i^*$. Mathematically this can be written as $\min_{\mathbf{w}} \frac{1}{2}\|\mathbf{w}\|^2 + C\sum_i \Delta(\mathbf{y}_i^*, \mathbf{z}_i^*, \widehat{\mathbf{y}}_i, \widehat{\mathbf{z}}_i)$ where $\mathbf{z}_i^* = \arg\max_{\mathbf{z}\in\mathcal{Z}_i} Score_{\mathbf{w}}(\mathbf{t}_i, \mathbf{h}_i, \mathbf{z}, \mathbf{y}_i^*)$ and Δ is the loss function between the predicted and the actual ranking and latent structure. We simplify the loss function and assume it to be independent of the hidden structure $(\Delta(\mathbf{y}_i^*, \mathbf{z}_i^*, \widehat{\mathbf{y}}_i, \widehat{\mathbf{z}}_i) = \Delta(\mathbf{y}_i^*, \widehat{\mathbf{y}}_i))$ and use a linear scoring function: $Score_{\mathbf{w}}(\mathbf{t}_i, \mathbf{h}_i, \mathbf{z}, \mathbf{y}) = \mathbf{w}^T\phi(\mathbf{t}_i, \mathbf{h}_i, \mathbf{z}, \mathbf{y})$ where ϕ is a feature map dependent on the text $\mathbf{t}_i$, the hypothesis set $\mathbf{h}_i$, an ordering of answers $\mathbf{y}$ and a hidden structure $\mathbf{z}$. We use a convex upper bound of the loss function (Yu and Joachims, 2009) to rewrite the objective:

$$\min_{\mathbf{w}} \frac{1}{2}\|\mathbf{w}\|^2 - C\sum_i \mathbf{w}^T\phi(\mathbf{t}_i, \mathbf{h}_i, \mathbf{z}_i^*, \mathbf{y}_i^*) \qquad (1)$$
$$+C\sum_{i=1}^{n} \max_{\mathbf{y}\in\mathcal{Y}_i, \mathbf{z}\in\mathcal{Z}_i} \{\mathbf{w}^T\phi(\mathbf{t}_i, \mathbf{h}_i, \mathbf{z}, \mathbf{y}) + \Delta(\mathbf{y}_i^*, \mathbf{y})\}$$

This problem can be solved using Concave-Convex Programming (Yuille and Rangarajan, 2003) with the cutting plane algorithm for structural SVM (Finley and Joachims, 2008). We use phi partial order (Joachims, 2006; Dubey et al., 2009) which has been used in previous structural ranking literature to incorporate ranking structure in the feature vector ϕ:

$$\phi(\mathbf{t}_i, \mathbf{h}_i, \mathbf{z}, \mathbf{y}) = \sum_{j:h_{ij}\neq h_i^*} c_j(\mathbf{y})(\psi(\mathbf{t}_i, h_i^*, z_i^*) - \psi(\mathbf{t}_i, h_{ij}, z_j)) \quad (2)$$

where, $c_j(\mathbf{y}) = 1$ if h_i^* is above $\mathbf{h}_{ij}$ in the ranking $\mathbf{y}$ else -1. We use pair preference (Chakrabarti et al., 2008) as the ranking loss $\Delta(\mathbf{y}_i^*, \mathbf{y})$. Here, ψ is the feature vector defined for a text, hypothesis and answer-entailing structure.

Solution: We substitute the feature map definition (2) into Equation 1, leading to our LSSVM formulation. We consider the optimization as an alternating minimization problem where we alternate between getting the best z_{ij} and ψ for each text-hypothesis pair given $\mathbf{w}$ (inference) and then solving for the weights $\mathbf{w}$ given ψ to obtain an optimal ordering of the hypothesis (learning). The step for solving for the weights is similar to rankSVM

(Joachims, 2002). Algorithm 1 describes our overall procedure Here, we use beam search for infer-

Algorithm 1 Alternate Minimization for LSSVM

1: Initialize $\mathbf{w}$
2: **repeat**
3: $z_{ij} = \arg\max_z \mathbf{w}^T \psi(\mathbf{t}_i, h_{ij}, z)\ \forall i, j$
4: Compute ψ for each i, j
5: $\mathcal{C}_i = \emptyset\ \forall i$
6: **repeat**
7: **for** $i = 1, \ldots, n$ **do**
8: $r(\mathbf{y}) = \mathbf{w}^T \phi(\mathbf{t}_i, \mathbf{h}_i, \mathbf{z}, \mathbf{y}) + \Delta(\mathbf{y}_i^*, \mathbf{y}) - \mathbf{w}^T \phi(\mathbf{t}_i, \mathbf{h}_i, \mathbf{z}_i^*, \mathbf{y}_i^*)$
9: $\widehat{\mathbf{y}}_i = \arg\max_{\mathbf{y} \in \mathcal{Y}_i} r(\mathbf{y})$
10: $\xi_i = \max\{0, \max_{\mathbf{y} \in \mathcal{U}_i} r(\mathbf{y})\}$
11: **if** $r(\widehat{\mathbf{y}}_i) > \xi_i + \epsilon$ **then**
12: $\mathcal{C}_i = \mathcal{C}_i \cup \widehat{\mathbf{y}}_i$

$$Solve: \quad \min_{\mathbf{w}, \xi} \frac{1}{2}\|\mathbf{w}\|^2 + C \sum_i \xi_i$$
$$\forall i, \forall \mathbf{y} \in \mathcal{C}_i : \mathbf{w}^T \phi(\mathbf{t}_i, \mathbf{h}_i, \mathbf{z}_i^*, \mathbf{y}_i^*) \geq \mathbf{w}^T \phi(\mathbf{t}_i, \mathbf{h}_i, \mathbf{z}, \mathbf{y}) + \Delta(\mathbf{y}_i^*, \mathbf{y}) - \xi_i$$

13: **until** no change in any $\mathcal{C}_i$
14: **until** Convergence

ring the latent structure z_{ij} in step 3. Also, note that in step 3, when the answer-entailing structures are "Subset" or "Subset+", we can always get a higher score by considering a larger subset of sentences. To discourage this, we add a penalty on the score proportional to the size of the subset.

Multi-task Latent Structured Learning: Machine comprehension is a complex task which often requires us to interpret questions, the kind of answers they seek as well as the kinds of inference required to solve them. Many approaches in QA (Moldovan et al., 2003; Ferrucci, 2012) solve this by having a top-level classifier that categorizes the complex task into a variety of sub-tasks. The subtasks can correspond to various categories of questions that can be asked or various facets of text understanding that are required to do well at machine comprehension in its entirety.It is well known that learning a sub-task together with other related subtasks leads to a better solution for each sub-task. Hence, we consider learning classifications of the sub-tasks and then using multi-task learning.

We extend our LSSVM to multi-task settings. Let S be the number of sub-tasks. We assume that the predictor $\mathbf{w}$ for each subtask s is partitioned into two parts: a parameter $\mathbf{w}_0$ that is globally shared across each subtasks and a parameter $\mathbf{v}_s$ that is locally used to provide for the variations within the particular subtask: $\mathbf{w} = \mathbf{w}_0 + \mathbf{v}_s$. Mathematically we define the scoring function for text $\mathbf{t}_i$, hypothesis set $\mathbf{h}_i$ of the subtask s to be $Score_{\mathbf{w}_0, \mathbf{v}, s}(\mathbf{t}_i, \mathbf{h}_i, \mathbf{z}, \mathbf{y}) = (\mathbf{w}_0 + \mathbf{v}_s)^T \phi(\mathbf{t}_i, \mathbf{h}_i, \mathbf{z}, \mathbf{y})$. The objective in this case is

$$\min_{\mathbf{w}_0, \mathbf{v}} \lambda_2 \|\mathbf{w}_0\|^2 + \frac{\lambda_1}{S} \sum_{s=1}^{S} \|\mathbf{v}_s\|^2 \qquad (3)$$
$$\sum_{s=1}^{S} \sum_{i=1}^{n} \max_{\mathbf{y} \in \mathcal{Y}_i, \mathbf{z} \in \mathcal{Z}_i} \{(\mathbf{w}_0 + \mathbf{v}_s)^T \phi(\mathbf{t}_i, \mathbf{h}_i, \mathbf{z}, \mathbf{y})$$
$$+ \Delta(\mathbf{y}_i^*, \mathbf{y})\} - C \sum_i (\mathbf{w}_0 + \mathbf{v}_s)^T \phi(\mathbf{t}, \mathbf{h}_i, \mathbf{z}_i^*, \mathbf{y}_i^*)$$

Now, we extend a trick that Evgeniou and Pontil (2004) used on linear SVM to reformulate this problem into an objective that looks like (1). Such reformulation will help in using algorithm 1 to solve the multi-task problem as well. Lets define a new feature map Φ_s, one for each sub-task s using the old feature map ϕ as:

$$\Phi_s(\mathbf{t}_i, \mathbf{h}_i, \mathbf{z}, \mathbf{y}) = (\frac{\phi(\mathbf{t}_i, \mathbf{h}_i, \mathbf{z}, \mathbf{y})}{\mu}, \underbrace{\mathbf{0}, \ldots, \mathbf{0}}_{s-1}, \phi(\mathbf{t}_i, \mathbf{h}_i, \mathbf{z}, \mathbf{y}), \underbrace{\mathbf{0}, \ldots, \mathbf{0}}_{S-s})$$

where $\mu = \frac{S\lambda_2}{\lambda_1}$ and the $\mathbf{0}$ denotes the zero vector of the same size as ϕ. Also define our new predictor as $\mathbf{w} = (\sqrt{\mu}\mathbf{w}_0, \mathbf{v}_1, \ldots, \mathbf{v}_S)$. Using this formulation we can show that $\mathbf{w}^T \Phi_s(\mathbf{t}_i, \mathbf{h}_i, \mathbf{z}, \mathbf{y}) = (\mathbf{w}_0 + \mathbf{v}_s)^T \phi(\mathbf{t}_i, \mathbf{h}_i, \mathbf{z}, \mathbf{y})$ and $\|\mathbf{w}\|^2 = \sum_s \|\mathbf{v}_s\|^2 + \mu\|\mathbf{w}_0\|^2$. Hence, if we now define the objective (1) but use the new feature map and $\mathbf{w}$ then we will get back our multitask objective (3). Thus we can use the same setup as before for multi-task learning after appropriately changing the feature map. We will explore a few definitions of sub-tasks in our experiments.

Features: Recall that our features had the form $\psi(\mathbf{t}, h, z)$ where the hypothesis h was itself formed from a question q and answer candidate a. Given an answer-entailing structure z, we induce the following features based on word level similarity of aligned words: (a) Limited word-level surface-form matching and (b) Semantic word form matching: Word similarity for synonymy using SENNA word vectors (Collobert et al., 2011),

"Antonymy" 'Class-Inclusion' or 'Is-A' relations using Wordnet (Fellbaum, 1998). We compute additional features of the aforementioned kinds to match named entities and events. We also add features for matching local neighborhood in the aligned structure: features for matching bigrams, trigrams, dependencies, semantic roles, predicate-argument structure as well as features for matching global structure: a tree kernel for matching syntactic representations of entire sentences using Srivastava and Hovy (2013). The local and global features can use the RST and coreference links enabling inference across sentences. For instance, in the example shown in figure 1, the coreference link connecting the two "restaurant" words brings the snippets "Alyssa enjoyed the" and "had a special on catfish" closer making these features more effective. The answer-entailing structures should be intuitively similar to the question but also the answer. Hence, we add features that are the product of features for the text-question match and text-answer match.

String edit Features: In addition to looking for features on exact word/phrase match, we also add features using two paraphrase databases ParaPara (Chan et al., 2011) and DIRT (Lin and Pantel, 2001). The ParaPara database contains strings of the form $\text{string}_1 \rightarrow \text{string}_2$ like "total lack of" $\rightarrow$ "lack of", "is one of" $\rightarrow$ "among", etc. Similarly, the DIRT database contains paraphrases of the form "If **X** decreases **Y** then **X** reduces **Y**", "If **X** causes **Y** then **X** affects **Y**", etc. Whenever we have a substring in the text can be transformed into another using these two databases, we keep match features for the substring with a higher score (according to $\mathbf{w}$) and ignore the other substring.

The sentences with discourse relations are related to each other by means of substitution, ellipsis, conjunction and lexical cohesion, etc (Mann and Thompson, 1988) and can help us answer certain kinds of questions (Jansen et al., 2014). As an example, the "cause" relation between sentences in the text can often give cues that can help us answer "why" or "how" questions. Hence, we add additional features - conjunction of the RST label and the question word - to our feature vector. Similarly, the entity and event co-reference relations can allows the system to reason about repeating entities or events through all the sentences they get mentioned in. Thus, we add additional features of the aforementioned types by replacing entity mentions with their first mentions.

Subset+ Features: We add an additional set of features which match the first sentence in the ordered set to the question and the last sentence in the ordered set to the answer. This helps in the case when a certain portion of the text is targeted by the question but then it must be used in combination with another sentence to answer the question. For instance, in Figure 1, sentence 2 mentions the target of the question but the answer can only be given when in combination with sentence 1.

Negation We empirically found that one key limitation in our formulation is its inability to handle negation (both in questions and text). Negation is especially hurtful to our model as it not only results in poor performance on questions that require us to reason with negated facts, it provides our model with a wrong signal (facts usually align well with their negated versions). We use a simple heuristic to overcome the negation problem. We detect negation (either in the hypothesis or a sentence in the text snippet aligned to it) using a small set of manually defined rules that test for presence of words such as "not", "n't", etc. Then, we flip the partial order - i.e. the correct hypothesis is now ranked below the other competing hypotheses. For inference at test time, we also invert the prediction rule i.e. we predict the hypothesis (answer) that has the least score under the model.

5 Experiments

Datasets: We use two datasets for our evaluation. **(1)** First is the MCTest-500 dataset [1], a freely available set of 500 stories (split into 300 train, 50 dev and 150 test) and associated questions (Richardson et al., 2013). The stories are fictional so the answers can be found only in the story itself. The stories and questions are carefully limited, thereby minimizing the world knowledge required for this task. Yet, the task is challenging for most modern NLP systems. Each story in MCTest has four multiple choice questions, each with four answer choices. Each question has only one correct answer. Furthermore, questions are also annotated with 'single' and 'multiple' labels. The questions annotated 'single' only require one sentence in the story to answer them. For 'multiple' questions it should not be possible to find the answer to the question in any individual sentence of the passage. In a sense, the 'multiple' questions are

[1] http://research.microsoft.com/mct

harder than the 'single' questions as they typically require complex lexical analysis, some inference and some form of limited reasoning. Cucerzan-converted questions can also be downloaded from the MCTest website.

(2) The second dataset is a synthetic dataset released under the *bAbI project*[2] (Weston et al., 2015). The dataset presents a set of 20 'tasks', each testing a different aspect of text understanding and reasoning in the QA setting, and hence can be used to test and compare capabilities of learning models in a fine-grained manner. For each 'task', 1000 questions are used for training and 1000 for testing. The 'tasks' refer to question categories such as questions requiring reasoning over single/two/three supporting facts or two/three arg. relations, yes/no questions, counting questions, etc. Candidate answers are not provided but the answers are typically constrained to a small set: either yes or no or entities already appearing in the text, etc. We write simple rules to convert the question and answer candidate pairs to hypotheses. [3]

Baselines: We have five baselines. (1) The first three baselines are inspired from Richardson et al. (2013). The first baseline (called *SW*) uses a sliding window and matches a bag of words constructed from the question and hypothesized answer to the text. (2) Since this ignores long range dependencies, the second baseline (called *SW+D*) accounts for intra-word distances as well. As far as we know, *SW+D* is the best previously published result on this task.[4] (3) The third baseline (called *RTE*) uses textual entailment to answer MCTest questions. For this baseline, MCTest is again re-casted as an RTE task by converting each question-answer pair into a statement (using Cucerzan and Agichtein (2005)) and then selecting the answer whose statement has the highest likelihood of being entailed by the story. [5] (4) The fourth baseline (called *LSTM*) is taken from Weston et al. (2015). The baseline uses LSTMs (Hochreiter and Schmidhuber, 1997) to accomplish the task. LSTMs have recently achieved state-of-the-art results in a variety of tasks due to their ability to model long-term context information as opposed to other neural networks based techniques. (5) The fifth baseline (called *QANTA*)[6] is taken from Iyyer et al. (2014). *QANTA* too uses a recursive neural network for question answering.

Task Classification for MultiTask Learning: We consider three alternative task classifications for our experiments. First, we look at question classification. We use a simple question classification based on the question word (what, why, what, etc.). We call this QClassification. Next, we also use a question/answer classification[7] from Li and Roth (2002). This classifies questions into different semantic classes based on the possible semantic types of the answers sought. We call this QAClassification. Finally, we also learn a classifier for the 20 tasks in the Machine Comprehension gamut described in Weston et al. (2015). The classification algorithm (called TaskClassification) was built on the *bAbI* training set. It is essentially a Naive-Bayes classifier and uses only simple unigram and bigram features for the question and answer. The tasks typically correspond to different strategies when looking for an answer in the machine comprehension setting. In our experiments we will see that learning these strategies is better than learning the question answer classification which is in turn better than learning the question classification.

Results: We compare multiple variants of our LSSVM[8] where we consider a variety of answer-entailing structures and our modification for negation and multi-task LSSVM, where we consider three kinds of task classification strategies against the baselines on the *MCTest* dataset. We consider two evaluation metrics: accuracy (proportion of questions correctly answered) and NDCG_4

[2]https://research.facebook.com/researchers/1543934539189348

[3]Note that the *bAbI* dataset is artificial and not meant for open-domain machine comprehension. It is a toy dataset generated from a simulated world. Due to its restrictive nature, we do not use it directly in evaluating our method vs. other open-domain machine comprehension methods. However, it provides benefit in identifying interesting subtasks of machine comprehension. As will be seen, we are able to leverage the dataset both to improve our multi-task learning algorithm, as well as to analyze the strengths and weaknesses of our model.

[4]We also construct two additional baselines (*LSTM* and *QUANTA*) for comparison in this paper both of which achieve superior performance to *SW+D*.

[5]The BIUTEE system (Stern and Dagan, 2012) available under the Excitement Open Platform http://hltfbk.github.io/Excitement-Open-Platform/ was used for recognizing textual entailment.

[6]http://cs.umd.edu/ miyyer/qblearn/

[7]http://cogcomp.cs.illinois.edu/Data/QA/QC/

[8]We tune the SVM regularization parameter C and the penalty factor on the subset size on the development set. We use a beam of size 5 in our experiments. We use Stanford CoreNLP and the HILDA parser (Feng and Hirst, 2014) for linguistic preprocessing.

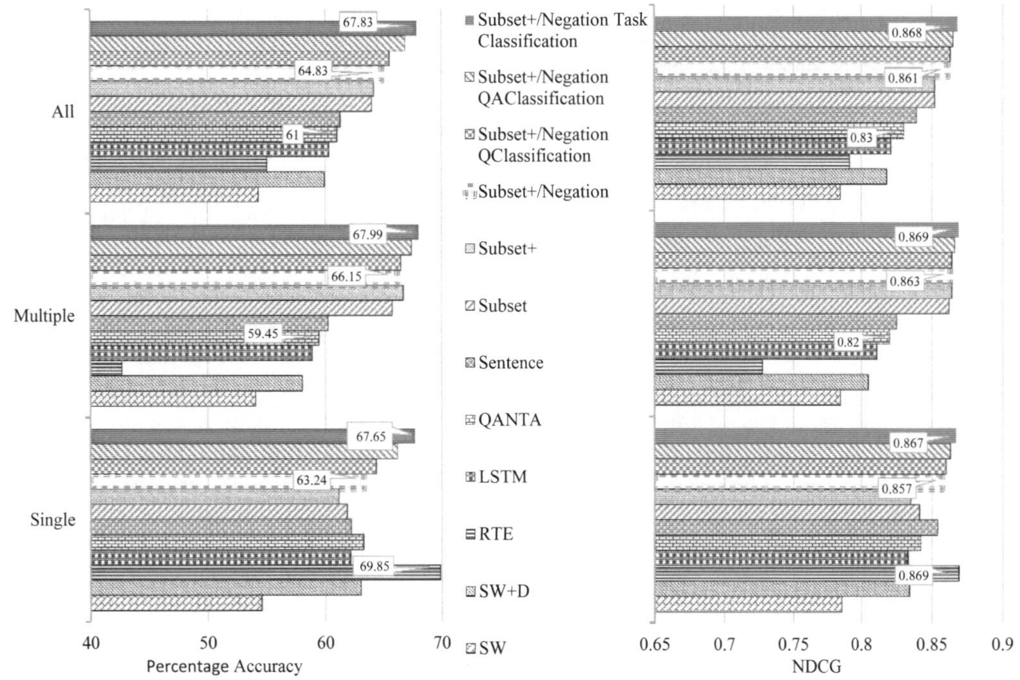

Figure 2: Comparison of variations of our method against several baselines on the MCTest-500 dataset. The figure shows two statistics, accuracy (on the left) and $NDCG_4$ (on the right) on the test set of MCTest-500. All differences between the baselines and LSSVMs, the improvement due to negation and the improvements due to multi-task learning are significant ($p < 0.01$) using the two-tailed paired T-test. The exact numbers are available in the supplementary.

(Järvelin and Kekäläinen, 2002). Unlike classification accuracy which evaluates if the prediction is correct or not, $NDCG_4$, being a measure of ranking quality, evaluates the position of the correct answer in our predicted ranking.

Figure 2 describes the comparison on *MCTest*. We can observe that all the LSSVM models have a better performance than all the five baselines (including LSTMs and RNNs which are state-of-the-art for many other NLP tasks) on both metrics. Very interestingly, LSSVMs have a considerable improvement over the baselines for "multiple" questions. We posit that this is because of our answer-entailing structure alignment strategy which is a weak proxy to the deep semantic inference procedure required for machine comprehension. The RTE baseline achieves the best performance on the "single" questions. This is perhaps because the RTE community has almost entirely focused on single sentence text hypothesis pairs for a long time. However, RTE fares pretty poorly on the "multiple" questions indicating that of-the-shelf RTE systems cannot perform inference across large texts.

Figure 2 also compares the performance of LSSVM variants when various answer-entailing structures are considered. Here we observe a clear benefit of using the alignment to the best subset structure over alignment to best sentence structure. We furthermore see improvements when the best subset alignment structure is augmented with the subset+ features. We can observe that the negation heuristic also helps, especially for "single" questions (majority of negation cases in the *MCTest* dataset are for the "single" questions).

It is also interesting to see that the multi-task learners show a substantial boost over the single task SSVM. Also, it can be observed that the multi-task learner greatly benefits if we can learn a separation between the various strategies needed to learn an overarching list of subtasks required to solve the machine comprehension task. [9] The multi-task method (TaskClassification) which uses the Weston style categorization does better

[9] Note that this is despite the fact that the classifier in not learned on the *MCTest* dataset but the *bAbI* detaset! This hints at the fact that the task classification proposed in Weston et al. (2015) is more general and broadly also makes sense for other machine comprehension settings such as *MCTest*.

than the multi-task method (QAClassification) that learns the question answer classification. QAClassification in turn performs better than multi-task method (QClassification) that learns the question classification only.

6 Strengths and Weaknesses

A good question to be asked is how good is structure alignment as a proxy to the semantics of the problem? In this section, we attempt to tease out the strengths and limitations of such a structure alignment approach for machine comprehension. To do so, we evaluate our methods on various tasks in the *bAbl* dataset.For the *bAbI* dataset, we add additional features inspired from the "task" distinction to handle specific "tasks".

In our experiments, we observed a similar general pattern of improvement of LSSVM over the baselines as well as the improvement due to multi-task learning. Again task classification helped the multi-task learner the most and the QA classification helped more than the QClassification. It is interesting here to look at the performance within the sub-tasks. Negation improved the performance for three sub-tasks, namely, the tasks of modelling "yes/no questions", "simple negations" and "indefinite knowledge" (the "Indefinite Knowledge" sub-task tests the ability to model statements that describe possibilities rather than certainties). Each of these sub-tasks contain a significant number of negation cases. Our models do especially well on questions requiring reasoning over one and two supporting facts, two arg. relations, indefinite knowledge, basic and compound coreference and conjunction. Our models achieve lower accuracy better than the baselines on two sub-tasks, namely "path finding" and "agent motivations". Our model along with the baselines do not do too well on the "counting" sub-task, although we get slightly better scores. The "counting" sub-task (which asks about the number of objects with a certain property) requires the inference to have an ability to perform simple counting operations. The "path finding" sub-task requires the inference to reason about the spatial path between locations (e.g. Pittsburgh is located on the west of New York). The "agents motivations" sub-task asks questions such as 'why an agent performs a certain action'. As inference is cheaply modelled via alignment structure, we lack the ability to deeply reason about facts or numbers. This is an important challenge for future work.

7 Related Work

The field of QA is quite rich. Most QA evaluations such as TREC have typically focused on short factoid questions. The solutions proposed have ranged from various IR based approaches (Mittal and Mittal, 2011) that treat this as a problem of retrieval from existing knowledge bases and perform some shallow inference to NLP approaches that learn a similarity between the question and a set of candidate answers (Yih et al., 2013). A majority of these approaches do not focus on doing any deeper inference. However, the task of machine comprehension requires an ability to perform inference over paragraph length texts to seek the answer. This is challenging for most IR and NLP techniques. In this paper, we presented a strategy for learning answer-entailing structures that helped us perform inference over much longer texts by treating this as a structured input-output problem.

The approach of treating a problem as one of mapping structured inputs to structured outputs is common across many NLP applications. Examples include word or phrase alignment for bitexts in MT (Blunsom and Cohn, 2006), text-hypothesis alignment in RTE (Sammons et al., 2009; MacCartney et al., 2008; Yao et al., 2013a; Sultan et al., 2014), question-answer alignment in QA (Berant et al., 2013; Yih et al., 2013; Yao and Van Durme, 2014), etc. Again all of these approaches align local parts of the input to local parts of the output. In this work, we extended the word alignment formalism to align multiple sentences in the text to the hypothesis. We also incorporated the document structure (rhetorical structures (Mann and Thompson, 1988)) and co-reference to help us perform inference over longer documents.

QA has had a long history of using pipeline models that extract a limited number of high-level features from induced representations of question-answer pairs, and then built a classifier using some labelled corpora. On the other hand we learnt these structures and performed machine comprehension jointly through a unified max-margin framework. We note that there exist some recent models such as Yih et al. (2013) that do model QA by automatically defining some kind of alignment between the question and answer snippets and use a similar structured input-output model. However, they are limited to single sentence answers.

Another advantage of our approach is its simple and elegant extension to multi-task settings. There has been a rich vein of work in multi-task learning for SVMs in the ML community. Evgeniou and Pontil (2004) proposed a multi-task SVM formulation assuming that the multi-task predictor $\mathbf{w}$ factorizes as the sum of a shared and a task-specific component. We used the same idea to propose a multi-task variant of Latent Structured SVMs. This allows us to use the single task SVM in the multi-task setting with a different feature mapping. This is much simpler than other competing approaches such as Zhu et al. (2011) proposed in the literature for multi-task LSSVM.

8 Conclusion

In this paper, we addressed the problem of machine comprehension which tests language understanding through multiple choice question answering tasks. We posed the task as an extension to RTE. Then, we proposed a solution by learning latent alignment structures between texts and the hypotheses in the equivalent RTE setting. The task requires solving a variety of sub-tasks so we extended our technique to a multi-task setting. Our technique showed empirical improvements over various IR and neural network baselines. The latent structures while effective are cheap proxies to the reasoning and language understanding required for this task and have their own limitations. We also discuss strengths and limitations of our model in a more fine-grained analysis. In the future, we plan to use logic-like semantic representations of texts, questions and answers and explore approaches to perform structured inference over richer semantic representations.

Acknowledgments

The authors would like to thank the anonymous reviewers, along with Sujay Jauhar and Snigdha Chaturvedi for their valuable comments and suggestions to improve the quality of the paper.

References

[Berant et al.2013] Jonathan Berant, Andrew Chou, Roy Frostig, and Percy Liang. 2013. Semantic parsing on freebase from question-answer pairs. In *EMNLP*, pages 1533–1544. ACL.

[Blunsom and Cohn2006] Phil Blunsom and Trevor Cohn. 2006. Discriminative word alignment with conditional random fields. In *Proceedings of the 21st International Conference on Computational Linguistics and the 44th annual meeting of the Association for Computational Linguistics*, pages 65–72. Association for Computational Linguistics.

[Burges2013] Christopher JC Burges. 2013. Towards the machine comprehension of text: An essay. Technical report, Microsoft Research Technical Report MSR-TR-2013-125, 2013, pdf.

[Chakrabarti et al.2008] Soumen Chakrabarti, Rajiv Khanna, Uma Sawant, and Chiru Bhattacharyya. 2008. Structured learning for non-smooth ranking losses. In *Proceedings of the 14th ACM SIGKDD International Conference on Knowledge Discovery and Data Mining*, pages 88–96.

[Chan et al.2011] Tsz Ping Chan, Chris Callison-Burch, and Benjamin Van Durme. 2011. Reranking bilingually extracted paraphrases using monolingual distributional similarity. In *Proceedings of the GEMS 2011 Workshop on GEometrical Models of Natural Language Semantics*, pages 33–42.

[Collobert et al.2011] Ronan Collobert, Jason Weston, Léon Bottou, Michael Karlen, Koray Kavukcuoglu, and Pavel Kuksa. 2011. Natural language processing (almost) from scratch. *The Journal of Machine Learning Research*, 12:2493–2537.

[Cucerzan and Agichtein2005] S. Cucerzan and E. Agichtein. 2005. Factoid question answering over unstructured and structured content on the web. In *Proceedings of TREC 2005*.

[Dubey et al.2009] Avinava Dubey, Jinesh Machchhar, Chiranjib Bhattacharyya, and Soumen Chakrabarti. 2009. Conditional models for non-smooth ranking loss functions. In *ICDM*, pages 129–138.

[Evgeniou and Pontil2004] Theodoros Evgeniou and Massimiliano Pontil. 2004. Regularized multi–task learning. In *Proceedings of the Tenth ACM SIGKDD International Conference on Knowledge Discovery and Data Mining*, pages 109–117.

[Fellbaum1998] Christiane Fellbaum. 1998. *WordNet: An Electronic Lexical Database*. Bradford Books.

[Feng and Hirst2014] Vanessa Wei Feng and Graeme Hirst. 2014. A linear-time bottom-up discourse parser with constraints and post-editing. In *Proceedings of the 52nd Annual Meeting of the Association for Computational Linguistics (Volume 1: Long Papers)*, pages 511–521.

[Ferrucci2012] David A Ferrucci. 2012. Introduction to this is watson. *IBM Journal of Research and Development*, 56(3.4):1–1.

[Finley and Joachims2008] T. Finley and T. Joachims. 2008. Training structural SVMs when exact inference is intractable. In *International Conference on Machine Learning (ICML)*, pages 304–311.

[Hochreiter and Schmidhuber1997] Sepp Hochreiter and Jürgen Schmidhuber. 1997. Long short-term memory. *Neural computation*, 9(8):1735–1780.

[Iyyer et al.2014] Mohit Iyyer, Jordan Boyd-Graber, Leonardo Claudino, Richard Socher, and Hal Daumé III. 2014. A neural network for factoid question answering over paragraphs. In *Empirical Methods in Natural Language Processing*.

[Jansen et al.2014] Peter Jansen, Mihai Surdeanu, and Peter Clark. 2014. Discourse complements lexical semantics for non-factoid answer reranking. In *Proceedings of the 52nd Annual Meeting of the Association for Computational Linguistics (Volume 1: Long Papers)*, pages 977–986.

[Järvelin and Kekäläinen2002] Kalervo Järvelin and Jaana Kekäläinen. 2002. Cumulated gain-based evaluation of ir techniques. *ACM Transactions on Information Systems (TOIS)*, 20(4):422–446.

[Joachims2002] Thorsten Joachims. 2002. Optimizing search engines using clickthrough data. In *Proceedings of the eighth ACM SIGKDD international conference on Knowledge discovery and data mining*, pages 133–142. ACM.

[Joachims2006] T. Joachims. 2006. Training linear SVMs in linear time. In *ACM SIGKDD International Conference On Knowledge Discovery and Data Mining (KDD)*, pages 217–226.

[Li and Roth2002] Xin Li and Dan Roth. 2002. Learning question classifiers. In *Proceedings of the 19th international conference on Computational linguistics-Volume 1*, pages 1–7.

[Lin and Pantel2001] Dekang Lin and Patrick Pantel. 2001. Dirt@ sbt@ discovery of inference rules from text. In *Proceedings of the seventh ACM SIGKDD international conference on Knowledge discovery and data mining*, pages 323–328.

[MacCartney et al.2008] Bill MacCartney, Michel Galley, and Christopher D Manning. 2008. A phrase-based alignment model for natural language inference. In *Proceedings of the conference on empirical methods in natural language processing*, pages 802–811.

[Mann and Thompson1988] William C Mann and Sandra A Thompson. 1988. {Rhetorical Structure Theory: Toward a functional theory of text organisation}. *Text*, 3(8):234–281.

[Mittal and Mittal2011] Sparsh Mittal and Ankush Mittal. 2011. Versatile question answering systems: seeing in synthesis. *International Journal of Intelligent Information and Database Systems*, 5(2):119–142.

[Moldovan et al.2003] Dan Moldovan, Marius Paşca, Sanda Harabagiu, and Mihai Surdeanu. 2003. Performance issues and error analysis in an open-domain question answering system. *ACM Transactions on Information Systems (TOIS)*, 21(2):133–154.

[Richardson et al.2013] Matthew Richardson, J.C. Christopher Burges, and Erin Renshaw. 2013. Mctest: A challenge dataset for the open-domain machine comprehension of text. In *Proceedings of the 2013 Conference on Empirical Methods in Natural Language Processing*, pages 193–203.

[Sammons et al.2009] M. Sammons, V. Vydiswaran, T. Vieira, N. Johri, M. Chang, D. Goldwasser, V. Srikumar, G. Kundu, Y. Tu, K. Small, J. Rule, Q. Do, and D. Roth. 2009. Relation alignment for textual entailment recognition. In *TAC*.

[Srivastava and Hovy2013] Shashank Srivastava and Dirk Hovy. 2013. A walk-based semantically enriched tree kernel over distributed word representations. In *Empirical Methods in Natural Language Processing*, pages 1411–1416.

[Stern and Dagan2012] Asher Stern and Ido Dagan. 2012. Biutee: A modular open-source system for recognizing textual entailment. In *Proceedings of the ACL 2012 System Demonstrations*, pages 73–78.

[Sultan et al.2014] Arafat Md Sultan, Steven Bethard, and Tamara Sumner. 2014. Back to basics for monolingual alignment: Exploiting word similarity and contextual evidence. *Transactions of the Association of Computational Linguistics – Volume 2, Issue 1*, pages 219–230.

[Weston et al.2014] Jason Weston, Sumit Chopra, and Antoine Bordes. 2014. Memory networks. *arXiv preprint arXiv:1410.3916*.

[Weston et al.2015] Jason Weston, Antoine Bordes, Sumit Chopra, and Tomas Mikolov. 2015. Towards ai-complete question answering: A set of prerequisite toy tasks.

[Yao and Van Durme2014] Xuchen Yao and Benjamin Van Durme. 2014. Information extraction over structured data: Question answering with freebase. In *Proceedings of the 52nd Annual Meeting of the Association for Computational Linguistics (Volume 1: Long Papers)*, pages 956–966. Association for Computational Linguistics.

[Yao et al.2013a] Xuchen Yao, Benjamin Van Durme, Chris Callison-Burch, and Peter Clark. 2013a. A lightweight and high performance monolingual word aligner. In *ACL (2)*, pages 702–707.

[Yao et al.2013b] Xuchen Yao, Benjamin Van Durme, Chris Callison-Burch, and Peter Clark. 2013b. Semi-markov phrase-based monolingual alignment. In *Proceedings of EMNLP*.

[Yih et al.2013] Wentau Yih, Ming-Wei Chang, Christopher Meek, and Andrzej Pastusiak. 2013. Question answering using enhanced lexical semantic models. In *Proceedings of the 51st Annual Meeting of the Association for Computational Linguistics*.

[Yu and Joachims2009] Chun-Nam Yu and T. Joachims. 2009. Learning structural svms with latent variables. In *International Conference on Machine Learning (ICML).*

[Yuille and Rangarajan2003] A. L. Yuille and Anand Rangarajan. 2003. The concave-convex procedure. *Neural Comput.*

[Zhang and Lee2003] Dell Zhang and Wee Sun Lee. 2003. Question classification using support vector machines. In *Proceedings of the 26th annual international ACM SIGIR conference on Research and development in informaion retrieval*, pages 26–32. ACM.

[Zhu et al.2011] Jun Zhu, Ning Chen, and Eric P Xing. 2011. Infinite latent svm for classification and multi-task learning. In *Advances in neural information processing systems*, pages 1620–1628.

Learning Continuous Word Embedding with Metadata for Question Retrieval in Community Question Answering

Guangyou Zhou[1], Tingting He[1], Jun Zhao[2], and Po Hu[1]
[1] School of Computer, Central China Normal University, Wuhan 430079, China
[2] National Laboratory of Pattern Recognition, CASIA, Beijing 100190, China
{gyzhou,tthe,phu}@mail.ccnu.edu.cn jzhao@nlpr.ia.ac.cn

Abstract

Community question answering (cQA) has become an important issue due to the popularity of cQA archives on the web. This paper is concerned with the problem of question retrieval. Question retrieval in cQA archives aims to find the existing questions that are semantically equivalent or relevant to the queried questions. However, the lexical gap problem brings about new challenge for question retrieval in cQA. In this paper, we propose to learn continuous word embeddings with metadata of category information within cQA pages for question retrieval. To deal with the variable size of word embedding vectors, we employ the framework of fisher kernel to aggregated them into the fixed-length vectors. Experimental results on large-scale real world cQA data set show that our approach can significantly outperform state-of-the-art translation models and topic-based models for question retrieval in cQA.

1 Introduction

Over the past few years, a large amount of user-generated content have become an important information resource on the web. These include the traditional Frequently Asked Questions (FAQ) archives and the emerging community question answering (cQA) services, such as Yahoo! Answers[1], Live QnA[2], and Baidu Zhidao[3]. The content in these web sites is usually organized as questions and lists of answers associated with metadata like user chosen categories to questions and askers' awards to the best answers. This data made cQA archives valuable resources for various tasks like question-answering (Jeon et al., 2005; Xue et al., 2008) and knowledge mining (Adamic et al., 2008), etc.

One fundamental task for reusing content in cQA is finding similar questions for queried questions, as questions are the keys to accessing the knowledge in cQA. Then the best answers of these similar questions will be used to answer the queried questions. Many studies have been done along this line (Jeon et al., 2005; Xue et al., 2008; Duan et al., 2008; Lee et al., 2008; Bernhard and Gurevych, 2009; Cao et al., 2010; Zhou et al., 2011; Singh, 2012; Zhang et al., 2014a). One big challenge for question retrieval in cQA is the lexical gap between the queried questions and the existing questions in the archives. Lexical gap means that the queried questions may contain words that are different from, but related to, the words in the existing questions. For example shown in (Zhang et al., 2014a), we find that for a queried question "how do I get knots out of my cats fur?", there are good answers under an existing question "how can I remove a tangle in my cat's fur?" in Yahoo! Answers. Although the two questions share few words in common, they have very similar meanings, it is hard for traditional retrieval models (e.g., BM25 (Robertson et al., 1994)) to determine their similarity. This lexical gap has become a major barricade preventing traditional IR models (e.g., BM25) from retrieving similar questions in cQA.

To address the lexical gap problem in cQA, previous work in the literature can be divided into two groups. The first group is the translation models, which leverage the question-answer pairs to learn the semantically related words to improve traditional IR models (Jeon et al., 2005; Xue et al., 2008; Zhou et al., 2011). The basic assumption is that question-answer pairs are "parallel texts" and relationship of words (or phrases) can be established through word-to-word (or phrase-to-phrase)

[1]http://answers.yahoo.com/
[2]http://qna.live.com/
[3]http://zhidao.baidu.com/

Proceedings of the 53rd Annual Meeting of the Association for Computational Linguistics and the 7th International Joint Conference on Natural Language Processing, pages 250–259, Beijing, China, July 26-31, 2015.

translation probabilities (Jeon et al., 2005; Xue et al., 2008; Zhou et al., 2011). Experimental results show that translation models obtain state-of-the-art performance for question retrieval in cQA. However, questions and answers are far from "parallel" in practice, questions and answers are highly asymmetric on the information they contain (Zhang et al., 2014a). The second group is the topic-based models (Cai et al., 2011; Ji et al., 2012), which learn the latent topics aligned across the question-answer pairs to alleviate the lexical gap problem, with the assumption that a question and its paired answers share the same topic distribution. However, questions and answers are heterogeneous in many aspects, they do not share the same topic distribution in practice.

Inspired by the recent success of continuous space word representations in capturing the semantic similarities in various natural language processing tasks, we propose to incorporate an embedding of words in a continuous space for question representations. Due to the ability of word embeddings, we firstly transform words in a question into continuous vector representations by looking up tables. These word embeddings are learned in advance using a continuous skip-gram model (Mikolov et al., 2013), or other continuous word representation learning methods. Once the words are embedded in a continuous space, one can view a question as a Bag-of-Embedded-Words (BoEW). Then, the variable-cardinality BoEW will be aggregated into a fixed-length vector by using the Fisher kernel (FK) framework of (Clinchant and Perronnin, 2013; Sanchez et al., 2013). Through the two steps, the proposed approach can map a question into a length invariable compact vector, which can be efficiently and effectively for large-scale question retrieval task in cQA.

We test the proposed approach on large-scale Yahoo! Answers data and Baidu Zhidao data. Yahoo! Answers and Baidu Zhidao represent the largest and most popular cQA archives in English and Chinese, respectively. We conduct both quantitative and qualitative evaluations. Experimental results show that our approach can significantly outperform state-of-the-art translation models and topic-based models for question retrieval in cQA.

Our contribution in this paper are three-fold: (1) we represent a question as a bag-of-embedded-words (BoEW) in a continuous space; (2) we introduce a novel method to aggregate the variable-cardinality BoEW into a fixed-length vector by using the FK. The FK is just one possible way to subsequently transform this bag representation into a fixed-length vector which is more amenable to large-scale processing; (3) an empirical verification of the efficacy of the proposed framework on large-scale English and Chinese cQA data.

The rest of this paper is organized as follows. Section 2 summarizes the related work. Section 3 describes our proposed framework for question retrieval. Section 4 reports the experimental results. Finally, we conclude the paper in Section 5.

2 Related Work

2.1 Question Retrieval in cQA

Significant research efforts have been conducted over the years in attempt to improve question retrieval in cQA (Jeon et al., 2005; Xue et al., 2008; Lee et al., 2008; Duan et al., 2008; Bernhard and Gurevych, 2009; Cao et al., 2010; Zhou et al., 2011; Singh, 2012; Zhang et al., 2014a). Most of these works focus on finding similar questions for the user queried questions. The major challenge for question retrieval in cQA is the lexical gap problem. Jeon et al. (2005) proposed a word-based translation model for automatically fixing the lexical gap problem. Xue et al. (2008) proposed a word-based translation language model for question retrieval. Lee et al. (2008) tried to further improve the translation probabilities based on question-answer pairs by selecting the most important terms to build compact translation models. Bernhard and Gurevych (2009) proposed to use as a parallel training data set the definitions and glosses provided for the same term by different lexical semantic resources. In order to improve the word-based translation model with some contextual information, Riezler et al. (2007) and Zhou et al. (2011) proposed a phrase-based translation model for question and answer retrieval. The phrase-based translation model can capture some contextual information in modeling the translation of phrases as a whole, thus the more accurate translations can better improve the retrieval performance. Singh (2012) addressed the lexical gap issues by extending the lexical word-based translation model to incorporate semantic information (entities).

In contrast to the works described above that assume question-answer pairs are "parallel text", our paper deals with the lexical gap by learning continuous word embeddings in capturing the similarities without any assumptions, which is much more reasonable in practice.

Besides, some other studies model the semantic relationship between questions and answers with deep linguistic analysis (Duan et al., 2008; Wang et al., 2009; Wang et al., 2010; Ji et al., 2012; Zhang et al., 2014a) or a learning to rank strategy (Surdeanu et al., 2008; Carmel et al., 2014). Recently, Cao et al. (2010) and Zhou et al. (2013) exploited the category metadata within cQA pages to further improve the performance. On the contrary, we focus on the representation learning for questions, with a different solution with those previous works.

2.2 Word Embedding Learning

Representation of words as continuous vectors has attracted increasing attention in the area of natural language processing (NLP). Recently, a series of works applied deep learning techniques to learn high-quality word representations. Bengio et al. (2003) proposed a probabilistic neural network language model (NNLM) for word representations. Furthermore, Mikolov et al. (2013) proposed efficient neural network models for learning word representations, including the continuous *skip-gram* model and the continuous bag-of-word model (CBOW), both of which are unsupervised models learned from large-scale text corpora. Besides, there are also a large number of works addressing the task of learning word representations (Huang et al., 2012; Maas et al., 2011; Turian et al., 2010).

Nevertheless, since most the existing works learned word representations mainly based on the word co-occurrence information, the obtained word embeddings cannot capture the relationship between two syntactically or semantically similar words if either of them yields very little context information. On the other hand, even though amount of context could be noisy or biased such that they cannot reflect the inherent relationship between words and further mislead the training process. Most recently, Yu et al. (2014) used semantic prior knowledge to improve word representations. Xu et al. (2014) used the knowledge graph to advance the learning of word embeddings. In contrast to all the aforementioned works, in this paper, we present a general method to leverage the metadata of category information within cQA pages to further improve the word embedding representations. To our knowledge, it is the first work to learn word embeddings with metadata on cQA data set.

3 Our Approach

In this Section, we describe the proposed approach: learning continuous word embedding with metadata for question retrieval in cQA. The proposed framework consists of two steps: (1) *word embedding learning* step: given a cQA data collection, questions are treated as the basic units. For each word in a question, we firstly transform it to a continuous word vector through the looking up tables. Once the word embeddings are learned, each question is represented by a variable-cardinality word embedding vector (also called BoEW); (2) *fisher vector generation* step: which uses a generative model in the FK framework to generate fisher vectors (FVs) by aggregating the BoEWs for all the questions. Question retrieval can be performed through calculating the similarity between the FVs of a queried question and an existing question in the archive.

From the framework, we can see that although the word embedding learning computations and generative model estimation are time consuming, they can run only once in advance. Meanwhile, the computational requirements of FV generation and similarity calculation are limited. Hence, the proposed framework can efficiently achieve the large-scale question retrieval task.

3.1 Word Embedding Learning

In this paper, we consider a context-aware predicting model, more specifically, the *Skip-gram* model (Mikolov et al., 2013) for learning word embeddings, since it is much more efficient as well as memory-saving than other approaches.[4] *Skip-gram* is recently proposed for learning word representations using a neural network model, whose underlying idea is that similar words should have similar contexts. In the *Skip-gram* model (see Figure 1), a sliding window is employed on the input text stream to generate the training data, and l indicates the context window size to be $2l + 1$. In each slide window, the model aims to use the central word w_k as input to predict the context words. Let $M_{d \times N}$ denote the learned embedding matrix,

[4] Note that although we use the skip-gram model as an example to illustrate our approach, the similar framework can be developed on the basis of any other word embedding models.

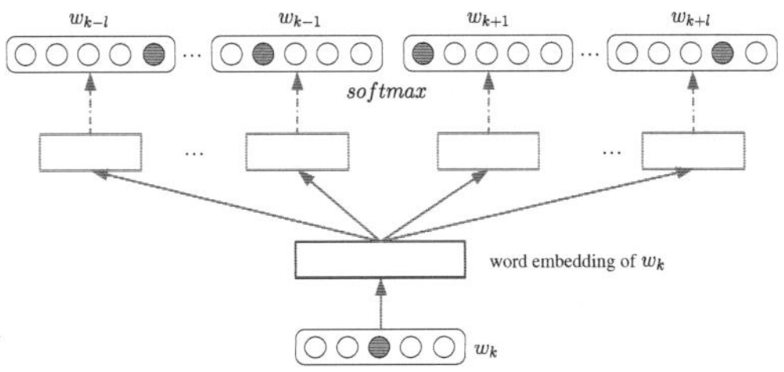

Figure 1: The continuous skip-gram model.

where N is the vocabulary size and d is the dimension of word embeddings. Each column of M represents the embedding of a word. Let w_k is first mapped to its embedding e_{w_k} by selecting the corresponding column vector of M. The probability of its context word w_{k+j} is then computed using a log-linear *softmax* function:

$$p(w_{k+j}|w_k;\theta) = \frac{\exp(e^T_{w_{k+j}} e_{w_k})}{\sum_{w=1}^{N} \exp(e^T_w e_{w_k})} \quad (1)$$

where θ are the parameters we should learned, $k = 1 \cdots d$, and $j \in [-l, l]$. Then, the log-likelihood over the entire training data can be computed as:

$$J(\theta) = \sum_{(w_k, w_{k+j})} \log p(w_{k+j}|w_k;\theta) \quad (2)$$

To calculate the prediction errors for back propagation, we need to compute the derivative of $p(w_{k+j}|w_k;\theta)$, whose computation cost is proportional to the vocabulary size N. As N is often very large, it is difficult to directly compute the derivative. To deal this problem, Mikolov et al. (2013) proposed a simple negative sampling method, which generates r noise samples for each input word to estimate the target word, in which r is a very small number compared with N. Therefore, the training time yields linear scale to the number of noise samples and it becomes independent of the vocabulary size. Suppose the frequency of word w is $u(w)$, then the probability of sampling w is usually set to $p(w) \propto u(w)^{3/4}$ (Mikolov et al., 2013).

3.2 Metadata Powered Model

After briefing the *skip-gram* model, we introduce how we equip it with the metadata information. In cQA sites, there are several metadata, such as "category","voting" and so on. In this paper, we only consider the metadata of category information for word embedding learning. All questions in cQA are usually organized into a hierarchy of categories. When an user asks a question, the user typically required to choose a category label for the question from a predefined hierarchy of categories (Cao et al., 2010; Zhou et al., 2013). Previous work in the literature has demonstrated the effectiveness of the category information for question retrieval (Cao et al., 2010; Zhou et al., 2013). On the contrary, we argue that the category information benefits the word embedding learning in this work. The basic idea is that category information encodes the attributes or properties of words, from which we can group similar words according to their categories. Here, a word's category is assigned based on the questions it appeared in. For example, a question "What are the security issues with *java?*" is under the category of "Computers & Internet → Security", we simply put the category of a word *java* as "Computers & Internet → Security". Then, we may require the representations of words that belong to the same category to be close to each other.

Let $s(w_k, w_i)$ be the similarity score between w_k and w_i. Under the above assumption, we use the following heuristic to constrain the similar scores:

$$s(w_k, w_i) = \begin{cases} 1 & \text{if } c(w_k) = c(w_i) \\ 0 & \text{otherwise} \end{cases} \quad (3)$$

where $c(w_k)$ denotes the category of w_k. If the central word w_k shares the same category with the word w_i, their similarity score will become 1, otherwise, we set to 0. Then we encode the category information using a regularization function E_c:

$$E_c = \sum_{k=1}^{N} \sum_{i=1}^{N} s(w_k, w_i) d(w_k, w_i) \quad (4)$$

where $d(w_k, w_i)$ is the distance for the words in the embedding space and $s(w_k, w_i)$ serves as a weighting function. Again, for simplicity, we define $d(w_k, w_i)$ as the Euclidean distance between w_k and w_i.

We combine the *skip-gram* objective function and the regularization function derived from the metadata of category information, we get the following combined objective J_c that incorporates category information into the word representation learning process:

$$J_c = J(\theta) + \beta E_c \quad (5)$$

where β is the combination coefficient. Our goal is to maximize the combined objective J_c, which

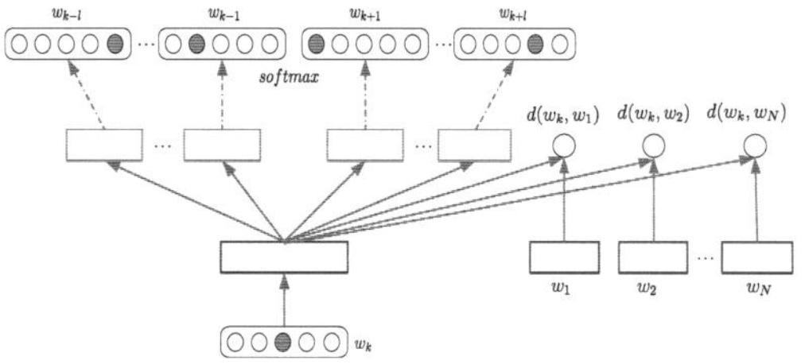

Figure 2: The continuous skip-gram model with metadata of category information, called M-NET.

can be optimized using back propagation neural networks. We call this model as metadata powered model (see Figure 2), and denote it by M-NET for easy of reference.

In the implementation, we optimize the regularization function derived from the metadata of category information along with the training process of the *skip-gram* model. During the procedure of learning word representations from the context words in the sliding window, if the central word w_k hits the category information, the corresponding optimization process of the metadata powered regularization function will be activated. Therefore, we maximize the weighted Euclidean distance between the representation of the central word and that of its similar words according to the objective function in Equation (5).

3.3 Fisher Vector Generation

Once the word embeddings are learned, questions can be represented by variable length sets of word embedding vectors, which can be viewed as BoEWs. Semantic level similarities between queried questions and the existing questions represented by BoEWs can be captured more accurately than previous bag-of-words (BoW) methods. However, since BoEWs are variable-size sets of word embeddings and most of the index methods in information retrieval field are not suitable for this kinds of issues, BoEWs cannot be directly used for large-scale question retrieval task.

Given a cQA data collection $\mathcal{Q} = \{q_i, 1 \leq i \leq |\mathcal{Q}|\}$, where q_i is the ith question and $|\mathcal{Q}|$ is the number of questions in the data collection. The ith question q_i is composed by a sequence of words $w_i = \{w_{ij}, 1 \leq j \leq N_i\}$, where N_i denotes the length of q_i. Through looking up table (word embedding matrix) of M, the ith question q_i can be represented by $E_{w_i} = \{e_{w_{ij}}, 1 \leq j \leq N_i\}$, where $e_{w_{ij}}$ is the word embedding of w_{ij}. According to the framework of FK (Clinchant and Perronnin, 2013; Sanchez et al., 2013; Zhang et al., 2014b), questions are modeled by a probability density function. In this work, we use Gaussian mixture model (GMM) to do it. We assume that the continuous word embedding E_{w_i} for question q_i have been generated by a "universal" (e.g., question-independent) probability density function (pdf). As is a common practice, we choose this pdf to be a GMM since any continuous distribution can be approximated with arbitrary precision by a mixture of Gaussian. In what follows, the pdf is denoted u_λ where $\lambda = \{\theta_i, \mu_i, \Sigma_i, i = 1 \cdots K\}$ is the set of parameters of the GMM. θ_i, μ_i and Σ_i denote respectively the mixture weight, mean vector and covariance matrix of Gaussian i. For computational reasons, we assume that the covariance matrices are diagonal and denote σ_i^2 the variance vector of Gaussian i, e.g., $\sigma_i^2 = \text{diag}(\sum_i)$. In real applications, the GMM is estimated offline with a set of continuous word embeddings extracted from a representative set of questions. The parameters λ are estimated through the optimization of a Maximum Likelihood (ML) criterion using the Expectation-Maximization (EM) algorithm. In the following, we follow the notations used in (Sanchez et al., 2013).

Given u_λ, one can characterize the question q_i using the following score function:

$$G_\lambda^{q_i} = \triangledown_\lambda^{N_i} \log u_\lambda(q_i) \quad (6)$$

where $G_\lambda^{q_i}$ is a vector whose size depends only on the number of parameters in λ. Assuming that the word embedding $e_{w_{ij}}$ is iid (a simplifying assumption), we get:

$$G_\lambda^{q_i} = \sum_{j=1}^{N_i} \triangledown_\lambda \log u_\lambda(e_{w_{ij}}) \quad (7)$$

Following the literature (Sanchez et al., 2013), we propose to measure the similarity between two questions q_i and q_j using the FK:

$$K(q_i, q_j) = G_\lambda^{q_i^T} F_\lambda^{-1} G_\lambda^{q_j} \quad (8)$$

where F_λ is the Fisher Information Matrix (FIM) of u_λ:

$$F_\lambda = E_{q_i \sim u_\lambda}\left[G_\lambda^{q_i} G_\lambda^{q_i^T}\right] \quad (9)$$

Since F_λ is symmetric and positive definite, F_λ^{-1} can be transformed to $L_\lambda^T L_\lambda$ based on the Cholesky decomposition. Hence, $K_{FK}(q_i, q_j)$ can rewritten as follows:

$$K_{FK}(q_i, q_j) = \mathcal{G}_\lambda^{q_i^T} \mathcal{G}_\lambda^{q_j} \quad (10)$$

where

$$\mathcal{G}_{\lambda}^{q_i} = L_{\lambda} G_{\lambda}^{q_i} = L_{\lambda} \nabla_{\lambda} \log u_{\lambda}(q_i) \tag{11}$$

In (Sanchez et al., 2013), $\mathcal{G}_{\lambda}^{q_i}$ refers to as the *Fisher Vector* (FV) of q_i. The dot product between FVs can be used to calculate the semantic similarities. Based on the specific probability density function, GMM, FV of q_i is respect to the mean μ and standard deviation σ of all the mixed Gaussian distributions. Let $\gamma_j(k)$ be the soft assignment of the jth word embedding $e_{w_{ij}}$ in q_i to Guassian k (u_k):

$$\gamma_j(k) = p(k|e_{w_{ij}}) \frac{\theta_i u_k(e_{w_{ij}})}{\sum_{j=1}^{K} \theta_k u_k(e_{w_{ij}})} \tag{12}$$

Mathematical derivations lead to:

$$\mathcal{G}_{\mu,k}^{q_i} = \frac{1}{N_i\sqrt{\theta_i}} \sum_{j=1}^{N_i} \gamma_j(k) \Big[\frac{e_{w_{ij}} - \mu_k}{\sigma_k}\Big] \tag{13}$$

$$\mathcal{G}_{\sigma,k}^{q_i} = \frac{1}{N_i\sqrt{2\theta_i}} \sum_{j=1}^{N_i} \gamma_j(k) \Big[\frac{(e_{w_{ij}} - \mu_k)^2}{\sigma_k^2} - 1\Big]$$

The division by the vector σ_k should be understood as a term-by-term operation. The final gradient vector $\mathcal{G}_{\lambda}^{q_i}$is the concatenation of the $\mathcal{G}_{\mu,k}^{q_i}$ and $\mathcal{G}_{\sigma,k}^{q_i}$ vectors for $k = 1 \cdots K$. Let d denote the dimensionality of the continuous word embeddings and K be the number of Gaussians. The final fisher vector $\mathcal{G}_{\lambda}^{q_i}$ is therefore $2Kd$-dimensional.

4 Experiments

In this section, we present the experiments to evaluate the performance of the proposed method for question retrieval.

4.1 Data Set and Evaluation Metrics

We collect the data sets from Yahoo! Answers and Baidu Zhidao. Yahoo! Answers and Baidu Zhidao represent the largest and the most popular cQA archives in English and Chinese, respectively. More specifically, we utilized the *resolved* questions at Yahoo! Answers and Baidu Zhidao. The questions include 10 million items from Yahoo! Answers and 8 million items from Baidu Zhidao (also called retrieval data). Each resolved question consists of three fields: "title", "description" and "answers", as well as some metadata, such as "category". For question retrieval, we use only the "title" field and "category" metadata. It is assumed that the titles of questions already provide enough semantic information for understanding users' information needs (Duan et al., 2008). We develop two test sets, one for "Yahoo data", and the other for "Baidu data". In order to create the test sets, we collect some extra questions that have been posted more recently than the retrieval data, and randomly sample $1,000$ questions for Yahoo! Answers and Baidu Zhidao, respectively. We take those questions as queries. All questions are lowercased and stemmed. Stopwords[5] are also removed.

	#queries	#candidate	#relevant
Yahoo data	1,000	13,000	2,671
Baidu data	1,000	8,000	2,104

Table 1: Statistics on the manually labeled data.

We separately index all data from Yahoo! Answers and Baidu Zhidao using an open source *Lucene* with the BM25 scoring function[6]. For each query from Yahoo! Answers and Baidu Zhidao, we retrieve the several candidate questions from the corresponding indexed data by using the BM25 ranking algorithm in *Lucene*. On average, each query from Yahoo! Answers has 13 candidate questions and the average number of candidate questions for Baidu Zhidao is 8.

We recruit students to label the relevance of the candidate questions regarding to the queries. Specifically, for each type of language, we let three native students. Given a candidate question, a student is asked to label it with "relevant" or "irrelevant". If a candidate question is considered semantically similar to the query, the student will label it as "relevant"; otherwise, the student will label it as "irrelevant". As a result, each candidate question gets three labels and the majority of the label is taken as the final decision for a query-candidate pair. We randomly split each of the two labeled data sets into a validation set and a test set with a ration $1:3$. The validation set is used for tuning parameters of different models, while the test set is used for evaluating how well the models ranked relevant candidates in contrast to irrelevant candidates. Table 1 presents the manually labeled data.

Please note that rather than evaluate both retrieval and ranking capability of different meth-

[5]http://truereader.com/manuals/onix/stopwords1.html

[6]We use the BM25 implementation provided by Apache Lucene (http://lucene.apache.org/), using the default parameter setting ($k_1 = 1.2, b = 0.75$)

ods like the existing work (Cao et al., 2010), we compare them in a ranking task. This may lose recall for some methods, but it can enable large-scale evaluation.

In order to evaluate the performance of different models, we employ Mean Average Precision (MAP), Mean Reciprocal Rank (MRR), R-Precision (R-Prec), and Precision at K (P@5) as evaluation measures. These measures are widely used in the literature for question retrieval in cQA (Cao et al., 2010).

4.2 Parameter Setting

In our experiments, we train the word embeddings on another large-scale data set from cQA sites. For English, we train the word embeddings on the Yahoo! Webscope dataset[7]. For Chinese, we train the word embeddings on a data set with 1 billion web pages from Baidu Zhidao. These two data sets do not intersect with the above mentioned retrieval data. Little pre-processing is conducted for the training of word embeddings. The resulting text is tokenized using the Stanford tokenizer,[8], and every word is converted to lowercase. Since the proposed framework has no limits in using which of the word embedding learning methods, we only consider the following two representative methods: *Skip-gram* (baseline) and *M-NET*. To train the word embedding using these two methods, we apply the same setting for their common parameters. Specifically, the count of negative samples r is set to 3; the context window size l is set to 5; each model is trained through 1 epoch; the learning rate is initialized as 0.025 and is set to decrease linearly so that it approached zero at the end of training.

Besides, the combination weight β used in *M-NET* also plays an important role in producing high quality word embedding. Overemphasizing the weight of the original objective of *Skip-gram* may result in weakened influence of metadata, while putting too large weight on metadata powered objective may hurt the generality of learned word embedding. Based on our experience, it is a better way to decode the objective combination weight of the *Skip-gram* model and metadata information based on the scale of their respective derivatives during optimization. Finally, we set $\beta = 0.001$ empirically. Note that if the parameter is optimized on the validation set, the final performance can be further improved.

For parameter K used in FV, we do an experiment on the validation data set to determine the best value among $1, 2, 4, \cdots, 64$ in terms of MAP. As a result, we set $K = 16$ in the experiments empirically as this setting yields the best performance.

4.3 Main Results

In this subsection, we present the experimental results on the test sets of Yahoo data and Baidu data. We compare the baseline word embedding trained by *Skip-gram* against this trained by *M-NET*. The dimension of word embedding is set as 50,100 and 300. Since the motivation of this paper attempts to tackle the lexical gap problem for queried questions and questions in the archive, we also compare them with the two groups of methods which also address the lexical gap in the literature. The first group is the translation models: word-based translation model (Jeon et al., 2005), word-based translation language model (Xue et al., 2008), and phrase-based translation model (Zhou et al., 2011). We implement those three translation models based on the original papers and train those models with (question, best answer) pairs from the Yahoo! Webscope dataset Yahoo answers and the 1 billion web pages of Baidu Zhidao for English and Chinese, respectively. Training the translation models with different pairs (e.g., question-best answer, question-description, question-answer) may achieve inconsistent performance on Yahoo data and Baidu data, but its comparison and analysis are beyond the scope of this paper. The second group is the topic-based methods: unsupervised question-answer topic model (Ji et al., 2012) and supervised question-answer topic model (Zhang et al., 2014a). We re-implement these two topic-based models and tune the parameter settings on our data set. Besides, we also introduce a baseline language model (LM) (Zhai and Lafferty, 2001) for comparison.

Table 2 shows the question retrieval performance by using different evaluation metrics. From this table, we can see that learning continuous word embedding representations (Skip-gram + FV, M-NET + FV) for question retrieval can outperform the translation-based approaches and topic-based approaches on all evaluation metrics. We conduct a statistical test (t-test), the results

[7] The Yahoo! Webscope dataset Yahoo answers comprehensive questions and answers version 1.0.2, available at http://reseach.yahoo.com/Academic_Relations.

[8] http://nlp.stanford.edu/software/tokenizer.shtml

Model	dim	Yahoo data				Baidu data			
		MAP	MRR	R-Prec	P@5	MAP	MRR	R-Prec	P@5
LM (baseline)	-	0.435	0.472	0.381	0.305	0.392	0.413	0.325	0.247
(Jeon et al., 2005)	-	0.463	0.495	0.396	0.332	0.414	0.428	0.341	0.256
(Xue et al., 2008)	-	0.518	0.560	0.423	0.346	0.431	0.435	0.352	0.264
(Zhou et al., 2011)	-	0.536	0.587	0.439	0.361	0.448	0.450	0.367	0.273
(Ji et al., 2012)	-	0.508	0.544	0.405	0.324	0.425	0.431	0.349	0.258
(Zhang et al., 2014a)	-	0.527	0.572	0.433	0.350	0.443	0.446	0.358	0.265
Skip-gram + FV	50	0.532	0.583	0.437	0.358	0.447	0.450	0.366	0.272
	100	0.544	$0.605^{\dagger}$	0.440	0.363	0.454	0.457	0.373	0.274
	300	$0.550^{\dagger}$	$0.619^{\dagger}$	0.444	0.365	$0.460^{\dagger}$	$0.464^{\dagger}$	0.374	0.277
M-NET + FV	50	$0.548^{\dagger}$	$0.612^{\dagger}$	0.441	0.363	$0.459^{\dagger}$	$0.462^{\dagger}$	0.374	0.276
	100	$0.562^{\ddagger}$	$0.628^{\ddagger}$	$0.452^{\dagger}$	$0.367^{\ddagger}$	$0.468^{\ddagger}$	0.471	$0.378^{\dagger}$	$0.280^{\dagger}$
	300	**$0.571^{\ddagger}$**	**$0.643^{\ddagger}$**	**$0.455^{\ddagger}$**	**$0.374^{\ddagger}$**	**$0.475^{\ddagger}$**	**$0.477^{\ddagger}$**	**$0.385^{\ddagger}$**	**$0.283^{\ddagger}$**

Table 2: Evaluation results on Yahoo data and Baidu data, where dim denotes the dimension of the word embeddings. The bold formate indicates the best results for question retrieval. † indicates that the difference between the results of our proposed approach (Skip-gram + FV, M-NET + FV) and other methods are mildly significant with $p < 0.08$ under a t-test; ‡ indicates the comparisons are statistically significant with $p < 0.05$.

show that the improvements between the proposed M-NET + FV and the two groups of compared methods (translation-based approaches and topic-based approaches) are statistically significant ($p < 0.05$), while the improvements between Skip-gram + FV and the translation-based approaches are mildly significant ($p < 0.08$). Moreover, the metadata of category information powered model (M-NET + FV) outperforms the baseline skip-gram model (Skip-gram + FV) and yields the largest improvements. These results can imply that the metadata powered word embedding is of higher quality than the baseline model with no metadata information regularization. Besides, we also note that setting higher dimension brings more improvements for question retrieval task.

Translation-based methods significantly outperform LM, which demonstrate that matching questions with the semantically related translation words or phrases from question-answer pairs can effectively address the word lexical gap problem. Besides, we also note that phrase-based translation model is more effective because it captures some contextual information in modeling the translation of phrases as a whole. More precise translation can be determined for phrases than for words. Similar observation has also been found in the previous work (Zhou et al., 2011).

On both data sets, topic-based models achieve comparable performance with the translation-based models and but they perform better than LM. The results demonstrate that learning the latent topics aligned across the question-answer pairs can be an alternative for bridging lexical gap problem for question retrieval.

5 Conclusion

This paper proposes to learn continuous vector representations for question retrieval in cQA. We firstly introduce a new metadata powered word embedding method, called M-NET, to leverage the category information within cQA pages to obtain word representations. Once the words are embedded in a continuous space, we treat each question as a BoEW. Then, the variable size BoEWs are aggregated into fixed-length vectors by using FK. Finally, the dot product between FVs are used to calculate the semantic similarities for question retrieval. Experiments on large-scale real world cQA data demonstrate that the efficacy of the proposed approach. For the future work, we will explore how to incorporate more types of metadata information, such as the *user ratings*, *like signals* and *Poll and Survey signals*, into the learning process to obtain more powerful word representations.

Acknowledgments

This work was supported by the National Natural Science Foundation of China (No. 61303180,

No. 61272332 and 61402191), the Beijing Natural Science Foundation (No. 4144087), the Major Project of National Social Science Found (No. 12&2D223), the Fundamental Research Funds for the Central Universities (No. CCNU15ZD003), and also Sponsored by CCF-Tencent Open Research Fund. We thank the anonymous reviewers for their insightful comments.

References

Lada A. Adamic, Jun Zhang, Eytan Bakshy, and Mark S. Ackerman. 2008. Knowledge sharing and yahoo answers: Everyone knows something. In *Proceedings of WWW*, pages 665–674.

Yoshua Bengio, Réjean Ducharme, Pascal Vincent, and Christian Janvin. 2003. A neural probabilistic language model. *J. Mach. Learn. Res.*, 3.

Delphine Bernhard and Iryna Gurevych. 2009. Combining lexical semantic resources with question & answer archives for translation-based answer finding. In *Proceedings of ACL-IJCNLP*.

Li Cai, Guangyou Zhou, Kang Liu, and Jun Zhao. 2011. Learning the latent topics for question retrieval in community qa. In *Proceedings of IJCNLP*, pages 273–281.

Xin Cao, Gao Cong, Bin Cui, and Christian S. Jensen. 2010. A generalized framework of exploring category information for question retrieval in community question answer archives. In *Proceedings of WWW*, pages 201–210.

David Carmel, Avihai Mejer, Yuval Pinter, and Idan Szpektor. 2014. Improving term weighting for community question answering search using syntactic analysis. In *Proceedings of CIKM*, pages 351–360.

Stephane Clinchant and Florent Perronnin. 2013. Aggregating continuous word embeddings for information retrieval. In *Proceedings of the Workshop on Continuous Vector Space Models and their Compositionality*, pages 100–109.

Huizhong Duan, Yunbo Cao, Chin yew Lin, and Yong Yu. 2008. Searching questions by identifying question topic and question focus. In *Proceedings of ACL*.

Eric H. Huang, Richard Socher, Christopher D. Manning, and Andrew Y. Ng. 2012. Improving word representations via global context and multiple word prototypes. In *Proceedings of ACL*, pages 873–882.

Jiwoon Jeon, W. Bruce Croft, and Joon Ho Lee. 2005. Finding similar questions in large question and answer archives. In *Proceedings of CIKM*.

Zongcheng Ji, Fei Xu, Bin Wang, and Ben He. 2012. Question-answer topic model for question retrieval in community question answering. In *Proceedings of CIKM*, pages 2471–2474.

Jung-Tae Lee, Sang-Bum Kim, Young-In Song, and Hae-Chang Rim. 2008. Bridging lexical gaps between queries and questions on large online q&a collections with compact translation models. In *Proceedings of EMNLP*, pages 410–418.

Andrew L. Maas, Raymond E. Daly, Peter T. Pham, Dan Huang, Andrew Y. Ng, and Christopher Potts. 2011. Learning word vectors for sentiment analysis. In *Proceedings of ACL*, pages 142–150.

Tomas Mikolov, Ilya Sutskever, Kai Chen, Greg S Corrado, and Jeff Dean. 2013. Distributed representations of words and phrases and their compositionality. In *Proceedings of NIPS*, pages 3111–3119.

Stefan Riezler, Er Vasserman, Ioannis Tsochantaridis, Vibhu Mittal, and Yi Liu. 2007. Statistical machine translation for query expansion in answer retrieval. In *Proceedings of ACL*.

S. Robertson, S. Walker, S. Jones, M. Hancock-Beaulieu, and M. Gatford. 1994. Okapi at trec-3. In *Proceedings of TREC*, pages 109–126.

Jorge Sanchez, Florent Perronnin, Thomas Mensink, and Jakob J. Verbeek. 2013. Image classification with the fisher vector: Theory and practice. *International Journal of Computer Vision*, pages 222–245.

A. Singh. 2012. Entity based q&a retrieval. In *Proceedings of EMNLP*, pages 1266–1277.

M. Surdeanu, M. Ciaramita, and H. Zaragoza. 2008. Learning to rank answers on large online qa collections. In *Proceedings of ACL*, pages 719–727.

Joseph Turian, Lev-Arie Ratinov, and Yoshua Bengio. 2010. Word representations: A simple and general method for semi-supervised learning. In *Proceedings of ACL*.

Kai Wang, Zhaoyan Ming, and Tat-Seng Chua. 2009. A syntactic tree matching approach to finding similar questions in community-based qa services. In *Proceedings of SIGIR*, pages 187–194.

B. Wang, X. Wang, C. Sun, B. Liu, and L. Sun. 2010. Modeling semantic relevance for question-answer pairs in web social communities. In *ACL*.

Chang Xu, Yalong Bai, Jiang Bian, Bin Gao, Gang Wang, Xiaoguang Liu, and Tie-Yan Liu. 2014. Rc-net: A general framework for incorporating knowledge into word representations. In *Proceedings of CIKM*, pages 1219–1228.

Xiaobing Xue, Jiwoon Jeon, and W. Bruce Croft. 2008. Retrieval models for question and answer archives. In *Proceedings of SIGIR*, pages 475–482.

Mo Yu and Mark Dredze. 2014. Improving lexical embeddings with semantic knowledge. In *Proceedings of ACL*, pages 545–550.

Chengxiang Zhai and John Lafferty. 2001. A study of smoothing methods for language models applied to ad hoc information retrieval. In *Proceedings of SIGIR*, pages 334–342.

Kai Zhang, Wei Wu, Haocheng Wu, Zhoujun Li, and Ming Zhou. 2014a. Question retrieval with high quality answers in community question answering. In *Proceedings of CIKM*, pages 371–380.

Qi Zhang, Jihua Kang, Jin Qian, and Xuanjing Huang. 2014b. Continuous word embeddings for detecting local text reuses at the semantic level. In *Proceedings of the 37th International ACM SIGIR Conference on Research & Development in Information Retrieval*, SIGIR '14, pages 797–806.

Guangyou Zhou, Li Cai, Jun Zhao, and Kang Liu. 2011. Phrase-based translation model for question retrieval in community question answer archives. In *Proceedings of ACL*, pages 653–662.

Guangyou Zhou, Yubo Chen, Daojian Zeng, and Jun Zhao. 2013. Towards faster and better retrieval models for question search. In *Proceedings of CIKM*, pages 2139–2148.

Question Answering over Freebase with Multi-Column Convolutional Neural Networks

Li Dong[†*] **Furu Wei**[‡] **Ming Zhou**[‡] **Ke Xu**[†]
[†]SKLSDE Lab, Beihang University, Beijing, China
[‡]Microsoft Research, Beijing, China
donglixp@gmail.com {fuwei,mingzhou}@microsoft.com
kexu@nlsde.buaa.edu.cn

Abstract

Answering natural language questions over a knowledge base is an important and challenging task. Most of existing systems typically rely on hand-crafted features and rules to conduct question understanding and/or answer ranking. In this paper, we introduce multi-column convolutional neural networks (MCCNNs) to understand questions from three different aspects (namely, answer path, answer context, and answer type) and learn their distributed representations. Meanwhile, we jointly learn low-dimensional embeddings of entities and relations in the knowledge base. Question-answer pairs are used to train the model to rank candidate answers. We also leverage question paraphrases to train the column networks in a multi-task learning manner. We use FREEBASE as the knowledge base and conduct extensive experiments on the WEBQUESTIONS dataset. Experimental results show that our method achieves better or comparable performance compared with baseline systems. In addition, we develop a method to compute the salience scores of question words in different column networks. The results help us intuitively understand what MCCNNs learn.

1 Introduction

Automatic question answering systems return the direct and exact answers to natural language questions. In recent years, the development of large-scale knowledge bases, such as FREEBASE (Bollacker et al., 2008), provides a rich resource to answer open-domain questions. However, how to understand questions and bridge the gap between natural languages and structured semantics of knowledge bases is still very challenging.

Up to now, there are two mainstream methods for this task. The first one is based on semantic parsing (Berant et al., 2013; Berant and Liang, 2014) and the other relies on information extraction over the structured knowledge base (Yao and Van Durme, 2014; Bordes et al., 2014a; Bordes et al., 2014b). The semantic parsers learn to understand natural language questions by converting them into logical forms. Then, the parse results are used to generate structured queries to search knowledge bases and obtain the answers. Recent works mainly focus on using question-answer pairs, instead of annotated logical forms of questions, as weak training signals (Liang et al., 2011; Krishnamurthy and Mitchell, 2012) to reduce annotation costs. However, some of them still assume a fixed and pre-defined set of lexical triggers which limit their domains and scalability capability. In addition, they need to manually design features for semantic parsers. The second approach uses information extraction techniques for open question answering. These methods retrieve a set of candidate answers from the knowledge base, and the extract features for the question and these candidates to rank them. However, the method proposed by Yao and Van Durme (2014) relies on rules and dependency parse results to extract hand-crafted features for questions. Moreover, some methods (Bordes et al., 2014a; Bordes et al., 2014b) use the summation of question word embeddings to represent questions, which ignores word order information and cannot process complicated questions.

In this paper, we introduce the multi-column convolutional neural networks (MCCNNs) to automatically analyze questions from multiple aspects. Specifically, the model shares the same word embeddings to represent question words.

[*]Contribution during internship at Microsoft Research.

Proceedings of the 53rd Annual Meeting of the Association for Computational Linguistics and the 7th International Joint Conference on Natural Language Processing, pages 260–269,
Beijing, China, July 26-31, 2015.

MCCNNs use different column networks to extract answer types, relations, and context information from the input questions. The entities and relations in the knowledge base (namely FREEBASE in our experiments) are also represented as low-dimensional vectors. Then, a score layer is employed to rank candidate answers according to the representations of questions and candidate answers. The proposed information extraction based method utilizes question-answer pairs to automatically learn the model without relying on manually annotated logical forms and hand-crafted features. We also do not use any pre-defined lexical triggers and rules. In addition, the question paraphrases are also used to train networks and generalize for the unseen words in a multi-task learning manner. We have conducted extensive experiments on WEBQUESTIONS. Experimental results illustrate that our method outperforms several baseline systems.

The contributions of this paper are three-fold:

- We introduce multi-column convolutional neural networks for question understanding without relying on hand-crafted features and rules, and use question paraphrases to train the column networks and word vectors in a multi-task learning manner;
- We jointly learn low-dimensional embeddings for the entities and relations in FREEBASE with question-answer pairs as supervision signals;
- We conduct extensive experiments on the WEBQUESTIONS dataset, and provide some intuitive interpretations for MCCNNs by developing a method to detect salient question words in the different column networks.

2 Related Work

The state-of-the-art methods for question answering over a knowledge base can be classified into two classes, i.e., semantic parsing based and information retrieval based.

Semantic parsing based approaches aim at learning semantic parsers which parse natural language questions into logical forms and then query knowledge base to lookup answers. The most important step is mapping questions into predefined logical forms, such as combinatory categorial grammar (Cai and Yates, 2013) and dependency-based compositional semantics (Liang et al., 2011). Some semantic parsing based systems required manually annotated logical forms to train the parsers (Zettlemoyer and Collins, 2005; Kwiatkowski et al., 2010). These annotations are relatively expensive. So recent works (Liang et al., 2011; Kwiatkowski et al., 2013; Berant et al., 2013; Berant and Liang, 2014; Bao et al., 2014; Reddy et al., 2014) mainly aimed at using weak supervision (question-answer pairs) to effectively train semantic parsers. These methods achieved comparable results without using logical forms annotated by experts. However, some methods relied on lexical triggers or manually defined features.

On the other hand, information retrieval based systems retrieve a set of candidate answers and then conduct further analysis to obtain answers. Their main difference is how to select correct answers from the candidate set. Yao and Van Durme (2014) used rules to extract question features from dependency parse of questions, and used relations and properties in the retrieved topic graph as knowledge base features. Then, the production of these two kinds of features was fed into a logistic regression model to classify the question's candidate answers into correct/wrong. In contrast, we do not use rules, dependency parse results, or hand-crafted features for question understanding. Some other works (Bordes et al., 2014a; Bordes et al., 2014b) learned low-dimensional vectors for question words and knowledge base constitutes, and used the sum of vectors to represent questions and candidate answers. However, simple vector addition ignores word order information and high-order n-grams. For example, the question representations of *who killed A* and *who A killed* are same in the vector addition model. We instead use multi-column convolutional neural networks which are more powerful to process complicated question patterns. Moreover, our multi-column network architecture distinguishes between information of answer type, answer path and answer context by learning multiple column networks, while the addition model mixes them together.

Another line of related work is applying deep learning techniques for the question answering task. Grefenstette et al. (2014) proposed a deep architecture to learn a semantic parser from annotated logic forms of questions. Iyyer et al. (2014) introduced dependency-tree recursive neural networks for the quiz bowl game which asked players to answer an entity for a given paragraph. Yu et al. (2014) proposed a bigram model based on convolutional neural networks to select answer sentences from text data. The model learned a similarity function between questions and answer sentences. Yih et al. (2014) used convolutional neural networks to answer single-relation questions on REVERB (Fader et al., 2011). However, the system worked on relation-entity triples instead of more structured knowledge bases. For instance, the question shown in Figure 1 is answered by using several triples in FREEBASE. Also, we can utilize richer information (such as entity types) in structured knowledge bases.

3 Setup

Given a natural language question $q = w_1 \ldots w_n$, we retrieve related entities and properties from FREEBASE and use them as the candidate answers C_q. Our goal is to score these candidates and predict answers. For instance, the correct output of the question *when did Avatar release in UK* is *2009-12-17*. It should be noted that there may be several correct answers for a question. In order to train the model, we use question-answer pairs without annotated logic forms. We further describe the datasets used in our work as follows:

WebQuestions This dataset (Berant et al., 2013) contains 3,778 training instances and 2,032 test instances. We further split the training instances into the training set and the development set by 80%/20%. The questions were collected by querying the Google Suggest API. A breadth-first search beginning with *wh-* was conducted. Then, answers were annotated in Amazon Mechanical Turk. All the answers can be found in FREEBASE.

Freebase It is a large-scale knowledge base that consists of general facts (Bollacker et al., 2008). These facts are organized as subject-property-object triples. For example, the fact *Avatar is directed by James Cameron* is represented by (/m/0bth54, film.film.directed_by, /m/03_gd) in RDF format. The preprocess method presented in (Bordes et al., 2014a) was used to make FREEBASE fit in memory. Specifically, we kept the triples where one of the entities appeared in the training/development set of WEBQUESTIONS or CLUEWEB extractions provided in (Lin et al., 2012), and removed the entities appearing less than five times. Then, we obtained 18M triples that contained 2.9M entities and 7k relation types. As described in (Bordes et al., 2014a), this preprocess method does not ease the task because WEBQUESTIONS only contains about 2k entities.

WikiAnswers Fader et al. (2013) extracted the similar questions on WIKIANSWERS and used them as question paraphrases. There are 350,000 paraphrase clusters which contain about two million questions. They are used to generalize for unseen words and question patterns.

4 Methods

The overview of our framework is shown in Figure 1. For instance, for the question *when did Avatar release in UK*, the related nodes of the entity *Avatar* are queried from FREEBASE. These related nodes are regarded as candidate answers (C_q). Then, for every candidate answer a, the model predicts a score $S(q, a)$ to determine whether it is a correct answer or not.

We use multi-column convolutional neural networks (MCCNNs) to learn representations of questions. The models share the same word embeddings, and have multiple columns of convolutional neural networks. The number of columns is set to three in our QA task. These columns are used to analyze different aspects of a question, i.e., answer path, answer context, and answer type. The vector representations learned by these columns are denoted as $\mathbf{f}_1(q), \mathbf{f}_2(q), \mathbf{f}_3(q)$. We also learn embeddings for the candidate answers appeared in FREEBASE. For every candidate answer a, we compute its vector representations and denote them as $\mathbf{g}_1(a), \mathbf{g}_2(a), \mathbf{g}_3(a)$. These three vectors correspond to the three aspects used in question understanding. Using these vector representations defined for questions and answers, we can compute the score for the question-answer pair (q, a). Specifically, the scoring function $S(q, a)$ is defined as:

$$S(q,a) = \underbrace{\mathbf{f}_1(q)^{\mathsf{T}}\mathbf{g}_1(a)}_{answer\ path} + \underbrace{\mathbf{f}_2(q)^{\mathsf{T}}\mathbf{g}_2(a)}_{answer\ context} + \underbrace{\mathbf{f}_3(q)^{\mathsf{T}}\mathbf{g}_3(a)}_{answer\ type} \tag{1}$$

where $\mathbf{f}_i(q)$ and $\mathbf{g}_i(a)$ have the same dimension. As shown in Figure 1, the score layer computes scores and adds them together.

4.1 Candidate Generation

The first step is to retrieve candidate answers from FREEBASE for a question. Questions should contain an identified entity that can be linked to the

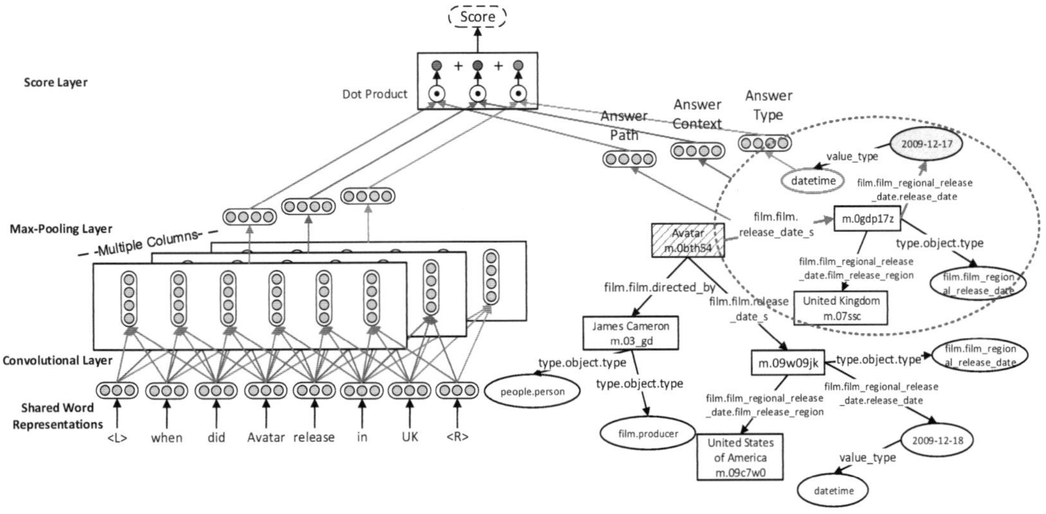

Figure 1: Overview for the question-answer pair *(when did Avatar release in UK, 2009-12-17)*. Left: network architecture for question understanding. Right: embedding candidate answers.

knowledge base. We use the Freebase Search API (Bollacker et al., 2008) to query named entities in a question. If there is not any named entity, noun phrases are queried. We use the top one entity in the ranked list returned by the API. This entity resolution method was also used in (Yao and Van Durme, 2014). Better methods can be developed, while it is not the focus of this paper. Then, all the 2-hops nodes of the linked entity are regarded as the candidate answers. We denote the candidate set for the question q as C_q.

4.2 MCCNNs for Question Understanding

MCCNNs use multiple convolutional neural networks to learn different aspects of questions from shared input word embeddings. For every single column, the network structure presented in (Collobert et al., 2011) is used to tackle the variable-length questions.

We present the model in the left part of Figure 1. Specifically, for the question $q = w_1 \dots w_n$, the lookup layer transforms every word into a vector $\mathbf{w}_j = \mathbf{W}_v \mathbf{u}(w_j)$, where $\mathbf{W}_v \in \mathbb{R}^{d_v \times |V|}$ is the word embedding matrix, $\mathbf{u}(w_j) \in \{0,1\}^{|V|}$ is the one-hot representation of w_j, and $|V|$ is the vocabulary size. The word embeddings are parameters, and are updated in the training process.

Then, the convolutional layer computes representations of the words in sliding windows. For the i-th column of MCCNNs, the convolutional layer computes n vectors for question q. The j-th vector is:

$$\mathbf{x}_j^{(i)} = \mathbf{h}\left(\mathbf{W}^{(i)}\left[\mathbf{w}_{j-s}^{\mathsf{T}} \dots \mathbf{w}_j^{\mathsf{T}} \dots \mathbf{w}_{j+s}^{\mathsf{T}}\right]^{\mathsf{T}} + \mathbf{b}^{(i)}\right) \tag{2}$$

where $(2s+1)$ is the window size, $\mathbf{W}^{(i)} \in \mathbb{R}^{d_q \times (2s+1)d_v}$ is the weight matrix of convolutional layer, $\mathbf{b}^{(i)} \in \mathbb{R}^{d_q \times 1}$ is the bias vector, and $\mathbf{h}(\cdot)$ is the nonlinearity function (such as softsign, tanh, and sigmoid). Paddings are used for left and right absent words.

Finally, a max-pooling layer is followed to obtain the fixed-size vector representations of questions. The max-pooling layer in the i-th column of MCCNNs computes the representation of the question q via:

$$\mathbf{f}_i(q) = \max_{j=1,\dots,n} \{\mathbf{x}_j^{(i)}\} \tag{3}$$

where $\max\{\cdot\}$ is an element-wise operator over vectors.

4.3 Embedding Candidate Answers

Vector representations $\mathbf{g}_1(a), \mathbf{g}_2(a), \mathbf{g}_3(a)$ are learned for the candidate answer a. The vectors are employed to represent different aspects of a. The embedding methods are described as follows:

Answer Path The answer path is the set of relations between the answer node and the entity asked in question. As shown in Figure 1, the 2-hops path between the entity *Avatar* and the correct answer is (film.film.release_date_s, film.film_regional_release_date.release_date). The vector representation $\mathbf{g}_1(a)$ is computed via $\mathbf{g}_1(a) = \frac{1}{\|\mathbf{u}_p(a)\|_1}\mathbf{W}_p\mathbf{u}_p(a)$, where $\|\cdot\|_1$ is 1-norm, $\mathbf{u}_p(a) \in \mathbb{R}^{|R|\times 1}$ is a binary vector which represents the presence or absence of every relation in the answer path, $\mathbf{W}_p \in \mathbb{R}^{d_q\times|R|}$ is the parameter matrix, and $|R|$ is the number of relations. In other words, the embeddings of relations that appear on the answer path are averaged.

Answer Context The 1-hop entities and relations connected to the answer path are regarded as the answer context. It is used to deal with constraints in questions. For instance, as shown in Figure 1, the release date of Avatar in UK is asked, so it is not enough that only the triples on answer path are considered. With the help of context information, the release date in UK has a higher score than in USA. The context representation is $\mathbf{g}_2(a) = \frac{1}{\|\mathbf{u}_c(a)\|_1}\mathbf{W}_c\mathbf{u}_c(a)$, where $\mathbf{W}_c \in \mathbb{R}^{d_q\times|C|}$ is the parameter matrix, $\mathbf{u}_c(a) \in \mathbb{R}^{|C|\times 1}$ is a binary vector expressing the presence or absence of context nodes, and $|C|$ is the number of entities and relations which appear in answer context.

Answer Type Type information in FREEBASE is an important clue to score candidate answers. As illustrated in Figure 1, the type of *2009-12-17* is datetime, and the type of *James Cameron* is people.person and film.producer. For the example question *when did Avatar release in UK*, the candidate answers whose types are datetime should be assigned with higher scores than others. The vector representation is defined as $\mathbf{g}_3(a) = \frac{1}{\|\mathbf{u}_t(a)\|_1}\mathbf{W}_t\mathbf{u}_t(a)$, where $\mathbf{W}_t \in \mathbb{R}^{d_q\times|T|}$ is the matrix of type embeddings, $\mathbf{u}_t(a) \in \mathbb{R}^{|T|\times 1}$ is a binary vector which indicates the presence or absence of answer types, and $|T|$ is the number of types. In our implementation, we use the relation common.topic.notable_types to query types. If a candidate answer is a property value, we instead use its value type (e.g., float, string, datetime).

4.4 Model Training

For every correct answer $a \in A_q$ of the question q, we randomly sample k wrong answers a' from the set of candidate answers C_q, and use them as negative instances to estimate parameters. To be more specific, the hinge loss is considered for pairs (q, a) and (q, a'):

$$l\left(q, a, a'\right) = \left(m - S(q, a) + S(q, a')\right)_+ \quad (4)$$

where $S(\cdot, \cdot)$ is the scoring function defined in Equation (1), m is the margin parameter employed to regularize the gap between two scores, and $(z)_+ = \max\{0, z\}$. The objective function is:

$$\min \sum_q \frac{1}{|A_q|} \sum_{a\in A_q} \sum_{a'\in R_q} l\left(q, a, a'\right) \quad (5)$$

where $|A_q|$ is the number of correct answers, and $R_q \subseteq C_q \setminus A_q$ is the set of k wrong answers.

The back-propagation algorithm (Rumelhart et al., 1986) is used to train the model. It back-propagates errors from top to the other layers. Derivatives are calculated and gathered to update parameters. The AdaGrad algorithm (Duchi et al., 2011) is then employed to solve this non-convex optimization problem. Moreover, the max-norm regularization (Srebro and Shraibman, 2005; Srivastava et al., 2014) is used for the column vectors of parameter matrices.

4.5 Inference

During the test, we retrieve all the candidate answers C_q for the question q. For every candidate $\hat{a}$, we compute its score $S(q, \hat{a})$. Then, the candidate answers with the highest scores are regarded as predicted results.

Because there may be more than one correct answers for some questions, we need a criterion to determine the score threshold. Specifically, the following equation is used to determine outputs:

$$\hat{A}_q = \{\hat{a} \mid \hat{a} \in C_q \ and \\ \max_{a'\in C_q}\{S(q, a')\} - S(q, \hat{a}) < m\} \quad (6)$$

where m is the margin defined in Equation (4). The candidates whose scores are not far from the best answer are regarded as predicted results.

Some questions may have a large set of candidate answers. So we use a heuristic method to prune their candidate sets. To be more specific, if the number of candidates on the same answer path is greater than 200, we randomly keep 200 candidates for this path. Then, we score and rank all these generated candidate answers together. If one of the candidates on the pruned path is regarded as a predicted answer, we further score the other candidates that are pruned on this path and determine the final results.

4.6 Question Paraphrases for Multi-Task Learning

We use the question paraphrases dataset WIKIANSWERS to generalize for words and question patterns which are unseen in the training set of question-answer pairs. The question understanding results of paraphrases should be same. Consequently, the representations of two paraphrases computed by the same column of MCCNNs should be similar. We use dot similarity to define the hinge loss $l_p(q_1, q_2, q_3)$ as:

$$l_p(q_1, q_2, q_3) = \sum_{i=1}^{3} \left(m_p - \mathbf{f}_i(q_1)^{\mathsf{T}} \mathbf{f}_i(q_2) + \mathbf{f}_i(q_1)^{\mathsf{T}} \mathbf{f}_i(q_3) \right)_+ \quad (7)$$

where q_1, q_2 are questions in the same paraphrase cluster P, q_3 is randomly sampled from another cluster, and m_p is the margin. The objective function is defined as:

$$\min \sum_{P} \sum_{q_1, q_2 \in P} \sum_{q_3 \in R_P} l_p(q_1, q_2, q_3) \quad (8)$$

where R_P contains k_p questions which are randomly sampled from other clusters. The same optimization algorithm described in Section 4.4 is used to update parameters.

5 Experiments

In order to evaluate the model, we use the dataset WEBQUESTIONS (Section 3) to conduct experiments.

Settings The development set is used to select hyper-parameters in the experiments. The nonlinearity function $f = \tanh$ is employed. The dimension of word vectors is set to 25. They are initialized by the pre-trained word embeddings provided in (Turian et al., 2010). The window size of MCCNNs is 5. The dimension of the pooling layers and the dimension of answer embeddings are set to 64. The parameters are initialized by the techniques described in (Bengio, 2012). The max value used for max-norm regularization is 3. The initial learning rate used in AdaGrad is set to 0.01. A mini-batch consists of 10 question-answer pairs, and every question-answer pair has k negative samples that are randomly sampled from its candidate set. The margin values in Equation (4) and Equation (7) is set to $m = 0.5$ and $m_p = 0.1$.

Method	F1	P@1
(Berant et al., 2013)	31.4	-
(Berant and Liang, 2014)	39.9	-
(Bao et al., 2014)	37.5	-
(Yao and Van Durme, 2014)	33.0	-
(Bordes et al., 2014a)	39.2	40.4
(Bordes et al., 2014b)	29.7	31.3
MCCNN (our)	**40.8**	**45.1**

Table 1: Evaluation results on the test split of WEBQUESTIONS.

5.1 Experimental Results

The evaluation metrics macro F1 score (Berant et al., 2013) and precision @ 1 (Bordes et al., 2014a) are reported. We use the official evaluation script provided by Berant et al. (2013) to compute the F1 score. Notably, the F1 score defined in (Yao and Van Durme, 2014) is slightly different from others (how to compute scores for the questions without predicted results). We instead use the original definition in experiments.

As shown in Table 1, our method achieves better or comparable results than baseline methods on WEBQUESTIONS. To be more specific, the first three rows are semantic parsing based methods, and the other baselines are information extraction based methods. These approaches except (Bordes et al., 2014a; Bordes et al., 2014b) rely on handcrafted features and predefined rules. The results show that automatically question understanding can be as good as the models using manually designed features. Besides, our multi-column convolutional neural networks based model outperforms the methods that use the sum of word embeddings as question representations (Bordes et al., 2014a; Bordes et al., 2014b).

5.2 Model Analysis

We also conduct ablation experiments to compare the results using different experiment settings. As shown in Table 2, the abbreviation *w/o* means removing a particular part from the model. We find that answer path information is most important among these three columns, and answer type information is more important than answer context information. The reason is that answer path and answer type are more direct clues for questions, but answer context is used to handle additional constraints in questions which are less common in the dataset. Moreover, we compare to the

Setting	F1	P@1
all	**40.8**	**45.1**
w/o path	32.5	37.1
w/o type	37.7	40.9
w/o context	39.1	41.0
w/o multi-column	38.4	41.8
w/o paraphrase	40.0	43.9
1-hop	29.3	32.2

Table 2: Evaluation results of different settings on the test split of WEBQUESTIONS. w/o path/type/context: without using the specific column. w/o multi-column: tying parameters of multiple columns. w/o paraphrase: without using question paraphrases for training. 1-hop: using 1-hop paths to generate candidate answers.

model using single-column networks (w/o multi-column), i.e., tying the parameters of different columns. The results indicate that using multiple columns to understand questions from different aspects improves the performance. Besides, we find that using question paraphrases in a multi-task learning manner contributes to the performance. In addition, we evaluate the results only using 1-hop paths to generate candidate answers. Compared to using 2-hops paths, we find that the performance drops significantly. This indicates only using the nodes directly connected to the queried entity in FREEBASE cannot handle many questions.

5.3 Salient Words Detection

In order to analyze the model, we detect salient words in questions. The salience score of a question word depends on how much the word affects the computation of question representation. In other words, if a word plays more important role in the model, its salience score should be larger.

We compute several salience scores for a same word to illustrate its importance in different columns of networks. For the i-th column, the salience score of word w_j in the question $q = w_1^n$ is defined as:

$$e_i(w_j) = \left\| \mathbf{f}_i \left(w_1^n \right) - \mathbf{f}_i \left(w_1^{j-1} w'_j w_{j+1}^n \right) \right\|_2 \quad (9)$$

where the word w_j is replaced with w'_j, and $\|\cdot\|_2$ denotes Euclidean norm. In practice, we replace w_j with several stop words (such as *is*, *to*, and *a*), and then compute their average score.

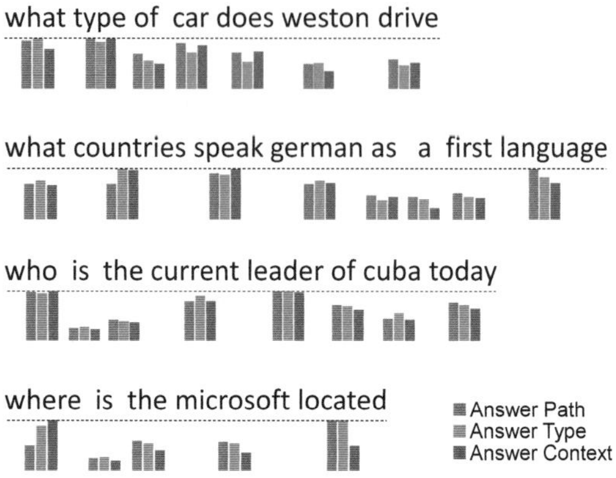

Figure 2: Salient words detection results for questions. From left to right, the three bars of every word correspond to salience scores in answer path column, answer type column, and answer context column, respectively. The salience scores are normalized by the max values of different columns.

As shown in Figure 2, we compute salience scores for several questions, and normalize them by the max values in different columns. We clearly see that these words play different roles in a question. The overall conclusion is that the *wh-* words (such as *what*, *who* and *where*) tend to be important for question understanding. Moreover, nouns dependent of the *wh-* words and verbs are important clues to obtain question representations. For instance, the figure demonstrates that the nouns *type/country/leader* and the verbs *speak/located* are salient in the columns of networks. These observations agree with previous works (Li and Roth, 2002). Some manually defined rules (Yao and Van Durme, 2014) used in the question answering task are also based on them.

5.4 Examples

Question representations computed by different columns of MCCNNs are used to query their most similar neighbors. We use cosine similarity in experiments. This experiment demonstrates whether the model learns different aspects of questions. For example, if a column of networks is employed to analyze answer types, the answer types of nearest questions should be same as the query.

As shown in Table 3, these three columns of table correspond to different columns of networks. To be more specific, the first column is used to process answer path. We find that the model learns different question patterns for the same

Column 1 (Answer Path)	Column 2 (Answer Type)	Column 3 (Answer Context)
what to do in hollywood can this weekend	**where be george washington originally from**	**where do charle draw go to college**
what to do in midland tx this weekend	where be george washington carver from	where do kevin love go to college
what to do in cancun with family	where be george bush from	where do pauley perrette go to college
what to do at fairfield can	where be the thame river source	where do kevin jame go to college
what to see in downtown asheville nc	where be the main headquarters of google	where do charle draw go to high school
what to see in toronto top 10	in what town do ned kelly and he family grow up	where do draw bree go to college wikianswer
who found collegehumor	**who be the leader of north korea today**	**who be judy garland father**
who found the roanoke settlement	who be the leader of syrium now	who be clint eastwood date
who own skywest	who be the leader of cuba 2012	who be emma stone father
who start mary kay	who be the leader of france 2012	who be robin robert father
who be the owner of kfc	who be the current leader of cuba today	who miley cyrus engage to
who own wikimedium foundation	who be the minority leader of the house of representative now	who be chri cooley marry to
what type of money do japanese use	**what be the two official language of paraguay**	**what be the timezone in vancouver**
what kind of money do japanese use	what be the local language of israel	what be my timezone in californium
what type of money do jamaica use	what be the four official language of nigerium	what be los angeles california time zone
what type of currency do brazil use	what be the official language of jamaica	what be my timezone in oklahoma
what type of money do you use in cuba	what be the dominant language of jamaica	what be my timezone in louisiana
what money do japanese use	what be the official language of brazil now	what be the time zone in france

Table 3: Using question representations obtained by different column networks to query the nearest neighbors. From left to right, the three columns are used to analyze information about answer path, answer type, and answer context, respectively. Lemmatization is used to better show question patterns.

path. For instance, the vector representations of "*who found/own/start* *" and "*who be the owner of* *" obtained by the first column are similar. The second column is employed to extract answer type information from questions. The answer types of example questions in Table 3 are same, while they may ask different relations. The third column learns to embed question information into answer context. We find that the similar questions are clustered together by this column.

5.5 Error Analysis

We investigate the predicted results on the development set, and show several error causes as follows.

Candidate Generation Some entity mentions in questions are linked incorrectly, hence we cannot obtain the desired candidate answers. As described in (Yao and Van Durme, 2014), the Freebase Search API returned correct entities for 86.4% of questions in top one results. Because some questions use the abbreviation or a part of its mention to express an entity. For example, it is not trivial to link *jfk* to *John F. Kennedy* in the question "*where did jfk and his wife live*". A better entity retrieval step should be developed for the open question answering scenario.

Time-Aware Questions We need to compare date values for some time-aware questions. For instance, to answer the question "*who is johnny cash's **first** wife*", we have to know the order of several marriages by comparing the marriage date. Its correct response should contain only one entity (*vivian liberto*). However, our system additionally outputs *june carter cash* who is his second wife, because both the candidate answers are connected to *johnny cash* by the relation people.person.spouse_s. In order to solve this issue, we need to define some ad-hoc operators used for comparisons or develop more advanced semantic representations.

Ambiguous Questions Some questions are ambiguous to obtain their correct representations. For example, the question *what has anna kendrick been in* is used to ask what movies she has played in. This question does not have explicit clue words to indicate the meanings, so it is difficult to rank the candidates. Moreover, the question *who is aidan quinn* is employed to ask what his occupation is. It also lacks sufficient clues for question understanding, and using *who is* to ask occupation is rare in the training data.

6 Conclusion and Future Work

This paper presents a method for question answering over FREEBASE using multi-column convolutional neural networks (MCCNNs). MCCNNs share the same word embeddings, and use multiple columns of convolutional neural networks to learn the representations of different aspects of questions. Accordingly, we use low-dimensional embeddings to represent multiple aspects of candidate answers, i.e., answer path, answer type, and answer context. We estimate the parameters from question-answer pairs, and use question paraphrases to train the columns of MCCNNs in a multi-task learning manner. Experimental results on WEBQUESTIONS show that our approach achieves better or comparable performance comparing with baselines. There are several interesting directions that are worth exploring in the future. For instance, we are integrating more external knowledge source, such as CLUEWEB (Lin et al., 2012), to train MCCNNs in a multi-task learning manner. Furthermore, as our model is capable of detecting the most important words in a question, it would be interesting to use the results to mine effective question patterns.

Acknowledgments

This research was supported by NSFC (Grant No. 61421003) and the fund of the State Key Lab of Software Development Environment (Grant No. SKLSDE-2015ZX-05).

References

Junwei Bao, Nan Duan, Ming Zhou, and Tiejun Zhao. 2014. Knowledge-based question answering as machine translation. In *Proceedings of the 52nd Annual Meeting of the Association for Computational Linguistics (Volume 1: Long Papers)*, pages 967–976. Association for Computational Linguistics.

Yoshua Bengio. 2012. Practical recommendations for gradient-based training of deep architectures. In *Neural Networks: Tricks of the Trade*, pages 437–478.

Jonathan Berant and Percy Liang. 2014. Semantic parsing via paraphrasing. In *Proceedings of the 52nd Annual Meeting of the Association for Computational Linguistics (Volume 1: Long Papers)*, pages 1415–1425. Association for Computational Linguistics.

Jonathan Berant, Andrew Chou, Roy Frostig, and Percy Liang. 2013. Semantic parsing on freebase from question-answer pairs. In *Proceedings of the 2013 Conference on Empirical Methods in Natural Language Processing*, pages 1533–1544. Association for Computational Linguistics.

Kurt D. Bollacker, Colin Evans, Praveen Paritosh, Tim Sturge, and Jamie Taylor. 2008. Freebase: a collaboratively created graph database for structuring human knowledge. In *International Conference on Management of Data*, pages 1247–1250.

Antoine Bordes, Sumit Chopra, and Jason Weston. 2014a. Question answering with subgraph embeddings. In *Proceedings of the 2014 Conference on Empirical Methods in Natural Language Processing (EMNLP)*, pages 615–620. Association for Computational Linguistics.

Antoine Bordes, Jason Weston, and Nicolas Usunier. 2014b. Open question answering with weakly supervised embedding models. In *Machine Learning and Knowledge Discovery in Databases - European Conference, ECML PKDD 2014, Nancy, France, September 15-19, 2014. Proceedings, Part I*, pages 165–180.

Qingqing Cai and Alexander Yates. 2013. Large-scale semantic parsing via schema matching and lexicon extension. In *Proceedings of the 51st Annual Meeting of the Association for Computational Linguistics (Volume 1: Long Papers)*, pages 423–433. Association for Computational Linguistics.

Ronan Collobert, Jason Weston, Léon Bottou, Michael Karlen, Koray Kavukcuoglu, and Pavel Kuksa. 2011. Natural language processing (almost) from scratch. *J. Mach. Learn. Res.*, 12:2493–2537, November.

John Duchi, Elad Hazan, and Yoram Singer. 2011. Adaptive subgradient methods for online learning and stochastic optimization. *JMLR*, 12:2121–2159, July.

Anthony Fader, Stephen Soderland, and Oren Etzioni. 2011. Identifying relations for open information extraction. In *Proceedings of the Conference on Empirical Methods in Natural Language Processing*, EMNLP '11, pages 1535–1545, Stroudsburg, PA, USA. Association for Computational Linguistics.

Anthony Fader, Luke Zettlemoyer, and Oren Etzioni. 2013. Paraphrase-driven learning for open question answering. In *Proceedings of the 51st Annual Meeting of the Association for Computational Linguistics (Volume 1: Long Papers)*, pages 1608–1618. Association for Computational Linguistics.

Edward Grefenstette, Phil Blunsom, Nando de Freitas, and Moritz Karl Hermann, 2014. *Proceedings of the ACL 2014 Workshop on Semantic Parsing*, chapter A Deep Architecture for Semantic Parsing, pages 22–27. Association for Computational Linguistics.

Mohit Iyyer, Jordan Boyd-Graber, Leonardo Claudino, Richard Socher, and Hal Daumé III. 2014. A neural network for factoid question answering over paragraphs. In *Proceedings of the 2014 Conference on Empirical Methods in Natural Language Processing (EMNLP)*, pages 633–644. Association for Computational Linguistics.

Jayant Krishnamurthy and Tom M Mitchell. 2012. Weakly supervised training of semantic parsers. In *Proceedings of the 2012 Joint Conference on Empirical Methods in Natural Language Processing and Computational Natural Language Learning*, pages 754–765. Association for Computational Linguistics.

Tom Kwiatkowski, Luke Zettlemoyer, Sharon Goldwater, and Mark Steedman. 2010. Inducing probabilistic ccg grammars from logical form with higher-order unification. In *Proceedings of the 2010 conference on empirical methods in natural language processing*, pages 1223–1233. Association for Computational Linguistics.

Tom Kwiatkowski, Eunsol Choi, Yoav Artzi, and Luke Zettlemoyer. 2013. Scaling semantic parsers with on-the-fly ontology matching. In *Proceedings of the 2013 Conference on Empirical Methods in Natural Language Processing*, pages 1545–1556. Association for Computational Linguistics.

Xin Li and Dan Roth. 2002. Learning question classifiers. In *COLING*, pages 1–7.

P. Liang, M. I. Jordan, and D. Klein. 2011. Learning dependency-based compositional semantics. In *Association for Computational Linguistics (ACL)*, pages 590–599.

Thomas Lin, Mausam, and Oren Etzioni. 2012. Entity linking at web scale. In *Proceedings of the Joint Workshop on Automatic Knowledge Base Construction and Web-scale Knowledge Extraction*, AKBC-WEKEX '12, pages 84–88, Stroudsburg, PA, USA. Association for Computational Linguistics.

Siva Reddy, Mirella Lapata, and Mark Steedman. 2014. Large-scale semantic parsing without question-answer pairs. *Transactions of the Association of Computational Linguistics – Volume 2, Issue 1*, pages 377–392.

D.E. Rumelhart, G.E. Hinton, and R.J. Williams. 1986. Learning representations by back-propagating errors. *Nature*, 323(6088):533–536.

Nathan Srebro and Adi Shraibman. 2005. Rank, trace-norm and max-norm. In *Proceedings of the 18th annual conference on Learning Theory*, pages 545–560. Springer-Verlag.

Nitish Srivastava, Geoffrey Hinton, Alex Krizhevsky, Ilya Sutskever, and Ruslan Salakhutdinov. 2014. Dropout: A simple way to prevent neural networks from overfitting. *Journal of Machine Learning Research*, 15:1929–1958.

Joseph Turian, Lev Ratinov, and Yoshua Bengio. 2010. Word representations: a simple and general method for semi-supervised learning. In *ACL*.

Xuchen Yao and Benjamin Van Durme. 2014. Information extraction over structured data: Question answering with freebase. In *Proceedings of the 52nd Annual Meeting of the Association for Computational Linguistics (Volume 1: Long Papers)*, pages 956–966. Association for Computational Linguistics.

Xuchen Yao, Jonathan Berant, and Benjamin Van Durme, 2014. *Proceedings of the ACL 2014 Workshop on Semantic Parsing*, chapter Freebase QA: Information Extraction or Semantic Parsing?, pages 82–86. Association for Computational Linguistics.

Wen-tau Yih, Xiaodong He, and Christopher Meek. 2014. Semantic parsing for single-relation question answering. In *Proceedings of the 52nd Annual Meeting of the Association for Computational Linguistics (Volume 2: Short Papers)*, pages 643–648. Association for Computational Linguistics.

Lei Yu, Karl Moritz Hermann, Phil Blunsom, and Stephen Pulman. 2014. Deep Learning for Answer Sentence Selection. In *NIPS Deep Learning Workshop*, December.

Luke S. Zettlemoyer and Michael Collins. 2005. Learning to map sentences to logical form: Structured classification with probabilistic categorial grammars. In *In Proceedings of the 21st Conference on Uncertainty in AI*, pages 658–666.

Hubness and Pollution: Delving into Cross-Space Mapping for Zero-Shot Learning

Angeliki Lazaridou   Georgiana Dinu   Marco Baroni
Center for Mind/Brain Sciences
University of Trento
{angeliki.lazaridou|georgiana.dinu|marco.baroni}@unitn.it

Abstract

Zero-shot methods in language, vision and other domains rely on a *cross-space mapping* function that projects vectors from the relevant feature space (e.g., visual-feature-based image representations) to a large semantic word space (induced in an unsupervised way from corpus data), where the entities of interest (e.g., objects images depict) are labeled with the words associated to the nearest neighbours of the mapped vectors. Zero-shot cross-space mapping methods hold great promise as a way to scale up annotation tasks well beyond the labels in the training data (e.g., recognizing objects that were never seen in training). However, the current performance of cross-space mapping functions is still quite low, so that the strategy is not yet usable in practical applications. In this paper, we explore some general properties, both theoretical and empirical, of the cross-space mapping function, and we build on them to propose better methods to estimate it. In this way, we attain large improvements over the state of the art, both in cross-linguistic (word translation) and cross-modal (image labeling) zero-shot experiments.

1 Introduction

In many supervised problems, the parameters of a classification function are estimated on $(\mathbf{x}, y)$ pairs, where $\mathbf{x}$ is a vector representing a training instance in some feature space, and y is the label assigned to the instance. For example, in image labeling $\mathbf{x}$ contains visual features extracted from a picture and y is the name of the object depicted in the picture (Grauman and Leibe, 2011). Since each label is treated as an unanalyzed primitive, this approach requires *ad-hoc* annotation for each label of interest, and it will not scale up to challenges where the potential label set is vast (for example, bilingual dictionary induction, where the label set corresponds to the full vocabulary of the target language).

Zero-shot methods (Palatucci et al., 2009) address the scalability problem by building on the observation that the labels of interest are often words (or longer linguistic expressions), which stand in a semantic similarity relation to each other. Moreover, distributional approaches allow us to estimate very large *semantic word spaces* in an efficient and unsupervised manner, using just unannotated text corpora as input (Turney and Pantel, 2010). Extensive evidence has shown that the similarity estimates obtained by representing words as vectors in such corpus-induced semantic spaces are extremely accurate (Baroni et al., 2014). Under the assumption that the domain of interest (e.g., objects in pictures, words in a source language) exhibits comparable similarity structure to that manifested in language, we can rephrase the learning task, from inducing multiple functions from the source feature space onto independent atomic labels, to that of estimating a single *cross-space mapping* function from vectors in the source feature space onto vectors for the corresponding word labels in distributional semantic space. The induced function can then also be applied to a data-point whose label was not used for training. The word corresponding to the nearest neighbour of the mapped vector in the latter space is used as the label of the data point. Zero-shot learning using distributional semantic spaces was originally proposed for brain signal decoding (Mitchell et al., 2008), but it has since been extensively applied in other domains, including image labeling (Frome et al., 2013; Lazaridou et al., 2014; Socher et al., 2013) and bilingual dictionary/phrase table induction (Dinu and Baroni, 2014; Mikolov et al.,

Proceedings of the 53rd Annual Meeting of the Association for Computational Linguistics and the 7th International Joint Conference on Natural Language Processing, pages 270–280,
Beijing, China, July 26-31, 2015.

2013a), the two applications we focus on here.

Effective zero-shot learning by cross-space mapping could get us through the manual annotation bottleneck that hampers many applications. However, in practice, the accuracy in label retrieval with current mapping methods is still too low for practical uses. In image labeling, when a search space of realistic size is considered, accuracy is just above 1% (which is still well above chance for large search spaces). In bilingual lexicon induction, accuracy reaches values around 30% (across words of varying frequency), which are definitely more encouraging, but still indicate that only 1 word in 3 will be translated correctly.

In this article, we look at some general properties of the linear cross-modal mapping function standardly used for zero-shot learning, in order to achieve a better understanding of its shortcomings, and improve its quality by devising methods to overcome them. First, when the mapping function is estimated with least-squares error techniques, we observe a systematic increase in *hubness* (Radovanović et al., 2010b), that is, in the tendency of some vectors ("hubs") to appear in the top neighbour lists of many test items. We connect hubness to least-squares estimation, and we show how it is greatly mitigated when the mapping function is estimated with a max-margin ranking loss instead. Still, switching to max-margin greatly improves accuracy in the cross-linguistic context, but not for vision-to-language mapping. In the cross-modal setting, we observe indeed a different problem, that we name (training instance) *pollution*: The neighbourhoods of mapped test items are "polluted" by the target vectors used in training. This suggests that cross-modal mapping suffers from overfitting issues, and consequently from poor generalization power. Taking inspiration from domain adaptation, which addresses similar generalization concerns, and self-learning, we propose a technique to augment the training data with automatically constructed examples that force the function to generalize better. Having shown the advantages of a ranking loss, our final contribution is the adaptation of some insights from the max-margin literature to our setting, in particular concerning the choice of negative examples. This leads to further accuracy improvements. We thus conclude the paper by reporting zero-shot performances in both cross-modal and cross-language settings that are well above the current state of the art. Table 1 provides a roadmap and summary of our results.

	cross-linguistic	cross-modal
former state of art	33.0	0.5
standard mapping	29.7	1.1
max-margin - §3	39.4	1.9
data augmentation - §4	NA	3.7
negative evidence - §5	40.2	5.6

Table 1: **Roadmap.** Proposed changes to cross-space mapping training and resulting percentage Precision @1 in our two experimental setups.

2 Experimental Setup

Cross-linguistic experiments In the cross-linguistic experiments, we learn a mapping from the semantic space of language A to the semantic space of language B, which can then be used for translating words outside the training set. Specifically, given the vector representation of a word in language A, we apply the mapping to obtain an estimate of the vector representation of its meaning in language B, returning the nearest neighbour of the mapped vector in the B space as candidate translation. We focus on translating from English to Italian and adopt the setup (word vectors, training and test data) of Dinu et al. (2015). For a set of 200K words, 300-dimensional vectors were built using the word2vec toolkit,[1] choosing the CBOW method.[2] CBOW, which learns to predict a target word from the ones surrounding it, produces state-of-the-art results in many linguistic tasks (Baroni et al., 2014). The word vectors were induced from corpora of 2.8 and 1.6 billion tokens, respectively, for English and Italian.[3] The train and test English-to-Italian translation pairs were extracted from a Europarl-derived dictionary (Tiedemann, 2012).[4] The 5K most frequent translation pairs were used for training, while the test set includes 1.5K English words equally split into 5 frequency bins. The search for the correct translation is performed in a semantic space of 200K

[1] `https://code.google.com/p/word2vec/`

[2] Other hyperparameters, which we adopted without further tuning, include a context window size of 5 words to either side of the target, setting the sub-sampling option to 1e-05 and estimating the probability of target words by negative sampling, drawing 10 samples from the noise distribution (Mikolov et al., 2013b).

[3] Corpus sources: `http://wacky.sslmit.unibo.it`, `http://www.natcorp.ox.ac.uk`

[4] `http://opus.lingfil.uu.se/`

Italian words.[5]

Cross-modal experiments In the cross-modal experiments, we induce a mapping from visual to linguistic space. Specifically, given an image, we apply the mapping to its visual vector representation to obtain an estimate of its representation in linguistic space, where the word associated to the nearest neighbour is retrieved as the image label. Similarly to translation pairs in the cross-linguistic setup, we create a list of "visual translation" pairs between images and their corresponding noun labels. Our starting point are the 5.1K labels in ImageNet (Deng et al., 2009) that occur at least 500 times in our English corpus and have concreteness score $\geq$5, according to Turney et al. (2011). For each label, we sample 100 pictures from its ImageNet entry, and associate each picture with the 4094-dimensional layer (fc7) at the top of the pre-trained convolutional neural network model of Krizhevsky et al. (2012), using the Caffe toolkit (Jia et al., 2014). The target word space is identical to the English space used in the cross-linguistic experiment. Finally, we use 75% of the labels (and the respective images) for training and the remaining 25% of the labels for testing.[6] From the 127.5K images corresponding to test labels, we sample 1K images as our test set. For zero-shot evaluation purposes, the search for the correct label is performed in the space of 5.1K possible labels, unless otherwise specified. However, when quantifying hubness and pollution, in order to have a setting comparable to that of cross-language mapping, we use the full set of 200K English words as search space.

Learning objectives We assume that we have cross-space "translation" pairs available for a set of $|Tr|$ items $(\mathbf{x}_i, \mathbf{y}_i) = \{\mathbf{x}_i \in \mathbb{R}^{d1}, \mathbf{y}_i \in \mathbb{R}^{d2}\}$. Moreover, following previous work, we assume that the mapping function is linear. For estimating its parameters $\mathbf{W} \in \mathbb{R}^{d1 \times d2}$, we consider two objectives. The first is L2-penalized least squares (**ridge**):

$$\hat{\mathbf{W}} = \underset{\mathbf{W} \in \mathbb{R}^{d1 \times d2}}{\text{argmin}} \|\mathbf{X}\mathbf{W} - \mathbf{Y}\| + \lambda \|\mathbf{W}\|,$$

which has an analytical solution.

The second objective is a margin-based ranking loss (**max-margin**) similar in spirit to the one used in similar cross-modal experiments with WSABIE (Weston et al., 2011) and DeViSE (Frome et al., 2013). The loss for a given pair of training items $(\mathbf{x}_i, \mathbf{y}_i)$ and the corresponding mapping-based prediction $\hat{\mathbf{y}}_i = \mathbf{W}\mathbf{x}_i$ is defined as

$$\sum_{j \neq i}^{k} \max\{0, \gamma + dist(\hat{\mathbf{y}}_i, \mathbf{y}_i) - dist(\hat{\mathbf{y}}_i, \mathbf{y}_j)\},$$

where $dist$ is a distance measure, in our case the inverse cosine, and γ and k are tunable hyperparameters denoting the margin and the number of negative examples, respectively. Intuitively, the goal of the max-margin objective is to rank the correct translation $\mathbf{y}_i$ of $\mathbf{x}_i$ higher than any other possible translation $\mathbf{y}_j$. In theory, the summation in the equation could range over all possible labels, but in practice this is too expensive (e.g., in the cross-linguistic experiments the search space contains 200K candidate labels!), and it is usually computed over just a portion of the label space. In Weston et al. (2011), the authors propose an efficient way of selecting negative examples, in which they randomly sample, for each training item, labels from the complete set, and pick as negative sample the first label violating the margin. This guarantees that there will be exactly as many weight updates as training items. Another possibility is proposed in Mikolov et al. (2013b), where negative samples are picked from a non-item specific distribution (e.g., the uniform distribution).[7] For the experiments in Sections 3 and 4, we follow a more general setup in which the size of the margin and number of negative samples is tuned for each task. In this way, for a sufficiently large margin and number of negative samples, we increase the probability of performing a weight update per training item. We estimate the mapping parameters $\mathbf{W}$ with stochastic gradient descent and per-parameter learning rates tuned with Adagrad (Duchi et al., 2011). The tuning of hyperparameters γ and k is performed on a random 25% subset of the training data.

[5]Faithful to the zero-shot setup, in our experiments there is never any overlap between train and test words; however, to make the task more challenging, we include the train words in the search space, except where expressly indicated.

[6]At training time, we average the 100 vectors associated to a label into a single representation, to reduce training set size while minimizing information loss. At test time, as normally done, we present the model with single image visual vectors.

[7]The notion of negative samples is not unique to margin-based learning; in Mikolov et al. (2013b), the authors used it to efficiently estimate a word probability distribution.

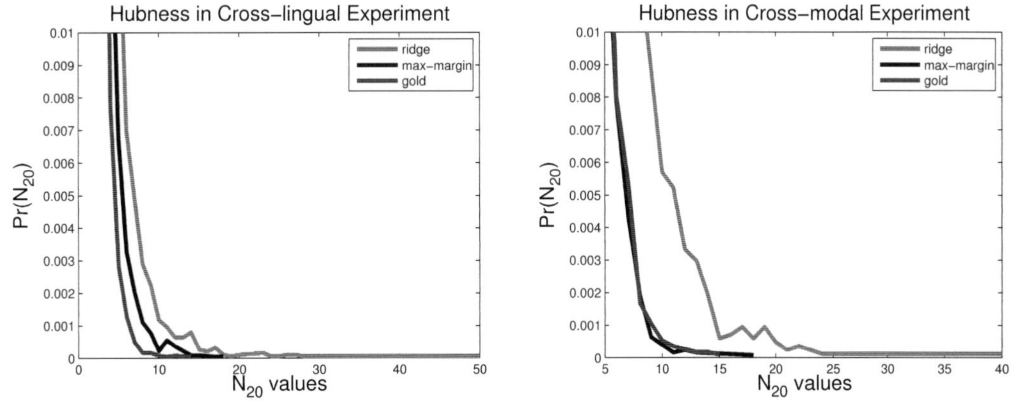

Figure 1: **Hubness distribution in cross-linguistic (left) and cross-modal (right) search spaces.** The hubness score (N_{20}) is computed on the top-20 neighbour lists of the test items, using their original (gold), ridge- or max-margin-mapped vectors as query terms.

3 Hubness

High-dimensional spaces are often affected by *hubness* (Radovanović et al., 2010b; Radovanović et al., 2010a), that is, they contain certain elements – *hubs* – that are near many other points in space without being similar to the latter in any meaningful way. As recently noted by Dinu et al. (2015), the hubness problem is greatly exacerbated when one looks at the nearest neighbours of vectors that have been mapped across spaces with **ridge**.[8] Given a set of query vectors with the corresponding top-k nearest neighbour lists, we can quantify the degree of hubness of an item in the search space (parameterized by k) by the number of lists in which it occurs. $N_k(y)$, the *hubness* at k of an item y, is computed as follows:

$$N_k(y) = |\{x \in T | y \in NN_k(x, S)\}|,$$

where S denotes the search space, T denotes the set of query items and $NN_k(x, S)$ denotes the k nearest neighbors of x in S.

Figure 1 reports N_{20} distributions across the cross-linguistic and cross-modal search spaces, using the respective test items as query vectors. The blue line shows the distributions for the "gold" vectors (that is, the vectors in the target space we would like to approximate). The red line shows the same distributions when neighbours are queried for the ridge-mapped test vectors (ignore black lines for now). In both spaces, when the query vectors are mapped, hubness increases dramatically. The largest hubs for the original test items occur in 15 neighbour lists or less. With the mapped vectors, we find hubs occurring in 40 lists or more. The figure also shows that, in both spaces, we observe more points with smaller but non-negligible N_{20} (e.g., around 10) when mapped vectors are queried. In both spaces, the difference in hubness is very significant according to a cross-tab test ($p<10^{-30}$). Finally, as Table 2 shows, the largest hubs are by no means terms that we might expect to occur as neighbours of many other items on semantic grounds (e.g., very general terms), but rather very specific and rare words whose high hubness cannot possibly be a genuine semantic property.

Cross-linguistic	Cross-modal
blockmonthon (50)	smilodon (40)
hashim (28)	pintle (33)
akayev (27)	knurled (27)
autogiustificazione (27)	handwheel (24)
limassol (26)	circlip (23)
regulars (26)	black-footed (23)
18 (25)	flatbread (22)

Table 2: **Top ridge hubs**, together with N_{20} scores. Note that cross-linguistic hubs are supposed to be *Italian* words.

Causes of hubness Why should the mapping function lead to an increase in hubness? We conjecture that this is due to an intrinsic property of least-squares estimation. Given the training ma-

[8]Dinu et al. (2015) observe, but do not attempt to understand hubness, as we do here. They propose to address it with methods to re-rank neighbour lists, which are less general and should be largely complementary to our effort to improve estimation of the cross-mapping function.

trices $\mathbf{X}$ and $\mathbf{Y}$, and the projection matrix $\mathbf{W}$ obtained by minimizing squared error, each column $\hat{\mathbf{y}}_{*,i}$ of $\hat{\mathbf{Y}} = \mathbf{XW}$ is the orthogonal projection of $\mathbf{y}_{*,i}$, the corresponding $\mathbf{Y}$ column onto the column space of $\mathbf{X}$ (Strang, 2003, Ch. 4). Consequently, $\mathbf{y}_{*,i} = \boldsymbol{\epsilon}_i + \hat{\mathbf{y}}_{*,i}$, where the $\boldsymbol{\epsilon}_i$ error vector is orthogonal to $\hat{\mathbf{y}}_{*,i}$. It follows that $||\mathbf{y}_{*,i}||^2 \geq= ||\hat{\mathbf{y}}_{*,i}||^2$. Since $\mathbf{y}_{*,i}$ and $\hat{\mathbf{y}}_{*,i}$ have equal means (because the error terms in $\boldsymbol{\epsilon}_i$ must sum to 0), it immediately follows from the squared length inequality that $\hat{\mathbf{y}}_{*,i}$ has lower or equal variance to $\mathbf{y}_{*,i}$. Since this holds for all columns of $\hat{\mathbf{Y}}$, it follows in turn that the set of mapped vectors in $\hat{\mathbf{Y}}$ has lower or equal variance to the corresponding set of original vectors in $\mathbf{Y}$. Coming back to hubness, a set of lower variance points (such as the mapped vectors) will result in higher hubness since the points will on average be closer to each other. The problem is likely to be further exacerbated by the property of least-squares to ignore relative distances between points (the objective only aims at making predicted and observed vectors look like each other),

Strictly, the theoretical result only holds for the training points. However, to the extent that the training set is representative of what will be encountered in the test set, it should also extend to test data (and if training and testing data are very different, the mapping function will generalize very poorly anyway). Moreover, the result holds for a pure least-squares solution, without the ridge L2 regularization term. Whether it also applies to ridge-based estimates will depend on the relative impact of the least-squares and L2 terms on the final solution (and it is not excluded that the L2 term might also independently reduce variance, of course). Empirically, we find that, indeed, lower variance also characterizes test vectors mapped with a ridge-estimated function.

Interestingly, in the literature on cross-space mapping we find that authors choose a different cost function than ridge, without motivating the choice. Socher et al. (2014) mention in passing that max-margin outperforms a least-squared-error cost for cross-modal mapping.

Max-margin as a solution to hubness Referring back to Figure 1, we see that when ridge estimation is replaced by max-margin (black line), there is a considerable decrease in hubness in both settings. This is directly reflected in a large increase in performance in our cross-linguistic (English-to-Italian) zero-shot task (left two columns of Table 3), with the largest improvement for the all important P@1 measure (equivalent to accuracy).[9] These results are well above the current best cross-language accuracy for cross-modal mapping without added orthographic cues (33%), attained by Mikolov et al. (2013a).[10] The absolute performance figures are low in the challenging cross-modal setting, but here too we observe a considerable improvement in accuracy when max-margin is applied. Indeed, we are already above the cross-modal zero-shot mapping state of the art for a search space of similar size (0.5% accuracy in Frome et al. (2013)). Still, the improvement over ridge (while present) is not as large for the less strict (higher ranks) performance scores.

Table 4 confirms that the improvement brought about by max-margin is indeed (at least partially) due to hubness reduction. A large proportion of vectors retrieved as top-1 predictions (translations/labels) are hubs when mapping is trained with ridge, but the proportion drops dramatically with max-margin. Still, more than 1/5 top predictions for cross-modal mapping with max-margin are hubs (vs. less than 1/10 for the original vectors). Now, the mathematical properties we reviewed above suggest that, for least-squares estimation, hubness is caused by general reduced variance of the space after mapping. Thus, hubs should be vectors that are near the mean of the space. The first row of Table 5 confirms that the hubs found in the neighbourhoods of ridge-mapped query terms are items that tend to be closer to the search space mean vector, and that this effect is radically reduced with max-margin estimation. However, the second row of the table shows another factor at play, that has a major role in the cross-modal setting, and it is only partially addressed by max-margin estimation: Namely, in vision-to-language mapping, there is a strong tendency for hubs (that, recall, have an important effect on performance, as they enter many nearest neighbour lists) to be close to a training data point.

[9] We have no realistic upper-bound estimate, but due to different word senses, synonymy, etc., it is certainly not 100%.

[10] Although the numbers are not fully comparable because of different language pairs and various methodological details, their method is essentially equivalent to our **ridge** approach we are clearly outperforming.

	Cross-linguistic		Cross-modal	
	ridge	**max-margin**	**ridge**	**max-margin**
P@1	29.7	38.4	1.1	1.9
P@5	44.2	54.2	4.8	5.4
P@10	49.1	60.4	7.9	9.0

Table 3: **Ridge vs. max-margin in zero-shot experiments.** Precision @N results cross-linguistically (test items: 1.5K, search space: 200K) and cross-modally (test items: 1K, search space: 5.1K).

Cross-linguistic			Cross-modal		
ridge	**max-margin**	**gold**	**ridge**	**max-margin**	**gold**
19.6	9.8	0.6	55.8	21.6	7.8

Table 4: **Hubs as top predictions**. Percentage of top-1 neighbours of test vectors in zero-shot experiments of Table 3 with $N_{20} > 5$.

	Cross-linguistic		Cross-modal	
cosine with	**ridge**	**max-margin**	**ridge**	**max-margin**
full-space mean	0.21	0.06	0.13	-0.01
training point	0.15	0.12	0.34	0.24

Table 5: **Properties of hubs.** Spearman ρ of N_{20} scores with cosines to mean vector of full search space (top) and nearest training item (bottom), across all search space elements. All correlations significant (p<0.001) except cross-modal **max-margin** hubness/full-space mean.

4 Pollution

The quantitative results and post-hoc analysis of hubs in Section 3 suggest that cross-modal mapping is facing a serious generalization problem. To get a better grasp of the phenomenon, we define a binary measure of *(training data) pollution* for a queried item x and parameterized by k, such that pollution is 1 if x has a (target) training item y among its k nearest neighbours, 0 otherwise. Formally:

$$N^{pol}_{k,S}(x) = [\![\exists y \in \mathbf{Y}^{Tr} : y \in NN_{k,S}(x)]\!],$$

where $\mathbf{Y}^{Tr}$ is the matrix of target vectors used in training, $NN_{k,S}(y)$ denotes the top k neighbors of y in search space S, and $[\![z]\!]$ is an indicator function.[11]

[11] Pollution is of course an effect of overfitting, but we use this more specific term to refer to the tendency of training vectors to "pollute" nearest neighbour lists of mapped vectors.

The average pollution $N^{pol}_{1,S}$ of all test items in the cross-modal experiment, when $|S|=200K$ is 18%, which indicates that in 1/5 of cases the returned label is that of a training point. The equivalent statistic in the cross-linguistic experiment drops to 8.7% (words tend to be more varied than the set of concrete, imageable concepts used for image annotation tasks, and so the cross-linguistic training set is probably less uniform than the one used in the vision-to-language setting).

The real extent of the generalization problem in the cross-modal setup becomes more obvious if we restrict the search space to labels effectively associated to an image in our data set ($|S|=5.1K$). In this case, the average pollution $N^{pol}_{1,S}$ across all test items jumps to 88%, that is, the vast majority of test images are annotated with a label coming from the training data. Clearly, there is a serious problem of overfitting to the training subspace. While we came to this observation by inspecting the properties of hubs, other work in zero-shot for image labeling has indirectly noted the same. Frome et al. (2013) empirically showed that the performance of the system is higher when removing training labels from the search space, while Norouzi et al. (2014) proposed a zero-shot method that avoids explicit cross-modal mapping.

Adapting to the full search space by data augmentation High training-data pollution indicates that cross-modal mapping does not generalize well beyond the kind of data points it encountered in learning. This is a special case of the *dataset bias* problem (Torralba and Efros, 2011) and, given that the latter has been addressed as a domain adaptation problem (Gong et al., 2012; Donahue et al., 2013), we adopt here a similar view. Self-training has been successfully used for domain adaptation in NLP, e.g., in syntactic parsing. Given the limited amount of syntactically annotated data coming from monotonous sources (e.g., the Wall Street Journal), parsers show a big drop in performance when applied to different domains (e.g., reviews), since training and test domains differ dramatically, thus affecting their generalization performance. In a nutshell, the idea behind self-training (McClosky et al., 2006; Reichart and Rappoport, 2007) is to use manually annotated data $(x^A_i, .., x^A_N, y^A_i, .., y^A_N)$ from domain A to train a parser, feed the trained parser with data $x^B_i, .., x^B_K$ from domain B in order to obtain their automated annotations $\hat{y}^B_i, .., \hat{y}^B_K$ and then retrain the parser

dolphin	tarantula	highland
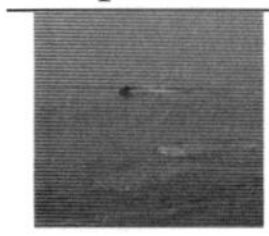		
whale	anteater	whisky
orca	arachnid	lowland
porpoise	spider	bagpipe
cetacean	opossum	glen
shark	scorpion	distillery

Table 6: **Visual chimeras** for *dolphin*, *tarantula* and *highland*.

	none	chimera-5	chimera-10
P@1	1.9	3.7	3.2
P@5	5.4	10.9	10.5
P@10	9.0	15.8	15.9

Table 7: **Cross-modal zero-shot experiment with data augmentation.** Labeling precision @N with no data augmentation (**none**) and when using top 5 (**chimera-5**) and top 10 (**chimera-10**) nearest neighbors from training set of each item in the search space to build the corresponding chimeras (1K test items, 5.1K search space).

with a combination of "clean" data from domain A and "noisy" data from domain B.

In our setup, self-training would be applied by labeling a larger set of images with a cross-modal mapping function estimated on the initial training data, and then using both sources of labeled data to retrain the function. Although the idea of self-training for inducing cross-modal mapping functions is appealing, especially given the vast amount of unlabeled data available out there, the very low performance of current cross-modal mapping functions makes the effort questionable. We would like to exploit unannotated data representative of the search space, *without* relying on the output of cross-modal mapping for their annotation. One way to achieve this is to use *data augmentation* techniques that are representative of the search space. Data augmentation is popular in computer vision, where it is performed (among others) by data jittering, visual sampling or image perturbations. It has proven beneficial for both "deep" (Krizhevsky et al., 2012; Zeiler and Fergus, 2014) and "shallow" (Chatfield et al., 2014) systems, and it was recently introduced to NLP tasks (Zhang and LeCun, 2015).

Specifically, in order to train the mapping function using both annotated data and points that are representative of the full search space, we rely on a form of data augmentation that we call *visual chimera* creation. For every item $\mathrm{y_i} \notin \mathbf{Y}^{Tr}$ in the search space S, we use linguistic similarity as a proxy of visual similarity, and create its *visual vector* $\hat{\mathrm{x}}_\mathrm{i}$ by averaging the visual vectors corresponding to the nearest words in language space that do occur as labels in the training set. Table 6 presents some examples of visual chimeras. For $\mathrm{y_i}$=*dolphin*, the visual vectors of other cetacean mammals are averaged to create the chimera $\hat{\mathrm{x}}_\mathrm{i}$. Since linguistic similarity is not always determined by visual factors, the method also produces noisy data points. For $\mathrm{y_i}$=*tarantula*, *opossums* enter the picture, while for $\mathrm{y_i}$=*highland* images of "topically" similar concepts are used (e.g., *bagpipe*).

Table 7 reports cross-modal zero-shot labeling when training with **max-margin** and data augmentation. We experiment with visual chimeras constructed using 5 vs. 10 nearest neighbours. While the examples above suggest that the process injects some noise in the training data, we also observe a decrease of pollution $\mathrm{N}^{\mathrm{pol}}_{1,\mathrm{S}}$ from 88% when using the "clean" training data, to 71% and 73% when expanding them with chimeras (for **chimera-5** and **chimera-10**, respectively). Reflecting this drop in pollution, we see large improvements in precision at all levels, when chimeras are used (no big differences between 5 or 10 neighbours).

The improvements brought about by the chimera method are robust. First, Table 8 reports performance when the search space excludes the training labels, showing that data augmentation is beneficial beyond mitigating the bias in favor of the latter. In this setup, **chimera-5** is clearly outperforming **chimera-10** (longer neighbour lists will include more noise), and we focus on it from here on.

All experiments up to here follow the standard cross-modal zero-shot protocol, in which the search space is given by the union of the test and training labels, or a subset thereof. Next, we make the task more challenging by increasing it with 1K extra elements acting as distractors. The distractors are either randomly sampled from our usual 200K English word space, or, in the most challenging scenario, picked among those words, in the same space, that are among the top-5 near-

	none	chimera-5	chimera-10
P@1	6.7	9.3	8.3
P@5	21.7	25.2	21.3
P@10	29.9	34.3	29.7

Table 8: **Cross-modal zero-shot experiment with data augmentation, disjoint train/search spaces.** Same setup as Table 8, but search space excludes training elements (1K test items, 1K search space).

	random		related	
	none	**chimera-5**	**none**	**chimera-5**
P@1	0.8	3.3	1.9	2.8
P@5	5.3	9.0	4.8	8.8
P@10	8.8	13.3	7.9	12.6

Table 9: **Cross-modal zero-shot experiment with data augmentation, enlarged search space.** Labeling precision @N with no data augmentation (**none**) and when using top 5 (**chimera-5**) nearest neighbors from training set of each item in the search space to build the corresponding chimeras. Test items: 1K. Search space: 5.1K+1K extra distractors from a 200K word space, either randomly picked (*random*), or *related* to the training items.

est neighbours of a training element. Again, we create one visual chimera for each label in the search space. Results are presented in Table 9. As expected, performance is negatively affected with both plain and data-augmented models, but the latter is still better in absolute terms. While **chimera-5** undergoes a larger drop when the search contains many elements similar to the training data ("related" column), which is explained by the fact that visual chimeras will often include the distractor items of this setup, it appears to be more resistant against random labels, which in many cases are words that bear no resemblance to the training data (e.g., *naushad, yamato, 13-14*). The picture when using no data augmentation is exactly the opposite, with the model being more harmed, at P@1, by the random labels.

Finally, Table 10 presents results in the cross-linguistic setup, when applying the same data augmentation technique. In this case, we augment the 5K training elements with 11.5K chimeras, for the 1.5K test elements and 10K randomly sampled distractors. For these 11.5K elements, we associate their Italian (target space) label y_i with a

	none	chimera-5
P@1	38.4	31.1
P@5	54.2	46.1
P@10	60.4	51.3

Table 10: **Cross-linguistic zero-shot experiment with data augmentation**. Translation precision @N when learning with **max-margin** and no data augmentation (**none**) or data augmentation using the top 5 (**chimera-5**) nearest neighbors of 11.5K items in the 200K-word search space (1.5K test items).

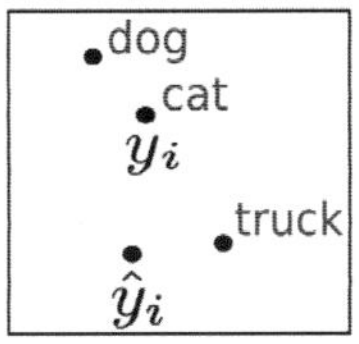

Figure 2: **Looking for intruders.** We pick *truck* rather than *dog* as negative example for *cat*.

"pseudo-translation" vector $\hat{x}_i$ obtained by averaging the vectors of the English (source space) translations of the nearest Italian words to y_i included in the training set. Results, in Table 10, show that in this case our data augmentation method is actually hampering performance. We saw that pollution affects the cross-linguistic setup much less than it affects the cross-modal one, and we conjecture that, consequently, in the translation task, there is not a large-enough generalization gain to make up for the extra noise introduced by augmentation.

5 Picking informative negative examples

An interesting feature of the ranking max-margin objective lies in its active use of negative examples. While previous work in cross-space mapping has paid little attention to the properties that negative samples should possess, this has not gone unnoticed in the NLP literature on structured prediction tasks. Smith and Eisner (2005) propose a contrastive estimation framework in the context of POS-tagging, in which positive evidence derived from gold sentence annotations is extended with negative evidence derived by various *neighbourhood functions* that corrupt the data in particular ways (e.g., by deleting 1 word).

Having shown the effectiveness of max-margin estimation in the previous sections, we now take

	Cross-linguistic		Cross-modal	
	random	**intruder**	**random**	**intruder**
P@1	38.4	40.2	3.7	5.6
P@5	54.2	55.5	10.9	12.4
P@10	60.4	61.8	15.8	17.8

Table 11: **Random vs. intruding negative examples.** Zero-shot precision @N results when cross-space function is estimated using **max-margin** with random or "intruder" negative examples, cross-linguistically (test items: 1.5K, search space: 200K) and cross-modally (test items: 1K, search space: 5.1K).

a first step towards engineering the negative evidence exploited by this method, in the context of inducing cross-space mapping functions. In particular, our idea is that, given a training instance x_i, an informative negative example would be *near* the mapped vector $\hat{y}_i$, but *far* from the actual gold target space vector y_i. Intuitively, such "intruders" correspond to cases where the mapping function is getting the predictions seriously wrong, and thus they should be very informative in "correcting" the function mapping trajectories. This can seen as a vector-space interpretation of the *max-loss* update protocol (Crammer et al., 2006) that picks negative samples expected to harm performance more. Figure 2 illustrates the idea with a cartoon example. If *cat* is the gold target vector y_i and $\hat{y}_i$ the corresponding mapped vector, then we are going to pick *truck* as negative example, since it is an intruder (near the mapped vector, far from the gold one).

More formally, at each step of stochastic gradient descent, given a source space vector x_i, its target gold label/translation y_i in $\mathbf{Y}^{Tr}$ and the mapped vector $\hat{y}_i$, we compute $s_j = \cos(\hat{y}_i, y_j) - \cos(y_i, y_j)$, for all vectors y_j in $\mathbf{Y}^{Tr}$ s.t. $j \neq i$, and pick as negative example for x_i the vector with the largest s_j.

Table 11 presents zero-shot mapping results when intruding negative examples are used for max-margin estimation. For cross-modal mapping, we apply data augmentation as described in the previous section. While the absolute performance increase is relatively small (less than 2% in both setups), it is consistent. Furthermore, the proposed protocol results in lower $N^{pol}_{1,S}$ pollution in the cross-modal setup (from 71% to 63%). Finally, we observe that the learning behaviour of the two

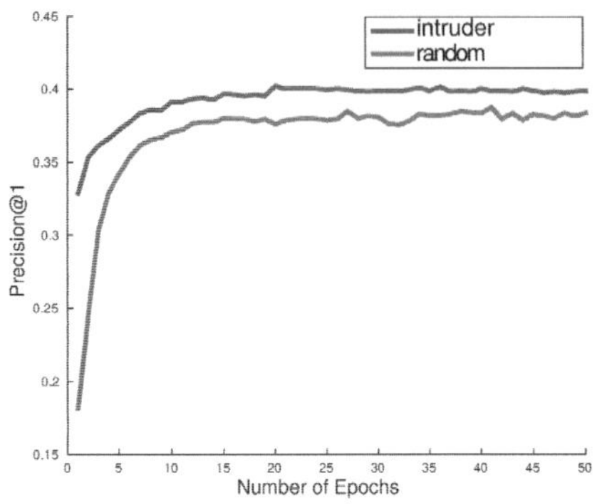

Figure 3: **Learning curve with random or intruding negative samples** in the cross-linguistic experiment.

protocols (intruders vs. random) is different; the **intruder** approach is already achieving good performance after just few training epochs, since it can rely on more informative negative samples (see Figure 3).

6 Conclusion

We have considered some general mathematical and empirical properties of linear cross-space mapping functions, suggesting one well-known (max-margin estimation) and two new (chimera augmentation and "intruder" negative sample adjustment) methods to improve their performance. With them, we achieve results well above the state of the art in both the cross-linguistic and the cross-modal setting. Both chimera and the intruder methods are flexible, and we plan to explore them further in future research. In particular, we want to devise more semantically-motivated methods to select chimera components and negative samples.

Acknowledgments

We thank Adam Liska, Yoav Goldberg and the anonymous reviewers for useful comments. We acknowledge ERC 2011 Starting Independent Research Grant n. 283554 (COMPOSES).

References

Marco Baroni, Georgiana Dinu, and Germán Kruszewski. 2014. Don't count, predict! a systematic comparison of context-counting vs. context-predicting semantic vectors. In *Proceedings of ACL*, pages 238–247, Baltimore, MD.

Ken Chatfield, Karen Simonyan, Andrea Vedaldi, and Andrew Zisserman. 2014. Return of the devil in the details: Delving deep into convolutional nets. *arXiv preprint arXiv:1405.3531*.

Koby Crammer, Ofer Dekel, Joseph Keshet, Shai Shalev-Shwartz, and Yoram Singer. 2006. Online passive-aggressive algorithms. *The Journal of Machine Learning Research*, 7:551–585.

Jia Deng, Wei Dong, Richard Socher, Lia-Ji Li, and Li Fei-Fei. 2009. Imagenet: A large-scale hierarchical image database. In *Proceedings of CVPR*, pages 248–255, Miami Beach, FL.

Georgiana Dinu and Marco Baroni. 2014. How to make words with vectors: Phrase generation in distributional semantics. In *Proceedings of ACL*, pages 624–633, Baltimore, MD.

Georgiana Dinu, Angeliki Lazaridou, and Marco Baroni. 2015. Improving zero-shot learning by mitigating the hubness problem. In *Proceedings of ICLR Workshop Track*, San Diego, CA. Published online: `http://www.iclr.cc/doku.php?id=iclr2015:main`.

Jeff Donahue, Judy Hoffman, Erik Rodner, Kate Saenko, and Trevor Darrell. 2013. Semi-supervised domain adaptation with instance constraints. In *In Proceedings of CVPR*, pages 668–675.

John Duchi, Elad Hazan, and Yoram Singer. 2011. Adaptive subgradient methods for online learning and stochastic optimization. *The Journal of Machine Learning Research*, 12:2121–2159.

Andrea Frome, Greg Corrado, Jon Shlens, Samy Bengio, Jeff Dean, Marc'Aurelio Ranzato, and Tomas Mikolov. 2013. DeViSE: A deep visual-semantic embedding model. In *Proceedings of NIPS*, pages 2121–2129, Lake Tahoe, NV.

Boqing Gong, Yuan Shi, Fei Sha, and Kristen Grauman. 2012. Geodesic flow kernel for unsupervised domain adaptation. In *In Proceedings of CVPR*, pages 2066–2073.

Kristen Grauman and Bastian Leibe. 2011. *Visual Object Recognition*. Morgan & Claypool, San Francisco.

Yangqing Jia, Evan Shelhamer, Jeff Donahue, Sergey Karayev, Jonathan Long, Ross Girshick, Sergio Guadarrama, and Trevor Darrell. 2014. Caffe: Convolutional architecture for fast feature embedding. *arXiv preprint arXiv:1408.5093*.

Alex Krizhevsky, Ilya Sutskever, and Geoffrey Hinton. 2012. ImageNet classification with deep convolutional neural networks. In *Proceedings of NIPS*, pages 1097–1105, Lake Tahoe, Nevada.

Angeliki Lazaridou, Elia Bruni, and Marco Baroni. 2014. Is this a wampimuk? cross-modal mapping between distributional semantics and the visual world. In *Proceedings of ACL*, pages 1403–1414, Baltimore, MD.

David McClosky, Eugene Charniak, and Mark Johnson. 2006. Effective self-training for parsing. In *Proceedings of HLT-NAACL*, pages 152–159.

Tomas Mikolov, Quoc V Le, and Ilya Sutskever. 2013a. Exploiting similarities among languages for machine translation. *arXiv preprint arXiv:1309.4168*.

Tomas Mikolov, Wen-tau Yih, and Geoffrey Zweig. 2013b. Linguistic regularities in continuous space word representations. In *Proceedings of NAACL*, pages 746–751, Atlanta, Georgia.

Tom Mitchell, Svetlana Shinkareva, Andrew Carlson, Kai-Min Chang, Vincente Malave, Robert Mason, and Marcel Just. 2008. Predicting human brain activity associated with the meanings of nouns. *Science*, 320:1191–1195.

Mohammad Norouzi, Tomas Mikolov, Samy Bengio, Yoram Singer, Jonathon Shlens, Andrea Frome, Greg S Corrado, and Jeffrey Dean. 2014. Zero-shot learning by convex combination of semantic embeddings. In *Proceedings of ICLR*.

Mark Palatucci, Dean Pomerleau, Geoffrey Hinton, and Tom Mitchell. 2009. Zero-shot learning with semantic output codes. In *Proceedings of NIPS*, pages 1410–1418, Vancouver, Canada.

Miloš Radovanović, Alexandros Nanopoulos, and Mirjana Ivanović. 2010a. Hubs in space: Popular nearest neighbors in high-dimensional data. *Journal of Machine Learning Research*, 11:2487–2531.

Milo˘s Radovanović, Alexandros Nanopoulos, and Mirjana Ivanović. 2010b. On the existence of obstinate results in vector space models. In *Proceedings of SIGIR*, pages 186–193, Geneva, Switzerland.

Roi Reichart and Ari Rappoport. 2007. Self-training for enhancement and domain adaptation of statistical parsers trained on small datasets. In *In Proceedings of ACL*, pages 616–623.

Noah A Smith and Jason Eisner. 2005. Contrastive estimation: Training log-linear models on unlabeled data. In *Proceedings of ACL*, pages 354–362.

Richard Socher, Milind Ganjoo, Christopher Manning, and Andrew Ng. 2013. Zero-shot learning through cross-modal transfer. In *Proceedings of NIPS*, pages 935–943, Lake Tahoe, NV.

Richard Socher, Quoc Le, Christopher Manning, and Andrew Ng. 2014. Grounded compositional semantics for finding and describing images with sentences. *Transactions of the Association for Computational Linguistics*, 2:207–218.

Gilbert Strang. 2003. *Introduction to linear algebra, 3d edition*. Wellesley-Cambridge Press, Wellesley, MA.

Jörg Tiedemann. 2012. Parallel data, tools and interfaces in OPUS. In *Proceedings of LREC*, pages 2214–2218.

Antonio Torralba and Alexei A Efros. 2011. Unbiased look at dataset bias. In *In Proceedings of CVPR*, pages 1521–1528.

Peter Turney and Patrick Pantel. 2010. From frequency to meaning: Vector space models of semantics. *Journal of Artificial Intelligence Research*, 37:141–188.

Peter Turney, Yair Neuman, Dan Assaf, and Yohai Cohen. 2011. Literal and metaphorical sense identification through concrete and abstract context. In *Proceedings of EMNLP*, pages 680–690, Edinburgh, UK.

Jason Weston, Samy Bengio, and Nicolas Usunier. 2011. Wsabie: Scaling up to large vocabulary image annotation. In *Proceedings of IJCAI*, pages 2764–2770.

Matthew Zeiler and Rob Fergus. 2014. Visualizing and understanding convolutional networks. In *Proceedings of ECCV (Part 1)*, pages 818–833, Zurich, Switzerland.

Xiang Zhang and Yann LeCun. 2015. Text understanding from scrath. *arXiv preprint arXiv:1502.01710*.

A Generalisation of Lexical Functions for Composition in Distributional Semantics

Antoine Bride
IRIT & Université de Toulouse
antoine.bride@irit.fr

Tim Van de Cruys
IRIT & CNRS, Toulouse
tim.vandecruys@irit.fr

Nicholas Asher
IRIT & CNRS, Toulouse
nicholas.asher@irit.fr

Abstract

Over the last two decades, numerous algorithms have been developed that successfully capture something of the semantics of single words by looking at their distribution in text and comparing these distributions in a vector space model. However, it is not straightforward to construct meaning representations beyond the level of individual words – i.e. the combination of words into larger units – using distributional methods. Our contribution is twofold. First of all, we carry out a large-scale evaluation, comparing different composition methods within the distributional framework for the cases of both adjective-noun and noun-noun composition, making use of a newly developed dataset. Secondly, we propose a novel method for composition, which generalises the approach by Baroni and Zamparelli (2010). The performance of our novel method is also evaluated on our new dataset and proves competitive with the best methods.

1 Introduction

In the course of the last two decades, there has been a growing interest in distributional methods for lexical semantics (Landauer and Dumais, 1997; Lin, 1998; Turney and Pantel, 2010). These methods are based on the distributional hypothesis (Harris, 1954), according to which words that appear in the same contexts tend to be similar in meaning. Inspired by Harris' hypothesis, numerous researchers have developed algorithms that try to capture the semantics of individual words by looking at their distribution in a large corpus.

Compared to manual studies common to formal semantics, distributional semantics offers substantially larger coverage since it is able to analyze massive amounts of empirical data. However, it is not trivial to combine the algebraic objects created by distributional semantics to get a sensible distributional representation for more complex expressions, consisting of several words. On the other hand, the formalism of the λ-calculus provides us with general, advanced and efficient methods for composition that can model meaning composition not only of simple phrases, but also more complex phenomena such as coercion or composition with fine-grained types (Asher, 2011; Luo, 2010; Bassac et al., 2010). Despite continued efforts to find a general method for composition and various approaches for the composition of specific syntactic structures (e.g. adjective-noun composition, or the composition of transitive verbs and direct objects (Mitchell and Lapata, 2008; Coecke et al., 2010; Baroni and Zamparelli, 2010)), the modeling of compositionality is still an important challenge for distributional semantics. Moreover, the validation of proposed methods for composition has used relatively small datasets of human similarity judgements (Mitchell and Lapata, 2008).[1] Although such studies comparing similarity judgements have their merits, it would be interesting to have studies that evaluate methods for composition on a larger scale, using a larger test set of different specific compositions. Such an evaluation would allow us to evaluate more thoroughly the different methods of composition that have been proposed. This is one of the goals of this paper.

To achieve this goal, we make use of two different resources. We have constructed a dataset for French containing a large number of pairs of a compositional expression (adjective-noun) and a single noun that is semantically close or identical to the composed expression. These pairs have been extracted semi-automatically from

[1] A notable exception is (Marelli et al., 2014), who propose a large-scale evaluation dataset for composition at the sentence level.

Proceedings of the 53rd Annual Meeting of the Association for Computational Linguistics and the 7th International Joint Conference on Natural Language Processing, pages 281–291,
Beijing, China, July 26-31, 2015.

the French Wiktionary. We have also used the Semeval 2013 dataset of phrasal similarity judgements for English with similar pairs extracted semi-automatically from the English Wiktionary to construct a dataset for English for both adjective-noun and noun-noun composition. This affords us a cross-linguistic comparison of the methods.

These data sets provide a substantial evaluation of the performance of different compositional methods. We have tested three different methods of composition proposed in the literature, viz. the additive and multiplicative model (Mitchell and Lapata, 2008), as well as the lexical function approach (Baroni and Zamparelli, 2010).

The two first methods are entirely general, and take as input automatically constructed vectors for adjectives and nouns. The method by Baroni and Zamparelli, on the other hand, requires the acquisition of a particular function for each adjective, represented by a matrix. The second goal of our paper is to generalise the functional approach in order to eliminate the need for an individual function for each adjective. To this goal, we automatically learn a generalised lexical function, based on Baroni and Zamparelli's approach. This generalised function combines with an adjective vector and a noun vector in a generalised way. The performance of our novel generalised lexical function approach is evaluated on our test sets and proves competitive with the best, extant methods.

Our paper is organized as follows. First, we discuss the different compositional models that we have evaluated in our study, briefly revisiting the different existing methods for composition, followed by a description of our generalisation of the lexical function approach. Next, we report on our evaluation method and its results. The results section is followed by a section that discusses work related to ours. Lastly, we draw conclusions and lay out some avenues for future work.

2 Composition methods

2.1 Simple Models of Composition

In this section, we describe the composition models for the adjective-noun case. The extension of these models to the noun-noun case is straightforward; one just needs to replace the adjective by the subordinate noun. Admittedly, choosing which noun is subordinate in noun-noun composition may be an interesting problem but it is outside the scope of this paper. We tested three simple models of composition: a baseline method that discounts the contribution of the adjective completely, and the additive and multiplicative models of composition. The baseline method is defined as follows:

$$\text{Comp}_{\text{baseline}}(\text{adj}, \text{noun}) = \mathbf{noun}$$

The additive model adds the point-wise values of the adjective vector **adj** and noun vector **noun** using independent coefficients to provide a result for the composition:

$$\text{Comp}_{\text{additive}}(\text{adj}, \text{noun}) = \alpha\,\mathbf{noun} + \beta\,\mathbf{adj}$$

The multiplicative model consists in a point-wise multiplication of the vectors **adj** and **noun**:

$$\begin{array}{l}\text{Comp}_{\text{multiplicative}}(\text{adj}, \text{noun}) = \mathbf{noun} \otimes \mathbf{adj} \\ \text{with} \quad (\mathbf{noun} \otimes \mathbf{adj})_i = \mathbf{noun}_i \times \mathbf{adj}_i\end{array}$$

2.2 The lexical function model

Baroni and Zamparelli's (2010) lexical function model (LF) is somewhat more complex. Adjective-noun composition is modeled as the functional application of an adjective meaning (represented as a matrix) to a noun meaning (represented as a vector). Thus, the combination of an adjective and noun is the product of the matrix **ADJ** and the vector **noun** as shown in Figure 1.

Baroni and Zamparelli propose learning an adjective's matrix from examples of the vectors for **adj_noun** obtained directly from the corpus. These vectors **adj_noun** are obtained in the same way as vectors representing a single word: when the adjective-noun combination occurs, we observe its context and construct the vector from those observations. As an illustration, consider the example in 2. The word *name* appears three times modified by an adjective in the following excerpt from Oscar Wilde's *The Importance of Being Earnest*. This informs us about the co-occurrence frequencies of three vectors: one for **divine_name**, another for **nice_name**, and one for **charming_name**.

Once the **adj_noun** vectors have been created for a given adjective, we are able to calculate the **ADJ** matrix using a least squares regression that minimizes the equation $\mathbf{ADJ} \times \mathbf{adj\_noun} - \mathbf{noun}$. More formally, the problem is the following:

Find **ADJ** s.t.
$\sum_{\text{noun}}(\mathbf{ADJ} \times \mathbf{noun} - \mathbf{adj\_noun})^2$
is minimal

$$\text{Composition}_{\text{LF}}(\text{adjective}, \text{noun}) = \boxed{\textbf{ADJECTIVE}} \times \boxed{\begin{array}{c}\textbf{n}\\\textbf{o}\\\textbf{u}\\\textbf{n}\end{array}}$$

Figure 1: Lexical Function Composition

Jack: Personally, darling, to speak quite candidly, I don't much care about the name of Ernest . . . I don't think the name suits me at all.
Gwendolen: It suits you perfectly. It is a divine [name]. It has a music of its own. It produces vibrations.
Jack: Well, really, Gwendolen, I must say that I think there are lots of other much nicer [names]. I think Jack, for instance, is a charming [name].

Figure 2: Excerpt from Oscar Wilde's *The Importance of Being Earnest*

For our example, we would minimize, among others **DIVINE**×**divine_name** − **name** to get the matrix for **DIVINE**.

LF requires a large corpus, because we have to observe a sufficient number of examples of the adjective and noun combined, which are perforce less exemplified than the presence of the noun or adjective in isolation. In Figure 2, each of the occurrences of 'name' can contribute to the information in the vector **name** but none can contribute to the vector **evanescent_name**.

Baroni and Zamparelli (2010) offer an explanation of how to cope with the potential sparse data problem for learning matrices for adjectives. Moreover, recent evaluations of LF show that existent corpora have enough data for it to provide a semantics for the most frequent adjectives and obtain better results than other methods (Dinu et al., 2013b).

Nevertheless, LF has limitations in treating relatively rare adjectives. For example, the adjective 'evanescent' appears 359 times in the UKWaC corpus (Baroni et al., 2009). This is enough to generate a vector for **evanescent**, but may not be sufficient to generate a sufficient number of vectors **evanescent_noun** to build the matrix **EVANESCENT**. More importantly, for noun-noun combinations, one may need to have a LF for a combination. To get the meaning of *blood donation campaign* in the LF approach, the matrix **BLOOD_DONATION** must be combined to the vector **campaign**. Learning this matrix would require to build vectors **blood_donation_noun** for many nouns. Even if it were possible, the issue would arise again for *blood donation campaign plan*, then for *blood donation campaign plan meeting* and so forth.

In addition, LF's approach to adjectival meaning and composition has a theoretical drawback. Like Montague Grammar, it supposes that the effect of an adjective on a noun meaning is specific to the adjective (Kamp, 1975). However, recent studies suggest that the Montague approach overgeneralises from the worst case, and that the vast majority of adjectives in the world's languages are subsective, suggesting that the modification of nominal meaning that results from their composition with a noun follows general principles (Partee, 2010; Asher, 2011) that are independent of the presence or absence of examples of association.

2.3 Generalised LF

To solve these problems, we generalise LF and replace individual matrices for adjectival meanings by a single lexical function: a tensor for adjectival composition $\mathscr{A}$.[2] Our proposal is that adjective-noun composition is carried out by multiplying the tensor $\mathscr{A}$ with the vector for the adjective **adj**, followed by a multiplication with the vector **noun**, *c.f.* Figure 3.

The product of the tensor $\mathscr{A}$ and the vector **adj** yields a matrix dependent of the adjective that is multiplied with the vector **noun**. This matrix corresponds to the LF matrix **ADJ**. As indicated in Figure 4, we obtain $\mathscr{A}$ with the help of matrices obtained from the LF approach, and from vectors for single words easily obtained in distributional semantics; we perform a least square regression minimizing the norm of the matrices generated by the equations in Figure 4. Formally, the problem is

[2] A tensor generalises a matrix to several dimensions. We use a tensor in three modes. For an introduction to tensors, see (Kolda and Bader, 2009).

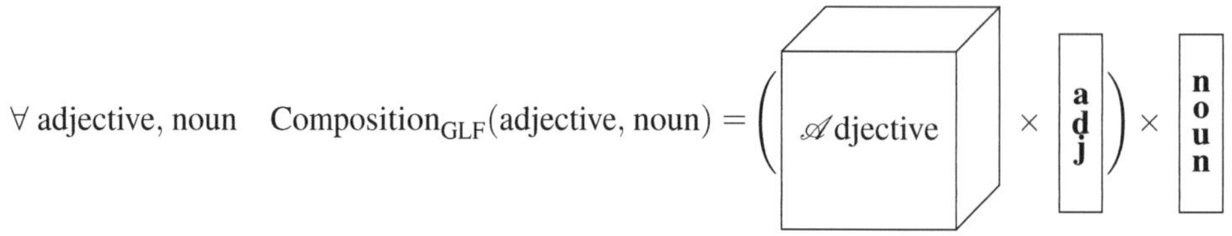

Figure 3: Composition in the generalised lexical function model

Find $\mathscr{A}$ s.t.
$\sum_{\text{adj}} (\mathscr{A} \times \mathbf{adj} - \mathbf{ADJ})^2$
is minimal

Note that our tensor is not just the compilation of the information found in the LF matrices: the adjective mode of our tensor has a limited number of dimensions, whereas the LF approach creates a separate matrix for each individual adjective. This reduction forces the model to generalise, and we hypothesise that this generalisation allows us to make proper noun modifications even in the light of sparse data.

Our approach requires learning a significant number of matrices **ADJ**. This is not a problem, since FRWaC and UKWaC provide sufficient data for the LF approach to generate matrices for a significant number of adjectives. For example, the 2000th most frequent adjective in FRWaC ('fasciste') has more than 4000 occurrences.

To return to our example of *blood donation campaign*, once the tensor $\mathscr{N}$ for noun-noun composition is learned, our approach requires only the knowledge of the vectors **blood**, **donation** and **campaign**. We would then perform the following computations:

$\mathbf{blood\_donation} = (\mathscr{N} \times \mathbf{blood}) \times \mathbf{donation}$
$\mathbf{blood\_donation\_campaign} =$
$(\mathscr{N} \times \mathbf{blood\_donation}) \times \mathbf{campaign}$

and this allows us to avoid the sparse data problem for the LF approach in generating the matrix **BLOOD_DONATION**.

Once we have obtained the tensor $\mathscr{A}$, we verify experimentally its relevance to composition, in order to check whether a tensor optimising the equations in Figure 4 would be semantically interesting.

3 Evaluation

3.1 Tasks description

In order to evaluate the different composition methods, we constructed test sets for French and English, inspired by the work of Zanzotto et al. (2010) and the SEMEVAL-2013 task *evaluating phrasal semantics* (Korkontzelos et al., 2013). The task is to make a judgement about the semantic similarity of a short word sequence (an adjective-noun combination) and a single noun. This is important, as composition models need to be able to treat word sequences of arbitrary length. Formally, the task is presented as:

With $\quad \mathbf{comp} = \text{composition}(\text{adj}, \text{noun}_1)$
Evaluate $\quad \text{similarity}(\mathbf{comp}, \mathbf{noun_2})$

where the 'composition' function is carried out by the different composition models. 'Similarity' needs to be a binary function, with return values 'similar' and 'non-similar'. Note, however, that the distributional approach yields a continuous similarity value (such as the cosine similarity between two vectors). In order to determine which cosine values correspond to 'similar' and which cosine values correspond to 'non-similar', we looked at a number of examples from a development set. More precisely, we carried out a logistic regression on 50 positive and 50 negative examples (separate from our test set) in order to automatically learn the threshold at which a pair is considered to be similar. Finally, we decided to use balanced test sets containing as many positive instances as negative ones.

The test set is constructed in a semi-automatic way, making use of the canonical phrasing of dictionary definitions. Take for example the definition of *bassoon* in the English Wiktionary[3], presented in Figure 5. It is quite straightforward to extract the pair (*musical_instrument*, *bassoon*) from this definition. Using a large dictionary (such as Wiktionary), it is then possible to extract a large number of positive – i.e. similar – (`adjective_noun`, `noun`) pairs.

For the construction of our test set for French, we downloaded all entries of the French Wiktionary (*Wiktionnaire*) and annotated them with

[3]`http://en.wiktionary.org/wiki/bassoon`, accessed on 26 February 2015.

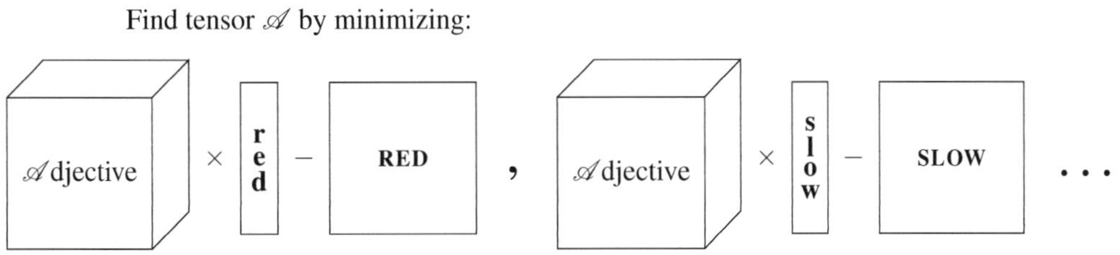

Figure 4: Learning the 𝒜djective tensor

bassoon /bəˈsuːn/ (plural bassoons)

1. A musical instrument in the woodwind family, having a double reed and, playing in the tenor and bass ranges.

Figure 5: Definition of *bassoon*, extracted from the English Wiktionary

part of speech tags, using the French part of speech tagger MElt (Denis et al., 2010). Next, we extracted all definitions that start with an adjective-noun combination. As a final step, we filtered all instances containing words that appear too infrequently in our FRWaC corpus.[4]

The automatically extracted instances were then checked manually, and all instances that were considered incorrect were rejected. This gave us a final test set of 714 positive examples.

We also created an initial set of negative examples, where we combined an existing combination of `adjective_noun1` (extracted from the French Wiktionary), with a randomly selected noun `noun2`. Again, we verified manually that the resulting (`adjective_noun1`, `noun2`) pairs constituted actual negative examples. We then created a second set of negative examples by randomly selecting two nouns (`noun1`,`noun2`) and one adjective `adjective`. The resulting pairs (`adjective_noun1`, `noun2`) were verified manually.

In addition to our new test set for French, we also experimented with the original test set of the SEMEVAL-2013 task *evaluation phrasal semantics* for English. However, the original test set lacked human oversight as 'manly behavior' was considered similar to 'testosterone' for example. We thus hand-checked the test set ourselves and extracted 652 positive pairs.

The negative pairs from the original SEMEVAL-2013 are a combination of a random noun and a random adjective-noun compositon found in the English Wiktionary. We used it as our first set of English negative examples as it is similar in construction to our first set of negative examples in French. In addition, we created a completely random negative test set for English in the same fashion we did for the second negative test set for French.

Finally, the original test set also contains noun-noun compounds so we also created a test set for that. This gave us 226 positive and negative pairs for the noun-noun composition.

3.2 Semantic space construction

In this section, we describe the construction of our semantic space. Our semantic space for French was built using the FRWaC corpus (Baroni et al., 2009) – about 1,6 billion words of web texts – which has been tagged with MElt tagger (Denis et al., 2010) and parsed with MaltParser (Nivre et al., 2006a), trained on a dependency-based version of the French treebank (Candito et al., 2010). Our semantic space for English has been built using the UKWaC corpus (Baroni et al., 2009), which consists of about 2 billion words extracted from the web. The corpus has been part of speech tagged and lemmatized with Stanford Part-Of-Speech Tagger (Toutanova and Manning, 2000; Toutanova et al., 2003), and parsed with Malt-Parser (Nivre et al., 2006b) trained on sections 2-21 of the Wall Street Journal section of the Penn Treebank extended with about 4000 ques-

[4] *i.e.* less than 200 times for adjectives and less than 1500 times for nouns

positive examples	random negative examples	Wiktionary-based negative examples
(*mot_court, abréviation*)	(*importance_fortuit, gamme*)	(*jugement_favorable, discorde*)
'short word', 'abbreviation'	'accidental importance', 'range'	'favorable judgement', 'discord'
(*ouvrage_littéraire, essai*)	(*penchant_autoritaire, ile*)	(*circonscription_administratif, fumier*)
'literary work', 'essay'	'authoritarian slope', isle'	'administrative district', 'manure'
(*compagnie_honorifique, ordre*)	(*auspice_aviaire, ponton*)	(*mention_honorable, renne*)
'honorary company', 'order'	'avian omen', 'pontoon'	'honorable mention', 'reindeer'

Table 1: A number of examples from our test set for French

tions from the QuestionBank[5].

For both corpora, we extracted the lemmas of all nouns, adjectives and (bag of words) context words. We only kept those lemmas that consist of alphabetic characters.[6] We then selected the 10K most frequent lemmas for each category (nouns, adjectives, context words), making sure to include all the words from the test set. As a final step, we created our semantic space vectors using adjectives and nouns as instances, and bag of words context words as features. The resulting vectors were weighted using *positive point-wise mutual information* (*ppmi*, (Church and Hanks, 1990)), and all vectors were normalized to unit length.

We then compared the different composition methods on different versions of the same semantic space (both for French and English): the full semantic space, a reduced version of the space to 300 dimensions using singular value decomposition (*svd*, (Golub and Van Loan, 1996)), and a reduced version of the space to 300 dimensions using non-negative matrix factorization (*nmf*, (Lee and Seung, 2000)). We did so in order to test each method in its optimal conditions. In fact:

- A non-reduced space contains more information. This might be beneficial for methods that are able to take advantage of the full semantic space (viz. the additive et multiplicative model). On the other hand, to be able to use the non-reduced space for the lexical function approach, one would have to learn matrices of size 10K ×10K for each adjective. This would be problematic in terms of computing time and data sparseness, as we previously noted. The same goes for our generalised approach.
- Previous research has indicated that the lexical function approach is able to achieve better results using a reduced space with *svd*. On the other hand, the negative values that result from *svd* are detrimental for the multiplicative approach.
- An *nmf*-reduced semantic space is not detrimental for the multiplicative approach.

In order to determine the best parameters for the additive model, we tested this model for different values of α and β where $\alpha + \beta = 1$[7] on a development set and kept the values with the best results: $\alpha = 0.4$, $\beta = 0.6$.

3.3 Data used for regression

The LF approach and its generalisation need data in order to perform the least square regression. We thus created a semantic space for **adjective_noun** and **noun_noun** vectors using the most frequent ones in a similar way to how we created them in 3.2. Then we solved the equations in 2.2 and forth. Even though the regression data were disjoint from the test sets, for each pair, we removed some of the data that may cause overfitting.

For the lexical function tests, we remove the **adjective_noun** vector corresponding to the test pair from the regression data. For example, we do not use **short_word** to learn **SHORT** for the (short_word, abbrevation) pair.

For the generalised lexical function tests, we use the full regression data to learn the lexical functions used to train the tensor. However, we remove the **ADJECTIVE** matrix corresponding to the test pair from the (tensor) regression data. For example, we do not use **SHORT** to learn $\mathscr{A}$ for the (short_word, abbreviation) pair.

[5] `http://maltparser.org/mco/english_parser/engmalt.html`

[6] This step generally filters out dates, numbers and punctuation, which have little interest for the distributional approach.

[7] Since the vectors are normalized (*cf.* 3.2), this condition does not affect the generality of our test.

Table 2: Percentage of correctly classified pairs for (adjective_noun1, noun2) for both French and English spaces.

	baseline		multiplicative		additive		LF		generalised LF	
	fr	**en**	**fr**	**en**	**fr**	**en**	**fr**	**en**	**fr**	**en**
non-reduced	0.83	0.81	0.86	0.86	0.88	0.86	N/A		N/A	
svd	0.79	0.79	0.55	0.59	0.84	0.78	**0.93**	**0.92**	0.91	0.88
nmf	0.78	0.78	0.83	0.77	0.79	0.84	0.90	0.86	0.88	0.85

(a) Negative examples are created randomly.

	baseline		multiplicative		additive		LF		generalised LF	
	fr	**en**	**fr**	**en**	**fr**	**en**	**fr**	**en**	**fr**	**en**
non-reduced	0.80	0.79	0.83	0.81	**0.85**	0.80	N/A		N/A	
svd	0.78	0.77	0.54	0.48	0.83	0.78	**0.84**	0.79	0.81	0.77
nmf	0.78	0.78	0.79	0.78	0.83	**0.82**	0.82	**0.82**	0.81	0.80

(b) Negative examples are created from existing pairs.

Table 3: Percentage of correctly classified pairs for (noun2_noun1, noun3) with negative examples from existing pairs. Only the English space is tested.

English space	baseline	multiplicative	additive	LF	generalised LF
non-reduced	0.77	0.80	0.84	N/A	N/A
svd	0.78	0.49	**0.86**	0.83	0.82
nmf	0.79	0.82	**0.86**	**0.85**	0.83

3.4 Results

In this section, we present how the various models perform on our test sets.

3.4.1 General results

Tables 2 & 3 give an overview of the results. Note first that the baseline approach, which compares only the two nouns and ignores the subordinate adjective or noun, does relatively well on the task ($\sim$ 80% accuracy). This reflects the fact that the head noun in our pairs extracted from definitions is close to (and usually a super type of) the noun to be defined.

In addition, we observe that the multiplicative method performs badly, as expected, on the semantic space reduced with *svd*. This confirms the incompatibility of this method with the negative values generated by *svd*. Indeed, multiplying two vectors with negative values term by term may yield a third vector very far away from the other two. Such a combination does not support the subsectivity of most our test pairs. Apart from that, *svd* and *nmf* reductions do not affect the methods much.

Moreover, we observe that the multiplicative model performs better than the baseline but is bested by the additive model. We also see that additive and lexical functions often yield similar performance.

Finally, the generalised lexical function is slightly less accurate than the lexical functions. This is an expected consequence of generalisation. Nevertheless, the generalised lexical function yields sound results confirming our intuition that we can represent adjective-noun (or noun-noun) combinations by one function.

3.4.2 Adjective-noun

With random negative pairs (Table 2a), we observe that the lexical function model obtains the best results for the *svd* space. This result is significantly better than any other method on any of the spaces—e.g.,for French space, $\chi^2 = 33.49$, $p < 0.01$ when compared to the additive model for the non-reduced space which performs second.

However, with non-random negative pairs (Table 2b), LF and the additive model obtain scores that are globally equivalent for their best respective conditions — in French 0.85 for the additive non-reduced model vs. 0.84 for the LF *svd* model, a difference that is not significant ($\chi^2 = 0.20$, $p < 0.05$).

This seems to indicate that LF is especially efficient at separating out nonsense combinations. This may be caused by the fact that lexical functions learn from actual pairs. Thus, when an adjective_noun combination is bizarre, the ADJECTIVE matrix has not been optimized to interact with the **noun** vector and may lead to complete non-sense — Which is a good thing because humans would analyze the combination as such.

Finally, similar results in French and English confirm the intuition that distributional methods (and its composition models) are independent of the idiosyncrasies of a particular language; in particular they are as efficient for French as for English.

3.4.3 Noun-noun

The noun-noun tests (Table 3) yields similar results to the adjective-noun tests. This is not so surprising since noun noun compounds in English also obey a roughly subsective property: a baseball field is still a field (though a cricket pitch is perhaps not so obviously a pitch). We can see that the accuracy increase from the baseline is higher compared to adjective-noun test on the same exact spaces (Table 2b, right values). This may be due to the fact that the subordinate noun in noun-noun combinations is more important than the adjective subordinate in adjective-noun combination.

4 Related work

Many researchers have already studied and evaluated different composition models within a distributional approach. One of the first studies evaluating compositional phenomena in a systematic way is Mitchell and Lapata's (2008) approach. They explore a number of different models for vector composition, of which vector addition (the sum of each feature) and vector multiplication (the element-wise multiplication of each feature) are the most important. They evaluate their models on a noun-verb phrase similarity task. Human annotators were asked to judge the similarity of two composed pairs (by attributing a certain score). The model's task is then to reproduce the human judgements. Their results show that the multiplicative model yields the best results, along with a weighted combination of the additive and multiplicative model. The authors redid their study using a larger test set in Mitchell and Lapata (2010) (adjective-noun composition was also included), and they confirmed their initial results.

Baroni and Zamparelli (2010) evaluate their lexical function model within a somewhat different context. They evaluated their model by looking at its capacity of reconstructing the **adjective_noun** vectors that have not been seen during training. Their results show that their lexical function model obtains the best results for the reconstruction of the original co-occurrence vectors, followed by the additive model. We observe the same tendency in our evaluation results for French, although our results for English show a different picture. We would like to explore this discordance further in future work.

Grefenstette et al. (2013) equally propose a generalisation of the lexical function model that uses tensors. Their goal is to model transitive verbs, and the way we acquire our tensor is similar to theirs. In fact, they use the LF approach in order to learn **VERB_OBJECT** matrices that may be multiplied by a **subject** vector to obtain the **subject_verb_object** vector. In a second step, they learn a tensor for each individual verb, which is similar to how we learn our adjective tensor $\mathscr{A}$.

Coecke et al. (2010) present an abstract theoretical framework in which a sentence vector is a function of the Kronecker product of its word vectors, which allows for greater interaction between the different word features. A number of instantiations of the framework – where the key idea is that relational words (e.g. adjectives or verbs) have a rich (multi-dimensional) structure that acts as a filter on their arguments – are tested experimentally in Grefenstette and Sadrzadeh (2011a) and Grefenstette and Sadrzadeh (2011b). The authors evaluated their models using a similarity task that is similar to the one used by Mitchell & Lapata. However, they use more complex compositional expressions: rather than using compositions of two words (such as a verb and an object), they use simple transitive phrases (subject-verb-object). They show that their instantiations of the categorical model reach better results than the additive and multiplicative models on their transitive similarity task.

Socher et al. (2012) present a compositional model based on a recursive neural network. Each node in a syntactic tree is assigned both a vector and a matrix; the vector captures the actual meaning of the constituent, while the matrix models the way it changes the meaning of neighbouring words and phrases. They use an extrinsic evaluation, using the model for a sentiment prediction task. They show that their model gets better results than the additive, multiplicative, and lexical function approach. Other researchers, however, have published different results. Blacoe and Lapata (2012) evaluated the additive and multiplicative model, as well as Socher et al.'s (2012) approach on two different tasks: Mitchell & Lapata's (2010) similarity task and a paraphrase detection task. They find that the additive and multiplicative models reach better scores than Socher et al.'s model.

Tensors have been used before to model different aspects of natural language. Giesbrecht (2010) describes a tensor factorization model for the construction of a distributional model that is sensitive to word order. And Van de Cruys (2010) uses a tensor factorization model in order to construct a three-way selectional preference model of verbs, subjects, and objects.

5 Conclusion

We have developed a new method of composition and tested it in comparison with different composition methods assuming a distributional approach. We developed a test set for French pairing nouns with adjective noun combinations very similar in meaning from the French Wiktionary. We also used an existing SEMEVAL-2013 set to create a similar test set for English both for adjective noun combination and noun noun combination. Our tests confirm that the lexical function approach by Baroni and Zamparelli performs well compared to other methods of composition, but only when the negative examples are constructed randomly. Our generalised lexical function approach fares almost equally well. It also has the advantage of being constructed from automatically acquired adjectival and noun vectors, and offers the additional advantage of countering data sparseness. However, the lexical function approach claims to perform well on more subtle cases — *e.g.* non-subsective combinations such as *stone lion*. Our test sets does not contain such cases, and so we cannot draw any conclusion on this claim.

In future work, we would like to test different sizes of dimensionality reduction, in order to optimize our generalised lexical function model. Moreover, it is possible that better results may be obtained by proposing multiple generalised lexical functions, rather than a single one. We could, e.g., try to separate the intersective adjectives from non-intersective adjectives. And finally, we would like to further explore the performance of the lexical function model and generalised lexical function model on different datasets, which involve more complex compositional phenomena.

6 Acknowledgments

We thank Dinu et al. (2013a) for their work on the DISSECT toolkit[8], which provides plenty of helpful functions for composition in distributional semantics. We also thank the OSIRIM platform[9] for allowing us to do the computations we needed. Finally, we thank the reviewers of this paper for their insightful comments.

This work is supported by a grant overseen by the French National Research Agency ANR (ANR-14-CE24-0014).

References

Nicholas Asher. 2011. *Lexical Meaning in Context: A Web of Words*. Cambridge University Press.

Marco Baroni and Roberto Zamparelli. 2010. Nouns are vectors, adjectives are matrices: Representing adjective-noun constructions in semantic space. In *Proceedings of the 2010 Conference on Empirical Methods in Natural Language Processing*, pages 1183–1193, Cambridge, MA, October. Association for Computational Linguistics.

Marco Baroni, Silvia Bernardini, Adriano Ferraresi, and Eros Zanchetta. 2009. The wacky wide web: A collection of very large linguistically processed web-crawled corpora. *Language Resources and Evaluation*, 43(3):209–226.

Christian Bassac, Bruno Mery, and Christian Retoré. 2010. Towards a Type-theoretical account of lexical semantics. *Journal of Logic, Language and Information*, 19(2):229–245.

William Blacoe and Mirella Lapata. 2012. A comparison of vector-based representations for semantic composition. In *Proceedings of the 2012 Joint Conference on Empirical Methods in Natural Language Processing and Computational Natural Language Learning*, pages 546–556, Jeju Island, Korea, July. Association for Computational Linguistics.

[8]http://clic.cimec.unitn.it/composes/toolkit/
[9]http://osirim.irit.fr/site/en

Marie Candito, Benoît Crabbé, Pascal Denis, et al. 2010. Statistical french dependency parsing: treebank conversion and first results. In *Proceedings of the Seventh International Conference on Language Resources and Evaluation (LREC 2010)*, pages 1840–1847.

Kenneth W. Church and Patrick Hanks. 1990. Word association norms, mutual information & lexicography. *Computational Linguistics*, 16(1):22–29.

Bob Coecke, Mehrnoosh Sadrzadeh, and Stephen Clark. 2010. Mathematical foundations for a compositional distributed model of meaning. *Lambek Festschrift, Linguistic Analysis, vol. 36*, 36.

Pascal Denis, Benoît Sagot, et al. 2010. Exploitation d'une ressource lexicale pour la construction d'un étiqueteur morphosyntaxique état-de-l'art du français. In *Traitement Automatique des Langues Naturelles: TALN 2010*.

Georgiana Dinu, Nghia The Pham, and Marco Baroni. 2013a. Dissect - distributional semantics composition toolkit. In *Proceedings of the 51st Annual Meeting of the Association for Computational Linguistics: System Demonstrations*, pages 31–36, Sofia, Bulgaria, August. Association for Computational Linguistics.

Georgiana Dinu, Nghia The Pham, and Marco Baroni. 2013b. General estimation and evaluation of compositional distributional semantic models. In *Proceedings of the Workshop on Continuous Vector Space Models and their Compositionality*, pages 50–58, Sofia, Bulgaria, August. Association for Computational Linguistics.

Eugenie Giesbrecht. 2010. Towards a matrix-based distributional model of meaning. In *Proceedings of the NAACL HLT 2010 Student Research Workshop*, pages 23–28. Association for Computational Linguistics.

Gene H. Golub and Charles F. Van Loan. 1996. *Matrix Computations (3rd Ed.)*. Johns Hopkins University Press, Baltimore, MD, USA.

Edward Grefenstette and Mehrnoosh Sadrzadeh. 2011a. Experimental support for a categorical compositional distributional model of meaning. In *Proceedings of the 2011 Conference on Empirical Methods in Natural Language Processing*, pages 1394–1404, Edinburgh, Scotland, UK., July. Association for Computational Linguistics.

Edward Grefenstette and Mehrnoosh Sadrzadeh. 2011b. Experimenting with transitive verbs in a discocat. In *Proceedings of the GEMS 2011 Workshop on GEometrical Models of Natural Language Semantics*, pages 62–66, Edinburgh, UK, July. Association for Computational Linguistics.

E. Grefenstette, G. Dinu, Y.-Z. Zhang, M. Sadrzadeh, and Baroni M. 2013. Multi-step regression learning for compositional distributional semantics. In *Proceedings of the 10th International Conference on Computational Semantics (IWCS)*, pages 131–142, East Stroudsburg PA. Association for Computational Linguistics.

Zellig S. Harris. 1954. Distributional structure. *Word*, 10(23):146–162.

Hans Kamp. 1975. Two theories about adjectives. *Formal semantics of natural language*, pages 123–155.

Tamara G. Kolda and Brett W. Bader. 2009. Tensor decompositions and applications. *SIAM Review*, 51(3):455–500, September.

Ioannis Korkontzelos, Torsten Zesch, Fabio Massimo Zanzotto, and Chris Biemann. 2013. Semeval-2013 task 5: Evaluating phrasal semantics. In *Second Joint Conference on Lexical and Computational Semantics (*SEM), Volume 2: Proceedings of the Seventh International Workshop on Semantic Evaluation (SemEval 2013)*, pages 39–47, Atlanta, Georgia, USA, June. Association for Computational Linguistics.

Thomas Landauer and Susan Dumais. 1997. A solution to Plato's problem: The Latent Semantic Analysis theory of the acquisition, induction, and representation of knowledge. *Psychology Review*, 104:211–240.

Daniel D. Lee and H. Sebastian Seung. 2000. Algorithms for non-negative matrix factorization. In *Advances in Neural Information Processing Systems 13*, pages 556–562.

Dekang Lin. 1998. Automatic retrieval and clustering of similar words. In *Proceedings of the 36th Annual Meeting of the Association for Computational Linguistics and 17th International Conference on Computational Linguistics (COLING-ACL98), Volume 2*, pages 768–774, Montreal, Quebec, Canada.

Zhaohui Luo. 2010. Type-theoretical semantics with coercive subtyping. *SALT20, Vancouver*.

Marco Marelli, Luisa Bentivogli, Marco Baroni, Raffaella Bernardi, S Menini, and Roberto Zamparelli. 2014. Semeval-2014 task 1: Evaluation of compositional distributional semantic models on full sentences through semantic relatedness and textual entailment. In *Proceedings of SemEval 2014: International Workshop on Semantic Evaluation*.

Jeff Mitchell and Mirella Lapata. 2008. Vector-based models of semantic composition. *proceedings of ACL-08: HLT*, pages 236–244.

J. Mitchell and M. Lapata. 2010. Composition in distributional models of semantics. *Cognitive Science*, 34(8):1388–1429.

J. Nivre, J. Hall, and J. Nilsson. 2006a. Maltparser: A data-driven parser-generator for dependency parsing. In *Proceedings of LREC-2006*, pages 2216–2219, Genoa, Italy.

Joakim Nivre, Johan Hall, and Jens Nilsson. 2006b. Maltparser: A data-driven parser-generator for dependency parsing. In *Proceedings of LREC-2006*, pages 2216–2219.

Barbara H Partee. 2010. Privative adjectives: subsective plus coercion. *BÄUERLE, R. et ZIMMERMANN, TE, éditeurs: Presuppositions and Discourse: Essays Offered to Hans Kamp*, pages 273–285.

Richard Socher, Brody Huval, Christopher D. Manning, and Andrew Y. Ng. 2012. Semantic compositionality through recursive matrix-vector spaces. In *Proceedings of the 2012 Joint Conference on Empirical Methods in Natural Language Processing and Computational Natural Language Learning*, pages 1201–1211, Jeju Island, Korea, July. Association for Computational Linguistics.

Kristina Toutanova and Christopher D. Manning. 2000. Enriching the knowledge sources used in a maximum entropy part-of-speech tagger. In *Proceedings of the Joint SIGDAT Conference on Empirical Methods in Natural Language Processing and Very Large Corpora (EMNLP/VLC-2000)*, pages 63–70.

Kristina Toutanova, Dan Klein, Christopher Manning, and Yoram Singer. 2003. Feature-rich part-of-speech tagging with a cyclic dependency network. In *Proceedings of HLT-NAACL 2003*, pages 252–259.

Peter Turney and Patrick Pantel. 2010. From frequency to meaning: Vector space models of semantics. *Journal of artificial intelligence research*, 37(1):141–188.

Tim Van de Cruys. 2010. A non-negative tensor factorization model for selectional preference induction. *Natural Language Engineering*, 16(4):417–437.

Fabio Massimo Zanzotto, Ioannis Korkontzelos, Francesca Fallucchi, and Suresh Manandhar. 2010. Estimating linear models for compositional distributional semantics. In *Proceedings of the 23rd International Conference on Computational Linguistics (Coling 2010)*, pages 1263–1271, Beijing, China, August. Coling 2010 Organizing Committee.

Simple Learning and Compositional Application of Perceptually Grounded Word Meanings for Incremental Reference Resolution

Casey Kennington
CITEC, Bielefeld University
Universitätsstraße 25
33615 Bielefeld, Germany
ckennington@cit-ec.uni-bielefeld.de

David Schlangen
CITEC, Bielefeld University
Universitätsstraße 25
33615 Bielefeld, Germany
david.schlangen@uni-bielefeld.de

Abstract

An elementary way of using language is to *refer* to objects. Often, these objects are physically present in the shared environment and reference is done via mention of perceivable properties of the objects. This is a type of language use that is modelled well neither by logical semantics nor by distributional semantics, the former focusing on inferential relations between expressed propositions, the latter on similarity relations between words or phrases. We present an account of word and phrase meaning that is perceptually grounded, trainable, compositional, and 'dialogue-plausible' in that it computes meanings word-by-word. We show that the approach performs well (with an accuracy of 65% on a 1-out-of-32 reference resolution task) on direct descriptions and target/landmark descriptions, even when trained with less than 800 training examples and automatically transcribed utterances.

1 Introduction

The most basic, fundamental site of language use is co-located dialogue (Fillmore, 1975; Clark, 1996) and referring to objects, as in Example (1), is a common occurrence in such a co-located setting.

(1) *The green book on the left next to the mug.*

Logical semantics (Montague, 1973; Gamut, 1991; Partee et al., 1993) has little to say about this process – its focus is on the construction of syntactically manipulable objects that model inferential relations; here, e.g. the inference that there are (at least) two objects. Vector space approaches to distributional semantics (Turney and Pantel, 2010) similarly focuses on something else, namely semantic similarity relations between words or phrases (e.g. finding closeness for "coloured tome on the right of the cup"). Neither approach by itself says anything about processing; typically, the assumption in applications is that fully presented phrases are being processed.

Lacking in these approaches is a notion of *grounding* of symbols in features of the world (Harnad, 1990).[1] In this paper, we present an account of word and phrase meaning that is (a) perceptually grounded in that it provides a link between words and (computer) vision features of real images, (b) trainable, as that link is learned from examples of language use, (c) compositional in that the meaning of phrases is a function of that of its parts and composition is driven by structural analysis, and (d) 'dialogue-plausible' in that it computes meanings incrementally, word-by-word and can work with noisy input from an automatic speech recogniser (ASR). We show that the approach performs well (with an accuracy of 65% on a reference resolution task out of 32 objects) on direct descriptions as well as target/landmark descriptions, even when trained with little data (less than 800 training examples).

In the following section we will give a background on reference resolution, followed by a description of our model. We will then describe the data we used and explain our evaluations. We finish by giving results, providing some additional analysis, and discussion.

2 Background: Reference Resolution

Reference resolution (RR) is the task of resolving referring expressions (REs; as in Example (1)) to a *referent*, the entity to which they are intended to refer. Following Kennington et al. (2015a), this can be formalised as a function f_{rr} that, given a representation U of the RE and a representation W

[1] But see discussion below of recent extensions of these approaches taking this into account.

Proceedings of the 53rd Annual Meeting of the Association for Computational Linguistics and the 7th International Joint Conference on Natural Language Processing, pages 292–301,
Beijing, China, July 26-31, 2015.

of the (relevant aspects of the) world, returns I^*, the identifier of one the objects in the world that is the referent of the RE. A number of recent papers have used stochastic models for f_{rr} where, given W and U, a distribution over a specified set of candidate entities in W is obtained and the probability assigned to each entity represents the strength of belief that it is the referent. The referent is then the argmax:

$$I^* = \underset{I}{\operatorname{argmax}} P(I|U, W) \quad (1)$$

Recently, generative approaches, including our own, have been presented (Funakoshi et al., 2012; Kennington et al., 2013; Kennington et al., 2014; Kennington et al., 2015b; Engonopoulos et al., 2013) which model U as words or ngrams and the world W as a set of objects in a virtual game board, represented as a set properties or concepts (in some cases, extra-linguistic or discourse aspects were also modelled in W, such as deixis). In Matuszek et al. (2014), W was represented as a distribution over properties of tangible objects and U was a Combinatory Categorical Grammar parse. In all of these approaches, the objects are distinct and represented via symbolically specified *properties*, such as colour and shape. The set of properties is either read directly from the world if it is virtual, or computed (i.e., discretised) from the real world objects.

In this paper, we learn a mapping from W to U directly, without mediating symbolic properties; such a mapping is a kind of perceptual grounding of meaning between W and U. Situated RR is a convenient setting for learning perceptually-grounded meaning, as objects that are referred to are physically present, are described by the RE, and have visual features that can be computationally extracted and represented.

Further comparison to related work will be discussed in Section 5.

3 Modelling Reference to Visible Objects

Overview As a representative of the kind of model explained above with formula (1), we want our model to compute a probability distribution over candidate objects, given a RE (or rather, possibly just a prefix of it). We break this task down into components: The basis of our model is a model of word meaning as a function from perceptual features of a given object to a judgement about how well a word and that object "fit together". (See Section 5 for discussion of prior uses of this "words as classifiers"-approach.) This can (loosely) be seen as corresponding to the *intension* of a word, which for example in Montague's approach is similarly modelled as a function, but from possible worlds to extensions (Gamut, 1991). We model two different types of words / word meanings: those picking out properties of single objects (e.g., "green" in "the green book"), following Kennington et al. (2015a), and those picking out relations of two objects (e.g., "next to" in (1)), going beyond Kennington et al. (2015a). These word meanings are learned from instances of language use.

The second component then is the application of these word meanings in the context of an actual reference and within a phrase. This application gives the desired result of a probability distribution over candidate objects, where the probability expresses the strength of belief in the object falling in the *extension* of the expression. Here we model two different types of composition, of what we call *simple references* and *relational references*. These applications are strictly compositional in the sense that the meanings of the more complex constructions are a function of those of their parts.

Word Meanings The first type of word (or rather, word meaning) we model picks out a single object via its visual properties. (At least, this is what we use here; any type of feature could be used.) To model this, we train for each word w from our corpus of REs a binary logistic regression classifier that takes a representation of a candidate object via visual features ($\mathbf{x}$) and returns a probability p_w for it being a good fit to the word (where $\mathbf{w}$ is the weight vector that is learned and σ is the logistic function):

$$p_w(\mathbf{x}) = \sigma(\mathbf{w}^\intercal \mathbf{x} + b) \quad (2)$$

Formalising the correspondence mentioned above, the *intension* of a word can in this approach then be seen as the classifier itself, a function from a representation of an object to a probability:

$$[\![w]\!]_{obj} = \lambda \mathbf{x}.p_w(\mathbf{x}) \quad (3)$$

(Where $[\![w]\!]$ denotes the meaning of w, and $\mathbf{x}$ is of the type of feature given by f_{obj}, the function computing a feature representation for a given object.)

We train these classifiers using a corpus of REs (further described in Section 4), coupled with representations of the scenes in which they were used and an annotation of the referent of that scene. The setting was restricted to reference to single objects. To get positive training examples, we pair each word of a RE with the features of the referent. To get negative training examples, we pair the word with features of (randomly picked) other objects present in the same scene, but *not* referred to by it. This selection of negative examples makes the assumption that the words from the RE apply only to the referent. This is wrong as a strict rule, as other objects could have similar visual features as the referent; for this to work, however, this has to be the case only more often than it is not.

The second type of word that we model expresses a relation between objects. Its meaning is trained in a similar fashion, except that it is presented a vector of features of a *pair* of objects, such as their euclidean distance, vertical and horizontal differences, and binary features denoting higher than/lower than and left/right relationships.

Application and Composition The model just described gives us a prediction for a pair of word and object (or pair of objects). What we wanted, however, is a distribution over all candidate objects in a given utterance situation, and not only for individual words, but for (incrementally growing) REs. Again as mentioned above, we model two types of application and composition. First, what we call '**simple references**'—which roughly corresponds to simple NPs—that refer only by mentioning properties of the referent (e.g. "the red cross on the left"). To get a distribution for a single word, we apply the word classifier (the *intension*) to all candidate objects and normalise; this can then be seen as the *extension* of the word in a given (here, visual) discourse universe W, which provides the candidate objects ($\mathbf{x}_i$ is the feature vector for object i, $normalize()$ vectorized normalisation, and I a random variable ranging over the candidates):

$$[\![w]\!]^W_{obj} = normalize(([\![w]\!]_{obj}(\mathbf{x}_1), \ldots, [\![w]\!]_{obj}(\mathbf{x}_k))) = normalize((p_w(\mathbf{x}_1), \ldots, p_w(\mathbf{x}_k))) = P(I|w) \quad (4)$$

In effect, this combines the individual classifiers into something like a multi-class logistic regression / maximum entropy model—but, *nota bene*, only for application. The training regime did not need to make any assumptions about the number of objects present, as it trained classifiers for a 2-class problem (how well does this given object fit to the word?). The multi-class nature is also indicated in Figure 1, which shows multiple applications of the logistic regression network for a word, and a normalisation layer on top.

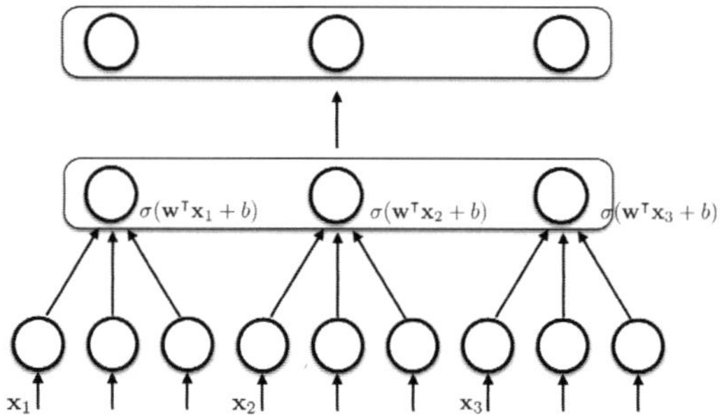

Figure 1: Representation as network with normalisation layer.

To compose the evidence from individual words $w_1, \ldots, w_k$ into a prediction for a 'simple' RE $[_{sr} w_1, \ldots, w_k]$ (where the bracketing indicates the structural assumption that the words belong to one, possibly incomplete, 'simple reference'), we average the contributions of its constituent words. The averaging function $avg()$ over distributions then is the contribution of the construction 'simple reference (phrase)', sr, and the meaning of the whole phrase is the application of the meaning of the construction to the meaning of the words:

$$[\![[_{sr} w_1, \ldots, w_k]]\!]^W = [\![sr]\!]^W [\![w_1, \ldots, w_k]\!]^W = avg([\![w_1]\!]^W, \ldots, [\![w_k]\!]^W) \quad (5)$$

where $avg()$ is defined as

$$avg([\![w_1]\!]^W, [\![w_2]\!]^W) = P_{avg}(I|w_1, w_2) \text{ with } P_{avg}(I = i|w_1, w_2) = \frac{1}{2}(P(I = i|w_1) + P(I = i|w_2)) \text{ for } i \in I \quad (6)$$

The averaging function is inherently incremental, in the sense that $avg(a, b, c) = avg(avg(a, b), c)$ and hence it can be extended "on the right". This represents an incremental model where new information from the current increment is added to what is already known, resulting in an intersective way of composing the meaning of the phrase. This cannot account for all constructions (such as negation or generally quantification), of course; we leave exploring other constructions that could occur even in our 'simple references' to future work.

Relational references such as in Example (1) from the introduction have a more complex structure, being a relation between a (simple) reference to a *landmark* and a (simple) reference to a *target*. This structure is indicated abstractly in the following 'parse': $[_{rel}[_{sr}w_1,\ldots,w_k][_r r_1,\ldots,r_n][_{sr}w'_1,\ldots,w'_m]]$, where the w are the target words, r the relational expression words, and w' the landmark words.

As mentioned above, the relational expression similarly is treated as a classifier (in fact, technically we contract expressions such as "to the left of" into a single token and learn one classifier for it), but expressing a judgement for pairs of objects. It can be applied to a specific scene with a set of candidate objects (and hence, candidate pairs) in a similar way by applying the classifier to all pairs and normalising, resulting in a distribution over pairs:

$$[\![r]\!]^W = P(R_1, R_2|r) \tag{7}$$

We expect the meaning of the phrase to be a function of the meaning of the constituent parts (the simple references, the relation expression, and the construction), that is:

$$[\![[_{rel}[_{sr}w_1,\ldots,w_k][_r r][_{sr}w'_1,\ldots,w'_m]]]\!] = [\![rel]\!]([\![sr]\!][\![w_1\ldots w_k]\!], [\![r]\!], [\![sr]\!][\![w'_1\ldots w'_m]\!]) \tag{8}$$

(dropping the indicator for concrete application, ^{W} on $[\![\ ]\!]$, for reasons of space and readability).

What is the contribution of the relational construction, $[\![rel]\!]$? Intuitively, what we want to express here is that the belief in an object being the intended referent should combine the evidence from the simple reference to the landmark object (e.g., "the mug" in (1)), from the simple (but presumably deficient) reference to the target object ("the green book on the left"), and that for the relation between them ("next to"). Instead of averaging (that is, combining additively), as for sr, we combine this evidence multiplicatively here: If the target constituent contributes $P(I_t|w_1,\ldots,w_k)$, the landmark constituent $P(I_l|w'_1,\ldots,w'_m)$, and the relation expression $P(R_1,R_2|r)$, with I_l, I_t, R_1 and R_2 all having the same domain, the set of all candidate objects, then the combination is

$$P(R_1|w_1,\ldots,w_k,r,w'_1,\ldots,w'_m) = \sum_{R_2}\sum_{I_l}\sum_{I_t} P(R_1,R_2|r) * P(I_l|w'_1,\ldots,w'_m) * P(I_t|w_1,\ldots,w_k) * P(R_1|I_t) * P(R_2|I_l) \tag{9}$$

The last two factors force identity on the elements of the pair and target and landmark, respectively (they are not learnt, but rather set to be 0 unless the values of R and I are equal), and so effectively reduce the summations so that all pairs need to be evaluated only once. The contribution of the construction then is this multiplication of the contributions of the parts, together with the factors enforcing that the pairs being evaluated by the relation expression consist of the objects evaluated by target and landmark expression, respectively.

In the following section, we will explain the data we collected and used to evaluate our model, the evaluation procedure, and the results.

4 Experiments

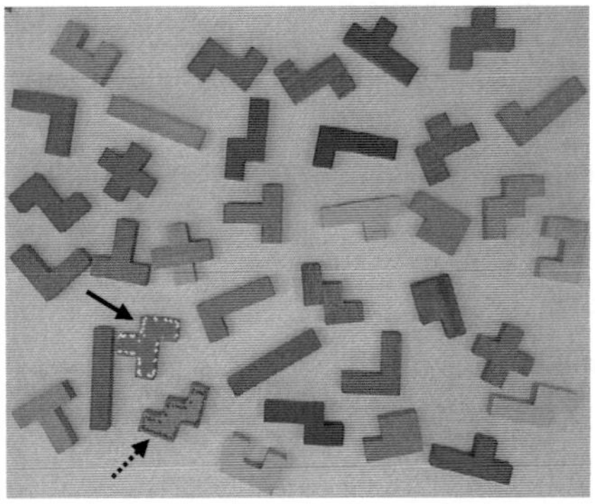

Figure 2: Example episode for *phase-2* where the target is outlined in green (solid arrow added here for presentation), the landmark outlined in blue (dashed arrow).

Data We evaluated our model using data we collected in a Wizard-of-Oz setting (that is, a human/computer interaction setting where parts of the functionality of the computer system were provided by a human experimentor). Participants were seated in front of a table with 36 Pentomino puzzle pieces that were randomly placed with some space between them, as shown in Figure 2. Above the table was a camera that recorded a video feed of the objects, processed using OpenCV (Pulli et al., 2012) to segment the objects (see below for details); of those, one (or one pair) was chosen randomly by the experiment software. The video image was presented to the participant on a display placed behind the table, but with the randomly selected piece (or pair of pieces) indicated by an overlay).

The task of the participant was to refer to that object using only speech, as if identifying it for a friend sitting next to the participant. The wizard (experimentor) had an identical screen depicting the scene but not the selected object. The wizard listened to the participant's RE and clicked on the object she thought was being referred on her screen. If it was the target object, a tone sounded and a new object was randomly chosen. This constituted a single *episode*. If a wrong object was clicked, a different tone sounded, the episode was flagged, and a new episode began. At varied intervals, the participant was instructed to "shuffle" the board between episodes by moving around the pieces.

The first half of the allotted time constituted phase-1. After phase-1 was complete, instructions for phase-2 were explained: the screen showed the target and also a landmark object, outlined in blue, near the target (again, see Figure 2). The participant was to refer to the target using the landmark. (In the instructions, the concepts of landmark and target were explained in general terms.) All other instructions remained the same as phase-1. The target's identifier, which was always known beforehand, was always recorded. For phase-2, the landmark's identifier was also recorded.

Nine participants (6 female, 3 male; avg. age of 22) took part in the study; the language of the study was German. Phase-1 for one participant and phase-2 for another participant were not used due to misunderstanding and a technical difficulty. This produced a corpus of 870 non-flagged episodes in total. Even though each episode had 36 objects in the scene, all objects were not always recognised by the computer vision processing. On average, 32 objects were recognized.

To obtain transcriptions, we used Google Web Speech (with a word error rate of 0.65, as determined by comparing to a hand transcribed sample) This resulted in 1587 distinct words, with 15.53 words on average per episode. The objects were not manipulated in any way during an episode, so the episode was guaranteed to remain static during a RE and a single image is sufficient to represent the layout of one episode's scene. Each scene was processed using computer vision techniques to obtain low-level features for each (detected) object in the scene which were used for the word classifiers.

We annotated each episode's RE with a simple tagging scheme that segmented the RE into words that directly referred to the target, words that directly referred to the landmark (or multiple landmarks, in some cases) and the relation words. For certain word types, additional information about the word was included in the tag if it described colour, shape, or spatial placement (denoted *contributing* REs in the evaluations below). The *direction* of certain relation words was normalised (e.g., *left-of* should always denote a landmark-target relation). This represents a minimal amount of "syntactic" information needed for the application of the classifiers and the composition of the phrase meanings. We leave applying a syntactic parser to future work. An example RE in the original German (as recognised by the ASR), English gloss, and tags for each word is given in (2).

(2)									
	a.	*grauer*	*stein*	*über*	*dem*	*grünen*	*m*	*unten*	*links*
	b.	gray	block	above	the	green	m	bottom	left
	c.	tc	ts	r		l	lc	ls tf	tf

To obtain visual features of each object, we used the same simple computer-vision pipeline of object segmentation and contour reconstruction as used by Kennington et al. (2015a), providing us with RGB representations for the colour and features such as skewness, number of edges etc. for the shapes.

Procedure We break down our data as follows: episodes where the target was referred directly via a 'simple reference' construction (DD; 410 episodes) and episodes where a target was referred via a landmark relation (RD; 460 episodes). We also test with either knowledge about structure (simple or relational reference) provided (ST) or not (WO, for "words-only"). All results shown are from 10-fold cross validations averaged over 10 runs; where for evaluations labelled RD the training data always includes all of DD plus 9 folds of RD, testing on RD. The sets address the following questions:

- how well does the sr model work on its own with just words? – DD.WO
- how well does the sr model work when it knows about REs? – DD.ST
- how well does the sr model work when it knows about REs, but not about relations? – RD.ST (sr)
- how well does the model learn relation words after it has learned about sr? RD.ST (r)
- how well does the rr model work (together with the sr)? RD.ST with DD.ST (rr)

Words were stemmed using the NLTK (Loper and Bird, 2002) Snowball Stemmer, reducing the vocabulary size to 1306. Due to sparsity, for relation words with a token count of less than 4 (found by ranging over values in a held-out set) relational features were piped into an UNK relation, which was used for unseen relations during evaluation (we assume the UNK relation would learn a general notion of 'nearness'). For the individual word classifiers, we always paired one negative example with one positive example.

For this evaluation, word classifiers for *sr* were given the following features: RGB values, HSV values, x and y coordinates of the centroids, euclidean distance of centroid from the center, and number of edges. The relation classifiers received information relating two objects, namely the euclidean distance between them, the vertical and horizontal distances, and two binary features that denoted if the landmark was higher than/lower than or left/right of the target.

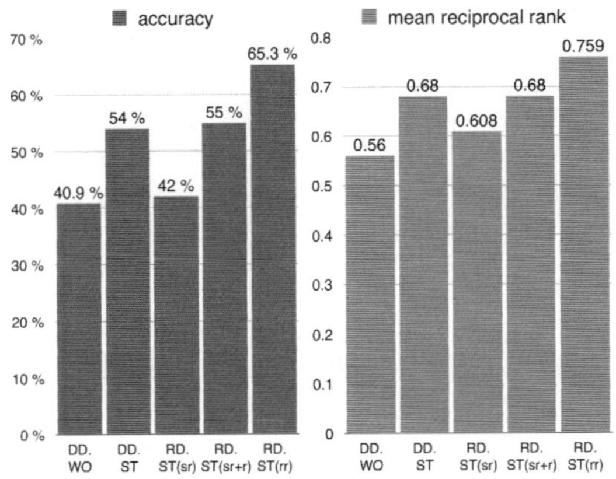

Figure 3: Results of our evaluation.

Metrics for Evaluation To give a picture of the overall performance of the model, we report **accuracy** (how often was the argmax the gold target) and **mean reciprocal rank** (MRR) of the gold target in the distribution over all the objects (like accuracy, higher MRR values are better; values range between 0 and 1). The use of MRR is motivated by the assumption that in general, a good rank for the correct object is desirable, even if it doesn't reach the first position, as when integrated in a dialogue system this information might still be useful to formulate clarification questions.

Results Figure 3 shows the results. (Random baseline of 1/32 or 3% not shown in plot.) DD.WO shows how well the *sr* model performs using the whole utterances and not just the REs. (Note that all evaluations are on noisy ASR transcriptions.) DD.ST adds structure by only considering words that are part of the actual RE, improving the results further. The remaining sets evaluate the contributions of the *rr* model. RD.ST (*sr*) does this indirectly, by including the target and landmark simple references, but not the model for the relations; the task here is to resolve target and landmark SRs as they are. This provides the baseline for the next two evaluations, which include the relation model. In RD.ST (*sr+r*), the model learns SRs from DD data and only relations from RD. The performance is substantially better than the baseline without the relation model. Performance is best finally for RD.ST (*rr*), where the landmark and target SRs in the training portion of RD also contribute to the word models.

The *mean reciprocal rank* scores follow a similar pattern and show that even though the target object was not the argmax of the distribution, on average it was high in the distribution. For all evaluations, the average standard deviation across the 10 runs was very small (0.01), meaning the model was fairly stable, despite the possibility of one run having randomly chosen more discriminating negative examples. Our conclusion from these experiments is that despite the small amount of training data and noise from ASR as well as the scene, the model is robust and yields respectable results.

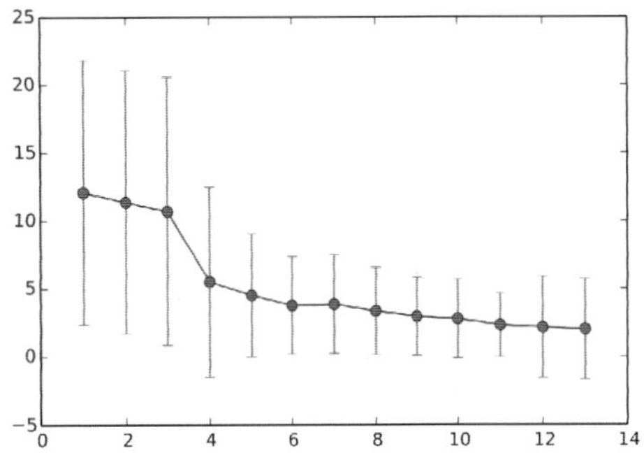

Figure 5: Incremental results: average rank improves over time

Incremental Results Figure 5 shows how our *rr* model processes incrementally, by giving the *average rank* of the (gold) target at each increment for the REs with the most common length in our data (13 words, of which there were 64 examples). A system that works incrementally would have a monotonically decreasing average rank as the utterance unfolds. The overall trend as shown in that

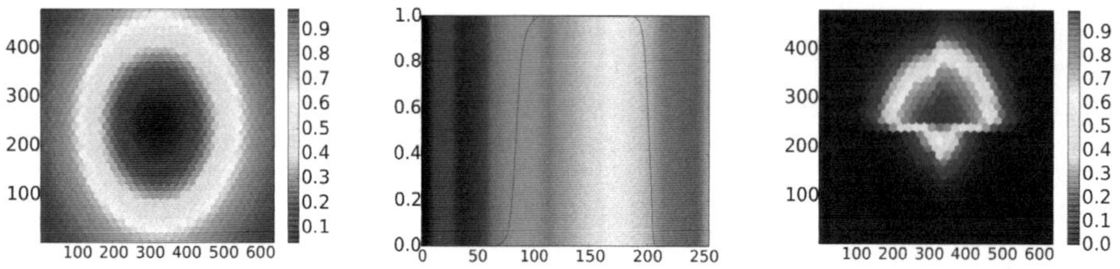

Figure 4: Each plot represents how well selected words fit assumptions about their lexical semantics: the leftmost plot *ecke* (*corner*) yields higher probabilities as objects are closer to the corner; the middle plot *grün* (*green*) yields higher probabilities when the colour spectrum values are nearer to green; the rightmost plot *über* (*above*) yields higher probabilities when targets are nearer to a landmark set in the middle.

Figure is as expected. There is a slight increase between 6-7, though very small (a difference of 0.09). Overall, these results seem to show that our model indeed works *intersectively* and "zooms in" on the intended referent.

4.1 Further Analysis

Analysis of Selected Words We analysed several individual word classifiers to determine how well their predictions match assumptions about their lexical semantics. For example, for the spatial word *Ecke* (*corner*), we would expect its classifier to return high probabilities if features related to an object's position (e.g., x and y coordinates, distance from the center) are near corners of the scene. The leftmost plot in Figure 4 shows that this is indeed the case; by holding all non-position features constant and ranging over all points on the screen, we can see that the classifier gives high probabilities around the edges, particularly in the four corners, and very low probabilities in the middle region. Similarly for the colour word *grün*, the centre plot in Figure 4 (overlaid with a colour spectrum) shows high probabilities are given when presented with the colour green, as expected. Similarly, for the relational word *über* (*above*), by treating the center point as the landmark and ranging over all other points on the plot for the target, the *über* classifier gives high probabilities when directly above the center point, with linear negative growth as the distance from the landmark increases.

Note that we selected the type of feature to vary here for presentation; all classifiers get the full feature set and learn automatically to "ignore" the irrelevant features (e.g., that for *grün* does not respond to variations in positional features). They do this wuite well, but we noticed some 'blurring', due to not all combinations of colours and shape being represented in the objects in the training set.

Analysis of Incremental Processing Figure 6 finally shows the interpretation of the RE in Example (2) in the scene from Figure 2. The top row depicts the distribution over objects (true target shown in red) after the relation word *unten* (bottom) is uttered; the second row that for landmark objects, after the landmark description begins (*dem grünen m / the green m*). The third row (target objects), ceases to change after the relational word is uttered, but continues again as additional target words are uttered (*unten links / bottom left*). While the true target is ranked highly already on the basis of the target SR alone, it is only when the relational information is added (top row) that it becomes argmax.

Discussion We did not explore how well our model could handle generalised quantifiers, such as *all* (e.g., *all the red objects*) or a specific number of objects (e.g., *the two green Ts*). We speculate that one could see as the contribution of words such as *all* or *two* a change to how the distribution is evaluated ("return the n top candidates"). Our model also doesn't yet directly handle more descriptive REs like *the cross in the top-right corner on the left*, as *left* is learned as a global term, or negation (*the cross that's not red*). We leave exploring such constructions to future work.

5 Related Work

Kelleher et al. (2005) approached RR using perceptually-grounded models, focusing on saliency and discourse context. In Gorniak and Roy (2004), descriptions of objects were used to learn a perceptually-grounded meaning with focus on spatial terms such as *on the left*. Steels and Belpaeme (2005) used neural networks to connect language with colour terms by interacting with humans. Larsson (2013) is closest in spirit to what we are attempting here; he provides a detailed

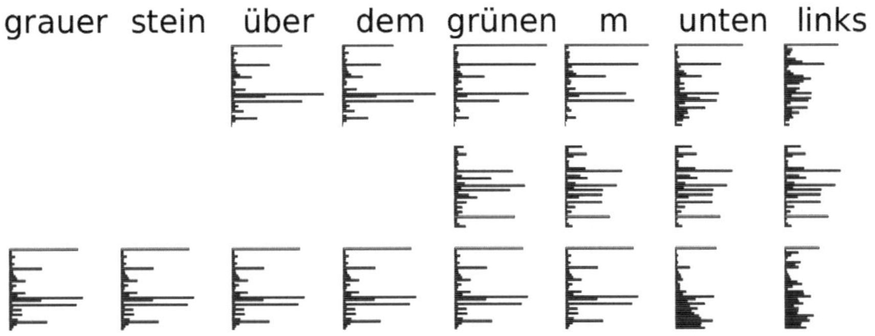

Figure 6: A depiction of the model working incrementally for the RE in Example (2): the distribution over objects for relation is row 1, landmark is row 2, target is row 3.

formal semantics for similarly descriptive terms, where parts of the semantics are modelled by a perceptual classifier. These approaches had limited lexicons (where we attempt to model all words in our corpus), and do not process incrementally, which we do here.

Recent efforts in multimodal distributional semantics have also looked at modelling word meaning based on visual context. Originally, vector space distributional semantics focused words in the context of other words (Turney and Pantel, 2010); recent multimodal approaches also consider low-level features from images. Bruni et al. (2012) and Bruni et al. (2014) for example model word meaning by word and visual context; each modality is represented by a vector, fused by concatenation. Socher et al. (2014) and Kiros et al. (2014) present approaches where words/phrases and images are mapped into the same high-dimensional space. While these approaches similarly provide a link between words and images, they are typically tailored towards a different setting (the words being descriptions of the whole image, and not utterance intended to perform a function within a visual situation). We leave more detailed exploration of similarities and differences to future work and only note for now that our approach, relying on much simpler classifiers (log-linear, basically), works with much smaller data sets and additionally seem to provide an easier interface to more traditional ways of composition (see Section 3 above).

The issue of semantic compositionality is also actively discussed in the distributional semantics literature (see, e.g., (Mitchell and Lapata, 2010; Erk, 2013; Lewis and Steedman, 2013; Paperno et al., 2014)), investigating how to combine vectors. This could be seen as composition on the level of intensions (if one sees distributional representations as intensions, as is variously hinted at, e.g. Erk (2013)). In our approach, composition is done on the extensional level (by interpolating distributions over candidate objects).

We do not see our approach as being in opposition to these attempts. Rather, we envision a system of semantics that combines traditional symbolic expressions (on which inferences can be modelled via syntactic calculi) with distributed representations (which model conceptual knowledge / semantic networks, as well as encyclopedic knowledge) and with our action-based (namely, identification in the environment via perceptual information) semantics. This line of approach is connected to a number of recent works (e.g., (Erk, 2013; Lewis and Steedman, 2013; Larsson, 2013)); for now, exploring its ramifications is left for future work.

6 Conclusion

In this paper, we presented a model of reference resolution that learns a perceptually-grounded meaning of words, including relational words. The model is simple, compositional, and robust despite low amounts of training data and noisy modalities. Our model is not without limitations; it so far only handles definite descriptions, yet there are other ways to refer to real-world objects, such as via pronouns and deixis. A unified model that can handle all of these, similar in spirit perhaps to Funakoshi et al. (2012), but with perceptual groundings, is left for future work. Our approach could also benefit from improved object segmentation and representation.

Our next steps with this model is to handle compositional structures without relying on our closed tag set (e.g., using a syntactic parser). We also plan to test our model in a natural, interactive dialogue system.

Acknowledgements We want to thank the anonymous reviewers for their comments. We also want to thank Spyros Kousidis for helping with data collection, Livia Dia for help with the computer vision processing, and Julian Hough for fruitful discussions on semantics, though we can't blame them for any problems of the work that may remain. This research/work was supported by the Cluster of Excellence Cognitive Interaction Technology 'CITEC' (EXC 277) at Bielefeld University, which is funded by the German Research Foundation (DFG).

References

Elia Bruni, Gemma Boleda, Marco Baroni, and Nam-Khanh Tran. 2012. Distributional semantics in technicolor. In *Proceedings of the 50th Annual Meeting of the Association for Computational Linguistics*, volume 1, pages 136–145.

Elia Bruni, Nam Khanh Tran, and Marco Baroni. 2014. Multimodal distributional semantics. *Journal of Artificial Intelligence Research*, 49:1–47.

Herbert H Clark. 1996. *Using Language*, volume 23. Cambridge University Press.

Nikos Engonopoulos, Martin Villalba, Ivan Titov, and Alexander Koller. 2013. Predicting the resolution of referring expressions from user behavior. In *Proceedings of EMLNP*, pages 1354–1359, Seattle, Washington, USA. Association for Computational Linguistics.

Katrin Erk. 2013. Towards a semantics for distributional representations. In *Proceedings of IWCS*, pages 1–11, Potsdam, Germany.

Charles J Fillmore. 1975. Pragmatics and the description of discourse. *Radical pragmatics*, pages 143–166.

Kotaro Funakoshi, Mikio Nakano, Takenobu Tokunaga, and Ryu Iida. 2012. A Unified Probabilistic Approach to Referring Expressions. In *Proceedings of SIGDial*, pages 237–246, Seoul, South Korea, July. Association for Computational Linguistics.

L T F Gamut. 1991. *Logic, Language and Meaning: Intensional Logic and Logical Grammar*, volume 2. Chicago University Press, Chicago.

Peter Gorniak and Deb Roy. 2004. Grounded semantic composition for visual scenes. *Journal of Artificial Intelligence Research*, 21:429–470.

Stevan Harnad. 1990. The Symbol Grounding Problem. *Physica D*, 42:335–346.

John Kelleher, Fintan Costello, and Jofsef Van Genabith. 2005. Dynamically structuring, updating and interrelating representations of visual and linguistic discourse context. *Artificial Intelligence*, 167(1–2):62–102.

Casey Kennington, Spyros Kousidis, and David Schlangen. 2013. Interpreting Situated Dialogue Utterances: an Update Model that Uses Speech, Gaze, and Gesture Information. In *Proceedings of SIGdial*.

Casey Kennington, Spyros Kousidis, and David Schlangen. 2014. Situated Incremental Natural Language Understanding using a Multimodal, Linguistically-driven Update Model. In *Proceedings of CoLing*.

Casey Kennington, Livia Dia, and David Schlangen. 2015a. A Discriminative Model for Perceptually-Grounded Incremental Reference Resolution. In *Proceedings of IWCS*. Association for Computational Linguistics.

Casey Kennington, Ryu Iida, Takenobu Tokunaga, and David Schlangen. 2015b. Incrementally Tracking Reference in Human/Human Dialogue Using Linguistic and Extra-Linguistic Information. In *NAACL*, Denver, U.S.A. Association for Computational Linguistics.

Ryan Kiros, Ruslan Salakhutdinov, and Richard S Zemel. 2014. Unifying Visual-Semantic Embeddings with Multimodal Neural Language Models. In *Proceedings of NIPS 2014 Deep Learning Workshop*, pages 1–13.

Staffan Larsson. 2013. Formal semantics for perceptual classification. *Journal of Logic and Computation*.

Mike Lewis and Mark Steedman. 2013. Combined Distributional and Logical Semantics. *Transactions of the ACL*, 1:179–192.

Edward Loper and Steven Bird. 2002. NLTK: The natural language toolkit. In *Proceedings of the ACL-02 Workshop on Effective tools and methodologies for teaching natural language processing and computational linguistics-Volume 1*, pages 63–70. Association for Computational Linguistics.

Cynthia Matuszek, Liefeng Bo, Luke Zettlemoyer, and Dieter Fox. 2014. Learning from Unscripted Deictic Gesture and Language for Human-Robot Interactions. In *AAAI*. AAAI Press.

Jeff Mitchell and Mirella Lapata. 2010. Composition in distributional models of semantics. *Cognitive science*, 34(8):1388–1429, November.

Richard Montague. 1973. The Proper Treatment of Quantifikation in Ordinary English. In J Hintikka, J Moravcsik, and P Suppes, editors, *Approaches to Natural Language: Proceedings of the 1970 Stanford Workshop on Grammar and Semantics*, pages 221–242, Dordrecht. Reidel.

Denis Paperno, Nghia The Pham, and Marco Baroni. 2014. A practical and linguistically-motivated approach to compositional distributional semantics. In *Proceedings of ACL*, pages 90–99.

Barbara H Partee, Alice ter Meuelen, and Robert E Wall. 1993. *Mathematical Methods in Linguistics*. Kluwer Academic Publishers, Dordrecht.

Kari Pulli, Anatoly Baksheev, Kirill Kornyakov, and Victor Eruhimov. 2012. Real-time computer vision with OpenCV. *Communications of the ACM*, 55(6):61–69.

Richard Socher, Andrej Karpathy, Quoc V Le, Christopher D Manning, and Andrew Y Ng. 2014. Grounded Compositional Semantics for Finding and Describing Images with Sentences. *Transactions of the Association for Computational Linguistics (TACL)*, 2:207–218.

Luc Steels and Tony Belpaeme. 2005. Coordinating perceptually grounded categories through language: a case study for colour. *The Behavioral and brain sciences*, 28(4):469–489; discussion 489–529.

Peter D Turney and Patrick Pantel. 2010. From Frequency to Meaning: Vector Space Models of Semantics. *Artificial Intelligence*, 37(1):141–188.

Neural CRF Parsing

Greg Durrett and **Dan Klein**
Computer Science Division
University of California, Berkeley
{gdurrett,klein}@cs.berkeley.edu

Abstract

This paper describes a parsing model that combines the exact dynamic programming of CRF parsing with the rich nonlinear featurization of neural net approaches. Our model is structurally a CRF that factors over anchored rule productions, but instead of linear potential functions based on sparse features, we use nonlinear potentials computed via a feedforward neural network. Because potentials are still local to anchored rules, structured inference (CKY) is unchanged from the sparse case. Computing gradients during learning involves backpropagating an error signal formed from standard CRF sufficient statistics (expected rule counts). Using only dense features, our neural CRF already exceeds a strong baseline CRF model (Hall et al., 2014). In combination with sparse features, our system[1] achieves 91.1 F_1 on section 23 of the Penn Treebank, and more generally outperforms the best prior single parser results on a range of languages.

1 Introduction

Neural network-based approaches to structured NLP tasks have both strengths and weaknesses when compared to more conventional models, such conditional random fields (CRFs). A key strength of neural approaches is their ability to learn nonlinear interactions between underlying features. In the case of unstructured output spaces, this capability has led to gains in problems ranging from syntax (Chen and Manning, 2014; Belinkov et al., 2014) to lexical semantics (Kalchbrenner et al., 2014; Kim, 2014). Neural methods are also powerful tools in the case of structured output spaces. Here, past work has often relied on recurrent architectures (Henderson, 2003; Socher et al., 2013; İrsoy and Cardie, 2014), which can propagate information through structure via real-valued hidden state, but as a result do not admit efficient dynamic programming (Socher et al., 2013; Le and Zuidema, 2014). However, there is a natural marriage of nonlinear induced features and efficient structured inference, as explored by Collobert et al. (2011) for the case of sequence modeling: feedforward neural networks can be used to score local decisions which are then "reconciled" in a discrete structured modeling framework, allowing inference via dynamic programming.

In this work, we present a CRF constituency parser based on these principles, where individual anchored rule productions are scored based on nonlinear features computed with a feedforward neural network. A separate, identically-parameterized replicate of the network exists for each possible span and split point. As input, it takes vector representations of words at the split point and span boundaries; it then outputs scores for anchored rules applied to that span and split point. These scores can be thought of as nonlinear potentials analogous to linear potentials in conventional CRFs. Crucially, while the network replicates are connected in a unified model, their computations factor along the same substructures as in standard CRFs.

Prior work on parsing using neural network models has often sidestepped the problem of structured inference by making sequential decisions (Henderson, 2003; Chen and Manning, 2014; Tsuboi, 2014) or by doing reranking (Socher et al., 2013; Le and Zuidema, 2014); by contrast, our framework permits exact inference via CKY, since the model's structured interactions are purely discrete and do not involve continuous hidden state. Therefore, we can exploit a neural net's capacity to learn nonlinear features without modifying

[1]System available at http://nlp.cs.berkeley.edu

Proceedings of the 53rd Annual Meeting of the Association for Computational Linguistics and the 7th International Joint Conference on Natural Language Processing, pages 302–312, Beijing, China, July 26-31, 2015.

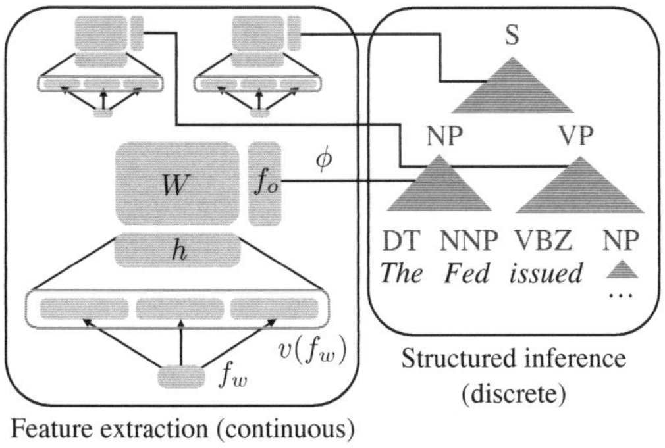

Figure 1: Neural CRF model. On the right, each anchored rule (r, s) in the tree is independently scored by a function ϕ, so we can perform inference with CKY to compute marginals or the Viterbi tree. On the left, we show the process for scoring an anchored rule with neural features: words in f_w (see Figure 2) are embedded, then fed through a neural network with one hidden layer to compute dense intermediate features, whose conjunctions with sparse rule indicator features f_o are scored according to parameters W.

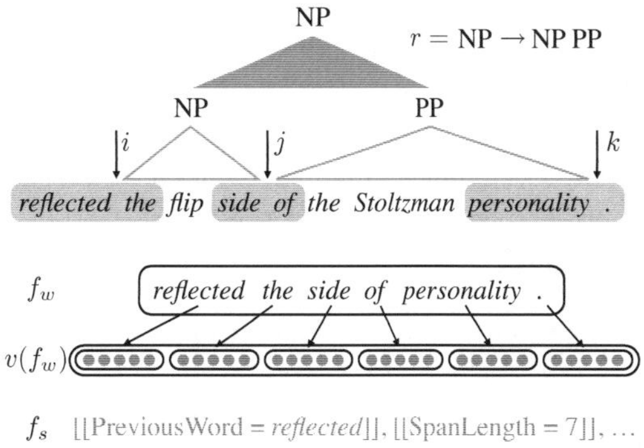

Figure 2: Example of an anchored rule production for the rule NP → NP PP. From the anchoring $s = (i, j, k)$, we extract either sparse surface features f_s or a sequence of word indicators f_w which are embedded to form a vector representation $v(f_w)$ of the anchoring's lexical properties.

our core inference mechanism, allowing us to use tricks like coarse pruning that make inference efficient in the purely sparse model. Our model can be trained by gradient descent exactly as in a conventional CRF, with the gradient of the network parameters naturally computed by backpropagating a difference of expected anchored rule counts through the network for each span and split point.

Using dense learned features alone, the neural CRF model obtains high performance, outperforming the CRF parser of Hall et al. (2014). When sparse indicators are used in addition, the resulting model gets 91.1 F_1 on section 23 of the Penn Treebank, outperforming the parser of Socher et al. (2013) as well as the Berkeley Parser (Petrov and Klein, 2007) and matching the discriminative parser of Carreras et al. (2008). The model also obtains the best single parser results on nine other languages, again outperforming the system of Hall et al. (2014).

2 Model

Figure 1 shows our neural CRF model. The model decomposes over anchored rules, and it scores each of these with a potential function; in a standard CRF, these potentials are typically linear functions of sparse indicator features, whereas in our approach they are nonlinear functions of word embeddings.[2] Section 2.1 describes our notation for anchored rules, and Section 2.2 talks about how they are scored. We then discuss specific choices of our featurization (Section 2.3) and the backbone grammar used for structured inference (Section 2.4).

2.1 Anchored Rules

The fundamental units that our parsing models consider are *anchored rules*. As shown in Figure 2, we define an anchored rule as a tuple (r, s), where r is an indicator of the rule's identity and $s = (i, j, k)$ indicates the span (i, k) and split point j of the rule.[3] A tree T is simply a collection of anchored rules subject to the constraint that those rules form a tree. All of our parsing models are CRFs that decompose over anchored rule productions and place a probability distribution over trees conditioned on a sentence $\mathbf{w}$ as follows:

$$P(T|\mathbf{w}) \propto \exp\left(\sum_{(r,s)\in T} \phi(\mathbf{w}, r, s)\right)$$

[2] Throughout this work, we will primarily consider two potential functions: linear functions of sparse indicators and nonlinear neural networks over dense, continuous features. Although other modeling choices are possible, these two points in the design space reflect common choices in NLP, and past work has suggested that nonlinear functions of indicators or linear functions of dense features may perform less well (Wang and Manning, 2013).

[3] For simplicity of exposition, we ignore unary rules; however, they are easily supported in this framework by simply specifying a null value for the split point.

where ϕ is a scoring function that considers the input sentence and the anchored rule in question. Figure 1 shows this scoring process schematically. As we will see, the module on the left can be be a neural net, a linear function of surface features, or a combination of the two, as long as it provides anchored rule scores, and the structured inference component is the same regardless (CKY).

A PCFG estimated with maximum likelihood has $\phi(\mathbf{w}, r, s) = \log P(r|\text{parent}(r))$, which is independent of the anchoring s and the words $\mathbf{w}$ except for preterminal productions; a basic discriminative parser might let this be a learned parameter but still disregard the surface information. However, surface features can capture useful syntactic cues (Finkel et al., 2008; Hall et al., 2014). Consider the example in Figure 2: the proposed parent NP is preceded by the word *reflected* and followed by a period, which is a surface context characteristic of NPs or PPs in object position. Beginning with *the* and ending with *personality* are typical properties of NPs as well, and the choice of the particular rule NP $\rightarrow$ NP PP is supported by the fact that the proposed child PP begins with *of*. This information can be captured with sparse features (f_s in Figure 2) or, as we describe below, with a neural network taking lexical context as input.

2.2 Scoring Anchored Rules

Following Hall et al. (2014), our baseline sparse scoring function takes the following bilinear form:

$$\phi_{\text{sparse}}(\mathbf{w}, r, s; W) = f_s(\mathbf{w}, s)^\top W f_o(r)$$

where $f_o(r) \in \{0, 1\}^{n_o}$ is a sparse vector of features expressing properties of r (such as the rule's identity or its parent label) and $f_s(\mathbf{w}, s) \in \{0, 1\}^{n_s}$ is a sparse vector of surface features associated with the words in the sentence and the anchoring, as shown in Figure 2. W is a $n_s \times n_o$ matrix of weights.[4] The scoring of a particular anchored rule is depicted in Figure 3a; note that surface features and rule indicators are conjoined in a systematic way.

The role of f_s can be equally well played by a vector of dense features learned via a neural net-

[4]A more conventional expression of the scoring function for a CRF is $\phi(\mathbf{w}, r, s) = \theta^\top f(\mathbf{w}, r, s)$, with a vector θ for the parameters and a single feature extractor f that jointly inspects the surface and the rule. However, when the feature representation conjoins each rule r with surface properties of the sentence in a systematic way (an assumption that holds in our case as well as for standard CRF models for POS tagging and NER), this is equivalent to our formalism.

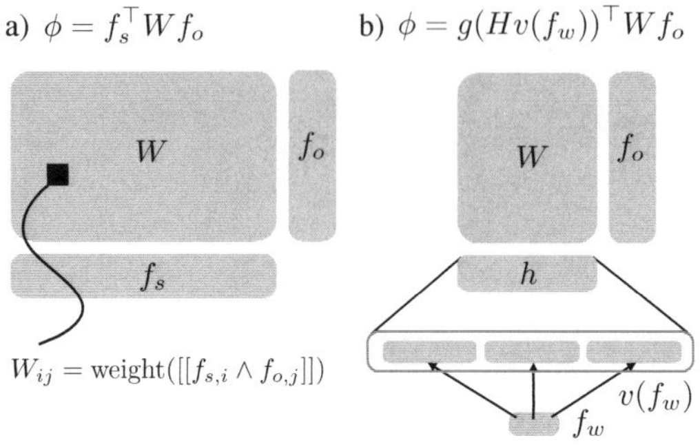

Figure 3: Our sparse (left) and neural (right) scoring functions for CRF parsing. f_s and f_w are raw surface feature vectors for the sparse and neural models (respectively) extracted over anchored spans with split points. (a) In the sparse case, we multiply f_s by a weight matrix W and then a sparse output vector f_o to score the rule production. (b) In the neural case, we first embed f_w and then transform it with a one-layer neural network in order to produce an intermediate feature representation h before combining with W and f_o.

work. We will now describe how to compute these features, which represent a transformation of surface lexical indicators f_w. Define $f_w(\mathbf{w}, s) \in \mathbb{N}^{n_w}$ to be a function that produces a fixed-length sequence of word indicators based on the input sentence and the anchoring. This vector of word identities is then passed to an embedding function $v : \mathbb{N} \rightarrow \mathbb{R}^{n_e}$ and the dense representations of the words are subsequently concatenated to form a vector we denote by $v(f_w)$.[5] Finally, we multiply this by a matrix $H \in \mathbb{R}^{n_h \times (n_w n_e)}$ of real-valued parameters and pass it through an elementwise nonlinearity $g(\cdot)$. We use rectified linear units $g(x) = \max(x, 0)$ and discuss this choice more in Section 6.

Replacing f_s with the end result of this computation $h(\mathbf{w}, s; H) = g(Hv(f_w(\mathbf{w}, s)))$, our scoring function becomes

$$\phi_{\text{neural}}(\mathbf{w}, r, s; H, W) = h(\mathbf{w}, s; H)^\top W f_o(r)$$

as shown in Figure 3b. For a fixed H, this model can be viewed as a basic CRF with dense input features. By learning H, we learn intermediate feature representations that provide the model with

[5]Embedding words allows us to use standard pre-trained vectors more easily and tying embeddings across word positions substantially reduces the number of model parameters. However, embedding features rather than words has also been shown to be effective (Chen et al., 2014).

more discriminating power. Also note that it is possible to use deeper networks or more sophisticated architectures here; we will return to this in Section 6.

Our two models can be easily combined:

$$\phi(\mathbf{w}, r, s; W_1, H, W_2) = \phi_{\text{sparse}}(\mathbf{w}, r, s; W_1) + \phi_{\text{neural}}(\mathbf{w}, r, s; H, W_2)$$

Weights for each component of the scoring function can be learned fully jointly and inference proceeds as before.

2.3 Features

We take f_s to be the set of features described in Hall et al. (2014). At the preterminal layer, the model considers prefixes and suffixes up to length 5 of the current word and neighboring words, as well as the words' identities. For nonterminal productions, we fire indicators on the words[6] before and after the start, end, and split point of the anchored rule (as shown in Figure 2) as well as on two other span properties, span length and span shape (an indicator of where capitalized words, numbers, and punctuation occur in the span).

For our neural model, we take f_w for all productions (preterminal and nonterminal) to be the words surrounding the beginning and end of a span and the split point, as shown in Figure 2; in particular, we look two words in either direction around each point of interest, meaning the neural net takes 12 words as input.[7] For our word embeddings v, we use pre-trained word vectors from Bansal et al. (2014). We compare with other sources of word vectors in Section 5. Contrary to standard practice, we do not update these vectors during training; we found that doing so did not provide an accuracy benefit and slowed down training considerably.

2.4 Grammar Refinements

A recurring issue in discriminative constituency parsing is the granularity of annotation in the base grammar (Finkel et al., 2008; Petrov and Klein, 2008; Hall et al., 2014). Using finer-grained symbols in our rules r gives the model greater capacity, but also introduces more parameters into W and increases the ability to overfit. Following Hall et al. (2014), we use grammars with very little annotation: we use no horizontal Markovization for any of experiments, and all of our English experiments with the neural CRF use no vertical Markovization ($V = 0$). This also has the benefit of making the system much faster, due to the smaller state space for dynamic programming. We do find that using parent annotation ($V = 1$) is useful on other languages (see Section 7.2), but this is the only grammar refinement we consider.

3 Learning

To learn weights for our neural model, we maximize the conditional log likelihood of our D training trees T^*:

$$\mathcal{L}(H, W) = \sum_{i=1}^{D} \log P(T_i^* | \mathbf{w}_i; H, W)$$

Because we are using rectified linear units as our nonlinearity, our objective is not everywhere differentiable. The interaction of the parameters and the nonlinearity also makes the objective nonconvex. However, in spite of this, we can still follow subgradients to optimize this objective, as is standard practice.

Recall that $h(\mathbf{w}, s; H)$ are the hidden layer activations. The gradient of W takes the standard form of log-linear models:

$$\frac{\partial \mathcal{L}}{\partial W} = \left(\sum_{(r,s) \in T^*} h(\mathbf{w}, s; H) f_o(r)^\top \right) - \left(\sum_T P(T|\mathbf{w}; H, W) \sum_{(r,s) \in T} h(\mathbf{w}, s; H) f_o(r)^\top \right)$$

Note that the outer products give matrices of feature counts isomorphic to W. The second expression can be simplified to be in terms of expected feature counts. To update H, we use standard backpropagation by first computing:

$$\frac{\partial \mathcal{L}}{\partial h} = \left(\sum_{(r,s) \in T^*} W f_o(r) \right) - \left(\sum_T P(T|\mathbf{w}; H, W) \sum_{(r,s) \in T} W f_o(r) \right)$$

Since h is the output of the neural network, we can then apply the chain rule to compute gradients for H and any other parameters in the neural network.

[6] The model actually uses the longest suffix of each word occurring at least 100 times in the training set, up to the entire word. Removing this abstraction of rare words harms performance.

[7] The sparse model did not benefit from using this larger neighborhood, so improvements from the neural net are not simply due to considering more lexical context.

Learning uses Adadelta (Zeiler, 2012), which has been employed in past work (Kim, 2014). We found that Adagrad (Duchi et al., 2011) performed equally well with tuned regularization and step size parameters, but Adadelta worked better out of the box. We set the momentum term $\rho = 0.95$ (as suggested by Zeiler (2012)) and did not regularize the weights at all. We used a minibatch size of 200 trees, although the system was not particularly sensitive to this. For each treebank, we trained for either 10 passes through the treebank or 1000 minibatches, whichever is shorter.

We initialized the output weight matrix W to zero. To break symmetry, the lower level neural network parameters H were initialized with each entry being independently sampled from a Gaussian with mean 0 and variance 0.01; Gaussian performed better than uniform initialization, but the variance was not important.

4 Inference

Our baseline and neural model both score anchored rule productions. We can use CKY in the standard fashion to compute either expected anchored rule counts $\mathbb{E}_{P(T|\mathbf{w})}[(r,s)]$ or the Viterbi tree $\arg\max_T P(T|\mathbf{w})$.

We speed up inference by using a coarse pruning pass. We follow Hall et al. (2014) and prune according to an X-bar grammar with head-outward binarization, ruling out any constituent whose max marginal probability is less than e^{-9}. With this pruning, the number of spans and split points to be considered is greatly reduced; however, we still need to compute the neural network activations for each remaining span and split point, of which there may be thousands for a given sentence.[8] We can improve efficiency further by noting that the same word will appear in the same position in a large number of span/split point combinations, and cache the contribution to the hidden layer caused by that word (Chen and Manning, 2014). Computing the hidden layer then simply requires adding n_w vectors together and applying the nonlinearity, instead of a more costly matrix multiply.

Because the number of rule indicators n_o is fairly large (approximately 4000 in the Penn Treebank), the multiplication by W in the model is also expensive. However, because only a small number of rules can apply to a given span and split point, f_o is sparse and we can selectively compute the terms necessary for the final bilinear product.

Our combined sparse and neural model trains on the Penn Treebank in 24 hours on a single machine with a parallelized CPU implementation. For reference, the purely sparse model with a parent-annotated grammar (necessary for the best results) takes around 15 hours on the same machine.

5 System Ablations

Table 1 shows results on section 22 (the development set) of the English Penn Treebank (Marcus et al., 1993), computed using `evalb`. Full test results and comparisons to other systems are shown in Table 4. We compare variants of our system along two axes: whether they use standard linear sparse features, nonlinear dense features from the neural net, or both, and whether any word representations (vectors or clusters) are used.

Sparse vs. neural The neural CRF (line (d) in Table 1) on its own outperforms the sparse CRF (a, b) even when the sparse CRF has a more heavily annotated grammar. This is a surprising result: the features in the sparse CRF have been carefully engineered to capture a range of linguistic phenomena (Hall et al., 2014), and there is no guarantee that word vectors will capture the same. For example, at the POS tagging layer, the sparse model looks at prefixes and suffixes of words, which give the model access to morphology for predicting tags of unknown words, which typically have regular inflection patterns. By contrast, the neural model must rely on the geometry of the vector space exposing useful regularities. At the same time, the strong performance of the combination of the two systems (g) indicates that not only are both featurization approaches high-performing on their own, but that they have complementary strengths.

Unlabeled data Much attention has been paid to the choice of word vectors for various NLP tasks, notably whether they capture more syntactic or semantic phenomena (Bansal et al., 2014; Levy and Goldberg, 2014). We primarily use vectors from Bansal et al. (2014), who train the skipgram model of Mikolov et al. (2013) using contexts from dependency links; a similar approach was also suggested by Levy and Goldberg (2014).

[8] One reason we did not choose to include the rule identity f_o as an input to the network is that it requires computing an even larger number of network activations, since we cannot reuse them across rules over the same span and split point.

	Sparse	Neural	V	Word Reps	F_1 len ≤ 40	F_1 all
	Hall et al. (2014), $V = 1$				90.5	
a	✓		0		89.89	89.22
b	✓		1		90.82	90.13
c	✓		1	Brown	90.80	90.17
d		✓	0	Bansal	90.97	90.44
e		✓	0	Collobert	90.25	89.63
f		✓	0	PTB	89.34	88.99
g	✓	✓	0	Bansal	**92.04**	**91.34**
h	✓	✓	0	PTB	91.39	90.91

Table 1: Results of our sparse CRF, neural CRF, and combined parsing models on section 22 of the Penn Treebank. Systems are broken down by whether local potentials come from sparse features and/or the neural network (the primary contribution of this work), their level of vertical Markovization, and what kind of word representations they use. The neural CRF (d) outperforms the sparse CRF (a, b) even when a more heavily annotated grammar is used, and the combined approach (g) is substantially better than either individual model. The contribution of the neural architecture cannot be replaced by Brown clusters (c), and even word representations learned just on the Penn Treebank are surprisingly effective (f, h).

		F_1 len ≤ 40	Δ
Neural CRF		90.97	—
Nonlinearity	ReLU	90.97	—
	Tanh	90.74	−0.23
	Cube	89.94	−1.03
Depth	0 HL	90.54	−0.43
	1 HL	90.97	—
	2 HL	90.58	−0.39
Embed output		88.81	−2.16

Table 2: Exploration of other implementation choices in the feedforward neural network on sentences of length ≤ 40 from section 22 of the Penn Treebank. Rectified linear units perform better than tanh or cubic units, a network with one hidden layer performs best, and embedding the output feature vector gives worse performance.

However, as these embeddings are trained on a relatively small corpus (BLLIP minus the Penn Treebank), it is natural to wonder whether less-syntactic embeddings trained on a larger corpus might be more useful. This is not the case: line (e) in Table 1 shows the performance of the neural CRF using the Wikipedia-trained word embeddings of Collobert et al. (2011), which do not perform better than the vectors of Bansal et al. (2014).

To isolate the contribution of continuous word representations themselves, we also experimented with vectors trained on just the text from the training set of the Penn Treebank using the skip-gram model with a window size of 1. While these vectors are somewhat lower performing on their own (f), they still provide a surprising and noticeable gain when stacked on top of sparse features (h), again suggesting that dense and sparse representations have complementary strengths. This result also reinforces the notion that the utility of word vectors does *not* come primarily from importing information about out-of-vocabulary words (Andreas and Klein, 2014).

Since the neural features incorporate information from unlabeled data, we should provide the sparse model with similar information for a true apples-to-apples comparison. Brown clusters have been shown to be effective vehicles in the past (Koo et al., 2008; Turian et al., 2010; Bansal et al., 2014). We can incorporate Brown clusters into the baseline CRF model in an analogous way to how embedding features are used in the dense model: surface features are fired on Brown cluster identities (we use prefixes of length 4 and 10) of key words. We use the Brown clusters from Koo et al. (2008), which are trained on the same data as the vectors of Bansal et al. (2014). However, Table 1 shows that these features provide no benefit to the baseline model, which suggests either that it is difficult to learn reliable weights for these as sparse features or that different regularities are being captured by the word embeddings.

6 Design Choices

The neural net design space is large, so we wish to analyze the particular design choices we made for this system by examining the performance of several variants of the neural net architecture used in our system. Table 2 shows development results from potential alternate architectural choices, which we now discuss.

Choice of nonlinearity The choice of nonlinearity g has been frequently discussed in the neural network literature. Our choice $g(x) = \max(x, 0)$, a rectified linear unit, is increasingly popular in computer vision (Krizhevsky et al., 2012). $g(x) = \tanh(x)$ is a traditional nonlinearity widely used throughout the history of neural nets (Bengio et al., 2003). $g(x) = x^3$ (cube) was found to be most successful by Chen and Manning (2014).

Table 2 compares the performance of these three nonlinearities. We see that rectified linear units perform the best, followed by $\tanh$ units, followed by cubic units.[9] One drawback of $\tanh$ as an activation function is that it is easily "saturated" if the input to the unit is too far away from zero, causing the backpropagation of derivatives through that unit to essentially cease; this is known to cause problems for training, requiring special purpose machinery for use in deep networks (Ioffe and Szegedy, 2015).

Depth Given that we are using rectified linear units, it bears asking whether or not our implementation is improving substantially over linear features of the continuous input. We can use the embedding vector of an anchored span $v(f_w)$ directly as input to a basic linear CRF, as shown in Figure 4a. Table 1 shows that the purely linear architecture (0 HL) performs surprisingly well, but is still less effective than the network with one hidden layer. This agrees with the results of Wang and Manning (2013), who noted that dense features typically benefit from nonlinear modeling. We also compare against a two-layer neural network, but find that this also performs worse than the one-layer architecture.

Densifying output features Overall, it appears beneficial to use dense representations of surface features; a natural question that one might ask is whether the same technique can be applied to the sparse output feature vector f_o. We can apply the approach of Srikumar and Manning (2014) and multiply the sparse output vector by a dense matrix K, giving the following scoring function (shown in Figure 4b):

$$\phi(\mathbf{w}, r, s; H, W, K) = g(Hv(f_w(\mathbf{w}, s)))^\top WKf_o(r)$$

where W is now $n_h \times n_{oe}$ and K is $n_{oe} \times n_o$. WK can be seen a low-rank approximation of the original W at the output layer, similar to low-rank factorizations of parameter matrices used in past

[9]The performance of cube decreased substantially late in learning; it peaked at around 90.52. Dropout may be useful for alleviating this type of overfitting, but in our experiments we did not find dropout to be beneficial overall.

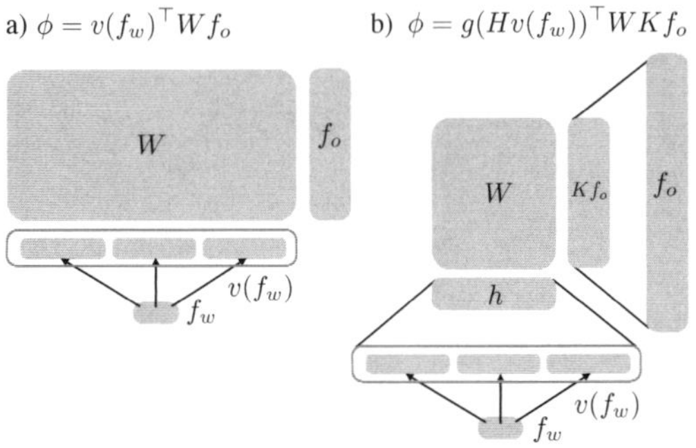

Figure 4: Two additional forms of the scoring function. a) Linear version of the dense model, equivalent to a CRF with continuous-valued input features. b) Version of the dense model where outputs are also embedded according to a learned matrix K.

work (Lei et al., 2014). This approach saves us from having to learn a separate row of W for every rule in the grammar; if rules are given similar embeddings, then they will behave similarly according to the model.

We experimented with $n_{oe} = 20$ and show the results in Table 2. Unfortunately, this approach does not seem to work well for parsing. Learning the output representation was empirically very unstable, and it also required careful initialization. We tried Gaussian initialization (as in the rest of our model) and initializing the model by clustering rules either randomly or according to their parent symbol. The latter is what is shown in the table, and gave substantially better performance. We hypothesize that blurring distinctions between output classes may harm the model's ability to differentiate between closely-related symbols, which is required for good parsing performance. Using pretrained rule embeddings at this layer might also improve performance of this method.

7 Test Results

We evaluate our system under two conditions: first, on the English Penn Treebank, and second, on the nine languages used in the SPMRL 2013 and 2014 shared tasks.

7.1 Penn Treebank

Table 4 reports results on section 23 of the Penn Treebank (PTB). We focus our comparison on single parser systems as opposed to rerankers, ensembles, or self-trained methods (though these are also mentioned for context). First, we compare against

	Arabic	Basque	French	German	Hebrew	Hungarian	Korean	Polish	Swedish	Avg
					Dev, all lengths					
Hall et al. (2014)	78.89	83.74	79.40	83.28	88.06	87.44	81.85	91.10	75.95	83.30
This work*	**80.68**	**84.37**	**80.65**	**85.25**	**89.37**	**89.46**	**82.35**	**92.10**	**77.93**	**84.68**
					Test, all lengths					
Berkeley	79.19	70.50	80.38	78.30	86.96	81.62	71.42	79.23	79.18	78.53
Berkeley-Tags	78.66	74.74	79.76	78.28	85.42	85.22	78.56	86.75	80.64	80.89
Crabbé and Seddah (2014)	77.66	85.35	79.68	77.15	86.19	87.51	79.35	91.60	82.72	83.02
Hall et al. (2014)	78.75	83.39	79.70	78.43	87.18	88.25	80.18	90.66	82.00	83.17
This work*	**80.24**	**85.41**	**81.25**	**80.95**	**88.61**	**90.66**	**82.23**	**92.97**	**83.45**	**85.08**
					Reranked ensemble					
2014 Best	**81.32**	**88.24**	**82.53**	**81.66**	**89.80**	**91.72**	**83.81**	**90.50**	**85.50**	**86.12**

Table 3: Results for the nine treebanks in the SPMRL 2013/2014 Shared Tasks; all values are F-scores for sentences of all lengths using the version of `evalb` distributed with the shared task. Our parser substantially outperforms the strongest single parser results on this dataset (Hall et al., 2014; Crabbé and Seddah, 2014). Berkeley-Tags is an improved version of the Berkeley parser designed for the shared task (Seddah et al., 2013). 2014 Best is a reranked ensemble of modified Berkeley parsers and constitutes the best published numbers on this dataset (Björkelund et al., 2013; Björkelund et al., 2014).

	F_1 all
Single model, PTB only	
Hall et al. (2014)	89.2
Berkeley	90.1
Carreras et al. (2008)	91.1
Shindo et al. (2012) single	91.1
Single model, PTB + vectors/clusters	
Zhu et al. (2013)	91.3
This work*	91.1
Extended conditions	
Charniak and Johnson (2005)	91.5
Socher et al. (2013)	90.4
Vinyals et al. (2014) single	90.5
Vinyals et al. (2014) ensemble	91.6
Shindo et al. (2012) ensemble	92.4

Table 4: Test results on section 23 of the Penn Treebank. We compare to several categories of parsers from the literatures. We outperform strong baselines such as the Berkeley Parser (Petrov and Klein, 2007) and the CVG Stanford parser (Socher et al., 2013) and we match the performance of sophisticated generative (Shindo et al., 2012) and discriminative (Carreras et al., 2008) parsers.

four parsers trained only on the PTB with no auxiliary data: the CRF parser of Hall et al. (2014), the Berkeley parser (Petrov and Klein, 2007), the discriminative parser of Carreras et al. (2008), and the single TSG parser of Shindo et al. (2012). To our knowledge, the latter two systems are the highest performing in this PTB-only, single parser data condition; we match their performance at 91.1 F_1, though we also use word vectors computed from unlabeled data. We further compare to the shift-reduce parser of Zhu et al. (2013), which uses unlabeled data in the form of Brown clusters. Our method achieves performance close to that of their parser.

We also compare to the compositional vector grammar (CVG) parser of Socher et al. (2013) as well as the LSTM-based parser of Vinyals et al. (2014). The conditions these parsers are operating under are slightly different: the former is a reranker on top of the Stanford Parser (Klein and Manning, 2003) and the latter trains on much larger amounts of data parsed by a product of Berkeley parsers (Petrov, 2010). Regardless, we outperform the CVG parser as well as the single parser results from Vinyals et al. (2014).

7.2 SPMRL

We also examine the performance of our parser on other languages, specifically the nine morphologically-rich languages used in the SPMRL 2013/2014 shared tasks (Seddah et al., 2013; Seddah et al., 2014). We train word vectors on the monolingual data distributed with the SPMRL 2014 shared task (typically 100M-200M tokens per language) using the skip-gram approach of `word2vec` with a window size of 1

(Mikolov et al., 2013).[10] Here we use $V = 1$ in the backbone grammar, which we found to be beneficial overall. Table 3 shows that our system improves upon the performance of the parser from Hall et al. (2014) as well as the top single parser from the shared task (Crabbé and Seddah, 2014), with robust improvements on all languages.

8 Conclusion

In this work, we presented a CRF parser that scores anchored rule productions using dense input features computed from a feedforward neural net. Because the neural component is modularized, we can easily integrate it into a preexisting learning and inference framework based around dynamic programming of a discrete parse chart. Our combined neural and sparse model gives strong performance both on English and on other languages.

Our system is publicly available at `http://nlp.cs.berkeley.edu`.

Acknowledgments

This work was partially supported by BBN under DARPA contract HR0011-12-C-0014, by a Facebook fellowship for the first author, and by a Google Faculty Research Award to the second author. Thanks to David Hall for assistance with the Epic parsing framework and for a preliminary implementation of the neural architecture, to Kush Rastogi for training word vectors on the SPMRL data, to Dan Jurafsky for helpful discussions, and to the anonymous reviewers for their insightful comments.

References

Jacob Andreas and Dan Klein. 2014. How much do word embeddings encode about syntax? In *Proceedings of the Association for Computational Linguistics*.

Mohit Bansal, Kevin Gimpel, and Karen Livescu. 2014. Tailoring Continuous Word Representations for Dependency Parsing. In *Proceedings of the Association for Computational Linguistics*.

Yonatan Belinkov, Tao Lei, Regina Barzilay, and Amir Globerson. 2014. Exploring Compositional Architectures and Word Vector Representations for Prepositional Phrase Attachment. *Transactions of the Association for Computational Linguistics*, 2:561–572.

[10]Training vectors with the SKIPDEP method of Bansal et al. (2014) did not substantially improve performance here.

Yoshua Bengio, Réjean Ducharme, Pascal Vincent, and Christian Janvin. 2003. A Neural Probabilistic Language Model. *Journal of Machine Learning Research*, 3:1137–1155, March.

Anders Björkelund, Ozlem Cetinoglu, Richárd Farkas, Thomas Mueller, and Wolfgang Seeker. 2013. (Re)ranking Meets Morphosyntax: State-of-the-art Results from the SPMRL 2013 Shared Task. In *Proceedings of the Fourth Workshop on Statistical Parsing of Morphologically-Rich Languages*.

Anders Björkelund, Özlem Çetinoğlu, Agnieszka Faleńska, Richárd Farkas, Thomas Mueller, Wolfgang Seeker, and Zsolt Szántó. 2014. Introducing the IMS-Wrocław-Szeged-CIS entry at the SPMRL 2014 Shared Task: Reranking and Morpho-syntax meet Unlabeled Data. In *Proceedings of the First Joint Workshop on Statistical Parsing of Morphologically Rich Languages and Syntactic Analysis of Non-Canonical Languages*.

Xavier Carreras, Michael Collins, and Terry Koo. 2008. TAG, Dynamic Programming, and the Perceptron for Efficient, Feature-rich Parsing. In *Proceedings of the Conference on Computational Natural Language Learning*.

Eugene Charniak and Mark Johnson. 2005. Coarse-to-Fine n-Best Parsing and MaxEnt Discriminative Reranking. In *Proceedings of the Association for Computational Linguistics*.

Danqi Chen and Christopher D Manning. 2014. A Fast and Accurate Dependency Parser using Neural Networks. In *Proceedings of Empirical Methods in Natural Language Processing*.

Wenliang Chen, Yue Zhang, and Min Zhang. 2014. Feature Embedding for Dependency Parsing. In *Proceedings of the International Conference on Computational Linguistics*.

Ronan Collobert, Jason Weston, Léon Bottou, Michael Karlen, Koray Kavukcuoglu, and Pavel Kuksa. 2011. Natural Language Processing (Almost) from Scratch. *Journal of Machine Learning Research*, 12:2493–2537.

Benoit Crabbé and Djamé Seddah. 2014. Multilingual Discriminative Shift-Reduce Phrase Structure Parsing for the SPMRL 2014 Shared Task. In *Proceedings of the First Joint Workshop on Statistical Parsing of Morphologically Rich Languages and Syntactic Analysis of Non-Canonical Languages*.

John Duchi, Elad Hazan, and Yoram Singer. 2011. Adaptive Subgradient Methods for Online Learning and Stochastic Optimization. *Journal of Machine Learning Research*, 12:2121–2159, July.

Jenny Rose Finkel, Alex Kleeman, and Christopher D. Manning. 2008. Efficient, Feature-based, Conditional Random Field Parsing. In *Proceedings of the Association for Computational Linguistics*.

David Hall, Greg Durrett, and Dan Klein. 2014. Less Grammar, More Features. In *Proceedings of the Association for Computational Linguistics*.

James Henderson. 2003. Inducing History Representations for Broad Coverage Statistical Parsing. In *Proceedings of the North American Chapter of the Association for Computational Linguistics*.

Sergey Ioffe and Christian Szegedy. 2015. Batch Normalization: Accelerating Deep Network Training by Reducing Internal Covariate Shift. *arXiv preprint*, arXiv:1502.03167.

Ozan İrsoy and Claire Cardie. 2014. Opinion Mining with Deep Recurrent Neural Networks. In *Proceedings of the Conference on Empirical Methods in Natural Language Processing*.

Nal Kalchbrenner, Edward Grefenstette, and Phil Blunsom. 2014. A Convolutional Neural Network for Modelling Sentences. In *Proceedings of the Association for Computational Linguistics*.

Yoon Kim. 2014. Convolutional Neural Networks for Sentence Classification. In *Proceedings of the Conference on Empirical Methods in Natural Language Processing*.

Dan Klein and Christopher D. Manning. 2003. Accurate Unlexicalized Parsing. In *Proceedings of the Association for Computational Linguistics*.

Terry Koo, Xavier Carreras, and Michael Collins. 2008. Simple Semi-supervised Dependency Parsing. In *Proceedings of the Association for Computational Linguistics*.

Alex Krizhevsky, Ilya Sutskever, and Geoffrey E. Hinton. 2012. ImageNet Classification with Deep Convolutional Neural Networks. In *Advances in Neural Information Processing Systems*.

Phong Le and Willem Zuidema. 2014. The inside-outside recursive neural network model for dependency parsing. In *Proceedings of the Conference on Empirical Methods in Natural Language Processing*.

Tao Lei, Yu Xin, Yuan Zhang, Regina Barzilay, and Tommi Jaakkola. 2014. Low-Rank Tensors for Scoring Dependency Structures. In *Proceedings of the Association for Computational Linguistics*.

Omer Levy and Yoav Goldberg. 2014. Dependency-Based Word Embeddings. In *Proceedings of the Association for Computational Linguistics*.

Mitchell P. Marcus, Beatrice Santorini, and Mary Ann Marcinkiewicz. 1993. Building a Large Annotated Corpus of English: The Penn Treebank. *Computational Linguistics*, 19(2).

Tomas Mikolov, Kai Chen, Greg Corrado, and Jeffrey Dean. 2013. Efficient Estimation of Word Representations in Vector Space. In *Proceedings of the International Conference on Learning Representations*.

Slav Petrov and Dan Klein. 2007. Improved Inference for Unlexicalized Parsing. In *Proceedings of the North American Chapter of the Association for Computational Linguistics*.

Slav Petrov and Dan Klein. 2008. Sparse Multi-Scale Grammars for Discriminative Latent Variable Parsing. In *Proceedings of the Conference on Empirical Methods in Natural Language Processing*.

Slav Petrov. 2010. Products of Random Latent Variable Grammars. In *Proceedings of the North American Chapter of the Association for Computational Linguistics*.

Djamé Seddah, Reut Tsarfaty, Sandra Kübler, Marie Candito, Jinho D. Choi, Richárd Farkas, Jennifer Foster, Iakes Goenaga, Koldo Gojenola Galletebeitia, Yoav Goldberg, Spence Green, Nizar Habash, Marco Kuhlmann, Wolfgang Maier, Joakim Nivre, Adam Przepiórkowski, Ryan Roth, Wolfgang Seeker, Yannick Versley, Veronika Vincze, Marcin Woliński, and Alina Wróblewska. 2013. Overview of the SPMRL 2013 Shared Task: A Cross-Framework Evaluation of Parsing Morphologically Rich Languages. In *Proceedings of the Fourth Workshop on Statistical Parsing of Morphologically-Rich Languages*.

Djamé Seddah, Sandra Kübler, and Reut Tsarfaty. 2014. Introducing the SPMRL 2014 Shared Task on Parsing Morphologically-rich Languages. In *Proceedings of the First Joint Workshop on Statistical Parsing of Morphologically Rich Languages and Syntactic Analysis of Non-Canonical Languages*.

Hiroyuki Shindo, Yusuke Miyao, Akinori Fujino, and Masaaki Nagata. 2012. Bayesian Symbol-refined Tree Substitution Grammars for Syntactic Parsing. In *Proceedings of the Association for Computational Linguistics*.

Richard Socher, John Bauer, Christopher D. Manning, and Andrew Y. Ng. 2013. Parsing With Compositional Vector Grammars. In *Proceedings of the Association for Computational Linguistics*.

Vivek Srikumar and Christopher D Manning. 2014. Learning Distributed Representations for Structured Output Prediction. In *Advances in Neural Information Processing Systems*.

Yuta Tsuboi. 2014. Neural Networks Leverage Corpus-wide Information for Part-of-speech Tagging. In *Proceedings of the Conference on Empirical Methods in Natural Language Processing*.

Joseph Turian, Lev Ratinov, and Yoshua Bengio. 2010. Word Representations: A Simple and General Method for Semi-supervised Learning. In *Proceedings of the Association for Computational Linguistics*.

Oriol Vinyals, Lukasz Kaiser, Terry Koo, Slav Petrov, Ilya Sutskever, and Geoffrey E. Hinton. 2014. Grammar as a Foreign Language. *CoRR*, abs/1412.7449.

Mengqiu Wang and Christopher D. Manning. 2013. Effect of Non-linear Deep Architecture in Sequence Labeling. In *Proceedings of the International Joint Conference on Natural Language Processing*.

Matthew D. Zeiler. 2012. ADADELTA: An Adaptive Learning Rate Method. *CoRR*, abs/1212.5701.

Muhua Zhu, Yue Zhang, Wenliang Chen, Min Zhang, and Jingbo Zhu. 2013. Fast and Accurate Shift-Reduce Constituent Parsing. In *Proceedings of the Association for Computational Linguistics*.

An Effective Neural Network Model for Graph-based Dependency Parsing

Wenzhe Pei **Tao Ge** **Baobao Chang***
Key Laboratory of Computational Linguistics, Ministry of Education,
School of Electronics Engineering and Computer Science, Peking University,
No.5 Yiheyuan Road, Haidian District, Beijing, 100871, China
Collaborative Innovation Center for Language Ability, Xuzhou, 221009, China.
{peiwenzhe,getao,chbb}@pku.edu.cn

Abstract

Most existing graph-based parsing models rely on millions of hand-crafted features, which limits their generalization ability and slows down the parsing speed. In this paper, we propose a general and effective Neural Network model for graph-based dependency parsing. Our model can automatically learn high-order feature combinations using only atomic features by exploiting a novel activation function *tanh-cube*. Moreover, we propose a simple yet effective way to utilize phrase-level information that is expensive to use in conventional graph-based parsers. Experiments on the English Penn Treebank show that parsers based on our model perform better than conventional graph-based parsers.

1 Introduction

Dependency parsing is essential for computers to understand natural languages, whose performance may have a direct effect on many NLP application. Due to its importance, dependency parsing, has been studied for tens of years. Among a variety of dependency parsing approaches (McDonald et al., 2005; McDonald and Pereira, 2006; Carreras, 2007; Koo and Collins, 2010; Zhang and Nivre, 2011), graph-based models seem to be one of the most successful solutions to the challenge due to its ability of scoring the parsing decisions on whole-tree basis. Typical graph-based models factor the dependency tree into subgraphs, ranging from the smallest edge (first-order) to a controllable bigger subgraph consisting of more than one single edge (second-order and third order), and score the whole tree by summing scores of the subgraphs. In these models, subgraphs are usually represented as a high-dimensional feature vectors which are fed into a linear model to learn the feature weight for scoring the subgraphs.

In spite of their advantages, conventional graph-based models rely heavily on an enormous number of hand-crafted features, which brings about serious problems. First, a mass of features could put the models in the risk of overfitting and slow down the parsing speed, especially in the high-order models where combinational features capturing interactions between head, modifier, siblings and (or) grandparent could easily explode the feature space. In addition, feature design requires domain expertise, which means useful features are likely to be neglected due to a lack of domain knowledge. As a matter of fact, these two problems exist in most graph-based models, which have stuck the development of dependency parsing for a few years.

To ease the problem of feature engineering, we propose a general and effective Neural Network model for graph-based dependency parsing in this paper. The main advantages of our model are as follows:

- Instead of using large number of hand-crafted features, our model only uses atomic features (Chen et al., 2014) such as word unigrams and POS-tag unigrams. Feature combinations and high-order features are automatically learned with our novel activation function *tanh-cube*, thus alleviating the heavy burden of feature engineering in conventional graph-based models (McDonald et al., 2005; McDonald and Pereira, 2006; Koo and Collins, 2010). Not only does it avoid the risk of overfitting but also it discovers useful new features that have never been used in conventional parsers.

- We propose to exploit phrase-level information through distributed representation for phrases (phrase embeddings). It not only en-

*Corresponding author

Proceedings of the 53rd Annual Meeting of the Association for Computational Linguistics and the 7th International Joint Conference on Natural Language Processing, pages 313–322,
Beijing, China, July 26-31, 2015.

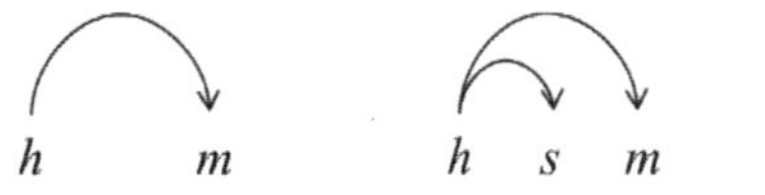

(a) First-order (b) Second-order

Figure 1: First-order and Second-order factorization strategy. Here h stands for head word, m stands for modifier word and s stands for the sibling of m.

ables our model to exploit richer context information that previous work did not consider due to the curse of dimension but also captures inherent correlations between phrases.

- Unlike other neural network based models (Chen et al., 2014; Le and Zuidema, 2014) where an additional parser is needed for either extracting features (Chen et al., 2014) or generating k-best list for reranking (Le and Zuidema, 2014), both training and decoding in our model are performed based on our neural network architecture in an effective way.

- Our model does not impose any change to the decoding process of conventional graph-based parsing model. First-order, second-order and higher order models can be easily implemented using our model.

We implement three effective models with increasing expressive capabilities. The first model is a simple first-order model that uses only atomic features and does not use any combinational features. Despite its simpleness, it outperforms conventional first-order model (McDonald et al., 2005) and has a faster parsing speed. To further strengthen our parsing model, we incorporate phrase embeddings into the model, which significantly improves the parsing accuracy. Finally, we extend our first-order model to a second-order model that exploits interactions between two adjacent dependency edges as in McDonald and Pereira (2006) thus further improves the model performance.

We evaluate our models on the English Penn Treebank. Experiment results show that both our first-order and second-order models outperform the corresponding conventional models.

2 Neural Network Model

A dependency tree is a rooted, directed tree spanning the whole sentence. Given a sentence x, graph-based models formulates the parsing process as a searching problem:

$$y^*(x) = \arg\max_{\hat{y} \in Y(x)} Score(x, \hat{y}(x); \theta) \quad (1)$$

where $y^*(x)$ is tree with highest score, $Y(x)$ is the set of all trees compatible with x, θ are model parameters and $Score(x, \hat{y}(x); \theta)$ represents how likely that a particular tree $\hat{y}(x)$ is the correct analysis for x. However, the size of $Y(x)$ is exponential large, which makes it impractical to solve equation (1) directly. Previous work (McDonald et al., 2005; McDonald and Pereira, 2006; Koo and Collins, 2010) assumes that the score of $\hat{y}(x)$ factors through the scores of subgraphs c of $\hat{y}(x)$ so that efficient algorithms can be designed for decoding:

$$Score(x, \hat{y}(x); \theta) = \sum_{c \in \hat{y}(x)} ScoreF(x, c; \theta) \quad (2)$$

Figure 1 gives two examples of commonly used factorization strategy proposed by Mcdonald et.al (2005) and Mcdonald and Pereira (2006). The simplest subgraph uses a first-order factorization (McDonald et al., 2005) which decomposes a dependency tree into single dependency arcs (Figure 1(a)). Based on the first-order model, second-order factorization (McDonald and Pereira, 2006) (Figure 1(b)) brings sibling information into decoding. Specifically, a sibling part consists of a triple of indices (h, m, s) where (h, m) and (h, s) are dependencies and s and m are successive modifiers to the same side of h.

The most common choice for $ScoreF(x, c; \theta)$, which is the score function for subgraph c in the tree, is a simple linear function:

$$ScoreF(x, c; \theta) = \boldsymbol{w} \cdot \boldsymbol{f}(x, c) \quad (3)$$

where $\boldsymbol{f}(x, c)$ is the feature representation of subgraph c and $\boldsymbol{w}$ is the corresponding weight vector. However, the effectiveness of this function relies heavily on the design of feature vector $\boldsymbol{f}(x, c)$. In previous work (McDonald et al., 2005; McDonald and Pereira, 2006), millions of hand-crafted features were used to capture context and structure information in the subgraph which not only limits the model's ability to generalize well but only slows down the parsing speed.

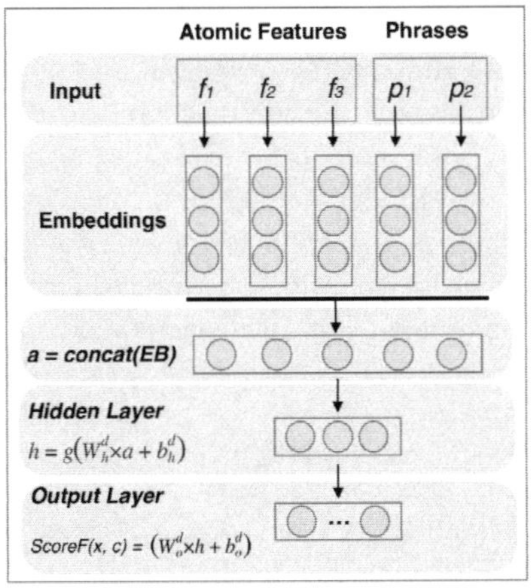

Figure 2: Architecture of the Neural Network

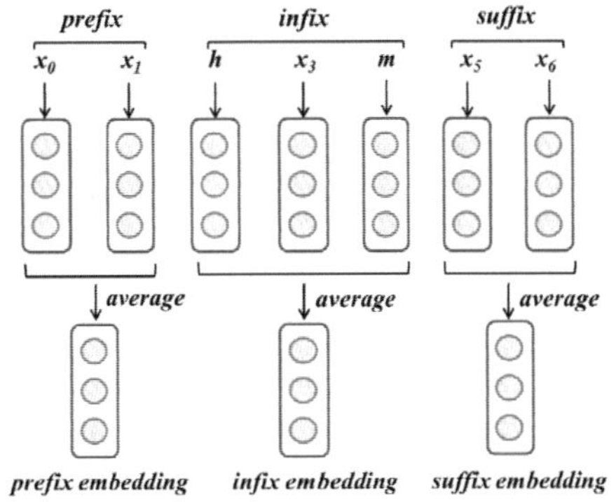

Figure 3: Illustration for phrase embeddings. h, m and x_0 to x_6 are words in the sentence.

In our work, we propose a neural network model for scoring subgraph c in the tree:

$$ScoreF(x, c; \theta) = \boldsymbol{NN}(x, c) \quad (4)$$

where $\boldsymbol{NN}$ is our scoring function based on neural network (Figure 2). As we will show in the following sections, it alleviates the heavy burden of feature engineering in conventional graph-based models and achieves better performance by automatically learning useful information in the data.

The effectiveness of our neural network depends on five key components: *Feature Embeddings*, *Phrase Embeddings*, *Direction-specific transformation*, *Learning Feature Combinations* and *Max-Margin Training*.

2.1 Feature Embeddings

As shown in Figure 2, part of the input to the neural network is feature representation of the subgraph. Instead of using millions of features as in conventional models, we only use use atomic features (Chen et al., 2014) such as word unigrams and POS-tag unigrams, which are less likely to be sparse. The detailed atomic features we use will be described in Section 3. Unlike conventional models, the atomic features in our model are transformed into their corresponding distributed representations (feature embeddings).

The idea of distributed representation for symbolic data is one of the most important reasons why neural network works in NLP tasks. It is shown that similar features will have similar embeddings which capture the syntactic and semantic information behind features (Bengio et al., 2003; Collobert et al., 2011; Schwenk et al., 2012; Mikolov et al., 2013; Socher et al., 2013; Pei et al., 2014).

Formally, we have a feature dictionary D of size $|D|$. Each feature $f \in D$ is represented as a real-valued vector (feature embedding) $Embed(f) \in \mathbb{R}^d$ where d is the dimensionality of the vector space. All feature embeddings stacking together forms the embedding matrix $M \in \mathbb{R}^{d \times |D|}$. The embedding matrix M is initialized randomly and trained by our model (Section 2.6).

2.2 Phrase Embeddings

Context information of word pairs[1] such as the dependency pair (h, m) has been widely believed to be useful in graph-based models (McDonald et al., 2005; McDonald and Pereira, 2006). Given a sentence x, the context for $\boldsymbol{h}$ and $\boldsymbol{m}$ includes three context parts: *prefix*, *infix* and *suffix*, as illustrated in Figure 3. We call these parts *phrases* in our work.

Context representation in conventional models are limited: First, phrases cannot be used as features directly because of the data sparseness problem. Therefore, phrases are backed off to low-order representation such as bigrams and trigrams. For example, Mcdonald et.al (2005) used tri-gram features of *infix* between head-modifier pair (h, m). Sometimes even tri-grams are expensive to use, which is the reason why Mcdonald and Pereira (2006) chose to ignore features over triples of words in their second-order model to prevent from exploding the size of the feature space. Sec-

[1]A word pair is not limited to the dependency pair (h, m). It could be any pair with particular relation (e.g., sibling pair (s, m) in Figure 1). Figure 3 only uses (h, m) as an example.

ond, bigrams or tri-grams are lexical features thus cannot capture syntactic and semantic information behind phrases. For instance, "*hit the ball*" and "*kick the football*" should have similar representations because they share similar syntactic structures, but lexical tri-grams will fail to capture their similarity.

Unlike previous work, we propose to use distributed representation (phrase embedding) of phrases to capture phrase-level information. We use a simple yet effective way to calculate phrase embeddings from word (POS-tag) embeddings. As shown in Figure 3, we average the word embeddings in *prefix*, *infix* and *suffix* respectively and get three global word-phrase embeddings. For pairs where no prefix or suffix exists, the corresponding embedding is set to zero. We also get three global POS-phrase embeddings which are calculated in the same way as words. These embeddings are then concatenated with feature embeddings and fed to the following hidden layer.

Phrase embeddings provide panorama representation of the context, allowing our model to capture richer context information compared with the back-off tri-gram representation. Moreover, as a distributed representation, phrase embeddings perform generalization over specific phrases, thus better capture the syntactic and semantic information than back-off tri-grams.

2.3 Direction-specific Transformation

In dependency representation of sentence, the edge direction indicates which one of the words is the head h and which one is the modifier m. Unlike previous work (McDonald et al., 2005; McDonald and Pereira, 2006) that models the edge direction as feature to be conjoined with other features, we model the edge direction with direction-specific transformation.

As shown in Figure 2, the parameters in hidden layer (W_h^d, b_h^d) and the output layer (W_o^d, b_o^d) are bound with index $d \in \{0, 1\}$ which indicates the direction between head and modifier (0 for left arc and 1 for right arc). In this way, the model can learn direction-specific parameters and automatically capture the interactions between edge direction and other features.

2.4 Learning Feature Combination

The key to the success of graph-based dependency parsing is the design of features, especially combinational features. Effective as these features are, as we have said in Section 1, they are prone to overfitting and hard to design. In our work, we introduce a new activation function that can automatically learn these feature combinations.

As shown in Figure 2, we first concatenate the embeddings into a single vector a. Then a is fed into the next layer which performs linear transformation followed by an element-wise activation function g:

$$h = g(W_h^d a + b_h^d) \tag{5}$$

Our new activation function g is defined as follows:

$$g(l) = tanh(l^3 + l) \tag{6}$$

where l is the result of linear transformation and *tanh* is the *hyperbolic tangent* activation function widely used in neural networks. We call this new activation function *tanh-cube*.

As we can see, without the cube term, *tanh-cube* would be just the same as the conventional non-linear transformation in most neural networks. The cube extension is added to enhance the ability to capture complex interactions between input features. Intuitively, the cube term in each hidden unit directly models feature combinations in a multiplicative way:

$$(w_1a_1 + w_2a_2 + ... + w_na_n + b)^3 =$$
$$\sum_{i,j,k}(w_iw_jw_k)a_ia_ja_k + \sum_{i,j} b(w_iw_j)a_ia_j...$$

These feature combinations are hand-designed in conventional graph-based models but our model learns these combinations automatically and encodes them in the model parameters.

Similar ideas were also proposed in previous works (Socher et al., 2013; Pei et al., 2014; Chen and Manning, 2014). Socher et.al (2013) and Pei et.al (2014) used a tensor-based activation function to learn feature combinations. However, tensor-based transformation is quite slow even with tensor factorization (Pei et al., 2014). Chen and Manning (2014) proposed to use cube function $g(l) = l^3$ which inspires our *tanh-cube* function. Compared with cube function, *tanh-cube* has three advantages:

- The cube function is unbounded, making the activation output either too small or too big if the norm of input l is not properly controlled, especially in deep neural network. On the contrary, *tanh-cube* is bounded by the *tanh* function thus safer to use in deep neural network.

- Intuitively, the behavior of cube function resembles the "polynomial kernel" in SVM. In fact, SVM can be seen as a special one-hidden-layer neural network where the kernel function that performs non-linear transformation is seen as a hidden layer and support vectors as hidden units. Compared with cube function, *tanh-cube* combines the power of "kernel function" with the *tanh* non-linear transformation in neural network.

- Last but not least, as we will show in Section 4, *tanh-cube* converges faster than the cube function although the rigorous proof is still open to investigate.

2.5 Model Output

After the non-linear transformation of hidden layer, the score of the subgraph c is calculated in the output layer using a simple linear function:

$$ScoreF(x, c) = W_o^d h + b_o^d \quad (7)$$

The output score $ScoreF(x, c) \in \mathbb{R}^{|L|}$ is a score vector where $|L|$ is the number of dependency types and each dimension of $ScoreF(x, c)$ is the score for each kind of dependency type of head-modifier pair (i.e. (h, m) in Figure 1).

2.6 Max-Margin Training

The parameters of our model are $\theta = \{W_h^d, b_h^d, W_o^d, b_o^d, M\}$. All parameters are initialized with uniform distribution within (-0.01, 0.01).

For model training, we use the Max-Margin criterion. Given a training instance (x, y), we search for the dependency tree with the highest score computed as equation (1) in Section 2. The object of Max-Margin training is that the highest scoring tree is the correct one: $y^* = y$ and its score will be larger up to a margin to other possible tree $\hat{y} \in Y(x)$:

$$Score(x, y; \theta) \geq Score(x, \hat{y}; \theta) + \triangle(y, \hat{y})$$

The structured margin loss $\triangle(y, \hat{y})$ is defined as:

$$\triangle(y, \hat{y}) = \sum_j^n \kappa \mathbf{1}\{h(y, x_j) \neq h(\hat{y}, x_j)\}$$

1-order-atomic	$h_{-2}.w$, $h_{-1}.w$, $h.w$, $h_1.w$, $h_2.w$ $h_{-2}.p$, $h_{-1}.p$, $h.p$, $h_1.p$, $h_2.p$ $m_{-2}.w$, $m_{-1}.w$, $m.w$, $m_1.w$, $m_2.w$ $m_{-2}.p$, $m_{-1}.p$, $m.p$, $m_1.p$, $m_2.p$ *dis(h, m)*
1-order-phrase	+ *hm_prefix.w*, *hm_infix.w*, *hm_suffix.w* + *hm_prefix.p*, *hm_infix.p*, *hm_suffix.p*
2-order-phrase	+ $s_{-2}.w$, $s_{-1}.w$, $s.w$, $s_1.w$, $s_2.w$ + $s_{-2}.p$, $s_{-1}.p$, $s.p$, $s_1.p$, $s_2.p$ + *sm_infix.w*, *sm_infix.p*

Table 1: Features in our three models. w is short for word and p for POS-tag. h indicates head and m indicates modifier. The subscript represents the relative position to the center word. $dis(h, m)$ is the distance between head and modifier. *hm_prefix*, *hm_infix* and *hm_suffix* are phrases for head-modifier pair (h, m). s indicates the sibling in second-order model. *sm_infix* is the *infix* phrase between sibling pair (s, m)

where n is the length of sentence x, $h(y, x_j)$ is the head (with type) for the j-th word of x in tree y and κ is a discount parameter. The loss is proportional to the number of word with an incorrect head and edge type in the proposed tree. This leads to the regularized objective function for m training examples:

$$\begin{aligned} J(\theta) &= \frac{1}{m} \sum_{i=1}^{m} l_i(\theta) + \frac{\lambda}{2} ||\theta||^2 \\ l_i(\theta) &= \max_{\hat{y} \in Y(x_i)} (Score(x_i, \hat{y}; \theta) + \triangle(y_i, \hat{y})) \\ &\quad - Score(x_i, y_i; \theta)) \end{aligned} \quad (8)$$

We use the diagonal variant of AdaGrad (Duchi et al., 2011) with minibatchs (batch size = 20) to minimize the object function. We also apply dropout (Hinton et al., 2012) with 0.5 rate to the hidden layer.

3 Model Implementation

Base on our Neural Network model, we present three model implementations with increasing expressive capabilities in this section.

3.1 First-order models

We first implement two first-order models: **1-order-atomic** and **1-order-phrase**. We use the Eisner (2000) algorithm for decoding. The first two rows of Table 1 list the features we use in these two models.

1-order-atomic only uses atomic features as shown in the first row of Table 1. Specifically, the

	Models	Dev		Test		Speed (sent/s)
		UAS	LAS	UAS	LAS	
First-order	MSTParser-1-order	92.01	90.77	91.60	90.39	20
	1-order-atomic-rand	92.00	90.71	91.62	90.41	**55**
	1-order-atomic	92.19	90.94	92.14	90.92	**55**
	1-order-phrase-rand	92.47	91.19	92.25	91.05	26
	1-order-phrase	**92.82**	**91.48**	**92.59**	**91.37**	26
Second-order	MSTParser-2-order	92.70	91.48	92.30	91.06	14
	2-order-phrase-rand	93.39	92.10	92.99	91.79	10
	2-order-phrase	**93.57**	**92.29**	**93.29**	**92.13**	10
Third-order	(Koo and Collins, 2010)	93.49	N/A	93.04	N/A	N/A

Table 2: Comparison with conventional graph-based models.

head word and its local neighbor words that are within the distance of 2 are selected as the head's word unigram features. The modifier's word unigram features is extracted in the same way. We also use the POS-tags of the corresponding word features and the distance between head and modifier as additional atomic features.

We then improved **1-order-atomic** to **1-order-phrase** by incorporating additional phrase embeddings. The three phrase embeddings of head-modifier pair (h, m): *hm_prefix*, *hm_infix* and *hm_suffix* are calculated as in Section 2.2.

3.2 Second-order model

Our model can be easily extended to a second-order model using the second-order decoding algorithm (Eisner, 1996; McDonald and Pereira, 2006). The third row of Table 1 shows the additional features we use in our second-order model.

Sibling node and its local context are used as additional atomic features. We also used the *infix embedding* for the *infix* between sibling pair (s, m), which we call *sm_infix*. It is calculated in the same way as *infix* between head-modifier pair (h, m) (i.e., *hm_infix*) in Section 2.2 except that the word pair is now s and m. For cases where no sibling information is available, the corresponding sibling-related embeddings are set to zero vector.

4 Experiments

4.1 Experiment Setup

We use the English Penn Treebank (PTB) to evaluate our model implementations and Yamada and Matsumoto (2003) head rules are used to extract dependency trees. We follow the standard splits of PTB3, using section 2-21 for training, section 22 as development set and 23 as test set. The Stanford POS Tagger (Toutanova et al., 2003) with ten-way jackknifing of the training data is used for assigning POS tags (accuracy $\approx 97.2\%$).

Hyper-parameters of our models are tuned on the development set and their final settings are as follows: embedding size d = 50, hidden layer (Layer 2) size = 200, regularization parameter $\lambda = 10^{-4}$, discount parameter for margin loss κ = 0.3, initial learning rate of AdaGrad alpha = 0.1.

4.2 Experiment Results

Table 2 compares our models with several conventional graph-based parsers. We use MSTParser[2] for conventional first-order model (McDonald et al., 2005) and second-order model (McDonald and Pereira, 2006). We also include the result of a third-order model of Koo and Collins (2010) for comparison[3]. For our models, we report the results with and without unsupervised pre-training. Pre-training only trains the word-based feature embeddings on Gigaword corpus (Graff et al., 2003) using *word2vec*[4] and all other parameters are still initialized randomly. In all experiments, we report unlabeled attachment scores (UAS) and labeled attachment scores (LAS) and punctuation[5] is excluded in all evaluation metrics. The parsing speeds are measured on a workstation with Intel Xeon 3.4GHz CPU and 32GB RAM.

As we can see, even with random initialization, **1-order-atomic-rand** performs as well as conventional first-order model and both **1-order-phrase-**

[2] `http://sourceforge.net/projects/mstparser`

[3] Note that Koo and Collins (2010)'s third-order model and our models are not strict comparable since their model is an unlabeled model.

[4] `https://code.google.com/p/word2vec/`

[5] Following previous work, a token is a punctuation if its POS tag is {“ ” : , .}

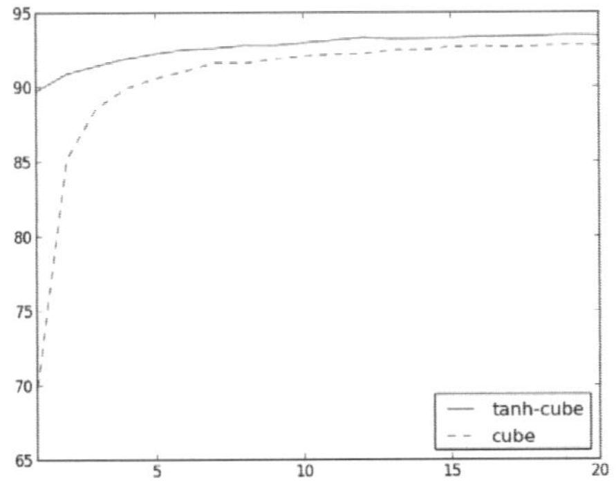

Figure 4: Convergence curve for *tanh-cube* and *cube* activation function.

Feature Type	Instance	Neighboors
Words (word2vec)	in	the, of, and, for, from
	his	himself, her, he, him, father
	which	its, essentially, similar, that, also
Words (Our model)	in	on, at, behind, among, during
	his	her, my, their, its, he
	which	where, who, whom, whose, though
POS-tags	NN	NNPS, NNS, EX, NNP, POS
	JJ	JJR, JJS, PDT, RBR, RBS

Table 4: Examples of similar words and POS-tags according to feature embeddings.

rand and **2-order-phrase-rand** perform better than conventional models in MSTParser. Pre-training further improves the performance of all three models, which is consistent with the conclusion of previous work (Pei et al., 2014; Chen and Manning, 2014). Moreover, **1-order-phrase** performs better than **1-order-atomic**, which shows that phrase embeddings do improve the model. **2-order-phrase** further improves the performance because of the more expressive second-order factorization. All three models perform significantly better than their counterparts in MSTParser where millions of features are used and **1-order-phrase** works surprisingly well that it even beats the conventional second-order model.

With regard to parsing speed, **1-order-atomic** is the fastest while other two models have similar speeds as MSTParser. Further speed up could be achieved by using pre-computing strategy as mentioned in Chen and Manning (2014). We did not try this strategy since parsing speed is not the main focus of this paper.

Model	*tanh-cube*	*cube*	*tanh*
1-order-atomic	**92.19**	91.97	91.73
1-order-phrase	**92.82**	92.25	92.13
2-order-phrase	**93.57**	92.95	92.91

Table 3: Model Performance of different activation functions.

We also investigated the effect of different activation functions. We trained our models with the same configuration except for the activation function. Table 3 lists the UAS of three models on development set.

As we can see, *tanh-cube* function outperforms *cube* function because of advantages we mentioned in Section 2.4. Moreover, both *tanh-cube* function and *cube* function performs better than *tanh* function. The reason is that the cube term can capture more interactions between input features.

We also plot the UAS of **2-order-phrase** during each iteration of training. As shown in Figure 4, *tanh-cube* function converges faster than *cube* function.

4.3 Qualitative Analysis

In order to see why our models work, we made qualitative analysis on different aspects of our model.

Ability of Feature Abstraction

Feature embeddings give our model the ability of feature abstraction. They capture the inherent correlations between features so that syntactic similar features will have similar representations, which makes our model generalizes well on unseen data.

Table 4 shows the effect of different feature embeddings which are obtained from **2-order-phrase** after training. For each kind of feature type, we list several features as well as top 5 features that are nearest (measured by Euclidean distance) to the corresponding feature according to their embeddings.

We first analysis the effect of word embeddings after training. For comparison, we also list the initial word embeddings in word2vec. As we can see, in word2vec word embeddings, words that are similar to *in* and *which* tends to be those

Phrase	Neighboor
On a Saturday morning	On Monday night football On Sunday On Saturday On Tuesday afternoon On recent Saturday morning
most of it	of it of it all some of it also most of these are only some of
big investment bank	great investment bank bank investment entire equity investment another cash equity investor real estate lending division

Table 5: Examples of similar phrases according to phrase embeddings.

co-occuring with them and for word *his*, similar words are morphologies of *he*. On the contrary, similar words measured by our embeddings have similar syntactic functions. This is helpful for dependency parsing since parsing models care more about the syntactic functions of words rather than their collocations or morphologies.

POS-tag embeddings also show similar behavior with word embeddings. As shown in Table 4, our model captures similarities between POS-tags even though their embeddings are initialized randomly.

We also investigated the effect of phrase embeddings in the same way as feature embeddings. Table 5 lists the examples of similar phrases. Our phrase embeddings work pretty well given that only a simple averaging strategy is used. Phrases that are close to each other tend to share similar syntactic and semantic information. By using phrase embeddings, our model sees panorama of the context rather than limited word tri-grams and thus captures richer context information, which is the reason why phrase embeddings significantly improve the performance.

Ability of Feature Learning

Finally, we try to unveil the mysterious hidden layer and investigate what features it learns. For each hidden unit of **2-order-phrase**, we get its connections with embeddings (i.e., W_h^d in Figure 2) and pick the connections whose weights have absolute value > 0.1. We sampled several hidden units and investigated which features their highly weighted connections belong to:

- Hidden 1: $h.w$, $m.w$, $h_{-1}.w$, $m_1.w$
- Hidden 2: $h.p$, $m.p$, $s.p$
- Hidden 3: *hm_infix.p, hm_infix.w, hm_prefix.w*
- Hidden 4: *hm_infix.w, hm_prefix.w, sm_infix.w*
- Hidden 5: *hm_infix.p, hm_infix.w, hm_suffix.w*

The samples above give qualitative results of what features the hidden layer learns:

- Hidden unit 1 and 2 show that atomic features of *head*, *modifier*, *sibling* and their local context words are useful in our model, which is consistent with our expectations since these features are also very important features in conventional graph-based models (McDonald and Pereira, 2006).
- Features in the same hidden unit will "combine" with each other through our *tanh-cube* activation function. As we can see, feature combination in hidden unit 2 were also used in Mcdonald and Pereira (2006). However, these feature combinations are automatically captured by our model without the labor-intensive feature engineering.
- Hidden unit 3 to 5 show that phrase-level information like *hm_prefix*, *hm_suffix* and *sm_infix* are effective in our model. These features are not used in conventional second-order model (McDonald and Pereira, 2006) because they could explode the feature space. Through our tanh-cube activation function, our model further captures the interactions between phrases and other features without the concern of overfitting.

5 Related Work

Models for dependency parsing have been studied with considerable effort in the NLP community. Among them, we only focus on the graph-based models here. Most previous systems address this task by using linear statistical models with carefully designed context and structure features. The types of features available rely on tree factorization and decoding algorithm. Mcdonald et.al (2005) proposed the first-order model which is also know as arc-factored model. Efficient decoding can be performed with Eisner (2000) algorithm in $O(n^3)$ time and $O(n^2)$ space. Mcdonald and Pereira (2006) further extend the first-order model to second-order model where sibling information is available during decoding. Eisner (2000) algorithm can be modified trivially for second-order decoding. Carreras (2007) proposed a more powerful second-order model that can score both sibling and grandchild parts with the cost of $O(n^4)$ time and $O(n^3)$ space. To exploit more structure information, Koo and Collins (2010) proposed three third-order models with computational requirements of $O(n^4)$ time and $O(n^3)$ space.

Recently, neural network models have been increasingly focused on for their ability to minimize the effort in feature engineering. Chen et.al (2014) proposed an approach to automatically learning feature embeddings for graph-based dependency parsing. The learned feature embeddings are used as additional features in conventional graph-based model. Le and Zuidema (2014) proprosed an infinite-order model based on recursive neural network. However, their model can only be used as an reranking model since decoding is intractable.

Compared with these work, our model is a general and standalone neural network model. Both training and decoding in our model are performed based on our neural network architecture in an effective way. Although only first-order and second-order models are implemented in our work, higher-order graph-based models can be easily implemented using our model.

6 Conclusion

In this paper, we propose a general and effective neural network model that can automatically learn feature combinations with our novel activation function. Moreover, we introduce a simple yet effect way to utilize phrase-level information, which greatly improves the model performance. Experiments on the benchmark dataset show that our model achieves better results than conventional models.

Acknowledgments

This work is supported by National Natural Science Foundation of China under Grant No. 61273318 and National Key Basic Research Program of China 2014CB340504. We want to thank Miaohong Chen and Pingping Huang for their valuable comments on the initial idea and helping pre-process the data.

References

Yoshua Bengio, Réjean Ducharme, Pascal Vincent, and Christian Jauvin. 2003. A neural probabilistic language model. *Journal of Machine Learning Research*, 3:1137–1155.

Xavier Carreras. 2007. Experiments with a higher-order projective dependency parser. In *EMNLP-CoNLL*, pages 957–961.

Danqi Chen and Christopher Manning. 2014. A fast and accurate dependency parser using neural networks. In *Proceedings of the 2014 Conference on Empirical Methods in Natural Language Processing (EMNLP)*, pages 740–750, Doha, Qatar, October. Association for Computational Linguistics.

Wenliang Chen, Yue Zhang, and Min Zhang. 2014. Feature embedding for dependency parsing. In *Proceedings of COLING 2014, the 25th International Conference on Computational Linguistics: Technical Papers*, pages 816–826, Dublin, Ireland, August. Dublin City University and Association for Computational Linguistics.

Ronan Collobert, Jason Weston, Léon Bottou, Michael Karlen, Koray Kavukcuoglu, and Pavel Kuksa. 2011. Natural language processing (almost) from scratch. *The Journal of Machine Learning Research*, 12:2493–2537.

John Duchi, Elad Hazan, and Yoram Singer. 2011. Adaptive subgradient methods for online learning and stochastic optimization. *The Journal of Machine Learning Research*, 999999:2121–2159.

Jason M Eisner. 1996. Three new probabilistic models for dependency parsing: An exploration. In *Proceedings of the 16th conference on Computational linguistics-Volume 1*, pages 340–345. Association for Computational Linguistics.

Jason Eisner. 2000. Bilexical grammars and their cubic-time parsing algorithms. In *Advances in probabilistic and other parsing technologies*, pages 29–61. Springer.

David Graff, Junbo Kong, Ke Chen, and Kazuaki Maeda. 2003. English gigaword. *Linguistic Data Consortium, Philadelphia.*

Geoffrey E Hinton, Nitish Srivastava, Alex Krizhevsky, Ilya Sutskever, and Ruslan R Salakhutdinov. 2012. Improving neural networks by preventing co-adaptation of feature detectors. *arXiv preprint arXiv:1207.0580.*

Terry Koo and Michael Collins. 2010. Efficient third-order dependency parsers. In *Proceedings of the 48th Annual Meeting of the Association for Computational Linguistics*, pages 1–11. Association for Computational Linguistics.

Phong Le and Willem Zuidema. 2014. The inside-outside recursive neural network model for dependency parsing. In *Proceedings of the 2014 Conference on Empirical Methods in Natural Language Processing (EMNLP)*, pages 729–739, Doha, Qatar, October. Association for Computational Linguistics.

Ryan T McDonald and Fernando CN Pereira. 2006. Online learning of approximate dependency parsing algorithms. In *EACL*. Citeseer.

Ryan McDonald, Koby Crammer, and Fernando Pereira. 2005. Online large-margin training of dependency parsers. In *Proceedings of the 43rd annual meeting on association for computational linguistics*, pages 91–98. Association for Computational Linguistics.

Tomas Mikolov, Kai Chen, Greg Corrado, and Jeffrey Dean. 2013. Efficient estimation of word representations in vector space. *arXiv preprint arXiv:1301.3781*.

Wenzhe Pei, Tao Ge, and Baobao Chang. 2014. Max-margin tensor neural network for chinese word segmentation. In *Proceedings of the 52nd Annual Meeting of the Association for Computational Linguistics (Volume 1: Long Papers)*, pages 293–303, Baltimore, Maryland, June. Association for Computational Linguistics.

Holger Schwenk, Anthony Rousseau, and Mohammed Attik. 2012. Large, pruned or continuous space language models on a gpu for statistical machine translation. In *Proceedings of the NAACL-HLT 2012 Workshop: Will We Ever Really Replace the N-gram Model? On the Future of Language Modeling for HLT*, pages 11–19. Association for Computational Linguistics.

Richard Socher, Alex Perelygin, Jean Wu, Jason Chuang, Christopher D. Manning, Andrew Ng, and Christopher Potts. 2013. Recursive deep models for semantic compositionality over a sentiment treebank. In *Proceedings of the 2013 Conference on Empirical Methods in Natural Language Processing*, pages 1631–1642, Seattle, Washington, USA, October. Association for Computational Linguistics.

Kristina Toutanova, Dan Klein, Christopher D Manning, and Yoram Singer. 2003. Feature-rich part-of-speech tagging with a cyclic dependency network. In *Proceedings of the 2003 Conference of the North American Chapter of the Association for Computational Linguistics on Human Language Technology-Volume 1*, pages 173–180. Association for Computational Linguistics.

Hiroyasu Yamada and Yuji Matsumoto. 2003. Statistical dependency analysis with support vector machines. In *Proceedings of IWPT*, volume 3, pages 195–206.

Yue Zhang and Joakim Nivre. 2011. Transition-based dependency parsing with rich non-local features. In *Proceedings of the 49th Annual Meeting of the Association for Computational Linguistics: Human Language Technologies*, pages 188–193, Portland, Oregon, USA, June. Association for Computational Linguistics.

Structured Training for Neural Network Transition-Based Parsing

David Weiss **Chris Alberti** **Michael Collins** **Slav Petrov**
Google Inc
New York, NY
{djweiss,chrisalberti,mjcollins,slav}@google.com

Abstract

We present structured perceptron training for neural network transition-based dependency parsing. We learn the neural network representation using a gold corpus augmented by a large number of automatically parsed sentences. Given this fixed network representation, we learn a final layer using the structured perceptron with beam-search decoding. On the Penn Treebank, our parser reaches 94.26% unlabeled and 92.41% labeled attachment accuracy, which to our knowledge is the best accuracy on Stanford Dependencies to date. We also provide in-depth ablative analysis to determine which aspects of our model provide the largest gains in accuracy.

1 Introduction

Syntactic analysis is a central problem in language understanding that has received a tremendous amount of attention. Lately, dependency parsing has emerged as a popular approach to this problem due to the availability of dependency treebanks in many languages (Buchholz and Marsi, 2006; Nivre et al., 2007; McDonald et al., 2013) and the efficiency of dependency parsers.

Transition-based parsers (Nivre, 2008) have been shown to provide a good balance between efficiency and accuracy. In transition-based parsing, sentences are processed in a linear left to right pass; at each position, the parser needs to choose from a set of possible actions defined by the transition strategy. In greedy models, a classifier is used to independently decide which transition to take based on local features of the current parse configuration. This classifier typically uses hand-engineered features and is trained on individual transitions extracted from the gold transition sequence. While extremely fast, these greedy models typically suffer from search errors due to the inability to recover from incorrect decisions. Zhang and Clark (2008) showed that a beam-search decoding algorithm utilizing the structured perceptron training algorithm can greatly improve accuracy. Nonetheless, significant manual feature engineering was required before transition-based systems provided competitive accuracy with graph-based parsers (Zhang and Nivre, 2011), and only by incorporating graph-based scoring functions were Bohnet and Kuhn (2012) able to exceed the accuracy of graph-based approaches.

In contrast to these carefully hand-tuned approaches, Chen and Manning (2014) recently presented a neural network version of a greedy transition-based parser. In their model, a feed-forward neural network with a hidden layer is used to make the transition decisions. The hidden layer has the power to learn arbitrary combinations of the atomic inputs, thereby eliminating the need for hand-engineered features. Furthermore, because the neural network uses a distributed representation, it is able to model lexical, part-of-speech (POS) tag, and arc label similarities in a continuous space. However, although their model outperforms its greedy hand-engineered counterparts, it is not competitive with state-of-the-art dependency parsers that are trained for structured search.

In this work, we combine the representational power of neural networks with the superior search enabled by structured training and inference, making our parser one of the most accurate dependency parsers to date. Training and testing on the Penn Treebank (Marcus et al., 1993), our transition-based parser achieves 93.99% unlabeled (UAS) / 92.05% labeled (LAS) attachment accuracy, outperforming the 93.22% UAS / 91.02% LAS of Zhang and McDonald (2014) and 93.27 UAS / 91.19 LAS of Bohnet and Kuhn (2012). In addition, by incorporating unlabeled data into training, we further improve the accuracy of our model to 94.26% UAS / 92.41% LAS (93.46%

Proceedings of the 53rd Annual Meeting of the Association for Computational Linguistics and the 7th International Joint Conference on Natural Language Processing, pages 323–333,
Beijing, China, July 26-31, 2015. ©2015 Association for Computational Linguistics

UAS / 91.49% LAS for our greedy model).

In our approach we start with the basic structure of Chen and Manning (2014), but with a deeper architecture and improvements to the optimization procedure. These modifications (Section 2) increase the performance of the greedy model by as much as 1%. As in prior work, we train the neural network to model the probability of individual parse actions. However, we do not use these probabilities directly for prediction. Instead, we use the activations from all layers of the neural network as the representation in a structured perceptron model that is trained with beam search and early updates (Section 3). On the Penn Treebank, this structured learning approach significantly improves parsing accuracy by 0.8%.

An additional contribution of this work is an effective way to leverage unlabeled data. Neural networks are known to perform very well in the presence of large amounts of training data; however, obtaining more expert-annotated parse trees is very expensive. To this end, we generate large quantities of high-confidence parse trees by parsing unlabeled data with two different parsers and selecting only the sentences for which the two parsers produced the same trees (Section 3.3). This approach is known as "tri-training" (Li et al., 2014) and we show that it benefits our neural network parser significantly more than other approaches. By adding 10 million automatically parsed tokens to the training data, we improve the accuracy of our parsers by almost ~1.0% on web domain data.

We provide an extensive exploration of our model in Section 5 through ablative analysis and other retrospective experiments. One of the goals of this work is to provide guidance for future refinements and improvements on the architecture and modeling choices we introduce in this paper.

Finally, we also note that neural network representations have a long history in syntactic parsing (Henderson, 2004; Titov and Henderson, 2007; Titov and Henderson, 2010); however, like Chen and Manning (2014), our network avoids any recurrent structure so as to keep inference fast and efficient and to allow the use of simple backpropagation to compute gradients. Our work is also not the first to apply structured training to neural networks (see e.g. Peng et al. (2009) and Do and Artires (2010) for Conditional Random Field (CRF) training of neural networks). Our paper extends this line of work to the setting of inexact search with beam decoding for dependency parsing; Zhou et al. (2015) concurrently explored a similar approach using a structured probabilistic ranking objective. Dyer et al. (2015) concurrently developed the Stack Long Short-Term Memory (S-LSTM) architecture, which does incorporate recurrent architecture and look-ahead, and which yields comparable accuracy on the Penn Treebank to our greedy model.

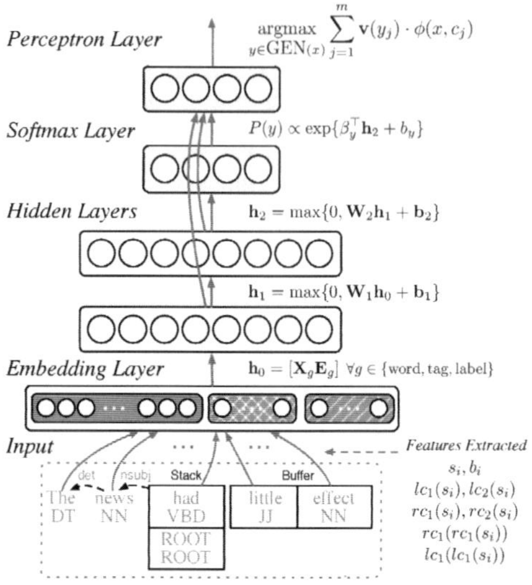

Figure 1: Schematic overview of our neural network model. Atomic features are extracted from the i'th elements on the stack (s_i) and the buffer (b_i); lc_i indicates the i'th leftmost child and rc_i the i'th rightmost child. We use the top two elements on the stack for the arc features and the top four tokens on stack and buffer for words, tags and arc labels.

2 Neural Network Model

In this section, we describe the architecture of our model, which is summarized in Figure 1. Note that we separate the embedding processing to a distinct "embedding layer" for clarity of presentation. Our model is based upon that of Chen and Manning (2014) and we discuss the differences between our model and theirs in detail at the end of this section. We use the *arc-standard* (Nivre, 2004) transition system.

2.1 Input layer

Given a parse configuration c (consisting of a stack s and a buffer b), we extract a rich set of discrete features which we feed into the neural network. Following Chen and Manning (2014), we group these features by their input source: words, POS tags, and arc labels. The features extracted for each group are represented as a sparse $F \times V$ matrix $\mathbf{X}$, where V is the size of the vocabulary of the feature group and F is the number of features. The value of element X_{fv} is 1 if the f'th feature takes on value v. We produce three input matrices: $\mathbf{X}_{\text{word}}$ for words features, $\mathbf{X}_{\text{tag}}$ for POS tag features, and $\mathbf{X}_{\text{label}}$ for arc labels, with $F_{\text{word}} = F_{\text{tag}} = 20$ and $F_{\text{label}} = 12$ (Figure 1).

For all feature groups, we add additional special values for "ROOT" (indicating the POS or word of the root token), "NULL" (indicating no valid feature value could be computed) or "UNK" (indicating an out-of-vocabulary item).

2.2 Embedding layer

The first learned layer h_0 in the network transforms the sparse, discrete features $\mathbf{X}$ into a dense, continuous embedded representation. For each feature group $\mathbf{X}_g$, we learn a $V_g \times D_g$ embedding matrix $\mathbf{E}_g$ that applies the conversion:

$$\mathbf{h}_0 = [\mathbf{X}_g \mathbf{E}_g \mid g \in \{\text{word}, \text{tag}, \text{label}\}], \quad (1)$$

where we apply the computation separately for each group g and concatenate the results. Thus, the embedding layer has $E = \sum_g F_g D_g$ outputs, which we reshape to a vector $\mathbf{h}_0$. We can choose the embedding dimensionality D for each group freely. Since POS tags and arc labels have much smaller vocabularies, we show in our experiments (Section 5.1) that we can use smaller D_{tag} and D_{label}, without a loss in accuracy.

2.3 Hidden layers

We experimented with one and two hidden layers composed of M rectified linear (Relu) units (Nair and Hinton, 2010). Each unit in the hidden layers is fully connected to the previous layer:

$$\mathbf{h}_i = \max\{0, \mathbf{W}_i \mathbf{h}_{i-1} + \mathbf{b}_i\}, \quad (2)$$

where $\mathbf{W}_1$ is a $M_1 \times E$ weight matrix for the first hidden layer and $\mathbf{W}_i$ are $M_i \times M_{i-1}$ matrices for all subsequent layers. The weights $\mathbf{b}_i$ are bias terms. Relu layers have been well studied in the neural network literature and have been shown to work well for a wide domain of problems (Krizhevsky et al., 2012; Zeiler et al., 2013). Through most of development, we kept $M_i = 200$, but we found that significantly increasing the number of hidden units improved our results for the final comparison.

2.4 Relationship to Chen and Manning (2014)

Our model is clearly inspired by and based on the work of Chen and Manning (2014). There are a few structural differences: (1) we allow for much smaller embeddings of POS tags and labels, (2) we use Relu units in our hidden layers, and (3) we use a deeper model with two hidden layers. Somewhat to our surprise, we found these changes combined with an SGD training scheme (Section 3.1) during the "pre-training" phase of the model to lead to an almost 1% accuracy gain over Chen and Manning (2014). This trend held despite carefully tuning hyperparameters for each method of training and structure combination.

Our main contribution from an algorithmic perspective is our training procedure: as described in the next section, we use the structured perceptron for learning the final layer of our model. We thus present a novel way to leverage a neural network representation in a structured prediction setting.

3 Semi-Supervised Structured Learning

In this work, we investigate a semi-supervised structured learning scheme that yields substantial improvements in accuracy over the baseline neural network model. There are two complementary contributions of our approach: (1) incorporating structured learning of the model and (2) utilizing unlabeled data. In both cases, we use the neural network to model the probability of each parsing action y as a soft-max function taking the final hidden layer as its input:

$$P(y) \propto \exp\{\beta_y^\top \mathbf{h}_i + b_y\}, \quad (3)$$

where β_y is a M_i dimensional vector of weights for class y and i is the index of the final hidden layer of the network. At a high level our approach can be summarized as follows:

- First, we pre-train the network's hidden representations by learning probabilities of parsing actions. Fixing the hidden representations, we learn an additional final output layer using the structured perceptron that uses the output of the network's hidden layers. In practice this improves accuracy by ~0.6% absolute.

- Next, we show that we can supplement the gold data with a large corpus of high quality automatic parses. We show that incorporating unlabeled data in this way improves accuracy by as much as 1% absolute.

3.1 Backpropagation Pretraining

To learn the hidden representations, we use mini-batched averaged stochastic gradient descent (ASGD) (Bottou, 2010) with momentum (Hinton, 2012) to learn the parameters Θ of the network, where $\Theta = \{\mathbf{E}_g, \mathbf{W}_i, \mathbf{b}_i, \beta_y \mid \forall g, i, y\}$. We use backpropagation to minimize the multinomial logistic loss:

$$L(\Theta) = -\sum_j \log P(y_j \mid c_j, \Theta) + \lambda \sum_i ||\mathbf{W}_i||_2^2, \quad (4)$$

where λ is a regularization hyper-parameter over the hidden layer parameters (we use $\lambda = 10^{-4}$ in all experiments) and j sums over all decisions and configurations $\{y_j, c_j\}$ extracted from gold parse trees in the dataset.

The specific update rule we apply at iteration t is as follows:

$$g_t = \mu g_{t-1} - \Delta L(\Theta_t), \quad (5)$$

$$\Theta_{t+1} = \Theta_t + \eta_t g_t, \quad (6)$$

where the descent direction g_t is computed by a weighted combination of the previous direction $g_{t-1}$and the current gradient $\Delta L(\Theta_t)$. The parameter $\mu \in [0, 1)$ is the momentum parameter while η_t is the traditional learning rate. In addition, since we did not tune the regularization parameter λ, we apply a simple exponential step-wise decay to η_t; for every γ rounds of updates, we multiply $\eta_t = 0.96\eta_{t-1}$.

The final component of the update is parameter averaging: we maintain averaged parameters $\bar{\Theta}_t = \alpha_t \bar{\Theta}_{t-1} + (1 - \alpha_t)\Theta_t$, where α_t is an averaging weight that increases from 0.1 to 0.9999 with $1/t$. Combined with averaging, careful tuning of the three hyperparameters μ, η_0, and γ using held-out data was crucial in our experiments.

3.2 Structured Perceptron Training

Given the hidden representations, we now describe how the perceptron can be trained to utilize these representations. The perceptron algorithm with early updates (Collins and Roark, 2004) requires a feature-vector definition ϕ that maps a sentence x together with a configuration c to a feature vector $\phi(x, c) \in \mathbb{R}^d$. There is a one-to-one mapping between configurations c and decision sequences $y_1 \ldots y_{j-1}$ for any integer $j \geq 1$: we will use c and $y_1 \ldots y_{j-1}$ interchangeably.

For a sentence x, define GEN(x) to be the set of parse trees for x. Each $y \in \text{GEN}(x)$ is a sequence of decisions $y_1 \ldots y_m$ for some integer m. We use $\mathcal{Y}$ to denote the set of possible decisions in the parsing model. For each decision $y \in \mathcal{Y}$ we assume a parameter vector $\mathbf{v}(y) \in \mathbb{R}^d$. These parameters will be trained using the perceptron.

In decoding with the perceptron-trained model, we will use beam search to attempt to find:

$$\operatorname*{argmax}_{y \in \text{GEN}(x)} \sum_{j=1}^{m} \mathbf{v}(y_j) \cdot \phi(x, y_1 \ldots y_{j-1}).$$

Thus each decision y_j receives a score:

$$\mathbf{v}(y_j) \cdot \phi(x, y_1 \ldots y_{j-1}).$$

In the perceptron with early updates, the parameters $\mathbf{v}(y)$ are trained as follows. On each training example, we run beam search until the gold-standard parse tree falls out of the beam.[1] Define j to be the length of the beam at this point. A structured perceptron update is performed using the gold-standard decisions $y_1 \ldots y_j$ as the target, and the highest scoring (incorrect) member of the beam as the negative example.

A key idea in this paper is to use the neural network to define the representation $\phi(x, c)$. Given the sentence x and the configuration c, assuming two hidden layers, the neural network defines values for $\mathbf{h}_1$, $\mathbf{h}_2$, and $P(y)$ for each decision y. We experimented with various definitions of ϕ (Section 5.2) and found that $\phi(x, c) = [\mathbf{h}_1 \; \mathbf{h}_2 \; P(y)]$ (the concatenation of the outputs from both hidden layers, as well as the probabilities for all decisions y possible in the current configuration) had the best accuracy on development data.

Note that it is possible to continue to use backpropagation to learn the representation $\phi(x, c)$ during perceptron training; however, we found using ASGD to pre-train the representation always led to faster, more accurate results in preliminary experiments, and we left further investigation for future work.

3.3 Incorporating Unlabeled Data

Given the high capacity, non-linear nature of the deep network we hypothesize that our model can

[1] If the gold parse tree stays within the beam until the end of the sentence, conventional perceptron updates are used.

be significantly improved by incorporating more data. One way to use unlabeled data is through unsupervised methods such as word clusters (Koo et al., 2008); we follow Chen and Manning (2014) and use pretrained word embeddings to initialize our model. The word embeddings capture similar distributional information as word clusters and give consistent improvements by providing a good initialization and information about words not seen in the treebank data.

However, obtaining more training data is even more important than a good initialization. One potential way to obtain additional training data is by parsing unlabeled data with previously trained models. McClosky et al. (2006) and Huang and Harper (2009) showed that iteratively re-training a single model ("self-training") can be used to improve parsers in certain settings; Petrov et al. (2010) built on this work and showed that a slow and accurate parser can be used to "up-train" a faster but less accurate parser.

In this work, we adopt the "tri-training" approach of Li et al. (2014): Two parsers are used to process the unlabeled corpus and only sentences for which both parsers produced the same parse tree are added to the training data. The intuition behind this idea is that the chance of the parse being correct is much higher when the two parsers agree: there is only one way to be correct, while there are many possible incorrect parses. Of course, this reasoning holds only as long as the parsers suffer from different biases.

We show that tri-training is far more effective than vanilla up-training for our neural network model. We use same setup as Li et al. (2014), intersecting the output of the BerkeleyParser (Petrov et al., 2006), and a reimplementation of ZPar (Zhang and Nivre, 2011) as our baseline parsers. The two parsers agree only 36% of the time on the tune set, but their accuracy on those sentences is 97.26% UAS, approaching the inter annotator agreement rate. These sentences are of course easier to parse, having an average length of 15 words, compared to 24 words for the tune set overall. However, because we only use these sentences to extract individual transition decisions, the shorter length does not seem to hurt their utility. We generate 10^7 tokens worth of new parses and use this data in the backpropagation stage of training.

4 Experiments

In this section we present our experimental setup and the main results of our work.

4.1 Experimental Setup

We conduct our experiments on two English language benchmarks: (1) the standard Wall Street Journal (WSJ) part of the Penn Treebank (Marcus et al., 1993) and (2) a more comprehensive union of publicly available treebanks spanning multiple domains. For the WSJ experiments, we follow standard practice and use sections 2-21 for training, section 22 for development and section 23 as the final test set. Since there are many hyperparameters in our models, we additionally use section 24 for tuning. We convert the constituency trees to Stanford style dependencies (De Marneffe et al., 2006) using version 3.3.0 of the converter. We use a CRF-based POS tagger to generate 5-fold jack-knifed POS tags on the training set and predicted tags on the dev, test and tune sets; our tagger gets comparable accuracy to the Stanford POS tagger (Toutanova et al., 2003) with 97.44% on the test set. We report unlabeled attachment score (UAS) and labeled attachment score (LAS) excluding punctuation on predicted POS tags, as is standard for English.

For the second set of experiments, we follow the same procedure as above, but with a more diverse dataset for training and evaluation. Following Vinyals et al. (2015), we use (in addition to the WSJ), the OntoNotes corpus version 5 (Hovy et al., 2006), the English Web Treebank (Petrov and McDonald, 2012), and the updated and corrected Question Treebank (Judge et al., 2006). We train on the union of each corpora's training set and test on each domain separately. We refer to this setup as the "Treebank Union" setup.

In our semi-supervised experiments, we use the corpus from Chelba et al. (2013) as our source of unlabeled data. We process it with the Berkeley-Parser (Petrov et al., 2006), a latent variable constituency parser, and a reimplementation of ZPar (Zhang and Nivre, 2011), a transition-based parser with beam search. Both parsers are included as baselines in our evaluation. We select the first 10^7 tokens for which the two parsers agree as additional training data. For our tri-training experiments, we re-train the POS tagger using the POS tags assigned on the unlabeled data from the Berkeley constituency parser. This increases POS

Method	UAS	LAS	Beam
Graph-based			
Bohnet (2010)	92.88	90.71	n/a
Martins et al. (2013)	92.89	90.55	n/a
Zhang and McDonald (2014)	93.22	91.02	n/a
Transition-based			
⋆Zhang and Nivre (2011)	93.00	90.95	32
Bohnet and Kuhn (2012)	93.27	91.19	40
Chen and Manning (2014)	91.80	89.60	1
S-LSTM (Dyer et al., 2015)	93.20	90.90	1
Our Greedy	93.19	91.18	1
Our Perceptron	**93.99**	**92.05**	8
Tri-training			
⋆Zhang and Nivre (2011)	92.92	90.88	32
Our Greedy	93.46	91.49	1
Our Perceptron	**94.26**	**92.41**	8

Table 1: Final WSJ test set results. We compare our system to state-of-the-art graph-based and transition-based dependency parsers. ⋆ denotes our own re-implementation of the system so we could compare tri-training on a competitive baseline. All methods except Chen and Manning (2014) and Dyer et al. (2015) were run using predicted tags from our POS tagger. For reference, the accuracy of the Berkeley constituency parser (after conversion) is 93.61% UAS / 91.51% LAS.

Method	News	Web	QTB
Graph-based			
Bohnet (2010)	91.38	85.22	91.49
Martins et al. (2013)	91.13	85.04	91.54
Zhang and McDonald (2014)	91.48	85.59	90.69
Transition-based			
⋆Zhang and Nivre (2011)	91.15	85.24	**92.46**
Bohnet and Kuhn (2012)	91.69	85.33	92.21
Our Greedy	91.21	85.41	90.61
Our Perceptron (B=16)	**92.25**	**86.44**	92.06
Tri-training			
⋆Zhang and Nivre (2011)	91.46	85.51	91.36
Our Greedy	91.82	86.37	90.58
Our Perceptron (B=16)	**92.62**	**87.00**	**93.05**

Table 2: Final Treebank Union test set results. We report LAS only for brevity; see Appendix for full results. For these tri-training results, we sampled sentences to ensure the distribution of sentence lengths matched the distribution in the training set, which we found marginally improved the ZPar tri-training performance. For reference, the accuracy of the Berkeley constituency parser (after conversion) is 91.66% WSJ, 85.93% Web, and 93.45% QTB.

accuracy slightly to 97.57% on the WSJ.

4.2 Model Initialization & Hyperparameters

In all cases, we initialized $\mathbf{W}_i$ and β randomly using a Gaussian distribution with variance 10^{-4}. We used fixed initialization with $b_i = 0.2$, to ensure that most Relu units are activated during the initial rounds of training. We did not systematically compare this random scheme to others, but we found that it was sufficient for our purposes.

For the word embedding matrix $\mathbf{E}_{\text{word}}$, we initialized the parameters using pretrained word embeddings. We used the publicly available `word2vec`[2] tool (Mikolov et al., 2013) to learn CBOW embeddings following the sample configuration provided with the tool. For words not appearing in the unsupervised data and the special "NULL" etc. tokens, we used random initialization. In preliminary experiments we found no difference between training the word embeddings on 1 billion or 10 billion tokens. We therefore trained the word embeddings on the same corpus we used for tri-training (Chelba et al., 2013).

We set $D_{\text{word}} = 64$ and $D_{\text{tag}} = D_{\text{label}} = 32$ for embedding dimensions and $M_1 = M_2 = 2048$ hidden units in our final experiments. For the perceptron layer, we used $\phi(x, c) = [\mathbf{h}_1\ \mathbf{h}_2\ P(y)]$ (concatenation of all intermediate layers). All hyperparameters (including structure) were tuned using Section 24 of the WSJ only. When not tri-training, we used hyperparameters of $\gamma = 0.2$, $\eta_0 = 0.05$, $\mu = 0.9$, early stopping after roughly 16 hours of training time. With the tri-training data, we decreased $\eta_0 = 0.05$, increased $\gamma = 0.5$, and decreased the size of the network to $M_1 = 1024$, $M_2 = 256$ for run-time efficiency, and trained the network for approximately 4 days. For the Treebank Union setup, we set $M_1 = M_2 = 1024$ for the standard training set and for the tri-training setup.

4.3 Results

Table 1 shows our final results on the WSJ test set, and Table 2 shows the cross-domain results from the Treebank Union. We compare to the best dependency parsers in the literature. For (Chen and Manning, 2014) and (Dyer et al., 2015), we use reported results; the other baselines were run by Bernd Bohnet using version 3.3.0 of the Stanford dependencies and our predicted POS tags for all datasets to make comparisons as fair as possible. On the WSJ and Web tasks, our parser outperforms all dependency parsers in our comparison by a substantial margin. The Question (QTB) dataset is more sensitive to the smaller beam size we use in order to train the models in a reasonable time; if we increase to $B = 32$ at inference

[2]http://code.google.com/p/word2vec/

time only, our perceptron performance goes up to 92.29% LAS.

Since many of the baselines could not be directly compared to our semi-supervised approach, we re-implemented Zhang and Nivre (2011) and trained on the tri-training corpus. Although tri-training did help the baseline on the dev set (Figure 4), test set performance did not improve significantly. In contrast, it is quite exciting to see that after tri-training, even our greedy parser is more accurate than any of the baseline dependency parsers and competitive with the Berkeley-Parser used to generate the tri-training data. As expected, tri-training helps most dramatically to increase accuracy on the Treebank Union setup with diverse domains, yielding 0.4-1.0% absolute LAS improvement gains for our most accurate model.

Unfortunately we are not able to compare to several semi-supervised dependency parsers that achieve some of the highest reported accuracies on the WSJ, in particular Suzuki et al. (2009), Suzuki et al. (2011) and Chen et al. (2013). These parsers use the Yamada and Matsumoto (2003) dependency conversion and the accuracies are therefore not directly comparable. The highest of these is Suzuki et al. (2011), with a reported accuracy of 94.22% UAS. Even though the UAS is not directly comparable, it is typically similar, and this suggests that our model is competitive with some of the highest reported accuries for dependencies on WSJ.

5 Discussion

In this section, we investigate the contribution of the various components of our approach through ablation studies and other systematic experiments. We tune on Section 24, and use Section 22 for comparisons in order to not pollute the official test set (Section 23). We focus on UAS as we found the LAS scores to be strongly correlated. Unless otherwise specified, we use 200 hidden units in each layer to be able to run more ablative experiments in a reasonable amount of time.

5.1 Impact of Network Structure

In addition to initialization and hyperparameter tuning, there are several additional choices about model structure and size a practitioner faces when implementing a neural network model. We explore these questions and justify the particular choices we use in the following. Note that we do not use a beam for this analysis and therefore do not train the final perceptron layer. This is done in order to reduce training times and because the trends persist across settings.

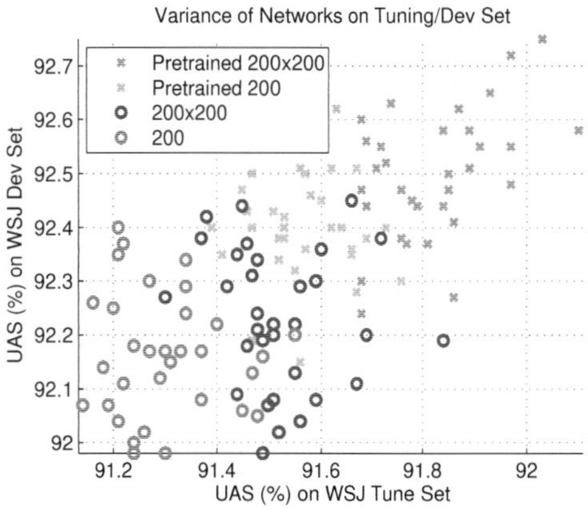

Figure 2: Effect of hidden layers and pre-training on variance of random restarts. Initialization was either completely random or initialized with `word2vec` embeddings ("Pretrained"), and either one or two hidden layers of size 200 were used ("200" vs "200x200"). Each point represents maximization over a small hyperparameter grid with early stopping based on WSJ tune set UAS score. $D_{\text{word}} = 64$, $D_{\text{tag}}, D_{\text{label}} = 16$.

Variance reduction with pre-trained embeddings. Since the learning problem is non-convex, different initializations of the parameters yield different solutions to the learning problem. Thus, for any given experiment, we ran multiple random restarts for every setting of our hyperparameters and picked the model that performed best using the held-out tune set. We found it important to allow the model to stop training early if tune set accuracy decreased.

We visualize the performance of 32 random restarts with one or two hidden layers and with and without pretrained word embeddings in Figure 2, and a summary of the figure in Table 3. While adding a second hidden layer results in a large gain on the tune set, there is no gain on the dev set if pre-trained embeddings are not used. In fact, while the overall UAS scores of the tune set and dev set are strongly correlated ($\rho = 0.64$, $p < 10^{-10}$), they are *not* significantly correlated if pre-trained embeddings are not used ($\rho = 0.12$, $p > 0.3$). This suggests that an additional benefit of pre-trained embeddings, aside from allowing learning to reach a more accurate solution, is to push learning towards a solution that generalizes to more data.

Pre	Hidden	WSJ §24 (Max)	WSJ §22
Y	200×200	92.10 ± 0.11	**92.58** ± 0.12
Y	200	91.76 ± 0.09	92.30 ± 0.10
N	200×200	91.84 ± 0.11	92.19 ± 0.13
N	200	91.55 ± 0.10	92.20 ± 0.12

Table 3: Impact of network architecture on UAS for greedy inference. We select the best model from 32 random restarts based on the tune set and show the resulting dev set accuracy. We also show the standard deviation across the 32 restarts.

# Hidden	64	128	256	512	1024	2048
1 Layer	91.73	92.27	92.48	92.73	92.74	**92.83**
2 Layers	91.89	92.40	92.71	92.70	92.96	**93.13**

Table 4: Increasing hidden layer size increases WSJ Dev UAS. Shown is the average WSJ Dev UAS across hyperparameter tuning and early stopping with 3 random restarts with a greedy model.

Diminishing returns with increasing embedding dimensions. For these experiments, we fixed one embedding type to a high value and reduced the dimensionality of all others to very small values. The results are plotted in Figure 3, suggesting larger embeddings do not significantly improve results. We also ran tri-training on a very compact model with $D_{\text{word}} = 8$ and $D_{\text{tag}} = D_{\text{label}} = 2$ ($8\times$ fewer parameters than our full model) which resulted in 92.33% UAS accuracy on the dev set. This is comparable to the full model without tri-training, suggesting that more training data can compensate for fewer parameters.

Increasing hidden units yields large gains. For these experiments, we fixed the embedding sizes $D_{\text{word}} = 64$, $D_{\text{tag}} = D_{\text{label}} = 32$ and tried increasing and decreasing the dimensionality of the hidden layers on a logarthmic scale. Improvements in accuracy did not appear to saturate even with increasing the number of hidden units by an order of magnitude, though the network became too slow to train effectively past $M = 2048$. These results suggest that there are still gains to be made by increasing the efficiency of larger networks, even for greedy shift-reduce parsers.

5.2 Impact of Structured Perceptron

We now turn our attention to the importance of structured perceptron training as well as the impact of different latent representations.

Bias reduction through structured training. To evaluate the impact of structured training, we compare using the estimates $P(y)$ from the neural network directly for beam search to using the activations from all layers as features in the structured perceptron. Using the probability estimates directly is very similar to Ratnaparkhi (1997), where a maximum-entropy model was used to model the distribution over possible actions at each parser state, and beam search was used to search for the highest probability parse. A known problem with beam search in this setting is the label-bias problem. Table 5 shows the impact of using structured perceptron training over using the softmax function during beam search as a function of the beam size used. For reference, our reimplementation of Zhang and Nivre (2011) is trained equivalently for each setting. We also show the impact on beam size when tri-training is used. Although the beam does marginally improve accuracy for the softmax model, much greater gains are achieved when perceptron training is used.

Beam	1	2	4	8	16	32
WSJ Only						
ZN'11	90.55	91.36	92.54	92.62	92.88	**93.09**
Softmax	92.74	93.07	93.16	**93.25**	93.24	93.24
Perceptron	92.73	93.06	93.40	93.47	93.50	**93.58**
Tri-training						
ZN'11	91.65	92.37	**93.37**	93.24	93.21	93.18
Softmax	93.71	93.82	93.86	**93.87**	93.87	93.87
Perceptron	93.69	94.00	94.23	**94.33**	94.31	94.32

Table 5: Beam search always yields significant gains but using perceptron training provides even larger benefits, especially for the tri-trained neural network model. The best result for each model is highlighted in bold.

$\phi(x, c)$	WSJ Only	Tri-training
$[\mathbf{h}_2]$	93.16	93.93
$[P(y)]$	93.26	93.80
$[\mathbf{h}_1\ \mathbf{h}_2]$	93.33	93.95
$[\mathbf{h}_1\ \mathbf{h}_2\ P(y)]$	**93.47**	**94.33**

Table 6: Utilizing all intermediate representations improves performance on the WSJ dev set. All results are with $B = 8$.

Using all hidden layers crucial for structured perceptron. We also investigated the impact of connecting the final perceptron layer to all prior hidden layers (Table 6). Our results suggest that all intermediate layers of the network are indeed discriminative. Nonetheless, aggregating all of their activations proved to be the most effective representation for the structured perceptron. This suggests that the representations learned by the network collectively contain the information re-

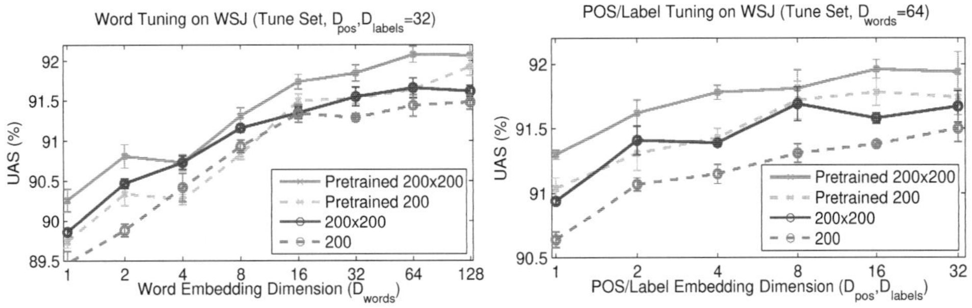

Figure 3: Effect of embedding dimensions on the WSJ tune set.

quired to reduce the bias of the model, but not when filtered through the softmax layer. Finally, we also experimented with connecting both hidden layers to the softmax layer during backpropagation training, but we found this did not significantly affect the performance of the greedy model.

5.3 Impact of Tri-Training

To evaluate the impact of the tri-training approach, we compared to up-training with the Berkely-Parser (Petrov et al., 2006) alone. The results are summarized in Figure 4 for the greedy and perceptron neural net models as well as our reimplementated Zhang and Nivre (2011) baseline.

For our neural network model, training on the output of the BerkeleyParser yields only modest gains, while training on the data where the two parsers agree produces significantly better results. This was especially pronounced for the greedy models: after tri-training, the greedy neural network model surpasses the BerkeleyParser in accuracy. It is also interesting to note that up-training improved results far more than tri-training for the baseline. We speculate that this is due to the a lack of diversity in the tri-training data for this model, since the same baseline model was intersected with the BerkeleyParser to generate the tri-training data.

5.4 Error Analysis

Regardless of tri-training, using the structured perceptron improved error rates on some of the common and difficult labels: `ROOT`, `ccomp`, `cc`, `conj`, and `nsubj` all improved by >1%. We inspected the learned perceptron weights **v** for the softmax probabilities $P(y)$ (see Appendix) and found that the perceptron reweights the softmax probabilities based on common confusions; e.g. a strong negative weight for the action RIGHT(`ccomp`) given the softmax model outputs RIGHT(`conj`). Note

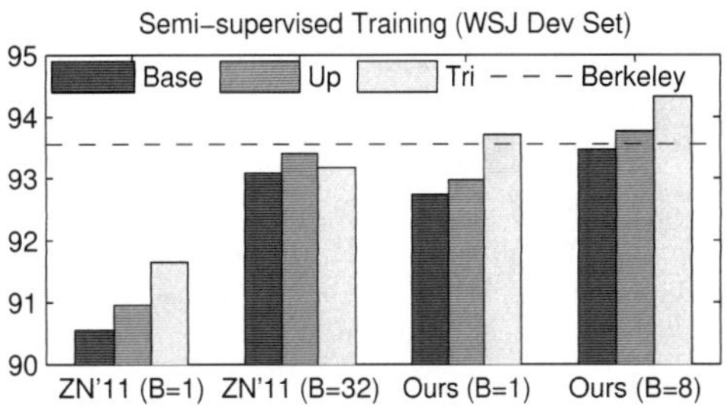

Figure 4: Semi-supervised training with 10^7 additional tokens, showing that tri-training gives significant improvements over up-training for our neural net model.

that this trend did not hold when $\phi(x, c) = [P(y)]$; without the hidden layer, the perceptron was not able to reweight the softmax probabilities to account for the greedy model's biases.

6 Conclusion

We presented a new state of the art in dependency parsing: a transition-based neural network parser trained with the structured perceptron and ASGD. We then combined this approach with unlabeled data and tri-training to further push state-of-the-art in semi-supervised dependency parsing. Nonetheless, our ablative analysis suggests that further gains are possible simply by scaling up our system to even larger representations. In future work, we will apply our method to other languages, explore end-to-end training of the system using structured learning, and scale up the method to larger datasets and network structures.

Acknowledgements

We would like to thank Bernd Bohnet for training his parsers and TurboParser on our setup. This paper benefitted tremendously from discussions with Ryan McDonald, Greg Coppola, Emily Pitler and Fernando Pereira. Finally, we are grateful to all members of the Google Parsing Team.

References

Bernd Bohnet and Jonas Kuhn. 2012. The best of both worlds: a graph-based completion model for transition-based parsers. In *Proc. EACL*, pages 77–87.

Bernd Bohnet. 2010. Top accuracy and fast dependency parsing is not a contradiction. In *Proc. 23rd International Conference on Computational Linguistics (Coling 2010)*, pages 89–97.

Léon Bottou. 2010. Large-scale machine learning with stochastic gradient descent. In *Proc. COMPSTAT*, pages 177–186.

Sabine Buchholz and Erwin Marsi. 2006. Conll-x shared task on multilingual dependency parsing. In *Proc. CoNLL*, pages 149–164.

Ciprian Chelba, Tomas Mikolov, Mike Schuster, Qi Ge, Thorsten Brants, and Phillipp Koehn. 2013. One billion word benchmark for measuring progress in statistical language modeling. *CoRR*.

Danqi Chen and Christopher D. Manning. 2014. A fast and accurate dependency parser using neural networks. In *Proc. EMNLP*, pages 740–750.

Wenliang Chen, Min Zhang, and Yue Zhang. 2013. Semi-supervised feature transformation for dependency parsing. In *Proc. 2013 EMNLP*, pages 1303–1313.

Michael Collins and Brian Roark. 2004. Incremental parsing with the perceptron algorithm. In *Proc. ACL, Main Volume*, pages 111–118, Barcelona, Spain.

Marie-Catherine De Marneffe, Bill MacCartney, and Christopher D. Manning. 2006. Generating typed dependency parses from phrase structure parses. In *Proc. LREC*, pages 449–454.

Trinh Minh Tri Do and Thierry Artires. 2010. Neural conditional random fields. In *AISTATS*, volume 9, pages 177–184.

Chris Dyer, Miguel Ballesteros, Wang Ling, Austin Matthews, and Noah A. Smith. 2015. Transition-based dependency parsing with stack long short-term memory. In *Proc. ACL*.

James Henderson. 2004. Discriminative training of a neural network statistical parser. In *Proc. ACL, Main Volume*, pages 95–102.

Geoffrey E. Hinton. 2012. A practical guide to training restricted boltzmann machines. In *Neural Networks: Tricks of the Trade (2nd ed.)*, Lecture Notes in Computer Science, pages 599–619. Springer.

Eduard Hovy, Mitchell Marcus, Martha Palmer, Lance Ramshaw, and Ralph Weischedel. 2006. Ontonotes: The 90% solution. In *Proc. HLT-NAACL*, pages 57–60.

Zhongqiang Huang and Mary Harper. 2009. Self-training PCFG grammars with latent annotations across languages. In *Proc. 2009 EMNLP*, pages 832–841, Singapore.

John Judge, Aoife Cahill, and Josef van Genabith. 2006. Questionbank: Creating a corpus of parse-annotated questions. In *Proc. ACL*, pages 497–504.

Terry Koo, Xavier Carreras, and Michael Collins. 2008. Simple semi-supervised dependency parsing. In *Proc. ACL-HLT*, pages 595–603.

Alex Krizhevsky, Ilya Sutskever, and Geoffrey E. Hinton. 2012. Imagenet classification with deep convolutional neural networks. In *Proc. NIPS*, pages 1097–1105.

Zhenghua Li, Min Zhang, and Wenliang Chen. 2014. Ambiguity-aware ensemble training for semi-supervised dependency parsing. In *Proc. ACL*, pages 457–467.

Mitchell P. Marcus, Beatrice Santorini, and Mary Ann Marcinkiewicz. 1993. Building a large annotated corpus of English: The Penn Treebank. *Computational Linguistics*, 19(2):313–330.

Andre Martins, Miguel Almeida, and Noah A. Smith. 2013. Turning on the turbo: Fast third-order non-projective turbo parsers. In *Proc. ACL*, pages 617–622.

David McClosky, Eugene Charniak, and Mark Johnson. 2006. Effective self-training for parsing. In *Proc. HLT-NAACL*, pages 152–159.

Ryan McDonald, Joakim Nivre, Yvonne Quirmbach-Brundage, Yoav Goldberg, Dipanjan Das, Kuzman Ganchev, Keith Hall, Slav Petrov, Hao Zhang, Oscar Täckström, Claudia Bedini, Núria Bertomeu Castelló, and Jungmee Lee. 2013. Universal dependency annotation for multilingual parsing. In *Proc. ACL*, pages 92–97.

Tomas Mikolov, Kai Chen, Greg Corrado, and Jeffrey Dean. 2013. Efficient estimation of word representations in vector space. *CoRR*, abs/1301.3781.

Vinod Nair and Geoffrey E. Hinton. 2010. Rectified linear units improve restricted boltzmann machines. In *Proc. 27th ICML*, pages 807–814.

Joakim Nivre, Johan Hall, Sandra Kübler, Ryan McDonald, Jens Nilsson, Sebastian Riedel, and Deniz Yuret. 2007. The CoNLL 2007 shared task on dependency parsing. In *Proc. CoNLL*, pages 915–932.

Joakim Nivre. 2004. Incrementality in deterministic dependency parsing. In *Proc. ACL Workshop on Incremental Parsing*, pages 50–57.

Joakim Nivre. 2008. Algorithms for deterministic incremental dependency parsing. *Computational Linguistics*, 34(4):513–553.

Jian Peng, Liefeng Bo, and Jinbo Xu. 2009. Conditional neural fields. In *Proc. NIPS*, pages 1419–1427.

Slav Petrov and Ryan McDonald. 2012. Overview of the 2012 shared task on parsing the web. Notes of the First Workshop on Syntactic Analysis of Non-Canonical Language (SANCL).

Slav Petrov, Leon Barrett, Romain Thibaux, and Dan Klein. 2006. Learning accurate, compact, and interpretable tree annotation. In *Proc. ACL*, pages 433–440.

Slav Petrov, Pi-Chuan Chang, Michael Ringgaard, and Hiyan Alshawi. 2010. Uptraining for accurate deterministic question parsing. In *Proc. EMNLP*, pages 705–713.

Adwait Ratnaparkhi. 1997. A linear observed time statistical parser based on maximum entropy models. In *Proc. EMNLP*, pages 1–10.

Jun Suzuki, Hideki Isozaki, Xavier Carreras, and Michael Collins. 2009. An empirical study of semi-supervised structured conditional models for dependency parsing. In *Proc. 2009 EMNLP*, pages 551–560.

Jun Suzuki, Hideki Isozaki, and Masaaki Nagata. 2011. Learning condensed feature representations from large unsupervised data sets for supervised learning. In *Proc. ACL-HLT*, pages 636–641.

Ivan Titov and James Henderson. 2007. Fast and robust multilingual dependency parsing with a generative latent variable model. In *Proc. EMNLP*, pages 947–951.

Ivan Titov and James Henderson. 2010. A latent variable model for generative dependency parsing. In *Trends in Parsing Technology*, pages 35–55. Springer.

Kristina Toutanova, Dan Klein, Christopher D. Manning, and Yoram Singer. 2003. Feature-rich part-of-speech tagging with a cyclic dependency network. In *NAACL*.

Oriol Vinyals, Lukasz Kaiser, Terry Koo, Slav Petrov, Ilya Sutskever, and Geoffrey E. Hinton. 2015. Grammar as a foreign language. *arXiv:1412.7449*.

Hiroyasu Yamada and Yuji Matsumoto. 2003. Statistical dependency analysis with support vector machines. In *Proc. IWPT*, pages 195–206.

Matthew D. Zeiler, Marc'Aurelio Ranzato, Rajat Monga, Mark Z. Mao, K. Yang, Quoc Viet Le, Patrick Nguyen, Andrew W. Senior, Vincent Vanhoucke, Jeffrey Dean, and Geoffrey E. Hinton. 2013. On rectified linear units for speech processing. In *IEEE International Conference on Acoustics, Speech and Signal Processing*, pages 3517–3521.

Yue Zhang and Stephen Clark. 2008. A tale of two parsers: investigating and combining graph-based and transition-based dependency parsing using beam-search. In *Proc. EMNLP*, pages 562–571.

Hao Zhang and Ryan McDonald. 2014. Enforcing structural diversity in cube-pruned dependency parsing. In *Proc. ACL*, pages 656–661.

Yue Zhang and Joakim Nivre. 2011. Transition-based dependency parsing with rich non-local features. In *Proc. ACL-HLT*, pages 188–193.

Hao Zhou, Yue Zhang, and Jiajun Chen. 2015. A neural probabilistic structured-prediction model for transition-based dependency parsing. In *Proc. ACL*.

Transition-Based Dependency Parsing with Stack Long Short-Term Memory

Chris Dyer[♣♠] **Miguel Ballesteros**[◇♠] **Wang Ling**[♠] **Austin Matthews**[♠] **Noah A. Smith**[♠]
[♣]Marianas Labs [◇]NLP Group, Pompeu Fabra University [♠]Carnegie Mellon University
chris@marianaslabs.com, miguel.ballesteros@upf.edu,
{lingwang,austinma,nasmith}@cs.cmu.edu

Abstract

We propose a technique for learning representations of parser states in transition-based dependency parsers. Our primary innovation is a new control structure for sequence-to-sequence neural networks—the stack LSTM. Like the conventional stack data structures used in transition-based parsing, elements can be pushed to or popped from the top of the stack in constant time, but, in addition, an LSTM maintains a continuous space embedding of the stack contents. This lets us formulate an efficient parsing model that captures three facets of a parser's state: (i) unbounded look-ahead into the buffer of incoming words, (ii) the complete history of actions taken by the parser, and (iii) the complete contents of the stack of partially built tree fragments, including their internal structures. Standard backpropagation techniques are used for training and yield state-of-the-art parsing performance.

1 Introduction

Transition-based dependency parsing formalizes the parsing problem as a series of decisions that read words sequentially from a buffer and combine them incrementally into syntactic structures (Yamada and Matsumoto, 2003; Nivre, 2003; Nivre, 2004). This formalization is attractive since the number of operations required to build any projective parse tree is linear in the length of the sentence, making transition-based parsing computationally efficient relative to graph- and grammar-based formalisms. The challenge in transition-based parsing is modeling which action should be taken in each of the unboundedly many states encountered as the parser progresses.

This challenge has been addressed by development of alternative transition sets that simplify the modeling problem by making better attachment decisions (Nivre, 2007; Nivre, 2008; Nivre, 2009; Choi and McCallum, 2013; Bohnet and Nivre, 2012), through feature engineering (Zhang and Nivre, 2011; Ballesteros and Nivre, 2014; Chen et al., 2014; Ballesteros and Bohnet, 2014) and more recently using neural networks (Chen and Manning, 2014; Stenetorp, 2013).

We extend this last line of work by learning representations of the parser state that are sensitive to the complete contents of the parser's state: that is, the complete input buffer, the complete history of parser actions, and the complete contents of the stack of partially constructed syntactic structures. This "global" sensitivity to the state contrasts with previous work in transition-based dependency parsing that uses only a narrow view of the parsing state when constructing representations (e.g., just the next few incoming words, the head words of the top few positions in the stack, etc.). Although our parser integrates large amounts of information, the representation used for prediction at each time step is constructed incrementally, and therefore parsing and training time remain linear in the length of the input sentence. The technical innovation that lets us do this is a variation of recurrent neural networks with long short-term memory units (LSTMs) which we call **stack LSTMs** (§2), and which support both reading (pushing) and "forgetting" (popping) inputs.

Our parsing model uses three stack LSTMs: one representing the input, one representing the stack of partial syntactic trees, and one representing the history of parse actions to encode parser states (§3). Since the stack of partial syntactic trees may contain both individual tokens and partial syntactic structures, representations of individual tree fragments are computed compositionally with recursive (i.e., similar to Socher et al., 2014) neural networks. The parameters are learned with backpropagation (§4), and we obtain state-of-the-art results on Chinese and English dependency parsing tasks (§5).

Proceedings of the 53rd Annual Meeting of the Association for Computational Linguistics and the 7th International Joint Conference on Natural Language Processing, pages 334–343,
Beijing, China, July 26-31, 2015.

2 Stack LSTMs

In this section we provide a brief review of LSTMs (§2.1) and then define stack LSTMs (§2.2).

Notation. We follow the convention that vectors are written with lowercase, boldface letters (e.g., $\mathbf{v}$ or $\mathbf{v}_w$); matrices are written with uppercase, boldface letters (e.g., $\mathbf{M}$, $\mathbf{M}_a$, or $\mathbf{M}_{ab}$), and scalars are written as lowercase letters (e.g., s or q_z). Structured objects such as sequences of discrete symbols are written with lowercase, bold, italic letters (e.g., $\boldsymbol{w}$ refers to a sequence of input words). Discussion of dimensionality is deferred to the experiments section below (§5).

2.1 Long Short-Term Memories

LSTMs are a variant of recurrent neural networks (RNNs) designed to cope with the vanishing gradient problem inherent in RNNs (Hochreiter and Schmidhuber, 1997; Graves, 2013). RNNs read a vector $\mathbf{x}_t$ at each time step and compute a new (hidden) state $\mathbf{h}_t$ by applying a linear map to the concatenation of the previous time step's state $\mathbf{h}_{t-1}$ and the input, and passing this through a logistic sigmoid nonlinearity. Although RNNs can, in principle, model long-range dependencies, training them is difficult in practice since the repeated application of a squashing nonlinearity at each step results in an exponential decay in the error signal through time. LSTMs address this with an extra memory "cell" ($\mathbf{c}_t$) that is constructed as a linear combination of the previous state and signal from the input.

LSTM cells process inputs with three multiplicative gates which control what proportion of the current input to pass into the memory cell ($\mathbf{i}_t$) and what proportion of the previous memory cell to "forget" ($\mathbf{f}_t$). The updated value of the memory cell after an input $\mathbf{x}_t$ is computed as follows:

$$\begin{aligned}
\mathbf{i}_t &= \sigma(\mathbf{W}_{ix}\mathbf{x}_t + \mathbf{W}_{ih}\mathbf{h}_{t-1} + \mathbf{W}_{ic}\mathbf{c}_{t-1} + \mathbf{b}_i) \\
\mathbf{f}_t &= \sigma(\mathbf{W}_{fx}\mathbf{x}_t + \mathbf{W}_{fh}\mathbf{h}_{t-1} + \mathbf{W}_{fc}\mathbf{c}_{t-1} + \mathbf{b}_f) \\
\mathbf{c}_t &= \mathbf{f}_t \odot \mathbf{c}_{t-1} + \\
&\qquad \mathbf{i}_t \odot \tanh(\mathbf{W}_{cx}\mathbf{x}_t + \mathbf{W}_{ch}\mathbf{h}_{t-1} + \mathbf{b}_c),
\end{aligned}$$

where σ is the component-wise logistic sigmoid function, and $\odot$ is the component-wise (Hadamard) product.

The value $\mathbf{h}_t$ of the LSTM at each time step is controlled by a third gate ($\mathbf{o}_t$) that is applied to the result of the application of a nonlinearity to the memory cell contents:

$$\begin{aligned}
\mathbf{o}_t &= \sigma(\mathbf{W}_{ox}\mathbf{x}_t + \mathbf{W}_{oh}\mathbf{h}_{t-1} + \mathbf{W}_{oc}\mathbf{c}_t + \mathbf{b}_o) \\
\mathbf{h}_t &= \mathbf{o}_t \odot \tanh(\mathbf{c}_t).
\end{aligned}$$

To improve the representational capacity of LSTMs (and RNNs generally), LSTMs can be stacked in "layers" (Pascanu et al., 2014). In these architectures, the input LSTM at higher layers at time t is the value of $\mathbf{h}_t$ computed by the lower layer (and $\mathbf{x}_t$ is the input at the lowest layer).

Finally, output is produced at each time step from the $\mathbf{h}_t$ value at the top layer:

$$\mathbf{y}_t = g(\mathbf{h}_t),$$

where g is an arbitrary differentiable function.

2.2 Stack Long Short-Term Memories

Conventional LSTMs model sequences in a left-to-right order.[1] Our innovation here is to augment the LSTM with a "stack pointer." Like a conventional LSTM, new inputs are always added in the right-most position, but in stack LSTMs, the current location of the stack pointer determines which cell in the LSTM provides $\mathbf{c}_{t-1}$ and $\mathbf{h}_{t-1}$ when computing the new memory cell contents.

In addition to adding elements to the end of the sequence, the stack LSTM provides a pop operation which moves the stack pointer to the previous element (i.e., the previous element that was extended, not necessarily the right-most element). Thus, the LSTM can be understood as a stack implemented so that contents are never overwritten, that is, push always adds a new entry at the end of the list that contains a back-pointer to the previous top, and pop only updates the stack pointer.[2] This control structure is schematized in Figure 1.

By querying the output vector to which the stack pointer points (i.e., the $\mathbf{h}_{\text{TOP}}$), a continuous-space "summary" of the contents of the current stack configuration is available. We refer to this value as the "stack summary."

What does the stack summary look like? Intuitively, elements near the top of the stack will

[1]Ours is not the first deviation from a strict left-to-right order: previous variations include bidirectional LSTMs (Graves and Schmidhuber, 2005) and multidimensional LSTMs (Graves et al., 2007).

[2]Goldberg et al. (2013) propose a similar stack construction to prevent stack operations from invalidating existing references to the stack in a beam-search parser that must (efficiently) maintain a priority queue of stacks.

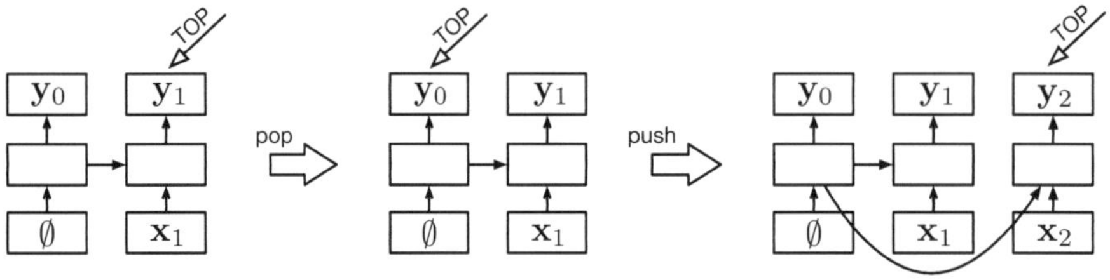

Figure 1: A stack LSTM extends a conventional left-to-right LSTM with the addition of a stack pointer (notated as TOP in the figure). This figure shows three configurations: a stack with a single element (left), the result of a pop operation to this (middle), and then the result of applying a push operation (right). The boxes in the lowest rows represent stack contents, which are the inputs to the LSTM, the upper rows are the outputs of the LSTM (in this paper, only the output pointed to by TOP is ever accessed), and the middle rows are the memory cells (the $\mathbf{c}_t$'s and $\mathbf{h}_t$'s) and gates. Arrows represent function applications (usually affine transformations followed by a nonlinearity), refer to §2.1 for specifics.

influence the representation of the stack. However, the LSTM has the flexibility to learn to extract information from arbitrary points in the stack (Hochreiter and Schmidhuber, 1997).

Although this architecture is to the best of our knowledge novel, it is reminiscent of the Recurrent Neural Network Pushdown Automaton (NNPDA) of Das et al. (1992), which added an external stack memory to an RNN. However, our architecture provides an embedding of the complete contents of the stack, whereas theirs made only the top of the stack visible to the RNN.

3 Dependency Parser

We now turn to the problem of learning representations of dependency parsers. We preserve the standard data structures of a transition-based dependency parser, namely a buffer of words (B) to be processed and a stack (S) of partially constructed syntactic elements. Each stack element is augmented with a continuous-space vector embedding representing a word and, in the case of S, any of its syntactic dependents. Additionally, we introduce a third stack (A) to represent the history of actions taken by the parser.[3] Each of these stacks is associated with a stack LSTM that provides an encoding of their current contents. The full architecture is illustrated in Figure 3, and we will review each of the components in turn.

3.1 Parser Operation

The dependency parser is initialized by pushing the words and their representations (we discuss word representations below in §3.3) of the input sentence in reverse order onto B such that the first word is at the top of B and the ROOT symbol is at the bottom, and S and A each contain an empty-stack token. At each time step, the parser computes a composite representation of the stack states (as determined by the current configurations of B, S, and A) and uses that to predict an action to take, which updates the stacks. Processing completes when B is empty (except for the empty-stack symbol), S contains two elements, one representing the full parse tree headed by the ROOT symbol and the other the empty-stack symbol, and A is the history of operations taken by the parser.

The parser state representation at time t, which we write $\mathbf{p}_t$, which is used to is determine the transition to take, is defined as follows:

$$\mathbf{p}_t = \max\left\{\mathbf{0}, \mathbf{W}[\mathbf{s}_t; \mathbf{b}_t; \mathbf{a}_t] + \mathbf{d}\right\},$$

where $\mathbf{W}$ is a learned parameter matrix, $\mathbf{b}_t$ is the stack LSTM encoding of the input buffer B, $\mathbf{s}_t$ is the stack LSTM encoding of S, $\mathbf{a}_t$ is the stack LSTM encoding of A, $\mathbf{d}$ is a bias term, then passed through a component-wise rectified linear unit (ReLU) nonlinearity (Glorot et al., 2011).[4]

Finally, the parser state $\mathbf{p}_t$ is used to compute

[3]The A stack is only ever pushed to; our use of a stack here is purely for implementational and expository convenience.

[4]In preliminary experiments, we tried several nonlinearities and found ReLU to work slightly better than the others.

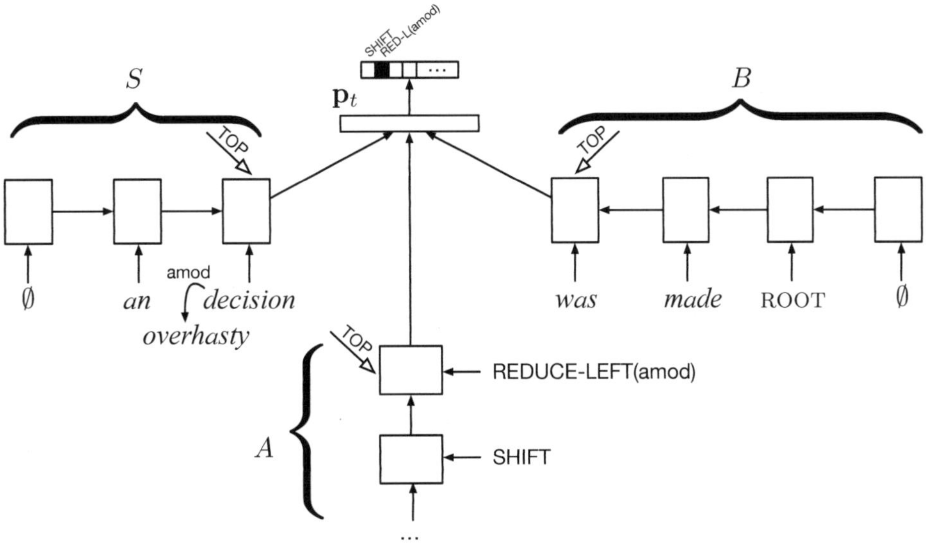

Figure 2: Parser state computation encountered while parsing the sentence "*an overhasty decision was made*." Here S designates the stack of partially constructed dependency subtrees and its LSTM encoding; B is the buffer of words remaining to be processed and its LSTM encoding; and A is the stack representing the history of actions taken by the parser. These are linearly transformed, passed through a ReLU nonlinearity to produce the parser state embedding $\mathbf{p}_t$. An affine transformation of this embedding is passed to a softmax layer to give a distribution over parsing decisions that can be taken.

the probability of the parser action at time t as:

$$p(z_t \mid \mathbf{p}_t) = \frac{\exp\left(\mathbf{g}_{z_t}^\top \mathbf{p}_t + q_{z_t}\right)}{\sum_{z' \in \mathcal{A}(S,B)} \exp\left(\mathbf{g}_{z'}^\top \mathbf{p}_t + q_{z'}\right)},$$

where $\mathbf{g}_z$ is a column vector representing the (output) embedding of the parser action z, and q_z is a bias term for action z. The set $\mathcal{A}(S, B)$ represents the valid actions that may be taken given the current contents of the stack and buffer.[5] Since $\mathbf{p}_t = f(\mathbf{s}_t, \mathbf{b}_t, \mathbf{a}_t)$ encodes information about all previous decisions made by the parser, the chain rule may be invoked to write the probability of any valid sequence of parse actions $\boldsymbol{z}$ conditional on the input as:

$$p(\boldsymbol{z} \mid \boldsymbol{w}) = \prod_{t=1}^{|\boldsymbol{z}|} p(z_t \mid \mathbf{p}_t). \tag{1}$$

3.2 Transition Operations

Our parser is based on the arc-standard transition inventory (Nivre, 2004), given in Figure 3.

[5]In general, $\mathcal{A}(S, B)$ is the complete set of parser actions discussed in §3.2, but in some cases not all actions are available. For example, when S is empty and words remain in B, a SHIFT operation is obligatory (Sartorio et al., 2013).

Why arc-standard? Arc-standard transitions parse a sentence from left to right, using a stack to store partially built syntactic structures and a buffer that keeps the incoming tokens to be parsed. The parsing algorithm chooses an action at each configuration by means of a score. In arc-standard parsing, the dependency tree is constructed bottom-up, because right-dependents of a head are only attached after the subtree under the dependent is fully parsed. Since our parser recursively computes representations of tree fragments, this construction order guarantees that once a syntactic structure has been used to modify a head, the algorithm will not try to find another head for the dependent structure. This means we can evaluate composed representations of tree fragments incrementally; we discuss our strategy for this below (§3.4).

3.3 Token Embeddings and OOVs

To represent each input token, we concatenate three vectors: a learned vector representation for each word type ($\mathbf{w}$); a fixed vector representation from a neural language model ($\tilde{\mathbf{w}}_{\text{LM}}$), and a learned representation ($\mathbf{t}$) of the POS tag of the token, provided as auxiliary input to the parser. A

$\textbf{Stack}_t$	$\textbf{Buffer}_t$	Action	$\textbf{Stack}_{t+1}$	$\textbf{Buffer}_{t+1}$	Dependency
$(\mathbf{u}, u), (\mathbf{v}, v), S$	B	REDUCE-RIGHT(r)	$(g_r(\mathbf{u}, \mathbf{v}), u), S$	B	$u \xrightarrow{r} v$
$(\mathbf{u}, u), (\mathbf{v}, v), S$	B	REDUCE-LEFT(r)	$(g_r(\mathbf{v}, \mathbf{u}), v), S$	B	$u \xleftarrow{r} v$
S	$(\mathbf{u}, u), B$	SHIFT	$(\mathbf{u}, u), S$	B	—

Figure 3: Parser transitions indicating the action applied to the stack and buffer and the resulting stack and buffer states. Bold symbols indicate (learned) embeddings of words and relations, script symbols indicate the corresponding words and relations.

linear map ($\mathbf{V}$) is applied to the resulting vector and passed through a component-wise ReLU,

$$\mathbf{x} = \max\left\{\mathbf{0}, \mathbf{V}[\mathbf{w}; \tilde{\mathbf{w}}_{\text{LM}}; \mathbf{t}] + \mathbf{b}\right\}.$$

This mapping can be shown schematically as in Figure 4.

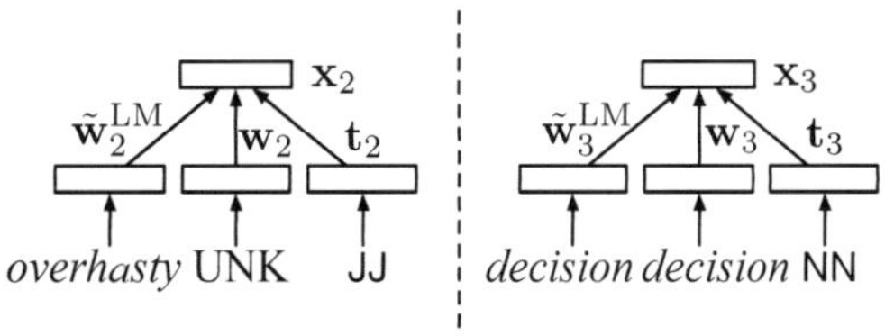

Figure 4: Token embedding of the words *decision*, which is present in both the parser's training data and the language model data, and *overhasty*, an adjective that is not present in the parser's training data but is present in the LM data.

This architecture lets us deal flexibly with out-of-vocabulary words—both those that are OOV in both the very limited parsing data but present in the pretraining LM, and words that are OOV in both. To ensure we have estimates of the OOVs in the parsing training data, we stochastically replace (with $p = 0.5$) each singleton word type in the parsing training data with the UNK token in each training iteration.

Pretrained word embeddings. A veritable cottage industry exists for creating word embeddings, meaning numerous pretraining options for $\tilde{\mathbf{w}}_{\text{LM}}$ are available. However, for syntax modeling problems, embedding approaches which discard order perform less well (Bansal et al., 2014); therefore we used a variant of the skip n-gram model introduced by Ling et al. (2015), named "structured skip n-gram," where a different set of parameters is used to predict each context word depending on its position relative to the target word. The hyperparameters of the model are the same as in the skip n-gram model defined in word2vec (Mikolov et al., 2013), and we set the window size to 5, used a negative sampling rate to 10, and ran 5 epochs through unannotated corpora described in §5.1.

3.4 Composition Functions

Recursive neural network models enable complex phrases to be represented compositionally in terms of their parts and the relations that link them (Socher et al., 2011; Socher et al., 2013c; Hermann and Blunsom, 2013; Socher et al., 2013b). We follow this previous line of work in embedding dependency tree fragments that are present in the stack S in the same vector space as the token embeddings discussed above.

A particular challenge here is that a syntactic head may, in general, have an arbitrary number of dependents. To simplify the parameterization of our composition function, we combine head-modifier pairs one at a time, building up more complicated structures in the order they are "reduced" in the parser, as illustrated in Figure 5. Each node in this expanded syntactic tree has a value computed as a function of its three arguments: the syntactic head ($\mathbf{h}$), the dependent ($\mathbf{d}$), and the syntactic relation being satisfied ($\mathbf{r}$). We define this by concatenating the vector embeddings of the head, dependent and relation, applying a linear operator and a component-wise non-linearity as follows:

$$\mathbf{c} = \tanh\left(\mathbf{U}[\mathbf{h}; \mathbf{d}; \mathbf{r}] + \mathbf{e}\right).$$

For the relation vector, we use an embedding of the parser action that was applied to construct the relation (i.e., the syntactic relation paired with the direction of attachment).

4 Training Procedure

We trained our parser to maximize the conditional log-likelihood (Eq. 1) of treebank parses given sentences. Our implementation constructs a computation graph for each sentence and runs forward- and backpropagation to obtain the gradients of this

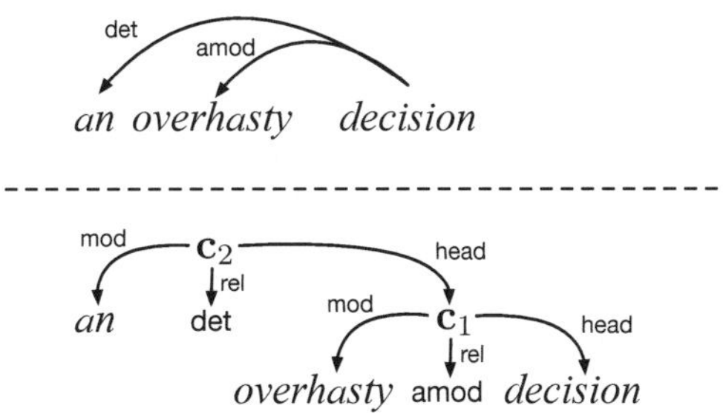

Figure 5: The representation of a dependency subtree (above) is computed by recursively applying composition functions to $\langle$head, modifier, relation$\rangle$ triples. In the case of multiple dependents of a single head, the recursive branching order is imposed by the order of the parser's reduce operations (below).

objective with respect to the model parameters. The computations for a single parsing model were run on a single thread on a CPU. Using the dimensions discussed in the next section, we required between 8 and 12 hours to reach convergence on a held-out dev set.[6]

Parameter optimization was performed using stochastic gradient descent with an initial learning rate of $\eta_0 = 0.1$, and the learning rate was updated on each pass through the training data as $\eta_t = \eta_0/(1 + \rho t)$, with $\rho = 0.1$ and where t is the number of epochs completed. No momentum was used. To mitigate the effects of "exploding" gradients, we clipped the ℓ_2 norm of the gradient to 5 before applying the weight update rule (Sutskever et al., 2014; Graves, 2013). An ℓ_2 penalty of 1×10^{-6} was applied to all weights.

Matrix and vector parameters were initialized with uniform samples in $\pm\sqrt{6/(r + c)}$, where r and c were the number of rows and columns in the structure (Glorot and Bengio, 2010).

Dimensionality. The full version of our parsing model sets dimensionalities as follows. LSTM hidden states are of size 100, and we use two layers of LSTMs for each stack. Embeddings of the parser actions used in the composition functions have 16 dimensions, and the output embedding size is 20 dimensions. Pretained word embeddings have 100 dimensions (English) and 80 dimensions (Chinese), and the learned word embeddings have 32 dimensions. Part of speech embeddings have 12 dimensions.

These dimensions were chosen based on intuitively reasonable values (words should have higher dimensionality than parsing actions, POS tags, and relations; LSTM states should be relatively large), and it was confirmed on development data that they performed well.[7] Future work might more carefully optimize these parameters; our reported architecture strikes a balance between minimizing computational expense and finding solutions that work.

5 Experiments

We applied our parsing model and several variations of it to two parsing tasks and report results below.

5.1 Data

We used the same data setup as Chen and Manning (2014), namely an English and a Chinese parsing task. This baseline configuration was chosen since they likewise used a neural parameterization to predict actions in an arc-standard transition-based parser.

- For English, we used the Stanford Dependencency (SD) treebank (de Marneffe et al., 2006) used in (Chen and Manning, 2014) which is the closest model published, with the same splits.[8] The part-of-speech tags are predicted by using the Stanford Tagger (Toutanova et al., 2003) with an accuracy of 97.3%. This treebank contains a negligible amount of non-projective arcs (Chen and Manning, 2014).

- For Chinese, we use the Penn Chinese Treebank 5.1 (CTB5) following Zhang and Clark (2008),[9] with gold part-of-speech tags which is also the same as in Chen and Manning (2014).

Language model word embeddings were generated, for English, from the AFP portion of the English Gigaword corpus (version 5), and from the complete Chinese Gigaword corpus (version 2),

[6] Software for replicating the experiments is available from `https://github.com/clab/lstm-parser`.

[7] We did perform preliminary experiments with LSTM states of 32, 50, and 80, but the other dimensions were our initial guesses.

[8] Training: 02-21. Development: 22. Test: 23.

[9] Training: 001–815, 1001–1136. Development: 886–931, 1148–1151. Test: 816–885, 1137–1147.

as segmented by the Stanford Chinese Segmenter (Tseng et al., 2005).

5.2 Experimental configurations

We report results on five experimental configurations per language, as well as the Chen and Manning (2014) baseline. These are: the full stack LSTM parsing model (S-LSTM), the stack LSTM parsing model without POS tags (−POS), the stack LSTM parsing model without pretrained language model embeddings (−pretraining), the stack LSTM parsing model that uses just head words on the stack instead of composed representations (−composition), and the full parsing model where rather than an LSTM, a classical recurrent neural network is used (S-RNN).

5.3 Results

Following Chen and Manning (2014) we exclude punctuation symbols for evaluation. Tables 1 and 2 show comparable results with Chen and Manning (2014), and we show that our model is better than their model in both the development set and the test set.

	Development		Test	
	UAS	LAS	UAS	LAS
S-LSTM	**93.2**	**90.9**	**93.1**	**90.9**
−POS	93.1	90.4	92.7	90.3
−pretraining	92.7	90.4	92.4	90.0
−composition	92.7	89.9	92.2	89.6
S-RNN	92.8	90.4	92.3	90.1
C&M (2014)	92.2	89.7	91.8	89.6

Table 1: English parsing results (SD)

	Dev. set		Test set	
	UAS	LAS	UAS	LAS
S-LSTM	**87.2**	**85.9**	**87.2**	**85.7**
−composition	85.8	84.0	85.3	83.6
−pretraining	86.3	84.7	85.7	84.1
−POS	82.8	79.8	82.2	79.1
S-RNN	86.3	84.7	86.1	84.6
C&M (2014)	84.0	82.4	83.9	82.4

Table 2: Chinese parsing results (CTB5)

5.4 Analysis

Overall, our parser substantially outperforms the baseline neural network parser of Chen and Manning (2014), both in the full configuration and in the various ablated conditions we report. The one exception to this is the −POS condition for the Chinese parsing task, which in which we underperform their baseline (which used gold POS tags), although we do still obtain reasonable parsing performance in this limited case. We note that predicted POS tags in English add very little value—suggesting that we can think of parsing sentences directly without first tagging them. We also find that using composed representations of dependency tree fragments outperforms using representations of head words alone, which has implications for theories of headedness. Finally, we find that while LSTMs outperform baselines that use only classical RNNs, these are still quite capable of learning good representations.

Effect of beam size. Beam search was determined to have minimal impact on scores (absolute improvements of $\leq 0.3\%$ were possible with small beams). Therefore, all results we report used greedy decoding—Chen and Manning (2014) likewise only report results with greedy decoding. This finding is in line with previous work that generates sequences from recurrent networks (Grefenstette et al., 2014), although Vinyals et al. (2015) did report much more substantial improvements with beam search on their "grammar as a foreign language" parser.[10]

6 Related Work

Our approach ties together several strands of previous work. First, several kinds of stack memories have been proposed to augment neural architectures. Das et al. (1992) proposed a neural network with an external stack memory based on recurrent neural networks. In contrast to our model, in which the entire contents of the stack are summarized in a single value, in their model, the network could only see the contents of the top of the stack. Mikkulainen (1996) proposed an architecture with a stack that had a summary feature, although the stack control was learned as a latent variable.

A variety of authors have used neural networks to predict parser actions in shift-reduce parsers. The earliest attempt we are aware of is due to Mayberry and Miikkulainen (1999). The resurgence of interest in neural networks has resulted

[10]Although superficially similar to ours, Vinyals et al. (2015) is a phrase-structure parser and adaptation to the dependency parsing scenario would have been nontrivial. We discuss their work in §6.

in in several applications to transition-based dependency parsers (Weiss et al., 2015; Chen and Manning, 2014; Stenetorp, 2013). In these works, the conditioning structure was manually crafted and sensitive to only certain properties of the state, while we are conditioning on the global state object. Like us, Stenetorp (2013) used recursively composed representations of the tree fragments (a head and its dependents). Neural networks have also been used to learn representations for use in chart parsing (Henderson, 2004; Titov and Henderson, 2007; Socher et al., 2013a; Le and Zuidema, 2014).

LSTMs have also recently been demonstrated as a mechanism for learning to represent parse structure.Vinyals et al. (2015) proposed a phrase-structure parser based on LSTMs which operated by first reading the entire input sentence in so as to obtain a vector representation of it, and then generating bracketing structures sequentially conditioned on this representation. Although superficially similar to our model, their approach has a number of disadvantages. First, they relied on a large amount of semi-supervised training data that was generated by parsing a large unannotated corpus with an off-the-shelf parser. Second, while they recognized that a stack-like shift-reduce parser control provided useful information, they only made the top word of the stack visible during training and decoding. Third, although it is impressive feat of learning that an entire parse tree be represented by a vector, it seems that this formulation makes the problem unnecessarily difficult.

Finally, our work can be understood as a progression toward using larger contexts in parsing. An exhaustive summary is beyond the scope of this paper, but some of the important milestones in this tradition are the use of cube pruning to efficiently include nonlocal features in discriminative chart reranking (Huang and Chiang, 2008), approximate decoding techniques based on LP relaxations in graph-based parsing to include higher-order features (Martins et al., 2010), and randomized hill-climbing methods that enable arbitrary nonlocal features in global discriminative parsing models (Zhang et al., 2014). Since our parser is sensitive to any part of the input, its history, or its stack contents, it is similar in spirit to the last approach, which permits truly arbitrary features.

7 Conclusion

We presented stack LSTMs, recurrent neural networks for sequences, with push and pop operations, and used them to implement a state-of-the-art transition-based dependency parser. We conclude by remarking that stack memory offers intriguing possibilities for learning to solve general information processing problems (Mikkulainen, 1996). Here, we learned from observable stack manipulation operations (i.e., supervision from a treebank), and the computed embeddings of final parser states were not used for any further prediction. However, this could be reversed, giving a device that learns to construct context-free programs (e.g., expression trees) given only observed outputs; one application would be unsupervised parsing. Such an extension of the work would make it an alternative to architectures that have an explicit external memory such as neural Turing machines (Graves et al., 2014) and memory networks (Weston et al., 2015). However, as with those models, without supervision of the stack operations, formidable computational challenges must be solved (e.g., marginalizing over all latent stack operations), but sampling techniques and techniques from reinforcement learning have promise here (Zaremba and Sutskever, 2015), making this an intriguing avenue for future work.

Acknowledgments

The authors would like to thank Lingpeng Kong and Jacob Eisenstein for comments on an earlier version of this draft and Danqi Chen for assistance with the parsing datasets. This work was sponsored in part by the U. S. Army Research Laboratory and the U. S. Army Research Office under contract/grant number W911NF-10-1-0533, and in part by NSF CAREER grant IIS-1054319. Miguel Ballesteros is supported by the European Commission under the contract numbers FP7-ICT-610411 (project MULTISENSOR) and H2020-RIA-645012 (project KRISTINA).

References

Miguel Ballesteros and Bernd Bohnet. 2014. Automatic feature selection for agenda-based dependency parsing. In *Proc. COLING*.

Miguel Ballesteros and Joakim Nivre. 2014. MaltOptimizer: Fast and effective parser optimization. *Natural Language Engineering*.

Mohit Bansal, Kevin Gimpel, and Karen Livescu. 2014. Tailoring continuous word representations for dependency parsing. In *Proc. ACL.*

Bernd Bohnet and Joakim Nivre. 2012. A transition-based system for joint part-of-speech tagging and labeled non-projective dependency parsing. In *Proc. EMNLP.*

Danqi Chen and Christopher D. Manning. 2014. A fast and accurate dependency parser using neural networks. In *Proc. EMNLP.*

Wenliang Chen, Yue Zhang, and Min Zhang. 2014. Feature embedding for dependency parsing. In *Proc. COLING.*

Jinho D. Choi and Andrew McCallum. 2013. Transition-based dependency parsing with selectional branching. In *Proc. ACL.*

Sreerupa Das, C. Lee Giles, and Guo-Zheng Sun. 1992. Learning context-free grammars: Capabilities and limitations of a recurrent neural network with an external stack memory. In *Proc. Cognitive Science Society.*

Marie-Catherine de Marneffe, Bill MacCartney, and Christopher D. Manning. 2006. Generating typed dependency parses from phrase structure parses. In *Proc. LREC.*

Xavier Glorot and Yoshua Bengio. 2010. Understanding the difficulty of training deep feedforward neural networks. In *Proc. ICML.*

Xavier Glorot, Antoine Bordes, and Yoshua Bengio. 2011. Deep sparse rectifier neural networks. In *Proc. AISTATS.*

Yoav Goldberg, Kai Zhao, and Liang Huang. 2013. Efficient implementation of beam-search incremental parsers. In *Proc. ACL.*

Alex Graves and Jürgen Schmidhuber. 2005. Framewise phoneme classification with bidirectional LSTM networks. In *Proc. IJCNN.*

Alex Graves, Santiago Fernández, and Jürgen Schmidhuber. 2007. Multi-dimensional recurrent neural networks. In *Proc. ICANN.*

Alex Graves, Greg Wayne, and Ivo Danihelka. 2014. Neural Turing machines. *CoRR*, abs/1410.5401.

Alex Graves. 2013. Generating sequences with recurrent neural networks. *CoRR*, abs/1308.0850.

Edward Grefenstette, Karl Moritz Hermann, Georgiana Dinu, and Phil Blunsom. 2014. New directions in vector space models of meaning. ACL Tutorial.

James Henderson. 2004. Discriminative training of a neural network discriminative parser. In *Proc. ACL.*

Karl Moritz Hermann and Phil Blunsom. 2013. The role of syntax in vector space models of compositional semantics. In *Proc. ACL.*

Sepp Hochreiter and Jürgen Schmidhuber. 1997. Long short-term memory. *Neural Computation*, 9(8):1735–1780.

Liang Huang and David Chiang. 2008. Forest reranking: Discriminative parsing with non-local features. In *Proc. ACL.*

Phong Le and Willem Zuidema. 2014. Inside-outside recursive neural network model for dependency parsing. In *Proc. EMNLP.*

Wang Ling, Chris Dyer, Alan Black, and Isabel Trancoso. 2015. Two/too simple adaptations of word2vec for syntax problems. In *Proc. NAACL.*

André F. T. Martins, Noah A. Smith, Eric P. Xing, Pedro M. Q. Aguiar, and Mário A. T. Figueiredo. 2010. Turboparsers: Dependency parsing by approximate variational inference. In *Proc. EMNLP.*

Marshall R. Mayberry and Risto Miikkulainen. 1999. SARDSRN: A neural network shift-reduce parser. In *Proc. IJCAI.*

Risto Mikkulainen. 1996. Subsymbolic case-role analysis of sentences with embedded clauses. *Cognitive Science*, 20:47–73.

Tomas Mikolov, Ilya Sutskever, Kai Chen, Greg S Corrado, and Jeff Dean. 2013. Distributed representations of words and phrases and their compositionality. In *Proc. NIPS.*

Joakim Nivre. 2003. An efficient algorithm for projective dependency parsing. In *Proc. IWPT.*

Joakim Nivre. 2004. Incrementality in deterministic dependency parsing. In *Proceedings of the Workshop on Incremental Parsing: Bringing Engineering and Cognition Together.*

Joakim Nivre. 2007. Incremental non-projective dependency parsing. In *Proc. NAACL.*

Joakim Nivre. 2008. Algorithms for deterministic incremental dependency parsing. *Computational Linguistics*, 34:4:513–553. MIT Press.

Joakim Nivre. 2009. Non-projective dependency parsing in expected linear time. In *Proc. ACL.*

Razvan Pascanu, Çaglar Gülçehre, Kyunghyun Cho, and Yoshua Bengio. 2014. How to construct deep recurrent neural networks. In *Proc. ICLR.*

Francesco Sartorio, Giorgio Satta, and Joakim Nivre. 2013. A transition-based dependency parser using a dynamic parsing strategy. In *Proc. ACL.*

Richard Socher, Eric H. Huang, Jeffrey Pennington, Andrew Y. Ng, and Christopher D. Manning. 2011. Dynamic pooling and unfolding recursive autoencoders for paraphrase detection. In *Proc. NIPS.*

Richard Socher, John Bauer, Christopher D. Manning, and Andrew Y. Ng. 2013a. Parsing with compositional vector grammars. In *Proc. ACL.*

Richard Socher, Andrej Karpathy, Quoc V. Le, Christopher D. Manning, and Andrew Y. Ng. 2013b. Grounded compositional semantics for finding and describing images with sentences. *TACL*.

Richard Socher, Alex Perelygin, Jean Y. Wu, Jason Chuang, Christopher D. Manning, Andrew Y. Ng, and Christopher Potts. 2013c. Recursive deep models for semantic compositionality over a sentiment treebank. In *Proc. EMNLP*.

Pontus Stenetorp. 2013. Transition-based dependency parsing using recursive neural networks. In *Proc. NIPS Deep Learning Workshop*.

Ilya Sutskever, Oriol Vinyals, and Quoc V. Le. 2014. Sequence to sequence learning with neural networks. In *Proc. NIPS*.

Ivan Titov and James Henderson. 2007. Constituent parsing with incremental sigmoid belief networks. In *Proc. ACL*.

Kristina Toutanova, Dan Klein, Christopher D. Manning, and Yoram Singer. 2003. Feature-rich part-of-speech tagging with a cyclic dependency network. In *Proc. NAACL*.

Huihsin Tseng, Pichuan Chang, Galen Andrew, Daniel Jurafsky, and Christopher Manning. 2005. A conditional random field word segmenter for SIGHAN bakeoff 2005. In *Proc. Fourth SIGHAN Workshop on Chinese Language Processing*.

Oriol Vinyals, Lukasz Kaiser, Terry Koo, Slav Petrov, Ilya Sutskever, and Geoffrey Hinton. 2015. Grammar as a foreign language. In *Proc. ICLR*.

David Weiss, Christopher Alberti, Michael Collins, and Slav Petrov. 2015. Structured training for neural network transition-based parsing. In *Proc. ACL*.

Jason Weston, Sumit Chopra, and Antoine Bordes. 2015. Memory networks. In *Proc. ICLR*.

Hiroyasu Yamada and Yuji Matsumoto. 2003. Statistical dependency analysis with support vector machines. In *Proc. IWPT*.

Wojciech Zaremba and Ilya Sutskever. 2015. Reinforcement learning neural Turing machines. *ArXiv e-prints*, May.

Yue Zhang and Stephen Clark. 2008. A tale of two parsers: Investigating and combining graph-based and transition-based dependency parsing. In *Proc. EMNLP*.

Yue Zhang and Joakim Nivre. 2011. Transition-based dependency parsing with rich non-local features. In *Proc. ACL*.

Yuan Zhang, Tao Lei, Regina Barzilay, and Tommi Jaakkola. 2014. Greed is good if randomized: New inference for dependency parsing. In *Proc. EMNLP*.

Leveraging Linguistic Structure For Open Domain Information Extraction

Gabor Angeli **Melvin Johnson Premkumar** **Christopher D. Manning**

Department of Computer Science
Stanford University
{angeli, melvinj, manning}@cs.stanford.edu

Abstract

Relation triples produced by open domain information extraction (open IE) systems are useful for question answering, inference, and other IE tasks. Traditionally these are extracted using a large set of patterns; however, this approach is brittle on out-of-domain text and long-range dependencies, and gives no insight into the substructure of the arguments. We replace this large pattern set with a few patterns for canonically structured sentences, and shift the focus to a classifier which learns to extract self-contained clauses from longer sentences. We then run natural logic inference over these short clauses to determine the maximally specific arguments for each candidate triple. We show that our approach outperforms a state-of-the-art open IE system on the end-to-end TAC-KBP 2013 Slot Filling task.

1 Introduction

Open information extraction (open IE) has been shown to be useful in a number of NLP tasks, such as question answering (Fader et al., 2014), relation extraction (Soderland et al., 2010), and information retrieval (Etzioni, 2011). Conventionally, open IE systems search a collection of patterns over either the surface form or dependency tree of a sentence. Although a small set of patterns covers most simple sentences (e.g., subject verb object constructions), relevant relations are often spread across clauses (see Figure 1) or presented in a non-canonical form.

Systems like Ollie (Mausam et al., 2012) approach this problem by using a bootstrapping method to create a large corpus of broad-coverage partially lexicalized patterns. Although this is effective at capturing many of these patterns, it can lead to unintuitive behavior on out-of-domain text. For instance, while *Obama is president* is extracted correctly by Ollie as *(Obama; is; president)*, replacing *is* with *are* in *cats are felines* produces no extractions. Furthermore, existing systems struggle at producing canonical argument forms – for example, in Figure 1 the argument *Heinz Fischer of Austria* is likely less useful for downstream applications than *Heinz Fischer*.

Born in Honolulu, Hawaii, Obama is a US Citizen.

Our System	Ollie
(Obama; is; US citizen)	(Obama; is; a US citizen)
(Obama; born in; Honolulu, Hawaii)	(Obama; be born in; Honolulu)
	(Honolulu; be born in; Hawaii)
	(Obama; is citizen of; US)

Friends give true praise.
Enemies give fake praise.

Our System	Ollie
(friends; give; true praise)	(friends; give; true praise)
(friends; give; praise)	
(enemies; give; fake praise)	(enemies; give; fake praise)

Heinz Fischer of Austria visits the US

Our System	Ollie
(Heinz Fischer; visits; US)	(Heinz Fischer of Austria; visits; the US)

Figure 1: Open IE extractions produced by the system, alongside extractions from the state-of-the-art Ollie system. Generating coherent clauses before applying patterns helps reduce false matches such as *(Honolulu; be born in; Hawaii)*. Inference over the sub-structure of arguments, in turn, allows us to drop unnecessary information (e.g., *of Austria*), but only when it is warranted (e.g., keep *fake* in *fake praise*).

In this paper, we shift the burden of extracting informative and broad coverage triples away from this large pattern set. Rather, we first pre-process the sentence in linguistically motivated ways to produce coherent clauses which are (1) logically

Proceedings of the 53rd Annual Meeting of the Association for Computational Linguistics and the 7th International Joint Conference on Natural Language Processing, pages 344–354,
Beijing, China, July 26-31, 2015. ©2015 Association for Computational Linguistics

entailed by the original sentence, and (2) easy to segment into open IE triples. Our approach consists of two stages: we first learn a classifier for splitting a sentence into shorter utterances (Section 3), and then appeal to natural logic (Sánchez Valencia, 1991) to maximally shorten these utterances while maintaining necessary context (Section 4.1). A small set of 14 hand-crafted patterns can then be used to segment an utterance into an open IE triple.

We treat the first stage as a greedy search problem: we traverse a dependency parse tree recursively, at each step predicting whether an edge should yield an independent clause. Importantly, in many cases naïvely yielding a clause on a dependency edge produces an incomplete utterance (e.g., *Born in Honolulu, Hawaii*, from Figure 1). These are often attributable to control relationships, where either the subject or object of the governing clause controls the subject of the subordinate clause. We therefore allow the produced clause to sometimes inherit the subject or object of its governor. This allows us to capture a large variety of long range dependencies with a concise classifier.

From these independent clauses, we then extract shorter sentences, which will produce shorter arguments more likely to be useful for downstream applications. A natural framework for solving this problem is natural logic – a proof system built on the syntax of human language (see Section 4.1). We can then observe that *Heinz Fischer of Austria visits China* entails that *Heinz Fischer visits China*. On the other hand, we respect situations where it is incorrect to shorten an argument. For example, *No house cats have rabies* should not entail that *cats have rabies*, or even that *house cats have rabies*.

When careful attention to logical validity is necessary – such as textual entailment – this approach captures even more subtle phenomena. For example, whereas *all rabbits eat fresh vegetables* yields *(rabbits; eat; vegetables)*, the apparently similar sentence *all young rabbits drink milk* does not yield *(rabbits; drink; milk)*.

We show that our new system performs well on a real world evaluation – the TAC KBP Slot Filling challenge (Surdeanu, 2013). We outperform both an official submission on open IE, and a baseline of replacing our extractor with Ollie, a state-of-the-art open IE systems.

2 Related Work

There is a large body of work on open information extraction. One line of work begins with TextRunner (Yates et al., 2007) and ReVerb (Fader et al., 2011), which make use of computationally efficient surface patterns over tokens. With the introduction of fast dependency parsers, Ollie (Mausam et al., 2012) continues in the same spirit but with learned dependency patterns, improving on the earlier WOE system (Wu and Weld, 2010). The Never Ending Language Learning project (Carlson et al., 2010) has a similar aim, iteratively learning more facts from the internet from a seed set of examples. Exemplar (Mesquita et al., 2013) adapts the open IE framework to n-ary relationships similar to semantic role labeling, but without the expensive machinery.

Open IE triples have been used in a number of applications – for example, learning entailment graphs for new triples (Berant et al., 2011), and matrix factorization for unifying open IE and structured relations (Yao et al., 2012; Riedel et al., 2013). In each of these cases, the concise extractions provided by open IE allow for efficient symbolic methods for entailment, such as Markov logic networks or matrix factorization.

Prior work on the KBP challenge can be categorized into a number of approaches. The most common of these are *distantly supervised* relation extractors (Craven and Kumlien, 1999; Wu and Weld, 2007; Mintz et al., 2009; Sun et al., 2011), and rule based systems (Soderland, 1997; Grishman and Min, 2010; Chen et al., 2010). However, both of these approaches require careful tuning to the task, and need to be trained explicitly on the KBP relation schema. Soderland et al. (2013) submitted a system to KBP making use of open IE relations and an easily constructed mapping to KBP relations; we use this as a baseline for our empirical evaluation.

Prior work has used natural logic for RTE-style textual entailment, as a formalism well-suited for formal semantics in neural networks, and as a framework for common-sense reasoning (MacCartney and Manning, 2009; Watanabe et al., 2012; Bowman et al., 2014; Angeli and Manning, 2013). We adopt the precise semantics of Icard and Moss (2014). Our approach of finding short entailments from a longer utterance is similar in spirit to work on textual entailment for information extraction (Romano et al., 2006).

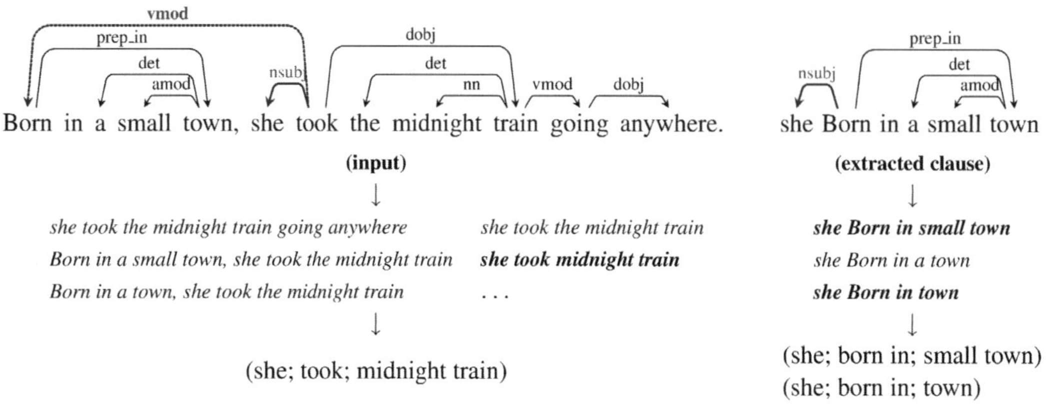

Figure 2: An illustration of our approach. From left to right, a sentence yields a number of independent clauses (e.g., *she Born in a small town* – see Section 3). From top to bottom, each clause produces a set of entailed shorter utterances, and segments the ones which match an atomic pattern into a relation triple (see Section 4.1).

3 Inter-Clause Open IE

In the first stage of our method, we produce a set of self-contained clauses from a longer utterance. Our objective is to produce a set of clauses which can stand on their own syntactically and semantically, and are entailed by the original sentence (see Figure 2). Note that this task is not specific to extracting open IE triples. Conventional relation extractors, entailment systems, and other NLP applications may also benefit from such a system.

We frame this task as a search problem. At a given node in the parse tree, we classify each outgoing arc $e = p \xrightarrow{l} c$, from the governor p to a dependent c with [collapsed] Stanford Dependency label l, into an action to perform on that arc. Once we have chosen an action to take on that arc, we can recurse on the dependent node. We decompose the action into two parts: (1) the action to take on the outgoing edge e, and (2) the action to take on the governor p. For example, in our motivating example, we are considering the arc: $e = took \xrightarrow{vmod} born$. In this case, the correct action is to (1) yield a new clause rooted at *born*, and (2) interpret the subject of *born* as the subject of *took*.

We proceed to describe this action space in more detail, followed by an explanation of our training data, and finally our classifier.

3.1 Action Space

The three actions we can perform on a dependency edge are:

Yield Yields a new clause on this dependency arc. A canonical case of this action is the arc $suggest \xrightarrow{ccomp} brush$ in *Dentists suggest that you should brush your teeth*, yielding *you should brush your teeth*.

Recurse Recurse on this dependency arc, but do not yield it as a new clause. For example, in the sentence *faeries are dancing in the field where I lost my bike*, we must recurse through the intermediate constituent *the field where I lost my bike* – which itself is not relevant – to get to the clause of interest: *I lost my bike*.

Stop Do not recurse on this arc, as the subtree under this arc is not entailed by the parent sentence. This is the case, for example, for most leaf nodes (*furry cats are cute* should not entail the clause *furry*), and is an important action for the efficiency of the algorithm.

With these three actions, a search path through the tree becomes a sequence of **Recurse** and **Yield** actions, terminated by a **Stop** action (or leaf node). For example, a search sequence $A \xrightarrow{Recurse} B \xrightarrow{Yield} C \xrightarrow{Stop} D$ would yield a clause rooted at C. A sequence $A \xrightarrow{Yield} B \xrightarrow{Yield} C \xrightarrow{Stop} D$ would yield clauses rooted at both B and C. Finding all such sequences is in general exponential in the size of the tree. In practice, during training we run breadth first search to collect the first 10 000 sequences. During inference we run uniform cost search until our classifier predictions fall below a given threshold.

For the **Stop** action, we do not need to further specify an action to take on the parent node. However, for both of the other actions, it is often the case that we would like to capture a controller in the higher clause. We define three such common actions:

Subject Controller If the arc we are considering is not already a subject arc, we can copy the subject of the parent node and attach it as a subject of the child node. This is the action taken in the example *Born in a small town, she took the midnight train.*

Object Controller Analogous to the subject controller action above, but taking the object instead. This is the intended action for examples like *I persuaded Fred to leave the room.*[1]

Parent Subject If the arc we are taking is the only outgoing arc from a node, we take the parent node as the (passive) subject of the child. This is the action taken in the example *Obama, our 44th president* to yield a clause with the semantics of *Obama [is] our 44th president.*

Although additional actions are easy to imagine, we found empirically that these cover a wide range of applicable cases. We turn our attention to the training data for learning these actions.

3.2 Training

We collect a noisy dataset to train our clause generation model. We leverage the *distant supervision* assumption for relation extraction, which creates a noisy corpus of sentences annotated with relation mentions (subject and object spans in the sentence with a known relation). Then, we take this annotation as itself distant supervision for a correct sequence of actions to take: any sequence which recovers the known relation is correct.

We use a small subset of the KBP source documents for 2010 (Ji et al., 2010) and 2013 (Surdeanu, 2013) as our distantly supervised corpus. To try to maximize the density of known relations in the training sentences, we take all sentences which have at least one known relation for every 10 tokens in the sentence, resulting in 43 155 sentences. In addition, we incorporate the 23 725 manually annotated examples from Angeli et al. (2014).

Once we are given a collection of labeled sentences, we assume that a sequence of actions which leads to a correct extraction of a known relation is a *positive sequence*. A correct extraction is any extraction we produce from our model (see Section 4) which has the same arguments as the known relation. For instance, if we know that Obama was born in Hawaii from the sentence *Born in Hawaii, Obama . . .*, and an action sequence produces the triple (Obama, born in, Hawaii), then we take that action sequence as a positive sequence.

Any sequence of actions which results in a clause which produces no relations is in turn considered a *negative sequence*. The third case to consider is a sequence of actions which produces a relation, but it is not one of the annotated relations. This arises from the *incomplete negatives* problem in distantly supervised relation extraction (Min et al., 2013): since our knowledge base is not exhaustive, we cannot be sure if an extracted relation is incorrect or correct but previously unknown. Although many of these unmatched relations are indeed incorrect, the dataset is sufficiently biased towards the STOP action that the occasional false negative hurts end-to-end performance. Therefore, we simply discard such sequences.

Given a set of noisy positive and negative *sequences*, we construct training data for our action classifier. All but the last action in a positive sequence are added to the training set with the label **Recurse**; the last action is added with the label **Split**. Only the last action in a negative sequence is added with the label **Stop**. We partition the feature space of our dataset according to the action applied to the parent node.

3.3 Inference

We train a multinomial logistic regression classifier on our noisy training data, using the features in Table 1. The most salient features are the label of the edge being taken, the incoming edge to the parent of the edge being taken, neighboring edges for both the parent and child of the edge, and the part of speech tag of the endpoints of the edge. The dataset is weighted to give 3× weight to examples in the **Recurse** class, as precision errors in this class are relatively harmless for accuracy, while recall errors are directly harmful to recall.

Inference now reduces to a search problem. Be-

[1]The system currently misses most most such cases due to insufficient support in the training data.

Feature Class	Feature Templates
Edge taken	$\{l, \text{short\_name}(l)\}$
Last edge taken	$\{\text{incoming\_edge}(p)\}$
Neighbors of parent	$\{\text{nbr}(p), (p, \text{nbr}(p))\}$
Grandchild edges	$\{\text{out\_edge}(c),$ $(e, \text{out\_edge}(c))\}$
Grandchild count	$\{\text{count}(\text{nbr}(e_{\text{child}}))$ $(e, \text{count}(\text{nbr}(e_{\text{child}})))\}$
Has subject/object	$\forall_{e \in \{e, e_{\text{child}}\}} \forall_{l \in \{subj, obj\}}$ $\mathbb{1}(l \in \text{nbr}(e))$
POS tag signature	$\{\text{pos}(p), \text{pos}(c),$ $(\text{pos}(p), \text{pos}(c))\}$
Features at root	$\{\mathbb{1}(p = root), \text{POS}(p)\}$

Table 1: Features for the clause splitter model, deciding to split on the arc $e = p \xrightarrow{l} c$. The feature class is a high level description of features; the feature templates are the particular templates used. For instance, the POS signature contains the tag of the parent, the tag of the child, and both tags joined in a single feature. Note that all features are joined with the action to be taken on the parent.

ginning at the root of the tree, we consider every outgoing edge. For every possible action to be performed on the parent (i.e., clone subject, clone root, no action), we apply our trained classifier to determine whether we (1) split the edge off as a clause, and recurse; (2) do not split the edge, and recurse; or (3) do not recurse. In the first two cases, we recurse on the child of the arc, and continue until either all arcs have been exhausted, or all remaining candidate arcs have been marked as not recursable.

We will use the scores from this classifier to inform the score assigned to our generated open IE extractions (Section 4). The score of a clause is the product of the scores of actions taken to reach the clause. The score of an extraction will be this score multiplied by the score of the extraction given the clause.

4 Intra-Clause Open IE

We now turn to the task of generating a maximally compact sentence which retains the core semantics of the original utterance, and parsing the sentence into a conventional open IE subject verb object triple. This is often a key component in downstream applications, where extractions need to be not only *correct*, but also *informative*. Whereas an argument like *Heinz Fischer of Austria* is often correct, a downstream application must apply further processing to recover information about either *Heinz Fischer*, or *Austria*. Moreover, it must do so without the ability to appeal to the larger context of the sentence.

4.1 Validating Deletions with Natural Logic

We adopt a subset of natural logic semantics dictating contexts in which lexical items can be removed. Natural logic as a formalism captures common logical inferences appealing directly to the form of language, rather than parsing to a specialized logical syntax. It provides a proof theory for lexical mutations to a sentence which either preserve or negate the truth of the premise.

For instance, if *all rabbits eat vegetables* then *all cute rabbits eat vegetables*, since we are allowed to mutate the lexical item *rabbit* to *cute rabbit*. This is done by observing that *rabbit* is in scope of the first argument to the operator *all*. Since *all* induces a *downward polarity* environment for its first argument, we are allowed to replace *rabbit* with an item which is more specific – in this case *cute rabbit*. To contrast, the operator *some* induces an *upward polarity* environment for its first argument, and therefore we may derive the inference from *cute rabbit* to *rabbit* in: *some cute rabbits are small* therefore *some rabbits are small*. For a more comprehensive introduction to natural logic, see van Benthem (2008).

We mark the scopes of all operators (*all*, *no*, *many*, etc.) in a sentence, and from this determine whether every lexical item can be replaced by something more general (has upward polarity), more specific (downward polarity), or neither. In the absence of operators, all items have upwards polarity.

Each dependency arc is then classified into whether deleting the dependent of that arc makes the governing constituent at that node more general, more specific (a rare case), or neither.[2] For example, removing the *amod* edge in *cute* $\xleftarrow{amod}$ *rabbit* yields the more general lexical item *rabbit*. However, removing the *nsubj* edge in *Fido* $\xleftarrow{nsubj}$ *runs* would yield the unentailed (and nonsensical) phrase *runs*. The last, rare, case is an edge that causes the resulting item to be more specific – e.g., *quantmod*: *about* $\xleftarrow{quantmod}$ *200* is more general than *200*.

[2]We use the Stanford Dependencies representation (de Marneffe and Manning, 2008).

For most dependencies, this semantics can be hard-coded with high accuracy. However, there are at least two cases where more attention is warranted. The first of these concerns non-subsective adjectives: for example a *fake gun* is not a gun. For this case, we make use of the list of non-subsective adjectives collected in Nayak et al. (2014), and prohibit their deletion as a hard constraint.

The second concern is with prepositional attachment, and direct object edges. For example, whereas *Alice went to the playground* $\xrightarrow{prep\_with}$ *Bob* entails that *Alice went to the playground*, it is not meaningful to infer that *Alice is friends* $\xrightarrow{prep\_with}$ *Bob* entails *Alice is friends*. Analogously, *Alice played* $\xrightarrow{dobj}$ *baseball on Sunday* entails that *Alice played on Sunday*; but, *Obama signed* $\xrightarrow{dobj}$ *the bill on Sunday* should not entail the awkward phrase **Obama signed on Sunday*.

We learn these attachment affinities empirically from the syntactic n-grams corpus of Goldberg and Orwant (2013). This gives us counts for how often object and preposition edges occur in the context of the governing verb and relevant neighboring edges. We hypothesize that edges which are frequently seen to co-occur are likely to be essential to the meaning of the sentence. To this end, we compute the probability of seeing an arc of a given type, conditioned on the most specific context we have statistics for. These contexts, and the order we back off to more general contexts, is given in Figure 3.

To compute a score s of *deleting* the edge from the affinity probability p collected from the syntactic n-grams, we simply cap the affinity and subtract it from 1:

$$s = 1 - \min(1, \frac{p}{K})$$

where K is a hyperparameter denoting the minimum fraction of the time an edge should occur in a context to be considered entirely unremovable. In our experiments, we set $K = \frac{1}{3}$.

The score of an extraction, then, is the product of the scores of each deletion multiplied by the score from the clause splitting step in Section 3.

4.2 Atomic Patterns

Once a set of short entailed sentences is produced, it becomes straightforward to segment them into conventional open IE triples. We employ 6 simple dependency patterns, given in Table 2, which cover the majority of atomic relations we are interested in.

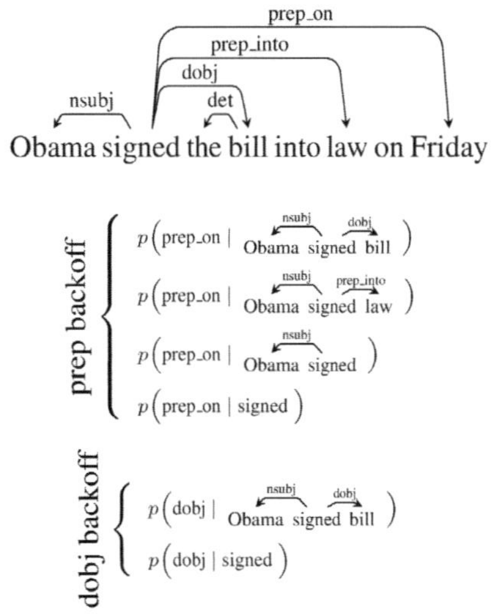

Figure 3: The ordered list of backoff probabilities when deciding to drop a prepositional phrase or direct object. The most specific context is chosen for which an empirical probability exists; if no context is found then we allow dropping prepositional phrases and disallow dropping direct objects. Note that this backoff arbitrarily orders contexts of the same size.

Input	**Extraction**
cats play with yarn	(cats; play with; yarn)
fish like to swim	(fish; like to; swim)
cats have tails	(cats; have; tails)
cats are cute	(cats; are; cute)
Tom and Jerry are fighting	(Tom; fighting; Jerry)
There are cats with tails	(cats; have; tails)

Table 2: The six dependency patterns used to segment an atomic sentence into an open IE triple.

When information is available to disambiguate the substructure of compound nouns (e.g., named entity segmentation), we extract additional relations with 5 dependency and 3 TokensRegex (Chang and Manning, 2014) surface form patterns. These are given in Table 3; we refer to these as *nominal relations*. Note that the constraint of named entity information is by no means required for the system. In other applications – for example, applications in vision – the otherwise trivial nominal relations could be quite useful.

KBP Relation	Open IE Relation	PMI^2	KBP Relation	Open IE Relation	PMI^2
Org:Founded	*found in*	1.17	Per:Date_Of_Birth	*be bear on*	1.83
	be found in	1.15		*bear on*	1.28
Org:Dissolved	**buy Chrysler in*	0.95	Per:Date_Of_Death	*die on*	0.70
	**membership in*	0.60		*be assassinate on*	0.65
Org:LOC_Of_HQ	*in*	2.12	Per:LOC_Of_Birth	*be bear in*	1.21
	base in	1.82	Per:LOC_Of_Death	**elect president of*	2.89
Org:Member_Of	**tough away game in*	1.80	Per:Religion	*speak about*	0.67
	**away game in*	1.80		*popular for*	0.60
Org:Parents	*'s bank*	1.65	Per:Parents	*daughter of*	0.54
	**also add to*	1.52		*son of*	1.52
Org:Founded_By	*invest fund of*	1.48	Per:LOC_Residence	*of*	1.48
	own stake besides	1.18		**independent from*	1.18

Table 4: A selection of the mapping from KBP to lemmatized open IE relations, conditioned on the types of the arguments being correct. The top one or two relations are shown for 7 person and 6 organization relations. Incorrect or dubious mappings are marked with an asterisk.

Input	Extraction
Durin, son of Thorin	(Durin; is son of; Thorin)
Thorin's son, Durin	(Thorin; 's son; Durin)
IBM CEO Rometty	(Rometty; is CEO of; IBM)
President Obama	(Obama; is; President)
Fischer of Austria	(Fischer; is of; Austria)
IBM's research group	(IBM; 's; research group)
US president Obama	(Obama; president of; US)
Our president, Obama,	(Our president; be; Obama)

Table 3: The eight patterns used to segment a noun phrase into an open IE triple. The first five are dependency patterns; the last three are surface patterns.

5 Mapping OpenIE to a Known Relation Schema

A common use case for open IE systems is to map them to a known relation schema. This can either be done manually with minimal annotation effort, or automatically from available training data. We use both methods in our TAC-KBP evaluation. A collection of relation mappings was constructed by a single annotator in approximately a day,[3] and a relation mapping was learned using the procedure described in this section.

We map open IE relations to the KBP schema by searching for co-occurring relations in a large distantly-labeled corpus, and marking open IE and KBP relation pairs which have a high PMI^2 value (Béatrice, 1994; Evert, 2005) conditioned on their type signatures matching. To compute PMI^2, we collect probabilities for the open IE and KBP relation co-occurring, the probability of the open IE relation occurring, and the probability of the KBP relation occurring. Each of these probabilities is conditioned on the type signature of the relation. For example, the joint probability of KBP relation r_k and open IE relation r_o, given a type signature of t_1, t_2, would be

$$p(r_k, r_o \mid t_1, t_2) = \frac{\text{count}(r_k, r_o, t_1, t_2)}{\sum_{r'_k, r'_o} \text{count}(r'_k, r'_o, t_1, t_2)}.$$

Omitting the conditioning on the type signature for notational convenience, and defining $p(r_k)$ and $p(r_o)$ analogously, we can then compute The PMI^2 value between the two relations:

$$\text{PMI}^2(r_k, r_o) = \log\left(\frac{p(r_k, r_o)^2}{p(r_k) \cdot p(r_o)}\right)$$

Note that in addition to being a measure related to PMI, this captures a notion similar to *alignment by agreement* (Liang et al., 2006); the formula can be equivalently written as $\log\left[p(r_k \mid r_o)p(r_o \mid r_k)\right]$. It is also functionally the same as the JC WordNet distance measure (Jiang and Conrath, 1997).

Some sample type checked relation mappings are given in Table 4. In addition to intuitive mappings (e.g., *found in* $\rightarrow$ Org:Founded), we can note some rare, but high precision pairs (e.g., *invest fund of* $\rightarrow$ Org:Founded_By). We can also see

[3]The official submission we compare against claimed two weeks for constructing their manual mapping, although a version of their system constructed in only 3 hours performs nearly as well.

the noise in distant supervision occasionally permeate the mapping, e.g., with *elect president of* → Per:LOC_Of_Death – a president is likely to die in his own country.

6 Evaluation

We evaluate our approach in the context of a real-world end-to-end relation extraction task – the TAC KBP Slot Filling challenge. In Slot Filling, we are given a large unlabeled corpus of text, a fixed schema of relations (see Section 5), and a set of query entities. The task is to find all relation triples in the corpus that have as a subject the query entity, and as a relation one of the defined relations. This can be viewed intuitively as populating Wikipedia Infoboxes from a large unstructured corpus of text.

We compare our approach to the University of Washington submission to TAC-KBP 2013 (Soderland et al., 2013). Their system used OpenIE v4.0 (a successor to Ollie) run over the KBP corpus and then they generated a mapping from the extracted relations to the fixed schema. Unlike our system, Open IE v4.0 employs a semantic role component extracting structured SRL frames, alongside a conventional open IE system. Furthermore, the UW submission allows for extracting relations and entities from substrings of an open IE triple argument. For example, from the triple *(Smith; was appointed; acting director of Acme Corporation)*, they extract that Smith is employed by Acme Corporation. We disallow such extractions, passing the burden of finding correct precise extractions to the open IE system itself (see Section 4).

For entity linking, the UW submission uses Tom Lin's entity linker (Lin et al., 2012); our submission uses the Illinois Wikifier (Ratinov et al., 2011) without the relational inference component, for efficiency. For coreference, UW uses the Stanford coreference system (Lee et al., 2011); we employ a variant of the simple coref system described in (Pink et al., 2014).

We report our results in Table 5.[4] UW Official refers to the official submission in the 2013 challenge; we show a 3.1 F_1 improvement (to 22.7 F_1) over this submission, evaluated using a comparable approach. A common technique in KBP systems but not employed by the official UW submission in 2013 is to add alternate names based on entity linking and coreference. Additionally, websites are often extracted using heuristic name-matching as they are hard to capture with traditional relation extraction techniques. If we make use of both of these, our end-to-end accuracy becomes 28.2 F_1.

System	P	R	F_1
UW Official*	**69.8**	11.4	19.6
Ollie†	57.4	4.8	8.9
+ Nominal Rels*	57.7	11.8	19.6
Our System			
- Nominal Rels†	64.3	8.6	15.2
+ Nominal Rels*	61.9	13.9	22.7
+ Alt. Name	57.8	17.8	27.1
+ Alt. Name + Website	58.6	**18.6**	**28.3**

Table 5: A summary of our results on the end-to-end KBP Slot Filling task. UW official is the submission made to the 2013 challenge. The second row is the accuracy of Ollie embedded in our framework, and of Ollie evaluated with nominal relations from our system. Lastly, we report our system, our system with nominal relations removed, and our system combined with an alternate names detector and rule-based website detector. Comparable systems are marked with a dagger† or asterisk*.

We attempt to remove the variance in scores from the influence of other components in an end-to-end KBP system. We ran the Ollie open IE system (Mausam et al., 2012) in an identical framework to ours, and report accuracy in Table 5. Note that when an argument to an Ollie extraction contains a named entity, we take the argument to be that named entity. The low performance of this system can be partially attributed to its inability to extract nominal relations. To normalize for this, we report results when the Ollie extractions are supplemented with the nominal relations produced by our system (Ollie + Nominal Rels in Table 5). Conversely, we can remove the nominal relation extractions from our system; in both cases we outperform Ollie on the task.

[4]All results are reported with the `anydoc` flag set to true in the evaluation script, meaning that only the truth of the extracted knowledge base entry and not the associated provenance is scored. In absence of human evaluators, this is in order to not penalize our system unfairly for extracting a new correct provenance.

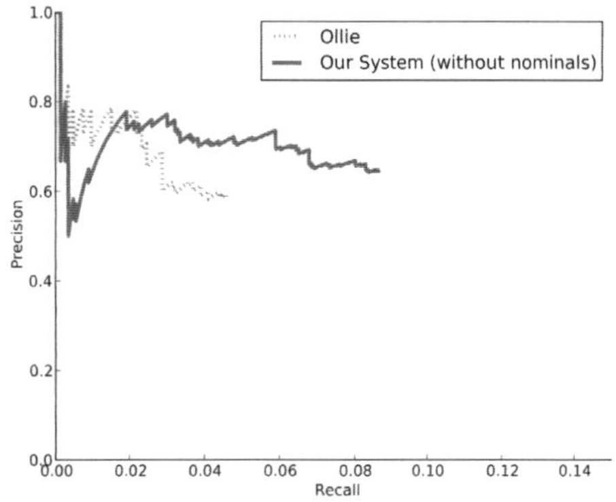

Figure 4: A precision/recall curve for Ollie and our system (without nominals). For clarity, recall is plotted on a range from 0 to 0.15.

6.1 Discussion

We plot a precision/recall curve of our extractions in Figure 4 in order to get an informal sense of the calibration of our confidence estimates. Since confidences only apply to standard extractions, we plot the curves without including any of the nominal relations. The confidence of a KBP extraction in our system is calculated as the sum of the confidences of the open IE extractions that support it. So, for instance, if we find (Obama; be bear in; Hawaii) n times with confidences $c_1 \ldots c_n$, the confidence of the KBP extraction would be $\sum_{i=0}^{n} c_i$. It is therefore important to note that the curve in Figure 4 necessarily conflates the confidences of individual extractions, and the frequency of an extraction.

With this in mind, the curves lend some interesting insights. Although our system is very high precision on the most confident extractions, it has a large dip in precision early in the curve. This suggests that the model is extracting multiple instances of a bad relation. Systematic errors in the clause splitter are the likely cause of these errors. While the approach of splitting sentences into clauses generalizes better to out-of-domain text, it is reasonable that the errors made in the clause splitter manifest across a range of sentences more often than the fine-grained patterns of Ollie would.

On the right half of the PR curve, however, our system achieves both higher precision and extends to a higher recall than Ollie. Furthermore, the curve is relatively smooth near the tail, suggesting that indeed we are learning a reasonable estimate of confidence for extractions that have only one supporting instance in the text – empirically, 46% of our extractions.

In total, we extract 42 662 862 open IE triples which link to a pair of entities in the corpus (i.e., are candidate KBP extractions), covering 1 180 770 relation types. 202 797 of these relation types appear in more than 10 extraction instances; 28 782 in more than 100 instances, and 4079 in more than 1000 instances. 308 293 relation types appear only once. Note that our system over-produces extractions when both a general and specific extraction are warranted; therefore these numbers are an overestimate of the number of semantically meaningful facts.

For comparison, Ollie extracted 12 274 319 triples, covering 2 873 239 relation types. 1 983 300 of these appeared only once; 69 010 appeared in more than 10 instances, 7951 in more than 100 instances, and 870 in more than 1000 instances.

7 Conclusion

We have presented a system for extracting open domain relation triples by breaking a long sentence into short, coherent clauses, and then finding the maximally simple relation triples which are warranted given each of these clauses. This allows the system to have a greater awareness of the context of each extraction, and to provide informative triples to downstream applications. We show that our approach performs well on one such downstream application: the KBP Slot Filling task.

Acknowledgments

We thank the anonymous reviewers for their thoughtful feedback. Stanford University gratefully acknowledges the support of a Natural Language Understanding-focused gift from Google Inc. and the Defense Advanced Research Projects Agency (DARPA) Deep Exploration and Filtering of Text (DEFT) Program under Air Force Research Laboratory (AFRL) contract no. FA8750-13-2-0040. Any opinions, findings, and conclusion or recommendations expressed in this material are those of the authors and do not necessarily reflect the view of the DARPA, AFRL, or the US government.

References

Gabor Angeli and Christopher D. Manning. 2013. Philosophers are mortal: Inferring the truth of unseen facts. In *CoNLL*.

Gabor Angeli, Julie Tibshirani, Jean Y. Wu, and Christopher D. Manning. 2014. Combining distant and partial supervision for relation extraction. In *EMNLP*.

DAILLE Béatrice. 1994. *Approche mixte pour l'extraction automatique de terminologie: statistique lexicale et filtres linguistiques*. Ph.D. thesis, Thèse de Doctorat. Université de Paris VII.

Jonathan Berant, Ido Dagan, and Jacob Goldberger. 2011. Global learning of typed entailment rules. In *Proceedings of ACL*, Portland, OR.

Samuel R. Bowman, Christopher Potts, and Christopher D. Manning. 2014. Recursive neural networks can learn logical semantics. *CoRR*, (arXiv:1406.1827).

Andrew Carlson, Justin Betteridge, Bryan Kisiel, Burr Settles, Estevam R Hruschka Jr, and Tom M Mitchell. 2010. Toward an architecture for never-ending language learning. In *AAAI*.

Angel X. Chang and Christopher D. Manning. 2014. TokensRegex: Defining cascaded regular expressions over tokens. Technical Report CSTR 2014-02, Department of Computer Science, Stanford University.

Zheng Chen, Suzanne Tamang, Adam Lee, Xiang Li, Wen-Pin Lin, Matthew Snover, Javier Artiles, Marissa Passantino, and Heng Ji. 2010. CUNY-BLENDER. In *TAC-KBP*.

Mark Craven and Johan Kumlien. 1999. Constructing biological knowledge bases by extracting information from text sources. In *AAAI*.

Marie-Catherine de Marneffe and Christopher D. Manning. 2008. The Stanford typed dependencies representation. In *Coling 2008: Proceedings of the workshop on Cross-Framework and Cross-Domain Parser Evaluation*.

Oren Etzioni. 2011. Search needs a shake-up. *Nature*, 476(7358):25–26.

Stefan Evert. 2005. *The statistics of word cooccurrences: word pairs and collocations*. Ph.D. thesis, Universit at Stuttgart.

Anthony Fader, Stephen Soderland, and Oren Etzioni. 2011. Identifying relations for open information extraction. In *EMNLP*.

Anthony Fader, Luke Zettlemoyer, and Oren Etzioni. 2014. Open question answering over curated and extracted knowledge bases. In *KDD*.

Yoav Goldberg and Jon Orwant. 2013. A dataset of syntactic-ngrams over time from a very large corpus of english books. In **SEM*.

Ralph Grishman and Bonan Min. 2010. New York University KBP 2010 slot-filling system. In *Proc. TAC 2010 Workshop*.

Thomas Icard, III and Lawrence Moss. 2014. Recent progress on monotonicity. *Linguistic Issues in Language Technology*.

Heng Ji, Ralph Grishman, Hoa Trang Dang, Kira Griffitt, and Joe Ellis. 2010. Overview of the tac 2010 knowledge base population track. In *Third Text Analysis Conference*.

Jay J Jiang and David W Conrath. 1997. Semantic similarity based on corpus statistics and lexical taxonomy. *Proceedings of the 10th International Conference on Research on Computational Linguistics*.

Heeyoung Lee, Yves Peirsman, Angel Chang, Nathanael Chambers, Mihai Surdeanu, and Dan Jurafsky. 2011. Stanford's multi-pass sieve coreference resolution system at the conll-2011 shared task. In *CoNLL Shared Task*.

Percy Liang, Ben Taskar, and Dan Klein. 2006. Alignment by agreement. In *NAACL-HLT*.

Thomas Lin, Mausam, and Oren Etzioni. 2012. No noun phrase left behind: detecting and typing unlinkable entities. In *EMNLP-CoNLL*.

Bill MacCartney and Christopher D Manning. 2009. An extended model of natural logic. In *Proceedings of the eighth international conference on computational semantics*.

Mausam, Michael Schmitz, Robert Bart, Stephen Soderland, and Oren Etzioni. 2012. Open language learning for information extraction. In *EMNLP*.

Filipe Mesquita, Jordan Schmidek, and Denilson Barbosa. 2013. Effectiveness and efficiency of open relation extraction. In *EMNLP*.

Bonan Min, Ralph Grishman, Li Wan, Chang Wang, and David Gondek. 2013. Distant supervision for relation extraction with an incomplete knowledge base. In *NAACL-HLT*.

Mike Mintz, Steven Bills, Rion Snow, and Dan Jurafsky. 2009. Distant supervision for relation extraction without labeled data. In *ACL*.

Neha Nayak, Mark Kowarsky, Gabor Angeli, and Christopher D. Manning. 2014. A dictionary of nonsubsective adjectives. Technical Report CSTR 2014-04, Department of Computer Science, Stanford University, October.

Glen Pink, Joel Nothman, and R. James Curran. 2014. Analysing recall loss in named entity slot filling. In *EMNLP*.

Lev Ratinov, Dan Roth, Doug Downey, and Mike Anderson. 2011. Local and global algorithms for disambiguation to wikipedia. In *ACL*.

Sebastian Riedel, Limin Yao, Andrew McCallum, and Benjamin M Marlin. 2013. Relation extraction with matrix factorization and universal schemas. In *NAACL-HLT*.

Lorenza Romano, Milen Kouylekov, Idan Szpektor, Ido Dagan, and Alberto Lavelli. 2006. Investigating a generic paraphrase-based approach for relation extraction. *EACL*.

Víctor Manuel Sánchez Sánchez Valencia. 1991. *Studies on natural logic and categorial grammar*. Ph.D. thesis, University of Amsterdam.

Stephen Soderland, Brendan Roof, Bo Qin, Shi Xu, Mausam, and Oren Etzioni. 2010. Adapting open information extraction to domain-specific relations. *AI Magazine*, 31(3):93–102.

Stephen Soderland, John Gilmer, Robert Bart, Oren Etzioni, and Daniel S. Weld. 2013. Open information extraction to KBP relations in 3 hours. In *Text Analysis Conference*.

Stephen G Soderland. 1997. *Learning text analysis rules for domain-specific natural language processing*. Ph.D. thesis, University of Massachusetts.

Ang Sun, Ralph Grishman, Wei Xu, and Bonan Min. 2011. New York University 2011 system for KBP slot filling. In *Proceedings of the Text Analytics Conference*.

Mihai Surdeanu. 2013. Overview of the tac2013 knowledge base population evaluation: English slot filling and temporal slot filling. In *Sixth Text Analysis Conference*.

Johan van Benthem. 2008. A brief history of natural logic. Technical Report PP-2008-05, University of Amsterdam.

Yotaro Watanabe, Junta Mizuno, Eric Nichols, Naoaki Okazaki, and Kentaro Inui. 2012. A latent discriminative model for compositional entailment relation recognition using natural logic. In *COLING*.

Fei Wu and Daniel S Weld. 2007. Autonomously semantifying wikipedia. In *Proceedings of the sixteenth ACM conference on information and knowledge management*. ACM.

Fei Wu and Daniel S Weld. 2010. Open information extraction using wikipedia. In *ACL*. Association for Computational Linguistics.

Limin Yao, Sebastian Riedel, and Andrew McCallum. 2012. Probabilistic databases of universal schema. In *Proceedings of the Joint Workshop on Automatic Knowledge Base Construction and Web-scale Knowledge Extraction*.

Alexander Yates, Michael Cafarella, Michele Banko, Oren Etzioni, Matthew Broadhead, and Stephen Soderland. 2007. TextRunner: Open information extraction on the web. In *ACL-HLT*.

Joint Information Extraction and Reasoning: A Scalable Statistical Relational Learning Approach

William Yang Wang
Language Technologies Institute
Carnegie Mellon University
Pittsburgh, PA 15213, USA
yww@cs.cmu.edu

William W. Cohen
Machine Learning Department
Carnegie Mellon University
Pittsburgh, PA 15213, USA
wcohen@cs.cmu.edu

Abstract

A standard pipeline for statistical relational learning involves two steps: one first constructs the knowledge base (KB) from text, and then performs the learning and reasoning tasks using probabilistic first-order logics. However, a key issue is that information extraction (IE) errors from text affect the quality of the KB, and propagate to the reasoning task. In this paper, we propose a statistical relational learning model for joint information extraction and reasoning. More specifically, we incorporate context-based entity extraction with structure learning (SL) in a scalable probabilistic logic framework. We then propose a latent context invention (LCI) approach to improve the performance. In experiments, we show that our approach outperforms state-of-the-art baselines over three real-world Wikipedia datasets from multiple domains; that joint learning and inference for IE and SL significantly improve both tasks; that latent context invention further improves the results.

1 Introduction

Information extraction (IE) is often an early stage in a pipeline that contains non-trivial downstream tasks, such as question answering (Mollá et al., 2006), machine translation (Babych and Hartley, 2003), or other applications (Wang and Hua, 2014; Li et al., 2014). Knowledge bases (KBs) populated by IE techniques have also been used as an input to systems that learn rules allowing further inferences to be drawn from the KB (Lao et al., 2011), a task sometimes called KB completion (Socher et al., 2013; Wang et al., 2014; West et al., 2014). Pipelines of this sort frequently suffer from error cascades, which reduces performance of the full system[1].

In this paper, we address this issue, and propose a joint model system for IE and KB completion in a statistical relational learning (SRL) setting (Sutton and McCallum, 2006; Getoor and Taskar, 2007). In particular, we outline a system which takes as input a partially-populated KB and a set of relation mentions in context, and jointly learns: 1) how to extract new KB facts from the relation mentions, and; 2) a set of logical rules that allow one to infer new KB facts. Evaluation of the KB facts inferred by the joint system shows that the joint model outperforms its individual components. We also introduce a novel extension of this model called Latent Context Invention (LCI), which associates latent states with context features for the IE component of the model. We show that LCI further improves performance, leading to a substantial improvement over prior state-of-the-art methods for joint relation-learning and IE.

To summarize our contributions:

- We present a joint model for IE and relational learning in a statistical relational learning setting which outperforms universal schemas (Riedel et al., 2013), a state-of-the-art joint method;
- We incorporate latent context into the joint SRL model, bringing additional improvements.

In next section, we discuss related work. We describe our approach in Section 3. The details of the datasets are introduced in Section 4. We show experimental results in Section 5, discuss in Section 6, and conclude in Section 7.

[1]For example, KBP slot filling is known for its complex pipeline, and the best overall F1 scores (Wiegand and Klakow, 2013; Angeli et al., 2014) for recent competitions are within the range of 30-40.

Proceedings of the 53rd Annual Meeting of the Association for Computational Linguistics and the 7th International Joint Conference on Natural Language Processing, pages 355–364,
Beijing, China, July 26-31, 2015.

2 Related Work

In NLP, our work clearly aligns with recent work on joint models of individual text processing tasks. For example, Finkel and Manning (2009) work on the problem of joint IE and parsing, where they use tree representations to combine named entities and syntactic chunks. Recently, Devlin et al. (Devlin et al., 2014) use a joint neural network model for machine translation, and obtain an impressive 6.3 BLEU point improvement over a hierarchical phrase-based system.

In information extraction, weak supervision (Craven et al., 1999; Mintz et al., 2009) is a common technique for extracting knowledge from text, without large-scale annotations. In extracting Infobox information from Wikipedia text, Wu and Weld (2007; 2010) also use a similar idea. In an open IE project, Banko et al. (2007) use a seed KB, and utilize weak supervision techniques to extend it. Note that weakly supervised extraction approaches can be noisy, as a pair of entities in context may be associated with one, none, or several of the possible relation labels, a property which complicates the application of distant supervision methods (Mintz et al., 2009; Riedel et al., 2010; Hoffmann et al., 2011; Surdeanu et al., 2012).

Lao et al. (2012) learned syntactic rules for finding relations defined by "lexico-semantic" paths spanning KB relations and text data. Wang et al. (2015) extends the methods used by Lao et al. to learn mutually recursive relations. Recently, Riedel et al. (2013) propose a matrix factorization technique for relation embedding, but their method requires a large amount of negative and unlabeled examples. Weston et al. (2013) connect text with KB embedding by adding a scoring term, though no shared parameters/embeddings are used. All these prior works make use of text and KBs. Unlike these prior works, our method is posed in an SRL setting, using a scalable probabilistic first-order logic, and allows learning of relational rules that are mutually recursive, thus allowing learning of multi-step inferences. Unlike some prior methods, our method also does not require negative examples, or large numbers of unlabeled examples.

3 Our Approach

In this section, we first briefly review the semantics, inference, and learning procedures of a newly proposed scalable probabilistic logic called ProPPR (Wang et al., 2013; Wang et al., 2014). Then, we describe the joint model for information extraction and relational learning. Finally, a latent context invention theory is proposed for enhancing the performance of the joint model.

about(X,Z) :- handLabeled(X,Z)	# base.
about(X,Z) :- sim(X,Y),about(Y,Z)	# prop.
sim(X,Y) :- links(X,Y)	# sim,link.
sim(X,Y) :- hasWord(X,W),hasWord(Y,W), linkedBy(X,Y,W)	# sim,word.
linkedBy(X,Y,W) :- true	# by(W).

Table 1: A simple program in ProPPR. See text for explanation.

3.1 ProPPR: Background

Below we will give an informal description of ProPPR, based on a small example. More formal descriptions can be found elsewhere (Wang et al., 2013).

ProPPR (for Programming with Personalized PageRank) is a stochastic extension of the logic programming language Prolog. A simple program in ProPPR is shown in Table 1. Roughly speaking, the upper-case tokens are variables, and the ":-" symbol means that the left-hand side (the *head* of a rule) is implied by the conjunction of conditions on the right-hand size (the *body*). In addition to the rules shown, a ProPPR program would include a *database* of *facts*: in this example, facts would take the form *handLabeled(page,label)*, *hasWord(page,word)*, or *linkedBy(page1,page2)*, representing labeled training data, a document-term matrix, and hyperlinks, respectively. The condition "true" in the last rule is "syntactic sugar" for an empty body.

In ProPPR, a user issues a query, such as "about(a,X)?", and the answer is a set of possible bindings for the free variables in the query (here there is just one such varable, "X"). To answer the query, ProPPR builds a *proof graph*. Each node in the graph is a list of conditions $R_1, \ldots, R_k$ that remain to prove, interpreted as a conjunction. To find the children of a node $R1, \ldots, Rk$, you look for either

1. database facts that match R_1, in which case the appropriate variables are bound, and R_1 is removed from the list, or;

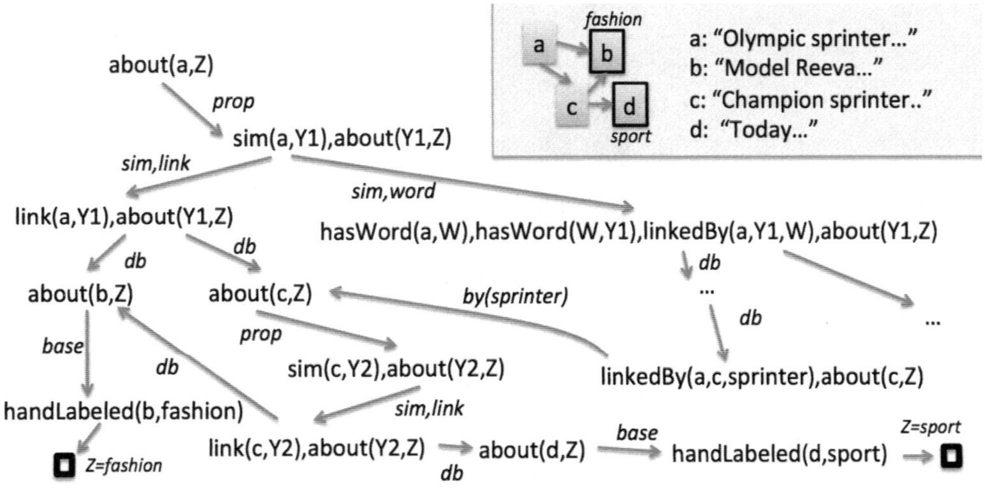

Figure 1: A partial proof graph for the query *about(a,Z)*. The upper right shows the link structure between documents a, b, c, and d, and some of the words in the documents. Restart links are not shown.

2. a rule $A \leftarrow B_1, \ldots, B_m$ with a head A that matches R_1, in which case again the appropriate variables are bound, and R_1 is replaced with the body of the rule, resulting in the new list $B_1, \ldots, B_m, R_2, \ldots, R_k$.

The procedures for "matching" and "appropriately binding variables" are illustrated in Figure 1.[2] An empty list of conditions (written □ in the figure) corresponds to a complete proof of the initial query, and by collecting the required variable bindings, this proof can be used to determine an answer to the initial query.

In Prolog, this proof graph is constructed on-the-fly in a depth-first, left-to-right way, returning the first solution found, and backtracking, if requested, to find additional solutions. In ProPPR, however, we will define a *stochastic process on the graph*, which will generate a score for each node, and hence a score for each answer to the query. The stochastic process used in ProPPR is *personalized PageRank* (Page et al., 1998; Csalogny et al., 2005), also known as random-walk-with-restart. Intuitively, this process upweights solution nodes that are reachable by *many short proofs* (i.e., short paths from the query node.) Formally, personalized PageRank is the fixed point of the iteration

$$\mathbf{p}^{t+1} = \alpha\chi_{v_0} + (1-\alpha)W\mathbf{p}^t \qquad (1)$$

[2] The edge annotations will be discussed later.

where $\mathbf{p}[u]$ is the weight assigned to u, v_0 is the seed (i.e., query) node, χ_{v_0} is a vector with $\chi_{v_0}[v_0] = 1$ and $\chi_{v_0}[u] = 0$ for $u \neq v$, and W is a matrix of transition probabilities, i.e., $W[v, u]$ is the probability of transitioning from node u to a child node v. The parameter α is the reset probability, and the transition probabilities we use will be discussed below.

Like Prolog, ProPPR's proof graph is also constructed on-the-fly, but rather than using depth-first search, we use PageRank-Nibble, a fast approximate technique for incrementally exploring a large graph from a an initial "seed" node (Andersen et al., 2008). PageRank-Nibble takes a parameter ϵ and will return an approximation $\hat{\mathbf{p}}$ to the personalized PageRank vector $\mathbf{p}$, such that each node's estimated probability is within ϵ of correct.

We close this background section with some final brief comments about ProPPR.

Scalability. ProPPR is currently limited in that it uses memory to store the fact databases, and the proof graphs constructed from them. ProPPR uses a special-purpose scheme based on sparse matrix representations to store facts which are triples, which allows it to accomodate databases with hundreds of millions of facts in tens of gigabytes.

With respect to run-time, ProPPR's scalability is improved by the fast approximate inference scheme used, which is often an order of magnitude faster than power iteration for moderate-sized problems (Wang et al., 2013). Experimen-

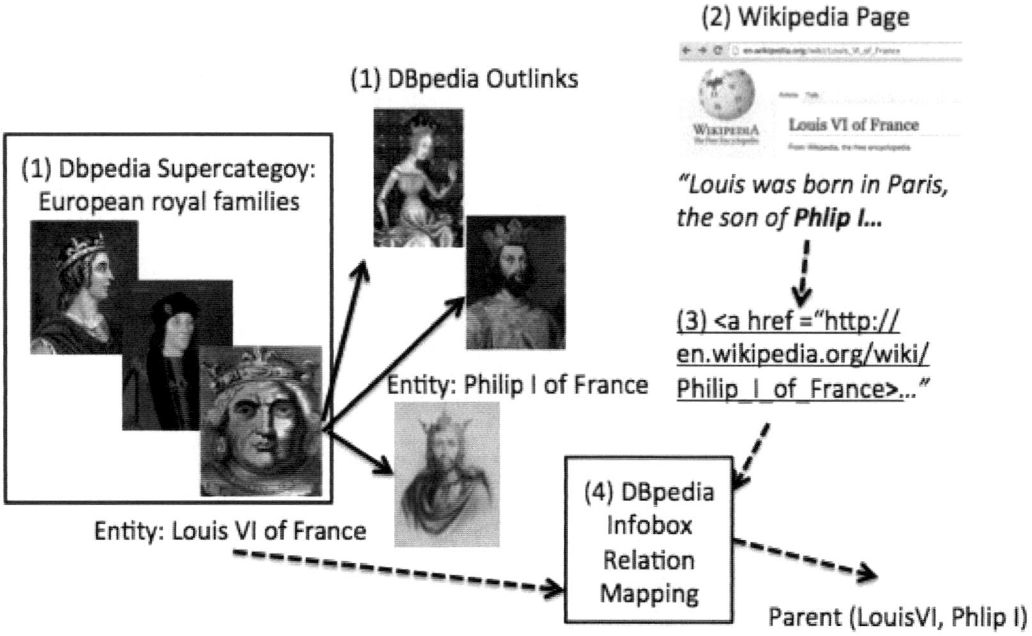

Figure 2: The data generation example as described in subsection 3.2.

tation and learning are also sped up because with PageRank-Nibble, each query is answered using a "small"—size $O(\frac{1}{\alpha\epsilon})$—proof graph. Many operations required in learning and experimentation can thus be easily parallized on a multi-core machine, by simply distributing different proof graphs to different threads.

Parameter learning. Personalized PageRank scores are defined by a transition probability matrix W, which is parameterized as follows. ProPPR allows "feature generators" to be attached to its rules, as indicated by the code after the hashtags in the example program.[3] Since edges in the proof graph correspond to rule matches, the edges can also be labeled by features, and a weighted combination of these features can be used to define a total weight for each edge, which finally can be normalized used to define the transition matrix W. Learning can be used to tune these weights to data; ProPPR's learning uses a parallelized SGD method, in which inference on different examples is performed in different threads, and weight updates are synchronized.

Structure learning. Prior work (Wang et al., 2014) has studied the problem of learning a ProPPR theory, rather than simply tuning parameters in an existing theory, a process called *structure learning* (SL). In particular, Wang et al. (2014) propose a scheme called the *structural gradient* which scores rules in some (possibly large) user-defined space $\mathcal{R}$ of potential rules, which can be viewed as instantiations of rule templates, such as the ones shown in the left-hand side of Table 2.

For completeness, we will summarize briefly the approach used in (Wang et al., 2014). The space of potential rules $\mathcal{R}$ is defined by a "second-order abductive theory", which conceptually is an interpreter that constructs proofs using all rules in $\mathcal{R}$. Each rule template is mapped to two clauses in the interpreter: one simulates the template (for any binding), and one "abduces" the specific binding (facts) from the KB. Associated with the use of the abductive rule is a feature corresponding to a particular binding for the template. The gradient of these features indicates which instantiated rules can be usefully added to the theory. More details can be found in (Wang et al., 2014).

[3]For instance, when matching the rule "sim(X,Y) :- links(X,Y)" to a condition such as "sim(a,X)" the two features "sim" and "link" are generated; likewise when matching the rule "linkedBy(X,Y,W) :- true" to the condition "linkedBy(a,c,sprinter)" the feature "by(sprinter)" is generated.

	Rule template	ProPPR clause
Structure learning		
(a)	P(X,Y) :- R(X,Y)	interp(P,X,Y) :- interp0(R,X,Y),abduce_if(P,R). abduce_if(P,R) :- true # f_if(P,R).
(b)	P(X,Y) :- R(Y,X)	interp(P,X,Y) :- interp0(R,Y,X),abduce_ifInv(P,R). abduce_ifInv(P,R) :- true # f_ifInv(P,R).
(c)	P(X,Y) :- R1(X,Z),R2(Z,Y)	interp(P,X,Y) :- interp0(R1,X,Z),interp0(R2,Z,Y), abduce_chain(P,R1,R2). abduce_chain(P,R1,R2) :- true # f_chain(P,R1,R2).
	base case for SL interpreter	interp0(P,X,Y) :- rel(R,X,Y).
	insertion point for learned rules	interp0(P,X,Y) :- *any rules learned by SL.*
Information extraction		
(d)	R(X,Y) :- link(X,Y,W), indicates(W,R).	interp(R,X,Y) :- link(X,Y,W),abduce_indicates(W,R). abduce_indicates(W,R) :- true #f_ind1(W,R).
(e)	R(X,Y) :- link(X,Y,W1), link(X,Y,W2), indicates(W1,W2,R).	interp(R,X,Y) :- link(X,Y,W1),link(X,Y,W2), abduce_indicates(W1,W2,R). abduce_indicates(W1,W2,R) :- true #f_ind2(W1,W2,R).
Latent context invention		
(f)	R(X,Y) :- latent(L), link(X,Y,W), indicates(W,L,R)	interp(R,X,Y) :- latent(L),link(X,Y,W),abduce_latent(W,L,R). abduce_latent(W,L,R) :- true #f_latent1(W,L,R).
(g)	R(X,Y) :- latent(L1),latent(L2) link(X,Y,W), indicates(W,L1,L2,R)	interp(R,X,Y) :- latent(L1),latent(L2),link(X,Y,W), abduce_latent(W,L1,L2,R). abduce_latent(W,L1,L2,R) :- true #f_latent2(W,L1,L2,R).

Table 2: The ProPPR template and clauses for joint structure learning and information extraction.

3.2 Joint Model for IE and SRL

Dataset Generation The KBs and text used in our experiments were derived from Wikipedia. Briefly, we choose a set of closely-related pages from a hand-selected Wikipedia list. These pages define a set of entities $\mathcal{E}$, and a set of commonly-used Infobox relations $\mathcal{R}$ between these entities define a KB. The relation mentions are hyperlinks between the pages, and the features of these relation mentions are words that appear nearby these links. This information is encoded in a single relation *link(X,Y,W)*, which indicates that there is hyperlink between Wikipedia pages X to Y which is near the context word W. The Infobox relation triples are stored in another relation, *rel(R,X,Y)*. [4]

Figure 2 shows an example. We first find the "*European royal families*" to find a list of entities $\mathcal{E}$. This list contains the page "*Louis VI of France*", the *source entity*, which contains an outlink to the *target entity page* "*Philip I of France*". On the source page, we can find the following text: "*Louis was born in Paris, the son of* ***Philip I*** *and his first wife, Bertha of Holland.*" From Infobox data, we also may know of a relationship between the source and target entities: in this case, the target entity is the *parent* of the source entity.

Theory for Joint IE and SL The structure learning templates we used are identical to those used in prior work (Wang et al., 2014), and are summarized by the clauses (a-c) in Table 2. In the templates in the left-hand side of the table, P, R, $R1$ and $R2$ are variables in the template, which will be bound to specific relations found to be useful in prediction. (The interpreter rules on the right-hand side are provided for completeness, and can be ignored by readers not deeply familiar with the work of (Wang et al., 2014).)

The second block of the table contains the templates used for IE. For example, to understand template (d), recall that the predicate *link* indicates a hyperlink from Wikipedia page X to

[4] In more detail, the extraction process was as follows. (1) We used a DBpedia dump of categories and hyperlink structure to find pages in a category; sometimes, this included crawling a supercategory page to find categories and then entities. (2) We used the DBpedia hyperlink graph to find the target entity pages, downloaded the most recent (2014) version of each of these pages, and collected relevant hyperlinks and anchor text, together with 80 characters of context to either side.

Y, which includes the context word W between two entities X and Y. The abductive predicate *abduce_indicates* activates a feature template, in which we learn the degree of association of a context word and a relation from the training data. These rules essentially act as a trainable classifier which classifies entity pairs based on the hyperlinks they that contain them, and classifies the hyperlinks according to the relation they reflect, based on context-word features.

Notice that the learner will attempt to tune word associations to match the gold *rel* facts used as training data, and that doing this does not require assigning labels to individual links, as would be done in a traditional distant supervision setting: instead these labels are essentially left latent in this model. Similar to "deep learning" approaches, the latent assignments are provided not by EM, but by hill-climbing search in parameter space.

A natural extension to this model is to add a bilexical version of this classifier in clause (e), where we learn a feature which conjoins word $W1$, word $W2$, and relation R.

Combining the clauses from (a) to (e), we derive a hybrid theory for joint SL and IE: the structure learning section involves a second-order probabilistic logic theory, where it searches the relational KB to form plausible first-order relational inference clauses. The information extraction section from (d) to (e) exploits the distributional similarity of contextual words for each relation, and extracts relation triples from the text, using distant supervision and latent labels for relation mentions (which in our case are hyperlinks). Training this theory as a whole trains it to perform joint reasoning to facts for multiple relations, based on relations that are known (from the partial KB) or inferred from the IE part of the theory. Both parameters for the IE portion of the theory and inference rules between KB relations are learned.[5]

Latent Context Invention Note that so far both the IE clauses (d-e) are fully observable: there are no latent predicates or variables. Recent work (Riedel et al., 2013) suggests that learning latent representations for words improves performance in predicting relations. Perhaps this is because such latent representations can better model the semantic information in surface forms, which are often ambiguous.

We call our method latent context invention (LCI), and it is inspired from literature in predicate invention (Kok and Domingos, 2007).[6] LCI applies the idea of predicate invention to the context space: instead of inventing new predicates, we now invent a *latent context property* that captures the regularities among the similar relational lexical items. To do this, we introduce some additional rules of the form *latent(1) :- true*, *latent(2) :- true*, etc, and allow the learner to find appropriate weights for pairing these arbitrarily-chosen values with specific words. This is implemented by template (f) in Table 2. Adding this to the joint theory means that we will learn to map surface-level lexical items (words) to the "invented" latent context values and also to relation.

Another view of LCI is that we are learning a latent embedding of words jointly with relations. In template (f) we model a single latent dimension, but to model higher-dimensional latent variables, we can add the clauses such as (g), which constructs a two-dimensional latent space. Below we will call this variant method hLCI.

4 Datasets

Using the data generation process that we described in subsection 3.2, we extract two datasets from the supercategories of "*European royal families*" and "*American people of English descent*, and third geographic dataset using three lists: "*List of countries by population*", "*List of largest cities and second largest cities by country*" and "*List of national capitals by population*".

For the *royal* dataset, we have 2,258 pages with 67,483 source-context-target mentions, and we use 40,000 for training, and 27,483 for testing. There are 15 relations[7]. In the *American* dataset, we have 679 pages with 11,726 mentions, and we use 7,000 for training, and 4,726 for testing. This dataset includes 30 relations[8]. As for the *Geo* dataset, there are 497

[5]In in addition to finding rules which instantiate the templates, weights on these rules are also learned.

[6]To give some background on this nomenclature, we note that the SL method is inspired by Cropper and Muggleton's Metagol system (Cropper and Muggleton, 2014), which includes predicate invention. In principle predicates could be invented by SL, by extending the interpreter to consider "invented" predicate symbols as binding to its template variables (e.g., P and R); however, in practice invented predicates leads to close dependencies between learned rules, and are highly sensitive to the level of noise in the data.

[7]birthPlace, child, commander, deathPlace, keyPerson, knownFor, monarch, parent, partner, predecessor, relation, restingPlace, spouse, successor, territory

[8]architect, associatedBand, associatedMusicalArtist, au-

pages with 43,475 mentions, and we use 30,000 for training, and 13,375 for testing. There are 10 relations[9]. The datasets are freely available for download at `http://www.cs.cmu.edu/~yww/data/jointIE+Reason.zip`.

5 Experiments

To evaluate these methods, we use the setting of Knowledge Base completion (Socher et al., 2013; Wang et al., 2014; West et al., 2014). We randomly remove a fixed percentage of facts in a training knowledge base, train the learner from the partial KB, and use the learned model to predict facts in the test KB. KB completion is a well-studied task in SRL, where multiple relations are often needed to fill in missing facts, and thus reconstruct the incomplete KB. Following prior work (Riedel et al., 2013; Wang et al., 2013), we use mean average precision (MAP) as the evaluation metric.

5.1 Baselines

To understand the performance of our joint model, we compare with three prior methods. **Structure Learning (SL)** includes the second-order relation learning templates (a-c) from Table 2. **Information Extraction (IE)** includes only templates (d) and (e). **Markov Logic Networks (MLN)** is the Alchemy's implementation[10] of Markov Logic Networks (Richardson and Domingos, 2006), using the first-order clauses learned from SL method[11]. We used conjugate gradient weight learning (Lowd and Domingos, 2007) with 10 iterations. Finally, **Universal Schema** is a state-of-the-art matrix factorization based universal method for jointly learning surface patterns and relations. We used the code and parameter settings for the best-performing model (NFE) from (Riedel et al., 2013).

As a final baseline method, we considered a simpler approach to clustering context words, which we called **Text Clustering**, which used the following template:

$$\begin{aligned}&R(X,Y) :\text{-}\\ &\quad clusterID(C), link(X,Y,W),\\ &\quad cluster(C,W), related(R,W).\end{aligned}$$

Here surface patterns are grouped to form latent clusters in a relation-*independent* fashion.

5.2 The Effectiveness of the Joint Model

Our experimental results are shown in 3. The leftmost part of the table concerns the Royal dataset. We see that the universal schema approach outperforms the MLN baseline in most cases, but ProPPR's SL method substantially improves over MLN's conjugated gradient learning method, and the universal schema approach. This is perhaps surprising, as the universal schema approach is also a joint method: we note that in our datasets, unlike the New York Times corpus used in (Riedel et al., 2013), large numbers of unlabeled examples are not available. The unigram and bilexical IE models in ProPPR also perform well—better than SL on this data. The joint model outperforms the baselines, as well as the separate models. The difference is most pronounced when the background KB gets noisier: the improvement with 10% missing setting is about 1.5 to 2.3% MAP, while with 50% missing data, the absolute MAP improvement is from 8% to 10%.

In the next few columns of Table 3, we show the KB completion results for the *Geo* dataset. This dataset has fewer relations, and the most common one is *country*. The overall MAP scores are much higher than the previous dataset. MLN's results are good, but still generally below the universal schema method. On this dataset, the universal schema method performs better than the IE only model for ProPPR in most settings. However, the ProPPRjoint model still shows large improvements over individual models and the baselines: the absolute MAP improvement is 22.4%.

Finally, in the rightmost columns of Table 3, we see that the overall MAP scores for the *American* dataset are relatively lower than other datasets, perhaps because it is the smallest of the three. The universal schema approach consistently outperforms the MLN model, but not ProPPR. On this dataset the SL-only model in ProPPR outperforms the IE-only models; however, the joint models still outperform individual ProPPR models from 1.5% to 6.4% in MAP.

thor, birthPlace, child, cinematography, deathPlace, director, format, foundationOrganisation, foundationPerson, influenced, instrument, keyPerson, knownFor, location, musicComposer, narrator, parent, president, producer, relation, relative, religion, restingPlace, spouse, starring, successor, writer

[9] archipelago, capital, country, daylightSavingTimeZone, largestSettlement, leaderTitle, mottoFor, timeZone, twinCity, twinCountry

[10] http://alchemy.cs.washington.edu/

[11] We also experimented with Alchemy's structure learning, but it was not able to generate results in 24 hours.

% missing	Royal 10%	20%	30%	40%	50%	Geo 10%	20%	30%	40%	50%	American 10%	20%	30%	40%	50%
Baselines															
MLN	60.8	43.7	44.9	38.8	38.8	80.4	79.2	68.1	66.0	68.0	54.0	56.0	51.2	41.0	13.8
Universal Schema	48.2	53.0	52.9	47.3	41.2	82.0	84.0	75.7	77.0	65.2	56.7	51.4	55.9	54.7	51.3
SL	79.5	77.2	74.8	65.5	61.9	83.8	80.4	77.1	72.8	67.2	73.1	70.0	71.3	67.1	61.7
IE only															
IE (U)	81.3	78.5	76.4	75.7	70.6	83.9	79.4	73.1	71.6	65.2	63.4	61.0	60.2	61.4	54.4
IE (U+B)	81.1	78.1	76.2	75.5	70.3	84.0	79.5	73.3	71.6	65.3	64.3	61.2	61.1	62.1	55.7
Joint															
SL+IE (U)	82.8	80.9	79.1	77.9	78.6	89.5	89.4	89.3	88.1	87.6	74.0	73.3	73.7	70.5	68.0
SL+IE (U+B)	83.4	82.0	80.7	79.7	80.3	89.6	89.6	89.5	88.4	87.7	**74.6**	73.5	74.2	70.9	68.4
Joint + Latent															
Joint + Clustering	**83.5**	82.3	81.2	80.2	80.7	89.8	89.6	89.5	88.8	88.4	**74.6**	73.9	74.4	71.5	69.7
Joint + LCI	**83.5**	**82.5**	81.5	80.6	81.1	**89.9**	**89.8**	**89.7**	89.1	89.0	**74.6**	74.1	74.5	72.3	70.3
Joint + LCI + hLCI	**83.5**	**82.5**	**81.7**	**81.0**	**81.3**	**89.9**	89.7	**89.7**	**89.6**	**89.5**	**74.6**	**74.4**	**74.6**	**73.6**	**72.1**

Table 3: The MAP results for KB completion on three datasets. U: unigram. B: bigram. Best result in each column is highlighted in **bold**.

The averaged training runtimes on an ordinary PC for unigram joint model on the above *Royal, Geo, American* datasets are 38, 36, and 29 seconds respectively, while the average testing times are 11, 10, and 9 seconds. For bilexical joint models, the averaged training times are 25, 10, and 10 minutes respectively, whereas the testing times are 111, 28, and 26 seconds respectively.

5.3 The Effectiveness of LCI

Finally we consider the latent context invention (LCI) approach. The last three rows of Table 3 show the performances of LCI and hHCI. We compare it here with the best previous approach, the joint IE + SL model, and text clustering approach.

For the *Royal* dataset, first, the LCI and hLCI models clearly improve over joint IE and SL. In noisy conditions of missing 50% facts, the biggest improvement of LCI/hLCI is 2.4% absolute MAP.

From the *Geo* dataset, we see that the joint models and joint+latent models have similar performances in relatively clean conditions (10%-30%) facts missing. However, in noisy conditions, we the LCI and hLCI model has an advantage of between 1.5% to 1.8% in absolute MAP.

Finally, the results for the *American* dataset show a consistent trend: again, in noisy conditions (missing 40% to 50% facts), the latent context models outperform the joint IE + SL models by 2.9% and 3.7% absolute MAP scores.

Although the LCI approach is inspired by predicate invention in inductive logic programming, our result is also consistent with theories of generalized latent variable modeling in probabilistic graphical models and statistics (Skrondal and Rabe-Hesketh, 2004): modeling hidden variables helps take into account the measurement (observation) errors (Fornell and Larcker, 1981) and results in a more robust model.

6 Discussions

Compared to state-of-the-art joint models (Riedel et al., 2013) that learn the latent factor representations, our method gives strong improvements in performance on three datasets with various settings. Our model is also trained to retrieve a target entity from a relation name plus a source entity, and does not require large samples of unlabeled or negative examples in training.

Another advantage of the ProPPR model is that they are explainable. For example, below are the features with the highest weights after joint learning from the *Royal* dataset, written as predicates or rules:

indicates("mother",parent)
indicates("king",parent)
indicates("spouse",spouse)
indicates("married",spouse)
indicates("succeeded",successor)
indicates("son",successor)

parent(X,Y) :- successor(Y,X)
successor(X,Y) :- parent(Y,X)
spouse(X,Y) :- spouse(Y,X)
parent(X,Y) :- predecessor(X,Y)
successor(Y,X) :- spouse(X,Y)
predecessor(X,Y) :- parent(X,Y)

Here we see that our model is able to learn that the keywords "mother" and "king" that are indicators of the relation *parent*, that the keywords "spouse" and "married" indicate the relation *spouse*, and the keywords "succeeded" and "son" indicate the relation *successor*. Interestingly, our joint model is also able to learn the inverse relation *successor* for the relation *parent*, as well as the similar relational predicate *predecessor* for *parent*.

7 Conclusions

In this paper, we address the issue of joint information extraction and relational inference. To be more specific, we introduce a holistic probabilistic logic programming approach for fusing IE contexts with relational KBs, using locally groundable inference on a joint proof graph. We then propose a latent context invention technique that learns relation-specific latent clusterings for words. In experiments, we show that joint modeling for IE and SRL improves over prior state-of-the-art baselines by large margins, and that the LCI model outperforms various fully baselines on three real-world Wikipedia dataset from different domains. In the future, we are interested in extending these techniques to also exploit unlabeled data.

Acknowledgment

This work was sponsored in part by DARPA grant FA87501220342 to CMU and a Google Research Award.

References

Reid Andersen, Fan R. K. Chung, and Kevin J. Lang. 2008. Local partitioning for directed graphs using pagerank. *Internet Mathematics*, 5(1):3–22.

Gabor Angeli, Julie Tibshirani, Jean Y Wu, and Christopher D Manning. 2014. Combining distant and partial supervision for relation extraction. In *Proceedings of the Conference on Empirical Methods in Natural Language Processing*.

Bogdan Babych and Anthony Hartley. 2003. Improving machine translation quality with automatic named entity recognition. In *Proceedings of the 7th International EAMT workshop on MT and other Language Technology Tools, Improving MT through other Language Technology Tools: Resources and Tools for Building MT*, pages 1–8. Association for Computational Linguistics.

Michele Banko, Michael J Cafarella, Stephen Soderland, Matthew Broadhead, and Oren Etzioni. 2007. Open information extraction for the web. In *IJCAI*, volume 7, pages 2670–2676.

Mark Craven, Johan Kumlien, et al. 1999. Constructing biological knowledge bases by extracting information from text sources. In *ISMB*, volume 1999, pages 77–86.

Andrew Cropper and Stephen H Muggleton. 2014. Can predicate invention in meta-interpretive learning compensate for incomplete background knowledge? *Proceedings of the 24th International Conference on Inductive Logic Programming*.

Kroly Csalogny, Dniel Fogaras, Balzs Rcz, and Tams Sarls. 2005. Towards scaling fully personalized PageRank: Algorithms, lower bounds, and experiments. *Internet Mathematics*, 2(3):333–358.

Jacob Devlin, Rabih Zbib, Zhongqiang Huang, Thomas Lamar, Richard Schwartz, and John Makhoul. 2014. Fast and robust neural network joint models for statistical machine translation. In *52nd Annual Meeting of the Association for Computational Linguistics, Baltimore, MD, USA, June*.

Jenny Rose Finkel and Christopher D Manning. 2009. Joint parsing and named entity recognition. In *Proceedings of Human Language Technologies: The 2009 Annual Conference of the North American Chapter of the Association for Computational Linguistics*, pages 326–334. Association for Computational Linguistics.

Claes Fornell and David F Larcker. 1981. Evaluating structural equation models with unobservable variables and measurement error. *Journal of marketing research*, pages 39–50.

Lise Getoor and Ben Taskar. 2007. *Introduction to statistical relational learning*. MIT press.

Raphael Hoffmann, Congle Zhang, Xiao Ling, Luke Zettlemoyer, and Daniel S Weld. 2011. Knowledge-based weak supervision for information extraction of overlapping relations. In *Proceedings of the 49th Annual Meeting of the Association for Computational Linguistics: Human Language Technologies-Volume 1*, pages 541–550. Association for Computational Linguistics.

Stanley Kok and Pedro Domingos. 2007. Statistical predicate invention. In *Proceedings of the 24th international conference on Machine learning*, pages 433–440. ACM.

Ni Lao, Tom M. Mitchell, and William W. Cohen. 2011. Random walk inference and learning in a large scale knowledge base. In *EMNLP*, pages 529–539. ACL.

Ni Lao, Amarnag Subramanya, Fernando C. N. Pereira, and William W. Cohen. 2012. Reading the web with learned syntactic-semantic inference rules. In *EMNLP-CoNLL*, pages 1017–1026. ACL.

Jiwei Li, Alan Ritter, and Eduard Hovy. 2014. Weakly supervised user profile extraction from twitter. ACL.

Daniel Lowd and Pedro Domingos. 2007. Efficient weight learning for markov logic networks. In *Knowledge Discovery in Databases: PKDD 2007*, pages 200–211. Springer.

Mike Mintz, Steven Bills, Rion Snow, and Dan Jurafsky. 2009. Distant supervision for relation extraction without labeled data. In *Proceedings of the Joint Conference of the 47th Annual Meeting of the ACL and the 4th International Joint Conference on Natural Language Processing of the AFNLP: Volume 2-Volume 2*, pages 1003–1011. Association for Computational Linguistics.

Diego Mollá, Menno Van Zaanen, and Daniel Smith. 2006. Named entity recognition for question answering. *Proceedings of ALTW*, pages 51–58.

Larry Page, Sergey Brin, R. Motwani, and T. Winograd. 1998. The PageRank citation ranking: Bringing order to the web. In *Technical Report, Computer Science department, Stanford University*.

Matthew Richardson and Pedro Domingos. 2006. Markov logic networks. *Mach. Learn.*, 62(1-2):107–136.

Sebastian Riedel, Limin Yao, and Andrew McCallum. 2010. Modeling relations and their mentions without labeled text. In *Machine Learning and Knowledge Discovery in Databases*, pages 148–163. Springer.

Sebastian Riedel, Limin Yao, Andrew McCallum, and Benjamin M Marlin. 2013. Relation extraction with matrix factorization and universal schemas. In *Proceedings of NAACL-HLT*, pages 74–84.

Anders Skrondal and Sophia Rabe-Hesketh. 2004. *Generalized latent variable modeling: Multilevel, longitudinal, and structural equation models*. CRC Press.

Richard Socher, Danqi Chen, Christopher D Manning, and Andrew Ng. 2013. Reasoning with neural tensor networks for knowledge base completion. In *Advances in Neural Information Processing Systems*, pages 926–934.

Mihai Surdeanu, Julie Tibshirani, Ramesh Nallapati, and Christopher D Manning. 2012. Multi-instance multi-label learning for relation extraction. In *Proceedings of the 2012 Joint Conference on Empirical Methods in Natural Language Processing and Computational Natural Language Learning*, pages 455–465. Association for Computational Linguistics.

Charles Sutton and Andrew McCallum. 2006. An introduction to conditional random fields for relational learning. *Introduction to statistical relational learning*, pages 93–128.

William Yang Wang and Zhenhao Hua. 2014. A semiparametric gaussian copula regression model for predicting financial risks from earnings calls. In *Proceedings of the 52th Annual Meeting of the Association for Computational Linguistics (ACL 2014)*, Baltimore, MD, USA, June. ACL.

William Yang Wang, Kathryn Mazaitis, and William W Cohen. 2013. Programming with personalized pagerank: a locally groundable first-order probabilistic logic. In *Proceedings of the 22nd ACM international conference on Conference on information & knowledge management*, pages 2129–2138. ACM.

William Yang Wang, Kathryn Mazaitis, and William W Cohen. 2014. Structure learning via parameter learning. *Proceedings of the 23rd ACM International Conference on Information and Knowledge Management (CIKM 2014)*.

William Yang Wang, Kathryn Mazaitis, Ni Lao, Tom Mitchell, and William W Cohen. 2015. Efficient inference and learning in a large knowledge base: Reasoning with extracted information using a locally groundable first-order probabilistic logic. *Machine Learning Journal*.

Robert West, Evgeniy Gabrilovich, Kevin Murphy, Shaohua Sun, Rahul Gupta, and Dekang Lin. 2014. Knowledge base completion via search-based question answering. In *Proceedings of the 23rd international conference on World wide web*, pages 515–526. International World Wide Web Conferences Steering Committee.

Jason Weston, Antoine Bordes, Oksana Yakhnenko, Nicolas Usunier, et al. 2013. Connecting language and knowledge bases with embedding models for relation extraction. In *Proceedings of the 2013 Conference on Empirical Methods in Natural Language Processing*, pages 1366–1371.

Benjamin Roth Tassilo Barth Michael Wiegand and Mittul Singh Dietrich Klakow. 2013. Effective slot filling based on shallow distant supervision methods. *Proceedings of NIST KBP workshop*.

Fei Wu and Daniel S Weld. 2007. Autonomously semantifying wikipedia. In *Proceedings of the sixteenth ACM conference on Conference on information and knowledge management*, pages 41–50. ACM.

Fei Wu and Daniel S Weld. 2010. Open information extraction using wikipedia. In *Proceedings of the 48th Annual Meeting of the Association for Computational Linguistics*, pages 118–127. Association for Computational Linguistics.

A Knowledge-Intensive Model for Prepositional Phrase Attachment

Ndapandula Nakashole
Carnegie Mellon University
5000 Forbes Avenue
Pittsburgh, PA, 15213
ndapa@cs.cmu.edu

Tom M. Mitchell
Carnegie Mellon University
5000 Forbes Avenue
Pittsburgh, PA, 15213
tom.mitchell@cs.cmu.edu

Abstract

Prepositional phrases (PPs) express crucial information that knowledge base construction methods need to extract. However, PPs are a major source of syntactic ambiguity and still pose problems in parsing. We present a method for resolving ambiguities arising from PPs, making extensive use of semantic knowledge from various resources. As training data, we use both labeled and unlabeled data, utilizing an expectation maximization algorithm for parameter estimation. Experiments show that our method yields improvements over existing methods including a state of the art dependency parser.

1 Introduction

Machine reading and information extraction (IE) projects have produced large resources with many millions of facts (Suchanek et al., 2007; Mitchell et al., 2015). This wealth of knowledge creates a positive feedback loop for automatic knowledge base construction efforts: the accumulated knowledge can be leveraged to improve machine reading; in turn, improved reading methods can be used to better extract knowledge expressed using complex and potentially ambiguous language. For example, prepositional phrases (PPs) express crucial information that IE methods need to extract. However, PPs are a major source of syntactic ambiguity. In this paper, we propose to use semantic knowledge to improve PP attachment disambiguation. PPs such as "in", "at", and "for" express details about the *where, when,* and *why* of relations and events. PPs also state attributes of nouns.

As an example, consider the following sentences: *S1.) Alice caught the butterfly with the spots. S2.) Alice caught the butterfly with the net.*

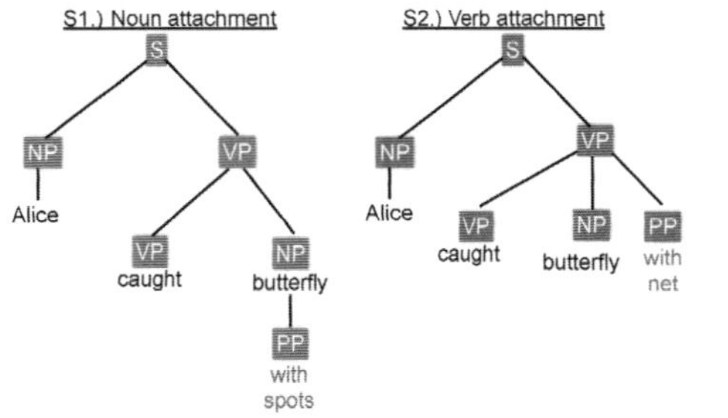

Figure 1: Parse trees where the prepositional phrase (PP) attaches to the noun, and to the verb.

Relations	Noun-Noun binary relations *(Paris, located in, France)* *(net, caught, butterfly)*
Nouns	Noun semantic categories *(butterfly, isA, animal)*
Verbs	Verb roles *caught(agent, patient, instrument)*
Prepositions	Preposition definitions *f(for)= used for, has purpose, ...* *f(with)= has, contains, ...*
Discourse	Context $n0 \in \{n0, v, n1, p, n2\}$

Table 1: Types of background knowledge used in this paper to determine PP attachment.

S1 and S2 are syntactically different, this is evident from their corresponding parse trees in Figure 1. Specifically, S1 and S2 differ in where their PPs attach. In S1, the butterfly has spots and therefore the PP, "with the spots", attaches to the *noun*. For relation extraction, we obtain a *binary* relation of the form: ⟨Alice⟩ caught ⟨butterfly with spots⟩. However, in S2, the net is the instrument used for catching and therefore the PP, "with the net", attaches to the *verb*. For relation extraction, we get a *ternary* extraction of the form: ⟨Alice⟩ caught ⟨butterfly⟩ with ⟨net⟩.

The PP attachment problem is often defined as follows: given a PP occurring within a sentence where there are multiple possible attachment sites

Proceedings of the 53rd Annual Meeting of the Association for Computational Linguistics and the 7th International Joint Conference on Natural Language Processing, pages 365–375,
Beijing, China, July 26-31, 2015.

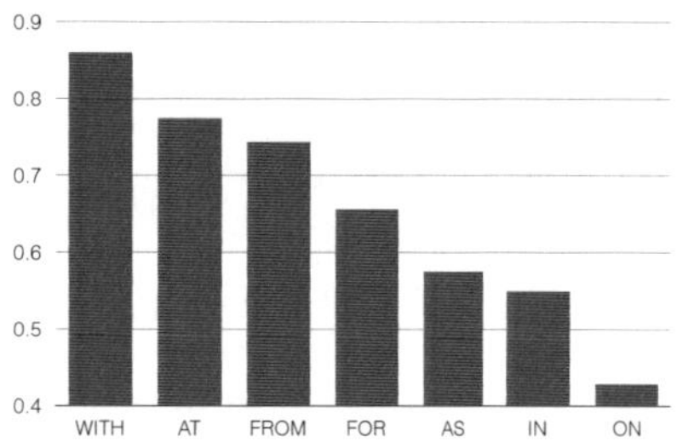

Figure 2: Dependency parser PP attachment accuracy for various frequent prepositions.

for the PP, choose the most plausible attachment site. In the literature, prior work going as far back as (Brill and Resnik, 1994; Ratnaparkhi et al., 1994; Collins and Brooks, 1995) has focused on the language pattern that causes most PP ambiguities, which is the 4-word sequence: $\{v, n1, p, n2\}$ (e.g., $\{$*caught, butterfly, with, spots*$\}$). The task is to determine if the prepositional phrase $(p, n2)$ attaches to the verb v or to the first noun $n1$. Following common practice, we focus on PPs occurring as $\{v, n1, p, n2\}$ quadruples — we shall refer to these as *PP quads*.

The approach we present here differs from prior work in two main ways. First, we make extensive use of semantic knowledge about nouns, verbs, prepositions, pairs of nouns, and the discourse context in which a PP quad occurs. Table 1 summarizes the types of knowledge we considered in our work. Second, in training our model, we rely on both labeled and unlabeled data, employing an expectation maximization (EM) algorithm (Dempster et al., 1977).

Contributions. In summary, our main contributions are:

1) Semantic Knowledge: Previous methods largely rely on corpus statistics. Our approach draws upon diverse sources of background knowledge, leading to performance improvements.

2) Unlabeled Data: In addition to training on labeled data, we also make use of a large amount of unlabeled data. This enhances our method's ability to generalize to diverse data sets.

3) Datasets: In addition to the standard Wall Street Journal corpus (WSJ) (Ratnaparkhi et al., 1994), we labeled two new datasets for testing purposes, one from Wikipedia (WKP), and another from the New York Times Corpus (NYTC). We make these datasets freely available for future research. In addition, we have applied our model to over 4 million 5-tuples of the form $\{n0, v, n1, p, n2\}$, and we also make this dataset available[1] for research into ternary relation extraction beyond spatial and temporal scoping.

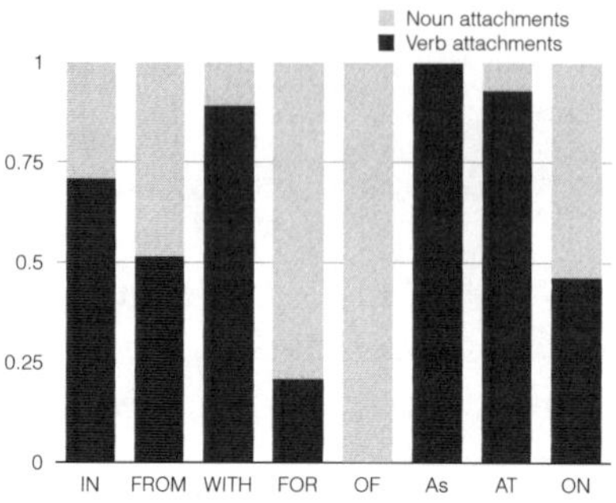

Figure 3: Noun vs. verb attachment proportions for frequent prepositions in the labeled NYTC dataset.

2 State of the Art

To quantitatively assess existing tools, we analyzed performance of the widely used Stanford parser[2] as of 2014, and the established baseline algorithm (Collins and Brooks, 1995), which has stood the test of time. We first manually labeled PP quads from the NYTC dataset, then prepended the noun phrase appearing before the quad, effectively creating sentences made up of 5 lexical items $(n0\ v\ n1\ p\ n2)$. We then applied the Stanford parser, obtaining the results summarized in Figure 2. The parser performs well on some prepositions, for example, "of", which tends to occur with noun attaching PPs as can be seen in Figure 3. However, for prepositions with an even distribution over verb and noun attachments, such as "on", precision is as low as 50%. The Collins baseline achieves 84% accuracy on the benchmark Wall Street Journal PP dataset. However, drawing a distinction in the precision of different prepositions provides useful insights on its performance. We re-implemented this baseline and found that when we remove the trivial preposition, "of", whose PPs are by default attached to the noun by this baseline, precision drops to 78%. This analysis suggests there is substantial room for improvement.

[1] http://rtw.ml.cmu.edu/resources/ppa

[2] http://nlp.stanford.edu:8080/parser/

3 Related Work

Statistics-based Methods. Prominent prior methods learn to perform PP attachment based on corpus co-occurrence statistics, gathered either from manually annotated training data (Collins and Brooks, 1995; Brill and Resnik, 1994) or from automatically acquired training data that may be noisy (Ratnaparkhi, 1998; Pantel and Lin, 2000). These models collect statistics on how often a given quadruple, $\{v, n1, p, n2\}$, occurs in the training data as a verb attachment as opposed to a noun attachment. The issue with this approach is sparsity, that is, many quadruples occuring in the test data might not have been seen in the training data. Smoothing techniques are often employed to overcome sparsity. For example, (Collins and Brooks, 1995) proposed a back-off model that uses subsets of the words in the quadruple, by also keeping frequency counts of triples, pairs and single words. Another approach to overcoming sparsity has been to use WordNet (Fellbaum, 1998) classes, by replacing nouns with their WordNet classes (Stetina and Nagao, 1997; Toutanova et al., 2004) to obtain less sparse corpus statistics. Corpus-derived clusters of similar nouns and verbs have also been used (Pantel and Lin, 2000).

Hindle and Rooth proposed a lexical association approach based on how words are associated with each other (Hindle and Rooth, 1993). Lexical preference is used by computing co-occurrence frequencies (lexical associations) of verbs and nouns, with prepositions. In this manner, they would discover that, for example, the verb "send" is highly associated with the preposition *from*, indicating that in this case, the PP is likely to be a verb attachment.

Structure-based Methods. These methods are based on high-level observations that are then generalized into heuristics for PP attachment decisions. (Kimball, 1988) proposed a right association method, whose premise is that a word tends to attach to another word immediately to its right. (Frazier, 1978) introduced a minimal attachment method, which posits that words attach to an existing non-terminal word using the fewest additional syntactic nodes. While simple, in practice these methods have been found to perform poorly (Whittemore et al., 1990).

Rule-based Methods. (Brill and Resnik, 1994) proposed methods that learn a set of transformation rules from a corpus. The rules can be too specific to have broad applicability, resulting in low recall. To address low recall, knowledge about nouns, as found in WordNet, is used to replace certain words in rules with their WordNet classes.

Parser Correction Methods. The quadruples formulation of the PP problem can be seen as a simplified setting. This is because, with quadruples, there is no need to deal with complex sentences but only well-defined quadruples of the form $\{v, n1, p, n2\}$. Thus in the quadruples setting, there are only two possible attachment sites for the PP, the v and $n1$. An alternative setting is to work in the context of full sentences. In this setting the problem is cast as a dependency parser correction problem (Atterer and Schütze, 2007; Agirre et al., 2008; Anguiano and Candito, 2011). That is, given a dependency parse of a sentence, with potentially incorrect PP attachments, rectify it such that the prepositional phrases attach to the correct sites. Unlike our approach, these methods do not take semantic knowledge into account.

Sense Disambiguation. In addition to prior work on prepositional phrase attachment, a highly related problem is preposition sense disambiguation (Hovy et al., 2011; Srikumar and Roth, 2013). Even a syntactically correctly attached PP can still be semantically ambiguous with respect to questions of machine reading such as *where, when,* and *why*. Therefore, when extracting information from prepositions, the problem of preposition sense disambiguation (semantics) has to be addressed in addition to prepositional phrase attachment disambiguation (syntax). In this paper, our focus is on the latter.

4 Methodology

Our approach consists of first generating features from background knowledge and then training a model to learn with these features. The types of features considered in our experiments are summarized in Table 2. The choice of features was motivated by our empirically driven characterization of the problem as follows:

(Verb attach) $\longrightarrow$ *v* $\langle$*has-slot-filler*$\rangle$ *n2*
(Noun attach a.) $\longrightarrow$ *n1* $\langle$*described-by*$\rangle$ *n2*
(Noun attach b.) $\longrightarrow$ *n2* $\langle$*described-by*$\rangle$ *n1*

Feature Type	#	Feature	Example
Noun-Noun Binary Relations		**Source: SVOs**	
	F1.	$svo(n2, v, n1)$	For q1; $(net, caught, butterfly)$
	F2.	$\forall i : \exists sv_io; svo(n1, v_i, n2)$	For q2; $(butterfly, has, spots)$
			For q2; $(butterfly, can\ see, spots)$
Noun Semantic Categories		**Source:** $\mathcal{T}$	
	F3.	$\forall t_i \in \mathcal{T}; isA(n1, t_i)$	For q1 $isA(butterlfy, animal)$
	F4.	$\forall t_i \in \mathcal{T}; isA(n2, t_i)$	For q2 $isA(net, device)$
Verb Role Fillers		**Source: VerbNet**	
	F5.	$hasRole(n2, r_i)$	For q1; $(net, instrument)$
Preposition Relational Definitions		**Source:** $\mathcal{M}$	
	F6.	$def(prep, v_i)\ \forall i : \exists sv_io; v_i \in \mathcal{M} \wedge svo(n1, v_i, n2)$	For q2; $def(with, has)$
Discourse Features		**Source: Sentence(s),** $\mathcal{T}$	
	F7.	$\forall t_i \in \mathcal{T}; isA(n0, t_i)$	$n0 \in \{n0, v, n1, p, n2\}$
Lexical Features		**Source: PP quads**	For q1;
	F8.	$(v, n1, p, n2)$	$(caught, butterfly, with, net)$
	F9.	$(v, n1, p)$	$(caught, butterfly, with)$
	F10.	$(v, p, n2)$	$(caught, with, net)$
	F11.	$(n1, p, n2)$	$(butterfly, with, net)$
	F12.	(v, p)	$(caught, with)$
	F13.	$(n1, p)$	$(butterfly, with)$
	F14.	$(p, n2)$	$(with, net)$
	F15.	(p)	$(with)$

Table 2: Types of features considered in our experiments. All features have values of 1 or 0. The PP quads used as running examples are: $q1 = \{caught, butterfly, with, net\} : V$, $q2 = \{caught, butterfly, with, spots\} : N$.

That is, we found that for verb-attaching PPs, $n2$ is usually a role filler for the verb, e.g., the net fills the role of an instrument for the verb *catch*. On the other hand, for noun-attaching PPs, one noun describes or elaborates on the other. In particular, we found two kinds of noun attachments. For the first kind of noun attachment, the second noun $n2$ describes the first noun $n1$, for example $n2$ might be an attribute or property of $n1$, as in the spots($n2$) are an attribute of the butterfly ($n1$). And for the second kind of noun attachment, the first noun $n1$ describes the second noun $n2$, as in the PP quad {*expect, decline, in, rates*}, where the PP "in rates", attaches to the *noun*. The decline:$n1$ that is expected:v is in the rates:$n2$. We sampled 50 PP quads from the WSJ dataset and found that every labeling could be explained using our characterization. We make this labeling available with the rest of the datasets.

We next describe in more detail how each type of feature is derived from the background knowledge in Table 1.

4.1 Feature Generation

We generate boolean-valued features for all the feature types we describe in this section.

4.1.1 Noun-Noun Binary Relations

The noun-noun binary relation features, F1-2 in Table 2, are boolean features $svo(n1, v_i, n2)$ (where v_i is any verb) and $svo(n2, v, n1)$ (where v is the verb in the PP quad, and the roles of $n2$ and $n1$ are reversed). These features describe diverse semantic relations between pairs of nouns (e.g., *butterfly-has-spots*, *clapton-played-guitar*). To obtain this type of knowledge, we dependency parsed all sentences in the 500 million English web pages of the ClueWeb09 corpus, then extracted subject-verb-object (SVO) triples from these parses, along with the frequency of each SVO triple in the corpus. The value of any given feature $svo(n1, v_i, n2)$ is defined to be 1 if that SVO triple was found at least 3 times in these SVO triples, and 0 otherwise. To see why these relations are relevant, let us suppose that we have the knowledge that *butterfly-has-spots*, $svo(n1, v_i, n2)$. From this, we can infer that the PP in $\{caught, butterfly, with, spots\}$ is likely to attach to the noun. Similarly, suppose we know that *net-caught-butterfly*, $svo(n2, v, n1)$. The fact that a net can be used to catch a butterfly can be used to predict that the PP in $\{caught, butterfly, with, net\}$ is likely to attach to the verb.

4.1.2 Noun Semantic Categories

Noun semantic type features, F3-4, are boolean features $isA(n1, t_i)$ and $isA(n2, t_i)$ where t_i is a noun category in a noun categorization scheme $\mathcal{T}$ such as WordNet classes. Knowledge about semantic types of nouns, for example that a butterfly is an animal, enables extrapolating predictions to other PP quads that contain nouns of the same type. We ran experiments with several noun categorizations including WordNet classes, knowledge base ontological types, and an unsupervised noun categorization produced by clustering nouns based on the verbs and adjectives with which they co-occur (distributional similarity).

4.1.3 Verb Role Fillers

The verb role feature, F5, is a boolean feature $hasRole(n2, r_i)$ where r_i is a role that $n2$ can fulfill for the verb v in the PP quad, according to background knowledge. Notice that if $n2$ fills a role for the verb, then the PP is a verb attachment. Consider the quad $\{caught, butterfly, with, net\}$, if we know that a net can play the role of an *instrument* for the verb *catch*, this suggests a likely verb attachment. We obtained background knowledge of verbs and their possible roles from the VerbNet lexical resource (Kipper et al., 2008). From VerbNet we obtained $2,573$ labeled sentences containing PP quads (verbs in the same VerbNet group are considered synonymous), and the labeled semantic roles filled by the second noun $n2$ in the PP quad. We use these example sentences to label similar PP quads, where similarity of PP quads is defined by verbs from the same VerbNet group.

4.1.4 Preposition Definitions

The preposition definition feature, $F6$, is a boolean feature $def(prep, v_i) = 1 \; if \; \exists v_i \in \mathcal{M} \wedge svo(n1, v_i, n2) = 1$, where $\mathcal{M}$ is a definition mapping of prepositions to verb phrases. This mapping defines prepositions, using verbs in our ClueWeb09 derived SVO corpus, in order to capture their senses using verbs; it contains definitions such as *def(with, *) = contains, accompanied by, ...* . If "with" is used in the sense of "contains" , then the PP is a likely noun attachment, as in $n1$ contains $n2$ in the quad $ate, cookies, with, cranberries$. However, if "with" is used in the sense of "accompanied by", then the PP is a likely verb attachment, as in the quad $visted, Paris, with, Sue$. To obtain the mapping, we took the labeled PP quads (WSJ, (Ratnaparkhi et al., 1994)) and computed a ranked list of verbs from SVOs, that appear frequently between pairs of nouns for a given preposition. Other sample mappings are: *def(for,*)= used for, def(in,*)= located in.* Notice that this feature $F6$ is a selective, more targeted version of $F2$.

4.1.5 Discourse and Lexical Features

The discourse feature, $F7$, is a boolean feature $isA(n0, t_i)$, for each noun category t_i found in a noun category ontology $\mathcal{T}$ such as WordNet semantic types. The context of the PP quad can contain relevant information for attachment decisions. We take into account the noun preceding a PP quad, in particular, its semantic type. This in effect makes the PP quad into a PP 5-tuple: $\{n0, v, n1, p, n2\}$, where the $n0$ provides additional context.

Finally, we use lexical features in the form of PP quads, features F8-15. To overcome sparsity of occurrences of PP quads, we also use counts of shorter sub-sequences, including triples, pairs and singles. We only use sub-sequences that contain the preposition, as the preposition has been found to be highly crucial in PP attachment decisions (Collins and Brooks, 1995).

4.2 Disambiguation Algorithm

We use the described features to train a model for making PP attachment decisions. Our goal is to compute $\mathbb{P}(y|x)$, the probability that the PP $(p, n2)$ in the tuple $\{v, n1, p, n2\}$ attaches to the *verb (v)* , $y = 1$ or to the $noun(n1)$, $y = 0$, given a feature vector x describing that tuple. As input to training the model, we are given a collection of PP quads, D where $d_i \in \mathcal{D} : d_i = \{v, n1, p, n2\}$. A small subset, $D^l \subset \mathcal{D}$ is labeled data, thus for each $d_i \in D^l$ we know the corresponding y_i. The rest of the quads, D^u, are unlabeled, hence their corresponding y_is are unknown. From each PP quad d_i, we extract a feature vector x_i according to the feature generation process discussed in Section 4.1.

4.2.1 Model

To model $\mathbb{P}(y|x)$, there a various possibilities. One could use a generative model (e.g., Naive Bayes) or a discriminative model (e.g., logistic regression). In our experiments we used both kinds of models, but found the discriminative model performed better. Therefore, we present details only for our discriminative model. We use the logistic function: $\mathbb{P}(y|x, \vec{\theta}) = \frac{e^{\vec{\theta}x}}{1+e^{\vec{\theta}x}}$, where $\vec{\theta}$ is a vector of model parameters. To estimate these parameters, we could use the labeled data as training data and use standard gradient descent to minimize the logistic regression cost function. However, we also leverage the unlabeled data.

4.2.2 Parameter Estimation

To estimate model parameters based on both labeled and unlabeled data, we use an Expectation Maximization (EM) algorithm. EM estimates model parameters that maximize the expected log likelihood of the full (observed and unobserved) data. Since we are using a discriminative model, our likelihood function is a conditional likelihood function:

$$\begin{aligned}\mathcal{L}(\theta) &= \sum_{i=1}^{N} \ln \mathbb{P}(y_i|x_i) \\ &= \sum_{i=1}^{N} y_i\theta^T x_i - \ln\left(1 + exp(\theta^T x_i)\right) \quad (1)\end{aligned}$$

where i indexes over the N training examples.

The EM algorithm produces parameter estimates that correspond to a local maximum in the expected log likelihood of the data under the posterior distribution of the labels, given by: $\arg\max_{\theta} E_{p(y|x,\theta)}[\ln \mathbb{P}(y|x,\theta)]$. In the E-step, we use the current parameters θ^{t-1} to compute the posterior distribution over the y labels, give by $\mathbb{P}(y|x, \theta^{t-1})$. We then use this posterior distribution to find the expectation of the log of the complete-data conditional likelihood, this expectation is given by $\mathcal{Q}(\theta, \theta^{\mathbf{t-1}})$, defined as:

$$\mathcal{Q}(\theta, \theta^{t-1}) = \sum_{i=1}^{N} E_{\theta^{t-1}}[\ln \mathbb{P}(y|x,\theta)] \quad (2)$$

In the M-step, a new estimate θ^t is then produced, by maximizing this Q function with respect to θ:

$$\theta^{\mathbf{t}} = \arg\max_{\theta} \mathcal{Q}(\theta, \theta^{\mathbf{t-1}}) \quad (3)$$

EM iteratively computes parameters $\theta^0, \theta^1, ...\theta^t$, using the above update rule at each iteration t, halting when there is no further improvement in the value of the Q function. Our algorithm is summarized in Algorithm 1. The M-step solution for θ^t is obtained using gradient ascent to maximize the Q function.

Algorithm 1 The EM algorithm for PP attachment

```
Input: X, D = D^l ∪ D^u
Output: θ^T
for t = 1 . . . T do
  E-Step:
  Compute p(y|x_i, θ^{t-1})
  x_i : d_i ∈ D^u; p(y|x_i, θ) = e^{θx} / (1+e^{θx})
  x_i : d_i ∈ D^l; p(y|x_i) = 1 if y = y_i, else 0
  M-Step:
  Compute new parameters, θ^t
  θ^t = arg max_θ Q(θ, θ^{t-1})

    Q(θ, θ^{t-1}) = Σ_{i=1}^{N} Σ_{y∈{0,1}} p(y|x_i, θ^{t-1}) ×
                    (yθ^T x_i − ln(1 + exp(θ^T x_i)))

  if convergence(L(θ), L(θ^{t-1})) then
    break
  end if
end for
return θ^T
```

5 Experimental Evaluation

We evaluated our method on several datasets containing PP quads of the form $\{v, n1, p, n2\}$. The task is to predict if the PP $(p, n2)$ attaches to the verb v or to the first noun $n1$.

5.1 Experimental Setup

Datasets. Table 3 shows the datasets used in our experiments. As labeled training data, we used the

DataSet	# Training quads	# Test quads
Labeled data		
WSJ	20,801	3,097
NYTC	0	293
WKP	0	381
Unlabeled data		
WKP	100,000	4,473,072

Table 3: Training and test datasets used in our experiments.

	PPAD	PPAD-NB	Coll-ins	Stan-ford
WKP	**0.793**	0.740	0.727	0.701
WKP \of	**0.759**	0.698	0.683	0.652
NYTC	**0.843**	0.792	0.809	0.679
NYTC \of	**0.815**	0.754	0.774	0.621
WSJ	**0.843**	0.816	0.841	N\A
WSJ \of	**0.779**	0.741	0.778	N\A

Table 4: PPAD vs. baselines.

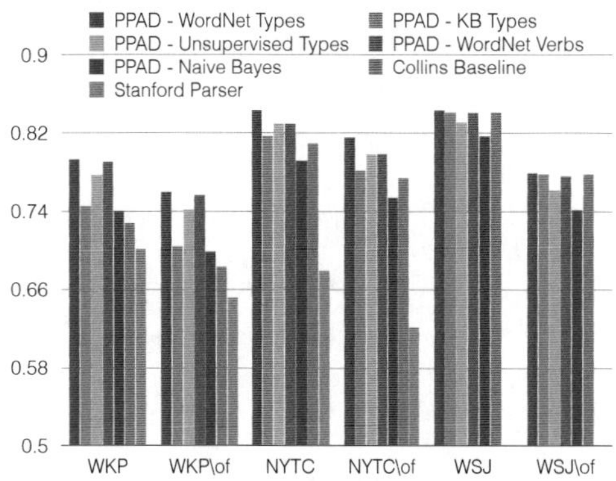

Figure 4: PPAD variations vs. baselines.

Wall Street Journal (WSJ) dataset. For the unlabeled training data, we extracted PP quads from Wikipedia (WKP) and randomly selected $100,000$ which we found to be a sufficient amount of unlabeled data. The largest labeled test dataset is WSJ but it is also made up of a large fraction, of "of" PP quads, 30% , which trivially attach to the noun, as already seen in Figure 3. The New York Times (NYTC) and Wikipedia (WKP) datasets are smaller but contain fewer proportions of "of" PP quads, 15%, and 14%, respectively. Additionally, we applied our model to over 4 million unlabeled 5-tuples from Wikipedia. We make this data available for download, along with our manually labeled NYTC and WKP datasets. For the WKP & NYTC corpora, each quad has a preceding noun, $n0$, as context, resulting in PP 5-tuples of the form: $\{n0, v, n1, p, n2\}$. The WSJ dataset was only available to us in the form of PP quads with no other sentence information.

Methods Under Comparison. *1) PPAD* (Prepositional Phrase Attachment Disambiguator) is our proposed method. It uses diverse types of semantic knowledge, a mixture of labeled and unlabeled data for training data, a logistic regression classifier, and expectation maximization (EM) for parameter estimation *2) Collins* is the established baseline among PP attachment algorithms (Collins and Brooks, 1995). *3) Stanford Parser* is a state-of-the-art dependency parser, the 2014 online version. *4) PPAD Naive Bayes(NB)* is the same as PPAD but uses a generative model, as opposed to the discriminative model used in PPAD.

5.2 PPAD vs. Baselines

Comparison results of our method to the three baselines are shown in Table 4. For each dataset, we also show results when the "of" quads are removed, shown as "WKP\of", "NYTC\of", and "WSJ\of". Our method yields improvements over the baselines. Improvements are especially significant on the datasets for which no labeled data was available (NYTC and WKP). On WKP, our method is 7% and 9% ahead of the Collins baseline and the Stanford parser, respectively. On NYTC, our method is 4% and 6% ahead of the Collins baseline and the Stanford parser, respectively. On WSJ, which is the source of the labeled data, our method is not significantly better than the Collins baseline. We could not evaluate the Stanford parser on the WSJ dataset. The parser requires well-formed sentences which we could not generate from the WSJ dataset as it was only available to us in the form of PP quads with no other sentence information. For the same reason, we could not generate discourse features,$F7$, for the WSJ PP quads. For the NYTC and WKP datasets, we generated well-formed short sentences containing only the PP quad and the noun preceding it.

Feature Type	Precision	Recall	F1
Noun-Noun Binary Relations (F1-2)	*low*	*high*	*low*
Noun Semantic Categories (F3-4)	*high*	*high*	**high**
Verb Role Fillers (F5)	*high*	*low*	*low*
Preposition Definitions (F6)	*low*	*low*	*low*
Discourse Features (F7)	*high*	*low*	**high**
Lexical Features (F8-15)	*high*	*high*	**high**

Table 5: An approximate characterization of feature knowledge sources in terms of precision/recall/F1

5.3 Feature Analysis

We found that features $F2$ and $F6$ did not improve performance, therefore we excluded them from the final model, PPAD. This means that binary noun-noun relations were not useful when used permissively, feature $F2$, but when used selectively, feature $F1$, we found them to be useful. Our attempt at mapping prepositions to verb definitions produced some noisy mappings, resulting in feature $F6$ producing mixed results. To analyze the impact of the unlabeled data, we inspected the features and their weights as produced by the PPAD model. From the unlabeled data, new lexical features were discovered that were not in the original labeled data. Some sample new features with high weights for verb attachments are: *(perform,song,for,*), (lose,*,by,*), (buy,property,in,*)*. And for noun attachments: *(*,conference,on,*), (obtain,degree,in,*), (abolish,taxes,on,*)*.

We evaluated several variations of PPAD, the results are shown in Figure 4. For "PPAD-WordNet Verbs", we expanded the data by replacing verbs in PP quads with synonymous WordNet verbs, ignoring verb senses. This resulted in more instances of features F1, F8-10, & F12.

We also used different types of noun categorizations: WordNet classes, semantic types from the NELL knowledge base (Mitchell et al., 2015) and unsupervised types. The KB types and the unsupervised types did not perform well, possibly due to the noise found in these categorizations. WordNet classes showed the best results, hence they were used in the final PPAD model for features F3-4 & F7. In Section 5.1, PPAD corresponds to the best model.

5.4 Discussion: The F1 Score of Knowledge

Why did we not reach 100% accuracy? Should relational knowledge not be providing a much bigger performance boost than we have seen in the results? To answer these questions, we characterize our features in terms precision and recall, and F1 measure of their knowledge sources in Table 5. A low recall feature means that the feature does not fire on many examples, the feature's knowledge source suffers from low coverage. A low precision feature means that when it fires, the feature could be incorrect, the feature's knowledge source contains a lot of errors.

From Table 5, the noun-noun binary relation features $(F1-2)$ have low precision, but high recall. This is because the SVO data, extracted from the ClueWeb09 corpus, that we used as our relational knowledge source is very noisy but it is high coverage. The low precision of the SVO data causes these features to be detrimental to performance. Notice that when we used a filtered version of the data, in feature $F2$, the data was no longer detrimental to performance. However, the $F2$ feature is low recall, and therefore it's impact on performance is also limited. The noun semantic category features $(F3-4)$ have high recall and precision, hence it to be expected that their impact on performance is significant. The verb role filler features $(F5)$, obtained from VerbNet have high precision but low recall, hence their marginal impact on performance is also to be expected. The preposition definition features $(F6)$ poor precision made them unusable. The discourse features $(F7)$ are based noun semantic types and lexical features $(F8-15)$, both of which have high recall and precision, hence they useful impact on performance.

In summary, low precision in knowledge is detrimental to performance. In order for knowledge to make even more significant contributions to language understanding, high precision, high recall knowledge sources are required for all features types. Success in ongoing efforts in knowledge base construction projects, will make performance of our algorithm better.

Relation	Prep.	Attachment accuracy	Example(s)
acquired	from	**99.97**	BNY Mellon *acquired* Insight *from* Lloyds.
hasSpouse	in	**91.54**	David *married* Victoria *in* Ireland.
worksFor	as	**99.98**	Shubert *joined* CNN *as* reporter.
playsInstrument	with	**98.40**	Kushner *played* guitar *with* rock band Weezer.

Table 6: Binary relations extended to ternary relations by mapping to verb-preposition pairs in PP 5-tuples. PPAD predicted verb attachments with accuracy >90% in all relations.

5.5 Application to Ternary Relations

Through the application of ternary relation extraction, we further tested PPAD's PP disambiguation accuracy and illustrated its usefulness for knowledge base population. Recall that a PP 5-tuple of the form $\{n0, v, n1, p, n2\}$, whose enclosed PP attaches to the verb v, denotes a ternary relation with arguments *n0, n1, & n2*. Therefore, we can extract a ternary relation from every 5-tuple for which our method predicts a verb attachment. If we have a mapping between verbs and binary relations from a knowledge base (KB), we can extend KB relations to ternary relations by augmenting the KB relations with a third argument $n2$.

We considered four KB binary relations and their instances such as $worksFor(TimCook, Apple)$, from the NELL KB. We then took the collection of 4 million 5-tuples that we extracted from Wikipedia. We mapped verbs in 5-tuples to KB relations, based on significant overlaps in the instances of the KB relations, noun pairs such as $(TimCook, Apple)$ with the $n0, n1$ pairs in the Wikipedia PP 5-tuple collection. We found that, for example, instances of the noun-noun KB relation "worksFor" match $n0, n1$ pairs in tuples where $v = joined$ and $p = as$, with $n2$ referring to the job title. Other binary relations extended are: "hasSpouse" extended by "in" with wedding location, "acquired" extended by "from" with the seller of the company being acquired. Examples are shown in Table 6. In all these mappings, the proportion of verb attachments in the corresponding PP quads is significantly high ($> 90\%$). PPAD is overwhelming making the right attachment decisions in this setting.

Efforts in temporal and spatial relation extraction have shown that higher N-ary relation extraction is challenging. Since prepositions specify details that transform binary relations to higher N-ary relations, our method can be used to read information that can augment binary relations already in KBs. As future work, we would like to incorporate our method into a pipeline for reading beyond binary relations. One possible direction is to read details about the *where,why, who* of events and relations, effectively moving from extracting only binary relations to reading at a more general level.

6 Conclusion

We have presented a knowledge-intensive approach to prepositional phrase (PP) attachment disambiguation, which is a type of syntactic ambiguity. Our method incorporates knowledge about verbs, nouns, discourse, and noun-noun binary relations. We trained a model using labeled data and unlabeled data, making use of expectation maximization for parameter estimation. Our method can be seen as an example of tapping into a positive feedback loop for machine reading, which has only become possible in recent years due to the progress made by information extraction and knowledge base construction techniques. That is, using background knowledge from existing resources to read better in order to further populate knowledge bases with otherwise difficult to extract knowledge. As future work, we would like to use our method to extract more than just binary relations.

Acknowledgments

We thank Shashank Srivastava and members of the NELL team at CMU for helpful comments. This research was supported by DARPA under contract number FA8750-13-2-0005.

References

Eneko Agirre, Timothy Baldwin, and David Martinez. 2008. Improving parsing and PP attachment performance with sense information. In *Proceedings of ACL-08: HLT*, pages 317–325.

Gerry Altmann and Mark Steedman. 1988. Interaction with context during human sentence processing. *Cognition*, 30:191–238.

Enrique Henestroza Anguiano and Marie Candito. 2011. Parse correction with specialized models for difficult attachment types. In *Proceedings of the 2011 Conference on Empirical Methods in Natural Language Processing, EMNLP*, pages 1222–1233.

Michaela Atterer and Hinrich Schütze. 2007. Prepositional phrase attachment without oracles. *Computational Linguistics*, 33(4):469–476.

Sören Auer, Christian Bizer, Georgi Kobilarov, Jens Lehmann, Richard Cyganiak, and Zachary G. Ives. 2007. Dbpedia: A nucleus for a web of open data. In *The Semantic Web, 6th International Semantic Web Conference, 2nd Asian Semantic Web Conference, ISWC 2007 + ASWC 2007, Busan, Korea, November 11-15, 2007.*, pages 722–735.

Michele Banko, Michael J Cafarella, Stephen Soderland, Matthew Broadhead, and Oren Etzioni. 2007. Open information extraction for the web. In *IJCAI*, volume 7, pages 2670–2676.

Kurt Bollacker, Colin Evans, Praveen Paritosh, Tim Sturge, and Jamie Taylor. 2008. Freebase: A collaboratively created graph database for structuring human knowledge. In *Proceedings of the 2008 ACM SIGMOD International Conference on Management of Data*, SIGMOD '08, pages 1247–1250.

Eric Brill and Philip Resnik. 1994. A rule-based approach to prepositional phrase attachment disambiguation. In *15th International Conference on Computational Linguistics, COLING*, pages 1198–1204.

Andrew Carlson, Justin Betteridge, Richard C. Wang, Estevam R. Hruschka, Jr., and Tom M. Mitchell. 2010. Coupled semi-supervised learning for information extraction. In *Proceedings of the Third ACM International Conference on Web Search and Data Mining*, WSDM '10, pages 101–110.

Michael Collins and James Brooks. 1995. Prepositional phrase attachment through a backed-off model. In *Proceedings of the Conference on Empirical Methods in Natural Language Processing*, pages 27–38.

Marie-Catherine de Marneffe, Bill MacCartney, and Christopher D. Manning. 2006. Generating typed dependency parses from phrase structure parses. In *Proceedings of the International Conference on Language Recources and Evaluation (LREC*, pages 449–454.

Luciano Del Corro and Rainer Gemulla. 2013. Clausie: Clause-based open information extraction. In *Proceedings of the 22Nd International Conference on World Wide Web*, WWW '13, pages 355–366.

A. P. Dempster, N. M. Laird, and D. B. Rubin. 1977. Maximum likelihood from incomplete data via the em algorithm. *Journal of the Royal Statistical Society, Series B*, 39(1):1–38.

Anthony Fader, Stephen Soderland, and Oren Etzioni. 2011a. Identifying relations for open information extraction. In *Proceedings of the Conference on Empirical Methods in Natural Language Processing*, EMNLP '11, pages 1535–1545.

Anthony Fader, Stephen Soderland, and Oren Etzioni. 2011b. Identifying relations for open information extraction. In *Proceedings of the Conference on Empirical Methods in Natural Language Processing*, pages 1535–1545. Association for Computational Linguistics.

Christiane Fellbaum, editor. 1998. *WordNet: an electronic lexical database*. MIT Press.

Lyn Frazier. 1978. *On comprehending sentences: Syntactic parsing strategies*. Ph.D. thesis, University of Connecticut.

Sanda M. Harabagiu and Marius Pasca. 1999. Integrating symbolic and statistical methods for prepositional phrase attachment. In *Proceedings of the Twelfth International Florida Artificial Intelligence Research Society ConferenceFLAIRS*, pages 303–307.

Donald Hindle and Mats Rooth. 1993. Structural ambiguity and lexical relations. *Computational Linguistics*, 19(1):103–120.

Dirk Hovy, Ashish Vaswani, Stephen Tratz, David Chiang, and Eduard Hovy. 2011. Models and training for unsupervised preposition sense disambiguation. In *Proceedings of the 49th Annual Meeting of the Association for Computational Linguistics: Human Language Technologies: Short Papers - Volume 2*, pages 323–328.

John Kimball. 1988. Seven principles of surface structure parsing in natural language. *Cognition*, 2:15–47.

Karin Kipper, Anna Korhonen, Neville Ryant, and Martha Palmer. 2008. A large-scale classification of english verbs. *Language Resources and Evaluation*, 42(1):21–40.

Dan Klein and Christopher D. Manning. 2003. Accurate unlexicalized parsing. In *Proceedings of the 41st Annual Meeting of the Association for Computational Linguistics,ACL*, pages 423–430.

Ni Lao, Tom Mitchell, and William W Cohen. 2011. Random walk inference and learning in a large scale knowledge base. In *Proceedings of the Conference on Empirical Methods in Natural Language Processing*, pages 529–539. Association for Computational Linguistics.

Jeff Mitchell and Mirella Lapata. 2008. Vector-based models of semantic composition. In *Proceedings of the 46th Annual Meeting of the Association for Computational Linguistics, ACL*, pages 236–244.

Tom M. Mitchell, William W. Cohen, Estevam R. Hruschka Jr., Partha Pratim Talukdar, Justin Betteridge, Andrew Carlson, Bhavana Dalvi Mishra, Matthew Gardner, Bryan Kisiel, Jayant Krishnamurthy, Ni Lao, Kathryn Mazaitis, Thahir Mohamed, Ndapandula Nakashole, Emmanouil Antonios Platanios, Alan Ritter, Mehdi Samadi, Burr Settles, Richard C. Wang, Derry Tanti Wijaya, Abhinav Gupta, Xinlei Chen, Abulhair Saparov, Malcolm Greaves, and Joel Welling. 2015. Never-ending learning. In *Proceedings of the Twenty-Ninth AAAI Conference on Artificial Intelligence, January 25-30, 2015, Austin, Texas, USA.*, pages 2302–2310.

Ndapandula Nakashole and Tom M. Mitchell. 2014. Language-aware truth assessment of fact candidates. In *Proceedings of the 52nd Annual Meeting of the Association for Computational Linguistics, ACL 2014, June 22-27, 2014, Baltimore, MD, USA, Volume 1: Long Papers*, pages 1009–1019.

Ndapandula Nakashole and Gerhard Weikum. 2012. Real-time population of knowledge bases: opportunities and challenges. In *Proceedings of the Joint Workshop on Automatic Knowledge Base Construction and Web-scale Knowledge Extraction*, pages 41–45. Association for Computational Linguistics.

Ndapandula Nakashole, Martin Theobald, and Gerhard Weikum. 2011. Scalable knowledge harvesting with high precision and high recall. In *Proceedings of the Fourth ACM International Conference on Web Search and Data Mining*, WSDM '11, pages 227–236.

Ndapandula Nakashole, Tomasz Tylenda, and Gerhard Weikum. 2013. Fine-grained semantic typing of emerging entities. In *Proceedings of the 51st Annual Meeting of the Association for Computational Linguistics, ACL*, pages 1488–1497.

Kamal Nigam, Andrew McCallum, Sebastian Thrun, and Tom M. Mitchell. 2000. Text classification from labeled and unlabeled documents using EM. *Machine Learning*, 39(2/3):103–134.

Patrick Pantel and Dekang Lin. 2000. An unsupervised approach to prepositional phrase attachment using contextually similar words. In *38th Annual Meeting of the Association for Computational Linguistics, ACL.*

Adwait Ratnaparkhi, Jeff Reynar, and Salim Roukos. 1994. A maximum entropy model for prepositional phrase attachment. In *Proceedings of the Workshop on Human Language Technology*, HLT '94, pages 250–255.

Adwait Ratnaparkhi. 1998. Statistical models for unsupervised prepositional phrase attachement. In *36th Annual Meeting of the Association for Computational Linguistics and 17th International Conference on Computational Linguistics, COLING-ACL*, pages 1079–1085.

Vivek Srikumar and Dan Roth. 2013. Modeling semantic relations expressed by prepositions. *TACL*, 1:231–242.

Jiri Stetina and Makoto Nagao. 1997. Prepositional phrase attachment through a backed-off model. In *Proceedings of the Conference on Empirical Methods in Natural Language Processing*, pages 66–80.

Fabian M Suchanek, Gjergji Kasneci, and Gerhard Weikum. 2007. Yago: a core of semantic knowledge. In *Proceedings of the 16th international conference on World Wide Web*, pages 697–706. ACM.

Kristina Toutanova, Christopher D. Manning, and Andrew Y. Ng. 2004. Learning random walk models for inducing word dependency distributions. In *Machine Learning, Proceedings of the Twenty-first International Conference, ICML.*

Olga van Herwijnen, Antal van den Bosch, Jacques M. B. Terken, and Erwin Marsi. 2003. Learning PP attachment for filtering prosodic phrasing. In *10th Conference of the European Chapter of the Association for Computational Linguistics,EACL*, pages 139–146.

Greg Whittemore, Kathleen Ferrara, and Hans Brunner. 1990. Empirical study of predictive powers od simple attachment schemes for post-modifier prepositional phrases. In *28th Annual Meeting of the Association for Computational Linguistics,ACL*, pages 23–30.

Derry Wijaya, Ndapandula Nakashole, and Tom Mitchell. 2014. Ctps: Contextual temporal profiles for time scoping facts via entity state change detection. In *Proceedings of the Conference on Empirical Methods in Natural Language Processing*. Association for Computational Linguistics.

Shaojun Zhao and Dekang Lin. 2004. A nearest-neighbor method for resolving pp-attachment ambiguity. In *Natural Language Processing - First International Joint Conference, IJCNLP*, pages 545–554.

A Convolution Kernel Approach to Identifying Comparisons in Text

Maksim Tkachenko
School of Information Systems
Singapore Management University
maksim.tkatchenko@gmail.com

Hady W. Lauw
School of Information Systems
Singapore Management University
hadywlauw@smu.edu.sg

Abstract

Comparisons in text, such as in online reviews, serve as useful decision aids. In this paper, we focus on the task of identifying whether a comparison exists between a specific pair of entity mentions in a sentence. This formulation is transformative, as previous work only seeks to determine whether a sentence is comparative, which is presumptuous in the event the sentence mentions multiple entities and is comparing only some, not all, of them. Our approach leverages not only lexical features such as salient words, but also structural features expressing the relationships among words and entity mentions. To model these features seamlessly, we rely on a dependency tree representation, and investigate the applicability of a series of tree kernels. This leads to the development of a new context-sensitive tree kernel: Skip-node Kernel (SNK). We further describe both its exact and approximate computations. Through experiments on real-life datasets, we evaluate the effectiveness of our kernel-based approach for comparison identification, as well as the utility of SNK and its approximations.

1 Introduction

When weighing various alternatives, users increasingly turn to the social media, by scouring online reviews, discussion forums, etc. Our goal is to extract from such corpora those text snippets where users make direct comparisons of entities. While sentiment analysis (Pang and Lee, 2008) may be helpful in evaluating individual entities, comparison by the same author within a sentence provides an unambiguous and more equitable basis for the relative positions of two entities on some aspect. For example, the sentence s_1 in Table 1, taken from an Amazon review about a digital camera, makes two distinct comparisons: #1) between "A630" and "A-series cameras" and #2) between "A630" and "its competition", with a clear sense of which entity mention is the *greater* on some aspect ("larger"). Moreover, comparisons may be objective (e.g., larger) or subjective (e.g., better), while sentiments are primarily subjective.

Problem Given a sentence and a specific pair of entity mentions, we seek to determine if a comparison exists between those two mentions. In previous work, the problem was formulated as identifying *comparative sentences*, i.e., those containing at least one comparison (Jindal and Liu, 2006a). This is not ideal because a sentence may contain more than two entity mentions, and may be comparing only some of them. For instance, s_1 is comparative with respect to the pair (A630, A-series cameras) and the pair (A630, its competition), but not the pair (A-series cameras, its competition).

We therefore postulate that the more appropriate formulation is *comparisons within sentences*. If a sentence compares two entities (A, B) with respect to some aspect Z, it should be possible to reformulate it into another sentence such as: "A is better than B with respect to Z" (Kessler and Kuhn, 2014a). Based on this definition, there is no comparison between (A-series cameras, its competition) in s_1. Here, we adopt this apt definition with a slight restriction to make it more practical, and seek to identify such comparisons automatically. We consider only sentences with at least two entity mentions involved in gradable comparisons, i.e., a clear sense of scaling in the comparison (e.g., A is better than B.). Such comparisons are more useful in investigating the pros and cons of entities, as opposed to equative comparisons expressing parity between two mentions (e.g., A is as good as B.), or superlative comparisons expressing the primacy of an entity with respect to unknown reference entities (e.g., A is the best.).

Proceedings of the 53rd Annual Meeting of the Association for Computational Linguistics and the 7th International Joint Conference on Natural Language Processing, pages 376–386,
Beijing, China, July 26-31, 2015.

ID	Sentence	Remarks
s_1	The A630 is slightly larger than previous generation A-series cameras, and also larger than much of its competition.	Contains two comparisons: (A630, A-series cameras) and (A630, its competition).
s_2	I got 30D for my wife because she wanted a better camera.	Includes comparative predicate "better", but contains no comparison.
s_3	I had D3100 and it was nice but the D5100 is truly amazing.	No comparative predicate, but has a comparison: (D3100, D5100).
s_4	D7000 and D7100 do better at high ISO than D300s.	Contains two comparisons: (D7000, D300s) and (D7100, D300s).

Table 1: Example Sentences with ≥ 2 Entity Mentions from Amazon.com Digital Cameras Reviews

Approach For English, there usually is a comparative predicate that anchors a comparison, such as "better" or "worse". However, many sentences with such predicate words are not comparisons. The sentence s_2 in Table 1 has the word "better", but does not contain any comparison between the entity mentions. Yet, other words (e.g., "amazing"), though not a comparative predicate, could signify a comparison, e.g., in s_3 in Table 1.

(Jindal and Liu, 2006a) considered the "context" around a predicate. A sentence is transformed into a sequence involving the predicate and the part of speech (POS) within a text window around the predicate (usually three words before and after). For instance, s_2 in Table 1 would be transformed into the sequence ⟨*PRP VBD DT better NN*⟩. Such sequences are labeled comparative or non-comparative, upon which (Jindal and Liu, 2006a) applies sequential pattern mining (Agrawal and Srikant, 1995; Ayres et al., 2002; Pei et al., 2001) to learn *class sequential rule* (CSR). These CSRs are then used as features in classifying comparative sentences.

While (Jindal and Liu, 2006a) makes some progress by considering context, its performance may be affected by several factors. First, CSRs are not sensitive to entity mentions. It may classify s_1 as comparative generally, missing the nuance that s_1 is not comparing the pair (A-series cameras, its competition). Second, as CSRs requires a list of comparative predicates, the quality and the completeness of the list are crucial. For instance, "amazing" is not in their list, and thus the comparison in s_3 may not be identifiable. Third, due to the windowing effect, CSRs has a limited ability to model long-range dependencies. For s_4, a window of three words around the predicate "better" excludes the word "than" that would have been very informative. Yet, enlarging the window might then bring in irrelevant associations.

What is important then is not so much whether a sentence is comparative as whether two entity mentions are related by a comparative relation. One insight we draw is how comparison identification is effectively a form of *relation extraction*. While there are diverse relation extraction formulations (Culotta and Sorensen, 2004; Bunescu and Mooney, 2005; Nguyen et al., 2009), our distinct relation type is comparison of two entity mentions.

Armed with this insight, we propose a kernel-based approach based on a dependency tree representation (Nivre, 2005), with significant innovations motivated by the comparative identification task. This proposed approach has several advantages over CSR. Most importantly, it models dependencies between any pair of words (including entity mentions), whereas CSR only relates a comparative predicate to nearby POS tags. For other advantages, unlike CSR, this approach is contingent on neither a pre-specified list of comparative predicates, nor a specific window length.

Contributions In this paper, we make the following contributions. *First*, we re-formulate the problem of automatic identification of comparative sentences into the more general task of identifying comparisons within sentences. *Second*, we propose to frame comparison identification as a relation extraction problem. This entails: #1) deriving an appropriate dependency tree representation of sentences to enable discrimination of comparison vs. non-comparison within the same sentence (see Section 2), and #2) a systematic exploration of the applicability of various tree kernel spaces to our task (see Section 3). *Third*, due to the limitation of the existing tree kernels, we propose a new tree kernel: Skip-node Kernel that is context-sensitive, and discuss both its exact and approximate computations (see Section 4). *Fourth*, we validate its effectiveness and efficiency through experiments on real-life datasets (see Section 5).

2 Overview

Task The input is a corpus of sentences $\mathcal{S}$ concerning a set of entities within a certain domain (e.g., digital cameras). Every sentence $s \in \mathcal{S}$ contains at least two entity mentions. The set of entity mentions in s is denoted M_s. For instance, the sentence s_4 in Table 1 contains three entity mentions: D7000, D7100, and D300s. The same entity may be mentioned more than once in a sentence, in which case every mention is a distinct instance.

As output, we seek to determine, for each pair of entity mentions $(m_i < m_j) \in M_s$ in a sentence $s \in \mathcal{S}$, a binary class label of whether s contains a comparison between m_i and m_j. For the pair (D7000, D7100) in s_4, the correct class is 0 (no comparison). For the other two pairs (D7000, D300s) and (D7100, D300s), the correct class is 1 (comparisons). We do not seek to identify the aspect of comparison, which is a different problem of independent research interest (see Section 6).

Dependency Tree In order to represent both the lexical units (words) as well their structural dependencies seamlessly, we represent each sentence s as a dependency tree T. For example, Figure 1(a) shows the dependency tree of s_4 in Table 1. The tree is rooted at the main verb ("do"), and each dependency relation associates a head word and a dependent word. To describe a tree or any of its substructures, we use the bracket notation. Figure 1(a) in this notation is `[do [D7000 [and] [D7100]] [better [at [ISO [high]]] [than [D300s]]]]`.

Here, we make two observations. First, there is one tree even for a sentence with multiple pairs of entity mentions. Second, the information signalling a comparison is borne by the structures around the mentions (e.g., `[better [than]]`, rather than the actual mentions (e.g., "D7000"). These lead us to introduce a *modified* dependency tree that is distinct for every pair of mentions, achieved by replacing each entity mention of interest by a placeholder token. Here, we use the token "#camera" for illustration. Figure 1(b) shows the modified tree for the pair (D7000, D7100). This enables learning in an entity-agnostic way, because the token ensures that sentences about different cameras are interpreted similarly.

Convolution Kernel Observe how the trees of the pair (D7000, D300s) in Figure 1(c) and the pair (D7100, D300s) in Figure 1(d), which are both comparisons, share certain substructures, such

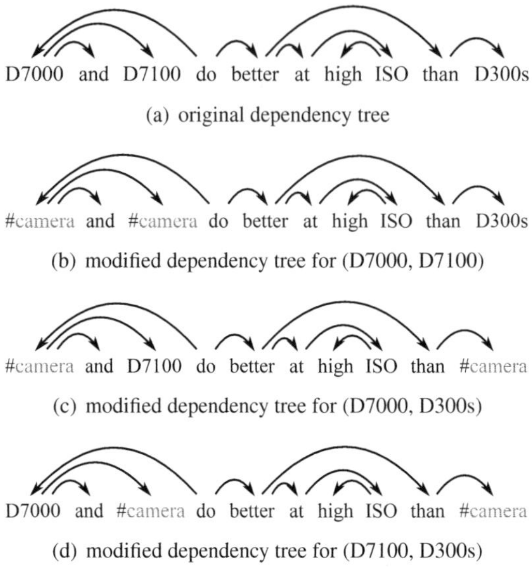

Figure 1: Modified dependency trees.

as `[do [better [than [#camera]]]]`. In contrast, the tree in Figure 1(b) for the pair (D7000, D7100), which is not a comparison, does not contain this substructure. What we need is a way to systematically examine tree substructures to determine the similarity between two trees.

Kernel methods offer a way to measure the similarity by exploring an implicit feature space without enumerating all substructures explicitly. Suppose that $\mathbf{T}$ denotes the space of all possible instances. A kernel function K is a symmetric and positive semidefinite function that maps the instance space $\mathbf{T} \times \mathbf{T}$ to a real value in the range of $[0, \infty)$ (Haussler, 1999). A tree kernel function can be reformulated into a *convolution kernel* (Collins and Duffy, 2001), shown in Equation 1.

$$K(T_1, T_2) = \sum_{n_i \in T_1} \sum_{n_j \in T_2} D(n_i, n_j) \qquad (1)$$

Here, n_i and n_j denote each node in their respective tree instances T_1 and T_2. $D(n_i, n_j)$ is the number of common substructure instances between the two sub-trees rooted in n_i and n_j respectively. The exact form of $D(n_i, n_j)$ depends on the specific definition of the tree kernel space. In Section 3, we systematically explore the applicability of various tree kernel spaces, leading to the introduction of the new *Skip-node Kernel*.

The appropriate kernel function can be embedded seamlessly in kernel methods for classification. In this work, we use the Support Vector Machines (SVM) (Steinwart and Christmann, 2008).

3 Tree Kernel Spaces

Tree kernels count substructures of a tree in some high-dimensional feature space. Different tree kernel spaces vary in the amount and the type of information they can capture, and thus may suit different purposes. To find a suitable tree kernel for the comparison identification task, we first systematically explore a progression of known tree kernel spaces, including Sub-tree, Subset Tree, and Partial Tree. Through the use of appropriate examples, we show how these existing tree kernel spaces may not be appropriate for certain instances. This section culminates in the introduction of a new feature space that we call Skip-node.

Sub-tree (ST) Space In this space, the basic substructure is a subgraph formed by a node along with all its descendants. Applying this kernel to two dependency trees of similar sentences may not be appropriate due to, for example, modifier words that change the dependency structure. To illustrate this, let us examine the two dependency parses in Figure 2. Both support comparisons, and ideally we can detect some level of similarity. However, if we consider only sub-trees, the two dependency trees share in common only two fragments: `[#camera]` and `[is]`. Neither of these fragments is indicative of a comparison.

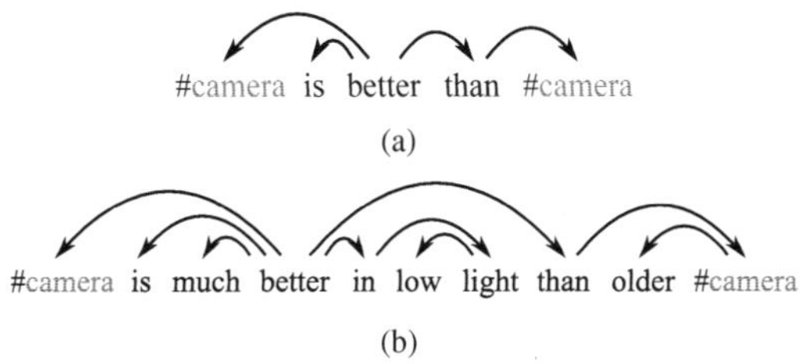

Figure 2: Dependency parses. Working example for the Sub-tree, Subset Tree, Partial Tree kernels.

Subset Tree (SST) Space We next consider the SST kernel, which computes similarity in a more general space of substructures than ST. Any subgraph of a tree that preserves production rules is counted. This definition suggests SST is intended more for a constituency parse (Moschitti, 2006a). In this feature space, the parses in Figure 2 now have in common the following fragments: `[#camera]`, `[is]`, `[than [#camera]]`. This representation is better than ST's, e.g., the fragment `[than [#camera]]` is informative. However, as a whole, the set of features are still insufficient to identify a comparison.

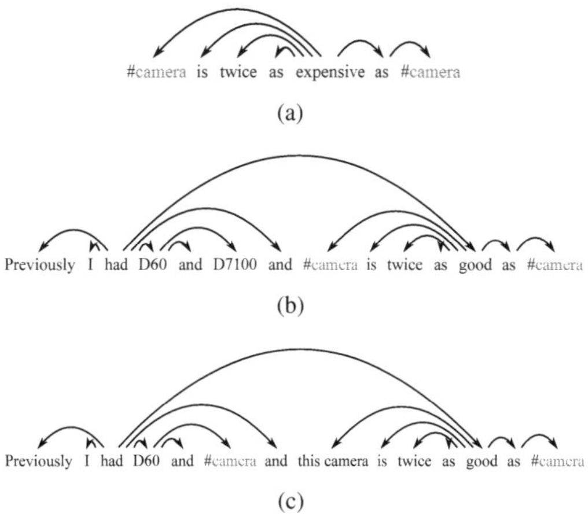

Figure 3: Dependency parses. Working example for the Partial Tree, Skip-node kernels.

Partial Tree (PT) Space In turn, the PT space allows breaking of production rules, making it a better choice than SST for dependency parses. PT kernel would find that the parse in Figure 2(a) with all its subgraphs can be matched as a whole within the parse in Figure 2(b), identifying a close match.

However, PT kernel is prone to two drawbacks. By generating an exponential feature space, it may overfit and degrade generalization (Cumby and Roth, 2003). More importantly, PT considers tree fragments independently from their contexts, resulting in features involving non-related parts of a sentence. This is particularly apparent when we consider multiple entities within a sentence.

Suppose that Figure 3(a) is in our training set, and we have the sentence below in the testing set:

> Previously, I had D60 and D7100, and this camera is twice as good as D60.

Figure 3(b) shows the parse for (this camera, D60), and Figure 3(c) for (D7100, D60). The former is a comparison, and should match Figure 3(a). The latter is not and should not match. PT kernel cannot resolve this ambiguity, computing the same similarity value to Figure 3(a) for both. The common features are: `[#camera]`, `[is]`, `[twice]`, `[as]`, and `[as [#camera]]`.

Skip-node (SN) Space Figures 3(a) and 3(b) share a similar substructure "twice as ... as", but because they use different words to express the comparisons ("expensive" vs. "good"), previous kernels treat their features disjointly, missing out on their similarity. To reduce this over-reliance on exact word similarity, we seek a feature space that

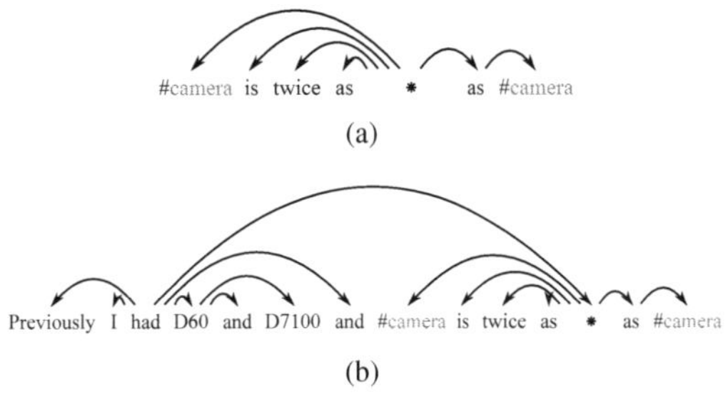

Figure 4: Dependency parses with skipped nodes.

would allow some degree of relaxation in determining the *structural* similarity between trees.

We therefore propose the Skip-node (SN) space, which represents a generalized space of tree fragments, where some nodes can be "skipped" or relabeled to a special symbol '$\star$' that would match nodes of any label. A restriction on this space is that each skip symbol must connect two non-skip (regular) nodes. The implication is that skips code for some notion of connecting distance between non-skip nodes. Moreover, the space would not include features such as `[* [* [#camera]]]` that serve only to indicate the presence of ancestors, and not any relationship of non-skip nodes.

Figure 4 resolves the ambiguity in Figure 3 by skipping the words "expensive" and "good", introducing a new set of features: `[* [#camera] [is] [twice] [as] [as [#camera]]]`. Note how in this case the skip symbol effectively serves as a "context" that pulls together the previously disjoint features identified by the PT kernel. These new context-sensitive features would allow a match between the earlier Figures 3(a) and 3(b), but not Figure 3(c).

Thus, SN space effectively generalizes over the PT space, and enriches it with context-sensitive features. To avoid overfitting, in addition to decay parameter λ used in PT kernel, we associate SN kernel with two other parameters. The SN space consists of rooted ordered trees where some nodes are labeled with a special skip symbol '$\star$', such that the number of regular nodes (not marked with '$\star$') is at most S, and each skip node is within a distance of L from a non-skip node. This engenders a graceful gradation of similarity as the number of skip nodes in a substructure grows, yet imposes a limit to the extent of relaxation.

4 Skip-node Kernel Computation

We now discuss the computation of Skip-node Kernel, first exactly, and thereafter approximately.

4.1 Exact Computation

We define the alignment of common fragments between two trees in the Skip-node space. When $S = 1$, only singleton nodes with the same labels contribute to the kernel, and alignment is straightforward. When aligning fragments with two regular nodes ($S > 1$), we consider their connection structure and the order of the child nodes to prevent over-counting substructures with the same labels (e.g., `[*[as][as]]` in Figure 4). To preserve the natural order of words in a sentence, we enumerate the tree nodes according to preorder, left-to-right depth-first search (DFS) traversal.

In turn, the connection structure is defined by the skip-node path connecting two regular nodes. This can be expressed as a sequence of upward (towards the root) and downward (towards the leaves) steps we need to perform to get from the leftmost to the rightmost regular node. Due to the natural ordering of regular nodes, upward steps are followed by downward steps. The sequence can be expressed as a pair of numbers: $\langle \rho(n_l, u), \rho(n_r, u)\rangle$, where n_l is the leftmost regular node of a fragment, n_r is the rightmost one, $u = \sigma(n_l, n_r)$ is the lowest common ancestor of nodes n_l, n_r, and ρ returns the number of edges in the shortest path connecting two nodes.

Suppose a rooted tree $T = (N, E)$ has preorder DFS enumeration $N = (n_1, n_2, ..., n_{|N|})$. For $i < j$, we define a function $\pi(n_i, n_j)$, which canonically represents the way two nodes are connected in a tree, as follows:

$$\pi(n_i, n_j) = \langle \rho(n_i, \sigma(n_i, n_j)), \rho(n_j, \sigma(n_i, n_j))\rangle.$$

DEFINITION 1 (STRUCTURAL ISOMORPHISM): Given two trees $T_1 = (N_1, E_1)$, $T_2 = (N_2, E_2)$, we say that pairs of nodes $(v_i, u_{i'}), (v_j, u_{j'}) \in N_1 \times N_2$ are *structurally isomorphic* and write $(v_i, u_{i'}) \leftrightsquigarrow (v_j, u_{j'})$ when $\pi(v_i, v_j) = \pi(u_{i'}, u_{j'})$ on the valid domain.

It can be shown that structural isomorphism is a transitive relation. This property allows us to grow aligned fragments by adding one node at a time:

$$(v_i, u_{i'}) \leftrightsquigarrow (v_j, u_{j'}) \wedge (v_j, v_{j'}) \leftrightsquigarrow (v_k, u_{k'}) \Rightarrow (v_i, u_{i'}) \leftrightsquigarrow (v_k, u_{k'}).$$

To compute the kernel, we use a graph-based approach to enumerate all the common substructures in the Skip-node space. Given two trees T_1 and T_2, we begin by aligning their nodes. The sets of nodes in T_1 and T_2 are N_1 and N_2 respectively. Let N_G be a set of pairs $(n_i, n_j) \in N_1 \times N_2$, where n_i and n_j have the same label. On top of N_G, we build a graph $G = (N_G, E_G)$. We draw an edge between two vertices $(v_i, v_k), (u_j, u_l) \in N_G$, if $(v_i, u_j) \leftrightsquigarrow (v_k, u_l)$ and $\rho(v_i, v_k) \leq L$.

Any connected subgraph of G represents a feature in the Skip-node space common to both T_1 and T_2. The kernel then needs to count the number of connected subgraphs of sizes not more than S. To see that this procedure is correct, we simply need to trace back the construction of graph G, and build an bijection from a subgraph of G to the corresponding fragments of T_1 and T_2.

Enumerating all the connected subgraphs of a given graph requires exponential time. The algorithm described above requires $\mathcal{O}(|N_1||N_2| + \sum_{i=1}^{S} \binom{|N_G|}{i})$ time, assuming that the distance between two nodes in a tree can be computed in $\mathcal{O}(1)$ with appropriate linear preprocessing. See (Bender and Farach-Colton, 2000) for insight. The exact computation is still tractable on the condition that S and L are not very large. This condition would probably hold in most realistic scenarios. Yet, to improve the practicality of the kernel, we propose a couple of approximations as follows.

4.2 Approximate Computation

One reason for the complexity of the Skip-node kernel is that although the graph G is formed by aligning two trees, by allowing connections through skips, G itself may not necessarily be in the form of a tree. In deriving an approximation, our strategy is to form G through alignment of linear substructures of the original two trees. A Skip-node space over linear structures can be computed in polynomial time using dynamic programming.

Linear Skip-node One approximation is to consider linear substructures in the form of root-paths. A root-path is a path from the root of a tree to a leaf. Given two trees T_1 and T_2, with DFS enumerated nodes $N_1 = (v_1, v_2, ..., v_{m_1})$ and $N_2 = (u_1, u_2, ..., u_{m_2})$ respectively. Here, v_1 and u_1 are roots, and v_{m_1} and u_{m_2} are the leaves. Starting with common fragments at the leaves, we grow them into larger common fragments towards the root. We call this approximation *Linear Skip-node*. Figure 5(a) shows examples of features considered by Linear Skip-node for the illustrated tree T in skip-node space ($S = 3, L = 2$).

The kernel function can be decomposed into:

$$K(T_1, T_2) = \sum_{v_i \in N_1} \sum_{u_j \in N_2} \sum_{s=1}^{S} \lambda^s D(v_i, u_j, s),$$

where $D(v_i, u_j, s)$ is the number of common substructures of size s with the leftmost regular nodes v_i and u_j. λ is a decay factor for substructure size.

The recursive definition of the kernel is:

$$D(v_i, u_j, s) = \sum_{i<k \leq m_1} \sum_{j<l \leq m_2} I(v_i, v_k, u_j, u_l) D(v_k, u_l, s-1),$$

$$D(v_i, u_j, 1) = \begin{cases} 1 & \text{if } label(v_i) = label(u_j), \\ 0 & \text{otherwise;} \end{cases}$$

$$I(v_i, v_k, u_j, u_l) = \mathbb{1}_{(v_i, u_j) \leftrightsquigarrow (v_k, u_l)} \mathbb{1}_{\rho(v_i, v_k) \leq L} \cdot \mathbb{1}_{(v_i \text{ is an ancestor of } v_k)},$$

where $\mathbb{1}_c$ equals 1 when constraint c is satisfied and 0 otherwise. Note that the first two factors of indicator function I just represent the general Skip-node space constraints, the last factor ensures that features are computed along the root-paths.

Lookahead Skip-node The second approximation, *Lookahead Skip-node*, is related to the observation that when growing a substructure, we do not have to confine the growth only towards ancestors, as DFS traversal already ensures iterative manner of computation. In other words, the constraint v_i is an ancestor of v_k can be dropped:

$$I(v_i, v_k, u_j, u_l) = \mathbb{1}_{(v_i, u_j) \leftrightsquigarrow (v_k, u_l)} \cdot \mathbb{1}_{\rho(v_i, v_k) \leq L}.$$

In addition to those features generated by Linear Skip-node in Figure 5(a), Lookahead Skip-node can generate additional tree substructures, shown in Figure 5(b). The approximation can be computed using different DFS enumerations, which may result in different feature sets. In our experiments, we used pre-order left-to-right enumeration. Given the enumeration of tree T as in Figure 5, we start to grow feature fragments from node n_4. According to the Skip-node space constraints, the growth can only proceed to nodes n_1 or n_2. Once any of these nodes is attached to n_4, we lose tree fragments containing n_3, as the procedure allows us to grow substructures only towards nodes with smaller (earlier) DFS enumer-

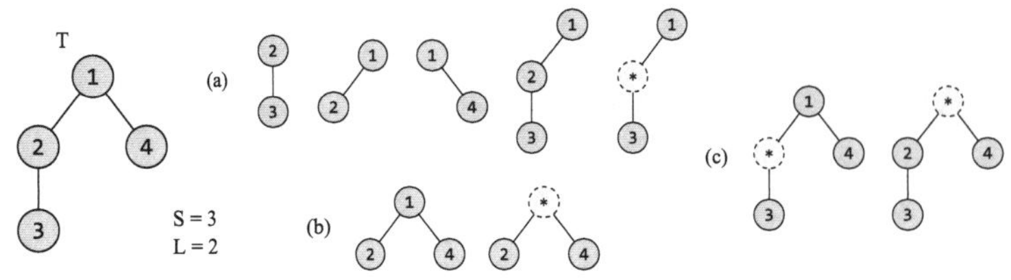

Figure 5: Features of T in skip-node space ($S = 3, L = 2$). Numbers indicates pre-order left-to-right DFS enumeration of T. Dashed circles represent skip nodes. Subfigures: (a) - modeled by all; (b) - modeled by Lookahead Skip-node, not by Linear Skip-node; (c) - modeled only by Exact Skip-node.

Domain	# sentences	% comp.	# pairs	% comp.
Camera	1716	59.4%	2170	49.9%
Cell	821	35.2%	1110	30.5%

Table 2: The dataset size for each domain.

ation numbers. Figure 5(c) shows the fragments that Lookahead Skip-node cannot capture[1].

The computation procedure is similar for both approximations and requires $\mathcal{O}(S|N_1|^2|N_2|^2)$.

5 Experiments

Data For experiments, we compiled two annotated datasets in two domains: Digital Camera and Cell Phone from online review sentences. The reviews were collected from *Amazon* and *Epinions*[2].

We identified the entity mentions through dictionary matching, followed by manual annotation to weed out false positives. Each dictionary entry is a product name (e.g., *Canon PowerShot D20, D7100*) or a common product reference (e.g., *this camera, that phone*). The dataset includes only sentences that contain at least two entity mentions. Every pair of entities within a sentence was annotated with a comparative label according to the definition given in Section 2. A sentence is comparative if at least one pair of entities within it is in a comparative relation. Table 2 shows the dataset properties, in terms of the number sentences and the percentage that are comparative sentences, as well as the number of pairs of entity mentions and the percentage that are comparative relations. There are more pairs than sentences, i.e., many sentences mention more than two entities.

This dataset subsumes the annotated gradable comparisons of (Kessler and Kuhn, 2014a) derived from *Epinions* reviews on Digital Cameras. (Jindal and Liu, 2006a)'s dataset is inapplicable, due to its lack of entity-centric comparison.

	Camera			Cell		
	P	R	F1	P	R	F1
CSR	74.3	52.3	61.3	48.9	**61.5***	54.3
BoW	76.9	**76.3**	76.6	62.2	58.0	59.8
BoW†	77.3	71.9	74.4	69.0	56.3	61.8
SNK	**80.5***	75.2	**77.7****	**77.2***	55.1	**64.1***

Table 3: Comparison identification task

Evaluation The experiments were carried out with SVM-light-TK framework[3] (Joachims, 1999; Moschitti, 2006b), into which we built Skip-node Kernel. We further release a separate standalone library that we built, called Tree-SVM[4], which does SVM optimization using the tree kernels described in this paper. The sentences were parsed and lemmatized with the use of the Stanford NLP software (Chen and Manning, 2014).

The experiments were done on 10 random data splits in 80:20 proportion of training vs. testing. Performance is measured by using F_1, which is the harmonic mean of precision P and recall R: $F_1 = \frac{2PR}{P+R}$. The statistical significance[5] is measured by randomization test (Yeh, 2000). The hyper-parameters, including the baselines', were optimized for F_1 through grid-search.

5.1 Comparison Identification

Our first and primary objective is to investigate the effectiveness of the proposed approach on the task of identifying comparisons between a pair of en-

[1]In this particular case, all features could have been computed by Lookahead Skip-node using preorder right-to-left DFS enumeration, although it may not be true in general.

[2]We used already available snapshots for *Epinions* dataset: http://groups.csail.mit.edu/rbg/code/precis/.

[3]http://disi.unitn.it/moschitti/Tree-Kernel.htm

[4]http://github.com/sitfoxfly/tree-svm

[5]When presenting the results, an asterisk indicates that the outperformance over the second-best result is significant at 0.05 level. Two asterisks indicate the same at 0.1 level.

	Camera			Cell		
	P	R	F1	P	R	F1
CSR	74.6	51.7	60.9	50.9	**61.2***	55.3
BoW	77.5	**76.3**	76.8	63.4	57.7	60.2
BoW†	77.6	72.4	74.9	70.9	57.3	63.2
SNK	**81.0***	75.2	**78.0****	**77.9***	54.8	**64.2**

Table 4: Comparative sentence identification task

tity mentions. Previous work focused on identifying comparative sentences. We compare to three baselines. One is CSR, implemented following the description in (Jindal and Liu, 2006a). Another is BoW, classification using bag-of-words as features. For the baselines, if a comparative sentence contains more than one pair of entities, we assume that every pair is in comparative relation. The third baseline, BoW†, considers only the words in between of the two target entities.

Table 3 shows the performance on the comparison identification task (best results are in bold). In terms of F_1, it is evident that SNK outperforms the baselines. This is achieved through significant gains in precision. It is expected that the baselines tend to have a high recall. CSR benefits from the human-constructed predefined list of comparative keywords and key phrases that a kernel-based method is unable to learn from a training split. BoW† tends to have a higher precision than the other baselines, as it is able to distinguish between different pairs of entities within one sentence.

While SNK may have an inherent advantage over CSR or BoW due to its entity orientation, to investigate the effectiveness of the method itself, we now compare them on the previous task of comparative sentence identification. Table 4 shows that even in this task, SNK still performs better than the baselines. Comparing Table 3 and Table 4, the results also concur with the intuition: once we fold up multiple entity pairs in a sentence into a comparative sentence, we observe a drop in recall and an increase in precision.

5.2 Tree Kernel Spaces

Our second objective is to explore the progression of feature spaces discussed in Section 3. Table 5 reports the results on comparison identification task. The F_1 columns show that the performance gradually increases from STK to SNK along with the increase in the complexity of feature space. PTK and SNK can be considered high-

	Camera			Cell		
	P	R	F1	P	R	F1
STK	67.5	64.0	64.9	43.7	41.9	42.6
SSTK	72.1	72.6	71.8	**79.6**	42.4	54.9
PTK	79.2	74.9	76.9	72.3	**56.0****	62.7
SNK	**80.5***	**75.2**	**77.7****	77.2	55.1	**64.1***

Table 5: Tree kernels

	Camera			Cell		
	P	R	F1	P	R	F1
STK_{BoW}	79.9	65.1	71.7	**77.5**	45.3	56.8
$SSTK_{BoW}$	78.0	73.5	75.6	71.8	54.5	61.6
PTK_{BoW}	78.6	74.1	76.2	71.0	53.8	60.8
SNK	**80.5**	**75.2****	**77.7***	77.2	**55.1**	**64.1****

Table 6: Tree kernels combined with bag-of-words

variance estimators due to the power of their feature spaces. The data is such that these kernels may not have fully modeled the feature space completely enough to show even sharper differences.

SNK's parameters were optimized to non-trivial cases ($S > 1$ and $L > 1$) by the grid-search, i.e., $S = 3$ and $L = 2$ for Digital Camera and $S = 2$ and $L = 3$ for Cell Phone. The trivial case $S = 1$ represents a standard bag-of-words feature space, i.e., this space is embedded into Skip-node space whenever $S > 1$. To show that SNK does not merely take advantage of this simple space to compete with structural kernels, we carried out another experiment where we combined STK, SSTK, and PTK with bag-of-word representation of a sentence. Table 6 shows that surprisingly this combination harms the quality of PTK. STK and SSTK gain more from bag-of-words features. Nevertheless, the overall outperformance by SNK remains.

5.3 Skip-node Kernel Approximations

Our third objective is to study the utility of the approximations of SNK described in Section 4. Table 7 reports the performance of the approximations. For Camera, the performance of Lookahead

	Camera			Cell		
	P	R	F1	P	R	F1
Linear SNK	78.9	**77.1***	**77.9**	71.8	**55.3**	62.2
Lookahead SNK	**80.5**	75.2	77.7	71.8	**55.3**	62.2
SNK	**80.5**	75.2	77.7	**77.2***	55.1	**64.1**

Table 7: Effectiveness: SNK vs. approximations

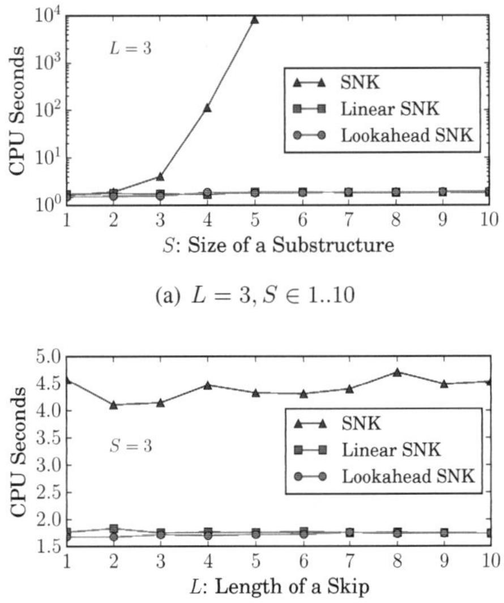

(a) $L = 3, S \in 1..10$

(b) $S = 3, L \in 1..10$

Figure 6: Efficiency: SNK vs. approximations

SNK and SNK are the same. In turn, Linear SNK represents more restricted features, yielding a drop in precision and a gain in recall, resulting in the best F_1. For Cell Phone, the approximations are close, but the original SNK has the best F_1.

To study the running time, we randomly select 500 sentences. Figure 6 shows the time for applying a kernel function to 250k pairs of sentences when we vary two parameters: S and L. When S varies, SNK running time has exponential behaviour, whereas the approximations show fairly linear curves. L seems to influence the computation time linearly for SNK and and its approximations. The experiments were carried out on a PC with Intel Core i5 CPU 3.2 GHz and 4Gb RAM.

This experiment shows that the original SNK is still tractable for small S and L, which turn out to be the case for optimal effectiveness. If efficiency is of paramount importance, the two approximations are significantly faster, without much degradation (none in some cases) of effectiveness.

6 Related Work

Exploiting comparisons in text begins with identifying comparisons within sentences. The previous state of the art for English is the baseline CSR approach (Jindal and Liu, 2006a). For scientific text, (Park and Blake, 2012) explored handcrafted syntactic rules that might not cross domains well. Comparisons are also studied in other languages, such as Chinese, Japanese, and Korean (Huang et al., 2008; Yang and Ko, 2009; Kurashima et al., 2008; Yang and Ko, 2009; Zhang and Jin, 2012).

A different task seeks to identify the "components" within comparative sentences, i.e., entities, aspect, comparative predicate (Jindal and Liu, 2006b; Hou and Li, 2008; Kessler and Kuhn, 2014b; Kessler and Kuhn, 2013; Feldman et al., 2007). Others are interested in yet another task to identify the direction of the comparisons (Ganapathibhotla and Liu, 2008; Tkachenko and Lauw, 2014), or the aggregated ranking (Kurashima et al., 2008; Zhang et al., 2013; Li et al., 2011). Our task precedes these tasks in the pipeline.

Other than comparison identification, dependency grammar has also found applications in natural language-related tasks, such as sentiment classification (Nakagawa et al., 2010), question answering (Punyakanok et al., 2004; Lin and Pantel, 2001), as well as relation extraction (Culotta and Sorensen, 2004; Bunescu and Mooney, 2005).

(Collins and Duffy, 2001) applied convolution kernels (Haussler, 1999; Watkins, 1999) to natural language objects, which evolved into tree kernels, e.g., sub-tree (Vishwanathan and Smola, 2004), subset tree (Collins and Duffy, 2002), descending-path kernel (Lin et al., 2014), partial tree (Moschitti, 2006a). Skip-node kernel joins the list of tree kernels applicable to dependency trees. These kernels may also apply to other types of trees, e.g., constituency trees (Zhou et al., 2007).

(Croce et al., 2011; Srivastava et al., 2013) proposed to capture semantic information along with tree structure, by allowing soft label matching via lexical similarity over distributional word representation. Skip-node gives another perspective on sparsity, using structural alignment of the tree fragments with non-matching labels. As lexical similarity can be incorporated into Skip-node kernel, we consider it orthogonal and complementary.

7 Conclusion

We study the effectiveness of a convolution kernel approach for the novel formulation of extracting comparisons within sentences. Our approach outperforms the baselines in identifying comparisons and comparative sentences. Skip-node kernel and its approximations are particularly effective for comparison identification, and potentially applicable to other relation extraction or natural-language tasks (the direction of our future work).

References

Rakesh Agrawal and Ramakrishnan Srikant. 1995. Mining sequential patterns. In *Proceedings of the International Conference on Data Engineering (ICDE)*, pages 3–14.

Jay Ayres, Jason Flannick, Johannes Gehrke, and Tomi Yiu. 2002. Sequential pattern mining using a bitmap representation. In *Proceedings of the ACM SIGKDD International Conference on Knowledge Discovery and Data Mining (KDD)*, pages 429–435.

Michael A. Bender and Martin Farach-Colton. 2000. The lca problem revisited. In *Proceedings of the Latin American Symposium on Theoretical Informatics*, LATIN '00, pages 88–94, London, UK, UK. Springer-Verlag.

Razvan C. Bunescu and Raymond J. Mooney. 2005. A shortest path dependency kernel for relation extraction. In *Proceedings of the Conference on Human Language Technology and Empirical Methods in Natural Language Processing (HLT)*, pages 724–731.

Danqi Chen and Christopher D Manning. 2014. A fast and accurate dependency parser using neural networks. In *Proceedings of the Conference on Empirical Methods in Natural Language Processing (EMNLP)*, pages 740–750.

Michael Collins and Nigel Duffy. 2001. Convolution kernels for natural language. In *Advances in Neural Information Processing Systems (NIPS)*, pages 625–632.

Michael Collins and Nigel Duffy. 2002. New ranking algorithms for parsing and tagging: Kernels over discrete structures, and the voted perceptron. In *Proceedings of the Annual Meeting on Association for Computational Linguistics (COLING)*, pages 263–270.

Danilo Croce, Alessandro Moschitti, and Roberto Basili. 2011. Structured lexical similarity via convolution kernels on dependency trees. In *Proceedings of the Conference on Empirical Methods in Natural Language Processing*, pages 1034–1046. Association for Computational Linguistics.

Aron Culotta and Jeffrey Sorensen. 2004. Dependency tree kernels for relation extraction. In *Proceedings of the Annual Meeting on Association for Computational Linguistics (COLING)*.

Chad Cumby and Dan Roth. 2003. On kernel methods for relational learning. In *Proceedings of the International Conference on Machine Learning (ICML)*, pages 107–114.

Ronen Feldman, Moshe Fresko, Jacob Goldenberg, Oded Netzer, and Lyle Ungar. 2007. Extracting product comparisons from discussion boards. In *Proceedings of the IEEE International Conference on Data Mining (ICDM)*, pages 469–474.

Murthy Ganapathibhotla and Bing Liu. 2008. Mining opinions in comparative sentences. In *Proceedings of the International Conference on Computational Linguistics (COLING)*, pages 241–248.

David Haussler. 1999. Convolution kernels on discrete structures. Technical report, Department of Computer Science, University of California at Santa Cruz.

Feng Hou and Guo-Hui Li. 2008. Mining Chinese comparative sentences by semantic role labeling. In *International Conference on Machine Learning and Cybernetics*, volume 5, pages 2563–2568.

Xiaojiang Huang, Xiaojun Wan, Jianwu Yang, and Jianguo Xiao. 2008. Learning to identify comparative sentences in Chinese text. In *Pacific Rim International Conference on Artificial Intelligence*, pages 187–198.

Nitin Jindal and Bing Liu. 2006a. Identifying comparative sentences in text documents. In *Proceedings of the International ACM SIGIR Conference on Research and Development in Information Retrieval (SIGIR)*, pages 244–251.

Nitin Jindal and Bing Liu. 2006b. Mining comparative sentences and relations. In *Proceedings of the AAAI Conference on Artificial Intelligence (AAAI)*, volume 22, pages 1331–1336.

Thorsten Joachims. 1999. Advances in kernel methods. chapter Making Large-scale Support Vector Machine Learning Practical, pages 169–184. MIT Press, Cambridge, MA, USA.

Wiltrud Kessler and Jonas Kuhn. 2013. Detection of product comparisons-how far does an out-of-the-box semantic role labeling system take you? In *Proceedings of the Conference on Empirical Methods on Natural Language Processing (EMNLP)*, pages 1892–1897.

Wiltrud Kessler and Jonas Kuhn. 2014a. A corpus of comparisons in product reviews. In *Proceedings of the International Conference on Language Resources and Evaluation (LREC)*, may.

Wiltrud Kessler and Jonas Kuhn. 2014b. Detecting comparative sentiment expressions – a case study in annotation design decisions. In *Proceedings of Konferenz zur Verarbeitung Natrlicher Sprache (KONVENS)*, October.

Takeshi Kurashima, Katsuji Bessho, Hiroyuki Toda, Toshio Uchiyama, and Ryoji Kataoka. 2008. Ranking entities using comparative relations. In *Database and Expert Systems Applications (DEXA)*, pages 124–133.

Si Li, Zheng-Jun Zha, Zhaoyan Ming, Meng Wang, Tat-Seng Chua, Jun Guo, and Weiran Xu. 2011. Product comparison using comparative relations. In *Proceedings of the International ACM SIGIR Conference on Research and Development in Information Retrieval (SIGIR)*, pages 1151–1152.

Dekang Lin and Patrick Pantel. 2001. Discovery of inference rules for question-answering. *Natural Language Engineering*, 7(04):343–360.

Chen Lin, Timothy Miller, Alvin Kho, Steven Bethard, Dmitriy Dligach, Sameer Pradhan, and Guergana Savova. 2014. Descending-path convolution kernel for syntactic structures. In *Proceedings of the 52nd Annual Meeting of the Association for Computational Linguistics*, pages 81–86. Association for Computational Linguistics.

Alessandro Moschitti. 2006a. Efficient convolution kernels for dependency and constituent syntactic trees. In *European Conference on Machine Learning (ECML)*, pages 318–329.

Alessandro Moschitti. 2006b. Making tree kernels practical for natural language learning. In *11th Conference of the European Chapter of the Association for Computational Linguistics*, pages 113–120.

Tetsuji Nakagawa, Kentaro Inui, and Sadao Kurohashi. 2010. Dependency tree-based sentiment classification using crfs with hidden variables. In *Human Language Technologies: Annual Conference of the North American Chapter of the Association for Computational Linguistics (NAACL-HLT)*, pages 786–794.

Truc-Vien T Nguyen, Alessandro Moschitti, and Giuseppe Riccardi. 2009. Convolution kernels on constituent, dependency and sequential structures for relation extraction. In *Proceedings of the Conference on Empirical Methods in Natural Language Processing (EMNLP)*, pages 1378–1387.

Joakim Nivre. 2005. Dependency grammar and dependency parsing. *MSI report*, 5133(1959):1–32.

Bo Pang and Lillian Lee. 2008. Opinion mining and sentiment analysis. *Foundations and Trends in Information Retrieval*, 2(1-2):1–135.

Dae Hoon Park and Catherine Blake. 2012. Identifying comparative claim sentences in full-text scientific articles. In *Proceedings of the Workshop on Detecting Structure in Scholarly Discourse*, pages 1–9.

Jian Pei, Jiawei Han, Behzad Mortazavi-Asl, Helen Pinto, Qiming Chen, Umeshwar Dayal, and Mei-Chun Hsu. 2001. Prefixspan: Mining sequential patterns efficiently by prefix-projected pattern growth. In *Proceedings of the International Conference on Data Engineering (ICDE)*, pages 0215–0215.

Vasin Punyakanok, Dan Roth, and Wen-tau Yih. 2004. Natural language inference via dependency tree mapping: An application to question answering. *Computational Linguistics*, 6(9).

Shashank Srivastava, Dirk Hovy, and Eduard Hovy. 2013. A walk-based semantically enriched tree kernel over distributed word representations. In *Proceedings of the 2013 Conference on Empirical Methods in Natural Language Processing*, pages 1411–1416. Association for Computational Linguistics.

Ingo Steinwart and Andreas Christmann. 2008. *Support vector machines*. Springer.

Maksim Tkachenko and Hady W Lauw. 2014. Generative modeling of entity comparisons in text. In *Proceedings of the ACM International Conference on Information and Knowledge Management (CIKM)*, pages 859–868.

SVN Vishwanathan and Alexander Johannes Smola. 2004. Fast kernels for string and tree matching. *Kernel Methods in Computational Biology*, pages 113–130.

Chris Watkins. 1999. Dynamic alignment kernels. *Advances in Neural Information Processing Systems (NIPS)*, pages 39–50.

Seon Yang and Youngjoong Ko. 2009. Extracting comparative sentences from Korean text documents using comparative lexical patterns and machine learning techniques. In *Proceedings of the ACL-IJCNLP Conference Short Papers*, pages 153–156.

Alexander Yeh. 2000. More accurate tests for the statistical significance of result differences. In *Proceedings of the Conference on Computational Linguistics (COLING)*, pages 947–953. Association for Computational Linguistics.

Runxiang Zhang and Yaohong Jin. 2012. Identification and transformation of comparative sentences in patent Chinese-English machine translation. In *International Conference on Asian Language Processing (IALP)*, pages 217–220.

Zhu Zhang, Chenhui Guo, and Paulo Goes. 2013. Product comparison networks for competitive analysis of online word-of-mouth. *ACM Transactions on Management Information Systems (TMIS)*, 3(4):20.

GuoDong Zhou, Min Zhang, Dong Hong Ji, and Qiaoming Zhu. 2007. Tree kernel-based relation extraction with context-sensitive structured parse tree information. *EMNLP-CoNLL*, page 728.

It Depends: Dependency Parser Comparison Using A Web-based Evaluation Tool

Jinho D. Choi
Emory University
400 Dowman Dr.
Atlanta, GA 30322, USA
jchoi31@emory.edu

Joel Tetreault
Yahoo Labs
229 West 43rd St.
New York, NY 10036, USA
tetreaul@yahoo-inc.com

Amanda Stent
Yahoo Labs
229 West 43rd St.
New York, NY 10036, USA
stent@yahoo-inc.com

Abstract

The last few years have seen a surge in the number of accurate, fast, publicly available dependency parsers. At the same time, the use of dependency parsing in NLP applications has increased. It can be difficult for a non-expert to select a good "off-the-shelf" parser. We present a comparative analysis of ten leading statistical dependency parsers on a multi-genre corpus of English. For our analysis, we developed a new web-based tool that gives a convenient way of comparing dependency parser outputs. Our analysis will help practitioners choose a parser to optimize their desired speed/accuracy tradeoff, and our tool will help practitioners examine and compare parser output.

1 Introduction

Dependency parsing is a valuable form of syntactic processing for NLP applications due to its transparent lexicalized representation and robustness with respect to flexible word order languages. Thanks to over a decade of research on statistical dependency parsing, many dependency parsers are now publicly available. In this paper, we report on a comparative analysis of leading statistical dependency parsers using a multi-genre corpus. Our purpose is not to introduce a new parsing algorithm but to assess the performance of existing systems across different genres of language use and to provide tools and recommendations that practitioners can use to choose a dependency parser. The contributions of this work include:

- A comparison of the accuracy and speed of ten state-of-the-art dependency parsers, covering a range of approaches, on a large multi-genre corpus of English.
- A new web-based tool, DEPENDABLE, for side-by-side comparison and visualization of the output from multiple dependency parsers.
- A detailed error analysis for these parsers using DEPENDABLE, with recommendations for parser choice for different factors.
- The release of the set of dependencies used in our experiments, the test outputs from all parsers, and the parser-specific models.

2 Related Work

There have been several shared tasks on dependency parsing conducted by CoNLL (Buchholz and Marsi, 2006; Nivre and others, 2007; Surdeanu and others, 2008; Hajič and others, 2009), SANCL (Petrov and McDonald, 2012), SPMRL (Seddah and others, 2013), and SemEval (Oepen and others, 2014). These shared tasks have led to the public release of numerous statistical parsers. The primary metrics reported in these shared tasks are: labeled attachment score (**LAS**) – the percentage of predicted dependencies where the arc and the label are assigned correctly; unlabeled attachment score (**UAS**) – where the arc is assigned correctly; label accuracy score (**LS**) – where the label is assigned correctly; and exact match (**EM**) – the percentage of sentences whose predicted trees are entirely correct.

Although shared tasks have been tremendously useful for advancing the state of the art in dependency parsing, most English evaluation has employed a single-genre corpus, the WSJ portion of the Penn Treebank (Marcus et al., 1993), so it is not immediately clear how these results gen-

Proceedings of the 53rd Annual Meeting of the Association for Computational Linguistics and the 7th International Joint Conference on Natural Language Processing, pages 387–396,
Beijing, China, July 26-31, 2015.

	BC	BN	MZ	NW	PT	TC	WB	ALL
Training	171,120	206,057	163,627	876,399	296,437	85,466	284,975	2,084,081
Development	29,962	25,274	15,422	147,958	25,206	11,467	36,351	291,640
Test	35,952	26,424	17,875	60,757	25,883	10,976	38,490	216,357
Training	10,826	10,349	6,672	34,492	21,419	8,969	12,452	105,179
Development	2,117	1,295	642	5,896	1,780	1,634	1,797	15,161
Test	2,211	1,357	780	2,327	1,869	1,366	1,787	11,697

Table 1: Distribution of data used for our experiments. The first three/last three rows show the number of tokens/trees in each genre. BC: broadcasting conversation, BN: broadcasting news, MZ: news magazine, NW: newswire, PT: pivot text, TC: telephone conversation, WB: web text, ALL: all genres combined.

eralize.[1] Furthermore, a detailed comparative error analysis is typically lacking. The most detailed comparison of dependency parsers to date was performed by McDonald and Nivre (2007; 2011); they analyzed accuracy as a function of sentence length, dependency distance, valency, non-projectivity, part-of-speech tags and dependency labels.[2] Since then, additional analyses of dependency parsers have been performed, but either with respect to specific linguistic phenomena (e.g. (Nivre et al., 2010; Bender et al., 2011)) or to downstream tasks (e.g. (Miwa and others, 2010; Petrov et al., 2010; Yuret et al., 2013)).

3 Data

3.1 OntoNotes 5

We used the English portion of the OntoNotes 5 corpus, a large multi-lingual, multi-genre corpus annotated with syntactic structure, predicate-argument structure, word senses, named entities, and coreference (Weischedel and others, 2011; Pradhan and others, 2013). We chose this corpus rather than the Penn Treebank used in most previous work because it is larger (2.9M vs. 1M tokens) and more diverse (7 vs. 1 genres). We used the standard data split used in CoNLL'12 [3], but removed sentences containing only one token so as not to artificially inflate accuracy.

Table 1 shows the distribution across genres of training, development, and test data. For the most strict and realistic comparison, we trained all ten parsers using automatically assigned POS tags from the tagger in ClearNLP (Choi and Palmer, 2012a), which achieved accuracies of 97.34 and 97.52 on the development and test data, respectively. We also excluded any "morphological" feature from the input, as these are often not available in non-annotated data.

3.2 Dependency Conversion

OntoNotes provides annotation of constituency trees only. Several programs are available for converting constituency trees into dependency trees. Table 2 shows a comparison between three of the most widely used: the LTH (Johansson and Nugues, 2007),[4], Stanford (de Marneffe and Manning, 2008),[5] and ClearNLP (Choi and Palmer, 2012b)[6] dependency converters. Compared to the Stanford converter, the ClearNLP converter produces a similar set of dependency labels but generates fewer unclassified dependencies (0.23% vs. 3.62%), which makes the training data less noisy.

Both the LTH and ClearNLP converters produce long-distance dependencies and use function tags for the generation of dependency relations, which allows one to generate rich dependency structures including non-projective dependencies. However, only the ClearNLP converter adapted the new Treebank guidelines used in OntoNotes. It can also produce secondary dependencies (e.g. right-node raising, referent), which can be used for further analysis. We used the ClearNLP converter to produce dependencies for our experiments.

	LTH	Stanford	ClearNLP
Long-distance	✓		✓
Secondary	1	2	4
Function tags	✓		✓
New TB format			✓

Table 2: Dependency converters. The "secondary" row shows how many types of secondary dependencies that can be produced by each converter.

[1] The SANCL shared task used OntoNotes and the Web Treebanks instead for better generalization.

[2] A detailed error analysis of constituency parsing was performed by (Kummerfeld and others, 2012).

[3] conll.cemantix.org/2012/download/ids/

[4] http://nlp.cs.lth.se/software

[5] http://nlp.stanford.edu/software

[6] http://www.clearnlp.com

Parser	Approach	Language	License
ClearNLP v2,3[7]	Transition-based, selectional branching (Choi and McCallum, 2013)	Java	Apache
GN13[8]	Easy-first, dynamic oracle (Goldberg and Nivre, 2013)	Python	GPL v2
LTDP v2.0.3[9]	Transition-based, beam-search + dynamic prog. (Huang et al., 2012)	Python	n/a
Mate v3.6.1[10]	Maximum spanning tree, 3rd-order features (Bohnet, 2010)	Java	GPL v2
RBG[11]	Tensor decomposition, randomized hill-climb (Lei et al., 2014)	Java	MIT
Redshift[12]	Transition-based, non-monotonic (Honnibal et al., 2013)	Cython	FOSS
spaCy[13]	Transition-based, greedy, dynamic oracle, Brown clusters	Cython	Dual
SNN[14]	Transition-based, word embeddings (Chen and Manning, 2014)	Java	GPL v2
Turbo v2.2[15]	Dual decomposition, 3rd-order features (Martins et al., 2013)	C++	GPL v2
Yara[16]	Transition-based, beam-search, dynamic oracle (Rasooli and Tetreault, 2015)	Java	Apache

Table 3: Dependency parsers used in our experiments.

4 Parsers

We compared ten state of the art parsers representing a wide range of contemporary approaches to statistical dependency parsing (Table 3). We trained each parser using the training data from OntoNotes. For all parsers we trained using the automatic POS tags generated during data preprocessing, as described above.

Training settings For most parsers, we used the default settings for training. For the SNN parser, following the recommendation of the developers, we used the word embeddings from (Collobert and others, 2011).

Development data ClearNLP, LTDP, SNN and Yara make use of the development data (for parameter tuning). Mate and Turbo self-tune parameter settings using the training data. The others were trained using their default/"standard" parameter settings.

Beam search ClearNLP, LTDP, Redshift and Yara have the option of different beam settings. The higher the beam size, the more accurate the parser usually becomes, but typically at the expense of speed. For LTDP and Redshift, we experimented with beams of 1, 8, 16 and 64 and found that the highest accuracy was achieved at beam 8.[17] For ClearNLP and Yara, a beam size of 64 produced the best accuracy, while a beam size of 1 for LTDT, ClearNLP, and Yara produced the best speed performance. Given this trend, we also include how those three parsers perform at beam 1 in our analyses.

Feature Sets RBG, Turbo and Yara have the options of different feature sets. A more complex or larger feature set has the advantage of accuracy, but often at the expense of speed. For RBG and Turbo, we use the "Standard" setting and for Yara, we use the default ("not basic") feature setting.

Output All the parsers other than LTDP output labeled dependencies. The ClearNLP, Mate, RBG, and Turbo parsers can generate non-projective dependencies.

5 DEPENDABLE: Web-based Evaluation and Visualization Tool

There are several very useful tools for evaluating the output of dependency parsers, including the venerable `eval.pl`[18] script used in the CoNLL shared tasks, and newer Java-based tools that support visualization of and search over parse trees such as TedEval (Tsarfaty et al., 2011),[19] MaltEval (Nilsson and Nivre, 2008)[20] and "What's wrong with my NLP?".[21] Recently, there is momentum towards web-based tools for annotation and visualization of NLP pipelines (Stenetorp and others, 2012). For this work, we used a new web-based tool, DEPENDABLE, developed by the first author of this paper. It requires no installation and so provides a convenient way to evaluate and compare dependency parsers. The following are key features of DEPENDABLE:

[7] www.clearnlp.com
[8] cs.bgu.ac.il/~yoavg/software/sdparser
[9] acl.cs.qc.edu/~lhuang
[10] code.google.com/p/mate-tools
[11] github.com/taolei87/RBGParser
[12] github.com/syllog1sm/Redshift
[13] honnibal.github.io/spaCy
[14] nlp.stanford.edu/software/nndep.shtml
[15] www.ark.cs.cmu.edu/TurboParser
[16] https://github.com/yahoo/YaraParser
[17] Due to memory limitations we were unable to train Redshift on a beam size greater than 8.

[18] ilk.uvt.nl/conll/software.html
[19] www.tsarfaty.com/unipar/
[20] www.maltparser.org/malteval.html
[21] whatswrong.googlecode.com

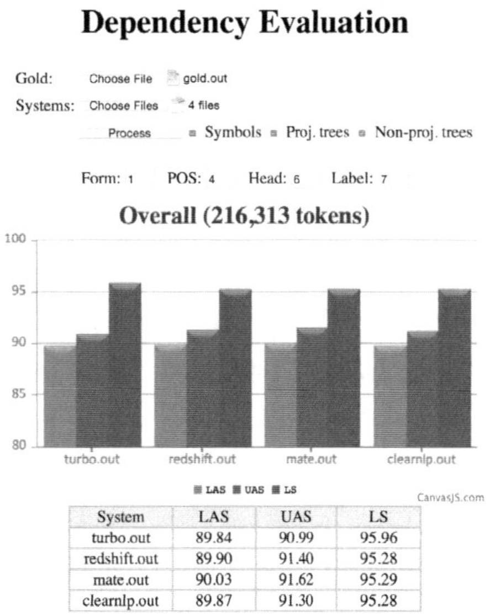

Figure 1: Screenshot of our evaluation tool.

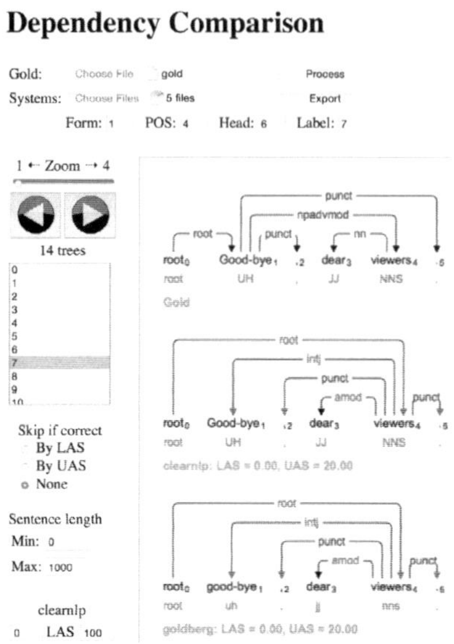

Figure 2: Screenshot of our visualization tool.

- It reads any type of Tab Separated Value (TSV) format, including the CoNLL formats.
- It computes LAS, UAS and LS for parse outputs from multiple parsers against gold (manual) parses.
- It computes exact match scores for multiple parsers, and "oracle ensemble" output, the upper bound performance obtainable by combining all parser outputs.
- It allows the user to exclude symbol tokens, projective trees, or non-projective trees.
- It produces detailed analyses by POS tags, dependency labels, sentence lengths, and dependency distances.
- It reports statistical significance values for all parse outputs (using McNemar's test).

DEPENDABLE can be also used for visualizing and comparing multiple dependency trees together (Figure 2). A key feature is that the user may select parse trees by specifying a range of accuracy scores; this enabled us to perform the error analyses in Section 6.5. DEPENDABLE allows one to filter trees by sentence length and highlights arc and label errors. The evaluation and comparison tools are publicly available at `http://nlp.mathcs.emory.edu/clearnlp/dependable`.

6 Results and Error Analysis

In this section, we report overall parser accuracy and speed. We analyze parser accuracy by sentence length, dependency distance, non-projectivity, POS tags and dependency labels, and genre. We report detailed manual error analyses focusing on sentences that multiple parsers parsed incorrectly.[22] All analyses, other than parsing speed, were conducted using the DEPENDABLE tool.[23] The full set of outputs from all parsers, as well as the trained models for each parser, available at `http://amandastent.com/dependable/`.

We also include the greedy parsing results of ClearNLP, LTDP, and Yara in two of our analyses to better illustrate the differences between the greedy and non-greedy settings. The greedy parsing results are denoted by the subscript '$_g$'. These two analyses are the overall accuracy results, presented in Section 6.1 (Table 4), and the overall speed results, presented in Section 6.2 ((Table 5 and Figure). All other analyses exclude the ClearNLP$_g$, LTDP$_g$ and Yara$_g$.

[22]For one sentence in the NW data, the LTDP parser failed to produce a complete parse containing all tokens, so we removed this sentence for all parsers, leaving 11,696 trees (216,313 tokens) in the test data.

[23]We compared the results produced by DEPENDABLE with those produced by `eval07.pl`, and verified that LAS, UAS, LA, and EM were the same when punctuation was included. Our tool uses a slightly different symbol set than `eval07.pl`: `!"#$%&'()*+,-./:;<=>?@[\]^_`{|}~`

	With Punctuation						Without Punctuation					
	Overall			Exact Match			Overall			Exact Match		
	LAS	UAS	LS	LAS	UAS	LS	LAS	UAS	LS	LAS	UAS	LS
ClearNLP$_g$	**89.19**	**90.63**	**94.94**	**47.65**	**53.00**	**61.17**	**90.09**	**91.72**	**94.29**	**49.12**	**55.01**	**61.31**
GN13	87.59	89.17	93.99	43.78	48.89	56.71	88.75	90.54	93.32	45.44	51.20	56.88
LTDP$_g$	n/a	85.75	n/a	n/a	46.38	n/a	n/a	87.16	n/a	n/a	48.01	n/a
SNN	86.42	88.15	93.54	42.98	48.53	55.87	87.63	89.59	92.70	43.96	49.83	55.91
spaCy	87.92	89.61	94.08	43.36	48.79	55.67	88.95	90.86	93.32	44.97	51.28	55.70
Yara$_g$	85.93	87.64	92.99	42.94	47.77	54.79	87.39	89.32	92.24	44.25	49.44	54.96
ClearNLP	89.87	91.30	95.28	49.38	55.18	63.18	90.64	92.26	**94.67**	50.61	56.88	63.24
LTDP	n/a	88.18	n/a	n/a	51.62	n/a	n/a	89.17	n/a	n/a	53.54	n/a
Mate	**90.03**	**91.62**	**95.29**	49.66	**56.44**	62.71	**90.70**	**92.50**	**94.67**	50.83	**58.36**	62.72
RBG	89.57	91.45	94.71	46.49	55.49	58.45	90.23	92.35	94.01	47.64	56.54	58.07
Redshift	89.48	91.01	95.04	49.71	55.82	62.70	90.27	92.00	94.42	50.88	57.28	62.78
Turbo	89.81	91.50	95.00	48.08	55.33	60.49	90.49	92.40	94.34	49.29	57.09	60.52
Yara	89.80	91.36	95.19	**50.07**	56.18	**63.36**	90.47	92.24	94.57	**51.02**	57.53	**63.42**

Table 4: Overall parsing accuracy. The top 6 rows and the bottom 7 rows show accuracies for greedy and non-greedy parsers, respectively.

6.1 Overall Accuracy

In Table 4, we report overall accuracy for each parser. For clarity, we report results separately for greedy and non-greedy versions of the parsers. Over all the different metrics, MATE is a clear winner, though ClearNLP, RBG, Redshift, Turbo and Yara are very close in performance. Looking at only the greedy parsers, ClearNLP$_g$ shows a significant advantage over the others.

We conducted a statistical significance test for the the parsers (greedy versions excluded). All LAS differences are statistically significant at $p < .01$ (using McNemar's test), except for: RBG vs. Redshift, Turbo vs. Yara, Turbo vs. ClearNLP and Yara vs. ClearNLP. All UAS differences are statistically significant at $p < .01$ (using McNemar's test), except for: SNN vs. LTDP, Turbo vs. Redshift, Yara vs. RBG and ClearNLP vs. Yara.

6.2 Overall Speed

We ran timing experiments on a 64 core machine with 16 Intel Xeon E5620 2.40 GHz processors and 24G RAM, and used the unix `time` command to time each run. Some parsers are multithreaded; for these, we ran in single-thread mode (since any parser can be externally parallelized). Most parsers do not report model load time, so we first ran each parser five times with a test set of 10 sentences, and then averaged the middle three times to get the average model load time.[24] Next, we ran each parser five times with the entire test set and derived the overall parse time by averaging the middle three parse times. We then subtracted the average model time from the average parse time and averaged over the number of sentences and tokens.

[24] Recall we exclude single-token sentences from our tests.

	Sent/Sec	Tokens/Sec	Language
ClearNLP$_g$	555	10,271	Java
GN13	95	1,757	Python
LTDP$_g$	232	4,287	Python
SNN	465	8,602	Java
spaCy	**755**	**13,963**	Cython
Yara$_g$	532	9,838	Java
ClearNLP	72	1,324	Java
LTDP	26	488	Python
Mate	30	550	Java
RBG	57	1,056	Java
Redshift	**188**	**3,470**	Cython
Turbo	19	349	C++
Yara	18	340	Java

Table 5: Overall parsing speed.

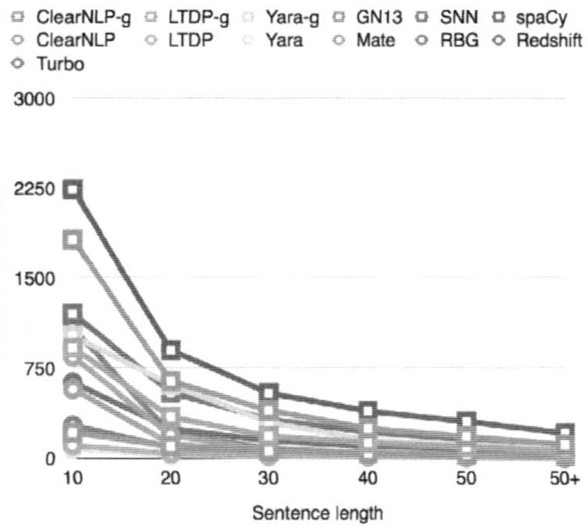

Figure 3: Number of sentences parsed per second by each parser with respect to sentence length.

Table 5 shows overall parsing speed for each parser. spaCy is the fastest greedy parser and Redshift is the fastest non-greedy parser. Figure 3 shows an analysis of parsing speed by sentence length in bins of length 10. As expected, as sentence length increases, parsing speed decreases remarkably.

6.3 Detailed Accuracy Analyses

For the following more detailed analyses, we used all tokens (including punctuation). As mentioned earlier, we exclude ClearNLP$_g$, LTDP$_g$ and Yara$_g$ from these analyses and instead use their respective non-greedy modes yielding higher accuracy.

Sentence Length We analyzed parser accuracy by sentence length in bins of length 10 (Figure 4). As expected, all parsers perform better on shorter sentences. For sentences under length 10, UAS ranges from 93.49 to 95.5; however, UAS declines to a range of 81.66 and 86.61 for sentence lengths greater than 50. The most accurate parsers (ClearNLP, Mate, RBG, Redshift, Turbo, and Yara) separate from the remaining when sentence length is more than 20 tokens.

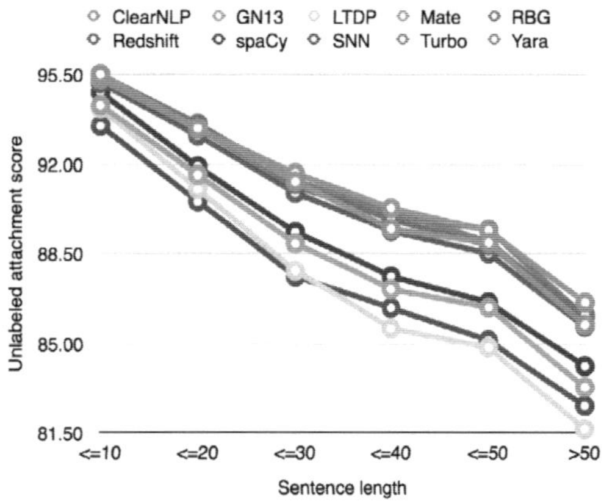

Figure 4: UAS by sentence length.

Dependency Distance We analyzed parser accuracy by dependency distance (depth from each dependent to its head; Figure 5). Accuracy falls off more slowly as dependency distance increases for the top 6 parsers vs. the rest.

Projectivity Some of our parsers only produce projective parses. Table 6 shows parsing accuracy for trees containing only projective arcs (11,231 trees, 202,521 tokens) and for trees containing non-projective arcs (465 trees, 13,792 tokens). As before, all differences are statistically significant at $p < .01$ except for: Redshift vs. RBG for overall LAS; LTDP vs. SNN for overall UAS; and Turbo vs. SpaCy for overall UAS. For strictly projective trees, the LTDP parser is 5th from the top in UAS. Apart from this, the grouping between "very good" and "good" parsers does not change.

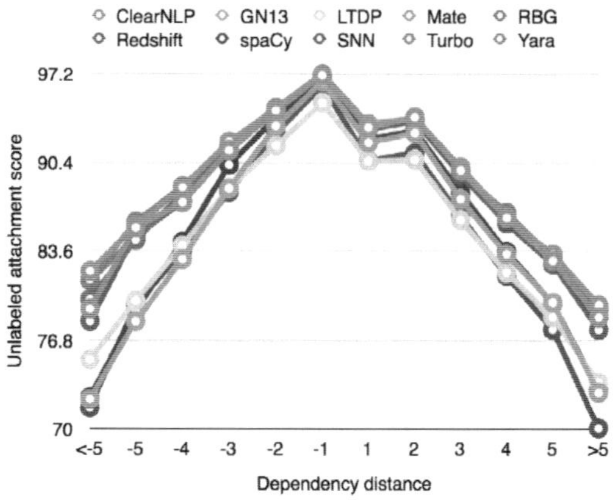

Figure 5: UAS by dependency distance.

	Projective only		Non-proj. only	
	LAS	UAS	LAS	UAS
ClearNLP	90.20	91.62	85.10	86.72
GN13	88.00	89.57	81.56	83.37
LTDP	n/a	90.24	n/a	57.83
Mate	**90.34**	**91.91**	**85.51**	**87.40**
RBG	89.86	91.72	84.83	86.94
Redshift	89.90	91.41	83.30	85.12
SNN	86.83	88.55	80.37	82.32
spaCy	88.31	89.99	82.15	84.08
Turbo	88.36	89.90	83.50	85.30
Yara	90.20	91.74	83.92	85.74

Table 6: Accuracy for proj. and non-proj. trees.

Dependency Relations We were interested in which dependency relations were computed with high/low overall accuracy, and for which accuracy varied between parsers. The dependency relations with the highest average LAS scores ($> 97\%$) were `possessive`, `hyph`, `expl`, `hmod`, `aux`, `det` and `poss`. These relations have strong lexical clues (e.g. `possessive`) or occur very often (e.g. `det`). Those with the lowest LAS scores ($< 50\%$) were `csubjpass`, `meta`, `dep`, `nmod` and `parataxis`. These either occur rarely or are very general (`dep`).

The most "confusing" dependency relations (those with the biggest range of accuracies across parsers) were `csubj`, `preconj`, `csubjpass`, `parataxis`, `meta` and `oprd` (all with a spread of $> 20\%$). The Mate and Yara parsers each had the highest accuracy for 3 out of the top 10 "confusing" dependency relations. The RBG parser had the highest accuracy for 4 out of the top 10 "most accurate" dependency relations. SNN had the lowest accuracy for 5 out of the top 10 "least accurate" dependency relations, while the RBG had the lowest accuracy for another 4.

POS Tags We also examined error types by part of speech tag of the dependent. The POS tags with the highest average LAS scores ($> 97\%$) were the highly unambiguous tags `POS`, `WP$`, `MD`, `TO`, `HYPH`, `EX`, `PRP` and `PRP$`. With the exception of `WP$`, these tags occur frequently. Those with the lowest average LAS scores ($< 75\%$) were punctuation markers ((,) and :, and the rare tags `AFX`, `FW`, `NFP` and `LS`.

Genres Table 7 shows parsing accuracy for each parser for each of the seven genres comprising the English portion of OntoNotes 5. Mate and ClearNLP are responsible for the highest accuracy for some genres, although accuracy differences among the top four parsers are generally small. Accuracy is highest for PT (pivot text, the Bible) and lowest for TC (telephone conversation) and WB (web data). The web data is itself multi-genre and includes translations from Arabic and Chinese, while telephone conversation data includes disfluencies and informal language.

6.4 Oracle Ensemble Performance

One popular method for achieving higher accuracy on a classification task is to use system combination (Björkelund and others, 2014; Le Roux and others, 2012; Le Roux et al., 2013; Sagae and Lavie, 2006; Sagae and Tsujii, 2010; Haffari et al., 2011). DEPENDABLE reports ensemble upper bound performance assuming that the best *tree* can be identified by an oracle (**macro**), or that the best *arc* can be identified by an oracle (**micro**). Table 8 provides an upper bound on ensemble performance for future work.

	LAS	UAS	LS
Macro	94.66	96.00	97.82
Micro	96.52	97.61	98.40

Table 8: Oracle ensemble performance.

The highest match was achieved between the RBG and Mate parser (62.22 UAS). ClearNLP, GN13 and LTDP all matched with Redshift the best, and RBG, Redshift and Turbo matched with Mate the best. SNN, spaCy and Turbo did not match well with other parsers; their respective "best match" score was never higher than 55.

6.5 Error Analysis

From the test data, we pulled out parses where only one parser achieved very high accuracy, and parses where only one parser had low accuracy (Table 9). As with the detailed performance analyses, we used the most accurate version of each parser for this analysis. Mate has the highest number of "generally good" parses, while the SNN parser has the highest number of "uniquely bad" parses. The SNN parser tended to choose the wrong root, but this did not appear to be tied to the number of verbs in the sentence - rather, the SNN parser just makes the earliest "reasonable" choice of root.

Parser UAS All others UAS	≥ 90 < 90	$= 100$ < 90	< 90 ≥ 90	< 90 $= 100$
ClearNLP	42	11	45	15
LTDP	29	12	182	36
GN13	26	8	148	65
Mate	**75**	19	44	10
RBG	49	21	49	15
Redshift	38	17	28	8
SNN	70	**23**	**417**	**142**
spaCy	48	17	218	73
Turbo	54	15	28	14
Yara	33	15	27	7

Table 9: Differential parsing accuracies.

To further analyze these results, we first looked at the parse trees for "errorful" sentences where the parsers agreed. From the test data, we extracted parses for sentences where at least two parsers got UAS of $< 50\%$. This gave us 253 sentences. The distribution of these errors across genres varied: PT - 2.8%, MZ - 3.5%, BN - 9.8%, NW - 10.3%, WB - 17.4%, BC - 25.3%, TC - 30.8%.

By manual comparison using the DEPENDABLE tool, we identified frequently occurring potential sources of error. We then manually annotated all sentences for these error types. Figure 6 shows the number of "errorful" sentences of each type. Punctuation attachment "errors" are prevalent. For genres with "noisy" text (e.g. broadcast conversation, telephone conversation) a significant proportion of errors come from fragmented sentences or those containing backchannels or disfluencies. There are also a number of sentences with what appeared to be manual dependency labeling errors in the gold annotation.

	BC		BN		MZ		NW		PT		TC		WB	
	LAS	**UAS**	**LAS**	**UAS**	**LAS**	**UAS**	**LAS**	**UAS**	**LAS**	**UAS**	**LAS**	**UAS**	**LAS**	**UAS**
ClearNLP	88.95	90.36	**89.59**	**91.01**	89.56	91.24	89.79	91.08	**95.88**	**96.68**	87.17	88.93	**87.93**	89.83
GN13	86.75	88.40	87.38	88.87	87.31	89.10	87.36	88.84	94.06	95.00	85.68	87.60	85.20	87.19
LTDP	n/a	86.81	n/a	87.43	n/a	88.87	n/a	88.40	n/a	93.52	n/a	85.85	n/a	86.37
Mate	**89.03**	**90.73**	89.30	90.82	**90.09**	**91.92**	**90.28**	**91.68**	95.71	96.64	**87.86**	**89.87**	87.86	**89.89**
RBG	88.64	90.58	88.99	90.86	89.28	91.45	89.85	91.47	95.27	96.41	87.36	89.65	87.12	89.61
Redshift	88.60	90.19	88.96	90.46	89.11	90.90	89.63	90.99	95.36	96.22	87.14	88.99	87.27	89.31
SNN	85.35	87.08	86.13	87.78	86.00	87.92	86.17	87.74	93.47	94.64	83.50	85.74	84.29	86.50
spaCy	87.27	89.05	87.70	89.31	87.37	89.29	88.00	89.52	94.28	95.27	85.67	87.65	85.16	87.40
Turbo	87.05	88.70	87.58	89.04	88.34	90.02	87.95	89.33	94.39	95.36	85.91	87.93	85.66	87.70
Yara	88.90	90.53	89.40	90.89	89.72	91.42	90.00	91.41	95.41	96.32	87.35	89.19	87.55	89.61
Total	2211		1357		780		2326		1869		1366		1787	

Table 7: Parsing accuracy by genre.

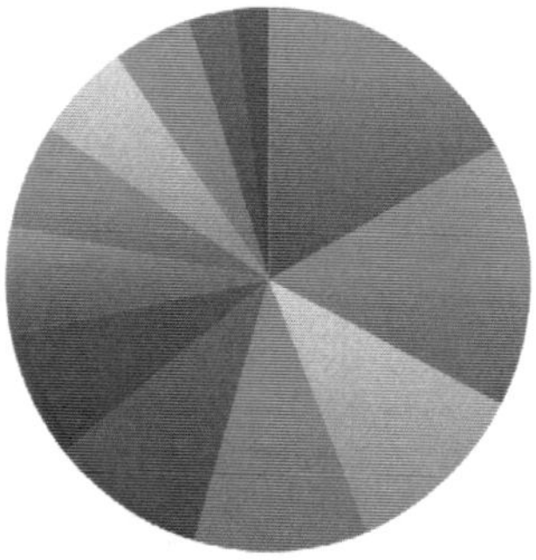

Figure 6: Common error types in erroneous trees.

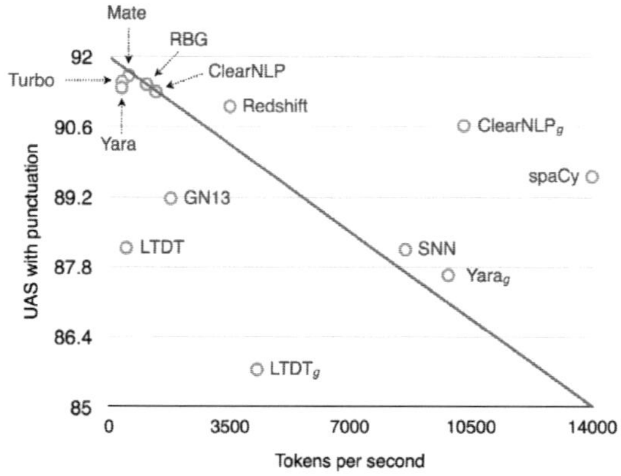

Figure 7: Speed with respect to accuracy.

6.6 Recommendations

Each of the transition-based parsers that was included in this evaluation can use varying beam widths to trade off speed vs. accuracy, and each parser has numerous other parameters that can be tuned. Notwithstanding all these variables, we can make some recommendations. Figure 7 illustrates the speed vs. accuracy tradeoff across the parsers. For highest accuracy (e.g. in dialog systems), Mate, RBG, Turbo, ClearNLP and Yara are good choices. For highest speed (e.g. in web-scale NLP), spaCy and ClearNLP$_g$ are good choices; SNN and Yara$_g$ are also good choices when accuracy is relatively not as important.

7 Conclusions and Future Work

In this paper we have: (a) provided a detailed comparative analysis of several state-of-the-art statistical dependency parsers, focusing on accuracy and speed; and (b) presented DEPENDABLE, a new web-based evaluation and visualization tool for analyzing dependency parsers. DEPENDABLE supports a wide range of useful functionalities. In the future, we plan to add regular expression search over parses, and sorting within results tables. Our hope is that the results from the evaluation as well as the tool will give non-experts in parsing better insight into which parsing tool works well under differing conditions. We also hope that the tool can be used to facilitate evaluation and be used as a teaching aid in NLP courses.

Supplements to this paper include the tool, the parse outputs, the statistical models for each parser, and the new set of dependency trees for OntoNotes 5 created using the ClearNLP dependency converter. We do recommend examining one's data and task before choosing and/or training a parser. Are non-projective parses likely or desirable? Does the data contain disfluencies, sentence fragments, and other "noisy text" phenomena? What is the average and standard deviation for sentence length and dependency length? The analyses in this paper can be used to select a parser if one has the answers to these questions.

In this work we did not implement an ensemble of parsers, partly because an ensemble necessarily entails complexity and/or speed delays that render it unusable by all but experts. However, our analyses indicate that it may be possible to achieve small but significant increases in accuracy of dependency parsing through ensemble methods. A good place to start would be with ClearNLP, Mate, or Redshift in combination with LTDP and Turbo, SNN or spaCy. In addition, it may be possible to achieve good performance in particular genres by doing "mini-ensembles" trained on general purpose data (e.g. WB) and genre-specific data. We leave this for future work. We also leave for future work the comparison of these parsers across languages.

It remains to be seen what downstream impact differences in parsing accuracy of 2-5% have on the goal task. If the impact is small, then speed and ease of use are the criteria to optimize, and here spaCy, ClearNLP$_g$, Yara$_g$ and SNN are good choices.

Acknowledgments

We would like to thank the researchers who have made available data (especially OntoNotes), parsers (especially those compared in this work), and evaluation and visualization tools. Special thanks go to Boris Abramzon, Matthew Honnibal, Tao Lei, Danqi Li and Mohammad Sadegh Rasooli for assistance in installation, trouble-shooting and general discussion. Additional thanks goes to the kind folks from the SANCL-SPMRL community for an informative discussion of evaluation and visualization tools. Finally, we would like to thank the three reviewers, as well as Martin Chodorow, Dean Foster, Joseph Le Roux and Robert Stine, for feedback on this paper.

References

Emily M. Bender, Dan Flickinger, Stephan Oepen, and Yi Zhang. 2011. Parser evaluation over local and non-local deep dependencies in a large corpus. In *Proceedings of EMNLP*.

Anders Björkelund et al. 2014. Introducing the IMS-Wrocław-Szeged-CIS entry at the SPMRL 2014 shared task: Reranking and morpho-syntax meet unlabeled data. In *Proceedings of the First Joint Workshop on Statistical Parsing of Morphologically Rich Languages and Syntactic Analysis of Non-Canonical Languages*.

Bernd Bohnet. 2010. Very high accuracy and fast dependency parsing is not a contradiction. In *Proceedings of COLING*.

Sabine Buchholz and Erwin Marsi. 2006. CoNLL-X shared task on multilingual dependency parsing. In *Proceedings of CoNLL*.

Danqi Chen and Christopher Manning. 2014. A fast and accurate dependency parser using neural networks. In *Proceedings of EMNLP*.

Jinho D. Choi and Andrew McCallum. 2013. Transition-based Dependency Parsing with Selectional Branching. In *Proceedings of the 51st Annual Meeting of the Association for Computational Linguistics*, ACL'13, pages 1052–1062.

Jinho D. Choi and Martha Palmer. 2012a. Fast and Robust Part-of-Speech Tagging Using Dynamic Model Selection. In *Proceedings of the 50th Annual Meeting of the Association for Computational Linguistics*, ACL'12, pages 363–367.

Jinho D. Choi and Martha Palmer. 2012b. Guidelines for the Clear Style Constituent to Dependency Conversion. Technical Report 01-12, Institute of Cognitive Science, University of Colorado Boulder, Boulder, CO, USA.

Ronan Collobert et al. 2011. Natural language processing (almost) from scratch. *Journal of Machine Learning Research*, 12:2493–2537.

Marie-Catherine de Marneffe and Christopher D. Manning. 2008. The Stanford typed dependencies representation. In *Proceedings of the COLING workshop on Cross-Framework and Cross-Domain Parser Evaluation*.

Yoav Goldberg and Joakim Nivre. 2013. Training deterministic parser with non-deterministic oracles. In *Proceedings of TACL*.

Gholamreza Haffari, Marzieh Razavi, and Anoop Sarkar. 2011. An ensemble model that combines syntactic and semantic clustering for discriminative dependency parsing. In *Proceedings of ACL-HLT*.

Jan Hajič et al. 2009. The CoNLL-2009 shared task: Syntactic and semantic dependencies in multiple languages. In *Proceedings of CoNLL*.

Matthew Honnibal, Yoav Goldberg, and Mark Johnson. 2013. A non-monotonic arc-eager transition system for dependency parsing. In *Proceedings of CoNLL*.

Liang Huang, Suphan Fayong, and Yang Guo. 2012. Structured perceptron with inexact search. In *Proceedings of the NAACL*.

Richard Johansson and Pierre Nugues. 2007. Extended constituent-to-dependency conversion for English. In *Proceedings of NODALIDA*.

Jonathan K. Kummerfeld et al. 2012. Parser showdown at the wall street corral: An empirical investigation of error types in parser output. In *Proceedings of EMNLP*.

Joseph Le Roux et al. 2012. DCU-Paris13 systems for the SANCL 2012 shared task. In *Proceedings of the First Workshop on Syntactic Analysis of Non-Canonical Language (SANCL)*.

Joseph Le Roux, Antoine Rozenknop, and Jennifer Foster. 2013. Combining PCFG-LA models with dual decomposition: A case study with function labels and binarization. In *Proceedings of EMNLP*.

Tao Lei, Yu Xin, Yuan Zhang, Regina Barzilay, and Tommi Jaakkola. 2014. Low-rank tensors for scoring dependency structures. In *Proceedings of the 52nd Annual Meeting of the Association for Computational Linguistics (Volume 1: Long Papers)*, pages 1381–1391, Baltimore, Maryland, June. Association for Computational Linguistics.

Mitchell P. Marcus, Mary Ann Marcinkiewicz, and Beatrice Santorini. 1993. Building a large annotated corpus of english: the Penn treebank. *Computational Linguistics*, 19(2):313–330.

André F. T. Martins, Miguel B. Almeida, and Noah A. Smith. 2013. Turning on the turbo: Fast third-order non-projective turbo parsers. In *Proceedings of the ACL*.

Ryan McDonald and Joakim Nivre. 2007. Characterizing the errors of data-driven dependency parsing models. In *Proceedings of EMNLP-CoNLL*.

Ryan McDonald and Joakim Nivre. 2011. Analyzing and integrating dependency parsers. *Computational Linguistics*, 37(1):197–230.

Makoto Miwa et al. 2010. A comparative study of syntactic parsers for event extraction. In *Proceedings of BioNLP*.

Jens Nilsson and Joakim Nivre. 2008. MaltEval: An evaluation and visualization tool for dependency parsing. In *Proceedings of LREC*.

Joakim Nivre et al. 2007. The CoNLL 2007 shared task on dependency parsing. In *Proceedings of CoNLL*.

Joakim Nivre, Laura Rimell, Ryan McDonald, and Carlos Gómez Rodríguez. 2010. Evaluation of dependency parsers on unbounded dependencies. In *Proceedings of the 23rd International Conference on Computational Linguistics (Coling 2010)*, pages 833–841, Beijing, China, August. Coling 2010 Organizing Committee.

Stephan Oepen et al. 2014. SemEval 2014 Task 8: Broad-Coverage Semantic Dependency Parsing. In *Proceedings of the 8th International Workshop on Semantic Evaluation (SemEval 2014)*, pages 63–72.

Slav Petrov and Ryan McDonald. 2012. Overview of the 2012 shared task on parsing the web. In *Proceedings of the First Workshop on Syntactic Analysis of Non-Canonical Language (SANCL) Shared Task*.

Slav Petrov, Pi-Chuan Chang, Michael Ringgaard, and Hiyan Alshawi. 2010. Uptraining for accurate deterministic question parsing. In *Proceedings of the 2010 Conference on Empirical Methods in Natural Language Processing*, pages 705–713, Cambridge, MA, October. Association for Computational Linguistics.

Sameer Pradhan et al. 2013. Towards robust linguistic analysis using OntoNotes. In *Proceedings of CoNLL*.

Mohammad Sadegh Rasooli and Joel R. Tetreault. 2015. Yara parser: A fast and accurate dependency parser. *CoRR*, abs/1503.06733.

Kenji Sagae and Alon Lavie. 2006. Parser combination by reparsing. In *Proceedings HLT-NAACL*.

Kenji Sagae and Jun'ichi Tsujii. 2010. Dependency parsing and domain adaptation with data-driven LR models and parser ensembles. In *Trends in Parsing Technology: Dependency Parsing, Domain Adaptation, and Deep Parsing*, pages 57–68. Springer.

Djamé Seddah et al. 2013. Overview of the SPMRL 2013 shared task: A cross-framework evaluation of parsing morphologically rich languages. In *Proceedings of the 4th Workshop on Statistical Parsing of Morphologically Rich Languages*.

Pontus Stenetorp et al. 2012. BRAT: A web-based tool for NLP-assisted text annotation. In *Proceedings of the EACL*.

Mihai Surdeanu et al. 2008. The CoNLL-2008 shared task on joint parsing of syntactic and semantic dependencies. In *Proceedings of CoNLL*.

Reut Tsarfaty, Joakim Nivre, and Evelina Andersson. 2011. Evaluating dependency parsing: Robust and heuristics-free cross-annotation evaluation. In *Proceedings of EMNLP*.

Ralph Weischedel et al. 2011. OntoNotes: A large training corpus for enhanced processing. In Joseph Olive, Caitlin Christianson, and John McCary, editors, *Handbook of Natural Language Processing and Machine Translation*. Springer.

Deniz Yuret, Laura Rimell, and Aydin Han. 2013. Parser evaluation using textual entailments. *Language Resources and Evaluation*, 47(3).

Generating High Quality Proposition Banks for Multilingual Semantic Role Labeling

Alan Akbik*
Technische Universität Berlin, Germany
alan.akbik@tu-berlin.de

Laura Chiticariu **Marina Danilevsky** **Yunyao Li**
Shivakumar Vaithyanathan **Huaiyu Zhu**
IBM Research - Almaden
650 Harry Road, San Jose, CA 95120, USA
{chiti,mdanile,yunyaoli,vaithyan,huaiyu}@us.ibm.com

Abstract

Semantic role labeling (SRL) is crucial to natural language understanding as it identifies the predicate-argument structure in text with semantic labels. Unfortunately, resources required to construct SRL models are expensive to obtain and simply do not exist for most languages. In this paper, we present a two-stage method to enable the construction of SRL models for resource-poor languages by exploiting monolingual SRL and multilingual parallel data. Experimental results show that our method outperforms existing methods. We use our method to generate Proposition Banks with high to reasonable quality for 7 languages in three language families and release these resources to the research community.

1 Introduction

Semantic role labeling (SRL) is the task of automatically labeling predicates and arguments in a sentence with shallow semantic labels. This level of analysis provides a more stable semantic representation across syntactically different sentences, thereby enabling a range of NLP tasks such as information extraction and question answering (Shen and Lapata, 2007; Maqsud et al., 2014). Projects such as the Proposition Bank (PropBank) (Palmer et al., 2005) spent considerable effort to annotate corpora with semantic labels, in turn enabling supervised learning of statistical SRL parsers for English. Unfortunately, due to the high costs of manual annotation, comparable SRL resources do not exist for most other languages, with few exceptions (Hajič et al., 2009; Erk et al., 2003; Zaghouani et al., 2010; Vaidya et al., 2011).

As a cost-effective alternative to manual annotation, previous work has investigated the *direct projection* of semantic labels from a resource rich language (English) to a resource poor target language (TL) in parallel corpora (Pado, 2007; Van der Plas et al., 2011). The underlying assumption is that original and translated sentences in parallel corpora are semantically broadly equivalent. Hence, if English sentences of a parallel corpus are automatically labeled using an SRL system, these labels can be projected onto aligned words in the TL corpus, thereby automatically labeling the TL corpus with semantic labels. This way, PropBank-like resources can automatically be created that enable the training of statistical SRL systems for new TLs.

However, as noted in previous work (Pado, 2007; Van der Plas et al., 2011), aligned sentences in parallel corpora often exibit issues such as *translation*

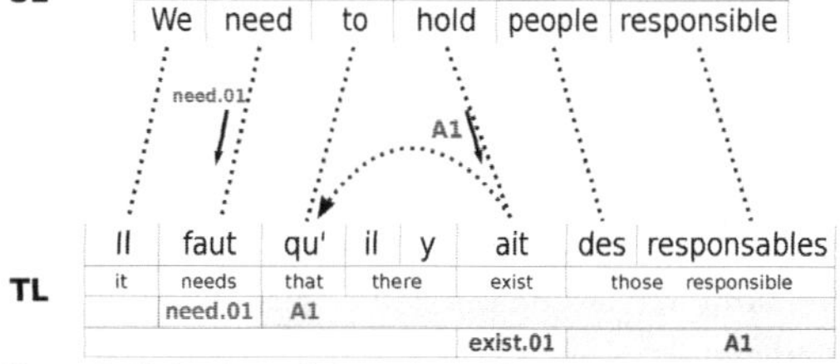

Figure 1: Pair of parallel sentences from $\texttt{French}_{gold}$ with word alignments (dotted lines), SRL labels for the English sentence, and gold SRL labels for the French sentence. Only two of the seven English SRL labels should be projected here.

*This work was conducted at IBM.

Proceedings of the 53rd Annual Meeting of the Association for Computational Linguistics and the 7th International Joint Conference on Natural Language Processing, pages 397–407,
Beijing, China, July 26-31, 2015.

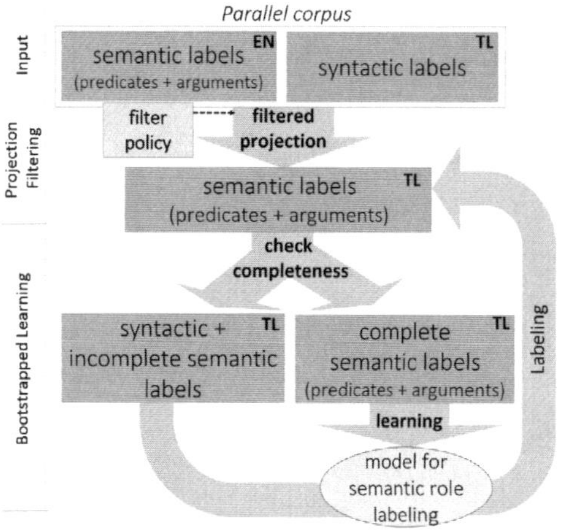

Figure 2: Overview of the proposed two-stage approach for projecting English (EN) semantic role labels onto a TL corpus.

shifts that go against this assumption. For example, in Fig. 1, the English sentence "*We need to **hold** people responsible*" is translated into a French sentence that literally reads as "*There need to **exist** those responsible*". Hence, the predicate label of the English word "*hold*" should not be projected onto the French verb, which has a different meaning. As the example in Fig. 1 shows, this means that only a subset of all SL labels can be directly projected.

In this paper, we aim to create PropBank-like resources for a range of languages from different language groups. To this end, we propose a two-stage approach to cross-lingual semantic labeling that addresses such errors, shown in Fig. 2: Given a parallel corpus in which the source language (SL) side is automatically labeled with PropBank labels and the TL side is syntactically parsed, we use a *filtered projection* approach that allows the projection only of high-confidence SL labels. This results in a TL corpus with low recall but high precision. In the second stage, we repeatedly sample a subset of complete TL sentences and train a classifier to iteratively add new labels, significantly increasing the recall in the TL corpus while retaining the improvement in precision.

Our contributions are: (1) We propose *filtered projection* focused specifically on raising the precision of projected labels, based on a detailed analysis of direct projection errors. (2) We propose a *bootstrap learning approach* to retrain the SRL to iteratively improve recall without a significant reduction of precision, especially for arguments; (3) We demonstrate the effectiveness and generalizability of our approach via an extensive set of experiments over 7 different language pairs. (4) We generate PropBanks for each of these languages and release them to the research community.[1]

2 Stage 1: Filtered Annotation Projection

Stage 1 of our approach (Fig. 2) is designed to create a TL corpus with high precision semantic labels.

Direct Projection The idea of direct annotation projection (Van der Plas et al., 2011) is to transfer semantic labels from SL sentences to TL sentences according to word alignments. Formally, for each pair of sentences s_{SL} and s_{TL} in the parallel corpus, the word alignment produces alignment pairs ($w_{\text{SL},i}$, $w_{\text{TL},i'}$), where $w_{\text{SL},i}$ and $w_{\text{TL},i'}$ are words from s_{SL} and s_{TL} respectively. Under direct projection, if $l_{\text{SL},i}$ is a predicate label for $w_{\text{SL},i}$ and ($w_{\text{SL},i}$, $w_{\text{TL},i'}$) is an alignment pair, then $l_{\text{SL},i}$ is transferred to $w_{\text{TL},i'}$; If $l_{\text{SL},j}$ is a predicate-argument label for ($w_{\text{SL},i}$, $w_{\text{SL},j}$), and ($w_{\text{SL},i}$, $w_{\text{TL},i'}$) and ($w_{\text{SL},j}$, $w_{\text{TL},j'}$) are alignment pairs, then $l_{\text{SL},j}$ is transferred to ($w_{\text{TL},i'}$, $w_{\text{TL},j'}$), as illustrated below.

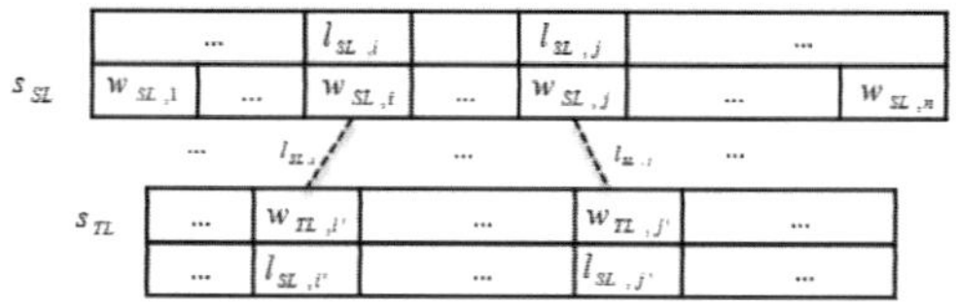

Filtered Projection As discussed earlier, direct projection is vulnerable to errors stemming from issues such as translation shifts. We propose *filtered projection* focused specifically on improving the precision of projected labels. Specifically, for a pair of sentences s_{SL} and s_{TL} in the parallel corpus, we retain the semantic label $l_{\text{SL},i}$ projected from $w_{\text{SL},i}$ onto $w_{\text{TL},i'}$ if and only if it satisfies the filtering policies. This results in a target corpus containing fewer labels but of higher precision compared to that obtained via direct projection.

In the rest of the section, we analyze typical errors in direct projection (Sec. 2.2), present a set of filters to handle such errors (Sec. 2.3), and experimentally evaluate their effectiveness (Sec. 2.4).

[1]The resources are available on request.

Error Class	Number
Translation Shift: Predicate Mismatch	37
Translation Shift: Verb→Non-verb	36
No English Equivalent	8
Gold Data Errors	6
SRL Errors	5
Verb (near-)Synonyms	4
Light Verb Construction	3
Alignment Errors	1
Total	100

Table 1: Breakdown of error classes in **predicate** projection.

Error Class	Number
Non-Argument Head	33
SRL Errors	31
No English Equivalent	12
Gold Data Errors	11
Translation Shift: Argument Function	6
Parsing Errors	4
Alignment Errors	3
Total	100

Table 2: Breakdown of error classes in **argument** projection.

2.1 Experimental Setup

Data For experiments in this section and Sec. 3, we used the gold data set compiled by (Van der Plas et al., 2011), referred to as $\texttt{French}_{\text{gold}}$. It consists of 1,000 sentence-pairs from the English-French `Europarl` corpus (Koehn, 2005) with French sentences manually labeled with predicate and argument labels from the English Propbank.

Evaluation In line with previous work (Van der Plas et al., 2010), we count synonymous predicate labels sharing the same VerbNet (Schuler, 2005) class as true positives.[2] In addition, we exclude modal verbs from the evaluation due to inconsistent annotation.

Source Language SRL Throughout the rest of the paper, we use ClearNLP (Choi and McCallum, 2013), a state-of-the-art SRL system, to produce semantic labels for English text.

2.2 Error Analysis

We observe that direct projection labels have both low precision and low recall (see Tab. 3 (*Direct*)).

Analysis of False Negatives The low recall of direct projection is not surprising; most semantic labels in the French sentences do not appear in the corresponding English sentences at all. Specifically, among 1,741 predicate labels in the French sentences, only 778 exist in the corresponding English sentences, imposing a 45% upper bound on the recall for projected predicates. Similarly, of the 5,061 argument labels in the French sentences, only 1,757 exist in the corresponding English sentences, resulting in a 35% upper bound on recall for arguments.[3]

[2] For instance, the French verb *sembler* may be correctly labeled as either of the synonyms: *seem.01* or *appear.02*.

[3] This upper bound is different from the one reported in (Van der Plas et al., 2011) which corresponds to the inter-annotator agreement over manual annotation of 100 sentences.

Analysis of False Positives While the recall produced by direct projection is close to the theoretical upper bound, the precision is far from the theoretical upper bound of 100%. To understand causes of false positives, we examine a random sample of 200 false positives, of which 100 are incorrect predicate labels, and 100 are incorrect argument labels belonging to correctly projected predicates. Tab. 1 and 2 show the detailed breakdown of errors for predicates and arguments, respectively. We first analyze the most common types of errors and discuss the residual errors later in Sec. 2.5.

• **Translation Shift: Predicate Mismatch** The most common predicate errors (37%) are translation shifts in which an English predicate is aligned to a French verb with a different meaning. Fig. 1 illustrates such a translation shift: label *hold.01* of English verb *hold* is wrongly projected onto the French verb *ait*, which is labeled as *exist.01* in $\texttt{French}_{\text{gold}}$.

• **Translation Shift: Verb→Non-Verb** is another common predicate error (36%). English verbs may be aligned with TL words other than verbs, which is often indicative of translation shifts. For instance, in the following sentence pair

s_{SL}	We	know	what	happened
s_{FR}	On	connait	la	suite
	We	know	the	result

the English verb *happen* is aligned to the French noun *suite (result)*, causing it to be wrongly projected with the English predicate label *happen.01*.

• **Non-Argument Head** The most common argument error (33%) is caused by the projection of argument labels onto words other than the syntactic head of a target verb's argument. For example, in Fig. 1 the label *A1* on the English *hold* is wrongly transferred to the French *ait*, which is not the syntactic head of the complement.

2.3 Filters

We consider the following filters to remove the most common types of false positives.

Verb Filter (VF) targets Verb→Non-Verb translation shift errors (Van der Plas et al., 2011). Formally, if direct projection transfers predicate label $l_{\text{SL},i}$ from $w_{\text{SL},i}$ onto $w_{\text{TL},i'}$, retain $l_{\text{SL},i}$ only if both $w_{\text{SL},i}$ and $w_{\text{TL},i'}$ are verbs.

Translation Filter (TF) handles both Predicate Mismatch and Verb→Non-Verb translation shift errors. It makes use of a translation dictionary and allows projection only if the TL verb is a valid translation of the SL verb. In addition, in order to ensure consistent predicate labels throughout the TL corpus, if a SL verb has several possible synonymous translations, it allows projection only for the most commonly observed translation.

Formally, for an aligned pair $(w_{\text{SL},i}, w_{\text{TL},i'})$ where $w_{\text{SL},i}$ has predicate label $l_{\text{SL},i}$, if $(w_{\text{SL},i}, w_{\text{TL},i'})$ is not a verb to verb translation from SL to TL, assign no label to $w_{\text{TL},i'}$. Otherwise, split the set of SL translations of $w_{\text{TL},i'}$ into synonym sets $S_1, S_2, \ldots$; For each k, let W^k be the subset of S_k most commonly aligned with $w_{\text{TL},i'}$; If $w_{\text{SL},i}$ is in one of these W^k, assign label $l_{\text{SL},i}$ to $w_{\text{TL},i'}$; Otherwise assign no label to $w_{\text{TL},i'}$.

Reattachment Heuristic (RH) targets non-argument head errors that occur if a TL argument is not the direct child of a verb in the dependency parse tree of its sentence.[4] Assume direct projection transfers the predicate-argument label $l_{\text{SL},j}$ from $(w_{\text{SL},i}, w_{\text{SL},j})$ onto $(w_{\text{TL},i'}, w_{\text{TL},j'})$. Find the immediate ancestor verb of $w_{\text{TL},j'}$ in the dependency parse tree. Denote as $w_{\text{TL},k}$ its child that is an ancestor of $w_{\text{TL},j'}$. Assign the label $l_{\text{SL},j}$ to $(w_{\text{TL},i'}, w_{\text{TL},k})$ instead of $(w_{\text{TL},i'}, w_{\text{TL},j'})$. An illustration is below:

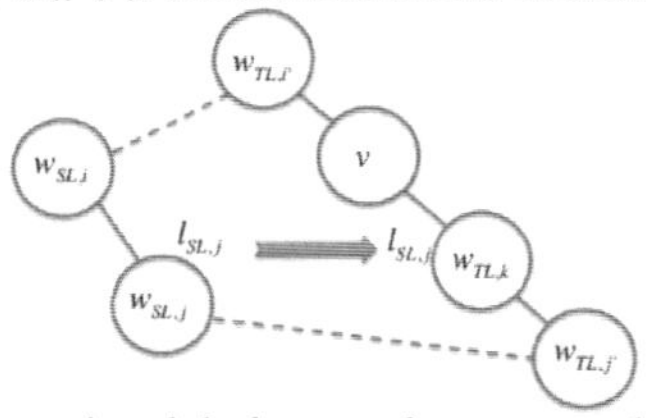

RH ensures that labels are always attached to the syntactic heads of their respective arguments, as determined by the dependency tree. An example of such reattachment is illustrated in Fig. 1 (curved arrow on TL sentence).

[4]In (Padó and Lapata, 2009), a similar filtering method is defined over constituent-based trees to reduce the set of viable nodes for argument labels to all nodes that are not a child of some ancestor of the predicate.

	PREDICATE			ARGUMENT		
PROJECTION	P	R	F1	P	R	F1
Direct	0.45	0.4	0.43	0.43	0.31	0.36
VF	0.59	0.4	0.48	0.53	0.31	0.39
TF	**0.88**	0.36	0.51	0.58	0.17	0.27
VF+RH	0.59	0.4	0.48	0.68	0.35	0.46
TF+RH	**0.88**	0.36	0.51	**0.75**	0.2	0.31
Upper Bound	1	0.45	0.62	1	0.35	0.51

Table 3: Quality of predicate and argument labels for different projection methods on $\texttt{French}_{\text{gold}}$, including upper bound.

2.4 Filter Effectiveness

We now present an initial validation on the effectiveness of the aforementioned filters by evaluating their contribution to annotation projection quality for $\texttt{French}_{\text{gold}}$, as summarized in Tab. 3.

VF reduces the number of wrongly projected predicate labels, resulting in an increase of predicate precision to 59% (↑14 pp), without impact to recall. As a side effect, argument precision also increases to 53% (↑10 pp), since, if a predicate label cannot be projected, none of its arguments can be projected.

TF[5] reduces the number of wrongly projected predicate labels even more significantly, increasing predicate precision to 88% (↑43 pp), at a small cost to recall. Again, argument precision increases as a side effect. However, as expected, argument recall decreases significantly (↓14 pp, to 17%), as many arguments can no longer be projected.

RH targets argument labels directly (unlike VF and TF), significantly increasing argument precision and slightly increasing argument recall.

In summary, initial experiments confirm that our proposed filters are effective in improving precision of projected labels at a small cost in recall. In fact, TF+RH results in nearly 100% improvement in predicate and argument labels precision with a much smaller drop in recall.

2.5 Residual Errors

Filtered projection removes the most common errors discussed in Sec. 2.2. Most of the remaining errors

[5]In all experiments in this paper, we derived the translation dictionaries from the WIKTIONARY project and used VERBNET and WORDNET to find SL synonym groups.

come from the following sources.

SRL Errors The most common residual errors in the remaining projected labels, especially for argument labels, are caused by mistakes made by the English SRL system. Any wrong label it assigns to an English sentence may be projected onto the TL sentence, resulting in false positives.

No English Equivalent A small number of errors occur due to French particularities that do not exist in English. Such errors include certain French verbs for which no appropriate English PropBank labels exists, and French-specific syntactic particularities.[6]

Gold Data Errors Our evaluation so far relies on $\texttt{French}_{\text{gold}}$ as ground truth. Unfortunately, $\texttt{French}_{\text{gold}}$ does contain a small number of errors (e.g. missing argument labels). As a result, some correctly projected labels are being mistaken as false positives, causing a drop in both precision and recall. We therefore expect the true precision and recall of the approach to be somewhat higher than the estimate based on $\texttt{French}_{\text{gold}}$.

3 Stage 2: Bootstrapped Training of SRL

As discussed earlier, the TL corpus generated via filtered projection suffers from low recall. We address this issue with the second stage of our method.

Relabeling The idea of relabeling (Van der Plas et al., 2011) is to first train an SRL system over a TL corpus labeled using direct projection (with VF filter) and then use this SRL to relabel the corpus, effectively overwriting the projected labels with potentially less noisy predicted labels.

We first present an analysis on relabeling in concert with our proposed filters (Sec. 3.1), which motivates our bootstrap algorithm (Sec. 3.2).

3.1 Analysis of Relabeling Approach

We use the same experimental setup as in Sec. 2, and produce a labeled French corpus for each filtered annotation method. We then train an off-the-shelf SRL system (Björkelund et al., 2009) on each generated corpus and use it to relabel the corpus.

We measure precision and recall of each resulting TL corpus against $\texttt{French}_{\text{gold}}$ (see Tab. 4). Across all experiments, relabeling consistently improves recall over projection. The results also show how different factors affect the performance of relabeling.

PROJECTION	PREDICATE			ARGUMENT		
SRL training	P	R	F1	P	R	F1
DIRECT						
–	0.45	0.40	0.43	0.43	0.31	0.36
relabel (SP)	0.49	0.57	0.53	0.52	0.43	0.47
relabel (OW)	0.66	0.60	0.63	0.71	0.37	0.49
VERB FILTER (VF)						
–	0.59	0.40	0.48	0.53	0.31	0.39
relabel (SP)	0.57	0.55	0.56	0.61	0.42	0.50
relabel (OW) (Van der Plas et al., 2011)	0.56	0.55	0.56	0.69	0.31	0.43
PROPOSED (TF+RH)						
–	0.88	0.36	0.51	0.75	0.20	0.31
$\text{relabel}_{\text{full data}}$(SP)	**0.83**	0.58	0.68	**0.75**	0.41	0.53
$\text{relabel}_{\text{full data}}$(OW)	0.78	0.51	0.62	0.73	0.35	0.47
$\text{relabel}_{\text{comp. sent.}}$(SP)	0.80	0.64	0.71	0.68	0.48	0.56
$\text{relabel}_{\text{comp. sent.}}$(OW)	0.62	0.60	0.61	0.55	0.40	0.47
bootstrap (iter. 3)	0.78	0.68	**0.73**	0.71	0.55	**0.62**
bootstrap (terminate)	0.77	**0.70**	**0.73**	0.64	**0.60**	**0.62**

Table 4: Experiments on $\texttt{French}_{\text{gold}}$, with different projection and SRL training methods. SP=Supplement; OW=Overwrite.

Supplement vs. Overwrite Projected Labels The labels produced by the trained SRL can be used to either *overwrite* projected labels as in (Van der Plas et al., 2011), or to *supplement* them (supplying labels only for words w/o projected labels). Whether to overwrite or supplement depends on whether labels produced by the trained SRL are of higher quality than the projected labels. We find that while predicted labels are of higher precision than directly projected labels, they are of lower precision than labels post filtered projection. Therefore, for filtered projection, it makes more sense to allow predicted labels to only *supplement* projected labels.

Impact of Sampling Method We are further interested in learning the impact of sampling the data on the quality of relabeling. For the best filter found earlier (TF+RH), we compare SRL trained on the entire data set ($_{\text{full data}}$) with SRL trained only on the subset of completely annotated sentences ($_{\text{comp. sent.}}$), where completeness is defined as:

Definition 1. *A direct component of a labeled sentence s_{TL} is either a verb in s_{TL} or a syntactic dependent of a verb. Then s_{TL} is **k-complete** if s_{TL} contains equal to or fewer than k unlabeled direct compo-*

[6] French negations, for instance, are split into a particle and a connegative. In the annotation scheme used in $\texttt{French}_{\text{gold}}$, particles and connegatives are labeled differently.

Algorithm 1 Bootstrap learning algorithm

Require: Corpus C_{TL} with initial set of labels L_{TL}, and resampling threshold function $k(i)$;
  for $i = 1$ to ∞ **do**
    Let $k_i = k(i)$;
    Let $C_{\text{TL}}{}^{\text{comp}} = \{w \in C_{\text{TL}} : w \in s_{\text{TL}}, s_{\text{TL}} \text{is } k_i\text{-complete}\}$;
    Let $L_{\text{TL}}{}^{\text{comp}}$ be subset of L_{TL} appearing on $C_{\text{TL}}{}^{\text{comp}}$;
    Train an SRL on $(C_{\text{TL}}{}^{\text{comp}}, L_{\text{TL}}{}^{\text{comp}})$;
    Use the SRL to produce label set $L_{\text{TL}}{}^{\text{new}}$ on C_{TL};
    Let $C_{\text{TL}}{}^{\text{no.lab}} = \{w \in C_{\text{TL}} : w \text{ not labelled by } L_{\text{TL}}\}$;
    Let $L_{\text{TL}}{}^{\text{suppl}}$ be subset of $L_{\text{TL}}{}^{\text{new}}$ appearing on $C_{\text{TL}}{}^{\text{no.lab}}$;
    if $L_{\text{TL}}{}^{\text{suppl}} = \emptyset$ **then**
      Return the SRL;
    end if
    Let $L_{\text{TL}} = L_{\text{TL}} \cup L_{\text{TL}}{}^{\text{suppl}}$;
  end for

nents. 0-complete is abbreviated as ***complete***.

We observe that for TF+RH, when new labels supplement projected labels, relabeling over complete sentences results in better recall at slightly reduced precision, while including incomplete sentences into the training data reduces recall, but improves precision. While this finding may seem counterintuitive, it can be explained by how statistical SRL works. A densely labeled training data (such as $_{\text{comp. sent.}}$) usually results in an SRL that generates densely labeled sentences, resulting in better recall but poorer precision. On the other hand, training data that is sparsely labeled results in an SRL that weighs the option of not assigning a label with higher probability, resulting in better precision and poorer recall. In short, one can control the trade-off between precision and recall of SRL output by manipulating the completeness of the training data.

3.2 Bootstrap Learning

Building on the observation that we can sample data in such a way as to either favor precision or recall, we propose a bootstrapping algorithm to train an SRL iteratively over *k-complete* subsets of the data which are supplemented by high precision labels produced from previous iteration. The detailed algorithm is depicted in Algorithm 1.

Resampling Threshold Our goal is to use bootstrap learning to improve recall without sacrificing too much precision.

Proposition 1. *Under any resampling threshold, the set of labels L_{TL} increases monotonically in each iteration of Algorithm 1.*

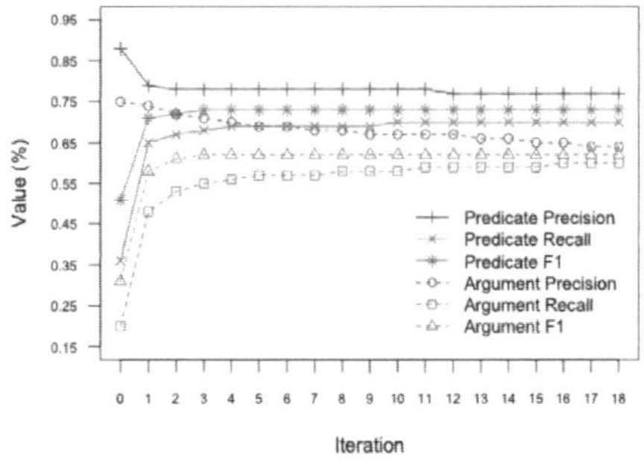

Figure 3: Values at each bootstrap iteration.

Since Prop. 1 guarantees the increase of the set of labels, we need to select a resampling function to favor precision while improving recall. Specifically, we use the formula $k(i) = \max(k_0 - i, 0)$, where k_0 is sufficiently large. Since the precision of labels generated by the SRL is lower than the precision of labels obtained from filtered projection, the precision of the training data is expected to decrease with the increase in recall. Therefore, starting with a high k seeks to ensure high precision labels are added to the training data in the first iterations. Decreasing k in each iteration seeks to ensure that resampling is done in an increasingly restrictive way to ensure that only high-quality annotated sentences are added to the training data, thus maintaining a high confidence in the learned SRL model.

3.3 Effectiveness of Bootstrapping

We experimentally evaluate the effectiveness of our model with $k_0 = 9$.[7] As shown in Tab 4, bootstrapping outperforms relabeling, producing labels with best overall quality in terms of F_1 measure and recall for both predicates and arguments, with a relatively small cost in precision.

While Algorithm 1 guarantees the increase of recall (Prop. 1), it provides no such guarantee on precision. Therefore, it is important to experimentally decide an early termination cutoff before the SRL gets overtrained. To do so, we evaluated the performance of the bootstrapping algorithm at each iteration (Fig. 3). We observe that for the first 3 iterations, F_1-measure for both predicates and arguments rises due to large increase in recall which offsets the smaller drop in precision. Then F_1-measure remains stable, with recall rising and pre-

[7]We found that setting k_0 to larger values had little impact on the final results .

LANGUAGE	DEP. PARSER	DATA SET	#SENTENCE
Arabic	STANFORD	UN	481K
Chinese	MATE-G	UN	2,986K
French	MATE-T	UN	2,542K
German	MATE-T	Europarl	560K
Hindi	MALT	Hindencorp	54K
Russian	MALT	UN	2,638K
Spanish	MATE-G	UN	2,304K

Table 5: Experimental setup .
Dependency parsers: STANFORD: (Green and Manning, 2010), MATE-G: (Bohnet, 2010), MATE-T: (Bohnet and Nivre, 2012), MALT: (Nivre et al., 2006). **Parallel corpora**: UN: (Rafalovitch et al., 2009), Europarl: (Koehn, 2005), Hindencorp: (Bojar et al., 2014). **Word alignment**: The UN corpus is already word-aligned. For others, we use the Berkeley Aligner (DeNero and Liang, 2007).

cision falling slightly at each iteration until convergence. To optimize precision and avoid overtraining, we set an iteration cutoff of 3. This combination of TF+RH filters, bootstrapping with $k_0 = 9$ and an iteration cutoff of 3 is used in the rest of our evaluation (Sec. 4), denoted as $\texttt{FB}_{best}$.

4 Multilingual Experiments

We use our method to generate Proposition Banks for 7 languages and evaluate the generated resources. We seek to answer the following questions: (1) What is the estimated quality for the generated PropBanks? How well does the approach work without language-specific adaptation? (2) Are there notable differences in quality from language to language; if so, why? We also present initial investigations on how different factors affect the performance of our method.

4.1 Experimental Setup

Data Tab. 5 lists the 7 different TLs and resources used in our experiments.[8] We chose these TLs because (1) they are among top 10 most influential languages in the world (Weber, 1997); and (2) we could find language experts to evaluate the results. English is used as SL in all our experiments.

Approach Tested For each TL, we used $\texttt{FB}_{best}$ (Sec. 3.3) to generate a corpus with semantic labels. From each TL corpus, we extracted all complete sentences to form the generated PropBanks.

[8]From each parallel corpus, we only keep sentences that are considered well-formed based on a set of standard heuristics. For example, we require a well-formed sentence to end in punctuation and not to contain certain special characters. For Arabic, as the dependency parser we use has relatively poor parsing accuracy, we additionally require sentences to be shorter than 100 characters.

		PREDICATE			ARGUMENT				
LANG.	Match	P	R	F1	P	R	F1	Agr	κ
Arabic	part.	0.97	0.89	0.93	0.86	0.69	0.77	0.92	0.87
	exact	0.97	0.89	0.93	0.67	0.63	0.65	0.85	0.77
Chinese	part.	0.97	0.88	0.92	0.93	0.83	0.88	0.95	0.91
	exact	0.97	0.88	0.92	0.83	0.81	0.82	0.92	0.86
French	part.	0.95	0.92	0.94	0.92	0.76	0.83	0.97	0.95
	exact	0.95	0.92	0.94	0.86	0.74	0.8	0.95	0.91
German	part.	0.96	0.92	0.94	0.95	0.73	0.83	0.95	0.91
	exact	0.96	0.92	0.94	0.91	0.73	0.81	0.92	0.86
Hindi	part.	0.91	0.68	0.78	0.93	0.66	0.77	0.94	0.88
	exact	0.91	0.68	0.78	0.58	0.54	0.56	0.81	0.69
Russian	part.	0.96	0.94	0.95	0.91	0.68	0.78	0.97	0.94
	exact	0.96	0.94	0.95	0.79	0.65	0.72	0.93	0.89
Spanish	part.	0.96	0.93	0.95	0.85	0.74	0.79	0.91	0.85
	exact	0.96	0.93	0.95	0.75	0.72	0.74	0.85	0.77

Table 6: Estimated precision and recall over seven languages.

Manual Evaluation While a gold annotated corpus for French ($\texttt{French}_{\text{gold}}$) was available for our experiments in the previous Sections, no such resources existed for the other TLs we wished to evaluate. We therefore chose to conduct a manual evaluation for each TL, each executed identically: For each TL we randomly selected 100 complete sentences with their generated semantic labels and assigned them to two language experts who were instructed to evaluate the semantic labels (based on their English descriptions) for the predicates and their core arguments. For each label, they were asked to determine (1) whether the label is correct; (2) if yes, then whether the boundary of the labeled constituent is correct: If also yes, mark the label as *fully correct*, otherwise as *partially correct*.

Metrics We used the standard measures of precision, recall, and F1 to measure the performance of the SRLs, with the following two schemes: (1) *Exact*: Only fully correct labels are considered as true positives; (2) *Partial*: Both fully and partially correct matches are considered as true positives.[9]

4.2 Experimental Results

Tab. 6 summarizes the estimated quality of semantic labels generated by our method for all seven TL. As can be seen, our method performed well for all

[9]Note that since the manually evaluated semantic labels are only a small fraction of the labels generated, the performance numbers obtained from manual evaluation is only an estimate of the actual quality for the generated resources.Thus the numbers obtained based on manual evaluation cannot be directly compared against the numbers computed over $\texttt{French}_{\text{gold}}$.

PROPBANK	#COMPLETE	%COMPLETE	#VERBS
Arabic	68.512	14%	330
Chinese	419,140	14%	1,102
French	248.256	10%	1145
German	44.007	8%	537
Hindi	1.623	3%	59
Russian	496.033	19%	1.349
Spanish	165.582	7%	909

Table 7: Characteristics of the generated PropBanks.

	PREDICATE			ARGUMENT		
SAMPLE SIZE	P	R	F1	P	R	F1
100%	0.87	0.81	0.84	0.86	0.74	0.8
10%	0.88	0.8	0.84	0.87	0.72	0.79
1%	0.9	**0.76**	0.83	0.89	**0.67**	0.76

Table 8: Estimated impact of downsampling parallel corpus.

	PREDICATE			ARGUMENT		
HEURISTIC	P	R	F1	P	R	F1
none*	0.87	0.81	0.84	0.86	0.74	0.8
none**	0.88	0.8	0.84	**0.76**	**0.65**	0.7
customization*	0.87	0.81	0.84	**0.9**	0.74	0.81

Table 9: Impact of English SRLs (*=CLEARNLP, **=MATE-SRL) and language-spec. customization (*filter synt. expletive*).

seven languages and generated high quality semantics labels across the board. For predicate labels, the precision is over 95% and the recall is over 85% for all languages except for Hindi. For argument labels, when considering partially correct matches, the precision is at least 85% (above 90% for most languages) and the recall is between 66% to 83% for all the languages. These encouraging results obtained from a diverse set of languages implies the generalizability of our method. In addition, the inter-annotator agreement is very high for all the languages, indicating that the results obtained based on manual evaluation are very reliable.

In addition, we make a number of interesting observations:

Dependency Parsing Accuracy The precision for exact argument labels is significantly below partial matches, particularly for Hindi (↓35 pp) and Arabic (↓19 pp). Since argument boundaries are determined syntactically, such errors are caused by dependency parsing. The fact that Hindi and Arbic suffer the most from this issue is consistent with the poorer performance of their dependency parsers compared to other languages (Nivre et al., 2006; Green and Manning, 2010).

Hindi as the Main Outlier The results for Hindi are much worse than the results for other languages. Besides the poorer dependency parser performance, the size of the parallel corpus used could be a factor: `Hindencorp` is one to two orders of magnitude smaller than the other corpora. The quality of the parallel corpus could be a reason as well: `Hindencorp` was collected from various sources, while both `UN` and `Europarl` were extracted from governmental proceedings.

Language-specific Errors Certain errors occur more frequently in some languages than others. An example are deverbal nouns in Chinese (Xue, 2006) in formal passive constructions with support verb 受. Since we currently only consider verbs for predicate labels, predicate labels are projected onto the support verbs instead of the deverbal nouns. Such errors appear for light verb constructions in all languages, but particularly affect Chinese due to the high frequency of this passive construction in the `UN` corpus.

Low Fraction of Complete Sentences As Tab. 7 shows, the fraction of complete sentences in the generated PropBanks is rather low, indicating the impact of moderate recall on the size of generated PropBanks. Especially for languages for which only small parallel corpora are available, such as Hindi, this points to the need to address recall issues in future work.

4.3 Additional Experiments

The observations made in Sec. 4.2 suggests a few factors that may potentially affect the performance of our method. To better understand their impact, we conducted the following initial investigation. SRL models produced in this set of experiments were evaluated using $\texttt{French}_{\text{gold}}$, sampled and evaluated in the same way as other experiments in this section for comparability.

Data Size We varied the data size for French by downsampling the `UN` corpus. As one can see from Tab. 8, downsampling the dataset by one order of magnitude (to 250k sentences) only slightly affects precision, while downsampling to 25k sentences has a more pronounced but still small impact on recall. It appears that data size does not have significant impact on the performance of our method.

Language-specific Customizations While our method is language-agnostic, intuitively language-specific customization can be helpful in addressing language-specific errors. As an initial experiment, we added a simple heuristic to filter out French verbs that are commonly used for "existential there" constructions, as one type of common errors for French involves the syntactic expletive *il* (Danlos, 2005) in "existential there" constructions such as *il faut* (see Fig. 1 (TL sentence) for an example) wrongly labeled with with role information. As shown in Tab. 9, this simple customization results in a small increase in precision, suggesting that language-specific customization can be helpful.

Quality of English SRL As noted in Sec. 2.5, errors made by English SRL are often prorogated to the TL via projection. To assess the impact of English SRL quality, we used two different English SRL systems: CLEARNLP and MATE-SRL. As can be seen from Tab. 9, the impact of English SRL quality is substantial on argument labeling.

4.4 Multilingual PropBanks

To facilitate future research on multilingual SRL, we release the created PropBanks for all 7 languages to the research community to encourage further research. Tab. 7 gives an overview over the resources.

5 Related Work

Annotation Projection in Parallel Corpora to train monolingual tools for new languages was introduced in the context of learning a PoS tagger (Yarowsky et al., 2001). Similar in spirit to our approach of using filters to increase the precision of projected labels, recent work (Täckström et al., 2013) uses token and type constraints to guide learning in cross-lingual PoS tagging.

Projection of Semantic Labels was considered for FrameNet (Baker et al., 1998) in (Padó and Lapata, 2009; Basili et al., 2009). Recently, however, most work in the area focuses on PropBank, which has been identified as a more suitable annotation scheme for joint syntactic-semantics settings due to broader coverage (Merlo and van der Plas, 2009), and was shown to be usable for languages other than English (Monachesi et al., 2007).

Direct projection of PropBank annotations was considered in (Van der Plas et al., 2011). Our approach significantly outperforms theirs in terms of recall and F_1 for both predicates and arguments (Section 3). A approach was proposed in (Van der Plas et al., 2014) in which information is aggregated at the corpus level, resulting in a significantly better SRL corpus for French. However, this approach has several practical limitations: (1) it does not consider the problem of argument identification of SRL systems, treating arguments as already given; (2) it generates rules for the argument classification step preferably from manually annotated data; (3) it has been demonstrated for a single language (French), and was not applied to any other language. In contrast, our approach trains an SRL system for both predicate and argument labels, in a completely automatic fashion. Furthermore, we have applied our approach to generate PropBanks for 7 languages and conducted experiments that indicate a high F_1 measure for all languages (Section 4).

Other Related Work A number of approaches such as model transfer (Kozhevnikov and Titov, 2013) and role induction (Titov and Klementiev, 2012) exist for the argument classification step in the SRL pipeline. In contrast, our work addresses the full SRL pipeline and seeks to generate SRL resources for TLs with English PropBank labels.

6 Conclusion

We proposed a two-staged method to construct multilingual SRL resources using monolingual SRL and parallel data and showed that our method outperforms previous approaches in both precision and recall. More importantly, through comprehensive experiments over seven languages from three language families, we show that our proposed method works well across different languages without any language specific customization. Preliminary results from additional experiments indicate that better English SRL and language-specific customization can further improve the results, which we aim to investigate in future work. A qualitative comparison against existing or under-construction PropBanks for Chinese (Xue, 2008), Hindi (Vaidya et al., 2011) or Arabic (Zaghouani et al., 2010) may be interesting, both for comparison of resources and for defining language-specific customizations. In addition, we plan to expand our experiments both to more languages as well as NomBank (Meyers et al., 2004)-style noun labels.

References

[Baker et al.1998] Collin F Baker, Charles J Fillmore, and John B Lowe. 1998. The berkeley framenet project. In *Proceedings of the 36th Annual Meeting of the Association for Computational Linguistics and 17th International Conference on Computational Linguistics-Volume 1*, pages 86–90. Association for Computational Linguistics.

[Basili et al.2009] Roberto Basili, Diego De Cao, Danilo Croce, Bonaventura Coppola, and Alessandro Moschitti. 2009. Cross-language frame semantics transfer in bilingual corpora. In *Computational Linguistics and Intelligent Text Processing*, pages 332–345. Springer.

[Björkelund et al.2009] Anders Björkelund, Love Hafdell, and Pierre Nugues. 2009. Multilingual semantic role labeling. In *Proceedings of the Thirteenth Conference on Computational Natural Language Learning: Shared Task*, pages 43–48. Association for Computational Linguistics.

[Bohnet and Nivre2012] Bernd Bohnet and Joakim Nivre. 2012. A transition-based system for joint part-of-speech tagging and labeled non-projective dependency parsing. In *Proceedings of the 2012 Joint Conference on Empirical Methods in Natural Language Processing and Computational Natural Language Learning*, pages 1455–1465. Association for Computational Linguistics.

[Bohnet2010] Bernd Bohnet. 2010. Very high accuracy and fast dependency parsing is not a contradiction. In *Proceedings of the 23rd International Conference on Computational Linguistics*, pages 89–97. Association for Computational Linguistics.

[Bojar et al.2014] Ondřej Bojar, Vojtěch Diatka, Pavel Rychlỳ, Pavel Straňák, Vít Suchomel, Aleš Tamchyna, Daniel Zeman, et al. 2014. Hindencorp–hindi-english and hindi-only corpus for machine translation. In *Proceedings of the Ninth International Conference on Language Resources and Evaluation*.

[Choi and McCallum2013] Jinho D. Choi and Andrew McCallum. 2013. Transition-based dependency parsing with selectional branching. In *Proceedings of the 51st Annual Meeting of the Association for Computational Linguistics*.

[Danlos2005] Laurence Danlos. 2005. Automatic recognition of french expletive pronoun occurrences. In *Natural language processing. Proceedings of the 2nd International Joint Conference on Natural Language Processing (IJCNLP-05)*, pages 73–78. Citeseer.

[DeNero and Liang2007] John DeNero and Percy Liang. 2007. The Berkeley Aligner. `http://code.google.com/p/berkeleyaligner/`.

[Erk et al.2003] K. Erk, A. Kowalski, S. Pado, and S. Pinkal. 2003. Towards a resource for lexical semantics: A large german corpus with extensive semantic annotation. In *ACL*.

[Green and Manning2010] Spence Green and Christopher D Manning. 2010. Better arabic parsing: Baselines, evaluations, and analysis. In *Proceedings of the 23rd International Conference on Computational Linguistics*, pages 394–402. Association for Computational Linguistics.

[Hajič et al.2009] Jan Hajič, Massimiliano Ciaramita, Richard Johansson, Daisuke Kawahara, Maria Antònia Martí, Lluís Màrquez, Adam Meyers, Joakim Nivre, Sebastian Padó, Jan Štěpánek, et al. 2009. The conll-2009 shared task: Syntactic and semantic dependencies in multiple languages. In *Proceedings of the Thirteenth Conference on Computational Natural Language Learning: Shared Task*, pages 1–18. Association for Computational Linguistics.

[Koehn2005] Philipp Koehn. 2005. Europarl: A parallel corpus for statistical machine translation. In *MT summit*, volume 5, pages 79–86.

[Kozhevnikov and Titov2013] Mikhail Kozhevnikov and Ivan Titov. 2013. Cross-lingual transfer of semantic role labeling models. In *ACL (1)*, pages 1190–1200.

[Maqsud et al.2014] Umar Maqsud, Sebastian Arnold, Michael Hülfenhaus, and Alan Akbik. 2014. Nerdle: Topic-specific question answering using wikia seeds. In Lamia Tounsi and Rafal Rak, editors, *COLING 2014, 25th International Conference on Computational Linguistics, Proceedings of the Conference System Demonstrations, August 23-29, 2014, Dublin, Ireland*, pages 81–85. ACL.

[Merlo and van der Plas2009] Paola Merlo and Lonneke van der Plas. 2009. Abstraction and generalisation in semantic role labels: Propbank, verbnet or both? In *ACL 2009*, pages 288–296.

[Meyers et al.2004] Adam Meyers, Ruth Reeves, Catherine Macleod, Rachel Szekely, Veronika Zielinska, Brian Young, and Ralph Grishman. 2004. Annotating noun argument structure for nombank. In *LREC*, volume 4, pages 803–806.

[Monachesi et al.2007] Paola Monachesi, Gerwert Stevens, and Jantine Trapman. 2007. Adding semantic role annotation to a corpus of written dutch. In *Proceedings of the Linguistic Annotation Workshop*, LAW '07, pages 77–84.

[Nivre et al.2006] Joakim Nivre, Johan Hall, and Jens Nilsson. 2006. Maltparser: A data-driven parser-generator for dependency parsing. In *Proceedings of LREC*, volume 6, pages 2216–2219.

[Padó and Lapata2009] Sebastian Padó and Mirella Lapata. 2009. Cross-lingual annotation projection for semantic roles. *Journal of Artificial Intelligence Research*, 36(1):307–340.

[Pado2007] Sebastian Pado. 2007. *Cross-Lingual Annotation Projection Models for Role-Semantic Information*. Ph.D. thesis, Saarland University. MP.

[Palmer et al.2005] Martha Palmer, Daniel Gildea, and Paul Kingsbury. 2005. The proposition bank: An annotated corpus of semantic roles. *Computational linguistics*, 31(1):71–106.

[Rafalovitch et al.2009] Alexandre Rafalovitch, Robert Dale, et al. 2009. United nations general assembly resolutions: A six-language parallel corpus. In *Proceedings of the MT Summit*, volume 12, pages 292–299.

[Schuler2005] Karin Kipper Schuler. 2005. *Verbnet: A Broad-coverage, Comprehensive Verb Lexicon*. Ph.D. thesis, University of Pennsylvania.

[Shen and Lapata2007] Dan Shen and Mirella Lapata. 2007. Using semantic roles to improve question answering. In *EMNLP-CoNLL*, pages 12–21. Citeseer.

[Täckström et al.2013] Oscar Täckström, Dipanjan Das, Slav Petrov, Ryan McDonald, and Joakim Nivre. 2013. Token and type constraints for cross-lingual part-of-speech tagging. *Transactions of the Association for Computational Linguistics*, 1:1–12.

[Titov and Klementiev2012] Ivan Titov and Alexandre Klementiev. 2012. Crosslingual induction of semantic roles. In *ACL*, pages 647–656.

[Vaidya et al.2011] Ashwini Vaidya, Jinho D Choi, Martha Palmer, and Bhuvana Narasimhan. 2011. Analysis of the hindi proposition bank using dependency structure. In *Proceedings of the 5th Linguistic Annotation Workshop*, pages 21–29. Association for Computational Linguistics.

[Van der Plas et al.2010] Lonneke Van der Plas, Tanja Samardžić, and Paola Merlo. 2010. Cross-lingual validity of propbank in the manual annotation of french. In *Proceedings of the Fourth Linguistic Annotation Workshop*, pages 113–117. Association for Computational Linguistics.

[Van der Plas et al.2011] Lonneke Van der Plas, Paola Merlo, and James Henderson. 2011. Scaling up automatic cross-lingual semantic role annotation. In *Proceedings of the 49th Annual Meeting of the Association for Computational Linguistics: Human Language Technologies: short papers-Volume 2*, pages 299–304. Association for Computational Linguistics.

[Van der Plas et al.2014] Lonneke Van der Plas, Marianna Apidianaki, Rue John von Neumann, and Chenhua Chen. 2014. Global methods for cross-lingual semantic role and predicate labelling. In *Proceedings of the 25th International Conference on Computational Linguistics (COLING 2014)*, pages 1279–1290. Association for Computational Linguistics.

[Weber1997] George Weber. 1997. Top languages: The world's 10 most influential languages. *Language Today*, December.

[Xue2006] Nianwen Xue. 2006. Semantic role labeling of nominalized predicates in chinese. In *Proceedings of the main conference on Human Language Technology Conference of the North American Chapter of the Association of Computational Linguistics*, pages 431–438. Association for Computational Linguistics.

[Xue2008] Nianwen Xue. 2008. Labeling chinese predicates with semantic roles. *Computational linguistics*, 34(2):225–255.

[Yarowsky et al.2001] David Yarowsky, Grace Ngai, and Richard Wicentowski. 2001. Inducing multilingual text analysis tools via robust projection across aligned corpora. In *Proceedings of the first international conference on Human language technology research*, pages 1–8. Association for Computational Linguistics.

[Zaghouani et al.2010] Wajdi Zaghouani, Mona Diab, Aous Mansouri, Sameer Pradhan, and Martha Palmer. 2010. The revised arabic propbank. In *Proceedings of the Fourth Linguistic Annotation Workshop*, pages 222–226. Association for Computational Linguistics.

Aligning Opinions: Cross-Lingual Opinion Mining with Dependencies

Mariana S. C. Almeida[*†] **Cláudia Pinto**[*] **Helena Figueira**[*]
Pedro Mendes[*] **André F. T. Martins**[*†]
[*]Priberam Labs, Alameda D. Afonso Henriques, 41, 2°, 1000-123 Lisboa, Portugal
[†]Instituto de Telecomunicações, Instituto Superior Técnico, 1049-001 Lisboa, Portugal
{mla,atm}@priberam.pt

Abstract

We propose a cross-lingual framework for fine-grained opinion mining using bitext projection. The only requirements are a running system in a source language and word-aligned parallel data. Our method projects opinion frames from the source to the target language, and then trains a system on the target language using the automatic annotations. Key to our approach is a novel dependency-based model for opinion mining, which we show, as a byproduct, to be on par with the current state of the art for English, while avoiding the need for integer programming or reranking. In cross-lingual mode (English to Portuguese), our approach compares favorably to a supervised system (with scarce labeled data), and to a delexicalized model trained using universal tags and bilingual word embeddings.

1 Introduction

The goal of **opinion mining** is to extract opinions and sentiments from text (Pang and Lee, 2008; Wilson, 2008; Liu, 2012). With the advent of social media and the increasing amount of data available on the Web, this has become a very active area of research, with applications in summarization of customer reviews (Hu and Liu, 2004; Wu et al., 2011), tracking of newswire and blogs (Ku et al., 2006), question answering (Yu and Hatzivassiloglou, 2003), and text-to-speech synthesis (Alm et al., 2005).

While early work has focused on determining sentiment at document and sentence level (Pang et al., 2002; Turney, 2002; Balog et al., 2006), research has gradually progressed towards **fine-grained opinion mining**, where rather than determining global sentiment, the goal is to parse text into **opinion frames**, identifying opinion expressions, agents, targets, and polarities (Ding et al., 2008), or addressing compositionality (Socher et al., 2013b). Since the release of the MPQA corpus[1] (Wiebe et al., 2005; Wilson, 2008), a standard corpus for fine-grained opinion mining of news documents, a long string of work has been produced (reviewed in §2). Despite the large volume of prior work, opinion mining has by and large been limited to monolingual approaches in English.[2] This is explained by the heavy effort of annotation necessary for current learning-based approaches to succeed, which delays the deployment of opinion miners for new languages.

We bridge the existing gap by proposing a cross-lingual approach to fine-grained opinion mining via **bitext projection**. This technique has been quite effective in several NLP tasks, such as part-of-speech (POS) tagging (Täckström et al., 2013), named entity recognition (Wang and Manning, 2014), syntactic parsing (Yarowsky and Ngai, 2001; Hwa et al., 2005), semantic role labeling (Padó and Lapata, 2009), and coreference resolution (Martins, 2015). Given a corpus of parallel sentences (bitext), the idea is to run a pre-trained system on the source side and then to use word alignments to transfer the produced annotations to the target side, creating an automatic training corpus for the impoverished language.

To alleviate the complexity of the task, we start by introducing a lightweight representation—called **dependency-based opinion mining**—and convert the MPQA corpus to this formalism (§3). We propose a simple arc-factored model that permits easy decoding (§4) and we show that, despite

[1]http://mpqa.cs.pitt.edu/corpora/mpqa_corpus.

[2]Besides English, monolingual systems have also been developed for Chinese and Japanese (Seki et al., 2007), German (Clematide et al., 2012) and Bengali (Das and Bandyopadhyay, 2010).

Proceedings of the 53rd Annual Meeting of the Association for Computational Linguistics and the 7th International Joint Conference on Natural Language Processing, pages 408–418, Beijing, China, July 26-31, 2015.

its simplicity, this model is on par with state-of-the-art opinion mining systems for English (§5). Then, through bitext projection, we transfer these dependency-based opinion frames to Portuguese (our target language), and train a system on the resulting corpus (§6).

As part of this work, a validation corpus in Portuguese with subjectivity annotations was created, along with a translation of the MPQA Subjectivity lexicon of Wilson et al. (2005).[3] Experimental evaluation (§7) shows that our cross-lingual approach surpasses a supervised system trained on a small corpus in the target language, as well as a delexicalized baseline trained using universal POS tags, bilingual word embeddings and a projected lexicon.

2 Related Work

A considerable amount of work on fine-grained opinion mining is based on the MPQA corpus. Kim and Hovy (2006) proposed a method for finding opinion holders and topics, with the aid of a semantic role labeler. Choi et al. (2005) and Breck et al. (2007) used CRFs for finding opinion holders and recognizing opinion expressions, respectively. The two things are predicted jointly by Choi et al. (2006), with integer programming, and Johansson and Moschitti (2010), via reranking. The same method was applied later for joint prediction of opinion expressions and their polarities (Johansson and Moschitti, 2011). The advantage of a joint model was also shown by Choi and Cardie (2010) and Yang and Cardie (2014). Yang and Cardie (2012) classified expressions with a semi-Markov decoder, outperforming a B-I-O tagger; in later work, the same authors proposed an ILP decoder to jointly retrieve opinion expressions, holders, and targets (Yang and Cardie, 2013). A more recent work (İrsoy and Cardie, 2014) proposes a recurrent neural network to identify opinion spans.

All the approaches above rely on a span-based representation of the opinion elements. This makes joint decoding procedures more complicated, since they must forbid overlap of opinion elements or add further constraints, leading to integer programming or reranking strategies. Besides, there is little consensus about what should be the correct span boundaries, the inter-annotator agreement being quite low (Wiebe et al., 2005). In constrast, we use dependencies to model opinion elements and relations, leading to a compact representation that does not depend on spans and which is tractable to decode. A dependency scheme was also used by Wu et al. (2011) for fine-grained opinion mining. Our work differs in which we mine opinions in news articles instead of product reviews, a considerably different task. In addition, the approach of Wu et al. (2011) relies on "span nodes" (instead of head words), requiring solving an ILP followed by an approximate heuristic.

Query-based multilingual opinion mining was addressed in several NTCIR shared tasks (Seki et al., 2007; Seki et al., 2010).[4] However, to our best knowledge, a cross-lingual approach has never been attempted. Some steps were taken by Mihalcea et al. (2007) and Banea et al. (2008), who translated an English lexicon and the MPQA corpus to Romanian and Spanish, but for the much simpler task of sentence-level subjectivity analysis. Cross-lingual sentiment classification was addressed by Wan (2009), Prettenhofer and Stein (2010) and Wei and Pal (2010) at document level, and by Lu et al. (2011) at sentence level. Recently, Gui et al. (2013) applied projection learning for opinion mining in Chinese. However, this work only addresses agent detection and requires translating the MPQA corpus. While all these works are relevant, none addresses fine-grained opinion mining in its full generality, where the goal is to predict full opinion frames.

3 Dependency-Based Opinion Mining

This work addresses various elements of subjectivity annotated in the MPQA corpus, namely:

- direct-subjective expressions (henceforth, **opinions**) that are direct mentions of a private state, *e.g.* opinions, beliefs, emotions, sentiments, speculations, goals, *etc.*;
- the opinion **agent**, *i.e.*, the holder of the opinion;
- the opinion **target**, *i.e.*, what is being argued about;
- the opinion **polarity**, *i.e.*, the sentiment (positive, negative or neutral) towards the target.

As an example, consider the sentence in Figure 1, which has two opinions, expressed by the

[3]The Portuguese corpus and the lexicon are available at `http://labs.priberam.com/Resources`.

[4]NTCIR-8 had a cross-lingual track but in a very different sense: there, queries and documents are in different languages; in contrast, we transfer a model accross languages.

spans "is believed" (O_1) and "are against" (O_2). The first opinion has an implicit agent and a neutral polarity toward the target "the rich elites" (T_1). This target is also the agent (A_2) of the second opinion, which has a negative polarity toward "Hugo Chávez" (T_2).

3.1 Motivation

As noted in prior work (Choi et al., 2005; Kim and Hovy, 2006; Johansson and Moschitti, 2010), one source of difficulty when learning opinion miners on MPQA is with the boundaries of the entity spans. The fact that no criterion for choosing these boundaries is explicitly defined in the annotation guidelines (Wiebe et al., 2005) leads to a low inter-annotator agreement. To circumvent this problem and make the learning task easier, we depart from the classical span-based approaches toward **dependency-based opinion mining**. This decision is inspired by the success of dependency models for syntax and semantics (Buchholz and Marsi, 2006; Surdeanu et al., 2008). These dependency relations can be further converted to opinion spans (as described in §3.3), or directly used as features in downstream applications. As we will see, a compact representation based on dependencies can achieve state-of-the-art results and has the advantage of being easily transferred to other languages through a parallel corpus.

3.2 Dependency Graph

Figure 1 depicts a sentence-level dependency representation for fine-grained opinion mining. The overall structure is a graph whose nodes are head words (plus two special nodes, `root` and `null`), connected by labeled arcs, as outlined below.

Determining head nodes. The three opinion elements that we want to detect (opinions, agents and targets) are each represented by a **head node**, which corresponds to a single word (underlined in Figure 1). When converting the MPQA corpus to dependencies, we determine this "representative" word automatically, by using the following simple heuristic: we first parse the sentence using the Stanford dependency parser (Socher et al., 2013a); then, we pick the last word in the span whose syntactic parent is outside the span (if the span is a syntactic phrase, there is only one word whose parent is outside the span, which is the lexical head). The same heuristic has been used for identifying the heads of mention spans in coreference resolution (Durrett and Klein, 2013).

Defining labeled arcs. The opinion relations are represented as **labeled arcs** that link these head nodes. Two artificial nodes are added: a `root` node, which links to all nodes that represent opinion words, with the label OPINION; and a `null` node, which is used for representing implicit relations. To represent opinion-agent relations, we draw an arc labeled AGENT toward the agent word. For opinion-target relations, the arc is toward the target word and has one of the labels TARGET:0, TARGET:+, or TARGET:-; this encodes the polarity in addition to the type of relation. We also include implicit arcs for opinion elements whose agent or target is not mentioned inside the sentence—these are modeled as arcs pointing to the `null` node.

Dependency opinion graph. We have the following requirements for a well-formed dependency opinion graph:

1. No self-arcs or arcs linking `root` to `null`.
2. An arc is labeled as OPINION if and only if it comes from the `root` node.
3. Arcs labeled as AGENT or TARGET must come from an opinion node (*i.e.*, a node with an incoming OPINION arc).
4. Every opinion node has exactly one AGENT and one TARGET outgoing arcs (possibly implicit).[5]

Similarly to prior work (Choi and Cardie, 2010; Johansson and Moschitti, 2011; Johansson and Moschitti, 2013), we map the MPQA's polarity into three levels: positive, negative and neutral, where the latter includes spans without polarity annotation or annotated as "both". As in Johansson and Moschitti (2013), we also ignore the "uncertain" aspect of the annotated polarities.

3.3 Dependency-to-Span Conversion

To evaluate the opinion miner against manual annotations and compare with other systems, we need a procedure to convert back from predicted dependencies to spans. In this work, we used a very simple procedure that we next describe,

[5]Even though this assumption is not always met in practice, it is typical in MPQA (only 10% of the opinions have multiple agents, typically coreferent; and only 13% have multiple targets). When multiple agents or targets exist, we keep the ones that are closest to the opinion expression.

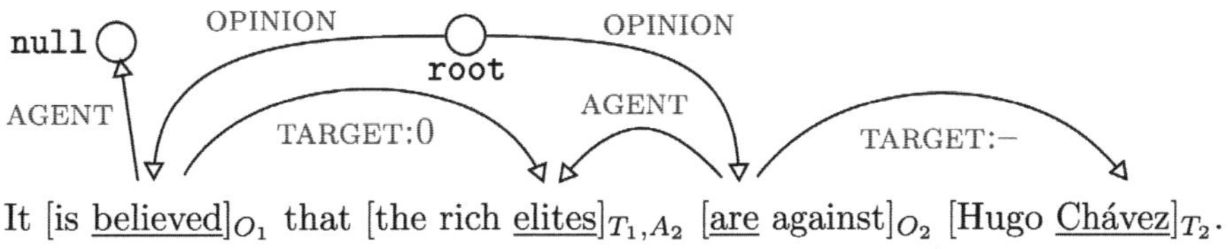

Figure 1: Example of an opinion mining graph in our dependency formalism. Heads are underlined.

which assumes the sentence was previously parsed using a syntactic dependency parser.

To generate agent and target spans, we compute the largest span, containing the head word, whose words are all descendants in the dependency parse tree and that are, simultaneously, not punctuations. To generate opinion spans, we start with the head word and expand the span by adding all neighbouring verbal words. In the case of English, we also allow adverbs, adjectives, modal verbs and the word *to*, when expanding to the left.

The application of this simple approach to the gold dependency graphs in the training partition of the MPQA leads to oracle F_1 scores of 86.0%, 95.8% and 93.0% in the reconstruction of opinion, agent and target spans, respectively, according to the proportional scores described in §5.2.

4 Arc-Factored Model

One of the advantages of the dependency representation is that we can easily decode opinion-agent-target relations without the need of complicated constrained sequence models or integer programming, as done in prior work (Choi et al., 2006; Yang and Cardie, 2012; Yang and Cardie, 2013).

4.1 Decoding

We model dependency-based opinion mining as a structured classification problem. Let x be a sentence and $y \in \mathcal{Y}(x)$ a set of well-formed dependency graphs, according to the constraints stated in §3. We define a score function that decomposes as a sum of labeled arc scores,

$$f(x, y) = \sum_{a \in y} f_a(x, y_a) \quad (1)$$

where y_a is a labeled arc and the sum is over the arcs of the graph y. We use a linear model with weight vector $\boldsymbol{w}$ and local features $\boldsymbol{\phi}_a(x, y_a)$:

$$f_a(x, y_a) = \boldsymbol{w} \cdot \boldsymbol{\phi}_a(x, y_a). \quad (2)$$

For making predictions, we need to compute

$$\widehat{y} = \arg\max_{y \in \mathcal{Y}(x)} f(x, y). \quad (3)$$

Under the assumptions stated in §3, this problem decouples into independent maximization problems (one for each possible opinion word in the sentence). The detailed procedure is as follows, where arcs a can take the form $o \rightarrow h$ (opinion to agent) and $o \rightarrow t$ (opinion to target). For every candidate opinion word o:

1. Obtain the most compatible agent word, $\widehat{h} := \arg\max_h f_{o \rightarrow h}(x, \text{AGENT})$;
2. Obtain the best target word and its polarity, $(\widehat{t}, \widehat{p}) := \arg\max_{t,p} f_{o \rightarrow t}(x, \text{TARGET:}p)$;
3. Compute the total score of this candidate opinion as $s_o := f_{\texttt{root} \rightarrow o}(x, \text{OPINION}) + f_{o \rightarrow \widehat{h}}(x, \text{AGENT}) + f_{o \rightarrow \widehat{t}}(x, \text{TARGET:}\widehat{p})$. Then, if $s_o \geq 0$, add the arcs $\texttt{root} \rightarrow o$, $o \rightarrow \widehat{h}$, and $o \rightarrow \widehat{t}$ to the dependency graph, respectively with labels OPINION, AGENT, and TARGET:$\widehat{p}$.

For a sentence with L words, this decoding procedure takes $O(L^2)$ time. In practice, we speed up this process by pruning from the candidate list arcs whose connected POS were not observed in the training set and whose length were larger than the ones observed in the training set.

4.2 Features

We now describe our features $\boldsymbol{\phi}_a$, which are computed after processing the sentence to predict POS tags, syntactic dependency trees, lemmas and voice (active or passive) information. For English, we used the Stanford dependency parser (Socher et al., 2013a) for the syntactic annotations, the Porter stemmer to compute word stems, and a set of rules for computing the voice of each word. Our Portuguese corpus include all these preprocessing elements (§6.3), with the exception of the voice information (features depending on voice were only used for English).

We also used the Subjectivity Lexicon[6] of Wilson et al. (2005) that we translated to Portuguese

[6] http://mpqa.cs.pitt.edu/lexicons/subj_lexicon/

(§6.3), and a set of negation words (*e.g. not, never, nor*) and quantity words (*e.g. very, much, less*) collected for both languages.

Our arc-factored features are described below; they are inspired by prior work on dependency parsing (Martins et al., 2013) and fine-grained opinion mining (Breck et al., 2007; Johansson and Moschitti, 2013).

Opinion features. We define a set of features that only look at the opinion word; special symbols are used if the opinion is connected to a `root` or `null` node. The features below are also conjoined with the arc label.

- OPINION WORD. The word itself, the lemma, the POS, and the voice. Conjunction of the word with the POS, and of the lemma with the POS.
- BIGRAMS. Bigrams of words and POS corresponding to the opinion word conjoined with its previous (and next) word.
- LEXICON (BASIC). Conjunction of the strength and polarity of the opinion word in the Subjectivity Lexicon[6] (e.g., "weaksubj+neg").
- LEXICON (COUNT). Number of subjective words (total, positive and negative) in a sentence, with and without being conjoined with the polarity of the opinion word in the lexicon.
- LEXICON (CONTEXT). For each word that is in the lexicon and within the 4-word context of the opinion, the form and the polarity of that word in the lexicon, with and without being conjoined with the form and the polarity in the lexicon of the opinion word. Besides the 4-word context, we also used the next/previous word in the sentence which is in the lexicon.
- NEGATION AND QUANTITY WORDS. Within the 4-word context, features indicating if a word is a negation or quantity word, conjoined with the word itself and the opinion word.
- SYNTACTIC PATH. The number of words up to the top of the syntactic dependency tree, and the sequence of POS tags in that path.

Opinion-Argument features. In case of arcs that neither connect to `null` nor `root`, the features above are also conjoined with the binned distance between the two words.For these arcs, we did not use the LEXICON (COUNT)/(CONTEXT) features, but we added features regarding the pair of opinion-argument words (below).

- OPINION-ARGUMENT WORD PAIR. Several conjunctions of word form, POS, voice and syntactic dependency relations corresponding to the pair opinion-argument.
- OPINION-ARGUMENT SYNTACTIC PATH. The syntactic path from the opinion word to the argument, conjoined with the POS and the dependency relations in the path (in Figure 1, for the agent "elites" headed by "are" with relation `nsuj`, we have: "VBP↓NNS" and "`nsuj`↓").

For arcs that neither connect to `null` or `root`, we conjoin voice features with the label, distance, and the direction of the arc. For these arcs, we also include back-off features where the polarity information is removed from the (target) labels.

5 English Monolingual Experiments

In a first set of experiments, we evaluated the performance of our dependency-based model for opinion mining (§3) in the MPQA English corpus.

5.1 Learning

We trained arc-factored models by running 25 epochs of max-loss MIRA (Crammer et al., 2006). Our cost function takes into account mismatches between predicted and gold dependencies, with a cost C_P on labeled arcs incorrectly predicted (false positives) and a cost $C_R = 1 - C_P$ on missed gold labeled arcs (false negatives). The cost C_P, the regularization constant, and the number of epochs were tuned in the development set.

5.2 Evaluation Metrics

Opinion spans (Op.) are evaluated with F_1 scores, according to two matching criteria commonly used in the literature: **overlap matching** (OM), where a predicted span is counted as correct if it overlaps a gold one, and **proportional matching** (PM), proposed by Johansson and Moschitti (2010). For the latter, we use the following formula for the recall, where we consider the sets of gold ($\mathcal{G}$) and predicted ($\mathcal{P}$) opinion spans:[7]

$$R(\mathcal{G}, \mathcal{P}) = \sum_{p \in \mathcal{P}} \max_{g \in \mathcal{G}} \frac{|g \bigcap p| / |p|}{|\mathcal{P}|}; \qquad (4)$$

[7]This metric is slightly different from the PM metric of Johansson and Moschitti (2010), in which recall was computed as $R(\mathcal{G}, \mathcal{P}) = \sum_{p \in \mathcal{P}} \sum_{g \in \mathcal{G}} \frac{|g \cap p| / |p|}{|\mathcal{P}|}$. The reason why we replace the "sum" by a "max" is that each predicted span p in (4) could contribute to the recall with a value greater than 1. Since most of the predicted spans only overlap a single gold span, this fix has a very small effect in the final scores.

the precision is $P(\mathcal{G}, \mathcal{P}) = R(\mathcal{P}, \mathcal{G})$. We also report metrics based on a **head matching** (HM) criterion, where a predicted span is considered correct if its syntactic head matches the head of the gold span. We consider that a pair opinion-agent (Op-Ag.) or opinion-target (Op-Tg.) is correctly extracted according to the OM or the HM criteria, if both the elements satisfy these criteria and the relation holds in the gold data. We also compute the metric described in Johansson and Moschitti (2010) which measures how well agents of opinions are predicted based on a proportional matching (PM) criterion. This metric is applied to evaluate the extraction of both agents and targets. Finally, to evaluate the opinions' polarities (Op-Pol. metric) we consider as correct opinions where the span and polarity both match the gold ones.

5.3 Results: Dependency-Based Model

We assess the quality of our monolingual dependency-based model by comparing it to the recent state-of-the-art approach of Johansson and Moschitti (2013), whose code is available online.[8] That paper reports the performance of a basic span-based pipeline system (which extracts opinions with a CRF, followed by two separate classifiers to detect polarities and agents), and of a more sophisticated system that applies a reranking procedure to account for more complex features that consider interactions accross opinion elements.

We ran experiments using the same data and MPQA partitions as Johansson and Moschitti (2013). However, since our system is designed for predicting opinion, agents and targets together, we removed the documents that were not annotated with targets. The final train/development/test sets have a total of 6,774/1,404/2,559 sentences and 3,834/881/1,426 opinions, respectively.

Table 1 reports the results; since the systems of Johansson and Moschitti (2013) do not predict targets, Table 1 omits target scores.[9] We observe that our dependency-based system achieves results competitive with the best results of Johansson and Moschitti (2013) and clearly above the ones reached by their basic system that does not use re-ranking features. Though the two systems are not fully comparable,[10] the results in Table 1 show that our dependency-based approach (§3.2) followed by a simple dependency-to-span conversion (§3.3) is, despite its simplicity, on par with a top-performing opinion mining system. We conjecture that this is due to the ability to extract opinions, agents, and targets jointly using exact decoding. Note that our proposed dependency scheme would also be able to include additional global features relating pairs of opinions (by adding scores to pairs of opinion arcs) or two opinions having the same agent (by adding scores to pairs of agent arcs sharing its argument), similar to the reranking features used by Johansson and Moschitti (2013). Similar second-order scores have been used in syntactic and semantic dependency parsing (Martins et al., 2013; Martins and Almeida, 2014), but with an increase in the complexity of the model and of the decoder.

6 Cross-Lingual Opinion Mining

We now turn to the problem of learning a opinion mining system for a resource-poor language (Portuguese), in a cross-lingual manner. We use a bitext projection approach (§6.1), whose only requirements are a model for a resource-rich language (English) and parallel data (§6.2).

6.1 Bitext Projection

Our methodology is outlined as Algorithm 1. For simplicity, we call the source and target languages English (e) and "foreign" (f), respectively. The procedure is inspired by the idea of bitext projection (Yarowsky and Ngai, 2001). We start by training an English system on the labeled data $\mathcal{L}^e$ (line 1), which in our case is the MPQA v.2.0 corpus. This system is then used to label the English side of the parallel data, automatically identifying opinion frames (line 2). The next step is to run a word aligner on the parallel data (line 3). The automatic alignments are then used to project the opinion frames to the target language (along with some filtering), yielding an automatic corpus $\widehat{\mathcal{D}}^{(f)}$ (line 4), which finally serves to train a system for the target language (line 5).

6.2 Parallel Data

We use an English-Portuguese parallel corpus based on the scientific news Brazilian magazine *Revista Pesquisa FAPESP*, collected by Aziz and

[8] `http://demo.spraakdata.gu.se/richard/unitn_opinion/details.html`

[9] We will report target scores later in §7.

[10] Our system makes use of target annotations to predict the opinion frames, while Johansson and Moschitti (2013) has access not only to *direct subjective* spans but also to *subjective expressions* annotations with their agents and polarity information.

	JM13, Basic			JM13, Reranking			Our System		
	HM	PM	OM	HM	PM	OM	HM	PM	OM
Op.	56.3	56.2	60.6	58.6	59.2	63.7	**61.6***	**59.8**	**65.1**
Op-Ag.	40.3	47.1	44.9	42.4	**51.4**	48.1	**45.7***	**51.4**	**50.3***
Op-Tg.	-	-	-	-	-	-	**31.3***	**48.3***	**48.3***
Op-Pol.	46.1	45.9	49.3	**48.5**	**48.9***	**52.5**	47.9	47.0	50.7

Table 1: Method comparison: F_1 scores obtained in the MPQA corpus, for our dependency based method and the approaches in Johansson and Moschitti (2013), with and without reranking. The symbol * indicates that the best system beats the other systems with statistical significance, with $p < 0.05$ and according to a bootstrap resampling test (Koehn, 2004).

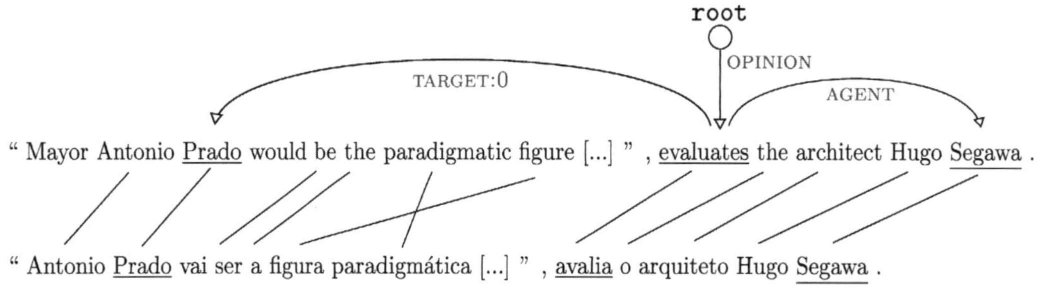

Figure 2: Excerpt of a bitext document from FAPESP, with automatic opinion dependencies. The annotations are directly projected to Portuguese via automatic word alignments.

Algorithm 1 Cross-Lingual Opinion Mining

Input: Labeled data $\mathcal{L}^e$, parallel data $\mathcal{D}^e$ and $\mathcal{D}^f$.
Output: Target opinion mining system $\mathcal{S}^f$.

$\mathcal{S}^e \leftarrow$ LearnOpinionMiner($\mathcal{L}^e$)
$\widehat{\mathcal{D}}^e \leftarrow$ RunOpinionMiner($\mathcal{S}^e, \mathcal{D}^e$)
$\mathcal{D}^{e\leftrightarrow f} \leftarrow$ RunWordAligner($\mathcal{D}^e, \mathcal{D}^f$)
$\widehat{\mathcal{D}}^f \leftarrow$ ProjectAndFilter($\mathcal{D}^{e\leftrightarrow f}, \widehat{\mathcal{D}}^e$)
$\mathcal{S}^f \leftarrow$ LearnOpinionMiner($\widehat{\mathcal{D}}^f$)

Specia (2011). Though this corpus is in Brazilian Portuguese (while our validation corpus is in European Portuguese), we preferred FAPESP over other commonly used parallel corpora (such as the Europarl and UN datasets), since it is closer to our newswire target domain, with a smaller prominence of direct speech. We computed word alignments using the Berkeley aligner (Liang et al., 2006), intersected them and filtered out all the alignments whose confidence is below 0.95.

After annotating the English side of FAPESP with the pre-trained system ($\widehat{\mathcal{D}}^e$ in Algorithm 1, with a total of 166,719 sentences and 81,492 opinions), the high confidence alignments ($D^{e\leftrightarrow f}$) are used to project the annotations to the Portuguese side of the corpus. The automatic annotations produced by our dependency-based system are easily transferred at a word level (for words with high confidence alignments), as illustrated in Figure 2. To improve the quality of the resulting corpus, we excluded sentences whose alignments cover less than 70% of the words in the target side of the corpus, or sentences whose opinion elements were not fully projected through high confidence alignments. At this point, we obtain an automatically annotated corpus in Portuguese ($\widehat{\mathcal{D}}^f$), with 106,064 sentences and 32,817 opinions.

6.3 Portuguese Opinion Mining Corpus

For validation purposes, we also created a Portuguese corpus with manually annotated fine-grained opinions. The corpus consists of a subset of the documents of the Priberam Compressive Summarization Corpus[11] (Almeida et al., 2014), which contains 80 news topics with 10 documents each, collected from several Portuguese newspapers, TV and radio websites in the biennia 2010–2011 and 2012–2013. In the scope of the current work, we selected and annotated one document of each of the 80 topics. The first biennium was selected as the test set and the second biennium was split into development and training sets (see Ta-

[11] http://labs.priberam.com/Resources/PCSC

ble 2 for statistics).

	#doc.	#sent.	#opin.
Train	20	441	240
Dev	20	225	197
Test	40	560	391

Table 2: Number of documents, sentences and opinions in the Portuguese Corpus.

	HM	PM	OM
Op.	77.0	76.7	79.2
Op-Ag.	69.1	72.3	73.5
Op-Tg.	61.9	65.4	71.4
Op-Pol.	49.4	49.1	50.7

Table 3: Inter-annotator agreement in the test partition (shown are F_1 scores).

The corpus was annotated in a similar vein as the MPQA (Wiebe et al., 2005), with the addition of the head node for each element of the opinion frame. It includes spans for direct-subjective expressions with intensity and polarity information; agent spans; and target spans. The annotation was carried out by three linguists, after reading the MPQA annotation guidelines (Wiebe et al., 2005; Wilson, 2008) and having a small practice period using the provided examples and some MPQA annotated sentences. Each document was annotated by two of the three linguists and then revised by the third linguist, who (in case of any doubts) discussed with the initial annotators to reach for the final consensus. Scores for inter-annotator agreement are shown in Table 3.

The corpus was annotated with automatic POS tags and dependency parse trees using TurboParser (Martins et al., 2013).[12] We used an in-house lemmatizer to obtain lemmas for each inflected word in the corpus. A Portuguese lexicon of subjectivity was created by translating the words in the Subjectivity Lexicon of Wilson et al. (2005). The annotated corpus and the translated subjectivity lexicon are available at `http://labs.priberam.com/Resources/Fine-Grained-Opinion-Corpus`, and `http://labs.priberam.com/Resources/Subjectivity-Lexicon-PT`, respectively.

[12]`http://www.ark.cs.cmu.edu/TurboParser`

	OUR SYSTEM			DELEXICALIZED		
	HM	PM	OM	HM	PM	OM
Op.	**65.7**	**63.5**	**69.8**	50.1	45.8	52.7
Op-Ag.	**47.6**	**48.8**	**51.1**	33.8	34.8	35.7
Op-Tg.	**34.9**	**44.8**	**50.3**	19.9	28.0	32.1
Op-Pol.	**51.5**	**50.2**	**54.4**	36.7	34.7	38.8

Table 4: F_1 scores obtained in English (MPQA), for our full system and the DELEXICALIZED one.

7 Cross-Lingual Experiments

In a final set of experiments, we compare three systems of fine-grained opinion mining for Portuguese. All were trained as described in §5.1.

7.1 System Description

Baseline #1: Supervised System. A SUPERVISED system was trained on the small Portuguese training set described in §6.3. Though being a small training corpus, this is, to the best of our knowledge, the only existing corpus with fine-grained opinions in Portuguese. We used the same arc-factored model and features described in §4.

Baseline #2: Delexicalized System with Bilingual Embeddings. This baseline consists of a direct model transfer: a DELEXICALIZED system is trained in the source language, without language specific features, so that it can be directly applied to the target language. Despite its simplicity, this strategy managed to provide a fairly strong baseline in several NLP tasks (Zeman and Resnik, 2008; McDonald et al., 2011; Søgaard, 2011).

To achieve a unified feature representation, we mapped all language-specific POS tags to universal tags (Petrov et al., 2012), and removed all features depending on the dependency relations, but maintained those depending on the syntactic path (but not on the dependency relations themselves). In addition, we replaced the lexical features by 128-dimensional cross-lingual word embeddings.[13] To obtain these bilingual neural embeddings, we ran the method of Hermann and Blunsom (2014) on the parallel data (§6.1). We scaled the embeddings by a factor of 2.0 (selected on the dev-set), following the procedure described in Turian et al. (2010).

We trained the English delexicalized system on the MPQA corpus, using the same test documents

[13]A delexicalized system trained without the word embeddings had a worse performance.

	BASELINE #1 (SUP.)			BASELINE #2 (DELEX.)			BITEXT PROJECTION		
	HM	PM	OM	HM	PM	OM	HM	PM	OM
Op.	49.4	48.7	50.8	33.1	32.1	34.3	**58.0***	**55.7***	**58.0***
Op-Ag.	23.5	27.2	31.5	14.3	18.8	20.0	**30.8***	**31.2***	**36.2***
Op-Tg.	23.0	24.9	30.6	11.0	15.7	19.0	**29.4***	**29.4***	**35.6***
Op-Pol.	24.1	23.8	24.7	16.6	16.4	17.6	**35.7***	**34.1***	**35.7***

Table 5: Comparison of cross-lingual approaches. F_1 scores obtained in our Portuguese validation corpus using: a SUPERVISED system trained on the small available data, a DELEXICALIZED system trained with universal POS tags and multilingual embeddings and our BITEXT PROJECTION OF DEPENDENCIES. The symbol * indicates that the best system beats the other systems with statistical significance, with $p < 0.05$ and according to a bootstrap resampling test (Koehn, 2004).

as Riloff and Wiebe (2003) and whose list is available with the corpus, but selecting only documents annotated with targets. We randomly split the remaining documents into train and development sets, respectively with a total of 6,471 and 782 sentences.[14] Table 4 shows the performance of the delexicalized baseline in English, compared with a lexicalized system. We will see how this model behaves in a cross-lingual setting in §7.2.

Our System: Bitext Projection of Opinion Dependencies. Finally, we implemented our cross-lingual BITEXT approach (§6). We trained the (lexicalized) English model on the MPQA corpus (the performance of this model is shown in Table 4). Then, we ran this model on the English side of the parallel corpus, generating automatic annotations, and projected these annotations to the Portuguese side, as described in §6.2. Finally, a Portuguese model was trained on these projected annotations using the arc-factored model and features described in §4.

7.2 Comparison

Table 5 shows the F_1 scores obtained by the three systems on the Portuguese test partition. We observe that the BITEXT approach outperformed the SUPERVISED and the DELEXICALIZED ones in all metrics with a considerable margin, which shows the effectiveness of our proposed method. The SUPERVISED system suffers from the fact that the training set is too small to allow good generalization; the bitext projection method, in contrast, can create arbitrarily large training corpora without any annotation effort. The performance of the DELEXICALIZED system is rather disappointing. This result is justified by a decrease of performance in English due to the delexicalization (cf. Table 4), followed by an extra loss of quality due to language differences.

Though our BITEXT approach scores the best, the scores are behind the range of values obtained for English (Table 4), and far from the inter-annotator agreement numbers (Table 3), suggesting room for improvement. The polarity scores in Table 5 appear to be relatively low. This fact is probably be justified with the annotator agreement scores (Table 3) which are considerably lower for these metrics.

8 Conclusions

We presented a cross-lingual framework for fine-grained opinion mining. We used a bitext projection technique to transfer dependency-based opinion frames from English to Portuguese. Experimentally, our dependency model achieved state-of-the-art results for English, and the Portuguese system trained with bitext projection outperformed two baselines: a supervised system trained on a small dataset, and a delexicalized model with bilingual word embeddings.

9 Acknowledgements

We would like to thank the anonymous reviewers for their insightful comments, and Richard Johansson for sharing his code and for answering several questions. This work was partially supported by the EU/FEDER programme, QREN/POR Lisboa (Portugal), under the Intelligo project (contract 2012/24803) and by a FCT grants UID/EEA/50008/2013 and PTDC/EEI-SII/2312/2012.

[14]Note that this split is different from the one we used in §5. There we used the same split as Johansson and Moschitti (2013), for a fair comparison with their system; here, we follow the standard MPQA test partition.

References

Cecilia Ovesdotter Alm, Dan Roth, and Richard Sproat. 2005. Emotions from text: machine learning for text-based emotion prediction. In *EMNLP*.

Miguel B. Almeida, Mariana S. C. Almeida, André F. T. Martins, Helena Figueira, Pedro Mendes, and Cláudia Pinto. 2014. Priberam compressive summarization corpus: A new multi-document summarization corpus for european portuguese. In *LREC*.

Wilker Aziz and Lucia Specia. 2011. Fully automatic compilation of a Portuguese-English parallel corpus for statistical machine translation. In *STIL*.

Krisztian Balog, Gilad Mishne, and Maarten de Rijke. 2006. Why are they excited?: Identifying and explaining spikes in blog mood levels. In *EACL*.

Carmen Banea, Rada Mihalcea, Janyce Wiebe, and Samer Hassan. 2008. Multilingual subjectivity analysis using machine translation. In *EMNLP*.

Eric Breck, Yejin Choi, and Claire Cardie. 2007. Identifying expressions of opinion in context. In *IJCAI*.

Sabine Buchholz and Erwin Marsi. 2006. CoNLL-X shared task on multilingual dependency parsing. In *CoNLL*.

Yejin Choi and Claire Cardie. 2010. Hierarchical sequential learning for extracting opinions and their attributes. In *ACL*.

Yejin Choi, Claire Cardie, Ellen Riloff, and Siddharth Patwardhan. 2005. Identifying sources of opinions with conditional random fields and extraction patterns. In *EMNLP*.

Yejin Choi, Eric Breck, and Claire Cardie. 2006. Joint extraction of entities and relations for opinion recognition. In *EMNLP*.

Simon Clematide, Stefan Gindl, Manfred Klenner, Stefanos Petrakis, Robert Remus, Josef Ruppenhofer, Ulli Waltinger, and Michael Wiegand. 2012. MLSA A Multilayered Reference Corpus for German Sentiment Analysis. In *LREC*.

Koby Crammer, Ofer Dekel, Joseph Keshet, Shai Shalev-Shwartz, and Yoram Singer. 2006. Online Passive-Aggressive Algorithms. *Journal of Machine Learning Research*.

Dipankar Das and Sivaji Bandyopadhyay. 2010. Labeling emotion in bengali blog corpus a fine grained tagging at sentence level. In *(ALR8), COLING*.

Xiaowen Ding, Bing Liu, and Philip S Yu. 2008. A holistic lexicon-based approach to opinion mining. In *WSDM*.

Greg Durrett and Dan Klein. 2013. Easy victories and uphill battles in coreference resolution. In *EMNLP*.

Lin Gui, Ruifeng Xu, Jun Xu, and Chenxiang Liu. 2013. A cross-lingual approach for opinion holder extraction. *Journal of Computational Information Systems*, 9(6).

Karl Moritz Hermann and Phil Blunsom. 2014. Multilingual Models for Compositional Distributional Semantics. In *ACL*.

Minqing Hu and Bing Liu. 2004. Mining opinion features in customer reviews. In *AAAI*.

Rebecca Hwa, Philip Resnik, Amy Weinberg, Clara Cabezas, and Okan Kolak. 2005. Bootstrapping parsers via syntactic projection across parallel texts. *Natural Language Engineering*, 11(3).

Ozan İrsoy and Claire Cardie. 2014. Opinion mining with deep recurrent neural networks. In *EMNLP*.

Richard Johansson and Alessandro Moschitti. 2010. Reranking models in fine-grained opinion analysis. In *COLING*.

Richard Johansson and Alessandro Moschitti. 2011. Extracting opinion expressions and their polarities: exploration of pipelines and joint models. In *ACL*.

Richard Johansson and Alessandro Moschitti. 2013. Relational features in fine-grained opinion analysis. *Computational Linguistics*, 39(3).

Soo-Min Kim and Eduard Hovy. 2006. Extracting opinions, opinion holders, and topics expressed in online news media text. In *SST*.

P. Koehn. 2004. Statistical signicance tests for machine translation evaluation. In *ACL*.

Lun-Wei Ku, Yu-Ting Liang, and Hsin-Hsi Chen. 2006. Opinion extraction, summarization and tracking in news and blog corpora. In *AAAI*.

Percy Liang, Ben Taskar, and Dan Klein. 2006. Alignment by agreement. In *NAACL*.

Bing Liu. 2012. Sentiment analysis and opinion mining. *Synthesis Lectures on Human Language Technologies*, 5(1).

Bin Lu, Chenhao Tan, Claire Cardie, and Benjamin K. Tsou. 2011. Joint bilingual sentiment classification with unlabeled parallel corpora. In *ACL*.

André F. T. Martins and M. S. C. Almeida. 2014. Priberam: A turbo semantic parser with second order features. In *SemEval*.

André F. T. Martins, Miguel B. Almeida, and Noah A. Smith. 2013. Turning on the turbo: Fast third-order non-projective turbo parsers. In *ACL*.

André F. T. Martins. 2015. Transferring coreference resolvers with posterior regularization. In *ACL*.

Ryan McDonald, Slav Petrov, and Keith Hall. 2011. Multi-source transfer of delexicalized dependency parsers. In *EMNLP*.

Rada Mihalcea, Carmen Banea, and Janyce Wiebe. 2007. Learning multilingual subjective language via cross-lingual projections. In *ACL*.

Sebastian Padó and Mirella Lapata. 2009. Cross-lingual annotation projection for semantic roles. *Journal of Artificial Intelligence Research*, 36(1).

Bo Pang and Lillian Lee. 2008. Opinion mining and sentiment analysis. *Foundations and Trends in Information Retrieval*, 2(1-2).

Bo Pang, Lillian Lee, and Shivakumar Vaithyanathan. 2002. Thumbs up?: Sentiment classification using machine learning techniques. In *EMNLP*.

Slav Petrov, Dipanjan Das, and Ryan McDonald. 2012. A universal part-of-speech tagset. In *LREC*.

Peter Prettenhofer and Benno Stein. 2010. Cross-language text classification using structural correspondence learning. In *ACL*.

Ellen Riloff and Janyce Wiebe. 2003. Learning extraction patterns for subjective expressions. In *EMNLP*.

Yohei Seki, David Kirk Evans, Lun-Wei Ku, Hsin-Hsi Chen, Noriko Kando, and Chin-Yew Lin. 2007. Overview of opinion analysis pilot task at NTCIR-6. In *NTCIR-6*.

Yohei Seki, Lun-Wei Ku, Le Sun, Hsin-Hsi Chen, and Noriko Kando. 2010. Overview of opinion analysis pilot task at NTCIR-8: A Step Toward Cross Lingual Opinion Analysis. In *NTCIR-8*.

Richard Socher, John Bauer, Christopher D. Manning, and Andrew Y. Ng. 2013a. Parsing with compositional vector grammars. In *ACL*.

Richard Socher, Alex Perelygin, Jean Y Wu, Jason Chuang, Christopher D Manning, Andrew Y Ng, and Christopher Potts. 2013b. Recursive deep models for semantic compositionality over a sentiment treebank. In *EMNLP*.

Anders Søgaard. 2011. Data point selection for cross-language adaptation of dependency parsers. In *ACL*.

Mihai Surdeanu, Richard Johansson, Adam Meyers, Luís Màrquez, and Joakim Nivre. 2008. The CoNLL-2008 Shared Task on Joint Parsing of Syntactic and Semantic Dependencies. In *CoNLL*.

Oscar Täckström, Dipanjan Das, Slav Petrov, Ryan McDonald, and Joakim Nivre. 2013. Token and type constraints for cross-lingual part-of-speech tagging. *Trans. of the Association for Computational Linguistics*.

Joseph Turian, Lev Ratinov, and Yoshua Bengio. 2010. Word representations: a simple and general method for semi-supervised learning. In *ACL*.

Peter D. Turney. 2002. Thumbs up or thumbs down?: Semantic orientation applied to unsupervised classification of reviews. In *ACL*.

Xiaojun Wan. 2009. Co-training for cross-lingual sentiment classification. In *ACL*.

Mengqiu Wang and Chris Manning. 2014. Cross-lingual projected expectation regularization for weakly supervised learning. *Trans. of the Association for Computational Linguistics*, 2.

Bin Wei and Christopher Pal. 2010. Cross lingual adaptation: an experiment on sentiment classifications. In *ACL*.

Janyce Wiebe, Theresa Wilson, and Claire Cardie. 2005. Annotating expressions of opinions and emotions in language. *Language Resources and Evaluation*, 39(2-3).

Theresa Wilson, Janyce Wiebe, and Paul Hoffmann. 2005. Recognizing contextual polarity in phrase-level sentiment analysis. In *EMNLP*.

Theresa Wilson. 2008. *Fine-Grained Subjectivity Analysis*. Ph.D. thesis, University of Pittsburgh.

Yuanbin Wu, Qi Zhang, Xuanjing Huang, and Lide Wu. 2011. Structural opinion mining for graph-based sentiment representation. In *EMNLP*.

Bishan Yang and Claire Cardie. 2012. Extracting opinion expressions with semi-markov conditional random fields. In *EMNLP*.

Bishan Yang and Claire Cardie. 2013. Joint inference for fine-grained opinion extraction. In *ACL*.

Bishan Yang and Claire Cardie. 2014. Joint modeling of opinion expression extraction and attribute classification. *Trans. of the Association for Computational Linguistics*.

David Yarowsky and Grace Ngai. 2001. Inducing multilingual pos taggers and np bracketers via robust projection across aligned corpora. In *NAACL*.

Hong Yu and Vasileios Hatzivassiloglou. 2003. Towards answering opinion questions: Separating facts from opinions and identifying the polarity of opinion sentences. In *EMNLP*.

Daniel Zeman and Philip Resnik. 2008. Cross-language parser adaptation between related languages. In *IJCNLP*.

Learning to Adapt Credible Knowledge in Cross-lingual Sentiment Analysis

Qiang Chen[*,†], **Wenjie Li**[†,⋆], **Yu Lei**[†], **Xule Liu**[*], **Yanxiang He**[*,‡]
[*]School of Computer Science, Wuhan University, China
[†]Department of Computing, The Hong Kong Polytechnic University, Hong Kong
[⋆]Hong Kong Polytechnic University Shenzhen Research Institute, China
[‡]The State Key Lab of Software Engineering, Wuhan University, China
[*]{qchen, xuleliu, yxhe}@whu.edu.cn
[†]{csqchen, cswjli, csylei}@comp.polyu.edu.hk

Abstract

Cross-lingual sentiment analysis is a task of identifying sentiment polarities of texts in a low-resource language by using sentiment knowledge in a resource-abundant language. While most existing approaches are driven by transfer learning, their performance does not reach to a promising level due to the transferred errors. In this paper, we propose to integrate into knowledge transfer a knowledge validation model, which aims to prevent the negative influence from the wrong knowledge by distinguishing highly credible knowledge. Experiment results demonstrate the necessity and effectiveness of the model.

1 Introduction

With the wide range of business value, sentiment analysis has drawn increasing attention in the past years. The extensive research and development efforts produce a variety of reliable sentiment resources for English, one of the most popular language in the world. These available rich resources become the treasure of knowledge to help conduct or enhance sentiment analysis in the other languages, which is a task known as cross-lingual sentiment analysis (CLSA). In the literature of CSLA, the language with abundant reliable resources is called the source language (e.g., English), while the low-resource language is referred to as the target language (e.g., Chinese). However, in this paper, the situation is a low resource language scenario, where the source language is English, and the target language is Chinese.

The main idea of existing CLSA researches is to first build up the connection between the source and target languages to overcome the language barrier, and then develop an appropriate knowledge transfer approach to leverage the annotated data from the source language to train a sentiment classification model in the target language, either supervised or semi-supervised. In particular, these approaches exploit and convert the knowledge learned from the source language to automatically generate and expand the pseudo-training data for the target language.

The machine translation (MT) service is one of the most common ways used to build the language connection (Wan, 2008; Banea et al., 2008; Wan, 2009; Wei and Pal, 2010; Gui et al., 2014). Although it is claimed in Duh et al. (2011) that the MT service is ripe for CLSA, the imperfect MT quality hinders existing MT-based CLSA approaches from the further advance. In our preliminary study, we find that even the Google translator[1] (i.e., one of the most widely used online MT service (Shankland 2013)) may unavoidably changes the sentiment polarity of the translated text, as illustrated below, with a percentage of around 10%.

*[**Original English Text**]: I am at home on bed rest and desperate for something good to read.*
*[Sentiment Label: **Negative**]*
*[**Translated Chinese Text**]:* 我在家卧床休息和绝望的东西很好看。 *{Meaning: I am in bed to rest at home and feel that desperate things are also good to read.}[Sentiment Label: **Positive**]*

The noisy data generated by MT errors for sure will weaken the contribution of the transferred knowledge and even worse may create conflicting knowledge. While it is a critical step in CLSA to localize the sentiment knowledge learned from the source language in the target language, to the best of our knowledge, hardly any previous research has focused on knowledge validation to filter out the noisy knowledge having sentiment changes caused by wrong translations during knowledge transfer.

[1] http://translate.google.com

Proceedings of the 53rd Annual Meeting of the Association for Computational Linguistics and the 7th International Joint Conference on Natural Language Processing, pages 419–429,
Beijing, China, July 26-31, 2015.

To reduce the noisy sentiment knowledge introduced into the target language, we are motivated to validate the knowledge transferred from the source language by checking its linguistic distributions and sentiment polarity consistency with the known knowledge in the target language. Different from previous co-training based approaches where two language views recommend knowledge to each other in the same manner, we consider the source language as the "supervisor" and the target language as the "learner". The "supervisor" boosts itself with its own accumulated labeled data (called knowledge) and meanwhile recommends its confident knowledge to the "learner". The "learner" tries to select trustworthy knowledge based on the recommendation to update and expand its training data. Adding a process to efficiently filter out noisy knowledge and retain the self-adaptive and interested new knowledge makes the subsequent boosting process more credible. This is why our approach can outperform state-of-the-art CLSA approaches.

The rest of this paper is organized as follows. Section 2 summarizes the related work. Section 3 explains the proposed model. Section 4 presents experimental results. Finally, Section 5 concludes the paper and suggests future work.

2 Related Work

2.1 Sentiment Analysis

Sentiment has been analyzed in different language granularity, e.g., entity, aspect, sentence and document. This paper focuses on sentiment analysis of online product reviews in the document level.

Existing approaches are generally categorized into lexicon-based and machine learning based approaches (Liu, 2012). Lexicon-based approaches highly depend on sentiment lexicons. Turney (2002) derives the overall phrase and document sentiment scores by averaging the sentiment scores provided in a lexicon over the words included. Similar idea is adopted in (Hiroshi et al., 2004; Kennedy and Inkpen, 2006). Machine learning based approaches, on the other hand, apply classification models. The task-specific features are designed to train sentiment polarity classifiers. Pang et al. (2002) compare the performance of NB, SVM and ME on movie reviews. SVM is found more effective. Gamon (2004) shows that SVM with deep linguistic features can further improve the performance. A variety of other machine learning approaches are also proposed to sentiment classification (Mullen and Collier, 2004; Read, 2005; Hassan and Radev, 2010; Socher et al., 2013).

Cross-domain sentiment classification (CDSC) shares certain common characteristics with cross-lingual sentiment classification (CLSC) (Tan et al., 2007; Li et al., 2009; Pan and Yang, 2010; He et al., 2011a; Glorot et al., 2011). Notice that the gap between source domain and target domain is the main difference between CDSC and CLSC. CLSC copes with two different datasets in two different languages. This difference makes CLSC a new challenge, drawing specific attention to researcher recently.

2.2 Cross-lingual Sentiment Analysis

There are two alternative solutions to cross-lingual sentiment analysis. One is ensemble learning that combines multiple classifiers. The other is transfer learning that develops strategies to adapt the knowledge from one language to the other. Wan (2008) is among the pioneers to develop the ensemble learning solutions, where multiple classifiers learned from different training datasets including those in original languages and translated languages are combined by voting. Most researches, on the other hand, explore transfer learning and focus on knowledge adaptation. For example, Wan (2009) applies a supervised co-training framework to iteratively adapt knowledge learned from the two languages by transferring translated texts to each other. Other similar work includes (Wei and Pal, 2010) and (He, 2011b). All these approaches rely on MT to build language connection.

Meanwhile, the unlabeled parallel data is also employed to fill the gap between two languages. To solve the feature coverage problem with the EM algorithm, Meng et al. (2012) leverage the unlabeled parallel data to learn unseen sentiment words. Similarly, Popat et al. (2013) use the unlabeled parallel data to cluster features in order to reduce the data sparsity problem. Meng et al. (2012) and Popat et al. (2013) also use the unlabeled parallel data to reduce the negative influence of the noisy and incorrect sentiment labels introduced by machine translation and knowledge transfer. However, the parallel data is also a scarce resource.

Some existing transfer learning based CLSA methods have attempted to address the noisy knowledge problem caused by wrong labels by checking label consistency. For example, to filter out the unconfident labels in Chinese, the supervised learning method proposed by (Xu et al., 2011) runs boosting in Chinese by checking consistency between the labels manually annotated in English and predicted by Chinese classifiers on translated Chinese. The work in (Gui et al., 2014) follows the same line although it considers knowledge transferring between two languages. On the contrary, the main focus of our work is to filter out the noisy knowledge having sentiment changes by wrong translations. Actually, both label consistency checking and linguistic distribution checking are important. Any one alone cannot work well. In fact, both of them are considered as the knowledge validation in our work, though the later is our focus.

3 Credible Boosting Model

In this paper, we propose a knowledge validation approach to improve the effectiveness of knowledge transfer without directly using extra parallel data. Our target is to filter out the noisy sentiment labels introduced by MT and the incorrect sentiment labels generated by imperfect classifier in the source language. Here, the knowledge is referred to as a collection of distributed document presentations with sentiment labels that have been verified to be robust in sentiment classification (Le and Mikolov, 2014). A novel credible boosting model, namely CredBoost is proposed to apply transfer-supervised learning with an added self-validation mechanism to guarantee the knowledge transferred highly credible and self-adaptive.

3.1 Problem Description

In a standard cross-lingual sentiment analysis setting, the training data includes labeled English reviews $L_{EN} = \{(x_i^{l_{en}}, y_i)\}_{i=1}^M$ and unlabeled Chinese reviews $U_{CN} = \{x_j^{u_{cn}}\}_{j=1}^N$, where x_i^k ($k = l_{en}\ or\ u_{cn}$) represents review i and $y_i \in \{-1, 1\}$ is the sentiment label of review x_i^l. The test data is Chinese reviews $T_{CN} = \{x_s^{t_{cn}}\}_{s=1}^S$.

We now introduce the unlabeled data into credBoost's setting. L_{EN} is divided into two disjoint parts L_{EN}^T and L_{EN}^B, where L_{EN}^T for basic training and L_{EN}^B for self-boosting. We translate L_{EN} into Chinese to obtain extra labeled Chinese pseudo-reviews $L_{TrCN} = \{(x_i^{l_{cnTr}}, y_i)\}_{i=1}^M$ and U_{CN} into English to obtain extra unlabeled English pseudo-reviews $U_{TrEN} = \{x_j^{l_{enTr}}\}_{j=1}^N$. Thereby, we obtain a pair of pseudo-parallel data (U_{CN}, U_{TrEN}).

The task is to use L_{EN} and U_{CN} to train a Chinese classifier to predict sentiment polarity for the test data T_{CN}. It is a standard transfer learning problem. We consider two language views, i.e., source language view D_S and target language view $D_\mathcal{T}$. D_S boosts itself with the labeled English data and recommend translated knowledge to $D_\mathcal{T}$, while D_t selects self-adaptive ones to boost itself.

3.2 Framework of CredBoost

The CredBoost model involves two synchronously boosting views for two languages respectively. During training, one view acts as a "supervisor" that recommends and passes the knowledge to the other view. The same knowledge is also added into its own view for boosting by automatically updating the weights of the labeled data. The other view acts as a "learner" that receives the recommended knowledge and selects the best-suited new knowledge to learn.

As mentioned before, the knowledge transferred through MT is not reliable. The source language view may also make wrong predictions and thus transfer the wrong knowledge to the target language even the translations are correct. Whether or not the "learner" can benefit from its "supervisor" and how much it benefits highly depends on the credibility and adaptiveness of the recommended knowledge accepted by the "learner". Knowledge validation is necessary to ensure the quality of learning. The objective of knowledge validation is to identify the new and acquired knowledge from recommendations. Both language views are iteratively trained until learning converges or reaches the iteration upper bound.

In the **source language view**, at iteration (t), the CredBoost model first uses $L_{EN}^{T(t)}$ to train a basic classifier $C_{EN}^{(t)}$ and then uses $C_{EN}^{(t)}$ to predict $L_{EN}^{B(t)}$ and $U_{TrEN}^{(t)}$. Top m and top n instances are sampled from $L_{EN}^{B(t)}$ and $U_{TrEN}^{(t)}$ respectively, by Formula (1) :

$$O_{EN}^{(t)} = \{(x_{i'}^{LB}, \hat{y}_{i'}^{LB})\}_{i'=1}^{m_{en}}$$
$$TR_{EN}^{(t)} = \{(x_i^{UTr}, \hat{y}_i^{UTr})\}_{i=1}^{n_{en}} \quad (1)$$

where $O_{EN}^{(t)}$ denotes the candidates to be added

into the training data, and $TR_{EN}^{(t)}$ the knowledge to be recommended to the target language view. We use the source knowledge validation function $V_S(O_{EN}^{(t)})$ to identify the acquired knowledge $K_{'Ac}^{(t)}$ learned in the previous learning process and the new knowledge $K_{'Nw}^{(t)}$ fresh to the current knowledge system from $O_{EN}^{(t)}$. The importance of each training instance is updated according to the performance of prediction by Formula (2) :

$$\begin{aligned}
\omega_{i'}^{'Ac} &= \begin{cases} e^{\epsilon(t)} \cdot \sqrt{\nu_{i'}^{(t)} \cdot c_{i'}^{(t)}} & \text{if } \hat{y}_{i'}^{'Ac} \neq y_{i'}^{'Ac} \\ \sqrt{\nu_{i'}^{(t)} \cdot c_{i'}^{(t)}} & \text{otherwise;} \end{cases} \\
\omega_{j'}^{'Nw} &= \begin{cases} e^{\epsilon(t)} \cdot \log(1+\sqrt{e}\cdot c_{j'}^{(t)}) & \text{if } \hat{y}_{j'}^{'Ac} \neq y_{j'}^{'Ac} \\ \log(1+\sqrt{e}\cdot c_{j'}^{(t)}) & \text{otherwise.} \end{cases}
\end{aligned} \tag{2}$$

where $c_{j'}^{(t)}$ is the confidence of an instance given by $\mathcal{C}_{EN}^{(t)}$, thus $\log(1+\sqrt{e}\cdot c_{j'}^{(t)}) > 1$ is to enhance the weight of new knowledge because of the higher significance contributing to the later learning. $\nu_{i'}^{(t)} (< 1)$ is the adaptiveness score given by the source knowledge validation function $V_S(O_{EN}^{(t)})$. $\epsilon_{(t)} (> 1)$ is the error rate of $\mathcal{C}_{EN}^{(t)}$, thus $e^{\epsilon(t)} > 1$ is to reward the wrongly predicted data in the next iteration. $\hat{y}_{i'}^{'Ac}$ is the label given by $\mathcal{C}_{EN}^{(t)}$ and $y_{i'}^{'Ac}$ is the manually annotated label. For the incorrectly predicted instance, the weight is boosted inversely to the performance of the current classifier. The instance identified as the new knowledge which contributes more to performance improvement is given a reward parameter to enhance its significant in the next training iteration. Data sets update by Formula (3). The training starts with iteration (1), the training data is initially set as $L_{EN}^{T(1)} = L_{EN}^{T}$.

$$\begin{aligned}
L_{EN}^{T(t+1)} &= L_{EN}^{T(t)} \cup K_{'Ac}^{(t)} \cup K_{'Nw}^{(t)} \\
L_{EN}^{B(t+1)} &= L_{EN}^{B(t)} - (K_{'Ac}^{(t)} \cup K_{'Nw}^{(t)})
\end{aligned} \tag{3}$$

In the **target language view**, at iteration (t), the CredBoost model receives the recommended knowledge $TR_{EN}^{(t)}$ and projects it to $O_{CN}^{(t)}$ from the unlabeled Chinese data $U_{CN}^{(t)}$ with the pseudo-parallel data $(U_{CN}^{(t)}, U_{TrEN}^{(t)})$. $O_{(t)}^{CN}$ is validated by the target knowledge validation function $V_\tau(O_{CN}^{(t)})$ to identify the acquired knowledge $K_{Ac}^{(t)}$ and the new knowledge $K_{Nw}^{(t)}$. $K_{Ac}^{(t)}$ and $K_{Nw}^{(t)}$ are projected to $K_{*Ac}^{(t)}$ and $K_{*Nw}^{(t)}$ from the unlabeled English pseudo-data $U_{TrEN}^{(t)}$. The weight of an instance is updated by Formula (4), and the parameter setting is similar to that in the source language view. The confidence $c_i^{(t)}$ is directly transferred from D_s. We reward the validated knowledge to raise their significance in the training data considering they are originally Chinese.

$$\begin{aligned}
\omega_i^{Ac} &= \sqrt{c_i^{(t)} \cdot \log(1+\sqrt{e}\cdot v_i^{(t)})} \\
\omega_j^{Nw} &= e^{\log(1+\sqrt{e}\cdot c_j^{(t)})} = 1+\sqrt{e}\cdot c_j^{(t)}
\end{aligned} \tag{4}$$

We update the data setting by Formula (5). The training data is initially set as $U_{CN}^{T(1)} = U_{CN}^{T}$. The CredBoost model is illustrated in Algorithm 1.

$$\begin{aligned}
L_{TrCN}^{(t+1)} &= L_{TrCN}^{(t)} \cup K_{Ac}^{(t)} \cup K_{Nw}^{(t)} \\
U_{CN}^{(t+1)} &= U_{CN}^{(t)} - (K_{Ac}^{(t)} \cup K_{Nw}^{(t)}) \\
U_{TrEN}^{(t+1)} &= U_{TrEN}^{(t)} - (K_{*Ac}^{(t)} \cup K_{*Nw}^{(t)})
\end{aligned} \tag{5}$$

Algorithm 1 CredBoost Model

Input: English labeled data L_{EN}^{T} and L_{EN}^{B}, translated English unlabeled data U_{TrEN}, translated Chinese data L_{TrCN} and unlabeled Chinese data U_{CN};
Initialize: Weights $W_{EN}^{(1)} = \{1\}^M$ for L_{EN}^{T} and $W_{TrCN}^{(1)} = \{1\}^M$ for L_{TrCN};
For $t = 1, \cdots, T$:
1. Use $L_{EN}^{T(t)}$ to learn English classifier $C_{EN(t)}$;
2. Use $\mathcal{C}_{EN}^{(t)}$ to predict $L_{EN}^{B(t)}$ and $U_{TrEN}^{(t)}$ sample top m and top n instances from $L_{EN}^{B(t)}$ and $U_{TrEN}^{(t)}$, $O_{EN}^{(t)}$ and $TR_{EN}^{(t)}$;
3. Validate $O_{EN}^{(t)}$ by knowledge validation function $V_S(O_{EN}^{(t)})$ to identify acquired knowledge $K_{'Ac}^{(t)}$ and new knowledge $K_{'Nw}^{(t)}$, generate the weights for them by Formula (2), then recommend $TR_{EN}^{(t)}$ to D_τ;
4. Project $TR_{EN}^{(t)}$ to $O_{CN}^{(t)}$ with pseudo-parallel data $(U_{CN}^{(t)}, U_{TrEN}^{(t)})$, and use knowledge validation function $V_\tau(O_{CN}^{(t)})$ to identify acquired knowledge $K_{Ac}^{(t)}$ and new knowledge $K_{Nw}^{(t)}$, then generate weights for them by Formula (4);
5. Update D_S by Formula (2) and D_τ by Formula (5);

End For.
Output: Chinese classifier $\mathcal{C}_{CN}^{(T)}$.

3.3 Knowledge Validation

Knowledge is familiarity, awareness or understanding of someone or something, such as facts, information or skills, which is acquired through experience or education by perceiving, discovering or learning[2]. It can be implicit or explicit.

In machine learning, natural language knowledge is a continuously improving hypothesis that consists of both semantic and significant domain

[2]Definition from Oxford Dictionary of English, available at: `http://oxforddictionaries.com/view/entry/m_en_us126`.

characters. While language is the expression of semantic, semantic is the carrier of sentiment. Using another word, two texts with more smaller semantic distance have higher probability to share the same sentiment polarity. Choi and Cardie (2008) assert that the sentiment polarity of natural language can be better inferred by compositional semantics. They also suggest that incorporating compositional semantics into learning can improve the performance of sentiment classifiers. Saif et al. (2012) also demonstrate that the addition of extra semantic features can further improve performance.

In order to filter out noisy and incorrect sentiment labels, we propose a knowledge validation approach to reduce these noisy data that hinder the improvement of learning performance. Knowledge validation is a way to identify the acquired knowledge implied in current knowledge system and also the new knowledge fresh to current knowledge system. The knowledge can be represented in the semantic space. (Le and Mikolov, 2014) project documents into a low-dimension semantic space with a deep learning approach, known as document-to-vector (Doc2Vec[3]). Considering that Dov2Vec has been verified to be efficient in many NLP tasks including sentiment analysis, we follow previous research to represent knowledge embedded in product reviews with the vectors generated by Doc2Vec.

Suppose distributed representations (i.e., low-dimensional vectors) of the all reviews including $\{L^T_{EN}, L^B_{EN}, U_{TrEN}\}$ and $\{L_{TrCN}, U_{CN}\}$ are $\{\mathcal{V}(L^T_{EN}), \mathcal{V}(L^B_{EN}), \mathcal{V}(U_{TrEN})\}$ and $\{\mathcal{V}(L_{TrCN}), \mathcal{V}(U_{CN})\}$ respectively. At iteration (t), $\mathcal{V}(L^{T(t)}_{EN})$ is the current knowledge system of the English view and $\mathcal{V}(L^{(t)}_{TrCN})$ is that of the Chinese. The knowledge validation runs separately in the source and target views.

In the **target language view**, at iteration (t), suppose the prediction confidence of the candidate $(x^U_i, \hat{y}^U_i) \in O^{(t)}_{CN}$ is $c^{(t)}_i$. We define the adaptiveness score as the average distance of top ζ_+ semantic distances between the instance x^{LB}_i and the positive cluster of $L^{(t)}_{TrCN}$, denoted as $L^{(t)+}_{TrCN}$, and top $\zeta^{(t)}_- = \zeta_+ \cdot \frac{\mathcal{L}^{(t)}_+}{\mathcal{L}^{(t)}_-}$ semantic distances between x^U_i and the negative cluster, denoted as $L^{(t)-}_{TrCN}$, where $\mathcal{L}^{(t)}_+$ and $\mathcal{L}^{(t)}_-$ are the numbers of the elements in $L^{(t)+}_{TrCN}$ and $L^{(t)-}_{TrCN}$ respectively. The validation parameters are defined by Formula (6), ω_r is the weight of training instance $\mathcal{V}(r)$, $\nu^{(t)}_i$ is the adaptiveness score, and $\mathcal{V}^{label}_* \in \{1, -1\}$ is the validated label which denotes the knowledge belonging to the positive cluster $L^{(t)+}_{TrCN}$ or the negative cluster $L^{(t)-}_{TrCN}$. The validation process is illustrated in Algorithm 2, where the acquired knowledge is $k^{(t)}_{Ac}$, and the new knowledge is $k^{(t)}_{Nw}$.

$$
\begin{aligned}
&\mathcal{D}(\mathcal{V}(x^{LB}_i), \mathcal{V}(r)) = \frac{\mathcal{V}(x^{LB}_i)^T \cdot \mathcal{V}(r)}{\| \mathcal{V}(x^{LB}_i) \| \cdot \| \mathcal{V}(r) \|} \\
&\Rightarrow \begin{cases} \nu^{(t)+}_i = \frac{1}{\zeta^+} \sum\limits_{r \in L^{(t)+}_{EN}} \omega_r \, \mathcal{D}(\mathcal{V}(x^{LB}_i), \mathcal{V}(r)) \\ \nu^{(t)-}_i = \frac{1}{\zeta^{(t)}_-} \sum\limits_{r' \in L^{(t)-}_{EN}} \omega_{r'} \, \mathcal{D}(\mathcal{V}(x^{LB}_i), \mathcal{V}(r')) \end{cases} \\
&\Rightarrow \quad \Delta(\nu^{(t)}_i) = \nu^{(t)+}_i - \nu^{(t)-}_i \\
&\Rightarrow \quad \delta^{(t)}_i = \frac{1}{e^{1+\Delta(\nu^{(t)}_i)}} \\
&\Rightarrow \quad \mathcal{V}^{label}_* = \begin{cases} 1 & \text{if } \delta^{(t)}_i > 0.5, \\ -1 & \text{if } \delta^{(t)}_i \leq 0.5. \end{cases} \\
&\Rightarrow \quad \nu^{(t)}_i = \begin{cases} \nu^{(t)+}_i & \text{if } \mathcal{V}^{label}_* = 1, \\ \nu^{(t)-}_i & \text{if } \mathcal{V}^{label}_* = -1. \end{cases}
\end{aligned} \tag{6}
$$

where $\mathcal{D}(\mathcal{V}(x^{LB}_i), \mathcal{V}(r))$ is the Cosine distance between the distributed representations of the two reviews. $\nu^{(t)+}_i$ and $\nu^{(t)-}_i$ are the weighted averages of the semantic distances. $\delta^{(t)}_i$ is the Sigmoid function which computes the probability that the data is distributed in the positive cluster $L^{(t)+}_{TrCN}$.

In the **source language view**, at iteration (t), let's suppose the prediction confidence of candidate $(x^{LB}_{i'}, \hat{y}^{LB}_{i'}) \in O^{(t)}_{EN}$ to be $c^{(t)}_{i'}$. The definitions of validation parameters are similar to those in the target language view. The validation process is illustrated in Algorithm 3. The validation is looser, because the training data and candidates are both in English. This differs from it in the target view.

4 Experiments

4.1 Experimental Setup

We evaluate the proposed CredBoost model on an open cross-lingual sentiment analysis task in NLP&CC 2013[4]. The data set provided is a

[3]Doc2Vec is one of the models implemented in the free python library ***Gensim*** which can be freely downloaded at: `https://pypi.python.org/pypi/gensim`.

[4]NLP&CC is an annual conference of Chinese information technology professional committee organized by Chinese computer Federation (CCF). It mainly focuses on the study and application novelty of natural language processing and Chinese computation. CLSA task is the task 3 of NLP&CC 2013. For more details and open

Algorithm 2 Knowledge Validation $V_\tau(D_\tau)$

Input: Labeled Chinese training data $L^{(t)}_{TrCN}$, weights of labeled data $W^{(t)}_{CN}$ and semantics vectors of all English data for iteration (t): $\{\mathcal{V}(L^{(t)}_{TrCN}), \mathcal{V}(U^{(t)}_{CN})\}$;
Initialize: $K'^{(1)}_{Ac} = \phi$, $K'^{(1)}_{Nw} = \phi$;
For x^U_i in $O^{(t)}_{CN}$:
1. Use $L^{(t)}_{TrCN}$ to train a classifier $\mathcal{C}^{(t)}_{CN}$, then use $\mathcal{C}^{(t)}_{CN}$ predict x^U_i, giving label y^{CN}_i;
2. Get validated label $\mathcal{V}^{label}_*$, positive and negative average distances $\nu^{(t)+}_i$, $\nu^{(t)-}_i$ of x^U_i by fomula (6);
3. **If** $\nu^{(t)+}_i < \psi$ and $\nu^{(t)-}_i < \psi$:
   If $\hat{y}^{LB}_i = \mathcal{V}^{label}_*$:
   Then $K^{(t)}_{Nw} \leftarrow K^{(t)}_{Nw} + x^U_i$;
   Else:
   If $\hat{y}^{LB}_i = \mathcal{V}^{label}_* = y^{CN}_i$:
   Then $K^{(t)}_{Ac} \leftarrow K^{(t)}_{Ac} + x^U_i$;

End For.
Output: $K^{(t)}_{Nw}$, $K^{(t)}_{Ac}$.

Algorithm 3 Knowledge Validation $V_S(D_S)$

Input: Weights of labeled data $W^{(1)}_{EN}$ and semantics vectors of all English data for iteration (t): $\{\mathcal{V}(L^{T(t)}_{EN}), \mathcal{V}(L^{B(t)}_{EN}), \mathcal{V}(U^{(t)}_{TrEN})\}$;
Initialize: $K'^{(1)}_{Ac} = \phi$, $K'^{(1)}_{Nw} = \phi$;
For $x^{LB}_{i'}$ in $O^{(t)}_{EN}$:
1. Get validated label $\mathcal{V}'^{label}$, positive and negative average distances $\nu^{(t)+}_{i'}$, $\nu^{(t)-}_{i'}$ of $x^{LB}_{i'}$ by fomula (6);
2. **If** $\nu^{(t)+}_{i'} < \psi$ and $\nu^{(t)-}_{i'} < \psi$:
   If $\hat{y}^{LB}_{i'} = \mathcal{V}'^{label}$:
   Then $K'^{(t)}_{Nw} \leftarrow K'^{(t)}_{Nw} + x^{LB}_{i'}$;
   Else:
   If $\hat{y}^{LB}_{i'} = \mathcal{V}'^{label}$:
   Then $K'^{(t)}_{Ac} \leftarrow K'^{(t)}_{Ac} + x^{LB}_{i'}$;

End For.
Output: $K'^{(t)}_{Nw}$, $K'^{(t)}_{Ac}$.

collection of bilingual Amazon product reviews in Books, DVD and Music domains. It contains 4,000 labeled English reviews, 4,000 Chinese test reviews, and 17,814, 47,071, 29,677 unlabeled Chinese reviews in three different domains. We randomly select 2,000 unlabeled Chinese reviews in each domain to train classifiers. Besides, the pseudo-data sets described in CredBoost model are translated with Google translator. The data set is summarized in Table 1.

Domain		English		Chinese	
		L	U	L	U
Books	Train	4,000	-	-	2,000
	Test	-	-	4,000	-
DVD	Train	4,000	-	-	2,000
	Test	-	-	4,000	-
Music	Train	4,000	-	-	2,000
	Test	-	-	4,000	-

Table 1: Experimental data sets. All data sets are balanced, L represents labeled data and U represents unlabeled data.

To better illustrate the significance of knowledge validation during knowledge transfer, we compare the proposed method with the following baseline methods:

Lexicon-based (LB): The standard English MPQA sentiment lexicons are translated into Chinese and then utilized together with a small number of Chinese turning words, negations and intensifiers to predict the sentiment polarities of the Chinese test reviews.

Basic SVM (BSVM-CN): The labeled English reviews are translated into Chinese, which are then used as the pseudo-training data to train a Chinese SVM classifier.

Primarily boost transfer learning (BTL-1): The labeled English reviews are used to train the English classifier, which is applied to label the English translations of the unlabeled Chinese reviews. These labeled Chinese reviews obtained via MT together with the Chinese translations of the labeled English reviews are then used as the pseudo-training data to train a Chinese sentiment classifier.

Best result in NLP&CC 2013 (BR2013): This is the best result reported in NLP&CC 2013. Unfortunately, the specification of the method is not available.

Self-boost (SB-CN) in Chinese: The labeled English reviews are translated into Chinese, which are used as the pseudo-training data to train a basic Chinese classifier. This classifier is iteratively refined by choosing the most confidently predicted English reviews to add into the Chinese training data until a predefined iteration number reaches. It can be also considered as a self-adaptive boosting approach.

Iteratively boost transfer learning (BTL-2): This is an enhanced transfer learning method sharing the same learning framework with CredBoost but it ignores knowledge validation. It iteratively transfers the knowledge from English to Chinese. The learning in both languages iteratively boosts themselves separately. The transfer size is 16, comparable to that in CredBoost.

Basic co-training (CoTr): The co-training method proposed in (Wan, 2009) is implemented. It is bidirectional transfer learning. In each

resource, you can available at: `http://tcci.ccf.org.cn/conference/2013/index.html`.

iteration, 10 positive and 10 negative reviews are transferred from one language to the other.

Doc2vec feature CredBoost (dCredB): This method is similar to CredBoost except that document-to-vector is used to generate features when training basic classifiers. The vectors are obtained from both original and translated reviews. The dimension of doc2vec is 300, while the other parameters are set as default.

The baseline methods described above are categorized into three classes: the first four which are preliminary methods, the middle three which are several state-of-the-art models being comparable to our proposed model, and the last one which is a comparison to suggest that the knowledge representation is not the answer to the performance improvement. For all the methods excluding LB and BR2013, we use support vector machines (SVMs) as basic classifiers. We use the Liblinear package (Fan et al., 2008) with the linear kernel[5]. All methods use Unigram+Bigram features to train the basic classifiers, except for dCredB.

4.2 Experimental Result

In this work, there are two main parameters that may significantly influence the performance of our proposed model. They are the new knowledge validation boundary ψ and the validation scale ζ_+ in the training data. We set the values of parameters with the grid search strategy. We first fix initial $\zeta_+ = 14$ to search the best new knowledge validation boundary ψ from an empirical value set $\{0.30, 0.35, 0.40, 0.45, 0.50\}$. We then fix the best $\psi = 0.40$ to check the suitable validation scale ζ_+ from the initial value set $\{6, 8, 9, 10, 11, 12, 14, 16\}$ in which values are comparable with the knowledge transfer scale of CoTr in the training data. Besides, the recommendation size m for English is set to 20 and the recommendation size n for Chinese is set to 40. The final settings are listed in Table 2. The performance is evaluated in terms of accuracy (Ac) defined by Formula (7).

$$Ac(f) = \frac{p^f}{P^f}, \quad Avg\_Ac = \frac{1}{3} \cdot \sum_{f' \in \mathcal{F}} Ac(f') \quad (7)$$

where p^f is the number of correct predictions and P^f is the total number of the test data; $\mathcal{F} \in \{Books, DVD, Music\}$ is the domain set.

[5]The parameter setting used in this paper is '*-s 7*'.

Domain	ψ	ζ_+	m	n
Books	0.45	12	20	40
DVD	0.40	12	20	40
Music	0.40	9	20	40

Table 2: Parameter settings of three domains in this paper.

Approaches	Domain			Avg_Ac
	Books	DVD	Music	
LB	0.7770	0.7832	0.7595	0.7709
BSVM-CN	0.7940	0.7995	0.7778	0.7904
BTL-1	0.8010	0.8058	0.7605	0.7891
BR2013	0.7850	0.7773	0.7513	0.7712
SB-CN	0.8400	0.8428	0.8012	0.8280
BTL-2	0.8105	0.8265	0.7980	0.8117
CoTr	0.8025	0.8508	0.7812	0.8115
dCredB	0.6485	0.6753	0.6700	0.6646
CredBoost	**0.8465**	**0.8518**	**0.8093**	**0.8359**

Table 3: Macro performance of all approaches in three domains. All values are accuracies and Avg-Ac represents the average accuracy in three domains.

The performances are reported in Tables 3 and 4. As shown, CredBoost outperforms all the other comparison methods. The first four baselines have poor performances compared to others. This suggests that the CLSA problem cannot be well solved by directly learning from the labeled translated data without any knowledge adaption or knowledge validation. SB-CN, BTL-2 and CoTr employ iterative boosting to adapt knowledge from the source English to the target Chinese without validating the transferred knowledge. They inevitably mis-recommend the massive noisy data into Chinese. CredBoost, in contrast, introduces knowledge validation into transfer learning with iterative boosting. It better adapts knowledge from English to Chinese and thus ensures the credibility of the accepted knowledge. Its best result justifies our assumption.

Specifically, SB-CN leverages both the Chinese training data translated from the labeled English data and the unlabeled Chinese data used for boosting. The boosting in Chinese iteratively selects the trustworthy data with the labels assigned by the Chinese classifier. Our proposed method, however, exploits two different languages simultaneously with an additional boosting step, i.e., it transfers knowledge from English to Chinese during boosting. We then use knowledge validation model to validate the unlabeled Chinese data whose labels are assigned by the English

Model (Books)	Positive			Negative			Ac
	P	R	F1	P	R	F1	
LB	0.7368	0.8400	0.7850	0.8140	0.7000	0.7527	0.7700
BSVM-CN	0.8249	0.7465	0.7837	0.7685	0.8415	0.8033	0.7940
BTL-1	**0.8537**	0.7265	0.7850	0.7620	0.8755	0.8148	0.8010
BR2013	-	-	-	-	-	-	0.7850
SB-CN	0.8716	0.7975	0.8329	0.8134	**0.8825**	0.8465	0.8400
BTL-2	0.7105	**0.8881**	0.7894	**0.9105**	0.7588	0.8278	0.8105
CoTr	0.8339	0.7555	0.7928	0.7765	0.8495	0.8114	0.8025
dCredB	0.5310	0.6941	0.6017	0.7660	0.6202	0.6854	0.6485
CredBoost	0.8225	0.8640	**0.8427**	0.8705	0.8306	**0.8501**	**0.8465**

Model (DVD)	Positive			Negative			Ac
	P	R	F1	P	R	F1	
LB	0.7648	0.8180	0.7905	0.8044	0.7485	0.7754	0.7832
BSVM-CN	0.7745	0.8450	0.8082	0.8295	0.7540	0.7900	0.7995
BTL-1	0.8282	0.7715	0.7988	0.7861	0.8400	0.8122	0.8058
BR2013	-	-	-	-	-	-	0.7773
SB-CN	**0.8853**	0.7875	0.8335	0.8086	**0.8980**	0.8510	0.8428
BTL-2	0.8525	0.8104	0.8309	0.8005	0.8444	0.8219	0.8265
CoTr	0.8374	0.8705	**0.8536**	**0.8652**	0.8310	0.8478	0.8508
dCredB	0.6070	0.7030	0.6515	0.7435	0.6542	0.6960	0.6753
CredBoost	0.8440	**0.8572**	0.8508	0.8595	0.8465	**0.8530**	**0.8518**

Model (Music)	Positive			Negative			Ac
	P	R	F1	P	R	F1	
LB	0.7387	0.8030	0.7695	0.7842	0.7160	0.7485	0.7595
BSVM-CN	0.8492	0.6755	0.7525	0.7306	0.8800	0.7984	0.7778
BTL-1	0.8437	0.6395	0.7275	0.7097	0.8815	0.7863	0.7605
BR2013	-	-	-	-	-	-	0.7513
SB-CN	**0.8787**	0.6990	0.7786	0.7501	**0.9035**	0.8197	0.8012
BTL-2	0.7285	0.8461	0.7829	0.8675	0.7616	0.8111	0.7980
CoTr	0.8536	0.6790	0.7564	0.7335	0.8835	0.8015	0.7812
dCredB	0.5860	0.7043	0.6397	0.7540	0.6455	0.6955	0.6700
CredBoost	0.7258	**0.8708**	**0.7917**	**0.8928**	0.7653	**0.8241**	**0.8093**

Table 4: Micro performance of all approaches in three domains. P: Precision, R: Recall, F1: micro-F measure, Ac: Accuracy, and - represents unknown. The model in BR2013 is unknown, thus its micro performance is unavailable.

classifier. It is reasonable that a Chinese classifier performs better on Chinese text than an English classifier performs on the translated English text due to the different language distributions and MT errors. However, as shown in Tables 3 and 4, the better performance of our proposed method compared with that of the self-boosting method further suggests the effectiveness of our proposed knowledge validation model.

Figure 1 illustrates the continuous changes of performances vs. the corresponding growth sizes of the training data sets for SB-CN, BTL-2, CoTr, and CredBoost. According to our common sense, noisy data have negative influence on performance improvement. Compared to the other three methods, CredBoost accepts less number of training instances during learning while it achieves more improvement. This verifies the ability of CredBoost that can filter out the noisy data recommended by the English sentiment classifier.

In Figure 1(a), the curves of BTL-2 and CoTr suggest that directly transferring the knowledge recommended from English imports many noisy data into Chinese. It is also obvious that the performance curve of CredBoost implies a stable improvement trend while the other three decrease after certain iterations because of the accumulated negative influence from the noisy data. Figure 1(b) shows CredBoost accepts decreased training instances after certain iterations because the number of "high-quality" instances decrease when learning proceeds. This finding suggests that knowledge validation would rather abandon "less-credible" knowledge with higher probability than easily accept it. Knowledge validation in the proposed model guarantees highly-credible learning when transferring knowledge from English to Chinese. The results also show that CredBoost has great potential to achieve better performance approaching to supervised approaches if more unlabeled Chinese data are available.

Another interesting finding is also observed.

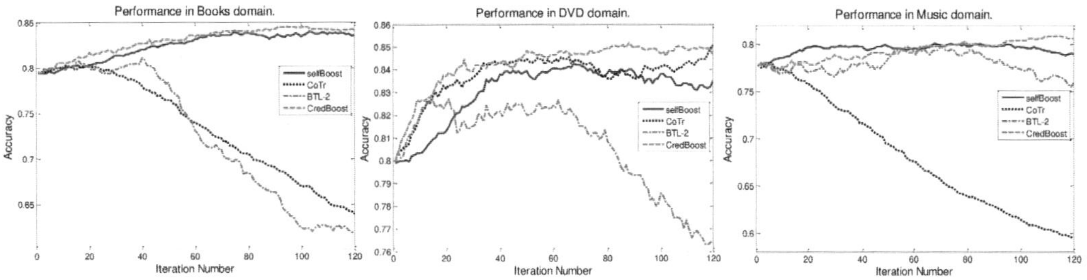

(a) Performances comparison in three domains

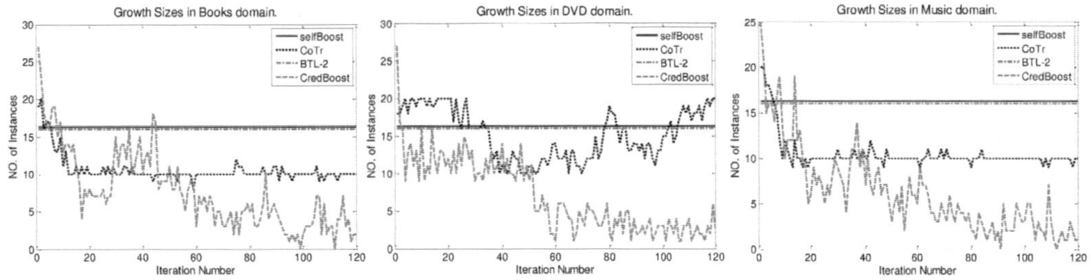

(b) Growth sizes comparison in three domains

Figure 1: Performances vs. Growth Sizes for SB-CN, CoTr, BTL-2, and CredBoost in three domains. The similar performance curves of CoTr is also reported in (Gui et al., 2014).

Although document-to-vector represents content semantic well, it cannot determine the sentiment polarity of text well, even when the document-to-vectors that are used to train basic classifiers are learned on the mixture of the translated and original reviews. The superior performance of CredBoost to dCredB suggests that the semantic representation is effective to identify highly-credible acquired knowledge and new knowledge but it alone may not be sufficient enough to model the sentiment information.

We also conduct some other experiments to study the sensitivity of the new knowledge validation boundary ψ and the validation scale ζ_+ in the training data. The experimental results show that the performances with different parameter settings fluctuate around the best result reported in Tables 3 and 4 in a small range. Our model is basically quite stable.

5 Conclusion

In this paper, we propose a semi-supervised learning model, called CredBoost, to address cross-lingual (English vs Chinese) sentiment analysis without direct labeled Chinese data nor direct parallel data. We propose to introduce knowledge validation during transfer learning to reduce the noisy data caused by machine translation errors or inevitable mistakes made by the source language sentiment classifier. The experimental result demonstrates the effectiveness of the proposed model. In the future, we will explore more suitable knowledge representations and knowledge validation in the CredBoost framework.

Acknowledgements

We thank all the anonymous reviewers for their detailed and insightful comments on this paper. The work described in this paper was supported by the Research Grants Council of Hong Kong project (PolyU 5202/12E and PolyU 152094/14E) and the grants from the National Natural Science Foundation of China (61272291, 61472290, 61472291 and 61303115).

References

Carmen Banea and Rada Mihalcea, Janyce Wiebe, Samer Hassan. 2008. Multilingual Subjectivity Analysis Using Machine Translation. In *Proceedings of the 2008 Conference on Empirical Methods in Natual Language Processing*, pages 127-135, Honolulu, October.

Carmen Banea, Yoonjung Choi, Lingjia Deng, Samer Hassan, Michael Mohler, Bishan Yang, Claire

Cardie, Rada Mihalcea, Janyce Wiebe. 2013. CPN-CORE: A Text Semantic Similarity System Infused with Opinion Knowledge. In *Proceedings of the Main Conference and the SHared Task in *SEM 2013*, pages 221-228, Atlanta, Georgia, June 13-14, 2013.

Yejin Choi and Claire Cardie. 2008. Learning with Compositional Semantics as Structural Inference for Subsentential Sentiment Analysis. In *Proceedings of the 2008 Conference on Empirical Methods in Natural Language Processing*, pages 792-801, Honolulu, October 2008.

Kevin Duh and Akinori Fujino and Masaaki Nagata. 2011. Is Machine Translation Ripe for Cross-lingual Sentiment Classification? In *Proceedings of the 49th Annual Meeting of the Association for Computational Linguistics: shortpapers*, pages 429-433, Portland, Oregon, June 19-24, 2011.

Rong-En Fan, Kai-Wei Chang, Cho-Jui Ksieh, Xiang-Rui Wang, Chih-Jen Lin. 2008. LIBLINEAR: A Library for Large Linear Classification. In *Journal of Machine Learning Research*, 9 (2008) 1871-1874.

Micheal Gamon. 2004. Sentiment Classification on Customer Feedback Data: Noisy Data, Large Feature Vectors and the Role of Linguistic Analysis. In *Proceedings of the 20th International Conference on Computational Linguistics*, pages 841-847, CH.

Xavier Glorot, Antoine Bordes, and Yoshua Bengio. 2011. Domain Adaptation for Large-scale Sentiment Classification: A Deep Learning Approach. In *Proceedings of the 28th International Conference on Machine Learning*, pages 513-520, Bellevue, Washington, USA.

Lin Gui, Ruifeng Xu, Qin Lu, Jun Xu, Jian Xu, Bin Liu, Xiaolong Wang. 2014. Cross-lingual Opinion Analysis via Negative Transfer Detection. In *Proceedings of the 52th Annual Meeting of the Association for Computational Linguistics (short paper)*, pages 860-865, Baltimore, Maryland, USA, June 23-25 2014.

Ahmed Hassan and Dragomir Radev. 2010. I-dentifying Text Polarity Using Random Walks. In *Proceedings of the 48th Annual Meeting on Association for Computational Linguistics*, pages 395-403, Uppsala, Sweden, 11-16 July 2010.

Yulan He, Chenghua Lin, Harith Alani. 2011a. Automatically Extracting Polarity-bearing Topics for Cross Domain Sentiment Classification. In *Proceedings of the 49th Annual Meeting of the Association for Computational Linguistics: Huamn Language Technologies*, pages 123-131, Portland, Oregon, USA.

Yulan He. 2011b. Latent Sentiment Model for Weakly-Supervised Cross-Lingual Sentiment Classification. In *Proceedings of the 33th European Conference on Information Retrieval(ECIR 2011)*, 18-21 Apr 2011, Dublin, Ireland.

KANAYAMA Hiroshi, NASUKAWAA Tetsuya, WATANABE Hideo. 2004. Deeper Sentiment Analysis Using Machine Translation Technology. In *Proceedings of the 20th International Conference on Computational Linguistics*, pages 494-500.

Alistair Kennedy and Diana Inkpen. 2006. Sentiment Classification of Movie and Product Reviews Using Contextual Valence Shifters. *Computational Intelligence*,22(2):110-125.

Quoc Le, Tomas Mikolov. 2014. Distributed Representations of Sentences and Documents. In *Proceedings of the 31th International Conference on Machine Learning*, Beijing, China, 2014. JMLR: W&CP volume 32.

Tao Li, Vikas Sindhwani, Chris Ding, and Yi Zhang. 2009. Knowledge Transformation for Cross-Domain Sentiment Classification. In *Proceedings of the 32th International ACM SIGIR Conference on Research and Development in Information Retrieval*, pages 716-717, Boston, MA, USA.

Bing Liu. May 2012. *Sentiment Analysis and Opinion Mining*. Morgan & Claypool Publisher.

Xinfan Meng, Furu Wei, Xiaohua Liu, Ming Zhou, Ge Xu, Houfeng Wang. 2012. Cross-Lingual Mixture Model for Sentiment Classification. In *Proceedings of the 50th Annual Meeting of the Association for Computational Linguistics*, pages 572-581, Jeju, Republic of Korea, 8-14 July 2012.

Tony Mullen and Nigel Collier. 2004. Sentiment analysis using support vector machines with diverse inoformation sources. In *Proceedings of the Conference on Empirical Methods in Natural Language Processing*, pages 412-418, (July 2004) poster paper.

Sinno Jialin Pan and Qiang Yang, Fellow, IEEE. 2010. A Survey on Transfer Learning. In *Journal of IEEE Transactions on Knowledge and Data Engineering*, Vol.22, NO.10, October 2010.

Bo Pang and Lillian Lee, Shivakumar Vaithyanathan. 2002. Thumps Up? Sentiment Classification using Machine Learning Techniques. In *Proceedings of the 2002 Conference on Empirical Methods in Natural Language Processing*, pages 79-86, Philadelphia, July 2002.

Kashyap Popat, Balamurali A R, Pushpak Bhattacharyya and Gholamreza Haffari. 2013. The Haves and the Have-Nots: Leverage Unlabeled Corpora for Sentiment Analysis. In *Proceedings of the 51th Annual Meeting of the Association for Computational Linguistics*, pages 412-422, Sofia, Bulgaria, 4-9 August 2013.

Jonathon Read. 2005. Using Emotions to reduce Dependency in Machine Learning Techniques for Sentiment Classification. In *Proceedings of the 43th Annual Meeting on Association for Computational Linguistics Student Research Workshop*, pages 43-48.

Hassan Saif, Yulan He and Harith Alani. 2012. Semantic Sentiment Analysis of Twitter. In *Proceedings of the 11th International Semantics Web Conference ISWC 2012*, Boston, USA.

Stephen Shankland. 2013. Google Translate now serves 200 millon people daily. In *CNET. CBS Interactive Inc*. May 18, 2013.

Richard Socher, Alex Perelygin, Jean Y. Wu, Jason Chuang, Chiristopher D. Manning, Andrew Y. Ng and Christopher Potts. 2013. Recursive Deep Models for Semantics Computationality Over a Sentiment Treebank. In *Proceedings of the Conference on Empirical Methods in Natural Language Processing*.

Songbo Tan, Gaowei Wu, Huifeng Tang and Xueqi Cheng. 2007. A Novel Scheme for Domain-transfer Problem in the context of Sentiment Analysis. In *CIKM 2007*, November 6-8, 2007, Lisboa, Portugal.

Peter D. Turney. 2002. Thumps Up or Thumps Down? Semantic Orientation Applied to Unsupervised Classification of Reviews. In *Proceedings of the 40th Annual Meeting of the Association for Computational Linguistics*, pages 417-424, Philadelphia, July 2002.

Xiaojun Wan. 2008. Using Bilingual Knowledge and Ensemble Technics for Unsupervised Chinese Sentiment Analysis. In *Proceedings of the 2008 Conference on Empirical Methods in Natual Language Processing*, pages 553-561, Honolulu, October 2008.

Xiaojun Wan. 2009. Co-Training for Cross-Lingual Sentiment Classification. In *Proceedings of the 47th Annual Meeting of the ACL and the 4th IJCNLP of the AFNLP*, pages 235-243, Suntec, Singapore, 2-7 August 2009.

Bin Wei and Christopher Pal. 2010. Cross Lingual Adaptation: An Experiment on Sentiment Classifications. In *Proceedings of the 48 Annual Meeting of the Association for Computational Linguistics (short paper)*, pages 258-262, Uppsala, Sweden, 11-16 July 2010.

Ruifeng Xu, Jun Xu and Xiaolong Wang. 2011. Instance Level Transfer Learning for Cross Lingual Opinion Analysis. In *Proceedings of the 2nd Workshop on Computational Approaches to Subjectivity and Sentiment Analysis, ACL-HLT 2011*, pages 182-188, 24 June, 2011, Portland, Oregon, USA.

Learning Bilingual Sentiment Word Embeddings for Cross-language Sentiment Classification

Huiwei Zhou, Long Chen, Fulin Shi, and Degen Huang
School of Computer Science and Technology
Dalian University of Technology, Dalian, P.R. China
{zhouhuiwei,huangdg}@dlut.edu.cn
{chenlong.415,shi_fl}@mail.dlut.edu.cn

Abstract

The sentiment classification performance relies on high-quality sentiment resources. However, these resources are imbalanced in different languages. Cross-language sentiment classification (CLSC) can leverage the rich resources in one language (source language) for sentiment classification in a resource-scarce language (target language). Bilingual embeddings could eliminate the semantic gap between two languages for CLSC, but ignore the sentiment information of text. This paper proposes an approach to learning bilingual sentiment word embeddings (BSWE) for English-Chinese CLSC. The proposed B-SWE incorporate sentiment information of text into bilingual embeddings. Furthermore, we can learn high-quality BSWE by simply employing labeled corpora and their translations, without relying on large-scale parallel corpora. Experiments on NLP&CC 2013 CLSC dataset show that our approach outperforms the state-of-the-art systems.

1 Introduction

Sentiment classification is a task of predicting sentiment polarity of text, which has attracted considerable interest in the NLP field. To date, a number of corpus-based approaches (Pang et al., 2002; Pang and Lee, 2004; Kennedy and Inkpen, 2006) have been developed for sentiment classification. The approaches heavily rely on quality and quantity of the labeled corpora, which are considered as the most valuable resources in sentiment classification task. However, such sentiment resources are imbalanced in different languages. To leverage resources in the source language to improve the sentiment classification performance in the target language, cross-language sentiment classification (CLSC) approaches have been investigated.

The traditional CLSC approaches employ machine translation (MT) systems to translate corpora in the source language into the target language, and train the sentiment classifiers in the target language (Banea et al., 2008). Directly employing the translated resources for sentiment classification in the target language is simple and could get acceptable results. However, the gap between the source language and target language inevitably impacts the performance of sentiment classification. To improve the classification accuracy, multi-view approaches have been proposed. In these approaches, the resources in the source language and their translations in the target language are both used to train sentiment classifiers in two independent views (Wan, 2009; Gui et al., 2013; Zhou et al., 2014a). The final results are determined by ensemble classifiers in these two views to overcome the weakness of monolingual classifiers. However, learning language-specific classifiers in each view fails to capture the common sentiment information of two languages during training process.

With the revival of interest in deep learning (Hinton and Salakhutdinov, 2006), shared deep representations (or embeddings) (Bengio et al., 2013) are employed for CLSC (Chandar A P et al., 2013). Usually, paired sentences from parallel corpora are used to learn word embeddings across languages (Chandar A P et al., 2013; Chandar A P et al., 2014), eliminating the need of MT systems. The learned bilingual embeddings could easily project the training data and test data into a common space, where training and testing are performed. However, high-quality bilingual embeddings rely on the large-scale task-related parallel corpora, which are not always readily available. Meanwhile, though semantic similarities across languages are captured during bilingual embedding learning process, sentiment information of

Proceedings of the 53rd Annual Meeting of the Association for Computational Linguistics and the 7th International Joint Conference on Natural Language Processing, pages 430–440,
Beijing, China, July 26-31, 2015.

text is ignored. That is, bilingual embeddings learned from unlabeled parallel corpora are not effective enough for CLSC because of a lack of explicit sentiment information. Tang and Wan (2014) first proposed a bilingual sentiment embedding model using the original training data and the corresponding translations through a linear mapping rather than deep learning technique.

This paper proposes a denoising autoencoder based approach to learning bilingual sentiment word embeddings (**BSWE**) for CLSC, which incorporates sentiment polarities of text into the bilingual embeddings. The proposed approach learns BSWE with the original labeled documents and their translations instead of parallel corpora. The BSWE learning process consists of two phases: the unsupervised phase of semantic learning and the supervised phase of sentiment learning. In the unsupervised phase, sentiment words and their negation features are extracted from the source training data and their translations to represent paired documents. These features are used as inputs for a denoising autoencoder to learn the bilingual embeddings. In the supervised phase, sentiment polarity labels of documents are used to guide BSWE learning for incorporating sentiment information into the bilingual embeddings.

The learned BSWE are applied to project English training data and Chinese test data into a common space. In this space, a linear support vector machine (SVM) is used to perform training and testing. The experiments are carried on NLP&CC 2013 CLSC dataset, including book, DVD and music categories. Experimental results show that our approach achieves 80.68% average accuracy, which outperforms the state-of-the-art systems on this dataset. Although the BSWE are only evaluated on English-Chinese CLSC here, it can be popularized to many other languages.

The major contributions of this work can be summarized as follows:

- We propose bilingual sentiment word embeddings (BSWE) for CLSC based on deep learning technique. Experimental results show that the proposed BSWE significantly outperform the bilingual embeddings by incorporating sentiment information.

- Instead of large-scale parallel corpora, only the labeled English corpora and English-to-Chinese translations are required for BSWE learning. It is proved that in spite of the small-scale of training set, our approach outperforms the state-of-the-art systems in NLP&CC 2013 CLSC share task.

- We employ sentiment words and their negation features rather than all words in documents to learn sentiment-specific embeddings, which significantly reduces the dimension of input vectors as well as improves sentiment classification performance.

2 Related Work

In this section, we review the literature related to this paper from two perspectives: cross-language sentiment classification and embedding learning for sentiment classification.

2.1 Cross-language Sentiment Classification (CLSC)

The critical problem of CLSC is how to bridge the gap between the source language and target language. Machine translations or parallel corpora are usually employed to solve this problem. We present a brief review of CLSC from two aspects: machine translation based approaches and parallel corpora based approaches.

Machine translation based approaches use MT systems to project training data into the target language or test data into the source language. Wan (2009) proposed a co-training approach for CLSC. The approach first translated Chinese test data into English, and English training data into Chinese. Then, they performed training and testing in two independent views: English view and Chinese view. Gui et al. (2013) combined self-training approach with co-training approach by estimating the confidence of each monolingual system. Li et al. (2013) selected the samples in the source language that were similar to those in the target language to decrease the gap between two languages. Zhou et al. (2014a) proposed a combination CLSC model, which adopted denoising autoencoders (Vincent et al., 2008) to enhance the robustness to translation errors of the input.

Most recently, a number of studies adopt deep learning technique to learn bilingual representations with parallel corpora. Bilingual representations have been successfully applied in many NLP tasks, such as machine translation (Zou et al., 2013), sentiment classification (Chandar A P et al., 2013; Zhou et al., 2014b), text classification (Chandar A P et al., 2014), etc.

Chandar A P et al. (2013) learned bilingual representations with aligned sentences throughout two phases: the language-specific representation learning phase and the shared representation learning phase. In the language-specific representation learning phase, they applied autoencoders to obtain a language-specific representation for each entity in two languages respectively. In shared representation learning phase, pairs of parallel language-specific representations were passed to an autoencoder to learn bilingual representations. To joint language-specific representations and bilingual representations, Chandar A P et al. (2014) integrated the two learning phases into a unified process to learn bilingual embeddings. Zhou et al. (2014b) employed bilingual representations for English-Chinese CLSC. The work mentioned above employed aligned sentences in bilingual embedding learning process. However, in the sentiment classification process, only representations in the source language are used for training, and representations in the target language are used for testing, which ignores the interactions of semantic information between the source language and target language.

2.2 Embedding Learning for Sentiment Classification

Bilingual embedding learning algorithms focus on capturing syntactic and semantic similarities across languages, but ignore sentiment information. To date, many embedding learning algorithms have been developed for sentiment classification problem by incorporating sentiment information into word embeddings. Maas et al. (2011) presented a probabilistic model that combined unsupervised and supervised techniques to learn word vectors, capturing semantic information as well as sentiment information. Wang et al. (2014) introduced sentiment labels into Neural Network Language Models (Bengio et al., 2003) to enhance sentiment expression ability of word vectors. Tang et al. (2014) theoretically and empirically analyzed the effects of the syntactic context and sentiment information in word vectors, and showed that the syntactic context and sentiment information were equally important to sentiment classification.

Recent years have seen a surge of interest in word embeddings with deep learning technique (Bespalov et al., 2011; Glorot et al., 2011; Socher et al., 2011; Socher et al., 2012), which have been empirically shown to preserve linguistic regularities (Mikolov et al., 2013). Our work focuses on learning bilingual sentiment word embeddings (BSWE) with deep learning technique. Unlike the work of Chandar A P et al. (2014) that adopted parallel corpora to learn bilingual embeddings, we only use training data and their translations to learn BSWE. More importantly, sentiment information is integrated into bilingual embeddings to improve their performance in CLSC.

3 Bilingual Sentiment Word Embeddings (BSWE) for Cross-language Sentiment Classification

3.1 Denoising Autoencoder

It has been demonstrated that the denoising autoencoder could decrease the effects of translation errors on the performance of CLSC (Zhou et al., 2014a). This paper proposes a deep learning based approach, which employs the denoising autoencoder to learn the bilingual embeddings for CLSC.

A denoising autoencoder is the modification of an autoencoder. The autoencoder (Bengio et al., 2007) includes an encoder f_θ and a decoder $g_{\theta'}$. The encoder maps a d-dimensional input vector $\mathbf{x} \in [0,1]^d$ to a hidden representation $\mathbf{y} \in [0,1]^{d'}$ through a deterministic mapping $\mathbf{y} = f_\theta(\mathbf{x}) = \sigma(\mathbf{W}\mathbf{x} + \mathbf{b})$, parameterized by $\theta = \{\mathbf{W}, \mathbf{b}\}$. $\mathbf{W}$ is a weight matrix, $\mathbf{b}$ is a bias term, and $\sigma(x)$ is the activation function. The decoder maps $\mathbf{y}$ back to a reconstructed vector $\hat{\mathbf{x}} = g_{\theta'}(\mathbf{y}) = \sigma(\mathbf{W}^T\mathbf{y} + \mathbf{c})$, parameterized by $\theta' = \{\mathbf{W}^T, \mathbf{c}\}$, where $\mathbf{c}$ is the bias term for reconstruction.

Through the process of encoding and decoding, the parameters θ and θ' of the autoencoder will be trained by gradient descent to minimize the loss function. The sum of reconstruction cross-entropies across the training set is usually used as the loss function:

$$l(x) = -\sum_{i=1}^{d}[\mathbf{x}_i \log \hat{\mathbf{x}}_i + (1-\mathbf{x}_i)\log(1-\hat{\mathbf{x}}_i)] \quad (1)$$

A denoising autoencoder enhances robustness to noises by corrupting the input $\mathbf{x}$ to a partially destroyed version $\tilde{\mathbf{x}}$. The desired noise level of the input $\mathbf{x}$ can be changed by adjusting the destruction fraction ν. For each input $\mathbf{x}$, a fixed number νd (d is the dimension of $\mathbf{x}$) of components are selected randomly, and their values are set to 0, while the others are left untouched. Like an autoencoder, the destroyed input $\tilde{\mathbf{x}}$ is mapped to a latent representation $\mathbf{y} = f_\theta(\tilde{\mathbf{x}}) = \sigma(\mathbf{W}\tilde{\mathbf{x}} + \mathbf{b})$. Then $\mathbf{y}$ is mapped back to a reconstructed vector $\hat{\mathbf{x}}$ through $\hat{\mathbf{x}} = g_{\theta'}(\mathbf{y}) = \sigma(\mathbf{W}^T\mathbf{y} + \mathbf{c})$. The loss function of a denoising autoencoder is the same as that of an autoencoder. Minimizing the loss makes $\hat{\mathbf{x}}$ close to the input $\mathbf{x}$ rather than $\tilde{\mathbf{x}}$.

Our BSWE learning process can be divided into two phases: the unsupervised phase of semantic learning and the supervised phase of sentiment learning. In the unsupervised phase, a denoising autoencoder is employed to learn the bilingual embeddings. In the supervised phase, the sentiment information is incorporated into the bilingual embeddings based on sentiment labels of documents to obtain BSWE.

3.2 Unsupervised Phase of the Bilingual Embedding Learning

In the unsupervised phase, the English training documents and their Chinese translations are employed to learn the bilingual embeddings (Sentiment polarity labels of documents are not employed in this phase). Based on the English documents, 2,000 English sentiment words in MPQA subjectivity lexicon[1] are extracted by the Chi-square method (Galavotti et al., 2000). Their corresponding Chinese translations are used as Chinese sentiment words. Besides, some sentiment words are often modified by negation words, which lead to inversion of their polarities. Therefore, negation features are introduced to each sentiment word to represent its negative form.

We take into account 14 frequently-used negation words in English such as *not* and *none*; 5 negation words in Chinese such as 不 (*no*/*not*) and 没有 (*without*). A sentiment word modified by these negation words in the window [-2, 2] is considered as its negative form in this paper, while sentiment word features remain the initial meaning. Negation features use binary expressions. If a sentiment word is not modified by negation words, the value of its negation features is set to 0. Thus, the sentiment words and their corresponding negation features in English and Chinese are adopted to represent the document pairs $(\mathbf{x}_E, \mathbf{x}_C)$.

We expect that pairs of documents could be forced to capture the common semantic information of two languages. To achieve this, a denoising autoencoder is used to perform the reconstructions of paired documents in both English and Chinese. Figure 1 shows the framework of bilingual embedding learning.

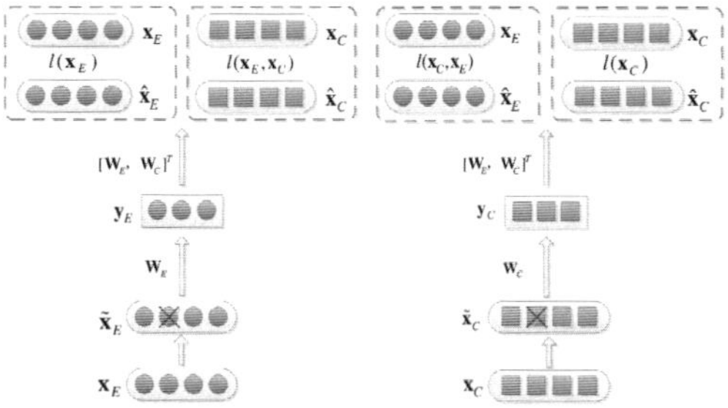

(a) reconstruction from $\mathbf{x}_E$ (b) reconstruction from $\mathbf{x}_C$

Figure 1: The framework of bilingual embedding learning.

For the corrupted versions $\tilde{\mathbf{x}}_E$ ($\tilde{\mathbf{x}}_C$) of the initial input vector $\mathbf{x}_E$ ($\mathbf{x}_C$), we use the sigmoid function as the activation function to extract latent representations:

$$\mathbf{y}_E = f_\theta(\tilde{\mathbf{x}}_E) = \sigma(\mathbf{W}_E\tilde{\mathbf{x}}_E + \mathbf{b}) \quad (2)$$

$$\mathbf{y}_C = f_\theta(\tilde{\mathbf{x}}_C) = \sigma(\mathbf{W}_C\tilde{\mathbf{x}}_C + \mathbf{b}) \quad (3)$$

where $\mathbf{W}_E$ and $\mathbf{W}_C$ are the language-specific word representation matrices, corresponding to English and Chinese respectively. Notice that the bias $\mathbf{b}$ is shared to ensure that the produced representations in two languages are on the same scale.

For the latent representations in either language, we would like two decoders to perform reconstructions in English and Chinese respectively. As shown in Figure 1(a), for the latent representation $\mathbf{y}_E$ in English, one decoder is used to map $\mathbf{y}_E$ back to a reconstruction $\hat{\mathbf{x}}_E$ in English, and the other is used to map $\mathbf{y}_E$ back to a reconstruction $\hat{\mathbf{x}}_C$ in Chinese such that:

$$\hat{\mathbf{x}}_E = g_{\theta'}(\mathbf{y}_E) = \sigma(\mathbf{W}_E^T\mathbf{y}_E + \mathbf{c}_E) \quad (4)$$

$$\hat{\mathbf{x}}_C = g_{\theta'}(\mathbf{y}_E) = \sigma(\mathbf{W}_C^T\mathbf{y}_E + \mathbf{c}_C) \quad (5)$$

where $\mathbf{c}_E$ and $\mathbf{c}_C$ are the biases of the decoders in English and Chinese, respectively. Similarly, the same steps repeat for the latent representation $\mathbf{y}_C$ in Chinese, which are shown in Figure 1(b).

The encoder and decoder structures allow us to learn a mapping within and across languages. Specifically, for a given document pair $(\mathbf{x}_E, \mathbf{x}_C)$, we can learn bilingual embeddings to reconstruct $\mathbf{x}_E$ from itself (loss $l(\mathbf{x}_E)$), reconstruct $\mathbf{x}_C$ from itself (loss $l(\mathbf{x}_C)$), construct $\mathbf{x}_C$ from

[1] http://mpqa.cs.pitt.edu/lexicons/subj_lexicon

$\mathbf{x}_E$ (loss $l(\mathbf{x}_E, \mathbf{x}_C)$), construct $\mathbf{x}_E$ from $\mathbf{x}_C$ (loss $l(\mathbf{x}_C, \mathbf{x}_E)$) and reconstruct the concatenation of $\mathbf{x}_E$ and $\mathbf{x}_C$ ($[\mathbf{x}_E, \mathbf{x}_C]$) from itself (loss $l([\mathbf{x}_E, \mathbf{x}_C], [\hat{\mathbf{x}}_E, \hat{\mathbf{x}}_C])$). The sum of 5 losses is used as the loss function of bilingual embeddings:

$$L = l(\mathbf{x}_E) + l(\mathbf{x}_C) + l(\mathbf{x}_E, \mathbf{x}_C) + l(\mathbf{x}_C, \mathbf{x}_E) + l([\mathbf{x}_E, \mathbf{x}_C], [\hat{\mathbf{x}}_E, \hat{\mathbf{x}}_C]) \tag{6}$$

3.3 Supervised Phase of Sentiment Learning

In the unsupervised phase, we have learned the bilingual embeddings, which could capture the semantic information within and across languages. However, the sentiment polarities of text are ignored in the unsupervised phase. Bilingual embeddings without sentiment information are not effective enough for sentiment classification task. This paper proposes an approach to learning B-SWE for CLSC, which introduces a supervised learning phase to incorporate sentiment information into the bilingual embeddings. The process of supervised phase is shown in Figure 2.

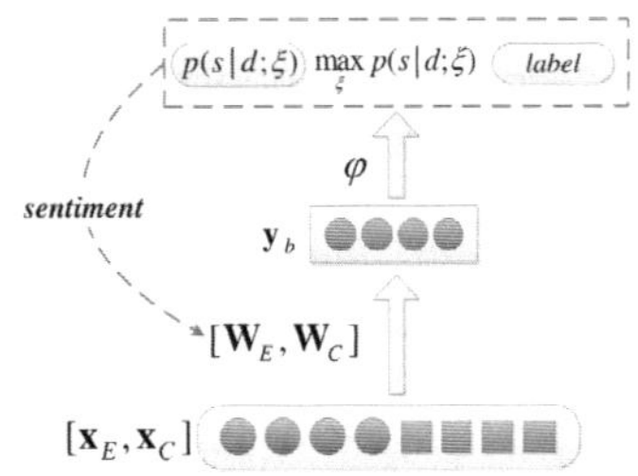

Figure 2: The supervised learning process.

For paired documents $[\mathbf{x}_E, \mathbf{x}_C]$, the sigmoid function is adopted as the activation function to extract latent bilingual representations $\mathbf{y}_b = \sigma([\mathbf{W}_E, \mathbf{W}_C][\mathbf{x}_E, \mathbf{x}_C] + \mathbf{b})$, where $[\mathbf{W}_E, \mathbf{W}_C]$ is the concatenation of $\mathbf{W}_E$ and $\mathbf{W}_C$.

The latent bilingual representation $\mathbf{y}_b$ is used to obtain the positive polarity probability $p(s = 1|d; \xi)$ of a document through a sigmoid function:

$$p(s = 1|d; \xi) = \sigma(\varphi^T \mathbf{y}_b + b_l) \tag{7}$$

where φ is the logistic regression weight vector and b_l is the bias of logistic regression. The sentiment label s is a Boolean value representing sentiment polarity of a document: $s = 0$ represents negative polarity and $s = 1$ represents positive polarity. Parameter $\xi^* = \{[\mathbf{W}_E, \mathbf{W}_C]^*, \mathbf{b}^*, \varphi^*, b_l^*\}$ is learned by maximizing the objective function according to the sentiment polarity label s_i of document d_i:

$$\xi^* = \arg\max_{\xi} \sum_{i=1} \log p(s_i|d_i; \xi) \tag{8}$$

Through the supervised learning phase, $[\mathbf{W}_E, \mathbf{W}_C]$ is optimized by maximizing sentiment polarity probability. Thus, rich sentiment information is encoded into the bilingual embeddings.

The following experiments will prove that the proposed BSWE outperform the traditional bilingual embeddings significantly in CLSC.

3.4 Bilingual Document Representation Method (BDR)

Once we have learned BSWE $[\mathbf{W}_E, \mathbf{W}_C]$, whose columns are representations for sentiment words, we can use them to represent documents in two languages.

Given an English training document d_E containing 2,000 sentiment word features $s_1, s_2, \cdots, s_{2,000}$ and 2,000 corresponding negation features, we represent it as the TF-IDF weighted sum of BSWE:

$$\phi_{d_E} = \sum_{i=1}^{4,000} TF - IDF(s_i)\mathbf{W}_{E.,s_i} \tag{9}$$

Similarly, for its Chinese translation d_C containing 2,000 sentiment word features $t_1, t_2, \cdots, t_{2,000}$ and 2,000 corresponding negation features, we represent it as:

$$\phi_{d_C} = \sum_{j=1}^{4,000} TF - IDF(t_j)\mathbf{W}_{C.,t_j} \tag{10}$$

We propose a bilingual document representation method (**BDR**) in this paper, which represents each document d_i with the concatenation of its English and Chinese representations $[\phi_{d_E}, \phi_{d_C}]$. B-DR is expected to enhance the ability of sentiment expression for further improving the classification performance. Such bilingual document representations are fed to a linear SVM to perform sentiment classification.

4 Experiment

4.1 Experimental Settings

Data Set. The proposed approach is evaluated on NLP&CC 2013 CLSC dataset[2] [3]. The dataset con-

[2]http://tcci.ccf.org.cn/conference/2013/dldoc/evsam03.zip
[3]http://tcci.ccf.org.cn/conference/2013/dldoc/evdata03.zip

sists of product reviews on three categories: book, DVD, and music. Each category contains 4,000 English labeled data as training data (the ratio of the number of positive and negative samples is 1:1) and 4,000 Chinese unlabeled data as test data.

Tools. In our experiments, Google Translate[4] is adopted for both English-to-Chinese and Chinese-to-English translation. ICTCLAS (Zhang et al., 2003) is used as Chinese word segmentation tool. A denoising autoencoder is developed based on Theano system (Bergstra et al., 2010). BSWE are trained for 50 and 30 epochs in unsupervised phase and supervised phases respectively. SVM^{light} (Joachims, 1999) is used to train linear SVM sentiment classifiers

Evaluation Metric. The performance is evaluated by the classification accuracy for each category, and the average accuracy of three categories, respectively. The category accuracy is defined as:

$$Accuracy_c = \frac{\#system\_correct_c}{\#system\_total_c} \tag{11}$$

where c is one of the three categories, and $\#system\_correct_c$ and $\#system\_total_c$ stand for the number of being correctly classified reviews and the number of total reviews in the category c, respectively.

The average accuracy is shown as:

$$Average = \frac{1}{3}\sum_c Accuracy_c \tag{12}$$

4.2 Evaluations on BSWE

In this section, we evaluate the quality of BSWE for CLSC. The dimension of bilingual embeddings d is set to 50, and destruction fraction ν is set to 0.2.

Effects of Bilingual Embedding Learning Methods

We first compare our unsupervised bilingual embedding learning method with the parallel corpora based method. The parallel corpora based method uses the paired documents in the parallel corpus[5] to learn bilingual embeddings, while our method only uses the English training documents and their Chinese translations (Sentiment polarity labels of documents are not employed here). The Boolean feature weight calculation method is adopted to represent documents for bilingual embedding learning and BDR is employed to represent training data and test data for sentiment classification. To represent the paired documents in the parallel corpus, 27,597 English words and 31,786 Chinese words are extracted for bilingual embedding learning. Our method only needs 2,000 English sentiment words, 2,000 Chinese sentiment words, and their negation features, which significantly reduces the dimension of input vectors.

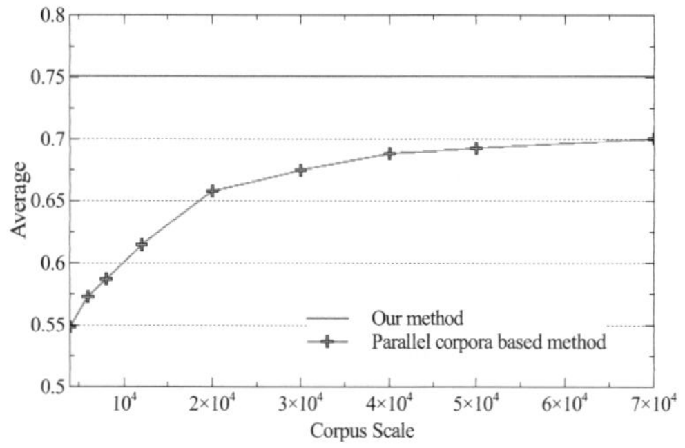

Figure 3: Our unsupervised bilingual embedding learning method vs. Parallel corpora based method.

The average accuracies on NLP&CC 2013 test data of the two bilingual embedding learning methods are shown in Figure 3. As can be seen from Figure 3, when the corpus scales of the two methods are the same (4,000 paired documents), our method (75.09% average accuracy) surpasses the parallel corpora method (54.82% average accuracy) by about 20%. With the scale of the parallel corpora increasing, the performance of parallel corpora based method is steadily improved. However, the performance is not as good as our bilingual embedding learning method. Though the document number of the parallel corpus is up to 70,000 , the average accuracy is only 70.05%. It is proved that our method is more suitable for learning bilingual embeddings for cross-language sentiment classification than the parallel corpora based method.

Effects of Feature Weight in Bilingual Embeddings

In this part, we compare the Boolean and TF-IDF feature weight calculation methods in bilingual embedding learning process.

Table 1 shows the classification accuracy with

[4] http://translate.google.cn/

[5] http://www.datatang.com/data/45485

Category	book	DVD	music	Average
Boolean	76.22%	74.30%	74.75%	75.09%
TF-IDF	76.65%	77.60%	74.50%	76.25%

Table 1: The classification accuracy with the Boolean and TF-IDF methods.

the Boolean and TF-IDF methods. Generally, the TF-IDF method performs better than the Boolean method. The average accuracy of the TF-IDF method is 1.16% higher than the Boolean method, which illustrates that the TF-IDF method could reflect the latent contribution of sentiment words to each document effectively. The TF-IDF weight calculation method is exploited in the following experiments. Notice that sentiment information is not yet introduced in the bilingual embeddings here.

Effects of Sentiment Information in BSWE

Incorporating sentiment information in the bilingual embeddings, the performance of bilingual embeddings (without sentiment information) and BSWE (with sentiment information) is compared in Figure 4.

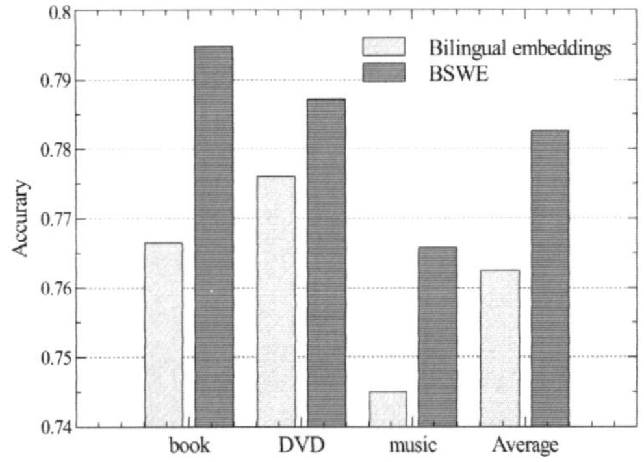

Figure 4: Performance comparison of the bilingual embeddings and BSWE.

As can be seen from Figure 4, by encoding sentiment information in the bilingual embeddings, the performance in book, DVD and music categories significantly improves to 79.47%, 78.72% and 76.58% respectively (2.82% increase in book, 1.12% in DVD, and 2.08% in music). The average accuracy reaches 78.26%, which is 2.01% higher than that of the bilingual embeddings. The experimental results indicate the effectiveness of sentiment information in the bilingual embedding learning. The BSWE learning approach is employed for CLSC in the following experiments.

Effects of Bilingual Document Representation Method

In this experiment, our bilingual document representation method (BDR) is compared with the following monolingual document representation methods.

En-En: This method represents training and test documents in English only with $\mathbf{W}_E$. English training documents and Chinese-to-English translations of test documents are both represented with $\mathbf{W}_E$.

Cn-Cn: This method represents training and test documents in Chinese only with $\mathbf{W}_C$. English-to-Chinese translations of training documents and Chinese test documents are both represented with $\mathbf{W}_C$.

En-Cn: This method represents English training documents with $\mathbf{W}_E$, while represents Chinese test documents with $\mathbf{W}_C$. Chandar A P et al. (2014) employed this method in their work.

BDR: This method adopts our bilingual document representation method, which represents training and test documents with both $\mathbf{W}_E$ and $\mathbf{W}_C$.

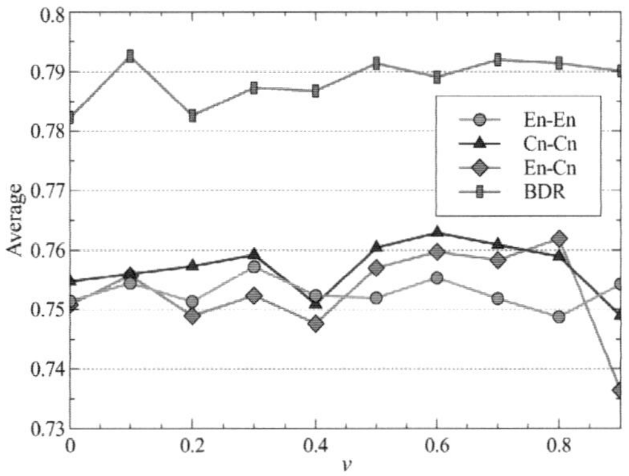

Figure 5: Effects of bilingual document representation method (BDR).

Figure 5 shows the average accuracy curves of different document representation methods with different destruction fraction ν. We vary ν from 0 to 0.9 with an interval of 0.1.

From Figure 5 we can see that En-En, Cn-Cn, and En-Cn get similar results. BDR performs constantly better than the other representation methods throughout the interval [0, 0.9]. The absolute superiority of BDR benefits from the enhanced ability of sentiment expression.

Meanwhile, when the input $\mathbf{x}$ is partially destroyed (ν varies from 0.1 to 0.9), the performance of En-En, Cn-Cn and En-Cn remains stable, which illustrates the robustness of the denoising autoencoder to corrupting noises. In addition, the average accuracies of BDR in the interval $\nu \in [0.1, 0.9]$ are all higher than the average accuracy under the condition $\nu = 0$ (78.23%). Therefore, adding noises properly to the training data could improve the performance of BSWE for CLSC.

4.3 Influences of Dimension d and Destruction Fraction ν

Figure 6 shows the relationship between accuracies and dimension d of BSWE as well as that between accuracies and destruction fraction ν in autoencoders in different categories. Dimension of embeddings d varies from 50 to 500, and destruction fraction ν varies from 0.1 to 0.9.

As shown in Figure 6, the average accuracies generally move upward as dimension of BSWE increasing. Generally, the average accuracies keep higher than 80% with ν varying from 0.1 to 0.5 as well as dimension varying from 300 to 500. When $\nu = 0.1$ and $d = 400$, the average accuracy reaches the peak value 80.68% (category accuracy of 81.05% in book, 81.60% in DVD, and 79.40% in music). The experimental results show that in BSWE learning process, increasing the dimension of embeddings or properly adding noises to the training data helps improve the performance of CLSC. In this paper, we only evaluate BSWE when dimension d varies from 50 to 500. However, there is still space for further improvement if d continues to increase.

4.4 Comparison with Related Work

Table 2 shows comparisons of the performance between our approach and some state-of-the-art systems on NLP&CC 2013 CLSC dataset. Our approach achieves the best performance with an 80.68% average accuracy. Compared with the recent related work, our approach is more effective and suitable for eliminating the language gap.

Chen et al. (2014) translated Chinese test data into English and then gave different weights to sentiment words according to the subject-predicate component of sentiment words. They got 77.09% accuracy and took the 2nd place in NLP&CC 2013 CLSC share task. The machine translation based approach was limited by the translation errors.

System	book	DVD	music	Average
Chen et al. (2014)	77.00%	78.33%	75.95%	77.09%
Gui et al. (2013)	78.70%	79.65%	78.30%	78.89%
Gui et al. (2014)	80.10%	81.60%	78.60%	80.10%
Zhou et al. (2014a)	80.63%	80.95%	78.48%	80.02%
Our approach	**81.05%**	**81.60%**	**79.40%**	**80.68%**

Table 2: Performance comparisons on the NLP&CC 2013 CLSC dataset.

Gui et al. (2013; 2014) and Zhou et al. (2014a) adopted the multi-view approach to bridge the language gap. Gui et al. (2013) proposed a mixed CLSC model by combining co-training and transfer learning strategies. They achieved the highest accuracy of 78.89% in NLP&CC CLSC share task. Gui et al. (2014) further improved the accuracy to 80.10% by removing noise from the transferred samples to avoid negative transfers. Zhou et al. (2014a) built denoising autoencoders in two independent views to enhance the robustness to translation errors in the inputs and achieved 80.02% accuracy. The multi-view approach learns language-specific classifiers in each view during training process, which is difficult to capture the common sentiment information of the two languages. Our approach integrates the bilingual embedding learning into a unified process, and outperforms Chen et al. (2014), Gui et al. (2013), Gui et al. (2014) and Zhou et al. (2014a) by 3.59%, 1.79%, 0.58%, and 0.66% respectively. The superiority of our approach benefits from the unified bilingual embedding learning process and the integration of semantic and sentiment information.

5 Conclusion and Future Work

This paper proposes an approach to learning BSWE by incorporating sentiment information into the bilingual embeddings for CLSC. The proposed approach learns BSWE with the labeled documents and their translations rather than parallel corpora. In addition, BDR is proposed to enhance the sentiment expression ability which combines English and Chinese representations. Experiments on the NLP&CC 2013 CLSC dataset show that our approach outperforms the previous state-of-the-art systems as well as traditional bilingual embedding systems. The proposed BSWE are only evaluated on English-Chinese CLSC in this paper, but it can be popularized to other languages.

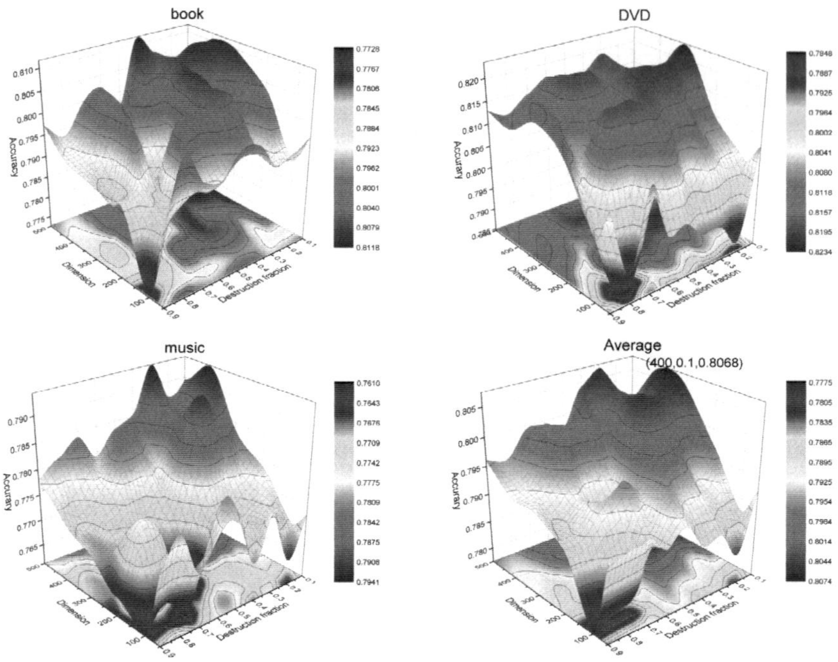

Figure 6: The relationship between accuracies and dimension d as well as that between accuracies and destruction fraction ν.

Both semantic and sentiment information play an important role in sentiment classification. In the following work, we will further investigate the relationship between semantic and sentiment information for CLSC, and balance their functions to optimize their combination for CLSC.

Acknowledgments

We wish to thank the anonymous reviewers for their valuable comments. This research is supported by National Natural Science Foundation of China (Grant No. 61272375).

References

Carmen Banea, Rada Mihalcea, Janyce Wiebe and Samer Hassan. 2008. Multilingual Subjectivity Analysis Using Machine Translation. In *Proceedings of the 2008 Conference on Empirical Methods in Natural Language Processing*, pages 127-135. Association for Computational Linguistics.

Yoshua Bengio, Réjean Ducharme, Pascal Vincent, and Christian Jauvin. 2003. A Neural Probabilistic Language Model. *The Journal of Machine Learning Research*, vol 3: 1137-1155.

Yoshua Bengio, Pascal Lamblin, Dan Popovici, and Hugo Larochelle. 2007. Greedy layer-wise training of deep networks. In *Proceedings of Advances in Neural Information Processing Systems 19 (NIPS 06)*, pages 153-160. MIT Press.

Yoshua Bengio, Aaron Courville, and Pascal Vincent. 2013. Representation learning: A review and new perspectives. *IEEE Transactions on Pattern Analysis and Machine Intelligence* 35(8): 1798-1828. IEEE.

James Bergstra, Olivier Breuleux, Frederic Bastien, Pascal Lamblin, Razvan Pascanu, Guillaume Desjardins, Joseph Turian, Yoshua Bengio. 2010. Theano: a CPU and GPU math expression compiler. In *Proceedings of the Python for scientific computing conference (SciPy)*.

Dmitriy Bespalov, Bing Bai, Yanjun Qi, and Ali Shokoufandeh. 2011. Sentiment classification based on supervised latent n-gram analysis. In *Proceedings of the Conference on Information and Knowledge Management*, pages 375-382. ACM.

Sarath Chandar A P, Mitesh M. Khapra, Balaraman Ravindran, Vikas Raykar and Amrita Saha. 2013. Multilingual deep learning. In *Deep Learning Workshop at NIPS 2013*.

Sarath Chandar A P, Stanislas Lauly, Hugo Larochelle, Mitesh M Khapra, Balaraman Ravindran, Vikas Raykar, and Amrita Saha. 2014. An autoencoder approach to learning bilingual word representations. In *Advances in Neural Information Processing Systems*, pages 1853-1861.

Qiang Chen, Yanxiang He, Xule Liu, Songtao Sun, Min Peng, and Fei Li. 2014. Cross-Language Sentiment Analysis Based on Parser (in Chinese). *Acta Scientiarum Naturalium Universitatis Pekinensis*, 50 (1): 55-60.

G. E. Hinton and R. R. Salakhutdinov. 2006. Reducing the Dimensionality of Data with Neural Networks. *Science*, vol 313: 504-507.

Luigi Galavotti, Fabrizio Sebastiani, and Maria Simi. 2000. Feature Selection and Negative Evidence in Automated Text Categorization. In *Proceedings of ECDL-00, 4th European Conference on Research and Advanced Technology for Digital Libraries*.

Xavier Glorot, Antoine Bordes, and Yoshua Bengio. 2011. Domain adaptation for large-scale sentiment classification: A deep learning approach. In *Proceedings of 28th International Conference on Machine Learning*, pages 513-520.

Lin Gui, Ruifeng Xu, Jun Xu, Li Yuan, Yuanlin Yao, Jiyun Zhou, Qiaoyun Qiu, Shuwei Wang, Kam-Fai Wong, and Ricky Cheung. 2013. A mixed model for cross lingual opinion analysis. In *Proceedings of Natural Language Processing and Chinese Computing*, pages 93-104. Springer Verlag.

Lin Gui, Ruifeng Xu, Qin Lu, Jun Xu, Jian Xu, Bin Liu, and Xiaolong Wang. 2014. Cross-lingual Opinion Analysis via Negative Transfer Detection. In *Proceedings of the 52nd Annual Meeting of the Association for Computational Linguistics (Short Papers)*, pages 860-865. Association for Computational Linguistics.

Thorsten Joachims. 1999. Making large-Scale SVM Learning Practical. Universität Dortmund.

Alistair Kennedy and Diana Inkpen. 2006. Sentiment classification of movie reviews using contextual valence shifters. *Computational intelligence*, 22(2): 110-125.

Shoushan Li, Rong Wang, Huanhuan Liu, and Chu-Ren Huang. 2013. Active learning for cross-lingual sentiment classification. In *Proceedings of Natural Language Processing and Chinese Computing*, pages 236-246. Springer Verlag.

Andrew L. Maas, Raymond E. Daly, Peter T. Pham, Dan Huang, Andrew Y. Ng, and Christopher Potts. 2011. Learning Word Vectors for Sentiment Analysis. In *Proceedings of the 49th Annual Meeting of the Association for Computational Linguistics*, pages 142-150. Association for Computational Linguistics.

Tomas Mikolov, Wen-tau Yih, and Geoffrey Zweig. 2013. Linguistic regularities in continuous space word representations. In *Proceedings of NAACL-HLT*, pages 746-751. Association for Computational Linguistics.

Bo Pang, Lillian Lee and Shivakumar Vaithyanathan. 2002. Thumbs up? Sentiment classification using machine learning techniques. In *Proceedings of the Conference on Empirical Methods in Natural Language Processing*, pages 79-86. ACM.

Bo Pang and Lillian Lee. 2004. A sentimental education: sentiment analysis using subjectivity summarization based on minimum cuts. In *Proceedings of the 42nd Annual Meeting on Association for Computational Linguistics*, pages 271-278. Association for Computational Linguistics.

Richard Socher, Cliff Chiung-Yu Lin, Andrew Y. Ng, and Christopher D. Manning. 2011. Parsing natural scenes and natural language with recursive neural networks. In *Proceedings of the International Conference on Machine Learning*, pages 129-136. Bellevue.

Richard Socher, Brody Huval, Christopher D. Manning, and Andrew Y. Ng. 2012. Semantic Compositionality through Recursive Matrix-Vector Spaces. In *Proceedings of the Conference on Empirical Methods in Natural Language Processing*, pages 1201-1211. Association for Computational Linguistics.

Duyu Tang, Furu Wei, Nan Yang, Ming Zhou, Ting Liu, and Bing Qin. 2014. Learning Sentiment-Specific Word Embedding for Twitter Sentiment Classification. In *Proceedings of the 52nd Annual Meeting of the Association for Computational Linguistic*, pages 1555-1565. Association for Computational Linguistics.

Xuewei Tang and Xiaojun Wan. 2014. Learning Bilingual Embedding Model for Cross-language Sentiment Classification. In *Proceedings of 2014 IEEE/WIC/ACM International Joint Conferences on Web Intelligence (WI) and Intelligent Agent Technologies (IAT)*, pages 134-141. IEEE.

Pascal Vincent, Hugo Larochelle, Yoshua Bengio, and Pierre-Antoine Manzagol. 2008. Extracting and composing robust features with denoising autoencoders. In *Proceedings of the 25th international conference on Machine learning*, pages 1096-1103. ACM.

Xiaojun Wan. 2009. Co-training for cross-lingual sentiment classification. In *Proceedings of the Joint Conference of the 47th Annual Meeting of the ACL and the 4th International Joint Conference on Natural Language Processing of the AFNLP*, pages 235-243. Association for Computational Linguistics.

Yuan Wang, Zhaohui Li, Jie Liu, Zhicheng He, Yalou Huang, and Dong Li. 2014. Word Vector Modeling for Sentiment Analysis of Product Reviews. In *Proceedings of Natural Language Processing and Chinese Computing*, pages 168-180. Springer Verlag.

Huaping Zhang, Hongkui Yu, Deyi Xiong, and Qun Liu. 2003. HHMM-based Chinese Lexical Analyzer ICTCLAS. In *2nd SIGHAN workshop affiliated with 41th ACL*, pages 184-187. Association for Computational Linguistics.

Guangyou Zhou, Tingting He, and Jun Zhao. 2014b. Bridging the Language Gap: Learning Distributed Semantics for Cross-Lingual Sentiment Classification. In *Proceedings of Natural Language Processing and Chinese Computing*, pages 138-149. Springer Verlag.

Huiwei Zhou, Long Chen, and Degen Huang. 2014a. Cross-lingual sentiment classification based on denoising autoencoder. In *Proceedings of Natural Language Processing and Chinese Computing*, pages 181-192. Springer Verlag.

Will Y. Zou, Richard Socher, Daniel Cer, and Christopher D. Manning. 2013. Bilingual Word Embedding for Phrase-Based Machine Translation. In *Proceedings of the 2013 Conference on Empirical Methods in Natural Language Processing*, pages 1393-1398.

Content Models for Survey Generation: A Factoid-Based Evaluation

Rahul Jha[⋆], **Catherine Finegan-Dollak**[⋆], **Reed Coke**[⋆], **Ben King**[⋆], **Dragomir Radev**[⋆†]

[⋆] Department of EECS, University of Michigan, USA
[†] School of Information, University of Michigan, USA
{rahuljha,cfdollak,reedcoke,benking,radev}@umich.edu

Abstract

We present a new factoid-annotated dataset for evaluating content models for scientific survey article generation containing 3,425 sentences from 7 topics in *natural language processing*. We also introduce a novel HITS-based content model for automated survey article generation called HITSUM that exploits the lexical network structure between sentences from citing and cited papers. Using the factoid-annotated data, we conduct a pyramid evaluation and compare HITSUM with two previous state-of-the-art content models: C-Lexrank, a network based content model, and TOPICSUM, a Bayesian content model. Our experiments show that our new content model captures useful survey-worthy information and outperforms C-Lexrank by 4% and TOPICSUM by 7% in pyramid evaluation.

Factoid	Weight
Question Answering	
answer extraction	6
question classification	6
definition of question answering	5
TREC QA track	5
information retrieval	5
Dependency Parsing	
non-projective dependency structures / trees	6
projectivity / projective dependency trees	6
deterministic parsing approaches: Nivre's algorithm	5
terminology: head - dependent	4
grammar driven approaches for dependency parsing	4

Table 1: Sample factoids from the topics of *question answering* and *dependency parsing* along with their factoid weights.

1 Introduction

Survey article generation is the task of automatically building informative surveys for scientific topics. Given the rapid growth of publications in scientific fields, the development of such systems is crucial as human-written surveys exist for a limited number of topics and get outdated quickly. In this paper, we investigate content models for extracting survey-worthy information from scientific papers. Such models are an essential component of any system for automatic survey article generation. Earlier work in the area of survey article generation has investigated content models based on lexical networks (Mohammad et al., 2009; Qazvinian and Radev, 2008). These models take as input citing sentences that describe important papers on the topic and assign them a salience score based on centrality in a lexical network formed by the input citing sentences. In this paper, we propose a new content model based on network structure previously unexplored for this task that exploits the lexical relationship between citing sentences and the sentences from the original papers that they cite. Our new formulation of the lexical network structure fits nicely with the hubs and authorities model for identifying important nodes in a network (Kleinberg, 1999), leading to a new content model called HITSUM. In addition to this new content model, we also describe how Bayesian content models previously explored in the news domain can be adapted for the content modeling task for survey generation.

For the task of evaluating various content models discussed in this paper, we have annotated a total of 3,425 sentences across 7 topics in the field of *natural language processing* with factoids from each of the topics. The factoids we use were extracted from existing survey articles and tutorials on each topic (Jha et al., 2013), and thus represent information that must be captured by a survey article on the corresponding topic. Each of the factoids is assigned a weight based on its frequency in the surveys/tutorials, which allows us to do pyra-

Proceedings of the 53rd Annual Meeting of the Association for Computational Linguistics and the 7th International Joint Conference on Natural Language Processing, pages 441–450,
Beijing, China, July 26-31, 2015.

Topic	# Sentences
dependency parsing	487
named entity recognition	383
question answering	452
semantic role labeling	466
sentiment analysis	613
summarization	507
word sense disambiguation	425

Table 2: List of seven NLP topics used in our experiments along with input size.

mid evaluation of our content models. Some sample factoids are shown in Table 1. Evaluation using factoids extracted from existing survey articles can help us understand the limits of automated survey article generation and how well these systems can be expected to perform. For example, if certain kinds of factoids are missing consistently from our input sentences, improvements in content models are unlikely to get us closer to the goal of generating survey articles that match those generated by humans, and effort must be directed to extracting text from other sources that will contain the missing information. On the other hand, if most of the factoids exist in the input sentences but important factoids are not found by the content models, we can think of strategies for improving these models by doing error analysis.

The main contributions of this paper are:

- HITSUM, a new HITS-based content model for automatic survey generation for scientific topics.
- A new dataset of 3,425 factoid-annotated sentences for scientific articles in 7 topics.
- Experimental results for pyramid evaluation comparing three existing content models (Lexrank, C-Lexrank, TOPICSUM) with HITSUM.

The rest of this paper is organized as follows. Section 2 describes the dataset used in our experiment and the factoid annotation process. Section 3 describes each of the content models used in our experiments including HITSUM. Section 4 describes our experiments and Section 5 summarizes the results. We summarize the related work in Section 6 and conclude in Section 7.

2 Data

Prior research in automatic survey generation has explored using text from different parts of scientific papers. Some of the recent work has treated survey generation as a direct extension of single paper summarization (Qazvinian and Radev, 2008) and used citing sentences to a set of relevant papers as the input for the summarizer (Mohammad et al., 2009; Qazvinian et al., 2013). However, in our prior work, we have observed that it's difficult to generate coherent and readable summaries using just citing sentences and have proposed the use of sentences from introductory texts of papers that cite a number of important papers on a topic (Jha et al., 2015). The use of full text allows for the use of discourse structure of these documents in framing coherent and readable surveys. Since the content models we explore are meant to be part of a larger system that should be able to generate coherent and readable survey articles, we use the introduction sentences for our experiments as well.

The corpus we used for extracting our experimental data was the ACL Anthology Network, a comprehensive bibliographic dataset that contains full text and citations for papers in most of the important venues in *natural language processing* (Radev et al., 2013). An oracle method is used for selecting the initial set of papers for each topic. For each topic, the bibliographies of at least three human-written surveys were extracted, and any papers that appeared in more than one survey were added to the target document set for the topic.

The text for summarization is extracted from introductory sections of papers that cite papers in the target document set. The intuition behind this is that the introductory sections of papers that cite these target document summarize the research in papers from the target document set as well as the relationships between these papers. Thus, these introductions can be thought of as mini-surveys for specific aspects of the topic; combining text from these introductory sections should allow us to generate good comprehensive survey articles for the topic[1]. For our experiments, we sort the citing papers based on the number of papers they cite

[1]Other sections of papers might have such information, e.g. related work. Initial data analysis showed, however, that not all papers in our corpus had related work sections. Thus for consistency, we decided to use introduction sections. The perfect system for this task would be able to extract "related work style" text segments from an entire paper.

Input sentence	Factoids
According to [1] , the corpus based supervised machine learning methods are the most successful approaches to WSD where contextual features have been used mainly to distinguish ambiguous words in these methods.	supervised wsd, corpus based wsd
Compared with supervised methods, unsupervised methods do not require tagged corpus, but the precision is usually lower than that of the supervised methods.	supervised wsd, unsupervised wsd
Word sense disambiguation (WSD) has been a hot topic in natural language processing, which is to determine the sense of an ambiguous word in a specific context.	definition of word sense disambiguation
Improvement in the accuracy of identifying the correct word sense will result in better machine translation systems, information retrieval systems, etc.	wsd for machine translation, wsd for information retrieval
The SENSEVAL evaluation framework (Kilgarriff 1998) was a DARPA-style competition designed to bring some conformity to the field of WSD, although it has yet to achieve that aim completely.	senseval

Table 3: Sample input sentences from the topic of *word sense disambiguation* annotated with factoids.

in the target document set, pick the top 20 papers, and extract sentences from their introductions to form the input text for the summarizer. The seven topics used in our experiments and input size for each topic are shown in Table 2.

Once the input text for each topic has been extracted, we annotate the sentences in the input text with factoids for that topic. Some annotated sentences in the topic of *word sense disambiguation* are shown in Table 3. Given this new annotated data, we can compare how the factoids are distributed across different citing sentences (as annotated by Jha et al. (2013)) and introduction sentences that we have annotated. For this, we divide the factoids into five categories: definitions, venue, resources, methodology, and applications. The fractional distribution of factoids in these categories is shown in Table 4. We can see that the distribution of factoids relating to venues, methodology and applications is similar for the two datasets. However, factoids related to definitional sentences are almost completely missing in the citing sentences data. This lack of background information in citing sentences is one of the motivations for using introduction sentences for survey article generation as opposed to previous work.

The complete set of factoids as well as annotated sentences for all the topics is available for download at `http://clair.si.umich.edu/corpora/Surveyor_CM_Data.tar.gz`.

3 Content Models

We now describe each of the content models used in our experiments.

Factoid category	% Citing	% Intro
definitions	0	4
venue	6	6
resources	18	2
methodology	70	83
applications	6	5

Table 4: Fractional distribution of factoids across various categories in citing sentences vs introduction sentences.

3.1 Lexrank

Lexrank is a network-based content selection algorithm that serves as a baseline for our experiments. Given an input set of sentences, it first creates a network using these sentences where each node represents a sentence and each edge represents the tf-idf cosine similarity between the sentences. Two methods for creating the network are possible. First, we can remove all edges that are lower than a certain threshold of similarity (generally set to 0.1). The Lexrank value for a node $p(u)$ in this case is calculated as:

$$\frac{1-d}{N} + d \sum_{v \in adj[u]} \frac{p(v)}{deg(v)}$$

Where N is the total number of sentences, d is the damping factor that controls the probability of a random jump (usually set to 0.85), $deg(v)$ is the degree of the node v, and $adj[u]$ is the set of nodes connected to the node u. A different way of creating the network is to treat the sentence similarities as edge weights and use the adjacency matrix as a transition matrix after normalizing the rows; the formula then becomes:

A dictionary such as the LDOCE has broad coverage of word senses, useful for WSD .
This paper describes a program that disambiguates English word senses in unrestricted text using statistical models of the major Roget's Thesaurus categories.
Our technique offers benefits both for online semantic processing and for the challenging task of mapping word senses across multiple MRDs in creating a merged lexical database.
The words in the sentences may be any of the 28,000 headwords in Longman's Dictionary of Contemporary English (LDOCE) and are disambiguated relative to the senses given in LDOCE.
This paper describes a heuristic approach to automatically identifying which senses of a machine-readable dictionary (MRD) headword are semantically related versus those which correspond to fundamentally different senses of the word.

Figure 1: A sentence from P_{citing} with a high hub score (bolded) and some of sentences from P_{cited} that it links to (italicised). The sentence from P_{citing} obtain a high hub score by being connected to the sentences with high authority scores.

$$\frac{1-d}{N} + d \sum_{v \in adj[u]} \frac{cos(u,v)}{TotalCos_v} p(v)$$

Where $cos(u, v)$ gives the tf-idf cosine similarity between sentence u and v and $TotalCos_v = \sum_{z \in adj[v]} cos(z, v)$. In our experiments, we employ this second formulation. The above equation can be solved efficiently using the power method (Newman, 2010) to obtain $p(u)$ for each node, which is then used as the score for ordering the sentences. The final Lexrank values $p(u)$ for a node represent the stationary distribution of the Markov chain represented by the transition matrix. Lexrank has been shown to perform well in summarization experiments (Erkan and Radev, 2004).

3.2 C-Lexrank

C-Lexrank is a clustering-based summarization system that was proposed by Qazvinian and Radev (2008) to summarize different perspectives in citing sentences that reference a paper or a topic. To create summaries, C-LexRank constructs a fully connected network in which vertices are sentences, and edges are cosine similarities calculated using the tf-idf vectors of citation sentences. It then employs a hierarchical agglomeration clustering algorithm proposed by Clauset et al. (2004) to find communities of sentences that discuss the same scientific contributions. Once the graph is clustered and communities are formed, the method extracts sentences from different clusters to build a summary. It iterates through the clusters from largest to smallest, choosing the most salient sentence of each cluster, until the summary length limit is reached. The salience of a sentence in its cluster is defined as its Lexrank value in the lexical network formed by sentences in the cluster.

3.3 HITSUM

The input set of sentences in our data come from introductory sections of papers that cite important papers on a topic. We'll refer to the set of citing papers that provide the input text for the summarizer as P_{citing} and the set of important papers that represent the research we are trying to summarize as P_{cited}. Both Lexrank and C-Lexrank work by finding central sentences in a network formed by the input sentences and thus, only use the lexical information present in P_{citing}, while ignoring additional lexical information from the papers in P_{cited}. We now present a formulation that uses the network structure that exists between the sentences in the two sets of papers to incorporate additional lexical information into the summarization system. This system is based on the hubs and authorities or the HITS model (Kleinberg, 1999) and hence is called HITSUM.

HITSUM, in addition to the sentences from the introductory sections of papers in P_{citing}, also uses sentences from the abstracts of P_{cited}. It starts by computing the tf-idf cosine similarity between the sentences of each paper $p_i \in P_{citing}$ with the sentences in the abstracts of each paper $p_j \in P_{cited}$ that is directly cited by p_i. A directed edge is created between every sentence s_i in p_i and s_j in p_j if $sim(s_i, s_j) > s_{min}$, where s_{min} is a similarity threshold (set to 0.1 for our experiments). Once this process has been completed for all papers in P_{citing}, we end up with a bipartite graph between sentences from P_{citing} and P_{cited}.

In this bipartite graph, sentences in P_{cited} that

ϕ_B		$\phi_{C/QA}$		$\phi_{D/J07-1005}$		$\phi_{C/NER}$		$\phi_{D/I08-1071}$	
the	0.066	question	0.044	metathesaurus	0.00032	ne	0.028	wikipedia	0.0087
of	0.040	questions	0.038	umls	0.00032	entity	0.022	pages	0.0053
and	0.034	answer	0.028	biomedical	0.00024	named	0.022	million	0.0018
a	0.029	answering	0.022	relevance	0.00024	entities	0.017	extracting	0.0018
in	0.027	qa	0.021	citation	0.00024	ner	0.014	articles	0.0018
to	0.027	answers	0.017	wykoff	0.00024	names	0.009	contributors	0.0018
is	0.017	2001	0.016	bringing	0.00016	location	0.008	version	0.0009
for	0.014	system	0.011	appropriately	0.00016	tagging	0.007	dakka	0.0009
that	0.012	trec	0.008	organized	0.00016	recognition	0.007	service	0.0009
we	0.011	factoid	0.008	foundation	0.00016	classes	0.007	academic	0.0009

Figure 2: Top words from different word distributions learned by TopicSum on our input document set of 15 topics. ϕ_B is the background word distribution that captures stop words. $\phi_{C/QA}$ and $\phi_{C/NER}$ are the word distributions for the topics of *question answering* and *named entity recognition* respectively. $\phi_{D/J07-1005}$ is the document-specific word distribution for a single paper in *question answering* that focuses on clinical question answering. $\phi_{D/I08-1071}$ is the document-specific word distribution for a single paper in *named entity recognition* that focuses on named entity recognition in Wikipedia articles.

have a lot of incoming edges represent sentences that presented important contributions in the field. Similarly, sentences in P_{citing} that have a lot of outgoing edges represent sentences that summarize a number of important contributions in the field. This suggests using the HITS algorithm, which, given a network, assigns hubs and authorities scores to each node in the network in a mutually reinforcing way. Thus, nodes with high authority scores are those that are pointed to by a number of good hubs, and nodes with high hub scores are those that point to a number of good authorities. This can be formalized with the following equation for the hub score of a node:

$$h(v) = \sum_{u \in successors(v)} a(u)$$

Where $h(v)$ is the hub score for node v, $successors(v)$ is the set of all nodes that v has an edge to, and $a(u)$ is the authority score for node u. Similarly, the authority score for each node is computed as:

$$a(v) = \sum_{u \in predecessors(v)} h(u)$$

Where $predecessors(v)$ is the set of all nodes that have an edge to v. The hub and authority score for each node can be computed using the power method that starts with an initial value and iteratively updates the scores for each node based on the above equations until the hub and authority scores for each node converge to within a tolerance value (set to 1E-08 for our experiments).

In our bipartite lexical network, we expect sentences in P_{cited} receiving high authority scores to be the ones reporting important contributions and sentences in P_{citing} that receive high hub scores to be sentences summarizing important contributions. Figure 1 shows an example of a sentence with a high hub score from the topic of *word sense disambiguation*, along with some of the sentences that it points to. HitSum computes the hub and authority score for each sentence in the lexical network and then uses the hub scores for sentences in P_{citing} as their relevance score. Sentences from P_{cited} are part of the lexical network, but are not used in the output summary.

3.4 TopicSum

TopicSum is a probabilistic content model presented in Haghighi and Vanderwende (2009) and is very similar to an earlier model called BayesSum proposed by Daumé and Marcu (2006). It is a hierarchical, LDA (Latent Dirichlet Allocation) style model that is based on the following generative story:[2] words in any sentence in the corpus can come from one of three word distributions: a background word distribution ϕ_B that flexibly models stop words, a content word distribution ϕ_C for each document set that models content relevant to the entire document set, and a document-specific word distribution ϕ_D. The word distributions are learned using Gibbs sampling. Given n document sets each with k doc-

[2]To avoid confusion in use of the term "topic," in this paper we refer to topics in the LDA sense as "word distributions." "Topics" in this paper refer to the natural language processing topics such as *question answering*, *word sense disambiguation*, etc.

Topic	Lexrank	C-Lexrank	TopicSum	HitSum
dependency parsing	0.47	0.76	0.62	1.00*
named entity recognition	0.80	0.89	0.90*	0.80
question answering	0.65	0.67	0.65	0.76*
sentiment analysis	0.64	0.62	0.75*	0.63
semantic role labeling	0.75*	0.67	0.65	0.69
summarization	0.52	0.75*	0.57	0.68
word sense disambiguation	0.78	0.66	0.67	0.79*
Average	**0.66**	**0.72**	**0.69**	**0.76***

Table 5: Pyramid scores obtained by different content models for each topic along with average scores for each model across all topics. For each topic as well as the average, the best performing method has been highlighted with a *.

uments, we get n content word distributions and $n * k$ document-specific distributions leading to a total of $1 + n + n * k$ word distributions.

To illustrate the kind of distributions TopicSum learns in our dataset, Figure 2 shows the top words along with their probabilities from the background word distribution, two content distributions and two document-specific word distributions. We see that the model effectively captures general content words for each topic. $\phi_{C/QA}$ is the word distribution for the topic of *question answering*, while $\phi_{D/J07-1005}$ is the document-specific word distribution for a specific paper in the document set for *question answering*[3] that focuses on clinical question answering. The word distribution $\phi_{D/J07-1005}$ contains words that are relevant to the specific subtopic in the paper, while $\phi_{C/QA}$ contains content words relevant to the general topic of *question answering*. Similar results can be seen in the word distributions for *named entity recognition* $\phi_{C/NER}$ and the document-specific word distribution for a specific paper in the topic $\phi_{D/I08-1071}$[4] that focuses on comparable entity mining.

These topics, learned using Gibbs sampling, can be used to select sentences for a summary in the following way. To summarize a document set, we greedily select sentences that minimize the KL-divergence of our summary to the document-set-specific topic. Thus, the score for each sentence s is $KL(\phi_C || P_s)$ where P_s is the sentence word distribution with add-one smoothing applied to both distributions. Using this objective, sentences that contain words from the content word distribution with high probability are more likely to be selected in the generated summary.

We implemented TopicSum in Python using Numpy and then optimized it using Scipy Weave. This code is available for use at `https://github.com/rahuljha/content-models`. The repository also contains Python code for HitSum.

4 Experiments

For evaluating our content models, we generated 2,000-character-long summaries using each of the systems (Lexrank, C-Lexrank, HitSum, and TopicSum) for each of the topics. The summaries are generated by ranking the input sentences using each content model and picking the top sentences till the budget of 2,000 characters is reached. Each of these summaries is then given a pyramid score (Nenkova and Passonneau, 2004) computed using the factoids assigned to each sentence.

For the pyramid evaluation, the factoids are organized in a pyramid of order n. The top tier in this pyramid contains the highest weighted factoids, the next tier contains the second highest weighted factoids, and so on. The score assigned to a summary is the ratio of the sum of the weights of the factoids it contains to the sum of weights of an optimal summary with the same number of factoids. Pyramid evaluation allows us to capture how each content model performs in terms of selecting sentences with the most highly weighted factoids. Since the factoids have been extracted from human-written surveys and tutorials on each of the topics, the pyramid score gives us an idea of the survey-worthiness of the sentences selected by

[3]Dina Demner-Fushman and Jimmy Lin. 2007. *Answering Clinical Questions with Knowledge-Based and Statistical Techniques.* Computational Linguistics.

[4]Wisam Dakka and Silviu Cucerzan. 2008. *Augmenting wikipedia with named entity tags.* In Proceedings of IJCNLP.

Question classification is a crucial component of modern question answering system.
A what-type question is defined as the one whose question word is 'what', 'which', 'name' or 'list'.
This metaclassifier beats all published numbers on standard question classification benchmarks [4.4].
Due to its challenge, this paper focuses on what-type question classification.
In this paper, we focus on fine-category classification.
The promise of a machine learning approach is that the QA system builder can now focus on designing features and providing labeled data, rather than coding and maintaining complex heuristic rule bases.

Figure 3: Part of the summary generated by HITSUM for the topic of *question answering*.

each content model.

5 Results and Discussion

The results of pyramid evaluation are summarized in Table 5. It shows the pyramid score obtained by each system on each of the topics as well as the average score. The highest performing system on average is HITSUM with an average performance of 76%. HITSUM does especially well for the topics of *dependency parsing*, *question answering*, and *word sense disambiguation*. The second best performing system is C-Lexrank, which is not surprising because it was developed specifically for the task of scientific paper summarization. However, HITSUM outperforms C-Lexrank on several topics and by 4% on average.

Figure 3 shows part of the summary generated by HITSUM for the topic of question answering. The summary contains mostly informative sentences about different aspects of question answering. One obvious drawback of this summary is that it's not very coherent and readable. However, previous work has shown how network based content models can be combined with discourse models to generate informative yet readable summaries (Jha et al., 2015). We looked at some of the network statistics of the lexical networks used by HITSUM. One of the things we noticed is that the lexical networks for topics where HITSUM performs well seem to have higher degree assortativity compared to the topics for which it doesn't perform well. High degree assortativity in lexical networks means sentences with high degree tend to be linked to other sentences with high degree. This suggests that HITS performs well for topics where a set of important factoids are mentioned in many citing and source sentences. A larger evaluation dataset is needed for a more thorough analysis of how the network properties of these lexical networks correlate with the performance of various content models.

TOPICSUM does well on the topics of *named entity recognition* and *sentiment analysis*, but does not do well on average. This can be attributed to the fact that it was developed as a content model for the domain of news summarization and does not translate well to our domain. All systems outperform Lexrank, which achieves the lowest average score. This result is also intuitive, because every other system in our evaluation uses additional information not used by Lexrank: C-Lexrank exploits the community structure in the input set of sentences, HITSUM exploits the lexical information from cited sentences, and TOPICSUM exploits information about global word distribution across all topics.

The different systems we tried in our evaluation depend on using different lexical information and seem to perform well for different topics. This suggests that further gains can be made by combining these systems. For example, C-Lexrank and HITSUM can be combined by utilizing both the network formed by citing sentences and the network between the citing sentences and the cited sentences into a larger lexical network. TOPICSUM scores can be combined with these network-based system by using the TOPICSUM scores as a prior for each node, and then running either Pagerank or HITS on top of it. We leave exploration of such hybrid systems to future work.

6 Related Work

The goal of content models in the context of summarization is to extract a representation from input text that can help in identifying important sentences that should be in the output summary. Our work is related to two main classes of content models: network-based methods and probabilistic methods. We summarize related work for each of these classes of content models, followed by a short summary of the related work in the domain of scientific summarization.

Network-based content models: Network-based content models (Erkan and Radev, 2004; Mihalcea and Tarau, 2004) work by converting the input sentences into a network. Each sentence is represented by a node in the network, and the edges between sentences are given weight based on the similarities of sentences. They then run Pagerank on this network, and sentences are selected based on their Pagerank score in the network. For computing Pagerank, the network can either be pruned by removing edges that have weights less than a certain threshold, or a weighted version of Pagerank can be run on the network. The method can also be modified for query-focused summarization (Otterbacher et al., 2009). C-Lexrank (Qazvinian and Radev, 2008) modifies Lexrank by first running a clustering algorithm on the network to partition the network into different communities and then selecting sentences from each community by running Lexrank on the sub-network within each community. C-Lexrank was also used in the task of automated survey generation with encouraging results (Mohammad et al., 2009).

Probabilistic content models: One of the first probabilistic content models seems to be BAYESSUM (Daumé and Marcu, 2006), designed for query-focused summarization. BAYESSUM models a set of document collections using a hierarchical LDA style model. Each word in a sentence can be generated using one of three language models: 1) a general English language model that captures English filler or background knowledge, 2) a document-specific language model, and 3) a query language model. These language models are inferred using expectation propagation, and then sentences are ranked based on their likelihood of being generated from the query language model. A similar model for general multidocument summarization called TOPICSUM was proposed by Haghighi and Vanderwende (2009), where the query language model is replaced by a document-collection-specific language model; thus sentences are selected based on how likely they are to contain information that summarizes the entire document collection instead of information pertaining to individual documents or background knowledge.

Barzilay and Lee (2004) present a Hidden Markov Model (HMM) based content model where the hidden states of the HMM represent the topics in the text. The transition probabilities are learned through Viterbi decoding. They show that the HMM model can be used for both reordering of sentences for coherence and discriminative scoring of sentences for extractive summarization. Fung and Ngai (2006) present a similar HMM-based model for multi-document summarization. Jiang and Zhai (2005) proposed an HMM-based model for the problem of extracting coherent passages relevant to a query from a relevant document. They learn an HMM with two background states (B_1 and B_2) and a query-relevant state (R), each associated with a language model. The HMM starts in background state B_1, switches to relevant state R and then switches to the next background state B_2. The sentences that the HMM emits while in R constitute the query-relevant passage from the document.

Scientific summarization: Early work in scientific summarization used abstracts of scientific articles to produce summaries of specific scientific papers (Kupiec et al., 1995). However, later work (Elkiss et al., 2008) showed that citation sentences are as important in understanding the main contributions of a paper.

Nanba and Okumura (1999) explored using reference information to build a system for supporting writing survey articles. Their system extracts citing sentences that describe a referred paper and identify the type of reference relationships. The type of references can be one of the three: 1) type B that base on other researcher's theory, 2) type C that compare with related works, or 3) type O representing relationships other than B or C. They posit that type C sentences are the most important for survey generation and can help show the similarities and differences among cited papers.

Teufel and Moens (2002) propose a method for summarizing scientific articles based on rhetorical status of sentences in scientific articles. They annotate sentences in a corpus of 80 scientific articles with rhetorical status, where the rhetorical status can be one of aim (specific research goal), textual (section structure), own (neutral description of own work), background (generally accepted background), contrast (comparison with other work), basis (agreement with or continuation of other work), and other (neutral description of other's work). They describe classifiers for tagging the rhetorical status of sentences automatically and present a method for using this to assign relevance score to sentences.

In other work, Kan et al. (2002) use a corpus of 2000 annotated bibliographies for scientific papers as a first step towards a supervised summarization system. They found that summaries in their corpus were mostly single-document abstractive summaries that were both indicative and informative and were organized around a "theme," making them ideal for query-based summarization. Mei and Zhai (2008) presented an impact-based summarization method for single-paper summarization that assigns relevance scores to sentences in a paper based on their similarity to the set of citing sentences that reference the paper.

More recently, Hoang and Kan (2010) present a method for automated related work generation. Their system takes as input a set of keywords arranged in a hierarchical fashion that describes a target paper's topic. They hypothesize that sentences in a related work provide either background information or specific contributions. They use two different models to extract these two kinds of sentences using the input tree and combines them to create the final output summary. Zhang et al. (2013) explore methods for biomedical summarization by identifying cliques in a network of semantic predications extracted from citations. These cliques are then clustered and labeled to identify different points of view represented in the summary.

7 Conclusion and Future Work

We have presented a new factoid-annotated dataset for evaluating content models for scientific survey article generation by annotating sentences from seven topics in *natural language processing*. We also introduce a new HITS-based content model called HitSum for survey article generation that exploits the lexical information from cited papers along with citing papers to rank input sentences for survey-worthiness. We conduct pyramid evaluation using our factoid dataset to compare HitSum with existing network-based methods (Lexrank, C-Lexrank) as well as methods based on Bayesian content modeling (TopicSum). On average, HitSum outperforms C-Lexrank by 4% and TopicSum by 7%. Since the different content models use different kinds of lexical information, further gains might be obtained by combining some of these models into a joint model. We plan to explore this in future work.

References

Regina Barzilay and Lillian Lee. 2004. Catching the drift: Probabilistic content models, with applications to generation and summarization. In Daniel Marcu Susan Dumais and Salim Roukos, editors, *HLT-NAACL 2004: Main Proceedings*, pages 113–120, Boston, Massachusetts, USA, May 2 - May 7. Association for Computational Linguistics.

Aaron Clauset, Mark E. J. Newman, and Cristopher Moore. 2004. Finding community structure in very large networks. *Phys. Rev. E*, 70(6):066111, Dec.

Hal Daumé, III and Daniel Marcu. 2006. Bayesian query-focused summarization. In *Proceedings of the 21st International Conference on Computational Linguistics and the 44th Annual Meeting of the Association for Computational Linguistics*, ACL-44, pages 305–312, Stroudsburg, PA, USA. Association for Computational Linguistics.

Aaron Elkiss, Siwei Shen, Anthony Fader, Güneş Erkan, David States, and Dragomir R. Radev. 2008. Blind men and elephants: What do citation summaries tell us about a research article? *Journal of the American Society for Information Science and Technology*, 59(1):51–62.

Güneş Erkan and Dragomir R. Radev. 2004. Lexrank: Graph-based centrality as salience in text summarization. *Journal of Artificial Intelligence Research (JAIR)*.

Pascale Fung and Grace Ngai. 2006. One story, one flow: Hidden markov story models for multilingual multidocument summarization. *ACM Trans. Speech Lang. Process.*, 3(2):1–16, July.

Aria Haghighi and Lucy Vanderwende. 2009. Exploring content models for multi-document summarization. In *Proceedings of Human Language Technologies: The 2009 Annual Conference of the North American Chapter of the Association for Computational Linguistics*, NAACL '09, pages 362–370, Stroudsburg, PA, USA. Association for Computational Linguistics.

Cong Duy Vu Hoang and Min-Yen Kan. 2010. Towards automated related work summarization. In *Proceedings of the 23rd International Conference on Computational Linguistics: Posters*, COLING '10, pages 427–435, Stroudsburg, PA, USA. Association for Computational Linguistics.

Rahul Jha, Amjad Abu-Jbara, and Dragomir R. Radev. 2013. A system for summarizing scientific topics starting from keywords. In *Proceedings of The Association for Computational Linguistics (short paper)*.

Rahul Jha, Reed Coke, and Dragomir R. Radev. 2015. Surveyor: A system for generating coherent survey articles for scientific topics. In *Proceedings of the Twenty-Ninth AAAI Conference*.

Jing Jiang and ChengXiang Zhai. 2005. Accurately extracting coherent relevant passages using hidden Markov models. pages 289–290.

Min-Yen Kan, Judith L. Klavans, and Kathleen R. McKeown. 2002. Using the Annotated Bibliography as a Resource for Indicative Summarization. In *The International Conference on Language Resources and Evaluation (LREC)*, Las Palmas, Spain.

Jon M. Kleinberg. 1999. Authoritative sources in a hyperlinked environment. *J. ACM*, 46:604–632, September.

Julian Kupiec, Jan Pedersen, and Francine Chen. 1995. A trainable document summarizer. In *Proceedings of the 18th Annual International ACM SIGIR Conference on Research and Development in Information Retrieval (SIGIR-95)*, pages 68–73.

Qiaozhu Mei and ChengXiang Zhai. 2008. Generating impact-based summaries for scientific literature. In *Proceedings of the 46th Annual Conference of the Association for Computational Linguistics (ACL-08)*, pages 816–824.

Rada Mihalcea and Paul Tarau. 2004. TextRank: Bringing order into texts. In *Proceedings of the Conference on Empirical Methods in Natural Language Processing (EMNLP-04)*, July.

Saif Mohammad, Bonnie Dorr, Melissa Egan, Ahmed Hassan, Pradeep Muthukrishan, Vahed Qazvinian, Dragomir Radev, and David Zajic. 2009. Using citations to generate surveys of scientific paradigms. In *Proceedings of Human Language Technologies: The 2009 Annual Conference of the North American Chapter of the Association for Computational Linguistics*, NAACL '09, pages 584–592, Stroudsburg, PA, USA. Association for Computational Linguistics.

Hidetsugu Nanba and Manabu Okumura. 1999. Towards multi-paper summarization using reference information. In *Proceedings of the 16th International Joint Conference on Artificial Intelligence (IJCAI-99)*, pages 926–931.

Ani Nenkova and Rebecca Passonneau. 2004. Evaluating content selection in summarization: The pyramid method. In *Proceedings of the North American Chapter of the Association for Computational Linguistics - Human Language Technologies (HLT-NAACL '04)*.

Mark E. J. Newman. 2010. *Networks: An Introduction*. Oxford University Press.

Jahna Otterbacher, Gunes Erkan, and Dragomir R. Radev. 2009. Biased lexrank: Passage retrieval using random walks with question-based priors. *Inf. Process. Manage.*, 45(1):42–54, January.

Vahed Qazvinian and Dragomir R. Radev. 2008. Scientific paper summarization using citation summary networks. In *Proceedings of the 22nd International Conference on Computational Linguistics (COLING-08)*, Manchester, UK.

Vahed Qazvinian, Dragomir R. Radev, Saif M. Mohammad, Bonnie Dorr, David Zajic, Michael Whidby, and Taesun Moon. 2013. Generating extractive summaries of scientific paradigms. *J. Artif. Int. Res.*, 46(1):165–201, January.

Dragomir R. Radev, Pradeep Muthukrishnan, Vahed Qazvinian, and Amjad Abu-Jbara. 2013. The acl anthology network corpus. *Language Resources and Evaluation*, pages 1–26.

Simone Teufel and Marc Moens. 2002. Summarizing scientific articles: experiments with relevance and rhetorical status. *Computational Linguistics*, 28(4):409–445.

Han Zhang, Marcelo Fiszman, Dongwook Shin, Bartlomiej Wilkowski, and Thomas C. Rindflesch. 2013. Clustering cliques for graph-based summarization of the biomedical research literature. *BMC Bioinformatics*, 14:182.

Training a Natural Language Generator From Unaligned Data

Ondřej Dušek and **Filip Jurčíček**
Charles University in Prague, Faculty of Mathematics and Physics
Institute of Formal and Applied Linguistics
Malostranské náměstí 25, CZ-11800 Prague, Czech Republic
{odusek,jurcicek}@ufal.mff.cuni.cz

Abstract

We present a novel syntax-based natural language generation system that is trainable from unaligned pairs of input meaning representations and output sentences. It is divided into sentence planning, which incrementally builds deep-syntactic dependency trees, and surface realization. Sentence planner is based on A* search with a perceptron ranker that uses novel differing subtree updates and a simple future promise estimation; surface realization uses a rule-based pipeline from the Treex NLP toolkit.

Our first results show that training from unaligned data is feasible, the outputs of our generator are mostly fluent and relevant.

1 Introduction

We present a novel approach to natural language generation (NLG) that does not require fine-grained alignment in training data and uses deep dependency syntax for sentence plans. We include our first results on the BAGEL restaurant recommendation data set of Mairesse et al. (2010).

In our setting, the task of a natural language generator is that of converting an abstract meaning representation (MR) into a natural language utterance. This corresponds to the sentence planning and surface realization NLG stages as described by Reiter and Dale (2000). It also reflects the intended usage in a spoken dialogue system (SDS), where the NLG component is supposed to translate a system output action into a sentence. While the content planning NLG stage has been used in SDS (e.g., Rieser and Lemon (2010)), we believe that deciding upon the contents of the system's utterance is generally a task for the dialogue manager. We focus mainly on the sentence planning part in this work, and reuse an existing rule-based surface realizer to test the capabilities of the generator in an end-to-end setting.

Current NLG systems usually require a separate training data alignment step (Mairesse et al., 2010; Konstas and Lapata, 2013). Many of them use a CFG or operate in a phrase-based fashion (Angeli et al., 2010; Mairesse et al., 2010), which limits their ability to capture long-range syntactic dependencies. Our generator includes alignment learning into sentence planner training and uses deep-syntactic trees with a rule-based surface realization step, which ensures grammatical correctness of the outputs. Unlike previous approaches to trainable sentence planning (e.g., Walker et al. (2001); Stent et al. (2004)), our generator does not require a handcrafted base sentence planner.

This paper is structured as follows: in Section 2, we describe the architecture of our generator. Sections 3 and 4 then provide further details on its main components. In Section 5, we describe our experiments on the BAGEL data set, followed by an analysis of the results in Section 6. Section 7 compares our generator to previous related works and Section 8 concludes the paper.

2 Generator Architecture

Our generator (see Figure 1) operates in two stages that roughly correspond to the traditional NLG stages of sentence planning and surface realization. In the first stage, a statistical sentence planner generates deep-syntactic dependency trees from the input meaning representation. These are converted into plain text sentences in the second stage by the (mostly rule-based) surface realizer.

We use deep-syntax dependency trees to represent the *sentence plan*, i.e. the intermediate data structure between the two aforementioned stages. These are ordered dependency trees that only contain nodes for content words (nouns, full verbs, adjectives, adverbs) and coordinating conjunctions.

Proceedings of the 53rd Annual Meeting of the Association for Computational Linguistics and the 7th International Joint Conference on Natural Language Processing, pages 451–461,
Beijing, China, July 26-31, 2015.

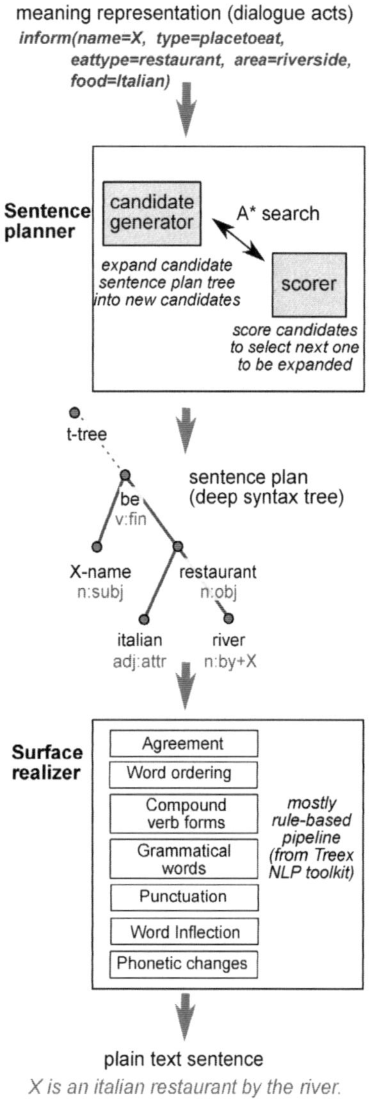

Figure 1: Overall structure of our generator

Each node has a *lemma* and a *formeme* – a concise description of its surface morphosyntactic form, which may include prepositions and/or subordinate conjunctions (Dušek et al., 2012). This structure is based on the deep-syntax trees of the Functional Generative Description (Sgall et al., 1986), but it has been simplified to fit our purposes (see Figure 1 in the middle).

There are several reasons for taking the traditional two-step approach to generation (as opposed to joint approaches, see Section 7) and using deep syntax trees as the sentence plan format: First, generating into deep syntax simplifies the task for the statistical sentence planner – the planner does not need to handle surface morphology and auxiliary words. Second, a rule-based syntactic realizer allows us to ensure grammatical correctness of the output sentences, which would be more difficult in a sequence-based and/or statistical approach.[1] And third, a rule-based surface realizer from our sentence plan format is relatively easy to implement and can be reused for any domain within the same language. As in our case, it is also possible to reuse and/or adapt an existing surface realizer (see Section 4).

Deep-syntax annotation of sentences in the training set is needed to train the sentence planner, but we assume automatic annotation and reuse an existing deep-syntactic analyzer from the Treex NLP framework (Popel and Žabokrtský, 2010).[2]

We use dialogue acts (DA) as defined in the BAGEL restaurant data set of Mairesse et al. (2010) as a MR in our experiments throughout this paper. Here, a DA consists of a dialogue act type, which is always "inform" in the set, and a list of slot-value pairs (SVPs) that contain information about a restaurant, such as food type or location (see the top of Figure 1). Our generator can be easily adapted to a different MR, though.

3 Sentence Planner

The sentence planner is based on a variant of the A* algorithm (Hart et al., 1968; Och et al., 2001; Koehn et al., 2003). It starts from an empty sentence plan tree and tries to find a path to the optimal sentence plan by iteratively adding nodes. It keeps two sets of hypotheses, i.e., candidate sentence plan trees, sorted by their score – hypotheses to expand (*open set*) and already expanded (*closed set*). It uses the following two subcomponents to guide the search:

- a *candidate generator* that is able to incrementally generate candidate sentence plan trees (see Section 3.1),
- a *scorer/ranker* that scores the appropriateness of these trees for the input MR (see Section 3.2).

[1] This issue would become more pressing in languages with richer morphology than English.

[2] See `http://ufal.mff.cuni.cz/treex`. Domain-independent deep syntax analysis for several languages is included in this framework; the English pipeline used here involves a statistical part-of-speech tagger (Spoustová et al., 2007) and a dependency parser (McDonald et al., 2005), followed by a rule-based conversion to deep syntax trees.

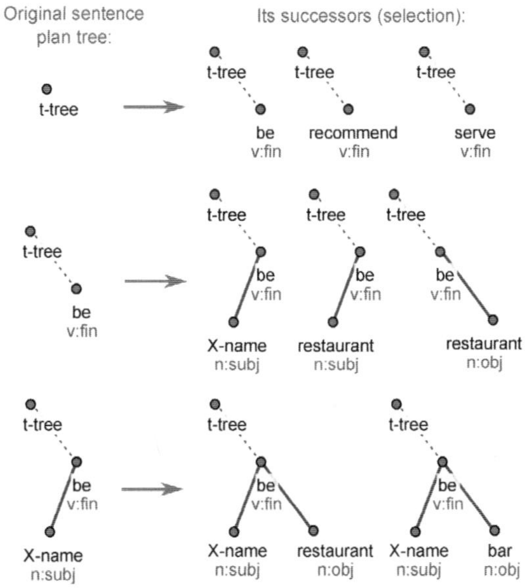

Figure 2: Candidate generator example inputs and outputs

The basic workflow of the sentence planner algorithm then looks as follows:

Init: Start from an *open set* with a single empty sentence plan tree and an empty *closed set*.

Loop:

1. Select the best-scoring candidate C from the *open set*. Add C to *closed set*.
2. The candidate generator generates **C**, a set of possible successors to C. These are trees that have more nodes than C and are deemed viable. Note that **C** may be empty.
3. The scorer scores all successors in **C** and if they are not already in the *closed set*, it adds them to the *open set*.
4. Check if the best successor in the *open set* scores better than the best candidate in the *closed set*.

Stop: The algorithm finishes if the top score in the *open set* is lower than the top score in the *closed set* for d consecutive iterations, or if there are no more candidates in the *open set*. It returns the best-scoring candidate from both sets.

3.1 Generating Sentence Plan Candidates

Given a sentence plan tree, which is typically incomplete and may be even empty, the candidate generator generates its successors by adding one new node in all possible positions and with all possible lemmas and formemes (see Figure 2). While a naive implementation – trying out any combination of lemmas and formemes found in the training data – works in principle, it leads to an unmanageable number of candidate trees even for a very small domain. Therefore, we include several rules that limit the number of trees generated:

1. Lemma-formeme compatibility – only nodes with a combination of lemma and formeme seen in the training data are generated.

2. Syntactic viability – the new node must be compatible with its parent node (i.e., this combination, including the dependency left/right direction, must be seen in the training data).

3. Number of children – no node can have more children than the maximum for this lemma-formeme combination seen in the training data.

4. Tree size – the generated tree cannot have more nodes than trees seen in the training data. The same limitation applies to the individual depth levels – the training data limit the number of nodes on the n-th depth level as well as the maximum depth of any tree.

   This is further conditioned on the input SVPs – the maximums are only taken from training examples that contain the same SVPs that appear on the current input.

5. Weak semantic compatibility – we only include nodes that appear in the training data alongside the elements of the input DA, i.e., nodes that appear in training examples containing SVPs from the current input,

6. Strong semantic compatibility – for each node (lemma and formeme), we make a "compatibility list" of SVPs and slots that are present in all training data examples containing this node. We then only allow generating this node if all of them are present in the current input DA. To allow for more generalization, this rule can be applied just to lemmas

(disregarding formemes), and a certain number of SVPs/slots from the compatibility list may be required at maximum.

Only Rules 4 (partly), 5, and 6 depend on the format of the input meaning representation. Using a different MR would require changing these rules to work with atomic substructures of the new MR instead of SVPs.

While especially Rules 5 and 6 exclude a vast number of potential candidate trees, this limitation is still much weaker than using hard alignment links between the elements of the MR and the output words or phrases. It leaves enough room to generate many combinations unseen in the training data (cf. Section 6) while keeping the search space manageable. To limit the space of potential tree candidates even further, one could also use automatic alignment scores between the elements of the input MR and the tree nodes (obtained using a tool such as GIZA++ (Och and Ney, 2003)).

3.2 Scoring Sentence Plan Trees

The scorer for the individual sentence plan tree candidates is a function that maps global features from the whole sentence plan tree t and the input MR m to a real-valued score that describes the fitness of t in the context of m.

We first describe the basic version of the scorer and then our two improvements – differing subtree updates and future promise estimation.

Basic perceptron scorer

The basic scorer is based on the linear perceptron ranker of Collins and Duffy (2002), where the score is computed as a simple dot product of the features and the corresponding weight vector:

$$\text{score}(t, m) = \mathbf{w}^\top \cdot \text{feat}(t, m)$$

In the training phase, the weights $\mathbf{w}$ are initialized to one. For each input MR, the system tries to generate the best sentence plan tree given current weights, t_{top}. The score of this tree is then compared to the score of the correct gold-standard tree t_{gold}.[3] If $t_{top} \neq t_{gold}$ and the gold-standard tree ranks worse than the generated one (score$(t_{top}, m) >$ score(t_{gold}, m)), the weight vector is updated by the feature value difference of the generated and the gold-standard tree:

$$\mathbf{w} = \mathbf{w} + \alpha \cdot (\text{feat}(t_{gold}, m) - \text{feat}(t_{top}, m))$$

where α is a predefined learning rate.

Differing subtree updates

In the basic version described above, the scorer is trained to score full sentence plan trees. However, it is also used to score incomplete sentence plans during the decoding. This leads to a bias towards bigger trees regardless of their fitness for the input MR. Therefore, we introduced a novel modification of the perceptron updates to improve scoring of incomplete sentence plans: In addition to updating the weights using the top-scoring candidate t_{top} and the gold-standard tree t_{gold} (see above), we also use their *differing subtrees* t^i_{top}, t^i_{gold} for additional updates.

Starting from the common subtree t_c of t_{top} and t_{gold}, pairs of differing subtrees t^i_{top}, t^i_{gold} are created by gradually adding nodes from t_{top} into t^i_{top} and from t_{gold} into t^i_{gold} (see Figure 3). To maintain the symmetry of the updates in case that the sizes of t_{top} and t_{gold} differ, more nodes may be added in one step.[4] The additional updates then look as follows:

$t^0_{top} = t^0_{gold} = t_c$
for i in $1, \ldots \min\{|t_{top}| - |t_c|, |t_{gold}| - |t_c|\} - 1$:
  $t^i_{top} = t^{i-1}_{top}$ + node(s) from t_{top}
  $t^i_{gold} = t^{i-1}_{gold}$ + node(s) from t_{gold}
  $\mathbf{w} = \mathbf{w} + \alpha \cdot (\text{feat}(t^i_{gold}, m) - \text{feat}(t^i_{top}, m))$

Future promise estimation

To further improve scoring of incomplete sentence plan trees, we incorporate a simple *future promise* estimation for the A* search intended to boost scores of sentence plans that are expected to further grow.[5] It is based on the expected number of children $E_c(n)$ of different node types (lemma-formeme pairs).[6] Given all nodes $n_1 \ldots n_{|t|}$ in a

[3]Note that the "gold-standard" sentence plan trees are actually produced by automatic annotation. For the purposes of scoring, they are, however, treated as gold standard.

[4]For example, if t_{gold} has 6 more nodes than t_c and t_{top} has 4 more, there will be 3 pairs of differing subtrees, with t^i_{gold} having 2, 4, and 5 more nodes than t_c and t^i_{top} having 1, 2, and 3 more nodes than t_c.

We have also evaluated a variant where both sets of subtrees t^i_{gold}, t^i_{top} were not equal in size, but this resulted in degraded performance.

[5]Note that this is not the same as future path cost in the original A* path search, but it plays an analogous role: weighing hypotheses of different size.

[6]$E_c(n)$ is measured as the average number of children over all occurrences of the given node type in the training data. It is expected to be domain-specific.

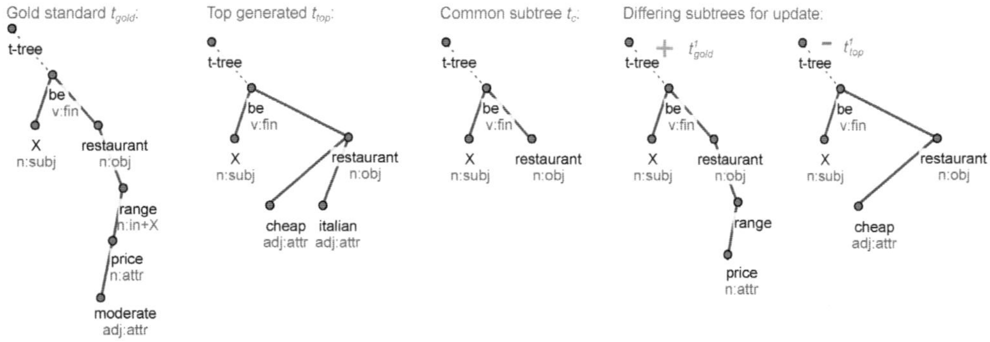

Figure 3: An example of differing subtrees

The gold standard tree t_{gold} has three more nodes than the common subtree t_c, while the top generated tree t_{top} has two more. Only one pair of differing subtrees t^1_{gold}, t^1_{top} is built, where two nodes are added into t^1_{gold} and one node into t^1_{top}.

sentence plan tree t, the future promise is computed in the following way:

$$\text{fp} = \lambda \cdot \sum \mathbf{w} \cdot \sum_{i=1}^{|t|} \max\{0, E_c(n_i) - c(n_i)\}$$

where $c(n_i)$ is the current number of children of node n_i, λ is a preset weight parameter, and $\sum \mathbf{w}$ is the sum of the current perceptron weights. Multiplying by the weights sum makes future promise values comparable to trees scores.

Future promise is added to tree scores throughout the tree generation process, but it is disregarded for the termination criterion in the *Stop* step of the generation algorithm and in perceptron weight updates.

Averaging weights and parallel training

To speed up training using parallel processing, we use the iterative parameter mixing approach of McDonald et al. (2010), where training data are split into several parts and weight updates are averaged after each pass through the training data. Following Collins (2002), we record the weights after each training pass, take an average at the end, and use this as the final weights for prediction.

4 Surface Realizer

We use the English surface realizer from the Treex NLP toolkit (cf. Section 2 and (Ptáček, 2008)). It is a simple pipeline of mostly rule-based blocks that gradually change the deep-syntactic trees into surface dependency trees, which are then linearized to sentences. It includes the following steps:

- *Agreement* – morphological attributes of some nodes are deduced based on agreement with other nodes (such as in subject-predicate agreement).
- *Word ordering* – the input trees are already ordered, so only a few rules for grammatical words are applied.
- *Compound verb forms* – additional verbal nodes are added for verbal particles (infinitive or phrasal verbs) and for compound expressions of tense, mood, and modality.
- *Grammatical words* – prepositions, subordinating conjunctions, negation particles, articles, and other grammatical words are added into the sentence.
- *Punctuation* – nodes for commas, final punctuation, quotes, and brackets are introduced.
- *Word Inflection* – words are inflected according to the information from formemes and agreement.
- *Phonetic changes* – English “a” becomes “an” based on the following word.

The realizer is designed as domain-independent and handles most English grammatical phenomena. A simple “round-trip” test – using automatic analysis with subsequent generation – reached a BLEU score (Papineni et al., 2002) of 89.79% against the original sentences on the whole BAGEL data set, showing only minor differences between the input sentence and generation output (mostly in punctuation).

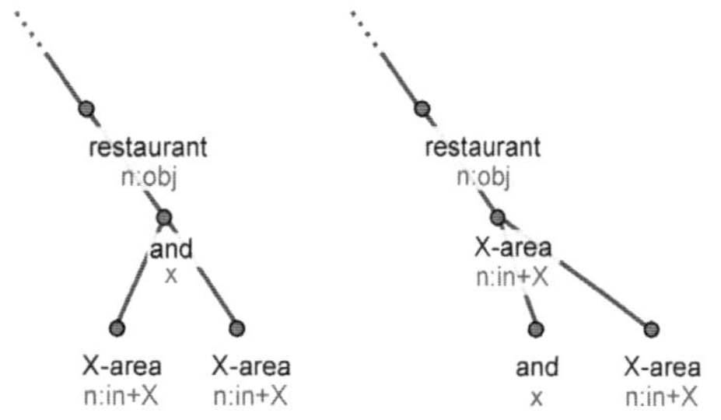

Figure 4: Coordination structures conversion: original (left) and our format (right).

5 Experimental Setup

Here we describe the data set used in our experiments, the needed preprocessing steps, and the settings of our generator specific to the data set.

5.1 Data set

We performed our experiments on the BAGEL data set of Mairesse et al. (2010), which fits our usage scenario in a spoken dialogue system and is freely available.[7] It contains a total of 404 sentences from a restaurant information domain (describing the restaurant location, food type, etc.), which correspond to 202 dialogue acts, i.e., each dialogue act has two paraphrases. Restaurant names, phone numbers, and other "non-enumerable" properties are abstracted – replaced by an "X" symbol – throughout the generation process. Note that while the data set contains alignment of source SVPs to target phrases, we do not use it in our experiments.

For sentence planner training, we automatically annotate all the sentences using the Treex deep syntactic analyzer (see Section 2). The annotation obtained from the Treex analyzer is further simplified for the sentence planner in two ways:

- Only lemmas and formemes are used in the sentence planner. Other node attributes are added in the surface realization step (see Section 5.2).
- We convert the representation of coordination structures into a format inspired by Universal Dependencies.[8] In the original Treex annotation style, the conjunction heads both conjuncts, whereas in our modification, the first conjunct is at the top, heading the coordination and the second conjunct (see Figure 4).

The coordinations can be easily converted back for the surface realizer, and the change makes the task easier for the sentence planner: it may first generate one node and then decide whether it will add a conjunction and a second conjunct.

5.2 Generator settings

In our candidate generator, we use all the limitation heuristics described in Section 3.1. For strong semantic compatibility (Rule 6), we use just lemmas and require at most 5 SVPs/slots from the lemma's compatibility list in the input DA.

We use the following feature types for our sentence planner scorer:

- current tree properties – tree depth, total number of nodes, number of repeated nodes
- tree and input DA – number of nodes per SVP and number of repeated nodes per repeated SVP,
- node features – lemma, formeme, and number of children of all nodes in the current tree, and combinations thereof,
- input features – whole SVPs (slot + value), just slots, and pairs of slots in the DA,
- combinations of node and input features,
- repeat features – occurrence of repeated lemmas and/or formemes in the current tree combined with repeated slots in the input DA,
- dependency features – parent-child pairs for lemmas and/or formemes, including and excluding their left-right order,
- sibling features – sibling pairs for lemmas and/or formemes, also combined with SVPs,
- bigram features – pairs of lemmas and/or formemes adjacent in the tree's left-right order, also combined with SVPs.

All feature values are normalized to have a mean of 0 and a standard deviation of 1, with normalization coefficients estimated from training data.

The feature set can be adapted for a different MR format – it only must capture all important parts of the MR, e.g., for a tree-like MR, the nodes and edges, and possibly combinations thereof.

[7] Available for download at: http://farm2.user.srcf.net/research/bagel/.

[8] http://universaldependencies.github.io

Setup	BLEU for training portion					NIST for training portion				
	10%	20%	30%	50%	100%	10%	20%	30%	50%	100%
Basic perc.	46.90	52.81	55.43	54.53	54.24	4.295	4.652	4.669	4.758	4.643
+ Diff-tree upd.	44.16	50.86	53.61	55.71	58.70	3.846	4.406	4.532	4.674	4.876
+ Future promise	37.25	53.57	53.80	58.15	59.89	3.331	4.549	4.607	5.071	5.231

Table 1: Evaluation on the BAGEL data set (averaged over all ten cross-validation folds)
"Training portion" denotes the percentage of the training data used in the experiment. "Basic perc." = basic perceptron updates, "+ Diff-tree upd." = with differing subtree perceptron updates, "+ Future promise" = with future promise estimation. BLEU scores are shown as percentages.

Based on our preliminary experiments, we use 100 passes over the training data and limit the number of iterations d that do not improve score to 3 for training and 4 for testing. We use a hard maximum of 200 sentence planner iterations per input DA. The learning rate α is set to 0.1. We use training data parts of 36 or 37 training examples (1/10th of the full training set) in parallel training. If future promise is used, its weight λ is set to 0.3.

The Treex English realizer expects not only lemmas and formemes, but also additional grammatical attributes for all nodes. In our experiments, we simply use the most common values found in the training data for the particular nodes as this is sufficient for our domain. In larger domains, some of these attributes may have to be also included in sentence plans.

6 Results

Same as Mairesse et al. (2010), we use 10-fold cross-validation where DAs seen at training time are never used for testing, i.e., both paraphrases or none of them are present in the full training set. We evaluate using BLEU and NIST scores (Papineni et al., 2002; Doddington, 2002) against both reference paraphrases for a given test DA.

The results of our generator are shown in Table 1, both for standard perceptron updates and our improvements – differing subtree updates and future promise estimation (see Section 3.2).

Our generator did not achieve the same performance as that of Mairesse et al. (2010) (ca. 67%).[9] However, our task is substantially harder since the generator also needs to learn the alignment of phrases to SVPs and determine whether all required information is present on the output (see also Section 7). Our differing tree updates clearly bring a substantial improvement over standard perceptron updates, and scores keep increasing with bigger amounts of training data used, whereas with plain perceptron updates, the scores stay flat. The increase with 100% is smaller since all training DAs are in fact used twice, each time with a different paraphrase.[10] A larger training set with different DAs should bring a bigger improvement. Using future promise estimation boosts the scores even further, by a smaller amount for BLEU but noticeably for NIST. Both improvements on the full training set are considered statistically significant at 95% confidence level by the paired bootstrap resampling test (Koehn, 2004). A manual inspection of a small sample of the results confirmed that the automatic scores reflect the quality of the generated sentences well.

If we look closer at the generated sentences (see Table 2), it becomes clear that the generator learns to produce meaningful utterances which mostly correspond well to the input DA. It is able to produce original paraphrases and generalizes to previously unseen DAs.

On the other hand, not all required information is always present, and some facts are sometimes repeated or irrelevant information appears. This mostly happens with input slot-value pairs that occur only rarely in the training data; we believe that a larger training set will solve this problem. Alternatively, one could introduce additional scorer features to discourage conflicting information. Another problem is posed by repeated slots in the input DA, which are sometimes not reflected properly in the generated sentence. This suggests that a further refinement of the scorer feature set may be needed.

[9] Mairesse et al. (2010) do not give a precise BLEU score number in their paper, they only show the values in a graph.

[10] We used the two paraphrases that come with each DA as independent training instances. While having two different gold-standard outputs for a single input is admittedly not ideal for a discriminative learner, it still brings an improvement in our case.

Input DA	inform(name=X-name, type=placetoeat, eattype=restaurant, near=X-near, food=Continental, food=French)
Reference	X is a French and continental restaurant near X.
Generated	X is a French and continental restaurant near X.
Input DA	inform(name=X-name, type=placetoeat, area=riverside, near=X-near, eattype=restaurant)
Reference	X restaurant is near X on the riverside.
Generated	X is a restaurant in the riverside area near X.
Input DA	inform(name=X-name, type=placetoeat, area=X-area, pricerange=moderate, eattype=restaurant)
Reference	X is a moderately priced restaurant in X.
Generated	X is a restaurant in the X area.
Input DA	inform(name=X-name, type=placetoeat, eattype=restaurant, area=riverside, food=French)
Reference	X is a French restaurant on the riverside.
Generated	X is a French restaurant in the riverside area which serves French food.
Input DA	inform(name=X-name, type=placetoeat, eattype=restaurant, pricerange=moderate, area=X-area, food=Contemporary, food=English)
Reference	X is a moderately priced English contemporary restaurant in X.
Generated	X is an English restaurant in the X area which serves expensive food in the moderate price range located in X.
Input DA	inform(name=X-name, type=placetoeat, eattype=restaurant, area=citycentre, near=X-near, food="Chinese takeaway", food=Japanese)
Reference	X is a Chinese takeaway and Japanese restaurant in the city centre near X.
Generated	X is a Japanese restaurant in the centre of town near X and X.
Input DA	inform(name=X-name, type=placetoeat, pricerange=moderate, eattype=restaurant)
Reference	X is a restaurant that offers moderate price range.
Generated	X is a restaurant in the moderate price range.

Table 2: Example generated sentences

Sentences generated when training on the full set and using differing subtree updates and future promise estimation.

7 Related Work

Previous trainable methods in sentence planning use in principle two techniques: First, in the overgeneration and ranking approach (Walker et al., 2001; Stent et al., 2004), many sentence plans are generated using a rule-based planner and then the best one is selected by a statistical ranker. Second, parameter optimization trains adjustable parameters of a handcrafted generator to produce outputs with desired properties (Paiva and Evans, 2005; Mairesse and Walker, 2008). As opposed to our approach, both methods require an existing handcrafted sentence planner.

Other previous works combine sentence planning and surface realization into a single step and do not require a handcrafted base module. Wong and Mooney (2007) experiment with a phrase-based machine translation system, comparing and combining it with an inverted semantic parser based on synchronous context-free grammars. Lu et al. (2009) use tree conditional random fields over hybrid trees that combine natural language phrases with formal semantic expressions. Angeli et al. (2010) generate text from database records through a sequence of classifiers, gradually selecting database records, fields, and corresponding textual realizations to describe them. Konstas and Lapata (2013) recast the whole NLG problem as parsing over a probabilistic context-free grammar estimated from database records and their descriptions. Mairesse et al. (2010) convert input DAs into "semantic stacks", which correspond to natural language phrases and contain slots and their values on top of each other. Their generation model uses two dynamic Bayesian networks: the first one performs an ordering of the input semantic stacks, inserting intermediary stacks which correspond to grammatical phrases, the second one then produces a concrete surface realization. Dethlefs et al. (2013) approach generation as a sequence labeling task and use a conditional random field classifier, assigning a word or a phrase to each input MR element.

Unlike our work, the joint approaches typically include the alignment of input MR elements to output words in a separate preprocessing step (Wong and Mooney, 2007; Angeli et al., 2010), or require pre-aligned training data (Mairesse et al., 2010; Dethlefs et al., 2013). In addition, their basic algorithm often requires a specific input MR format, e.g., a tree (Wong and Mooney, 2007; Lu et al., 2009) or a flat database (Angeli et al., 2010; Konstas and Lapata, 2013; Mairesse et al., 2010).

While dependency-based deep syntax has been used previously in statistical NLG, the approaches known to us (Bohnet et al., 2010; Belz et al., 2012; Ballesteros et al., 2014) focus only on the surface realization step and do not include a sentence planner, whereas our work is mainly focused on statistical sentence planning and uses a rule-based realizer.

Our approach to sentence planning is most similar to Zettlemoyer and Collins (2007), which use a candidate generator and a perceptron ranker for CCG parsing. Apart from proceeding in the inverse direction and using dependency trees, we use only very generic rules in our candidate generator instead of language-specific ones, and we incorporate differing subtree updates and future promise estimation into our ranker.

8 Conclusions and Further Work

We have presented a novel natural language generator, capable of learning from unaligned pairs of input meaning representation and output utterances. It consists of a novel, A*-search-based sentence planner and a largely rule-based surface realizer from the Treex NLP toolkit. The sentence planner is, to our knowledge, first to use dependency syntax and learn alignment of semantic elements to words or phrases jointly with sentence planning.

We tested our generator on the BAGEL restaurant information data set of Mairesse et al. (2010). We have achieved very promising results, the utterances produced by our generator are mostly fluent and relevant. They did not surpass the BLEU score of the original authors; however, our task is substantially harder as our generator does not require fine-grained alignments on the input. Our novel feature of the sentence planner ranker – using differing subtrees for perceptron weight updates – has brought a significant performance improvement.

The generator source code, along with configuration files for experiments on the BAGEL data set, is available for download on Github.[11]

In future work, we plan to evaluate our generator on further domains, such as geographic information (Kate et al., 2005), weather reports (Liang et al., 2009), or flight information (Dahl et al., 1994). In order to improve the performance of our generator and remove the dependency on domain-specific features, we plan to replace the perceptron ranker with a neural network. We also want to experiment with removing the dependency on the Treex surface realizer by generating directly into dependency trees or structures into which dependency trees can be converted in a language-independent way.

[11] `https://github.com/UFAL-DSG/tgen`

Acknowledgments

This work was funded by the Ministry of Education, Youth and Sports of the Czech Republic under the grant agreement LK11221 and core research funding, SVV project 260 104, and GAUK grant 2058214 of Charles University in Prague. It used language resources stored and distributed by the LINDAT/CLARIN project of the Ministry of Education, Youth and Sports of the Czech Republic (project LM2010013).

The authors would like to thank Lukáš Žilka, Ondřej Plátek, and the anonymous reviewers for helpful comments on the draft.

References

G. Angeli, P. Liang, and D. Klein. 2010. A simple domain-independent probabilistic approach to generation. In *Proc. of the 2010 Conference on Empirical Methods in Natural Language Processing*, page 502–512.

M. Ballesteros, S. Mille, and L. Wanner. 2014. Classifiers for data-driven deep sentence generation. In *Proceedings of the 8th International Natural Language Generation Conference*, pages 108–112, Philadelphia.

A. Belz, B. Bohnet, S. Mille, L. Wanner, and M. White. 2012. The Surface Realisation Task: Recent Developments and Future Plans. In *INLG 2012*, pages 136–140.

B. Bohnet, L. Wanner, S. Mille, and A. Burga. 2010. Broad coverage multilingual deep sentence generation with a stochastic multi-level realizer. In *Proc. of the 23rd International Conference on Computational Linguistics*, page 98–106.

M. Collins and N. Duffy. 2002. New ranking algorithms for parsing and tagging: Kernels over discrete structures, and the voted perceptron. In *Proceedings of the 40th Annual Meeting on Association for Computational Linguistics*, page 263–270, Stroudsburg, PA, USA. Association for Computational Linguistics.

M. Collins. 2002. Discriminative training methods for hidden Markov models: Theory and experiments with perceptron algorithms. In *Proceedings of the ACL-02 conference on Empirical methods in natural language processing-Volume 10*, page 1–8. Association for Computational Linguistics.

D. A. Dahl, M. Bates, M. Brown, W. Fisher, K. Hunicke-Smith, D. Pallett, E. Rudnicky, and E. Shriberg. 1994. Expanding the scope of the ATIS task: the ATIS-3 corpus. In *in Proc. ARPA Human Language Technology Workshop '92, Plainsboro, NJ*, pages 43–48. Morgan Kaufmann.

N. Dethlefs, H. Hastie, H. Cuayáhuitl, and O. Lemon. 2013. Conditional Random Fields for Responsive Surface Realisation using Global Features. In *Proceedings of ACL*, Sofia.

G. Doddington. 2002. Automatic evaluation of machine translation quality using N-gram co-occurrence statistics. In *Proceedings of the Second International Conference on Human Language Technology Research*, pages 138–145, San Francisco, CA, USA. Morgan Kaufmann Publishers Inc.

O. Dušek, Z. Žabokrtský, M. Popel, M. Majliš, M. Novák, and D. Mareček. 2012. Formemes in English-Czech deep syntactic MT. In *Proceedings of the Seventh Workshop on Statistical Machine Translation*, page 267–274, Montreal.

P. E. Hart, N. J. Nilsson, and B. Raphael. 1968. A formal basis for the heuristic determination of minimum cost paths. *IEEE Transactions on Systems Science and Cybernetics*, 4(2):100–107.

R. J. Kate, Y. W. Wong, and R. J. Mooney. 2005. Learning to transform natural to formal languages. In *Proceedings of the National Conference on Artificial Intelligence*, volume 20. Menlo Park, CA; Cambridge, MA; London; AAAI Press; MIT Press; 1999.

P. Koehn, F. J. Och, and D. Marcu. 2003. Statistical phrase-based translation. In *Proceedings of NAACL-HLT - Volume 1*, page 48–54, Stroudsburg, PA, USA. Association for Computational Linguistics.

P. Koehn. 2004. Statistical significance tests for machine translation evaluation. In *Proceedings of EMNLP*, page 388–395.

I. Konstas and M. Lapata. 2013. A global model for concept-to-text generation. *Journal of Artificial Intelligence Research*, 48:305–346.

P. Liang, M. I. Jordan, and D. Klein. 2009. Learning semantic correspondences with less supervision. In *Proceedings of the Joint Conference of the 47th Annual Meeting of the ACL and the 4th International Joint Conference on Natural Language Processing of the AFNLP: Volume 1-Volume 1*, page 91–99.

W. Lu, H. T. Ng, and W. S. Lee. 2009. Natural language generation with tree conditional random fields. In *Proc. of the 2009 Conference on Empirical Methods in Natural Language Processing: Volume 1-Volume 1*, page 400–409.

F. Mairesse and M. Walker. 2008. Trainable generation of big-five personality styles through data-driven parameter estimation. In *Proc. of the 46th Annual Meeting of the ACL (ACL)*, page 165–173.

F. Mairesse, M. Gašić, F. Jurčíček, S. Keizer, B. Thomson, K. Yu, and S. Young. 2010. Phrase-based statistical language generation using graphical models and active learning. In *Proc. of the 48th Annual Meeting of the ACL*, page 1552–1561.

R. McDonald, F. Pereira, K. Ribarov, and J. Hajič. 2005. Non-projective dependency parsing using spanning tree algorithms. In *Proceedings of the conference on Human Language Technology and Empirical Methods in Natural Language Processing*, page 523–530.

R. McDonald, K. Hall, and G. Mann. 2010. Distributed training strategies for the structured perceptron. In *Human Language Technologies: The 2010 Annual Conference of the North American Chapter of the Association for Computational Linguistics*, pages 456–464. Association for Computational Linguistics.

F. J. Och and H. Ney. 2003. A systematic comparison of various statistical alignment models. *Computational Linguistics*, 29(1):19–51.

F. J. Och, N. Ueffing, and H. Ney. 2001. An efficient A* search algorithm for statistical machine translation. In *Proceedings of the Workshop on Data-driven Methods in Machine Translation - Volume 14*, page 1–8, Stroudsburg, PA, USA. Association for Computational Linguistics.

D. S. Paiva and R. Evans. 2005. Empirically-based control of natural language generation. In *Proc. of the 43rd Annual Meeting of ACL*, page 58–65, Stroudsburg, PA, USA. ACL.

K. Papineni, S. Roukos, T. Ward, and W.-J. Zhu. 2002. BLEU: a method for automatic evaluation of machine translation. In *Proceedings of the 40th annual meeting of the Association for Computational Linguistics*, page 311–318.

M. Popel and Z. Žabokrtský. 2010. TectoMT: modular NLP framework. In *Proceedings of IceTAL, 7th International Conference on Natural Language Processing*, page 293–304, Reykjavík.

J. Ptáček. 2008. Two tectogrammatical realizers side by side: Case of English and Czech. In *Fourth International Workshop on Human-Computer Conversation*, Bellagio, Italy.

E. Reiter and R. Dale. 2000. *Building Natural Language Generation Systems*. Cambridge Univ. Press.

V. Rieser and O. Lemon. 2010. Natural language generation as planning under uncertainty for spoken dialogue systems. In *Empirical methods in natural language generation*, page 105–120.

P. Sgall, E. Hajičová, and J. Panevová. 1986. *The meaning of the sentence in its semantic and pragmatic aspects*. D. Reidel, Dordrecht.

D. J. Spoustová, J. Hajič, J. Votrubec, P. Krbec, and P. Květoň. 2007. The Best of Two Worlds: Cooperation of Statistical and Rule-based Taggers for Czech. In *Proceedings of the Workshop on Balto-Slavonic Natural Language Processing: Information Extraction and Enabling Technologies*, pages 67–74. Association for Computational Linguistics.

A. Stent, R. Prasad, and M. Walker. 2004. Trainable sentence planning for complex information presentation in spoken dialog systems. In *Proceedings of the 42nd Annual Meeting on Association for Computational Linguistics*, pages 79–86.

M. A. Walker, O. Rambow, and M. Rogati. 2001. SPoT: a trainable sentence planner. In *Proc. of 2nd meeting of NAACL*, page 1–8, Stroudsburg, PA, USA. ACL.

Y. W. Wong and R. J. Mooney. 2007. Generation by inverting a semantic parser that uses statistical machine translation. In *Proc. of Human Language Technologies: The Conference of the North American Chapter of the ACL (NAACL-HLT-07)*, page 172–179.

L. S. Zettlemoyer and M. Collins. 2007. Online learning of relaxed CCG grammars for parsing to logical form. In *Proceedings of the 2007 Joint Conference on Empirical Methods in Natural Language Processing and Computational Natural Language Learning*, pages 678–687, Prague.

Event-Driven Headline Generation

Rui Sun[†], **Yue Zhang**[‡], **Meishan Zhang**[‡] **and Donghong Ji**[†]
[†] Computer School, Wuhan University, China
[‡] Singapore University of Technology and Design
{ruisun, dhji}@whu.edu.cn
{yue_zhang, meishan_zhang}@sutd.edu.sg

Abstract

We propose an event-driven model for headline generation. Given an input document, the system identifies a key event chain by extracting a set of structural events that describe them. Then a novel multi-sentence compression algorithm is used to fuse the extracted events, generating a headline for the document. Our model can be viewed as a novel combination of extractive and abstractive headline generation, combining the advantages of both methods using event structures. Standard evaluation shows that our model achieves the best performance compared with previous state-of-the-art systems.

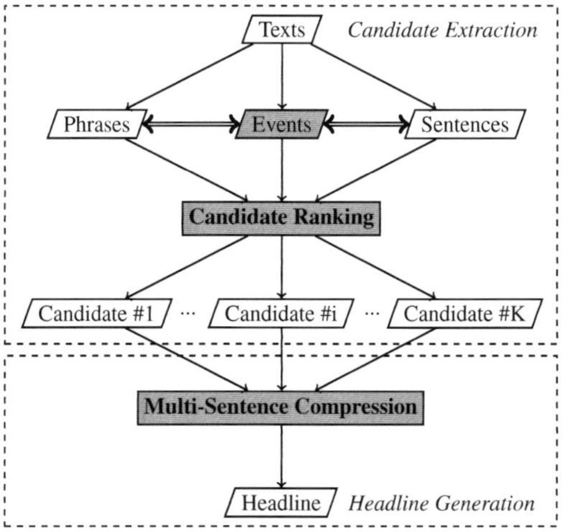

Figure 1: System framework.

1 Introduction

Headline generation (HG) is a text summarization task, which aims to describe an article (or a set of related paragraphs) using a single short sentence. The task is useful in a number of practical scenarios, such as compressing text for mobile device users (Corston-Oliver, 2001), generating table of contents (Erbs et al., 2013), and email summarization (Wan and McKeown, 2004). This task is challenging in not only informativeness and readability, which are challenges to common summarization tasks, but also the length reduction, which is unique for headline generation.

Previous headline generation models fall into two main categories, namely extractive HG and abstractive HG (Woodsend et al., 2010; Alfonseca et al., 2013). Both consist of two steps: candidate extraction and headline generation. Extractive models choose a set of salient sentences in candidate extraction, and then exploit sentence compression techniques to achieve headline generation (Dorr et al., 2003; Zajic et al., 2005). Abstractive models choose a set of informative phrases for candidate extraction, and then exploit sentence synthesis techniques for headline generation (Soricut and Marcu, 2007; Woodsend et al., 2010; Xu et al., 2010).

Extractive HG and abstractive HG have their respective advantages and disadvantages. Extractive models can generate more readable headlines, because the final title is derived by tailoring human-written sentences. However, extractive models give less informative titles (Alfonseca et al., 2013), because sentences are very sparse, making high-recall candidate extraction difficult. In contrast, abstractive models use phrases as the basic processing units, which are much less sparse. However, it is more difficult for abstractive HG to ensure the grammaticality of the generated titles, given that sentence synthesis is still very inaccurate based on a set of phrases with little grammatical information (Zhang, 2013).

In this paper, we propose an event-driven model for headline generation, which alleviates the

Proceedings of the 53rd Annual Meeting of the Association for Computational Linguistics and the 7th International Joint Conference on Natural Language Processing, pages 462–472,
Beijing, China, July 26-31, 2015.

disadvantages of both extractive and abstractive HG. The framework of the proposed model is shown in Figure 1. In particular, we use *events* as the basic processing units for candidate extraction. We use structured tuples to represent the subject, predicate and object of an event. This form of event representation is widely used in open information extraction (Fader et al., 2011; Qiu and Zhang, 2014). Intuitively, events can be regarded as a trade-off between sentences and phrases. Events are meaningful structures, containing necessary grammatical information, and yet are much less sparse than sentences. We use salience measures of both sentences and phrases for event extraction, and thus our model can be regarded as a combination of extractive and abstractive HG.

During the headline generation step, A graph-based multi-sentence compression (MSC) model is proposed to generate a final title, given multiple events. First a directed acyclic word graph is constructed based on the extracted events, and then a beam-search algorithm is used to find the best title based on path scoring.

We conduct experiments on standard datasets for headline generation. The results show that headline generation can benefit not only from exploiting events as the basic processing units, but also from the proposed graph-based MSC model. Both our candidate extraction and headline generation methods outperform competitive baseline methods, and our model achieves the best results compared with previous state-of-the-art systems.

2 Background

Previous extractive and abstractive models take two main steps, namely candidate extraction and headline generation. Here, we introduce these two types of models according to the two steps.

2.1 Extractive Headline Generation

Candidate Extraction. Extractive models exploit sentences as the basic processing units in this step. Sentences are ranked by their salience according to specific strategies (Dorr et al., 2003; Erkan and Radev, 2004; Zajic et al., 2005). One of the state-of-the-art approaches is the work of Erkan and Radev (2004), which exploits centroid, position and length features to compute sentence salience. We re-implemented this method as our baseline sentence ranking method. In this paper, we use `SentRank` to denote this method.

Headline Generation. Given a set of sentences, extractive models exploit sentence compression techniques to generate a final title. Most previous work exploits single-sentence compression (SSC) techniques. Dorr et al. (2003) proposed the Hedge Trimmer algorithm to compress a sentence by making use of handcrafted linguistically-based rules. Alfonseca et al. (2013) introduce a multi-sentence compression (MSC) model into headline generation, using it as a baseline in their work. They indicated that the most important information is distributed across several sentences in the text.

2.2 Abstractive Headline Generation

Candidate Extraction. Different from extractive models, abstractive models exploit phrases as the basic processing units. A set of salient phrases are selected according to specific principles during candidate extraction (Schwartz, 01; Soricut and Marcu, 2007; Xu et al., 2010; Woodsend et al., 2010). Xu et al. (2010) propose to rank phrases using background knowledge extracted from Wikipedia. Woodsend et al. (2010) use supervised models to learn the salience score of each phrase. Here, we use the work of Soricut and Marcu (2007) , namely `PhraseRank`, as our baseline phrase ranking method, which is an unsupervised model without external resources. The method exploits unsupervised topic discovery to find a set of salient phrases.

Headline Generation. In the headline generation step, abstractive models exploit sentence synthesis technologies to accomplish headline generation. Zajic et al. (2005) exploit unsupervised topic discovery to find key phrases, and use the Hedge Trimmer algorithm to compress candidate sentences. One or more key phrases are added into the compressed fragment according to the length of the headline. Soricut and Marcu (2007) employ WIDL-expressions to generate headlines. Xu et al. (2010) employ keyword clustering based on several bag-of-words models to construct a headline. Woodsend et al. (2010) use quasi-synchronous grammar (QG) to optimize phrase selection and surface realization preferences jointly.

3 Our Model

Similar to extractive and abstractive models, the proposed event-driven model consists of two steps, namely candidate extraction and headline generation.

3.1 Candidate Extraction

We exploit events as the basic units for candidate extraction. Here an event is a tuple (S, P, O), where S is the subject, P is the predicate and O is the object. For example, for the sentence *"Ukraine Delays Announcement of New Government"*, the event is *(Ukraine, Delays, Announcement)*. This type of event structures has been used in open information extraction (Fader et al., 2011), and has a range of NLP applications (Ding et al., 2014; Ng et al., 2014).

A sentence is a well-formed structure with complete syntactic information, but can contain redundant information for text summarization, which makes sentences very sparse. Phrases can be used to avoid the sparsity problem, but with little syntactic information between phrases, fluent headline generation is difficult. Events can be regarded as a trade-off between sentences and phrases. They are meaningful structures without redundant components, less sparse than sentences and containing more syntactic information than phrases.

In our system, candidate event extraction is performed on a bipartite graph, where the two types of nodes are lexical chains (Section 3.1.2) and events (Section 3.1.1), respectively. Mutual Reinforcement Principle (Zha, 2002) is applied to jointly learn chain and event salience on the bipartite graph for a given input. We obtain the top-*k* candidate events by their salience measures.

3.1.1 Extracting Events

We apply an open-domain event extraction approach. Different from traditional event extraction, for which types and arguments are pre-defined, open event extraction does not have a closed set of entities and relations (Fader et al., 2011). We follow Hu's work (Hu et al., 2013) to extract events.

Given a text, we first use the Stanford dependency parser[1] to obtain the Stanford typed dependency structures of the sentences (Marneffe and Manning, 2008). Then we focus on

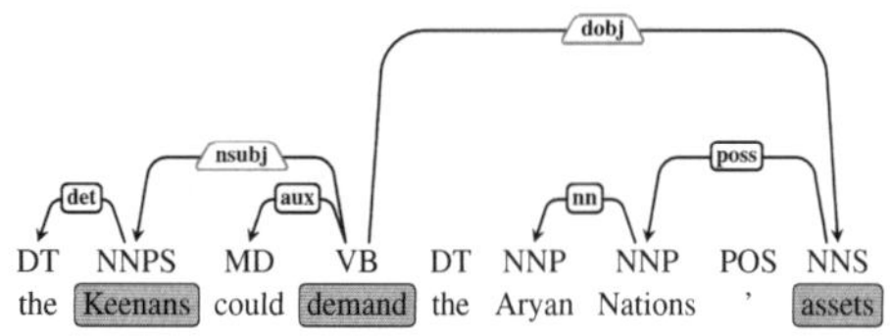

Figure 2: Dependency tree for the sentence *"the Keenans could demand the Aryan Nations' assets"*.

two relations, *nsubj* and *dobj*, for extracting event arguments. Event arguments that have the same predicate are merged into one event, represented by tuple (*Subject, Predicate, Object*). For example, given the sentence, *"the Keenans could demand the Aryan Nations' assets"*, Figure 2 present its partial parsing tree. Based on the parsing results, two event arguments are obtained: *nsubj(demand, Keenans)* and *dobj(demand, assets)*. The two event arguments are merged into one event: *(Keenans, demand, assets)*.

3.1.2 Extracting Lexical Chains

Lexical chains are used to link semantically-related words and phrases (Morris and Hirst, 1991; Barzilay and Elhadad, 1997). A lexical chain is analogous to a semantic synset. Compared with words, lexical chains are less sparse for event ranking.

Given a text, we follow Boudin and Morin (2013) to construct lexical chains based on the following principles:

1. All words that are identical after stemming are treated as one word;

2. All NPs with the same head word fall into one lexical chain;[2]

3. A pronoun is added to the corresponding lexical chain if it refers to a word in the chain (The coreference resolution is performed using the Stanford Coreference Resolution system);[3]

4. Lexical chains are merged if their main words are in the same synset of WordNet.[4]

[1] http://nlp.stanford.edu/software/lex-parser.shtml

[2] NPs are extracted according to the dependency relations *nn* and *amod*. As shown in Figure 2, we can extract the noun phrase *Aryan Nations* according to the dependency relation *nn(Nations, Aryan)*.

[3] http://nlp.stanford.edu/software/dcoref.shtml

[4] http://wordnet.princeton.edu/

At initialization, each word in the document is a lexical chain. We repeatedly merge existing chains by the four principles above until convergence. In particular, we focus on content words only, including verbs, nouns and adjective words. After the merging, each lexical chain represents a word cluster, and the first occuring word in it can be used as the main word of chain.

3.1.3 Learning Salient Events

Intuitively, one word should be more important if it occurs in more important events. Similarly, one event should be more important if it includes more important words. Inspired by this, we construct a bipartite graph between lexical chains and events, shown in Figure 3, and then exploit MRP to jointly learn the salience of lexical chains and events. MRP has been demonstrated effective for jointly learning the vertex weights of a bipartite graph (Zhang et al., 2008; Ventura et al., 2013).

Given a text, we construct bipartite graph between the lexical chains and events, with an edge being constructed between a lexical chain and an event if the event contains a word in the lexical chain. Suppose that there are n events $\{e_1, \cdots, e_n\}$ and m lexical chains: $\{l_1, \cdots, l_m\}$ in the bipartite graph G_{bi}. Their scores are represented by $sal(e) = \{sal(e_1), \cdots, sal(e_n)\}$ and $sal(l) = \{sal(l_1), \cdots, sal(l_m)\}$, respectively. We compute the final $sal(e)$ and $sal(l)$ iteratively by MRP. At each step, $sal(e_i)$ and $sal(l_j)$ are computed as follows:

$$
\begin{aligned}
sal(e_i) &\propto \sum_{j=1}^{m} r_{ij} \times sal(l_j) \\
sal(l_j) &\propto \sum_{i=1}^{n} r_{ij} \times sal(e_i) \\
r_{ij} &= \frac{\sum_{(l_j, e_i) \in G_{bi}} w(l_j) \cdot w(e_i)}{A}
\end{aligned} \tag{1}
$$

where $r_{ij} \in R$ denotes the cohesion between lexicon chain l_i and event e_j, A is a normalization factor, $sal(\cdot)$ denotes the salience, and the initial values of $sal(e)$ and $sal(t)$ can be assigned randomly.

The remaining problem is how to define the salience score of a given lexicon chain l_i and a given event e_j. In this work, we use the guidance of abstractive and extractive models to compute

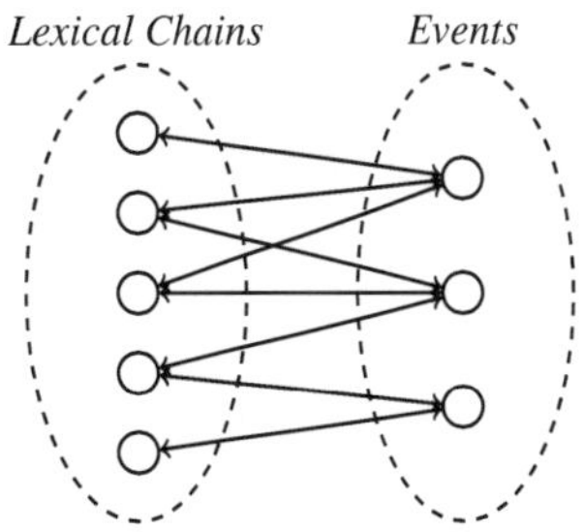

Figure 3: Bipartite graph where two vertex sets denote lexical chains and events, respectively.

$sal(l_j)$ and $sal(e_i)$, respectively, as shown below:

$$
\begin{aligned}
w(l_j) &= \sum_{w \in l_j} sal_{abs}(w) \\
w(e_i) &= \sum_{s \in Sen(e_i)} sal_{ext}(s)
\end{aligned} \tag{2}
$$

where $sal_{abs}(\cdot)$ denotes the word salience score of an abstractive model, $sal_{ext}(\cdot)$ denotes the sentence salience score of an extractive model, and $Sen(e_i)$ denotes the sentence set where e_i is extracted from. We exploit our baseline sentence ranking method, `SentRank`, to obtain the sentence salience score, and use our baseline phrase ranking method, `PhraseRank`, to obtain the phrase salience score.

3.2 Headline Generation

We use a graph-based multi-sentence compression (MSC) model to generate the final title for the proposed event-driven model. The model is inspired by Filippova (2010). First, a weighted directed acyclic word graph is built, with a start node and an end node in the graph. A headline can be obtained by any path from the start node to the end node. We measure each candidate path by a scoring function. Based on the measurement, we exploit a beam-search algorithm to find the optimum path.

3.2.1 Word-Graph Construction

Given a set of candidate events CE, we extract all the sentences that contain the events. In particular, we add two artificial words, $\langle S \rangle$ and $\langle E \rangle$, to the start position and end position of all sentences, respectively. Following Filippova (2010), we extract all words in the sentences as graph vertexes, and then construct edges based on these words. Filippova (2010) adds edges

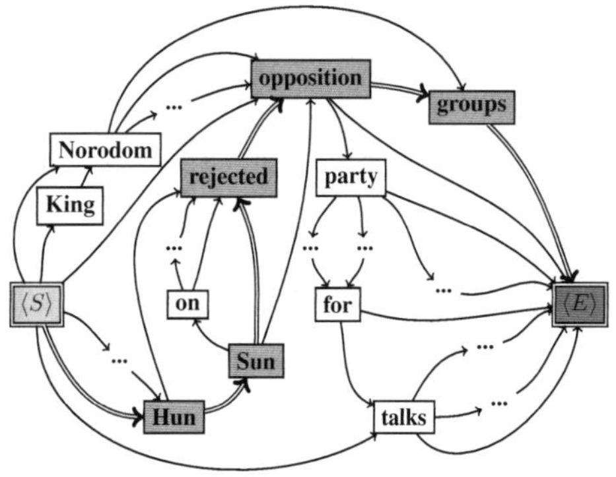

Figure 4: Word graph generated from candidates and a possible compression path.

for all the word pairs that are adjacent in one sentence. The title generated using this strategy can mistakenly contain common word bigrams(i.e. adjacent words) in different sentences. To address this, we change the strategy slightly, by adding edges for **a**ll word pairs of one sentence in the original order. In another words, if word w_j occurs after w_i in one sentence, then we add an edge $w_i \rightarrow w_j$ for the graph. Figure 4 gives an example of the word graph. The search space of the graph is larger compared with that of Filippova (2010) because of more added edges.

Different from Filippova (2010), salience information is introduced into the calculation of the weights of vertexes. One word that occurs in more salient candidate should have higher weight. Given a graph $G = (\mathcal{V}, \mathcal{E})$, where $\mathcal{V} = \{V_1, \cdots, V_n\}$ denotes the word nodes and $\mathcal{E} = \{E_{ij} \in \{0,1\}, i,j \in [1,n]\}$ denotes the edges. The vertex weight is computed as follows:

$$w(V_i) = \sum_{e \in CE} sal(e) \exp\{-dist(V_i.w, e)\} \quad (3)$$

where $sal(e)$ is the salience score of an event from the candidate extraction step, $V_i.w$ denotes the word of vertex V_i, and $dist(w, e)$ denotes the distance from the word w to the event e, which are defined by the minimum distance from w to all the related words of e in a sentence by the dependency path[5] between them. Intuitively, equation 3 demonstrates that a vertex is salient when its corresponding word is close to salient events. It is worth noting that the formula can adapt to extractive and abstractive models as well, by replacing events with sentences and phrases. We use them for the `SentRank` and `PhraseRank` baseline systems in Section 4.3, respectively.

The equation to compute the edge weight is adopted from Filippova (2010):

$$\begin{aligned} w'(E_{ij}) &= \sum_s rdist(V_i.w, V_j.w) \\ w(E_{ij}) &= \frac{w(V_i)w(V_j) \cdot w'(E_{ij})}{w(V_i) + w(V_j)} \end{aligned} \quad (4)$$

where $w'(E_{ij})$ refers to the sum of $rdist(V_i.w, V_j.w)$ over all sentences, and $rdist(\cdot)$ denotes the reciprocal distance of two words in a sentence by the dependency path. By the formula, an edge is salient when the corresponding vertex weights are large or the corresponding words are close.

3.2.2 Scoring Method

The key to our MSC model is the path scoring function. We measure a candidate path based on two aspects. Besides the sum edge score of the path, we exploit a trigram language model to compute a fluency score of the path. Language models have been commonly used to generate more readable titles.

The overall score of a path is compute by:

$$\begin{aligned} score(p) &= edge(p) + \lambda \times flu(p) \\ edge(p) &= \frac{\sum_{E_{ij} \in p} \ln\{w(E_{ij})\}}{n} \\ flu(p) &= \frac{\sum_i \ln\{p(w_i | w_{i-2}w_{i-1})\}}{n} \end{aligned} \quad (5)$$

where p is a candidate path and the corresponding word sequence of p is $w_1 \cdots w_n$. A trigram language model is trained using SRILM[6] on English Gigaword (LDC2011T07).

3.2.3 Beam Search

Beam search has been widely used aiming to find the sub optimum result (Collins and Roark, 2004; Zhang and Clark, 2011), when exact inference is extremely difficult. Assuming our word graph has a vertex size of n, the worst computation complexity is $O(n^4)$ when using a trigram language model, which is time consuming.

[5]The distance is $+\infty$ when e and w are not in one sentence.

[6]http://www.speech.sri.com/projects/srilm/

```
Input: G ← (𝒱, ℰ), LM, B
Output: best
candidates ← { {⟨S⟩} }
loop do
  beam ← { }
  for each candidate in candidates
    if candidate endwith ⟨E⟩
      AddToBeam(beam, candidate)
      continue
    for each V_i in 𝒱
      candidate ← AddVertex(candidate, V_i)
      ComputeScore(candidate, LM)
      AddToBeam(beam, candidate)
    end for
  end for
  candidates ← Top-K(beam, B)
  if candidates all endwith ⟨E⟩ : break
end loop
best ← Best(candidates)
```

Figure 5: The beam-search algorithm.

Using beam search, assuming the beam size is B, the time complexity decreases to $O(Bn^2)$.

Pseudo-code of our beam search algorithm is shown in Figure 5. During search, we use *candidates* to save a fixed size (B) of partial results. For each iteration, we generate a set of new candidates by adding one vertex from the graph, computing their scores, and maintaining the top B candidates for the next iteration. If one candidate reaches the end of the graph, we do not expand it, directly adding it into the new candidate set according to its current score. If all the candidates reach the end, the searching algorithm terminates and the result path is the candidate from *candidates* with the highest score.

4 Experiment

4.1 Settings

We use the standard HG test dataset to evaluate our model, which consists of 500 articles from DUC–04 task 1[7], where each article is provided with four reference headlines. In particular, we use the first 100 articles from DUC–07 as our development set. There are averaged 40 events per article in the two datasets. All the pre-processing steps, including POS tagging, lemma analysis, dependency parsing and anaphora resolution, are conducted using the Stanford NLP tools (Marneffe and Manning, 2008). The MRP iteration number is set to 10.

We use ROUGE (Lin, 2004) to automatically measure the model performance, which has been widely used in summarization tasks (Wang et al., 2013; Ng et al., 2014). We focus on Rouge1 and Rouge2 scores, following Xu et al. (2010). In addition, we conduct human evaluations, using the same method as Woodsend et al. (2010). Four participants are asked to rate the generated headlines by three criteria: informativeness (how much important information in the article does the headline describe?), fluency (is it fluent to read?) and coherence (does it capture the topic of article?). Each headline is given a subjective score from 0 to 5, with 0 being the worst and 5 being the best. The first 50 documents from the test set and their corresponding headlines are selected for human rating. We conduct significant tests using t-test.

4.2 Development Results

There are three important parameters in the proposed event-driven model, including the beam size B, the fluency weight λ and the number of candidate events N. We find the optimum parameters on development dataset in this section. For efficiency, the three parameters are optimized separately. The best performance is achieved with $B = 8$, $\lambda = 0.4$ and $N = 10$. We report the model results on the development dataset to study the influences of the three parameters, respectively, with the other two parameters being set with their best value.

4.2.1 Influence of Beam Size

We perform experiments with different beam widths. Figure 6 shows the results of the proposed model with beam sizes of 1, 2, 4, 8, 16, 32, 64. As can be seen, our model can achieve the best performances when the beam size is set to 8. Larger beam sizes do not bring better results.

4.2.2 Influence of Fluency Weight

The fluency score is used for generating readable titles, while the edge score is used for generating informative titles. The balance between them is important. By default, we set one to the weight of edge score, and find the best weight λ for the fluency score. We set λ ranging from 0 to 1 with and interval of 0.1, to investigate the influence of

[7]http://duc.nist.gov/duc2004/tasks.html

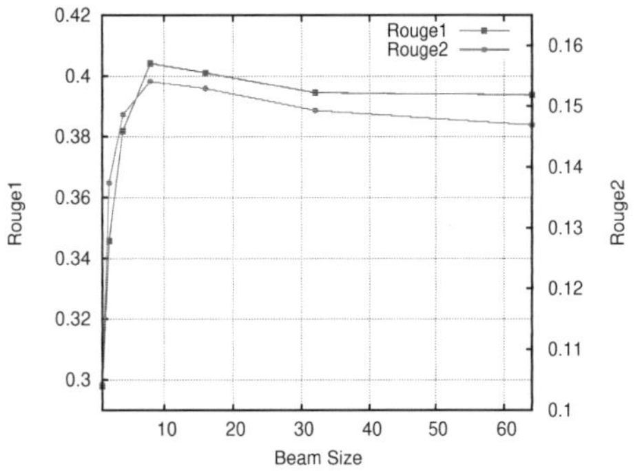

Figure 6: Results with different beam sizes.

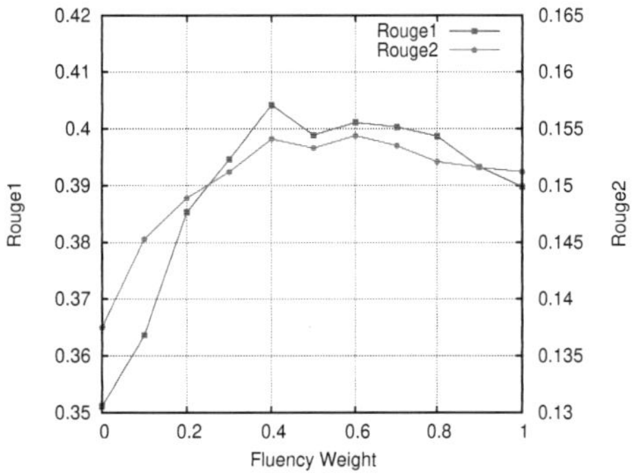

Figure 7: Results using different fluency weights.

this parameter[8]. Figure 7 shows the results. The best result is obtained when $\lambda = 0.4$.

4.2.3 Influence of Candidate Event Count

Ideally, all the sentences of an original text should be considered in multi-sentence compression. But an excess of sentences would bring more noise. We suppose that the number of candidate events N is important as well. To study its influence, we report the model results with different N, from 1 to 15 with an interval of 1. As shown in Figure 8, the performance increases significantly from 1 to 10, and no more gains when $N > 10$. The performance decreases drastically when M ranges from 12 to 15.

4.3 Final Results

Table 1 shows the final results on the test dataset. The performances of the proposed event-driven model are shown by `EventRank`. In addition, we use our graph-based MSC model to

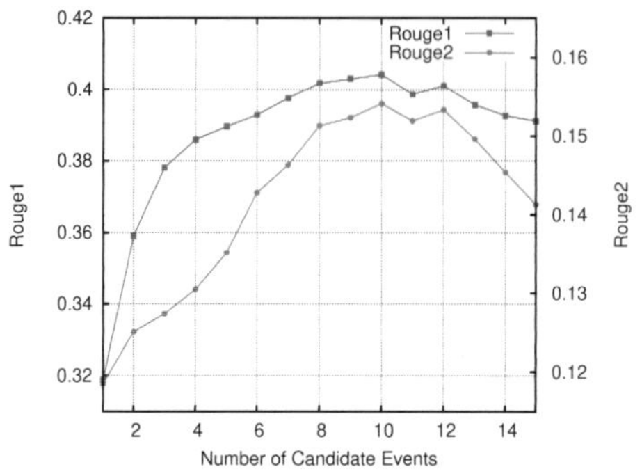

Figure 8: Results using different numbers of candidate events.

Method	Model Type	Rouge1	Rouge2
Our SalMSC			
SentRank	Extractive	0.3511	0.1375
PhraseRank	Abstractive	0.3706	0.1415
EventRank	Event-driven	**0.4247**‡	**0.1484**‡
Using MSC			
SentRank	Extractive	0.2773	0.0980
PhraseRank	Abstractive	0.3652	0.1299
EventRank	Event-driven	**0.3822**‡	**0.1380**‡
Other work			
SentRank+SSC	Extractive	0.2752	0.0855
Topiary	Abstractive	0.2835	0.0872
Woodsend	Abstractive	0.26*	0.06*[9]

Table 1: Performance comparison for automatic evaluation. The mark ‡ denotes that the result is significantly better with a p-value below 0.01.

generate titles for `SentRank` and `PhraseRank`, respectively, as mentioned in Section 3.2.1. By comparison with the two models, we can examine the effectiveness of the event-driven model. As shown in Table 1, the event-driven model achieves the best scores on both Rouge1 and Rouge2, demonstrating events are more effective than sentences and phrases.

Further, we compare our proposed MSC method with the MSC proposed by Filippova (2010), to study the effectiveness of our novel MSC. We use `MSC`[10] and `SalMSC`[11] to

[8] Preliminary results show that λ is better below one.

[9] The mark $*$ denotes the results are inaccurate, which are guessed from the figures in the published paper.

[10] The MSC source code, published by Boudin and Morin (2013), is available at https://github.com/boudinfl/takahe.

[11] Our source code is available at https://github.com/dram218/WordGraphCompression.

Method	Info.	Infu.	Cohe.
SentRank	4.13	2.85	2.54
PhraseRank	4.21	3.25	2.62
EventRank	**4.35**‡	**3.41**‡	**3.22**‡

Table 2: Results from the manual evaluation. The mark ‡ denotes the result is significantly better with a p-value below 0.01.

`SentRank`, `PhraseRank` and `EventRank` to denote their MSC method and our proposed MSC, respectively, applying them, respectively. As shown in Table 1, better performance is achieved by our MSC, demonstrating the effectiveness of our proposed MSC. Similarly, the event-driven model can achieve the best results.

We report results of previous state-of-the-art systems as well. `SentRank+SSC` denotes the result of Erkan and Radev (2004), which uses our SentRank and SSC to obtain the final title. `Topiary` denotes the result of Zajic et al. (2005), which is an early abstractive model. `Woodsend` denotes the result of Woodsend et al. (2010), which is an abstractive model using a quasi-synchronous grammar to generate a title. As shown in Table 1, MSC is significantly better than SSC, and our event-driven model achieves the best performance, compared with state-of-the-art systems.

Following Alfonseca et al. (2013), we conduct human evaluation also. The results are shown in Table 2, by three aspects: informativeness, fluency and coherence. The overall tendency is similar to the results, and the event-driven model achieves the best results.

4.4 Example Outputs

We show several representative examples of the proposed event-driven model, in comparison with the extractive and abstractive models. The examples are shown in Table 3.

In the first example, the results of both `SentRank` and `PhraseRank` contain the redundant phrase "catastrophe Tuesday". The output of `PhraseRank` is less fluent compared with that of `SentRank`. The preposition "for" is not recovered by the headline generation system `PhraseRank`. In contrast, the output of `EventRank` is better, capturing the major event in the reference title.

Method	Generated Headlines
Reference	Honduras, other Caribbean countries brace for the wrath of Hurricane Mitch
SentRank	Honduras braced for potential catastrophe Tuesday as Hurricane Mitch roared through northwest Caribbean
PhraseRank	Honduras braced catastrophe Tuesday Hurricane Mitch roared northwest Caribbean
EventRank	Honduras braced for Hurricane Mitch roared through northwest Caribbean
Reference	At Ibero-American summit Castro protests arrest of Pinochet in London
SentRank	Castro disagreed with the arrest Augusto Pinochet calling international meddling
PhraseRank	Cuban President Fidel Castro disagreed arrest London Chilean dictator Augusto Pinochet
EventRank	Fidel Castro disagreed with arrest in London of Chilean dictator Augusto Pinochet
Reference	Cambodian leader Hun Sen rejects opposition demands for talks in Beijing
SentRank	Hun Sen accusing opposition parties of internationalize the political crisis
PhraseRank	opposition parties demands talks internationalize political crisis
EventRank	Cambodian leader Hun Sen rejected opposition parties demands for talks

Table 3: Comparison of headlines generated by the different methods.

In the second example, the outputs of three systems all lose the phrase "Ibero-American summit". `SentRank` gives different additional information compared with `PhraseRank` and `EventRank`. Overall, the three outputs can be regarded as comparable. `PhraseRank` also has a fluency problem by ignoring some function words.

In the third example, `SentRank` does not capture the information on "demands for talks". `PhraseRank` discards the preposition word "for". The output of `EventRank` is better, being both more fluent and more informative.

From the three examples, we can see that `SentRank` tends to generate more readable titles, but may lose some important information. `PhraseRank` tends to generate a title with more important words, but the fluency is relatively weak even with MSC. `EventRank` combines the advantages of both `SentRank` and `PhraseRank`, generating titles that contain more important events with complete structures. The observation verifies our hypothesis in the introduction — that extractive models have the problem of low information coverage, and abstractive models have the problem of poor grammaticality. The event-driven mothod can alleviate both issues since event offer a trade-off between sentence and phrase.

5 Related Work

Our event-driven model is different from traditional extractive (Dorr et al., 2003; Erkan and Radev, 2004; Alfonseca et al., 2013) and abstractive models (Zajic et al., 2005; Soricut and Marcu, 2007; Woodsend et al., 2010; Xu et al., 2010) in that events are used as the basic processing units instead of sentences and phrases. As mentioned above, events are a trade-off between sentences and phrases, avoiding sparsity and structureless problems. In particular, our event-driven model can interact with sentences and phrases, thus is a light combination for two traditional models.

The event-driven model is mainly inspired by Alfonseca et al. (2013), who exploit events for multi-document headline generation. They leverage titles of sub-documents for supervised training. In contrast, we generate a title for a single document using an unsupervised model. We use novel approaches for event ranking and title generation.

In recent years, sentence compression (Galanis and Androutsopoulos, 2010; Yoshikawa and Iida, 2012; Wang et al., 2013; Li et al., 2014; Thadani, 2014) has received much attention. Some methods can be directly applied for multi-document summarization (Wang et al., 2013; Li et al., 2014). To our knowledge, few studies have been explored on applying them in headline generation.

Multi-sentence compression based on word graph was first proposed by Filippova (2010). Some subsequent work was presented recently. Boudin and Morin (2013) propose that the key phrase is helpful to sentence generation. The key phrases are extracted according to syntactic pattern and introduced to identify shortest path in their work. Mehdad et al. (2013; Mehdad et al. (2014) introduce the MSC based on word graph into meeting summarization. Tzouridis et al. (2014) cast multi-sentence compression as a structured predication problem. They use a large-margin approach to adapt parameterised edge weights to the data in order to acquire the shortest path. In their work, the sentences introduced to a word graph are treated equally, and the edges in the graph are constructed according to the adjacent order in original sentence.

Our MSC model is also inspired by Filippova (2010). Our approach is more aggressive than their approach, generating compressions with arbitrary length by using a different edge construction strategy. In addition, our search algorithm is also different from theirs. Our graph-based MSC model is also similar in spirit to sentence fusion, which has been used for multi-document summarization (Barzilay and McKeown, 2005; Elsner and Santhanam, 2011).

6 Conclusion and Future Work

We proposed an event-driven model headline generation, introducing a graph-based MSC model to generate the final title, based on a set of events. Our event-driven model can incorporate sentence and phrase salience, which has been used in extractive and abstractive HG models. The proposed graph-based MSC model is not limited to our event-driven model. It can be applied on extractive and abstractive models as well. Experimental results on DUC–04 demonstrate that event-driven model can achieve better results than extractive and abstractive models, and the proposed graph-based MSC model can bring improved performances compared with previous MSC techniques. Our final event-driven model obtains the best result on this dataset.

For future work, we plan to explore two directions. Firstly, we plan to introduce event relations to learning event salience. In addition, we plan to investigate other methods about multi-sentence compression and sentence fusion, such as supervised methods.

Acknowledgments

We thank all reviewers for their detailed comments. This work is supported by the State Key Program of National Natural Science Foundation of China (Grant No.61133012), the National Natural Science Foundation of China (Grant No.61373108, 61373056), the National Philosophy Social Science Major Bidding Project of China (Grant No.11&ZD189), and the Key Program of Natural Science Foundation of Hubei, China (Grant No.2012FFA088). The corresponding authors of this paper are Meishan Zhang and Donghong Ji.

References

Enrique Alfonseca, Daniele Pighin and Guillermo Garrido. 2013. HEADY: News headline abstraction through event pattern clustering. In *Proceedings of ACL 2013*,pages 1243–1253.

Regina Barzilay and Michael Elhadad. 1997. Using Lexical Chains for Text Summarization. In *Proceedings of the Intelligent Scalable Text Summarization Workshop(ISTS'97), Madrid.*

Regina Barzilay and Kathleen R. McKeown. 2005. Sentence fusion for multidocument news summarization. *Computational Linguistics*, 31(3), pages 297–328.

Florian Boudin and Emmanuel Morin. 2013. Keyphrase Extraction for N-best Reranking in Multi-Sentence Compression. In *Proccedings of the NAACL HLT 2013 conference*, page 298–305.

James Clarke and Mirella Lapata. 2010. Discourse Constraints for Document Compression. *Computational Linguistics*, 36(3), pages 411–441.

Michael Collins and Brian Roark. 2004. Incremental Parsing with the Perceptron Algorithm. In *Proceedings of ACL 2004*, pages 111-118.

Corston-Oliver, Simon. 2001. Text compaction for display on very small screens. In *Proceedings of the NAACL Workshop on Automatic Summarization*, Pittsburg, PA, 3 June 2001, pages 89–98.

Xiao Ding, Yue Zhang, Ting Liu, Junwen Duan. 2014. Using Structured Events to Predict Stock Price Movement : An Empirical Investigation. In *Proceedings of EMNLP 2014*, pages 1415–1425.

Bonnie Dorr, David Zajic, and Richard Schwartz. 2003. Hedge trimmer: A parse-and-trim approach to headline generation. In *proceedings of the HLT-NAACL 03 on Text summarization workshop*, volume 5, pages 1–8.

Micha Elsner and Deepak Santhanam. 2011. Learning to fuse disparate sentences. In *Proceedings of ACL 2011*, pages 54–63.

Nicolai Erbs, Iryna Gurevych and Torsten Zesch. 2013. Hierarchy Identification for Automatically Generating Table-of-Contents. In *Proceedings of Recent Advances in Natural Language Processing*, Hissar, Bulgaria, pages 252–260.

Gunes Erkan and Dragomir R Radev. 2004. LexRank : Graph-based Lexical Centrality as Salience in Text Summarization. *Journal of Artificial Intelligence Research 22*, 2004, pages 457–479.

Fader A, Soderland S, Etzioni O. 2011. Identifying relations for open information extraction. In *Proceedings of EMNLP 2011*, pages 1535–1545.

Katja Filippova. 2010. Multi-sentence compression: Finding shortest paths in word graphs. In *Proceedings of Coling 2010*, pages 322–330.

Dimitrios Galanis and Ion Androutsopoulos. 2010. An extractive supervised two-stage method for sentence compression. In *Proceedings of NAACL 2010*, pages 885–893.

Barbara J. Grosz and Scott Weinstein and Aravind K. Joshi. 1995. Centering: A framework for modeling the local coherence of discourse. *Computational Linguistics*, volume 21, pages 203–225.

Zhichao Hu, Elahe Rahimtoroghi, Larissa Munishkina, Reid Swanson and Marilyn A.Walker. 2013. Unsupervised Induction of Contingent Event Pairs from Film Scenes. In *Proceedings of EMNLP 2013*, pages 369–379.

Chen Li,Yang Liu, Fei Liu, Lin Zhao, Fuliang Weng. 2014. Improving Multi-documents Summarization by Sentence Compression based on Expanded Constituent Parse Trees. In *Proceedings of EMNLP 2014*, pages 691–701.

Chin-Yew Lin. 2004. Rouge: A package for automatic evaluation of summaries. In *Text Summarization Branckes Out: Proceedings of the ACL–04 Workshop*, pages 74–81.

Andre F.T. Martins and Noah A. Smith. 2009. Summarization with a joint model for sentence extraction and compression. In *Proceedings of the Workshop on Integer Linear Programming for Natural Language Processing*, pages 1–9.

Yashar Mehdad, Giuseppe Carenini, Frank W.Tompa and Raymond T.Ng. 2013. Abstractive Meeting Summarization with Entailment and Fusion. In *Proceedings of the 14th European Workshop on Natural Language Generation*, pages 136–146.

Yashar Mehdad, Giuseppe Carenini and Raymond T.Ng. 2014. Abstractive Summarization of Spoken and Written Conversations Based on Phrasal Queries. In *Proceedings of ACL 2014*, pages 1220–1230.

Jane Morris and Graeme Hirst. 1991. Lexical cohesion computed by thesaural relations as an indicator of the structure of text. *Computational Linguistics*, 17(1), pages 21–48.

Marie-Catherine de Marneffe and Christopher D. Manning. 2008. The stanford typed dependencies representation. In *COLING 2008 Workshop on Cross-framework and Cross-domain Parser Evaluation.*

Jun-Ping Ng, Yan Chen, Min-Yen Kan, Zhoujun Li. 2014. Exploiting Timelines to Enhance Multi-document Summarization. *Proceedings of ACL 2014*, pages 923–933.

Likun Qiu and Yue Zhang. 2014. ZORE: A Syntax-based System for Chinese Open Relation Extraction. *Proceedings of EMNLP 2014*, pages 1870–1880.

Robert G. Sargent. 1988. Polynomial Time Joint Structural Inference for Sentence Compression. *Management Science*, 34(10), pages 1231–1251.

Schwartz R. 1988. Unsupervised topic discovery. In *Proceedings of workshop on language modeling and information retrieval*, pages 72–77.

R. Soricut, and D. Marcu. 2007. Abstractive headline generation using WIDL-expressions. *Information Processing and Management*, 43(6), pages 1536–1548.

Kapil Thadani. 2014. Approximation Strategies for Multi-Structure Sentence Compression. *Proceedings of ACL 2014*, pages 1241–1251.

Emmanouil Tzouridis, Jamal Abdul Nasir and Ulf Brefeld. 2014. Learning to Summarise Related Sentences. *Proceedings of COLING 2014*,Dublin, Ireland, August 23-29 2014. pages 1636–1647.

Carles Ventura, Xavier Giro-i-Nieto, Veronica Vilaplana, Daniel Giribet, and Eusebio Carasusan. 2013. Automatic keyframe selection based on Mutual Reinforcement Algorithm. In *Proceedings of 11th international workshop on content-based multimedia indexing(CBMI)*, pages 29–34.

Stephen Wan and Kathleen McKeown. 2004. Generating overview summaries of ongoing email thread discussions. In *Proceedings of COLING 2004*, Geneva, Switzerland, 2004, pages 1384–1394.

Lu Wang, Hema Raghavan, Vittorio Castelli, Radu Florian, Claire Cardie. 2013. A sentence compression based framework to query-focused mutli-document summarization. In *Proceedings of ACL 2013*, Sofia, Bulgaria, August 4-9 2013, pages 1384–1394.

Kristian Woodsend, Yansong Feng and Mirella Lapata. 2010. Title generation with quasi-synchronous grammar. In *Proceedings of EMNLP 2010*, pages 513–523.

Songhua Xu, Shaohui Yang and Francis C.M. Lau. 2010. Keyword extraction and headline generation using novel work features. In *Proceedings of AAAI 2010*, pages 1461–1466.

Katsumasa Yoshikawa and Ryu Iida. 2012. Sentence Compression with Semantic Role Constraints. In *Proceedings of ACL 2012*, pages 349–353.

David Zajic, Bonnie Dorr and Richard Schwartz. 2005. Headline generation for written and broadcast news. *lamp-tr-120, cs-tr-4698.*

Hongyuan Zha. 2002. Generic summarization and keyphrase extraction using mutual reinforement principle and sentence clustering. In *Proceedings of SIGIR 2002*, pages 113–120.

Qi Zhang, Xipeng Qiu, Xuanjing Huang, Wu Lide. 2008. Learning semantic lexicons using graph mutual reinforcement based bootstrapping. *Acta Automatica Sinica*, 34(10), pages 1257–1261.

Yue Zhang, Stephen Clark. 2011. Syntactic Processing Using the Generalized Perceptron and Beam Search. *Computational Linguistics*, 37(1), pages 105–150.

Yue Zhang. 2013. Partial-Tree Linearization: Generalized Word Ordering for Text Synthesis. In *Proceedings of IJCAI 2013*, pages 2232–2238.

New Transfer Learning Techniques for Disparate Label Sets

Young-Bum Kim[†] **Karl Stratos**[‡] **Ruhi Sarikaya**[†] **Minwoo Jeong**[†]

[†]Microsoft Corporation, Redmond, WA
[‡]Columbia University, New York, NY
{ybkim, ruhi.sarikaya, minwoo.jeong}@microsoft.com
stratos@cs.columbia.edu

Abstract

In natural language understanding (NLU), a user utterance can be labeled differently depending on the domain or application (e.g., weather vs. calendar). Standard domain adaptation techniques are not directly applicable to take advantage of the existing annotations because they assume that the label set is invariant. We propose a solution based on label embeddings induced from canonical correlation analysis (CCA) that reduces the problem to a standard domain adaptation task and allows use of a number of transfer learning techniques. We also introduce a new transfer learning technique based on pretraining of hidden-unit CRFs (HUCRFs). We perform extensive experiments on slot tagging on eight personal digital assistant domains and demonstrate that the proposed methods are superior to strong baselines.

1 Introduction

The main goal of NLU is to automatically extract the meaning of spoken or typed queries. In recent years, this task has become increasingly important as more and more speech-based applications have emerged. Recent releases of personal digital assistants such as Siri, Google Now, Dragon Go and Cortana in smart phones provide natural language based interface for a variety of domains (e.g. places, weather, communications, reminders). The NLU in these domains are based on statistical machine learned models which require annotated training data. Typically each domain has its own schema to annotate the words and queries. However the meaning of words and utterances could be different in each domain. For example, "sunny" is considered a weather condition in the weather domain but it may be a song title in a music domain. Thus every time a new application is developed or a new domain is built, a significant amount of resources is invested in creating annotations specific to that application or domain.

One might attempt to apply existing techniques (Blitzer et al., 2006; Daumé III, 2007) in domain adaption to this problem, but a straightforward application is not possible because these techniques assume that the label set is invariant.

In this work, we provide a simple and effective solution to this problem by abstracting the label types using the canonical correlation analysis (CCA) by Hotelling (Hotelling, 1936) a powerful and flexible statistical technique for dimensionality reduction. We derive a low dimensional representation for each label type that is maximally correlated to the average context of that label via CCA. These shared label representations, or label embeddings, allow us to map label types across different domains and reduce the setting to a standard domain adaptation problem. After the mapping, we can apply the standard transfer learning techniques to solve the problem.

Additionally, we introduce a novel pretraining technique for hidden-unit CRFs (HUCRFs) to effectively transfer knowledge from one domain to another. In our experiments, we find that our pretraining method is almost always superior to strong baselines such as the popular domain adaptation method of Daumé III (2007).

2 Problem description and related work

Let $\mathcal{D}$ be the number of distinct domains. Let X_i be the space of observed samples for the i-th domain. Let Y_i be the space of possible labels for the i-th domain. In most previous works in domain adaptation (Blitzer et al., 2006; Daumé III, 2007), observed data samples may vary but label space is

Proceedings of the 53rd Annual Meeting of the Association for Computational Linguistics and the 7th International Joint Conference on Natural Language Processing, pages 473–482, Beijing, China, July 26-31, 2015.

invariant[1]. That is,

$$Y_i = Y_j \qquad \forall i, j \in \{1 \dots \mathcal{D}\}$$

but $X_i \neq X_j$ for some domains i and j. For example, in part-of-speech (POS) tagging on newswire and biomedical domains, the observed data sample may be radically different but the POS tag set remains the same.

In practice, there are cases, where the same query is labeled differently depending on the domain or application and the context. For example, *Fred Myer* can be tagged differently; "send a text message to *Fred Myer*" and "get me driving direction to *Fred Myer* ". In the first case, *Fred Myer* is person in user's contact list but it is a grocery store in the second one.

So, we relax the constraint that label spaces must be the same. Instead, we assume that surface forms (i.e words) are similar. This is a natural setting in developing multiple applications on speech utterances; input spaces (service request utterances) do not change drastically but output spaces (slot tags) might.

Multi-task learning differs from our task. In general multi-task learning aims to improve performance across all domains while our domain adaptation objective is to optimize the performance of semantic slot tagger on the target domain.

Below, we review related work in domain adaption and natural language understanding (NLU).

2.1 Related Work

Domain adaptation has been widely used in many natural language processing (NLP) applications including part-of-speech tagging (Schnabel and Schütze, 2014), parsing (McClosky et al., 2010), and machine translation (Foster et al., 2010). Most of the work can be classified either supervised domain adaptation (Chelba and Acero, 2006; Blitzer et al., 2006; Daume III and Marcu, 2006; Daumé III, 2007; Finkel and Manning, 2009; Chen et al., 2011) or semi-supervised adaptation (Ando and Zhang, 2005; Jiang and Zhai, 2007; Kumar et al., 2010; Huang and Yates, 2010). Our problem setting falls into the former.

Multi-task learning has become popular in NLP. Sutton and McCallum (2005) showed that joint learning and/or decoding of sub-tasks helps to improve performance. Collobert and Weston (2008) proved the similar claim in a deep learning architecture. While our problem resembles their settings, there are two clear distinctions. First, we aim to optimize performance on the target domain by minimizing the gap between source and target domain while multi-task learning jointly learns the shared tasks. Second, in our problem the domains are different, but they are closely related. On the other hand, prior work focuses on multiple subtasks of the same data.

Despite the increasing interest in NLU (De Mori et al., 2008; Xu and Sarikaya, 2013; Sarikaya et al., 2014; Xu and Sarikaya, 2014; Anastasakos et al., 2014; El-Kahky et al., 2014; Liu and Sarikaya, 2014; Marin et al., 2014; Celikyilmaz et al., 2015; Ma et al., 2015; Kim et al., 2015), transfer learning in the context of NLU has not been much explored. The most relevant previous work is Tur (2006) and Li et al. (2011), which described both the effectiveness of multi-task learning in the context of NLU. For multi-task learning, they used shared slots by associating each slot type with aggregate active feature weight vector based on an existing domain specific slot tagger. Our empirical results shows that these vector representation might be helpful to find shared slots across domain, but cannot find bijective mapping between domains.

Also, Jeong and Lee (2009) presented a transfer learning approach in multi-domain NLU, where the model jointly learns slot taggers in multiple domains and simultaneously predicts domain detection and slot tagging results.[2] To share parameters across domains, they added an additional node for domain prediction on top of the slot sequence. However, this framework also limited to a setting in which the label set remains invariant. In contrast, our method is restricted to this setting without any modification of models.

3 Sequence Modeling Technique

The proposed techniques in Section 4 and 5 are generic methodologies and not tied to any particular models such as any sequence models and instanced based models. However, because of superior performance over CRF, we use a hidden unit CRF (HUCRF) of Maaten et al. (2011).

[1] Multilingual learning (Kim et al., 2011; Kim and Snyder, 2012; Kim and Snyder, 2013) has same setting.

[2] Jeong and Lee (2009) pointed out that if the domain is given, their method is the same as that of Daumé III (2007).

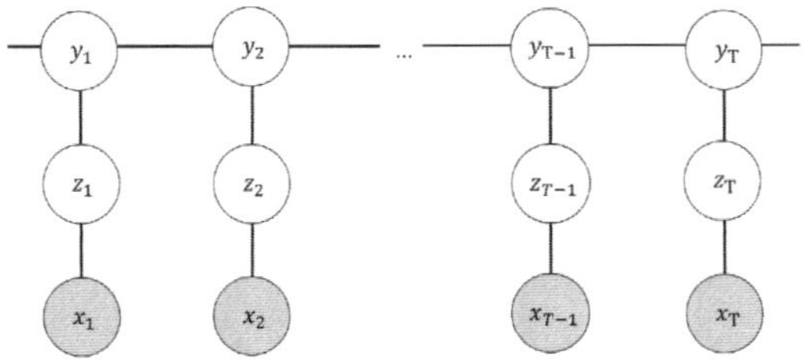

Figure 1: Graphical representation of hidden unit CRFs.

While popular and effective, a CRF is still a linear model. In contrast, a HUCRF benefits from nonlinearity, leading to superior performance over CRF (Maaten et al., 2011). Thus we will focus on HUCRFs to demonstrate our techniques in experiments.

3.1 Hidden Unit CRF (HUCRF)

A HUCRF introduces a layer of binary-valued hidden units $z = z_1 \ldots z_n \in \{0,1\}$ for each pair of label sequence $y = y_1 \ldots y_n$ and observation sequence $x = x_1 \ldots x_n$. A HUCRF parametrized by $\theta \in \mathbb{R}^d$ and $\gamma \in \mathbb{R}^{d'}$ defines a joint probability of y and z conditioned on x as follows:

$$p_{\theta,\gamma}(y,z|x) = \frac{\exp(\theta^\top \Phi(x,z) + \gamma^\top \Psi(z,y))}{\sum_{\substack{z' \in \{0,1\}^n \\ y' \in \mathcal{Y}(x,z')}} \exp(\theta^\top \Phi(x,z') + \gamma^\top \Psi(z',y'))} \tag{1}$$

where $\mathcal{Y}(x,z)$ is the set of all possible label sequences for x and z, and $\Phi(x,z) \in \mathbb{R}^d$ and $\Psi(z,y) \in \mathbb{R}^{d'}$ are global feature functions that decompose into local feature functions:

$$\Phi(x,z) = \sum_{j=1}^{n} \phi(x,j,z_j)$$

$$\Psi(z,y) = \sum_{j=1}^{n} \psi(z_j,y_{j-1},y_j)$$

HUCRF forces the interaction between the observations and the labels at each position j to go through a latent variable z_j: see Figure 1 for illustration. Then the probability of labels y is given by marginalizing over the hidden units,

$$p_{\theta,\gamma}(y|x) = \sum_{z \in \{0,1\}^n} p_{\theta,\gamma}(y,z|x)$$

As in restricted Boltzmann machines (Larochelle and Bengio, 2008), hidden units are conditionally independent given observations and labels. This allows for efficient inference with HUCRFs despite their richness (see Maaten et al. (2011) for details). We use a perceptron-style algorithm of Maaten et al. (2011) for training HUCRFs.

4 Transfer learning between domains with different label sets

In this section, we describe three methods for utilizing annotations in domains with different label types. First two methods are about transferring features and last method is about transferring model parameters. Each of these methods requires some sort of *mapping* for label types. A fine-grained label type needs to be mapped to a coarse one; a label type in one domain needs to be mapped to the corresponding label type in another domain. We will provide a solution to obtaining these label mappings automatically in Section 5.

4.1 Coarse-to-fine prediction

This approach has some similarities to the method of Li et al. (2011) in that shared slots are used to transfer information between domains. In this two-stage approach, we train a model on the source domain, make predictions on the target domain, and then use the predicted labels as additional features to train a final model on the target domain. This can be helpful if there is some correlation between the label types in the source domain and the label types in the target domain.

However, it is not desirable to directly use the label types in the source domain since they can be highly specific to that particular domain. An effective way to combat this problem is to reduce the original label types such `start-time`, `contract-info`, and `restaurant` as to a set of coarse label types such as `name`, `date`, `time`, and `location` that are universally shared across all domains. By doing so, we can use the first model to predict generic labels such as `time` and then use the second model to use this information to predict fine-grained labels such as `start-time` and `end-time`.

4.2 Method of Daumé III (2007)

In this popular technique for domain adaptation, we train a model on the union of the source domain data and the target domain data but with the following preprocessing step: each feature is duplicated and the copy is conjoined with a domain indicator. For example, in a `WEATHER` domain dataset, a feature that indicates the identity of the string "Sunny" will generate both $w(0) = Sunny$ and $(w(0) = Sunny) \wedge (domain = WEATHER)$ as feature types. This preprocessing allows the model to utilize all data through the common features and at the same time specialize to specific domains through the domain specific features. This is especially helpful when there is label ambiguity on particular features (e.g., "Sunny" might be a `weather-condition` in a `WEATHER` domain dataset but a `music-song-name` in a `MUSIC` domain dataset).

Note that a straightforward application of this technique is in general not feasible in our situation. This is because we have features conjoined with label types and our domains do *not* share label types. This breaks the sharing of features across domains: many feature types in the source domain are disjoint from those in the target domain due to different labeling.

Thus it is necessary to first map source domain label types to target domain label type. After the mapping, features are shared across domains and we can apply this technique.

4.3 Transferring model parameter

In this approach, we train HUCRF on the source domain and transfer the learned parameters to initialize the training process on the target domain. This can be helpful for at least two reasons:

1. The resulting model will have parameters for feature types observed in the source domain as well as the target domain. Thus it has better feature coverage.

2. If the training objective is non-convex, this initialization can be helpful in avoiding bad local optima.

Since the training objective of HUCRFs is non-convex, both benefits can apply. We show in our experiments that this is indeed the case: the model benefits from both better feature coverage and better initialization.

Note that in order to use this approach, we need to map source domain label types to target domain label type so that we know which parameter in

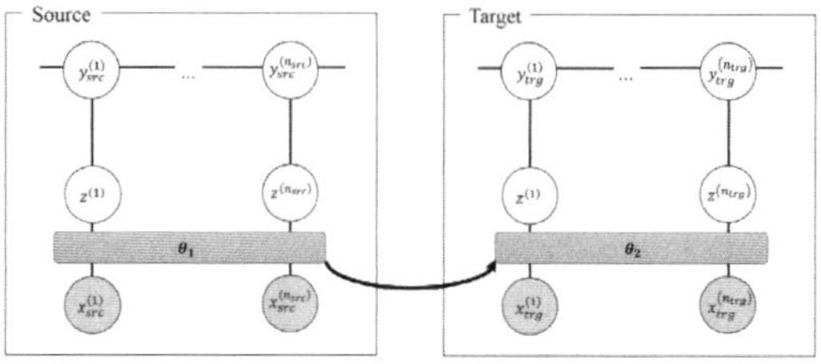

Figure 2: Illustration of a pretraining scheme for HUCRFs.

the source domain corresponds to which parameter in the target domain. This can be a many-to-one, one-to-many, one-to-one mapping depending on the label sets.

4.3.1 Pretraining with HUCRFs

In fact, pretraining HUCRFs in the source domain can be done in various ways. Recall that there are two parameter types: $\theta \in \mathbb{R}^d$ for scoring observations and hidden states and $\gamma \in \mathbb{R}^{d'}$ for scoring hidden states and labels (Eq. (1)). In pretraining, we first train a model (θ_1, γ_1) on the source data $\{(x_{src}^{(i)}, y_{src}^{(i)})\}_{i=1}^{n_{src}}$:

$$(\theta_1, \gamma_1) \approx \arg\max_{\theta,\gamma} \sum_{i=1}^{n_{src}} \log p_{\theta,\gamma}(y_{src}^{(i)} | x_{src}^{(i)})$$

Then we train a model (θ_2, γ_2) on the target data $\{(x_{trg}^{(i)}, y_{trg}^{(i)})\}_{i=1}^{n_{trg}}$ by initializing $(\theta_2, \gamma_2) \leftarrow (\theta_1, \gamma_1)$:

$$(\theta_2, \gamma_2) \approx \arg\max_{\theta,\gamma} \sum_{i=1}^{n_{trg}} \log p_{\theta,\gamma}(y_{trg}^{(i)} | x_{trg}^{(i)})$$

Here, we can choose to initialize only $\theta_2 \leftarrow \theta_1$ and discard the parameters for hidden states and labels since they may not be the same. The θ_1 parameters model the hidden structures in the source domain data and serve as a good initialization point for learning the θ_2 parameters in the target domain. This can be helpful if the mapping between the label types in the source data and the label types in the target data is unreliable. This process is illustrated in Figure 2.

5 Automatic generation of label mappings

All methods described in Section 4 require a way to propagate the information in label types across different domains. A straightforward solution would be to manually construct such mappings by inspection. For instance, we can specify that `start-time` and `end-time` are grouped as the same label `time`, or that the label `public-transportation-route` in the `PLACES` domain maps to the label `implicit-location` in the `CALENDAR` domain.

Instead, we propose a technique that automatically generates the label mappings. We induce vector representations for all label types through canonical correlation analysis (CCA) — a powerful and flexible technique for deriving low-dimensional representation. We give a review of CCA in Section 5.1 and describe how we use the technique to construct label mappings in Section 5.2.

5.1 Canonical Correlation Analysis (CCA)

CCA is a general technique that operates on a pair of multi-dimensional variables. CCA finds k dimensions (k is a parameter to be specified) in which these variables are maximally correlated.

Let $x_1 \ldots x_n \in \mathbb{R}^d$ and $y_1 \ldots y_n \in \mathbb{R}^{d'}$ be n samples of the two variables. For simplicity, assume that these variables have zero mean. Then CCA computes the following for $i = 1 \ldots k$:

$$\underset{\substack{u_i \in \mathbb{R}^d,\, v_i \in \mathbb{R}^{d'}: \\ u_i^\top u_{i'} = 0 \;\; \forall i' < i \\ v_i^\top v_{i'} = 0 \;\; \forall i' < i}}{\arg\max} \frac{\sum_{l=1}^{n} (u_i^\top x_l)(v_i^\top y_l)}{\sqrt{\sum_{l=1}^{n} (u_i^\top x_l)^2} \sqrt{\sum_{l=1}^{n} (v_i^\top y_l)^2}}$$

In other words, each (u_i, v_i) is a pair of projection vectors such that the *correlation* between the projected variables $u_i^\top x_l$ and $v_i^\top y_l$ (now scalars) is maximized, under the constraint that this projection is *uncorrelated* with the previous $i - 1$ projections.

This is a non-convex problem due to the interaction between u_i and v_i. Fortunately, a method based on singular value decomposition (SVD) provides an efficient and exact solution to this problem (Hotelling, 1936). The resulting solution $u_1 \ldots u_k \in \mathbb{R}^d$ and $v_1 \ldots v_k \in \mathbb{R}^{d'}$ can be used to project the variables from the original d- and d'-dimensional spaces to a k-dimensional space:

$$x \in \mathbb{R}^d \longrightarrow \bar{x} \in \mathbb{R}^k : \bar{x}_i = u_i^\top x$$
$$y \in \mathbb{R}^{d'} \longrightarrow \bar{y} \in \mathbb{R}^k : \bar{y}_i = v_i^\top y$$

The new k-dimensional representation of each variable now contains information about the other variable. The value of k is usually selected to be much smaller than d or d', so the representation is typically also low-dimensional.

5.2 Inducing label embeddings

We now describe how to use CCA to induce vector representations for label types. Using the same notation, let n be the number of instances of labels in the entire data. Let $x_1 \ldots x_n$ be the original representations of the label samples and $y_1 \ldots y_n$ be the original representations of the associated words set contained in the labels.

We employ the following definition for the original representations for reasons we explain below. Let d be the number of distinct label types and d' be the number of distinct word types.

- $x_l \in \mathbb{R}^d$ is a zero vector in which the entry corresponding to the label type of the l-th instance is set to 1.
- $y_l \in \mathbb{R}^{d'}$ is a zero vector in which the entries corresponding to words spanned by the label are set to 1.

The motivation for this definition is that similar label types often have similar or same word.

For instance, consider two label types `start-time`, (start time of a calendar event) and `end-time`, meaning (the end time of a calendar event). Each type is frequently associated with phrases about time. The phrases {"9 pm", "7", "8 am"} might be labeled as `start-time`; the phrases {"9 am", "7 pm"} might be labeled as `end-time`. In these examples, both label types share words "am", "pm", "9", and "7" even though phrases may not match exactly.

Figure 3 gives the CCA algorithm for inducing label embeddings. It produces a k-dimensional vector for each label type corresponding to the CCA projection of the one-hot encoding of that label.

5.3 Discussion on alternative label representations

We point out that there are other options for inducing label representations besides CCA. For instance, one could simply use the sparse feature vector representation of each label. However, CCA's low-dimensional projection is computationally more convenient and arguably more generalizable. One can also consider training a predictive model similar to `word2vec` (Mikolov

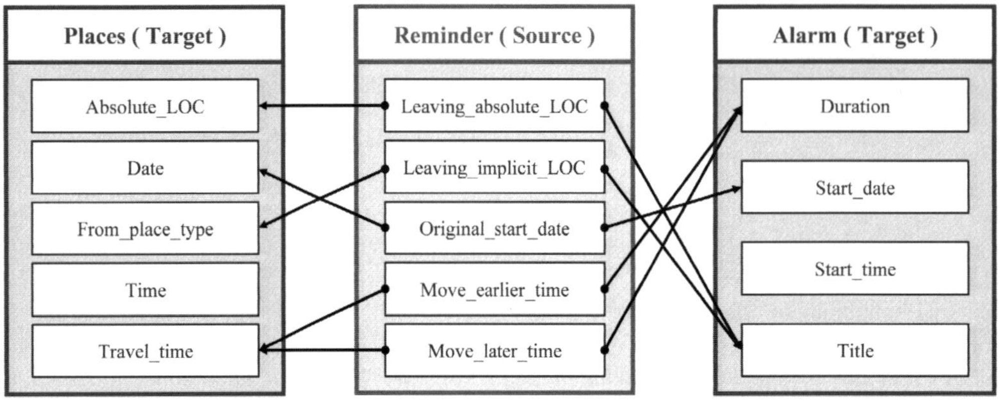

Figure 4: Bijective mapping: labels in `REMINDER` domain (orange box) are mapped into those in `PLACES` and `ALARM` domains.

CCA-LABEL
Input: labeled sequences $\{(x^{(i)}, y^{(i)})\}_{i=1}^{n}$, dimension k
Output: label vector $v \in \mathbb{R}^k$ for each label type

1. For each label type $l \in \{1 \ldots d\}$ and word type $w \in \{1 \ldots d\}$ present in the sequences, calculate
   - **count**(l) = number of times label l occurs
   - **count**(w) = number of times word w occurs
   - **count**(l, w) = number of times word w occurs under label l
2. Define a matrix $\Omega \in \mathbb{R}^{d \times d'}$ where:
$$\Omega_{l,w} = \frac{\textbf{count}(l, w)}{\sqrt{\textbf{count}(l)\textbf{count}(w)}}$$
3. Perform rank-k SVD on Ω. Let $U \in \mathbb{R}^{d \times k}$ be a matrix where the i-th column is the left singular vector of Ω corresponding to the i-th largest singular value.
4. For each label l, set the l-th normalized row of U to be its vector representation.

Figure 3: CCA algorithm for inducing label embeddings.

et al., 2013). But this requires significant efforts in implementation and also very long training time. In contrast, CCA is simple, efficient, and effective and can be readily implemented. Also, CCA is theoretically well understood while methods inspired by neural networks are not.

5.4 Constructing label mappings

Vector representations of label types allow for natural solutions to the task of constructing label mappings.

5.4.1 Mapping to a coarse label set

Given a domain and the label types that occur in the domain, we can reduce the number of label types by simply clustering their vector representations. For instance, if the embeddings for `start-time` and `end-time` are close together, they will be grouped as a single label type. We run the k-means algorithm on the label embeddings to obtain this coarse label set.

Table 1 shows examples of this clustering. It demonstrates that the CCA representations obtained by the procedure described in Section 5.2 are indeed informative of the labels' properties.

Cluster	Labels	Cluster	Labels
Time	start_time end_time original_start_time travel_time	Person	contact_info artist from_contact_name relationship_name
Loc	absolute_loc leaving_loc from_loc position_ref	Loc_ATTR	prefer_route public_trans_route nearby distance

Table 1: Some of cluster examples

5.4.2 Bijective mapping between label sets

Given a pair of domains and their label sets, we can create a bijective label mapping by finding the nearest neighbor of each label type. Figure 4 shows some actual examples of CCA-based bijective maps, where the label set in the `REMINDER` domain is mapped to the `PLACES` and `ALARM` domains. One particularly interesting example is that `move_earlier_time` in `REMINDER` domain is mapped to `Travel_time` in `PLACES` and `Duration` in `ALARM` domain. This is a tag used in a user utterance requesting to move an

Domains	# of label	Source Training	Test	Description
Alarm	7	27865	3334	Set alarms
Calendar	20	50255	7017	Set appointments & meetings in the calendar
Communication	18	104881	14484	Make calls, send texts, and communication related user request
Note	4	17445	2342	Note taking
Ondevice	7	60847	9704	Phone settings
Places	32	150348	20798	Find places & get direction
Reminder	16	62664	8235	Setting time, person & place based reminder
Weather	9	53096	9114	Weather forecasts & historical information about weather patterns

Table 2: Size of number of label, labeled data set size and description for Alarm, Calendar, Communication, Note, Ondevice, Places, Reminder and Weather domains partitioned into training and test set.

appointment to an earlier time. For example, in the query "move the dentist's appointment up by 30 minutes.", the phrase "30 minutes" is tagged with `move_earlier_time`. The role of this tag is very similar to the role of `Travel_time` in `PLACES` (not `Time`) and `Duration` in `ALARMS` (not `Start_date`), and CCA is able to recover this relation.

6 Experiments

In this section, we turn to experimental findings to provide empirical support for our proposed methods.

6.1 Setup

To test the effectiveness of our approach, we apply it to a suite of eight Cortana personal assistant domains for slot sequence tagging tasks, where the goal is to find the correct semantic tagging of the words in a given user utterance.

The data statistics and short descriptions are shown in Table 2. As the table indicates, the domains have very different granularity and diverse semantics.

6.2 Baselines

In all our experiments, we trained HUCRF and only used n-gram features, including unigram, bigram, and trigram within a window of five words (± 2 words) around the current word as binary feature functions. With these features, we compare the following methods for slot tagging:

- *NoAdapt*: train only on target training data.
- *Union*: train on the union of source and target training data.
- *Daume*: train with the feature duplication method described in 4.2.
- *C2F*: train with the coarse-to-fine prediction method described in 4.1.
- *Pretrain*: train with the pretraining method described in 4.3.1.

To apply these methods except for *Target*, we treat each of the eight domains in turn as the test domain, with one of remaining seven domain as the source domain. As in general domain adaptation setting, we assume that the source domain has a sufficient amount of labeled data but the target domain has an insufficient amount of labeled data. Specifically, For each test or target domain, we only use 10% of the training examples to simulate data scarcity. In the following experiments, we report the slot F-measure, using the standard CoNLL evaluation script [3]

6.3 Results on mappings

	Mapping technique		
Adaptation technique	Manual	Li et al. (2011)	CCA
Union	68.16	64.7	70.51
Daume	73.42	67.32	75.85
C2F	75.47	75.69	76.29
Pretrain	77.72	76.99	78.76
NoAdapt		75.13	

Table 3: Comparison of slot F1 scores using the proposed CCA-derived mapping versus other mapping methods combined with different adaptation techniques.

To assess the quality of our automatic mapping methods via CCA described in Section 5, we compared against manually established mappings and also the mapping method of Li et al. (2011). The method of Li et al. (2011) is to associate each slot type with the aggregate active feature weight vectors based on an existing domain specific slot tagger (a CRF). Manual mapping were performed

[3]http://www.cnts.ua.ac.be/conll2000/chunking/output.html

Target Domain	Source Nearest Domain	NoAdapt	Minimum distance domain performance: Union	Daume	C2F	Pretrain
Alarm	Calendar	74.82	84.46	**84.97**	81.54	84.88
Calendar	Reminder	70.51	73.94	73.07	72.82	**77.08**
Note	Reminder	65.38	56.39	**69.89**	66.6	69.55
Ondevice	Weather	70.86	66.66	71.17	71.49	**73.5**
Reminder	Calendar	77.3	**83.38**	82.19	81.29	83.22
Communication	Reminder	79.31	74.28	80.33	79.66	**82.96**
Places	Weather	73.93	73.74	75.86	73.73	**80.11**
Weather	Places	92.78	92.88	94.43	93.75	**97.18**
Average	-	75.61	75.72	78.99	77.61	**81.06**

Table 4: Slot F1 scores on each target domain using adapted models from the nearest source domain.

Source \ Target		Alarm	Calendar	Note	Ondevice	Reminder	Communication	Places	Weather	Average
NoAdapt		74.82	70.51	65.38	70.86	77.3	79.31	73.93	92.78	75.61
Alarm	Union	-	72.26	59.92	67.32	79.45	77.91	73.78	92.67	74.76
	Daume	-	72.77	66.28	70.94	81.12	80.38	75.62	93.12	77.18
	C2F	-	70.59	64.06	71	78.8	79.5	74.29	92.75	75.86
	Pretrain	-	**76.68**	**68.12**	**71.8**	**81.25**	**81.5**	**77.1**	**95.03**	**78.78**
Calendar	Union	84.46	-	50.64	64.7	**83.38**	75.02	71.13	93.2	74.65
	Daume	**84.97**	-	65.43	70.12	82.19	79.78	75.21	93.1	78.69
	C2F	81.54	-	66.08	71.22	81.29	80.11	73.75	93.18	78.17
	Pretrain	84.88	-	**69.21**	**72.3**	83.22	**82.75**	**77.89**	**95.8**	**80.86**
Note	Union	60.26	60.42	-	65.79	69.81	76.85	70.56	90.02	70.53
	Daume	66.03	67.38	-	69.54	76.65	77.83	73.49	92.09	74.72
	C2F	74.68	70.51	-	71.34	77.49	79.48	74.17	92.89	77.22
	Pretrain	**75.52**	**72.4**	-	**71.4**	**80.1**	**82.06**	**76.53**	**94.22**	**78.89**
Ondevice	Union	63.72	66.28	55.67	-	75.16	74.85	70.59	90.7	71.00
	Daume	71.01	69.39	64.02	-	75.75	77.92	74.41	92.62	75.02
	C2F	74.02	70.33	64.99	-	77.43	79.53	73.84	92.71	76.12
	Pretrain	**76.27**	**71.59**	**67.21**	-	**78.67**	**82.34**	**77.45**	**95.04**	**78.37**
Reminder	Union	84.74	73.94	56.39	61.27	-	74.28	68.14	92.22	73.00
	Daume	84.66	73.07	**69.89**	67.94	-	80.33	73.36	93.19	77.49
	C2F	80.42	72.82	66.6	71.36	-	79.66	74.35	92.38	76.80
	Pretrain	**84.75**	**77.08**	69.55	**71.9**	-	**82.96**	**78.57**	**95.37**	**80.03**
Communication	Union	58.25	54.69	65.28	62.95	63.98	-	68.16	87.13	65.78
	Daume	70.4	67.41	69.14	69.26	77.67	-	73.33	92.82	74.29
	C2F	74.54	70.84	65.48	70.81	77.68	-	74.15	92.79	75.18
	Pretrain	**76.04**	**74.01**	**68.76**	**73.2**	**80.74**	-	**76.83**	**94.58**	**77.74**
Places	Union	71.7	67.56	45.37	53.93	67.78	63.67	-	92.88	66.13
	Daume	75.69	69.01	66.11	65.46	79.01	78.42	-	94.43	75.45
	C2F	**78.9**	71.64	66.93	71.26	79.2	79.19	-	93.75	77.27
	Pretrain	76.8	**74.12**	**67.5**	**72.7**	**81**	**81.89**	-	**97.18**	**78.74**
Weather	Union	69.43	58.53	56.76	66.66	74.98	77.53	73.74	-	68.23
	Daume	75	71.73	66.54	71.17	**79.36**	80.57	75.86	-	74.32
	C2F	**77.61**	71.47	63.24	71.49	78.44	79.43	73.73	-	73.63
	Pretrain	77.37	**74.5**	**68.23**	**73.5**	80.96	**82.05**	**80.11**	-	**76.67**
Average	Union	70.37	64.81	55.72	63.23	73.51	74.3	70.87	91.26	70.51
	Daume	75.4	70.23	66.77	69.2	78.32	79.32	74.47	93.05	75.85
	C2F	77.39	71.17	65.4	71.21	78.62	79.56	74.04	92.92	76.29
	Pretrain	**78.80**	**74.34**	**68.37**	**72.40**	**80.85**	**82.22**	**77.78**	**95.32**	**78.76**

Table 5: Slot F1 scores of using Union, Daume, Coarse-to-Fine and pretraining on all pairs of source and target data. The numbers in boldface are the best performing adaptation technique in each pair.

by two experienced annotators who have PhD in linguistics and machine learning. Each annotator first assigned mapping slot labels independently and then both annotators collaborated to reduce disagreement of their mapping results. Initially, the disagreement of their mapping rate between two annotators was about 30% because labels of slot tagging are very diverse; furthermore, in some cases it is not clear for human annotators if there exists a valid mapping.

The results are shown at Table 3. Vector representation of Li et al. (2011) increases the F1 score slightly from 75.13 to 75.69 in *C2F*, but it does not help as much in cases that require bijective mapping: *Daume*, *Union* and *Pretrain*.

In contrast, the proposed CCA based technique consistently outperforms the *NoAdapt* baselines by significant margins. More importantly, it also outperforms manual results under all conditions. It is perhaps not so surprising – the CCA derived mapping is completely data driven, while human annotators have nothing but the prior linguistic knowledge about the slot tags and the domain.

6.4 Main Results

The full results are shown in Table 5, where all pairs of source and target languages are considered for domain adaptation. It is clear from the table that we can always achieve better results using adaptation techniques than the non-adapted models trained only on the target data. Also, our proposed pretraining method outperforms other types of adaptation in most cases.

The overall result of our experiments are shown in Table 4. In this experiment, we compare different adaptation techniques using our suggested CCA-based mapping. Here, except for *NoAdapt*, we use both the target and the nearest source domain data. To find the nearest domain, we first map fine grained label set to coarse label set by using the method described in Section 5.4.1 and then count how many coarse labels are used in a domain. And then we can find the nearest source domain by calculating the l_2 distance between the multinomial distributions of the source domain and the target domain over the set of coarse labels.

For example, for `CALENDAR`, we identify `REMINDER` as the nearest domain and vice versa because most of their labels are attributes related to `time`. In all experiments, the domain adapted models perform better than using only target domain data which achieves 75.1% F1 score. Simply combining source and target domain using our automatically mapped slot labels performs slightly better than baseline. *C2F* boosts the performance up to 77.61% and *Daume* is able to reach 78.99%.[4] Finally, our proposed method, *pretrain* achieves nearly 81.02% F1 score.

7 Conclusion

We presented an approach to take advantage of existing annotations when the data are similar but the label sets are different. This approach was based on label embeddings from CCA, which reduces the setting to a standard domain adaptation problem. Combined with a novel pretraining scheme applied to hidden-unit CRFs, our approach is shown to be superior to strong baselines in extensive experiments for slot tagging on eight distinct personal assistant domains.

[4] It is known that *Daume* is less beneficial when the source and target domains are similar due to the increased number of features.

References

Tasos Anastasakos, Young-Bum Kim, and Anoop Deoras. 2014. Task specific continuous word representations for mono and multi-lingual spoken language understanding. In *Proceeding of the ICASSP*, pages 3246–3250. IEEE.

Rie Kubota Ando and Tong Zhang. 2005. A framework for learning predictive structures from multiple tasks and unlabeled data. *The Journal of Machine Learning Research*, 6:1817–1853.

John Blitzer, Ryan McDonald, and Fernando Pereira. 2006. Domain adaptation with structural correspondence learning. In *Proceedings of the EMNLP*, pages 120–128. Association for Computational Linguistics.

Asli Celikyilmaz, Dilek Hakkani-Tur, Panupong Pasupat, and Ruhi Sarikaya. 2015. Enriching word embeddings using knowledge graph for semantic tagging in conversational dialog systems. AAAI - Association for the Advancement of Artificial Intelligence.

Ciprian Chelba and Alex Acero. 2006. Adaptation of maximum entropy capitalizer: Little data can help a lot. *Computer Speech & Language*, 20(4):382–399.

Minmin Chen, Kilian Q Weinberger, and John Blitzer. 2011. Co-training for domain adaptation. In *Advances in neural information processing systems*, pages 2456–2464.

Ronan Collobert and Jason Weston. 2008. A unified architecture for natural language processing: Deep neural networks with multitask learning. In *Proceedings of the ICML*, pages 160–167. ACM.

Hal Daume III and Daniel Marcu. 2006. Domain adaptation for statistical classifiers. *Journal of Artificial Intelligence Research*, pages 101–126.

Hal Daumé III. 2007. Frustratingly easy domain adaptation. *proceedings of the ACL*, page 256.

Renato De Mori, Frédéric Bechet, Dilek Hakkani-Tur, Michael McTear, Giuseppe Riccardi, and Gokhan Tur. 2008. Spoken language understanding. *Signal Processing Magazine, IEEE*, 25(3):50–58.

Ali El-Kahky, Derek Liu, Ruhi Sarikaya, Gokhan Tur, Dilek Hakkani-Tur, and Larry Heck. 2014. Extending domain coverage of language understanding systems via intent transfer between domains using knowledge graphs and search query click logs. IEEE, Proceedings of the ICASSP.

Jenny Rose Finkel and Christopher D Manning. 2009. Hierarchical bayesian domain adaptation. In *Proceedings of the ACL*, pages 602–610. Association for Computational Linguistics.

George Foster, Cyril Goutte, and Roland Kuhn. 2010. Discriminative instance weighting for domain adaptation in statistical machine translation. In *Proceedings of the EMNLP*, pages 451–459. Association for Computational Linguistics.

Harold Hotelling. 1936. Relations between two sets of variates. *Biometrika*, 28(3/4):321–377.

Fei Huang and Alexander Yates. 2010. Exploring representation-learning approaches to domain adaptation. In *Proceedings of the 2010 Workshop on Domain Adaptation for Natural Language Processing*, pages 23–30. Association for Computational Linguistics.

Minwoo Jeong and Gary Geunbae Lee. 2009. Multi-domain spoken language understanding with transfer learning. *Speech Communication*, 51(5):412–424.

Jing Jiang and ChengXiang Zhai. 2007. Instance weighting for domain adaptation in nlp. In *Proceedings of the ACL*, volume 7, pages 264–271. Association for Computational Linguistics.

Young-Bum Kim and Benjamin Snyder. 2012. Universal grapheme-to-phoneme prediction over latin alphabets. In *Proceedings of the EMNLP*, pages 332–343, Jeju Island, South Korea, July. Association for Computational Linguistics.

Young-Bum Kim and Benjamin Snyder. 2013. Unsupervised consonant-vowel prediction over hundreds of languages. In *Proceedings of the ACL*, pages 1527–1536. Association for Computational Linguistics.

Young-Bum Kim, João V Graça, and Benjamin Snyder. 2011. Universal morphological analysis using structured nearest neighbor prediction. In *Proceedings of the EMNLP*, pages 322–332. Association for Computational Linguistics.

Young-Bum Kim, Minwoo Jeong, Karl Stratos, and Ruhi Sarikaya. 2015. Weakly supervised slot tagging with partially labeled sequences from web search click logs. In *Proceedings of the NAACL*. Association for Computational Linguistics.

Abhishek Kumar, Avishek Saha, and Hal Daume. 2010. Co-regularization based semi-supervised domain adaptation. In *Advances in Neural Information Processing Systems*, pages 478–486.

Hugo Larochelle and Yoshua Bengio. 2008. Classification using discriminative restricted boltzmann machines. In *Proceedings of the ICML*.

Xiao Li, Ye-Yi Wang, and Gökhan Tür. 2011. Multi-task learning for spoken language understanding with shared slots. In *Proceeding of the INTERSPEECH*, pages 701–704. IEEE.

Xiaohu Liu and Ruhi Sarikaya. 2014. A discriminative model based entity dictionary weighting approach for spoken language understanding. IEEE Institute of Electrical and Electronics Engineers.

Yi Ma, Paul A. Crook, Ruhi Sarikaya, and Eric Fosler-Lussier. 2015. Knowledge graph inference for spoken dialog systems. In *Proceedings of the ICASSP*. IEEE.

Laurens Maaten, Max Welling, and Lawrence K Saul. 2011. Hidden-unit conditional random fields. In *International Conference on Artificial Intelligence and Statistics*.

Alex Marin, Roman Holenstein, Ruhi Sarikaya, and Mari Ostendorf. 2014. Learning phrase patterns for text classification using a knowledge graph and unlabeled data. ISCA - International Speech Communication Association.

David McClosky, Eugene Charniak, and Mark Johnson. 2010. Automatic domain adaptation for parsing. In *Proceedings of the NAACL*, pages 28–36. Association for Computational Linguistics.

Tomas Mikolov, Kai Chen, Greg Corrado, and Jeffrey Dean. 2013. Efficient estimation of word representations in vector space. *arXiv preprint arXiv:1301.3781*.

Ruhi Sarikaya, Asli C, Anoop Deoras, and Minwoo Jeong. 2014. Shrinkage based features for slot tagging with conditional random fields. Proceeding of ISCA - International Speech Communication Association, September.

Tobias Schnabel and Hinrich Schütze. 2014. Flors: Fast and simple domain adaptation for part-of-speech tagging. *Transactions of the Association for Computational Linguistics*, 2:15–26.

Charles Sutton and Andrew McCallum. 2005. Composition of conditional random fields for transfer learning. In *Proceedings of the EMNLP*, pages 748–754. Association for Computational Linguistics.

Gokhan Tur. 2006. Multitask learning for spoken language understanding. In *Proceedings of the ICASSP*, Toulouse, France. IEEE.

Puyang Xu and Ruhi Sarikaya. 2013. Convolutional neural network based triangular crf for joint intent detection and slot filling. In *Automatic Speech Recognition and Understanding (ASRU)*, pages 78–83. IEEE.

Puyang Xu and Ruhi Sarikaya. 2014. Targeted feature dropout for robust slot filling in natural language understanding. ISCA - International Speech Communication Association.

Matrix Factorization with Knowledge Graph Propagation for Unsupervised Spoken Language Understanding

Yun-Nung Chen, William Yang Wang, Anatole Gershman, and Alexander I. Rudnicky
School of Computer Science, Carnegie Mellon University
5000 Forbes Aveue, Pittsburgh, PA 15213-3891, USA
{yvchen, yww, anatoleg, air}@cs.cmu.edu

Abstract

Spoken dialogue systems (SDS) typically require a predefined semantic ontology to train a spoken language understanding (SLU) module. In addition to the annotation cost, a key challenge for designing such an ontology is to define a coherent slot set while considering their complex relations. This paper introduces a novel matrix factorization (MF) approach to learn latent feature vectors for utterances and semantic elements without the need of corpus annotations. Specifically, our model learns the semantic slots for a domain-specific SDS in an unsupervised fashion, and carries out semantic parsing using latent MF techniques. To further consider the global semantic structure, such as inter-word and inter-slot relations, we augment the latent MF-based model with a knowledge graph propagation model based on a slot-based semantic graph and a word-based lexical graph. Our experiments show that the proposed MF approaches produce better SLU models that are able to predict semantic slots and word patterns taking into account their relations and domain-specificity in a joint manner.

1 Introduction

A key component of a spoken dialogue system (SDS) is the spoken language understanding (SLU) module—it parses the users' utterances into semantic representations; for example, the utterance "*find a cheap restaurant*" can be parsed into (price=*cheap*, target=*restaurant*) (Pieraccini et al., 1992). To design the SLU module of a SDS, most previous studies relied on predefined slots[1] for training the decoder (Seneff, 1992; Dowding et al., 1993; Gupta et al., 2006; Bohus and Rudnicky, 2009). However, these predefined semantic slots may bias the subsequent data collection process, and the cost of manually labeling utterances for updating the ontology is expensive (Wang et al., 2012).

In recent years, this problem led to the development of unsupervised SLU techniques (Heck and Hakkani-Tür, 2012; Heck et al., 2013; Chen et al., 2013b; Chen et al., 2014b). In particular, Chen et al. (2013b) proposed a frame-semantics based framework for automatically inducing semantic slots given raw audios. However, these approaches generally do not explicitly learn the latent factor representations to model the measurement errors (Skrondal and Rabe-Hesketh, 2004), nor do they jointly consider the complex lexical, syntactic, and semantic relations among words, slots, and utterances.

Another challenge of SLU is the inference of the hidden semantics. Considering the user utterance "*can i have a cheap restaurant*", from its surface patterns, we can see that it includes explicit semantic information about "price (cheap)" and "target (restaurant)"; however, it also includes hidden semantic information, such as "food" and "seeking", since the SDS needs to infer that the user wants to "find" some cheap "food", even though they are not directly observed in the surface patterns. Nonetheless, these implicit semantics are important semantic concepts for domain-specific SDSs. Traditional SLU models use discriminative classifiers (Henderson et al., 2012) to predict whether the predefined slots occur in the utterances or not, ignoring the unobserved concepts and the hidden semantic information.

In this paper, we take a rather radical approach: we propose a novel matrix factorization (MF) model for learning latent features for SLU, taking account of additional information such as the word relations, the induced slots, and the slot relations. To further consider the global coherence of induced slots, we combine the MF model with

[1] A slot is defined as a basic semantic unit in SLU, such as "price" and "target" in the example.

Proceedings of the 53rd Annual Meeting of the Association for Computational Linguistics and the 7th International Joint Conference on Natural Language Processing, pages 483–494,
Beijing, China, July 26-31, 2015.

a knowledge graph propagation based model, fusing both a word-based lexical knowledge graph and a slot-based semantic graph. In fact, as it is shown in the Netflix challenge, MF is credited as the most useful technique for recommendation systems (Koren et al., 2009). Also, the MF model considers the unobserved patterns and estimates their probabilities instead of viewing them as negative examples. However, to the best of our knowledge, the MF technique is not yet well understood in the SLU and SDS communities, and it is not very straight-forward to use MF methods to learn latent feature representations for semantic parsing in SLU. To evaluate the performance of our model, we compare it to standard discriminative SLU baselines, and show that our MF-based model is able to produce strong results in semantic decoding, and the knowledge graph propagation model further improves the performance. Our contributions are three-fold:

- We are among the first to study matrix factorization techniques for unsupervised SLU, taking account of additional information;
- We augment the MF model with a knowledge graph propagation model, increasing the global coherence of semantic decoding using induced slots;
- Our experimental results show that the MF-based unsupervised SLU outperforms strong discriminative baselines, obtaining promising results.

In the next section, we outline the related work in unsupervised SLU and latent variable modeling for spoken language processing. Section 3 introduces our framework. The detailed MF approach is explained in Section 4. We then introduce the global knowledge graphs for MF in Section 5. Section 6 shows the experimental results, and Section 7 concludes.

2 Related Work

Unsupervised SLU Tur et al. (2011; 2012) were among the first to consider unsupervised approaches for SLU, where they exploited query logs for slot-filling. In a subsequent study, Heck and Hakkani-Tür (2012) studied the Semantic Web for an unsupervised intent detection problem in SLU, showing that results obtained from the unsupervised training process align well with the performance of traditional supervised learning. Following their success of unsupervised SLU, recent studies have also obtained interesting results on the tasks of relation detection (Hakkani-Tür et al., 2013; Chen et al., 2014a), entity extraction (Wang et al., 2014), and extending domain coverage (El-Kahky et al., 2014; Chen and Rudnicky, 2014). However, most of the studies above do not explicitly learn latent factor representations from the data—while we hypothesize that the better robustness in noisy data can be achieved by explicitly modeling the measurement errors (usually produced by automatic speech recognizers (ASR)) using latent variable models and taking additional local and global semantic constraints into account.

Latent Variable Modeling in SLU Early studies on latent variable modeling in speech included the classic hidden Markov model for statistical speech recognition (Jelinek, 1997). Recently, Celikyilmaz et al. (2011) were the first to study the intent detection problem using query logs and a discrete Bayesian latent variable model. In the field of dialogue modeling, the partially observable Markov decision process (POMDP) (Young et al., 2013) model is a popular technique for dialogue management, reducing the cost of hand-crafted dialogue managers while producing robustness against speech recognition errors. More recently, Tur et al. (2013) used a semi-supervised LDA model to show improvement on the slot filling task. Also, Zhai and Williams (2014) proposed an unsupervised model for connecting words with latent states in HMMs using topic models, obtaining interesting qualitative and quantitative results. However, for unsupervised learning for SLU, it is not obvious how to incorporate additional information in the HMMs. To the best of our knowledge, this paper is the first to consider MF techniques for learning latent feature representations in unsupervised SLU, taking various local and global lexical, syntactic, and semantic information into account.

3 The Proposed Framework

This paper introduces a matrix factorization technique for unsupervised SLU,. The proposed framework is shown in Figure 1(a). Given the utterances, the task of the SLU model is to decode their surface patterns into semantic forms and differentiate the target semantic concepts from the generic semantic space for task-oriented SDSs simultaneously. Note that our model does not require any human-defined slots and domain-specific semantic representations for utterances.

In the proposed model, we first build a feature matrix to represent the training utterances, where each row represents an utterance, and each column refers to an observed surface pattern or a induced slot candidate. Figure 1(b) illustrates an example

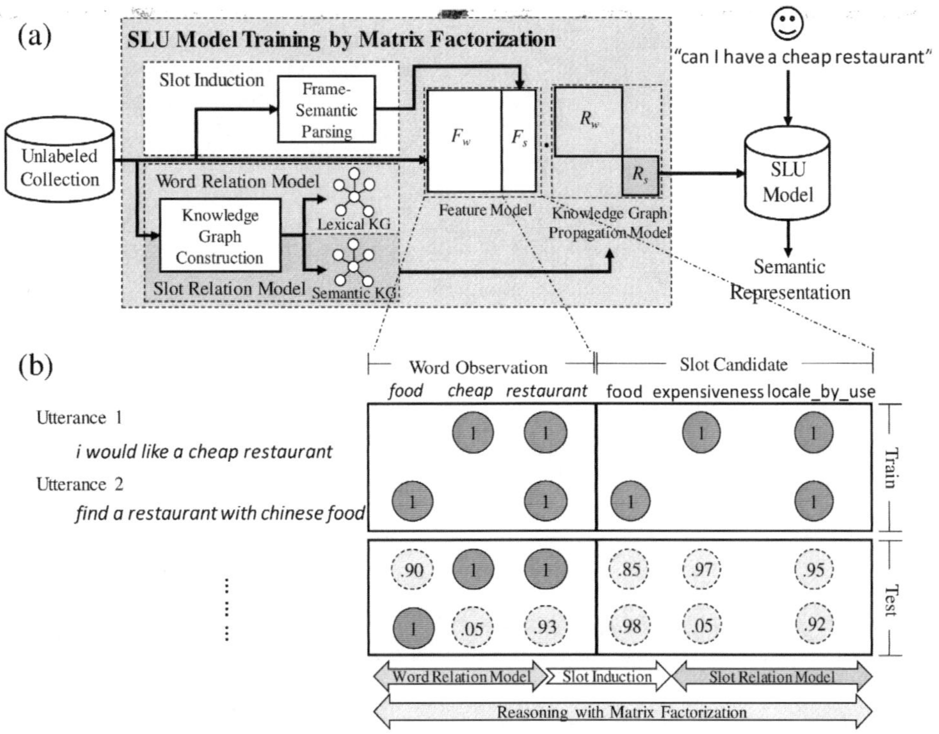

Figure 1: (a): The proposed framework. (b): Our matrix factorization method completes a partially-missing matrix for implicit semantic parsing. Dark circles are observed facts, shaded circles are inferred facts. The slot induction maps (yellow arrow) observed surface patterns to semantic slot candidates. The word relation model (blue arrow) constructs correlations between surface patterns. The slot relation model (pink arrow) learns the slot-level correlations based on propagating the automatically derived semantic knowledge graphs. Reasoning with matrix factorization (gray arrow) incorporates these models jointly, and produces a coherent, domain-specific SLU model.

of the matrix. Given a testing utterance, we convert it into a vector based on the observed surface patterns, and then fill in the missing values of the slots. In the first utterance in the figure, although the semantic slot food is not observed, the utterance implies the meaning facet food. The MF approach is able to learn the latent feature vectors for utterances and semantic elements, inferring implicit semantic concepts to improve the decoding process—namely, by filling the matrix with probabilities (lower part of the matrix).

The feature model is built on the observed word patterns and slot candidates, where the slot candidates are obtained from the slot induction component through frame-semantic parsing (the yellow block in Figure 1(a)) (Chen et al., 2013b). Section 4.1 explains the detail of the feature model.

In order to consider the additional inter-word and inter-slot relations, we propose a knowledge graph propagation model based on two knowledge graphs, which includes a word relation model (blue block) and a slot relation model (pink block), described in Section 4.2. The method of automatic knowledge graph construction is introduced in Section 5, where we leverage distributed word embeddings associated with typed syntactic dependencies to model the relations (Mikolov et al., 2013b; Mikolov et al., 2013c; Levy and Goldberg, 2014; Chen et al., 2015).

Finally, we train the SLU model by learning latent feature vectors for utterances and slot candidates through MF techniques. Combining with a knowledge graph propagation model based on word/slot relations, the trained SLU model estimates the probability that each semantic slot occurs in the testing utterance, and how likely each slot is domain-specific simultaneously. In other words, the SLU model is able to transform the testing utterances into domain-specific semantic representations without human involvement.

4 The Matrix Factorization Approach

Considering the benefits brought by MF techniques, including 1) modeling the noisy data, 2) modeling hidden semantics, and 3) modeling the

Figure 2: An example of probabilistic frame-semantic parsing on ASR output. FT: frame target. FE: frame element. LU: lexical unit.

long-range dependencies between observations, in this work we apply an MF approach to SLU modeling for SDSs. In our model, we use U to denote the set of input utterances, W as the set of word patterns, and S as the set of semantic slots that we would like to predict. The pair of an utterance $u \in U$ and a word pattern/semantic slot $x \in \{W + S\}$, $\langle u, x \rangle$, is a *fact*. The input to our model is a set of observed facts $\mathcal{O}$, and the observed facts for a given utterance is denoted by $\{\langle u, x \rangle \in \mathcal{O}\}$. The goal of our model is to estimate, for a given utterance u and a given word pattern/semantic slot x, the probability, $p(M_{u,x} = 1)$, where $M_{u,x}$ is a binary random variable that is true if and only if x is the word pattern/domain-specific semantic slot in the utterance u. We introduce a series of exponential family models that estimate the probability using a natural parameter $\theta_{u,x}$ and the logistic sigmoid function:

$$p(M_{u,x} = 1 \mid \theta_{u,x}) = \sigma(\theta_{u,x}) = \frac{1}{1 + \exp(-\theta_{u,x})} \quad (1)$$

We construct a matrix $M_{|U| \times (|W| + |S|)}$ as observed facts for MF by integrating a feature model and a knowledge graph propagation model below.

4.1 Feature Model

First, we build a word pattern matrix F_w with binary values based on observations, where each row represents an utterance and each column refers to an observed unigram. In other words, F_w carries the basic word vectors for the utterances, which is illustrated as the left part of the matrix in Figure 1(b).

To induce the semantic elements, we parse all ASR-decoded utterances in our corpus using SEMAFOR[2], a state-of-the-art semantic parser for frame-semantic parsing (Das et al., 2010; Das et al., 2013), and extract all frames from semantic parsing results as slot candidates (Chen et al., 2013b; Dinarelli et al., 2009). Figure 2 shows an example of an ASR-decoded output parsed by SEMAFOR. Three FrameNet-defined frames (capability, expensiveness, and locale_by_use) are generated for the utterance, which we consider as slot candidates for a domain-specific dialogue system (Baker et al., 1998). Then we build a slot matrix F_s with binary values based on the induced slots, which also denotes the slot features for the utterances (right part of the matrix in Figure 1(b)).

To build the feature model M_F, we concatenate two matrices:

$$M_F = [\ F_w \quad F_s\ ], \quad (2)$$

which is the upper part of the matrix in Figure 1(b) for training utterances. Note that we do not use any annotations, so all slot candidates are included.

4.2 Knowledge Graph Propagation Model

Since SEMAFOR was trained on FrameNet annotation, which has a more generic frame-semantic context, not all the frames from the parsing results can be used as the actual slots in the domain-specific dialogue systems. For instance, in Figure 2, we see that the frames "expensiveness" and "locale_by_use" are essentially the key slots for the purpose of understanding in the restaurant query domain, whereas the "capability" frame does not convey particularly valuable information for SLU.

Assuming that domain-specific concepts are usually related to each other, considering global relations between semantic slots induces a more coherent slot set. It is shown that the relations on knowledge graphs help make decisions on domain-specific slots (Chen et al., 2015). Considering two directed graphs, semantic and lexical knowledge graphs, each node in the semantic knowledge graph is a slot candidate s_i generated by the frame-semantic parser, and each node in the lexical knowledge graph is a word w_j.

- **Slot-based semantic knowledge graph** is built as $G_s = \langle V_s, E_{ss} \rangle$, where $V_s = \{s_i \in S\}$ and $E_{ss} = \{e_{ij} \mid s_i, s_j \in V_s\}$.
- **Word-based lexical knowledge graph** is built as $G_w = \langle V_w, E_{ww} \rangle$, where $V_w = \{w_i \in W\}$ and $E_{ww} = \{e_{ij} \mid w_i, w_j \in V_w\}$.

The edges connect two nodes in the graphs if there is a typed dependency between them. Figure 3 is a simplified example of a slot-based semantic knowledge graph. The structured graph helps define a coherent slot set. To model the relations between words/slots based on the knowledge graphs, we define two relation models below.

[2] http://www.ark.cs.cmu.edu/SEMAFOR/

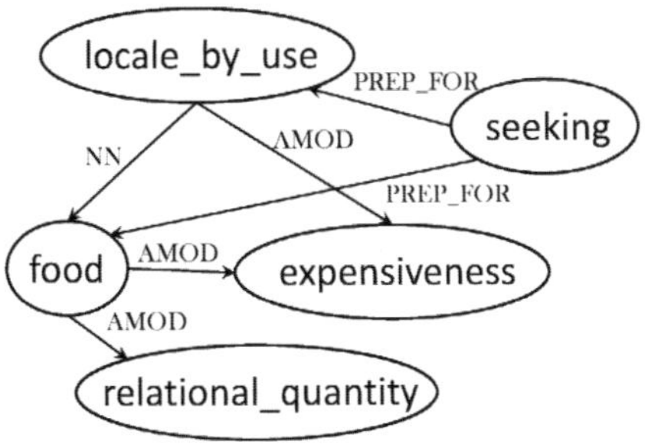

Figure 3: A simplified example of the automatically derived knowledge graph.

- Semantic Relation
  For modeling word semantic relations, we compute a matrix $R_w^S = [Sim(w_i, w_j)]_{|W| \times |W|}$, where $Sim(w_i, w_j)$ is the cosine similarity between the dependency embeddings of the word patterns w_i and w_j after normalization. For slot semantic relations, we compute $R_s^S = [Sim(s_i, s_j)]_{|S| \times |S|}$ similarly[3]. The matrices R_w^S and R_s^S model not only the semantic but functional similarity since we use dependency-based embeddings (Levy and Goldberg, 2014).

- Dependency Relation
  Assuming that important semantic slots are usually mutually related to each other, that is, connected by syntactic dependencies, our automatically derived knowledge graphs are able to help model the dependency relations. For word dependency relations, we compute a matrix $R_w^D = [\hat{r}(w_i, w_j)]_{|W| \times |W|}$, where $\hat{r}(w_i, w_j)$ measures the dependency between two word patterns w_i and w_j based on the word-based lexical knowledge graph, and the detail is described in Section 5. For slot dependency relations, we similarly compute $R_s^D = [\hat{r}(s_i, s_j)]_{|S| \times |S|}$ based on the slot-based semantic knowledge graph.

With the built word relation models (R_w^S and R_w^D) and slot relation models (R_s^S and R_s^D), we combine them as a knowledge graph propagation matrix M_R[4].

$$M_R = \begin{bmatrix} R_w^{SD} & 0 \\ 0 & R_s^{SD} \end{bmatrix}, \quad (3)$$

where $R_w^{SD} = R_w^S + R_w^D$ and $R_s^{SD} = R_s^S + R_s^D$ to integrate semantic and dependency relations. The goal of this matrix is to propagate scores between nodes according to different types of relations in the knowledge graphs (Chen and Metze, 2012).

4.3 Integrated Model

With a feature model M_F and a knowledge graph propagation model M_R, we integrate them into a single matrix.

$$\begin{aligned} M &= M_F \cdot (\alpha I + \beta M_R) \\ &= \begin{bmatrix} \alpha F_w + \beta F_w R_w & 0 \\ 0 & \alpha F_s + \beta F_s R_s \end{bmatrix}, \end{aligned} \quad (4)$$

where M is the final matrix and I is the identity matrix. α and β are the weights for balancing original values and propagated values, where $\alpha + \beta = 1$. The matrix M is similar to M_F, but some weights are enhanced through the knowledge graph propagation model, M_R. The word relations are built by $F_w R_w$, which is the matrix with internal weight propagation on the lexical knowledge graph (the blue arrow in Figure 1(b)). Similarly, $F_s R_s$ models the slot correlations, and can be treated as the matrix with internal weight propagation on the semantic knowledge graph (the pink arrow in Figure 1(b)). The propagation models can be treated as running a random walk algorithm on the graphs.

F_s contains all slot candidates generated by SEMAFOR, which may include some generic slots (such as capability), so the original feature model cannot differentiate the domain-specific and generic concepts. By integrating with R_s, the semantic and dependency relations can be propagated via the knowledge graph, and the domain-specific concepts may have higher weights based on the assumption that the slots for dialogue systems are often mutually related (Chen et al., 2015). Hence, the structure information can be automatically involved in the matrix. Also, the word relation model brings the same function, but now on the word level. In conclusion, for each utterance, the integrated model not only predicts the probability that semantic slots occur but also considers whether the slots are domain-specific. The following sections describe the learning process.

4.4 Parameter Estimation

The proposed model is parameterized through weights and latent component vectors, where the parameters are estimated by maximizing the log

[3] For each column in R_w^S and R_s^S, we only keep top 10 highest values, which correspond the top 10 semantically similar nodes.

[4] The values in the diagonal of M_R are 0 to model the propagation from other entries.

likelihood of observed data (Collins et al., 2001).

$$\begin{aligned}\theta^* &= \arg\max_\theta \prod_{u\in U} p(\theta \mid M_u) \\ &= \arg\max_\theta \prod_{u\in U} p(M_u \mid \theta)p(\theta) \\ &= \arg\max_\theta \sum_{u\in U} \ln p(M_u \mid \theta) - \lambda_\theta,\end{aligned} \tag{5}$$

where M_u is the vector corresponding to the utterance u from $M_{u,x}$ in (1), because we assume that each utterance is independent of others.

To avoid treating unobserved facts as designed negative facts, we consider our positive-only data as *implicit feedback*. Bayesian Personalized Ranking (BPR) is an optimization criterion that learns from implicit feedback for MF, which uses a variant of the ranking: giving observed true facts higher scores than unobserved (true or false) facts (Rendle et al., 2009). Riedel et al. (2013) also showed that BPR learns the implicit relations for improving the relation extraction task.

4.4.1 Objective Function

To estimate the parameters in (5), we create a dataset of *ranked pairs* from M in (4): for each utterance u and each observed fact $f^+ = \langle u, x^+\rangle$, where $M_{u,x} \geq \delta$, we choose each word pattern/slot x^- such that $f^- = \langle u, x^-\rangle$, where $M_{u,x} < \delta$, which refers to the word pattern/slot we have not observed to be in utterance u. That is, we construct the observed data $\mathcal{O}$ from M. Then for each pair of facts f^+ and f^-, we want to model $p(f^+) > p(f^-)$ and hence $\theta_{f^+} > \theta_{f^-}$ according to (1). BPR maximizes the summation of each ranked pair, where the objective is

$$\sum_{u\in U} \ln p(M_u \mid \theta) = \sum_{f^+\in\mathcal{O}} \sum_{f^-\notin\mathcal{O}} \ln \sigma(\theta_{f^+} - \theta_{f^-}). \tag{6}$$

The BPR objective is an approximation to the per utterance AUC (area under the ROC curve), which directly correlates to what we want to achieve – well-ranked semantic slots per utterance.

4.4.2 Optimization

To maximize the objective in (6), we employ a stochastic gradient descent (SGD) algorithm (Rendle et al., 2009). For each randomly sampled observed fact $\langle u, x^+\rangle$, we sample an unobserved fact $\langle u, x^-\rangle$, which results in $|\mathcal{O}|$ fact pairs $\langle f^-, f^+\rangle$. For each pair, we perform an SGD update using the gradient of the corresponding objective function for matrix factorization (Gantner et al., 2011).

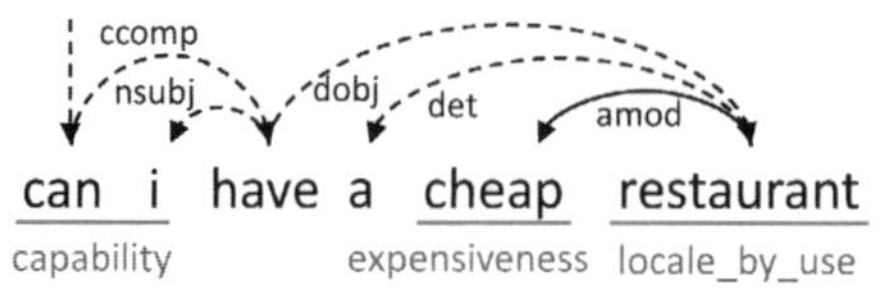

Figure 4: The dependency parsing result.

5 Knowledge Graph Construction

This section introduces the procedure of constructing knowledge graphs in order to estimate $\hat{r}(w_i, w_j)$ for building R_w^D and $\hat{r}(s_i, s_j)$ for R_s^D in Section 4.2. Considering the relations in the knowledge graphs, the edge weights for E_{ww} and E_{ss} are measured as $\hat{r}(w_i, w_j)$ and $\hat{r}(s_i, s_j)$ based on the dependency parsing results respectively.

The example utterance "*can i have a cheap restaurant*" and its dependency parsing result are illustrated in Figure 4. The arrows denote the dependency relations from headwords to their dependents, and words on arcs denote types of the dependencies. All typed dependencies between two words are encoded in triples and form a word-based dependency set $\mathcal{T}_w = \{\langle w_i, t, w_j\rangle\}$, where t is the typed dependency between the headword w_i and the dependent w_j. For example, Figure 4 generates $\langle$*restaurant*, AMOD, *cheap*$\rangle$, $\langle$*restaurant*, DOBJ, *have*$\rangle$, etc. for $\mathcal{T}_w$. Similarly, we build a slot-based dependency set $\mathcal{T}_s = \{\langle s_i, t, s_j\rangle\}$ by transforming dependencies between slot-fillers into ones between slots. For example, $\langle$*restaurant*, AMOD, *cheap*$\rangle$ from $\mathcal{T}_w$ is transformed into $\langle$locale_by_use, AMOD, expensiveness$\rangle$ for building $\mathcal{T}_s$, because both sides of the non-dotted line are parsed as slot-fillers by SEMAFOR.

5.1 Relation Weight Estimation

For the edges in the knowledge graphs, we model the relations between two connected nodes x_i and x_j as $\hat{r}(x_i, x_j)$, where x is either a slot s or a word pattern w. Since the weights are measured based on the relations between nodes regardless of the directions, we combine the scores of two directional dependencies:

$$\hat{r}(x_i, x_j) = r(x_i \to x_j) + r(x_j \to x_i), \tag{7}$$

where $r(x_i \to x_j)$ is the score estimating the dependency including x_i as a head and x_j as a dependent. We propose a scoring function for $r(\cdot)$ using dependency-based embeddings.

Table 1: The example contexts extracted for training dependency-based word/slot embeddings.

	Typed Dependency Relation	Target Word	Contexts
Word	⟨*restaurant*, AMOD, *cheap*⟩	*restaurant*	*cheap*/AMOD
		cheap	*restaurant*/AMOD^{-1}
Slot	⟨locale_by_use, AMOD, expensiveness⟩	locale_by_use	expensiveness/AMOD
		expansiveness	locale_by_use/AMOD^{-1}

5.1.1 Dependency-Based Embeddings

Most neural embeddings use linear bag-of-words contexts, where a window size is defined to produce contexts of the target words (Mikolov et al., 2013c; Mikolov et al., 2013b; Mikolov et al., 2013a). However, some important contexts may be missing due to smaller windows, while larger windows capture broad topical content. A dependency-based embedding approach was proposed to derive contexts based on the syntactic relations the word participates in for training embeddings, where the embeddings are less topical but offer more functional similarity compared to original embeddings (Levy and Goldberg, 2014).

Table 1 shows the extracted dependency-based contexts for each target word from the example in Figure 4, where headwords and their dependents can form the contexts by following the arc on a word in the dependency tree, and -1 denotes the directionality of the dependency. After replacing original bag-of-words contexts with dependency-based contexts, we can train dependency-based embeddings for all target words (Yih et al., 2014; Bordes et al., 2011; Bordes et al., 2013).

For training dependency-based word embeddings, each target x is associated with a vector $\mathbf{v_x} \in \mathbb{R}^d$ and each context c is represented as a context vector $\mathbf{v_c} \in \mathbb{R}^d$, where d is the embedding dimensionality. We learn vector representations for both targets and contexts such that the dot product $\mathbf{v_x} \cdot \mathbf{v_c}$ associated with "good" target-context pairs belonging to the training data $\mathcal{D}$ is maximized, leading to the objective function:

$$\arg\max_{\mathbf{v_x},\mathbf{v_c}} \sum_{(w,c)\in\mathcal{D}} \log \frac{1}{1+\exp(-\mathbf{v_c}\cdot\mathbf{v_x})}, \quad (8)$$

which can be trained using stochastic-gradient updates (Levy and Goldberg, 2014). Then we can obtain the dependency-based slot and word embeddings using $\mathcal{T}_s$ and $\mathcal{T}_w$ respectively.

5.1.2 Embedding-Based Scoring Function

With trained dependency-based embeddings, we estimate the probability that x_i is the headword and x_j is its dependent via the typed dependency t as

$$P(x_i \xrightarrow[t]{} x_j) = \frac{Sim(x_i, x_j/t) + Sim(x_j, x_i/t^{-1})}{2}, \quad (9)$$

where $Sim(x_i, x_j/t)$ is the cosine similarity between word/slot embeddings $\mathbf{v_{x_i}}$ and context embeddings $\mathbf{v_{x_j/t}}$ after normalizing to $[0, 1]$.

Based on the dependency set $\mathcal{T}_x$, we use $t^*_{x_i\to x_j}$ to denote the most possible typed dependency with x_i as a head and x_j as a dependent.

$$t^*_{x_i\to x_j} = \arg\max_t C(x_i \xrightarrow[t]{} x_j), \quad (10)$$

where $C(x_i \xrightarrow[t]{} x_j)$ counts how many times the dependency $\langle x_i, t, x_j\rangle$ occurs in the dependency set $\mathcal{T}_x$. Then the scoring function $r(\cdot)$ in (7) that estimates the dependency $x_i \to x_j$ is measured as

$$r(x_i \to x_j) = C(x_i \xrightarrow[t^*_{x_i\to x_j}]{} x_j)\cdot P(x_i \xrightarrow[t^*_{x_i\to x_j}]{} x_j), \quad (11)$$

which is equal to the highest observed frequency of the dependency $x_i \to x_j$ among all types from $\mathcal{T}_x$ and additionally weighted by the estimated probability. The estimated probability smoothes the observed frequency to avoid overfitting due to the smaller dataset. Figure 3 is a simplified example of an automatically derived semantic knowledge graph with the most possible typed dependencies as edges based on the estimated weights. Then the relation weights $\hat{r}(x_i, x_j)$ can be obtained by (7) in order to build R_w^D and R_s^D matrices.

6 Experiments

6.1 Experimental Setup

In this experiment, we used the Cambridge University SLU corpus, previously used on several other SLU tasks (Henderson et al., 2012; Chen et al., 2013a). The domain of the corpus is about restaurant recommendation in Cambridge; subjects were asked to interact with multiple SDSs in an in-car setting. The corpus contains a total number of 2,166 dialogues, including 15,453 utterances (10,571 for self-training and 4,882 for

Table 2: The MAP of predicted slots (%); † indicates that the result is significantly better than the Logistic Regression (row (b)) with $p < 0.05$ in t-test.

Approach				ASR		Manual	
				w/o	w/ Explicit	w/o	w/ Explicit
Explicit		SVM	(a)	32.48		36.62	
		MLR	(b)	33.96		38.78	
Implicit	Baseline	Random	(c)	3.43	22.45	2.63	25.09
		Majority	(d)	15.37	32.88	16.43	38.41
	MF	Feature	(e)	24.24	37.61†	22.55	45.34†
		Feature + KGP	(f)	**40.46†**	**43.51†**	**52.14†**	**53.40†**

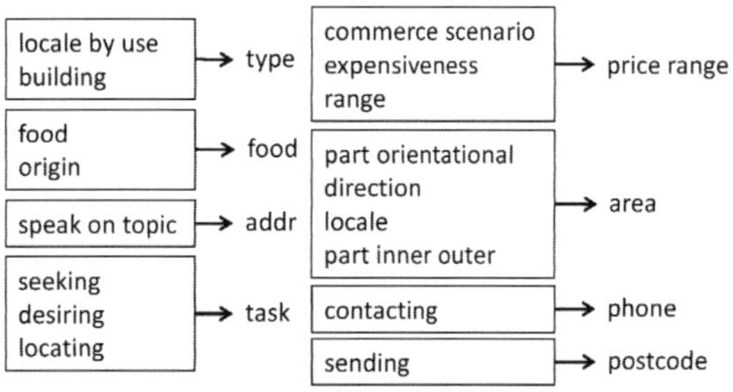

Figure 5: The mappings from induced slots (within blocks) to reference slots (right sides of arrows).

testing). The data is gender-balanced, with slightly more native than non-native speakers. The vocabulary size is 1868. An ASR system was used to transcribe the speech; the word error rate was reported as 37%. There are 10 slots created by domain experts: addr, area, food, name, phone, postcode, price range, signature, task, and type.

For parameter setting, the weights for balancing feature models and propagation models, α and β, are set as 0.5 to give the same influence, and the threshold for defining the unobserved facts δ is set as 0.5 for all experiments. We use the Stanford Parser[5] to obtain the collapsed typed syntactic dependencies (Socher et al., 2013) and set the dimensionality of embeddings $d = 300$ in all experiments.

6.2 Evaluation Metrics

To evaluate the accuracy of the automatically decoded slots, we measure their quality as the proximity between predicted slots and reference slots. Figure 5 shows the mappings that indicate semantically related induced slots and reference slots (Chen et al., 2013b).

To eliminate the influence of threshold selection when predicting semantic slots, in the following metrics, we take the whole ranking list into account and evaluate the performance by the metrics that are independent of the selected threshold. For each utterance, with the predicted probabilities of all slot candidates, we can compute an average precision (AP) to evaluate the performance of SLU by treating the slots with mappings as positive. AP scores the ranking result higher if the correct slots are ranked higher, which also approximates to the area under the precision-recall curve (Boyd et al., 2012). Mean average precision (MAP) is the metric for evaluating all utterances. For all experiments, we perform a paired t-test on the AP scores of the results to test the significance.

6.3 Evaluation Results

Table 2 shows the MAP performance of predicted slots for all experiments on ASR and manual transcripts. For the first baseline using explicit semantics, we use the observed data to self-train models for predicting the probability of each semantic slot by support vector machine (SVM) with a linear kernel and multinomial logistic regression (MLR) (row (a)-(b)) (Pedregosa et al., 2011; Henderson et al., 2012). It is shown that SVM and MLR perform similarly, and MLR is slightly better than SVM because it has better capability of estimating probabilities. For modeling implicit semantics, two baselines are performed as references, Random (row (c)) and Majority (row (d)), where the former assigns random probabilities for all slots, and the later assigns probabilities for the slots based on their frequency distribution. To improve probability estimation, we further integrate the results from implicit semantics with the better result from explicit approaches, MLR (row (b)), by averaging the probability distribution from two results.

Two baselines, Random and Majority, cannot model the implicit semantics, producing poor results. The results of Random integrated with MLR significantly degrades the performance of

[5] http://nlp.stanford.edu/software/lex-parser.shtml

Table 3: The MAP of predicted slots using different types of relation models in M_R (%); † indicates that the result is significantly better than the feature model (column (a)) with $p < 0.05$ in t-test.

Model	Feature	Knowledge Graph Propagation Model				
Rel.	(a) None	(b) Semantic	(c) Dependency	(d) Word	(e) Slot	(f) All
M_R	-	$\begin{bmatrix} R_w^S & 0 \\ 0 & R_s^S \end{bmatrix}$	$\begin{bmatrix} R_w^D & 0 \\ 0 & R_s^D \end{bmatrix}$	$\begin{bmatrix} R_w^{SD} & 0 \\ 0 & 0 \end{bmatrix}$	$\begin{bmatrix} 0 & 0 \\ 0 & R_s^{SD} \end{bmatrix}$	$\begin{bmatrix} R_w^{SD} & 0 \\ 0 & R_s^{SD} \end{bmatrix}$
ASR	37.61	41.39†	41.63†	39.19†	42.10†	**43.51**†
Manual	45.34	51.55†	49.04†	45.18	49.91†	**53.40**†

MLR for both ASR and manual transcripts. Also, the results of Majority integrated with MLR does not produce any difference compared to the MLR baseline. Among the proposed MF approaches, only using feature model for building the matrix (row (e)) achieves 24.2% and 22.6% of MAP for ASR and manual results respectively, which are worse than two baselines using explicit semantics. However, with the combination of explicit semantics, using only the feature model significantly outperforms the baselines, where the performance comes from about 34.0% to 37.6% and from 38.8% to 45.3% for ASR and manual results respectively. Additionally integrating a knowledge graph propagation (KGP) model (row (e)) outperforms the baselines for both ASR and manual transcripts, and the performance is further improved by combining with explicit semantics (achieving MAP of 43.5% and 53.4%). The experiments show that the proposed MF models successfully learn the implicit semantics and consider the relations and domain-specificity simultaneously.

6.4 Discussion and Analysis

With promising results obtained by the proposed models, we analyze the detailed difference between different relation models in Table 3.

6.4.1 Effectiveness of Semantic and Dependency Relation Models

To evaluate the effectiveness of semantic and dependency relations, we consider each of them individually in M_R of (3) (columns (b) and (c) in Table 3). Comparing to the original model (column (a)), both modeling semantic relations and modeling dependency relations significantly improve the performance for ASR and manual results. It is shown that semantic relations help the SLU model infer the implicit meaning, and then the prediction becomes more accurate. Also, dependency relations successfully differentiate the generic concepts from the domain-specific concepts, so that the SLU model is able to predict more coherent set of semantic slots (Chen et al., 2015). Integrating two types of relations (column (f)) further improves the performance.

6.4.2 Comparing Word/ Slot Relation Models

To analyze the performance results from inter-word and inter-slot relations, the columns (d) and (e) show the results considering only word relations and only slot relations respectively. It can be seen that the inter-slot relation model significantly improves the performance for both ASR and manual results. However, the inter-word relation model only performs slightly better results for ASR output (from 37.6% to 39.2%), and there is no difference after applying the inter-word relation model on manual transcripts. The reason may be that inter-slot relations carry high-level semantics that align well with the structure of SDSs, but inter-word relations do not. Nevertheless, combining two relations (column (f)) outperforms both results for ASR and manual transcripts, showing that different types of relations can compensate each other and then benefit the SLU performance.

7 Conclusions

This paper presents an MF approach to self-train the SLU model for semantic decoding in an unsupervised way. The purpose of the proposed model is not only to predict the probability of each semantic slot but also to distinguish between generic semantic concepts and domain-specific concepts that are related to an SDS. The experiments show that the MF-based model obtains promising results, outperforming strong discriminative baselines.

Acknowledgments

We thank anonymous reviewers for their useful comments and Prof. Manfred Stede for his mentoring. We are also grateful to MetLife's support. Any opinions, findings, and conclusions expressed in this publication are those of the authors and do not necessarily reflect the views of funding agencies.

References

Collin F Baker, Charles J Fillmore, and John B Lowe. 1998. The Berkeley FrameNet project. In *Proceedings of COLING*, pages 86–90.

Dan Bohus and Alexander I Rudnicky. 2009. The RavenClaw dialog management framework: Architecture and systems. *Computer Speech & Language*, 23(3):332–361.

Antoine Bordes, Jason Weston, Ronan Collobert, Yoshua Bengio, et al. 2011. Learning structured embeddings of knowledge bases. In *Proceedings of AAAI*.

Antoine Bordes, Nicolas Usunier, Alberto Garcia-Duran, Jason Weston, and Oksana Yakhnenko. 2013. Translating embeddings for modeling multi-relational data. In *Proceedings of Advances in Neural Information Processing Systems*, pages 2787–2795.

Kendrick Boyd, Vitor Santos Costa, Jesse Davis, and C David Page. 2012. Unachievable region in precision-recall space and its effect on empirical evaluation. In *Machine learning: proceedings of the International Conference. International Conference on Machine Learning*, volume 2012, page 349. NIH Public Access.

Asli Celikyilmaz, Dilek Hakkani-Tür, and Gokhan Tür. 2011. Leveraging web query logs to learn user intent via bayesian discrete latent variable model. In *Proceedings of ICML*.

Yun-Nung Chen and Florian Metze. 2012. Two-layer mutually reinforced random walk for improved multi-party meeting summarization. In *Proceedings of The 4th IEEE Workshop on Spoken Language Tachnology*, pages 461–466.

Yun-Nung Chen and Alexander I. Rudnicky. 2014. Dynamically supporting unexplored domains in conversational interactions by enriching semantics with neural word embeddings. In *Proceedings of 2014 IEEE Spoken Language Technology Workshop (SLT)*, pages 590–595. IEEE.

Yun-Nung Chen, William Yang Wang, and Alexander I. Rudnicky. 2013a. An empirical investigation of sparse log-linear models for improved dialogue act classification. In *Proceedings of ICASSP*, pages 8317–8321.

Yun-Nung Chen, William Yang Wang, and Alexander I Rudnicky. 2013b. Unsupervised induction and filling of semantic slots for spoken dialogue systems using frame-semantic parsing. In *Proceedings of 2013 IEEE Workshop on Automatic Speech Recognition and Understanding (ASRU)*, pages 120–125. IEEE.

Yun-Nung Chen, Dilek Hakkani-Tür, and Gokan Tur. 2014a. Deriving local relational surface forms from dependency-based entity embeddings for unsupervised spoken language understanding. In *Proceedings of 2014 IEEE Spoken Language Technology Workshop (SLT)*, pages 242–247. IEEE.

Yun-Nung Chen, William Yang Wang, and Alexander I. Rudnicky. 2014b. Leveraging frame semantics and distributional semantics for unsupervised semantic slot induction in spoken dialogue systems. In *Proceedings of 2014 IEEE Spoken Language Technology Workshop (SLT)*, pages 584–589. IEEE.

Yun-Nung Chen, William Yang Wang, and Alexander I. Rudnicky. 2015. Jointly modeling inter-slot relations by random walk on knowledge graphs for unsupervised spoken language understanding. In *Proceedings of the 2015 Conference of the North American Chapter of the Association for Computational Linguistics - Human Language Technologies*. ACL.

Michael Collins, Sanjoy Dasgupta, and Robert E Schapire. 2001. A generalization of principal components analysis to the exponential family. In *Proceedings of Advances in Neural Information Processing Systems*, pages 617–624.

Dipanjan Das, Nathan Schneider, Desai Chen, and Noah A Smith. 2010. Probabilistic frame-semantic parsing. In *Proceedings of The Conference of the North American Chapter of the Association for Computational Linguistics: Human Language Technologies*, pages 948–956.

Dipanjan Das, Desai Chen, André F. T. Martins, Nathan Schneider, and Noah A. Smith. 2013. Frame-semantic parsing. *Computational Linguistics*.

Marco Dinarelli, Silvia Quarteroni, Sara Tonelli, Alessandro Moschitti, and Giuseppe Riccardi. 2009. Annotating spoken dialogs: from speech segments to dialog acts and frame semantics. In *Proceedings of the 2nd Workshop on Semantic Representation of Spoken Language*, pages 34–41. ACL.

John Dowding, Jean Mark Gawron, Doug Appelt, John Bear, Lynn Cherny, Robert Moore, and Douglas Moran. 1993. Gemini: A natural language system for spoken-language understanding. In *Proceedings of ACL*, pages 54–61.

Ali El-Kahky, Derek Liu, Ruhi Sarikaya, Gökhan Tür, Dilek Hakkani-Tür, and Larry Heck. 2014. Extending domain coverage of language understanding systems via intent transfer between domains using knowledge graphs and search query click logs. In *Proceedings of ICASSP*.

Zeno Gantner, Steffen Rendle, Christoph Freudenthaler, and Lars Schmidt-Thieme. 2011. Mymedialite: A free recommender system library. In *Proceedings of the fifth ACM conference on Recommender systems*, pages 305–308. ACM.

Narendra Gupta, Gökhan Tür, Dilek Hakkani-Tür, Srinivas Bangalore, Giuseppe Riccardi, and Mazin Gilbert. 2006. The AT&T spoken language understanding system. *IEEE Transactions on Audio, Speech, and Language Processing*, 14(1):213–222.

Dilek Hakkani-Tür, Larry Heck, and Gokhan Tur. 2013. Using a knowledge graph and query click logs for unsupervised learning of relation detection. In *Proceedings of ICASSP*, pages 8327–8331.

Larry Heck and Dilek Hakkani-Tür. 2012. Exploiting the semantic web for unsupervised spoken language understanding. In *Proceedings of SLT*, pages 228–233.

Larry P Heck, Dilek Hakkani-Tür, and Gokhan Tur. 2013. Leveraging knowledge graphs for web-scale unsupervised semantic parsing. In *Proceedings of INTERSPEECH*, pages 1594–1598.

Matthew Henderson, Milica Gasic, Blaise Thomson, Pirros Tsiakoulis, Kai Yu, and Steve Young. 2012. Discriminative spoken language understanding using word confusion networks. In *Proceedings of SLT*, pages 176–181.

Frederick Jelinek. 1997. *Statistical methods for speech recognition*. MIT press.

Yehuda Koren, Robert Bell, and Chris Volinsky. 2009. Matrix factorization techniques for recommender systems. *Computer*, (8):30–37.

Omer Levy and Yoav Goldberg. 2014. Dependency-based word embeddings. In *Proceedings of ACL*.

Tomas Mikolov, Kai Chen, Greg Corrado, and Jeffrey Dean. 2013a. Efficient estimation of word representations in vector space. In *Proceedings of Workshop at ICLR*.

Tomas Mikolov, Ilya Sutskever, Kai Chen, Greg S Corrado, and Jeff Dean. 2013b. Distributed representations of words and phrases and their compositionality. In *Proceedings of Advances in Neural Information Processing Systems*, pages 3111–3119.

Tomas Mikolov, Wen-tau Yih, and Geoffrey Zweig. 2013c. Linguistic regularities in continuous space word representations. In *HLT-NAACL*, pages 746–751. Citeseer.

Fabian Pedregosa, Gaël Varoquaux, Alexandre Gramfort, Vincent Michel, Bertrand Thirion, Olivier Grisel, Mathieu Blondel, Peter Prettenhofer, Ron Weiss, Vincent Dubourg, et al. 2011. Scikit-learn: Machine learning in python. *The Journal of Machine Learning Research*, 12:2825–2830.

Roberto Pieraccini, Evelyne Tzoukermann, Zakhar Gorelov, J Gauvain, Esther Levin, Chin-Hui Lee, and Jay G Wilpon. 1992. A speech understanding system based on statistical representation of semantics. In *Proceedings of 1992 IEEE International Conference on Acoustics, Speech, and Signal Processing (ICASSP)*, volume 1, pages 193–196. IEEE.

Steffen Rendle, Christoph Freudenthaler, Zeno Gantner, and Lars Schmidt-Thieme. 2009. BPR: Bayesian personalized ranking from implicit feedback. In *Proceedings of the Twenty-Fifth Conference on Uncertainty in Artificial Intelligence*, pages 452–461. AUAI Press.

Sebastian Riedel, Limin Yao, Andrew McCallum, and Benjamin M Marlin. 2013. Relation extraction with matrix factorization and universal schemas. In *Proceedings of NAACL-HLT*, pages 74–84.

Stephanie Seneff. 1992. TINA: A natural language system for spoken language applications. *Computational linguistics*, 18(1):61–86.

Anders Skrondal and Sophia Rabe-Hesketh. 2004. *Generalized latent variable modeling: Multilevel, longitudinal, and structural equation models*. Crc Press.

Richard Socher, John Bauer, Christopher D Manning, and Andrew Y Ng. 2013. Parsing with compositional vector grammars. In *Proceedings of the ACL conference*. Citeseer.

Gokhan Tur, Dilek Z Hakkani-Tür, Dustin Hillard, and Asli Celikyilmaz. 2011. Towards unsupervised spoken language understanding: Exploiting query click logs for slot filling. In *Proceedings of INTERSPEECH*, pages 1293–1296.

Gokhan Tur, Minwoo Jeong, Ye-Yi Wang, Dilek Hakkani-Tür, and Larry P Heck. 2012. Exploiting the semantic web for unsupervised natural language semantic parsing. In *Proceedings of INTERSPEECH*.

Gokhan Tur, Asli Celikyilmaz, and Dilek Hakkani-Tur. 2013. Latent semantic modeling for slot filling in conversational understanding. In *Proceedings of 2013 IEEE International Conference on Acoustics, Speech and Signal Processing (ICASSP)*, pages 8307–8311. IEEE.

William Yang Wang, Dan Bohus, Ece Kamar, and Eric Horvitz. 2012. Crowdsourcing the acquisition of natural language corpora: Methods and observations. In *Proceedings of SLT*, pages 73–78.

Lu Wang, Dilek Hakkani-Tür, and Larry Heck. 2014. Leveraging semantic web search and browse sessions for multi-turn spoken dialog systems. In *Proceedings of 2014 IEEE International Conference on Acoustics, Speech and Signal Processing (ICASSP)*, pages 4082–4086. IEEE.

Wen-tau Yih, Xiaodong He, and Christopher Meek. 2014. Semantic parsing for single-relation question answering. In *Proceedings of ACL*.

Steve Young, Milica Gasic, Blaise Thomson, and Jason D Williams. 2013. POMDP-based statistical spoken dialog systems: A review. *Proceedings of the IEEE*, 101(5):1160–1179.

Ke Zhai and Jason D Williams. 2014. Discovering latent structure in task-oriented dialogues. In *Proceedings of the Association for Computational Linguistics*.

Efficient Disfluency Detection with Transition-based Parsing

Shuangzhi Wu[†] **, Dongdong Zhang**[‡] **, Ming Zhou**[‡] **, Tiejun Zhao**[†]
[†]Harbin Institute of Technology
[‡]Microsoft Research
{v-shuawu, dozhang, mingzhou}@microsoft.com
tjzhao@hit.edu.cn

Abstract

Automatic speech recognition (ASR) outputs often contain various disfluencies. It is necessary to remove these disfluencies before processing downstream tasks. In this paper, an efficient disfluency detection approach based on right-to-left transition-based parsing is proposed, which can efficiently identify disfluencies and keep ASR outputs grammatical. Our method exploits a global view to capture long-range dependencies for disfluency detection by integrating a rich set of syntactic and disfluency features with linear complexity. The experimental results show that our method outperforms state-of-the-art work and achieves a 85.1% f-score on the commonly used English Switchboard test set. We also apply our method to in-house annotated Chinese data and achieve a significantly higher f-score compared to the baseline of CRF-based approach.

1 Introduction

With the development of the mobile internet, speech inputs have become more and more popular in applications where automatic speech recognition (ASR) is the key component to convert speech into text. ASR outputs often contain various disfluencies which create barriers to subsequent text processing tasks like parsing, machine translation and summarization. Usually, disfluencies can be classified into uncompleted words, filled pauses (e.g. "uh", "um"), discourse markers (e.g. "I mean"), editing terms (e.g. "you know") and repairs. To identify and remove disfluencies, straightforward rules can be designed to tackle the former four classes of disfluencies since they often belong to a closed set. However, the repair type disfluency poses particularly more difficult problems as their form is more arbitrary. Typically, as shown in Figure 1, a repair disfluency type consists of a reparandum ("to Boston") and a filled pause ("um"), followed by its repair ("to Denver"). This special structure of disfluency constraint, which exists in many languages such as English and Chinese, reflects the scenarios of spontaneous speech and conversation, where people often correct preceding words with following words when they find that the preceding words are wrong or improper. This procedure might be interrupted and inserted with filled pauses when people are thinking or hesitating. The challenges of detecting repair disfluencies are that reparandums vary in length, may occur everywhere, and are sometimes nested.

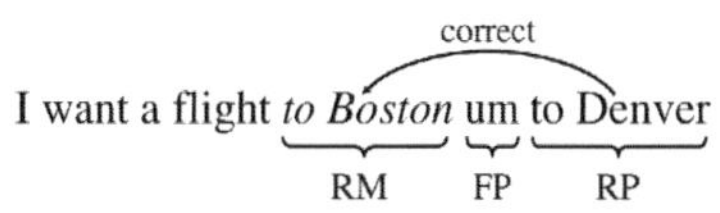

Figure 1: A typical example of repair type disfluency consists of FP (Filled Pause), RM (Reparandum), and RP (Repair). The preceding RM is corrected by the following RP.

There are many related works on disfluency detection, that mainly focus on detecting repair type of disfluencies. Straightforwardly, disfluency detection can be treated as a sequence labeling problem and solved by well-known machine learning algorithms such as conditional random fields (CRF) or max-margin markov network (M^3N) (Liu et al., 2006; Georgila, 2009; Qian and Liu, 2013), and prosodic features are also concerned in (Kahn et al., 2005; Zhang et al., 2006). These methods achieve good performance, but are not powerful enough to capture complicated disfluencies with longer spans or distances. Recently, syntax-based models such as transition-based parser have been used for detecting disflu-

Proceedings of the 53rd Annual Meeting of the Association for Computational Linguistics and the 7th International Joint Conference on Natural Language Processing, pages 495–503, Beijing, China, July 26-31, 2015.

encies (Honnibal and Johnson, 2014; Rasooli and Tetreault, 2013). These methods can jointly perform dependency parsing and disfluency detection. But in these methods, great efforts are made to distinguish normal words from disfluent words as decisions cannot be made imminently from left to right, leading to inefficient implementation as well as performance loss.

In this paper, we propose detecting disfluencies using a right-to-left transition-based dependency parsing (R2L parsing), where the words are consumed from right to left to build the parsing tree based on which the current word is predicted to be either disfluent or normal. The proposed models cater to the disfluency constraint and integrate a rich set of features extracted from contexts of lexicons and partial syntactic tree structure, where the parsing model and disfluency predicting model are jointly calculated in a cascaded way. As shown in Figure 2(b), while the parsing tree is being built, disfluency tags are predicted and attached to the disfluency nodes. Our models are quite efficient with linear complexity of $2 * N$ (N is the length of input).

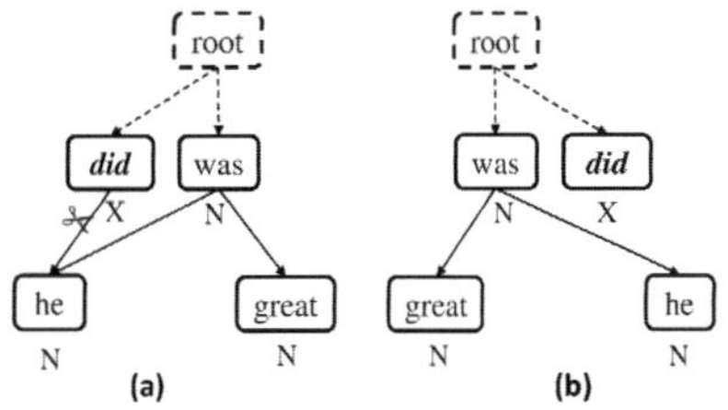

Figure 2: An instance of the detection procedure where 'N' stands for a normal word and 'X' a disfluency word. Words with italic font are Reparandums. (a) is the L2R detecting procedure and (b) is the R2L procedure.

Intuitively, compared with previous syntax-based work such as (Honnibal and Johnson, 2014) that uses left-to-right transition-based parsing (L2R parsing) model, our proposed approach simplifies disfluency detection by sequentially processing each word, without going back to modify the pre-built tree structure of disfluency words. As shown in Figure 2(a), the L2R parsing based joint approach needs to cut the pre-built dependency link between "did" and "he" when "was" is identified as the repair of "did", which is never needed in our method as Figure 2(b). Furthermore, our method overcomes the deficiency issue in decoding of L2R parsing based joint method, meaning the number of parsing transitions for each hypothesis path is not identical to $2 * N$, which leads to the failure of performing optimal search during decoding. For example, the involvement of the extra cut operation in Figure 2(a) destroys the competition scoring that accumulates over $2 * N$ transition actions among hypotheses in the standard transition-based parsing. Although the heuristic score, such as the normalization of transition count (Honnibal and Johnson, 2014), can be introduced, the total scores of all hypotheses are still not statistically comparable from a global view.

We conduct the experiments on English Switchboard corpus. The results show that our method can achieve a 85.1% f-score with a gain of 0.7 point over state-of-the-art M^3N labeling model in (Qian and Liu, 2013) and a gain of 1 point over state-of-the-art joint model proposed in (Honnibal and Johnson, 2014). We also apply our method on Chinese annotated data. As there is no available public data in Chinese, we annotate 25k Chinese sentences manually for training and testing. We achieve 71.2% f-score with 15 points gained compared to the CRF-based baseline, showing that our models are robust and language independent.

2 Transition-based dependency parsing

In a typical transition-based parsing, the Shift-Reduce decoding algorithm is applied and a queue and stack are maintained (Zhang and Clark, 2008). The queue stores the stream of the input and the front of the queue is indexed as the current word. The stack stores the unfinished words which may be linked to the current word or a future word in the queue. When words in the queue are consumed in sequential order, a set of transition actions is applied to build a parsing tree. There are four kinds of transition actions in the parsing process (Zhang and Clark, 2008), as described below.

- *Shift* : Removes the front of the queue and pushes it to the stack.
- *Reduce* : Pops the top of the stack.
- *LeftArc* : Pops the top of the stack, and links the popped word to the front of the queue.
- *RightArc* : Links the front of the queue to the top of the stack and, removes the front of the queue and pushes it to the stack.

The choice of each transition action during parsing is scored by a generalized perceptron (Collins,

2002) which can be trained over a rich set of non-local features. In decoding, beam search is performed to search the optimal sequence of transition actions. As each word must be pushed to the stack once and popped off once, the number of actions needed to parse a sentence is always $2 * N$, where N is the length of the sentence.

Transition-based dependency parsing (Zhang and Clark, 2008) can be performed in either a left-to-right or a right-to-left way, both of which have a performance that is comparable as illustrated in Section 4. However, when they are applied to disfluency detection, their behaviors are very different due to the disfluency structure constraint. We prove that right-to-left transition-based parsing is more efficient than left-to-right transition-based parsing for disfluency detection.

3 Our method

3.1 Model

Unlike previous joint methods (Honnibal and Johnson, 2014; Rasooli and Tetreault, 2013), we introduce dependency parsing into disfluency detection from theory. In the task of disfluency detection, we are given a stream of unstructured words from automatic speech recognition (ASR). We denote the word sequence with $W_1^n := w_1$, w_2,w_3,...,w_n, which is actually the inverse order of ASR words that should be w_n, w_{n-1},w_{n-2},...,w_1. The output of the task is a sequence of binary tags denoted as $D_1^n = d_1$, d_2,d_3,...,d_n, where each d_i corresponds to w_i, indicating whether w_i is a disfluency word (X) or not (N).[1]

Our task can be modeled as formula (1), which is to search the best sequence D^* given the stream of words W_1^n.

$$D^* = argmax_D P(D_1^n|W_1^n) \quad (1)$$

The dependency parsing tree is introduced into model (1) to guide detection. The rewritten formula is shown below:

$$D^* = argmax_D \sum_T P(D_1^n, T|W_1^n) \quad (2)$$

We jointly optimize disfluency detection and parsing with form (3), rather than considering all possible parsing trees:

$$(D^*, T^*) = argmax_{(D,T)} P(D_1^n, T|W_1^n) \quad (3)$$

[1]We just use tag 'N' to represent a normal word, in practice normal words will not be tagged anything by default.

As both the dependency tree and the disfluency tags are generated word by word, we decompose formula (3) into:

$$(D^*, T^*) = argmax_{(D,T)} \prod_{i=1}^{n} P(d_i, T_1^i|W_1^i, T_1^{i-1}) \quad (4)$$

where T_1^i is the partial tree after word w_i is consumed, d_i is the disfluency tag of w_i.

We simplify the joint optimization in a cascaded way with two different forms (5) and (6).

$$(D^*, T^*) = argmax_{(D,T)} \prod_{i=1}^{n} P(T_1^i|W_1^i, T_1^{i-1}) \times P(d_i|W_1^i, T_1^i) \quad (5)$$

$$(D^*, T^*) = argmax_{(D,T)} \prod_{i=1}^{n} P(d_i|W_1^i, T_1^{i-1}) \times P(T_1^i|W_1^i, T_1^{i-1}, d_i) \quad (6)$$

Here, $P(T_1^i|.)$ is the parsing model, and $P(d_i|.)$ is the disfluency model used to predict the disluency tags on condition of the contexts of partial trees that have been built.

In (5), the parsing model is calculated first, followed by the calculation of the disfluency model. Inspired by (Zhang et al., 2013), we associate the disfluency tags to the transition actions so that the calculation of $P(d_i|W_1^i, T_1^i)$ can be omitted as d_i can be inferred from the partial tree T_1^i. We then get

$$(D^*, T^*) = argmax_{(D,T)} \prod_{i=1}^{n} P(d_i, T_1^i|W_1^i, T_1^{i-1}) \quad (7)$$

Where the parsing and disfluency detection are unified into one model. We refer to this model as the Unified Transition(UT) model.

While in (6), the disfluency model is calculated first, followed by the calculation of the parsing model. We model $P(d_i|.)$ as a binary classifier to classify whether a word is disfluent or not. We refer to this model as the binary classifier transition (BCT) model.

3.2 Unified transition-based model (UT)

In model (7), in addition to the standard 4 transition actions mentioned in Section 2, the UT model adds 2 new transition actions which extend the original *Shift* and *RightArc* transitions as shown below:

- *Dis_Shift*: Performs what *Shift* does then marks the pushed word as disfluent.
- *Dis_RightArc*: Adds a virtual link from the front of the queue to the top of the stack which is similar to *Right_Arc*, marking the front of the queue as disfluenct and pushing it to the stack.

Figure 3 shows an example of how the UT model works. Given an input "*he did great was great*", the optimal parsing tree is predicted by the UT model. According to the parsing tree, we can get the disfluency tags "N X X N N" which have been attached to each word. To ensure the normal words are built grammatical in the parse tree, we apply a constraint to the UT model.

UT model constraint: When a word is marked disfluent, all the words in its left and right subtrees will be marked disfluent and all the links of its descendent offsprings will be converted to virtual links, no matter what actions are applied to these words.

For example, the italic word "*great*" will be marked disfluent, no matter what actions are performed on it.

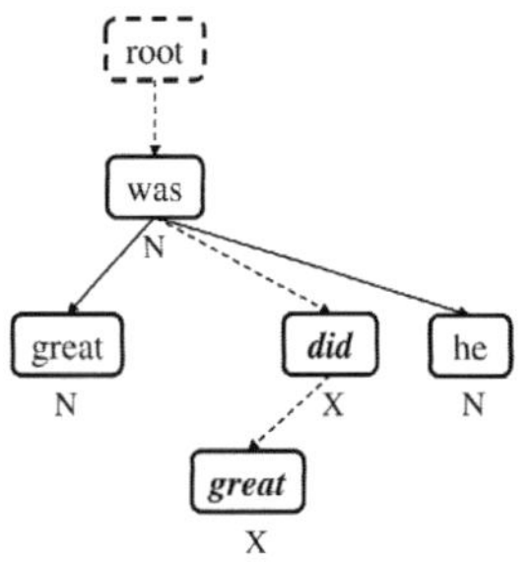

Figure 3: An example of UT model, where 'N' means the word is a fluent word and 'X' means it is disfluent. Words with italic font are Reparandums.

3.3 A binary classifier transition-based model (BCT)

In model (6), we perform the binary classifier and the parsing model together by augmenting the Shift-Reduce algorithm with a binary classifier transition(BCT) action:

- *BCT* : Classifies whether the current word is disfluent or not. If it is, remove it from the queue, push it into the stack which is similar to *Shift* and then mark it as disfluent, otherwise the original transition actions will be used.

It is noted that when BCT is performed, the next action must be *Reduce*. This constraint guarantees that any disfluent word will not have any descendent offspring. Figure 2(b) shows an example of the BCT model. When the partial tree "*great was*" is built, the next word "*did*" is obviously disfluent. Unlike UT model, the BCT will not link the word "*did*" to any word. Instead only a virtual link will add it to the virtual root.

3.4 Training and decoding

In practice, we use the same linear model for both models (6) and (7) to score a parsing tree as:

$$Score(T) = \sum_{action} \phi(action) \cdot \vec{\lambda}$$

Where $\phi(action)$ is the feature vector extracted from partial hypothesis T for a certain $action$ and $\vec{\lambda}$ is the weight vector. $\phi(action) \cdot \vec{\lambda}$ calculates the score of a certain transition action. The score of a parsing tree T is the sum of $action$ scores.

In addition to the basic features introduced in (Zhang and Nivre, 2011) that are defined over bag of words and POS-tags as well as tree-based context, our models also integrate three classes of new features combined with Brown cluster features (Brown et al., 1992) that relate to the right-to-left transition-based parsing procedure as detailed below.

Simple repetition function

- $\delta_I(a, b)$: A logic function which indicates whether a and b are identical.

Syntax-based repetition function

- $\delta_L(a, b)$: A logic function which indicates whether a is a left child of b.
- $\delta_R(a, b)$: A logic function which indicates whether a is a right child of b.

Longest subtree similarity function

- $N_I(a, b)$: The count of identical children on the left side of the root node between subtrees rooted at a and b.
- $N_\#(a_{0..n}, b)$: The count of words among a_0 .. a_n that are on the right of the subtree rooted at b.

Table 1 summarizes the features we use in the model computation, where w_s denotes the top word of the stack, w_0 denotes the front word of the queue and $w_{0..2}$ denotes the top three words of the queue. Every p_i corresponds to the POS-tag of w_i and $p_{0..2}$ represents the POS-tags of $w_{0..2}$. In addition, $w_i c$ means the Brown cluster of w_i. With these symbols, several new feature templates are defined in Table 1. Both our models have the same feature templates.

Basic features	All templates in (Zhang and Nivre, 2011)
New disfluency features	
Function unigrams	$\delta_I(w_s, w_0)$;$\delta_I(p_s, p_0)$; $\delta_L(w_0, w_s)$;$\delta_L(p_0, p_s)$; $\delta_R(w_0, w_s)$;$\delta_R(p_0, p_s)$; $N_I(w_0, w_s)$;$N_I(p_0, p_s)$; $N_\#(w_{0..2}, w_s)$;$N_\#(p_{0..2}, p_s)$;
Function bigrams	$\delta_I(w_s, w_0)\delta_I(p_s, p_0)$; $\delta_L(w_0, w_s)\delta_L(p_0, p_s)$; $\delta_R(w_0, w_s)\delta_R(p_0, p_s)$; $N_I(w_0, w_s)N_I(p_0, p_s)$; $N_\#(w_{0..2}, w_s)N_\#(p_{0..2}, p_s)$; $\delta_I(w_s, w_0)w_s c$; $\delta_I(w_s, w_0)w_0 c$;
Function trigrams	$w_s w_0 \delta_I(w_s, w_0)$; $w_s w_0 \delta_I(p_s, p_0)$;

Table 1: Feature templates designed for disfluency detection and dependency parsing.

Similar to the work in (Zhang and Clark, 2008; Zhang and Nivre, 2011), we train our models by averaged perceptron (Collins, 2002). In decoding, beam search is performed to get the optimal parsing tree as well as the tag sequence.

4 Experiments

4.1 Experimental setup

Our training data is the Switchboard portion of the English Penn Treebank (Marcus et al., 1993) corpus, which consists of telephone conversations about assigned topics. As not all the Switchboard data has syntactic bracketing, we only use the subcorpus of PAESED/MRG/SWBD. Following the experiment settings in (Charniak and Johnson, 2001), the training subcorpus contains directories 2 and 3 in PAESED/MRG/SWBD and directory 4 is split into test and development sets. We use the Stanford dependency converter (De Marneffe et al., 2006) to get the dependency structure from the Switchboard corpus, as Honnibal and Johnson (2014) prove that Stanford converter is robust to the Switchboard data.

For our Chinese experiments, no public Chinese corpus is available. We annotate about 25k spoken sentences with only disfluency annotations according to the guideline proposed by Meteer et al. (1995). In order to generate similar data format as English Switchboard corpus, we use Chinese dependency parsing trained on the Chinese Treebank corpus to parse the annotated data and use these parsed data for training and testing . For our Chinese experiment setting, we respectively select about 2k sentences for development and testing. The rest are used for training.

To train the UT model, we create data format adaptation by replacing the original *Shift* and *RightArc* of disfluent words with *Dis_Shift* and *Dis_RightArc*, since they are just extensions of *Shift* and *RightArc*. For the BCT model, disfluent words are directly depended to the root node and all their links and labels are removed. We then link all the fluent children of disfluent words to parents of disfluent words. We also remove partial words and punctuation from data to simulate speech recognizer results where such information is not available (Johnson and Charniak, 2004). Additionally, following Honnibal and Johnson (2014), we remove all one token sentences as these sentences are trivial for disfluency detection, then lowercase the text and discard filled pauses like "um" and "uh".

The evaluation metrics of disfluency detection are precision (Prec.), recall (Rec.) and f-score (F1). For parsing accuracy metrics, we use unlabeled attachment score (UAS) and labeled attachment score (LAS). For our primary comparison, we evaluate the widely used CRF labeling model, the state-of-the-art M^3N model presented by Qian and Liu (2013) which has been commonly used as baseline in previous works and the state-of-the-art L2R parsing based joint model proposed by Honnibal and Johnson (2014).

4.2 Experimental results

4.2.1 Performance of disfluency detection on English Swtichboard corpus

The evaluation results of both disfluency detection and parsing accuracy are presented in Table 2. The accuracy of M^3N directly refers to the re-

	Disfluency detection accuracy			Parsing accuracy	
Method	Prec.	Rec.	F1	UAS	LAS
CRF(BOW)	81.2%	44.9%	57.8%	88.7%	84.7%
CRF(BOW+POS)	88.3%	62.2%	73.1%	89.2%	85.6%
M^3N	N/A	N/A	84.1%	N/A	N/A
$M^3N^\dagger$	90.5%	79.1%	84.4%	91%	88.2%
H&J	N/A	N/A	84.1%	90.5%	N/A
UT(basic features)	86%	72.5%	78.7%	91.9%	89.0%
UT(+new features)	88.8%	75.1%	81.3%	92.1%	89.4%
BCT(basic features)	88.2%	77.9%	82.7%	92.1%	89.3%
BCT(+new features)	90.3%	80.5%	85.1%	92.2%	89.6%

Table 2: Disfluency detection and parsing accuracies on English Switchboard data. The accuracy of M^3N refers to the result reported in (Qian and Liu, 2013). H&J is the L2R parsing based joint model in (Honnibal and Johnson, 2014). The results of $M^3N^\dagger$ come from the experiments with toolkit released by Qian and Liu (2013) on our pre-processed corpus.

sults reported in (Qian and Liu, 2013). The results of $M^3N^\dagger$ come from our experiments with the toolkit[2] released by Qian and Liu (2013) which uses our data set with the same pre-processing. It is comparable between our models and the L2R parsing based joint model presented by Honnibal and Johnson (2014), as we all conduct experiments on the same pre-processed data set. In order to compare parsing accuracy, we use the CRF and $M^3N^\dagger$ model to pre-process the test set by removing all the detected disfluencies, then evaluate the parsing performance on the processed set. From the table, our BCT model with new disfluency features achieves the best performance on disfluency detection as well as dependency parsing.

The performance of the CRF model is low, because the local features are not powerful enough to capture long span disfluencies. Our main comparison is with the $M^3N^\dagger$ labeling model and the L2R parsing based model by Honnibal and Johnson (2014). As illustrated in Table 2, the BCT model outperforms the $M^3N^\dagger$ model (we got an accuracy of 84.4%, though 84.1% was reported in their paper) and the L2R parsing based model respectively by 0.7 point and 1 point on disfluency detection, which shows our method can efficiently tackle disfluencies. This is because our method can cater extremely well to the disfluency constraint and perform optimal search with identical transition counts over all hypotheses in beam search. Furthermore, our global syntactic and disfluency features can help capture long-range dependencies for disfluency detection. However, the UT model does not perform as well as BCT. This is because the UT model suffers from the risk that normal words may be linked to disfluencies which may bring error propagation in decoding. In addition our models with only basic features respectively score about 3 points below the models adding new features, which shows that these features are important for disfluency detection. In comparing parsing accuracy, our BCT model outperforms all the other models, showing that this model is more robust on disfluent parsing.

[2]The toolkit is available at https://code.google.com/p/disfluency-detection/downloads.

4.2.2 Performance of disfluency detection on different part-of-speeches

In this section, we further analyze the frequency of different part-of-speeches in disfluencies and test the performance on different part-of-speeches. Five classes of words take up more than 73% of all disfluencies as shown in Table 3, which are pronouns (contain PRP and PRP$), verbs (contain VB,VBD,VBP,VBZ,VBN), determiners (contain DT), prepositions (contain IN) and conjunctions (contain CC). Obviously, these classes of words appear frequently in our communication.

	Pron.	Verb	Dete.	Prep.	Conj.	Others
Dist.	30.2%	14.7%	13%	8.7%	6.7%	26.7%

Table 3: Distribution of different part-of-speeches in disfluencies. Conj.=conjunction; Dete.=determiner; Pron.=pronoun; Prep.= preposition.

Table 4 illustrates the performance (f-score) on these classes of words. The results of L2R parsing based joint model in (Honnibal and Johnson, 2014) are not listed because we cannot get such detailed data.

	CRF (BOW)	CRF (BOW +POS)	$M^3N^\dagger$	UT (+feat.)	BCT (+feat.)
Pron.	73.9%	85%	92%	91.5%	93.8%
Verb	38.2%	64.8%	84.2%	82.3%	84.7%
Dete.	66.8%	80%	88%	83.7%	87%
Prep.	60%	71.5%	79.1%	76.1%	79.3%
Conj.	75.2%	82.2%	81.6%	79.5%	83.2%
Others	43.2%	61%	78.4%	72.3%	79.1%

Table 4: Performance on different classes of words. Dete.=determiner; Pron.=pronoun; Conj.=conjunction; Prep.= preposition. feat.=new disfluency features

As shown in Table 4, our BCT model outperforms all other models except that the performance on determiner is lower than $M^3N^\dagger$, which shows that our algorithm can significantly tackle common disfluencies.

4.2.3 Performance of disfluency detection on Chinese annotated corpus

In addition to English experiments, we also apply our method on Chinese annotated data. As there is no standard Chinese corpus, no Chinese experimental results are reported in (Honnibal and Johnson, 2014; Qian and Liu, 2013). We only use the CRF-based labeling model with lexical and POS-tag features as baselines. Table 5 shows the results of Chinese disfluency detection.

Model	Prec.	Rec.	F1
CRF(BOW)	89.5%	35.6%	50.9%
CRF(BOW+POS)	83.4%	41.6%	55.5%
UT(+new features)	86.7%	59.5%	70.6%
BCT(+new features)	85.5%	61%	71.2%

Table 5: Disfluency detection performance on Chinese annotated data.

Our models outperform the CRF model with bag of words and POS-tag features by more than 15 points on f-score which shows that our method is more effective. As shown latter in 4.2.4, the standard transition-based parsing is not robust in parsing disfluent text. There are a lot of parsing errors in Chinese training data. Even though we are still able to get promising results with less data and un-golden parsing annotations. We believe that if we were to have the golden Chinese syntactic annotations and more data, we would get much better results.

4.2.4 Performance of transition-based parsing

In order to show whether the advantage of the BCT model is caused by the disfluency constraint or the difference between R2L and L2R parsing models, in this section, we make a comparison between the original left-to-right transition-based parsing and right-to-left parsing. These experiments are performed with the Penn Treebank (PTB) Wall Street Journal (WSJ) corpus. We follow the standard approach to split the corpus as 2-21 for training, 22 for development and section 23 for testing (McDonald et al., 2005). The features for the two parsers are basic features in Table 1. The POS-tagger model that we implement for a pre-process before parsing also uses structured perceptron for training and can achieve a competitive accuracy of 96.7%. The beam size for both POS-tagger and parsing is set to 5. Table 6 presents the results on WSJ test set and Switchboard (SWBD) test set.

Data sets	Model	UAS	LAS
WSJ	L2R Parsing	92.1%	89.8%
	R2L Parsing	92.0%	89.6%
SWBD	L2R Parsing	88.4%	84.4%
	R2L Parsing	88.7%	84.8%

Table 6: Performance of our parsers on different test sets.

The parsing accuracy on SWBD is lower than WSJ which means that the parsers are more robust on written text data. The performances of R2L and L2R parsing are comparable on both SWBD and WSJ test sets. This demonstrates that the effectiveness of our disfluency detection model mainly relies on catering to the disfluency constraint by using R2L parsing based approach, instead of the difference in parsing models between L2R and R2L parsings.

5 Related work

In practice, disfluency detection has been extensively studied in both speech processing field and natural language processing field. Noisy channel models have been widely used in the past to detect disfluencies. Johnson and Charniak (2004) proposed a TAG-based noisy channel model where the TAG model was used to find rough copies. Thereafter, a language model and MaxEnt reranker were added to the noisy channel model by Johnson et al. (2004). Following their framework, Zwarts and Johnson (2011) extended this model using minimal expected f-loss oriented n-best reranking with additional corpus for language model training.

Recently, the max-margin markov networks (M^3N) based model has achieved great improvement in this task. Qian and Liu (2013) presented a multi-step learning method using weighted M^3N model for disfluency detection. They showed that M^3N model outperformed many other labeling models such as CRF model. Following this work, Wang et al. (2014) used a beam-search decoder to combine multiple models such as M^3N and language model, they achieved the highest f-score. However, direct comparison with their work is difficult as they utilized the whole SWBD data while we only use the subcorpus with syntactic annotation which is only half the SWBD corpus and they also used extra corpus for language model training.

Additionally, syntax-based approaches have been proposed which concern parsing and disfluency detection together. Lease and Johnson (2006) involved disfluency detection in a PCFG parser to parse the input along with detecting disfluencies. Miller and Schuler (2008) used a right corner transform of syntax trees to produce a syntactic tree with speech repairs. But their performance was not as good as labeling models. There exist two methods published recently which are similar to ours. Rasooli and Tetreault (2013) designed a joint model for both disfluency detection and dependency parsing. They regarded the two tasks as a two step classifications. Honnibal and Johnson (2014) presented a new joint model by extending the original transition actions with a new "Edit" transition. They achieved the state-of-the-art performance on both disfluency detection and parsing. But this model suffers from the problem that the number of transition actions is not identical for different hypotheses in decoding, leading to the failure of performing optimal search. In contrast, our novel right-to-left transition-based joint method caters to the disfluency constraint which can not only overcome the decoding deficiency in previous work but also achieve significantly higher performance on disfluency detection as well as dependency parsing.

6 Conclusion and Future Work

In this paper, we propose a novel approach for disfluency detection. Our models jointly perform parsing and disfluency detection from right to left by integrating a rich set of disfluency features which can yield parsing structure and difluency tags at the same time with linear complexity. The algorithm is easy to implement without complicated backtrack operations. Experiential results show that our approach outperforms the baselines on the English Switchboard corpus and experiments on the Chinese annotated corpus also show the language independent nature of our method. The state-of-the-art performance on disfluency detection and dependency parsing can benefit the downstream tasks of text processing.

In future work, we will try to add new classes of features to further improve performance by capturing the property of disfluencies. We would also like to make an end-to-end MT test over transcribed speech texts with disfluencies removed based on the method proposed in this paper.

Acknowledgments

We are grateful to the anonymous reviewers for their insightful comments. We also thank Mu Li, Shujie Liu, Lei Cui and Nan Yang for the helpful discussions.

References

Peter F Brown, Peter V Desouza, Robert L Mercer, Vincent J Della Pietra, and Jenifer C Lai. 1992. Class-based n-gram models of natural language. *Computational linguistics*, 18(4):467–479.

Eugene Charniak and Mark Johnson. 2001. Edit detection and parsing for transcribed speech. In *Proceedings of the second meeting of the North American Chapter of the Association for Computational Linguistics on Language technologies*, pages 1–9. Association for Computational Linguistics.

Michael Collins. 2002. Discriminative training methods for hidden markov models: Theory and experiments with perceptron algorithms. In *Proceedings of the ACL-02 conference on Empirical methods in natural language processing-Volume 10*, pages 1–8. Association for Computational Linguistics.

Marie-Catherine De Marneffe, Bill MacCartney, Christopher D Manning, et al. 2006. Generating typed dependency parses from phrase structure parses. In *Proceedings of LREC*, volume 6, pages 449–454.

Kallirroi Georgila. 2009. Using integer linear programming for detecting speech disfluencies. In *Proceedings of Human Language Technologies: The 2009 Annual Conference of the North American Chapter of the Association for Computational Linguistics, Companion Volume: Short Papers*, pages 109–112. Association for Computational Linguistics.

Matthew Honnibal and Mark Johnson. 2014. Joint incremental disfluency detection and dependency parsing. *Transactions of the Association for Computational Linguistics*, 2:131–142.

Mark Johnson and Eugene Charniak. 2004. A tag-based noisy channel model of speech repairs. In *Proceedings of the 42nd Annual Meeting on Association for Computational Linguistics*, page 33. Association for Computational Linguistics.

Mark Johnson, Eugene Charniak, and Matthew Lease. 2004. An improved model for recognizing disfluencies in conversational speech. In *Proceedings of Rich Transcription Workshop*.

Jeremy G Kahn, Matthew Lease, Eugene Charniak, Mark Johnson, and Mari Ostendorf. 2005. Effective use of prosody in parsing conversational speech. In *Proceedings of the conference on human language technology and empirical methods in natural language processing*, pages 233–240. Association for Computational Linguistics.

Matthew Lease and Mark Johnson. 2006. Early deletion of fillers in processing conversational speech. In *Proceedings of the Human Language Technology Conference of the NAACL, Companion Volume: Short Papers*, pages 73–76. Association for Computational Linguistics.

Yang Liu, Elizabeth Shriberg, Andreas Stolcke, Dustin Hillard, Mari Ostendorf, and Mary Harper. 2006. Enriching speech recognition with automatic detection of sentence boundaries and disfluencies. *Audio, Speech, and Language Processing, IEEE Transactions on*, 14(5):1526–1540.

Mitchell P Marcus, Mary Ann Marcinkiewicz, and Beatrice Santorini. 1993. Building a large annotated corpus of english: The penn treebank. *Computational linguistics*, 19(2):313–330.

Ryan McDonald, Koby Crammer, and Fernando Pereira. 2005. Online large-margin training of dependency parsers. In *Proceedings of the 43rd annual meeting on association for computational linguistics*, pages 91–98. Association for Computational Linguistics.

Marie W Meteer, Ann A Taylor, Robert MacIntyre, and Rukmini Iyer. 1995. *Dysfluency annotation stylebook for the switchboard corpus*. University of Pennsylvania.

Tim Miller and William Schuler. 2008. A unified syntactic model for parsing fluent and disfluent speech. In *Proceedings of the 46th Annual Meeting of the Association for Computational Linguistics on Human Language Technologies: Short Papers*, pages 105–108. Association for Computational Linguistics.

Xian Qian and Yang Liu. 2013. Disfluency detection using multi-step stacked learning. In *HLT-NAACL*, pages 820–825.

Mohammad Sadegh Rasooli and Joel R Tetreault. 2013. Joint parsing and disfluency detection in linear time. In *EMNLP*, pages 124–129.

Xuancong Wang, Hwee Tou Ng, and Khe Chai Sim. 2014. A beam-search decoder for disfluency detection. In *Proc. of COLING*.

Yue Zhang and Stephen Clark. 2008. A tale of two parsers: investigating and combining graph-based and transition-based dependency parsing using beam-search. In *Proceedings of the Conference on Empirical Methods in Natural Language Processing*, pages 562–571. Association for Computational Linguistics.

Yue Zhang and Joakim Nivre. 2011. Transition-based dependency parsing with rich non-local features. In *Proceedings of the 49th Annual Meeting of the Association for Computational Linguistics: Human Language Technologies: short papers-Volume 2*, pages 188–193. Association for Computational Linguistics.

Qi Zhang, Fuliang Weng, and Zhe Feng. 2006. A progressive feature selection algorithm for ultra large feature spaces. In *Proceedings of the 21st International Conference on Computational Linguistics and the 44th annual meeting of the Association for Computational Linguistics*, pages 561–568. Association for Computational Linguistics.

Dongdong Zhang, Shuangzhi Wu, Nan Yang, and Mu Li. 2013. Punctuation prediction with transition-based parsing. In *ACL (1)*, pages 752–760.

Simon Zwarts and Mark Johnson. 2011. The impact of language models and loss functions on repair disfluency detection. In *Proceedings of the 49th Annual Meeting of the Association for Computational Linguistics: Human Language Technologies-Volume 1*, pages 703–711. Association for Computational Linguistics.

S-MART: Novel Tree-based Structured Learning Algorithms Applied to Tweet Entity Linking

Yi Yang
School of Interactive Computing
Georgia Institute of Technology
yiyang@gatech.edu

Ming-Wei Chang
Microsoft Research
minchang@microsoft.com

Abstract

Non-linear models recently receive a lot of attention as people are starting to discover the power of statistical and embedding features. However, tree-based models are seldom studied in the context of structured learning despite their recent success on various classification and ranking tasks. In this paper, we propose S-MART, a tree-based structured learning framework based on multiple additive regression trees. S-MART is especially suitable for handling tasks with dense features, and can be used to learn many different structures under various loss functions.

We apply S-MART to the task of tweet entity linking — a core component of tweet information extraction, which aims to identify and link name mentions to entities in a knowledge base. A novel inference algorithm is proposed to handle the special structure of the task. The experimental results show that S-MART significantly outperforms state-of-the-art tweet entity linking systems.

1 Introduction

Many natural language processing (NLP) problems can be formalized as structured prediction tasks. Standard algorithms for structured learning include Conditional Random Field (CRF) (Lafferty et al., 2001) and Structured Supported Vector Machine (SSVM) (Tsochantaridis et al., 2004). These algorithms, usually equipped with a linear model and sparse lexical features, achieve state-of-the-art performances in many NLP applications such as part-of-speech tagging, named entity recognition and dependency parsing.

This classical combination of linear models and sparse features is challenged by the recent emerging usage of dense features such as statistical and embedding features. Tasks with these low dimensional dense features require models to be more sophisticated to capture the relationships between features. Therefore, non-linear models start to receive more attention as they are often more expressive than linear models.

Tree-based models such as boosted trees (Friedman, 2001) are flexible non-linear models. They can handle categorical features and count data better than other non-linear models like Neural Networks. Unfortunately, to the best of our knowledge, little work has utilized tree-based methods for structured prediction, with the exception of TreeCRF (Dietterich et al., 2004).

In this paper, we propose a novel structured learning framework called S-MART (**S**tructured **M**ultiple **A**dditive **R**egression **T**rees). Unlike TreeCRF, S-MART is very versatile, as it can be applied to tasks beyond sequence tagging and can be trained under various objective functions. S-MART is also powerful, as the high order relationships between features can be captured by non-linear regression trees.

We further demonstrate how S-MART can be applied to tweet entity linking, an important and challenging task underlying many applications including product feedback (Asur and Huberman, 2010) and topic detection and tracking (Mathioudakis and Koudas, 2010). We apply S-MART to entity linking using a simple logistic function as the loss function and propose a novel inference algorithm to prevent overlaps between entities.

Our contributions are summarized as follows:

- We propose a novel structured learning framework called S-MART. S-MART combines non-linearity and efficiency of tree-based models with structured prediction, leading to a family of new algorithms. (Section 2)

Proceedings of the 53rd Annual Meeting of the Association for Computational Linguistics and the 7th International Joint Conference on Natural Language Processing, pages 504–513,
Beijing, China, July 26-31, 2015.

- We apply S-MART to tweet entity linking. Building on top of S-MART, we propose a novel inference algorithm for non-overlapping structure with the goal of preventing conflicting entity assignments. (Section 3)

- We provide a systematic study of evaluation criteria in tweet entity linking by conducting extensive experiments over major data sets. The results show that S-MART significantly outperforms state-of-the-art entity linking systems, including the system that is used to win the NEEL 2014 challenge (Cano and others, 2014). (Section 4)

2 Structured Multiple Additive Regression Trees

The goal of a structured learning algorithm is to learn a joint scoring function S between an input $\mathbf{x}$ and an output structure $\mathbf{y}$, $S : (\mathbf{x}, \mathbf{y}) \rightarrow \mathbb{R}$. The structured output $\mathbf{y}$ often contains many interdependent variables, and the number of the possible structures can be exponentially large with respect to the size of $\mathbf{x}$. At test time, the prediction $\mathbf{y}$ for $\mathbf{x}$ is obtained by

$$\arg\max_{\mathbf{y} \in Gen(\mathbf{x})} S(\mathbf{x}, \mathbf{y}),$$

where $Gen(\mathbf{x})$ represents the set of all valid output structures for $\mathbf{x}$.

Standard learning algorithms often directly optimize the model parameters. For example, assume that the joint scoring function S is parameterized by θ. Then, gradient descent algorithms can be used to optimize the model parameters θ iteratively. More specifically,

$$\theta_m = \theta_{m-1} - \eta_m \frac{\partial L(\mathbf{y}^*, S(\mathbf{x}, \mathbf{y}; \theta))}{\partial \theta_{m-1}}, \quad (1)$$

where $\mathbf{y}^*$ is the gold structure, $L(\mathbf{y}^*, S(\mathbf{x}, \mathbf{y}; \theta))$ is a loss function and η_m is the learning rate of the m-th iteration.

In this paper, we propose a framework called **Structured Multiple Additive Regression Trees (S-MART)**, which generalizes Multiple Additive Regression Trees (MART) for structured learning problems. Different from Equation (1), S-MART does *not* directly optimize the model parameters; instead, it approximates the optimal scoring function that minimize the loss by adding (weighted) regression tree models iteratively.

Due to the fact that there are exponentially many input-output pairs in the training data, S-MART assumes that the joint scoring function can be decomposed as

$$S(\mathbf{x}, \mathbf{y}) = \sum_{k \in \Omega(\mathbf{x})} F(\mathbf{x}, \mathbf{y}_k),$$

where $\Omega(\mathbf{x})$ contains the set of the all factors for input $\mathbf{x}$ and $\mathbf{y}_k$ is the sub-structure of $\mathbf{y}$ that corresponds to the k-th factor in $\Omega(\mathbf{x})$. For instance, in the task of word alignment, each factor can be defined as a pair of words from source and target languages respectively. Note that we can recover $\mathbf{y}$ from the union of $\{\mathbf{y}_k\}_1^K$.

The factor scoring function $F(\mathbf{x}, \mathbf{y}_k)$ can be optimized by performing gradient descent in the function space in the following manner:

$$F_m(\mathbf{x}, \mathbf{y}_k) = F_{m-1}(\mathbf{x}, \mathbf{y}_k) - \eta_m g_m(\mathbf{x}, \mathbf{y}_k) \quad (2)$$

where function $g_m(\mathbf{x}, \mathbf{y}_k)$ is the functional gradient.

Note that g_m is a *function* rather than a vector. Therefore, modeling g_m theoretically requires an infinite number of data points. We can address this difficulty by approximating g_m with a finite number of point-wise functional gradients

$$g_m(\mathbf{x}, \mathbf{y}_k = u_k) = \quad (3)$$
$$\left[\frac{\partial L(\mathbf{y}^*, S(\mathbf{x}, \mathbf{y}_k = u_k))}{\partial F(\mathbf{x}, \mathbf{y}_k = u_k)}\right]_{F(\mathbf{x}, \mathbf{y}_k) = F_{m-1}(\mathbf{x}, \mathbf{y}_k)}$$

where u_k index a valid sub-structure for the k-th factor of $\mathbf{x}$.

The key point of S-MART is that it approximates $-g_m$ by modeling the point-wise negative functional gradients using a regression tree h_m. Then the factor scoring function can be obtained by

$$F(\mathbf{x}, \mathbf{y}_k) = \sum_{m=1}^{M} \eta_m h_m(\mathbf{x}, \mathbf{y}_k),$$

where $h_m(\mathbf{x}, \mathbf{y}_k)$ is also called a basis function and η_m can be simply set to 1 (Murphy, 2012).

The detailed S-MART algorithm is presented in Algorithm 1. The factor scoring function $F(\mathbf{x}, \mathbf{y}_k)$ is simply initialized to zero at first (line 1). After this, we iteratively update the function by adding regression trees. Note that the scoring function is shared by all the factors. Specifically, given the current decision function F_{m-1}, we can consider line 3 to line 9 a process of generating the pseudo

Algorithm 1 S-MART: A family of structured learning algorithms with multiple additive regression trees

1: $F_0(\mathbf{x}, \mathbf{y}_k) = 0$
2: **for** $m = 1$ to M **do**: ▷ going over all trees
3: $D \leftarrow \emptyset$
4: **for** all examples **do**: ▷ going over all examples
5: **for** $\mathbf{y}_k \in \Omega(\mathbf{x})$ **do**: ▷ going over all factors
6: For all u_k, obtain g_{ku} by Equation (3)
7: $D \leftarrow D \cup \{(\Phi(\mathbf{x}, \mathbf{y}_k = u_k), -g_{ku})\}$
8: **end for**
9: **end for**
10: $h_m(\mathbf{x}, \mathbf{y}_k) \leftarrow \texttt{TrainRegressionTree}(D)$
11: $F_m(\mathbf{x}, \mathbf{y}_k) = F_{m-1}(\mathbf{x}, \mathbf{y}_k) + h_m(\mathbf{x}, \mathbf{y}_k)$
12: **end for**

training data D for modeling the regression tree. For each training example, S-MART first computes the point-wise functional gradients according to Equation (3) (line 6). Here we use g_{ku} as the abbreviation for $g_m(\mathbf{x}, \mathbf{y}_k = u_k)$. In line 7, for each sub-structure u_k, we create a new training example for the regression problem by the feature vector $\Phi(\mathbf{x}, \mathbf{y}_k = u_k)$ and the negative gradient $-g_{ku}$. In line 10, a regression tree is constructed by minimizing differences between the prediction values and the point-wise negative gradients. Then a new basis function (modeled by a regression tree) will be added into the overall F (line 11).

It is crucial to note that S-MART is *a family of algorithms* rather than a single algorithm. S-MART is flexible in the choice of the loss functions. For example, we can use either logistic loss or hinge loss, which means that S-MART can train probabilistic models as well as non-probabilistic ones. Depending on the choice of factors, S-MART can handle various structures such as linear chains, trees, and even the semi-Markov chain (Sarawagi and Cohen, 2004).

S-MART versus MART There are two key differences between S-MART and MART. First, S-MART decomposes the joint scoring function $S(\mathbf{x}, \mathbf{y})$ into factors to address the problem of the exploding number of input-output pairs for structured learning problems. Second, S-MART models a single scoring function $F(\mathbf{x}, \mathbf{y}_k)$ over inputs and output variables directly rather than O different functions $F^o(\mathbf{x})$, each of which corresponds to a label class.

S-MART versus TreeCRF TreeCRF can be viewed as a special case of S-MART, and there are two points where S-MART improves upon TreeCRF. First, the model designed in (Dietterich et al., 2004) is tailored for sequence tagging problems. Similar to MART, for a tagging task with O tags, they choose to model O functions $F^o(\mathbf{x}, o')$ instead of directly modeling the joint score of the factor. This imposes limitations on the feature functions, and TreeCRF is consequently unsuitable for many tasks such as entity linking.[1] Second, S-MART is more general in terms of the objective functions and applicable structures. In the next section, we will see how S-MART can be applied to a non-linear-chain structure and various loss functions.

3 S-MART for Tweet Entity Linking

We first formally define the task of tweet entity linking. As *input*, we are given a tweet, an entity database (*e.g.*, Wikipedia where each article is an entity), and a lexicon[2] which maps a surface form into a set of entity candidates. For each incoming tweet, all n-grams of this tweet will be used to find matches in the lexicon, and each match will form a mention candidate. As *output*, we map every mention candidate (*e.g.*, "new york giants") in the message to an entity (*e.g.*, NEW YORK GIANTS) or to **Nil** (*i.e.*, a non-entity). A mention candidate can often potentially link to multiple entities, which we call possible *entity assignments*.

This task is a structured learning problem, as the final entity assignments of a tweet should not overlap with each other.[3] We decompose this learning problem as follows: we make each mention candidate a factor, and the score of the entity assignments of a tweet is the sum of the score of each entity and mention candidate pair. Although all mention candidates are decomposed, the non-overlapping constraint requires the system to perform global inference.

Consider the example tweet in Figure 1, where we show the tweet with the mention candidates in brackets. To link the mention candidate "new york giants" to a non-**Nil** entity, the system has to link previous overlapping mention candidates to **Nil**. It is important to note that this is **not** a linear chain problem because of the non-overlapping constraint, and the inference algorithm needs to be

[1] For example, entity linking systems need to model the similarity between an entity and the document. The TreeCRF formulation does not support such features.

[2] We use the standard techniques to construct the lexicon from anchor texts, redirect pages and other information resources.

[3] We follow the common practice and do not allow embedded entities.

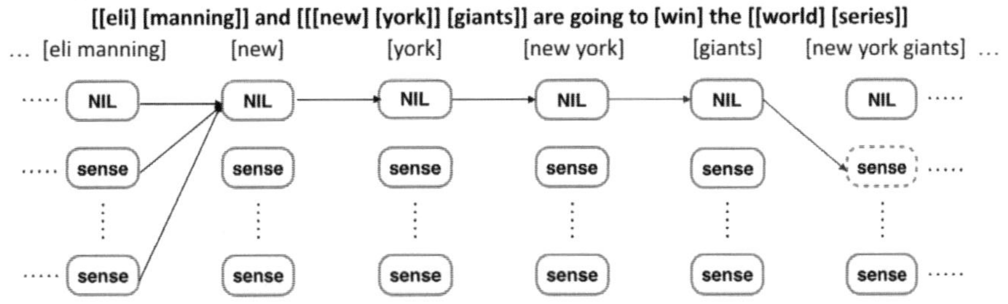

Figure 1: Example tweet and its mention candidates. Each mention candidate is marked as a pair of brackets in the original tweet and forms a column in the graph. The graph demonstrates the non-overlapping constraint. To link the mention candidate "new york giants" to a non-**Nil** entity, the system has to link previous four overlapping mention candidates to **Nil**. The mention candidate "eli manning" is not affected by "new york giants". **Note that this is not a standard linear chain problem.**

carefully designed.

3.1 Applying S-MART

We derive specific model for tweet entity linking task with S-MART and use logistic loss as our running example. The hinge loss version of the model can be derived in a similar way.

Note that the tweet and the mention candidates are given. Let x be the tweet, u_k be the entity assignment of the k-th mention candidate. We use function $F(\mathbf{x}, y_k = u_k)$ to model the score of the k-th mention candidate choosing entity u_k.[4] The overall scoring function can be decomposed as follows:

$$S(\mathbf{x}, \mathbf{y} = \{u_k\}_{k=1}^{K}) = \sum_{k=1}^{K} F(\mathbf{x}, y_k = u_k)$$

S-MART utilizes regression trees to model the scoring function $F(\mathbf{x}, y_k = u_k)$, which requires point-wise functional gradient for each entity of every mention candidate. Let's first write down the logistic loss function as

$$\begin{aligned} L(\mathbf{y}^*, S(\mathbf{x}, \mathbf{y})) &= -\log P(\mathbf{y}^*|\mathbf{x}) \\ &= \log Z(\mathbf{x}) - S(\mathbf{x}, \mathbf{y}^*) \end{aligned}$$

where $Z(\mathbf{x}) = \sum_{\mathbf{y}} \exp(S(\mathbf{x}, \mathbf{y}))$ is the potential function. Then the point-wise gradients can be computed as

$$\begin{aligned} g_{ku} &= \frac{\partial L}{\partial F(\mathbf{x}, y_k = u_k)} \\ &= P(y_k = u_k|\mathbf{x}) - \mathbf{1}[y_k^* = u_k], \end{aligned}$$

where $\mathbf{1}[\cdot]$ represents an indicator function. The conditional probability $P(y_k = u_k|\mathbf{x})$ can be computed by a variant of the forward-backward algorithm, which we will detail in the next subsection.

[4]Note that each mention candidate has different own entity sets.

3.2 Inference

The non-overlapping structure is distinct from linear chain and semi-Markov chain (Sarawagi and Cohen, 2004) structures. Hence, we propose a carefully designed forward-backward algorithm to calculate $P(y_k = u_k|\mathbf{x})$ based on current scoring function $F(\mathbf{x}, y_k = u_k)$ given by the regression trees. The non-overlapping constraint distinguishes our inference algorithm from other forward-backward variants.

To compute the forward probability, we sort[5] the mention candidates by their end indices and define forward recursion by

$$\begin{aligned} \alpha(u_1, 1) &= \exp(F(\mathbf{x}, y_1 = u_1)) \\ \alpha(u_k, k) &= \exp(F(\mathbf{x}, y_k = u_k)) \\ &\quad \cdot \prod_{p=1}^{P-1} \exp(F(\mathbf{x}, y_{k-p} = \textbf{Nil})) \\ &\quad \cdot \sum_{u_{k-P}} \alpha(u_{k-P}, k - P) \end{aligned} \quad (4)$$

where $k - P$ is the index of the previous non-overlapping mention candidate. Intuitively, for the k-th mention candidate, we need to identify its nearest non-overlapping fellow and recursively compute the probability. The overlapping mention candidates can only take the **Nil** entity.

Similarly, we can sort the mention candidates by their start indices and define backward recur-

[5]Sorting helps the algorithms find non-overlapping candidates.

sion by

$$\beta(u_K, K) = 1$$
$$\beta(u_k, k) = \sum_{u_{k+Q}} \exp(F(\mathbf{x}, y_{k+Q} = u_{k+Q})) \cdot \prod_{q=1}^{Q-1} \exp(F(\mathbf{x}, y_{k+q} = \textbf{Nil})) \cdot \beta(u_{k+Q}, k+Q) \quad (5)$$

where $k + Q$ is the index of the next non-overlapping mention candidate. Note that the third terms of equation (4) or (5) will vanish if there are no corresponding non-overlapping mention candidates.

Given the potential function can be computed by $Z(\mathbf{x}) = \sum_{u_k} \alpha(u_k, k)\beta(u_k, k)$, for entities that are not **Nil**,

$$P(y_k = u_k|\mathbf{x}) = \frac{\exp(F(\mathbf{x}, y_k = u_k)) \cdot \beta(u_k, k)}{Z(\mathbf{x})} \cdot \prod_{p=1}^{P-1} \exp(F(\mathbf{x}, y_{k-p} = \textbf{Nil})) \cdot \sum_{u_{k-P}} \alpha(u_{k-P}, k-P) \quad (6)$$

The probability for the special token **Nil** can be obtained by

$$P(y_k = \textbf{Nil}|\mathbf{x}) = 1 - \sum_{u_k \neq \textbf{Nil}} P(y_k = u_k|\mathbf{x}) \quad (7)$$

In the worst case, the total cost of the forward-backward algorithm is $\mathcal{O}(\max\{TK, K^2\})$, where T is the number of entities of a mention candidate.[6]

Finally, at test time, the decoding problem $\arg\max_{\mathbf{y}} S(\mathbf{x}, \mathbf{y})$ can be solved by a variant of the Viterbi algorithm.

3.3 Beyond S-MART: Modeling entity-entity relationships

It is important for entity linking systems to take advantage of the entity-to-entity information while making local decisions. For instance, the identification of entity "eli manning" leads to a strong clue for linking "new york giants" to the NFL team.

Instead of defining a more complicated structure and learning everything jointly, we employ a two-stage approach as the solution for modeling entity-entity relationships after we found that S-MART achieves high precision and reasonable recall. Specifically, in the first stage, the system identifies all possible entities with basic features, which enables the extraction of entity-entity features. In the second stage, we re-train S-MART on a union of basic features and entity-entity features. We define entity-entity features based on the Jaccard distance introduced by Guo et al. (2013).

Let $\Gamma(e_i)$ denotes the set of Wikipedia pages that contain a hyperlink to an entity e_i and $\Gamma(t_{-i})$ denotes the set of pages that contain a hyperlink to any identified entity e_j of the tweet t in the first stage excluding e_i. The Jaccard distance between e_i and t is

$$Jac(e_i, t) = \frac{|\Gamma(e_i) \cap \Gamma(t_{-i})|}{|\Gamma(e_i) \cup \Gamma(t_{-i})|}.$$

In addition to the Jaccard distance, we add one additional binary feature to indicate if the current entity has the highest Jaccard distance among all entities for this mention candidate.

4 Experiments

Our experiments are designed to answer the following three research questions in the context of tweet entity linking:

- Do non-linear learning algorithms perform better than linear learning algorithms?
- Do structured entity linking models perform better than non-structured ones?
- How can we best capture the relationships between entities?

4.1 Evaluation Methodology and Data

We evaluate each entity linking system using two evaluation policies: Information Extraction (IE) driven evaluation and Information Retrieval (IR) driven evaluation. For both evaluation settings, precision, recall and F1 scores are reported. Our data is constructed from two publicly available sources: Named Entity Extraction & Linking (NEEL) Challenge (Cano et al., 2014) datasets, and the datasets released by Fang and Chang (2014). Note that we gather two datasets from Fang and Chang (2014) and they are used in two different evaluation settings. We refer to these two datasets as TACL-IE and TACL-IR, respectively. We perform some data cleaning and unification on

[6] The cost is $\mathcal{O}(K^2)$ only if every mention candidate of the tweet overlaps other mention candidates. In practice, the algorithm is nearly linear w.r.t K.

these sets.[7] The statistics of the datasets are presented in Table 1.

IE-driven evaluation The IE-driven evaluation is the standard evaluation for an end-to-end entity linking system. We follow Carmel et al. (2014) and relax the definition of the correct mention boundaries, as they are often ambiguous. A mention boundary is considered to be correct if it overlaps (instead of being the same) with the gold mention boundary. Please see (Carmel et al., 2014) for more details on the procedure of calculating the precision, recall and F1 score.

The NEEL and TACL-IE datasets have different annotation guidelines and different choices of knowledge bases, so we perform the following procedure to clean the data and unify the annotations. We first filter out the annotations that link to entities excluded by our knowledge base. We use the same knowledge base as the ERD 2014 competition (Carmel et al., 2014), which includes the union of entities in Wikipedia and Freebase. Second, we follow NEEL annotation guideline and re-annotate TACL-IE dataset. For instance, in order to be consistent with NEEL, all the user tags (e.g. @BarackObama) are re-labeled as entities in TACL-IE.

We train all the models with NEEL Train dataset and evaluate different systems on NEEL Test and TACL-IE datasets. In addition, we sample 800 tweets from NEEL Train dataset as our development set to perform parameter tuning.

IR-driven evaluation The IR-driven evaluation is proposed by Fang and Chang (2014). It is motivated by a key application of entity linking — retrieval of relevant tweets for target entities, which is crucial for downstream applications such as product research and sentiment analysis. In particular, given a query entity we can search for tweets based on the match with some potential surface forms of the query entity. Then, an entity linking system is evaluated by its ability to correctly identify the presence or absence of the query entity in every tweet. Our IR-driven evaluation is based on the TACL-IR set, which includes 980 tweets sampled for ten query entities of five entity types (roughly 100 tweets per entity). About 37% of the sampled tweets did not mention the query entity due to the anchor ambiguity.

[7] We plan to release the cleaned data and evaluation code if license permitted.

Data	#Tweet	#Entity	Date
NEEL Train	2340	2202	Jul. ~Aug. 11
NEEL Test	1164	687	Jul. ~Aug. 11
TACL-IE	500	300	Dec. 12
TACL-IR	980	NA	Dec. 12

Table 1: Statistics of data sets.

4.2 Experimental Settings

Features We employ a total number of 37 dense features as our basic feature set. Most of the features are adopted from (Guo et al., 2013)[8], including various statistical features such as the probability of the surface to be used as anchor text in Wikipedia. We also add additional Entity Type features correspond to the following entity types: Character, Event, Product and Brand. Finally, we include several NER features to indicate each mention candidate belongs to one the following NER types: Twitter user, Twitter hashtag, Person, Location, Organization, Product, Event and Date.

Algorithms Table 2 summarizes all the algorithms that are compared in our experiments. First, we consider two linear structured learning algorithms: Structured Perceptron (Collins, 2002) and Linear Structured SVM (SSVM) (Tsochantaridis et al., 2004).

For non-linear models, we consider polynomial SSVM, which employs polynomial kernel inside the structured SVM algorithm. We also include LambdaRank (Quoc and Le, 2007), a neural-based learning to rank algorithm, which is widely used in the information retrieval literature. We further compare with MART, which is designed for performing multiclass classification using log loss without considering the structured information. Finally, we have our proposed log-loss S-MART algorithm, as described in Section 3. [9]

Note that our baseline systems are quite strong. Linear SSVM has been used in one of the state-of-the-art tweet entity linking systems (Guo et al., 2013), and the system based on MART is the winning system of the 2014 NEEL Challenge (Cano and others, 2014)[10].

Table 2 summarizes several properties of the algorithms. For example, most algorithms are struc-

[8] We consider features of Base, Capitalization Rate, Popularity, Context Capitalization and Entity Type categories.

[9] Our pilot experiments show that the log-loss S-MART consistently outperforms the hinge-loss S-MART.

[10] Note that the numbers we reported here are different from the results in NEEL challenge due to the fact that we have cleaned the datasets and the evaluation metrics are slightly different in this paper.

Model	Structured	Non-linear	Tree-based
Structured Perceptron	✓		
Linear SSVM	✓		
Polynomial SSVM	✓	✓	
LambdaRank		✓	
MART		✓	✓
S-MART	✓	✓	✓

Table 2: Included algorithms and their properties.

tured (e.g. they perform dynamic programming at test time) except for MART and LambdaRank, which treat mention candidates independently.

Parameter tuning All the hyper-parameters are tuned on the development set. Then, we re-train our models on full training data (including the dev set) with the best parameters. We choose the soft margin parameter C from $\{0.5, 1, 5, 10\}$ for two structured SVM methods. After a preliminary parameter search, we fixed the number of trees to 300 and the minimum number of documents in a leaf to 30 for all tree-based models. For LambdaRank, we use a two layer feed forward network. We select the number of hidden units from $\{10, 20, 30, 40\}$ and learning rate from $\{0.1, 0.01, 0.001\}$.

It is widely known that F1 score can be affected by the trade-off between precision and recall. In order to make the comparisons between all algorithms fairer in terms of F1 score, we include a post-processing step to balance precision and recall for all the systems. Note the tuning is only conducted for the purpose of robust evaluation. In particular, we adopt a simple tuning strategy that works well for all the algorithms, in which we add a bias term b to the scoring function value of **Nil**:

$$F(\mathbf{x}, y_k = \textbf{Nil}) \leftarrow F(\mathbf{x}, y_k = \textbf{Nil}) + b.$$

We choose the bias term b from values between -3.0 to 3.0 on the dev set and apply the same bias term at test time.

4.3 Results

Table 3 presents the empirical findings for S-MART and competitive methods on tweet entity linking task in both IE and IR settings. In the following, we analyze the empirical results in details.

Linear models vs. non-linear models Table 3 clearly shows that linear models perform worse than non-linear models when they are restricted to the IE setting of the tweet entity linking task. The story is similar in IR-driven evaluation, with the exception of LambdaRank. Among the linear models, linear SSVM demonstrates its superiority over Structured Perceptron on all datasets, which aligns with the results of (Tsochantaridis et al., 2005) on the named entity recognition task.

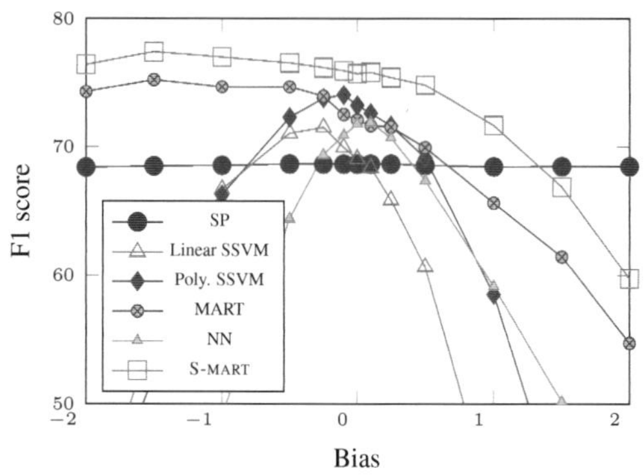

Figure 2: Balance precisions and recalls. X-axis corresponds to values of the bias terms for the special token **Nil**. Note that S-MART is still the overall winning system without tuning the threshold.

We have many interesting observations on the non-linear models side. First, by adopting a polynomial kernel, the non-linear SSVM further improves the entity linking performances on the NEEL datasets and TACL-IR dataset. Second, LambdaRank, a neural network based model, achieves better results than linear models in IE-driven evaluation, but the results in IR-driven evaluation are worse than all the other methods. We believe the reason for this dismal performance is that the neural-based method tends to overfit the IR setting given the small number of training examples. Third, both MART and S-MART significantly outperform alternative linear and non-linear methods in IE-driven evaluation and performs better or similar to other methods in IR-driven evaluation. This suggests that tree-based non-linear models are suitable for tweet entity linking task. Finally, S-MART outperforms previous state-of-the-art method Structured SVM by a surprisingly large margin. In the NEEL Test dataset, the difference is more than 10% F1. Overall, the results show that the shallow linear models are not expressive enough to capture the complex patterns in the data, which are represented by a few dense features.

Structured learning models To showcase structured learning technique is crucial for entity linking with non-linear models, we compare S-MART against MART directly. As shown in

Model	NEEL Dev			NEEL Test			TACL-IE			TACL-IR		
	P	R	F1	P	R	F1	P	R	F1	P	R	F1
Structured Perceptron	75.8	62.8	68.7	79.1	64.3	70.9	74.4	63.0	68.2	86.2	43.8	58.0
Linear SSVM	78.0	66.1	71.5	80.5	67.1	73.2	**78.2**	64.7	70.8	86.7	48.5	62.2
Polynomial SSVM	77.7	70.7	74.0	81.3	69.0	74.6	76.8	64.0	69.8	91.1	48.8	63.6
LambdaRank	75.0	69.0	71.9	80.3	71.2	75.5	77.8	66.7	71.8	85.8	42.4	56.8
MART	76.2	74.3	75.2	76.8	78.0	77.4	73.4	71.0	72.2	**98.1**	46.4	63.0
S-MART	**79.1**	**75.8**	**77.4**	**83.2**	**79.2**	**81.1**	76.8	**73.0**	**74.9**	95.1	**52.2**	**67.4**
+ entity-entity	79.2	75.8	77.5	81.5	76.4	78.9	77.3	73.7	75.4	95.5	56.7	71.1

Table 3: IE-driven and IR-driven evaluation results for different models. The best results with basic features are in **bold**. The results are underlined if adding entity-entity features gives the overall best results.

Table 3, S-MART can achieve higher precision and recall points compared to MART on all datasets in terms of IE-driven evaluation, and can improve F1 by 4 points on NEEL Test and TACL-IR datasets. The task of entity linking is to produce non-overlapping entity assignments that match the gold mentions. By adopting structured learning technique, S-MART is able to automatically take into account the non-overlapping constraint during learning and inference, and produce global optimal entity assignments for mention candidates of a tweet. One effect is that S-MART can easily eliminate some common errors caused by popular entities (e.g. new york in Figure 1).

Modeling entity-entity relationships Entity-entity relationships provide strong clues for entity disambiguation. In this paper, we use the simple two-stage approach described in Section 3.3 to capture the relationships between entities. As shown in Table 3, the significant improvement in IR-driven evaluation indicates the importance of incorporating entity-entity information.

Interestingly, while IR-driven results are significantly improved, IE-driven results are similar or even worse given entity-entity features. We believe the reason is that IE-driven and IR-driven evaluations focus on different aspects of tweet entity linking task. As Guo et al. (2013) shows that most mentions in tweets should be linked to the most popular entities, IE setting actually pays more attention on mention detection sub-problem. In contrast to IE setting, IR setting focuses on entity disambiguation, since we only need to decide whether the tweet is relevant to the query entity. Therefore, we believe that both evaluation policies are needed for tweet entity linking.

Balance Precision and Recall Figure 2 shows the results of tuning the bias term for balancing precision and recall on the dev set. The results show that S-MART outperforms competitive approaches without any tuning, with similar margins to the results after tuning. Balancing precision and recall improves F1 scores for all the systems, which suggests that the simple tuning method performs quite well. Finally, we have an interesting observation that different methods have various scales of model scores.

5 Related Work

Linear structured learning methods have been proposed and widely used in the literature. Popular models include Structured Perceptron (Collins, 2002), Conditional Random Field (Lafferty et al., 2001) and Structured SVM (Taskar et al., 2004; Tsochantaridis et al., 2005). Recently, many structured learning models based on neural networks have been proposed and are widely used in language modeling (Bengio et al., 2006; Mikolov et al., 2010), sentiment classification (Socher et al., 2013), as well as parsing (Socher et al., 2011). Cortes et al. (2014) recently proposed a boosting framework which treats different structured learning algorithms as base learners to ensemble structured prediction results.

Tree-based models have been shown to provide more robust and accurate performances than neural networks in some tasks of computer vision (Roe et al., 2005; Babenko et al., 2011) and information retrieval (Li et al., 2007; Wu et al., 2010), suggesting that it is worth to investigate tree-based non-linear models for structured learning problems. To the best of our knowledge, TreeCRF (Dietterich et al., 2004) is the only work that explores tree-based methods for structured learning problems. The relationships between TreeCRF and our work have been discussed in Section 2.

Early research on entity linking has focused on well written documents (Bunescu and Pasca, 2006; Cucerzan, 2007; Milne and Witten, 2008). Due to the raise of social media, many techniques have been proposed or tailored to short texts including tweets, for the problem of entity linking (Ferragina and Scaiella, 2010; Meij et al., 2012; Guo et al., 2013) as well as the related problem of named entity recognition (NER) (Ritter et al., 2011). Recently, non-textual information such as spatial and temporal signals have also been used to improve entity linking systems (Fang and Chang, 2014). The task of entity linking has attracted a lot of attention, and many shared tasks have been hosted to promote entity linking research (Ji et al., 2010; Ji and Grishman, 2011; Cano and others, 2014; Carmel et al., 2014).

Building an end-to-end entity linking system involves in solving two interrelated sub-problems: mention detection and entity disambiguation. Earlier research on entity linking has been largely focused on the entity disambiguation problem, including most work on entity linking for well-written documents such as news and encyclopedia articles (Cucerzan, 2007) and also few for tweets (Liu et al., 2013). Recently, people have focused on building systems that consider mention detection and entity disambiguation jointly. For example, Cucerzan (2012) delays the mention detection decision and consider the mention detection and entity linking problem jointly. Similarly, Sil and Yates (2013) proposed to use a reranking approach to obtain overall better results on mention detection and entity disambiguation.

6 Conclusion and Future Work

In this paper, we propose S-MART, a family of structured learning algorithms which is flexible on the choices of the loss functions and structures. We demonstrate the power of S-MART by applying it to tweet entity linking, and it significantly outperforms the current state-of-the-art entity linking systems. In the future, we would like to investigate the advantages and disadvantages between tree-based models and other non-linear models such as deep neural networks or recurrent neural networks.

Acknowledgments We thank the reviewers for their insightful feedback. We also thank Yin Li and Ana Smith for their valuable comments on earlier version of this paper.

References

S. Asur and B.A. Huberman. 2010. Predicting the future with social media. *arXiv preprint arXiv:1003.5699.*

Boris Babenko, Ming-Hsuan Yang, and Serge Belongie. 2011. Robust object tracking with online multiple instance learning. *Pattern Analysis and Machine Intelligence, IEEE Transactions on*, pages 1619–1632.

Yoshua Bengio, Holger Schwenk, Jean-Sébastien Senécal, Fréderic Morin, and Jean-Luc Gauvain. 2006. Neural probabilistic language models. In *Innovations in Machine Learning*, pages 137–186.

R. C Bunescu and M. Pasca. 2006. Using encyclopedic knowledge for named entity disambiguation. In *Proceedings of the European Chapter of the ACL (EACL)*, pages 9–16.

AE Cano et al. 2014. Microposts2014 neel challenge. In *Microposts2014 NEEL Challenge.*

Amparo E Cano, Giuseppe Rizzo, Andrea Varga, Matthew Rowe, Milan Stankovic, and Aba-Sah Dadzie. 2014. Making sense of microposts (# microposts2014) named entity extraction & linking challenge. *Making Sense of Microposts (# Microposts2014).*

David Carmel, Ming-Wei Chang, Evgeniy Gabrilovich, Bo-June Paul Hsu, and Kuansan Wang. 2014. Erd'14: entity recognition and disambiguation challenge. In *ACM SIGIR Forum*, pages 63–77.

Michael Collins. 2002. Discriminative training methods for hidden markov models: Theory and experiments with perceptron algorithms. In *Proceedings of the conference on Empirical methods in natural language processing (EMNLP)*, pages 1–8.

Corinna Cortes, Vitaly Kuznetsov, and Mehryar Mohri. 2014. Learning ensembles of structured prediction rules. In *Proceedings of ACL.*

Silviu Cucerzan. 2007. Large-scale named entity disambiguation based on wikipedia data. In *Proceedings of the Conference on Empirical Methods in Natural Language Processing (EMNLP)*, pages 708–716.

Silviu Cucerzan. 2012. The msr system for entity linking at tac 2012. In *Text Analysis Conference.*

Thomas G Dietterich, Adam Ashenfelter, and Yaroslav Bulatov. 2004. Training conditional random fields via gradient tree boosting. In *Proceedings of the twenty-first international conference on Machine learning (ICML)*, pages 28–35.

Yuan Fang and Ming-Wei Chang. 2014. Entity linking on microblogs with spatial and temporal signals. *Transactions of the Association for Computational Linguistics (ACL)*, pages 259–272.

P. Ferragina and U. Scaiella. 2010. TAGME: on-the-fly annotation of short text fragments (by Wikipedia entities). In *Proceedings of ACM Conference on Information and Knowledge Management (CIKM)*, pages 1625–1628.

Jerome H Friedman. 2001. Greedy function approximation: a gradient boosting machine. *Annals of Statistics*, pages 1189–1232.

Stephen Guo, Ming-Wei Chang, and Emre Kiciman. 2013. To link or not to link? a study on end-to-end tweet entity linking. In *Proceedings of the North American Chapter of the Association for Computational Linguistics (NAACL)*, pages 1020–1030.

Heng Ji and Ralph Grishman. 2011. Knowledge base population: Successful approaches and challenges. In *Proceedings of the 49th Annual Meeting of the Association for Computational Linguistics*, pages 1148–1158.

Heng Ji, Ralph Grishman, Hoa Trang Dang, Kira Griffitt, and Joe Ellis. 2010. Overview of the tac 2010 knowledge base population track. In *Third Text Analysis Conference (TAC)*.

John Lafferty, Andrew McCallum, and Fernando CN Pereira. 2001. Conditional random fields: Probabilistic models for segmenting and labeling sequence data. In *Proceedings of the 18th international conference on Machine learning (ICML)*, pages 282–289.

Ping Li, Qiang Wu, and Christopher J Burges. 2007. Mcrank: Learning to rank using multiple classification and gradient boosting. In *Advances in neural information processing systems (NIPS)*, pages 897–904.

Xiaohua Liu, Yitong Li, Haocheng Wu, Ming Zhou, Furu Wei, and Yi Lu. 2013. Entity linking for tweets. In *Proceedings of the Association for Computational Linguistics (ACL)*, pages 1304–1311.

Michael Mathioudakis and Nick Koudas. 2010. Twittermonitor: trend detection over the twitter stream. In *Proceedings of the 2010 ACM SIGMOD International Conference on Management of data (SIGMOD)*, pages 1155–1158.

E. Meij, W. Weerkamp, and M. de Rijke. 2012. Adding semantics to microblog posts. In *Proceedings of International Conference on Web Search and Web Data Mining (WSDM)*, pages 563–572.

Tomas Mikolov, Martin Karafiát, Lukas Burget, Jan Cernockỳ, and Sanjeev Khudanpur. 2010. Recurrent neural network based language model. In *INTERSPEECH*, pages 1045–1048.

D. Milne and I. H. Witten. 2008. Learning to link with Wikipedia. In *Proceedings of ACM Conference on Information and Knowledge Management (CIKM)*, pages 509–518.

Kevin P Murphy. 2012. *Machine learning: a probabilistic perspective*. MIT press.

C Quoc and Viet Le. 2007. Learning to rank with nonsmooth cost functions. pages 193–200.

A. Ritter, S. Clark, Mausam, and O. Etzioni. 2011. Named entity recognition in tweets: an experimental study. In *Proceedings of the Conference on Empirical Methods for Natural Language Processing (EMNLP)*, pages 1524–1534.

Byron P Roe, Hai-Jun Yang, Ji Zhu, Yong Liu, Ion Stancu, and Gordon McGregor. 2005. Boosted decision trees as an alternative to artificial neural networks for particle identification. *Nuclear Instruments and Methods in Physics Research Section A: Accelerators, Spectrometers, Detectors and Associated Equipment*, pages 577–584.

Sunita Sarawagi and William W Cohen. 2004. Semi-markov conditional random fields for information extraction. In *Advances in Neural Information Processing Systems (NIPS)*, pages 1185–1192.

Avirup Sil and Alexander Yates. 2013. Re-ranking for joint named-entity recognition and linking. In *Proceedings of ACM Conference on Information and Knowledge Management (CIKM)*, pages 2369–2374.

Richard Socher, Cliff C Lin, Chris Manning, and Andrew Y Ng. 2011. Parsing natural scenes and natural language with recursive neural networks. In *Proceedings of the 28th International Conference on Machine Learning (ICML)*, pages 129–136.

Richard Socher, Alex Perelygin, Jean Y Wu, Jason Chuang, Christopher D Manning, Andrew Y Ng, and Christopher Potts. 2013. Recursive deep models for semantic compositionality over a sentiment treebank. In *Proceedings of the Conference on Empirical Methods in Natural Language Processing (EMNLP)*, pages 1631–1642.

Ben Taskar, Carlos Guestrin, and Daphne Roller. 2004. Max-margin markov networks. *Advances in neural information processing systems*, 16:25.

Ioannis Tsochantaridis, Thomas Hofmann, Thorsten Joachims, and Yasemin Altun. 2004. Support vector machine learning for interdependent and structured output spaces. In *Proceedings of the twenty-first international conference on Machine learning (ICML)*, page 104.

Ioannis Tsochantaridis, Thorsten Joachims, Thomas Hofmann, and Yasemin Altun. 2005. Large margin methods for structured and interdependent output variables. In *Journal of Machine Learning Research*, pages 1453–1484.

Qiang Wu, Christopher JC Burges, Krysta M Svore, and Jianfeng Gao. 2010. Adapting boosting for information retrieval measures. *Information Retrieval*, pages 254–270.

Entity Retrieval via Entity Factoid Hierarchy*

Chunliang Lu, Wai Lam, Yi Liao
Key Laboratory of High Confidence Software Technologies
Ministry of Education (CUHK Sub-Lab)
Department of Systems Engineering and Engineering Management
The Chinese University of Hong Kong
{cllu,wlam,yliao}@se.cuhk.edu.hk

Abstract

We propose that entity queries are generated via a two-step process: users first select entity facts that can distinguish target entities from the others; and then choose words to describe each selected fact. Based on this query generation paradigm, we propose a new entity representation model named as entity factoid hierarchy. An entity factoid hierarchy is a tree structure composed of factoid nodes. A factoid node describes one or more facts about the entity in different information granularities. The entity factoid hierarchy is constructed via a factor graph model, and the inference on the factor graph is achieved by a modified variant of Multiple-try Metropolis algorithm. Entity retrieval is performed by decomposing entity queries and computing the query likelihood on the entity factoid hierarchy. Using an array of benchmark datasets, we demonstrate that our proposed framework significantly improves the retrieval performance over existing models.

1 Introduction

Entity retrieval, which aims at returning specific entities to directly answer a user's query, has drawn much attention these years. Various entity retrieval tasks have been proposed, such as TREC Entity (Balog et al., 2012; Wang et al., 2011) and INEX-LD (Wang et al., 2012; Wang and Kang, 2012). Many existing entity retrieval models follow the document retrieval assumption: when issuing queries, users choose the words that may appear in the "entity pseudo-document". Based on the assumption, these models construct internal entity representations by combining various entity descriptions, and use these representations to compute the rank of the candidate entities for a given entity query. These models include fielded versions of BM25 and Mixture of Language Models (Neumayer et al., 2012), Entity Language Model (Raghavan et al., 2004), Hierarchical Expert Model (Petkova and Croft, 2006), Structured Positional Entity Language Model (Lu et al., 2013).

However, a closer examination of entity queries reveals that most of them are not simple uniform word samples from the "entity pseudo-document". Instead, they can be decomposed into multiple parts, where each part describes a fact about target entities. For example, the query "National capitals situated on islands" describes two facts regarding a target entity: it is a national capital; it is located on an island. Compared to the assumption in document retrieval models, where query terms are assumed to be generated from a single document, these query terms can be regarded to be independently generated from two underlying documents. According to this observation, we propose that an entity query is generated via a two-step process: users first select facts that can distinguish target entities from the others; and then choose words that describe the selected facts. Based on the proposed query generation paradigm, we design a new entity retrieval framework. On one hand, an entity is modeled to have multiple internal representations, each regarding one or more closely related facts. On the other hand, an entity query is decomposed into one or more subqueries, each describing a fact about target entities. In this way, entity retrieval can be performed by combining the probabilities of subqueries being satisfied for each candidate entity.

One of the central components of our proposed

* The work described in this paper is substantially supported by grants from the Research Grant Council of the Hong Kong Special Administrative Region, China (Project Codes: 413510 and 14203414) and the Direct Grant of the Faculty of Engineering, CUHK (Project Code: 4055034).

Proceedings of the 53rd Annual Meeting of the Association for Computational Linguistics and the 7th International Joint Conference on Natural Language Processing, pages 514–523,
Beijing, China, July 26-31, 2015.

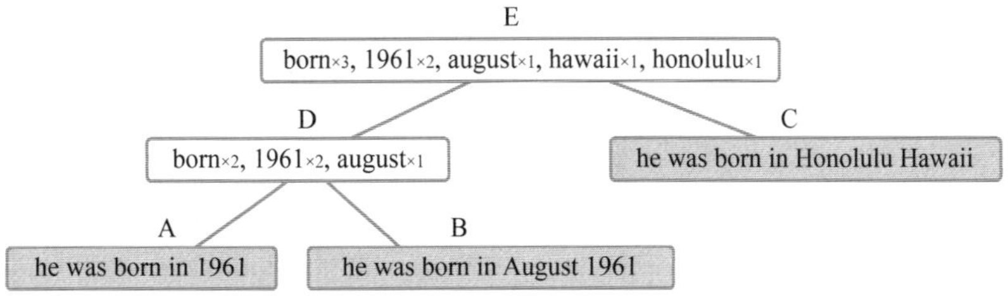

Figure 1: An example of entity factoid hierarchy containing two factoids about Barack Obama

retrieval framework is a novel entity representation known as entity factoid hierarchy. An entity factoid hierarchy is a tree structure composed of factoid nodes, which is automatically constructed from a collection of entity descriptions. We abuse the term "factoid" to denote a single piece of information regarding an entity. A factoid node in the hierarchy describes one or more factoids. Factoid nodes in different levels capture the information of different levels of detail (referred to as information granularities hereafter), where lower level nodes contain more detailed information and higher level nodes abstract the details away. The entity factoid hierarchy is constructed via a factor graph model, and the inference on the factor graph is achieved by a modified variant of Multiple-try Metropolis algorithm. Each factoid node is indexed separately as a pseudo-document. During retrieval, the query likelihood for a candidate entity are computed by transversing the factoid hierarchy. Compared to exiting entity retrieval models, our proposed framework exhibits two advantages:

- By organizing entity descriptions in a hierarchical structure, detailed entity information is preserved and we can return finer confidence value. Suppose that the entity "Barack Obama" is only described by one sentence: "born in 1961". Traditional entity models, which model an entity as a pseudo-document, would return high confidence value for the query "who is born in 1961". However, as we add more and more sentences to describe "Barack Obama", the confidence value returned for the query decreases due to the longer entity pseudo-document. This result is not desirable for entity retrieval, since adding more descriptions about other facts should not affect the confidence of existing facts. Our factoid hierarchy avoids this problem by preserving all the entity descriptions in a hierarchical structure. When performing retrieval, entity factoid hierarchy can be traversed to locate the best supporting description for the query.

- By separating entity facts in different factoid nodes, our model prevent ambiguity caused by mixing terms describing different facts. Suppose "Barack Obama" is described by two sentences: "Barack Obama is a president of United States" and "Barack Obama is a graduate of Harvard Law School", and our query is "Who is a president of Harvard Law School". A traditional document retrieval model with a bag-of-word entity pseudo-document would return "Barack Obama" with high confidence, since all the query terms appear in the entity descriptions. But obviously, this result is not correct. In our factoid hierarchy, these two facts are separated in lower level factoid nodes. While higher level nodes are still mixed with terms from child nodes, they are penalized to avoid giving high confidence value.

2 Factoid Hierarchy

2.1 Hierarchy Representation

As mentioned in the previous section, all the information regarding an entity is organized in a particular factoid hierarchy. We denote the term "factoid" as a single piece of information regarding an entity, such as the birth date of Barack Obama. A factoid node in the hierarchy describes one or more factoids. Each factoid node is associated with a bag-of-words vector to represent the factoid description. Factoid nodes in different depth encode information in different granularities.

An example of an entity factoid hierarchy, regarding two factoids (birth date and birth place) about Barack Obama, is given in Figure 1. The example hierarchy is constructed from three sentences about Barack Obama: he was born in 1961; he was born in August 1961; he was born in Honolulu Hawaii. These three sentences correspond to the leaf nodes A, B, and C respectively in Figure 1. In general, a leaf node in the factoid hierarchy comes directly from a sentence or a RDF triple describing the entity. Since it is extracted either from human written texts or from manually crafted structured databases, a leaf node represents the most exact representation regarding one or more factoids. During the construction of the hierarchy, intermediate nodes are formed as parents for nodes that contain closely related factoids. The factoid description for an intermediate node is the sum of bag-of-words vectors of its child nodes. In this way, intermediate nodes capture the words that are used more frequently with higher weights to describe the underlying factoids in a more general form. As we merge more nodes and move up in the hierarchy, intermediate nodes become blended with more different factoids. Node D in Figure 1 is an intermediate factoid node, as a parent node for nodes A and B both describing the birth date. The root node in an entity factoid hierarchy summarizes all the descriptions regarding an entity, which is similar to the "entity pseudo-document" used in some existing entity retrieval models. Each entity factoid hierarchy has only one root node. For example, node E in Figure 1 is the root node, and it contains words from all the three sentences.

Note that the depth of a leaf node varies with the number of descriptions associated with the factoids. Some factoids may be associated with lots of detailed information and are expressed in many sentences, while others are only expressed in one or two sentences. For example, the factoid that Obama is elected president in 2008 may be described in many sentences and in different contexts; while the factoid that Obama is born in Kapiolani Maternity & Gynecological Hospital is only mentioned in a few sentences. In this case, factoid nodes associated with more details may have deeper hierarchical structure.

2.2 Factor Graph Model

To construct the entity factoid hierarchy, we make use of a hierarchical discriminative factor graph model. A similar factor graph model has been proposed to solve the coreference resolution in (Singh et al., 2011; Wick et al., 2012). Here we design a factor graph model corresponding to the entity factoid hierarchy, together with new factor types and inference mechanism.

Generally speaking, a factor graph is composed of two parts: a set of random variables and a set of factors that model the dependencies between random variables. An example of the factor graph construction corresponding to the factoid hierarchy involved in Figure 1 is given in Figure 2. In our factor graph approach, each factoid is represented as a random variable f_i, corresponding to a rounded square node in Figure 2. The pairwise binary decision variable y_{ij}, denotes whether a factoid f_i is a child of another factoid f_j corresponding to a circle node in Figure 2. The set of factoids F plus the set of decision variables $\mathbf{y}$ are the random variables in our factor graph model. To model the dependency between factoids, we consider two types of factors. Ψ_p is the set of factors that consider the compatibility between two factoid nodes, i.e., to indicate whether two nodes have parent-child relationship. Ψ_u is the set of factors that measure the compatibility of the factoid node itself. Such factor is used to check whether a new intermediate node should be created. Factors are represented as square nodes in Figure 2. Given a factor graph model $\mathbf{m}$, our target is to find the best assignments for the decision variable $\mathbf{y}$ that maximizes the objective function in Equation (1).

$$P(\mathbf{y}, F|\mathbf{m}) = \prod_{f \in \mathcal{F}} \Psi_p(f, f^p)\Psi_u(f) \quad (1)$$

2.3 Factors Design

The pairwise factors Ψ_p and unit-wise factors Ψ_u compute the compatibility scores among factoid nodes. Each factor type is associated with a weight w to indicate the importance of the factor during inference. For the notation, the bag-of-words representation for a factoid node is denoted as d. We use superscripts p and c to denote the variables of parent nodes and child nodes. To capture the interrelations between factoid nodes, the following factors are used in our factor graph model.

Bag-of-words similarity To check whether two factoid nodes refer to the same fact, we compare the similarity between their bag-of-words descriptions. We choose Kullback-Leibler divergence (KL divergence) as the similarity measure. By definition, the KL divergence of Q from P, denoted $D_{KL}(P||Q)$, is a measure of the informa-

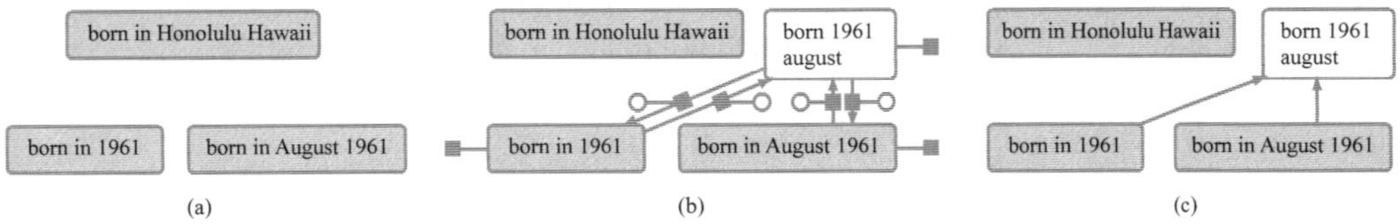

Figure 2: Generation of an factoid hierarchy via factor graph inference. Factoid nodes are initialized as singletons in (a). During one step of sampling in (b), two factoid nodes are selected and one proposal is to add a common parent. If we accept the proposal, we end up with the factoid hierarchy in (c).

tion lost when Q is used to approximate P. It is a non-symmetric measure and fits in our problem nicely, i.e., measuring whether a parent node is a more abstract representation of its child node. The compatibility score is computed as:

$$\begin{aligned} & -w_1 \cdot D_{KL}(d^p||d^q) \\ =& -w_1 \cdot \sum_{i=1}^{m} d_i^p \times \log\left(\frac{d_i^p}{d_i^c}\right), \end{aligned} \tag{2}$$

where d_i^p is the smoothed term frequency of the factoid description for the parent node; d_i^c is for the child node; w_1 is a global weighting parameter among different factors. In fact, we have also explored other popular text similarity metrics summarized in (Huang, 2008), and find that KL divergence performs the best.

Entropy penalty We penalize the entropy of the factoid description to encourage a smaller vocabulary of words describing the underlying factoids:

$$-w_2 \cdot \frac{H(d)}{\log ||d||_0}, \tag{3}$$

where $H(d)$ denotes the Shannon entropy for the bag-of-words representation of the factoid description d; $||d||_0$ is the number of unique terms in the factoid description.

Structure penalty The depth of a factoid node indicates the level of information granularity. However, we also need to control the depth of the factoid hierarchy. A factoid node should not have too many levels. We define the depth penalty as:

$$-w_3 \cdot |n_d - \frac{||d||_0}{s}|, \tag{4}$$

where n_d is the depth of a factoid node and s is the parameter that controls the average depth of factoid nodes per term. In this way, we can control the average depth of factoid nodes in the entity factoid hierarchy.

2.4 Inference

Exact inference is impossible for our factor graph model due to the large state space. Here we adopt a modified variant of Multiple-try Metropolis algorithm to conduct maximum probability estimation for inference, following the work in (Wick et al., 2013). At each sampling step, multiple changes to the current setting are proposed. The acceptance probability for a given proposal is equal to the likelihood ratio of the proposed hypothesis to the current hypothesis. In our case, we initialize the MCMC procedure to the singleton configuration, where each entity description, such as a sentence or a RDF triple, forms its own factoid hierarchy initially. At each sampling step, we randomly select two nodes and propose several alternative local modifications. If f_i and f_j are not connected, i.e., sharing no common child nodes, the following changes are proposed:

- Add factoid f_i as the parent of f_j, if f_j has no parent node;
- Remove f_j from its current parent, if f_j has a parent;
- Create a new common parent for f_i and f_j, if both f_i and f_j have no parent.

Otherwise, if f_i and f_j are in the same cluster, the following changes are proposed:

- Remove f_j from its current parent;
- Move f_j's children to f_j's parent and delete f_j, if f_j is an intermediate node.

A sampling step of the inference process is illustrated in Figure 2. Initially, all the decision variables $\mathbf{y}$ are set to zero. That is, each factoid node is regarded as forming its own factoid hierarchy, as illustrated in Figure 2(a). During the inference, local modifications are proposed to the current factor graph hypothesis. For example, in Figure 2(b), the two factoid nodes at the bottom are selected and proposed to add a new intermediate factoid as their common parent. If we accept the proposal, we get an intermediate factoid hierarchy as illustrated in Figure 2(c).

The sampling process is iterated until no proposal has been accepted in a certain number of successive steps, or a maximum number of steps has been reached. Each entity factoid hierarchy is inferred separately, allowing us to parallelize the inference across multiple machines.

3 Entity Retrieval

3.1 Retrieval Model

After we preprocess available information sources and construct the entity factoid hierarchy, we are ready to answer entity queries. Our retrieval model is based on the query likelihood model. Using Bayes' rule, the probability that an entity e is a target entity for a query q can be written as:

$$p(e|q) = \frac{p(q|e)p(e)}{p(q)}. \tag{5}$$

The probability of the query $p(q)$ is the same for all entities and can be ignored. Furthermore, we assume that the prior probability of an entity being a target entity is uniform. Thus, $p(e)$ can also be ignored. The task is to rank an entity e in response to a query q by estimating the query generation probability $p(q|e)$.

To compute $p(q|e)$, recall that our two-step query generation process assumes that users generate queries by first selecting facts and then choosing query words for each fact. Based on the query generation process, we first decompose the query q into m subqueries q_i (discussed in Section 3.2). Then the probability $p(q|e)$ can be computed as:

$$\begin{aligned} p(q|e) &= \prod_{i=1}^{m} p(q_i|e) & (6) \\ &= \prod_{i=1}^{m}\sum_{k=1}^{n} p(q_i|f_k)p(f_k|e) & (7) \\ &\simeq \prod_{i=1}^{m} \max_k p(q_i|f_k). & (8) \end{aligned}$$

Equation (6) decomposes the query into subqueries, assuming that all the subqueries are independent. Equation (7) iterates through all the factoid nodes f_k in the factoid hierarchy of an entity e. Equation (8) simplifies the computation by assuming that the underlying factoid generating subquery q_i is the factoid f_k with the highest query generation probability.

To compute $p(q_i|f_k)$, the probability of the factoid f_k generating the subquery q_i, we use the multinomial unigram language model:

$$p(q_i|f_k) = e(f_k)\prod_j p(t_i^j|f_k), \tag{9}$$

where t_i^j is the term j in the subquery q_i. $e(f_k)$ is the penalty term for factoids containing many children:

$$e(f_k) = w \cdot \frac{1}{c(f_k)}, \tag{10}$$

where $c(f_k)$ is the number of child nodes for f_k. To understand why we add this penalty term, consider a query "who is born in 2008". Suppose "Barack Obama" is described by two sentences: "born in 1961" and "elected president in 2008". When computing $p(q_i|f_k)$ for the root node, although it contains both the terms "born" and "2008", it should be penalized since the terms come from two different child nodes.

3.2 Query analysis

As mentioned earlier, we decompose the original query q into multiple factoid subqueries q_i. For long queries issued in a verbose sentence, such as "which presidents were born in 1945", dependency parsing is performed (Klein and Manning, 2003) and the resulting dependency tree is used to split the original query. For short queries issued in keywords, such as "vietnam war movies", we decompose it based on possible key concepts expressed in the query. Usually a short query only contains a single entity, which is used to segment the original query into subqueries.

Furthermore, stop structures in verbose queries is removed, following the method proposed in (Huston and Croft, 2010). Here a stop structure is defined as a phrase which provides no information regarding the information needs, such as "tell me the". We also inject target entity type information by replacing the leading "who " as "person", and "where" as "place" for all the queries.

3.3 Retrieval Process

For the purpose of retrieval, each node in the entity factoid hierarchy is regarded as a pseudo-document describing one or more factoids about the entity, and is indexed as a bag-of-words document during the preprocessing. The retrieval is performed in a two-step process. First, for each individual subquery, we retrieve top 1000 candidate entities by performing retrieval on all root nodes. This gives us an initial pool of candidate entities by merging the returned entities for subqueries. After that, for each candidate entity, we traverse its factoid hierarchy and compute the query generation probability $p(q|e)$ using Equations (8) and (9). Top ranked entities are returned as retrieval results.

4 Experiments

4.1 Dataset

We perform entity retrieval experiments using the DBpedia-Entity dataset used in (Balog and Neumayer, 2013). The dataset is a mixture of multiple entity retrieval datasets, covering entity queries of various styles such as keyword queries like "vietnam war movies" and verbose queries like "What is the capital of Canada". Some query statistics are shown in Table 2.

Query set	#query	avg($\|q\|$)	avg(#rel)
INEX-XER	55	5.5	29.7
TREC Entity	17	6.7	12.9
SemSearch ES	130	2.7	8.6
SemSearch LS	43	5.4	12.5
QALD-2	140	7.9	41.2
INEX-LD	100	4.8	36.8
Total	485	5.3	26.7

Table 2: DBpedia-Entity dataset statistics

The data corpus we use are DBpedia 3.9 and the corresponding English Wikipedia data dump on April 4, 2013. It should be noted that the original DBpedia-Entity benchmark only uses DBpedia for entity modeling (Balog and Neumayer, 2013). In our experiments, we also conducted another set of experiments which include full-text Wikipedia articles as additional entity descriptions, to evaluate the capacity of different models on handling free texts as information sources.

4.2 Comparison models and variants of our model

For comparison, we have implemented the following two existing models:

- **BM25**. BM25 is a popular document retrieval method and also used to perform entity retrieval (Balog and Neumayer, 2013). All the descriptions about an entity are aggregated into an entity pseudo-document. We use $k_1 = 1.2, b = 0.8$ for the model parameter, similar to the original papers.

- **MLM-tc**. The Mixture of Language Model represents an entity as a document with multiple fields, where each field is given a different weight for generating the query terms. MLM is often adopted to do entity retrieval (Neumayer et al., 2012). Here we adopt the MLM-tc model used in (Balog and Neumayer, 2013), where two fields are considered: title and content fields (described in Section 4.3). The parameters used are 0.8 for the title field and 0.2 for the content field.

Note that both MLM-tc and BM25 are also compared in (Balog and Neumayer, 2013), and have shown the best MAP performances among all the compared models.

For our models, the following two variants are implemented and compared.

- **Factoid Retrieval Model with Hierarchy (FRMwH)**. Our full model uses entity factoid graph as entity representation. Each factoid node is indexed as a bag-of-words document. The retrieval model described in Section 3 is employed.

- **Factoid Retrieval Model (FRM)**. This model does not use entity factoid hierarchy as entity representation. Instead, K-Means clustering algorithm is used to cluster the sentences into text clusters. Each text cluster is then indexed as a document. Compared to the FRMwH model, an entity only has a flat cluster of factoid descriptions. The same retrieval model is used.

All the four models use the same query preprocessing techniques.

4.3 Setup

The entity descriptions come from texts in Wikipedia articles and structured information from DBpedia. For DBpedia information, we consider top 1000 most frequent predicates as fields. We convert RDF predicates to free text by breaking the camelcase predicate name to terms, for example "birthPlace" is converted to "birth place". For Wikipedia texts, we first remove all markup text such as images, categories. Infoboxes are also

Model	INEX-XER		TREC Entity		SemSearch ES		SemSearch LS		QALD-2		INEX-LD		Total	
	MAP	P@10	MAP	P@10	MAP	P@10	MAP	P@10	MAP	P@10	MAP	P@10	MAP	P@10
Experiments with only DBpedia information														
BM25	.1890	.2706	.1257	.1571	.2732	.2426	.2050	.2286	.2211	.1976	.1104	.2158	.1806	.1901
MLM-tc	.1439	.2176	.1138	.1143	.2962	.2641	.1755	.1976	.1789	.1598	.1093	.2144	.1720	.1792
FRM	.2186	.2186	.1548	.1548	.2430	.2430	.2088	.2088	.2462	.2462	.1178	.1178	.1854	.1965
FRMwH	.2260	.2260	.1742	.1742	.2270	.2270	.1642	.1642	.2286	.2286	.1358	.1358	.1905	.2004
Experiments with both DBpedia and Wikipedia information														
BM25	.1313	.1887	.1374	.1667	.2916	.2526	.1867	.1833	.1552	.1253	.1698	.2680	.1848	.1821
MLM-tc	.0777	.0981	.0942	.0875	.2794	.2398	.1071	.1071	.1024	.0771	.1501	.2370	.1515	.1452
FRM	.1922	.1922	.1601	.1601	.2279	.2279	.1729	.1729	.1965	.1965	.1793	.1793	.1934	.1998
FRMwH	.2634	.2634	.1770	.1770	.2267	.2267	.1910	.1910	.2491	.2491	.1554	.1554	.2092	.2130

Table 1: Retrieval performance for various models

removed since the information is already well captured in DBpedia. Each Wikipedia article is then segmented to a list of sentences, which are considered as factoid descriptions regarding the entity.

For the BM25 model, all the descriptions about an entity are aggregated into an entity pseudo-document. For the MLMtc model, the *title* field is constructed by combining DBpedia properties whose property names are ending with "title", "name" or "label", such as "fullName" (Neumayer et al., 2012), and the *content* field is the same as the entity pseudo-document used in the BM25 model.

The inference algorithm for the entity factoid hierarchy is implemented based on the factorie package (McCallum et al., 2009). The parameters used in the inference are manually tuned on a small set of entities. The retrieval algorithms, including BM25 and Language Modeling, are implemented based on Apache Lucene[1]. For language models, Bayesian smoothing with Dirichlet priors is used, with parameter $\mu = 2000$. For FRM, to cluster the entity descriptions, we use the K-Means clustering algorithm implemented in Carrot2[2].

4.4 Results

We report two standard retrieval measures: mean average precision (MAP) and precision at 10 (P@10). Top 100 ranked entities are evaluated for each query. Two set of experiments are conducted: experiments with only DBpedia information; experiments with both DBpedia and Wikipedia information. The experiment result is shown in Table 1. To conduct the statistical significance analysis, we use two-tailed paired t-test at the 0.05 level. The symbols underline and wave underline are used to indicate significant improvement of our model compared with the BM25 and MLM-tc models respectively.

The first set of rows in Table 1 show the performance of four models using only DBpedia information. Both of our models have better overall performance. On datasets with verbose queries, such as INEX-XER and TREC Entity, both our models outperform the baseline models. One reason is that our retrieval model relies on the assumption that verbose queries can be decomposed into multiple subqueries. The second set of rows show the performance of four models using both DBpedia and Wikipedia information. After adding the additional information from Wikipedia articles, MLM-tc attains much worse performance, while BM25 performs roughly the same. One possible reason is that Wikipedia articles contain much irrelevant information regarding entities, and these two existing models cannot easily make use of additional information. In contrast, with Wikipedia full-text available, both of our proposed models achieve obviously better performances.

Our full model, FRMwH, has shown consistently better overall performance compared with the FRM model. It demonstrates that it is worthwhile to employ our proposed entity hierarchical structure for entity representation.

4.5 Analysis

For the retrieval performance, we also perform a topic-level analysis between our model FRMwH and the baseline model BM25, shown in Figure 3. The X-axis represents individual query topics, ordered by average precision difference (shown on the Y-axis). Positive Y value indicates that FRMwH performs better than the BM25 model for the query. From the figure, most of

[1] Apache Lucene: http://lucene.apache.org/

[2] Carrot^2: http://www.carrot2.org/

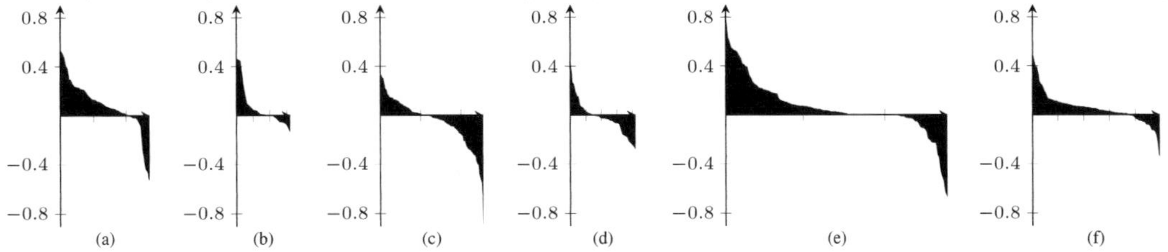

Figure 3: Topic-level differences between FRMwH and BM25. Positive values mean FRMwH is better. (a) INEX-XER; (b) TREC Entity; (c) SemSearch ES; (d) SemSearch LS; (e) QALD-2; (f) INEX-LD.

queries are affected by using FRMwH model. On the datasets with verbose queries, such as INEX-XER and TREC Entity, we can see most of the query are improved. FRMwH performs slightly worse for datasets like SemSearch ES which is mostly composed of keyword queries. For the queries that show little or no performance differences, manual inspection shows that both models fail to find any relevant results, due to the lack of supporting descriptions in Wikipedia and DBpedia.

5 Related Work

Besides the entity retrieval models reviewed in Section 1, there are models that do not maintain an explicit entity representation. Instead, they compute the entity relevance score based on the co-occurance between entities and query terms in the documents directly. Most of these models are originally proposed for expertise retrieval, where the appearance of a person name indicates the association with the expertise mentioned in the same document. Typical models include voting model (Macdonald and Ounis, 2006), graph model (Serdyukov et al., 2008), etc. However, it is not easy to generalize these models for open domain entity retrieval.

Entity models are also used in other fields besides entity retrieval. For example, entity topic models are used to perform entity prediction, classification of entity pairs, construction of entity-entity network (Newman et al., 2006), as well as entity linking (Han and Sun, 2012). These models are not suitable for our retrieval framework.

The decomposing of entity queries into factoid queries is related to query segmentation. Query segmentation has been used by search engines to support inverse lookup of words and phrases (Risvik et al., 2003; Bergsma and Wang, 2007). Our use of query decomposition is quite different compared to query segmentation. Besides query segmentation, query decomposition has also been used to facilitate the acquisition and optimization of high-order contextual term associations (Song et al., 2012).

Our work is also related to the information extraction and knowledge representation field since our framework involves extraction and aggregation of knowledge from free texts. However, most existing approaches takes two extreme ways: either extract relations based on pre-defined ontology, such as DBpedia (Lehmann et al., 2014); or cluster relation without referring to some ontology, such as OpenIE (Etzioni et al., 2011). Though our main goal is not on constructing a complete knowledge base, we do leverage both existing knowledge bases as well as free text data.

Semantic search also targets on returning answers directly (Pound et al., 2010; Blanco et al., 2011; Tonon et al., 2012; Kahng and Lee, 2012). However, they are mainly based on structured linked data, as well as structured query language like SPARQL. While this is an effective approach if we have a powerful thorough knowledge base, in practice many facts cannot be effectively represented as linked data. Only a small set of relations (thousands in DBpedia) have been defined in the ontology, such as "birthPlace". Furthermore, even if we can define a formal representation of human knowledge, retrieve them effectively is still a problem due to the difficulty of transforming the human query into a structured query on a knowledge base.

6 Conclusions

We propose that an entity query is generated in a two-step process: users first select the facts that can distinguish target entities from the others; then choose words to express those facts. Following this motivation, we propose a retrieval framework by decomposing the original query into factoid queries. We also propose to construct an entity factoid hierarchy as the entity model for the purpose of entity retrieval. Our entity factoid hierarchy can integrate information of different granularities from both free text and structured data. Extensive experiments demonstrate the effectiveness of our framework.

References

Krisztian Balog and Robert Neumayer. 2013. A test collection for entity search in DBpedia. In *Proceedings of the 36th International ACM SIGIR conference on Research and Development in Information Retrieval*, pages 737–740.

K. Balog, P. Serdyukov, and A. P. de Vries. 2012. Overview of the TREC 2011 entity track. In *Proceedings of the Twentieth Text REtrieval Conference.*

Shane Bergsma and Qin Iris Wang. 2007. Learning noun phrase query segmentation. In *Proc. EMNLP-CoNLL*, pages 819–826.

Roi Blanco, Harry Halpin, Daniel M. Herzig, Peter Mika, Jeffrey Pound, and Henry S. Thompson. 2011. Entity search evaluation over structured web data. In *Proceedings of the 1st International Workshop on Entity-Oriented Search*, EOS '11.

Oren Etzioni, Anthony Fader, Janara Christensen, Stephen Soderland, and Mausam Mausam. 2011. Open information extraction: The second generation. In *Proceedings of the Twenty-Second International Joint Conference on Artificial Intelligence*, pages 3–10.

Xianpei Han and Le Sun. 2012. An entity-topic model for entity linking. In *Proceedings of the 2012 Joint Conference on Empirical Methods in Natural Language Processing and Computational Natural Language Learning*, EMNLP-CoNLL '12, pages 105–115.

Anna Huang. 2008. Similarity measures for text document clustering. In *Proceedings of the Sixth New Zealand Computer Science Research Student Conference*, pages 49–56.

Samuel Huston and W. Bruce Croft. 2010. Evaluating verbose query processing techniques. In *Proceedings of the 33rd International ACM SIGIR Conference on Research and Development in Information Retrieval*, pages 291–298.

Minsuk Kahng and Sang-goo Lee. 2012. Exploiting paths for entity search in rdf graphs. In *Proceedings of the 35th international ACM SIGIR conference on Research and development in information retrieval*, SIGIR '12, pages 1027–1028.

Dan Klein and Christopher D. Manning. 2003. Accurate unlexicalized parsing. In *Proceedings of the 41st Annual Meeting on Association for Computational Linguistics - Volume 1*, ACL '03, pages 423–430.

Jens Lehmann, Robert Isele, Max Jakob, Anja Jentzsch, Dimitris Kontokostas, Pablo N. Mendes, Sebastian Hellmann, Mohamed Morsey, Patrick van Kleef, Sören Auer, and Christian Bizer. 2014. DBpedia - a large-scale, multilingual knowledge base extracted from wikipedia. *Semantic Web Journal*, 6(2):167–195.

Chunliang Lu, Lidong Bing, and Wai Lam. 2013. Structured positional entity language model for enterprise entity retrieval. In *Proceedings of the 22Nd ACM International Conference on Conference on Information & Knowledge Management*, CIKM '13, pages 129–138.

Craig Macdonald and Iadh Ounis. 2006. Voting for candidates: adapting data fusion techniques for an expert search task. In *Proceedings of the 15th ACM International Conference on Information and Knowledge Management*, pages 387–396.

Andrew McCallum, Karl Schultz, and Sameer Singh. 2009. FACTORIE: Probabilistic programming via imperatively defined factor graphs. In *Neural Information Processing Systems (NIPS)*, pages 1249–1257.

Robert Neumayer, Krisztian Balog, and Kjetil Nrvg. 2012. When simple is (more than) good enough: Effective semantic search with (almost) no semantics. In *Advances in Information Retrieval*, pages 540–543.

David Newman, Chaitanya Chemudugunta, and Padhraic Smyth. 2006. Statistical entity-topic models. In *Proceedings of the 12th ACM SIGKDD International Conference on Knowledge Discovery and Data Mining*, pages 680–686.

D. Petkova and W.B. Croft. 2006. Hierarchical language models for expert finding in enterprise corpora. In *Tools with Artificial Intelligence, 2006. ICTAI '06. 18th IEEE International Conference on*, pages 599–608, Nov.

Jeffrey Pound, Peter Mika, and Hugo Zaragoza. 2010. Ad-hoc object retrieval in the web of data. In *Proceedings of the 19th international conference on World wide web*, WWW '10, pages 771–780.

Hema Raghavan, James Allan, and Andrew Mccallum. 2004. An exploration of entity models, collective classification and relation description. In *Proceedings of KDD Workshop on Link Analysis and Group Detection*, pages 1–10.

K. M. Risvik, T. Mikolajewski, and P. Boros. 2003. Query segmentation for web search. In *Proceedings of the Twelfth International World Wide Web Conference (Poster session).*

Pavel Serdyukov, Henning Rode, and Djoerd Hiemstra. 2008. Modeling multi-step relevance propagation for expert finding. In *Proceeding of the 17th ACM Conference on Information and Knowledge Mining*, pages 1133–1142.

Sameer Singh, Amarnag Subramanya, Fernando Pereira, and Andrew McCallum. 2011. Large-scale cross-document coreference using distributed inference and hierarchical models. In *Proceedings of the 49th Annual Meeting of the Association for Computational Linguistics: Human Language Technologies*, pages 793–803.

Dawei Song, Qiang Huang, Peter Bruza, and Raymond Lau. 2012. An aspect query language model based on query decomposition and high-order contextual term associations. *Comput. Intell.*, 28(1):1–23, February.

Alberto Tonon, Gianluca Demartini, and Philippe Cudré-Mauroux. 2012. Combining inverted indices and structured search for ad-hoc object retrieval. In *Proceedings of the 35th international ACM SIGIR conference on Research and development in information retrieval*, SIGIR '12, pages 125–134.

Qiuyue Wang and Jinglin Kang. 2012. Integrated retrieval over structured and unstructured data. In Pamela Forner, Jussi Karlgren, and Christa Womser-Hacker, editors, *CLEF (Online Working Notes/Labs/Workshop)*, pages 42–44.

Zhanyi Wang, Wenlong Lv, Heng Li, Wenyuan Zhou, Li Zhang, Xiao Mo, Liaoming Zhou, Weiran Xu, Guang Chen, and Jun Guo. 2011. PRIS at TREC 2011 entity track: Related entity finding and entity list completion. In *TREC*.

Qiuyue Wang, Jaap Kamps, Georgina Ramírez Camps, Maarten Marx, Anne Schuth, Martin Theobald, Sairam Gurajada, and Arunav Mishra. 2012. Overview of the inex 2012 linked data track. In *CLEF (Online Working Notes/Labs/Workshop)*.

Michael Wick, Sameer Singh, and Andrew McCallum. 2012. A discriminative hierarchical model for fast coreference at large scale. In *Proceedings of the 50th Annual Meeting of the Association for Computational Linguistics*, pages 379–388.

Michael Wick, Sameer Singh, Harshal Pandya, and Andrew McCallum. 2013. A joint model for discovering and linking entities. In *CIKM 2013 Workshop on Automated Knowledge Base Construction*, pages 67–72.

Encoding Distributional Semantics into Triple-Based Knowledge Ranking for Document Enrichment

Muyu Zhang[1]*, Bing Qin[1], Mao Zheng[1], Graeme Hirst[2], and Ting Liu[1]
[1]Research Center for Social Computing and Information Retrieval
Harbin Institute of Technology, Harbin, China
[2]Department of Computer Science, University of Toronto, Toronto, ON, Canada
{myzhang,qinb,mzheng,tliu}@ir.hit.edu.cn
gh@cs.toronto.edu

Abstract

Document enrichment focuses on retrieving relevant knowledge from external resources, which is essential because text is generally replete with gaps. Since conventional work primarily relies on special resources, we instead use triples of *Subject, Predicate, Object* as knowledge and incorporate distributional semantics to rank them. Our model first extracts these triples automatically from raw text and converts them into real-valued vectors based on the word semantics captured by Latent Dirichlet Allocation. We then represent these triples, together with the source document that is to be enriched, as a graph of triples, and adopt a global iterative algorithm to propagate relevance weight from source document to these triples so as to select the most relevant ones. Evaluated as a ranking problem, our model significantly outperforms multiple strong baselines. Moreover, we conduct a task-based evaluation by incorporating these triples as additional features into document classification and enhances the performance by 3.02%.

1 Introduction

Document enrichment is the task of acquiring relevant background knowledge from external resources for a given document. This task is essential because, during the writing of text, some basic but well-known information is usually omitted by the author to make the document more concise. For example, *Baghdad is the capital of Iraq* is omitted in Figure 1a. A human will fill these gaps automatically with the background knowledge in his mind. However, the machine lacks both the necessary background knowledge and the ability to select. The task of document enrichment is proposed to tackle this problem, and has been proved helpful in many NLP tasks such as web search (Pantel and Fuxman, 2011), coreference resolution (Bryl et al., 2010), document cluster (Hu et al., 2009) and entity disambiguation (Sen, 2012).

We can classify previous work into two classes according to the resources they rely on. The first line of work uses *Wikipedia*, the largest on-line encyclopedia, as a resource and introduces the content of Wikipedia pages as external knowledge (Cucerzan, 2007; Kataria et al., 2011; He et al., 2013). Most research in this area relies on the text similarity (Zheng et al., 2010; Hoffart et al., 2011) and structure information (Kulkarni et al., 2009; Sen, 2012; He et al., 2013) between the mention and the Wikipedia page. Despite the apparent success of these methods, most Wikipedia pages contain too much information, most of which is not relevant enough to the source document, and this causes a noise problem. Another line of work tries to improve the accuracy by introducing ontologies (Fodeh et al., 2011; Kumar and Salim, 2012) and structured knowledge bases such as WordNet (Nastase et al., 2010), which provide semantic information about words such as synonym (Sun et al., 2011) and antonym (Sansonnet and Bouchet, 2010). However, these methods primarily rely on special resources constructed with supervision or even manually, which are difficult to expand and in turn limit their applications in practice.

In contrast, we wish to seek the benefits of both coverage and accuracy from a better representation of background knowledge: triples of *Subject, Predicate, Object* (SPO). According to Hoffart et al. (2013), these triples, such as *LeonardCohen, wasBornIn, Montreal*, can be extracted automatically from Wikipedia and other sources, which is compatible with the RDF data model (Staab and Studer, 2009). Moreover, by extracting these

* This work was partly done while the first author was visiting University of Toronto.

Proceedings of the 53rd Annual Meeting of the Association for Computational Linguistics and the 7th International Joint Conference on Natural Language Processing, pages 524–533,
Beijing, China, July 26-31, 2015.

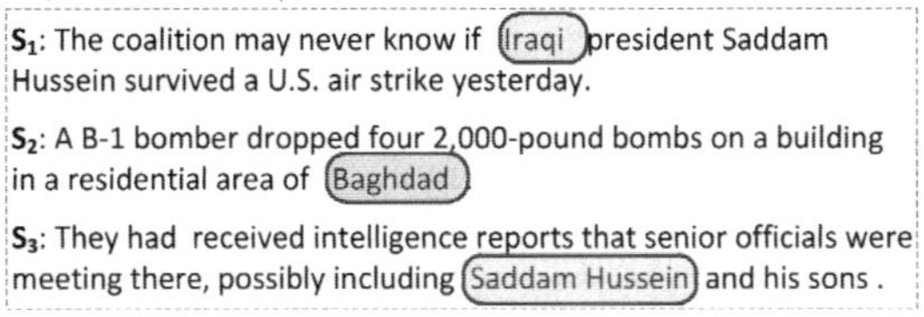

(a) Source document: air strike aiming at Saddam in Baghdad

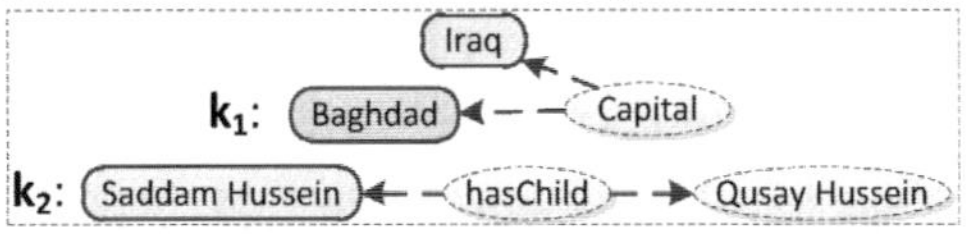

(b) Two omitted relevant pieces of background knowledge

Figure 1: An example of document enrichment: A source document about a U.S. air strike omitting two important pieces of background knowledge which are acquired by our framework.

triples from multiple sources, we also get better coverage. Therefore, one can expect that this representation is helpful for better document enrichment by incorporating both accuracy and coverage. In fact, there is already evidence that this representation is helpful. Zhang et al. (2014) proposed a triple-based document enrichment framework which uses triples of SPO as background knowledge. They first proposed a search engine–based method to evaluate the relatedness between every pair of triples, and then an iterative propagation algorithm was introduced to select the most relevant triples to a given source document (see Section 2), which achieved a good performance.

However, to evaluate the semantic relatedness between two triples, Zhang et al. (2014) primarily relied on the text of triples and used search engines, which makes their method difficult to re-implement and in turn limits its application in practice. Moreover, they did not carry out any task-based evaluation, which makes it uncertain whether their method will be helpful in real applications. Therefore, we instead use topic models, especially *Latent Dirichlet Allocation* (LDA), to encode distributional semantics of words and convert every triple into a real-valued vector, which is then used to evaluate the relatedness between a pair of triples. We then incorporate these triples into the given source document and represent them together as a graph of triples. Then a modified iterative propagation is carried out over the entire graph to select the most relevant triples of background knowledge to the given source document.

To evaluate our model, we conduct two series of experiments: (1) evaluation as a ranking problem, and (2) task-based evaluation. We first treat this task as a ranking problem which inputs one document and outputs the top N most-relevant triples of background knowledge. Second, we carry out a task-based evaluation by incorporating these relevant triples acquired by our model into the original model of document classification as additional features. We then perform a direct comparison between the classification models with and without these triples, to determine whether they are helpful or not. On the first series of experiments, we achieve a *MAP* of 0.6494 and a *P@N* of 0.5597 in the best situation, which outperforms the strongest baseline by 5.87% and 17.21%. In the task-based evaluation, the enriched model derived from the triples of background knowledge performs better by 3.02%, which demonstrates the effectiveness of our framework in real NLP applications.

2 Background

The most closely related work in this area is our own (Zhang et al., 2014), which used the triples of *SPO* as background knowledge. In that work, we first proposed a *triple graph* to represent the source document and then used a search engine–based iterative algorithm to rank all the triples. We describe this work in detail below.

Triple graph Zhang et al. (2014) proposed the *triple graph* as a document representation, where the triples of *SPO* serve as nodes, and the edges between nodes indicate their semantic relatedness. There are two kinds of nodes in the triple graph: (1) source document nodes (*sd-nodes*), which are triples extracted from source documents, and (2) background knowledge nodes (*bk-nodes*), which are triples extracted from external sources. Both of them are extracted automatically with *Reverb*, a well-known *Open Information Extraction* system (Etzioni et al., 2011). There are also two kinds of edges: (1) an edge between a pair of sd-nodes, and (2) an edge between one sd-node and another bk-node, both of which are unidirectional. In the original representation, there are no edges between two bk-nodes because they treat the bk-nodes as recipients of relevance weight only. In this paper, we modify this setup and connect every pair of bk-nodes with an edge, so the bk-nodes serve as intermediate nodes during the iterative propagation process and contribute to the final performance too as shown in our experiments (see Section 5.1).

Relevance evaluation To compute the weight of a edge, Zhang et al. (2014) evaluate the semantic relatedness between two nodes with a search engine–based method. They first convert every node, which is a triple of *SPO*, into a query by combining the text of *Subject* and *Object* together. Then for every pair of nodes t_i and t_j, they construct three queries: p, q, and $p \cap q$, which correspond to the queries of t_i, t_j, and $t_j \cap t_j$, the combination of t_i and t_j. All these queries are put into a search engine to get $H(p)$, $H(q)$, and $H(p \cap q)$, the numbers of returned pages for query p, p, and $p \cap q$. Then the *WebJaccard Coefficient* (Bollegala et al., 2007) is used to evaluate $r(i,j)$, the relatedness between t_i and t_j, according to Formula 1.

$$r(i,j) = WebJaccard(p,q) = \begin{cases} 0 & \text{if } H(p \cap q) \leq C \\ \dfrac{H(p \cap q)}{H(p) + H(q) - H(p \cap q)} & \text{otherwise.} \end{cases} \quad (1)$$

Using $r(i,j)$, Zhang et al. (2014) further define $p(i,j)$, the probability of t_i and t_j propagating to each other, as shown in Formula 2. Here N is the set of all nodes, and $\delta(i,j)$ denotes whether an edge exists between two nodes or not.

$$p(i,j) = \frac{r(i,j) \times \delta(i,j)}{\sum_{n \in N} r(n,j) \times \delta(n,j)} \quad (2)$$

Iterative propagation Considering that the source document D is represented as a graph of sd-nodes, so the relevance of background knowledge t_b to D is naturally converted into that of t_b to the graph of sd-nodes. Zhang et al. (2014) evaluate this relevance by propagating relevance weight from sd-nodes to t_b iteratively. After convergence, the relevance weight of t_b will be treated as the final relevance to D. There are in total $n \times n$ pairs of nodes, and their $p(i,j)$ are stored in a matrix P. Zhang et al. (2014) use $\vec{W} = (w_1, w_2, \ldots, w_n)$ to denote the relevance weights of nodes, where w_i indicates the relevance of t_i to D. At the beginning, each w_i of bk-nodes is initialized to 0, and each that of sd-nodes is initialized to its importance to D. Then $\vec{W}$ is updated to $\vec{W}'$ after every iteration according to Formula 3. They keep updating the weights of both sd-nodes and bk-nodes until convergence and do not distinguish them explicitly.

$$\begin{aligned} \vec{W}' &= \vec{W} \times P \\ &= \vec{W} \times \begin{bmatrix} p(1,1) & p(1,2) & \ldots & p(1,n) \\ p(2,1) & p(2,2) & \ldots & p(2,n) \\ \ldots & \ldots & \ldots & \ldots \\ p(n,1) & p(n,2) & \ldots & p(n,n) \end{bmatrix} \end{aligned} \quad (3)$$

3 Methodology

The key idea behind this work is that every document is composed of several units of information, which can be extracted into triples automatically. For every unit of background knowledge b, the more units that are relevant to b and the more relevant they are, the more relevant b will be to the source document. Based on this intuition, we first present both source document information and background knowledge together as a document-level triple graph as illustrated in Section 2. Then we use LDA to capture the distributional semantics of a triple by representing it as a vector of distributional probabilities over k topics and evaluate the relatedness between two triples with cosine-similarity. Finally, we propose a modified iterative process to propagate the relevance score from the source document information to the background knowledge and select the top n relevant ones.

3.1 Encoding distributional semantics

LDA LDA is a popular generative probabilistic model, which was first introduced by Blei et al. (2003). LDA views every document as a mixture over underlying topics, and each topic as a distribution over words. Both the document-topic and the topic-word distributions are assumed to have a *Dirichlet prior*. Given a set of documents and a number of topics, the model returns θ_d, the topic distribution for each document d, and ϕ_z, the word distribution for every topic z.

LDA assumes the following generative process for each document in a corpus D:

1. Choose $N \sim Poisson(\xi)$.
2. Choose $\theta \sim Dir(\alpha)$.
   (a) Choose a topic $z_n \sim Multinomial(\theta)$.
   (b) Choose a word w_n from $p(w_n | z_n, \beta)$ conditioned on the topic z_n.

Here the dimensionality k of the Dirichlet distribution (and thus the dimensionality of the topic vari-

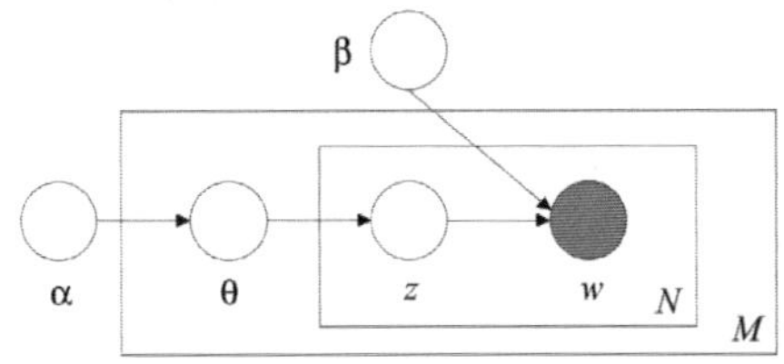

Figure 2: Graphical representation of LDA. The boxes represents replicates, where the inner box represents the repeated choice of N topics and words within a document, while the outer one represents the repeated generation of M documents.

able z) is assumed to be known and fixed; θ is a k-dimensional Dirichlet random variable, where the parameter α is a k-vector with components $\alpha_i > 0$; and the β indicates the word probabilities over topics, which is a matrix with $\beta_{ij} = p(w^j = 1|z^i = 1)$. Figure 2 shows the representation of LDA as a probabilistic graphical model with three levels. There are two corpus-level parameters α and β , which are assumed to be sampled once in the process of generating a corpus; one document-level variable θ_d, which is sampled once per document; and two word-level variables z_{dn} and w_{dn}, which are sampled once for each word in each document.

We employ the publicly available implementation of LDA, JGibbLDA2[1] (Phan et al., 2008), which has two main execution methods: parameter estimation (model building) and inference for new data (classification of a new document).

Relevance evaluation Given a set of documents and the number of topics k, LDA will return ϕ_z, the word distribution over the topic z. So for every word w_n, we get k distributional probabilities over k topics. We use $p_{w_n z_i}$ to denote the probability that w_n appears in the ith topic z_i, where $i \leq k$, $z_i \in Z$, the set of k topics. Then we combine these k possibilities together as a real-valued vector $\vec{v}_{w_n}$ to represent w_n as shown in Formula 4.

$$\vec{v}_{w_n} = (p_{w_n z_1}, p_{w_n z_2}, \cdots, p_{w_n z_k}) \quad (4)$$

After getting the vectors of words, we employ an intuitive method to compute the vector of a triple t, by accumulating all the corresponding vectors of words appearing in t according to Formula 5. Considering that the elements of this newly generated vector indicate the distributional probabilities of t over k topics, we then normalize it according to Formula 6 so that its elements sum to 1. This gives us $\vec{v}_t$, the real-valued vector of triple t, which captures its distributional probabilities over k topics. Here t corresponds to a triple of background knowledge or of source document, p_{tz_i} indicates the possibility of t to appear in the ith topic z_i, and $w_n \in t$ means that w_n appears in t.

$$p_{tz_i} = \sum_{w_n \in t} p_{w_n z_i} \quad (5)$$

$$\vec{v}_t = \frac{(p_{tz_1}, p_{tz_2}, \cdots, p_{tz_k})}{\sum_{i=1}^{k} p_{tz_i}} \quad (6)$$

Using the vectors of triples, we can easily compute the semantic relatedness between a pair of triples as their cosine-similarity according to Formula 7. Here A, B correspond to the real-valued vectors of two triples, $r(A,B)$ denotes their semantic relatedness, and k is the number of topics, which is also the length of A (or B). A high value of $r(A,B)$ usually indicates a close relatedness between A and B, and thus a higher probability of propagating to each other in the following modified iterative propagation illustrated in Section 3.2.

$$r(A,B) = \cos(A,B) = \frac{AB}{\|A\|\|B\|} = \frac{\sum_{i=1}^{k} A_i B_i}{\sqrt{\sum_{i=1}^{k} (A_i)^2}\sqrt{\sum_{i=1}^{k} (B_i)^2}} \quad (7)$$

3.2 Modified iterative propagation

In this part, we propose a modified iterative propagation based ranking model to select the most-relevant triples of background knowledge. There are three primary modifications to the original model of Zhang et al. (2014), all of which are shown more powerful in our experiments.

First of all, the original model (Zhang et al., 2014) does not reset the relevance weight of sd-nodes after every iteration. This results in a continued decrease of the relevance weight of sd-nodes, which weakens the effect of sd-nodes during the iterative propagation and in turn affects the final performance. To tackle this problem, we decrease the relevance weight of bk-nodes and increase that of sd-nodes according to a fixed ratio after every iteration, so as to ensure that the total weight of sd-nodes is always higher than that of bk-nodes. Note that although the relevance weights of bk-nodes are changed after the redistribution, the corresponding ranking of them is not changed because the redistribution is carried out

[1] http://jgibblda.sourceforge.net/

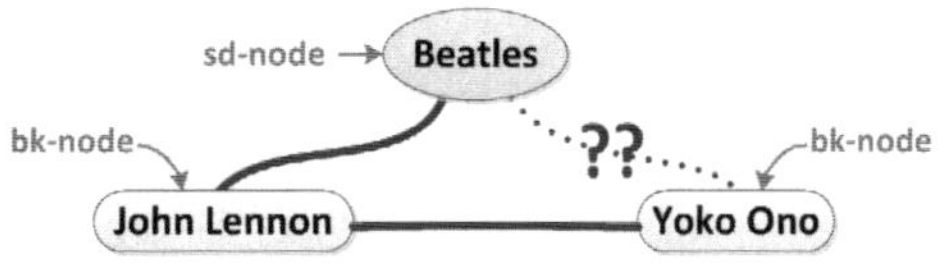

Figure 3: The edge between two bk-nodes helps in the better evaluation of relatedness between the bk-node *Yoko Ono* and the sd-node *Beatles*.

over all nodes accordingly. In our experiments, we tried different ratios and finally chose 10:1, with sd-nodes corresponding to 10 and bk-nodes to 1, which achieved the best performance.

In addition, we also modify the triple graph, the representation of a document illustrated in Section 2, by connecting every pair of bk-nodes with an edge, which is not allowed in the original model. This modification was motivated by the intuition that the relatedness between bk-nodes also contributes to the better evaluation of relevance to the source document, because the bk-nodes can serve as the intermediate nodes during the iterative propagation over the entire graph. Figure 3 shows an example, where the bk-node *John Lennon* is close to both the sd-node *Beatles* and to another bk-node *Yoko Ono*, so the relatedness between two bk-nodes *John Lennon* and *Yoko Ono* helps in better evaluation of the relatedness between the bk-node *Yoko Ono* and the sd-node *Beatles*.

We also modify the definition of $p(i, j)$, the probability of two nodes t_i and t_j propagating to each other. Zhang et al. (2014) compute this probability according to Formula 2, which highlights the number of neighbors, but weakens the relatedness between nodes, due to the normalization. For instance, if a node t_x has only one neighbor t_y, no matter how low their relatedness is, their $p(x, y)$ will still be equal to 1 in the original model, while another node with two equally but closely related neighbors will only get a probability of 0.5 for each neighbor. We modify this setup by removing the normalization process and computing $p(i, j)$ as the relatedness between t_i and t_j directly, which is evaluated according to Formula 1 .

4 Encoding background knowledge into document classification

In this part, we demonstrate that the introduction of relevant knowledge could be helpful to real NLP applications. In particular, we choose the *document classification* task as a demonstration, which aims to classify documents into predefined categories automatically (Sebastiani, 2002). We choose this task for two reasons: (1) This task has witnessed a booming interest in the last 20 years, due to the increased availability of documents in digital form and the ensuing need to organize them, so it is important in both research and application. (2) The state-of-the-art performance of this task is achieved by a series of topic model–based methods, which rely on the same model as we do, but make use of source document information only. However, there is always some omitted information and relevant knowledge, which cannot be captured from the source document. Intuitively, the recovery of this information will be helpful. If we can improve the performance by introducing extra background knowledge into existing framework of document classification, we can inference naturally that the improvement benefits from the introduction of this knowledge.

Traditional methods primarily use topic models to represent a document as a topic vector. Then a *SVM* classifier takes this vector as input and outputs the class of the document. In this work, we propose a new framework for document classification to incorporate extra knowledge. Given a document to be classified, we select the top N most-relevant triples of background knowledge with our model introduced in Section 3, all of which are represented as vectors of $\vec{v}_t = (p_{tz_1}, p_{tz_2}, \ldots, p_{tz_k})$. Then we combine these N triples as a new vector $\vec{v}_t'$, which is then incorporated into the original framework of document classification. Another *SVM* classifier takes $\vec{v}_t'$, together with the original features extracted from the source document, as input and outputs the category of the source document. To combine N triples as one, we employ an intuitive method by computing the average of N corresponding vectors in every dimension.

One possible problem is how to decide N, the number of triples to be introduced. We first introduce a fixed amount of triples for every document. Moreover, we also select the triples according to their relevance weight to the source document (see Section 3.2) by setting a threshold of relevance weight first and selecting the triples whose weights are higher than the threshold. We further discuss the impact of different thresholds in Section 5.2.

5 Experiments

To evaluate our model, we conduct two series of experiments: (1) We first treat this task as a ranking problem, which takes a document as input and outputs the ranked triples of background knowledge, and evaluate the ranking performance by computing the scores of *MAP* and *P@N*. (2) We also conduct a task-based evaluation, where document classification (see Section 4) is chosen as a demonstration, by enriching the background knowledge to the original framework as additional features and performing a direct comparison.

5.1 Evaluation as a ranking problem

Data preparation The data is composed of two parts: source documents and background knowledge. For source documents, we use a publicly available Chinese corpus which consists of 17,199 documents and 13,719,428 tokens extracted from Internet news[2] including 9 topics: *Finance, IT, Health, Sports, Travel, Education, Jobs, Art, Military*. We then randomly but equally select 600 articles as the set of source documents from 9 topics without data bias. We use all the other 16,599 documents of the same corpus as the source of background knowledge, and then introduce a well-known Chinese open source tool (Che et al., 2010) to extract the triples of background knowledge from the raw text automatically. So the background knowledge also distributes evenly across the same 9 topics. We use the same tool to extract the triples of source documents too.

Baseline systems As Zhang et al. (2014) argued, it is difficult to use the methods in traditional ranking tasks, such as information retrieval (Manning et al., 2008) and entity linking (Han et al., 2011; Sen, 2012), as baselines in this task, because our model takes triples as basic input and thus lacks some crucial information such as link structure. For better comparison, we implement three methods as baselines, which have been proved effective in relevance evaluation: (1) *Vector Space Model* (VSM), (2) *Word Embedding* (WE), and (3) *Latent Dirichlet Allocation* (LDA). Note that our model captures the distributional semantics of triples with LDA, while WE serves as a baseline only, where the word embeddings are acquired over the same corpus mentioned previously with the publicly available tool *word2vec*[3].

Here we use t_i, D, and w_i to denote a triple of background knowledge, a source document, and the relevance of t_i to D. For *VSM*, we represent both t_i and D with a *tf-idf* scheme first (Salton and McGill, 1986) and compute w_i as their cosine-similarity. For *WE*, we first convert both t_i and the triples extracted from D into real-valued vectors with WE and then compute w_i by accumulating all the cosine-similarities between t_i and every triple from D. For *LDA*, we represent t_i as a vector with our model introduced in Section 3.1 and get the vector of D directly with LDA. Then we evaluate their relevance of t_i to D by computing the cosine-similarity of two corresponding vectors.

Moreover, to determine whether our modified iterative propagation is helpful or not, we also compare our full model (*Ours*) against a simplified version without *iterative propagation* (*Ours-S*). In *Ours-S*, we represent both t_i and the triples extracted from D as real-valued vectors with our model introduced in Section 3.1. Then we compute w_i by accumulating all the cosine-similarities between t_i and the triples extracted from D. For all the baselines, we rank the triples of background knowledge according to w_i, their relevance to D.

Experimental setup Previous research relies on manual annotation to evaluate the ranking performance (Zhang et al., 2014), which costs a lot, and in which it is difficult to get high consistency. In this paper, we carry out an automatic evaluation. The corpus we used consists of 9 different classes, from which we extract triples of background knowledge. So correspondingly, there will be 9 sets of triples too. Then we randomly select 200 triples from every class and mix $200 \times 9 = 1800$ triples together as S, the set of triples of background knowledge. For every document D to be enriched, our model selects the top N most-relevant triples from S and returns them to D as enrichments. We treat a triple t_i selected by our model as positive only if t_i is extracted from the same class as D. We evaluate the performance of our model with two well-known criteria in ranking problem: *MAP* and *P@N* (Voorhees et al., 2005). Statistically significant differences of performance are determined using the two-tailed paired t-test computed at a 95% confidence level based on the average performance per source document.

[2]http://www.sogou.com/labs/dl/c.html

[3]https://code.google.com/p/word2vec/

Model	MAP_5	P@5	MAP_10	P@10
VSM	0.4968	0.3435	0.4752	0.3841
WE	0.4356	0.3354	0.4624	0.3841
LDA	0.6134	0.4775	0.6071	0.5295
Ours-S	0.5325	0.3762	0.5012	0.4054
Ours	**0.6494**	**0.5597**	**0.6338**	**0.5502**

Table 1: The performance evaluated as a ranking task. Here *Ours* corresponds to our full model, while *Ours-S* is a simplified version of our model without *iterative propagation* (see Section 3.2).

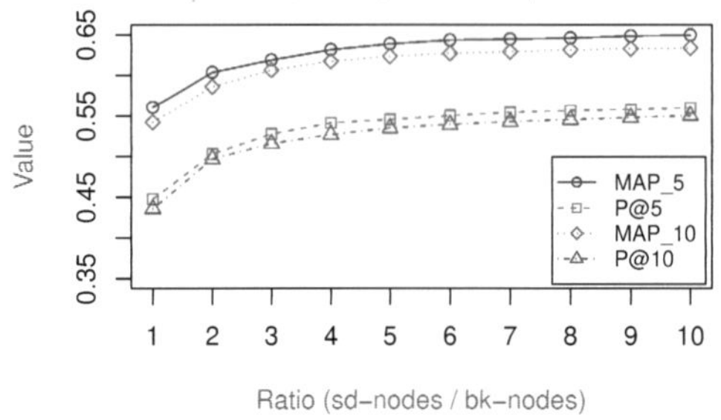

Figure 4: The performance of our model with different ratios between sd-nodes and bk-nodes.

Results The performance of multiple models is shown in Table 1. Overall, our full model *Ours* outperforms all the baseline systems significantly in every metric. When evaluating the top 10 triples with the highest relevance weight, our framework outperforms the best baseline *LDA* by 4.4% in *MAP* and by 3.91% in *P@N*. When evaluating the top 5 triples, our framework performs even better and significantly outperforms the best baseline by 5.87% in *MAP* and by 17.21% in *P@N*.

To analyze the results further, *Ours-S*, the simplified version of our model without *iterative propagation*, outperforms two strong baselines *VSM* and *WE*, which indicates the effectiveness of encoding distributional semantics. However, the performance of this simplified model is not as good as that of *LDA*, because *Ours-S* evaluates the relevance with simple accumulation, which fails to capture the relatedness between multiple triples from the source document. We tackle this problem by incorporating the modified iterative propagation over the entire triple graph into *Ours*, which achieves the best performance. One possible problem is why *WE* has a poor performance, the reason of which lies in the setup of our evaluation, where we label positive and negative instances according to the class information of triples and documents. This is better fit for topic model–based methods.

Discussion We further analyze the impact of the three modifications we made to the original model (see Section 3.2). We first focus on the impact of decreasing the relevance weight of bk-nodes and increasing that of sd-nodes after every iteration. As mentioned previously, we change their relevance weight according to a fixed ratio, which is important to the performance. Figure 4 shows the performance of models with different ratios. With any increase of the ratio, our model improves its performance in every metric, which shows the effectiveness of this setup. The performance remains stable from the value of 10:1, which is thus chosen as the final value in our experiments. We then turn to the other two modifications about the edges between bk-nodes and the setup of propagation probability. Table 2 shows the performance of our full model and the simplified models without these two modifications. With the edges between bk-nodes, our model improves the performance by 1.48% in *MAP_5* and by 1.82% in *P@5*. With the modified iterative propagation, we achieve a even greater improvement of 13.99% in *MAP_5* and 24.27% in *P@5*. All these improvements are statistically significant, which indicates the effectiveness of these modifications to the original model.

Model	MAP_5	P@5	MAP_10	P@10
Full	**0.6494**	**0.5597**	**0.6338**	**0.5502**
Full−bb	0.6399	0.5497	0.6254	0.5404
Full−p	0.5697	0.4504	0.5485	0.4409

Table 2: The performance of our full model (*Full*) and two simplified models without modifications: (1) without edges between bk-nodes (*Full−bb*), (2) without the newly proposed definition of propagation probability between nodes (*Full−p*).

5.2 Task-based evaluation

Data preparation To carry out the task-based evaluation, we use the same Chinese corpus as that in previous experiments, which consists of 17,199 documents extracted from Internet news in 9 topics. We also use the same tool (Che et al., 2010) to extract triples of both source document and background knowledge. For every document D to be classified, we first use our model to get the top N most-relevant triples to D, and then use them as extra features for the original model. We conduct a direct comparison between the models with and

Model	P	R	F
VSM+one-hot	0.8214	0.8146	0.8168
VSM+tf-idf	0.8381	0.8333	0.8336
LDA+SVM	0.8512	0.8422	0.8436
LDA+SVM+Ours-S	0.8584	0.8489	0.8501
LDA+SVM+Ours	**0.8748**	**0.8689**	**0.8691**

Table 3: The performance of document classification with (*LDA+SVM+Ours-S, LDA+SVM+Ours*) and without (*others*) background knowledge.

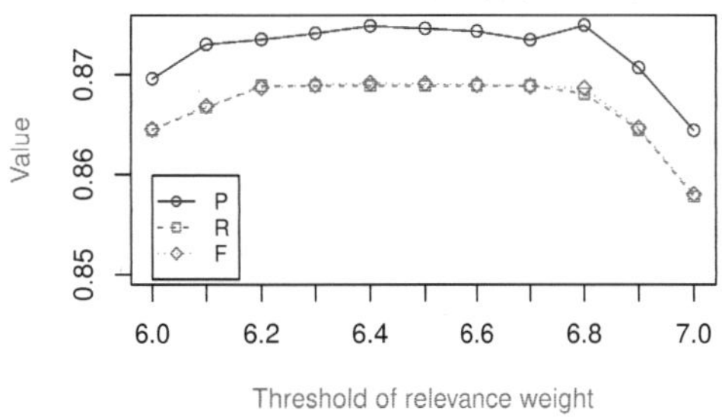

Figure 5: The performance of document classification models with different thresholds. The knowledge whose relevance weight to the source document exceeds the threshold will be introduced as background knowledge.

without background knowledge to evaluate the impact of introducing background knowledge.

Baseline systems We first illustrate two baselines without background knowledge based on VSM and LDA. For VSM, the test document D is represented as a bag of words, where the word distribution over candidate topics is trained on the same corpus mentioned previously. Then we evaluate the similarity between D and a candidate topic with cosine-similarity directly, where the topic with the highest similarity will be chosen as the final class. We use two setups: (1) *VSM-one-hot* represents a word as 1 if it appears in a document or topic, or 0 if not. (2) *VSM-tf-idf* represents a word as the value of tf-idf. For LDA, we re-implement the state-of-the-art system as another baseline, which represents D as a topic vector $\vec{v}_d$ in the parameter estimation step, and then introduces a SVM classifier to take $\vec{v}_d$ as input and decide the final class in the inference step.

We also evaluate the impact of knowledge quality by proposing two different models to introduce background knowledge: our full model introduced in Section 3 (*Ours*), and a simplified version of our model without iterative propagation (*Ours-S*). They have different performances on introducing background knowledge as shown in previous experiments (see Section 5.1). We then conduct a direct comparison between the document classification models with these conditions, whose differing performances demonstrates the impact of different qualities of background knowledge on this task.

Results Table 3 shows the results. We use P, R, F to evaluate the performance, which are computed as the micro-average over 9 topics. Both models with background knowledge (*LDA+SVM+Ours-S, LDA+SVM+Ours*) outperform systems without knowledge, which shows that the introduction of background knowledge helps in better classification of documents. The system with the simplified version of our model without iterative propagation (*LDA+SVM+Ours-S*) achieves a F-value of 0.8501, which outperforms the other baselines without knowledge too. Moreover, the system with our full model (*LDA+SVM+Ours*) achieves the best performance, a F-value of 0.8691, and outperforms the best baseline *LDA+SVM* significantly. This shows that introducing better quality of background knowledge is helpful to the better classification of documents. Statistical significance is also verified using the two-tailed paired t-test computed at a 95% confidence level based on the results of classification over the test set.

Discussion One important question here is how much background knowledge to include. As mentioned in Section 4, we have tried two different solutions: (1) introducing a fixed amount of background knowledge for every document, and (2) setting a threshold and selecting knowledge whose relevance weight exceeds the threshold. The results are shown in Table 4, where the systems with threshold outperform that with fixed amount, which shows that the threshold helps in better introduction of background knowledge.

Model	P	R	F
Ours-S+Top5	0.8522	0.8444	0.8456
Ours-S+ThreD	**0.8584**	**0.8489**	**0.8501**
Ours+Top5	0.8769	0.8667	0.8677
Ours+ThreD	**0.8748**	**0.8689**	**0.8691**

Table 4: The performance of document classification with the full model (*Ours*) and the simplified model (*Ours-S*) to introduce knowledge.

We also evaluate the impact of different thresholds as shown in Figure 5. The performance keeps improving as the threshold increases up to 6.4 and becomes steady from 6.4 to 6.7, while it begins to decline sharply from 6.7. This is reasonable because at the beginning, as the threshold increases, we recall more background knowledge and provide more information. However, with the further increase of the threshold, we introduce more noise, which decreases the performance. In our experiments, we choose 6.4 as the final threshold.

6 Conclusion and Future Work

This study encodes distributional semantics into the triple-based background knowledge ranking model (Zhang et al., 2014) for better document enrichment. We first use LDA to represent every triple as a real-valued vector, which is used to evaluate the relatedness between triples, and then propose a modified iterative propagation model to rank all the triples of background knowledge. For evaluation, we conduct two series of experiments: (1) evaluation as ranking problem, and (2) task-based evaluation, especially for document classification. In the first set of experiments, our model outperforms multiple strong baselines based on VSM, LDA, and WE. In the second set of experiments, our full model with background knowledge outperforms the state-of-the-art systems significantly. Moreover, we also explore the impact of knowledge quality and show its importance.

In our future work, we wish to explore a better way to encode distributional semantics by proposing a modified LDA for better triples representation. In addition, we also want to explore the effect of introducing background knowledge in conjunction with other NLP tasks, especially with discourse parsing (Marcu, 2000; Pitler et al., 2009).

Acknowledgments

We would like to thank our colleagues for their great help. This work was partly supported by National Natural Science Foundation of China via grant 61133012, the National 863 Leading Technology Research Project via grant 2015AA015407, and the National Natural Science Foundation of China Surface Project via grant 61273321.

References

David M Blei, Andrew Y Ng, and Michael I Jordan. 2003. Latent Dirichlet allocation. *Journal of Machine Learning Research*, 3:993–1022.

Danushka Bollegala, Yutaka Matsuo, and Mitsuru Ishizuka. 2007. Measuring semantic similarity between words using web search engines. *Proceedings of the 16th International Conference on World Wide Web*, 7:757–766.

Volha Bryl, Claudio Giuliano, Luciano Serafini, and Kateryna Tymoshenko. 2010. Using background knowledge to support coreference resolution. In *Proceedings of the 2010 Conference on ECAI 2010: 19th European Conference on Artificial Intelligence*, volume 10, pages 759–764.

Wanxiang Che, Zhenghua Li, and Ting Liu. 2010. Ltp: A Chinese language technology platform. In *Proceedings of the 23rd International Conference on Computational Linguistics: Demonstrations*, pages 13–16. Association for Computational Linguistics.

Silviu Cucerzan. 2007. Large-scale named entity disambiguation based on Wikipedia data. In *Proceedings of the 2007 Joint Conference on Empirical Methods in Natural Language Processing and Computational Natural Language Learning*, volume 7, pages 708–716.

Oren Etzioni, Anthony Fader, Janara Christensen, Stephen Soderland, and Mausam Mausam. 2011. Open information extraction: The second generation. In *Proceedings of the Twenty-Second international joint conference on Artificial Intelligence-Volume Volume One*, pages 3–10. AAAI Press.

Samah Fodeh, Bill Punch, and Pang-Ning Tan. 2011. On ontology-driven document clustering using core semantic features. *Knowledge and Information Systems*, 28(2):395–421.

Xianpei Han, Le Sun, and Jun Zhao. 2011. Collective entity linking in web text: a graph-based method. In *Proceedings of the 34th international ACM SIGIR conference on Research and development in Information Retrieval*, pages 765–774. ACM.

Zhengyan He, Shujie Liu, Mu Li, Ming Zhou, Longkai Zhang, and Houfeng Wang. 2013. Learning entity representation for entity disambiguation. *Proceedings of the 51st Annual Meeting of the Association for Computational Linguistics (Volume 2: Short Papers)*, August.

Johannes Hoffart, Mohamed Amir Yosef, Ilaria Bordino, Hagen Fürstenau, Manfred Pinkal, Marc Spaniol, Bilyana Taneva, Stefan Thater, and Gerhard Weikum. 2011. Robust disambiguation of named entities in text. In *Proceedings of the Conference on Empirical Methods in Natural Language Processing*, pages 782–792. Association for Computational Linguistics.

Johannes Hoffart, Fabian M Suchanek, Klaus Berberich, and Gerhard Weikum. 2013. Yago2: a spatially and temporally enhanced knowledge base from Wikipedia. *Artificial Intelligence*, 194:28–61.

Xiaohua Hu, Xiaodan Zhang, Caimei Lu, Eun K Park, and Xiaohua Zhou. 2009. Exploiting Wikipedia as external knowledge for document clustering. In *Proceedings of the 15th International Conference on Knowledge Discovery and Data Mining*, pages 389–396. ACM.

Saurabh S Kataria, Krishnan S Kumar, Rajeev R Rastogi, Prithviraj Sen, and Srinivasan H Sengamedu. 2011. Entity disambiguation with hierarchical topic models. In *Proceedings of the 17th International Conference on Knowledge Discovery and Data Mining*, pages 1037–1045. ACM.

Sayali Kulkarni, Amit Singh, Ganesh Ramakrishnan, and Soumen Chakrabarti. 2009. Collective annotation of Wikipedia entities in web text. In *Proceedings of the 15th International Conference on Knowledge Discovery and Data Mining*, pages 457–466. ACM.

Yogan Jaya Kumar and Naomie Salim. 2012. Automatic multi document summarization approaches. *Journal of Computer Science*, 8(1).

Christopher D Manning, Prabhakar Raghavan, and Hinrich Schütze. 2008. *Introduction to information retrieval*, volume 1. Cambridge University Press Cambridge.

Daniel Marcu. 2000. The rhetorical parsing of unrestricted texts: A surface-based approach. *Computational Linguistics*, 26(3):395–448.

Vivi Nastase, Michael Strube, Benjamin Börschinger, Cäcilia Zirn, and Anas Elghafari. 2010. Wikinet: A very large scale multi-lingual concept network. In *Proceeding of the 7th International Conference on Language Resources and Evaluation.*

Patrick Pantel and Ariel Fuxman. 2011. Jigs and lures: Associating web queries with structured entities. In *Proceedings of the 49th Annual Meeting of the Association for Computational Linguistics: Human Language Technologies-Volume 1*, pages 83–92. Association for Computational Linguistics.

Xuan-Hieu Phan, Le-Minh Nguyen, and Susumu Horiguchi. 2008. Learning to classify short and sparse text & web with hidden topics from large-scale data collections. In *Proceedings of the 17th International Conference on World Wide Web*, pages 91–100. ACM.

Emily Pitler, Annie Louis, and Ani Nenkova. 2009. Automatic sense prediction for implicit discourse relations in text. In *Proceedings of the Joint Conference of the 47th Annual Meeting of the ACL and the 4th International Joint Conference on Natural Language Processing of the AFNLP: Volume 2-Volume 2*, pages 683–691. Association for Computational Linguistics.

Gerard Salton and Michael J. McGill. 1986. *Introduction to Modern Information Retrieval*. McGraw-Hill, Inc., New York, NY, USA.

Jean-Paul Sansonnet and François Bouchet. 2010. Extraction of agent psychological behaviors from glosses of WordNet personality adjectives. In *Proc. of the 8th European Workshop on Multi-Agent Systems (EUMAS10).*

Fabrizio Sebastiani. 2002. Machine learning in automated text categorization. *ACM Computing Surveys*, 34(1):1–47, March.

Prithviraj Sen. 2012. Collective context-aware topic models for entity disambiguation. In *Proceedings of the 21st International Conference on World Wide Web*, pages 729–738. ACM.

Steffen Staab and Rudi Studer. 2009. *Handbook on Ontologies*. Springer Publishing Company, Incorporated, 2nd edition.

Koun-Tem Sun, Yueh-Min Huang, and Ming-Chi Liu. 2011. A WordNet-based near-synonyms and similar-looking word learning system. *Educational Technology & Society*, 14(1):121–134.

Ellen M Voorhees, Donna K Harman, et al. 2005. *TREC: Experiment and evaluation in information retrieval*, volume 63. MIT press Cambridge.

Muyu Zhang, Bing Qin, Ting Liu, and Mao Zheng. 2014. Triple based background knowledge ranking for document enrichment. In *Proceedings of COLING 2014, the 25th International Conference on Computational Linguistics: Technical Papers*, pages 917–927, Dublin, Ireland, August. Dublin City University and Association for Computational Linguistics.

Zhicheng Zheng, Fangtao Li, Minlie Huang, and Xiaoyan Zhu. 2010. Learning to link entities with knowledge base. In *Human Language Technologies: The 2010 Annual Conference of the North American Chapter of the Association for Computational Linguistics*, pages 483–491. Association for Computational Linguistics.

A Strategic Reasoning Model for Generating Alternative Answers

Jon Scott Stevens
Center for General Linguistics, Berlin
stevens@zas.gwz-berlin.de
Anton Benz
Center for General Linguistics, Berlin

Sebastian Reuße
Ruhr University Bochum
sebastian.reusse@rub.de
Ralf Klabunde
Ruhr University Bochum

Abstract

We characterize a class of indirect answers to yes/no questions, *alternative answers*, where information is given that is not directly asked about, but which might nonetheless address the underlying motivation for the question. We develop a model rooted in game theory that generates these answers via *strategic reasoning* about possible unobserved domain-level user requirements. We implement the model within an interactive question answering system simulating real estate dialogue. The system learns a prior probability distribution over possible user requirements by analyzing training dialogues, which it uses to make strategic decisions about answer selection. The system generates pragmatically natural and interpretable answers which make for more efficient interactions compared to a baseline.

1 Introduction

In natural language dialogue, questions are often answered indirectly. This is particularly apparent for yes/no questions, where a wide range of responses beyond literal "yes" and "no" answers is available. Sometimes indirect answers serve to anticipate the next step of the hearer's *plan*, as in (1) (Allen and Perrault, 1980), where the literal answer is entailed by the supplied answer, and sometimes indirect answers leave it to the hearer to infer the literal answer from common contextual assumptions, as in (2) (de Marneffe et al., 2009).

(1) Q: Has the train to Windsor left yet?
A: It's leaving soon from gate 7.

(2) Q: Is Sue at work?
A: She's sick with the flu.

But other times there is no semantic link between the question and the supplied answer. Rather, the answer must be interpreted in light of the task-specific goals of the interlocutors. Consider (3) in a context where a customer is posing questions to a real estate agent with the aim of renting an apartment.

(3) Q: Does the apartment have a garden?
A: Well, it has a large balcony.

Whether there is a balcony has no logical bearing on whether there is a garden. Intuitively, the realtor is inferring that the customer's question might have been motivated by a more general requirement (perhaps the customer wants a place to grow flowers) and supplying an alternative attribute to satisfy that requirement. In this case the answerer must reason about which attributes of an apartment might satisfy a customer who would ask about a garden. Note that multiple motivating requirements are possible (perhaps the customer just wants to relax outside), such that the answerer might just as easily have said, "It has a large balcony, and there is a park close by." In either case, the hearer can infer from the lack of a direct answer that the apartment must not have a garden, because if it did, to say so would have been more obviously helpful.

This paper focuses on this class of answers, which we call *alternative answers*. We characterize these as indirect answers to yes/no questions that offer attributes of an object under discussion which might satisfy an unobserved domain-level *requirement* of the questioner. We conceive of a requirement as a set of *satisfying conditions*, such that a particular domain-related need would be met by any one member of the set. For example, in the context of (3) we can encode a possible customer requirement of a place to grow flowers in an apartment, FLOWERS = {GARDEN, BALCONY}, such that *either* GARDEN *or* BALCONY would suffice to satisfy the requirement.

Proceedings of the 53rd Annual Meeting of the Association for Computational Linguistics and the 7th International Joint Conference on Natural Language Processing, pages 534–542,
Beijing, China, July 26-31, 2015.

In order to generate alternative answers automatically, we must first solve two problems: (i) how does one learn and represent a space of likely user requirements?, and (ii) how does one use such a space to select indirect answers? To do this in a natural, pragmatically interpretable way, we must not only derive answers like in (3), but crucially, also rule out infelicitous responses like the following, where a logically possible alternative leads to incoherence due to the low probability of an appropriate requirement like {GARDEN, BASEMENT}. (In other words, wanting a garden has little effect on the probability of wanting a basement.)

(4) Q: Does the apartment have a garden?
A: #Well, it has a large basement.

To solve these problems, we propose an approach rooted in decision-theoretic and game-theoretic analyses of indirectness in natural language (van Rooij, 2003; Benz and van Rooij, 2007; Benz et al., 2011; Stevens et al., 2014) whereby a system uses *strategic reasoning* to derive an optimal response to a yes/no question given certain domain assumptions. The model operates by assuming that both the questioner and the answerer are *rational*, i.e. that both participants want to further their own goals, and will behave so as to maximize the probability of success at doing so.

One appeal of the strategic approach is its relative simplicity: the model utilizes a learned probability distribution over possible domain-level requirements of the questioner and applies simple probabilistic reasoning to feed content selection during online answer generation. Unlike plan inference approaches, we do not need to represent any complex taxonomies of stimulus conditions (Green and Carberry, 1994) or coherence relations (Green and Carberry, 1999; Asher and Lascarides, 2003).

By implementing the strategic reasoning model within a simple interactive question answering system (Konstantinova and Orasan, 2012), simulating real estate dialogues with exchanges like in (3), we are able to evaluate the current approach quantitatively in terms of dialogue efficiency, perceived coherence of the supplied answers, and ability of users to draw natural pragmatic inferences. We conclude that strategic reasoning provides a promising framework for developing answer generation methods by starting with principled theoretical analyses of human dialogue.

The following section presents the model, including a concrete content selection algorithm used for producing answers to questions, and then walks through a simple illustrative example. Section 3 describes our implementation, addresses the problem of learning requirement probabilities, and presents the results of our evaluation, providing quantitative support for our approach. Section 4 concludes with a general summary.

2 Model

2.1 Overview

We derive our model beginning with a simple description of the discourse situation. In our case, this is an exchange of questions and answers where a *user* poses questions to be answered by an *expert* who has access to a *database* of information that the user wants. The expert has no advance knowledge of the database, and thus must *look up* information as needed. Each user question is motivated by a *requirement*, conceived of as a (possibly singleton) set of database attributes (restricted for current purposes to boolean attributes), any one of which satisfies a user need (e.g. {GARDEN, BALCONY} in the previous section). Only the user has direct access to her own requirements, and only the expert can query the database to inform the user whether her requirements can be satisfied. For current purposes we assume that each question and answer in the dialogue pertains to a specific object o from the database which is designated as the *object under discussion*. This way we can represent answers and question denotations with attributes, like GARDEN, where the queried/supplied attribute is assumed to predicate over o. In these terms, the expert can either ASSERT an attribute (if it holds of o) or DENY an attribute (if it does not hold of o) in response to a user query.

Now we describe the goals of the interlocutors. The user wants her requirements to be satisfied, and will not accept an object until she is sure this is the case. If it is clear that an object cannot satisfy one or more requirements, the user will ask to discuss a different object from the database. We can thus characterize the set of possible user responses as follows: the user may ACCEPT the object as one that meets all requirements, the user may REJECT the object and ask to see something else, or the user may FOLLOW UP, continuing to pose questions about the current object. The user's goal, then, is ultimately to accept an object that in fact satisfies her requirements, and to reject any object that does not.

The expert's goal is to help the user find an optimal object as efficiently as possible. Given this goal, the expert does better to provide alternative attributes (like BALCONY for GARDEN in (3)) in place of simple "no" answers only when those attributes are relevant to the user's underlying requirements. To use some economic terminology, we can define the *benefit* (B) of looking up a potential alternative attribute a in the database as a binary function indicating whether a is relevant to (i.e. a member of) the user requirement ρ which motivated the user's question. For example, in (3), if the user's question is motivated by requirement {GARDEN, BALCONY}, then the benefit of looking up whether there is a balcony is 1, because if that attribute turns out to hold of o, then the customer's requirement is satisfied. If, on the other hand, the questioner has requirement {GARDEN}, then the benefit of looking up BALCONY is 0, because this attribute cannot satisfy this requirement.

$$B(a|\rho) = 1 \text{ if } a \in \rho \text{ and } 0 \text{ otherwise} \quad (1)$$

Regardless of benefit, the expert incurs a *cost* by looking up information. To fully specify what cost means in this context, first assume a small, fixed effort cost associated with looking up an attribute. Further assume a larger cost incurred when the user has to ask a follow-up question to find out whether a requirement is satisfied. What really matters are not the raw cost amounts, which may be very small, but rather the *relative cost* of looking up an attribute compared to that of receiving a follow-up. We can represent the ratio of look-up cost to follow-up cost as a constant κ, which encodes the reluctance of the expert to look up new information. Intuitively, if κ is close to 1 (i.e. if follow-ups are not much more costly than simple look-ups), the expert should give mostly literal answers, and if κ is close to 0, (i.e. if relative follow-up cost is very high), the expert should look up all potentially beneficial attributes. With this, let the *utility* (U) of looking up a be the benefit of looking up a minus the relative cost.

$$U(a|\rho) = B(a|\rho) - \kappa \quad (2)$$

The expert is utility-maximizing under game-theoretic assumptions, and (assuming a baseline utility of zero for doing nothing) should aim to look up attributes for which U is positive, i.e. for which benefit outweighs cost. But the expert has a problem: ρ, on which U depends, is known only to the user. Therefore, the best the expert can do is to reason probabilistically, based on the user's question, to maximize *expected utility*, or the weighted average of $U(a|\rho)$ for all possible values of ρ. The expected utility of looking up an attribute a can be written as the *expected benefit* of a—the weighted average of $B(a|\rho)$ for all ρ—minus the relative cost. Let REQS be the set of all possible user requirements and let q be the user's question.

$$EU(a|q, \text{REQS}) = EB(a|q, \text{REQS}) - \kappa \quad (3)$$

$$EB(a|q, \text{REQS}) = \sum_{\rho \in \text{REQS}} P(\rho|q) \times B(a|\rho) \quad (4)$$

The probability of a user requirement $P(\rho|q)$ is calculated via Bayes' rule, assuming that users will choose their questions randomly from the set of questions whose denotations are in their requirement set. This yields the following.

$$P(\rho|q) = \frac{P(q|\rho) \times P(\rho)}{\sum_{\rho' \in \text{REQS}} P(q|\rho') \times P(\rho')} \quad (5)$$

$$P(q|\rho) = \frac{1}{|\rho|} \text{ if } [\![q]\!] \in \rho \text{ and } 0 \text{ otherwise} \quad (6)$$

The prior probability of a user requirement, $P(\rho)$, is given as input to the model. We will see in the next section that it is possible to learn a prior probability distribution from training dialogues.

We have now fully characterized the expected benefit (EB) of looking up an attribute in the database. As per Eq.3, the expert should only bother looking up an attribute if EB is greater than the relative cost κ, since that is when EU is positive. The final step is to give the expert a sensible way to iteratively look up attributes to potentially produce multiple alternatives. To this end, we first point out that if an alternative has been found which satisfies a certain requirement, then it no longer adds any benefit to consider that requirement when selecting further alternatives. For example, in the context of example (3), when the realtor queries the database to find the apartment has a balcony, she no longer needs to consider the probability of a requirement {BALCONY, GARDEN} when considering additional attributes, since that is already satisfied. Given this consideration, the order in which database attributes are looked up can make a difference to the outcome. So, we need a consistent and principled criterion for determining the order in which to look up attributes. The most efficient method is to start with the attribute with the highest possible EB value and then iteratively move down to the next best attribute until EB is less than or equal to cost.

Note that the attribute that was asked about will always have an EB value of 1. Consider again the QA exchange in (3). Recall that the expert assumes that the user's query is relevant to an underlying requirement ρ. This means that ρ must contain the attribute GARDEN. Therefore, by definition, supplying GARDEN will always yield positive benefit. We can use this fact to explain how alternative answers are interpreted by the user. The user knows that the most beneficial attribute to look up (in terms of EB) is the one asked about. If that attribute is not included in the answer, the user is safe to assume that it does not hold of the object under discussion. By reasoning about the expert's reasoning, the user can derive the implicature that the literal answer to her question is "no". In fact, this is what licenses the expert to leave the negation of the garden attribute out of the answer: the expert knows that the user knows that the expert would have included it if it were true. This type of "I know that you know" reasoning is characteristic of game-theoretic analysis.[1]

2.2 Algorithm and example

Our algorithm for generating alternative answers (Algorithm 1), which simulates strategic reasoning by the expert in our dialogue situation, is couched in a simple information state update (ISU) framework (Larsson and Traum, 2000; Traum and Larsson, 2003), whereby the answerer keeps track of the current object under discussion (o) as well as a history of attributes looked up for o (HIST_o). The output of the algorithm takes the form of a dialogue move, either an assertion (or set of assertions) or denial that an attribute holds of o. These dialogue moves can then be translated into natural language with simple sentence templates. The answerer uses HIST_o to make sure redundant alternatives aren't given across QA exchanges. If

[1]It can be shown that the answer selection algorithm presented in this section, combined with a simple user interpretation model, constitutes a *perfect Bayesian equilibrium* (Harsanyi, 1968; Fudenberg and Tirole, 1991) in a signaling game (Lewis, 1969) with private hearer types which formally describes this kind of dialogue.

Requirement set	$P(\rho)$	$P(q\|\rho)$	$P(\rho\|q)$
ρ_G ={GARDEN}	0.5	1	0.67
ρ_F ={GARDEN, BALCONY}	0.25	0.5	0.17
ρ_P ={GARDEN, PARK}	0.2	0.5	0.13
ρ_S ={GARDEN, BASEMENT}	0.05	0.5	0.03

Table 1: A toy example of a customer requirement space with probabilities for q = 'Does the apartment have a garden?'

all possible answers are redundant, the answerer falls back on a direct yes/no response.

To illustrate how the algorithm works, consider a simple toy example. Table 1 gives a hypothetical space of possible requirements along with a distribution of priors, likelihoods and Bayesian posteriors. We imagine that a customer might want a garden (ρ_G), or more generally a place to grow flowers (ρ_F), a place for their child to play outside (ρ_P), or, in rare cases, either a garden or a basement to use as storage space (ρ_S). The rather odd nature of ρ_S is reflected in its low prior. Consider a variant of (3) where HIST_o is empty, and where DB_o contains BALCONY, PARK and BASEMENT.

(5) Q: Does the apartment have a garden?
A: It has a balcony, and there is a park very close by.

To start, let REQS contain the requirements in Table 1, and let $\kappa = 0.1$. The algorithm derives the answer as follows. First, the algorithm looks up whether GARDEN holds of o. It does not hold, so GARDEN is not added to the answer; it is only added to the history of looked up attributes.

$a = \text{GARDEN};\ EB(\text{GARDEN}) = 1;$
$\text{HIST}_o = \{\text{GARDEN}\}$

Then, the system finds the next best attribute, BALCONY, which does hold of o, appends it to the answer as well as the history, and removes the relevant requirement from consideration.

$a = \text{BALCONY};\ EB(\text{BALCONY}) = 0.17;$
$\text{HIST}_o = \{\text{GARDEN, BALCONY}\};$
$\text{ANSWER} = \{\text{BALCONY}\};$
$\text{REQS} = \{\rho_G, \rho_P, \rho_S\}$

The attribute PARK is similarly added.

$a = \text{PARK};\ EB(\text{PARK}) = 0.13;$
$\text{HIST}_o = \{\text{GARDEN, BALCONY, PARK}\};$
$\text{ANSWER} = \{\text{BALCONY, PARK}\};$
$\text{REQS} = \{\rho_G, \rho_S\}$

The attribute BASEMENT is next in line. However, its EB value is below the threshold of 0.1 due

Algorithm 1 An algorithm for generating alternative answers

Input: A set of attributes Φ, an object under discussion o, a database DB_o of attributes which hold of o, a history HIST_o of attributes that have been looked up in the database, a set of possible user requirements REQS, a prior probability distribution over REQS, a user-supplied question q with denotation $[\![q]\!]$ and a relative cost threshold $\kappa \in (0, 1)$

Initialize: $\text{ANSWER} = \{\}$; $\text{LOOKUP} = \text{TRUE}$

while LOOKUP **do**
    $\Phi' = (\Phi \setminus \text{HIST}_o) \cup \{[\![q]\!]\}$ ▷ Only consider alternatives once per object per dialogue.
    $a = \arg\max_{\phi \in \Phi'} \text{EB}(\phi | q, \text{REQS})$ ▷ Find the best candidate answer.
    if $\text{EB}(a|q, \text{REQS}) > \kappa$ **then** ▷ Check whether expected benefit outweighs cost.
        $\text{HIST}_o = \text{HIST}_o \cup \{a\}$ ▷ Log which attribute has been looked up.
        if $a \in \text{DB}_o$ **then**
            $\text{ANSWER} = \text{ANSWER} \cup \{a\}$ ▷ Add to answer if attribute holds.
            $\text{REQS} = \text{REQS} \setminus \{\rho \in \text{REQS} \mid \rho \cap \text{ANSWER} \neq \emptyset\}$ ▷ Don't consider requirements that are already satisfied.
        end if
    else
        $\text{LOOKUP} = \text{FALSE}$ ▷ Stop querying the database when there are no promising candidates left.
    end if
end while
if $\text{ANSWER} \neq \emptyset$ **then** ASSERT(ANSWER),
else DENY($[\![q]\!]$)
end if

to its low prior probability, and thus the iteration stops there, and BASEMENT is never looked up.

$a = \text{BASEMENT}$; $EB(\text{BASEMENT}) = 0.03$;
$EB < \kappa$; exit loop

3 Implementation and evaluation

3.1 Setup

A simple interactive question answering system was built using a modified version of the PyTrindiKit toolkit[2] with a database back end implemented using an adapted version of PyKE, a Horn logic theorem prover.[3] The system was set up to emulate the behavior of a real estate agent answering customers' yes/no questions about a range of attributes pertaining to individual apartments. A set of 12 attributes was chosen for the current evaluation experiment. The system generates answers by first selecting a discourse move (i.e. assertion or denial of an attribute) and then translating the move into natural language with simple sentence templates like, "It has a(n) X" or "There is a(n) X nearby". When answers are indirect (i.e. not asserting or denying the attribute asked about), the system begins its reply with the discourse connective "well" as in example (3).[4]

Subjects interacted with our system by means of an online text-based interface accessible remotely through a web browser. At the outset of the experiment, subjects were told to behave as if they were finding an apartment for a hypothetical friend, and given a list of requirements for that friend. The task required them to identify which from among a sequence of presented apartments would satisfy the given set of requirements. One out of four lists, each containing three requirements (one of which was a singleton), was assigned to subjects at random. The requirements were constructed by the researchers to be plausible desiderata for users looking for a place to rent or buy (e.g. connection to public transit, which could be satisfied either by a nearby bus stop, or by a nearby train station).

The apartments presented by the system were individually generated for each experiment such that there was an apartment satisfying one attribute for each possible combination of the three requirements issued to subjects, plus two additional apartments that each satisfied two of the conditions ($2^3 + 2 = 10$ apartments overall). Attributes outside a subject's requirement sets were added at random to assess the effect of "unhelpful" alternative answers.

Subject interacted with one of two answer generation models: a *literal* model, which only produced direct yes/no answers, and the *strategic*

[2]https://code.google.com/p/py-trindikit

[3]http://pyke.sourceforge.net/

[4]Early feedback indicated that alternative answers were more natural when preceded by such a discourse connective. To assess this effect, we ran a separate evaluation experiment with an earlier version of the system that produced alternative answers without "well". Dialogue lengths and coherence scores were not very different from what is reported in this section; however, in contrast with the current evaluation, we found a large effect of model type (a 69% decrease for strategic vs. literal) on whether the subjects successfully completed the task (z=-2.19, p=0.03). This is consistent with the early feedback.

model as outlined above. Crucially, in both conditions, the sequence in which objects were presented was fixed so that the last apartment offered would be the sole object satisfying all of the desired criteria. Also, we set the strategic model's κ parameter high enough ($1/7$) that only single-attribute answers were ever given. These two properties of the task, taken together, allow us to obtain an apples-to-apples comparison of the models with respect to average dialogue length. If subjects failed to accept the optimal solution, the interaction was terminated. After completing interaction with our system, subjects were asked to complete a short survey designed to get at the perceived coherence of the system's answers. Subjects were asked to rate, on a seven-point Likert scale, the relevance of the system's answers to the questions asked, overall helpfulness, the extent to which questions seemed to be left open, and the extent to which the system seemed evasive.

We predict that the strategic system will improve overall efficiency of dialogue over that of the literal system by (i) offering helpful alternatives to satisfy the customer's needs, and (ii) allowing customers to infer implicit "no" answers from alternative answers, leading to rejections of sub-optimal apartments. If, contrary to our hypothesis, subjects fail to draw inferences/implicatures from alternative answers, then we expect unhelpful alternatives (i.e. alternatives not in the user's requirement set) to prompt repeated questions and/or failures to complete the task.

With respect to the questionnaire items, the literal system is predicted to be judged maximally coherent, since only straightforward yes/no answers are offered. The question is whether the pragmatic system also allows for coherent dialogue. If subjects judge alternative answers to be incoherent, then we expect any difference in average Likert scale ratings between strategic and literal system to reflect the proportion of alternative answers that are given.

3.2 Learning prior probabilities

Before presenting our results, we explain how prior probabilities can be learned within this framework. One of the assumptions of the strategic reasoning model is that users ask questions that are motivated by specific requirements. Moreover, we should assume that users employ a reasonable questioning strategy for finding out whether

S:	An apartment in the north of town might suit you. I have an additional offer for you there.
U:	Does the apartment have a garden?
S:	The apartment does not have a garden.
U:	Does the apartment have a balcony?
S:	The apartment does not have a balcony.
U:	I'd like to see something else

Figure 1: An example of the negation-rejection sequence $\langle$GARDEN, BALCONY$\rangle$

requirements hold, which is tailored to the system they are interacting with. For example, if a user interacts with a system that only produces literal yes/no answers, the user should take all answers at face value, not drawing any pragmatic inferences. In such a scenario, we expect the user's questioning strategy to be roughly as follows: for $a_1, a_2, \cdots, a_n$ in requirement ρ, ask about a_1, then if a_1 is asserted, accept (or move on to the next requirement if there are multiple requirements), and if not, ask about a_2; if a_2 is asserted, accept, and if not, ask about a_3, and so on, until a_n is asked about. If a_n is denied, then reject the object under discussion. If you need a place to grow flowers, ask if there is a balcony or garden, then, if the answer is no, ask about the other attribute. If no "yes" answers are given, reject.

Such a strategy predicts that potential user requirements should be able to be gleaned from dialogues with a literal system by analyzing *negation-rejection sequences* (NRSs). A negation-rejection sequence is a maximal observed sequence of questions which all receive "no" answers, without any intervening "yes" answers or any other intervening dialogue moves, such that at the end of that sequence of questions, the user chooses to reject the current object under discussion. Such a sequence is illustrated in Fig.1. By hypothesis, the NRS $\langle$GARDEN, BALCONY$\rangle$ indicates a possible user requirement $\{$GARDEN, BALCONY$\}$.

By considering NRSs, the system can learn from training data a reasonable prior probability distribution over possible customer requirements. This obviates the need to pre-supply the system with complex world knowledge. If customer requirements can in principle be learned, then the strategic approach could be expanded to dialogue situations where the distribution of user requirements could not sensibly be pre-supplied. While the system in its current form is not guaranteed to scale up in this way, its success here provides us with a promising proof of concept.

Using the dialogues with the literal system as training data, we were able to gather frequencies of observed negation-rejection sequences. By transforming the sequences into unordered sets and then normalizing the frequencies of those sets, we obtained a prior probability distribution over possible customer requirements. In the training dialogues, subjects were given the same lists of requirements as was given for the evaluation of the strategic model. If successful, the system should use the yes/no dialogue data to learn high probabilities for requirements which customers actually had, and low probabilities for any others, allowing us to evaluate the system without giving it any prior clues as to which customer requirements were assigned.

Because we know in advance which requirements the subjects wanted to fulfill, we have a gold standard against which we can compare the question-alternative answer pairs that different variants of the model are able to produce. For example, we know that if a subject asked whether the apartment had a balcony and received an answer about a nearby café, that answer could not have been beneficial, since no one was assigned the requirement $\{\text{CAFÉ}, \text{BALCONY}\}$.

Table 2 compares three variant models: (i) the system we use in our evaluation, which sets prior probabilities proportional to NRS frequency, (ii) a system with flat priors, where probability is zero if NRS frequency is zero, but where all observed NRSs are taken to correspond to equiprobable requirements, and finally (iii) a baseline which does not utilize an EB threshold, but rather simply randomly selects alternatives which were observed at least once in an NRS with the queried attribute. These models are compared by the maximum benefit of their possible outputs using best-case values for κ. We see that there is a good match between the answers given by the strategic model with learned priors and the actual requirements that users were told to fulfill.

Though it remains to be seen whether this would scale up to more complex requirement spaces, this result suggests that NRSs can in fact be indicative of disjunctive requirement sets, and can indeed be useful in learning what possible alternatives might be. For purposes of our evaluation, we will see that the method was successful.

Model	Precision	Recall	F1
Frequency-based	1	0.92	0.96
Flat	0.88	0.92	0.90
Baseline	0.23	1	0.37

Table 2: Comparison of best-case output with respect to potential benefit of alternative answer types to subjects. Precision = hits / hits+misses, and Recall = hits / possible hits. A "hit" is a QA pair which is a possible output of the model, such that A could be a beneficial answer to a customer asking Q, and a "miss" is such a QA pair such that A is irrelevant to Q.

3.3 Evaluation results

We obtained data from a total of 115 subjects via Amazon Mechanical Turk; 65 subjects interacted with the literal comparison model, and 50 subjects interacted with the strategic model. We excluded a total of 13 outliers across both conditions who asked too few or too many questions (1.5 interquartile ranges below the 1st or above the 3rd quartile). These subjects either quit the task early or simply asked all available questions even for apartments that were obviously not a good fit for their requirements. Two subjects were excluded for not filling out the post-experiment questionnaire. This left 100 subjects (59 literal/41 strategic), of which 86 (49/37) successfully completed the task, accepting the object which met all assigned requirements. There was no statistically significant difference between the literal and strategic models with respect to task success.

We first compare the literal and strategic models with regard to dialogue length, looking only at the subjects who successfully completed the task. Due to the highly structured nature of the experiment it was always the case that a successful dialogue consisted of 10 apartment proposals, some number of QA pairs, where each question was given a single answer, 9 rejections and, finally, one acceptance. This allows us to use the number of questions asked as a proxy for dialogue length. Figure 2 shows the comparison. The strategic model yields 27.4 questions on average, more than four fewer than the literal model's 31.6. Standard statistical tests show the effect to be highly significant, with a one-way ANOVA yielding $F=16.2$, $p = 0.0001$, and a mixed effects regression model with a random slope for item (the items in this case being the set of requirements assigned to the sub-

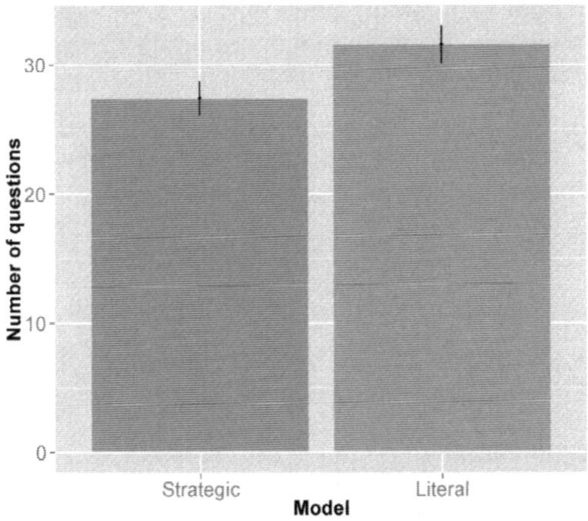

Figure 2: Avg. number of QA pairs by model

S:	How about an apartment in the east of the city? I have an offer for you there.
U:	Does the apartment have a café nearby?
S:	Well, there is a restaurant nearby.
U:	I'd like to see something else

Figure 3: A QA exchange from a dialogue where the user was instructed to find an apartment with a café nearby

ject) yielding t=4, p=0.0001.

We now ask whether the observed effect is due only to the presence of helpful alternatives which preclude the need for follow-up questions, or whether the ability of users to draw pragmatic inferences from *unhelpful* alternatives (i.e. alternatives that don't actually satisfy the user's requirement) also contributes to dialogue efficiency. Figure 3, taken from a real dialogue with our system, illustrates such an inference. The subject specifically wants a café nearby, and infers from the alternative answer that this requirement cannot be satisfied, and therefore rejects. The subject could have asked the question again to get a direct answer, which would have had a negative effect on dialogue efficiency, but this did not happen. We want to know if subjects' aggregate behavior reflects this example.

First, take the null hypothesis to be that subjects do *not* reliably draw such negative implicatures. In that case we would expect a certain proportion of questions to be repeated. Subjects are allowed to ask questions multiple times, and alternatives are never presented twice, such that repeating questions will ultimately lead to a direct yes/no answer. We do see some instances of this behavior in the

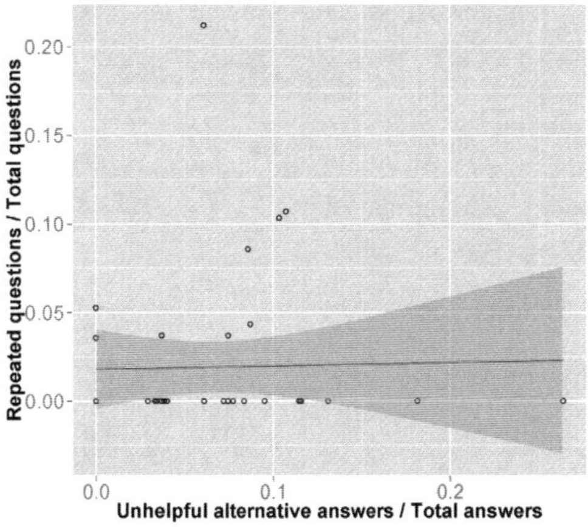

Figure 4: Proportion unhelpful alternatives vs. proportion repeated questions

dialogues. If this is indicative of an overall difficulty in drawing pragmatic inferences from an online dialogue system, then we expect the number of such repetitions to reflect the number of unhelpful alternatives that are offered. Instead, we find that when we plot a linear regression of repeated questions vs. unhelpful alternatives, we get a flat line with no observable correlation (Fig.4). Moreover, we also find no effect of unhelpful alternatives on whether the task was successfully completed. This suggests that the correct inferences are being drawn, as in Fig.3.

We now look at the perceived coherence of the dialogues as assessed by our post-experiment questionnaire. We obtain a composite *coherence score* from all coherence-related items on the seven point Likert scale by summing all per-item scores for each subject and normalizing them to a unit interval, where 1 signifies the upper bound of perceived coherence. Although there is a difference in mean coherence score between the strategic and literal models, with the strategic model exhibiting 88% perceived coherence and the literal model 93%, the difference is not statistically significant. Moreover, we can rule out the possibility that the strategic model is judged to be coherent only when the number of alternative answers is low. To rule this out, we calculate the expected coherence score under the null hypothesis that coherence is directly proportional to the proportion of literal answers. Taking the literal model's average score of 0.93 as a ceiling, we multiply this by the proportion of literal answers to obtain a null hypothesis expected score of about 0.75 for the strategic model. This null hypothesis is disconfirmed (F=12.5, t=30.6, p<0.01). The strategic model is judged, by the criteria assessed by our post-experiment questionnaire, to be pragmatically coherent independently of the rate of indirect answers given.

4 Conclusion

We have characterized the class of alternative answers to yes/no questions and proposed a content selection model for generating these answers in dialogue. The model is based on strategic reasoning about unobserved user requirements, and is based on work in game-theoretic pragmatics (Benz and van Rooij, 2007; Stevens et al., 2014). The model was implemented as an answer selection algorithm within an interactive question answering system in a real estate domain. We have presented an evaluation of this system against a baseline which produces only literal answers. The results show that the strategic reasoning approach leads to efficient dialogues, allows pragmatic inferences to be drawn, and does not dramatically reduce the overall perceived coherence or naturalness of the produced answers. Although the strategic model requires a form of world knowledge—knowledge of possible user requirements and their probabilities—we have shown that there is a simple method, the analysis of negation-rejection sequences in yes/no QA exchanges, that can be used to learn this knowledge with positive results. Further research is required to address issues of scalability and generalizability, but the current model represents a promising step in the direction of pragmatically competent dialogue systems with solid basis in formal pragmatic theory.

Acknowledgments

This work has been supported by the Deutsche Forschungsgemeinschaft (DFG) (Grant nrs. BE 4348/3-1 and KL 1109/6-1, project 'Pragmatic Requirements for Answer Generation in a Sales Dialogue'), and by the Bundesministerium für Bildung und Forschung (BMBF) (Grant nr. 01UG0711).

References

James F. Allen and C. Raymond Perrault. 1980. Analyzing intention in utterances. *Artificial Intelligence*, 15(3):143–178.

N. Asher and A. Lascarides. 2003. *Logics of Conversation*. Studies in Natural Language Processing. Cambridge University Press.

Anton Benz and Robert van Rooij. 2007. Optimal assertions, and what they implicate. a uniform game theoretic approach. *Topoi*, 26(1):63–78.

Anton Benz, Nuria Bertomeu, and Alexandra Strekalova. 2011. A decision-theoretic approach to finding optimal responses to over-constrained queries in a conceptual search space. In *Proceedings of the 15th Workshop on the Semantics and Pragmatics of Dialogue*, pages 37–46.

Marie-Catherine de Marneffe, Scott Grimm, and Christopher Potts. 2009. Not a simple yes or no. In *Proceedings of the SIGDIAL 2009 Conference: The 10th Annual Meeting of the Special Interest Group on Discourse and Dialogue*, pages 136–143.

Dan Fudenberg and Jean Tirole. 1991. Perfect Bayesian equilibrium and sequential equilibrium. *Journal of Economic Theory*, 53(2):236–260.

Nancy Green and Sandra Carberry. 1994. Generating indirect answers to yes-no questions. In *Proceedings of the Seventh International Workshop on Natural Language Generation*, pages 189–198.

Nancy Green and Sandra Carberry. 1999. Interpreting and generating indirect answers. *Computational Linguistics*, 25(3):389–435.

John C. Harsanyi. 1968. Games of incomplete information played by 'Bayesian' players, part II. *Management Science*, 14(5):320–334.

Natalia Konstantinova and Constantin Orasan. 2012. Interactive question answering. *Emerging Applications of Natural Language Processing: Concepts and New Research*, pages 149–169.

Staffan Larsson and David R. Traum. 2000. Information state and dialogue management in the TRINDI dialogue move engine toolkit. *Natural Language Engineering*, 6(3&4):323–340.

David Lewis. 1969. *Convention: A Philosophical Study*. Cambridge University Press, Cambridge.

Jon Scott Stevens, Anton Benz, Sebastian Reuße, Ronja Laarmann-Quante, and Ralf Klabunde. 2014. Indirect answers as potential solutions to decision problems. In *Proceedings of the 18th Workshop on the Semantics and Pragmatics of Dialogue*, pages 145–153.

David R. Traum and Staffan Larsson. 2003. The information state approach to dialogue management. In Jan van Kuppevelt and Ronnie W. Smith, editors, *Current and new directions in discourse and dialogue*, pages 325–353. Springer.

Robert van Rooij. 2003. Questioning to resolve decision problems. *Linguistics and Philosophy*, 26(6):727–763.

Modeling Argument Strength in Student Essays

Isaac Persing and **Vincent Ng**
Human Language Technology Research Institute
University of Texas at Dallas
Richardson, TX 75083-0688
{persingq,vince}@hlt.utdallas.edu

Abstract

While recent years have seen a surge of interest in automated essay grading, including work on grading essays with respect to particular dimensions such as prompt adherence, coherence, and technical quality, there has been relatively little work on grading the essay dimension of argument strength, which is arguably the most important aspect of argumentative essays. We introduce a new corpus of argumentative student essays annotated with argument strength scores and propose a supervised, feature-rich approach to automatically scoring the essays along this dimension. Our approach significantly outperforms a baseline that relies solely on heuristically applied sentence argument function labels by up to 16.1%.

1 Introduction

Automated essay scoring, the task of employing computer technology to evaluate and score written text, is one of the most important educational applications of natural language processing (NLP) (see Shermis and Burstein (2003) and Shermis et al. (2010) for an overview of the state of the art in this task). A major weakness of many existing scoring engines such as the Intelligent Essay Assessor™(Landauer et al., 2003) is that they adopt a holistic scoring scheme, which summarizes the quality of an essay with a single score and thus provides very limited feedback to the writer. In particular, it is not clear which dimension of an essay (e.g., style, coherence, relevance) a score should be attributed to. Recent work addresses this problem by scoring a particular dimension of essay quality such as coherence (Miltsakaki and Kukich, 2004), technical errors, relevance to prompt (Higgins et al., 2004; Persing and Ng, 2014), organization (Persing et al., 2010), and thesis clarity (Persing and Ng, 2013). Essay grading software that provides feedback along multiple dimensions of essay quality such as E-*rater*/Criterion (Attali and Burstein, 2006) has also begun to emerge.

Our goal in this paper is to develop a computational model for scoring the essay dimension of *argument strength*, which is arguably the most important aspect of argumentative essays. Argument strength refers to the strength of the argument an essay makes for its thesis. An essay with a high argument strength score presents a strong argument for its thesis and would convince most readers. While there has been work on *designing* argument schemes (e.g., Burstein et al. (2003), Song et al. (2014), Stab and Gurevych (2014a)) for *annotating* arguments manually (e.g., Song et al. (2014), Stab and Gurevych (2014b)) and automatically (e.g., Falakmasir et al. (2014), Song et al. (2014)) in student essays, little work has been done on scoring the argument strength of student essays. It is worth mentioning that some work has investigated the use of automatically determined argument labels for heuristic (Ong et al., 2014) and learning-based (Song et al., 2014) essay scoring, but their focus is *holistic* essay scoring, not argument strength essay scoring.

In sum, our contributions in this paper are two-fold. First, we develop a scoring model for the argument strength dimension on student essays using a *feature-rich* approach. Second, in order to stimulate further research on this task, we make our data set consisting of argument strength annotations of 1000 essays publicly available. Since progress in argument strength modeling is hindered in part by the lack of a publicly annotated corpus, we believe that our data set will be a valuable resource to the NLP community.

2 Corpus Information

We use as our corpus the 4.5 million word International Corpus of Learner English (ICLE) (Granger

Proceedings of the 53rd Annual Meeting of the Association for Computational Linguistics and the 7th International Joint Conference on Natural Language Processing, pages 543–552,
Beijing, China, July 26-31, 2015.

Topic	Languages	Essays
Most university degrees are theoretical and do not prepare students for the real world. They are therefore of very little value.	13	131
The prison system is outdated. No civilized society should punish its criminals: it should rehabilitate them.	11	80
In his novel *Animal Farm*, George Orwell wrote "All men are equal but some are more equal than others." How true is this today?	10	64

Table 1: Some examples of writing topics.

et al., 2009), which consists of more than 6000 essays on a variety of different topics written by university undergraduates from 16 countries and 16 native languages who are learners of English as a Foreign Language. 91% of the ICLE texts are written in response to prompts that trigger argumentative essays. We select 10 such prompts, and from the subset of argumentative essays written in response to them, we select 1000 essays to annotate for training and testing of our essay argument strength scoring system. Table 1 shows three of the 10 topics selected for annotation. Fifteen native languages are represented in the set of annotated essays.

3 Corpus Annotation

We ask human annotators to score each of the 1000 argumentative essays along the argument strength dimension. Our annotators were selected from over 30 applicants who were familiarized with the scoring rubric and given sample essays to score. The six who were most consistent with the expected scores were given additional essays to annotate. Annotators evaluated the argument strength of each essay using a numerical score from one to four at half-point increments (see Table 2 for a description of each score).[1] This contrasts with previous work on essay scoring, where the corpus is annotated with a binary decision (i.e., *good* or *bad*) for a given scoring dimension (e.g., Higgins et al. (2004)). Hence, our annotation scheme not only provides a finer-grained distinction of argument strength (which can be important in practice), but also makes the prediction task more challenging.

[1]See our website at http://www.hlt.utdallas.edu/~persingq/ICLE/ for the complete list of argument strength annotations.

Score	Description of Argument Strength
4	essay makes a **strong argument** for its thesis and would convince most readers
3	essay makes a **decent argument** for its thesis and could convince some readers
2	essay makes a **weak argument** for its thesis or sometimes even **argues against it**
1	essay **does not make an argument** or it is often **unclear what the argument is**

Table 2: Descriptions of the meaning of scores.

To ensure consistency in annotation, we randomly select 846 essays to have graded by multiple annotators. Though annotators exactly agree on the argument strength score of an essay only 26% of the time, the scores they apply fall within 0.5 points in 67% of essays and within 1.0 point in 89% of essays. For the sake of our experiments, whenever the two annotators disagree on an essay's argument strength score, we assign the essay the average the two scores rounded down to the nearest half point. Table 3 shows the number of essays that receive each of the seven scores for argument strength.

score	1.0	1.5	2.0	2.5	3.0	3.5	4.0
essays	2	21	116	342	372	132	15

Table 3: Distribution of argument strength scores.

4 Score Prediction

We cast the task of predicting an essay's argument strength score as a regression problem. Using regression captures the fact that some pairs of scores are more similar than others (e.g., an essay with an argument strength score of 2.5 is more similar to an essay with a score of 3.0 than it is to one with a score of 1.0). A classification system, by contrast, may sometimes believe that the scores 1.0 and 4.0 are most likely for a particular essay, even though these scores are at opposite ends of the score range. In the rest of this section, we describe how we train and apply our regressor.

Training the regressor. Each essay in the training set is represented as an instance whose label is the essay's gold score (one of the values shown in Table 3), with a set of baseline features (Section 5) and up to seven other feature types we propose (Section 6). After creating training instances, we train a linear regressor with regularization parameter c for scoring test essays using the linear SVM regressor implemented in the LIBSVM software package (Chang and Lin, 2001). All SVM-specific learning parameters are set to their default values except c, which we tune to maximize performance on held-out validation data.[2]

Applying the regressor. After training the regressor, we use it to score the test set essays. Test instances are created in the same way as the training instances. The regressor may assign an essay any score in the range of 1.0–4.0.

5 Baseline Systems

In this section, we describe two baseline systems for predicting essays' argument strength scores.

5.1 Baseline 1: Most Frequent Baseline

Since there is no existing system specifically for scoring argument strength, we begin by designing a simple baseline. When examining the score distribution shown in Table 3, we notice that, while there exist at least a few essays having each of the seven possible scores, the essays are most densely clustered around scores 2.5 and 3.0. A system that always predicts one of these two scores will very frequently be right. For this reason, we develop a *most frequent* baseline. Given a training set, Baseline 1 counts the number of essays assigned to each of the seven scores. From these counts, it determines which score is most frequent and assigns this most frequent score to each test essay.

5.2 Baseline 2: Learning-based Ong et al.

Our second baseline is a learning-based version of Ong et al.'s (2014) system. Recall from the introduction that Ong et al. presented a rule-based approach to predict the holistic score of an argumentative essay. Their approach was composed of two steps. First, they constructed eight heuristic rules for automatically labeling each of the sentences in their corpus with exactly one of the following argument labels: OPPOSES, SUPPORTS, CITATION, CLAIM, HYPOTHESIS, CURRENT STUDY, or NONE. After that, they employed these sentence labels to construct five heuristic rules to holistically score a student essay.

We create Baseline 2 as follows, employing the methods described in Section 4 for training, parameter tuning, and testing. We employ Ong et al.'s method to tag each sentence of our essays with an argument label, but modify their method to accommodate differences between their and our corpus. In particular, our more informal corpus

#	Rule
1	Sentences that begin with a comparison discourse connective or contain any string prefixes from "conflict" or "oppose" are tagged OPPOSES.
2	Sentences that begin with a contingency connective are tagged SUPPORTS.
3	Sentences containing any string prefixes from "suggest", "evidence", "shows", "Essentially", or "indicate" are tagged CLAIM.
4	Sentences in the first, second, or last paragraph that contain string prefixes from "hypothes", or "predict", but do not contain string prefixes from "conflict" or "oppose" are tagged HYPOTHESIS.
5	Sentences containing the word "should" that contain no contingency connectives or string prefixes from "conflict" or "oppose" are also tagged HYPOTHESIS.
6	If the previous sentence was tagged hypothesis and this sentence begins with an expansion connective, it is also tagged HYPOTHESIS.
7	Do not apply a label to this sentence.

Table 4: Sentence labeling rules.

does not contain CURRENT STUDY or CITATION sentences, so we removed portions of rules that attempt to identify these labels (e.g. portions of rules that search for a four-digit number, as would appear as the year in a citation). Our resulting rule set is shown in Table 4. If more than one of these rules applies to a sentence, we tag it with the label from the earliest rule that applies.

After labeling all the sentences in our corpus, we then convert three of their five heuristic scoring rules into features for training a regressor.[3] The resulting three features describe (1) whether an essay contains at least one sentence labeled HYPOTHESIS, (2) whether it contains at least one sentence labeled OPPOSES, and (3) the sum of CLAIM sentences and SUPPORTS sentences divided by the number of paragraphs in the essay. If the value of the last feature exceeds 1, we instead assign it a value of 1. These features make sense because, for example, we would expect essays containing lots of SUPPORTS sentences to offer stronger arguments.

6 Our Approach

Our approach augments the feature set available to Baseline 2 with seven types of novel features.

1. POS N-grams (POS) Word n-grams, though commonly used as features for training text classifiers, are typically not used in automated essay

[2] For parameter tuning, we employ the following c values: 10^0 10^1, 10^2, 10^3, 10^4, 10^5, or 10^6.

[3] We do not apply the remaining two of their heuristic scoring rules because they deal solely with current studies and citations.

grading. The reason is that any list of word n-gram features automatically compiled from a given set of training essays would be contaminated with prompt-specific n-grams that may make the resulting regressor generalize less well to essays written for new prompts.

To generalize our feature set in a way that does not risk introducing prompt-dependent features, we introduce POS n-gram features. Specifically, we construct one feature from each sequence of 1−5 part-of-speech tags appearing in our corpus. In order to obtain one of these features' values for a particular essay, we automatically label each essay with POS tags using the Stanford CoreNLP system (Manning et al., 2014), then count the number of times the POS tag sequence occurs in the essay. An example of a useful feature of this type is "CC NN ,", as it is able to capture when a student writes either "for instance," or "for example,". We normalize each essay's set of POS n-gram features to unit length.

2. Semantic Frames (SFR) While POS n-grams provide syntactic generalizations of word n-grams, FrameNet-style semantic role labels provide semantic generalizations. For each essay in our data set, we employ SEMAFOR (Das et al., 2010) to identify each semantic frame occurring in the essay as well as each frame element that participates in it. For example, a semantic frame may describe an event that occurs in a sentence, and the event's frame elements may be the people or objects that participate in the event. For a more concrete example, consider the sentence "I said that I do not believe that it is a good idea". This sentence contains a Statement frame because a statement is made in it. One of the frame elements participating in the frame is the Speaker "I". From this frame, we would extract a feature pairing the frame together with its frame element to get the feature "Statement-Speaker-I". We would expect this feature to be useful for argument strength scoring because we noticed that essays that focus excessively on the writer's personal opinions and experiences tended to receive lower argument strength scores.

As with POS n-grams, we normalize each essay's set of Semantic Frame features to unit length.

3. Transitional Phrases (TRP) We hypothesize that a more cohesive essay, being easier for a reader to follow, is more persuasive, and thus makes a stronger argument. For this reason, it would be worthwhile to introduce features that measure how cohesive an essay is. Consequently, we create features based on the 149 transitional phrases compiled by Study Guides and Strategies[4]. Study Guides and Strategies collected these transitions into lists of phrases that are useful for different tasks (e.g. a list of transitional phrases for restating points such as "in essence" or "in short"). There are 14 such lists, which we use to generalize transitional features. Particularly, we construct a feature for each of the 14 phrase type lists. For each essay, we assign the feature a value indicating the average number of transitions from the list that occur in the essay per sentence. Despite being phrase-based, transitional phrases features are designed to capture only *prompt-independent* information, which as previously mentioned is important in essay grading.

4. Coreference (COR) As mentioned in our discussion of transitional phrases, a strong argument must be cohesive so that the reader can understand what is being argued. While the transitional phrases already capture one aspect of this, they cannot capture when transitions are made via repeated mentions of the same entities in different sentences. We therefore introduce a set of 19 coreference features that capture information such as the fraction of an essay's sentences that mention entities introduced in the prompt, and the average number of total mentions per sentence.[5] Calculating these feature values, of course, requires that the text be annotated with coreference information. We automatically coreference-annotate the essays using the Stanford CoreNLP system.

5. Prompt Agreement (PRA) An essay's prompt is always either a single statement, or can be split up into multiple statements with which a writer may AGREE STRONGLY, AGREE SOMEWHAT, be NEUTRAL, DISAGREE SOMEWHAT, DISAGREE STRONGLY, NOT ADDRESS, or explicitly have NO OPINION on. We believe information regarding which of these categories a writer's opinion falls into has some bearing on the strength of her argument because, for example, a writer who explicitly mentions having no opinion has probably not made a persuasive argument.

For this reason, we annotate a subset of 830 of our ICLE essays with these agreement labels. We then train a multiclass maximum entropy classifier

[4] `http://www.studygs.net/wrtstr6.htm`

[5] See our website at `http://www.hlt.utdallas.edu/~persingq/ICLE/` for a complete list of coreference features.

using MALLET (McCallum, 2002) for identifying which one of these seven categories an author's opinion falls into. The feature set we use for this task includes POS n-gram and semantic frame features as described earlier in this section, lemmatized word 1-3 grams, the keyword and prompt adherence keyword features we described in Persing and Ng (2013) and Persing and Ng (2014), respectively, and a feature indicating which statement in the prompt we are attempting to classify the author's agreement level with respect to.

Our classifier's training set in this case is the subset of prompt agreement annotated essays that fall within the training set of our 1000 essay argument strength annotated data. We then apply the trained classifier to our entire 1000 essay set in order to obtain predictions from which we can then construct features for argument strength scoring. For each prediction, we construct a feature indicating which of the seven classes the classifier believes is most likely, as well as seven additional features indicating the probability the classifier associates with each of the seven classes.

We produce additional related annotations on this 830 essay set in cases when the annotated opinion was neither AGREE STRONGLY nor DISAGREE STRONGLY, as the reason the annotator chose one of the remaining five classes may sometimes offer insight into the writer's argument. The classes of reasons we annotate include cases when the writer: (1) offered CONFLICTING OPINIONS, (2) EXPLICITLY STATED an agreement level, (3) gave only a PARTIAL RESPONSE to the prompt, (4) argued a SUBTLER POINT not capturable by extreme opinions, (5) did not make it clear that the WRITER'S POSITION matched the one she argued, (6) only BRIEFLY DISCUSSED the topic, (7) CONFUSINGLY PHRASED her argument, or (8) wrote something whose RELEVANCE to the topic was not clear. We believe that knowing which reason(s) apply to an argument may be useful for argument strength scoring because, for example, the CONFLICTING OPINIONS class indicates that the author wrote a confused argument, which probably deserves a lower argument strength score.

We train eight binary maximum entropy classifiers, one for each of these reasons, using the same training data and feature set we use for agreement level prediction. We then use the trained classifiers to make predictions for these eight reasons on all 1000 essays. Finally, we generate features for our argument strength regressor from these predictions by constructing two features from each of the eight reasons. The first binary feature is turned on whenever the maximum entropy classifier believes that the reason applies (i.e., when it assigns the reason a probability of over 0.5). The second feature's value is the probability the classifier assigns for this reason.

6. Argument Component Predictions (ACP) Many of our features thus far do not result from an attempt to build a deep understanding of the structure of the arguments within our essays. To introduce such an understanding into our system, we follow Stab and Gurevych (2014a), who collected and annotated a corpus of 90 persuasive essays (not from the ICLE corpus) with the understanding that the arguments contained therein consist of three types of argument components. In one essay, these argument components typically include a MAJOR CLAIM, several lesser CLAIMs which usually support or attack the major claim, and PREMISEs which usually underpin the validity of a claim or major claim.

Stab and Gurevych (2014b) trained a system to identify these three types of argument components within their corpus given the components' boundaries. Since our corpus does not contain annotated argument components, we modify their approach in order to simultaneously identify argument components and their boundaries.

We begin by implementing a maximum entropy version of their system using MALLET for performing the argument component identification task. We feed our system the same structural and lexical features they described. We then augment the system in the following ways.

First, since our corpus is not annotated with argument component boundaries, we construct a set of low precision, high recall heuristics for identifying the locations in each sentence where an argument component's boundaries might occur. The majority of these rules depend primarily on a syntactic parse tree we automatically generated for the sentence using the Stanford CoreNLP system. Since a large majority of annotated argument components are substrings of a simple declarative clause (an S node in the parse tree), we begin by identifying each S node in the sentence's tree.

Given one of these clauses, we collect a list of left and right boundaries where an argument component may begin or end. The rules we used to

(a) Potential left boundary locations

#	Rule
1	Exactly where the S node begins.
2	After an initial explicit connective, or if the connective is immediately followed by a comma, after the comma.
3	After nth comma that is an immediate child of the S node.
4	After nth comma.

(b) Potential right boundary locations

#	Rule
5	Exactly where the S node ends, or if S ends in a punctuation, immediately before the punctuation.
6	If the S node ends in a (possibly nested) SBAR node, immediately before the nth shallowest SBAR.[6]
7	If the S node ends in a (possibly nested) PP node, immediately before the nth shallowest PP.

Table 5: Rules for extracting candidate argument component boundary locations.

find these boundaries are summarized in Table 5.

Given an S node, we use our rules to construct up to $l \times r$ argument component candidate instances to feed into our system by combining each left boundary with each right boundary that occurs after it, where l is the number of potential left boundaries our rules found, and r is the number of right boundaries they found.

The second way we augment the system is by adding a boundary rule feature type. Whenever we generate an argument component candidate instance, we augment its normal feature set with two binary features indicating which heuristic rule was used to find the candidate's left boundary, and which rule was used to find its right boundary. If two rules can be used to find the same left or right boundary position, the first rule listed in the table is the one used to create the boundary rule feature. This is why, for example, the table contains multiple rules that can find boundaries at comma locations. We would expect some types of commas (e.g., ones following an explicit connective) to be more significant than others.

A last point that requires additional explanation is that several of the rules contain the word "nth". This means that, for example, if a sentence contains multiple commas, we will generate multiple left boundary positions for it using rule 4, and the left boundary rule feature associated with each position will be different (e.g., there is a unique feature for the first comma, and for the the second comma, etc.).

The last augmentation we make to the system is that we apply a NONE label to all argument component candidates whose boundaries do not exactly match those of a gold standard argument component. While Stab and Gurevych also did this, their list of such argument component candidates consisted solely of sentences containing no argument components at all. We could not do this, however, since our corpus is not annotated with argument components and we therefore do not know which sentences these would be.

We train our system on all the instances we generated from the 90 essay corpus and apply it to label all the instances we generated in the same way from our 1000 essay ICLE corpus. As a result, we end up with a set of automatically generated argument component annotations on our 1000 essay corpus. We use these annotations to generate five additional features for our argument strength scoring SVM regressor. These features' values are the number of major claims in the essay, the number of claims in the essay, the number of premises in the essay, the fraction of paragraphs that contain either a claim or a major claim, and the fraction of paragraphs that contain at least one argument component of any kind.

7. Argument Errors (ARE) We manually identified three common problems essays might have that tend to result in weaker arguments, and thus lower argument strength scores. We heuristically construct three features, one for each of these problems, to indicate to the learner when we believe an essay has one of these problems.

It is difficult to make a reasonably strong argument in an essay that is too short. For this reason, we construct a feature that encodes whether the essay has 15 or fewer sentences, as only about 7% of our essays are this short.

In the Stab and Gurevych corpus, only about 5% of paragraphs have no claims or major claims in them. We believe that an essay that contains too many of these claim or major claim-less paragraphs may have an argument that is badly structured, as it is typical for a paragraph to contain one or two (major) claim(s). For this reason, we construct a feature that encodes whether more than half of the essay's paragraphs contain no claims or major claims, as indicated by the previously generated automatic annotations.

[6] The S node may end in an SBAR node which itself has an SBAR node as its last child, and so on. In this case, the S node could be said to end with any of these "nested" SBARS, so we use the position before each (nth) one as a right boundary.

Similarly, only 5% of the Stab and Gurevych essays contain no argument components at all. We believe that an essay that contains too many of these component-less paragraphs is likely to have taken too much space discussing issues that are not relevant to the main argument of the essay. For this reason, we construct a feature that encodes whether more than one of the essay's paragraphs contain no components, as indicated by the previously generated automatic annotations.

7 Evaluation

In this section, we evaluate our system for argument strength scoring. All the results we report are obtained via five-fold cross-validation experiments. In each experiment, we use 60% of our labeled essays for model training, another 20% for parameter tuning and feature selection, and the final 20% for testing. These correspond to the training set, held-out validation data, and test set mentioned in Section 4.

7.1 Scoring Metrics

We employ four evaluation metrics. As we will see below, $S1$, $S2$, and $S3$ are *error* metrics, so lower scores on them imply better performance. In contrast, PC is a *correlation* metric, so higher correlation implies better performance.

The simplest metric, $S1$, measures the frequency at which a system predicts the wrong score out of the seven possible scores. Hence, a system that predicts the right score only 25% of the time would receive an $S1$ score of 0.75.

The $S2$ metric measures the average distance between a system's predicted score and the actual score. This metric reflects the idea that a system that predicts scores close to the annotator-assigned scores should be preferred over a system whose predictions are further off, even if both systems estimate the correct score at the same frequency.

The $S3$ metric measures the average square of the distance between a system's score predictions and the annotator-assigned scores. The intuition behind this metric is that not only should we prefer a system whose predictions are close to the annotator scores, but we should also prefer one whose predictions are not too frequently very far away from the annotated scores. The three error metric scores are given by:

$$\frac{1}{N}\sum_{A_j \neq E'_j} 1, \quad \frac{1}{N}\sum_{j=1}^{N} |A_j - E_j|, \quad \frac{1}{N}\sum_{j=1}^{N} (A_j - E_j)^2$$

System	$S1$	$S2$	$S3$	PC
Baseline 1	.668	.428	.321	.000
Baseline 2	.652	.418	.267	.061
Our System	.618	.392	.244	.212

Table 6: Five-fold cross-validation results for argument strength scoring.

where A_j, E_j, and E'_j are the annotator assigned, system predicted, and rounded system predicted scores[7] respectively for essay j, and N is the number of essays.

The last metric, PC, computes Pearson's correlation coefficient between a system's predicted scores and the annotator-assigned scores. PC ranges from -1 to 1. A positive (negative) PC implies that the two sets of predictions are positively (negatively) correlated.

7.2 Results and Discussion

Five-fold cross-validation results on argument strength score prediction are shown in Table 6. The first two rows show our baseline systems' performances. The best baseline system (Baseline 2), which recall is a learning-based version of Ong et al.'s (2014) system, predicts the wrong score 65.2% of the time. Its predictions are off by an average of .418 points, the average squared error of its predictions is .267, and its average Pearson correlation coefficient with the gold argument strength score across the five folds is .061.

Results of our system are shown on the third row of Table 6. Rather than using all of the available features (i.e., Baseline 2's features and the novel features described in Section 6), our system uses only the feature subset selected by the backward elimination feature selection algorithm (Blum and Langley, 1997) that achieves the best performance on the validation data (see Section 7.3 for details). As we can see, our system predicts the wrong score only 61.8% of the time, predicts scores that are off by an average of .392 points, the average squared error of its predictions is .244, and its average Pearson correlation coefficient with the gold scores is .212. These numbers correspond to relative error reductions[8] of 5.2%,

[7]We round all predictions to 1.0 or 4.0 if they fall outside the 1.0–4.0 range and round $S1$ predictions to the nearest half point.

[8]These numbers are calculated $\frac{B-O}{B-P}$ where B is the baseline system's score, O is our system's score, and P is a perfect score. Perfect scores for error measures and PC are 0 and 1 respectively.

6.2%, 8.6%, and 16.1% over Baseline 2 for S1, S2, S3, and PC, respectively, the last three of which are significant improvements[9]. The magnitudes of these improvements suggest that, while our system yields improvements over the best baseline by all four measures, its greatest contribution is that its predicted scores are best-correlated with the gold standard argument strength scores.

7.3 Feature Ablation

To gain insight into how much impact each of the feature types has on our system, we perform feature ablation experiments in which we remove the feature types from our system one-by-one.

We show the results of the ablation experiments on the held-out validation data as measured by the four scoring metrics in Table 7. The top line of each subtable shows what a system that uses all available features's score would be if we removed just one of the feature types. So to see how our system performs by the PC metric if we remove only prompt agreement (PRA) features, we would look at the first row of results of Table 7(d) under the column headed by PRA. The number here tells us that the resulting system's PC score is .303. Since our system that uses all feature types obtains $S1$, $S2$, $S3$, and PC scores of .521, .366, .218, and .341 on the validation data respectively, the removal of PRA features costs the complete system .038 PC points, and thus we can infer that the inclusion of PRA features has a beneficial effect.

From row 1 of Table 7(a), we can see that removing the Baseline 2 feature set (BAS) yields a system with the best $S1$ score in the presence of the remaining feature types in this row. For this reason, we permanently remove the BAS features from the system before we generate the results on line 2. We iteratively remove the feature type that yields a system with the best performance in this way until we get to the last line, where only one feature type is used to generate each result.

Since the feature type whose removal yields the best system is always the rightmost entry in a line, the order of column headings indicates the relative importance of the feature types, with the leftmost feature types being most important to performance and the rightmost feature types being least important in the presence of the other feature types. The score corresponding to the best system is boldfaced for emphasis, indicating that all feature types appearing to its left are included in the best system.[10]

(a) Results using the $S1$ metric

SFR	ACP	TRP	PRA	POS	COR	ARE	BAS
.534	.594	.530	.524	.522	.532	.529	**.521**
.530	.554	.526	.529	.526	.528	.525	
.534	.555	.525	.531	.528	.522		
.543	.558	.536	.530	.527			
.565	.561	.536	.529				
.563	.547	.539					
.592	.550						

(b) Results using the $S2$ metric

POS	PRA	ACP	TRP	BAS	SFR	COR	ARE
.370	.369	.375	.367	.367	.366	.366	.365
.369	.369	.375	.366	.366	.365	.365	
.370	.371	.372	.367	.366	**.365**		
.374	.374	.376	.368	.366			
.377	.375	.374	.368				
.381	.377	.376					
.385	.382						

(c) Results using the $S3$ metric

POS	PRA	ACP	TRP	BAS	COR	ARE	SFR
.221	.220	.225	.219	.218	.217	.217	.211
.220	.219	.221	.214	.212	.211	.211	
.218	.218	.220	.212	.211	**.209**		
.221	.216	.218	.212	.210			
.224	.217	.218	.212				
.228	.220	.219					
.229	.225						

(d) Results using the PC metric

POS	ACP	PRA	TRP	BAS	ARE	COR	SFR
.302	.270	.303	.326	.324	.347	.347	.356
.316	.300	.327	.344	.361	.366	.371	
.346	.331	.341	.356	.367	**.378**		
.325	.331	.345	.362	.375			
.297	.331	.339	.360				
.280	.320	.321					
.281	.281						

Table 7: Feature ablation results. In each subtable, the first row shows how our system would perform on the validation set essays if each feature type was removed. We then remove the least important feature type, and show in the next row how the adjusted system would perform without each remaining type.

It is interesting to note that while the relative importance of different feature types does not remain exactly the same if we measure performance in different ways, we can see that some feature types tend to be more important than others in a majority of the four scoring metrics.

From these tables, it is clear that POS n-grams

[9]All significance tests are paired t-tests with $p < 0.05$.

[10]The reason the performances shown in these tables appear so much better than those shown previously is that in these tables we tune parameters and display results on the validation set in order to make it clearer why we chose to remove each feature type. In Table 6, by contrast, we tune parameters on the validation set, but display results using those parameters on the test set.

	$S1$			$S2$			$S3$			PC		
Gold	.25	.50	.75	.25	.50	.75	.25	.50	.75	.25	.50	.75
1.0	2.90	2.90	2.90	2.74	2.74	2.74	2.74	2.74	2.74	2.74	2.74	2.74
1.5	2.69	2.78	2.89	2.36	2.67	2.78	2.52	2.63	2.71	2.52	2.63	2.81
2.0	2.61	2.72	2.85	2.54	2.69	2.79	2.60	2.69	2.78	2.60	2.70	2.80
2.5	2.64	2.71	2.85	2.65	2.75	2.86	2.66	2.75	2.85	2.69	2.79	2.89
3.0	2.73	2.84	2.92	2.71	2.81	2.91	2.70	2.80	2.90	2.72	2.83	2.90
3.5	2.74	2.85	2.97	2.78	2.89	3.02	2.79	2.90	3.00	2.81	2.90	2.98
4.0	2.75	2.87	3.10	2.76	2.85	3.09	2.76	2.83	3.08	2.81	2.86	3.19

Table 8: Distribution of regressor scores for our system.

(POS), prompt agreement features (PRA), and argument component predictions (ACP) are the most generally important feature types in roughly that order. They all appear in the leftmost three positions under the tables for metrics $S2$, $S3$, and PC, the three metrics by which our system significantly outperforms Baseline 2. Furthermore, removing any of them tends to have a larger negative impact on our system than removing any of the other feature types.

Transitional phrase features (TRP) and Baseline 2 features (BAS), by contrast, are of more middling importance. While both appear in the best feature sets for the aforementioned metrics (i.e., they appear to the left of the boldfaced entry in the corresponding ablation tables), the impact of their removal is relatively less than that of POS, PRA, or ACP features.

Finally, while the remaining three feature types might at first glance seem unimportant to argument strength scoring, it is useful to note that they all appear in the best performing feature set as measured by at least one of the four scoring metrics. Indeed, semantic frame features (SFR) appear to be the most important feature type as measured by the $S1$ metric, despite being one of the least useful feature types as measured by the other performance metrics. From this we learn that when designing an argument strength scoring system, it is important to understand what the ultimate goal is, as the choice of performance metric can have a large impact on what type of system will seem ideal.

7.4 Analysis of Predicted Scores

To more closely examine the behavior of our system, in Table 8 we chart the distributions of scores it predicts for essays having each gold standard score. As an example of how to read this table, consider the number 2.60 appearing in row 2.0 in the .25 column of the $S3$ region. This means that 25% of the time, when our system with parameters tuned for optimizing $S3$ (including the $S3$ feature set as selected in Table 7(c)) is presented with a test essay having a gold standard score of 2.0, it predicts that the essay has a score less than or equal to 2.60.

From this table, we see that our system has a bias toward predicting more frequent scores as the smallest entry in the table is 2.36 and the largest entry is 3.19, and as we saw in Table 3, 71.4% of essays have gold scores in this range. Nevertheless, our system does not rely entirely on bias, as evidenced by the fact that each column in the table has a tendency for its scores to ascend as the gold standard score increases, implying that our system has some success at predicting lower scores for essays with lower gold standard argument strength scores and higher scores for essays with higher gold standard argument strength scores. The major exception to this rule is line 1.0, but this is to be expected since there are only two essays having this gold score, so the sample from which the numbers on this line are calculated is very small.

8 Conclusion

We proposed a feature-rich approach to the new problem of predicting argument strength scores on student essays. In an evaluation on 1000 argumentative essays selected from the ICLE corpus, our system significantly outperformed a baseline system that relies solely on features built from heuristically labeled sentence argument function labels by up to 16.1%. To stimulate further research on this task, we make all of our annotations publicly available.

Acknowledgments

We thank the three anonymous reviewers for their detailed comments. This work was supported in part by NSF Grants IIS-1147644 and IIS-1219142. Any opinions, findings, conclusions or recommendations expressed in this paper are those of the authors and do not necessarily reflect the views or official policies, either expressed or implied, of NSF.

References

Yigal Attali and Jill Burstein. 2006. Automated essay scoring with E-rater v.2.0. *Journal of Technology, Learning, and Assessment*, 4(3).

Avrim Blum and Pat Langley. 1997. Selection of relevant features and examples in machine learning. *Artificial Intelligence*, 97(1–2):245–271.

Jill Burstein, Daniel Marcu, and Kevin Knight. 2003. Finding the WRITE stuff: Automatic identification of discourse structure in student essays. *IEEE Intelligent Systems*, 18(1):32–39.

Chih-Chung Chang and Chih-Jen Lin, 2001. *LIBSVM: A library for support vector machines*. Software available at `http://www.csie.ntu.edu.tw/~cjlin/libsvm`.

Dipanjan Das, Nathan Schneider, Desai Chen, and Noah A. Smith. 2010. Probabilistic frame-semantic parsing. In *Human Language Technologies: The 2010 Annual Conference of the North American Chapter of the Association for Computational Linguistics*, pages 948–956.

Mohammad Hassan Falakmasir, Kevin D. Ashley, Christian D. Schunn, and Diane J. Litman. 2014. Identifying thesis and conclusion statements in student essays to scaffold peer review. In *Intelligent Tutoring Systems*, pages 254–259. Springer International Publishing.

Sylviane Granger, Estelle Dagneaux, Fanny Meunier, and Magali Paquot. 2009. *International Corpus of Learner English (Version 2)*. Presses universitaires de Louvain.

Derrick Higgins, Jill Burstein, Daniel Marcu, and Claudia Gentile. 2004. Evaluating multiple aspects of coherence in student essays. In *Human Language Technologies: The 2004 Annual Conference of the North American Chapter of the Association for Computational Linguistics*, pages 185–192.

Thomas K. Landauer, Darrell Laham, and Peter W. Foltz. 2003. Automated scoring and annotation of essays with the Intelligent Essay Assessor™. In *Automated Essay Scoring: A Cross-Disciplinary Perspective*, pages 87–112. Lawrence Erlbaum Associates, Inc., Mahwah, NJ.

Christopher D. Manning, Mihai Surdeanu, John Bauer, Jenny Finkel, Steven J. Bethard, and David McClosky. 2014. The Stanford CoreNLP natural language processing toolkit. In *Proceedings of 52nd Annual Meeting of the Association for Computational Linguistics: System Demonstrations*, pages 55–60.

Andrew Kachites McCallum. 2002. MALLET: A Machine Learning for Language Toolkit. `http://mallet.cs.umass.edu`.

Eleni Miltsakaki and Karen Kukich. 2004. Evaluation of text coherence for electronic essay scoring systems. *Natural Language Engineering*, 10(1):25–55.

Nathan Ong, Diane Litman, and Alexandra Brusilovsky. 2014. Ontology-based argument mining and automatic essay scoring. In *Proceedings of the First Workshop on Argumentation Mining*, pages 24–28.

Isaac Persing and Vincent Ng. 2013. Modeling thesis clarity in student essays. In *Proceedings of the 51st Annual Meeting of the Association for Computational Linguistics (Volume 1: Long Papers)*, pages 260–269.

Isaac Persing and Vincent Ng. 2014. Modeling prompt adherence in student essays. In *Proceedings of the 52nd Annual Meeting of the Association for Computational Linguistics (Volume 1: Long Papers)*, pages 1534–1543.

Isaac Persing, Alan Davis, and Vincent Ng. 2010. Modeling organization in student essays. In *Proceedings of the 2010 Conference on Empirical Methods in Natural Language Processing*, pages 229–239.

Mark D. Shermis and Jill C. Burstein. 2003. *Automated Essay Scoring: A Cross-Disciplinary Perspective*. Lawrence Erlbaum Associates, Inc., Mahwah, NJ.

Mark D. Shermis, Jill Burstein, Derrick Higgins, and Klaus Zechner. 2010. Automated essay scoring: Writing assessment and instruction. In *International Encyclopedia of Education (3rd edition)*. Elsevier, Oxford, UK.

Yi Song, Michael Heilman, Beata Beigman Klebanov, and Paul Deane. 2014. Applying argumentation schemes for essay scoring. In *Proceedings of the First Workshop on Argumentation Mining*, pages 69–78.

Christian Stab and Iryna Gurevych. 2014a. Annotating argument components and relations in persuasive essays. In *Proceedings of the 25th International Conference on Computational Linguistics: Technical Papers*, pages 1501–1510.

Christian Stab and Iryna Gurevych. 2014b. Identifying argumentative discourse structures in persuasive essays. In *Proceedings of the 2014 Conference on Empirical Methods in Natural Language Processing*, pages 46–56.

Summarization of Multi-Document Topic Hierarchies using Submodular Mixtures

Ramakrishna B Bairi
IITB-Monash Research Academy
IIT Bombay
Mumbai, 40076, India
bairi@cse.iitb.ac.in

Rishabh Iyer
University of Washington
Seattle, WA-98175, USA
rkiyer@u.washington.edu

Ganesh Ramakrishnan
IIT Bombay
Mumbai, 40076, India
ganesh@cse.iitb.ac.in

Jeff Bilmes
University of Washington
Seattle, WA-98175, USA
bilmes@uw.edu

Abstract

We study the problem of summarizing DAG-structured topic hierarchies over a given set of documents. Example applications include automatically generating Wikipedia disambiguation pages for a set of articles, and generating candidate multi-labels for preparing machine learning datasets (e.g., for text classification, functional genomics, and image classification). Unlike previous work, which focuses on clustering the set of documents using the topic hierarchy as features, we directly pose the problem as a submodular optimization problem on a topic hierarchy using the documents as features. Desirable properties of the chosen topics include document coverage, specificity, topic diversity, and topic homogeneity, each of which, we show, is naturally modeled by a submodular function. Other information, provided say by unsupervised approaches such as LDA and its variants, can also be utilized by defining a submodular function that expresses coherence between the chosen topics and this information. We use a large-margin framework to learn convex mixtures over the set of submodular components. We empirically evaluate our method on the problem of automatically generating Wikipedia disambiguation pages using human generated clusterings as ground truth. We find that our framework improves upon several baselines according to a variety of standard evaluation metrics including the Jaccard Index, F1 score and NMI, and moreover, can be scaled to extremely large scale problems.

1 Introduction

Several real world machine learning applications involve hierarchy based categorization of topics for a set of objects. Objects could be, e.g., a set of documents for text classification, a set of genes in functional genomics, or a set of images in computer vision. One can often define a natural topic hierarchy to categorize these objects. For example, in text and image classification problems, each document or image is assigned a hierarchy of labels — a baseball page is assigned the labels "baseball" and "sports." Moreover, many of these applications, naturally have an existing topic hierarchy generated on the entire set of objects (Rousu et al., 2006; Barutcuoglu et al., 2006; ling Zhang and hua Zhou, 2007; Silla and Freitas, 2011; Tsoumakas et al., 2010).

Given a DAG-structured topic hierarchy and a subset of objects, we investigate the problem of finding a subset of DAG-structured topics that are induced by that subset (of objects). This problem arises naturally in several real world applications. For example, consider the problem of identifying appropriate label sets for a collection of articles. Several existing text collection datasets such as 20 Newsgroup[1], Reuters-21578[2] work with a predefined set of topics. We observe that these topic names are highly abstract[3] for the articles categorized under them. On the other hand, techniques proposed by systems such as Wikipedia Miner (Milne, 2009) and TAGME (Ferragina and Scaiella, 2010) generate several labels for each article in the dataset that are highly specific to the article. Collating all labels from all articles to create a label

[1] http://qwone.com/~jason/20Newsgroups/

[2] http://www.daviddlewis.com/resources/testcollections/reuters21578/

[3] Topic *Concept* is more abstract than the topic *Science* which is more abstract than the topic *Chemistry*

Proceedings of the 53rd Annual Meeting of the Association for Computational Linguistics and the 7th International Joint Conference on Natural Language Processing, pages 553–563,
Beijing, China, July 26-31, 2015.

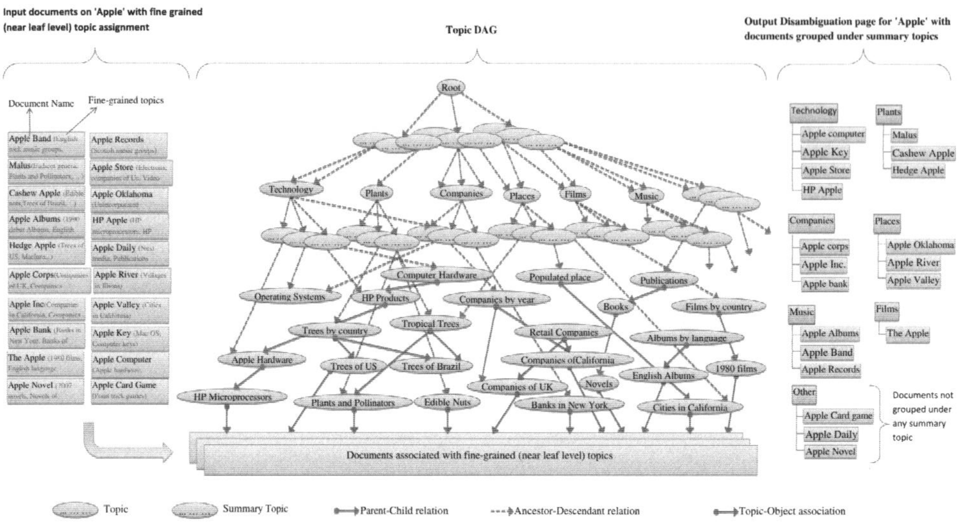

Figure 1: Topic Summarization overview. On the left, we show many documents related to Apple. In the middle, a Wikipedia category hierarchy shown as a topic DAG, links these documents at the leaf level. On the right, we show the output of our summarization process, which creates a set of summary topics (Plants, Technology, Companies, Films, Music and Places in this example) with the input documents classified under them.

set for the dataset can result in a large number of labels and become unmanageable. Our proposed techniques can summarize such large sets of labels into a smaller and more meaningful label sets using a DAG-structured topic hierarchy. This also holds for image classification problems and datasets like ImageNet (Deng et al., 2009). We use the term *summarize* to highlight the fact that the smaller label set semantically covers the larger label set. For example, the topics *Physics*, *Chemistry*, and *Mathematics* can be summarized into a topic *Science*.

A particularly important application of our work (and the one we use for our evaluations in Section 4) is the following: Given a collection of articles spanning different topics, but with similar titles, automatically generate a disambiguation page for those titles using the Wikipedia category hierarchy[4] as a topic DAG. Disambiguation pages[5] on Wikipedia are used to resolve conflicts in article titles that occur when a title is naturally associated with multiple articles on distinct topics. Each disambiguation page organizes articles into several groups, where the articles in each group pertain only to a specific topic. Disambiguations may be seen as paths in a hierarchy leading to different articles that arguably could have the same title. For example, the title *Apple*[6] can refer to a plant, a company, a film, a television show, a place, a technology, an album, a record label, and a newspaper daily. The problem then, is to organize the articles into multiple groups where each group contains articles of similar nature (topics) and has an appropriately discerned group heading. Figure 1 describes the topic summarization process for creation of the disambiguation page for "Apple".

All the above mentioned problems can be modeled as the problem of finding the most representative subset of topic nodes from a DAG-Structured topic hierarchy. We argue that many formulations of this problem are natural instances of submodular maximization, and provide a learning framework to create submodular mixtures to solve this problem. A set function $\mathrm{f}(.)$ is said to be submodular if for any element v and sets $A \subseteq B \subseteq V \setminus \{v\}$, where V represents the ground set of elements, $\mathrm{f}(A \cup \{v\}) - \mathrm{f}(A) \geq \mathrm{f}(B \cup \{v\}) - \mathrm{f}(B)$. This is called the diminishing returns property and states, informally, that adding an element to a smaller set increases the function value more than adding that element to a larger set. Submodular functions naturally model notions of coverage and diversity in applications, and therefore, a number of machine learning problems can be modeled as forms of submodular optimization (Kempe et al., 2003; Krause and Guestrin, 2005; Narasimhan and Bilmes, 2004; Iyer et al., 2013; Lin and Bilmes, 2012; Lin and Bilmes, 2010). In this paper, we investigate structured prediction methods for learn-

[4] http://en.wikipedia.org/wiki/Help:Categories

[5] http://en.wikipedia.org/wiki/Wikipedia:Disambiguation

[6] http://en.wikipedia.org/wiki/Apple_(disambiguation)

ing weighted mixtures of submodular functions to summarize topics for a collection of objects using DAG-structured topic hierarchies. Throughout this paper we use the terms "topic" and "category" interchangeably.

1.1 Related Work

To the best of our knowledge, the specific problem we consider here is new. Previous work on identifying topics can be broadly categorized into one of the following types: a) cluster the objects and then identify names for the clusters; or b) dynamically identify topics (including hierarchical) for a set of objects. LDA (Blei et al., 2003) clusters the documents and simultaneously produces a set of topics into which the documents are clustered. In LDA, each document may be viewed as a mixture of various topics and the topic distribution is assumed to have a Dirichlet prior. LDA associates a group of high probability words to each identified topic. A name can be assigned to a topic by manually inspecting the words or using additional algorithms like (Mei et al., 2007; Maiya et al., 2013). LDA does not make use of existing topic hierarchies and correlation between topics. The Correlated Topic Model (Blei and Lafferty, 2006) induces a correlation structure between topics by using the logistic normal distribution instead of the Dirichlet. Another extension is the hierarchical LDA (Blei et al., 2004), where topics are joined together in a hierarchy by using the nested Chinese restaurant process. Nonparametric extensions of LDA include the Hierarchical Dirichlet Process (Teh et al., 2006) mixture model, which allows the number of topics to be unbounded and learnt from data and the Nested Chinese Restaurant Process which allows topics to be arranged in a hierarchy whose structure is learnt from data. In each of these approaches, unlike our proposed approach, an existing topic hierarchy is not used, nor is any additional object-topic information leveraged.

The pachinko allocation model (PAM)(Li and McCallum, 2006) captures arbitrary, nested, and possibly sparse correlations between topics using a DAG. The leaves of the DAG represent individual words in the vocabulary, while each interior node represents a correlation among its children, which may be words or other interior nodes (topics). PAM learns the probability distributions of words in a topic, subtopics in a topic, and topics in a document. We cannot, however, generate a subset of topics from a large existing topic DAG that can act as summary topics, using PAM.

HSLDA (Perotte et al., 2011) introduces a hierarchically supervised LDA model to infer hierarchical labels for a document. It assumes an existing label hierarchy in the form of a tree. The model infers one or more labels such that, if a label l is inferred as relevant to a document, then all the labels from l to the root of the tree are also inferred as relevant to the document. Our approach differs from HSLDA since: (1) we use the label hierarchy to infer a set of labels for a *group* of documents; (2) we do not enforce the label hierarchy to be a tree as it can be a DAG; and (3) generalizing HSLDA to use a DAG structured hierarchy and infer labels for a *group* of documents (e.g., combining into one big document) also may not help in solving our problem. HSLDA will apply *all* the relevant labels to the documents as per the classifier that it learns for every label. Moreover, the "root" label is always applied and it is very likely that many labels near the top level of the label hierarchy are also classified as relevant to the group of documents.

Wei and James (Bi and Kwok, 2011) present a hierarchical multi-label classification algorithm that can be used on both tree and DAG structured hierarchies. They formulate a search for the optimal consistent multi-label as the finding of the best subgraph in a tree/DAG. In our approach, we assume, individual documents are already associated with one or more topics and we find a consistent label set for a group of documents using the DAG structured topic hierarchy.

Medelyan et al. (Medelyan et al., 2008) and Ferragina et al. (Ferragina and Scaiella, 2010) detect topics for a document using Wikipedia article names and category names as the topic vocabulary. These systems are able to extract signals from a text document and identify Wikipedia articles and/or categories that optimally match the document and assign those article/category names as topics for the document. When run on a large collection of documents, these approaches generate enormous numbers of topics, a problem our proposed approach addresses.

1.2 Our Contributions

While most prior work discussed above focuses on the underlying set of documents, (*e.g.*, by clustering documents), we focus directly on the topics. In particular, we formulate the problem as subset selection on the set of topics within a DAG while simultaneously considering the documents to be categorized. Our method can scale to the colossal size of the DAG (1 million topics and 3 million correlation links between topics in Wikipedia). Moreover, our approach can naturally incorporate outputs from many of the aforementioned algorithms. Our approach is based on submodular maximization and mixture learning, which has been successfully used in applications such as document summarization (Lin, 2012) and image summarization (Tschiatschek et al., 2014), but has never been applied to topic identification tasks or, more generally, DAG summarization.

We introduce a family of submodular functions to identify an appropriate set of topics from a DAG structured hierarchy of topics for a group of documents. We characterize this topic appropriateness through a set of desirable properties such as coverage, diversity, specificity, clarity, and relevance. Each of the submodular function components we consider are monotone, thereby ensuring a near optimal performance obtainable via a simple greedy algorithm for optimization.[7]. We also show how our technique naturally embodies outputs of other algorithms such as LDA, clustering, and classifications. Finally, we utilize a large margin formulation for learning mixtures of these submodular functions, and show how we can optimally learn them from training data.

Our approach demonstrates how to utilize the features collectively in the document space and the topic space to infer a set of topics. From an empirical perspective, we introduce and evaluate our approach on a dataset of around 8000 disambiguations that was extracted from Wikipedia and subsequently cleaned using the methods described in the experimentation section. We show that our learning framework outperforms many of the baselines, and is practical enough to be used on large corpora.

2 Problem Formulation

Let $G\,(V, E)$ be the DAG structured topic hierarchy with V topics. These topics are observed to have a parent child (*isa*) relationship forming a DAG. Let D be the set of documents that are associated with one or more of these topics. The middle portion of Figure 1 depicts a topic hierarchy with associated documents. The association links between the documents and topics can be hard or soft. In case of a hard link, a document is attached to a set of topics. Examples include multi-labeled documents. In case of a soft link, a document is associated with a topic with some degree of confidence (or probability). Furthermore, if a document is attached to a topic t, we assume that all the ancestor topics of t are also relevant for that document. This assumption has been employed in earlier works (Blei et al., 2004; Bi and Kwok, 2011; Rousu et al., 2006) as well. Given a budget of K, our objective is to choose a set of K topics from V, which best describe the documents in D. The notion of best describing topics is characterized through a set of desirable properties - coverage, diversity, specificity, clarity, relevance and fidelity - that K topics have to satisfy. The submodular functions that we introduce in the next section ensure these properties are satisfied. Formally, we solve the following discrete optimization problem:

$$S^* \in \underset{S \subseteq V : |S| \leq K}{\operatorname{argmax}} \sum_i w_i f_i(S) \qquad (1)$$

where, f_i are monotone submodular mixture components and $w_i \geq 0$ are the weights associated with those mixture components. Set S^* is the summary topics scored best.

It is easy to find massive (i.e., size in the order of million) DAG structured topic hierarchies in practice. Wikipedia's category hierarchy consists of more than 1M categories (topics) arranged hierarchically. In fact, they form a cyclic graph (Zesch and Gurevych, 2007). However, we can convert it to a DAG by eliminating the cycles as described in the supplementary material. YAGO (Suchanek et al., 2007) and Freebase (Bollacker et al., 2008) are other instances of massive topic hierarchies. The association of the documents with the existing topic hierarchy is also well studied. Systems such as WikipediaMiner (Milne, 2009), TAGME (Ferragina and Scaiella, 2010) and several annotation systems such as (Dill et al., 2003; Mihalcea and Csomai, 2007; Bunescu and Pasca, 2006) attach topics from Wikipedia (and other catalogs) to the documents by establishing the hard or soft links mentioned above.

Our goal is the following: Given a (ground set) collection V of topics organized in a pre-existing hierarchical DAG structure, and a collection D of documents, chose a size $K \in \mathbb{Z}_+$ representative subset of topics. Our approach is distinct from earlier work (e.g., (Kanungo et al., 2002; Blei et al., 2003)) where typically only a set of documents is classified and categorized in some way. We next provide a few definitions needed later in the paper.

Definition 1: Transitive Cover Γ**):** A topic t is said to cover a set of documents $\Gamma(t)$, called the transitive cover of the topic t, if for all documents $i \in \Gamma(t)$, either i is associated directly with topic t or with any of the descendant topics of t in the topic DAG. A natural extension of this definition to a set of topics T is defined as $\Gamma(T) = \cup_{t \in T} \Gamma(t)$.

[7]A simple greedy algorithm (Nemhauser et al., 1978) obtains a $1 - 1/e$ approximation guarantee for monotone submodular function maximization

Definition 2: Truncated Transitive Cover (Γ^α): This is a transitive cover of topic t, but with the limitation that the path length between a document and the topic t is not more than α. Hence, $|\Gamma^\alpha(t)| \leq |\Gamma(t)|$.

While our problem is closely related to clustering approaches, which consider the set of documents directly, there are some crucial differences. In particular, we focus on producing a clustering of documents where clusters are encouraged to honor a pre-defined DAG structured topic hierarchy. Existing agglomerative clustering algorithms focusing on the coverage of documents may not produce the desired clustering. To understand this, consider six documents d1, d2 ... d6 to be grouped into three clusters. There may be multiple ways to do this depending upon multiple aggregation paths present in the topic DAG: ((d1, d2), (d3, d4), (d5, d6)) or ((d1, d2, d3), (d4, d5), (d6)) or ((d1, d2, d3, d4), (d5), (d6)) or something else. Hence, we need more stringent measures to prefer one clustering over the others. Our work addresses this with a variety of quality criteria (coverage, diversity, specificity, clarity, relevance and fidelity, which are explained later in this paper) that are organically derived from well established submodular functions. And, most importantly, we learn the right mixture of these qualities to be enforced from the data itself. Furthermore, our approach also generalizes these clustering approaches, since one of the components in our mixture of submodular functions is defined via these unsupervised approaches, and maps a given clustering to a set of topics in the hierarchy.

3 Submodular Components and Learning

Summarization is the task of extracting information from a source that is both small in size but still representative. Our problem is different from traditional summarization tasks since we have an underlying DAG as a topic hierarchy that we wish to summarize in response to a subset of documents. Thus, a critical part of our problem is to take the graph structure into account while creating the summaries. Below, we identify properties we wish our summaries to posses.

Coverage: A summary set of topics should cover most of the documents. A document is said to be covered by a topic if there exists a path from the topic, going through intermediary descendant topics, to the document, i.e., the document is within the transitive cover of the topic.

Diversity: Summaries should be as diverse as possible, i.e., each summary topic should cover a unique set of documents. When a document is covered by more than one topic, that document is redundantly covered, e.g., "Finance" and "Banking" would be unlikely members of the same summary.

Summary qualities also involve "quality" notions, including:

Specificity/Clarity/Relevance/Coherence: These quality measures help us choose a set of topics that are neither too abstract nor overly specific. They ensure that the topics are clear and relevant to the documents that they represent. When additional information such as clustering (from LDA or other sources) and tagging (manual) documents is available, these quality criteria encourage the chosen topics to show resemblance (coherence) to those clustering/tagging in terms of transitive cover of documents they produce.

In the below, we define a variety of submodular functions that capture the above properties, and we then describe a large margin learning framework for learning convex mixtures of such components.

3.1 Submodular Components

3.1.1 Coverage Based Functions

Coverage components capture "coverage" of a set of documents.

Weighted Set Cover Function: Given a set of categories, $S \subseteq V$, define $\Gamma(S)$ as the set of documents covered — for each topic $s \in S$, $\Gamma(s) \subseteq D$ represents the documents covered by topic s and $\Gamma(S) = \cup_{s \in S}\Gamma(s)$. The weighted set cover function, defined as $f(S) = \sum_{d \in \Gamma(S)} w_d = w(\Gamma(S))$, assigns weights to the documents based on their relative importance (e.g., in Wikipedia disambiguation, the different documents could be ranked based on their priority).

Feature-based Functions: This class of function represents coverage in feature space. Given a set of categories $S \subseteq V$, and a set of features U, define $m_u(S)$ as the score associated with the set of categories S for feature $u \in U$. The feature set could represent, for example, the documents, in which case $m_u(S)$ represents the number of times document u is covered by the set S. U could also represent more complicated features. For example, in the context of Wikipedia disambiguation, U could represent TFIDF features over the documents. Feature based are then defined as $f(S) = \sum_{u \in U} \psi(m_u(S))$, where ψ is a concave (e.g., the square root) function. This function class has been successfully used in several applications (Kirchhoff and Bilmes, 2014; Wei et al., 2014a; Wei et al., 2014b).

3.1.2 Similarity based Functions

Similarity functions are defined through a similarity matrix $\mathbf{S} = \{s_{ij}\}_{i,j \in V}$. Given categories $i, j \in V$, similarity s_{ij} in our case can be defined as $s_{ij} = |\Gamma(i) \cap \Gamma(j)|$, i.e the number of documents commonly covered by both i and j.

Facility Location: The facility location function, defined as $f(S) = \sum_{i \in V} \max_{j \in S} s_{ij}$, is a natural model for k-medoids and exemplar based clustering, and has been used in several summarization problems (Tschiatschek et al., 2014; Wei et al., 2014a).

Penalty based diversity: A similarity matrix may be used to express a form of coverage of a set S but that is then penalized with a redundancy term, as in the following difference: $f(S) = \sum_{i \in V, j \in S} s_{ij} - \lambda \sum_{i \in S} \sum_{j \in S,} s_{i,j}$ (Lin and Bilmes, 2011)). Here $\lambda \in [0, 1]$. This function is submodular, but is not in general monotone, and has been used in document summarization (Lin and Bilmes, 2011), as a dispersion function (Borodin et al., 2012), and in image summarization (Tschiatschek et al., 2014).

3.1.3 Quality Control (QC) Functions

QC functions ensure a quality criteria is met by a set S of topics. We define the quality score of the set S as $F_q(S) = \sum_{s \in S} f_q(s)$, where $f_q(s)$ is the quality score of topic s for quality q. Therefore, $F_q(S)$ is a modular function in S. We investigate three types of quality control functions: Topic Specificity, Topic Clarity, and Topic Relevance.

Topic Specificity: The farther a topic is from the root of the DAG, the more specific it becomes. Topics higher up in the hierarchy are abstract and less specific. We therefore prefer topics low in the DAG, but lower topics also have less coverage. We define $f_{\text{specificity}}(s) = s_h$ where s_h is the height of topic s in the DAG. The root topic has height zero and the "height" increases as we move down the DAG in Figure 1.

Topic Clarity: Topic clarity is the fraction of descendant topics that cover one or more documents. If a topic has many descendant topics that do not cover any documents, it has less clarity. Formally, $f_{\text{clarity}}(s) = \frac{\sum_{t \in \text{descendants}(s)} [\![\Gamma(t) > 0]\!]}{|\text{descendants}(s)|}$, where $[\![\cdot]\!]$ is the indicator function.

Topic Relevance: A topic is considered to be better related to a document if the number of hops needed to reach the document from that topic is lower. Given any set $A \subseteq D$ of document, and any topic $s \in V$, we can define $f_{\text{relevance}}(s|A) = \operatorname{argmin}_{\alpha}\{\alpha : A \subseteq \Gamma^{\alpha}(s)\}$.

QC Functions As Barrier Modular Mixtures: We introduce a modular function for every QC function as follows

$$f^{\alpha}_{\text{specificity}}(s) = \begin{cases} 1 & \text{if the height of topic } s \text{ is at least } \alpha \\ 0 & \text{otherwise} \end{cases}$$

for every possible value of α. This creates a submodular mixture with as many components as the number of possible values of α. In our experiments with Wikipedia, we had α varying from 1 to 120 stepping by 1, adding 120 modular mixture components. Similarly, we define,

$$f^{\beta}_{\text{clarity}}(s) = \begin{cases} 1 & \text{if the clarity of topic } s \text{ is at least } \beta \\ 0 & \text{otherwise} \end{cases}$$

for every possible (discretized to make it countably finite) value of β. And,

$f^{\gamma}_{\text{relevance}}(s) = f_{\text{cov}}(s|\Gamma^{\gamma}(s))$, where $f_{\text{cov}}(\cdot)$ is the coverage submodular function and $s|X$ indicates coverage of a topic s over a set of documents X. All these functions (modular and submodular terms) are added as mixture components in our learning framework to learn suitable weights for them. We then use these weights in our inference procedure to obtain a subset of topics as described in 3.2. We show from our experiments that this approach performs better than all other approaches and baselines.

3.1.4 Fidelity Functions

A function representing the fidelity of a set S to another reference set R is one that gets a large value when the set S represents the set R. Such a function scores inferred topics high when it resembles a reference set of topics and/or item clusters. The reference set in this case can be produced from other algorithms such as k-means, LDA and its variants or from a manually tagged corpus. Next we describe one such fidelity function.

Topic Coherence: This function scores a set of topics S high when the transitive cover (Definition 1) produced by the topics in S resembles the clusters of documents produced by an external source (k-means, LDA or manual). Given an external source that clusters the documents, producing T clusters $L_1, L_2, ..., L_T$ (for T topics), topic coherence is defined as: $f(S) = \sum_{t \in T} \max_{k \in S} w_{k,t}$ where $w_{k,t} = \text{harmonic\_mean}(w^p_{k,t}, w^r_{k,t})$ and $w^p_{k,t} = \frac{|\Gamma(k) \cap L_t|}{|\Gamma(k)|}$ and $w^r_{k,t} = \frac{|\Gamma(k) \cap L_t|}{|L_t|}$. Note that, $w^p_{k,t} \geq 0$ and $w^r_{k,t} \geq 0$ are the precision on recall of the resemblance and $w_{k,t}$ is the F1 measure. If the transitive cover of topics in S resembles the reference clusters L_t exactly, we attain maximum coherence (or fidelity). As the resemblance diminishes, the score decreases. The above function $f(S)$ is monotone submodular.

3.1.5 Mixture of Submodular Components:

Given the different classes of submodular functions above, we construct our submodular scoring functions $F_w(\cdot)$ as a convex combinations of these different submodular functions $f_1, f_2, \ldots, f_m$, above. In other words,

$$F_w(S) = \sum_{i=1}^{m} w_i f_i(S), \tag{2}$$

where $w = (w_1, \ldots, w_m)$, $w_i \geq 0, \sum_i w_i = 1$. The components f_i are submodular and assumed to be normalized: i.e., $f_i(\emptyset) = 0$, and $f_i(V) = 1$ for monotone functions and $\max_{A \subseteq V} f_i(A) \leq 1$ for non-monotone functions. A simple way to normalize a monotone submodular function is to define the component as $f_i(S)/f_i(V)$. This ensures that the components are *compatible* with each other. Obviously, the merit of the scoring function $F_w(\cdot)$ depends on the selection of the components.

3.2 Large Margin Learning

We optimize the weights w of the scoring function $F_w(\cdot)$ in a large-margin structured prediction framework. In this setting, we assume we have training data in the form of pairs of a set of documents, and a human generated summary as a set of topics. For example, in the case of Wikipedia disambiguation, we use the human generated disambiguation pages as the ground truth summary. We represent the set of ground-truth summaries as $\mathcal{S} = \{S_1, S_2, \cdots, S_N\}$. In large margin training, the weights are optimized such that ground-truth summaries $\mathcal{S}$ are separated from competitor summaries by a loss-dependent margin:

$$F_w(S) \geq F_w(S') + \mathcal{L}(S'), \quad \forall S \in \mathcal{S}, S' \in \mathcal{Y} \setminus \mathcal{S}, \tag{3}$$

where $\mathcal{L}(\cdot)$ is the loss function, and where $\mathcal{Y}$ is a structured output space (for example $\mathcal{Y}$ is the set of summaries that satisfy a certain budget B, i.e., $\mathcal{Y} = \{S' \subseteq V : |S'| \leq B\}$). We assume the loss to be normalized, $0 \leq \mathcal{L}(S') \leq 1, \forall S' \subseteq V$, to ensure that mixture and loss are calibrated. Equation (3) can be stated as $F_w(S) \geq \max_{S' \in \mathcal{Y}} [F_w(S') + \mathcal{L}(S')], \forall S \in \mathcal{S}$ which is called *loss-augmented inference*. We introduce slack variables and minimize the regularized sum of slacks (Lin and Bilmes, 2012):

$$\min_{w \geq 0, \|w\|_1 = 1} \sum_{S \in \mathcal{S}} \left[\max_{S' \in \mathcal{Y}} [F_w(S') + \mathcal{L}(S')] - F_w(S) \right] + \frac{\lambda}{2} \|w\|_2^2, \tag{4}$$

where the non-negative orthant constraint, $w \geq 0$, ensures that the final mixture is submodular. Note a 2-norm regularizer is used on top of a 1-norm constraint $\|w\|_1 = 1$ which we interpret as a prior to encourage higher entropy, and thus more diverse mixture distributions. Tractability depends on the choice of the loss function. The parameters w are learnt using stochastic gradient descent as in (Tschiatschek et al., 2014).

3.3 Loss Functions

A natural choice of loss functions for our case can be derived from cluster evaluation metrics. Every inferred topic s induces a subset of documents, namely the transitive cover $\Gamma(s)$ of s. We compare these clusters with the clusters induced from the true topics in the training set and compute the loss.

In this paper, we use the Jaccard Index (JI) as a loss function. Let S be the inferred topics and T be the true topics. The Jaccard loss is defined as $\mathcal{L}_{\text{jaccard}}(S, T) = 1 - \frac{1}{k} \sum_{s \in S} \max_{t \in T} \frac{|\Gamma(s) \cap \Gamma(t)|}{|\Gamma(s) \cup \Gamma(t)|}$, where $k = |S| = |T|$ is the number of topics. When the clustering produced by the inferred and the true topics are similar, Jaccard loss is 0. When they are completely dissimilar, the loss is maximum, i.e., 1. Jaccard loss is a modular function.

3.4 Inference Algorithm: Greedy

Having learnt the weights for the mixture components, the resulting function $F_w(S) = \sum_{i=1}^{m} w_i f_i(S)$ is a submodular function. In the case when the individual components are themselves monotone (all our functions in fact are), $F_w(S)$ can be optimized by the accelerated greedy algorithm (Minoux, 1978). Thanks to submodularity, we can obtain near optimal solutions very efficiently. In case the functions are all monotone submodular, we can guarantee that the solution is within $1 - 1/e$ factor from the optimal solution.

4 Experimental Results

To validate our approach, we make use of Wikipedia category structure as a topic DAG and apply our technique to the task of automatic generation of Wikipedia disambiguation pages. We pre-processed the category graph to eliminate the cycles in order to make it a DAG. Each Wikipedia disambiguation page is manually created by Wikipedia editors by grouping a collection of Wikipedia articles into several groups. Each group is then assigned a name, which serves as a topic for the group. Typically, a disambiguation page segregates around 20-30 articles into 5-6 groups. Our goal is to measure how accurately we can recreate the groups for a disambiguation page and label them, given only the collection of articles mentioned in that disambiguation page (when actual groupings and labels are hidden).

4.1 Datasets

We parsed the contents of Wikipedia disambiguation pages and extracted disambiguation page names, article groups and group names. We collected about 8000 disambiguation pages that had at least four groups on them. Wikipedia category structure is used as the topic DAG. We eliminated few administrative categories such as "Hidden Categories", "Articles needing cleanup", and the like. The final DAG had about 1M topics and 3M links.

4.2 Evaluation Metrics

Every group of articles on the Wikipedia disambiguation page is assigned a name by the editors. Unfortunately, these names may not correspond to the Wikipedia category (topic) names. For example, one of the groups on the "Matrix" disambiguation page has a name "Business and government" and there is no Wikipedia category by that name. However, the group names generated by our (and baseline) method are from the Wikipedia categories (which forms our topic DAG). In addition, there can be multiple relevant names for a group. For example, a group on a disambiguation page may be called "Calculus", but an algorithm may rightly generate "Vector Calculus". Hence we cannot evaluate the accuracy of an algorithm just by matching the generated group names to those on the disambiguation page. To alleviate this problem, we adopt cluster-based evaluation metrics. We treat every group of articles generated by an algorithm under a topic for a disambiguation page as a cluster of articles. These are considered as *inferred* clusters for a disambiguation page. We compare them against the actual grouping of articles on the Wikipedia disambiguation page by treating those groups as *true* clusters. We can now adopt Jaccard Index, F1-measure, and NMI (Normalized Mutual Information) based cluster evaluation metrics described in (Manning et al., 2008). For each disambiguation page in the test set, we compute every metric score and then average it over all the disambiguation pages.

4.3 Methods Compared

We validated our approach by comparing against several baselines described below. We also compared two variations of our approach as described next. For each of these cases (baselines and two variations) we generated and compared the metrics (Jaccard Index, F1-measure and NMI) as described in the previous section.

KM$_{docs}$: K-Means algorithm run on articles as TF-IDF vectors of words. The number of clusters K is set to the number of true clusters on the Wikipedia disambiguation page.

KMed$_{docs}$: K-Medoids algorithm with articles as TF-IDF vectors of words. The number of clusters are set as in KM$_{docs}$.

KMed$_{topics}$: K-Medoids run on topics as TF-IDF vectors of words. The words for each topic is taken from the articles that are in the transitive cover of the topic.

LDA$_{docs}$: LDA algorithm with the number of topics set to the number of true clusters on the Wikipedia disambiguation page. Each article is then grouped under the highest probability topic.

SMML$_{cov}$: This is the submodular mixture learning case explained in section 3.1.5. Here we consider a mixture of all the submodular functions governing coverage, diversity, fidelity and QC functions. However, we exclude the similarity based functions described in section 3.1.2. Coverage based functions have a time complexity of $O(n)$ whereas similarity based functions are $O(n^2)$. By excluding similarity based functions, we can compare the quality of the results with and without $O(n^2)$ functions. We learn the mixture weights from the training set and use them during inference on the test set to subset K topics through the submodular maximization (Equation 1).

SMML$_{cov+sim}$: This case is similar to SMML$_{cov}$ except that, we include similarity based submodular mixture components. This makes the inference time complexity $O(n^2)$.

We do not compare against HSLDA, PAM and few other techniques cited in the related work sections because they do not produce a subset of K summary topics — these are not directly comparable with our work.

4.4 Evaluation Results

We show that the submodular mixture learning and maximization approaches, i.e., SMML$_{cov}$ and SMML$_{cov+sim}$ outperform other approaches in various metrics. In all these experiments, we performed 5 fold cross validation to learn the parameters from 80% of the disambiguation pages and evaluated on the rest of the 20%, in each fold.

In Figure 2a we summarize the results of the comparison of the methods mentioned above on Jaccard Index, F1 measure and NMI. Our proposed techniques SMML$_{cov}$ and SMML$_{cov+sim}$ outperform other techniques consistently.

In Figures 2b and 2c we measure the number of test instances (i.e., disambiguation queries) in which each of the algorithms dominate (win) in evaluation metrics. In 60% of the disambiguation queries, SMML$_{cov}$ and SMML$_{cov+sim}$ approaches

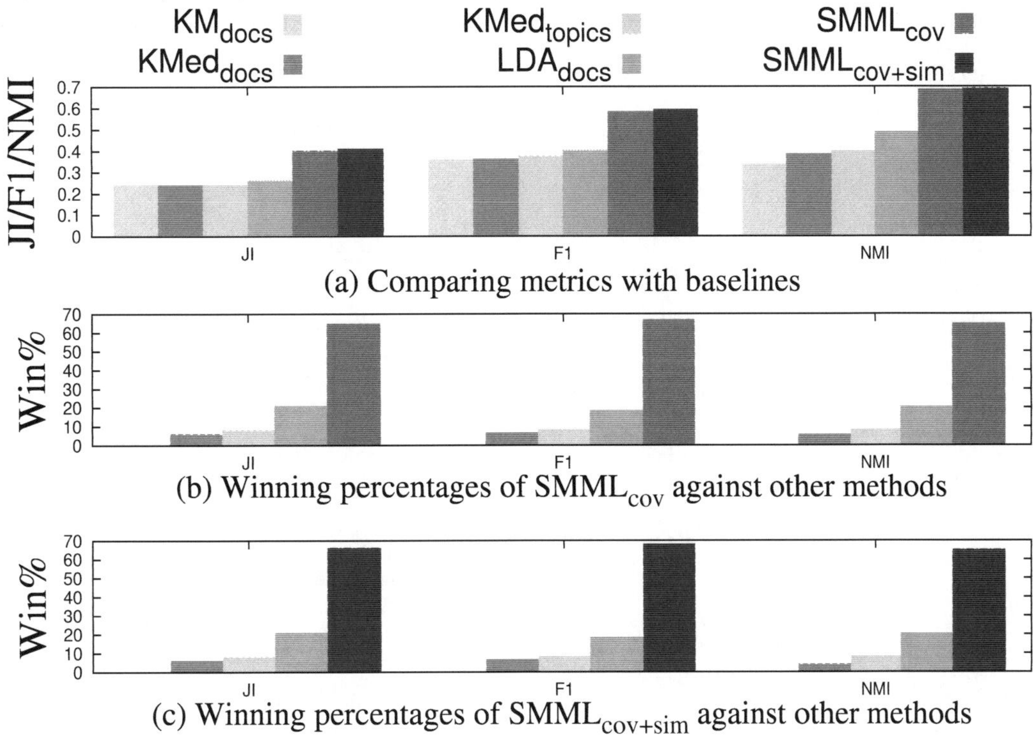

Figure 2: Comparison of techniques

produce higher JI, F1 and NMI than all other methods. This indicates that the clusters of articles produced by our technique resembles the clusters of articles present on the disambiguation page better than other techniques.

From Figures 2b and 2c it is clear that $O(n)$ time complexity based submodular mixture functions (SMML$_{cov}$) perform on par with $O(n^2)$ based functions (SMML$_{cov+sim}$), but at a greatly reduced execution time, demonstrating the sufficiency of $O(n)$ functions for our task. On the average, for each disambiguation query, SMML$_{cov}$ took around 40 seconds (over 1M topics and 3M edges DAG) to infer the topics, whereas SMML$_{cov+sim}$ took around 35 minutes. Both these experiments were carried on a machine with 32 GB RAM, Eight-Core AMD Opteron(tm) Processor 2427.

5 Conclusions

We investigated a problem of summarizing topics over a massive topic DAG such that the summary set of topics produced represents the objects in the collection. This representation is characterized through various classes of submodular (and monotone) functions that captured coverage, similarity, diversity, specificity, clarity, relevance and fidelity of the topics. Currently we assume that the number of topics K is given as an input to our algorithm. It would be an interesting future problem to estimate the value of K automatically in our setting. As future work, we also plan to extend our techniques to produce a hierarchical summary of topics and scale it across heterogeneous collection of objects (from different domains) to bring all of them under the same topic DAG and investigate interesting cases thereon.

Acknowledgements: This material is based upon work supported by the National Science Foundation under Grant No. IIS-1162606, and by a Google, a Microsoft, and an Intel research award. Rishabh Iyer acknowledges support from the Microsoft Research Ph.D Fellowship.

References

Zafer Barutcuoglu, Robert E. Schapire, and Olga G. Troyanskaya. 2006. Hierarchical multi-label prediction of gene function. *Bioinformatics*, 22(7):830–836, April.

W. Bi and J. T. Kwok. 2011. Multi-label classification on tree-and DAG-structured hierarchies. In *ICML*. ICML.

David M. Blei and John D. Lafferty. 2006. Correlated topic models. In *In Proceedings of the 23rd International Conference on Machine Learning*, pages 113–120. MIT Press.

David M. Blei, Andrew Y. Ng, and Michael I. Jordan. 2003. Latent dirichlet allocation. *J. Mach. Learn. Res.*, 3:993–1022, March.

David M. Blei, Thomas L. Griffiths, Michael I. Jordan, and Joshua B. Tenenbaum. 2004. Hierarchical topic models and the nested chinese restaurant process. In *Advances in Neural Information Processing Systems*, page 2003. MIT Press.

Kurt Bollacker, Colin Evans, Praveen Paritosh, Tim Sturge, and Jamie Taylor. 2008. Freebase: A collaboratively created graph database for structuring human knowledge. In *Proceedings of the 2008 ACM SIGMOD International Conference on Management of Data*, SIGMOD '08, pages 1247–1250, New York, NY, USA. ACM.

Allan Borodin, Hyun Chul Lee, and Yuli Ye. 2012. Max-sum diversification, monotone submodular functions and dynamic updates. In *Proceedings of Principles of Database Systems*, pages 155–166. ACM.

Razvan Bunescu and Marius Pasca. 2006. Using encyclopedic knowledge for named entity disambiguation. In *Proceedings of the 11th Conference of the European Chapter of the Association for Computational Linguistics (EACL-06), Trento, Italy*, pages 9–16, April.

Jia Deng, Wei Dong, Richard Socher, Li-Jia Li, Kai Li, and Li Fei-Fei. 2009. Imagenet: A large-scale hierarchical image database. In *Computer Vision and Pattern Recognition, 2009. CVPR 2009. IEEE Conference on*, pages 248–255. IEEE.

Stephen Dill, Nadav Eiron, David Gibson, Daniel Gruhl, R. Guha, Anant Jhingran, Tapas Kanungo, Sridhar Rajagopalan, Andrew Tomkins, John A. Tomlin, and Jason Y. Zien. 2003. Semtag and seeker: Bootstrapping the semantic web via automated semantic annotation. In *Proceedings of the 12th International Conference on World Wide Web*, WWW '03, pages 178–186, New York, NY, USA. ACM.

Paolo Ferragina and Ugo Scaiella. 2010. Tagme: On-the-fly annotation of short text fragments (by wikipedia entities). In *Proceedings of the 19th ACM International Conference on Information and Knowledge Management*, CIKM '10, pages 1625–1628, New York, NY, USA.

R. Iyer, S. Jegelka, and J. Bilmes. 2013. Fast semidifferential-based submodular function optimization. ICML.

Tapas Kanungo, David M. Mount, Nathan S. Netanyahu, Christine D. Piatko, Ruth Silverman, Angela Y. Wu, Senior Member, and Senior Member. 2002. An efficient k-means clustering algorithm: Analysis and implementation. *IEEE Transactions on Pattern Analysis and Machine Intelligence*, 24:881–892.

D. Kempe, J. Kleinberg, and E. Tardos. 2003. Maximizing the spread of influence through a social network. In *SIGKDD*.

Katrin Kirchhoff and Jeff Bilmes. 2014. Submodularity for data selection in machine translation. October.

A. Krause and C. Guestrin. 2005. Near-optimal nonmyopic value of information in graphical models. In *Proceedings of Uncertainity in Artificial Intelligence*. UAI.

Wei Li and Andrew McCallum. 2006. Pachinko allocation: Dag-structured mixture models of topic correlations. In *Proceedings of the 23rd International Conference on Machine Learning*, ICML '06, pages 577–584, New York, NY, USA. ACM.

H. Lin and J. Bilmes. 2010. Multi-document summarization via budgeted maximization of submodular functions. In *NAACL*.

Hui Lin and Jeff Bilmes. 2011. A class of submodular functions for document summarization. In *The 49th Meeting of the Assoc. for Comp. Ling. Human Lang. Technologies (ACL/HLT-2011)*, Portland, OR, June.

H. Lin and J. Bilmes. 2012. Learning mixtures of submodular shells with application to document summarization. In *Conference on Uncertainty in Artificial Intelligence (UAI)*, page 479490.

Hui Lin. 2012. *Submodularity in Natural Language Processing: Algorithms and Applications*. Ph.D. thesis, University of Washington, Dept. of EE.

Min ling Zhang and Zhi hua Zhou. 2007. Ml-knn: A lazy learning approach to multi-label learning. *PATTERN RECOGNITION*, 40:2007.

Arun S. Maiya, John P. Thompson, Francisco Loaiza-Lemos, and Robert M. Rolfe. 2013. Exploratory analysis of highly heterogeneous document collections. In *Proceedings of the 19th ACM SIGKDD International Conference on Knowledge Discovery and Data Mining*, KDD '13, pages 1375–1383, New York, NY, USA. ACM.

Christopher D. Manning, Prabhakar Raghavan, and Hinrich Schütze. 2008. *Introduction to Information Retrieval*. Cambridge University Press, New York, NY, USA.

Olena Medelyan, Ian H. Witten, and David Milne. 2008. Topic indexing with Wikipedia. In *Proceedings of the Wikipedia and AI workshop at AAAI-08*. AAAI.

Qiaozhu Mei, Xuehua Shen, and ChengXiang Zhai. 2007. Automatic labeling of multinomial topic models. In *Proceedings of the 13th ACM SIGKDD International Conference on Knowledge Discovery and Data Mining*, KDD '07, pages 490–499, New York, NY, USA. ACM.

Rada Mihalcea and Andras Csomai. 2007. Wikify!: Linking documents to encyclopedic knowledge. In *Proceedings of the Sixteenth ACM Conference on Conference on Information and Knowledge Management*, CIKM '07, pages 233–242, New York, NY, USA. ACM.

David Milne. 2009. An open-source toolkit for mining wikipedia. In *In Proc. New Zealand Computer Science Research Student Conf*, page 2009.

Michel Minoux. 1978. Accelerated greedy algorithms for maximizing submodular set functions. In J. Stoer, editor, *Optimization Techniques*, volume 7 of *Lecture Notes in Control and Information Sciences*, chapter 27, pages 234–243. Springer Berlin Heidelberg, Berlin/Heidelberg.

Mukund Narasimhan and Jeff Bilmes. 2004. PAC-learning bounded tree-width graphical models. In *Uncertainty in Artificial Intelligence: Proceedings of the Twentieth Conference (UAI-2004)*. Morgan Kaufmann Publishers, July.

George L Nemhauser, Laurence A Wolsey, and Marshall L Fisher. 1978. An analysis of approximations for maximizing submodular set functionsi. *Mathematical Programming*, 14(1):265–294.

Adler J. Perotte, Frank Wood, Noemie Elhadad, and Nicholas Bartlett. 2011. Hierarchically supervised latent dirichlet allocation. In John Shawe-Taylor, Richard S. Zemel, Peter L. Bartlett, Fernando C. N. Pereira, and Kilian Q. Weinberger, editors, *NIPS*, pages 2609–2617.

Juho Rousu, Craig Saunders, Sndor Szedmk, and John Shawe-Taylor. 2006. Kernel-based learning of hierarchical multilabel classification models. *Journal of Machine Learning Research*, 7:1601–1626.

Jr. Silla, CarlosN. and AlexA. Freitas. 2011. A survey of hierarchical classification across different application domains. *Data Mining and Knowledge Discovery*, 22(1-2):31–72.

Fabian M. Suchanek, Gjergji Kasneci, and Gerhard Weikum. 2007. Yago: A core of semantic knowledge. In *Proceedings of the 16th International Conference on World Wide Web*, WWW '07, pages 697–706, New York, NY, USA. ACM.

Yee Whye Teh, Michael I. Jordan, Matthew J. Beal, and David M. Blei. 2006. Hierarchical dirichlet processes. *Journal of the American Statistical Association*, 101(476):1566–1581.

Sebastian Tschiatschek, Rishabh Iyer, Hoachen Wei, and Jeff Bilmes. 2014. Learning Mixtures of Submodular Functions for Image Collection Summarization. In *Neural Information Processing Systems (NIPS)*.

Grigorios Tsoumakas, Ioannis Katakis, and Ioannis Vlahavas. 2010. Mining multi-label data. In Oded Maimon and Lior Rokach, editors, *Data Mining and Knowledge Discovery Handbook*, pages 667–685. Springer US.

Kai Wei, Rishabh Iyer, and Jeff Bilmes. 2014a. Fast multi-stage submodular maximization. In *ICML*.

Kai Wei, Yuzong Liu, Katrin Kirchhoff, Chris Bartels, and Jeff Bilmes. 2014b. Submodular subset selection for large-scale speech training data. *Proceedings of ICASSP, Florence, Italy*.

Torsten Zesch and Iryna Gurevych. 2007. Analysis of the wikipedia category graph for nlp applications. In *Proceedings of the TextGraphs-2 Workshop (NAACL-HLT)*, pages 1–8, Rochester, April. Association for Computational Linguistics.

Learning to Explain Entity Relationships in Knowledge Graphs

Nikos Voskarides*
University of Amsterdam
n.voskarides@uva.nl

Edgar Meij
Yahoo Labs, London
emeij@yahoo-inc.com

Manos Tsagkias
904Labs, Amsterdam
manos@904labs.com

Maarten de Rijke
University of Amsterdam
derijke@uva.nl

Wouter Weerkamp
904Labs, Amsterdam
wouter@904labs.com

Abstract

We study the problem of explaining relationships between pairs of knowledge graph entities with human-readable descriptions. Our method extracts and enriches sentences that refer to an entity pair from a corpus and ranks the sentences according to how well they describe the relationship between the entities. We model this task as a learning to rank problem for sentences and employ a rich set of features. When evaluated on a large set of manually annotated sentences, we find that our method significantly improves over state-of-the-art baseline models.

1 Introduction

Knowledge graphs are a powerful tool for supporting a large spectrum of search applications including ranking, recommendation, exploratory search, and web search (Dong et al., 2014). A knowledge graph aggregates information around entities across multiple content sources and links these entities together, while at the same time providing entity-specific properties (such as age or employer) and types (such as actor or movie).

Although there is a growing interest in automatically constructing knowledge graphs, e.g., from unstructured web data (Weston et al., 2013; Craven et al., 2000; Fan et al., 2012), the problem of providing evidence on why two entities are related in a knowledge graph remains largely unaddressed. Extracting and presenting evidence for linking two entities, however, is an important aspect of knowledge graphs, as it can enforce trust between the user and a search engine, which in turn can improve long-term user engagement, e.g., in the context of related entity recommendation (Blanco et al., 2013). Although knowledge graphs exist that provide this functionality to a certain degree (e.g., when hovering over Google's suggested entities, see Figure 1), to the best of our knowledge there is no previously published research on methods for entity relationship explanation.

Figure 1: Part of Google's search result page for the query "barack obama". When hovering over the related entity "Michelle Obama", an explanation of the relationship between her and "Barack Obama" is shown.

In this paper we propose a method for explaining the relationship between two entities, which we evaluate on a newly constructed annotated dataset that we make publicly available. In particular, we consider the task of explaining relationships between pairs of Wikipedia entities. We aim to infer a human-readable description for an entity pair given a relationship between the two entities. Since Wikipedia does not explicitly define relationships between entities we use a knowledge graph to obtain these relations. We cast our task as a sentence ranking problem: we automatically extract sentences from a corpus and rank

*This work was carried out while this author was visiting Yahoo Labs.

Proceedings of the 53rd Annual Meeting of the Association for Computational Linguistics and the 7th International Joint Conference on Natural Language Processing, pages 564–574,
Beijing, China, July 26-31, 2015. ©2015 Association for Computational Linguistics

them according to how well they describe a given relationship between a pair of entities. For ranking purposes, we extract a rich set of features and use learning to rank to effectively combine them. Our feature set includes both traditional information retrieval and natural language processing features that we augment with entity-dependent features. These features leverage information from the structure of the knowledge graph. On top of this, we use features that capture the presence in a sentence of the relationship of interest. For our evaluation we focus on "people" entities and we use a large, manually annotated dataset of sentences.

The research questions we address are the following. First, we ask what the effectiveness of state-of-the-art sentence retrieval models is for explaining a relationship between two entities (RQ1). Second, we consider whether we can improve over sentence retrieval models by casting the task in a learning to rank framework (RQ2). Third, we examine whether we can further improve performance by using relationship-dependent models instead of a relationship-independent one (RQ3). We complement these research questions with an error and feature analysis.

Our main contributions are a robust and effective method for explaining entity relationships, detailed insights into the performance of our method and features, and a manually annotated dataset.

2 Related Work

We combine ideas from sentence retrieval, learning to rank, and question answering to address the task of explaining relationships between entities.

Previous work that is closest to the task we address in this paper is that of Blanco and Zaragoza (2010) and Fang et al. (2011). First, Blanco and Zaragoza (2010) focus on finding and ranking sentences that explain the relationship between an entity and a query. Our work is different in that we want to explain the relationship between two entities, rather than a query. Fang et al. (2011) explore the generation of a ranked list of knowledge base relationships for an entity pair. Instead, we try to select sentences that describe a particular relationship, assuming that this is given.

Our approach builds on sentence retrieval, where one retrieves sentences rather than documents that answer an information need. Document retrieval models such as tf-idf, BM25, and language modeling (Baeza-Yates et al., 1999) have been extended to tackle sentence retrieval. Three of the most successful sentence retrieval methods are TFISF (Allan et al., 2003), which is a variant of the vector space model with tf-idf weighting, language modeling with local context (Murdock, 2006; Fernández et al., 2011), and a recursive version of TFISF that accounts for local context (Doko et al., 2013). TFISF is very competitive compared to document retrieval models tuned specifically for sentence retrieval (e.g., BM25 and language modeling (Losada, 2008)) and we therefore include it as a baseline.

Sentences that are suitable for explaining relationships can have attributes that are important for ranking but cannot be captured by term-based retrieval models. One way to combine a wide range of ranking features is learning to rank (LTR). Recent years have witnessed a rapid increase in the work on learning to rank, and it has proven to be a very successful method for combining large numbers of ranking features, for web search, but also other information retrieval applications (Burges et al., 2011; Surdeanu et al., 2011; Agarwal et al., 2012). We use learning to rank and represent each sentence with a set of features that aim to capture different dimensions of the sentence.

Question answering (QA) is the task of providing direct and concise answers to questions formed in natural language (Hirschman and Gaizauskas, 2001). QA can be regarded as a similar task to ours, assuming that the combination of entity pair and relationship form the "question" and that the "answer" is the sentence describing the relationship of interest. Even though we do not follow the QA paradigm in this paper, some of the features we use are inspired by QA systems. In addition, we employ learning to rank to combine the devised features, which has recently been successfully applied for QA (Surdeanu et al., 2011; Agarwal et al., 2012).

3 Problem Statement

We address the problem of explaining relationships between pairs of entities in a knowledge graph. We operationalize the problem as a problem of ranking sentences from documents in a corpus that is related to the knowledge graph. More specifically, given two entities e_i and e_j that form an entity pair $\langle e_i, e_j \rangle$, and a relation r between them, the task is to extract a set of candidate sentences $S_{ij} = \{s_{ij_1}, \ldots, s_{ij_k}\}$ that refer to $\langle e_i, e_j \rangle$ and to impose a ranking on the sentences in S_{ij}. The relation r has the general form $\langle type(e_i), terms(r), type(e_j) \rangle$, where $type(e)$ is the type of the entity e (e.g., `Person` or `Actor`) and $terms(r)$ are the terms of the relation (e.g., `CoCastsWith` or `IsSpouseOf`).

We are left with two specific tasks: (1) extracting candidate sentences S_{ij}, and (2) ranking S_{ij}, where the goal is to have sentences that provide a perfect explanation of the relationship at the top position of the ranking. The next section describes our methods for both tasks.

4 Explaining Entity Relationships

We follow a two-step approach for automatically explaining relationships between entity pairs. First, in Section 4.1, we extract and enrich sentences that refer to an entity pair $\langle e_i, e_j \rangle$ from a corpus in order to construct a set of candidate sentences. Second, in Section 4.2, we extract a rich set of features describing the entities' relationship r and use supervised machine learning in order to rank the sentences in S_{ij} according to how well they describe the relationship r.

4.1 Extracting candidate sentences

To create a set of candidate sentences for a given entity pair and relationship, we require a corpus of documents that is pertinent to the entities at hand. Although any kind of document collection can be used, we focus on Wikipedia in this paper, as it provides good coverage for the majority of entities in our knowledge graph.

First, we extract surface forms for the given entities: the title of the entity's Wikipedia article (e.g., "Barack Obama"), the titles of all redirect pages linking to that article (e.g., "Obama"), and all anchor text associated with hyperlinks to the article within Wikipedia (e.g., "president obama"). We then split all Wikipedia articles into sentences and consider a sentence as a candidate if (i) the sentence is part of either entities' Wikipedia article and contains a surface form of, or a link to, the other entity; or (ii) the sentence contains surface forms of, or links to, both entities in the entity pair.

Next, we apply two sentence enrichment steps for (i) making sentences self-contained and readable outside the context of the source document and (ii) linking the sentences to entities. For (i), we replace pronouns in candidate sentences with the title of the entity. We apply a simple heuristic for the people entities, inspired by (Wu and Weld, 2010):[1] we count the frequency of the terms "he" and "she" in the article for determining the gender of the entity, and we replace the first appearance of "he" or "she" in each sentence with the entity's title. We skip this step if any surface form of the entity occurs in the sentence.

For (ii), we apply entity linking to provide links from the sentence to additional entities (Milne and Witten, 2008). This need arises from the fact that not every sentence in an article contains explicit links to the entities it mentions, as Wikipedia guidelines only allow one link to another article in the article's text.[2] The algorithm takes a sentence as input and iterates over n-grams that are not yet linked to an entity. If an n-gram matches a surface form of an entity, we establish a link between the n-gram and the entity. We restrict our search space to entities that are linked from within the source article of the sentence and from within articles to which the source article links. This way, our entity linking method achieves high precision as almost no disambiguation is necessary.

As an example, consider the sentence "He gave critically acclaimed performances in the crime thriller Seven…" on the Wikipedia page for Brad Pitt. After applying our enrichment steps, we obtain "`Brad_Pitt` gave critically acclaimed performances in the crime thriller `Seven`…", making the sentence human readable and link to the entities `Brad_Pitt` and `Seven_(1995_film)`.

4.2 Ranking sentences

After extracting candidate sentences, we rank them by how well they describe the relationship of interest r between entities e_i and e_j. There are many signals beyond simple term statistics that can indicate relevance. Automatically constructing a ranking model using supervised machine learning techniques is therefore an obvious choice. For ranking we use learning to rank (LTR) and represent each sentence with a rich set of features. Table 1 lists the features we use. Below we provide

[1] We experimented with the Stanford co-reference resolution system (Lee et al., 2011) and Apache OpenNLP and found that they were not able to consistently achieve the level of effectiveness that we require.

[2] `http://en.Wikipedia.org/wiki/Wikipedia:Manual_of_Style/Linking`

#	Name	Gloss
Text features		
1	Sentence length	Length of s in words
2	Sum of idf	Sum of IDF of terms of s in Wikipedia
3	Average idf	Average IDF of terms of s in Wikipedia
4	Sentence density	Lexical density of s, see Equation 1 (Lee et al., 2001)
5–8	POS fractions	Fraction of verbs, nouns, adjectives, others in s (Mintz et al., 2009)
Entity features		
9	#entities	Total number of entities in s
10	Link to e_i	Whether s contains a link to the entity e_i
11	Link to e_j	Whether s contains a link to the entity e_j
12	Links to e_i and e_j	Whether s contains links to both entities e_i and e_j
13	Entity first	Is e_i or e_j the first entity in the sentence?
14	Spread of e_i, e_j	Distance between the last match of e_i and e_j in s (Blanco and Zaragoza, 2010)
15–22	POS fractions left/right	Fraction of verbs, nouns, adjectives, others to the left/right window of e_i and e_j in s (Mintz et al., 2009)
23–25	#entities left/right/between	Number of entities to the left/right or between entities e_i and e_j in s
26	common links e_i, e_j	Whether s contains any common link of e_i and e_j
27	#common links	The number of common links of e_i and e_j in s
28	Score common links e_i, e_j	Sum of the scores of the common links of e_i and e_j in s
29–30	#common links prev/next	The number of common links of e_i and e_j in previous/next sentence of s
Relationship features		
31	Match $terms(r)$?	Whether s contains any term in $terms(r)$
32	Match $wordnet(r)$?	Whether s contains any phrase in $wordnet(r)$
33	Match $word2vec(r)$?	Whether s contains any phrase in $word2vec(r)$
34–36	or's	Boolean OR of feature 31 and one or both of features 32 and 33
37–38	or(31, 32, 33) prev/next	Boolean OR of features 31, 32, 33 for the previous/next sentence of s
39	Average $word2vec(r)$	Average cosine similarity of phrases in $word2vec(r)$ that are matched in s
40	Maximum $word2vec(r)$	Maximum cosine similarity of phrases in $word2vec(r)$ that are matched in s
41	Sum $word2vec(r)$	Sum of cosine similarity of phrases in $word2vec(r)$ that are matched in s
42	Score LC	Lucene score of s with $titles(e_i, e_j)$, $terms(r)$, $wordnet(r)$, $word2vec(r)$ as query
43	Score R-TFISF	R-TFISF score of s with queries constructed as above
Source features		
44	Sentence position	Position of s in document from which it originates
45	From e_i or e_j?	Does s originate from the Wikipedia article of e_i or e_j?
46	#(e_i or e_j)	Number of occurrences of e_i or e_j in document from which s originates, inspired by document smoothing for sentence retrieval (Murdock and Croft, 2005)

Table 1: Features used for sentence ranking.

a brief description of the more complex ones.

Text features This feature type regards the importance of the sentence s at the term level. We compute the density of s (feature 4) as:

$$density(s) = \frac{1}{K \cdot (K+1)} \sum_{j=1}^{n} \frac{idf(t_j) \cdot idf(t_{j+1})}{distance(t_j, t_{j+1})^2}, \quad (1)$$

where K is the number of keyword terms in s and $distance(t_j, t_{j+1})$ is the number of non-keyword terms between keyword terms t_j and t_{j+1}. We treat stop words and numbers in s as non-keywords and the remaining terms as keywords. Features 5–8 capture the distribution of part-of-speech tags in the sentence.

Entity features These features partly build on (Tsagkias et al., 2011; Meij et al., 2012) and describe the entities and are dependent on the knowledge graph. Whether e_i or e_j is the first appearing entity in a sentence might be an indicator of importance (feature 13). The spread of e_i and e_j in the sentence (feature 14) might be an indicator of their centrality in the sentence (Blanco and Zaragoza, 2010). Features 15–22 capture the distribution of part-of-speech tags in the sentence in a window of four words around e_i or e_j in s (Mintz et al., 2009), complemented by the number of entities between, to the left of, and to the right of the entity pair (features 23–25).

We assume that two articles that have many common articles that point to them are strongly related (Witten and Milne, 2008). We hypothesize that, if a sentence contains common inlinks from e_i and e_j, the sentence might contain important information about their relationship. Hence, we add whether the sentence contains a common link (feature 26) and the number of common links (feature 27) as features. We score a common link l between e_i and e_j using:

$$score(l, e_i, e_j) = sim(l, e_i) \cdot sim(l, e_j), \quad (2)$$

where $sim(\cdot, \cdot)$ is defined as the similarity between two Wikipedia articles, computed using a variant of Normalized Google Distance (Witten and Milne, 2008). Feature 28 then measures the sum of the scores of the common links.

Previous research shows that using surrounding sentences is beneficial for sentence retrieval (Doko et al., 2013). We therefore consider the number of common links in the previous and next sentence (features 29–30).

Relationship features Feature 31 indicates whether any of the relationship-specific terms occurs in the sentence. Only matching the terms in the relationship may have low coverage since terms such as "spouse" may have many synonyms and/or highly related terms, e.g., "husband" or "married". Therefore, we use WordNet to find synonym phrases of r (feature 32); we refer to this method as $wordnet(r)$.

Alternatively, we use word embeddings to find such similar phrases (Mikolov et al., 2013). Such embeddings take a text corpus as input and learn vector representations of words and phrases consisting of real numbers. Given the set V_r consisting of the vector representations of all the relationship terms and the set V which consists of the vector representations of all the candidate phrases in the data, we calculate the distance between a candidate phrase represented by a vector $\mathbf{v}_i \in V$ and the vectors in V_r as:

$$distance(\mathbf{v}_i, V) = \cos\left(\mathbf{v}_i, \sum_{\mathbf{v}_j \in V_r} \mathbf{v}_j\right), \quad (3)$$

where $\sum_{\mathbf{v}_j \in V_r} \mathbf{v}_j$ is the element-wise sum of the vectors in V_r and the distance between two vectors $\mathbf{v}_1$ and $\mathbf{v}_2$ is measured using cosine similarity. The candidate phrases in V are then ranked using Equation 3 and the top-m phrases are selected, resulting in features 33, 39, 40, and 41; we refer to the ranked set of phrases that are selected using this procedure as $word2vec(r)$.

In addition, we employ state-of-the-art retrieval functions and include the scores for queries that are constructed using the entities e_i and e_j, the relation r, $wordnet(r)$, and $word2vec(r)$. We use the titles of the entity articles $titles(e)$ to represent the entities in the query and two ranking functions, Recursive TFISF (R-TFISF) and LC,[3] (features 42–43). TFISF is a sentence retrieval model that determines the level of relevance of a sentence s given a query q as:

$$R(s, q) = \sum_{t \in q} \log(tf_{t,q} + 1) \cdot \log(tf_{t,s} + 1) \cdot \log\left(\frac{n+1}{0.5 + sf_t}\right), \quad (4)$$

where $tf_{t,q}$ and $tf_{t,s}$ are the number of occurrences of term t in the query q and the sentence s respectively, sf_t is the number of sentences in which t appears, and n is the number of sentences in the collection. R-TFISF is an improved extension of the TFISF method (Doko et al., 2013), which incorporates context from neighboring sentences in the ranking function:

$$R_c(s, q) = (1 - \mu) R(s, q) + \mu[R_c(s_{prev}(s), q) + R_c(s_{next}(s), q)], \quad (5)$$

where μ is a free parameter and $s_{prev}(s)$ and $s_{next}(s)$ indicate functions to retrieve the previous and next sentence, respectively. We use a maximum of three recursive calls.

Source features Here, we refer to features that are dependent on the source document of the sentences. We have three such features.

5 Experimental setup

In this section we describe the dataset, manual annotations, learning to rank algorithm, and evaluation metrics that we use to answer our research questions.

5.1 Dataset

We draw entities and their relationships from a proprietary knowledge graph that is created from Wikipedia, Freebase, IMDB, and other sources, and that is used by the Yahoo web search engine. We focus on "people" entities and relationships between them.[4] For our experiments we need to select a manageable set of entities, which we obtain as follows. We consider a year of query logs

[3] In preliminary experiments R-TFISF and LC were the best performing among a pool of sentence retrieval methods.

[4] Note that, except for the co-reference resolution step described in Section 4.1, our method does not depend on this restriction.

from a large commercial search engine, count the number of times a user clicks on a Wikipedia article of an entity in the results page and perform stratified sampling of entities according to this distribution. As we are bounded by limited resources for our manual assessments, we sample 1 476 entity pairs that together with nine unique relationship types form our experimental dataset.

We use an English Wikipedia dump dated July 8, 2013, containing approximately 4M articles, of which 50 638 belong to "people" entities that are also in our knowledge graph. We extract sentences using the approach described in Section 4.1, resulting in 36 823 candidate sentences for our entities. On average we have 24.94 sentences per entity pair (maximum 423 and minimum 0). Because of the large variance, it is not feasible to obtain exhaustive annotations for all sentences. We rank the sentences using R-TFISF and keep the top-10 sentences per entity pair for annotation. This results in a total of 5 689 sentences.

Five human annotators provided relevance judgments, manually judging sentences based on how well they describe the relationship for an entity pair, for which we use a five-level graded relevance scale (perfect, excellent, good, fair, bad).[5] Of all relevance grades 8.1% is perfect, 15.69% excellent, 19.98% good, 8.05% fair, and 48.15% bad. Out of 1 476 entity pairs, 1 093 have at least one sentence annotated as fair. As is common in information retrieval evaluation, we discard entity pairs that have only "bad" sentences. We examine the difficulty of the task for human annotators by measuring inter-annotator agreement on a subset of 105 sentences that are judged by 3 annotators. Fleiss' kappa is $k = 0.449$, which is considered to be moderate agreement.

5.2 Machine learning

For ranking sentences we use a Random Forest (RF) classifier (Breiman, 2001).[6] We set the number of iterations to 300 and the sampling rate to 0.3. Experiments with varying these two parameters did not show any significant differences. We also tried several feature normalization methods, none of them being able to significantly outperform the runs without feature normalization.

We obtain POS tags using the Stanford part-of-speech tagger and filter out a standard list of 33 English stopwords. For the word embeddings we use *word2vec* and train our model on all text in Wikipedia using negative sampling and the continuous bag of words architecture. We set the size of the phrase vectors to 500 and $m = 30$.

Baseline	NDCG@1	NDCG@10	ERR@1	ERR@10
B1	0.7508	0.8961	0.3577	0.4531
B2	0.7511	0.8958	0.3584	0.4530
B3	0.7595	0.8997	0.3696	0.4600
B4	0.7767	0.9070	0.3774	0.4672
B5	**0.7801**	**0.9093**	**0.3787**	**0.4682**

Table 2: Results for five baseline variants. See text for their description and significant differences.

5.3 Evaluation metrics

We employ two main evaluation metrics in our experiments, NDCG (Järvelin and Kekäläinen, 2002) and ERR (Chapelle et al., 2009). The former measures the total accumulated gain from the top of the ranking that is discounted at lower ranks and is normalized by the ideal cumulative gain. The latter models user behavior and measures the expected reciprocal rank at which a user will stop her search. We consider these ranking-based graded evaluation metrics at two cut-off points: position 1, corresponding to showing a single sentence to a user, and 10, which accounts for users who might look at more results. We report on NDCG@1, NDCG@10, ERR@1, ERR@10, and Exc@1, which indicates whether we have an "excellent" or "perfect" sentence at the top of the ranking. Likewise, Per@1 indicates whether we have a "perfect" sentence at the top of the ranking (not all entity pairs have an excellent or a perfect sentence).

We perform 5-fold cross validation and test for statistical significance using a paired two-tailed t-test. We depict a significant difference in performance for $p < 0.01$ with $^{\blacktriangle}$ (gain) and $^{\blacktriangledown}$ (loss) and for $p < 0.05$ with $^{\vartriangle}$ (gain) and $^{\triangledown}$ (loss). Boldface indicates the best score for a metric.

6 Results and Analysis

We compare the performance of typical document retrieval models and state-of-the-art sentence retrieval models in order to answer RQ1. We consider five sentence retrieval models: Lucene ranking (LC), language modeling with Dirichlet

[5] `https://github.com/nickvosk/acl2015-dataset-learning-to-explain-entity-relationships`

[6] In preliminary experiments, we contrasted RF with gradient boosted regression trees and LambdaMART and found that RF consistently outperformed other methods.

Has one	# pairs	# sentences	Method	NDCG@1	NDCG@10	ERR@1	ERR@10	Exc@1	Per@1
fair	1 093	4 435	B5	0.7801	0.9093	0.3787	0.4682	–	–
			LTR	**0.8489**▲	**0.9375**▲	**0.4242**▲	**0.4980**▲	–	–
good	1 038	4 285	B5	0.7742	0.9078	0.3958	0.4894	–	–
			LTR	**0.8486**▲	**0.9374**▲	**0.4438**▲	**0.5208**▲	–	–
excellent	752	3 387	B5	0.7455	0.8999	0.4858	0.5981	0.7314	–
			LTR	**0.8372**▲	**0.9340**▲	**0.5500**▲	**0.6391**▲	**0.8298**▲	–
perfect	339	1 687	B5	0.7082	0.8805	0.6639	0.7878	0.7729	0.6136
			LTR	**0.8150**▲	**0.9245**▲	**0.7640**▲	**0.8518**▲	**0.8909**▲	**0.7227**▲

Table 3: Results for the best baseline (B5) and the learning to rank method (LTR).

smoothing (LM), BM25, TFISF, and Recursive TF-ISF (R-TFISF). We follow related work and set $\mu = 0.1$ for R-TFISF, $k = 1$ and $b = 0$ for BM25 and $\mu = 250$ for LM (Fernández et al., 2011).

In our experiments, a query q is constructed using various combinations of surface forms of the two entities e_i and e_j and the relationship r. Each entity in the entity pair can be represented by its title, the titles of any redirect pages pointing to the entity's article, the n-grams used as anchors in Wikipedia to link to the article of the entity, or the union of them all. The relationship r can be represented by the terms in the relationship, synonyms in $wordnet(r)$, or by phrases in $word2vec(r)$.

First, we fix the way we represent r. Baseline B1 does not include any representation of r in the query. B2 includes the relationship terms of r, while B3 includes the relationship terms of r and the synonyms in $wordnet(r)$. B4 includes the terms of r and the phrases in $word2vec(r)$, and B5 includes the relationship terms of r, the synonyms in $wordnet(r)$ and the phrases in $word2vec(r)$. Combining these variations with the entity representations, we find that all combinations that use the titles as representation and R-TFISF as the retrieval function outperform all other combinations.[7] This can be explained by the fact that titles are least ambiguous, thus reducing the possibility of accidentally referring to other entities. BM25 and LC perform almost as well as R-TFISF, with only insignificant differences in performance.

Table 2 shows the best performing combination of each baseline, i.e., varying the representation of r and using titles and R-TFISF. B4 and B5 are the best performing baselines, suggesting that $word2vec(r)$ and $wordnet(r)$ are beneficial. B5 significantly outperforms all baselines except B4.

We also experiment with a supervised combination of the baseline rankers using LTR. Here, we consider each baseline ranker as a separate feature and train a ranking model. The trained model is not able to outperform the best individual baseline, however.

6.1 Learning to rank sentences

Next, we provide the results of our method using the features described in Section 4.2, exploring whether our learning to rank (LTR) approach improves over sentence retrieval models (RQ2). We compare an LTR model using Table 1's features against the best baseline (B5). Table 3 shows the results. Each group in the table contains the results for the entity pairs that have at least one candidate sentence of that relevance grade for B5 and LTR.

We find that LTR significantly outperforms B5 by a large margin. The absolute performance difference between LTR and B5 becomes larger for all metrics as we move from "fair" to "perfect," which shows that LTR is more robust than the baseline for entity pairs that have at least one high quality candidate sentence. LTR ranks the best possible sentence at the top of the ranking for ~83% of the cases for entity pairs that contain an "excellent" sentence and for ~72% of the cases for entity pairs that contain a "perfect" sentence.

Note that, as indicated in Section 5.1, we discard entity pairs that have only "bad" sentences in our experiments. For the sake of completeness, we report on the results for all entity pairs in our dataset—including those without any relevant sentences—in Table 4.

6.2 Relationship-dependent models

Relevant sentences may have different properties for different relationship types. For example, a sentence describing two entities being partners would have a different form than one describing that two entities costar in a movie. A similar

[7] We omit a full table of results due to space constraints.

Has one	# pairs	# sentences	Method	NDCG@1	NDCG@10	ERR@1	ERR@10	Exc@1	Per@1
-	1 476	5 689	B5	0.5776	0.6733	0.2804	0.3467	–	–
			LTR	**0.6285**▲	**0.6940**▲	**0.3155**▲	**0.3694**▲	–	–

Table 4: Results for the best baseline (B5) and the learning to rank method (LTR), using all entity pairs in the dataset, including those without any relevant sentences.

Relationship	# pairs	# sentences	NDCG@1	NDCG@10	ERR@1	ERR@10
⟨*MovieActor*, *CoCastsWith*, *MovieActor*⟩	410	1 403	0.8604	0.9436	0.3809	0.4546
⟨*TvActor*, *CoCastsWith*, *TvActor*⟩	210	626	0.8729	0.9482	0.3271	0.3845
⟨*MovieActor*, *IsDirectedBy*, *MovieDirector*⟩ ⟨*MovieDirector*, *Directs*, *MovieActor*⟩	112	492	0.8795	0.9396	0.4709	0.5261
⟨*Person*, *isChildOf*, *Person*⟩ ⟨*Person*, *isParentOf*, *Person*⟩	108	716	0.8428	0.9081	0.6395	0.7136
⟨*Person*, *isPartnerOf*, *Person*⟩ ⟨*Person*, *isSpouseOf*, *Person*⟩	155	877	0.8623	0.9441	0.6153	0.6939
⟨*Athlete*, *PlaysSameSportTeamAs*, *Athlete*⟩	98	321	0.8787	0.9535	0.3350	0.3996
Average results over all data	1 093	4 435	**0.8661**	**0.9395**	**0.4615**	**0.5287**
LTR (Table 3; fair)			0.8489	0.9375	0.4242	0.4980

Table 5: Results for relationship-dependent models. Similar relationships are grouped together.

idea was investigated in the context of QA for associating question and answer types (Yao et al., 2013). To answer (RQ3) we examine whether learning a relationship-dependent model improves over learning a single model for all types. We split our dataset per relationship type and train a model per type using 5-fold cross-validation within each. Table 5 shows the results.[8] Our method is robust across different relationships in terms of NDCG. However, we observe some variation in ERR as this metric is more sensitive to the distribution of relevant items than NDCG—the distribution over relevance grades varies per relationship type. For example, it is much more likely to find candidate sentences that have a high relevance grade for ⟨*Person*, *isSpouseOf*, *Person*⟩ than for ⟨*Athlete*, *PlaysSameSportTeamAs*, *Athlete*⟩ in our dataset. We plan to address this issue by exploring other corpora in the future.

The second-to-last row in Table 5 shows the averaged results over the different relationship types, which is a significant improvement over LTR at $p < 0.01$ for all metrics. This method ranks the best possible sentence at the top of the ranking for ~85% of the cases for entity pairs that contain an "excellent" sentence (~2% absolute improvement over LTR) and for ~75% of the cases for entity pairs that contain a "perfect" sentence (~3% absolute improvement over LTR).

[8] We omit Exc@1 and Per@1 due to space constraints.

6.3 Feature type analysis

Next, we analyze the impact of the feature types. Table 6 shows how performance varies when removing one feature type at a time from the full feature set. Relationship type features are the most important, although entity type features are important as well. This indicates that introducing features based on entities identified in the sentences and the relationship is beneficial for this task. Furthermore, the limited dependency on the source feature type indicates that our method might be able to generalize in other domains. Finally, text type features do contribute to retrieval effectiveness, although not significantly. Note that calculating the sentence features is straightforward, as none of our features requires heavy linguistic analysis.

Features	NDCG@1	NDCG@10	ERR@1	ERR@10
All	**0.8661**	**0.9395**	**0.4615**	**0.5287**
All∖text	0.8620	0.9372	0.4606	0.5274
All∖source	0.8598	0.9372	0.4582	0.5261
All∖entity	0.8421▽	0.9282▼	0.4497	0.5202▽
All∖relation	0.8183▼	0.9201▼	0.4352▼	0.5112▼

Table 6: Results using relationship-dependent models, removing individual feature types.

6.4 Error analysis

When looking at errors made by the system, we find that some are due to the fact that entity pairs might have more than one relationship (e.g., actors that costar in movies also being partners) but the selected sentence covers only one of the relationships.[9] For example, `Liza Minnelli` is the daughter of `Judy Garland`, but they have also costarred in a movie, which is the relationship of interest. The model ranks the sentence "Liza Minnelli is the daughter of singer and actress Judy Garland..." at the top, while the most relevant sentence is: "Judy Garland performed at the London Palladium with her then 18-year-old daughter Liza Minnelli in November 1964."

Sentences that contain the relationship in which we are interested, but for which this cannot be directly inferred, are another source of error. Consider, for example, the following sentence, which explains director `Christopher Nolan` directed actor `Christian Bale`: "Jackman starred in the 2006 film The Prestige, directed by Christopher Nolan and costarring Christian Bale, Michael Caine, and Scarlett Johansson". Even though the sentence contains the relationship of interest, it focuses on actor `Hugh Jackman`. The sentence "In 2004, after completing filming for The Machinist, Bale won the coveted role of Batman and his alter ego Bruce Wayne in Christopher Nolan's Batman Begins...", in contrast, refers to the two entities and the relationship of interest directly, resulting in a higher relevance grade. Our method, however, ranks the first sentence on top, as it contains more phrases that refer to the relationship.

7 Conclusions and Future Work

We have presented a method for explaining relationships between knowledge graph entities with human-readable descriptions. We first extract and enrich sentences that refer to an entity pair and then rank the sentences according to how well they describe the relationship. For ranking, we use learning to rank with a diverse set of features. Evaluation on a manually annotated dataset of "people" entities shows that our method significantly outperforms state-of-the-art sentence retrieval models for this task. Experimental results also show that using relationship-dependent models is beneficial.

In future work we aim to evaluate how our method performs on entities and relationships of any type and popularity, including tail entities and miscellaneous relationships. We also want to investigate moving beyond Wikipedia and extract candidate sentences from documents that are not related to the knowledge graph, such as web pages or news articles. Employing such documents also implies an investigation into more advanced coreference resolution methods.

Our analysis showed that sentences may cover different relationships between entities or different aspects of a single relationship—we aim to account for such cases in follow-up work. Furthermore, sentences may contain unnecessary information for explaining the relation of interest between two entities. Especially when we want to show the obtained results to end users, we may need to apply further processing of the sentences to improve their quality and readability. We would like to explore sentence compression techniques to address this. Finally, relationships between entities have an inherit temporal nature and we aim to explore ways to explain entity relationships and their changes over time.

Acknowledgments

This research was partially supported by the European Community's Seventh Framework Programme (FP7/2007-2013) under grant agreement nr 312827 (VOX-Pol), the Netherlands Organisation for Scientific Research (NWO) under project nrs 727.011.005, 612.001.116, HOR-11-10, 640.006.013, 612.066.930, CI-14-25, SH-322-15, Amsterdam Data Science, the Dutch national program COMMIT, the ESF Research Network Program ELIAS, the Elite Network Shifts project funded by the Royal Dutch Academy of Sciences (KNAW), the Netherlands eScience Center under project nr 027.012.105, the Yahoo! Faculty Research and Engagement Program, the Microsoft Research PhD program, and the HPC Fund.

References

Arvind Agarwal, Hema Raghavan, Karthik Subbian, Prem Melville, Richard D. Lawrence, David C. Gondek, and James Fan. 2012. Learning to rank for robust question answering. In *Proceedings of the 21st ACM international conference on Information and knowledge management*, pages 833–842. ACM.

James Allan, Courtney Wade, and Alvaro Bolivar. 2003. Retrieval and novelty detection at the sentence level. In *Proceedings of the 26th annual international ACM SIGIR conference on Research and*

[9] The annotators marked sentences that do not refer to the relationship of interest as "bad" but indicated whether they describe another relationship or not. We plan to account for such cases in future work.

development in informaion retrieval, pages 314–321. ACM.

Ricardo Baeza-Yates, Berthier Ribeiro-Neto, et al. 1999. *Modern information retrieval*, volume 463. ACM press New York.

Roi Blanco and Hugo Zaragoza. 2010. Finding support sentences for entities. In *Proceedings of the 33rd international ACM SIGIR conference on Research and development in information retrieval*, pages 339–346. ACM.

Roi Blanco, Berkant Barla Cambazoglu, Peter Mika, and Nicolas Torzec. 2013. Entity recommendations in web search. In *The Semantic Web–ISWC 2013*, pages 33–48. Springer.

Leo Breiman. 2001. Random forests. *Mach. Learn.*, 45(1):5–32.

Christopher J.C. Burges, Krysta Marie Svore, Paul N. Bennett, Andrzej Pastusiak, and Qiang Wu. 2011. Learning to rank using an ensemble of lambda-gradient models. In *Yahoo! Learning to Rank Challenge*, pages 25–35.

Olivier Chapelle, Donald Metzler, Ya Zhang, and Pierre Grinspan. 2009. Expected reciprocal rank for graded relevance. In *Proceedings of the 18th ACM conference on Information and knowledge management*, pages 621–630. ACM.

Mark Craven, Dan DiPasquo, Dayne Freitag, Andrew McCallum, Tom Mitchell, Kamal Nigam, and Seán Slattery. 2000. Learning to construct knowledge bases from the world wide web. *Artificial Intelligence*, 118(1–2):69–113.

Alen Doko, Maja Štula, and Darko Stipaničev. 2013. A recursive TF-ISF based sentence retrieval method with local context. *International Journal of Machine Learning and Computing*, 3(2):195–200.

Xin Dong, Evgeniy Gabrilovich, Geremy Heitz, Wilko Horn, Ni Lao, Kevin Murphy, Thomas Strohmann, Shaohua Sun, and Wei Zhang. 2014. Knowledge vault: A web-scale approach to probabilistic knowledge fusion. In *Proceedings of the 20th ACM SIGKDD International Conference on Knowledge Discovery and Data Mining*, KDD '14, pages 601–610. ACM.

James Fan, Raphael Hoffman, Aditya Kalyanpur, Sebastian Riedel, Fabian Suchanek, and Pratim Partha Talukdar, 2012. *Proceedings of the Joint Workshop on Automatic Knowledge Base Construction and Web-scale Knowledge Extraction (AKBC-WEKEX)*, chapter Proceedings of the Joint Workshop on Automatic Knowledge Base Construction and Web-scale Knowledge Extraction (AKBC-WEKEX). Association for Computational Linguistics.

Lujun Fang, Anish Das Sarma, Cong Yu, and Philip Bohannon. 2011. Rex: explaining relationships between entity pairs. *Proceedings of the VLDB Endowment*, 5(3):241–252.

Ronald T Fernández, David E. Losada, and Leif Azzopardi. 2011. Extending the language modeling framework for sentence retrieval to include local context. *Information Retrieval*, 14(4):355–389.

Lynette Hirschman and Robert Gaizauskas. 2001. Natural language question answering: the view from here. *Natural Language Engineering*, 7(04):275–300.

Kalervo Järvelin and Jaana Kekäläinen. 2002. Cumulated gain-based evaluation of IR techniques. *ACM Transactions on Information Systems (TOIS)*, 20(4):422–446.

Gary Geunbae Lee, Jungyun Seo, Seungwoo Lee, Hanmin Jung, Bong-Hyun Cho, Changki Lee, Byung-Kwan Kwak, Jeongwon Cha, Dongseok Kim, JooHui An, et al. 2001. SiteQ: Engineering high performance QA system using lexico-semantic pattern matching and shallow NLP. In *TREC*.

Heeyoung Lee, Yves Peirsman, Angel Chang, Nathanael Chambers, Mihai Surdeanu, and Dan Jurafsky. 2011. Stanford's multi-pass sieve coreference resolution system at the CoNLL-2011 shared task. In *Proceedings of the Fifteenth Conference on Computational Natural Language Learning: Shared Task*, pages 28–34. Association for Computational Linguistics.

David E. Losada. 2008. A study of statistical query expansion strategies for sentence retrieval. In *Proceedings of the SIGIR 2008 Workshop on Focused Retrieval*, pages 37–44.

Edgar Meij, Wouter Weerkamp, and Maarten de Rijke. 2012. Adding semantics to microblog posts. In *Proceedings of the fifth ACM international conference on Web search and data mining*, pages 563–572. ACM.

Tomas Mikolov, Ilya Sutskever, Kai Chen, Greg S. Corrado, and Jeff Dean. 2013. Distributed representations of words and phrases and their compositionality. In *Advances in Neural Information Processing Systems*, pages 3111–3119.

David Milne and Ian H. Witten. 2008. Learning to link with Wikipedia. In *Proceedings of the 17th ACM conference on Information and knowledge management*, pages 509–518. ACM.

Mike Mintz, Steven Bills, Rion Snow, and Dan Jurafsky. 2009. Distant supervision for relation extraction without labeled data. In *Proceedings of the Joint Conference of the 47th Annual Meeting of the ACL and the 4th International Joint Conference on Natural Language Processing of the AFNLP: Volume 2-Volume 2*, pages 1003–1011. Association for Computational Linguistics.

Vanessa Murdock and W. Bruce Croft. 2005. A translation model for sentence retrieval. In *Proceedings of the conference on Human Language Technology and Empirical Methods in Natural Language Processing*, pages 684–691. Association for Computational Linguistics.

Vanessa Graham Murdock. 2006. *Aspects of Sentence Retrieval*. Ph.D. thesis, University of Massachusetts Amherst.

Mihai Surdeanu, Massimiliano Ciaramita, and Hugo Zaragoza. 2011. Learning to rank answers to non-factoid questions from web collections. *Computational Linguistics*, 37(2):351–383.

Manos Tsagkias, Maarten de Rijke, and Wouter Weerkamp. 2011. Linking online news and social media. In *WSDM 2011: Fourth ACM International Conference on Web Search and Data Mining*. ACM, February.

Jason Weston, Antoine Bordes, Oksana Yakhnenko, and Nicolas Usunier. 2013. Connecting language and knowledge bases with embedding models for relation extraction. In *Proceedings of the 2013 Conference on Empirical Methods in Natural Language Processing, EMNLP 2013*.

Ian Witten and David Milne. 2008. An effective, low-cost measure of semantic relatedness obtained from wikipedia links. In *Proceeding of AAAI Workshop on Wikipedia and Artificial Intelligence: an Evolving Synergy, AAAI Press, Chicago, USA*, pages 25–30.

Fei Wu and Daniel S Weld. 2010. Open information extraction using wikipedia. In *Proceedings of the 48th Annual Meeting of the Association for Computational Linguistics*, pages 118–127. Association for Computational Linguistics.

Xuchen Yao, Benjamin Van Durme, and Peter Clark. 2013. Automatic coupling of answer extraction and information retrieval. In *Proceedings of the 51st Annual Meeting of the Association for Computational Linguistics (Volume 2: Short Papers)*, pages 159–165. Association for Computational Linguistics.

Bring you to the past: Automatic Generation of Topically Relevant Event Chronicles

Tao Ge[1,2], Wenzhe Pei[1], Heng Ji[3], Sujian Li[1,2], Baobao Chang[1,2], Zhifang Sui[1,2]
[1]Key Laboratory of Computational Linguistics, Ministry of Education,
School of EECS, Peking University, Beijing, 100871, China
[2]Collaborative Innovation Center for Language Ability, Xuzhou, Jiangsu, 221009, China
[3]Computer Science Department, Rensselaer Polytechnic Institute, Troy, NY 12180, USA
getao@pku.edu.cn, wenzhepei@pku.edu.cn, jih@rpi.edu,
lisujian@pku.edu.cn, chbb@pku.edu.cn, szf@pku.edu.cn

Abstract

An event chronicle provides people with an easy and fast access to learn the past. In this paper, we propose the first novel approach to automatically generate a topically relevant event chronicle during a certain period given a reference chronicle during another period. Our approach consists of two core components – a time-aware hierarchical Bayesian model for event detection, and a learning-to-rank model to select the salient events to construct the final chronicle. Experimental results demonstrate our approach is promising to tackle this new problem.

1 Introduction

Human civilization has developed for thousands of years. During the long period, history witnessed the changes of societies and dynasties, the revolution of science and technology, as well as the emergency of celebrities, which are great wealth for later generations. Even nowadays, people usually look back through history either for their work or interests. Among various ways to learn history, many people prefer reading an event chronicle summarizing important events in the past, which saves much time and efforts.

The left part of Figure 1 shows a disaster event chronicle from Infoplease[1], by which people can easily learn important disaster events in 2009. Unfortunately, almost all the available event chronicles are created and edited manually, which requires editors to learn everything that happened in the past. Even if an editor tries her best to generate an event chronicle, she still cannot guarantee that all the important events are included. Moreover, when new events happen in the future, she needs to update the chronicle in time, which is laborious. For example, the event chronicle of 2010 in Wikipedia[2] has been edited 8,488 times by 3,211 distinct editors since this page was created. In addition, event chronicles can vary according to topic preferences. Some event chronicles are mainly about disasters while others may focus more on sports. For people interested in sports, the event chronicle in Figure 1 is undesirable. Due to the diversity of event chronicles, it is common that an event chronicle regarding a specific topic for some certain period is unavailable. If editing an event chronicle can be done by computers, people can have an overview of any period according to their interests and do not have to wait for human editing, which will largely speed up knowledge acquisition and popularization.

Based on this motivation, we propose a new task of automatic event chronicle generation, whose goal is to generate a topically relevant event chronicle for some period based on a reference chronicle of another period. For example, if an disaster event chronicle during 2009 is available, we can use it to generate a disaster chronicle during 2010 from a news collection, as shown in Figure 1.

To achieve this goal, we need to know what events happened during the target period, whether these events are topically relevant to the chronicle, and whether they are important enough to be included, since an event chronicle has only a limited number of entries. To tackle these challenges, we propose an approach consisting of two core components – an event detection component based on a novel time-aware hierarchical Bayesian model and a learning-to-rank component to select the salient events to construct the final chronicle. Our event detection model can not only learn topic preferences of the reference chronicle and measure topical relevance of an event to the chronicle

[1]http://www.infoplease.com/world/disasters/2009.html

[2]http://en.wikipedia.org/wiki/2010

Proceedings of the 53rd Annual Meeting of the Association for Computational Linguistics and the 7th International Joint Conference on Natural Language Processing, pages 575–585,
Beijing, China, July 26-31, 2015. ©2015 Association for Computational Linguistics

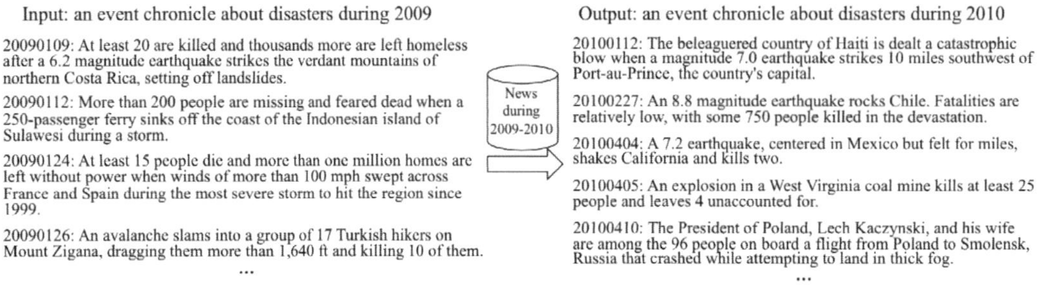

Figure 1: Example for automatic generation of a topically relevant event chronicle.

but also can effectively distinguish similar events by taking into account time information and event-specific details. Experimental results show our approach significantly outperforms baseline methods and that is promising to tackle this new problem.

The major novel contributions of this paper are:

- We propose a new task automatic generation of a topically relevant event chronicle, which is meaningful and has never been studied to the best of our knowledge.

- We design a general approach to tackle this new problem, which is language-independent, domain-independent and scalable to any arbitrary topics.

- We design a novel event detection model. It outperforms the state-of-the-art event detection model for generating topically relevant event chronicles.

2 Terminology and Task Overview

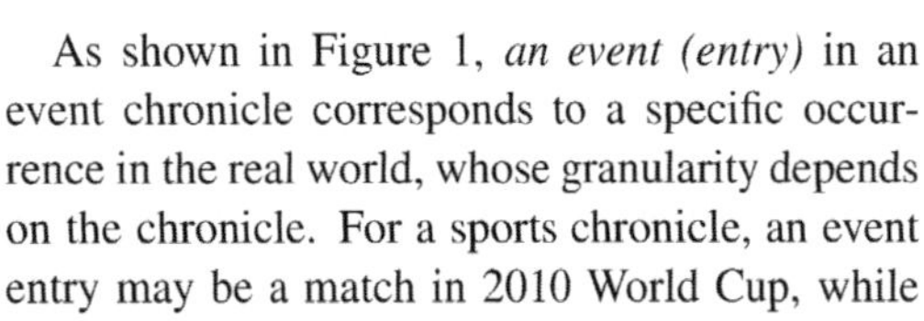

Figure 2: An example of relevance-topic-event hierarchical structure for a disaster event chronicle.

As shown in Figure 1, *an event (entry)* in an event chronicle corresponds to a specific occurrence in the real world, whose granularity depends on the chronicle. For a sports chronicle, an event entry may be a match in 2010 World Cup, while for a comprehensive chronicle, the World Cup is regarded as one event. In general, an event can be represented by a cluster of documents related to it. *The topic* of an event can be considered as the event class. For example, we can call the topic of MH17 crash as air crash (fine-grained) or disaster (coarse-grained). The relation between topic and event is shown through the example in Figure 2.

An event chronicle is a set of important events occurring in the past. Event chronicles vary according to topic preferences. For the disaster chronicle shown in Figure 1, earthquakes and air crashes are relevant topics while election is not. Hence, we can use a hierarchical structure to organize documents in a corpus, as Figure 2 shows.

Formally, we define an event chronicle $\mathbb{E} = \{e_1, e_2, ..., e_n\}$ where e_i is an event entry in $\mathbb{E}$ and it can be represented by a tuple $e_i = \langle D_{e_i}, t_{e_i}, z_{e_i} \rangle$. D_{e_i} denotes the set of documents about e_i, t_{e_i} is e_i's time and z_{e_i} is e_i's topic. Specially, we use Λ to denote the time period (interval) covered by $\mathbb{E}$, and θ to denote the topic distribution of $\mathbb{E}$, which reflects $\mathbb{E}$'s topic preferences.

As shown in Figure 1, the goal of our task is to generate an (target) event chronicle $\mathbb{E}_T$ during Λ_T based on a reference chronicle $\mathbb{E}_R$ during Λ_R. The topic distributions of $\mathbb{E}_T$ and $\mathbb{E}_R$ (i.e., θ_T and θ_R) should be consistent.

3 Event Detection

3.1 Challenges of Event Detection

(d_1) A magnitude-6.1 earthquake in southern China's Yunnan province destroyed thousands of home on Sunday, killing at least 367 people. (Aug 2014)

(d_2) A massive earthquake devastated Sichuan province in southwest China, leaving five million people homeless and taking some 87,000 lives. (May 2008)

(d_3) A 3.4-magnitude earthquake occurred in and around the city of Napa, California on Sunday, killing one person and injuring about 200. (Aug 2014)

Figure 3: Documents that are lexically similar but refer to different events. The underlined words are event-specific words.

For our task, the first step is to detect topically relevant events from a corpus. A good event detection model should be able to

(1) measure the topical relevance of a detected event to the reference chronicle.

(2) consider document time information.

(3) look into a document's event-specific details.

The first requirement is to identify topically relevant events since we want to generate a topically relevant chronicle. The second and third requirements are for effectively distinguishing events, especially similar events like the example in Figure 3. To distinguish the similar events, we must consider document time information (for distinguishing events in d_1 and d_2) and look into the document's event-specific details (the underlined words in Figure 3) (for distinguishing events in d_1 and d_3).

3.2 TaHBM: A Time-aware Hierarchical Bayesian Model

To tackle all the above challenges mentioned in Section 3.1, which cannot be tackled by conventional detection methods (e.g., agglomerative clustering), we propose a **T**ime-**a**ware **H**ierarchical **B**ayesian **M**odel (TaHBM) for detecting events.

Model Overview

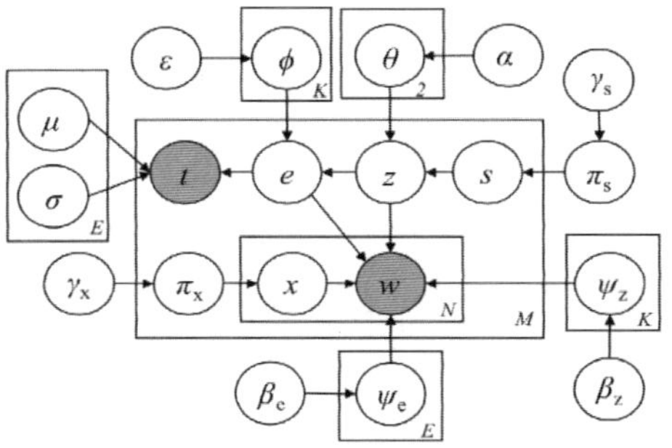

Figure 4: The plate diagram of TaHBM. The shaded nodes are observable nodes.

The plate diagram and generative story of TaHBM are depicted in Figure 4 and Figure 5 respectively. For a corpus with M documents, TaHBM assumes each document has three labels – s, z, and e. s is a binary variable indicating a document's topical relevance to the reference event chronicle, whose distribution is a Bernoulli distribution π_s drawn from a Beta distribution with symmetric hyperparameter γ_s. s=1 indicates the document is topically relevant to the chronicle while s=0 means not. z is a document's topic label drawn from a K-dimensional multinomial distribution θ, and e is a document's event label drawn from an E-dimensional multinomial distribution ϕ. θ and ϕ are drawn from Dirichlet distributions with symmetric hyperparameter α and ε respectively. For an event e', it can be represented by a set of documents whose event label is e'.

Draw $\pi_s \sim Beta(\gamma_s)$
For each $s \in \{0, 1\}$: draw $\theta^{(s)} \sim Dir(\alpha)$
For each $z = 1, 2, 3, ..., K$: draw $\phi^{(z)} \sim Dir(\varepsilon)$, $\psi_z^{(z)} \sim Dir(\beta_z)$
For each $e = 1, 2, 3, ..., E$: draw $\psi_e^{(e)} \sim Dir(\beta_e)$
For each document $m = 1, 2, 3, ..., M$:
    Draw $s \sim Bernoulli(\pi_s)$
    Draw $z \sim Multi(\theta^{(s)})$
    Draw $e \sim Multi(\phi^{(z)})$
    Draw $t' \sim Gaussian(\mu_e, \sigma_e), t \leftarrow \lfloor t' \rfloor$
    Draw $\pi_x \sim Beta(\gamma_x)$
    For each word w in document m:
        Draw $x \sim Bernoulli(\pi_x)$
        If $x = 0$: draw $w \sim \psi_z^{(z)}$
        Else: draw $w \sim \psi_e^{(e)}$

Figure 5: The generative story of TaHBM

In TaHBM, the relations among s, z and e are similar to the hierarchical structure in Figure 2. Based on the dependencies among s, z and e, we can compute the topical relevance of an event to the reference chronicle by Eq (1) where $P(e|z)$, $P(e)$, $P(s)$ and $P(z|s)$ can be estimated using Bayesian inference (some details of estimation of $P(s)$ and $P(s|z)$ will be discussed in Section 3.3) and thus we solve the first challenge in Section 3.1 (i.e., topical relevance measure problem).

$$P(s|e) = \frac{P(s) \times P(z|s) \times P(e|z)}{P(e)} \quad (1)$$

Now, we introduce how to tackle the second challenge – how to take into account a document's time information for distinguishing events. In TaHBM, we introduce t, document timestamps. We assume $t = \lfloor t' \rfloor$ where t' is drawn from a Gaussian distribution with mean μ and variance σ^2. Each event e corresponds to a specific Gaussian distribution which serves as a temporal constraint for e. A Gaussian distribution has only one peak around where the probability is concentrated. Its value trends to zero if a point lies far away from the mean. For this reason, a Gaussian distribution is suitable to describe an event's temporal distribution whose probability usually concentrates around the event's burst time and it will be close to zero if time lies far from the burst time. Figure 6 shows the temporal distribution of *the July 2009 Urumqi riots*[3]. The probability of this event concentrates around the 7th day. If we use a Gaussian distribution (the dashed curve in Figure 6) to constrain this event's time scope, the documents whose timestamps are beyond this scope are unlikely to be grouped into this event's cluster.

Now that the problems of topical relevance measure and temporal constraints have been solved, we discuss how to identify event-specific details of a document for distinguishing events. By analyzing the documents shown in Figure 3, we find that general words (e.g., *earthquake, kill, injury, devastate*) indicate the document's topic while words about event-specific details (e.g., *Napa, California, 3.4-magnitude*) are helpful to determine what events the document talks about. Assuming a person is asked to analyze what event a document discusses, it would be a natural way to first determine topic of the document based its general words, and then determine what event it talks about given its topic, timestamp and event-specific details, which is exactly the way our TaHBM works.

For simplicity, we call the general words as **topic words** and call the words describing event-specific information as **event words**. Inspired by the idea of Chemudugunta et al. (2007), given the different roles these two kinds of words play, we assume words in a document are generated by two distributions: topic words are generated by a topic word distribution ψ_z while event words are generated by an event word distribution ψ_e. ψ_z and ψ_e are $|V|$-dimensional multinomial distributions drawn from Dirichlet distributions with symmetric hyperparameter β_z and β_e respectively, where $|V|$ denotes the size of vocabulary V. A binary indicator x, which is generated by a Bernoulli distribution π_x drawn from a Beta distribution with symmetric hyperparameter γ_x, determines whether a word is generated by ψ_z or ψ_e. Specifically, if $x = 0$, a word is drawn from ψ_z; otherwise the

[3]http://en.wikipedia.org/wiki/July_2009_Urumqi_riots

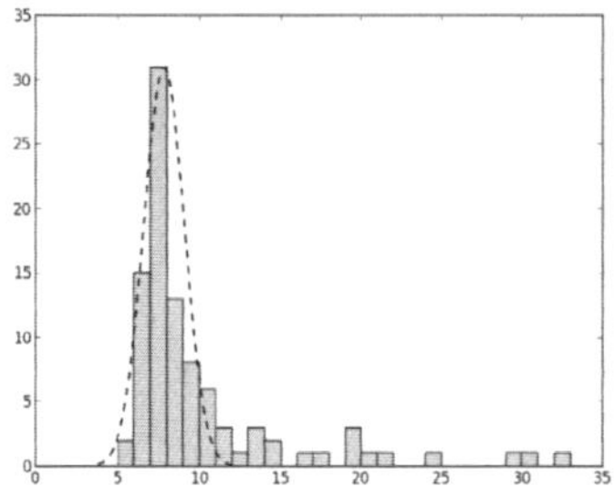

Figure 6: The temporal distribution of documents about the Urumqi riots, which can be described by a Gaussian distribution (the dashed curve). The horizontal axis is time (day) and the vertical axis is the number of documents about this event.

word is drawn from ψ_e. Since ψ_z is shared by all events of one topic, it can be seen as a background word distribution which captures general aspects. In contrast, ψ_e tends to describe the event-specific aspects. In this way, we can model a document's general and specific aspects and use the information to better distinguish similar events[4].

Model Inference

Like most Bayesian models, we use collapsed Gibbs sampling for model inference in TaHBM. For a document m, we present the conditional probability of its latent variables s, z and x for sampling:

$$P(s_m|\vec{s}_{\neg m}, \vec{z}, \gamma_s, \alpha) = \frac{c_s + \gamma_s}{\sum_s (c_s + \gamma_s)} \times \frac{c_{s,z_m} + \alpha}{\sum_z (c_{s,z} + \alpha)} \quad (2)$$

$$\begin{aligned} &P(z_m|\vec{z}_{\neg m}, \vec{e}, \vec{s}, \vec{w}_m, \vec{x}_m, \alpha, \varepsilon, \beta_z) \\ &= \frac{c_{s_m,z} + \alpha}{\sum_z (c_{s_m,z} + \alpha)} \times \frac{c_{z,e_m} + \varepsilon}{\sum_e (c_{z,e} + \varepsilon)} \\ &\times \prod_{n=1}^{N_m} \left(\frac{c_{z,w_{m,n}} + \sum_{i=1}^{n-1} \mathbf{1}(w_{m,i} = w_{m,n}) + \beta_z}{\sum_{w \in V} (c_{z,w} + \beta_z) + n - 1}\right)^{(1-x_{m,n})} \end{aligned} \quad (3)$$

$$\begin{aligned} &P(x_{m,n}|\vec{w}_m, \vec{x}_{\neg m,n}, z_m, e_m, \gamma_x) \\ &= \frac{c_{m,x} + \gamma_x}{N_m + 2\gamma_x} \times \left(\frac{c_{z_m,w_{m,n}} + \beta_z}{\sum_{w \in V} (c_{z_m,w} + \beta_z)}\right)^{(1-x)} \\ &\times \left(\frac{c_{e_m,w_{m,n}} + \beta_e}{\sum_{w \in V} (c_{e_m,w} + \beta_e)}\right)^{x} \end{aligned} \quad (4)$$

where V denotes the vocabulary, $w_{m,n}$ is the nth word in a document m, c_s is the count of documents with topic relevance label s, $c_{s,z}$ is the count

[4]TaHBM is language-independent, which can identify event words without name tagging. But if name tagging results are available, we can also exploit them (e.g., we can fix x of a named entity specific to an event to 1 during inference.).

of documents with topic relevance label s and topic label z, $c_{z,w}$ is the count of word w whose document's topic label is z, $c_{m,x}$ is the count of words with binary indicator label x in m and $\mathbf{1}(\cdot)$ is an indicator function.

Specially, for variable e which is dependent on the Gaussian distribution, its conditional probability for sampling is computed as Eq (5):

$$\begin{aligned} & P(e_m|\vec{e}_{\neg m},\vec{z},\vec{w}_m,\vec{x}_m,t_m,\varepsilon,\beta_e,\mu_e,\sigma_e) \\ & = \frac{c_{z_m,e}+\varepsilon}{\sum_e(c_{z_m,e}+\varepsilon)} \times \int_{t_m}^{t_m+1} p_G(t_m;\mu_e,\sigma'_e) \\ & \times \prod_{n=1}^{N_m} \left(\frac{c_{e,w_{m,n}}+\sum_{i=1}^{n-1}\mathbf{1}(w_{m,i}=w_{m,n})+\beta_e}{\sum_{w\in V}(c_{e,w}+\beta_e)+n-1}\right)^{x_{m,n}} \end{aligned} \quad (5)$$

where $p_G(x;\mu,\sigma)$ is a Gaussian probability mass function with parameter μ and σ.

The function $p_G(\cdot)$ can be seen as the temporal distribution of an event, as discussed before. In this sense, the temporal distribution of the whole corpus can be considered as a mixture of Gaussian distributions of events. As a natural way to estimate parameters of mixture of Gaussians, we use EM algorithm (Bilmes, 1998). In fact, Eq (5) can be seen as the E-step. The M-step of EM updates μ and σ as follows:

$$\mu_e = \frac{\sum_{d\in D_e} t_d}{|D_e|}, \sigma_e = \sqrt{\frac{\sum_{d\in D_e}(t_d-\mu_e)^2}{|D_e|}} \quad (6)$$

where t_d is document d's timestamp and D_e is the set of documents with event label e.

Specially, for sampling e we use σ'_e defined as $\sigma'_e = \sigma_e + \tau$ (τ is a small number for smoothing[5]) because when σ is very small (e.g., $\sigma = 0$), an event's temporal scope will be strictly constrained. Using σ'_e can help the model overcome this "trap" for better parameter estimation.

Above all, the model inference and parameter estimation procedure can be summarized by algorithm 1.

Algorithm 1 Model inference for TaHBM

```
Initialize parameters in TaHBM;
for each iteration do
    for each document d in the corpus do
        sample s according to Eq (2)
        sample z according to Eq (3)
        sample e according to Eq (5)
        for each word w in d do
            sample x according to Eq (4)
        end for
    end for
    for each event e do
        update μ_e, σ_e according to Eq (6)
    end for
end for
```

3.3 Learn Topic Preferences of the Event Chronicle

A prerequisite to use Eq (1) to compute an event's topical relevance to an event chronicle is that we know $P(s)$ and $P(z|s)$ which reflects topic preferences of the event chronicle. Nonetheless, $P(s)$ and $P(z|s)$ vary according to different event chronicles. Hence, we cannot directly estimate them in an unsupervised manner; instead, we provide TaHBM some "supervision". As we mentioned in section 3.2, the variable s indicates a document's topical relevance to the event chronicle. For some documents, s label can be easily derived with high accuracy so that we can exploit the information to learn the topic preferences.

To obtain the labeled data, we use the description of each event entry in the reference chronicle $\mathbb{E}_R$ during period Λ_R as a query to retrieve relevant documents in the corpus using Lucene (Jakarta, 2004) which is an information retrieval software library. We define $\mathscr{R}$ as the set of documents in hits of any event entry in the reference chronicle returned by Lucene:

$$\mathscr{R} = \cup_{e\in\mathbb{E}_R} Hit(e)$$

where $Hit(e)$ is the complete hit list of event e returned by Lucene. For document d with timestamp t_d, if $d \notin \mathscr{R}$ and $t_d \in \Lambda_R$, then d is considered irrelevant to the event chronicle and thus it would be labeled as a negative example.

To generate positive examples, we use a strict criterion since we cannot guarantee that all the documents in $\mathscr{R}$ are actually relevant. To precisely generate positive examples, a document d is labeled as positive only if it satisfies the **positive condition** which is defined as follows:

$$\exists_{e\in\mathbb{E}_R} 0 \le t_d - t_e \le 10 \wedge sim(d,e) \ge 0.4$$

where t_e is time[6] of event e, provided by the reference chronicle. $sim(d,e)$ is Lucene's score of d given query e. According to the positive condition, a positive document example must be lexi-

[5] τ is set to 0.5 in our experiments.

[6] The time unit of t_d and t_e is one day.

cally similar to some event in the reference chronicle and its timestamp is close to the event's time.

As a result, we can use the labeled data to learn topic preferences of the event chronicle. For the labeled documents, s is fixed during model inference. In contrast, for documents that are not labeled, s is sampled by Eq (2). In this manner, TaHBM can learn topic preferences (i.e., $P(z|s)$) without any manually labeled data and thus can measure the topical relevance between an event and the reference chronicle.

4 Event Ranking

Generating an event chronicle is beyond event detection because we cannot use all detected events to generate the chronicle with a limited number of entries. We propose to use learning-to-rank techniques to select the most salient events to generate the final chronicle since we believe the reference event chronicle can teach us the principles of selecting salient events. Specifically, we use SVM-Rank (Joachims, 2006).

4.1 Training and Test Set Generation

The event detection component returns many document clusters, each of which represents an event. As Section 3.2 shows, each event has a Gaussian distribution whose mean indicates its burst time in TaHBM. We use the events whose burst time is during the reference chronicle's period as training examples and treat those during the target chronicle's period as test examples. Formally, the training set and test set are defined as follows:

$$Train = \{e|\mu_e \in \Lambda_R\}, Test = \{e|\mu_e \in \Lambda_T\}$$

In the training set, events containing at least one positive document (i.e. relevant to the event chronicle) in Section 3.3 are labeled as high rank priority while those without positive documents are labeled as low priority.

4.2 Features

We use the following features to train the ranking model, all of which can be provided by TaHBM.

- $P(s=1|e)$: the probability that an event e is topically relevant to the reference chronicle.
- $P(e|z)$: the probability reflects an event's impact given its topic.
- σ_e: the parameter of an event e's Gaussian distribution. It determines the 'bandwidth' of the Gaussian distribution and thus can be considered as the time span of e.
- $|D_e|$: the number of documents related to event e, reflecting the impact of e.
- $\frac{|D_e|}{\sigma_e}$: For an event with a long time span (e.g., Premier League), the number of relevant documents is large but its impact may not be profound. Hence, we use $\frac{|D_e|}{\sigma_e}$ to normalize $|D_e|$, which may better reflect the impact of e.

5 Experiments

5.1 Experiment Setting

Data: We use various event chronicles during 2009 as references to generate their counterparts during 2010. Specifically, we collected disaster, sports, war, politics and comprehensive chronicles during 2009 from mapreport[7], infoplease and Wikipedia[8]. To generate chronicles during 2010, we use 2009-2010 APW and Xinhua news in English Gigaword (Graff et al., 2003) and remove documents whose titles and first paragraphs do not include any burst words. We detect burst words using Kleinberg algorithm (Kleinberg, 2003), which is a 2-state finite automaton model and widely used to detect bursts. In total, there are 140,557 documents in the corpus.

Preprocessing: We remove stopwords and use Stanford CoreNLP (Manning et al., 2014) to do lemmatization.

Parameter setting: For TaHBM, we empirically set $\alpha = 0.05$, $\beta_z = 0.005$, $\beta_e = 0.0001$, $\gamma_s = 0.05$, $\gamma_x = 0.5$, $\varepsilon = 0.01$, the number of topics $K = 50$, and the number of events $E = 5000$. We run Gibbs sampler for 2000 iterations with burn-in period of 500 for inference. For event ranking, we set regularization parameter of SVMRank $c = 0.1$.

Chronicle display: We use a heuristic way to generate the description of each event. Since the first paragraph of a news article is usually a good summary of the article and the earliest document in a cluster usually explicitly describes the event, for an event represented by a document cluster, we choose the first paragraph of the earliest document written in 2010 in the cluster to generate the event's description. The earliest document's timestamp is considered as the event's time.

[7] http://www.mapreport.com

[8] http://en.wikipedia.org/wiki/2009

5.2 Evaluation Methods and Baselines

Since there is no existing evaluation metric for the new task, we design a method for evaluation.

Although there are manually edited event chronicles on the web, which may serve as references for evaluation, they are often incomplete. For example, the 2010 politics event chronicle on Wikipedia has only two event entries. Hence, we first pool all event entries of existing chronicles on the web and chronicles generated by approaches evaluated in this paper and then have 3 human assessors judge each event entry for generating a ground truth based on its topical relevance, impact and description according to the standard of the reference chronicles. An event entry will be included in the ground-truth only if it is selected as a candidate by at least two human judges. On average, the existing event chronicles on the web cover 50.3% of event entries in the ground-truth.

Given the ground truth, we can use *Precision@k* to evaluate an event chronicle's quality.

$$Precision@k = |\mathbb{E}_G \cap \mathbb{E}_{topk}|/k$$

where $\mathbb{E}_G$ and $\mathbb{E}_{topk}$ are ground-truth chronicle and the chronicle with top k entries generated by an approach respectively. If there are multiple event entries corresponding to one event in the ground-truth, only one is counted.

For comparison, we choose several baseline approaches. Note that event detection models except TaHBM do not provide features used in learning-to-rank model. For these detection models, we use a criterion that considers both relevance and importance to rank events:

$$rankscore_{basic}(e) = \sum_{d \in D_e} max_{e' \in \mathbb{E}_R} sim(d, e')$$

where $\mathbb{E}_R$ is the reference chronicle and $sim(d, e')$ is Lucene's score of document d given query e'. We call this ranking criterion as **basic criterion**.

- Random: We randomly select k documents to generate the chronicle.
- NB+basic: Since TaHBM is essentially an extension of NB, we use Naive Bayes (NB) to detect events and basic ranking criterion to rank events.
- B-HAC+basic: We use hierarchical agglomerative clustering (HAC) based on BurstVSM schema (Zhao et al., 2012) to detect events, which is the state-of-the-art event detection method for general domains.
- TaHBM+basic: we use this baseline to verify the effectiveness of learning-to-rank.

As TaHBM, the number of clusters in NB is set to 5000 for comparison. For B-HAC, we adopt the same setting with (Zhao et al., 2012).

5.3 Experiment Results

Using the evaluation method introduced above, we can conduct a quantitative evaluation for event chronicle generation approaches[9].

Table 1 shows the overall performance. Our approach outperforms the baselines for all chronicles. TaHBM beats other detection models for chronicle generation owing to its ability of incorporating the temporal information and identification of event-specific details of a document. Moreover, learning-to-ranking is proven more effective to rank events than the basic ranking criterion.

Among these 5 chronicles, almost all approaches perform best on disaster event chronicle while worst on sports event chronicle. We analyzed the results and found that many event entries in the sports event chronicle are about the opening match, or the first-round match of a tournament due to the display method described in Section 5.1. According to the reference sport event chronicle, however, only matches after quarterfinals in a tournament are qualified to be event entries. In other words, a sports chronicle should provide information about the results of semi-final and final, and the champion of the tournament instead of the first-round match's result, which accounts for the poor performance. In contrast, the earliest document about a disaster event always directly describes the disaster event while the following reports usually concern responses to the event such as humanitarian aids and condolence from the world leaders. The patterns of reporting war events are similar to those of disasters, thus the quality of war chronicle is also good. Politics is somewhat complex because some political events (e.g., election) are arranged in advance while others (e.g., government shutdown) are unexpected. It is notable that for generating comprehensive event chronicles, learning-to-rank does

[9]Due to the space limitation, we display chronicles generated by our approach in the supplementary notes.

	sports		politics		disaster		war		comprehensive	
	P@50	P@100	P@50	P@100	P@50	P@100	P@50	P@100	P@50	P@100
Random	0.02	0.08	0	0	0.02	0.04	0	0	0.02	0.03
NB+basic	0.08	0.12	0.18	0.19	0.42	0.36	0.18	0.17	0.38	0.31
B-HAC+basic	0.10	0.13	0.30	0.26	0.50	0.47	0.30	0.22	0.36	0.32
TaHBM+basic	0.18	**0.15**	0.30	0.29	0.50	0.43	0.46	0.36	0.38	**0.33**
Our approach	**0.20**	**0.15**	**0.38**	**0.36**	**0.64**	**0.53**	**0.54**	**0.41**	**0.40**	**0.33**

Table 1: Performance of event chronicle generation.

	Topically Irrelevant	Trivial Events	Indirect Description	Redundant Entries
disaster	31.91%	17.02%	44.68%	6.38%
sports	38.82%	55.29%	3.52%	2.35%
comp	-	67.16%	31.34%	1.49%

Table 2: Proportion of errors in disaster, sports and comprehensive event chronicles.

not show significant improvement. A possible reason is that a comprehensive event chronicle does not care the topical relevance of a event. In other words, its ranking problem is simpler so that the learning-to-rank does not improve the basic ranking criterion much.

Moreover, we analyze the incorrect entries in the chronicles generated by our approaches. In general, there are four types of errors.

Topically irrelevant: the topic of an event entry is irrelevant to the event chronicle.

Minor events: the event is not important enough to be included. For example, "*20100828: Lebanon beat Canada 81-71 in the opening round of the basketball world championships*" is a minor event in the sports chronicle because it is about an opening-round match and not important enough.

Indirect description: the entry does not describe a major event directly. For instance, "*20100114: Turkey expressed sorrow over the Haiti earthquake*" is an incorrect entry in the disaster chronicle though it mentions the Haiti earthquake.

Redundant entries: multiple event entries describe the same event.

We analyze the errors of the disaster, sports and comprehensive event chronicle since they are representative, as shown in Table 2.

Topical irrelevance is a major error source for both disaster and sports event chronicles. This problem mainly arises from incorrect identification of topically relevant events during detection. Moreover, disaster and sports chronicles have their own more serious problems. Disaster event chronicles suffer from the indirect description problem since there are many responses (e.g., humanitarian aids) to a disaster. These responses are topically relevant and contain many documents, and thus appear in the top list. One possible solution might be to increase the event granularity by adjusting parameters of the detection model so that the documents describing a major event and those discussing in response to this event can be grouped into one cluster (i.e., one event). In contrast, the sports event chronicle's biggest problem is on minor events, as mentioned before. Like the sports chronicle, the comprehensive event chronicle also has many minor event entries but its main problem results from its strict criterion. Since comprehensive chronicles can include events of any topic, only extremely important events can be included. For example, "*Netherlands beat Uruguay to reach final in the World Cup 2010*" may be a correct event entry in sports chronicles but it is not a good entry in comprehensive chronicles. Compared with comprehensive event chronicles, events in other chronicles tend to describe more details. For example, a sports chronicle may regard each match in the World Cup as an event while comprehensive chronicles consider the World Cup as one event, which requires us to adapt event granularity for different chronicles.

Also, we evaluate the time of event entries in these five event chronicles because event's happening time is not always equal to the timestamp of the document creation time (UzZaman et al., 2012; Ge et al., 2013). We collect existing manually edited 2010 chronicles on the web and use their event time as gold standard. We define a metric to evaluate if the event entry's time in our chronicle is accurate:

$$diff = \sum_{e \in \mathbb{E} \cap \mathbb{E}^*} |(t_e - t_e^*)| / |\mathbb{E} \cap \mathbb{E}^*|$$

where $\mathbb{E}$ and $\mathbb{E}^*$ are our chronicle and the manually edited event chronicle respectively. t_e is e's time labeled by our method and t_e^* is e's correct time. Note that for multiple entries referring the same event in event chronicles, the earliest entry's time is used as the event's time to compute *diff*.

sports	politics	disaster	war	comprehensive
0.800	3.363	1.042	1.610	2.467

Table 3: Difference between an event's actual time and the time in our chronicles. Time unit is a day.

Table 3 shows the performance of our approach in labeling event time. For disaster, sports and war, the accuracy is desirable since important events about these topics are usually reported in time. In contrast, the accuracy of political event time is the lowest. The reason is that some political events may be confidential and thus they are not reported as soon as they happen; on the other hand, some political events (e.g., a summit) are reported several days before the events happen. The comprehensive event chronicle includes many political events, which results in a lower accuracy.

6 Related Work

To the best of our knowledge, there was no previous end-to-end topically relevant event chronicle generation work but there are some related tasks.

Event detection, sometimes called topic detection (Allan, 2002), is an important part of our approach. Yang et al. (1998) used clustering techniques for event detection on news. He et al. (2007) and Zhao et al. (2012) designed burst feature representations for detecting bursty events. Compared with our TaHBM, these methods lack the ability of distinguishing similar events.

Similar to event detection, event extraction focuses on finding events from documents. Most work regarding event extraction (Grishman et al., 2005; Ahn, 2006; Ji and Grishman, 2008; Chen and Ji, 2009; Liao and Grishman, 2010; Hong et al., 2011; Li et al., 2012; Chen and Ng, 2012; Li et al., 2013) was developed under Automatic Content Extraction (ACE) program. The task only defines 33 event types and events are in much finer grain than those in our task. Moreover, there was work (Verhagen et al., 2005; Chambers and Jurafsky, 2008; Bethard, 2013; Chambers, 2013; Chambers et al., 2014) about temporal event extraction and tracking. Like ACE, the granularity of events in this task is too fine to be suitable for our task.

Also, timeline generation is related to our work. Most previous work focused on generating a timeline for a document (Do et al., 2012), a centroid entity (Ji et al., 2009) or one major event (Hu et al., 2011; Yan et al., 2011; Lin et al., 2012; Li and Li, 2013). In addition, Li and Cardie (2014) generated timelines for users in microblogs. The most related work to ours is Swan and Allan (2000). They used a timeline to show bursty events along the time, which can be seen as an early form of event chronicles. Different from their work, we generate a topically relevant event chronicle based on a reference event chronicle.

7 Conclusions and Future Work

In this paper, we propose a novel task – automatic generation of topically relevant event chronicles. It can serve as a new framework to combine the merits of Information Retrieval, Information Extraction and Summarization techniques, to rapidly extract and rank salient events. This framework is also able to rapidly and accurately capture a user's interest and needs based on the reference chronicle (instead of keywords as in Information Retrieval or event templates as in Guided Summarization) which can reflect diverse levels of granularity.

As a preliminary study of this new challenge, this paper focuses on event detection and ranking. There are still many challenges for generating high-quality event chronicles. In the future, we plan to investigate automatically adapting an event's granularity and learn the principle of summarizing the event according to the reference event chronicle. Moreover, we plan to study the generation of entity-driven event chronicles, leveraging more fine-grained entity and event extraction approaches.

Acknowledgments

We thank the anonymous reviewers for their thought-provoking comments. This work is supported by National Key Basic Research Program of China 2014CB340504, NSFC project 61375074, China Scholarship Council (CSC, No. 201406010174) and USA ARL NS-CTA No. W911NF-09-2-0053. The contact author of this paper is Zhifang Sui.

References

David Ahn. 2006. The stages of event extraction. In *Workshop on Annotating and Reasoning about Time and Events*.

James Allan. 2002. *Topic detection and tracking: event-based information organization*, volume 12. Springer Science & Business Media.

Steven Bethard. 2013. Cleartk-timeml: A minimalist approach to tempeval 2013. In *Second Joint Conference on Lexical and Computational Semantics*.

Jeff A Bilmes. 1998. A gentle tutorial of the em algorithm and its application to parameter estimation for gaussian mixture and hidden markov models. *International Computer Science Institute*, 4(510):126.

Nathanael Chambers and Dan Jurafsky. 2008. Jointly combining implicit constraints improves temporal ordering. In *EMNLP*.

Nathanael Chambers, Taylor Cassidy, Bill McDowell, and Steven Bethard. 2014. Dense event ordering with a multi-pass architecture. *TACL*, 2:273–284.

Nathanael Chambers. 2013. Navytime: Event and time ordering from raw text. Technical report, DTIC Document.

Chaitanya Chemudugunta and Padhraic Smyth Mark Steyvers. 2007. Modeling general and specific aspects of documents with a probabilistic topic model. In *NIPS*.

Zheng Chen and Heng Ji. 2009. Language specific issue and feature exploration in chinese event extraction. In *NAACL*.

Chen Chen and Vincent Ng. 2012. Joint modeling for chinese event extraction with rich linguistic features. In *COLING*.

Quang Xuan Do, Wei Lu, and Dan Roth. 2012. Joint inference for event timeline construction. In *EMNLP*.

Tao Ge, Baobao Chang, Sujian Li, and Zhifang Sui. 2013. Event-based time label propagation for automatic dating of news articles. In *EMNLP*.

David Graff, Junbo Kong, Ke Chen, and Kazuaki Maeda. 2003. English gigaword. *Linguistic Data Consortium, Philadelphia*.

Ralph Grishman, David Westbrook, and Adam Meyers. 2005. Nyu's english ace 2005 system description. In *ACE 2005 Evaluation Workshop*.

Qi He, Kuiyu Chang, and Ee-Peng Lim. 2007. Using burstiness to improve clustering of topics in news streams. In *ICDM*.

Yu Hong, Jianfeng Zhang, Bin Ma, Jian-Min Yao, Guodong Zhou, and Qiaoming Zhu. 2011. Using cross-entity inference to improve event extraction. In *ACL*.

Po Hu, Minlie Huang, Peng Xu, Weichang Li, Adam K Usadi, and Xiaoyan Zhu. 2011. Generating breakpoint-based timeline overview for news topic retrospection. In *ICDM*.

Apache Jakarta. 2004. Apache lucene-a high-performance, full-featured text search engine library.

Heng Ji and Ralph Grishman. 2008. Refining event extraction through cross-document inference. In *ACL*.

Heng Ji, Ralph Grishman, Zheng Chen, and Prashant Gupta. 2009. Cross-document event extraction and tracking: Task, evaluation, techniques and challenges. In *RANLP*.

Thorsten Joachims. 2006. Training linear svms in linear time. In *SIGKDD*.

Jon Kleinberg. 2003. Bursty and hierarchical structure in streams. *Data Mining and Knowledge Discovery*, 7(4):373–397.

Jiwei Li and Claire Cardie. 2014. Timeline generation: Tracking individuals on twitter. In *WWW*.

Jiwei Li and Sujian Li. 2013. Evolutionary hierarchical dirichlet process for timeline summarization. In *ACL*.

Peifeng Li, Guodong Zhou, Qiaoming Zhu, and Libin Hou. 2012. Employing compositional semantics and discourse consistency in chinese event extraction. In *EMNLP*.

Qi Li, Heng Ji, and Liang Huang. 2013. Joint event extraction via structured prediction with global features. In *ACL*.

Shasha Liao and Ralph Grishman. 2010. Using document level cross-event inference to improve event extraction. In *ACL*.

Chen Lin, Chun Lin, Jingxuan Li, Dingding Wang, Yang Chen, and Tao Li. 2012. Generating event storylines from microblogs. In *CIKM*.

Christopher D Manning, Mihai Surdeanu, John Bauer, Jenny Finkel, Steven J Bethard, and David McClosky. 2014. The stanford corenlp natural language processing toolkit. In *ACL System Demonstrations*.

Russell Swan and James Allan. 2000. Automatic generation of overview timelines. In *SIGIR*.

Naushad UzZaman, Hector Llorens, James Allen, Leon Derczynski, Marc Verhagen, and James Pustejovsky. 2012. Tempeval-3: Evaluating events, time expressions, and temporal relations. *arXiv preprint arXiv:1206.5333*.

Marc Verhagen, Inderjeet Mani, Roser Sauri, Robert Knippen, Seok Bae Jang, Jessica Littman, Anna Rumshisky, John Phillips, and James Pustejovsky. 2005. Automating temporal annotation with tarsqi. In *ACL demo*.

Rui Yan, Xiaojun Wan, Jahna Otterbacher, Liang Kong, Xiaoming Li, and Yan Zhang. 2011. Evolutionary timeline summarization: a balanced optimization framework via iterative substitution. In *SIGIR*.

Yiming Yang, Tom Pierce, and Jaime Carbonell. 1998. A study of retrospective and on-line event detection. In *SIGIR*.

Wayne Xin Zhao, Rishan Chen, Kai Fan, Hongfei Yan, and Xiaoming Li. 2012. A novel burst-based text representation model for scalable event detection. In *ACL*.

Context-aware Entity Morph Decoding

Boliang Zhang[1], Hongzhao Huang[1], Xiaoman Pan[1], Sujian Li[2], Chin-Yew Lin[3]
Heng Ji[1], Kevin Knight[4], Zhen Wen[5], Yizhou Sun[6], Jiawei Han[7], Bulent Yener[1]
[1]Rensselaer Polytechnic Institute, [2]Peking University, [3]Microsoft Research Asia, [4]University of Southern California
[5]IBM T. J. Watson Research Center, [6]Northeastern University, [7]Univerisity of Illinois at Urbana-Champaign
[1]{zhangb8,huangh9,panx2,jih,yener}@rpi.edu, [2]lisujian@pku.edu.cn, [3]cyl@microsoft.com
[4]hanj@illinois.edu, [5]zhenwen@us.ibm.com, [6]yzsun@ccs.neu.edu, [7]hanj@illinois.edu

Abstract

People create morphs, a special type of fake alternative names, to achieve certain communication goals such as expressing strong sentiment or evading censors. For example, "*Black Mamba*", the name for a highly venomous snake, is a morph that *Kobe Bryant* created for himself due to his agility and aggressiveness in playing basketball games. This paper presents the first end-to-end context-aware entity morph decoding system that can automatically identify, disambiguate, verify morph mentions based on specific contexts, and resolve them to target entities. Our approach is based on an absolute "*cold-start*" - it does not require any candidate morph or target entity lists as input, nor any manually constructed morph-target pairs for training. We design a semi-supervised collective inference framework for morph mention extraction, and compare various deep learning based approaches for morph resolution. Our approach achieved significant improvement over the state-of-the-art method (Huang et al., 2013), which used a large amount of training data. [1]

1 Introduction

Morphs (Huang et al., 2013; Zhang et al., 2014) refer to the fake alternative names created by social media users to entertain readers or evade censors. For example, during the World Cup in 2014, a morph "*Su-tooth*" was created to refer to the Uruguay striker "*Luis Suarez*" for his habit of biting other players. Automatically decoding human-generated morphs in text is critical for downstream deep language understanding tasks such as entity linking and event argument extraction.

However, even for human, it is difficult to decode many morphs without certain historical, cultural, or political background knowledge (Zhang et al., 2014). For example, "*The Hutt*" can be used to refer to a fictional alien entity in the *Star Wars* universe ("*The Hutt stayed and established himself as ruler of Nam Chorios*"), or the governor of New Jersey, *Chris Christie* ("*The Hutt announced a bid for a seat in the New Jersey General Assembly*"). Huang et al. (2013) did a pioneering pilot study on morph resolution, but their approach assumed the entity morphs were already extracted and used a large amount of labeled data. In fact, they resolved morphs on corpus-level instead of mention-level and thus their approach was context-independent. A practical morph decoder, as depicted in Figure 1, consists of two problems: (1) Morph Extraction: given a corpus, extract morph mentions; and (2). Morph Resolution: For each morph mention, figure out the entity that it refers to.

In this paper, we aim to solve the fundamental research problem of end-to-end morph decoding and propose a series of novel solutions to tackle the following challenges.

Challenge 1: Large-scope candidates

Only a very small percentage of terms can be used as morphs, which should be interesting and fun. As we annotate a sample of 4,668 Chinese weibo tweets, only 450 out of 19,704 unique terms are morphs. To extract morph mentions, we propose a

[1]The data set and programs are publicly available at: http://nlp.cs.rpi.edu/data/morphdecoding.zip and http://nlp.cs.rpi.edu/software/morphdecoding.tar.gz

Proceedings of the 53rd Annual Meeting of the Association for Computational Linguistics and the 7th International Joint Conference on Natural Language Processing, pages 586–595,
Beijing, China, July 26-31, 2015.

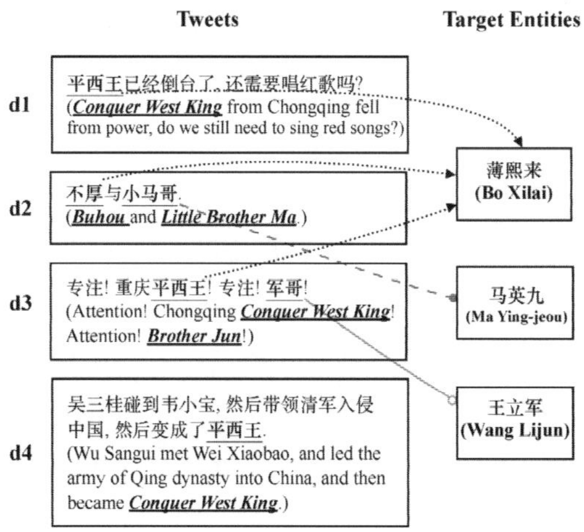

Figure 1: An Illustration of Morph Decoding Task.

two-step approach to first identify individual mention candidates to narrow down the search scope, and then verify whether they refer to morphed entities instead of their original meanings.

Challenge 2: Ambiguity, Implicitness, Informality

Compared to regular entities, many morphs contain informal terms with hidden information. For example, "不厚 *(not thick)*" is used to refer to "薄熙来 *(Bo Xilai)*" whose last name "薄 *(Bo)*" means "thin". Therefore we attempt to model the rich contexts with careful considerations for morph characteristics both globally (e.g., language models learned from a large amount of data) and locally (e.g. phonetic anomaly analysis) to extract morph mentions.

For morph resolution, the main challenge lies in that the surface forms of morphs usually appear quite different from their target entity names. Based on the distributional hypothesis (Harris, 1954) which states that words that often occur in similar contexts tend to have similar meanings, we propose to use deep learning techniques to capture and compare the deep semantic representations of a morph and its candidate target entities based on their contextual clues. For example, the morph "平西王*(Conquer West King)*" and its target entity "薄熙来 *(Bo Xilai)*" share similar implicit contextual representations such as "重庆*(Chongqing)*" (Bo was the governor of Chongqing) and "倒台 *(fall from power)*".

Challenge 3: Lack of labeled data

To the best of our knowledge, no sufficient mention-level morph annotations exist for training an end-to-end decoder. Manual morph annotations require native speakers who have certain cultural background (Zhang et al., 2014). In this paper we focus on exploring novel approaches to save annotation cost in each step. For morph extraction, based on the observation that morphs tend to share similar characteristics and appear together, we propose a semi-supervised collective inference approach to extract morph mentions from multiple tweets simultaneously. Deep learning techniques have been successfully used to model word representation in an unsupervised fashion. For morph resolution, we make use of a large amount of unlabeled data to learn the semantic representations of morphs and target entities based on the unsupervised continuous bag-of-words method (Mikolov et al., 2013b).

2 Problem Formulation

Following the recent work on morphs (Huang et al., 2013; Zhang et al., 2014), we use Chinese Weibo tweets for experiments. Our goal is to develop an end-to-end system that automatically extract morph mentions and resolve them to their target entities. Given a corpus of tweets $D = \{d_1, d_2, ..., d_{|D|}\}$, we define a candidate *morph* m_i as a unique term t_j in T, where $T = \{t_1, t_2, ..., t_{|T|}\}$ is the set of unique terms in D. To extract T, we first apply several well-developed Natural Language Processing tools, including Stanford Chinese word segmenter (Chang et al., 2008), Stanford part-of-speech tagger (Toutanova et al., 2003) and Chinese lexical analyzer ICTCLAS (Zhang et al., 2003), to process the tweets and identify noun phrases. Then we define a *morph mention* m_i^p of m_i as the p-th occurrence of m_i in a specific document d_j. Note that a mention with the same surface form as m_i but referring to its original entity is not considered as a morph mention. For instance, the "平西王 *(Conquer West King)*" in d_1 and d_3 in Figure 1 are morph mentions since they refer to the modern politician "薄熙来 *(Bo Xilai)*", while the one in d_4 is not a morph mention since it refers to the original entity, who was king "吴三桂 *(Wu Sangui)*".

For each morph mention, we discover a list of target candidates $E = \{e_1, e_2, ..., e_{|E|}\}$ from Chinese web data for morph mention resolution. We design an end-to-end morph decoder which consists of the following procedure:

- ***Morph Mention Extraction***
  - ***Potential Morph Discovery***: This first step aims to obtain a set of potential entity-level morphs $M = \{m_1, m_2, ...\}(M \subseteq T)$. Then, we only verify and resolve the mentions of these potential morphs, instead of all the terms in T in a large corpus.
  - ***Morph Mention Verification***: In this step, we aim to verify whether each mention m_i^p of the potential morph $m_i(m_i \in M)$ from a specific context d_j is a morph mention or not.
- ***Morph Mention Resolution***: The final step is to resolve each morph mention m_i^p to its target entity (e.g., "薄熙来 *(Bo Xilai)*" for the morph mention "平西王 *(Conquer West King)*" in d_1 in Figure 1).

3 Morph Mention Extraction

3.1 Why Traditional Entity Mention Extraction doesn't Work

In order to automatically extract morph mentions from any given documents, our first reflection is to formulate the task as a sequence labeling problem, just like labeling regular entity mentions. We adopted the commonly used conditional random fields (CRFs) (Lafferty et al., 2001) and got only 6% F-score. Many morphs are not presented as regular entity mentions. For example, the morph "天线 *(Antenna)*" refers to "温家宝 *(Wen Jiabao)*" because it shares one character "宝 *(baby)*" with the famous children's television series "天线宝宝 *(Teletubbies)*". Even when they are presented as regular entity mentions, they must refer to new target entities which are different from the regular ones. So we propose the following novel two-step solution.

3.2 Potential Morph Discovery

We first introduce the first step of our approach – potential morph discovery, which aims to narrow down the scope of morph candidates without losing recall. This step takes advantage of the common characteristics shared among morphs and identifies the potential morphs using a supervised method, since it is relatively easy to collect a certain number of corpus-level morphs as training data compared to labeling morph mentions. Through formulating this task as a binary classification problem, we adopt the Support Vector Machines (SVMs) (Cortes and Vapnik, 1995) as the learning model. We propose the following four categories of features.

Basic: (i) character unigram, bigram, trigram, and surface form; (ii) part-of-speech tags; (iii) the number of characters; (iv) whether some characters are identical. These basic features will help identify several common characteristics of morph candidates (e.g., they are very likely to be nouns, and very unlikely to contain single characters).

Dictionary: Many morphs are non-regular names derived from proper names while retaining some characteristics. For example, the morphs "薄督 *(Governor Bo)*" and "吃省 *(Gourmand Province)*" are derived from their target entity names "薄熙来 *(Bo Xilai)*" and "广东省 *(Guandong Province)*", respectively. Therefore, we adopt a dictionary of proper names (Li et al., 2012) and propose the following features: (i) Whether a term occurs in the dictionary. (ii) Whether a term starts with a commonly used last name, and includes uncommonly used characters as its first name. (iii) Whether a term ends with a geo-political entity or organization suffix word, but it's not in the dictionary.

Phonetic: Many morphs are created based on phonetic (Chinese pinyin in our case) modifications. For instance, the morph "饭饼饼 *(Rice Cake)*" has the same phonetic transcription as its target entity name "范冰冰 *(Fan Bingbing)*". To extract phonetic-based features, we compile a dictionary composed of ⟨phonetic transcription, term⟩ pairs from the Chinese Gigaword corpus [2]. Then for each term, we check whether it has the same phonetic transcription as any entry in the dictionary but they include different characters.

Language Modeling: Many morphs rarely appear in a general news corpus (e.g., "六步郎 *(Six Step Man)*" refers to the NBA baseketball player "勒布朗·詹姆斯 *(Lebron James)*".). Therefore, we use the character-based language models trained from Gigaword to calculate the occurrence probabilities of each term, and use n-gram probabilities ($n \in [1:5]$) as features.

3.3 Morph Mention Verification

The second step is to verify whether a mention of the discovered potential morphs is indeed used as a morph in a specific context. Based on the ob-

[2]https://catalog.ldc.upenn.edu/LDC2011T07

servation that closely related morph mentions often occur together, we propose a semi-supervised graph-based method to leverage a small set of labeled seeds, coreference and correlation relations, and a large amount of unlabeled data to perform collective inference and thus save annotation cost. According to our observation of morph mentions, we propose the following two hypotheses:

Hypothesis 1: *If two mentions are coreferential, then they both should either be morph mentions or non-morph mentions.* For instance, the morph mentions "平西王 *(Conquer West King)*" in d_1 and d_3 in Figure 1 are coreferential, they both refer to the modern politician "薄熙来 *(Bo Xilai)*".

Hypothesis 2: *Those highly correlated mentions tend to either be morph mentions or non-morph mentions.* From our annotated dataset, 49% morph mentions co-occur on tweet level. For example, "平西王*(Conquer West King)*" and "军哥*(Brother Jun)*" are used together in d_3 in Figure 1.

Based on these hypotheses, we aim to design an effective approach to compensate for the limited annotated data. Graph-based semi-supervised learning approaches (Zhu et al., 2003; Smola and Kondor, 2003; Zhou et al., 2004) have been successfully applied many NLP tasks (Niu et al., 2005; Chen et al., 2006; Huang et al., 2014). Therefore we build a mention graph to capture the semantic relatedness (weighted arcs) between potential morph mentions (nodes) and propose a semi-supervised graph-based algorithm to collectively verify a set of relevant mentions using a small amount of labeled data. We now describe the detailed algorithm as follows.

Mention Graph Construction

First, we construct a mention graph that can reflect the association between all the mentions of potential morphs. According to the above two hypotheses, *mention coreference* and *correlation* relations are the basis to build our mention graph, which is represented by a matrix.

In Chinese Weibo, their exist rich and clean social relations including *authorship*, *replying*, *retweeting*, or *user mentioning* relations. We make use of these social relations to judge the possibility of two mentions of the same potential morph being coreferential. If there exists one social relation between two mentions m_i^p and m_i^q of the morph m_i, they are usually coreferential and assigned an association score 1. We also detect coreferential relations by performing content similarity analysis. The cosine similarity is adopted with the tf-idf representation for the contexts of two mentions. Then we get a coreference matrix W^1:

$$W^1_{m_i^p, m_i^q} = \begin{cases} 1.0 & \text{if } m_i^p \text{ and } m_i^q \text{ are linked} \\ & \text{with certain social relation} \\ cos(m_i^p, m_i^q) & \text{else if } q \in kNN(p) \\ 0 & \text{Otherwise} \end{cases}$$

where m_i^p and m_i^q are two mentions from the same potential morph m_i, and kNN means that each mention is connected to its k nearest neighboring mentions.

Users tend to use morph mentions together to achieve their communication goals. To incorporate such evidence, we measure the correlation between two mentions m_i^p and m_j^q of two different potential morphs m_i and m_j as $corr(m_i^p, m_j^q) = 1.0$ if there exists a certain social relation between them. Otherwise, $corr(m_i^p, m_j^q) = 0$. Then we can obtain the correlation matrix: $W^2_{m_i^p, m_j^q} = corr(m_i^p, m_j^q)$.

To tune the balance of coreferential relation and correlation relation during learning, we first get two matrices $\hat{W}^1$ and $\hat{W}^2$ by row-normalizing W^1 and W_2, respectively. Then we obtain the final mention matrix W with a linear combination of $\hat{W}^1$ and $\hat{W}^2$: $W = \alpha\hat{W}^1 + (1-\alpha)\hat{W}^2$, where α is the coefficient between 0 and 1 [3].

Graph-based Semi-supervised Learning

Intuitively, if two mentions are strongly connected, they tend to hold the same label. The label of 1 indicates a mention is a morph mention, and 0 means a non-morph mention. We use $Y = \begin{bmatrix} Y_l & Y_u \end{bmatrix}^T$ to denote the label vector of all mentions, where the first l nodes are verified mentions labeled as 1 or 0, and the remaining u nodes need to be verified and initialized with the label 0.5. Our final goal is to obtain the final label vector Y_u by incorporating evidence from initial labels and the mention graph.

Following the graph-based semi-supervised learning algorithm (Zhu et al., 2003), the mention verification problem is formulated to optimize the objective function $\mathcal{Q}(\mathcal{Y}) = \mu \sum_{i=1}^{l}(y_i - y_i^0)^2 + \frac{1}{2}\sum_{i,j} W_{ij}(y_i - y_j)^2$ where y_i^0 denotes the initial

[3] α is set to 0.8 in this paper, optimized from the development set.

label, and μ is a regularization parameter that controls the trade-off between initial labels and the consistency of labels on the mention graph. Zhu et al. (2003) has proven that this formula has both closed-form and iterative solutions.

4 Morph Mention Resolution

The final step is to resolve the extracted morph mentions to their target entities.

4.1 Candidate Target Identification

We start from identifying a list of target candidates for each morph mention from the comparable corpora including Sina Weibo, Chinese News and English Twitter. After preprocessing the corpora using word segmentation, noun phrase chunking and name tagging, the name entity list is still too large and too noisy for candidate ranking. To clean the name entity list, we adopt the temporal Distribution Assumption proposed in our recent work (Huang et al., 2013). It assumes that a morph m and its real target e should have similar temporal distributions in terms of their occurrences. Following the same heuristic we assume that an entity is a valid candidate for a morph if and only if the candidate appears fewer than seven days after the morph's appearance.

4.2 Candidate Target Ranking

Motivations of Using Deep Learning

Compared to regular entity linking tasks (Ji et al., 2010; Ji et al., 2011; Ji et al., 2014), the major challenge of ranking a morph's candidate target entities lies in that the surface features such as the orthographic similarity between morph and target candidates have been proven inadequate (Huang et al., 2013). Therefore, it is crucial to capture the semantics of both mentions and target candidates. For instance, in order to correctly resolve "平西王 *(Conquer West King)*" from d_1 and d_3 in Figure 1 to the modern politician "薄熙来*(Bo Xilai)*" instead of the ancient king "吴三桂 *(Wu Sangui)*", it is important to model the surrounding contextual information effectively to capture important information (e.g., "重庆 *(Chongqing)*", "倒台 *(fall from power)*", and "唱红歌 *(sing red songs)*") to represent the mentions and target entity candidates. Inspired by the recent success achieved by deep learning based techniques on learning semantic representations for various NLP tasks (e.g., (Bengio et al., 2003; Collobert et al., 2011; Mikolov et al., 2013b; He et al., 2013)), we design and compare the following two approaches to employ hierarchical architectures with multiple hidden layers to extract useful features and map morphs and target entities into a latent semantic space.

Pairwise Cross-genre Supervised Learning

Ideally, we hope to obtain a large amount of coreferential entity mention pairs for training. A natural knowledge resource is Wikipedia which includes anchor links. We compose an anchor's surface string and the title of the entity it's linked to as a positive training pair. Then we randomly sample negative training instances from those pairs that don't share any links.

Our approach consists of the following steps: (1) generating high quality embedding for each training instance; (2) pre-training with the stacked denoising auto-encoder (Bengio et al., 2003) for feature dimension reduction; and (3) supervised fine-tuning to optimize the neural networks towards a similarity measure (e.g., dot product). Figure 2 depicts the overall architecture of this approach.

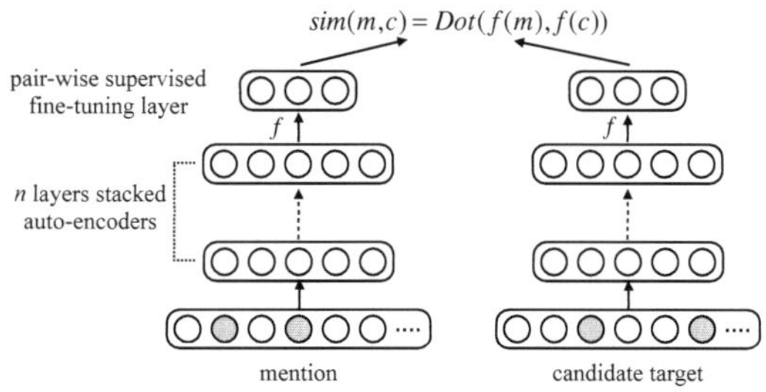

Figure 2: Overall Architecture of Pairwise Cross-genre Supervised Learning

However, morph resolution is significantly different from the traditional entity linking task since the latter mainly focuses on formal and explicit entities (e.g., "薄熙来 *(Bo Xilai)*") which tend to have stable referents in Wikipedia. In contrast, morphs tend to be informal, implicit and have newly emergent meanings which evolve over time. In fact, these morph mentions rarely appear in Wikipedia. For example, almost all "平西王 *(Conquer West King)*" mentions in Wikipedia refer to the ancient king instead of the modern politician "薄熙来 *(Bo Xilai)*". In addition, the contextual words in Wikipedia used to describe entities are quite different from those in social media. For example, to describe a death event, Wikipedia usually uses a formal expression “去世 (pass away)” while an informal expression “挂了 (hang up)” is used more often in tweets. Therefore this approach suffers from the knowledge discrepancy between these two genres.

Within-genre Unsupervised Learning

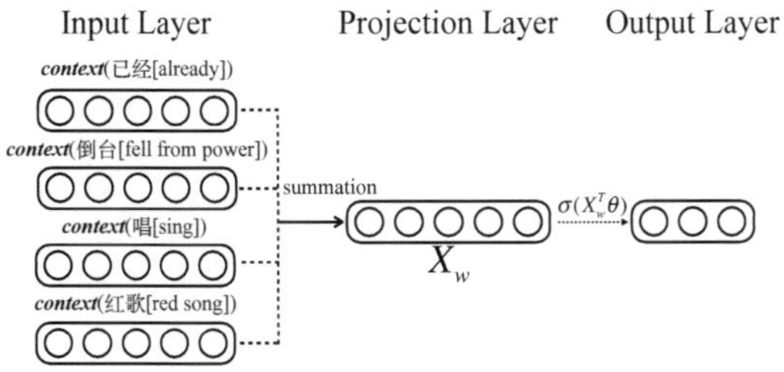

Figure 3: Continuous Bag-of-Words Architecture

To address the above challenge, we propose the second approach to learn semantic embeddings of both morph mentions and entities directly from tweets. Also we prefer unsupervised learning methods due to the lack of training data. Following (Mikolov et al., 2013a), we develop a continuous bag-of-words (CBOW) model that can effectively model the surrounding contextual information. CBOW is discriminatively trained by maximizing the conditional probability of a term w_i given its contexts $c(w_i) = \{w_{i-n}, ..., w_{i-1}, w_{i+1}, ..., w_{i+n}\}$, where n is the contextual window size, and w_i is a term obtained using the preprocessing step introduced in Section 2 [4]. The architecture of CBOW is depicted in Figure 3. We obtain a vector X_{w_i} through the projection layer by summing up the embedding vectors of all terms in $c(w_i)$, and then use the sigmoid activation function to obtain the final embedding of w_i in $c(w_i)$ in the output layer.

Formally, the objective function of CBOW can be formulated as $\mathcal{L}(\theta) = \sum_{w_i \in W} \sum_{w_j \in W} \log p(w_j|c(w_i))$, where W is the set of unique terms obtained from the whole training corpus. $p(w_j|c(w_i))$ is the conditional likelihood of w_j given the context $c(w_i)$ and it is formulated as follows:

$$p(w_j|c(w_i)) = [\sigma(X_{w_i}^T \theta^{w_j})]^{L^{w_i}(w_j)} \times [1 - \sigma(X_{w_i}^T \theta^{w_j})]^{1-L^{w_i}(w_j)},$$

[4]Each w_i is not limited to noun phrases we consider as candidate morphs.

Data	Training	Development	Testing
# Tweets	1,500	500	2,688
# Unique Terms	10,098	4, 848	15,108
# Morphs	250	110	341
# Morph Mentions	1,342	487	2,469

Table 1: Data Statistics

where $L^{w_i}(w_j) = \begin{cases} 1, & w_i = w_j \\ 0, & Otherwise \end{cases}$, σ is the sigmoid activation function, and θ^{w_i} is the embeddings of w_i to be learned with back-propagation during training.

5 Experiments

5.1 Data

We retrieved 1,553,347 tweets from Chinese Sina Weibo from May 1 to June 30, 2013 and 66, 559 web documents from the embedded URLs in tweets for experiments. We then randomly sampled 4,688 non-redundant tweets and asked two Chinese native speakers to manually annotate morph mentions in these tweets. The annotated dataset is randomly split into training, development, and testing sets, with detailed statistics shown in Table 1 [5]. We used 225 positive instances and 225 negative instances to train the model in the first step of potential morph discovery.

We collected a Chinese Wikipedia dump of October 9th, 2014, which contains 2,539,355 pages. We pulled out person, organization and geopolitical pages based on entity type matching with DBpedia [6]. We also filter out the pages with fewer than 300 words. For training the model, we use 60,000 mention-target pairs along with one negative sample randomly generated for each pair, among which, 20% pairs are reserved for parameter tuning.

5.2 Overall: End-to-End Decoding

In this subsection, we first study the end-to-end decoding performance of our best system, and compare it with the state-of-the-art supervised learning-to-rank approach proposed by (Huang et al., 2013) based on information networks construction and traverse with meta-paths. We use the 225 extracted morphs as input to feed (Huang et al., 2013) system. The experiment setting, implementation and evaluation process are similar to (Huang et al., 2013).

[5]We will make all of these annotations and other resources available for research purposes if this paper gets accepted.

[6]http://dbpedia.org

The overall performance of our approach using within-genre learning for resolution is shown in Table 2. We can see that our system achieves significantly better performance (95.0% confidence level by the Wilcoxon Matched-Pairs Signed-Ranks Test) than the approach proposed by (Huang et al., 2013). We found that (Huang et al., 2013) failed to resolve many unpopular morphs (e.g., "小马 *(Little Ma)*" is a morph referring to Ma Yingjiu, and it only appeared once in the data), because it heavily relies on aggregating contextual and temporal information from multiple instances of each morph. In contrast, our unsupervised resolution approach only leverages the pre-trained word embeddings to capture the semantics of morph mentions and entities.

Model	Precision	Recall	F_1
Huang et al., 2013	40.2	33.3	36.4
Our Approach	**41.1**	**35.9**	**38.3**

Table 2: End-to-End Morph Decoding (%)

5.3 Diagnosis: Morph Mention Extraction

The first step discovered 888 potential morphs (80.1% of all morphs, 5.9% of all terms), which indicates that this step successfully narrowed down the scope of candidate morphs.

Method	Precision	Recall	F_1
Naive	58.0	83.1	68.3
SVMs	61.3	80.7	69.7
Our Approach	88.2	77.2	**82.3**

Table 3: Morph Mention Verification (%)

Now we evaluate the performance of morph mention verification. We compare our approach with two baseline methods: (i) *Naive*, which considers all mentions as morph mentions; (ii) *SVMs*, a fully supervised model using Support Vector Machines (Cortes and Vapnik, 1995) based on unigrams and bigrams features. Table 3 shows the results. We can see that our approach achieves significantly better performance than the baseline approaches. In particular it can verify the mentions of newly emergent morphs. For instance, "棒棒棒 *(Good Good Good)*" is mistakenly identified by the first step as a potential morph, but the second step correctly filters it out.

5.4 Diagnosis: Morph Mention Resolution

The target candidate identification step successfully filters 86% irrelevant entities with high precision (98.5% of morphs retain their target entitis). For candidate ranking, we compare with several baseline approaches as follows:

- ***BOW***: We compute cosine similarity over bag-of-words vectors with tf-idf values to measure the context similarity between a mention and its candidates.
- ***Pair-wise Cross-genre Supervised Learning***: We first construct a vocabulary by choosing the top 100,000 frequent terms. Then we randomly sample 48,000 instances for training and 12,000 instances for development. At the pre-training step, we set the number of hidden layers as 3, the size of each hidden layer as 1000, the masking noise probability for the first layer as 0.7, and a Gaussian noise with standard deviation of 0.1 for higher layers. The learning rate is set to be 0.01. At the fine-tuning stage, we add a 200 units layer on top of auto-encoders and optimize the neural network models based on the training data.
- ***Within-genre Unsupervised Learning***: We directly train morph mention and entity embeddings from the large-scale tweets and web documents that we collect. We set the window size as 10 and the vector dimension as 800 based on the development set.

The overall performance of various resolution approaches using perfect morph mentions is shown in Figure 4. We can clearly see that our second within-genre learning approach achieves the best performance. Figure 5 demonstrates the differences between our two deep learning based methods. When learning semantic embeddings directly from Wikipedia, we can see that the top 10 closest entities of the mention "平西王*(Conquer West King)*" are all related to the ancient king "吴三桂*(Wu Sangui)*". Therefore this method is only able to capture the original meanings of morphs. In contrast, when we learn embeddings directly from tweets, most of the closest entities are relevant to its target entity "薄熙来 *(Bo Xilai)*".

6 Related Work

The first morph decoding work (Huang et al., 2013) assumed morph mentions are already discovered and didn't take contexts into account. To the best of our knowledge, this is the first work on context-aware end-to-end morph decoding.

Morph decoding is related to several traditional

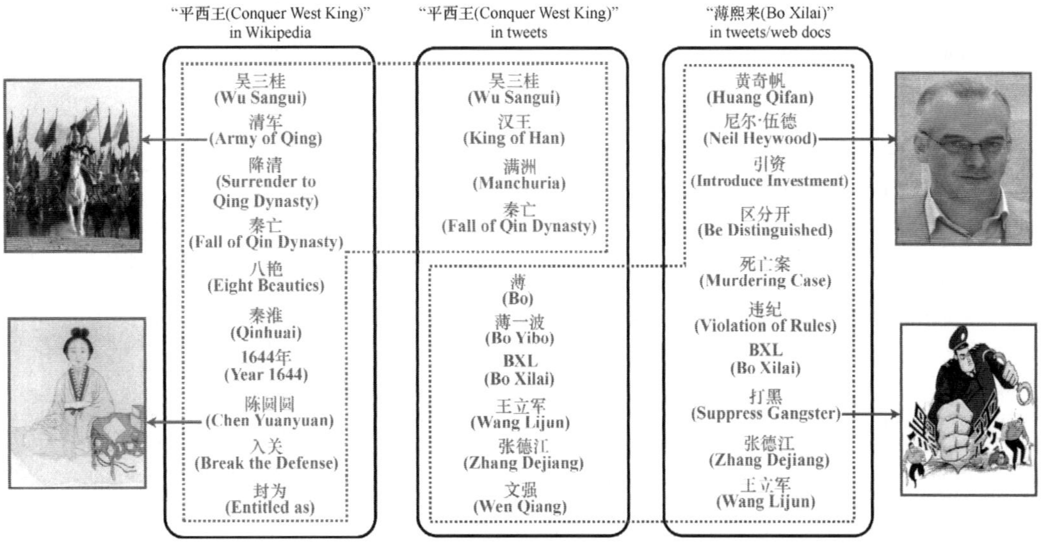

Figure 5: Top 10 closest entities to morph and target in different genres

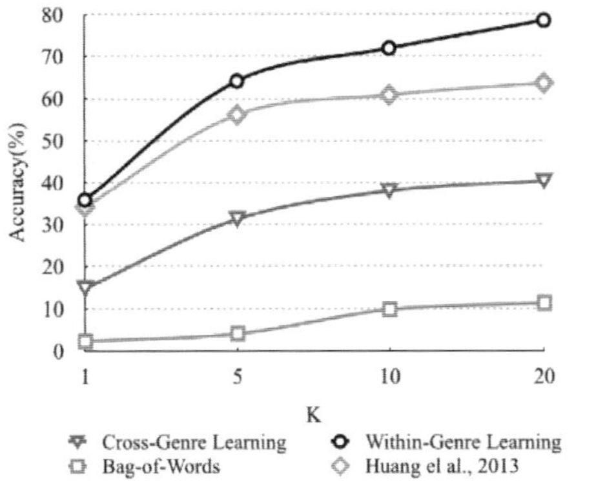

Figure 4: Resolution Acc@K for Perfect Morph Mentions

NLP tasks: entity mention extraction (e.g., (Zitouni and Florian, 2008; Ohta et al., 2012; Li and Ji, 2014)), metaphor detection (e.g., (Wang et al., 2006; Tsvetkov, 2013; Heintz et al., 2013)), word sense disambiguation (WSD) (e.g., (Yarowsky, 1995; Mihalcea, 2007; Navigli, 2009)), and entity linking (EL) (e.g., (Mihalcea and Csomai, 2007; Ji et al., 2010; Ji et al., 2011; Ji et al., 2014). However, none of these previous techniques can be applied directly to tackle this problem. As mentioned in section 3.1, entity morphs are fundamentally different from regular entity mentions. Our task is also different from metaphor detection because morphs cover a much wider range of semantic categories and can include either abstractive or concrete information. Some common features for detecting metaphors (e.g. (Tsvetkov, 2013)) are not effective for morph extraction: (1). Semantic categories. Metaphors usually fall into certain semantic categories such as noun.animal and noun.cognition. (2). Degree of abstractness. If the subject or an object of a concrete verb is abstract then the verb is likely to be a metaphor. In contrast, morphs can be very abstract (e.g., "函数 *(Function)*" refers to "杨幂 *(Yang Mi)*" because her first name "幂 *(Mi)*" means the Power Function) or very concrete (e.g., "薄督 *(Governor Bo)*" refers to "薄熙来 *(Bo Xilai)*"). In contrast to traditional WSD where the senses of a word are usually quite stable, the "sense" (target entity) of a morph may be newly emergent or evolve over time rapidly. The same morph can also have multiple senses. The EL task focuses more on explicit and formal entities (e.g., named entities), while morphs tend to be informal and convey implicit information.

Morph mention detection is also related to malware detection (e.g., (Firdausi et al., 2010; Chandola et al., 2009; Firdausi et al., 2010; Christodorescu and Jha, 2003)) which discovers abnormal behavior in code and malicious software. In contrast our task tackles anomaly texts in semantic context.

Deep learning-based approaches have been demonstrated to be effective in disambiguation related tasks such as WSD (Bordes et al., 2012), entity linking (He et al., 2013) and question linking (Yih et al., 2014; Bordes et al., 2014; Yang et al., 2014). In this paper we proved that it's crucial to keep the genres consistent between learning embeddings and applying embeddings.

7 Conclusions and Future Work

This paper describes the first work of context-aware end-to-end morph decoding. By conducting deep analysis to identity the common characteristics of morphs and the unique challenges of this task, we leverage a large amount of unlabeled data and the coreferential and correlation relations to perform collective inference to extract morph mentions. Then we explore deep learning-based techniques to capture the semantics of morph mentions and entities and resolve morph mentions on the fly. Our future work includes exploiting the profiles of target entities as feedback to refine the results of morph mention extraction. We will also extend the framework for event morph decoding.

Acknowledgments

This work was supported by the US ARL NS-CTA No. W911NF-09-2-0053, DARPA DEFT No. FA8750-13-2-0041, NSF Awards IIS-1523198, IIS-1017362, IIS-1320617, IIS-1354329 and HDTRA1-10-1-0120, gift awards from IBM, Google, Disney and Bosch. The views and conclusions contained in this document are those of the authors and should not be interpreted as representing the official policies, either expressed or implied, of the U.S. Government. The U.S. Government is authorized to reproduce and distribute reprints for Government purposes notwithstanding any copyright notation here on.

References

Y. Bengio, R. Ducharme, P. Vincent, and C. Janvin. 2003. A neural probabilistic language model. *Journal of Machine Learning Research*, 3:1137–1155, March.

A. Bordes, X. Glorot, J. Weston, and Y. Bengio. 2012. Joint learning of words and meaning representations for open-text semantic parsing. In *Proc. of the 15th International Conference on Artificial Intelligence and Statistics (AISTATS2012)*.

A. Bordes, S. Chopra, and J. Weston. 2014. Question answering with subgraph embeddings. In *Proc. of the 2014 Conference on Empirical Methods in Natural Language Processing (EMNLP2014)*.

V. Chandola, A. Banerjee, and V. Kumar. 2009. Anomaly detection: A survey. *ACM Computing Surveys (CSUR)*, 41(3):15.

P. Chang, M. Galley, and D. Manning. 2008. Optimizing chinese word segmentation for machine translation performance. In *Proc. of the Third Workshop on Statistical Machine Translation (StatMT 2008)*.

J. Chen, D. Ji, C Tan, and Z. Niu. 2006. Relation extraction using label propagation based semi-supervised learning. In *Proc. of the 21st International Conference on Computational Linguistics and 44th Annual Meeting of the Association for Computational Linguistics (ACL2006)*.

M. Christodorescu and S. Jha. 2003. Static analysis of executables to detect malicious patterns. In *Proc. of the 12th Conference on USENIX Security Symposium (SSYM2003)*.

R. Collobert, J. Weston, L. Bottou, M. Karlen, K. Kavukcuoglu, and P. Kuksa. 2011. Natural language processing (almost) from scratch. *Journal of Machine Learning Research*, 12:2493–2537, November.

C. Cortes and V. Vapnik. 1995. Support-vector networks. *Machine Learning*, 20:273–297, September.

I. Firdausi, C. Lim, A. Erwin, and A. Nugroho. 2010. Analysis of machine learning techniques used in behavior-based malware detection. In *Proc. of the 2010 Second International Conference on Advances in Computing, Control, and Telecommunication Technologies (ACT2010)*.

Z. Harris. 1954. Distributional structure. *Word*, 10:146–162.

Z. He, S. Liu, M. Li, M. Zhou, L. Zhang, and H. Wang. 2013. Learning entity representation for entity disambiguation. In *Proc. of the 51st Annual Meeting of the Association for Computational Linguistics (ACL2013)*.

I. Heintz, R. Gabbard, M. Srivastava, D. Barner, D. Black, M. Friedman, and R. Weischedel. 2013. Automatic extraction of linguistic metaphors with lda topic modeling. In *Proc. of the ACl2013 Workshop on Metaphor in NLP*.

H. Huang, Z. Wen, D. Yu, H. Ji, Y. Sun, J. Han, and H. Li. 2013. Resolving entity morphs in censored data. In *Proc. of the 51st Annual Meeting of the Association for Computational Linguistics (ACL2013)*.

H. Huang, Y. Cao, X. Huang, H. Ji, and C. Lin. 2014. Collective tweet wikification based on semi-supervised graph regularization. In *Proc. of the 52nd Annual Meeting of the Association for Computational Linguistics (ACL2014)*.

H. Ji, R. Grishman, H.T. Dang, K. Griffitt, and J. Ellis. 2010. Overview of the tac 2010 knowledge base population track. In *Proc. of the Text Analysis Conference (TAC2010)*.

H. Ji, R. Grishman, and H.T. Dang. 2011. Overview of the tac 2011 knowledge base population track. In *Proc. of the Text Analysis Conference (TAC2011)*.

H. Ji, J. Nothman, and H. Ben. 2014. Overview of tac-kbp2014 entity discovery and linking tasks. In *Proc. of the Text Analysis Conference (TAC2014)*.

J. Lafferty, A. McCallum, and F. Pereira. 2001. Conditional random fields: Probabilistic models for segmenting and labeling sequence data. In *Proc. of the Eighteenth International Conference on Machine Learning (ICML2001)*.

Q. Li and H. Ji. 2014. Incremental joint extraction of entity mentions and relations. In *Proc. of the 52nd Annual Meeting of the Association for Computational Linguistics (ACL2014)*.

Q. Li, H. Li, H. Ji, W. Wang, J. Zheng, and F. Huang. 2012. Joint bilingual name tagging for parallel corpora. In *Proc. of the 21st ACM International Conference on Information and Knowledge Management (CIKM2012)*.

R. Mihalcea and A. Csomai. 2007. Wikify!: linking documents to encyclopedic knowledge. In *Proc. of the sixteenth ACM conference on Conference on information and knowledge management (CIKM2007)*.

R. Mihalcea. 2007. Using wikipedia for automatic word sense disambiguation. In *Proc. of the Conference of the North American Chapter of the Association for Computational Linguistics (HLT-NAACL2007)*.

T. Mikolov, K. Chen, G. Corrado, and J. Dean. 2013a. Efficient estimation of word representations in vector space. *CoRR*, abs/1301.3781.

T. Mikolov, I. Sutskever, K. Chen, S.G. Corrado, and J. Dean. 2013b. Distributed representations of words and phrases and their compositionality. In *Advances in Neural Information Processing Systems 26*.

R. Navigli. 2009. Word sense disambiguation: A survey. *ACM Computing Surveys*, 41:10:1–10:69, February.

Z. Niu, D. Ji, and C. Tan. 2005. Word sense disambiguation using label propagation based semi-supervised learning. In *Proc. of the 43rd Annual Meeting of the Association for Computational Linguistics (ACL2005)*.

T. Ohta, S. Pyysalo, J. Tsujii, and S. Ananiadou. 2012. Open-domain anatomical entity mention detection. In *Proc. of the ACL2012 Workshop on Detecting Structure in Scholarly Discourse*.

A. Smola and R. Kondor. 2003. Kernels and regularization on graphs. In *Proc. of the Annual Conference on Computational Learning Theory and Kernel Workshop (COLT2003)*.

K. Toutanova, D. Klein, C. D. Manning, and Y. Singer. 2003. Feature-rich part-of-speech tagging with a cyclic dependency network. In *Proc. of the 2003 Conference of the North American Chapter of the Association for Computational Linguistics on Human Language Technology (NAACL2003)*.

Y. Tsvetkov. 2013. Cross-lingual metaphor detection using common semantic features. In *Proc. of the ACL2013 Workshop on Metaphor in NLP*.

Z. Wang, H. Wang, H. Duan, S. Han, and S. Yu. 2006. Chinese noun phrase metaphor recognition with maximum entropy approach. In *Proc. of the Seventh International Conference on Intelligent Text Processing and Computational Linguistics (CICLing2006)*.

M. Yang, N. Duan, M. Zhou, and H. Rim. 2014. Joint relational embeddings for knowledge-based question answering. In *Proc. of the 2014 Conference on Empirical Methods in Natural Language Processing (EMNLP2014)*.

D. Yarowsky. 1995. Unsupervised word sense disambiguation rivaling supervised methods. In *Proc. of the 33rd Annual Meeting on Association for Computational Linguistics (ACL1995)*.

W. Yih, X. He, and C. Meek. 2014. Semantic parsing for single-relation question answering. In *Proc. of the 52nd Annual Meeting of the Association for Computational Linguistics (ACL2014)*.

H. Zhang, H. Yu, D. Xiong, and Q. Liu. 2003. Hhmm-based chinese lexical analyzer ictclas. In *Proc. of the second SIGHAN workshop on Chinese language processing (SIGHAN2003)*.

B. Zhang, H. Huang, X. Pan, H. Ji, K. Knight, Z. Wen, Y. Sun, J. Han, and B. Yener. 2014. Be appropriate and funny: Automatic entity morph encoding. In *Proc. of the 52nd Annual Meeting of the Association for Computational Linguistics (ACL2014)*.

D. Zhou, O. Bousquet, T. Lal, J. Weston, and B. Schölkopf. 2004. Learning with local and global consistency. In *Advances in Neural Information Processing Systems 16*, pages 321–328.

X. Zhu, Z. Ghahramani, and J. Lafferty. 2003. Semi-supervised learning using gaussian fields and harmonic functions. In *Proc. of the International Conference on Machine Learning (ICML2003)*.

I. Zitouni and R. Florian. 2008. Mention detection crossing the language barrier. In *Proc. of the Conference on Empirical Methods in Natural Language Processing (EMNLP2008)*.

Multi-Objective Optimization for the Joint Disambiguation of Nouns and Named Entities

Dirk Weissenborn, Leonhard Hennig, Feiyu Xu and Hans Uszkoreit
Language Technology Lab, DFKI
Alt-Moabit 91c
Berlin, Germany
{dirk.weissenborn, leonhard.hennig, feiyu, uszkoreit}@dfki.de

Abstract

In this paper, we present a novel approach to joint word sense disambiguation (WSD) and entity linking (EL) that combines a set of complementary objectives in an extensible multi-objective formalism. During disambiguation the system performs continuous optimization to find optimal probability distributions over candidate senses. The performance of our system on nominal WSD as well as EL improves state-of-the-art results on several corpora. These improvements demonstrate the importance of combining complementary objectives in a joint model for robust disambiguation.

1 Introduction

The task of automatically assigning the correct meaning to a given word or entity mention in a document is called word sense disambiguation (WSD) (Navigli, 2009) or entity linking (EL) (Bunescu and Pasca, 2006), respectively. Successful disambiguation requires not only an understanding of the topic or domain a document is dealing with, but also a deep analysis of how an individual word is used within its local context. For example, the meanings of the word "newspaper", as in the company or the physical product, often cannot be distinguished by the global topic of the document it was mentioned in, but by recognizing which type of meaning fits best into the local context of its mention. On the other hand, for an ambiguous entity mention such as a person name, e.g., "Michael Jordan", it is important to recognize the domain or topic of the wider context to distinguish, e.g., between the basketball player and the machine learning expert.

The combination of the two most commonly employed reference knowledge bases for WSD and EL, WordNet (Fellbaum, 1998) and Wikipedia, in BabelNet (Navigli and Ponzetto, 2012), has enabled a new line of research towards the joint disambiguation of words and named entities. *Babelfy* (Moro et al., 2014) has shown the potential of combining these two tasks in a purely knowledge-driven approach that jointly finds connections between potential word senses on a global, document level. On the other hand, typical supervised methods (Zhong and Ng, 2010) trained on sense-annotated datasets are usually quite successful in dealing with individual words in their local context on a sentence level. Hoffart et al. (2011) recognize the importance of combining both local and global context for robust disambiguation. However, their approach is limited to EL and optimization is performed in a discrete setting.

We present a system that combines disambiguation objectives for both global and local contexts into a single multi-objective function. The resulting system is flexible and easily extensible with complementary objectives. In contrast to prior work (Hoffart et al., 2011; Moro et al., 2014) we model the problem in a continuous setting based on probability distributions over candidate meanings instead of a binary treatment of candidate meanings during disambiguation. Our approach combines knowledge from various sources in one robust model. The system uses lexical and encyclopedic knowledge for the joint disambiguation of words and named entities, and exploits local context information of a mention to infer the type of its meaning. We integrate prior statistics from surface strings to candidate meanings in a "natural" way as starting probability distributions for each mention.

The contributions of our work are the following:

- a model for joint nominal WSD and EL that outperforms previous state-of-the-art systems on both tasks
- an extensible framework for multi-objective

Proceedings of the 53rd Annual Meeting of the Association for Computational Linguistics and the 7th International Joint Conference on Natural Language Processing, pages 596–605,
Beijing, China, July 26-31, 2015.

disambiguation

- an extensive evaluation of the approach on multiple standard WSD and EL datasets
- the first work that employs continuous optimization techniques for disambiguation (to our knowledge)
- publicly available code, resources and models at `https://bitbucket.org/dfki-lt-re-group/mood`

2 Approach

Our system detects mentions in texts and disambiguates their meaning to one of the candidate senses extracted from a reference knowledge base. The integral parts of the system, namely *mention detection*, *candidate search* and *disambiguation* are described in detail in this section. The model requires a tokenized, lemmatized and POS-tagged document as input; the output are sense-annotated mentions.

2.1 Knowledge Source

We employ BabelNet 2.5.1 as our reference knowledge base (KB). BabelNet is a multilingual semantic graph of concepts and named entities that are represented by synonym sets, called *Babel synsets*. It is composed of lexical and encyclopedic resources, such as WordNet and Wikipedia. Babel synsets comprise several Babel senses, each of which corresponds to a sense in another knowledge base. For example the Babel synset of "Neil Armstrong" contains multiple senses including for example "armstrong#n#1" (WordNet), "Neil_Armstrong" (Wikipedia). All synsets are interlinked by conceptual-semantic and lexical relations from WordNet and semantic relations extracted from links between Wikipedia pages.

2.2 Mention Extraction & Entity Detection

We define a mention to be a sequence of tokens in a given document. The system extracts mentions for all content words (nouns, verbs, adjectives, adverbs) and multi-token units of up to 7 tokens that contain at least one noun. In addition, we apply a NER-tagger to identify named entity (NE) mentions. Our approach distinguishes NEs from common nouns because there are many common nouns also referring to NEs, making disambiguation unnecessarily complicated. For example, the word "moon" might refer to songs, films, video games, etc., but we should only consider these meanings if the occurrence suggests that it is used as a NE.

2.3 Candidate Search

After potential mentions are extracted, the system tries to identify their candidate meanings, i.e., the appropriate synsets. Mentions without any candidates are discarded. There are various resources one can exploit to map surface strings to candidate meanings. However, existing methods or resources especially for NEs are either missing many important mappings[1] or contain many noisy mappings[2]. Therefore, we created a candidate mapping strategy that tries to avoid noisy mappings while including all potentially correct candidates. Our approach employs several heuristics that aim to avoid noise. Their union yields an almost complete mapping that includes the correct candidate meaning for 97-100% of the examples in the test datasets. Candidate mentions are mapped to synsets based on similarity of their surface strings or lemmas. If the surface string or lemma of a mention matches the lemma of a synonym in a synset that has the same part of speech, the synset will be considered as a candidate meaning. We allow partial matches for BabelNet synonyms derived from Wikipedia titles or redirections. However, partial matching is restricted to synsets that belong either to the semantic category "Place" or "Agent". We make use of the semantic category information provided by the DBpedia ontology[3]. A partial match allows the surface string of a mention to differ by up to 3 tokens from the Wikipedia title (excluding everything in parentheses) if the partial string occurred at least once as an anchor for the corresponding Wikipedia page. E.g., for the Wikipedia title Armstrong_School_District_(Pennsylvania), the following surface strings would be considered matches: "Armstrong School District (Pennsylvania)", "Armstrong School District", "Armstrong", but not "School" or "District", since they were never used as an anchor. If there is no match we try the same procedure applied to the lowercase forms of the surface string or the lemma. For persons we allow matches to all partial names, e.g., only first name, first and middle name, last name, etc.

In addition to the aforementioned candidate extraction we also match surface strings to candidate entities mentioned on their respective disambigua-

[1] e.g., using only the synonyms of a synset

[2] e.g., partial matches for all synonyms of a synset

[3] `http://wiki.dbpedia.org/Ontology`

tion pages in Wikipedia[4]. For cases where adjectives should be disambiguated as nouns, e.g., "English" as a country to "England", we allow candidate mappings through the *pertainment* relation from WordNet. Finally, frequently annotated surface strings in Wikipedia are matched to their corresponding entities, where we stipulate "frequently" to mean that the surface string occurs at least 100 times as anchor in Wikipedia and the entity was either at least 100 times annotated by this surface string or it was annotated above average.

The distinction between nouns and NEs imposes certain restrictions on the set of potential candidates. Candidate synsets for nouns are noun synsets considered as "Concepts" in BabelNet (as opposed to "Named Entities") in addition to all synsets of WordNet senses. On the other hand, candidate synsets for NEs comprise all nominal Babel synsets. Thus, the range of candidate sets for NEs properly contains the one for nouns. We include all nominal synsets as potential candidates for NEs because the distinction of NEs and simple concepts is not always clear in BabelNet. For example the synset for "UN" (United Nations) is considered a concept whereas it could also be considered a NE. Finally, if there is no candidate for a potential nominal mention, we try to find NE candidates for it before discarding it.

2.4 Multi-Objective Disambiguation

We formulate the disambiguation as a continuous, multi-objective optimization problem. Individual objectives model different aspects of the disambiguation problem. Maximizing these objectives means assigning high probabilities to candidate senses that contribute most to the combined objective. After maximization, we select the candidate meaning with the highest probability as the disambiguated sense. Our model is illustrated in Figure 1.

Given a set of objectives $\mathfrak{O}$ the overall objective function $\mathbf{O}$ is defined as the sum of all normalized objectives $O \in \mathfrak{O}$ given a set of mentions M:

$$\mathbf{O}(M) = \sum_{O \in \mathfrak{O}} \frac{|M_O|}{|M|} \cdot \frac{O(M)}{O_{max}(M) - O_{min}(M)}. \tag{1}$$

The continuous approach has several advantages over a discrete setting. First, we can exploit well established continuous optimization algorithms, such as conjugate gradient or LBFGS. Second, by optimizing upon probability distributions we are optimizing the actually desired result, in contrast to densest sub-graph algorithms where normalized confidence scores are calculated afterwards, e.g., Moro et al. (2014). Third, discrete optimization usually works on a single candidate per iteration whereas in a continuous setting, probabilities are adjusted for each candidate, which is computationally advantageous for highly ambiguous documents.

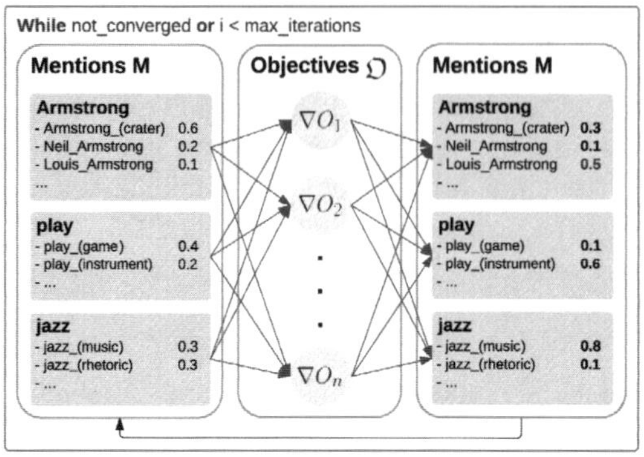

Figure 1: Illustration of our multi-objective approach to WSD & EL for the example sentence: *Armstrong plays jazz.* Mentions are disambiguated by iteratively updating probability distributions over their candidate senses with respect to the given objective gradients ∇O_i.

We normalize each objective using the difference of its maximum and minimum value for a given document, which makes the weighting of the objectives different for each document. The maximum/minimum values can be calculated analytically or, if this is not possible, by running the optimization algorithm with only the given objective for an approximate estimate for the maximum and with its negated form for an approximate minimum. Normalization is important for optimization because it ensures that the individual gradients have similar norms on average for each objective. Without normalization, optimization is biased towards objectives with large gradients.

Given that one of the objectives can be applied to only a fraction of all mentions (e.g., only nominal mentions), we scale each objective by the fraction of mentions it is applied to.

Note that our formulation could easily be extended to using additional coefficients for each ob-

[4]provided by DBpedia at `http://wiki.dbpedia.org/Downloads2014`

jective. However, these hyper-parameters would have to be estimated on development data and therefore, this method could hurt generalization.

Prior Another advantage of working with probability distributions over candidates is the easy integration of prior information. For example, the word "Paris" without further context has a strong prior on its meaning as a city instead of a person. Our approach utilizes prior information in form of frequency statistics over candidate synsets for a mention's surface string. These priors are derived from annotation frequencies provided by WordNet and Wikipedia. We make use of occurrence frequencies extracted by DBpedia Spotlight (Daiber et al., 2013) for synsets containing Wikipedia senses in case of NE disambiguation. For nominal WSD, we employ frequency statistics from WordNet for synsets containing WordNet senses. Laplace-smoothing is applied to all prior frequencies. The priors serve as initialization for the probability distributions over candidate synsets. Note that we use priors "naturally", i.e., as actual priors for initialization only and not during disambiguation itself. They should not be applied during disambiguation because these priors can be very strong and are not domain independent. However, they provide a good initialization which is important for successful continuous optimization.

3 Disambiguation Objectives

3.1 Coherence Objective

Jointly disambiguating all mentions within a document has been shown to have a large impact on disambiguation quality, especially for named entities (Kulkarni et al., 2009). It requires a measurement of semantic relatedness between concepts that can for example be extracted from a semantic network like BabelNet. However, semantic networks usually suffer from data sparsity where important links between concepts might be missing. To deal with this issue, we adopt the idea of using *semantic signatures* from Moro et al. (2014). Following their approach, we create *semantic signatures* for concepts and named entities by running a random walk with restart (RWR) in the semantic network. We count the times a vertex is visited during RWR and define all frequently visited vertices to be the *semantic signature* (i.e., a set of highly related vertices) of the starting concept or named entity vertex.

Our coherence objective aims at maximizing the semantic relatedness among selected candidate senses based on their semantic signatures S_c. We define the continuous objective using probability distributions $p_m(c)$ over the candidate set C_m of each mention $m \in M$ in a document as follows:

$$O_{\text{coh}}(M) = \sum_{\substack{m \in M \\ c \in C_m}} \sum_{\substack{m' \in M \\ m' \neq m \\ c' \in C_{m'}}} s(m, c, m', c')$$

$$s(m, c, m', c') = p_m(c) \cdot p_{m'}(c') \cdot \mathbb{1}((c, c') \in S)$$

$$p_m(c) = \frac{e^{w_{m,c}}}{\sum_{c' \in C_m} e^{w_{m,c'}}} \quad , \qquad (2)$$

where $\mathbb{1}$ denotes the indicator function and $p_m(c)$ is a softmax function. The only free, optimizable parameters are the softmax weights $\mathbf{w_m}$. This objective includes all mentions, i.e., $M_{O_{\text{coh}}} = M$. It can be interpreted as finding the densest subgraph where vertices correspond to mention-candidate pairs and edges to semantic signatures between candidate synsets. However, in contrast to a discrete setup, each vertex is now weighted by its probability and therefore each edge is weighted by the product of its adjacent vertex probabilities.

3.2 Type Objective

One of the biggest problems for supervised approaches to WSD is the limited size and synset coverage of available training datasets such as SemCor (Miller et al., 1993). One way to circumvent this problem is to use a coarser set of semantic classes that groups synsets together. Previous studies on using semantic classes for disambiguation showed promising results (Izquierdo-Beviá et al., 2006). For example, WordNet provides a mapping, called lexnames, of synsets into 45 types, which is based on the syntactic categories of synsets and their logical groupings[5]. In WordNet 13.5% of all nouns are ambiguous with an average ambiguity of 2.79 synsets per lemma. Given a noun and a type (lexname), the percentage of ambiguous nouns drops to 7.1% for which the average ambiguity drops to 2.33. This indicates that exploiting type classification for disambiguation can be very useful.

Similarly, for EL it is important to recognize the type of an entity mention in a local context.

[5] `http://wordnet.princeton.edu/man/lexnames.5WN.html`

For example, in the phrase "London beats Manchester" it is very likely that the two city names refer to sports clubs and not to the cities. We utilize an existing mapping from Wikipedia pages to types from the DBpedia ontology, restricting the set of target types to the following: "Activity", "Organisation", "Person", "Event", "Place" and "Misc" for the rest.

We train a multi-class logistic regression model for each set of types that calculates probability distributions $q_m(t)$ over WN- or DBpedia-types t given a noun- or a NE-mention m, respectively. The features used as input to the model are the following:

- word embedding of mention's surface string
- sum of word embeddings of all sentence words excluding stopwords
- word embedding of the dependency parse parent
- collocations of surrounding words as in Zhong et al. (2010)
- POS tags with up to 3 tokens distance to m
- possible types of candidate synsets

We employed pre-trained word embeddings from Mikolov et al. (2013) instead of the words themselves to increase generalization.

Type classification is included as an objective in the model as defined in equation 3. It puts type specific weights derived from type classification on candidate synsets, enforcing candidates of fitting type to have higher probabilities. The objective is only applied to noun, NE and verb mentions, i.e., $M_{O_{\text{typ}}} = M_n \cup M_{NE} \cup M_v$.

$$O_{\text{typ}}(M) = \sum_{m \in M_{O_{\text{typ}}}} \sum_{c \in C_m} q_m(t_c) \cdot p_m(c) \quad (3)$$

3.3 Regularization Objective

Because candidate priors for NE mentions can be very high, we add an additional L2-regularization objective for NE mentions:

$$O_{L2}(M) = -\frac{\lambda}{2} \sum_{m \in M_{NE}} \|\mathbf{w_m}\|_2^2 \quad (4)$$

The regularization objective is integrated in the overall objective function as it is, i.e., it is not normalized.

Dataset	|D|	|M|	KB
SemEval-2015-13 (*Sem15*) (to be published)	4	757	BN
SemEval-2013-12 (*Sem13*)	13	1931	BN
SemEval-2013-12 (*Sem13*) (Navigli et al., 2013)	13	1644	WN
SemEval-2007-17 (*Sem07*) (Pradhan et al., 2007)	3	159	WN
Senseval 3 (*Sen3*) (Snyder and Palmer, 2004)	4	886	WN
AIDA-CoNLL-testb (*AIDA*) (Hoffart et al., 2011)	216	4530	Wiki
KORE50 (*KORE*) (Hoffart et al., 2012)	50	144	Wiki

Table 1: List of datasets used in experiments with information about their number of documents (D), annotated noun and/or NE mentions (M), and their respective target knowledge base (KB): *BN-BabelNet, WN-WordNet, Wiki-Wikipedia.*

4 Experiments

4.1 Datasets

We evaluated our approach on 7 different datasets, comprising 3 WSD datasets annotated with WordNet senses, 2 datasets annotated with Wikipedia articles for EL and 2 more recent datasets annotated with Babel synsets. Table 1 contains a list of all datasets.

Besides these test datasets we used SemCor (Miller et al., 1993) as training data for WSD and the training part of the AIDA CoNLL dataset for EL.

4.2 Setup

For the creation of semantic signatures we choose the same parameter set as defined by Moro et al. (2014). We run the random walk with a restart probability of 0.85 for a total of 1 million steps for each vertex in the semantic graph and keep vertices visited at least 100 times as semantic signatures.

The L2-regularization objective for named entities is employed with $\lambda = 0.001$, which we found to perform best on the training part of the AIDA-CoNLL dataset.

We trained the multi-class logistic regression model for WN-type classification on SemCor and for DBpedia-type classification on the training part of the AIDA-CoNLL dataset using LBFGS and L2-Regularization with $\lambda = 0.01$ until convergence.

Our system optimizes the combined multi-objective function using Conjugate Gradient

System	KB	Description
IMS (Zhong and Ng, 2010)	WN	supervised, SVM
KPCS (Hoffart et al., 2011)	Wiki	greedy densest-subgraph on combined mention-entity, entity-entity measures
KORE (Hoffart et al., 2012)	Wiki	extension of KPCS with keyphrase relatedness measure between entities
MW (Milne and Witten, 2008)	Wiki	Normalized Google Distance
Babelfy (Moro et al., 2014)	BN	greedy densest-subgraph on semantic signatures

Table 2: Systems used for comparison during evaluation.

(Hestenes and Stiefel, 1952) with up to a maximum of 1000 iterations per document.

We utilized existing implementations from FACTORIE version 1.1 (McCallum et al., 2009) for logistic regression, NER tagging and Conjugate Gradient optimization. For NER tagging we used a pre-trained stacked linear-chain CRF (Lafferty et al., 2001).

4.3 Systems

We compare our approach to state-of-the-art results on all datasets and a most frequent sense (MFS) baseline. The MFS baseline selects the candidate with the highest prior as described in section 2.4. Table 2 contains a list of all systems we compared against. We use *Babelfy* as our main baseline, because of its state-of-the-art performance on all datasets and because it also employed BabelNet as its sense inventory. Note that Babelfy achieved its results with different setups for WSD and EL, in contrast to our model, which uses the same setup for both tasks.

4.4 General Results

We report the performance of all systems in terms of F1-score. To ensure fairness we restricted the candidate sets of the target mentions in each dataset to candidates of their respective reference KB. Note that our candidate mapping strategy ensures for all datasets a $97\% - 100\%$ chance that the target synset is within a mention's candidate set.

This section presents results on the evaluation datasets divided by their respective target KBs: WordNet, Wikipedia and BabelNet.

WordNet Table 3 shows the results on three datasets for the disambiguation of nouns to WordNet. Our approach exhibits state-of-the-art results outperforming all other systems on two of the three datasets. The model performs slightly worse on the Senseval 3 dataset because of one document in particular where the F1 score is very low compared to the MFS baseline. On the other three documents, however, it performs as good or even better. In general, results from the literature are always worse than the MFS baseline on this dataset. A strong improvement can be seen on the SemEval 2013 Task 12 dataset (Sem13), which is also the largest dataset. Our system achieves an improvement of nearly 7% F1 over the best other system, which translates to an error reduction of roughly 20% given that every word mention gets annotated. Besides the results presented in Table 3, we also evaluated the system on the SemEval 2007 Task 7 dataset for coarse grained WSD, where it achieved 85.5% F1 compared to the best previously reported result of 85.5% F1 from Ponzetto et al. (2010) and Babelfy with 84.6%.

System	Sens3	Sem07	Sem13
MFS	**72.6**	65.4	62.8
IMS	71.2	63.3	65.7
Babelfy	68.3	62.7	65.9
Our	68.8	**66.0**	**72.8**

Table 3: Results for nouns on WordNet annotated datasets.

System	AIDA	KORE
MFS	70.1	35.4
KPCS	82.2	55.6
KORE-LSH-G	81.8	64.6
MW	82.3	57.6
Babelfy	82.1	**71.5**
Our	**85.1**	67.4

Table 4: Results for NEs on Wikipedia annotated datasets.

Wikipedia The performance on entity linking was evaluated against state-of-the-art systems on two different datasets. The results in Table 4 demonstrate that our model can compete with the best existing models, showing superior results especially on the large AIDA CoNLL[6] test dataset comprising 216 news texts, where we achieve an error reduction of about 16%, resulting in a new state-of-the-art of 85.1% F1. On the other hand, our system is slightly worse on the KORE dataset compared to Babelfy (6 errors more in total), which might be due to the strong priors and

[6]the largest, freely available dataset for EL.

System	Sem13	Sem15
MFS	66.7	71.1
Babelfy	69.2	–
Best other	–	64.8
Our	**71.5**	**75.4**

Table 5: Results for nouns and NEs on BabelNet annotated datasets.

System	Sem13	Sem15	AIDA
MFS	66.7	71.1	70.1
O_{typ}	68.1	73.8	78.0
$O_{coh} + O_{L2}$	68.1	69.6	82.7
$O_{coh} + O_{typ} + O_{L2}$	**71.5**	**75.4**	**85.1**

Table 6: Detailed results for nouns and NEs on BabelNet annotated datasets and AIDA CoNLL.

the small context. However, the dataset is rather small, containing only 50 sentences, and has been artificially tailored to the use of highly ambiguous entity mentions. For example, persons are most of the time only mentioned by their first names. It is an interesting dataset because it requires the system to employ a lot of background knowledge about mentioned entities.

BabelNet Table 5 shows the results on the 2 existing BabelNet annotated datasets. To our knowledge, our system shows the best performance on both datasets in the literature. An interesting observation is that the F1 score on SemEval 2013 with BabelNet as target KB is lower compared to WordNet as target KB. The reason is that ambiguity rises for nominal mentions by including concepts from Wikipedia that do not exist in WordNet. For example, the Wikipedia concept "formal language" becomes a candidate for the surface string "language".

4.5 Detailed Results

We also experimented with different objective combinations, namely "type only" (O_{typ}), "coherence only" ($O_{coh} + O_{L2}$) and "all" ($O_{coh} + O_{typ} + O_{L2}$), to evaluate the impact of the different objectives. Table 6 shows results of employing individual configurations compared to the MFS baseline.

Results for only using coherence or type exhibit varying performance on the datasets, but still consistently exceed the strong MFS baseline. Combining both objectives always yields better results compared to all other configurations. This finding is important because it proves that the objectives proposed in this work are indeed complementary, and thus demonstrates the significance of combining complementary approaches in one robust framework such as ours.

An additional observation was that DBpedia-type classification slightly overfitted on the AIDA CoNLL training part. When removing DBpedia-type classification from the type objective, results increased marginally on some datasets except for the AIDA CoNLL dataset, where results decreased by roughly 3% F1. The improvements of using DBpedia-type classification are mainly due to the fact that the classifier is able to correctly classify names of places in tables consisting of sports scores not to the "Place" type but to the "Organization" type. Note that the AIDA CoNLL dataset (train and test) contains many of those tables. This shows that including supervised objectives into the system helps when data is available for the domain.

4.6 Generalization

We evaluated the ability of our system to generalize to different domains based on the SemEval 2015 Task 13 dataset. It includes documents from the bio-medical, the math&computer and general domains. Our approach performs particularly well on the bio-medical domain with 86.3% F1 (MFS: 77.3%). Results on the math&computer domain (58.8% F1, MFS: 57.0%), however, reveal that performance still strongly depends on the document topic. This indicates that either the employed resources do not cover this domain as well as others, or that it is generally more difficult to disambiguate. Another potential explanation is that enforcing only pairwise coherence does not take the hidden concepts *computer* and *maths* into account, which connect all concepts, but are never actually mentioned. An interesting point for future research might be the introduction of an additional objective or the extension of the coherence objective to allow indirect connections between candidate meanings through shared topics or categories.

Besides these very specific findings, the model's ability to generalize is strongly supported by its good results across all datasets, covering a variety of different topics.

5 Related Work

WSD Approaches to WSD can be distinguished by the kind of resource exploited. The two main resources for WSD are sense annotated datasets and knowledge bases. Typical supervised approaches like IMS (Zhong and Ng, 2010) train classifiers that learn from existing, annotated examples. They suffer from the sparsity of sense annotated datasets that is due to the data acquisition bottleneck (Pilehvar and Navigli, 2014). There have been approaches to overcome this issue through the automatic generation of such resources based on bootstrapping (Pham et al., 2005), sentences containing unambiguous relatives of senses (Martinez et al., 2008) or exploiting Wikipedia (Shen et al., 2013). On the other hand, knowledge-based approaches achieve good performances rivaling state-of-the-art supervised systems (Ponzetto and Navigli, 2010) by using existing structured knowledge (Lesk, 1986; Agirre et al., 2014), or take advantage of the structure of a given semantic network through connectivity or centrality measures (Tsatsaronis et al., 2007; Navigli and Lapata, 2010). Such systems benefit from the availability of numerous KBs for a variety of domains. We believe that both knowledge-based approaches and supervised methods have unique, complementary abilities that need to be combined for sophisticated disambiguation.

EL Typical EL systems employ supervised machine learning algorithms to classify or rank candidate entities (Bunescu and Pasca, 2006; Milne and Witten, 2008; Zhang et al., 2010). Common features include popularity metrics based on Wikipedia's graph structure or on name mention frequency (Dredze et al., 2010; Han and Zhao, 2009), similarity metrics exploring Wikipedia's concept relations (Han and Zhao, 2009), and string similarity features. Mihalcea and Csomai (2007) disambiguate each mention independently given its sentence level context only. In contrast, Cucerzan (2007) and Kulkarni et al. (Kulkarni et al., 2009) recognize the interdependence between entities in a wider context. The most similar work to ours is that of Hoffart et al. (2011) which was the first that combined local and global context measures in one robust model. However, objectives and the disambiguation algorithm differ from our work. They represent the disambiguation task as a densest subgraph problem where the least connected entity is eliminated in each iteration. The discrete treatment of candidate entities can be problematic especially at the beginning of disambiguation where it is biased towards mentions with many candidates.

Babelfy (Moro et al., 2014) is a knowledge-based approach for joint WSD and EL that also uses a greedy densest subgraph algorithm for disambiguation. It employs a single coherence model based on semantic signatures similar to our coherence objective. The system's very good performance indicates that the semantic signatures provide a powerful resource for joint disambiguation. However, because we believe it is not sufficient to only enforce semantic agreement among nouns and entities, our approach includes an objective that also focuses on the local context of mentions, making it more robust.

6 Conclusions & Future Work

We have presented a novel approach for the joint disambiguation of nouns and named entities based on an extensible framework. Our system employs continuous optimization on a multi-objective function during disambiguation. The integration of complementary objectives into our formalism demonstrates that robust disambiguation can be achieved by considering both the local and the global context of a mention. Our model outperforms previous state-of-the-art systems for nominal WSD and for EL. It is the first system that achieves such results on various WSD and EL datasets using a single setup.

In future work, new objectives should be integrated into the framework and existing objectives could be enhanced. For example, it would be interesting to express semantic relatedness continuously rather than in a binary setting for the coherence objective. Additionally, using the entire model during training could ensure better compatibility between the different objectives. At the moment, the model itself is composed of different pre-trained models that are only combined during disambiguation.

Acknowledgment

This research was partially supported by the German Federal Ministry of Education and Research (BMBF) through the projects ALL SIDES (01IW14002), BBDC (01IS14013E), and by the German Federal Ministry of Economics and Energy (BMWi) through the project SD4M (01MD15007B), and by Google through a Focused Research Award granted in July 2013.

References

[Agirre et al.2014] Eneko Agirre, Oier Lopez de Lacalle, and Aitor Soroa. 2014. Random walks for knowledge-based word sense disambiguation. *Computational Linguistics*, 40(1):57–84.

[Bunescu and Pasca2006] Razvan C Bunescu and Marius Pasca. 2006. Using encyclopedic knowledge for named entity disambiguation. In *EACL*, volume 6, pages 9–16.

[Cucerzan2007] Silviu Cucerzan. 2007. Large-scale named entity disambiguation based on wikipedia data. In *EMNLP-CoNLL*, volume 7, pages 708–716.

[Daiber et al.2013] Joachim Daiber, Max Jakob, Chris Hokamp, and Pablo N Mendes. 2013. Improving efficiency and accuracy in multilingual entity extraction. In *Proceedings of the 9th International Conference on Semantic Systems*, pages 121–124. ACM.

[Dredze et al.2010] Mark Dredze, Paul McNamee, Delip Rao, Adam Gerber, and Tim Finin. 2010. Entity disambiguation for knowledge base population. In *Proc. of the 23rd International Conference on Computational Linguistics*, pages 277–285. Association for Computational Linguistics.

[Fellbaum1998] Christiane Fellbaum. 1998. *WordNet*. Wiley Online Library.

[Han and Zhao2009] Xianpei Han and Jun Zhao. 2009. Named entity disambiguation by leveraging wikipedia semantic knowledge. In *Proc. of the 18th ACM conference on Information and knowledge management*, pages 215–224. ACM.

[Hestenes and Stiefel1952] Magnus Rudolph Hestenes and Eduard Stiefel. 1952. *Methods of conjugate gradients for solving linear systems*, volume 49. National Bureau of Standards Washington, DC.

[Hoffart et al.2011] Johannes Hoffart, Mohamed Amir Yosef, Ilaria Bordino, Hagen Fürstenau, Manfred Pinkal, Marc Spaniol, Bilyana Taneva, Stefan Thater, and Gerhard Weikum. 2011. Robust disambiguation of named entities in text. In *Proc. of the Conference on Empirical Methods in Natural Language Processing*, pages 782–792. Association for Computational Linguistics.

[Hoffart et al.2012] Johannes Hoffart, Stephan Seufert, Dat Ba Nguyen, Martin Theobald, and Gerhard Weikum. 2012. Kore: keyphrase overlap relatedness for entity disambiguation. In *Proc. of the 21st ACM international conference on Information and knowledge management*, pages 545–554. ACM.

[Izquierdo-Beviá et al.2006] Rubén Izquierdo-Beviá, Lorenza Moreno-Monteagudo, Borja Navarro, and Armando Suárez. 2006. Spanish all-words semantic class disambiguation using cast3lb corpus. In *MICAI 2006: Advances in Artificial Intelligence*, pages 879–888. Springer.

[Kulkarni et al.2009] Sayali Kulkarni, Amit Singh, Ganesh Ramakrishnan, and Soumen Chakrabarti. 2009. Collective annotation of wikipedia entities in web text. In *Proc. of the 15th ACM SIGKDD international conference on Knowledge discovery and data mining*, pages 457–466. ACM.

[Lafferty et al.2001] John D. Lafferty, Andrew McCallum, and Fernando C. N. Pereira. 2001. Conditional random fields: Probabilistic models for segmenting and labeling sequence data. In *Proceedings of the Eighteenth International Conference on Machine Learning*, ICML '01, pages 282–289, San Francisco, CA, USA. Morgan Kaufmann Publishers Inc.

[Lesk1986] Michael Lesk. 1986. Automatic sense disambiguation using machine readable dictionaries: how to tell a pine cone from an ice cream cone. In *Proc. of the 5th annual international conference on Systems documentation*, pages 24–26. ACM.

[Martinez et al.2008] David Martinez, Oier Lopez De Lacalle, and Eneko Agirre. 2008. On the use of automatically acquired examples for all-nouns word sense disambiguation. *J. Artif. Intell. Res.(JAIR)*, 33:79–107.

[McCallum et al.2009] Andrew McCallum, Karl Schultz, and Sameer Singh. 2009. FACTORIE: Probabilistic programming via imperatively defined factor graphs. In *Neural Information Processing Systems (NIPS)*.

[Mihalcea and Csomai2007] Rada Mihalcea and Andras Csomai. 2007. Wikify!: linking documents to encyclopedic knowledge. In *Proc. of the sixteenth ACM conference on Conference on information and knowledge management*, pages 233–242. ACM.

[Mikolov et al.2013] Tomas Mikolov, Ilya Sutskever, Kai Chen, Greg S Corrado, and Jeff Dean. 2013. Distributed representations of words and phrases and their compositionality. In *Advances in Neural Information Processing Systems*, pages 3111–3119.

[Miller et al.1993] George A Miller, Claudia Leacock, Randee Tengi, and Ross T Bunker. 1993. A semantic concordance. In *Proc. of the workshop on Human Language Technology*, pages 303–308. Association for Computational Linguistics.

[Milne and Witten2008] David Milne and Ian H Witten. 2008. Learning to link with wikipedia. In *Proc. of the 17th ACM conference on Information and knowledge management*, pages 509–518. ACM.

[Moro et al.2014] Andrea Moro, Alessandro Raganato, and Roberto Navigli. 2014. Entity linking meets word sense disambiguation: A unified approach. *Transactions of the Association for Computational Linguistics*, 2.

[Navigli and Lapata2010] Roberto Navigli and Mirella Lapata. 2010. An experimental study of graph connectivity for unsupervised word sense disambiguation. *Pattern Analysis and Machine Intelligence, IEEE Transactions on*, 32(4):678–692.

[Navigli and Ponzetto2012] Roberto Navigli and Simone Paolo Ponzetto. 2012. Babelnet: The automatic construction, evaluation and application of a wide-coverage multilingual semantic network. *Artificial Intelligence*, 193:217–250.

[Navigli et al.2013] Roberto Navigli, David Jurgens, and Daniele Vannella. 2013. Semeval-2013 task 12: Multilingual word sense disambiguation. In *Second Joint Conference on Lexical and Computational Semantics (SEM)*, volume 2, pages 222–231.

[Navigli2009] Roberto Navigli. 2009. Word sense disambiguation: A survey. *ACM Computing Surveys (CSUR)*, 41(2):10.

[Pham et al.2005] Thanh Phong Pham, Hwee Tou Ng, and Wee Sun Lee. 2005. Word sense disambiguation with semi-supervised learning. In *Proc. of the national conference on artificial intelligence*, volume 20, page 1093. Menlo Park, CA; Cambridge, MA; London; AAAI Press; MIT Press; 1999.

[Pilehvar and Navigli2014] Mohammad Taher Pilehvar and Roberto Navigli. 2014. A large-scale pseudoword-based evaluation framework for state-of-the-art word sense disambiguation. *Computational Linguistics*, 40(4):837–881.

[Ponzetto and Navigli2010] Simone Paolo Ponzetto and Roberto Navigli. 2010. Knowledge-rich word sense disambiguation rivaling supervised systems. In *Proc. of the 48th annual meeting of the association for computational linguistics*, pages 1522–1531. Association for Computational Linguistics.

[Pradhan et al.2007] Sameer S Pradhan, Edward Loper, Dmitriy Dligach, and Martha Palmer. 2007. Semeval-2007 task 17: English lexical sample, srl and all words. In *Proc. of the 4th International Workshop on Semantic Evaluations*, pages 87–92. Association for Computational Linguistics.

[Shen et al.2013] Hui Shen, Razvan Bunescu, and Rada Mihalcea. 2013. Coarse to fine grained sense disambiguation in wikipedia. *Proc. of SEM*, pages 22–31.

[Snyder and Palmer2004] Benjamin Snyder and Martha Palmer. 2004. The english all-words task. In *Senseval-3: Third International Workshop on the Evaluation of Systems for the Semantic Analysis of Text*, pages 41–43.

[Tsatsaronis et al.2007] George Tsatsaronis, Michalis Vazirgiannis, and Ion Androutsopoulos. 2007. Word sense disambiguation with spreading activation networks generated from thesauri. In *IJCAI*, volume 7, pages 1725–1730.

[Zhang et al.2010] Wei Zhang, Jian Su, Chew Lim Tan, and Wen Ting Wang. 2010. Entity linking leveraging: automatically generated annotation. In *Proc. of the 23rd International Conference on Computational Linguistics*, pages 1290–1298. Association for Computational Linguistics.

[Zhong and Ng2010] Zhi Zhong and Hwee Tou Ng. 2010. It makes sense: A wide-coverage word sense disambiguation system for free text. In *Proc. of the ACL 2010 System Demonstrations*, pages 78–83. Association for Computational Linguistics.

Building a Scientific Concept Hierarchy Database (SCHBASE)

Eytan Adar
University of Michigan
Ann Arbor, MI 48104
eadar@umich.edu

Srayan Datta
University of Michigan
Ann Arbor, MI 48104
srayand@umich.edu

Abstract

Extracted keyphrases can enhance numerous applications ranging from search to tracking the evolution of scientific discourse. We present SCHBASE, a hierarchical database of keyphrases extracted from large collections of scientific literature. SCHBASE relies on a tendency of scientists to generate new abbreviations that "extend" existing forms as a form of signaling novelty. We demonstrate how these keyphrases/concepts can be extracted, and their viability as a database in relation to existing collections. We further show how keyphrases can be placed into a semantically-meaningful "phylogenetic" structure and describe key features of this structure. The complete SCHBASE dataset is available at: http://cond.org/schbase.html.

1 Introduction

Due to the immense practical value to Information Retrieval and other text mining applications, keyphrase extraction has become an extremely popular topic of research. Extracted keyphrases, specifically those derived from scientific literature, support search tasks (Anick, 2003), classification and tagging (Medelyan et al., 2009), information extraction (Wu and Weld, 2008), and higher-level analysis such as the tracking of influence and dynamics of information propagation (Shi et al., 2010; Ohniwa et al., 2010). In our own work we use the extracted hierarchies to predict scientific emergence based on how rapidly new variants emerge. Keyphrases themselves capture a diverse set of scientific language (e.g., methods, techniques, materials, phenomena, processes, diseases, devices).

Keyphrases, and their uses, have been studied extensively (Gil-Leiva and Alonso-Arroyo, 2007). However, automated keyphrase *extraction* work has often focused on large-scale statistical techniques and ignored the scientific communication literature. This literature points to the complex ways in which keyphrases are created in light of competing demands: expressiveness, findability, succinct writing, signaling novelty, signaling community membership, and so on (Hartley and Kostoff, 2003; Ibrahim, 1989; Grange and Bloom, 2000; Gil-Leiva and Alonso-Arroyo, 2007). Furthermore, the tendency to extract keyphrases through statistical mechanisms often leads to flat keyphrase spaces that make analysis of evolution and emergence difficult.

Our contention, and the main motivation behind our work, is that we can do better by leveraging explicit mechanisms adopted by authors in keyphrase generation. Specifically, we focus on a tendency to expand keyphrases by adding terms, coupled with a pressure to abbreviate to retain succinctness. As we argue below, scientific communication has evolved the use of abbreviations to deal with various constraints. Abbreviations, and acronyms specifically, are relatively new in many scientific domains (Grange and Bloom, 2000; Fandrych, 2008) but are now ubiquitous (Ibrahim, 1989; Cheng, 2010).

Keyphrase selection is often motivated by increasing article findability within a domain (thereby increasing citation). This strategy leads to keyphrase reuse. A competing pressure, however, is to signal novelty in an author's work which is often done by creating new terminology (e.g., creating a "brand" around a system or idea). For

Proceedings of the 53rd Annual Meeting of the Association for Computational Linguistics and the 7th International Joint Conference on Natural Language Processing, pages 606–615, Beijing, China, July 26-31, 2015.

example, a machine learning expert working on a new type of Support Vector Machine will want their article found when someone searches for "Support Vector Machine," but will also want to add their own unique brand. In response, they will often augment the original keyphrase (e.g., "Least-Squares Support Vector Machine") rather than inventing a completely new one. Unfortunately, continuous expansion will soon render a paper unreadable (e.g., one of many extensions to *Polymerase Chain Reaction* is *Standard Curve Quantitative Competitive Reverse Transcription Polymerase Chain Reaction*). Thus emerges a second strategy: abbreviation.

Our assertion is that abbreviations are a key mechanism for resolving competing demands. Authors can simultaneously expand keyphrases, thus maintaining both findability and novelty, while at the same time addressing the need to be succinct and non-repetitive. Of interest to us is the phenomena that if a new keyphrase expands an existing keyphrase that has an established abbreviation, the new keyphrase will also be abbreviated (e.g., LS-SVM and SVM). This tendency allows us to construct hierarchies of evolved keyphrases (rather than assuming a flat keyphrase space) which can be leveraged to identify emergence, keyphrase "mash-ups," and perform other high level analysis. As we demonstrate below, edges represent the rough semantic of EXTENDS or ISSUBTYPEOF. So if keyphrase *A* is connected to *B*, we can say *A* is a subtype of *B* (e.g., *A* is "Least-Squares Support Vector Machine" and *B* is "Support Vector Machine").

In this paper we introduce SCHBASE, a hierarchical database of keyphrases. We demonstrate how we can simply, but effectively, extract keyphrases by mining abbreviations from scientific literature and composing those keyphrases into semantically-meaningful hierarchies. We further show that abbreviations are a viable mechanism for building a domain-specific keyphrase database by comparing our extracted keyphrases to a number of author-defined and automatically-created keyphrase corpora. Finally, we illustrate how authors build upon each others' terminology over time to create new keyphrases.[1]

[1]Full database available at: http://cond.org/schbase.html

2 Related Work

Initial work in keyphrase extraction utilized heuristics that were based on the understood structure of scientific documents (Edmundson, 1969). As more data became available, it was possible to move away from heuristic cues and to leverage statistical techniques (Paice and Jones, 1993; Turney, 2000; Frank et al., 1999) that could identify keyphrases within, and between, documents. The guiding model in this approach is that phrases that appear as statistical "anomalies" (by some measure) are effective for summarizing a document or corpus. This style of keyphrase extraction represents much of the current state-of-the-art (Kim et al., 2010). Specific extensions in this space involve the use of network structures (Mihalcea and Tarau, 2004; Litvak and Last, 2008; Das Gollapalli and Caragea, 2014), part-of-speech features (Barker and Cornacchia, 2000; Hulth, 2003), or more sophisticated metrics (Tomokiyo and Hurst, 2003).

However, as we note above, these statistical approaches largely ignore the underlying tensions in scientific communication that lead to the creation of new keyphrases and how they are signaled to others. The result is that these techniques often find statistically "anomalous" phrases which often are not valid scientific concepts (but are simply uncommon phrasing), are unstructured and disconnected, and inflexible to size variance (as in the case of fixed length n-grams), and fail to capture extremely rare terminology.

The idea that abbreviations may be useful for keyphrase extraction has been partially realized. Nguyen et al., (2007) found that they could produce better keyphrases by extending existing models (Frank et al., 1999) to include an acronym indicator as a feature. That is, if a candidate phrase had an associated parenthetical acronym associated with it in the text a binary feature would be set. This approach has been implemented by others (Bordea and Buitelaar, 2010). We propose to expand on this idea by implementing a simple, but effective, solution by performing abbreviation extraction to build a hierarchical keyphrase database – a form of open-information extraction (Etzioni et al., 2008) on large scientific corpora.

3 Keyphrases and Hierarchies

Our high level strategy for finding an initial set of keyphrases is to mine a corpus for abbreviation expansions. This is a simple strategy, but as we show below, highly effective. Though the idea that abbreviations and keyphrases are linked fits within our understanding of scientific writing, we confirmed our intuition through a small experiment. Specifically, we looked at the 85 unique keyphrases (in this case, article titles) listed in the Wikipedia entry for *List of Machine Learning Concepts* (Wikipedia, 2014). These ranged from well known terms (e.g., *Support Vector Machines* and *Autoencoders*) to less known (e.g., *Information fuzzy networks*). In *all* 85 cases we were able to find an abbreviation on the Web (using Google) alongside the expansion (e.g., searching for the phrases *"Support Vector Machines (SVMs)"* or *"Information Fuzzy Networks (IFN)"*). Though there may be bias in the use of abbreviations in the Machine Learning literature, our experience has been that this holds in other domains as well. When a scientific keyphrase is used often enough, someone, somewhere, will have abbreviated it.

3.1 Abbreviation Extraction

To find all abbreviation expansions we use the unsupervised SaRAD algorithm (Adar, 2004). This algorithm is simple to implement, does not require extremely large amounts of data, works for both acronyms and more general abbreviations, and has been demonstrated as effective in various contexts (Adar, 2004; Schwartz and Hearst, 2003). However, our solution does not depend on a specific implementation, only that we are able to accurately identify abbreviation expansions.

Adar (2004) presents the full details for the algorithm, but for completeness we present the high level details. The algorithm progresses by identifying abbreviations inside of parentheses (defined as single words with at least one capital letter). The algorithm then extracts a "window" of text preceding the parenthesis, up to n words long (where n is the character length of the abbreviation plus padding). This window does not cross sentence boundaries. Within the window all possible "explanations" of the abbreviation are derived.

An explanation consists of a continuous subsequence of words that contain all the characters of the original abbreviation *in order*. For example, the window "determine the geographical distribution of ribonucleic acid" preceding the abbreviation "RNA" includes the explanations: "dete*r*mi*n*e the geogr*a*phical," "g*r*aphical distributio*n* of ribonucleic *a*cid" and "*r*ibo*n*ucleic *a*cid" (matching characters in italics). In the example above there are ten explanations (five unique). Each explanation is scored heuristically: 1 point for each abbreviation character at the start of a word; 1 point subtracted for every word between the explanation and the parenthesis; 1 point bonus if the explanation is adjacent to the parenthesis; 1 point subtracted for each extra word beyond the abbreviation length. For the explanations above, the scores are -4, 0, and 3 respectively. The highest scoring match (we require a minimum of 1 point) is returned as the mostly likely expansion.

In practice, pairs of extracted abbreviations/expansions are pulled from a large textual corpus. This both allows us to identify variants of expansions (e.g., different pluralization, spelling, hyphenation, etc.) as well as finding more plausible expansions (those that are repeated multiple times in a corpus). Thus, each expansion/abbreviation pair has an associated count which can be used to threshold and filter for increased quality. To discard units of measurement, single letter abbreviations and single word expansions are removed. We return to this decision later, but our experience is also that single word keyphrases are rare. Additionally, expansions containing brackets are not considered as they usually represent mathematical formulae.

3.1.1 The AbbrevCorpus

In our experiments we utilize the ACM Digital Library (ACMDL) as our main corpus. Though the ACMDL is more limited than other collections, it has a number of desirable properties: spanning nearly the entire history (1954-2011) of a domain (Computer Science) with full-text and clean metadata. The corpus itself contains both journal and conference articles (77k and 197k, respectively).

In addition to the filtering rules described above, we manually constructed a set of filter terms to remove publication venues, agencies, and other institutions: 'university', 'conference', 'symposium', 'journal', 'foundation', 'consortium', 'agency', 'institute' and 'school' are discarded. We further normalize our keyphrases by lowercasing, removing hyphens, and using the Snowball stemmer (Porter, 2001) to merge plural variants. After stemming and normalizing, we found a total of 155,957 unique abbreviation expansions. Among these, 48,890 expansions occur more than once, 25,107 expansions thrice or more and 16,916 expansions four or more times. We refer to this collection as the ABBREVCORPUS.

For each keyphrase we search within the full-text corpus to identify set of documents containing the keyphrase. This allowed us to find both the earliest mention of the keyphrase (the expansion, not the abbreviation) as well as overall popularity of keyphrases. We do not argue that abbreviations are the norm in the introduction of new keyphrases and may, in fact, only happen much later when the domain is familiar enough with the phrase.

To find the expansions in the full-text we utilize a modified suffix-tree that greedily finds the longest-matching phrase and avoids "double-counting". For example, if the text contains the phrase, "...we utilize a Least-Squares Support Vector Machine for ..." it will match against *Least-Squares Support Vector Machine* but not *Least Squares*, *Support Vector Machines*, or *Support Vector* (also keyphrases in our collection). The distribution of keyphrase frequency is a power-law (many keyphrases appearing once with a long tail) with exponent (α) of 2.17 (fit using Clauset et al., (2009)).

3.2 Building Keyphrase Hierarchies

We employ a very simple method of text containment to build keyphrase hierarchies from ABBREVCORPUS. If a keyphrase A is a *substring* of keyphrase B, A is said to be contained by B ($B \rightarrow A$). If a third keyphrase, C, *contains* B and is *contained* by A, the containment link between A and B is dropped and two new ones ($A \rightarrow C$ and $C \rightarrow B$) are added. For example for the keyphrases, *circuit switching*, *optical circuit switching* and *dynamic optical circuit switching*, there are links from *optical circuit switching* to *circuit switching*, and *dynamic optical circuit switching* to *optical circuit switching*, but there is no link from *dynamic optical circuit switching* to *circuit switching*. The hierarchies formed in this manner are mostly trees, but in rare cases a keyphrase can have links to multiple branches. Example hierarchies are displayed in Figure 1.

For efficiency we sort all keyphrases by length (from largest to shortest) and iterate over each one, testing for containment in all previously "seen" keyphrases. This is computationally intensive, $O(n^2)$, but can be parallelized.

A potential issue with string containment is that negating prefixes can also appear (e.g., *non-monotonic reasoning* and *monotonic reasoning*). Our algorithm uses a dictionary of negations and can annotate the results. However, in practice we find that only .6% of our data has a leading negating-prefix ("internal" negating prefixes can also be caught in this way, but are similarly rare). It is an application-specific question if we want to consider such pairs as "siblings" or "parent-child" (with both supported).

4 Overlap with Keyphrase Corpora

To test our newly-constructed keyphrase database we generate a mixture of human- and machine-built datasets to compare. Our goal is to characterize both the intersection (keyphrases appearing in our corpus as well as the external datasets) as well as those keyphrases uniquely captured by each dataset.

4.1 ACM Author keyphrases (ACMCORPUS)

The metadata for articles in ACM corpus contain author-provided keyphrases. In the corpus described above, we found 145,373 unique author-provided keyphrases after stemming and normalization. We discard 16,418 single-word keywords and those that do not appear in the full-text of any document. We retain 116,246 keyphrases which we refer to as the ACMCORPUS.

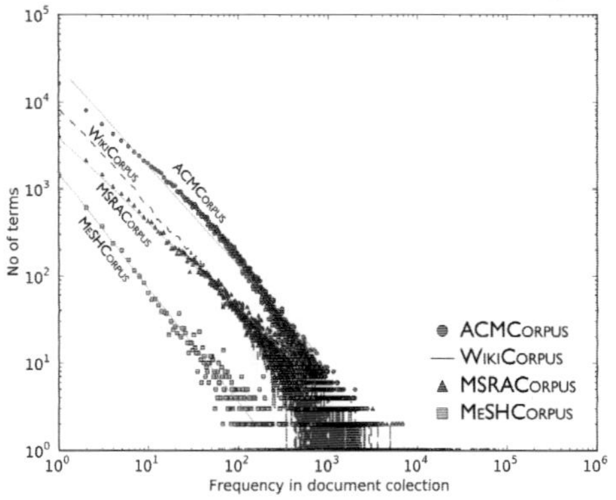

Figure 2: Keyphrase counts for the ACMCORPUS (powerlaw $\alpha = 2.36$), WIKICORPUS (2.49), MSRACORPUS (2.55) and MESHCORPUS (2.7) within the ACM full-text.

4.2 Microsoft Academic (MSRACORPUS)

Our second keyphrase dataset comes from the Microsoft Academic (MSRA) search corpus (Microsoft, 2015). While particularly focused on

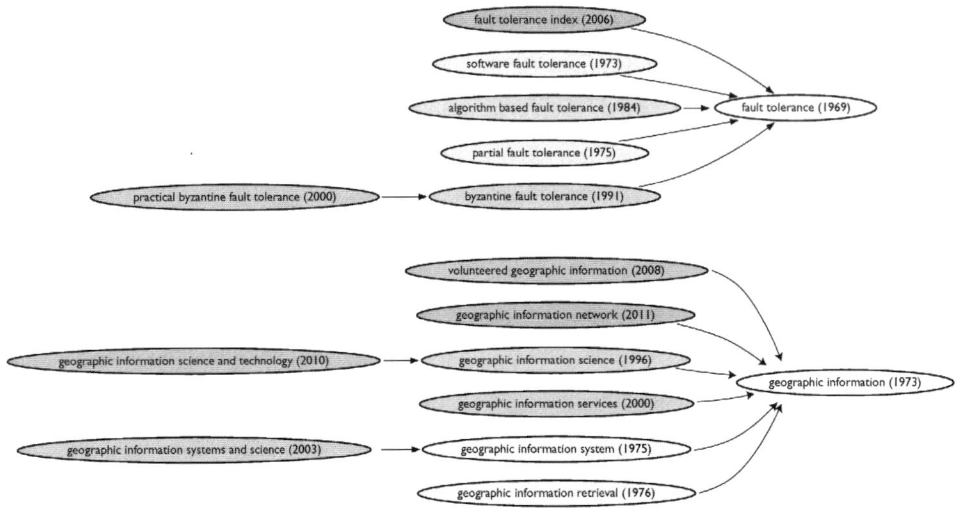

Figure 1: Keyphrase hierarchy for *Fault Tolerance* (top) and *Geographic Information* (Bottom). Colors encode earliest appearance (brighter green is earlier)

Computer Science, this collection contains articles and keyphrases from over a dozen domains[2]. MSRA provides a list of keyphrases with unique IDs and different stemming variations of each keyphrase. There are a total of 46,978 (without counting stemming variations) of which 30,477 keyphrases occur in ACM full-text corpus after stemming and normalization (64% coverage).

4.3 MeSH (MESHCORPUS)

Medical Subject Headings (MeSH) (Lipscomb, 2000) is set of subject headings or descriptors in the life sciences domain. For the purpose of our work, we use the 27,149 keyphrases from the 2014 MeSH dataset. Similar to the other keyphrase lists we only use stemmed and normalized multi-word keywords that occur in in the ACM full-text corpus, which is 4,363 in case of MeSH.

4.4 Wikipedia (WIKICORPUS)

Scientific article headings in Wikipedia can often be used as a proxy for keyphrases. To collect relevant titles, we find Wikipedia articles that exactly match (in title name) existing MeSH and MSRA keyphrases. For these "seed" articles, we compile their categories and mark all the articles in these categories as potentially "relevant." However, as this also captures scientist names (e.g., a researcher's page may be placed under the "Computer Science" category), research institutes and other non-keyphrase matches, we use the page's infobox as a further filter. Pages containing "person," "place," infoboxes, in "book," "video game," "TV show" or other related "media" category, and those with geographical coordinates are removed. After applying these filters, we obtain 110,102 unique article titles (after stemming) which we treat as keyphrases. Of these, 39,974 occur in the ACM full-text corpus.

[2]We know these keyphrases are algorithmically derived, but the details are not disclosed.

4.5 Results

The total overlap for ACMCORPUS, MESHCORPUS, MSRACORPUS and WIKICORPUS are 14.12%, 12.28%, 32.33% and 17.41% respectively. While these numbers seem low, it is worth noting that many of these terms only appear *once* in the ACM full-text corpus (see Figure 2).

Figure 3 illustrates the relationship between the number of times a keyphrase appears in the full-text and the probability that it will appear in ABBREVCORPUS. In all cases, the more often a keyphrase appears in the corpus, the more likely it is to have an abbreviation. If we qualitatively examine popular phrases that do not appear in ABBREVCORPUS we find mathematical forms (e.g., *of-the-form*, *well-defined* or *a priori*), and nouns/entities that are largely unrelated to scientific keyphrases (e.g., *New Jersey*, *Government Agency*, and *Private Sector*). More importantly, the majority of phrases that are never abbreviated are simply not Computer Science keyphrases (we return to this in Section 4.6).

We were somewhat surprised by the poor overlap of the ACMCORPUS, even for terms that were very common in the full-text. We found that the cause was a large set of "bad" keyphrases. Specifically, 69.3k (69.5%) of author-defined keyphrases (occurring in ACMCORPUS *but not* in ABBREVCORPUS) are used as a keyword in only one paper. However, they appear more than once in the full-text – often many times. For example, one author (and only one) used *if and only if* as a keyphrase, which matched a great many articles. The result is that there is little correlation between the number of times a keyphrase appears in the full-text and how many times it used explicitly as a keyphrase in the document metadata. Because these will never be found as an abbreviation, they "pull" the mean probability down.

Instead of counting the number of times a keyphrase occurs in the full-text we generate a frequency count based on the number of times authors explicitly use it in the metadata. This new curve, labeled as ACMCORPUS (KEY) in Figure 3 displays a very different tendency, with a rapid upward slope that peaks at 100% for frequently-occurring keyphrases. Notably, only 16k (16%) keyphrases appear once in full-text but are never abbreviated (far fewer than the 69.5% above).

It is worth briefly considering those terms that appear in ABBREVCORPUS and not in the other keyphrases lists. We find roughly 17.6k, 24.7k, 19.4k, and 21.4k terms that appear in ABBREVCORPUS (with a threshold of 2 to eliminate "noisy" expansions), but not in ACMCORPUS, MESHCORPUS, MSRACORPUS, and WIKICORPUS respectively. As MeSH keyphrases tend to be focused on the biological keyphrases this is perhaps unsurprising but the high numbers for the author-provided ACM keyphrases is unexpected. We find that some of the keyphrases that are in ABBREVCORPUS but not in ACMCORPUS are highly specific (e.g., *Multi-object Evolutionary Algorithm Based on Decomposition* or *Stochastic Variable Graph Model*). However, many are also extremely generic terms that one *would* expect to find in a computer science corpus: *Run-Time Error Detection*, *Parallel Execution Tree*, and *Little Endian*. Our hypothesis is that these are often not the focus of a paper and are unlikely to be selected

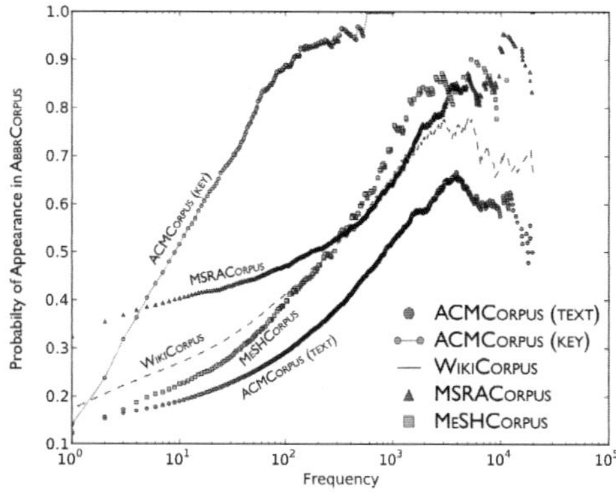

Figure 3: The probability of inclusion of keyphrases in ABBREVCORPUS based on frequency of appearance in full text or, in the case if ACMCORPUS (KEY), frequency of use as a keyword. At frequency x, the y value represents probability of appearence in ABBREVCORPUS if we only consider terms that appear at least x times in the other corpus.

by the author. We believe this provides further evidence of the viability of the abbreviation approach to generating good keyphrase lists.

4.6 Domain keyphrases

When looking at keyphrases that appear in MESHCORPUS but not in the ABBREVCORPUS we find that many phrases do, in fact, appear in the full text but are never abbreviated. For example, *Color Perception* and *Blood Cell* both appear in ACM articles but are not abbreviated. Our hypothesis—which is motivated by the tendency of scientists to abbreviate terms that are deeply familiar to their community (Grange and Bloom, 2000)—is that terms that are possibly distant from the core domain focus tend not to be abbreviated. This is supported by the fact that these terms *are* abbreviated in other collections (e.g., one can find CP as an abbreviation for Color Perception in psychology and cognition work and BC, for Blood Cell, in medical and biological journals). Additional evidence is apparent in Figure 3 which shows that ACMCORPUS keyphrases are more likely to be abbreviated (with far fewer repeats necessary). MSRACORPUS, which contains many Computer Science articles, also has higher probabilities (though not nearly matching the ACM).

To test this systematically, we calculated semantic similarity between each keyphrase in the *WikiCorpus* dataset to "computer science." Specifically, we utilize Explicit Semantic Analysis (Gabrilovich and Markovitch, 2009) to calculate similarity. In this method, every segment of text is represented in a very high dimensional space in terms of keyphrases (based on Wikipedia categories). The similarity score for each term is between 0 (unrelated) and 1 (very similar).

Figure 4 demonstrates that with increasing similarity, the likelihood of abbreviation increases. From this, one may infer that to generate a domain-specific database that excludes unrelated keyphrases, the abbreviation-derived corpus is highly appropriate. Conversely, to get coverage of keyphrases from all scientific domains it is insufficient to mine for abbreviations in one specific domain's text. Even though a keyphrase may appear in the full-text it will simply never be abbreviated.

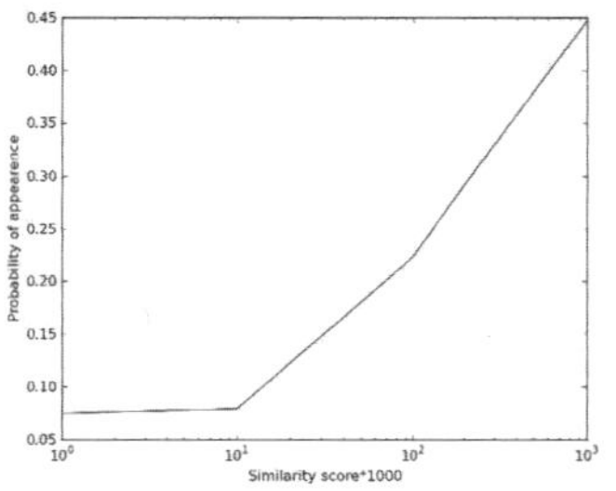

Figure 4: Probability of a keyphrase appearing in ABBREVCORPUS (y-axis) based on semantic similarity of the keyphrase to "Computer Science" (x-axis, binned exponentially for readability).

4.7 Keyphrase Hierarchies

Our hierarchy generation process (see Section 3.2) generated 1716 hierarchies accounting for 8661 unique keyphrases. Most of the hierarchies (1002 or 58%) only contained two nodes (a root and one child). The degree distribution, aggregated across all hierarchies, is again power-law ($\alpha = 2.895$). Hierarchy sizes are power-law distributed ($\alpha = 2.807$) and an average "diameter" (max height) of 1.135. The hierarchies contain a giant component with 2302 nodes and 2436 edges.

While most of our hierarchies are trees, keyphrases can connect to two independent branches. For example, *Least-Squares Support Vector Machines (LS-SVMs)* appears in both the *Least Squares* and *Support Vector* hierarchies. In total, 649 keyphrases appear in multiple hierarchies, the majority appearing 2. Only 17 keyphrases appear in 3 hierarchies. For example, the particularly long *Single Instruction Multiple Thread Evolution Strategy Pattern Search* appears in the *Evolution(ary) Strategy*, *Pattern Search*, and *Single-Instruction-Multiple-Thread* hierarchies. These collisions are interesting in that they reflect a mash-ups of different concepts, and by extension, different sub-disciplines or techniques. In some situations, where there is an overlap in many sub-keyphrases, this may indicate that two root keyphrases are in fact equivalent or highly related (e.g., *likelihood ratio* and *log likelihood*). We do not currently handle such ambiguity in SCHBASE.

To test the semantic interpretation of edges as EXTENDS/ISSUBTYPEOF we randomly sampled 200 edges and manually checked these. We found that in 92% (184) this interpretation was correct. The remaining 16 were largely an artifact of normalization errors rather than a wrong "type" (e.g., "session identifier" and "session id" where clearly a more accurate interpretation is ISEXPANSIONOF). We believe it is fair to say that the hierarchies we construct are the "skeleton" of a full EXTENDS hierarchy but one that is nonetheless fairly encompassing. Our qualitative analysis is that most keyphrases that share a type also share a root keyphrase (e.g., "classifier").

It is interesting to consider if edges which are derived by "containment" reflect a temporal pattern. That is, if keyphrase A EXTENDS B, does the first mention of A in the literature happen after B? We find that this is almost always the case. Among the 7136 edges generated by our algorithm only 165 (2.3%) are "reversed." Qualitatively, we find that these instances appear either due to missing data (the parent keyphrase first appeared outside the ACM) or publication ordering (in some cases the difference in first-appearance is only a year). In most situations the date is only 1-2 years apart. This high degree of consistency lends further support to the tendency of scientists to expand upon keyphrases over time.

Figure 5 depicts the mean change in length of "children" in keyphrase hierarchies. The numbers depicted are relative change. Thus, at year "0", the year the root keyphrase is introduced, there is no relative increase. Within 1 year, new children of that root are 50% larger in character length and after that children continue to "grow" as authors add additional keyphrases. A particularly obvious example of this is the branch for *Petri Net (PN)* which was extended as *Queueing Petri Net (QPN)* and then *Hierarchically Combined Queueing Petri Nets (HCQPN)* and finally *Extended Hierarchically Combined Queueing Petri Nets (EHCQPN)*. Notably, this may have implications to other extractors that assume fixed-sized entities over the history of the collection.

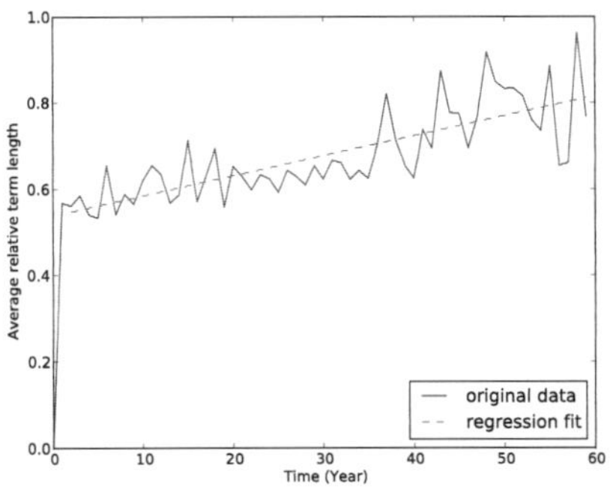

Figure 5: Average increase in character length of sub-keyphrases over time

5 Discussion and Future Work

Our decision to eliminate single-word keyphrases from consideration is an explicit one. Of the 145k keyphrases in the original ACMCORPUS (pre-filtering), 16,418 (11.29%) were single-word keyphrases. Our experience with the ACM author-defined keyphrases is that such terms are too generic to be useful as "scientific" keyphrases. For example, In all the ACM proceedings, the top-5 most common single-word keyphrases are *security*, *visualization*, *evaluation*, *design*, and *privacy*. Even in specific sub-domains, such as recommender systems (Proceedings of Recsys), the most popular single-word keyphrases are *personalization*, *recommendation*, *evaluation*, and *trust*. Contrast these to the most popular multi-word terms: *recommender system(s)*, *collaborative filtering*, *matrix factorization*, and *social network(s)*.

Notably, in the MSRA corpus, which is algorithmically filtered, only .46% (226 keyphrases) were single word. MeSH, in contrast, has a full 37% of keyphrases as single-term. In most situations these reflect chemical names (e.g., 382 single-word enzymes) or biological structures. In such a domain, and if these keyphrases are desirable, it may be advisable to retain single-word abbreviations. While it may seem surprising, even single words are often abbreviated (e.g., *Transaldolase* is "T" and *Ultrafiltration* is "U" or "U/F").

A second key observation is that while the ACM full-text corpus is large, it is by no means "big." We selected to use it because it controlled and "clean." However, we have also run our algorithms on the MSRA Corpus (which contains only abstracts) and CiteSeer (which contains full-text). Because the corpora contain more text we find significantly higher overlap with the different keyphrase corpora. However, this comes at the cost of not being able to isolate the domain-specific keyphrases. To put it differently, the broader full-text collections enable to us generate a more fleshed out keyphrase hierarchies that tracks keyphrases across all domains but which may not be appropriate for certain workloads.

Finally, it is worth considering the possibility of building hierarchies (and connecting them) by relations other than "containment." We have begun to utilize metrics such as co-occurrence of keyphrases (e.g., PMI) as well as higher level citation and co-citation structure in the corpora. Thus, we are able to connect terms that are highly related but are textually dissimilar. When experimenting with PMI, for example, we have found a diverse set of edge types including ISUSEDFOR (e.g., "n-gram language model" and "machine translation") or ISUSEDIN (e.g., "Expectation Maximization" and "Baum-Welch" or "euclidean algorithm" and "k-means"). By necessity, edges generated by this technique require an additional classification.

6 Summary

We have introduced SCHBASE, a simple, robust, and highly effective system and database of scientific concepts/keyphrases. By leveraging the incentive structure of scientists to expand existing ideas while simultaneously signaling novelty we are able to construct semantically-meaningful hierarchies of related keyphrases. The further tendency by authors to succinctly describe new keyphrases results in a general habit of utilizing abbreviations. We have demonstrated a mechanism to identify these keyphrases by extracting abbreviation expansions and have shown that these keyphrases cover the bulk of "useful" keyphrases within the domain of the corpus. We believe that SCHBASE will enable a number of applications ranging from search, categorization, and analysis of scientific communication patterns.

Acknowledgments

The authors thank the Microsoft Academic team, Jaime Teevan, Susan Dumais, and Carl Lagoze for providing us with data and advice. This work is supported by the Intelligence Advanced Research Projects Activity (IARPA) via Department of Interior National Business Center contract number D11PC20155. The U.S. government is authorized to reproduce and distribute reprints for Governmental purposes notwithstanding any copyright annotation thereon. Disclaimer: The views and conclusions contained herein are those of the authors and should not be interpreted as necessarily representing the official policies or endorsements, either expressed or implied, of IARPA, DoI/NBC, or the U.S. Government.

References

Eytan Adar. 2004. SaRAD: a simple and robust abbreviation dictionary. *Bioinformatics*, 20(4):527–533.

Peter Anick. 2003. Using terminological feedback for web search refinement: A log-based study. In *Proceedings of the 26th Annual International ACM SIGIR Conference on Research and Development in Informaion Retrieval*, SIGIR '03, pages 88–95, New York, NY, USA. ACM.

Ken Barker and Nadia Cornacchia. 2000. Using noun phrase heads to extract document keyphrases. In Howard J. Hamilton, editor, *Advances in Artificial Intelligence*, volume 1822 of *Lecture Notes in Computer Science*, pages 40–52. Springer Berlin Heidelberg.

Georgeta Bordea and Paul Buitelaar. 2010. Deriunlp: A context based approach to automatic keyphrase extraction. In *Proceedings of the 5th international workshop on semantic evaluation*, pages 146–149. Association for Computational Linguistics.

Tsung O. Cheng. 2010. What's in a name? another unexplained acronym! *International Journal of Cardiology*, 144(2):291 – 292.

Aaron Clauset, Cosma Rohilla Shalizi, and Mark EJ Newman. 2009. Power-law distributions in empirical data. *SIAM Review*, 51(4):661–703.

Sujatha Das Gollapalli and Cornelia Caragea. 2014. Extracting keyphrases from research papers using citation networks. In *Twenty-Eighth AAAI Conference on Artificial Intelligence*.

Harold P Edmundson. 1969. New methods in automatic extracting. *Journal of the ACM*, 16(2):264–285, April.

Oren Etzioni, Michele Banko, Stephen Soderland, and Daniel S. Weld. 2008. Open information extraction from the web. *Communications of the ACM*, 51(12):68–74, December.

Ingrid Fandrych. 2008. Submorphemic elements in the formation of acronyms, blends and clippings 147. *Lexis*, page 105.

Eibe Frank, Gordon W. Paynter, Ian H. Witten, Carl Gutwin, and Craig G. Nevill-Manning. 1999. Domain-specific keyphrase extraction. In *Proceedings of the 16th International Joint Conference on Artificial Intelligence - Volume 2*, IJCAI'99, pages 668–673, San Francisco, CA, USA. Morgan Kaufmann Publishers Inc.

Evgeniy Gabrilovich and Shaul Markovitch. 2009. Wikipedia-based semantic interpretation for natural language processing. *Journal of Artificial Intelligence Research*, 34(1):443–498, March.

Isidoro Gil-Leiva and Adolfo Alonso-Arroyo. 2007. Keywords given by authors of scientific articles in database descriptors. *Journal of the American Society for Information Science and Technology*, 58(8):1175–1187.

Bob Grange and D.A. Bloom. 2000. Acronyms, abbreviations and initialisms. *BJU International*, 86(1):1–6.

James Hartley and Ronald N. Kostoff. 2003. How useful are 'key words' in scientific journals? *Journal of Information Science*, 29(5):433–438.

Anette Hulth. 2003. Improved automatic keyword extraction given more linguistic knowledge. In *Proceedings of the 2003 Conference on Empirical Methods in Natural Language Processing*, EMNLP '03, pages 216–223, Stroudsburg, PA, USA. Association for Computational Linguistics.

A.M. Ibrahim. 1989. Acronyms observed. *Professional Communication, IEEE Transactions on*, 32(1):27–28, Mar.

Su Nam Kim, Olena Medelyan, Min-Yen Kan, and Timothy Baldwin. 2010. Semeval-2010 task 5: Automatic keyphrase extraction from scientific articles. In *Proceedings of the 5th International Workshop on Semantic Evaluation*, pages 21–26. Association for Computational Linguistics.

Carolyn E. Lipscomb. 2000. Medical subject headings (mesh). *Bull Med Libr Assoc.* 88(3): 265266.

Marina Litvak and Mark Last. 2008. Graph-based keyword extraction for single-document summarization. In *Proceedings of the Workshop on Multi-source Multilingual Information Extraction and Summarization*, MMIES '08, pages 17–24, Stroudsburg, PA, USA. Association for Computational Linguistics.

Olena Medelyan, Eibe Frank, and Ian H. Witten. 2009. Human-competitive tagging using automatic keyphrase extraction. In *Proceedings of the 2009 Conference on Empirical Methods in Natural Language Processing: Volume 3 - Volume 3*, EMNLP '09, pages 1318–1327, Stroudsburg, PA, USA. Association for Computational Linguistics.

Microsoft. 2015. Microsoft academic search. http://academic.research.microsoft.com. Accessed: 2015-2-26.

Rada Mihalcea and Paul Tarau. 2004. Textrank: Bringing order into texts. In Dekang Lin and Dekai Wu, editors, *Proceedings of EMNLP 2004*, pages 404–411, Barcelona, Spain, July. Association for Computational Linguistics.

ThuyDung Nguyen and Min-Yen Kan. 2007. Keyphrase extraction in scientific publications. In Dion Hoe-Lian Goh, Tru Hoang Cao, Ingeborg Torvik Sølvberg, and Edie Rasmussen, editors, *Asian Digital Libraries. Looking Back 10 Years and Forging New Frontiers*, volume 4822 of *Lecture Notes in Computer Science*, pages 317–326. Springer Berlin Heidelberg.

Ryosuke L. Ohniwa, Aiko Hibino, and Kunio Takeyasu. 2010. Trends in research foci in life science fields over the last 30 years monitored by emerging topics. *Scientometrics*, 85(1):111–127.

Chris D. Paice and Paul A. Jones. 1993. The identification of important concepts in highly structured technical papers. In *Proceedings of the 16th Annual International ACM SIGIR Conference on Research and Development in Information Retrieval*, SIGIR '93, pages 69–78, New York, NY, USA. ACM.

Martin F. Porter. 2001. Snowball: A language for stemming algorithms. http://snowball.tartarus.org/texts/introduction.html. Accessed: 2015-2-26.

Ariel S Schwartz and Marti A Hearst. 2003. A simple algorithm for identifying abbreviation definitions in biomedical text. *Pacific Symposium on Biocomputing. Pacific Symposium on Biocomputing*, page 451462.

Xiaolin Shi, Jure Leskovec, and Daniel A. McFarland. 2010. Citing for high impact. In *Proceedings of the 10th Annual Joint Conference on Digital Libraries*, JCDL '10, pages 49–58, New York, NY, USA. ACM.

Takashi Tomokiyo and Matthew Hurst. 2003. A language model approach to keyphrase extraction. In *Proceedings of the ACL 2003 Workshop on Multiword Expressions: Analysis, Acquisition and Treatment - Volume 18*, MWE '03, pages 33–40, Stroudsburg, PA, USA. Association for Computational Linguistics.

Peter D. Turney. 2000. Learning algorithms for keyphrase extraction. *Information Retrieval*, 2(4):303–336, May.

Wikipedia. 2014. Wikipedia: List of machine learning concepts. http://en.wikipedia.org/wiki/List_of_machine_learning_concepts. Accessed: 2015-2-26.

Fei Wu and Daniel S. Weld. 2008. Automatically refining the wikipedia infobox ontology. In *Proceedings of the 17th International Conference on World Wide Web*, WWW '08, pages 635–644, New York, NY, USA. ACM.

Sentiment-Aspect Extraction based on Restricted Boltzmann Machines

Linlin Wang[1], Kang Liu[2*], Zhu Cao[1], Jun Zhao[2] and Gerard de Melo[1]
[1]Institute for Interdisciplinary Information Sciences, Tsinghua University, Beijing, China
[2]National Laboratory of Pattern Recognition, Institute of Automation,
Chinese Academy of Sciences, Beijing, China
{ll-wang13, cao-z13}@mails.tsinghua.edu.cn,
{kliu, jzhao}@nlpr.ia.ac.cn, gdm@demelo.org

Abstract

Aspect extraction and sentiment analysis of reviews are both important tasks in opinion mining. We propose a novel sentiment and aspect extraction model based on Restricted Boltzmann Machines to jointly address these two tasks in an unsupervised setting. This model reflects the generation process of reviews by introducing a heterogeneous structure into the hidden layer and incorporating informative priors. Experiments show that our model outperforms previous state-of-the-art methods.

1 Introduction

Nowadays, it is commonplace for people to express their opinion about various sorts of entities, e.g., products or services, on the Internet, especially in the course of e-commerce activities. Analyzing online reviews not only helps customers obtain useful product information, but also provide companies with feedback to enhance their products or service quality. Aspect-based opinion mining enables people to consider much more fine-grained analyses of vast quantities of online reviews, perhaps from numerous different merchant sites. Thus, automatic identification of aspects of entities and relevant sentiment polarities in Big Data is a significant and urgent task (Liu, 2012; Pang and Lee, 2008; Popescu and Etzioni, 2005).

Identifying aspect and analyzing sentiment words from reviews has the ultimate goal of discerning people's opinions, attitudes, emotions, etc. towards entities such as products, services, organizations, individuals, events, etc. In this context, *aspect-based opinion mining*, also known as *feature-based opinion mining*, aims at extracting and summarizing particular salient aspects of entities and determining relevant sentiment polarities from reviews (Hu and Liu, 2004). Consider reviews of computers, for example. A given computer's components (e.g., *hard disk*, *screen*) and attributes (e.g., *volume*, *size*) are viewed as aspects to be extracted from the reviews, while sentiment polarity classification consists in judging whether an opinionated review expresses an overall positive or negative opinion.

Regarding aspect identification, previous methods can be divided into three main categories: rule-based, supervised, and topic model-based methods. For instance, association rule-based methods (Hu and Liu, 2004; Liu et al., 1998) tend to focus on extracting product feature words and opinion words but neglect connecting product features at the aspect level. Existing rule-based methods typically are not able to group the extracted aspect terms into categories. Supervised (Jin et al., 2009; Choi and Cardie, 2010) and semi-supervised learning methods (Zagibalov and Carroll, 2008; Mukherjee and Liu, 2012) were introduced to resolve certain aspect identification problems. However, supervised training requires hand-labeled training data and has trouble coping with domain adaptation scenarios.

Hence, unsupervised methods are often adopted to avoid this sort of dependency on labeled data. Latent Dirichlet Allocation, or LDA for short, (Blei et al., 2003) performs well in automatically extracting aspects and grouping corresponding representative words into categories. Thus, a number of LDA-based aspect identification approaches have been proposed in recent years (Brody and Elhadad, 2010; Titov and McDonald, 2008; Zhao et al., 2010). Still, these methods have several important drawbacks. First, inaccurate approximations of the distribution over topics may reduce the computational accuracy. Second, mixture models are unable to exploit the co-occurrence of topics to yield high probability predictions for words that are sharper than the distributions predicted by in-

*Corresponding Author: Kang Liu (kliu@nlpr.ia.ac.cn)

Proceedings of the 53rd Annual Meeting of the Association for Computational Linguistics and the 7th International Joint Conference on Natural Language Processing, pages 616–625,
Beijing, China, July 26-31, 2015.

dividual topics (Hinton and Salakhutdinov, 2009).

To overcome the weaknesses of existing methods and pursue the promising direction of jointly learning aspect and sentiment, we present the novel Sentiment-Aspect Extraction RBM (SERBM) model to simultaneously extract aspects of entities and relevant sentiment-bearing words. This two-layer structure model is inspired by conventional Restricted Boltzmann machines (RBMs). In previous work, RBMs with shared parameters (RSMs) have achieved great success in capturing distributed semantic representations from text (Hinton and Salakhutdinov, 2009).

Aiming to make the most of their ability to model latent topics while also accounting for the structured nature of aspect opinion mining, we propose replacing the standard hidden layers of RBMs with a novel heterogeneous structure. Three different types of hidden units are used to represent aspects, sentiments, and background words, respectively. This modification better reflects the generative process for reviews, in which review words are generated not only from the aspect distribution but also affected by sentiment information. Furthermore, we blend background knowledge into this model using priors and regularization to help it acquire more accurate feature representations. After m-step Contrastive Divergence for parameter estimation, we can capture the required data distribution and easily compute the posterior distribution over latent aspects and sentiments from reviews. In this way, aspects and sentiments are jointly extracted from reviews, with limited computational effort. This model is hence a promising alternative to more complex LDA-based models presented previously. Overall, our main contributions are as follows:

1. Compared with previous LDA-based methods, our model avoids inaccurate approximations and captures latent aspects and sentiment both adequately and efficiently.

2. Our model exploits RBMs' advantage in properly modeling distributed semantic representations from text, but also introduces heterogeneous structure into the hidden layer to reflect the generative process for online reviews. It also uses a form of regularization to incorporate prior knowledge into the model. Due these modifications, our model is very well-suited for solving aspect-based opinion mining tasks.

3. The optimal weight matrix of this RBM model can exactly reflect individual word features toward aspects and sentiment, which is hard to achieve with LDA-based models due to the mixture model sharing mechanism.

4. Last but not the least, this RBM model is capable of jointly modeling aspect and sentiment information together.

2 Related Work

We summarize prior state-of-the-art models for aspect extraction. In their seminal work, Hu and Liu (2004) propose the idea of applying classical information extraction to distinguish different aspects in online reviews. Methods following their approach exploit frequent noun words and dependency relations to extract product features without supervision (Zhuang et al., 2006; Liu et al., 2005; Somasundaran and Wiebe, 2009). These methods work well when the aspect is strongly associated with a single noun, but obtain less satisfactory results when the aspect emerges from a combination of low frequency items. Additionally, rule-based methods have a common shortcoming in failing to group extracted aspect terms into categories.

Supervised learning methods (Jin et al., 2009; Choi and Cardie, 2010; Jakob and Gurevych, 2010; Kobayashi et al., 2007) such as Hidden Markov Models, one-class SVMs, and Conditional Random Fields have been widely used in aspect information extraction. These supervised approaches for aspect identification are generally based on standard sequence labeling techniques. The downside of supervised learning is its requirement of large amounts of hand-labeled training data to provide enough information for aspect and opinion identification.

Subsequent studies have proposed unsupervised learning methods, especially LDA-based topic modeling, to classify aspects of comments. Specific variants include the Multi-Grain LDA model (Titov and McDonald, 2008) to capture local rateable aspects, the two-step approach to detect aspect-specific opinion words (Brody and Elhadad, 2010), the joint sentiment/topic model (JST) by Lin and He (2009), the topic-sentiment mixture model with domain adaption (Mei et al., 2007), which treats sentiment as different topics, and MaxEnt-LDA (Zhao et al., 2010), which integrates a maximum entropy approach into LDA.

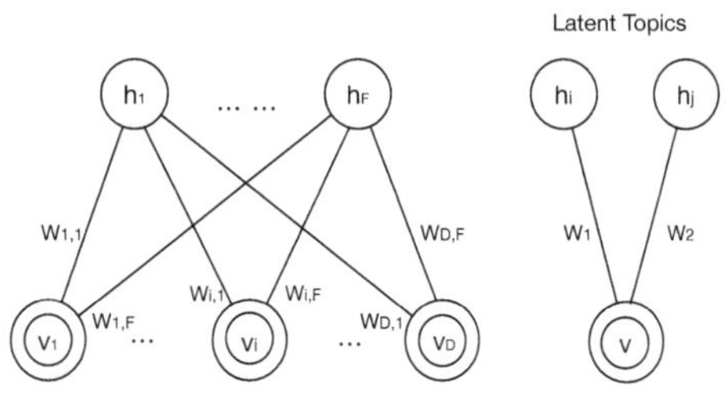

Figure 1: RBM Schema

However, these LDA-based methods can only adopt inaccurate approximations for the posterior distribution over topics rather than exact inference. Additionally, as a mixture model, LDA suffers from the drawbacks mentioned in Section 1 that are common to all mixture models.

3 Model

In order to improve over previous work, we first introduce a basic RBM-based model and then describe our modified full model.

3.1 Basic RBM-based Model

Restricted Boltzmann Machines can be used for topic modeling by relying on the structure shown in Figure 1. As shown on the left side of the figure, this model is a two-layer neural network composed of one visible layer and one hidden layer. The visible layer consists of a softmax over discrete visible units for words in the text, while the hidden layer captures its topics. More precisely, the visible layer is represented as a $K \times D$ matrix **v**, where K is the dictionary size, and D is the document length. Here, if visible unit i in **v** takes the k-th value, we set $v_i^k = 1$. The hidden layer can be expressed as $h \in \{0,1\}^F$, where F is the number of hidden layer nodes, corresponding to topics. The right side of Figure 1 is another way of viewing the network, with a single multinomial visible unit (Hinton and Salakhutdinov, 2009).

The energy function of the model can be defined as

$$E(\mathbf{v},h) = -\sum_{i=1}^{D}\sum_{j=1}^{F}\sum_{k=1}^{K} W_{ij}^k h_j v_i^k - \sum_{i=1}^{D}\sum_{k=1}^{K} v_i^k b_i^k - \sum_{j=1}^{F} h_j a_j, \quad (1)$$

where W_{ij}^k specifies the connection weight from the i-th visible node of value k to the j-th hidden node, b_i^k corresponds to a bias of v_i^k, and a_j corresponds to a bias of h_j.

The probability of the input layer **v** is defined as

$$P(\mathbf{v}) = \frac{1}{Z}\sum_h \exp(-E(\mathbf{v},h)), \quad (2)$$

where Z is the partition function to normalize the probability.

The conditional probabilities from the hidden to the visible layer and from the visible to the hidden one are given in terms of a softmax and logistic function, respectively, i.e.

$$P(v_i^k = 1 \mid h) = \frac{\exp\left(b_i^k + \sum_{j=1}^{F} h_j W_{ij}^k\right)}{\sum_{q=1}^{K}\exp\left(b_i^q + \sum_{j=1}^{F} h_j W_{ij}^q\right)},$$

$$P(h_j = 1 \mid \mathbf{v}) = \sigma\left(a_j + \sum_{i=1}^{D}\sum_{k=1}^{K} v_i^k W_{ij}^k\right), \quad (3)$$

where $\sigma(x) = 1/(1+\exp(-x))$ is the logistic function.

3.2 Our Sentiment-Aspect Extraction model

While the basic RBM-based method provides a simple model of latent topics, real online reviews require a more fine-grained model, as they consist of opinion aspects and sentiment information. Therefore, aspect identification is a different task from regular topic modeling and the basic RBM-based model may not perform well in aspect extraction for reviews.

To make the most of the ability of the basic RBM-based model in extracting latent topics, and obtain an effective method that is well-suited to solve aspect identification tasks, we present our novel Sentiment-Aspect Extraction RBM model.

3.2.1 Generative Perspective

From a generative perspective, product reviews can be regarded as follows. Every word in a review text may describe a specific aspect (e.g. "expensive" for the *price* aspect), or an opinion (e.g. "amazing" for a positive sentiment and "terrible" for a negative one), or some irrelevant background information (e.g. "Sunday"). In a generative model, a word may be generated from a latent aspect variable, a sentiment variable, or a background variable. Also, there may exist certain relations between such latent variables.

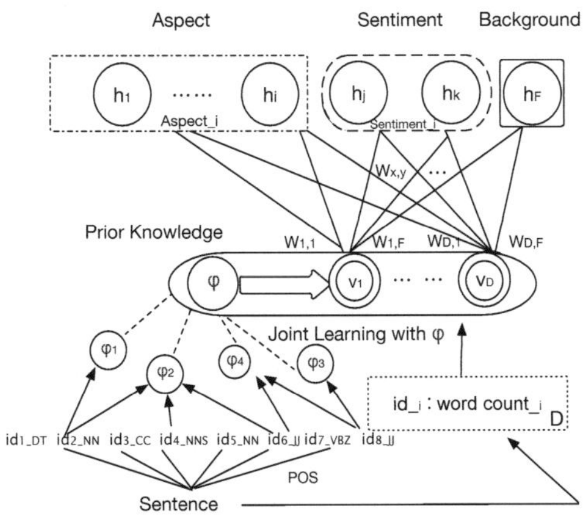

Figure 2: Sentiment-Aspect Extraction Model

3.2.2 Structure

To simulate this generative process for reviews, we adapt the standard RBM structure to reflect the aspect-sentiment identification task.

Undirected Model. Our Sentiment-Aspect Extraction model structure is illustrated in Figure 2.

Compared to standard RBMs, a crucial difference is that hidden units now have a heterogeneous structure instead of being homogeneous as in the standard basic RBM model. In particular, we rely on three types of hidden units, representing aspect, sentiment, and background, respectively. The first two types are self-explanatory, while the background units are intended to reflect the kind of words that do not contribute much to the aspect or sentiment information of review documents. Since the output of the hidden units is a re-encoding of the information in the visible layer, we obtain a deeper representation and a more precise expression of information in the input reviews. Thus, this approach enables the model to learn multi-faceted information with a simple yet expressive structure.

To formalize this, we denote $\widehat{v}^k = \sum_{i=1}^{D} v_i^k$ as the count for the k-th word, where D is the document length. The energy function can then be defined as follows:

$$E(\mathbf{v}, h) = -\sum_{j=1}^{F}\sum_{k=1}^{K} W_j^k h_j \widehat{v}^k - \sum_{k=1}^{K} \widehat{v}^k b^k - \sum_{j=1}^{F} h_j a_j, \tag{4}$$

where W_j^k denotes the weight between the k-th visible unit and the j-th hidden unit.

The conditional probability from visible to hidden unit can be expressed as:

$$P(h_j = 1|\mathbf{v}) = \sigma(a_j + \sum_{k=1}^{K} \widehat{v}^k W_j^k). \tag{5}$$

In an RBM, every hidden unit can be activated or restrained by visible units. Thus, every visible unit has a potential contribution towards the activation of a given hidden unit. The probability of whether a given visible unit affects a specific hidden unit is described as follows (cf. appendix for details):

$$\begin{aligned} P(h_j = 1 \mid \widehat{v}^k) =& P(h_j = 1 \mid h_{-j}, \widehat{v}^k) \\ =& \sigma(a_j + W_j^k \widehat{v}^k). \end{aligned} \tag{6}$$

Under this architecture, this equation can be explained as the conditional probability from visible unit k to hidden unit j (softmax of words to aspect or sentiment). According to Eq. 6, the conditional probability for the k-th word feature towards the j-th aspect or sentiment $p(h_j = 1 \mid v_k)$ is a monotone function of W_j^k, the (k, j)-th entry of the optimal weight matrix. Thus, the optimal weight matrix of this RBM model can directly reflect individual word features toward aspects and sentiment.

Informative Priors. To improve the ability of the model to extract aspects and identify sentiments, we capture priors for words in reviews and incorporate this information into the learning process of our Sentiment-Aspect Extraction model. We regularize our model based on these priors to constrain the aspect modeling and improve its accuracy. Figure 3 provides an example of how such priors can be applied to a sentence, with ϕ_i representing the prior knowledge.

Research has found that most aspect words are nouns (or noun phrases), and sentiment is often expressed with adjectives. This additional information has been utilized in previous work on aspect extraction (Hu and Liu, 2004; Benamara et al., 2007; Pang et al., 2002). Inspired by this, we first rely on Part of Speech (POS) Tagging to identify nouns and adjectives. For all noun words, we first calculate their term frequency (TF) in the review corpus, and then compute their inverse document frequency (IDF) from an external Google n-gram corpus[1]. Finally, we rank their TF∗IDF

[1] http://books.google.com/ngrams/datasets

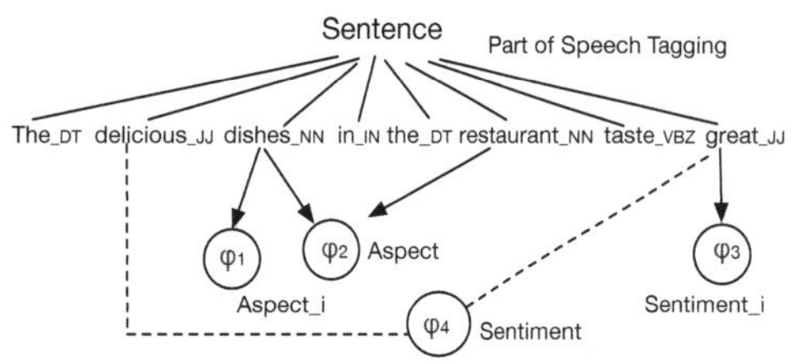

Figure 3: Prior Feature Extraction

values and assign them an aspect prior probability p_{A,v_k}, indicating their general probability of being an aspect word. This TF-IDF approach is motivated by the following intuitions: the most frequently mentioned candidates in reviews have the highest probability of being an opinion target and false target words are non-domain specific and frequently appear in a general text corpus (Liu et al., 2012; Liu et al., 2013). For all adjective words, if the words are also included in the online sentiment resource SentiWordNet[2], we assign prior probability p_{s,v_k} to suggest that these words are generally recognized as sentiment words.

Apart from these general priors, we obtain a small amount of fine-grained information as another type of prior knowledge. This fine-grained prior knowledge serves to indicate the probability of a known aspect word belonging to a specific aspect, denoted as p_{A_j,v_k} and an identified sentiment word bearing positive or negative sentiment, denoted as p_{S_j,v_k}. For instance, "salad" is always considered as a general word that belongs to the specific aspect *food*, and "great" is generally considered a *positive* sentiment word.

To extract p_{A_j,v_k}, we apply regular LDA on the review dataset. Since the resulting topic clusters are unlabeled, we manually assign top k words from the topics to the target aspects. We thus obtain fine-grained prior probabilities to suggest these words as belonging to specific aspects. To obtain p_{S_j,v_k}, we rely on SentiWordNet and sum up the probabilities of an identified sentiment word being positive or negative sentiment-bearing, respectively. Then we adopt the corresponding percentage value as a fine-grained specific sentiment prior.

It is worthwhile to mention that the priors are not a compulsory component. However, the procedure for obtaining priors is generic and can easily be applied to any given dataset. Furthermore, we only obtain such fine-grained prior knowledge for a small amount of words in review sentences and rely on the capability of model itself to deal with the remaining words.

[2]http://sentiwordnet.isti.cnr.it

3.2.3 Objective Function

We now construct an objective function for our SERBM model that includes regularization based on the priors defined above in Section 3.2.2. Suppose that the training set is $S = \mathbf{v}^1, \mathbf{v}^2, \ldots, \mathbf{v}^{n_s}$, where n_s is the number of training objects. Each element has the form $\mathbf{v}^i = (v_1^i, v_2^i, \ldots, v_K^i)^D$, where $i = 1, 2, \ldots, n_s$, and these data points are assumed to be independent and identically distributed.

We define the following novel log-likelihood function $\ln L_S$, with four forms of regularization corresponding to the four kinds of priors:

$$\ln L_S = \ln \prod_{i=1}^{n_s} P(\mathbf{v}^i) - \sum_{i=1}^{n_s} \Bigg[\lambda_1 \ln \prod_{j=1}^{F_1-1} \prod_{k \in R_1} \left[P(h_j = 1 \mid \widehat{v}^k) - p_{A_j,v_k} \right]^2 + \lambda_2 \ln \prod_{k \in R_2} \left[\sum_{j=1}^{F_1} P(h_j = 1 \mid \widehat{v}^k) - p_{A,v_k} \right]^2 + \lambda_3 \ln \prod_{j=F_2}^{F_2+1} \prod_{k \in R_3} \left[P(h_j = 1 \mid \widehat{v}^k) - p_{S_j,v_k} \right]^2 + \lambda_4 \ln \prod_{k \in R_4} \left[\sum_{j=F_2}^{F_2+1} P(h_j = 1 \mid \widehat{v}^k) - p_{S,v_k} \right]^2 \Bigg] \quad (7)$$

Here, $P(h_j = 1 \mid \widehat{v}^k)$ stands for the probability of a given input word belonging to a specific hidden unit. We assume all $\lambda_i > 0$ for $i = 1 \ldots 4$, while F_1 and F_2 are integers for the offsets within the hidden layer. Units up to index F_1 capture aspects, with the last one reserved for miscellaneous *Other Aspects*, while units from F_2 capture the sentiment (with $F_1 = F_2 + 1 < F$ for convenience).

Our goal will be to maximize the log-likelihood $\ln L_S$ in order to adequately model the data, in accordance with the regularization.

3.2.4 Training

We use Stochastic Gradient Descent (SGD) to find suitable parameters that maximize the objective function. Given a single training instance $\mathbf{v}$ from the training set S, we obtain

$$\frac{\partial \ln L}{\partial \theta} = \frac{\partial \ln P(\mathbf{v})}{\partial \theta}$$
$$- \lambda_1 \sum_{j=1}^{F_1-1} \sum_{k \in R_1} \frac{\partial \ln \left[P(h_j = 1 \mid \widehat{v}^k) - p_{A_j,v_k}\right]^2}{\partial \theta}$$
$$- \lambda_2 \sum_{k \in R_2} \frac{\partial \ln \left[\sum_{j=1}^{F_1} P(h_j = 1 \mid \widehat{v}^k) - p_{A,v_k}\right]^2}{\partial \theta}$$
$$- \lambda_3 \sum_{j=F_2}^{F_2+1} \sum_{k \in R_3} \frac{\partial \ln \left[P(h_j = 1 \mid \widehat{v}^k) - p_{S_j,v_k}\right]^2}{\partial \theta}$$
$$- \lambda_4 \sum_{k \in R_4} \frac{\partial \ln \left[\sum_{j=F_2}^{F_2+1} P(h_j = 1 \mid \widehat{v}^k) - p_{S,v_k}\right]^2}{\partial \theta} \quad (8)$$

where $\theta = \{W, a_j, b_i\}$ stands for the parameters. Given N documents $\{\mathbf{v}^n\}_{n=1}^N$, the first term in the log-likelihood function with respect to W is:

$$\frac{1}{N} \sum_{n=1}^{N} \frac{\partial \ln P(\mathbf{v}^n)}{\partial W_j^k} = E_{D_1}[\hat{v}^k h_j] - E_{D_2}[\hat{v}^k h_j]. \quad (9)$$

Here, $D_1[\cdot]$ and $D_2[\cdot]$ represent the expectation with respect to the data distribution and the distribution obtained by this model, respectively. We use Contrastive Divergence (CD) to approximate $E_{D_2}[\hat{v}^k h_j]$ (Hinton and Salakhutdinov, 2009). Due to the m steps of transfer between input and hidden layers in a CD-m run of the algorithm, the two types of hidden units, aspect and sentiment, will jointly affect input reviews together with the connection matrix between the two layers.

Finally, we consider the partial derivative of the entire log-likelihood function with respect to the parameter W. Denoting $\ln \frac{\partial L}{\partial W}$ as ∇W, in each step we update ∇W_j^k by adding

$$\lambda \left[P(h_j = 1|\mathbf{v}^{(0)})v_k^{(0)} - P(h_j = 1|\mathbf{v}^{(\mathrm{cdm})})v_k^{(\mathrm{cdm})}\right]$$
$$- \lambda_1 \sum_{j=1}^{F_1-1} \sum_{k \in R_1} \frac{2G_j \widehat{v}^k}{(1+G_j)^2(\frac{1}{1+G_j} - p_{A_j,v_k})}$$
$$- \lambda_2 \sum_{k \in R_2} \frac{2\widehat{v}^k}{\sum_{j=1}^{F_1} \frac{1}{(1+G_j)} - p_{A,v_k}} \sum_{j=1}^{F_1} \frac{G_j}{(1+G_j)^2}$$
$$- \lambda_3 \sum_{j=F_2}^{F_2+1} \sum_{k \in R_3} \frac{2G_j \widehat{v}^k}{(1+G_j)^2(\frac{1}{1+G_j} - p_{S_j,v_k})}$$
$$- \lambda_4 \sum_{k \in R_4} \frac{2\widehat{v}^k}{\sum_{j=F_2}^{F_2+1} \frac{1}{(1+G_j)} - p_{S,v_k}} \sum_{j=F_2}^{F_2+1} \frac{G_j}{(1+G_j)^2},$$

where $G_j = e^{-(a_j + W_j^k \widehat{v}^k)}$ for convenience, and $v^{(\mathrm{cdm})}$ is the result from the CD-m steps.

4 Experiments

We present a series of experiments to evaluate our model's performance on the aspect identification and sentiment classification tasks.

4.1 Data

For this evaluation, we rely on a restaurant review dataset widely adopted by previous work (Ganu et al., 2009; Brody and Elhadad, 2010; Zhao et al., 2010), which contains 1,644,923 tokens and 52,574 documents in total. Documents in this dataset are annotated with one or more labels from a gold standard label set $S = \{$*Food*, *Staff*, *Ambience*, *Price*, *Anecdote*, *Miscellaneous*$\}$. Following the previous studies, we select reviews with less than 50 sentences and remove stop words. The Stanford POS Tagger[3] is used to distinguish noun and adjective words from each other.

We later also rely on the Polarity dataset v2.0[4] to conduct an additional experiment on sentiment classification in order to better assess the model's overall performance. This dataset focuses on movie reviews and consists of 1000 positive review documents and 1000 negative ones. It has also been used in the experiments by Lin & He (2009), among others.

4.2 Aspect Identification

We first apply our novel model to identify aspects from documents in the restaurant review dataset.

4.2.1 Experimental Setup

For the experimental setup, we use ten hidden units in our Sentiment-Aspect Extraction RBM (SERBM), where units 0–6 capture aspects, units 7–8 capture sentiment information, and unit 9 stores background information. In particular, we fix hidden units 0–6 to represent the target aspects *Food*, *Staff*, *Ambience*, *Price*, *Ambience*, *Miscellaneous*, and *Other Aspects*, respectively. Units 7–8 represent *positive* and *negative* sentiment, respectively. The remaining hidden unit is intended to capture irrelevant background information.

Note that the structure of our model needs no modifications for new reviews. There are two cases for datasets from a new domain. If the new

[3] http://nlp.stanford.edu/software/tagger.shtml

[4] http://www.cs.cornell.edu/people/pabo/movie-review-data/

Method	RBM	RSM	SERBM
PPL	49.73	39.19	21.18

Table 1: Results in terms of perplexity

dataset has a gold standard label set, then we assign one hidden unit to represent each label in the gold standard set. If not, our model only obtains the priors p_{A,v_k} and p_{S,v_k}, and the aspect set can be inferred as in the work of Zhao et al. (2010).

For evaluation, following previous work, the annotated data is fed into our unsupervised model, without any of the corresponding labels. The model is then evaluated in terms of how well its prediction matches the true labels. As for hyperparameter optimization, we use the perplexity scores as defined in Eq. 10 to find the optimal hyperparameters.

As a baseline, we also re-implement standard RBMs and the RSM model (Hinton and Salakhutdinov, 2009) to process this same restaurant review dataset and identify aspects for every document in this dataset under the same experimental conditions. We recall that RSM is a similar undirected graphical model that models topics from raw text.

Last but not the least, we conduct additional comparative experiments, including with LocLDA (Brody and Elhadad, 2010), MaxEnt-LDA (Zhao et al., 2010) and the SAS model (Mukherjee and Liu, 2012) to extract aspects for this restaurant review dataset under the same experimental conditions. In the following, we use the abbreviated name MELDA to stand for the MaxEnt LDA method.

4.2.2 Evaluation

Brody and Elhadad (2010) and Zhao et al. (2010) utilize three aspects to perform a quantitative evaluation and only use sentences with a single label for evaluation to avoid ambiguity. The three major aspects chosen from the gold standard labels are $S = \{Food, Staff, Ambience\}$. The evaluation criterion essentially is to judge how well the prediction matches the true label, resulting in Precision, Recall, and F_1 scores. Besides these, we consider perplexity (PPL) as another evaluation metric to analyze the aspect identification quality. The average test perplexity PPL over words is defined as:

$$\exp\left(-\frac{1}{N}\sum_{n=1}^{N}\frac{1}{D_n}\log P(v_n)\right), \quad (10)$$

Aspect	Method	Precision	Recall	F_1
food	RBM	0.753	0.680	0.715
	RSM	0.718	0.736	0.727
	LocLDA	**0.898**	0.648	0.753
	MELDA	0.874	0.787	0.828
	SAS	0.867	0.772	0.817
	SERBM	0.891	**0.854**	**0.872**
staff	RBM	0.436	0.567	0.493
	RSM	0.430	0.310	0.360
	LocLDA	0.804	**0.585**	0.677
	MELDA	0.779	0.540	0.638
	SAS	0.774	0.556	0.647
	SERBM	**0.819**	0.582	**0.680**
ambi -ence	RBM	0.489	0.439	0.463
	RSM	0.498	0.441	0.468
	LocLDA	0.603	**0.677**	0.638
	MELDA	0.773	0.588	0.668
	SAS	0.780	0.542	0.640
	SERBM	**0.805**	0.592	**0.682**

Table 2: Aspect identification results in terms of precision, recall, and F_1 scores on the restaurant reviews dataset

where N is the number of documents, D_n represents the word number, and v_n stands for the word-count of document n.

Average perplexity results are reported in Table 1, while Precision, Recall, and F_1 evaluation results for aspect identification are given in Table 2. Some LDA-based methods require manual mappings for evaluation, which causes difficulties in obtaining a fair PPL result, so a few methods are only considered in Table 2.

To illustrate the differences, in Table 3, we list representative words for aspects identified by various models and highlight words without an obvious association or words that are rather unspecific in bold.

4.2.3 Discussion

Considering the results from Table 1 and the RBM, RSM, and SERBM-related results from Table 2, we find that the RSM performs better than the regular RBM model on this aspect identification task. However, the average test perplexity is greatly reduced even further by the SERBM method, resulting in a relative improvement by 45.96% over the RSM model. Thus, despite the elaborate modification, our SERBM inherits RBMs' ability in modeling latent topics, but significantly outperforms other RBM family models

Aspect	RSM	RBM	Loc-LDA	ME-LDA	SAS	SERBM
Food	**great**	menu,drink	chicken	chocolate	food,menu	salad,cheese
	dessert	food,pizza	menu,salad	dessert	dessert	dessert
	beef	chicken	**good**	cream	drinks	chicken
	drink,BBQ	seafood	fish	ice,cake	chicken	sauce
	menu	**good**	drinks	desserts	cheeses	rice,pizza
	delicious	sandwich	wine,sauce	**good**	beers,salad	food
	good	soup	rice	bread	delicious	dish
	fish	flavor	cheese	cheese	rice	sushi,menu
Staff	service	staff	service	service	staff,**slow**	service
	room	**helpful**	staff,waiter	staff,**food**	waitress	staff,friendly
	slow	waiter	attentive	wait,waiters	attentive	waitress
	table	friendly	**busy**	waiter	**helpful**	waitstaff
	quick	**good**,attentive	**slow**,friendly	**place**	service	attentive
	waitress	**slow**,service	**table**	restaurant	**minutes**	waitresses
	friendly	restaurant	wait	waitress	wait,friendly	servers
	waiter	**minutes**	**minutes**	waitstaff	waiter	**minutes**
Ambience	atmosphere	place	**great**	room	place	atmosphere
	music	atmosphere	atmosphere	**dining**	decor	atmosphere
	place	cozy	**wonderful**	tables	**great**	scene
	dinner	**door**	**music**	**bar**	**good**	place
	romantic	**cute**	**seating**	place	romantic	**tables**
	room	**bar**	experience	decor	**tables**	outside
	comfortable	**great**	relaxed	scene	bar	area
	tables	**seating**	**bar**	space	decor	ambiance
	good	experience	room	area	**great**	outdoor
	ambiance	romantic	outside	**table**	**music**	romantic,cozy

Table 3: Aspects and representative words

on the aspect identification task.

In Table 2, we also observe that SERBM achieves a higher accuracy compared with other state-of-the-art aspect identification methods. More specifically, it is evident that our SERBM model outperforms previous methods' F_1 scores. Compared with MELDA, the F_1 scores for the SERBM lead to relative improvements of 5.31%, 6.58%, and 2.10%, respectively, for the *Food*, *Staff*, and *Ambience* aspects. Compared with SAS, the F_1 scores yield relative improvements by 6.73%, 5.10%, and 6.56%, respectively, on those same aspects. As for Precision and Recall, the SERBM also achieves a competitive performance compared with other methods in aspect identification.

Finally, we conclude from Table 3 that the SERBM method has the capability of extracting word with obvious aspect-specific features and makes less errors compared with other models.

4.3 Sentiment Classification

We additionally conduct two experiments to evaluate the model's performance on sentiment classification.

4.3.1 Comparison with SentiWordNet

We assign a sentiment score to every document in the restaurant review dataset based on the output of SERBM's sentiment-type hidden units. To analyze SERBM's performance in sentiment classification, we compare these results with SentiWordNet[5], a well-known sentiment lexicon. For this SentiWordNet baseline, we consult the resource to obtain a sentiment label for every word and aggregate these to judge the sentiment information of an entire review document in terms of the sum of word-specific scores. Table 4 provides a comparison between SERBM and SentiWordNet, with Accuracy as the evaluation metric.

We observe in Table 4 that the sentiment

[5]http://sentiwordnet.isti.cnr.it

Method	SentiWordNet	SERBM
Accuracy	0.703	**0.788**

Table 4: Accuracy for SERBM and SentiWordNet

classification accuracy on the restaurant review dataset sees a relative improvement by 12.1% with SERBM over the SentiWordNet baseline.

4.3.2 Comparison with JST

We additionally utilize the Polarity dataset v2.0 to conduct an additional sentiment classification experiment in order to assess SERBM's performance more thoroughly. We compare SERBM with the advanced joint sentiment/topic model (JST) by Lin & He (2009). For the JST and the Trying-JST methods only, we use the filtered subjectivity lexicon (subjective MR) as prior information, containing 374 positive and 675 negative entries, which is the same experimental setting as in Lin & He (2009). For SERBM, we use the same general setup as before except for the fact that aspect-specific priors are not used here.

Table 5 provides the sentiment classification accuracies on both the overall dataset and on the subsets for each polarity, where pos. and neg. refer to the positive and negative reviews in the dataset, respectively.

Method	overall	pos.	neg.
JST(%)	84.6	96.2	73
Trying-JST(%)	82	89.2	74.8
SERBM(%)	**89.1**	**92.0**	**86.2**

Table 5: Accuracy for SERBM and JST

In Table 5, we observe that SERBM outperforms JST both in terms of the overall accuracy and for the positive/negative-specific subsets. SERBM yields a relative improvement in the overall accuracy by 5.31% over JST and by 8.66% over Trying-JST.

5 Conclusion

In this paper, we have proposed the novel Sentiment-Aspect Extraction RBM (SERBM) model to jointly extract review aspects and sentiment polarities in an unsupervised setting. Our approach modifies the standard RBM model by introducing a heterogeneous structure into the hidden layer and incorporating informative priors into the model. Our experimental results show that this model can outperform LDA-based methods.

Hence, our work opens up the avenue of utilizing RBM-based undirected graphical models to solve aspect extraction and sentiment classification tasks as well as other unsupervised tasks with similar structure.

Appendix

The joint probability distribution is defined as

$$p_\theta(\mathbf{v}, h) = \frac{1}{Z_\theta} e^{E_\theta(\mathbf{v}, h)}, \tag{11}$$

where Z_θ is the partition function. In conjunction with Eq. 1, we obtain

$$E_\theta(\widehat{v}_k, h) = -b_i \widehat{v}^k - \sum_{j=1}^{F} a_j h_j - \sum_{j=1}^{F} h_j W_j^k \widehat{v}^k \tag{12}$$

Then, we can obtain the derivation in Eq. 6.

$$\begin{aligned}
&P(h_j = 1 \mid \widehat{v}^k) \\
=&P(h_j = 1 \mid h_{-j}, \widehat{v}^k) \\
=&\frac{P(h_j = 1, h_{-j}, \widehat{v}^k)}{P(h_{-j}, \widehat{v}^k)} \\
=&\frac{P(h_j = 1, h_{-j}, \widehat{v}^k)}{P(h_j = 1, h_{-j}, \widehat{v}^k) + P(h_j = 0, h_{-j}, \widehat{v}^k)} \\
=&\frac{\frac{1}{Z} e^{-E(h_j=1, h_{-j}, \widehat{v}^k)}}{\frac{1}{Z} e^{-E(h_j=1, h_{-j}, \widehat{v}^k)} + \frac{1}{Z} e^{-E(h_j=0, h_{-j}, \widehat{v}^k)}} \\
=&\frac{e^{-E(h_j=1, h_{-j}, \widehat{v}^k)}}{e^{-E(h_j=1, h_{-j}, \widehat{v}^k)} + e^{-E(h_j=0, h_{-j}, \widehat{v}^k)}} \\
=&\frac{1}{1 + e^{-E(h_j=0, h_{-j}, \widehat{v}^k) + E(h_j=1, h_{-j}, \widehat{v}^k)}} \\
=&\sigma(a_j + W_j^k \widehat{v}^k)
\end{aligned} \tag{13}$$

Acknowledgments

The research at IIIS was supported by China 973 Program Grants 2011CBA00300, 2011CBA00301 and NSFC Grants 61033001, 61361136003, 61450110088. The research at CASIA was supported by the National Basic Research Program of China Grant No. 2012CB316300 and NSFC Grants 61272332 and 61202329.

References

Farah Benamara, Carmine Cesarano, Antonio Picariello, Diego Reforgiato Recupero, and Venkatramana Subrahmanian. 2007. Sentiment analysis: Adjectives and adverbs are better than adjectives alone. In *Proceedings of ICWSM 2007*.

David Blei, Andrew Ng, and Michael Jordan. 2003. Latent dirichlet allocation. *Journal of Machine Learning Research*, 3:993–1022.

Samuel Brody and Noemie Elhadad. 2010. An unsupervised aspect-sentiment model for online reviews. In *Proceedings of NAACL-HLT 2010*, pages 804–812. Association for Computational Linguistics.

Yejin Choi and Claire Cardie. 2010. Hierarchical sequential learning for extracting opinions and their attributes. In *Proceedings of ACL 2010*, pages 269–274. Association for Computational Linguistics.

Gayatree Ganu, Noemie Elhadad, and Amélie Marian. 2009. Beyond the stars: Improving rating predictions using review text content. In *Proceedings of WebDB 2009*, pages 1–6.

Geoffrey Hinton and Ruslan Salakhutdinov. 2009. Replicated softmax: an undirected topic model. In *Advances in Neural Information Processing Systems (NIPS 2009)*, pages 1607–1614.

Minqing Hu and Bing Liu. 2004. Mining and summarizing customer reviews. In *Proceedings of KDD 2004*, pages 168–177, New York, NY, USA. ACM.

Niklas Jakob and Iryna Gurevych. 2010. Extracting opinion targets in a single-and cross-domain setting with Conditional Random Fields. In *Proceedings of EMNLP 2010*, pages 1035–1045. Association for Computational Linguistics.

Wei Jin, Hung Hay Ho, and Rohini K Srihari. 2009. A novel lexicalized HMM-based learning framework for Web opinion mining. In *Proceedings of ICML 2009*, pages 465–472.

Nozomi Kobayashi, Kentaro Inui, and Yuji Matsumoto. 2007. Extracting aspect-evaluation and aspect-of relations in opinion mining. In *Proceedings of EMNLP-CoNLL*, pages 1065–1074.

Chenghua Lin and Yulan He. 2009. Joint sentiment/topic model for sentiment analysis. In *Proceedings of the 18th ACM Conference on Information and Knowledge Management (CIKM 2009)*, pages 375–384. ACM.

Bing Liu, Wynne Hsu, and Yiming Ma. 1998. Integrating classification and association rule mining. In *Proceedings of KDD 1998*, pages 80–86. AAAI Press.

Bing Liu, Minqing Hu, and Junsheng Cheng. 2005. Opinion observer: analyzing and comparing opinions on the Web. In *Proceedings of the 14th international conference on World Wide Web*, pages 342–351. ACM.

Kang Liu, Liheng Xu, and Jun Zhao. 2012. Opinion target extraction using word-based translation model. In *Proceedings of EMNLP-CoNLL 2012*, pages 1346–1356.

Kang Liu, Liheng Xu, Yang Liu, and Jun Zhao. 2013. Opinion target extraction using partially-supervised word alignment model. In *Proceedings of the 23rd International Joint Conference on Artificial Intelligence (IJCAI 2013)*, pages 2134–2140. AAAI Press.

Bing Liu. 2012. Sentiment analysis and opinion mining. *Synthesis Lectures on Human Language Technologies*, 5(1):1–167.

Qiaozhu Mei, Xu Ling, Matthew Wondra, Hang Su, and ChengXiang Zhai. 2007. Topic sentiment mixture: modeling facets and opinions in weblogs. In *Proceedings of the 16th international conference on the World Wide Web (WWW 2007)*, pages 171–180. ACM.

Arjun Mukherjee and Bing Liu. 2012. Aspect extraction through semi-supervised modeling. In *Proceedings of ACL 2012*, pages 339–348.

Bo Pang and Lillian Lee. 2008. Opinion mining and sentiment analysis. *Foundations and trends in information retrieval*, 2(1-2):1–135.

Bo Pang, Lillian Lee, and Shivakumar Vaithyanathan. 2002. Thumbs up?: Sentiment classification using machine learning techniques. In *Proceedings of EMNLP 2002*, pages 79–86. Association for Computational Linguistics.

Ana-Maria Popescu and Orena Etzioni. 2005. Extracting product features and opinions from reviews. In *Proceedings of HLT/EMNLP 2005*. Springer.

Swapna Somasundaran and Janyce Wiebe. 2009. Recognizing stances in online debates. In *Proceedings of ACL-IJCNLP 2009*, pages 226–234. Association for Computational Linguistics.

Ivan Titov and Ryan McDonald. 2008. Modeling online reviews with multi-grain topic models. In *Proceedings of the 17th international conference on the World Wide Web (WWW 2008)*, pages 111–120. ACM.

Taras Zagibalov and John Carroll. 2008. Automatic seed word selection for unsupervised sentiment classification of Chinese text. In *Proceedings of COLING 2008*, pages 1073–1080.

Wayne Xin Zhao, Jing Jiang, Hongfei Yan, and Xiaoming Li. 2010. Jointly modeling aspects and opinions with a MaxEnt-LDA hybrid. In *Proceedings of EMNLP 2010*, pages 56–65. Association for Computational Linguistics.

Li Zhuang, Feng Jing, and Xiao-Yan Zhu. 2006. Movie review mining and summarization. In *Proceedings of the 15th ACM international Conference on Information and Knowledge Management (CIKM 2006)*, pages 43–50. ACM.

Classifying Relations by Ranking with Convolutional Neural Networks

Cícero Nogueira dos Santos
IBM Research
138/146 Av. Pasteur
Rio de Janeiro, RJ, Brazil
cicerons@br.ibm.com

Bing Xiang
IBM Watson
1101 Kitchawan
Yorktown Heights, NY, USA
bingxia@us.ibm.com

Bowen Zhou
IBM Watson
1101 Kitchawan
Yorktown Heights, NY, USA
zhou@us.ibm.com

Abstract

Relation classification is an important semantic processing task for which state-of-the-art systems still rely on costly handcrafted features. In this work we tackle the relation classification task using a convolutional neural network that performs classification by ranking (CR-CNN). We propose a new pairwise ranking loss function that makes it easy to reduce the impact of artificial classes. We perform experiments using the the SemEval-2010 Task 8 dataset, which is designed for the task of classifying the relationship between two nominals marked in a sentence. Using CR-CNN, we outperform the state-of-the-art for this dataset and achieve a F1 of 84.1 without using any costly handcrafted features. Additionally, our experimental results show that: (1) our approach is more effective than CNN followed by a softmax classifier; (2) omitting the representation of the artificial class *Other* improves both precision and recall; and (3) using only word embeddings as input features is enough to achieve state-of-the-art results if we consider only the text between the two target nominals.

1 Introduction

Relation classification is an important Natural Language Processing (NLP) task which is normally used as an intermediate step in many complex NLP applications such as question-answering and automatic knowledge base construction. Since the last decade there has been increasing interest in applying machine learning approaches to this task (Zhang, 2004; Qian et al., 2009; Rink and Harabagiu, 2010). One reason is the availability of benchmark datasets such as the SemEval-2010 task 8 dataset (Hendrickx et al., 2010), which encodes the task of classifying the relationship between two nominals marked in a sentence. The following sentence contains an example of the *Component-Whole* relation between the nominals *"introduction"* and *"book"*.

The [introduction]$_{e_1}$ in the [book]$_{e_2}$ is a summary of what is in the text.

Some recent work on relation classification has focused on the use of deep neural networks with the aim of reducing the number of handcrafted features (Socher et al., 2012; Zeng et al., 2014; Yu et al., 2014). However, in order to achieve state-of-the-art results these approaches still use some features derived from lexical resources such as WordNet or NLP tools such as dependency parsers and named entity recognizers (NER).

In this work, we propose a new convolutional neural network (CNN), which we name Classification by Ranking CNN (CR-CNN), to tackle the relation classification task. The proposed network learns a distributed vector representation for each relation class. Given an input text segment, the network uses a convolutional layer to produce a distributed vector representation of the text and compares it to the class representations in order to produce a score for each class. We propose a new pairwise ranking loss function that makes it easy to reduce the impact of artificial classes. We perform an extensive number of experiments using the the SemEval-2010 Task 8 dataset. Using CR-CNN, and without the need for any costly handcrafted feature, we outperform the state-of-the-art for this dataset. Our experimental results are evidence that: (1) CR-CNN is more effective than CNN followed by a softmax classifier; (2) omitting the representation of the artificial class *Other* improves both precision and recall; and (3) using only word embeddings as input features is enough to achieve state-of-the-art results if we consider only the text between the two target nominals.

Proceedings of the 53rd Annual Meeting of the Association for Computational Linguistics and the 7th International Joint Conference on Natural Language Processing, pages 626–634,
Beijing, China, July 26-31, 2015.

The remainder of the paper is structured as follows. Section 2 details the proposed neural network. In Section 3, we present details about the setup of experimental evaluation, and then describe the results in Section 4. In Section 5, we discuss previous work in deep neural networks for relation classification and for other NLP tasks. Section 6 presents our conclusions.

2 The Proposed Neural Network

Given a sentence x and two target nouns, CR-CNN computes a score for each relation class $c \in C$. For each class $c \in C$, the network learns a distributed vector representation which is encoded as a column in the class embedding matrix $W^{classes}$. As detailed in Figure 1, the only input for the network is the tokenized text string of the sentence. In the first step, CR-CNN transforms words into real-valued feature vectors. Next, a convolutional layer is used to construct a distributed vector representations of the sentence, r_x. Finally, CR-CNN computes a score for each relation class $c \in C$ by performing a dot product between $r_x^\intercal$ and $W^{classes}$.

2.1 Word Embeddings

The first layer of the network transforms words into representations that capture syntactic and semantic information about the words. Given a sentence x consisting of N words $x = \{w_1, w_2, ..., w_N\}$, every word w_n is converted into a real-valued vector r^{w_n}. Therefore, the input to the next layer is a sequence of real-valued vectors $emb_x = \{r^{w_1}, r^{w_2}, ..., r^{w_N}\}$

Word representations are encoded by column vectors in an embedding matrix $W^{wrd} \in \mathbb{R}^{d^w \times |V|}$, where V is a fixed-sized vocabulary. Each column $W_i^{wrd} \in \mathbb{R}^{d^w}$ corresponds to the word embedding of the i-th word in the vocabulary. We transform a word w into its word embedding r^w by using the matrix-vector product:

$$r^w = W^{wrd} v^w$$

where v^w is a vector of size $|V|$ which has value 1 at index w and zero in all other positions. The matrix W^{wrd} is a parameter to be learned, and the size of the word embedding d^w is a hyperparameter to be chosen by the user.

2.2 Word Position Embeddings

In the task of relation classification, information that is needed to determine the class of a relation

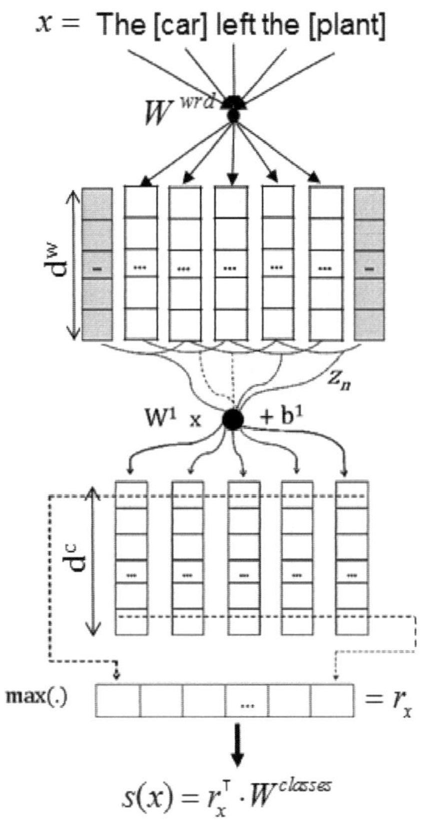

Figure 1: CR-CNN: a Neural Network for classifying by ranking.

between two target nouns normally comes from words which are close to the target nouns. Zeng et al. (2014) propose the use of *word position embeddings* (position features) which help the CNN by keeping track of how close words are to the target nouns. These features are similar to the position features proposed by Collobert et al. (2011) for the Semantic Role Labeling task.

In this work we also experiment with the word position embeddings (WPE) proposed by Zeng et al. (2014). The WPE is derived from the relative distances of the current word to the target $noun_1$ and $noun_2$. For instance, in the sentence shown in Figure 1, the relative distances of *left* to *car* and *plant* are -1 and 2, respectively. As in (Collobert et al., 2011), each relative distance is mapped to a vector of dimension d^{wpe}, which is initialized with random numbers. d^{wpe} is a hyperparameter of the network. Given the vectors wp_1 and wp_2 for the word w with respect to the targets $noun_1$ and $noun_2$, the position embedding of w is given by the concatenation of these two vectors, $wpe^w = [wp_1, wp_2]$.

In the experiments where word position embeddings are used, the word embedding and the word position embedding of each word are concatenated to form the input for the convolutional layer, $emb_x = \{[r^{w_1}, wpe^{w_1}], [r^{w_2}, wpe^{w_2}], ..., [r^{w_N}, wpe^{w_N}]\}$.

2.3 Sentence Representation

The next step in the NN consists in creating the distributed vector representation r_x for the input sentence x. The main challenges in this step are the sentence size variability and the fact that important information can appear at any position in the sentence. In recent work, convolutional approaches have been used to tackle these issues when creating representations for text segments of different sizes (Zeng et al., 2014; Hu et al., 2014; dos Santos and Gatti, 2014) and character-level representations of words of different sizes (dos Santos and Zadrozny, 2014). Here, we use a convolutional layer to compute distributed vector representations of the sentence. The convolutional layer first produces local features around each word in the sentence. Then, it combines these local features using a max operation to create a fixed-sized vector for the input sentence.

Given a sentence x, the convolutional layer applies a matrix-vector operation to each window of size k of successive windows in $emb_x = \{r^{w_1}, r^{w_2}, ..., r^{w_N}\}$. Let us define the vector $z_n \in \mathbb{R}^{d^w k}$ as the concatenation of a sequence of k word embeddings, centralized in the n-th word:

$$z_n = (r^{w_{n-(k-1)/2}}, ..., r^{w_{n+(k-1)/2}})^\intercal$$

In order to overcome the issue of referencing words with indices outside of the sentence boundaries, we augment the sentence with a special *padding* token replicated $\frac{k-1}{2}$ times at the beginning and the end.

The convolutional layer computes the j-th element of the vector $r_x \in \mathbb{R}^{d^c}$ as follows:

$$[r_x]_j = \max_{1<n<N} \left[f\left(W^1 z_n + b^1\right) \right]_j$$

where $W^1 \in \mathbb{R}^{d^c \times d^w k}$ is the weight matrix of the convolutional layer and f is the hyperbolic tangent function. The same matrix is used to extract local features around each word window of the given sentence. The fixed-sized distributed vector representation for the sentence is obtained by using the max over all word windows. Matrix W^1 and vector b^1 are parameters to be learned. The number of convolutional units d^c, and the size of the word context window k are hyperparameters to be chosen by the user. It is important to note that d^c corresponds to the size of the sentence representation.

2.4 Class embeddings and Scoring

Given the distributed vector representation of the input sentence x, the network with parameter set θ computes the score for a class label $c \in C$ by using the dot product

$$s_\theta(x)_c = r_x^\intercal [W^{classes}]_c$$

where $W^{classes}$ is an embedding matrix whose columns encode the distributed vector representations of the different class labels, and $[W^{classes}]_c$ is the column vector that contains the embedding of the class c. Note that the number of dimensions in each class embedding must be equal to the size of the sentence representation, which is defined by d^c. The embedding matrix $W^{classes}$ is a parameter to be learned by the network. It is initialized by randomly sampling each value from an uniform distribution: $\mathcal{U}(-r, r)$, where $r = \sqrt{\frac{6}{|C| + d^c}}$.

2.5 Training Procedure

Our network is trained by minimizing a pairwise ranking loss function over the training set D. The input for each training round is a sentence x and two different class labels $y^+ \in C$ and $c^- \in C$, where y^+ is a correct class label for x and c^- is not. Let $s_\theta(x)_{y^+}$ and $s_\theta(x)_{c^-}$ be respectively the scores for class labels y^+ and c^- generated by the network with parameter set θ. We propose a new logistic loss function over these scores in order to train CR-CNN:

$$\begin{aligned} L = \; & log(1 + exp(\gamma(m^+ - s_\theta(x)_{y^+})) \\ & + log(1 + exp(\gamma(m^- + s_\theta(x)_{c^-})) \end{aligned} \quad (1)$$

where m^+ and m^- are margins and γ is a scaling factor that magnifies the difference between the score and the margin and helps to penalize more on the prediction errors. The first term in the right side of Equation 1 decreases as the score $s_\theta(x)_{y^+}$ increases. The second term in the right side decreases as the score $s_\theta(x)_{c^-}$ decreases. Training CR-CNN by minimizing the loss function in Equation 1 has the effect of training to give scores greater than m^+ for the correct class and (negative) scores smaller than $-m^-$ for incorrect classes. In our experiments we set γ to 2, m^+ to 2.5 and m^- to 0.5. We use $L2$ regularization by adding the term $\beta\|\theta\|^2$ to Equation 1. In our experiments we set β to 0.001. We use stochastic gradient descent (SGD) to minimize the loss function with respect to θ.

Like some other ranking approaches that only update two classes/examples at every training round (Weston et al., 2011; Gao et al., 2014), we can efficiently train the network for tasks which have a very large number of classes. This is an advantage over softmax classifiers.

On the other hand, sampling informative negative classes/examples can have a significant impact in the effectiveness of the learned model. In the case of our loss function, more informative negative classes are the ones with a score larger than $-m^-$. The number of classes in the relation classification dataset that we use in our experiments is small. Therefore, in our experiments, given a sentence x with class label y^+, the incorrect class c^- that we choose to perform a SGD step is the one with the highest score among all incorrect classes $c^- = \underset{c \in C;\, c \neq y^+}{\arg\max}\ s_\theta(x)_c$.

For tasks where the number of classes is large, we can fix a number of negative classes to be considered at each example and select the one with the largest score to perform a gradient step. This approach is similar to the one used by Weston et al. (2014) to select negative examples.

We use the backpropagation algorithm to compute gradients of the network. In our experiments, we implement the CR-CNN architecture and the backpropagation algorithm using Theano (Bergstra et al., 2010).

2.6 Special Treatment of *Artificial* Classes

In this work, we consider a class as *artificial* if it is used to group items that do not belong to any of the *actual* classes. An example of artificial class is the class *Other* in the SemEval 2010 relation classification task. In this task, the artificial class *Other* is used to indicate that the relation between two nominals does not belong to any of the nine relation classes of interest. Therefore, the class *Other* is very noisy since it groups many different types of relations that may not have much in common.

An important characteristic of CR-CNN is that it makes it easy to reduce the effect of artificial classes by omitting their embeddings. If the embedding of a class label c is omitted, it means that the embedding matrix $W^{classes}$ does not contain a column vector for c. One of the main benefits from this strategy is that the learning process focuses on the "natural" classes only. Since the embedding of the artificial class is omitted, it will not influence the prediction step, i.e., CR-CNN does not produce a score for the artificial class.

In our experiments with the SemEval-2010 relation classification task, when training with a sentence x whose class label $y = Other$, the first term in the right side of Equation 1 is set to zero. During prediction time, a relation is classified as *Other* only if all actual classes have negative scores. Otherwise, it is classified with the class which has the largest score.

3 Experimental Setup

3.1 Dataset and Evaluation Metric

We use the SemEval-2010 Task 8 dataset to perform our experiments. This dataset contains 10,717 examples annotated with 9 different relation types and an artificial relation Other, which is used to indicate that the relation in the example does not belong to any of the nine main relation types. The nine relations are *Cause-Effect, Component-Whole, Content-Container, Entity-Destination, Entity-Origin, Instrument-Agency, Member-Collection, Message-Topic* and *Product-Producer.* Each example contains a sentence marked with two nominals e_1 and e_2, and the task consists of predicting the relation between the two nominals taking into consideration the directionality. That means that the relation Cause-Effect(e1,e2) is different from the relation Cause-Effect(e2,e1), as shown in the examples below. More information about this dataset can be found in (Hendrickx et al., 2010).

The [war]$_{e_1}$ resulted in other collateral imperial [conquests]$_{e_2}$ as well. ⇒ Cause-Effect(e1,e2)

The [burst]$_{e_1}$ has been caused by water hammer [pressure]$_{e2}$. ⇒ Cause-Effect(e2,e1)

The SemEval-2010 Task 8 dataset is already partitioned into 8,000 training instances and 2,717 test instances. We score our systems by using the SemEval-2010 Task 8 official scorer, which computes the macro-averaged F1-scores for the nine actual relations (excluding Other) and takes the directionality into consideration.

3.2 Word Embeddings Initialization

The word embeddings used in our experiments are initialized by means of unsupervised pre-training. We perform pre-training using the skip-gram NN architecture (Mikolov et al., 2013) available in the `word2vec` tool. We use the December 2013 snapshot of the English Wikipedia corpus to train word embeddings with `word2vec`. We preprocess the Wikipedia text using the steps described in (dos Santos and Gatti, 2014): (1) removal of paragraphs that are not in English; (2) substitution of non-western characters for a special character; (3) tokenization of the text using the tokenizer available with the Stanford POS Tagger (Toutanova et al., 2003); (4) removal of sentences that are less than 20 characters long (including white spaces) or have less than 5 tokens. (5) lowercase all words and substitute each numerical digit by a 0. The resulting clean corpus contains about 1.75 billion tokens.

3.3 Neural Network Hyper-parameter

We use 4-fold cross-validation to tune the neural network hyperparameters. Learning rates in the range of 0.03 and 0.01 give relatively similar results. Best results are achieved using between 10 and 15 training epochs, depending on the CR-CNN configuration. In Table 1, we show the selected hyperparameter values. Additionally, we use a learning rate schedule that decreases the learning rate λ according to the training epoch t. The learning rate for epoch t, λ_t, is computed using the equation: $\lambda_t = \frac{\lambda}{t}$.

Parameter	Parameter Name	Value
d^w	Word Emb. size	400
d^{wpe}	Word Pos. Emb. size	70
d^c	Convolutinal Units	1000
k	Context Window size	3
λ	Initial Learning Rate	0.025

Table 1: CR-CNN Hyperparameters

4 Experimental Results

4.1 Word Position Embeddings and Input Text Span

In the experiments discussed in this section we assess the impact of using word position embeddings (WPE) and also propose a simpler alternative approach that is almost as effective as WPEs. The main idea behind the use of WPEs in relation classification task is to give some hint to the convolutional layer of how close a word is to the target nouns, based on the assumption that closer words have more impact than distant words.

Here we hypothesize that most of the information needed to classify the relation appear between the two target nouns. Based on this hypothesis, we perform an experiment where the input for the convolutional layer consists of the word embeddings of the word sequence $\{w_{e_1} - 1, ..., w_{e_2} + 1\}$ where e_1 and e_2 correspond to the positions of the first and the second target nouns, respectively.

In Table 2 we compare the results of different CR-CNN configurations. The first column indicates whether the full sentence was used (*Yes*) or whether the text span between the target nouns was used (*No*). The second column informs if the WPEs were used or not. It is clear that the use of WPEs is essential when the full sentence is used, since F1 jumps from 74.3 to 84.1. This effect of WPEs is reported by (Zeng et al., 2014). On the other hand, when using only the text span between the target nouns, the impact of WPE is much smaller. With this strategy, we achieve a F1 of 82.8 using only word embeddings as input, which is a result as good as the previous state-of-the-art F1 of 83.0 reported in (Yu et al., 2014) for the SemEval-2010 Task 8 dataset. This experimental result also suggests that, in this task, the CNN works better for short texts.

All experiments reported in the next sections use CR-CNN with full sentence and WPEs.

Full Sentence	Word Position	Prec.	Rec.	F1
Yes	Yes	**83.7**	**84.7**	**84.1**
No	Yes	83.3	83.9	83.5
No	No	83.4	82.3	82.8
Yes	No	78.1	71.5	74.3

Table 2: Comparison of different CR-CNN configurations.

4.2 Impact of Omitting the Embedding of the artificial class *Other*

In this experiment we assess the impact of omitting the embedding of the class *Other*. As we mentioned above, this class is very noisy since it groups many different infrequent relation types. Its embedding is difficult to define and therefore brings noise into the classification process of the natural classes. In Table 3 we present the results comparing the use and omission of embedding for the class *Other*. The two first lines of results present the official F1, which does not take into account the results for the class *Other*. We can see that by omitting the embedding of the class *Other* both precision and recall for the other classes improve, which results in an increase of 1.4 in the F1. These results suggest that the strategy we use in CR-CNN to avoid the noise of artificial classes is effective.

Use embedding of class *Other*	Class	Prec.	Rec.	F1
No	All	**83.7**	**84.7**	**84.1**
Yes	All	81.3	84.3	82.7
No	Other	52.0	48.7	50.3
Yes	Other	60.1	48.7	53.8

Table 3: Impact of not using an embedding for the artificial class Other.

In the two last lines of Table 3 we present the results for the class *Other*. We can note that while the recall for the cases classified as *Other* remains 48.7, the precision significantly decreases from 60.1 to 52.0 when the embedding of the class *Other* is not used. That means that more cases from natural classes (all) are now been classified as *Other*. However, as both the precision and the recall of the natural classes increase, the cases that are now classified as *Other* must be cases that are also wrongly classified when the embedding of the class *Other* is used.

4.3 CR-CNN versus CNN+Softmax

In this section we report experimental results comparing CR-CNN with CNN+Softmax. In order to do a fair comparison, we've implemented a CNN+Softmax and trained it with the same data, word embeddings and WPEs used in CR-CNN. Concretely, our CNN+Softmax consists in getting the output of the convolutional layer, which is the vector r_x in Figure 1, and giving it as input for a softmax classifier. We tune the parameters of CNN+Softmax by using a 4-fold cross-validation with the training set. Compared to the hyperparameter values for CR-CNN presented in Table 1, the only difference for CNN+Softmax is the number of convolutional units d^c, which is set to 400.

In Table 4 we compare the results of CR-CNN and CNN+Softmax. CR-CNN outperforms CNN+Softmax in both precision and recall, and improves the F1 by 1.6. The third line in Table 4 shows the result reported by Zeng et al. (2014) when only word embeddings and WPEs are used as input to the network (similar to our CNN+Softmax). We believe that the word embeddings employed by them is the main reason their result is much worse than that of CNN+Softmax. We use word embeddings of size 400 while they use word embeddings of size 50, which were trained using much less unlabeled data than we did.

Neural Net.	Prec.	Rec.	F1
CR-CNN	**83.7**	**84.7**	**84.1**
CNN+SoftMax	82.1	83.1	82.5
CNN+SoftMax (Zeng et al., 2014)	-	-	78.9

Table 4: Comparison of results of CR-CNN and CNN+Softmax.

4.4 Comparison with the State-of-the-art

In Table 5 we compare CR-CNN results with results recently published for the SemEval-2010 Task 8 dataset. Rink and Harabagiu (2010) present a support vector machine (SVM) classifier that is fed with a rich (traditional) feature set. It obtains an F1 of 82.2, which was the best result at SemEval-2010 Task 8. Socher et al. (2012) present results for a recursive neural network (RNN) that employs a matrix-vector representation to every node in a parse tree in order to compose the distributed vector representation for the complete sentence. Their method is named the matrix-vector recursive neural network (MVRNN) and achieves a F1 of 82.4 when POS, NER and WordNet features are used. In (Zeng et al., 2014), the authors present results for a CNN+Softmax classifier which employs lexical and sentence-level features. Their classifier achieves a F1 of 82.7 when adding a handcrafted feature based on the WordNet. Yu et al. (2014) present the Factor-based Compositional Embedding Model (FCM), which achieves a F1 of 83.0 by deriving sentence-level and substructure embeddings from word embeddings utilizing dependency trees and named entities.

As we can see in the last line of Table 5, CR-CNN using the full sentence, word embeddings and WPEs outperforms all previous reported results and reaches a new state-of-the-art F1 of 84.1. This is a remarkable result since we do not use any complicated features that depend on external lexical resources such as WordNet and NLP tools such as named entity recognizers (NERs) and dependency parsers.

We can see in Table 5 that CR-CNN[1] also achieves the best result among the systems that use word embeddings as the only input features. The closest result (80.6), which is produced by the FCM system of Yu et al. (2014), is 2.2 F1 points behind CR-CNN result (82.8).

4.5 Most Representative Trigrams for each Relation

In Table 6, for each relation type we present the five trigrams in the test set which contributed the most for scoring correctly classified examples. Remember that in CR-CNN, given a sentence x the score for the class c is computed by $s_\theta(x)_c = r_x^\intercal[W^{classes}]_c$. In order to compute the most representative trigram of a sentence x, we trace back each position in r_x to find the trigram responsible for it. For each trigram t, we compute its particular contribution for the score by summing the terms in score that use positions in r_x that trace back to t. The most *representative* trigram in x is the one with the largest contribution to the improvement of the score. In order to create the results presented in Table 6, we rank the trigrams which were selected as the most representative of any sentence in decreasing order of contribution value. If a trigram appears as the largest contributor for more than one sentence, its contribuition value becomes the sum of its contribution for each sentence.

We can see in Table 6 that for most classes, the trigrams that contributed the most to increase the score are indeed very informative regarding the relation type. As expected, different trigrams play an important role depending on the direction of the relation. For instance, the most informative trigram for *Entity-Origin(e1,e2)* is *"away from the"*, while reverse direction of the relation, *Entity-Origin(e2,e1)* or *Origin-Entity*, has *"the source of"* as the most informative trigram. These results are a step towards the extraction of meaningful knowledge from models produced by CNNs.

[1]This is the result using only the text span between the target nouns.

5 Related Work

Over the years, various approaches have been proposed for relation classification (Zhang, 2004; Qian et al., 2009; Hendrickx et al., 2010; Rink and Harabagiu, 2010). Most of them treat it as a multi-class classification problem and apply a variety of machine learning techniques to the task in order to achieve a high accuracy.

Recently, deep learning (Bengio, 2009) has become an attractive area for multiple applications, including computer vision, speech recognition and natural language processing. Among the different deep learning strategies, convolutional neural networks have been successfully applied to different NLP task such as part-of-speech tagging (dos Santos and Zadrozny, 2014), sentiment analysis (Kim, 2014; dos Santos and Gatti, 2014), question classification (Kalchbrenner et al., 2014), semantic role labeling (Collobert et al., 2011), hashtag prediction (Weston et al., 2014), sentence completion and response matching (Hu et al., 2014).

Some recent work on deep learning for relation classification include Socher et al. (2012), Zeng et al. (2014) and Yu et al. (2014). In (Socher et al., 2012), the authors tackle relation classification using a recursive neural network (RNN) that assigns a matrix-vector representation to every node in a parse tree. The representation for the complete sentence is computed bottom-up by recursively combining the words according to the syntactic structure of the parse tree Their method is named the matrix-vector recursive neural network (MVRNN).

Zeng et al. (2014) propose an approach for relation classification where sentence-level features are learned through a CNN, which has word embedding and position features as its input. In parallel, lexical features are extracted according to given nouns. Then sentence-level and lexical features are concatenated into a single vector and fed into a softmax classifier for prediction. This approach achieves state-of-the-art performance on the SemEval-2010 Task 8 dataset.

Yu et al. (2014) propose a Factor-based Com-

Classifier	Feature Set	F1
SVM (Rink and Harabagiu, 2010)	POS, prefixes, morphological, WordNet, dependency parse, Levin classes, ProBank, FrameNet, NomLex-Plus, Google n-gram, paraphrases, TextRunner	82.2
RNN (Socher et al., 2012)	word embeddings	74.8
	word embeddings, POS, NER, WordNet	77.6
MVRNN (Socher et al., 2012)	word embeddings	79.1
	word embeddings, POS, NER, WordNet	82.4
CNN+Softmax (Zeng et al., 2014)	word embeddings	69.7
	word embeddings, word position embeddings, word pair, words around word pair, WordNet	82.7
FCM (Yu et al., 2014)	word embeddings	80.6
	word embeddings, dependency parse, NER	83.0
CR-CNN	word embeddings	82.8
	word embeddings, word position embeddings	**84.1**

Table 5: Comparison with results published in the literature.

Relation	(e1,e2)	(e2,e1)
Cause-Effect	$e1$ resulted in, $e1$ caused a, had caused the, poverty cause $e2$, caused a $e2$	$e2$ caused by, was caused by, are caused by, been caused by, $e2$ from $e1$
Component-Whole	$e1$ of the, of the $e2$, part of the, in the $e2$, $e1$ on the	$e2$'s $e1$, with its $e1$, $e2$ has a, $e2$ comprises the, $e2$ with $e1$
Content-Container	was in a, was hidden in, were in a, was inside a, was contained in	$e2$ full of, $e2$ with $e1$, $e2$ was full, $e2$ contained a, $e2$ with cold
Entity-Destination	$e1$ into the, $e1$ into a, $e1$ to the, was put inside, imported into the	-
Entity-Origin	away from the, derived from a, had left the, derived from an, $e1$ from the	the source of, $e2$ grape $e1$, $e2$ butter $e1$
Instrument-Agency	are used by, $e1$ for $e2$, is used by, trade for $e2$, with the $e2$	with a $e1$, by using $e1$, $e2$ finds a, $e2$ with a, $e2$, who
Member-Collection	of the $e2$, in the $e2$, of this $e2$, the political $e2$, $e1$ collected in	$e2$ of $e1$, of wild $e1$, of elven $e1$, $e2$ of different, of 0000 $e1$
Message-Topic	$e1$ is the, $e1$ asserts the, $e1$ that the, on the $e2$, $e1$ inform about	described in the, discussed in the, featured in numerous, discussed in cabinet, documented in two,
Product-Producer	$e1$ by the, by a $e2$, of the $e2$, by the $e2$, from the $e2$	$e2$ of the, $e2$ has constructed, $e2$'s $e1$, $e2$ came up, $e2$ who created

Table 6: List of most representative trigrams for each relation type.

positional Embedding Model (FCM) by deriving sentence-level and substructure embeddings from word embeddings, utilizing dependency trees and named entities. It achieves slightly higher accuracy on the same dataset than (Zeng et al., 2014), but only when syntactic information is used.

There are two main differences between the approach proposed in this paper and the ones proposed in (Socher et al., 2012; Zeng et al., 2014; Yu et al., 2014): (1) CR-CNN uses a pair-wise ranking method, while other approaches apply multi-class classification by using the softmax function on the top of the CNN/RNN; and (2) CR-CNN employs an effective method to deal with artificial classes by omitting their embeddings, while other approaches treat all classes equally.

6 Conclusion

In this work we tackle the relation classification task using a CNN that performs classification by ranking. The main contributions of this work are: (1) the definition of a new state-of-the-art for the SemEval-2010 Task 8 dataset without using any costly handcrafted features; (2) the proposal of a new CNN for classification that uses class embeddings and a new rank loss function; (3) an effective method to deal with artificial classes by omitting their embeddings in CR-CNN; (4) the demonstration that using only the text between target nominals is almost as effective as using WPEs; and (5) a method to extract from the CR-CNN model the most representative contexts of each relation type. Although we apply CR-CNN to relation classification, this method can be used for any classification task.

Acknowledgments

The authors would like to thank Nina Wacholder for her valuable suggestions to improve the final version of the paper.

References

Yoshua Bengio. 2009. Learning deep architectures for ai. *Foundations and Trends Machine Learning*, 2(1):1–127.

James Bergstra, Olivier Breuleux, Frédéric Bastien, Pascal Lamblin, Razvan Pascanu, Guillaume Desjardins, Joseph Turian, David Warde-Farley, and Yoshua Bengio. 2010. Theano: a CPU and GPU math expression compiler. In *Proceedings of the Python for Scientific Computing Conference*.

R. Collobert, J. Weston, L. Bottou, M. Karlen, K. Kavukcuoglu, and P. Kuksa. 2011. Natural language processing (almost) from scratch. *Journal of Machine Learning Research*, 12:2493–2537.

Cícero Nogueira dos Santos and Maíra Gatti. 2014. Deep convolutional neural networks for sentiment analysis of short texts. In *Proceedings of the 25th International Conference on Computational Linguistics (COLING)*, Dublin, Ireland.

Cícero Nogueira dos Santos and Bianca Zadrozny. 2014. Learning character-level representations for part-of-speech tagging. In *Proceedings of the 31st International Conference on Machine Learning (ICML), JMLR: W&CP volume 32*, Beijing, China.

Jianfeng Gao, Patrick Pantel, Michael Gamon, Xiaodong He, and Li Deng. 2014. Modeling interestingness with deep neural networks. In *Proceedings of the Conference on Empirical Methods in Natural Language Processing (EMNLP)*.

Iris Hendrickx, Su Nam Kim, Zornitsa Kozareva, Preslav Nakov, Diarmuid Ó. Séaghdha, Sebastian Padó, Marco Pennacchiotti, Lorenza Romano, and Stan Szpakowicz. 2010. Semeval-2010 task 8: Multi-way classification of semantic relations between pairs of nominals. In *Proceedings of the 5th International Workshop on Semantic Evaluation*, pages 33–38.

Baotian Hu, Zhengdong Lu, Hang Li, and Qingcai Chen. 2014. Convolutional neural network architectures for matching natural language sentences. In *Proceedings of the Conference on Neural Information Processing Systems*, pages 2042–2050.

Nal Kalchbrenner, Edward Grefenstette, and Phil Blunsom. 2014. A convolutional neural netork for modelling sentences. In *Proceedings of the 52th Annual Meeting of the Association for Computational Linguistics*, pages 655–665, Baltimore, Maryland.

Yoon Kim. 2014. Convolutional neural networks for sentence classification. In *Proceedings of the 2014 Conference on Empirical Methods for Natural Language Processing*, pages 1746–1751, Doha, Qatar.

Tomas Mikolov, Kai Chen, Greg Corrado, and Jeffrey Dean. 2013. Efficient estimation of word representations in vector space. In *In Proceedings of Workshop at ICLR*.

Longhua Qian, Guodong Zhou, Fang Kong, and Qiaoming Zhu. 2009. Semi-supervised learning for semantic relation classification using stratified sampling strategy. In *Proceedings of the Conference on Empirical Methods in Natural Language Processing*, pages 1437–1445.

Bryan Rink and Sanda Harabagiu. 2010. Utd: Classifying semantic relations by combining lexical and semantic resources. In *Proceedings of International Workshop on Semantic Evaluation*, pages 256–259.

Richard Socher, Brody Huval, Christopher D. Manning, and Andrew Y. Ng. 2012. Semantic compositionality through recursive matrix-vector spaces. In *Proceedings of the Joint Conference on Empirical Methods in Natural Language Processing and Computational Natural Language Learning*, pages 1201–1211.

Kristina Toutanova, Dan Klein, Christopher D Manning, and Yoram Singer. 2003. Feature-rich part-of-speech tagging with a cyclic dependency network. In *Proceedings of the Conference of the North American Chapter of the Association for Computational Linguistics on Human Language Technology*, pages 173–180.

Jason Weston, Samy Bengio, and Nicolas Usunier. 2011. Wsabie: Scaling up to large vocabulary image annotation. In *Proceedings of the Twenty-Second International Joint Conference on Artificial Intelligence*, pages 2764–2770.

Jason Weston, Sumit Chopra, and Keith Adams. 2014. #tagspace: Semantic embeddings from hashtags. In *Proceedings of the Conference on Empirical Methods in Natural Language Processing (EMNLP)*, pages 1822–1827.

Mo Yu, Matthew Gormley, and Mark Dredze. 2014. Factor-based compositional embedding models. In *Proceedings of the 2nd Workshop on Learning Semantics*, Montreal, Canada.

Daojian Zeng, Kang Liu, Siwei Lai, Guangyou Zhou, and Jun Zhao. 2014. Relation classification via convolutional deep neural network. In *Proceedings of the 25th International Conference on Computational Linguistics (COLING)*, pages 2335–2344, Dublin, Ireland.

Zhu Zhang. 2004. Weakly-supervised relation classification for information extraction. In *Proceedings of the ACM International Conference on Information and Knowledge Management*, pages 581–588, New York, NY, USA.

Semantic Representations for Domain Adaptation: A Case Study on the Tree Kernel-based Method for Relation Extraction

Thien Huu Nguyen[†], **Barbara Plank**[§] **and Ralph Grishman**[†]
[†] Computer Science Department, New York University, New York, NY 10003, USA
[§] Center for Language Technology, University of Copenhagen, Denmark
thien@cs.nyu.edu,bplank@cst.dk,grishman@cs.nyu.edu

Abstract

We study the application of word embeddings to generate semantic representations for the domain adaptation problem of relation extraction (RE) in the tree kernel-based method. We systematically evaluate various techniques to generate the semantic representations and demonstrate that they are effective to improve the generalization performance of a tree kernel-based relation extractor across domains (up to 7% relative improvement). In addition, we compare the tree kernel-based and the feature-based method for RE in a compatible way, on the same resources and settings, to gain insights into which kind of system is more robust to domain changes. Our results and error analysis shows that the tree kernel-based method outperforms the feature-based approach.

1 Introduction

Relation Extraction (RE) is an important aspect of information extraction that aims to discover the semantic relationships between two entity mentions appearing in the same sentence. Previous research on RE has followed either the kernel-based approach (Zelenko et al., 2003; Bunescu and Mooney, 2005; Zhao and Grishman, 2005; Zhang et al., 2006; Bunescu, 2007; Qian et al., 2008; Nguyen et al., 2009) or the feature-based approach (Kambhatla, 2004; Grishman et al., 2005; Zhou et al., 2005; Jiang and Zhai, 2007a; Chan and Roth, 2010; Sun et al., 2011). Usually, in such supervised machine learning systems, it is assumed that the training data and the data to which the RE system is applied to are sampled independently and identically from the same distribution. This assumption is often violated in reality and exemplified in the fact that the performance of the traditional RE techniques degrades significantly in such a domain mismatch case (Plank and Moschitti, 2013). To alleviate this performance loss, we need to resort to domain adaptation (DA) techniques to adapt a system trained on some *source domain* to perform well on new *target domains*. We here focus on the *unsupervised domain adaptation* (i.e., no labeled target data) and *single-system* DA (Petrov and McDonald, 2012; Plank and Moschitti, 2013), i.e., building a single system that is able to cope with different, yet related target domains.

While DA has been investigated extensively in the last decade for various natural language processing (NLP) tasks, the examination of DA for RE is only very recent. To the best of our knowledge, there have been only three studies on DA for RE (Plank and Moschitti, 2013; Nguyen and Grishman, 2014; Nguyen et al., 2014). Of these, Nguyen et al. (2014) follow the supervised DA paradigm and assume some labeled data in the target domains. In contrast, Plank and Moschitti (2013) and Nguyen and Grishman (2014) work on the unsupervised DA. In our view, unsupervised DA is more challenging, but more realistic and practical for RE as we usually do not know which target domains we need to work on in advance, thus cannot expect to possess labeled data of the target domains. Our current work therefore focuses on the single-system *unsupervised* DA. Besides, note that this setting tries to construct a single system that can work robustly with different but related domains (multiple target domains), thus being different from most previous studies on DA (Blitzer et al., 2006; Blitzer et al., 2007) which have attempted to design a specialized system for every specific target domain.

Plank and Moschitti (2013) propose to embed word clusters and latent semantic analysis (LSA) of words into tree kernels for DA of RE, while Nguyen and Grishman (2014) studies the appli-

Proceedings of the 53rd Annual Meeting of the Association for Computational Linguistics and the 7th International Joint Conference on Natural Language Processing, pages 635–644,
Beijing, China, July 26-31, 2015.

cation of word clusters and word embeddings for DA of RE on the feature-based method. Although word clusters (Brown et al., 1992) have been employed by both studies to improve the performance of relation extractors across domains, the application of word embeddings (Bengio et al., 2003; Mnih and Hinton, 2008; Turian et al., 2010) for DA of RE is only examined in the feature-based method and never explored in the tree kernel-based method so far, giving rise to the first question we want to address in this paper:

(i) Can word embeddings help the tree kernel-based methods on DA for RE and more importantly, in which way can we do it effectively?

This question is important as word embeddings are real valued vectors, while the tree kernel-based methods rely on the symbolic matches or mismatches of concrete labels in the parse trees to compute the kernels. It is unclear at the first glance how to encode word embeddings into the tree kernels effectively so that word embeddings could help to improve the generalization performance of RE. One way is to use word embeddings to compute similarities between words and embed these similarity scores into the kernel functions, e.g., by resembling the method of Plank and Moschitti (2013) that exploited LSA (in the semantic syntactic tree kernel (SSTK), cf. §2.1). We explore various methods to apply word embeddings to generate the semantic representations for DA of RE and demonstrate that semantic representations are very effective to significantly improve the portability of the relation extractors based on the tree kernels, bringing us to the second question:

(ii) Between the feature-based method in Nguyen and Grishman (2014) and the SSTK method in Plank and Moschitti (2013), which method is better for DA of RE, given the recent discovery of word embeddings for both methods?

It is worth noting that besides the approach difference, these two works employ rather different resources and settings in their evaluation, making it impossible to directly compare their performance. In particular, while Plank and Moschitti (2013) only use the path-enclosed trees induced from the constituent parse trees as the representation for relation mentions, Nguyen and Grishman (2014) include a rich set of features extracted from multiple resources such as constituent trees, dependency trees, gazetteers, semantic resources in the representation. Besides, Plank and Moschitti (2013) consider the direction of relations in their evaluation (i.e, distinguishing between relation classes and their inverses) but Nguyen and Grishman (2014) disregard this relation direction. Finally, we note that although both studies evaluate their systems on the ACE 2005 dataset, they actually have different dataset partitions. In order to overcome this limitation, we conduct an evaluation in which the two methods are directed to use the same resources and settings, and are thus compared in a *compatible* manner to achieve an insight on their effectiveness for DA of RE. In fact, the problem of incompatible comparison is unfortunately very common in the RE literature (Wang, 2008; Plank and Moschitti, 2013) and we believe there is a need to tackle this increasing confusion in this line of research. Therefore, this is actually the first attempt to compare the two methods (tree kernel-based and feature-based) on the same settings. To ease the comparison for future work and circumvent the *Zigglebottom* pitfall (Pedersen, 2008), the entire setup and package is available.[1]

2 Relation Extraction Approaches

In the following, we introduce the two relation extraction systems further examined in this study.

2.1 Tree kernel-based Method

In the tree kernel-based method (Moschitti, 2006; Moschitti, 2008; Plank and Moschitti, 2013), a relation mention (the two entity mentions and the sentence containing them) is represented by the path-enclosed tree (PET), the smallest constituency-based subtree including the two target entity mentions (Zhang et al., 2006). The syntactic tree kernel (STK) is then defined to compute the similarity between two PET trees (where target entities are marked) by counting the common sub-trees, without enumerating the whole fragment space (Moschitti, 2006; Moschitti, 2008). STK is then applied in the support vector machines (SVMs) for RE. The major limitation of STK is its inability to match two trees that share the same substructure, but involve different though semantically related terminal nodes (words). This is caused by the hard matches between words, and consequently between sequences containing them. For instance, in the following example taken from Plank and Moschitti (2013), the two fragments "*governor from Texas*" and "*head of Mary-*

[1] https://bitbucket.org/nycphre/limo-re

land' would not match in STK although they have very similar syntactic structures and basically convey the same relationship.

Plank and Moschitti (2013) propose to resolve this issue for STK using the semantic syntactic tree kernel (SSTK) (Bloehdorn and Moschitti, 2007) and apply it to the domain adaptation problem of RE. The two following techniques are utilized to activate the SSTK: (i) replace the part-of-speech nodes in the PET trees by the new ones labeled by the word clusters of the corresponding terminals (words); (ii) replace the binary similarity scores between words (i.e, either 1 or 0) by the similarities induced from the latent semantic analysis (LSA) of large corpus. The former generalizes the part-of-speech similarity to the semantic similarity on word clusters; the latter, on the other hand, allows soft matches between words that have the same latent semantic but differ in symbolic representation. Both techniques emphasize the invariants of word semantics in different domains, thus being helpful to alleviate the vocabulary difference across domains.

2.2 Feature-based Method

In the feature-based method (Zhou et al., 2005; Sun et al., 2011; Nguyen and Grishman, 2014), relation mentions are first transformed into rich feature vectors that capture various characteristics of the relation mentions (i.e, lexicon, syntax, semantics etc). The resulting vectors are then fed into the statistical classifiers such as Maximum Entropy (MaxEnt) to perform classification for RE.

The main reason for the performance loss of the feature-based systems on new domains is the behavioral changes of the features when domains shift. Some features might be very informative in the source domain but become less relevant in the target domains. For instance, some words, that are very indicative in the source domain might not appear in the target domains (lexical sparsity). Consequently, the models putting high weights on such words (features) in the source domain will fail to perform well on the target domains. Nguyen and Grishman (2014) address this problem for the feature-based method in DA of RE by introducing word embeddings as additional features. The rationale is based on the fact that word embeddings are low dimensional and real valued vectors, capturing latent syntactic and semantic properties of words (Bengio et al., 2003; Mnih and Hinton, 2008; Turian et al., 2010). The embeddings of symbolically different words are often close to each other if they have similar semantic and syntactic functions. This again helps to mitigate the lexical sparsity or the vocabulary difference between the domains and has proven helpful for, amongst others, the feature-based method in DA of RE.

2.3 Tree Kernel-based vs Feature-based

The feature-based method explicitly encapsulates the linguistic intuition and domain expertise for RE into the features, while the tree kernel-based method avoids the complicated feature engineering and implicitly encode the features into the computation of the tree kernels. Which method is better for DA of RE?

In order to ensure the two methods (Plank and Moschitti, 2013; Nguyen and Grishman, 2014) are compared compatibly on the same resources, we make sure the two systems have access to the same amount of information. Thus, we follow Plank and Moschitti (2013) and use the PET trees (beside word clusters and word embeddings) as the only resource the two methods can exploit.

For the feature-based method, we utilize all the features extractable from the PET trees that are standardly used in the state-of-the-art feature-based systems for DA of RE (Nguyen and Grishman, 2014). Specifically, the feature set employed in this paper (denoted by FET) includes: the lexical features, i.e., the context words, the head words, the bigrams, the number of words, the lexical path, the order of mention (Zhou et al., 2005; Sun et al., 2011); and the syntactic features, i.e., the path connecting the two mentions in PET and the unigrams, bigrams, trigrams along this path (Zhou et al., 2005; Jiang and Zhai, 2007a).

Hypothesis: Assuming identical settings and resources, we hypothesize that the tree kernel-based method is better than the feature-based method for DA of RE. This is motivated because of at least two reasons: (i) the tree kernel-based method implicitly encodes a more comprehensive feature set (involving all the sub-trees in the PETs), thus potentially captures more domain-independent features to be useful for DA of RE; (ii) the tree kernel-based method avoids the inclusion of fine-tuned and domain-specific features originated from the excessive feature engineering (i.e., hand-designing feature sets based on the linguistic intuition for specific domains) of the feature-based method.

3 Word Embeddings & Tree Kernels

In this section, we first give the intuition that guides us in designing the proposed methods. In particular, one limitation of the syntactic semantic tree kernel presented in Plank and Moschitti (2013) (§2.1) is that semantics is highly tied to syntax (the PET trees) in the kernel computation, limiting the generalization capacity of semantics to the extent of syntactic matches. If two relation mentions have different syntactic structures, the two relation mentions will not match, although they share the same semantic representation and express the same relation class. For instance, the two fragments "*Tom is the CEO of the company*" and "*the company, headed by Tom*" express the same relationship between "*Tom*" and "*company*" based on the semantics of their context words, but cannot be matched in SSTK as their syntactic structures are different. In such a case, it is desirable to have a representation of relation mentions that is grounded on the semantics of the context words and reflects the latent semantics of the whole relation mentions. This representation is expected to be general enough to be effective on different domains. Once the semantic representation of relation mentions is established, we can use it in conjunction with the traditional tree kernels to extend their coverage. The benefit is mutual as both semantics and syntax help to generalize relation mentions to improve the recall, but also constrain each other to support precision. This is the basic idea of our approach, which we compare to the previous methods.

3.1 Methods

We propose to utilize word embeddings of the context words as the principal components to obtain semantic representations for relation mentions in the tree kernel-based methods. Besides more traditional approaches to exploit word embeddings, we investigate representations that go beyond the word level and use compositionality embeddings for domain adaptation for the first time.

In general, suppose we are able to acquire an additional real-valued vector V_i from word embeddings to semantically represent a relation mention R_i (along with the PET tree T_i), leading to the new representation of $R_i = (T_i, V_i)$. The new kernel function in this case is then defined by:

$$K_{new}(R_i, R_j) = (1 - \alpha)\text{SSTK}(T_i, T_j) + \alpha K_{vec}(V_i, V_j)$$

where $K_{vec}(V_i, V_j)$ is some standard vector kernel like the polynomial kernels. α is a trade-off parameter and indicates whether the system attributes more weight to the traditional SSTK or the new semantic kernel K_{vec}.

In this work, we consider the following methods to obtain the semantic representation V_i from the word embeddings of the context words of R_i (assuming d is the dimensionality of the word embeddings):

HEAD: V_i = the concatenation of the word embeddings of the two entity mention heads of R_i. This representation is inherited from Nguyen and Grishman (2014) that only examine embeddings at the word level separately for the feature-based method without considering the compositionality embeddings of relation mentions. The dimensionality of HEAD is $2d$.

According to the principle of compositionality (Werning et al., 2006; Baroni and Zamparelli, 2010; Paperno et al., 2014), the meaning of a complex expression is determined by the meanings of its components and the rules to combine them. We study the following two compositionality embeddings for relation mentions that can be generated from the embeddings of the context words:

PHRASE: V_i = the mean of the embeddings of the words contained in the PET tree T_i of R_i. Although this composition is simple, it is in fact competitive to the more complicated methods based on recursive neural networks (Socher et al., 2012b; Blacoe and Lapata, 2012; Sterckx et al., 2014) on representing phrase semantics.

TREE: This is motivated by the training of recursive neural networks (Socher et al., 2012a) for semantic compositionality and attempts to aggregate the context words embeddings syntactically. In particular, we compute an embedding for every node in the PET tree in a bottom-up manner. The embeddings of the leaves are the embeddings of the words associated with them while the embeddings of the internal nodes are the means of the embeddings of their children nodes. We use the embeddings of the root of the PET tree to represent the relation mention in this case. Both PHRASE and TREE have d dimensions.

It is also interesting to examine combinations of these three representations (cf., Table 1).

SIM: Finally, for completeness, we experiment with a more obvious way to introduce word embeddings into tree kernels, resembling more closely the approach of Plank and Moschitti (2013). In particularly, the SIM method simply replaces the similarity scores between word pairs obtained from LSA by the cosine similarities between the word embeddings to be used in the SSTK kernel.

4 Experiments

4.1 Dataset, Resources and Parameters

We use the word clusters trained by Plank and Moschitti (2013) on the ukWaC corpus (Baroni et al., 2009) with 2 billion words, and the C&W word embeddings from Turian el al. (2010)[2] with 50 dimensions following Nguyen and Grishman (2014). In order to make the comparisons compatible, we introduce word embeddings into the tree kernel by extending the package provided by Plank and Moschitti (2013), which uses the Charniak parser to obtain the constituent trees, the SVM-light-TK for the SSTK kernel in SVM, the directional relation classes, etc. We utilize the default vector kernel in the SVM-light-TK package (`d=3`). For the feature-based method, we apply the MaxEnt classifier in the MALLET[3] package with the L2 regularizer on the hierarchical architecture for relation extraction as in Nguyen and Grishman (2014).

Following prior work, we evaluate the systems on the ACE 2005 dataset which involves 6 domains: broadcast news (bn), newswire (nw), broadcast conversation (bc), telephone conversation (cts), weblogs (wl) and usenet (un). The union of **bn** and **nw** (**news**) is used as the source domain while **bc**, **cts** and **wl** play the role of the target domains. We take half of bc as the only target development set, and use the remaining data and domains for testing. The dataset partition is exactly the same as in Plank and Moschitti (2013). As described in their paper, the target domains quite differ from the source domain in the relation distributions and vocabulary.

4.2 Word Embeddings for Tree Kernel

We investigate the effectiveness of different semantic representations (§3.1) in tree kernels by taking the PET tree as the baseline[4], and evaluate the performance of the representations when combined with the baseline on the bc development set.

[2] `http://metaoptimize.com/projects/wordreprs/`

[3] `http://mallet.cs.umass.edu/`

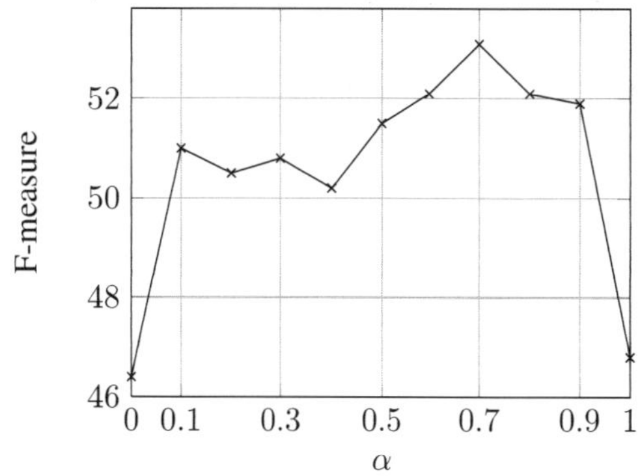

Figure 1: α vs F-measure on PET+HEAD+PHRASE

Method	P	R	F1
PET (Plank and Moschitti, 2013)	52.2	41.7	46.4
PET+SIM	39.4	37.2	38.3
PET+HEAD	60.4	44.9	51.5
PET+PHRASE	58.4	40.7	48.0
PET+TREE	59.8	42.2	49.5
PET+HEAD+PHRASE	63.2	46.2	**53.4**
PET+HEAD+TREE	61.0	45.7	52.3
PET+PHRASE+TREE	59.2	42.4	49.4
PET+HEAD+PHRASE+TREE	60.8	45.2	51.9

Table 1: Performance on the bc dev set for PET. Best combination (HEAD+PHRASE) is denoted WED in Table 2

Table 1 shows the results. The main conclusions include:

(i) The substitution of LSA similarity scores with the word embedding cosine similarities (SIM) does not help to improve the performance of the tree kernel method.

(ii) When employed independently, both the word level embeddings (HEAD) and the compositionality embeddings (PHRASE, TREE) are effective for the tree kernel-based method on DA for RE, showing a slight advantage for HEAD.

(iii) Thus, the compositionality embeddings PHRASE and TREE seem to capture different information with respect to the word level embeddings HEAD. We expect the combination of HEAD with either PHRASE or TREE to further improve performance. This is the case when adding one of them at a time. PHRASE and TREE seem to capture similar information, combining all (last row in Table 1) is not the overall best system. The best performance is achieved when the HEAD and PHRASE embeddings are utilized at

[4] By using their system we obtained the same results.

#	System:	nw+bn (in-dom.) P:	R:	F1:	bc P:	R:	F1:	cts P:	R:	F1:	wl P:	R:	F1:
1	PET (Plank and Moschitti, 2013)	50.6	42.1	46.0	51.2	40.6	45.3	51.0	37.8	43.4	35.4	32.8	34.0
2	PET+WED	55.8	48.7	52.0	57.3	45.7	50.8	54.0	38.1	44.7	40.1	36.5	38.2
3	PET_WC	55.4	44.6	49.4	54.3	41.4	47.0	55.9	37.1	44.6	40.0	32.7	36.0
4	PET_WC+WED	56.3	48.2	51.9	57.0	44.3	49.8	56.1	38.1	45.4	40.7	36.1	38.2
5	PET_LSA	52.3	44.1	47.9	51.4	41.7	46.0	49.7	36.5	42.1	38.1	36.5	37.3
6	PET_LSA+WED	55.2	48.5	51.6	58.8	45.8	51.5	54.1	38.1	44.7	40.9	38.5	39.6
7	PET+PET_WC	55.0	46.5	50.4	54.4	43.4	48.3	54.1	38.1	44.7	38.4	34.5	36.3
8	PET+PET_WC+WED	56.3	50.3	53.1	57.5	46.6	51.5	55.6	39.8	**46.4**	41.5	37.9	39.6
9	PET+PET_LSA	52.7	46.6	49.5	53.9	45.2	49.2	49.9	37.6	42.9	37.9	38.3	38.1
10	PET+PET_LSA+WED	55.5	49.9	52.6	56.8	45.8	50.8	52.5	38.6	44.5	41.6	39.3	**40.5**
11	PET+PET_WC+PET_LSA	55.1	45.9	50.1	55.3	43.1	48.5	53.1	37.0	43.6	39.9	35.8	37.8
12	PET+PET_WC+PET_LSA+WED	55.0	48.8	51.7	58.5	47.3	**52.3**	52.6	38.8	44.7	42.3	38.9	**40.5**

Table 2: In-domain (first column) and out-of-domain performance (columns two to four) on ACE 2005. Systems of the rows not in gray come from Plank and Moschitti (2013) (the baselines). WED means HEAD+PHRASE.

the same time, reaching an F1 of 53.4% (compared to 46.4% of the baseline) on the development set.

The results in Table 1 are obtained using the trade-off parameter $\alpha = 0.7$. Figure 1 additionally shows the variation of the performance with changing α (for the best system on dev, i.e., for the representation PET+HEAD+PHRASE). As we can see, the performance for $\alpha > 0.5$ is in general better, suggesting a preference for the semantic representation over the syntactic representation in DA for RE. The performance reaches its peak when the suitable amounts of semantics and syntax are combined (i.e, $\alpha = 0.7$).

In the following experiments, we use the embedding combination (HEAD+PHRASE) with $\alpha = 0.7$ for the tree kernels, denoted WED.

4.3 Domain Adaptation Experiments

In this section, we examine the semantic representation for DA of RE in the tree kernel-based method. In particular, we take the systems using the PET trees, word clusters and LSA in Plank and Moschitti (2013) as the baselines and augment them with the embeddings WED = HEAD+PHRASE. We report the performance of these augmented systems in Table 2 for the two scenarios: (i) in-domain: both training and testing are performed on the source domain via 5-fold cross validation and (ii) out-of-domain: models are trained on the source domain but evaluated on the three target domains. To summarize, we find:

First, word embeddings seem to subsume word clusters in the tree kernel-based method (comparing rows 2 and 4, and except domain cts) while word embeddings and LSA actually encode different information (comparing rows 2 and 6 for the out-of-domain experiments) and their combination would be helpful for DA of RE.

Second, regarding composite kernels, given word embeddings, the addition of the baseline kernel (PET) is in general useful for the augmented kernels PET_WC and PET_LSA (comparing rows 4 and 8, rows 6 and 10) although it is less pronounced for PET_LSA.

Third and most importantly, for all the systems in Plank and Moschitti (2013) (the baselines) and for all the target domains, whether word clusters and LSA are utilized or not, we consistently witness the performance improvement of the baselines when combined with word embedding (comparing systems X and X+WED where X is some baseline system). The best out-of-domain performance is achieved when word embeddings are employed in conjunction with the composite kernels (PET+PET_WC+PET_LSA for the target domains bc and wl, and PET+PET_WC for the target domain cts). To be more concrete, the best system with word embeddings (row 12 in Table 2) significantly outperforms the best system in Plank and Moschitti (2013) with $p < 0.05$, an improvement of 3.7%, 1.1% and 2.7% on the target domains bc, cts and wl respectively, demonstrating the benefit of word embeddings for DA of RE in the tree kernel-based method.

4.4 Tree Kernel-based vs Feature-based DA of RE

This section aims to compare the tree kernel-based method in Plank and Moschitti (2013) and the feature-based method in Nguyen and Grishman (2014) for DA of RE on the same settings (i.e, same dataset partition, the same pre-processing

System:	nw+bn (in-dom.) P:	R:	F1:	bc P:	R:	F1:	cts P:	R:	F1:	wl P:	R:	F1:
Tree kernel-based:												
PET+PET_WC+HEAD+PHRASE	56.3	50.3	**53.1**	57.5	46.6	**51.5**	55.6	39.8	**46.4**	41.5	37.9	**39.6**
Feature-based:												
FET+WC+HEAD	44.5	51.0	47.5	46.5	49.3	47.8	44.5	40.0	42.1	35.4	39.5	37.3
FET+WC+TREE	44.4	50.2	47.1	46.4	48.7	47.6	43.7	40.3	41.9	32.7	36.7	34.6
FET+WC+HEAD+PHRASE	44.9	51.6	48.0	46.0	49.1	47.5	45.2	41.5	43.3	34.7	39.2	36.8
FET+WC+HEAD+TREE	45.1	51.0	47.8	46.9	48.4	47.6	43.8	39.5	41.5	34.7	38.8	36.6

Table 3: Tree kernel-based in Plank and Moschitti (2013) vs feature-based in Nguyen and Grishman (2014). All the comparisons between the tree kernel-based method and the feature-based method in this table are significant with $p < 0.05$.

procedure, the same model of directional relation classes, the same PET trees for tree kernels and feature extraction, the same word clusters and the same word embeddings). We first evaluate the feature-based system with different combinations of embeddings (i.e, HEAD, PHRASE and TREE) on the bc development set. Based on the evaluation results, we then discuss the effect of the semantic representations on the feature-based system and the tree kernel-based system, and then compare the performance of the two methods when they are augmented with their best corresponding embedding combinations.

System	P	R	F1
B	51.2	49.4	50.3
B+HEAD	55.8	52.4	**54.0**
B+PHRASE	50.7	46.2	48.4
B+TREE	53.6	51.1	**52.3**
B+HEAD+PHRASE	53.2	50.1	51.6
B+HEAD+TREE	54.9	51.4	**53.1**
B+PHRASE+TREE	50.7	48.4	49.5
B+HEAD+PHRASE+TREE	52.7	49.4	51.0

Table 4: Performance of the feature-based method (dev).

Table 4 presents the evaluation results on the bc development for the feature-based system where B is the baseline feature set consisting of FET and word clusters (WC) (Nguyen and Grishman, 2014).

The Role of Semantic Representations Considering Table 4 for the feature-based method and Table 1 for the tree kernel-based method, we see that when combined with the HEAD embeddings, the compositionality embedding TREE is more effective for the feature-based method, in contrast to the tree kernel-based method, where the PHRASE embeddings are better. This can be partly explained by the fact that the tree kernel-based method emphasizes the syntactic structure of the relation mentions, while the feature-based method exploits the sequential structure more. Consequently, the syntactic semantics of TREE are more helpful for the feature-based method, whereas the sequential semantics of PHRASE are more useful for the tree kernel-based method.

Performance Comparison The three best embedding combinations for the feature-based system in Table 4 are (listed by performance order): (HEAD), (HEAD+TREE) and (TREE), where (HEAD) is also the best word level method employed in Nguyen and Grishman (2014). In order to enable a fairer and clearer evaluation, when doing comparison, we use both the three best embedding combinations in the feature-based method and the best embedding combination (HEAD+PHRASE) in the tree kernel-based method. In the tree kernel-based method, we do not employ the LSA information as it comes in the form of similarity scores between pairs of words, and it is not clear how to encode this information into the feature-based method effectively. Finally, we utilize the composite kernel for its demonstrated effectiveness in Section 4.3.

The most important observation from the experimental results (shown in Table 3) is that over all the target domains, the tree kernel-based system is significantly better than the feature-based systems with $p < 0.05$ (assuming the same resources and settings mentioned above). In fact, there are large margins between the tree kernel-based and the feature-based methods in this case (i.e, about 3.7% for bc, 3.1% for cts and 2.3% for wl), clearly confirming the hypothesis about the advantage of the tree kernel-based method over the feature-based method on DA for RE in Section 2.3.

5 Analysis

This section analyzes the output of the systems to gain more insights into their operation.

Word Embeddings for the Tree-kernel based Method We focus on the comparison of the best model in Plank and Moschitti (2013) (row 11 in Table 2) (called P) with the same model but augmented with the embedding WED (row 12 in Tabel 2) (called P+WED). One of the most interesting insights is that the embedding WED helps to semantically generalize the phrases connecting the two target entity mentions beyond the syntactic constraints. For instance, model P fails to discover the relation between "*Chuck Hagel*" and "*Vietnam*" in the sentence (of the target domain bc): "*Sergeant Chuck Hagel was seriously wounded twice in Vietnam.*" (i.e, it returns the NONE relation as the prediction) as the substructure associated with "*seriously wounded twice*" does not appear with any relation in the source domain. Model P+WED, on the other hand, correctly predicts the PHYS (Located) relation between the two entities as the PHRASE embedding of "*Chuck Hagel was seriously wounded twice in Vietnam.*" (phrase X1) is very close to the embedding of the source domain phrase: "*Stewart faces up to 30 years in prison*" (phrase X2) (annotated with the PHYS relation between "*Stewart*" and "*prison*").

In fact, X2 is only the 9th closest phrase in the source domain of X1. The closest phrase of X1 in the source domain is X3: the phrase between "*Iraqi soldiers*" and "*herself*" in the sentence "*The Washington Post is reporting she shot several* ***Iraqi soldiers before she was captured and she was shot herself****, too.*". However, as the syntactical structure of X1 is more similar to X2's, and is remarkably different from X3 as well as the other closest phrases (ranked from 2nd to 8th), the new kernel function K_{new} would still prefer X2 due to its trade-off between syntax and semantics.

Tree Kernel-based vs Feature-based From the analysis of the systems in Table 3, we find that, among others, the tree kernel-based method improves the precision significantly via the semantic and syntactic refinement it maintains. Let us consider the following phrase of the target domain bc: "*troops have dislodged stubborn Iraqi soldiers*" (called Y1). The feature-based systems in Table 3 incorrectly predict the ORG-AFF relation (Employment or Membership) between "*Iraqi soldiers*" and "*troops*". This is mainly due to the high weights of the features linking the words "*troop*" and "*soldiers*" with the relation type ORG-AFF in the feature-based models, which is, in turn, originated from the high correlation of these words and the relation type in the training data of the source domain (domain bias). The tree kernel-based model in Table 3 successfully recognizes the NONE relation in this case. A closer examination shows that the phrase with the closest embedding to Y1 in the source domain is Y2: "*Iraqi soldiers abandoned their posts*",[5] which is annotated with the NONE relation between "*Iraqi soldiers*" and "*their posts*". As the syntactic structure of Y2 is also very similar to Y1, it is not surprising that Y1 is closest to Y2 in the new kernel function, consequently helping the tree kernel-based method work correctly in this case.

6 Related work

Word embeddings are only applied to RE recently. Socher et al. (2012b) use word embeddings as input for matrix-vector recursive neural networks in relation classification while Zeng et al. (2014), and Nguyen and Grishman (2015) employ word embeddings in the framework of convolutional neural networks for relation classification and extraction, respectively. Sterckx et al. (2014) utilize word embeddings to reduce noise of training data in distant supervision. Kuksa et al. (2010) present a string kernel for bio-relation extraction with word embeddings, and Yu et al. (2014; 2015) study the factor-based compositional embedding models. However, none of this work examines word embeddings for tree kernels as well as domain adaptation as we do.

Regarding DA, in the unsupervised DA setting, Huang and Yates (2010) attempt to learn multi-dimensional feature representations while Blitzer et al. (2006) introduce structural correspondence learning. Daumé (2007) proposes an easy adaptation framework (EA) while Xiao and Guo (2013) present a log-bilinear language adaptation technique in the supervised DA setting. Unfortunately, all of this work assumes some prior (in the form of either labeled or unlabeled data) on the target domains for the sequential labeling tasks, in contrast to our single-system unsupervised DA setting for relation extraction. An alternative method that is also popular to DA is instance weighting (Jiang and Zhai, 2007b). However, as shown by Plank and Moschitti (2013), instance weighting is not

[5]The full sentence is: "*After today's air strikes, Iraqi soldiers abandoned their posts and surrendered to Kurdish fighters.*".

very useful for DA of RE.

7 Conclusion

In order to improve the generalization of relation extractors, we propose to augment the semantic syntactic tree kernels with the semantic representation of relation mentions, generated from the word embeddings of the context words. The method demonstrates strong promise for the DA of RE, i.e, it significantly improves the best system of Plank and Moschitti (2013) (up to 7% relative improvement). Moreover, we perform a compatible comparison between the tree kernel-based method and the feature-based method on the same settings and resources, which suggests that the tree kernel-based method (Plank and Moschitti, 2013) is better than the feature-based method (Nguyen and Grishman, 2014) for DA of RE. An error analysis is conducted to get a deeper comprehension of the systems. Our future plan is to investigate other syntactic and semantic structures (such as dependency trees, abstract meaning representation etc) for DA of RE, as well as continue the comparison between the kernel-based method and the feature-based method when they are allowed to exploit more resources.

References

Marco Baroni and Roberto Zamparelli. 2010. Nouns are vectors, adjectives are matrices: Representing adjective-noun constructions in semantic space. In *EMNLP*.

Marco Baroni, Silvia Bernardini, Adriano Ferraresi, and Eros Zanchetta. 2009. The WaCky wide web: a collection of very large linguistically processed web-crawled corpora. In *Language Resources and Evaluation*, pages 209–226.

Yoshua Bengio, Réjean Ducharme, Pascal Vincent, and Christian Jauvin. 2003. A neural probabilistic language model. In *Journal of Machine Learning Research 3*, pages 1137–1155.

William Blacoe and Mirella Lapata. 2012. A comparison of vector-based representations for semantic composition. In *EMNLP*.

John Blitzer, Ryan McDonald, and Fernando Pereira. 2006. Domain adaptation with structural correspondence learning. In *EMNLP*.

John Blitzer, Mark Dredze, and Fernando Pereira. 2007. Biographies, bollywood, boom-boxes and blenders: Domain adaptation for sentiment classification. In *ACL*.

Stephan Bloehdorn and Alessandro Moschitti. 2007. Exploiting Structure and Semantics for Expressive Text Kernels. In *CIKM*.

Peter F. Brown, Peter V. deSouza, Robert L. Mercer, Vincent J. Della Pietra, and Jenifer C. Lai. 1992. Class-based n-gram models of natural language. In *Computational Linguistics*, pages 467–479.

Razvan C. Bunescu and Raymond J. Mooney. 2005. A shortest path dependency kernel for relation extraction. In *EMNLP*.

Razvan C. Bunescu. 2007. Learning to extract relations from the web using minimal supervision. In *ACL*.

Yee Seng Chan and Dan Roth. 2010. Exploiting background knowledge for relation extraction. In *COLING*.

Hal Daume. 2007. Frustratingly easy domain adaptation. In *ACL*.

Ralph Grishman, David Westbrook, and Adam Meyers. 2005. Nyu's english ace 2005 system description. In *The ACE 2005 Evaluation Workshop*.

Fei Huang and Alexander Yates. 2010. Exploring representation-learning approaches to domain adaptation. In *The ACL Workshop on Domain Adaptation for Natural Language Processing (DANLP)*.

Jing Jiang and ChengXiang Zhai. 2007a. A systematic exploration of the feature space for relation extraction. In *NAACL-HLT*.

Jing Jiang and ChengXiang Zhai. 2007b. Instance weighting for domain adaptation in nlp. In *ACL*.

Nanda Kambhatla. 2004. Combining lexical, syntactic, and semantic features with maximum entropy models for information extraction. In *ACL*.

Pavel Kuksa, Yanjun Qi, Bing Bai, Ronan Collobert, Jason Weston, Vladimir Pavlovic, and Xia Ning. 2010. Semi-supervised abstraction-augmented string kernel for multi-level bio-relation extraction. In *ECML PKDD*.

Andriy Mnih and Geoffrey Hinton. 2008. A scalable hierarchical distributed language model. In *NIPS*.

Alessandro Moschitti. 2006. Efficient convolution kernels for dependency and constituent syntactic trees. In *ECML*.

Alessandro Moschitti. 2008. Kernel methods, syntax and semantics for relational text categorization. In *CIKM*.

Thien Huu Nguyen and Ralph Grishman. 2014. Employing word representations and regularization for domain adaptation of relation extraction. In *ACL*.

Thien Huu Nguyen and Ralph Grishman. 2015. Relation extraction: Perspective from convolutional neural networks. In *The NAACL Workshop on Vector Space Modeling for NLP (VSM)*.

T. Truc-Vien Nguyen, Alessandro Moschitti, and Giuseppe Riccardi. 2009. Convolution kernels on constituent, dependency and sequential structures for relation extraction. In *EMNLP*.

Luan Minh Nguyen, W. Ivor Tsang, A. Kian Ming Chai, and Leong Hai Chieu. 2014. Robust domain adaptation for relation extraction via clustering consistency. In *ACL*.

Denis Paperno, The Nghia Pham, and Marco Baroni. 2014. A practical and linguistically-motivated approach to compositional distributional semantics. In *ACL*.

Ted Pedersen. 2008. Empiricism is not a matter of faith. In *Computational Linguistics 3*, pages 465–470.

Slav Petrov and Ryan McDonald. 2012. Overview of the 2012 shared task on parsing the web. In *The First Workshop on Syntactic Analysis of Non-Canonical Language (SANCL)*.

Barbara Plank and Alessandro Moschitti. 2013. Embedding semantic similarity in tree kernels for domain adaptation of relation extraction. In *ACL*.

Longhua Qian, Guodong Zhou, Fang Kong, Qiaoming Zhu, and Peide Qian. 2008. Exploiting constituent dependencies for tree kernel-based semantic relation extraction. In *COLING*.

Richard Socher, Alex Perelygin, Jean Y. Wu, Jason Chuang, Christopher D. Manning, Andrew Y. Ng, and Christopher Potts. 2012a. Recursive deep models for semantic compositionality over a sentiment treebank. In *EMNLP-CoNLL*.

Richard Socher, Brody Huval, Christopher D. Manning, and Andrew Y. Ng. 2012b. Semantic compositionality through recursive matrix-vector spaces. In *EMNLP*.

Lucas Sterckx, Thomas Demeester, Johannes Deleu, and Chris Develder. 2014. Using active learning and semantic clustering for noise reduction in distant supervision. In *AKBC*.

Ang Sun, Ralph Grishman, and Satoshi Sekine. 2011. Semi-supervised relation extraction with large-scale word clustering. In *ACL*.

Joseph Turian, Lev-Arie Ratinov, and Yoshua Bengio. 2010. Word representations: A simple and general method for semi-supervised learning. In *ACL*.

Mengqiu Wang. 2008. A re-examination of dependency path kernels for relation extraction. In *IJCNLP*.

Markus Werning, Edouard Machery, and Gerhard Schurz. 2006. Compositionality of meaning and content: Foundational issues (linguistics & philosophy). In *Linguistics & philosophy*.

Min Xiao and Yuhong Guo. 2013. Domain adaptation for sequence labeling tasks with a probabilistic language adaptation model. In *ICML*.

Mo Yu, Matthew Gormley, and Mark Dredze. 2014. Factor-based compositional embedding models. In *The NIPS workshop on Learning Semantics*.

Mo Yu, Matthew Gormley, and Mark Dredze. 2015. Combining word embeddings and feature embeddings for fine-grained relation extraction. In *NAACL*.

Dmitry Zelenko, Chinatsu Aone, and Anthony Richardella. 2003. Kernel methods for relation extraction. In *Journal of Machine Learning Research 3*, pages 1083–1106.

Daojian Zeng, Kang Liu, Siwei Lai, Guangyou Zhou, and Jun Zhao. 2014. Relation classification via convolutional deep neural network. In *COLING*.

Min Zhang, Jie Zhang, Jian Su, and Guodong Zhou. 2006. A composite kernel to extract relations between entities with both flat and structured features. In *COLING-ACL*.

Shubin Zhao and Ralph Grishman. 2005. Extracting relations with integrated information using kernel methods. In *ACL*.

GuoDong Zhou, Jian Su, Jie Zhang, and Min Zhang. 2005. Exploring various knowledge in relation extraction. In *ACL*.

Omnia Mutantur, Nihil Interit: Connecting Past with Present by Finding Corresponding Terms across Time

Yating Zhang[*], **Adam Jatowt**[*], **Sourav S Bhowmick**[+], **Katsumi Tanaka**[*]
[*]School of Informatics, Kyoto University
[+]School of Computer Engineering, Nanyang Technological University
{zhang,adam,tanaka}@dl.kuis.kyoto-u.ac.jp
assourav@ntu.edu.sg

Abstract

In the current fast-paced world, people tend to possess limited knowledge about things from the past. For example, some young users may not know that Walkman played similar function as iPod does nowadays. In this paper, we approach the *temporal correspondence problem* in which, given an input term (e.g., *iPod*) and the target time (e.g. 1980s), the task is to find the counterpart of the query that existed in the target time. We propose an approach that transforms word contexts across time based on their neural network representations. We then experimentally demonstrate the effectiveness of our method on the New York Times Annotated Corpus.

1 Introduction

What music device 30 years ago played similar role as iPod does nowadays? Who are today's Beatles? Who was a counterpart of President Chirac in 1988? These and many other similar questions may be difficult to answer by average users (especially, by young ones). This is because people tend to possess less knowledge about the past than about the contemporary time.

In this work we propose an effective method to solve the problem of finding counterpart terms across time. In particular, for an input pair of a term (e.g., *iPod*) and the target time (e.g. 1980s), we find the corresponding term that existed in the target time (*walkman*). We consider temporal counterparts to be terms which are semantically similar, yet, which existed in different time.

Knowledge of temporal counterparts can help to alleviate the problem of terminology gap for users searching within temporal document collections such as archives. For example, given a user's query and the target time frame, a new modified query that represents the same meaning could be suggested to improve search results. Essentially, it would mean letting searchers use the knowledge they possess on the current world to perform search within unknown collections such as ones containing documents from the distant past. Furthermore, solving temporal correspondence problem can help timeline construction, temporal summarization, reference forecasting and can have applications in education.

The problem of temporal counterpart detection is however not trivial. The key difficulty comes from the change of the entire context that results in low overlap of context across time. In other words, it is difficult to find temporal counterpart terms by directly comparing context vectors across time. This fact is nicely portrayed by the Latin proverb: "omnia mutantur, nihil interit" (in English: "everything changes, nothing perishes") which indicates that there are no completely static things, yet, many things and concepts are still similar across time. Another challenge is the lack of training data. If we have had enough training pairs of input terms and their temporal counterparts, then it would have become possible to represent the task as a typical machine learning problem. However, it is difficult to collect multiple training pairs over various domains and for arbitrary time.

In view of the challenges mentioned above, we propose an approach that transforms term representations from one vector space (e.g., one derived from the present documents) to another vector space (e.g., one obtained from the past documents). Terms in both the vector spaces are represented by the distributed vector representation (Mikolov et al. 2013a; Mikolov et al. 2013c). Our method then matches the terms by comparing their relative positions in the vector spaces of different time periods alleviating the problem of low overlap between word contexts over time. It also does not require to manually prepare seed pairs of temporal counterparts. We further improve this method by automatically generating reference points that more precisely represent target terms in the form of local graphs. In result, our approach consists of finding *global* and *local* correspondence between terms over time.

Proceedings of the 53rd Annual Meeting of the Association for Computational Linguistics and the 7th International Joint Conference on Natural Language Processing, pages 645–655,
Beijing, China, July 26-31, 2015.

To sum up, we make the following contributions in this paper: (1) we propose an efficient method to find temporal counterparts by transforming the representation of terms within different temporal spaces, (2) we then enhance the *global correspondence* method by considering also the local context of terms (*local correspondence*) and (3) we perform extensive experiments on the New York Times Annotated Corpus (Sandhaus, 2008), including the search from the present to the past and vice versa, which prove the effectiveness of our approach.

2 Global Correspondence Across Time

Let the *base time* denoted as T^B mean the time period associated with the input term and let the *target time, T^T*, mean the time period in which we want to find this term's counterparts. Typically, for users, the base time is the present time and the target time is some selected time period in the past. Note however, that we do not impose any restriction on the order and the distance of the both times. Hence, it is possible to search for present counterparts of terms that existed in the past.

In our approach we first represent all the terms in the base time and in the target time within their respective semantic vector spaces, χ^B and χ^T. Then, we construct a transformation matrix to bridge the two vector spaces. Algorithm 1 summarizes the procedures needed to compute the global transformation. We will explain it in Section 2.1 and 2.2.

Algorithm 1 Overview of Global Transformation

Input: query q, base time T^B and target time T^T

1. Construct word representation model for corpus in the base time, $D(T^B)$, and in the target time, $D(T^T)$. (**Section 2.1**)
2. Construct transformation matrix $\boldsymbol{M}$ between $D(T^B)$ and $D(T^T)$ by first collecting ***CFTs*** as training pairs and then learning $\boldsymbol{M}$ using **Eq. 1**. (**Section 2.2**)
3. Rank the words in target time by their correspondence scores (**Eq. 2**)

Output: ranked list of temporal counterparts

2.1 Vector space word representations

Distributed representation of words by neural network was first proposed by Rumelhart et al. (1986). More recently, Mikolov et al. (2013a, 2013c) introduced the *Skip-gram model* which utilizes a simplified neural network architecture for learning vector representations of words from unstructured text data. We apply this model due to its advantages: (1) it can capture precise semantic word relationships; (2) due to the simplified neural network architecture, the model can easily scale to millions of words. After applying the Skip-gram model, the documents in the base time, $D(T^B)$, are converted to a $m \times p$ matrix where n is the vocabulary size and p are the dimensions of feature vectors. Similarly, the documents in the target time, $D(T^T)$, are represented as a $n \times q$ matrix (as shown in Fig. 1).

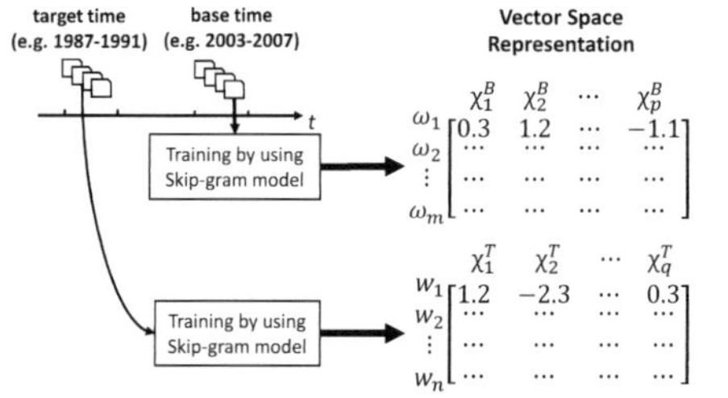

Figure 1: Word vector representations for the base and the target time.

2.2 Transformation across vector spaces

Our goal is to compare words in the base time and the target time in order to find temporal counterparts. However, it is impossible to directly compare words in two different semantic vector spaces, as the features in both spaces have no direct correspondence between each other (as can be seen in Fig. 1). To solve this problem, we propose to train a transformation matrix in order to build the connection between different vector spaces. The key idea is that the relative positions of words in each vector space should remain more or less stable. In other words, a temporal counterpart term should have similar relative position in its own vector space as the position of the queried term in the base time space. Fig. 2 conceptually portrays this idea as the correspondence between the context of *Walkman* and the context of *iPod* (only two dimensions are shown for simplicity).

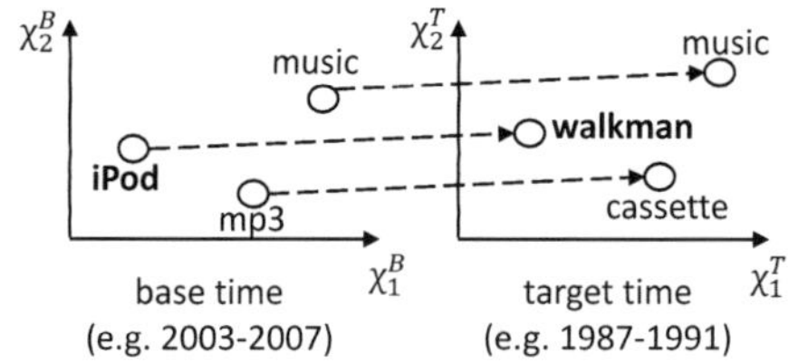

Figure 2: Conceptual view of the across-time transformation by matching similar relative geometric positions in each space.

Our task is then to train the transformation matrix to automatically "rotate" the base vector space into the target vector space. Suppose we have K pairs of temporal counterparts $\{(\omega_1, w_1),\ldots,(\omega_k, w_k,)\}$ where ω_i is a base time term and w_i is its counterpart in the target time. Then the transformation matrix $\boldsymbol{M}$ can be computed by minimizing the differences between $\boldsymbol{M}\cdot\omega_i$ and w_i as given in Eq. 1. The latter part of Eq. 1 is added as regularization to overcome the problem of overfitting. Intuitively, matrix M is obtained by making sure that the sum of Euclidean 2-norms between transformed query vectors and their counterparts is minimal on K seed query-counterpart pairs. Eq.1 is used for solving regularized least squares problem (γ equals to 0.02).

$$M = \arg\min_{M} \sum_{i=1}^{K} \|M \cdot \omega_i - w_i\|_2^2 + \gamma\|M\|_2^2 \qquad (1)$$

However, as mentioned before, the other challenge is that the training pairs are difficult to be obtained. It is non-trivial to prepare large enough training data that would also cover various domains and any possible combinations of the base and target time periods. We apply here a simple trick that performs reasonably well. We select terms that (a) have the same syntactic forms in the base and the target time periods and (b) are frequent in the both time periods. Such *Common Frequent Terms (CFTs)* are then used as the training data. Essentially, we assume here that very frequent terms (e.g., *man, women, water, dog, see, three*) change their meanings only to small extent. The reasoning is that the more frequently the word is used, the harder is to change its dominant meaning (or the longer time it takes to make the meaning shift) as the word is commonly used by many people. The phenomenon that words used more often in everyday language had evolved more slowly has been observed in several languages including English, Spanish, Russian and Greek (Pargel et al., 2007; Lieberman et al. 2007). Then, using the common frequent terms as the training pairs, we solve Eq. 1 as the least squares problem. Note that the number of *CFT*s is heuristically decided. In Sec. 5 we discuss transformation performance with regards to different numbers of *CFT*s.

After obtaining matrix $\boldsymbol{M}$, we can then transform the base time term, q, first by multiplying its vector representation with the transformation matrix $\boldsymbol{M}$, and then by calculating the cosine similarity between such transformed vector and the vectors of all the terms in the target time. We call the result of this similarity comparison the *correspondence score* between the input term q in the base time and a given term w in the target time (see Eq. 2). A term which has the highest correspondence score could be then considered as temporal counterpart of q.

$$Correspondence(q, w) = \cos(M \cdot q, w) \qquad (2)$$

3 Local Correspondence across Time

The method described above computes "global similarity" between terms across time. In result, the discovered counterparts can be similar to the query term for variety of reasons, some of which may not always lead to the best results. For instance, the global transformation finds *VCR* as the temporal counterpart of *iPod* in 1980s simply because both of them can have recording and playback functions. *Macintosh* is another term judged to be strongly corresponding to *iPod* since both are produced by *Apple*. Clearly, although *VCR* and *Macintosh* are somewhat similar to *iPod*, they are far from being its counterparts. The global transformation, as presented in the previous section, may thus fail to find correct counterparts due to neglecting fundamental relations between a query term and its context.

Inspired by these observations, we propose another method for leveraging the informative context terms of an input query term called *reference points*. They are used to help mapping the query to its correct temporal counterpart by considering the relation between the query and the reference points. We call this kind of similarity matching as *local correspondence* in contrast to *global correspondence* described in Sec. 2. In the following sub-sections, we first introduce the desired characteristics of the *reference points* and we then propose three computation methods for selecting them. Finally, we describe how to find temporal counterparts using the selected reference points. Algorithm 2 shows the process of computing the local transformation.

Algorithm 2 Overview of Local Transformation

Input: query q, base time T^B and target time T^T

1. Construct the local graph of q by detecting the reference points in the context of q. (**Section 3.1**)
2. Compute similarity of the local graph of q with all the local graphs of candidate temporal counterparts in the target time. (**Section 3.2**)
3. Rank the candidate temporal counterparts in the target time by graph similarity score (**Eq. 4**).

Output: ranked list of temporal counterparts

3.1 Reference points detection

Reference points are terms in the query's context which help to build connection between the query and its temporal counterparts. Reference points should have at least some of the following characteristics: (a) have high relation with the query (b) be sufficiently general and (c) be independent from each other.

Note that it does not mean that the selected reference point should have exactly same surface form across time. Let us consider the previous example query *iPod* and 1980s as the target time. The term *music* could be a candidate reference point for this query. Its temporal counterpart has exactly the same syntax form in the target time (*music*). However, *mp3* could be another reference point. Even though *mp3* did not exist in 1980s, it can still be referred to storage devices at the target time such as *cassette* or *disk* helping thus to find the correct counterparts of *iPod*, that is, *walkman* and *CD player*.

Since different reference points will lead to different answers, we propose three methods for selecting the reference points. Each one considers the previously mentioned characteristics of reference points to different extent. Note that, if necessary, the choice of the references points can be left to users.

Term co-occurrence. The first approach satisfies the reference points' characteristics of being related to the query. To select reference points using this approach we rank context terms by multiplying two factors: *tf(c)* and *relatedness(q,c)*, where *tf(c)* is the frequency of a context term *c*, while *relatedness(q,c)* is the relation strength of *q* and *c* measured by the χ^2 test. The test is conducted based on the hypothesis that $P(c|q)=P(c|\bar{q})$, according to which the term *c* has the same probability of occurring in documents containing query *q* and in the documents not containing *q*. We then use the inverse of the p-value obtained from the test as *relatedness(q,c)*.

Lexico-syntactic patterns. As the second approach we propose using hypernyms of terms. This corresponds to the characteristic of reference points to be general words. General terms are preferred rather than specific or detailed ones since the former are more probable to be associated with correct temporal counterparts[1]. This is because detailed or specific terms are less likely to have corresponding terms in the target time. To detect hypernyms on the fly, we adopt the method proposed by Ohshima et al. (2010) that uses bi-directional lexico-syntactic patterns due to its high speed and the lack of requirements for using external ontologies. The latter is important since, to the best of our knowledge, there are no ready ontology resources for arbitrary periods in the past (e.g., there seems to be no Wordnet for the past).

Semantic clustering. The last method chooses reference points from clusters of context terms. The purpose of applying clustering is to avoid choosing semantically similar reference points. Clustering helps to select typical terms from different sematic clusters to provide diverse informative context.

For grouping the context terms we utilize the bisecting k-means algorithm. It is superior over k-means and the agglomerative approach (Steinbach et al., 2000) in terms of accuracy. The procedure of bisecting k-means is to, first, select a cluster to split and then to utilize the basic k-means to form two sub-clusters. These two steps are repeated until the desired number of clusters is obtained. The distance between any two terms w_1, w_2 is the inverse of cosine similarity between their vector representations.

$$Dist(w_1, w_2) = 1 - \cos(w_1, w_2) \tag{3}$$

3.2 Local graph matching

Formulation. The local graph of query *q* is a star shaped graph, denoted as $S_q^{F_B}$, in which *q* is the internal node, and the set of reference points, $F_B = \{f_1, f_2, ..., f_u\}$, are leaf nodes where *u* is the number of reference points. Our objective is to find a local graph $S_w^{F_T}$ in the target vector space that is most similar to $S_q^{F_B}$ in the base vector space. *w* denotes here the temporal counterpart of *q* and F_T is the set of terms in the target vector space that corresponds to F_B.

Algorithm. *Step (1)*: to compare the similarity between two graphs in different vector spaces, every node (i.e. term) in $S_q^{F_B}$ is required to be transformed first to allow for comparison under the same vector space. So the transformed vector representation of *q* becomes $\boldsymbol{M}\cdot q$ and F_B is transformed to $\{\boldsymbol{M}\cdot f_1, \boldsymbol{M}\cdot f_2 ..., \boldsymbol{M}\cdot f_u\}$ (recall that $\boldsymbol{M}$ is the transformation matrix). *Step (2)*: for each node in $S_q^{F_B}$, we then choose the top *k* candidate terms with the highest correspondence score in the target space. Note that we would need to perform $k \cdot k^u$

[1] We have experimented with hyponyms and coordinate terms used as reference points and found the results are worse than when using hypernyms.

combinations of nodes (or candidate local graphs) in total, to find the best graph with the highest graph similarity. The computation time becomes then an issue as the number of comparisons grows in polynomial way with the increase in the number of candidate terms. However, we manage to reduce the number of combinations to $k \cdot k \cdot u$ by assuming the reference points be independent of each other. Then, for every selected candidate temporal counterpart, we only choose the set of corresponding terms F_T which maximizes the current graph similarity. By default we set k equal to 1000. The process is shown in Algorithm 3.

Algorithm 3 Local Graph Matching

Input: local graph of q, $S_q^{F_B}$
W = top k corresponding terms of q (by **Eq. 2**)
FF = {top k corresponding terms of each f in reference points F_B={ $f_0, f_1, ..., f_u$}} (by **Eq. 2**)
for w = *W[1:k]* **do**:
  sum_cos = 0 *# total graph similarity score*
  for F = *FF[1:u]* **do:**
    max_cos = 0 *# current maximum similarity*
    for c = *F[1:k]* **do:**
      find c which maximizes current graph similarity
    end for
    sum_cos += max_cos
  end for
end for
sort W by sum_cos of each w in W.
Output: sorted W as ranked list of temporal counterparts

Graph similarity computation. To compute the similarity of two star shaped graphs, we take both the *semantic* and *relational similarities* into consideration. Fig. 3 conceptually portrays this idea. Since all the computation is done under the same vector space (after transformation), the semantic meaning is represented by the absolute position of the term, that is, by its vector representation in the vector space. On the other hand, the relation is described by the difference of two term vectors. Finally, the graph similarity function $g(S_q^{F_B}, S_w^{F_T})$ is defined as the combination of the *relational similarity function*, $h(S_q^{F_B}, S_w^{F_T})$, and *semantic similarity function*, $z(S_q^{F_B}, S_w^{F_T})$, as follows:

$$\begin{aligned} g(S_q^{F_B}, S_w^{F_T}) &= (1-\lambda)\cdot h(S_q^{F_B}, S_w^{F_T}) + \lambda \cdot z(S_q^{F_B}, S_w^{F_T}) \\ &= (1-\lambda)\cdot \sum_{f_B \in F_B, f_T \in F_T} \max(R_q^{f_B} \cdot R_w^{f_T}) \\ &+ \lambda \cdot \max(\sum_{f_B \in F_B, f_T \in F_T} \cos(f_B, f_T) + \cos(q, w)) \end{aligned} \quad (4)$$

where $R_q^{f_B}$ is the difference of vectors between q and f_B in F_B represented as $[q\text{-}f_B]$. $R_w^{f_T}$ is the difference of vectors between w and f_T in F_T, $[w\text{-}f_T]$, where f_T is selected from k candidates corresponding terms of f_B. f_T maximizes the cosine similarity between $[q\text{-} f_B]$ and $[w\text{-} f_T]$. λ is set to 0.5 by default. Intuitively, $S_q^{F_B}$ is a graph composed of query and its reference points, while $S_w^{F_T}$ is a graph containing candidate word w and its reference points. The first maximum in Eq. 4 finds for each reference point in the base time, f_B, the top-k candidate terms corresponding to f_B in the target time. Next, it finds within k such f_T that similarity between $[q\text{-} f_B]$ and $[w\text{-} f_T]$ is maximum (relational similarity). The second maximum in Eq. 4 is same as the first one with the exception that it computes the semantic similarity instead of the relational similarity. The two summations in Eq. 4 aggregate both the similarity scores over all the reference points.

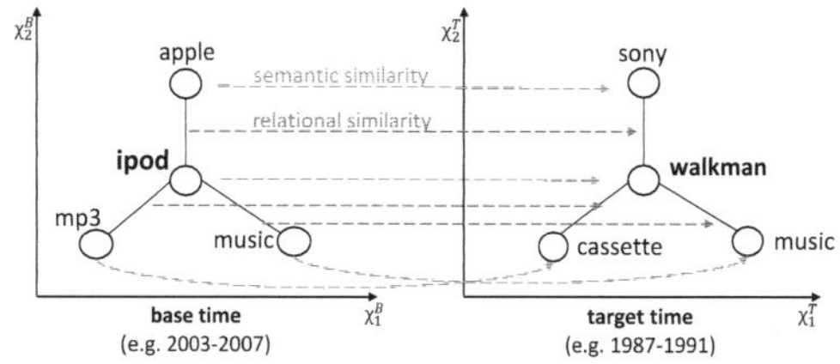

Figure 3: The concept of computing semantic and relational similarity in matching local graphs.

4 Experimental Setup

4.1 Training sets

For the experiments we use the New York Times Annotated Corpus (Sandhaus, 2008). This dataset contains over 1.8 million newspaper articles published between 1987 and 2007. We first divide it into four parts according to article publication time: [1987-1991], [1992-1996], [1997-2001] and [2002-2007]. Each time period contains then around half a million articles. We next train the model of distributed vector representation separately for each time period. The vocabulary size of the entire corpus is 360k, while the vocabulary size of each time period is around 300k.

In the experiments, we first focus on the pair of time periods separated by the longest time gap, that is, [2002, 2007] as the base time and [1987, 1991] as the target time. We also repeat the experiment using more recent target time: [1992, 1996].

q [2002,2007]	*tc* [1987,1991]	BOW (baseline)	LSI-Com (baseline)	LSI-Tran (baseline)	GT (proposed)	LT-Cooc (proposed)	LT-Lex (proposed)	LT-Clust (proposed)
Putin	Yeltsin	1000+	252	353	24	**1**	**1**	**1**
Chirac	Mitterrand	1000+	8	**1**	7	19	**1**	3
iPod	Walkman	1000+	20	131	3	13	**1**	16
Merkel	Kohl	1000+	1000+	537	142	76	**7**	102
Facebook	Usenet	1000+	1000+	1000+	**1**	**1**	**1**	**1**
Linux	Unix	1000+	11	**1**	20	**1**	**1**	**1**
email	letter	1000+	1000+	464	**1**	35	**1**	17
email	mail	1000+	**1**	9	7	**2**	6	11
email	fax	1000+	1000+	10	3	**1**	4	2
Pixar	Tristar	1000+	549	**1**	**1**	**1**	**1**	**1**
Pixar	Disney	1000+	4	4	3	**2**	**2**	4
Serbia	Yugoslavia	1000+	15	1000+	**1**	**1**	**1**	**1**
mp3	compact disk	1000+	56	44	58	**17**	19	22
Rogge	Samaranch	1000+	**4**	22	42	82	34	44
Berlin	Bonn	1000+	43	265	62	**40**	48	56
Czech	Czechoslovakia	1000+	**1**	3	4	**3**	7	4
USB	floppy disk	1000+	209	1000+	20	**1**	**1**	4
spam	junk mail	1000+	1000+	37	5	61	**1**	**1**
Kosovo	Yugoslavia	1000+	59	1000+	14	10	**6**	11

Table 1: Example results where *q* is the input term and *tc* is the matching temporal counterpart. The numbers are the ranks of the correct temporal counterpart in the results ranked by each method. Since we output only the top 1000 results, ranks lower than 1000 are represented as 1000+.

4.2 Test sets

As far as we know there is no standard test bench for temporal correspondence finding. We then had to manually create test sets containing queries in the base time and their correct temporal counterparts in the target time. In this process we used external resources including the Wikipedia, a Web search engine and several historical textbooks. The test terms cover three types of entities: persons, locations and objects.

The examples of the test queries and their temporal counterparts for [1987, 1991] are shown in Table 1 where *q* denotes the input term and *tc* is the correct counterpart. Note that the expected answer is not required to be single neither exhaustive. For example, there can be many answers for the same query term, such as *letter*, *mail*, *fax*, all being commonly used counterparts in 1980s for *email*. Furthermore, as we do not care for recall in this research, we do not require all the correct counterpart terms to be found. In total, there are 95 pairs of terms (query and its counterpart) resulting from 54 input query terms for the task of mapping [2002, 2007] with [1987, 1991], and 50 term pairs created from 25 input query terms for matching [2002, 2007] and [1992, 1996].

4.3 Evaluation measures and baselines

We use the *Mean Reciprocal Rank* (*MRR*) as a main metric to evaluate the ranked search results for each method. MRR is expressed as the mean of the inverse ranks for each test where a correct result appears. It is calculated as follows:

$$MRR = \frac{1}{N}\sum_{i=1}^{N}\frac{1}{rank_i} \quad (5)$$

where $rank_i$ is the rank of a correct counterpart at the *i-th* test. *N* is the number of query-answer pairs. MRR's values range between [0,1]. The higher the value, the more correct the method is. Besides MRR, we also report precision @1, @5, @10 and @20. They are equal to the rates of tests in which the correct counterpart term *tc* was found in the top 1, 5, 10 and 20 results, respectively.

Baselines. We prepare three baselines:

(1) ***Bag of words approach*** (***BOW***) without transformation: this method directly compares the context of the query in the base time with the context of the candidate term in the target time. We use it to examine whether the distributed vector representation and transformation are necessary.

(2) ***Latent Semantic Indexing (LSI)*** **without transformation (LSI-Com)**: we first merge the documents in the base time and the documents in the target time. Then, we train LSI (Deerwester, 1988) on such combined collection to represent each term by the same distribution of detected topics. We next search for the terms that exist in the target period and that are also semantically similar to the queried terms by comparing their vector

representations. The purpose of using LSI-Com is to check the need for the transformation over time.

(3) ***Latent Semantic Indexing (LSI) with transformation* (LSI-Tran)**: we train two LSI models separately on the documents in the base time and the documents in the target time. Then we train the *transformation matrix* in the same way as we did for our proposed methods. Lastly, for a given input query, we compare its transformed vector representation with terms in the target time. LSI-Tran is used to investigate if LSI can be an alternative for the vector representation under our transformation scenario.

Proposed Methods. All our methods use the neural network based term representation. The first one is the method without considering the local context graph called **GT** (see Sec. 2). By testing it we want to investigate the necessity of transforming the context of the query in the target time.

We also test the three variants of the proposed approach that applies the local graph (explained in Sec. 3). The first one, **LT-Lex**, constructs the local graph by using the hypernyms of terms. **LT-Cooc** applies term co-occurrence to select the reference points. Finally, **LT-Clust** clusters the context terms by their semantic meanings and selects the most common term from each cluster.

4.4 Parameter settings

We set the parameters as follows:
(1) *num_of_dim*: we experimentally set the number of dimensions of the Skip-gram model and the number of topics of LSI to be 200.
(2) *num_of_CFTs*: we utilize the top 5% (18k words) of Common Frequent Terms to train the transformation matrix. We have tried other numbers but we found 5% to perform best (see Fig. 4).
(3) u: the number of reference points (same as the number of semantic clusters) is set to be 5. According to the results, we found that increasing the number of reference points does not always improve the results. The performance depends rather on whether the reference points are general enough, as too detailed ones hurt the results.

5 Experimental Results

First, we look at the results of finding temporal counterparts in [1987, 1991]. The average scores for each method are shown in Table 2. Table 1 shows detailed results for few example queries.

The main finding is that all our methods outperform the baselines when measured by MRR and by the precisions at different ranks. In the following subsections we discuss the results in detail.

5.1 Context change over time

The first observation is that the task is quite difficult as evidenced by extremely poor performance of the bag of words approach (**BOW**). The correct answers in **BOW** approach are usually found at ranks 10k-30k (recall that the vocabulary size is 360k). This suggests little overlap in the contexts of query and counterpart terms. The fact that all our methods outperform the baselines suggests that the across-time transformation is helpful.

5.2 Using local context graph

We can observe from Table 2 that, in general, using the local context graph improves the results. The best performing approach, **LT-Lex**, improves **GT** method, which uses only global similarity matching, by 24% when measured using MRR. It increases the precision at certain levels of top ranks, especially, at the top 1, where it boosts the performance by 44%. **LT-Lex** uses the hypernyms of query as reference points in the local graph. This suggests that using generalized context terms as reference points is most helpful for finding correct temporal counterparts. On the other hand, **LT-Cooc** and **LT-Clust** usually fail to improve **GT**. It may be because the term co-occurrence and semantic clustering approaches detect less general terms that tend to capture too detailed information which is then poorly related to the temporal counterpart. For example, **LT-Cooc** detects *{music, Apple, computer, digital, iTunes}* as the reference points of the query *iPod*. While *music* is shared by *iPod*'s counterpart (*walkman*) and *Apple* can be considered analogical to *Sony*, other terms (i.e., *computer, digital, iTunes*) are rather too specific and unique for *iPod*.

5.3 Using neural network model

When comparing the results of **LSI-Com** and **LSI-Tran** in Table 2, we can see that using the *transformation* does not help LSI to enhance the performance but, on the contrary, it makes the results worse.

Method	MRR	P@1	P@5	P@10	P@20
BOW	4.1E-5	0	0	0	0
LSI-Com	0.206	15.8	27.3	29.5	38.6
LSI-Tran	0.112	7.9	13.6	21.6	22.7
GT	0.298	16.8	44.2	56.8	**73.7**
LT-Cooc	0.283	18.8	35.3	50.6	62.4
LT-Lex	**0.369**	**24.2**	**49.5**	**63.2**	71.6
LT-Clust	0.285	14.7	42.1	55.1	65.2

Table 2: Results of searching from present to past (present: 2002-2007; past: 1987-1991).

Yet, as discussed above, applying the *transformation* is good idea in the case of the Neural Network Model. We believe the reason for this is because it is difficult to perform the global transformation between topics underling the dimensions of LSI, in contrast to transforming "semantic dimensions" of Neural Network Model.

5.4 Effect of the number of CFTs

Fig. 4 shows MRR results for different numbers of *Common Frequent Terms* (*CFTs*) when applying **GT** method. Note that the level of 0.10% (the first point) corresponds to using 658 stop words as seed pairs. As mentioned before, 5% of CFTs allows to obtain the best results.

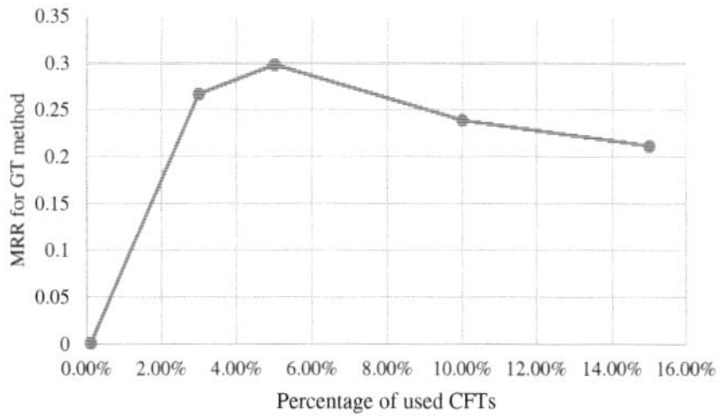

Figure 4: Results of MRR for **GT** method depending on number of used *CFTs*.

5.5 Searching from past to present

We next analyze the case of searching from the past to the present. This scenario may apply to the case of a user (perhaps, an older person) who possesses knowledge about the past term but does not know its modern counterparts.

Table 3 shows the performance. We can see that, again, all our approaches outperform all the baselines using all the measures. **LT-Lex** is the best performing approach, when measured by MRR and P@1 and P@20. **LT-Cooc** this time returns the best results at P@5 and P@10.

Method	MRR	P@1	P@5	P@10	P@20
BOW	3.4E-5	0	0	0	0
LSI-Com	0.181	13.2	19.7	28.9	35.5
LSI-Tran	0.109	5.3	17.1	21.1	23.7
GT	0.226	15.2	27.3	33.3	45.5
LT-Cooc	0.231	14.7	**30.7**	**36**	46.7
LT-Lex	**0.235**	**16.7**	28.8	31.8	**48.5**
LT-Clust	0.228	13.6	28.8	31.8	47

Table 3: Average scores of searching from past to present (present: 2002-2007; past: 1987-1991).

The objective of testing the search from the past to present is to prove our methods work in both directions. As for now, we can only conclude the performance is asymmetrical. Yet, we might speculate that, along with the increase in distance, searching from past to present could be harder due to present world becoming relatively more diverse when seen from the distant past.

5.6 Results using different time period

Finally, we perform additional experiment using another target time period [1992, 1996] to verify whether our approach is still superior on different target time. For the experiment we use the best performing baseline listed in Table 2, **LSI-Com**, and the best proposed approach, **LT-Lex**, as well as **GT**. The results are shown in Tables 4 and 5. **LT-Lex** outperforms the other baselines in both the search from the present to the past (Table 4) and from the past to the present (Table 5). Note that since the query-answers pairs for [1992, 1996] are different than ones for [1987, 1991], their results cannot be directly compared.

Method	MRR	P@1	P@5	P@10	P@20
LSI-Com	0.115	10.6	14.9	21.3	23.4
GT	0.132	8.5	27.7	40.4	53.2
LT-Lex	**0.169**	**10.6**	**34.1**	**48.9**	**55.3**

Table 4: Results of searching from present to past (present: 2002-2007; past: 1992-1996).

Method	MRR	P@1	P@5	P@10	P@20
LSI-Com	0.148	11.6	18.6	23.3	30.2
GT	0.184	11.6	23.3	30.2	44.2
LT-Lex	**0.212**	**14**	**28**	**32.6**	**44.2**

Table 5: Results of searching from past to present (present: 2002-2007; past: 1992-1996).

5.7 Confidence of Results

The approach described in this paper will always try to output some matching terms to a query in the target time period. However in some cases, no term corresponding to the one in the base time existed in the target time (e.g. when the semantic concept behind the term was not yet born or, on the contrary, it has already felt out of use). For example, junk mail may not have any equivalent in texts created around 1800s. A simple solution to this problem would be to use Eqs. 2 and 4 to serve as measures of confidence behind each result in order to decide whether the found counterparts should or not be shown to users. Note however that the scores returned by Eqs. 2 and 4 need to be first normalized according to the distance between the target time and the base time periods.

6 Related Work

Temporal changes in word meaning have been an important topic of study within historical linguistics (Aitchison, 2001; Campbell 2004; Labov, 2010; Hughes, 1988). Some researchers employed computational methods for analyzing changes in word senses over time (Mihalcea and Nastase, 2012; Kim et al., 2014; Jatowt and Duh, 2014; Kulkarni et al., 2015). For example, Mihalcea and Nastase (2012) classified words to one of three past epochs based on words' contexts. Kim et al. (2014) and Kulkarni et al. (2015) computed the degree of meaning change by applying neural networks for word representation. Jatowt and Duh (2014) used also sentiment analysis and word pair comparison for meaning change estimation. Our objective is different as we search for corresponding terms across time, and, in our case, temporal counterparts can have different syntactic forms.

Some works considered computing term similarity across time (Kalurachchi et al., 2010; Kanhabua et al. 2010; Tahmasebi et al. 2012, Berberich et al. 2009). Kalurachchi et al. (2010) proposed to discover semantically identical temporally altering concepts by applying association rule mining, assuming that the concepts referred by similar events (verbs) are semantically related. Kanhabua et al. (2010) discovered the change of terms through the comparison of temporal Wikipedia snapshots. Berberich et al. (2009) approached the problem by introducing a HMM model and measuring the across-time sematic similarity between two terms by comparing the contexts captured by co-occurrence measures. Tahmasebi et al. (2012) improved their approach by first detecting the periods of name change and then by analyzing the contexts during the change periods to find the temporal co-references of different names. There are important differences between those works and ours. First, the previous works mainly focused on detecting changes of the names of the same, single entity over time. For example, the objective was to look for the previous name of Pope Benedict (i.e. Joseph Ratzinger) or the previous name of St. Petersburg (i.e. Leningrad). Second, these approaches relied on applying the co-occurrence statistics according to the intuition that if two terms share similar contexts, then these terms are semantically similar. In our work, we do not require the context to be literally same but to have the same meaning.

Transfer Learning (Pan et al., 2010) is related to some extent to our work. It has been mainly used in tasks such as POS tagging (Blitzer et al., 2006), text classification (Blitzer et al., 2007; Ling et al., 2008; Wang et al., 2011; Xue et al., 2008), learning to rank (Cai et al., 2011; Gao et al., 2010; Wang et al., 2009) and content-based retrieval (Kato et al., 2012). The temporal correspondence problem can be also understood as a transfer learning as it is a search process that uses samples in the base time for inferring correspondent instances existing in the target time. However, the difference is that we do not only consider the structural correspondence but we also utilize the semantic similarity across time.

The idea of distance-preserving projections is also used in automatic translation (Mikolov et al., 2013b). Our research problem is however more difficult and is still unexplored. In the traditional language translation, languages usually share same concepts, while in the across-time translation concepts evolve and thus may be similar but not always same. Furthermore, the lack of training data is another key problem.

7 Conclusions and Future Work

This work approaches the problem of finding temporal counterparts as a way to build a "bridge" across different times. Knowing corresponding terms across time can have direct usage in supporting search within longitudinal document collections or be helpful for constructing evolution timelines. We first discuss the key challenge of the temporal counterpart detection – the fact that contexts of terms change, too. We then propose the global correspondence method using transformation between two vector spaces. Based on this, we then introduce more refined approach of computing the local correspondence. Through experiments we demonstrate that the local correspondence using hypernyms outperforms both the baselines and the global correspondence approach.

In the future, we plan to test our approaches over longer time spans and to design the way to automatically "explain" temporal counterparts by outputting "evidence" terms for clarifying the similarity between the counterparts.

Acknowledgments

We thank Makoto P. Kato for valuable comments. This work was supported in part by Grants-in-Aid for Scientific Research (Nos. 15H01718, 15K12158) from MEXT of Japan and by the JST Research Promotion Program Sakigake: "Analyzing Collective Memory and Developing Methods for Knowledge Extraction from Historical Documents".

References

J. Aitchison, Language Change, Progress or Decay? Cambridge University Press, 2001.

K. Berberich, S. J. Bedathur, M. Sozio and G. Weikum, Bridging the Terminology Gap in Web Archive Search, In *Proc. of WebDB '09*, 2009.

J. Blitzer, M. Dredze, and F. Pereira. Biographies, Bollywood, Boom-boxes and Blenders: Domain Adaption for Sentiment Classification. In *Proc. of ACL*, pages 440-447, 2007.

J. Blitzer, R. McDonald, and F. Pereira. Domain adaption with structural correspondence learning. In *Proceedings of the 2006 conference on empirical methods in natural language processing. Association for Computational Linguistics (EMNLP)*, pages 120-128, 2006.

P. Cai, W. Gao, A. Zhou et al. Relevant knowledge helps in choosing right teacher: active query selection for ranking adaptation. *In Proceedings of the 34th international ACM SIGIR conference on Research and development in Information Retrieval*, pages 115-124, 2001.

L. Campbell, Historical Linguistics, 2nd edition, MIT Press, 2004.

S. Deerwester et al., Improving Information Retrieval with Latent Semantic Indexing, In *Proceedings of the 51st Annual Meeting of the American Society for Information Science*, 25, pages 36–40, 1988.

W. Gao, P. Cai, K.F. Wong et al. Learning to rank only using training data from related domain. In *Proceedings of the 33rd international ACM SIGIR conference on Research and development in information retrieval*, pages 162-169, 2010.

G. Hughes, Words in Time: A Social History of the English Vocabulary. Basil Blackwell, 1988.

A. Jatowt and K. Duh. A framework for analyzing semantic change of words across time. In *Proc. of JCDL*, pages 229-238, 2014.

A. Kalurachchi, A. S. Varde, S. Bedathur, G. Weikum, J. Peng and A. Feldman, Incorporating Terminology Evolution for Query Translation in Text Retrieval with Association Rules, In *Proceedings of the 19th ACM international Conference on Information and Knowledge Management (CIKM)*, pages 1789-1792, 2010.

N. Kanhabua, K. Nørvåg, Exploiting Time-based Synonyms in Searching Document Archives, In *Proceedings of the 10th annual joint conference on Digital libraries (JCDL)*, pages 79-88, 2010.

M. P. Kato, H. Ohshima and K. Tanaka. Content-based Retrieval for Heterogeneous Domains: Domain Adaption by Relative Aggregation Points. In *Proceedings of the 35th international ACM SIGIR conference on Research and development in information retrieval*, pages 811-820, 2012.

Y. Kim, Y-I. Chiu, K. Hanaki, D. Hegde and S. Petrov. Temporal Analysis of Language through Neural Language Models. In *Proceedings of the ACL 2014 Workshop on Language Technologies and Computational Social Science*, pp. 61-65, 2014.

V. Kulkarni, R. Al-Rfou, B. Perozzi, and S. Skiena. 2014. Statistically Significant Detection of Linguistic Change. In *Proc. of WWW*, pages 625-635, 2015.

W. Labov. Principles of Linguistic Change (Social Factors), Wiley-Blackwell, 2010.

E. Lieberman, J.-B. Michel, J. Jackson, T. Tang, M. A. Nowak. Quantifying the evolutionary dynamics of language. *Nature*, 449, 713-716, 2007.

X. Ling, W. Dai, G. R. Xue, Q. Yang and Y. Yu. Spectral domain-transfer learning. In *Proceedings of the 14th ACM SIGKDD international conference on Knowledge discovery and data mining,* pages 488-496, 2008.

R. Mihalcea, and V. Nastase, "Word Epoch Disambiguation: Finding How Words Change Over Time" in Proceedings of ACL (2) 2012, pp. 259-263, 2012.

T. Mikolov, K. Chen, G. Corrado and J. Dean. Efficient Estimation of Word Representations in Vector Space. In *ICLR Workshop*, 2013a.

T. Mikolov, QV. Le, I. Sutskever. Exploiting similarities among languages for machine translation. CoRR, abs/1309.4168, 2013b.

T. Mikolov, I. Sutskever, K. Chen, G. Corrado, and J. Dean. Distributed Representation of Phrases and Their Compositionality. In *Advances in Neural Information Processing Systems (NIPS)*, pages 3111-3119, 2013c.

H. Ohshima and K. Tanaka. High-speed Detection of Ontological Knowledge and Bi-directional Lexico-Syntactic Patterns from the Web. *Journal of Software*, 5(2): 195-205, 2010.

S. Pan and Q. Yang. A survey on transfer learning. *IEEE Transactions on Knowledge and Data Engineering*, 22(10): 1345-1359, 2010.

M. Pargel, Q. D. Atkinson and A. Meade. Frequency of word-use predicts rates of lexical evolution throughout Indo-European history. *Nature*, 449, 717-720, 2007.

D. E. Rumelhart, G. E. Hinton, R.J. Williams. Learning internal representations by error propagation. California Univ, San Diego La Jolla Inst. For Cognitive Science, 1985.

E. Sandhaus. The New York Times Annotated Corpus Overview. The New York Times Company, Research and Development, pp. 1-22, 2008. https://catalog.ldc.upenn.edu/docs/LDC2008T19/new_york_times_annotated_corpus.pdf

M. Steinbach, G. Karypis, V. Kumar. A comparison of document clustering techniques. In *Proc. of KDD workshop on text mining*. 2000, 400(1): 525-526.

N. Tahmasebi, G. Gossen, N. Kanhabua, H. Holzmann, and T. Risse. NEER: An Unsupervised Method for Named Entity Evolution Recognition, In *Proc. of Coling*, pages 2553-2568, 2012.

H. Wang, H. Huang, F. Nie, and C. Ding. Cross-language web page classification via dual knowledge transfer using nonnegative matrix tri-factorization. In *Proceedings of the 34th international ACM SIGIR conference on Research and development in Information Retrieval*, pages 933-942, 2011.

B. Wang, J. Tang, W. Fan, S. Chen, Z. Yang and Y. Liu. Heterogeneous cross domain ranking in latent space. In *Proceedings of the 18th ACM conference on Information and knowledge management (CIKM)*, pages 987-996, 2009.

G. Xue, W. Dai, Q. Yang, and Y. Yu. Topic-bridged plsa for cross-domain text classification. In *Proceedings of the 31st annual international ACM SIGIR conference on Research and development in information retrieval*, pages 627-634, 2008.

Negation and Speculation Identification in Chinese Language

Bowei Zou **Qiaoming Zhu** **Guodong Zhou***

Natural Language Processing Lab, School of Computer Science and Technology
Soochow University, Suzhou, 215006, China
zoubowei@gmail.com, {qmzhu, gdzhou}@suda.edu.cn

Abstract

Identifying negative or speculative narrative fragments from fact is crucial for natural language processing (NLP) applications. Previous studies on negation and speculation identification in Chinese language suffers much from two problems: corpus scarcity and the bottleneck in fundamental Chinese information processing. To resolve these problems, this paper constructs a Chinese corpus which consists of three sub-corpora from different resources. In order to detect the negative and speculative cues, a sequence labeling model is proposed. Moreover, a bilingual cue expansion method is proposed to increase the coverage in cue detection. In addition, this paper presents a new syntactic structure-based framework to identify the linguistic scope of a cue, instead of the traditional chunking-based framework. Experimental results justify the usefulness of our Chinese corpus and the appropriateness of our syntactic structure-based framework which obtained significant improvement over the state-of-the-art on negation and speculation identification in Chinese language.

1 Introduction

Negation and speculation are ubiquitous phenomena in natural language. While negation is a grammatical category which comprises various kinds of devices to reverse the truth value of a proposition, speculation is a grammatical category which expresses the attitude of a speaker towards a statement in terms of degree of certainty, reliability, subjectivity, sources of information, and perspective (Morante and Sporleder, 2012).

Current studies on negation and speculation identification mainly focus on two tasks: 1) cue detection, which aims to detect the signal of a negative or speculative expression, and 2) scope resolution, which aims to determine the linguistic coverage of a cue in sentence, in distinguishing unreliable or uncertain information from facts. For example, (E1) and (E2) include a negative cue and a speculative cue respectively, both denoted in **boldface** with their linguistic scopes denoted in square brackets (adopted hereinafter). In sentence (E1), the negative cue "不(not)" triggers the scope of "不会追究酒店的这次管理失职(would not investigate the dereliction of hotel)", within which the fragment "investigate the dereliction of hotel" is the part that is repudiated; While the speculative cue "有望(expected)" in sentence (E2) triggers the scope "后期仍有望反弹(is still expected to rebound in the late)", within which the fragment "the benchmark Shanghai Composite Index will rebound in the late" is the speculative part.

(E1) *所有住客均表示[**不**会追究酒店的这次管理失职].*
*(All of guests said that they [would **not** investigate the dereliction of hotel].)*

(E2) *尽管上周五沪指盘中还受创业板的下跌所拖累,但[后期仍**有望**反弹].*
*(Although dragged down by GEM last Friday, the benchmark Shanghai Composite Index [is still **expected** to rebound in the late].)*

Negation and speculation identification is very relevant for almost all NLP applications involving text understanding which need to discriminate between factual and non-factual information. The treatment of negation and speculation in computational linguistics has been shown to be

* Corresponding author

Proceedings of the 53rd Annual Meeting of the Association for Computational Linguistics and the 7th International Joint Conference on Natural Language Processing, pages 656–665,
Beijing, China, July 26-31, 2015.

useful for biomedical text processing (Morante et al., 2008; Chowdhury and Lavelli, 2013), information retrieval (Averbuch, 2004), sentiment analysis (Councill et al., 2010; Zhu et al., 2014), recognizing textual entailment (Snow et al., 2006), machine translation (Baker et al., 2010; Wetzel and Bond, 2012), and so forth.

The research on negation and speculation identification in English has received a noticeable boost. However, in contrast to the significant achievements concerning English, the research progress in Chinese language is quite limited. The main reason includes the following two aspects: First, the scarcity of linguistic resource seriously limits the advance of related research. To the best of our knowledge, there are no publicly available standard Chinese corpus of reasonable size annotated with negation and speculation. Second, this may be attributed to the limitations of Chinese information processing.

The contributions of this paper are as follows:

- To address the aforementioned first issue, this paper seeks to fill this gap by presenting the Chinese negation and speculation corpus which consists of three kind of sub-corpora annotated for negative and speculative cues, and their linguistic scopes. The corpus has been made publicly available for research purposes and it is freely downloadable from http://nlp.suda.edu.cn/corpus.
- For cue detection, we propose a feature-based sequence labeling model to identify cues. It is worth noting that the morpheme feature is employed to better represent the compositional semantics inside Chinese words. Moreover, for improving the low recall rate which suffers from the unknown cues, we propose a cross-lingual cue expansion strategy based on parallel corpora.
- For scope resolution, we present a new syntactic structure-based framework on dependency tree. Evaluation justifies the appropriateness and validity of this framework on Chinese scope resolution, which outperforms the chunking-based framework that widely used in mainstream scope resolution systems.

The layout of the rest paper is organized as follows. Section 2 describes related work. Section 3 provides details about annotation guidelines and also presents statistics about corpus characteristics. Section 4 describes our approach in detail. Section 5 reports and discusses our experimental results. Finally, we conclude our work and indicate some future work in Section 6.

2 Related Work

Currently, both cue detection task and scope resolution task are always modeled as a classification problem with the purpose of predicting whether a token is inside or outside the cue and its scope. Among them, feature-based and kernel-based approaches are most popular.

In the feature-based framework, Agarwal and Yu (2010) employed a conditional random fields (CRFs) model to detect speculative cues and their scopes on the BioScope corpus. The CRFs-based model achieved an F1-meature of 88% in detecting speculative cues. We train this model on our corpus as the baseline system for cue detection. Our work is different from theirs in that we employ a new feature (morpheme feature) which is particularly appropriate for Chinese.

Besides, kernel-based approaches exploit the structure of the tree that connects cue and its corresponding scope. Zou et al. (2013) developed a tree kernel-based system to resolve the scope of negation and speculation, which captures the structured information in syntactic parsing trees. To the best of our knowledge, this system is the best English scope resolution system. For this reason, we train this system on our corpus as the baseline system for scope resolution.

Compared with a fair amount of works on English negation and speculation identification, unfortunately, few works has been published on Chinese. Ji et al. (2010) developed a system to detect speculation in Chinese news texts. However, only the speculative sentences have been found out, with no more fine-grained information such as scope. The insufficient study on Chinese negation and speculation identification drives us to construct a high-quality corpus and investigate how to find an approach that is particularly appropriate for Chinese language.

3 Corpus Construction

In this section, we elaborate on the overall characteristics of the Chinese Negation and Speculation (abbr., CNeSp) corpus we constructed, including a brief description of the sources that constitute our corpus, general guidelines which illustrated with lots of examples and some special cases, and statistics on the overall results of our corpus.

3.1 Sources

To capture the heterogeneity of language use in texts, the corpus consists of three different sources and types, including scientific literature, product reviews, and financial articles.

Vincze et al. (2008) described that it is necessary to separate negative and speculative information from factual especially in science articles, because conclusions of science experiment are always described by using diversity of expressions and include hypothetical asserts or viewpoints. For this reason, we adopt the 19 articles from Chinese Journal of Computers (Vol.35(11)), an authoritative academic journal in Chinese, to construct the Scientific Literature sub-corpus.

Another part of the corpus consists of 311 articles from “股市及时雨(timely rain for stock market)” column from Sina.com in April, 2013. There are 22.3% and 40.2% sentences in the Financial Article sub-corpus containing negation and speculation respectively.

Many researches have investigated the role of negation in sentiment analysis task, as an important linguistic qualifier which leads to a change in polarity. For example, Councill et al. (2010) investigated the problem of determining the polarity of sentiment in movie reviews when negation words occur in the sentences. On the other hand, speculation is a linguistic expression that tends to correlate with subjectivity which is also crucial for sentiment analysis. Pang and Lee (2004) showed that subjectivity detection in the review domain helps to improve polarity classification. Therefore, the Product Review sub-corpus consists of 821 comments of hotel service from the website Ctrip.com.

3.2 Annotation Guidelines

The guidelines of our CNeSp corpus have partly referred to the existing Bioscope corpus guidelines (BioScope, 2008) in order to fit the needs of the Chinese language. In annotation process, negative or speculative cues and their linguistic scopes in sentence are annotated. There are several general principles below:

(G1) Cue is contained in its scope.

(G2) The minimal unit that expresses negation or speculation is annotated as a cue.

(E3) *该股极有**可能**再度出现涨停.*
*(The stock is very **likely** to hit limit up.)*

To G2, the modifiers such as prepositions, determiners, or adverbs are not annotated as parts of the cue. For example, in Sentence (E3), “极(very)” is only a modifier of the speculative cue “可能(likely)”, but not a constituent of the cue.

For the drawbacks of the Bioscope corpus guidelines either on itself or for Chinese language, we introduced some modifications. These main changes are summarized below:

(G3) A cue is annotated only relying on its actual semantic in context.

(E4) *大盘**不可能**再次出现高开低走.*
*(It is **not possible** that the broader market opens high but slips later again.)*

To G3, “不可能(not possible)” means that the author denies the possibility of the situation that “the broader market opens high but slips later again”, which contains negative meanings than speculative. Thus, the phrase “不可能(not possible)” should be labeled as a negative cue.

(G4) A scope should contain the subject which contributes to the meaning of the content being negated or speculated if possible.

(E5) **Once again, the Disorder module does [**not** contribute positively to the prediction].*

The BioScope corpus suggests that the scope of negative adverbs usually starts with the cue and ends at the end of the phrase, clause or sentence (E5). However, in our view, the scope should contain the subject for the integrity of meaning. Following is an exceptional case.

(G5) Scope should be a continuous fragment in sentence.

(E6) *酒店有高档的配套设施,然而却[**不能**多给我们提供一个枕头].*
*(The hotel are furnished with upscale facilities, but [**cannot** offer us one more pillow].)*

Some rhetoric in Chinese language, such as parallelism or ellipsis, often gives rise to separation of some sentence constituents from others. For example, in Sentence (E6), the subject of the second clause should be “酒店(the hotel)”, which is omitted. In this situation, we only need to identify the negative or speculative part in sentence than all semantic constituents which can be completed through other NLP technologies, such as zero subject anaphora resolution or semantic role labeling.

(G6) A negative or speculative character or word may not be a cue.

(E7) *早茶的种类之多不得不赞.*
(We are difficult not to give credit to the variety of morning snack.)

We have come across several cases where the presence of a negative or speculative character or word does not denote negative or speculative meaning. For example, there are lots of double negatives in Chinese language only for emphasizing than negative meanings. In Sentence (E7), obviously, the author wants to emphasis the praise of the variety of breakfast buffet by using the phrase "不得不(be difficult not to)" which does not imply a negative meaning.

The CNeSp corpus is annotated by two independent annotators who are not allowed to communicate with each other. A linguist expert resolves the differences between the two annotators and modified the guidelines when they are confronted with problematic issues, yielding the gold standard labeling of the corpus.

3.3 Statistics and Agreement Analysis

Table 1 summarizes the chief characteristics of the three sub-corpora, including Scientific Literature (Sci., for short), Financial Article (Fin.), and Product Review (Prod.). As shown in Table 1, out of the total amount of 16,841 sentences more than 20% contained negation or speculation, confirming the availability for corpus.

Item	Sci.	Fin.	Prod.
#Documents	19	311	821
#Sentences	4,630	7,213	4,998
Avg. Length of Sentences	30.4	30.7	24.1
Negation			
%Sentence	13.2	17.5	52.9
Avg. Length of Scopes	9.1	7.2	5.1
Speculation			
%Sentence	21.6	30.5	22.6
Avg. Length of Scopes	12.3	15.0	6.9

(Avg. Length: The average number of Chinese characters.)

Table 1. Statistics of corpus.

Type		Sci.	Fin.	Prod.
Negation	Cue	0.96	0.96	0.93
	Cue & Scope	0.90	0.91	0.88
Speculation	Cue	0.94	0.90	0.93
	Cue & Scope	0.93	0.85	0.89

Table 2. Inter-annotator agreement.

We measured the inter-annotator agreement of annotating cues and their linguistic scope for all of three sub-corpora between the two independent annotators in terms of Kappa (Cohen, 1960). The results are shown in Table 2. The 2nd and 4th rows of the table show the kappa value of only cue annotation for negation and speculation, respectively. The 3rd and 5th rows show the agreement rate for both cue and its full scope. The most obvious conclusions here are that the identification of speculation is more complicated than negation even for humans because of the higher ambiguity of cues and the longer average length of scopes in speculation.

4 Chinese Negation and Speculation Identification

As a pipeline task, negation and speculation identification generally consists of two basic stages, cue detection and scope resolution. The former detects whether a word or phrase implies negative or speculative meanings, while the latter determines the sequences of terms which are dominated by the corresponding cue in sentence.

In this section, we improve our cue detection system by using the morpheme features of Chinese characters and expanding the cue clusters based on bilingual parallel corpora. Then, we present a new syntactic structure-based framework for Chinese language, which regards the sub-structures of dependency tree selected by a heuristic rule as scope candidates.

4.1 Cue Detection

Most of the existing cue detection approaches are proposed from feature engineering perspective. They formulate cue detection as a classification issue, which is to classify each token in sentence as being the element of cue or not.

Feature-based sequence labeling model

At the beginning, we explore the performance of an English cue detection system, as described in Agarwal and Yu (2010), which employs a conditional random fields (abbr., CRFs) model with lexical and syntactic features. Unfortunately, the performance is very low on Chinese texts (Section 5.1). This may be attributed to the different characteristic of Chinese language, for example, no word boundaries and lack of morphologic variations. Such low performance drives us to investigate new effective features which are particularly appropriate for Chinese. We employed three kinds of features for cue detection:

1) N-gram features

For each character c_i, assuming its 5-windows characters are $c_{i-2}\ c_{i-1}\ c_i\ c_{i+1}\ c_{i+2}$, we adopt following features: c_{i-2}, c_{i-1}, c_i, c_{i+1}, c_{i+2}, $c_{i-1}c_i$, c_ic_{i+1}, $c_{i-2}c_{i-1}c_i$, $c_{i-1}c_ic_{i+1}$, $c_ic_{i+1}c_{i+2}$.

2) Lexical features

To achieve high performance as much as possible, we also use some useful basic features which are widely used in other NLP tasks on Chinese. The basic feature set consists of POS tag, the left/right character and its PoS tag. It is worth noting that the cue candidates in our model are characters. Thus, in order to get these features, we substitute them with corresponding features of the words which contain the characters.

3) Morpheme features

The word-formation of Chinese implies that almost all of the meanings of a word are made up by the morphemes, a minimal meaningful unit in Chinese language contained in words. This more fine-grained semantics are the compositional semantics inside Chinese words namely. We assume that the morphemes in a given cue are also likely to be contained in other cues. For example, “猜测(guess)” is a given speculative cue which consists of “猜(guess)” and “测(speculate)”, while the morpheme “猜(guess)” could be appeared in “猜想(suppose)”. In consideration of the Chinese characteristics, we use every potential character in cues to get the morpheme feature.

A Boolean feature is taken to represent the morpheme information. Specifically, the characters which appear more than once within different cues in training corpus were selected as the features. The morpheme feature is set to 1, if the character is a negative or speculative morpheme.

For the ability of capturing the local information around a cue, we choose CRFs, a conditional sequence model which represents the probability of a hidden state sequence given some observations, as classifier to label each character with a tag indicating whether it is out of a cue (O), the beginning of the cue (B) or a part of the cue except the beginning one (I). In this way, our CRFs-based cue identifier performs sequential labeling by assigning each character one of the three tags and a character assigned with tag B is concatenated with following characters with tag I to form a cue.

Cross-lingual Cue Expansion Strategy

The feature-based cue detection approach mentioned above shows that a bottleneck lies in low recall (see Table 4). This is probably due to the absence of about 12% negation cues and 17% speculation cues from the training data. It is a challenging task to identify unknown cues with the limited amount of training data. Hence, we propose a cross-lingual cue expansion strategy.

In the approach, we take use of the top 5 Chinese cues in training corpus as our “anchor set”. For each cue, we search its automatically aligned English words from a Chinese-English parallel corpus to construct an English word cluster. The parallel corpus consisting of 100,000 sentence pairs is built by using Liu's approach (Liu et al., 2014), which combines translation model with language model to select high-quality translation pairs from 16 million sentence pairs. The word alignment was obtained by running Giza++ (Och and Ney, 2003). In each cluster, we record the frequency of each unique English word. Considering the word alignment errors in cross-lingual clusters, we filter the clusters by word alignment probability which is formulated as below:

$$\begin{aligned} P_A &= \alpha P(w_E \mid w_C) + (1-\alpha) P(w_C \mid w_E) \\ &= \alpha \frac{P(w_E, w_C)}{P(w_C)} + (1-\alpha) \frac{P(w_E, w_C)}{P(w_E)} \\ &= \alpha \frac{align(w_E, w_C)}{\sum_i align(w_{Ei}, w_C)} + (1-\alpha) \frac{align(w_E, w_C)}{\sum_i align(w_{Ci}, w_E)} \end{aligned} \quad (1)$$

where $P(w_E \mid w_C)$ is the translation probability of English word w_E conditioned on Chinese word w_C, reversely, while $P(w_C \mid w_E)$ is the translation probability of Chinese word w_C conditioned on English word w_E. $align(w_m, w_n)$ is the number of alignments of word w_m and word w_n in parallel corpus. $\sum_i align(w_{mi}, w_n)$ is the sum of the number of alignments which contain word w_n. The parameter $\alpha \in [0,1]$ is the coefficient controlling the relative contributions from the two directions of translation probability.

Then we conduct the same procedure in the other direction to construct Chinese word clusters anchored by English cues, until no new word comes about. For example, applying the above approach from the cue “可能(may)”, we obtain 59 Chinese speculative cues. All of words in the final expansion cluster are identified as cues.

4.2 Scope Resolution

Currently, mainstream approaches formulated the scope resolution as a chunking problem, which classifies every word of a sentence as being inside or outside the scope of a cue. However, unlike in English, we found that plenty of errors occurred in Chinese scope resolution by using words as the basic identifying candidate.

In this paper we propose a new framework using the sub-structures of dependency tree as scope candidates. Specifically, given a cue, we adopt the following heuristic rule to get the scope candidates in the dependency tree.

Setting constituent X and its siblings as the root nodes of candidate structure of scope, X should be the ancestor node of cue or cue itself.

For example, in the sentence “所有住客均表示不会追究酒店的这次管理失职(All of guests said that they would not investigate the dereliction of hotel)”, the negative cue “不(not)” has four constituent Xs and seven scope candidates, as shown in Figure 1. According to the above rule, three ancestor nodes {Xa: “表示(said)”, Xb: “追究(investigate)”, and Xc: “会(would)”} correspond to three scope candidates (a, b1, and c),

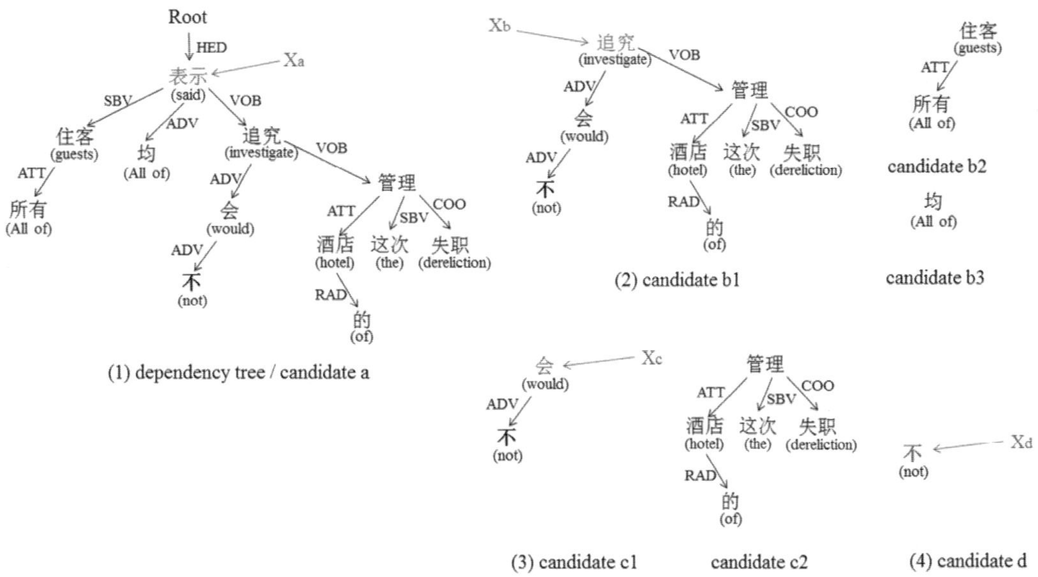

Figure 1. Examples of a negative cue and its seven scope candidates in dependency tree.

Feature	Description	Instantiation
Cue:		
C1: Itself	Tokens of cue	不(not)
C2: PoS	PoS of cue	d(adverb)
Scope candidate:		
S1: Itself	Tokens of headword	追究(investigate)
S2: PoS	PoS of headword	v(verb)
S3: Dependency type	Dependency type of headword	VOB
S4: Dependency type of child nodes	Dependency type of child nodes of headword	ADV+VOB
S5: Distance<candidate, left word>	Number of dependency arcs between the first word of candidate and its left word	3
S6: Distance<candidate, right word>	Number of dependency arcs between the last word of candidate and its right word	0
Relationship between cue and scope candidate:		
R1: Path	Dependency relation path from cue to headword	ADV-ADV
R2: Distance<cue, headword>	Number of dependency arcs between cue and headword	2
R3: Compression path	Compression version of path	ADV
R4: Position	Positional relationship of cue with scope candidate	L_N(Left-nested)

Table 3. Features and their instantiations for scope resolution.

and the cue itself is certainly a scope candidate (d). In addition, the Xb node has two siblings in dependency tree { "住客(guests)" and "均(all of)" }. Therefore, the two scope candidates corresponding to them are b2 and b3, respectively. Similarly, the sibling of the Xc node is labeled as candidate c2.

A binary classifier is applied to determine each candidate as either part of scope or not. In this paper, we employ some lexical and syntactic features about cue and candidate. Table 3 lists all of the features for scope resolution classification (with candidate b1 as the focus constituent (i.e., the scope candidate) and "不(not)" as the given cue, regarding candidate b1 in Figure 1(2)).

For clarity, we categorize the features into three groups according to their relevance with the given cue (C, in short), scope candidate (S, in short), and the relationship between cue andcandidate (R, in short). Figure 2 shows four kinds of positional features between cue and scope candidate we defined (R4).

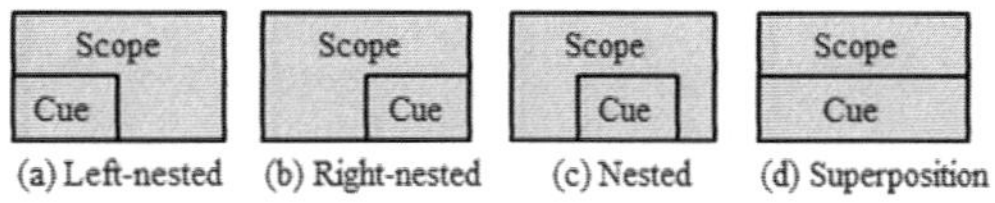

Figure 2. Positional features.

Some features proposed above may not be effective in classification. Therefore, we adopt a greedy feature se-lection algorithm as described in (Jiang and Ng, 2006) to pick up positive features incrementally according to their contributions on the development data. Additionally, a cue should have one continuous block as its scope, but the scope identifier may result in discontinuous scope due to independent candidate in classification. For this reason, we employ a post-processing algorithm as described in Zhu et al. (2010) to identify the boundaries.

5 Experimentation

In this section, we evaluate our feature-based sequence labeling model and cross-lingual cue expansion strategy on cue detection, and report the experimental results to justify the appropriateness of our syntactic structure-based framework on scope resolution in Chinese language.

The performance is measured by Precision (P), Recall (R), and F1-score (F). In addition, for scope resolution, we also report the accuracy in PCS (Percentage of Correct Scopes), within which a scope is fully correct if the output of scope resolution system and the correct scope have been matched exactly.

5.1 Cue Detection

Results of the Sequence Labeling Model

Every sub-corpus is randomly divided into ten equal folds so as to perform ten-fold cross validation. Lexical features are gained by using an open-source Chinese language processing platform, LTP[1](Che et al., 2010) to perform word segmentation, POS tagging, and syntactic parsing. CRF++0.58[2] toolkit is employed as our sequence labeling model for cue detection.

Table 4 lists the performances of cue detection systems using a variety of features. It shows that the morpheme features derived from the word-formation of Chinese improve the performance for both negation and speculation cue detection systems on all kinds of sub-corpora. However, the one exception occurs in negation cue detection on the Product Review sub-corpus, in which the performance is decreased about 4.55% in precision. By error analysis, we find out the main reason is due to the pseudo cues. For example, "非常(very)" is identified by the negative morpheme "非(-un)", which is a pseudo cue.

Table 4 also shows a bottleneck of our sequence labeling model, which lies in low recall. Due to the diversity of Chinese language, many cues only appear a few times in corpus. For example, 83% (233/280) of speculative cues appear less than ten times in Financial Article sub-corpus. This data sparse problem directly leads to the low recall of cue detection.

	Negation			Speculation		
Sci.	P	R	F1	P	R	F1
Agarwal's	48.75	36.44	41.71	46.16	33.49	38.82
N-gram	64.07	49.64	55.94	62.15	42.87	50.74
+Lexical	76.68	57.36	65.63	70.47	48.31	57.32
+Morpheme	**81.37**	**59.11**	**68.48**	**76.91**	**50.77**	**61.16**
Fin.						
Agarwal's	41.93	39.15	40.49	50.39	42.80	46.29
N-gram	56.05	45.48	50.21	60.37	44.16	51.01
+Lexical	71.61	50.12	58.97	68.96	48.72	57.10
+Morpheme	**78.94**	**53.37**	**63.68**	**75.43**	**51.29**	**61.06**
Prod.						
Agarwal's	58.47	47.31	52.30	45.88	34.13	39.14
N-gram	71.33	54.69	61.91	49.38	39.31	43.77
+Lexical	**86.76**	65.41	**74.59**	64.85	44.63	52.87
+Morpheme	82.21	**66.82**	73.72	**70.06**	**45.31**	**55.03**

Table 4. Contribution of features to cue detection.

Results of the Cross-lingual Cue Expansion Strategy

Before cue expansion, we select the parameter α as defined in formula (1) by optimizing the F1-measure score of on Financial Article sub-corpus. Figure 3 shows the effect on F1-measure of varying the coefficient from 0 to 1. We can see that the best performance can be obtained by selecting parameter 0.6 for negation and 0.7 for speculation. Then we apply these parameter values directly for cue expansion.

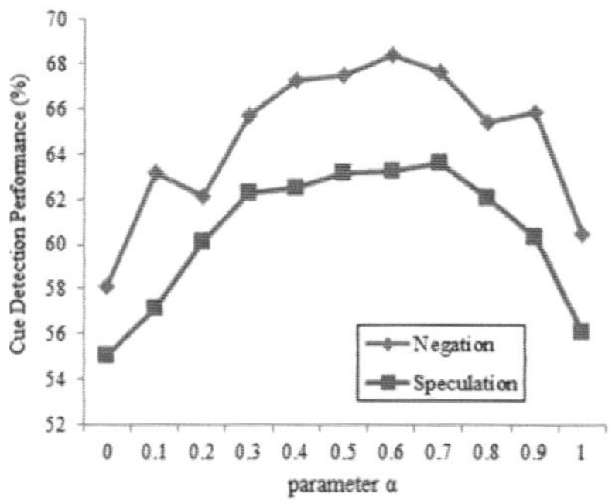

Figure 3. The effect of varying the value of parameter α on Financial Article sub-corpus.

Table 5 lists the performances of feature-based system, expansion-based system, and the combined system. A word is identified as a cue by combined system if it is identified by one of the above systems (Feat-based or Exp-based) at least.

For both negation and speculation, the cross-lingual cue expansion approach provides significant improvement over the feature-based sequence labeling model, achieving about 15-20%

[1] http://www.ltp-cloud.com
[2] https://crfpp.googlecode.com/svn/trunk/doc/index.html

better recall with little loss in precision. More importantly, the combined system obtains the best performance.

	Negation			Speculation		
Sci.	P	R	F1	P	R	F1
Feat-based	81.37	59.11	68.48	76.91	50.77	61.16
Exp-based	68.29	76.24	72.05	62.74	68.07	65.30
Combined	75.17	78.91	**76.99**	70.98	75.71	**73.27**
Fin.						
Feat-based	78.94	53.37	63.68	75.43	51.29	61.06
Exp-based	70.31	64.49	67.27	67.46	68.78	68.11
Combined	72.77	67.02	**69.78**	71.60	69.03	**70.29**
Prod.						
Feat-based	82.21	66.82	73.72	70.06	45.31	55.03
Exp-based	78.30	86.47	82.18	62.18	63.47	62.82
Combined	81.94	89.23	**85.43**	67.56	69.61	**68.57**

Table 5. Performance of cue detection.

5.2 Syntactic Structure-based Scope Resolution

Considering the effectiveness of different features, we divide the Financial Article sub-corpus into 5 equal parts, within which 2 parts are used for feature selection. Then, the feature selection data are divided into 5 equal parts, within which 4 parts for training and the rest for developing. On this data set, a greedy feature selection algorithm (Jiang and Ng, 2006) is adopted to pick up positive features proposed in Table 3. In addition, SVM^{Light}[3] with the default parameter is selected as our classifier.

Table 6 lists the performance of selected features. 7 features {C1, C2, S4, S5, S6, R1, R4} are selected consecutively for negation scope resolution, while 9 features {C2, S1, S3, S4, S5, R1, R2, R3, R4} are selected for speculation scope resolution. We will include those selected features in all the remaining experiments.

Type	Feature set	Sci.	Fin.	Prod.
Negation	Selected features	62.16	56.07	60.93
	All features	59.74	54.20	55.42
Speculation	Selected features	54.16	49.64	52.89
	All features	52.33	46.27	48.07

Table 6. Feature selection for scope resolution on golden cues (PCS %).

The feature selection experiments suggest that the feature C2 (POS of cue) plays a critical role for both negation and speculation scope resolution. It may be due to the fact that cues of different POS usually undertake different syntactic roles. Thus, there are different characteristics in triggering linguistic scopes. For example, an adjective cue may treat a modificatory structure as its scope, while a conjunction cue may take the two connected components as its scope.

As a pipeline task, the negation and speculation identification could be regarded as a combination of two sequential tasks: first, cue detection, and then scope resolution. Hence, we turn to a more realistic scenario in which cues are automatically recognized.

Type	Corpus	P	R	F1	PCS
Negation	Sci.	55.32	53.06	54.17	59.08
	Fin.	42.14	46.37	44.15	49.24
	Prod.	50.57	48.55	49.54	52.17
Speculation	Sci.	45.68	47.15	46.40	48.36
	Fin.	34.21	31.80	32.96	41.33
	Prod.	32.64	33.59	33.11	39.78

Table 7. Performance of scope resolution with automatic cue detection.

Table 7 lists the performance of scope resolution by using automatic cues. It shows that automatic cue detection lowers the performance by 3.08, 6.83, and 8.76 in PCS for the three sub-corpora, respectively; while it lowers the performance by 5.80, 8.31 and 13.11 in PCS for speculation scope resolution on the three sub-corpora, respectively (refer to Table 6). The main reason of performance lost is the error propagation from the automatic cue detection.

We employ a start-of-the-art chunking-based scope resolution system (described in Zou et al., (2013)) as a baseline, in which every word in sentence has been labelled as being the element of the scope or not. Table 8 compares our syntactic structure-based framework with the chunking-based framework on scope resolution. Note that all the performances are achieved on Financial Article sub-corpus by using golden cues. The results in Table 8 shows that our scope resolution system outperforms the chunking ones both on negation and speculation, improving 8.75 and 7.44 in PCS, respectively.

Type	System	PCS
Negation	Chunking-based	47.32
	Ours	56.07
Speculation	Chunking-based	42.20
	Ours	49.64

Table 8. Comparison with the chunking-based system on Financial Article sub-corpus.

6 Conclusion

In this paper we construct a Chinese corpus for negation and speculation identification, which annotates cues and their linguistic scopes. For cue detection, we present a feature-based sequence labeling model, in which the morpheme

[3] http://svmlight.joachims.org

feature is employed to better catch the composition semantics inside the Chinese words. Complementally, a cross-lingual cue expansion strategy is pro-posed to increase the coverage in cue detection. For scope resolution, we present a new syntactic structure-based framework to identify the linguistic scope of a cue. Evaluation justifies the usefulness of our Chinese corpus and the appropriateness of the syntactic structure-based framework. It also shows that our approach outperforms the state-of-the-art chunking ones on negation and speculation identification in Chinese language.

In the future we will explore more effective features to improve the negation and speculation identification in Chinese language, and focus on joint learning of the two subtasks.

Acknowledgments

This research is supported by the National Natural Science Foundation of China, No.61272260, No.61331011, No.61273320, No.61373097, and the Major Project of College Natural Science Foundation of Jiangsu Province, No.11KJA520003. The authors would like to thank the anonymous reviewers for their insightful comments and suggestions.

Reference

Shashank Agarwal and Hong Yu. 2010. Detecting hedge cues and their scope in biomedical text with conditional random fields. *Journal of Biomedical Informatics*, 43, 953-961.

Mordechai Averbuch, Tom H. Karson, Benjamin Ben-Ami, Oded Maimon, and Lior Rokach. 2004. Context-sensitive medical information retrieval. In *Proceedings of the 11th World Congress on Medical Informatics (MEDINFO'04)*, 1-8.

Kathrin Baker, Michael Bloodgood, Bonnie Dorr, Nathaniel W. Filardo, Lori Levin, and Christine Piatko. 2010. A modality lexicon and its use in automatic tagging. In *Proceedings of the Seventh Conference on International Language Resources and Evaluation (LREC'10)*, 1402-1407.

BioScope. 2008. Annotation guidelines. http://www.inf.u-szeged.hu/rgai/project/nlp/bioscope/Annotation guidelines2.1.pdf

Wanxiang Che, Zhenghua Li, Ting Liu. 2010. LTP: A Chinese language technology platform. In *Proceedings of the 23rd International Conference on Computational Linguistics (COLING'10): Demonstrations*, 13-16.

Md. Faisal Mahbub Chowdhury and Alberto Lavelli. 2013. Exploiting the scope of negations and heterogeneous features for relation extraction: A case study for drug-drug interaction extraction. In *Proceedings of the 2013 Conference of the North American Chapter of the Association for Computational Linguistics: Human Language Technologies (NAACL-HLT'13)*, 765-771.

Jacob Cohen. 1960. A coefficient of agreement for nominal scales. *Educational and Psychological Measurement*, 20, 37-46.

Isaac Councill, Ryan McDonald, and Leonid Velikovich. 2010. What's great and what's not: Learning to classify the scope of negation for improved sentiment analysis. In *Proceedings of the Workshop on Negation and Speculation in Natural Language Processing*, 51-59.

Zhengping Jiang and Hwee T. Ng. 2006. Semantic role labeling of NomBank: A maximum entropy approach. In *Proceedings of the Human Language Technology Conference and Conference on Empirical Methods in Natural Language Processing (EMNLP'06)*, 138-145.

Le Liu, Yu Hong, Hao Liu, Xing Wang, and Jianmin Yao. 2014. Effective selection of translation model training data. In *Proceedings of the 52nd Annual Meeting of the Association for Computational Linguistics (ACL'14)*, Short Papers, 569-573.

Feng Ji, Xipeng Qiu, Xuanjing Huang. 2010. Exploring uncertainty sentences in Chinese. In Proceedings of the 16th China Conference on Information Retreval, 594-601.

Roser Morante, Anthony Liekens, and Walter Daelemans. 2008. Learning the scope of negation in biomedical texts. In *Proceedings of the Human Language Technology Conference and Conference on Empirical Methods in Natural Language Processing (EMNLP'08)*, 715-724.

Roser Morante and Caroline Sporleder. 2012. Modality and negation: an introduction to the special issue. *Comput. Linguist. 38*, 2, 223-260.

Franz Josef Och and Hermann Ney. 2003. A systematic comparison of various statistical alignment models. *Comput. Linguist.* 29, 1, 19-51.

Bo Pang and Lillian Lee. 2004. A sentimental education: sentiment analysis using subjectivity. In *Proceedings of the 42nd Annual Meeting of the Association for Computational Linguistics (ACL'04)*, 271-278.

Rion Snow, Lucy Vanderwende, and Arul Menezes. 2006. Effectively using syntax for recognizing false entailment. In *Proceedings of the Main Conference on Human Language Technology Conference of the North American Chapter of the Associ-*

ation of Computational Linguistics (HLT-NAACL'06), 33-40.

Veronika Vincze, György Szarvas, Richárd Farkas, György Móra and János Csirik. 2008. The BioScope corpus: biomedical texts annotated for uncertainty, negation and their scopes. *BMC Bioinformatics*, 9(Suppl 11):S9.

Dominikus Wetzel, and Francis Bond. 2012. Enriching parallel corpora for statistical machine translation with semantic negation rephrasing. In *Proceedings of the 6th Workshop on Syntax, Semantics and Structure in Statistical Translation*, 20-29.

Qiaoming Zhu, Junhui Li, Hongling Wang, and Guodong Zhou. 2010. A Unified Framework for Scope Learning via Simplified Shallow Semantic Parsing. In *Proceedings of the 2010 Conference on Empirical Methods in Natural Language Processing (EMNLP'10)*, 714-724.

Xiaodan Zhu, Hongyu Guo, Saif Mohammad, and Svetlana Kiritchenko. 2014. An empirical study on the effect of negation words on sentiment. In *Proceedings of the 52nd Annual Meeting of the Association for Computational Linguistics (ACL'14)*, 304-313.

Bowei Zou, Guodong Zhou, and Qiaoming Zhu. 2013. Tree kernel-based negation and speculation scope detection with structured syntactic parse features. In *Proceedings of the 2013 Conference on Empirical Methods in Natural Language Processing (EMNLP'13)*, 968-976.

Learning Relational Features with Backward Random Walks

Ni Lao
Google Inc.
nlao@google.com

Einat Minkov
University of Haifa
einatm@is.haifa.ac.il

William W. Cohen
Carnegie Mellon University
wcohen@cs.cmu.edu

Abstract

The path ranking algorithm (PRA) has been recently proposed to address relational classification and retrieval tasks at large scale. We describe Cor-PRA, an enhanced system that can model a larger space of relational rules, including longer relational rules and a class of first order rules with constants, while maintaining scalability. We describe and test faster algorithms for searching for these features. A key contribution is to leverage backward random walks to efficiently discover these types of rules. An empirical study is conducted on the tasks of graph-based knowledge base inference, and person named entity extraction from parsed text. Our results show that learning paths with constants improves performance on both tasks, and that modeling longer paths dramatically improves performance for the named entity extraction task.

1 Introduction

Structured knowledge about entities and the relationships between them can be represented as an edge-typed graph, and relational learning methods often base predictions on connectivity patterns in this graph. One such method is the Path Ranking Algorithm (PRA), a random-walk based relational learning and inference framework due to Lao and Cohen (2010b). PRA is highly scalable compared with other statistical relational learning approaches, and can therefore be applied to perform inference in large knowledge bases (KBs). Several recent works have applied PRA to link prediction in semantic KBs, as well as to learning syntactic relational patterns used in information extraction from the Web (Lao et al., 2012; Gardner et al., 2013; Gardner et al., 2014; Dong et al., 2014).

A typical relational inference problem is illustrated in Figure 1. Having relational knowledge represented as a graph, it is desired to infer additional relations of interest between entity pairs. For example, one may wish to infer whether an *AthletePlaysInLeague* relation holds between nodes *HinesWard* and *NFL*. More generally, link prediction involves queries of the form: which entities are linked to a source node s (*HinesWard*) over a relation of interest r (e.g., r is *AlthletePlaysInLeague*)?

PRA gauges the relevance of a target node t with respect to the source node s and relation r based on a set of relation paths (i.e., sequences of edge labels) that connect the node pair. Each path π_i is considered as feature, and the value of feature π_i for an instance (s, t) is the probability of reaching t from s following path π_i. A classifier is learned in this feature space, using logistic regression.

PRA's candidate paths correspond closely to a certain class of Horn clauses: for instance, the path $\pi = \langle AthletePlaysForTeam, TeamPlaysInLeague\rangle$, when used as a feature for the relation $r = AthletePlaysForLeague$, corresponds to the Horn clause

$$AthletePlaysForTeam(s,z) \wedge TeamPlaysInLeague(z,t) \rightarrow AthletePlaysForLeague(s,t)$$

One difference between PRA's features and more traditional logical inference is that random-walk weighting means that not all inferences instantiated by a clause will be given the same weight. Another difference is that PRA is very limited in terms of expressiveness. In particular, inductive logic programming

Proceedings of the 53rd Annual Meeting of the Association for Computational Linguistics and the 7th International Joint Conference on Natural Language Processing, pages 666–675,
Beijing, China, July 26-31, 2015.

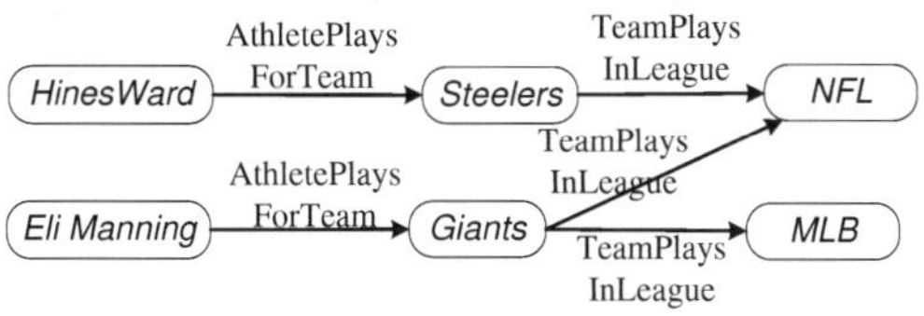

Figure 1: An example knowledge graph

(ILP) methods such as FOIL (Quinlan and Cameron-Jones, 1993) learn first-order Horn rules that may involve constants. Consider the following rules as motivating examples.

$$EmployeedByAgent(s,t) \wedge IsA(t, SportsTeam) \rightarrow AthletePlaysForTeam(s,t)$$

$$t = NFL \rightarrow AthletePlaysForTeam(s,t)$$

The first rule includes *SportsTeam* as a constant, corresponding to a particular graph node, which is a the semantic class (hypernym) of the target node t. The second rule simply assigns *NFL* as the target node for the *AthletePlaysForTeam* relation; if used probabilistically, this rule can serve as a prior. Neither feature can be expressed in PRA, as PRA features are restricted to edge type sequences.

We are interested in extending the range of relational rules that can be represented within the PRA framework, including rules with constants. A key challenge is that this greatly increases the space of candidate rules. Knowledge bases such as Freebase (Bollacker et al., 2008), YAGO (Suchanek et al., 2007), or NELL (Carlson et al., 2010a), may contain thousands of predicates and millions of concepts. The number of features involving concepts as constants (even if limited to simple structures such as the example rules above) will thus be prohibitively large. Therefore, it is necessary to search the space of candidate paths π very efficiently. More efficient candidate generation is also necessary if one attempts to use a looser bound on the length of candidate paths.

To achieve this, we propose using *backward random walks*. Given target nodes that are known to be relevant for relation r, we perform backward random walks (up to finite length ℓ) originating at these target nodes, where every graph node c reachable in this random walk process is considered as a potentially useful constant. Consequently, the relational paths that connect nodes c and t are evaluated as possible random walk features. As we will show, such paths provide informative class priors for relational classification tasks.

Concretely, this paper makes the following contributions. First, we outline and discuss a new and larger family of relational features that may be represented in terms of random walks within the PRA framework. These features represent paths with constants, expanding the expressiveness of PRA. In addition, we propose to encode bi-directional random walk probabilities as features; we will show that accounting for this sort of directionality provides useful information about graph structure.

Second, we describe the learning of this extended set of paths by means of backward walks from relevant target nodes. Importantly, the search and computation of the extended set of features is performed efficiently, maintaining high scalability of the framework. Concretely, using backward walks, one can compute random walk probabilities in a bi-directional fashion; this means that for paths of length $2M$, the time complexity of path finding is reduced from $O(|V|^{2M})$ to $O(|V|^{M})$, where $|V|$ is the number of edge types in graph.

Finally, we report experimental results for relational inference tasks in two different domains, including knowledge base link prediction and person named entity extraction from parsed text (Minkov and Cohen, 2008). It is shown that the proposed extensions allow one to effectively explore a larger feature space, significantly improving model quality over previously published results in both domains. In particular, incorporating paths with constants significantly improves model quality on both tasks. Bi-directional walk probability computation also enables the learning of longer predicate chains, and the modeling of long paths is shown to substantially improve performance on the person name extraction task. Importantly, learning and inference remain highly efficient in both these settings.

2 Related Work

ILP complexity stems from two main sources—the complexity of searching for clauses, and of evaluating them. First-order learning systems (e.g. FOIL, FOCL (Pazzani et al., 1991)) mostly rely on hill-climbing search, i.e., incrementally expanding existing patterns to explore the combinatorial model space, and are thus often vulnerable to local maxima. PRA takes another approach, generating features using efficient random graph walks, and selecting a subset of those features which pass precision and frequency thresholds. In this respect, it resembles a stochastic approach to ILP used in earlier work (Sebag and Rouveirol, 1997).The idea of sampling-based inference and induction has been further explored by later systems (Kuželka and Železný, 2008; Kuželka and Železný, 2009).

Compared with conventional ILP or relational learning systems, PRA is limited to learning from binary predicates, and applies random-walk semantics to its clauses. Using sampling strategies (Lao and Cohen, 2010a), the computation of clause probabilities can be done in time that is independent of the knowledge base size, with bounded error rate (Wang et al., 2013). Unlike in FORTE and similar systems, in PRA, sampling is also applied to the induction path-finding stage. The *relational feature construction* problem (or propositionalization) has previously been addressed in the ILP community—*e.g.*, the RSD system (Železný and Lavrač, 2006) performs explicit first-order feature construction guided by an precision heuristic function. In comparison, PRA uses precision and recall measures, which can be readily read off from random walk results.

Bi-directional search is a popular strategy in AI, and in the ILP literature. The *Aleph* algorithm (Srinivasan, 2001) combines top-down with bottom-up search of the refinement graph, an approach inherited from Progol. FORTE (Richards and Mooney, 1991) was another early ILP system which enumerated paths via a bi-directional seach. Computing backward random walks for PRA can be seen as a particular way of bi-directional search, which is also assigned a random walk probability semantics. Unlike in prior work, we will use this probability semantics directly for feature selection.

3 Background

We first review the Path Ranking Algorithm (PRA) as introduced by (Lao and Cohen, 2010b), paying special attention to its random walk feature estimation and selection components.

3.1 Path Ranking Algorithm

Given a directed graph G, with nodes N, edges E and edge types R, we assume that all edges can be traversed in both directions, and use r^{-1} to denote the reverse of edge type $r \in R$. A *path type* π is defined as a sequence of edge types $r_1 \dots r_\ell$. Such path types may be indicative of an extended relational meaning between graph nodes that are linked over these paths; for example, the path $\langle$*AtheletePlaysForTeam*, *TeamPlaysInLeague*$\rangle$ implies the relationship "the league a certain player plays for". PRA encodes $P(s \rightarrow t; \pi_j)$, the probability of reaching target node t starting from source node s and following path π_j, as a feature that describes the semantic relation between s and t. Specifically, provided with a set of selected path types up to length ℓ, $\mathcal{P}_\ell = \{\pi_1, \dots, \pi_m\}$, the relevancy of target nodes t with respect to the query node s and the relationship of interest is evaluated using the following scoring function

$$score(s,t) = \sum_{\pi_j \in \mathcal{P}_\ell} \theta_j P(s \rightarrow t; \pi_j), \qquad (1)$$

where θ are appropriate weights for the features, estimated in the following fashion.

Given a relation of interest r and a set of annotated node pairs $\{(s,t)\}$, for which it is known whether $r(s,t)$ holds or not, a training data set $\mathcal{D} = \{(\mathbf{x}, y)\}$ is constructed, where $\mathbf{x}$ is a vector of all the path features for the pair (s,t)—i.e., the j-th component of $\mathbf{x}$ is $P(s \rightarrow t; \pi_j)$, and y is a boolean variable indicating whether $r(s,t)$ is true. We adopt the closed-world assumption—a set of relevant target nodes G_i is specified for every example source node s_i and relation r, and all other nodes are treated as negative target nodes. A biased sampling procedure selects only a small subset of negative samples to be included in the objective function (Lao and Cohen, 2010b). The parameters θ are estimated from both positive and negative examples using a regularized logistic regression model.

3.2 PRA Features–Generation and Selection

PRA features are of the form $P(s \rightarrow t; \pi_j)$, denoting the probability of reaching target node t, originating random walk at node s and following edge type sequence π_j. These path probabilities need to be estimated for every node pair, as part of both training and inference. High scalability is achieved due to efficient path probability estimation. In addition, feature selection is applied so as to allow efficient learning and avoid overfitting.

Concretely, the probability of reaching t from s following path type π can be recursively defined as

$$P(s \rightarrow t; \pi) = \sum_{z} P(s \rightarrow z; \pi')P(z \rightarrow t; r), \tag{2}$$

where r is the last edge type in path π, and π' is its prefix, such that adding r to π' gives π. In the terminal case that π' is the empty path ϕ, $P(s \rightarrow z; \phi)$ is defined to be 1 if $s = z$, and 0 otherwise. The probability $P(z \rightarrow t; r)$ is defined as $1/|r(z)|$ if $r(z,t)$, and 0 otherwise, where $r(z)$ is the set of nodes linked to node z over edge type r. It has been shown that $P(s \rightarrow t; \pi)$ can be effectively estimated using random walk sampling techniques, with bounded complexity and bounded error, for all graph nodes that can be reached from s over path type π (Lao and Cohen, 2010a).

Due to the exponentially large feature space in relational domains, candidate path features are first generated using a dedicated particle filtering path-finding procedure (Lao et al., 2011), which is informed by training signals. Meaningful features are then selected using the following *goodness measures*, considering path precision and coverage:

$$precision(\pi) = \frac{1}{n} \sum_{i} P(s_i \rightarrow G_i; \pi), \tag{3}$$

$$coverage(\pi) = \sum_{i} I(P(s_i \rightarrow G_i; \pi) > 0). \tag{4}$$

where $P(s_i \rightarrow G_i; \pi) \equiv \sum_{t \in G_i} P(s_i \rightarrow t; \pi)$. The first measure prefers paths that lead to correct nodes with high average probability. The second measure reflects the number of queries for which some correct node is reached over path π. In order for a path type π to be included in the PRA model, it is required that the respective scores pass thresholds, $precision(\pi) \geq a$ and $coverage(\pi) \geq h$, where the thresholds a and h are tuned empirically using training data.

4 Cor-PRA

We will now describe the enhanced system, which we call Cor-PRA, for the Constant and Reversed Path Ranking Algorithm. Our goal is to enrich the space of relational rules that can be represented using PRA, while maintaining the scalability of this framework.

4.1 Backward random walks

We first introduce *backward* random walks, which are useful for generating and evaluating the set of proposed relational path types, including paths with constants. As discussed in Sec.4.4, the use of backward random walks also enables the modeling of long relational paths within Cor-PRA.

A key observation is that the path probability $P(s \rightarrow t; \pi)$ may be computed using forward random walks (Eq. (2)), or alternatively, it can be recursively defined in a *backward* fashion:

$$P(t \leftarrow s; \pi) = \sum_{z} P(t \leftarrow z; \pi'^{-1})P(z \leftarrow s; r^{-1}) \tag{5}$$

where π'^{-1} is the path that results from removing the last edge type r in π'. Here, in the terminal condition that $\pi'^{-1} = \phi$, $P(t \leftarrow z; \pi'^{-1})$ is defined to be 1 for $z = t$, and 0 otherwise. In what follows, the starting point of the random walk calculation is indicated at the left side of the arrow symbol; i.e., $P(s \rightarrow t; \pi)$ denotes the probability of reaching t from s computed using forward random walks, and $P(t \leftarrow s; \pi)$ denotes the same probability, computed in a backward fashion.

4.2 Relational paths with constants

As stated before, we wish to model relational rules that may include constants, denoting related entities or concepts. Main questions are, how can relational rules with constants be represented as path probability features? and, how can meaningful rules with constants be generated and selected efficiently?

In order to address the first question, let us assume that a set of *constant nodes* $\{c\}$, which are known to be useful with respect to relation r, has been already identified. The relationship between each constant c and target node t may be represented in terms of path probability features, $P(c \rightarrow t; \pi)$. For example, the rule *IsA*$(t, $*SportsTeam*$)$ corresponds to a path originating at constant *SportsTeam*, and reaching target node t over a direct edge typed *IsA*$^{-1}$. Such paths, which are independent of the source node s, readily represent the semantic type, or other characteristic attributes of relevant target nodes. Similarly, a feature (c, ϕ), designating a constant and an empty path, forms a prior for the target node identity.

The remaining question is how to identify meaningful constant features. Apriori, candidate constants range over all of the graph nodes, and searching for useful paths that originate at arbitrary constants is generally intractable. Provided with labeled examples, we apply the path-finding procedure for this purpose, where rather than search for high-probability paths from source node s to target t, paths are explored in a backward fashion, initiating path search at the known relevant target nodes $t \in G_i$ per each labeled query. This process identifies candidate (c, π) tuples, which give high $P(c \leftarrow t; \pi^{-1})$ values, at bounded computation cost. As a second step, $P(c \rightarrow t; \pi)$ feature values are calculated, where useful path features are selected using the *precision* and *coverage* criteria. Further details are discussed in Section 4.4.

4.3 Bi-directional Random Walk Features

The PRA algorithm only uses features of the form $P(s \rightarrow t; \pi)$. In this study we also consider graph walk features in the inverse direction of the form $P(s \leftarrow t; \pi^{-1})$. Similarly, we consider both $P(c \rightarrow t; \pi)$ and $P(c \leftarrow t; \pi^{-1})$. While these path feature pairs represent the same logical expressions, the directional random walk probabilities may greatly differ. For example, it may be highly likely for a random walker to reach a target node representing a sports team t from node s denoting a player over a path π that describes the functional *AthletePlaysForTeam* relation, but unlikely to reach a particular player node s from the multiplayer team t via the reversed path π^{-1}.

In general, there are six types of random walk probabilities that may be modeled as relational features following the introduction of constant paths and inverse path probabilities. The random walk probabilities between s and constant nodes c, $P(s \rightarrow c; \pi)$ and $P(s \leftarrow c; \pi)$, do not directly affect the ranking of candidate target nodes, so we do not use them in this study. It is possible, however, to generate random walk features that combine these probabilities with random walks starting or ending with t through conjunction.

Algorithm 1 Cor-PRA Feature Induction[1]

Input training queries $\{(s_i, G_i)\}, i = 1...n$
for each query (s, G) **do**
  1. Path exploration
  (i). Apply *path-finding* to generate paths $\mathcal{P}_s$ up to length ℓ that originate at s_i.
  (ii). Apply *path-finding* to generate paths $\mathcal{P}_t$ up to length ℓ that originate at every $t_i \in G_i$.
  2. Calculate random walk probabilities:
  for each $\pi_s \in \mathcal{P}_s$: **do**
    compute $P(s \rightarrow x; \pi_s)$ and $P(s \leftarrow x; \pi_s^{-1})$
  end for
  for each $\pi_t \in \mathcal{P}_t$: **do**
    compute $P(G \rightarrow x; \pi_t)$ and $P(G \leftarrow x; \pi_t^{-1})$
  end for
  3. Generate constant paths candidates:
  for each $(x \in N, \pi \in \mathcal{P}_t)$ with $P(G \rightarrow x|\pi_t) > 0$ **do**
    propose path feature $P(c \leftarrow t; \pi_t^{-1})$ setting $c = x$, and update its statistics by $coverage$ += 1.
  end for
  for each $(x \in N, \pi \in \mathcal{P}_t)$ with $P(G \leftarrow x|\pi_t^{-1}) > 0$ **do**
    propose $P(c \rightarrow t; \pi_t)$ setting $c = x$ and update its statistics by $coverage$ += 1
  end for
  4. Generate long (concatenated) path candidates:
  for each $(x \in N, \pi_s \in \mathcal{P}_s, \pi_t \in \mathcal{P}_t)$ with $P(s \rightarrow x|\pi_s) > 0$ and $P(G \leftarrow x|\pi_t^{-1}) > 0$ **do**
    propose long path $P(s \rightarrow t; \pi_s.\pi_t^{-1})$ and update its statistics by $coverage$ += 1, and $precision$ += $P(s \rightarrow x|\pi_s)P(G \leftarrow x|\pi_t^{-1})/n$.
  end for
  for each $(x \in N, \pi_s \in \mathcal{P}_s, \pi_t \in \mathcal{P}_t)$ with $P(s \leftarrow x|\pi_s^{-1}) > 0$ and $P(G \rightarrow x|\pi_t) > 0$ **do**
    propose long path $P(s \leftarrow t; \pi_t.\pi_s^{-1})$ and update its statistics by $coverage$ += 1, and $precision$ += $P(s \leftarrow x|\pi_s^{-1})P(G \rightarrow x|\pi_t)/n$.
  end for
end for

4.4 Cor-PRA feature induction and selection

The proposed feature induction procedure is outlined in Alg. 1. Given labeled node pairs, the particle-filtering path-finding procedure is first applied to identify edge type sequences up to length ℓ that originate at either source nodes s_i or relevant target nodes t_i (step 1). Bi-directional path probabilities are then calculated over these paths, recording the terminal graph nodes x (step 2). Note that since the set of nodes x may be large, path probabilities are all computed with respect to s or t as starting points. As a result of the induction process, candidate relational paths involving constants are identified, and are associated with precision and coverage statistics (step 3). Further, long paths up to length 2ℓ are formed between the source and target nodes as the combination of paths π_s from the source side and path π_t from the target side, updating accuracy and coverage statistics for the concatenated paths $\pi_s\pi_t$

(step 4).

Following feature induction, feature selection is applied. First, random walks are performed for all the training queries, so as to obtain complete (rather than sampled) precision and coverage statistics per path. Then relational paths, which pass respective tuned thresholds are added to the model. We found, however, that applying this strategy for paths with constants often leads to over-fitting. We therefore select only the top K constant features in terms of F_1[2], where K is tuned using training examples.

Finally, at test time, random walk probabilities are calculated for the selected paths, starting from either s or c nodes per query–since the identity of relevant targets t is unknown, but rather has to be revealed.

5 Experiments

In this section, we report the results of applying Cor-PRA to the tasks of knowledge base inference and person named entity extraction from parsed text.

We performed 3-fold cross validation experiments, given datasets of labeled queries. For each query node in the evaluation set, a list of graph nodes ranked by their estimated relevancy to the query node s and relation r is generated. Ideally, relevant nodes should be ranked at the top of these lists. Since the number of correct answers is large for some queries, we report results in terms of mean average precision (MAP), a measure that reflects both precision and recall (Turpin and Scholer, 2006).

The *coverage* and *precision* thresholds of Cor-PRA were set to $h = 2$ and $a = 0.001$ in all of the experiments, following empirical tuning using a small subset of the training data. The particle filtering path-finding algorithm was applied using the parameter setting $w_g = 10^6$, so as to find useful paths with high probability and yet constrain the computational cost.

Our results are compared against the FOIL algorithm[3], which learns first-order horn clauses. In order to evaluate FOIL using MAP, its candidate beliefs are first ranked by the number of FOIL rules they match. We further report results using *Random Walks with Restart* (RWR), also known as personalized PageRank (Haveliwala, 2002), a popular random walk based graph similarity measure, that has been shown to be fairly successful for many types of tasks (e.g., (Agirre and Soroa, 2009; Moro et al., 2014)). Finally, we compare against PRA, which models relational paths in the form of edge-sequences (no constants), using only uni-directional path probabilities, $P(s \to t; \pi)$.

All experiments were run on a machine with a 16 core Intel Xeon 2.33GHz CPU and 24Gb of memory. All methods are trained and tested with the same data splits. We report the total training time of each method, measuring the efficiency of inference and induction as a whole.

Table 1: MAP and training time [sec] on KB inference and NE extraction tasks. $const_i$ denotes constant paths up to length i.

	KB inference		NE extraction	
	Time	MAP	Time	MAP
RWR	25.6	0.429	7,375	0.017
FOIL	18918.1	0.358	366,558	0.167
PRA	10.2	0.477	277	0.107
CoR-PRA-*no-const*	16.7	0.479	449	0.167
CoR-PRA-$const_2$	23.3	0.524	556	0.186
CoR-PRA-$const_3$	27.1	**0.530**	643	**0.316**

5.1 Knowledge Base Inference

We first consider relational inference in the context of NELL, a semantic knowledge base constructed by continually extracting facts from the Web (Carlson et al., 2010b). This work uses a snapshot of the NELL knowledge base graph, which consists of ~1.6M edges comprised of 353 edge types, and ~750K nodes. Following Lao et al. (2011), we test our approach on 16 link prediction tasks, targeting relations such as *Athlete-plays-in-league*, *Team-plays-in-league* and *Competes-with*.

Table 1 reports MAP results and training times for all of the evaluated methods. The maximum path length of RWR, PRA, and CoR-PRA are set to 3 since longer path lengths do not result in better MAPs. As shown, RWR performance is inferior to PRA; unlike the other approaches, RWR is merely associative and does not involve path learning. PRA is significantly faster than FOIL due to its particle filtering approach in feature induction and inference. It also results in a better MAP performance due to its ability to combine random walk features in a discriminative model.

[2] F_1 is the harmonic mean of precision and recall, where the latter is defined as $\frac{coverage}{total\_number\_targets\_in\_training\_queries}$

[3] http://www.rulequest.com/Personal/

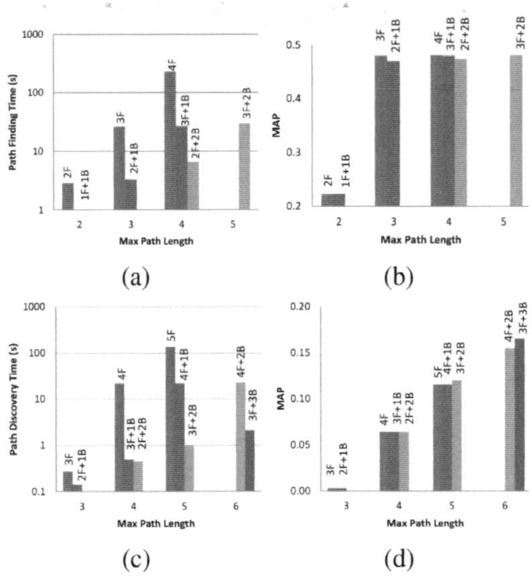

Figure 2: Path finding time (a) and MAP (b) for the KB inference (top) and name extraction (bottom) tasks. A marker $iF + jB$ indicates the maximum path exploration depth i from query node s and j from target node t–so that the combined path length is up to $i + j$. No paths with constants were used.

Table 1 further displays the evaluation results of several variants of CoR-PRA. As shown, modeling features that encode random walk probabilities in both directions (CoR-PRA-*no-const*), yet no paths with constants, requires longer training times, but results in slightly better performance compared with PRA. Note that for a fixed path length, CoR-PRA has "forward" features of the form $P(s \rightarrow t; \pi)$, the probability of reaching target node t from source node s over path π (similarly to PRA), as well as backward features of the form $P(s \leftarrow t; \pi^{-1})$, the probability of reaching s from t over the backward path π^{-1}. As mentioned earlier these probabilities are not the same; for example, a player usually plays for one team, whereas a team is linked to many players.

Performance improves significantly, however, when paths with constants are further added. The table includes our results using constant paths up to length $\ell = 2$ and $\ell = 3$ (denoted as CoR-PRA-$const_\ell$). Based on tuning experiments on one fold of the data, $K = 20$ top-rated constant paths were included in the models.[4] We found that these paths provide informative class priors;

[4] MAP performance peaked at roughly $K = 20$, and gradually decayed as K increased.

Table 2: Example paths with constants learnt for the knowledge base inference tasks. (ϕ denotes empty paths.)

Constant path	Interpretation
r=athletePlaysInLeague	
$P(mlb \rightarrow t; \phi)$	Bias toward *MLB*.
$P(boston\_braves \rightarrow t; \langle athletePlaysForTeam^{-1}, athletePlaysInLeague \rangle)$	The leagues played by *Boston Braves* university team members.
r=competesWith	
$P(google \rightarrow t; \phi)$	Bias toward *Google*.
$P(google \rightarrow t; \langle competesWith, competesWith \rangle)$	Companies which compete with Google's competitors.
r=teamPlaysInLeague	
$P(ncaa \rightarrow t; \phi)$	Bias toward *NCAA*.
$P(boise\_state \rightarrow t; \langle teamPlaysInLeague \rangle)$	The leagues played by *Boise State* university teams.

example paths and their interpretation are included in Table 2.

Figure 2(a) shows the effect of increasing the maximal path length on path finding and selection time. The leftmost (blue) bars show baseline performance of PRA, where only forward random walks are applied. It is clearly demonstrated that the time spent on path finding grows exponentially with ℓ. Due to memory limitations, we were able to execute forward-walk models only up to 4 steps. The bars denoted by $iF + jB$ show the results of combining forward walks up to length i with backward walks of up to $j = 1$ or $j = 2$ steps. Time complexity using bidirectional random walks is dominated by the longest path segment (either forward or backward)—e.g., the settings $3F$, $3F + 1B$, $3F + 2B$ have similar time complexity. Using bidirectional search, we were able to consider relational paths up to length 5. Figure 2(b) presents MAP performance, where it is shown that extending the maximal explored path length did not improve performance in this case. This result indicates that meaningful paths in this domain are mostly short. Accordingly, path length was set to 3 in the respective main experiments.

5.2 Named Entity Extraction

We further consider the task of named entity extraction from a corpus of parsed texts, following previous work by Minkov and Cohen (2008).

In this case, an entity-relation graph schema is used to represent a corpus of parsed sentences, as illustrated in Figure 3. Graph nodes denoting word mentions (in round edged boxes) are linked over edges typed with dependency relations. The parsed sentence structures are connected via nodes that denote word lemmas, where every word lemma is linked to all of its mentions in the corpus via the special edge type W. We represent part-of-speech tags as another set of graph nodes, where word mentions are connected to the relevant tag over POS edge type.

In this graph, task-specific word similarity measures can be derived based on the lexico-syntactic paths that connect word types (Minkov and Cohen, 2014). The task defined in the experiments is to retrieve a ranked list of *person names* given a small set of seeds. This task is implemented in the graph as a query, where we let the query distribution be uniform over the given seeds (and zero elsewhere). That is, our goal is to find target nodes that are related to the query nodes over the relation r =*similar-to*, or, *coordinate-term*. We apply link prediction in this case with the expected result of generating a ranked list of graph nodes, which is populated with many additional person names. The named entity extraction task we consider is somewhat similar to the one adopted by FIGER (Ling and Weld, 2012), in that a finer-grain category is being assigned to proposed named entities. Our approach follows however set expansion settings (Wang and Cohen, 2007), where the goal is to find new instances of the specified type from parsed text.

In the experiments, we use the training set portion of the MUC-6 data set (MUC, 1995), represented as a graph of 153k nodes and 748K edges. We generated 30 labeled queries, each comprised of 4 person names selected randomly from the person names mentioned in the data set. The MUC corpus is fully annotated with entity names, so that relevant target nodes (other person names) were readily sampled. Extraction performance was evaluated considering the tagged *person names*, which were not included in the query, as the correct answer set. The maximum path length of RWR, PRA, and CoR-PRA are set to 6 due to memory limitation.

Table 1 shows that PRA is much faster than RWR or FOIL on this data set, giving competitive MAP performance to FOIL. RWR is generally ineffective on this task, because similarity in this domain is represented by a relatively small set of long paths, whereas RWR express local node associations in the

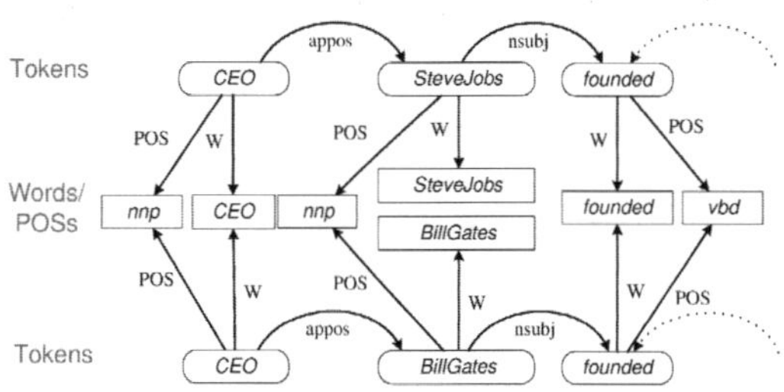

Figure 3: Part of a typed graph representing a corpus of parsed sentences.

Table 3: Highly weighted paths with constants learnt for the person name extraction task.

Constant path	Interpretation
$P(said \leftarrow t; W^{-1}, nsubj, W)$	The subjects of 'said' or 'say'
$P(says \leftarrow t; W^{-1}, nsubj, W)$	are likely to be a person name.
$P(vbg \leftarrow t; POS^{-1}, nsubj, W)$	Subjects, proper nouns, and
$P(nnp \leftarrow t; POS^{-1}, W)$	nouns with apposition or
$P(nn \leftarrow t; POS^{-1}, appos^{-1}, W)$	possessive constructions, are
$P(nn \leftarrow t; POS^{-1}, poss, W)$	likely to be person names.

graph (Minkov and Cohen, 2008). Modeling inverse path probabilities improves performance substantially, and adding relational features with constants boosts performance further. The constant paths learned encode lexical features, as well as provide useful priors, mainly over different part-of-speech tags. Example constant paths that were highly weighted in the learned models and their interpretation are given in Table 3.

Figure 2(c) shows the effect of modeling long relational paths using bidirectional random walks in the language domain. Here, forward path finding was applied to paths up to length 5 due to memory limitation. The figure displays the results of exploring paths up to a total length of 6 edges, performing backward search from the target nodes of up to $j = 1, 2, 3$ steps. MAP performance (Figure 2(d)) using paths of varying lengths shows significant improvements as the path length increases. Top weighted long features include:

$P(s \rightarrow t; W^{-1}, conj\_and^{-1}, W, W^{-1}, conj\_and, W)$

$P(s \rightarrow t; W^{-1}, nn, W, W^{-1}, appos^{-1}, W)$

$P(s \rightarrow t; W^{-1}, appos, W, W^{-1}, appos^{-1}, W)$

These paths are similar to the top ranked paths found in previous work (Minkov and Cohen, 2008). In comparison, their results on this dataset using paths of up to 6 steps measured 0.09 in MAP. Our results reach roughly 0.16 in MAP due to modeling of inverse paths; and, when constant paths are incorporated, MAP reaches 0.32.

Interestingly, in this domain, FOIL generates fewer yet more complex rules, which are characterised with low recall and high precision, such as: $W(B, A) \wedge POS(B, nnp) \wedge nsubj(D, B) \wedge W(D, said) \wedge appos(B, F) \rightarrow person(A)$. Note that subsets of these rules, namely, $POS(B, nnp)$, $nsubj(D, B) \wedge W(D, said)$ and $appos(B, F)$ have been discovered by PRA as individual features assigned with high weights (Table 3). This indicates an interesting future work, where products of random walk features can be used to express their conjunctions.

6 Conclusion

We have introduced CoR-PRA, extending an existing random walk based relational learning paradigm to consider relational paths with constants, bi-directional path features, as well as long paths. Our experiments on knowledge base inference and person name extraction tasks show significant improvements over previously published results, while maintaining efficiency. An interesting future direction is to use products of these random walk features to express their conjunctions.

Acknowledgments

We thank the reviewers for their helpful feedback. This work was supported in part by BSF grant No. 2010090 and a grant from Google Research.

References

Eneko Agirre and Aitor Soroa. 2009. Personalizing pagerank for word sense disambiguation. In *Proceedings of the 12th Conference of the European Chapter of the Association for Computational Linguistics.*

Kurt Bollacker, Colin Evans, Praveen Paritosh, Tim Sturge, and Jamie Taylor. 2008. Freebase: a collaboratively created graph database for structuring human knowledge. In *Proceedings of the 2008 ACM SIGMOD international conference on Management of data*, pages 1247–1250. ACM.

A. Carlson, J. Betteridge, B. Kisiel, B. Settles, E. Hruschka Jr., and T. Mitchell. 2010a. Toward an architecture for never-ending language learning. In *AAAI*.

Andrew Carlson, Justin Betteridge, Bryan Kisiel, Burr Settles, Estevam R. Hruschka Jr., and Tom M. Mitchell. 2010b. Toward an Architecture for Never-Ending Language Learning. In *AAAI*.

Xin Dong, Evgeniy Gabrilovich, Geremy Heitz, Wilko Horn, Ni Lao, Kevin Murphy, Thomas Strohmann, Shaohua Sun, and Wei Zhang. 2014. Knowledge vault: a web-scale approach to probabilistic knowledge fusion. In *The 20th ACM SIGKDD International Conference on Knowledge Discovery and Data Mining, KDD '14, New York, NY, USA - August 24 - 27, 2014*, pages 601–610.

Matt Gardner, Partha Pratim Talukdar, Bryan Kisiel, and Tom Mitchell. 2013. Improving learning and inference in a large knowledge-base using latent syntactic cues. In *EMNLP*.

Matt Gardner, Partha Talukdar, Jayant Krishnamurthy, and Tom Mitchell. 2014. Incorporating Vector Space Similarity in Random Walk Inference over Knowledge Bases. In *EMNLP*.

Taher H. Haveliwala. 2002. Topic-sensitive pagerank. In *WWW*, pages 517–526.

Ondřej Kuželka and Filip Železný. 2008. A restarted strategy for efficient subsumption testing. *Fundam. Inf.*, 89(1):95–109, January.

Ondřej Kuželka and Filip Železný. 2009. Block-wise construction of acyclic relational features with monotone irreducibility and relevancy properties. In *Proceedings of the 26th Annual International Conference on Machine Learning*, ICML '09, pages 569–576, New York, NY, USA. ACM.

Ni Lao and William W. Cohen. 2010a. Fast query execution for retrieval models based on path-constrained random walks. In *Proceedings of the 16th ACM SIGKDD International Conference on Knowledge Discovery and Data Mining*, KDD '10, pages 881–888, New York, NY, USA. ACM.

Ni Lao and William W. Cohen. 2010b. Relational retrieval using a combination of path-constrained random walks. In *Machine Learning*, volume 81, pages 53–67, July.

Ni Lao, Tom M. Mitchell, and William W. Cohen. 2011. Random Walk Inference and Learning in A Large Scale Knowledge Base. In *EMNLP*, pages 529–539.

Ni Lao, Amarnag Subramanya, Fernando Pereira, and William W. Cohen. 2012. Reading the web with learned syntactic-semantic inference rules. In *Proceedings of the 2012 Joint Conference on Empirical Methods in Natural Language Processing and Computational Natural Language Learning*, EMNLP-CoNLL '12, pages 1017–1026, Stroudsburg, PA, USA. Association for Computational Linguistics.

X. Ling and D.S. Weld. 2012. Fine-grained entity recognition. In *Proceedings of the 26th Conference on Artificial Intelligence (AAAI)*.

Einat Minkov and William W Cohen. 2008. Learning Graph Walk Based Similarity Measures for Parsed Text. *EMNLP*.

Einat Minkov and William W. Cohen. 2014. Adaptive graph walk-based similarity measures for parsed text. *Natural Language Engineering*, 20(3).

Andrea Moro, Alessandro Raganato, and Roberto Navigli. 2014. Entity Linking meets Word Sense Disambiguation: a Unified Approach. *Transactions of the Association for Computational Linguistics (TACL)*, 2.

1995. *MUC6 '95: Proceedings of the 6th Conference on Message Understanding*, Stroudsburg, PA, USA. Association for Computational Linguistics.

Michael Pazzani, Cliff Brunk, and Glenn Silverstein. 1991. A Knowledge-Intensive Approach to Learning Relational Concepts. In *Proceedings of the Eighth International Workshop on Machine Learning*, pages 432–436. Morgan Kaufmann.

J. Ross Quinlan and R. Mike Cameron-Jones. 1993. FOIL: A Midterm Report. In *ECML*, pages 3–20.

B L Richards and R J Mooney. 1991. First-Order Theory Revision. In *Proceedings of the 8th International Workshop on Machine Learning*, pages 447–451. Morgan Kaufmann.

Michele Sebag and Celine Rouveirol. 1997. Tractable induction and classification in first order logic via stochastic matching. In *Proceedings of the Fifteenth International Joint Conference on Artifical Intelligence - Volume 2*, IJCAI'97, pages 888–893, San Francisco, CA, USA. Morgan Kaufmann Publishers Inc.

Ashwin Srinivasan. 2001. The Aleph Manual. In *http://web.comlab.ox.ac.uk/oucl/research/areas/machlearn/Aleph/*.

F. Suchanek, G. Kasneci, and G. Weikum. 2007. YAGO - A Core of Semantic Knowledge. In *WWW*.

Andrew Turpin and Falk Scholer. 2006. User performance versus precision measures for simple search tasks. In *PProceedings of the international ACM SIGIR conference on Research and development in information retrieval (SIGIR)*.

Filip Železný and Nada Lavrač. 2006. Propositionalization-based relational subgroup discovery with rsd. *Mach. Learn.*, 62(1-2):33–63, February.

Richard C Wang and William W Cohen. 2007. Language-independent set expansion of named entities using the web. In *Proceedings of the IEEE International Conference on Data Mining (ICDM)*.

William Yang Wang, Kathryn Mazaitis, and William W Cohen. 2013. Programming with personalized pagerank: A locally groundable first-order probabilistic logic. *Proceedings of the 22nd ACM International Conference on Information and Knowledge Management (CIKM 2013)*.

Learning the Semantics of Manipulation Action

Yezhou Yang[†] and **Yiannis Aloimonos**[†] and **Cornelia Fermüller**[†] and **Eren Erdal Aksoy**[‡]
[†] UMIACS, University of Maryland, College Park, MD, USA
{yzyang, yiannis, fer}@umiacs.umd.edu
[‡] Karlsruhe Institute of Technology, Karlsruhe, Germany
eren.aksoy@kit.edu

Abstract

In this paper we present a formal computational framework for modeling manipulation actions. The introduced formalism leads to semantics of manipulation action and has applications to both observing and understanding human manipulation actions as well as executing them with a robotic mechanism (e.g. a humanoid robot). It is based on a Combinatory Categorial Grammar. The goal of the introduced framework is to: (1) represent manipulation actions with both syntax and semantic parts, where the semantic part employs λ-calculus; (2) enable a probabilistic semantic parsing schema to learn the $lambda$-calculus representation of manipulation action from an annotated action corpus of videos; (3) use (1) and (2) to develop a system that visually observes manipulation actions and understands their meaning while it can reason beyond observations using propositional logic and axiom schemata. The experiments conducted on a public available large manipulation action dataset validate the theoretical framework and our implementation.

1 Introduction

Autonomous robots will need to learn the actions that humans perform. They will need to recognize these actions when they see them and they will need to perform these actions themselves. This requires a formal system to represent the action semantics. This representation needs to store the semantic information about the actions, be encoded in a machine readable language, and inherently be in a programmable fashion in order to enable reasoning beyond observation. A formal representation of this kind has a variety of other applications such as intelligent manufacturing, human robot collaboration, action planning and policy design, etc.

In this paper, we are concerned with manipulation actions, that is actions performed by agents (humans or robots) on objects, resulting in some physical change of the object. However most of the current AI systems require manually defined semantic rules. In this work, we propose a computational linguistics framework, which is based on probabilistic semantic parsing with Combinatory Categorial Grammar (CCG), to learn manipulation action semantics (lexicon entries) from annotations. We later show that this learned lexicon is able to make our system reason about manipulation action goals beyond just observation. Thus the intelligent system can not only imitate human movements, but also imitate action goals.

Understanding actions by observation and executing them are generally considered as dual problems for intelligent agents. The sensori-motor bridge connecting the two tasks is essential, and a great amount of attention in AI, Robotics as well as Neurophysiology has been devoted to investigating it. Experiments conducted on primates have discovered that certain neurons, the so-called mirror neurons, fire during both observation and execution of identical manipulation tasks (Rizzolatti et al., 2001; Gazzola et al., 2007). This suggests that the same process is involved in both the observation and execution of actions. From a functionalist point of view, such a process should be able to first build up a semantic structure from observations, and then the decomposition of that same structure should occur when the intelligent agent executes commands.

Additionally, studies in linguistics (Steedman, 2002) suggest that the language faculty develops in humans as a direct adaptation of a more primitive apparatus for planning goal-directed action in the world by composing affordances of tools and consequences of actions. It is this more primitive

Proceedings of the 53rd Annual Meeting of the Association for Computational Linguistics and the 7th International Joint Conference on Natural Language Processing, pages 676–686,
Beijing, China, July 26-31, 2015.

apparatus that is our major interest in this paper. Such an apparatus is composed of a "syntax part" and a "semantic part". In the syntax part, every linguistic element is categorized as either a function or a basic type, and is associated with a syntactic category which either identifies it as a function or a basic type. In the semantic part, a semantic translation is attached following the syntactic category explicitly.

Combinatory Categorial Grammar (CCG) introduced by (Steedman, 2000) is a theory that can be used to represent such structures with a small set of combinators such as functional application and type-raising. What do we gain though from such a formal description of action? This is similar to asking what one gains from a formal description of language as a generative system. Chomskys contribution to language research was exactly this: the formal description of language through the formulation of the Generative and Transformational Grammar (Chomsky, 1957). It revolutionized language research opening up new roads for the computational analysis of language, providing researchers with common, generative language structures and syntactic operations, on which language analysis tools were built. A grammar for action would contribute to providing a common framework of the syntax and semantics of action, so that basic tools for action understanding can be built, tools that researchers can use when developing action interpretation systems, without having to start development from scratch. The same tools can be used by robots to execute actions.

In this paper, we propose an approach for learning the semantic meaning of manipulation action through a probabilistic semantic parsing framework based on CCG theory. For example, we want to learn from an annotated training action corpus that the action "Cut" is a function which has two arguments: a subject and a patient. Also, the action consequence of "Cut" is a separation of the patient. Using formal logic representation, our system will learn the semantic representations of "Cut":

$$Cut := (AP\backslash NP)/NP : \lambda x.\lambda y.cut(x, y) \rightarrow divided(y)$$

Here $cut(x, y)$ is a primitive function. We will further introduce the representation in Sec. 3. Since our action representation is in a common calculus form, it enables naturally further logical reasoning beyond visual observation.

The advantage of our approach is twofold: 1) Learning semantic representations from annotations helps an intelligent agent to enrich automatically its own knowledge about actions; 2) The formal logic representation of the action could be used to infer the object-wise consequence after a certain manipulation, and can also be used to plan a set of actions to reach a certain action goal. We further validate our approach on a large publicly available manipulation action dataset (MANIAC) from (Aksoy et al., 2014), achieving promising experimental results. Moreover, we believe that our work, even though it only considers the domain of manipulation actions, is also a promising example of a more closely intertwined computer vision and computational linguistics system. The diagram in Fig.1 depicts the framework of the system.

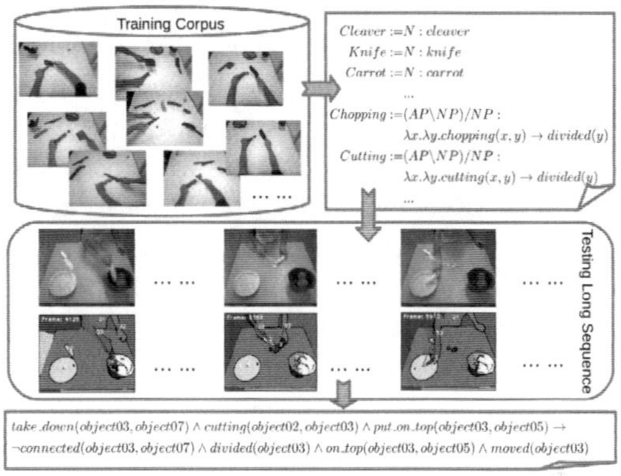

Figure 1: A CCG based semantic parsing framework for manipulation actions.

2 Related Works

Reasoning beyond appearance: The very small number of works in computer vision, which aim to reason beyond appearance models, are also related to this paper. (Xie et al., 2013) proposed that beyond state-of-the-art computer vision techniques, we could possibly infer implicit information (such as functional objects) from video, and they call them "Dark Matter" and "Dark Energy". (Yang et al., 2013) used stochastic tracking and graph-cut based segmentation to infer manipulation consequences beyond appearance. (Joo et al., 2014) used a ranking SVM to predict the persuasive motivation (or the intention) of the photographer who captured an image. More recently, (Pirsiavash et al., 2014) seeks to infer the motivation of the person in the image by mining knowledge stored in a large corpus using natural language processing techniques. Different from these fairly general investigations about reasoning beyond appearance, our paper seeks to learn manipulation actions semantics in logic forms through CCG, and further infer hidden action consequences beyond appearance through reasoning.

Action Recognition and Understanding: Human activity recognition and understanding has been studied heavily in Computer Vision recently, and there is a large range of applications for this work in areas like human-computer interactions, biometrics, and video surveillance. Both visual recognition methods, and the non-visual description methods using motion capture systems have been used. A few good surveys of the former can be found in (Moeslund et al., 2006) and (Turaga et al., 2008). Most of the focus has been on recognizing single human actions like walking, jumping, or running etc. (Ben-Arie et al., 2002; Yilmaz and Shah, 2005). Approaches to more complex actions have employed parametric approaches, such as HMMs (Kale et al., 2004) to learn the transition between feature representations in individual frames e.g. (Saisan et al., 2001; Chaudhry et al., 2009). More recently, (Aksoy et al., 2011; Aksoy et al., 2014) proposed a semantic event chain (SEC) representation to model and learn the semantic segment-wise relationship transition from spatial-temporal video segmentation.

There also have been many syntactic approaches to human activity recognition which used the concept of context-free grammars, because such grammars provide a sound theoretical basis for modeling structured processes. Tracing back to the middle 90's, (Brand, 1996) used a grammar to recognize disassembly tasks that contain hand manipulations. (Ryoo and Aggarwal, 2006) used the context-free grammar formalism to recognize composite human activities and multi-person interactions. It is a two level hierarchical approach where the lower-levels are composed of HMMs and Bayesian Networks while the higher-level interactions are modeled by CFGs. To deal with errors from low-level processes such as tracking, stochastic grammars such as stochastic CFGs were also used (Ivanov and Bobick, 2000; Moore and Essa, 2002). More recently, (Kuehne et al., 2014) proposed to model goal-directed human activities using Hidden Markov Models and treat subactions just like words in speech. These works proved that grammar based approaches are practical in activity recognition systems, and shed insight onto human manipulation action understanding. However, as mentioned, thinking about manipulation actions solely from the viewpoint of recognition has obvious limitations. In this work we adopt principles from CFG based activity recognition systems, with extensions to a CCG grammar that accommodates not only the hierarchical structure of human activity but also action semantics representations. It enables the system to serve as the core parsing engine for both manipulation action recognition and execution.

Manipulation Action Grammar: As mentioned before, (Chomsky, 1993) suggested that a minimalist generative grammar, similar to the one of human language, also exists for action understanding and execution. The works closest related to this paper are (Pastra and Aloimonos, 2012; Summers-Stay et al., 2013; Guha et al., 2013). (Pastra and Aloimonos, 2012) first discussed a Chomskyan grammar for understanding complex actions as a theoretical concept, and (Summers-Stay et al., 2013) provided an implementation of such a grammar using as perceptual input only objects. More recently, (Yang et al., 2014) proposed a set of context-free grammar rules for manipulation action understanding, and (Yang et al., 2015) applied it on unconstrained instructional videos. However, these approaches only consider the syntactic structure of manipulation actions without coupling semantic rules using λ expressions, which limits the capability of doing reasoning and prediction.

Combinatory Categorial Grammar and Semantic Parsing: CCG based semantic parsing originally was used mainly to translate natural language sentences to their desired semantic representations as λ-calculus formulas (Zettlemoyer and Collins, 2005; Zettlemoyer and Collins, 2007). (Mooney, 2008) presented a framework of grounded language acquisition: the interpretation of language entities into semantically informed structures in the context of perception and actuation. The concept has been applied successfully in tasks such as robot navigation (Matuszek et al., 2011), forklift operation (Tellex et al., 2014) and of human-robot interaction (Matuszek et al., 2014). In this work, instead of grounding natural language sentences directly, we ground information obtained from visual perception into semantically informed structures, specifically in the domain of manipulation actions.

3 A CCG Framework for Manipulation Actions

Before we dive into the semantic parsing of manipulation actions, a brief introduction to the Combinatory Categorial Grammar framework in Linguistics is necessary. We will only introduce related concepts and formalisms. For a complete background reading, we would like to refer readers to (Steedman, 2000). We will first give a brief introduction to CCG and then introduce a fundamental combinator, i.e., functional application. The introduction is followed by examples to show how the combinator is applied to parse actions.

3.1 Manipulation Action Semantics

The semantic expression in our representation of manipulation actions uses a typed λ-calculus language. The formal system has two basic types: entities and functions. Entities in manipulation actions are Objects or Hands, and functions are the Actions. Our $lambda$-calculus expressions are formed from the following items:

Constants: Constants can be either entities or functions. For example, *Knife* is an entity (i.e., it is of type N) and *Cucumber* is an entity too (i.e., it is of type N). *Cut* is an action function that maps entities to entities. When the event *Knife Cut Cucumber* happened, the expression *cut(Knife, Cucumber)* returns an entity of type AP, aka. Action Phrase. Constants like *divided* are status functions that map entities to truth values. The expression $divided(cucumber)$ returns a true value after the event (*Knife Cut Cucumber*) happened.

Logical connectors: The λ-calculus expression has logical connectors like conjunction ($\wedge$), disjunction ($\vee$), negation($\neg$) and implication($\rightarrow$).

For example, the expression

$$connected(tomato, cucumber) \wedge$$
$$divided(tomato) \wedge divided(cucumber)$$

represents the joint status that the sliced *tomato* merged with the sliced *cucumber*. It can be regarded as a simplified goal status for "making a cucumber tomato salad". The expression $\neg connected(spoon, bowl)$ represents the status after the *spoon* finished stirring the *bowl*.

$$\lambda x.cut(x, cucumber) \rightarrow divided(cucumber)$$

represents that if the *cucumber* is cut by x, then the status of the *cucumber* is divided.

λ **expressions**: $lambda$ expressions represent functions with unknown arguments. For example, $\lambda x.cut(knife, x)$ is a function from entities to entities, which is of type NP after any entities of type N that is cut by *knife*.

3.2 Combinatory Categorial Grammar

The semantic parsing formalism underlying our framework for manipulation actions is that of combinatory categorial grammar (CCG) (Steedman, 2000). A CCG specifies one or more logical forms for each element or combination of elements for manipulation actions. In our formalism, an element of Action is associated with a syntactic "category" which identifies it as functions, and specifies the type and directionality of their arguments and the type of their result. For example, action "Cut" is a function from patient object phrase (NP) on the right into predicates, and into functions from subject object phrase (NP) on the left into a sub action phrase (AP):

$$Cut := (AP \backslash NP)/NP. \quad (1)$$

As a matter of fact, the pure categorial grammar is a conext-free grammar presented in the accepting, rather than the producing direction. The expression (1) is just an accepting form for Action "Cut" following the context-free grammar. While it is now convenient to write derivations as follows, they are equivalent to conventional tree structure derivations in Figure. 3.2.

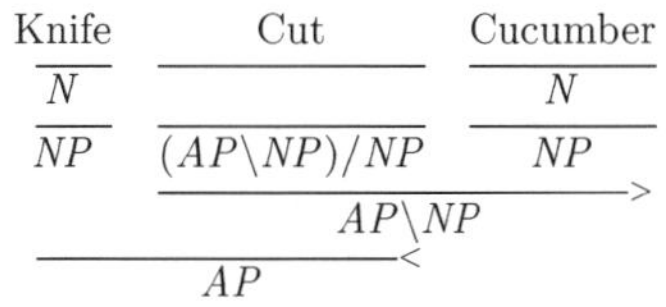

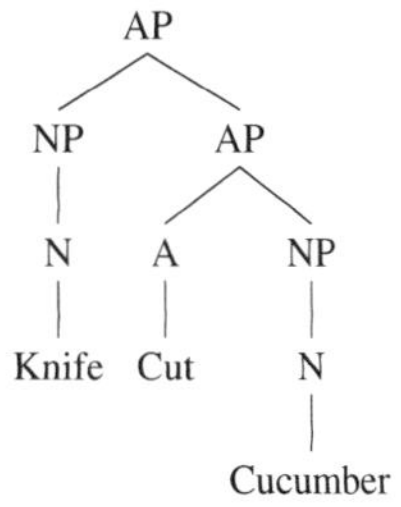

Figure 2: Example of conventional tree structure.

The semantic type is encoded in these categories, and their translation can be made explicit in an expanded notation. Basically a λ-calculus expression is attached with the syntactic category. A colon operator is used to separate syntactical and semantic expressions, and the right side of the colon is assumed to have lower precedence than the left side of the colon. Which is intuitive as any explanation of manipulation actions should first obey syntactical rules, then semantic rules. Now the basic element, Action "Cut", can be further represented by:

$$Cut := (AP\backslash NP)/NP : \lambda x.\lambda y.cut(x,y) \rightarrow divided(y).$$

$(AP\backslash NP)/NP$ denotes a phrase of type AP, which requires an element of type NP to specify what object was cut, and requires another element of type NP to further complement what effector initiates the cut action. $\lambda x.\lambda y.cut(x,y)$ is the λ-calculus representation for this function. Since the functions are closely related to the state update, $\rightarrow divided(y)$ further points out the status expression after the action was performed.

A CCG system has a set of combinatory rules which describe how adjacent syntatic categories in a string can be recursively combined. In the setting of manipulation actions, we want to point out that similar combinatory rules are also applicable. Especially the functional application rules are essential in our system.

3.3 Functional application

The functional application rules with semantics can be expressed in the following form:

$$A/B : f \quad B : g => A : f(g) \tag{2}$$

$$B : g \quad A\backslash B : f => A : f(g) \tag{3}$$

Rule. (2) says that a string with type A/B can be combined with a right-adjacent string of type B to form a new string of type A. At the same time, it also specifies how the semantics of the category A can be compositionally built out of the semantics for A/B and B. Rule. (3) is a symmetric form of Rule. (2).

In the domain of manipulation actions, following derivation is an example CCG parse. This parse shows how the system can parse an observation ("Knife Cut Cucumber") into a semantic representation $(cut(knife, cucumber) \rightarrow divided(cucumber))$ using the functional application rules.

$$\begin{array}{ccc}
\text{Knife} & \text{Cut} & \text{Cucumber} \\
\hline
N & & N \\
\hline
NP & (AP\backslash NP)/NP & NP \\
knife & \lambda x.\lambda y.cut(x,y) & cucumber \\
knife & \rightarrow divided(y) & cucumber \\
\hline
& \multicolumn{2}{c}{AP\backslash NP \quad (>)} \\
& \multicolumn{2}{c}{\lambda x.cut(x, cucumber)} \\
& \multicolumn{2}{c}{\rightarrow divided(cucumber)} \\
\hline
\multicolumn{3}{c}{AP \quad (<)} \\
\multicolumn{3}{c}{cut(knife, cucumber)} \\
\multicolumn{3}{c}{\rightarrow divided(cucumber)}
\end{array}$$

4 Learning Model and Semantic Parsing

After having defined the formalism and application rule, instead of manually writing down all the possible CCG representations for each entity, we would like to apply a learning technique to derive them from the paired training corpus. Here we adopt the learning model of (Zettlemoyer and Collins, 2005), and use it to assign weights to the semantic representation of actions. Since an action may have multiple possible syntactic and semantic representations assigned to it, we use the probabilistic model to assign weights to these representations.

4.1 Learning Approach

First we assume that complete syntactic parses of the observed action are available, and in fact a manipulation action can have several different parses. The parsing uses a probabilistic combinatorial categorial grammar framework similar to the one given by (Zettlemoyer and Collins, 2007). We assume a probabilistic categorial grammar (PCCG) based on a log linear model. M denotes a manipulation task, L denotes the semantic representation of the task, and T denotes its parse tree. The probability of a particular syntactic and semantic parse is given as:

$$P(L, T|M; \Theta) = \frac{e^{f(L,T,M)\cdot\Theta}}{\sum_{(L,T)} e^{f(L,T,M)\cdot\Theta}} \tag{4}$$

where f is a mapping of the triple (L, T, M) to feature vectors $\in R^d$, and the $\Theta \in R^d$ represents the weights to be learned. Here we use only lexical features, where each feature counts the number of times a lexical entry is used in T. Parsing a manipulation task under PCCG equates to finding L such that $P(L|M; \Theta)$ is maximized:

$$\begin{aligned} & argmax_L P(L|M; \Theta) \\ = & argmax_L \sum_T P(L, T|M; \Theta). \end{aligned} \tag{5}$$

We use dynamic programming techniques to calculate the most probable parse for the manipulation task. In this paper, the implementation from (Baral et al., 2011) is adopted, where an inverse-λ technique is used to generalize new semantic representations. The generalization of lexicon rules are essential for our system to deal with unknown actions presented during the testing phase.

5 Experiments

5.1 Manipulation Action (MANIAC) Dataset

(Aksoy et al., 2014) provides a manipulation action dataset with 8 different manipulation actions (cutting, chopping, stirring, putting, taking, hiding, uncovering, and pushing), each of which consists of 15 different versions performed by 5 different human actors[1]. There are in total 30 different objects manipulated in all demonstrations. All manipulations were recorded with the Microsoft Kinect sensor and serve as **training** data here.

The MANIAC data set contains another 20 long and complex chained manipulation sequences (e.g. "making a sandwich") which consist of a total of 103 different versions of these 8 manipulation tasks performed in different orders with novel objects under different circumstances. These serve as **testing** data for our experiments.

(Aksoy et al., 2014; Aksoy and Wörgötter, 2015) developed a semantic event chain based model free decomposition approach. It is an unsupervised probabilistic method that measures the frequency of the changes in the spatial relations embedded in event chains, in order to extract the subject and patient visual segments. It also decomposes the long chained complex testing actions into their primitive action components according to the spatio-temporal relations of the manipulator. Since the visual recognition is not the core of this work, we omit the details here and refer the interested reader to (Aksoy et al., 2014; Aksoy and Wörgötter, 2015). All these features make the MANIAC dataset a great testing bed for both the theoretical framework and the implemented system presented in this work.

5.2 Training Corpus

We first created a training corpus by annotating the 120 training clips from the MANIAC dataset, in the format of observed triplets (subject action patient) and a corresponding semantic representation of the action as well as its consequence. The semantic representations in λ-calculus format are given by human annotators after watching each action clip. A set of sample training pairs are given in Table.1 (one from each action category in the training set). Since every training clip contains one single full execution of each manipulation action considered, the training corpus thus has a total of 120 paired training samples.

Snapshot	triplet	semantic representation
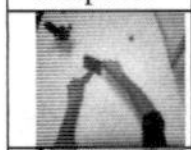	cleaver chopping carrot	$chopping(cleaver, carrot)$ $\rightarrow divided(carrot)$
	spatula cutting pepper	$cutting(spatula, pepper)$ $\rightarrow divided(pepper)$
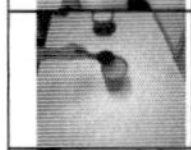	spoon stirring bucket	$stirring(spoon, bucket)$
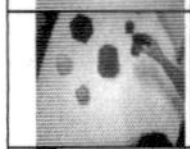	cup take_down bucket	$take\_down(cup, bucket)$ $\rightarrow \neg connected(cup, bucket)$ $\wedge moved(cup)$
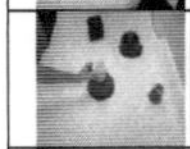	cup put_on_top bowl	$put\_on\_top(cup, bowl)$ $\rightarrow on\_top(cup, bowl)$ $\wedge moved(cup)$
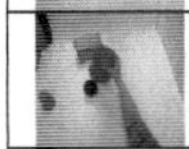	bucket hiding ball	$hiding(bucket, ball)$ $\rightarrow contained(bucket, ball)$ $\wedge moved(bucket)$
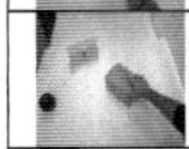	hand pushing box	$pushing(hand, box)$ $\rightarrow moved(box)$
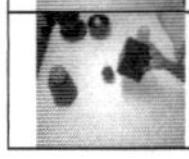	box uncover apple	$uncover(box, apple)$ $\rightarrow appear(apple)$ $\wedge moved(box)$

Table 1: Example annotations from training corpus, one per manipulation action category.

We also assume the system knows that every "object" involved in the corpus is an entity of its own type, for example:

$$Knife := N : knife$$
$$Bowl := N : bowl$$
$$......$$

Additionally, we assume the syntactic form of each "action" has a main type $(AP\backslash NP)/NP$ (see Sec. 3.2). These two sets of rules form the initial seed lexicon for learning.

5.3 Learned Lexicon

We applied the learning technique mentioned in Sec. 4, and we used the NL2KR implementation from (Baral et al., 2011). The system learns and generalizes a set of lexicon entries (syntactic and semantic) for each action categories from the training corpus accompanied with a set of weights.

[1]Dataset available for download at `https://fortknox.physik3.gwdg.de/cns/index.php?page=maniac-dataset`.

We list the one with the largest weight for each action here respectively:

$$\begin{aligned}
Chopping &:= (AP\backslash NP)/NP : \lambda x.\lambda y.chopping(x,y) \\
&\quad \rightarrow divided(y) \\
Cutting &:= (AP\backslash NP)/NP : \lambda x.\lambda y.cutting(x,y) \\
&\quad \rightarrow divided(y) \\
Stirring &:= (AP\backslash NP)/NP : \lambda x.\lambda y.stirring(x,y) \\
Take_down &:= (AP\backslash NP)/NP : \lambda x.\lambda y.take_down(x,y) \\
&\quad \rightarrow \neg connected(x,y) \wedge moved(x) \\
Put_on_top &:= (AP\backslash NP)/NP : \lambda x.\lambda y.put_on_top(x,y) \\
&\quad \rightarrow on_top(x,y) \wedge moved(x) \\
Hiding &:= (AP\backslash NP)/NP : \lambda x.\lambda y.hiding(x,y) \\
&\quad \rightarrow contained(x,y) \wedge moved(x) \\
Pushing &:= (AP\backslash NP)/NP : \lambda x.\lambda y.pushing(x,y) \\
&\quad \rightarrow moved(y) \\
Uncover &:= (AP\backslash NP)/NP : \lambda x.\lambda y.uncover(x,y) \\
&\quad \rightarrow appear(y) \wedge moved(x).
\end{aligned}$$

The set of seed lexicon and the learned lexicon entries are further used to probabilistically parse the detected triplet sequences from the 20 long manipulation activities in the testing set.

5.4 Deducing Semantics

Using the decomposition technique from (Aksoy et al., 2014; Aksoy and Wörgötter, 2015), the reported system is able to detect a sequence of action triplets in the form of (Subject Action Patient) from each of the testing sequence in MANIAC dataset. Briefly speaking, the event chain representation (Aksoy et al., 2011) of the observed long manipulation activity is first scanned to estimate the main manipulator, i.e. the hand, and manipulated objects, e.g. knife, in the scene without employing any visual feature-based object recognition method. Solely based on the interactions between the hand and manipulated objects in the scene, the event chain is partitioned into chunks. These chunks are further fragmented into subunits to detect parallel action streams. Each parsed Semantic Event Chain (SEC) chunk is then compared with the model SECs in the library to decide whether the current SEC sample belongs to one of the known manipulation models or represents a novel manipulation. SEC models, stored in the library, are learned in an on-line unsupervised fashion using the semantics of manipulations derived from a given set of training data in order to create a large vocabulary of single atomic manipulations.

For the different testing sequence, the number of triplets detected ranges from two to seven. In total, we are able to collect 90 testing detections and they serve as the testing corpus. However, since many of the objects used in the testing data are not present in the training set, an object model-free approach is adopted and thus "subject" and "patient" fields are filled with segment IDs instead of a specific object name. Fig. 3 and 4 show several examples of the detected triplets accompanied with a set of key frames from the testing sequences. Nevertheless, the method we used here can 1) generalize the unknown segments into the category of object entities and 2) generalize the unknown actions (those that do not exist in the training corpus) into the category of action function. This is done by automatically generalizing the following two types of lexicon entries using the inverse-λ technique from (Baral et al., 2011):

$$\begin{aligned}
Object_[ID] &:= N : object_[ID] \\
Unknown &:= (AP\backslash NP)/NP : \lambda x.\lambda y.unknown(x,y)
\end{aligned}$$

Among the 90 detected triplets, using the learned lexicon we are able to parse all of them into semantic representations. Here we pick the representation with the highest probability after parsing as the individual action semantic representation. The "parsed semantics" rows of Fig. 3 and 4 show several example action semantics on testing sequences. Taking the fourth sub-action from Fig. 4 as an example, the visually detected triplets based on segmentation and spatial decomposition is $(Object\_014, Chopping, Object\_011)$. After semantic parsing, the system predicts that $divided(Object\_011)$. The complete training corpus and parsed results of the testing set will be made publicly available for future research.

5.5 Reasoning Beyond Observations

As mentioned before, because of the use of λ-calculus for representing action semantics, the obtained data can naturally be used to do logical reasoning beyond observations. This by itself is a very interesting research topic and it is beyond this paper's scope. However by applying a couple of common sense Axioms on the testing data, we can provide some flavor of this idea.

Case study one: See the "final action consequence and reasoning" row of Fig. 3 for case one. Using propositional logic and axiom schema, we can represent the common sense statement ("if an object x is contained in object y, and object z is on top of object y, then object z is on top of object x") as follows:

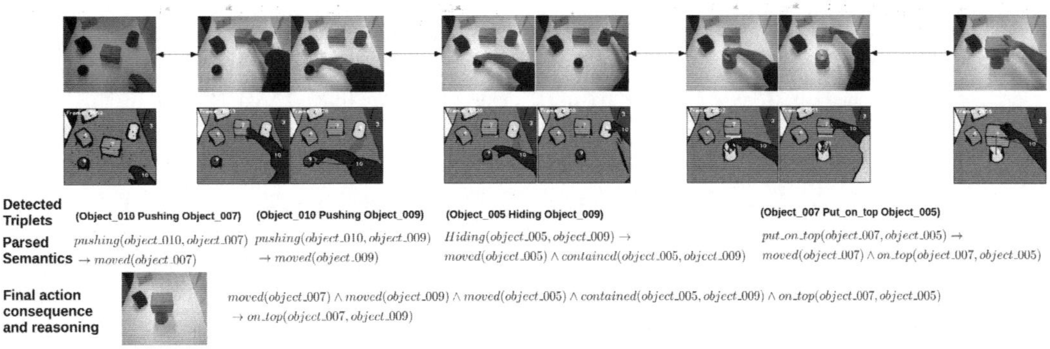

Figure 3: System output on complex chained manipulation testing sequence one. The segmentation output and detected triplets are from (Aksoy and Wörgötter, 2015)

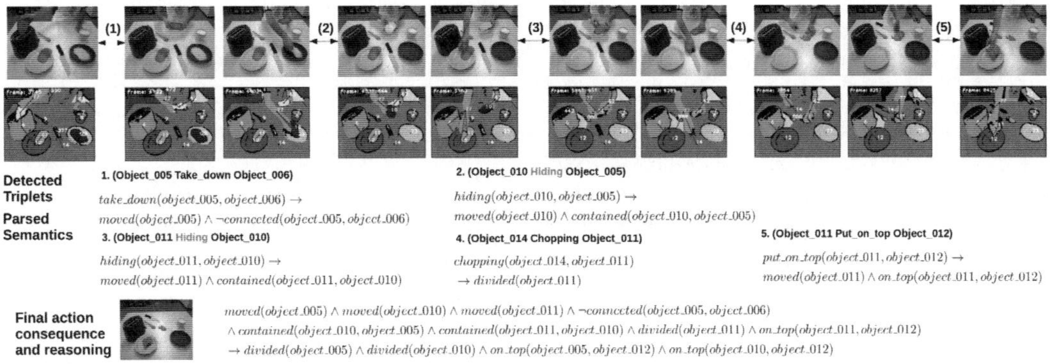

Figure 4: System output on the 18th complex chained manipulation testing sequence. The segmentation output and detected triplets are from (Aksoy and Wörgötter, 2015)

Axiom (1): $\exists x, y, z, contained(y, x) \wedge on\_top(z, y) \rightarrow on\_top(z, x)$.

Then it is trivial to deduce an additional final action consequence in this scenario that ($on\_top(object\_007, object\_009)$). This matches the fact: the yellow box which is put on top of the red bucket is also on top of the black ball.

Case study two: See the "final action consequence and reasoning" row of Fig. 4 for a more complicated case. Using propositional logic and axiom schema, we can represent three common sense statements:

1) "if an object y is contained in object x, and object z is contained in object y, then object z is contained in object x";

2) "if an object x is contained in object y, and object y is divided, then object x is divided";

3) "if an object x is contained in object y, and object y is on top of object z, then x is on top of object z" as follows:

Axiom (2): $\exists x, y, z, contained(y, x) \wedge contained(z, y) \rightarrow contained(z, x)$.

Axiom (3): $\exists x, y, contained(y, x) \wedge divided(y) \rightarrow divided(x)$.

Axiom (4): $\exists x, y, z, contained(y, x) \wedge on\_top(y, z) \rightarrow on\_top(x, z)$.

With these common sense Axioms, the system is able to deduce several additional final action consequences in this scenario:

$$divided(object\_005) \wedge divided(object\_010) \\ \wedge on\_top(object\_005, object\_012) \\ \wedge on\_top(object\_010, object\_012).$$

From Fig. 4, we can see that these additional consequences indeed match the facts: 1) the bread and cheese which are covered by ham are also divided, even though from observation the system only detected the ham being cut; 2) the divided bread and cheese are also on top of the plate, even though from observation the system only detected the ham being put on top of the plate.

We applied the four Axioms on the 20 testing action sequences and deduced the "hidden" consequences from observation. To evaluate our system performance quantitatively, we first annotated all the final action consequences (both obvious and "hidden" ones) from the 20 testing sequences as ground-truth facts. In total there are 122 consequences annotated. Using perception only (Aksoy and Wörgötter, 2015), due to the decomposition errors (such as the red font ones in Fig. 4) the system can detect 91 consequences correctly, yielding a 74% correct rate. After applying the four Axioms and reasoning, our system is able to detect 105 consequences correctly, yielding a 86% correct rate. Overall, this is a 15.4% of improvement.

Here we want to mention a caveat: there are definitely other common sense Axioms that we are not able to address in the current implementation. However, from the case studies presented, we can see that using the presented formal framework, our system is able to reason about manipulation action goals instead of just observing what is happening visually. This capability is essential for intelligent agents to imitate action goals from observation.

6 Conclusion and Future Work

In this paper we presented a formal computational framework for modeling manipulation actions based on a Combinatory Categorial Grammar. An empirical study on a large manipulation action dataset validates that 1) with the introduced formalism, a learning system can be devised to deduce the semantic meaning of manipulation actions in λ-schema; 2) with the learned schema and several common sense Axioms, our system is able to reason beyond just observation and deduce "hidden" action consequences, yielding a decent performance improvement.

Due to the limitation of current testing scenarios, we conducted experiments only considering a relatively small set of seed lexicon rules and logical expressions. Nevertheless, we want to mention that the presented CCG framework can also be extended to learn the formal logic representation of more complex manipulation action semantics. For example, the temporal order of manipulation actions can be modeled by considering a seed rule such as $AP\backslash AP : \lambda f.\lambda g.before(f(\cdot), g(\cdot))$, where $before(\cdot,\cdot)$ is a temporal predicate. For actions in this paper we consider seed main type $(AP\backslash NP)/NP$. For more general manipulation scenarios, based on whether the action is transitive or intransitive, the main types of action can be extended to include $AP\backslash NP$.

Moreover, the logical expressions can also be extended to include universal quantification $\forall$ and existential quantification $\exists$. Thus, manipulation action such as "knife cut every tomato" can be parsed into a representation as $\forall x.tomato(x) \wedge cut(knife, x) \rightarrow divided(x)$ (the parse is given in the following chart). Here, the concept "every" has a main type of $NP\backslash NP$ and semantic meaning of $\forall x.f(x)$. The same framework can also extended to have other combinatory rules such as **composition** and **type-raising** (Steedman, 2002). These are parts of the future work along the line of the presented work.

Knife	Cut	every	Tomato
N			N
NP	$(AP\backslash NP)/NP$	$NP\backslash NP$	NP
$knife$	$\lambda x.\lambda y.cut(x,y)$	$\forall x.f(x)$	$tomato$
$knife$	$\rightarrow divided(y)$	$\forall x.f(x)$	$tomato$

$$\text{every Tomato} \Rightarrow_{>} NP: \forall x.tomato(x)$$

$$\text{Cut every Tomato} \Rightarrow_{>} AP\backslash NP: \forall y.\lambda x.tomato(y) \wedge cut(x,y) \rightarrow divided(y)$$

$$\text{Knife Cut every Tomato} \Rightarrow_{<} AP: \forall y.tomato(y) \wedge cut(knife,y) \rightarrow divided(y)$$

The presented computational linguistic framework enables an intelligent agent to predict and reason action goals from observation, and thus has many potential applications such as human intention prediction, robot action policy planning, human robot collaboration etc. We believe that our formalism of manipulation actions bridges computational linguistics, vision and robotics, and opens further research in Artificial Intelligence and Robotics. As the robotics industry is moving towards robots that function safely, effectively and autonomously to perform tasks in real-world unstructured environments, they will need to be able to understand the meaning of actions and acquire human-like common-sense reasoning capabilities.

7 Acknowledgements

This research was funded in part by the support of the European Union under the Cognitive Systems program (project POETICON++), the National Science Foundation under INSPIRE grant SMA 1248056, and by DARPA through U.S. Army grant W911NF-14-1-0384 under the Project: Shared Perception, Cognition and Reasoning for Autonomy.

References

E E. Aksoy and F. Wörgötter. 2015. Semantic decomposition and recognition of long and complex manipulation action sequences. *International Journal of Computer Vision*, page Under Review.

E.E. Aksoy, A. Abramov, J. Dörr, K. Ning, B. Dellen, and F. Wörgötter. 2011. Learning the semantics of object–action relations by observation. *The International Journal of Robotics Research*, 30(10):1229–1249.

E E. Aksoy, M. Tamosiunaite, and F. Wörgötter. 2014. Model-free incremental learning of the semantics of manipulation actions. *Robotics and Autonomous Systems*, pages 1–42.

Chitta Baral, Juraj Dzifcak, Marcos Alvarez Gonzalez, and Jiayu Zhou. 2011. Using inverse λ and generalization to translate english to formal languages. In *Proceedings of the Ninth International Conference on Computational Semantics*, pages 35–44. Association for Computational Linguistics.

Jezekiel Ben-Arie, Zhiqian Wang, Purvin Pandit, and Shyamsundar Rajaram. 2002. Human activity recognition using multidimensional indexing. *Pattern Analysis and Machine Intelligence, IEEE Transactions on*, 24(8):1091–1104.

Matthew Brand. 1996. Understanding manipulation in video. In *Proceedings of the Second International Conference on Automatic Face and Gesture Recognition*, pages 94–99, Killington,VT. IEEE.

R. Chaudhry, A. Ravichandran, G. Hager, and R. Vidal. 2009. Histograms of oriented optical flow and binet-cauchy kernels on nonlinear dynamical systems for the recognition of human actions. In *Proceedings of the 2009 IEEE Intenational Conference on Computer Vision and Pattern Recognition*, pages 1932–1939, Miami,FL. IEEE.

N. Chomsky. 1957. *Syntactic Structures*. Mouton de Gruyter.

Noam Chomsky. 1993. *Lectures on government and binding: The Pisa lectures*. Walter de Gruyter.

V Gazzola, G Rizzolatti, B Wicker, and C Keysers. 2007. The anthropomorphic brain: the mirror neuron system responds to human and robotic actions. *Neuroimage*, 35(4):1674–1684.

Anupam Guha, Yezhou Yang, Cornelia Fermüller, and Yiannis Aloimonos. 2013. Minimalist plans for interpreting manipulation actions. *Proceedings of the 2013 IEEE/RSJ International Conference on Intelligent Robots and Systems*, pages 5908–5914.

Yuri A. Ivanov and Aaron F. Bobick. 2000. Recognition of visual activities and interactions by stochastic parsing. *IEEE Transactions on Pattern Analysis and Machine Intelligence*, 22(8):852–872.

Jungseock Joo, Weixin Li, Francis F Steen, and Song-Chun Zhu. 2014. Visual persuasion: Inferring communicative intents of images. In *Computer Vision and Pattern Recognition (CVPR), 2014 IEEE Conference on*, pages 216–223. IEEE.

A. Kale, A. Sundaresan, AN Rajagopalan, N.P. Cuntoor, A.K. Roy-Chowdhury, V. Kruger, and R. Chellappa. 2004. Identification of humans using gait. *IEEE Transactions on Image Processing*, 13(9):1163–1173.

Hilde Kuehne, Ali Arslan, and Thomas Serre. 2014. The language of actions: Recovering the syntax and semantics of goal-directed human activities. In *Computer Vision and Pattern Recognition (CVPR), 2014 IEEE Conference on*, pages 780–787. IEEE.

Cynthia Matuszek, Nicholas FitzGerald, Luke Zettlemoyer, Liefeng Bo, and Dieter Fox. 2011. A joint model of language and perception for grounded attribute learning. In *International Conference on Machine learning (ICML)*.

Cynthia Matuszek, Liefeng Bo, Luke Zettlemoyer, and Dieter Fox. 2014. Learning from unscripted deictic gesture and language for human-robot interactions. In *Twenty-Eighth AAAI Conference on Artificial Intelligence*.

T.B. Moeslund, A. Hilton, and V. Krüger. 2006. A survey of advances in vision-based human motion capture and analysis. *Computer vision and image understanding*, 104(2):90–126.

Raymond J Mooney. 2008. Learning to connect language and perception. In *AAAI*, pages 1598–1601.

Darnell Moore and Irfan Essa. 2002. Recognizing multitasked activities from video using stochastic context-free grammar. In *Proceedings of the National Conference on Artificial Intelligence*, pages 770–776, Menlo Park, CA. AAAI.

K. Pastra and Y. Aloimonos. 2012. The minimalist grammar of action. *Philosophical Transactions of the Royal Society B: Biological Sciences*, 367(1585):103–117.

Hamed Pirsiavash, Carl Vondrick, and Antonio Torralba. 2014. Inferring the why in images. *arXiv preprint arXiv:1406.5472*.

Giacomo Rizzolatti, Leonardo Fogassi, and Vittorio Gallese. 2001. Neurophysiological mechanisms underlying the understanding and imitation of action. *Nature Reviews Neuroscience*, 2(9):661–670.

Michael S Ryoo and Jake K Aggarwal. 2006. Recognition of composite human activities through context-free grammar based representation. In *Proceedings of the 2006 IEEE Conference on Computer Vision and Pattern Recognition*, volume 2, pages 1709–1718, New York City, NY. IEEE.

P. Saisan, G. Doretto, Y.N. Wu, and S. Soatto. 2001. Dynamic texture recognition. In *Proceedings of the 2001 IEEE Intenational Conference on Computer Vision and Pattern Recognition*, volume 2, pages 58–63, Kauai, HI. IEEE.

Mark Steedman. 2000. *The syntactic process*, volume 35. MIT Press.

Mark Steedman. 2002. Plans, affordances, and combinatory grammar. *Linguistics and Philosophy*, 25(5-6):723–753.

D. Summers-Stay, C.L. Teo, Y. Yang, C. Fermüller, and Y. Aloimonos. 2013. Using a minimal action grammar for activity understanding in the real world. In *Proceedings of the 2013 IEEE/RSJ International Conference on Intelligent Robots and Systems*, pages 4104–4111, Vilamoura, Portugal. IEEE.

Stefanie Tellex, Pratiksha Thaker, Joshua Joseph, and Nicholas Roy. 2014. Learning perceptually grounded word meanings from unaligned parallel data. *Machine Learning*, 94(2):151–167.

P. Turaga, R. Chellappa, V.S. Subrahmanian, and O. Udrea. 2008. Machine recognition of human activities: A survey. *IEEE Transactions on Circuits and Systems for Video Technology*, 18(11):1473–1488.

Dan Xie, Sinisa Todorovic, and Song-Chun Zhu. 2013. Inferring "dark matter" and "dark energy" from videos. In *Computer Vision (ICCV), 2013 IEEE International Conference on*, pages 2224–2231. IEEE.

Yezhou Yang, Cornelia Fermüller, and Yiannis Aloimonos. 2013. Detection of manipulation action consequences (MAC). In *Proceedings of the 2013 IEEE Conference on Computer Vision and Pattern Recognition*, pages 2563–2570, Portland, OR. IEEE.

Y. Yang, A. Guha, C. Fermuller, and Y. Aloimonos. 2014. A cognitive system for understanding human manipulation actions. *Advances in Cognitive Sysytems*, 3:67–86.

Yezhou Yang, Yi Li, Cornelia Fermuller, and Yiannis Aloimonos. 2015. Robot learning manipulation action plans by "watching" unconstrained videos from the world wide web. In *The Twenty-Ninth AAAI Conference on Artificial Intelligence (AAAI-15)*.

A. Yilmaz and M. Shah. 2005. Actions sketch: A novel action representation. In *Proceedings of the 2005 IEEE Intenational Conference on Computer Vision and Pattern Recognition*, volume 1, pages 984–989, San Diego, CA. IEEE.

Luke S Zettlemoyer and Michael Collins. 2005. Learning to map sentences to logical form: Structured classification with probabilistic categorial grammars. In *UAI*.

Luke S Zettlemoyer and Michael Collins. 2007. Online learning of relaxed ccg grammars for parsing to logical form. In *EMNLP-CoNLL*, pages 678–687.

Knowledge Graph Embedding via Dynamic Mapping Matrix

Guoliang Ji, Shizhu He, Liheng Xu, Kang Liu and Jun Zhao
National Laboratory of Pattern Recognition (NLPR)
Institute of Automation Chinese Academy of Sciences, Beijing, 100190, China
{guoliang.ji,shizhu.he,lhxu,kliu,jzhao}@nlpr.ia.ac.cn

Abstract

Knowledge graphs are useful resources for numerous AI applications, but they are far from completeness. Previous work such as TransE, TransH and TransR/CTransR regard a relation as translation from head entity to tail entity and the CTransR achieves state-of-the-art performance. In this paper, we propose a more fine-grained model named TransD, which is an improvement of TransR/CTransR. In TransD, we use two vectors to represent a named symbol object (entity and relation). The first one represents the meaning of a(n) entity (relation), the other one is used to construct mapping matrix dynamically. Compared with TransR/CTransR, TransD not only considers the diversity of relations, but also entities. TransD has less parameters and has no matrix-vector multiplication operations, which makes it can be applied on large scale graphs. In Experiments, we evaluate our model on two typical tasks including triplets classification and link prediction. Evaluation results show that our approach outperforms state-of-the-art methods.

1 Introduction

Knowledge Graphs such as WordNet (Miller 1995), Freebase (Bollacker et al. 2008) and Yago (Suchanek et al. 2007) have been playing a pivotal role in many AI applications, such as relation extraction(RE), question answering(Q&A), etc. They usually contain huge amounts of structured data as the form of triplets (*head entity*, *relation*, *tail entity*)(denoted as (h, r, t)), where relation models the relationship between the two entities. As most knowledge graphs have been built either collaboratively or (partly) automatically, they often suffer from incompleteness. Knowledge graph completion is to predict relations between entities based on existing triplets in a knowledge graph. In the past decade, much work based on symbol and logic has been done for knowledge graph completion, but they are neither tractable nor enough convergence for large scale knowledge graphs. Recently, a powerful approach for this task is to encode every element (entities and relations) of a knowledge graph into a low-dimensional embedding vector space. These methods do reasoning over knowledge graphs through algebraic operations (see section "Related Work").

Among these methods, TransE (Bordes et al. 2013) is simple and effective, and also achieves state-of-the-art prediction performance. It learns low-dimensional embeddings for every entity and relation in knowledge graphs. These vector embeddings are denoted by the same letter in boldface. The basic idea is that every relation is regarded as translation in the embedding space. For a golden triplet (h, r, t), the embedding $\mathbf{h}$ is close to the embedding $\mathbf{t}$ by adding the embedding $\mathbf{r}$, that is $\mathbf{h} + \mathbf{r} \approx \mathbf{t}$. TransE is suitable for 1-to-1 relations, but has flaws when dealing with 1-to-N, N-to-1 and N-to-N relations. TransH (Wang et al. 2014) is proposed to solve these issues. TransH regards a relation as a translating operation on a relation-specific hyperplane, which is characterized by a norm vector $\mathbf{w}_r$ and a translation vector $\mathbf{d}_r$. The embeddings $\mathbf{h}$ and $\mathbf{t}$ are first projected to the hyperplane of relation r to obtain vectors $\mathbf{h}_\perp = \mathbf{h} - \mathbf{w}_r^\top \mathbf{h} \mathbf{w}_r$ and $\mathbf{t}_\perp = \mathbf{t} - \mathbf{w}_r^\top \mathbf{t} \mathbf{w}_r$, and then $\mathbf{h}_\perp + \mathbf{d}_r \approx \mathbf{t}_\perp$. Both in TransE and TransH, the embeddings of entities and relations are in the same space. However, entities and relations are different types objects, it is insufficient to model them in the same space. TransR/CTransR (Lin et al. 2015) set a mapping matrix $\mathbf{M}_r$ and a vector $\mathbf{r}$ for every relation r. In TransR, $\mathbf{h}$ and $\mathbf{t}$ are projected to the aspects that relation r focuses on through the ma-

Proceedings of the 53rd Annual Meeting of the Association for Computational Linguistics and the 7th International Joint Conference on Natural Language Processing, pages 687–696,
Beijing, China, July 26-31, 2015.

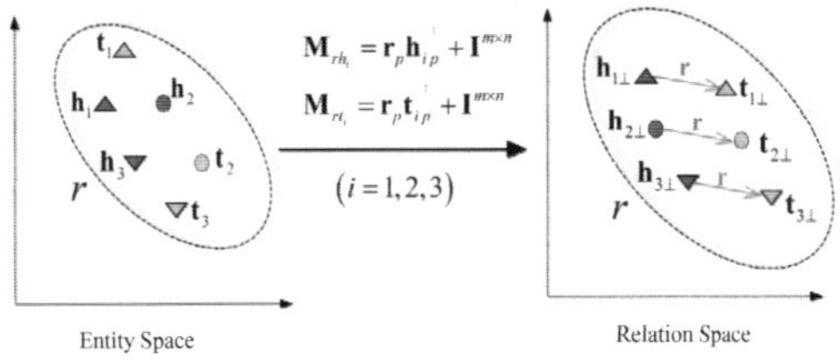

Figure 1: Simple illustration of TransD. Each shape represents an entity pair appearing in a triplet of relation r. $\mathbf{M}_{rh}$ and $\mathbf{M}_{rt}$ are mapping matrices of $\mathbf{h}$ and $\mathbf{t}$, respectively. $\mathbf{h}_{ip}$, $\mathbf{t}_{ip}(i = 1, 2, 3)$, and $\mathbf{r}_p$ are projection vectors. $\mathbf{h}_{i\perp}$ and $\mathbf{t}_{i\perp}(i = 1, 2, 3)$ are projected vectors of entities. The projected vectors satisfy $\mathbf{h}_{i\perp} + \mathbf{r} \approx \mathbf{t}_{i\perp}(i = 1, 2, 3)$.

trix $\mathbf{M}_r$ and then $\mathbf{M}_r\mathbf{h} + \mathbf{r} \approx \mathbf{M}_r\mathbf{t}$. CTransR is an extension of TransR by clustering diverse head-tail entity pairs into groups and learning distinct relation vectors for each group. TransR/CTransR has significant improvements compared with previous state-of-the-art models. However, it also has several flaws: (1) For a typical relation r, all entities share the same mapping matrix $\mathbf{M}_r$. However, the entities linked by a relation always contains various types and attributes. For example, in triplet (*friedrich_burklein, nationality, germany*), *friedrich_burklein* and *germany* are typical different types of entities. These entities should be projected in different ways; (2) The projection operation is an interactive process between an entity and a relation, it is unreasonable that the mapping matrices are determined only by relations; and (3) Matrix-vector multiplication makes it has large amount of calculation, and when relation number is large, it also has much more parameters than TransE and TransH. As the complexity, TransR/CTransR is difficult to apply on large-scale knowledge graphs.

In this paper, we propose a novel method named TransD to model knowledge graphs. Figure 1 shows the basic idea of TransD. In TransD, we define *two* vectors for each entity and relation. The first vector represents the meaning of an entity or a relation, the other one (called *projection vector*) represents the way that how to project a entity embedding into a relation vector space and it will be used to construct mapping matrices. Therefore, every entity-relation pair has an unique mapping matrix. In addition, TransD has no matrix-by-vector operations which can be replaced by vectors operations. We evaluate TransD with the task of triplets classification and link prediction. The experimental results show that our method has significant improvements compared with previous models.

Our contributions in this paper are: (1)We propose a novel model TransD, which constructs a dynamic mapping matrix for each entity-relation pair by considering the diversity of entities and relations simultaneously. It provides a flexible style to project entity representations to relation vector space; (2) Compared with TransR/CTransR, TransD has fewer parameters and has no matrix-vector multiplication. It is easy to be applied on large-scale knowledge graphs like TransE and TransH; and (3) In experiments, our approach outperforms previous models including TransE, TransH and TransR/CTransR in link prediction and triplets classification tasks.

2 Related Work

Before proceeding, we define our mathematical notations. We denote a triplet by (h, r, t) and their column vectors by bold lower case letters $\mathbf{h}, \mathbf{r}, \mathbf{t}$; matrices by bold upper case letters, such as $\mathbf{M}$; tensors by bold upper case letters with a hat, such as $\widehat{\mathbf{M}}$. Score function is represented by $f_r(\mathbf{h}, \mathbf{t})$. For a golden triplet (h, r, t) that corresponds to a true fact in real world, it always get a relatively higher score, and lower for an negative triplet. Other notations will be described in the appropriate sections.

2.1 TransE, TransH and TransR/CTransR

As mentioned in Introduction section, TransE (Bordes et al. 2013) regards the relation $\mathbf{r}$ as translation from $\mathbf{h}$ to $\mathbf{t}$ for a golden triplet (h, r, t). Hence, $(\mathbf{h}+\mathbf{r})$ is close to $(\mathbf{t})$ and the score function is

$$f_r(\mathbf{h}, \mathbf{t}) = -\|\mathbf{h} + \mathbf{r} - \mathbf{t}\|_2^2. \tag{1}$$

TransE is only suitable for 1-to-1 relations, there remain flaws for 1-to-N, N-to-1 and N-to-N relations.

To solve these problems, TransH (Wang et al. 2014) proposes an improved model named translation on a hyperplane. On hyperplanes of different relations, a given entity has different representations. Similar to TransE, TransH has the score function as follows:

$$f_r(\mathbf{h}, \mathbf{t}) = -\|\mathbf{h}_\perp + \mathbf{r} - \mathbf{t}_\perp\|_2^2. \tag{2}$$

Model	#Parameters	# Operations (Time complexity)
Unstructured (Bordes et al. 2012; 2014)	$O(N_e m)$	$O(N_t)$
SE (Bordes et al. 2011)	$O(N_e m + 2N_r n^2)(m = n)$	$O(2m^2 N_t)$
SME(linear) (Bordes et al. 2012; 2014)	$O(N_e m + N_r n + 4mk + 4k)(m = n)$	$O(4mkN_t)$
SME (bilinear) (Bordes et al. 2012; 2014)	$O(N_e m + N_r n + 4mks + 4k)(m = n)$	$O(4mksN_t)$
LFM (Jenatton et al. 2012; Sutskever et al. 2009)	$O(N_e m + N_r n^2)(m = n)$	$O((m^2 + m)N_t)$
SLM (Socher et al. 2013)	$O(N_e m + N_r(2k + 2nk))(m = n)$	$O((2mk + k)N_t)$
NTN (Socher et al. 2013)	$O(N_e m + N_r(n^2 s + 2ns + 2s))(m = n)$	$O(((m^2 + m)s + 2mk + k)N_t)$
TransE (Bordes et al. 2013)	$O(N_e m + N_r n)(m = n)$	$O(N_t)$
TransH (Wang et al. 2014)	$O(N_e m + 2N_r n)(m = n)$	$O(2mN_t)$
TransR (Lin et al. 2015)	$O(N_e m + N_r(m + 1)n)$	$O(2mnN_t)$
CTransR (Lin et al. 2015)	$O(N_e m + N_r(m + d)n)$	$O(2mnN_t)$
TransD (this paper)	$O(2N_e m + 2N_r n)$	$O(2nN_t)$

Table 1: Complexity (the number of parameters and the number of multiplication operations in an epoch) of several embedding models. N_e and N_r represent the number of entities and relations, respectively. N_t represents the number of triplets in a knowledge graph. m is the dimension of entity embedding space and n is the dimension of relation embedding space. d denotes the average number of clusters of a relation. k is the number of hidden nodes of a neural network and s is the number of slice of a tensor.

In order to ensure that $\mathbf{h}_\perp$ and $\mathbf{t}_\perp$ are on the hyperplane of r, TransH restricts $\|\mathbf{w}_r\| = 1$.

Both TransE and TransH assume that entities and relations are in the same vector space. But relations and entities are different types of objects, they should not be in the same vector space. TransR/CTransR (Lin et al. 2015) is proposed based on the idea. TransR set a mapping matrix $\mathbf{M}_r$ for each relation r to map entity embedding into relation vector space. Its score function is:

$$f_r(\mathbf{h}, \mathbf{t}) = -\|\mathbf{M}_r\mathbf{h} + \mathbf{r} - \mathbf{M}_r\mathbf{t}\|_2^2. \tag{3}$$

where $\mathbf{M}_r \in \mathbb{R}^{m \times n}$, $\mathbf{h}, \mathbf{t} \in \mathbb{R}^n$ and $\mathbf{r} \in \mathbb{R}^m$. CTransR is an extension of TransR. As head-tail entity pairs present various patterns in different relations, CTransR clusters diverse head-tail entity pairs into groups and sets a relation vector for each group.

2.2 Other Models

Unstructured. Unstructured model (Bordes et al. 2012; 2014) ignores relations, only models entities as embeddings. The score function is

$$f_r(\mathbf{h}, \mathbf{t}) = -\|\mathbf{h} - \mathbf{t}\|_2^2. \tag{4}$$

It's a simple case of TransE. Obviously, Unstructured model can not distinguish different relations.

Structured Embedding (SE). SE model (Bordes et al. 2011) sets two separate matrices $\mathbf{M}_{rh}$ and $\mathbf{M}_{rt}$ to project head and tail entities for each relation. Its score function is defined as follows:

$$f_r(\mathbf{h}, \mathbf{t}) = -\|\mathbf{M}_{rh}\mathbf{h} - \mathbf{M}_{rt}\mathbf{t}\|_1 \tag{5}$$

Semantic Matching Energy (SME). SME model (Bordes et al. 2012; 2014) encodes each named symbolic object (entities and relations) as a vector. Its score function is a neural network that captures correlations between entities and relations via matrix operations. Parameters of the neural network are shared by all relations. SME defines two semantic matching energy functions for optimization, a linear form

$$\mathbf{g}_\eta = \mathbf{M}_{\eta 1}\mathbf{e}_\eta + \mathbf{M}_{\eta 2}\mathbf{r} + \mathbf{b}_\eta \tag{6}$$

and a bilinear form

$$\mathbf{g}_\eta = (\mathbf{M}_{\eta 1}\mathbf{e}_\eta) \otimes (\mathbf{M}_{\eta 2}\mathbf{r}) + \mathbf{b}_\eta \tag{7}$$

where $\eta = \{left, right\}$, $\mathbf{e}_{left} = \mathbf{h}$, $\mathbf{e}_{right} = \mathbf{t}$ and $\otimes$ is the Hadamard product. The score function is

$$f_r(\mathbf{h}, \mathbf{t}) = \mathbf{g}_{left}{}^\top \mathbf{g}_{right} \tag{8}$$

In (Bordes et al.2014), matrices of the bilinear form are replaced by tensors.

Latent Factor Model (LFM). LFM model (Jenatton et al. 2012; Sutskever et al. 2009) encodes each entity into a vector and sets a matrix for every relation. It defines a score function $f_r(\mathbf{h}, \mathbf{t}) = \mathbf{h}^\top \mathbf{M}_r \mathbf{t}$, which incorporates the interaction of the two entity vectors in a simple and effecitve way.

Single Layer Model (SLM). SLM model is designed as a baseline of Neural Tensor Network (Socher et al. 2013). The model constructs a nonlinear neural network to represent the score function defined as follows.

$$f_r(\mathbf{h}, \mathbf{t}) = \mathbf{u}_r^\top f(\mathbf{M}_{r1}\mathbf{h} + \mathbf{M}_{r2}\mathbf{t} + \mathbf{b}_r) \tag{9}$$

where $\mathbf{M}_{r1}$, $\mathbf{M}_{r2}$ and $\mathbf{b}_r$ are parameters indexed by relation r, $f()$ is $tanh$ operation.

Neural Tensor Network (NTN). NTN model (Socher et al. 2013) extends SLM model by considering the second-order correlations into nonlinear neural networks. The score function is

$$f_r(\mathbf{h}, \mathbf{t}) = \mathbf{u}_r^\top f(\mathbf{h}^\top \widehat{\mathbf{W}}_r \mathbf{t} + \mathbf{M}_r \begin{bmatrix} \mathbf{h} \\ \mathbf{t} \end{bmatrix} + \mathbf{b}_r) \quad (10)$$

where $\widehat{\mathbf{W}}_r$ represents a 3-way tensor, $\mathbf{M}_r$ denotes the weight matrix, $\mathbf{b}_r$ is the bias and $f()$ is $tanh$ operation. NTN is the most expressive model so far, but it has so many parameters that it is difficult to scale up to large knowledge graphs.

Table 1 lists the complexity of all the above models. The complexity (especially for time) of TransD is much less than TransR/CTransR and is similar to TransE and TransH. Therefore, TransD is effective and train faster than TransR/CTransR. Beyond these embedding models, there is other related work of modeling multi-relational data, such as matrix factorization, recommendations, etc. In experiments, we refer to the results of **RESCAL** presented in (Lin et al. 2015) and compare with it.

3 Our Method

We first define notations. Triplets are represented as $(h_i, r_i, t_i)(i = 1, 2, \ldots, n_t)$, where h_i denotes a head entity, t_i denotes a tail entity and r_i denotes a relation. Their embeddings are denoted by $\mathbf{h}_i, \mathbf{r}_i, \mathbf{t}_i (i = 1, 2, \ldots, n_t)$. We use Δ to represent golden triplets set, and use Δ' to denote negative triplets set. Entities set and relations set are denoted by E and R, respectively. We use $\mathbf{I}^{m \times n}$ to denote the identity matrix of size $m \times n$.

3.1 Multiple Types of Entities and Relations

Considering the diversity of relations, CTransR segments triplets of a specific relation r into several groups and learns a vector representation for each group. However, entities also have various types. Figure 2 shows several kinds of head and tail entities of relation *location.location.partially_containedby* in FB15k. In both TransH and TransR/CTransR, all types of entities share the same mapping vectors/matrices. However, different types of entities have different attributes and functions, it is insufficient to let them share the same transform parameters of a relation. And for a given relation, similar entities should have similar mapping matrices and otherwise for dissimilar entities. Furthermore, the mapping process is a transaction between entities and relations that both have various types. Therefore, we propose a more fine-grained model TransD, which considers different types of both entities and relations, to encode knowledge graphs into embedding vectors via dynamic mapping matrices produced by projection vectors.

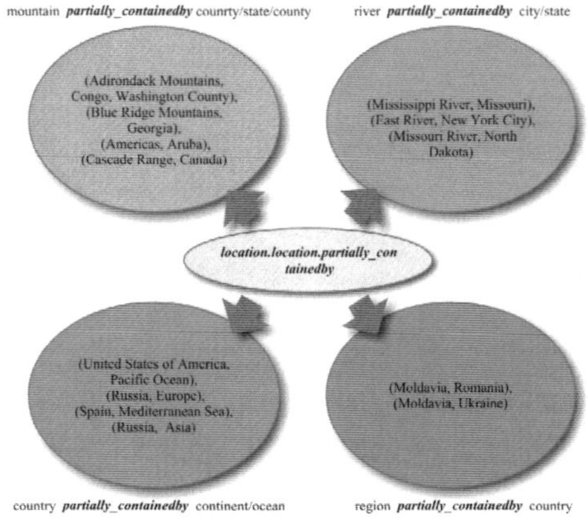

Figure 2: Multiple types of entities of relation *location.location.partially_containedby*.

3.2 TransD

Model In TransD, each named symbol object (entities and relations) is represented by *two* vectors. The first one captures the meaning of entity (relation), the other one is used to construct mapping matrices. For example, given a triplet (h, r, t), its vectors are $\mathbf{h}, \mathbf{h}_p, \mathbf{r}, \mathbf{r}_p, \mathbf{t}, \mathbf{t}_p$, where subscript p marks the projection vectors, $\mathbf{h}, \mathbf{h}_p, \mathbf{t}, \mathbf{t}_p \in \mathbb{R}^n$ and $\mathbf{r}, \mathbf{r}_p \in \mathbb{R}^m$. For each triplet (h, r, t), we set two mapping matrices $\mathbf{M}_{rh}, \mathbf{M}_{rt} \in \mathbb{R}^{m \times n}$ to project entities from entity space to relation space. They are defined as follows:

$$\mathbf{M}_{rh} = \mathbf{r}_p \mathbf{h}_p^\top + \mathbf{I}^{m \times n} \quad (11)$$

$$\mathbf{M}_{rt} = \mathbf{r}_p \mathbf{t}_p^\top + \mathbf{I}^{m \times n} \quad (12)$$

Therefore, the mapping matrices are determined by both entities and relations, and this kind of operation makes the two projection vectors interact sufficiently because each element of them can meet every entry comes from another vector. As we initialize each mapping matrix with an identity matrix, we add the $\mathbf{I}^{m \times n}$ to $\mathbf{M}_{rh}$ and $\mathbf{M}_{rh}$. With the mapping matrices, we define the projected vectors as follows:

$$\mathbf{h}_\perp = \mathbf{M}_{rh} \mathbf{h}, \quad \mathbf{t}_\perp = \mathbf{M}_{rt} \mathbf{t} \quad (13)$$

Then the score function is

$$f_r(\mathbf{h}, \mathbf{t}) = -\|\mathbf{h}_\perp + \mathbf{r} - \mathbf{t}_\perp\|_2^2 \quad (14)$$

In experiments, we enforce constrains as $\|\mathbf{h}\|_2 \leq 1, \|\mathbf{t}\|_2 \leq 1, \|\mathbf{r}\|_2 \leq 1, \|\mathbf{h}_\perp\|_2 \leq 1$ and $\|\mathbf{t}_\perp\|_2 \leq 1$.

Training Objective We assume that there are n_t triplets in training set and denote the ith triplet by $(h_i, r_i, t_i)(i = 1, 2, \ldots, n_t)$. Each triplet has a label y_i to indicate the triplet is positive ($y_i = 1$) or negative ($y_i = 0$). Then the golden and negative triplets are denoted by $\Delta = \{(h_j, r_j, t_j) \mid y_j = 1\}$ and $\Delta' = \{(h_j, r_j, t_j) \mid y_j = 0\}$, respectively. Before training, one important trouble is that knowledge graphs only encode positive training triplets, they do not contain negative examples. Therefore, we obtain Δ from knowledge graphs and generate Δ' as follows: $\Delta' = \{(h_l, r_k, t_k) \mid h_l \neq h_k \wedge y_k = 1\} \cup \{(h_k, r_k, t_l) \mid t_l \neq t_k \wedge y_k = 1\}$. We also use two strategies "unif" and "bern" described in (Wang et al. 2014) to replace the head or tail entity.

Let us use ξ and ξ' to denote a golden triplet and a corresponding negative triplet, respectively. Then we define the following margin-based ranking loss as the objective for training:

$$L = \sum_{\xi \in \Delta} \sum_{\xi' \in \Delta'} [\gamma + f_r(\xi') - f_r(\xi)]_+ \quad (15)$$

where $[x]_+ \triangleq \max(0, x)$, and γ is the margin separating golden triplets and negative triplets. The process of minimizing the above objective is carried out with stochastic gradient descent (SGD). In order to speed up the convergence and avoid overfitting, we initiate the entity and relation embeddings with the results of TransE and initiate all the transfer matrices with identity matrices.

3.3 Connections with TransE, TransH and TransR/CTransR

TransE is a special case of TransD when the dimension of vectors satisfies $m = n$ and all projection vectors are set zero.

TransH is related to TransD when we set $m = n$. Under the setting, projected vectors of entities can be rewritten as follows:

$$\mathbf{h}_\perp = \mathbf{M}_{rh}\mathbf{h} = \mathbf{h} + \mathbf{h}_p^\top \mathbf{h} \mathbf{r}_p \quad (16)$$

$$\mathbf{t}_\perp = \mathbf{M}_{rt}\mathbf{t} = \mathbf{t} + \mathbf{t}_p^\top \mathbf{t} \mathbf{r}_p \quad (17)$$

Hence, when $m = n$, the difference between TransD and TransH is that projection vectors are determinded only by relations in TransH, but TransD's projection vectors are determinded by both entities and relations.

As to TransR/CTransR, TransD is an improvement of it. TransR/CTransR directly defines a mapping matrix for each relation, TransD consturcts two mapping matrices dynamically for each triplet by setting a projection vector for each entity and relation. In addition, TransD has no matrix-vector multiplication operation which can be replaced by vector operations. Without loss of generality, we assume $m \geq n$, the projected vectors can be computed as follows:

$$\mathbf{h}_\perp = \mathbf{M}_{rh}\mathbf{h} = \mathbf{h}_p^\top \mathbf{h} \mathbf{r}_p + \left[\ \mathbf{h}^\top, \mathbf{0}^\top\ \right]^\top \quad (18)$$

$$\mathbf{t}_\perp = \mathbf{M}_{rt}\mathbf{t} = \mathbf{t}_p^\top \mathbf{t} \mathbf{r}_p + \left[\ \mathbf{t}^\top, \mathbf{0}^\top\ \right]^\top \quad (19)$$

Therefore, TransD has less calculation than TransR/CTransR, which makes it train faster and can be applied on large-scale knowledge graphs.

4 Experiments and Results Analysis

We evaluate our apporach on two tasks: triplets classification and link prediction. Then we show the experiments results and some analysis of them.

4.1 Data Sets

Triplets classification and link prediction are implemented on two popular knowledge graphs: WordNet (Miller 1995) and Freebase (Bollacker et al. 2008). WordNet is a large lexical knowledge graph. Entities in WordNet are synonyms which express distinct concepts. Relations in WordNet are conceptual-semantic and lexical relations. In this paper, we use two subsets of WordNet: WN11 (Socher et al. 2013) and WN18 (Bordes et al. 2014). Freebase is a large collaborative knowledge base consists of a large number of the world facts, such as triplets (*anthony_asquith, location, london*) and (*nobuko_otowa, profession, actor*). We also use two subsets of Freebase: FB15k (Bordes et al. 2014) and FB13 (Socher et al. 2013). Table 2 lists statistics of the 4 datasets.

Dataset	#Rel	#Ent	#Train	#Valid	#Test
WN11	11	38,696	112,581	2,609	10,544
WN18	18	40,943	141,442	5,000	5,000
FB13	13	75,043	316,232	5908	23,733
FB15k	1,345	14,951	483,142	50,000	59,071

Table 2: Datasets used in the experiments.

4.2 Triplets Classification

Triplets classification aims to judge whether a given triplet (h, r, t) is correct or not, which is a binary classification task. Previous work (Socher et al. 2013; Wang et al. 2014; Lin et al. 2015) had explored this task. In this paper ,we use three datasets WN11, FB13 and FB15k to evaluate our approach. The test sets of WN11 and FB13 provided by (Socher et al. 2013) contain golden and negative triplets. As to FB15k, its test set only contains correct triplets, which requires us to construct negative triplets. In this parper, we construct negative triplets following the same setting used for FB13 (Socher et al. 2013).

For triplets classification, we set a threshold δ_r for each relation r. δ_r is obtained by maximizing the classification accuracies on the valid set. For a given triplet (h, r, t), if its score is larger than δ_r, it will be classified as positive, otherwise negative.

We compare our model with several previous embedding models presented in Related Work section. As we construct negative triplets for FB15k by ourselves, we use the codes of TransE, TransH and TransR/CTransR provied by (Lin et al. 2015) to evaluate the datasets instead of reporting the results of (Wang et al.2014; Lin et al. 2015) directly.

In this experiment, we optimize the objective with ADADELTA SGD (Zeiler 2012). We select the margin γ among $\{1, 2, 5, 10\}$, the dimension of entity vectors m and the dimension of relation vectors n among $\{20, 50, 80, 100\}$, and the mini-batch size B among $\{100, 200, 1000, 4800\}$. The best configuration obtained by valid set are:$\gamma = 1, m, n = 100, B = 1000$ and taking L_2 as dissimilarity on WN11; $\gamma = 1, m, n = 100, B = 200$ and taking L_2 as dissimilarity on FB13; $\gamma = 2, m, n = 100, B = 4800$ and taking L_1 as dissimilarity on FB15k. For all the three datasets, We traverse to training for 1000 rounds. As described in Related Work section, TransD trains much faster than TransR (On our PC, TransR needs 70 seconds and TransD merely spends 24 seconds a round on FB15k).

Table 3 shows the evaluation results of triplets classification. On WN11, we found that there are 570 entities appearing in valid and test sets but not appearing in train set, we call them "NULL Entity". In valid and test sets, there are 1680 (6.4%) triplets containing "NULL Entity". In NTN(+E), these entity embeddings can be obtained by word embedding. In TransD, however, they are only initialized randomly. Therefore, it is not fair for TransD, but we also achieve the accuracy 86.4% which is higher than that of NTN(+E) (86.2%). From Table 3, we can conclude that: (1) On WN11, TransD outperforms any other previous models including TransE, TransH and TransR/CTransR, especially NTN(+E); (2) On FB13, the classification accuracy of TransD achieves 89.1%, which is significantly higher than that of TransE, TransH and TransR/CTransR and is near to the performance of NTN(+E) (90.0%); and (3) Under most circumstances, the "bern" sampling method works better than "unif".

Data sets	WN11	FB13	FB15K
SE	53.0	75.2	-
SME(bilinear)	70.0	63.7	-
SLM	69.9	85.3	-
LFM	73.8	84.3	-
NTN	70.4	87.1	68.2
NTN(+E)	86.2	**90.0**	-
TransE(unif)	75.9	70.9	77.3
TransE(bern)	75.9	81.5	79.8
TransH(unif)	77.7	76.5	74.2
TransH(bern)	78.8	83.3	79.9
TransR(unif)	85.5	74.7	81.1
TransR(bern)	85.9	82.5	82.1
CTransR(bern)	85.7	-	84.3
TransD(unif)	85.6	85.9	86.4
TransD(bern)	**86.4**	89.1	**88.0**

Table 3: Experimental results of Triplets Classification(%). "+E" means that the results are combined with word embedding.

Figure 3 shows the prediction accuracy of different relations. On the three datasets, different relations have different prediction accuracy: some are higher and the others are lower. Here we focus on the relations which have lower accuracy. On WN11, the relation *similar_to* obtains accuracy 51%, which is near to random prediction accuracy. In the view of intuition, *similar_to* can be inferred from other information. However, the number of entity pairs linked by relation *similar_to* is only 1672, which accounts for 1.5% in all train data, and prediction of the relation needs much information about entities. Therefore, the insufficient of train data is the main cause. On FB13, the accuracies of relations *cuase_of_death* and *gender* are lower than that of other relations because they are difficult to infer from other imformation, especially *cuase_of_death*. Relation *gender* may be inferred from a person's name (Socher et al. 2013), but we learn a vector for each name, not for the words included in the names, which makes the

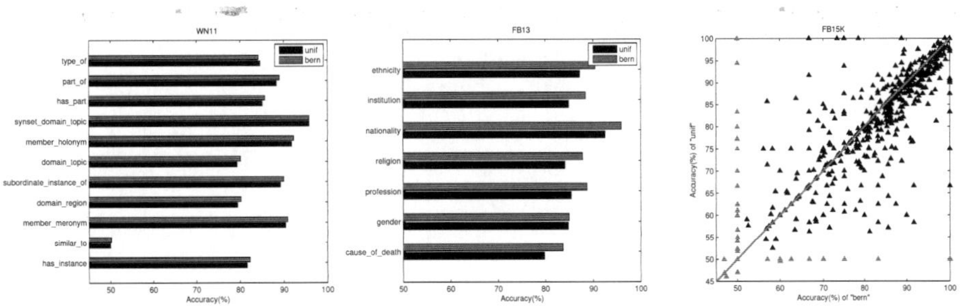

Figure 3: Classification accuracies of different relations on the three datasets. For FB15k, each triangle represent a relation, in which the red triangles represent the relations whose accuracies of "bern" or "unif" are lower than 50% and the blacks are higher than 50%. The red line represents the function $y = x$. We can see that the most relations are in the lower part of the red line.

names information useless for *gender*. On FB15k, accuracies of some relations are lower than 50%, for which some are lack of train data and some are difficult to infer. Hence, the ability of reasoning new facts based on knowledge graphs is under a certain limitation, and a complementary approach is to extract facts from plain texts.

4.3 Link Prediction

Link prediction is to predict the missing h or t for a golden triplet (h, r, t). In this task, we remove the head or tail entity and then replace it with all the entities in dictionary in turn for each triplet in test set. We first compute scores of those corrupted triplets and then rank them by descending order; the rank of the correct entity is finally stored. The task emphasizes the rank of the correct entity instead of only finding the best one entity. Similar to (Bordes et al. 2013), we report two measures as our evaluation metrics: the average rank of all correct entites (*Mean Rank*) and the proportion of correct entities ranked in top 10 (*Hits@10*). A lower *Mean Rank* and a higher *Hits@10* should be achieved by a good embedding model. We call the evaluation setting "Raw'. Noting the fact that a corrupted triplet may also exist in knowledge graphs, the corrupted triplet should be regard as a correct triplet. Hence, we should remove the corrupted triplets included in train, valid and test sets before ranking. We call this evaluation setting "Filter". In this paper, we will report evaluation results of the two settings .

In this task, we use two datasets: WN18 and FB15k. As all the data sets are the same, we refer to their experimental results in this paper. On WN18, we also use ADADELTA SGD (Zeiler 2012) for optimization. We select the margin γ among $\{0.1, 0.5, 1, 2\}$, the dimension of entity vectors m and the dimension of relation vectors n among $\{20, 50, 80, 100\}$, and the mini-batch size B among $\{100, 200, 1000, 1400\}$. The best configuration obtained by valid set are:$\gamma = 1, m, n = 50, B = 200$ and taking L_2 as dissimilarity. For both the two datasets, We traverse to training for 1000 rounds.

Experimental results on both WN18 and FB15k are shown in Table 4. From Table 4, we can conclude that: (1) TransD outperforms other baseline embedding models (TransE, TransH and TransR/CTransR), especially on sparse dataset, i.e., FB15k; (2) Compared with CTransR, TransD is a more fine-grained model which considers the multiple types of entities and relations simultaneously, and it achieves a better performance. It indicates that TransD handles complicated internal correlations of entities and relations in knowledge graphs better than CTransR; (3) The "bern" sampling trick can reduce false negative labels than "unif".

For the comparison of *Hits@10* of different kinds of relations, Table 5 shows the detailed results by mapping properties of relations[1] on FB15k. From Table 5, we can see that TransD outperforms TransE, TransH and TransR/CTransR significantly in both "unif" and "bern" settings. TransD achieves better performance than CTransR in all types of relations (1-to-1, 1-to-N, N-to-1 and N-to-N). For N-to-N relations in predicting both head and tail, our approach improves the *Hits@10* by almost 7.4% than CTransR. In particular, for

[1]Mapping properties of relations follows the same rules in (Bordes et al. 2013)

Data sets	WN18				FB15K			
Metric	Mean Rank		Hits@10		Mean Rank		Hits@10	
	Raw	Filt	Raw	Filt	Raw	Filt	Raw	Filt
Unstructured (Bordes et al. 2012)	315	304	35.3	38.2	1,074	979	4.5	6.3
RESCAL (Nickle, Tresp, and Kriegel 2011)	1,180	1,163	37.2	52.8	828	683	28.4	44.1
SE (Bordes et al. 2011)	1,011	985	68.5	80.5	273	162	28.8	39.8
SME (linear) (Bordes et al.2012)	545	533	65.1	74.1	274	154	30.7	40.8
SME (Bilinear) (Bordes et al. 2012)	526	509	54.7	61.3	284	158	31.3	41.3
LFM (Jenatton et al. 2012)	469	456	71.4	81.6	283	164	26.0	33.1
TransE (Bordes et al. 2013)	263	251	75.4	89.2	243	125	34.9	47.1
TransH (unif) (Wang et al. 2014)	318	303	75.4	86.7	211	84	42.5	58.5
TransH (bern) (Wang et al. 2014)	401	388	73.0	82.3	212	87	45.7	64.4
TransR (unif) (Lin et al. 2015)	232	219	78.3	91.7	226	78	43.8	65.5
TransR (bern) (Lin et al. 2015)	238	225	**79.8**	92.0	198	77	48.2	68.7
CTransR (unif) (Lin et al. 2015)	243	230	78.9	92.3	233	82	44.0	66.3
CTransR (bern) (Lin et al. 2015)	231	218	79.4	92.3	199	75	48.4	70.2
TransD (unif)	242	229	79.2	**92.5**	211	**67**	**49.4**	**74.2**
TransD (bern)	**224**	**212**	79.6	92.2	**194**	91	**53.4**	**77.3**

Table 4: Experimental results on link prediction.

Tasks	Prediction Head (Hits@10)				Prediction Tail (Hits@10)			
Relation Category	1-to-1	1-to-N	N-to-1	N-to-N	1-to-1	1-to-N	N-to-1	N-to-N
Unstructured (Bordes et al. 2012)	34.5	2.5	6.1	6.6	34.3	4.2	1.9	6.6
SE (Bordes et al. 2011)	35.6	62.6	17.2	37.5	34.9	14.6	68.3	41.3
SME (linear) (Bordes et al.2012)	35.1	53.7	19.0	40.3	32.7	14.9	61.6	43.3
SME (Bilinear) (Bordes et al. 2012)	30.9	69.6	19.9	38.6	28.2	13.1	76.0	41.8
TransE (Bordes et al. 2013)	43.7	65.7	18.2	47.2	43.7	19.7	66.7	50.0
TransH (unif) (Wang et al. 2014)	66.7	81.7	30.2	57.4	63.7	30.1	83.2	60.8
TransH (bern) (Wang et al. 2014)	66.8	87.6	28.7	64.5	65.5	39.8	83.3	67.2
TransR (unif) (Lin et al. 2015)	76.9	77.9	38.1	66.9	76.2	38.4	76.2	69.1
TransR (bern) (Lin et al. 2015)	78.8	89.2	34.1	69.2	79.2	37.4	90.4	72.1
CTransR (unif) (Lin et al. 2015)	78.6	77.8	36.4	68.0	77.4	37.8	78.0	70.3
CTransR (bern) (Lin et al. 2015)	81.5	89.0	34.7	71.2	80.8	38.6	90.1	73.8
TransD (unif)	80.7	85.8	**47.1**	**75.6**	80.0	**54.5**	80.7	**77.9**
TransD (bern)	**86.1**	**95.5**	**39.8**	**78.5**	**85.4**	**50.6**	**94.4**	**81.2**

Table 5: Experimental results on FB15K by mapping properities of relations (%).

N-to-1 relations (predicting head) and 1-to-N relations (predicting tail), TransD improves the accuracy by 9.0% and 14.7% compared with previous state-of-the-art results, respectively. Therefore, the diversity of entities and relations in knowledge grahps is an important factor and the dynamic mapping matrix is suitable for modeling knowledge graphs.

5 Properties of Projection Vectors

As mentioned in Section "Introduction", TransD is based on the motivation that each mapping matrix is determined by entity-relation pair dynamically. These mapping matrices are constructed with projection vectors of entities and relations. Here, we analysis the properties of projection vectors. We seek the similar objects (entities and relations) for a given object (entities and relations) by projection vectors. As WN18 has the most entities (40,943 entities which contains various types of words. FB13 also has many entities, but the most are person's names) and FB15k has the most relations (1,345 relations), we show the similarity of projection vectors on them. Table 6 and 7 show that the same category objects have similar projection vectors. The similarity of projection vectors of different types of entities and relations indicates the rationality of our method.

6 Conclusions and Future Work

We introduced a model TransD that embed knowledge graphs into continues vector space for their completion. TransD has less complexity and more flexibility than TransR/CTransR. When learning embeddings of named symbol objects (entities or relations), TransD considers the diversity of them both. Extensive experiments show that TransD outperforms TrasnE, TransH and TransR/CTransR on two tasks including triplets classification and link prediction.

As shown in Triplets Classification section, not all new facts can be deduced from the exist-

Datesets	WN18			
Entities and Definitions	*_upset_VB_4*	cause to overturn from an upright or normal position	*_srbija_NN_1*	a historical region in central and northern Yugoslavia
Similar Entities and Definitions	*_sway_VB_4*	cause to move back and forth	*_montenegro_NN_1*	a former country bordering on the Adriatic Sea
	_shift_VB_2	change place or direction	*_constantina_NN_1*	a Romanian resort city on the Black Sea
	_flap_VB_3	move with a thrashing motion	*_lappland_NN_1*	a region in northmost Europe inhabited by Lapps
	_fluctuate_VB_1	cause to fluctuate or move in a wave-like pattern	*_plattensee_NN_1*	a large shallow lake in western Hungary
	_leaner_NN_1	(horseshoes) the throw of a horse-shoe so as to lean against (but not encircle) the stake	*_brasov_NN_1*	a city in central Romania in the foothills of the Transylvanian Alps

Table 6: Entity projection vectors similarity (in descending order) computed on WN18. The similarity scores are computed with $cosine$ function.

Datesets	FB15k
Relation	*/location/statistical_region/rent50_2./measurement_unit/dated_money_value/currency*
Similar relations	*/location/statistical_region/rent50_3./measurement_unit/dated_money_value/currency* */location/statistical_region/rent50_1./measurement_unit/dated_money_value/currency* */location/statistical_region/rent50_4./measurement_unit/dated_money_value/currency* */location/statistical_region/rent50_0./measurement_unit/dated_money_value/currency* */location/statistical_region/gdp_nominal./measurement_unit/dated_money_value/currency*
Relation	*/sports/sports_team/roster./soccer/football_roster_position/player*
Similar relations	*/soccer/football_team/current_roster./sports/sports_team_roster/player* */soccer/football_team/current_roster./soccer/football_roster_position/player* */sports/sports_team/roster./sports/sports_team_roster/player* */basketball/basketball_team/historical_roster./sports/sports_team_roster/player* */sports/sports_team/roster./basketball/basketball_historical_roster_position/player*

Table 7: Relation projection vectors similarity computed on FB15k. The similarity scores are computed with $cosine$ function.

ing triplets in knowledge graphs, such as relations *gender, place of place, parents* and *children*. These relations are difficult to infer from all other information, but they are also useful resource for practical applications and incomplete, i.e. the *place of birth* attribute is missing for 71% of all people included in FreeBase (Nickel, et al. 2015). One possible way to obtain these new triplets is to extract facts from plain texts. We will seek methods to complete knowledge graphs with new triplets whose entities and relations come from plain texts.

Acknowledgments

This work was supported by the National Basic Research Program of China (No. 2014CB340503) and the National Natural Science Foundation of China (No. 61272332 and No. 61202329).

References

George A. Miller. 1995. WordNet: A lexical database for english. *Communications of the ACM*, 38(11):39-41.

Bollacker K., Evans C., Paritosh P., Sturge T., and Taylor J. 2008. Freebase: A collaboratively created graph database for structuring human knowledge. In *Proceedings of the 2008 ACM SIGMOD International Conference on Management of Data.* pages 1247-1250.

Fabian M. Suchanek, Kasneci G., Weikum G. 2007. YAGO: A core of semantic Knowledge Unifying WordNet and Wikipedia. In *Proceedings of the 16th international conference on World Wide Web.*

Bordes A., Usunier N., Garcia-Durán A. 2013. Translating Embeddings for Modeling Multi-relational Data. In *Proceedings of NIPS.* pags:2787-2795.

Wang Z., Zhang J., Feng J. and Chen Z. 2014. Knowledge graph embedding by translating on hyperplanes. In *Proceedings of AAAI.* pags:1112-1119.

Lin Y., Zhang J., Liu Z., Sun M., Liu Y., Zhu X. 2015. Learning Entity and Relation Embeddings for Knowledge Graph Completion. In *Proceedings of AAAI.*

Bordes A., Glorot X., Weston J., and Bengio Y. 2012. Joint learning of words and meaning representations for open-text semantic parsing. In *Proceedings of AISTATS.* pags:127-135.

Bordes A., Glorot X., Weston J., and Bengio Y. 2014. A semantic matching energy function for learing with multirelational data. *Machine Learning.* 94(2):pags:233-259.

Bordes A., Weston J., Collobert R., and Bengio Y. 2011. Learning structured embeddings of knowledge bases. In *Proceedings of AAAI.* pags:301-306.

Jenatton R., Nicolas L. Roux, Bordes A., and Obozinaki G. 2012. A latent factor model for highly multi-relational data. In *Proceedings of NIPS.* pags:3167-3175.

Sutskever I., Salakhutdinov R. and Joshua B. Tenenbaum. 2009. Modeling Relational Data using Bayesian Clustered Tensor Factorization. In *Proceedings of NIPS.* pags:1821-1828.

Socher R., Chen D., Christopher D. Manning and Andrew Y. Ng. 2013. Reasoning With Neural Tensor Networks for Knowledge Base Completion. In *Proceedings of NIPS.* pags:926-934.

Weston J., Bordes A., Yakhnenko O. Manning and Ununier N. 2013. Connecting language and knowledge bases with embedding models for relation extraction. In *Proceedings of EMNLP.* pags:1366-1371.

Matthew D. Zeiler. 2012. ADADELTA: AN ADAPTIVE LEARNING RATE METHOD. In *Proceedings of CVPR.*

Socher R., Huval B., Christopher D Manning. Manning and Andrew Y. Ng. 2012. Semantic Compositionality through Recursive Matrix-vector Spaces. In *Proceedings of EMNLP.*

Nickel M., Tresp V., Kriegel H-P. 2011. A three-way model for collective learning on multi-relational data. In *Proceedings of ICML.* pages:809-816.

Nickel M., Tresp V., Kriegel H-P. 2012. Factorizing YAGO: Scalable Machine Learning for Linked Data. In *Proceedings of WWW.*

Nickel M., Tresp V. 2013a. An Analysis of Tensor Models for Learning from Structured Data. *Machine Learning and Knowledge Discovery in Databases, Springer.*

Nickel M., Tresp V. 2013b. Tensor Factorization for Multi-Relational Learning. *Machine Learning and Knowledge Discovery in Databases, Springer.*

Nickel M., Murphy K., Tresp V., Gabrilovich E. 2015. A Review of Relational Machine Learning for Knowledge Graphs. In *Proceedings of IEEE.*

How Far are We from Fully Automatic High Quality Grammatical Error Correction?

Christopher Bryant
Department of Computer Science
National University of Singapore
13 Computing Drive
Singapore 117417
bryant@comp.nus.edu.sg

Hwee Tou Ng
Department of Computer Science
National University of Singapore
13 Computing Drive
Singapore 117417
nght@comp.nus.edu.sg

Abstract

In this paper, we first explore the role of inter-annotator agreement statistics in grammatical error correction and conclude that they are less informative in fields where there may be more than one correct answer. We next created a dataset of 50 student essays, each corrected by 10 different annotators for all error types, and investigated how both human and GEC system scores vary when different combinations of these annotations are used as the gold standard. Upon learning that even humans are unable to score higher than 75% $F_{0.5}$, we propose a new metric based on the ratio between human and system performance. We also use this method to investigate the extent to which annotators agree on certain error categories, and find that similar results can be obtained from a smaller subset of just 10 essays.

1 Introduction

Interest in grammatical error correction (GEC) systems has grown considerably in the past few years, thanks mainly to the success of the recent Helping Our Own (HOO) (Dale and Kilgarriff, 2011; Dale et al., 2012) and Conference on Natural Language Learning (CoNLL) (Ng et al., 2013; Ng et al., 2014) shared tasks. Despite this increasing attention, however, one of the most significant challenges facing GEC today is the lack of a robust evaluation practice. In fact Chodorow et al. (2012) even go as far to say that it is sometimes "hard to draw meaningful comparisons between different approaches, even when they are evaluated on the same corpus."

One of the reasons for this is that, traditionally, system performance has only ever been evaluated against the gold standard annotations of a single native speaker (rarely, two native speakers). As such, system output is not actually scored on the basis of grammatical acceptability alone, but rather is also constrained by the idiosyncrasies of the particular annotators.

The obvious solution to this problem would be to compare systems against the gold standard annotations of multiple annotators, in an effort to dilute the effect of individual annotator bias, however creating manual annotations is often considered too time consuming and expensive. In spite of this, while other studies have instead elected to use crowdsourcing to produce multiply-corrected annotations, often concerning only a limited number of error types (Madnani et al., 2011; Pavlick et al., 2014; Tetreault et al., 2014), one of the main contributions of this paper is the provision of a dataset of 10 human expert annotations, annotated in the tradition of CoNLL-2014, that is moreover annotated for all error types.[1]

With this new dataset, we have, for the first time, been able to compare system output against the gold standard annotations of a larger group of human annotators, in a realistic grammar checking scenario, and consequently been able to quantify the extent to which additional annotators affect system performance. Additionally, we also noticed that some annotators tend to agree on certain error categories more than others and so attempt to explain this.

In light of the results, we also explore how human annotators themselves compare against the combined annotations of the remaining annotators and thus calculate an upper bound $F_{0.5}$ score for the given dataset and number of annotators; e.g., if one human versus nine other humans is only able to score a maximum of 70% $F_{0.5}$, then it is unreasonable to expect a machine to do better. For this reason, we propose a more informative method of

[1] http://www.comp.nus.edu.sg/~nlp/sw/10gec_annotations.zip

Proceedings of the 53rd Annual Meeting of the Association for Computational Linguistics and the 7th International Joint Conference on Natural Language Processing, pages 697–707,
Beijing, China, July 26-31, 2015.

evaluating a system based on the ratio of that system's $F_{0.5}$ score against the equivalent human $F_{0.5}$ score.

Section 2 contains an overview of some of the latest research in both GEC and SMT that makes use of IAA statistics. Section 3 shows an example sentence from our dataset and qualitatively analyses how individual annotator bias affects their choice of corrections. Section 4 describes the data collection process and presents some preliminary results. Section 5 discusses the main quantitative results of the paper, formalizing the formulas used and introducing the more informative method of ratio scoring for GEC, while Section 6 summarizes the results from our additional experiments on category agreement and essay subsets. Section 7 concludes the paper.

2 Inter-Annotator Agreement (IAA)

Whenever we discuss multiple annotators, researchers invariably raise the issue of inter-annotator agreement (IAA), or rather the extent to which annotators agree with each other. This is because data which shows a higher level of agreement is often believed to be in some way more reliable than data which has a lower agreement score. Within GEC, agreement has often been reported in terms of Cohen's-κ (Cohen, 1960), although other agreement statistics could also be used.[2]

In the rest of this section, however, we wish to challenge the use of IAA statistics in GEC and question their value in this field. Specifically, while IAA statistics may be informative in areas where items can be classified into single, well-defined categories, such as in part-of-speech tagging, we argue that they are less well-suited to GEC and SMT, where there is often more than one correct answer. For example, two annotators may correct or translate a given sentence in two completely different yet valid ways, but IAA statistics are only able to interpret the alternative answers as disagreements.

2.1 Inter-Annotator Agreement in GEC

One important study that made use of κ as a measure of agreement between raters is by Tetrault and Chodorow (2008) (also in Tetreault et al. (2014)), who asked two native English speakers to insert a missing preposition into 200 randomly chosen, well-formed sentences from which a single preposition had been removed.

Despite the simplicity of this correction task, the authors reported κ-agreement of just 0.7, noting that in cases where the raters disagreed, their disagreements were often "licensed by context" and thus actually "acceptable alternatives". This led them to conclude that they would "expect even more disagreement when the task is preposition error detection in 'noisy' learner texts" and, by extension, imply that detection of *all* error types in 'noisy' texts would show more disagreement still.

The most important question to ask then, as a result of this study, is whether low κ-scores in 'noisy' texts are truly indicative of real disagreement, or whether, as in this preposition test, the disagreement is actually the result of multiple correct answers, and therefore not disagreement at all.

In a related study, and aware of the fact that there are often multiple ways to correct individual words in sentence, Rozovskaya and Roth (2010) instead chose to compute agreement at the sentence level. Specifically, three raters were asked simply to decide whether they thought 200 sentences were correct or not.

This time, despite operating at the more general sentence level, the authors reported κ scores of just 0.16, 0.4 and 0.23, surmising that "the low numbers reflect the difficulty of the task and the variability of the native speakers' judgments about acceptable usage." If that is the case, then true disagreement may be indistinguishable from native variability, and we should be wary of using IAA statistics as a measure of agreement or evaluation in GEC.

2.2 Inter-Annotator Agreement in SMT

In fact, the issues regarding the reliability of IAA metrics are not unique to GEC and we can also draw a parallel with the field of statistical machine translation (SMT). In the same way that there is often more than one way to correct a sentence in GEC, it is also well known that there is often more than one way to translate a sentence in SMT.

Nevertheless, while several papers have successfully discussed ways to minimize annotator bias effects in SMT (Snover et al., 2006; Madnani et al., 2008), IAA metrics such as κ still unhelpfully play a role in the field and have, for example, been reported almost every year in the Workshop on Machine Translation (WMT) conference.

[2]See Hayes and Krippendorff (2007) or Artstein and Poesio (2008) for the pros and cons of different IAA metrics.

Source:	**To put it in the nutshell**, I believe that people should **have the obligation** to tell their relatives about **the** genetic **testing result** for the good of their health.
A1	To put it in **a** nutshell, I believe that people should **be obliged** to tell their relatives about **their** genetic **test results** for the good of their health.
A2	**In a nutshell**, I believe that people should have **an** obligation to tell their relatives about the genetic testing result for the good of their health.
A3	**In summary**, I believe that people should have the obligation to tell their relatives about the genetic testing result for the good of their health.
A4	**In a nutshell**, I believe that people should **be obligated** to tell their relatives about the genetic testing result for the good of their health.
A5	To put it in **a** nutshell, I believe that people should **be obligated** to tell their relatives about the genetic testing **results** for the good of their health.
A6	To put it in the nutshell, I believe that people should have **an** obligation to tell their relatives about **their** genetic **test results** for the good of their health.
A7	To put it in **a** nutshell, I believe that people should have the obligation to tell their relatives about the genetic testing result for the good of their health.
A8	To put it in **a** nutshell, I believe that people should **be obligated** to tell their relatives about the genetic testing result for the good of their health.
A9	To put it in **a** nutshell, I believe that people should have the obligation to tell their relatives about the genetic **test** result for the good of their health.
A10	To put it in **a** nutshell, I believe that people should have the obligation to tell their relatives about the genetic **test results** for the good of their health.

Table 1: Table showing how each of the 10 annotators edited the same source sentence in Essay 25. The words in the source sentence that were changed are highlighted in bold.

This is in spite of the fact that the average inter-annotator κ score across all language pairs over the past five years has never been higher than 0.4 (Bojar et al., 2014).

One important paper that attempts to explain why IAA metrics score so poorly in SMT is by Lommel et al. (2014), who asked annotators to highlight and categorize sections of automatically translated text they believed to be erroneous. Their results showed that while annotators were often able to agree on the rough locations of errors, they often disagreed as to the specific boundaries of those errors: for instance, given the phrase "had go", some annotators considered just the participle "go" $\rightarrow$ "gone" to be the minimal error, while others considered the whole verbal unit, "had go" $\rightarrow$ "had gone", to be the minimal error. Similarly, the authors also noted that annotators sometimes had problems categorizing ambiguous errors which could be classified into more than one error category.

In short, while annotators already vary as to what they consider an error, these observations show that even when they do apparently agree, there is no guarantee that every annotator will define the error in exactly the same terms. This poses a problem for IAA statistics, which rely on an exact match to measure agreement.

Finally, it is also worth mentioning that a related study, by Denkowski and Lavie (2010), suggested that "annotators also have difficulty agreeing with themselves" (shown from *intra*-annotator agreement κ scores of about 0.6), and so we should be especially wary of using IAA metrics to validate datasets that may even be unreliable for a single annotator.

3 Annotator Bias

In an effort to better understand how annotators' judgments might differ, we first carried out a small-scale qualitative analysis on a handful of random sentences corrected by the 10 human annotators in our dataset. One such sentence, and all its various corrections, is shown in Table 1.

It is interesting to note that, for even as short an idiom as "To put it in the nutshell', there are still multiple alternative edits. Although 8 out of the 10 annotators elected to replace the article "the" with "a", among them, A2 and A4 also deleted "To put it" from the expression. Of the remaining 2 annotators, A3 chose to replace the idiom entirely with "In summary", while A6 made no correction at all. Although no correction appears to be unacceptable to the majority of annotators, it is also not completely ungrammatical (just idiomatically awkward) so it may be that A6 has a higher tolerance for this kind of error than the other annotators. Alternatively, there is also always the possibility that, given such a large amount of text to correct, this error was simply overlooked.

Another noteworthy difference is that annotators A1, A4, A5, and A8 all elected to change the verb "have the obligation" from active to passive, although A1 still disagreed with the others on the form of the participle. Similarly, there is also a great difference of opinion on whether "testing result" should be corrected or not, and if so, how. While half of the annotators left the phrase unchanged, A1, A6, and A10 all changed both words to "test results". Meanwhile, somewhere in between, A5 decided to change "result" to "results", but not "testing" to "test", while, conversely, A9 decided to do the opposite. This would suggest that error correction of even minor phrases falls along a continuum governed by each annotator's natural bias.

Finally, one of the most important results of this qualitative evaluation is that even though all 10 annotators edited the same sentence to a level they deemed grammatical, not one single annotator agreed with another exactly. This fact alone suggests IAA statistics are not a good way to evaluate GEC data and that a more robust agreement metric must take into account the possibility of alternative correct answers.

4 Data Collection

The raw text data in our dataset was originally produced by 25 students at the National University of Singapore (NUS) who were non-native speakers of English. They were asked to write two essays on the topics of genetic testing and social media respectively. All essays were of similar length and quality. This was important because varying the skill level of the essays is likely to further affect the natural bias of the annotators, who may then consistently over- or under-correct essays. These raw essays also formed the basis of the CoNLL-2014 test data (Ng et al., 2014). See Table 2 for some basic statistics on the resulting 50 essays.

	Total	Average per essay
# Paragraphs	252	5.0
# Sentences	1312	26.2
# Tokens	30144	602.9

Table 2: Statistics for the 50 unannotated essays.

The 10 annotators who annotated all 50 essays include: the 2 official annotators of CoNLL-2014, the first author of this paper, and 7 freelancers who were recruited via online recruitment website, Elance.[3] All annotators are native British English speakers, many of whom also have backgrounds in English language teaching, proofreading, and/or Linguistics.

All annotations were made using an online annotation platform, WAMP, especially designed for annotating ESL errors (Dahlmeier et al., 2013). Using this platform, annotators were asked to highlight a minimal error string in the source text, provide an appropriate correction, and then categorize their selection according to the same 28-category error framework used by CoNLL-2014. Before commencing annotation, however, each annotator was given detailed instructions on how to use the tool, along with an explanation of each of the error categories. In cases of uncertainty, annotators were also encouraged to ask questions.

As it was slightly harder to control the quality of the 7 independently recruited annotators via Elance, they were each preliminarily asked to annotate only the first two essays before being given detailed feedback on their work. The main purpose of this feedback was to make sure that they a) understood the error category framework, and b) knew how to deal with more complicated cases such as word insertions, punctuation, etc. Unless it was felt that they had overlooked an obvious error in these first two essays, the feedback did not go so far as to tell annotators what they should and should not highlight in an effort to preserve individual annotator bias.

In all, while the specific time taken to complete annotation of all 50 essays was not calculated, all annotators completed the task over a period of about 3 weeks, at a rate of about 45 minutes per essay.

4.1 Early Observations

To investigate the extent to which different annotators have different biases, we first counted the total number of edits made by each annotator and sorted them by error category (Table 3).

As can be seen, there is quite a difference between the annotator who made the most edits (A1) and the annotator who made the fewest edits (A7), with A1 making more than twice the number of edits as A7. This just goes to show how varied judgments on grammaticality can be. Incidentally, annotators A3 and A7, who are among those who made the fewest edits, were also the two official gold standard annotators in CoNLL-2014.

There is also a large difference between edits in

[3] http://www.elance.com

Category	A1	A2	A3	A4	A5	A6	A7	A8	A9	A10	Total
ArtOrDet	879	639	443	503	665	620	331	358	390	624	5452
Cit	0	0	0	0	0	1	0	2	0	0	3
Mec	227	376	493	325	411	336	228	733	598	780	4507
Nn	404	290	228	264	360	300	215	254	277	365	2957
Npos	21	21	15	21	31	28	19	25	29	23	233
Others	42	186	49	116	95	43	44	34	125	105	839
Pform	431	52	18	57	30	83	47	53	19	18	808
Pref	4	79	153	18	223	53	96	92	250	180	1148
Prep	755	488	390	421	502	556	211	276	362	459	4420
Rloc–	488	308	199	331	187	244	94	174	296	240	2561
Sfrag	1	5	1	3	1	5	13	2	12	2	45
Smod	1	4	5	0	1	0	0	3	1	1	16
Spar	0	18	24	0	2	11	3	2	8	0	68
Srun	157	38	21	16	17	18	7	15	17	37	343
Ssub	74	54	10	4	25	81	68	21	18	82	437
SVA	162	123	154	95	140	114	105	132	144	144	1313
Trans	248	100	78	147	118	81	93	199	87	95	1246
Um	5	12	42	25	25	12	12	19	7	8	167
V0	137	35	37	50	81	69	31	58	51	85	634
Vform	388	168	91	100	156	125	132	78	122	124	1484
Vm	71	48	37	67	119	24	49	39	4	62	520
Vt	100	209	150	200	82	237	133	234	117	188	1650
Wa	0	1	1	3	1	1	0	2	4	2	15
Wci	623	476	479	446	456	595	340	250	212	346	4223
Wform	126	107	103	150	136	145	77	103	107	81	1135
WOadv	23	48	27	23	61	76	12	94	41	62	467
WOinc	187	67	54	78	53	74	22	24	87	103	749
Wtone	6	30	15	65	38	27	9	10	12	15	227
Total	5560	3982	3317	3528	4016	3959	2391	3286	3397	4231	37667

Table 3: Table showing how many annotations each annotator made in terms of error category. See Ng et al. (2014) Table 1 for a more detailed description of error categories.

terms of category use, with almost half of all edits falling into the categories for article or determiner (ArtOrDet), spelling or punctuation (Mec), preposition (Prep), or word choice (Wci) errors.

5 Quantitative Analysis

In the main phase of experimentation, we first investigated how different numbers of annotators affected the performance of various systems in the context of the CoNLL-2014 shared task. To do this, we downloaded the official system output of all the participating teams[4] and then the *Max-Match* (M2) Scorer[5] (Dahlmeier and Ng, 2012), which was the official scorer of the previous CoNLL-2013 and CoNLL-2014 shared tasks.

This scorer evaluates a system at the sentence level in terms of correct edits, proposed edits, and gold edits, and uses these to calculate an F-score for each team. When more than one set of gold standard annotations is available, the scorer will calculate F-scores for each alternative gold-standard *sentence* and choose the one from whichever annotator scored the highest. As in CoNLL-2014, we calculate $F_{0.5}$, which weights precision twice as much as recall, because it is more important for a system to be accurate than to correct every possible error. See (Ng et al., 2014) for more details on how $F_{0.5}$ is calculated.

5.1 Pairwise Evaluation

In order to quantify how much the F-score can vary in a realistic grammar checking scenario when there is only one gold standard annotator, we first computed the scores for a participating system vs each annotator in a pairwise fashion. Table 4 hence shows how the top team in CoNLL-2014, CAMB (Felice et al., 2014), performed against each of the 10 human annotators individually.

While Tetrault and Chodorow (2008) and Tetreault et al. (2014) reported a difference of 10% precision and 5% recall between their two individual annotators in their simplified preposition correction task, Table 4 shows this difference can actually be as much as almost 15% precision (A1 vs A7) and 6% recall (A1 vs A3) in a more realistic full scale correction task. This equates to a differ-

[4] http://www.comp.nus.edu.sg/~nlp/conll14st/official_submissions.tar.gz

[5] http://www.comp.nus.edu.sg/~nlp/sw/m2scorer.tar.gz

CAMB	P	R	$F_{0.5}$
A1	39.64	14.06	29.06
A2	35.73	17.35	29.48
A3	35.22	20.29	30.70
A4	32.69	17.88	28.04
A5	35.74	17.26	29.43
A6	35.76	17.73	29.72
A7	24.96	19.62	23.67
A8	29.17	16.92	25.48
A9	32.03	18.28	27.84
A10	35.52	16.26	28.72

Table 4: Table showing the $F_{0.5}$ scores for the top team in CoNLL-2014, CAMB, against each of the 10 annotators individually.

ence of over 7% $F_{0.5}$ (A3 vs A7) and once again shows how varied annotator's judgments can be.

5.2 All Combinations

5.2.1 Human vs Human

Whereas previously we could only calculate $F_{0.5}$ scores on a system vs human basis, when there are two or more annotators, we can also calculate scores on a human vs human basis. In fact, as the number of annotators increases, we can also start to calculate scores against different combinations of gold standard annotations.[6]

To give an example, since we have 10 annotators, a subset of these annotators, say annotators a2–a8, could be chosen as the gold standard annotations. We could then evaluate how each of the remaining annotators (i.e., annotator a1, a9, and a10) performs against this gold standard, by computing the M2 score for annotator a1 against annotators a2–a8, annotator a9 against annotators a2–a8, and annotator a10 against annotators a2–a8. We then average these 3 M2 scores, to determine how, on average, an annotator performs when measured against gold standard annotators a2–a8.

It is worth reiterating, however, that when more than one annotator is used as the gold standard, the M2 scorer will choose whichever annotator for the given *sentence* produces the highest F-score; i.e., if a2–a8 are the gold standard and we want to compute the F-score for a9, the M2 scorer will compute a9 vs a2, a9 vs a3, ..., a9 vs a8 separately *for each sentence*, and choose the highest.

[6]Note that by combinations of annotators, we mean simply that the M2 scorer has access to a larger number of alternative gold standard corrections; we do not attempt to merge annotations in any way.

The above calculations can be formalized as Equation 1:

$$g(X) = \frac{1}{|A| - |X|} \sum_{a \in A \setminus X} f(a, X) \qquad (1)$$

where A is the set of all annotators ($|A| = 10$ in our case) and X is a non-empty and proper subset of A, denoting the set of annotators chosen to be in the gold standard. The function $f(a, X)$ is the score computed by the M2 scorer to evaluate annotator a against each set of gold standard annotators X. $g(X)$ is thus the average M2 scores for the remaining annotators against the input gold standard combination X.

So far, in our example, we have chosen annotators a2–a8 to be the gold standard. There are, however, many other different ways of choosing 7 annotators to serve as the gold standard. For example, we could have chosen { a1, a2, ..., a7 }, { a1, a3, a4, ..., a8 }, etc. In fact, there are $\binom{10}{7} = 120$ different combinations of 7 annotators. As such, we can also compute how an individual human annotator performs when measured against any combination of 7 gold standard annotators, by averaging these 120 M2 scores. The above calculation is formalized in the general case in Equation 2:

$$h_i = \frac{1}{\binom{|A|}{|X|}} \sum_{X:|X|=i} g(X) \qquad (2)$$

where $\binom{|A|}{|X|}$ is the binomial coefficient for $|A|$ choose $|X|$ and $1 \leq i < |A|$. The function $g(X)$ is defined in Equation 1.

The resulting h_i values are hence the average $F_{0.5}$ scores achieved by any human against any combination of i other humans, and so, in some ways, also represent the upper bound of human performance on the current dataset. The specific values for h_i are shown in the second column of Table 5.

5.2.2 Caveat

One caveat regarding this method is that the number of *all* possible combinations of annotators is of the order $2^{|A|}$, which quickly becomes computationally expensive for large values of $|A|$. Fortunately however, in a realistic GEC evaluation scenario, it is only the last row of Table 5 that we are most interested in, and so it is actually only necessary to calculate a much more manageable $\binom{|A|}{|A|-1}$ gold standard combinations, which is conveniently

Gold Annotators (i)	Human (h_i)	AMU		CAMB		CUUI	
	Avg $F_{0.5}$	Avg $F_{0.5}$	Ratio	Avg $F_{0.5}$	Ratio	Avg $F_{0.5}$	Ratio
1	45.91	24.20	52.71%	28.22	61.46%	26.76	58.29%
2	56.68	33.47	59.05%	37.77	66.64%	36.04	63.59%
3	61.83	38.35	62.03%	42.68	69.03%	40.76	65.92%
4	65.05	41.53	63.85%	45.87	70.51%	43.77	67.29%
5	67.33	43.84	65.11%	48.17	71.54%	45.94	68.23%
6	69.07	45.62	66.06%	49.93	72.29%	47.60	68.92%
7	70.45	47.06	66.80%	51.34	72.87%	48.94	69.46%
8	71.60	48.26	67.40%	52.50	73.32%	50.05	69.89%
9	72.58	49.28	67.90%	53.47	73.67%	50.99	70.25%

Table 5: Table showing average human $F_{0.5}$ scores over all combinations of $1 \leq i < 10$ gold annotators compared to the same averages for the top 3 systems in CoNLL-2014, and the ratio percentage of each team's average score versus the human average score.

equal to the total number of annotators. We only compute all combinations here in order to quantify, for the first time, how much each additional annotator affects performance.

5.2.3 System vs Human

In addition to calculating scores on a human vs human basis, we also calculated the F-scores for the top three CoNLL-2014 teams, AMU (Junczys-Dowmunt and Grundkiewicz, 2014), CAMB (Felice et al., 2014), and CUUI (Rozovskaya et al., 2014), versus all the combinations of humans (Equation 3).

$$s_i = \frac{1}{\binom{|A|}{|X|}} \sum_{X:|X|=i} f(s, X) \qquad (3)$$

Specifically, $s \in S$, where S is the set of all three shared task systems, i.e., $\{$AMU, CAMB, CUUI$\}$, and $f(s, X)$ is the same function in Equation 1 which is the score computed by the M2 scorer to evaluate system s against the set of annotators X chosen to be in the gold standard. The average $F_{0.5}$ scores for each of the team's systems versus increasing numbers of i annotators are also shown in Table 5.

We notice from these scores that, as expected, both system and human performance increases as more annotators are used in a gold standard. We do now, however, have data that quantifies exactly how much each additional annotator affects the score. This effect can be more clearly seen in Figure 1.

It is important to note, however, that even with 9 annotators, human output itself does not reach close to 100% $F_{0.5}$ and instead, the difference between the systems and the humans is about 20% $F_{0.5}$. Furthermore, the curves for humans and systems also remain roughly parallel, suggesting human corrections gain as much benefit as system corrections from larger sets of gold standard annotations.

5.3 Ratio Scoring

In light of the above observation that even humans vs humans are unable to score 100% $F_{0.5}$, it thus seems unreasonable to expect machines to do the same. As such, we propose that it is much more informative to score system output against the average performance of humans instead of against the theoretical maximum score. The ratio values for the three CoNLL-2014 teams against the human gold standards of various sizes are hence also reported in Table 5. The most important thing to note is that these figures are not only much higher than the low $F_{0.5}$ values currently reported in the literature, they are also more representative of the state of the art. For instance, it is highly significant that we can report that the top system in CoNLL-2014, CAMB, is actually able to perform 73% as reliably as a human, which suggests GEC may actually be a more viable technology than was previously thought.

6 Additional Experiments

6.1 Error Categories

As well as carrying out experiments at the system level, we also carried out similar experiments at the error category level. More specifically, we recalculated the values of Equation 1 and 2 for cases where the set of annotations consisted of only a

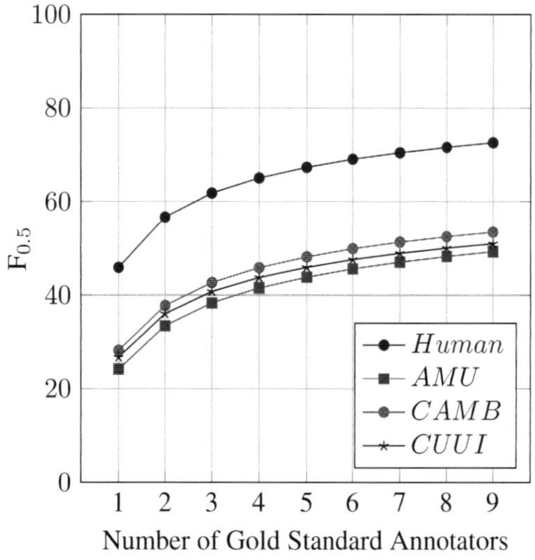

Figure 1: Graph showing how average $F_{0.5}$ scores for humans and systems increase as the number of gold standard annotators also increases (*all error types, 50 Essays*).

single specific error type. Since the participating teams in CoNLL-2014 were not asked to classify the type of errors their systems corrected, we were only able to calculate these new values using the 10 sets of human annotations.

Like Figure 1, we can see from Figure 2 that the $F_{0.5}$ performance of individual error types increases diminishingly as the number of annotators in the gold standard also increases. More importantly, however, we notice that some error types achieve much higher scores than others, which suggests some annotators agree on certain categories more than others.

In particular, noun number (Nn) and subject-verb agreement (SVA) errors achieve the highest scores, at just under 90% $F_{0.5}$, which is also not far from the 100% $F_{0.5}$ that would be achieved if we had gold standard answers for all possible alternative corrections of this type. The most likely reason for this is that, as the correction of these error types typically only involves the addition or removal of an -s suffix, i.e., a minor change in number morphology, there is very little room for annotators to disagree.

In contrast, the next highest category, article and determiner errors (ArtOrDet), has a slightly larger confusion set, {the, a/an, ϵ}, which may account for the slightly lower score. Similarly, the next group of error categories, spelling and punctuation

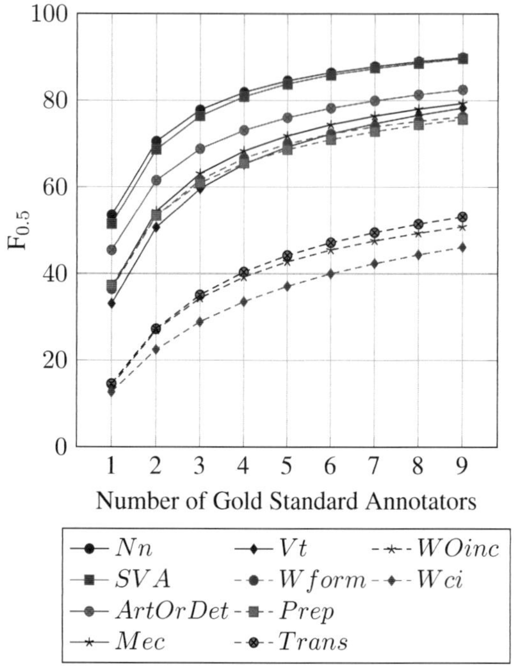

Figure 2: Graph showing how average $F_{0.5}$ scores for various error categories increase as the number of gold standard annotators also increases (*50 essays*). Calculations based on human annotations only.

(Mec), verb tense (Vt), and word form (Wform), which all often involve a similar type of edit operation to a word lemma, likewise have slightly larger confusion sets that include a larger variety of possible morphological inflections. It is likely that the next category, prepositions (Prep), also has a confusion set of a similar size.

The last three categories, conjunctions (all-types) (Trans), word order (WOinc) and word choice (Wci), are all notable because they perform significantly worse than the hitherto mentioned categories. The main reason for this is that these error types all typically have a scope much larger than most other categories in that they often involve changes at the structural or semantic level; e.g., changing an active to a passive or choosing a synonym. For this reason, there are often many more alternative ways to correct them, meaning they are also much more likely to be affected by annotator bias.

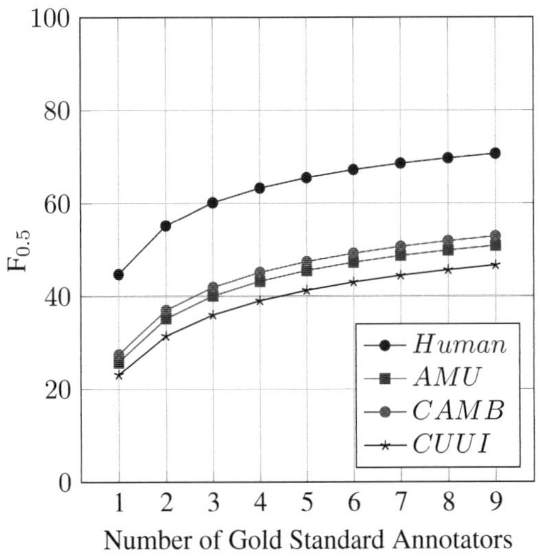

Figure 3: Graph showing how average $F_{0.5}$ scores for humans and systems increase as the number of gold standard annotators also increases (*all error types, 10 Essays*).

6.2 Essay Subsets

Now that we had empirical evidence showing how $F_{0.5}$ scores varied with the number of annotators, an additional question to ask was whether the same trends for 50 essays were also present in a smaller subset of essays. We therefore repeated the main experiment with all error types, but this time used just 10 essays (specifically, essays 1–10) in both the hypothesis and gold standard. The results are shown in Figure 3.

Compared to Figure 1, the most significant difference between these two graphs is that the ranking for AMU and CUUI has changed, although not by much in terms of $F_{0.5}$. The most likely reason for this is that the distribution of error types in the smaller subset of essays is better suited to AMU's more general SMT approach than to CUUI's more targeted classifier based approach. For instance, see Table 9 in Ng et al. (2014) to compare each team's performance on different error types in the CoNLL-2014 shared task.

In other words, while the overall relationship between the system and human scores on 10 and 50 essays remains more or less the same, researchers must be aware that smaller datasets may have more skewed error distributions, which in turn may affect system performance, dependent upon correction strategy. With a balanced test set though, it would seem feasible to carry out future evaluation research on as few as 10 essays (about 6000 words).

7 Conclusion

To summarize, we first showed that 10 individual annotators can all correct the same sentence in 10 different ways, yet also all produce valid alternatives. This implies that inter-annotator agreement statistics, which rely on exact matching, are not well-suited to grammatical error correction, because it may not be the case that annotators truly disagree, but rather that they have a bias towards a particular type of alternative answer.

We next showed that, as has long been suspected, increasing the number of annotators in the gold standard also leads to an increase in $F_{0.5}$, although at a diminishing rate. This data can be used to help researchers decide how many gold standard annotations should be used in GEC evaluation.

The main result of this paper however, is that by computing scores for human against human, we determined that it is *not* true that any human correction is able to score 100% $F_{0.5}$. Instead, we found that the human upper bound is roughly 73% $F_{0.5}$ and that the top 3 teams from CoNLL-2014 actually perform, on average, between 67-73% as reliably as this human upper bound. This result is highly significant, because it suggests GEC systems may actually be more viable than their previously low $F_{0.5}$ scores would suggest.

In addition to the above, we also found that humans tend to agree on some error categories more than others, and suggest that one of the main reasons for this concerns the size of the confusion set of the particular error type.

Finally, not only are we making the corrections by 10 annotators of all 50 essays available with this paper, we also showed that the trends found in the data are also consistent with the annotations of just 10 essays, allowing future research to be conducted on much less text.

Acknowledgments

This research is supported by Singapore Ministry of Education Academic Research Fund Tier 2 grant MOE2013-T2-1-150. We would also like to thank the three anonymous reviewers for their comments.

References

Ron Artstein and Massimo Poesio. 2008. Inter-coder agreement for computational linguistics. *Computational Linguistics*, 34(4):555–596.

Ondrej Bojar, Christian Buck, Christian Federmann, Barry Haddow, Philipp Koehn, Johannes Leveling, Christof Monz, Pavel Pecina, Matt Post, Herve Saint-Amand, Radu Soricut, Lucia Specia, and Aleš Tamchyna. 2014. Findings of the 2014 Workshop on Statistical Machine Translation. In *Proceedings of the Ninth Workshop on Statistical Machine Translation*, pages 12–58, Baltimore, Maryland, USA, June. Association for Computational Linguistics.

Martin Chodorow, Markus Dickinson, Ross Israel, and Joel R. Tetreault. 2012. Problems in evaluating grammatical error detection systems. In *COLING*, pages 611–628.

Jacob Cohen. 1960. A coefficient of agreement for nominal scales. *Educational and Psychological Measurement*, 20(1):37–46.

Daniel Dahlmeier and Hwee Tou Ng. 2012. Better evaluation for grammatical error correction. In *HLT-NAACL*, pages 568–572.

Daniel Dahlmeier, Hwee Tou Ng, and Siew Mei Wu. 2013. Building a large annotated corpus of learner English: The NUS Corpus of Learner English. In *Proceedings of the Eighth Workshop on Innovative Use of NLP for Building Educational Applications*, pages 22–31, Atlanta, Georgia, USA.

Robert Dale and Adam Kilgarriff. 2011. Helping Our Own: The HOO 2011 pilot shared task. In *Proceedings of the Generation Challenges Session at the 13th European Workshop on Natural Language Generation*, pages 242–249.

Robert Dale, Ilya Anisimoff, and George Narroway. 2012. Helping Our Own: HOO 2012: A report on the preposition and determiner error correction shared task. In *Proceedings of the Seventh Workshop on Innovative Use of NLP for Building Educational Applications*, pages 54–62.

Michael Denkowski and Alon Lavie. 2010. Choosing the right evaluation for machine translation: an examination of annotator and automatic metric performance on human judgment tasks. *Proceedings of AMTA*.

Mariano Felice, Zheng Yuan, Øistein E Andersen, Helen Yannakoudakis, and Ekaterina Kochmar. 2014. Grammatical error correction using hybrid systems and type filtering. In *Proceedings of the Eighteenth Conference on Computational Natural Language Learning: Shared Task*, pages 15–24.

Andrew F Hayes and Klaus Krippendorff. 2007. Answering the call for a standard reliability measure for coding data. *Communication Methods and Measures*, 1(1):77–89.

Marcin Junczys-Dowmunt and Roman Grundkiewicz. 2014. The AMU system in the CoNLL-2014 shared task: Grammatical error correction by data-intensive and feature-rich statistical machine translation. In *Proceedings of the Eighteenth Conference on Computational Natural Language Learning: Shared Task*, pages 25–33.

Arle Richard Lommel, Maja Popovic, and Aljoscha Burchardt. 2014. Assessing inter-annotator agreement for translation error annotation. In *MTE: Workshop on Automatic and Manual Metrics for Operational Translation Evaluation*.

Nitin Madnani, Philip Resnik, Bonnie J. Dorr, and Richard Schwartz. 2008. Are multiple reference translations necessary? Investigating the value of paraphrased reference translations in parameter optimization. *Proceedings of the Eighth Conference of the Association for Machine Translation in the Americas, October*.

Nitin Madnani, Martin Chodorow, Joel R. Tetreault, and Alla Rozovskaya. 2011. They can help: Using crowdsourcing to improve the evaluation of grammatical error detection systems. In *Proceedings of the 49th Annual Meeting of the Association for Computational Linguistics*, pages 508–513.

Hwee Tou Ng, Siew Mei Wu, Yuanbin Wu, Christian Hadiwinoto, and Joel R. Tetreault. 2013. The CoNLL-2013 shared task on grammatical error correction. In *Proceedings of the Seventeenth Conference on Computational Natural Language Learning: Shared Task*, pages 1–12, Sofia, Bulgaria. ACL.

Hwee Tou Ng, Siew Mei Wu, Ted Briscoe, Christian Hadiwinoto, Raymond Hendy Susanto, and Christopher Bryant. 2014. The CoNLL-2014 shared task on grammatical error correction. In *Proceedings of the Eighteenth Conference on Computational Natural Language Learning: Shared Task*, pages 1–14, Baltimore, Maryland, USA. ACL.

Ellie Pavlick, Rui Yan, and Chris Callison-Burch. 2014. Crowdsourcing for grammatical error correction. In *Proceedings of the Companion Publication of the 17th ACM Conference on Computer Supported Cooperative Work and Social Computing*, CSCW Companion '14, pages 209–212, New York, NY, USA. ACM.

Alla Rozovskaya and Dan Roth. 2010. Annotating ESL errors: Challenges and rewards. In *NAACL Workshop on Innovative Use of NLP for Building Educational Applications*, pages 28–36.

Alla Rozovskaya, Kai-Wei Chang, Mark Sammons, Dan Roth, and Nizar Habash. 2014. The Illinois-Columbia system in the CoNLL-2014 shared task. In *Proceedings of the Eighteenth Conference on Computational Natural Language Learning: Shared Task*, pages 34–42.

Matthew Snover, Bonnie Dorr, Richard Schwartz, Linnea Micciulla, and Ralph Weischedel. 2006. A study of translation error rate with targeted human annotation. In *Proceedings of the Association for Machine Transaltion in the Americas*.

Joel R. Tetrault and Martin Chodorow. 2008. Native judgments of non-native usage: Experiments in preposition error detection. In *COLING Workshop on Human Judgments in Computational Linguistics*, pages 24–32, Manchester, UK.

Joel R. Tetreault, Martin Chodorow, and Nitin Madnani. 2014. Bucking the trend: improved evaluation and annotation practices for ESL error detection systems. *Language Resources and Evaluation*, 48(1):5–31.

Knowledge Portability with Semantic Expansion of Ontology Labels

Mihael Arcan[1] **Marco Turchi**[2] **Paul Buitelaar**[1]

[1] Insight Centre for Data Analytics, National University of Ireland, Galway
firstname.lastname@insight-centre.org

[2] FBK- Fondazione Bruno Kessler, Via Sommarive 18, 38123 Trento, Italy
turchi@fbk.eu

Abstract

Our research focuses on the multilingual enhancement of ontologies that, often represented only in English, need to be translated in different languages to enable knowledge access across languages. Ontology translation is a rather different task then the classic document translation, because ontologies contain highly specific vocabulary and they lack contextual information. For these reasons, to improve automatic ontology translations, we first focus on identifying relevant unambiguous and domain-specific sentences from a large set of generic parallel corpora. Then, we leverage Linked Open Data resources, such as DBPedia, to isolate ontology-specific bilingual lexical knowledge. In both cases, we take advantage of the semantic information of the labels to select relevant bilingual data with the aim of building an ontology-specific statistical machine translation system. We evaluate our approach on the translation of a medical ontology, translating from English into German. Our experiment shows a significant improvement of around 3 BLEU points compared to a generic as well as a domain-specific translation approach.

1 Introduction

Currently, most of the semantically structured data, i.e. ontologies or taxonomies, has labels expressed in English only.[1] On the one hand, the increasing amount of ontologies offers an excellent opportunity to link this knowledge together (Gómez-Pérez et al., 2013). On the other hand, non-English users may encounter difficulties when using the ontological knowledge represented only in English. Furthermore, applications in information retrieval, question answering or knowledge management, that use monolingual ontologies are therefore limited to the language in which the ontology labels are stored. To make the ontological knowledge language-independent and accessible beyond language borders, these monolingual resources need to be transformed into multilingual knowledge bases. This multilingual enhancement can enable queries on documents beyond English, e.g. for cross-lingual business intelligence in the financial domain (O'Riain et al., 2013), providing information related to an ontology label, e.g. *other intangible assets*,[2] in Spanish, German or Italian. The main challenge involved in building multilingual knowledge bases is, however, to bridge the gap between language-specific information and the language-independent semantic content of ontologies or taxonomies (Gracia et al., 2012).

Since manual multilingual enhancement of ontologies is a very time consuming and expensive process, we engage an ontology-specific statistical machine translation (SMT) system to automatically translate the ontology labels. Due to the fact that ontology labels are usually highly domain-specific and stored only in knowledge representations (Chandrasekaran et al., 1999), the labels appear infrequent in parallel corpora, which are needed to build a domain-specific translation system with accurate translation candidates. Additionally, ambiguous labels built out of only a few words do often not express enough semantic or contextual information to guide the SMT system to translate a label into the targeted domain. This can be observed by domain-unadapted SMT systems, e.g. Google Translate, where ambiguous expressions, such as *vessel* stored in an medical ontology, are often translated into a generic do-

[1]Based on (Gracia et al., 2012), around 80% of ontology labels indexed in Watson are English.

[2]ontology label stored in FINREP - FINancial REPorting

Proceedings of the 53rd Annual Meeting of the Association for Computational Linguistics and the 7th International Joint Conference on Natural Language Processing, pages 708–718,
Beijing, China, July 26-31, 2015.

main as *Schiff*[3] in German (meaning *ship* or *boat*), but not into the targeted medical domain as *Gefäß*. Since ontologies may change over time, keeping up with these changes can be challenging for a human translator. Having in place an SMT system adapted to an ontology can therefore be very beneficial.

In this work, we propose an approach to select the most relevant (parallel) sentences from a pool of generic sentences based on the lexical and semantic overlap with the ontology labels. The goal is to identify sentences that are domain-specific in respect of the target domain and contain as much as possible relevant words that can allow the SMT system to learn the translations of the monolingual ontology labels. For instance, with the sentence selection we aim to retain only parallel sentences where the English word *injection* is translated into the German language as *Impfung* in the medical domain, but not into *Eindüsung*, belonging to the technical domain. This selection process aims to reduce the semantic noise in the translation process, since we try to avoid learning translation candidates that do not belong to the targeted domain. Nonetheless, some of the domain-specific ontology labels may not be automatically translatable with SMT, due to the fact that the bilingual information is missing and cannot be learned from the parallel sentences. Therefore we use the information contained in the DBpedia knowledge base (Lehmann et al., 2015) to improve the translation of expressions which are not known to the SMT system. We tested our approach on the medical domain translating from English to German, showing improvements of around 3 BLEU points compared to a generic as well as a domain-specific translation model.

The remainder of this paper is organized as follows: Section 2 gives an overview of the related work done in the field of ontology translation within SMT. In Section 3, we present the methodology of parallel data selection and terminology identification to improve ontology label translation. Furthermore we show different methods of embedding domain-specific knowledge into SMT. In Experimental Setting, Section 4, we describe the ontology to be translated along the training data needed for SMT. Moreover we introduce existing approaches and give a description of metrics for automatic translation evaluation. Section 5 presents the automatic and manual evaluation of the translated labels. Finally, conclusions and future work are shown in Section 6.

[3]Translation performed on 25.02.2015

2 Related Work

The task of ontology translation involves the finding of an appropriate translation for the lexical layer, i.e. labels, of the ontology. Most of the previous work tackled this problem by accessing multilingual lexical resources, e.g. EuroWordNet or IATE (Declerck et al., 2006; Cimiano et al., 2010). Their work focuses on the identification of the lexical overlap between the ontology and the multilingual resource. Since the replacement of the source and target vocabulary guarantees a high precision but a low recall, external translation services, e.g. BabelFish, SDL FreeTranslation tool or Google Translate, were used to overcome this issue (Fu et al., 2009; Espinoza et al., 2009). Additionally, ontology label disambiguation was performed by (Espinoza et al., 2009) and (McCrae et al., 2011), where the structure of the ontology along with existing multilingual ontologies was used to annotate the labels with their semantic senses. Differently to the aforementioned approaches, which rely on external knowledge or services, we focus on how to gain adequate translations using a small, but ontology-specific SMT system. We learned that using external SMT services often results in wrong translations of labels, because the external SMT services are not able to adapt to the specificity of the ontology. Avoiding existing multilingual resources, which enables a simple replacement of source and target labels, showed the possibility of improving label translations without manually generated lexical resources, since not every ontology may benefit of current multilingual resources.

Due to the specificity of the labels, previous research (Wu et al., 2008; Haddow and Koehn, 2012) showed that generic SMT systems, which merge all accessible data together, cannot be used to translate domain-specific vocabulary. To avoid unsatisfactory translations of specific vocabulary we have to provide the SMT system domain-specific bilingual knowledge, from where it can learn specific translation candidates. (Eck et al., 2004) used for the language model adaptation within SMT the information retrieval technique *tf-idf*. Similarly, (Hildebrand et al., 2005) and (Lü et al., 2007) utilized this approach to select relevant sentences from available parallel text to adapt translation models. The results confirmed that large amounts of generic training data cannot compensate for the requirement of domain-specific training sentences. Another approach is taken by (Moore and Lewis, 2010), where, based on source and target language models, the authors calculated the difference of the cross-entropy values for a given sentence. (Axelrod et al., 2011) extend this work using the bilingual difference of cross-entropy on in-domain and out-of-domain language models for training sentence selection for SMT. (Wuebker et al., 2014) reused the cross-entropy approach and applied it to the translation of video lectures. (Kirchhoff and Bilmes, 2014) introduce submodular optimization using complex features for parallel sentence selection. In their experiments they use the source and target side of the text to be translated, and show significant improvements over the widely used cross-entropy method. A different approach for sentence selection is shown in (Cuong and Sima'an, 2014), where the authors propose a latent domain translation model to distinguish between hidden in- and out-of-domain data. (Gascó et al., 2012) and (Bicici and Yuret, 2011) sub-sample sentence pairs whose source has most overlap with the evaluation dataset. Different from these approaches, we do not embed any specific in-domain knowledge to the generic corpus, from which sentence selection is performed. Furthermore, none of these methods explicitly exploit the ontological hierarchy for label disambiguation and are not specifically designed to deal with the characteristics of ontology labels.

As a lexical resource, Wikipedia with its rich semantic knowledge was used as a resource for bilingual term identification in the context of SMT. (Tyers and Pieanaar, 2008) extracts bilingual dictionary entries from Wikipedia to support the machine translation system. Based on exact string matching they query Wikipedia with a list of around 10,000 noun lemmas to generate the bilingual dictionary. Besides the interwiki link system, (Erdmann et al., 2009) enhance their bilingual dictionary by using redirection page titles and anchor text within Wikipedia. To cast the problem of ambiguous Wikipedia titles, (Niehues and Waibel, 2011; Arcan et al., 2014a) use the information of Wikipedia categories and the text of the articles to provide the SMT system domain-specific bilingual knowledge. This research showed that using the lexical information stored in this knowledge base improves the translation of highly domain-specific vocabulary. However, we do not rely on category annotations of Wikipedia articles, but perform domain-specific dictionary generation based on the overlap between related words from the ontology label and the abstract of a Wikipedia article.

3 Methodology

We propose an approach that uses the ontology labels to be translated to select the most relevant parallel sentences from a generic parallel corpus. Since ontology labels tend to be short (McCrae et al., 2011), we expand the label representation with its semantically related words. This expansion enables a larger semantic overlap between a label and the (parallel) sentences, which gives us more information to distinguish between related and unrelated sentences. Our approach reduces the ambiguity of expressions in the selected parallel sentences, which consequently gives more preference to translation candidates of the targeted domain. Furthermore, we access the DBpedia knowledge base to identify bilingual terminology belonging to the domain of the ontology. Once the domain-specific parallel sentences and lexical knowledge is available, we use different techniques to embed this knowledge into the SMT system. These methods are detailed in the following subsections.

3.1 Domain-Specific Parallel Sentence Selection

In order to generate the best translation system we select only sentences from the generic parallel corpus which are most relevant to the labels to be translated. The first criteria for relevance was the *n-gram overlap* between a label and a source sentence coming from the generic corpus. Therefore we calculate the cosine similarity between the n-grams extracted from a label and the n-grams of each source sentence in the generic corpus. The similarity between the label and the sentence is defined as the cosine of the angle between the two vectors. The calculated similarity score allows us to distinguish between more and less relevant sentences.

Due to the specificity of ontology labels, the *n-gram overlap* approach is not able to select useful sentences in the presence of short labels. For this reason, we improve it by extending the semantic information of labels using a technique for computing vector representations of words. The technique is based on a neural network that analyses the textual data provided as input and provides as output a list of semantically related words (Mikolov et al., 2013). Each input string is vectorized using the surrounding context and compared to other vectorized sets of words (from the training data) in a multi-dimensional vector space. For obtaining the vector representations we used a distributional semantic model trained on the Wikipedia articles,[4] containing more than 3 billion words. Word relatedness is measured through the cosine similarity between two word vectors. A score of 1 would represent a perfect word similarity; e.g. *cholera* equals *cholera*, while the medical expression *medicine* has a cosine distance of 0.678 to *cholera*. Since words, which occur in similar contexts tend to have similar meanings (Harris, 1954), this approach enables to group related words together. The output of this technique is the analysed label with a vector attached to it, e.g. for the medical label *cholera* it provides related words with its relatedness value, e.g. *typhus* (0.869), *smallpox* (0.849), *epidemic* (0.834), *dysentery* (0.808) ... In our experiments, this method is implemented by the use of Word2Vec.[5]

To additionally disambiguate short labels, the related words of the current label are combined with the related words of its direct parent in the ontology. The usage of the ontology hierarchy allows us to take advantage of the specific vocabulary of the related words in the computation of the cosine similarity. Given a label and a source sentence from the generic corpus, related words and their weights are extracted from both of them and used as entries of the vectors passed to the cosine similarity. The most similar source sentence and the label should share the largest number of related words (largest cosine similarity).

3.2 Bilingual Terminology Identification

The automatic translation of domain-specific vocabulary can be a hard task for a generic SMT system, if the bilingual knowledge is not present in the parallel dataset. To complement the previous approaches we access DBpedia[6] as a multilingual lexical resource.

We engage the idea of (Arcan et al., 2012) where the authors provide to the SMT system unambiguous terminology identified in Wikipedia to improve the translations of labels in the financial domain. To disambiguate Wikipedia entries with translations into different domains, they query the repository for analysing the n-gram overlap between the financial labels and the Wikipedia entries and store the frequency of categories which are associated with the matched entry. In a final step they extract only bilingual Wikipedia entries, which are associated with the most frequent Wikipedia categories identified in the previous step.

Since the Wikipedia entries are often associated only with a few categories, this limited vocabulary may give only a small contribution for this disambiguation of different meanings or topics of the same Wikipedia entry. For this reason, we use for each Wikipedia entry the extended abstract, which contains more information about the entry compared to the previous approach. For ambiguous Wikipedia entries, which overlap with a medical label, we therefore calculate the cosine similarity between the related words associated with the label and the lexical information of the Wikipedia abstract. Among different ambiguous entries, the cosine similarity gives more weight to the Wikipedia entry, which is closer to our preferred domain. Finally, if the Wikipedia entry has an equivalent in the target language, i.e. German, we use the bilingual information for the lexical enhancement of the SMT system.

3.3 Integration of Domain-Specific Knowledge into SMT

After the identification of domain-specific bilingual knowledge, it has to be integrated into the workflow of the SMT system. The injection of new obtained knowledge can be performed by retraining the domain-specific knowledge with the generic parallel corpus (Langlais, 2002; Ren et al., 2009; Haddow and Koehn, 2012) or by adding new entries directly to the translation system (Pinnis et al., 2012; Bouamor et al., 2012). These methods have the drawback that the bilingual domain specificity may get lost due to the usually larger generic parallel corpora. Giving more priority to domain-specific translations than generic ones, we focus on two techniques, i.e. the Fill-Up model (Bisazza et al., 2011) and the Cache-Based

[4]Wikipedia dump id enwiki-20141106

[5]https://code.google.com/p/word2vec/

[6]http://wiki.dbpedia.org/Downloads2014

Model (Bertoldi et al., 2013) approach.

The Fill-Up model has been developed to address a common scenario where a large generic background model exists, and only a small quantity of domain-specific data can be used to build a translation model. Its goal is to leverage the large coverage of the background model, while preserving the domain-specific knowledge coming from the domain-specific data. For this purpose the generic and the domain-specific translation models are merged. For those translation candidates that appear in both models, only one instance is reported in the Fill-Up model with the largest probabilities according to the translation models. To keep track of a translation candidate's provenance, a binary feature is added that gives preference to a translation candidate if it comes from the domain-specific translation model. We engage the idea of the Fill-Up model to combine the domain-specific parallel knowledge from the selected sentences with the generic (1.9M) parallel corpus.

Furthermore, for embedding bilingual lexical knowledge into the SMT system, we engage the idea of cache-based translation and language models (Bertoldi et al., 2013). The main idea behind these models is to combine a large static global model with a small, but dynamic local model. This approach has already shown its potential of injecting domain-specific knowledge into a generic SMT system (Arcan et al., 2014b). For our experiments we inject the bilingual lexical knowledge identified in DBpedia and IATE into the cache-based models. The cache-based model relies on a local translation model (CBTM) and language model (CBLM). The first is implemented as an additional table in the translation model providing one score. All entries are associated with an 'age' (initially set to 1), corresponding to the time when they were actually inserted. Each new insertion causes an ageing of the existing translation candidates and hence their re-scoring; in case of re-insertion of a phrase pair, the old value is set to the initial value. Similarly to the CBTM, the local language model is built to give preference to the provided target expressions. Each entry stored in CBLM is associated with a decaying function of the age of insertion into the model. Both models are used as additional features of the log-linear model in the SMT system.

4 Experimental Setting

In this Section, we give an overview on the dataset and the translation toolkit used in our experiment. Furthermore, we describe the existing approaches and give insights into the SMT evaluation techniques, considering the translation direction from English to German.

Evaluation Dataset For our experiments we used the International Classification of Diseases (ICD) ontology as the gold standard,[7] whereby the considered translation direction is from English to German. The ICD ontology, translated into 43 languages, is used to monitor diseases and to report the general health situation of the population in a country. This stored information also provides an overview of the national mortality rate and appearance of diseases of WHO member countries.

For our experiment we used 2000 English labels from the ICD-10 dataset, which were aligned to their German equivalents (Table 1). To identify the best set of sentences we experiment with different values of τ, which is the percentage of all the sentences that are considered relevant (domain-specific) by the sentence extraction approach. The value that allows the SMT system to achieve the best performance on the *development dataset 1* is used on the *evaluation set*, which is used for the translation evaluation of ontology labels reported in this paper. The parameters within the SMT system are optimized on the *development dataset 2*.

Statistical Machine Translation and Training Dataset For our translation task, we use the statistical translation toolkit Moses (Koehn et al., 2007), where the word alignments were built with the GIZA++ toolkit (Och and Ney, 2003). The SRILM toolkit (Stolcke, 2002) was used to build the 5-gram language model.

For a broader domain coverage of the generic training dataset necessary for the SMT system, we merged parts of JRC-Acquis 3.0[8] (Steinberger et al., 2006), Europarl v7[9] (Koehn, 2005) and OpenSubtitles2013[10] (Tiedemann, 2012), obtaining a training corpus of 1.9M sentences, con-

[7] http://www.who.int/classifications/icd/en/

[8] https://ec.europa.eu/jrc/en/language-technologies/jrc-acquis

[9] http://www.statmt.org/europarl/

[10] http://opus.lingfil.uu.se/OpenSubtitles2013.php

		English	German
Generic Dataset (out-domain)	Sentences	1.9M	
	Running Words	39.8M	37.1M
	Vocabulary	195,912	446,068
EMEA Dataset (domain-specific)	Sentences	1.1M	
	Running Words	13.8M	12.7M
	Vocabulary	58,935	115,754
Development Dataset 1	Labels	500	
	Running Words	3,025	2,908
	Vocabulary	889	951
Development Dataset 2	Labels	500	
	Running Words	3,003	3,020
	Vocabulary	938	1,027
Evaluation Dataset	Labels	1,000	
	Running Words	5,677	5,514
	Vocabulary	1,255	1,489

Table 1: Statistics for the bilingual training, development and evaluation datasets. ('Vocabulary' denotes the number of unique words in the dataset)

taining around 38M running words (Table 1).[11] The generic SMT system, trained on the concatenated 1.9 sentences, is used as a baseline, which we compare against the domain-specific models generated with different sentence selection methods. Furthermore we use the generic SMT system in combination with the smaller domain-specific models to evaluate different approaches when combining generic and domain-specific data together.

We additionally compare our results to an SMT system built on an existing domain-specific parallel dataset, i.e. EMEA[12] (Tiedemann, 2009), which holds specific medical parallel data extracted from the European Medicines Agency documents and websites.

Comparison to Existing Approaches We compare our approach on knowledge expansion for sentence selection with similar methods that distinguish between more important sentences and less important ones. First, we sort 1.9M sentences from the generic corpus based on the *perplexity* of the ontology vocabulary. The perplexity score gives a notion of how well the probability model based on the ontology vocabulary predicts a sample, which is in our case each sentence in the generic corpus.

Second, we use the method shown in (Hildebrand et al., 2005), where the authors use a method based on *tf-idf*[13] to select the most relevant sentences. This widely-used method in information retrieval tells us how important a word is to a document, whereby each sentence from the generic corpus is treated as a document.

Finally, we compare our approach with the *infrequent n-gram recovery* method, described in (Gascó et al., 2012). Their technique consists of selection of relevant sentences from the generic corpus, which contain infrequent n-grams based on their test data. They consider an n-gram as infrequent if it appears in the generic corpus less times than an infrequent threshold *t*.

Furthermore we enrich and evaluate our proposed ontology-specific SMT system with the lexical information coming from the terminological database IATE[14] (Inter-Active Terminology for Europe). IATE is the institutional terminology database of the EU and is used for the collection, dissemination and shared management of specific terminology and contains approximately 1.4 million multilingual entries.

Evaluation Metrics The automatic translation evaluation is based on the correspondence between the SMT output and reference translation (gold standard). For the automatic evaluation we used the BLEU (Papineni et al., 2002) and METEOR (Denkowski and Lavie, 2014) algorithms.[15]

BLEU (Bilingual Evaluation Understudy) is calculated for individual translated segments (n-grams) by comparing them with a dataset of reference translations. Considering the shortness of the labels, we report scores based on the bi-gram overlap (BLEU-2) and the standard four-gram overlap (BLEU-4). Those scores, between 0 and 100 (perfect translation), are then averaged over the whole *evaluation dataset* to reach an estimate of the translation's overall quality.

METEOR (Metric for Evaluation of Translation with Explicit ORdering) is based on the harmonic mean of precision and recall, whereby recall is weighted higher than precision. Along with standard exact word (or phrase) matching it has additional features, i.e. stemming, paraphrasing and synonymy matching. Differently to BLEU, the metric produces good correlation with human judgement at the sentence or segment level.

[11] For reproducibility and future evaluation we take the first one-third part of each corpus.

[12] `http://opus.lingfil.uu.se/EMEA.php`

[13] *tf-idf* – term frequency-inverse document frequency

[14] `http://iate.europa.eu/downloadTbx.do`

[15] METEOR configuration: exact, stem, paraphrase

The approximate randomization approach in MultEval (Clark et al., 2011) is used to test whether differences among system performances are statistically significant with a p-value < 0.05.

5 Evaluation of Ontology Labels

In this Section, we report the translation quality of ontology labels based on translation systems learned from different sentence selection methods. Additionally, we perform experiments training an SMT system on the combination of in- and out-domain knowledge. The final approach enhances a domain-specific translation system with lexical knowledge identified in IATE or DBpedia.

5.1 Automatic Translation Evaluation

We report the automatic evaluation based on BLEU and METEOR for the sentence selection techniques, the combination of in- and out-domain data and the lexical enhancement of SMT.

Sentence Selection Techniques As a first evaluation, we automatically compare the quality of the ICD labels translated with different SMT systems trained on specific sentences by the aforementioned selection techniques (Table 2). Due to the in-domain bilingual knowledge, the translation system trained using the EMEA dataset performs slightly better compared to the large generic baseline system. Among the different sentence selection approaches, the *infrequent n-gram recovery* method (infreq. in Table 2) outperforms the baselines and all the other techniques. This is due to the very strict criteria of selecting relevant sentences that allows the *infrequent n-gram recovery* method to identify a limited number (20,000) of highly ontology-specific bilingual sentences. The *related words* and the *n-gram overlap* models perform slightly better than the baseline, with a usage of 81,000 and 59,000 relevant sentences, and perform similarly to the in-domain EMEA translation system.

Further translation quality improvement is possible, if sentence selection methods are combined together (last four rows in Table 2). The cosine similarities of the methods are combined together, whereby new thresholds τ are computed on the *development dataset 1* and applied on the ICD *evaluation dataset*. Each combined method showed improvement compared to the stand-alone method. The best overall performance is obtained

Dataset Type	Size	BLEU-2	BLEU-4	METEOR
Generic dataset	1.9M	17.2	6.6	24.7
EMEA dataset	1.1M	18.5	7.0	25.8
(1) perplexity	89K	17.5	6.8	24.8
(2) tf-idf	21K	12,6	4.9	18,7
(3) infreq.	20K	19.1	8.1	25.3
(4) related w.	81K	18.9	7.0	25.8
(5) n-gram	59K	17.7	7.1	23.3
(5) ∧ (3)	22K	18.9	8.2*	25.1
(5) ∧ (4)	24K	17.3	7.3	23.9
(3) ∧ (4)	24K	18.4	8.4*	25.5*
(5) ∧ (4) ∧ (3)	30K	**20.1**	**8.9***	**27.2***

Table 2: Automatic translation evaluation on the evaluation dataset of the ICD ontology (Size = amount of selected sentences from the generic parallel corpus. bold results = best performance; *statistically significant compared to baseline)

when combining the *n-gram overlap*, the semantic *related words* and *infrequent n-gram recovery* methods. With this combination, we reduce the amount of parallel sentences by 98% compared to the generic corpus and significantly outperform the baseline by 2.3 BLEU score points. These two factors confirm the capability of the combined approach of selecting only few ontology-specific bilingual sentences (30,000) that allows the SMT system to identify the correct translations in the target ontology domain. This is due to the fact that the three combined methods are quite complementary. In fact, the *n-gram overlap* method selects a relatively large amount of bilingual sentences with few words in common with the label, the *related words* approach identifies bilingual sentences in the ontology target domain, and the infrequent n-gram recovery technique selects few bilingual sentences with only specific n-grams in common with the labels balancing the effect of the n-gram overlap method.

Combining In- and Out-Domain Data Considering the relatively small amount of parallel data extracted with the sentence selecting methods for the SMT community, we evaluate different approaches that combine a large generic translation model with domain-specific data. For this purpose, we use the sentences selected by the best approach ((5)∧(4)∧(3)) in the previous experiments and combine them with the generic parallel dataset. We evaluate the translation performance when *(i)* concatenating the selected domain-specific parallel dataset with the generic

Dataset Type	BLEU-2	BLEU-4	METEOR
Generic dataset	17.2	6.6	24.7
(5)∧(4)∧(3) sent. selec.	20.1	8.9*	27.2*
Data Concatenation *(i)*	18.1	6.8	24.1
Log-linear Models *(ii)*	18.9	8.1*	25.3
Fill-Up Model *(iii)*	17.7	7.0	24.7
(5)∧(4)∧(3) + IATE	19.8	9.0*	27.8*
(5)∧(4)∧(3) + DBpedia$^{(1)}$	20.6	9.1*	27.3*
(5)∧(4)∧(3) + DBpedia$^{(2)}$	**21.0**	**9.6**$^{*\diamond}$	**28.2**$^{*\diamond}$

Table 3: Evaluation of the ICD ontology evaluation dataset combining domain-specific with generic parallel knowledge and lexical enhancement of SMT using IATE and DBpedia (bold results = best performance; *statistically significant compared to baseline; $^{\diamond}$statistically significant compared to best sentence selection model)

parallel one, *(ii)* combining the generated translation models from the selected domain-specific parallel dataset and the generic corpus and *(iii)* applying the Fill-Up model to emphasise the domain-specific data in a single translation model. The translation performance of the combination methods are shown in Table 3. It is interesting to notice that none of them benefits from the use of the additional generic parallel data showing translation performance smaller than the domain-specific model. Although all methods outperform the generic translation model, only the log-linear approach, keeping in- and out-domain translation models separated, shows significant improvement. Comparing it to the combined sentence selection technique ((5)∧(4)∧(3)) does not show any statistical significant differences between the approaches. We conclude that the generic corpus is too large compared to the selected in-domain corpus, nullifying the influence of the extracted domain-specific parallel knowledge.

Lexical enhancement for SMT Since the out-of-vocabulary problem can be only mitigated with sentence selection, we accessed lexical resources IATE and DBpedia to further improve the translations of the medical labels. Based on the word overlap between labels and entries in IATE we extracted 11,641 English lexical entries with its equivalent in German. The DBpedia$^{(1)}$ approach, which disambiguates DBpedia entries based on the (Wikipedia article) categories (Arcan et al., 2012), identified 7,911 English-German expression for the targeted domain, while the abstract based disambiguation approach, marked as DBpedia$^{(2)}$ in Table 3 identified 3,791 bilingual entries. The lexical enhanced models further improved the translations of the medical labels (last three rows in Table 3) due to the additional bilingual information from the lexical resources, which is missing in the standalone sentence selection model. Comparing the ICD *evaluation dataset* and the translations generated with the DBpedia$^{(2)}$ lexical enhanced model we observed that more than 80 labels benefit from the additional lexical knowledge, e.g. correcting the mistranslated "adrenal gland" into "Nebenniere". The lexical extraction and disambiguation of bilingual knowledge based on the abstract of the article compared to the article categories further improves the lexical choice, helping SMT systems to improve the translation of ontology labels.

5.2 Manual Evaluation of Translated Labels

Since ontologies store specific vocabulary about a domain, this vocabulary is adapted to a concrete language and culture community (Cimiano et al., 2010). In order to investigate to what extent the automatically generated translations differ from a translator's adapted point of view, we manually inspected the translations produced by the sentence selection approaches described in Section 5.1.

While analysing the English and German part of the ICD ontology gold standard we noticed significant differences in the translations of the medical labels. As a result of the language and cultural adaptation, many labels in the ICD ontology were not always translated literally, i.e. parts of a label were semantically merged, omitted or new information was added while crossing the language border. For example, the ICD label "acute kidney failure and chronic kidney disease" is stored in the German part of the ontology as "Niereninsuffizienz".[16] Although none of the translation systems can generate the compounded medical expression for German, the SMT system generated nevertheless an acceptable translation, i.e. "akutes Nierenversagen und chronischer Nierenerkrankungen".[17] A more extreme example is the English label "slipping, tripping, stumbling and falls", in the German ICD ontology represented as

[16] Niereninsuffizienz←kidney insufficiency

[17] akutes←acute, Nierenversagen←kidney failure, und←and, chronischer←chronic, Nierenerkrankungen←kidney disease

"sonstige Stürze auf gleicher Ebene".[18] The language and cultural adaptation is very active for this example, where the whole English label is semantically merged into the word "Stürze", meaning "falls". Additionally, the German part holds more information within the label, i.e. "auf gleicher Ebene" (en. "at the same level"), which is not represented on the English side. Since the SMT system will always try to translate every phrase (word or word segments) into the target language, an automatic translation evaluation cannot reflect the overall SMT performance.

Further we detected a large error class caused by compounding, a common linguistic feature of German. Although the phrase "heart diseases" with its reference translation "Herzkrankheiten" appears frequent in the generic training dataset, the SMT system prefers to translate it word by word into "Herz Krankheiten". [19] Similar observations were made with "upper arm" (German "Oberarm") with the SMT word to word translation "oberen Arm".

Finally, we analysed the impact of the semantically enriched sentence selection with *related words* coming from Word2Vec compared to the surface based sentence selection, e.g. *perplexity*, *infrequent n-gram recovery* or *n-gram overlap*. Since semantically enriched selection stored the most relevant sentences, we observed the correct translation of the label "blood vessels" into "Blutgefäße". The generic and other surface based selections translated the expression individually into "Blut Schiffe", where "Schiffe" refers to the more common English word "ship", but not to 'part of the system transporting blood throughout our body'. The last example illustrates further the semantic mismatch between the training domain and the test domain. Using the generic model, built mainly out of European laws and parliament discussions (JRC-Acquis/Europarl) the word "head" inside the label "injury of head" is wrongly translated into the word "Leiter", meaning "leader" in the legal domain. Nevertheless, the additional semantic information prevents storing wrong parallel sentences and guides the SMT to the correct translation, i.e. "Schädigung des Kopfes".[20]

[18] sonstige←other, Stürze←falls, auf←on, gleicher←same, Ebene←level

[19] Herz←heart, Krankheiten←diseases

[20] Schädigung←injury, des←of, Kopfes←head

6 Conclusion

In this paper we presented an approach to identify the most relevant sentences from a large generic parallel corpus, giving the possibility to translate highly specific ontology labels without particular in-domain parallel data. We enhanced furthermore the translation system build on the in-domain parallel knowledge with additional lexical knowledge accessing DBpedia. With the aim to better select relevant bilingual knowledge for SMT, we extend previous sentence and lexical selection techniques with additional semantic knowledge. Our proposed ontology-specific SMT system showed a statistical significant improvement (up to 3 BLEU points) of ontology label translation over the compared translation approaches.

In future, we plan to integrate a larger diversity of surface, semantic and linguistic information for relevant sentence selection. Although the SMT system is capable of translating several words into a compound word, the small amount of the selected sentences limits this capability. To improve the ontology label translations, we therefore see the need to focus more on the German compound feature. Additionally we observed that more than 25% of the identified lexical knowledge consists of multi-word-expressions, e.g. "fatal familial insomnia". For this reason, our ongoing work focuses on the alignment of nested knowledge inside those expressions. To move further in this direction, we plan to focus on exploiting morphological term variations taking advantage of the alternative terms provided by DBpedia.

Acknowledgments

This publication has emanated from research supported in part by a research grant from Science Foundation Ireland (SFI) under Grant Number SFI/12/RC/2289 (Insight) and the European Union supported projects LIDER (ICT-2013.4.1-610782) and MixedEmotions (H2020-644632).

References

Arcan, M., Federmann, C., and Buitelaar, P. (2012). Experiments with term translation. In *Proceedings of the 24th International Conference on Computational Linguistics*, Mumbai, India.

Arcan, M., Giuliano, C., Turchi, M., and Buitelaar, P. (2014a). Identification of Bilingual Terms from Monolingual Documents for Statistical Machine Translation. In *Proceedings of the 4th International Workshop on Computational Terminology (Computerm)*, Dublin, Ireland.

Arcan, M., Turchi, M., Tonelli, S., and Buitelaar, P. (2014b). Enhancing statistical machine translation with bilingual terminology in a cat environment. In *Proceedings of the 11th Conference of the Association for Machine Translation in the Americas*, Vancouver, Canada.

Axelrod, A., He, X., and Gao, J. (2011). Domain adaptation via pseudo in-domain data selection. In *Proceedings of the Conference on Empirical Methods in Natural Language Processing*, EMNLP '11, Stroudsburg, PA, USA.

Bertoldi, N., Cettolo, M., and Federico, M. (2013). Cache-based Online Adaptation for Machine Translation Enhanced Computer Assisted Translation. In *Proceedings of Machine Translation Summit XIV*, Nice, France.

Bicici, E. and Yuret, D. (2011). Instance selection for machine translation using feature decay algorithms. In *Proceedings of the Sixth Workshop on Statistical Machine Translation*, Edinburgh, Scotland.

Bisazza, A., Ruiz, N., and Federico, M. (2011). Fill-up versus Interpolation Methods for Phrase-based SMT Adaptation. In *Proceedings of IWSLT*.

Bouamor, D., Semmar, N., and Zweigenbaum, P. (2012). Identifying bilingual multi-word expressions for statistical machine translation. In *Proceedings of the Eight International Conference on Language Resources and Evaluation*, Istanbul, Turkey.

Chandrasekaran, B., Josephson, J. R., and Benjamins, V. R. (1999). What are ontologies, and why do we need them? *IEEE Intelligent Systems*, 14(1):20–26.

Cimiano, P., Montiel-Ponsoda, E., Buitelaar, P., Espinoza, M., and Gómez-Pérez, A. (2010). A note on ontology localization. *Appl. Ontol.*, 5(2):127–137.

Clark, J., Dyer, C., Lavie, A., and Smith, N. (2011). Better Hypothesis Testing for Statistical Machine Translation: Controlling for Optimizer Instability . In *Proceedings of the Association for Computational Lingustics*.

Cuong, H. and Sima'an, K. (2014). Latent domain translation models in mix-of-domains haystack. In *Proceedings of the 25th International Conference on Computational Linguistics*, Dublin, Ireland.

Declerck, T., Pérez, A. G., Vela, O., Gantner, Z., Manzano, D., and D-Saarbrücken (2006). Multilingual lexical semantic resources for ontology translation. In *In Proceedings of the 5th International Conference on Language Resources and Evaluation*.

Denkowski, M. and Lavie, A. (2014). Meteor universal: Language specific translation evaluation for any target language. In *Proceedings of the EACL 2014 Workshop on Statistical Machine Translation*.

Eck, M., Vogel, S., and Waibel, A. (2004). Language model adaptation for statistical machine translation based on information retrieval. In *Proc. of LREC*.

Erdmann, M., Nakayama, K., Hara, T., and Nishio, S. (2009). Improving the extraction of bilingual terminology from wikipedia. *ACM Trans. Multimedia Comput. Commun. Appl.*, 5(4).

Espinoza, M., Montiel-Ponsoda, E., and Gómez-Pérez, A. (2009). Ontology localization. In *Proceedings of the Fifth International Conference on Knowledge Capture*, K-CAP '09, New York, NY, USA. ACM.

Fu, B., Brennan, R., and O'Sullivan, D. (2009). Cross-lingual ontology mapping - an investigation of the impact of machine translation. In Gómez-Pérez, A., Yu, Y., and Ding, Y., editors, *ASWC*, volume 5926 of *Lecture Notes in Computer Science*. Springer.

Gascó, G., Rocha, M.-A., Sanchis-Trilles, G., Andrés-Ferrer, J., and Casacuberta, F. (2012). Does more data always yield better translations? In *Proceedings of the 13th Conference of the European Chapter of the Association for Computational Linguistics*, EACL '12, Stroudsburg, PA, USA.

Gómez-Pérez, A., Vila-Suero, D., Montiel-Ponsoda, E., Gracia, J., and Aguado-de Cea, G. (2013). Guidelines for multilingual linked data. In *Proceedings of the 3rd International Conference on Web Intelligence, Mining and Semantics*. ACM.

Gracia, J., Montiel-Ponsoda, E., Cimiano, P., Gómez-Pérez, A., Buitelaar, P., and McCrae, J. (2012). Challenges for the multilingual web of data. *Web Semantics: Science, Services and Agents on the World Wide Web*, 11.

Haddow, B. and Koehn, P. (2012). Analysing the Effect of Out-of-Domain Data on SMT Systems. In *Proceedings of the Seventh Workshop on Statistical Machine Translation*, Montréal, Canada.

Harris, Z. (1954). Distributional structure. *Word*, 10(23).

Hildebrand, A. S., Eck, M., Vogel, S., and Waibel, A. (2005). Adaptation of the translation model for statistical machine translation based on information retrieval. In *Proceedings of the 10th Conference of the European Association for Machine Translation (EAMT)*, Budapest.

Kirchhoff, K. and Bilmes, J. (2014). Submodularity for data selection in machine translation. In *Empirical Methods in Natural Language Processing (EMNLP)*.

Koehn, P. (2005). Europarl: A Parallel Corpus for Statistical Machine Translation. In *Conference Proceedings: the tenth Machine Translation Summit*, pages 79–86. AAMT.

Koehn, P., Hoang, H., Birch, A., Callison-Burch, C., Federico, M., Bertoldi, N., Cowan, B., Shen, W., Moran, C., Zens, R., Dyer, C., Bojar, O., Constantin, A., and Herbst, E. (2007). Moses: Open source toolkit for statistical machine translation. In *Proceedings of the 45th Annual Meeting of the ACL on Interactive Poster and Demonstration Sessions*, Stroudsburg, PA, USA.

Langlais, P. (2002). Improving a general-purpose statistical translation engine by terminological lexicons. In *Proceedings of the 2nd International Workshop on Computational Terminology (COMPUTERM) '2002, Taipei, Taiwan*.

Lehmann, J., Isele, R., Jakob, M., Jentzsch, A., Kontokostas, D., Mendes, P. N., Hellmann, S., Morsey, M., van Kleef, P., Auer, S., and Bizer, C. (2015). DBpedia - a large-scale, multilingual knowledge base extracted from wikipedia. *Semantic Web Journal*, 6(2):167–195.

Lü, Y., Huang, J., and Liu, Q. (2007). Improving statistical machine translation performance by training data selection and optimization. In *Proceedings of the 2007 Joint Conference on Empirical Methods in Natural Language Processing and Computational Natural Language Learning (EMNLP-CoNLL)*.

McCrae, J., Espinoza, M., Montiel-Ponsoda, E., Aguado-de Cea, G., and Cimiano, P. (2011). Combining statistical and semantic approaches to the translation of ontologies and taxonomies. In *Fifth workshop on Syntax, Structure and Semantics in Statistical Translation (SSST-5)*.

Mikolov, T., Chen, K., Corrado, G., and Dean, J. (2013). Efficient estimation of word representations in vector space. *CoRR*, abs/1301.3781.

Moore, R. C. and Lewis, W. (2010). Intelligent selection of language model training data. In *Proceedings of the ACL 2010 Conference Short Papers*, ACLShort '10, Stroudsburg, PA, USA.

Niehues, J. and Waibel, A. (2011). Using Wikipedia to Translate Domain-specific Terms in SMT. In *International Workshop on Spoken Language Translation*, San Francisco, CA, USA.

Och, F. J. and Ney, H. (2003). A systematic comparison of various statistical alignment models. *Computational Linguistics*, 29.

O'Riain, S., Coughlan, B., Buitelaar, P., Declerck, T., Krieger, U., and Thomas, S. M. (2013). Cross-lingual querying and comparison of linked financial and business data. In Cimiano, P., Fernández, M., Lopez, V., Schlobach, S., and Völker, J., editors, *ESWC (Satellite Events)*, volume 7955 of *Lecture Notes in Computer Science*. Springer.

Papineni, K., Roukos, S., Ward, T., and Zhu, W.-J. (2002). BLEU: a method for automatic evaluation of machine translation. In *Proceedings of the 40th Annual Meeting on Association for Computational Linguistics*, ACL '02, pages 311–318.

Pinnis, M., Ljubešić, N., Ştefănescu, D., Skadiņa, I., Tadić, M., and Gornostay, T. (2012). Term extraction, tagging, and mapping tools for under-resourced languages. In *Proceedings of the Terminology and Knowledge Engineering (TKE2012) Conference*.

Ren, Z., Lü, Y., Cao, J., Liu, Q., and Huang, Y. (2009). Improving statistical machine translation using domain bilingual multiword expressions. In *Proceedings of the Workshop on Multiword Expressions: Identification, Interpretation, Disambiguation and Applications*, MWE '09, Stroudsburg, PA, USA.

Steinberger, R., Pouliquen, B., Widiger, A., Ignat, C., Erjavec, T., Tufis, D., and Varga, D. (2006). The JRC-Acquis: A multilingual aligned parallel corpus with 20+ languages. In *Proceedings of the 5th International Conference on Language Resources and Evaluation (LREC'2006)*.

Stolcke, A. (2002). SRILM - An extensible language modeling toolkit. In *Proceedings International Conference on Spoken Language Processing*.

Tiedemann, J. (2009). News from OPUS - A collection of multilingual parallel corpora with tools and interfaces. In Nicolov, N., Bontcheva, K., Angelova, G., and Mitkov, R., editors, *Recent Advances in Natural Language Processing*, volume V. John Benjamins, Amsterdam/Philadelphia, Borovets, Bulgaria.

Tiedemann, J. (2012). Parallel data, tools and interfaces in opus. In Chair), N. C. C., Choukri, K., Declerck, T., Doğan, M. U., Maegaard, B., Mariani, J., Odijk, J., and Piperidis, S., editors, *Proceedings of the Eight International Conference on Language Resources and Evaluation*, Istanbul, Turkey.

Tyers, F. M. and Pieanaar, J. A. (2008). Extracting bilingual word pairs from wikipedia. In *Collaboration: interoperability between people in the creation of language resources for less-resourced languages (A SALTMIL workshop)*.

Wu, H., Wang, H., and Zong, C. (2008). Domain adaptation for statistical machine translation with domain dictionary and monolingual corpora. In *Proceedings of the 22nd International Conference on Computational Linguistics - Volume 1*, COLING '08.

Wuebker, J., Ney, H., Martínez-Villaronga, A., Giménez, A., , Juan, A., Servan, C., Dymetman, M., and Mirkin, S. (2014). Comparison of Data Selection Techniques for the Translation of Video Lectures. In *Proc. of the Eleventh Biennial Conf. of the Association for Machine Translation in the Americas (AMTA-2014)*, Vancouver (Canada).

Automatic disambiguation of English puns

Tristan Miller and Iryna Gurevych
Ubiquitous Knowledge Processing Lab (UKP-TUDA)
Department of Computer Science, Technische Universität Darmstadt
`https://www.ukp.tu-darmstadt.de/`

Abstract

Traditional approaches to word sense disambiguation (WSD) rest on the assumption that there exists a single, unambiguous communicative intention underlying every word in a document. However, writers sometimes intend for a word to be interpreted as simultaneously carrying multiple distinct meanings. This deliberate use of lexical ambiguity—*i.e.*, punning—is a particularly common source of humour. In this paper we describe how traditional, language-agnostic WSD approaches can be adapted to "disambiguate" puns, or rather to identify their double meanings. We evaluate several such approaches on a manually sense-annotated collection of English puns and observe performance exceeding that of some knowledge-based and supervised baselines.

1 Introduction

Word sense disambiguation, or WSD, is the task of identifying a word's meaning in context. No matter whether it is performed by a human or a machine, WSD usually rests on the assumption that there is a single unambiguous communicative intention underlying each word in the document.[1] However, there exists a class of language constructs known as *paronomasia* and *syllepsis*, or more generally as *puns*, in which homonymic (*i.e.*, coarse-grained) lexical-semantic ambiguity is a *deliberate* effect of the communication act. That is, the writer intends for a certain word or other lexical item to be interpreted as simultaneously carrying two or more separate meanings, or alternatively for it to be unclear which meaning is the intended one. There are a variety of motivations writers have for employing such constructions, and in turn for why such uses are worthy of scholarly investigation.

Perhaps surprisingly, this sort of intentional lexical ambiguity has attracted little attention in the fields of computational linguistics and natural language processing. What little research has been done is confined largely to computational mechanisms for pun generation (in the context of natural language generation for computational humour) and to computational analysis of phonological properties of puns. A fundamental problem which has not yet been as widely studied is the automatic detection and identification of intentional lexical ambiguity—that is, given a text, does it contain any lexical items which are used in a deliberately ambiguous manner, and if so, what are the intended meanings?

We consider these to be important research questions with a number of real-world applications. For instance, puns are particularly common in advertising, where they are used not only to create humour but also to induce in the audience a valenced attitude toward the target (Valitutti et al., 2008). Recognizing instances of such lexical ambiguity and understanding their affective connotations would be of benefit to systems performing sentiment analysis on persuasive texts. Wordplay is also a perennial topic of scholarship in literary criticism and analysis. To give just one example, puns are one of the most intensively studied aspects of Shakespeare's rhetoric, and laborious manual counts have shown their frequency in certain

[1] Under this assumption, lexical ambiguity arises due to there being a plurality of words with the same surface form but different meanings, and the task of the interpreter is to select correctly among them. An alternative view is that each word is a single lexical entry whose specific meaning is *underspecified* until it is activated by the context (Ludlow, 1996). In the case of *systematically polysemous* terms (*i.e.*, words that have several related senses shared in a systematic way by a group of similar words), it may not be necessary to disambiguate them at all in order to interpret the communication (Buitelaar, 2000). While there has been some research in modelling intentional lexical-semantic underspecification (Jurgens, 2014), it is intended for closely related senses such as those of systematically polysemous terms, not those of coarser-grained homonyms which are the subject of this paper.

Proceedings of the 53rd Annual Meeting of the Association for Computational Linguistics and the 7th International Joint Conference on Natural Language Processing, pages 719–729,
Beijing, China, July 26-31, 2015.

of his plays to range from 17 to 85 instances per thousand lines (Keller, 2009). It is not hard to image how computer-assisted detection, classification, and analysis of puns could help scholars in the digital humanities. Finally, computational pun detection and understanding hold tremendous potential for machine-assisted translation. Some of the most widely disseminated and translated popular discourses—particularly television shows and movies—feature puns and other forms of wordplay as a recurrent and expected feature (Schröter, 2005). These pose particular challenges for translators, who need not only to recognize and comprehend each instance of humour-provoking ambiguity, but also to select and implement an appropriate translation strategy.[2] NLP systems could assist translators in flagging intentionally ambiguous words for special attention, and where they are not directly translatable (as is usually the case), the systems may be able to propose ambiguity-preserving alternatives which best match the original pun's double meaning.

In the present work, we discuss the adaptation of automatic word sense disambiguation techniques to intentionally ambiguous text and evaluate these adaptations in a controlled setting. We focus on humorous puns, as these are by far the most commonly encountered and more readily available in (and extractable from) existing text corpora.

The remainder of this paper is structured as follows: In the following section we give a brief introduction to puns, WSD, and related previous work on computational detection and comprehension of humour. In §3 we describe the data set produced for our experiments. In §§4 and 5 we describe how disambiguation algorithms, evaluation metrics, and baselines from traditional WSD can be adapted to the task of pun identification, and in §6 we report and discuss the performance of our adapted systems. Finally, we conclude in §7 with a review of our research contributions and an outline of our plans for future work.

2 Background

2.1 Puns

Punning is a form of wordplay where a word is used in such a way as to evoke several independent meanings simultaneously. Humorous and non-humorous puns have been the subject of extensive study in the humanities and social sciences, which has led to insights into the nature of language-based humour and wordplay, including their role in commerce, entertainment, and health care; how they are processed in the brain; and how they vary over time and across cultures (Monnot, 1982; Culler, 1988; Lagerwerf, 2002; Bell et al., 2011; Bekinschtein et al., 2011). Study of literary puns imparts a greater understanding of the cultural or historical context in which the literature was produced, which is often necessary to properly interpret and translate it (Delabastita, 1997).

Puns can be classified in various ways (Attardo, 1994), though from the point of view of our particular natural language processing application the most important distinction is between homographic and homophonic puns. A *homographic* pun exploits distinct meanings of the same written word, and a *homophonic* pun exploits distinct meanings of the same spoken word. Puns can be homographic, homophonic, both, or neither, as the following examples illustrate:

(1) A lumberjack's world revolves on its axes.

(2) She fell through the window but felt no pane.

(3) A political prisoner is one who stands behind her convictions.

(4) The sign at the nudist camp read, "Clothed until April."

In (1), the pun on *axes* is homographic but not homophonic, since the two meanings ("more than one axe" and "more than one axis") share the same spelling but have different pronunciations. In (2), the pun on *pane* ("sheet of glass") is homophonic but not homographic, since the word for the secondary meaning ("feeling of injury") is properly spelled *pain* but pronounced the same. The pun on *convictions* ("strongly held beliefs" and "findings of criminal guilt") in (3) is both homographic and homophonic. Finally, the pun on *clothed* in (4) is neither homographic nor homophonic, since the word for the secondary meaning, *closed*, differs in both spelling and pronunciation. Such puns are commonly known as *imperfect* puns.

Other characteristics of puns important for our work include whether they involve compounds, multiword expressions, or proper names, and whether the pun's multiple meanings involve mul-

[2]The problem is compounded in audio-visual media such as films; often one or both of the pun's meanings appears in the visual channel, and thus cannot be freely substituted.

tiple parts of speech. We elaborate on the significance of these characteristics in the next section.

2.2 Word sense disambiguation

Word sense disambiguation (WSD) is the task of determining which sense of a polysemous term is the one intended when that term is used in a given communicative act. Besides the target term itself, a WSD system generally requires two inputs: the *context* (*i.e.*, the running text containing the target), and a *sense inventory* which specifies all possible senses of the target.

Approaches to WSD can be categorized according to the type of knowledge sources used to help discriminate senses. *Knowledge-based* approaches restrict themselves to using pre-existing lexical-semantic resources (LSRs), or such additional information as can be automatically extracted or mined from raw text corpora. *Supervised* approaches, on the other hand, use manually sense-annotated corpora as training data for a machine learning system, or as seed data for a bootstrapping process. Supervised WSD systems generally outperform their knowledge-based counterparts, though this comes at the considerable expense of having human annotators manually disambiguate hundreds or thousands of example sentences. Moreover, supervised approaches tend to be such that they can disambiguate only those words for which they have seen sufficient training examples to cover all senses. That is, most of them cannot disambiguate words which do not occur in the training data, nor can they select the correct sense of a known word if that sense was never observed in the training data.

Regardless of the approach, all WSD systems work by extracting contextual information for the target word and comparing it against the sense information stored for that word. A seminal knowledge-based example is the Lesk algorithm (Lesk, 1986) which disambiguates a pair of target terms in context by comparing their respective dictionary definitions and selecting the two with the greatest number of words in common. Though simple, the Lesk algorithm performs surprisingly well, and has frequently served as the basis of more sophisticated approaches. In recent years, Lesk variants in which the contexts and definitions are supplemented with entries from a distributional thesaurus (Lin, 1998) have achieved state-of-the-art performance for knowledge-based systems on standard data sets (Miller et al., 2012; Basile et al., 2014).

In traditional word sense disambiguation, the part of speech and lemma of the target word are usually known *a priori*, or can be determined with high accuracy using off-the-shelf natural language processing tools. The pool of candidate senses can therefore be restricted to those whose lexicalizations exactly match the target lemma and part of speech. No such help is available for puns, at least not in the general case. Take the following two examples:

(5) Tom moped.

(6) "I want a scooter," Tom moped.

In the first of these sentences, the word *moped* is unambiguously a verb with the lemma *mope*, and would be correctly recognized as such by any automatic lemmatizer and part-of-speech tagger. The *moped* of the second example is a pun, one of whose meanings is the same inflected form of the verb *mope* ("to sulk") and the other of which is the noun *moped* ("motorized scooter"). For such cases an automated pun identifier would therefore need to account for all possible lemmas for all possible parts of speech of the target word. The situation becomes even more onerous for heterographic and imperfect puns, which may require the use of pronunciation dictionaries, and application of phonological theories of punning, in order to recover the lemmas (Hempelmann, 2003).

As our research interests are in lexical semantics rather than phonology, we focus on puns which are homographic and monolexemic. This allows us to investigate the problem of pun identification in as controlled a setting as possible.

2.3 Previous work

2.3.1 Computational humour

There is some previous research on computational detection and comprehension of humour, though by and large it is not concerned specifically with puns; those studies which do analyze puns tend to have a phonological or syntactic rather than semantic bent. In this subsection we briefly review some prior work which is relevant to ours.

Yokogawa (2002) describes a system for detecting the presence of puns in Japanese text. However, this work is concerned only with puns which are both imperfect and ungrammatical, relying on syntactic cues rather than the lexical-semantic information we propose to use. Taylor and Mazlack (2004) describe an n-gram–based approach for recognizing when imperfect puns are used for humorous effect in a certain narrow class of English knock-knock jokes. Their focus on imperfect puns and their use of a fixed syntactic context makes their approach largely inapplicable to perfect puns in running text. Mihalcea and Strapparava (2005) treat humour recognition as a classification task, employing various machine learning techniques on humour-specific stylistic features such as alliteration and antonymy. Of particular interest is their follow-up analysis (Mihalcea and Strapparava, 2006), where they specifically point to their system's failure to resolve lexical-semantic ambiguity as a stumbling block to better accuracy, and speculate that deeper semantic analysis of the text, such as via word sense disambiguation or domain disambiguation, could aid in the detection of humorous incongruity and opposition.

The previous work which is perhaps most relevant to ours is that of Mihalcea et al. (2010). They build a data set consisting of 150 joke set-ups, each of which is followed by four possible "punchlines", only one of which is actually humorous (but not necessarily due to a pun). They then compare the set-ups against the punchlines using various models of incongruity detection, including many exploiting knowledge-based semantic relatedness such as Lesk. The Lesk model had an accuracy of 56%, which is lower than that of a naïve polysemy model which simply selects the punchline with the highest mean polysemy (66%) and even of a random-choice baseline (62%). However, it should be stressed here that the Lesk model did not directly account for the possibility that any given word might be ambiguous. Rather, for every word in the setup, the Lesk measure was used to select a word in the punchline such that the lexical overlap between each *one* of their possible definitions was maximized. The overlap scores for all word pairs were then averaged, and the punchline with the lowest average score selected as the most humorous.

2.3.2 Corpora

There are a number of English-language corpora of intentional lexical ambiguity which have been used in past work, usually in linguistics or the social sciences. In their work on computer-generated humour, Lessard et al. (2002) use a corpus of 374 "Tom Swifty" puns taken from the Internet, plus a well-balanced corpus of 50 humorous and non-humorous lexical ambiguities generated programmatically (Venour, 1999). Hong and Ong (2009) also study humour in natural language generation, using a smaller data set of 27 punning riddles derived from a mix of natural and artificial sources. In their study of wordplay in religious advertising, Bell et al. (2011) compile a corpus of 373 puns taken from church marquees and literature, and compare it against a general corpus of 1515 puns drawn from Internet websites and a specialized dictionary. Zwicky and Zwicky (1986) conduct a phonological analysis on a corpus of several thousand puns, some of which they collected themselves from advertisements and catalogues, and the remainder of which were taken from previously published collections. Two studies on cognitive strategies used by second language learners (Kaplan and Lucas, 2001; Lucas, 2004) used a data set of 58 jokes compiled from newspaper comics, 32 of which rely on lexical ambiguity. Bucaria (2004) conducts a linguistic analysis of a set of 135 humorous newspaper headlines, about half of which exploit lexical ambiguity.

Such data sets—particularly the larger ones—provided us good evidence that intentionally lexical ambiguous exemplars exist in sufficient numbers to make a rigorous evaluation of our task feasible. Unfortunately, none of the above-mentioned corpora have been published in full, and moreover many of them contain (sometimes exclusively) the sort of imperfect or otherwise heterographic puns which we mean to exclude from consideration. This has motivated us to produce our own corpus of puns, the construction and analysis of which is described in the following section.

3 Data set

As in traditional WSD, a prerequisite for our research is a corpus of examples, where one or more human annotators have already identified the ambiguous words and marked up their various meanings with reference to a given sense inventory. Such a corpus is sufficient for evaluating what we term *pun identification* or *pun disambiguation*—that is, identifying the senses of a term known *a priori* to be a pun.

3.1 Construction

Though several prior studies have produced corpora of puns, none of them are systematically sense-annotated. We therefore compiled our own corpus by pooling together some of the aforementioned corpora, the user-submitted puns from the Pun of the Day website,[3] and private collections provided to us by some professional humorists. This raw collection of 7750 one-liners was then filtered by trained human annotators to those instances meeting the following four criteria:

One pun per instance: Of all the lexical units in the instance, one and only one may be a pun. (This criterion simplifies the task detecting the presence and location of puns in a text, a classification task which we intend to investigate in future work.)

One content word per pun: The lexical unit that forms the pun must consist of, or contain, only a single content word (*i.e.*, a noun, verb, adjective, or adverb), excepting adverbial particles of phrasal verbs. This criterion is important because, in our observations, it is often only one word which carries ambiguity in puns on compounds and multi-word expressions. Accepting lexical units containing more than one content word would have required our annotators to laboriously partition the pun into (possibly overlapping) sense-bearing units and to assign sense sets to each of them, inflating the complexity of the annotation task to unacceptable levels.

Two meanings per pun: The pun must have exactly two distinct meanings. Though many sources state that puns have only two senses (Redfern, 1984; Attardo, 1994), our annotators identified a handful of corpus examples where the pun could plausibly be analyzed as carrying three distinct meanings. To simplify our manual annotation procedure and our evaluation metrics we excluded these rare outliers.

Weak homography: The lexical units corresponding to the two distinct meanings must be spelled exactly the same way, except that particles and inflections may be disregarded. This somewhat softer definition of homography allows us to admit a good many morphologically interesting cases which were nonetheless readily recognized by our human annotators.

The filtering reduced the number of instances to 1652, whose puns two human judges annotated with sense keys from WordNet 3.1 (Fellbaum, 1998). Using an online annotation tool specially constructed for this study, the annotators applied two sets of sense keys to each instance, one for each of the two meanings of the pun. For cases where the distinction between WordNet's fine-grained senses was irrelevant, the annotators had the option of labelling the meaning with more than one sense key. Annotators also had the option of marking a meaning as unassignable if WordNet had no corresponding sense key. Further details of our annotation tool and its use can be found in Miller and Turković (2015).

3.2 Analysis

Our judges agreed on which word was the pun in 1634 out of 1652 cases, a raw agreement of 98.91%. For the agreed cases, we used DKPro Agreement (Meyer et al., 2014) to compute Krippendorff's α (Krippendorff, 1980) for the sense annotations. This is a chance-correcting metric of inter-annotator agreement ranging in $(-1,1]$, where 1 indicates perfect agreement, -1 perfect disagreement, and 0 the expected score for random labelling. Our distance metric for α is a straightforward adaptation of the MASI set comparison metric (Passonneau, 2006). Whereas standard MASI, $d_M(A,B)$, compares two annotation sets A and B, our annotations take the form of unordered *pairs* of sets $\{A_1,A_2\}$ and $\{B_1,B_2\}$. We therefore find the mapping between elements of the two pairs that gives the lowest total distance, and halve it: $d_{M'}(\{A_1,A_2\},\{B_1,B_2\}) = \frac{1}{2}\min(d_M(A_1,B_1) + d_M(A_2,B_2), d_M(A_1,B_2) + d_M(A_2,B_1))$. With this method we observe a Krippendorff's α of 0.777; this is only slightly below the 0.8 threshold recommended by Krippendorff, and far higher than what has been reported in other sense annotation studies (Passonneau et al., 2006; Jurgens and Klapaftis, 2013).

Where possible, we resolved sense annotation disagreements automatically by taking the intersection of corresponding sense sets. Where the annotators' sense sets were disjoint or contradictory (including the cases where the annotators disagreed on the pun word), we had a human adjudicator attempt to resolve the disagreement in favour of one annotator or the other. This left us with 1607 instances,[4] of which we retained only the 1298 that had successful (*i.e.*, not marked as unassignable)

[3] http://www.punoftheday.com/

[4] Pending clearance of the distribution rights, we will make some or all of our annotated data set available on our website at https://www.ukp.tu-darmstadt.de/data/.

annotations for the present study. The contexts in this data set range in length from 3 to 44 words, with an average length of 11.9. The 2596 meanings carry sense key annotations corresponding to anywhere from one to seven WordNet synsets, with an average of 1.08. As expected, then, WordNet's sense granularity proved to be somewhat finer than necessary to characterize the meanings in the data set, though only marginally so.

Of the 2596 individual meanings, 1303 (50.2%) were annotated with noun senses only, 877 (33.8%) with verb senses only, 340 (13.1%) with adjective senses only, and 41 (1.6%) with adverb senses only. Only 35 individual meanings (1.3%) carry sense annotations corresponding to multiple parts of speech. However, for 297 (22.9%) of our puns, the two meanings had different parts of speech. Similarly, sense annotations for each individual meaning correspond to anywhere from one to four different lemmas, with a mean of 1.25. These observations confirm the concerns we raised in §2.2 that pun disambiguators, unlike traditional WSD systems, cannot always rely on the output of a lemmatizer or part-of-speech tagger to narrow down the list of sense candidates.

4 Pun disambiguation

It has long been observed that gloss overlap–based WSD systems, such as those based on the Lesk algorithm, fail to distinguish between candidate senses when their definitions have a similar overlap with the target word's context. In some cases this is because the overlap is negligible or nonexistent; this is known as the *lexical gap* problem, and various solutions to it are discussed in (*inter alia*) Miller et al. (2012). In other cases, the indecision arises because the definitions provided by the sense inventory are too fine-grained; this problem has been addressed, with varying degrees of success, through sense clustering or coarsening techniques (a short but reasonably comprehensive survey of which appears in Matuschek et al. (2014)). A third condition under which senses cannot be discriminated is when the target word is used in an underspecified or intentionally ambiguous manner. We hold that for this third scenario a disambiguator's inability to discriminate senses should not be seen as a failure condition, but rather as a limitation of the WSD task as traditionally defined. By reframing the task so as to permit the assignment of multiple senses (or groups of senses), we can allow disambiguation systems to sense-annotate intentionally ambiguous constructions such as puns.

Many approaches to WSD, including Lesk-like algorithms, involve computing some score for all possible senses of a target word, and then selecting the single highest-scoring one as the "correct" sense. The most straightforward modification of these techniques to pun disambiguation, then, is to have the systems select the *two* top-scoring senses, one for each meaning of the pun. Accordingly we applied this modification to the following knowledge-based WSD algorithms:

Simplified Lesk (Kilgarriff and Rosenzweig, 2000) disambiguates a target word by examining the definitions[5] for each of its candidate senses and selecting the single sense—or in our case, the two senses—which have the greatest number of words in common with the context. As we previously demonstrated that puns often transcend part of speech, our pool of candidate senses is constructed as follows: we apply a morphological analyzer to recover all possible lemmas of the target word without respect to part of speech, and for each lemma we add all its senses to the pool.

Simplified extended Lesk (Ponzetto and Navigli, 2010) is similar to simplified Lesk, except that the definition for each sense is concatenated with those of neighbouring senses in WordNet's semantic network.

Simplified lexically expanded Lesk (Miller et al., 2012) is also based on simplified Lesk, with the extension that every word in the context and sense definitions is expanded with up to 100 entries from a large distributional thesaurus.

The above algorithms fail to make a sense assignment when more than two senses are tied for the highest lexical overlap, or when there is a single highest-scoring sense but multiple senses are tied for the second-highest overlap. We therefore devised two pun-specific tie-breaking strategies. The first is motivated by the informal observation that, though the two meanings of a pun may have different parts of speech, at least one of the parts

[5]In our implementation, the sense definitions are formed by concatenating the synonyms, gloss, and example sentences provided by WordNet.

of speech is grammatical in the context of the sentence, and so would probably be the one assigned by a stochastic or rule-based POS tagger. Our "POS" tie-breaker therefore preferentially selects the best sense, or pair of senses, whose POS matches the one applied to the target by the Stanford POS tagger (Toutanova et al., 2003). For our second tie-breaking strategy, we posit that since humour derives from the resolution of semantic incongruity (Raskin, 1985; Attardo, 1994), puns are more likely to exploit coarse-grained homonymy than than fine-grained systematic polysemy. Thus, following Matuschek et al. (2014), we induced a clustering of WordNet senses by aligning WordNet to the more coarse-grained OmegaWiki LSR.[6] Our "cluster" fallback works the same as the "POS" one, with the addition that any remaining ties among senses with the second-highest overlap are resolved by preferentially selecting those which are not in the same induced cluster as, and which in WordNet's semantic network are at least three edges distant from, the sense with the highest overlap.

5 Evaluation

5.1 Scoring

In traditional word sense disambiguation, *in vitro* evaluations are conducted by comparing the senses assigned by the disambiguation system to the gold-standard senses assigned by the human annotators. For the case that the system and gold-standard assignments consist of a single sense each, the exact-match criterion is used: the system receives a score of 1 if it chose the sense specified by the gold standard, and 0 otherwise. Where the system selects a single sense for an instance for which there is more than one correct gold standard sense, the multiple tags are interpreted disjunctively—that is, the system receives a score of 1 if it chose any one of the gold-standard senses, and 0 otherwise. Overall performance is reported in terms of coverage (the number of targets for which a sense assignment was attempted), precision (the sum of scores divided by the number of attempted targets), recall (the sum of scores divided by the total number of targets in the data set), and F_1 (the harmonic mean of precision and recall) (Palmer et al., 2006).

The traditional approach to scoring individual targets is not usable as-is for pun disambiguation, because each pun carries two disjoint but equally valid sets of sense annotations. Instead, since our systems assign exactly one sense to each of the pun's two sense sets, we count this as a match (scoring 1) only if each chosen sense can be found in one of the gold-standard sense sets, and no two gold-standard sense sets contain the same chosen sense. (As with traditional WSD scoring, various approaches could be used to assign credit for partially correct assignments, though we leave exploration of these to future work.)

5.2 Baselines

System performance in WSD is normally interpreted with reference to one or more baselines. To our knowledge, ours is the very first study of automatic pun disambiguation on any scale, so at this point there are no previous systems against which to compare our results. However, traditional WSD systems are often compared with two naïve baselines (Gale et al., 1992) which can be adapted for our purposes.

The first of these naïve baselines is to randomly select from among the candidate senses. In traditional WSD, the score for a random disambiguator which selects a single sense for a given target t is the number of gold-standard senses divided by the number of candidate senses: $\text{score}(t) = g(t) \div \delta(t)$. In our pun disambiguation task, however, a random disambiguator must select *two* senses—one for each of the sense sets $g_1(t)$ and $g_2(t)$—and these senses must be distinct. There are $\binom{\delta(t)}{2}$ possible ways of selecting two unique senses, so the random score for any given instance is $\text{score}(t) = g_1(t) \cdot g_2(t) \div \binom{\delta(t)}{2}$.

The second naïve baseline for WSD, known as *most frequent sense* (MFS), is a supervised baseline, meaning that it depends on a manually sense-annotated background corpus. As its name suggests, it involves always selecting from the candidates that sense which has the highest frequency in the corpus. As with our test algorithms, we adapt this technique to pun disambiguation by having it select the two most frequent senses (according to WordNet's built-in sense frequency counts). In traditional WSD, MFS baselines are notoriously difficult to beat, even for supervised disambiguation systems, and since they rely on expensive sense-tagged data they are not normally considered a benchmark for the performance of knowledge-based disambiguators.

[6] http://www.omegawiki.org/

system	C	P	R	F_1
SL	35.52	19.74	7.01	10.35
SEL	42.45	19.96	8.47	11.90
SLEL	**98.69**	13.43	13.25	13.34
SEL+POS	59.94	**21.21**	12.71	15.90
SEL+cluster	68.10	20.70	**14.10**	**16.77**
random	100.00	9.31	9.31	9.31
MFS	100.00	13.25	13.25	13.25

Table 1: Coverage, precision, recall, and F_1 for various pun diasmbiguation algorithms.

6 Results

Using the freely available DKPro WSD framework (Miller et al., 2013), we implemented our pun disambiguation algorithms, ran them on our full data set, and compared their annotations against those of our manually produced gold standard. Table 1 shows the coverage, precision, recall, and F_1 for simplified Lesk (SL), simplified extended Lesk (SEL), simplified lexically expanded Lesk (SLEL), and the random and most frequent sense baselines; for SEL we also report results for each of our pun-specific tie-breaking strategies. All metrics are reported as percentages, and the highest score for each metric (excluding baseline coverage, which is always 100%) is highlighted in boldface.

Accuracy for the random baseline annotator was about 9%; for the MFS baseline it was just over 13%. These figures are considerably lower than what is typically seen with traditional WSD corpora, where random baselines achieve accuracies of 30 to 60%, and MFS baselines 65 to 80% (Palmer et al., 2001; Snyder and Palmer, 2004; Navigli et al., 2007). Our baselines' low figures are the result of them having to consider senses from every possible lemmatization and part of speech of the target, and underscore the difficulty of our task.

The simplest knowledge-based algorithm we tested, simplified Lesk, was over twice as accurate as the random baseline in terms of precision (19.74%), but predictably had very low coverage (35.52%), leading in turn to very low recall (7.01%). Manual examination of the unassigned instances confirmed that failure was usually due to the lack of any lexical overlap whatsoever between the context and definitions. The use of a tie-breaking strategy would not help much here, though some way of bridging the lexical gap would. This is, in fact, the strategy employed by the extended and lexically expanded variants of simplified Lesk, and we observed that both were successful to some degree. Simplified lexically expanded Lesk almost completely closed the lexical gap, with nearly complete coverage (98.69%), though this came at the expense of a large drop in precision (to 13.43%). Given the near-total coverage, use of a tie-breaking strategy here would have no appreciable effect on the accuracy.

Simplified extended Lesk, on the other hand, saw significant increases in coverage, precision, and recall (to 42.45%, 19.96%, and 8.47%, respectively). Its recall is statistically indistinguishable[7] from the random baseline, though spot-checks of its unassigned instances show that the problem is very frequently not the lexical gap but rather multiple senses tied for the greatest overlap with the context. We therefore tested our two pun-specific backoff strategies to break this system's ties. Using the "POS" strategy increased coverage by 41%, relatively speaking, and gave us our highest observed precision of 21.21%. Our "cluster" strategy effected a relative increase in coverage of over 60%, and gave us the best recall (14.10%). This strategy also had the best tradeoff between precision and recall, with an F_1 of 16.77%.

Significance testing shows the recall scores for SLEL, SEL+POS, and SEL+cluster to be significantly better than the random baseline, and statistically indistinguishable from that of MFS. This is excellent news, especially in light of the fact that supervised approaches (even baselines like MFS) usually outperform their knowledge-based counterparts. Though the three knowledge-based systems are not statistically distinguishable from each other in terms of recall, they do show a statistically significant improvement over SL and SEL, and the two implementing pun-specific tie-breaking strategies were markedly more accurate than SLEL for those targets where they attempted an assignment. These two systems would therefore be preferable for applications where precision is more important than recall.

We also examined the results of our generally best-performing system, SEL+cluster, to see whether there was any relationship with the targets' part of speech. We filtered the results according to whether both gold-standard meanings of the pun contain senses for nouns only, verbs only, adjec-

[7] All significance statements in this section are based on McNemar's test at a confidence level of 5%.

POS	C	P	R	R_{rand}
noun	66.60	20.89	13.91	10.44
verb	65.61	14.54	9.54	5.12
adj.	68.87	39.73	27.36	16.84
adv.	100.00	75.00	75.00	46.67
pure	66.77	21.44	14.31	9.56
mult.	72.58	18.43	13.38	12.18

Table 2: Coverage, precision, and recall for SEL+cluster, and random baseline recall, according to part of speech.

tives only, or adverbs only; these amounted to 539, 346, 106, and 8 instances, respectively. These results are shown in Table 2. Also shown there is a row which aggregates the 999 targets with "pure" POS, and another for the remaining 608 instances ("mult."), where one or both of the two meanings contain senses for multiple parts of speech, or where the two meanings have different parts of speech. The last column of each row shows the recall of the random baseline for comparison.

Accuracy was lowest on the verbs, which had the highest candidate polysemy (21.6) and are known to be particularly difficult to disambiguate even in traditional WSD. Still, as with all the other single parts of speech, performance of SEL+cluster exceeded the random baseline. While recall was lower on targets with mixed POS than those with pure POS, coverage was significantly higher. Normally such a disparity could be attributed to a difference in polysemy: Lesk-like systems are more likely to attempt a sense assignment for highly polysemous targets, since there is a greater likelihood of one of the candidate definitions matching the context, though the probability of the assignment being correct is reduced. In this case, however, the multi-POS targets actually had lower average polysemy than the single-POS ones (13.2 *vs.* 15.8).

7 Conclusion

In this paper we have introduced the novel task of pun disambiguation and have proposed and evaluated several computational approaches for it. The major contributions of this work are as follows: First, we have produced a new data set consisting of manually sense-annotated homographic puns. The data set is large enough, and the manual annotations reliable enough, for a principled evaluation of automatic pun disambiguation systems. Second, we have shown how evaluation metrics, baselines, and disambiguation algorithms from traditional WSD can be adapted to the task of pun disambiguation, and we have tested these adaptations in a controlled experiment. The results show pun disambiguation to be a particularly challenging task for NLP, with baseline results far below what is commonly seen in traditional WSD. We showed that knowledge-based disambiguation algorithms naïvely adapted from traditional WSD perform poorly, but that extending them with strategies that rely on pun-specific features brings about dramatic improvements in accuracy: their recall becomes comparable to that of a supervised baseline, and their precision greatly exceeds it.

There are a number of avenues we intend to explore in future work. First, we would like to try adapting and evaluating some additional WSD algorithms for use with puns. Though our data set is probably too small to use with machine learning–based approaches, we are particularly interested in testing knowledge-based disambiguators which rely on measures of graph connectivity rather than gloss overlaps. Second, we would like to investigate alternative tie-breaking strategies, such as the domain similarity measures used by Mihalcea et al. (2010). Finally, whereas in this paper we have treated only the task of sense disambiguation for the case where a word is known *a priori* to be a pun, we are interested in exploring the requisite problem of *pun detection*, where the object is to determine whether or not a given context contains a pun, and more precisely whether any given word in a context is a pun.

Acknowledgments

The work described in this paper is supported by the Volkswagen Foundation as part of the Lichtenberg Professorship Program under grant No. I/82806. The authors thank John Black, Matthew Collins, Don Hauptman, Christian F. Hempelmann, Stan Kegel, Andrew Lamont, Beatrice Santorini, Mladen Turković, and Andreas Zimpfer for helping us build our data set.

References

Salvatore Attardo. 1994. *Linguistic Theories of Humor*. Mouton de Gruyter.

Pierpaolo Basile, Annalina Caputo, and Giovanni Semeraro. 2014. An enhanced Lesk word sense disambiguation algorithm through a distributional semantic model. In *Proceedings of the 25th International Conference on Computational Linguistics (COLING 2014)*, pages 1591–1600.

Tristan A. Bekinschtein, Matthew H. Davis, Jennifer M. Rodd, and Adrian M. Owen. 2011. Why clowns taste funny: The relationship between humor and semantic ambiguity. *The Journal of Neuroscience*, 31(26):9665–9671, June.

Nancy D. Bell, Scott Crossley, and Christian F. Hempelmann. 2011. Wordplay in church marquees. *Humor: International Journal of Humor Research*, 24(2):187–202, April.

Chiara Bucaria. 2004. Lexical and syntactic ambiguity as a source of humor: The case of newspaper headlines. *Humor: International Journal of Humor Research*, 17(3):279–309.

Paul Buitelaar. 2000. Reducing lexical semantic complexity with systematic polysemous classes and underspecification. In *Proceedings of the 2000 NAACL-ANLP Workshop on Syntactic and Semantic Complexity in Natural Language Processing Systems*, volume 1, pages 14–19.

Jonathan D. Culler, editor. 1988. *On Puns: The Foundation of Letters*. Basil Blackwell, Oxford.

Dirk Delabastita, editor. 1997. *Traductio: Essays on Punning and Translation*. St. Jerome, Manchester.

Christiane Fellbaum, editor. 1998. *WordNet: An Electronic Lexical Database*. MIT Press, Cambridge, MA.

William Gale, Kenneth Ward Church, and David Yarowsky. 1992. Estimating upper and lower bounds on the performance of word-sense disambiguation programs. In *Proceedings of the 30th Annual Meeting of the Association of Computational Linguistics (ACL 1992)*, pages 249–256.

Christian F. Hempelmann. 2003. *Paronomasic Puns: Target Recoverability Towards Automatic Generation*. Ph.D. thesis, Purdue University.

Bryan Anthony Hong and Ethel Ong. 2009. Automatically extracting word relationships as templates for pun generation. In *Proceedings of the 1st Workshop on Computational Approaches to Linguistic Creativity (CALC 2009)*, pages 24–31, June.

David Jurgens and Ioannis Klapaftis. 2013. SemEval-2013 Task 13: Word sense induction for graded and non-graded senses. In *Proceedings of the 7th International Workshop on Semantic Evaluation (SemEval 2013)*, pages 290–299, June.

David Jurgens. 2014. An analysis of ambiguity in word sense annotations. In *Proceedings of the 9th International Conference on Language Resources and Evaluation (LREC 2014)*, pages 3006–3012, May.

Nora Kaplan and Teresa Lucas. 2001. Comprensión del humorismo en inglés: Estudio de las estrategias de inferencia utilizadas por estudiantes avanzados de inglés como lengua extranjera en la interpretación de los retruécanos en historietas cómicas en lengua inglesa. *Anales de la Universidad Metropolitana*, 1(2):245–258.

Stefan Daniel Keller. 2009. *The Development of Shakespeare's Rhetoric: A Study of Nine Plays*, volume 136 of *Swiss Studies in English*. Narr, Tübingen.

Adam Kilgarriff and Joseph Rosenzweig. 2000. Framework and results for English SENSEVAL. *Computers and the Humanities*, 34:15–48.

Klaus Krippendorff. 1980. *Content Analysis: An Introduction to its Methodology*. Sage, Beverly Hills, CA.

Luuk Lagerwerf. 2002. Deliberate ambiguity in slogans: Recognition and appreciation. *Document Design*, 3(3):245–260.

Michael Lesk. 1986. Automatic sense disambiguation using machine readable dictionaries: How to tell a pine cone from a ice cream cone. In *Proceedings of the 5th Annual International Conference of Systems Documentation (SIGDOC 1986)*, pages 24–26.

Greg Lessard, Michael Levison, and Chris Venour. 2002. Cleverness versus funniness. In *Proceedings of the 20th Twente Workshop on Language Technology*, pages 137–145.

Dekang Lin. 1998. Automatic retrieval and clustering of similar words. In *Proceedings of the 36th Annual Meeting of the Association for Computational Linguistics (ACL 1998) and the 17th International Conference on Computational Linguistics (COLING 1998)*, volume 2, pages 768–774.

Teresa Lucas. 2004. *Deciphering the Meaning of Puns in Learning English as a Second Language: A Study of Triadic Interaction*. Ph.D. thesis, Florida State University.

Peter J. Ludlow. 1996. *Semantic Ambiguity and Underspecification* (review). *Computational Linguistics*, 3(23):476–482.

Michael Matuschek, Tristan Miller, and Iryna Gurevych. 2014. A language-independent sense clustering approach for enhanced WSD. In *Proceedings of the 12th Konferenz zur Verarbeitung natürlicher Sprache (KONVENS 2014)*, pages 11–21, October.

Christian M. Meyer, Margot Mieskes, Christian Stab, and Iryna Gurevych. 2014. DKPro Agreement: An open-source Java library for measuring inter-rater agreement. In *Proceedings of the 25th International Conference on Computational Linguistics (System Demonstrations) (COLING 2014)*, pages 105–109, August.

Rada Mihalcea and Carlo Strapparava. 2005. Making computers laugh: Investigations in automatic humor recognition. In *Proceedings of the 11th Human Language Technology Conference and the 10th Conference on Empirical Methods in Natural Language Processing (HLT-EMNLP 2005)*, pages 531–538, October.

Rada Mihalcea and Carlo Strapparava. 2006. Learning to laugh (automatically): Computational models for humor recognition. *Computational Intelligence*, 22(2):126–142.

Rada Mihalcea, Carlo Strapparava, and Stephen Pulman. 2010. Computational models for incongruity detection in humour. In *Proceedings of the 11th International Conference on Computational Linguistics and Intelligent Text Processing (CICLing 2010)*, volume 6008 of *Lecture Notes in Computer Science*, pages 364–374. Springer, March.

Tristan Miller and Mladen Turković. 2015. Towards the automatic detection and identification of English puns. *European Journal of Humour Research*. To appear.

Tristan Miller, Chris Biemann, Torsten Zesch, and Iryna Gurevych. 2012. Using distributional similarity for lexical expansion in knowledge-based word sense disambiguation. In *Proceedings of the 24th International Conference on Computational Linguistics (COLING 2012)*, pages 1781–1796, December.

Tristan Miller, Nicolai Erbs, Hans-Peter Zorn, Torsten Zesch, and Iryna Gurevych. 2013. DKPro WSD: A generalized UIMA-based framework for word sense disambiguation. In *Proceedings of the 51st Annual Meeting of the Association for Computational Linguistics (System Demonstrations) (ACL 2013)*, pages 37–42, August.

Michel Monnot. 1982. Puns in advertising: Ambiguity as verbal aggression. *Maledicta*, 6:7–20.

Roberto Navigli, Kenneth C. Litkowski, and Orin Hargraves. 2007. SemEval-2007 Task 07: Coarse-grained English All-words Task. In *Proceedings of the 4th International Workshop on Semantic Evaluations (SemEval-2007)*, pages 30–35, June.

Martha Palmer, Christiane Fellbaum, Scott Cotton, Lauren Delfs, and Hoa Trang Dang. 2001. English tasks: All-words and verb lexical sample. In *Proceedings of Senseval-2: 2nd International Workshop on Evaluating Word Sense Disambiguation Systems*, pages 21–24, July.

Martha Palmer, Hwee Tou Ng, and Hoa Trang Dang. 2006. Evaluation of WSD systems. In Eneko Agirre and Philip Edmonds, editors, *Word Sense Disambiguation: Algorithms and Applications*, volume 33 of *Text, Speech, and Language Technology*. Springer.

Rebecca J. Passonneau, Nizar Habash, and Owen Rambow. 2006. Inter-annotator agreement on a multilingual semantic annotation task. In *Proceedings of the 5th International Conference on Language Resources and Evaluations (LREC 2006)*, pages 1951–1956.

Rebecca J. Passonneau. 2006. Measuring agreement on set-valued items (MASI) for semantic and pragmatic annotation. In *Proceedings of the 5th International Conference on Language Resources and Evaluations (LREC 2006)*, pages 831–836.

Simone Paolo Ponzetto and Roberto Navigli. 2010. Knowledge-rich word sense disambiguation rivaling supervised systems. In *Proceedings of the 48th Annual Meeting of the Association for Computational Linguistics (ACL 2010)*, pages 1522–1531.

Vitor Raskin. 1985. *Semantic Mechanisms of Humor*. D. Reidel, Dordrecht, the Netherlands.

Walter Redfern. 1984. *Puns*. Basil Blackwell, Oxford.

Thorsten Schröter. 2005. *Shun the Pun, Rescue the Rhyme? The Dubbing and Subtitling of Language-Play in Film*. Ph.D. thesis, Karlstad University.

Benjamin Snyder and Martha Palmer. 2004. The English all-words task. In *Proceedings of the 3rd International Workshop on the Evaluation of Systems for the Semantic Analysis of Text (Senseval-3)*, pages 41–43, July.

Julia M. Taylor and Lawrence J. Mazlack. 2004. Computationally recognizing wordplay in jokes. In *Proceedings of the 26th Annual Conference of the Cognitive Science Society (CogSci 2004)*, pages 1315–1320, August.

Kristina Toutanova, Dan Klein, Christopher Manning, and Yoram Singer. 2003. Feature-rich part-of-speech tagging with a cyclic dependency network. In *Proceedings of the 3rd Conference of the North American Chapter of the Association for Computational Linguistics and the 9th Human Language Technologies Conference (HLT-NAACL 2003)*, pages 252–259.

Alessandro Valitutti, Carlo Strapparava, and Oliviero Stock. 2008. Textual affect sensing for computational advertising. In *Proceedings of the AAAI Spring Symposium on Creative Intelligent Systems*, pages 117–122, March.

Chris Venour. 1999. The computational generation of a class of puns. Master's thesis, Queen's University, Kingston, ON.

Toshihiko Yokogawa. 2002. Japanese pun analyzer using articulation similarities. In *Proceedings of the 11th IEEE International Conference on Fuzzy Systems (FUZZ 2002)*, volume 2, pages 1114–1119, May.

Arnold M. Zwicky and Elizabeth D. Zwicky. 1986. Imperfect puns, markedness, and phonological similarity: With fronds like these, who needs anemones? *Folia Linguistica*, 20(3–4):493–503.

Unsupervised Cross-Domain Word Representation Learning

Danushka Bollegala danushka.bollegala@liverpool.ac.uk University of Liverpool
Takanori Maehara maehara.takanori@shizuoka.ac.jp Shizuoka University
Ken-ichi Kawarabayashi k_keniti@nii.ac.jp National Institute of Informatics
JST, ERATO, Kawarabayashi Large Graph Project.

Abstract

Meaning of a word varies from one domain to another. Despite this important domain dependence in word semantics, existing word representation learning methods are bound to a single domain. Given a pair of *source-target* domains, we propose an unsupervised method for learning domain-specific word representations that accurately capture the domain-specific aspects of word semantics. First, we select a subset of frequent words that occur in both domains as *pivots*. Next, we optimize an objective function that enforces two constraints: (a) for both source and target domain documents, pivots that appear in a document must accurately predict the co-occurring non-pivots, and (b) word representations learnt for pivots must be similar in the two domains. Moreover, we propose a method to perform domain adaptation using the learnt word representations. Our proposed method significantly outperforms competitive baselines including the state-of-the-art domain-insensitive word representations, and reports best sentiment classification accuracies for all domain-pairs in a benchmark dataset.

1 Introduction

Learning semantic representations for words is a fundamental task in NLP that is required in numerous higher-level NLP applications (Collobert et al., 2011). Distributed word representations have gained much popularity lately because of their accuracy as semantic representations for words (Mikolov et al., 2013a; Pennington et al., 2014). However, the meaning of a word often varies from one domain to another. For example, the phrase *lightweight* is often used in a positive sentiment in the portable electronics domain because a lightweight device is easier to carry around, which is a positive attribute for a portable electronic device. However, the same phrase has a negative sentiment assocition in the *movie* domain because movies that do not invoke deep thoughts in viewers are considered to be lightweight (Bollegala et al., 2014). However, existing word representation learning methods are agnostic to such domain-specific semantic variations of words, and capture semantics of words only within a single domain. To overcome this problem and capture domain-specific semantic orientations of words, we propose a method that learns separate distributed representations for each domain in which a word occurs.

Despite the successful applications of distributed word representation learning methods (Pennington et al., 2014; Collobert et al., 2011; Mikolov et al., 2013a) most existing approaches are limited to learning only a single representation for a given word (Reisinger and Mooney, 2010). Although there have been some work on learning multiple *prototype* representations (Huang et al., 2012; Neelakantan et al., 2014) for a word considering its multiple senses, such methods do not consider the semantics of the domain in which the word is being used.

If we can learn separate representations for a word for each domain in which it occurs, we can use the learnt representations for domain adaptation tasks such as cross-domain sentiment classification (Bollegala et al., 2011b), cross-domain POS tagging (Schnabel and Schütze, 2013), cross-domain dependency parsing (McClosky et al., 2010), and domain adaptation of relation extractors (Bollegala et al., 2013a; Bollegala et al., 2013b; Bollegala et al., 2011a; Jiang and Zhai, 2007a; Jiang and Zhai, 2007b).

We introduce the *cross-domain word represen-*

Proceedings of the 53rd Annual Meeting of the Association for Computational Linguistics and the 7th International Joint Conference on Natural Language Processing, pages 730–740,
Beijing, China, July 26-31, 2015.

tation learning task, where given two domains, (referred to as the *source* ($\mathcal{S}$) and the *target* ($\mathcal{T}$)) the goal is to learn two separate representations $\boldsymbol{w}_{\mathcal{S}}$ and $\boldsymbol{w}_{\mathcal{T}}$ for a word w respectively from the source and the target domain that capture *domain-specific* semantic variations of w. In this paper, we use the term *domain* to represent a collection of documents related to a particular topic such as user-reviews in Amazon for a product category (e.g. *books*, *dvds*, *movies*, etc.). However, a domain in general can be a field of study (e.g. *biology*, *computer science*, *law*, etc.) or even an entire source of information (e.g. *twitter*, *blogs*, *news articles*, etc.). In particular, we do not assume the availability of any labeled data for learning word representations.

This problem setting is closely related to unsupervised domain adaptation (Blitzer et al., 2006), which has found numerous useful applications such as, sentiment classification and POS tagging. For example, in unsupervised cross-domain sentiment classification (Blitzer et al., 2006; Blitzer et al., 2007), we train a binary sentiment classifier using positive and negative labeled user reviews in the source domain, and apply the trained classifier to predict sentiment of the target domain's user reviews. Although the distinction between the source and the target domains is not important for the word representation learning step, it is important for the domain adaptation tasks in which we subsequently evaluate the learnt word representations. Following prior work on domain adaptation (Blitzer et al., 2006), high-frequent features (unigrams/bigrams) common to both domains are referred to as *domain-independent* features or *pivots*. In contrast, we use *non-pivots* to refer to features that are specific to a single domain.

We propose an unsupervised cross-domain word representation learning method that jointly optimizes two criteria: (a) given a document d from the source or the target domain, we must accurately predict the non-pivots that occur in d using the pivots that occur in d, and (b) the source and target domain representations we learn for pivots must be similar. The main challenge in domain adaptation is *feature mismatch*, where the features that we use for training a classifier in the source domain do not necessarily occur in the target domain. Consequently, prior work on domain adaptation (Blitzer et al., 2006; Pan et al., 2010) learn lower-dimensional mappings from non-pivots to pivots, thereby overcoming the feature mismatch problem. Criteria (a) ensures that word representations for domain-specific non-pivots in each domain are related to the word representations for domain-independent pivots. This relationship enables us to discover pivots that are similar to target domain-specific non-pivots, thereby overcoming the feature mismatch problem.

On the other hand, criteria (b) captures the prior knowledge that high-frequent words common to two domains often represent domain-independent semantics. For example, in sentiment classification, words such as *excellent* or *terrible* would express similar sentiment about a product irrespective of the domain. However, if a pivot expresses different semantics in source and the target domains, then it will be surrounded by dissimilar sets of non-pivots, and reflected in the first criteria. Criteria (b) can also be seen as a regularization constraint imposed on word representations to prevent overfitting by reducing the number of free parameters in the model.

Our contributions in this paper can be summarized as follows.

- We propose a distributed word representation learning method that learns separate representations for a word for each domain in which it occurs. To the best of our knowledge, ours is the first-ever *domain-sensitive distributed* word representation learning method.

- Given domain-specific word representations, we propose a method to learn a cross-domain sentiment classifier.

  Although word representation learning methods have been used for various related tasks in NLP such as similarity measurement (Mikolov et al., 2013c), POS tagging (Collobert et al., 2011), dependency parsing (Socher et al., 2011a), machine translation (Zou et al., 2013), sentiment classification (Socher et al., 2011b), and semantic role labeling (Roth and Woodsend, 2014), to the best of our knowledge, word representations methods have not yet been used for cross-domain sentiment classification.

Experimental results for cross-domain sentiment classification on a benchmark dataset show that the word representations learnt using the proposed method statistically significantly outperform a state-of-the-art domain-insensitive word representation learning method (Pennington et al., 2014), and several competitive baselines. In particular, our proposed cross-domain word representation learning method is not specific to a particular task such as sentiment classification, and in principle, can be in applied to a wide-range of domain adaptation tasks. Despite this task-independent nature of the proposed method, it achieves the best sentiment classification accuracies on all domain-pairs, reporting statistically comparable results to the current state-of-the-art unsupervised cross-domain sentiment classification methods (Pan et al., 2010; Blitzer et al., 2006).

2 Related Work

Representing the semantics of a word using some algebraic structure such as a vector (more generally a tensor) is a common first step in many NLP tasks (Turney and Pantel, 2010). By applying algebraic operations on the word representations, we can perform numerous tasks in NLP, such as composing representations for larger textual units beyond individual words such as phrases (Mitchell and Lapata, 2008). Moreover, word representations are found to be useful for measuring semantic similarity, and for solving proportional analogies (Mikolov et al., 2013c). Two main approaches for computing word representations can be identified in prior work (Baroni et al., 2014): *counting-based* and *prediction-based*.

In counting-based approaches (Baroni and Lenci, 2010), a word w is represented by a vector $\boldsymbol{w}$ that contains other words that co-occur with w in a corpus. Numerous methods for selecting co-occurrence contexts such as proximity or dependency relations have been proposed (Turney and Pantel, 2010). Despite the numerous successful applications of co-occurrence counting-based distributional word representations, their high dimensionality and sparsity are often problematic in practice. Consequently, further post-processing steps such as dimensionality reduction, and feature selection are often required when using counting-based word representations.

On the other hand, prediction-based approaches first assign each word, for example, with a d-dimensional real-vector, and learn the elements of those vectors by applying them in an auxiliary task such as language modeling, where the goal is to predict the next word in a given sequence. The dimensionality d is fixed for all the words in the vocabulary, and, unlike counting-based word representations, is much smaller (e.g. $d \in [10, 1000]$ in practice) compared to the vocabulary size. The neural network language model (NNLM) (Bengio et al., 2003) uses a multi-layer feed-forward neural network to predict the next word in a sequence, and uses backpropagation to update the word vectors such that the prediction error is minimized.

Although NNLMs learn word representations as a by-product, the main focus on language modeling is to predict the next word in a sentence given the previous words, and not learning word representations that capture semantics. Moreover, training multi-layer neural networks using large text corpora is time consuming. To overcome those limitations, methods that specifically focus on learning word representations that model word co-occurrences in large corpora have been proposed (Mikolov et al., 2013a; Mnih and Kavukcuoglu, 2013; Huang et al., 2012; Pennington et al., 2014). Unlike the NNLM, these methods use *all* the words in a contextual window in the prediction task. Methods that use one or no hidden layers are proposed to improve the scalability of the learning algorithms. For example, the skip-gram model (Mikolov et al., 2013b) predicts the words c that appear in the local context of a word w, whereas the continuous bag-of-words model (CBOW) predicts a word w conditioned on all the words c that appear in w's local context (Mikolov et al., 2013a). Methods that use global co-occurrences in the entire corpus to learn word representations have shown to outperform methods that use only local co-occurrences (Huang et al., 2012; Pennington et al., 2014). Overall, prediction-based methods have shown to outperform counting-based methods (Baroni et al., 2014).

Despite their impressive performance, existing methods for word representation learning do not consider the semantic variation of words across different domains. However, as described in Section 1, the meaning of a word vary from one domain to another, and must be considered. To the best of our knowledge, the only prior work studying the problem of word representation variation across domains is due to Bollegala et al. (2014). Given a source and a target domain, they first select a set of pivots using pointwise mutual information, and create two distributional representations for each pivot using their co-occurrence contexts in a particular domain. Next, a projection matrix from the source to the target domain feature spaces is learnt using partial least squares regression. Finally, the learnt projection matrix is used to find the nearest neighbors in the source domain for each target domain-specific features. However, unlike our proposed method, their method *does not* learn domain-specific word representations, but simply uses co-occurrence counting when creating in-domain word representations.

Faralli et al. (2012) proposed a domain-driven word sense disambiguation (WSD) method where they construct glossaries for several domain using a pattern-based bootstrapping technique. This work demonstrates the importance of considering the domain specificity of word senses. However, the focus of their work is not to learn representations for words or their senses in a domain, but to construct glossaries. It would be an interesting future research direction to explore the possibility of using such domain-specific glossaries for learning domain-specific word representations.

Neelakantan et al. (2014) proposed a method that jointly performs WSD and word embedding learning, thereby learning multiple embeddings per word type. In particular, the number of senses per word type is automatically estimated. However, their method is limited to a single domain, and does not consider how the representations vary across domains. On the other hand, our proposed method learns a single representation for a particular word for each domain in which it occurs.

Although in this paper we focus on the monolingual setting where source and target domains belong to the same language, the related setting where learning representations for words that are translational pairs across languages has been studied (Hermann and Blunsom, 2014; Klementiev et al., 2012; Gouws et al., 2015). Such representations are particularly useful for cross-lingual information retrieval (Duc et al., 2010). It will be an interesting future research direction to extend our proposed method to learn such cross-lingual word representations.

3 Cross-Domain Representation Learning

We propose a method for learning word representations that are sensitive to the semantic variations of words across domains. We call this problem *cross-domain word representation learning*, and provide a definition in Section 3.1. Next, in Section 3.2, given a set of pivots that occurs in both a source and a target domain, we propose a method for learning cross-domain word representations. We defer the discussion of pivot selection methods to Section 3.4. In Section 3.5, we propose a method for using the learnt word representations to train a cross-domain sentiment classifier.

3.1 Problem Definition

Let us assume that we are given two sets of documents $\mathcal{D}_\mathcal{S}$ and $\mathcal{D}_\mathcal{T}$ respectively for a source ($\mathcal{S}$) and a target ($\mathcal{T}$) domain. We do not consider the problem of retrieving documents for a domain, and assume such a collection of documents to be given. Then, given a particular word w, we define cross-domain representation learning as the task of learning two separate representations $\boldsymbol{w}_\mathcal{S}$ and $\boldsymbol{w}_\mathcal{T}$ capturing w's semantics in respectively the source $\mathcal{S}$ and the target $\mathcal{T}$ domains.

Unlike in domain adaptation, where there is a clear distinction between the source (i.e. the domain on which we train) vs. the target (i.e. the domain on which we test) domains, for representation learning purposes we do not make a distinction between the two domains. In the *unsupervised* setting of the cross-domain representation learning that we study in this paper, we do not assume the availability of labeled data for any domain for the purpose of learning word representations. As an extrinsic evaluation task, we apply the trained word representations for classifying sentiment related to user-reviews (Section 3.5). However, for this evaluation task we require sentiment-labeled user-reviews from the source domain.

Decoupling of the word representation learning from any tasks in which those representations are subsequently used, simplifies the problem as well as enables us to learn *task-independent* word representations with potential generic applicability. Although we limit the discussion to a pair of domains for simplicity, the proposed method can be easily extended to jointly learn word representations for more than two domains. In fact, prior work on cross-domain sentiment analysis show that incorporating multiple source domains improves sentiment classification accuracy on a target domain (Bollegala et al., 2011b; Glorot et al., 2011).

3.2 Proposed Method

To describe our proposed method, let us denote a pivot and a non-pivot feature respectively by c and w. Our proposed method does not depend on a specific pivot selection method, and can be used with all previously proposed methods for selecting pivots as explained later in Section 3.4. A pivot c is represented in the source and target domains respectively by vectors $\boldsymbol{c}_{\mathcal{S}} \in \mathbb{R}^n$ and $\boldsymbol{c}_{\mathcal{T}} \in \mathbb{R}^n$. Likewise, a source specific non-pivot w is represented by $\boldsymbol{w}_{\mathcal{S}}$ in the source domain, whereas a target specific non-pivot w is represented by $\boldsymbol{w}_{\mathcal{T}}$ in the target domain. By definition, a non-pivot occurs only in a single domain. For notational convenience we use w to denote non-pivots in both domains when the domain is clear from the context. We use $\mathcal{C}_{\mathcal{S}}$, $\mathcal{W}_{\mathcal{S}}, \mathcal{C}_{\mathcal{T}}$, and $\mathcal{W}_{\mathcal{T}}$ to denote the sets of word representation vectors respectively for the source pivots, source non-pivots, target pivots, and target non-pivots.

Let us denote the set of documents in the source and the target domains respectively by $\mathcal{D}_{\mathcal{S}}$ and $\mathcal{D}_{\mathcal{T}}$. Following the bag-of-features model, we assume that a document D is represented by the set of pivots and non-pivots that occur in D ($w \in d$ and $c \in d$). We consider the co-occurrences of a pivot c and a non-pivot w within a fixed-size contextual window in a document. Following prior work on representation learning (Mikolov et al., 2013a), in our experiments, we set the window size to 10 tokens, without crossing sentence boundaries. The notation $(c, w) \in d$ denotes the co-occurrence of a pivot c and a non-pivot w in a document d.

We learn domain-specific word representations by maximizing the prediction accuracy of the non-pivots w that occur in the local context of a pivot c. The hinge loss, $L(\mathcal{C}_{\mathcal{S}}, \mathcal{W}_{\mathcal{S}})$, associated with predicting a non-pivot w in a source document $d \in \mathcal{D}_{\mathcal{S}}$ that co-occurs with pivots c is given by:

$$\sum_{d \in \mathcal{D}_{\mathcal{S}}} \sum_{(c,w) \in d} \sum_{w^* \sim p(w)} \max\left(0, 1 - {\boldsymbol{c}_{\mathcal{S}}}^\top \boldsymbol{w}_{\mathcal{S}} + {\boldsymbol{c}_{\mathcal{S}}}^\top \boldsymbol{w}^*_{\mathcal{S}}\right) \quad (1)$$

Here, $\boldsymbol{w}^*_{\mathcal{S}}$ is the source domain representation of a non-pivot w^* that *does not occur* in d. The loss function given by Eq. 1 requires that a non-pivot w that co-occurs with a pivot c in the document d is assigned a higher ranking score as measured by the inner-product between $\boldsymbol{c}_{\mathcal{S}}$ and $\boldsymbol{w}_{\mathcal{S}}$ than a non-pivot w^* that does not occur in d. We randomly sample k non-pivots from the set of all source domain non-pivots that do not occur in d as w^*.

Specifically, we use the marginal distribution of non-pivots $p(w)$, estimated from the corpus counts, as the sampling distribution. We raise $p(w)$ to the $3/4$-th power as proposed by Mikolov et al. (2013a), and normalize it to unit probability mass prior to sampling k non-pivots w^* per each co-occurrence of $(c, w) \in d$. Because non-occurring non-pivots w^* are randomly sampled, prior work on noise contrastive estimation has found that it requires more negative samples than positive samples to accurately learn a prediction model (Mnih and Kavukcuoglu, 2013). We experimentally found $k = 5$ to be an acceptable trade-off between the prediction accuracy and the number of training instances.

Likewise, the loss function $L(\mathcal{C}_{\mathcal{T}}, \mathcal{W}_{\mathcal{T}})$ for predicting non-pivots using pivots in the target domain is given by:

$$\sum_{d \in \mathcal{D}_{\mathcal{T}}} \sum_{(c,w) \in d} \sum_{w^* \sim p(w)} \max\left(0, 1 - {\boldsymbol{c}_{\mathcal{T}}}^\top \boldsymbol{w}_{\mathcal{T}} + {\boldsymbol{c}_{\mathcal{T}}}^\top \boldsymbol{w}^*_{\mathcal{T}}\right) \quad (2)$$

Here, w^* denotes target domain non-pivots that *do not occur* in d, and are randomly sampled from $p(w)$ following the same procedure as in the source domain.

The source and target loss functions given respectively by Eqs. 1 and 2 can be used on their own to independently learn source and target domain word representations. However, by definition, pivots are common to both domains. We use this property to relate the source and target word representations via a *pivot-regularizer*, $R(\mathcal{C}_{\mathcal{S}}, \mathcal{C}_{\mathcal{T}})$, defined as:

$$R(\mathcal{C}_{\mathcal{S}}, \mathcal{C}_{\mathcal{T}}) = \frac{1}{2} \sum_{i=1}^{K} ||\boldsymbol{c}^{(i)}_{\mathcal{S}} - \boldsymbol{c}^{(i)}_{\mathcal{T}}||^2 \quad (3)$$

Here, $||\boldsymbol{x}||$ represents the l_2 norm of a vector $\boldsymbol{x}$, and $c^{(i)}$ is the i-th pivot in a total collection of K pivots. Word representations for non-pivots in the source and target domains are linked via the pivot regularizer because, the non-pivots in each domain are predicted using the word representations for the pivots in each domain, which in turn are regularized by Eq. 3. The overall objective function, $L(\mathcal{C}_{\mathcal{S}}, \mathcal{W}_{\mathcal{S}}, \mathcal{C}_{\mathcal{T}}, \mathcal{W}_{\mathcal{T}})$, we minimize is the sum[1] of

[1]Weighting the source and target loss functions by the respective dataset sizes did not result in any significant increase in performance. We believe that this is because the benchmark dataset contains approximately equal numbers of documents for each domain.

the source and target loss functions, regularized via Eq. 3 with coefficient λ, and is given by:

$$L(\mathcal{C}_S, \mathcal{W}_S,) + L(\mathcal{C}_T, \mathcal{W}_T) + \lambda R(\mathcal{C}_S, \mathcal{C}_T) \quad (4)$$

3.3 Training

Word representations of pivots c and non-pivots w in the source ($\boldsymbol{c}_S$, $\boldsymbol{w}_S$) and the target ($\boldsymbol{c}_T$, $\boldsymbol{w}_T$) domains are parameters to be learnt in the proposed method. To derive parameter updates, we compute the gradients of the overall loss function in Eq. 4 w.r.t. to each parameter as follows:

$$\frac{\partial L}{\partial \boldsymbol{w}_S} = \begin{cases} 0 & \text{if } {\boldsymbol{c}_S}^\top(\boldsymbol{w}_S - \boldsymbol{w}_S^*) \geq 1 \\ -\boldsymbol{c}_S & \text{otherwise} \end{cases} \quad (5)$$

$$\frac{\partial L}{\partial \boldsymbol{w}_S^*} = \begin{cases} 0 & \text{if } {\boldsymbol{c}_S}^\top(\boldsymbol{w}_S - \boldsymbol{w}_S^*) \geq 1 \\ \boldsymbol{c}_S & \text{otheriwse} \end{cases} \quad (6)$$

$$\frac{\partial L}{\partial \boldsymbol{w}_T} = \begin{cases} 0 & \text{if } {\boldsymbol{c}_T}^\top(\boldsymbol{w}_T - \boldsymbol{w}_T^*) \geq 1 \\ -\boldsymbol{c}_T & \text{otherwise} \end{cases} \quad (7)$$

$$\frac{\partial L}{\partial \boldsymbol{w}_T^*} = \begin{cases} 0 & \text{if } {\boldsymbol{c}_T}^\top(\boldsymbol{w}_T - \boldsymbol{w}_T^*) \geq 1 \\ \boldsymbol{c}_T & \text{otherwise} \end{cases} \quad (8)$$

$$\frac{\partial L}{\partial \boldsymbol{c}_S} = \begin{cases} \lambda(\boldsymbol{c}_S - \boldsymbol{c}_T) & \text{if } {\boldsymbol{c}_S}^\top(\boldsymbol{w}_S - \boldsymbol{w}_S^*) \geq 1 \\ \boldsymbol{w}_S^* - \boldsymbol{w}_S + \lambda(\boldsymbol{c}_S - \boldsymbol{c}_T) & \text{otherwise} \end{cases} \quad (9)$$

$$\frac{\partial L}{\partial \boldsymbol{c}_T} = \begin{cases} \lambda(\boldsymbol{c}_T - \boldsymbol{c}_S) & \text{if } {\boldsymbol{c}_T}^\top(\boldsymbol{w}_T - \boldsymbol{w}_T^*) \geq 1 \\ \boldsymbol{w}_T^* - \boldsymbol{w}_T + \lambda(\boldsymbol{c}_T - \boldsymbol{c}_S) & \text{otherwise} \end{cases} \quad (10)$$

Here, for simplicity, we drop the arguments inside the loss function and write it as L. We use mini batch stochastic gradient descent with a batch size of 50 instances. AdaGrad (Duchi et al., 2011) is used to schedule the learning rate. All word representations are initialized with n dimensional random vectors sampled from a zero mean and unit variance Gaussian. Although the objective in Eq. 4 is not jointly convex in all four representations, it is convex w.r.t. the representation of a particular feature (pivot or non-pivot) when the representations for all the other features are held fixed. In our experiments, the training converged in all cases with less than 100 epochs over the dataset.

The rank-based predictive hinge loss (Eq. 1) is inspired by the prior work on word representation learning for a single domain (Collobert et al., 2011). However, unlike the multilayer neural network in Collobert et al. (2011), the proposed method uses a computationally efficient single layer to reduce the number of parameters that must be learnt, thereby scaling to large datasets. Similar to the skip-gram model (Mikolov et al., 2013a), the proposed method predicts occurrences of contexts (non-pivots) w within a fixed-size contextual window of a target word (pivot) c.

Scoring the co-occurrences of two words c and w by the bilinear form given by the inner-product is similar to prior work on domain-insensitive word-representation learning (Mnih and Hinton, 2008; Mikolov et al., 2013a). However, unlike those methods that use the softmax function to convert inner-products to probabilities, we directly use the inner-products without any further transformations, thereby avoiding computationally expensive distribution normalizations over the entire vocabulary.

3.4 Pivot Selection

Given two sets of documents $\mathcal{D}_S$, $\mathcal{D}_T$ respectively for the source and the target domains, we use the following procedure to select pivots and non-pivots. First, we tokenize and lemmatize each document using the Stanford CoreNLP toolkit[2]. Next, we extract unigrams and bigrams as features for representing a document. We remove features listed as stop words using a standard stop words list. Stop word removal increases the effective co-occurrence window size for a pivot. Finally, we remove features that occur less than 50 times in the entire set of documents.

Several methods have been proposed in the prior work on domain adaptation for selecting a set of pivots from a given pair of domains such as the minimum frequency of occurrence of a feature in the two domains, mutual information (MI), and the entropy of the feature distribution over the documents (Pan et al., 2010). In our preliminary experiments, we discovered that a normalized version of the PMI (NPMI) (Bouma, 2009) to work consistently well for selecting pivots from different pairs of domains. NPMI between two features x and y is given by:

$$\text{NPMI}(x, y) = \log\left(\frac{p(x, y)}{p(x)p(y)}\right)\frac{1}{-\log(p(x, y))} \quad (11)$$

Here, the joint probability $p(x, y)$, and the marginal probabilities $p(x)$ and $p(y)$ are estimated using the number of co-occurrences of x and y in the sentences in the documents. Eq. 11 normalizes both the upper and lower bounds of the PMI.

[2] http://nlp.stanford.edu/software/corenlp.shtml

We measure the appropriateness of a feature as a pivot according to the score given by:

$$\text{score}(x) = \min\left(\text{NPMI}(x, \mathcal{S}), \text{NPMI}(x, \mathcal{T})\right). \quad (12)$$

We rank features that are common to both domains in the descending order of their scores as given by Eq. 12, and select the top $N_{\mathcal{P}}$ features as pivots. We rank features x that occur only in the source domain by $\text{NPMI}(x, \mathcal{S})$, and select the top ranked $N_{\mathcal{S}}$ features as source-specific non-pivots. Likewise, we rank the features x that occur only in the target domain by $\text{NPMI}(x, \mathcal{T})$, and select the top ranked $N_{\mathcal{T}}$ features as target-specific non-pivots.

The pivot selection criterion described here differs from that of Blitzer et al. (2006; 2007), where pivots are defined as features that behave similarly both in the source and the target domains. They compute the mutual information between a feature (i.e. unigrams or bigrams) and the sentiment labels using source domain labeled reviews. This method is useful when selecting pivots that are closely associated with positive or negative sentiment in the source domain. However, in unsupervised domain adaptation we do not have labeled data for the target domain. Therefore, the pivots selected using this approach are not guaranteed to demonstrate the same sentiment in the target domain as in the source domain. On the other hand, the pivot selection method proposed in this paper focuses on identifying a subset of features that are closely associated with both domains.

It is noteworthy that our proposed cross-domain word representation learning method (Section 3.2) *does not* assume any specific pivot/non-pivot selection method. Therefore, in principle, our proposed word representation learning method could be used with any of the previously proposed pivot selection methods. We defer a comprehensive evaluation of possible combinations of pivot selection methods and their effect on the proposed word representation learning method to future work.

3.5 Cross-Domain Sentiment Classification

As a concrete application of cross-domain word representations, we describe a method for learning a cross-domain sentiment classifier using the word representations learnt by the proposed method. Existing word representation learning methods that learn from only a single domain are typically evaluated for their accuracy in measuring semantic similarity between words, or by solving word analogy problems. Unfortunately, such gold standard datasets capturing cross-domain semantic variations of words are unavailable. Therefore, by applying the learnt word representations in a cross-domain sentiment classification task, we can conduct an indirect extrinsic evaluation.

The train data available for unsupervised cross-domain sentiment classification consists of unlabeled data for both the source and the target domains as well as labeled data for the source domain. We train a binary sentiment classifier using those train data, and apply it to classify sentiment of the target test data.

Unsupervised cross-domain sentiment classification is challenging due to two reasons: *feature-mismatch*, and *semantic variation*. First, the sets of features that occur in source and target domain documents are different. Therefore, a sentiment classifier trained using source domain labeled data is likely to encounter unseen features during test time. We refer to this as the feature-mismatch problem. Second, some of the features that occur in both domains will have different sentiments associated with them (e.g. *lightweight*). Therefore, a sentiment classifier trained using source domain labeled data is likely to incorrectly predict similar sentiment (as in the source) for such features. We call this the semantic variation problem. Next, we propose a method to overcome both problems using cross-domain word representations.

Let us assume that we are given a set $\{(\boldsymbol{x}_{\mathcal{S}}^{(i)}, y^{(i)})\}_{i=1}^{n}$ of n labeled reviews $\boldsymbol{x}_{\mathcal{S}}^{(i)}$ for the source domain $\mathcal{S}$. For simplicity, let us consider binary sentiment classification where each review $\boldsymbol{x}^{(i)}$ is labeled either as positive (i.e. $y^{(i)} = 1$) or negative (i.e. $y^{(i)} = -1$). Our cross-domain binary sentiment classification method can be easily extended to multi-class classification. First, we lemmatize each word in a source domain labeled review $\boldsymbol{x}_{\mathcal{S}}^{(i)}$, and extract unigrams and bigrams as features to represent $\boldsymbol{x}_{\mathcal{S}}^{(i)}$ by a binary-valued feature vector. Next, we train a binary linear classifier, $\boldsymbol{\theta}$, using those feature vectors. Any binary classification algorithm can be used for this purpose. We use $\boldsymbol{\theta}(z)$ to denote the weight learnt by the classifier for a feature z. In our experiments, we used l_2 regularized logistic regression.

At test time, we represent a test target review by a binary-valued vector $\boldsymbol{h}$ using a the set of unigrams and bigrams extracted from that review. Then, the activation score, $\psi(\boldsymbol{h})$, of $\boldsymbol{h}$ is defined by:

$$\psi(\boldsymbol{h}) = \sum_{c \in \boldsymbol{h}} \sum_{c' \in \boldsymbol{\theta}} \boldsymbol{\theta}(c') f(\boldsymbol{c}'_{\mathcal{S}}, \boldsymbol{c}_{\mathcal{S}}) + \sum_{w \in \boldsymbol{h}} \sum_{w' \in \boldsymbol{\theta}} \boldsymbol{\theta}(w') f(\boldsymbol{w}'_{\mathcal{S}}, \boldsymbol{w}_{\mathcal{T}}) \quad (13)$$

Here, f is a similarity measure between two vectors. If $\psi(\boldsymbol{h}) > 0$, we classify $\boldsymbol{h}$ as positive, and negative otherwise. Eq. 13 measures the similarity between each feature in $\boldsymbol{h}$ against the features in the classification model $\boldsymbol{\theta}$. For pivots $c \in \boldsymbol{h}$, we use the the source domain representations to measure similarity, whereas for the (target-specific) non-pivots $w \in \boldsymbol{h}$, we use their target domain representations. We experimented with several popular similarity measures for f and found cosine similarity to perform consistently well. We can interpret Eq. 13 as a method for *expanding* a test target document using nearest neighbor features from the source domain labeled data. It is analogous to query expansion used in information retrieval to improve document recall (Fang, 2008). Alternatively, Eq. 13 can be seen as a linearly-weighted additive kernel function over two feature spaces.

4 Experiments and Results

For train and evaluation purposes, we use the Amazon product reviews collected by Blitzer et al. (2007) for the four product categories: books (**B**), DVDs (**D**), electronic items (**E**), and kitchen appliances (**K**). There are 1000 positive and 1000 negative sentiment labeled reviews for each domain. Moreover, each domain has on average $17,547$ unlabeled reviews. We use the standard split of 800 positive and 800 negative labeled reviews from each domain as training data, and the rest (200+200) for testing. For validation purposes we use *movie* (source) and *computer* (target) domains, which were also collected by Blitzer et al. (2007), but not part of the train/test domains.

Experiments conducted using this validation dataset revealed that the performance of the proposed method is relatively insensitive to the value of the regularization parameter $\lambda \in [10^{-3}, 10^{3}]$. For the non-pivot prediction task we generate positive and negative instances using the procedure described in Section 3.2. As a typical example, we have $88,494$ train instances from the books source domain and $141,756$ train instances from the target domain (1:5 ratio between positive and negative instances in each domain). The number of pivots and non-pivots are set to $N_{\mathcal{P}} = N_{\mathcal{S}} = N_{\mathcal{T}} = 500$.

In Figure 1, we compare the proposed method against two baselines (**NA**, **InDomain**), current state-of-the-art methods for unsupervised cross-domain sentiment classification (**SFA**, **SCL**), word representation learning (**GloVe**), and cross-domain similarity prediction (**CS**). The **NA** (no-adapt) lower baseline uses a classifier trained on source labeled data to classify target test data without any domain adaptation. The **InDomain** baseline is trained using the labeled data for the target domain, and simulates the performance we can expect to obtain if target domain labeled data were available. Spectral Feature Alignment (**SFA**) (Pan et al., 2010) and Structural Correspondence Learning (**SCL**) (Blitzer et al., 2007) are the state-of-the-art methods for cross-domain sentiment classification. However, those methods do not learn word representations.

We use Global Vector Prediction (**GloVe**) (Pennington et al., 2014), the current state-of-the-art word representation learning method, to learn word representations separately from the source and target domain unlabeled data, and use the learnt representations in Eq. 13 for sentiment classification. In contrast to the *joint* word representations learnt by the proposed method, **GloVe** simulates the level of performance we would obtain by learning representations *independently*. **CS** denotes the cross-domain vector prediction method proposed by Bollegala et al. (2014). Although **CS** can be used to learn a vector-space translation matrix, it *does not* learn word representations. Vertical bars represent the classification accuracies (i.e. percentage of the correctly classified test instances) obtained by a particular method on target domain's test data, and Clopper-Pearson 95% binomial confidence intervals are superimposed.

Differences in data pre-processing (tokenization/lemmatization), selection (train/test splits), feature representation (unigram/bigram), pivot selection (MI/frequency), and the binary classification algorithms used to train the final classifier make it difficult to directly compare results published in prior work. Therefore, we re-run the original algorithms on the same processed dataset under the same conditions such that any differences reported in Figure 1 can be directly attributable to the domain adaptation, or word-representation learning methods compared.

All methods use l_2 regularized logistic regression as the binary sentiment classifier, and the reg-

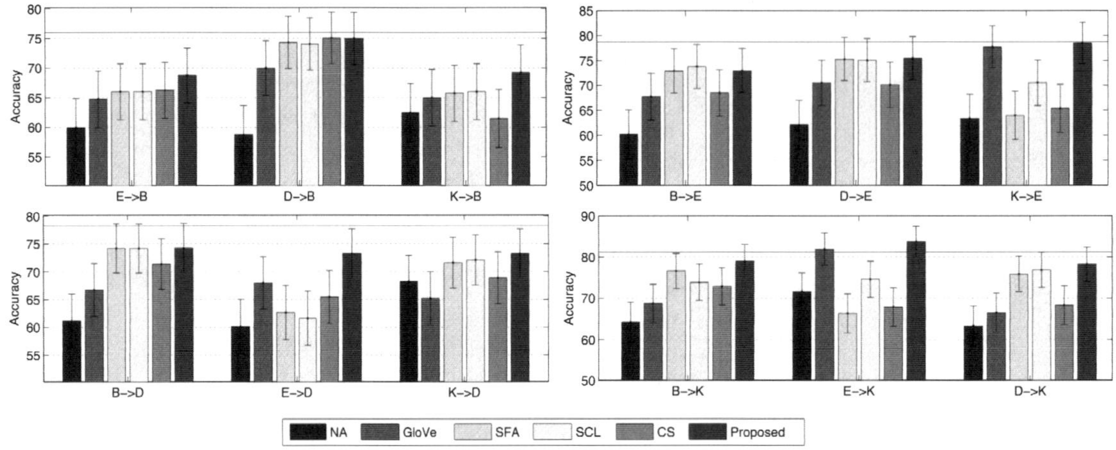

Figure 1: Accuracies obtained by different methods for each source-target pair in cross-domain sentiment classification.

ularization coefficients are set to their optimal values on the validation dataset. **SFA**, **SCL**, and **CS** use the same set of 500 pivots as used by the proposed method selected using NPMI (Section 3.4). Dimensionality n of the representation is set to 300 for both **GloVe** and the proposed method.

From Fig. 1 we see that the proposed method reports the highest classification accuracies in all 12 domain pairs. Overall, the improvements of the proposed method over **NA**, **GloVe**, and **CS** are statistically significant, and is comparable with **SFA**, and **SCL**. The proposed method's improvement over **CS** shows the importance of *predicting* word representations instead of *counting*. The improvement over **GloVe** shows that it is inadequate to simply apply existing word representation learning methods to learn independent word representations for the source and target domains.

We must consider the correspondences between the two domains as expressed by the pivots to jointly learn word representations. As shown in Fig. 2, the proposed method reports superior accuracies over **GloVe** across different dimensionalities. Moreover, we see that when the dimensionality of the representations increases, initially accuracies increase in both methods and saturates after 200 − 600 dimensions. However, further increasing the dimensionality results in unstable and some what poor accuracies due to overfitting when training high-dimensional representations. Although our word representations learnt by the proposed method are not specific to sentiment classification, the fact that it clearly outperforms **SFA** and **SCL** in all domain pairs is encouraging, and implies the wider-applicability of the proposed method for domain adaptation tasks beyond sentiment classification.

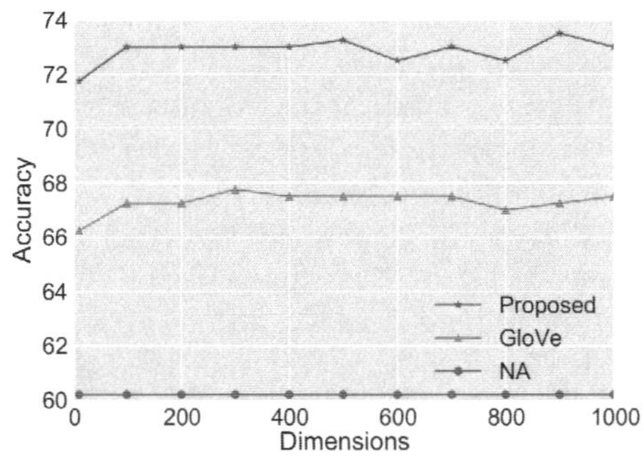

Figure 2: Accuracy vs. dimensionality of the representation.

5 Conclusion

We proposed an unsupervised method for learning cross-domain word representations using a given set of pivots and non-pivots selected from a source and a target domain. Moreover, we proposed a domain adaptation method using the learnt word representations.

Experimental results on a cross-domain sentiment classification task showed that the proposed method outperforms several competitive baselines and achieves best sentiment classification accuracies for all domain pairs. In future, we plan to apply the proposed method to other types of domain adaptation tasks such as cross-domain part-of-speech tagging, named entity recognition, and relation extraction.

Source code and pre-processed data etc. for this publication are publicly available[3].

[3] www.csc.liv.ac.uk/~danushka/prj/darep

References

Marco Baroni and Alessandro Lenci. 2010. Distributional memory: A general framework for corpus-based semantics. *Computational Linguistics*, 36(4):673 – 721.

Marco Baroni, Georgiana Dinu, and Germán Kruszewski. 2014. Don't count, predict! a systematic comparison of context-counting vs. context-predicting semantic vectors. In *Proc. of ACL*, pages 238–247.

Yoshua Bengio, Réjean Ducharme, Pascal Vincent, and Christian Jauvin. 2003. A neural probabilistic language model. *Journal of Machine Learning Research*, 3:1137 – 1155.

John Blitzer, Ryan McDonald, and Fernando Pereira. 2006. Domain adaptation with structural correspondence learning. In *Proc. of EMNLP*, pages 120 – 128.

John Blitzer, Mark Dredze, and Fernando Pereira. 2007. Biographies, bollywood, boom-boxes and blenders: Domain adaptation for sentiment classification. In *Proc. of ACL*, pages 440 – 447.

Danushka Bollegala, Yutaka Matsuo, and Mitsuru Ishizuka. 2011a. Relation adaptation: Learning to extract novel relations with minimum supervision. In *Proc. of IJCAI*, pages 2205 – 2210.

Danushka Bollegala, David Weir, and John Carroll. 2011b. Using multiple sources to construct a sentiment sensitive thesaurus for cross-domain sentiment classification. In *ACL/HLT*, pages 132 – 141.

Danushka Bollegala, Mitsuru Kusumoto, Yuichi Yoshida, and Ken ichi Kawarabayashi. 2013a. Mining for analogous tuples from an entity-relation graph. In *Proc. of IJCAI*, pages 2064 – 2070.

Danushka Bollegala, Yutaka Matsuo, and Mitsuru Ishizuka. 2013b. Minimally supervised novel relation extraction using latent relational mapping. *IEEE Transactions on Knowledge and Data Engineering*, 25(2):419 – 432.

Danushka Bollegala, David Weir, and John Carroll. 2014. Learning to predict distributions of words across domains. In *Proc. of ACL*, pages 613 – 623.

Gerlof Bouma. 2009. Normalized (pointwsie) mutual information in collocation extraction. In *Proc. of GSCL*, pages 31 – 40.

Ronan Collobert, Jason Weston, Leon Bottou, Michael Karlen, Koray Kavukcuoglu, and Pavel Kuska. 2011. Natural language processing (almost) from scratch. *Journal of Machine Learning Research*, 12:2493 – 2537.

Nguyen Tuan Duc, Danushka Bollegala, and Mitsuru Ishizuka. 2010. Using relational similarity between word pairs for latent relational search on the web. In *IEEE/WIC/ACM International Conference on Web Intelligence and Intelligent Agent Technology*, pages 196 – 199.

John Duchi, Elad Hazan, and Yoram Singer. 2011. Adaptive subgradient methods for online learning and stochastic optimization. *Journal of Machine Learning Research*, 12:2121 – 2159, July.

Hui Fang. 2008. A re-examination of query expansion using lexical resources. In *Proc. of ACL*, pages 139–147.

Stefano Faralli and Roberto Navigli. 2012. A new minimally-supervised framework for domain word sense disambiguation. In *EMNLP*, pages 1411 – 1422.

Xavier Glorot, Antoine Bordes, and Yoshua Bengio. 2011. Domain adaptation for large-scale sentiment classification: A deep learning approach. In *Proc. of ICML*.

Stephan Gouws, Yoshua Bengio, and Greg Corrado. 2015. Bilbowa: Fast bilingual distributed representations without word alignments. In *Proc. of ICML*.

Karl Moritz Hermann and Phil Blunsom. 2014. Multilingual distributed representations without word alignment. In *Proc. of ICLR*.

Eric H. Huang, Richard Socher, Christopher D. Manning, and Andrew Y. Ng. 2012. Improving word representations via global context and multiple word prototypes. In *Proc. of ACL*, pages 873 – 882.

Jing Jiang and ChengXiang Zhai. 2007a. Instance weighting for domain adaptation in nlp. In *ACL 2007*, pages 264 – 271.

Jing Jiang and ChengXiang Zhai. 2007b. A two-stage approach to domain adaptation for statistical classifiers. In *CIKM 2007*, pages 401–410.

Alexandre Klementiev, Ivan Titov, and Binod Bhattarai. 2012. Inducing crosslingual distributed representations of words. In *Proc. of COLING*, pages 1459 – 1474.

David McClosky, Eugene Charniak, and Mark Johnson. 2010. Automatic domain adaptation for parsing. In *Proc. of NAACL/HLT*, pages 28 – 36.

Tomas Mikolov, Kai Chen, and Jeffrey Dean. 2013a. Efficient estimation of word representation in vector space. *CoRR*.

Tomas Mikolov, Ilya Sutskever, Kai Chen, Gregory S. Corrado, and Jeffrey Dean. 2013b. Distributed representations of words and phrases and their compositionality. In *Proc. of NIPS*, pages 3111 – 3119.

Tomas Mikolov, Wen tau Yih, and Geoffrey Zweig. 2013c. Linguistic regularities in continous space word representations. In *NAACL'13*, pages 746 – 751.

Jeff Mitchell and Mirella Lapata. 2008. Vector-based models of semantic composition. In *Proc. of ACL-HLT*, pages 236 – 244.

Andriy Mnih and Geoffrey E. Hinton. 2008. A scalable hierarchical distributed language model. In *Proc. of NIPS*, pages 1081–1088.

Andriy Mnih and Koray Kavukcuoglu. 2013. Learning word embeddings efficiently with noise-contrastive estimation. In *Proc. of NIPS*.

Arvind Neelakantan, Jeevan Shankar, Alexandre Passos, and Andrew McCallum. 2014. Efficient non-parametric estimation of multiple embeddings per word in vector space. In *Proc. of EMNLP*, pages 1059–1069.

Sinno Jialin Pan, Xiaochuan Ni, Jian-Tao Sun, Qiang Yang, and Zheng Chen. 2010. Cross-domain sentiment classification via spectral feature alignment. In *Proc. of WWW*, pages 751 – 760.

Jeffery Pennington, Richard Socher, and Christopher D. Manning. 2014. Glove: global vectors for word representation. In *Proc. of EMNLP*.

Joseph Reisinger and Raymond J. Mooney. 2010. Multi-prototype vector-space models of word meaning. In *Proc. of HLT-NAACL*, pages 109 – 117.

Michael Roth and Kristian Woodsend. 2014. Composition of word representations improves semantic role labelling. In *Proc. of EMNLP*, pages 407–413.

Tobias Schnabel and Hinrich Schütze. 2013. Towards robust cross-domain domain adaptation for part-of-speech tagging. In *Proc. of IJCNLP*, pages 198 – 206.

Richard Socher, Cliff Chiung-Yu Lin, Andrew Ng, and Chris Manning. 2011a. Parsing natural scenes and natural language with recursive neural networks. In *ICML'11*.

Richard Socher, Jeffrey Pennington, Eric H. Huang, Andrew Y. Ng, and Christopher D. Manning. 2011b. Semi-supervised recursive autoencoders for predicting sentiment distributions. In *Proc. of EMNLP*, pages 151–161.

Peter D. Turney and Patrick Pantel. 2010. From frequency to meaning: Vector space models of semantics. *Journal of Aritificial Intelligence Research*, 37:141 – 188.

Will Y. Zou, Richard Socher, Daniel Cer, and Christopher D. Manning. 2013. Bilingual word embeddings for phrase-based machine translation. In *Proc. of EMNLP'13*, pages 1393 – 1398.

A Unified Multilingual Semantic Representation of Concepts

José Camacho-Collados, Mohammad Taher Pilehvar and **Roberto Navigli**
Department of Computer Science
Sapienza University of Rome
{collados,pilehvar,navigli}@di.uniroma1.it

Abstract

Semantic representation lies at the core of several applications in Natural Language Processing. However, most existing semantic representation techniques cannot be used effectively for the representation of individual word senses. We put forward a novel multilingual concept representation, called MUFFIN, which not only enables accurate representation of word senses in different languages, but also provides multiple advantages over existing approaches. MUFFIN represents a given concept in a unified semantic space irrespective of the language of interest, enabling cross-lingual comparison of different concepts. We evaluate our approach in two different evaluation benchmarks, semantic similarity and Word Sense Disambiguation, reporting state-of-the-art performance on several standard datasets.

1 Introduction

Semantic representation, i.e., the task of representing a linguistic item (such as a word or a word sense) in a mathematical or machine-interpretable form, is a fundamental problem in Natural Language Processing (NLP). The Vector Space Model (VSM) is a prominent approach for semantic representation, with widespread popularity in numerous NLP applications. The prevailing methods for the computation of a vector space representation are based on distributional semantics (Harris, 1954). However, these approaches, whether in their conventional co-occurrence based form (Salton et al., 1975; Turney and Pantel, 2010; Landauer and Dooley, 2002), or in their newer predictive branch (Collobert and Weston, 2008; Mikolov et al., 2013; Baroni et al., 2014), suffer from a major drawback: they are unable to model individual word senses or concepts, as they conflate different meanings of a word into a single vectorial representation. This hinders the functionality of this group of vector space models in tasks such as Word Sense Disambiguation (WSD) that require the representation of individual word senses. There have been several efforts to adapt and apply distributional approaches to the representation of word senses (Pantel and Lin, 2002; Brody and Lapata, 2009; Reisinger and Mooney, 2010; Huang et al., 2012). However, none of these techniques provides representations that are already linked to a standard sense inventory, and consequently such mapping has to be carried out either manually, or with the help of sense-annotated data. Chen et al. (2014) addressed this issue and obtained vectors for individual word senses by leveraging WordNet glosses. NASARI (Camacho-Collados et al., 2015) is another approach that obtains accurate sense-specific representations by combining the complementary knowledge from WordNet and Wikipedia. Graph-based approaches have also been successfully utilized to model individual words (Hughes and Ramage, 2007; Agirre et al., 2009; Yeh et al., 2009), or concepts (Pilehvar et al., 2013; Pilehvar and Navigli, 2014), drawing on the structural properties of semantic networks. The applicability of all these techniques, however, is usually either constrained to a single language (usually English), or to a specific task.

We put forward MUFFIN (Multilingual, UniFied and Flexible INterpretation), a novel method that exploits both structural knowledge derived from semantic networks and distributional statistics from text corpora, to produce effective representations of individual word senses or concepts. Our approach provides multiple advantages in comparison to the previous VSM techniques:

1. *Multilingual*: it enables sense representation in dozens of languages;
2. *Unified*: it represents a linguistic item, irrespective of its language, in a unified seman-

Proceedings of the 53rd Annual Meeting of the Association for Computational Linguistics and the 7th International Joint Conference on Natural Language Processing, pages 741–751,
Beijing, China, July 26-31, 2015.

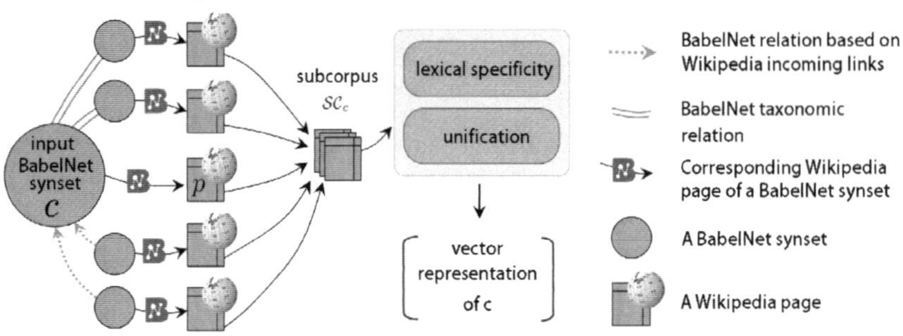

Figure 1: Our procedure for constructing a multilingual vector representation for a concept c.

tic space having concepts as its dimensions, permitting direct comparison of different representations across languages, and hence enabling cross-lingual applications;

3. *Flexible*: it can be readily applied to different NLP tasks with minimal adaptation.

We evaluate our semantic representation on two different tasks in lexical semantics: semantic similarity and Word Sense Disambiguation. To assess the multilingual capability of our approach, we also perform experiments on languages other than English on both tasks, and across languages for semantic similarity. We report state-of-the-art performance on multiple datasets and settings in both frameworks, which confirms the reliability and flexibility of our representations.

2 Methodology

Figure 1 illustrates our procedure for constructing the vector representation of a given concept. We use BabelNet[1] (version 2.5) as our main sense repository. BabelNet (Navigli and Ponzetto, 2012a) is a multilingual encyclopedic dictionary which merges WordNet with other lexical resources, such as Wikipedia and Wiktionary, thanks to its use of an automatic mapping algorithm. BabelNet extends the WordNet synset model to take into account multilinguality: a BabelNet synset contains the words that, in the various languages, express the given concept.

Our approach for modeling a BabelNet synset consists of two main steps. First, for the given synset we gather contextual information from Wikipedia by exploiting knowledge from the BabelNet semantic network (Section 2.1). Then, by analyzing the corresponding contextual information and comparing and contrasting it with the whole Wikipedia corpus, we obtain a vectorial representation of the given synset (Section 2.2).

2.1 A Wikipedia sub-corpus for each concept

Let c be a concept, which in our setting is a BabelNet synset, and let $\mathcal{W}_c$ be the set containing the Wikipedia page p corresponding to the concept c and all the Wikipedia pages having an outgoing link to p. We further enrich $\mathcal{W}_c$ with the corresponding Wikipedia pages of the hypernyms and hyponyms of c in the BabelNet network. $\mathcal{W}_c$ is the set of Wikipedia pages whose contents are exploited to build a representation for the concept c. We refer to the bag of content words in all the Wikipedia pages in $\mathcal{W}_c$ as the sub-corpus $\mathcal{SC}_c$ for the concept c.

2.2 Vector construction: lexical specificity

Lexical specificity (Lafon, 1980) is a statistical measure based on the hypergeometric distribution. Due to its efficiency in extracting a set of highly relevant words from a sub-corpus, the measure has recently gained popularity in different NLP applications, such as textual data analysis (Lebart et al., 1998), term extraction (Drouin, 2003), and domain-based term disambiguation (Camacho-Collados et al., 2014; Billami et al., 2014). We leverage lexical specificity to compute the weights in our vectors. In our earlier work (Camacho-Collados et al., 2015), we conducted different experiments which demonstrated the improvement that lexical specificity can provide over the popular term frequency-inverse document frequency weighting scheme (Jones, 1972, *tf-idf*). Lexical specificity computes the vector weights for an item, i.e., a word or a set of words, by comparing and contrasting its contextual information with a reference corpus. In our setting, we take the whole Wikipedia as our reference corpus $\mathcal{RC}$ (we use the October 2012 Wikipedia dump).

[1] http://www.babelnet.org

Let T and t be the respective total number of tokens in $\mathcal{RC}$ and $\mathcal{SC}_c$, while F and f denote the frequency of a given item in $\mathcal{RC}$ and $\mathcal{SC}_c$, respectively. Our goal is to compute a weight denoting the association of an item to the concept c. For notational brevity, we use the following expression to refer to positive lexical specificity:

$$\textit{specificity}(T, t, F, f) = -\log_{10} P(X \geq f) \quad (1)$$

where X represents a random variable following a hypergeometric distribution of parameters F, t and T. As we are only interested in a set of items that are representative of the concept being modeled, we follow Billami et al. (2014) and only consider in our final vector the items which are relevant to $\mathcal{SC}_c$ with a confidence higher than 99% according to the hypergeometric distribution $(P(X \geq f) \leq 0.01)$.

On the basis of lexical specificity we put forward two types of representations: *lexical* and *unified*. The lexical vector representation lex_c of a concept c has lemmas as its individual dimensions. To this end, we apply lexical specificity to every lemma in $\mathcal{SC}_c$ in order to estimate the relevance of each lemma to our concept c. We use the lexical representation for the task of WSD (see Section 3.2). We describe the unified representation in the next subsection.

2.3 Unified representation

Unlike the lexical version, our *unified* representation has concepts as individual dimensions. Algorithm 1 shows the construction process of a concept's unified vector. The algorithm first clusters together those words that have a sense sharing the same hypernym (h in the algorithm) according to the BabelNet taxonomy (lines 2-4). Next, the specificity is computed for the set of all the hyponyms of h, even those that do not appear in the sub-corpus $\mathcal{SC}_c$ (lines 6-14). Here, F and f denote the aggregated frequencies of all the hyponyms of h in the whole Wikipedia (i.e., reference corpus $\mathcal{RC}$) and the sub-corpus $\mathcal{SC}_c$, respectively.

Our binding of a set of sibling words into a single cluster represented by their common hypernym provides two advantages. Firstly, it transforms the representations to a unified semantic space. This space has concepts as its dimensions, enabling their comparability across languages. Secondly, the clustering can be viewed as an implicit disambiguation process, whereby a set of potentially ambiguous words are disambiguated into their intended sense on the basis of the contextual clues of the neighbouring content words, resulting in more accurate representations of meaning.

Algorithm 1 Unified Vector Construction

Input: a concept c
Output: the unified vector u_c where $u_c(h)$ is the dimension corresponding to concept h

1: $H \leftarrow \emptyset$
2: **for each** lemma $l \in \mathcal{SC}_c$
3:     **for each** hypernym h of l in BabelNet
4:         $H \leftarrow H \cup \{h\}$
5: vector $u_c \leftarrow$ null vector
6: **for each** $h \in H$
7:     **if** $\exists\, l_1, l_2 \in \mathcal{SC}_c$: l_1, l_2 hyponyms of h and $l_1 \neq l_2$ **then**
8:         $F \leftarrow 0$
9:         $f \leftarrow 0$
10:         **for each** hyponym $hypo$ of h
11:             **for each** lexicalization lex of $hypo$
12:                 $F \leftarrow F + \textit{freq}(lex, \mathcal{RC})$
13:                 $f \leftarrow f + \textit{freq}(lex, \mathcal{SC}_c)$
14:         $u_c(h) \leftarrow \textit{specificity}(T, t, F, f))$
15: **return** vector u_c

Example. Table 1 lists the top-weighted concepts, represented by their relevant lexicalizations, in the unified vectors generated for the bird and machine senses of the noun *crane* and for three different languages.[2] A comparison of concepts across the two senses indicates the effectiveness of our representation in identifying relevant concepts in different languages, while guaranteeing a clear distinction between the two meanings.

3 Applications

Thanks to their VSM nature and the sense-level functionality, our concept representations are highly flexible, allowing us to adapt and apply them to different NLP tasks with minimal adaptation. In this section we explain how we use our representations in the tasks of semantic similarity (Section 3.1) and WSD (Section 3.2).

Associating concepts with words. Given that our representations are for individual word senses, a preliminary step for both tasks would be to associate the set of concepts, i.e., BabelNet synsets, $\mathcal{C}_w = \{c_1, ..., c_n\}$ with a given word w. In the case when w exists in the BabelNet dictionary, we obtain the set of associated senses of the word as defined in the BabelNet sense inventory.

In order to enhance the coverage in the case of

[2]We use the sense notation of Navigli (2009): $\textit{word}^p_n$ is the nth sense of the *word* with part of speech p.

Crane (bird)			Crane (machine)		
English	French	German	English	French	German
shore_bird$^{1}_{n}$	‡famille_des_oiseaux$^{1}_{n}$	‡vogel-familie$^{1}_{n}$	∗lifting device$^{1}_{n}$	∗dispositif de levage$^{1}_{n}$	∗hebevorrichtung$^{1}_{n}$
bird$^{1}_{n}$	∗limicole$^{1}_{n}$	∗charadrii$^{1}_{n}$	‡construction$^{4}_{n}$	navire$^{1}_{n}$	radfahrzeug$^{1}_{n}$
∗wading_bird$^{1}_{n}$	oiseau_aquatique$^{2}_{n}$	†vogel_gattung$^{1}_{n}$	platform$^{1}_{n}$	limicole$^{1}_{n}$	†lenkfahrzeug$^{1}_{n}$
oscine_bird$^{1}_{n}$	tollé$^{2}_{n}$	wirbeltiere$^{2}_{n}$	warship$^{1}_{n}$	⋄vaisseau$^{2}_{n}$	regler$^{3}_{n}$
†bird_genus$^{1}_{n}$	gallinacé$^{1}_{n}$	fleisch$^{1}_{n}$	electric circuit$^{1}_{n}$	spationef$^{1}_{n}$	reisebus$^{1}_{n}$
‡bird_family$^{1}_{n}$	⋄classe$^{1}_{n}$	tier um$^{1}_{n}$	⋄vessel$^{2}_{n}$	‡construction$^{2}_{n}$	charadrii$^{1}_{n}$
⋄taxonomic_group$^{1}_{n}$	occurence$^{1}_{n}$	reiher$^{1}_{n}$	boat$^{1}_{n}$	†véhicule$^{3}_{n}$	güterwagen$^{2}_{n}$

Table 1: Top-weighted concepts, i.e., BabelNet synsets, for the bird and machine senses of the noun *crane*. We represent each synset by one of its word senses. Word senses marked with the same symbol across languages correspond to the same BabelNet synset.

words that are not defined in the BabelNet dictionary, we also exploit the so-called Wikipedia piped links. A piped link is a hyperlink appearing in the body of a Wikipedia article, providing a link to another Wikipedia article. For example, the piped link [[dockside_crane|Crane_(machine)]] is a hyperlink that appears as *dockside_crane* in the text, but takes the user to the Wikipedia page titled *Crane_(machine)*. These links provide Wikipedia editors with the ability to represent a Wikipedia article through a suitable lexicalization that preserves the grammatical structure, contextual coherency, and flow of the sentence. This property provides an effective means of obtaining a set of concepts for the words not covered by BabelNet. For the case of our example, the BabelNet out-of-vocabulary word w = *dockside_crane* will have in its set of associated concepts $\mathcal{C}_w$ the BabelNet synset corresponding to the Wikipedia page titled *Crane_(machine)*.

3.1 Semantic Similarity

Once we have the set $\mathcal{C}_w$ of concepts associated with each word w, we first retrieve the set of corresponding unified vector representations. We then follow Camacho-Collados et al. (2015) and use square-rooted Weighted Overlap (Pilehvar et al., 2013, WO) as our vector comparison method, a metric that has been shown to suit specificity-based vectors more than the conventional cosine. WO compares two vectors on the basis of their overlapping dimensions, which are harmonically weighted by their relative ranking:

$$WO(v_1, v_2) = \frac{\sum_{q \in O} \left(rank(q, v_1) + rank(q, v_2) \right)^{-1}}{\sum_{i=1}^{|O|} (2i)^{-1}} \quad (2)$$

where O is the set of overlapping dimensions (i.e. concepts) between the two vectors and $rank(q, v_i)$ is the rank of dimension q in the vector v_i.

Finally, the similarity between two words w_1 and w_2 is calculated as the similarity of their closest senses, a prevailing approach in the literature (Resnik, 1995; Budanitsky and Hirst, 2006):

$$sim(w_1, w_2) = \max_{v_1 \in \mathcal{C}_{w_1}, v_2 \in \mathcal{C}_{w_2}} \sqrt{WO(v_1, v_2)} \quad (3)$$

where w_1 and w_2 can belong to different languages. This cross-lingual similarity measurement is possible thanks to the unified language-independent space of concepts of our semantic representations.

3.2 Multilingual Word Sense Disambiguation

In order to be able to apply our approach to WSD, we use the lexical vector lex_c for each concept c. The reason for our choice of lexical vectors in this setting is that they enable a direct comparison of a candidate sense's representation with the context, which is also in the same lexical form. Algorithm 2 summarizes the general framework of our approach. Given a target word w to disambiguate, our approach proceeds by the following steps:

1. Retrieve $\mathcal{C}_w$, the set of associated concepts with the target word w (line 1);
2. Obtain the lexical vector lex_c for each concept $c \in \mathcal{C}_w$ (cf. Section 2);
3. Calculate, for each candidate concept c, a confidence score ($score_c$) based on the harmonic sum of the ranks of the overlapping words between its lexical vector lex_c and the context of the target word (line 5 in Algorithm 2).

Algorithm 2 MUFFIN for WSD

Input: a target word w and a document d (context of w)
Output: $\hat{c}$, the intended sense of w

for each concept $c \in \mathcal{C}_w$
  $score_c \leftarrow 0$
  for each lemma $l \in d$
    if $l \in lex_c$ **then**
      $score_c \leftarrow score_c + \big(rank(l, lex_c)\big)^{-1}$
$\hat{c} \leftarrow \arg\max_{c \in \mathcal{C}_w} score_c$
return $\hat{c}$

Thanks to the use of BabelNet, our approach is applicable to arbitrary languages. For the task of WSD, we focus on two major sense inventories integrated in BabelNet: Wikipedia and WordNet.

Wikipedia sense inventory. In this case, we obtain the set of candidate senses for a target word by following the procedure described in the beginning of this Section (i.e., associating concepts with words). However, we do not consider those BabelNet synsets that are not associated with Wikipedia pages.

WordNet sense inventory. Similarly, when restricted to the WordNet inventory, we discard those BabelNet synsets that do not contain a WordNet synset. In this setting, we also leverage relations from WordNet's semantic network and its disambiguated glosses[3] in order to obtain a richer set of Wikipedia articles in the sub-corpus construction. The enrichment of the semantic network with the disambiguated glosses has been shown to be beneficial in various graph-based disambiguation tasks (Navigli and Velardi, 2005; Agirre and Soroa, 2009; Pilehvar et al., 2013).

4 Experiments

We assess the reliability of MUFFIN in two standard evaluation benchmarks: semantic similarity (Section 4.1) and Word Sense Disambiguation (Section 4.2).

4.1 Semantic Similarity

As our semantic similarity experiment we opted for word similarity, which is one of the most popular evaluation frameworks in lexical semantics. Given a pair of words, the task in word similarity is to automatically judge their semantic similarity and, ideally, this judgement should be close to that given by humans.

4.1.1 Datasets

Monolingual. We picked the RG-65 dataset (Rubenstein and Goodenough, 1965) as our monolingual word similarity dataset. The dataset comprises 65 English word pairs which have been manually annotated by several annotators according to their similarity on a scale of 0 to 4. We also perform evaluations on the French (Joubarne and Inkpen, 2011) and German (Gurevych, 2005) adaptations of this dataset.

Cross-lingual. Hassan and Mihalcea (2009) developed two sets of cross-lingual datasets based on the English MC-30 (Miller and Charles, 1991) and WordSim-353 (Finkelstein et al., 2002) datasets, for four different languages: English, German, Romanian, and Arabic. However, the construction procedure they adopted, consisting of translating the pairs to other languages while preserving the original similarity scores, has led to inconsistencies in the datasets. For instance, the Spanish dataset contains the identical pair *mediodia-mediodia* with a similarity score of 3.42 (in the scale [0,4]). Additionally, the datasets contain several orthographic errors, such as *despliege* and *grua* (instead of *despliegue* and *grúa*) and incorrect translations (e.g., the English noun *implement* translated into the Spanish verb *implementar*).

Kennedy and Hirst (2012) proposed a more reliable procedure that leverages two existing aligned monolingual word similarity datasets for the construction of a new cross-lingual dataset. To this end, for each two word pairs *a-b* and *a'-b'* in the two datasets, if the difference in the corresponding scores is greater than one, the pairs are discarded. Otherwise, two new pairs *a-b'* and *a'-b* are created with a score equal to the average of the two original pairs' scores. In the case of repeated pairs, we merge them into a single pair with a similarity equal to their average scores. Using this procedure as a basis, Kennedy and Hirst (2012) created an English-French dataset consisting of 100 pairs. We followed the same procedure and built two datasets for English-German (consisting of 125 pairs) and German-French (comprising 96 pairs) language pairs.[4]

4.1.2 Comparison systems

Monolingual. We benchmark our system against four other approaches that exploit

[3]http://wordnet.princeton.edu/glosstag.shtml

[4]The cross-lingual datasets are available at http://lcl.uniroma1.it/sim-datasets/.

English	ρ	r	German	ρ	r	French	ρ	r
MUFFIN	0.83	0.84	MUFFIN	**0.77**	**0.76**	MUFFIN	**0.71**	**0.77**
SOC-PMI	–	0.61	SOC-PMI	–	0.27	SOC-PMI	–	0.19
PMI	–	0.41	PMI	–	0.40	PMI	–	0.34
Retrofitting	0.74	–	Retrofitting	0.60	–	Retrofitting	0.61	–
LSA-Wiki	0.69	0.65	–	–	–	LSA-Wiki	0.52	0.57
Wiki-wup	–	0.59	Wiki-wup	–	0.65			
SSA	0.83	**0.86**	Resnik	–	0.72			
NASARI	0.84	0.82	Lesk_hyper	–	0.69			
ADW	**0.87**	0.81						
Word2Vec	–	0.84						
PMI-SVD	–	0.74						
ESA	–	0.72						

Table 2: Spearman (ρ) and Pearson (r) correlation performance of different systems on the English, German and French RG-65 datasets.

Wikipedia as their main knowledge resource: SSA[5] (Hassan and Mihalcea, 2011), ESA (Gabrilovich and Markovitch, 2007), Wiki-wup (Ponzetto and Strube, 2007), and LSA-Wiki (Granada et al., 2014). We also provide results for systems that use distributional semantics for modeling words, both the conventional co-occurrence based approach, i.e., PMI-SVD (Baroni et al., 2014), PMI and SOC-PMI (Joubarne and Inkpen, 2011), and Retrofitting (Faruqui et al., 2015), and the newer word embeddings, i.e., Word2Vec (Mikolov et al., 2013). For Word2Vec and PMI-SVD, we use the pre-trained models obtained by Baroni et al. (2014).[6] As for WordNet-based approaches, we report results for Resnik (Resnik, 1995) and ADW (Pilehvar et al., 2013), which take advantage of its structural information, and Lesk_hyper (Gurevych, 2005), which leverages definitional information in WordNet for similarity computation. Finally, we also report the performance of our earlier work NASARI (Camacho-Collados et al., 2015), which combines knowledge from WordNet and Wikipedia for the English language in its setting without the Wiktionary synonyms module.

Cross-lingual. We compare the performance of our approach against the best configuration of the CL-MSR-2.0 system (Kennedy and Hirst, 2012), which exploits Pointwise Mutual Information (PMI) on a parallel corpus obtained from the English and French versions of WordNet. Since two of our cross-lingual datasets are newly-created, we developed three baseline systems to enable a more meaningful comparison. To this end, we first use Google Translate to translate the non-English side of the dataset to the English language. Accordingly, three state-of-the-art graph-based and corpus-based approaches were used to measure the similarity of the resulting English pairs. As English similarity measurement systems, we opted for ADW (Pilehvar et al., 2013), and the best predictive (Mikolov et al., 2013, Word2Vec) and co-occurrence (i.e., PMI-SVD) models obtained by Baroni et al. (2014).[7] In our experiments we refer to these systems as *pivot*, since they use English as a pivot for computing semantic similarity. As a comparison, we also show results for MUFFIN$_{pivot}$, which is the variant of our system applied to the same automatically translated monolingual datasets.

4.1.3 Results

Monolingual. We show in Table 2 the performance of different systems in terms of Spearman and Pearson correlations on the English, German, and French RG-65 datasets. On the German and French datasets, our system outperforms the comparison systems according to both evaluation measures. It achieves considerable Spearman and Pearson correlation leads of 0.1 and 0.2, respectively, on the French dataset in comparison to the best system. Also on the English RG-65 dataset, our system attains competitive performance according to both Spearman and Pearson correla-

[5]SSA involves several parameters tuned on datasets that are constructed on the basis of MC-30 and RG-65.

[6]We report the best configuration of the systems on the RG-65 dataset out of their 48 configurations. The corpus used to train the models contained 2.8 billion tokens, including Wikipedia (Baroni et al., 2014).

[7]`http://clic.cimec.unitn.it/composes/semantic-vectors.html`

Measure	FR-EN	EN-DE	DE-FR
MUFFIN	**0.83**	**0.76**	**0.83**
MUFFIN$_{pivot}$	**0.83**	0.73	0.79
ADW$_{pivot}$	0.80	0.73	0.72
Word2Vec$_{pivot}$	0.75	0.69	0.77
PMI-SVD$_{pivot}$	0.76	0.72	0.65
CL-MSR-2.0	0.30	–	–

Table 3: Pearson correlation performance of different similarity measures on the three cross-lingual RG-65 datasets.

tions. We note that most state-of-the-art systems on the dataset (e.g., ADW) are restricted to the English language only.

Cross-lingual. Pearson correlation results on the three cross-lingual RG-65 datasets are presented in Table 3. Similarly to the monolingual experiments, our system proves highly reliable in the cross-lingual setting, improving the performance of the comparison systems on all three language pairs. Moreover, MUFFIN$_{pivot}$ attains the best results among the *pivot* systems on all datasets, confirming the reliability of our system in the monolingual setting. We note that since the cross-lingual datasets were built by translating the word pairs in the original English RG-65 dataset, the pivot-based comparison systems proved to be highly competitive, outperforming the CL-MSR-2.0 system by a considerable margin.

4.2 Word Sense Disambiguation

4.2.1 Wikipedia

In this setting, we selected the SemEval 2013 all-words WSD task (Navigli et al., 2013) as our evaluation benchmark. The task provides datasets for five different languages: Italian, English, French, Spanish and German. There are on average 1123 words to disambiguate in each language's dataset. As comparison system, we provide results for the best-performing participating system on each language. We also show results for the state-of-the-art WSD system of Moro et al. (2014, Babelfy), which relies on random walks on the BabelNet semantic network and a set of graph heuristic algorithms. Finally, we also report results for the Most Frequent Sense (MFS) baseline provided by the task organizers.

We follow Moro et al. (2014) and back off to the MFS baseline in the case when our system's judgement does not meet a threshold θ. Similarly to Babelfy, we tuned the value of the threshold θ on the trial dataset provided by the organizers of the task. We tuned θ with step size 0.05 (hence, 21 possible values in [0,1]), obtaining an optimal value of 0.85 in the trial set, a value which we use across all languages.

Table 4 lists the F1 percentage performance of different systems on the five datasets of the SemEval-2013 all-words WSD task. Despite not being tuned to the task, our representations provide competitive results on all datasets, outperforming the sophisticated Babelfy system on the Spanish and German languages. The variant of our system not utilizing the MFS information in the disambiguation process ($\theta = 0$), i.e., MUFFIN⋆, also shows competitive results, outperforming the best system in the SemEval-2013 dataset on all languages. Interestingly, MUFFIN⋆ proves highly effective on the French language, surpassing not only the performance of our system using the MFS information, but also attaining the best overall performance.

4.2.2 WordNet

As regards the WordNet disambiguation task, we take as our benchmark the two recent SemEval English all-words WSD tasks: the SemEval-2013 task on Multilingual WSD (Navigli et al., 2013) and the SemEval-2007 English Lexical Sample, SRL and All-Words task (Pradhan et al., 2007). The all-words datasets of the two tasks contain 1644 instances (SemEval-2013) and 162 noun instances (SemEval-2007), respectively.

As comparison system, we report the performance of the best configuration of the top-performing system in the SemEval-2013 task, i.e., UMCC-DLSI (Gutiérrez et al., 2013). We also show results for the state-of-the-art supervised system (Zhong and Ng, 2010, IMS), as well as for two graph-based approaches that are based on random walks on the WordNet graph (Agirre and Soroa, 2009, UKB w2w) and the BabelNet semantic network (Moro et al., 2014, Babelfy). We follow Babelfy and also exploit the WordNet's sense frequency information from the SemCor sense-annotated corpus (Miller et al., 1993). However, instead of simply backing off to the most frequent sense, we propose a more meaningful exploitation of this information. To this end, we compute the relevance of a specific sense as the average of its normalized sense frequency and its corresponding

System	MFS Back off	Italian	English	French	Spanish	German
MUFFIN	✓	81.9	84.5	71.4	**85.1**	**83.1**
MUFFIN⋆		67.9	73.5	**72.3**	81.1	76.1
Babelfy	✓	**84.3**	**87.4**	71.6	83.8	81.6
Best SemEval 2013 system	✓	58.3	54.8	60.5	58.1	61.0
MFS	-	82.2	80.2	69.1	82.1	83.0

Table 4: F1 percentage performance on the SemEval-2013 Multilingual WSD datasets using Wikipedia as sense inventory.

score ($score_c$ in Algorithm 2) given by our system. The sense with the highest overall relevance value is then picked as the intended sense.

Additionally, we put forward a hybrid system that combines our system with IMS, hence benefiting from the judgements made by two systems that utilize complementary information. Our system makes judgements based on global contexts, whereas IMS exploits the local context of the target word. To this end, we compute the relevance of a specific sense as the average of the normalized scores given by IMS and our system ($score_c$ in Algorithm 2). We refer to this hybrid system as MUFFIN+IMS.

Table 5 reports the F1 percentage performance of different systems on the datasets of SemEval-2013 and SemEval-2007 English all-words WSD tasks. We also report the results for the MFS baseline, which always picks the most frequent sense of a word. Similarly to the disambiguation task on the Wikipedia sense inventory, MUFFIN proves to be quite competitive on the WordNet disambiguation task, while surpassing the performance of all the comparison systems on the SemEval-2013 dataset. On the SemEval-2007 dataset, IMS achieves the best performance, thanks to its usage of large amounts of manually and semi-automatically tagged data. Finally, our hybrid system, MUFFIN+IMS, provides the best overall performance on the two datasets, showing that our combination of the two WSD systems that utilize different types of knowledge was beneficial.

System	SemEval-2013	SemEval-2007
MUFFIN	**66.0**	66.0
UKB	61.3	56.0
UMCC-DLSI	64.7	–
IMS	65.3	**67.3**
Babelfy	65.9	62.7
MFS	63.2	65.8
MUFFIN+IMS	66.9	68.5

Table 5: F1 percentage performance on the SemEval-2013 and SemEval-2007 (noun instances) English All-words WSD datatets using WordNet as sense inventory.

5 Related work

We briefly review the recent literature on the two NLP tasks to which we applied our representations, i.e., Word Sense Disambiguation and semantic similarity.

WSD. There are two main categories of WSD techniques: knowledge-based and supervised (Navigli, 2009). Supervised systems such as IMS (Zhong and Ng, 2010) analyze sense-annotated data and model the context in which the various senses of a word usually appear. Despite their accuracy for the words that are provided with suitable amounts of sense-annotated data, their applicability is limited to those words and languages for which such data is available, practically limiting them to a small subset of words mainly in the English language. Knowledge-based approaches (Sinha and Mihalcea, 2007; Navigli and Lapata, 2007; Agirre and Soroa, 2009) significantly improve the coverage of supervised systems. However, similarly to their supervised counterparts, knowledge-based techniques are usually limited to the English language.

Recent years have seen a growing interest in cross-lingual and multilingual WSD (Lefever and Hoste, 2010; Lefever and Hoste, 2013; Navigli et al., 2013). Multilinguality is usually offered by methods that exploit the structural information of large-scale multilingual lexical resources such as Wikipedia (Gutiérrez et al., 2013; Manion and Sainudiin, 2013; Hovy et al., 2013). Babelfy (Moro et al., 2014) is an approach with state-of-the-art performance that relies on random walks on BabelNet multilingual semantic network (Navigli and Ponzetto, 2012a) and densest subgraph heuristics. However, the approach is limited to the WSD and Entity Linking tasks. In contrast, our approach is global as it can be used in different NLP tasks, including WSD.

Semantic similarity. Semantic similarity of word pairs is usually computed either on the basis of the structural properties of lexical databases and thesauri, or by comparing vectorial representations of words learned from massive text corpora. Structural approaches usually measure the similarity on the basis of the distance information on semantic networks, such as WordNet (Budanitsky and Hirst, 2006), or thesauri, such as Roget's (Morris and Hirst, 1991; Jarmasz and Szpakowicz, 2003). The semantic network of WordNet has also been used in more sophisticated techniques such as those based on random graph walks (Ramage et al., 2009; Pilehvar et al., 2013), or coupled with the complementary knowledge from Wikipedia (Camacho-Collados et al., 2015). However, these techniques are either limited in the languages to which they can be applied, or in their applicability to tasks other than semantic similarity (Navigli and Ponzetto, 2012b).

Corpus-based techniques are more flexible, enabling the training of models on corpora other than English. However, these approaches, either in their conventional co-occurrence based form (Gabrilovich and Markovitch, 2007; Landauer and Dumais, 1997; Turney and Pantel, 2010; Bullinaria and Levy, 2012), or the more recent predictive models (Mikolov et al., 2013; Collobert and Weston, 2008; Pennington et al., 2014), are restricted in two ways: (1) they cannot be used to compare word senses; and (2) they cannot be directly applied to cross-lingual semantic similarity. Though the first problem has been solved by multi-prototype models (Huang et al., 2012), or by the sense-specific representations obtained as a result of exploiting WordNet glosses (Chen et al., 2014), the second problem remains unaddressed. In contrast, our approach models word senses and concepts effectively, while providing a unified representation for different languages that enables cross-lingual semantic similarity.

6 Conclusions

This paper presented MUFFIN, a new multilingual, unified and flexible representation of individual word senses. Thanks to its effective combination of distributional statistics and structured knowledge, the approach can compute efficient representations of arbitrary word senses, with high coverage and irrespective of their language. We evaluated our representations on two different NLP tasks, i.e., semantic similarity and Word Sense Disambiguation, reporting state-of-the-art performance on several datasets. Experimental results demonstrated the reliability of our unified representation approach, while at the same time also highlighting its main advantages: multilinguality, owing to its effective application within and across multiple languages; and flexibility, owing to its robust performance on two different tasks.

Acknowledgments

The authors gratefully acknowledge the support of the ERC Starting Grant MultiJEDI No. 259234.

References

Eneko Agirre and Aitor Soroa. 2009. Personalizing PageRank for Word Sense Disambiguation. In *Proceedings of EACL*, pages 33–41.

Eneko Agirre, Enrique Alfonseca, Keith Hall, Jana Kravalova, Marius Paşca, and Aitor Soroa. 2009. A study on similarity and relatedness using distributional and WordNet-based approaches. In *Proceedings of NAACL*, pages 19–27.

Marco Baroni, Georgiana Dinu, and Germán Kruszewski. 2014. Don't count, predict! a systematic comparison of context-counting vs. context-predicting semantic vectors. In *Proceedings of ACL*, pages 238–247.

Mokhtar-Boumeyden Billami, José Camacho-Collados, Evelyne Jacquey, and Laurence Kister. 2014. Semantic annotation and terminology validation in full scientific articles in social sciences and humanities (annotation sémantique et validation terminologique en texte intégral en shs) [in french]. In *Proceedings of TALN 2014*, pages 363–376.

Samuel Brody and Mirella Lapata. 2009. Bayesian Word Sense Induction. In *Proceedings of EACL*, pages 103–111.

Alexander Budanitsky and Graeme Hirst. 2006. Evaluating WordNet-based measures of Lexical Semantic Relatedness. *Computational Linguistics*, 32(1):13–47.

John A. Bullinaria and Joseph P. Levy. 2012. Extracting semantic representations from word co-occurrence statistics: stop-lists, stemming, and SVD. *Behavior Research Methods*, 44(3):890–907.

José Camacho-Collados, Mokhtar Billami, Evelyne Jacquey, and Laurence Kister. 2014. Approche statistique pour le filtrage terminologique des occurrences de candidats termes en texte intégral. In *JADT*, pages 121–133.

José Camacho-Collados, Mohammad Taher Pilehvar, and Roberto Navigli. 2015. NASARI: a Novel Approach to a Semantically-Aware Representation of Items. In *Proceedings of NAACL*, pages 567–577.

Xinxiong Chen, Zhiyuan Liu, and Maosong Sun. 2014. A unified model for word sense representation and disambiguation. In *Proceedings of EMNLP*, pages 1025–1035.

Ronan Collobert and Jason Weston. 2008. A unified architecture for natural language processing: Deep neural networks with multitask learning. In *Proceedings of ICML*, pages 160–167.

Patrick Drouin. 2003. Term extraction using non-technical corpora as a point of leverage. *Terminology*, 9(1):99–115.

Manaal Faruqui, Jesse Dodge, Sujay K. Jauhar, Chris Dyer, Eduard Hovy, and Noah A. Smith. 2015. Retrofitting word vectors to semantic lexicons. In *Proceedings of NAACL*, pages 1606–1615.

Lev Finkelstein, Gabrilovich Evgeniy, Matias Yossi, Rivlin Ehud, Solan Zach, Wolfman Gadi, and Ruppin Eytan. 2002. Placing search in context: The concept revisited. *ACM Transactions on Information Systems*, 20(1):116–131.

Evgeniy Gabrilovich and Shaul Markovitch. 2007. Computing semantic relatedness using Wikipedia-based explicit semantic analysis. In *Proceedings of IJCAI*, pages 1606–1611.

Roger Granada, Cassia Trojahn, and Renata Vieira. 2014. Comparing semantic relatedness between word pairs in Portuguese using Wikipedia. In *Computational Processing of the Portuguese Language*, pages 170–175.

Iryna Gurevych. 2005. Using the structure of a conceptual network in computing semantic relatedness. In *Proceedings of IJCNLP*, pages 767–778.

Yoan Gutiérrez, Yenier Castañeda, Andy González, Rainel Estrada, D. Dennys Piug, I. Jose Abreu, Roger Pérez, Antonio Fernández Orquín, Andrés Montoyo, Rafael Muñoz, and Franc Camara. 2013. UMCC_DLSI: Reinforcing a ranking algorithm with sense frequencies and multidimensional semantic resources to solve multilingual word sense disambiguation. In *Proceedings of SemEval 2013*, pages 241–249.

Zellig Harris. 1954. Distributional structure. *Word*, 10:146–162.

Samer Hassan and Rada Mihalcea. 2009. Cross-lingual semantic relatedness using encyclopedic knowledge. In *Proceedings of EMNLP*, pages 1192–1201.

Samer Hassan and Rada Mihalcea. 2011. Semantic relatedness using salient semantic analysis. In *Proceedings of AAAI*, pages 884,889.

Eduard H. Hovy, Roberto Navigli, and Simone Paolo Ponzetto. 2013. Collaboratively built semi-structured content and Artificial Intelligence: The story so far. *Artificial Intelligence*, 194:2–27.

Eric H. Huang, Richard Socher, Christopher D. Manning, and Andrew Y. Ng. 2012. Improving word representations via global context and multiple word prototypes. In *Proceedings of ACL*, pages 873–882.

Thad Hughes and Daniel Ramage. 2007. Lexical semantic relatedness with random graph walks. In *Proceedings of EMNLP-CoNLL*, pages 581–589.

Mario Jarmasz and Stan Szpakowicz. 2003. Roget's thesaurus and semantic similarity. In *Proceedings of RANLP*, pages 212–219.

Karen Spärck Jones. 1972. A statistical interpretation of term specificity and its application in retrieval. *Journal of Documentation*, 28:11–21.

Colette Joubarne and Diana Inkpen. 2011. Comparison of semantic similarity for different languages using the Google n-gram corpus and second-order co-occurrence measures. In *Advances in Artificial Intelligence*, pages 216–221.

Alistair Kennedy and Graeme Hirst. 2012. Measuring semantic relatedness across languages. In *Proceedings of xLiTe: Cross-Lingual Technologies Workshop at the Neural Information Processing Systems Conference*.

Pierre Lafon. 1980. Sur la variabilité de la fréquence des formes dans un corpus. *Mots*, 1:127–165.

Tom Landauer and Scott Dooley. 2002. Latent semantic analysis: theory, method and application. In *Proceedings of CSCL*, pages 742–743.

Thomas K Landauer and Susan T Dumais. 1997. A solution to Plato's problem: The latent semantic analysis theory of acquisition, induction, and representation of knowledge. *Psychological Review*, 104(2):211.

Ludovic Lebart, A Salem, and Lisette Berry. 1998. *Exploring textual data*. Kluwer Academic Publishers.

Els Lefever and Veronique Hoste. 2010. SemEval-2010 Task 3: Cross-lingual Word Sense Disambiguation. In *Proceedings of SemEval 2010*, pages 82–87, Uppsala, Sweden.

Els Lefever and Veronique Hoste. 2013. SemEval-2013 Task 10: Cross-lingual Word Sense Disambiguation. In *Proceedings of SemEval 2013*, pages 158–166, Atlanta, USA.

Steve L. Manion and Raazesh Sainudiin. 2013. Daebak!: Peripheral diversity for multilingual Word Sense Disambiguation. In *Proceedings of SemEval 2013*, pages 250–254.

Tomas Mikolov, Kai Chen, Greg Corrado, and Jeffrey Dean. 2013. Efficient estimation of word representations in vector space. *CoRR*, abs/1301.3781.

George A. Miller and Walter G. Charles. 1991. Contextual correlates of semantic similarity. *Language and Cognitive Processes*, 6(1):1–28.

George A. Miller, Claudia Leacock, Randee Tengi, and Ross Bunker. 1993. A semantic concordance. In *Proceedings of the 3rd DARPA Workshop on Human Language Technology*, pages 303–308, Plainsboro, N.J.

Andrea Moro, Alessandro Raganato, and Roberto Navigli. 2014. Entity Linking meets Word Sense Disambiguation: a Unified Approach. *Transactions of the Association for Computational Linguistics (TACL)*, 2:231–244.

Jane Morris and Graeme Hirst. 1991. Lexical cohesion computed by thesaural relations as an indicator of the structure of text. *Computational Linguistics*, 17(1).

Roberto Navigli and Mirella Lapata. 2007. Graph connectivity measures for unsupervised Word Sense Disambiguation. In *Proceedings of IJCAI*, pages 1683–1688.

Roberto Navigli and Simone Paolo Ponzetto. 2012a. BabelNet: The automatic construction, evaluation and application of a wide-coverage multilingual semantic network. *Artificial Intelligence*, 193:217–250.

Roberto Navigli and Simone Paolo Ponzetto. 2012b. BabelRelate! a joint multilingual approach to computing semantic relatedness. In *Proceedings of AAAI*, pages 108–114.

Roberto Navigli and Paola Velardi. 2005. Structural Semantic Interconnections: a knowledge-based approach to Word Sense Disambiguation. *IEEE Transactions on Pattern Analysis and Machine Intelligence*, 27(7):1075–1088.

Roberto Navigli, David Jurgens, and Daniele Vannella. 2013. SemEval-2013 Task 12: Multilingual Word Sense Disambiguation. In *Proceedings of SemEval 2013*, pages 222–231.

Roberto Navigli. 2009. Word Sense Disambiguation: A survey. *ACM Computing Surveys*, 41(2):1–69.

Patrick Pantel and Dekang Lin. 2002. Discovering word senses from text. In *Proceedings of KDD*, pages 613–619.

Jeffrey Pennington, Richard Socher, and Christopher D Manning. 2014. GloVe: Global vectors for word representation. In *Proceedings of EMNLP*, pages 1532–1543.

Mohammad Taher Pilehvar and Roberto Navigli. 2014. A robust approach to aligning heterogeneous lexical resources. In *Proceedings of ACL*, pages 468–478.

Mohammad Taher Pilehvar, David Jurgens, and Roberto Navigli. 2013. Align, Disambiguate and Walk: a Unified Approach for Measuring Semantic Similarity. In *Proceedings of ACL*, pages 1341–1351.

Simone Paolo Ponzetto and Michael Strube. 2007. Knowledge derived from Wikipedia for computing semantic relatedness. *Journal of Artificial Intelligence Research (JAIR)*, 30:181–212.

Sameer Pradhan, Edward Loper, Dmitriy Dligach, and Martha Palmer. 2007. SemEval-2007 task-17: English lexical sample, SRL and all words. In *Proceedings of SemEval*, pages 87–92.

Daniel Ramage, Anna N. Rafferty, and Christopher D. Manning. 2009. Random walks for text semantic similarity. In *Proceedings of the 2009 Workshop on Graph-based Methods for Natural Language Processing*, pages 23–31.

Joseph Reisinger and Raymond J. Mooney. 2010. Multi-prototype vector-space models of word meaning. In *Proceedings of ACL*, pages 109–117.

Philip Resnik. 1995. Using information content to evaluate semantic similarity in a taxonomy. In *Proceedings of IJCAI*, pages 448–453.

Herbert Rubenstein and John B. Goodenough. 1965. Contextual correlates of synonymy. *Communications of the ACM*, 8(10):627–633.

Gerard Salton, A. Wong, and C. S. Yang. 1975. A vector space model for automatic indexing. *Communications of the ACM*, 18(11):613–620.

Ravi Sinha and Rada Mihalcea. 2007. Unsupervised graph-based Word Sense Disambiguation using measures of word semantic similarity. In *Proceedings of ICSC*, pages 363–369.

Peter D. Turney and Patrick Pantel. 2010. From frequency to meaning: Vector space models of semantics. *Journal of Artificial Intelligence Research*, 37:141–188.

Eric Yeh, Daniel Ramage, Christopher D. Manning, Eneko Agirre, and Aitor Soroa. 2009. WikiWalk: random walks on Wikipedia for semantic relatedness. In *Proceedings of the Workshop on Graph-based Methods for Natural Language Processing*, pages 41–49.

Zhi Zhong and Hwee Tou Ng. 2010. It Makes Sense: A wide-coverage Word Sense Disambiguation system for free text. In *Proceedings of the ACL System Demonstrations*, pages 78–83.

Demographic Factors Improve Classification Performance

Dirk Hovy
Center for Language Technology
University of Copenhagen, Denmark
Njalsgade 140
dirk@cst.dk

Abstract

Extra-linguistic factors influence language use, and are accounted for by speakers and listeners. Most natural language processing (NLP) tasks to date, however, treat language as uniform. This assumption can harm performance. We investigate the effect of including demographic information on performance in a variety of text-classification tasks. We find that by including age or gender information, we consistently and significantly improve performance over demographic-agnostic models. These results hold across three text-classification tasks in five languages.

1 Introduction

When we use language, we take demographic factors of the speakers into account. In other words, we do have certain expectations as to who uses "super cute," "rather satisfying," or "rad, dude." Sociolinguistics has long since studied the interplay between demographic factors and language use (Labov, 1964; Milroy and Milroy, 1992; Holmes, 1997; Macaulay, 2001; Macaulay, 2002; Barbieri, 2008; Wieling et al., 2011; Rickford and Price, 2013, inter alia).[1] These factors greatly influence word choice, syntax, and even semantics.

In natural language processing (NLP), however, we have largely ignored demographic factors, and treated language as a uniform medium. It was irrelevant, (and thus not modeled) whether a text was produced by a middle-aged man, an elderly lady, or a teenager. These three groups, however, differ along a whole host of demographic axes, and these differences are reflected in their language use.

[1]Apart from the demographic factors, other factors such as mood, interpersonal relationship, authority, language attitude, etc. contribute to our perception of language.

A model that is agnostic to demographic differences will lose these distinctions, and performance suffers whenever the model is applied to a new demographic. Historically, the demographics of training and test data (newswire) were relatively homogenous, language was relatively uniform, and information the main objective. Under these uniform conditions, the impact of demographics on performance was small.

Lately, however, NLP is increasingly applied to other domains, such as social media, where language is less canonical, demographic information about the author is available, and the authors' goals are no longer purely informational. The influence of demographic factors in this medium is thus much stronger than on the data we have traditionally used to induce models. The resulting performance drops have often been addressed via various domain adaptation approaches (Blitzer et al., 2006; Daume III and Marcu, 2006; Reichart and Rappoport, 2007; Chen et al., 2009; Daumé et al., 2010; Chen et al., 2011; Plank and Moschitti, 2013; Plank et al., 2014; Hovy et al., 2015b, inter alia). However, the authors and target demographics of social media differ radically from those in newswire text, and domain might in some case be a secondary effect to demographics. In this paper, we thus ask whether we also need *demographic adaptation.*

Concretely, we investigate

1. how we can encode demographic factors, and
2. what effect they have on the performance of text-classification tasks

We focus on **age** and **gender**, and similarly to Bamman et al. (2014a), we use distributed word representations (embeddings) conditioned on these demographic factors (see Section 2.1) to incorporate the information.

We evaluate the effect of demographic information on classification performance in three NLP

Proceedings of the 53rd Annual Meeting of the Association for Computational Linguistics and the 7th International Joint Conference on Natural Language Processing, pages 752–762,
Beijing, China, July 26-31, 2015.

tasks: sentiment analysis (Section 2.2), topic detection (Section 2.3), and author attribute classification (Section 2.4). [2]

We compare F_1-performance of classifiers a) trained with access to demographic information, or b) under agnostic conditions. We find that demographic-aware models consistently outperform their agnostic counterparts in all tasks.

Our contributions

We investigate the effect of demographic factors on classification performance. We show that NLP systems benefit from demographic awareness, i.e., that information about age and gender can lead to significant performance improvements in three different NLP tasks across five different languages.

2 Data

We use data from an international user review website, Trustpilot. It contains information both about the review (text and star rating), as well as the reviewer, in form of a profile. The profile included a screen name, and potentially information about gender and birth year.

Since demographic factors are extra-linguistic, we assume that the same effects hold irrespective of language. To investigate this hypothesis, we use data from several languages (Danish, French, and German) and varieties (American English, British English).

We use data from the countries with most users, i.e., Great Britain, Denmark, Germany, France, and the US. The selection was made based on the availability of sufficient amounts of training data (see Table 1 for more details). The high number of users in Denmark (one tenth of the country's population) might be due to the fact that Trustpilot is a Danish company and thus existed there longer than in other countries. Danish users also provide (in relative terms) more information about themselves than users of any other country, so that even in absolute numbers, there is oftentimes more information available than for larger countries like France or Germany, where users are more reluctant to disclose information.

While most of this profile information is voluntary, we have good coverage for both age and gender. In case of missing gender values, we base a guess on the first name (if given), by choosing the gender most frequently associated with that name in the particular language. We do require that one gender is prevalent (accounting for 95% of all mentions), and that there is enough support (at least 3 attributed instances), though. For age, coverage is less dense, so the resulting data sets are smaller, but still sufficient.

[2] We selected these tasks to represent a range of text-classification applications, and based on the availability of suitable data with respect to target and demographic variables.

	USERS	AGE	GENDER	PLACE	ALL
UK	1,424k	7%	62%	5%	4%
France	741k	3%	53%	2%	1%
Denmark	671k	23%	87%	17%	16%
US	648k	8%	59%	7%	4%
Germany	329k	8%	47%	6%	4%

Table 1: Number of users and % per variable per country (after applying augmentations).

For more information on Trustpilot as a resource, see Hovy et al. (2015a).

We split each review into sentences, tokenize, replace numbers with a 0, lowercase the data, and join frequent bigrams with an underscore to form a single token.

For each language, we collect four sub-corpora, namely two for gender (male and female) and two for age (under 35 and over 45). The sub-corpora for the discrete variable gender are relatively straightforward (although see (Bamman et al., 2014b)), but the split for the continuous age variable are less clear. While the effect of age on language use is undisputed (Barke, 2000; Barbieri, 2008; Rickford and Price, 2013), providing a clear cut-off is hard. We therefore use age ranges that result in roughly equally sized data sets for both groups, and that are not contiguous.

For each independent variable (age and gender), we induce embeddings for the two sub-groups (see section 2.1), as well as a "mixed" setting. We also extract labeled data for each task (see sections 2.2, 2.3, and 2.4). Each of these data sets is randomly split into training and test data, 60:40. Note that we do *not* set any parameters on development data, but instead use off-the-shelf software with default parameters for classification. Table 2 gives an overview of the number of training and test instances for each task and both variables (gender and age).

Note that this setup is somewhat artificial: the vocabulary of the embeddings can subsume the

		GENDER		AGE	
TASK	COUNTRY	TRAIN	TEST	TRAIN	TEST
TOPIC	Denmark	72.48k	48.32k	26.89k	17.93k
	France	33.34k	22.23k	3.67k	2.45k
	Germany	18.35k	12.23k	4.82k	3.22k
	UK	110.40k	73.60k	13.26k	8.84k
	US	36.95k	24.63k	7.25k	4.84k
SENTIMENT	Denmark	150.29k	100.19k	45.18k	30.12k
	France	40.38k	26.92k	3.94k	2.63k
	Germany	17.35k	11.57k	3.52k	2.35k
	UK	93.98k	62.65k	15.80k	10.53k
	US	43.36k	28.91k	3.90k	2.60k
ATTRIBUTES	Denmark	180.31k	120.20k	180.31k	120.20k
	France	10.69k	7.12k	10.69k	7.12k
	Germany	11.47k	7.64k	11.47k	7.64k
	UK	70.87k	47.25k	70.87k	47.25k
	US	28.10k	18.73k	28.10k	18.73k
total		918.32k	612.20k	429.66k	286.43k

Table 2: Number of sentences per task for **gender** and **age** as independent variable

vocabulary of the tasks (there is some loss due to frequency cut-offs in `word2vec`). The out-of-vocabulary rate on the tasks is thus artificially low and can inflate results. In a standard "improvement over baseline"-setup, this would be problematic. However, the results should not be interpreted with respect to their absolute value on the respective tasks, but with respect to the relative differences.

2.1 Conditional Embeddings

COUNTRY	AGE	GENDER
Denmark	495k	1.6m
France	36k	490k
Germany	47k	211k
UK	232k	1.63m
US	70k	576k
total	880k	4.51m

Table 3: Number of sentences used to induce embeddings

Embeddings are distributed representations of words in a vector space, capturing syntactic and semantic regularities among the words. We learn our word embeddings by using `word2vec`[3] (Mikolov et al., 2013) on unlabeled review data. Our corpora are relatively small, compared to the language modeling tasks the tool was developed for (see Table 3 for the number of instances used for each language and variable). We thus follow the suggestions in the `word2vec` documentation and use the skip-gram model and hierarchical softmax rather than the standard continuous-bag-of-words model. This setting penalizes low-frequent words less. All out-of-vocabulary (OOV) words are replaced with an "unknown" token, which is represented as the averaged vector over all other words.

In this paper, we want to use embeddings to capture group-specific differences. We therefore train embeddings on each of the sub-corpora (e.g., *male*, *female*, and *U35*, *O45*) separately. As comparison, we create a mixed setting. For each variable, we combine half of both sub-corpora (say, men and women) to form a third corpus with no demographic distinction. We also train embeddings on this data. This setting assumes that there are no demographic differences, which is the common approach in NLP to date.

Since embeddings depend crucially on the

[3] `https://code.google.com/p/word2vec/`

size of the available training data, and since we want to avoid modeling size effects, we balance the three corpora we use to induce embeddings such that all three contain the same number of instances.[4]

Note that while we condition the embeddings on demographic variables, they are *not* task-specific. While general-purpose embeddings are widely used in the NLP community, task-specific embeddings are known to lead to better results for various tasks, including sentiment analysis (Tang et al., 2014). Inducing task-specific embeddings carries the risk of overfitting to a task and data set, though, and would make it harder to attribute performance differences to demographic factors.

Since we are only interested in the *relative* difference between demographic-aware and unaware systems, not in the absolute performance on the tasks, we do not use task-specific embeddings.

2.2 Sentiment Analysis

Sentiment analysis is the task of determining the polarity of a document. In our experiments, we use three polarity values: positive, negative, and neutral. To collect data for the sentiment analysis task, we select all reviews that contain the target variable (gender or age), and a star-rating. Following previous work on similar data (Blitzer et al., 2007; Hardt and Wulff, 2012; Elming et al., 2014), we use one, three, or five star ratings, corresponding to negative, neutral, and positive sentiment, respectively.

We balance the data sets so that both training and test set contain equal amounts of all three labels. We do this in order to avoid demographic-specific label distributions (women and people over 45 tend to give more positive ratings than men and people under 35, see Section 3.1).

2.3 Topic Identification

Topic identification is the task of assigning a high-level concept to a document that captures its content. In our case, the topic labels are taken from the Trustpilot taxonomy for companies (e.g., *Electronics*, *Pets*, etc.). Again, there is a strong gender bias: the most common topic for men is *Computer & Accessories*, the most common topic among women is *Pets*. There is thus considerably less overlap between the groups than for the other tasks. In order not to model gender-specific topic bias and to eliminate topic frequency as a confounding factor, we restrict ourselves to the five most frequent labels that occur in both groups. We also ensure that we have the same number of examples for each label in both groups. However, in the interest of data size, we do not enforce a uniform distribution over the five labels (i.e., the classes are not balanced).

2.4 Author Attribute Identification

Author attribute identification is the task of inferring demographic factors from linguistic features (Alowibdi et al., 2013; Ciot et al., 2013; Liu and Ruths, 2013). It is often used in author profiling (Koppel et al., 2002) and stylometrics (Goswami et al., 2009; Sarawgi et al., 2011). Rosenthal and McKeown (2011) have shown that these attributes are correlated.

In this paper, we restrict ourselves to using gender to predict age, and age to predict gender. This serves as an additional test case. Again, we balance the class labels to minimize the effect of any confounding factors.

3 Experiments

3.1 Data Analysis

Before we analyze the effect of demographic differences on NLP performance, we investigate whether there is an effect on the non-linguistic correlates, i.e., ratings and topics. To measure the influence of demographic factors on these values, we quantify the distributions over the three sentiment labels and the five topic labels. We analyze both gender and age groups separately, but in the interest of space average across all languages.

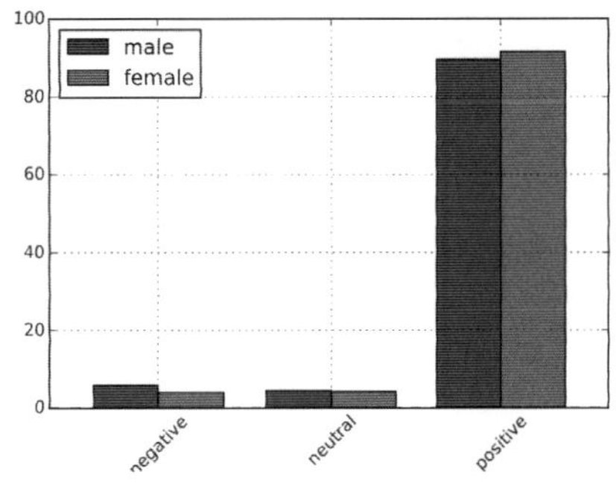

Figure 1: Label distribution for gender

[4]Note, however, that the vocabulary sizes still vary among languages and between age and gender.

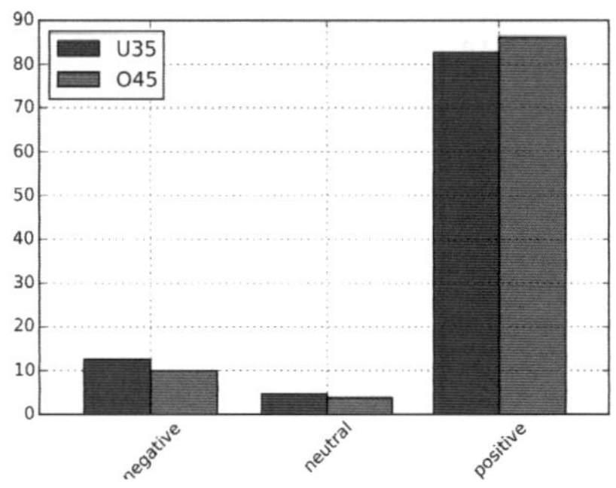

Figure 2: Label distribution for age groups

Figures 1 and 2 show the distributions over sentiment labels. We note that men give more negative and fewer positive ratings than women. The same holds for people in the younger group, who are more skewed towards negative ratings than people in the older group. While the differences are small, they suggest that demographics correlate with rating behavior have a measurable effect on model performance.

The gender distributions over categories exhibit a very different tendency. Table 3 shows that the review categories (averaged over all languages) are highly gender-specific. With the exception of *Hotels* and *Fashion Accessories*, the two distributions are almost bimodal opposites. However, they are still significantly correlated (Spearman ρ is 0.49 at $p < 0.01$).

The difference in the two distributions illustrates why we need to control for topic frequency in our experiments.

3.2 Models

Classifiers For all tasks, we use logistic regression models[5] with standard parameter settings. In order to isolate the effect of demographic differences on performance in all text classification tasks, we need to represent variable length documents based *only* upon the embeddings of the words they contain.

We follow Tang et al. (2014) in using convolutional layers over word embeddings (Collobert et al., 2011) to generate fixed-length input representations. Figure 4 schematically shows the procedure for the minimum of a 4-dimensional toy example. For each instance, we collect five N-dimensional statistics over the t by N input matrix, where N is the dimensionality of the embeddings (here: 100), and t is the sentence length in words.

From the matrix representation, we compute the dimension-wise minimum, maximum, and mean representation, as well as one standard deviation above and below the mean. We then concatenate those five 100-dimensional vectors to a 500-dimensional vector thats represents each instance (i.e., review) as input to the logistic regression classifier.

Taking the maximum and minimum across all embedding dimensions is equivalent to representing the exterior surface of the "instance manifold" (the volume in embedding space within which all words in the instance reside). Adding the mean and standard deviation summarizes the density per-dimension within the manifold. This way, we can represent any input sentence solely based on the embeddings, and with the same feature vector dimensionality.

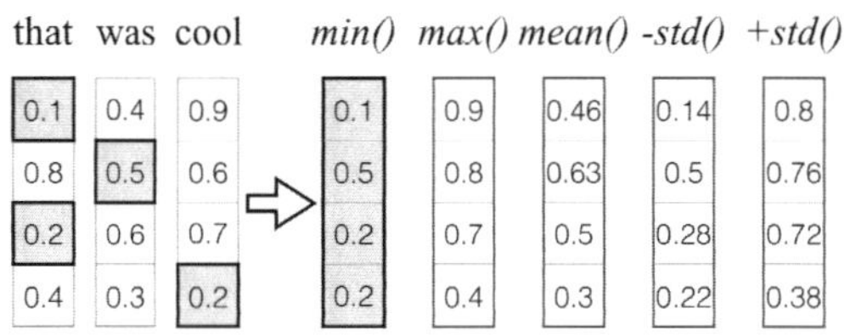

Figure 4: Example for deriving embedding statistics from sentence in 4-dimensional space. Minimum shaded

The approach is the same for all three tasks, and we did not tune any parameters to maximize performance. The results are thus maximally comparable to each other, albeit far from state-of-the-art. Overall performance could be improved with task-specific features and more sophisticated models, but it would make the results less comparable, and complicate identifying the source of performance differences. We leave this for future research.

Comparison In order to compare demographic-aware and agnostic models, we use the following setup for each task and language:

1. In the *"agnostic"* setting, we train a logistic-regression model using the joint embeddings (i.e., embeddings induced on the corpus containing both sub-groups, e.g. male and fe-

[5] http://scikit-learn.org/stable/modules/generated/sklearn.linear_model.LogisticRegression.html

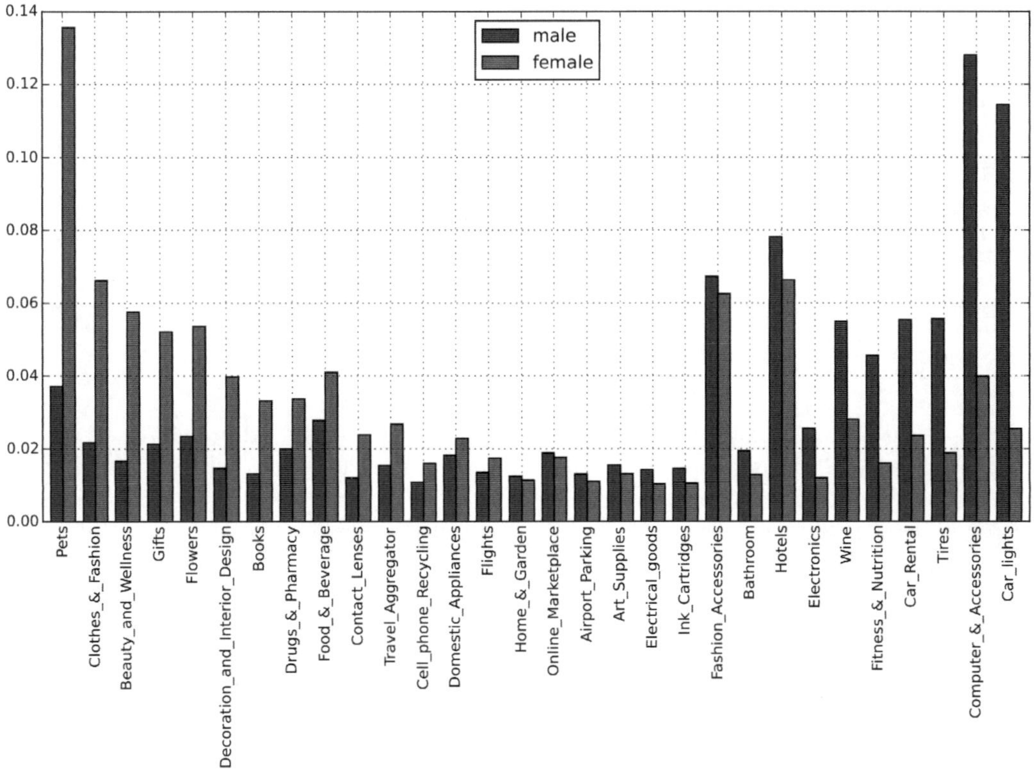

Figure 3: Distribution of the 30 most frequent categories per gender over all languages

male) and group-agnostic training data (i.e., data that contains an equal amount of instances from either sub-group).

2. In the *demographic-aware* setting, we train a logistic-regression model for each of the two sub-groups (e.g., male and female). For each sub-group, we use the group-specific embeddings (i.e., embeddings induced on, say, male data) and group-specific training data (i.e., instances collected from male data).

We measure F_1-performance for both settings (agnostic and demographic-aware) on the test set. The test data contains an equal amount of instances from both sub-groups (say, male and female). We use the demographic-aware classifier appropriate for each instance (e.g., male classifier for male instances), i.e., we assume that the model has access to this information. For many user-generated content settings, this is realistic, since demographic information *is* available. However, we only predict the target variable (sentiment, topic, or author attribute). We do *not* require the model to predict the sub-group (age or gender group).

We assume that demographic factors hold irrespective of language. We thus compute a *macro-*F_1 over all languages. *Micro-*F_1 would favor languages for which there is more data available, i.e., performance on those languages would dominate the average performance. Since we do not want to ascribe more importance to any particular language, macro-F_1 is more appropriate.

Even if there is a difference in performance between the agnostic and aware settings, this difference could still be due to the specific data set. In order to test whether the difference is also statistically significant, we use a *bootstrap-sampling test*. In a bootstrap-sampling test, we sample subsets of the predictions of both settings (with replacement) 10,000 times. For each sample, we measure F_1 of both systems, and compare the winning system of the sample to the winning system on the entire data set. The number of times

	SENTIMENT ANALYSIS		TOPIC CLASSIFICATION		AGE CLASSIFICATION	
COUNTRY	AGNOSTIC	AWARE	AGNOSTIC	AWARE	AGNOSTIC	AWARE
Denmark	61.75	***62.00**	49.19	***50.08**	59.94	***60.22**
France	**61.21**	61.09	38.45	***39.33**	53.85	**54.21**
Germany	60.50	**61.36**	60.45	**61.11**	60.19	**60.20**
UK	**65.22**	65.12	66.02	**66.26**	59.78	***60.35**
US	60.94	**61.24**	**65.64**	65.37	61.97	**62.68**
avg	61.92	**62.16**	55.95	**56.43**	59.15	**59.53**

Table 4: F_1 for **gender**-aware and agnostic models on tasks. Averages are macro average. * : $p < 0.05$

the sample winner differs from the entire data set, divided by $10,000$, is the reported p-value. Bootstrap-sampling essentially simulates runs of the two systems on different data sets. If one system outperforms the other under most of these conditions (i.e., the test returns a low p-value), we can be reasonably sure that the difference is not due to chance.

As discussed in Berg-Kirkpatrick et al. (2012) and Søgaard et al. (2014), this test is the most appropriate for NLP data, since it does not make any assumptions about the underlying distributions, and directly takes performance into account. Note that the test still depends on data size, though, so that small differences in performance on larger data sets can be significant, while larger differences on small sets might not.

We test for significance with the standard cutoff of $p < 0.05$. However, even under a bootstrap-sampling test, we can only limit the number of likely false positives. If we run enough tests, we increase the chance of reporting a type-I error. In order to account for this effect, we use Bonferroni corrections for each of the tasks.

4 Results

For each task, we compare the demographic-aware setting to an agnostic setting. The latter is equivalent to the currently common approach in NLP. For each task and language, the setting with the higher performance is marked in bold. Statistically significant differences (at $p < 0.05$) are marked with a star (*). Note that for the macro-averaged scores, we cannot perform bootstrap significance testing.

4.1 Gender

Table 4 shows the F_1 scores for the different tasks. In the left column of each task (labeled AGNOSTIC), the system is trained on embeddings and data from *both* genders, in the same ratios as in the test data. This column is similar to the configuration normally used in NLP to date, where – at least in theory – data comes from a uniformly distributed sample.

In the right column (labeled AWARE), the classification is based on the classifier trained on embeddings and data from the respective gender.

While the improvements are small, they are consistent. We do note some variance in consistency across tasks.

The largest average improvement among the three tasks is on topic classification. This improvement is interesting, since we have seen stark differences for the topic distribution between genders. Note, however that we controlled for this factor in our experiments (cf. Table 3). The results thus show that taking gender into account improves topic classification performance even *after* controlling for prior topic distribution as a confounding factor.

The improvements in age classification are the most consistent. This consistency is likely due to the fact that author attributes are often correlated. The fact that the attributes are related can be exploited in stacking approaches, where the attributes are predicted together.

Analyzing the errors, the misclassifications for sentiment analysis (the weakest task) seem to be system-independent. Mistakes are mainly due to the simplicity of the system. Since we do not explicitly model negation, we incur errors such as "I will never order anywhere else again" classified as negative, even though it is in fact rather positive.

	Sentiment Analysis		Topic Classification		Gender Classification	
COUNTRY	AGNOSTIC	AWARE	AGNOSTIC	AWARE	AGNOSTIC	AWARE
Denmark	58.74	**59.12**	45.11	**46.00**	58.82	**58.97**
France	**53.50**	53.40	**43.54**	42.64	54.64	**54.24**
Germany	51.91	**52.83**	***56.91**	55.41	54.04	**54.51**
UK	59.72	***60.83**	59.40	***60.88**	57.69	***58.25**
US	55.57	**56.00**	61.14	**61.38**	60.05	**60.97**
avg	55.89	**56.44**	53.22	**53.26**	57.05	**57.59**

Table 5: F_1 for **age**-aware and agnostic models on tasks. Averages are macro average. $^*: p < 0.05$

4.2 Age

Table 5 presents the results for systems with age as independent demographic variable. Again, we show the difference between the agnostic and age-aware setting in parallel columns for each task.

The improvements are similar to the ones for gender. The smaller magnitude across tasks indicates that knowledge of age offers less discriminative power than knowledge of gender. This in itself is an interesting result, suggesting that the age gap is much smaller than the gender gap when it comes to language variation (i.e., older people's language is more similar to younger people than the language of men is to women). The difference between groups could be a domain-effect, though, caused by the fact that all subjects are using a form of "reviewese" when leaving their feedback. Why this effect would be more prevalent across ages than across genders is not obvious from the data.

When averaged over all languages, the age-aware setup again consistently outperforms the agnostic setup, as it did for gender. While the final numbers are lower than in the gender setting, average improvements tend to be just as decisive.

5 Related Work

Most work in NLP that has dealt with demographic factors has either a) looked at the correlation of socio-economic attributes with linguistic features (Eisenstein et al., 2011; Eisenstein, 2013a; Eisenstein, 2013b; Doyle, 2014; Bamman et al., 2014a; Eisenstein, to appear), or b) used linguistic features to infer socio-economic attributes (Rosenthal and McKeown, 2011; Nguyen et al., 2011; Alowibdi et al., 2013; Ciot et al., 2013; Liu and Ruths, 2013; Bergsma et al., 2013; Volkova et al., 2015).

Our approach is related to the work by Eisenstein (2013a) and Doyle (2014), in that we investigate the influence of extralinguistic factors. Both of them work on Twitter and use geocoding information, whereas we focus on age and gender. Also, rather than correlating with census-level statistics, as in (Eisenstein et al., 2011; Eisenstein, 2013a; Eisenstein, to appear), we take individual information of each author into account.

Volkova et al. (2013) also explore the influence of gender and age on text-classification. They include demographic-specific features into their model and show improvements on sentiment analysis in three languages. Our work extends to more languages and three different text-classification tasks. We also use word representations trained on corpora from the various demographic groups, rather than incorporating the differences explicitly as features in our model.

Recently, Bamman et al. (2014a) have shown how regional lexical differences (i.e., *situated language*) can be learned and represented via distributed word representations (embeddings). They evaluate the conditional embeddings intrinsically, to show that the regional representatives of sports teams, parks, etc. are more closely associated with the respective hypernyms than other representatives. We also use embeddings conditioned on demographic factors (age and gender instead of location), but evaluate their effect on performance extrinsically, when used as input to an NLP system, rather than intrinsically (i.e., for discovering correlations between language use and demographic statistics).

Tang et al. (2014) learn embeddings for sentiment analysis by splitting up their data by rating.

We follow their methodology in using embeddings to represent variable length inputs for classification.

The experiments on author attribute identification are inspired by a host of previous work (Rosenthal and McKeown, 2011; Nguyen et al., 2011; Alowibdi et al., 2013; Ciot et al., 2013; Liu and Ruths, 2013; Volkova et al., 2015, inter alia). The main difference is that we use embeddings trained on another demographic variable rather than n-gram based features, and that our goal is not to build a state-of-the-art system.

6 Discussion

The results in Section 4 have shown that incorporating information on age and gender improves performance across a host of text-classification tasks. Even though the improvements are small and vary from task to task, they hold consistently across three tasks and languages. The magnitude of the improvements could be improved by using task-specific embeddings, additional features, and more sophisticated models. This would obscure the influence of the individual factors, though.

The observed improvements are solely due to the fact that different demographic groups use language quite differently. Sociolinguistic research suggests that younger people and women tend to be more creative in their language use than men and older groups. The former are thus often the drivers of language change (Holmes, 2013; Nguyen et al., 2014). Modeling language as uniform loses these distinctions, and thus causes performance drops.

As NLP systems are increasingly used for business intelligence and decision making, systematic performance differences carry the danger of disadvantaging minority groups whose language use differs from the norm.

7 Conclusion

In this paper, we investigate the influence of age and gender on topic identification, sentiment analysis, and author attribute identification. We induce embeddings conditioned on the respective demographic variable and use those embeddings as sole input to classifiers to build both demographic-agnostic and aware models. We evaluate our models on five languages.

Our results show that the models using demographic information perform on average better than the agnostic models. The improvements are small, but consistent, and in 8/30 cases, also statistically significant at $p < 0.05$, according to bootstrap sampling tests.

The results indicate that NLP systems can improve classification performance by incorporating demographic information, where available. In most of situated texts (social media, etc.), this is the case. While the improvements vary among tasks, the results suggest that similar to domain adaptation, we should start addressing the problem of *demographic* adaptation in NLP.

Acknowledgements

Thanks to Željko Agić, David Bamman, Jacob Eisenstein, Stephan Gouws, Anders Johannsen, Barbara Plank, Anders Søgaard, and Svitlana Volkova for their invaluable feedback, as well as to the anonymous reviewers, whose comments helped improve the paper. The author was supported under ERC Starting Grant LOWLANDS No. 313695.

References

Jalal S Alowibdi, Ugo A Buy, and Philip Yu. 2013. Empirical evaluation of profile characteristics for gender classification on twitter. In *Machine Learning and Applications (ICMLA), 2013 12th International Conference on*, volume 1, pages 365–369. IEEE.

David Bamman, Chris Dyer, and Noah A. Smith. 2014a. Distributed representations of geographically situated language. In *Proceedings of the 52nd Annual Meeting of the Association for Computational Linguistics*, pages 828–834. Proceedings of ACL.

David Bamman, Jacob Eisenstein, and Tyler Schnoebelen. 2014b. Gender identity and lexical variation in social media. *Journal of Sociolinguistics*, 18(2):135–160.

Federica Barbieri. 2008. Patterns of age-based linguistic variation in American English. *Journal of sociolinguistics*, 12(1):58–88.

Andrew J Barke. 2000. The Effect of Age on the Style of Discourse among Japanese Women. In *Proceedings of the 14th Pacific Asia Conference on Language, Information and Computation*, pages 23–34.

Taylor Berg-Kirkpatrick, David Burkett, and Dan Klein. 2012. An empirical investigation of statistical significance in NLP. In *Proceedings of EMNLP*.

Shane Bergsma, Mark Dredze, Benjamin Van Durme, Theresa Wilson, and David Yarowsky. 2013.

Broadly improving user classification via communication-based name and location clustering on twitter. In *HLT-NAACL*, pages 1010–1019.

John Blitzer, Ryan McDonald, and Fernando Pereira. 2006. Domain adaptation with structural correspondence learning. In *Proceedings of EMNLP*.

John Blitzer, Mark Dredze, and Fernando Pereira. 2007. Biographies, Bollywood, Boom-boxes and Blenders: Domain Adaptation for Sentiment Classification. In *Proceedings of ACL*.

Bo Chen, Wai Lam, Ivor Tsang, and Tak-Lam Wong. 2009. Extracting discriminative concepts for domain adaptation in text mining. In *KDD*.

Minmin Chen, Killiang Weinberger, and John Blitzer. 2011. Co-training for domain adaptation. In *NIPS*.

Morgane Ciot, Morgan Sonderegger, and Derek Ruths. 2013. Gender inference of twitter users in non-english contexts. In *Proceedings of the 2013 Conference on Empirical Methods in Natural Language Processing, Seattle, Wash*, pages 18–21.

Ronan Collobert, Jason Weston, Léon Bottou, Michael Karlen, Koray Kavukcuoglu, and Pavel Kuksa. 2011. Natural language processing (almost) from scratch. *The Journal of Machine Learning Research*, 12:2493–2537.

Hal Daumé, Abhishek Kumar, and Avishek Saha. 2010. Frustratingly easy semi-supervised domain adaptation. In *ACL Workshop on Domain Adaptation for NLP*.

Hal Daume III and Daniel Marcu. 2006. Domain adaptation for statistical classifiers. *Journal of Artificial Intelligence Research*, 26:101–126.

Gabriel Doyle. 2014. Mapping dialectal variation by querying social media. In *EACL*.

Jacob Eisenstein, Noah Smith, and Eric Xing. 2011. Discovering sociolinguistic associations with structured sparsity. In *Proceedings of ACL*.

Jacob Eisenstein. 2013a. Phonological factors in social media writing. In *Workshop on Language Analysis in Social Media, NAACL*.

Jacob Eisenstein. 2013b. What to do about bad language on the internet. In *Proceedings of NAACL*.

Jacob Eisenstein. to appear. Systematic patterning in phonologically-motivated orthographic variation. *Journal of Sociolinguistics*.

Jakob Elming, Barbara Plank, and Dirk Hovy. 2014. Robust cross-domain sentiment analysis for low-resource languages. In *Proceedings of the 5th Workshop on Computational Approaches to Subjectivity, Sentiment and Social Media Analysis*, pages 2–7, Baltimore, Maryland, June. Association for Computational Linguistics.

Sumit Goswami, Sudeshna Sarkar, and Mayur Rustagi. 2009. Stylometric analysis of bloggers' age and gender. In *Third International AAAI Conference on Weblogs and Social Media*.

Daniel Hardt and Julie Wulff. 2012. What is the meaning of 5*'s? an investigation of the expression and rating of sentiment. In *Empirical Methods in Natural Language Processing*, page 319.

Janet Holmes. 1997. Women, language and identity. *Journal of Sociolinguistics*, 1(2):195–223.

Janet Holmes. 2013. *An introduction to sociolinguistics*. Routledge.

Dirk Hovy, Anders Johannsen, and Anders Søgaard. 2015a. User review-sites as a source for large-scale sociolinguistic studies. In *Proceedings of WWW*.

Dirk Hovy, Barbara Plank, Héctor Martínez Alonso, and Anders Søgaard. 2015b. Mining for unambiguous instances to adapt pos taggers to new domains. In *Proceedings of NAACL-HLT*.

Moshe Koppel, Shlomo Argamon, and Anat Rachel Shimoni. 2002. Automatically categorizing written texts by author gender. *Literary and Linguistic Computing*, 17(4):401–412.

William Labov. 1964. *The social stratification of English in New York City*. Ph.D. thesis, Columbia university.

Wendy Liu and Derek Ruths. 2013. What's in a name? using first names as features for gender inference in twitter. In *Analyzing Microtext: 2013 AAAI Spring Symposium*.

Ronald Macaulay. 2001. You're like 'why not?' the quotative expressions of glasgow adolescents. *Journal of Sociolinguistics*, 5(1):3–21.

Ronald Macaulay. 2002. Extremely interesting, very interesting, or only quite interesting? adverbs and social class. *Journal of Sociolinguistics*, 6(3):398–417.

Tomas Mikolov, Kai Chen, Greg Corrado, and Jeffrey Dean. 2013. Efficient estimation of word representations in vector space. *arXiv preprint arXiv:1301.3781*.

Lesley Milroy and James Milroy. 1992. Social network and social class: Toward an integrated sociolinguistic model. *Language in society*, 21(01):1–26.

Dong Nguyen, Noah A Smith, and Carolyn P Rosé. 2011. Author age prediction from text using linear regression. In *Proceedings of the 5th ACL-HLT Workshop on Language Technology for Cultural Heritage, Social Sciences, and Humanities*, pages 115–123. Association for Computational Linguistics.

Dong Nguyen, Dolf Trieschnigg, A. Seza Dogruöz, Rilana Gravel, Mariet Theune, Theo Meder, and Franciska De Jong. 2014. Predicting Author Gender and Age from Tweets: Sociolinguistic Theories and Crowd Wisdom. In *Proceedings of COLING 2014*.

Barbara Plank and Alessandro Moschitti. 2013. Embedding semantic similarity in tree kernels for domain adaptation of relation extraction. In *Proceedings of ACL*.

Barbara Plank, Dirk Hovy, Ryan McDonald, and Anders Søgaard. 2014. Adapting taggers to twitter with not-so-distant supervision. In *Proceedings of COLING*. COLING.

Roi Reichart and Ari Rappoport. 2007. Self-training for enhancement and domain adaptation of statistical parsers trained on small datasets. In *Proceedings of ACL*.

John Rickford and Mackenzie Price. 2013. Girlz ii women: Age-grading, language change and stylistic variation. *Journal of Sociolinguistics*, 17(2):143–179.

Sara Rosenthal and Kathleen McKeown. 2011. Age prediction in blogs: A study of style, content, and online behavior in pre-and post-social media generations. In *Proceedings of the 49th Annual Meeting of the Association for Computational Linguistics: Human Language Technologies-Volume 1*, pages 763–772. Association for Computational Linguistics.

Ruchita Sarawgi, Kailash Gajulapalli, and Yejin Choi. 2011. Gender attribution: tracing stylometric evidence beyond topic and genre. In *Proceedings of the Fifteenth Conference on Computational Natural Language Learning*, pages 78–86. Association for Computational Linguistics.

Anders Søgaard, Anders Johannsen, Barbara Plank, Dirk Hovy, and Héctor Martínez Alonso. 2014. What's in a p-value in nlp? In *Proceedings of the Eighteenth Conference on Computational Natural Language Learning*, pages 1–10, Ann Arbor, Michigan, June. Association for Computational Linguistics.

Duyu Tang, Furu Wei, Nan Yang, Ming Zhou, Ting Liu, and Bing Qin. 2014. Learning sentiment-specific word embedding for twitter sentiment classification. In *Proceedings of the 52nd Annual Meeting of the Association for Computational Linguistics*, pages 1555–1565.

Svitlana Volkova, Theresa Wilson, and David Yarowsky. 2013. Exploring demographic language variations to improve multilingual sentiment analysis in social media. In *Proceedings of EMNLP*, pages 1815–1827.

Svitlana Volkova, Yoram Bachrach, Michael Armstrong, and Vijay Sharma. 2015. Inferring latent user properties from texts published in social media (demo). In *Proceedings of the Twenty-Ninth Conference on Artificial Intelligence (AAAI)*, Austin, TX, January.

Martijn Wieling, John Nerbonne, and R Harald Baayen. 2011. Quantitative social dialectology: Explaining linguistic variation geographically and socially. *PloS one*, 6(9):e23613.

Vector-space calculation of semantic surprisal for predicting word pronunciation duration

Asad Sayeed, Stefan Fischer, and Vera Demberg
Computational Linguistics and Phonetics/M²CI Cluster of Excellence
Saarland University
66123 Saarbrücken, Germany
{asayeed,sfischer,vera}@coli.uni-saarland.de

Abstract

In order to build psycholinguistic models of processing difficulty and evaluate these models against human data, we need highly accurate language models. Here we specifically consider *surprisal*, a word's predictability in context. Existing approaches have mostly used n-gram models or more sophisticated syntax-based parsing models; this largely does not account for effects specific to semantics. We build on the work by Mitchell et al. (2010) and show that the semantic prediction model suggested there can successfully predict spoken word durations in naturalistic conversational data.

An interesting finding is that the training data for the semantic model also plays a strong role: the model trained on in-domain data, even though a better language model for our data, is not able to predict word durations, while the out-of-domain trained language model does predict word durations. We argue that this at first counter-intuitive result is due to the out-of-domain model better matching the "language models" of the speakers in our data.

1 Introduction

The Uniform Information Density (UID) hypothesis holds that speakers tend to maintain a relatively constant rate of information transfer during speech production (e.g., Jurafsky et al., 2001; Aylett and Turk, 2006; Frank and Jaeger, 2008). The rate of information transfer is thereby quantified using as each words' *Surprisal* (Hale, 2001), that is, a word's negative log probability in context.

$$Surprisal(w_i) = -\log P(w_i|w_1..w_{i-1})$$

This work makes use of an existing measure of semantic surprisal calculated from a distributional space in order to test whether this measure accounts for an effect of UID on speech production. Our hypothesis is that a word in a semantically surprising context is pronounced with a slightly longer duration than the same word in a semantically less-expected context. In this way, a more uniform rate of information transfer is achieved, because the higher information content of the unexpected word is stretched over a slightly longer time. To our knowledge, the use of this form of surprisal as a pronunciation predictor has never been investigated.

The intuition is thus: in a sentence like *the sheep ate the long grass*, the word *grass* will have relatively high surprisal if the context only consists of *the long*. However, a distributional representation that retains the other content words in the sentence, thus representing the contextual similarity of *grass* to *sheep ate*, would able to capture the relevant context for content word prediction more easily. In the approach taken here, both types of models are combined: a standard language model is reweighted with semantic similarities in order to capture both short- and more long-distance dependency effects within the sentence.

The semantic surprisal model, a re-implementation of Mitchell (2011), uses a word vector w and a history or context vector h to calculate the language model $p(w|h)$, defining this probability in vector space via cosine similarity. Words that have a higher distributional similarity to their context are thus represented as having a higher probability than words that do not. Thus, we calculate probabilities for words in the context of a sentence in a framework of distributional semantics.

Regarding our main hypothesis—that speakers adapt their speech rate as a function of a word's information content—it is particularly important to

Proceedings of the 53rd Annual Meeting of the Association for Computational Linguistics and the 7th International Joint Conference on Natural Language Processing, pages 763–773,
Beijing, China, July 26-31, 2015.

us to test this hypothesis on fully "natural" conversational data. Therefore, we use the AMI corpus, which contains transcripts of English-language conversations with orthographically correct transcriptions and precise word pronunciation boundaries in terms of time.

We will explain the calculation of semantic surprisal in section 4 (this is so far only described in Mitchell's 2011 PhD thesis), and then evaluate the effect of an in-domain semantic surprisal model in section 7. Next, we will compare this to the effect of an out-of-domain semantic surprisal model in section 8. The hypothesis is only confirmed for the out-of-domain model, which we argue is due to this model being more similar to the speaker's internal "model" than the in-domain model.

2 Background

2.1 Surprisal and UID

Surprisal is defined in terms of the negative logarithm of the probability of a word in context: $S(w) = -\log P(w|context)$, where $P(w|context)$ is the probability of a word given its previous (linguistic) context. It is a measure of information content in which a high surprisal implies low predictability. The use of surprisal in psycholinguistic research goes back to Hale (2001), who used a probabilistic Earley Parser to model the difficulty in parsing so-called garden path sentences (e.g. "The horse raced past the barn fell"), wherein the unexpectedness of an upcoming word or structure influences the language processor's difficulty. Recent work in psycholinguistics has provided increasing support (e.g., Levy (2008); Demberg and Keller (2008); Smith and Levy (2013); Frank et al. (2013)) for the hypothesis that the surprisal of a word is proportional to the processing difficulty (measured in terms of reading times and EEG event-related potentials) it causes to a human.

The Uniform Information Density (UID) hypothesis (Frank and Jaeger, 2008) holds that speakers tend distribute information uniformly across an utterance (in the limits of grammaticality). Information density is quantified in terms of the surprisal of each word (or other linguistic unit) in the utterance. These notions go back to Shannon (1948), who showed that conveying information uniformly close to channel capacity is optimal for communication through a (noisy) communication channel.

Frank and Jaeger (2008) investigated UID effects in the SWITCHBOARD corpus at a morphosyntactic level wherein speakers avoid using English contracted forms ("you are" vs. "you're") when the contractible phrase is also transmitting a high degree of information in context. In this case, n-gram surprisal was used as the information density measure. Related hypotheses have been suggested by Jurafsky et al. (2001), who related speech durations to bigram probabilities on the Switchboard corpus, and Aylett and Turk (2006), who investigated information density effects at the syllable level. They used a read-aloud English speech synthesis corpus, and they found that there is an inverse relationship between the pronunciation duration and the N-gram predictability. Demberg et al. (2012) also use the AMI corpus used in this work, and show that syntactic surprisal (i.e., the surprisal estimated from Roark's (2009) PCFG parser) can predict word durations in natural speech.

Our work expands upon the existing efforts in demonstrating the UID hypothesis by applying surprisal to the level of lexical semantics.

2.2 Distributional semantics

Given a means of evaluating the similarity of linguistic units (e.g., words, sentences, texts) in some numerical space that represents the contexts in which they appear, it is possible to approximate the semantics in distributional terms. This is usually done by collecting statistics from a corpus using techniques developed for information retrieval. Using these statistics as a model of semantics is justified in terms of the "distributional hypothesis", which holds that words used in similar contexts have similar meanings (Harris, 1954).

A simple and widely-used type of distributional semantic model is the vector space model (Turney and Pantel, 2010). In such a model, all words are represented each in terms of vectors in a single high-dimensional space. The semantic similarity of words can then be calculated via the cosine of the angle between the vectors in this manner: $\cos(\varphi) = \frac{\vec{a}\cdot\vec{b}}{|\vec{a}||\vec{b}|}$. Closed-class function words are usually excluded from this calculation. Until relatively recently (Erk, 2012), distributional semantic models did not take into account the fine-grained details of syntactic and semantic structure construed in formal terms.

3 Corpus

The AMI Meeting Corpus (Carletta, 2007) is a multimodal English-language corpus. It contains videos and transcripts of simulated workgroup meetings accompanied by various kinds of annotations. The corpus is available along with its annotations under a free license[1].

Two-thirds of the videos contain simulated meetings of 4-person design teams assigned to talk about the development of a fictional television remote control. The remaining meetings discuss various other topics. The majority of speakers were non-native speakers of English, although all the conversations were held in English. The corpus contains about 100 hours of material.

An important characteristic of this corpus for our work is that the transcripts make use of consistent English orthography (as opposed to being phonetic transcripts). This enables the use of natural language processing techniques that require the reliable identification of words. Grammatical errors, however, remain in the corpus. The corpus includes other annotations such as gesture and dialog acts. Most important for our work are the time spans of word pronunciation, which are precise to the hundredth of a second.

We removed interjections, incomplete words, and transcriptions that were still misspelled from the corpus, and we took out all incomplete sentences. This left 951,769 tokens (15,403 types) remaining in the corpus.

4 Semantic surprisal model

We make use of a re-implementation of the semantic surprisal model presented in Mitchell et al. (2010). As this paper does not provide a detailed description of how to calculate semantic surprisal, our re-implementation is based on the description in Mitchell's PhD thesis (2011).

In order to calculate surprisal, we need to be able to obtain a good estimate of a word given previous context. Mitchell uses the following concepts in his model:

- h_{n-1} is the *history* and represents all the previous words in the sentence. If w_n is the current word, then $h_{n-1} = w_1 \dots w_{n-1}$. The vector-space semantic representation of h_{n-1} is calculated from the composition of individual word vectors, which we call $\vec{h}_{n-1}$.
- *context words* represent the dimensions of the word vectors. The value of a word vector's component is the co-occurrence of that word with a context word. The context words consist of the most frequent words in the corpus.
- we use *word class* and distinguish between content words and function words, for which we use open and closed classes as a proxy.

4.1 Computing the vector components

The proportion between two probabilities $\frac{p(c_i|w)}{p(c_i)}$ is used for calculating vector components, where c_i is the ith context dimension and w is the given word in the current position. We can calculate each vector component v_i for a word vector $\vec{v}$ according to the following equation:

$$v_i = \frac{p(c_i|w)}{p(c_i)} = \frac{f_{c_i w} f_{total}}{f_w f_{c_i}} \quad (1)$$

where $f_{c_i w}$ is the cooccurrence frequency of w and c_i together, f_{total} is the total corpus size, and c_i represents the unigram frequencies of w. All future steps in calculating our language model rely on this definition of v_i.

4.2 Semantic probabilities

For the goal of computing $p(w|h)$, we use the basic idea that the more "semantically coherent" a word is with its history, the more likely it is. Cosine similarity is a common way to define this similarity mathematically in a distributional space, producing a value in the interval $[-1, 1]$. We use the following definitions, wherein φ is the angle between $\vec{w}$ and $\vec{h}$:

$$\cos(\varphi) = \frac{\vec{w} \cdot \vec{h}}{|\vec{w}||\vec{h}|} \quad (2)$$

$$\vec{w} \cdot \vec{h} = \sum_i w_i h_i \quad (3)$$

Mitchell notes that there are at least three problems with using cosine similarity in connection with the construction of a probabilistic model: (a) the sum of all cosine values is not unity, (b) word frequency does not pay a role in the calculation, such that a rare synonym of a frequent word might get a high similarity rating, despite low predictability, and (c) the calculation can result in negative values.

[1] http://groups.inf.ed.ac.uk/ami/download/

This problem is addressed by two changes to the notion of dot product used in the calculation of the cosine:

$$\vec{w} \cdot \vec{h} = \sum_i \frac{p(c_i|w)}{p(c_i)} \frac{p(c_i|h)}{p(c_i)} \quad (4)$$

The influence of word frequencies is then restored using $p(w)$ and $p(c_i)$:

$$p(w|h) = p(w) \sum_i \frac{p(c_i|w)}{p(c_i)} \frac{p(c_i|h)}{p(c_i)} p(c_i) \quad (5)$$

This expression reweights the new scalar product with the likelihood of the given words and the context words. We refer the reader to Mitchell (2011) in order to see that this is a true probability. The application of Bayes' Rule allows us to rewrite the formula as $p(w|h) = \sum_i p(w|c_i)p(c_i|h)$. Nevertheless, equation (5) is better suited to our task, as it operates directly over our word vectors.

4.3 Incremental processing

Equation (5) provides a conditional probability for a word w and its history h. To calculate the product $\frac{p(c_i|w)}{p(c_i)} \frac{p(c_i|h)}{p(c_i)}$, we need the components of the vectors for w and h at the current position in the sentence. We can get $\vec{w}$ from directly from the vector space of words. However, $\vec{h}$ does not have a direct representation in that space, and it must be constructed compositionally:

$$\vec{h}_1 = \vec{w}_1 \qquad \text{Initialization} \quad (6)$$

$$\vec{h}_n = f(\vec{h}_{n-1}, \vec{w}_n) \qquad \text{Composition} \quad (7)$$

f is a vector composition function that can be chosen independently from the model. The history is initialized using the vector of the first word and combined step-by-step with the vectors of the following words. History vectors that arise from the composition step are normalized[2]:

$$h_i = \frac{\hat{h}_i}{\sum_j \hat{h}_j p(c_j)} \qquad \text{Normalization} \quad (8)$$

The equations (5), (6), (7), and (8) represent a simple language model, assuming calculation of vector components with equation (1).

[2]This equation is slightly different from what appears in Mitchell (2011). We present here a corrected formula based on private communication with the author.

4.4 Accounting for word order

The model described so far is based on semantic coherence and mostly ignores word order. Consequently, it has poor predictive power. In this section, we describe how a notion of word order is included in the model through the integration of an n-gram language model.

Specifically, equation (5) can be represented as the product of two factors:

$$p(w|h) = p(w)\Delta(w, h) \quad (9)$$

$$\Delta(w, h) = \sum_i \frac{p(c_i|w)}{p(c_i)} \frac{p(c_i|h)}{p(c_i)} p(c_i) \quad (10)$$

where Δ is the semantic component that scales $p(w)$ in function of the context. A word w that has a close semantic similarity to a history h should receive higher or lower probability depending on whether Δ is higher or lower than 1. In order to make this into a prediction, $p(w)$ is replaced with a trigram probability.

$$\hat{p}(w_n, h_{n-1}, w_{n-2}^{n-1}) = p(w_n|w_{n-2}^{n-1})\Delta(w_n, h_{n-1}) \quad (11)$$

However, this change means that the result is no longer a true probability. Instead, equation 11 can be seen as an estimate of semantic similarity. In order to restore its status as a probability, Mitchell includes another normalization step:

$$p(w_n|h_{n-3}, w_{n-2}^{n-1}) = \begin{cases} p(w_n|w_{n-2}^{n-1}) & \text{Function words} \\ \frac{\hat{p}(w_n, h_{n-3}, w_{n-2}^{n-1})}{\sum_{w_c} \hat{p}(w_c, h_{n-3}, w_{n-2}^{n-1})} \sum_{w_c} p(w_c|w_{n-2}^{n-1}) & \text{Content words} \end{cases} \quad (12)$$

The model hence simply uses the trigram model probability for function words, making the assumption that the distributional representation of such words does not include useful information. On the other hand, content words obtain a portion of the probability mass whose size depends on its similarity estimate $\hat{p}(w_n, h_{n-3}, w_{n-2}^{n-1})$ relative to the similarity estimates of all other words $\sum_{w_c} \hat{p}(w_c, h_{n-3}, w_{n-2}^{n-1})$. The factor $\sum_{w_c} p(w_c|w_{n-2}^{n-1})$ ensures that not all of the probability mass is divided up among the content words w_c; rather, only the mass assigned by the n-gram model at position w_{n-2}^{n-1} is re-distributed. The probability mass of the function words remains unchanged.

Mitchell (2011) restricts the history so that only words outside the trigram window are taken into account in order to keep the n-gram model and the semantic similarity model independent. Thus, the n-gram model represents local dependencies, and the semantic model represents longer-distance dependencies.

The final model that we use in our experiment consists of equations (1), (6), (7), (8) and (12).

5 Evaluation Methods

Our goal is to test whether semantically reweighted surprisal can explain spoken word durations over and above more simple factors that are known to influence word durations, such as word length, frequency and predictability using a simpler language model. Our first experiment tests whether semantic surprisal based on a model trained using in-domain data is predictive of word pronunciation duration, considering the UID hypothesis. For our in-domain model, we estimate surprisal using 10-fold cross-validation over the AMI corpus: we divide the corpus into ten equally-sized segments and produce surprisal values for each word in each segment based on a model trained from the other nine segments. We then use linear mixed effects modeling (LME) via the lme4 package in R (Pinheiro and Bates, 2000; Bates et al., 2014) in order to account for word pronunciation length. We follow the approach of Demberg et al. (2012).

Linear mixed effects modelling is a generalization of linear regression modeling and includes both fixed effects and random effects. This is particularly useful when we have a statistical units (e.g., speakers) each with their own set of repeated measures (e.g., word duration), but each such unit has its own particular characteristics (e.g., some speakers naturally speak more slowly than others). These are the random effects. The fixed effects are those characteristics that are expected not to vary across such units. LME modeling learns coefficients for all of the predictors, defining a regression equation that should account for the data in the dependent variable (in our case, word pronunciation duration). The variance in the data that a model cannot explain is referred to as the residual. We denote statistical significances in the following way: *** means a p-value ≤ 0.001, ** means $p \leq 0.01$, * means $p \leq 0.05$, and no stars means that the predictor is not significant ($p > 0.05$).

In our regression models, all the variables are centered and scaled to reduce effects of correlations between predictors. Furthermore, we log-transformed the response variable (actual spoken word durations from the corpus) as well as the duration estimates from the MARY speech synthesis system to obtain more normal distributions, which are prerequisite for applying the LME models. All conclusions drawn here also hold for versions of the model where no log transformation is used.

From the AMI corpus, we filter out data points (words) that have a pronunciation duration of zero or those that are longer than two seconds, the latter in order to avoid including such things as pauses for thought. We also remove items that are not represented in Gigaword. That leaves us with 790,061 data points for further analysis. However, in our semantic model, function words are not affected by the Δ semantic similarity adjustment and are therefore not analyzable for the effect of semantically-weighted trigram predictability. That leaves 260k data points for analysis in the models.

6 Baseline model

As a first step, we estimate a baseline model which does not include the in-domain semantic surprisal. The response variable in this model are the word durations observed in the corpus. Predictor variables include D_{MARY} (the context-dependent spoken word duration as estimated by the MARY speech synthesis system), word frequency estimates from the same domain as well as the GigaWord corpus (F_{AMI} and F_{Giga}, both as log relative frequencies), the interaction between estimated word durations and in-domain frequency, (D_{MARY}:F_{AMI}) and a domain-general trigram model ($S_{AMI\text{-}3}$). Our model also includes a random intercept for each speaker, as well as random slopes under speaker for D_{MARY} and $S_{AMI\text{-}3}$. The baseline model is shown in Table 1.

All predictors in the baseline model shown in Table 1 significantly improve model fit. We can see that the MARY-TTS estimated word durations are a positive highly significant predictor in the model. Furthermore, the word frequency estimates from the domain general corpus as well as the in-domain frequency estimates are significant negative predictors of word durations, this means

Predictor	Coefficient	t-value	Sig.
(Intercept)	0.034	4.90	***
D_{MARY}	0.427	143.97	***
F_{AMI}	-0.137	-60.26	***
F_{Giga}	-0.051	-18.92	***
$S_{Giga\text{-}3gram}$	0.032	10.94	***
D_{MARY}:F_{AMI}	-0.003	-2.12	*

Table 1: Fixed effects of a baseline model including the data points for which we could calculate semantic surprisal.

that as expected, words durations are shorter for more frequent words. We can furthermore see that n-gram surprisal is a significant positive predictor of spoken word durations; i.e., more unexpected words have longer durations than otherwise predicted. Finally, there is also a significant interaction between estimated word durations and in-domain word frequency, which means that the duration of long and frequent words is corrected slightly downward.

7 Experiment 1: in-domain model

The AMI corpus contains spoken conversations, and is thus quite different from the written corpora we have available. When we train an n-gram model in domain (using 10-fold cross validation), perplexities for the in-domain model (67.9) are much lower than for a language model trained on gigaword (359.7), showing that the in-domain model is a better language model for the data[3].

In order to see the effect of semantic surprisal estimated based on the in-domain language model and reweighted for semantic similarity within the same sentence as described in Section 3, we then expand the baseline model, adding $S_{Semantics}$ as a predictor. Table 2 shows the fixed effects of this expanded model. The predictor for semantic surprisal is significant, but the coefficient is negative. This apparently contradicts our hypothesis that semantic surprisal has a UID effect on pronunciation duration, so that higher $S_{Semantics}$ means higher D_{AMI}. We found that these results are very stable—in particular, the same results also hold if we estimate a separate model with $S_{Semantics}$ as a predictor and residuals of the baseline model as a response variable, and when we include in-domain semantic surprisal in a model where there ngram surprisal on the out of domain corpus is not included as a predictor variable.

Predictor	Coefficient	t-value	Sig.
(Intercept)	0.031	4.53	**
D_{MARY}	0.428	144.06	***
F_{AMI}	-0.148	-59.15	***
F_{Giga}	-0.043	-15.10	***
$S_{Giga\text{-}3gram}$	0.047	14.60	***
$S_{Semantics}$	-0.028	-9.78	***
D_{MARY}:F_{AMI}	-0.003	-2.27	*

Table 2: Fixed effects of the baseline model with semantic surprisal (including also a random slope for semantic surprisal under subject).

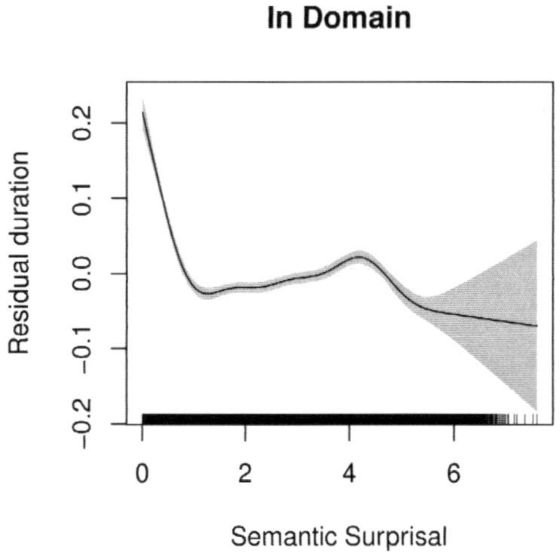

Figure 1: GAM-calculated spline for $S_{Semantics}$ for the in-domain model.

In order to understand the unexpected behaviour of $S_{Semantics}$, we make use of a generalized additive model (GAM) with the R package mgcv. Compared to LME models, GAMs are parameter-free and do not assume a linear form of the predictors. Instead, for every predictor, GAMs can fit a spline. We learn a GAM using the residuals of the baseline model as a response variable and fitting semantic surprisal based on the in-domain model; see Table 2.

In figure 1, we see that $S_{Semantics}$ is poorly fit by a linear function. In particular, there are two intervals in the curve. Between surprisal values 0

[3]Low perplexity estimates are reflective of the spoken conversational domain. Perplexities on content words are much higher: 357.3 for the in-domain model and 2169.8 for the out of domain model.

and 1.5, the curve falls, but between 1.5 and 4, it rises. (For high surprisal values, there are too few data points from which to draw conclusions.)

Therefore, we decided to divide the data up into datapoints with $S_{\text{Semantics}}$ above 1.5 and below 1.5. We then modelled the effect of $S_{\text{Semantics}}$ on the residuals of the baseline model, with $S_{\text{Semantics}}$ as a random effect. This is to remove a possible effect of collinearity between $S_{\text{Semantics}}$ and the other predictors.

Interval of $S_{\text{Semantics}}$	Predictor	Coef.	t-value	Sig.
$[0, \infty[$	(Intercept)	0	0	
	$S_{\text{Semantics}}$	-0.013	-7.01	***
$[0, 1.5[$	(Intercept)	0	0	
	$S_{\text{Semantics}}$	-0.06	-18.56	***
$[1.5, \infty[$	(Intercept)	0	0	
	$S_{\text{Semantics}}$	0.013	5.50	***

Table 3: Three models of $S_{\text{Semantics}}$ as a random effect over the residuals of baseline models learned from the remaining fixed effects. The first model is over the entire range.

Table 3 shows that the random effect of semantic surprisal is positive and significant in the range of semantic surprisal above 1.5. That low surprisals have the opposite effect compared to what we expect suggests to us that using the AMI corpus as an in-domain source of training data presents a problem. The observed result for the relationship between semantic surprisal and spoken word durations does not only hold for the semantic surprisal model, but also for the standard non-weight-adjusted in-domain trigram model. We therefore hypothesize that our semantic surprisal model is producing surprisal values that are low because they are common in this domain (both higher frequency and higher similarities), but speakers are coming to the AMI task with "models" trained on out-of-domain data. Thus, words that are apparently very low-surprisal display longer pronunciation durations as an artifact of the model. To test this, we conducted a second experiment, for which we built a model with out-of-domain data.

8 Experiment 2: out-of-domain training

In order to test for the effect of possible underestimation of surprisal due to in-domain training, we also tested the semantic surprisal model when trained on more domain-general text. As training data for our semantic model, we use a randomly selected 1% (by sentence) of the English Gigaword 5.0 corpus. This is lowercased, with hapax legomena treated as unknown words. We test the model against the entire AMI corpus. Furthermore, we also compare our semantic surprisal values to the syntactic surprisal values calculated by Demberg et al. (2012) for the AMI corpus, which we obtained from the authors. As noted above, the out-of-domain language model has higher perplexity on the AMI corpus—that is, it is a lower-performing language model. On the other hand, it may represent overall speaker experience more accurately than the in-domain model; in other words, it may be a better model of the speaker.

8.1 Results

Once again, the semantic surprisal model is only different from a general n-gram model on content words. We therefore first compare whether the model that is reweighted for semantic surprisal can explain more of the variance than the same model without semantic reweighting.

We again use the same baseline model as for the in-domain experiment, see table 1. As the semantic surprisal model represents a reweighted trigram model, there is a high correlation between the trigram model and the semantic surprisal model. We thus need to know whether the semantically reweighted model is **better** than the simple trigram model. When we compare a model that contains both trigram surprisal and semantic surprisal as a predictor, we find that this model is significantly better than the model including only trigram surprisal (AIC of baseline model: 618427; AIC of model with semantic surprisal: 618394; $\chi^2 = 35.8; p < 0.00001$). On the other hand, the model including both predictors is only marginally better than the model including semantic surprsial (AIC of semantic surprisal model: 618398). This means that the simpler trigram surprisal model does not contribute anything over the semantic model, and that the semantic model fits the word duration data better. Table 4 shows the model with semantic surprisal as a predictor.

Furthermore, we wanted to check whether our hypothesis about the negative result for the in-domain model was indeed due to an under-estimation of surprisal of in-domain words for the

Predictor	Coefficient	t-value	Sig.
(Intercept)	0.034	4.90	***
D_{MARY}	0.427	144.36	***
F_{AMI}	-0.135	-58.76	***
F_{Giga}	-0.053	-19.99	***
$S_{Semantics}$	0.034	11.70	***
D_{MARY}:F_{AMI}	-0.003	-2.09	*

Table 4: Model of spoken word durations, with random intercept and random slopes for D_{MARY} and $S_{Semantics}$ under speaker.

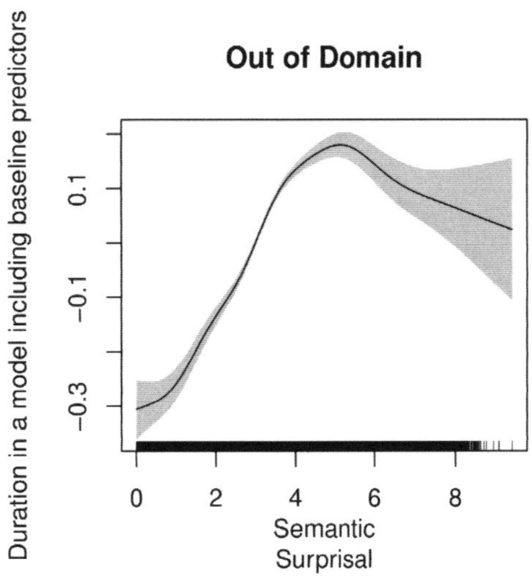

Figure 2: GAM-calculated spline for $S_{Semantics}$ for the ouf-of-domain model.

in-domain model. We again calculate a GAM model showing the effect of out-of-domain semantic surprisal in a model containing also the baseline predictors, see figure 2.

We can see that word durations increase with increasing semantic surprisal, and that there is in particular no effect of longer word durations for low surprisal words. This result is also confirmed by LME models splitting up the data in small and large surprisal values, as done for the in-domain model in Table 3; semantic surprisal based on the out-of-domain model is a significant positive predictor in both data ranges.

Next, we tested whether the semantic similarity model improves model fit over and above a model also containing syntactic surprisal as a predictor. We find that syntactic surprisal improves model fit over and above the model including semantic surprisal ($\chi^2 = 309.5; p < 0.00001$), and that semantic surprisal improves model fit over and above a model including syntactic surprisal and trigram surprisal ($\chi^2 = 28.5; p < 0.00001$). Table 5 shows the model containing both syntactic based on the Roark parser ((Roark et al., 2009); see also Demberg et al. (2012) for use of syntactic surprisal for estimating spoken word durations) and semantic surprisal.

Predictor	Coefficient	t-value	Sig.
(Intercept)	-0.058	-6.58	***
D_{MARY}	0.425	144.04	***
F_{AMI}	-0.131	-57.04	***
F_{Giga}	-0.051	-19.41	***
S_{Syntax}	0.011	17.61	***
$S_{Semantics}$	0.015	4.99	***
D_{MARY}:F_{AMI}	-0.007	-4.44	***

Table 5: Linear mixed effects model for spoken word durations in the AMI corpus, for a model including both syntactic and semantic surprisal as a predictor as well as a random intercept and slope for D_{MARY} and $S_{Semantics}$ under speaker.

Finally, we split our dataset into data from native and non-native speakers of English (305 native speakers, vs. 376 non-native speakers). Table 6 shows generally larger effects for native than non-native speakers. In particular, the interaction between duration estimates and word frequencies, and semantic surprisal were not significant predictors in the non-native speaker model (however, random slopes for semantic surprisal under speaker still improved model fit very strongly, showing that non-native speakers differ in whether and how they take into account semantic surprisal during language production).

9 Discussion

Our analysis shows that high information density at one linguistic level of description (for example, syntax or semantics) can lead to a compensatory effect at a different linguistic level (here, spoken word durations). Our data also shows however, that the choice of training data for the models is important. A language model trained exclusively in a specific domain, while a good language model, may not be representative of speaker's overall language experience. This is particularly relevant for the AMI corpus, in which groups of

	Native Speaker			Non-native Speaker		
Predictor	Coefficient	t-value	Sig.	Coefficient	t-value	Sig.
(Intercept)	-0.1706	-13.76	***	0.035	3.42	***
D_{MARY}	0.4367	105.43	***	0.415	104.09	***
F_{AMI}	-0.1407	-42.54	***	-0.122	-38.66	***
F_{Giga}	-0.0421	-11.07	***	-0.063	-18.70	***
S_{Syntax}	0.0132	14.22	***	0.009	11.96	***
$S_{Semantics}$	0.0246	5.89	***			***
D_{MARY}:F_{AMI}	-0.0139	-6.12	***			***

Table 6: Linear mixed effects models for spoken word durations in the AMI corpus, for native as well as non-native speakers of English separately. The models include both syntactic and semantic surprisal as a fixed effect, and a random intercept and slope for D_{MARY} and $S_{Semantics}$ under speaker.

researchers are discussing the design of a remote control, but where it is not necessarily the case that these people discuss remote controls very frequently. Furthermore, none of the speakers were present in the whole corpus, and most of the > 600 speakers participated only in very few meetings. This means that the in-domain language model strongly over-estimates people's familiarity with the domain.

Words that are highly predictable for the in-domain model (but which are not highly predictable in general) were not pronounced faster, as evident in our first analysis. When semantic surprisal is however estimated based on a more domain-general text like Gigaword, we find a significant positive effect of semantic surprisal on spoken word durations across the complete spectrum from very predictable to unpredictable words.

These results also point to an interesting scientific question: to what extent to people use their domain-general model for adapting their language and speech production in a specific situation, and to what extent do they use a domain-specific model for adaptation? Do people adapt during a conversation, such that in-domain models would be more relevant for language production in situations where speakers are more versed in the domain?

10 Conclusions and future work

We have described a method by which it is possible to connect a semantic level of representation (estimated using a distributional model) to observations about speech patterns at the word level. From a language science or psycholinguistic perspective, we have shown that semantic surprisal affects spoken word durations in natural conversational speech, thus providing additional supportive evidence for the uniform information density hypothesis. In particular, we find evidence that UID effects connect linguistic levels of representation, providing more information about the architecture of the human processor or generator.

This work also has implications for designers of speech synthesis systems: our results point towards using high-level information about the rate of information transfer measured in terms of surprisal for estimating word durations in order to make artificial word pronunciation systems sound more natural.

Finally, the strong effect of training data domain raises scientific questions about how speakers use domain-general and -specific knowledge in communicative cooperation with listeners at the word pronunciation level.

One possible next step would be to expand this work to more complex semantic spaces which include stronger notions of compositionality, semantic roles, and so on, such as the distributional approaches of Baroni and Lenci (2010), Sayeed and Demberg (2014), and Greenberg et al. (2015) that contain grammatical information but rely on vector operations.

Acknowledgements

This research was funded by the German Research Foundation (DFG) as part of SFB 1102 "Information Density and Linguistic Encoding".

References

Aylett, M. and Turk, A. (2006). Language redundancy predicts syllabic duration and the spectral characteristics of vocalic syllable nuclei. *The Journal of the Acoustical Society of America*, 119(5):3048–3058.

Baroni, M. and Lenci, A. (2010). Distributional memory: A general framework for corpus-based semantics. *Comput. Linguist.*, 36(4):673–721.

Bates, D., Mächler, M., Bolker, B. M., and Walker, S. C. (2014). Fitting linear mixed-effects models using lme4. ArXiv e-print; submitted to *Journal of Statistical Software*.

Carletta, J. (2007). Unleashing the killer corpus: experiences in creating the multi-everything AMI meeting corpus. *Language Resources and Evaluation*, 41(2):181–190.

Demberg, V. and Keller, F. (2008). Data from eye-tracking corpora as evidence for theories of syntactic processing complexity. *Cognition*, 109(2):193–210.

Demberg, V., Sayeed, A., Gorinski, P., and Engonopoulos, N. (2012). Syntactic surprisal affects spoken word duration in conversational contexts. In *Proceedings of the 2012 Joint Conference on Empirical Methods in Natural Language Processing and Computational Natural Language Learning*, pages 356–367, Jeju Island, Korea. Association for Computational Linguistics.

Erk, K. (2012). Vector space models of word meaning and phrase meaning: A survey. *Language and Linguistics Compass*, 6(10):635–653.

Frank, A. F. and Jaeger, T. F. (2008). Speaking rationally: Uniform information density as an optimal strategy for language production. In Love, B. C., McRae, K., and Sloutsky, V. M., editors, *Proceedings of the 30th Annual Conference of the Cognitive Science Society*, pages 939–944. Cognitive Science Society.

Frank, S. L., Otten, L. J., Galli, G., and Vigliocco, G. (2013). Word surprisal predicts n400 amplitude during reading. In *ACL (2)*, pages 878–883.

Greenberg, C., Sayeed, A., and Demberg, V. (2015). Improving unsupervised vector-space thematic fit evaluation via role-filler prototype clustering. In *Proceedings of the 2015 Conference of the North American Chapter of the Association for Computational Linguistics Human Language Technologies (NAACL HLT)*.

Hale, J. (2001). A probabilistic Earley parser as a psycholinguistic model. In *Proceedings of the Second Meeting of the North American Chapter of the Association for Computational Linguistics on Language Technologies*, NAACL '01, pages 1–8, Stroudsburg, PA, USA. Association for Computational Linguistics.

Harris, Z. S. (1954). Distributional structure. *Word*, 10(2-3):146–162.

Jurafsky, D., Bell, A., Gregory, M., and Raymond, W. D. (2001). Probabilistic relations between words: Evidence from reduction in lexical production. *Typological studies in language*, 45:229–254.

Levy, R. (2008). Expectation-based syntactic comprehension. *Cognition*, 106(3):1126–1177.

Mitchell, J., Lapata, M., Demberg, V., and Keller, F. (2010). Syntactic and semantic factors in processing difficulty: An integrated measure. In *Proceedings of the 48th Annual Meeting of the Association for Computational Linguistics*, pages 196–206. Association for Computational Linguistics.

Mitchell, J. J. (2011). *Composition in distributional models of semantics*. PhD thesis, The University of Edinburgh.

Pinheiro, J. C. and Bates, D. M. (2000). *Mixed-Effects Models in S and S-PLUS*. Statistics and Computing. Springer.

Roark, B., Bachrach, A., Cardenas, C., and Pallier, C. (2009). Deriving lexical and syntactic expectation-based measures for psycholinguistic modeling via incremental top-down parsing. In *Proceedings of the 2009 Conference on Empirical Methods in Natural Language Processing*, pages 324–333, Singapore. Association for Computational Linguistics.

Sayeed, A. and Demberg, V. (2014). Combining unsupervised syntactic and semantic models of thematic fit. In *Proceedings of the first Italian Conference on Computational Linguistics (CLiC-it 2014)*.

Shannon, C. E. (1948). A mathematical theory of communication. *Bell System Technical Journal*, 27(379-423):623–656.

Smith, N. J. and Levy, R. (2013). The effect of word predictability on reading time is logarithmic. *Cognition*, 128(3):302–319.

Turney, P. D. and Pantel, P. (2010). From frequency to meaning: Vector space models of semantics. *Journal of Artificial Intelligence Research*, 37:141–188.

Efficient Methods for Inferring Large Sparse Topic Hierarchies

Doug Downey, Chandra Sekhar Bhagavatula, Yi Yang
Electrical Engineering and Computer Science
Northwestern University
ddowney@eecs.northwestern.edu, {csb, yiyang}@u.northwestern.edu

Abstract

Latent variable topic models such as Latent Dirichlet Allocation (LDA) can discover topics from text in an unsupervised fashion. However, scaling the models up to the many distinct topics exhibited in modern corpora is challenging. "Flat" topic models like LDA have difficulty modeling sparsely expressed topics, and richer hierarchical models become computationally intractable as the number of topics increases.

In this paper, we introduce efficient methods for inferring large topic hierarchies. Our approach is built upon the Sparse Backoff Tree (SBT), a new prior for latent topic distributions that organizes the latent topics as leaves in a tree. We show how a document model based on SBTs can effectively infer accurate topic spaces of over a million topics. We introduce a collapsed sampler for the model that exploits sparsity and the tree structure in order to make inference efficient. In experiments with multiple data sets, we show that scaling to large topic spaces results in much more accurate models, and that SBT document models make use of large topic spaces more effectively than flat LDA.

1 Introduction

Latent variable topic models, such as Latent Dirichlet Allocation (Blei et al., 2003), are popular approaches for automatically discovering topics in document collections. However, learning models that capture the large numbers of distinct topics expressed in today's corpora is challenging. While efficient methods for learning large topic models have been developed (Li et al., 2014; Yao et al., 2009; Porteous et al., 2008), these methods have focused on "flat" topic models such as LDA. Flat topic models over large topic spaces are prone to overfitting: even in a Web-scale corpus, some words are expressed rarely, and many documents are brief. Inferring a large topic distribution for each word and document given such sparse data is challenging. As a result, LDA models in practice tend to consider a few thousand topics at most, even when training on billions of words (Mimno et al., 2012).

A promising alternative to flat topic models is found in recent *hierarchical* topic models (Paisley et al., 2015; Blei et al., 2010; Li and McCallum, 2006; Wang et al., 2013; Kim et al., 2013; Ahmed et al., 2013). Topics of words and documents can be naturally arranged into hierarchies. For example, an article on the topic of the *Chicago Bulls* is also relevant to the more general topics of *NBA*, *Basketball*, and *Sports*. Hierarchies can combat data sparsity: if data is too sparse to place the term "Pau Gasol" within the Chicago Bulls topic, perhaps it can be appropriately modeled at somewhat less precision within the Basketball topic. A hierarchical model can make fine-grained distinctions where data is plentiful, and back-off to more coarse-grained distinctions where data is sparse. However, current hierarchical models are hindered by computational complexity. The existing inference methods for the models have runtimes that increase at least linearly with the number of topics, making them intractable on large corpora with large numbers of topics.

In this paper, we present a hierarchical topic model that can scale to large numbers of distinct topics. Our approach is built upon a new prior for latent topic distributions called a Sparse Backoff Tree (SBT). SBTs organize the latent topics as leaves in a tree, and smooth the distributions for each topic with those of similar topics nearby in the tree. SBT priors use absolute discounting and learned backoff distributions for

Proceedings of the 53rd Annual Meeting of the Association for Computational Linguistics and the 7th International Joint Conference on Natural Language Processing, pages 774–784,
Beijing, China, July 26-31, 2015.

smoothing sparse observation counts, rather than the fixed additive discounting utilized in Dirichlet and Chinese Restaurant Process models. We show how the SBT's characteristics enable a novel collapsed sampler that exploits the tree structure for efficiency, allowing SBT-based document models (SBTDMs) that scale to hierarchies of over a million topics.

We perform experiments in text modeling and hyperlink prediction, and find that SBTDM is more accurate compared to LDA and the recent nested Hierarchical Dirichlet Process (nHDP) (Paisley et al., 2015). For example, SBTDMs with a hundred thousand topics achieve perplexities 28-52% lower when compared with a standard LDA configuration using 1,000 topics. We verify that the empirical time complexity of inference in SBTDM increases sub-linearly in the number of topics, and show that for large topic spaces SBTDM is more than an order of magnitude more efficient than the hierarchical Pachinko Allocation Model (Mimno et al., 2007) and nHDP. Lastly, we release an implementation of SBTDM as open-source software.[1]

2 Previous Work

The intuition in SBTDM that topics are naturally arranged in hierarchies also underlies several other models from previous work. Paisley et al. (2015) introduce the nested Hierarchical Dirichlet Process (nHDP), which is a tree-structured generative model of text that generalizes the nested Chinese Restaurant Process (nCRP) (Blei et al., 2010). Both the nCRP and nHDP model the tree structure as a random variable, defined over a flexible (potentially infinite in number) topic space. However, in practice the infinite models are truncated to a maximal size. We show in our experiments that SBTDM can scale to larger topic spaces and achieve greater accuracy than nHDP. To our knowledge, our work is the first to demonstrate a hierarchical topic model that scales to more than one million topics, and to show that the larger models are often much more accurate than smaller models. Similarly, compared to other recent hierarchical models of text and other data (Petinot et al., 2011; Wang et al., 2013; Kim et al., 2013; Ahmed et al., 2013; Ho et al., 2010), our focus is on scaling to larger data sets and topic spaces.

The Pachinko Allocation Model (PAM) introduced by Li & McCallum (Li and McCallum, 2006) is a general approach for modeling correlations among topic variables in latent variable models. Hierarchical organizations of topics, as in SBT, can be considered as a special case of a PAM, in which inference is particularly efficient. We show that our model is much more efficient than an existing PAM topic modeling implementation in Section 5.

Hu and Boyd-Graber (2012) present a method for augmenting a topic model with known hierarchical correlations between words (taken from e.g. WordNet synsets). By contrast, our focus is on automatically learning a hierarchical organization of topics from data, and we demonstrate that this technique improves accuracy over LDA. Lastly, SparseLDA (Yao et al., 2009) is a method that improves the efficiency of inference in LDA by only generating portions of the sampling distribution when necessary. Our collapsed sampler for SBTDM utilizes a related intuition at each level of the tree in order to enable fast inference.

3 Sparse Backoff Trees

In this section, we introduce the Sparse Backoff Tree, which is a prior for a multinomial distribution over a latent variable. We begin with an example showing how an SBT transforms a set of observation counts into a probability distribution. Consider a latent variable topic model of text documents, similar to LDA (Blei et al., 2003) or pLSI (Hofmann, 1999). In the model, each token in a document is generated by first sampling a discrete latent topic variable Z from a document-specific topic distribution, and then sampling the token's word type from a multinomial conditioned on Z.

We will focus on the document's distribution over topics, ignoring the details of the word types for illustration. We consider a model with 12 latent topics, denoted as integers from the set $\{1, \ldots, 12\}$. Assume we have assigned latent topic values to five tokens in the document, specifically the topics $\{1, 4, 4, 5, 12\}$. We indicate the number of times topic value z has been selected as n_z (Figure 1).

Given the five observations, the key question faced by the model is: what is the topic distribution over a sixth topic variable from the same document? In the case of the Dirichlet prior utilized for the topic distribution in LDA, the probability

[1] http://websail.cs.northwestern.edu/projects/sbts/

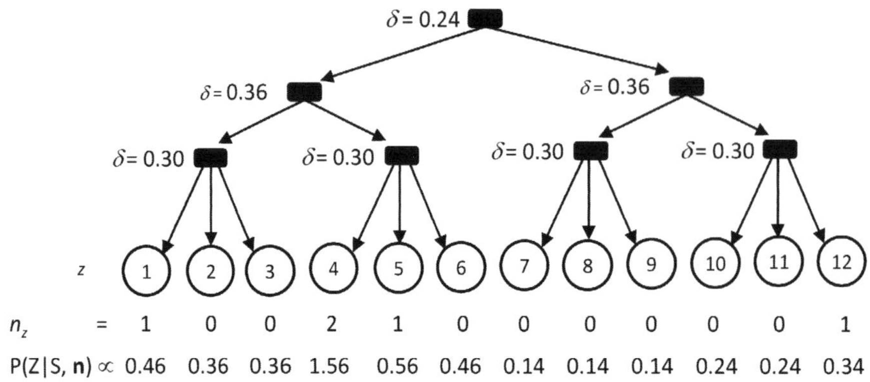

Figure 1: An example Sparse Backoff Tree over 12 latent variable values.

that the sixth topic variable has value z is proportional to $n_z + \alpha$, where α is a hyperparameter of the model.

SBT differs from LDA in that it organizes the topics into a tree structure in which the topics are leaves (see Figure 1). In this paper, we assume the tree structure, like the number of latent topics, is manually selected in advance. With an SBT prior, the estimate of the probability of a topic z is increased when nearby topics in the tree have positive counts. Each interior node a of the SBT has a *discount* δ_a associated with it. The SBT transforms the observation counts n_z into pseudo-counts (shown in the last row in the figure) by subtracting δ_a from each non-zero descendent of each interior node a, and re-distributing the subtracted value uniformly among the descendants of a. For example, the first state has a total of 0.90 subtracted from its initial count $n_1 = 1$, and then receives $0.30/3$ from its parent, $1.08/6$ from its grandparent, and $0.96/12$ from the root node for a total pseudo-count of 0.46. The document's distribution over a sixth topic variable is then proportional to these pseudo-counts.

When each document tends to discuss a set of related topics, the SBT prior will assign a higher likelihood to the data when related topics are located nearby in the tree. Thus, by inferring latent variable values to maximize likelihood, nearby leaves in the tree will come to represent related topics. SBT, unlike LDA, encodes the intuition that a topic becomes more likely in a document that also discusses other, related topics. In the example, the pseudo-count the SBT produces for topic six (which is related to other topics that occur in the document) is almost three times larger than that of topic eight, even though the observation counts are zero in each case. In LDA, topics six and eight would have equal pseudo-counts (proportional to α).

3.1 Definitions

Let Z be a discrete random variable that takes integer values in the set $\{1, \ldots, L\}$. Z is drawn from a multinomial parameterized by a vector θ of length L.

Definition 1 *A Sparse Backoff Tree $SBT(\mathcal{T}, \delta^\theta, Q(z))$ for the discrete random variable Z consists of a rooted tree $\mathcal{T}$ containing L leaves, one for each value of Z; a coefficient $\delta_a > 0$ for each interior node a of $\mathcal{T}$; and a backoff distribution $Q(z)$.*

Figure 1 shows an example SBT. The example includes simplifications we also utilize in our experiments, namely that all nodes at a given depth in the tree have the same number of children and the same δ value. However, the inference techniques we present in Section 4 are applicable to any tree $\mathcal{T}$ and set of coefficients $\{\delta_a\}$.

For a given SBT S, let $\Delta_S(z)$ indicate the sum of all δ_a values for all ancestors a of leaf node z (i.e., all interior nodes on the path from the root to z). For example, in the figure, $\Delta_S(z) = 0.90$ for all z. This amount is the total absolute discount that the SBT applies to the random variable value z.

We define the SBT prior implicitly in terms of the posterior distribution it induces on a random variable Z drawn from a multinomial θ with an SBT prior, after θ is integrated out. Let the vector $\mathbf{n} = [n_1, \ldots, n_L]$ denote the sufficient statistics for any given observations drawn from θ, where n_z is the number of times value z has been observed. Then, the distribution over a subsequent draw of Z

given SBT prior S and observations $\mathbf{n}$ is defined as:

$$P(Z = z|S, \mathbf{n}) \equiv \frac{\max(n_z - \Delta_S(z), 0) + B(S, z, \mathbf{n})Q(z)}{K(S, \sum_i n_i)} \quad (1)$$

where $K(S, \sum_i n_i)$ is a normalizing constant that ensures the distribution sums to one for any fixed number of observations $\sum_i n_i$, and $B(S, z, \mathbf{n})$ and $Q(z)$ are defined as below.

The quantity $B(S, z, \mathbf{n})$ expresses how much of the discounts from all other leaves z' contribute to the probability of z. For an interior node a, let $desc(a)$ indicate the number of leaves that are descendants of a, and let $desc^+(a)$ indicate the number of leaf descendants z of a that have non-zero values n_z. Then the contribution of the discount δ_a of node a to *each* of its descendent leaves is $b(a, \mathbf{n}) = \delta_a desc^+(a)/desc(a)$. We then define $B(S, z, \mathbf{n})$ to be the sum of $b(a, \mathbf{n})$ over all interior nodes a on the path from the root to z.

The function $Q(z)$ is a *backoff distribution*. It allows the portion of the discount probability mass that is allocated to z to vary with a proposed distribution $Q(z)$. This is useful because in practice the SBT is used as a prior for a conditional distribution, for example the distribution $P(Z|w)$ over topic Z given a word w in a topic model of text. In that case, an estimate of $P(Z|w)$ for a rare word w may be improved by "mixing in" the marginal topic distribution $Q(z) = P(Z = z)$, analogous to backoff techniques in language modeling. Our document model described in the following section utilizes two different Q functions, one uniform ($Q(z) = 1/T$) and another related to the marginal topic distribution $P(z)$.

4 The SBT Document Model

We now present the SBT document model, a probabilistic latent variable model of text documents that utilizes SBT priors. We then provide a collapsed sampler for the model that exploits the tree structure to make inference more efficient.

Our document model follows the Latent Dirichlet Allocation (LDA) Model (Blei et al., 2003), illustrated graphically in Figure 2 (left). In LDA, a corpus of documents is generated by sampling a topic distribution θ_d for each document d, and also a distribution over words ϕ_z for each topic. Then, in document d each token w is generated by first sampling a topic z from the multinomial $P(Z|\theta_d)$, and then sampling w from the multinomial $P(W|Z, \phi_z)$.

The SBTDM is the same as LDA, with one significant difference. In LDA, the parameters θ and ϕ are sampled from two Dirichlet priors, with separate hyperparameters α and β. In SBTDM, the parameters are instead sampled from particular SBT priors. Specifically, the generative model is:

$$\begin{aligned} \theta &\sim SBT(\mathcal{T}, \delta^\theta, Q_\theta(z) = 1/T) \\ \phi' &\sim SBT(\mathcal{T}, \delta^\phi, Q_\phi(z) = P^*(z)) \\ \lambda &\sim \text{Dirichlet}(\alpha') \\ Z|\theta &\sim \text{Discrete}(\theta) \\ W|z, \phi', \lambda &\sim \text{Discrete}(\lambda\phi'_{.,z}/P(z|\phi')) \end{aligned}$$

The variable ϕ' represents the distribution of topics given words, $P(Z|W)$. The SBTDM samples a distribution ϕ'_w over topics for each word type w in the vocabulary (of size V). In SBTDM, the random variable ϕ'_w has dimension L, rather than V for ϕ_z as in LDA. We also draw a prior word frequency distribution, $\lambda = \{\lambda_w\}$ for each word w. [2] We then apply Bayes Rule to obtain the conditional distributions $P(W|Z, \phi')$ required for inference. The expression $\lambda\phi'_{.,z}/P(z|\phi')$ denotes the normalized element-wise product of two vectors of length V: the prior distribution λ over words, and the vector of probabilities $P(z|w) = \phi'_{w,z}$ over words w for the given topic z.

The SBT priors for ϕ' and θ share the same tree structure $\mathcal{T}$, which is fixed in advance. The SBTs have different discount factors, denoted by the hyperparameters δ^θ and δ^ϕ. Finally, the backoff distribution for θ is uniform, whereas ϕ's backoff distribution P^* is defined below.

4.1 Backoff distribution $P^*(z)$

SBTDM requires choosing a backoff distribution $P^*(z)$ for ϕ'. As we now show, it is possible to select a natural backoff distribution $P^*(z)$ that enables scalable inference.

Given a set of observations $\mathbf{n}$, we will set $P^*(z)$ proportional to $P(z|S^\phi, \mathbf{n})$. This is a recursive definition, because $P(z|S^\phi, \mathbf{n})$ depends on $P^*(z)$. Thus, we define:

$$P^*(z) \equiv \frac{\sum_w \max(n_z^w - \Delta_S(z), 0)}{C - \sum_w B_w(S^\phi, z, \mathbf{n})} \quad (2)$$

[2] The word frequency distribution does not impact the inferred topics (because words are always observed), and in our experiments we simply use maximum likelihood estimates for λ_w (i.e., setting α' to be negligibly small). Exploring other word frequency distributions is an item of future work.

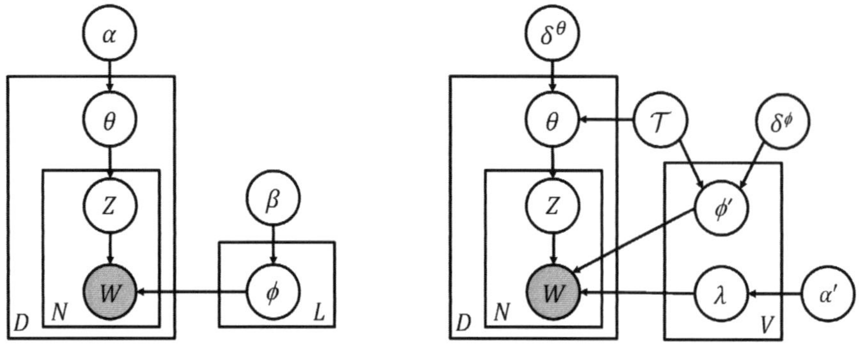

Figure 2: The Latent Dirichlet Allocation Model (left) and our SBT Document Model (right).

where $C > \sum_w B_w(S^\phi, z, \mathbf{n})$ is a hyperparameter, n_z^w is the number of observations of topic z for word w in $\mathbf{n}$, and B_w indicates the function $B(S^\phi, z, \mathbf{n})$ defined in Section 3.1, for the particular word w. That is, $\sum_w B_w(S^\phi, z, \mathbf{n})$ is the total quantity of smoothing distributed to topic z across all words, *before* the backoff distribution $P^*(z)$ is applied.

The form of $P^*(z)$ has two key advantages. The first is that setting $P^*(z)$ proportional to the marginal topic probability allows SBTDM to back-off toward marginal estimates, a successful technique in language modeling (Katz, 1987) (where it has been utilized for word probabilities, rather than topic probabilities). Secondly, setting the backoff distribution in this way allows us to simplify inference, as described below.

Algorithm 1 Compute the sampling distribution for a product of two multinomials with SBT priors with $Q(z) = 1$

```
function INTERSECT(SBT Node a_r, SBT Node a_l)
    if a_r, a_l are leaves then
        τ(i) ← τ(a_r)τ(a_l)
        return i
    end if
    i.r ← a_r
    r(i) ← b(a_l) * τ(a_r)
    i.l ← a_l ; b(i.l) ← 0
    l(i) ← b(a_r) * τ(a_l) − b(a_r)b(a_l)desc(a_r)
    τ(i)+ = r(i) + l(i)
    for all child c non-zero for a_r and a_l do
        i_c ← INTERSECT(a_r.c, a_l.c)
        i.children += i_c
        τ(i) += τ(i_c)
    end for
    return i
end function
```

4.2 Inference with Collapsed Sampling

Given a corpus of documents D, we infer the values of the hidden variables Z using the collapsed Gibbs sampler popular in Latent Dirichlet Allocation models (Griffiths and Steyvers, 2004). Each variable Z_i is sampled given the settings of all other variables (denoted as $\mathbf{n}_{-i}$):

$$P(Z_i = z|\mathbf{n}_{-i}, D) \propto P(z|\mathbf{n}_{-i}, \mathcal{T}, \delta^\theta) \cdot P(w_i|z, \mathbf{n}_{-i}, \mathcal{T}, \delta^\phi) \quad (3)$$

The first term on the right-hand side is given by Equation 1. The second can be rewritten as:

$$P(w_i|z, \mathbf{n}_{-i}, \mathcal{T}, \delta^\phi) = \frac{P(z, w_i|\mathbf{n}_{-i}, \mathcal{T}, \delta^\phi)}{P(z|\mathbf{n}_{-i}, \mathcal{T}, \delta^\phi)} \quad (4)$$

4.3 Efficient Inference Implementation

The primary computational cost when scaling to large topic spaces involves constructing the sampling distribution. Both LDA with collapsed sampling and SBTDM share an advantage in space complexity: the model parameters are specified by a sparse set of non-zero counts denoting how often tokens of each word or document are assigned to each topic. However, in general the sampling distribution for SBTDM has non-uniform probabilities for each of L different latent variable values. Thus, even if many parameters are zero, a naive approach that computes the complete sampling distribution will still take time linear in L.

However, in SBTs the sampling distribution can be constructed efficiently using a simple recursive algorithm that exploits the structure of the tree. The result is an inference algorithm that often requires far less than linear time in L, as we verify in our experiments.

First, we note that $P(z, w_i|\mathbf{n}_{-i}, \mathcal{T}, \delta^\phi)$ is proportional to the sum of two quantities: the discounted count $\max(n_z - \Delta_S, 0)$ and the smoothing probability mass $B(S, z, \mathbf{n})Q(z)$. By choosing $Q(z) = P^*(z)$, we can be ensured that $P^*(z)$ normalizes this sum. Thus, the backoff distribution cancels through the normalization. This means we can normalize the SBT for ϕ' in advance by scaling the non-zero counts by a factor of $1/P^*(z)$, and then at inference time we need only multiply pointwise two multinomials with SBT priors and *uniform* backoff distributions.

The intersection of two multinomials drawn from SBT priors with uniform backoff distributions can be performed efficiently for sparse trees. The algorithm relies on two quantities defined for each node of each tree. The first, $b(a, \mathbf{n})$, was defined in Section 3. It denotes the smoothing that the interior node a distributes (uniformly) to each of its descendent leaves. We denote $b(a, \mathbf{n})$ as $b(a)$ in this section for brevity. The second quantity, $\tau(a)$, expresses the total count mass of all leaf descendants of a, *excluding* the smoothing from ancestors of a.

With the quantities $b(a)$ and $\tau(a)$ for all a, we can efficiently compute the sampling distribution of the product of two SBT-governed multinomials (which we refer to as an SBTI). The method is shown in Algorithm 1. It takes two SBT nodes as arguments; these are corresponding nodes from two SBT priors that share the same tree structure $\mathcal{T}$. It returns an SBTI, a data structure representing the sampling distribution.

The efficiency of Algorithm 1 is reflected in the fact that the algorithm only recurses for child nodes c with non-zero $\tau(c)$ for *both* of the SBT node arguments. Because such cases will be rare for sparse trees, often Algorithm 1 only needs to traverse a small portion of the original SBTs in order to compute the sampling distribution exactly. Our experiments illustrate the efficiency of this algorithm in practice.

Finally, we can efficiently sample from either an SBTI or a single SBT-governed multinomial. The sampling methods are straightforward recursive methods, supplied in Algorithms 2 and 3.

Algorithm 2 Sample(SBT Node a)

```
procedure SAMPLE(SBT Node a)
    if a is a leaf then return a
    end if
    Sample from {b(a)desc(a), τ(a) − b(a)desc(a)}.
    if back-off distribution b(a)desc(a) selected then
        return Uniform[a's descendents]
    else
        Sample a's child c ~ τ(c)
        return SAMPLE(c)
    end if
end procedure
```

Algorithm 3 Sampling from an SBTI

```
function SAMPLE(SBTI Node i)
    if i is a leaf then return i
    end if
    Sample from {r(i), l(i), τ(i) − r(i) − l(i)}
    if right distribution r(i) selected then
        return SAMPLE(i.r)
    else
        if left distribution l(i) selected then
            return SAMPLE(i.l)
        else
            Sample i's child c ~ τ(c)
            return SAMPLE(c)
        end if
    end if
end function
```

4.4 Expansion

Much of the computational expense encountered in inference with SBTDM occurs shortly after initialization. After a slow first several sampling passes, the conditional distributions over topics for each word and document become concentrated on a sparse set of paths through the SBT. From that point forward, sampling is faster and requires much less memory.

We utilize the hierarchical organization of the topic space in SBTs to side-step this computational complexity by adding new leaves to the SBTs of a trained SBTDM. This is a "coarse-to-fine" (Petrov and Charniak, 2011) training approach that we refer to as *expansion*. Using expansion, the initial sampling passes of the larger model can be much more time and space efficient, because they leverage the already-sparse structure of the smaller trained SBTDM.

Our expansion method takes as input an inferred sampling distribution $\mathbf{n}$ for a given tree $\mathcal{T}$. The algorithm adds k new branches to each leaf of $\mathcal{T}$ to obtain a larger tree $\mathcal{T}'$. We then transform the sampling state by replacing each $n_i \in \mathbf{n}$ with one of its children in $\mathcal{T}'$. For example, in Figure 1, expanding with $k = 3$ would result in a new tree containing 36 topics, and the single observation of topic 4 in $\mathcal{T}$ would be re-assigned randomly to one of the topics $\{10, 11, 12\}$ in $\mathcal{T}'$.

5 Experiments

We now evaluate the efficiency and accuracy of SBTDM. We evaluate SBTs on two data sets, the RCV1 Reuters corpus of newswire text (Lewis et al., 2004), and a distinct data set of Wikipedia links, WPL. We consider two disjoint subsets of RCV1, a small training set (RCV1s) and a larger training set (RCV1).

We compare the accuracy and efficiency of SBTDM against flat LDA and two existing hierarchical models, the Pachinko Allocation Model (PAM) and nested Hierarchical Dirichlet Process (nHDP).

To explore how the SBT structure impacts modeling performance, we experiment with two different SBTDM configurations. **SBTDM-wide** is a shallow tree in which the branching factor increases from the root downward in the sequence $3, 6, 6, 9, 9, 12, 12$. Thus, the largest model we consider has $3 \cdot 6 \cdot 6 \cdot 9 \cdot 9 \cdot 12 \cdot 12 =$ 1,259,712 distinct latent topics. **SBTDM-tall** has lower branching factors of either 2 or 3 (so in our evaluation its depth ranges from 3 to 15). As in SBTDM-wide, in SBTDM-tall the lower branching factors occur toward the root of the tree. We vary the number of topics by considering balanced subtrees of each model. For nHDP, we use the same tree structures as in SBT-wide. In preliminary experiments, using the tall structure in nHDP yielded similar accuracy but was somewhat slower.

Similar to our LDA implementation, SBTDM optimizes hyperparameter settings as sampling proceeds. We use local beam search to choose new hyperparameters that maximize leave-one-out likelihood for the distributions $P(Z|d)$ and $P(Z|w)$ on the training data, evaluating the parameters against the current state of the sampler.

We trained all models by performing 100 sampling passes through the full training corpus (i.e., approximately 10 billion samples for RCV1, and 8 billion samples for WPL). We evaluate performance on held-out test sets of 998 documents for RCV1 (122,646 tokens), and 200 documents for WPL (84,610 tokens). We use the left-to-right algorithm (Wallach et al., 2009) over a randomized word order with 20 particles to compute perplexity. We re-optimize the LDA hyperparameters at regular intervals during sampling.

5.1 Small Corpus Experiments

We begin with experiments over a small corpus to highlight the efficiency advantages of SBTDM.

Data Set	Tokens	Vocabulary	Documents
RCV1s	2,669,093	46,130	22,149
RCV1	101,184,494	283,911	781,262
WPL	82,154,551	1,141,670	199,000

Table 1: Statistics of the three training corpora.

As argued above, existing hierarchical models require inference that becomes expensive as the topic space increases in size. We illustrate this by comparing our model with PAM and nHDP. We also compare against a fast "flat" LDA implementation, SparseLDA, from the MALLET software package (McCallum, 2002).

For SBTDM we utilize a parallel inference approach, sampling all variables using a fixed estimate of the counts $\mathbf{n}$, and then updating the counts after each full sampling pass (as in (Wang et al., 2009)). The SparseLDA and nHDP implementations are also parallel. All parallel methods use 15 threads. The PAM implementation provided in MALLET is single-threaded.

Our efficiency measurements are shown in Figure 3. We plot the mean wall-clock time to perform 100 sampling passes over the RCV1s corpus, starting from randomly initialized models (i.e. *without* expansion in SBTDM). For the largest plotted topic sizes for PAM and nHDP, we estimate total runtime using a small number of iterations. The results show that SBTDM's time to sample increases well below linear in the number of topics. Both SBTDM methods have runtimes that increase at a rate substantially below that of the square root of the number of topics (plotted as a blue line in the figure for reference). For the largest numbers of topics in the plot, when we increase the number of topics by a factor of 12, the time to sample increases by less than a factor of 1.7 for both SBT configurations.

We also evaluate the accuracy of the models on the small corpus. We do not compare against PAM, as the MALLET implementation lacks a method for computing perplexity for a PAM model. The results are shown in Table 3. The SBT models tend to achieve lower perplexity than LDA, and SBTDM-tall performs slightly better than SBTDM-wide for most topic sizes. The best model, SBT-wide with 8,748 topics, achieves perplexity 14% lower than the best LDA model and 2% lower than the best SBTDM-tall model. The LDA model overfits for the largest topic configuration, whereas at that size both SBT models remain at least as accurate as any of the LDA models in Table 3.

We also evaluated using the topic coherence measure from (Mimno et al., 2011), which reflects how well the learned topics reflect word co-occurrence statistics in the training data. Follow-

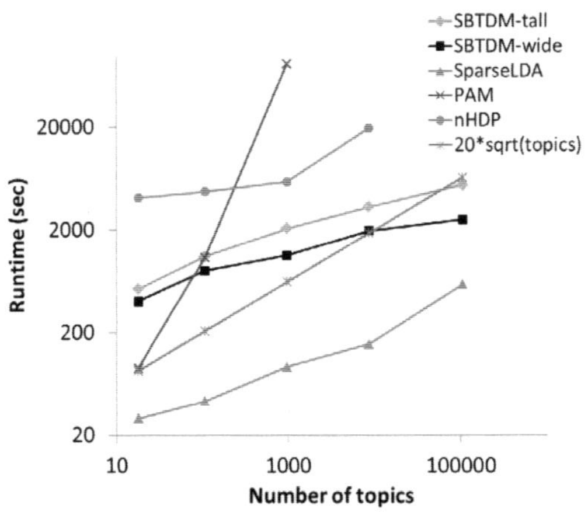

Figure 3: Time (in seconds) to perform a sampling pass over the RCV1s corpus as number of topics varies, plotted on a log-log scale. The SBT models scale sub-linearly in the number of topics.

ing recent experiments with the measure (Stevens et al., 2012), we use $\epsilon = 10^{-12}$ pseudo-co-occurrences of each word pair and we evaluate the average coherence using the top 10 words for each topic. Table 2 shows the results. PAM, LDA, and nHDP have better coherence at smaller topic sizes, but SBT maintains higher coherence as the number of topics increases.

Topics	LDA	PAM	nHDP	SBTDM -wide	SBTDM -tall
18	-420.8	-421.2	-422.9	-444.3	-440.2
108	-434.8	-430.9	-554.3	-445.4	-445.8
972	-451.2	-	-548.1	-443.3	-443.8
8748	-615.3	-	-	-444.3	-444.1

Table 2: Average topic coherence on the small RCV1s corpus.

5.1.1 Evaluating Expansion

The results discussed above do not utilize expansion in SBTDM. To evaluate expansion, we performed separate experiments in which we expanded a 972-topic model trained on RCV1s to initialize a 8,748-topic model. Compared to random initialization, expansion improved efficiency and accuracy. Inference in the expanded model executed approximately 30% faster and used 70% less memory, and the final 8,748-topic models had approximately 10% lower perplexity.

5.2 Large Corpus Results

Our large corpus experiments are reported in Table 4. Here, we compare the test set perplexity of a single model for each topic size and model type. We focus on SBTDM-tall for the large corpora. We utilize expansion (see Section 4.4) for SBTDM-tall models with more than a thousand topics on each data set. The results show that on both data sets, SBTDM-tall utilizes larger numbers of topics more effectively. On RCV1, LDA improves only marginally between 972 and 8,748 topics, whereas SBTDM-tall improves dramatically. For 8,748 topics, SBTDM-tall achieves a perplexity score 17% lower than LDA model on RCV1, and 29% lower on WPL. SBT improves even further in larger topic configurations. Training and testing LDA with our implementation using over a hundred thousand topics was not tractable on our data sets due to space complexity (the MALLET implementation exceeded our maximum 250G of heap space). As discussed above, expansion enables SBTDM to dramatically reduce space complexity for large topic spaces.

The results highlight the accuracy improvements found from utilizing larger numbers of topics than are typically used in practice. For example, an SBTDM with 104,976 topics achieves perplexity 28-52% lower when compared with a standard LDA configuration using only 1,000 topics.

	RCV1		WPL	
# Topics	LDA	SBTDM-tall	LDA	SBTDM-tall
108	**1,121**	1,148	**7,049**	7,750
972	**820**	841	2,598	**2,095**
8,748	772	**637**	1,730	**1,236**
104,976	-	593	-	1,242
1,259,712	-	626	-	-

Table 4: Model accuracy on large corpora (corpus perplexity measure). The SBT model utilizes larger numbers of topics more effectively.

5.3 Exploring the Learned Topics

Lastly, we qualitatively examine whether the SBTDM's learned topics reflect meaningful hierarchical relationships. From an SBTDM of 104,976 topics trained on the Wikipedia links data set, we examined the first 108 leaves (these are contained in a single subtree of depth 5). 760 unique terms (i.e. Wikipedia pages) had positive counts for the topics, and 500 of these terms were related to radio stations.

The leaves appear to encode fine-grained subcategorizations of the terms. In Figure 4, we provide examples from one subtree of six topics (topics 13-18). For each topic t, we list the top three

	Number of Topics				
Model	18	108	972	8,748	104,976
LDA	**1420** (16.3)	**1016** (9.8)	844 (1.8)	845 (3.3)	1058 (4.1)
nHDP	1433 (19.6)	1446 (53.3)	1583 (157.7)	-	-
SBTDM-wide	1510 (31.5)	1091 (31.8)	797 (3.5)	**723** (18.2)	844 (60.1)
SBTDM-tall	1480 (13.5)	1051 (9.1)	**787** (10.5)	736 (3.2)	**776** (14.1)

Table 3: Small training corpus (RCV1s) performance. Shown is perplexity averaged over three runs for each method and number of topics, with standard deviation in parens. Both SBTDM models achieve lower perplexity than LDA and nHDP for the larger numbers of topics.

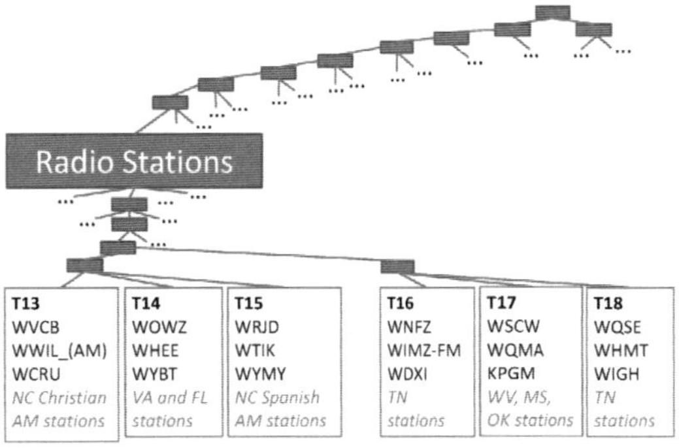

Figure 4: An example of topics from a 104,976-topic SBTDM defined over Wikipedia pages.

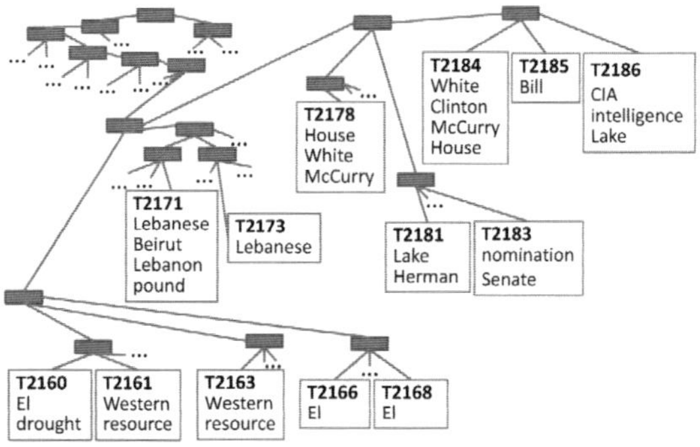

Figure 5: An example of topics from an 8,748-topic SBTDM defined over the RCV1 corpus.

terms w (ranked by symmetric conditional probability, $P(w|t)P(t|w)$), and a specific categorization that applies to the three terms. Interestingly, as shown in the figure, the top terms for the six topics we examined were all four-character "call letters" for particular radio stations. Stations with similar content or in nearby locations tend to cluster together in the tree. For example, the two topics focused on radio stations in Tennessee (TN) share the same parent, as do the topics focused on North Carolina (NC) AM stations. More generally, all six topics focus on radio stations in the southern US.

Figure 5 shows a different example, from a model trained on the RCV1 corpus. In this example, we first select only those terms that occur at least 2,000 times in the corpus and have a statistical association with their topic that exceeds a threshold, and we again rank terms by symmetric conditional probability. The 27-topic subtree detailed in the figure appears to focus on terms from major storylines in United States politics in early 1997, including El Niño, Lebanon, White House Press Secretary Mike McCarry, and the Senate confirmation hearings of CIA Director nominee Tony Lake.

6 Conclusion and Future Work

We introduced the Sparse Backoff Tree (SBT), a prior for latent topic distributions that organizes the latent topics as leaves in a tree. We presented and experimentally analyzed a document model based on the SBT, called an SBTDM. The SBTDM was shown to utilize large topic spaces more effectively than previous techniques.

There are several directions of future work. One limitation of the current work is that the SBT is defined only implicitly. We plan to investigate explicit representations of the SBT prior or related variants. Other directions include developing methods to learn the SBT structure from data, as well as applying the SBT prior to other tasks, such as sequential language modeling.

Acknowledgments

This research was supported in part by NSF grants IIS-1065397 and IIS-1351029, DARPA contract D11AP00268, and the Allen Institute for Artificial Intelligence. We thank the anonymous reviews for their helpful comments.

References

[Ahmed et al.2013] Amr Ahmed, Liangjie Hong, and Alexander Smola. 2013. Nested chinese restaurant franchise process: Applications to user tracking and document modeling. In *Proceedings of the 30th International Conference on Machine Learning (ICML-13)*, pages 1426–1434.

[Blei et al.2003] David M Blei, Andrew Y Ng, and Michael I Jordan. 2003. Latent dirichlet allocation. *the Journal of machine Learning research*, 3:993–1022.

[Blei et al.2010] David M Blei, Thomas L Griffiths, and Michael I Jordan. 2010. The nested chinese restaurant process and bayesian nonparametric inference of topic hierarchies. *Journal of the ACM (JACM)*, 57(2):7.

[Griffiths and Steyvers2004] Thomas L Griffiths and Mark Steyvers. 2004. Finding scientific topics. *Proceedings of the National academy of Sciences of the United States of America*, 101(Suppl 1):5228–5235.

[Ho et al.2010] Qirong Ho, Ankur P Parikh, Le Song, and Eric P Xing. 2010. Infinite hierarchical mmsb model for nested communities/groups in social networks. *arXiv preprint arXiv:1010.1868*.

[Hofmann1999] Thomas Hofmann. 1999. Probabilistic latent semantic indexing. In *Proceedings of the 22nd annual international ACM SIGIR conference on Research and development in information retrieval*, pages 50–57. ACM.

[Hu and Boyd-Graber2012] Yuening Hu and Jordan Boyd-Graber. 2012. Efficient tree-based topic modeling. In *Proceedings of the 50th Annual Meeting of the Association for Computational Linguistics: Short Papers-Volume 2*, pages 275–279. Association for Computational Linguistics.

[Katz1987] Slava Katz. 1987. Estimation of probabilities from sparse data for the language model component of a speech recognizer. *Acoustics, Speech and Signal Processing, IEEE Transactions on*, 35(3):400–401.

[Kim et al.2013] Suin Kim, Jianwen Zhang, Zheng Chen, Alice Oh, and Shixia Liu. 2013. A hierarchical aspect-sentiment model for online reviews. In *Proceedings of AAAI*.

[Lewis et al.2004] David D Lewis, Yiming Yang, Tony G Rose, and Fan Li. 2004. Rcv1: A new benchmark collection for text categorization research. *The Journal of Machine Learning Research*, 5:361–397.

[Li and McCallum2006] Wei Li and Andrew McCallum. 2006. Pachinko allocation: Dag-structured mixture models of topic correlations. In *Proceedings of the 23rd International Conference on Machine Learning*, ICML '06, pages 577–584, New York, NY, USA. ACM.

[Li et al.2014] Aaron Q Li, Amr Ahmed, Sujith Ravi, and Alexander J Smola. 2014. Reducing the sampling complexity of topic models. In *Proceedings of the 20th ACM SIGKDD international conference on Knowledge discovery and data mining*, pages 891–900. ACM.

[McCallum2002] Andrew Kachites McCallum. 2002. Mallet: A machine learning for language toolkit. http://mallet.cs.umass.edu.

[Mimno et al.2007] David Mimno, Wei Li, and Andrew McCallum. 2007. Mixtures of hierarchical topics with pachinko allocation. In *Proceedings of the 24th international conference on Machine learning*, pages 633–640. ACM.

[Mimno et al.2011] David Mimno, Hanna M Wallach, Edmund Talley, Miriam Leenders, and Andrew McCallum. 2011. Optimizing semantic coherence in topic models. In *Proceedings of the Conference on Empirical Methods in Natural Language Processing*, pages 262–272. Association for Computational Linguistics.

[Mimno et al.2012] David Mimno, Matt Hoffman, and David Blei. 2012. Sparse stochastic inference for latent dirichlet allocation. *arXiv preprint arXiv:1206.6425*.

[Paisley et al.2015] J. Paisley, C. Wang, D.M. Blei, and M.I. Jordan. 2015. Nested hierarchical dirichlet processes. *Pattern Analysis and Machine Intelligence, IEEE Transactions on*, 37(2):256–270, Feb.

[Petinot et al.2011] Yves Petinot, Kathleen McKeown, and Kapil Thadani. 2011. A hierarchical model of web summaries. In *Proceedings of the 49th Annual Meeting of the Association for Computational Linguistics: Human Language Technologies: short papers-Volume 2*, pages 670–675. Association for Computational Linguistics.

[Petrov and Charniak2011] Slav Petrov and Eugene Charniak. 2011. *Coarse-to-fine natural language processing*. Springer Science & Business Media.

[Porteous et al.2008] Ian Porteous, Arthur Asuncion, David Newman, Padhraic Smyth, Alexander Ihler, and Max Welling. 2008. Fast collapsed gibbs sampling for latent dirichlet allocation. In *In Proceedings of the 14th ACM SIGKDD International Conference on Knowledge Discovery and Data Mining*, pages 569–577.

[Stevens et al.2012] Keith Stevens, Philip Kegelmeyer, David Andrzejewski, and David Buttler. 2012. Exploring topic coherence over many models and many topics. In *Proceedings of the 2012 Joint Conference on Empirical Methods in Natural Language Processing and Computational Natural Language Learning*, pages 952–961. Association for Computational Linguistics.

[Wallach et al.2009] Hanna M Wallach, Iain Murray, Ruslan Salakhutdinov, and David Mimno. 2009. Evaluation methods for topic models. In *Proceedings of the 26th Annual International Conference on Machine Learning*, pages 1105–1112. ACM.

[Wang et al.2009] Yi Wang, Hongjie Bai, Matt Stanton, Wen-Yen Chen, and Edward Y Chang. 2009. Plda: Parallel latent dirichlet allocation for large-scale applications. In *Algorithmic Aspects in Information and Management*, pages 301–314. Springer.

[Wang et al.2013] Chi Wang, Marina Danilevsky, Nihit Desai, Yinan Zhang, Phuong Nguyen, Thrivikrama Taula, and Jiawei Han. 2013. A phrase mining framework for recursive construction of a topical hierarchy. In *Proceedings of the 19th ACM SIGKDD International Conference on Knowledge Discovery and Data Mining*, KDD '13, pages 437–445, New York, NY, USA. ACM.

[Yao et al.2009] Limin Yao, David Mimno, and Andrew McCallum. 2009. Efficient methods for topic model inference on streaming document collections. In *Proceedings of the 15th ACM SIGKDD international conference on Knowledge discovery and data mining*, pages 937–946. ACM.

Trans-dimensional Random Fields for Language Modeling

Bin Wang[1], **Zhijian Ou**[1], **Zhiqiang Tan**[2]
[1]Department of Electronic Engineering, Tsinghua University, Beijing 100084, China
[2]Department of Statistics, Rutgers University, Piscataway, NJ 08854, USA
wangbin12@mails.tsinghua.edu.cn, ozj@tsinghua.edu.cn,
ztan@stat.rutgers.edu

Abstract

Language modeling (LM) involves determining the joint probability of words in a sentence. The conditional approach is dominant, representing the joint probability in terms of conditionals. Examples include n-gram LMs and neural network LMs. An alternative approach, called the random field (RF) approach, is used in whole-sentence maximum entropy (WSME) LMs. Although the RF approach has potential benefits, the empirical results of previous WSME models are not satisfactory. In this paper, we revisit the RF approach for language modeling, with a number of innovations. We propose a trans-dimensional RF (TDRF) model and develop a training algorithm using joint stochastic approximation and trans-dimensional mixture sampling. We perform speech recognition experiments on Wall Street Journal data, and find that our TDRF models lead to performances as good as the recurrent neural network LMs but are computationally more efficient in computing sentence probability.

1 Introduction

Language modeling is crucial for a variety of computational linguistic applications, such as speech recognition, machine translation, handwriting recognition, information retrieval and so on. It involves determining the joint probability $p(x)$ of a sentence x, which can be denoted as a pair $x = (l, x^l)$, where l is the length and $x^l = (x_1, \dots, x_l)$ is a sequence of l words.

Currently, the dominant approach is conditional modeling, which decomposes the joint probability of x^l into a product of conditional probabilities [1] by using the chain rule,

$$p(x_1, \dots, x_l) = \prod_{i=1}^{l} p(x_i | x_1, \dots, x_{i-1}). \quad (1)$$

To avoid degenerate representation of the conditionals, the history of x_i, denoted as $h_i = (x_1, \cdots, x_{i-1})$, is reduced to equivalence classes through a mapping $\phi(h_i)$ with the assumption

$$p(x_i | h_i) \approx p(x_i | \phi(h_i)). \quad (2)$$

Language modeling in this conditional approach consists of finding suitable mappings $\phi(h_i)$ and effective methods to estimate $p(x_i|\phi(h_i))$. A classic example is the traditional n-gram LMs with $\phi(h_i) = (x_{i-n+1}, \dots, x_{i-1})$. Various smoothing techniques are used for parameter estimation (Chen and Goodman, 1999). Recently, neural network LMs, which have begun to surpass the traditional n-gram LMs, also follow the conditional modeling approach, with $\phi(h_i)$ determined by a neural network (NN), which can be either a feedforward NN (Schwenk, 2007) or a recurrent NN (Mikolov et al., 2011).

Remarkably, an alternative approach is used in whole-sentence maximum entropy (WSME) language modeling (Rosenfeld et al., 2001). Specifically, a WSME model has the form:

$$p(x; \lambda) = \frac{1}{Z} \exp\{\lambda^T f(x)\} \quad (3)$$

Here $f(x)$ is a vector of features, which can be arbitrary computable functions of x, λ is the corresponding parameter vector, and Z is the global normalization constant. Although WSME models have the potential benefits of being able to naturally express sentence-level phenomena and integrate features from a variety of knowledge

[1]And the joint probability of x is modeled as $p(x) = p(x^l)p(\langle EOS\rangle | x_l)$, where $\langle EOS\rangle$ is a special token placed at the end of every sentence. Thus the distribution of the sentence length is implicitly modeled.

Proceedings of the 53rd Annual Meeting of the Association for Computational Linguistics and the 7th International Joint Conference on Natural Language Processing, pages 785–794,
Beijing, China, July 26-31, 2015.

sources, their performance results ever reported are not satisfactory (Rosenfeld et al., 2001; Amaya and Benedí, 2001; Ruokolainen et al., 2010).

The WSME model defined in (3) is basically a Markov random field (MRF). A substantial challenge in fitting MRFs is that evaluating the gradient of the log likelihood requires high-dimensional integration and hence is difficult even for moderately sized models (Younes, 1989), let alone the language model (3). The sampling methods previously tried for approximating the gradient are the Gibbs sampling, the Independence Metropolis-Hasting sampling and the importance sampling (Rosenfeld et al., 2001). Simple applications of these methods are hardly able to work efficiently for the complex, high-dimensional distribution such as (3), and hence the WSME models are in fact poorly fitted to the data. This is one of the reasons for the unsatisfactory results of previous WSME models.

In this paper, we propose a new language model, called the trans-dimensional random field (TDRF) model, by explicitly taking account of the empirical distributions of lengths. This formulation subsequently enables us to develop a powerful Markov chain Monte Carlo (MCMC) technique, called trans-dimensional mixture sampling and then propose an effective training algorithm in the framework of stochastic approximation (SA) (Benveniste et al., 1990; Chen, 2002). The SA algorithm involves jointly updating the model parameters and normalization constants, in conjunction with trans-dimensional MCMC sampling. Section 2 and 3 present the model definition and estimation respectively.

Furthermore, we make several additional innovations, as detailed in Section 4, to enable successful training of TDRF models. First, the diagonal elements of hessian matrix are estimated during SA iterations to rescale the gradient, which significantly improves the convergence of the SA algorithm. Second, word classing is introduced to accelerate the sampling operation and also improve the smoothing behavior of the models through sharing statistical strength between similar words. Finally, multiple CPUs are used to parallelize the training of our RF models.

In Section 5, speech recognition experiments are conducted to evaluate our TDRF LMs, compared with the traditional 4-gram LMs and the recurrent neural network LMs (RNNLMs) (Mikolov et al., 2011) which have emerged as a new state-of-art of language modeling. We explore the use of a variety of features based on word and class information in TDRF LMs. In terms of word error rates (WERs) for speech recognition, our TDRF LMs alone can outperform the KN-smoothing 4-gram LM with 9.1% relative reduction, and perform comparably to the RNNLM with a slight 0.5% relative reduction. To our knowledge, this result represents the first strong empirical evidence supporting the power of using the whole-sentence language modeling approach. Our open-source TDRF toolkit is released publicly [2].

2 Model Definition

Throughout, we denote [3] by $x^l = (x_1, \dots, x_l)$ a sentence (i.e., word sequence) of length l ranging from 1 to m. Each element of x^l corresponds to a single word. For $l = 1, \dots, m$, we assume that sentences of length l are distributed from an exponential family model:

$$p_l(x^l; \lambda) = \frac{1}{Z_l(\lambda)} e^{\lambda^T f(x^l)}, \tag{4}$$

where $f(x^l) = (f_1(x^l), f_2(x^l), \dots, f_d(x^l))^T$ is the feature vector and $\lambda = (\lambda_1, \lambda_2, \dots, \lambda_d)^T$ is the corresponding parameter vector, and $Z_l(\lambda)$ is the normalization constant:

$$Z_l(\lambda) = \sum_{x^l} e^{\lambda^T f(x^l)} \tag{5}$$

Moreover, we assume that length l is associated with probability π_l for $l = 1, \dots, m$. Therefore, the pair (l, x^l) is jointly distributed as

$$p(l, x^l; \lambda) = \pi_l \, p_l(x^l; \lambda). \tag{6}$$

We provide several comments on the above model definition. First, by making explicit the role of lengths in model definition, it is clear that the model in (6) is a mixture of random fields on sentences of different lengths (namely on subspaces of different dimensions), and hence will be called a trans-dimensional random field (TDRF). Different from the WSME model (3), a crucial aspect of the TDRF model (6) is that the mixture weights π_l can be set to the empirical length probabilities in the training data. The WSME

[2] `http://oa.ee.tsinghua.edu.cn/~ouzhijian/software.htm`

[3] We add sup or subscript l, e.g. in $x^l, p_l()$, to make clear that the variables and distributions depend on length l.

model (3) is essentially also a mixture of RFs, but the mixture weights implied are proportional to the normalizing constants $Z_l(\lambda)$:

$$p(l, x^l; \lambda) = \frac{Z_l(\lambda)}{Z(\lambda)} \frac{1}{Z_l(\lambda)} e^{\lambda^T f(x^l)}, \qquad (7)$$

where $Z(\lambda) = \sum_{l=1}^{m} Z_l(\lambda)$.

A motivation for proposing (6) is that it is very difficult to sample from (3), namely (7), as a mixture distribution with unknown weights which typically differ from each other by orders of magnitudes, e.g. 10^{40} or more in our experiments. Setting mixture weights to the known, empirical length probabilities enables us to develop a very effective learning algorithm, as introduced in Section 3. Basically, the empirical weights serve as a control device to improve sampling from multiple distributions (Liang et al., 2007; Tan, 2015) .

Second, it can be shown that if we incorporate the length features [4] in the vector of features $f(x)$ in (3), then the distribution $p(x; \lambda)$ in (3) under the maximum entropy (ME) principle will take the form of (6) and the probabilities $(\pi_1, \ldots, \pi_m)$ in (6) implied by the parameters for the length features are exactly the empirical length probabilities.

Third, a feature $f_i(x^l)$, $1 \le i \le d$, can be any computable function of the sentence x^l, such as n-grams. In our current experiments, the features $f_i(x^l)$ and their corresponding parameters λ_i are defined to be position-independent and length-independent. For example, $f_i(x^l) = \sum_k f_i(x^l, k)$, where $f_i(x^l, k)$ is a binary function of x^l evaluated at position k. As a result, the feature $f_i(x^l)$ takes values in the non-negative integers.

3 Model Estimation

We develop a stochastic approximation algorithm using Markov chain Monte Carlo to estimate the parameters λ and the normalization constants $Z_1(\lambda), \ldots, Z_m(\lambda)$ (Benveniste et al., 1990; Chen, 2002). The core algorithms newly designed in this paper are the joint SA for simultaneously estimating parameters and normalizing constants (Section 3.2) and trans-dimensional mixture sampling (Section 3.3) which is used as Step I of the joint SA. The most relevant previous works that we borrowed from are (Gu and Zhu, 2001) on SA for fitting a single RF, (Tan, 2015) on sampling and estimating normalizing constants from multiple RFs of the same dimension, and (Green, 1995) on trans-dimensional MCMC.

3.1 Maximum likelihood estimation

Suppose that the training dataset consists of n_l sentences of length l for $l = 1, \ldots, m$. First, the maximum likelihood estimate of the length probability π_l is easily shown to be n_l/n, where $n = \sum_{l=1}^{m} n_l$. By abuse of notation, we set $\pi_l = n_l/n$ hereafter. Next, the log-likelihood of λ given the empirical length probabilities is

$$L(\lambda) = \frac{1}{n} \sum_{l=1}^{m} \sum_{x^l \in D_l} \log p_l(x^l; \lambda), \qquad (8)$$

where D_l is the collection of sentences of length l in the training set. By setting to 0 the derivative of (8) with respect to λ, we obtain that the maximum likelihood estimate of λ is determined by the following equation:

$$\frac{\partial L(\lambda)}{\partial \lambda} = \tilde{p}[f] - p_\lambda[f] = 0, \qquad (9)$$

where $\tilde{p}[f]$ is the expectation of the feature vector f with respect to the empirical distribution:

$$\tilde{p}[f] = \frac{1}{n} \sum_{l=1}^{m} \sum_{x^l \in D_l} f(x^l), \qquad (10)$$

and $p_\lambda[f]$ is the expectation of f with respect to the joint distribution (6) with $\pi_l = n_l/n$:

$$p_\lambda[f] = \sum_{l=1}^{m} \frac{n_l}{n} p_{\lambda,l}[f], \qquad (11)$$

and $p_{\lambda,l}[f] = \sum_{x^l} f(x^l) p_l(x^l; \lambda)$. Eq.(9) has the form of equating empirical expectations $\tilde{p}[f]$ with theoretical expectations $p_\lambda[f]$, as similarly found in maximum likelihood estimation of single random field models.

3.2 Joint stochastic approximation

Training random field models is challenging due to numerical intractability of the normalizing constants $Z_l(\lambda)$ and expectations $p_{\lambda,l}[f]$. We propose a novel SA algorithm for estimating the parameters λ by (9) and, simultaneously, estimating the log ratios of normalization constants:

$$\zeta_l^*(\lambda) = \log \frac{Z_l(\lambda)}{Z_1(\lambda)}, \quad l = 1, \ldots, m \qquad (12)$$

[4] The length feature corresponding to length l is a binary feature that takes one if the sentence x is of length l, and otherwise takes zero.

Algorithm 1 Joint stochastic approximation

Input: training set

set initial values $\lambda^{(0)} = (0, \dots, 0)^T$ and $\zeta^{(0)} = \zeta^*(\lambda^{(0)}) - \zeta_1^*(\lambda^{(0)})$
for $t = 1, 2, \dots, t_{max}$ **do**
  set $B^{(t)} = \emptyset$
  set $(L^{(t,0)}, X^{(t,0)}) = (L^{(t-1,K)}, X^{(t-1,K)})$
  Step I: MCMC sampling
  for $k = 1 \rightarrow K$ **do**
    sampling (See Algorithm 3)
    $(L^{(t,k)}, X^{(t,k)}) = SAMPLE(L^{(t,k-1)}, X^{(t,k-1)})$
    set $B^{(t)} = B^{(t)} \cup \{(L^{(t,k)}, X^{(t,k)})\}$
  end for
  Step II: SA updating
  Compute $\lambda^{(t)}$ based on (14)
  Compute $\zeta^{(t)}$ based on (15) and (16)
end for

where $Z_1(\lambda)$ is chosen as the reference value and can be calculated exactly. The algorithm can be obtained by combining the standard SA algorithm for training single random fields (Gu and Zhu, 2001) and a trans-dimensional extension of the self-adjusted mixture sampling algorithm (Tan, 2015).

Specifically, consider the following joint distribution of the pair (l, x^l):

$$p(l, x^l; \lambda, \zeta) \propto \frac{\pi_l}{e^{\zeta_l}} e^{\lambda^T f(x^l)}, \qquad (13)$$

where π_l is set to n_l/n for $l = 1, \dots, m$, but $\zeta = (\zeta_1, \dots, \zeta_m)^T$ with $\zeta_1 = 0$ are hypothesized values of the truth $\zeta^*(\lambda) = (\zeta_1^*(\lambda), \dots, \zeta_m^*(\lambda))^T$ with $\zeta_1^*(\lambda) = 0$. The distribution $p(l, x^l; \lambda, \zeta)$ reduces to $p(l, x^l; \lambda)$ in (6) if ζ were identical to $\zeta^*(\lambda)$. In general, $p(l, x^l; \lambda, \zeta)$ differs from $p(l, x^l; \lambda)$ in that the marginal probability of length l is not necessarily π_l.

The joint SA algorithm, whose pseudo-code is shown in Algorithm 1, consists of two steps at each time t as follows.

Step I: MCMC sampling. Generate a sample set $B^{(t)}$ with $p(l, x^l; \lambda^{(t-1)}, \zeta^{(t-1)})$ as the stationary distribution (see Section 3.3).

Step II: SA updating. Compute

$$\lambda^{(t)} = \lambda^{(t-1)} + \gamma_\lambda \left\{ \tilde{p}[f] - \frac{\sum_{(l,x^l)\in B^{(t)}} f(x^l)}{K} \right\} \qquad (14)$$

where γ_λ is a learning rate of λ; compute

$$\zeta^{(t-\frac{1}{2})} = \zeta^{(t)} + \gamma_\zeta \left\{ \frac{\delta_1(B^{(t)})}{\pi_1}, \dots, \frac{\delta_m(B^{(t)})}{\pi_m} \right\} \qquad (15)$$

$$\zeta^{(t)} = \zeta^{(t-\frac{1}{2})} - \zeta_1^{(t-\frac{1}{2})} \qquad (16)$$

where γ_ζ is a learning rate of ζ, and $\delta_l(B^{(t)})$ is the relative frequency of length l appearing in $B^{(t)}$:

$$\delta_l(B^{(t)}) = \frac{\sum_{(j,x^j)\in B^{(t)}} 1(j = l)}{K}. \qquad (17)$$

The rationale in (15) is to adjust ζ based on how the relative frequencies of lengths $\delta_l(B^{(t)})$ are compared with the desired length probabilities π_l. Intuitively, if the relative frequency of some length l in the sample set $B^{(t)}$ is greater (or respectively smaller) than the desired length probability π_l, then the hypothesized value $\zeta_l^{(t-1)}$ is an underestimate (or overestimate) of $\zeta_l^*(\lambda^{(t-1)})$ and hence should be increased (or decreased).

Following Gu & Zhu (2001) and Tan (2015), we set the learning rates in two stages:

$$\gamma_\lambda = \begin{cases} t^{-\beta_\lambda} & \text{if } t \le t_0 \\ \frac{1}{t - t_0 + t_0^{\beta_\lambda}} & \text{if } t > t_0 \end{cases} \qquad (18)$$

$$\gamma_\zeta = \begin{cases} (0.1t)^{-\beta_\zeta} & \text{if } t \le t_0 \\ \frac{1}{0.1(t-t_0) + (0.1t_0)^{\beta_\zeta}} & \text{if } t > t_0 \end{cases} \qquad (19)$$

where $0.5 < \beta_\lambda, \beta_\zeta < 1$. In the first stage ($t \le t_0$), a slow-decaying rate of $t^{-\beta}$ is used to introduce large adjustments. This forces the estimates $\lambda^{(t)}$ and $\zeta^{(t)}$ to fall reasonably fast into the true values. In the second stage ($t > t_0$), a fast-decaying rate of t^{-1} is used. The iteration number t is multiplied by 0.1 in (19), to make the the learning rate of ζ decay more slowly than λ. Commonly, t_0 is selected to ensure there is no more significant adjustment observed in the first stage.

3.3 Trans-dimensional mixture sampling

We describe a trans-dimensional mixture sampling algorithm to simulate from the joint distribution $p(l, x^l; \lambda, \zeta)$, which is used with $(\lambda, \zeta) = (\lambda^{(t-1)}, \zeta^{(t-1)})$ at time t for MCMC sampling in the joint SA algorithm. The name "mixture sampling" reflects the fact that $p(l, x^l; \lambda, \zeta)$ represents a labeled mixture, because l is a label indicating that x^l is associated with the distribution $p_l(x^l; \zeta)$. With fixed (λ, ζ), this sampling algorithm can be seen as formally equivalent to reversible jump MCMC (Green, 1995), which was originally proposed for Bayes model determination.

The trans-dimensional mixture sampling algorithm consists of two steps at each time t: local jump between lengths and Markov move of sentences for a given length. In the following, we denote by $L^{(t-1)}$ and $X^{(t-1)}$ the length and sequence before sampling, but use the short notation (λ, ζ) for $(\lambda^{(t-1)}, \zeta^{(t-1)})$.

Step I: Local jump. The Metropolis-Hastings method is used in this step to sample the length. Assuming $L^{(t-1)} = k$, first we draw a new length $j \sim \Gamma(k, \cdot)$. The jump distribution $\Gamma(k, l)$ is defined to be uniform at the neighborhood of k :

$$\Gamma(k,l) = \begin{cases} \frac{1}{3}, \text{if } k \in [2, m-1], l \in [k-1, k+1] \\ \frac{1}{2}, \text{if } k = 1, l \in [1,2] \text{ or } k = m, l \in [m-1, m] \\ 0, \text{otherwise} \end{cases} \tag{20}$$

where m is the maximum length. Eq.(20) restricts the difference between j and k to be no more than one. If $j = k$, we retain the sequence and perform the next step directly, i.e. set $L^{(t)} = k$ and $X^{(t)} = X^{(t-1)}$. If $j = k + 1$ or $j = k - 1$, the two cases are processed differently.

If $j = k + 1$, we first draw an element (i.e., word) Y from a proposal distribution: $Y \sim g_{k+1}(y|X^{(t-1)})$. Then we set $L^{(t)} = j\,(= k + 1)$ and $X^{(t)} = \{X^{(t-1)}, Y\}$ with probability

$$\min\left\{1, \frac{\Gamma(j,k)}{\Gamma(k,j)} \frac{p(j, \{X^{(t-1)}, Y\}; \lambda, \zeta)}{p(k, X^{(t-1)}; \lambda, \zeta) g_{k+1}(Y|X^{(t-1)})}\right\} \tag{21}$$

where $\{X^{(t-1)}, Y\}$ denotes a sequence of length $k + 1$ whose first k elements are $X^{(t-1)}$ and the last element is Y.

If $j = k - 1$, we set $L^{(t)} = j\,(= k - 1)$ and $X^{(t)} = X^{(t-1)}_{1:j}$ with probability

$$\min\left\{1, \frac{\Gamma(j,k)}{\Gamma(k,j)} \frac{p(j, X^{(t-1)}_{1:j}; \lambda, \zeta) g_k(X^{(t-1)}_k | X^{(t-1)}_{1:j})}{p(k, X^{(t-1)}; \lambda, \zeta)}\right\} \tag{22}$$

where $X^{(t-1)}_{1:j}$ is the first j elements of $X^{(t-1)}$ and $X^{(t-1)}_k$ is the kth element of $X^{(t-1)}$.

In (21) and (22), $g_{k+1}(y|x^k)$ can be flexibly specified as a proper density function in y. In our application, we find the following choice works reasonably well:

$$g_{k+1}(y|x^k) = \frac{p(k+1, \{x^k, y\}; \lambda, \zeta)}{\sum_w p(k+1, \{x^k, w\}; \lambda, \zeta)}. \tag{23}$$

Step II: Markov move. After the step of local jump, we obtain

$$X^{(t)} = \begin{cases} X^{(t-1)} & \text{if } L^{(t)} = k \\ \{X^{(t-1)}, Y\} & \text{if } L^{(t)} = k+1 \\ X^{(t-1)}_{1:k-1} & \text{if } L^{(t)} = k-1 \end{cases} \tag{24}$$

Then we perform Gibbs sampling on $X^{(t)}$, from the first element to the last element (Algorithm 2)

Algorithm 2 Markov Move

```
1: for i = 1 → L^(t) do
2:     draw W ~ p(L^(t), {X^(t)_{1:i-1}, w, X^(t)_{i+1:L^(t)}}; λ, ζ)
3:     set X^(t)_i = W
4: end for
```

4 Algorithm Optimization and Acceleration

The joint SA algorithm may still suffer from slow convergence, especially when λ is high-dimensional. We introduce several techniques for improving the convergence of the algorithm and reducing computational cost.

4.1 Improving SA recursion

We propose two techniques to effectively improve the convergence of SA recursion.

The first technique is to incorporate Hessian information, similarly as in related works on s-tochastic approximation (Gu and Zhu, 2001) and stochastic gradient descent algorithms (Byrd et al., 2014). But we only use the diagonal elements of the Hessian matrix to re-scale the gradient, due to high-dimensionality of λ.

Taking the second derivatives of $L(\lambda)$ yields

$$H_i = -\frac{d^2 L(\lambda)}{d\lambda_i^2} = p[f_i^2] - \sum_{l=1}^{m} \pi_l (p_l[f_i])^2 \tag{25}$$

where H_i denotes the ith diagonal element of Hessian matrix. At time t, before updating the parameter λ (Step II in Section 3.2), we compute

$$H_i^{(t-\frac{1}{2})} = \frac{1}{K} \sum_{(l,x^l) \in B^{(t)}} f_i(x^l)^2 - \sum_{l=1}^{m} \pi_l (\bar{p}_l[f_i])^2, \tag{26}$$

$$H_i^{(t)} = H_i^{(t-1)} + \gamma_H (H_i^{(t-\frac{1}{2})} - H_i^{(t-1)}), \tag{27}$$

where $\bar{p}_l[f_i] = |B_l^{(t)}|^{-1} \sum_{(l,x^l) \in B_l^{(t)}} f_i(x^l)$, and $B_l^{(t)}$ is the subset, of size $|B_l^{(t)}|$, containing all sentences of length l in $B^{(t)}$.

The second technique is to introduce the "mini-batch" on the training set. At each iteration, a subset $D^{(t)}$ of K sentences are randomly selected from the training set. Then the gradient is approximated with the overall empirical expectation $\tilde{p}[f]$ being replaced by the empirical expectation over the subset $D^{(t)}$. This technique is reminiscent of stochastic gradient descent using a random sub-sample of training data to achieve fast convergence

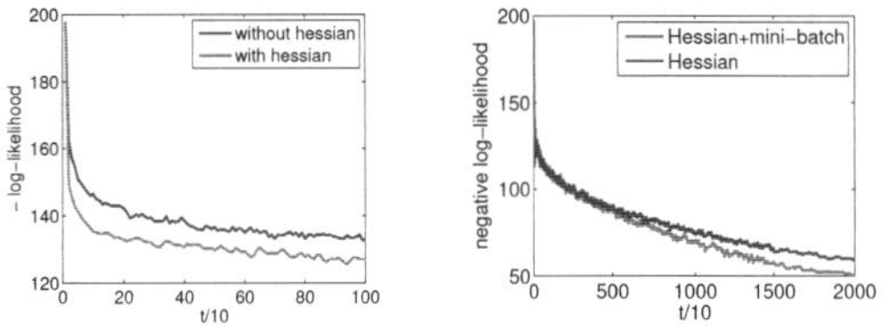

(a) (b)

Figure 1: Examples of convergence curves on training set after introducing hessian and training set mini-batching.

of optimization algorithms (Bousquet and Bottou, 2008).

By combining the two techniques, we revise the updating equation (14) of λ to

$$\lambda_i^{(t)} = \lambda_i^{(t-1)} + \frac{\gamma_\lambda}{\max(H_i^{(t)}, h)} \times \left\{ \frac{\sum_{(l,x^l)\in D^{(t)}} f_i(x^l)}{K} - \frac{\sum_{(l,x^l)\in B^{(t)}} f_i(x^l)}{K} \right\} \tag{28}$$

where $0 < h < 1$ is a threshold to avoid $H_i^{(t)}$ being too small or even zero. Moreover, a constant t_c is added to the denominator of (18), to avoid too large adjustment of λ, i.e.

$$\gamma_\lambda = \begin{cases} \frac{1}{t_c + t^{\beta_\lambda}} & \text{if } t \le t_0, \\ \frac{1}{t_c + t - t_0 + t_0^{\beta_\lambda}} & \text{if } t > t_0. \end{cases} \tag{29}$$

Fig.1(a) shows the result after introducing hessian estimation, and Fig.1(b) shows the effect of training set mini-batching.

4.2 Sampling acceleration

For MCMC sampling in Section 3.3, the Gibbs sampling operation of drawing $X_i^{(t)}$ (Step 2 in Algorithms 2) involves calculating the probabilities of all the possible elements in position i. This is computationally costly, because the vocabulary size $|\mathcal{V}|$ is usually 10 thousands or more in practice. As a result, the Gibbs sampling operation presents a bottleneck limiting the efficiency of sampling algorithms.

We propose a novel method of using class information to effectively reduce the computational cost of Gibbs sampling. Suppose that each word in vocabulary $\mathcal{V}$ is assigned to a single class. If the total class number is $|\mathcal{C}|$, then there are, on average, $|\mathcal{V}|/|\mathcal{C}|$ words in each class. With the class information, we can first draw the class of $X_i^{(t)}$, denoted by $c_i^{(t)}$, and then draw a word belonging to class $c_i^{(t)}$. The computational cost is reduced from $|\mathcal{V}|$ to $|\mathcal{C}| + |\mathcal{V}|/|\mathcal{C}|$ on average.

Algorithm 3 Class-based MCMC sampling

1: **function** SAMPLE($(L^{(t-1)}, X^{(t-1)})$)
2: set $k = L^{(t-1)}$
3: init $(L^{(t)}, X^{(t)}) = (k, X^{(t-1)})$
Step I: Local jump
4: generate $j \sim \Gamma(k, \cdot)$ (Eq.(20))
5: **if** $j = k+1$ **then**
6: generate $C \sim Q_{k+1}(c)$
7: generate $Y \sim \breve{g}_{k+1}(y|X^{(t-1)}, C)$ (Eq.31)
8: set $L^{(t)} = j$ and $X^{(t)} = \{X^{(t-1)}, Y\}$ with probability (Eq.21) and (Eq.32)
9: **end if**
10: **if** $j = k-1$ **then**
11: set $L^{(t)} = j$ and $X^{(t)} = X_{1:k-1}^{(t-1)}$ with probability Eq.(22) and (Eq.32)
12: **end if**
Step II: Markov move
13: **for** $i = 1 \to L^{(t)}$ **do**
14: draw $C \sim Q_i(c)$
15: set $c_i^{(t)} = C$ with probability (Eq.30)
16: draw $W \in \mathcal{V}_{c_i^{(t)}}$
17: set $X_i^{(t)} = W$
18: **end for**
19: **return** $(L^{(t)}, X^{(t)})$
20: **end function**

The idea of using class information to accelerate training has been proposed in various contexts of language modeling, such as maximum entropy models (Goodman, 2001b) and RNN LMs (Mikolov et al., 2011). However, the realization of this idea is different for training our models.

The pseudo-code of the new sampling method is shown in Algorithm 3. Denote by $\mathcal{V}_c$ the subset of $\mathcal{V}$ containing all the words belonging to class c. In the Markov move step (Step 13 to 18 in Algorithm 3), at each position i, we first generate a class C from a proposal distribution $Q_i(c)$ and then accept C as the new $c_i^{(t)}$ with probability

$$\min\left\{1, \frac{Q_i(c_i^{(t)})}{Q_i(C)} \frac{p_i(C)}{p_i(c_i^{(t)})}\right\} \tag{30}$$

where

$$p_i(c) = \sum_{w \in \mathcal{V}_c} p(L^{(t)}, \{X_{1:i-1}^{(t)}, w, X_{i+1:L^{(t)}}^{(t)}\}; \lambda, \zeta).$$

The probabilities $Q_i(c)$ and $p_i(c)$ depend on $\{X_{1:i-1}^{(t)}, X_{i+1:L^{(t)}}^{(t)}\}$, but this is suppressed in the notation. Then we normalize the probabilities of words belonging to class $c_i^{(t)}$ and draw a word as the new $X_i^{(t)}$ from the class $c_i^{(t)}$.

Similarly, in the local jump step with $k = L^{(t-1)}$, if the proposal $j = k+1$ (Step 5 to 9 in Algorithm 3), we first generate $C \sim Q_{k+1}(c)$ and then generate Y from class C by

$$\breve{g}_{k+1}(y|x^k, C) = \frac{p(k+1, \{x^k, y\}; \lambda, \zeta)}{\sum_{w \in \mathcal{V}_C} p(k+1, \{x^k, w\}; \lambda, \zeta)} \quad (31)$$

with $x^k = X^{(t-1)}$. Then we set $L^{(t)} = j$ and $X^{(t)} = \{X^{(t-1)}, Y\}$ with probability as defined in (21), by setting

$$g_{k+1}(y|x^k) = Q_{k+1}(C)\breve{g}_{k+1}(y|x^k, C). \quad (32)$$

If the proposal $j = k - 1$, similarly we use acceptance probability (22) with (32).

In our application, we construct $Q_i(c)$ dynamically as follows. Write x^l for $\{X^{(t-1)}, Y\}$ in Step 8 or for $X^{(t)}$ in Step 11 of Algorithm 3. First, we construct a reduced model $p_l^c(x^l)$, by including only the features that depend on x_i^l through its class and retaining the corresponding parameters in $p_l(x^l; \lambda, \zeta)$. Then we define the distribution

$$Q_i(c) = p_l^c(\{x_{1:i-1}^l, c, x_{i+1:l}^l\}),$$

which can be directly calculated without knowing the value of x_i^l.

4.3 Parallelization of sampling

The sampling operation can be easily parallelized in SA Algorithm 1. At each time t, both the parameters λ and log normalization constants ζ are fixed at $\lambda^{(t-1)}$ and $\zeta^{(t-1)}$. Instead of simulating one Markov Chain, we simulate J Markov Chains on J CPU cores separately. As a result, to generate a sample set $B^{(t)}$ of size K, only K/J sampling steps need to be performed on each CPU core. By parallelization, the sampling operation is completed J times faster than before.

5 Experiments

5.1 PTB perplexity results

In this section, we evaluate the performance of LMs by perplexity (PPL). We use the Wall Street Journal (WSJ) portion of Penn Treebank (PTB). Sections 0-20 are used as the training data (about 930K words), sections 21-22 as the development data (74K) and section 23-24 as the test data (82K). The vocabulary is limited to 10K words, with one special token $\langle UNK \rangle$ denoting words not in the vocabulary. This setting is the same as that used in other studies (Mikolov et al., 2011).

The baseline is a 4-gram LM with modified Kneser-Ney smoothing (Chen and Goodman, 1999), denoted by KN4. We use the RNNLM toolkit[5] to train a RNNLM (Mikolov et al., 2011). The number of hidden units is 250 and other configurations are set by default[6].

Type	Features
w	$(w_{-3}w_{-2}w_{-1}w_0)(w_{-2}w_{-1}w_0)(w_{-1}w_0)(w_0)$
c	$(c_{-3}c_{-2}c_{-1}c_0)(c_{-2}c_{-1}c_0)(c_{-1}c_0)(c_0)$
ws	$(w_{-3}w_0)(w_{-3}w_{-2}w_0)(w_{-3}w_{-1}w_0)(w_{-2}w_0)$
cs	$(c_{-3}c_0)(c_{-3}c_{-2}c_0)(c_{-3}c_{-1}c_0)(c_{-2}c_0)$
wsh	$(w_{-4}w_0)$ $(w_{-5}w_0)$
csh	$(c_{-4}c_0)$ $(c_{-5}c_0)$
cpw	$(c_{-3}c_{-2}c_{-1}w_0)$ $(c_{-2}c_{-1}w_0)(c_{-1}w_0)$

Table 1: Feature definition in TDRF LMs

Word classing has been shown to be useful in conditional ME models (Chen, 2009). For our TDRF models, we consider a variety of features as shown in Table 1, mainly based on word and class information. Each word is deterministically assigned to a single class, by running the automatic clustering algorithm proposed in (Martin et al., 1998) on the training data.

In Table 1, $w_i, c_i, i = 0, -1, \ldots, -5$ denote the word and its class at different position offset i, e.g. w_0, c_0 denotes the current word and its class. We first introduce the classic word/class n-gram features (denoted by "w"/"c") and the word/class skipping n-gram features (denoted by "ws"/"cs") (Goodman, 2001a). Second, to demonstrate that long-span features can be naturally integrated in TDRFs, we introduce higher-order features "wsh"/"csh", by considering two words/classes separated with longer distance. Third, as an example of supporting heterogenous features that combine different information, the crossing features "cpw" (meaning class-predict-word) are introduced. Note that for all the feature types in Table 1, only the features observed in the training data are used.

The joint SA (Algorithm 1) is used to train the TDRF models, with all the acceleration methods described in Section 4 applied. The minibatch size $K = 300$. The learning rates γ_λ and γ_ζ are configured as (29) and (19) respectively with $\beta_\lambda = \beta_\zeta = 0.6$ and $t_c = 3000$. For t_0, it is first initialized to be 10^4. During iterations, we monitor the smoothed log-likelihood (moving average of 1000 iterations) on the PTB development data.

[5] http://rnnlm.org/

[6] Minibatch size=10, learning rate=0.1, BPTT steps=5. 17 sweeps are performed before stopping, which takes about 25 hours. No word classing is used, since classing in RNNLMs reduces computation but at cost of accuracy. RNNLMs were experimented with varying numbers of hidden units (100-500). The best result from using 250 hidden units is reported.

models	PPL (± std. dev.)
KN4	142.72
RNN	128.81
TDRF w+c	130.69±1.64

Table 2: The PPLs on the PTB test data. The class number is 200.

We set t_0 to the current iteration number once the rising percentage of the smoothed log-likelihoods within 100 iterations is below 20%, and then continue 5000 further iterations before stopping. The configuration of hessian estimation (Section 4.1) is $\gamma_H = \gamma_\lambda$ and $h = 10^{-4}$. L_2 regularization with constant 10^{-5} is used to avoid over-fitting. 8 CPU cores are used to parallelize the algorithm, as described in Section 4.3, and the training of each TDRF model takes less than 20 hours.

The perplexity results on the PTB test data are given in Table 2. As the normalization constants of TDRF models are estimated stochastically, we report the Monte Carlo mean and standard deviation from the last 1000 iterations for each PPL. The TDRF model using the basic "w+c" features performs close to the RNNLM in perplexity. To be compact, results with more features are presented in the following WSJ experiment.

5.2 WSJ speech recognition results

In this section, we continue to use the LMs obtained above (using PTB training and development data), and evaluate their performance measured by WERs in speech recognition, by rescoring 1000-best lists from WSJ'92 test data (330 sentences). The oracle WER of the 1000-best lists is 3.4%, which are generated from using the Kaldi toolkit[7] with a DNN-based acoustic model.

TDRF LMs using a variety of features and different number of classes are tested. The results are shown in Table 3. Different types of features, like the skipping features, the higher-order features and the crossing features can all be easily supported in TDRF LMs, and the performance is improved to varying degrees. Particularly, the TDRF using the "w+c+ws+cs+cpw" features with class number 200 performs comparable to the RNNLM in both perplexity and WER. Numerically, the relative reduction is 9.1% compared with the KN4 LMs, and 0.5% compared with the RNN LM.

[7] http://kaldi.sourceforge.net/

model	WER	PPL (± std. dev.)	#feat
KN4	8.71	295.41	1.6M
RNN	7.96	256.15	5.1M
WSMEs (200c)			
w+c+ws+cs	8.87	$\approx 2.8 \times 10^{12}$	5.2M
w+c+ws+cs+cpw	8.82	$\approx 6.7 \times 10^{12}$	6.4M
TDRFs (100c)			
w+c	8.56	268.25±3.52	2.2M
w+c+ws+cs	8.16	265.81±4.30	4.5M
w+c+ws+cs+cpw	8.05	265.63±7.93	5.6M
w+c+ws+cs+wsh+csh	8.03	276.90±5.00	5.2M
TDRFs (200c)			
w+c	8.46	257.78±3.13	2.5M
w+c+ws+cs	8.05	257.80±4.29	5.2M
w+c+ws+cs+cpw	**7.92**	264.86±8.55	6.4M
w+c+ws+cs+wsh+csh	**7.94**	266.42±7.48	5.9M
TDRFs (500c)			
w+c	8.72	261.02±2.94	2.8M
w+c+ws+cs	8.29	266.34±6.13	5.9M

Table 3: The WERs and PPLs on the WSJ'92 test data. "#feat" denotes the feature number. Different TDRF models with class number 100/200/500 are reported (denoted by "100c"/"200c"/"500c")

5.3 Comparison and discussion

TDRF vs WSME. For comparison, Table 3 also presents the results from our implementation of the WSME model (3), using the same features as in Table 1. This WSME model is the same as in (Rosenfeld, 1997), but different from (Rosenfeld et al., 2001), which uses the traditional n-gram LM as the priori distribution p_0.

For the WSME model (3), we can still use a SA training algorithm, similar to that developed in Section 3.2, to estimate the parameters λ. But in this case, there is no need to introduce ζ_l, because the normalizing constants $Z_l(\lambda)$ are canceled out as seen from (7). Specifically, the learning rate γ_λ and the L_2 regularization are configured the same as in TDRF training. A fixed number of iterations with $t_0 = 5000$ is performed. The total iteration number is 10000, which is similar to the iteration number used in TDRF training.

In order to calculate perplexity, we need to estimate the global normalizing constant $Z(\lambda) = \sum_{l=1}^{m} Z_l(\lambda)$ for the WSME model. Similarly as in (Tan, 2015), we apply the SA algorithm in Section 3.2 to estimate the log normalizing constants ζ, while fixing the parameters λ to be those already estimated from the WSME model and using uniform probabilities $\pi_l \equiv m^{-1}$.

The resulting PPLs of these WSME models are extremely poor. The average test log-likelihoods per sentence for these two WSME models are

−494 and −509 respectively. However, the WERs from using the trained WSME models in hypothesis re-ranking are not as poor as would be expected from their PPLs. This appears to indicate that the estimated WSME parameters are not so bad for relative ranking. Moreover, when the estimated λ and ζ are substituted into our TDRF model (6) with the empirical length probabilities π_l, the "corrected" average test log-likelihoods per sentence for these two sets of parameters are improved to be −152 and −119 respectively. The average test log-likelihoods are both −96 for the two corresponding TDRF models in Table 3. This is some evidence for the model deficiency of the WSME distribution as defined in (3), and introducing the empirical length probabilities gives a more reasonable model assumption.

TDRF vs conditional ME. After training, TDRF models are computationally more efficient in computing sentence probability, simply summing up weights for the activated features in the sentence. The conditional ME models (Khudanpur and Wu, 2000; Roark et al., 2004) suffer from the expensive computation of local normalization factors. This computational bottleneck hinders their use in practice (Goodman, 2001b; Rosenfeld et al., 2001). Partly for this reason, although building conditional ME models with sophisticated features as in Table 1 is theoretically possible, such work has not been pursued so far.

TDRF vs RNN. The RNN models suffer from the expensive softmax computation in the output layer [8]. Empirically in our experiments, the average time costs for re-ranking of the 1000-best list for a sentence are 0.16 sec vs 40 sec, based on TDRF and RNN respectively (no GPU used).

6 Related Work

While there has been extensive research on conditional LMs, there has been little work on the whole-sentence LMs, mainly in (Rosenfeld et al., 2001; Amaya and Benedí, 2001; Ruokolainen et al., 2010). Although the whole-sentence approach has potential benefits, the empirical results of previous WSME models are not satisfactory, almost the same as traditional n-gram models. After incorporating lexical and syntactic information, a mere relative improvement of 1% and 0.4% respectively in perplexity and in WER is reported for the resulting WSEM (Rosenfeld et al., 2001). Subsequent studies of using WSEMs with grammatical features, as in (Amaya and Benedí, 2001) and (Ruokolainen et al., 2010), report perplexity improvement above 10% but no WER improvement when using WSEMs alone.

Most RF modeling has been restricted to fixed-dimensional spaces [9]. Despite recent progress, fitting RFs of moderate or large dimensions remains to be challenging (Koller and Friedman, 2009; Mizrahi et al., 2013). In particular, the work of (Pietra et al., 1997) is inspiring to us, but the improved iterative scaling (IIS) method for parameter estimation and the Gibbs sampler are not suitable for even moderately sized models. Our TDRF model, together with the joint SA algorithm and trans-dimensional mixture sampling, are brand new and lead to encouraging results for language modeling.

7 Conclusion

In summary, we have made the following contributions, which enable us to successfully train TDRF models and obtain encouraging performance improvement.

- The new TDRF model and the joint SA training algorithm, which simultaneously updates the model parameters and normalizing constants while using trans-dimensional mixture sampling.
- Several additional innovations including accelerating SA iterations by using Hessian information, introducing word classing to accelerate the sampling operation and improve the smoothing behavior of the models, and parallelization of sampling.

In this work, we mainly explore the use of features based on word and class information. Future work with other knowledge sources and larger-scale experiments is needed to fully exploit the advantage of TDRFs to integrate richer features.

8 Acknowledgments

This work is supported by Toshiba Corporation, National Natural Science Foundation of China (NSFC) via grant 61473168, and Tsinghua Initiative. We thank the anonymous reviewers for helpful comments on this paper.

[8] This deficiency could be partly alleviated with some speed-up methods, e.g. using word clustering (Mikolov, 2012) or noise contrastive estimation (Mnih and Kavukcuoglu, 2013).

[9] Using local fixed-dimensional RFs in sequential models was once explored, e.g. temporal restricted Boltzmann machine (TRBM) (Sutskever and Hinton, 2007).

References

Fredy Amaya and José Miguel Benedí. 2001. Improvement of a whole sentence maximum entropy language model using grammatical features. In *Association for Computational Linguistics (ACL)*.

Albert Benveniste, Michel Métivier, and Pierre Priouret. 1990. *Adaptive algorithms and stochastic approximations*. New York: Springer.

Olivier Bousquet and Leon Bottou. 2008. The tradeoffs of large scale learning. In *NIPS*, pages 161–168.

Richard H Byrd, SL Hansen, Jorge Nocedal, and Yoram Singer. 2014. A stochastic quasi-newton method for large-scale optimization. *arXiv preprint arXiv:1401.7020*.

Stanley F. Chen and Joshua Goodman. 1999. An empirical study of smoothing techniques for language modeling. *Computer Speech & Language*, 13:359–394.

Hanfu Chen. 2002. *Stochastic approximation and its applications*. Springer Science & Business Media.

Stanley F. Chen. 2009. Shrinking exponential language models. In *Proc. of Human Language Technologies: The 2009 Annual Conference of the North American Chapter of the Association for Computational Linguistics*.

Joshua Goodman. 2001a. A bit of progress in language modeling. *Computer Speech & Language*, 15:403–434.

Joshua Goodman. 2001b. Classes for fast maximum entropy training. In *Proc. of International Conference on Acoustics, Speech, and Signal Processing (ICASSP)*.

Peter J. Green. 1995. Reversible jump markov chain monte carlo computation and bayesian model determination. *Biometrika*, 82:711–732.

Ming Gao Gu and Hong-Tu Zhu. 2001. Maximum likelihood estimation for spatial models by markov chain monte carlo stochastic approximation. *Journal of the Royal Statistical Society: Series B (Statistical Methodology)*, 63:339–355.

Sanjeev Khudanpur and Jun Wu. 2000. Maximum entropy techniques for exploiting syntactic, semantic and collocational dependencies in language modeling. *Computer Speech & Language*, 14:355–372.

Daphne Koller and Nir Friedman. 2009. *Probabilistic graphical models: principles and techniques*. MIT press.

Faming Liang, Chuanhai Liu, and Raymond J Carroll. 2007. Stochastic approximation in monte carlo computation. *Journal of the American Statistical Association*, 102(477):305–320.

Sven Martin, Jörg Liermann, and Hermann Ney. 1998. Algorithms for bigram and trigram word clustering. *Speech Communication*, 24:19–37.

Tomas Mikolov, Stefan Kombrink, Lukas Burget, Jan H Cernocky, and Sanjeev Khudanpur. 2011. Extensions of recurrent neural network language model. In *Proc. of International Conference on Acoustics, Speech and Signal Processing (ICASSP)*.

Tomáš Mikolov. 2012. Statistical language models based on neural networks. *Ph.D. thesis, Brno University of Technology*.

Yariv Dror Mizrahi, Misha Denil, and Nando de Freitas. 2013. Linear and parallel learning of markov random fields. *arXiv preprint arXiv:1308.6342*.

Andriy Mnih and Koray Kavukcuoglu. 2013. Learning word embeddings efficiently with noise-contrastive estimation. In *Neural Information Processing Systems (NIPS)*.

Stephen Della Pietra, Vincent Della Pietra, and John Lafferty. 1997. Inducing features of random fields. *IEEE Transactions on Pattern Analysis and Machine Intelligence*, 19:380–393.

Brian Roark, Murat Saraclar, Michael Collins, and Mark Johnson. 2004. Discriminative language modeling with conditional random fields and the perceptron algorithm. In *Proceedings of the 42nd Annual Meeting on Association for Computational Linguistics (ACL)*, page 47.

Ronald Rosenfeld, Stanley F. Chen, and Xiaojin Zhu. 2001. Whole-sentence exponential language models: a vehicle for linguistic-statistical integration. *Computer Speech & Language*, 15:55–73.

Ronald Rosenfeld. 1997. A whole sentence maximum entropy language model. In *Proc. of Automatic Speech Recognition and Understanding (ASRU)*.

Teemu Ruokolainen, Tanel Alumäe, and Marcus Dobrinkat. 2010. Using dependency grammar features in whole sentence maximum entropy language model for speech recognition. In *Baltic HLT*.

Holger Schwenk. 2007. Continuous space language models. *Computer Speech & Language*, 21:492–518.

Ilya Sutskever and Geoffrey E Hinton. 2007. Learning multilevel distributed representations for high-dimensional sequences. In *International Conference on Artificial Intelligence and Statistics (AISTATS)*.

Zhiqiang Tan. 2015. Optimally adjusted mixture sampling and locally weighted histogram. In *Technical Report, Department of Statistics, Rutgers University.*

Laurent Younes. 1989. Parametric inference for imperfectly observed gibbsian fields. *Probability theory and related fields*, 82:625–645.

Gaussian LDA for Topic Models with Word Embeddings

Rajarshi Das*, Manzil Zaheer*, Chris Dyer
School of Computer Science
Carnegie Mellon University
Pittsburgh, PA, 15213, USA
{rajarshd, manzilz, cdyer} @cs.cmu.edu

Abstract

Continuous space word embeddings learned from large, unstructured corpora have been shown to be effective at capturing semantic regularities in language. In this paper we replace LDA's parameterization of "topics" as categorical distributions over opaque word types with multivariate Gaussian distributions on the embedding space. This encourages the model to group words that are *a priori* known to be semantically related into topics. To perform inference, we introduce a fast collapsed Gibbs sampling algorithm based on Cholesky decompositions of covariance matrices of the posterior predictive distributions. We further derive a scalable algorithm that draws samples from stale posterior predictive distributions and corrects them with a Metropolis–Hastings step. Using vectors learned from a domain-general corpus (English Wikipedia), we report results on two document collections (20-newsgroups and NIPS). Qualitatively, Gaussian LDA infers different (but still very sensible) topics relative to standard LDA. Quantitatively, our technique outperforms existing models at dealing with OOV words in held-out documents.

1 Introduction

Latent Dirichlet Allocation (LDA) is a Bayesian technique that is widely used for inferring the topic structure in corpora of documents. It conceives of a document as a mixture of a small number of topics, and topics as a (relatively sparse) distribution over word types (Blei et al., 2003). These priors are remarkably effective at producing useful results. However, our intuitions tell us that while documents may indeed be conceived of as a mixture of topics, we should further expect topics to be *semantically coherent*. Indeed, standard human evaluations of topic modeling performance are designed to elicit assessment of semantic coherence (Chang et al., 2009; Newman et al., 2009). However, this prior preference for semantic coherence is not encoded in the model, and any such observation of semantic coherence found in the inferred topic distributions is, in some sense, accidental. In this paper, we develop a variant of LDA that operates on continuous space embeddings of words—rather than word types—to impose a prior expectation for semantic coherence. Our approach replaces the opaque word types usually modeled in LDA with continuous space embeddings of these words, which are generated as draws from a multivariate Gaussian.

How does this capture our preference for semantic coherence? Word embeddings have been shown to capture lexico-semantic regularities in language: words with similar syntactic and semantic properties are found to be close to each other in the embedding space (Agirre et al., 2009; Mikolov et al., 2013). Since Gaussian distributions capture a notion of centrality in space, and semantically related words are localized in space, our Gaussian LDA model encodes a prior preference for semantically coherent topics. Our model further has several advantages. Traditional LDA assumes a fixed vocabulary of word types. This modeling assumption drawback as it cannot handle *out of vocabulary* (OOV) words in "held out" documents. Zhai and Boyd-Graber (2013) proposed an approach to address this problem by drawing topics from a Dirichlet Process with a base distribution over all possible character strings (i.e., words). While this model can in principle handle unseen words, the only bias toward being included in a particular topic comes from the topic assignments in the rest

*Both student authors had equal contribution.

Proceedings of the 53rd Annual Meeting of the Association for Computational Linguistics and the 7th International Joint Conference on Natural Language Processing, pages 795–804,
Beijing, China, July 26-31, 2015.

of the document. Our model can exploit the contiguity of semantically similar words in the embedding space and can assign high topic probability to a word which is similar to an existing topical word even if it has never been seen before.

The main contributions of our paper are as follows: We propose a new technique for topic modeling by treating the document as a collection of word embeddings and topics itself as multivariate Gaussian distributions in the embedding space (§3). We explore several strategies for collapsed Gibbs sampling and derive scalable algorithms, achieving asymptotic speed-up over the naïve implementation (§4). We qualitatively show that our topics make intuitive sense and quantitatively demonstrate that our model captures a better representation of a document in the topic space by outperforming other models in a classification task (§5).

2 Background

Before going to the details of our model we provide some background on two topics relevant to our work: vector space word embeddings and LDA.

2.1 Vector Space Semantics

According to the **distributional hypothesis** (Harris, 1954), words occurring in similar contexts tend to have similar meaning. This has given rise to data-driven learning of word vectors that capture lexical and semantic properties, which is now a technique of central importance in natural language processing. These word vectors can be used for identifying semantically related word pairs (Turney, 2006; Agirre et al., 2009) or as features in downstream text processing applications (Turian et al., 2010; Guo et al., 2014). Word vectors can either be constructed using low rank approximations of cooccurrence statistics (Deerwester et al., 1990) or using internal representations from neural network models of word sequences (Collobert and Weston, 2008). We use a recently popular and fast tool called `word2vec`[1], to generate skip-gram word embeddings from unlabeled corpus. In this model, a word is used as an input to a log-linear classifier with continuous projection layer and words within a certain window before and after the words are predicted.

[1] https://code.google.com/p/word2vec/

2.2 Latent Dirichlet Allocation (LDA)

LDA (Blei et al., 2003) is a probabilistic topic model of corpora of documents which seeks to represent the underlying thematic structure of the document collection. They have emerged as a powerful new technique of finding useful structure in an unstructured collection as it learns distributions over words. The high probability words in each distribution gives us a way of understanding the contents of the corpus at a very high level. In LDA, each document of the corpus is assumed to have a distribution over K topics, where the discrete topic distributions are drawn from a symmetric dirichlet distribution. The generative process is as follows.

1. for $k = 1$ to K
   (a) Choose topic $\boldsymbol{\beta}_k \sim \mathsf{Dir}(\boldsymbol{\eta})$
2. for each document d in corpus D
   (a) Choose a topic distribution $\boldsymbol{\theta}_d \sim \mathsf{Dir}(\boldsymbol{\alpha})$
   (b) for each word index n from 1 to N_d
      i. Choose a topic $z_n \sim \mathsf{Categorical}(\boldsymbol{\theta}_d)$
      ii. Choose word $w_n \sim \mathsf{Categorical}(\boldsymbol{\beta}_{z_n})$

As it follows from the definition above, a topic is a discrete distribution over a fixed vocabulary of word types. This modeling assumption precludes new words to be added to topics. However modeling topics as a continuous distribution over word embeddings gives us a way to address this problem. In the next section we describe Gaussian LDA, a straightforward extension of LDA that replaces categorical distributions over word types with multivariate Gaussian distributions over the word embedding space.

3 Gaussian LDA

As with multinomial LDA, we are interested in modeling a collection of documents. However, we assume that rather than consisting of sequences of word types, documents consist of sequences of word embeddings. We write $\mathbf{v}(w) \in \mathbb{R}^M$ as the embedding of word of type w or $\mathbf{v}_{d,i}$ when we are indexing a vector in a document d at position i.

Since our observations are no longer discrete values but continuous vectors in an M-dimensional space, we characterize each topic k as a multivariate Gaussian distribution with mean $\boldsymbol{\mu}_k$ and covariance $\boldsymbol{\Sigma}_k$. The choice of a Gaussian parameterization is justified by both analytic convenience and observations that Euclidean distances

$$p(z_{d,i} = k \mid \boldsymbol{z}_{-(d,i)}, \mathbf{V}_d, \boldsymbol{\zeta}, \boldsymbol{\alpha}) \propto (n_{k,d} + \alpha_k) \times t_{\nu_k - M+1}\left(\mathbf{v}_{d,i} \middle| \boldsymbol{\mu}_k, \frac{\kappa_k + 1}{\kappa_k}\boldsymbol{\Sigma}_k\right) \quad (1)$$

Figure 1: Sampling equation for the collapsed Gibbs sampler; refer to text for a description of the notation.

between embeddings correlate with semantic similarity (Collobert and Weston, 2008; Turney and Pantel, 2010; Hermann and Blunsom, 2014). We place conjugate priors on these values: a Gaussian centered at zero for the mean and an inverse Wishart distribution for the covariance. As before, each document is seen as a mixture of topics whose proportions are drawn from a symmetric Dirichlet prior. The generative process can thus be summarized as follows:

1. for k = 1 to K
   (a) Draw topic covariance $\boldsymbol{\Sigma}_k \sim \mathcal{W}^{-1}(\boldsymbol{\Psi}, \nu)$
   (b) Draw topic mean $\boldsymbol{\mu}_k \sim \mathcal{N}(\boldsymbol{\mu}, \frac{1}{\kappa}\boldsymbol{\Sigma}_k)$
2. for each document d in corpus D
   (a) Draw topic distribution $\boldsymbol{\theta}_d \sim \mathsf{Dir}(\boldsymbol{\alpha})$
   (b) for each word index n from 1 to N_d
      i. Draw a topic $z_n \sim \mathsf{Categorical}(\boldsymbol{\theta}_d)$
      ii. Draw $\mathbf{v}_{d,n} \sim \mathcal{N}(\boldsymbol{\mu}_{z_n}, \boldsymbol{\Sigma}_{z_n})$

This model has previously been proposed for obtaining indexing representations for audio retrieval (Hu et al., 2012). They use variational/EM method for posterior inference. Although we don't do any experiment to compare the running time of both approaches, the per-iteration computational complexity is same for both inference methods. We propose a faster inference technique using Cholesky decomposition of covariance matrices which can be applied to both the Gibbs and variational/EM method. However we are not aware of any straightforward way of applying the aliasing trick proposed by (Li et al., 2014) on the variational/EM method which gave us huge improvement on running time (see Figure 2). Another work which combines embedding with topic models is by (Wan et al., 2012) where they jointly learn the parameters of a neural network and a topic model to capture the topic distribution of low dimensional representation of images.

4 Posterior Inference

In our application, we observe documents consisting of word vectors and wish to infer the posterior distribution over the topic parameters, proportions, and the topic assignments of individual words. Since there is no analytic form of the posterior, approximations are required. Because of our choice of conjugate priors for topic parameters and proportions, these variables can be analytically integrated out, and we can derive a collapsed Gibbs sampler that resamples topic assignments to individual word vectors, similar to the collapsed sampling scheme proposed by Griffiths and Steyvers (2004).

The conditional distribution we need for sampling is shown in Figure 1. Here, $\boldsymbol{z}_{-(d,i)}$ represents the topic assignments of all word embeddings, excluding the one at i^{th} position of document d; $\mathbf{V}_d$ is the sequence of vectors for document d; $t_{\nu'}(\mathbf{x} \mid \boldsymbol{\mu}', \boldsymbol{\Sigma}')$ is the multivariate t - distribution with ν' degrees of freedom and parameters $\boldsymbol{\mu}'$ and $\boldsymbol{\Sigma}'$. The tuple $\boldsymbol{\zeta} = (\boldsymbol{\mu}, \kappa, \boldsymbol{\Sigma}, \nu)$ represents the parameters of the prior distribution.

It should be noted that the first part of the equation which expresses the probability of topic k in document d is the same as that of LDA. This is because the portion of the model which generates a topic for each word (vector) from its document topic distribution is still the same. The second part of the equation which expresses the probability of assignment of topic k to the word vector $\mathbf{v}_{d,i}$ given the current topic assignments (aka posterior predictive) is given by a multivariate t distribution with parameters $(\boldsymbol{\mu}_k, \kappa_k, \boldsymbol{\Sigma}_k, \nu_k)$. The parameters of the posterior predictive distribution are given as (Murphy, 2012):

$$\begin{aligned} \kappa_k &= \kappa + N_k & \boldsymbol{\mu}_k &= \frac{\kappa\boldsymbol{\mu} + N_k\bar{\mathbf{v}}_k}{\kappa_k} \\ \nu_k &= \nu + N_k & \boldsymbol{\Sigma}_k &= \frac{\boldsymbol{\Psi}_k}{(\nu_k - M + 1)} \\ \boldsymbol{\Psi}_k &= \boldsymbol{\Psi} + \mathbf{C}_k + \frac{\kappa N_k}{\kappa_k}(\bar{\mathbf{v}}_k - \boldsymbol{\mu})(\bar{\mathbf{v}}_k - \boldsymbol{\mu})^\top \end{aligned} \quad (2)$$

where $\bar{\mathbf{v}}_k$ and $\mathbf{C}_k$ are given by,

$$\bar{\mathbf{v}}_k = \frac{\sum_d \sum_{i:z_{d,i}=k}(\mathbf{v}_{d,i})}{N_k}$$

$$\mathbf{C}_k = \sum_d \sum_{i:z_{d,i}=k} (\mathbf{v}_{d,i} - \bar{\mathbf{v}}_k)(\mathbf{v}_{d,i} - \bar{\mathbf{v}}_k)^\top$$

Here $\bar{\mathbf{v}}_k$ is the sample mean and $\mathbf{C}_k$ is the scaled form of sample covariance of the vectors with topic assignment k. N_k represents the count of words assigned to topic k across all documents. Intuitively the parameters $\boldsymbol{\mu}_k$ and $\boldsymbol{\Sigma}_k$ represents the posterior mean and covariance of the topic distribution and κ_k, ν_k represents the strength of the prior for mean and covariance respectively.

Analysis of running time complexity

As can be seen from (1), for computation of the posterior predictive we need to evaluate the determinant and inverse of the posterior covariance matrix. Direct naïve computation of these terms require $O(M^3)$ operations. Moreover, during sampling as words get assigned to different topics, the parameters $(\boldsymbol{\mu}_k, \kappa_k, \boldsymbol{\Psi}_k, \nu_k)$ associated with a topic changes and hence we have to recompute the determinant and inverse matrix. Since these step has to be recomputed several times (as many times as number of words times number of topics in one Gibbs sweep, in the worst case), it is critical to make the process as efficient as possible. We speed up this process by employing a combination of modern computational techniques and mathematical (linear algebra) tricks, as described in the following subsections.

4.1 Faster sampling using Cholesky decomposition of covariance matrix

Having another look at the posterior equation for $\boldsymbol{\Psi}_k$, we can re-write the equation as:

$$\begin{aligned}\boldsymbol{\Psi}_k &= \boldsymbol{\Psi} + \mathbf{C}_k + \frac{\kappa N_k}{\kappa_k}(\bar{\mathbf{v}}_k - \boldsymbol{\mu})(\bar{\mathbf{v}}_k - \boldsymbol{\mu})^\top \\ &= \boldsymbol{\Psi} + \sum_d \sum_{i:z_{d,i}=k} \mathbf{v}_{d,i}\mathbf{v}_{d,i}^\top - \kappa_k \boldsymbol{\mu}_k \boldsymbol{\mu}_k^\top \\ &\quad + \kappa \boldsymbol{\mu}\boldsymbol{\mu}^\top. \end{aligned} \tag{3}$$

During sampling when we are computing the assignment probability of topic k to $\mathbf{v}_{d,i}$, we need to calculate the updated parameters of the topic. Using (3) it can be shown that $\boldsymbol{\Psi}_k$ can be updated from current value of $\boldsymbol{\Psi}_k$, after updating $\kappa_k.\nu_k$ and μ_k, as follows:

$$\boldsymbol{\Psi}_k \leftarrow \boldsymbol{\Psi}_k + \frac{\kappa_k}{\kappa_k - 1}(\boldsymbol{\mu}_k - \mathbf{v}_{d,i})(\boldsymbol{\mu}_k - \mathbf{v}_{d,i})^\top. \tag{4}$$

This equation has the form of a rank 1 update, hinting towards use of Cholesky decomposition. If we have the Cholesky decomposition of $\boldsymbol{\Psi}_k$ computed, then we have tools to update $\boldsymbol{\Psi}_k$ cheaply. Since $\boldsymbol{\Psi}_k$ and $\boldsymbol{\Sigma}_k$ are off by only a scalar factor, we can equivalently talk about $\boldsymbol{\Sigma}_k$. Equation (4) can also be understood in the following way. During sampling, when a word embedding $\mathbf{v}_{d,i}$ gets a new assignment to a topic, say k, then the new value of the topic covariance can be computed from the current one using just a rank 1 update.[2] We next describe how to exploit the Cholesky decomposition representation to speed up computations.

For sake of completeness, any symmetric $M \times M$ real matrix $\boldsymbol{\Sigma}_k$ is said to be positive definite if $\forall \mathbf{z} \in \mathbb{R}^M : \mathbf{z}^\top \boldsymbol{\Sigma}_k \mathbf{z} > 0$. The Cholesky decomposition of such a symmetric positive definite matrix $\boldsymbol{\Sigma}_k$ is nothing but its decomposition into the product of some lower triangular matrix $\mathbf{L}$ and its transpose, i.e.

$$\boldsymbol{\Sigma}_k = \mathbf{L}\mathbf{L}^\top.$$

Finding this factorization also take cubic operation. However given Cholesky decomposition of $\boldsymbol{\Sigma}_k$, after a rank 1 update (or downdate), i.e. the operation:

$$\boldsymbol{\Sigma}_k \leftarrow \boldsymbol{\Sigma}_k + \mathbf{z}\mathbf{z}^\top$$

we can find the factorization of new $\boldsymbol{\Sigma}_k$ in just quadratic time (Stewart, 1998). We will use this trick to speed up the computations[3]. Basically, instead of computing determinant and inverse again in cubic time, we will use such rank 1 update (downdate) to find new determinant and inverse in an efficient manner as explained in details below.

To compute the density of the posterior predictive $t-$distribution, we need to compute the determinant $|\boldsymbol{\Sigma}_k|$ and the term of the form $(\mathbf{v}_{d,i} - \boldsymbol{\mu}_k)^\top \boldsymbol{\Sigma}_k^{-1}(\mathbf{v}_{d,i} - \boldsymbol{\mu}_k)$. The Cholesky decomposition of the covariance matrix can be used for efficient computation of these expression as shown below.

[2]Similarly the covariance of the old topic assignment of the word w can be computed using a rank 1 downdate

[3]For our experiments, we set the prior covariance to be $3*\mathcal{I}$, which is a positive definite matrix.

Computation of determinant: The determinant of $\mathbf{\Sigma}_k$ can be computed from from its Cholesky decomposition $\mathbf{L}$ as:

$$\log(|\mathbf{\Sigma}_k|) = 2 \times \sum_{i=1}^{M} \log\left(\mathbf{L}_{i,i}\right).$$

This takes linear time in the order of dimension and is clearly a significant gain from cubic time complexity.

Computation of $(\mathbf{v}_{d,i} - \boldsymbol{\mu}_k)^\top \mathbf{\Sigma}_k^{-1}(\mathbf{v}_{d,i} - \boldsymbol{\mu})$: Let $\mathbf{b} = (\mathbf{v}_{d,i} - \boldsymbol{\mu}_k)$. Now $\mathbf{b}^\top \mathbf{\Sigma}^{-1}\mathbf{b}$ can be written as

$$\begin{aligned} \mathbf{b}^\top \mathbf{\Sigma}^{-1}\mathbf{b} &= \mathbf{b}^\top (\mathbf{L}\mathbf{L}^\top)^{-1}\mathbf{b} \\ &= \mathbf{b}^T (\mathbf{L}^{-1})^\top \mathbf{L}^{-1}\mathbf{b} \\ &= (\mathbf{L}^{-1}\mathbf{b})^\top (\mathbf{L}^{-1}\mathbf{b}) \end{aligned}$$

Now $(\mathbf{L}^{-1}\mathbf{b})$ is the solution of the equation $\mathbf{L}\mathbf{x} = \mathbf{b}$. Also since $\mathbf{L}$ is a lower triangular matrix, this equation can be solved easily using forward substitution. Lastly we will have to take an inner product of $\mathbf{x}$ and $\mathbf{x}^\top$ to get the value of $(\mathbf{v}_{d,i} - \boldsymbol{\mu}_k)^\top \mathbf{\Sigma}^{-1}(\mathbf{v}_{d,i} - \boldsymbol{\mu}_k)$. This step again takes quadratic time and is again a savings from the cubic time complexity.

4.2 Further reduction of sampling complexity using Alias Sampling

Although Cholesky trick helps us to reduce the sampling complexity of a embedding to $O(KM^2)$, it can still be impractical.In Gaussian LDA, the Gibbs sampling equation (1) can be split into two terms. The first term $n_{k,d} \times t_{\nu_k - M+1}\left(\mathbf{v}_{d,i} \,\middle|\, \boldsymbol{\mu}_k, \frac{\kappa_k+1}{\kappa_k}\mathbf{\Sigma}_k\right)$ denotes the document contribution and the second term $\alpha_k \times t_{\nu_k - M+1}\left(\mathbf{v}_{d,i} \,\middle|\, \boldsymbol{\mu}_k, \frac{\kappa_k+1}{\kappa_k}\mathbf{\Sigma}_k\right)$ denotes the language model contribution. Empirically one can make two observations about these terms. First, $n_{k,d}$ is often a sparse vector, as a document most likely contains only a few of the topics. Secondly, topic parameters (μ_k, Σ_k) captures global phenomenon, and rather change relatively slowly over the iterations. We can exploit these findings to avoid the naive approach to draw a sample from (1).

In particular, we compute the document-specific sparse term exactly and for the remainder language model term we borrow idea from (Li et al., 2014). We use a slightly stale distribution for the language model. Then Metropolis Hastings (MH) algorithm allows us to convert the stale sample into a fresh one, provided that we compute ratios between successive states correctly. It is sufficient to run MH for a few number of steps because the stale distribution acting as the proposal is very similar to the target. This is because, as pointed out earlier, the language model term does not change too drastically whenever we resample a single word. The number of words is huge, hence the amount of change per word is concomitantly small. (Only if one could convert stale bread into fresh one, it would solve world's food problem!)

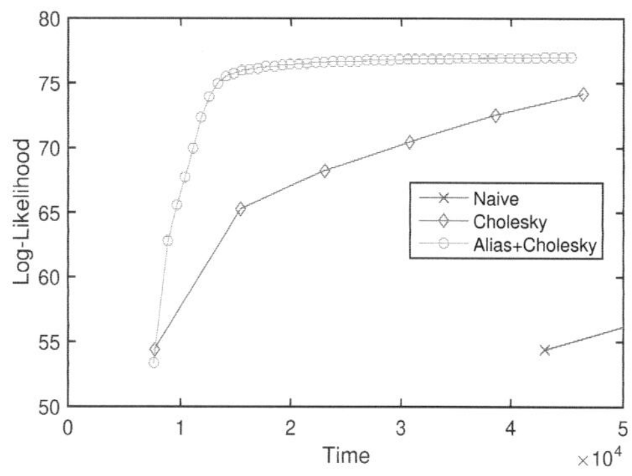

Figure 2: Plot comparing average log-likelihood vs time (in sec) achieved after applying each trick on the NIPS dataset. The shapes on each curve denote end of each iteration.

The exercise of using stale distribution and MH steps is advantageous because sampling from it can be carried out in $O(1)$ amortized time, thanks to alias sampling technique (Vose, 1991). Moreover, the task of building the alias tables can be outsourced to other cores.

With the combination of both Cholesky and Alias tricks, the sampling complexity can thus be brought down to $O(K_d M^2)$ where K_d represents the number of actually instantiated topics in the document and $K_d \ll K$. In particular, we plot the sampling rate achieved naively, with Cholesky (CH) trick and with Cholesky+Alias (A+CH) trick in figure 2 demonstrating better likelihood at much less time. Also after initial few iterations, the time per iteration of A+CH trick is 9.93 times less than CH and 53.1 times less than naive method. This is because initially we start with random initialization of words to topics, but after few iterations the $n_{k,d}$ vector starts to become sparse.

5 Experiments

In this section we evaluate our Word Vector Topic Model on various experimental tasks. Specifically we wish to determine:

- Is our model is able to find coherent and meaningful topics?
- Is our model able to infer the topic distribution of a held-out document even when the document contains words which were previously unseen?

We run our experiments[4] on two datasets 20-NEWSGROUP[5] and NIPS[6]. All the datasets were tokenized and lowercased with `cdec` (Dyer et al., 2010).

5.1 Topic Coherence

Quantitative Analysis Typically topic models are evaluated based on the likelihood of held-out documents. But in this case, it is not correct to compare perplexities with models which do topic modeling on words. Since our topics are continuous distributions, the probability of a word vector is given by its density w.r.t the normal distribution based on its topic assignment, instead of a probability mass from a discrete topic distribution. Moreover, (Chang et al., 2009) showed that higher likelihood of held-out documents doesn't necessarily correspond to human perception of topic coherence. Instead to measure topic coherence we follow (Newman et al., 2009) to compute the Pointwise Mutual Information (PMI) of topic words w.r.t wikipedia articles. We extract the document co-occurrence statistics of topic words from Wikipedia and compute the score of a topic by averaging the score of the top 15 words of the topic. A higher PMI score implies a more coherent topic as it means the topic words usually co-occur in the same document. In the last line of Table 1, we present the PMI score for some of the topics for both Gaussian LDA and traditional multinomial LDA. It can be seen that Gaussian LDA is a clear winner, achieving an average 275% higher score on average.

However, we are using embeddings trained on Wikipedia corpus itself, and the PMI measure is computed from co-occurrence in the Wikipedia corpus. As a result, our model is definitely biased towards producing higher PMI. Nevertheless Wikipedia PMI is a believed to be a good measure of semantic coherence.

Qualitative Analysis Table 1 shows some top words from topics from Gaussian-LDA and LDA on the 20-news dataset for $K = 50$. The words in Gaussian-LDA are ranked based on their density assigned to them by the posterior predictive distribution in the final sample. As shown, Gaussian LDA is able to capture several intuitive topics in the corpus such as sports, government, 'religion', 'universities', 'tech', 'finance' etc. One interesting topic discovered by our model (on both 20-news and NIPS dataset) is the collection of human names, which was not captured by classic LDA. While one might imagine that names associated with particular topics might be preferable to a 'names-in-general' topic, this ultimately is a matter of user preference. More substantively, classic LDA failed to identify the 'finance' topics. We also noticed that there were certain words ('don', 'writes', etc) which often came as a top word in many topics in classic LDA. However our model was not able to capture the 'space' topics which LDA was able to identify.

Also we visualize a part of the continuous space where the word embedding is performed. For this task we performed the Principal Component Analysis (PCA) over all the word vectors and plot the first two components as shown in Figure 3. We can see clear separations between some of the clusters of topics as depicted. The other topics would be separated in other dimensions.

5.2 Performance on document containing new words

In this experiment we evaluate the performance of our model on documents which contains previously unseen words. It should be noted that traditional topic modeling algorithms will typically ignore such words while inferring the topic distribution and hence might miss out important words. The continuous topic distributions of the Word Vector Topic Model on the other hand, will be able

[4] Our implementation is available at `https://github.com/rajarshd/Gaussian_LDA`

[5] A collection of newsgroup documents partitioned into 20 news groups. After pre-processing we had 18768 documents. We randomly selected 2000 documents as our test set. This dataset is publicly available at `http://qwone.com/~jason/20Newsgroups/`

[6] A collection of 1740 papers from the proceedings of Neural Information Processing System. The dataset is available at `http://www.cs.nyu.edu/~roweis/data.html`

Gaussian LDA topics								
hostile	play	government	people	university	hardware	scott	market	gun
murder	round	state	god	program	interface	stevens	buying	rocket
violence	win	group	jews	public	mode	graham	sector	military
victim	players	initiative	israel	law	devices	walker	purchases	force
testifying	games	board	christians	institute	rendering	tom	payments	machine
provoking	goal	legal	christian	high	renderer	russell	purchase	attack
legal	challenge	bill	great	research	user	baker	company	operation
citizens	final	general	jesus	college	computers	barry	owners	enemy
conflict	playing	policy	muslims	center	monitor	adams	paying	fire
victims	hitting	favor	religion	study	static	jones	corporate	flying
rape	match	office	armenian	reading	encryption	joe	limited	defense
laws	ball	political	armenians	technology	emulation	palmer	loans	warning
violent	advance	commission	church	programs	reverse	cooper	credit	soldiers
trial	participants	private	muslim	level	device	robinson	financing	guns
intervention	scores	federal	bible	press	target	smith	fees	operations
0.8302	0.9302	0.4943	2.0306	0.5216	2.3615	2.7660	1.4999	1.1847
Multinomial LDA topics								
turkish	year	people	god	university	window	space	ken	gun
armenian	writes	president	jesus	information	image	nasa	stuff	people
people	game	mr	people	national	color	gov	serve	law
armenians	good	don	bible	research	file	earth	line	guns
armenia	team	money	christian	center	windows	launch	attempt	don
turks	article	government	church	april	program	writes	den	state
turkey	baseball	stephanopoulos	christ	san	display	orbit	due	crime
don	don	time	christians	number	jpeg	moon	peaceful	weapons
greek	games	make	life	year	problem	satellite	article	firearms
soviet	season	clinton	time	conference	screen	article	served	police
time	runs	work	don	washington	bit	shuttle	warrant	control
genocide	players	tax	faith	california	files	lunar	lotsa	writes
government	hit	years	good	page	graphics	henry	occurred	rights
told	time	ll	man	state	gif	data	writes	article
killed	apr	ve	law	states	writes	flight	process	laws
0.3394	0.2036	0.1578	0.7561	0.0039	1.3767	1.5747	-0.0721	0.2443

Table 1: Top words of some topics from Gaussian-LDA and multinomial LDA on 20-newsgroups for $K = 50$. Words in Gaussian LDA are ranked based on density assigned to them by the posterior predictive distribution. The last row for each method indicates the PMI score (w.r.t. Wikipedia co-occurence) of the topics fifteen highest ranked words.

to assign topics to an unseen word, if we have the vector representation of the word. Given the recent development of fast and scalable methods of estimating word embeddings, it is possible to train them on huge text corpora and hence it makes our model a viable alternative for topic inference on documents with new words.

Experimental Setup: Since we want to capture the strength of our model on documents containing unseen words, we select a subset of documents and replace words of those documents by its synonyms if they haven't occurred in the corpus before. We obtain the synonym of a word using two existing resources and hence we create two such datasets. For the first set, we use the Paraphrase Database (Ganitkevitch et al., 2013) to get the lexical paraphrase of a word. The paraphrase database[7] is a semantic lexicon containing around 169 million paraphrase pairs of which 7.6 million are lexical (one word to one word) paraphrases. The dataset comes in varying size ranges starting from S to XXXL in increasing order of size and decreasing order of paraphrasing confidence. For our experiments we selected the L size of the paraphrase database.

The second set was obtained using WordNet (Miller, 1995), a large human annotated lexicon for English that groups words into sets of synonyms called synsets. To obtain the synonym of a word, we first label the words with their part-of-speech using the Stanford POS tagger (Toutanova et al., 2003). Then we use the WordNet database

[7] http://www.cis.upenn.edu/~ccb/ppdb/

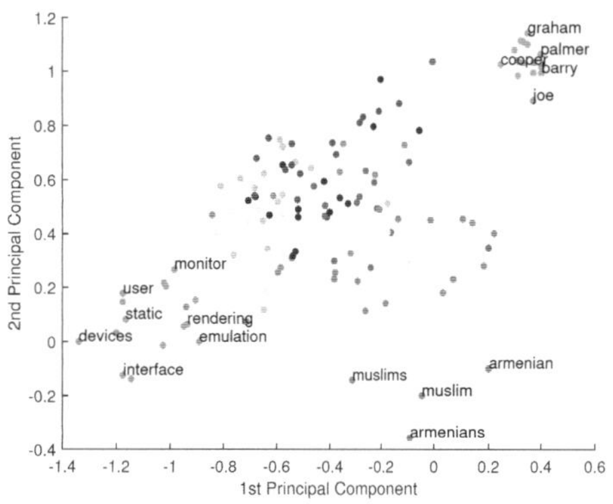

Figure 3: The first two principal components for the word embeddings of the top words of topics shown in Table 1 have been visualized. Each blob represents a word color coded according to its topic in the Table 1.

to get the synonym from its sysnset.[8] We select the first synonym from the synset which hasn't occurred in the corpus before. On the 20-news dataset (vocab size = 18,179 words, test corpus size = 188,694 words), a total of 21,919 words (2,741 distinct words) were replaced by synonyms from PPDB and 38,687 words (2,037 distinct words) were replaced by synonyms from Wordnet.

Evaluation Benchmark: As mentioned before traditional topic model algorithms cannot handle OOV words. So comparing the performance of our document with those models would be unfair. Recently (Zhai and Boyd-Graber, 2013) proposed an extension of LDA (*infvoc*) which can incorporate new words. They have shown better performances in a document classification task which uses the topic distribution of a document as features on the 20-news group dataset as compared to other fixed vocabulary algorithms. Even though, the *infvoc* model can handle OOV words, it will most likely not assign high probability to a new topical word when it encounters it for the first time since it is directly proportional to the number of times the word has been observed On the other hand, our model could assign high probability to the word if its corresponding embedding gets a high probability from one of the topic gaussians. With the experimental setup mentioned before, we want to evaluate performance of this property of our model. Using the topic distribution of a document as features, we try to classify the document into one of the 20 news groups it belongs to. If the document topic distribution is modeled well, then our model should be able to do a better job in the classification task.

To infer the topic distribution of a document we follow the usual strategy of fixing the learnt topics during the training phase and then running Gibbs sampling on the test set (G-LDA (*fix*) in table 2). However *infvoc* is an online algorithm, so it would be unfair to compare our model which observes the entire set of documents during test time. Therefore we implement the online version of our algorithm using Gibbs sampling following (Yao et al., 2009). We input the test documents in batches and do inference on those batches independently also sampling for the topic parameter, along the lines of *infvoc*. The batch size for our experiments are mentioned in parentheses in table 2. We classify using the multi class logistic regression classifier available in `Weka` (Hall et al., 2009).

It is clear from table 2 that we outperform *infvoc* in all settings of our experiments. This implies that even if new documents have significant amount of new words, our model would still do a better job in modeling it. We also conduct an experiment to check the actual difference between the topic distribution of the original and synthetic documents. Let h and h' denote the topic vectors of the original and synthetic documents. Table 3 shows the average l_1, l_2 and l_∞ norm of $(h - h')$ of the test documents in the NIPS dataset. A low value of these metrics indicates higher similarity. As shown in the table, Gaussian LDA performs better here too.

6 Conclusion and Future Work

While word embeddings have been incorporated to produce state-of-the-art results in numerous supervised natural language processing tasks from the word level to document level ; however, they have played a more minor role in unsupervised learning problems. This work shows some of the promise that they hold in this domain. Our model can be extended in a number of potentially useful, but straightforward ways. First, DPMM models of word emissions would better model the fact that identical vectors will be generated multiple times, and perhaps add flexibility to the topic distributions that can be captured, without sacrificing our

[8] We use the `JWI` toolkit (Finlayson, 2014)

Model	Accuracy	
	PPDB	WordNet
infvoc	28.00%	19.30%
G-LDA (*fix*)	44.51%	43.53%
G-LDA (*1*)	44.66%	43.47%
G-LDA (*100*)	43.63%	43.11%
G-LDA (*1932*)	44.72%	42.90%

Table 2: Accuracy of our model and *infvoc* on the synthetic datasets. In Gaussian LDA *fix*, the topic distributions learnt during training were fixed; G-LDA(*1, 100, 1932*) is the online implementation of our model where the documents comes in mini-batches. The number in parenthesis denote the size of the batch. The full size of the test corpus is 1932.

Model	PPDB (Mean Deviation)		
	L_1	L_2	L_∞
infvoc	94.95	7.98	1.72
G-LDA (*fix*)	15.13	1.81	0.66
G-LDA (*1*)	15.71	1.90	0.66
G-LDA (*10*)	15.76	1.97	0.66
G-LDA (*174*)	14.58	1.66	0.66

Table 3: This table shows the Average L_1 Deviation, Average L_2 Deviation, Average L_∞ Deviation for the difference of the topic distribution of the actual document and the synthetic document on the NIPS corpus. Compared to *infvoc*, G-LDA achieves a lower deviation of topic distribution inferred on the synthetic documents with respect to actual document. The full size of the test corpus is 174.

preference for topical coherence. More broadly still, running LDA on documents consisting of different modalities than just text is facilitated by using the *lingua franca* of vector space representations, so we expect numerous interesting applications in this area. An interesting extension to our work would be the ability to handle polysemous words based on multi-prototype vector space models (Neelakantan et al., 2014; Reisinger and Mooney, 2010) and we keep this as an avenue for future research.

Acknowledgments

We thank the anonymous reviewers and Manaal Faruqui for helpful comments and feedback.

References

Eneko Agirre, Enrique Alfonseca, Keith Hall, Jana Kravalova, Marius Paşca, and Aitor Soroa. 2009. A study on similarity and relatedness using distributional and wordnet-based approaches. In *Proceedings of NAACL*.

David M. Blei, Andrew Y. Ng, and Michael I. Jordan. 2003. Latent dirichlet allocation. *J. Mach. Learn. Res.*, 3:993–1022, March.

Jonathan Chang, Jordan Boyd-Graber, Chong Wang, Sean Gerrish, and David M. Blei. 2009. Reading tea leaves: How humans interpret topic models. In *Neural Information Processing Systems*.

Ronan Collobert and Jason Weston. 2008. A unified architecture for natural language processing: deep neural networks with multitask learning. In *Proceedings of ICML*.

S. C. Deerwester, S. T. Dumais, T. K. Landauer, G. W. Furnas, and R. A. Harshman. 1990. Indexing by latent semantic analysis. *Journal of the American Society for Information Science*.

Chris Dyer, Adam Lopez, Juri Ganitkevitch, Johnathan Weese, Ferhan Ture, Phil Blunsom, Hendra Setiawan, Vladimir Eidelman, and Philip Resnik. 2010. cdec: A decoder, alignment, and learning framework for finite-state and context-free translation models. In *Proceedings of ACL*.

Mark Finlayson, 2014. *Proceedings of the Seventh Global Wordnet Conference*, chapter Java Libraries for Accessing the Princeton Wordnet: Comparison and Evaluation, pages 78–85.

Juri Ganitkevitch, Benjamin Van Durme, and Chris Callison-Burch. 2013. PPDB: The paraphrase database. In *Proceedings of NAACL-HLT*, pages 758–764, Atlanta, Georgia, June. Association for Computational Linguistics.

T. L. Griffiths and M. Steyvers. 2004. Finding scientific topics. *Proceedings of the National Academy of Sciences*, 101:5228–5235, April.

Jiang Guo, Wanxiang Che, Haifeng Wang, and Ting Liu. 2014. Revisiting embedding features for simple semi-supervised learning. In *Proceedings of EMNLP*.

Mark Hall, Eibe Frank, Geoffrey Holmes, Bernhard Pfahringer, Peter Reutemann, and Ian H. Witten. 2009. The weka data mining software: An update. *SIGKDD Explor. Newsl.*, 11(1):10–18, November.

Zellig Harris. 1954. Distributional structure. *Word*, 10(23):146–162.

Karl Moritz Hermann and Phil Blunsom. 2014. Multilingual models for compositional distributed semantics. *arXiv preprint arXiv:1404.4641*.

Pengfei Hu, Wenju Liu, Wei Jiang, and Zhanlei Yang. 2012. Latent topic model based on Gaussian-LDA for audio retrieval. In *Pattern Recognition*, volume 321 of *CCIS*, pages 556–563. Springer.

Aaron Q. Li, Amr Ahmed, Sujith Ravi, and Alexander J. Smola. 2014. Reducing the sampling complexity of topic models. In *Proceedings of the 20th ACM SIGKDD International Conference on Knowledge Discovery and Data Mining*, KDD '14.

Tomas Mikolov, Wen-tau Yih, and Geoffrey Zweig. 2013. Linguistic regularities in continuous space word representations. In *Proceedings of the 2013 Conference of the North American Chapter of the Association for Computational Linguistics: Human Language Technologies*, pages 746–751, Atlanta, Georgia, June. Association for Computational Linguistics.

George A. Miller. 1995. Wordnet: A lexical database for english. *Commun. ACM*, 38(11):39–41, November.

Kevin P. Murphy. 2012. *Machine Learning: A Probabilistic Perspective*. The MIT Press.

Arvind Neelakantan, Jeevan Shankar, Alexandre Passos, and Andrew McCallum. 2014. Efficient non-parametric estimation of multiple embeddings per word in vector space. In *Proceedings of the 2014 Conference on Empirical Methods in Natural Language Processing, EMNLP 2014, October 25-29, 2014, Doha, Qatar, A meeting of SIGDAT, a Special Interest Group of the ACL*.

David Newman, Sarvnaz Karimi, and Lawrence Cavedon. 2009. External evaluation of topic models. pages 11–18, December.

Joseph Reisinger and Raymond J. Mooney. 2010. Multi-prototype vector-space models of word meaning. In *Human Language Technologies: The 2010 Annual Conference of the North American Chapter of the Association for Computational Linguistics*, HLT '10.

G. Stewart. 1998. *Matrix Algorithms*. Society for Industrial and Applied Mathematics.

Kristina Toutanova, Dan Klein, Christopher D. Manning, and Yoram Singer. 2003. Feature-rich part-of-speech tagging with a cyclic dependency network. In *Proceedings of the 2003 Conference of the North American Chapter of the Association for Computational Linguistics on Human Language Technology - Volume 1*, NAACL '03, pages 173–180, Stroudsburg, PA, USA. Association for Computational Linguistics.

Joseph Turian, Lev Ratinov, and Yoshua Bengio. 2010. Word representations: a simple and general method for semi-supervised learning. In *Proc. of ACL*.

Peter D. Turney and Patrick Pantel. 2010. From frequency to meaning : Vector space models of semantics. *JAIR*, pages 141–188.

Peter D. Turney. 2006. Similarity of semantic relations. *Comput. Linguist.*, 32(3):379–416, September.

Michael D. Vose. 1991. A linear algorithm for generating random numbers with a given distribution. *Software Engineering, IEEE Transactions on*.

Li Wan, Leo Zhu, and Rob Fergus. 2012. A hybrid neural network-latent topic model. In Neil D. Lawrence and Mark A. Girolami, editors, *Proceedings of the Fifteenth International Conference on Artificial Intelligence and Statistics (AISTATS-12)*, volume 22, pages 1287–1294.

Limin Yao, David Mimno, and Andrew McCallum. 2009. Efficient methods for topic model inference on streaming document collections. In *Proceedings of the 15th ACM SIGKDD International Conference on Knowledge Discovery and Data Mining*, KDD '09, pages 937–946, New York, NY, USA. ACM.

Ke Zhai and Jordan L. Boyd-Graber. 2013. Online latent dirichlet allocation with infinite vocabulary. In *ICML (1)*, volume 28 of *JMLR Proceedings*, pages 561–569. JMLR.org.

Pairwise Neural Machine Translation Evaluation

Francisco Guzmán **Shafiq Joty** **Lluís Màrquez** and **Preslav Nakov**
ALT Research Group
Qatar Computing Research Institute — HBKU, Qatar Foundation
{fguzman,sjoty,lmarquez,pnakov}@qf.org.qa

Abstract

We present a novel framework for machine translation evaluation using neural networks in a pairwise setting, where the goal is to select the better translation from a pair of hypotheses, given the reference translation. In this framework, lexical, syntactic and semantic information from the reference and the two hypotheses is compacted into relatively small distributed vector representations, and fed into a multi-layer neural network that models the interaction between each of the hypotheses and the reference, as well as between the two hypotheses. These compact representations are in turn based on word and sentence embeddings, which are learned using neural networks. The framework is flexible, allows for efficient learning and classification, and yields correlation with humans that rivals the state of the art.

1 Introduction

Automatic machine translation (MT) evaluation is a necessary step when developing or comparing MT systems. *Reference*-based MT evaluation, i.e., comparing the system output to one or more human reference translations, is the most common approach. Existing MT evaluation measures typically output an absolute quality score by computing the similarity between the machine and the human translations. In the simplest case, the similarity is computed by counting word n-gram matches between the translation and the reference. This is the case of BLEU (Papineni et al., 2002), which has been the standard for MT evaluation for years. Nonetheless, more recent evaluation measures take into account various aspects of linguistic similarity, and achieve better correlation with human judgments.

Having absolute quality scores at the sentence level allows to rank alternative translations for a given source sentence. This is useful, for instance, for statistical machine translation (SMT) parameter tuning, for system comparison, and for assessing the progress during MT system development. The quality of automatic MT evaluation metrics is usually assessed by computing their correlation with human judgments. To that end, quality rankings of alternative translations have been created by human judges. It is known that assigning an absolute score to a translation is a difficult task for humans. Hence, ranking-based evaluations, where judges are asked to rank the output of 2 to 5 systems, have been used in recent years, which has yielded much higher inter-annotator agreement (Callison-Burch et al., 2007).

These human quality judgments can be used to train automatic metrics. This supervised learning can be oriented to predict absolute scores, e.g., using regression (Albrecht and Hwa, 2008), or rankings (Duh, 2008; Song and Cohn, 2011). A particular case of the latter is used to learn in a pairwise setting, i.e., given a reference and two alternative translations (or hypotheses), the task is to decide which one is better. This setting emulates closely how human judges perform evaluation assessments in reality, and can be used to produce rankings for an arbitrarily large number of hypotheses. In this pairwise setting, the challenge is to learn, from a pair of hypotheses, which are the features that help to discriminate the better from the worse translation. Although the pairwise setting does not produce absolute quality scores (i.e., it is not an evaluation metric applicable to a single translation), it is useful and arguably sufficient for most evaluation and MT development scenarios.[1]

[1] We do not argue that the pairwise approach is better than the direct estimation of human quality scores. Both approaches have pros and cons; we see them as complementary.

Proceedings of the 53rd Annual Meeting of the Association for Computational Linguistics and the 7th International Joint Conference on Natural Language Processing, pages 805–814,
Beijing, China, July 26-31, 2015.

Recently, Guzmán et al. (2014a) presented a learning framework for this pairwise setting, based on preference kernels and support vector machines (SVM). They obtained promising results using syntactic and discourse-based structures. However, using convolution kernels over complex structures comes at a high computational cost both at training and at testing time because the use of kernels requires that the SVM operate in the much slower dual space. Thus, some simplification is needed to make it practical. While there are some solutions in the kernel-based learning framework to alleviate the computational burden, in this paper we explore an entirely different direction.

We present a novel neural-based architecture for learning in the pairwise setting for MT evaluation. Lexical, syntactic and semantic information from the reference and the two hypotheses is compacted into relatively small distributed vector representations and fed into the input layer, together with a set of individual real-valued features coming from simple pre-existing MT evaluation metrics. A hidden layer, motivated by our intuitions on the pairwise ranking problem, is used to capture interactions between the relevant input components. Finally, we present a task-oriented cost function, specifically tailored for this problem.

Our evaluation results on the *WMT12 metrics task* benchmark datasets (Callison-Burch et al., 2012) show very high correlation with human judgments. These results clearly surpass (Guzmán et al., 2014a) and are comparable to the best previously reported results for this dataset, achieved by DiscoTK (Joty et al., 2014), which is a much heavier combination-based metric.

Another advantage of the proposed architecture is efficiency. Due to the vector-based compression of the linguistic structure and the relatively reduced size of the network, testing is fast, which would greatly facilitate the practical use of this approach in real MT evaluation and development. Finally, we empirically show that syntactically- and semantically-oriented embeddings can be incorporated to produce sizeable and cumulative gains in performance over a strong combination of pre-existing MT evaluation measures (BLEU, NIST, METEOR, and TER). This is promising evidence towards our longer-term goal of defining a general platform for integrating varied linguistic information and for producing more informed MT evaluation measures.

2 Related Work

Contemporary MT evaluation measures have evolved beyond simple lexical matching, and now take into account various aspects of linguistic structures, including synonymy and paraphrasing (Lavie and Denkowski, 2009), syntax (Giménez and Màrquez, 2007; Popović and Ney, 2007; Liu and Gildea, 2005), semantics (Giménez and Màrquez, 2007; Lo et al., 2012), and even discourse (Comelles et al., 2010; Wong and Kit, 2012; Guzmán et al., 2014b; Joty et al., 2014). The combination of several of these aspects has led to improved results in metric evaluation campaigns, such as the *WMT metrics task* (Bojar et al., 2014).

In this paper, we present a general framework for learning to rank translations in the pairwise setting, using information from several linguistic representations of the translations and references. This work has connections with the ranking-based approaches for learning to reproduce human judgments of MT quality. In particular, our setting is similar to that of Duh (2008), but differs from it both in terms of the feature representation and of the learning framework. For instance, we integrate several layers of linguistic information, while Duh (2008) only used lexical and POS matches as features. Secondly, we use information about both the reference and the two alternative translations simultaneously in a neural-based learning framework capable of modeling complex interactions between the features.

Another related work is that of Kulesza and Shieber (2004), in which lexical and syntactic features, together with other metrics, e.g., BLEU and NIST, are used in an SVM classifier to discriminate good from bad translations. However, their setting is not pairwise comparison, but a classification task to distinguish *human-* from *machine-produced* translations. Moreover, in their work, using syntactic features decreased the correlation with human judgments dramatically (although classification accuracy improved), while in our case the effect is positive.

In our previous work (Guzmán et al., 2014a), we introduced a learning framework for the pairwise setting, based on preference kernels and SVMs. We used lexical, POS, syntactic and discourse-based information in the form of tree-like structures to learn to differentiate better from worse translations.

However, in that work we used convolution kernels, which is computationally expensive and does not scale well to large datasets and complex structures such as graphs and enriched trees. This inefficiency arises both at training and testing time. Thus, here we use neural embeddings and multilayer neural networks, which yields an efficient learning framework that works significantly better on the same datasets (although we are not using exactly the same information for learning).

To the best of our knowledge, the application of structured neural embeddings and a neural network learning architecture for MT evaluation is completely novel. This is despite the growing interest in recent years for deep neural nets (NNs) and word embeddings with application to a myriad of NLP problems. For example, in SMT we have observed an increased use of neural nets for language modeling (Bengio et al., 2003; Mikolov et al., 2010) as well as for improving the translation model (Devlin et al., 2014; Sutskever et al., 2014).

Deep learning has spread beyond language modeling. For example, recursive NNs have been used for syntactic parsing (Socher et al., 2013a) and sentiment analysis (Socher et al., 2013b). The increased use of NNs by the NLP community is in part due to *(i)* the emergence of tools such as word2vec (Mikolov et al., 2013a) and GloVe (Pennington et al., 2014), which have enabled NLP researchers to learn word embeddings, and *(ii)* unified learning frameworks, e.g., (Collobert et al., 2011), which cover a variety of NLP tasks such as part-of-speech tagging, chunking, named entity recognition, and semantic role labeling.

While in this work we make use of widely available pre-computed structured embeddings, the novelty of our work goes beyond the type of information considered as input, and resides on the way it is integrated to a neural network architecture that is inspired by our intuitions about MT evaluation.

3 Neural Ranking Model

Our motivation for using neural networks for MT evaluation is twofold. First, to take advantage of their ability to model complex non-linear relationships efficiently. Second, to have a framework that allows for easy incorporation of rich syntactic and semantic representations captured by word embeddings, which are in turn learned using deep learning.

3.1 Learning Task

Given two translation hypotheses t_1 and t_2 (and a reference translation r), we want to tell which of the two is better.[2] Thus, we have a binary classification task, which is modeled by the class variable y, defined as follows:

$$y = \begin{cases} 1 & \text{if } t_1 \text{ is better than } t_2 \text{ given } r \\ 0 & \text{if } t_1 \text{ is worse than } t_2 \text{ given } r \end{cases} \tag{1}$$

We model this task using a feed-forward neural network (NN) of the form:

$$p(y|t_1, t_2, r) = \text{Ber}(y|f(t_1, t_2, r)) \tag{2}$$

which is a Bernoulli distribution of y with parameter $\sigma = f(t_1, t_2, r)$, defined as follows:

$$f(t_1, t_2, r) = \text{sig}(\mathbf{w_v^T} \phi(t_1, t_2, r) + b_v) \tag{3}$$

where sig is the sigmoid function, $\phi(x)$ defines the transformations of the input x through the hidden layer, $\mathbf{w_v}$ are the weights from the hidden layer to the output layer, and b_v is a bias term.

3.2 Network Architecture

In order to decide which hypothesis is *better* given the tuple (t_1, t_2, r) as input, we first map the hypotheses and the reference to a fixed-length vector $[\mathbf{x}_{t_1}, \mathbf{x}_{t_2}, \mathbf{x}_r]$, using syntactic and semantic embeddings. Then, we feed this vector as input to our neural network, whose architecture is shown in Figure 1.

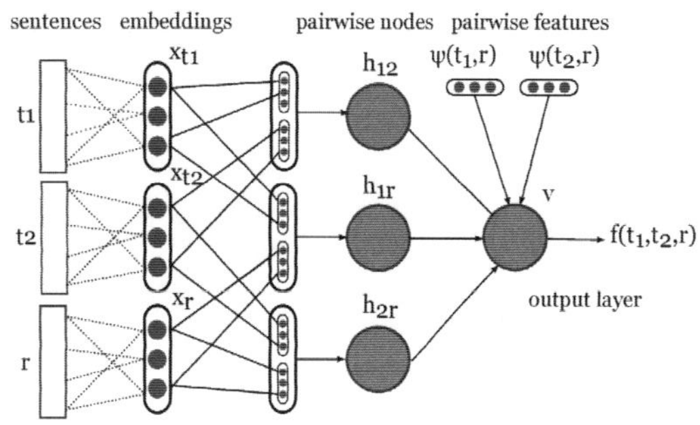

Figure 1: Overall architecture of the neural network.

In our architecture, we model three types of interactions, using different groups of nodes in the hidden layer. We have two *evaluation* groups $\mathbf{h_{1r}}$ and $\mathbf{h_{2r}}$ that model how similar each hypothesis t_i is to the reference r.

[2]In this work, we do not learn to predict ties, and ties are excluded from our training data.

The vector representations of the hypothesis (i.e., $\mathbf{x}_{t1}$ or $\mathbf{x}_{t2}$) together with the reference (i.e., $\mathbf{x}_r$) constitute the input to the hidden nodes in these two groups. The third group of hidden nodes $\mathbf{h_{12}}$, which we call *similarity* group, models how close t_1 and t_2 are. This might be useful as highly similar hypotheses are likely to be comparable in quality, irrespective of whether they are good or bad in absolute terms.

The input to each of these groups is represented by concatenating the vector representations of the two components participating in the interaction, i.e., $\mathbf{x_{1r}} = [\mathbf{x}_{t_1}, \mathbf{x}_r]$, $\mathbf{x_{2r}} = [\mathbf{x}_{t_2}, \mathbf{x}_r]$, $\mathbf{x_{12}} = [\mathbf{x}_{t_1}, \mathbf{x}_{t_2}]$. In summary, the transformation $\phi(t_1, t_2, r) = [\mathbf{h_{12}}, \mathbf{h_{1r}}, \mathbf{h_{2r}}]$ in our NN architecture can be written as follows:

$$\begin{aligned} \mathbf{h_{1r}} &= g(\mathbf{W_{1r}} \mathbf{x_{1r}} + \mathbf{b_{1r}}) \\ \mathbf{h_{2r}} &= g(\mathbf{W_{2r}} \mathbf{x_{2r}} + \mathbf{b_{2r}}) \\ \mathbf{h_{12}} &= g(\mathbf{W_{12}} \mathbf{x_{12}} + \mathbf{b_{12}}) \end{aligned}$$

where $g(.)$ is a non-linear activation function (applied component-wise), $\mathbf{W} \in \mathbb{R}^{H \times N}$ are the associated weights between the input layer and the hidden layer, and $\mathbf{b}$ are the corresponding bias terms. In our experiments, we used $\tanh$ as an activation function, rather than sig, to be consistent with how parts of our input vectors were generated.[3]

In addition, our model allows to incorporate external sources of information by enabling *skip arcs* that go directly from the input to the output, skipping the hidden layer. In our setting, these arcs represent pairwise similarity features between the translation hypotheses and the reference (e.g., the BLEU scores of the translations). We denote these pairwise external feature sets as $\psi_{1r} = \psi(t_1, r)$ and $\psi_{2r} = \psi(t_2, r)$. When we include the external features in our architecture, the activation at the output, i.e., eq. (3), can be rewritten as follows:

$$f(t_1, t_2, r) = \text{sig}(\mathbf{w_v^T}[\phi(t_1, t_2, r), \psi_{1r}, \psi_{2r}] + b_v)$$

3.3 Network Training

The negative log likelihood of the training data for the model parameters $\theta = (\mathbf{W_{12}}, \mathbf{W_{1r}}, \mathbf{W_{2r}}, \mathbf{w_v}, \mathbf{b_{12}}, \mathbf{b_{1r}}, \mathbf{b_{2r}}, b_v)$ can be written as follows:

$$J_\theta = -\sum_n y_n \log \hat{y}_{n\theta} + (1 - y_n) \log (1 - \hat{y}_{n\theta}) \tag{4}$$

[3]Many of our input representations consist of word embeddings trained with neural networks that used tanh as an activation function.

In the above formula, $\hat{y}_{n\theta} = f_n(t_1, t_2, r)$ is the activation at the output layer for the n-th data instance. It is also common to use a regularized cost function by adding a weight decay penalty (e.g., L_2 or L_1 regularization) and to perform maximum aposteriori (MAP) estimation of the parameters. We trained our network with stochastic gradient descent (SGD), mini-batches and adagrad updates (Duchi et al., 2011), using Theano (Bergstra et al., 2010).

4 Experimental Setup

In this section, we describe the different aspects of our general experimental setup (we will discuss some extensions thereof in Section 6), starting with a description of the input representations we use to capture the syntactic and semantic characteristics of the two hypothesis translations and the corresponding reference, as well as the datasets used to evaluate the performance of our model.

4.1 Word Embedding Vectors

Word embeddings play a crucial role in our model, since they allow us to model complex relations between the translations and the reference using syntactic and semantic vector representations.

Syntactic vectors. We generate a syntactic vector for each sentence using the Stanford neural parser (Socher et al., 2013a), which generates a 25-dimensional vector as a by-product of syntactic parsing using a recursive NN. Below we will refer to these vectors as SYNTAX25.

Semantic vectors. We compose a semantic vector for a given sentence using the average of the embedding vectors for the words it contains (Mitchell and Lapata, 2010). We use pre-trained, fixed-length word embedding vectors produced by (*i*) GloVe (Pennington et al., 2014), (*ii*) COMPOSES (Baroni et al., 2014), and (*iii*) word2vec (Mikolov et al., 2013b).

Our primary representation is based on 50-dimensional GloVe vectors, trained on Wikipedia 2014+Gigaword 5 (6B tokens), to which below we will refer as WIKI-GW25.

Furthermore, we experiment with WIKI-GW300, the 300-dimensional GloVe vectors trained on the same data, as well as with the CC-300-42B and CC-300-840B, 300-dimensional GloVe vectors trained on 42B and on 840B tokens from Common Crawl.

We also experiment with the pre-trained, 300-dimensional word2vec embedding vectors, or WORD2VEC300, trained on 100B words from Google News. Finally, we use COMPOSES400, the 400-dimensional COMPOSES vectors trained on 2.8 billion tokens from ukWaC, the English Wikipedia, and the British National Corpus.

4.2 Tuning and Evaluation Datasets

We experiment with datasets of segment-level human rankings of system outputs from the WMT11, WMT12 and WMT13 Metrics shared tasks (Callison-Burch et al., 2011; Callison-Burch et al., 2012; Macháček and Bojar, 2013). We focus on translating into English, for which the WMT11 and WMT12 datasets can be split by source language: Czech (cs), German (de), Spanish (es), and French (fr); WMT13 also has Russian (ru).

4.3 Evaluation Score

We evaluate our metrics in terms of correlation with human judgments measured using Kendall's τ. We report τ for the individual languages as well as macro-averaged across all languages.

Note that there were different versions of τ at WMT over the years. Prior to 2013, WMT used a strict version, which was later relaxed at WMT13 and further revised at WMT14. See (Macháček and Bojar, 2014) for a discussion. Here we use the strict version used at WMT11 and WMT12.

4.4 Experimental Settings

Datasets: We train our neural models on WMT11 and we evaluate them on WMT12. We further use a random subset of 5,000 examples from WMT13 as a validation set to implement early stopping.
Early stopping: We train on WMT11 for up to 10,000 epochs, and we calculate Kendall's τ on the development set after each epoch. We then select the model that achieves the highest τ on the validation set; in case of ties for the best τ, we select the latest epoch that achieved the highest τ.
Network parameters: We train our neural network using SGD with adagrad, an initial learning rate of $\eta = 0.01$, mini-batches of size 30, and L_2 regularization with a decay parameter $\lambda = 1e^{-4}$. We initialize the weights for our matrices by sampling from a uniform distribution following (Bengio and Glorot, 2010). We further set the size of each of our pairwise hidden layers H to four nodes, and we normalize the input data using min-max to map the feature values to the range $[-1, 1]$.

5 Experiments and Results

The main findings of our experiments are shown in Table 1. Section I of Table 1 shows the results for four commonly-used metrics for MT evaluation that compare a translation hypothesis to the reference(s) using primarily lexical information like word and n-gram overlap (even though some allow paraphrases): BLEU, NIST, TER, and METEOR (Papineni et al., 2002; Doddington, 2002; Snover et al., 2006; Denkowski and Lavie, 2011). We will refer to the set of these four metrics as 4METRICS. These metrics are not tuned and achieve Kendall's τ between 18.5 and 23.5.

Section II of Table 1 shows the results for multi-layer neural networks trained on vectors from word embeddings only: SYNTAX25 and WIKI-GW25. These networks achieve modest τ values around 10, which should not be surprising: they use very general vector representations and have no access to word or n-gram overlap or to length information, which are very important features to compute similarity against the reference. However, as will be discussed below, their contribution is complementary to the four previous evaluation metrics and will lead to significant improvements in combination with them.

Section III of Table 1 shows the results for neural networks that combine the four metrics from 4METRICS with SYNTAX25 and WIKI-GW25. We can see that just combining the four metrics in a flat neural net (i.e., no hidden layer), which is equivalent to a logistic regression, yields a τ of 27.06, which is better than the best of the four metrics by 3.5 points absolute, and also better by over 1.5 points absolute than the best metric that participated at the WMT12 metrics task competition (SPEDE07PP with $\tau = 25.4$). Indeed, 4METRICS is a strong mix that involves not only simple lexical overlap but also approximate matching, paraphrases, edit distance, lengths, etc. Yet, adding to 4METRICS the embedding vectors yields sizeable further improvements: +1.5 and +2.0 points absolute when adding SYNTAX25 and WIKI-GW25, respectively. Finally, adding both yields even further improvements close to τ of 30 (+2.64 τ points), showing that lexical semantics and syntactic representations are complementary.

Section IV of Table 1 puts these numbers in perspective: it lists the τ for the top three systems that participated at WMT12, whose scores ranged between 22.9 and 25.4.

	System	Details	Kendall's τ				
I	**4METRICS: commonly-used individual metrics**		**cz**	**de**	**es**	**fr**	**AVG**
	BLEU	no learning	15.88	18.56	18.57	20.83	18.46
	NIST	no learning	19.66	23.09	20.41	22.21	21.34
	TER	no learning	17.80	25.31	22.86	21.05	21.75
	METEOR	no learning	20.82	26.79	23.81	22.93	23.59
II	**NN using embedding vectors: syntactic & semantic**						
	SYNTAX25	multi-layer NN	8.00	13.03	12.11	7.42	10.14
	WIKI-GW25	multi-layer NN	14.31	11.49	9.24	4.99	10.01
III	**NN using 4METRICS+ embedding vectors**						
	4METRICS	logistic regression	23.46	29.95	27.49	27.36	27.06
	4METRICS+SYNTAX25	multi-layer NN	26.09	30.58	29.30	28.07	28.51
	4METRICS+WIKI-GW25	multi-layer NN	25.67	32.50	29.21	28.92	29.07
	4METRICS+SYNTAX25+WIKI-GW25	multi-layer NN	26.30	33.19	30.38	28.92	**29.70**
IV	**Comparison to previous results on WMT12**						
	DiscoTK (Joty et al., 2014)	Best on the WMT12 dataset	*na*	*na*	*na*	*na*	30.5
	SPEDE07PP	1st at the WMT12 competition	21.2	27.8	26.5	26.0	25.4
	METEOR*	2nd at WMT12 the competition	21.2	27.5	24.9	25.1	24.7
	(Guzmán et al., 2014a)	Preference kernel approach	23.1	25.8	22.6	23.2	23.7
	AMBER	3rd at the WMT12 competition	19.1	24.8	23.1	24.5	22.9

Table 1: Kendall's tau (τ) on the WMT12 dataset for various metrics. Notes: (*i*) the version of METEOR that took part in the WMT12 competition (marked with * in section IV of the table) is different from the one used in our experiments (section I of the table), (*ii*) values marked as *na* were not reported by the authors.

We can see that 4METRICS is much stronger than the winner at WMT12, and thus arguably a baseline hard to improve upon. While our results are slightly behind those of DiscoTK (Joty et al., 2014), we should note that we only combine four metrics, plus the vectors, while DiscoTK combines over 20 metrics, many of which are costly to compute.

On the other hand, we work in a ranking framework, i.e., we are not interested in producing an absolute score, but in making pairwise decisions only. Mapping these pairwise decisions into an absolute score is challenging and in our experiments it leads to a slight drop in τ (results omitted here to save space).

The only other result on WMT12 by authors working with our pairwise framework is our own previous work (Guzmán et al., 2014a), where we used a preference kernel approach to combine syntactic and discourse trees with lexical information; as we can see, our earlier results are 6 absolute points lower than those we achieve here. Moreover, our NN approach offers advantages over SVMs in terms of computational cost.

Based on these results, we can conclude that word embeddings, whether syntactic or semantic, offer generalizations that efficiently complement very strong metric combinations, and thus should be considered when designing future MT evaluation metrics.

6 Discussion

In this section, we explore how different parts of our framework can be modified to improve its performance, or how it can be extended for further generalization. First, we explore variations of the feature sets from the perspective of both the pairwise features and the embeddings. Then, we analyze the role of the network architecture and of the cost function used for learning.

6.1 Fine-Grained Pairwise Features

We have shown that our NN can integrate syntactic and semantic vectors with scores from other metrics. In fact, ours is a more general framework, where one can integrate the *components of a metric* instead of its score, which could yield better learning. Below, we demonstrate this for BLEU.

BLEU has different components: the n-gram precisions, the n-gram matches, the total number of n-grams (n=1,2,3,4), the lengths of the hypotheses and of the reference, the length ratio between them, and BLEU's brevity penalty. We will refer to this decomposed BLEU as BLEUCOMP. Some of these features were previously used in SIMPBLEU (Song and Cohn, 2011).

The results of using the components of BLEUCOMP as features are shown in Table 2. We see that using a single-layer neural network, which is equivalent to logistic regression, outperforms BLEU by more than +1 τ points absolute.

System	Details	Kendall's τ				
		cz	de	es	fr	AVG
BLEU	no learning	15.88	18.56	18.57	20.83	18.46
BLEUCOMP	logistic regression	18.18	21.13	19.79	19.91	19.75
BLEUCOMP+SYNTAX25	multi-layer NN	20.75	25.32	24.85	23.88	23.70
BLEUCOMP+WIKI-GW25	multi-layer NN	22.96	26.63	25.99	24.10	24.92
BLEUCOMP+SYNTAX25+WIKI-GW25	multi-layer NN	22.84	28.92	27.95	24.90	**26.15**
BLEU+SYNTAX25+WIKI-GW25	*multi-layer NN*	*20.03*	*25.95*	*27.07*	*23.16*	*24.05*

Table 2: Kendall's τ on WMT12 for neural networks using BLEUCOMP, a decomposed version of BLEU. For comparison, the last line shows a combination using BLEU instead of BLEUCOMP.

Source	Alone	Comb.
WIKI-GW25	*10.01*	*29.70*
WIKI-GW300	9.66	**29.90**
CC-300-42B	**12.16**	29.68
CC-300-840B	**11.41**	**29.88**
WORD2VEC300	7.72	29.13
COMPOSES400	**12.35**	28.54

Table 3: Average Kendall's τ on WMT12 for semantic vectors trained on different text collections. Shown are results (*i*) when using the semantic vectors alone, and (*ii*) when combining them with 4METRICS and SYNTAX25. The improvements over WIKI-GW25 are marked in bold.

As before, adding SYNTAX25 and WIKI-GW25 improves the results, but now by a more sizable margin: +4 for the former and +5 for the latter. Adding both yields +6.5 improvement over BLEUCOMP, and almost 8 points over BLEU.

We see once again that the syntactic and semantic word embeddings are complementary to the information sources used by metrics such as BLEU, and that our framework can learn from richer pairwise feature sets such as BLEUCOMP.

6.2 Larger Semantic Vectors

One interesting aspect to explore is the effect of the dimensionality of the input embeddings. Here, we studied the impact of using semantic vectors of bigger sizes, trained on different and larger text collections. The results are shown in Table 3. We can see that, compared to the 50-dimensional WIKI-GW25, 300-400 dimensional vectors are generally better by 1-2 τ points absolute when used in isolation; however, when used in combination with 4METRICS+SYNTAX25, they do not offer much gain (up to +0.2), and in some cases, we observe a slight drop in performance. We suspect that the variability across the different collections is due to a domain mismatch. Yet, we defer this question for future work.

Details	Kendall's τ				
	cz	de	es	fr	AVG
single-layer	25.86	32.06	30.03	28.45	29.10
multi-layer	26.30	33.19	30.38	28.92	**29.70**

Table 4: Kendall's tau (τ) on the WMT12 dataset for alternative architectures using 4METRICS+SYNTAX25+WIKI-GW25 as input.

6.3 Deep vs. Flat Neural Network

One interesting question is how much of the learning is due to the rich input representations, and how much happens because of the architecture of the neural network. To answer this, we experimented with two settings: a single-layer neural network, where all input features are fed directly to the output layer (which is logistic regression), and our proposed multi-layer neural network.

The results are shown in Table 4. We can see that switching from our multi-layer architecture to a single-layer one yields an absolute drop of 0.6 τ. This suggests that there is value in using the deeper, pairwise layer architecture.

6.4 Task-Specific Cost Function

Another question is whether the log-likelihood cost function $J(\theta)$ (see Section 3.3) is the most appropriate for our ranking task, provided that it is evaluated using Kendall's τ as defined below:

$$\tau = \frac{concord. - disc. - ties}{concord + disc. + ties} \tag{5}$$

where *concord.*, *disc.* and *ties* are the number of concordant, disconcordant and tied pairs.

Given an input tuple (t_1, t_2, r), the logistic cost function yields larger values of $\sigma = f(t_1, t_2, r)$ if $y = 1$, and smaller if $y = 0$, where $0 \leq \sigma \leq 1$ is the parameter of the Bernoulli distribution. However, it does not model *directly* the probability when the order of the hypotheses in the tuple is reversed, i.e., $\sigma' = f(t_2, t_1, r)$.

Details	Kendall's τ cz	de	es	fr	AVG
Logistic	26.30	33.19	30.38	28.92	29.70
Kendall	27.04	33.60	29.48	28.54	29.53
Log.+Ken.	26.90	33.17	30.40	29.21	**29.92**

Table 5: Kendall's tau (τ) on WMT12 for alternative cost functions using 4METRICS+SYNTAX25+WIKI-GW25.

For our specific task, given an input tuple (t_1, t_2, r), we want to make sure that the difference between the two output activations $\Delta = \sigma - \sigma'$ is positive when $y = 1$, and negative when $y = 0$. Ensuring this would take us closer to the actual objective, which is Kendall's τ. One possible way to do this is to introduce a task-specific cost function that penalizes the disagreements similarly to the way Kendall's τ does.[4] In particular, we define a new *Kendall cost* as follows:

$$J_\theta = -\sum_n y_n \operatorname{sig}(-\gamma\Delta_n) + (1 - y_n) \operatorname{sig}(\gamma\Delta_n) \tag{6}$$

where we use the sigmoid function sig as a differentiable approximation to the step function.

The above cost function penalizes disconcordances, i.e., cases where (*i*) $y = 1$ but $\Delta < 0$, or (*ii*) when $y = 0$ but $\Delta > 0$. However, we also need to make sure that we discourage *ties*. We do so by adding a zero-mean Gaussian regularization term $\exp(-\beta\Delta^2/2)$ that penalizes the value of Δ getting close to zero. Note that the specific values for γ and β are not really important, as long as they are large. In particular, in our experiments, we used $\gamma = \beta = 100$.

Table 5 shows a comparison of the two cost functions: (*i*) the standard logistic cost, and (*ii*) our Kendall cost. We can see that using the Kendall cost enables effective learning, although it is eventually outperformed by the logistic cost. Our investigation revealed that this was due to a combination of slower convergence and poor initialization. Therefore, we further experimented with a setup where we first used the logistic cost to pretrain the neural network, and then we switched to the Kendall cost in order to perform some finer tuning. As we can see in Table 5 (last row), doing so yielded a sizable improvement over using the Kendall cost only; it also improved over using the logistic cost only.

[4]Other variations for ranking tasks are possible, e.g., (Yih et al., 2011).

7 Conclusions and Future Work

We have presented a novel framework for learning a tunable MT evaluation metric in a pairwise ranking setting, given pre-existing pairwise human preference judgments.

In particular, we used a neural network, where the input layer encodes lexical, syntactic and semantic information from the reference and the two translation hypotheses, which is efficiently compacted into relatively small embeddings. The network has a hidden layer, motivated by our intuition about the problem, which captures the interactions between the relevant input components. Unlike previously proposed kernel-based approaches, our framework allows us to do both training and inference efficiently. Moreover, we have shown that it can be trained to optimize a task-specific cost function, which is more appropriate for the pairwise MT evaluation setting.

The evaluation results have shown that our NN model yields state-of-the-art results when using lexical, syntactic and semantic features (the latter two based on compact embeddings). Moreover, we have shown that the contribution of the different information sources is additive, thus demonstrating that the framework can effectively integrate complementary information. Furthermore, the framework is flexible enough to exploit different granularities of features such as n-gram matches and other components of BLEU (which individually work better than using the aggregated BLEU score). Finally, we have presented evidence suggesting that using the pairwise hidden layers is advantageous over simpler flat models.

In future work, we would like to experiment with an extension that allows for multiple references. We further plan to incorporate features from the *source* sentence. We believe that our framework can support learning similarities between the two translations and the source, for an improved MT evaluation. Variations of this architecture might be useful for related tasks such as Quality Estimation and hypothesis re-ranking for Machine Translation, where no references are available.

Other aspects worth studying as a complement to the present work include (*i*) the impact of the quality of the syntactic analysis (translations are often just a "word salad"), (*ii*) differences across language pairs, and (*iii*) the relevance of the domain the semantic representations are trained on.

References

Joshua Albrecht and Rebecca Hwa. 2008. Regression for machine translation evaluation at the sentence level. *Machine Translation*, 22(1-2):1–27.

Marco Baroni, Georgiana Dinu, and Germán Kruszewski. 2014. Don't count, predict! A systematic comparison of context-counting vs. context-predicting semantic vectors. In *Proceedings of the 52nd Annual Meeting of the Association for Computational Linguistics*, ACL '14, pages 238–247, Baltimore, Maryland, USA.

Yoshua Bengio and Xavier Glorot. 2010. Understanding the difficulty of training deep feedforward neural networks. In *Proceedings of AI & Statistics 2010*, volume 9, pages 249–256, Chia Laguna Resort, Sardinia, Italy.

Yoshua Bengio, Réjean Ducharme, Pascal Vincent, and Christian Janvin. 2003. A neural probabilistic language model. *Journal of Machine Learning Research*, 3:1137–1155.

James Bergstra, Olivier Breuleux, Frédéric Bastien, Pascal Lamblin, Razvan Pascanu, Guillaume Desjardins, Joseph Turian, David Warde-Farley, and Yoshua Bengio. 2010. Theano: a CPU and GPU math expression compiler. In *Proceedings of the Python for Scientific Computing Conference*, SciPy '10, Austin, Texas.

Ondrej Bojar, Christian Buck, Christian Federmann, Barry Haddow, Philipp Koehn, Johannes Leveling, Christof Monz, Pavel Pecina, Matt Post, Herve Saint-Amand, Radu Soricut, Lucia Specia, and Aleš Tamchyna. 2014. Findings of the 2014 workshop on statistical machine translation. In *Proceedings of the Ninth Workshop on Statistical Machine Translation*, WMT '14, pages 12–58, Baltimore, Maryland, USA.

Chris Callison-Burch, Cameron Fordyce, Philipp Koehn, Christof Monz, and Josh Schroeder. 2007. (Meta-) evaluation of machine translation. In *Proceedings of the Second Workshop on Statistical Machine Translation*, WMT '07, pages 136–158, Prague, Czech Republic.

Chris Callison-Burch, Philipp Koehn, Christof Monz, and Omar Zaidan. 2011. Findings of the 2011 workshop on statistical machine translation. In *Proceedings of the Sixth Workshop on Statistical Machine Translation*, WMT '11, pages 22–64, Edinburgh, Scotland.

Chris Callison-Burch, Philipp Koehn, Christof Monz, Matt Post, Radu Soricut, and Lucia Specia. 2012. Findings of the 2012 Workshop on Statistical Machine Translation. In *Proceedings of the Seventh Workshop on Statistical Machine Translation*, WMT '12, pages 10–51, Montréal, Canada.

Ronan Collobert, Jason Weston, Léon Bottou, Michael Karlen, Koray Kavukcuoglu, and Pavel Kuksa. 2011. Natural language processing (almost) from scratch. *Journal of Machine Learning Research*, 12:2493–2537.

Elisabet Comelles, Jesús Giménez, Lluís Màrquez, Irene Castellón, and Victoria Arranz. 2010. Document-level automatic MT evaluation based on discourse representations. In *Proceedings of the Joint Fifth Workshop on Statistical Machine Translation and MetricsMATR*, WMT '10, pages 333–338, Uppsala, Sweden.

Michael Denkowski and Alon Lavie. 2011. Meteor 1.3: Automatic metric for reliable optimization and evaluation of machine translation systems. In *Proceedings of the Sixth Workshop on Statistical Machine Translation*, WMT '11, pages 85–91, Edinburgh, Scotland.

Jacob Devlin, Rabih Zbib, Zhongqiang Huang, Thomas Lamar, Richard Schwartz, and John Makhoul. 2014. Fast and robust neural network joint models for statistical machine translation. In *Proceedings of the 52nd Annual Meeting of the Association for Computational Linguistics*, ACL '14, pages 1370–1380, Baltimore, Maryland, USA.

George Doddington. 2002. Automatic evaluation of machine translation quality using n-gram cooccurrence statistics. In *Proceedings of the Second International Conference on Human Language Technology Research*, HLT '02, pages 138–145, San Francisco, California, USA. Morgan Kaufmann Publishers.

John Duchi, Elad Hazan, and Yoram Singer. 2011. Adaptive subgradient methods for online learning and stochastic optimization. *Journal of Machine Learning Research*, 12:2121–2159.

Kevin Duh. 2008. Ranking vs. regression in machine translation evaluation. In *Proceedings of the Third Workshop on Statistical Machine Translation*, WMT '08, pages 191–194, Columbus, Ohio, USA.

Jesús Giménez and Lluís Màrquez. 2007. Linguistic features for automatic evaluation of heterogenous MT systems. In *Proceedings of the Second Workshop on Statistical Machine Translation*, WMT '07, pages 256–264, Prague, Czech Republic.

Francisco Guzmán, Shafiq Joty, Lluís Màrquez, Alessandro Moschitti, Preslav Nakov, and Massimo Nicosia. 2014a. Learning to differentiate better from worse translations. In *Proceedings of the 2014 Conference on Empirical Methods in Natural Language Processing*, EMNLP '14, pages 214–220, Doha, Qatar.

Francisco Guzmán, Shafiq Joty, Lluís Màrquez, and Preslav Nakov. 2014b. Using discourse structure improves machine translation evaluation. In *Proceedings of 52nd Annual Meeting of the Association for Computational Linguistics*, ACL '14, pages 687–698, Baltimore, Maryland, USA.

Shafiq Joty, Francisco Guzmán, Lluís Màrquez, and Preslav Nakov. 2014. DiscoTK: Using discourse structure for machine translation evaluation. In *Proceedings of the Ninth Workshop on Statistical Machine Translation*, WMT '14, pages 402–408, Baltimore, Maryland, USA.

Alex Kulesza and Stuart M. Shieber. 2004. A learning approach to improving sentence-level MT evaluation. In *Proceedings of the 10th International Conference on Theoretical and Methodological Issues in Machine Translation*.

Alon Lavie and Michael Denkowski. 2009. The METEOR metric for automatic evaluation of machine translation. *Machine Translation*, 23(2–3):105–115.

Ding Liu and Daniel Gildea. 2005. Syntactic features for evaluation of machine translation. In *Proceedings of the ACL Workshop on Intrinsic and Extrinsic Evaluation Measures for Machine Translation and/or Summarization*, pages 25–32, Ann Arbor, Michigan, USA.

Chi-kiu Lo, Anand Karthik Tumuluru, and Dekai Wu. 2012. Fully automatic semantic MT evaluation. In *Proceedings of the Seventh Workshop on Statistical Machine Translation*, WMT '12, pages 243–252, Montréal, Canada.

Matouš Macháček and Ondřej Bojar. 2013. Results of the WMT13 metrics shared task. In *Proceedings of the Eighth Workshop on Statistical Machine Translation*, WMT '13, pages 45–51, Sofia, Bulgaria.

Matouš Macháček and Ondřej Bojar. 2014. Results of the WMT14 metrics shared task. In *Proceedings of the Ninth Workshop on Statistical Machine Translation*, WMT '14, pages 293–301, Baltimore, Maryland, USA.

Tomas Mikolov, Martin Karafiát, Lukas Burget, Jan Cernocký, and Sanjeev Khudanpur. 2010. Recurrent neural network based language model. In *11th Annual Conference of the International Speech Communication Association*, pages 1045–1048, Makuhari, Chiba, Japan.

Tomas Mikolov, Ilya Sutskever, Kai Chen, Greg S. Corrado, and Jeff Dean. 2013a. Distributed representations of words and phrases and their compositionality. In *Advances in Neural Information Processing Systems 26*, NIPS '13, pages 3111–3119. Lake Tahoe, California, USA.

Tomas Mikolov, Wen-tau Yih, and Geoffrey Zweig. 2013b. Linguistic regularities in continuous space word representations. In *Proceedings of the 2013 Conference of the North American Chapter of the Association for Computational Linguistics: Human Language Technologies*, NAACL-HLT '13, pages 746–751, Atlanta, Georgia, USA.

Jeff Mitchell and Mirella Lapata. 2010. Composition in distributional models of semantics. *Cognitive Science*, 34(8):1388–1439.

Kishore Papineni, Salim Roukos, Todd Ward, and Wei-Jing Zhu. 2002. BLEU: a method for automatic evaluation of machine translation. In *Proceedings of 40th Annual Meting of the Association for Computational Linguistics*, ACL '02, pages 311–318, Philadelphia, Pennsylvania, USA.

Jeffrey Pennington, Richard Socher, and Christopher Manning. 2014. Glove: Global vectors for word representation. In *Proceedings of the Conference on Empirical Methods in Natural Language Processing*, EMNLP '14, pages 1532–1543, Doha, Qatar.

Maja Popović and Hermann Ney. 2007. Word error rates: Decomposition over POS classes and applications for error analysis. In *Proceedings of the Second Workshop on Statistical Machine Translation*, WMT '07, pages 48–55, Prague, Czech Republic.

Matthew Snover, Bonnie Dorr, Richard Schwartz, Linnea Micciulla, and John Makhoul. 2006. A study of translation edit rate with targeted human annotation. In *Proceedings of the 7th Biennial Conference of the Association for Machine Translation in the Americas*, AMTA '06, Cambridge, Massachusetts, USA.

Richard Socher, John Bauer, Christopher D. Manning, and Ng Andrew Y. 2013a. Parsing with compositional vector grammars. In *Proceedings of the 51st Annual Meeting of the Association for Computational Linguistics (Volume 1: Long Papers)*, ACL '13, pages 455–465, Sofia, Bulgaria.

Richard Socher, Alex Perelygin, Jean Wu, Jason Chuang, Christopher D. Manning, Andrew Ng, and Christopher Potts. 2013b. Recursive deep models for semantic compositionality over a sentiment treebank. In *Proceedings of the 2013 Conference on Empirical Methods in Natural Language Processing*, EMNLP '13, pages 1631–1642, Seattle, Washington, USA.

Xingyi Song and Trevor Cohn. 2011. Regression and ranking based optimisation for sentence-level MT evaluation. In *Proceedings of the Sixth Workshop on Statistical Machine Translation*, WMT '11, pages 123–129, Edinburgh, Scotland.

Ilya Sutskever, Oriol Vinyals, and Quoc V. Le. 2014. Sequence to sequence learning with neural networks. In *Proceedings of the Neural Information Processing Systems*, NIPS '14, Montreal, Canada.

Billy Wong and Chunyu Kit. 2012. Extending machine translation evaluation metrics with lexical cohesion to document level. In *Proceedings of the 2012 Joint Conference on Empirical Methods in Natural Language Processing and Computational Natural Language Learning*, EMNLP-CoNLL '12, pages 1060–1068, Jeju Island, Korea.

Wen-tau Yih, Kristina Toutanova, John C. Platt, and Christopher Meek. 2011. Learning discriminative projections for text similarity measures. In *Proceedings of the Fifteenth Conference on Computational Natural Language Learning*, CoNLL '11, pages 247–256, Portland, Oregon, USA.

String-to-Tree Multi Bottom-up Tree Transducers

Nina Seemann and **Fabienne Braune** and **Andreas Maletti**
Institute for Natural Language Processing, University of Stuttgart
Pfaffenwaldring 5b, 70569 Stuttgart, Germany
{seemanna,braunefe,maletti}@ims.uni-stuttgart.de

Abstract

We achieve significant improvements in several syntax-based machine translation experiments using a string-to-tree variant of multi bottom-up tree transducers. Our new parameterized rule extraction algorithm extracts string-to-tree rules that can be discontiguous and non-minimal in contrast to existing algorithms for the tree-to-tree setting. The obtained models significantly outperform the string-to-tree component of the Moses framework in a large-scale empirical evaluation on several known translation tasks. Our linguistic analysis reveals the remarkable benefits of discontiguous and non-minimal rules.

1 Introduction

We present an application of a variant of local multi bottom-up tree transducers (ℓMBOTs) as proposed in Maletti (2011) to statistical machine translation. ℓMBOTs allow discontinuities on the target language side since they have a sequence of target tree fragments instead of a single tree fragment in their rules. The original approach makes use of syntactic information on both the source and the target side (*tree-to-tree*) and a corresponding minimal rule extraction is presented in (Maletti, 2011). Braune et al. (2013) implemented it as well as a decoder inside the Moses framework (Koehn et al., 2007) and demonstrated that the resulting tree-to-tree ℓMBOT system significantly improved over its tree-to-tree baseline using minimal rules. We can see at least two drawbacks in this approach. First, experiments investigating the integration of syntactic information on both sides generally report quality deterioration. For example, Lavie et al. (2008), Liu et al. (2009), and Chiang (2010) noted that translation quality tends to decrease in tree-to-tree systems because the rules become too restrictive. Second, minimal rules (i.e., rules that cannot be obtained from other extracted rules) typically consist of a few lexical items only and are thus not the most suitable to translate idiomatic expressions and other fixed phrases. To overcome these drawbacks, we abolish the syntactic information for the source side and develop a string-to-tree variant of ℓMBOTs. In addition, we develop a new rule extraction algorithm that can also extract non-minimal rules. In general, the number of extractable rules explodes, so our rule extraction places parameterized restrictions on the extracted rules in the same spirit as in (Chiang, 2007). In this manner, we combine the advantages of the hierarchical phrase-based approach on the source side and the tree-based approach with discontinuiety on the target side.

We evaluate our new system in 3 large-scale experiments using translation tasks, in which we expect discontinuiety on the target. MBOTs are powerful but asymmetric models since discontinuiety is available only on the target. We chose to translate from English to German, Arabic, and Chinese. In all experiments our new system significantly outperforms the string-to-tree syntax-based component (Hoang et al., 2009) of Moses. The (potentially) discontiguous rules of our model are very useful in these setups, which we confirm in a quantitative and qualitative analysis.

2 Related work

Modern statistical machine translation systems (Koehn, 2009) are based on different translation models. Syntax-based systems have become widely used because of their ability to handle non-local reordering and other linguistic phenomena better than phrase-based models (Och and Ney, 2004). Synchronous tree substitution grammars (STSGs) of Eisner (2003) use a single source and target tree fragment per rule. In contrast, an ℓMBOT rule contains a single source tree

Proceedings of the 53rd Annual Meeting of the Association for Computational Linguistics and the 7th International Joint Conference on Natural Language Processing, pages 815–824,
Beijing, China, July 26-31, 2015.

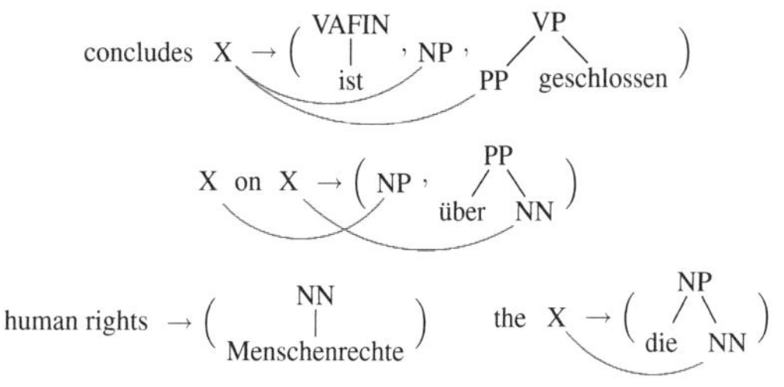

Figure 1: Several valid rules for our MBOT.

fragment and a sequence of target tree fragments. ℓMBOTs can also be understood as a restriction of the non-contiguous STSSGs of Sun et al. (2009), which allow a sequence of source tree fragments and a sequence of target tree fragments. ℓMBOT rules require exactly one source tree fragment.

While the mentioned syntax-based models use tree fragments for source and target (tree-to-tree), Galley et al. (2004) and Galley et al. (2006) use syntactic annotations only on the target language side (*string-to-tree*). Further research by DeNeefe et al. (2007) revealed that adding non-minimal rules improves translation quality in this setting. Here we improve statistical machine translation in this setting even further using non-minimal ℓMBOT rules.

3 Theoretical Model

As our translation model, we use a string-to-tree variant of the shallow local multi bottom-up tree transducer of Braune et al. (2013). We will call our variant MBOT for simplicity. Our MBOT is a synchronous grammar (Chiang, 2006) similar to a synchronous context-free grammar (SCFG), but instead of a single source and target fragment per rule, our rules are of the form $s \rightarrow (t_1, \ldots, t_n)$ with a single *source string* s and potentially several *target tree fragments* $t_1, \ldots, t_n$. Besides lexical items the source string can contain (several occurrences of) the placeholder X, which links to non-lexical leaves in the target tree fragments. In contrast to an SCFG each placeholder can have several such links. However, each non-lexical leaf in a target tree fragment has exactly one such link to a placeholder X. An MBOT is simply a finite collection of such rules. Several valid rules are depicted in Figure 1.

The sentential forms of our MBOTs, which occur during derivations, have exactly the same shape as our rules and each rule is a sentential

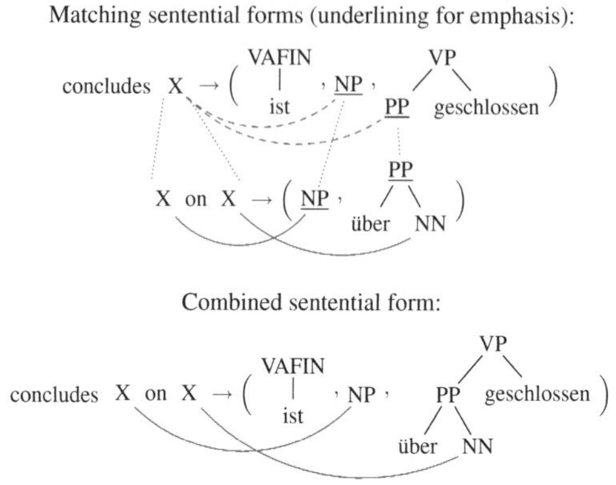

Figure 2: Substitution of sentential forms.

form. We can combine sentential forms with the help of substitution (Chiang, 2006). Roughly speaking, in a sentential form ξ we can replace a placeholder X that is linked (left-to-right) to non-lexical leaves $C_1, \ldots, C_k$ in the target tree fragments by the source string of any sentential form ζ, whose roots of the target tree fragments (left-to-right) read $C_1, \ldots, C_k$. The target tree fragments of ζ will replace the respective linked leaves in the target tree fragments of the sentential form ξ. In other words, substitution has to respect the symbols in the linked target tree fragments and all linked leaves are replaced at the same time. We illustrate substitution in Figure 2, where we replace the placeholder X in the source string, which is linked to the underlined leaves NP and PP in the target tree fragments. The rule below (also in Figure 1) is also a sentential form and matches since its (underlined) root labels of the target tree fragments read "NP PP". Thus, we can substitute the latter sentential form into the former and obtain the sentential form shown at the bottom of Figure 2. Ideally, the substitution process is repeated until the complete source sentence is derived.

4 Rule Extraction

The rule extraction of Maletti (2011) extracts minimal tree-to-tree rules, which are rules containing both source and target tree fragments, from sentence pairs of a word-aligned and bi-parsed parallel corpus. In particular, this requires parses for both the source and the target language sentences which adds a source for errors and specificity potentially leading to lower translation performance and lower coverage (Wellington et al., 2006). Chiang (2010) showed that string-to-tree systems—

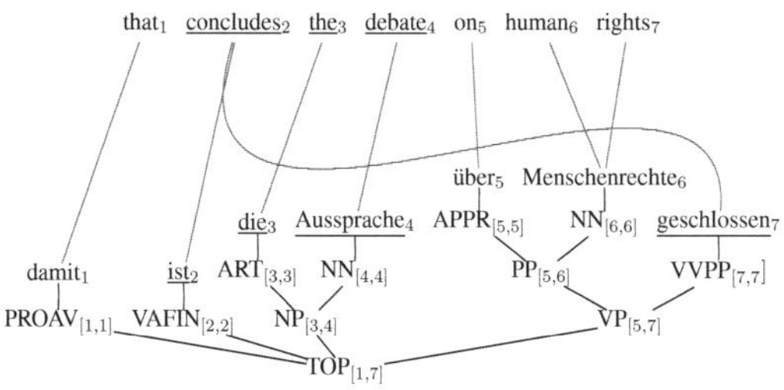

Figure 3: Word-aligned sentence pair with target-side parse.

which he calls fuzzy tree-to-tree-systems— generally yield higher translation quality compared to corresponding tree-to-tree systems.

For efficiency reasons the rule extraction of Maletti (2011) only extracts *minimal* rules, which are the smallest tree fragments compatible with the given word alignment and the parse trees. Similarly, non-minimal rules are those that can be obtained from minimal rules by substitution. In particular, each lexical item of a sentence pair occurs in exactly one minimal rule extracted from that sentence pair. However, minimal rules are especially unsuitable for fixed phrases consisting of rare words because minimal rules encourage small fragments and thus word-by-word translation. Consequently, such fixed phrases will often be assembled inconsistently by substitution from small fragments. Non-minimal rules encourage a consistent translation by covering larger parts of the source sentence.

Here we want to develop an efficient rule extraction procedure for our string-to-tree MBOTs that avoids the mentioned drawbacks. Naturally, we could substitute minimal rules into each other to obtain non-minimal rules, but performing substitution for all combinations is clearly intractable. Instead we essentially follow the approach of Koehn et al. (2003), Och and Ney (2004), and Chiang (2007), which is based on consistently aligned phrase pairs. Our training corpus contains *word-aligned sentence pairs* $\langle e, A, f\rangle$, which contain a source language sentence e, a target language sentence f, and an alignment $A \subseteq [1, \ell_e] \times [1, \ell_f]$, where ℓ_e and ℓ_f are the lengths of the sentences e and f, respectively, and $[i, i'] = \{j \in \mathbb{Z} \mid i \leq j \leq i'\}$ is the span (closed interval of integers) from i to i' for all positive integers $i \leq i'$. Rules are extracted for each pair of the corpus, so in the following let $\langle e, A, f\rangle$ be a word-aligned sentence pair. A *source phrase* is simply a span $[i, i'] \subseteq [1, \ell_e]$ and correspondingly, a *target phrase* is a span $[j, j'] \subseteq [1, \ell_f]$. A *rule span* is a pair $\langle p, \varphi\rangle$ consisting of a source phrase p and a sequence $\varphi = p_1 \cdots p_n$ of (non-overlapping) target phrases $p_1, \ldots, p_n$. Spans overlap if their intersection is non-empty. If $n = 1$ (i.e., there is exactly one target phrase in φ) then $\langle p, \varphi\rangle$ is also a phrase pair (Koehn et al., 2003). We want to emphasize that formally phrases are spans and not the substrings occuring at that span.

Next, we lift the notion of consistently aligned phrase pairs to our rule spans. Simply put, for a consistently aligned rule span $\langle p, p_1 \cdots p_n\rangle$ we require that it respects the alignment A in the sense that the origin i of an alignment $(i, j) \in A$ is covered by p if and only if the destination j is covered by $p_1, \ldots, p_n$. Formally, the rule span $\langle p, p_1 \cdots p_n\rangle$ is *consistently aligned* if for every $(i, j) \in A$ we have $i \in p$ if and only if $j \in \bigcup_{k=1}^{n} p_k$. For example, given the word-aligned sentence pair in Figure 3, the rule span $\langle [2,4],\ [2,4]\,[7,7]\rangle$ is consistently aligned, whereas the phrase pair $\langle [2,4],\ [2,7]\rangle$ is not.

Our MBOTs use rules consisting of a source string and a sequence of target tree fragments. The target trees are provided by a parser for the target language. For each word-aligned sentence pair $\langle e, A, f\rangle$ we thus have a parse tree t for f. An example is provided in Figure 3. We omit a formal definition of trees, but recall that each node η of the parse tree t *governs* a (unique) target phrase. In Figure 3 we have indicated those target phrases (spans) as subscript to the non-lexical node labels. A consistently aligned rule span $\langle p, p_1 \cdots p_n\rangle$ of $\langle e, A, f\rangle$ is *compatible with* t if there exist nodes $\eta_1, \ldots, \eta_n$ of t such that η_k governs p_k for all $1 \leq k \leq n$. For example, given the word-aligned sentence pair and parse tree t in Figure 3, the consistently aligned rule span $\langle [2,4],\ [2,4]\,[7,7]\rangle$ is not compatible with t because there is no node in t that governs $[2,4]$. However, for the same data, the rule span $\langle [2,4],\ [2,2]\,[3,4]\,[7,7]\rangle$ is consistently aligned and compatible with t. The required nodes of t are labeled VAFIN, NP, VVPP.

Now we are ready to start the rule extraction. For each consistently aligned rule span $\langle p, p_1 \cdots p_n\rangle$ that is compatible with t and each selection of nodes $\eta_1, \ldots, \eta_n$ of t such that n_k governs p_k for each $1 \leq k \leq n$, we can extract the rule $e(p) \to \big(\mathrm{flat}(t_{\eta_1}), \ldots, \mathrm{flat}(t_{\eta_n})\big)$, where

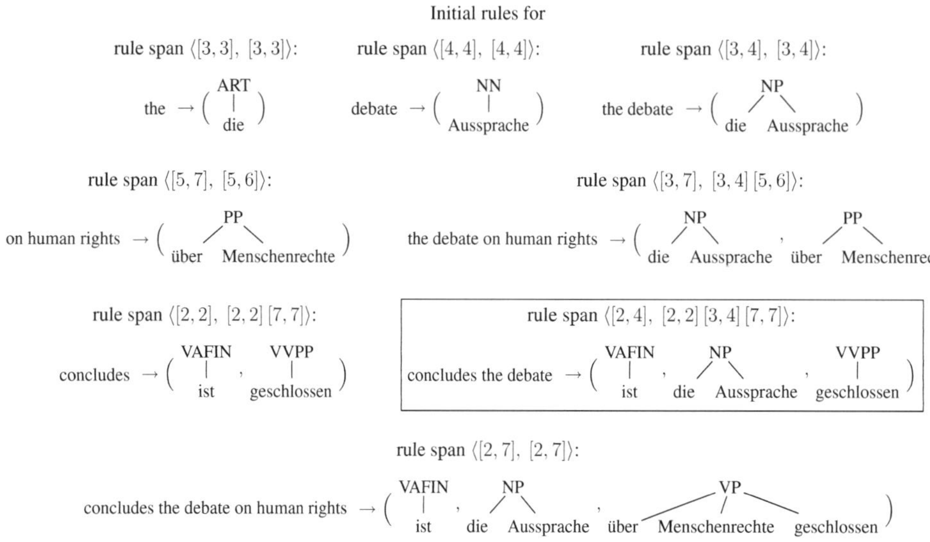

Figure 4: Some initial rules extracted from the word-aligned sentence pair and parse of Figure 3.

- $e(p)$ is the substring of e at span p,[1]
- $\text{flat}(u)$ removes all internal nodes from u (all nodes except the root and the leaves), and
- t_η is the subtree rooted in η for node η of t.

The rules obtained in this manner are called *initial rules for* $\langle e, A, f\rangle$ *and* t. For example, for the rule span $\langle [2,4],\ [2,2]\ [3,4]\ [7,7]\rangle$ we can extract only one initial rule. More precisely, we have

- $e([2,4]) =$ concludes the debate
- $t_{\eta_1} =$ (VAFIN ist)
- $t_{\eta_2} = \big($NP (ART die) (NN Aussprache)$\big)$,
- and $t_{\eta_3} =$ (VVPP geschlossen).

The function flat leaves t_{η_1} and t_{η_3} unchanged, but $\text{flat}(t_{\eta_2}) =$ (NP die Aussprache). Thus, we obtain the boxed rule of Figure 4.

Clearly, the initial rules are just the start because they are completely lexical in the sense that they never contain the placeholder X in the source string nor a non-lexical leaf in any output tree fragment. We introduce non-lexical rules using the same approach as for the hierarchical rules of Chiang (2007). Roughly speaking, we obtain a new rule r'' by "excising" an initial rule r from another rule r' and replacing the removed part by

- the placeholder X in the source string,
- the root label of the removed tree fragment in the target tree fragments, and
- linking the removed parts appropriately,

so that the flatted substitution of r into r'' can yield r'. This "excision" process is illustrated in Figure 5, where we remove the middle initial rule from the topmost initial rule. The result is displayed at the bottom in Figure 5. Formally, the set of *extractable rules* R for a given word-aligned sentence pair $\langle e, A, f\rangle$ with parse tree t for f is the smallest set subject to the following two conditions:

- Each initial rule is in R and thus extractable.
- For every initial rule r and extractable rule $r' \in R$, any flat rule r'', into which we can substitute r to obtain ρ with $\text{flat}(\rho) = r'$, is in R and thus extractable.[2]

For our running example depicted in Figure 3 we display some extractable rules in Figure 6.

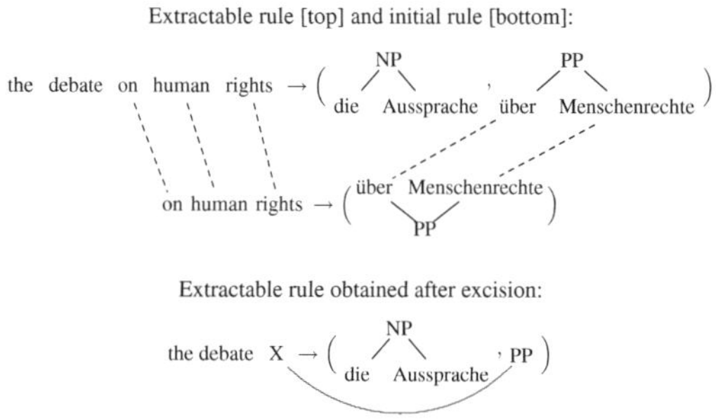

Figure 5: Excision of the middle initial rule from the topmost initial rule. Substituting the middle rule into the result yields the topmost rule.

[1] If $p = [i, i']$, then $e(p) = e[i, i']$ is the substring of e ranging from the i-th token to the i'-th token.

[2] A rule $\rho = s \to (t_1, \dots, t_n)$ is *flat* if $\text{flat}(\rho) = \rho$, where $\text{flat}(\rho) = s \to (\text{flat}(t_1), \dots, \text{flat}(t_n))$.

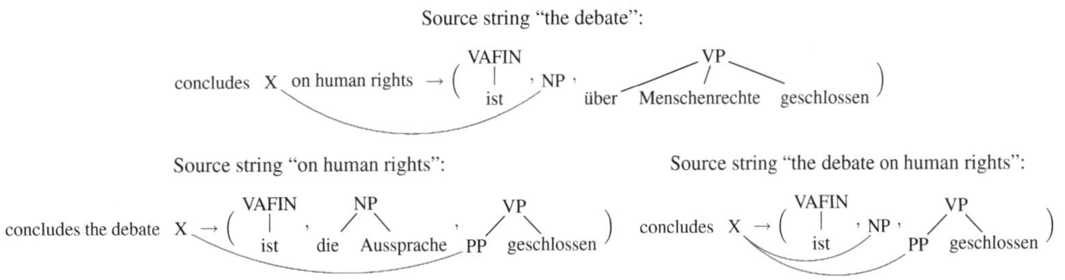

Figure 6: Extractable rules obtained by excising various initial rules (see Figure 4) from the initial rule displayed at the bottom of Figure 4.

Unfortunately, already Chiang (2007) points out that the set of all extractable rules is generally too large and keeping all extractable rules leads to slow training, slow decoding, and spurious ambiguity. Our MBOT rules are restricted by the parse tree for the target sentence, but the MBOT model permits additional flexibility due to the presence of multiple target tree fragments. Overall, we experience the same problems, and consequently, in the experiments we use the following additional constraints on rules $s \to (t_1, \ldots, t_n)$:

(a) We only consider source phrases p of length at most 10 (i.e., $i' - i < 10$ for $p = [i, i']$).[3]
(b) The source string s contains at most 5 occurrences of lexical items or X (i.e. $\ell_s \leq 5$).
(c) The source string s cannot have consecutive Xs (i.e., XX is not a substring of s).
(d) The source string contains at least one lexical item that was aligned in $\langle e, A, f \rangle$.
(e) The left-most token of the source string s cannot be X (i.e., $s[1,1] \neq$ X).

Our implementation can easily be modified to handle other constraints. Figure 7 shows extractable rules violating those additional constraints.

Table 1 gives an overview on how many rules are extracted. Our string-to-tree variant extracts 12–17 times more rules than the minimal tree-to-tree rule extraction. For our experiments (see Section 6), we filter all rule tables on the given input. The decoding times for the minimal ℓMBOT and our MBOT share the same order of magnitude.

5 Model Features

For each source language sentence e, we want to determine its most likely translation $\hat{f}$ given by

$$\hat{f} = \arg\max_f p(f \mid e) = \arg\max_f p(e \mid f) \cdot p(f)$$

for some unknown probability distributions p. We estimate $p(e \mid f) \cdot p(f)$ by a log-linear combination of features $h_i(\cdot)$ with weights λ_i scored on sentential forms $e \to (t)$ of our extracted MBOT M such that the leaves of t read (left-to-right) f.

We use the decoder provided by MBOT-Moses of Braune et al. (2013) and its standard features, which includes all the common features (Koehn, 2009) and a gap penalty 100^{1-c}, where c is the number of target tree fragments that contributed to t. This feature discourages rules with many target tree fragments. As usual, all features are obtained as the product of the corresponding rule features for the rules used to derive $e \to (t)$ by means of substitution. The rule weights for the translation weights are obtained as relative frequencies normalized over all rules with the same right- and left-hand side. Good-Turing smoothing (Good, 1953) is applied to all rules that were extracted at most 10 times. The lexical translation weights are obtained as usual.

6 Experimental Results

We considered three reasonable baselines: (i) minimal ℓMBOT, (ii) non-contiguous STSSG (Sun et al., 2009), or (iii) a string-to-tree Moses system. We decided against the minimal ℓMBOT as a baseline since tree-to-tree systems generally get lower BLEU scores than string-to-tree systems. We nevertheless present its BLEU scores (see Table 3). Unfortunately, we could not compare to Sun et al. (2009) because their decoder and rule extraction algorithms are not publicly available. Furthermore, we have the impression that their system does not scale well:

- Only around 240,000 training sentences were used. Our training data contains between 1.8M and 5.7M sentence pairs.
- The development and test set were length-

[3]Note that this restricts the set of initial rules.

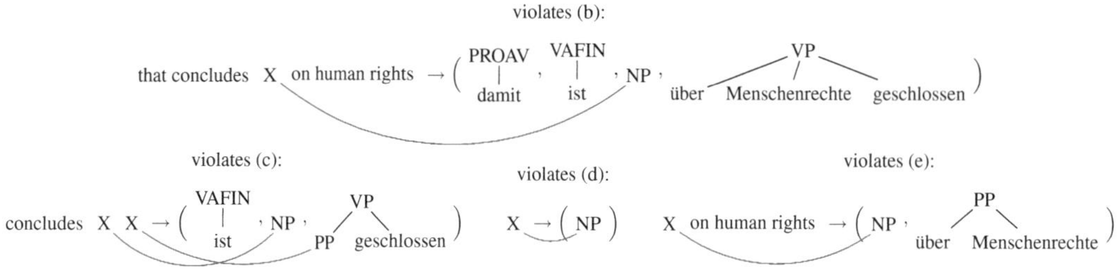

Figure 7: Showing extractable rules violating the restrictions.

System	number of extracted rules		
	English-To-German	English-To-Arabic	English-To-Chinese
minimal tree-to-tree ℓMBOT	12,478,160	28,725,229	10,162,325
non-minimal string-to-tree MBOT	143,661,376	491,307,787	162,240,663
string-to-tree Moses	14,092,729	55,169,043	17,047,570

Table 1: Overview of numbers of extracted rules with respect to the different extraction algorithms.

ratio filtered to sentences up to 50 characters. We do not modify those sets.

- Only rules with at most one gap were allowed which would be equivalent to restrict the number of target tree fragments to 2 in our system.

Hence we decided to use a string-to-tree Moses system as baseline (see Section 6.1).

6.1 Setup

As a baseline system for our experiments we use the syntax-based component (Hoang et al., 2009) of the Moses toolkit (Koehn et al., 2007). Our system is the presented translation system based on MBOTs. We use the MBOT-Moses decoder (Braune et al., 2013) which – similar to the baseline decoder – uses a CYK+ chart parsing algorithm using a standard X-style parse tree which is sped up by cube pruning (Chiang, 2007) with integrated language model scoring.

Our and the baseline system use linguistic syntactic annotation (parses) only on the target side (*string-to-tree*). During rule extraction we impose the restrictions of Section 4. Additional glue-rules that concatenate partial translations without performing any reordering are used in all systems.

For all experiments (English-to-German, English-to-Arabic, and English-to-Chinese), the training data was length-ratio filtered. The word alignments were generated by GIZA++ (Och and Ney, 2003) with the *grow-diag-final-and* heuristic (Koehn et al., 2005). The following language-specific processing was performed. The German text was true-cased and the functional and morphological annotations were removed from the parse. The Arabic text was tokenized with MADA (Habash et al., 2009) and transliterated according to Buckwalter (2002). Finally, the Chinese text was word-segmented using the Stanford Word Segmenter (Chang et al., 2008).

In all experiments the feature weights λ_i of the log-linear model were trained using minimum error rate training (Och, 2003). The remaining information for the experiments is presented in Table 2.

6.2 Quantitative Analysis

The overall translation quality was measured with 4-gram BLEU (Papineni et al., 2002) on true-cased data for German, on transliterated data for Arabic, and on word-segmented data for Chinese. Significance was computed with Gimpel's implementation (Gimpel, 2011) of pairwise bootstrap resampling with 1,000 samples. Table 3 lists the evaluation results. In all three setups the MBOT system significantly outperforms the baseline. For German we obtain a BLEU score of 15.90 which is a gain of 0.68 points. For Arabic we get an increase of 0.78 points which results in 49.10 BLEU. For Chinese we obtain a score of 18.35 BLEU gaining 0.66 points.[4] We also trained a vanilla phrase-based system for each language pair on the same data as described in Table 2.

To demonstrate the usefulness of the multiple

[4]NIST-08 also shows BLEU for word-segmented output (`http://www.itl.nist.gov/iad/mig/tests/mt/2008/doc/mt08_official_results_v0.html`). Best constrained system: 17.69 BLEU; best unconstrained system: 19.63 BLEU.

	English to German	English to Arabic	English to Chinese
training data	7th EuroParl corpus (Koehn, 2005)	MultiUN corpus (Eisele and Chen, 2010)	
training data size	≈ 1.8M sentence pairs	≈ 5.7M sentence pairs	≈ 1.9M sentence pairs
target-side parser	BitPar (Schmid, 2004)	Berkeley parser (Petrov et al., 2006)	
language model	5-gram SRILM (Stolcke, 2002)		
add. LM data	WMT 2013	Arabic in MultiUN	Chinese in MultiUN
LM data size	≈ 57M sentences	≈ 9.7M sentences	≈ 9.5M sentences
tuning data	WMT 2013	cut from MultiUN	NIST 2002, 2003, 2005
tuning size	3,000 sentences	2,000 sentences	2,879 sentences
test data	WMT 2013 (Bojar et al., 2013)	cut from MultiUN	NIST 2008 (NIST, 2010)
test size	3,000 sentences	1,000 sentences	1,859 sentences

Table 2: Summary of the performed experiments.

Language pair	System	BLEU
English-to-German	Moses Baseline	15.22
	MBOT	*15.90
	minimal ℓMBOT	14.09
	Phrase-based Moses	16.73
English-to-Arabic	Moses Baseline	48.32
	MBOT	*49.10
	minimal ℓMBOT	32.88
	Phrase-based Moses	50.27
English-to-Chinese	Moses Baseline	17.69
	MBOT	*18.35
	minimal ℓMBOT	12.01
	Phrase-based Moses	18.09

Table 3: Evaluation results. The starred results are statistically significant improvements over the baseline (at confidence $p < 1\%$).

target tree fragments of MBOTs, we analyzed the MBOT rules that were used when decoding the test set. We distinguish several types of rules. A rule is *contiguous* if it has only 1 target tree fragment. All other rules are (potentially) *discontiguous*. Moreover, *lexical* rules are rules whose leaves are exclusively lexical items. All other rules (i.e., those that contain at least one non-lexical leaf) are *structural*. Table 4 reports how many rules of each type are used during decoding for both our MBOT system and the minimal ℓMBOT. Below, we focus on analyzing our MBOT system. Out of the rules used for German, 27% were (potentially) discontiguous and 5% were structural. For Arabic, we observe 67% discontiguous rules and 26% structural rules. For translating into Chinese 30% discontiguous rules were used and the structural rules account to 18%. These numbers show that the usage of discontiguous rules tunes to the specific language pair. For instance, Arabic utilizes them more compared to German and Chinese. Furthermore, German uses a lot of lexical rules which is probably due to the fact that it is a morphologically rich language. On the other hand, Arabic and Chinese make good use of structural rules. In addition, Table 4 presents a finer-grained analysis based on the number of target tree fragments. Only rules with at most 8 target tree fragments were used. While German and Arabic seem to require some rules with 6 target tree fragments, Chinese probably does not. We conclude that the number of target tree fragments can be restricted to a language-pair specific number during rule extraction.

6.3 Qualitative Analysis

In this section, we inspect some English-to-German translations generated by the Moses baseline and our MBOT system in order to provide some evidence for linguistic constructions that our system handles better. We identified (a) the realization of reflexive pronouns, relative pronouns, and particle verbs, (b) the realization of verbal material, and (c) local and long distance reordering to be better throughout than in the baseline system. All examples are (parts of) translations of sentences from the test data. Ungrammatical constructions are enclosed in brackets and marked with a star. We focus on instances that seem relevant to the new ability to use non-minimal rules.

We start with an example showing the realization of a reflexive pronoun.

Source: Bitcoin *differs* from other types of virtual currency.
Reference: Bitcoin *unterscheidet sich* von anderen Arten virtueller Währungen.
Baseline: Bitcoin [*unterscheidet*]* von anderen Arten [der virtuellen Währung]*.

Language pair	System	Type	Lex	Struct	Total	Target tree fragments				
						2	3	4	5	≥ 6
English-to-German	our MBOT	cont.	27,351	635	27,986					
		discont.	9,336	1,110	10,446	5,565	3,441	1,076	312	52
	minimal ℓMBOT	cont.	55,910	4,492	60,402					
		discont.	2,167	7,386	9,553	6,458	2,589	471	34	1
English-to-Arabic	our MBOT	cont.	1,839	651	2,490					
		discont.	3,670	1,324	4,994	3,008	1,269	528	153	36
	minimal ℓMBOT	cont.	18,389	2,855	21,244					
		discont.	1,138	1,920	3,058	2,525	455	67	8	3
English-to-Chinese	our MBOT	cont.	17,135	1,585	18,720					
		discont.	4,822	3,341	8,163	6,411	1,448	247	55	2
	minimal ℓMBOT	cont.	34,275	8,820	43,095					
		discont.	516	4,292	4,808	3,816	900	82	6	4

Table 4: Number of rules per type used when decoding test (Lex = lexical rules; Struct = structural rules; [dis]cont. = [dis]contiguous).

MBOT: Bitcoin *unterscheidet sich* von anderen Arten [der virtuellen Währung]*.

Here the baseline drops the reflexive pronoun *sich*, which is correctly realized by the MBOT system. The rule used is displayed in Figure 8.

Figure 8: Rule realizing the reflexive pronoun.

Next, we show a translation in which our system correctly generates a whole verbal segment.

Source: *It turned out that* not only ...
Reference: *Es stellte sich heraus, dass* nicht nur ...
Baseline: [*Heraus,*]* nicht nur ...
MBOT: *Es stellte sich heraus, dass* nicht nur ...

The baseline drops the verbal construction whereas the large non-minimal rule of Figure 9 allows our MBOT to avoid that drop. Again, the required reflexive pronoun *sich* is realized as well as the necessary comma before the conjunction *dass*.

Figure 9: MBOT rule for the verbal segment.

Another feature of MBOT is its power to perform long distance reordering with the help of several discontiguous output fragments.

Source: ...weapons factories now, *which do not endure competition on the international market* and ...
Reference: ...Rüstungsfabriken, *die der internationalen Konkurrenz nicht standhalten* und ...
Baseline: ...[Waffen in den Fabriken nun]*, *die nicht einem Wettbewerb auf dem internationalen Markt* []* und ...
MBOT: ...[Waffen Fabriken nun]*, *die Konkurrenz auf dem internationalen Markt nicht ertragen* und ...

Figure 10 shows the rules which enable the MBOT system to produce the correct reordering.

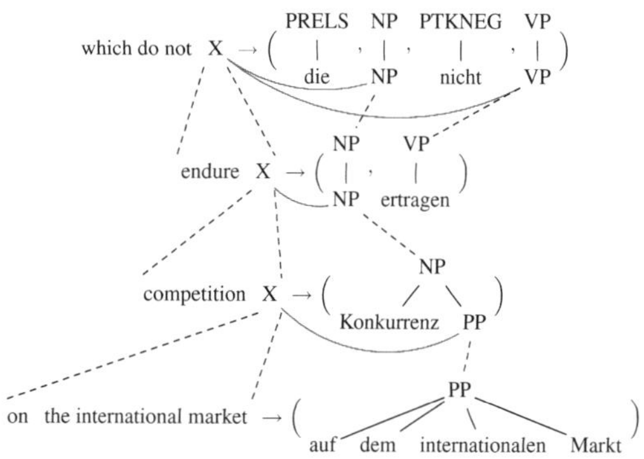

Figure 10: Long distance reordering.

7 Conclusion

We present an application of a string-to-tree variant of local multi bottom-up tree transducers, which are tree-to-tree models, to statistical machine translation. Originally, only minimal rules were extracted, but to overcome the typically lower translation quality of tree-to-tree systems and minimal rules, we abolish the syntactic annotation on the source side and develop a string-to-tree variant. In addition, we present a new parameterized rule extraction that can extract non-minimal rules, which are particularly helpful for translating fixed phrases. It would be interesting to know how much can be gained when using only one contribution at a time. Hence, we will explore the impact of string-to-tree and non-minimal rules in isolation.

We demonstrate that our new system significantly outperforms the standard Moses string-to-tree system on three different large-scale translation tasks (English-to-German, English-to-Arabic, and English-to-Chinese) with a gain between 0.53 and 0.87 BLEU points. An analysis of the rules used to decode the test sets suggests that the usage of discontiguous rules is tuned to each language pair. Furthermore, it shows that only discontiguous rules with at most 8 target tree fragments are used. Thus, further research could investigate a hard limit on the number of target tree fragments during rule extraction. We also perform a manual inspection of the obtained translations and confirm that our string-to-tree MBOT rules can adequately handle discontiguous phrases, which occur frequently in German, Arabic, and Chinese. Other languages that exhibit such phenomena include Czech, Dutch, Russian, and Polish. Thus, we hope that our approach can also be applied successfully to other language pairs.

To support further experimentation by the community, we publicly release our developed software and complete tool-chain (`http://www.ims.uni-stuttgart.de/forschung/ressourcen/werkzeuge/mbotmoses.html`).

Acknowledgement

The authors would like to express their gratitude to the reviewers for their helpful comments and Robin Kurtz for preparing the Arabic corpus.

All authors were financially supported by the German Research Foundation (DFG) grant MA 4959 / 1-1.

References

Ondřej Bojar, Christian Buck, Chris Callison-Burch, Christian Federmann, Barry Haddow, Philipp Koehn, Christof Monz, Matt Post, Radu Soricut, and Lucia Specia. 2013. Findings of the 2013 Workshop on Statistical Machine Translation. In *Proc. 8th WMT*, pages 1–44. Association for Computational Linguistics.

Fabienne Braune, Nina Seemann, Daniel Quernheim, and Andreas Maletti. 2013. Shallow local multi bottom-up tree transducers in statistical machine translation. In *Proc. 51st ACL*, pages 811–821. Association for Computational Linguistics.

Timothy Buckwalter. 2002. Arabic transliteration. `http://www.qamus.org/transliteration.htm`.

Pi-Chuan Chang, Michel Galley, and Christopher D. Manning. 2008. Optimizing Chinese word segmentation for machine translation performance. In *Proc. 3rd WMT*, pages 224–232. Association for Computational Linguistics.

David Chiang. 2006. An introduction to synchronous grammars. In *Proc. 44th ACL*. Association for Computational Linguistics. Part of a tutorial given with Kevin Knight.

David Chiang. 2007. Hierarchical phrase-based translation. *Computational Linguistics*, 33(2):201–228.

David Chiang. 2010. Learning to translate with source and target syntax. In *Proc. 48th ACL*, pages 1443–1452. Association for Computational Linguistics.

Steve DeNeefe, Kevin Knight, Wei Wang, and Daniel Marcu. 2007. What can syntax-based MT learn from phrase-based MT? In *Proc. 2007 EMNLP*, pages 755–763. Association for Computational Linguistics.

Andreas Eisele and Yu Chen. 2010. MultiUN: A multilingual corpus from United Nation documents. In *Proc. 7th LREC*, pages 2868–2872. European Language Resources Association.

Jason Eisner. 2003. Learning non-isomorphic tree mappings for machine translation. In *Proc. 41st ACL*, pages 205–208. Association for Computational Linguistics.

Michel Galley, Mark Hopkins, Kevin Knight, and Daniel Marcu. 2004. What's in a translation rule? In *Proc. 2004 NAACL*, pages 273–280. Association for Computational Linguistics.

Michel Galley, Jonathan Graehl, Kevin Knight, Daniel Marcu, Steve DeNeefe, Wei Wang, and Ignacio Thayer. 2006. Scalable inference and training of context-rich syntactic translation models. In *Proc. 44th ACL*, pages 961–968. Association for Computational Linguistics.

Kevin Gimpel. 2011. Code for statistical significance testing for MT evaluation metrics. `http://www.ark.cs.cmu.edu/MT/`.

Irving J. Good. 1953. The population frequencies of species and the estimation of population parameters. *Biometrika*, 40(3–4):237–264.

Nizar Habash, Owen Rambow, and Ryan Roth. 2009. MADA+TOKAN: A toolkit for Arabic tokenization, diacritization, morphological disambiguation, POS tagging, stemming and lemmatization. In *Proc. 2nd MEDAR*, pages 102–109. Association for Computational Linguistics.

Hieu Hoang, Philipp Koehn, and Adam Lopez. 2009. A unified framework for phrase-based, hierarchical, and syntax-based statistical machine translation. In *Proc. 6th IWSLT*, pages 152–159.

Philipp Koehn, Franz Josef Och, and Daniel Marcu. 2003. Statistical phrase-based translation. In *Proc. 2003 NAACL*, pages 48–54. Association for Computational Linguistics.

Philipp Koehn, Amittai Axelrod, Alexandra Birch Mayne, Chris Callison-Burch, Miles Osborne, and David Talbot. 2005. Edinburgh system description for the 2005 IWSLT Speech Translation Evaluation. In *Proc. 2nd IWSLT*, pages 68–75.

Philipp Koehn, Hieu Hoang, Alexandra Birch, Chris Callison-Burch, Marcello Federico, Nicola Bertoldi, Brooke Cowan, Wade Shen, Christine Moran, Richard Zens, Chris Dyer, Ondrej Bojar, Alexandra Constantin, and Evan Herbst. 2007. Moses: Open source toolkit for statistical machine translation. In *Proc. 45th ACL*, pages 177–180. Association for Computational Linguistics.

Philipp Koehn. 2005. Europarl: A parallel corpus for statistical machine translation. In *Proc. 10th MT Summit*, pages 79–86. Association for Machine Translation in the Americas.

Philipp Koehn. 2009. *Statistical Machine Translation*. Cambridge University Press.

Alon Lavie, Alok Parlikar, and Vamshi Ambati. 2008. Syntax-driven learning of sub-sentential translation equivalents and translation rules from parsed parallel corpora. In *Proc. 2nd SSST*, pages 87–95. Association for Computational Linguistics.

Yang Liu, Yajuan Lü, and Qun Liu. 2009. Improving tree-to-tree translation with packed forests. In *Proc. 47th ACL*, pages 558–566. Association for Computational Linguistics.

Andreas Maletti. 2011. How to train your multi bottom-up tree transducer. In *Proc. 49th ACL*, pages 825–834. Association for Computational Linguistics.

NIST. 2010. NIST 2002 [2003, 2005, 2008] open machine translation evaluation. Linguistic Data Consortium. LDC2010T10 [T11, T14, T21].

Franz J. Och and Hermann Ney. 2003. A systematic comparison of various statistical alignment models. *Computational Linguistics*, 29(1):19–51.

Franz J. Och and Hermann Ney. 2004. The alignment template approach to statistical machine translation. *Computational Linguistics*, 30(4):417–449.

Franz J. Och. 2003. Minimum error rate training in statistical machine translation. In *Proc. 41st ACL*, pages 160–167. Association for Computational Linguistics.

Kishore Papineni, Salim Roukos, Todd Ward, and Wei jing Zhu. 2002. BLEU: a method for automatic evaluation of machine translation. In *Proc. 40th ACL*, pages 311–318. Association for Computational Linguistics.

Slav Petrov, Leon Barrett, Romain Thibaux, and Dan Klein. 2006. Learning accurate, compact, and interpretable tree annotation. In *Proc. 44th ACL*, pages 433–440. Association for Computational Linguistics.

Helmut Schmid. 2004. Efficient parsing of highly ambiguous context-free grammars with bit vectors. In *Proc. 20th COLING*, pages 162–168. Association for Computational Linguistics.

Andreas Stolcke. 2002. SRILM — an extensible language modeling toolkit. In *Proc. 7th INTERSPEECH*, pages 257–286.

Jun Sun, Min Zhang, and Chew Lim Tan. 2009. A noncontiguous tree sequence alignment-based model for statistical machine translation. In *Proc. 47th ACL*, pages 914–922. Association for Computational Linguistics.

Benjamin Wellington, Sonjia Waxmonsky, and I. Dan Melamed. 2006. Empirical lower bounds on the complexity of translational equivalence. In *Proc. 44th ACL*, pages 977–984. Association for Computational Linguistics.

Non-linear Learning for Statistical Machine Translation

Shujian Huang, Huadong Chen, Xinyu Dai and Jiajun Chen
State Key Laboratory for Novel Software Technology
Nanjing University
Nanjing 210023, China
{huangsj, chenhd, daixy, chenjj}@nlp.nju.edu.cn

Abstract

Modern statistical machine translation (SMT) systems usually use a linear combination of features to model the quality of each translation hypothesis. The linear combination assumes that all the features are in a linear relationship and constrains that each feature interacts with the rest features in an linear manner, which might limit the expressive power of the model and lead to a under-fit model on the current data. In this paper, we propose a non-linear modeling for the quality of translation hypotheses based on neural networks, which allows more complex interaction between features. A learning framework is presented for training the non-linear models. We also discuss possible heuristics in designing the network structure which may improve the non-linear learning performance. Experimental results show that with the basic features of a hierarchical phrase-based machine translation system, our method produce translations that are better than a linear model.

1 Introduction

One of the core problems in the research of statistical machine translation is the modeling of translation hypotheses. Each modeling method defines a score of a target sentence $\mathbf{e} = e_1 e_2 ... e_i ... e_I$, given a source sentence $\mathbf{f} = f_1 f_2 ... f_j ... f_J$, where each e_i is the ith target word and f_j is the jth source word. The well-known modeling method starts from the Source-Channel model (Brown et al., 1993)(Equation 1). The scoring of $\mathbf{e}$ decomposes to the calculation of a translation model and a language model.

$$Pr(\mathbf{e}|\mathbf{f}) = Pr(\mathbf{e})Pr(\mathbf{f}|\mathbf{e})/Pr(\mathbf{f}) \quad (1)$$

The modeling method is extended to log-linear models by Och and Ney (2002), as shown in Equation 2, where $h_m(\mathbf{e}|\mathbf{f})$ is the mth feature function and λ_m is the corresponding weight.

$$\begin{aligned} Pr(\mathbf{e}|\mathbf{f}) &= p_{\lambda_1^M}(\mathbf{e}|\mathbf{f}) \\ &= \frac{exp[\sum_{m=1}^{M} \lambda_m h_m(\mathbf{e}|\mathbf{f})]}{\sum_{\mathbf{e}'} exp[\sum_{m=1}^{M} \lambda_m h_m(\mathbf{e}'|\mathbf{f})]} \end{aligned} \quad (2)$$

Because the normalization term in Equation 2 is the same for all translation hypotheses of the same source sentence, the score of each hypothesis, denoted by s_L, is actually a linear combination of all features, as shown in Equation 3.

$$s_L(\mathbf{e}) = \sum_{m=1}^{M} \lambda_m h_m(\mathbf{e}|\mathbf{f}) \quad (3)$$

The log-linear models are flexible to incorporate new features and show significant advantage over the traditional source-channel models, thus become the state-of-the-art modeling method and are applied in various translation settings (Yamada and Knight, 2001; Koehn et al., 2003; Chiang, 2005; Liu et al., 2006).

It is worth noticing that log-linear models try to separate good and bad translation hypotheses using a linear hyper-plane. However, complex interactions between features make it difficult to linearly separate good translation hypotheses from bad ones (Clark et al., 2014).

Taking common features in a typical phrase-based (Koehn et al., 2003) or hierarchical phrase-based (Chiang, 2005) machine translation system as an example, the language model feature favors shorter hypotheses; the word penalty feature encourages longer hypotheses. The phrase translation probability feature selects phrases that occurs more frequently in the training corpus, which sometimes is long with a lower translation probability, as in translating named entities or idioms;

Proceedings of the 53rd Annual Meeting of the Association for Computational Linguistics and the 7th International Joint Conference on Natural Language Processing, pages 825–835,
Beijing, China, July 26-31, 2015.

sometimes is short but with a high translation probability, as in translating verbs or pronouns. These three features jointly decide the choice of translations. Simply use the weighted sum of their values may not be the best choice for modeling translations. As a result, log-linear models may under-fit the data. This under-fitting may prevents the further improvement of translation quality.

In this paper, we propose a non-linear modeling of translation hypotheses based on neural networks. The traditional features of a machine translation system are used as the input to the network. By feeding input features to nodes in a hidden layer, complex interactions among features are modeled, resulting in much stronger expressive power than traditional log-linear models. (Section 3)

Employing a neural network for SMT modeling has two issues to be tackled. The first issue is the parameter learning. Log-linear models rely on minimum error rate training (MERT) (Och, 2003) to achieve best performance. When the scoring function become non-linear, the intersection points of these non-linear functions could not be effectively calculated and enumerated. Thus MERT is no longer suitable for learning the parameters. To solve the problem, we present a framework for effective training including several criteria to transform the training problem into a binary classification task, a unified objective function and an iterative training algorithm. (Section 4)

The second issue is the structure of neural network. Single layer neural networks are equivalent to linear models; two-layer networks with sufficient nodes are capable of learning any continuous function (Bishop, 1995). Adding more layers into the network could model complex functions with less nodes, but also brings the problem of vanishing gradient (Erhan et al., 2009). We adapt a two-layer feed-forward neural network to keep the training process efficient. We notice that one major problem that prevents a neural network training reaching a good solution is that there are too many local minimums in the parameter space. Thus we discuss how to constrain the learning of neural networks with our intuitions and observations of the features. (Section 5)

Experiments are conducted to compare various settings and verify the effectiveness of our proposed learning framework. Experimental results show that our framework could achieve better translation quality even with the same traditional features as previous linear models. (Section 6)

2 Related work

Many research has been attempting to bring non-linearity into the training of SMT. These efforts could be roughly divided into the following three categories.

The first line of research attempted to re-interpret original features via feature transformation or additional learning. For example, Maskey and Zhou (2012) use a deep belief network to learn representations of the phrase translation and lexical translation probability features. Clark et al. (2014) used discretization to transform real-valued dense features into a set of binary indicator features. Lu et al. (2014) learned new features using a semi-supervised deep auto encoder. These work focus on the explicit representation of the features and usually employ extra learning procedure. Our proposed method only takes the original features, with no transformation, as the input. Feature transformation or combination are performed implicitly during the training of the network and integrated with the optimization of translation quality.

The second line of research attempted to use non-linear models instead of log-linear models, which is most similar in spirit with our work. Duh and Kirchhoff (2008) used the boosting method to combine several results of MERT and achieved improvement in a re-ranking setting. Liu et al. (2013) proposed an additive neural network which employed a two-layer neural network for embedding-based features. To avoid local minimum, they still rely on a pre-training and post-training from MERT or PRO. Comparing to these efforts, our proposed method takes a further step that it is integrated with iterative training, instead of re-ranking, and works without the help of any pre-trained linear models.

The third line of research attempted to add non-linear features/components into the log-linear learning framework. Neural network based models are trained as language models (Vaswani et al., 2013; Auli and Gao, 2014), translation models (Gao et al., 2014) or joint language and translation models (Auli et al., 2013; Devlin et al., 2014). Liu et al. (2013) also introduced word embedding for source and target sides of the translation

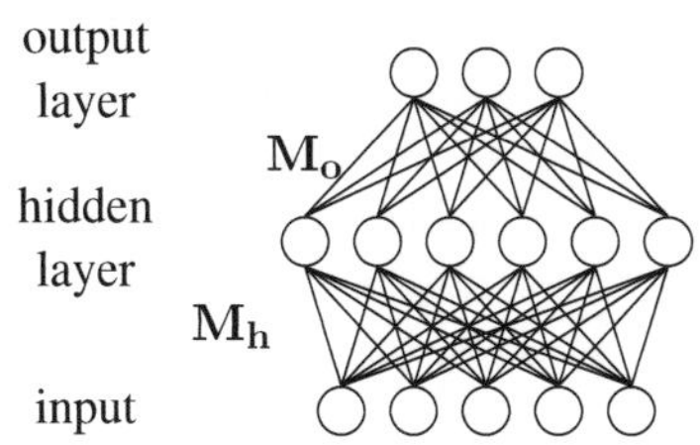

Figure 1: A two-layer feed-forward neural network.

rules as local features. In this paper, we focus on enhancing the expressive power of the modeling, which is independent of the research of enhancing translation systems with new designed features. We believe additional improvement could be achieved by incorporating more features into our framework.

3 Non-linear Translation

The non-linear modeling of translation hypotheses could be used in both phrase-based system and syntax-based systems. In this paper, we take the hierarchical phrase based machine translation system (Chiang, 2005) as an example and introduce how we fit the non-linearity into the system.

3.1 Two-layer Neural Networks

We employ a two-layer neural network as the non-linear model for scoring translation hypotheses. The structure of a typical two-layer feed-forward neural network includes an input layer, a hidden layer, and a output layer (as shown in Figure 1).

We use the input layer to accept input features, the hidden layer to combine different input features, the output layer with only one node to output the model score for each translation hypothesis based on the value of hidden nodes. More specifically, the score of hypothesis $\mathbf{e}$, denoted as s_N, is defined as:

$$s_N(\mathbf{e}) = \sigma_o(M_o \cdot \sigma_h(M_h \cdot h_1^m(\mathbf{e}|\mathbf{f}) + b_h) + b_o) \quad (4)$$

where M, b is the weight matrix, bias vector of the neural nodes, respectively; σ is the activation function, which is often set to non-linear functions such as the tanh function or sigmoid function; subscript h and o indicates the parameters of hidden layer and output layer, respectively.

3.2 Features

We use the standard features of a typical hierarchical phrase based translation system(Chiang, 2005). Adding new features into the framework is left as a future direction. The features as listed as following:

- $p(\alpha|\gamma)$ and $p(\gamma|\alpha)$: conditional probability of translating α as γ and translating α as γ, where α and γ is the left and right hand side of a initial phrase or hierarchical translation rule, respectively;
- $p_w(\alpha|\gamma)$ and $p_w(\gamma|\alpha)$: lexical probability of translating words in α as words in γ and translating words in γ as words in α;
- p_{lm}: language model probability;
- wc: accumulated count of individual words generated during translation;
- pc: accumulated count of initial phrases used;
- rc: accumulated count of hierarchical rule phrases used;
- gc: accumulated count of glue rule used in this hypothesis;
- uc: accumulated count of unknown source word. which has no entry in the translation table;
- nc: accumulated count of source phrases that translate into null;

3.3 Decoding

The basic decoding algorithm could be kept almost the same as traditional phrase-based or syntax-based translation systems (Yamada and Knight, 2001; Koehn et al., 2003; Chiang, 2005; Liu et al., 2006). For example, in the experiments of this paper, we use a CKY style decoding algorithm following Chiang (2005).

Our non-linear translation system is different from traditional systems in the way to calculate the score for each hypothesis. Instead of calculating the score as a linear combination, we use neural networks (Section 3.1) to perform a non-linear combination of feature values.

We also use the cube-pruning algorithm (Chiang, 2005) to keep the decoding efficient. Although the non-linearity in model scores may cause more search errors (Huang and Chiang,

2007) finding the highest scoring hypothesis, in practice it still achieves reasonable results.

4 Non-linear Learning Framework

Traditional machine translation systems rely on MERT to tune the weights of different features. MERT performs efficient search by enumerating the score function of all the hypotheses and using intersections of these linear functions to form the "upper-envelope" of the model score function (Och, 2003). When the scoring function is non-linear, it is not feasible to find the intersections of these functions. In this section, we discuss alternatives to train the parameters for non-linear models.

4.1 Training Criteria

The task of machine translation is a complex problem with structural output space. Decoding algorithms search for the translation hypothesis with the highest score, according to a given scoring function, from an exponentially large set of candidate hypotheses. The purpose of training is to select the scoring function, so that the function score the hypotheses "correctly". The correctness is often introduced by some extrinsic metrics, such as BLEU (Papineni et al., 2002).

We denote the scoring function as $s(\mathbf{f}, \mathbf{e}; \vec{\theta})$, or simply s, which is parameterized by $\vec{\theta}$; denote the set of all translation hypotheses as C; denote the extrinsic metric as $eval(\cdot)$ [1]. Note that, in linear cases, s is a linear function as in Equation 3, while in the non-linear case described in this paper, s is the scoring function in Equation 4.

Ideally, the training objective is to select a scoring function $\hat{s}$, from all functions $\mathcal{S}$, that scores the correct translation (or references) $\hat{\mathbf{e}}$, higher than any other hypotheses (Equation 5).

$$\hat{s} = \{s \in \mathcal{S} | s(\hat{\mathbf{e}}) > s(\mathbf{e})\, \forall \mathbf{e} \in C\} \quad (5)$$

In practice, the candidate set C is exponentially large and hard to enumerate; the correct translation $\hat{\mathbf{e}}$ may not even exist in the current search space for various reasons, e.g. unknown source word. As a result, we use the n-best set C_{nbest} to approximate C, use the extrinsic metric $eval(\cdot)$ to evaluate the quality of hypotheses in C_{nbest} and use the following three alternatives as approximations to the ideal objective.

Best v.s. Rest (BR) To score the best hypothesis in the n-best set $\tilde{\mathbf{e}}$ higher than the rest hypotheses. This objective is very similar to MERT in that it tries to optimize the score of $\tilde{\mathbf{e}}$ and doesn't concern about the ranking of rest hypotheses. In this case, $\tilde{\mathbf{e}}$ is an approximation of $\hat{\mathbf{e}}$.

Best v.s. Worst (BW) To score the best hypothesis higher than the worst hypothesis in the n-best set. This objective is motivated by the practice of separating the "hope" and "fear" translation hypotheses (Chiang, 2012). We take a simpler strategy which uses the best and worst hypothesis in C_{nbest} as the "hope" and "fear" hypothesis, respectively, in order to avoid multi-pass decoding.

Pairwise (PW) To score the better hypothesis in sampled hypothesis pairs higher than the worse one in the same pair. This objective is adapted from the Pairwise Ranking Optimization (PRO) (Hopkins and May, 2011), which tries to ranking all the hypotheses instead of selecting the best one. We use the same sampling strategy as their original paper.

Note that each of the above criteria transforms the original problem of selecting best hypotheses from an exponential space to a certain pairwise comparison problem, which could be easily trained using binary classifiers.

4.2 Training Objective

For the binary classification task, we use a hinge loss following Watanabe (2012). Because the network has a lot of parameters compared with the linear model, we use a L_1 norm instead of L_2 norm as the regularization term, to favor sparse solutions. We define our training objective function in Equation 6.

$$\begin{aligned} & arg \min_{\theta} \frac{1}{N} \sum_{\mathbf{f} \in D} \sum_{(\mathbf{e}_1, \mathbf{e}_2) \in T(f)} \delta(\mathbf{f}, \mathbf{e}_1, \mathbf{e}_2; \theta) \\ & \qquad + \lambda \cdot ||\theta||_1 \\ & \text{with} \\ & \delta(\cdot) = max\{s(\mathbf{f}, \mathbf{e}_1; \theta) - s(\mathbf{f}, \mathbf{e}_2; \theta) + 1, 0\} \end{aligned} \quad (6)$$

where D is the given training data; $(\mathbf{e}_1, \mathbf{e}_2)$ is a training hypothesis-pair, with $\mathbf{e}_1$ to be the one with

[1] In our experiments, we use sentence level BLEU with +1 smoothing as the evaluation metric.

higher $eval(\cdot)$ score; N is the total number of hypothesis-pairs in D; $T(f)$, or simply T, is the set of hypothesis-pairs for each source sentence f.

The set T is decided by the criterion used for training. For the BR setting, the best hypothesis is paired with every other hypothesis in the n-best list (Equation 7); while for the BW setting, it is only paired with the worst hypothesis (Equation 8). The generation of T in PW setting is the same with PRO sampling, we refer the readers to the original paper of Hopkins and May (2011).

$$T_{BR} = \{(\mathbf{e}_1, \mathbf{e}_2) | \mathbf{e}_1 = arg \max_{\mathbf{e} \in C_{nbest}} eval(\mathbf{e}), \\ \mathbf{e}_2 \in C_{nbest} \text{ and } \mathbf{e}_1 \neq \mathbf{e}_2\} \tag{7}$$

$$T_{BW} = \{(\mathbf{e}_1, \mathbf{e}_2) | \mathbf{e}_1 = arg \max_{\mathbf{e} \in C_{nbest}} eval(\mathbf{e}), \\ \mathbf{e}_2 = arg \min_{\mathbf{e} \in C_{nbest}} eval(\mathbf{e})\} \tag{8}$$

4.3 Training Procedure

In standard training algorithm for classification, the training instances stays the same in each iteration. In machine translation, decoding algorithms usually return a very different n-best set with different parameters. This is due to the exponentially large size of search space. MERT and PRO extend the current n-best set by merging the n-best set of all previous iterations into a pool (Och, 2003; Hopkins and May, 2011). In this way, the enlarged n-best set may give a better approximation of the true hypothesis set C and may lead to better and more stable training results.

We argue that the training should still focus on hypotheses obtained in current round, because in each iteration the searching for the n-best set is independent of previous iterations. To compromise the above two goals, in our practice, training hypothesis pairs are first generated from the current n-best set, then merged with the pairs generated from all previous iterations. In order to make the model focus more on pairs from current iteration, we assign pairs in previous iterations a small constant weight and assign pairs in current iteration a relatively large constant weight [2]. This is inspired by the AdaBoost algorithm (Schapire, 1999) in weighting instances.

Following the spirit of MERT, we propose a iterative training procedure (Algorithm 1). The

[2] In our experiments, we empirically set the constants to be 0.1 and 0.9, respectively.

Algorithm 1 Iterative Training Algorithm

Input: the set of training sentences D, max number of iteration I

```
1:  θ^0 ← RandomInit(),
2:  for i = 0 to I do
3:      T_i ← ∅;
4:      for each f ∈ D do
5:          C_nbest ← NbestDecode(f ; θ^i)
6:          T ← GeneratePair(C_nbest)
7:          T_i ← T_i ∪ T
8:      end for
9:      T_all ← WeightedCombine(∪_{k=0}^{i-1} T_k, T_i)
10:     θ^{i+1} ← Optimize(T_all, θ^i)
11: end for
```

training starts by randomly initialized model parameters θ^0 (line 1). In ith iteration, the decoding algorithm decodes each sentence $\mathbf{f}$ to get the n-best set C_{nbest} (line 5). Training hypothesis pairs T are extracted from C_{nbest} according to the training criterion described in Section 4.2 (line 6). Newly collected pairs T_i are combined with pairs from previous iterations before used for training (line 9). θ^{i+1} is obtained by solving Equation 6 using the Conjugate Sub-Gradient method (Le et al., 2011) (line 10).

5 Structure of the Network

Although neural networks bring strong expressive power to the modeling of translation hypothesis, training a neural network is prone to resulting in local minimum which may affect the training results. We speculate that one reason for these local minimums is that the structure of a well-connected network has too many parameters. Take a neural network with k nodes in the input layer and m nodes in the hidden layer as an example. Every node in the hidden layer is connected to each of the k input nodes. This simple structure resulting in at least $k \times m$ parameters.

In Section 4.2, we use L_1 norm in the objective function in order to get sparser solutions. In this section, we propose some constrained network structures according to our prior knowledge of the features. These structures have much less parameters or simpler structures comparing to original neural networks, thus reduce the possibility of getting stuck in local minimums.

5.1 Network with two-degree Hidden Layer

We find the first pitfall of the standard two-layer neural network is that each node in the hidden layer receives input from every input layer node. Features used in SMT are usually manually designed, which has their concrete meanings. For a network of several hidden nodes, combining every features into every hidden node may be redundant and not necessary to represent the quality of a hypothesis.

As a result, we take a harsh step and constrain the nodes in hidden layer to have a in-degree of two, which means each hidden node only accepts inputs from two input nodes. We do not use any other prior knowledge about features in this setting. So for a network with k nodes in the input layer, the hidden layer should contain $C_k^2 = k(k-1)/2$ nodes to accept all combinations from the input layer. We name this network structure as Two-Degree Hidden Layer Network (TDN).

It is easy to see that a TDN has $C_k^2 \times 2 = k(k-1)$ parameters for the hidden layer because of the constrained degree. This is one order of magnitude less than a standard two-layer network with the same number of hidden nodes, which has $C_k^2 \times k = k^2(k-1)/2$ parameters.

Note that we perform a 2-degree combination that looks similar in spirit with those combination of atomic features in large scale discriminative learning for other NLP tasks, such as POS tagging and parsing. However, unlike the practice in these tasks that directly combines values of different features to generate a new feature type, we first linearly combine the value of these features and perform non-linear transformation on these values via an activation function.

5.2 Network with Grouped Features

It might be a too strong constraint to require the hidden node have in-degree of 2. In order to relax this constraint, we need more prior knowledge from the features.

Our first observation is that there are different types of features. These types are different from each other in terms of value ranges, sources, importance, etc. For example, language model features usually take a very small value of probability, and word count feature takes a integer value and usually has a much higher weight in linear case than other count features.

The second observation is that features of the same type may not have complex interaction with each other. For example, it is reasonable to combine language model features with word count features in a hidden node. But it may not be necessary to combine the count of initial phrases and the count of unknown words into a hidden node.

Based on the above two intuitions, we design a new structure of network that has the following constraints: given a disjoint partition of features: $G_1, G_2, \ldots, G_k$, every hidden node takes input from a set of input nodes, where any two nodes in this set come from two different feature groups. Under this constraint, the in-degree of a hidden node is at most k. We name this network structure as Grouped Network (GN).

In practice, we divide the basic features in Section 3.2 into five groups: language model features, translation probability features, lexical probability features, the word count feature, and the rest of count features. This division considers not only the value ranges, but also types of features and the possibility of them interact with each other.

6 Experiments and Results

6.1 General Settings

We conduct experiments on a large scale machine translation tasks. The parallel data comes from LDC, including LDC2002E18, LDC2003E14, LDC2004E12, LDC2004T08, LDC2005T10, LDC2007T09, which consists of 8.2 million of sentence pairs. Monolingual data includes Xinhua portion of Gigaword corpus. We use multi-references data MT03 as training data, MT02 as development data, and MT04, MT05 as test data. These data are mainly in the same genre, avoiding the extra consideration of domain adaptation.

Data	Usage	Sents.
LDC	TM train	8,260,093
Gigaword	LM train	14,684,074
MT03	train	919
MT02	dev	878
MT04	test	1,789
MT05	test	1,083

Table 1: Experimental data and statistics.

The Chinese side of the corpora is word segmented using ICTCLAS[3]. Our translation sys-

[3]http://ictclas.nlpir.org/

Criteria	MT03(train)	MT02(dev)	MT04	MT05
BR_c	35.02	36.63	34.96	34.15
BR	38.66	40.04	38.73	37.50
BW	39.55	39.36	38.72	37.81
PW	38.61	38.85	38.73	37.98

Table 2: BLEU4 in percentage on different training criteria ("BR", "BW" and "PW" refer to experiments with "Best v.s. Rest", "Best v.s. Worst" and "Pairwise" training criteria, respectively. "BR_c" indicates generate hypothesis pairs from n-best set of current iteration only presented in Section 4.3.

tem is an in-house implementation of the hierarchical phrase-based translation system(Chiang, 2005). We set the beam size to 20. We train a 5-gram language model on the monolingual data with MKN smoothing(Chen and Goodman, 1998). For each parameter tuning experiments, we ran the same training procedure 3 times and present the average results. The translation quality is evaluated use 4-gram case-insensitive BLEU (Papineni et al., 2002). Significant test is performed using bootstrap re-sampling implemented by Clark et al. (2011). We employ a two-layer neural network with 11 input layer nodes, corresponding to features listed in Section 3.2 and 1 output layer node. The number of nodes in the hidden layer varies in different settings. The sigmoid function is used as the activation function for each node in the hidden layer. For the output layer we use a linear activation function. We try different λ for the L_1 norm from 0.01 to 0.00001 and use the one with best performance on the development set. We solve the optimization problem with ALGLIB package[4].

6.2 Experiments of Training Criteria

This set experiments evaluates different training criteria discussed in Section 4.1. We generate hypothesis-pair according to BW, BR and PW criteria, respectively, and perform training with these pairs. In the PW criterion, we use the sampling method of PRO (Hopkins and May, 2011) and get the 50 hypothesis pairs for each sentence. We use 20 hidden nodes for all three settings to make a fair comparison.

The results are presented in Table 2. The first two rows compare training with and without the weighted combination of hypothesis pairs we discussed in Section 4.3. As the result suggested, with the weighted combination of hypothesis pairs from previous iterations, the performance improves significantly on both test sets.

[4]http://www.alglib.net/

Although the system performance on the dev set varies, the performance on test sets are almost comparable. This suggest that although the three training criteria are based on different assumptions, their are basically equivalent for training translation systems.

Criteria	Pairs/iteration	Accuracy(%)
BR	19	70.7
BW	1	79.5
PW	100	67.3

Table 3: Comparison of different training criteria in number of new instances per iteration and training accuracy.

We also compares the three training criteria in their number of new instances per iteration and final training accuracy (Table 3). Compared to BR which tries to separate the best hypothesis from the rest hypotheses in the n-best set, and PW which tries to obtain a correct ranking of all hypotheses, BW only aims at separating the best and worst hypothesis of each iteration, which is a easier task for learning a classifiers. It requires the least training instances and achieves the best performance in training. Note that, the accuracy for each system in Table 3 are the accuracy each system achieves after training stops. They are not calculated on the same set of instances, thus not directly comparable. We use the differences in accuracy as an indicator for the difficulties of the corresponding learning task.

For the rest of this paper, we use the BW criterion because it is much simpler compared to sampling method of PRO (Hopkins and May, 2011).

6.3 Experiments of Network Structures

We make several comparisons of the network structures and compare them with a baseline hierarchical phrase-based translation system (HPB).

Table 4 shows the translation performance of

Systems	MT03(train)	MT02(dev)	MT04	MT05	Test Average
HPB	39.25	39.07	38.81	38.01	38.41
TLayer_{20}	39.55^*	39.36^*	38.72	37.81	38.27(-0.14)
TLayer_{30}	39.70^+	39.71^*	38.89	37.90	38.40(-0.01)
TLayer_{50}	39.26	38.97	38.72	38.79^+	38.76(+0.35)
TLayer_{100}	39.42	38.77	38.65	38.65^+	38.69(+0.28)
TLayer_{200}	39.69	38.68	38.72	38.80^+	38.74(+0.32)
TDN	39.60^+	38.94	38.99^*	38.13	38.56(+0.15)
GN	**39.73**$^+$	**39.41**$^+$	**39.45**$^+$	**38.51**$^+$	**38.98(+0.57)**

Table 4: BLEU4 in percentage for comparing of systems using different network structures (HPB refers to the baseline hierarchical phrase-based system. TLayer, TDN, GN refer to the standard 2-layer network, Two-Degree Hidden Layer Network, Grouped Network, respectively. Subscript of TLayer indicates the number of nodes in the hidden layer.) $^+$, * marks results that are significant better than the baseline system with $p < 0.01$ and $p < 0.05$.

Systems	# Hidden Nodes	# Parameters	Training Time per iter.(s)
HPB	-	11	1041
TLayer_{20}	20	261	671
TLayer_{30}	30	391	729
TLayer_{50}	50	651	952
TLayer_{100}	100	1,301	1,256
TLayer_{200}	200	2,601	2,065
TDN	55	221	808
GN	214	1,111	1,440

Table 5: Comparison of network scales and training time of different systems, including the number of nodes in the hidden layer, the number of parameters, the average training time per iteration (15 iterations). The notations of systems are the same as in Table4.

different systems[5]. All 5 two-layer feed forward neural networks models could achieve comparable or better performance comparing to the baseline system. We can see that training a larger network may lead to better translation quality (from TLayer_{20} and TLayer_{30} to TLayer_{50}). However, increasing the number of hidden node to 100 and 200 does not bring further improvement. One possible reason is that training a larger network with arbitrary connections brings in too many parameters which may be difficult to train with limited training data.

TDN and GN are the two network structures proposed in Section 5. With the constraint that all input to the hidden node should be of degree 2, TDN performs comparable to the baseline system. With the grouped feature, we could design networks such as GN, which shows significant improvement over the baseline systems (+0.57) and achieves the best performance among all neural systems.

[5] TLayer_{20} is the same system as BW in Table 2

Table 4 shows statistics related to the efficiency issue of different systems. The baseline system (HPB) uses MERT for training. HPB has a very small number of parameters and searches for the best parameters exhaustively in each iteration. The non-linear systems with few nodes (TLayer_{20} and TLayer_{30}) train faster than HPB in each iteration because they perform back-propagation instead of exhaustive search. We iterate 15 iterations for each non-linear system, while MERT takes about 10 rounds to reach its best performance.

When the number of nodes in the hidden layer increases (from 20 to 200), the number of parameters in the system also increases, which requires longer time to compute the score for each hypothesis and to update the parameters through back-propagation. The network with 200 hidden nodes takes about twice the time to train for each iteration, compared to the linear system[6].

TDN and GN have larger numbers of hidden

[6] Matrix operation is CPU intensive. The cost will increase when multiple tasks are running.

nodes. However, because of our intuitions in designing the structure of the networks, the degree of the hidden node is constrained. So these two networks are sparser in parameters and take significant less training time than standard neural networks. For example, GN has a comparable number of hidden nodes with TLayer_{200}, but only has half of its parameters and takes about 70% time to train in each iteration. In other words, our proposed network structure provides more efficient training in these cases and achieve better results.

7 Conclusion

In this paper, we discuss a non-linear framework for modeling translation hypothesis for statistical machine translation system. We also present a learning framework including training criterion and algorithms to integrate our modeling into a state of the art hierarchical phrase based machine translation system. Compared to previous effort in bringing in non-linearity into machine translation, our method uses a single two-layer neural networks and performs training independent with any previous linear training methods (e.g. MERT). Our method also trains its parameters without any pre-training or post-training procedure. Experiment shows that our method could improve the baseline system even with the same feature as input, in a large scale Chinese-English machine translation task.

In training neural networks with hidden nodes, we use heuristics to reduce the complexity of network structures and obtain extra advantages over standard networks. It shows that heuristics and intuitions of the data and features are still important to a machine translation system.

Neural networks are able to perform feature learning by using hidden nodes to model the interaction among a large vector of raw features, as in image and speech processing (Krizhevsky et al., 2012; Hinton et al., 2012). We are trying to model the interaction between hand-crafted features, which is indeed similar in spirit with learning features from raw features. Although our features already have concrete meaning, e.g. the probability of translation, the fluency of target sentence, etc. Combining these features may have extra advantage in modeling the translation process.

As future work, it is necessary to integrate more features into our learning framework. It is also interesting to see how the non-linear modeling fits in to more complex learning tasks which involves domain specific learning techniques.

Acknowledgments

The authors would like to thank Yue Zhang and the anonymous reviewers for their valuable comments. This work is supported by the National Natural Science Foundation of China (No. 61300158, 61223003), the Jiangsu Provincial Research Foundation for Basic Research (No. BK20130580).

References

Michael Auli and Jianfeng Gao. 2014. Decoder integration and expected BLEU training for recurrent neural network language models. In *Proceedings of the 52nd Annual Meeting of the Association for Computational Linguistics, ACL 2014, June 22-27, 2014, Baltimore, MD, USA, Volume 2: Short Papers*, pages 136–142.

Michael Auli, Michel Galley, Chris Quirk, and Geoffrey Zweig. 2013. Joint language and translation modeling with recurrent neural networks. In *Proceedings of the 2013 Conference on Empirical Methods in Natural Language Processing, EMNLP 2013, 18-21 October 2013, Grand Hyatt Seattle, Seattle, Washington, USA, A meeting of SIGDAT, a Special Interest Group of the ACL*, pages 1044–1054.

Christopher M. Bishop. 1995. *Neural Networks for Pattern Recognition*. Oxford University Press, Inc., New York, NY, USA.

Peter F. Brown, Stephen Della Pietra, Vincent J. Della Pietra, and Robert L. Mercer. 1993. The mathematic of statistical machine translation: Parameter estimation. *Computational Linguistics*, 19(2):263–311.

S. F. Chen and J. T. Goodman. 1998. An empirical study of smoothing techniques for language modeling. Technical report, Computer Science Group, Harvard University, Technical Report TR-10-98.

David Chiang. 2005. A hierarchical phrase-based model for statistical machine translation. In *annual meeting of the Association for Computational Linguistics*.

David Chiang. 2012. Hope and fear for discriminative training of statistical translation models. *J. Mach. Learn. Res.*, 13(1):1159–1187, April.

Jonathan H. Clark, Chris Dyer, Alon Lavie, and Noah A. Smith. 2011. Better hypothesis testing for statistical machine translation: Controlling for optimizer instability. In *Proceedings of the 49th Annual*

Meeting of the Association for Computational Linguistics: Human Language Technologies: Short Papers - Volume 2, HLT '11, pages 176–181, Stroudsburg, PA, USA. Association for Computational Linguistics.

Jonathan Clark, Chris Dyer, and Alon Lavie. 2014. Locally non-linear learning for statistical machine translation via discretization and structured regularization. *Transactions of the Association for Computational Linguistics*, 2:393–404.

Jacob Devlin, Rabih Zbib, Zhongqiang Huang, Thomas Lamar, Richard M. Schwartz, and John Makhoul. 2014. Fast and robust neural network joint models for statistical machine translation. In *Proceedings of the 52nd Annual Meeting of the Association for Computational Linguistics, ACL 2014, June 22-27, 2014, Baltimore, MD, USA, Volume 1: Long Papers*, pages 1370–1380.

Kevin Duh and Katrin Kirchhoff. 2008. Beyond log-linear models: Boosted minimum error rate training for n-best re-ranking. In *Proceedings of the 46th Annual Meeting of the Association for Computational Linguistics on Human Language Technologies: Short Papers*, HLT-Short '08, pages 37–40, Stroudsburg, PA, USA. Association for Computational Linguistics.

Dumitru Erhan, Pierre antoine Manzagol, Yoshua Bengio, Samy Bengio, and Pascal Vincent. 2009. The difficulty of training deep architectures and the effect of unsupervised pre-training. In David V. Dyk and Max Welling, editors, *Proceedings of the Twelfth International Conference on Artificial Intelligence and Statistics (AISTATS-09)*, volume 5, pages 153–160. Journal of Machine Learning Research - Proceedings Track.

Jianfeng Gao, Xiaodong He, Wen-tau Yih, and Li Deng. 2014. Learning continuous phrase representations for translation modeling. In *Proceedings of the 52nd Annual Meeting of the Association for Computational Linguistics, ACL 2014, June 22-27, 2014, Baltimore, MD, USA, Volume 1: Long Papers*, pages 699–709.

Geoffrey Hinton, Li Deng, Dong Yu, George E Dahl, Abdel-rahman Mohamed, Navdeep Jaitly, Andrew Senior, Vincent Vanhoucke, Patrick Nguyen, Tara N Sainath, et al. 2012. Deep neural networks for acoustic modeling in speech recognition: The shared views of four research groups. *Signal Processing Magazine, IEEE*, 29(6):82–97.

Mark Hopkins and Jonathan May. 2011. Tuning as ranking. In *Proceedings of the Conference on Empirical Methods in Natural Language Processing*, EMNLP '11, pages 1352–1362, Stroudsburg, PA, USA. Association for Computational Linguistics.

Liang Huang and David Chiang. 2007. Forest rescoring: Faster decoding with integrated language models. In *Proceedings of the 45th Annual Meeting of the Association of Computational Linguistics*, pages 144–151, Prague, Czech Republic, June. Association for Computational Linguistics.

Philipp Koehn, Franz Josef Och, and Daniel Marcu. 2003. Statistical phrase-based translation. In *HLT-NAACL*.

Alex Krizhevsky, Ilya Sutskever, and Geoffrey E. Hinton. 2012. Imagenet classification with deep convolutional neural networks. In F. Pereira, C.J.C. Burges, L. Bottou, and K.Q. Weinberger, editors, *Advances in Neural Information Processing Systems 25*, pages 1097–1105. Curran Associates, Inc.

Quoc V. Le, Jiquan Ngiam, Adam Coates, Ahbik Lahiri, Bobby Prochnow, and Andrew Y. Ng. 2011. On optimization methods for deep learning. In *Proceedings of the 28th International Conference on Machine Learning, ICML 2011, Bellevue, Washington, USA, June 28 - July 2, 2011*, pages 265–272.

Yang Liu, Qun Liu, and Shouxun Lin. 2006. Tree-to-string alignment template for statistical machine translation. In *Proceedings of the 44th Annual Meeting of the Association of Computational Linguistics*. The Association for Computer Linguistics.

Lemao Liu, Taro Watanabe, Eiichiro Sumita, and Tiejun Zhao. 2013. Additive neural networks for statistical machine translation. In *Proceedings of the 51st Annual Meeting of the Association for Computational Linguistics, ACL 2013, 4-9 August 2013, Sofia, Bulgaria, Volume 1: Long Papers*, pages 791–801.

Shixiang Lu, Zhenbiao Chen, and Bo Xu. 2014. Learning new semi-supervised deep auto-encoder features for statistical machine translation. In *Proceedings of the 52nd Annual Meeting of the Association for Computational Linguistics (Volume 1: Long Papers)*, pages 122–132, Baltimore, Maryland, June. Association for Computational Linguistics.

Sameer Maskey and Bowen Zhou. 2012. Unsupervised deep belief features for speech translation. In *INTERSPEECH 2012, 13th Annual Conference of the International Speech Communication Association, Portland, Oregon, USA, September 9-13, 2012*.

Franz Josef Och and Hermann Ney. 2002. Discriminative training and maximum entropy models for statistical machine translation. pages 295–302.

Franz Josef Och. 2003. Minimum error rate training in statistical machine translation. In *ACL '03: Proceedings of the 41st Annual Meeting on Association for Computational Linguistics*, pages 160–167, Morristown, NJ, USA. Association for Computational Linguistics.

Kishore Papineni, Salim Roukos, Todd Ward, and Wei-Jing Zhu. 2002. Bleu: a method for automatic evaluation of machine translation. In *ACL '02: Proceedings of the 40th Annual Meeting on Association for*

Computational Linguistics, pages 311–318, Morristown, NJ, USA. Association for Computational Linguistics.

Robert E. Schapire. 1999. A brief introduction to boosting. In *Proceedings of the 16th International Joint Conference on Artificial Intelligence - Volume 2*, IJCAI'99, pages 1401–1406, San Francisco, CA, USA. Morgan Kaufmann Publishers Inc.

Ashish Vaswani, Yinggong Zhao, Victoria Fossum, and David Chiang. 2013. Decoding with large-scale neural language models improves translation. In *Proceedings of the 2013 Conference on Empirical Methods in Natural Language Processing, EMNLP 2013, 18-21 October 2013, Grand Hyatt Seattle, Seattle, Washington, USA, A meeting of SIGDAT, a Special Interest Group of the ACL*, pages 1387–1392.

Taro Watanabe. 2012. Optimized online rank learning for machine translation. In *Proceedings of the 2012 Conference of the North American Chapter of the Association for Computational Linguistics: Human Language Technologies*, NAACL HLT '12, pages 253–262, Stroudsburg, PA, USA. Association for Computational Linguistics.

Kenji Yamada and Kevin Knight. 2001. A syntax-based statistical translation model. In *Proceedings of the 39th Annual Meeting of the Association of Computational Linguistics*, pages 523–530.

Unifying Bayesian Inference and Vector Space Models for Improved Decipherment

Qing Dou[*], **Ashish Vaswani**[*], **Kevin Knight**
Information Sciences Institute
Department of Computer Science
University of Southern California
{qdou,avaswani,knight}@isi.edu

Chris Dyer
School of Computer Science
Carnegie Mellon University
cdyer@cs.cmu.edu

Abstract

We introduce into Bayesian decipherment a base distribution derived from similarities of word embeddings. We use Dirichlet multinomial regression (Mimno and McCallum, 2012) to learn a mapping between ciphertext and plaintext word embeddings from *non-parallel* data. Experimental results show that the base distribution is highly beneficial to decipherment, improving state-of-the-art decipherment accuracy from 45.8% to 67.4% for Spanish/English, and from 5.1% to 11.2% for Malagasy/English.

1 Introduction

Tremendous advances in Machine Translation (MT) have been made since we began applying automatic learning techniques to learn translation rules automatically from parallel data. However, reliance on parallel data also limits the development and application of high-quality MT systems, as the amount of parallel data is far from adequate in low-density languages and domains.

In general, it is easier to obtain non-parallel monolingual data. The ability to learn translations from monolingual data can alleviate obstacles caused by insufficient parallel data. Motivated by this idea, researchers have proposed different approaches to tackle this problem. They can be largely divided into two groups.

The first group is based on the idea proposed by Rapp (1995), in which words are represented as context vectors, and two words are likely to be translations if their context vectors are similar. Initially, the vectors contained only context words. Later extensions introduced more features (Haghighi et al., 2008; Garera et al., 2009; Bergsma and Van Durme, 2011; Daumé and Jagarlamudi, 2011; Irvine and Callison-Burch, 2013b; Irvine and Callison-Burch, 2013a), and used more abstract representation such as word embeddings (Klementiev et al., 2012).

Another promising approach to solve this problem is decipherment. It has drawn significant amounts of interest in the past few years (Ravi and Knight, 2011; Nuhn et al., 2012; Dou and Knight, 2013; Ravi, 2013) and has been shown to improve end-to-end translation. Decipherment views a foreign language as a cipher for English and finds a translation table that converts foreign texts into sensible English.

Both approaches have been shown to improve quality of MT systems for domain adaptation (Daumé and Jagarlamudi, 2011; Dou and Knight, 2012; Irvine et al., 2013) and low density languages (Irvine and Callison-Burch, 2013a; Dou et al., 2014). Meanwhile, they have their own advantages and disadvantages. While context vectors can take larger context into account, it requires high quality seed lexicons to learn a mapping between two vector spaces. In contrast, decipherment does not depend on any seed lexicon, but only looks at a limited n-gram context.

In this work, we take advantage of both approaches and combine them in a joint inference process. More specifically, we extend previous work in large scale Bayesian decipherment by introducing a better base distribution derived from similarities of word embedding vectors. The main contributions of this work are:

- We propose a new framework that combines the two main approaches to finding translations from monolingual data only.

[*] Equal contribution

Proceedings of the 53rd Annual Meeting of the Association for Computational Linguistics and the 7th International Joint Conference on Natural Language Processing, pages 836–845,
Beijing, China, July 26-31, 2015.

- We develop a new base-distribution technique that improves state-of-the art decipherment accuracy by a factor of two for Spanish/English and Malagasy/English.
- We make our software available for future research, functioning as a kind of GIZA for non-parallel data.

2 Decipherment Model

In this section, we describe the previous decipherment framework that we build on. This framework follows Ravi and Knight (2011), who built an MT system using only non-parallel data for translating movie subtitles; Dou and Knight (2012) and Nuhn et al. (2012), who scaled decipherment to larger vocabularies; and Dou and Knight (2013), who improved decipherment accuracy with dependency relations between words.

Throughout this paper, we use f to denote target language or ciphertext tokens, and e to denote source language or plaintext tokens. Given ciphertext $\mathbf{f}: f_1...f_n$, the task of decipherment is to find a set of parameters $P(f_i|e_i)$ that convert f to sensible plaintext. The ciphertext $\mathbf{f}$ can either be full sentences (Ravi and Knight, 2011; Nuhn et al., 2012) or simply bigrams (Dou and Knight, 2013). Since using bigrams and their counts speeds up decipherment, in this work, we treat $\mathbf{f}$ as bigrams, where $\mathbf{f} = \{\mathbf{f}^n\}_{n=1}^N = \{f_1^n, f_2^n\}_{n=1}^N$.

Motivated by the idea from Weaver (1955), we model an observed cipher bigram $\mathbf{f}^n$ with the following generative story:

- First, a language model $P(\mathbf{e})$ generates a sequence of two plaintext tokens e_1^n, e_2^n with probability $P(e_1^n, e_2^n)$.
- Then, substitute e_1^n with f_1^n and e_2^n with f_2^n with probability $P(f_1^n \mid e_1^n) \cdot P(f_2^n \mid e_2^n)$.

Based on the above generative story, the probability of any cipher bigram $\mathbf{f^n}$ is:

$$P(\mathbf{f}^n) = \sum_{e_1 e_2} P(e_1 e_2) \prod_{i=1}^{2} P(f_i^n \mid e_i)$$

The probability of the ciphertext corpus,

$$P(\{\mathbf{f}^n\}_{n=1}^N) = \prod_{n=1}^{N} P(\mathbf{f}^n)$$

There are two sets of parameters in the model: the channel probabilities $\{P(f \mid e)\}$ and the bigram language model probabilities $\{P(e' \mid e)\}$, where f ranges over the ciphertext vocabulary and e, e' range over the plaintext vocabulary. Given a plaintext bigram language model, the training objective is to learn $P(f \mid e)$ that maximize $P(\{\mathbf{f}^n\}_{n=1}^N)$. When formulated like this, one can directly apply EM to solve the problem (Knight et al., 2006). However, EM has time complexity $O(N \cdot V_e^2)$ and space complexity $O(V_f \cdot V_e)$, where V_f, V_e are the sizes of ciphertext and plaintext vocabularies respectively, and N is the number of cipher bigrams. This makes the EM approach unable to handle long ciphertexts with large vocabulary size.

An alternative approach is Bayesian decipherment (Ravi and Knight, 2011). We assume that $P(f \mid e)$ and $P(e' \mid e)$ are drawn from a Dirichet distribution with hyper-parameters $\alpha_{f,e}$ and $\alpha_{e,e'}$, that is:

$$P(f \mid e) \sim Dirichlet(\alpha_{f,e})$$
$$P(e \mid e') \sim Dirichlet(\alpha_{e,e'}).$$

The remainder of the generative story is the same as the noisy channel model for decipherment. In the next section, we describe how we learn the hyper parameters of the Dirichlet prior. Given $\alpha_{f,e}$ and $\alpha_{e,e'}$, The joint likelihood of the complete data and the parameters,

$$\begin{aligned}
&P(\{\mathbf{f}^n, \mathbf{e}^n\}_{n=1}^N, \{P(f \mid e)\}, \{P(e \mid e')\}) \\
&= P(\{\mathbf{f}^n \mid \mathbf{e}^n\}_{n=1}^N, \{P(f \mid e)\}) \\
&P(\{\mathbf{e}^n\}_{n=1}^N, P(e \mid e')) \\
&= \prod_e \frac{\Gamma\left(\sum_f \alpha_{f,e}\right)}{\prod_f \Gamma\left(\alpha_{e,f}\right)} \prod_f P(f \mid e)^{\#(e,f)+\alpha_{e,f}-1} \\
&\prod_e \frac{\Gamma\left(\sum_{e'} \alpha_{e,e'}\right)}{\prod_{e'} \Gamma\left(\alpha_{e,e'}\right)} \prod_f P(e \mid e')^{\#(e,e')+\alpha_{e,e'}-1},
\end{aligned} \quad (1)$$

where $\#(e, f)$ and $\#(e, e')$ are the counts of the translated word pairs and plaintext bigram pairs in the complete data, and $\Gamma(\cdot)$ is the Gamma function. Unlike EM, in Bayesian decipherment, we no longer search for parameters $P(f \mid e)$ that maximize the likelihood of the observed ciphertext. Instead, we draw samples from posterior distribution of the plaintext sequences given the ciphertext. Under the above Bayesian decipherment model, it turns out that the probability of a particular cipher word f_j having a value k, given the current plaintext word e_j, and the samples for all the other ciphertext and plaintext words, $\mathbf{f}_{-j}$ and $\mathbf{e}_{-j}$, is:

$$P(f_j = k \mid e_j, \mathbf{f}_{-j}, \mathbf{e}_{-j}) = \frac{\#(k, e_j)_{-j} + \alpha_{e_j,k}}{\#(e_j)_{-j} + \sum_f \alpha_{e_j,f}}.$$

Where, $\#(k, e_j)_{-j}$ and $\#(e_j)_{-j}$ are the counts of the ciphertext, plaintext word pair and plaintext word in the samples excluding f_j and e_j. Similarly, the probability of a plaintext word e_j taking a value l given samples for all other plaintext words,

$$P(e_j = l \mid \mathbf{e}_{-j}) = \frac{\#(l, e_{j-1})_{-j} + \alpha_{l,e_{j-1}}}{\#(e_{j-1})_{-j} + \sum_e \alpha_{e,e_{j-1}}}. \quad (2)$$

Since we have large amounts of plaintext data, we can train a high-quality dependency-bigram language model, $P_{LM}(e \mid e')$ and use it to guide our samples and learn a better posterior distribution. For that, we define $\alpha_{e,e'} = \alpha P_{LM}(e \mid e')$, and set α to be very high. The probability of a plaintext word (Equation 2) is now

$$P(e_j = l \mid \mathbf{e}_{-j}) \approx P_{LM}(l \mid e_{j-1}). \quad (3)$$

To sample from the posterior, we iterate over the observed ciphertext bigram tokens and use equations 2 and 3 to sample a plaintext token with probability

$$P(e_j \mid \mathbf{e}_{-j}, \mathbf{f}) \propto P_{LM}(e_j \mid e_{j-1})$$
$$P_{LM}(e_{j+1} \mid e_j) P(f_j \mid e_j, \mathbf{f}_{-j}, \mathbf{e}_{-j}). \quad (4)$$

In previous work (Dou and Knight, 2012), the authors use symmetric priors over the channel probabilities, where $\alpha_{e,f} = \alpha \frac{1}{V_f}$, and they set α to 1. Symmetric priors over word translation probabilities are a poor choice, as one would not a-priori expect plaintext words and ciphertext words to cooccur with equal frequency. Bayesian inference is a powerful framework that allows us to inject useful prior information into the sampling process, a feature that we would like to use. In the next section, we will describe how we model and learn better priors using distributional properties of words. In subsequent sections, we show significant improvements over the baseline by learning better priors.

3 Base Distribution with Cross-Lingual Word Similarities

As shown in the previous section, the base distribution in Bayesian decipherment is given independent of the inference process. A better base distribution can improve decipherment accuracy. Ideally, we should assign higher base distribution probabilities to word pairs that are similar.

One straightforward way is to consider orthographic similarities. This works for closely related languages, e.g., the English word "new" is translated as "neu" in German and "nueva" in Spanish. However, this fails when two languages are not closely related, e.g., Chinese/English. Previous work aims to discover translations from comparable data based on word context similarities. This is based on the assumption that words appearing in similar contexts have similar meanings. The approach straightforwardly discovers monolingual synonyms. However, when it comes to finding translations, one challenge is to draw a mapping between the different context spaces of the two languages. In previous work, the mapping is usually learned from a seed lexicon.

There has been much recent work in learning distributional vectors (embeddings) for words. The most popular approaches are the skip-gram and continuous-bag-of-words models (Mikolov et al., 2013a). In Mikolov et al. (2013b), the authors are able to successfully learn word translations using *linear transformations* between the source and target word vector-spaces. However, unlike our learning setting, their approach relied on large amounts of translation pairs learned from *parallel* data to train their linear transformations. Inspired by these approaches, we aim to exploit high-quality monolingual word embeddings to help learn better posterior distributions in unsupervised decipherment, without any parallel data.

In the previous section, we incorporated our pre-trained language model in $\alpha_{e,e'}$ to steer our sampling. In the same vein, we model $\alpha_{e,f}$ using pre-trained word embeddings, enabling us to improve our estimate of the posterior distribution. In Mimno and McCallum (2012), the authors develop topic models where the base distribution over topics is a log-linear model of observed document features, which permits learning better priors over topic distributions for each document. Similarly, we introduce a latent cross-lingual linear mapping M and define:

$$\alpha_{f,e} = \exp\{v_e^T M v_f\}, \tag{5}$$

where v_e and v_f are the pre-trained plaintext word and ciphertext word embeddings. M is the similarity matrix between the two embedding spaces. $\alpha_{f,e}$ can be thought of as the affinity of a plaintext word to be mapped to a ciphertext word. Rewriting the channel part of the joint likelihood in equation 1,

$$\begin{aligned} & P(\{\mathbf{f}^n \mid \mathbf{e}^n\}_{n=1}^N, \{P(f \mid e)\}) \\ & = \prod_e \frac{\Gamma\left(\sum_f \exp\{v_e^T M v_f\}\right)}{\prod_f \Gamma\left(\exp\{v_e^T M v_f\}\right)} \\ & \prod_f P(f \mid e)^{\#(e,f)+\exp\{v_e^T M v_f\}-1} \end{aligned}$$

Integrating out the channel probabilities, the complete data log-likelihood of the observed ciphertext bigrams and the sampled plaintext bigrams,

$$\begin{aligned} & P(\{\mathbf{f}^n \mid \mathbf{e}^n\}) \\ & = \prod_e \frac{\Gamma\left(\sum_f \exp\{v_e^T M v_f\}\right)}{\prod_f \Gamma\left(\exp\{v_e^T M v_f\}\right)} \\ & \prod_e \frac{\prod_f \Gamma\left(\exp\{v_e^T M v_f\} + \#(e,f)\right)}{\Gamma\left(\sum_f \exp\{v_e^T M v_f\} + \#(e)\right)}. \end{aligned}$$

We also add a $L2$ regularization penalty on the elements of M. The derivative of $\log P(\{\mathbf{f}^n \mid \mathbf{e}^n\} - \frac{\lambda}{2}\sum_{i,j} M_{i,j}^2$, where λ is the regularization weight, with respect to M,

$$\begin{aligned} & \frac{\partial \log P(\{\mathbf{f}^n \mid \mathbf{e}^n\} - \frac{\lambda}{2}\sum_{i,j} M_{i,j}^2}{\partial M} \\ & = \sum_e \sum_f \exp\{v_e^T M v_f\} v_e v_f^T (\\ & \Psi\left(\sum_{f'} \exp\{v_e^T M v_{f'}\}\right) - \\ & \Psi\left(\sum_{f'} \exp\{v_e^T M v_{f'}\} + \#(e)\right) + \\ & + \Psi\left(\exp\{v_e^T M v_f\} + \#(e,f)\right) - \\ & \Psi\left(exp\{v_e^T M v_f\}\right) - \lambda M, \end{aligned}$$

where we use

$$\begin{aligned} & \frac{\partial \exp\{v_e^T M v_f\}}{\partial M} \\ & = \exp\{v_e^T M v_f\} \frac{\partial v_e^T M v_f}{\partial M} \\ & = \exp\{v_e^T M v_f\} v_e v_f^T. \end{aligned}$$

$\Psi(\cdot)$ is the Digamma function, the derivative of $\log \Gamma(\cdot)$. Again, following Mimno and McCallum (2012), we train the similarity matrix M with stochastic EM. In the E-step, we sample plaintext words for the observed ciphertext using equation 4 and in the M-step, we learn M that maximizes $\log P(\{\mathbf{f}^n \mid \mathbf{e}^n\})$ with stochastic gradient descent. The time complexity of computing the gradient is $\mathcal{O}(V_e V_f)$. However, significant speedups can be achieved by precomputing $v_e v_f^T$ and exploiting GPUs for Matrix operations.

After learning M, we can set

$$\begin{aligned} \alpha_{e,f} &= \sum_{f'} \exp\{v_e^T M v_{f'}\} \frac{\exp\{v_e^T M v_f\}}{\sum_{f''} \exp\{v_e^T M v_{f''}\}} \\ &= \alpha_e m_{e,f}, \end{aligned} \tag{6}$$

where $\alpha_e = \sum_{f'} \exp\{v_e^T M v_{f'}\}$ is the concentration parameter and $m_{e,f} = \frac{\exp\{v_e^T M v_f\}}{\sum_{f''} \exp\{v_e^T M v_{f''}\}}$ is an element of the base measure $\mathbf{m}_e$ for plaintext word e. In practice, we find that α_e can be very large, overwhelming the counts from sampling when we only have a few ciphertext bigrams. Therefore, we use $\mathbf{m}_e$ and set α_e proportional to the data size.

4 Deciphering Spanish Gigaword

In this section, we describe our data and experimental conditions for deciphering Spanish into English.

4.1 Data

In our Spanish/English decipherment experiments, we use half of the Gigaword corpus as monolingual data, and a small amount of parallel data from Europarl *for evaluation*. We keep only the 10k most frequent word types for both languages and replace all other word types with "UNK". We also exclude sentences longer than 40 tokens, which significantly slow down our parser. After preprocessing, the size of data for each language is shown in Table 1. While we use all the monolingual data shown in Table 1 to learn word embeddings, we only parse the AFP (Agence France-Presse) section of the Gigaword corpus to extract

	Spanish	English
Training	992 million (Gigaword)	940 million (Gigaword)
Evaluation	1.1 million (Europarl)	1.0 million (Europarl)

Table 1: Size of data in tokens used in Spanish/English decipherment experiment

cipher dependency bigrams and build a plaintext language model. We also use GIZA (Och and Ney, 2003) to align Europarl parallel data to build a dictionary for evaluating our decipherment.

4.2 Systems

We implement a baseline system based on the work described in Dou and Knight (2013). The baseline system carries out decipherment on dependency bigrams. Therefore, we use the Bohnet parser (Bohnet, 2010) to parse the AFP section of both Spanish and English versions of the Gigaword corpus. Since not all dependency relations are shared across the two languages, we do not extract all dependency bigrams. Instead, we only use bigrams with dependency relations from the following list:

- Verb / Subject
- Verb / Object
- Preposition / Object
- Noun / Noun-Modifier

We denote the system that uses our new method as **DMRE** (Dirichlet Multinomial Regression with Embedings). The system is the same as the baseline except that it uses a base distribution derived from word embeddings similarities. Word embeddings are learned using word2vec (Mikolov et al., 2013a).

For all the systems, language models are built using the SRILM toolkit (Stolcke, 2002). We use the modified Kneser-Ney (Kneser and Ney, 1995) algorithm for smoothing.

4.3 Sampling Procedure

Motivated by the previous work, we use multiple random restarts and an iterative sampling process to improve decipherment (Dou and Knight, 2012). As shown in Figure 1, we start a few sampling processes each with a different random sample. Then results from different runs are combined to initiate the next sampling iteration. The details of the sampling procedure are listed below:

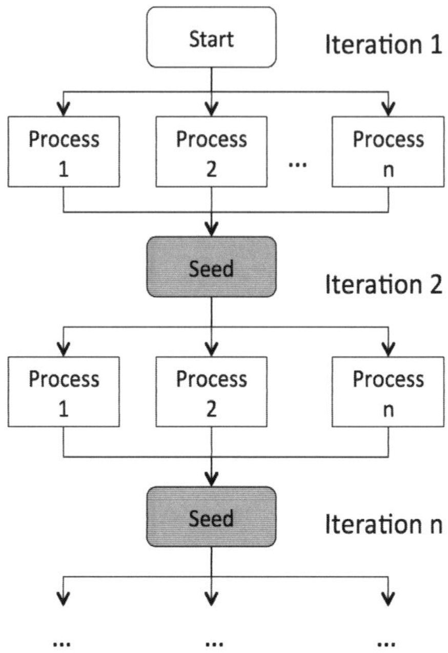

Figure 1: Iterative sampling procedures

1. Extract dependency bigrams from parsing outputs and collect their counts.
2. Keep bigrams whose counts are greater than a threshold t. Then start N different randomly seeded and initialized sampling processes. Perform sampling.
3. At the end of sampling, extract word translation pairs (f, e) from the final sample. Estimate translation probabilities $P(e|f)$ for each pair. Then construct a translation table by keeping translation pairs (f, e) seen in more than one decipherment and use the average $P(e|f)$ as the new translation probability.
4. Start N different sampling processes again. Initialize the first samples with the translation pairs obtained from the previous step (for each dependency bigram f_1, f_2, find an English sequence e_1, e_2, whose $P(e_1|f_1) \cdot P(e_2|f_2) \cdot P(e_1, e_2)$is the highest). Initialize similarity matrix M with one learned by previous sampling process whose posterior probability is highest. Go to the third step, repeat until it converges.
5. Lower the threshold t to include more bigrams into the sampling process. Go to the second step, and repeat until $t = 1$.

The sampling process consists of sampling and learning of similarity matrix M. The sampling process creates training examples for learning M, and the new M is used to update the base distribution for sampling. In our Spanish/English decipherment experiments, we use 10 different random starts. As pointed out in section 3, setting α_e to it's theoretical value (equation 6) gives poor results as it can be quite large. In experiments, we set α_e to a small value for the smaller data sets and increase it as more ciphtertext becomes available. We find that using the learned base distribution always improves decipherment accuracy, however, certain ranges are better for a given data size. We use α_e values of $1, 2$, and 5 for ciphertexts with 100k, 1 million, and 10 million tokens respectively. We leave automatic learning of α_e for future work.

5 Deciphering Malagasy

Despite spoken in Africa, Malagasy has its root in Asia, and belongs to the Malayo-Polynesian branch of the Austronesian language family. Malagasy and English have very different word order (VOS versus SVO). Generally, Malagasy is a typical head-initial language: Determiners precede nouns, while other modifiers and relative clauses follow nouns (e.g. ny "the" ankizilahy "boy" kely "little"). The significant differences in word order pose great challenges for both parsing and decipherment.

5.1 Data

Table 2 lists the sizes of monolingual and parallel data used in this experiment, released by Dou et al. (2014). The monolingual data in Malagasy contains news text collected from Madagascar websites. The English monolingual data contains Gigaword and an additional 300 million tokens of African news. Parallel data (used for evaluation) is collected from GlobalVoices, a multilingual news website, where volunteers translate news into different languages.

5.2 Systems

The baseline system is the same as the baseline used in Spanish/English decipherment experiments. We use data provided in previous work (Dou et al., 2014) to build a Malagasy dependency parser. For English, we use the Turbo parser, trained on the Penn Treebank (Martins et al., 2013).

	Malagasy	English
Training	16 million (Web)	1.2 billion (Gigaword and Web)
Evaluation	2.0 million (GlobalVoices)	1.8 million (GlobalVoices)

Table 2: Size of data in tokens used in Malagasy/English decipherment experiment. GlobalVoices is a parallel corpus.

Because the Malagasy parser does not predict dependency relation types, we use the following head-child part-of-speech (POS) tag patterns to select a subset of dependency bigrams for decipherment:

- Verb / Noun
- Verb / Proper Noun
- Verb / Personal Pronoun
- Preposition / Noun
- Preposision / Proper Noun
- Noun / Adjective
- Noun / Determiner
- Noun / Verb Particle
- Noun / Verb Noun
- Noun / Cardinal
- Noun / Noun

5.3 Sampling Procedure

We use the same sampling protocol designed for Spanish/English decipherment. We double the number of random starts to 20. Further more, compared with Spanish/English decipherment, we find the base distribution plays a more important role in achieving higher decipherment accuracy for Malagasy/English. Therefore, we set α_e to 10, 50, and 200 when deciphering 100k, 1 million, and 20 million token ciphtertexts, respectively.

6 Results

In this section, we first compare decipherment accuracy of the baseline with our new approach. Then, we evaluate the quality of the base distribution through visualization.

We use top-5 type accuracy as our evaluation metric for decipherment. Given a word type f in Spanish, we find top-5 translation pairs (f, e) ranked by $P(e|f)$ from the learned decipherent translation table. If any pair (f, e) can also be found in a gold translation lexicon T_{gold}, we treat

	Spanish/English				Malagasy/English			
Top	5k		10k		5k		10k	
System	Baseline	DMRE	Baseline	DMRE	Baseline	DMRE	Baseline	DMRE
100k	1.9	12.4	1.1	7.1	1.2	2.7	0.6	1.4
1 million	7.3	37.7	4.2	23.6	2.5	5.8	1.3	3.2
10 million	29.0	64.7	23.4	43.7	5.4	11.2	3.0	6.9
100 million	45.8	67.4	39.4	58.1	N/A	N/A	N/A	N/A

Table 3: Spanish/English, Malagasy/English decipherment top-5 accuracy (%) of 5k and 10k most frequent word types

the word type f as correctly deciphered. Let $|C|$ be the number of word types correctly deciphered, and $|V|$ be the total number of word types evaluated. We define type accuracy as $\frac{|C|}{|V|}$.

To create T_{gold}, we use GIZA to align a small amount of Spanish/English parallel text (1 million tokens for each language), and use the lexicon derived from the alignment as our gold translation lexicon. T_{gold} contains a subset of 4233 word types in the 5k most frequent word types, and 7479 word types in the top 10k frequent word types. We decipher the 10k most frequent Spanish word types to the 10k most frequent English word types, and evaluate decipherment accuracy on both the 5k most frequent word types as well as the full 10k word types.

We evaluate accuracy for the 5k and 10k most frequent word types for each language pair, and present them in Table 3.

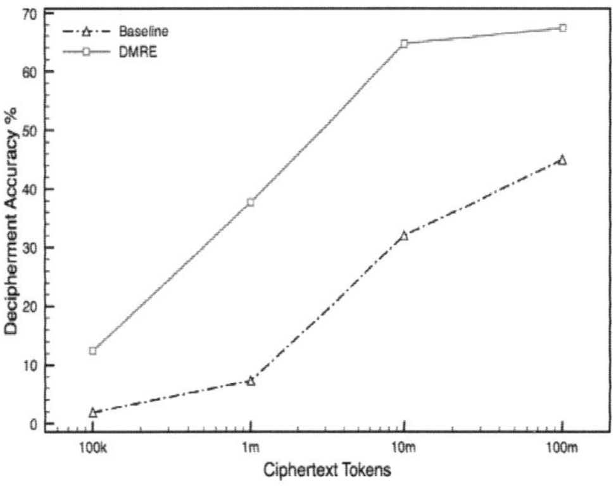

Figure 2: Learning curves of top-5 accuracy evaluated on 5k most frequent word types for Spanish/English decipherment.

We also present the learning curves of decipherment accuracy for the 5k most frequent word types. Figure 2 compares the baseline with **DMRE** in deciphering Spanish into English. Performance of the baseline is in line with previous work (Dou and Knight, 2013). (The accuracy reported here is higher as we evaluate top-5 accuracy for each word type.) With 100k tokens of Spanish text, the baseline achieves 1.9% accuracy, while **DMRE** reaches 12.4% accuracy, improving the baseline by over 6 times. Although the gains attenuate as we increase the number of ciphertext tokens, they are still large. With 100 million cipher tokens, the baseline achieves 45.8% accuracy, while **DMRE** reaches 67.4% accuracy.

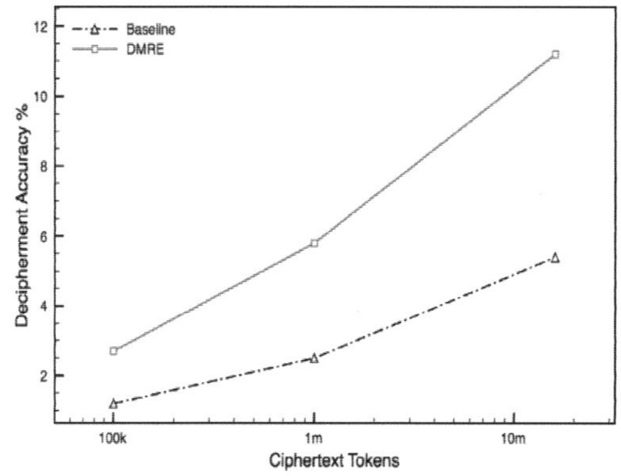

Figure 3: Learning curves of top-5 accuracy evaluated on 5k most frequent word types for Malagasy/English decipherment.

Figure 3 compares the baseline with our new approach in deciphering Malagasy into English. With 100k tokens of data, the baseline achieves 1.2% accuracy, and **DMRE** improves it to 2.4%. We observe consistent improvement throughout the experiment. In the end, the baseline accuracy obtains 5.8% accuracy, and **DMRE** improves it to 11.2%.

Low accuracy in Malagasy-English decipherment is attributed to the following factors: First, compared with the Spanish parser, the Malagasy parser has lower parsing accuracy. Second, word alignment between Malagasy and English is more challenging, producing less correct translation pairs. Last but not least, the domain of the English language model is much closer to the domain of the Spanish monolingual text compared with that of Malagasy.

Overall, we achieve large consistent gains across both language pairs. We hypothesize the gain comes from a better base distribution that considers larger context information. This helps prevent the language model driving deicpherment to a wrong direction.

Since our learned transformation matrix M significantly improves decipherment accuracy, it's likely that it is *translation preserving*, that is, plaintext words are transformed from their native vector space to points in the ciphertext such that translations are close to each other. To visualize this effect, we take the $5k$ most frequent plaintext words and transform them into new embeddings in the ciphertext embedding space $v_{e'} = v_e^T M$, where M is learned from 10 million Spanish bigram data. We then project the $5k$ most frequent ciphertext words and the projected plaintext words from the joint embedding space into a $2-$dimensional space using t-sne (?).

In Figure 4, we see an instance of a recurring phenomenon, where translation pairs are very close and sometimes even overlap each other, for example (judge, jueces), (secret, secretos). The word "magistrado" does not appear in our evaluation set. However, it is placed close to its possible translations. Thus, our approach is capable of learning word translations that cannot be discovered from limited parallel data.

We often also see *translation clusters*, where translations of groups of words are close to each other. For example, in Figure 5, we can see that time expressions in Spanish are quite close to their translations in English. Although better quality translation visualizations (Mikolov et al., 2013b) have been presented in previous work, they exploit large amounts of parallel data to learn the mapping between source and target words, while our transformation is learned on *non-parallel* data.

These results show that our approach can achieve high decipherment accuracy and discover novel word translations from non-parallel data.

Figure 4: Translation pairs are often close and sometimes overlap each other. Words in spanish have been appended with _spanish

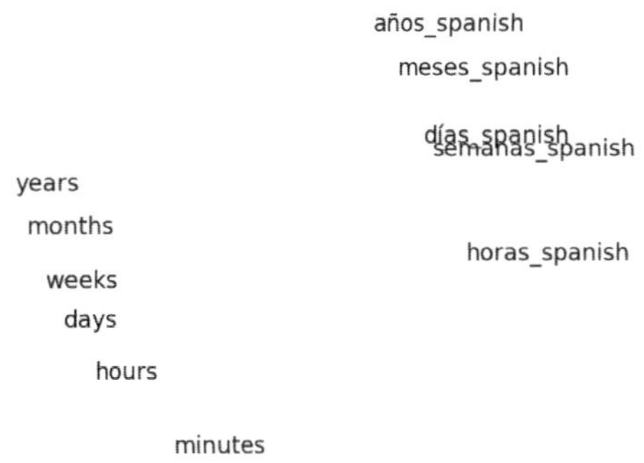

Figure 5: Semantic groups of word-translations appear close to each other.

7 Conclusion and Future Work

We proposed a new framework that simultaneously performs decipherment and learns a cross-lingual mapping of word embeddings. Our method is both theoretically appealing and practically powerful. The mapping is used to give decipherment a better base distribution.

Experimental results show that our new algorithm improved state-of-the-art decipherment accuracy significantly: from 45.8% to 67.4% for Spanish/English, and 5.1% to 11.2% for Malagasy/English. This improvement could lead to further advances in using monolingual data to improve end-to-end MT.

In the future, we will work on making the our approach scale to much larger vocabulary sizes using noise contrastive estimation (?), and apply it to improve MT systems.

Acknowledgments

This work was supported by ARL/ARO (W911NF-10-1-0533) and DARPA (HR0011-12-C-0014).

References

Shane Bergsma and Benjamin Van Durme. 2011. Learning bilingual lexicons using the visual similarity of labeled web images. In *Proceedings of the Twenty-Second international joint conference on Artificial Intelligence - Volume Volume Three*. AAAI Press.

Bernd Bohnet. 2010. Top accuracy and fast dependency parsing is not a contradiction. In *Proceedings of the 23rd International Conference on Computational Linguistics*. Coling.

Hal Daumé, III and Jagadeesh Jagarlamudi. 2011. Domain adaptation for machine translation by mining unseen words. In *Proceedings of the 49th Annual Meeting of the Association for Computational Linguistics: Human Language Technologies*. Association for Computational Linguistics.

Qing Dou and Kevin Knight. 2012. Large scale decipherment for out-of-domain machine translation. In *Proceedings of the 2012 Joint Conference on Empirical Methods in Natural Language Processing and Computational Natural Language Learning*. Association for Computational Linguistics.

Qing Dou and Kevin Knight. 2013. Dependency-based decipherment for resource-limited machine translation. In *Proceedings of the 2013 Conference on Empirical Methods in Natural Language Processing*. Association for Computational Linguistics.

Qing Dou, Ashish Vaswani, and Kevin Knight. 2014. Beyond parallel data: Joint word alignment and decipherment improves machine translation. In *Proceedings of the 2014 Conference on Empirical Methods in Natural Language Processing (EMNLP)*. Association for Computational Linguistics.

Nikesh Garera, Chris Callison-Burch, and David Yarowsky. 2009. Improving translation lexicon induction from monolingual corpora via dependency contexts and part-of-speech equivalences. In *Proceedings of the Thirteenth Conference on Computational Natural Language Learning*. Association for Computational Linguistics.

Aria Haghighi, Percy Liang, Taylor Berg-Kirkpatrick, and Dan Klein. 2008. Learning bilingual lexicons from monolingual corpora. In *Proceedings of ACL-08: HLT*. Association for Computational Linguistics.

Ann Irvine and Chris Callison-Burch. 2013a. Combining bilingual and comparable corpora for low resource machine translation. In *Proceedings of the Eighth Workshop on Statistical Machine Translation*. Association for Computational Linguistics, August.

Ann Irvine and Chris Callison-Burch. 2013b. Supervised bilingual lexicon induction with multiple monolingual signals. In *Proceedings of the 2013 Conference of the North American Chapter of the Association for Computational Linguistics: Human Language Technologies*. Association for Computational Linguistics.

Ann Irvine, Chris Quirk, and Hal Daume III. 2013. Monolingual marginal matching for translation model adaptation. In *Proceedings of the Conference on Empirical Methods in Natural Language Processing (EMNLP)*. Association for Computational Linguistics.

Alexandre Klementiev, Ivan Titov, and Binod Bhattarai. 2012. Inducing crosslingual distributed representations of words. In *Proceedings of COLING 2012*. The COLING 2012 Organizing Committee.

Reinhard Kneser and Hermann Ney. 1995. Improved backing-off for m-gram language modeling. *IEEE International Conference on Acoustics, Speech, and Signal Processing (ICASSP)*.

Kevin Knight, Anish Nair, Nishit Rathod, and Kenji Yamada. 2006. Unsupervised analysis for decipherment problems. In *Proceedings of the COLING/ACL 2006 Main Conference Poster Sessions*. Association for Computational Linguistics.

Andre Martins, Miguel Almeida, and Noah A. Smith. 2013. Turning on the turbo: Fast third-order non-projective turbo parsers. In *Proceedings of the 51st Annual Meeting of the Association for Computational Linguistics (Volume 2: Short Papers)*. Association for Computational Linguistics.

Tomas Mikolov, Kai Chen, Greg Corrado, and Jeffrey Dean. 2013a. Efficient estimation of word representations in vector space. *arXiv preprint arXiv:1301.3781*.

Tomas Mikolov, Quoc V Le, and Ilya Sutskever. 2013b. Exploiting similarities among languages for machine translation. *arXiv preprint arXiv:1309.4168*.

David Mimno and Andrew McCallum. 2012. Topic models conditioned on arbitrary features with dirichlet-multinomial regression. *arXiv preprint arXiv:1206.3278*.

Malte Nuhn, Arne Mauser, and Hermann Ney. 2012. Deciphering foreign language by combining language models and context vectors. In *Proceedings of the 50th Annual Meeting of the Association for Computational Linguistics: Long Papers - Volume 1*. Association for Computational Linguistics.

Franz Josef Och and Hermann Ney. 2003. A systematic comparison of various statistical alignment models. *Computational Linguistics*.

Reinhard Rapp. 1995. Identifying word translations in non-parallel texts. In *Proceedings of the 33rd annual meeting on Association for Computational Linguistics*. Association for Computational Linguistics.

Sujith Ravi and Kevin Knight. 2011. Deciphering foreign language. In *Proceedings of the 49th Annual Meeting of the Association for Computational Linguistics: Human Language Technologies*. Association for Computational Linguistics.

Sujith Ravi. 2013. Scalable decipherment for machine translation via hash sampling. In *Proceedings of the 51th Annual Meeting of the Association for Computational Linguistics*. Association for Computational Linguistics.

Andreas Stolcke. 2002. SRILM - an extensible language modeling toolkit. In *Proceedings of the International Conference on Spoken Language Processing*.

Warren Weaver, 1955. *Translation (1949). Reproduced in W.N. Locke, A.D. Booth (eds.).* MIT Press.

Non-projective Dependency-based Pre-Reordering with Recurrent Neural Network for Machine Translation

Antonio Valerio Miceli-Barone
Università di Pisa
Largo B. Pontecorvo, 3
56127 Pisa, Italy
`miceli@di.unipi.it`

Giuseppe Attardi
Università di Pisa
Largo B. Pontecorvo, 3
56127 Pisa, Italy
`attardi@di.unipi.it`

Abstract

The quality of statistical machine translation performed with phrase based approaches can be increased by permuting the words in the source sentences in an order which resembles that of the target language. We propose a class of recurrent neural models which exploit source-side dependency syntax features to reorder the words into a target-like order. We evaluate these models on the German-to-English and Italian-to-English language pairs, showing significant improvements over a phrase-based Moses baseline. We also compare with state of the art German-to-English pre-reordering rules, showing that our method obtains similar or better results.

1 Introduction

Statistical machine translation is typically performed using phrase-based systems (Koehn et al., 2007). These systems can usually produce accurate local reordering but they have difficulties dealing with the long-distance reordering that tends to occur between certain language pairs (Birch et al., 2008).

The quality of phrase-based machine translation can be improved by reordering the words in each sentence of source-side of the parallel training corpus in a "target-like" order and then applying the same transformation as a pre-processing step to input strings during execution.

When the source-side sentences can be accurately parsed, pre-reordering can be performed using hand-coded rules. This approach has been successfully applied to German-to-English (Collins et al., 2005) and other languages. The main issue with it is that these rules must be designed for each specific language pair, which requires considerable linguistic expertise.

Fully statistical approaches, on the other hand, learn the reordering relation from word alignments. Some of them learn reordering rules on the constituency (Dyer and Resnik, 2010) (Khalilov and Fonollosa, 2011) or projective dependency (Genzel, 2010), (Lerner and Petrov, 2013) parse trees of source sentences. The permutations that these methods can learn can be generally non-local (i.e. high distance) on the sentences but local (parent-child or sibling-sibling swaps) on the parse trees. Moreover, constituency or projective dependency trees may not be the ideal way of representing the syntax of non-analytic languages such as German or Italian, which could be better described using non-projective dependency trees (Bosco and Lombardo, 2004). Other methods, based on recasting reordering as a combinatorial optimization problem (Tromble and Eisner, 2009), (Visweswariah et al., 2011), can learn to generate in principle arbitrary permutations, but they can only make use of minimal syntactic information (part-of-speech tags) and therefore can't exploit the potentially valuable structural syntactic information provided by a parser.

In this work we propose a class of reordering models which attempt to close this gap by

Proceedings of the 53rd Annual Meeting of the Association for Computational Linguistics and the 7th International Joint Conference on Natural Language Processing, pages 846–856,
Beijing, China, July 26-31, 2015.

exploiting rich dependency syntax features and at the same time being able to process non-projective dependency parse trees and generate permutations which may be non-local both on the sentences and on the parse trees.
We represent these problems as sequence prediction machine learning tasks, which we address using recurrent neural networks.

We applied our model to reorder German sentences into an English-like word order as a pre-processing step for phrase-based machine translation, obtaining significant improvements over the unreordered baseline system and quality comparable to the hand-coded rules introduced by Collins et al. (2005). We also applied our model to Italian-to-English pre-reordering, obtaining a considerable improvement over the unreordered baseline.

2 Reordering as a walk on a dependency tree

In order to describe the non-local reordering phenomena that can occur between language pairs such as German-to-English and Italian-to-English, we introduce a reordering framework similar to (Miceli Barone and Attardi, 2013), based on a *graph walk* of the dependency parse tree of the source sentence. This framework doesn't restrict the parse tree to be projective, and allows the generation of arbitrary permutations.

Let $f \equiv (f_1, f_2, \ldots, f_{L_f})$ be a source sentence, annotated by a rooted dependency parse tree: $\forall j \in 1, \ldots, L_f, h_j \equiv PARENT(j)$

We define a *walker* process that walks from word to word across the edges of the parse tree, and at each steps optionally *emits* the current word, with the constraint that each word must be eventually emitted exactly once.
Therefore, the final string of emitted words f' is a permutation of the original sentence f, and any permutation can be generated by a suitable walk on the parse tree.

2.1 Reordering automaton

We formalize the walker process as a non-deterministic finite-state automaton.
The state v of the automaton is the tuple $v \equiv (j, E, a)$ where $j \in 1, \ldots, L_f$ is the current vertex (word index), E is the set of emitted vertices, a is the last action taken by the automaton.
The initial state is: $v(0) \equiv (root_f, \{\}, null)$ where $root_f$ is the root vertex of the parse tree.

At each step t, the automaton chooses one of the following actions:

- *EMIT*: emit the word f_j at the current vertex j. This action is enabled only if the current vertex has not been already emitted:

$$\frac{j \notin E}{(j, E, a) \overset{EMIT}{\to} (j, E \cup \{j\}, EMIT)} \tag{1}$$

- *UP*: move to the parent of the current vertex. Enabled if there is a parent and we did not just come down from it:

$$\frac{h_j \neq null, a \neq DOWN_j}{(j, E, a) \overset{UP}{\to} (h_j, E, UP_j)} \tag{2}$$

- $DOWN_{j'}$: move to the child j' of the current vertex. Enabled if the subtree $s(j')$ rooted at j' contains vertices that have not been already emitted and if we did not just come up from it:

$$\frac{h_{j'} = j, a \neq UP_{j'}, \exists k \in s(j') : k \notin E}{(j, E, a) \overset{DOWN_{j'}}{\to} (j', E, DOWN_{j'})} \tag{3}$$

The execution continues until all the vertices have been emitted.

We define the sequence of states of the walker automaton during one run as an *execution* $\bar{v} \in GEN(f)$. An execution also uniquely specifies the sequence of actions performed by the automation.

The preconditions make sure that all execution of the automaton always end generating a permutation of the source sentence. Furthermore, no cycles are possible: progress is made at every step, and it is not possible to enter in an execution that later turns out to be invalid.
Every permutation of the source sentence can be generated by some execution. In fact, each permutation f' can be generated by exactly one execution, which we denote as $\bar{v}(f')$.

We can split the execution $\bar{v}(f')$ into a sequence of L_f *emission fragments* $\bar{v}_j(f')$, each ending with an $EMIT$ action.
The first fragment has zero or more $DOWN_*$ actions followed by one $EMIT$ action, while each other fragment has a non-empty sequence of UP and $DOWN_*$ actions (always zero or more UPs followed by zero or more DOWNs) followed by one $EMIT$ action.

Finally, we define an action in an execution as *forced* if it was the only action enabled at the step where it occurred.

2.2 Application

Suppose we perform reordering using a typical syntax-based system which processes source-side projective dependency parse trees and is limited to swaps between pair of vertices which are either in a parent-child relation or in a sibling relation. In such execution the UP actions are always forced, since the "walker" process never leaves a subtree before all its vertices have been emitted.

Suppose instead that we could perform reordering according to an "oracle". The executions of our automaton corresponding to these permutations will in general contain *unforced* UP actions. We define these actions, and the execution fragments that exhibit them, as *non-tree-local*.

In practice we don't have access to a reordering "oracle", but for sentences pairs in a parallel corpus we can compute heuristic "pseudo-oracle" reference permutations of the source sentences from word-alignments.

Following (Al-Onaizan and Papineni, 2006), (Tromble and Eisner, 2009), (Visweswariah et al., 2011), (Navratil et al., 2012), we generate word alignments in both the source-to-target and the target-to-source directions using IBM model 4 as implemented in GIZA++ (Och et al., 1999) and then we combine them into a symmetrical word alignment using the "grow-diag-final-and" heuristic implemented in Moses (Koehn et al., 2007).

Given the symmetric word-aligned corpus, we assign to each source-side word an integer index corresponding to the position of the leftmost target-side word it is aligned to (attaching unaligned words to the following aligned word) and finally we perform a stable sort of source-side words according to this index.

2.3 Reordering example

Consider the segment of a German sentence shown in fig. 1. The English-reordered segment "**die Währungsreserven anfangs lediglich dienen sollten zur Verteidigung**" corresponds to the English: "**the reserve assets were originally intended to provide protection**".

In order to compose this segment from the original German, the reordering automaton described in our framework must perform a complex sequence of moves on the parse tree:

- Starting from "**sollten**", descend to "**dienen**", descent to "**Währungsreserven**" and finally to "**die**". Emit it, then go up to "**Währungsreserven**", emit it and go up to "**dienen**" and up again to "**sollten**". Note that the last UP is *unforced* since "**dienen**" has not been emitted at that point and has also unemitted children. This unforced action indicates non-tree-local reordering.

- Go down to "**anfangs**". Note that the in the parse tree edge crosses another edge, indicating non-projectivity. Emit "**anfangs**" and go up (forced) back to "**sollten**".

- Go down to "**dienen**", down to "**zur**", down to "**lediglich**" and emit it. Go up (forced) to "**zur**", up (unforced) to "**dienen**", emit it, go up (unforced) to "**sollten**", emit it. Go down to "**dienen**", down to "**zur**" emit it, go down to "**Verteidigung**" and emit it.

Correct reordering of this segment would be difficult both for a phrase-based system (since the words are further apart than both the typical maximum distortion distance and maximum phrase length) and for a syntax-based system (due to the presence of non-projectivity and non-tree-locality).

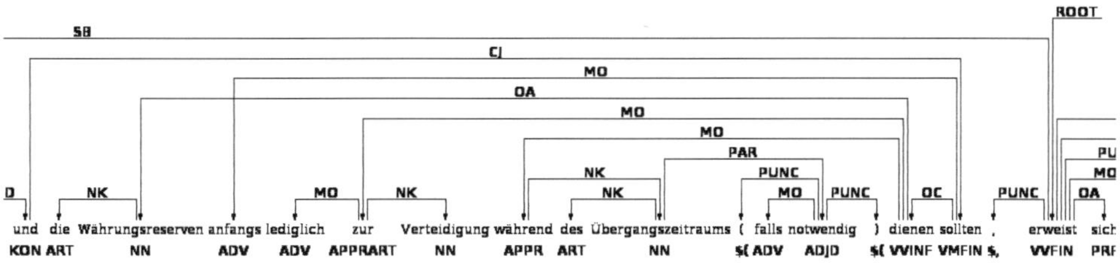

Figure 1: Section of the dependency parse tree of a German sentence.

3 Recurrent Neural Network reordering models

Given the reordering framework described above, we could try to directly predict the executions as Miceli Barone and Attardi (2013) attempted with their version of the framework. However, the executions of a given sentence can have widely different lengths, which could make incremental inexact decoding such as beam search difficult due to the need to prune over partial hypotheses that have different numbers of emitted words.

Therefore, we decided to investigate a different class of models which have the property that state transition happen only in correspondence with word emission. This enables us to leverage the technology of incremental *language models*.

Using language models for reordering is not something new (Feng et al., 2010), (Durrani et al., 2011), (Bisazza and Federico, 2013), but instead of using a more or less standard n-gram language model, we are going to base our model on *recurrent neural network language models* (Mikolov et al., 2010).

Neural networks allow easy incorporation of multiple types of features and can be trained more specifically on the types of sequences that will occur during decoding, hence they can avoid wasting model space to represent the probabilities of non-permutations.

3.1 Base RNN-RM

Let $f \equiv (f_1, f_2, \ldots, f_{L_f})$ be a source sentence. We model the reordering system as a deterministic single hidden layer recurrent neural network:

$$v(t) = \tau(\Theta^{(1)} \cdot x(t) + \Theta^{REC} \cdot v(t-1)) \quad (4)$$

where $x(t) \in \mathcal{R}^n$ is a feature vector associated to the t-th word in a permutation f', $v(0) \equiv v_{init}, \Theta^{(1)}$ and Θ^{REC} are parameters[1] and $\tau(\cdot)$ is the hyperbolic tangent function.

If we know the first $t-1$ words of the permutation f' in order to compute the probability distribution of the t-th word we do the following:

- Iteratively compute the state $v(t-1)$ from the feature vectors $x(1), \ldots, x(t-1)$.
- For the all the indices of the words that haven't occurred in the permutation so far $j \in J(t) \equiv ([1, L_f] - \bar{i}_{t-1:})$, compute a score $h_{j,t} \equiv h_o(v(t-1), x_o(j))$, where $x_o(\cdot)$ is the feature vector of the candidate target word.
- Normalize the scores using the logistic softmax function: $P(\bar{I}_t = j | f, \bar{i}_{t-1:}, t) = \frac{\exp(h_{j,t})}{\sum_{j' \in J(t)} \exp(h_{j',t})}$.

The scoring function $h_o(v(t-1), x_o(j))$ applies a feed-forward hidden layer to the feature inputs $x_o(j)$, and then takes a weighed inner product between the activation of this layer and the state $v(t-1)$. The result is then linearly combined to an additional feature equal to the logarithm of the remaining words in the permutation $(L_f - t)$,[2] and to a bias feature:

$$h_{j,t} \equiv < \tau(\Theta^{(o)} \cdot x_o(j)), \theta^{(2)} \odot v(t-1) > + \theta^{(\alpha)} \cdot \log(L_f - t) + \theta^{(bias)} \quad (5)$$

where $h_{j,t} \equiv h_o(v(t-1), x_o(j))$.

[1] we don't use a bias feature since it is redundant when the layer has input features encoded with the "one-hot" encoding

[2] since we are then passing this score to a softmax of variable size $(L_f - t)$, this feature helps the model to keep the score already approximately scaled.

We can compute the probability of an entire permutation f' just by multiplying the probabilities for each word: $P(f'|f) = P(\bar{I} = \bar{i}|f) = \prod_{t=1}^{L_f} P(\bar{I}_t = \bar{i}_t|f,t)$

3.1.1 Training

Given a training set of pairs of sentences and reference permutations, the training problem is defined as finding the set of parameters $\theta \equiv (v_{init}, \Theta^{(1)}, \theta^{(2)}, \Theta^{REC}, \Theta^{(o)}, \theta^{(\alpha)}, \theta^{(bias)})$ which minimize the per-word empirical cross-entropy of the model w.r.t. the reference permutations in the training set. Gradients can be efficiently computed using *backpropagation through time* (BPTT).

In practice we used the following training architecture:
Stochastic gradient descent, with each training pair (f, f') considered as a single minibatch for updating purposes. Gradients computed using the automatic differentiation facilities of Theano (Bergstra et al., 2010) (which implements a generalized BPTT). No truncation is used. L2-regularization [3]. Learning rates dynamically adjusted per scalar parameter using the *AdaDelta* heuristic (Zeiler, 2012). Gradient clipping heuristic to prevent the "exploding gradient" problem (Graves, 2013). Early stopping w.r.t. a validation set to prevent overfitting. Uniform random initialization for parameters other than the recurrent parameter matrix Θ^{REC}. Random initialization with *echo state property* for Θ^{REC}, with contraction coefficient $\sigma = 0.99$ (Jaeger, 2001), (Gallicchio and Micheli, 2011).

Training time complexity is $O(L_f^2)$ per sentence, which could be reduced to $O(L_f)$ using truncated BTTP at the expense of update accuracy and hence convergence speed. Space complexity is $O(L_f)$ per sentence.

3.1.2 Decoding

In order to use the RNN-RM model for pre-reordering we need to compute the most likely permutation $\overset{*}{f'}$ of the source sentence f:

$$\overset{*}{f'} \equiv \operatorname*{argmax}_{f' \in GEN(f)} P(f'|f) \qquad (6)$$

Solving this problem to the global optimum is computationally hard[4], hence we solve it to a local optimum using a *beam search* strategy.

We generate the permutation incrementally from left to right. Starting from an initial state consisting of an empty string and the initial state vector v_{init}, at each step we generate all possible successor states and retain the B-most probable of them (histogram pruning), according to the probability of the entire prefix of permutation they represent.

Since RNN state vectors do not decompose in a meaningful way, we don't use any hypothesis recombination.
At step t there are $L_f - t$ possible successor states, and the process always takes exactly L_f steps[5], therefore time complexity is $O(B \cdot L_f^2)$ and space complexity is $O(B)$.

3.1.3 Features

We use two different feature configurations: *unlexicalized* and *lexicalized*.

In the *unlexicalized* configuration, the state transition input feature function $x(j)$ is composed by the following features, all encoded using the "one-hot" encoding scheme:

- Unigram: $POS(j)$, $DEPREL(j)$, $POS(j) * DEPREL(j)$. Left, right and parent unigram: $POS(k)$, $DEPREL(k)$, $POS(k) * DEPREL(k)$, where k is the index of respectively the word at the left (in the original sentence), at the right and the dependency parent of word j. Unique tags are used for padding.

- Pair features: $POS(j) * POS(k)$, $POS(j) * DEPREL(k)$, $DEPREL(j) * POS(k)$, $DEPREL(j) * DEPREL(k)$, for k defined as above.

- Triple features $POS(j) * POS(left_j) * POS(right_j)$, $POS(j) * POS(left_j) * POS(parent_j)$, $POS(j) * POS(right_j) * POS(parent_j)$.

- Bigram: $POS(j) * POS(k)$, $POS(j) * DEPREL(k)$, $DEPREL(j) * POS(k)$ where k is the previous emitted word in the permutation.

[3] $\lambda = 10^{-4}$ on the recurrent matrix, $\lambda = 10^{-6}$ on the final layer, per minibatch.

[4] NP-hard for at least certain choices of features and parameters

[5] actually, $L_f - 1$, since the last choice is forced

- Topological features: three binary features which indicate whether word j and the previously emitted word are in a parent-child, child-parent or sibling-sibling relation, respectively.

The target word feature function $x_0(j)$ is the same as $x(j)$ except that each feature is also conjoined with a quantized signed distance[6] between word j and the previous emitted word. Feature value combinations that appear less than 100 times in the training set are replaced by a distinguished "rare" tag.

The *lexicalized* configuration is equivalent to the unlexicalized one except that $x(j)$ and $x_0(j)$ also have the surface form of word j (not conjoined with the signed distance).

3.2 Fragment RNN-RM

The *Base RNN-RM* described in the previous section includes dependency information, but not the full information of reordering fragments as defined by our automaton model (sec. 2). In order to determine whether this rich information is relevant to machine translation pre-reordering, we propose an extension, denoted as *Fragment RNN-RM*, which includes reordering fragment features, at expense of a significant increase of time complexity.

We consider a hierarchical recurrent neural network. At top level, this is defined as the previous RNN. However, the $x(j)$ and $x_0(j)$ vectors, in addition to the feature vectors described as above now contain also the final states of another recurrent neural network.

This internal RNN has a separate clock and a separate state vector. For each step t of the top-level RNN which transitions between word $f'(t-1)$ and $f'(t)$, the internal RNN is reinitialized to its own initial state and performs multiple internal steps, one for each action in the fragment of the execution that the walker automaton must perform to walk between words $f'(t-1)$ and $f'(t)$ in the dependency parse (with a special shortcut of length one if they are adjacent in f with monotonic relative order).

[6]values greater than 5 and smaller than 10 are quantized as 5, values greater or equal to 10 are quantized as 10. Negative values are treated similarly.

The state transition of the inner RNN is defined as:

$$v_r(t) = \tau(\Theta^{(r_1)} \cdot x_r(t_r) + \Theta^{r_{REC}} \cdot v_r(t_r - 1)) \quad (7)$$

where $x_r(t_r)$ is the feature function for the word traversed at inner time t_r in the execution fragment. $v_r(0) = v_r^{init}$, $\Theta^{(r_1)}$ and $\Theta^{r_{REC}}$ are parameters.

Evaluation and decoding are performed essentially in the same was as in Base RNN-RM, except that the time complexity is now $O(L_f^3)$ since the length of execution fragments is $O(L_f)$.

Training is also essentially performed in the same way, though gradient computation is much more involved since gradients propagate from the top-level RNN to the inner RNN. In our implementation we just used the automatic differentiation facilities of Theano.

3.2.1 Features

The *unlexicalized* features for the inner RNN input vector $x_r(t_r)$ depend on the current word in the execution fragment (at index t_r), the previous one and the action label: UP, $DOWN$ or $RIGHT$ (shortcut). $EMIT$ actions are not included as they always implicitly occur at the end of each fragment.

Specifically the features, encoded with the "one-hot" encoding are: $A * POS(t_r) * POS(t_r - 1)$, $A * POS(t_r) * DEPREL(t_r - 1)$, $A * DEPREL(t_r) * POS(t_r - 1)$, $A * DEPREL(t_r) * DEPREL(t_r - 1)$.

These features are also conjoined with the quantized signed distance (in the original sentence) between each pair of words.

The *lexicalized* features just include the surface form of each visited word at t_r.

3.3 Base GRU-RM

We also propose a variant of the Base RNN-RM where the standard recurrent hidden layer is replaced by a *Gated Recurrent Unit* layer, recently proposed by Cho et al. (2014) for machine translation applications.

The Base GRU-RM is defined as the Base RNN-RM of sec. 3.1, except that the recurrence relation 4 is replaced by fig. 2

Features are the same of unlexicalized Base RNN-RM (we experienced difficulties training the Base GRU-RM with lexicalized features).

$$\begin{aligned} v_{rst}(t) &= \pi(\Theta^{(1)}_{rst} \cdot x(t) + \Theta^{REC}_{rst} \cdot v(t-1)) \\ v_{upd}(t) &= \pi(\Theta^{(1)}_{upd} \cdot x(t) + \Theta^{REC}_{upd} \cdot v(t-1)) \\ v_{raw}(t) &= \tau(\Theta^{(1)} \cdot x(t) + \Theta^{REC} \cdot v(t-1) \odot v_{upd}(t)) \\ v(t) &= v_{rst}(t) \odot v(t-1) + (1 - v_{rst}(t)) \odot v_{raw}(t) \end{aligned} \quad (8)$$

Figure 2: GRU recurrence equations. $v_{rst}(t)$ and $v_{upd}(t)$ are the activation vectors of the "reset" and "update" gates, respectively, and $\pi(\cdot)$ is the logistic sigmoid function.

Training is also performed in the same way except that we found more beneficial to convergence speed to optimize using *Adam* (Kingma and Ba, 2014) [7] rather than AdaDelta.
In principle we could also extend the Fragment RNN-RM into a Fragment GRU-RM, but we did not investigate that model in this work.

4 Experiments

We performed German-to-English pre-reordering experiments with Base RNN-RM (both unlexicalized and lexicalized), Fragment RNN-RM and Base GRU-RM.

In order to validate the experimental results on a different language pair, we additionally performed an Italian-to-English pre-reordering experiment with the Base GRU-RM, after assessing that this was the model that obtained the largest improvement on German-to-English.

4.1 Setup

The German-to-English baseline phrase-based system was trained on the Europarl v7 corpus (Koehn, 2005). We randomly split it in a 1,881,531 sentence pairs training set, a 2,000 sentence pairs development set (used for tuning) and a 2,000 sentence pairs test set. The English language model was trained on the English side of the parallel corpus augmented with a corpus of sentences from AP News, for a total of 22,891,001 sentences.
The baseline system is phrase-based Moses in a default configuration with maximum distortion distance equal to 6 and lexicalized reordering enabled. Maximum phrase size is equal to 7.
The language model is a 5-gram IRSTLM/KenLM.
The pseudo-oracle system was trained on the training and tuning corpus obtained by permuting the German source side using the heuristic described in section 2.2 and is otherwise equal to the baseline system.
In addition to the test set extracted from Europarl, we also used a 2,525 sentence pairs test set ("news2009") a 3,000 sentence pairs "challenge" set used for the WMT 2013 translation task ("news2013").

The Italian-to-English baseline system was trained on a parallel corpus assembled from Europarl v7, JRC-ACQUIS v2.2 (Steinberger et al., 2006) and additional bilingual articles crawled from online newspaper websites[8], totaling 3,081,700 sentence pairs, which were split into a 3,075,777 sentence pairs phrase-table training corpus, a 3,923 sentence pairs tuning corpus, and a 2,000 sentence pairs test corpus.

Non-projective dependency parsing for our models, both for German and Italian was performed with the DeSR transition-based parser (Attardi, 2006).

We also trained a German-to-English Moses system with pre-reordering performed by Collins et al. (2005) rules, implemented by Howlett and Dras (2011).
Constituency parsing for Collins et al. (2005) rules was performed with the Berkeley parser (Petrov et al., 2006). For Italian-to-English we did not compare with a hand-coded reordering system as we are not aware of any strong pre-reordering baseline for this language pair.

For our experiments, we extract approxi-

[7] with learning rate $2 \cdot 10^{-5}$ and all the other hyper-parameters equal to the default values in the article.

[8] Corriere.it and Asianews.it

mately 300,000 sentence pairs from the Moses training set based on a heuristic confidence measure of word-alignment quality (Huang, 2009), (Navratil et al., 2012). We randomly removed 2,000 sentences from this filtered dataset to form a validation set for early stopping, the rest were used for training the pre-reordering models.

4.2 Results

The hidden state size s of the RNNs was set to 100 while it was set to 30 for the GRU model, validation was performed every 2,000 training examples. After 50 consecutive validation rounds without improvement, training was stopped and the set of training parameters that resulted in the lowest validation cross-entropy were saved.
Training took approximately 1.5 days for the unlexicalized Base RNN-RM, 2.5 days for the lexicalized Base RNN-RM and for the unlexicalized Base GRU-RM and 5 days for the unlexicalized Fragment RNN-RM on a 24-core machine without GPU (CPU load never rose to more than 400%).

Decoding was performed with a beam size of 4. Decoding the whole German corpus took about 1.0-1.2 days for all the models except Fragment RNN-RM for which it took about 3 days. Decoding for the Italian corpus for the Base GRU-RM took approximately 1.5 days.

Effects on monolingual reordering score are shown in fig. 3 (German) and fig. 4 (Italian), effects on translation quality are shown in fig. 5 (German-to-English) and fig. 6 (Italian-to-English)[9].

4.3 Discussion and analysis

All our German-to-English models significantly improved over the phrase-based baseline, performing as well as or almost as well as (Collins et al., 2005), which is an interesting result since our models doesn't require any specific linguistic expertise.

Surprisingly, the lexicalized version of Base RNN-RM performed worse than the unlexicalized one. This goes contrary to expectation as neural language models are usually lexicalized and in fact often use nothing but lexical features.

The unlexicalized Fragment RNN-RM was quite accurate but very expensive both during training and decoding, thus it may not be practical.

The unlexicalized Base GRU-RM performed very well, especially on the Europarl dataset (where all the scores are much higher than the other datasets) and it never performed significantly worse than the unlexicalized Fragment RNN-RM which is much slower.

We also performed exploratory experiments with different feature sets (such as lexical-only features) but we couldn't obtain a good training error. Larger network sizes should increase model capacity and may possibly enable training on simpler feature sets.

The Italian-to-English experiment with Base GRU-RM confirmed that this model performs very well on a language pair with different reordering phenomena than German-to-English.

5 Conclusions

We presented a class of statistical syntax-based, non-projective, non-tree-local pre-reordering systems for machine translation.
Our systems processes source sentences parsed with non-projective dependency parsers and permutes them into a target-like word order, suitable for translation by an appropriately trained downstream phrase-based system.

The models we proposed are completely trained with machine learning approaches and is, in principle, capable of generating arbitrary permutations, without the hard constraints that are commonly present in other statistical syntax-based pre-reordering methods.
Practical constraints depend on the choice of features and are therefore quite flexible, allowing a trade-off between accuracy and speed.

In our experiments with the RNN-RM and GRU-RM models we managed to achieve translation quality improvements compara-

[9] Although the baseline systems were trained on the same datasets used in Miceli Barone and Attardi (2013), the results are different since we used a different version of Moses

Reordering	BLEU	improvement
none	62.10	
unlex. Base RNN-RM	64.03	+1.93
lex. Base RNN-RM	63.99	+1.89
unlex. Fragment RNN-RM	64.43	+2.33
unlex. Base GRU-RM	64.78	+2.68

Figure 3: German "Monolingual" reordering scores (upstream system output vs. "oracle"-permuted German) on the Europarl test set. All improvements are significant at 1% level.

Reordering	BLEU	improvement
none	73.11	
unlex. Base GRU-RM	81.09	+7.98

Figure 4: Italian "Monolingual" reordering scores on the Europarl test set. All improvements are significant at 1% level.

Test set	system	BLEU	improvement
Europarl	baseline	33.00	
Europarl	"oracle"	41.80	+8.80
Europarl	Collins	33.52	+0.52
Europarl	unlex. Base RNN-RM	33.41	+0.41
Europarl	lex. Base RNN-RM	33.38	+0.38
Europarl	unlex. Fragment RNN-RM	33.54	+0.54
Europarl	**unlex. Base GRU-RM**	34.15	**+1.15**
news2013	baseline	18.80	
news2013	Collins	NA	NA
news2013	unlex. Base RNN-RM	19.19	+0.39
news2013	lex. Base RNN-RM	19.01	+0.21
news2013	unlex. Fragment RNN-RM	19.27	+0.47
news2013	**unlex. Base GRU-RM**	19.28	**+0.48**
news2009	baseline	18.09	
news2009	**Collins**	18.74	**+0.65**
news2009	unlex. Base RNN-RM	18.50	+0.41
news2009	lex. Base RNN-RM	18.44	+0.35
news2009	unlex. Fragment RNN-RM	18.60	+0.51
news2009	unlex. Base GRU-RM	18.58	+0.49

Figure 5: German-to-English RNN-RM translation scores. All improvements are significant at 1% level.

Test set	system	BLEU	improvement
Europarl	baseline	29.58	
Europarl	**unlex. Base GRU-RM**	30.84	**+1.26**

Figure 6: Italian-to-English RNN-RM translation scores. Improvement is significant at 1% level.

ble to those of the best hand-coded pre-reordering rules.

References

Yaser Al-Onaizan and Kishore Papineni. 2006. Distortion models for statistical machine translation. In *Proceedings of the 21st International Conference on Computational Linguistics and the 44th Annual Meeting of the Association for Computational Linguistics*, ACL-44, pages 529–536, Stroudsburg, PA, USA. Association for Computational Linguistics.

Giuseppe Attardi. 2006. Experiments with a multilanguage non-projective dependency parser. In *Proceedings of the Tenth Conference on Computational Natural Language Learning*, CoNLL-X '06, pages 166–170, Stroudsburg, PA, USA. Association for Computational Linguistics.

James Bergstra, Olivier Breuleux, Frédéric Bastien, Pascal Lamblin, Razvan Pascanu, Guillaume Desjardins, Joseph Turian, David Warde-Farley, and Yoshua Bengio. 2010. Theano: a CPU and GPU math expression compiler. In *Proceedings of the Python for Scientific Computing Conference (SciPy)*, June. Oral Presentation.

Alexandra Birch, Miles Osborne, and Philipp Koehn. 2008. Predicting success in machine translation. In *Proceedings of the Conference on Empirical Methods in Natural Language Processing*, EMNLP '08, pages 745–754, Stroudsburg, PA, USA. Association for Computational Linguistics.

Arianna Bisazza and Marcello Federico. 2013. Efficient solutions for word reordering in German-English phrase-based statistical machine translation. In *Proceedings of the Eighth Workshop on Statistical Machine Translation*, pages 440–451, Sofia, Bulgaria, August. Association for Computational Linguistics.

Cristina Bosco and Vincenzo Lombardo. 2004. Dependency and relational structure in treebank annotation. In *COLING 2004 Recent Advances in Dependency Grammar*, pages 1–8.

Kyunghyun Cho, Bart van Merriënboer, Dzmitry Bahdanau, and Yoshua Bengio. 2014. On the properties of neural machine translation: Encoder-decoder approaches. *arXiv preprint arXiv:1409.1259*.

Michael Collins, Philipp Koehn, and Ivona Kučerová. 2005. Clause restructuring for statistical machine translation. In *Proceedings of the 43rd annual meeting on association for computational linguistics*, pages 531–540. Association for Computational Linguistics.

Nadir Durrani, Helmut Schmid, and Alexander Fraser. 2011. A joint sequence translation model with integrated reordering. In *Proceedings of the 49th Annual Meeting of the Association for Computational Linguistics: Human Language Technologies-Volume 1*, pages 1045–1054. Association for Computational Linguistics.

Chris Dyer and Philip Resnik. 2010. Context-free reordering, finite-state translation. In *Human Language Technologies: The 2010 Annual Conference of the North American Chapter of the Association for Computational Linguistics*, HLT '10, pages 858–866, Stroudsburg, PA, USA. Association for Computational Linguistics.

Minwei Feng, Arne Mauser, and Hermann Ney. 2010. A source-side decoding sequence model for statistical machine translation. In *Conference of the Association for Machine Translation in the Americas (AMTA)*.

C. Gallicchio and A. Micheli. 2011. Architectural and markovian factors of echo state networks. *Neural Networks*, 24(5):440 - 456.

Dmitriy Genzel. 2010. Automatically learning source-side reordering rules for large scale machine translation. In *Proceedings of the 23rd International Conference on Computational Linguistics*, COLING '10, pages 376–384, Stroudsburg, PA, USA. Association for Computational Linguistics.

Alex Graves. 2013. Generating sequences with recurrent neural networks. *arXiv preprint arXiv:1308.0850*.

Susan Howlett and Mark Dras. 2011. Clause restructuring for SMT not absolutely helpful. In *Proceedings of the 49th Annual Meeting of the Assocation for Computational Linguistics: Human Language Technologies*, pages 384–388.

Fei Huang. 2009. Confidence measure for word alignment. In *Proceedings of the Joint Conference of the 47th Annual Meeting of the ACL and the 4th International Joint Conference on Natural Language Processing of the AFNLP: Volume 2-Volume 2*, pages 932–940. Association for Computational Linguistics.

Herbert Jaeger. 2001. The echo state approach to analysing and training recurrent neural networks-with an erratum note. *Bonn, Germany: German National Research Center for Information Technology GMD Technical Report*, 148:34.

Maxim Khalilov and José AR Fonollosa. 2011. Syntax-based reordering for statistical machine translation. *Computer speech & language*, 25(4):761–788.

Diederik Kingma and Jimmy Ba. 2014. Adam: A method for stochastic optimization. *arXiv preprint arXiv:1412.6980*.

Philipp Koehn, Hieu Hoang, Alexandra Birch, Chris Callison-Burch, Marcello Federico, Nicola Bertoldi, Brooke Cowan, Wade Shen, Christine Moran, Richard Zens, Chris Dyer, Ondřej Bojar, Alexandra Constantin, and Evan Herbst. 2007. Moses: open source toolkit for statistical machine translation. In *Proceedings of the 45th Annual Meeting of the ACL on Interactive Poster and Demonstration Sessions*, ACL '07, pages 177–180, Stroudsburg, PA, USA. Association for Computational Linguistics.

Philipp Koehn. 2005. Europarl: A parallel corpus for statistical machine translation. In *Conference Proceedings: the tenth Machine Translation Summit*, pages 79–86, Phuket, Thailand. AAMT, AAMT.

Uri Lerner and Slav Petrov. 2013. Source-side classifier preordering for machine translation. In *Proceedings of the 2014 Conference on Empirical Methods in Natural Language Processing (EMNLP '13)*.

Antonio Valerio Miceli Barone and Giuseppe Attardi. 2013. Pre-reordering for machine translation using transition-based walks on dependency parse trees. In *Proceedings of the Eighth Workshop on Statistical Machine Translation*, pages 164–169, Sofia, Bulgaria, August. Association for Computational Linguistics.

Tomas Mikolov, Martin Karafiát, Lukas Burget, Jan Cernockỳ, and Sanjeev Khudanpur. 2010. Recurrent neural network based language model. In *INTERSPEECH*, pages 1045–1048.

Jiri Navratil, Karthik Visweswariah, and Ananthakrishnan Ramanathan. 2012. A comparison of syntactic reordering methods for english-german machine translation. In *COLING*, pages 2043–2058.

Franz Josef Och, Christoph Tillmann, Hermann Ney, et al. 1999. Improved alignment models for statistical machine translation. In *Proc. of the Joint SIGDAT Conf. on Empirical Methods in Natural Language Processing and Very Large Corpora*, pages 20–28.

Slav Petrov, Leon Barrett, Romain Thibaux, and Dan Klein. 2006. Learning accurate, compact, and interpretable tree annotation. In *Proceedings of the 21st International Conference on Computational Linguistics and the 44th annual meeting of the Association for Computational Linguistics*, pages 433–440. Association for Computational Linguistics.

Ralf Steinberger, Bruno Pouliquen, Anna Widiger, Camelia Ignat, Tomaz Erjavec, Dan Tufis, and Dniel Varga. 2006. The jrc-acquis: A multilingual aligned parallel corpus with 20+ languages. In *Proceedings of the 5th International Conference on Language Resources and Evaluation (LREC'2006)*, Genoa, Italy.

Roy Tromble and Jason Eisner. 2009. Learning linear ordering problems for better translation. In *Proceedings of the 2009 Conference on Empirical Methods in Natural Language Processing: Volume 2 - Volume 2*, EMNLP '09, pages 1007–1016, Stroudsburg, PA, USA. Association for Computational Linguistics.

Karthik Visweswariah, Rajakrishnan Rajkumar, Ankur Gandhe, Ananthakrishnan Ramanathan, and Jiri Navratil. 2011. A word reordering model for improved machine translation. In *Proceedings of the Conference on Empirical Methods in Natural Language Processing*, EMNLP '11, pages 486–496, Stroudsburg, PA, USA. Association for Computational Linguistics.

Matthew D Zeiler. 2012. Adadelta: An adaptive learning rate method. *arXiv preprint arXiv:1212.5701*.

Detecting Deceptive Groups Using Conversations and Network Analysis

Dian Yu[1], **Yulia Tyshchuk**[2], **Heng Ji**[1], **William Wallace**[2]

[1]Computer Science Department, Rensselaer Polytechnic Institute
[2]Department of Industrial and Systems Engineering, Rensselaer Polytechnic Institute
[1,2]{yud2,tyshcy,jih,wallaw}@rpi.edu

Abstract

Deception detection has been formulated as a supervised binary classification problem on single documents. However, in daily life, millions of fraud cases involve detailed conversations between deceivers and victims. Deceivers may dynamically adjust their deceptive statements according to the reactions of victims. In addition, people may form groups and collaborate to deceive others. In this paper, we seek to identify deceptive groups from their conversations. We propose a novel subgroup detection method that combines linguistic signals and signed network analysis for dynamic clustering. A social-elimination game called *Killer Game* is introduced as a case study[1]. Experimental results demonstrate that our approach significantly outperforms human voting and state-of-the-art subgroup detection methods at dynamically differentiating the deceptive groups from truth-tellers.

1 Introduction

Deception generally entails messages and information intentionally transmitted to create a false conclusion (Buller et al., 1994). Deception detection is an important task for a wide range of applications including law enforcement, intelligence gathering, and financial fraud. Most of the previous work (*e.g.*, (Ott et al., 2011; Feng et al., 2012)) focused on content analysis of a single document in isolation (*e.g.*, a product review). The promoters of a product may post fake complimentary reviews, while their competitors may hire people to write fake negative reviews (Ott et al., 2011).

However, when we want to detect deception from text or voice conversations, the deception behavior may be affected by the following factors beyond textual statements.

1. *Dynamic*. Recent research in social science suggests that deception communication is dynamic and involves interactions among people (*e.g.*, (Buller and Burgoon, 1996)). Additionally, the research postulates that human's capacity to learn by observation enables him to acquire large, integrated units of behavior by example (Bandura, 1971). Therefore, a person's behavior concerning deception or truth-telling can change constantly, while he learns from others' statements during conversations.
2. *Global*. People may form groups for purpose of deception. Research in social psychology has shown that an individual's object-related behavior may be affected by the attitudes of other people due to group dynamics (Friedkin, 2010).

Recent studies typically have been conducted over "*static*" written or oral deceptive statements. There is no obligatory requirement for communication between the author and the readers of these statements (Yancheva and Rudzicz, 2013). As a result, a victim of deception tends to trust the story mainly based on the statement he reads (Ott et al., 2011). However, in daily life, millions of fraud cases involve detailed conversations between deceivers and victims. A deceiver may make a statement, which is partially true in order to deceive or mislead victims and adjust his deceptive strategies based on the reactions of victims (Zhou et al., 2004). Therefore, it is more challenging to identity a deceiver in an interactive process of deception.

Most deception detection research addressed individual deceivers, but deceivers often act in pairs or larger groups (Vrij et al., 2010). The interac-

[1]The data set is publicly available for research purposes at: http://nlp.cs.rpi.edu/data/killer.zip

Proceedings of the 53rd Annual Meeting of the Association for Computational Linguistics and the 7th International Joint Conference on Natural Language Processing, pages 857–866,
Beijing, China, July 26-31, 2015.

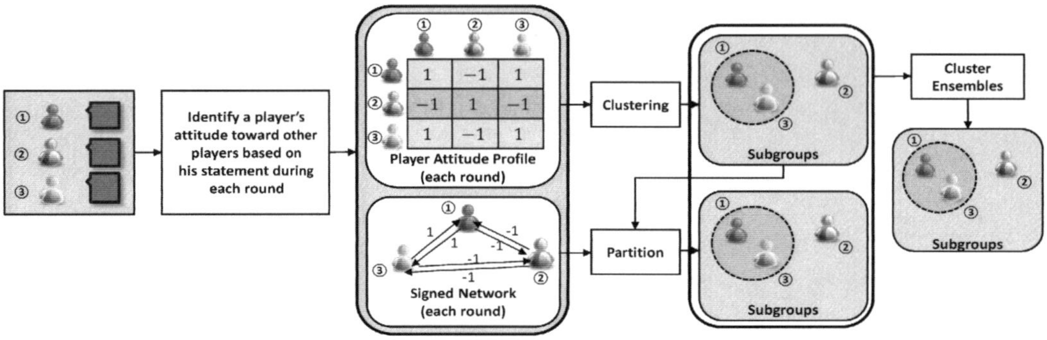

Figure 1: Deceptive group detection for a single round.

tions within a deceptive group have been ignored. For example, a product review from a deceiver may be supported by his teammates so that his deceptive comments can be read by more potential buyers. In this case, we can identify a deceptive group based on their collaborations and common characteristics, which is more promising than the typical methods of classifying individual statements as deceptive or trustworthy.

In order to identify deceptive groups by analyzing the evolution of a person's deception strategy during his interactions with victims and the interactions within the deceptive group from conversations, we use a social-elimination game called *Killer Game* which contains the ground-truth of subgroups.

The killer game has many variants that involve different roles and skills. We choose a classical version played by three roles/teams: detectives, citizens, and killers. The role of each *player* (game participant) is randomly assigned by a third-party game judge. Every killer/detective is given the identities of his teammates. There are two alternating phases of the game: "*night*", when killers may covertly "*murder*" a player and detectives may learn one player's role; and "*day*", when surviving players are informed of who was killed last "*night*" and then asked to speculate about the roles of other surviving players. Before a "*day*" ends, every surviving player should vote for a suspect. The candidate with the most votes is eliminated. A player's identity is not exposed after his "*death*". The game continues until all killers have been eliminated or all detectives have been killed. The killers are treated as deceivers, and citizens and detectives as truth-tellers.

In this paper, we present an unsupervised approach for differentiating the deceptive groups from truth-tellers in a game. During each round, we use Natural Language Processing (NLP) techniques to identify a player's attitude toward other players (Section 2), which are used to construct a vector of attitudes for each surviving player (Section 3.1) and a signed social network representation (Section 3.2) for the discussions. Then we use a clustering algorithm to cluster the attitude vector space and obtain results for each round (Section 3.1). We also implement a greedy optimization algorithm to partition the singed network based on the attitude clustering result (Section 3.2). Finally, we apply a pairwise-similarity approach that makes use of the predicted co-occurrence relations between players to combine all results from each round (Section 3.3). Figure 1 provides an overview of our system pipeline.

The major novel contributions of this paper are as follows.

- This is the first study to investigate conversations and deceptive groups for computerized deception detection.
- The proposed clustering technique is shown to be successful in separating deceptive groups from truth-tellers.
- The method can be applied to dynamically detect subgroups in a network with discussants who tend to change their opinions.

2 Attitude Identification

In this section, we describe how we take a player's statement in a single round as input to extract his attitudes toward other players and represent them by an attitude 3-tuple (speaker, target, polarity) list. For this work, the polarity of attitudes (Balahur et al., 2009) can be positive (1), negative (-1) or neutral (0). A game log from a single round will be used as our illustrative example, as shown in Figure 2.

C: CITIZEN; D: DETECTIVE; K: KILLER

System: First Round.
System: 15 was killed last night. 15, please leave your last words.
15(C): I'm a citizen. Over.
16(K): I'm a good person. 11 and 2 are suspicious.
1(K): I'm a good person. It has been a long time since I played as a killer. I'm a citizen. 11 is suspicious and I don't want to comment on 16's statement.
2(C): I'm a detective. 6 was proved as a killer last night. Over.
3(C): I don't know 2's identity. It's hard to judge 16's statement. 1 seems to be a good person. I'm a citizen.
4(C): Citizen. I cannot find a killer. I trust 2 since 2 sounds a good person. 16 is suspicious. I regard 16 as a killer. I'm 2's teammate.
5(D): I'm a detective. I verify 2's identity and 2 is a killer. 13 is good.
6(C): Why do you want to attack 2? I don't understand. 14 is suspicious.
7(K): It's hard to define 6's identity. 4 may be a citizen. I will vote for 2. 6 sounds very weird and I found 6 very suspicious. I will follow the detective 5 to vote for 2.
8(C): We should calm down. 7 seems to be a bad person.
9(C): 1 and 7 seem to be killers. There is no evidence to support 2 as a detective. 3 is a citizen. 4 is possibly a detective. 6 is also good.
10(D): I agree with you. 7 must be a killer. 2 and 7 should debate.
11(C): I don't know 2 but I think 2 is good. 3 is good. There should be one or two killers among 1, 4 and 7.
12(K): 11 sounds like a killer. 2 is a killer. I'm a citizen. Vote for 2.
13(D): 15 is a citizen. 16 is logically good. I think 1, 8, 9, 10 are OK. I don't think 2 is a killer. I doubt 7's intention. Please vote for 7.
14(D): 10, 13, 16 are good. I don't think 7 must be a killer. 2 is obviously bad. I'm a citizen.
System: 16, 11, 14, 7, 1, 3, 8, 12, 4 vote for 2 ··· 10, 13, 5, 2 vote for 7 ··· 9, 6 vote for 11 ··· *2 is out.*

Figure 2: Killer game sample log (the 1st round).

2.1 Target and Attitude Word Identification

We start by identifying targets and attitude words from conversations. In the killer game, a target is represented by his unique ID[2] and game terms are regarded as attitude words. We collected 41 terms in total from the game's website [3] and related discussion forum posts. ICTCLAS (Zhang et al., 2003) is used for word segmentation and part-of-speech (POS) tagging. There are two kinds of game terms: positive and negative. Positive terms include "*citizen*", "*good person*", "*good person certified by the detectives*" and "*detective*". Negative terms include "*killer*", "*killer verified by the detectives*" and "*a killer who claimed himself/herself to be a detective*". We assign the polarity score +1, -1 to positive and negative terms respectively.

[2]Each player has a game ID, assigned by the online game system based on when he entered the game room.

[3]e.g., http://www.3j3f.com/how/

2.2 Attitude-Target Pairing

Then we associate each attitude word with its corresponding target. We remove interrogative and exclamatory sentences and only keep the sentences that include at least one attitude word from a player's statement during each round.

We develop a rule-based approach for attitude-target pairing: if there is at least one ID in the sentence, we associate all attitude words in that sentence with it. Otherwise, if "I" is the only subject or there are no subjects at all, we associate attitude words with the ID of the speaker. We reverse the polarity of an attitude word if it appears in a negation context.

Previous methods pair a target and an attitude word if they satisfy at least one dependency rule (*e.g.*, (Somasundaran and Wiebe, 2009)). We check the POS tag sequence between them. For each attitude-target pair, if there exists an attitude word, a belief-oriented verb such as "*think*", "*believe*", "*feel*", or more than two verbs in the sequence, we will discard this pair. The assumption is that POS tag sequences can be used to summarize dependency rules when statements are relatively short.

For those targets, the speaker didn't mention or there is no positive/negative attitude word used when they are mentioned, the attitude polarity score is set to 0. For instance, given Player 16's statement in Figure 2, its attitude tuple list is: [(16, 16, +1), (16, 11, -1), (16, 2, -1), (16, 1, 0), (16, 3, 0), . . . , (16, 15, 0)].

3 Clustering

Since the statements in conversations are relatively short and concise, it is difficult to identify which one is deceptive, even using deep linguistic features such as the language style.

In this section, we introduce a method to construct an attitude profile for each player and a signed network based on the attitude tuple list in Section 2, and combine them to analyze a dynamic network with discussants telling lies and truths.

3.1 Clustering based on Attitude Profile

We use a vector containing numerical values to represent each player's attitude toward identified targets in each round. The values correspond to the polarity scores in a player's attitude tuple list. For example, the polarity score of player 16's attitude toward target 11 is -1 as shown in Figure 2.

We call this vector as the discussant attitude profile (DAP) following (Abu-Jbara et al., 2012a).

Suppose there are n players who participate in a single game. Since a player's identity is not exposed to the public after his death[4], people can still analyze the identity of a "*dead*" player. Therefore, the number of possibly mentioned targets in each round equals to n. Given all the statements from m surviving players in a single round, each player's DAP has $n+1$ dimensions including his vote and thus we can have a $m \times (n+1)$ attitude matrix A where A_{ij} represents the attitude polarity of i toward j we got from Section 2. $A_{i(n+1)}$ represents i's vote.

In a certain round, given a set of m surviving players $X = \{x_1, x_2, \cdots, x_m\}$ to be clustered and their respective DAPs, we can modify the Euclidean metric to compute the differences in attitudes and get an $m \times m$ distance matrix M:

$$M_{ij} = \sqrt{\sum_{k=1}^{n}(A_{ik} - A_{jk})^2 + (2 - 2\delta_{A_{i(n+1)},A_{j(n+1)}})^2} \quad (1)$$

The Kronecker delta function δ is:

$$\delta_{ij} = \begin{cases} 1 & i = j \\ 0 & i \neq j \end{cases} \quad (2)$$

We use this function to compare the votes of two players separately because a player's vote can be inconsistent with his previous statements. We assume that there is a larger distance between two players when they vote for different suspects.

A common assumption in previous research was that a member is more likely to show a positive attitude toward other members in the same group, and a negative attitude toward the opposing groups (Abu-Jbara et al., 2012a). However, a deceiver may pretend to be innocent by supporting those truth-tellers and attacking his teammates, whose identities have already been exposed. Therefore, it is not enough to judge the relationship between two players by simply measuring the distance between their DAPs.

In addition to comparing DAPs between players i and j, we also consider the attitudes of other players toward i and j, as well as their attitudes toward each other. We modify M_{ij} as follows and show it in Figure 3:

$$M'_{ij} = M_{ij} + \sqrt{\sum_{k=1}^{m}(A_{ki} - A_{kj})^2 + (h(A_{ij}) + h(A_{ji}))^2} \quad (3)$$

where the function h detects the negative attitudes. $h(x) = 0$ if $x \geq 0$ and $h(x) = -1$ otherwise.

We perform hierarchical clustering on the condensed distance matrix of M and use the complete linkage method to compute the distance between two clusters (Voorhees, 1986). We set the number of clusters as 3 since there are three natural groups in the game. We focus on separating deceivers (killers) from truth-tellers (citizens and detectives).

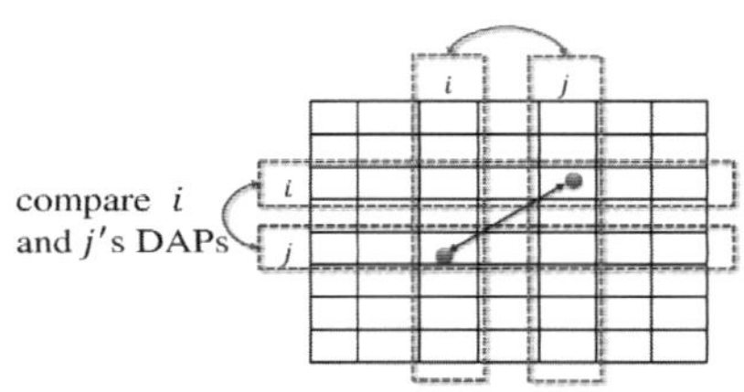

Figure 3: Computation of the distance between player i and j based on the attitude matrix.

3.2 Signed Network Partition

When we computed the distance between two players in Section 3.1, we did not consider the network structure among all the players. For example, if A supports C, B supports D and C and D dislike each other, A and B may belong to different groups. Thus, we propose to capture the interactions in the social network to further improve the attitude-profile-based clustering result.

We can easily convert the attitude matrix A into a signed network by adding a directed edge $i \rightarrow j$ between i and j if $A_{ij} \neq 0$. We denote a directed graph corresponding to a signed network as $G = (V, S, N, W)$, where V is the set of nodes, S is the set of positive edges, N is the set of negative edges and $W : (V \times V) \rightarrow \{-1, 1\}$ is a function that maps every directed edge to a value, $W(i,j) = A_{ij}$.

We use a greedy optimization algorithm (Doreian and Mrvar, 1996) to find partitions. A criterion function for an optimal partitioning procedure

[4]Each round, the player killed by killers and the player with the most votes are out.

is constructed such that positive links are dense within groups and negative links are dense between groups. For any potential partition $\mathbb{C}$, we seek to minimize the following error function:

$$E(\mathbb{C}) = \sum_{C \in \mathbb{C}} [(1-\gamma) \sum_{\substack{i \in C \\ j \notin C}} W(i,j) S_{i,j} - \gamma \sum_{i,j \in C} W(i,j) N_{i,j}] \quad (4)$$

where $\gamma \in [0, 1]$ controls the balance of the penalty difference between putting a positive edge across and a negative edge within a group. We regard these two types of errors as equally important and set $\gamma = 0.5$ for our experiments.

Initially, we use the clustering result in Section 3.1 to partition nodes into three different groups and an error function, E, is evaluated for that cluster. Every cluster has a set of neighbor clusters in the cluster space. A neighbor cluster is obtained by moving a node from one group to another, or exchanging two nodes in two different groups. E is evaluated for all the neighbor clusters of the current cluster and the one with the lowest value is set as the new cluster. The algorithm is repeated until it finds a minimal solution[5]. We set the upper limit for the number of subgroups to 3.

3.3 Cluster Ensembles

The relationships between players are dynamic throughout the game. For example, a killer tends to hide his identity and pretends to be friendly to others at later stages in order to survive. Thus, it is insufficient to rely on a single round's discussion to cluster players. In addition, for each single round, we also need to combine the clustering results from the attitude profiles of the players and the signed network.

In a game with information gathered from up to r rounds, let $P = \{P_1, P_2, \cdots, P_r\}$ be the set of r clusterings (partitionings) based on attitude profiles and $P' = \{P'_1, P'_2, \cdots, P'_r\}$ be the set of r clusterings based on the signed network.

Using the co-occurrence relations between players, we can generate a $n \times n$ pairwise similarity matrix T based on the information of all r rounds:

$$T^r_{ij} = \frac{\lambda \cdot vote_{ij} + (1-\lambda) \cdot vote'_{ij}}{r_{ij}} \quad (5)$$

where $vote_{ij}$, $vote'_{ij}$ are the number of times that player i and j are assigned to the same cluster in P and P' respectively. r_{ij} denotes the number of rounds when both of them survived ($r_{ij} \leq r$). $T^r_{ij} \in [0, 1]$. We assign a higher weight to the result of P_1 and set $\lambda = 2/3$ in our experiments.

Given the input in Figure 2, x_3 and x_4 are assigned to the same cluster in P_1 ($vote_{34} = 1$) and in P'_1 ($vote'_{34} = 1$) respectively as shown in Figure 4. x_3 and x_4 co-occurred in the first round ($r_{34} = 1$). $T^1_{34} = (2/3 \times 1 + 1/3 \times 1)/1 = 1$.

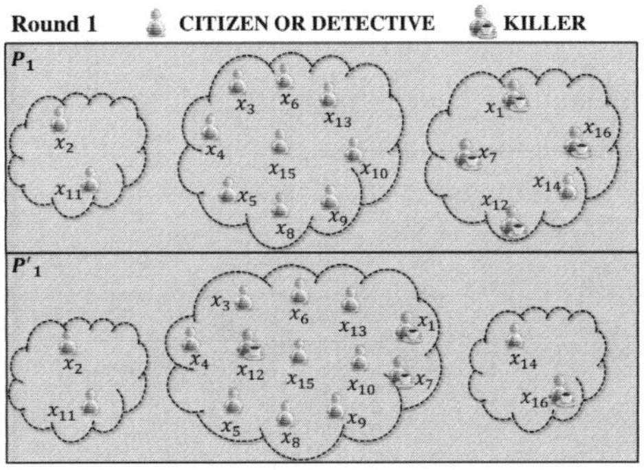

Figure 4: Example of cluster ensemble for a single round.

We apply hierarchical clustering (Voorhees, 1986) to the similarity matrix above to obtain the final global clustering results.

4 Experiments

4.1 Dataset Construction

We recorded 10 games from 3J3F[6], one of the most popular Chinese online killer game websites [7]. A screenshot of the game system interface is shown in Figure 5. There are 16 participating players per game: 4 detectives, 4 killers and 8 citizens. Each player occupies a position in ①. All the surviving players can express their attitudes via a voice channel using ②, while detectives and killers can also communicate with teammates in their respective private team channels ③ via texts. The system provides real-time updates on the game progress, voting results, and so on using the public channel ④. We manually transcribed speech and stored the text information in the public channel, which contains the voting and death information. The average game length

[5] Since our graphs are small, we search through all partitions. We repeated 1000 times in our experiment.

[6] http://www.3j3f.com

[7] All data sets and resources will be made available for research purposes upon the acceptance of the paper.

Game	*Purity* (%)					*Entropy*				
#	D	N	H	eD	$eD+N$	D	N	H	eD	$eD+N$
1	68.8	75.0	75.0	68.8	75.0	0.48	0.50	0.78	0.63	0.50
2	75.0	68.8	68.8	43.8	81.3	0.71	0.69	0.81	0.73	0.43
3	43.8	81.3	56.3	75.0	75.0	0.77	0.67	0.81	0.72	0.72
4	75.0	62.5	75.0	93.8	93.8	0.78	0.68	0.74	0.28	0.28
5	62.5	75.0	81.3	75.0	75.0	0.61	0.50	0.61	0.72	0.72
6	81.3	81.3	75.0	81.3	81.3	0.64	0.38	0.74	0.60	0.60
7	81.3	75.0	81.3	81.3	87.5	0.65	0.70	0.68	0.51	0.51
8	87.5	75.0	75.0	93.8	93.8	0.41	0.73	0.78	0.23	0.23
9	75.0	43.8	75.0	81.3	87.5	0.76	0.80	0.78	0.67	0.49
10	62.5	75.0	87.5	81.3	81.3	0.78	0.60	0.51	0.61	0.67
Average	71.3	71.3	75.0	77.5	**83.2**	0.66	0.62	0.72	0.57	**0.51**

Table 1: Results on subgroup detection. D refers to *DAPC*, N refers to *Network*, H refers to *Human Voting*, and eD refers to *extended DAPC*.

is about 76.3 minutes and there are on average 5 rounds and 411 sentences per game. Note that our method is language-independent and could easily be adapted to other languages.

Figure 5: Screenshot of the online killer game interface.

4.2 Evaluation Metrics

We use two metrics to evaluate the clustering accuracy: Purity and Entropy. Purity (Manning et al., 2008) is a metric in which each cluster is assigned to the class with the majority vote in the cluster, and then the accuracy of this assignment is measured by dividing the number of correctly assigned instances by the total number of instances N. More formally:

$$purity(\Omega, C) = \frac{1}{N}\sum_{k} max_j |w_k \cap c_j| \quad (6)$$

where $\Omega = \{w_1, w_2, \cdots, w_k\}$ is the set of clusters and $C = \{c_1, c_2, \cdots, c_j\}$ is the set of classes. w_k is interpreted as the set of instances in w_k and c_j is the set of instances in c_j. The purity increases as the quality of clustering improves.

Entropy (Steinbach et al., 2000) measures the uniformity of a cluster. The entropy for all clusters is defined by the weighted sum of the entropy of each cluster:

$$Entropy = -\sum^{j} \frac{n_j}{n} \sum^{i} P(i,j) \times log_2 P(i,j) \quad (7)$$

where $P(i,j)$ is the probability of finding an element from the category i in the cluster j, n_j is the number of items in cluster j and n is the total number of items in the distribution. The entropy decreases as the quality of clustering improves.

4.3 Overall Performance

We compare our approach with two state-of-the-art subgroup detection methods and human performance as follows:

1. DAPC: In Section 3.1, we introduced our implementation of the discussant attitude profile clustering (DAPC) method proposed in (Abu-Jbara et al., 2012a). In the original DAPC method, for each opinion target, there are 3 dimensions in the feature vector, corresponding to (1) the number of positive expressions, (2) negative expressions toward the target from the online posts and (3) the number of times the discussant mentioned the target. For our experiment, we only keep one dimension representing the discussant's attitude (positive, negative, neutral) toward the target since a discussant attitude remains the same in his statement within a single round.
2. Network: We also implemented the signed network partition method for subgroup detection proposed by (Hassan et al., 2012). To determine the number of subgroups t, we set an upper limit of $t = 3$ in order to minimize the optimization function.

3. Human_Voting: We also compare our methods with human voting results. There are two subgroups based on the voting results. The players with the highest votes each round belong to one subgroup and the rest of the players are in the other subgroup.

Table 1 shows the overall performance of various methods on subgroup detection and Figure 6 depicts the average performance. We can see that our method significantly outperforms two baseline methods and human voting. The human performance is not satisfying, which indicates it's very challenging even for a human to identify a deceiver whose deceptive statement is mixed with plenty of truthful opinions (Xu and Zhao, 2012).

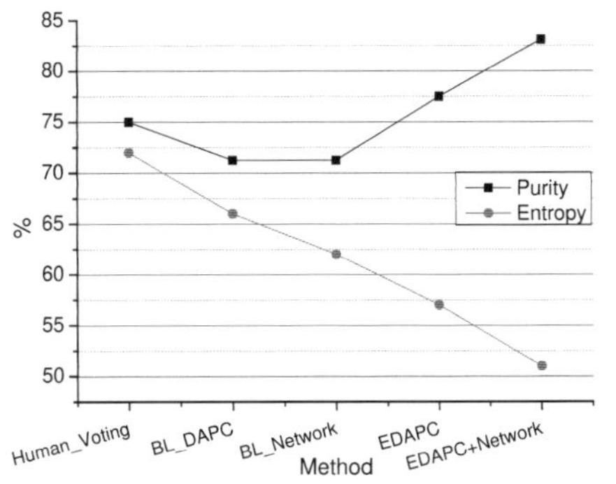

Figure 6: An overview of the average performance of all the methods.

By extending the DAPC method (EDPAC), we can estimate the distance between two players more accurately by considering the attitudes of other players toward them and their attitudes toward each other. Given the log in Figure 2 as input, players 5 (detective) and 7 (killer) are clustered into one group when DAPC is applied since they don't have conflicting views on the identities of other players. However, 5 voted for 7 and is supported by more players compared with 7, which indicates that they are less likely to be teammates. We can successfully separate them after re-computing the distance between them.

Adding network information provided 5.7% further gain in Purity. In some cases, the performance remains the same when EDAPC clustering result is already optimal with the minimum value of the criterion function.

4.4 Dynamic Subgroup Detection

As shown in Figure 7, the performance of our approach improves as the game proceeds. Players seldom maintain their opinions throughout a game. Figure 2 shows that most killers (16,1,12) insisted that citizen 11 should be a killer except 7. As a response to the group pressure (Asch, 1951), 7 changed his opinion and stated that 11 could be a killer in the following round.

In reality, a discussant who participates in an online discussion tends to change his opinions about a target as he learns more information, which shows both the necessity and importance of the dynamic detection of subgroups. Our method can be applied to detect subgroups dynamically by grouping posts into multiple discussion *"rounds"* based on their timestamps.

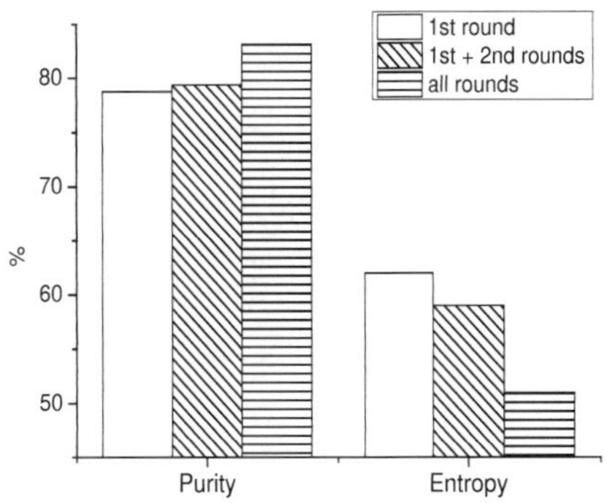

Figure 7: Average performance based on different rounds.

5 Related Work

5.1 Opinion Analysis

Our work on mining a player's attitude toward other players is related to opinion mining. Attitudes and opinions are related and can be regarded as the same in our task. Compared with the previous work (*e.g.*,(Qiu et al., 2011; Kim and Hovy, 2006)), the opinion words and targets in our task are relatively easier to recognize due to the simplicity of statements. Some recent work (*e.g.*, (Somasundaran and Wiebe, 2009; Abu-Jbara et al., 2012a)) developed syntactic rules to pair an opinion word and a target if they satisfy at least one specific dependency rule. We use POS tag sequences to efficiently help us filter out irrelevant pairs.

5.2 Deception Detection

Most of the previous computational work for deception detection used supervised/semi-supervised classification methods (Li et al., 2013b). Besides lexical and syntactical features (Ott et al., 2011; Feng et al., 2012; Yancheva and Rudzicz, 2013), Feng and Hirst (2013) proposed using profile compatibility to distinguish fake and genuine reviews. Xu and Zhao (2012) used deep linguistic features such as text genre to detect deceptive opinion spams. Banerjee et al. (2014) used extended linguistic signals such as keystroke patterns. Li et al. (2013a) used topic models to detect the difference between deceptive and truthful topic-word distribution. Researchers have began to realize the importance of analyzing computer-mediated communication in deception detection. Zhou and Sung (2008) conducted an empirical study on deception cues using the killer game as a task scenario and obtained many interesting findings (*e.g.*, deceivers send fewer messages than truth-tellers).

Our work is most related to the work of Chittaranjan and Hung (2010) on detecting deceptive roles in the Werewolf Game which is another variant of the killer game. They created a Werewolf data set by audio-visual recording 8 games played by 2 groups of people face-to-face and extracted audio features and interaction features for their experiments. However, we should note that non face-to-face deception detection emphasizes verbal and linguistic cues over less controllable non-verbal communication cues (Walther, 1996).

5.3 Subgroup Detection

In online discussions, people usually split into subgroups based on various topics. The member of a subgroup is more likely to show positive attitude to the members of the same subgroup, and negative attitude to the members of opposing subgroups (Abu-Jbara et al., 2012a). Previous work also studied subgroup detection in social media sites. Abu-Jbara et al. (2012a) constructed a discussant attitude profile (DAP) for each discussant and then used clustering techniques to cluster their attitudes. Hassan et al. (2012; 2012b; 2013) proposed various methods to automatically construct a signed social network representation of discussions and then identify subgroups by partitioning their signed networks. Qiu et al. (2013) applied collaborative filtering through Probabilistic Matrix Factorization (PMF) to generalize and improve extracted opinion matrices.

An underlying assumption of the previous work was that a participant will not tell lies nor hide his own stance. Moreover, their work did not take into account that a person's attitude or stance will change as he learns more by reading the comments from others and acquiring more background knowledge (Bandura, 1971). Our contribution is that we extend the DAP method and combine it with the signed network partition in order to cluster the hidden group members. We also develop a novel cluster ensemble approach in order to analyze the dynamic network.

6 Conclusions and Future Work

Using the killer game as a case study, we present an effective clustering method to detect subgroups from dynamic conversations with lies and truths. This is the first work to utilize the dynamics of group conversations for deception detection. Experiments demonstrated that truth-tellers and deceptive groups are separable and the proposed method significantly outperforms baseline approaches and human voting.

Our work builds a pathway to future work in deception detection in content-rich dynamic environments such as electronic commerce and repeated interrogation which will require sophisticated content and network analysis. In real-life suspects may be interrogated about particular events on numerous occasions. Our method can potentially be modified to find criminals who act in groups based on their statements. Other applications of this research include law enforcement, financial fraud, fraudulent ad campaigns and social engineering.

This study focuses on analyzing the verbal content in conversations. It will be interesting to study non-verbal features such as blink rate, gaze aversion and pauses (Granhag and Strömwall, 2002) when people play this game face-to-face and combine the non-verbal and verbal features for deception detection. In addition, it is worth exploring the impact of cross-cultural analysis in detecting deception. When attempting to detect deceit in people of other ethnic origin than themselves, people perform even worse in terms of lie detection accuracy than when judging people of their own ethnic origin (Vrij, 2000). For the future work, we aim to use automatic prediction of deceivers to help truth-tellers win games more easily.

Acknowledgement

This work was supported by the U.S. DARPA DEFT Program No. FA8750-13-2-0041, ARL NS-CTA No. W911NF-09-2-0053, NSF Awards IIS-0953149 and IIS-1523198, AFRL DREAM project, gift awards from IBM, Google, Disney and Bosch. The views and conclusions contained in this document are those of the authors and should not be interpreted as representing the official policies, either expressed or implied, of the U.S. Government. The U.S. Government is authorized to reproduce and distribute reprints for Government purposes notwithstanding any copyright notation here on.

References

A. Abu-Jbara, M. Diab, P. Dasigi, and D. Radev. 2012a. Subgroup detection in ideological discussions. In *Proc. Annual Meeting of the Association for Computational Linguistics (ACL 2012)*.

A. Abu-Jbara, A. Hassan, and D. Radev. 2012b. Attitudeminer: mining attitude from online discussions. In *Proc. North American Chapter of the Association for Computational Linguistics - Human Language Technologies (NAACL HLT 2012)*.

A. Abu-Jbara, B. King, M. Diab, and D. Radev. 2013. Identifying opinion subgroups in arabic online discussions. In *Proc. Association for Computational Linguistics (ACL 2013)*.

S. Asch. 1951. Effects of group pressure upon the modification and distortion of judgments. *Groups, leadership, and men. S.*

A. Balahur, R. Steinberger, E. Goot, B. Pouliquen, and M. Kabadjov. 2009. Opinion mining on newspaper quotations. In *IEEE/WIC/ACM International Joint Conferences on Web Intelligence and Intelligent Agent Technologies (WI-IAT 2009)*.

A. Bandura. 1971. *Social Learning Theory*. General Learning Corporation.

R. Banerjee, S. Feng, J. Kang, and Y. Choi. 2014. Keystroke patterns as prosody in digital writings: A case study with deceptive reviews and essays. In *Proc. Empirical Methods on Natural Language Processing (EMNLP 2014)*.

D. Buller and J. Burgoon. 1996. Interpersonal deception theory. *Communication theory*.

David B Buller, Judee K Burgoon, JA Daly, and JM Wiemann. 1994. Deception: Strategic and nonstrategic communication. *Strategic interpersonal communication*.

G. Chittaranjan and H. Hung. 2010. Are you awerewolf? detecting deceptive roles and outcomes in a conversational role-playing game. In *IEEE International Conference on Acoustics Speech and Signal Processing (ICASSP 2010)*.

P. Doreian and A. Mrvar. 1996. A partitioning approach to structural balance. *Social networks*.

V. Feng and G. Hirst. 2013. Detecting deceptive opinions with profile compatibility. In *Proc. International Joint Conference on Natural Language Processing (IJCNLP 2013)*.

S. Feng, R. Banerjee, and Y. Choi. 2012. Syntactic stylometry for deception detection. In *Proc. Association for Computational Linguistics (ACL 2012)*.

N. E. Friedkin. 2010. The attitude-behavior linkage in behavioral cascades. *Social Psychology Quarterly*.

P. Granhag and L. Strömwall. 2002. Repeated interrogations: verbal and non-verbal cues to deception. *Applied Cognitive Psychology*.

A. Hassan, A. Abu-Jbara, and D. Radev. 2012. Detecting subgroups in online discussions by modeling positive and negative relations among participants. In *Proc. Empirical Methods in Natural Language Processing and Computational Natural Language Learning (EMNLP-CoNLL 2012)*.

S. Kim and E. Hovy. 2006. Extracting opinions, opinion holders, and topics expressed in online news media text. In *Proc. ACL-COLING 2006 Workshop on Sentiment and Subjectivity in Text*.

J. Li, C. Cardie, and S. Li. 2013a. Topicspam: a topic-model based approach for spam detection. In *Proc. Association for Computational Linguistics (ACL 2013)*.

J. Li, M. Ott, and C. Cardie. 2013b. Identifying manipulated offerings on review portals. In *Proc. Empirical Methods on Natural Language Processing (EMNLP 2013)*.

C. Manning, P. Raghavan, and H. Schütze. 2008. *Introduction to information retrieval*. Cambridge university press Cambridge.

M. Ott, Y. Choi, C. Cardie, and J. Hancock. 2011. Finding deceptive opinion spam by any stretch of the imagination. In *Proc. Association for Computational Linguistics (ACL 2011)*.

G. Qiu, B. Liu, J. Bu, and C. Chen. 2011. Opinion word expansion and target extraction through double propagation. *Computational linguistics*.

M. Qiu, L. Yang, and J. Jiang. 2013. Mining user relations from online discussions using sentiment analysis and probabilistic matrix factorization. In *Proc. North American Chapter of the Association for Computational Linguistics - Human Language Technologies (NAACL HLT 2013)*.

S. Somasundaran and J. Wiebe. 2009. Recognizing stances in online debates. In *Proc. Joint Conference of the Annual Meeting of the ACL and the 4th International Joint Conference on Natural Language Processing of the AFNLP*.

M. Steinbach, G. Karypis, V. Kumar, et al. 2000. A comparison of document clustering techniques. In *Proc. KDD 2000 workshop on text mining*.

E. Voorhees. 1986. Implementing agglomerative hierarchic clustering algorithms for use in document retrieval. *Information Processing & Management*.

A. Vrij, P. Granhag, and S. Porter. 2010. Pitfalls and opportunities in nonverbal and verbal lie detection. *Psychological Science in the Public Interest*.

A. Vrij. 2000. *Detecting lies and deceit: The psychology of lying and implications for professional practice*. Wiley.

J. Walther. 1996. Computer-mediated communication impersonal, interpersonal, and hyperpersonal interaction. *Communication research*.

Q. Xu and H. Zhao. 2012. Using deep linguistic features for finding deceptive opinion spam. In *Proc. International Conference on Computational Linguistics (COLING 2012)*.

M. Yancheva and F. Rudzicz. 2013. Automatic detection of deception in child-produced speech using syntactic complexity features. In *Proc. Association for Computational Linguistics (ACL 2013)*.

H. Zhang, H. Yu, D. Xiong, and Q. Liu. 2003. Hhmm-based chinese lexical analyzer ictclas. In *Proc. SIGHAN 2003 workshop on Chinese language processing*.

L. Zhou and Y. Sung. 2008. Cues to deception in online chinese groups. In *Proc. Hawaii International Conference on System Sciences (HICSS 2008)*.

L. Zhou, J Burgoon, J. Nunamaker, and D. Twitchell. 2004. Automating linguistics-based cues for detecting deception in text-based asynchronous computer-mediated communications. *Group decision and negotiation*.

WikiKreator: Improving Wikipedia Stubs Automatically

Siddhartha Banerjee
The Pennsylvania State University
Information Sciences and Technology
University Park, PA, USA
sub253@ist.psu.edu

Prasenjit Mitra
Qatar Computing Research Institute
Hamad Bin Khalifa University
Doha, Qatar
pmitra@qf.org.qa

Abstract

Stubs on Wikipedia often lack comprehensive information. The huge cost of editing Wikipedia and the presence of only a limited number of active contributors curb the consistent growth of Wikipedia. In this work, we present WikiKreator, a system that is capable of generating content automatically to improve existing stubs on Wikipedia. The system has two components. First, a text classifier built using topic distribution vectors is used to assign content from the web to various sections on a Wikipedia article. Second, we propose a novel abstractive summarization technique based on an optimization framework that generates section-specific summaries for Wikipedia stubs. Experiments show that WikiKreator is capable of generating well-formed informative content. Further, automatically generated content from our system have been appended to Wikipedia stubs and the content has been retained successfully proving the effectiveness of our approach.

1 Introduction

Wikipedia provides comprehensive information on various topics. However, a significant percentage of the articles are stubs[1] that require extensive effort in terms of adding and editing content to transform them into complete articles. Ideally, we would like to create an automatic Wikipedia content generator, which can generate a comprehensive overview on any topic using available information from the web and append the generated content to the stubs. Addition of automatically generated content can provide a useful starting point for contributors on Wikipedia, which can be improved upon later.

Several approaches to automatically generate Wikipedia articles have been explored (Sauper and Barzilay, 2009; Banerjee et al., 2014; Yao et al., 2011). To the best of our knowledge, all the above mentioned methods identify information sources from the web using keywords and directly use the most relevant excerpts in the final article. Information from the web cannot be directly copied into Wikipedia due to copyright violation issues (Banerjee et al., 2014). Further, keyword search does not always satisfy information requirements (Baeza-Yates et al., 1999). To address the above-mentioned issues, we present WikiKreator – a system that can automatically generate content for Wikipedia stubs. First, WikiKreator does not operate using keyword search. Instead, we use a classifier trained using topic distribution features to identify relevant content for the stub. Topic-distribution features are more effective than keyword search as they can identify relevant content based on word distributions (Song et al., 2010). Second, we propose a novel abstractive summarization (Dalal and Malik, 2013) technique to summarize content from multiple snippets of relevant information.[2]

Figure 1 shows a stub that we attempt to improve using WikiKreator. Generally, in stubs, only the introductory content is available; other sections ($s_1, ..., s_r$) are absent. The stub also belongs to several categories (C_1,C_2, etc. in Figure) on Wikipedia. In this work, we address the following research question: *Given the introductory content, the title of the stub and information on the categories - how can we transform the stub into a com-*

[1] https://en.wikipedia.org/wiki/Wikipedia:Stub

[2] An example of our system's output can be found here – https://en.wikipedia.org/wiki/2014_Enterovirus_D68_outbreak – content was added on 5th Jan, 2015. The sections on *Epidemiology*, *Causes* and *Prevention* have been added using content automatically generated by our method.

Proceedings of the 53rd Annual Meeting of the Association for Computational Linguistics and the 7th International Joint Conference on Natural Language Processing, pages 867–877,
Beijing, China, July 26-31, 2015.

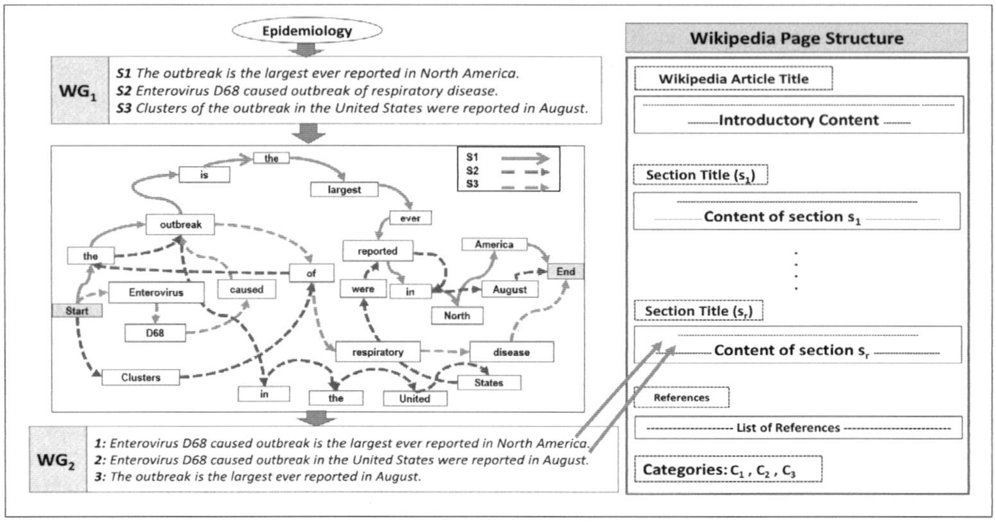

Figure 1: Overview of our word-graph based generation (left) to populate Wikipedia template (right)

prehensive Wikipedia article?

Our proposed approach consists of two stages. First, a text classifier assigns content retrieved from the web into specific sections of the Wikipedia article. We train the classifier using a set of articles within the same category. Currently, we limit the system to learn and assign content into the 10 most frequent sections in any given category. The training set includes content from the most frequent sections as instances and their corresponding section titles as the class labels. We extract topic distribution vectors using Latent Dirichlet Allocation (LDA) (Blei et al., 2003) and use the features to train a Random Forest (RF) Classifier (Liaw and Wiener, 2002). To gather web content relevant to the stub, we formulate queries and retrieve top 20 search results (pages) from Google. We use boilerplate detection (Kohlschütter et al., 2010) to retain the important excerpts (text elements) from the pages. The RF classifier classifies the excerpts into one of the most frequent classes (section titles). Second, we develop a novel Integer Linear Programming (ILP) based abstractive summarization technique to generate text from the classified content. Previous work only included the most informative excerpt in the article (Sauper and Barzilay, 2009); in contrast, our abstractive summarization approach minimizes loss of information that should ideally be in an Wikipedia article by fusing content from several sentences. As shown in Figure 1, we construct a word-graph (Filippova, 2010) using all the sentences (WG_1) assigned to a specific class (*Epidemiology*) by the classifier. Multiple paths (sentences) between the *start* and *end* nodes in the graph are generated (WG_2). We represent the generated paths as variables in the ILP problem. The coefficients of each variable in the objective function of the ILP problem is obtained by combining the information score and the linguistic quality score of the path. We introduce several constraints into our ILP model. We limit the summary for each section to a maximum of 5 sentences. Further, we avoid redundant sentences in the summary that carry similar information. The solution to the optimization problem decides the paths that are selected in the final section summary. For example, in Figure 1, the final paths determined by the ILP solution, – 1 and 2 in WG_2, are assigned to a section (s_r), where (s_r) is the section title *Epidemiology*.

To the best of our knowledge, this work is the first to address the issue of generating content automatically to transform Wikipedia stubs into comprehensive articles. Further, we address the issue of abstractive text summarization for Wikipedia content generation. We evaluate our approach by generating articles in three different categories: *Diseases and Disorders*[3], *American Mathematicians*[4] and *Software companies of the United States*[5]. Our LDA-based classi-

[3] https://en.wikipedia.org/wiki/Category:Diseases_and_disorders

[4] https://en.wikipedia.org/wiki/Category:American_mathematicians

[5] https://en.wikipedia.org/wiki/Category:Software_companies_of_the_United_States

fier outperforms a TFIDF-based classifier in all the categories. We use ROUGE (Lin, 2004) to compare content generated by WikiKreator and the corresponding Wikipedia articles. The results of our evaluation confirm the benefits of using abstractive summarization for content generation over approaches that do not use summarization. WikiKreator outperforms other comparable approaches significantly in terms of content selection. On ROUGE-1 scores, WikiKreator outperforms the perceptron-based baseline (Sauper and Barzilay, 2009) by ~20%. We also analyze reviewer reactions, by appending content into several stubs on Wikipedia, most of which (~77%) have been retained by reviewers.

2 Related Work

Wikipedia has been used to compute semantic relatedness (Gabrilovich and Markovitch, 2007), index topics (Medelyan et al., 2008), etc. However, the problem of enhancing the content of a Wikipedia article has not been addressed adequately. Learning structures of templates from the Wikipedia articles have been attempted in the past (Sauper and Barzilay, 2009; Yao et al., 2011). Both these efforts use queries to extract excerpts from the web and the excerpts ranked as the most relevant are added into the article. However, as already pointed out, current standards of Wikipedia requires rewriting of web content to avoid copyright violation issues.

To address the issue of copyright violation, multi-document abstractive summarization is required. Various abstractive approaches have been proposed till date (Nenkova et al., 2011). However, these methods suffer from severe deficiencies. Template-based summarization methods work well, but, it assumes prior domain knowledge (Li et al., 2013). Writing style across articles vary widely; hence learning templates automatically is difficult. In addition, such techniques require handcrafted rules for sentence realization (Gerani et al., 2014). Alternatively, we can use text-to-text generation (T2T) (Ganitkevitch et al., 2011) techniques. WikiKreator constructs a word-graph structure similar to (Filippova, 2010) using all the sentences that are assigned to a particular section by a text classifier. Multiple paths (sentences) from the graph are generated. WikiKreator selects few sentences from this set of paths using an optimization problem formulation that jointly maximizes the informativeness and readability of section-specific snippets and generates output that is informative, well-formed and readable.

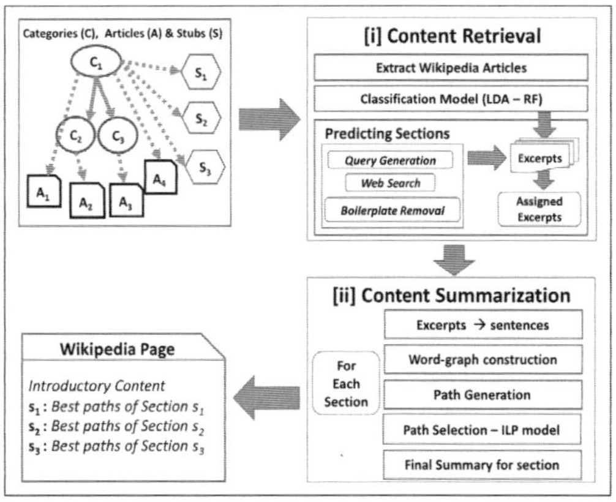

Figure 2: WikiKreator System Architecture: Content Retrieval and Content Summarization

3 Proposed Approach

Figure 2 shows the system architecture of WikiKreator. We are required to generate content to populate sections of the stubs (S_1, S_2, etc.) that belong to category C_1. Categories on Wikipedia group together pages on similar subjects. Hence, categories characterize Wikipedia articles surprisingly well (Zesch and Gurevych, 2007). Naturally, we leverage knowledge existing in the categories to build our text classifier. To learn category specific templates, the system should learn from articles contained within the same or similar categories. WikiKreator learns category-specific templates using all the articles that can be reached using a top-down approach from the particular category. For example, in addition to C_1, WikiKreator also learns templates from articles in C_2 and C_3 (the subcategories of C_1). As shown in the Figure 2, we deploy a two stage process to generate content for a stub:

[i] Content Retrieval and

[ii] Content Summarization.

In the first stage, our focus is to retrieve content that is relevant to the stub, say, S_1 that belongs to C_1. We extract all the articles that belong to C_1 and the subcategories, namely, C_2 and C_3. A training set is created with the contents in the sections of the articles as instances and the section titles as the corresponding classes. Topic distribution vectors for each section content are generated using LDA (Blei et al., 2003). We train a Random Forest

(RF) classifier using the topic distribution vectors. As mentioned earlier, only the top 10 most frequent sections are considered for the multi-class classification task. We retrieve relevant excerpts from the web by formulating queries. The topic model infers the topic distribution features of each excerpt and the RF classifier predicts the section (s_1, s_2, etc.) of the excerpt. All web automation tasks are performed using HTMLUnit[6]. In the second stage, our ILP based summarization approach synthesizes information from multiple excerpts assigned to a section and presents the most informative and linguistically well-formed summary as the corresponding content for each section. A word-graph is constructed that generates several sentences; only a few of the sentences are retained based on the ILP solution. The predicted section is entered in the stub article along with the final sentences selected by the ILP solution as the corresponding section-specific content on Wikipedia.

3.1 Content Retrieval

Article Extraction: Wikipedia provides an API[7] to download articles in the XML format. Given a category, the API is capable of extracting all the articles under it. We recursively extract articles by identifying all the categories in the hierarchy that can be reached by the crawler using top-down traversal. We use a simple python script[8] to extract the section titles and the corresponding text content from the XML dump.

Classification model: WikiKreator uses Latent Dirichlet Allocation (LDA) to represent each document as a vector of topic distributions. Each topic is further represented as a vector of probabilities of word distributions. Our intuition is that the topic distribution vectors of the same sections across different articles would be similar. Our objective is to learn these topic representations, such that we can accurately classify any web excerpt by inferring the topics in the text. Say C, a category on Wikipedia, has k Wikipedia articles (W).

$$(C) = \{W_1, W_2, W_3, W_4, ..., W_k\}$$

Each article W_j has several sections denoted as $s_{ji}c_{ji}$ where s_{ji} and c_{ji} refer to the section title and content of the ith section in the jth article, respectively. We concentrate on the 10 most frequent sections in any category. Training using content from sections that are not frequent might result in sub-optimal classification models. In our experiments, each frequent section had enough instances to optimally train a classifier. Let us denote the 10 most frequent sections in any category as $\boldsymbol{S}$. If any s_{ji} from W_j exists in $\boldsymbol{S}$, the content (c_{ji}) is included in the training set along with the section title (s_{ji}) as the corresponding class label. These steps are repeated for all the articles in the category. Each instance is then represented as:

$$c_{ji} = \{p_{ji}(t_1), p_{ji}(t_2), p_{ji}(t_3), \ldots, p_{ji}(t_m)\}$$

where m is the number of topics. s_{ji} is the corresponding label for this training instance. The set of topics are t_1, t_2, t_3,..., t_m while $p_{ji}(t_m)$ refers to the probability of topic m of content c_{ji}. Contents from the most frequent sections are each considered as a document and LDA is applied to generate document-topic distributions. We experiment with several values of m and use the value that generates the best classification model in each category. The topic vectors and the corresponding labels are used to train a Random Forest (RF) classifier. As the classes might be unbalanced, we apply resampling on the training set.

Predicting sections: In this step, we search the web for relevant content on the stub and assign them to their respective sections. We formulate search queries to retrieve web pages using a search engine. We extract multiple excerpts from the pages and then the RF classifier predicts the class (section label) for each excerpt.

(i) Query Generation: To search the web, we formulate queries by combining the stub title and keyphrases extracted from the first sentence of the introductory content of the stub. The first sentence generally contains the most important keywords that represent the article. Focused queries increases relevance of extraction as well as helps in disambiguation of content. We use the topia term extractor (Chatti et al., 2014) to extract keyphrases. For example, the query generated for a stub on *Hereditary hyperbilirubinemia* is *Hereditary hyperbilirubinemia bilirubin metabolic disorder* where *bilirubin metabolic disorder* are the keyphrases generated from the first sentence of the stub from Wikipedia. The query is used to identify the top 20 URLs (search results) from Google[9].

(ii) Boilerplate removal: Web content from the search results obtained in the previous step re-

[6] http://htmlunit.sourceforge.net/

[7] https://en.wikipedia.org/wiki/Special:Export

[8] http://medialab.di.unipi.it/wiki/Wikipedia_Extractor

[9] http://www.google.com

quires cleaning to retain only the relevant information. Removal of irrelevant content is done using boilerplate detection (Kohlschütter et al., 2010). The web pages contain several excerpts (text elements) in between the HTML tags. Only the excerpts that are classified as relevant by the boilerplate detection technique are retained.

(iii) Classification and assignment of excerpts: The LDA model generated earlier infers topic distribution of each excerpt based on word distributions. The RF classifier predicts the class (section title) for each excerpt based on the topic distribution. However, predictions that do not have a high level of confidence might lead to excerpts being appended to inappropriate sections. Therefore, we set the minimum confidence level at 0.5. If the prediction confidence of the RF classifier for a particular excerpt is above the minimum confidence level, the excerpt is assigned to the class; otherwise, the excerpt is discarded.

In the next step, we apply summarization on the excerpts assigned to each section.

3.2 Content Summarization

To summarize content for Wikipedia effectively, we formulate an ILP problem to generate abstractive summaries for each section with the objective of maximizing linguistic quality and information content.

Word-graph: A word-graph is constructed using all the sentences included in the excerpts assigned to a particular section. We used the same technique to construct the word-graph as (Filippova, 2010) where the nodes represent the words (along with parts-of-speech (POS)) and directed edges between the nodes are added if the words are adjacent in the input sentences. Each sentence is connected to dummy *start* and *end* nodes to mark the beginning and ending of the sentences. The sentences from the excerpts are added to the graph in an iterative fashion. Once the first sentence is added, words from the following sentences are mapped onto a node in the graph provided that they have the exact same word form and the same POS tag. Inclusion of POS information prevents ungrammatical mappings. The words are added to the graph in the following order:

- Content words are added for which there are no candidates in the existing graph;
- Content words for which multiple mappings are possible or such words that occur more than once in the sentence;
- Stopwords.

If multiple mappings are possible, the context of the word is checked using word overlaps to the left and right within a window of two words. Eventually, the word is mapped to that node that has the highest context. We also changed Filippova's method by adding punctuations as nodes to the graph. Figure 1 shows a simple example of the word-graph generation technique. We do not show POS and punctuations in the figure for the sake of clarity. The Figure also shows that several possible paths (sentences) exist between the dummy *start* and *end* nodes in the graph. Ideally, excerpts for any section would contain multiple common words as they belong to the same topic and have been assigned the same section. The presence of common words ensure that new sentences can be generated from the graph by fusing original set of sentences in the graph. Figure 1 shows an illustration of our approach where the set of sentences assigned to a particular section (WG_1) are used to create the word-graph. The word-graph generates several possible paths between the dummy nodes; we show only three such paths (WG_2). To obtain abstractive summaries, we remove generated paths from the graph that are same or very similar to any of the original sentences. If the cosine similarity of a generated path to any of the original sentences is greater than 0.8, we do not retain the path. We compute cosine similarity after applying stopword removal. However, we do not apply stemming as our graph construction is based on words existing in the same form in multiple sentences. Similar to Filippova's work, we set the minimum path length (in words) to eight to avoid incomplete sentences. Paths without verbs are discarded. The final set of generated paths after discarding the ineligible ones are used in the next step of summary generation.

3.2.1 ILP based Path Selection

Our goal is to select paths that maximize the informativeness and linguistic quality of the generated summaries. To select the best multiple possible sentences, we apply an *overgenerate and select* (Walker et al., 2001) strategy. We formulate an optimization problem that 'selects' a few of the many generated paths in between the dummy nodes from the word-graph. Let p_i denote each path obtained from the word-graph. We introduce three different factors to judge the relevance of a path – *Local informativeness* ($I^{loc}(p_i)$), *Global informativeness* ($I^{glob}(p_i)$) and *Linguistic quality* ($LQ(p_i)$). Any sentence path should be relevant to the central topic of the article; this relevance is tackled using $I^{glob}(p_i)$. $I^{loc}(p_i)$ models the importance of a sentence among several possible sentences that are generated from the word-graph. Linguistic quality ($LQ(p_i)$) is computed using a trigram language model (Song and Croft, 1999) that assigns a logarithmic score of probabilities of occurrences of three word sequences in the sentences.

Local Informativeness: In principle, we can use any existing method that computes sentence importance to account for *Local Informativeness.* In our model, we use TextRank scores (Mihalcea and Tarau, 2004) to generate an importance value of each path. TextRank creates a graph of words from the sentences. The score of each node in the graph is calculated as shown in Equation (1):

$$S(V_i) = (1-d) + d \times \sum_{V_j \in adj(V_i)} \frac{w_{ji}}{\sum_{V_k \in adj(V_i)} w_{jk}} S(V_i) \tag{1}$$

where V_i represents the words and $adj(V_i)$ denotes the adjacent nodes of V_i. Setting d to 0.80 in our experiments provided the best content selection results. The computation convergences to return final word importance scores. The informativeness score of a path $I^{loc}(p_i)$ is obtained by adding the importance scores of the individual words in the path.

Global Informativeness: To compute global informativeness, we compute the relevance of a sentence with respect to the query to assign higher weights to sentences that explicitly mention the main title or mention certain keywords that are relevant to the article. We compute the cosine similarity using TFIDF features between each sentence and the original query that was formulated during the web search stage. We define global informativeness as follows:

$$I^{glob}(p_i) = CosineSimilarity(Q, p_i) \tag{2}$$

where Q denotes the formulated query.

Linguistic Quality: In order to compute *Linguistic quality*, we use a language model that assigns probabilities to sequence of words to compute linguistic quality. Suppose a path contains a sequence of q words $\{w_1, w_2, ..., w_q\}$. The score $LQ(p_i)$ assigned to each path is defined as follows:

$$LQ(p_i) = \frac{1}{1 - LL(w_1, w_2, ..., w_q)}, \tag{3}$$

where $LL(w_1, w_2, ..., w_q)$ is defined as:

$$LL(w_1, \ldots, w_q) = \frac{1}{L} \cdot \log_2 \prod_{t=3}^{q} P(w_t | w_{t-1} w_{t-2}). \tag{4}$$

As can be seen from Equation (4), we combine the conditional probability of different sets of 3-grams (trigrams) in the sentence and averaged the value by L – the number of conditional probabilities computed. The $LL(w_1, w_2, \ldots, w_q)$ scores are negative; with higher magnitude implying lower importance. Therefore, in Equation (3), we take the reciprocal of the logarithmic value with smoothing to compute $LQ(p_i)$. In our experiments, we used a 3-gram model[10] that is trained on the English Gigaword corpus. Trigram models have been successfully used in several text-to-text generation tasks (Clarke and Lapata, 2006; Filippova and Strube, 2008) earlier.

ILP Formulation: To select the best paths, we combine all the above mentioned factors $I^{loc}(p_i)$, $I^{glob}(p_i)$ and linguistic quality $LQ(p_i)$ in an optimization framework. We maximize the following objective function:

$$F(p_1, \ldots, p_K) = \sum_{i=1}^{K} \frac{1}{T(p_i)} \cdot I^{loc}(p_i) \cdot I^{glob}(p_i) \cdot LQ(p_i) \cdot p_i \tag{5}$$

where K represents the total number of generated paths. Each p_i represents a binary variable, that can be either 0 or 1, depending on whether the path is selected in the final summary or not. In addition, $T(p_i)$ – the number of tokens in a path, is included in the objective function. The term $\frac{1}{T(p_i)}$ normalizes the Textrank scores by the length of the sentences. First, we ensure that a maximum of S_{max} sentences are selected in the summary using Equation (6).

$$\sum_{i=1}^{K} p_i \leq S_{max} \tag{6}$$

In our experiments, we set S_{max} to 5 to generate short concise summaries in each section. Using a length constraint enables us to only populate the sections using the most informative content. We introduce Equation (7) to prevent similar information (cosine similarity ≥ 0.5) from being conveyed

[10] The model is available here: `http://www.keithv.com/software/giga/`. We used the VP 20K vocab version.

Category	Most Frequent Sections
American Mathematicians	*Awards, Awards and honors, Biography, Books, Career, Education, Life, Publications, Selected publications, Work*
Diseases and Disorders	*Causes, Diagnosis, Early life, Epidemiology, History, Pathophysiology, Prognosis, Signs and symptoms, Symptoms, Treatment*
US Software companies	*Awards, Criticism, Features, Games, History, Overview, Products, Reception, Services, Technology*

Table 1: Data characteristics of three domains on Wikipedia

Category	#Articles	#Instances
American Mathematicians	~ 2100	1493
Diseases and Disorders	~ 7000	9098
US Software companies	~ 3600	2478

Table 2: Dataset used for classification

by different sentences. This constraint reduces redundancy. If two sentences have a high degree of similarity, only one out of the two can be selected in the summary.

$$\forall i, i' \in [1, K], i \neq i', \\ p_i + p_{i'} \leq 1 \text{ if } sim(p_i, p_{i'}) \geq 0.5. \quad (7)$$

The ILP problem is solved using the Gurobi optimizer (2015). The solution to the problem decides the paths that should be included in the final summary. We populate the sections on Wikipedia using the final summaries generated for each section along with the section title. All the references that have been used to generate the sentences are appended along with the content generated on Wikipedia.

4 Experimental Results

To evaluate the effectiveness of our proposed technique, we conduct several experiments. First, we evaluate our content generation approach by generating content for comprehensive articles that already exist on Wikipedia. Second, we analyze reviewer reactions on our system generated articles by adding content to several stubs on Wikipedia. Our experiments were designed to answer the following questions:

(i)*What are the optimal number of topic distribution features for each category? What are the classification accuracies in each domain?*

(ii)*To what extent can our technique generate the content for articles automatically?*

(iii)*What are the general reviewer reactions on Wikipedia and what percentage of automatically generated content on Wikipedia is retained?*

Dataset Construction: As mentioned earlier in Section 3.1, we crawl Wikipedia articles by traversing the category graph. Articles that contain at least three sections were included in the training set; other articles having lesser number of sections are generally labeled as stubs and hence not used for training. Table 1 shows the most frequent sections in each category. Further, Table 2 shows the total number of articles retrieved from Wikipedia in each category. The total number of instances are also shown. The number of instances denotes the total number of the most frequent sections in each category. As can be seen from the table, the number of instances is higher than the number of articles only in case of the category on *diseases*. This implies that there are generally more common sections in the diseases category than the other categories.

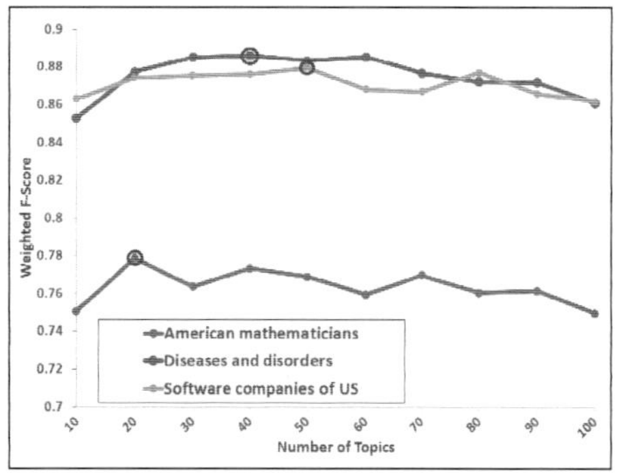

Figure 3: Performance of Classifier in the three categories based on the number of topics.

In each category, the content from only the most frequent sections were used to generate a topic model. The topic model is further used to infer topic distribution vectors from the training instances. We used the MALLET toolkit (McCallum, 2002) for generating topic distribution vectors and the WEKA package (Hall et al., 2009) for the classification tasks.

Optimal number of topics: The LDA model requires a pre-defined number of topics. We experiment with several values of the number of topics ranging from 10 to 100. The topic distribution features of the content of the instances are used to train a Random Forest Classifier with the corresponding section titles as the class labels. As can be seen in the Figure 3, the classification performance varies across domains as well as on the number of topics. The optimal number of topics based on the dataset are marked in *blue* cir-

Category	LDA-RF	SVM-WV
American Mathematicians	**0.778**	0.478
Diseases and Disorders	**0.886**	0.801
US Software companies	**0.880**	0.537

Table 3: Classification: Weighted F-Scores

Category	System	ROUGE-1	ROUGE-2
American Mathematicians	WikiKreator	**0.522**	**0.311**
	Perceptron	0.431	0.193
	Extractive	0.471	0.254
Diseases and Disorders	WikiKreator	**0.537**	**0.323**
	Perceptron	0.411	0.197
	Extractive	0.473	0.232
US Software companies	WikiKreator	**0.521**	**0.321**
	Perceptron	0.421	0.228
	Extractive	0.484	0.257

Table 4: ROUGE-1 and 2 Recall values – Comparing system generated articles to model articles

cles (40, 50 and 20 topics for *Diseases*, *Software Companies in US* and *American mathematicians*, respectively) in the Figure. We classify web excerpts using the best performing classifiers trained using the optimal number of topic features in each category.

Classification performance: We use 10-fold cross validation to evaluate the accuracy of our classifier. According to the F-Scores, our classifier **(LDA-RF)** performs similarly in the categories on *Diseases* and *US Software companies*. However, the accuracy is lower in the *American Mathematicians* category. We also experimented with a baseline classifier, that is trained on TFIDF features (upto trigrams). A Support vector machine (Cortes and Vapnik, 1995) classifier obtained the best performance using the TFIDF features. The baseline system is referred to as **SVM-WV**. We experimented with several other combinations of classifiers; however, we show only the best performing systems using the LDA and TFIDF features. As can be seen from the Table 3, our classifier **(LDA-RF)** outperforms **SVM-WV** significantly in all the domains. **SVM-WV** performs better in the category on diseases than the other two categories and the performance is comparable to **(LDA-RF)**. The diseases category has more uniformity in terms of the section titles, hence specific words or phrases characterize the sections well. In contrast, word distributions (LDA) work significantly better than TFIDF features in the other two categories.

Error Analysis: We performed error analysis to understand the reason for misclassifications. As can be seen from the Table 1, all the categories have several overlapping sections. For example, *Awards and honors* and *Awards* contain similar content. Authors use various section names for similar content in the articles within the same category. We analyzed the confusion matrices, and found that multiple instances in *Awards* were classified into the class of *Awards and honors*. Similar observations are made on the *Books* and *Publications* classes – which are related sections in the context of academic biographies. In future, we plan to use semantic measures to relate similar classes automatically and group them in the same class during classification.

Content Selection Evaluation: To evaluate the effectiveness of our content generation process, we generated the content of 500 randomly selected articles that already exist on Wikipedia in each of the categories. We compare WikiKreator's output against the current content of those articles on Wikipedia using ROUGE (Lin, 2004). ROUGE matches N-gram sequences that exist in both the system generated articles and the original Wikipedia articles (gold standard). We also compare WikiKreator's output with an existing Wikipedia generation system [**Perceptron**] of Sauper and Barzilay (2009)[11] that employs a perceptron learning framework to learn topic specific extractors. Queries devised using the conjunction of the document title and the section title were used to obtain excerpts from the web using a search engine, which were used in the perceptron model. In *Perceptron*, the most important sections in the category was determined using a bisectioning algorithm to identify clusters of similar sections. To understand the effectiveness of our abstractive summarizer, we design a system (**Extractive**) that uses an extractive summarization module. In *Extractive*, we use LexRank (Erkan and Radev, 2004) as the summarizer instead of our ILP based abstractive summarization model. We restrict the extractive summaries to 5 sentences for accurate comparison of both the systems. The same content was received as input from the classifier by the *Extractive* as well as our ILP-based system.

As can be seen from the Table 4, the ROUGE scores obtained by WikiKreator is higher than that of the other comparable systems in all the categories. The higher ROUGE scores imply that *WikiKreator* is generally able to retrieve useful information from the web, synthesize them and present the important information in the article.

[11]The system is available here: `https://github.com/csauper/wikipedia`

Statistics	Count
Number of stubs edited	40
Number of stubs retained without any changes	21
Number of stubs that required minor editing	6
Number of stubs where edits were modified by reviewers	4
Number of stubs in which content was removed	9
Average change in size of stubs	515 bytes
Average number of edits made post content-addition	~3

Table 5: Statistics of Wikipedia generation

However, it may also be noted that the *Extractive* system outperforms the Perceptron framework. Summarization from multiple sources generates more informative summaries and is more effective than 'selection' of the most informative excerpt, which is often inadequate due to potential loss of information. WikiKreator performs better than the extractive system on all the categories. Our ILP-based abstractive summarization system fuses and selects content from multiple sentences, thereby aggregating information successfully from multiple sources. In contrast, LexRank 'extracts' the top 5 sentences that results in some information loss.

Analysis of Wikipedia Reviews: To compare our method with the other techniques, it is necessary to generate content and append to Wikipedia stubs using all the techniques. However, recent work on article generation (Banerjee et al., 2014) has already shown that content directly copied from web sources cannot be used on Wikipedia. Further, bots using copyrighted content might be banned and real-users would have to read sub-standard articles due to the internal tests we perform. Due to the above mentioned reasons, we appended content generated only using our abstractive summarization technique.

We published content generated by WikiKreator on Wikipedia and appended the content to 40 randomly selected stubs. As can be seen from the Table 5, the content generated using our system was generally accepted by the reviewers. Half of the articles did not require any further changes; while in 6 cases (15%) the reviewers asked us to fix grammatical issues. In 9 stubs, the reliability of the cited references was questioned. Information sources on Wikipedia need to satisfy a minimum reliability standard, which our algorithm currently cannot determine. On an average, 3 edits were made to the Wikipedia articles that we generated. In general, there is an average increase in the content size of the stubs that we edited showing that our method is capable of producing content that generally satisfy Wikipedia criterion.

Analysis of section assignment: We manually inspected generated content of 20 articles in each category. Generated summaries are both informative and precise. However, in certain cases, the generated section title is not the same as the section title in the original Wikipedia article. For example, we generated content for the section "Causes" for the article on Middle East Respiratory Syndrome (MERS)[12]:

Milk or meat may play a role in the transmission of the virus . People should avoid drinking raw camel milk or meat that has not been properly cooked . There is growing evidence that contact with live camels or meat is causing MERS.

The corresponding content on the Wikipedia is in a section labeled as "Transmission". Section titles at the topmost level in a category might not be relevant to all the articles. Instead of using a top-down approach of traversing the category-graph, we can also use a bottom-up approach where we learn from all the categories that an article belongs to. For example, the article on MERS belongs to two categories: *Viral respiratory tract infection* and *Zoonoses*. Training using all the categories will allow context-driven section identification. Most frequent sections at a higher level in the category graph might not always be relevant to all the articles within a category.

5 Conclusions and Future Work

In this work, we presented WikiKreator that can generate content automatically to improve Wikipedia stubs. Our technique employs a topic-model based text classifier that assigns web excerpts into various sections on an article. The excerpts are summarized using a novel abstractive summarization technique that maximizes informativeness and linguistic quality of the generated summary. Our experiments reveal that WikiKreator is capable of generating well-formed informative content. The summarization step ensures that we avoid any copyright violation issues. The ILP based sentence generation strategy ensures that we generate novel content by synthesizing information from multiple sources and thereby improve content selection. In future, we plan to cluster related sections using semantic relatedness measures. We also plan to estimate reliabilities of sources to retrieve information only from reliable sources.

[12]https://en.wikipedia.org/wiki/Middle_East_respiratory_syndrome

References

Ricardo Baeza-Yates, Berthier Ribeiro-Neto, et al. 1999. *Modern information retrieval*, volume 463. ACM press New York.

Siddhartha Banerjee, Cornelia Caragea, and Prasenjit Mitra. 2014. Playscript classification and automatic wikipedia play articles generation. In *Pattern Recognition (ICPR), 2014 22nd International Conference on*, pages 3630–3635, Aug.

David M Blei, Andrew Y Ng, and Michael I Jordan. 2003. Latent dirichlet allocation. *the Journal of machine Learning research*, 3:993–1022.

Mohamed Amine Chatti, Darko Dugoija, Hendrik Thus, and Ulrik Schroeder. 2014. Learner modeling in academic networks. In *Advanced Learning Technologies (ICALT), 2014 IEEE 14th International Conference on*, pages 117–121. IEEE.

James Clarke and Mirella Lapata. 2006. Constraint-based sentence compression an integer programming approach. In *Proceedings of the COLING/ACL on Main conference poster sessions*, pages 144–151. Association for Computational Linguistics.

Corinna Cortes and Vladimir Vapnik. 1995. Support-vector networks. *Machine learning*, 20(3):273–297.

Vipul Dalal and Latesh Malik. 2013. A survey of extractive and abstractive text summarization techniques. In *Emerging Trends in Engineering and Technology (ICETET), 2013 6th International Conference on*, pages 109–110. IEEE.

Günes Erkan and Dragomir R Radev. 2004. Lexrank: Graph-based lexical centrality as salience in text summarization. *J. Artif. Intell. Res.(JAIR)*, 22(1):457–479.

Katja Filippova and Michael Strube. 2008. Sentence fusion via dependency graph compression. In *Proceedings of the Conference on Empirical Methods in Natural Language Processing*, pages 177–185. Association for Computational Linguistics.

Katja Filippova. 2010. Multi-sentence compression: Finding shortest paths in word graphs. In *Proceedings of the 23rd International Conference on Computational Linguistics*, pages 322–330. Association for Computational Linguistics.

Evgeniy Gabrilovich and Shaul Markovitch. 2007. Computing semantic relatedness using wikipedia-based explicit semantic analysis. In *IJCAI*, volume 7, pages 1606–1611.

Juri Ganitkevitch, Chris Callison-Burch, Courtney Napoles, and Benjamin Van Durme. 2011. Learning sentential paraphrases from bilingual parallel corpora for text-to-text generation. In *Proceedings of the Conference on Empirical Methods in Natural Language Processing*, pages 1168–1179. Association for Computational Linguistics.

Shima Gerani, Yashar Mehdad, Giuseppe Carenini, T. Raymond Ng, and Bita Nejat. 2014. Abstractive summarization of product reviews using discourse structure. In *Proceedings of the 2014 Conference on Empirical Methods in Natural Language Processing (EMNLP)*, pages 1602–1613. Association for Computational Linguistics.

Inc. Gurobi Optimization. 2015. Gurobi optimizer reference manual.

Mark Hall, Eibe Frank, Geoffrey Holmes, Bernhard Pfahringer, Peter Reutemann, and Ian H Witten. 2009. The weka data mining software: an update. *ACM SIGKDD explorations newsletter*, 11(1):10–18.

Christian Kohlschütter, Peter Fankhauser, and Wolfgang Nejdl. 2010. Boilerplate detection using shallow text features. In *Proceedings of the third ACM international conference on Web search and data mining*, pages 441–450. ACM.

Peng Li, Yinglin Wang, and Jing Jiang. 2013. Automatically building templates for entity summary construction. *Information Processing & Management*, 49(1):330–340.

Andy Liaw and Matthew Wiener. 2002. Classification and regression by randomforest. *R news*, 2(3):18–22.

Chin-Yew Lin. 2004. Rouge: A package for automatic evaluation of summaries. In *Text Summarization Branches Out: Proceedings of the ACL-04 Workshop*, pages 74–81.

Andrew K McCallum. 2002. {MALLET: A Machine Learning for Language Toolkit}.

Olena Medelyan, Ian H Witten, and David Milne. 2008. Topic indexing with wikipedia. In *Proceedings of the AAAI WikiAI workshop*, pages 19–24.

Rada Mihalcea and Paul Tarau. 2004. Textrank: Bringing order into texts. Association for Computational Linguistics.

Ani Nenkova, Sameer Maskey, and Yang Liu. 2011. Automatic summarization. In *Proceedings of the 49th Annual Meeting of the Association for Computational Linguistics: Tutorial Abstracts of ACL 2011*, page 3. Association for Computational Linguistics.

Christina Sauper and Regina Barzilay. 2009. Automatically generating wikipedia articles: A structure-aware approach. In *Proceedings of the Joint Conference of the 47th Annual Meeting of the ACL and the 4th International Joint Conference on Natural Language Processing of the AFNLP: Volume 1-Volume 1*, pages 208–216. Association for Computational Linguistics.

Fei Song and W Bruce Croft. 1999. A general language model for information retrieval. In *Proceedings of the eighth international conference on Information and knowledge management*, pages 316–321. ACM.

Wei Song, Yu Zhang, Ting Liu, and Sheng Li. 2010. Bridging topic modeling and personalized search. In *Proceedings of the 23rd International Conference on Computational Linguistics: Posters*, pages 1167–1175. Association for Computational Linguistics.

Marilyn A Walker, Owen Rambow, and Monica Rogati. 2001. Spot: A trainable sentence planner. In *Proceedings of the second meeting of the North American Chapter of the Association for Computational Linguistics on Language technologies*, pages 1–8. Association for Computational Linguistics.

Conglei Yao, Xu Jia, Sicong Shou, Shicong Feng, Feng Zhou, and HongYan Liu. 2011. Autopedia: automatic domain-independent wikipedia article generation. In *Proceedings of the 20th international conference companion on World wide web*, pages 161–162. ACM.

Torsten Zesch and Iryna Gurevych. 2007. Analysis of the wikipedia category graph for nlp applications. In *Proceedings of the TextGraphs-2 Workshop (NAACL-HLT 2007)*, pages 1–8.

Language to Code: Learning Semantic Parsers for If-This-Then-That Recipes

Chris Quirk
Microsoft Research
Redmond, WA, USA
chrisq@microsoft.com

Raymond Mooney*
UT Austin
Austin TX, USA
mooney@cs.utexas.edu

Michel Galley
Microsoft Research
Redmond, WA, USA
mgalley@microsoft.com

Abstract

Using natural language to write programs is a touchstone problem for computational linguistics. We present an approach that learns to map natural-language descriptions of simple "if-then" rules to executable code. By training and testing on a large corpus of naturally-occurring programs (called "recipes") and their natural language descriptions, we demonstrate the ability to effectively map language to code. We compare a number of semantic parsing approaches on the highly noisy training data collected from ordinary users, and find that loosely synchronous systems perform best.

1 Introduction

The ability to program computers using natural language would clearly allow novice users to more effectively utilize modern information technology. Work in *semantic parsing* has explored mapping natural language to some formal domain-specific programming languages such as database queries (Woods, 1977; Zelle and Mooney, 1996; Berant et al., 2013), commands to robots (Kate et al., 2005), operating systems (Branavan et al., 2009), smartphones (Le et al., 2013), and spreadsheets (Gulwani and Marron, 2014). Developing such language-to-code translators has generally required specific dedicated efforts to manually construct parsers or large corpora of suitable training examples.

An interesting subset of the possible program space is if-then "recipes," simple rules that allow users to control many aspects of their digital life including smart devices. Automatically parsing these recipes represents a step toward complex natural language programming, moving beyond single commands toward compositional statements with control flow.

Several services, such as Tasker and IFTTT, allow users to create simple programs with "triggers" and "actions." For example, one can program their Phillips Hue light bulbs to flash red and blue when the Cubs hit a home run. A somewhat complicated GUI allows users to construct these recipes based on a set of information "channels." These channels represent many types of information. Weather, news, and financial services have provided constant updates through web services. Home automation sensors and controllers such as motion detectors, thermostats, location sensors, garage door openers, etc. are also available. Users can then describe the recipes they have constructed in natural language and publish them.

Our goal is to build semantic parsers that allow users to describe recipes in natural language and have them automatically mapped to executable code. We have collected 114,408 recipe-description pairs from the http://ifttt.com website. Because users often provided short or incomplete English descriptions, the resulting data is extremely noisy for the task of training a semantic parser. Therefore, we have constructed semantic-parser learners that utilize and adapt ideas from several previous approaches (Kate and Mooney, 2006; Wong and Mooney, 2006) to learn an effective interpreter from such noisy training data. We present results on our collected IFTTT corpus demonstrating that our best approach produces more accurate programs than several competing baselines. By exploiting such "found data" on the web, semantic parsers for natural-language programming can potentially be developed with minimal effort.

*Work performed while visiting Microsoft Research.

Proceedings of the 53rd Annual Meeting of the Association for Computational Linguistics and the 7th International Joint Conference on Natural Language Processing, pages 878–888, Beijing, China, July 26-31, 2015.

2 Background

We take an approach to semantic parsing that directly exploits the formal grammar of the target meaning representation language, in our case IFTTT recipes. Given supervised training data in the form of natural-language sentences each paired with their corresponding IFTTT recipe, we learn to introduce productions from the formal-language grammar into the derivation of the target program based on expressions in the natural-language input. This approach originated with the SILT system (Kate et al., 2005) and was further developed in the WASP (Wong and Mooney, 2006; Wong and Mooney, 2007b) and KRISP (Kate and Mooney, 2006) systems.

WASP casts semantic parsing as a syntax-based *statistical machine translation* (SMT) task, where a *synchronous context-free grammar* (SCFG) (Wu, 1997; Chiang, 2005; Galley et al., 2006) is used to model the translation of natural language into a formal meaning representation. It uses statistical models developed for syntax-based SMT for lexical learning and parse disambiguation. Productions in the formal-language grammar are used to construct synchronous rules that simultaneously model the generation of the natural language. WASP was subsequently "inverted" to use the same synchronous grammar to generate natural language from the formal language (Wong and Mooney, 2007a).

KRISP uses classifiers trained using a Support-Vector Machine (SVM) to introduce productions in the derivation of the formal translation. The productions of the formal-language grammar are treated like semantic concepts to be recognized from natural-language expressions. For each production, an SVM classifier is trained using a *string subsequence kernel* (Lodhi et al., 2002). Each classifier can then estimate the probability that a given natural-language substring introduces a production into the derivation of the target representation. During semantic parsing, these classifiers are employed to estimate probabilities on different substrings of the sentence to compositionally build the most probable meaning representation for the sentence. Unlike WASP whose synchronous grammar needs to be able to directly parse the input, KRISP's approach to "soft matching" productions allows it to produce a parse for *any* input sentence. Consequently, KRISP was shown to be much more robust to noisy training data than previous approaches to semantic parsing (Kate and Mooney, 2006).

Since our "found data" for IFTTT is extremely noisy, we have taken an approach similar to KRISP; however, we use a probabilistic log-linear text classifier rather than an SVM to recognize productions.

This method of assembling well-formed programs guided by a natural language query bears some resemblance to Keyword Programming (Little and Miller, 2007). In that approach, users enter natural language queries in the middle of an existing program; this query drives a search for programs that are relevant to the query and fit within the surrounding program. However, the function used to score derivations is a simple matching heuristic relying on the overlap between query terms and program identifiers. Our approach uses machine learning to build a correspondence between queries and recipes based on parallel data.

There is also a large body of work applying Combinatory Categorical Grammars to semantic parsing, starting with Zettlemoyer and Collins (2005). Depending on the set of combinators used, this approach can capture more expressive languages than synchronous context-free MT. In practice, however, synchronous MT systems have competitive accuracy scores (Andreas et al., 2013). Therefore, we have not yet evaluated CCG on this task.

3 If-this-then-that recipes

The recipes considered in this paper are diverse and powerful despite being simple in structure. Each recipe always contains exactly one trigger and one action. Whenever the conditions of the trigger are satisfied, the action is performed. The resulting recipes can perform tasks such as home automation ("turn on my lights when I arrive home"), home security ("text me if the door opens"), organization ("add receipt emails to a spreadsheet"), and much more ("remind me to drink water if I've been at a bar for more than two hours"). Triggers and actions are drawn from a wide range of channels that must be activated by each user. These channels can represent many entities and services, including devices (such as Android devices or WeMo light switches) and knowledge sources (such as ESPN or Gmail). Each channel exposes a set of functions for both trigger and action.

Several services such as IFTTT, Tasker, and Llama allow users to author if-this-then-that recipes. IFTTT is unique in that it hosts a large set of recipes along with descriptions and other metadata. Users of this site construct recipes using a GUI interface to select the trigger, action, and the parameters for both trigger and action. After the recipe is authored, the user must provide a description and optional set of notes for this recipe and publish the recipe. Other users can browse and use these published recipes; if a user particularly likes a recipe, they can mark it as a favorite.

As of January 2015, we found 114,408 recipes on http://ifttt.com. Among the available recipes we encountered a total of 160 channels. In total, we found 552 trigger functions from 128 of those channels, and 229 action functions from 99 channels, for a total of 781 functions. Each recipe includes a number of pieces of information: description[1], note, author, number of uses, etc. 99.98% of the entries have a description, and 35% contain a note. Based on availability, we focused primarily on the description, though there are cases where the note is a more explicit representation of program intent.

The recipes at http://ifttt.com are represented as HTML forms, with combo boxes, inline maps, and other HTML UI components allowing end users to select functions and their parameters. This is convenient for end users, but difficult for automated approaches. We constructed a *formal grammar* of possible program structures, and from each HTML form we extracted an abstract syntax tree (AST) conforming to this grammar. We model this as a context-free grammar, though this assumption is violated in some cases. Consider the program in Figure 1, where some of the parameters used the action are provided by the trigger.

This data could be used in a variety of ways. Recipes could be suggested to users based on their activities or interests, for instance, or one could train a natural language generation system to give a readable description of code.

In this paper, the paired natural language descriptions and abstract syntax trees serve as training data for semantic parsing. Given a description, a system must produce the AST for an IFTTT recipe. We note in passing that the data was constructed in the opposite direction: users first implemented the recipe and then provided a description afterwards. Ideal data for our application would instead start with the description and construct the recipe based on this description. Yet the data is unusually large and diverse, making it interesting training data for mapping natural language to code.

[1]The IFTTT site refers to this as "title".

4 Program synthesis methods

We consider a number of methods to map the natural language description of a problem into its formal program representation.

4.1 Program retrieval

One natural baseline is retrieval. Multiple users could potentially have similar needs and therefore author similar or even identical programs. Given a novel description, we can search for the closest description in a table of program-description pairs, and return the associated program. We explored several text-similarity metrics, and found that string edit distance over the unmodified character sequence achieved best performance on the development set. As the corpus of program-description pairs becomes larger, this baseline should increase in quality and coverage.

4.2 Machine Translation

The downside to retrieval is that it cannot generalize. Phrase-based SMT systems(Och et al., 1999; Koehn et al., 2003) can be seen as an incremental step beyond retrieval: they segment the training data and attempt to match and assemble those segments at runtime. If the phrase length is unbounded, retrieval is almost a special case: it could return whole programs from the training data when the description matches exactly. In addition, they can find subprograms that are relevant to portions of the input, and assemble those subprograms into whole programs.

As a baseline, we adopt a recent approach (Andreas et al., 2013) that casts semantic parsing as phrasal translation. First, the ASTs are converted into flat sequences of code tokens using a pre-order left-to-right traversal. The tokens are annotated with their arity, which is sufficient to reconstruct the tree given a well formed sequence of tokens using a simple stack algorithm. Given this parallel corpus of language and code tokens, we train a conventional statistical machine translation system that is similar in structure and performance to Moses (Koehn et al., 2007). We gather the k-best translations, retaining the first such output that can be successfully converted into a well-formed program according to the formal grammar. Integration of the well-formedness constraint into decoding would likely produce better translations, but would require more modifications to the MT system.

Approaches to semantic parsing inspired by machine translation have proven effective when the

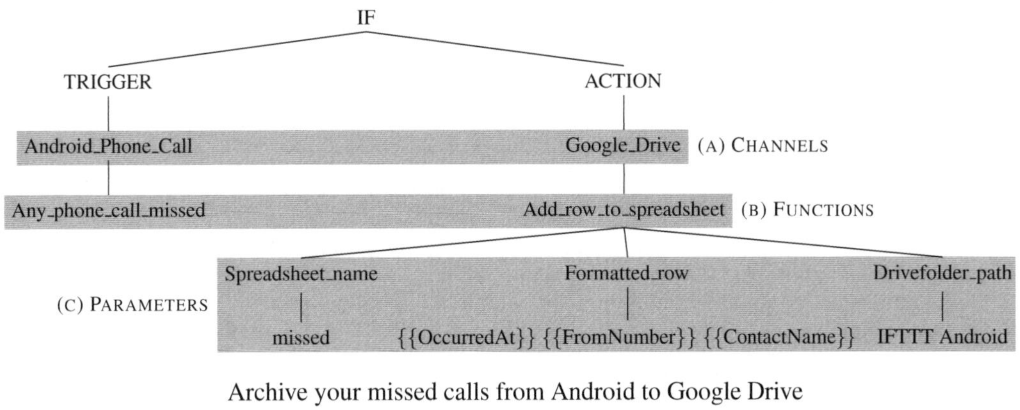

Figure 1: Example recipe with description, with nodes corresponding to (a) Channels, (b) Functions, and (c) Parameters indicated with specific boxes. Note how some of the fields in braces, such as OccurredAt, depend on the trigger.

data is very parallel. In the IFTTT dataset, however, the available pairs are not particularly clean. Word alignment quality suffers, and production extraction suffers in turn. Descriptions in this corpus are often quite telegraphic (e.g., "Instagram to Facebook") or express unnecessary pieces of information, or are downright unintelligible ("_2Mrl14"). Approaches that rely heavily on lexicalized information and assume a one-to-one correspondence between source and target (at the phrase, if not the word level) struggle in this setting.

4.3 Generation without alignment

An alternate approach is to treat the source language as context and a general direction, rather than a hard constraint. The target derivation can be produced primarily according to the formal grammar while guided by features from the source language.

For each production in the formal grammar, we can train a binary classifier intended to predict whether that production should be present in the derivation. This classifier uses general features of the source sentence. Note how this allows productions to be inferred based on context: although a description might never explicitly say that a production is necessary, the surrounding context might strongly imply it.

We assign probabilities to derivations by looking at each production independently. A derivation either uses or does not use each production. For each production used in the derivation, we multiply by the probability of its inclusion. Likewise for each production *not* used in the derivation, we multiply by one minus the probability of its inclusion.

Let $G = (V, \Sigma, R, S)$ be the formal grammar with non-terminals V, terminal vocabulary Σ, productions R and start symbol S. E represents a source sentence, and D, a formal derivation tree for that sentence. $R(D)$ is the set of productions in that derivation. The score of a derivation is the following product:

$$P(D|E) = \prod_{r \in R(D)} P(r|E) \prod_{r \in R \setminus R(D)} P(\neg r|E)$$

The binary classifiers are log-linear models over features, F, of the input string: $P(r|E) \propto \exp\left(\theta_r^\top F(E)\right)$.

4.3.1 Training

For each production, we train a binary classifier predicting its presence or absence. Given a training set of parallel descriptions and programs, we create $|R|$ binary classifier training sets, one for each classifier. We currently use a small set of simple features: word unigrams and bigrams, and character trigrams.

4.3.2 Inference

When presented with a novel utterance, E, our system must find the best code corresponding to that utterance. We use a top-down, left-to-right generation strategy, where each search node contains a stack of symbols yet to be expanded and a log probability. The initial node is $\langle [S], 0 \rangle$; and a node is complete when its stack of non-terminals is empty.

Given a search node with a non-terminal as its first symbol on the stack, we expand with any production for that symbol, putting its yield onto the stack and updating the node cost to include its derivation score:

$$\frac{\langle [X, \alpha], p \rangle \quad (X \to \beta) \in R}{\langle [\beta, \alpha], p + \log P(X \to \beta | E) \rangle \rangle}$$

If the first stack item is a terminal, it is scanned:

$$\frac{\langle [a, \alpha], p \rangle \quad a \in \Sigma}{\langle [\alpha], p \rangle}$$

Using these inference rules, we utilize a simple greedy approach that only accounts for the productions included in the derivation. To account for the negative $\prod_{r \in R \setminus R(D)} P(\neg r | E)$ factors, we use a beam search, and rerank the n-best final outcomes from this search based on the probability of all productions that are not included. Partial derivations are grouped into beams according to the number of productions in that derivation.

4.4 Loosely synchronous generation

The above method learns distributions over productions given the input, but treats the sentence as an undifferentiated bag of linguistic features. The syntax of the source sentence is not leveraged at all, nor is any correspondence between the language syntax and the program structure used. Often the pairs are not in sufficient correspondence to suggest synchronous approaches, but some loose correspondence to maintain at least a notion of coverage could be helpful.

We pursue an approach similar to KRISP (Kate and Mooney, 2006), with several differences. First, rather than a string kernel SVM, we use a log-linear model with character and word n-gram features. [2] Second, we allow the model to consider both span-internal features and contextual features.

This approach explicitly models the correspondence between nodes in the code side and tokens in the language. Unlike standard MT systems, word alignment is not used as a hard constraint. Instead, this phrasal correspondence is induced as part of model training.

We define a semantic derivation D of a natural language sentence E as a program AST where each production in the AST is augmented with a span. The substrings covered by the children of a production must not overlap, and the substring covered by the parent must be the concatenation of the substrings covered by the children. Figure 2 shows a sample semantic derivation.

[2]We have a preference for log-linear models given their robustness to hyperparameter settings, ease of optimization, and flexible incorporation of features. An SVM trained with similar features should have similar performance, though.

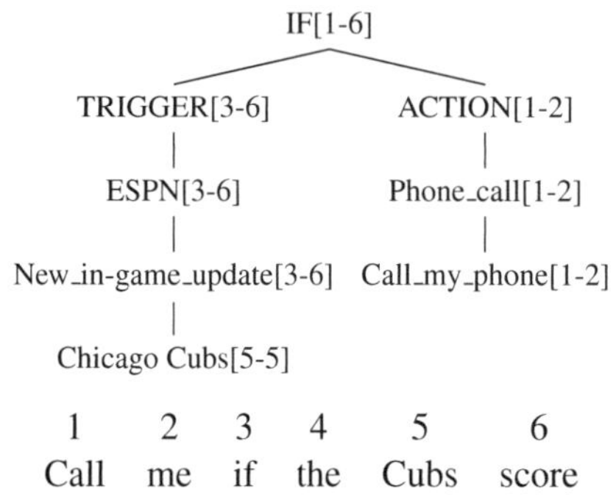

Figure 2: An example training pair with its semantic derivation. Note the correspondence between formal language and natural language denoted with indices and spans.

The core components of KRISP are string-kernel classifiers $P(r, i..j|E)$ denoting the probability that a production r in the AST covers the span of words $i..j$ in the sentence E. Here, $i < j$ are positions in the sentence indicating the span of tokens most relevant to this production. In other words, the substring $E[i..j]$ denotes the production r with probability $P(r, i..j|E)$. The probability of a semantic derivation D is defined as follows:

$$P(D|E) = \prod_{(r,i..j) \in D} P(r, i..j|E)$$

That is, we assume that each production is independent of all others, and is conditioned only on the string to which it is aligned. This can be seen as a refinement of the above production classification approach using a notion of correspondence.

Rather than using string kernels, we use logistic regression classifiers with word unigram, word bigram, and character trigram features. Unlike KRISP, we include features from both inside and outside the substring. Consider the production "Phone_call → Call_my_phone" with span 1-2 from Figure 2. Word unigram features indicate that "call" and "me" are inside the span; the remaining words are outside the span. Word bigram features indicate that "call me" is inside the span, "me if" is on the boundary of the span, and all remaining bigrams are outside the span.

4.4.1 Training

These classifiers are trained in an iterative EM-like manner (Kate and Mooney, 2006). Starting with some initial classifiers and a training set of NL and AST pairs, we search for the most likely derivation. If the AST underlying this derivation matches the gold AST, then this derivation is added to the set of positive instances. Otherwise, it is added to the set of negative instances, and the best derivation constrained to match the gold standard AST is found and added to the positive instances. Given this revised training data, the classifiers are retrained. After each pass through the training data, we evaluate the current model on the development set. This procedure is repeated until development-set performance begins to fall.

4.4.2 Inference

To find the most probable derivation according to the grammar, KRISP uses a variation on Earley parsing. This is similar to the inference method from Section 4.3.2, but each item now additionally maintains a position and a span. Inference proceeds left-to-right through the source string. The natural language may present information in a different order than the formal language, so all permutations of rules are considered during inference.

We found this inference procedure to be quite slow for larger data sets, especially because wide beams were needed to prevent search failure. To speed up inference, we used scores from the position-independent classifiers as completion-cost estimates.

The completion-cost estimate for a given symbol is defined recursively. Terminals have a cost of zero. Productions have a completion cost of the log probability of the production given the sentence, plus the completion cost of all non-terminal symbols. The completion cost for a non-terminal is the max cost of any production rooted in that non-terminal. Computing this cost requires traversing all productions in the grammar for each sentence.

Given a partial hypothesis, we use exact scores for the left-corner subtree that has been fully constructed, and completion estimates for all the symbols and productions whose left and right spans are not yet fully instantiated.

5 Experimental Evaluation

Next we evaluate the accuracy of these approaches. The 114,408 recipes described in Section 3 were first cleaned and tokenized. We kept only one recipe per unique description, after mapping to lowercase and normalizing punctuation.[3] Finally the recipes were split by author, randomly assigning each to training, development, or test, to prevent overfitting to the linguistic style of a particular author. Table 1 presents summary statistics for the resulting data.

		Language	Code
Train	Recipes	77,495	77,495
	Tokens	527,368	1,776,010
	Vocabulary	58,102	140,871
Dev	Recipes	5,171	5,171
	Tokens	37,541	110,074
	Vocabulary	7,741	14,804
Test	Recipes	4,294	4,294
	Tokens	28,214	94,367
	Vocabulary	6,782	13,969

Table 1: Statistics of the data after cleaning and separating into training, development, and test sets. In each case, the number of recipes, tokens (including punctuation, etc.) and vocabulary size are included.

Although certain trigger-action pairs occur much more often than others, the recipes in this data are quite diverse. The top 10 trigger-action pairs account for 14% of the recipes; the top 100 account for 37%; the top 1000 account for 72%.

5.1 Metrics

To evaluate system performance, several different measures are employed. Ideally a system would output exactly the correct abstract syntax tree. One measure is to count the number of exact matches, though almost all methods receive a score of 0.[4]

Alternatively, we can look at the AST as a set of productions, computing balanced F-measure. This is a much more forgiving measure, giving partial credit for partially correct results, though it has the caveat that all errors are counted equally.

Correctly assigning the trigger and action is the most important, especially because some of the parameter values are tailored for particular users. For example, "turn off my lights when I leave home" requires a "home" location, which varies for each user. Therefore, we also measure accuracy at identifying the correct trigger and action, both at the channel and function level.

5.2 Human comparison

One remaining difficulty is that multiple programs may be equally correct. Some descriptions are very difficult to interpret, even for humans. Second,

[3]We found many recipes with the same description, likely copies of some initial recipe made by different users. We selected one representative using a deterministic heuristic.

[4]Retrieval gets an exact match 3.7% of the time, likely due to near-duplicates from copied recipes.

multiple channels may provide similar functionality: both Phillips Hue and WeMo channels provide the ability to turn on lights. Even a well-authored description may not clarify which channel should be used. Finally, many descriptions are underspecified. For instance, the description "notify me if it rains" does not specify whether the user should receive an Android notification, an iOS notification, an email, or an SMS. This is difficult to capture with an automatic metric.

To address the prevalence and impact of underspecification and ambiguity in descriptions, we asked humans to perform a very similar task. Human annotators on Amazon Mechanical Turk ("turkers") were presented with recipe descriptions and asked to identify the correct channel and function (but not parameters). Turkers received careful instructions and several sample description-recipe pairs, then were asked to specify the best recipe for each input. We requested they try their best to find an action and a trigger even when presented with vague or ambiguous descriptions, but they could tag inputs as 'unintelligible' if they were unable to make an educated guess. Turkers created recipes only for English descriptions, applying the label 'non-English' otherwise. Five recipes were gathered for each description. The resulting recipes are not exactly gold, as they have limited training at the task. However, we imposed stringent qualification requirements to control the annotation quality.[5]

Our workers were in fair agreement with one another and the gold standard, producing high quality annotation at wages calibrated to local minimum wage. We measure turker agreement with Krippendorff's α (Krippendorff, 1980), which is a statistical measure of agreement between any number of coders. Unlike Cohen's κ (Cohen, 1960), the α statistic does not require that coders be the same for each unit of analysis. This property is particularly desirable in our case, since turkers generally differ across HITs. A value of $\alpha = 1$ indicates perfect agreement, while $\alpha \leq 0$ suggests the absence of agreement or systematic disagreement. Agreement measures on the Mechanical Turk data are shown in Table 2. This shows encouraging levels of agreement for both the trigger and the action, especially considering the large number of categories. Krippendorff (1980) advocates a 0.67 cutoff to allow

[5]Turkers must have 95% HIT approval rating and be native speakers of English (As an approximation of the latter, we required Turkers be from the U.S.). Manual inspection of annotation on a control set drawn from the training data ensured there was no apparent spam.

	Trigger		Action	
	C	C+F	C	C+F
# of categories	*128*	*552*	*99*	*229*
all	.592	.492	.596	.532
Intelligible English	.687	.528	.731	.627

Table 2: Annotator agreement as measured by Krippendorff's α coefficient (Krippendorff, 1980). Agreement is measured on either channel (C) or channel and function (C+F), and on either the full test set (4294 recipes) or its English and intelligible subset (2262 recipes).

"tentative conclusion" of agreement, and turkers are relatively close to that level for both trigger and action channels. However, it is important to note that the coding scheme used by turkers is not mutually exclusive, as several triggers and actions (e.g., "SMS" vs. "Android SMS" actions) accomplish similar effects. Thus, our levels of agreement are likely to be greater than suggested by measures in the table. Finally, we also measured agreement on the English and intelligible subset of the data, as we found that confusion between the two labels "non-English" and "unintelligible" was relatively high. As shown in the table, this substantially increased levels of agreement, up to the point where α for both trigger and action channels are above the 0.67 cutoff drawing tentative conclusion of agreement.

5.3 Systems and baselines

The **retrieval** method searches for the closest description in the training data based on character string-edit-distance and returns the recipe for that training program. The **phrasal** method uses phrase-based machine translation to generate candidate outputs, searching the resulting n-best candidates for the first well-formed recipe. After exploring multiple word alignment approaches, we found that an unsupervised feature-rich method (Berg-Kirkpatrick et al., 2010) worked best, leveraging features of string similarity between the description and the code. We ran MERT on the development data to tune parameters. We used a phrasal decoder with performance similar to Moses. The **synch**ronous grammar method, a recreation of WASP, uses the same word alignment as above, but extracts a synchronous grammar rules from the parallel data (Wong and Mooney, 2006). The **classifier** approach described in Section 4.3 is independent of word alignment. Finally, the **posclass** approach from Section 4.4 derives its own derivation structure from the data.

The human annotations are used to establish the **mturk** human-performance baseline by taking the majority selection of the trigger and action over 5 HITs for each description and comparing the result to the gold standard. The **oracleturk** human-performance baseline shows how often at least one of the turkers agreed with the gold standard.

In addition, we evaluated all systems on a subset of the test data where at least three human-generated recipes agreed with the gold standard. This subset represents those programs that are easily reproducible by human workers. A good method should strive to achieve 100% accuracy on this set, and we should perhaps not be overly concerned about the remaining examples where humans disagree about the correct interpretation.

5.4 Results and discussion

Table 3 summarizes the main evaluation results. Most of the measures are in concordance.

Interestingly, retrieval outperforms the phrasal MT baseline. With a sufficiently long phrase limit, phrasal MT approaches retrieval, but with a few crucial differences. First, phrasal requires an exact match of some substring of the input to some substring of the training data, where retrieval can skip over words. Second, the phrases are heavily dependent on word alignment; we find the word alignment techniques struggle with the noisy IFTTT descriptions. Sync performs similarly to phrasal. The underspecified descriptions challenge assumptions in synchronous grammars: much of the target structure is implied rather than stated.

In contrast, the classification method performs quite well. Some productions may be very likely given a prior alone, or may be inferred given other productions and the need for a well-formed derivation. Augmenting this information with positional information as in posclass can help with the attribution problem. Consider the input "Download Facebook Photos you're tagged in to Dropbox": we would like the token "Facebook" to invoke only the trigger, not the action. We believe further gains could come from better modeling of the correspondence between derivation and natural language.

We find that semantic parsing systems have accuracy nearly as high or even higher than turkers in certain conditions. There are several reasons for this. First, many of the channels overlap in functionality (Gmail vs. email, or Android SMS vs. SMS); likewise functions may be very closely related (Post a tweet vs. Post a tweet with an image). All the systems with access to thousands of training pairs are at a strong advantage; they can, for

	Channel	+Func	Prod F1
(a) All: 4,294 recipes			
retrieval	28.2	19.3	40.8
phrasal	17.3	10.0	34.8
sync	16.2	9.5	34.9
classifier	46.3	33.0	47.3
posclass	**47.4**	**34.5**	**48.0**
mturk	33.4	22.6	–n/a–
oracleturk	48.8	37.8	–n/a–
(b) Omit non-English: 3,741 recipes			
retrieval	28.9	20.2	41.7
phrasal	19.3	11.3	35.3
sync	18.1	10.6	35.1
classifier	48.8	35.2	48.4
posclass	**50.0**	**36.9**	**49.3**
mturk	38.4	26.0	–n/a–
oracleturk	56.0	43.5	–n/a–
(c) Omit non-English & unintelligible: 2,262 recipes			
retrieval	36.8	25.4	49.0
phrasal	27.8	16.4	39.9
sync	26.7	15.5	37.6
classifier	64.8	47.2	56.5
posclass	**67.2**	**50.4**	**57.7**
mturk	59.0	41.5	–n/a–
oracleturk	86.2	59.4	–n/a–
(d) $\geq$3 turkers agree with gold: 758 recipes			
retrieval	43.3	32.3	56.2
phrasal	37.2	23.5	45.5
sync	36.5	24.1	42.8
classifier	79.3	66.2	65.0
posclass	**81.4**	**71.0**	**66.5**
mturk	100.0	100.0	–n/a–
oracleturk	100.0	100.0	–n/a–

Table 3: Evaluation results. The first column measures how often the channels are selected correctly for both trigger and action (e.g. Android_Phone_Call and Google_Drive in Figure 1). The next column measures how often *both* the channel *and* function are correctly selected for both trigger and action (e.g. Android_Phone_Call::Any_phone_call_missed and Google_Drive::Add_row_to_spreadsheet). The last column shows balanced F-measure against the gold tree over all productions in the proposed derivation, from the root production down to the lowest parameter. We show results on (a) the full test data; (b) omitting descriptions marked as non-English by a majority of the crowdsourced workers; (c) omitting descriptions marked as either non-English or unintelligible by the crowd; and (d) only recipes where at least three of five workers agreed with the gold standard.

(a)	INPUT	Park in garage when snow tomorrow	
	IFTTT	Weather : Tomorrow's_forecast_calls_for	⟹ SMS : Send_me_an_SMS
	OUTPUT	Weather : Tomorrow's_forecast_calls_for	⟹ SMS : Send_me_an_SMS
(b)	INPUT	Suas fotos do instagr.am salvas no dropbox	
	IFTTT	Instagram : Any_new_photo_by_you	⟹ Dropbox : Add_file_from_URL
	OUTPUT	Instagram : Any_new_photo_by_you	⟹ Dropbox : Add_file_from_URL
(c)	INPUT	Foursquare check-in archive	
	IFTTT	Foursquare : Any_new_check-in	⟹ Evernote : Create_a_note
	OUTPUT	Foursquare : Any_new_check-in	⟹ Google_Drive : Add_row_to_spreadsheet
(d)	INPUT	if i post something on blogger it will post it to wordpress	
	IFTTT	Blogger : Any_new_post	⟹ WordPress : Create_a_post
	OUTPUT	Feed : New_feed_item	⟹ Blogger : Create_a_post
(e)	INPUT	Endless loop!	
	IFTTT	Gmail : New_email_in_inbox_from	⟹ Gmail : Send_an_email
	OUTPUT	SMS : Send_IFTTT_any_SMS	⟹ Philips_hue : Turn_on_color_loop

Table 4: Example output from the posclass system. For each input instance, we show the original query, the recipe originally authored through IFTTT, and our system output. Instance (a) demonstrates a case where the correct program is produced even though the input is rather tricky. Even the Portuguese query of (b) is correctly predicted, though keywords help here. In instance (c), the query is underspecified, and the system predicts that archiving should be done in Google Drive rather than evernote. Instance (d) shows how we sometimes confuse the trigger and action. Certain queries, such as (e), would require very deep inference: the IFTTT recipe sets up an endless email loop, where our system assembles a strange interpretation based on keyword match.

instance, more effectively break such ties by learning a prior over which channels are more likely. Turkers, on the other hand, have neither specific training at this job nor a background corpus and more frequently disagree with the gold standard. Second, there are a number of non-English and unintelligible descriptions. Although the turkers were asked to skip these sentences, the machine-learning systems may still correctly predict the channel and action, since the training set also contains non-English and cryptic descriptions. For the cases where humans agree with each other and with the gold standard, the best automated system (posclass) does fairly well, getting 81% channel and 71% function accuracy.

Table 4 has some sample outputs from the posclass system, showing both examples where the system is effective and where it struggles to find the intended interpretation.

6 Conclusions

The primary goal of this paper is to highlight a new application and dataset for semantic parsing. Although if-this-then-that recipes have a limited structure, many potential recipes are possible. This is a small step toward broad program synthesis from natural language, but is driven by real user data for modern hi-tech applications. To encourage further exploration, we are releasing the URLs of recipes along with turker annotations at http://research.microsoft.com/lang2code/.

The best performing results came from a loosely synchronous approach. We believe this is a very promising direction: most work inspired by parsing or machine translation has assumed a strong connection between the description and the operable semantic representation. In practical situations, however, many elements of the semantic representation may only be implied by the description, rather than explicitly stated. As we tackle domains with greater complexity, identifying implied but necessary information will be even more important.

Underspecified descriptions open up new interface possibilities as well. This paper considered only single-turn interactions, where the user describes a request and the system responds with an interpretation. An important next step would be to engage the user in an interactive dialogue to confirm and refine the user's intent and develop a fully-functional correct program.

Acknowledgments

The authors would like to thank William Dolan and the anonymous reviewers for their helpful advice and suggestions.

References

Jacob Andreas, Andreas Vlachos, and Stephen Clark. 2013. Semantic parsing as machine translation. In *Proceedings of the 51st Annual Meeting of the Association for Computational Linguistics (Volume 2: Short Papers)*, pages 47–52, Sofia, Bulgaria, August. Association for Computational Linguistics.

Jonathan Berant, Andrew Chou, Roy Frostig, and Percy Liang. 2013. Semantic parsing on Freebase from question-answer pairs. In *Proceedings of Conference on Empirical Methods in Natural Language Processing (EMNLP-13)*.

Taylor Berg-Kirkpatrick, Alexandre Bouchard-Côté, John DeNero, and Dan Klein. 2010. Painless unsupervised learning with features. In *Human Language Technologies: The 2010 Annual Conference of the North American Chapter of the Association for Computational Linguistics*, pages 582–590, Los Angeles, California, June. Association for Computational Linguistics.

S.R.K. Branavan, Harr Chen, Luke S. Zettlemoyer, and Regina Barzilay. 2009. Reinforcement learning for mapping instructions to actions. In *Joint Conference of the 47th Annual Meeting of the Association for Computational Linguistics and the 4th International Joint Conference on Natural Language Processing of the Asian Federation of Natural Language Processing (ACL-IJCNLP)*, Singapore.

David Chiang. 2005. A hierarchical phrase-based model for statistical machine translation. In *Proceedings of the 43nd Annual Meeting of the Association for Computational Linguistics (ACL)*, pages 263–270, Ann Arbor, MI.

J. Cohen. 1960. A coefficient of agreement for nominal scales. *Educational and Psychological Measurement*, 20(1):37 – 46.

Michel Galley, Jonathan Graehl, Kevin Knight, Daniel Marcu, Steve DeNeefe, Wei Wang, and Ignacio Thayer. 2006. Scalable inference and training of context-rich syntactic translation models. In *Proceedings of the 21st International Conference on Computational Linguistics and 44th Annual Meeting of the Association for Computational Linguistics (COLING/ACL)*, pages 961–968, Sydney, Australia, July.

Sumit Gulwani and Mark Marron. 2014. Nlyze: Interactive programming by natural language for spreadsheet data analysis and manipulation. In *SIGMOD*.

Rohit J. Kate and Raymond J. Mooney. 2006. Using string-kernels for learning semantic parsers. In *Proceedings of the 21st International Conference on Computational Linguistics and 44th Annual Meeting of the Association for Computational Linguistics*, pages 913–920, Sydney, Australia, July. Association for Computational Linguistics.

R. J. Kate, Y. W. Wong, and R. J. Mooney. 2005. Learning to transform natural to formal languages. In *Proceedings of the Twentieth National Conference on Artificial Intelligence (AAAI-05)*, pages 1062–1068, Pittsburgh, PA, July.

Philipp Koehn, Franz Josef Och, and Daniel Marcu. 2003. Statistical phrase-based translation. In *Proceedings of the 2003 Conference of the North American Chapter of the Association for Computational Linguistics on Human Language Technology - Volume 1*, NAACL '03, pages 48–54, Stroudsburg, PA, USA. Association for Computational Linguistics.

Philipp Koehn, Hieu Hoang, Alexandra Birch, Chris Callison-Burch, Marcello Federico, Nicola Bertoldi, Brooke Cowan, Wade Shen, Christine Moran, Richard Zens, Chris Dyer, Ondrej Bojar, Alexandra Constantin, and Evan Herbst. 2007. Moses: Open source toolkit for statistical machine translation. In *Annual Meeting of the Association for Computational Linguistics (ACL), demonstration session*, Prague, Czech Republic, June.

Klaus Krippendorff. 1980. *Content Analysis: an Introduction to its Methodology*. Sage Publications, Beverly Hills, CA.

Vu Le, Sumit Gulwani, and Zhendong Su. 2013. Smartsynth: Synthesizing smartphone automation scripts from natural language. In *MobiSys*.

Greg Little and Robert C. Miller. 2007. Keyword programming in java. In *Proceedings of the Twenty-second IEEE/ACM International Conference on Automated Software Engineering*, ASE '07, pages 84–93, New York, NY, USA. ACM.

Huma Lodhi, Craig Saunders, John Shawe-Taylor, Nello Cristianini, and Chris Watkins. 2002. Text classification using string kernels. *Journal of Machine Learning Research*, 2:419–444.

Franz Josef Och, Christoph Tillmann, and Hermann Ney. 1999. Improved alignment models for statistical machine translation. In *Proc. of the Conference on Empirical Methods in Natural Language Processing and Very Large Corpora*, pages 20–28, University of Maryland, College Park, MD, June.

Yuk Wah Wong and Raymond Mooney. 2006. Learning for semantic parsing with statistical machine translation. In *Proceedings of the Human Language Technology Conference of the NAACL, Main Conference*, pages 439–446, New York City, USA, June. Association for Computational Linguistics.

Yuk Wah Wong and Raymond J. Mooney. 2007a. Generation by inverting a semantic parser that uses statistical machine translation. In *Proceedings of Human Language Technologies: The Conference of the North American Chapter of the Association for Computational Linguistics (NAACL-HLT)*, pages 172–179, Rochester, NY.

Yuk Wah Wong and Raymond J. Mooney. 2007b. Learning synchronous grammars for semantic parsing with lambda calculus. In *Proceedings of the 45th Annual Meeting of the Association for Computational Linguistics (ACL)*, pages 960–967, Prague, Czech Republic, June.

William A. Woods. 1977. Lunar rocks in natural English: Explorations in natural language question answering. In Antonio Zampoli, editor, *Linguistic Structures Processing*. Elsevier North-Holland, New York.

Dekai Wu. 1997. Stochastic inversion transduction grammars and bilingual parsing of parallel corpora. *Computational Linguistics*, 23(3):377–403.

John M. Zelle and Raymond J. Mooney. 1996. Learning to parse database queries using inductive logic programming. In *Proceedings of the Thirteenth National Conference on Artificial Intelligence (AAAI-96)*, pages 1050–1055, Portland, OR, August.

Luke S. Zettlemoyer and Michael Collins. 2005. Learning to map sentences to logical form: Structured classification with probabilistic categorial grammars. In *In Proceedings of the 21st Conference on Uncertainty in AI*, pages 658–666.

Deep Questions without Deep Understanding

Igor Labutov
Cornell University
124 Hoy Road
Ithaca, NY
iil4@cornell.edu

Sumit Basu
Microsoft Research
One Microsoft Way
Redmond, WA
sumitb@microsoft.com

Lucy Vanderwende
Microsoft Research
One Microsoft Way
Redmond, WA
lucyv@microsoft.com

Abstract

We develop an approach for generating deep (i.e, high-level) comprehension questions from novel text that bypasses the myriad challenges of creating a full semantic representation. We do this by decomposing the task into an *ontology-crowd-relevance* workflow, consisting of first representing the original text in a low-dimensional ontology, then crowd-sourcing candidate question templates aligned with that space, and finally ranking potentially relevant templates for a novel region of text. If ontological labels are not available, we infer them from the text. We demonstrate the effectiveness of this method on a corpus of articles from Wikipedia alongside human judgments, and find that we can generate relevant deep questions with a precision of over 85% while maintaining a recall of 70%.

1 Introduction

Questions are a fundamental tool for teachers in assessing the understanding of their students. Writing good questions, though, is hard work, and harder still when the questions need to be deep (i.e., high-level) rather than factoid-oriented. These deep questions are the sort of open-ended queries that require deep thinking and recall rather than a rote response, that span significant amounts of content rather than a single sentence. Unsurprisingly, it is these deep questions that have the greatest educational value (Anderson, 1975; Andre, 1979; McMillan, 2001). They are thus a key assessment mechanism for a spectrum of online educational options, from MOOCs to interactive tutoring systems. As such, the problem of automatic question generation has long been of interest to the online education community (Mitkov and Ha, 2003; Schwartz, 2004), both as a means of providing self-assessments directly to students and as a tool to help teachers with question authoring. Much work to date has focused on questions based on a single sentence of the text (Becker et al., 2012; Lindberg et al., 2013; Mazidi and Nielsen, 2014), and the ideal of creating deep, conceptual questions has remained elusive. In this work, we hope to take a significant step towards this challenge by approaching the problem in a somewhat unconventional way.

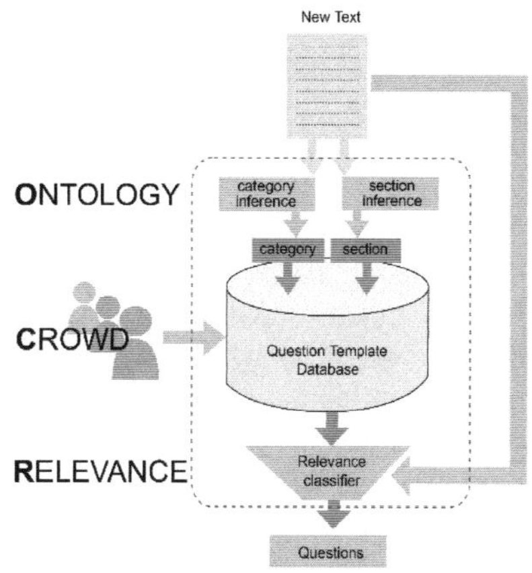

Figure 1: Overview of our ontology-crowd-relevance approach.

While one might expect the natural path to generating deep questions to involve first extracting a semantic representation of the entire text, the state-of-the-art in this area is at too early a stage to achieve such a representation effectively. Rather we take a step back from full understanding, and instead propose an *ontology-crowd-relevance* workflow for generating high-level questions, shown in Figure 1. This involves 1) decomposing a text into a meaningful, intermediate, low-dimensional *ontology*, 2) soliciting high-level templates from the *crowd*, aligned with this intermediate representation, and 3) for a target text segment, retrieving a subset of the collected templates based

Proceedings of the 53rd Annual Meeting of the Association for Computational Linguistics and the 7th International Joint Conference on Natural Language Processing, pages 889–898,
Beijing, China, July 26-31, 2015.

on its ontological categories and then ranking these questions by estimating the relevance of each to the text at hand.

In this work, we apply the proposed workflow to the Wikipedia corpus. For our ontology, we use a Cartesian product of article categories (derived from Freebase) and article section names (directly from Wikipedia) as the intermediate representation (e.g. category: *Person*, section: *Early life*), henceforth referred to as *category-section pairs*. We use these pairs to prompt our crowd workers to create relevant templates; for instance, *(Person, Early Life)* might lead a worker to generate the question "Who were the key influences on <*Person*> in their childhood?", a good example of the sort of deep question that can't be answered from a single sentence in the article. We also develop classifiers for inferring these categories when explicit or matching labels are not available. Given a database of such *category-section*-specific question templates, we then train a binary classifier that can estimate the relevance of each to a new document. We hypothesize that the resulting ranked questions will be both high-level and relevant, without requiring full machine understanding of the text – in other words, deep questions without deep understanding.

In the sections that follow, we detail the various components of this method and describe the experiments showing their efficacy at generating high-quality questions. We begin by motivating our choice of ontology and demonstrating its coverage properties (Section 3). We then describe our crowdsourcing methodology for soliciting questions and question-article relevance judgments (Section 4), and outline our model for determining the relevance of these questions to new text (Section 5). After this we describe the two datasets that we construct for the evaluation of our approach and present quantitative results (Section 6) as well as examples of our output and an error analysis (Section 7) before concluding (Section 8).

2 Related Work

We consider three aspects of past research in automatic question generation: work that focuses on the grammaticality of natural language question generation, work that focuses on the semantic quality of generated questions, i.e. the "what to ask about" rather than "how to ask it," and finally work that builds a semantic representation of text in order to generate higher-level questions.

Approaches focusing on the grammaticality of question generation date back to the AUTOQUEST system (Wolfe, 1976), which examined the generation of Wh-questions from single sentences. Later systems addressing the same goal include methods that use transformation rules (Mitkov and Ha, 2003), template-based generation (Chen et al., 2009; Curto et al., 2011) and overgenerate-and-rank methods (Heilman and Smith, 2010a). Another approach has been to create fill-in-the-blank questions from single sentences to ensure grammaticality (Agarwal et al. 2011, Becker et al. 2012).

More relevant to our direction is work on the semantic aspect of question generation, which has become a more active research area in the past several years. Several authors (Mazidi and Nielsen 2014; Linberg et al. 2013) generate questions according to the semantic role patterns extracted from the source sentence. Becker et al. (2012) also leverage semantic role labeling within a sentence in a supervised setting. We hope to continue in this direction of semantic focus, but extend the capabilities of question generation to include open-ended questions that go far beyond the scope of a single sentence.

Other work has taken on the challenge of deeper questions by attempting to build a semantic representation of arbitrary text. This has included work using concept maps over keywords (Olney et al. 2012) and minimal recursion semantics (Yao 2010) to reason over concepts in the text. While the work of (Olney et al. 2012) is impressive in its possibilities, the range of the types of questions that can be generated is restricted by a relatively specific set of relations (e.g. Is-A, Part-Of) captured in the ontology of the domain (biology textbook). Mannem et al. (2010) observe as we have that "capturing the exact true meaning of a paragraph is beyond the reach of current NLP systems;" thus, in their system for Shared Task A (for paragraph-level questions (Rus et al. 2010)) they make use of predicate argument structures along with semantic role labeling. However, the generation of these questions is restricted to the first sentence of the paragraph. Though motivated by the same noble impulses of these authors to achieve higher-level questions, our hope is that we can bypass the challenges and constraints of semantic parsing and generate deep questions via a more holistic approach.

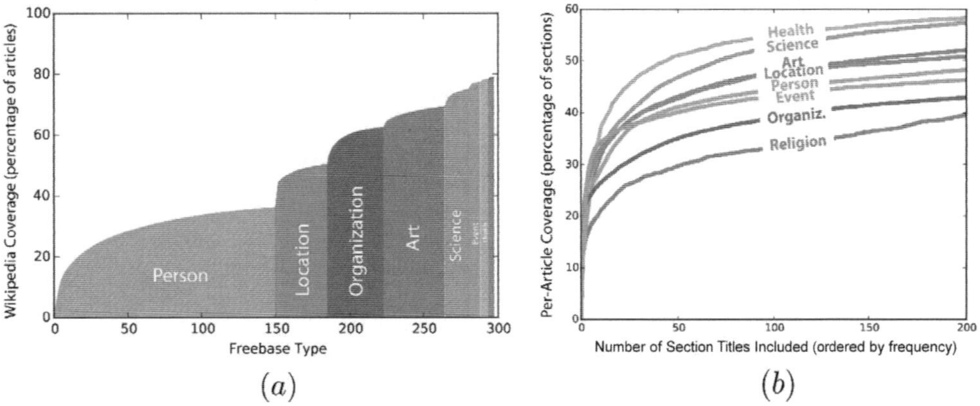

Figure 2: Coverage properties of our *category-section* representation: (a) fraction of Wikipedia articles covered by the top *j* most common Freebase types, grouped by our eight higher-level categories. (b) Average fraction of sections covered per document if only the top *k* most frequent sections are used; each line represents one of our eight categories.

3 An Ontology of Categories and Sections

The key insight of our approach is that we can leverage an easily interpretable (for crowd workers), low-dimensional ontology for text segments in order to crowdsource a set of high-level, reusable templates that generalize well to many documents. The choice of this representation must strike a balance between domain coverage and the crowdsourcing effort required to obtain that coverage. Inasmuch as Wikipedia is deemed to have broad coverage of human knowledge, we can estimate domain coverage by measuring what fraction of that corpus is covered by the proposed representation. In our work, we have developed a *category-section* ontology using annotations from Freebase and Wikipedia (English), and now describe its structure and coverage in detail.

For the high-level *categories*, we make use of the Freebase "notable type" for each Wikipedia article. In contrast to the noisy default Wikipedia categories, the Freebase "notable types" provide a clean high-level encapsulation of the topic or entity discussed in a Wikipedia article. As we wish to maximize coverage, we compute the histogram by type and take the 300 most common ones across Wikipedia. We further merge these into eight broad categories to reduce crowdsourcing effort: *Person, Location, Event, Organization, Art, Science, Health,* and *Religion*. These eight categories cover 78% of Wikipedia articles (see Figure 2a); the mapping between Freebase types and our categories will be made available as part of our corpus (see Section 8).

To achieve greater specificity of questions within the articles, we make use of Wikipedia *sections*, which offer a high-level segmentation of the content. The Cartesian product of our *categories* from above and the most common Wikipedia *section* titles (per category) then yield an interpretable, low-dimensional representation of the article. For instance, the set of *category-section* pairs for an article about *Albert Einstein* contains (*Person, Early_life*), (*Person, Awards*), and (*Person, Political_views*) as well as several others.

For each category, the section titles that occur most frequently represent central themes in articles belonging to that category. We therefore hypothesize that question templates authored for such high-coverage titles are likely to generalize to a large number of articles in that category. Table 1 below shows the four most frequent sections for each of our eight categories.

Person	**Location**	**Organization**	**Art**
Early life	History	History	Plot
Career	Geography	Geography	Reception
Pers. life	Economy	Academics	History
Biography	Demographics	Demographics	Production
Science	**Event**	**Health**	**Religion**
Descript.	Background	Treatment	Etymology
Taxonomy	Aftermath	Diagnosis	Icongraphy
History	Battle	Causes	Worship
Distributn.	Prelude	History	Mythology

Table 1: Most frequent section titles by category.

As the crowdsourcing effort is directly proportional to the size of the ontology, our goal is to select the smallest set of pairs that will provide sufficient coverage. As with *categories*, the cutoff for the number of *sections* used for each *category* is guided by the trade-off between coverage and crowdsourcing costs. Figure 2b plots the average fraction of an article covered by the top k sections from each category. We found that the top 50 sections cover 30% to 55% of the sections of an individual article (on average) across our categories. This implies that by only crowdsourcing question templates for those 50 sections per category, we would be able to ask questions about a third to a half of the sections of any article.

Of course, if we were to limit ourselves to only segments with these labels at runtime, we would completely miss many articles as well as texts outside of Wikipedia. To extend our reach, we also develop the means for category and section *inference* from raw text in Section 5 below, for cases in which ontological labels are either not available or are not contained within our limited set.

4 Crowdsourcing Methodology

We designed a two-stage crowdsourcing pipeline to 1) collect templates targeted to a set of *category-section* pairs and 2) obtain binary relevance judgments for the generated templates in relation to a set of article *segments* (for Wikipedia, these are simply sections) that match in *category-section* labels. We recruit Mechanical Turk workers for both stages of the pipeline, filtering for workers from the United States due to native English proficiency. A total of 307 unique workers participated in the two tasks combined (78 and 229 workers for the generation and ratings tasks respectively).

> You are reading an article about an important Person named **X**.
>
> You have just finished reading the **Legacy** section in this article.
>
> Your task
>
> Write a follow-up test question about the **Legacy** section in this article about **X**.

Figure 3: Prompt for the generation task for the *category-section* pair (*Person, Legacy*).

4.1 Question generation task

Following the coverage analysis above, we select the 50 most frequent sections for the top two categories, *Person* and *Location*, yielding 100 *category-section* pairs. As these two *categories* cover nearly 50% of all articles on Wikipedia, we believe that they suffice in demonstrating the effectiveness of the proposed methodology. For each *category-section* pair, we instructed 10 (median) workers to generate a question regarding a hypothetical entity belonging to the target with the prompt in Figure 3. Additional instructions and an interactive tutorial were pre-administered, guiding the workers to formulate appropriately deep questions, i.e. questions that are likely to generalize to many articles, while avoiding factoid questions like "When was X born?"

In total, 995 question templates were added to our question database using this methodology (only 0.5% of all generated questions were exact repeats of existing questions). We confirm in section 4.2 that workers were able to formulate deep, interesting and relevant questions whose answers spanned more than a single sentence and that generalized to many articles using this prompt.

In earlier pilots, we tried an alternative prompt which also presented the text of a specific article segment. In Figure 4, we show the average scope and relevance of questions generated by workers under both prompt conditions. As the figure demonstrates, the alternative prompt showing specific article text resulted in questions that generalized less well (workers' questions were found to be relevant to fewer articles), likely because the details in the text distracted the workers from thinking broadly about the domain. These questions also had a smaller scope on average, i.e., answers to these questions were contained in shorter spans in the text. The differences in scope and relevance between the two prompt designs were both significant (p-values: 0.006 and 4.5e-11 respectively, via two-sided Welch's t-tests).

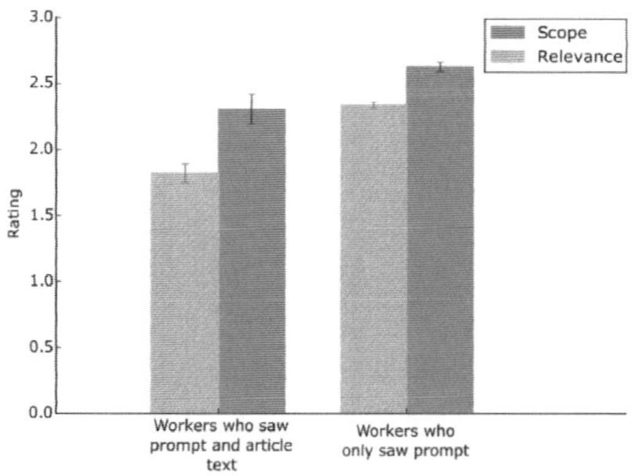

Figure 4: Average relevance and scope of worker-generated questions versus how the workers were prompted.

4.2 Question relevance rating task

For our 100 *category-section* pairs, 4 (median) article segments within reasonable length for a Mechanical Turk task (200-1000 tokens) were drawn at random from the Wikipedia corpus; this resulted in a set of 513 article segments. Each worker was then presented with one of these segments alongside at most 10 questions from the question template database matching in *category-section*; templates were converted into questions by filling in the article-specific entity extracted from the title. Workers were requested to rate each question along three dimensions: *relevance, quality*, and *scope,* as detailed below. Quality and scope ratings were only requested when the worker determined the question to be relevant.

- **Relevance:** *1 (not relevant) – 4 (relevant)*
  Does the article answer the question?
- **Quality:** *1 (poor) – 4 (excellent)*
  Is this question well-written?
- **Scope:** *1 (single-sentence) – 4 (multi-sentence/paragraph)*
  How long is the answer to this question?

A median of 3 raters provided an independent judgment for each question-article pair. The mean relevance, quality and scope ratings across the 995 questions were 2.3 (sd=0.83), 3.5 (sd=.65) and 2.6 (sd=1.0) respectively. Note that the sample sizes for scope and quality were smaller, 774 and 778 respectively, as quality/scope judgments were not gathered for questions deemed irrelevant. We note that 80% of the relevant crowd-sourced questions had a median scope rating larger than 1 sentence, and 23% had a median scope rating of 4, defined as "the answer to this question can be found in many sentences and paragraphs," corresponding to the maximum attainable scope rating. Note that while in this work, we have only used the scope judgments to report summary statistics about the generated questions, in future work these ratings could be used to build a scope classifier to filter out questions targeting short spans of text.

As described in Section 5.2, the relevance judgments are converted to binary relevance ratings for training the relevance classifier (we consider relevance ratings {1, 2} as "not relevant" and {3, 4} as "relevant"). In terms of agreement between raters for these binary relevance labels, we obtained a Fleiss' Kappa of 0.33, indicating fair agreement.

5 Model

There are two key models to our system: the first is for category and section inference of a novel article segment, which allows us to infer the keys to our question database when explicit labels are not available. The second is for question relevance prediction, which lets us decide which question templates from the database's store for that *category-section* actually apply to the text at hand.

5.1 Category/section inference

Both category and section inference were cast as standard text-classification problems. *Category* inference is performed on the whole article, while *section* inference is performed on the individual article segments (i.e., sections). We trained individual logistic regression classifiers for the eight categories and the 50 top section types for each one (a total of 400) using the default L2 regularization parameter in LIBLINEAR (Fan, 2008). For section inference, a total of 736,947 article segments were sampled from Wikipedia (June 2014 snapshot), each belonging to one of the 400 section types and within the same length bounds from Section 4.2 (200-1000 tokens). For category inference, we sampled a total of 86,348 articles with at least 10 sentences and belonging to one of our eight categories.

In both cases, a binary dataset was constructed for a one-against-all evaluation, where the negative instances were sampled randomly from the negative categories or sections (there was an average 17% and 32% positive skew in the section and category datasets, respectively). Basic tf-idf features (using a vocabulary of 200,000 after eliminating stopwords) were used in both text classification tasks. Applying the category/section inference to held-out portions of the dataset (30% for each category/section) resulted in balanced accuracies of 83%/95% respectively, which gave us confidence in the inference. Keep in mind that this is not a strict bound on our question generation performance, since the inferred category/section, while not matching the label perfectly, could still be sufficiently close to produce relevant questions (for instance, we could misrecognize "Childhood" as "Early Life"). We explore the ramifications of this in our end-to-end experiments in Section 6.

5.2 Relevance Classification

We also cast the problem of question/article relevance prediction as one of binary classification, where we map a question-article pair to a relevance score; as such our features had to combine aspects of both the question and the article. Our core approach was to use a vector of the component-wise Euclidean distances between individual features of the question and article segment, i.e., the ith feature vector component f_i is given by $f_i = (q_i - a_i)^2$, where q_i and a_i are the components of the question and article feature vectors. For the feature representation, we utilized a concatenation of continuous embedding features: 300 features from a Word2Vec embedding (Mikolov, 2013) and 200,000 tfidf features (as with category/section classification above).

As question templates are typically short, though, we found that this representation alone performed poorly. As a result, we augmented the vector by concatenating additional distance features between the target article segment and one specific instance of an entire article for which the question applied. This augmenting article was selected at random from all those for which the template was judged to be relevant. The resulting feature vector was thus doubled in length, where the first k distances were between the question template and the target segment, and the next k were between the augmenting article and the target segment. Note that the augmenting article segments were removed from the training/test sets.

To train this classifier, we assumed that we would be able to acquire at least n positive relevance labels for each question template, i.e., n article segments judged to be relevant to each template for inclusion in the training set. We explore the effect of increasing values of n, from 0 (where no relevance labels are available) to 3 (referred to as conditions T0..T3 in Figure 5). We then trained and evaluated the relevance classifier, a single logistic regression model using LIBLINEAR with default L2 regularization, using 10-fold cross-validation on DATASET I (see Section 6).

Figure 5 depicts a series of ROC curves summarizing the performance of our template relevance classifier on unseen article segments. As expected, we see increasing performance with increasing n. However, the benefit drops off after 3 instances (i.e., T4 is only marginally better than T3). While the character of the curves is modest, keep in mind we are already filtering questions by retrieving them from the database for the inferred category-section (which by itself gives us a precision of .74 – see green bars in Figure 6); this ROC represents the "lift" achieved by further filtering the questions with our relevance classifier, resulting in far higher precision (.85 to .95 – see blue bars in Figure 6).

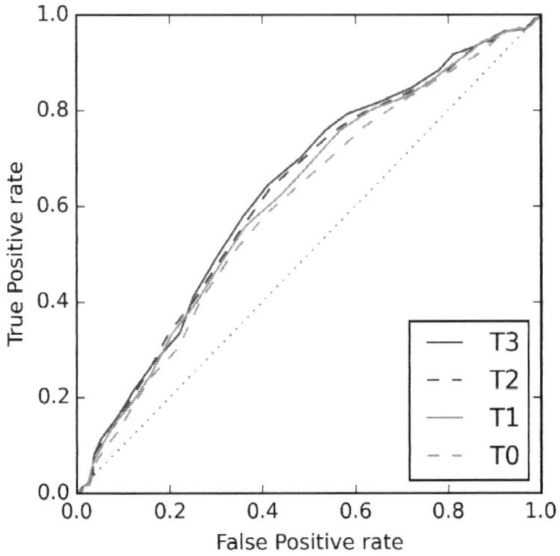

Figure 5: ROC curves for the task of question-to-article relevance prediction. Tn means that n positively labeled article segments were available for each question template during training.

6 Experiments and Results

In this section, we describe the datasets used for training the relevance classifier in Section 5.2 (DATASET I) as well as for end-to-end performance on unlabeled text segments (DATASET II). We then evaluate the performance on this second dataset under three settings: first, when the category and section are known, second, when those labels are unavailable, and third, when neither the labels nor the relevance classifier are available.

6.1 DATASET I: for the Relevance Classifier

The first dataset (DATASET I) was intended for training and evaluating the relevance classifier, and for this we assumed the category and section labels were known. As such, judgments were collected only for questions templates authored for a given article's actual category and section labels. After filtering out annotations from unreliable workers (based on their pre-test results) as well as those with inter-annotator agreement below 60%, we were left with a set of 995 rated questions, spanning across two categories (*Person* and *Location*) and 50 sections per category (100 *category-section* pairs total). This corresponded to a total of 4439 relevance tuples (*label, question, article*) where *label* is a binary relevance rating aggregated via majority vote across multiple raters. The relevance labels were skewed towards the positive (relevant) class with 63% relevant instances.

This is of course a mostly unrealistic data setting for applications of question generation (known category and section labels), but greatly useful in developing and evaluating the relevance classifier; we thus used this dataset only for that purpose (see Section 5.2 and Figure 5).

6.2 DATASET II: for End-to-End Evaluation

For an end-to-end evaluation we need to examine situations where the category and section labels are not available and we must rely on inference instead. As this is the more typical use case for our method, it is critical to understand how the performance will be affected. For DATASET II, then, we first sampled articles from the Wikipedia corpus at random (satisfying the constraints described in Section 3) and then performed category and section inference on the article segments. The category c with the highest posterior probability was chosen as the inferred category, while all section types s_i with a posterior probability greater than 0.6 were considered as sources for templates. Only articles whose inferred category was *Person* or *Location* were considered, but given the noise in inference there was no guarantee that the true labels were of these categories. We continued this process until we retrieved a total of 12 articles. For each article segment in these 12, we drew a random subset of at most 20 question templates from our database matching the inferred category and section(s), then ordered them by their estimated relevance for presentation to judges.

We then solicited an additional 62 Mechanical Turk workers to a rating task set up according to the same protocol as for DATASET I. After aggregation and filtering in the same way, the second dataset contained a total 256 (*label, question, article*) relevance tuples, skewed towards the positive class with 72% relevant instances.

6.3 Information Retrieval–based Evaluation

As our end-to-end task is framed as the retrieval of a set of relevant questions for a given article segment, we can measure performance in terms of an information retrieval-based metric. Consider a user who supplies an article segment (the "query" in IR terms) for which she wants to generate a quiz: the system then presents a ranked list of retrieved questions, ordered according to their estimated relevance to the article. As she makes her way down this ranked list of questions, adding a question at a time to the quiz (set Q), the behavior of the precision and recall (with respect to relevance to the article segment) of the questions in Q, summarizes the performance of the retrieval system (i.e. the Precision-Recall (PR) curve (Manning, 2008)). We summarize the performance of our system by averaging the individual article segments' PR curves (linearly interpolated) from DATASET II, and present the average precision over bins of recall values in Figure 6. We consider the following experimental conditions:

- **Known category/section, using relevance classifier (red):** This is the case in which the actual category and section labels of the query article are known, and only the questions that match exactly in category and section are considered for relevance classification (i.e. added to Q if found relevant by the classifier). Recall is computed with respect to the total number of relevant questions in DATASET II, including those corresponding to sections different from the section label of the article.
- **Inferred category/section, using relevance classifier (blue):** This is the expected use case, where the category/section labels are not known. Questions matching in category and section(s) to the inferred category and section of each article are considered and ranked in Q by their score from the relevance classifier. Recall is computed with respect to the total number of relevant questions in DATASET II.
- **Inferred category/section, ignoring relevance classifier (green):** This is a baseline where we only use category/section inference and then retrieve questions from the database without filtering: all questions that match in inferred category and section(s) of the article are added to Q in a random ranking order, without performing relevance classification.

As we examine Figure 6, it is important to point out a subtlety in our choice to calculate recall of the **known category/section** condition (red bars) with respect to the set of *all* relevant questions, including those that are matched to sections different from the original (labeled) sections. While this condition by construction does not have access to questions of any other section, the resulting limitation in recall underlines the importance of performing section inference: without inference, we achieve a recall of no greater than 0.4.

As we had hypothesized, while the labels of the sections play an instrumental role in instructing the crowd to generate relevant questions, the resulting questions often tend to be relevant to content found under different but semantically related sections as well. Leveraging the available questions of these related sections (by performing inference) boosts recall at the expense of only a small degree of precision (blue bars). If we forgo relevance classification entirely, we get a constant precision of 0.74 (green bars) as mentioned in

Section 5.2; it is clear that the relevance classifier results in a significant advantage.

While there is a slight drop in precision when using inference, this is at least partly due to the constraints that were imposed during data-collection and relevance classifier training, i.e., all pairs of articles and questions belonged to the same category and section. While this constraint made the crowdsourcing methodology proposed in this work tractable, it also prevented the inclusion of training examples for sections that could potentially be inferred at test time. One possible approach to remedy this would be sample from article segments that are similar in text (in terms of our distance metric) as opposed to only segments exactly matching in category and section.

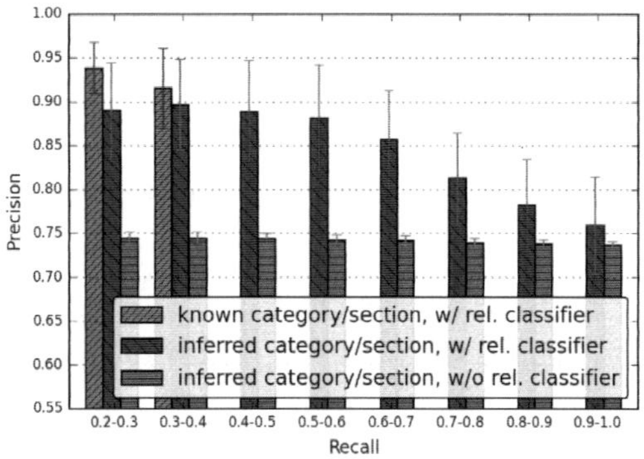

Figure 6: Precision-recall results for the end-to-end experiment, grouped in bins of recall ranges.

7 Examples and Error Analysis

In Table 2 we show a set of sample retrieved questions and the corresponding correctness of the relevance classifier's decision with respect to the judgment labels; examining the errors yields some interesting insights. Consider the false positive example shown in row 8, where the category correctly inferred as *Location*, but section title was inferred as *Transportation* instead of *Services*. This mismatch resulted in the following template authored for (*Location*, *Transportation*) being retrieved: "*What geographic factors influence the preferred transport methods in <entity>?*" To the relevance classifier, this particular template (containing the word "transport") appears to be relevant on the surface level to the text of an article segment about schedules (*Services*) at a railway station. However, as this template never appeared to judges in the context of a *Services* segment – a section that differs considerably in theme from the inferred section (*Transportation*) – the relevance classifier unsurprisingly makes the wrong call.

True section	Inferred section	Result	Generated Question
Honours	Later Life	TP	What accomplishments characterized the later career of Colin Cowdrey?
Acting Career	Television	TP	How did Corbin Bernstein's television career evolve over time?
Route Description	Geography	TP	What are some unique geographic features of Puerto Rico Highway 10?
Athletics	Athletics	TN	How much significance do people of DeMartha Catholic High School place on athletics?
Route Description	Geography	TN	How does the geography of Puerto Rico Highway 10 impact its resources?
Work	Reception	FN	What type of reaction did Thornton Dial receive?
Acting Career	Later Career	FP	What were the most important events in the later career of Corbin Berstein?
Services	Transportation	FP	What geographic factors influence the preferred transport methods in Weymouth Railway Station?
Later Career	Legacy	FP	How has Freddy Mitchell's legacy shaped current events?

Table 2: Examples of retrieved questions. TP, TN, FP, FN stand for true/false positive/negative with respect to the relevance classification.

In considering additional sources of relevance classification errors, recall that we employ a single relevant article segment for the purpose of augmenting a template's feature representation. In the case of the false negative example (row 6 in Table 2), the sensitivity of the classifier to the particular augmenting article used is apparent. Upon inspecting the target article segment (article: *Thornton Dial*, section: *Work*), and the augmenting article segment (article: *Syed Masood*, section: *Reception*), it's clear that the inferred section *Reception* is a reasonable title for the *Work* section of the article on *Thornton Dial*, making the question "What type of reaction did Thornton Dial receive?" a relevant question to the target article (as reflected in the human judgment). However, although both segments generally talk about "reception," the language across the two segments is distinct: the critical reception of Thornton Dial the visual artist is described in a different way from the reception of Syed Masood the actor, resulting in little overlap in surface text, and as a result the relevance classifier falsely rejects the question.

Reasonable substitutions for inferred sections can also lead to false positives, as in row 9, for the article *Freddy Mitchell*. In this case, while *Legacy* (the inferred section) is a believable substitute for the true label of *Later Career,* in this case the article segment did not discuss his legacy. However, there was a good match between the augmenting article for this template and the section. We hypothesize that in both this and the previous examples a broader sample of augmenting article segments for each category/section is likely to be effective at mitigating these types of errors.

8 Conclusion

We have presented an approach for generating relevant, deep questions that are broad in scope and apply to a wide range of documents, all without constructing a detailed semantic representation of the text. Our three primary contributions are 1) our insight that a low-dimensional ontological document representation can be used as an intermediary for retrieving and generalizing high-level question templates to new documents, 2) an efficient crowdsourcing scheme for soliciting such templates and relevance judgments (of templates to article) from the crowd in order to train a relevance classification model, and 3) using category/section inference and relevance prediction to retrieve and rank relevant deep questions for new text segments. Note that the approach and workflow presented here constitute a general framework that could potentially be useful in other language generation applications. For example, a similar setup could be used for high-level summarization, where question templates would be replaced with "summary snippets."

Finally, to encourage the community to further explore this approach as well as to compare it with others, we are releasing all of our data (category mappings, generated templates, and relevance judgments) at http://research.microsoft.com/~sumitb/questiongeneration .

References

Manish Agarwal, Rakshit Shah, and Prashanth Mannem. 2011. Automatic Question Generation Using Discourse Cues. In *Proceedings of the 6th Workshop on Innovative Use of NLP for Building Educational Applications*.

Richard C. Anderson and W. Barry Biddle. 1975. On Asking People Questions About What they are Reading. *Psychology of Learning and Motivation.* 9:90-132.

Thomas Andre. 1979. Does Answering Higher-level Questions while Reading Facilitate Productive Learning? *Review of Educational Research* 49(2): 280-318.

Lee Becker, Sumit Basu, and Lucy Vanderwende. 2012. Mind the Gap: Learning to Choose Gaps for Question Generation. In *Proceedings of the 2012 Conference of the North American Chapter of the Association for Computational Linguistics: Human Language Technologies*.

Wei Chen, Gregory Aist, and Jack Mostow. 2009. Generating Questions Automatically from Informational Text. In S. Craig & S. Dicheva (Ed.), *Proceedings of the 2nd Workshop on Question Generation*.

Sérgio Curto, Ana Cristina Mendes, and Luisa Coheur. 2011. Exploring Linguistically-rich Patterns for Question Generation. In *Proceedings of the UCNLG+Eval: Language Generation and Evaluation Workshop*.

Rong-En Fan, Kai-Wei Chang, Cho-Jui Hsieh, Xiang-Rui Wang, Chih-Jen Lin. 2008. LIBLINEAR: A library for large linear classification. *Journal of Machine Learning Research* 9: 1871-1874.

Michael Heilman and Noah Smith. 2010. Good Question! Statistical Ranking for Question Generation. In Proceedings of *NAACL/HLT*.

David Lindberg, Fred Popowich, John Nesbit, and Phil Winne. 2013. Generating Natural Language Questions to Support Learning On-line. In *Proceedings of the 14th European Workshop on Natural Language Generation*.

Prashanth Mannem, Rashmi Prasad, and Aravind Joshi. 2010. Question generation from paragraphs at UPenn: QGSTEC system description. In *Proceedings of the Third Workshop on Question Generation*.

Christopher D. Manning, Prabhakar Raghavan, and Hinrich Schutze. 2008. *Introduction to Information Retrieval.* Cambridge: Cambridge university press

Karen Mazidi and Rodney D. Nielsen. 2014. Linguistic Considerations in Automatic Question Generation. In *Proceedings of ACL*.

James H. McMillan. 2001. Secondary Teachers' Classroom Assessment and Grading Practices." *Educational Measurement: Issues and Practice* 20(1): 20-32.

Tomas Mikolov, Ilya Sutskever, Kai Chen, Greg S. Corrado, and Jeff Dean. 2013. Distributed Representations of Words and Phrases and their Compositionality. In *Proceedings of Advances in Neural Information Processing Systems*.

Ruslan Mitkov and Le An Ha. 2003. Computer-Aided Generation of Multiple-Choice Tests. In *Proceed-*

ings of the HLT-NAACL 2003 Workshop on Building Educational Applications Using Natural Language Processing.

Andrew M. Olney, Arthur C. Graesser, and Natalie K. Person. 2012. Question Generation from Concept Maps. *Dialogue & Discourse* 3(2): 75-99.

Daniel Ramage, David Hall, Ramesh Nallapati, and Christopher D. Manning. 2009. Labeled LDA: A Supervised Topic Model for Credit Attribution in Multi-labeled Corpora. In *Proceedings of the 2009 Conference on Empirical Methods in Natural Language Processing.*

Vasile Rus, Brendan Wyse, Paul Piwek, Mihai Lintean, Svetlana Stoyanchev, and Cristian Moldovan. 2010. Overview of The First Question Generation Shared Task Evaluation Challenge. In *Proceedings of the Third Workshop on Question Generation.*

Lee Schwartz, Takako Aikawa, and Michel Pahud. 2004. Dynamic Language Learning Tools. In Proceedings of *STIL/ICALL Symposium on Computer Assisted Learning.*

John H. Wolfe. 1976. Automatic Question Generation from Text - an Aid to Independent Study. In *Proceedings of ACM SIGCSE-SIGCUE Joint Symposium on Computer Science Education.*

Xuchen Yao and Yi Zhang. 2010. Question generation with minimal recursion semantics. In *Proceedings of QG2010: The Third Workshop on Question Generation.*

The NL2KR Platform for building Natural Language Translation Systems

Nguyen H. Vo, Arindam Mitra and Chitta Baral
School of Computing, Informatics and Decision Systems Engineering
Arizona State University
{nguyen.h.vo, amitra7, chitta }@asu.edu

Abstract

This paper presents the NL2KR platform to build systems that can translate text to different formal languages. It is freely-available[1], customizable, and comes with an Interactive GUI support that is useful in the development of a translation system. Our key contribution is a user-friendly system based on an interactive multistage learning algorithm. This effective algorithm employs Inverse-λ, Generalization and user provided dictionary to learn new meanings of words from sentences and their representations. Using the learned meanings, and the Generalization approach, it is able to translate new sentences. NL2KR is evaluated on two standard corpora, Jobs and GeoQuery and it exhibits state-of-the-art performance on both of them.

1 Introduction and Related Work

For natural language interaction with systems one needs to translate natural language text to the input language of that system. Since different systems (such as a robot or database system) may have different input language, we need a way to translate natural language to different formal languages as needed by the application. We have developed a user friendly platform, NL2KR, that takes examples of sentences and their translations (in a desired target language that varies with the application), and some bootstrap information (an initial lexicon), and constructs a translation system from text to that desired target language.

[1]http://nl2kr.engineering.asu.edu/

Our approach to translate natural language text to formal representation is inspired by Montague's work (Montague, 1974) where the meanings of words and phrases are expressed as λ-calculus expressions and the meaning of a sentence is built from semantics of constituent words through appropriate λ-calculus (Church, 1936) applications. A major challenge in using this approach has been the difficulty of coming up with the λ-calculus representation of words.

Montague's approach has been widely used in (Zettlemoyer and Collins, 2005; Kwiatkowski et al., 2010) to translate natural language to formal languages. In ZC05 (Zettlemoyer and Collins, 2005) the learning algorithm requires the user to provide the semantic templates for all words. A semantic template is a λ-expression (e.g. $\lambda x.p(x)$ for an arity one predicate), which describes a particular pattern of representation in that formal language. With all these possible templates, the learning algorithm extracts the semantic representation of the words from the formal representation of a sentence. It then associates the extracted meanings to the words of the sentence in all possible ways and ranks the associations according to some goodness measure. While manually coming up with semantic templates for one target language is perhaps reasonable, manually doing it for different target languages corresponding to different applications may not be a good idea as manual creation of semantic templates requires deep understanding of translation to the target language. This calls for automating this process. In UBL (Kwiatkowski et al., 2010) this process is automated by restricting the choices of formal representation and learning the meanings in a brute force manner. Given, a sentence S and its representation M in the restricted formal language,

Proceedings of the 53rd Annual Meeting of the Association for Computational Linguistics and the 7th International Joint Conference on Natural Language Processing, pages 899–908,
Beijing, China, July 26-31, 2015.

it breaks the sentence into two smaller substrings $S1, S2$ and uses higher-order unification to compute two λ-terms $M1, M2$ which combines to produce M. It then recursively learns the meanings of the words, from the sub-instance $< S1, M1 >$ and $< S2, M2 >$. Since, there are many ways to split the input sentence S and the choice of $M1, M2$ can be numerous, it needs to consider all possible splittings and their combinations; which produces many spurious meanings. Most importantly, their higher-order unification algorithm imposes various restrictions (such as limited number of conjunctions in a sentence, limited forms of functional application) on the meaning representation language which severely limits its applicability to new applications. Another common drawback of these two algorithms is that they both suffer when the test sentence contains words that are not part of the training corpus.

Our platform NL2KR uses a different automated approach based on Inverse-λ (section 2.1) and Generalization (section 2.2) which does not impose such restrictions enforced by their higher-order unification algorithm. Also, Generalization algorithm along with Combinatory Categorical Grammar (Steedman, 2000) parser, allows NL2KR to go beyond the training dictionary and translate sentences which contain previously unseen words. The main aspect of our approach is as follows: given a sentence, its semantic representation and an initial dictionary containing the meaning of some words, NL2KR first obtains several derivation of the input sentence in Combinatory Categorical Grammar (CCG). Each CCG derivation tree describes the rules of functional application through which constituents combine with each other. With the user provided initial dictionary, NL2KR then traverses the tree in a bottom-up fashion to compute the semantic expressions of intermediate nodes. It then traverses the augmented tree in a top-down manner to learn the meaning of missing words using Inverse-λ (section 2.1). If Inverse-λ is not sufficient to learn the meaning of all unknown words, it employs Generalization (section 2.2) to guess the meanings of unknown words with the meaning of known similar words. It then restarts the learning process with the updated knowledge. The learning process stops if it learns the meanings of all words or fails to learn any new meaning in an iteration. In the latter case, it shows the augmented tree to the user. The user can then provide meanings of some unknown words and resumes the learning process.

Another distinguishing feature of NL2KR is its user-friendly interface that helps users in creating their own translation system. The closest system to NL2KR is the UW Semantic Parsing Framework (UW SPF) (Artzi and Zettlemoyer, 2013) which incorporates the algorithms in (Zettlemoyer and Collins, 2005; Kwiatkowski et al., 2010) . However, to use UW SPF for the development of a new system, the user needs to learn their coding guidelines and needs to write new code in their system. NL2KR does not require the users to write new code and guides the development process with its rich user interface.

We have evaluated NL2KR on two standard datasets: GeoQuery (Tang and Mooney, 2001) and Jobs (Tang and Mooney, 2001). GeoQuery is a database of geographical questions and Jobs contains sentences with job related query. Experiments demonstrate that NL2KR can exhibit state-of-the-art performance with fairly small initial dictionary. The rest of the paper is organized as follows: we first present the algorithms and architecture of the NL2KR platform in section 2; we discuss about the experiments in section 3; and finally, we conclude in section 4.

2 Algorithms and Architecture

The NL2KR architecture (Figure 1) has two subparts which depend on each other (1) NL2KR-L for learning and (2) NL2KR-T for translation. The NL2KR-L sub-part takes the following as input: (1) a set of training sentences and their target formal representations, and (2) an initial lexicon or dictionary consisting of some words, their CCG categories, and their meanings in terms of λ-calculus expressions. It then constructs the CCG parse trees and uses them for learning of word meanings.

Learning of word meanings is done by using Inverse-λ and Generalization (Baral et al., 2012; Baral et al., 2011) and ambiguity is addressed by a Parameter Learning module that learns the weights of the meanings. The learned meanings update the lexicon. The translation sub-part uses this updated lexicon to get the meaning of all the words in a new sentence, and combines them to get the meaning of the new sentence. Details of each module will be presented in the following subsections.

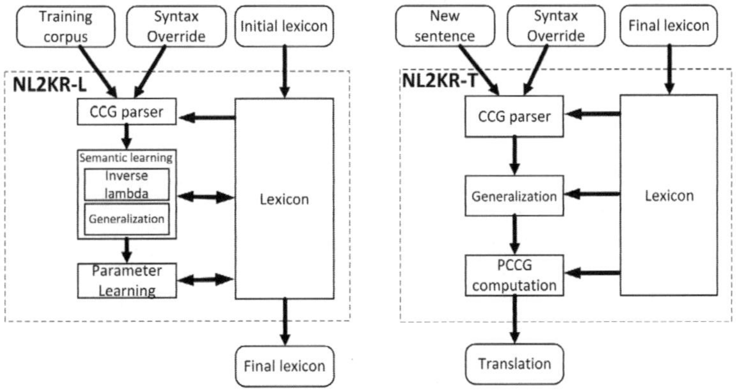

Figure 1: Architecture of NL2KR

The NL2KR platform provides a GUI (Figure 2) with six features: λ-application, Inverse-λ, Generalization, CCG-Parser, NL2KR-L and NL2KR-T. The fourth feature is a stand-alone CCG parser and the first four features can help on user with constructing the initial lexicon. The user can then use NL2KR-L to update the lexicon using training data and the NL2KR-T button then works as a translation system.

2.1 Inverse-λ

Inverse-λ plays a key role in the learning process. Formally, given two λ-expressions H and G with $H = F@G$ or $H = G@F$, the Inverse-λ operation computes the λ expression F. For example, given the meaning of "is texas" as $\lambda x2.x2@stateid(texas)$ and the meaning of "texas" as $stateid(texas)$, with the additional information that "is" acts as the function while "texas" is the argument, the Inverse-λ algorithm computes the meaning of "is" as $\lambda x3.\lambda x2.x2@x3$ (Figure 4). NL2KR implements the Inverse-λ algorithm specified in (Baral et al., 2012). The Inverse-λ module is separately accessible through the main GUI (Figure 2).

2.2 Generalization

Generalization (Baral et al., 2012; Baral et al., 2011) is used when Inverse-λ is not sufficient to learn new semantic representation of words. In contrast to Inverse-λ which learns the exact meaning of a word in a particular context, Generalization learns the meanings of a word from similar words with existing representations. Thus, Generalization helps NL2KR to learn meanings of words that are not even present in the training data set. In the current implementation, two words are considered as similar if they have the exact same CCG category. As an example, if we want to generalize the meaning of the word "plays" with CCG category $(S\backslash NP)/NP)$ and the lexicon already contains an entry for "eats" with the same CCG category, and the meaning $\lambda y.\lambda x.eats(x, y)$, the algorithm will extract the template $\lambda y.\lambda x.WORD(x, y)$ and apply the template to $plays$ to get the meaning $\lambda y.\lambda x.plays(x, y)$.

2.3 Combinatory Categorial Grammar

Derivation of a sentence in Combinatory Categorial Grammar (CCG) determines the way the constituents combine together to establish the meaning of the whole. CCG is a type of phrase structure grammar and clearly describes the predicate-argument structure of constituents.

Figure 3 shows an example output of NL2KR's CCG parser. In the figure, "John" and "home" have the category [N] (means noun) and can change to [NP] (means noun phrase). The phrase"walk home" has the category [S\NP], which means that it can combine with a constituent with category [NP] ("John" in this case) from left with the *backward application* to form category [S] (sentence). The word "walk" has the category [(S\NP)/NP], which means it can combine with a constituent with category [NP] ("home") from right through the *forward application* combinator to form category [S\NP] (of "walk home").

A detailed description on CCG goes beyond the scope of this paper (see (Steedman, 2000) for more details). Since, natural language sentences can have various CCG parse trees, each expressing a different meaning of the sentence, a key challenge

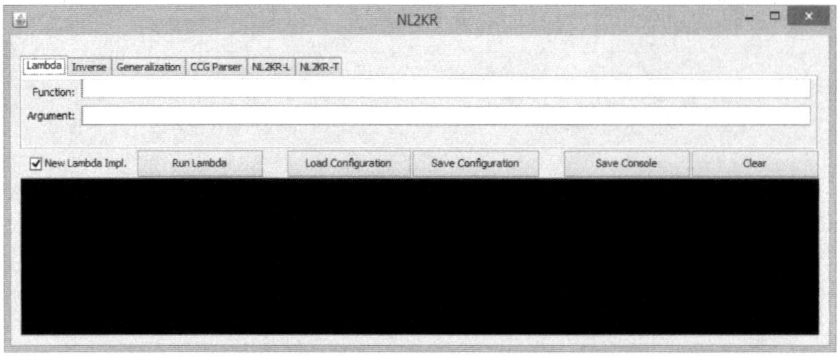

Figure 2: NL2KR's main GUI, Version 1.7.0001

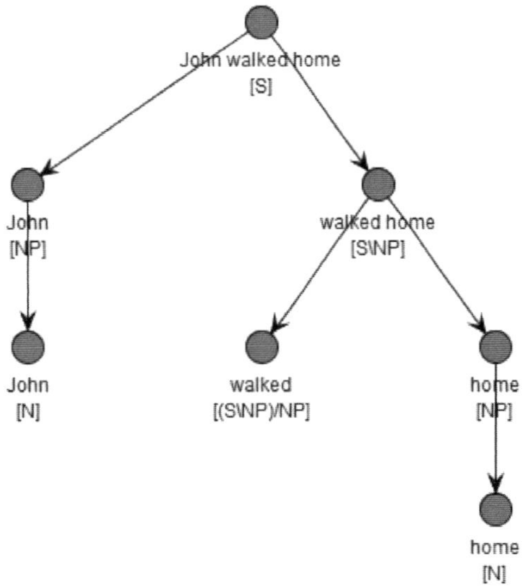

Figure 3: CCG parse tree of "John walked home".

in the learning and the translation process is to find a suitable CCG parse tree for a sentence in natural language. We overcome this impediment by allowing our learning and translation subsystem to work with multiple weighted parse trees for a given sentence and determining on the fly, the one that is most suitable. We discuss more on this in sections 2.4-2.6.

Existing CCG parsers (Curran et al., 2007; Lierler and Schüller, 2012) either return a single best parse tree for a given sentence or parse it in all possible ways with no preferential ordering among them. In order to overcome this shortcoming and generate more than one weighted candidate parse trees, we have developed a new parser using beam search with Cocke-Younger-Kasami(CYK) algorithm. NL2KRs CCG parser uses the C&C model (Curran et al., 2007) and constraints from the Stanford parser (Socher et al., 2013; Toutanova et al., 2003) to guide the derivation of a sentence. The output of the CCG parser is a set of k weighted parse trees, where the parameter k is provided by the user.

NL2KR system allows one to use the CCG parser independently through the interactive GUI. The output graphs look like the one in Figure 3. It can be zoomed in/out and its nodes can be moved around, making it easier to work with complex sentences.

2.4 Multistage learning approach

Learning meanings of words is the major component of our system. The inputs to the learning module are a list of training sentences, their target formal representations and an initial lexicon consisting of triplets of the form *<word, CCG category, meaning>*, where meanings are represented in terms of λ-calculus expressions. The output of the algorithm is a final dictionary containing a set of 4-tuples *(word, CCG category, meaning, weight)*.

Interactive Multistage Learning Algorithm (IMLA) NL2KR employs an Interactive Multistage Learning Algorithm (Algorithm 1) that runs many iterations on the input sentences. In each iteration, it goes through one or more of the following stages:

Stage 1 In Stage 1, it gets all the unfinished sentences. It then employs *Bottom Up-Top Down* algorithm (Algorithm 2) to learn new meanings (by Inverse-λ). For a sentence, if it has computed the meanings of all its constituents, which can be combined to produce the given representation, that sentence is considered as learned. Each

Algorithm 1 IMLA algorithm

```
function IMLA(initLexicon,sentences, sentsMeanings)
  regWords ← ∅
  generalize ← false
  lexicon ← initLexicon
  repeat
    repeat
      repeat
        for all s ∈ sentences do
          newMeanings ← BT(s,lexicon,sentsMeanings)
          lexicon ← lexicon ∪ newMeanings
          for all n ∈ newMeanings do
            ms ← GENERALIZE(regWords, n)
            lexicon ← lexicon ∪ ms
          end for
        end for
      until newMeanings = ∅
      if generalize=false then
        generalize ← true
        for all t ∈ unfinishedSents do
          words ← GETALLWORDS(t)
          ms ← GENERALIZE(words)
          lexicon ← lexicon ∪ ms
          regWords ← regWords ∪ words
        end for
      end if
    until newMeanings = ∅
    INTERATIVELEARNING
  until unfinishedSents = ∅ OR userBreak
  lexicon ← PARAMETERESTIMATION(lexicon,sentences)
  return lexicon
end function
```

new meaning learned by this process is used to generalize the words in a waiting list. Initially, this waiting list is empty and is updated in stage 2. When no more new meaning can be learned by *Bottom Up-Top Down* algorithm, IMLA (Algorithm 1) enters stage 2.

Stage 2 In this stage, it takes all the sentences for which the learning is not yet finished and applies Generalization process on all the words of those sentences. At the same time, it populates those words into the waiting list, so that from now on, *Bottom Up-Top Down* will try to generalize new meanings for them when it learns some new meanings. It then goes back to stage 1. Next time, after exiting stage 1, it directly goes to stage 3.

Stage 3 When both aforementioned stages can not learn all the sentences, the *Interactive Learning* process is invoked and all the unfinished sentences are shown on the interactive GUI (Figure 4). Users can either skip or provide more information on the GUI and the learning process is continued.

After finishing all stages, IMLA (Algorithm 1) calls Parameter Estimation (section 2.5) algorithm to compute the weight of each lexicon tuple.

Bottom Up-Top Down learning For a given sentence, the CCG parser is used for the CCG parse trees like the one of *how big is texas* in Figure 4. For each parse tree, two main processes are called, namely "bottom up" and "top down". In the first process, all the meanings of the words in the sentences are retrieved from the lexicon. These meanings are populated in the leaf nodes of a parse tree (see Figure 4), which are combined in a bottom-up manner to compute the meanings of phrases and full sentences. We call these meanings, the *current meanings*.

In the "top down" process, using Inverse-λ algorithm, the given meaning of the whole sentence (called the *expected meaning* of the sentence) and the current meanings of the phrases, we calculate the expected meanings of each of the phrases from the root of the tree to the leaves. For example, given the expected meaning of *how big is texas* and the current meaning of *how big*, we use Inverse-λ algorithm to get the meaning (expected) of *is texas*. This expected meaning is used together with current meanings of *is* (*texas*) to calculate the expected meanings of *texas* (*is*). The expected meanings of the leaf nodes we have just learned will be saved to the lexicon and will be used in the other sentences and in subsequent learning iteration. The "top down" process is stopped when the expected meanings are same as the current meanings. And in both "bottom up" and "top-down" processes, the beam search algorithm is used to speed-up the learning process.

Interactive learning In the interactive learning process it opens a GUI which shows the unfinished sentences. Users can see the current and expected meanings for the unfinished sentences. When the user gives additional meanings of word(s), the λ-application or Inverse-λ operation is automatically performed to update the new meaning(s) to related

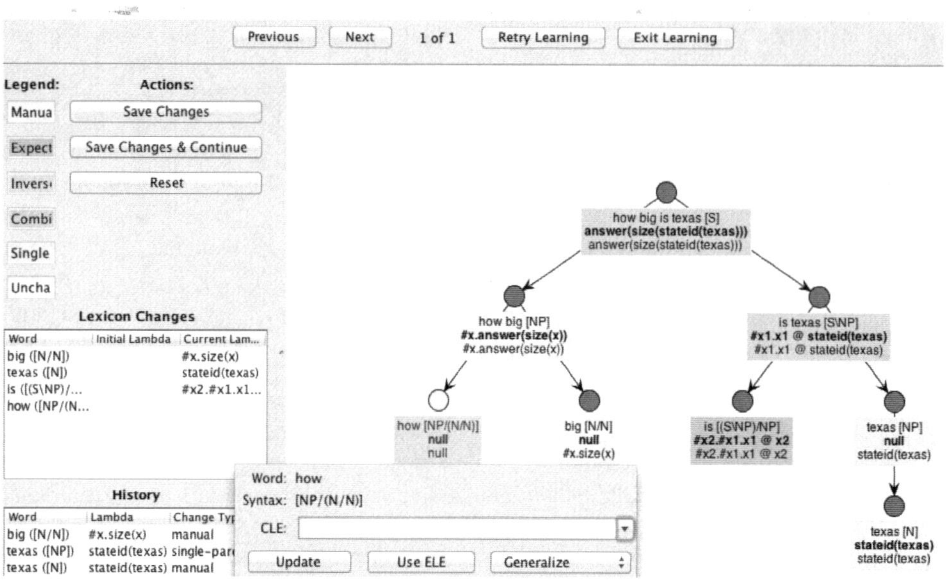

Figure 4: Interactive learning GUI. The box under each node show: the corresponding phrases [CCG category], the expected meanings and the current meanings. Click on the red node will show the window to change the current meaning (CLE)

Algorithm 2 BottomUp-TopDown (BT) algorithm

```
function BT(
    sentence, lexicon, sentsMeanings)
  parseTrees ← CCGPARSER(sentence)
  for all tree ∈ parseTrees do
    t ← BOTTOMUP(tree,lexicon)
    TOPDOWN(t,sentsMeanings)
  end for
end function
```

word(s). Once satisfied, the user can switch back to the automated learning mode.

Example Let us consider the question "How big is texas?" with meaning $answer(size(stateid(texas)))$ (see Figure 4).

Let us assume that the initial dictionary has the following entries: *how* $:= NP/(N/N) : \lambda x.\lambda y.answer(x@y)$, *big* $:= N/N : \lambda x.size(x)$ and *texas* $:= NP : stateid(texas)$. The algorithm then proceeds as follows.

First, the meanings of "*how*" and "*big*" are combined to compute the current meaning of "*how big*" $:= NP : \lambda x.answer(size(x))$ in the "bottom up" process. Since the meaning of "*is*" is unknown, the current meaning of "*is texas*" still remains unknown.

It then starts the "top down" process where it knows the expected meaning of "*How big is texas*" $:= S : answer(size(stateid(texas)))$ and the current meaning of "*how big*". Using them in the Inverse-λ algorithm, it then compute the meaning of "*is texas*" $:= S\backslash NP : \lambda x1.x1@stateid(texas)$. Using this expected meaning and current meaning of "*texas*" $:= NP : stateid(texas)$, it then calculates the expected meaning of "*is*" as "*is*" $:= (S\backslash NP)/NP : \lambda x2.\lambda x1.x1@x2$. This newly learned expected meaning is then saved into the lexicon.

Since the meaning of all the words in the question are known, the learning algorithm stops here and the *Interactive Learning* is never called.

If initially, the dictionary contains only two meanings: "*big*" $:= N/N : \lambda x.size(x)$ and "*texas*" $:= NP : stateid(texas)$, NL2KR tries to first learn the sentence but fails to learn the complete sentence and switches to *Interactive Learning* which shows the interactive GUI (see Figure 4). If the user specifies that "*how*" means $\lambda x.\lambda y.answer(x@y)$, NL2KR combines its meaning with the meaning of "*big*" to get the meaning "*how big*" $:= NP : \lambda x.answer(size(x))$. It will then use Inverse-λ to figure out the meaning of "*is texas*" and then the meaning of "*is*". Now all the meanings are combined to compute the current meaning $answer(size(stateid(texas)))$ of "*How big is texas*". This meaning is same as the expected meaning, so we know that the sentence is successfully learned. Now, the user can press *Retry Learning* to switch back to automated learning.

2.5 Parameter Estimation

The Parameter Estimation module estimates a weight for each word-meaning pair such that the joint probability of the training sentences getting translated to their given representation is maximized. It implements the algorithm described in Zettlemoyer et. al.(2005).

2.6 Translation

The goal of this module is to convert input sentences into the target formalism using the lexicon previously learned. The algorithm used in Translation module (Algorithm 3) is similar to the bottom-up process in the learning algorithm. It first obtains several weighted CCG parse trees of the input sentence. It then computes a formal representation for each of the parse trees using the learned dictionary. Finally, it ranks the translations according to the weights of word-meaning pairs and the weights of the CCG parse trees. However, test sentences may contain words which were not present in the training set. In such cases, Generalization is used to guess the meanings of those unknown words from the meanings of the similar words present in the dictionary.

Algorithm 3 Translation algorithm

function TRANSLATE($sentence$, $lexicon$)
  $candidates \leftarrow \emptyset$
  $parseTrees \leftarrow$ CCGPARSER($sentence$)
  for all $tree \in parseTrees$ **do**
    GENERALIZE($tree$);
    $t \leftarrow$ BOTTOMUP($tree$)
    $candidates \leftarrow candidates \cup t$
  end for
  $output \leftarrow$ VERIFY-RANK($candidates$)
  return $output$
end function

3 Experimental Evaluation

We have evaluated NL2KR on two standard corpora: GeoQuery and Jobs. For both the corpus, the output generated by the learned system has been considered correct if it is an exact replica of the logical formula described in the corpus.

We report the performance in terms of precision (percentage of returned logical-forms that are correct), recall (percentage of sentences for which the correct logical-form was returned), F1-measure (harmonic mean of precision and recall) and the size of the initial dictionary.

We compare the performance of our system with recently published, directly-comparable works, namely, FUBL (Kwiatkowski et al., 2011), UBL (Kwiatkowski et al., 2010), λ-WASP (Wong and Mooney, 2007), ZC07 (Zettlemoyer and Collins, 2007) and ZC05 (Zettlemoyer and Collins, 2005) systems.

3.1 Corpora

GeoQuery GeoQuery (Tang and Mooney, 2001) is a corpus containing questions on geographical facts about the United States. It contains a total of 880 sentences written in natural language, paired with their meanings in a formal query language, which can be executed against a database of the geographical information of the United States. We follow the standard training/testing split of 600/280. An example sentence meaning pair is shown below.

Sentence: *How long is the Colorado river?*
Meaning: *answer(A,(len(B,A),const(B, riverid(colorado)), river(B)))*

Jobs The Jobs (Tang and Mooney, 2001) dataset contains a total of 640 job related queries written in natural language. The Prolog programming language has been used to represent the meaning of a query. Each query specifies a list of job criteria and can be directly executed against a database of job listings. An example sentence meaning pair from the corpus is shown below.

Question: *What jobs are there for programmers that know assembly?*
Meaning: *answer(J,(job(J),title(J,T), const(T,'Programmer'),language(J,L), const(L,'assembly'))))*

The dataset contains a training split of 500 sentences and a test split of 140 sentences.

3.2 Initial Dictionary Formulation

GeoQuery For GeoQuery corpus, we manually selected a set of 100 structurally different sentences from the training set and initiated the learning process with a dictionary containing the repre-

	GUI Driven	Initial Dictionary	Learned Dictionary
♯ <word, category >	31	118	401
♯ <word, category, meaning>	36	127	1572
♯ meaning	30	89	819

Table 1: Comparison of Initial and Learned dictionary for GeoQuery corpus on the basis of the number of entries in the dictionary, number of unique <word, CCG category> pairs and the number of unique meanings across all the entries. "GUI Driven" denotes the amount of the total meanings given through interactive GUI and is a subset of the Initial dictionary.

	GUI Driven	Initial Dictionary	Learned Dictionary
♯ <word, category>	58	103	226
♯ <word, category, meaning>	74	119	1793
♯ meaning	57	71	940

Table 2: Comparison of Initial and Learned dictionary for Jobs corpus.

sentation of the nouns and question words. These meanings were easy to obtain as they follow simple patterns. We then trained the translation system on those selected sentences. The output of this process was used as the initial dictionary for training step. Further meanings were provided on demand through interactive learning. A total of 119 word meanings tuples (Table 1, ♯ *<word, category, meaning >*) were provided from which the NL2KR system learned 1793 tuples. 45 of the 119 were representation of nouns and question words that were obtained using simple patterns. The remaining 74 were obtained by a human using the NL2KR GUI. These numbers illustrate the usefulness of the NL2KR GUI as well as the NL2KR learning component. One of our future goals is to further automate the process and reduce the GUI interaction part.

Table 1 compares the initial and learned dictionary for GeoQuery on the basis of number of unique *<word, category, meaning>* entries in dictionary, number of unique *<word, category>* pairs and the number of unique meanings across all the entries in the dictionary. Since each unique <word, CCG category> pair must have at least one meaning, the total number of unique *<word, category>* pairs in the training corpus provides a lower bound on the size of the ideal output dictionary. However, one *<word, category>* pair may have multiple meanings, so the ideal dictionary can be much bigger than the number of unique *<word, category>* pairs. Indeed, there were many words such as "of", "in" that had multiple meanings for the same CCG category. Table 1 clearly describes that the amount of initial effort is substantially less compared to the return.

Jobs For the Jobs dataset, we followed a similar process as in the GeoQuery dataset. A set of 120 structurally different sentences were selected and a dictionary was created which contained the representation of the nouns and the question words from the training corpus. A total of 127 word meanings were provided in the process. Table 2 compares the initial and learned dictionary for Jobs. Again, we can see that the amount of initial effort is substantially less in comparison to the return.

3.3 Precision, Recall and F1-measure

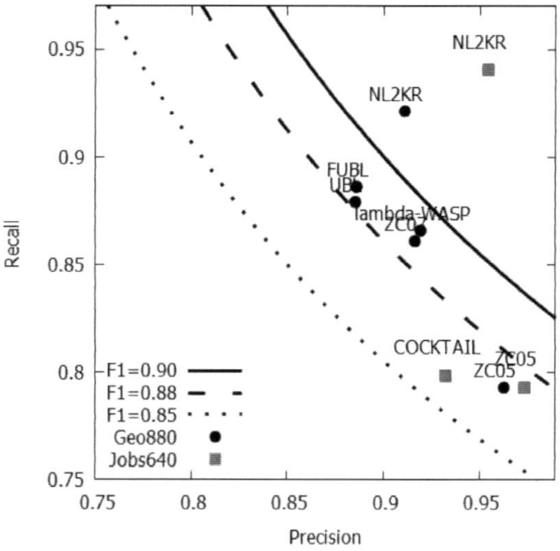

Figure 5: Comparison of Precision, Recall and F1-measure on GeoQuery and Jobs dataset.

Table 3, Table 4 and Figure 5 present the comparison of the performance of NL2KR on the GeoQuery and Jobs domain with other recent works. NL2KR obtained 91.1% precision value, 92.1%

System	Precision	Recall	F1
ZC05	0.963	0.793	0.87
ZC07	0.916	0.861	0.888
λ-WASP	0.9195	0.8659	0.8919
UBL	0.885	0.879	0.882
FUBL	0.886	0.886	0.886
NL2KR	0.911	0.921	0.916

Table 3: Comparison of Precision, Recall and F1-measure on GeoQuery dataset.

recall value and a F1-measure of 91.6% on GeoQuery (Figure 5, Geo880) dataset. For Jobs corpus, the precision, recall and F1-measure were 95.43%, 94.03% and 94.72% respectively. In all cases, NL2KR achieved state-of-the-art recall and F1 measures and it significantly outperformed FUBL (the latest work on translation systems) on GeoQuery.

For both GeoQuery and Jobs corpus, our recall is significantly higher than existing systems because meanings discovered by NL2KRs learning algorithm is more general and reusable. In other words, meanings learned from a particular sentence are highly likely to be applied again in the context of other sentences. It may be noted that, larger lexicons do not necessarily imply higher recall as lambda expressions for two phrases may not be suitable for functional application, thus failing to generate any translation for the whole. Moreover, the use of a CCG parser maximizes the recall by exhibiting consistency and providing a set of weighted parse trees. By consistency, we mean that the order of the weighted parse tree remains same over multiple parses of the same sentence and the sentences having similar syntactic structures have identical ordering of the derivations, thus making Generalization to be more effective in the process of translation.

The sentences for which NL2KR did not have a translation are the ones having structural difference with the sentences present in the training dataset. More precisely, their structure was not identical with any of the sentences present in the training dataset or could not be constructed by combining the structures observed in the training sentences.

We analyzed the sentences for which the translated meaning did not match the correct one and observed that the translation algorithm selected the wrong meaning, even though it discovered the correct one as one of the possible meanings the

System	Precision	Recall	F1
ZC05	0.9736	0.7929	0.8740
COCKTAIL	0.9325	0.7984	0.8603
NL2KR	0.9543	0.9403	0.9472

Table 4: Comparison of Precision, Recall and F1-measure on Jobs dataset.

sentence could have had in the target formal language. Among the sentences for which NL2KR returned a translation, there were very few instances where it did not discover the correct meaning in the set of possible meanings.

It may be noted that even though our precision is lower than ZC05 and very close to ZC07 and WASP; we have achieved significantly higher F1 measure than all the related systems. In fact, ZC05, which achieves the best precision for both the datasets, is better by a margin of only 0.019 on the Jobs dataset and 0.052 on the GeoQuery dataset. We think one of the main reasons is that it uses manually predefined lambda-templates, which we try to automate as much as possible.

4 Conclusion

NL2KR is a freely available[2], user friendly, rich graphical platform for building translation systems to convert sentences from natural language to their equivalent formal representations in a wide variety of domains. We have described the system algorithms and architecture and its performance on the GeoQuery and Jobs datasets. As mentioned earlier, the NL2KR GUI and the NL2KR learning module help in starting from a small initial lexicon (for example, 119 in Table 2) and learning a much larger lexicon (1793 in Table 2). One of our future goals is to reduce the initial lexicon to be even smaller by further automating the NL2KR GUI interaction component .

Acknowledgements

We thank NSF for the DataNet Federation Consortium grant OCI-0940841 and ONR for their grant N00014-13-1-0334 for partially supporting this research.

[2]More examples and a tutorial to use NL2KR are available in the download package.

References

Yoav Artzi and Luke Zettlemoyer. 2013. UW SPF: The University of Washington Semantic Parsing Framework. *arXiv preprint arXiv:1311.3011*.

Chitta Baral, Juraj Dzifcak, Marcos Alvarez Gonzalez, and Jiayu Zhou. 2011. Using inverse λ and generalization to translate english to formal languages. In *Proceedings of the Ninth International Conference on Computational Semantics*, pages 35–44. Association for Computational Linguistics.

Chitta Baral, Juraj Dzifcak, Marcos Alvarez Gonzalez, and Aaron Gottesman. 2012. Typed answer set programming lambda calculus theories and correctness of inverse lambda algorithms with respect to them. *TPLP*, 12(4-5):775–791.

Alonzo Church. 1936. An Unsolvable Problem of Elementary Number Theory. *American Journal of Mathematics*, 58(2):345–363, April.

James Curran, Stephen Clark, and Johan Bos. 2007. Linguistically Motivated Large-Scale NLP with C&C and Boxer. In *Proceedings of the 45th Annual Meeting of the Association for Computational Linguistics Companion Volume Proceedings of the Demo and Poster Sessions*, pages 33–36, Prague, Czech Republic, June. Association for Computational Linguistics.

Tom Kwiatkowski, Luke Zettlemoyer, Sharon Goldwater, and Mark Steedman. 2010. Inducing probabilistic CCG grammars from logical form with higher-order unification. In *Proceedings of the 2010 conference on empirical methods in natural language processing*, pages 1223–1233. Association for Computational Linguistics.

Tom Kwiatkowski, Luke Zettlemoyer, Sharon Goldwater, and Mark Steedman. 2011. Lexical generalization in ccg grammar induction for semantic parsing. In *Proceedings of the Conference on Empirical Methods in Natural Language Processing*, pages 1512–1523. Association for Computational Linguistics.

Yuliya Lierler and Peter Schüller. 2012. Parsing combinatory categorial grammar via planning in answer set programming. In *Correct Reasoning*, pages 436–453. Springer.

Richard Montague. 1974. English as a Formal Language. In Richmond H. Thomason, editor, *Formal Philosophy: Selected Papers of Richard Montague*, pages 188–222. Yale University Press, New Haven, London.

Richard Socher, John Bauer, Christopher D. Manning, and Andrew Y. Ng. 2013. Parsing with Compositional Vector Grammars. In *ACL (1)*, pages 455–465.

Mark Steedman. 2000. *The syntactic process*, volume 35. MIT Press.

Lappoon R Tang and Raymond J Mooney. 2001. Using multiple clause constructors in inductive logic programming for semantic parsing. In *Machine Learning: ECML 2001*, pages 466–477. Springer.

Kristina Toutanova, Dan Klein, Christopher D. Manning, and Yoram Singer. 2003. Feature-rich part-of-speech tagging with a cyclic dependency network. In *Proceedings of the 2003 Conference of the North American Chapter of the Association for Computational Linguistics on Human Language Technology - Volume 1*.

Yuk Wah Wong and Raymond J Mooney. 2007. Learning synchronous grammars for semantic parsing with lambda calculus. In *Annual Meeting-Association for computational Linguistics*, volume 45, page 960. Citeseer.

Luke S. Zettlemoyer and Michael Collins. 2005. Learning to Map Sentences to Logical Form: Structured Classification with Probabilistic Categorial Grammars. In *UAI*, pages 658–666. AUAI Press.

Luke S Zettlemoyer and Michael Collins. 2007. Online learning of relaxed CCG grammars for parsing to logical form. In *In Proceedings of the 2007 Joint Conference on Empirical Methods in Natural Language Processing and Computational Natural Language Learning (EMNLP-CoNLL-2007)*.

Author Index

Adar, Eytan, 606
Aggarwal, Varun, 1085
Agić, Željko, 1713
Akbik, Alan, 397
Aksoy, Eren Erdal, 676
Alberti, Chris, 323
Aletras, Nikolaos, 1754
Almeida, Mariana S. C., 408
Aloimonos, Yiannis, 676
Amir, Silvio, 1074
Angeli, Gabor, 344, 982
ARAMAKI, Eiji, 1660
Arcan, Mihael, 708
Asher, Nicholas, 281
Astudillo, Ramón, 1074
Attardi, Giuseppe, 846

Bairi, Ramakrishna, 553
Baldridge, Jason, 1385
Ballesteros, Miguel, 334
Banerjee, Siddhartha, 867
Baral, Chitta, 899
Baroni, Marco, 270, 971
Barzilay, Regina, 1253
Basu, Sumit, 889
Beller, Charley, 1512
Bengio, Yoshua, 1
Bentor, Yinon, 177
Benz, Anton, 534
Berant, Jonathan, 1332
Besançon, Romaric, 188
Bhagavatula, Chandra, 774
Bhowmick, Sourav, 645
Bilmes, Jeff, 553
Bing, Lidong, 1587
Bisk, Yonatan, 1395
Bohnet, Bernd, 1713
Bollegala, Danushka, 730
Börschinger, Benjamin, 1460
Bos, Johan, 1512
Boyd-Graber, Jordan, 1438, 1650, 1681
Braune, Fabienne, 815
Bride, Antoine, 281
Bryant, Christopher, 697
Buitelaar, Paul, 708

C. de Souza, José G., 219
Calacci, Dan, 1629
Callison-Burch, Chris, 1512
Camacho-Collados, José, 741
Cao, Zhu, 616
Carreras, Xavier, 126
Chai, Qinghua, 1263
Chang, Angel, 53
Chang, Baobao, 313, 575
Chang, Ming-Wei, 504, 1321
Chao, Jiayuan, 1783
Charniak, Eugene, 1035
Che, Wanxiang, 1234
Chen, Huadong, 825
Chen, Jiajun, 825, 1213
Chen, Long, 430
Chen, Qian, 106
Chen, Qiang, 419
Chen, Wenliang, 1783
Chen, Xiaoping, 106
Chen, Xinchi, 1159, 1744
Chen, Yubo, 167
Chen, Yun-Nung, 483
Chen, Zhigang, 106
Cheng, Xueqi, 136
chiticariu, laura, 397
Cho, Kyunghyun, 1
Choe, Do Kook, 1035, 1223
Choi, Eunsol, 1311
Choi, Jinho D., 387
Ciaramita, Massimiliano, 1460
Clark, Alexander, 1618
Clark, Kevin, 1405
Clavel, Chloé, 1064
Cohen, William, 666
Cohen, William W, 355
Cohen, William W., 1449
Coke, Reed, 441
Collins, Michael, 323, 1282
Curran, James R., 1148

Da San Martino, Giovanni, 1003

Dai, Xin-Yu, 825, 1054
Danescu-Niculescu-Mizil, Cristian, 1650
Daniele, Falavigna, 1095
Danilevsky, Marina, 397
Das, Rajarshi, 795
Datta, Srayan, 606
Daumé III, Hal, 1639, 1681
de Melo, Gerard, 616, 950
de Rijke, Maarten, 564
de Vries, Arjen, 42
Demberg, Vera, 763
Deng, Yuntian, 1292
Deulofeu, José, 1116
Devlin, Jacob, 31
Diaz, Fernando, 1608
Dinu, Georgiana, 270
Dong, Daxiang, 1723
Dong, Li, 260
dos Santos, Cicero, 626
Dou, Qing, 836
Downey, Doug, 774
Dragut, Eduard, 1024
Du, Lan, 1460
Du, Yantao, 1545
Dubey, Kumar, 239
Duh, Kevin, 961
Durrett, Greg, 302
Dušek, Ondřej, 451
Dyer, Chris, 334, 795, 836, 1491

Eger, Steffen, 909
Elhadad, Noémie, 1375
Elliott, Desmond, 42

Faruqui, Manaal, 1491
Feldman, Naomi, 1639
Fermuller, Cornelia, 676
Fernández-González, Daniel, 1523
Ferret, Olivier, 188
Figueira, Helena, 408
Filice, Simone, 1003
Finegan-Dollak, Catherine, 441
Fischer, Stefan, 763
Foulds, James, 74, 116
Friedrich, Annemarie, 1272

Galley, Michel, 878
Gao, Jianfeng, 1321
Gao, Yingkai, 1292
Ge, Tao, 313, 575
Gershman, Anatole, 483
Getoor, Lise, 74, 116
Gleize, Martin, 939
Graham, Yvette, 1804
Grau, Brigitte, 939
Grave, Edouard, 1375
Grishman, Ralph, 635
Groschwitz, Jonas, 1481
Guo, Jiafeng, 136
Guo, Jiang, 1234
Guo, Li, 84
Guo, Shu, 84
Guo, Weiwei, 1587
Gurevych, Iryna, 719
Guzmán, Francisco, 805

H. Kumar, Shachi, 74
Han, Jiawei, 586
Han, Xianpei, 229
He, Shizhu, 687
He, Tingting, 250
He, Wei, 1723
He, Xiaodong, 1321
He, Yanxiang, 419
Hearst, Marti A., 1245
Hennig, Leonhard, 596
Herder, Eelco, 1598
Hinrichs, Erhard, 1733
Hirst, Graeme, 524
Hockenmaier, Julia, 1395
Hoi, Steven, 1692
Hovy, Dirk, 752
Hsu, Daniel, 1282
Hu, Po, 250
Hu, Yu, 1501
Hu, Zhiting, 1292
Huang, Bert, 116
Huang, Degen, 430
Huang, Hongzhao, 586
Huang, Lei, 1045
Huang, Minlie, 1365
Huang, Poyao, 1292
Huang, Shujian, 825, 1213
Huang, Xuanjing, 1159, 1744
Huang, Zhongqiang, 31

Iacobacci, Ignacio, 95
Ishikawa, Hiroshi, 1660
Iyer, Rishabh, 553
Iyyer, Mohit, 1681

Jalalvand, Shahab, 1095
Jatowt, Adam, 645
Jean, Sébastien, 1

Jeong, Minwoo, 473
Jha, Rahul, 441
Ji, Donghong, 462
Ji, Guoliang, 687
Ji, Heng, 575, 586, 857
Jiang, Hui, 106, 1501
Jiang, Wenbin, 20, 1567
Johannsen, Anders, 1713
Johnson Premkumar, Melvin Jose, 344
Johnson, Mark, 1460
Joty, Shafiq, 805
Jurafsky, Dan, 1106
Jurcicek, Filip, 451

Kanouchi, Shin, 1660
Kawarabayashi, Ken-ichi, 730
Kedzie, Chris, 1608
Keller, Frank, 1191
Kennington, Casey, 292
Kiagias, Emmanouil, 1702
Kim, Young-Bum, 473
King, Ben, 441
Klabunde, Ralf, 534
Klein, Dan, 302
Knight, Kevin, 586, 836
Koller, Alexander, 1481
Komachi, Mamoru, 1660
Konstas, Ioannis, 1191
Kruszewski, Germán, 971
Kumar, Srijan, 1650
Kwiatkowski, Tom, 1311

Labutov, Igor, 889
Lam, Wai, 514, 1587
Lamar, Thomas, 31
Lampos, Vasileios, 1754
Lan, Yanyan, 136
Langlet, Caroline, 1064
Lao, Ni, 666
Lappin, Shalom, 1618
Lau, Jey Han, 1618
Lauw, Hady, 376
Lavrenko, Victor, 1765
Lazaridou, Angeliki, 270, 971
Lazer, David, 1629
Le, Quoc, 11
Lee, Chin-Hui, 920
Lei, Yu, 419
Li, Chen, 929
Li, Hang, 20, 1567, 1577
Li, Jiwei, 1106
Li, Piji, 1587
Li, Ru, 1263
Li, Shoushan, 1045
Li, Sujian, 575, 586
Li, Tao, 1054
Li, Wenjie, 419
Li, Yunyao, 397
Li, Zhenghua, 1783
Liang, Percy, 992, 1332, 1470
Liao, Yi, 514, 1587
Lin, Chin-Yew, 586
Lin, Hongyu, 229
Lin, Wei, 106
Ling, Wang, 334, 1074
Ling, Zhen-Hua, 1501
Liu, Kang, 167, 616, 687
Liu, Quan, 1501
Liu, Qun, 20, 1567
Liu, Ting, 524, 1014, 1234
Liu, Xule, 419
Liu, Yang, 229, 929, 1180, 1365
Liu, Yuanchao, 1343
Lu, Chunliang, 514
Lu, Zhengdong, 20, 1567, 1577
Luong, Thang, 11, 1106

Ma, Jianqiang, 1733
Maehara, Takanori, 730
Maier, Wolfgang, 1202
Makhoul, John, 31
Maletti, Andreas, 815
Manjunatha, Varun, 1681
Manning, Christopher D., 53, 344, 982, 1405, 1556
Markert, Katja, 1598
Màrquez, Lluís, 805
Martínez Alonso, Héctor, 1713
Martins, André F. T., 408, 1427, 1523
Matsumoto, Yuji, 961
Matthews, Austin, 334
McCallum, Andrew, 146, 156
McClosky, David, 1223
McKeown, Kathleen, 1608
Meij, Edgar, 564
Memisevic, Roland, 1
Mendes, Pedro, 408
Meng, Fandong, 20
Mi, Haitao, 1138
Miceli Barone, Antonio Valerio, 846
Mielens, Jason, 1385
Miler, Kristina, 1438
Miller, Tristan, 719
Minkov, Einat, 666
Misra, Dipendra Kumar, 992

Mitchell, Jeff, 1301
Mitchell, Tom M., 365
Mitra, Arindam, 899
Mitra, Prasenjit, 867
Miyao, Yusuke, 1534
Mochihashi, Daichi, 1774
Monroe, Will, 53
Mooney, Raymond, 177, 878
Moschitti, Alessandro, 1003
Movshovitz-Attias, Dana, 1449

Nakagawa, Tetsuji, 208
Nakamura, Satoshi, 198
Nakashole, Ndapandula, 365
Nakov, Preslav, 805
Narasimhan, Karthik, 1253
Nasr, Alexis, 1116
Navigli, Roberto, 95, 741
Neelakantan, Arvind, 156
Negri, Matteo, 219, 1095
Neubig, Graham, 198
Ng, Dominick, 1148
Ng, Hwee Tou, 697
Ng, Vincent, 543
Nguyen, Kiem-Hieu, 188
Nguyen, Thien Hai, 1354
Nguyen, Thien Huu, 635
Nguyen, Viet-An, 1438
Niculae, Vlad, 1650
Nissim, Malvina, 1512
Noji, Hiroshi, 1534

Oda, Yusuke, 198
Okazaki, Naoaki, 1660
Orita, Naho, 1639
Osborne, Miles, 1765
Ou, Zhijian, 785
Ouchi, Hiroki, 961

Pan, Xiaoman, 586
Pandey, Nishant, 1085
Passonneau, Rebecca, 1587
Pasupat, Panupong, 1470
Pate, John K, 1460
Pavlick, Ellie, 1512
Pei, Wenzhe, 313, 575
Persing, Isaac, 543
Petrov, Slav, 323
Pham, Nghia The, 971
Pilehvar, Mohammad Taher, 95, 741
Pinkal, Manfred, 1272
Pinto, Claudia, 408
Plank, Barbara, 635, 1713
Potts, Christopher, 53
Preoţiuc-Pietro, Daniel, 1754
Primadhanty, Audi, 126

Qian, Qiao, 1365
Qian, Xian, 1180
Qin, Bing, 524, 1014
Qiu, Xipeng, 1159, 1744
Quattoni, Ariadna, 126
Quirk, Chris, 878

Radev, Dragomir, 441
Rajani, Nazneen Fatema, 177
Ramakrishnan, Ganesh, 553
Ramesh, Arti, 74
Ramisch, Carlos, 1116
Resnik, Philip, 1438
Reuße, Sebastian, 534
Ricci, Elisa, 219
Richardson, Matthew, 239
Rose, Carolyn, 1671
Roth, Benjamin, 156
Rothe, Sascha, 1793
Rousseau, Francois, 1702
Rudnicky, Alexander, 483
Rush, Alexander M., 1416

Sachan, Mrinmaya, 239
Sakti, Sakriani, 198
Sarikaya, Ruhi, 473
Savva, Manolis, 53
Saxena, Ashutosh, 992
Sayeed, Asad, 763
Schlangen, David, 292
Schneider, Andrew, 1024
Schütze, Hinrich, 63, 1793
Schwartz, Richard, 31
Seemann, Nina, 815
Setiawan, Hendra, 31
Søgaard, Anders, 1713
Shang, Lifeng, 1577
Shashidhar, Vinay, 1085
Shi, Fulin, 430
Shieber, Stuart, 1416
Shindo, Hiroyuki, 961
Shirai, Kiyoaki, 1354
Shutova, Ekaterina, 950
Silva, Mario, 1074
Silverstein, Kate, 146
Smith, Noah A., 334, 1491
Socher, Richard, 1556

Sridhar, Dhanya, 116
Steedman, Mark, 1301, 1460
Stent, Amanda, 387
Stevens, Jon, 534
Stratos, Karl, 473, 1282
Strubell, Emma, 146
Su, Jinsong, 229
Sui, Zhifang, 575
Sumita, Eiichiro, 1169
SUN, Chengjie, 1343
Sun, Fei, 136
Sun, Liang, 1385
Sun, Rui, 462
Sun, Weiwei, 1545
Sun, Yizhou, 586
Sutskever, Ilya, 11

Tai, Kai Sheng, 1556
Tan, Zhiqiang, 785
Tanaka, Katsumi, 645
Tandon, Niket, 950
Tang, Duyu, 1014
Tannier, Xavier, 188
Tao, Kejia, 992
Teichmann, Christoph, 1481
Tetreault, Joel, 387
Thang, Le Quang, 1534
Tian, Bo, 1365
Tkachenko, Maksim, 376
Toda, Tomoki, 198
Tran, Giang, 1598
Trancoso, Isabel, 1074
Tsagkias, Manos, 564
Tsukahara, Hiroshi, 1774
Tsur, Oren, 1629
Tsvetkov, Yulia, 1491
Turchi, Marco, 219, 708, 1095
Tyshchuk, Yulia, 857

Uchiumi, Kei, 1774
Uszkoreit, Hans, 596

Vaithyanathan, Shivakumar, 397
Valli, André, 1116
Van de Cruys, Tim, 281
Van Durme, Benjamin, 1512
Vanderwende, Lucy, 889
Vaswani, Ashish, 836
Vazirgiannis, Michalis, 1702
Vilnis, Luke, 146
Vinyals, Oriol, 11
Viswanathan, Vidhoon, 177
Vo, Nguyen, 899
Vornov, Eliana, 1639
Voskarides, Nikos, 564

Walker, Marilyn, 116
Wallace, Byron C., 1035
Wallace, William, 857
Wan, Ji, 1692
Wan, Xiaojun, 1545
Wang, Baoxun, 1343
Wang, Bin, 84, 785
Wang, Cheng, 1054
Wang, Haifeng, 1234, 1723
Wang, Jialei, 1692
Wang, Lihong, 84
Wang, Linlin, 616
Wang, Mingxuan, 20, 1567
Wang, Quan, 84
Wang, Rong, 1045
Wang, William Yang, 355, 483
Wang, Xiaolong, 1343
Wang, Xin, 1343
Wang, Yushi, 1332
Wang, Zhiguo, 1138
Wang, Zhiqiang, 1263
Watanabe, Taro, 1169
Weerkamp, Wouter, 564
Wei, Furu, 260
Wei, Si, 106, 1501
Weiss, David, 323
Weissenborn, Dirk, 596
Wen, Miaomiao, 1671
Wen, Zhen, 586
Werling, Keenon, 982
Weston, Jason, 1416
Wiseman, Sam, 1416
Wu, Hua, 1723
Wu, Juan, 1263
Wu, Shuangzhi, 495
Wurzer, Dominik, 1765

Xia, Rui, 1054
Xia, Yunqing, 920
Xiang, Bing, 626
Xing, Eric, 239, 1292
Xiong, Deyi, 229
Xu, Feiyu, 596
Xu, Jun, 136
Xu, Ke, 260, 920
Xu, Liheng, 167, 687
Xu, Wei, 1127
Xue, Nianwen, 1138

Yang, Diyi, 1671
Yang, Yezhou, 676
Yang, Yi, 504, 774
Yao, Junfeng, 229
Yarowsky, David, 1234
Yener, Bulent, 586
Yih, Wen-tau, 1321
Yin, Wenpeng, 63
Yogatama, Dani, 1491
Yu, Dian, 857
Yu, Dianhai, 1723

Zaheer, Manzil, 795
Zaremba, Wojciech, 11
Zbib, Rabih, 31
Zeng, Daojian, 167
Zettlemoyer, Luke, 1311
Zhang, Boliang, 586
Zhang, Dongdong, 495
Zhang, Meishan, 462
Zhang, Min, 229, 1783
Zhang, Muyu, 524
Zhang, Yating, 645
Zhang, Yongdong, 1692
Zhang, Yue, 462, 1213
Zhao, Jun, 167, 250, 616, 687
Zhao, Tiejun, 495
Zhao, Zhendong, 1460
Zheng, Mao, 524
Zhou, Bowen, 626
Zhou, Guangyou, 250
Zhou, Guodong, 656, 1045
Zhou, Hao, 1213
Zhou, HuiWei, 430
Zhou, Jie, 1127
Zhou, Ming, 260, 495
Zhu, Chenxi, 1159, 1744
Zhu, Huaiyu, 397
Zhu, Qiaoming, 656
Zhu, Xiaodan, 106
Zhu, Xiaoyan, 1365
Zhu, Xuan, 1365
Zou, Bowei, 656

53rd Annual Meeting of the Association for Computational Linguistics and 7th International Joint Conference on Natural Language Processing of the Asian Federation of Natural Language Processing

(ACL-IJCNLP 2015)

Long Papers

Beijing, China
26 – 31 July 2015

Volume 2 of 2

ISBN: 978-1-5108-0842-3

Printed from e-media with permission by:

Curran Associates, Inc.
57 Morehouse Lane
Red Hook, NY 12571

Some format issues inherent in the e-media version may also appear in this print version.

Printed by Curran Associates, Inc. (2015)

Association for Computational Linguistics
209 N. Eighth Street
Stroudsburg, Pennsylvania 18360

Phone: 1-570-476-8006
Fax: 1-570-476-0860

acl@aclweb.org

Additional copies of this publication are available from:

Curran Associates, Inc.
57 Morehouse Lane
Red Hook, NY 12571 USA
Phone: 845-758-0400
Fax: 845-758-2634
Email: curran@proceedings.com
Web: www.proceedings.com

ACL-IJCNLP July 26-31 2015

The 53rd Annual Meeting of the Association for Computational Linguistics and the 7th International Joint Conference on Natural Language Processing of the Asian Federation of Natural Language Processing

Proceedings of the Conference

Long Papers

ACL 2015
July 26-31
Beijing, China

Platinum Sponsors:

Gold Sponsors:

Silver Sponsors:

Bronze Sponsor:

Best Paper Sponsor:

Preface: General Chair

It was fifteen years ago when ACL first came to Asia in 2000. The conference in Hong Kong was a very excited one and attracted lots of people. It was a great opportunity for a number of Asian NLP researchers to meet face-to-face in such a large scale meeting. Establishment of AFNLP (Asian Federation of Natural Language Processing) was discussed soon after this wonderful event, and then AFNLP started IJCNLP (the International Joint Conference of Natural Language Processing) as a biennial flagship conference of AFNLP. ACL's three year regional rotation and IJCNLP's two year cycle meet every six years, and this is the second joint ACL-IJCNLP conference following the first held in Singapore in 2009. ACL meetings in Asia and IJNCLPs are now a propelling force of NLP research in Asian regions, and provide valuable experiences especially to young researchers and students who first attend this size of a big conference.

The success of ACL-IJCNLP owes a great deal to the hard work and dedication of many people. I would like to thank all of them for their time and contribution to this joint ACL-AFNLP conference.

Priscilla Rasmussen (the ACL Business Manager), Gertjan van Noord (ACL Past President), Chris Manning (ACL President), Graeme Hirst (ACL Treasurer), Dragomir Radev (ACL Secretary), Keh-Yih Su (AFNLP Past President), Fam-Fai Wong (AFNLP President), all other ACL and AFNLP Executive Committee members and ACL-AFNLP Conference Coordinating Committee members (forgive me for not listing all their names) have always been very helpful and guided me anytime I missed something or was behind the schedule, and given me appropriate advice. Without their help, I could not fulfill even half my duty.

I was very lucky to have a wonderful team of chairs, who have done a fantastic job for leading this conference to an invaluable one. I would like to express my deepest gratitude to Michael Strube and Chengqing Zong (Program Committee Co-Chairs), Le Sun and Yang Liu (Local Arrangement Co-Chairs), Hang Li and Sebastian Riedel (Workshop Co-Chairs), Kevin Duh and Eneko Agirre (Tutorial Co-Chairs), Hsin-His Chen and Katja Markert (System Demonstration Co-Chairs), Wanxiang Che and Guodong Zhou (Publications Co-Chairs), Stephan Oepen, Chin-Yew Lin and Emily Bender (Student Research Workshop Faculty Advisors), Kuan-Yu Chen, Angelina Ivanova and Ellie Pavlick (Student Research Workshop Co-Chairs), Francis Bond (Mentoring Chair), Xianpei Han and Kang Liu (Publicity Co-Chairs), Zhiyuan Liu (Webmaster), and all the team members of the Local Organizing Committee. Thanks to their dedicated efforts, we now have a great conference consisting of the Presidential Address (by Chris Manning), two Keynote Addresses (by Marti Hearst and Jiawei Han), 173 long and 145 short papers, 12 TACL papers, 7 Student Research Workshop papers, 25 system demonstrations, 8 tutorials, 15 workshops, one collocated conference (CoNLL-2015), and a not yet known Lifetime Achievement Awardee's speech.

I am also grateful to our sponsors for their generous contributions. ACL-IJCNLP-2015 is supported by six Platinum Sponsors (CreditEase, Baidu, Tencent, Alibaba Group, SAMSUNG, and Microsoft), four Gold Sponsors (Google, Facebook, SinoVoice, and Huawei), three Silver Sponsors (Nuance, Amazon, and Sogou), one Bronze Sponsor (Yandex), one Oversea Student Fellowship Sponsor (Baobab), and one Best Paper Sponsor (IBM). I would express special thanks to Yiqun Liu (Local Sponsorship Chair) and all members of the International Sponsorship Committee (Ting Liu, Hideto Kazawa, Asli Celikyilmaz, Julia Hochenmaier, and Alessandro Moschitti).

Finally, I would like to thank two keynote speakers, the area chairs of the main conference, the workshop organizers, the tutorial presenters, the authors of main conference and demo papers, the reviewers for their contribution, and all the attendees for participation. I hope everyone have a great time and enjoy this conference.

ACL-IJCNLP 2015 General Chair
Yuji Matsumoto
Nara Institute of Science and Technology

Preface: Program Committee Co-Chairs

Welcome to the 53rd Annual Meeting of the Association for Computational Linguistics and the 7th International Joint Conference on Natural Language Processing of the Asian Federation of Natural Language Processing (ACL-IJCNLP)! This year ACL-IJCNLP received 692 long paper submissions and 648 short paper submissions which sets a new record for ACL for both long and short papers! We are pleased to observe that our community continues to grow. Of the long papers, 173 were accepted for presentation at ACL-IJCNLP – 105 as oral and 68 as poster presentations. 145 short papers were accepted – 50 as oral and 95 as poster presentations. In addition, ACL-IJCNLP also features 12 presentations of papers accepted in the Transactions of the Association for Computational Linguistics (TACL).

The submissions were reviewed under different categories and using different review forms for empirical/data-driven, theoretical, applications/tools, resources/evaluation, and survey papers. This year we introduced the item "MENTORING" to the review form to indicate whether a paper needs the help of a mentor in its writing, organization or presentation. For short papers, following up on last year's successful experiences, we also welcomed submissions describing negative results. We are glad to see that the community is becoming more open towards negative results so that such papers have the chance to be published, so that other researchers do not fall in the same trap.

We view posters as an integral part of ACL-IJCNLP. Half of the papers have been accepted as posters. Hence, we spent a great deal of time to ensure that the poster session will be a good experience for poster presenters and their audience. Following last year's exciting poster session, we also organized the posters in two large poster sessions to accommodate the high-quality submissions accepted in poster presentation format. We hope attendees and authors will benefit from this additional time to present and have more time to discuss with each other.

ACL-IJCNLP 2015 will have two distinguished invited speakers. Marti Hearst (professor at UC Berkeley in the School of Information and EECS) and Jiawei Han (Abel Bliss Professor at University of Illinois at Urbana-Champaign). We are grateful that they accepted our invitation.

There are many individuals to thank for their contributions to ACL-IJCNLP 2015. We would like to thank the 37 area chairs for their hard work on recruiting reviewers, leading the discussion process, and carefully ranking the submissions. We would also like to thank the 749 primary and the 137 secondary reviewers on whose efforts we depended to select high-quality and timely scientific work. This year we specifically acknowledge around 18.2% of the reviewers who went the extra mile and provided extremely helpful reviews (their names are marked with a * in the organization section of the proceedings). The ACL coordinating committee members, including Dragomir Radev, Graeme Hirst, Jian Su, and Gertjan van Noord were invaluable on various issues relating to the organization. We would like to thank the prior conference chairs Kristina Toutanova and Hua Wu and their predecessors for their advice. We are very grateful for the guidance and support of the general chair Yuji Matsumoto, to the ACL Business Manager Priscilla Rasmussen who knew practically everything, to the local chairs Le Sun and Yang Liu, the publication chairs Wanxiang Che and Guodong Zhou, and webmaster Zhiyuan Liu. We would also like to thank Jiajun Zhang who helped with reviewer assignment and numerous other tasks. Rich Gerber and Paolo Gai from Softconf were extremely responsive to all of our requests, and we are grateful for that.

We are indebted to the best paper award committee which consisted of Eneko Agirre, Tim Baldwin, Philipp Koehn, Joakim Nivre, and Yue Zhang. They read the candidate papers, ranked them and provided comments on a very short notice.

We hope you will enjoy ACL-IJCNLP 2015 in Beijing!

ACL-IJCNLP 2015 Program Co-Chairs
Chengqing Zong, Chinese Academy of Sciences
Michael Strube, Heidelberg Institute for Theoretical Studies

Organizing Committee

General Chair

Yuji Matsumoto, Nara Institute of Science and Technology

Program Committee Co-Chairs

Chengqing Zong, Institute of Automation, Chinese Academy of Sciences
Michael Strube, Heidelberg Institute for Theoretical Studies

Local Co-Chairs

Le Sun, Institute of Software, Chinese Academy of Sciences
Yang Liu, Tsinghua University

Workshop Co-Chairs

Hang Li, Huawei
Sebastian Riedel, University College London

Tutorial Co-Chairs

Kevin Duh, Nara Institute of Science and Technology
Eneko Agirre, University of the Basque Country

Publications Chairs

Wanxiang Che, Harbin Institute of Technology
Guodong Zhou, Suzhou University

Demonstration Co-Chairs

Hsin-Hsi Chen, National Taiwan University
Katja Markert, University of Leeds

Sponsorship Chair

Yiqun Liu, Tsinghua University

Publicity Co-Chairs

Xianpei Han, Institute of Software, Chinese Academy of Sciences
Kang Liu, Institute of Automation, Chinese Academy of Sciences

Student Research Workshop Faculty Advisors

Stephan Oepen, University of Oslo
Chin-Yew Lin, Microsoft Research Asia
Emily Bender, University of Washington

Student Co-Chairs (Student Research Workshop)

Kuan-Yu Chen, National Taiwan University
Angelina Ivanova, University of Oslo
Ellie Pavlick, University of Pennsylvania

Mentoring Chair

Francis Bond, Nanyang Technological University

Student Volunteer Co-Chairs

Erhong Yang, Beijing Language and Culture University
Dong Yu, Beijing Language and Culture University

Webmasters

Zhiyuan Liu, Tsinghua University
Qi Zhang, Fudan University

Entertainment Chair

Binyang Li, University of International Relations

Space Management Co-Chairs

Jiajun Zhang, Institute of Automation, Chinese Academy of Sciences
Wenbin Jiang, Institute of Computing Technology, Chinese Academy of Sciences
Qiuye Zhao, Institute of Computing Technology, Chinese Academy of Sciences

Graphic Design

Yi Han, Tsinghua University
Ying Lin, Beijing University of Posts and Telecommunications

Program Committee

Program Committee Co-Chairs

Chengqing Zong, Institute of Automation, Chinese Academy of Sciences
Michael Strube, Heidelberg Institute for Theoretical Studies

Area Chairs

Srinivas Bangalore, Interactions
Regina Barzilay, MIT
Steven Bethard, University of Alabama at Birmingham
Chris Biemann, TU Darmstadt
Razvan Bunescu, Ohio University
Pascal Denis, INRIA Lille
Mark Dras, Macquarie University
James Fan
Raquel Fernandez, University of Amsterdam
Jianfeng Gao, Microsoft Research
Julia Hirschberg, Columbia University
Fei Huang, Facebook
Mausam, IIT Dehli
Jing Jiang, Singapore Management University
John Kelleher, Dublin Institute of Technology
Jin-Dong Kim, Research Organization of Information and Systems
Greg Kondrak, University of Alberta
Zornitsa Kozareva, Yahoo! Labs
Lun-Wei Ku, Academia Sinica
Tom Kwiatkowski, Google Research
Mirella Lapata, University of Edinburgh
Shou-De Lin, National Taiwan University
Qin Lu, The Hong Kong Polytechnic University
Yusuke Miyao, National Institute of Informatics
Daichi Mochihashi, The Institute of Statistical Mathematics
Jian-Yun Nie, Université de Montréal
Alice Oh, KAIST
Rashmi Prasad, University of Wisconsin-Milwaukee
Marta Recasens, Google Research
David Schlangen, University of Bielefeld
Anders Søgaard, University of Copenhagen
Suzanne Stevenson, University of Toronto
Joel Tetreault, Yahoo! Labs
Xiaojun Wan, Peking University
Taro Watanabe, Google
Eric Xing, Carnegie Mellon University
Min Zhang, Soochow University

Primary Reviewers

Reviewers who are acknowledged by the program committee for providing one or more outstanding reviews are marked with "*".

Ahmed Abbasi, Omri Abend*, Stergos Afantenos, Eneko Agirre*, Željko Agić*, Cem Akkaya, Jan

Alexandersson, Enrique Alfonseca*, Afra Alishahi, Yiannis Aloimonos, David Alvarez-Melis*, Richard Andersson, Ion Androutsopoulos*, Gabor Angeli*, Yuki Arase*, Cedric Archambeau, Yasuo Ariki, Ron Artstein*, Yoav Artzi*, Nicholas Asher, Giuseppe Attardi, Michael Auli, AiTi Aw, Necip Fazil Ayan

Olga Babko-Malaya, JinYeong Bak, Niranjan Balasubramanian, Timothy Baldwin*, Miguel Ballesteros, David Bamman, Carmen Banea, Srinivas Bangalore, Mohit Bansal, Ken Barker, Marco Baroni, Loïc Barrault, Regina Barzilay, Roberto Basili, Timo Baumann, Frederic Bechet, Barend Beekhuizen*, Núria Bel, Anja Belz, Jose Miguel Benedi, Jonathan Berant, Taylor Berg-Kirkpatrick, Steven Bethard, Suma Bhat*, Archna Bhatia*, Klinton Bicknell, Chris Biemann, Anders Björkelund*, Alan W Black, Nate Blaylock, John Blitzer, Bernd Bohnet, Dan Bohus*, Ondrej Bojar, Gemma Boleda*, Kalina Bontcheva, Antoine Bordes, Mihaela Bornea, Johan Bos, Alexandre Bouchard, Johan Boye, Kristy Boyer, S.R.K. Branavan, António Branco, Chris Brew, Ted Briscoe, Chris Brockett*, Julian Brooke, Eric Brown, Elia Bruni, Paul Buitelaar, Razvan Bunescu, Harry Bunt, Jill Burstein, Miriam Butt

Elena Cabrio, Aoife Cahill*, Nicoletta Calzolari, Erik Cambria, Marie Candito, Yunbo Cao, Xavier Carreras*, Tommaso Caselli, Taylor Cassidy, Vittorio Castelli, Asli Celikyilmaz, Daniel Cer, Christophe Cerisara, Nathanael Chambers*, Yee Seng Chan, Yi Chang, Wanxiang Che, Boxing Chen, Chen Chen, Wenliang Chen, Colin Cherry*, David Chiang, Christian Chiarcos, Laura Chiticariu*, Eunsol Choi, Jinho D. Choi, Key-Sun Choi, Yejin Choi, Monojit Choudhury, Munmun De Choudhury, Grzegorz Chrupała, Jennifer Chu-Carroll, Cindy Chung, Alexander Clark, Stephen Clark, Ann Clifton, Moreno Coco*, Shay B. Cohen, Trevor Cohn, Nigel Collier, Gao Cong, Miriam Connor, John Conroy, Paul Cook*, Bonaventura Coppola, Anna Corazza, Mark Core, Marta R. Costa-jussà, Danilo Croce, Paul Crook, Tim Van De Cruys, Xiaodong Cui

Robert Daland*, Bharath Dandala, Kareem Darwish, Dipanjan Das, Thierry Declerck, Estelle Delpech, Vera Demberg, John DeNero, Pascal Denis, Leon Derczynski, David DeVault*, Jacob Devlin, Mona Diab, Marco Dinarelli, Georgiana Dinu, Stefanie Dipper, Dmitriy Dligach, Simon Dobnik*, Bill Dolan, Mathew Magimai Doss, Doug Downey, Mark Dras, Mark Dredze*, Markus Dreyer, Gregory Druck*, Lan Du, Xiangyu Duan, Ewan Dunbar*, Benjamin Van Durme*, Greg Durrett*, Chris Dyer

Matthias Eck, Jens Edlund, Koji Eguchi, Yo Ehara*, Patrick Ehlen, Vladimir Eidelman, Jacob Eisenstein, Michael Elhadad*, Desmond Elliott, Klaus-Peter Engelbrecht, Erkut Erdem*, Katrin Erk*, Maxine Eskenazi

Giuseppe Di Fabbrizio, Anthony Fader*, James Fan, Benoit Favre*, Anna Feldman, Naomi Feldman, Raquel Fernandez, Katja Filippova, Nicholas FitzGerald, Darja Fišer, Margaret Fleck, Radu Florian, Antske Fokkens*, David Forsyth, Karën Fort, George Foster, Jennifer Foster, James Foulds*, Stella Frank, Alexander Fraser, Dayne Freitag*, Guohong Fu

Michel Galley, Michael Gamon*, Kuzman Ganchev, Juri Ganitkevitch, Jianfeng Gao, Qin Gao, Wei Gao, Yue Gao, Claire Gardent, Albert Gatt*, Maria Gavrilidou, Kallirroi Georgila*, Daniel Gildea, Alastair Gill, Jennifer Gillenwater*, Kevin Gimpel*, Filip Ginter, Roxana Girju, Adrià De Gispert, Alfio Gliozzo, Amir Globerson, Yoav Goldberg, Dan Goldwasser, Matthew R. Gormley, Cyril Goutte, Amit Goyal, Joao Graca, Brigitte Grau, Agustin Gravano, Edouard Grave*, Spence Green, Edward Grefenstette, Gregory Grefenstette, Ralph Grishman, Marco Guerini, Curry Guinn*, Weiwei Guo, Yuhong Guo, Rahul Gupta*, Sonal Gupta, Carlos Gómez-Rodríguez*

Ben Hachey, Barry Haddow, Gholamreza Haffari, Hannaneh Hajishirzi, Dilek Hakkani-Tur, John Hale, David Hall, Keith Hall, Bo Han, Xianpei Han, Mark Hasegawa-Johnson*, Hany Hassan, Kenneth Heafield*, Peter Heeman, Ulrich Heid, James Henderson, John Henderson, Karl Moritz Hermann, Tsutomu Hirao, Keikichi Hirose, Julia Hirschberg, Graeme Hirst, Anna Hjalmarsson, Hieu Hoang, Julia Hockenmaier, Johannes Hoffart, Veronique Hoste, Dirk Hovy*, Yuening Hu, Fei Huang (Facebook), Fei Huang (Temple University), Liang Huang, Ruihong Huang, Xuanjing

Huang, Zhongqiang Huang, Mans Hulden, Gerhard Van Huyssteen, Rebecca Hwa*, Young-Sook Hwang

Nancy Ide, Ryu Iida, Hal Daumé III*, Shajith Ikbal, Iustina Ilisei, Diana Inkpen, Kentaro Inui, Hitoshi Isahara, Abe Ittycheriah, Mohit Iyyer

Jagadeesh Jagarlamudi, Yacine Jernite, Rahul Jha, Heng Ji, Yangfeng Ji, Jing Jiang, Richard Johansson*, Mark Johnson, Michael Johnston, Kristiina Jokinen, Arne Jonsson, Shafiq Joty

Kyo Kageura, Min-Yen Kan*, Pallika Kanani, Daisuke Kawahara, Tatsuya Kawahara, Hideto Kazawa, Simon Keizer, John Kelleher, Frank Keller*, Emre Kiciman, Bernd Kiefer, Dongwoo Kim, Jin-Dong Kim, Seungyeon Kim, Su Nam Kim, Suin Kim, Tracy Holloway King, Brian Kingsbury, Kevin Knight, Alistair Knott, Philipp Koehn, Oleksandr Kolomiyets, Mamoru Komachi, Kazunori Komatani, Grzegorz Kondrak, Stefan Kopp, Parisa Kordjamshidi, Valia Kordoni, Anna Korhonen, Milen Kouylekov*, Zornitsa Kozareva, Emiel Krahmer, Jayant Krishnamurthy, Lun-Wei Ku*, Marco Kuhlmann, Roland Kuhn*, Tsung-Ting Kuo, Nate Kushman*, Polina Kuznetsova, Tom Kwiatkowski, Sandra Kübler

Wai Lam, Patrik Lambert, Guy Lapalme, Mirella Lapata, Shalom Lappin, Dominique Laurent, Alan Lee, Kenton Lee, Sungjin Lee, Yoong Keok Lee, Young-Suk Lee, Els Lefever, Fabrice Lefevre, Tao Lei, Alessandro Lenci, James Lester, Rivka Levitan, Gina-Anne Levow, Omer Levy*, Mike Lewis, Cheng-Te Li, Haibo Li, Hang Li, Jiwei Li, Lishuang Li, Mu Li, Qi Li*, Shoushan Li, Tao Li, Wenjie Li, Zhenghua Li, Chin-Yew Lin*, Shou-de Lin, Keith Vander Linden, Bing Liu, Fei Liu, Jing Liu, Kang Liu, Lemao Liu, Qun Liu, Ting Liu, Xiaohua Liu, Yang Liu (University Of Texas At Dallas), Yang Liu (Tsinghua University), Yiqun Liu, Zhanyi Liu, Zhiyuan Liu, Annie Louis, Wei Lu, Marco Lui, Xiaoqiang Luo, Franco M. Luque, Yajuan Lv

Klaus Macherey, Wolfgang Macherey, Nitin Madnani*, Daniel Marcu*, Marco Marelli, Anna Margolis, Joseph Mariani, Marie-Catherine De Marneffe, Erwin Marsi, Toni Marti, James H. Martin, Scott Martin*, André F. T. Martins, Vivien Mast*, Yuji Matsumoto, Takuya Matsuzaki, Mausam, Arne Mauser, Jonathan May*, David McClosky, Kathy McCoy*, Ryan McDonald, Tara McIntosh, Kathy McKeown, Susan McRoy, Alexander Mehler, Edgar Meij, Yelena Mejova, Gerard De Melo, Arul Menezes, Helen Meng, Florian Metze, Christian M. Meyer*, Adam Meyers, Haitao Mi, Rada Mihalcea, Timothy Miller*, Tristan Miller*, Bonan Min, Wolfgang Minker, Margaret Mitchell, Yusuke Miyao, Daichi Mochihashi, Marie-Francine Moens, Saif Mohammad, Karo Moilanen, Christian Monson, Manuel Montes, Christof Monz, Robert Moore, Roser Morante, Andrea Moro, Alessandro Moschitti, Arjun Mukherjee*, Philippe Muller*, Yugo Murawaki*, Smaranda Muresan

Seiichi Nakagawa, Mikio Nakano, Ndapandula Nakashole, Preslav Nakov, Jason Naradowsky*, Karthik Narasimhan, Shashi Narayan, Tahira Naseem, Vivi Nastase, Borja Navarro, Roberto Navigli, Mark-Jan Nederhof, Matteo Negri, Aida Nematzadeh, Ani Nenkova*, Graham Neubig*, Hwee Tou Ng, Vincent Ng, Dong Nguyen, Truc-Vien T. Nguyen, Viet-An Nguyen, Jian-Yun NIE, Joakim Nivre, Scott Nowson

Douglas O'Shaughnessy, Douglas Oard*, Stephan Oepen, Kemal Oflazer, Alice Oh, Jong-Hoon Oh, Naoaki Okazaki, Manabu Okumura, Constantin Orasan, Miles Osborne, Petya Osenova, Mari Ostendorf, Ekaterina Ovchinnikova

Ulrike Pado, John Paisley, Alexis Palmer, Martha Palmer*, Patrick Pantel, Aasish Pappu, Ankur P. Parikh, Cecile Paris, Souneil Park, Patrick Paroubek, Kristen Parton, Marius Pasca, Katerina Pastra*, Siddharth Patwardhan, Michael J. Paul, Adam Pauls, Bolette Pedersen, Edgar Gonzàlez Pellicer, Marco Pennacchiotti, Wim Peters, Slav Petrov, Anselmo Peñas, Maciej Piasecki, Olivier Pietquin, Juan Pino, Yuval Pinter*, Emily Pitler, Paul Piwek, Barbara Plank, Massimo Poesio, Simone Paolo Ponzetto, Hoifung Poon, Fred Popowich*, Christopher Potts*, Sameer Pradhan, Rashmi Prasad, Daniel Preoţiuc-Pietro, Emily Prud'hommeaux, Adam Przepiórkowski, Laurent Prévot, Stephen Pulman, Matthew Purver*, Sampo Pyysalo*, Verónica Pérez-Rosas

Guojun Qi, Xian Qian, Lu Qin, Xipeng Qiu, Ariadna Quattoni

Stephan Raaijmakers, Altaf Rahman, Jonathan Raiman, Ganesh Ramakrishnan, Owen Rambow, Ari Rappoport, Antoine Raux*, Sujith Ravi*, Marta Recasens, Siva Reddy, Sravana Reddy*, Roi Reichart, Joseph Reisinger, Ehud Reiter, Norbert Reithinger, David Reitter, Steffen Remus, Matthew Richardson, Sebastian Riedel, Martin Riedl*, German Rigau, Laura Rimell*, Alan Ritter, Brian Roark*, Andrew Rosenberg, Robert Ross, Paolo Rosso, Michael Roth, Joseph Le Roux, Alla Rozovskaya*, Frank Rudzicz, Alexander M. Rush, Christopher Ré

Mrinmaya Sachan, Markus Saers*, Kenji Sagae, Saurav Sahay, Patrick Saint-dizier, Murat Saraclar, Felix Sasaki, Roser Saurí, David Schlangen, Helmut Schmid, Nathan Schneider*, William Schuler*, Lane Schwartz*, Roy Schwartz*, Holger Schwenk, Djamé Seddah*, Frederique Segond, Satoshi Sekine, Pavel Serdyukov, Violeta Seretan*, Hendra Setiawan*, Serge Sharoff, Shuming Shi, Xiaodong Shi, Hiroyuki Shindo, Szymon Sidor, Avirup Sil, Fabrizio Silvestri, Yanchuan Sim, Khalil Sima'an, Sameer Singh, Gabriel Skantze, Ielka Van Der Sluis, Kevin Small*, Alan Smeaton, Noah A. Smith*, Richard Socher, Stephen Soderland, Eduardo Lleida Solano, Thamar Solorio*, Sa-kwang Song, Lucia Specia, Caroline Sporleder*, Rachele Sprugnoli, Vivek Srikumar, Edward Stabler, Maria Staudte, Georg Stemmer, Suzanne Stevenson, Svetlana Stoyanchev*, Veselin Stoyanov, Keh-Yih Su*, L V Subramaniam, Ke SUN, Le Sun, Weiwei Sun, Xu Sun, Mihai Surdeanu, Jun Suzuki*, Marc Swerts*, Stan Szpakowicz, Idan Szpektor, Diarmuid Ó Séaghdha, Anders Søgaard

Marko Tadić, Hiroya Takamura, Partha P. Talukdar, Akihiro Tamura, Kumiko Tanaka-Ishii, Joel Tetreault, Kapil Thadani, Ran Tian, Jörg Tiedemann, Christoph Tillmann, Ivan Titov, Takenobu Tokunaga*, Sara Tonelli, Kentaro Torisawa*, Kristina Toutanova, Isabel Trancoso, David Traum*, Richard Tzong-Han Tsai, Reut Tsarfaty, Masashi Tsubaki, Oren Tsur, Yoshimasa Tsuruoka, Oscar Täckström

Olga Uryupina, Masao Utiyama

Lucy Vanderwende*, Ashish Vaswani, Eva Maria Vecchi, Paola Velardi, Marc Verhagen, Yannick Versley*, Renata Vieira, Laure Vieu, David Vilar, Aline Villavicencio*, Andreas Vlachos, Svitlana Volkova, Piek Vossen

Michael Walsh, Stephen Wan, Xiaojun Wan, Bin Wang, Chong Wang, Haifeng Wang, Hongning Wang, Hsin-Min Wang, Jun Wang, Lu Wang, Leo Wanner, Nigel Ward, Taro Watanabe, Bonnie Webber, Ingmar Weber, Furu Wei, Gerhard Weikum, Michael White*, Janyce Wiebe*, Jason D Williams*, Theresa Wilson, Shuly Wintner, Derek F. Wong, Kristian Woodsend, Hua Wu, Joern Wuebker*

Fei Xia, Bing Xiang, Tong Xiao, Pengtao Xie, Eric Xing, Deyi Xiong, Ruifeng Xu*, Wei Xu, Ying Xu

Bishan Yang, Charles Yang, Muyun Yang, Yi Yang*, Xuchen Yao, Mark Yatskar, Xing Yi, Wentau Yih, Anssi Yli-Jyrä, Dani Yogatama, Steve Young, Bei Yu, Liang-Chih Yu, Nicholas Yuan, François Yvon

David Zajic*, Alessandra Zarcone, Xiaodong Zeng, Torsten Zesch, Luke Zettlemoyer, Deniz Zeyrek, Congle Zhang*, Dongdong Zhang, Hao Zhang, Jiajun Zhang*, Joy Ying Zhang, Min Zhang, Qi Zhang, Yu Zhang, Yuan Zhang, Yue Zhang, Zhe Zhang, Dongyan Zhao, Jun Zhao, Shiqi Zhao, Tiejun Zhao, Yanyan Zhao, Bowen Zhou, Guangyou Zhou, Ming Zhou, Yu Zhou, Jingbo Zhu, Jun Zhu

Secondary Reviewers

Nitish Aggarwal, Zejlko Agic, Henry Anaya-Sanchez, Héctor Martínez Alonso, Shunsuke Aoki, Kartik Asooja, Isabelle Augenstein, Wilker Aziz

Gianni Barlacchi, Lisa Beinborn, Adrian Benton, Georgeta Bordea, Fethi Bougares, Tim vor der Brück

Ming-Lun Cai, Hailong Cao, Houwei Cao, Giuseppe Castellucci, Kehai Chen, Xiao Chen, Edgar Chávez, James Cross, Lei Cui

Dezhong Deng, Aliya Deri, Anton Dil, Xiao Ding, Li Dong, Qing Dou, Avinava Dubey

Bradley Ellert, Aykut Erdem

Yang Feng, Francis Ferraro, Tiziano Flati, Marc Franco-Salvador

Michael Glass, Martin Gleize, Genevieve Gorrell, James Gung, Jiang Guo, Parth Gupta

Patrick Haffner, Wei He, Zhongjun He, Daniel Hershcovich, Cong Duy Vu Hoang, Hao Hu

Ruben Izquierdo

Anders Johannsen

Savvas Karagiannidis, Ghazaleh Kazeminejad, Daniel Khashabi, Jooyeon Kim, Wu Kui, Mikael Kågebäck

Oier Lopez de Lacalle, Gianluca Lebani, Chen Li, Jing Li, Peng Li, Rui Li, Sujian Li, Jianxun Lian, Anne-Laure Ligozat, Chen Lin, Xiao Ling, Alessandro Lopopolo, Michal Lukasik, Andy Lücking

Wei-Yun Ma, Todor Milanov

Steven Neale, Massimo Nicosia, Hiroshi Noji

Tim O'Gorman, Lydia Odilinye, Alexander Ororbia

Umashanthi Pavalanathan, Benjamin Piwowarski

Preethi Raghavan, Balamurali ANDIYAKKAL RAJENDRAN, Pushpendre Rastogi, Alex Ratner, Paul Reisert, Marco Tulio Ribeiro

Benoit Sagot, Christer Samuelsson, Fernando Sanchez Vega, Maarten Sap, Daniele Sartiano, Aliaksei Severyn, Lifeng Shang, Huaxing Shi, Parinaz Sobhani, Sanja Stajner, Jinsong Su, Elior Sulem

Kaveh Taghipour, Zhixing Tan, Irina Temnikova, Milan Tofiloski, Marco Del Tredici, William Trimble, Marco del Tredici

Jorrig Vogels, Greg Vorsanger, Hoang Cong Duy Vu

Baoxun Wang, Longyue Wang, Quan Wang, Xuancong Wang, Yingzi Wang, Zhongyu Wei, Travis Wolfe, Shumin Wu

Rui Xia, Xinyan Xiao, Wang Xuancong

Mo Yu

Jia Zeng, Ke Zhai, Ce Zhang, Chunyue Zhang, Meng Zhang, Muyu Zhang, Renxian Zhang, Xi Zhang, Xiaojun Zhang, Kai Zhao, Kaiqi Zhao, Zhou Zhao, Junguo Zhu, Xiaoning Zhu

Invited Talk: Can Natural Language Processing Become Natural LanguageCoaching?

Marti A. Hearst

School of Information and EECS, UC Berkeley

Abstract

How we teach and learn is undergoing a revolution, due to changes in technology and connectivity. Education may be one of the best application areas for advanced NLP techniques, and NLP researchers have much to contribute to this problem, especially in the areas of learning to write, mastery learning, and peer learning. In this talk I consider what happens when we convert natural language processors into natural language coaches.

Biography

Marti Hearst is a Professor at UC Berkeley in the School of Information and EECS. She received her PhD in CS from UC Berkeley in 1994 and was a member of the research staff at Xerox PARC form 1994-1997. Her research is in computational linguistics, search user interfaces, information visualization, and improving learning at scale. Her NLP work includes automatic acquisition of hypernym relations ("Hearst Patterns"), TextTiling discourse segmentation, abbreviation recognition, and multiword semantic relations. She wrote the book "Search User Interfaces" (Cambridge) in 2009, co-founded the ACM Conference on Learning at Scale in 2014, and was named an ACM Fellow in 2013. She has received four student-initiated Excellence in Teaching Awards, including in 2014 and 2015.

Invited Talk: Construction and Mining of Heterogeneous Information Networks from Text Data

Jiawei Han

Department of Computer Science, University of Illinois at Urbana-Champaign

Abstract

The real-world data are unstructured but interconnected. The majority of such data is in the form of natural language text. One of the grand challenges is to turn such massive data into actionable knowledge. In this talk, we present our vision on how to turn massive unstructured, text-rich, but interconnected data into knowledge. We propose a data-to-network-to-knowledge (i.e., D2N2K) paradigm, which is to first turn data into relatively structured heterogeneous information networks, and then mine such text-rich and structure-rich heterogeneous networks to generate useful knowledge. We show why such a paradigm represents a promising direction and present some recent progress on the development of effective methods for construction and mining of structured heterogeneous information networks from text data.

Biography

Jiawei Han is Abel Bliss Professor in the Department of Computer Science, University of Illinois at Urbana-Champaign. He has been researching into data mining, information network analysis, database systems, and data warehousing, with over 600 journal and conference publications. He has chaired or served on many program committees of international conferences, including PC co-chair for KDD, SDM, and ICDM conferences, and Americas Coordinator for VLDB conferences. He also served as the founding Editor-In-Chief of ACM Transactions on Knowledge Discovery from Data and is serving as the Director of Information Network Academic Research Center supported by U.S. Army Research Lab, and Director of KnowEnG, an NIH funded Center of Excellence in Big Data Computing. He is a Fellow of ACM and Fellow of IEEE, and received 2004 ACM SIGKDD Innovations Award, 2005 IEEE Computer Society Technical Achievement Award, 2009 IEEE Computer Society Wallace McDowell Award, and 2011 Daniel C. Drucker Eminent Faculty Award at UIUC. His co-authored book "Data Mining: Concepts and Techniques" has been adopted as a textbook popularly worldwide.

Table of Contents

On Using Very Large Target Vocabulary for Neural Machine Translation
Sébastien Jean, Kyunghyun Cho, Roland Memisevic and Yoshua Bengio 1

Addressing the Rare Word Problem in Neural Machine Translation
Thang Luong, Ilya Sutskever, Quoc Le, Oriol Vinyals and Wojciech Zaremba 11

Encoding Source Language with Convolutional Neural Network for Machine Translation
Fandong Meng, Zhengdong Lu, Mingxuan Wang, Hang Li, Wenbin Jiang and Qun Liu 20

Statistical Machine Translation Features with Multitask Tensor Networks
Hendra Setiawan, Zhongqiang Huang, Jacob Devlin, Thomas Lamar, Rabih Zbib, Richard Schwartz and John Makhoul 31

Describing Images using Inferred Visual Dependency Representations
Desmond Elliott and Arjen de Vries 42

Text to 3D Scene Generation with Rich Lexical Grounding
Angel Chang, Will Monroe, Manolis Savva, Christopher Potts and Christopher D. Manning 53

MultiGranCNN: An Architecture for General Matching of Text Chunks on Multiple Levels of Granularity
Wenpeng Yin and Hinrich Schütze 63

Weakly Supervised Models of Aspect-Sentiment for Online Course Discussion Forums
Arti Ramesh, Shachi H. Kumar, James Foulds and Lise Getoor 74

Semantically Smooth Knowledge Graph Embedding
Shu Guo, Quan Wang, Bin Wang, Lihong Wang and Li Guo 84

SensEmbed: Learning Sense Embeddings for Word and Relational Similarity
Ignacio Iacobacci, Mohammad Taher Pilehvar and Roberto Navigli 95

Revisiting Word Embedding for Contrasting Meaning
Zhigang Chen, Wei Lin, Qian Chen, Xiaoping Chen, Si Wei, Hui Jiang and Xiaodan Zhu 106

Joint Models of Disagreement and Stance in Online Debate
Dhanya Sridhar, James Foulds, Bert Huang, Lise Getoor and Marilyn Walker 116

Low-Rank Regularization for Sparse Conjunctive Feature Spaces: An Application to Named Entity Classification
Audi Primadhanty, Xavier Carreras and Ariadna Quattoni 126

Learning Word Representations by Jointly Modeling Syntagmatic and Paradigmatic Relations
Fei Sun, Jiafeng Guo, Yanyan Lan, Jun Xu and Xueqi Cheng 136

Learning Dynamic Feature Selection for Fast Sequential Prediction
Emma Strubell, Luke Vilnis, Kate Silverstein and Andrew McCallum 146

Compositional Vector Space Models for Knowledge Base Completion
Arvind Neelakantan, Benjamin Roth and Andrew McCallum 156

Event Extraction via Dynamic Multi-Pooling Convolutional Neural Networks
Yubo Chen, Liheng Xu, Kang Liu, Daojian Zeng and Jun Zhao 167

Stacked Ensembles of Information Extractors for Knowledge-Base Population
Vidhoon Viswanathan, Nazneen Fatema Rajani, Yinon Bentor and Raymond Mooney 177

Generative Event Schema Induction with Entity Disambiguation
Kiem-Hieu Nguyen, Xavier Tannier, Olivier Ferret and Romaric Besançon 188

Syntax-based Simultaneous Translation through Prediction of Unseen Syntactic Constituents
Yusuke Oda, Graham Neubig, Sakriani Sakti, Tomoki Toda and Satoshi Nakamura 198

Efficient Top-Down BTG Parsing for Machine Translation Preordering
Tetsuji Nakagawa 208

Online Multitask Learning for Machine Translation Quality Estimation
José G. C. de Souza, Matteo Negri, Elisa Ricci and Marco Turchi 219

A Context-Aware Topic Model for Statistical Machine Translation
Jinsong Su, Deyi Xiong, Yang Liu, Xianpei Han, Hongyu Lin, Junfeng Yao and Min Zhang . . . 229

Learning Answer-Entailing Structures for Machine Comprehension
Mrinmaya Sachan, Kumar Dubey, Eric Xing and Matthew Richardson 239

Learning Continuous Word Embedding with Metadata for Question Retrieval in Community Question Answering
Guangyou Zhou, Tingting He, Jun Zhao and Po Hu 250

Question Answering over Freebase with Multi-Column Convolutional Neural Networks
Li Dong, Furu Wei, Ming Zhou and Ke Xu 260

Hubness and Pollution: Delving into Cross-Space Mapping for Zero-Shot Learning
Angeliki Lazaridou, Georgiana Dinu and Marco Baroni 270

A Generalisation of Lexical Functions for Composition in Distributional Semantics
Antoine Bride, Tim Van de Cruys and Nicholas Asher 281

Simple Learning and Compositional Application of Perceptually Grounded Word Meanings for Incremental Reference Resolution
Casey Kennington and David Schlangen 292

Neural CRF Parsing
Greg Durrett and Dan Klein 302

An Effective Neural Network Model for Graph-based Dependency Parsing
Wenzhe Pei, Tao Ge and Baobao Chang 313

Structured Training for Neural Network Transition-Based Parsing
David Weiss, Chris Alberti, Michael Collins and Slav Petrov 323

Transition-Based Dependency Parsing with Stack Long Short-Term Memory
Chris Dyer, Miguel Ballesteros, Wang Ling, Austin Matthews and Noah A. Smith 334

Leveraging Linguistic Structure For Open Domain Information Extraction
Gabor Angeli, Melvin Jose Johnson Premkumar and Christopher D. Manning 344

Joint Information Extraction and Reasoning: A Scalable Statistical Relational Learning Approach
William Yang Wang and William W Cohen 355

A Knowledge-Intensive Model for Prepositional Phrase Attachment
Ndapandula Nakashole and Tom M. Mitchell 365

A Convolution Kernel Approach to Identifying Comparisons in Text
Maksim Tkachenko and Hady Lauw 376

It Depends: Dependency Parser Comparison Using A Web-based Evaluation Tool
Jinho D. Choi, Joel Tetreault and Amanda Stent 387

Generating High Quality Proposition Banks for Multilingual Semantic Role Labeling
Alan Akbik, laura chiticariu, Marina Danilevsky, Yunyao Li, Shivakumar Vaithyanathan and Huaiyu Zhu 397

Aligning Opinions: Cross-Lingual Opinion Mining with Dependencies
Mariana S. C. Almeida, Claudia Pinto, Helena Figueira, Pedro Mendes and André F. T. Martins 408

Learning to Adapt Credible Knowledge in Cross-lingual Sentiment Analysis
Qiang Chen, Wenjie Li, Yu Lei, Xule Liu and Yanxiang He 419

Learning Bilingual Sentiment Word Embeddings for Cross-language Sentiment Classification
HuiWei Zhou, Long Chen, Fulin Shi and Degen Huang 430

Content Models for Survey Generation: A Factoid-Based Evaluation
Rahul Jha, Catherine Finegan-Dollak, Ben King, Reed Coke and Dragomir Radev 441

Training a Natural Language Generator From Unaligned Data
Ondřej Dušek and Filip Jurcicek 451

Event-Driven Headline Generation
Rui Sun, Yue Zhang, Meishan Zhang and Donghong Ji 462

New Transfer Learning Techniques for Disparate Label Sets
Young-Bum Kim, Karl Stratos, Ruhi Sarikaya and Minwoo Jeong 473

Matrix Factorization with Knowledge Graph Propagation for Unsupervised Spoken Language Understanding
Yun-Nung Chen, William Yang Wang, Anatole Gershman and Alexander Rudnicky 483

Efficient Disfluency Detection with Transition-based Parsing
Shuangzhi Wu, Dongdong Zhang, Ming Zhou and Tiejun Zhao 495

S-MART: Novel Tree-based Structured Learning Algorithms Applied to Tweet Entity Linking
Yi Yang and Ming-Wei Chang 504

Entity Retrieval via Entity Factoid Hierarchy
Chunliang Lu, Wai Lam and Yi Liao 514

Encoding Distributional Semantics into Triple-Based Knowledge Ranking for Document Enrichment
Muyu Zhang, Bing Qin, Mao Zheng, Graeme Hirst and Ting Liu 524

A Strategic Reasoning Model for Generating Alternative Answers
Jon Stevens, Anton Benz, Sebastian Reuße and Ralf Klabunde 534

Modeling Argument Strength in Student Essays
Isaac Persing and Vincent Ng 543

Summarization of Multi-Document Topic Hierarchies using Submodular Mixtures
Ramakrishna Bairi, Rishabh Iyer, Ganesh Ramakrishnan and Jeff Bilmes 553

Learning to Explain Entity Relationships in Knowledge Graphs
Nikos Voskarides, Edgar Meij, Manos Tsagkias, Maarten de Rijke and Wouter Weerkamp 564

Bring you to the past: Automatic Generation of Topically Relevant Event Chronicles
Tao Ge, Wenzhe Pei, Heng Ji, Sujian Li, Baobao Chang and Zhifang Sui 575

Context-aware Entity Morph Decoding
Boliang Zhang, Hongzhao Huang, Xiaoman Pan, Sujian Li, Chin-Yew Lin, Heng Ji, Kevin Knight, Zhen Wen, Yizhou Sun, Jiawei Han and Bulent Yener 586

Multi-Objective Optimization for the Joint Disambiguation of Nouns and Named Entities
Dirk Weissenborn, Leonhard Hennig, Feiyu Xu and Hans Uszkoreit 596

Building a Scientific Concept Hierarchy Database (SCHBase)
Eytan Adar and Srayan Datta 606

Sentiment-Aspect Extraction based on Restricted Boltzmann Machines
Linlin Wang, Kang Liu, Zhu Cao, Jun Zhao and Gerard de Melo 616

Classifying Relations by Ranking with Convolutional Neural Networks
Cicero dos Santos, Bing Xiang and Bowen Zhou 626

Semantic Representations for Domain Adaptation: A Case Study on the Tree Kernel-based Method for Relation Extraction
Thien Huu Nguyen, Barbara Plank and Ralph Grishman 635

Omnia Mutantur, Nihil Interit: Connecting Past with Present by Finding Corresponding Terms across Time
Yating Zhang, Adam Jatowt, Sourav Bhowmick and Katsumi Tanaka 645

Negation and Speculation Identification in Chinese Language
Bowei Zou, Qiaoming Zhu and Guodong Zhou 656

Learning Relational Features with Backward Random Walks
Ni Lao, Einat Minkov and William Cohen 666

Learning the Semantics of Manipulation Action
Yezhou Yang, Yiannis Aloimonos, Cornelia Fermuller and Eren Erdal Aksoy 676

Knowledge Graph Embedding via Dynamic Mapping Matrix
Guoliang Ji, Shizhu He, Liheng Xu, Kang Liu and Jun Zhao 687

How Far are We from Fully Automatic High Quality Grammatical Error Correction?
Christopher Bryant and Hwee Tou Ng 697

Knowledge Portability with Semantic Expansion of Ontology Labels
Mihael Arcan, Marco Turchi and Paul Buitelaar 708

Automatic disambiguation of English puns
Tristan Miller and Iryna Gurevych 719

Unsupervised Cross-Domain Word Representation Learning
Danushka Bollegala, Takanori Maehara and Ken-ichi Kawarabayashi 730

A Unified Multilingual Semantic Representation of Concepts
José Camacho-Collados, Mohammad Taher Pilehvar and Roberto Navigli 741

Demographic Factors Improve Classification Performance
Dirk Hovy 752

Vector-space calculation of semantic surprisal for predicting word pronunciation duration
Asad Sayeed, Stefan Fischer and Vera Demberg 763

Efficient Methods for Inferring Large Sparse Topic Hierarchies
Doug Downey, Chandra Bhagavatula and Yi Yang 774

Trans-dimensional Random Fields for Language Modeling
Bin Wang, Zhijian Ou and Zhiqiang Tan 785

Gaussian LDA for Topic Models with Word Embeddings
Rajarshi Das, Manzil Zaheer and Chris Dyer 795

Pairwise Neural Machine Translation Evaluation
Francisco Guzmán, Shafiq Joty, Lluís Màrquez and Preslav Nakov......................... 805

String-to-Tree Multi Bottom-up Tree Transducers
Nina Seemann, Fabienne Braune and Andreas Maletti 815

Non-linear Learning for Statistical Machine Translation
Shujian Huang, Huadong Chen, Xin-Yu Dai and Jiajun Chen.............................. 825

Unifying Bayesian Inference and Vector Space Models for Improved Decipherment
Qing Dou, Ashish Vaswani, Kevin Knight and Chris Dyer 836

Non-projective Dependency-based Pre-Reordering with Recurrent Neural Network for Machine Translation
Antonio Valerio Miceli Barone and Giuseppe Attardi.................................... 846

Detecting Deceptive Groups Using Conversations and Network Analysis
Dian Yu, Yulia Tyshchuk, Heng Ji and William Wallace 857

WikiKreator: Improving Wikipedia Stubs Automatically
Siddhartha Banerjee and Prasenjit Mitra 867

Language to Code: Learning Semantic Parsers for If-This-Then-That Recipes
Chris Quirk, Raymond Mooney and Michel Galley.. 878

Deep Questions without Deep Understanding
Igor Labutov, Sumit Basu and Lucy Vanderwende... 889

The NL2KR Platform for building Natural Language Translation Systems
Nguyen Vo, Arindam Mitra and Chitta Baral 899

Multiple Many-to-Many Sequence Alignment for Combining String-Valued Variables: A G2P Experiment
Steffen Eger... 909

Tweet Normalization with Syllables
Ke Xu, Yunqing Xia and Chin-Hui Lee 920

Improving Named Entity Recognition in Tweets via Detecting Non-Standard Words
Chen Li and Yang Liu 929

A Unified Kernel Approach for Learning Typed Sentence Rewritings
Martin Gleize and Brigitte Grau 939

Perceptually Grounded Selectional Preferences
Ekaterina Shutova, Niket Tandon and Gerard de Melo 950

Joint Case Argument Identification for Japanese Predicate Argument Structure Analysis
Hiroki Ouchi, Hiroyuki Shindo, Kevin Duh and Yuji Matsumoto 961

Jointly optimizing word representations for lexical and sentential tasks with the C-PHRASE model
Nghia The Pham, Germán Kruszewski, Angeliki Lazaridou and Marco Baroni 971

Robust Subgraph Generation Improves Abstract Meaning Representation Parsing
Keenon Werling, Gabor Angeli and Christopher D. Manning 982

Environment-Driven Lexicon Induction for High-Level Instructions
Dipendra Kumar Misra, Kejia Tao, Percy Liang and Ashutosh Saxena 992

Structural Representations for Learning Relations between Pairs of Texts
Simone Filice, Giovanni Da San Martino and Alessandro Moschitti 1003

Learning Semantic Representations of Users and Products for Document Level Sentiment Classification
Duyu Tang, Bing Qin and Ting Liu 1014

Towards Debugging Sentiment Lexicons
Andrew Schneider and Eduard Dragut 1024

Sparse, Contextually Informed Models for Irony Detection: Exploiting User Communities, Entities and Sentiment
Byron C. Wallace, Do Kook Choe and Eugene Charniak 1035

Sentence-level Emotion Classification with Label and Context Dependence
Shoushan Li, Lei Huang, Rong Wang and Guodong Zhou 1045

Co-training for Semi-supervised Sentiment Classification Based on Dual-view Bags-of-words Representation
Rui Xia, Cheng Wang, Xin-Yu Dai and Tao Li 1054

Improving social relationships in face-to-face human-agent interactions: when the agent wants to know user's likes and dislikes
Caroline Langlet and Chloé Clavel 1064

Learning Word Representations from Scarce and Noisy Data with Embedding Subspaces
Ramón Astudillo, Silvio Amir, Wang Ling, Mario Silva and Isabel Trancoso 1074

Automatic Spontaneous Speech Grading: A Novel Feature Derivation Technique using the Crowd
Vinay Shashidhar, Nishant Pandey and Varun Aggarwal 1085

Driving ROVER with Segment-based ASR Quality Estimation
Shahab Jalalvand, Matteo Negri, Falavigna Daniele and Marco Turchi 1095

A Hierarchical Neural Autoencoder for Paragraphs and Documents
Jiwei Li, Thang Luong and Dan Jurafsky 1106

Joint Dependency Parsing and Multiword Expression Tokenization
Alexis Nasr, Carlos Ramisch, José Deulofeu and André Valli 1116

End-to-end learning of semantic role labeling using recurrent neural networks
Jie Zhou and Wei Xu 1127

Feature Optimization for Constituent Parsing via Neural Networks
Zhiguo Wang, Haitao Mi and Nianwen Xue 1138

Identifying Cascading Errors using Constraints in Dependency Parsing
Dominick Ng and James R. Curran 1148

A Re-ranking Model for Dependency Parser with Recursive Convolutional Neural Network
Chenxi Zhu, Xipeng Qiu, Xinchi Chen and Xuanjing Huang 1159

Transition-based Neural Constituent Parsing
Taro Watanabe and Eiichiro Sumita 1169

Feature Selection in Kernel Space: A Case Study on Dependency Parsing
Xian Qian and Yang Liu 1180

Semantic Role Labeling Improves Incremental Parsing
Ioannis Konstas and Frank Keller 1191

Discontinuous Incremental Shift-reduce Parsing
Wolfgang Maier 1202

A Neural Probabilistic Structured-Prediction Model for Transition-Based Dependency Parsing
Hao Zhou, Yue Zhang, Shujian Huang and Jiajun Chen 1213

Parsing Paraphrases with Joint Inference
Do Kook Choe and David McClosky 1223

Cross-lingual Dependency Parsing Based on Distributed Representations
Jiang Guo, Wanxiang Che, David Yarowsky, Haifeng Wang and Ting Liu 1234

Can Natural Language Processing Become Natural Language Coaching?
Marti A. Hearst 1245

Machine Comprehension with Discourse Relations
Karthik Narasimhan and Regina Barzilay 1253

Implicit Role Linking on Chinese Discourse: Exploiting Explicit Roles and Frame-to-Frame Relations
Ru Li, Juan Wu, Zhiqiang Wang and Qinghua Chai 1263

Discourse-sensitive Automatic Identification of Generic Expressions
Annemarie Friedrich and Manfred Pinkal 1272

Model-based Word Embeddings from Decompositions of Count Matrices
Karl Stratos, Michael Collins and Daniel Hsu 1282

Entity Hierarchy Embedding
Zhiting Hu, Poyao Huang, Yuntian Deng, Yingkai Gao and Eric Xing.................... 1292

Orthogonality of Syntax and Semantics within Distributional Spaces
Jeff Mitchell and Mark Steedman 1301

Scalable Semantic Parsing with Partial Ontologies
Eunsol Choi, Tom Kwiatkowski and Luke Zettlemoyer 1311

Semantic Parsing via Staged Query Graph Generation: Question Answering with Knowledge Base
Wen-tau Yih, Ming-Wei Chang, Xiaodong He and Jianfeng Gao 1321

Building a Semantic Parser Overnight
Yushi Wang, Jonathan Berant and Percy Liang 1332

Predicting Polarities of Tweets by Composing Word Embeddings with Long Short-Term Memory
Xin Wang, Yuanchao Liu, Chengjie SUN, Baoxun Wang and Xiaolong Wang 1343

Topic Modeling based Sentiment Analysis on Social Media for Stock Market Prediction
Thien Hai Nguyen and Kiyoaki Shirai 1354

Learning Tag Embeddings and Tag-specific Composition Functions in Recursive Neural Network
Qiao Qian, Bo Tian, Minlie Huang, Yang Liu, Xuan Zhu and Xiaoyan Zhu 1365

A convex and feature-rich discriminative approach to dependency grammar induction
Edouard Grave and Noémie Elhadad 1375

Parse Imputation for Dependency Annotations
Jason Mielens, Liang Sun and Jason Baldridge 1385

Probing the Linguistic Strengths and Limitations of Unsupervised Grammar Induction
Yonatan Bisk and Julia Hockenmaier 1395

Entity-Centric Coreference Resolution with Model Stacking
Kevin Clark and Christopher D. Manning 1405

Learning Anaphoricity and Antecedent Ranking Features for Coreference Resolution
Sam Wiseman, Alexander M. Rush, Stuart Shieber and Jason Weston 1416

Transferring Coreference Resolvers with Posterior Regularization
André F. T. Martins 1427

Tea Party in the House: A Hierarchical Ideal Point Topic Model and Its Application to Republican Legislators in the 112th Congress
Viet-An Nguyen, Jordan Boyd-Graber, Philip Resnik and Kristina Miler 1438

KB-LDA: Jointly Learning a Knowledge Base of Hierarchy, Relations, and Facts
Dana Movshovitz-Attias and William W. Cohen 1449

A Computationally Efficient Algorithm for Learning Topical Collocation Models
Zhendong Zhao, Lan Du, Benjamin Börschinger, John K Pate, Massimiliano Ciaramita, Mark Steedman and Mark Johnson 1460

Compositional Semantic Parsing on Semi-Structured Tables
Panupong Pasupat and Percy Liang 1470

Graph parsing with s-graph grammars
Jonas Groschwitz, Alexander Koller and Christoph Teichmann 1481

Sparse Overcomplete Word Vector Representations
Manaal Faruqui, Yulia Tsvetkov, Dani Yogatama, Chris Dyer and Noah A. Smith 1491

Learning Semantic Word Embeddings based on Ordinal Knowledge Constraints
Quan Liu, Hui Jiang, Si Wei, Zhen-Hua Ling and Yu Hu 1501

Adding Semantics to Data-Driven Paraphrasing
Ellie Pavlick, Johan Bos, Malvina Nissim, Charley Beller, Benjamin Van Durme and Chris Callison-Burch 1512

Parsing as Reduction
Daniel Fernández-González and André F. T. Martins 1523

Optimal Shift-Reduce Constituent Parsing with Structured Perceptron
Le Quang Thang, Hiroshi Noji and Yusuke Miyao 1534

A Data-Driven, Factorization Parser for CCG Dependency Structures
Yantao Du, Weiwei Sun and Xiaojun Wan 1545

Improved Semantic Representations From Tree-Structured Long Short-Term Memory Networks
Kai Sheng Tai, Richard Socher and Christopher D. Manning 1556

genCNN: A Convolutional Architecture for Word Sequence Prediction
Mingxuan Wang, Zhengdong Lu, Hang Li, Wenbin Jiang and Qun Liu 1567

Neural Responding Machine for Short-Text Conversation
Lifeng Shang, Zhengdong Lu and Hang Li 1577

Abstractive Multi-Document Summarization via Phrase Selection and Merging
Lidong Bing, Piji Li, Yi Liao, Wai Lam, Weiwei Guo and Rebecca Passonneau 1587

Joint Graphical Models for Date Selection in Timeline Summarization
Giang Tran, Eelco Herder and Katja Markert 1598

Predicting Salient Updates for Disaster Summarization
Chris Kedzie, Kathleen McKeown and Fernando Diaz 1608

Unsupervised Prediction of Acceptability Judgements
Jey Han Lau, Alexander Clark and Shalom Lappin 1618

A Frame of Mind: Using Statistical Models for Detection of Framing and Agenda Setting Campaigns
Oren Tsur, Dan Calacci and David Lazer 1629

Why discourse affects speakers' choice of referring expressions
Naho Orita, Eliana Vornov, Naomi Feldman and Hal Daumé III 1639

Linguistic Harbingers of Betrayal: A Case Study on an Online Strategy Game
Vlad Niculae, Srijan Kumar, Jordan Boyd-Graber and Cristian Danescu-Niculescu-Mizil 1650

Who caught a cold ? - Identifying the subject of a symptom
Shin Kanouchi, Mamoru Komachi, Naoaki Okazaki, Eiji ARAMAKI and Hiroshi Ishikawa .. 1660

Weakly Supervised Role Identification in Teamwork Interactions
Diyi Yang, Miaomiao Wen and Carolyn Rose 1671

Deep Unordered Composition Rivals Syntactic Methods for Text Classification
Mohit Iyyer, Varun Manjunatha, Jordan Boyd-Graber and Hal Daumé III 1681

SOLAR: Scalable Online Learning Algorithms for Ranking
Jialei Wang, Ji Wan, Yongdong Zhang and Steven Hoi 1692

Text Categorization as a Graph Classification Problem
Francois Rousseau, Emmanouil Kiagias and Michalis Vazirgiannis 1702

Inverted indexing for cross-lingual NLP
Anders Søgaard, Željko Agić, Héctor Martínez Alonso, Barbara Plank, Bernd Bohnet and Anders Johannsen 1713

Multi-Task Learning for Multiple Language Translation
Daxiang Dong, Hua Wu, Wei He, Dianhai Yu and Haifeng Wang 1723

Accurate Linear-Time Chinese Word Segmentation via Embedding Matching
Jianqiang Ma and Erhard Hinrichs 1733

Gated Recursive Neural Network for Chinese Word Segmentation
Xinchi Chen, Xipeng Qiu, Chenxi Zhu and Xuanjing Huang 1744

An analysis of the user occupational class through Twitter content
Daniel Preoţiuc-Pietro, Vasileios Lampos and Nikolaos Aletras 1754

Tracking unbounded Topic Streams
Dominik Wurzer, Victor Lavrenko and Miles Osborne 1765

Inducing Word and Part-of-Speech with Pitman-Yor Hidden Semi-Markov Models
Kei Uchiumi, Hiroshi Tsukahara and Daichi Mochihashi 1774

Coupled Sequence Labeling on Heterogeneous Annotations: POS Tagging as a Case Study
Zhenghua Li, Jiayuan Chao, Min Zhang and Wenliang Chen 1783

AutoExtend: Extending Word Embeddings to Embeddings for Synsets and Lexemes
Sascha Rothe and Hinrich Schütze 1793

Improving Evaluation of Machine Translation Quality Estimation
Yvette Graham 1804

Conference Program

Sunday, July 26

18:00–21:00 Welcome Reception

Monday, July 27

07:30–18:00 Registration

08:45–09:00 Welcome to ACL-IJCNLP 2015

09:00–09:40 Presidential Address: Christopher D. Manning

09:40–10:10 Coffee Break

10:10–11:50 Session 1: TACL and Long Papers

Session 1A: 10:10–11:50 Machine Translation: Neural Networks

On Using Very Large Target Vocabulary for Neural Machine Translation
Sébastien Jean, Kyunghyun Cho, Roland Memisevic and Yoshua Bengio

Addressing the Rare Word Problem in Neural Machine Translation
Thang Luong, Ilya Sutskever, Quoc Le, Oriol Vinyals and Wojciech Zaremba

Encoding Source Language with Convolutional Neural Network for Machine Translation
Fandong Meng, Zhengdong Lu, Mingxuan Wang, Hang Li, Wenbin Jiang and Qun Liu

Statistical Machine Translation Features with Multitask Tensor Networks
Hendra Setiawan, Zhongqiang Huang, Jacob Devlin, Thomas Lamar, Rabih Zbib, Richard Schwartz and John Makhoul

Session 1B: 10:10–11:50 Language and Vision/NLP Applications

Describing Images using Inferred Visual Dependency Representations
Desmond Elliott and Arjen de Vries

Text to 3D Scene Generation with Rich Lexical Grounding
Angel Chang, Will Monroe, Manolis Savva, Christopher Potts and Christopher D. Manning

MultiGranCNN: An Architecture for General Matching of Text Chunks on Multiple Levels of Granularity
Wenpeng Yin and Hinrich Schütze

Weakly Supervised Models of Aspect-Sentiment for Online Course Discussion Forums
Arti Ramesh, Shachi H. Kumar, James Foulds and Lise Getoor

Session 1C: 10:10–11:50 Semantics: Embeddings

[TACL] Improving Distributional Similarity with Lessons Learned from Word Embeddings
Omer Levy, Yoav Goldberg, Ido Dagan

Semantically Smooth Knowledge Graph Embedding
Shu Guo, Quan Wang, Bin Wang, Lihong Wang and Li Guo

SensEmbed: Learning Sense Embeddings for Word and Relational Similarity
Ignacio Iacobacci, Mohammad Taher Pilehvar and Roberto Navigli

Revisiting Word Embedding for Contrasting Meaning
Zhigang Chen, Wei Lin, Qian Chen, Xiaoping Chen, Si Wei, Hui Jiang and Xiaodan Zhu

Session 1D: 10:10–11:50 Machine Learning

Joint Models of Disagreement and Stance in Online Debate
Dhanya Sridhar, James Foulds, Bert Huang, Lise Getoor and Marilyn Walker

Low-Rank Regularization for Sparse Conjunctive Feature Spaces: An Application to Named Entity Classification
Audi Primadhanty, Xavier Carreras and Ariadna Quattoni

Learning Word Representations by Jointly Modeling Syntagmatic and Paradigmatic Relations
Fei Sun, Jiafeng Guo, Yanyan Lan, Jun Xu and Xueqi Cheng

Learning Dynamic Feature Selection for Fast Sequential Prediction
Emma Strubell, Luke Vilnis, Kate Silverstein and Andrew McCallum

Session 1E: 10:10–11:50 Information Extraction 1

Compositional Vector Space Models for Knowledge Base Completion
Arvind Neelakantan, Benjamin Roth and Andrew McCallum

Event Extraction via Dynamic Multi-Pooling Convolutional Neural Networks
Yubo Chen, Liheng Xu, Kang Liu, Daojian Zeng and Jun Zhao

Stacked Ensembles of Information Extractors for Knowledge-Base Population
Vidhoon Viswanathan, Nazneen Fatema Rajani, Yinon Bentor and Raymond Mooney

Generative Event Schema Induction with Entity Disambiguation
Kiem-Hieu Nguyen, Xavier Tannier, Olivier Ferret and Romaric Besançon

11:50–13:20 Lunch Break; Student Lunch

13:20–15:00 Session 2: TACL and Long Papers

Session 2A: 13:20–15:00 Machine Translation

Syntax-based Simultaneous Translation through Prediction of Unseen Syntactic Constituents
Yusuke Oda, Graham Neubig, Sakriani Sakti, Tomoki Toda and Satoshi Nakamura

Efficient Top-Down BTG Parsing for Machine Translation Preordering
Tetsuji Nakagawa

Online Multitask Learning for Machine Translation Quality Estimation
José G. C. de Souza, Matteo Negri, Elisa Ricci and Marco Turchi

A Context-Aware Topic Model for Statistical Machine Translation
Jinsong Su, Deyi Xiong, Yang Liu, Xianpei Han, Hongyu Lin, Junfeng Yao and Min Zhang

Session 2B: 13:20–15:00 Question Answering

Learning Answer-Entailing Structures for Machine Comprehension
Mrinmaya Sachan, Kumar Dubey, Eric Xing and Matthew Richardson

Learning Continuous Word Embedding with Metadata for Question Retrieval in Community Question Answering
Guangyou Zhou, Tingting He, Jun Zhao and Po Hu

Question Answering over Freebase with Multi-Column Convolutional Neural Networks
Li Dong, Furu Wei, Ming Zhou and Ke Xu

[TACL] Higher-order Lexical Semantic Models for Non-factoid Answer Reranking
Daniel Fried, Peter Jansen, Gustave Hahn-Powell, Mihai Surdeanu, Peter Clark

Session 2C: 13:20–15:00 Semantics: Distributional Approaches

Hubness and Pollution: Delving into Cross-Space Mapping for Zero-Shot Learning
Angeliki Lazaridou, Georgiana Dinu and Marco Baroni

[TACL] Learning a Compositional Semantics for Freebase with an Open Predicate Vocabulary
Jayant Krishnamurthy and Tom M. Mitchell

A Generalisation of Lexical Functions for Composition in Distributional Semantics
Antoine Bride, Tim Van de Cruys and Nicholas Asher

Simple Learning and Compositional Application of Perceptually Grounded Word Meanings for Incremental Reference Resolution
Casey Kennington and David Schlangen

Session 2D: 13:20–15:00 Parsing: Neural Networks

Neural CRF Parsing
Greg Durrett and Dan Klein

An Effective Neural Network Model for Graph-based Dependency Parsing
Wenzhe Pei, Tao Ge and Baobao Chang

Structured Training for Neural Network Transition-Based Parsing
David Weiss, Chris Alberti, Michael Collins and Slav Petrov

Transition-Based Dependency Parsing with Stack Long Short-Term Memory
Chris Dyer, Miguel Ballesteros, Wang Ling, Austin Matthews and Noah A. Smith

Session 2E: 13:20–15:00 Information Extraction 2

Leveraging Linguistic Structure For Open Domain Information Extraction
Gabor Angeli, Melvin Jose Johnson Premkumar and Christopher D. Manning

Joint Information Extraction and Reasoning: A Scalable Statistical Relational Learning Approach
William Yang Wang and William W Cohen

A Knowledge-Intensive Model for Prepositional Phrase Attachment
Ndapandula Nakashole and Tom M. Mitchell

A Convolution Kernel Approach to Identifying Comparisons in Text
Maksim Tkachenko and Hady Lauw

15:00–15:30 Coffee Break

15:30–16:45 Session 3: TACL and Long Papers

Session 3A: 15:30–16:45 Language Resources

[TACL] A New Corpus and Imitation Learning Framework for Context-Dependent Semantic Parsing
Andreas Vlachos and Stephen Clark

It Depends: Dependency Parser Comparison Using A Web-based Evaluation Tool
Jinho D. Choi, Joel Tetreault and Amanda Stent

Generating High Quality Proposition Banks for Multilingual Semantic Role Labeling
Alan Akbik, laura chiticariu, Marina Danilevsky, Yunyao Li, Shivakumar Vaithyanathan and Huaiyu Zhu

Session 3B: 15:30–16:45 Sentiment Analysis: Cross-/Multi Lingual

Aligning Opinions: Cross-Lingual Opinion Mining with Dependencies
Mariana S. C. Almeida, Claudia Pinto, Helena Figueira, Pedro Mendes and André F. T. Martins

Learning to Adapt Credible Knowledge in Cross-lingual Sentiment Analysis
Qiang Chen, Wenjie Li, Yu Lei, Xule Liu and Yanxiang He

Learning Bilingual Sentiment Word Embeddings for Cross-language Sentiment Classification
HuiWei Zhou, Long Chen, Fulin Shi and Degen Huang

Session 3C: 15:30–16:45 Natural Language Generation

Content Models for Survey Generation: A Factoid-Based Evaluation
Rahul Jha, Catherine Finegan-Dollak, Ben King, Reed Coke and Dragomir Radev

Training a Natural Language Generator From Unaligned Data
Ondřej Dušek and Filip Jurcicek

Event-Driven Headline Generation
Rui Sun, Yue Zhang, Meishan Zhang and Donghong Ji

Session 3D: 15:30–16:45 Spoken Language Processing and Understanding

New Transfer Learning Techniques for Disparate Label Sets
Young-Bum Kim, Karl Stratos, Ruhi Sarikaya and Minwoo Jeong

Matrix Factorization with Knowledge Graph Propagation for Unsupervised Spoken Language Understanding
Yun-Nung Chen, William Yang Wang, Anatole Gershman and Alexander Rudnicky

Efficient Disfluency Detection with Transition-based Parsing
Shuangzhi Wu, Dongdong Zhang, Ming Zhou and Tiejun Zhao

Session 3E: 15:30–16:45 Information Extraction 3/Information Retrieval

S-MART: Novel Tree-based Structured Learning Algorithms Applied to Tweet Entity Linking
Yi Yang and Ming-Wei Chang

[TACL] Design Challenges for Entity Linking
Xiao Ling, Sameer Singh, Daniel S. Weld

Entity Retrieval via Entity Factoid Hierarchy
Chunliang Lu, Wai Lam and Yi Liao

16:45–17:00 Short Break

17:00–18:00 Session 4: Short Papers

18:00–21:00 Poster and Dinner Session 1: TACL Papers, Long Papers, System Demonstrations

Session P1.01: 18:00–21:00 Poster: Pragmatics

Encoding Distributional Semantics into Triple-Based Knowledge Ranking for Document Enrichment
Muyu Zhang, Bing Qin, Mao Zheng, Graeme Hirst and Ting Liu

A Strategic Reasoning Model for Generating Alternative Answers
Jon Stevens, Anton Benz, Sebastian Reuße and Ralf Klabunde

Modeling Argument Strength in Student Essays
Isaac Persing and Vincent Ng

Session P1.02: 18:00–21:00 Poster: Information Retrieval

Summarization of Multi-Document Topic Hierarchies using Submodular Mixtures
Ramakrishna Bairi, Rishabh Iyer, Ganesh Ramakrishnan and Jeff Bilmes

Learning to Explain Entity Relationships in Knowledge Graphs
Nikos Voskarides, Edgar Meij, Manos Tsagkias, Maarten de Rijke and Wouter Weerkamp

Session P1.03: 18:00–21:00 Poster: Information Extraction

[TACL] Exploiting Parallel News Streams for Unsupervised Event Extraction
Congle Zhang, Stephen Soderland, Daniel Weld

Bring you to the past: Automatic Generation of Topically Relevant Event Chronicles
Tao Ge, Wenzhe Pei, Heng Ji, Sujian Li, Baobao Chang and Zhifang Sui

Context-aware Entity Morph Decoding
Boliang Zhang, Hongzhao Huang, Xiaoman Pan, Sujian Li, Chin-Yew Lin, Heng Ji, Kevin Knight, Zhen Wen, Yizhou Sun, Jiawei Han and Bulent Yener

Multi-Objective Optimization for the Joint Disambiguation of Nouns and Named Entities
Dirk Weissenborn, Leonhard Hennig, Feiyu Xu and Hans Uszkoreit

Building a Scientific Concept Hierarchy Database (SCHBase)
Eytan Adar and Srayan Datta

Sentiment-Aspect Extraction based on Restricted Boltzmann Machines
Linlin Wang, Kang Liu, Zhu Cao, Jun Zhao and Gerard de Melo

Classifying Relations by Ranking with Convolutional Neural Networks
Cicero dos Santos, Bing Xiang and Bowen Zhou

Semantic Representations for Domain Adaptation: A Case Study on the Tree Kernel-based Method for Relation Extraction
Thien Huu Nguyen, Barbara Plank and Ralph Grishman

Omnia Mutantur, Nihil Interit: Connecting Past with Present by Finding Corresponding Terms across Time
Yating Zhang, Adam Jatowt, Sourav Bhowmick and Katsumi Tanaka

Negation and Speculation Identification in Chinese Language
Bowei Zou, Qiaoming Zhu and Guodong Zhou

Learning Relational Features with Backward Random Walks
Ni Lao, Einat Minkov and William Cohen

Session P1.04: 18:00–21:00 Poster: Language and Vision

Learning the Semantics of Manipulation Action
Yezhou Yang, Yiannis Aloimonos, Cornelia Fermuller and Eren Erdal Aksoy

Session P1.05: 18:00–21:00 Poster: Language Resources

Knowledge Graph Embedding via Dynamic Mapping Matrix
Guoliang Ji, Shizhu He, Liheng Xu, Kang Liu and Jun Zhao

How Far are We from Fully Automatic High Quality Grammatical Error Correction?
Christopher Bryant and Hwee Tou Ng

Session P1.06: 18:00–21:00 Poster: Lexical Semantics and Ontology

Knowledge Portability with Semantic Expansion of Ontology Labels
Mihael Arcan, Marco Turchi and Paul Buitelaar

Automatic disambiguation of English puns
Tristan Miller and Iryna Gurevych

Unsupervised Cross-Domain Word Representation Learning
Danushka Bollegala, Takanori Maehara and Ken-ichi Kawarabayashi

A Unified Multilingual Semantic Representation of Concepts
José Camacho-Collados, Mohammad Taher Pilehvar and Roberto Navigli

Session P1.07: 18:00–21:00 Poster: Linguistic and Psycholinguistic Aspects of CL

Demographic Factors Improve Classification Performance
Dirk Hovy

Vector-space calculation of semantic surprisal for predicting word pronunciation duration
Asad Sayeed, Stefan Fischer and Vera Demberg

Session P1.08: 18:00–21:00 Poster: Machine Learning and Topic Modeling

Efficient Methods for Inferring Large Sparse Topic Hierarchies
Doug Downey, Chandra Bhagavatula and Yi Yang

Trans-dimensional Random Fields for Language Modeling
Bin Wang, Zhijian Ou and Zhiqiang Tan

Gaussian LDA for Topic Models with Word Embeddings
Rajarshi Das, Manzil Zaheer and Chris Dyer

Session P1.09: 18:00–21:00 Poster: Machine Translation

Pairwise Neural Machine Translation Evaluation
Francisco Guzmán, Shafiq Joty, Lluís Màrquez and Preslav Nakov

String-to-Tree Multi Bottom-up Tree Transducers
Nina Seemann, Fabienne Braune and Andreas Maletti

Non-linear Learning for Statistical Machine Translation
Shujian Huang, Huadong Chen, Xin-Yu Dai and Jiajun Chen

Unifying Bayesian Inference and Vector Space Models for Improved Decipherment
Qing Dou, Ashish Vaswani, Kevin Knight and Chris Dyer

Non-projective Dependency-based Pre-Reordering with Recurrent Neural Network for Machine Translation
Antonio Valerio Miceli Barone and Giuseppe Attardi

Session P1.10: 18:00–21:00 Poster: NLP Applications

Detecting Deceptive Groups Using Conversations and Network Analysis
Dian Yu, Yulia Tyshchuk, Heng Ji and William Wallace

WikiKreator: Improving Wikipedia Stubs Automatically
Siddhartha Banerjee and Prasenjit Mitra

Language to Code: Learning Semantic Parsers for If-This-Then-That Recipes
Chris Quirk, Raymond Mooney and Michel Galley

Deep Questions without Deep Understanding
Igor Labutov, Sumit Basu and Lucy Vanderwende

The NL2KR Platform for building Natural Language Translation Systems
Nguyen Vo, Arindam Mitra and Chitta Baral

Session P1.12: 18:00–21:00 Poster: Morphology

Multiple Many-to-Many Sequence Alignment for Combining String-Valued Variables: A G2P Experiment
Steffen Eger

Session P1.11: 18:00–21:00 Poster: NLP for the Web and Social Media

Tweet Normalization with Syllables
Ke Xu, Yunqing Xia and Chin-Hui Lee

Improving Named Entity Recognition in Tweets via Detecting Non-Standard Words
Chen Li and Yang Liu

Session P1.13: 18:00–21:00 Poster: Question Answering

A Unified Kernel Approach for Learning Typed Sentence Rewritings
Martin Gleize and Brigitte Grau

Session P1.14: 18:00–21:00 Poster: Semantics

[TACL] From Visual Attributes to Adjectives through Decompositional Distributional Semantics
Angeliki Lazaridou, Georgiana Dinu, Adam Liska, Marco Baroni

Perceptually Grounded Selectional Preferences
Ekaterina Shutova, Niket Tandon and Gerard de Melo

Joint Case Argument Identification for Japanese Predicate Argument Structure Analysis
Hiroki Ouchi, Hiroyuki Shindo, Kevin Duh and Yuji Matsumoto

Jointly optimizing word representations for lexical and sentential tasks with the C-PHRASE model
Nghia The Pham, Germán Kruszewski, Angeliki Lazaridou and Marco Baroni

Robust Subgraph Generation Improves Abstract Meaning Representation Parsing
Keenon Werling, Gabor Angeli and Christopher D. Manning

Environment-Driven Lexicon Induction for High-Level Instructions
Dipendra Kumar Misra, Kejia Tao, Percy Liang and Ashutosh Saxena

Structural Representations for Learning Relations between Pairs of Texts
Simone Filice, Giovanni Da San Martino and Alessandro Moschitti

Session P1.15: 18:00–21:00 Poster: Sentiment Analysis

[TACL] Joint Modeling of Opinion Expression Extraction and Attribute Classification
Bishan Yang and Claire Cardie

Learning Semantic Representations of Users and Products for Document Level Sentiment Classification
Duyu Tang, Bing Qin and Ting Liu

Towards Debugging Sentiment Lexicons
Andrew Schneider and Eduard Dragut

Sparse, Contextually Informed Models for Irony Detection: Exploiting User Communities, Entities and Sentiment
Byron C. Wallace, Do Kook Choe and Eugene Charniak

Sentence-level Emotion Classification with Label and Context Dependence
Shoushan Li, Lei Huang, Rong Wang and Guodong Zhou

Co-training for Semi-supervised Sentiment Classification Based on Dual-view Bags-of-words Representation
Rui Xia, Cheng Wang, Xin-Yu Dai and Tao Li

Improving social relationships in face-to-face human-agent interactions: when the agent wants to know user's likes and dislikes
Caroline Langlet and Chloé Clavel

Learning Word Representations from Scarce and Noisy Data with Embedding Subspaces
Ramón Astudillo, Silvio Amir, Wang Ling, Mario Silva and Isabel Trancoso

Session P1.16: 18:00–21:00 Poster: Spoken Language Processing

Automatic Spontaneous Speech Grading: A Novel Feature Derivation Technique using the Crowd
Vinay Shashidhar, Nishant Pandey and Varun Aggarwal

Driving ROVER with Segment-based ASR Quality Estimation
Shahab Jalalvand, Matteo Negri, Falavigna Daniele and Marco Turchi

Session P1.17: 18:00–21:00 Poster: Natural Language Generation

A Hierarchical Neural Autoencoder for Paragraphs and Documents
Jiwei Li, Thang Luong and Dan Jurafsky

Session P1.18: 18:00–21:00 Poster: Tagging, Chunking, Parsing

[TACL]Domain Adaptation for Syntactic and Semantic Dependency Parsing Using Deep Belief Networks
Haitong Yang, Tao Zhuang, Chengqing Zong

Joint Dependency Parsing and Multiword Expression Tokenization
Alexis Nasr, Carlos Ramisch, José Deulofeu and André Valli

End-to-end learning of semantic role labeling using recurrent neural networks
Jie Zhou and Wei Xu

Feature Optimization for Constituent Parsing via Neural Networks
Zhiguo Wang, Haitao Mi and Nianwen Xue

Identifying Cascading Errors using Constraints in Dependency Parsing
Dominick Ng and James R. Curran

A Re-ranking Model for Dependency Parser with Recursive Convolutional Neural Network
Chenxi Zhu, Xipeng Qiu, Xinchi Chen and Xuanjing Huang

Transition-based Neural Constituent Parsing
Taro Watanabe and Eiichiro Sumita

Monday, July 27 (continued)

Feature Selection in Kernel Space: A Case Study on Dependency Parsing
Xian Qian and Yang Liu

Semantic Role Labeling Improves Incremental Parsing
Ioannis Konstas and Frank Keller

Discontinuous Incremental Shift-reduce Parsing
Wolfgang Maier

A Neural Probabilistic Structured-Prediction Model for Transition-Based Dependency Parsing
Hao Zhou, Yue Zhang, Shujian Huang and Jiajun Chen

Parsing Paraphrases with Joint Inference
Do Kook Choe and David McClosky

Cross-lingual Dependency Parsing Based on Distributed Representations
Jiang Guo, Wanxiang Che, David Yarowsky, Haifeng Wang and Ting Liu

Tuesday, July 28

07:30–18:00 Registration

09:00–10:00 Keynote Address: "Can Natural Language Processing Become Natural Language Coaching?" - Marti A. Hearst

Can Natural Language Processing Become Natural Language Coaching?
Marti A. Hearst

10:00–10:30 Coffee Break

10:30–12:00 Session 5: Short Papers

12:00–13:30 Lunch Break

13:30–14:45 Session 6: Long Papers

Session 6A: 13:30–14:45 Discourse, Pragmatics

Machine Comprehension with Discourse Relations
Karthik Narasimhan and Regina Barzilay

Implicit Role Linking on Chinese Discourse: Exploiting Explicit Roles and Frame-to-Frame Relations
Ru Li, Juan Wu, Zhiqiang Wang and Qinghua Chai

Discourse-sensitive Automatic Identification of Generic Expressions
Annemarie Friedrich and Manfred Pinkal

Session 6B: 13:30–14:45 Machine Learning: Embeddings

Model-based Word Embeddings from Decompositions of Count Matrices
Karl Stratos, Michael Collins and Daniel Hsu

Entity Hierarchy Embedding
Zhiting Hu, Poyao Huang, Yuntian Deng, Yingkai Gao and Eric Xing

Orthogonality of Syntax and Semantics within Distributional Spaces
Jeff Mitchell and Mark Steedman

Session 6C: 13:30–14:45 Semantics: Semantic Parsing

Scalable Semantic Parsing with Partial Ontologies
Eunsol Choi, Tom Kwiatkowski and Luke Zettlemoyer

Semantic Parsing via Staged Query Graph Generation: Question Answering with Knowledge Base
Wen-tau Yih, Ming-Wei Chang, Xiaodong He and Jianfeng Gao

Building a Semantic Parser Overnight
Yushi Wang, Jonathan Berant and Percy Liang

Session 6D: 13:30–14:45 Sentiment Analysis: Learning

Predicting Polarities of Tweets by Composing Word Embeddings with Long Short-Term Memory
Xin Wang, Yuanchao Liu, Chengjie SUN, Baoxun Wang and Xiaolong Wang

Topic Modeling based Sentiment Analysis on Social Media for Stock Market Prediction
Thien Hai Nguyen and Kiyoaki Shirai

Learning Tag Embeddings and Tag-specific Composition Functions in Recursive Neural Network
Qiao Qian, Bo Tian, Minlie Huang, Yang Liu, Xuan Zhu and Xiaoyan Zhu

Session 6E: 13:30–14:45 Grammar Induction and Annotation

A convex and feature-rich discriminative approach to dependency grammar induction
Edouard Grave and Noémie Elhadad

Parse Imputation for Dependency Annotations
Jason Mielens, Liang Sun and Jason Baldridge

Probing the Linguistic Strengths and Limitations of Unsupervised Grammar Induction
Yonatan Bisk and Julia Hockenmaier

14:45–15:15 Coffee Break

15:15–16:30 Session 7: TACL and Long Papers

Session 7A: 15:15–16:30 Discourse, Coreference

Entity-Centric Coreference Resolution with Model Stacking
Kevin Clark and Christopher D. Manning

Learning Anaphoricity and Antecedent Ranking Features for Coreference Resolution
Sam Wiseman, Alexander M. Rush, Stuart Shieber and Jason Weston

Transferring Coreference Resolvers with Posterior Regularization
André F. T. Martins

Session 7B: 15:15–16:30 Topic Modeling

Tea Party in the House: A Hierarchical Ideal Point Topic Model and Its Application to Republican Legislators in the 112th Congress
Viet-An Nguyen, Jordan Boyd-Graber, Philip Resnik and Kristina Miler

KB-LDA: Jointly Learning a Knowledge Base of Hierarchy, Relations, and Facts
Dana Movshovitz-Attias and William W. Cohen

A Computationally Efficient Algorithm for Learning Topical Collocation Models
Zhendong Zhao, Lan Du, Benjamin Börschinger, John K Pate, Massimiliano Ciaramita, Mark Steedman and Mark Johnson

Session 7C: 15:15–16:30 Semantics: Semantic Parsing

[TACL] Efficient Inference and Structured Learning for Semantic Role Labeling
Oscar Täckström, Kuzman Ganchev, Dipanjan Das

Compositional Semantic Parsing on Semi-Structured Tables
Panupong Pasupat and Percy Liang

Graph parsing with s-graph grammars
Jonas Groschwitz, Alexander Koller and Christoph Teichmann

Session 7D: 15:15–16:30 Lexical Semantics

Sparse Overcomplete Word Vector Representations
Manaal Faruqui, Yulia Tsvetkov, Dani Yogatama, Chris Dyer and Noah A. Smith

Learning Semantic Word Embeddings based on Ordinal Knowledge Constraints
Quan Liu, Hui Jiang, Si Wei, Zhen-Hua Ling and Yu Hu

Adding Semantics to Data-Driven Paraphrasing
Ellie Pavlick, Johan Bos, Malvina Nissim, Charley Beller, Benjamin Van Durme and Chris Callison-Burch

Session 7E: 15:15–16:30 Parsing

Parsing as Reduction
Daniel Fernández-González and André F. T. Martins

Optimal Shift-Reduce Constituent Parsing with Structured Perceptron
Le Quang Thang, Hiroshi Noji and Yusuke Miyao

A Data-Driven, Factorization Parser for CCG Dependency Structures
Yantao Du, Weiwei Sun and Xiaojun Wan

Tuesday, July 28 (continued)

16:30–19:30 **Poster and Dinner Session 2: Short Papers, Student Research Workshop Papers**

19:45–22:00 **Social Event**

Wednesday, July 29

07:30–18:00 **Registration**

09:00–10:00 **Keynote Address: "Construction and Mining of Heterogenous Information Networks from Data" - Jiawei Han**

10:00–10:30 **Coffee Break**

10:30–11:45 **Session 8: Long Papers**

Session 8A: 10:30–11:45 Machine Learning: Neural Networks

Improved Semantic Representations From Tree-Structured Long Short-Term Memory Networks
Kai Sheng Tai, Richard Socher and Christopher D. Manning

genCNN: A Convolutional Architecture for Word Sequence Prediction
Mingxuan Wang, Zhengdong Lu, Hang Li, Wenbin Jiang and Qun Liu

Neural Responding Machine for Short-Text Conversation
Lifeng Shang, Zhengdong Lu and Hang Li

Wednesday, July 29 (continued)

Session 8B: 10:30–11:45 Automatic Summarization

Abstractive Multi-Document Summarization via Phrase Selection and Merging
Lidong Bing, Piji Li, Yi Liao, Wai Lam, Weiwei Guo and Rebecca Passonneau

Joint Graphical Models for Date Selection in Timeline Summarization
Giang Tran, Eelco Herder and Katja Markert

Predicting Salient Updates for Disaster Summarization
Chris Kedzie, Kathleen McKeown and Fernando Diaz

Session 8C: 10:30–11:45 Linguistic and Psycholinguistic Aspects of NLP

Unsupervised Prediction of Acceptability Judgements
Jey Han Lau, Alexander Clark and Shalom Lappin

A Frame of Mind: Using Statistical Models for Detection of Framing and Agenda Setting Campaigns
Oren Tsur, Dan Calacci and David Lazer

Why discourse affects speakers' choice of referring expressions
Naho Orita, Eliana Vornov, Naomi Feldman and Hal Daumé III

Session 8D: 10:30–11:45 NLP for the Web: Social Media

Linguistic Harbingers of Betrayal: A Case Study on an Online Strategy Game
Vlad Niculae, Srijan Kumar, Jordan Boyd-Graber and Cristian Danescu-Niculescu-Mizil

Who caught a cold ? - Identifying the subject of a symptom
Shin Kanouchi, Mamoru Komachi, Naoaki Okazaki, Eiji ARAMAKI and Hiroshi Ishikawa

Weakly Supervised Role Identification in Teamwork Interactions
Diyi Yang, Miaomiao Wen and Carolyn Rose

Session 8E: 10:30–11:45 Text Categorization/Information Retrieval

Deep Unordered Composition Rivals Syntactic Methods for Text Classification
Mohit Iyyer, Varun Manjunatha, Jordan Boyd-Graber and Hal Daumé III

SOLAR: Scalable Online Learning Algorithms for Ranking
Jialei Wang, Ji Wan, Yongdong Zhang and Steven Hoi

Text Categorization as a Graph Classification Problem
Francois Rousseau, Emmanouil Kiagias and Michalis Vazirgiannis

11:45–13:00 **Lunch Break**

13:00–14:30 **ACL Business Meeting**

14:35–15:25 **Session 9: TACL and Long papers**

Session 9A: 14:35–15:25 Multilinguality

Inverted indexing for cross-lingual NLP
Anders Søgaard, Željko Agić, Héctor Martínez Alonso, Barbara Plank, Bernd Bohnet and Anders Johannsen

Multi-Task Learning for Multiple Language Translation
Daxiang Dong, Hua Wu, Wei He, Dianhai Yu and Haifeng Wang

Session 9B: 14:35–15:25 Word Segmentation

Accurate Linear-Time Chinese Word Segmentation via Embedding Matching
Jianqiang Ma and Erhard Hinrichs

Gated Recursive Neural Network for Chinese Word Segmentation
Xinchi Chen, Xipeng Qiu, Chenxi Zhu and Xuanjing Huang

Session 9C: 14:35–15:25 Morphology, Phonology

[TACL] An Unsupervised Method for Uncovering Morphological Chains
Karthik Narasimhan, Regina Barzilay, Tommi Jaakkola

[TACL] Modeling Word Forms Using Latent Underlying Morphs and Phonology
Ryan Cotterell, Nanyun Peng, Jason Eisner

Session 9D: 14:35–15:25 NLP for the Web: Twitter

An analysis of the user occupational class through Twitter content
Daniel Preoţiuc-Pietro, Vasileios Lampos and Nikolaos Aletras

Tracking unbounded Topic Streams
Dominik Wurzer, Victor Lavrenko and Miles Osborne

Session 9E: 14:35–15:25 POS Tagging

Inducing Word and Part-of-Speech with Pitman-Yor Hidden Semi-Markov Models
Kei Uchiumi, Hiroshi Tsukahara and Daichi Mochihashi

Coupled Sequence Labeling on Heterogeneous Annotations: POS Tagging as a Case Study
Zhenghua Li, Jiayuan Chao, Min Zhang and Wenliang Chen

15:25–15:55 Coffee Break

Session BP: 15:55–17:10 Best Paper Session

AutoExtend: Extending Word Embeddings to Embeddings for Synsets and Lexemes
Sascha Rothe and Hinrich Schütze

Improving Evaluation of Machine Translation Quality Estimation
Yvette Graham

17:10–18:30 Lifetime Achievement Award

18:30–19:00 Closing Session

Day Date

Session Ses Code: Ses Time–Ses End Time Ses Title

Gen *Time–Gen End Time Gen Title*
Gen Presenter

Multiple Many-to-Many Sequence Alignment for Combining String-Valued Variables: A G2P Experiment

Steffen Eger
Text Technology Lab
Goethe University Frankfurt am Main
Frankfurt am Main, Germany
steeger@em.uni-frankfurt.de

Abstract

We investigate *multiple many-to-many alignments* as a primary step in integrating supplemental information strings in string transduction. Besides outlining DP based solutions to the multiple alignment problem, we detail an approximation of the problem in terms of multiple sequence segmentations satisfying a coupling constraint. We apply our approach to boosting baseline G2P systems using homogeneous as well as heterogeneous sources of supplemental information.

1 Introduction

String-to-string translation (string transduction) is the problem of converting one string $\mathbf{x}$ over an alphabet Σ into another string $\mathbf{y}$ over a possibly different alphabet Γ. The most prominent applications of string-to-string translation in natural language processing (NLP) are grapheme-to-phoneme conversion, in which $\mathbf{x}$ is a letter-string and $\mathbf{y}$ is a string of phonemes, transliteration (Sherif and Kondrak, 2007), lemmatization (Dreyer et al., 2008), and spelling error correction (Brill and Moore, 2000). The classical learning paradigm in each of these settings is to train a model on pairs of strings $\{(\mathbf{x}, \mathbf{y})\}$ and then to evaluate model performance on test data. Thereby, all state-of-the-art modelings we are aware of (e.g., (Jiampojamarn et al., 2007; Bisani and Ney, 2008; Jiampojamarn et al., 2008; Jiampojamarn et al., 2010; Novak et al., 2012)) proceed by first *aligning* the string pairs $(\mathbf{x}, \mathbf{y})$ in the training data. Also, these modelings acknowledge that alignments may typically be of a rather complex nature in which several $\mathbf{x}$ sequence characters may be matched up with several $\mathbf{y}$ sequence characters; Table 1 illustrates. Once the training data is aligned, since $\mathbf{x}$ and $\mathbf{y}$ sequences are then segmented into equal number of segments, string-to-string translation may be seen as a sequence labeling (tagging) problem in which $\mathbf{x}$ (sub-)sequence characters are observed variables and $\mathbf{y}$ (sub-)sequence characters are hidden states (Jiampojamarn et al., 2007; Jiampojamarn et al., 2010).

ph	oe	n	i	x
f	i	n	ɪ	ks

Table 1: Sample monotone many-to-many alignment between $\mathbf{x} =$ phoenix and $\mathbf{y} =$ finɪks.

In this work, we extend the problem of classical string-to-string translation by assuming that, at training time, we have available $(M+2)$-tuples of strings $\{(\mathbf{x}, \hat{\mathbf{y}}^{(1)}, \ldots, \hat{\mathbf{y}}^{(M)}, \mathbf{y})\}$, where $\mathbf{x}$ is the input string, $\hat{\mathbf{y}}^{(m)}$, for $1 \leq m \leq M$, are *supplemental information* strings, and $\mathbf{y}$ is the desired output string; at test time, we wish to predict $\mathbf{y}$ from $(\mathbf{x}, \hat{\mathbf{y}}^{(1)}, \ldots, \hat{\mathbf{y}}^{(M)})$. Generally, we may think of $\hat{\mathbf{y}}^{(1)}, \ldots, \hat{\mathbf{y}}^{(M)}$ as arbitrary strings over arbitrary alphabets $\Sigma^{(m)}$, for $1 \leq m \leq M$. For example, $\mathbf{x}$ might be a letter-string and $\hat{\mathbf{y}}^{(m)}$ might be a transliteration of $\mathbf{x}$ in language L_m (cf. Bhargava and Kondrak (2012)). Alternatively, and this is our model scenario in the current work, $\mathbf{x}$ might be a letter input string and $\hat{\mathbf{y}}^{(m)}$ might be the predicted string of phonemes, given $\mathbf{x}$, produced by an (offline) system T_m. This situation is outlined in Table 3. In the table, we also illustrate a *multiple (monotone) many-to-many alignment* of $(\mathbf{x}, \hat{\mathbf{y}}^{(1)}, \ldots, \hat{\mathbf{y}}^{(M)}, \mathbf{y})$. By this, we mean an alignment where (1) *subsequences* of all $M+2$ strings may be matched up with each other (many-

Proceedings of the 53rd Annual Meeting of the Association for Computational Linguistics and the 7th International Joint Conference on Natural Language Processing, pages 909–919,
Beijing, China, July 26-31, 2015.

to-many alignments), and where (2) the matching up of subsequences obeys monotonicity. Note that such a multiple alignment generalizes classical monotone many-to-many alignments between *pairs* of strings, as shown in Table 1. Furthermore, such an alignment may apparently be quite useful. For instance, while none of the strings $\hat{\mathbf{y}}^{(m)}$ in the table equals the true phonetic transcription $\mathbf{y}$ of $\mathbf{x}$, taking a position-wise majority vote of the multiple alignment of $(\hat{\mathbf{y}}^{(1)}, \ldots, \hat{\mathbf{y}}^{(M)})$ yields $\mathbf{y}$. Moreover, analogously as in the case of pairs of aligned strings, we may perceive the so extended string-to-string translation problem as a sequence labeling task once $(\mathbf{x}, \hat{\mathbf{y}}^{(1)}, \ldots, \hat{\mathbf{y}}^{(M)}, \mathbf{y})$ are multiply aligned, but now, with *additional observed variables* (or *features*), namely, (sub-)sequence characters of each string $\hat{\mathbf{y}}^{(m)}$.

To further motivate our approach, consider the situation of training a new G2P system on the basis of, e.g., Combilex (Richmond et al., 2009). For each letter form in its database, Combilex provides a corresponding phonetic transcription. Now, suppose that, in addition, we can poll an external knowledge source such as Wiktionary for (its) phonetic transcriptions of the respective Combilex letter words as outlined in Table 2. The central question we want to answer is: can we train a system using this *additional* information which performs better than the 'baseline' system that ignores the extra information? Clearly, a system with more information should not perform worse than a system with less information (unless the additional information is highly noisy), but it is a priori not clear at all how the extra information can be included, as Bhargava and Kondrak (2012) note: output predictions may be in distinct alphabets and/or follow different conventions, and simple rule-based conversions may even deteriorate a baseline system's performance. Their solution to the problem is to let the baseline system output its n-best phonetic transcriptions, and then to re-rank these n-best predictions via an SVM reranker trained on the supplemental representations (see their figure 2). Our approach is much different from this: we character (or substring) align the supplemental information strings with the input letter strings and then sequentially transduce input character substrings as in the standard G2P approach, but where the sequential transducer is aware of the corresponding subsequences of the supplemental information strings.

Input form	Wiktionary	Combilex
neutrino	njuːtɹiːnoʊ	nutrinF
wooded	wʊdɪd	wUd@d
wrench	ɹɛntʃ	rEn<

Table 2: Input letter words, Wiktionary and Combilex transcriptions.

$\mathbf{x}$ = schizo	s	ch	i	z	o
$\hat{\mathbf{y}}^{(1)}$ = skaɪzəʊ	s	k	aɪ	z	əʊ
$\hat{\mathbf{y}}^{(2)}$ = saɪzəʊ	s	-	aɪ	z	əʊ
$\hat{\mathbf{y}}^{(3)}$ = skɪtsə	s	k	ɪ	ts	ə
$\hat{\mathbf{y}}^{(4)}$ = ʃitsəʊ	ʃ	-	i	ts	əʊ
$\hat{\mathbf{y}}^{(5)}$ = skɪtsə	s	k	ɪ	ts	ə
$\mathbf{y}$ = skɪtsəʊ	s	k	ɪ	ts	əʊ

Table 3: Left: Input string $\mathbf{x}$, predictions of 5 systems, and output string $\mathbf{y}$. Right: A multiple many-to-many alignment of $(\mathbf{x}, \hat{\mathbf{y}}^{(1)}, \ldots, \hat{\mathbf{y}}^{(5)}, \mathbf{y})$. Skips are marked by a dash ('-').

Our goals in the current work are first, in Section 2, to formally introduce the multiple many-to-many alignment problem, which, to our knowledge, has not yet been formally considered, and to indicate how it can be solved (by standard extensions of well-known DP recursions). Secondly, we outline an 'approximation algorithm', also in Section 2, with much better runtime complexity, to solving the multiple many-to-many alignment problem. This proceeds by optimally *segmenting* individual strings to align *under the global constraint that the number of segments must agree* across strings. Thirdly, we demonstrate experimentally, in Section 5, that multiple many-to-many alignments may be an extremely useful first step in boosting the performance of a G2P model. In particular, we show that by conjoining a base system with additional systems very high performance increases can be achieved. We also investigate the effects of using our introduced approximation algorithm instead of 'exactly' determining alignments. We discuss related work in Section 3, present data and systems in Section 4 and conclude in Section 6.

2 Mult. Many-to-Many Alignm. Models

We now formally define the problem of multiply aligning several strings in a *monotone and many-to-many alignment* manner. For notational convenience, in this section, let the N strings to align be denoted by $\mathbf{w}_1, \ldots, \mathbf{w}_N$ (rather than $\mathbf{x}, \hat{\mathbf{y}}^{(m)}, \mathbf{y}$, etc.). Let each $\mathbf{w}_n$, for $1 \leq n \leq N$, be an arbitrary string over some alphabet $\Sigma^{(n)}$. Let $\ell_n = |\mathbf{w}_n|$ denote the length of $\mathbf{w}_n$. Moreover, assume that a set $S \subseteq \prod_{n=1}^{N}\{0, \ldots, \ell_n\} \backslash \{\mathbf{0}_N\}$ of *allowable steps* is specified, where $\mathbf{0}_N = (\underbrace{0, \ldots, 0}_{N \text{ times}})$.[1] We interpret the elements of S as follows: if $(s_1, s_2, \ldots, s_N) \in S$, then subsequences of $\mathbf{w}_1$ of length s_1, subsequences of $\mathbf{w}_2$ of length s_2, ..., subsequences of $\mathbf{w}_N$ of length s_N may be matched up with each other. In other words, S defines the types of valid 'many-to-many match-up operations'.[2] While we could drop S from consideration and simply allow every possible matching up of character subsequences, it is convenient to introduce S because algorithmic complexity may then be specified in terms of S, and by choosing particular S, one may retrieve special cases otherwise considered in the literature (see next section).

As indicated, for us, a multiple alignment of $(\mathbf{w}_1, \ldots, \mathbf{w}_N)$ is any scheme

$$\begin{matrix} \mathbf{w}_{1,1} & \mathbf{w}_{1,2} & \cdots & \mathbf{w}_{1,k} \\ \mathbf{w}_{2,1} & \mathbf{w}_{2,2} & \cdots & \mathbf{w}_{2,k} \\ \vdots & \vdots & \ddots & \vdots \\ \mathbf{w}_{N,1} & \mathbf{w}_{N,2} & \cdots & \mathbf{w}_{N,k} \end{matrix}$$

such that $(|\mathbf{w}_{1,i}|, \ldots, |\mathbf{w}_{N,i}|) \in S$, for all $i = 1, \ldots, k$, and such that $\mathbf{w}_n = \mathbf{w}_{n,1} \cdots \mathbf{w}_{n,k}$, for all $1 \leq n \leq N$. Let $A_S = A_S(\mathbf{w}_1, \ldots, \mathbf{w}_N)$ denote the set of all multiple alignments of $(\mathbf{w}_1, \ldots, \mathbf{w}_N)$. For an alignment $a \in A_S$, denote by $\text{score}(a) = f(a)$ the *score* of alignment a under *alignment model* f, where $f : A_S(\mathbf{w}_1, \ldots, \mathbf{w}_N) \to \mathbb{R}$. We now investigate solutions to the *problem of finding the alignment with maximal score* under different choices of alignment models f, i.e., we search to efficiently solve

$$\max_{a \in A_S(\mathbf{w}_1, \ldots, \mathbf{w}_N)} f(a). \tag{1}$$

Unigram alignment model For our first alignment model f, we assume that $f(a)$, for $a \in A_S$, is the score

$$f(a) = \sum_{i=1}^{k} \mathsf{sim}_1(\mathbf{w}_{1,i}, \ldots, \mathbf{w}_{N,i}) \tag{2}$$

for a real-valued similarity function $\mathsf{sim}_1 : \prod_{n=1}^{N}(\Sigma^{(n)})^* \to \mathbb{R}$. We call the model f in (2) a *unigram model* because $f(a)$ is the sum of the similarity scores of the matched-up subsequences $(\mathbf{w}_{1,i}, \ldots, \mathbf{w}_{N,i})$, ignoring context. Due to this independence assumption, solving maximization problem in Eq. (1) under specification (2) is straightforward via a dynamic programming (DP) recursion. To do so, define by $M_{S,\mathsf{sim}_1}(i_1, i_2, \ldots, i_N)$ the score of the best alignment, under alignment model $f = \sum \mathsf{sim}_1$ and set of steps S, of $(\mathbf{w}_1(1 : i_1), \ldots, \mathbf{w}_N(1 : i_N))$.[3] Then, $M_{S,\mathsf{sim}_1}(i_1, \ldots, i_N)$ is equal to

$$\max_{(j_1,\ldots,j_N)\in S} M_{S,\mathsf{sim}_1}(i_1 - j_1, \ldots, i_N - j_N) + \mathsf{sim}_1\big(\mathbf{w}(i_1 - j_1 + 1 : i_1), \ldots, \mathbf{w}(i_N - j_N + 1 : j_N)\big). \tag{3}$$

This recurrence directly leads to a DP algorithm, shown in Algorithm 1, for computing the *score* of the best alignment of $(\mathbf{w}_1, \ldots, \mathbf{w}_N)$; the actual alignment can be found by storing pointers to the maximizing steps taken. If similarity evaluations $\mathsf{sim}_1(\mathbf{w}_{1,i}, \ldots, \mathbf{w}_{N,i})$ are thought of as taking constant time, this algorithm's run time is $\mathcal{O}(\prod_{n=1}^{N} \ell_n \cdot |S|)$. When $\ell = \ell_1 = \cdots = \ell_n$ and $|S| = \ell^N - 1$ ('worst case' size of S), then the algorithm's runtime is thus $\mathcal{O}(\ell^{2N})$, which quickly becomes untractable as N, the number of strings to align, increases.

Of course, the unigram alignment model could be generalized to an m-gram alignment model. An m-gram alignment model would exhibit worst-case runtime complexity of $\mathcal{O}(\ell^{(m+1)N})$ under analogous DP recursions as for the unigram model.

Algorithm 1

procedure UNIGRAM-ALIGN($\mathbf{w}_1, \ldots, \mathbf{w}_N$; S, sim_1)
  $M(i_1, \ldots, i_N) \leftarrow -\infty$ for all $(i_1, \ldots, i_N) \in \mathbb{Z}^N$
  $M(\mathbf{0}_N) \leftarrow 0$
  for $i_1 = 0 \ldots \ell_1$ **do**
    for $\cdots$ **do**
      for $i_N = 0 \ldots \ell_N$ **do**
        if $(i_1, \ldots, i_N) \neq \mathbf{0}_N$ **then**
          $M(i_1, \ldots, i_N) \leftarrow$ Eq. (3)
  return $M(\ell_1, \ldots, \ell_N)$

Separable alignment models For our second model class, assume that, for any $a \in$

[1] Here, $\prod$ denotes the Cartesian product of sets.

[2] In the case of two strings, this is sometimes denoted in the manner M-N (e.g., 3-2, 1-0), indicating that M characters of one string may be matched up with N characters of the other string. Analogously, we could write here s_1-s_2-s_3-$\cdots$.

[3] We denote by $\mathbf{x}(a : b)$ the substring $x_a x_{a+1} \cdots x_b$ of the string $x_1 x_2 \cdots x_t$.

$A_S(\mathbf{w}_1,\ldots,\mathbf{w}_N)$, $f(a)$ decomposes into

$$f(a) = \Psi\Big(f_{\mathbf{w}_1}(\mathbf{w}_{1,1}\cdots\mathbf{w}_{1,k}),\ldots,f_{\mathbf{w}_N}(\mathbf{w}_{N,1}\cdots\mathbf{w}_{N,k})\Big) \tag{4}$$

for some models $f_{\mathbf{w}_1},\ldots,f_{\mathbf{w}_N}$ and where $\Psi : \mathbb{R}^N \to \mathbb{R}$ is non-decreasing in its arguments (e.g., $\Psi(f_{\mathbf{w}_1},\ldots,f_{\mathbf{w}_N}) = \sum_{n=1}^N f_{\mathbf{w}_n}$). If $f(a)$ decomposes in such a manner, then $f(a)$ is called *separable*.[4] The advantage with separable models is that we can solve the 'subproblems' $f_{\mathbf{w}_1},\ldots,f_{\mathbf{w}_N}$ independently. Thus, in order to find optimal multiple alignments of $(\mathbf{w}_1,\ldots,\mathbf{w}_N)$ under such a specification, we would only have to find the best *segmentations* of sequences $\mathbf{w}_n$ under models $f_{\mathbf{w}_n}$, for $1 \leq n \leq N$, subject to the constraint that the segmentations must agree in their *number* of segments (the *coupling variable*). Let $S_{\mathbf{w}_n} \subseteq \{0,1,\ldots,\ell_n\}$ denote the constraints on *segment lengths*, similar to the interpretation of steps in S. If $f_{\mathbf{w}_n}$ is a unigram segmentation model then the problem of finding the best segmentation of $\mathbf{w}_n$ with exactly j segments can be solved in time $\mathcal{O}(\ell_n\,|S_{\mathbf{w}_n}|\,j)$. Thus, if each $f_{\mathbf{w}_n}$ is a unigram segmentation model, worst-case time complexity for each subproblem would be $\mathcal{O}(\ell_n^3)$ (if string $\mathbf{w}_n$ can be segmented into at most ℓ_n segments) and then the overall problem (1) under specification (4) is solvable in worst-case time $N \cdot \mathcal{O}(\ell^3)$. More generally, if each $f_{\mathbf{w}_n}$ is an m-gram segmentation model, then worst-case time complexity amounts to $N \cdot \mathcal{O}(\ell^{m+2})$. Importantly, this scales *linearly* with the number N of strings to align, rather than *exponentially* as the $\mathcal{O}(\ell^{(m+1)N})$ under the (non-separable) m-gram alignment model discussed above.

Unsupervised alignments The algorithms presented may be applied iteratively in order to induce multiple alignments in an unsupervised (EM-like) fashion in which sim_1 is gradually learnt (e.g., starting from a uniform initialization of sim_1). *We skip details of this, as we do not make us of it in our current experiments.* Rather, in our experiments below, we directly specify sim_1 as a sum of pairwise similarity scores which we extract from alignments produced by an off-the-shelf *pairwise* aligner.

[4]Note the difference between Eqs. (2) and (4). While each $f_{\mathbf{w}_n}$ in (4) operates on a 'row' of an alignment scheme, sim_1 in (2) acts on the 'columns'. In other words, the unigram alignment model correlates the multiply matched-up subsequences, while the separable alignment model assumes independence here.

3 Related work

Monotone alignments have a long tradition, both in NLP and bioinformatics. The classical Needleman-Wunsch algorithm (Needleman and Wunsch, 1970) computes the optimal alignment between two sequences when only single character matches, mismatches, and skips are allowed. It is a special case of the unigram model (2) in optimization problem (1) for which $N = 2$, $S = \{(1,0),(0,1),(1,1)\}$ and sim_1 takes on values from $\{0,-1\}$, depending on whether compared input subsequences match or not. As is well-known, this alignment specification is equivalent to the edit distance problem (Levenshtein, 1966) in which the minimal number of insertions, deletions and substitutions is sought that transforms one string into another. *Substring-to-substring edit operations* — or equivalently, (monotone) many-to-many alignments — have appeared in the NLP context, e.g., in (Deligne et al., 1995), (Brill and Moore, 2000), (Jiampojamarn et al., 2007), (Bisani and Ney, 2008), (Jiampojamarn et al., 2010), or, significantly earlier, in (Ukkonen, 1985), (Véronis, 1988). *Learning* edit distance/monotone alignments in an *unsupervised* manner has been the topic of, e.g., (Ristad and Yianilos, 1998), (Cotterell et al., 2014), besides the works already mentioned. All of these approaches are special cases of our unigram model outlined in Section 2 — i.e., they consider particular S (most prominently, $S = \{(1,0),(0,1),(1,1)\}$) and/or restrict attention to only $N = 2$ strings.[5]

Alignments between multiple sequences, i.e., multiple sequence alignment, has also been an issue both in NLP (e.g., Covington (1998), Bhargava and Kondrak (2009)) and bioinformatics (e.g., Durbin et al. (1998)). An interesting application of alignments of multiple sequences is to determine what has been called *median string* (Kohonen, 1985) or *Steiner consensus string* (Gusfield, 1997), defined as the string $\bar{\mathbf{s}}$ that minimizes the sum of distances, for a given distance function $d(\mathbf{x},\mathbf{y})$, to a list of strings $\mathbf{s}_1,\ldots,\mathbf{s}_N$ (Jiang et al., 2012); typically, d is the standard edit distance. As Gusfield (1997) shows, the Steiner consensus string may be retrieved from a multiple align-

[5]In Cotterell et al. (2014), context influences alignments, so that the approach goes beyond the unigram model sketched in (2), but there, too, the focus is on the situation $N = 2$ and $S = \{(1,0),(0,1),(1,1)\}$.

ment of $\mathbf{s}_1, \ldots, \mathbf{s}_N$ by concatenating the columnwise majority characters in the alignment, ignoring skips. Since median string computation (and hence also the multiple many-to-many alignment problem, as we consider) is an NP-hard problem (Sim and Park, 2003), designing approximations is an active field of research. For example, Marti and Bunke (2001) ignore part of the search space by declaring matches-up of distant characters as unlikely, and Jiang et al. (2012) apply an approximation based on string embeddings in vector spaces. Paul and Eisner (2012) apply dual decomposition to compute Steiner consensus strings. Via the approach taken in this paper, median strings may be computed in case d is a (distance) function taking *substring-to-substring edit operations* into account, a seemingly straightforward, yet extremely useful generalization in several NLP applications, as indicated in the introduction.

Our approach may also be seen in the context of classifier combination for string-valued variables. While ensemble methods for structured prediction have been considered in several works (see, e.g., Nguyen and Guo (2007), Cortes et al. (2014), and references therein), a typical assumption in this situation is that the sequences to be combined have equal length, which clearly cannot be expected to hold when, e.g., the outputs of several G2P, transliteration, etc., systems must be combined. In fact, the multiple many-to-many alignment models investigated in this work could act as a preprocessing step in this setup, since the alignment precisely serves the functionality of segmenting the strings into equal number of segments/substructures. Of course, combining outputs with varying number of elements is also an issue in machine translation (e.g., Macherey and Och (2007), Heafield et al. (2009)), but, there, the problem is harder due to the potential non-monotonicities in the ordering of elements, which typically necessitates (additional) heuristics. One approach for constructing multiple alignments is here *progressive multiple alignment* (Feng and Doolittle, 1987) in which a multiple (typically one-to-one) alignment is iteratively constructed from successive pairwise alignments (Bangalore et al., 2001). Matusov et al. (2006) apply word reordering and subsequent pairwise monotone one-to-one alignments for MT system combination.

4 Data and systems

4.1 Data

We conduct experiments on the General American (GA) variant of the Combilex data set (Richmond et al., 2009). This contains about 144,000 grapheme-phoneme pairs as exemplarily illustrated in Table 2. In our experiments, we split the data into two disjoint parts, one for testing (about 28,000 word pairs) and one for training/development (the remainder).

4.2 Systems

BASELINE Our baseline system is a linear-chain conditional random field model (CRF)[6] (Lafferty et al., 2001) which we apply in the manner indicated in the introduction: after many-to-many aligning the training data as in Table 1, at *training time*, we use the CRF as a tagging model that is trained to label each input character subsequence with an output character subsequence. As *features* for the CRF, we use all n-grams of subsequences of $\mathbf{x}$ that fit inside a window of size 5 centered around the current subsequence (*context features*). We also include *linear-chain features* which allow previously generated output character subsequences to influence current output character subsequences. In essence, our baseline model is a standard discriminative approach to G2P. It is, all in all, the same approach as described in Jiampojamarn et al. (2010), except that we do not include joint n-gram features. At *test time*, we first segment a new input string $\mathbf{x}$ and then apply the CRF. Thereby, we train the segmentation module on the segmented $\mathbf{x}$ sequences, as available from the aligned training data.[7]

BASELINE+X As competitors for the baseline system, we introduce systems that rely on the predictions of one or several additional (black box/offline) systems. *At training time*, we first multiply many-to-many align the input string $\mathbf{x}$, the predictions $\hat{\mathbf{y}}^{(1)}, \ldots, \hat{\mathbf{y}}^{(M)}$ and the true transcription $\mathbf{y}$ as illustrated in Table 3 (see Section 4.3 for details). Then, as for the baseline system, we train a CRF to label each input character

[6] We made use of the CRF++ package available at https://code.google.com/p/crfpp/.

[7] To be more precise on the training of the segmentation module, in an alignment as in Table 1, we consider the segmented $\mathbf{x}$ string — ph-oe-n-i-x — and then encode this segmentation in a binary string where 1's indicate splits. Thus, segmentation becomes, again, a sequence labling task; see, e.g., Bartlett et al. (2008) or Eger (2013) for details.

subsequence with the corresponding output character subsequence. However, this time, the CRF has access to the subsequence suggestions (as the alignments indicate) produced by the offline systems. As *features* for the extended models, we additionally include context features for all predicted strings $\hat{\mathbf{y}}^{(m)}$ (all n-grams in a window of size 3 centered around the current subsequence prediction). We also include a joint feature firing on the tuple of the current subsequence value of $\mathbf{x}$, $\hat{\mathbf{y}}^{(1)}, \ldots, \hat{\mathbf{y}}^{(M)}$. To illustrate, when BASELINE+X tags position 2 in the (split up) input string in Table 3, it sees that its value is *ch*, that the previous input position contains *s*, that the next contains *i*, that the next two contain (*i,z*), that the prediction of the first system at position 2 is k, that the first system's next prediction is ai, and so forth. *At test time*, we first multiply many-to-many align $\mathbf{x}, \hat{\mathbf{y}}^{(1)}, \ldots, \hat{\mathbf{y}}^{(M)}$, and then apply the enhanced CRF.

4.3 Alignments

To induce multiple monotone many-to-many alignments of input strings, offline system predictions and output strings, we proceed in one of two manners.

Exact alignments *Firstly*, we specify sim_1 in Eq. (2), as $\mathsf{sim}_1(\mathbf{x}_i, \hat{\mathbf{y}}_i^{(1)}, \ldots, \hat{\mathbf{y}}_i^{(M)}, \mathbf{y}_i) =$

$$\Big(\sum_{m=1}^{M} \mathsf{psim}(\mathbf{x}_i, \hat{\mathbf{y}}_i^{(m)})\Big) + \mathsf{psim}(\mathbf{x}_i, \mathbf{y}_i),$$

where psim is a pair-similarity function. The advantage with this specification is that the similarity of a tuple of subsequences is defined as the sum of *pairwise* similarity scores, which we can directly estimate from pairwise alignments of $(\mathbf{x}, \hat{\mathbf{y}}^{(m)})$ that an off-the-shelf pairwise aligner can produce (we use the Phonetisaurus aligner for this). We set $\mathsf{psim}(\mathbf{u}, \mathbf{v})$ as log-probability of observing the tuple $(\mathbf{u}, \mathbf{v})$ in the training data of pairwise aligned sequences. To illustrate, we define the similarity of (o,əʊ,əʊ,ə,əʊ,ə,əʊ) in the example in Table 3 as the pairwise similarity of (o,əʊ) (as inferred from pairwise alignments of $\mathbf{x}$ strings and system 1 transcriptions) plus the pairwise similarity of (o,əʊ) (as inferred from pairwise alignments of $\mathbf{x}$ strings and system 2 transcriptions), etc. At test time, we use the same procedure but drop the term $\mathsf{psim}(\mathbf{x}_i, \mathbf{y}_i)$ when inducing alignments. For our current purposes, we label the outlined modus as **exact (alignment) modus**.

Approx. alignments *Secondly*, we derive the optimal multiple many-to-many alignment of the strings in question by choosing an alignment that satisfies the condition that (1) each individual string $\mathbf{x}, \hat{\mathbf{y}}^{(1)}, \ldots, \hat{\mathbf{y}}^{(M)}, \mathbf{y}$ is optimally *segmented* (e.g., *ph-oe-n-i-x* rather than *pho-eni-x*, f-i-n-ɪ-ks rather than f-inɪk-s) subject to the global constraint that (2) the number of segments must agree across the strings to align. This constitutes a separable alignment model as discussed in Section 2, and thus has much lower runtime complexity as the first model. Segmentation models can be directly learned from the pairwise alignments that Phonetisaurus produces by focusing on either the segmented $\mathbf{x}$ or $\mathbf{y}/\hat{\mathbf{y}}^{(m)}$ sequences; we choose to implement bigram individual segmentation models. This second model type may be considered an *approximation* of the first, since in a good alignment, we would not only expect individually good segmentations and agreement of segment numbers but also that subsegments are *likely correlations* of each other, precisely as our first model type captures. Therefore, we shall call this alignment modus **approximate (alignment) modus**, for our present purposes.

5 Experiments

We now describe two sets of experiments, a **controlled experiment** on the Combilex data set where we can design our offline/black box systems ourselves and where the black box systems are trained on a similar distribution as the baseline and the extended baseline systems. In particular, the black box systems operate on the same output alphabet as the extended baseline systems, which constitutes an 'ideal' situation. Thereafter, we investigate how our extended baseline system performs in a **'real-world' scenario**: we train a system on Combilex that has as supplemental information corresponding Wiktionary (and PTE, as explained below) transcriptions.

Throughout, we use as accuracy measures for all our systems **word accuray** (WACC). Word accuracy is defined as the number of correctly transcribed strings among all transcribed strings in a test sample. WACC is a strict measure that penalizes even tiny deviations from the gold-standard transcriptions, but has nowadays become standard in G2P.

5.1 A controlled experiment

In our first set of experiments, we let our offline/black box systems be the Sequitur G2P modeling toolkit (Bisani and Ney, 2008) (S) and the Phonetisaurus modeling toolkit (Novak et al., 2012) (P). We train them on *disjoint sets* of 20,000 grapheme-to-phoneme Combilex string pairs each. The performance of these two systems, on the test set of size 28,000, is indicated in Table 4. Next, we train BASELINE on *disjoint* sets (disjoint from both the training sets of P and S) of size 2,000, 5,000, 10,000 and 20,000. Making BASELINE's training sets disjoint from the training sets of the offline systems is both realistic (since a black box system would typically follow a partially distinct distribution from one's own training set distribution) and also prevents the extended baseline systems from fully adapting to the predictions of either P or S, whose training set accuracy is an upward biased representation of their true accuracy. As baseline extensions, we consider the systems BASELINE+P (+P), and BASELINE+P+S (+P+S).[8]

	Phonetisaurus	Sequitur
WACC	72.12	71.70

Table 4: Word-accuracy (in %) on the test data, for the two systems indicated.

Results are shown in Figures 1 and 2. We see that conjoining the base system with the predictions of the offline Phonetisaurus and Sequitur models substantially increases the baseline WACC, *especially in the case of little training data*. In fact, WACC increases here by almost 100% when the baseline system is complemented by $\hat{\mathbf{y}}^{(P)}$ and $\hat{\mathbf{y}}^{(S)}$. As training set size increases, differences become less and less pronounced. Eventually, we would expect them to drop to zero, since beyond some training set size, the additional features may provide no new information.[9] We also note that conjoining the two systems is more valuable than conjoining only one system, and, in Figure 2, that the models which are based on exact multiple alignments outperform the models based on approximate alignments, but not by a wide margin.

[8] We omit BASELINE+S since it yielded similar results as BASELINE+P.

[9] In fact, in follow-up work, we find that the additional information may also confuse the base system when training set sizes are large enough.

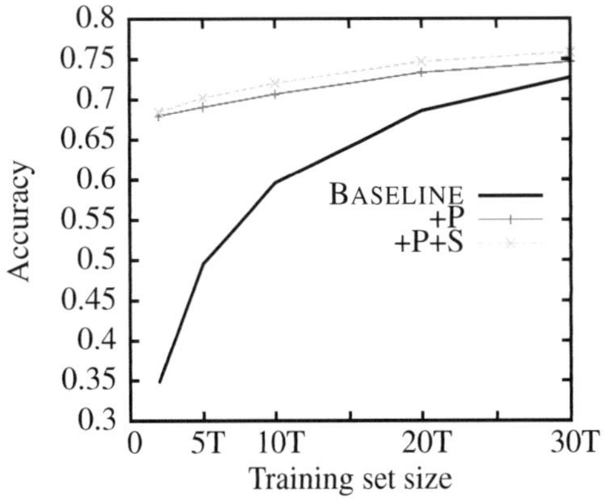

Figure 1: WACC as a function of training set size for the system indicated. Exact align. modus.

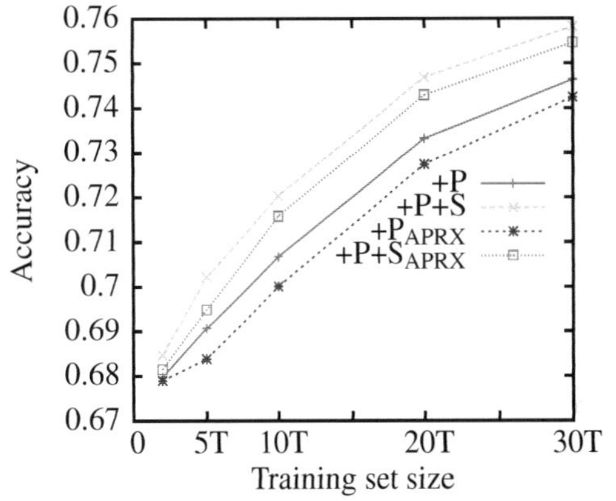

Figure 2: Comparison of models based on exact and approximate alignments; WACC as a function of training set size. APRX denotes the approximation alignment model.

Concerning differences in *alignments* between the two alignment types, exact vs. approximate, an illustrative example where the approximate model fails and the exact model does not is ('false' alignment based on the approximate model indicated):

r	ee	n	t	e	r	e	d
r	i	E	n	t	@'	r	d
r	i	E	n	t	@'	r	d

which nicely captures the inability of the approximate model to account for correlations between the matched-up subsequences. That is, while the segmentations of the three shown sequences appear acceptable, a matching of graphemic *t* with phonemic n, etc., seems quite unlikely. Still, it is very promising to see that these differences in alignment quality translate into very small differences in overall string-to-string translation model performance, as Figure 2 outlines. Namely, differences in WACC are typically on the level of 1% or less (always in favor of the exact alignment model). This is a very important finding, as it indicates that string-to-string translation need not be (severely) negatively impacted by switching to the approximate alignment model, a tractable alternative to the exact models, which quickly become practically infeasible as the number of strings to align increases.

5.2 Real-world experiments

To test whether our approach may also succeed in a 'real-world setting', we use as offline/black box systems GA Wiktionary transcriptions of our input forms as well as PhotoTransEdit (PTE) transcriptions,[10] a lexicon-based G2P system which offers both GA and RP (received pronunciation) transcription of English strings. *We train and test on input strings for which both Combilex and PTE transcriptions are available, and for which both Combilex and Wiktionary transcriptions are available.*[11] Test set sizes are about 1,500 in the case of PTE and 3,500 in the case of Wiktionary. We only test here the performance of the exact alignment method, noting that, as before, approximate alignments produced slightly weaker results.

Clearly, Wiktionary and PTE differ from the Combilex data. First, both Wiktionary and PTE use different numbers of phonemic symbols than Combilex, as Table 5 illustrates. Some differences

Dataset	$\|\Sigma\|$
Combilex	54
$\text{Wiktionary}_{\text{GA}}$	107
$\text{Wiktionary}_{\text{RP}}$	116
PTE_{GA}	44
PTE_{RP}	57

Table 5: Sizes of phonetic inventaries of different data sets.

arise from the fact that, e.g., lengthening of vowels is indicated by two output letters in some data sets and only one in others. Also, phonemic transcription conventions differ, as becomes most strikingly evident in the case of RP vs. GA transcriptions — Table 6 illustrates. Finally, Wiktionary has many more phonetic symbols than the other datasets, a finding that we attribute to its crowd-sourced nature and lacking of normalization. Despite these differences in phonemic annotation standards between Combilex, Wiktionary and PTE, we observe that conjoining input strings with predicted Wiktionary or PTE transcriptions via multiple alignments leads to very good improvements in WACC over only using the input string as information source. Indeed, as shown in Table 7, for PTE, WACC increases by as much as 80% in case of small training sample (1,099 string pairs) and as much as 37% in case of medium-sized training sample (2,687 string pairs). Thus, comparing with the previous situation of homogenous systems, we also observe that the gain from including heterogeneous system is relatively weaker, as we would expect due to distinct underlying assumptions, but still impressive. Performance increases when including Wiktionary are slightly lower, most likely because it constitutes a very heterogenous source of phonetic transcriptions with user-idiosyncratic annotations (however, training set sizes are also different).[12]

	BASEL.	BASEL.+PTE_{GA}	BASEL.+PTE_{RP}
1,099	31.34	56.47	50.22
2,687	45.75	60.80	62.80

	BASEL.	BASEL.+Wik_{GA}	BASEL.+Wik_{RP}
2,000	38.44	60.71	62.18
5,000	51.69	65.81	65.96
10,000	58.97	67.30	68.66

Table 7: Top: WACC in % for baseline CRF model and the models that integrate PTE in the GA versions and RP versions, respectively. Bottom: BASELINE and BASELINE+Wiktionary.

6 Conclusion

We have generalized the task description of string transduction to include supplemental information strings. Moreover, we have suggested multiple

[10] Downloadable from http://www.photransedit.com/.

[11] This yields a clear method of comparison. An alternative would be to provide predictions for missing transcriptions. In any case, by our task definition, all systems must provide a hypothesis for an input string.

[12] To provide, for the interested reader, a comparison with Phonetisaurus and Sequitur: for the Wiktionary GA data, performance of Phonetisaurus is 41.80% (training set size 2,000), 55.70% (5,000) and 62.47% (10,000). Respective numbers for Sequitur are 40.58%, 54.84%, and 61.58%. On PTE, results are, similarly, slightly higher than our baseline, but substantially lower than the extended baseline.

b	o	t	ch	i	ng		b	a	rr	ed		a	s	th	m	a	t	i	c	s
b	o	t	ʃ	ɪ	ŋ		b	a	-	d		æ	s	-	m	æ	t	ɪ	k	s
b	A	-	tS	I	N		b	A	r	d		a	z	0	m	a	t	I	k	s

Table 6: Multiple alignments of input string, predicted PTE transcription and true (Combilex) transcription. Differences may be due to alternative phonemic conventions (e.g., Combilex has a single phonemic character representing the sound tʃ) and/or due to differences in pronunciation in GA and RP, resp.

many-to-many alignments — and a subsequent standardly extended discriminative approach — for solving string transduction (here, G2P) in this generalized setup. We have shown that, in a real-world setting, our approach may significantly beat a standard discriminative baseline, e.g., when we add Wiktionary transcriptions or predictions of a rule-based system as additional information to the input strings. The appeal of this approach lies in the fact that almost *any sort of external knowledge source may be integrated to improve the performance of a baseline system*. For example, supplemental information strings may appear in the form of transliterations of an input string in other languages; they may be predictions of other G2P systems, whether carefully manually crafted or learnt from data; they might even appear in the form of phonetic transcriptions of the input string in other dialects or languages. What distinguishes our solution to integrating supplemental information strings in string transduction settings from other research (e.g., (Bhargava and Kondrak, 2011; Bhargava and Kondrak, 2012)) is that rather than integrating systems on the *global* level of *strings*, we integrate them on the *local* level of smaller units, namely, *substrings* appropriated to the domain of application (e.g., in our context, phonemes/grapheme substructures). Both approaches may be considered complementary. Finally, another important contribution of our work is to outline an 'approximation algorithm' to inducing multiple many-to-many alignments of strings, which is otherwise an NP-hard problem for which (most likely) no efficient exact solutions exist, and to investigate its suitability for the problem task. In particular, we have seen that exact alignments lead to better overall model performance, but that the margin over the approximation is not wide.

The scope for future research of our modeling is huge: multiple many-to-many alignments may be useful in aligning cognates in linguistic research; they may be the first necessary step for many other ensemble techniques in string transduction as we have considered (Cortes et al., 2014), and they may allow, on a large scale, to boost G2P (transliteration, lemmatization, etc.) systems by integrating them with many traditional (or modern) knowledge resources such as rule- and dictionary-based lemmatizers, crowd-sourced phonetic transcriptions (e.g., based on Wiktionary), etc., with the outlook of significantly outperforming current state-of-the-art models which are based solely on input string information.

Finally, we note that we have thus far shown that supplemental information strings may be beneficial in case of overall little training data and that improvements decrease with data size. Further investigating this relationship will be of importance. Morevoer, it will be insightful to compare the exact and approximate alignment algorithms presented here with other (heuristic) alignment methods, such as iterative pairwise alignments as employed in machine translation, and to investigate how alignment quality of multiple strings impacts overall G2P performance in the setup of additional information strings.

References

S. Bangalore, G. Bodel, and G. Riccardi. 2001. Computing consensus translation from multiple machine translation systems. In *In Proceedings of IEEE Automatic Speech Recognition and Understanding Workshop (ASRU-2001*, pages 351–354.

Susan Bartlett, Grzegorz Kondrak, and Colin Cherry. 2008. Automatic syllabification with structured svms for letter-to-phoneme conversion. In Kathleen McKeown, Johanna D. Moore, Simone Teufel, James Allan, and Sadaoki Furui, editors, *ACL*, pages 568–576. The Association for Computer Linguistics.

Aditya Bhargava and Grzegorz Kondrak. 2009. Multiple word alignment with Profile Hidden Markov Models. In *Proceedings of Human Language Technologies: The 2009 Annual Conference of the North American Chapter of the Association for Computational Linguistics, Companion Volume: Student Research Workshop and Doctoral Consortium*, pages

43–48, Boulder, Colorado, June. Association for Computational Linguistics.

Aditya Bhargava and Grzegorz Kondrak. 2011. How do you pronounce your name?: Improving g2p with transliterations. In *Proceedings of the 49th Annual Meeting of the Association for Computational Linguistics: Human Language Technologies - Volume 1*, HLT '11, pages 399–408, Stroudsburg, PA, USA. Association for Computational Linguistics.

Aditya Bhargava and Grzegorz Kondrak. 2012. Leveraging supplemental representations for sequential transduction. In *HLT-NAACL*, pages 396–406. The Association for Computational Linguistics.

Maximilian Bisani and Hermann Ney. 2008. Joint-sequence models for grapheme-to-phoneme conversion. *Speech Communication*, 50(5):434–451.

Eric Brill and Robert C. Moore. 2000. An improved error model for noisy channel spelling correction. In *Proceedings of the 38th Annual Meeting on Association for Computational Linguistics*, ACL '00, pages 286–293, Stroudsburg, PA, USA. Association for Computational Linguistics.

Corinna Cortes, Vitaly Kuznetsov, and Mehryar Mohri. 2014. Ensemble methods for structured prediction. In *Proceedings of the 31th International Conference on Machine Learning, ICML 2014, Beijing, China, 21-26 June 2014*, pages 1134–1142.

Ryan Cotterell, Nanyun Peng, and Jason Eisner. 2014. Stochastic contextual edit distance and probabilistic FSTs. In *Proceedings of the 52nd Annual Meeting of the Association for Computational Linguistics (ACL)*, Baltimore, June. 6 pages.

Michael A. Covington. 1998. Alignment of multiple languages for historical comparison. In *Proceedings of the 36th Annual Meeting of the Association for Computational Linguistics and 17th International Conference on Computational Linguistics, Volume 1*, pages 275–279, Montreal, Quebec, Canada, August. Association for Computational Linguistics.

Sabine Deligne, Franois Yvon, and Frédéric Bimbot. 1995. Variable-length sequence matching for phonetic transcription using joint multigrams. In *EUROSPEECH*. ISCA.

Markus Dreyer, Jason Smith, and Jason Eisner. 2008. Latent-variable modeling of string transductions with finite-state methods. In *EMNLP*, pages 1080–1089. ACL.

Richard Durbin, Sean R. Eddy, Anders Krogh, and Graeme Mitchison. 1998. *Biological Sequence Analysis: Probabilistic Models of Proteins and Nucleic Acids*. Cambridge University Press.

Steffen Eger. 2013. Sequence segmentation by enumeration: An exploration. *Prague Bull. Math. Linguistics*, 100:113–132.

D. F. Feng and R. F. Doolittle. 1987. Progressive sequence alignment as a prerequisite to correct phylogenetic trees. *Journal of molecular evolution*, 25(4):351–360.

Dan Gusfield. 1997. *Algorithms on Strings, Trees, and Sequences - Computer Science and Computational Biology*. Cambridge University Press.

Kenneth Heafield, Greg Hanneman, and Alon Lavie. 2009. Machine translation system combination with flexible word ordering. In *Proceedings of the EACL 2009 Fourth Workshop on Statistical Machine Translation*, pages 56–60, Athens, Greece, March.

Sittichai Jiampojamarn, Grzegorz Kondrak, and Tarek Sherif. 2007. Applying many-to-many alignments and hidden markov models to letter-to-phoneme conversion. In *Human Language Technologies 2007: The Conference of the North American Chapter of the Association for Computational Linguistics; Proceedings of the Main Conference*, pages 372–379, Rochester, New York, April. Association for Computational Linguistics.

Sittichai Jiampojamarn, Colin Cherry, and Grzegorz Kondrak. 2008. Joint processing and discriminative training for letter-to-phoneme conversion. In *Proceedings of ACL-08: HLT*, pages 905–913, Columbus, Ohio, June. Association for Computational Linguistics.

Sittichai Jiampojamarn, Colin Cherry, and Grzegorz Kondrak. 2010. Integrating joint n-gram features into a discriminative training framework. In *HLT-NAACL*, pages 697–700. The Association for Computational Linguistics.

Xiaoyi Jiang, Jran Wentker, and Miquel Ferrer. 2012. Generalized median string computation by means of string embedding in vector spaces. *Pattern Recognition Letters*, 33(7):842–852.

T. Kohonen. 1985. Median strings. *Pattern Recognition Letters*, 3:309–313.

John Lafferty, Andrew McCallum, and Fernando Pereira. 2001. Conditional random fields: Probabilistic models for segmenting and labeling sequence data. In *Proc. 18th International Conf. on Machine Learning*, pages 282–289. Morgan Kaufmann, San Francisco, CA.

VI Levenshtein. 1966. Binary Codes Capable of Correcting Deletions, Insertions and Reversals. *Soviet Physics Doklady*, 10:707.

Wolfgang Macherey and Franz Josef Och. 2007. An empirical study on computing consensus translations from multiple machine translation systems. In *EMNLP-CoNLL*, pages 986–995. ACL.

Urs-Viktor Marti and Horst Bunke. 2001. Use of positional information in sequence alignment for multiple classifier combination. In Josef Kittler and Fabio Roli, editors, *Multiple Classifier Systems*, volume

2096 of *Lecture Notes in Computer Science*, pages 388–398. Springer.

Evgeny Matusov, Nicola Ueffing, and Hermann Ney. 2006. Computing consensus translation from multiple machine translation systems using enhanced hypotheses alignment. In *Conference of the European Chapter of the Association for Computational Linguistics*, pages 33–40, Trento, Italy, April.

Saul B. Needleman and Christian D. Wunsch. 1970. A general method applicable to the search for similarities in the amino acid sequence of two proteins. *Journal of Molecular Biology*, 48(3):443–453, March.

Nam Nguyen and Yunsong Guo. 2007. Comparisons of sequence labeling algorithms and extensions. In Zoubin Ghahramani, editor, *ICML*, volume 227 of *ACM International Conference Proceeding Series*, pages 681–688. ACM.

Josef R. Novak, Nobuaki Minematsu, and Keikichi Hirose. 2012. WFST-based grapheme-to-phoneme conversion: Open source tools for alignment, model-building and decoding. In *Proceedings of the 10th International Workshop on Finite State Methods and Natural Language Processing*, pages 45–49, Donostia–San Sebastin, July. Association for Computational Linguistics.

Michael J. Paul and Jason Eisner. 2012. Implicitly intersecting weighted automata using dual decomposition. In *HLT-NAACL*, pages 232–242. The Association for Computational Linguistics.

Korin Richmond, Robert A. J. Clark, and Susan Fitt. 2009. Robust LTS rules with the Combilex speech technology lexicon. In *INTERSPEECH*, pages 1295–1298. ISCA.

Eric Sven Ristad and Peter N. Yianilos. 1998. Learning string-edit distance. *IEEE Trans. Pattern Anal. Mach. Intell.*, 20(5):522–532.

Tarek Sherif and Grzegorz Kondrak. 2007. Substring-based transliteration. In John A. Carroll, Antal van den Bosch, and Annie Zaenen, editors, *ACL*. The Association for Computational Linguistics.

Jeong Seop Sim and Kunsoo Park. 2003. The consensus string problem for a metric is np-complete. *J. of Discrete Algorithms*, 1(1):111–117, February.

Esko Ukkonen. 1985. Algorithms for approximate string matching. *Information and Control*, 64:100–118.

Jean Véronis. 1988. Computerized correction of phonographic errors. *Computers and the Humanities*, 22(1):43–56.

Tweet Normalization with Syllables

Ke Xu
School of Software Eng.
Beijing U. of Posts & Telecom.
Beijing 100876, China
xxukez2@gmail.com

Yunqing Xia
STCA
Microsoft
Beijing 100084, China
yxia@microsoft.com

Chin-Hui Lee
School of Electr. & Comp. Eng.
Georgia Institute of Technology
Atlanta, GA 30332-0250, USA
chl@ece.gatech.edu

Abstract

In this paper, we propose a syllable-based method for tweet normalization to study the cognitive process of non-standard word creation in social media. Assuming that syllable plays a fundamental role in forming the non-standard tweet words, we choose syllable as the basic unit and extend the conventional noisy channel model by incorporating the syllables to represent the word-to-word transitions at both word and syllable levels. The syllables are used in our method not only to suggest more candidates, but also to measure similarity between words. Novelty of this work is three-fold: First, to the best of our knowledge, this is an early attempt to explore syllables in tweet normalization. Second, our proposed normalization method relies on unlabeled samples, making it much easier to adapt our method to handle non-standard words in any period of history. And third, we conduct a series of experiments and prove that the proposed method is advantageous over the state-of-art solutions for tweet normalization.

1 Introduction

Due to the casual nature of social media, there exists a large number of non-standard words in text expressions which make it substantially different from formal written text. It is reported in (Liu et al., 2011) that more than 4 million distinct out-of-vocabulary (OOV) tokens are found in the Edinburgh Twitter corpus (Petrovic et al., 2010). This variation poses challenges when performing natural language processing (NLP) tasks (Sproat et al., 2001) based on such texts. Tweet normalization, aiming at converting these OOV non-standard words into their in-vocabulary (IV) formal forms, is therefore viewed as a very important pre-processing task.

Researchers focus their studies in tweet normalization at different levels. A character-level tagging system is used in (Pennell and Liu, 2010) to solve deletion-based abbreviation. It was further extended in (Liu et al., 2012) using more characters instead of `Y` or `N` as labels. The character-level machine translation (MT) approach (Pennell and Liu, 2011) was modified in (Li and Liu, 2012a) into character-block. While a string edit distance method was introduced in (Contractor et al., 2010) to represent word-level similarity, and this orthographical feature has been adopted in (Han and Baldwin, 2011), and (Yang and Eisenstein, 2013).

Challenges are encountered in these different levels of tweet normalization. In the character-level sequential labeling systems, features are required for every character and their combinations, leading to much more noise into the later reverse table look-up process (Liu et al., 2012). In the character-block level MT systems equal number of blocks and their corresponding phonetic symbols are required for alignment (Li and Liu, 2012b). This strict restriction can result in a great difficulty in training set construction and a loss of useful information. Finally, word-level normalization methods cannot properly model how non-standard words are formed, and some patterns or consistencies within words can be omitted and altered.

We observe the cognitive process that, given non-standard words like `tmr`, people tend to first segment them into syllables like `t-m-r`. Then they will find the corresponding standard word with syllables like `to-mor-row`. Inspired by this cognitive observation, we propose a syllable based tweet normalization method, in which non-standard words are first segmented into syllables. Since we cannot predict the writers deterministic intention in using `tmr` as a segmentation of `tm-r`

Proceedings of the 53rd Annual Meeting of the Association for Computational Linguistics and the 7th International Joint Conference on Natural Language Processing, pages 920–928,
Beijing, China, July 26-31, 2015. ©2015 Association for Computational Linguistics

(representing `tim-er`) or `t-m-r` (representing `to-mor-row`), every possible segmentation form is considered. Then we represent similarity of standard syllables and non-standard *syllables* using an exponential potential function. After every transition probabilities of standard syllable and non-standard syllable are assigned, we then use noisy channel model and Viterbi decoder to search for the most possible standard candidate in each tweet sentence.

Our empirical study reveals that syllable is a proper level for tweet normalization. The syllable is similar to character-block but it represents phonetic features naturally because every word is pronounced with syllables. Our syllable-based tweet normalization method utilizes effective features of both character- and word-level: (1) Like character-level, it can capture more detailed information about how non-standard words are generated; (2) Similar to word-level, it reduces a large amount of noisy candidates. Instead of using domain-specific resources, our method makes good use of standard words to extract linguistic features. This makes our method extendable to new normalization tasks or domains.

The rest of this paper is organized as follows: previous work in tweet normalization are reviewed and discussed in Section 2. Our approach is presented in Section 3. In Section 4 and Section 5, we provide implementation details and results. Then we make some analysis of the results in Section 6. This work is finally concluded in Section 7.

2 Related Work

Non-standard words exhibit different forms and change rapidly, but people can still figure out their original standard words. To properly model this human ability, researchers are studying what remain unchanged under this dynamic characteristic. Human normalization of an non-standard word can be as follows: After realizing the word is non-standard, people usually first figure out standard candidate words in various manners. Then they replace the non-standard words with the standard candidates in the sentence to check whether the sentence can carry a meaning. If not, they switch to a different candidate until a good one is found. Most normalization methods in existence follow the same procedure: candidates are first generated, and then put into the sentence to check whether a reasonable sentence can be formed. Differences lie in how the candidates are generated and weighted. Related work can be classified into three groups.

2.1 Orthographical similarity

Orthographical similarity is built upon the assumption that the non-standard words *look like* its standard counterparts, leading to a high *Longest Common Sequence* (LCS) and low *Edit Distance* (ED). This method is widely used in spell checker, in which the LCS and ED scores are calculated for weighting possible candidates. However, problems are that the correct word cannot always be the most *looked like* one. Taking the non-standard word `nite` for example, `note` looks more likely than the correct form `night`. To overcome this problem, an *exception dictionary* of strongly-associated word pairs are constructed in (Gouws et al., 2011). Further, these pairs are added into a unified log-linear model in (Yang and Eisenstein, 2013) and Monte Carlo sampling techniques are used to estimate parameters.

2.2 Phonetic similarity

The assumption underlying the phonetic similarity is that during transition, non-standard words *sound like* the standard counterparts, thus the pronunciation of non-standard words can be traced back to a standard dictionary. The challenge is the algorithm to annotate pronunciation of the non-standard words. Double Metaphone algorithm (Philips, 2000) is used to decode pronunciation and then to represent phonetic similarity by edit distance of these transcripts (Han and Baldwin, 2011). IPA symbols are utilized in (Li and Liu, 2012b) to represent sound of words and then word alignment-based machine translation is applied to generate possible pronunciation of non-standard words. And also, phoneme is used in (Liu et al., 2012) as one kind of features to train their CRF model.

2.3 Contextual similarity

It is accepted that after standard words are transformed into non-standard words, the meaning of a sentence remains unchanged. So the normalized standard word must carry a meaning. Most researchers use n-gram language model to normalize a sentence, and several researches use more contextual information. For example, training pairs are generated in (Liu et al., 2012) by a cosine contextual similarity formula whose items are defined by TF-IDF scheme. A bipartite graph is constructed in (Hassan and Menezes, 2013) to represent tokens (both non-standard and standard words) and their context. Thus, random walks on the graph can represent contextual-similarity between non-standard and standard words. Very recently, word-embedding (Mikolov et al., 2010; Mikolov et al., 2013) is utilized in (Li and Liu, 2014) to represent more complex contextual relationship.

In word-to-word candidate selection, most researches use orthographical similarity and phonetic similarity separately. In the log-linear model (Yang and Eisenstein, 2013), edit distance is modeled as major feature. In the character- and phone-based approaches (Li and Liu, 2012b), orthographical information and phonetic information were treated separately to generate candidates.

In (Han and Baldwin, 2011), candidates from lexical edit distance and phonemic edit distance are merged together. Then an up to 16% increasing recall was reported when adding candidates from phonetic measure. But improper processing level makes it difficult to model the two types of information simultaneously: (1) Single character can hardly reflect orthographical features of one word. (2) As fine-grained reasonable restrictions are lacked, as showed in (Han and Baldwin, 2011), several times of candidates are included when adding phonetic candidates and this will bring much more noise. To combine orthographical and phonetic measure in a fine-grained level, we proposed the syllable-level approach.

3 Approach

3.1 Framework

The framework of the proposed tweet normalization method is presented in Figure 1. The proposed method extends the basic HMM channel model (Choudhury et al., 2007; Cook and Stevenson, 2009) into syllable level. And the following four characteristics are very intersting.

(1) **Combination**: When reading a sentence, fast subvocalization will occur in our mind. In the process, some non-standard words generated by phonetic substitution are correctly pronounced and then normalized. And also, because subvocalization is fast, people tend to ignore some minor flaws in spelling intentionally or unintentionally. As this often occurs in people's real-life interacting with these social media language, we believe the combination of phonetic and orthographical information is of great significance.

(2) **Syllable level**: Inspired by Chinese normalization (Xia et al., 2006) using pinyin (phonetic transcripts of Chinese), syllable can be seen as basic unit when processing pronunciation. Different from mono-syllable Chinese words, English words can be multi-syllable; this will bring changes in our method that extra layers of syllables must be put into consideration. Thus, apart from word-based noisy-channel model, we extend it into a syllable-level framework.

(3) **Priori knowledge**: Priori knowledge is acquired from standard words, meaning that both standard syllabification and pronunciation can shed some lights to non-standard words. This assumption makes it possible to obtain non-standard syllables by standard syllabification and gain pronunciation of syllables by standard words and rules generated with them.

(4) **General patterns**: Social media language changes rapidly while labeled data is expensive thus limited. To effectively solve the problem, linguistic features instead of statistical features should be emphasized. We exploit standard words of their syllables, pronunciation and possible transition patterns and proposed the four-layer HMM-based model (see Figure 1).

In our method, non-standard words c_i are first segmented into syllables $sc_i^{(1)} \dots sc_i^{(k)}$, and for standard syllable $sw_i^{(j)}$ mapping to non-standard syllable $sw_i^{(j)}$, we calculate their similarity by combining the orthographical and phonetic measures. Standard syllables $sw_i^{(1)} \dots sw_i^{(k)}$ make up one standard candidates. Since candidates are generated and weighted, we can use Viterbi decoder to perform sentence normalization. Table 1 shows some possible candidates for the non-standard word `tmr`.

3.2 Method

We extend the noisy channel model to syllable-level as follows:

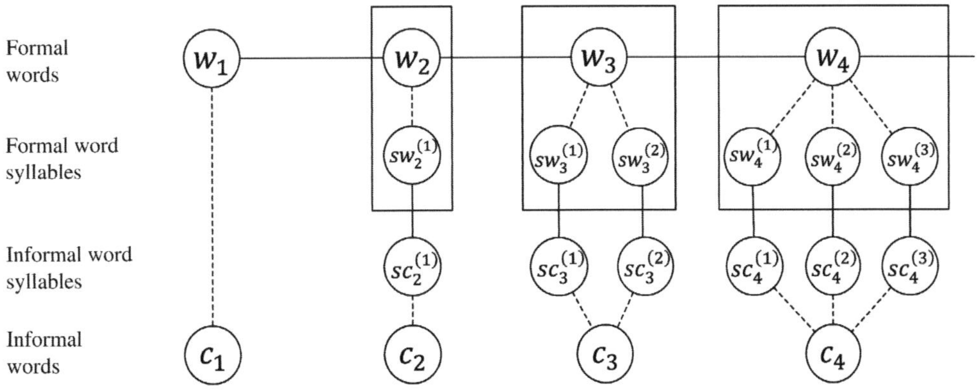

Figure 1: Framework of the propose tweet normalization method.

$$\begin{aligned}\widehat{w} &= argmax \quad p(w|c) \\ &= argmax \quad p(c|w) \times p(w) \\ &= argmax \quad p(\vec{sc}|\vec{sw}) \times p(\vec{sw}),\end{aligned} \quad (1)$$

where w indicates the standard word and c the non-standard word, and sw and sc represent their syllabic form, respectively. To simplify the problem, we restrict the number of standard syllables equals to the number of non-standard syllables in our method.

Assuming that syllables are independent of each other in transforming, we obtain:

$$p(\vec{sc}|\vec{sw}) = \prod_{j=1}^{k} p(sc_j|sw_j). \quad (2)$$

For syllable similarity, we use an exponential potential function to combine orthographical distance and phonetic distance. Because pronunciation can be represented using letter-to-phone transcripts, we can treat string similarity of these transcripts as phonetic similarity. Thus the syllable similarity can be calculated as follows.

$$p(sc_j|sw_j, \lambda) = \frac{\Phi(sc_j, sw_j)}{Z(sw_j)} \quad (3)$$

$$Z(sw_j) = \sum_{sc_j} \Phi(sc_j, sw_j) \quad (4)$$

$$\begin{aligned}\Phi(sc, sw) = exp(&\lambda(LCS(sc, sw) - ED(sc, sw)) \\ &+(1-\lambda)(PLCS(sc, sw) - PED(sc, sw)))\end{aligned} \quad (5)$$

Exponential function grows tremendously as its argument increases, so much more weight can be assigned if syllables are more similar. The parameter λ here is used to empirically adjust relative contribution of letters and sounds. Longest common sequence (LCS) and edit distance (ED) are used to measure orthographical similarity, while phonetic longest common sequence (PLCS) and phonetic edit distant (PED) are used to measure phonetic similarity but based on letter-to-sound transcripts. The PLCS are defined as basic LCS but PED here is slightly different.

When performing phonetic similarity calculation based on syllables, we follow (Xia et al., 2006) in treating consonant and vowels separately because transition of consonants can make a totally different pronunciation. So if consonants of sc_j and sw_j are exactly the same or fit rules listed in Table 2, $PED(sc_j, sw_j)$ equals to edit

tmr	t-mr	tm-r	t-m-r
tamer	ta-mer	tim-er	to-mor-row
	ti-mor	tim-ber	tri-mes-ter
	ti-more	ton-er	tor-men-tor
	tu-mor	tem-per	ta-ma-ra
	...	...	...

Table 1: Standard candidates of *tmr* in syllable level. The first row gives the different segmentations and the second row presents the candidates.

Description	Rules	Examples
1. -ng as suffix: g-dropping	-n/-ng	do-in/do-ing, go-in/go-ing, talk-in/talk-ing, mak-in/mak-ing
2. -ng as suffix: n-dropping	-g/-ng	tak-ig/tak-ing, likig/lik-ing
3. suffix: z/s equaling	-z/-s, -s/-z	jamz/james, plz/please
4. suffix: n/m equaling	-m/-n, -n/-m	in-portant/im-portant, get-tim/get-ting
5. suffix: t/d equaling	-t/-d, -d/-t	shid/shit, shult/should
6. suffix: t-dropping	-/-t	jus/just, wha/what, mus/must, ain/ain't
7. suffix: r-dropping	-/-r	holla/holler, t-m-r/tomorrow
8. prefix: th-/d- equaling	d-/th-, th-/d-	de/the, dat/that, dats/that's, dey/they

Table 2: The consonant rules.

distance of letter-to-phone transcripts, or it will be assigned infinity to indicate that their pronunciation are so different that this transition can seldom happen. For example, as consonantal transition between suffix `z` and `s` can always happen, PED(`plz`,`please`) equals string edit distance of their transcripts. But as consonatal transition of `f` and `d` is rare, phonetic distance of `fly` and `sky` is assigned infinity. Note the consonant rules in Table 2 are manually defined in our empirical study, which represent the most commonly used ones.

3.3 Parameter

Parameter in the proposed method is only the λ in Equation (5), which represents the relative contribution of orthographical similarity and phonetic similarity. Because the limited number of annotated corpus, we have to enumerate the parameter in $\{0, 0.1, 0.2, ..., 1\}$ in the experiment to find the optimal setting.

4 Implementation

The method described in the previous section are implemented with the following details.

4.1 Preprocessing

Before performing normalization, we need to process several types of non-standard words:

- **Words containing numbers**: People usually substitute some kind of sounds with numbers like `4/four`, `2/two` and `8/eight` or numbers can be replacement of some letters like `1/i`, `4/a`. So we replace numbers with its words or characters and then use them to generate possible candidates.

- **Words with repeating letters**: As our method is syllable-based, repeating letters for sentiment expressing (like `cooool`, (Brody and Diakopoulos, 2011)) can cause syllabifying failure. For repeating letters, we reduce it to both two and one to generate candidate separately. Then the two lists are merged together to form the whole candidate list.

4.2 Letter-to-sound conversion

Syllable in this work refers to orthographic syllables. For example, we convert word `tomorrow` into `to-mor-row`. However, when comparing the syllable of a standard word and that of a non-standard word, sound (i.e., phones) of the syllables are considered. Thus letter-to-sound conversion tools are required.

Several TTS system can perform the task according to some linguistic rules, even for non-standard words. The Double Metaphone algorithm used in (Han and Baldwin, 2011) is one of them. But it uses consonants to encode a word, which gives less information than we need. In our method, we use freeTTS (Walker et al., 2002) with CMU lexicon[1] to transform words into APRAbet[2] symbols. For example, word `tomorrow` is transcribed to {`T-UW M-AA R-OW`} and `tmr` to {`T M R`}.

4.3 Dictionary preparation

- **Dictionary #1: In-vocabulary (IV) words**

  Following (Yang and Eisenstein, 2013), our set of IV words is also based on the GNU aspell dictionary (v0.60.6). Differently, we use a collection of 100 million tweets (roughly the same size of Edinburgh Twitter corpus) because the Edinburgh Twitter corpus is no longer available due to Twitter policies. The

[1] http://www.speech.cs.cmu.edu/cgi-bin/cmudict
[2] http://en.wikipedia.org/wiki/Arpabet

final IV dictionary contains 51,948 standard words.

- **Dictionary #2: Syllables for the standard words**

  Following (Pennell and Liu, 2010), we use the online dictionary[3] to extract syllables for each standard words. We encountered same problem when accessing words with prefixes or suffixes, which are not syllabified in the same format as the base words on the website. To address the issue, we simply regard these prefixes and suffixes as syllables.

- **Dictionary #3: Pronunciation of the syllables**

  Using the CMU pronouncing dictionary (Weide, 1998) and dictionary 2, and knowing all possible APRAbet symbol for all consonant characters, we can program to capture every possible pronunciation of all syllables in the standard dictionary.

4.4 Automatic syllabification of non-standard words

Automatic syllabification of non-standard words is a supervised problem. A straightforward idea is to train a CRF model on manually labeled syllables of non-standard words. Unfortunately, such a corpus is not available and very expensive to produce.

We assume that both standard and non-standard forms follow the same syllable rules (i.e., the cognitive process). Thus we propose to train the CRF model on the corpus of syllables of standard words (which is easy to obtain) to construct an automatic annotation system based on CRF++ (Kudo, 2005). In this work, we extract syllables of standard words from Dictionary #2 as training set. Annotations follow (Pennell and Liu, 2010) to identify boundaries of syllables and in our work, CRF++ can suggest several candidate solutions, rather than an optimal segmentation solution for syllable segmentation of the non-standard words. In the HMM channel model, the candidate solutions are included as part of the search space.

4.5 Language model

Using Tweets from our corpus that contain no OOV words besides hashtags and username mentions (following (Han and Baldwin, 2011)), the Kneser-Ney smoothed tri-gram language model is estimated using SRILM toolkit (Stolcke, 2002). Note that punctuations, hashtags, and username mentions have some syntactic value (Kaufmann and Kalita, 2010) to some extent, we replace them with '<PUNCT>', '<TOPIC>' and '<USER>'.

[3] http://www.dictionary.com

5 Evaluation

5.1 Datasets

We use two labeled twitter datasets in existence to evaluate our tweet normalization method.

- **LexNorm1.1** contains 549 complete tweets with 1184 non-standard tokens (558 unique word type) (Han and Baldwin, 2011).

- **LexNorm1.2** is a revised version of LexNorm1.1 (Yang and Eisenstein, 2013). Some inconsistencies and errors in LexNorm1.1 are corrected and some more non-standard words are properly recovered.

In both datasets, to-be-normalized non-standard words are detected manually as well as the corresponding standard words.

5.2 Evaluation criteria

Here we use precision, recall and F-score to evaluate our method. As normalization methods on these datasets focused on the labeled non-standard words (Yang and Eisenstein, 2013), recall is the proportion of words requiring normalization which are normalized correctly; precision is the proportion of normalizations which are correct. When we perform the tweet normalization methods, every error is both a false positive and false negative, so in the task, precision equals to recall.

5.3 Sentence level normalization

We choose the following prior normalization methods:

- (Liu et al., 2012): the extended character-level CRF tagging system;

- (Yang and Eisenstein, 2013): log-linear model using string edit distance and longest common sequence measures as major features;

- (Hassan and Menezes, 2013): bipartite graph major exploit contextual similarity;

Method	Dataset	Precision	Recall	F-measure
(Han and Baldwin, 2011)		75.30	75.30	75.30
(Liu et al., 2012)		84.13	78.38	81.15
(Hassan and Menezes, 2013)	LexNorm 1.1	85.37	56.4	69.93
(Yang and Eisenstein, 2013)		82.09	82.09	82.09
Syllable-based method		85.30	85.30	85.30
(Yang and Eisenstein, 2013)	LexNorm 1.2	82.06	82.06	82.06
Syllable-based method		86.08	86.08	86.08

Table 3: Experiment results of the tweet normalization methods.

- (Han and Baldwin, 2011): the orthography-phone combined system using lexical edit distance and phonemic edit distance.

In our method, we set λ=0.7 because it is found best in our experiments (see Figure 2). The experimental results are presented in Table 3, which indicate that our method outperforms the state-of-the-art methods. Details on how to adjust parameter is given in Section 5.4.

Recall we argue that combination of three similarity is necessary when performing sentence-level normalization. Apart from contextual similarity like language model or graphic model, methods in (Yang and Eisenstein, 2013) or (Hassan and Menezes, 2013) do not include phonetic measure, causing loss of important phonetic information. Though using phoneme, morpheme boundary and syllable boundary as features (Liu et al., 2012), the character-level reversed approach will bring much more noise into the later reversed look-up table, and also, features of whole word are omitted.

Like (Han and Baldwin, 2011), we also use lexical measure and phonetic measure. Great difference between the two approaches is the processing level: word level and syllable level. In their work, average candidates number suffers times of increase when adding phonetic measure. This is because when introducing phonemic edit distance, important pronunciations can be altered (phonemic edit distance of `night-need` and `night-kite` is equal). Syllable level allows us to reflect consistencies during transition in a finer-grained level. Thus the phonetic similarity can be more precisely modeled.

5.4 Contributions of phone and orthography

In our method, the parameter λ in Equation 5 is used to represent the relatively contributions of both phonetic and orthographical information. But as the lack of prior knowledge, we cannot judge an optimal λ. We choose to conduct experiments varying $\lambda = \{0, 0.1, ..., 1\}$ to find out how this adjustment can affect performance. The experimental results are presented in Figure 2.

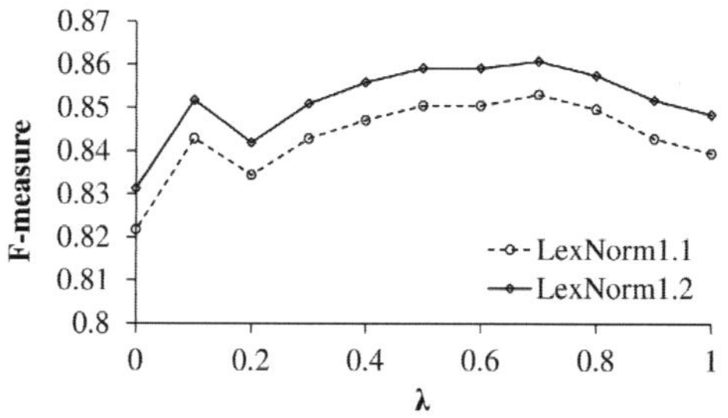

Figure 2: Contribution of phone and orthography.

As shown in Figure 2, when λ is set 0 or 1 (indicating no contribution of either orthographical or phonetic in assigning weight to candidates), our method performs much worse. In our experiment, when $\lambda = 0.7$, the models performs best, showing that orthographical measure makes relatively more contribution over phonetic measure, but the latter is indispensable. This justifies the effectiveness of combining orthographical and phonetic measure, indicating that human normalization process is properly modeled.

6 Analysis

6.1 Our exceptions

Deeper observation of our normalization results shows that there are several types of exceptions beyond our consonant-based rules. For example, `thanks` fails to be selected as a candidate for the non-standard word `thx` because the pronunciation of `thanks` contains an `N` but `thx` does not. The same situation happens when we process `stong/strong` because of the lacking `R`. We believe some more consonant should be exploited and more precisely described.

6.2 Non-standard words involving multiple syllables

There are one type of transition that we cannot solve like `acc/accelerate` and `bio/biology` because the mapping is between single-syllable word and multi-syllable word. We add possible standard syllable $sw_0^{(i)}$ and $sw_{k+1}^{(i)}$ to the head and tail of origin syllables, but this extended form failed to be assigned high probability because the string edit distances are too large. We leave this problem for further research.

6.3 Annotation issue

Though similar, our results of LexNorm1.2 is better than LexNorm1.1. After scrutinizing, we notice that several issues in LexNorm1.1 are fixed in LexNorm1.2. So our results like `meh/me` (meaning the non-standard word `meh` are corrected to `me`) in LexNorm1.1 is wrong but in LexNorm1.2 is right. Even in LexNorm1.2, there exist some inconsistencies and errors. For example, our result `buyed/bought` is wrong for both datasets, which is actually correct. For another example, `til` is normalized to `until` in some cases but to `till` in other cases. We show that the LexNorm test corpus is still imperfect. We appeal for systematic efforts to produce a standard dataset under a widely-accepted guideline.

6.4 Conventions

Social media language often contains words that are culture-specific and widely used in daily life. Some word like `congrats`, `tv` and `pic` are included into several dictionaries. We also observed several transitions like `atl/atlanta` or `wx/weather` in the datasets. These kinds of conventional abbreviations pose great difficulty to us. Normalization of those conventional non-standard words still needs further study.

7 Conclusion

In this paper, a syllable-based tweet normalization method is proposed for social media text normalization. Results on publicly available standard datasets justify our assumption that syllable plays a fundamental role in social media non-standard words. Advantage of our proposed method lies in that syllable is viewed as the basic processing unit and syllable-level similarity. This accords to the human cognition in creating and understanding the social non-standard words. Our method is domain independent. It is robust on non-standard words in any period of history. Furthermore, give the syllable transcription tool, our method can be easily adapted to a new language.

Acknowledgement

This research work was carried out when the authors worked at Tsinghua University. We acknowledge the financial support from Natural Science Foundation of China (NSFC: 61272233, 61373056, 61433018). We thank the anonymous reviewers for the insightful comments.

References

Samuel Brody and Nicholas Diakopoulos. 2011. Cooooooooooooooollllllllllllll!!!!!!!!!!!!!! using word lengthening to detect sentiment in microblogs. In *EMNLP*, pages 562–570. ACL.

Monojit Choudhury, Rahul Saraf, Vijit Jain, Animesh Mukherjee, Sudeshna Sarkar, and Anupam Basu. 2007. Investigation and modeling of the structure of texting language. *International Journal of Document Analysis and Recognition (IJDAR)*, 10(3-4):157–174.

Danish Contractor, Tanveer A. Faruquie, and L. Venkata Subramaniam. 2010. Unsupervised cleansing of noisy text. In Chu-Ren Huang and Dan Jurafsky, editors, *COLING (Posters)*, pages 189–196. Chinese Information Processing Society of China.

Paul Cook and Suzanne Stevenson. 2009. An unsupervised model for text message normalization. In *CALC '09: Proceedings of the Workshop on Computational Approaches to Linguistic Creativity*, pages 71–78, Morristown, NJ, USA. Association for Computational Linguistics.

Stephan Gouws, Dirk Hovy, and Donald Metzler. 2011. Unsupervised mining of lexical variants from noisy text. In *Proceedings of the First workshop on Unsupervised Learning in NLP*, pages 82–90. Association for Computational Linguistics.

Bo Han and Timothy Baldwin. 2011. Lexical normalisation of short text messages: Makn sens a #twitter. In Dekang Lin, Yuji Matsumoto, and Rada Mihalcea, editors, *ACL*, pages 368–378. The Association for Computer Linguistics.

Hany Hassan and Arul Menezes. 2013. Social text normalization using contextual graph random walks. In *ACL (1)*, pages 1577–1586. The Association for Computer Linguistics.

Max Kaufmann and Jugal Kalita. 2010. Syntactic normalization of Twitter messages. In *International conference on natural language processing, Kharagpur, India*.

Taku Kudo. 2005. Crf++: Yet another crf toolkit. *Software available at http://crfpp. sourceforge. net*.

Chen Li and Yang Liu. 2012a. Improving text normalization using character-blocks based models and system combination. In *COLING 2012, 24th International Conference on Computational Linguistics, Proceedings of the Conference: Technical Papers, 8-15 December 2012, Mumbai, India*, pages 1587–1602.

Chen Li and Yang Liu. 2012b. Normalization of text messages using character- and phone-based machine translation approaches. In *INTERSPEECH*. ISCA.

Chen Li and Yang Liu. 2014. Improving text normalization via unsupervised model and discriminative reranking. In *Proceedings of the 52nd Annual Meeting of the Association for Computational Linguistics, ACL 2014, June 22-27, 2014, Baltimore, MD, USA, Student Research Workshop*, pages 86–93.

Fei Liu, Fuliang Weng, Bingqing Wang, and Yang Liu. 2011. Insertion, deletion, or substitution?: normalizing text messages without precategorization nor supervision. In *Proceedings of the 49th Annual Meeting of the Association for Computational Linguistics: Human Language Technologies: short papers-Volume 2*, pages 71–76. Association for Computational Linguistics.

Fei Liu, Fuliang Weng, and Xiao Jiang. 2012. A broad-coverage normalization system for social media language. In *In Proceedings of ACL: Long Papers-Volume 1*, pages 1035–1044. Association for Computational Linguistics.

Tomáš Mikolov, Martin Karafiát, Luk Burget, Jan ernock, and Sanjeev Khudanpur. 2010. Recurrent neural network based language model. In *Interspeech*, pages 1045–1048.

Tomáš Mikolov, Kai Chen, Greg Corrado, and Jeffrey Dean. 2013. Efficient estimation of word representations in vector space. *CoRR*, abs/1301.3781.

Deana Pennell and Yang Liu. 2010. Normalization of text messages for text-to-speech. In *ICASSP*, pages 4842–4845. IEEE.

Deana Pennell and Yang Liu. 2011. A character-level machine translation approach for normalization of sms abbreviations. In *IJCNLP*, pages 974–982.

S. Petrovic, M. Osborne, and V. Lavrenko. 2010. The edinburgh twitter corpus. In *Proceedings of the NAACL HLT Workshop on Computational Linguistics in a World of Social Media*, pages 25–26.

Lawrence Philips. 2000. The double metaphone search algorithm. *C/C++ Users Journal*, 18(5), June.

Richard Sproat, Alan W. Black, Stanley F. Chen, Shankar Kumar, Mari Ostendorf, and Christopher Richards. 2001. Normalization of non-standard words. *Computer Speech & Language*, 15(3):287–333.

Andreas Stolcke. 2002. Srilm-an extensible language modeling toolkit. In *Proceedings International Conference on Spoken Language Processing*, pages 257–286, November.

Willie Walker, Paul Lamere, and Philip Kwok. 2002. Freetts: a performance case study.

Robert L Weide. 1998. The cmu pronouncing dictionary. *URL: http://www. speech. cs. cmu. edu/cgibin/cmudict*.

Yunqing Xia, Kam-Fai Wong, and Wenjie Li. 2006. A phonetic-based approach to chinese chat text normalization. In Nicoletta Calzolari, Claire Cardie, and Pierre Isabelle, editors, *ACL*. The Association for Computer Linguistics.

Yi Yang and Jacob Eisenstein. 2013. A log-linear model for unsupervised text normalization. In *EMNLP*, pages 61–72. ACL.

Improving Named Entity Recognition in Tweets via Detecting Non-Standard Words

Chen Li and **Yang Liu**
Computer Science Department, The University of Texas at Dallas
Richardson, Texas 75080, USA
{chenli,yangl@hlt.utdallas.edu}

Abstract

Most previous work of text normalization on informal text made a strong assumption that the system has already known which tokens are non-standard words (NSW) and thus need normalization. However, this is not realistic. In this paper, we propose a method for NSW detection. In addition to the information based on the dictionary, e.g., whether a word is out-of-vocabulary (OOV), we leverage novel information derived from the normalization results for OOV words to help make decisions. Second, this paper investigates two methods using NSW detection results for named entity recognition (NER) in social media data. One adopts a pipeline strategy, and the other uses a joint decoding fashion. We also create a new data set with newly added normalization annotation beyond the existing named entity labels. This is the first data set with such annotation and we release it for research purpose. Our experiment results demonstrate the effectiveness of our NSW detection method and the benefit of NSW detection for NER. Our proposed methods perform better than the state-of-the-art NER system.

1 Introduction

Short text messages or comments from social media websites such as Facebook and Twitter have become one of the most popular communication forms in recent years. However, abbreviations, misspelled words and many other non-standard words are very common in short texts for various reasons (e.g., length limitation, need to convey much information, writing style). They post problems to many NLP techniques in this domain.

There are many ways to improve language processing performance on the social media data. One is to leverage normalization techniques to automatically convert the non-standard words into the corresponding standard words (Aw et al., 2006; Cook and Stevenson, 2009; Pennell and Liu, 2011; Liu et al., 2012a; Li and Liu, 2014; Sonmez and Ozgur, 2014). Intuitively this will ease subsequent language processing modules. For example, if '2mr' is converted to 'tomorrow', a text-to-speech system will know how to pronounce it, a part-of-speech (POS) tagger can label it correctly, and an information extraction system can identify it as a time expression. This normalization task has received an increasing attention in social media language processing.

However, most of previous work on normalization assumed that they already knew which tokens are NSW that need normalization. Then different methods are applied only to these tokens. To our knowledge, Han and Baldwin (2011) is the only previous work which made a pilot research on NSW detection. One straight forward method to do this is to use a dictionary to classify a token into in-vocabulary (IV) words and out-of-vocabulary (OOV) words, and just treat all the OOV words as NSW. The shortcoming of this method is obvious. For example, tokens like 'iPhone', 'PES'(a game name) and 'Xbox' will be considered as NSW, however, these words do not need normalization. Han and Baldwin (2011) called these OOV words correct-OOV, and named those OOV words that do need normalization as ill-OOV. We will follow their naming convention and use these two terms in our study. In this paper, we propose two methods to classify tokens in informal text into three classes: IV, correct-OOV, and ill-OOV. In the following, we call this task the NSW detection task, and these three labels NSW labels or classes. The novelty of our work is that we incorporate a token's normalization information to assist this clas-

Proceedings of the 53rd Annual Meeting of the Association for Computational Linguistics and the 7th International Joint Conference on Natural Language Processing, pages 929–938,
Beijing, China, July 26-31, 2015.

sification process. Our experiment results demonstrate that our proposed system gives a significant performance improvement on NSW detection compared with the dictionary baseline system.

On the other hand, the impact of normalization or NSW detection on NER has not been well studied in social media domain. In this paper, we propose two methods to incorporate the NSW detection information: one is a pipeline system that just uses the predicted NSW labels as additional features in an NER system; the other one uses joint decoding, where we can simultaneously decide a token's NSW and NER labels. Our experiment results show that our proposed joint decoding performs better than the pipeline method, and it outperforms the state-of-the-art NER system.

Our contributions in this paper are as follows: (1) We proposed a NSW detection model by leveraging normalization information of the OOV tokens. (2) We created a data set with new NSW and normalization information, in addition to the existing NER labels. (3) It is the first time to our knowledge that an effective and joint approach is proposed to combine the NSW detection and NER techniques to improve the performance of these two tasks at the same time on social media data. (4) We demonstrate the effectiveness of our proposed method. Our proposed NER system outperforms the state-of-the-art system.

2 Related Work

There has been a surge of interest in lexical normalization with the advent of social media data. Lots of approaches have been developed for this task, from using edit distance (Damerau, 1964; Levenshtein, 1966), to the noisy channel model (Cook and Stevenson, 2009; Pennell and Liu, 2010; Liu et al., 2012a) and machine translation method (Aw et al., 2006; Pennell and Liu, 2011; Li and Liu, 2012b; Li and Liu, 2012a). Normalization performance on some benchmark data has been improved a lot. Currently, unsupervised models are widely used to extract latent relationship between non-standard words and correct words from a huge corpus. Hassan and Menezes (2013) applied the random walk algorithm on a contextual similarity bipartite graph, constructed from n-gram sequences on a large unlabeled text corpus to build relation between non-standard tokens and correct words. Yang and Eisenstein (2013) presented a unified unsupervised statistical model, in which the relationship between the standard and non-standard words is characterized by a log-linear model, permitting the use of arbitrary features. Chrupała (2014) proposed a text normalization model based on learning edit operations from labeled data while incorporating features induced from unlabeled data via recurrent network derived character-level neural text embeddings.

These studies only focused on how to normalize a given ill-OOV word and did not address the problem of detecting an ill-OOV word. Han and Baldwin (2011) is the only previous study that conducted the detection work. For any OOV word, they replaced it with its possible correct candidate, then if the possible candidate together with OOV's original context adheres to the knowledge they learned from large formal corpora, the replacement could be considered as a better choice and that OOV token is classified as ill-OOV. In this paper, we propose a different method for NSW detection. Similar to (Han and Baldwin, 2011), we also use normalization information for OOV words, but we use a feature based learning approach.

In order to improve robustness of NLP modules in social media domain, some works chose to design specific linguistic information. For example, by designing or annotating POS, chunking and capitalized information on tweets, (Ritter et al., 2011) proposed a system which reduced the POS tagging error by 41% compared with Stanford POS Tagger, and by 50% in NER compared with the baseline systems. Gimpel et al. (2011) created a specific set of POS tags for twitter data. With this tag set and word cluster information extracted from a huge Twitter corpus, their proposed system obtained significant improvement on POS tagging accuracy in Twitter data.

At the same time, increasing research work has been done to integrate lexical normalization into the NLP tasks in social media data. Kaji and Kitsuregawa (2014) combined lexical normalization, word segmentation and POS tagging on Japanese microblog. They used rich character-level and word-level features from the state-of-the-art models of joint word segmentation and POS tagging in Japanese (Kudo et al., 2004; Neubig et al., 2011). Their model can also be trained on a partially annotated corpus. Li and Liu (2015) conducted a similar research on joint POS tagging and text normalization for English. Wang and Kan

(2013) proposed a method of joint ill-OOV word recognition and word segmentation in Chinese Microblog. But with their method, ill-OOV words are merely recognized and not normalized. Therefore, they did not investigate how to exploit the information that may be derived from normalization to increase word segmentation accuracy. Liu et al. (2012b) studied the problem of named entity normalization (NEN) for tweets. They proposed a novel graphical model to simultaneously conduct NER and NEN on multiple tweets. Although this work involved text normalization, it only focused on the NER task, and there was no reported result for normalization. On Turkish tweets, Kucuk and Steinberger (2014) adapted NER rules and resources to better fit Twitter language by relaxing its capitalization constraint, expanding its lexical resources based on diacritics, and using a normalization scheme on tweets. These showed positive effect on the overall NER performance. Rangarajan Sridhar et al. (2014) decoupled the SMS translation task into normalization followed by translation. They exploited bi-text resources, and presented a normalization approach using distributed representation of words learned through neural networks.

In this study, we propose new methods to effectively integrate information of OOV words and their normalization for the NER task. In particular, by adopting joint decoding for both NSW detection and NER, we are able to outperform state-of-the-art results for both tasks. This is the first study that systematically evaluates the effect of OOV words and normalization on NER in social media data.

3 Proposed Method

3.1 NSW Detection Methods

The task of NSW detection is to find those words that indeed need normalization. Note that in this study we only consider single-token ill-OOV words (both before and after normalization). For example, we would consider *snds* (*sounds*) as ill-OOV, but not *smh* (*shaking my head*).

For a data set, our annotation process is as follows. We first manually label whether a token is ill-OOV and if so its corresponding standard word. We only consider tokens consisting of *alphanumeric* characters. Then based on a dictionary, the tokes that are not labeled as ill-OOV can be categorized into IV and OOV words. These OOV words will be considered as correct-OOV. Therefore all the tokens will have these three labels: IV, ill-OOV, and correct-OOV.

Throughout this paper, we use GNU spell dictionary (v0.60.6.1) to determine whether a token is OOV.[1] Twitter mentions (e.g., @twitter), hashtags and urls are excluded from consideration for OOV. Dictionary lookup of Internet slang[2] is performed to filter those ill-OOV words whose correct forms are not single words.

We propose two methods for NSW detection. The first one is a two-step method, where we first label a token as IV or OOV based on the given dictionary and some filter rules, then a statistical classifier is applied on those OOV tokens to further decide their classes: ill-OOV or correct-OOV. We use a maximum entropy classifier for this. The second model directly does 3-way classification to predict a token's label to be IV, correct-OOV, or ill-OOV. We use a CRF model in this method.[3]

Table 1 shows the features used in these two methods. The first dictionary feature is not applicable for the two-step method because all the instances in that process have the same feature value 'OOV'. However, this dictionary feature is an important feature for the 3-way classification model – a token with a feature value 'IV' has a very high probability of being 'IV'. Lexical features focus on a token's surface information to judge whether it is a regular English word or not. It is because most of correct-OOV words (e.g., location and person names) are still some regular words, complying with the general rules of word formation. For example, features 5-8 consider English word formation rules that at least one vowel character is needed for a correct word[4]. Feature 9 considers that a correct English word does not contain more than three consecutive same character. The character level language model used in Feature 10 is trained from a dictionary. A higher probability may indicate that it is a correct word.

The motivation for the normalization features is

[1] We remove all the one-character tokens, except *a* and *I*.

[2] 5452 items are collected from http://www.noslang.com.

[3] We can also use a maximum entropy classifier to implement this model. Our experiments showed that using CRFs has slightly better results. But the main reason we adopt CRFs is because we use CRFs for NER, therefore we can easily integrate the two models in joint decoding in Section 3.2 for NER and NSW detection. We do not use CRFs in the two-step system because the labeling is performed on a subset of the words, not the entire sequence.

[4] Although some exceptions exist, this rule applies to most words.

Dictionary Feature
1. is token categorized as IV or OOV by the given dictionary (Only used in 3-way classification)
Lexical Features
2. word identity 3. whether token's first character is capitalized 4. token's length 5. how many vowel character chunks does this token have 6. how many consonant character chunks does this token have 7. the length of longest consecutive vowel character chunk 8. the length of longest consecutive consonant character chunk 9. whether this token contains more than 3 consecutive same character 10. character level probability of this token based on a character level language model
Normalization Features
11. whether each individual candidate list has any candidates for this token 12. how many candidates each individual candidate list has 13. whether each individual list's top 10 candidates contain this token itself 14. the max number of lists that have the same top one candidate 15. the similarity value between each individual normalization system's first candidate w and this token t, calculated by $\frac{longest\_common\_string(w,t)}{length(t)}$ 16. the similarity value between each individual normalization system's first candidate w and this token t, calculated by $\frac{longest\_common\_sequence(w,t)}{length(t)}$

Table 1: Features used in NSW detection system.

to leverage the normalization result of an OOV token to help its classification. Before we describe the reason why normalization information could benefit this task, we first introduce the normalization system we used. We apply a state-of-the-art normalization system proposed by (Li and Liu, 2014). Briefly, in this normalization system there are three supervised and two unsupervised subsystems for each OOV token, resulting in six candidate lists (one system provides two lists). Then a maximum entropy reranking model is adopted to combine and rerank these candidate lists, using a rich set of features. Please refer to (Li and Liu, 2014) for more details. By analyzing each individual system, we find that for ill-OOV words most normalization systems can generate many candidates, which may contain a correct candidate; for correct-OOV words, many normalization systems have few candidates or may not provide any candidates. For example, only two of the six lists have candidates for the token *Newsfeed* and *Metropcs*. Therefore, we believe the patterns of these normalization results contain useful information to classify OOVs. Note that this kind of feature is only applicable for those tokens that are judged as OOV by the given dictionary (normalization is done on these OOV words). The bottom of Table 1 shows the normalization features we designed.

3.2 NER Methods

The NER task we study in this paper is just about segmenting named entities, without identifying their types (e.g., person, location, organization). Following most previous work, we model it as a sequence-labeling task and use the BIO encoding method (each word either begins, is inside, or outside of a named entity).

Intuitively, NSW detection has an impact on NER, because many named entities may have the correct-OOV label. Therefore, we investigate if we can leverage NSW label information for NER. First, we adopt a pipeline method, where we first perform NSW detection and the results are used as features in the NER system. Table 2 shows the features we designed. One thing worth mentioning is that the POS tags we used are from (Gimpel et al., 2011). This POS tag set consists of 25 coarse-grained tags designed for social media text. We use CRFs for this NER system.

The above method simply incorporates a token's predicted NSW label as features in the NER model. Obviously it has an unavoidable limitation – the errors from the NSW detection model would affect the downstream NER process. Therefore we propose a second method, a joint decoding process to determine a token's NSW and NER label at the same time. The 3-way classification method for NSW detection and the above NER system both use CRFs. The decoding process for these two tasks is performed separately, using their corresponding trained models. The motivation of our proposed joint decoding process is to combine the two processes together, therefore we can avoid the error propagation in the pipeline system, and allow the two models to benefit from each other.

Part (A) and (B) of Figure 1 show the trellis for decoding word sequence 'Messi is well-known' in the NER and NSW detection systems respectively. As shown in (A), every black box with dashed line is a hidden state (possible BIO tag) for the corresponding token. Two sources of information are used in decoding. One is the label transition probability $p(y_i|y_j)$, from the trained model, where y_i and y_j are two BIO tags. The other is $p(y_i|t_i)$, where y_i is a BIO label for token t_i. Similarly, during decoding in NSW detection, we need the probability of $p(o_i|o_j)$ and $p(o_i|t_i)$. The only difference is that o_i is a NSW label. Part (C) of Figure 1 shows the trellis used in our proposed joint decoding approach for NSW detection and NER. In this figure, three places are worth pointing out: (1) the label is a combination of NSW and NER labels, and thus there are nine in total; (2) the label transition probability is a linear sum of the previous two transition probabilities: $p(y_i\_o_i|y_j\_o_j) = p(y_i|y_j) + \beta * p(o_i|o_j)$, where y_i and y_j are BIO tags and o_i and o_j are NSW tags; (3) similarly, $p(y_i\_o_i|t_i)$ equals to $p(y_i|t_i) + \alpha * p(o_i|t_i)$. Please note all these probabilities are log probabilities and they are trained separately from each system.

Basic Features
1. Lexical features (word n-gram): Unigram: $W_i(i = 0)$ Bigram: $W_iW_{i+1}(i = -2, -1, 0, 1)$ Trigram: $W_{i-1}W_iW_{i+1}(i = -2, -1, 0, 1)$ 2. POS features (POS n-gram): Unigram: $P_i(i = 0)$ Bigram: $P_iP_{i+1}(i = -2, -1, 0, 1)$ Trigram: $P_{i-1}P_iP_{i+1}(i = -2, -1, 0, 1)$ 3. Token's capitalization information: Trigram: $C_{i-1}C_iC_{i+1}(i = 0)$ ($C_i = 1$ means this token's first character is capitalized.)
Additional Features by Incorporating Predicted NSW Label
4. Token's dictionary categorization label: Unigram: $D_i(i = 0)$ Bigram: $D_iD_{i+1}(i = -2, -1, 0, 1)$ Trigram: $D_{i-1}D_iD_{i+1}(i = -2, -1, 0, 1)$ 5. Token's predicted NSW label: Unigram: $L_i(i = 0)$ Bigram: $L_iL_{i+1}(i = -2, -1, 0, 1)$ Trigram: $L_{i-1}L_iL_{i+1}(i = -2, -1, 0, 1)$ 6. Compound features using lexical and NSW labels: $W_iD_i, W_iL_i, W_iD_iL_i(i = 0)$ 7. Compound features using POS and NSW labels: $P_iD_i, P_iL_i, P_iD_iL_i(i = 0)$ 8. Compound features using word, POS, and NSW labels: $W_iP_iD_iL_i(i = 0)$

Table 2: Features used in the NER System. W and P represent word and POS. D and L represent labels classified by the dictionary and 3-way NSW detection system. Subscripts i, $i - 1$ and $i + 1$ indicate the word position. For example, when i equals to -1, $i + 1$ means the current word.

4 Data and Experiment

4.1 Data Set and Experiment Setup

The NSW detection model is trained using the data released by (Li and Liu, 2014). It has 2,577 Twitter messages (selected from the Edinburgh Twitter corpus (Petrovic et al., 2010)), in which there are 2,333 unique pairs of NSW and their standard words. This data is used for training the different normalization models. We labeled this data set using the given dictionary for NSW detection. 4,121 tokens are labeled as ill-OOV, 1,455 as correct-OOV, and the rest 33,740 tokens are IV words.

We have two test sets for evaluating the NSW detection system. One is from (Han and Baldwin, 2011), which includes 549 tweets. Each tweet contains at least one ill-OOV and the corresponding correct word. We call it Test set 1 in the following. The other is from (Li and Liu, 2015), who further processed the tweets data from (Owoputi et al., 2013). Briefly, Owoputi et al. (2013) released 2,347 tweets with their designed POS tags for social media text, and then Li and Liu (2015) further annotated this data with normalization information for each token. The released data by (Li and Liu, 2015) contains 798 tweets with ill-OOV. We use these 798 tweets as the second data set for NSW detection, and call it Test set 2 in the following. In addition, we use all of these 2,347 tweets to train a POS model which then is used to predict tokens' POS tags for NER (see Section 3.2 about the POS tags). The CRF model is implemented using the pocket-CRF toolkit[5]. The SRILM toolkit (Stolcke, 2002) is used to build the character-level language model (LM) for generating the LM features in NSW detection system.

[5]http://sourceforge.net/projects/pocket-crf-1/

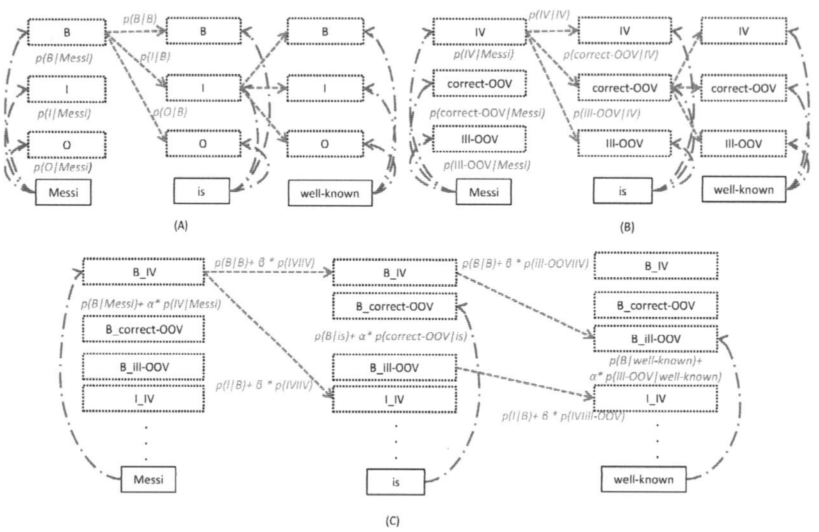

Figure 1: Trellis Viterbi decoding for different systems.

The data with the NER labels are from (Ritter et al., 2011) who annotated 2,396 tweets (34K tokens) with named entities, but there is no information on the tweets' ill-OOV words. In order to evaluate the impact of ill-OOV on NER, we ask six annotators to annotate the ill-OOV words and the corresponding standard words in this data. There are only 1,012 sentences with ill-OOV words. We use all the sentences (2,396) for the NER experiments. This data set,[6] to our knowledge, is the first one having both ill-OOV and NER annotation in social media domain. For joint decoding, the parameters α and β are empirically set as 0.95 and 0.5.

4.2 Experiment Results

4.2.1 NSW Detection Results

For NSW detection, we compared our two proposed systems on the two test sets described above, and also conducted different experiments to investigate the effectiveness of different features. We use the categorization of words by the dictionary as the baseline for this task. Table 3 shows the results for three NSW detection systems. We use Recall, Precision and F value for the ill-OOV class as the evaluation metrics. The Dictionary baseline can only recognize the token as IV and OOV, and thus label all the OOV words as ill-OOV. Both the two-step and the 3-way classification methods in Table 3 leverage all the features described in Table 1. First note because of the property of the two-step method (it further divides the OOV words from the dictionary-based method into ill-OOV and correct-OOV), the upper bound of its recall is the recall of the dictionary based method. We can see that in Test set 1, both the two-step and the 3-way classification methods have a significant improvement compared to the Dictionary method. However, in Test set 2, the two-step method performs much worse than that of the 3-way classification method, although it outperforms the dictionary method. This can be attributed to the characteristics of that data set and also the system's upper bounded recall. We will provide a more detailed analysis in the following feature analysis part..

Table 4 and 5 show the performance of the two systems on the two test sets with different features. Note that the dictionary feature is not applicable to the two-step method, and the results for the two-step method using dictionary feature (feature 1, first line in the tables) are the same as the dictionary baseline in Table 3. From these two tables, we can see that: (1) For both systems, normalization features (11$\sim$16) and lexical features (2$\sim$10) both perform better than the dictionary feature. (2) In general, the combination of any two kinds of features has better performance than any one feature type. Using all the features (results shown in Table 3) yields the best performance, which significantly improves the performance compared with the baseline. (3) There are some differences across

[6] http://www.hlt.utdallas.edu/~chenli/normalization_ner

the two data sets in terms of the feature effectiveness on the two methods. On Test set 2, when lexical features are combined with other features (forth and fifth line of Table 5), the 3-way classification method significantly outperforms the two-step method. It is because this data set has a large number of ill-OOV words that are dictionary words. For example, token 'its' appears 31 times as ill-OOV, 'ya' 13 times, and 'bro' 10 times. Such ill-OOV words occur more than two hundred times in total. Since these tokens are included in the dictionary, they are already classified as IV by the dictionary, and their label will not change in the second step. This is also the reason why in Table 3, the performance of 3-way classification is significantly better than that of the two-step method using all the features. However, we also find that when we only use lexical features (2∼10), the two methods have similar performance on Test set 2, but the two-step method has much better performance than the 3-way classifier method on Test set 1. We believe this shows that lexical features themselves are not reliable for the NSW detection task, and other information such as normalization features may be more stable.

System	Test Set 1			Test Set 2		
	R	P	F	R	P	F
Dictionary	88.73	72.35	79.71	67.87	69.59	68.72
Two-step	81.66	88.74	85.05	57.60	90.04	70.26
3-way	87.63	83.49	**85.51**	73.53	90.42	**81.10**

Table 3: NSW detection results.

Features	Two-Step			3-way Classification		
	R	P	F	R	P	F
1	88.73	72.35	79.71	87.13	70.04	77.66
2∼10	87.21	77.44	82.04	82.59	67.49	74.28
11∼16	86.45	78.77	82.43	91.75	74.97	82.51
1∼10	76.78	92.87	84.07	77.12	93.09	84.36
2∼16	81.16	89.02	84.90	87.13	86.54	85.30
1,11∼16	78.30	91.00	84.17	78.55	93.77	85.48

Table 4: Feature impact on NSW detection on Test Set 1. The feature number corresponds to that in Table 1.

4.2.2 NER Results

For the NER task, in order to make a fair comparison with (Ritter et al., 2011), we conducted 4-fold cross validation experiments as they did. First we present the result on the NSW detection task on this date set when using our proposed joint decoding method integrating NER and NSW. This is done using the 1,012 sentences that contain ill-OOV words. Table 6 shows such results on the NER data described in Section 4.1. The 3-way classification method for NSW detection is used as a baseline here. It is the same model as used in the previous section, and applied to the entire NER data. For each cross validation experiment of the joint decoding method, the NSW detection model is kept the same (from 3-way classification method), but NER model is tested on 1/4 of the data and trained from the remaining 3/4 of the data. From the Table 6, we can see that joint decoding yields some marginal improvement for the NSW detection task.

Features	Two-Step			3-way Classification		
	R	P	F	R	P	F
1	67.86	69.59	68.72	66.45	64.27	65.34
2∼10	64.33	79.52	71.12	69.56	76.26	72.76
11∼16	53.78	91.34	67.70	54.35	91.42	68.17
1∼10	63.12	81.53	71.16	78.41	81.65	80.00
2∼16	56.40	89.02	69.06	72.32	90.28	80.31
1,11∼16	56.40	92.35	70.03	56.68	92.81	70.38

Table 5: Feature impact on NSW detection on Test Set 2.

System	R	P	F
3-way classification	58.65	72.83	64.97
Joint decoding w all features	59.53	72.96	**65.56**

Table 6: NSW detection results on the data from (Ritter et al., 2011) with our new NSW annotation.

In the following, we will focus on the impact of NSW detection on NER. Table 7 shows the NER performance from different systems on the data with NER and NSW labels. From this table, we can see that when using our pipeline system, adding NSW label features has a significant improvement compared to the basic features. The F value of 67.4% when using all the features is even higher than the state-of-the-art performance from (Ritter et al., 2011). Please note that Ritter et al. (2011) used much more information than us for this task, such as dictionaries including a set of type lists gathered from Freebase, brown clusters, and outputs of their specifically designed chunk and capitalization labels components[7]. Then they

[7]The chunk and capitalization components are specially created by them for social media domain data. Then they created a data set to train these models.

improved their baseline performance from 65% to the reported best one at 67%. However, we only added our predicted NSW labels and related features, and we already achieved similar or slightly better results. Using joint decoding can further boost the performance to 69%.

System	R	P	F
Pipeline w basic features	55.85	74.33	63.76
Pipeline w all features	60.00	77.09	67.40
Joint decoding w all features	73.56	65.02	**69.00**
(Ritter et al., 2011)	73.00	61.00	67.00

Table 7: NER results from different systems on data from (Ritter et al., 2011).

Table 8 shows the impact of different features. This analysis is based on the pipeline system. First, we can see that adding feature 4 and 5 (Uni-, Bi- and Tri-gram of the dictionary and predicted NSW labels) yields the most improvement compared with other features, and between these two kinds of features, using predicted NSW labels is better than the dictionary labels. It also shows the effectiveness of our NSW detection system. Second, comparing adding feature 6 and 7, it shows that combination of word/POS and its dictionary or NSW label is not as good as only considering the label's n-gram. We also explored various other n-gram features, but did not find any that outperformed feature 4 or 5. Another finding is that the POS related features are not as good as that of words.

Features	R	P	F
Basic	55.85	74.33	63.76
Basic + 4	57.71	75.04	65.23
Basic + 5	57.47	75.87	65.37
Basic + 6	56.53	74.20	64.12
Basic + 7	56.13	74.66	64.06
Basic + 8	57.14	74.55	64.66

Table 8: Pipeline NER performance using different features. The feature number corresponds to that in Table 2.

4.2.3 Error Analysis

A detailed error analysis further shows what improvement our proposed method makes and what errors it is still making. For example, for the tweet *'Watching the VMA pre-show again ...'*, the token *VMA* is annotated as *B-tvshow* in NER labels. Without using predicted NSW labels, the baseline system labels this token as *O* (outside of named entity). However, after using the NSW predicted label *correct-OOV* and related features, the pipeline NER system predicts its label as *B*. We noticed that joint decoding can solve some complicated cases that are hard for the pipeline system, especially for some OOVs, or when there are consecutive named entity tokens. For example, in a tweet, *'Let's hope the Serie A continues to be on the tv schedule next week'*, *Seria A* is a proper noun (meaning Italian soccer league). The annotation for *Seria* and *A* is correct-OOV/*B* and IV/*I*. We find the joint decoding system successfully labels *A* as *I* after *Seria* is labeled as *B*. However, the pipeline system labels *A* as *O* even it correctly labels *Seria*. Take another example, in a tweet *'I was gonna buy a Zune HD ...'*, *Zune HD* is consecutive named entities. The pipeline system recognized *Zune* as correct-OOV and *HD* as ill-OOV, then labeled both them as *O*. But the joint decoding system identified *HD* as correct-OOV and labeled *'Zune HD'* as *B* and *I*. These changes may have happened because of adjusting the transition probability and observation probability during Viterbi decoding.

5 Conclusion and Future Work

In this paper, we proposed an approach to detect NSW. This makes the lexical normalization task as a complete applicable process. The proposed NSW detection system leveraged normalization information of an OOV and other useful lexical information. Our experimental results show both kinds of information can help improve the prediction performance on two different data sets. Furthermore, we applied the predicted labels as additional information for the NER task. In this task, we proposed a novel joint decoding approach to label every token's NSW and NER label in a tweet at the same time. Again, experimental results demonstrate that the NSW label has a significant impact on NER performance and our proposed method improves performance on both tasks and outperforms the best previous results in NER.

In future work, we propose to pursue a number of directions. First, we plan to consider how to conduct NSW detection and normalization at the same time. Second, we like to try a joint method to simultaneously train the NSW detection and NER models, rather than just combining models in decoding. Third, we want to investigate the impact of NSW and normalization on other NLP tasks such as parsing in social media data.

Acknowledgments

We thank the anonymous reviewers for their detailed and insightful comments on earlier drafts of this paper. The work is partially supported by DARPA Contract No. FA8750-13-2-0041. Any opinions, findings, and conclusions or recommendations expressed are those of the authors and do not necessarily reflect the views of the funding agencies.

References

Aiti Aw, Min Zhang, Juan Xiao, Jian Su, and Jian Su. 2006. A phrase-based statistical model for sms text normalization. In *Processing of COLING/ACL*.

Grzegorz Chrupała. 2014. Normalizing tweets with edit scripts and recurrent neural embeddings. In *Proceedings of ACL*.

Paul Cook and Suzanne Stevenson. 2009. An unsupervised model for text message normalization. In *Proceedings of NAACL*.

Fred J Damerau. 1964. A technique for computer detection and correction of spelling errors. *Communications of the ACM*, 7(3):171–176.

Kevin Gimpel, Nathan Schneider, Brendan O'Connor, Dipanjan Das, Daniel Mills, Jacob Eisenstein, Michael Heilman, Dani Yogatama, Jeffrey Flanigan, and Noah A. Smith. 2011. Part-of-speech tagging for twitter: Annotation, features, and experiments. In *Proceedings of ACL*.

Bo Han and Timothy Baldwin. 2011. Lexical normalisation of short text messages: Makn sens a #twitter. In *Proceeding of ACL*.

Hany Hassan and Arul Menezes. 2013. Social text normalization using contextual graph random walks. In *Proceedings of ACL*.

Nobuhiro Kaji and Masaru Kitsuregawa. 2014. Accurate word segmentation and pos tagging for Japanese microblogs: Corpus annotation and joint modeling with lexical normalization. In *Proceedings of EMNLP*.

Dilek Kucuk and Ralf Steinberger. 2014. Experiments to improve named entity recognition on turkish tweets. In *Proceedings of Workshop on Language Analysis for Social Media (LASM) on EACL*.

Taku Kudo, Kaoru Yamamoto, and Yuji Matsumoto. 2004. Applying conditional random fields to Japanese morphological analysis. In *Proceedings of EMNLP*.

Vladimir I Levenshtein. 1966. Binary codes capable of correcting deletions, insertions and reversals. In *Soviet physics doklady*, volume 10, page 707.

Chen Li and Yang Liu. 2012a. Improving text normalization using character-blocks based models and system combination. In *Proceedings of COLING 2012*.

Chen Li and Yang Liu. 2012b. Normalization of text messages using character- and phone-based machine translation approaches. In *Proceedings of 13th Interspeech*.

Chen Li and Yang Liu. 2014. Improving text normalization via unsupervised model and discriminative reranking. In *Proceedings of ACL*.

Chen Li and Yang Liu. 2015. Joint POS tagging and text normalization for informal text. In *Proceedings of IJCAI*.

Fei Liu, Fuliang Weng, and Xiao Jiang. 2012a. A broad-coverage normalization system for social media language. In *Proceedings of ACL*.

Xiaohua Liu, Ming Zhou, Xiangyang Zhou, Zhongyang Fu, and Furu Wei. 2012b. Joint inference of named entity recognition and normalization for tweets. In *Proceedings of ACL*.

Graham Neubig, Yosuke Nakata, and Shinsuke Mori. 2011. Pointwise prediction for robust, adaptable Japanese morphological analysis. In *Proceedings of ACL*.

Olutobi Owoputi, Brendan O'Connor, Chris Dyer, Kevin Gimpel, Nathan Schneider, and Noah A. Smith. 2013. Improved part-of-speech tagging for online conversational text with word clusters. In *Proceedings of NAACL*.

Deana Pennell and Yang Liu. 2010. Normalization of text messages for text-to-speech. In *ICASSP*.

Deana Pennell and Yang Liu. 2011. A character-level machine translation approach for normalization of sms abbreviations. In *Proceedings of IJCNLP*.

Sasa Petrovic, Miles Osborne, and Victor Lavrenko. 2010. The Edinburgh twitter corpus. In *Proceedings of NAACL*.

Vivek Kumar Rangarajan Sridhar, John Chen, Srinivas Bangalore, and Ron Shacham. 2014. A framework for translating SMS messages. In *Proceedings of COLING*.

Alan Ritter, Sam Clark, and Oren Etzioni. 2011. Named entity recognition in tweets: an experimental study. In *Proceedings of EMNLP*.

Cagil Sonmez and Arzucan Ozgur. 2014. A graph-based approach for contextual text normalization. In *Proceedings of EMNLP*.

Andreas Stolcke. 2002. SRILM-an extensible language modeling toolkit. In *Proceedings International Conference on Spoken Language Processing*.

Aobo Wang and Min-Yen Kan. 2013. Mining informal language from Chinese microtext: Joint word recognition and segmentation. In *Proceedings of ACL*.

Yi Yang and Jacob Eisenstein. 2013. A log-linear model for unsupervised text normalization. In *Proceedings of EMNLP*.

A Unified Kernel Approach for Learning Typed Sentence Rewritings

Martin Gleize
LIMSI-CNRS, Orsay, France
Université Paris-Sud, Orsay, France
gleize@limsi.fr

Brigitte Grau
LIMSI-CNRS, Orsay, France
ENSIIE, Evry, France
bg@limsi.fr

Abstract

Many high level natural language processing problems can be framed as determining if two given sentences are a rewriting of each other. In this paper, we propose a class of kernel functions, referred to as type-enriched string rewriting kernels, which, used in kernel-based machine learning algorithms, allow to learn sentence rewritings. Unlike previous work, this method can be fed external lexical semantic relations to capture a wider class of rewriting rules. It also does not assume preliminary syntactic parsing but is still able to provide a unified framework to capture syntactic structure and alignments between the two sentences. We experiment on three different natural sentence rewriting tasks and obtain state-of-the-art results for all of them.

1 Introduction

Detecting implications of sense between statements stands as one of the most sought-after goals in computational linguistics. Several high level tasks look for either one-way rewriting between single sentences, like recognizing textual entailment (RTE) (Dagan et al., 2006), or two-way rewritings like paraphrase identification (Dolan et al., 2004) and semantic textual similarity (Agirre et al., 2012). In a similar fashion, selecting sentences containing the answer to a question can be seen as finding the best rewritings of the question among answer candidates. These problems are naturally framed as classification tasks, and as such most current solutions make use of supervised machine learning. They have to tackle several challenges: picking an adequate language representation, aligning semantically equivalent elements and extracting relevant features to learn the final decision. Bag-of-words and by extension bag-of-ngrams are traditionally the most direct approach and features rely mostly on lexical matching (Wan et al., 2006; Lintean and Rus, 2011; Jimenez et al., 2013). Moreover, a good solving method has to account for typically scarce labeled training data, by enriching its model with lexical semantic resources like WordNet (Miller, 1995) to bridge gaps between surface forms (Mihalcea et al., 2006; Islam and Inkpen, 2009; Yih et al., 2013). Models based on syntactic trees remain the typical choice to account for the structure of the sentences (Heilman and Smith, 2010; Wang and Manning, 2010; Socher et al., 2011; Calvo et al., 2014). Usually the best systems manage to combine effectively different methods, like Madnani et al.'s meta-classifier with machine translation metrics (Madnani et al., 2012).

A few methods (Zanzotto et al., 2007; Zanzotto et al., 2010; Bu et al., 2012) use kernel functions to learn what makes two sentence pairs similar. Building on this work, we present a type-enriched string rewriting kernel giving the opportunity to specify in a fine-grained way how words match each other. Unlike previous work, rewriting rules learned using our framework account for syntactic structure, term alignments and lexico-semantic typed variations in a unified approach. We detail how to efficiently compute our kernel and lastly experiment on three different high-level NLP tasks, demonstrating the vast applicability of our method. Our system based on type-enriched string rewriting kernels obtains state-of-the-art results on paraphrase identification and answer sentence selection and outperforms comparable methods on RTE.

2 Type-Enriched String Rewriting Kernel

Kernel functions measure the similarity between two elements. Used in machine learning methods

Proceedings of the 53rd Annual Meeting of the Association for Computational Linguistics and the 7th International Joint Conference on Natural Language Processing, pages 939–949,
Beijing, China, July 26-31, 2015.

like SVM, they allow complex decision functions to be learned in classification tasks (Vapnik, 2000). The goal of a well-designed kernel function is to have a high value when computed on two instances of same label, and a low value for two instances of different label.

2.1 String rewriting kernel

String rewriting kernels (Bu et al., 2012) count the number of common rewritings between two pairs of sentences seen as sequences of words. The rewriting rule (A) in Figure 1 can be viewed as a kind of phrasal paraphrase with linked variables (Madnani and Dorr, 2010). Rule (A) rewrites (B)'s first sentence into its second but it does not however rewrite the sentences in (C), which is what we try to fix in this paper.

Following the terminology of string kernels, we use the term *string* and *character* instead of *sentence* and *word*. We denote $(s,t) \in (\Sigma^* \times \Sigma^*)$ an instance of string rewriting, with a source string s and a target string t, both finite sequences of elements in Σ the finite set of characters. Suppose that we are given training data of such instances labeled in $\{+1, -1\}$, for paraphrase/non-paraphrase or entailment/non-entailment in applications. We can use a kernel method to train on this data and learn to automatically classify unlabeled instances. A kernel on string rewriting instances is a map:

$$K : (\Sigma^* \times \Sigma^*) \times (\Sigma^* \times \Sigma^*) \rightarrow \mathbb{R}$$

such that for all $(s_1, t_1), (s_2, t_2) \in \Sigma^* \times \Sigma^*$,

$$K((s_1,t_1),(s_2,t_2)) = \langle \Phi(s_1,t_1), \Phi(s_2,t_2) \rangle \quad (1)$$

where Φ maps each instance into a high dimension feature space. Kernels allow us to avoid the potentially expensive explicit representation of Φ through the inner product space they define. The purpose of the string rewriting kernels is to measure the similarity between two pairs of strings in term of the number of rewriting rules of a set R that they share. Φ is thus naturally defined by $\Phi(s,t) = (\phi_r(s,t))_{r \in R}$ with $\phi_r(s,t) = n$ the number of contiguous substring pairs of (s,t) that rewriting rule r matches.

2.2 Typed rewriting rules

Let the wildcard domain $D \subseteq \Sigma^*$ be the set of strings which can be replaced by wildcards. We now present the formal framework of the type-enriched string rewriting kernels.

Let Γ_p be the set of *pattern types* and Γ_v the set of *variable types*.

To a type $\gamma_p \in \Gamma_p$, we associate the *typing relation* $\overset{\gamma_p}{\approx} \subseteq \Sigma \times \Sigma$.

To a type $\gamma_v \in \Gamma_v$,we associate the *typing relation* $\overset{\gamma_v}{\rightsquigarrow} \subseteq D \times D$.

Together with the typing relations, we call the association of Γ_p and Γ_v the *typing scheme* of the kernel. Let Σ_p be defined as

$$\Sigma_p = \bigcup_{\gamma \in \Gamma} \{[a|b] \mid \exists a, b \in \Sigma, a \overset{\gamma}{\approx} b\} \quad (2)$$

We finally define typed rewriting rules. A *typed rewriting rule* is a triple $r = (\beta_s, \beta_t, \tau)$, where $\beta_s, \beta_t \in (\Sigma_p \cup \{*\})^*$ denote source and target string typed patterns and $\tau \subseteq ind_*(\beta_s) \times ind_*(\beta_t)$ denotes the alignments between the wildcards in the two string patterns. Here $ind_*(\beta)$ denotes the set of indices of wildcards in β.

We say that a rewriting rule (β_s, β_t, τ) *matches* a pair of strings (s,t) if and only if the following conditions are true:

- string patterns β_s, resp. β_t, can be turned into s, resp. t, by:
  - substituting each element $[a|b]$ of Σ_p in the string pattern with an a or b ($\in \Sigma$)
  - substituting each wildcard in the string pattern with an element of the wildcard domain D
- $\forall (i,j) \in \tau$, s, resp. t, substitutes the wildcards at index i, resp. j, by $s_* \in D$, resp. t_*, such that there exists a variable type $\gamma \in \Gamma_v$ with $s_* \overset{\gamma}{\rightsquigarrow} t_*$.

A *type-enriched string rewriting kernel* (TESRK) is simply a string rewriting kernel as defined in Equation 1 but with R a set of typed rewriting rules. This class of kernels depends on wildcard domain D and the typed rewriting rules R which can be tuned to allow for more flexibility in the matching of pairs of characters in a rewriting rule. Within this framework, the k-gram bijective string rewriting kernel (kb-SRK) is defined by the wildcard domain $D = \Sigma$ and the ruleset

$$R = \{(\beta_s, \beta_t, \tau) \mid \beta_s, \beta_t \in (\Sigma_p \cup \{*\})^k, \tau \text{ bijective}\}$$

under $\Gamma_p = \Gamma_v = \{id\}$ with $a \overset{id}{\approx} b$, resp. $a \overset{id}{\rightsquigarrow} b$, if and only if $a = b$.

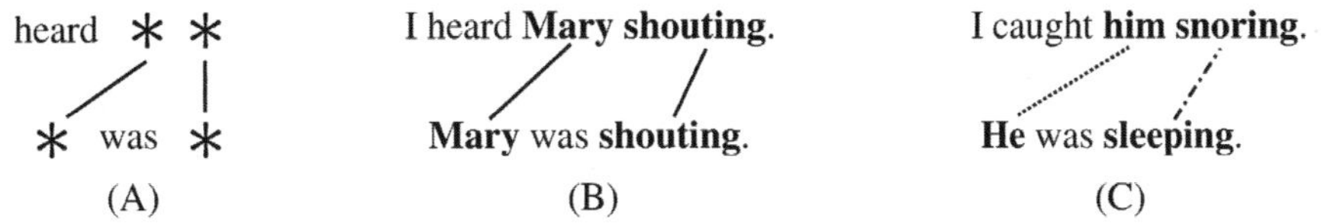

Figure 1: Rewriting rule (A) matches pair of strings (B) but does not match (C).

We now present an example of how kb-SRK is applied to real pairs of sentences, what its limitations are and how we can deal with them by reworking its typing scheme. Let us consider again Figure 1, (A) is a rewriting rule with $\beta_s =$ (*heard*, $*$, $*$), $\beta_t = (*$, *was*, $*)$, $\tau = \{(2,1);(3,3)\}$. Each string pattern has the same length, and pairs of wildcards in the two patterns are aligned bijectively. This is a valid rule for kb-SRK. It matches the pair of strings (B): each aligned pair of wildcards is substituted in source and target sentences by the same word and string patterns of (A) can indeed be turned into pairs of substrings of the sentences. However, it cannot match the pair of sentences (C) in the original kb-SRK. We change Γ_p to {hypernym, id} where $a \overset{hypernym}{\approx} b$ if and only if a and b have a common hypernym in WordNet. And we change Γ_v to $\Gamma_v =$ {same_pronoun, entailment, id} where $a \overset{same\_pronoun}{\rightsquigarrow} b$ if and only if a and b are a pronoun of the same person and same number, and $a \overset{entailment}{\rightsquigarrow} b$ if and only if verb a has a relation of entailment with b in WordNet.
By redefining the typing scheme, rule (A) can now match (C).

3 Computing TESRK

3.1 Formulation

The k-gram bijective string rewriting kernel can be computed efficiently (Bu et al., 2012). We show that we can compute its type-enriched equivalent at the price of a seemingly insurmountable loosening of theoretical complexity boundaries. Experiments however show that its computing time is of the same order as the original kernel.
A type-enriched kb-SRK is parameterized by k the length of k-grams, and its typing scheme the sets Γ_p and Γ_v and their associated relations. The annotations of Γ_p and Γ_v to K_k and $\bar{K}_k$ will be omitted for clarity and because they typically will not change while we test different values for k.
We rewrite the inner product in Equation 1 to better fit the k-gram framework:

$$K_k((s_1,t_1),(s_2,t_2)) = \sum_{\substack{\alpha_{s_1} \in \text{k-grams}(s_1) \\ \alpha_{t_1} \in \text{k-grams}(t_1)}} \sum_{\substack{\alpha_{s_2} \in \text{k-grams}(s_2) \\ \alpha_{t_2} \in \text{k-grams}(t_2)}} \bar{K}_k((\alpha_{s_1},\alpha_{t_1}),(\alpha_{s_2},\alpha_{t_2})) \quad (3)$$

where $\bar{K}_k$ is the number of different rewriting rules which match two pairs of k-grams (the same rule cannot trigger twice in k-gram substrings):

$$\bar{K}_k((\alpha_{s_1},\alpha_{t_1}),(\alpha_{s_2},\alpha_{t_2})) = \sum_{r \in R} \mathbb{1}_r(\alpha_{s_1},\alpha_{t_1}) \mathbb{1}_r(\alpha_{s_2},\alpha_{t_2}) \quad (4)$$

with $\mathbb{1}_r$ the indicator function of rule r: 1 if r matches the pair of k-grams, 0 otherwise.
Computing K_k as defined in Equation 3 is obviously intractable. There is $\mathcal{O}((n-k+1)^4)$ terms in the sum, where n is the length of the longest string, and each term involves enumerating every rewriting rule in R.

3.2 Computing $\bar{K}_k$ in type-enriched kb-SRK

Enumerating all rewriting rules in Equation 4 is itself intractable: there are more than $|\Sigma|^{2k}$ rules without wildcards, where $|\Sigma|$ is conceivably the size of a typical lexicon. In fact, we just have to constructively generate the rules which substitute their string patterns correctly to simultaneously produce both pairs of k-grams $(\alpha_{s_1},\alpha_{t_1})$ and $(\alpha_{s_2},\alpha_{t_2})$.

Let the operator $\otimes$ be such that $\alpha_1 \otimes \alpha_2 = ((\alpha_1[1],\alpha_2[1]),...,(\alpha_1[k],\alpha_2[k]))$. This operation is generally known as *zipping* in functional programming. We use the function *CountPerfectMatchings* computed by Algorithm 1 to recursively count the number of rewriting rules matching both $(\alpha_{s_1},\alpha_{t_1})$ and $(\alpha_{s_2},\alpha_{t_2})$. The workings of the algorithm will make clearer why we can compute $\bar{K}_k$ with the following formula:

$$\bar{K}_k((\alpha_{s_1},\alpha_{t_1}),(\alpha_{s_2},\alpha_{t_2})) = \text{CountPerfectMatchings}(\alpha_{s_1} \otimes \alpha_{s_2}, \alpha_{t_1} \otimes \alpha_{t_2}) \quad (5)$$

Algorithm 1 takes as input remaining character pairs in $\alpha_{s_1} \otimes \alpha_{s_2}$ and $\alpha_{t_1} \otimes \alpha_{t_2}$, and outputs the number of ways they can substitute aligned wildcards in a matching rule.
First (lines 2 and 3) we have the base case where both remaining sets are empty. There is exactly 1 way the empty set's wildcards can be aligned with each other: nothing is aligned. In lines 4 to 9, there is no source pairs anymore, so the algorithm continues to deplete target pairs as long as they have a common pattern type, i.e. as long as they do not have to substitute a wildcard. If a candidate wildcard is found, as the opposing set is empty, we cannot align it and we return 0. In the general case (lines 11 to 19), consider the first character pair (a_1, a_2) in the reminder of $\alpha_{s_1} \otimes \alpha_{s_2}$ in line 12. What follows in the computation depends on its types. Every character pair in $\alpha_{t_1} \otimes \alpha_{t_2}$ that can be paired through variable types with (a_1, a_2) (lines 15 to 19) is a new potential wildcard alignment, so we try all the possible alignment and recursively continue the computation after removing both aligned pairs. And if (a_1, a_2) does not need to substitute a wildcard because it has common pattern types (lines 13 and 14), we can choose to not create any wildcard pairing with it and ignore it in the recursive call.
This algorithm enumerates all configurations such that each character pair has a common pattern type or is matched 1-for-1 with a character pair with common variable types, which is exactly the definition of a rewriting rule in TESRK.

This problem is actually equivalent to counting the perfect matchings of the bipartite graph of potential wildcards. It has been shown intractable (Valiant, 1979) and Algorithm 1 is a naive recursive algorithm to solve it. In our implementation we represent the graph with its bi-adjacency matrix, and if our typing relations are independent of k, the function has a $\mathcal{O}(k)$ time complexity without including its recursive calls. The number of recursive calls can be greater than $k!^2$ which is the number of perfect matchings in a complete bipartite graph of $2k$ vertices. In our experiments on linguistic data however, we observed a linear number of recursive calls for low values of k, and up to a quadratic number for $k > 10$ –which is way past the point where the kernel becomes ineffective.

As an example, Figure 2 shows the zipped k-grams for source and target as a bipartite graph

Algorithm 1: Counting perfect matchings

1 `CountPerfectMatchings` (*remS, remT*)
  Data: *remS*: remaining char. pairs in source
  remT: remaining char. pairs in target
  graph: $\alpha_{s_1} \otimes \alpha_{s_2}$ and $\alpha_{t_1} \otimes \alpha_{t_2}$ as a bipartite graph, not added in the arguments to avoid cluttering the recursive calls
  ruleSet: Γ_p and Γ_v
  Result: Number of rewriting rules matching $(\alpha_{s_1}, \alpha_{t_1})$ and $(\alpha_{s_2}, \alpha_{t_2})$
2 **if** *remS* == $\emptyset$ **and** *remT* == $\emptyset$ **then**
3   return 1;
4 **else if** *remS* == $\emptyset$ **then**
5   (b_1, b_2) = remT.first();
6   **if** $\exists \gamma \in \Gamma_p \mid b_1 \overset{\gamma}{\approx} b_2$ **then**
7   return CountPerfectMatchings($\emptyset$, remT - $\{(b_1, b_2)\}$);
8   **else**
9   return 0;
10 **else**
11   result = 0;
12   (a_1, a_2) = remS.first();
13   **if** $\exists \gamma \in \Gamma_p \mid a_1 \overset{\gamma}{\approx} a_2$ **then**
14   res += CountPerfectMatchings(remS - $\{(a_1, a_2)\}$, remT);
15   **for** $(b_1, b_2) \in$ remT
16     $\mid \exists \gamma \in \Gamma_v \mid a_1 \overset{\gamma}{\rightsquigarrow} b_1$ and $a_2 \overset{\gamma}{\rightsquigarrow} b_2$ **do**
17   res += CountPerfectMatchings(
18   remS - $\{(a_1, a_2)\}$,
19   remT - $\{(b_1, b_2)\}$
20   );

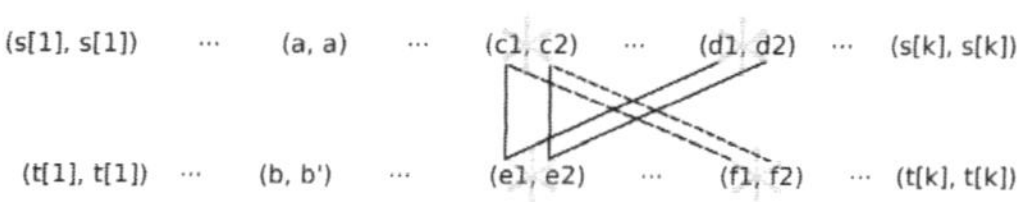

Figure 2: Bipartite graph of character pairs, with edges between potential wildcards

with $2k$ vertices and potential wildcard edges. Assuming that vertices (a, a) and (b, b') have common pattern types, they can be ignored as in lines 7 and 14. (c_1, c_2) to (f_1, f_2) however must substitute wildcards in a matching rewriting rule. If we align (c_1, c_2) with (e_1, e_2) in line 16, the recursive call will return 0 because the other two pairs cannot be aligned. A valid rule is generated if c's are paired with f's and d's with e's. This kind of choices is the main source of computational cost.

This problem did not arise in the original kb-SRK because of the transitivity of its only type (*identity*). In type-enriched kb-SRK, wildcard pairing is less constrained.

3.3 Computing K_k

Even with an efficient method for computing $\bar{K}_k$, implementing K_k directly by applying Equation 3 remains impractical. The main idea is to efficiently compute a reasonably sized set $\mathbb{C}$ of elements $((\alpha_{s_1}, \alpha_{t_1}), (\alpha_{s_2}, \alpha_{t_2}))$ which has the essential property of including all elements such that $\bar{K}_k((\alpha_{s_1}, \alpha_{t_1}), (\alpha_{s_2}, \alpha_{t_2})) \neq 0$.
By definition of $\mathbb{C}$, we can compute efficiently

$$K_k((s_1, t_1), (s_2, t_2)) = \sum_{((\alpha_{s_1}, \alpha_{s_2}), (\alpha_{t_1}, \alpha_{t_2})) \in \mathbb{C}} \bar{K}_k((\alpha_{s_1}, \alpha_{t_1}), (\alpha_{s_2}, \alpha_{t_2})) \quad (6)$$

There are a number of ways to do it, with a trade-off between computation time and number of elements in the reduced domain $\mathbb{C}$. The main idea of our own algorithm is that $\bar{K}_k((\alpha_{s_1}, \alpha_{t_1}), (\alpha_{s_2}, \alpha_{t_2})) = 0$ if the character pairs $(a_1, a_2) \in \alpha_{s_1} \otimes \alpha_{s_2}$ with no common pattern type are not **all** matched with pairs $(b_1, b_2) \in \alpha_{t_1} \otimes \alpha_{t_2}$ such that $a_1 \overset{\gamma}{\rightsquigarrow} b_1$ and $a_2 \overset{\gamma}{\rightsquigarrow} b_2$ for some $\gamma \in \Gamma_v$. This is conversely true for character pairs in $\alpha_{t_1} \otimes \alpha_{t_2}$ with no common pattern type. More simply, character pairs with no common pattern type are mismatched and have to substitute a wildcard in a rewriting rule matching both $(\alpha_{s_1}, \alpha_{t_1})$ and $(\alpha_{s_2}, \alpha_{t_2})$. But introducing a wildcard on one side of the rule means that there is a matching wildcard on the other side, so we can eliminate k-gram quadruples that do not fill this wildcard inclusion. This filtering can be done efficiently and yields a manageable number of quadruples on which to compute $\bar{K}_k$.

Algorithm 2 computes a set $\mathbb{C}$ to be used in Equation 6 for computing the final value of kernel K_k. In our experiments, it efficiently produces a reasonable number of inputs. All maps in the algorithm are maps to multisets, and multisets are used extensively throughout. *Multisets* are an extension of sets where elements can appear multiple times, the number of times being called the *multiplicity*. Typically implemented as hash tables from set elements to integers, they allow for constant-time retrieval of the number of a given element. Union ($\cup$) and intersection ($\cap$) have special definitions on multisets. If $\mathbb{1}_A(x)$ is the multiplicity of x in A, we have $\mathbb{1}_{A \cup B}(x) = max(\mathbb{1}_A(x), \mathbb{1}_B(x))$ and $\mathbb{1}_{A \cap B}(x) = min(\mathbb{1}_A(x), \mathbb{1}_B(x))$.

Algorithm 2: Computing a set including all elements on which $\bar{K}_k \neq 0$

Data: s_1, t_1, s_2, t_2 strings, and k an integer
Result: Set $\mathbb{C}$ which include all inputs such that $\bar{K}_k \neq 0$

1 Initialize maps $e^i_{s \to t}$ and maps $e^i_{t \to s}$, for $i \in \{1, 2\}$;
2 **for** $i \in \{1, 2\}$ **do**
3   **for** $a \in s_i, b \in t_i \mid a \overset{\gamma}{\rightsquigarrow} b, \gamma \in \Gamma_v$ **do**
4         $e^i_{s \to t}[a]$ += (b, γ); $e^i_{t \to s}[b]$ += (a, γ);
5 $w_{s \to t}, aP_t =$ OneWayInclusion$(s_1, s_2, t_1, t_2, e^1_{s \to t}, e^2_{s \to t})$;
6 $w_{t \to s}, aP_s =$ OneWayInclusion$(t_1, t_2, s_1, s_2, e^1_{t \to s}, e^2_{t \to s})$;
7 Initialize multiset res;
8 **for** $(\alpha_{s_1}, \alpha_{s_2}) \in aP_s$ **do**
9   **for** $(\alpha_{t_1}, \alpha_{t_2}) \in aP_t$ **do**
10   res += $((\alpha_{s_1}, \alpha_{s_2}), (\alpha_{t_1}, \alpha_{t_2}))$;
11 res = res $\cup w_{s \to t} \cup w_{t \to s}.map(swap)$;
12 return res;
13 ---
14 `OneWayInclusion` $(s_1, s_2, t_1, t_2, e^1, e^2)$
Initialize map d multisets resWildcards, resAllPatterns;
15 **for** $(\alpha_{s_1}, \alpha_{s_2}) \in$ *kgrams*$(s_1) \times$ *kgrams*(s_2) **do**
16   **for** $(b_1, b_2) \mid \exists \gamma \in \Gamma_v, (a_1, a_2) \in \alpha_{s_1} \otimes \alpha_{s_2}, (b_i, \gamma) \in e^i[a_i]\ \forall i \in \{1, 2\}$ **do**
17         $d[(b_1, b_2)]$ += $(\alpha_{s_1}, \alpha_{s_2})$;
18 **for** $(\alpha_{t_1}, \alpha_{t_2}) \in$ *kgrams*$(t_1) \times$ *kgrams*(t_2) **do**
19   **for** $(b_1, b_2) \in \alpha_{t_1} \otimes \alpha_{t_2} \mid b_1 \overset{\gamma}{\not\rightsquigarrow} b_2 \forall \gamma \in \Gamma_p$ **do**
20   **if** *compatWkgrms not initialized* **then**
21   Initialize multiset compatWkgrms = $d[(b_1, b_2)]$;
22   compatWkgrms = compatWkgrms $\cap\, d[(b_1, b_2)]$;
23   **if** *compatWkgrms not initialized* **then**
24   resAllPatterns += $(\alpha_{t_1}, \alpha_{t_2})$;
25   **for** $(\alpha_{s_1}, \alpha_{s_2}) \in$ *compatWkgrms* **do**
26   resWildcards+=$((\alpha_{s_1}, \alpha_{s_2}), (\alpha_{t_1}, \alpha_{t_2}))$;
27 return (resWildcards, resAllPatterns);

Let us now comment on how the algorithm unfolds. In lines 1 to 4, we index characters in source strings by characters in target strings which have common variable types, and vice versa. It allows in lines 15 to 19 to quickly map a character pair to the set of opposing k-gram pairs with a matching –in the sense of variable types– character pair, i.e. potential aligned wildcards. In lines 20 to 28 we keep only the k-gram quadruples whose wildcard candidates (character pairs with no common pattern) from one side **all** find matches on the other side. We do not check for the other inclusion, hence the name of the function *OneWayInclusion*. At line 26, we did not find any character pair with no common pattern, so we save the k-gram pair as "all-pattern". All-pattern k-grams will be paired in lines 8 to 10 in the result. Finally, in line 11, we add the union of one-way compatible k-gram quadruples; calling swap on all the pairs of one set is necessary to consistently have sources on the left side and targets on the right side in the result.

4 Experiments

4.1 Systems

We experimented on three tasks: paraphrase identification, recognizing textual entailment and answer sentence selection. The setup we used for all experiments was the same save for the few parameters we explored such as: k, and typing scheme. We implemented 2 kernels, kb-SRK, henceforth simply denoted *SRK*, and the type-enriched kb-SRK, denoted *TESRK*. All sentences were tokenized and POS-tagged using OpenNLP (Morton et al., 2005). Then they were stemmed using the Porter stemmer (Porter, 2001) in the case of SRK. Various other pre-processing steps were applied in the case of TESRK: they are considered as types in the model and are detailed in Table 1. We used LIBSVM (Chang and Lin, 2011) to train a binary SVM classifier on the training data with our two kernels. The default SVM algorithm in LIBSVM uses a parameter C, roughly akin to a regularization parameter. We 10-fold cross-validated this parameter on the training data, optimizing with a grid search for f-score, or MRR for question-answering. All kernels were normalized using $\tilde{K}(x,y) = \frac{K(x,y)}{\sqrt{K(x,x)}\sqrt{K(y,y)}}$. We denote by "+" a sum of kernels, with normalizations applied both before and after summing. Following Bu et al. (Bu et al., 2012) experimental setup, we introduced an auxiliary vector kernel denoted *PR* of features named *unigram precision* and *recall*, defined in (Wan et al., 2006). In our experiments a linear kernel seemed to yield the best results. Our Scala implementation of kb-SRKs has an average throughput of about 1500 original kb-SRK computations per second, versus 500 type-enriched kb-SRK computations per second on a 8-core machine. It typically takes a few hours on a 32-core machine to train, cross-validate and test on a full dataset.

Finally, Table 1 presents an overview of our types with how they are defined and implemented. Every type can be used both as a pattern type or as a variable type, but the two roles are different. Pattern types are useful to unify different surface forms of rewriting rules that are semantically equivalent, i.e. having semantically similar patterns. Variable types are useful for when the semantic relation between 2 entities across the same rewriting is more important than the entities themselves. That is why some types in Table 1 are inherently more fitted to be used for one role rather than the other. For example, it is unlikely that replacing a word in a pattern of a rewriting rule by one of its holonyms will yield a semantically similar rewriting rule, so *holonym* would not be a good pattern type for most applications. On the contrary, it can be very useful in a rewriting rule to type a wildcard link with the relation holonym, as this provides constrained semantic roles to the linked wildcards in the rule, thus *holonym* would be a good variable type.

4.2 Paraphrase identification

Paraphrase identification asks whether two sentences have the same meaning. The dataset we used to evaluate our systems is the MSR Paraphrase Corpus (Dolan and Brockett, 2005), containing 4,076 training pairs of sentences and 1,725 testing pairs. For example, the sentences *"An injured woman co-worker also was hospitalized and was listed in good condition."* and *"A woman was listed in good condition at Memorial's HealthPark campus, he said."* are paraphrases in this corpus. On the other hand, *"'There are a number of locations in our community, which are essentially vulnerable,' Mr Ruddock said."* and *"'There are a range of risks which are being seriously examined by competent authorities,' Mr Ruddock said."* are not paraphrases.

We report in Table 2 our best results, the system *TESRK + PR*, defined by the sum of PR and typed-enriched kb-SRKs with k from 1 to 4, with types $\Gamma_p = \Gamma_v = \{stem, synonym\}$. We observe

Type	Typing relation on words (a, b)	Tool/resources
id	words have same surface form and tag	OpenNLP tagger
idMinusTag	words have same surface form	OpenNLP tokenizer
lemma	words have same lemma	WordNetStemmer
stem	words have same stem	Porter stemmer
synonym, antonym	words are [type]	WordNet
hypernym, hyponym entailment, holonym	b is a [type] of a	WordNet
ne	a and b are both tagged with the same Named Entity	BBN Identifinder
lvhsn	words are at edit distance of 1	Levenshtein distance

Table 1: Types

Paraphrase system	Accuracy	F-score
All paraphrase	66.5	79.9
Wan et al. (2006)	75.6	83.0
Bu et al. (2012)	76.3	N/A
Socher et al. (2011)	76.8	83.6
Madnani et al. (2012)	**77.4**	**84.1**
PR	73.5	82.1
SRK + PR	76.2	83.6
TESRK	76.6	83.7
TESRK + PR	**77.2**	**84.0**

Table 2: Evaluation results on MSR Paraphrase

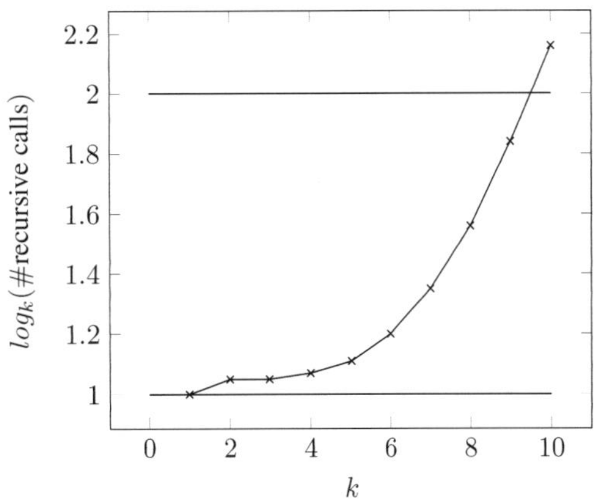

Figure 3: Evolution of the number of recursive calls to CountPerfectMatchings with k

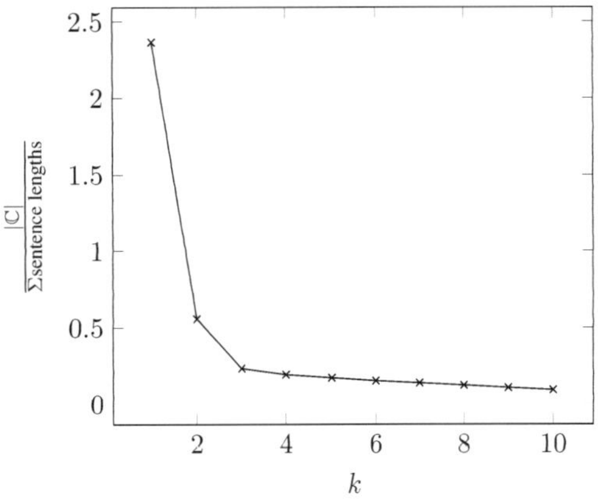

Figure 4: Evolution of the size of $\mathbb{C}$ with k

that our results are state-of-the-art and in particular, they improve on the orignal kb-SRK by a good margin. We tried other combinations of types but it did not yield good results, this is probably due to the nature of the MSR corpus, which did not contain much more advanced variations from WordNet. The only statistically significant improvement we obtained was between *TESRK + PR* and our PR baseline ($p < 0.05$). The performances obtained by all the cited systems and ours are not significantly different in any statistical sense. We made a special effort to try to reproduce as best as we could the original kb-SRK performances (Bu et al., 2012), although our implementation and theirs should theoretically be equivalent.

Figure 3 plots the average number of recursive calls to CountPerfectMatchings (algorithm 1) during a kernel computation, as a function of k. Composing with log_k, we can observe whether the empiric number of recursive calls is closer to $\mathcal{O}(k)$ or $\mathcal{O}(k^2)$. We conclude that this element of complexity is linear for low values of k, but tends to explode past $k = 7$. Thankfully, counting common rewriting rules on pairs of 7-to-10-grams rarely yields non-zero results, so in practice using high values of k is not interesting.

Figure 4 plots the average size of set $\mathbb{C}$ computed by algorithm 2, as a function of k (divided by the sum of lengths of the 4 sentences involved in the kernel computation). We can observe that this

RTE system	Accuracy
All entailments	51.2
Heilman and Smith (2010)	62.8
Bu et al. (2012)	65.1
Zanzotto et al. (2007)	65.8
Hickl et al. (2006)	**80.0**
PR	61.8
TESRK (All)	62.1
SRK + PR	63.8
TESRK (Syn) + PR	64.1
TESRK (All) + PR	66.1

Table 3: Evaluation results on RTE-3

quantity is small, except for a peak at low values of k, which is not an issue because the computation of $\bar{K}_k$ is very fast for those values of k.

4.3 Recognizing textual entailment

Recognizing Textual Entailment asks whether the meaning of a sentence *hypothesis* can be inferred by reading a sentence *text*. The dataset we used to evaluate our systems is RTE-3. Following similar work (Heilman and Smith, 2010; Bu et al., 2012), we took as training data (text, hypothesis) pairs from RTE-1 and RTE-2's whole datasets and from RTE-3's training data, which amounts to 3,767 sentence pairs. We tested on RTE-3 testing data containing 800 sentence pairs. For example, a valid textual entailment in this dataset is the pair of sentences *"In a move widely viewed as surprising, the Bank of England raised UK interest rates from 5% to 5.25%, the highest in five years."* and *"UK interest rates went up from 5% to 5.25%."*: the first entails the second. On the other hand, the pair *"Former French president General Charles de Gaulle died in November. More than 6,000 people attended a requiem mass for him at Notre Dame cathedral in Paris."* and *"Charles de Gaulle died in 1970."* does not constitute a textual entailment.

We report in Table 3 our best results, the system *TESRK (All) + PR*, defined by the sum of PR, 1b-SRK and typed-enriched kb-SRKs with k from 2 to 4, with types $\Gamma_p = \{\text{stem, synonym}\}$ and $\Gamma_v = \{\text{stem, synonym, hypernym, hyponym, entailment, holonym}\}$. Our results are to be compared with systems using techniques and resources of similar nature, but as reference the top performance at RTE-3 is still reported. This time we did not manage to fully reproduce Bu et al. 2012's performance, but we observe that type-enriched kb-SRK greatly improves upon our original implementation of kb-SRK and outperforms their system anyway. Combining TESRK and the PR baseline yields significantly better results than either one alone ($p < 0.05$), and performs significantly better than the system of (Heilman and Smith, 2010), the only one which was evaluated on the same three tasks as us ($p < 0.10$). We tried with less types in our system *TESRK (Syn) + PR* by removing all WordNet types but synonyms but got lower performance. This seems to indicate that rich types indeed help capturing more complex sentence rewritings. Note that we needed for $k = 1$ to replace the type-enriched kb-SRK by the original kernel in the sum, otherwise the performance dropped significantly. Our conclusion is that including richer types is only beneficial if they are captured within a context of a couple of words and that including all those variations on unigrams only add noise.

4.4 Answer sentence selection

Answer sentence selection is the problem of selecting among single candidate sentences the ones containing the correct answer to an open-domain factoid question. The dataset we used to evaluate our system on this task was created by (Wang et al., 2007) based on the QA track of past Text REtrieval Conferences (TREC-QA)[1]. The training set contains 4718 question/answer pairs, for 94 questions, originating from TREC 8 to 12. The testing set contains 1517 pairs for 89 questions. As an example, a correct answer to the question *"What do practitioners of Wicca worship?"* is *"An estimated 50,000 Americans practice Wicca, a form of polytheistic nature worship."* On the other hand, the answer candidate *"When people think of Wicca, they think of either Satanism or silly mumbo jumbo."* is incorrect. Sentences with more than 40 words and questions with only positive or only negative answers were filtered out (Yao et al., 2013). The average fraction of correct answers per question is 7.4% for training and 18.7% for testing. Performances are evaluated as for a re-ranking problem, in term of Mean Average Precision (MAP) and Mean Reciprocal Rank (MRR). We report our results in Table 4. We evaluated several combinations of features. *IDF word-count* (IDF) is a baseline of

[1] Available at `http://nlp.stanford.edu/mengqiu/data/qg-emnlp07-data.tgz`

System	MAP	MRR
Random baseline	0.397	0.493
Wang et al. (2007)	0.603	0.685
Heilman and Smith (2010)	0.609	0.692
Wang and Manning (2010)	0.595	0.695
Yao et al. (2013)	0.631	0.748
Yih et al. (2013) LCLR	**0.709**	**0.770**
IDF word-count (IDF)	0.596	0.650
SRK	0.609	0.669
SRK + IDF	0.620	0.677
TESRK (WN)	0.642	0.725
TESRK (WN+NE)	0.656	0.744
TESRK (WN) + IDF	0.678	0.759
TESRK (WN+NE) + IDF	0.672	**0.768**

Table 4: Evaluation results on QA

IDF-weighted common word counting, integrated in a linear kernel. Then we implemented SRK and TESRK (with k from 1 to 5) with two typing schemes: *WN* stands for $\Gamma_p = \{\text{stem, synonym}\}$ and $\Gamma_v = \{\text{stem, synonym, hypernym, hyponym, entailment, holonym}\}$, and *WN+NE* adds type ne to both sets of types. We finally summed our kernels with the IDF baseline kernel. We observe that types which make use of WordNet variations seem to increase the most our performance. Our assumption was that named entities would be useful for question answering and that we could learn associations between question type and answer type through variations: NE does seem to help a little when combined with WN alone, but is less useful once TESRK is combined with our baseline of IDF-weighted common words. Overall, typing capabilities allow TESRK to obtain way better performances than SRK in both MAP and MRR, and our best system combining all our features is comparable to state-of-the-art systems in MRR, and significantly outperforms *SRK + IDF*, the system without types ($p < 0.05$).

5 Related work

Lodhi et al. (Lodhi et al., 2002) were among the first in NLP to use kernels: they apply *string kernels* which count common subsequences to text classification. Sentence pair classification however require the capture of 2 types of links: the link between sentences within a pair, and the link between pairs. Zanzotto et al. (Zanzotto et al., 2007) used a kernel method on syntactic tree pairs. They expanded on graph kernels in (Zanzotto et al., 2010). Their method first aligns tree nodes of a pair of sentences to form a single tree with placeholders. They then use *tree kernel* (Moschitti, 2006) to compute the number of common subtrees of those trees. Bu et al. (Bu et al., 2012) introduced a string rewriting kernel which can capture at once lexical equivalents and common syntactic dependencies on pair of sentences. All these kernel methods require an exact match or assume prior partial matches between words, thus limiting the kind of learned rewriting rules. Our contribution addresses this issue with a type-enriched string rewriting kernel which can account for lexico-semantic variations of words. Limitations of our rewriting rules include the impossibility to skip a pattern word and to replace wildcards by multiple words.

Some recent contributions (Chang et al., 2010; Wang and Manning, 2010) also provide a uniform way to learn both intermediary representations and a decision function using potentially rich feature sets. They use heuristics in the joint learning process to reduce the computational cost, while our kernel approach with a simple sequential representation of sentences has the benefit of efficiently computing an exact number of common rewriting rules between rewriting pairs. This in turn allows to precisely fine-tune the shape of desired rewriting rules through the design of the typing scheme.

6 Conclusion

We developed a unified kernel-based framework for solving sentence rewriting tasks. Types allow for an increased flexibility in counting common rewriting rules, and can also add a semantic layer to the rewritings. We show that we can efficiently compute a kernel which takes types into account, called type-enriched k-gram bijective string rewriting kernel. A SVM classifier with this kernel yields state-of-the-art results in paraphrase identification and answer sentence selection and outperforms comparable systems in recognizing textual entailment.

References

Eneko Agirre, Mona Diab, Daniel Cer, and Aitor Gonzalez-Agirre. 2012. Semeval-2012 task 6: A pilot on semantic textual similarity. In *Proceedings of the First Joint Conference on Lexical and Computational Semantics-Volume 1: Proceedings of the main conference and the shared task, and Volume*

2: *Proceedings of the Sixth International Workshop on Semantic Evaluation*, pages 385–393. Association for Computational Linguistics.

Fan Bu, Hang Li, and Xiaoyan Zhu. 2012. String re-writing kernel. In *Proceedings of the 50th Annual Meeting of the Association for Computational Linguistics: Long Papers-Volume 1*, pages 449–458. Association for Computational Linguistics.

Hiram Calvo, Andrea Segura-Olivares, and Alejandro García. 2014. Dependency vs. constituent based syntactic n-grams in text similarity measures for paraphrase recognition. *Computación y Sistemas*, 18(3):517–554.

Chih-Chung Chang and Chih-Jen Lin. 2011. Libsvm: a library for support vector machines. *ACM Transactions on Intelligent Systems and Technology (TIST)*, 2(3):27.

Ming-Wei Chang, Dan Goldwasser, Dan Roth, and Vivek Srikumar. 2010. Discriminative learning over constrained latent representations. In *Human Language Technologies: The 2010 Annual Conference of the North American Chapter of the Association for Computational Linguistics*, pages 429–437. Association for Computational Linguistics.

Ido Dagan, Oren Glickman, and Bernardo Magnini. 2006. The pascal recognising textual entailment challenge. In *Machine learning challenges. evaluating predictive uncertainty, visual object classification, and recognising tectual entailment*, pages 177–190. Springer.

William B Dolan and Chris Brockett. 2005. Automatically constructing a corpus of sentential paraphrases. In *Proc. of IWP*.

Bill Dolan, Chris Quirk, and Chris Brockett. 2004. Unsupervised construction of large paraphrase corpora: Exploiting massively parallel news sources. In *Proceedings of the 20th international conference on Computational Linguistics*, page 350. Association for Computational Linguistics.

Michael Heilman and Noah A Smith. 2010. Tree edit models for recognizing textual entailments, paraphrases, and answers to questions. In *Human Language Technologies: The 2010 Annual Conference of the North American Chapter of the Association for Computational Linguistics*, pages 1011–1019. Association for Computational Linguistics.

Aminul Islam and Diana Inkpen. 2009. Semantic similarity of short texts. *Recent Advances in Natural Language Processing V*, 309:227–236.

Sergio Jimenez, Claudia Becerra, Alexander Gelbukh, Av Juan Dios Bátiz, and Av Mendizábal. 2013. Softcardinality: hierarchical text overlap for student response analysis. In *Proceedings of the 2nd joint conference on lexical and computational semantics*, volume 2, pages 280–284.

Mihai C Lintean and Vasile Rus. 2011. Dissimilarity kernels for paraphrase identification. In *FLAIRS Conference*.

Huma Lodhi, Craig Saunders, John Shawe-Taylor, Nello Cristianini, and Chris Watkins. 2002. Text classification using string kernels. *The Journal of Machine Learning Research*, 2:419–444.

Nitin Madnani and Bonnie J Dorr. 2010. Generating phrasal and sentential paraphrases: A survey of data-driven methods. *Computational Linguistics*, 36(3):341–387.

Nitin Madnani, Joel Tetreault, and Martin Chodorow. 2012. Re-examining machine translation metrics for paraphrase identification. In *Proceedings of the 2012 Conference of the North American Chapter of the Association for Computational Linguistics: Human Language Technologies*, pages 182–190. Association for Computational Linguistics.

Rada Mihalcea, Courtney Corley, and Carlo Strapparava. 2006. Corpus-based and knowledge-based measures of text semantic similarity. In *AAAI*, volume 6, pages 775–780.

George A Miller. 1995. Wordnet: a lexical database for english. *Communications of the ACM*, 38(11):39–41.

Thomas Morton, Joern Kottmann, Jason Baldridge, and Gann Bierner. 2005. Opennlp: A java-based nlp toolkit. http://opennlp.sourceforge.net.

Alessandro Moschitti. 2006. Efficient convolution kernels for dependency and constituent syntactic trees. In *Machine Learning: ECML 2006*, pages 318–329. Springer.

Martin F Porter. 2001. Snowball: A language for stemming algorithms.

Richard Socher, Eric H Huang, Jeffrey Pennin, Christopher D Manning, and Andrew Y Ng. 2011. Dynamic pooling and unfolding recursive autoencoders for paraphrase detection. In *Advances in Neural Information Processing Systems*, pages 801–809.

Leslie G Valiant. 1979. The complexity of enumeration and reliability problems. *SIAM Journal on Computing*, 8(3):410–421.

Vladimir Vapnik. 2000. *The nature of statistical learning theory*. Springer Science & Business Media.

Stephen Wan, Mark Dras, Robert Dale, and Cécile Paris. 2006. Using dependency-based features to take the para-farce out of paraphrase. In *Proceedings of the Australasian Language Technology Workshop*, volume 2006.

Mengqiu Wang and Christopher D Manning. 2010. Probabilistic tree-edit models with structured latent variables for textual entailment and question answering. In *Proceedings of the 23rd International Conference on Computational Linguistics*, pages 1164–1172. Association for Computational Linguistics.

Mengqiu Wang, Noah A Smith, and Teruko Mitamura. 2007. What is the jeopardy model? a quasi-synchronous grammar for qa. In *EMNLP-CoNLL*, volume 7, pages 22–32.

Xuchen Yao, Benjamin Van Durme, Chris Callison-Burch, and Peter Clark. 2013. Answer extraction as sequence tagging with tree edit distance. In *HLT-NAACL*, pages 858–867. Citeseer.

Wen-tau Yih, Ming-Wei Chang, Christopher Meek, and Andrzej Pastusiak. 2013. Question answering using enhanced lexical semantic models. In *Proceedings of the 26rd International Conference on Computational Linguistics*. Association for Computational Linguistics.

Fabio Massimo Zanzotto, Marco Pennacchiotti, and Alessandro Moschitti. 2007. Shallow semantics in fast textual entailment rule learners. In *Proceedings of the ACL-PASCAL workshop on textual entailment and paraphrasing*, pages 72–77. Association for Computational Linguistics.

Fabio Massimo Zanzotto, Lorenzo DellArciprete, and Alessandro Moschitti. 2010. Efficient graph kernels for textual entailment recognition. *Fundamenta Informaticae*.

Perceptually grounded selectional preferences

Ekaterina Shutova
Computer Laboratory
University of Cambridge, UK
es407@cam.ac.uk

Niket Tandon
Max Planck Institute
for Informatics, Germany
ntandon@mpi-inf.mpg.de

Gerard de Melo
IIIS
Tsinghua University, China
gdm@demelo.org

Abstract

Selectional preferences (SPs) are widely used in NLP as a rich source of semantic information. While SPs have been traditionally induced from textual data, human lexical acquisition is known to rely on both linguistic and perceptual experience. We present the first SP learning method that simultaneously draws knowledge from text, images and videos, using image and video descriptions to obtain visual features. Our results show that it outperforms linguistic and visual models in isolation, as well as the existing SP induction approaches.

1 Introduction

Selectional preferences (SPs) are the semantic constraints that a predicate places onto its arguments. This means that certain classes of entities are more likely to fill the predicate's argument slot than others. For instance, while the sentences "*The authors wrote a new paper.*" and "*The cat is eating your sausage!*" sound natural and describe plausible real-life situations, the sentences "*The carrot ate the keys.*" and "*The law sang a driveway.*" appear implausible and difficult to interpret, as the arguments do not satisfy the verbs' common preferences. SPs provide generalisations about word meaning and use and find a wide range of applications in natural language processing (NLP), including word sense disambiguation (Resnik, 1997; McCarthy and Carroll, 2003; Wagner et al., 2009), resolving ambiguous syntactic attachments (Hindle and Rooth, 1993), semantic role labelling (Gildea and Jurafsky, 2002; Zapirain et al., 2010), natural language inference (Zanzotto et al., 2006; Pantel et al., 2007), and figurative language processing (Fass, 1991; Mason, 2004; Shutova et al., 2013; Li et al., 2013). Automatic acquisition of SPs from linguistic data has thus become an active area of research. The community has investigated a range of techniques to tackle data sparsity and to perform generalisation from observed arguments to their underlying types, including the use of WordNet synsets as SP classes (Resnik, 1993; Li and Abe, 1998; Clark and Weir, 1999; Abney and Light, 1999; Ciaramita and Johnson, 2000), word clustering (Rooth et al., 1999; Bergsma et al., 2008; Sun and Korhonen, 2009), distributional similarity metrics (Erk, 2007; Peirsman and Padó, 2010), latent variable models (Ó Séaghdha, 2010; Ritter et al., 2010), and neural networks (Van de Cruys, 2014).

Little research, however, has been concerned with the sources of knowledge that underlie the learning of SPs. There is ample evidence in cognitive and neurolinguistics that our concept learning and semantic representation are grounded in perception and action (Barsalou, 1999; Glenberg and Kaschak, 2002; Barsalou, 2008; Aziz-Zadeh and Damasio, 2008). This suggests that word meaning and relational knowledge are acquired not only from linguistic input but also from our experiences in the physical world. Multi-modal models of word meaning have thus enjoyed a growing interest in semantics (Bruni et al., 2014), outperforming purely text-based models in tasks such as similarity estimation (Bruni et al., 2014; Kiela et al., 2014), predicting compositionality (Roller and Schulte im Walde, 2013), and concept categorization (Silberer and Lapata, 2014). However, to date these approaches relied on low-level image features such as color histograms or SIFT keypoints to represent the meaning of isolated words. To the best of our knowledge, there has not yet been a multimodal semantic approach performing extraction of

Proceedings of the 53rd Annual Meeting of the Association for Computational Linguistics and the 7th International Joint Conference on Natural Language Processing, pages 950–960,
Beijing, China, July 26-31, 2015.

predicate-argument relations from visual data. In this paper, we propose the first SP model integrating information about predicate-argument interactions from text, images, and videos. We expect it to outperform purely text-based models of SPs, which suffer from two problems: topic bias and figurative uses of words. Such bias stems from the fact that we typically write about abstract topics and events, resulting in high coverage of abstract senses of words and comparatively lower coverage of the original physical senses (Shutova, 2011). For instance, the verb *cut* is used predominantly in the domains of economics and finance and its most frequent direct objects are *cost* and *price*, according to the British National Corpus (BNC) (Burnard, 2007). Predicate-argument distributions acquired from text thus tend to be skewed in favour of abstract domains and figurative uses, inadequately reflecting our daily experiences with *cutting*, which guide human acquisition of meaning. Integrating predicate-argument relations observed in the physical world (in the form of image and video descriptions) with the more abstract text-based relations is likely to yield a more realistic semantic model, with real prospects of improving the performance of NLP applications that rely on SPs.

We use the BNC as an approximation of linguistic knowledge and a large collection of tagged images and videos from Flickr (`www.flickr.com`) as an approximation of perceptual knowledge. The human-annotated labels that accompany media on Flickr enable us to acquire predicate-argument co-occurrence information. Our experiments focus on verb preferences for their subjects and direct objects. In summary, our method (1) performs word sense disambiguation and part-of-speech (PoS) tagging of Flickr tag sequences to extract verb-noun co-occurrence; (2) clusters nouns to induce SP classes using linguistic and visual features; (3) quantifies the strength of preference of a verb for a given class by interpolating linguistic and visual SP distributions. We investigate the impact of perceptual information at different levels – from none (purely text-based model) to 100% (purely visual model). We evaluate our model directly against a dataset of human plausibility judgements of verb-noun pairs, as well as in the context of a semantic task: metaphor interpretation. Our results show that the interpolated model combining linguistic and visual relations outperforms the purely linguistic model in both evaluation settings.

2 Related work

2.1 Selectional preference induction

The widespread interest in automatic acquisition of SPs was triggered by the work of Resnik (1993), who treated SPs as probability distributions over all potential arguments of a predicate, rather than a single argument class assigned to the predicate. The original study used WordNet to define SP classes and to map the words in the corpus to those classes. Since then, the field has moved toward automatic induction of SP classes from corpus data. Rooth et al. (1999) presented a probabilistic latent variable model of verb preferences. In their approach, verb-argument pairs are generated from a latent variable, which represents a cluster of verb-argument interactions. The latent variable distribution and the probabilities that a latent variable generates the verb and the argument are learned from the data using Expectation Maximization (EM). The latent variables enable the model to recognise previously unseen verb-argument pairs. Ó Séaghdha (2010) and Ritter et al. (2010) similarly model SPs within a latent variable framework, but use Latent Dirichlet Allocation (LDA) to learn the probability distributions, for single-argument and multi-argument preferences respectively.

Padó et al. (2007) and Erk (2007) used similarity metrics to approximate selectional preference classes. Their underlying hypothesis is that a predicate-argument combination (p, a) is felicitous if the predicate p is frequently observed in the data with the arguments a' similar to a. The systems compute similarities between distributional representations of arguments in a vector space.

Bergsma et al. (2008) trained an SVM classifier to discriminate between felicitous and infelicitous verb-argument pairs. Their training data consisted of observed verb-argument pairs (positive examples) with unobserved, randomly-generated ones (negative examples). They classified nominal arguments of verbs, using their verb co-occurrence probabilities and information about their semantic classes as features. Bergsma and Goebel (2011) extended this method by incorporating image-driven noun features. They extract color and SIFT keypoint features from images found for a particular noun via Google image searches and add them to the feature vectors to classify nouns as felicitous or infelicitous arguments of a given verb. This method is the closest in spirit to ours and the only one so far to investigate the relevance of visual features to lexical preference learning. However, our work casts the problem in a different framework: rather than relying on low-level visual properties of nouns in isolation, we explicitly model interactions of predicates and arguments within an image or a video frame.

Van de Cruys (2014) recently presented a deep learning approach to SP acquisition. He trained a neural network to discriminate between felicitous and infelicitous arguments using the data constructed of positive (observed) and negative (randomly-generated) examples for training. The network weights were optimized by requiring the model to assign a higher score to an observed pair than to the unobserved one by a given margin.

2.2 Multi-modal methods in semantics

Previous work has used multimodal data to determine distributional similarity or to learn multimodal embeddings that project multiple modalities into the same vector space. Some studies rely on extensions of LDA to obtain correlations between words and visual features (Feng and Lapata, 2010; Roller and Schulte im Walde, 2013). Bruni et al. (2012) integrated visual features into distributional similarity models using simple vector concatenation. Instead of generic visual features, Silberer et al. (2013) relied on supervised learning to train 412 higher-level visual attribute classifiers.

Applications of multimodal embeddings include zero-shot object detection, i.e. recognizing objects in images without training data for the object class (Socher et al., 2013; Frome et al., 2013; Lazaridou et al., 2014), and automatic generation of image captions (Kulkarni et al., 2013), video descriptions (Rohrbach et al., 2013), or tags (Srivastava et al., 2014). Other applications of multimodal data include language modeling (Kiros et al., 2014) and knowledge mining from images (Chen et al., 2013; Divvala et al., 2014). Young et al. (2014) apply simplification rules to image captions, showing that the resulting hierarchy of mappings between natural language expressions and images can be used for entailment tasks.

3 Experimental data

Textual data. We extract linguistic features for our model from the BNC. In particular, we parse the corpus using the RASP parser (Briscoe et al., 2006) and extract subject–verb and verb–object relations from its dependency output. These relations are then used as features for clustering to obtain SP classes, as well as to quantify the strength of association between a particular verb and a particular argument class.

Visual data. For the visual features of our model, we mine the Yahoo! Webscope Flickr-100M dataset (Shamma, 2014). Flickr-100M contains 99.3 million images and 0.7 million videos with language tags annotated by users, enabling us to generalise SPs at a large scale. The tags reflect how humans describe objects and actions from a visual perspective. We first stem the tags and remove words that are absent in WordNet (typically named entities and misspellings), then identify their PoS based on their visual context and extract verb–noun co-occurrences.

4 Identifying visual verb-noun co-occurrence

In the Flickr-100M dataset, tags are assigned to images and videos in the form of sets of words, rather than grammatically coherent sentences. However, the roles that individual words play are still discernible from their visual context, as manifested by the other words in a given set. In order to identify verbs and nouns co-occurring in the same images, we propose a *list sense disambiguation* method that first maps each word to a set of possible WordNet senses (accompanied by PoS information) and then performs a joint optimization on the space of candidate word senses, such that their overall similarity is maximized. This amounts to assigning those senses and PoS tags to the words in the set that best fit together.

For a given word i and one of its candidate WordNet senses j, we consider an assignment variable x_{ij} and compute a sense frequency-based prior for it as $P_{ij} = \frac{1}{1+R}$, where R is the WordNet rank of the sense. We then compute a similarity score $S_{ij,i'j'}$ between all pairs of sense choices for two words i,i' and their respective candidate senses j,j'. For these, we rely on WordNet's taxonomic path-based similarities (Pedersen et al., 2004) in the case of noun-noun sense pairs, the Adapted Lesk similarity measure for adjective-adjective pairs, and finally, WordNet verb-groups and VerbNet class membership (Kipper-Schuler, 2005) for verb-verb pairs. Note that even parts of speech that are disregarded later on can still be helpful at this stage, as we aim at a joint optimization over all words. After the similarities have been obtained for all relevant sense pairs, we maximize the coherence of the senses of the words in the set as an Integer Linear Program, using the Gurobi Optimizer (Gurobi Optimization, 2014) and solving

maximize

$$\sum_i P_{ij}x_{ij} + \sum_{ij}\sum_{i'j'} S_{ij,i'j'}B_{ij,i'j'}$$

subject to

$$\sum_j x_{ij} \leq 1\ \forall i,\quad x_{ij} \in \{0,1\}\ \forall i,j,$$
$$B_{ij,i'j'} \leq x_{ij},\quad B_{ij,i'j'} \leq x_{i'j'},$$
$$B_{ij,i'j'} \in \{0,1\}\ \ \forall i,j,i'j'.$$

The binary variables $B_{ij,i'j'}$ are 1 iff $x_{ij} = 1$ and $x_{i'j'} = 1$, indicating that both senses were simultaneously chosen. The optimizer disambiguates the input words by selecting sense tuples $x_{1j}, x_{2j}, \ldots$, from which we can directly obtain the corresponding PoS information. Verb-noun co-occurrence information is then extracted from the PoS-tagged sets.

5 Selectional preference model

5.1 Acquisition of argument classes

To address the issue of data sparsity, we generalise selectional preferences over argument classes, as opposed to individual arguments. We obtain SP classes by means of spectral clustering of nouns with lexico-syntactic features, which has been shown effective in previous lexical classification tasks (Brew and Schulte im Walde, 2002; Sun and Korhonen, 2009).

Spectral clustering partitions the data, relying on a similarity matrix that records similarities between all pairs of data points. We use *Jensen-Shannon divergence* to measure the similarity between feature vectors for two nouns, w_i and w_j, defined as follows:

$$d_{\mathrm{JS}}(w_i, w_j) = \frac{1}{2}d_{\mathrm{KL}}(w_i||m) + \frac{1}{2}d_{\mathrm{KL}}(w_j||m), \tag{1}$$

where d_{KL} is the Kullback-Leibler divergence, and m is the average of w_i and w_j. We construct the similarity matrix S computing similarities S_{ij} as $S_{ij} = \exp(-d_{\mathrm{JS}}(w_i, w_j))$. The matrix S then encodes a similarity graph G (over our nouns), where S_{ij} are the adjacency weights. The clustering problem can then be defined as identifying the optimal partition, or *cut*, of the graph into clusters, such that the intra-cluster weights are high and the inter-cluster weights are low. We use the multiway normalized cut (MNCut) algorithm of Meila and Shi (2001) for this purpose. The algorithm transforms S into a stochastic matrix P containing transition probabilities between the vertices in the graph as

$$P = D^{-1}S, \tag{2}$$

where the degree matrix D is a diagonal matrix with $D_{ii} = \sum_{j=1}^{N} S_{ij}$. It then computes the K leading eigenvectors of P, where K is the desired number of clusters. The graph is partitioned by finding approximately equal elements in the eigenvectors using a simpler clustering algorithm, such as *k-means*. Meila and Shi (2001) have shown that the partition I derived in this way minimizes the MNCut criterion:

$$\mathrm{MNCut}(I) = \sum_{k=1}^{K}(1 - P(I_k \to I_k|I_k)), \tag{3}$$

which is the sum of transition probabilities across different clusters. Since k-means starts from a random cluster assignment, we run the algorithm multiple times and select the partition that minimizes the cluster distortion, i.e. distances to cluster centroid.

We cluster nouns using linguistic and visual features in two independent experiments.

Clustering with linguistic features: We first cluster the 2,000 most frequent nouns in the BNC, using their grammatical relations as features. The features consist of verb lemmas appearing in the subject, direct object and indirect object relations with the given nouns in the RASP-parsed BNC, indexed by relation type. The feature vectors are first constructed from the corpus counts, and subsequently normalized by the sum of the feature values.

Clustering with visual features: We also cluster the 2,000 most frequent nouns in the Flickr data. Since our goal is to create argument classes for verb preferences, we extract co-occurrence features that map to verb-noun relations from PoS-disambiguated image tags. We use the verb lemmas co-occurring with the noun in the same images and videos as features for clustering. The feature values are again normalised by their sum.

SP classes: Example clusters produced using linguistic and visual features are shown in Figures 1 and 2. Our cluster analysis reveals that the image-derived clusters tend to capture scene-like relations (e.g. *beach* and *ocean*; *guitar* and *concert*), as opposed to types of entities, yielded by the linguistic features and better suited to generalise over

desire hostility anxiety passion doubt fear curiosity enthusiasm impulse instinct emotion feeling suspicion
official officer inspector journalist detective constable police policeman reporter
book statement account draft guide advertisement document report article letter

Figure 1: Clusters obtained using linguistic features

pilot aircraft plane airline landing flight wing arrival departure airport
concert festival music guitar alternative band instrument audience event performance rock benjamin
cost benefit crisis debt credit customer consumer

Figure 2: Clusters obtained using visual features

predicate-argument structure. In addition, the image features tend to be sparse for abstract concepts, reducing both the quality and the coverage of abstract clusters. We thus use the noun clusters derived with linguistic features as an approximation of SP classes.

5.2 Quantifying selectional preferences

Once the SP classes have been obtained, we need to quantify the strength of association of a given verb with each of the classes. We adopt an information theoretic measure proposed by Resnik (1993) for this purpose. Resnik first measures *selectional preference strength* (SPS) of a verb in terms of Kullback-Leibler divergence between the distribution of noun classes occurring as arguments of this verb, $p(c|v)$, and the prior distribution of the noun classes, $p(c)$.

$$\mathrm{SPS}_R(v) = \sum_c p(c|v) \log \frac{p(c|v)}{p(c)}, \qquad (4)$$

where R is the grammatical relation for which SPs are computed. SPS measures how strongly the predicate constrains its arguments. Selectional association of the verb with a particular argument class is then defined as a relative contribution of that argument class to the overall SPS of the verb.

$$\mathrm{Ass}_R(v,c) = \frac{1}{\mathrm{SPS}_R(v)} p(c|v) \log \frac{p(c|v)}{p(c)} \qquad (5)$$

We use this measure to quantify verb SPs based on linguistic and visual co-occurrence information. We first extract verb-subject and verb-direct object relations from the RASP-parsed BNC, map the argument heads to SP classes and quantify selectional association of a given verb with each SP class, thus acquiring its *base* preferences. Since visual verb-noun co-occurrences do not contain information about grammatical relations, we rely on linguistic data to provide a set of base arguments of the verb for a given grammatical relation. We then interpolate the verb-argument probabilities from linguistic and visual models for the base arguments of the verb, thus preserving information about grammatical relations.

5.3 Linguistic and visual model interpolation

We investigate two model interpolation techniques: simple linear interpolation and predicate-driven linear interpolation.

Linear interpolation combines information from component models by computing a weighted average of their probabilities. The interpolated probability of an event e is derived as $p^{\mathrm{LI}}(e) = \sum_i \lambda_i p_i(e)$, where $p_i(e)$ is the probability of e in the model i and λ_i is the interpolation weight defined such that $\sum_i \lambda_i = 1$; and $\lambda_i \in [0,1]$. In our experiments, we interpolate the probabilities $p(c)$ and $p(c|v)$ in the linguistic (LM) and visual (VM) models, as follows:

$$p^{\mathrm{LI}}(c) = \lambda_{\mathrm{LM}} p_{\mathrm{LM}}(c) + \lambda_{\mathrm{VM}} p_{\mathrm{VM}}(c) \qquad (6)$$

$$p^{\mathrm{LI}}(c|v) = \lambda_{\mathrm{LM}} p_{\mathrm{LM}}(c|v) + \lambda_{\mathrm{VM}} p_{\mathrm{VM}}(c|v) \qquad (7)$$

We experiment with a number of parameter settings for λ_{LM} and λ_{VM}.

Predicate-driven linear interpolation derives predicate-specific interpolation weights directly from the data, as opposed to pre-setting them universally for all verbs. For each predicate v, we compute the interpolation weights based on its prominence in the respective corpus, as follows:

$$\lambda_i(v) = \frac{\mathrm{rel}_i(v)}{\sum_k \mathrm{rel}_k(v)}, \qquad (8)$$

where rel is the relevance function of model i for verb v, computed as its relative frequency in the respective corpus: $\mathrm{rel}_i(v) = \frac{f_i(v)}{\sum_V f_i(v)}$. The interpolation weights for LM and VM are then computed as

$$\lambda_{\mathrm{LM}}(v) = \frac{\mathrm{rel}_{\mathrm{LM}}(v)}{\mathrm{rel}_{\mathrm{LM}}(v) + \mathrm{rel}_{\mathrm{VM}}(v)} \qquad (9)$$

$$\lambda_{\mathrm{VM}}(v) = \frac{\mathrm{rel}_{\mathrm{VM}}(v)}{\mathrm{rel}_{\mathrm{LM}}(v) + \mathrm{rel}_{\mathrm{VM}}(v)}. \qquad (10)$$

The motivation for this approach comes from the fact that not all verbs are represented equally well in linguistic and visual data. For instance, while concrete verbs, such as *run, push* or *throw*, are more likely to be prominent in visual data, abstract verbs, such as *understand* or *speculate*, are best represented in text. Relative linguistic and visual frequencies of a verb provide a way to estimate the relevance of linguistic and visual features to its SP learning.

6 Direct evaluation and data analysis

We evaluate the predicate-argument scores assigned by our models against a dataset of human plausibility judgements of verb-direct object pairs collected by Keller and Lapata (2003). Their dataset is balanced with respect to the frequency of verb-argument relations, as well as their plausibility and implausibility, thus creating a realistic SP evaluation task. Keller and Lapata selected 30 predicates and matched each of them to three arguments from different co-occurrence frequency bands according to their BNC counts, e.g. *divert attention* (high frequency), *divert water* (medium) and *divert fruit* (low). This constituted their dataset of *Seen* verb-noun pairs, 90 in total. Each of the predicates was then also paired with three randomly selected arguments with which it did not occur in the BNC, creating the *Unseen* dataset. The pairs in both datasets were then rated for their plausibility by 27 human subjects, and their judgements were aggregated into a gold standard. We compare the verb-argument scores generated by our linguistic (LSP), visual (VSP) and interpolated (ISP) SP models against these two datasets in terms of Pearson correlation coefficient, r, and Spearman rank correlation coefficient, ρ. The selectional association score of the cluster to which a given noun belongs is taken to represent the preference score of the verb for this noun. If a noun is not present in our argument clusters, we match it to its nearest cluster, as determined by its distributional similarity to the cluster centroid in terms of Jensen-Shannon divergence.

We first compare LSP, VSP and ISP with static and predicate-driven interpolation weights. The results, presented in Table 1, demonstrate that the interpolated model outperforms both LSP and VSP used on their own. The best performance is attained with the static interpolation weights of $\lambda_{LM} = 0.8$ ($r = 0.540$; $\rho = 0.728$) and $\lambda_{LM} = 0.9$ ($r = 0.548$; $\rho = 0.699$). This suggests that while linguistic input plays a crucial role in SP induction (by providing both semantic and syntactic information), visual features further enhance the quality of SPs, as we expected. Figure 3 shows LSP- and VSP-acquired direct object preferences of the verb

	Seen		Unseen	
	r	ρ	r	ρ
VSP	0.180	0.126	0.118	0.132
ISP: $\lambda_{LM} = 0.1$	0.279	0.532	0.220	0.371
ISP: $\lambda_{LM} = 0.2$	0.349	0.556	0.278	0.411
ISP: $\lambda_{LM} = 0.3$	0.385	0.558	0.305	0.423
ISP: $\lambda_{LM} = 0.4$	0.410	0.571	0.320	0.428
ISP: $\lambda_{LM} = 0.5$	0.448	0.579	0.329	0.430
ISP: $\lambda_{LM} = 0.6$	0.461	0.591	0.330	0.431
ISP: $\lambda_{LM} = 0.7$	0.523	0.713	0.335	0.431
ISP: $\lambda_{LM} = 0.8$	0.540	**0.728**	0.339	0.430
ISP: $\lambda_{LM} = 0.9$	**0.548**	0.699	0.342	0.429
ISP: Predicate-driven	0.476	0.597	0.391	0.551
LSP	0.512	0.688	**0.412**	**0.559**

Table 1: Model comparison on the plausibility data of Keller and Lapata (2003)

LSP: (1) 0.309 expenditure cost risk expense emission budget spending; **(2)** 0.201 dividend price rate premium rent rating salary wages; **(3)** 0.088 employment investment growth supplies sale import export production [..]

ISP predicate-driven $\lambda_{LM} = 0.65$
(1) 0.346 expenditure cost risk expense emission budget spending; **(2)** 0.211 dividend price rate premium rent rating salary wages; **(3)** 0.126 tail collar strand skirt trousers hair curtain sleeve

VSP: (1) 0.224 tail collar strand skirt trousers hair curtain sleeve; **(2)** 0.098 expenditure cost risk expense emission budget spending; **(3)** 0.090 management delivery maintenance transport service housing [..]

Figure 3: Top three direct object classes for *cut* and their association scores, assigned by different models

cut, as well as the effects of merging the features in the interpolated model – the verbs' experiential arguments (e.g. *hair* or *fabric*) are emphasized by the visual features.

However, the model based on visual features alone performs poorly on the dataset of Keller and Lapata (2003). This is partly explained by the fact that a number of verbs in this dataset are abstract verbs, whose visual representations in the Flickr data are sparse. In addition, VSP (as other visual models used in isolation from text) is not syntax-aware and is unable to discriminate between different types of semantic relations. VSP thus acquires sets of verb-argument relations that are closer in nature to scene descriptions and semantic frames than to lexico-syntactic paradigms. Figure 4 shows the differences between linguistic and visual arguments of the verb *kill* ranked by LSP and VSP. While LSP produces mainly semantic objects of *kill*, VSP output contains other types of arguments, such as *weapon* (instrument) and *death* (consequence).

Taking the argument classes produced by the linguistic model as a basis and then re-ranking

LSP: (1) 0.523 girl other woman child person people; **(2)** 0.164 fleet soldier knight force rebel guard troops crew army pilot; **(3)** 0.133 sister daughter parent relative lover cousin friend wife mother husband brother father; **(4)** 0.048 being species sheep animal creature horse baby human fish male lamb bird rabbit [..]; **(5)** 0.045 victim bull teenager prisoner hero gang enemy rider offender youth killer thief [..]

VSP: (1) 0.180 defeat fall death tragedy loss collapse decline [..]; **(2)** 0.141 girl other woman child person people; **(3)** 0.128 abuse suicide killing offence murder breach crime; **(4)** 0.113 handle weapon horn knife blade stick sword [..]; **(5)** 0.095 victim bull teenager prisoner hero gang enemy rider offender youth killer thief [..]

Figure 4: Top five arguments of *kill* and their association scores, assigned by LSP and VSP

(1) 0.442 drink coffee champagne pint wine beer; **(2)** 0.182 mixture dose substance drug milk cream alcohol chemical [..]; **(3)** 0.091 girl other woman child person people; **(4)** 0.053 sister daughter parent relative lover cousin friend wife mother husband brother father; **(5)** 0.050 drop tear sweat paint blood water juice

Figure 5: Error analysis: Mixed subjects and direct objects of *drink*, assigned by the predicate-driven ISP

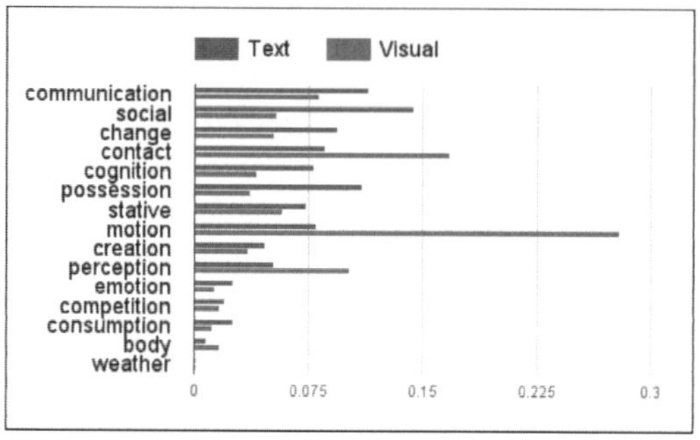

Figure 6: WordNet top level class distributions for verbs in the visual and textual corpora

	Seen		Unseen	
	r	ρ	r	ρ
Rooth et al. (1999)*	0.455	0.487	0.479	0.520
Padó et al. (2007)*	0.484	0.490	0.398	0.430
O'Seaghdha (2010)	0.520	0.548	**0.564**	**0.605**
VSP	0.180	0.126	0.118	0.132
ISP (best)	**0.548**	**0.699**	0.342	0.429
LSP	0.512	0.688	0.412	0.559

Table 2: Comparison to other SP induction methods. * Results reported in O'Seaghdha (2010).

them to incorporate visual statistics helps to avoid the above problem for the interpolated models, whose output corresponds to grammatical relations. However, static interpolation weights (emphasizing linguistic features over the visual ones for all verbs equally) outperformed the predicate-driven interpolation technique, attaining correlations of $r = 0.548$ and $r = 0.476$ respectively. This is mainly due to the fact that some verbs are over-represented in the visual data (e.g. the predicate-driven interpolation weight for the verb *drink* is $\lambda_{LM} = 0.08$). As a result, candidate argument classes (selected based on syntactically-parsed linguistic input) are ranked predominantly based on visual statistics. This makes it possible to emphasize incorrectly parsed arguments (such as subject relations in the direct object SP distribution and vice versa). The predicate-driven ISP output for direct object SPs of *drink*, for instance, contains a mixture of subject and direct object classes, as shown in Figure 5. Using a static model with a high λ_{LM} weight helps to avoid such errors and, therefore, leads to a better performance.

In order to investigate the composition of the visual and linguistic datasets, we assess the average level of concreteness of the verbs and nouns present in the datasets. We use the concreteness ratings from the MRC Psycholinguistic Database (Wilson, 1988) for this purpose. In this database, nouns and verbs are rated for concreteness on a scale from 100 (highly abstract) to 700 (highly concrete). We map the verbs and nouns in our textual and visual corpora to their MRC concreteness scores. We then calculate a dataset-wide concreteness score as an average of the concreteness scores of individual verbs and nouns weighted by their frequency in the respective corpus. The average concreteness scores in the visual dataset were 506.4 (nouns) and 498.1 (verbs). As expected, they are higher than the respective scores in the textual data: 433.1 (nouns) and 363.4 (verbs). In order to compare the types of actions that are common in each of the datasets, we map the verbs to their corresponding top level classes in WordNet. Figure 6 shows the comparison of prominent verb classes in visual and textual data. One can see from the Figure that the visual dataset is well suited for representing *motion, perception* and *contact*, while abstract verbs related to e.g. *communication, cognition, possession* or *change* are more common in textual data.

We also compare the performance of our models to existing SP induction methods: the EM-based clustering method of Rooth et al. (1999), the vector space similarity-based method of Padó et al. (2007) and the LDA topic modelling approach of Ó Séaghdha (2010)[1]. The best ISP configuration

[1]Since Rooth et al.'s (1999) and Padó et al.'s (2007) models were not originally evaluated on the same dataset, we use the

($\lambda_{\text{LM}} = 0.9$) outperforms all of these methods, as well as our own LSP, on the *Seen* dataset, confirming the positive contribution of visual features. However, it achieves less success on the *Unseen* data, where the methods of Ó Séaghdha (2010) and Rooth et al. (1999) are leading. This result speaks in favour of latent variable models for acquisition of SP estimates for rarely attested predicate-argument pairs. In turn, this suggests that integrating our ISP model (that currently outperforms others on more common pairs) with such techniques is likely to improve SP prediction across frequency bands.

7 Task-based evaluation

In order to investigate the applicability of perceptually grounded SPs in wider NLP, we evaluate them in the context of an external semantic task – that of metaphor interpretation. Since metaphor is based on transferring imagery and knowledge across domains – typically from more familiar domains of physical experiences to the sphere of vague and elusive abstract thought – metaphor interpretation provides an ideal framework for testing perceptually grounded SPs. Our experiments rely on the metaphor interpretation method of Shutova (2010), in which text-derived SPs are a central component of the system. We replace the SP component with our LSP and ISP ($\lambda_{\text{LM}} = 0.8$) models and compare their performance in the context of metaphor interpretation.

Shutova (2010) defined metaphor interpretation as a paraphrasing task, where literal paraphrases for metaphorical expressions are derived from corpus data using a set of statistical measures. For instance, their system interprets the metaphor "a carelessly *leaked* report" as "a carelessly disclosed report". Focusing on metaphorical verbs in subject and direct object constructions, Shutova first applies a maximum likelihood model to extract and rank candidate paraphrases for the verb given the context, as follows:

$$P(i, w_1, ..., w_N) = \frac{\prod_{n=1}^{N} f(w_n, i)}{(f(i))^{N-1} \cdot \sum_k f(i_k)}, \quad (11)$$

where $f(i)$ is the frequency of the paraphrase on its own and $f(w_n, i)$ the co-occurrence frequency of the paraphrase with the context word w_n. This model favours paraphrases that match the given context best. These candidates are then filtered based on the presence of shared features with the metaphorical verb, as defined by their location and distance in the WordNet hierarchy. All the candidates that have a common hypernym with the metaphorical verb within three levels of the WordNet hierarchy are selected. This results in a set of paraphrases retaining the meaning of the metaphorical verb. However, some of them are still figuratively used. Shutova further applies an SP model to discriminate between figurative and literal paraphrases, treating a strong selectional preference fit as a likely indicator of literalness. The candidates are re-ranked by the SP model, emphasizing the verbs whose preferences the noun in the context matches best. We use LSP and ISP scores to perform this re-ranking step.

We evaluate the performance of our models on this task using the metaphor paraphrasing gold standard of Shutova (2010). The dataset consists of 52 verb metaphors and their human-produced literal paraphrases. Following Shutova, we evaluate the performance in terms of mean average precision (MAP), which measures the ranking quality of GS paraphrases across the dataset. MAP is defined as follows:

$$\text{MAP} = \frac{1}{M} \sum_{j=1}^{M} \frac{1}{N_j} \sum_{i=1}^{N_j} P_{ji},$$

where M is the number of metaphorical expressions, N_j is the number of correct paraphrases for the metaphorical expression j, P_{ji} is the precision at each correct paraphrase (the number of correct paraphrases among the top i ranks). As compared to the gold standard, ISP attains a MAP score of 0.65, outperforming both the LSP (MAP = 0.62) and the original system of Shutova (2010) (MAP = 0.62), demonstrating the positive contribution of visual features.

8 Conclusion

We have presented the first SP induction method that simultaneously draws knowledge from text, images and videos. Our experiments show that it outperforms linguistic and visual models in isolation, as well as the previous approaches to SP learning. We believe that this model has a wide applicability in NLP, where many systems already rely on automatically induced SPs. It can also benefit image caption generation systems, which

results for their re-implementation reported by O'Seaghdha (2010), who conducted a comprehensive evaluation of SP models on the plausibility data of Keller and Lapata (2003).

typically focus on objects rather than actions, by providing information about predicate-argument structure.

In the future, it would be interesting to derive the information about predicate-argument relations from low-level visual features directly. However, to our knowledge, reliably mapping images to actions (i.e. verbs) at a large-scale is still a challenging task. Human-annotated image and video descriptions allow us to investigate what types of verb–noun relations are in principle present in the visual data and the ways in which they are different from the ones found in text. Our results show that visual data is better suited for capturing physical properties of concepts as well as containing relations not explicitly described in text.

The presented interpolation techniques are also applicable outside multi-modal semantics. For instance, they can be generalised to acquire SPs from unbalanced corpora of different sizes (e.g. for languages lacking balanced corpora) or to perform domain adaptation of SPs. In the future, we would like to apply SP interpolation to multilingual SP learning, i.e. integrating data from multiple languages for more accurate SP induction and projecting universal semantic relations to low-resource languages. It is also interesting to investigate SP learning at the level of semantic predicates (e.g. automatically inducing FrameNet-style frames), where combining the visual and linguistic knowledge is likely to outperform text-based models on their own.

Acknowledgements

Ekaterina Shutova's research is funded by the University of Cambridge and the Leverhulme Trust Early Career Fellowship. Gerard de Melo's work is funded by China 973 Program Grants 2011CBA00300, 2011CBA00301, and NSFC Grants 61033001, 61361136003, 61450110088. We are grateful to the ACL reviewers for their insightful feedback.

References

Steven Abney and Marc Light. 1999. Hiding a Semantic Hierarchy in a Markov Model. In *Proceedings of the Workshop on Unsupervised Learning in Natural Language Processing, ACL*, pages 1–8.

Lisa Aziz-Zadeh and Antonio Damasio. 2008. Embodied semantics for actions: Findings from functional brain imaging. *Journal of Physiology – Paris*, 102(1-3).

Lawrence W. Barsalou. 1999. Perceptual symbol systems. *Behavioral and Brain Sciences*, 22(4):577–609.

Lawrence W. Barsalou. 2008. Grounded cognition. *Annual Review of Psychology*, 59(1):617–645.

Shane Bergsma and Randy Goebel. 2011. Using visual information to predict lexical preference. In *Proceedings of RANLP*.

Shane Bergsma, Dekang Lin, and Randy Goebel. 2008. Discriminative learning of selectional preference from unlabeled text. In *Proceedings of EMNLP 2008*, EMNLP '08, pages 59–68, Honolulu, Hawaii.

Chris Brew and Sabine Schulte im Walde. 2002. Spectral clustering for German verbs. In *Proceedings of EMNLP*, pages 117–124.

Ted Briscoe, John Carroll, and Rebecca Watson. 2006. The second release of the RASP system. In *Proceedings of the COLING/ACL on Interactive presentation sessions*, pages 77–80.

Elia Bruni, Gemma Boleda, Marco Baroni, and Nam Khanh Tran. 2012. Distributional semantics in Technicolor. In *Proceedings of ACL 2012*, pages 136–145, Jeju Island, Korea, July. ACL.

Elia Bruni, Nam Khanh Tran, and Marco Baroni. 2014. Multimodal distributional semantics. *Journal of Artificial Intelligence Research*, 49:1–47.

Lou Burnard. 2007. *Reference Guide for the British National Corpus (XML Edition)*.

Xinlei Chen, Abhinav Shrivastava, and Abhinav Gupta. 2013. NEIL: Extracting Visual Knowledge from Web Data. In *Proceedings of ICCV 2013*.

Massimiliano Ciaramita and Mark Johnson. 2000. Explaining away ambiguity: Learning verb selectional preference with Bayesian networks. In *Proceedings of COLING 2000*, pages 187–193.

Stephen Clark and David Weir. 1999. An iterative approach to estimating frequencies over a semantic hierarchy. In *Proceedings of EMNLP/VLC 1999*, pages 258–265.

Santosh Divvala, Ali Farhadi, and Carlos Guestrin. 2014. Learning everything about anything: Webly-supervised visual concept learning. In *Proceedings of CVPR 2014*.

Katrin Erk. 2007. A simple, similarity-based model for selectional preferences. In *Proceedings of ACL 2007*.

Dan Fass. 1991. met*: A method for discriminating metonymy and metaphor by computer. *Computational Linguistics*, 17(1):49–90.

Yansong Feng and Mirella Lapata. 2010. Visual information in semantic representation. In *Proceedings of NAACL 2010*, pages 91–99. ACL.

Andrea Frome, Greg Corrado, Jon Shlens, Samy Bengio, Jeffrey Dean, Marc'Aurelio Ranzato, and Tomas Mikolov. 2013. DeViSE: A deep visual-semantic embedding model. In *Proceedings of NIPS 2013*.

Daniel Gildea and Daniel Jurafsky. 2002. Automatic labeling of semantic roles. *Computational Linguistics*, 28.

Arthur M. Glenberg and Michael P. Kaschak. 2002. Grounding language in action. *Psychonomic Bulletin and Review*, pages 558–565.

Gurobi Optimization. 2014. Gurobi optimizer reference manual, version 5.6. Houston, TX, USA.

Donald Hindle and Mats Rooth. 1993. Structural ambiguity and lexical relations. *Computational Linguistics*, 19:103–120.

Frank Keller and Mirella Lapata. 2003. Using the web to obtain frequencies for unseen bigrams. *Computational Linguistics*, 29(3):459–484.

Douwe Kiela, Felix Hill, Anna Korhonen, and Stephen Clark. 2014. Improving multi-modal representations using image dispersion: Why less is sometimes more. In *Proceedings of ACL 2014*, Baltimore, Maryland.

Karin Kipper-Schuler. 2005. *VerbNet: A broad-coverage, comprehensive verb lexicon*. Ph.D. thesis, University of Pennsylvania, PA.

Ryan Kiros, Ruslan Salakhutdinov, and Richard S. Zemel. 2014. Multimodal neural language models. In *Proceedings of ICML 2014*, pages 595–603.

Girish Kulkarni, Visruth Premraj, Vicente Ordonez, Sagnik Dhar, Siming Li, Yejin Choi, Alexander C. Berg, and Tamara L. Berg. 2013. Babytalk: Understanding and generating simple image descriptions. *IEEE Trans. Pattern Anal. Mach. Intell.*, 35(12):2891–2903.

Angeliki Lazaridou, Elia Bruni, and Marco Baroni. 2014. Is this a wampimuk? cross-modal mapping between distributional semantics and the visual world. In *Proceedings of ACL 2014*, pages 1403–1414. ACL.

Hang Li and Naoki Abe. 1998. Generalizing case frames using a thesaurus and the mdl principle. *Computational Linguistics*, 24(2):217–244.

Hongsong Li, Kenny Q. Zhu, and Haixun Wang. 2013. Data-driven metaphor recognition and explanation. *Transactions of the Association for Computational Linguistics*, 1:379–390.

Zachary Mason. 2004. Cormet: a computational, corpus-based conventional metaphor extraction system. *Computational Linguistics*, 30(1):23–44.

Diana McCarthy and John Carroll. 2003. Disambiguating nouns, verbs, and adjectives using automatically acquired selectional preferences. *Computational Linguistics*, 29(4):639–654.

Marina Meila and Jianbo Shi. 2001. A random walks view of spectral segmentation. In *Proceedings of AI-STATS*.

Diarmuid Ó Séaghdha. 2010. Latent variable models of selectional preference. In *Proceedings of ACL 2010*.

Sebastian Padó, Ulrike Padó, and Katrin Erk. 2007. Flexible, corpus-based modelling of human plausibility judgements. In *Proceedings of EMNLP-CoNLL*.

P. Pantel, R. Bhagat, T. Chklovski, and E. Hovy. 2007. Isp: Learning inferential selectional preferences. In *Proceedings of NAACL 2007*.

Ted Pedersen, Siddharth Patwardhan, and Jason Michelizzi. 2004. Wordnet:: Similarity: measuring the relatedness of concepts. In *Demonstration Papers at HLT-NAACL 2004*, pages 38–41.

Y. Peirsman and S. Padó. 2010. Cross-lingual induction of selectional preferences with bilingual vector spaces. In *Proceedings of NAACL 2010*, pages 921–929.

Philip Resnik. 1993. Selection and information: A class-based approach to lexical relationships. Technical report, University of Pennsylvania.

Philip Resnik. 1997. Selectional preference and sense disambiguation. In *ACL SIGLEX Workshop on Tagging Text with Lexical Semantics*, Washington, D.C.

Alan Ritter, Mausam Etzioni, and Oren Etzioni. 2010. A latent dirichlet allocation method for selectional preferences. In *Proceedings ACL 2010*, pages 424–434.

Marcus Rohrbach, Wei Qiu, Ivan Titov, Stefan Thater, Manfred Pinkal, and Bernt Schiele. 2013. Translating video content to natural language descriptions. In *Proceedings of ICCV 2013*.

Stephen Roller and Sabine Schulte im Walde. 2013. A Multimodal LDA Model integrating Textual, Cognitive and Visual Modalities. In *Proceedings of EMNLP 2013*, pages 1146–1157, Seattle, WA.

Mats Rooth, Stefan Riezler, Detlef Prescher, Glenn Carroll, and Franz Beil. 1999. Inducing a semantically annotated lexicon via EM-based clustering. In *Proceedings of ACL 1999*, pages 104–111.

David Shamma. 2014. One hundred million Creative Commons Flickr images for research. `http://labs.yahoo.com/news/yfcc100m/`.

Ekaterina Shutova, Simone Teufel, and Anna Korhonen. 2013. Statistical Metaphor Processing. *Computational Linguistics*, 39(2).

Ekaterina Shutova. 2010. Automatic metaphor interpretation as a paraphrasing task. In *Proceedings of NAACL 2010*, pages 1029–1037, Los Angeles, USA.

Ekaterina Shutova. 2011. *Computational Approaches to Figurative Language*. Ph.D. thesis, University of Cambridge, UK.

Carina Silberer and Mirella Lapata. 2014. Learning grounded meaning representations with autoencoders. In *Proceedings of ACL 2014*, Baltimore, Maryland.

Carina Silberer, Vittorio Ferrari, and Mirella Lapata. 2013. Models of semantic representation with visual attributes. In *Proceedings of ACL 2013*, pages 572–582.

Richard Socher, Milind Ganjoo, Christopher D. Manning, and Andrew Ng. 2013. Zero-shot learning through cross-modal transfer. In *Proceedings of NIPS 2013*, pages 935–943.

Nitish Srivastava, Geoffrey Hinton, Alex Krizhevsky, Ilya Sutskever, and Ruslan Salakhutdinov. 2014. Dropout: A simple way to prevent neural networks from overfitting. *Journal of Machine Learning Research*, 15:1929–1958.

Lin Sun and Anna Korhonen. 2009. Improving verb clustering with automatically acquired selectional preferences. In *Proceedings of EMNLP 2009*.

Tim Van de Cruys. 2014. A neural network approach to selectional preference acquisition. In *Proceedings of EMNLP 2014*.

Wiebke Wagner, Helmut Schmid, and Sabine Schulte Im Walde. 2009. Verb sense disambiguation using a predicate-argument clustering model. In *Proceedings of the CogSci Workshop on Semantic Space Models (DISCO)*.

M.D. Wilson. 1988. The MRC Psycholinguistic Database: Machine Readable Dictionary, Version 2. *Behavioural Research Methods, Instruments and Computers*, 20:6–11.

Peter Young, Alice Lai, Micah Hodosh, and Julia Hockenmaier. 2014. From image descriptions to visual denotations. *Transactions of the Association of Computational Linguistics – Volume 2, Issue 1*, pages 67–78.

Fabio Massimo Zanzotto, Marco Pennacchiotti, and Maria Teresa Pazienza. 2006. Discovering asymmetric entailment relations between verbs using selectional preferences. In *Proceedings of COLING/ACL*, pages 849–856.

Beñat Zapirain, Eneko Agirre, Lluís Màrquez, and Mihai Surdeanu. 2010. Improving semantic role classification with selectional preferences. In *Proceedings of NAACL HLT 2010*, pages 373–376.

Joint Case Argument Identification for Japanese Predicate Argument Structure Analysis

Hiroki Ouchi **Hiroyuki Shindo** **Kevin Duh** **Yuji Matsumoto**
Graduate School of Information and Science
Nara Institute of Science and Technology
8916-5, Takayama, Ikoma, Nara, 630-0192, Japan
{ ouchi.hiroki.nt6, shindo, kevinduh, matsu }@is.naist.jp

Abstract

Existing methods for Japanese predicate argument structure (PAS) analysis identify case arguments of each predicate without considering interactions between the target PAS and others in a sentence. However, the argument structures of the predicates in a sentence are semantically related to each other. This paper proposes new methods for Japanese PAS analysis to jointly identify case arguments of all predicates in a sentence by (1) modeling multiple PAS interactions with a bipartite graph and (2) approximately searching optimal PAS combinations. Performing experiments on the NAIST Text Corpus, we demonstrate that our joint analysis methods substantially outperform a strong baseline and are comparable to previous work.

1 Introduction

Predicate argument structure (PAS) analysis is a shallow semantic parsing task that identifies basic semantic units of a sentence, such as *who does what to whom*, which is similar to semantic role labeling (SRL)[1].

In Japanese PAS analysis, one of the most problematic issues is that arguments are often omitted in the surface form, resulting in so-called *zero-pronouns*. Consider the sentence of Figure 1.

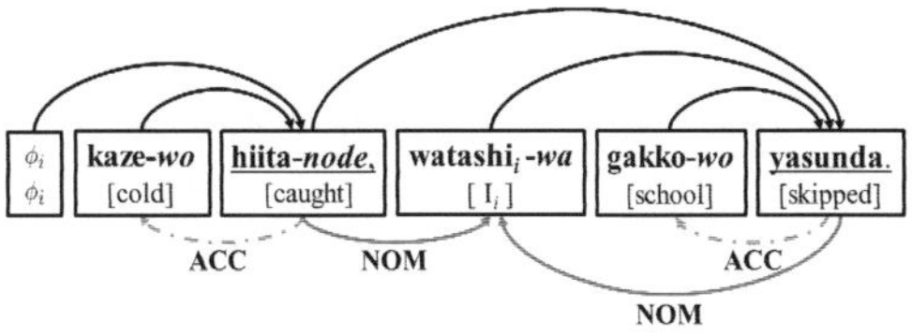

Figure 1: An example of Japanese PAS. The English translation is "Because ϕ_i caught a cold, I$_i$ skipped school.". The upper edges are dependency relations, and the under edges are case arguments. "NOM" and "ACC" represents the nominative and accusative arguments, respectively. "ϕ_i" is a *zero-pronoun*, referring to the *antecedent* "watashi$_i$".

The case role label "NOM" and "ACC" respectively represents the nominative and accusative roles, and ϕ_i represents a zero-pronoun. There are two predicates "hiita (caught)" and "yasunda (skipped)". For the predicate "yasunda (skipped)", "watashi$_i$-*wa* (I$_i$)" is the "skipper", and "gakko-*wo* (school)" is the "entity skipped". It is easy to identify these arguments, since syntactic dependency between an argument and its predicate is a strong clue. On the other hand, the nominative argument of the predicate "hiita (caught)" is "watashi$_i$-*wa* (I$_i$)", and this identification is more difficult because of the lack of the direct syntactic dependency with "hiita (caught)". The original nominative argument appears as a zero-pronoun, so that we have to explore the *antecedent*, an element referred to by a zero-pronoun, as the argument. As the example sentence shows, we cannot use effective syntactic information for identifying such arguments. This type of arguments is known as **implicit arguments**, a very problematic language

[1] We use "PAS analysis" in this paper following previous work on Japanese PAS analysis.

Proceedings of the 53rd Annual Meeting of the Association for Computational Linguistics and the 7th International Joint Conference on Natural Language Processing, pages 961–970,
Beijing, China, July 26-31, 2015.

phenomenon for PAS analysis (Gerber and Chai, 2010; Laparra and Rigau, 2013).

Previous work on Japanese PAS analysis attempted to solve this problem by identifying arguments per predicate without considering ***interactions*** between multiple predicates and arguments (Taira et al., 2008; Imamura et al., 2009). However, implicit arguments are likely to be shared by semantically-related predicates. In the above example (Figure 1), the implicit argument of the predicate "hiita (caught)" is shared by the other predicate "yasunda (skipped)" as its nominative argument "watashi$_i$ (I$_i$)".

Based on this intuition, we propose methods to jointly identify optimal case arguments of all predicates in a sentence taking their interactions into account. We represent the interactions as a bipartite graph that covers all predicates and candidate arguments in a sentence, and factorize the whole relation into the second-order relations. This interaction modeling results in a hard combinatorial problem because it is required to select the optimal PAS combination from all possible PAS combinations in a sentence. To solve this issue, we extend the randomized hill-climbing algorithm (Zhang et al., 2014) to search all possible PAS in the space of bipartite graphs.

We perform experiments on the NAIST Text Corpus (Iida et al., 2007), a standard benchmark for Japanese PAS analysis. Experimental results show that compared with a strong baseline, our methods achieve an improvement of 1.0-1.2 points in F-measure for total case argument identification, and especially improve performance for implicit argument identification by 2.0-2.5 points. In addition, although we exploit no external resources, we get comparable results to previous work exploiting large-scale external resources (Taira et al., 2008; Imamura et al., 2009; Sasano and Kurohashi, 2011). These results suggest that there is potential for more improvement by adding external resources.

The main contributions of this work are: (1) We present new methods to jointly identify case arguments of all predicates in a sentence. (2) We propose global feature templates that capture interactions over multiple PAS. (3) Performing experiments on the NAIST Text Corpus, we demonstrate our methods are superior to a strong baseline and comparable to the methods of representative previous work.

2 Japanese Predicate Argument Structure Analysis

2.1 Task Overview

In Japanese PAS analysis, we identify arguments taking part in the three major case roles, **nominative** (NOM), **accusative** (ACC) and **dative** (DAT) cases, for each predicate. Case arguments can be divided into three categories according to the positions relative to their predicates (Hayashibe et al., 2011):

Dep**:** The arguments that have direct syntactic dependency with the predicate.

Zero**:** The implicit arguments whose antecedents appear in the same sentence and have no direct syntactic dependency with the predicate.

Inter-Zero**:** The implicit arguments whose antecedents do not appear in the same sentence.

For example, in Figure 1, the accusative argument "gakko-*wo* (school)" of the predicate "yasunda (skipped)" is regarded as *Dep*, and the nominative argument "watashi$_i$-*wa* (I)" (the antecedent of zero-pronoun "ϕ_i") of the predicate "hiita (caught)" is *Zero*.

In this paper, we focus on the analysis for intra-sentential arguments (*Dep* and *Zero*). In order to identify inter-sentential arguments (*Inter-Zero*), it is required to search a much broader space, such as the whole document, resulting in a much harder analysis than intra-sentential arguments.[2] Therefore, we believe that quite different approaches are necessary to realize an inter-sentential PAS analysis with high accuracy, and leave it for future work.

2.2 Related Work

For Japanese PAS analysis research, the NAIST Text Corpus has been used as a standard benchmark (Iida et al., 2007). One of the representative researches using the NAIST Text Corpus is Imamura et al. (2009). They built three distinct models corresponding to the three case roles by extracting features defined on each pair of a predicate and a candidate argument. Using each model, they select the best candidate argument for each case per predicate. Their models are based on maximum entropy model and can easily incorporate various features, resulting in high accuracy.

[2]Around 10-20% in F measure has been achieved in previous work (Taira et al., 2008; Imamura et al., 2009; Sasano and Kurohashi, 2011).

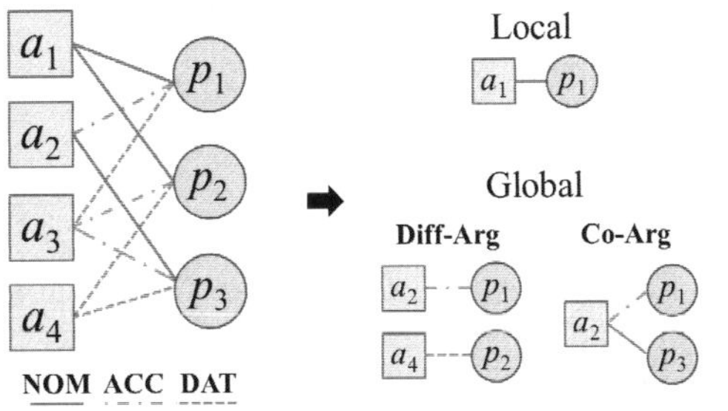

Figure 2: Intuitive image of a *predicate-argument graph*. This graph is factorized into the local and global features. The different line color/style indicate different cases.

While in Imamura et al. (2009) one case argument is identified at a time per predicate, the method proposed by Sasano and Kurohashi (2011) simultaneously determines all the three case arguments per predicate by exploiting large-scale case frames obtained from large raw texts. They focus on identification of implicit arguments (*Zero* and *Inter-Zero*), and achieves comparable results to Imamura et al. (2009).

In these approaches, case arguments were identified per predicate without considering interactions between multiple predicates and candidate arguments in a sentence. In the semantic role labeling (SRL) task, Yang and Zong (2014) pointed out that information of different predicates and their candidate arguments could help each other for identifying arguments taking part in semantic roles. They exploited a reranking method to capture the interactions between multiple predicates and candidate arguments, and jointly determine argument structures of all predicates in a sentence (Yang and Zong, 2014). In this paper, we propose new joint analysis methods for identifying case arguments of all predicates in a sentence capturing interactions between multiple predicates and candidate arguments.

3 Graph-Based Joint Models

3.1 A Predicate-Argument Graph

We define predicate argument relations by exploiting a bipartite graph, illustrated in Figure 2. The nodes of the graph consist of two disjoint sets: the left one is a set of *candidate arguments* and the right one is a set of *predicates*. In this paper, we call it a **predicate-argument (PA) graph**.

Each predicate node has three distinct edges corresponding to nominative (NOM), accusative (ACC), and dative (DAT) cases. Each edge with a case role label joins a candidate argument node with a predicate node, which represents a case argument of a predicate. For instance, in Figure 2 a_1 is the nominative argument of p_1, and a_3 is the accusative argument of p_2.

Formally, a PA graph is a bipartite graph $\langle A, P, E \rangle$, where A is the node set consisting of candidate arguments, P the node set consisting of predicates, and E the set of edges subject to that there is exactly one edge e with a case role label c outgoing from each of the predicate nodes p to a candidate argument node a. A PA graph is defined as follows:

$$A = \{a_1, ..., a_n, a_{n+1} = \mathtt{NULL}\}$$
$$P = \{p_1, ..., p_m\}$$
$$E = \{\langle a, p, c \rangle \mid deg(p, c) = 1, \; \forall a \in A, \forall p \in P, \forall c \in C\}$$

where $deg(p, c)$ is the number of edges with a case role c outgoing from p, and C is the case role label set. We add a dummy node a_{n+1}, which is defined for the cases where the predicate requires no case argument or the required case argument does not appear in the sentence. An edge $e \in E$ is represented by a tuple $\langle a, p, c \rangle$, indicating the edge with a case role c joining a candidate argument node a and a predicate node p. An admissible PA graph satisfies the constraint $deg(p, c) = 1$, representing that each predicate node p has only one edge with a case role c.

To identify the whole PAS for a sentence x, we predict the PA graph with an edge set corresponding to the correct PAS from the admissible PA graph set $G(x)$ based on a **score** associated with a PA graph y as follows:

$$\tilde{y} = \underset{y \in G(x)}{\operatorname{argmax}} \; Score(x, y)$$

A scoring function $Score(x, y)$ receives a sentence x and a candidate graph y as its input, and returns a scalar value.

In this paper, we propose two scoring functions as analysis models based on different assumptions: (1) **Per-Case Joint Model** assumes the interaction between multiple predicates (***predicate interaction***) and the independence between case roles, and (2) **All-Cases Joint Model** assumes the interaction between case roles (***case interaction***) as well as the *predicate interaction*.

3.2 Per-Case Joint Model

Per-Case Joint Model assumes that different case roles are independent from each other. However, for each case, interactions between multiple predicates are considered jointly.

We define the score of a PA graph y to be the sum of the scores for each case role c of the set of the case roles C:

$$Score_{per}(x, y) = \sum_{c \in C} Score_c(x, y) \quad (1)$$

The scores for each case role are defined as the dot products between a weight vector $\boldsymbol{\theta_c}$ and a feature vector $\boldsymbol{\phi_c}(x, E(y, c))$:

$$Score_c(x, y) = \boldsymbol{\theta_c} \cdot \boldsymbol{\phi_c}(x, E(y, c)) \quad (2)$$

where $E(y, c)$ is the edge set associated with a case role c in the candidate graph y, and the feature vector is defined on the edge set.

The edge set $E(y, c)$ in the equation (2) is utilized for the two types of features, the **local features** and **global features**, inspired by (Huang, 2008), defined as follows:

$$\boldsymbol{\theta_c} \cdot \boldsymbol{\phi_c}(x, E(y, c)) =$$
$$\sum_{e \in E(y,c)} \boldsymbol{\theta_c}\, \boldsymbol{\phi_l}(x, e) + \boldsymbol{\theta_c}\, \boldsymbol{\phi_g}(x, E(y, c)) \quad (3)$$

where $\boldsymbol{\phi_l}(x, e)$ denotes the local feature vector, and $\boldsymbol{\phi_g}(x, E(y, c))$ the global feature vector. The local feature vector $\boldsymbol{\phi_l}(x, e)$ is defined on each edge e in the edge set $E(y, c)$ and a sentence x, which captures a predicate-argument pair. Consider the example of Figure 2. For Per-Case Joint Model, we use edges, $e_{a_1p_1}$, $e_{a_1p_2}$, and $e_{a_2p_3}$, as local features to compute the score of the edge set with the nominative case.

In addition, the global feature vector $\boldsymbol{\phi_g}(x, E(y, c))$ is defined on the edge set $E(y, c)$, and enables the model to utilize linguistically richer information over multiple predicate-argument pairs. In this paper, we exploit *second-order* relations, similar to the second-order edge factorization of dependency trees (McDonald and Pereira, 2006). We make a set of edge pairs E_{pair} by combining two edges e_i, e_j in the edge set $E(y, c)$, as follows:

$$E_{pair} = \{\, \{e_i, e_j\} \mid \forall e_i, e_j \in E(y, c),\ e_i \neq e_j \,\}$$

For instance, in the PA graph in Figure 2, to compute the score of the nominative arguments, we make three edge pairs:

$$\{\{e_{a_1p_1}, e_{a_1p_2}\}, \{e_{a_1p_1}, e_{a_2p_3}\}, \{e_{a_1p_2}, e_{a_2p_3}\}\}$$

Then, features are extracted from these edge pairs and utilized for the score computation. For the accusative and dative cases, their scores are computed in the same manner. Then, we obtain the resulting score of the PA graph by summing up the scores of the local and global features. If we do not consider the global features, the model reduces to a per-case local model similar to previous work (Imamura et al., 2009).

3.3 All-Cases Joint Model

While Per-Case Joint Model assumes the *predicate interaction* with the independence between case roles, All-Cases Joint Model assumes the *case interaction* together with the *predicate interaction*. Our graph-based formulation is very flexible and easily enables the extension of Per-Case Joint Model to All-Cases Joint Model. Therefore, we extend Per-Case Joint Model to All-Cases Joint Model to capture the interactions between predicates and all case arguments in a sentence.

We define the score of a PA graph y based on the local and global features as follows:

$$Score_{all}(x, y) =$$
$$\sum_{e \in E(y)} \boldsymbol{\theta} \cdot \boldsymbol{\phi_l}(x, e) + \boldsymbol{\theta} \cdot \boldsymbol{\phi_g}(x, E(y)) \quad (4)$$

where $E(y)$ is the edge set associated with all the case roles on the candidate graph y, $\boldsymbol{\phi_l}(x, e)$ is the local feature vector defined on each edge e in the edge set $E(y)$, and $\boldsymbol{\phi_g}(x, E(y))$ is the global feature vector defined on the edge set $E(y)$.

Consider the PA graph in Figure 2. The local features are extracted from each edge:

Nominative : $e_{a_1p_1}, e_{a_1p_2}, e_{a_2p_3}$
Accusative : $e_{a_2p_1}, e_{a_3p_2}, e_{a_3p_3}$
Dative : $e_{a_3p_1}, e_{a_4p_2}, e_{a_4p_3}$

For the global features, we make a set of edge pairs E_{pair} by combining two edges e_i, e_j in the edge set $E(y)$, like Per-Case Joint Model. However, in the All-Cases Joint Model, the global features may involve different cases (i.e. mixing edges with different case roles). For the PA graph in Figure 2, we make the edge pairs $\{e_{a_1p_1}, e_{a_2p_1}\}$, $\{e_{a_3p_1}, e_{a_1p_2}\}$, $\{e_{a_3p_2}, e_{a_4p_3}\}$, and so on. From these edge pairs, we extract information as global features to compute a graph score.

Structure	Name	Description
Diff-Arg	**PAIR**	$\langle\, p_i$.rf $\circ$ p_j.rf $\circ$ p_i.vo $\circ$ p_j.vo $\rangle$, $\langle\, a_i$.ax $\circ$ a_i.rp $\circ$ p_i.ax $\circ$ p_i.vo $\rangle$, $\langle\, a_j$.ax $\circ$ a_j.rp $\circ$ p_j.ax $\circ$ p_j.vo $\rangle$
	TRIANGLE	$\langle\, a_i$.ax $\circ$ a_i.ax $\circ$ a_i.rp $\circ$ a_j.rp $\circ$ p_i.ax $\circ$ p_i.vo $\rangle$, $\langle\, a_i$.ax $\circ$ a_j.ax $\circ$ a_i.rp $\circ$ a_j.rp $\circ$ p_j.ax $\circ$ p_j.vo $\rangle$,
	QUAD	$\langle\, a_i$.ax $\circ$ a_j.ax $\circ$ a_i.rp $\circ$ a_j.rp $\circ$ p_i.vo $\circ$ p_j.vo $\rangle$ $\langle\, a_i$.ax $\circ$ a_j.ax $\circ$ p_i.ax $\circ$ p_j.ax $\circ$ a_i.rp $\circ$ a_j.rp $\circ$ p_i.vo $\circ$ p_j.vo $\rangle$ $\langle\, a_i$.ax $\circ$ a_j.ax $\circ$ p_i.rf $\circ$ p_j.rf $\circ$ a_i.rp $\circ$ a_i.rp $\circ$ p_i.vo $\circ$ p_i.vo $\rangle$
Co-Arg	**BI-PREDS**	$\langle\, a_i$.rp $\circ$ p_i.rf $\circ$ p_j.rf $\rangle$, $\langle\, a_i$.ax $\circ$ a_i.rp $\circ$ p_i.rf $\circ$ p_j.rf $\rangle$
	DEP-REL	$\langle\, a_i$.ax $\circ$ a_i.rp $\circ$ p_i.ax $\circ$ p_j.ax $\circ$ p_i.vo $\circ$ p_j.vo $\circ$ (x, y).dep $\rangle$ if x depends on y for x,y in (p_i,p_j), (a_i,p_i), (a_i,p_j), (p_i,a_i), (p_j,a_i)

Table 1: Global feature templates. p_i, p_j is a predicate, a_i is the argument connected with p_i, and a_j is the argument connected with p_j. Feature conjunction is indicated by $\circ$; ax=auxiliary, rp=relative position, vo=voice, rf=regular form, dep=dependency. All the features are conjoined with the relative position and the case role labels of the two predicates.

4 Global Features

Features are extracted based on **feature templates**, which are functions that draw information from the given entity. For instance, one feature template $\phi_{100} = a.ax \circ p.vo$ is a conjunction of two atomic features $a.ax$ and $p.vo$, representing an auxiliary word attached to a candidate argument ($a.ax$) and the voice of a predicate ($p.vo$). We design several feature templates for characterizing each specific PA graph. Consider the PA graph constructed from the sentence in Figure 1, and a candidate argument "kaze-*wo* (a cold)" and a predicate "hiita (caught)" are connected with an edge. To characterize the graph, we draw some linguistic information associated with the edge. Since the auxiliary word attached to the candidate argument is "*wo*" and the voice of the predicate is "*active*", the above feature template ϕ_{100} will generate a feature instance as follows.

$$(a.ax = wo) \circ (p.vo = active)$$

Such features are utilized for the local and global features in the joint models.

We propose the *global feature* templates that capture multiple PAS interactions based on the **Diff-Arg** and **Co-Arg** structures, depicted in the right part of Figure 1. The Diff-Arg structure represents that the two predicates have different candidate arguments, and the Co-Arg structure represents that the two predicates share the same candidate argument. Based on these structures, we define the global feature templates that receive a pair of edges in a PA graph as input and return a feature vector, shown in Table 1.

4.1 Diff-Arg Features

The feature templates based on the Diff-Arg structure are three types: **PAIR** (a pair of predicate-argument relation), **TRIANGLE** (a predicate and its two arguments relation), and **QUAD** (two predicate-argument relations).

PAIR These feature templates denote where the target argument is located relative to another argument and the two predicates in the Diff-Arg structure. We combine the relative position information (rp) with the auxiliary words (ax) and the voice of the two predicates (vo).

TRIANGLE This type of feature templates captures the interactions between three elements: two candidate arguments and a predicate. Like the PAIR feature templates, we encode the relative position information of two candidate arguments and a predicate with the auxiliary words and voice.

QUAD When we judge if a candidate argument takes part in a case role of a predicate, it would be beneficial to grasp information of another predicate-argument pair. The QUAD feature templates capture the mutual relation between four elements: two candidate arguments and predicates. We encode the relative position information, the auxiliary words, and the voice.

4.2 Co-Arg Features

To identify predicates that take implicit (*Zero*) arguments, we set two feature types, **BI-PREDS** and **DEP-REL**, based on the Co-Arg structure.

BI-PREDS For identifying an implicit argu-

Input: the set of cases to be analyzed C, parameter $\boldsymbol{\theta_c}$, sentence x
Output: a locally optimal PA graph $\tilde{y}$

1: Sample a PA graph $y^{(0)}$ from $G(x)$
2: $t \leftarrow 0$
3: **for** each case $c \in C$ **do**
4:   **repeat**
5:     $Y_c \leftarrow NeighborG(y^{(t)}, c) \cup y^{(t)}$
6:     $y^{(t+1)} \leftarrow \underset{y \in Y_c}{\text{argmax}}\, \boldsymbol{\theta_c} \cdot \boldsymbol{\phi_c}(x, E(y, c))$
7:     $t \leftarrow t + 1$
8:   **until** $y^{(t)} = y^{(t+1)}$
9: **end for**
10: **return** $\tilde{y} \leftarrow y^{(t)}$

Figure 3: Hill-Climbing for Per-Case Joint Model

Input: the set of cases to be analyzed C, parameter $\boldsymbol{\theta}$, sentence x
Output: a locally optimal PA graph $\tilde{y}$

1: Sample a PA graph $y^{(0)}$ from $G(x)$
2: $t \leftarrow 0$
3: **repeat**
4:   $Y \leftarrow NeighborG(y^{(t)}) \cup y^{(t)}$
5:   $y^{(t+1)} \leftarrow \underset{y \in Y}{\text{argmax}}\, \boldsymbol{\theta} \cdot \boldsymbol{\phi}(x, E(y))$
6:   $t \leftarrow t + 1$
7: **until** $y^{(t)} = y^{(t+1)}$
8: **return** $\tilde{y} \leftarrow y^{(t)}$

Figure 4: Hill-Climbing for All-Cases Joint Model

ment of a predicate, information of another semantically-related predicate in the sentence could be effective. We utilize bi-grams of the regular forms (rf) of the two predicates in the Co-Arg structure to capture the predicates that are likely to share the same argument in the sentence.

DEP-REL We set five distinct feature templates to capture dependency relations (dep) between the shared argument and the two predicates. If two elements have a direct dependency relation, we encode its dependency relation with the auxiliary words and the voice.

5 Inference and Training

5.1 Inference for the Joint Models

Global features make the inference of finding the maximum scoring PA graph more difficult. For searching the graph with the highest score, we propose two greedy search algorithms by extending the *randomized hill-climbing* algorithm proposed in (Zhang et al., 2014), which has been shown to achieve the state-of-the-art performance in dependency parsing.

Figure 3 describes the pseudo code of our proposed algorithm for Per-Case Joint Model. Firstly, we set an initial PA graph $y^{(0)}$ sampled uniformly from the set of admissible PA graphs $G(x)$ (line 1 in Figure 3). Then, the union Y_c is constructed from the set of neighboring graphs with a case $NeighborG(y^{(t)}, c)$, which is a set of admissible graphs obtained by changing one edge with the case c in $y^{(t)}$, and the current graph $y^{(t)}$ (line 5). The current graph $y^{(t)}$ is updated to a higher scoring graph $y^{(t+1)}$ selected from the union Y_c (line 6). The algorithm continues until no more score improvement is possible by changing an edge with the case c in $y^{(t)}$ (line 8). This repetition is executed for other case roles in the same manner. As a result, we can get a locally optimal graph $\tilde{y}$.

Figure 4 describes the pseudo code of the algorithm for All-Cases Joint Model. The large part of the algorithm is the same as that for Per-Case Joint Model. The difference is that the union Y consists of the current graph $y^{(t)}$ and the neighboring graph set obtained by changing one edge in $y^{(t)}$ regardless of case roles (line 4 in Figure 4), and that the iteration process for each case role (line 3 in Figure 3) is removed. The algorithm also continues until no more score improvement is possible by changing an edge in $y^{(t)}$, resulting in a locally optimal graph $\tilde{y}$.

Following Zhang et al. (2014), for a given sentence x, we repeatedly run these algorithms with K consecutive restarts. Each run starts with initial graphs randomly sampled from the set of admissible PA graphs $G(x)$, so that we obtain K local optimal graphs by K restarts. Then the highest scoring one of K graphs is selected for the sentence x as the result. Each run of the algorithms is independent from each other, so that multiple runs are easily executable in parallel.

5.2 Training

Given a training data set $D = \{(\hat{x}, \hat{y})\}_i^N$, the weight vectors $\boldsymbol{\theta}$ ($\boldsymbol{\theta_c}$) in the scoring functions of the joint models are estimated by using machine learning techniques. We adopt averaged perceptron (Collins, 2002) with a max-margin technique:

$$\forall i \in \{1, ..., N\},\ y \in G(x_i),$$
$$Score(\hat{x}_i, \hat{y}_i) \geq Score(\hat{x}_i, y) + \|\hat{y}_i - y\|_1 - \xi_i$$

where $\xi_i \geq 0$ is the slack variable and $\|\hat{y}_i - y\|_1$ is the Hamming distance between the gold PA graph $\hat{y}_i$ and a candidate PA graph y of the admissible PA graphs $G(x_i)$. Following Zhang et al. (2014), we select the highest scoring graph $\tilde{y}$ as follows:

$$\text{TRAIN}: \tilde{y} = \underset{y \in G(\hat{x}_i)}{\text{argmax}}\{Score(\hat{x}_i, y) + \|\hat{y}_i - y\|_1\}$$
$$\text{TEST}: \tilde{y} = \underset{y \in G(x)}{\text{argmax}}\{Score(x, y)\}$$

Using the weight vector tuned by the training, we perform analysis on a sentence x in the test set.

6 Experiment

6.1 Experimental Settings

Data Set We evaluate our proposed methods on the NAIST Text Corpus 1.5, which consists of 40,000 sentences of Japanese newspaper text (Iida et al., 2007). While previous work has adopted the version 1.4 beta, we adopt the latest version. The major difference between version 1.4 beta and 1.5 is revision of dative case (corresponding to Japanese case particle "ni"). In 1.4 beta, most of adjunct usages of "ni" are mixed up with the argument usages of "ni", making the identification of dative cases seemingly easy. Therefore, our results are not directly comparable with previous work.

We adopt standard train/dev/test split (Taira et al., 2008) as follows:

Train	Articles: Jan 1-11,	Editorials: Jan-Aug
Dev	Articles: Jan 12-13,	Editorials: Sept
Test	Articles: Jan 14-17,	Editorials: Oct-Dec

We exclude inter-sentential arguments (*Inter-Zero*) in our experiments. Our features make use of the annotated POS tags, phrase boundaries, and dependency relations annotated in the NAIST Text Corpus. We do not use any external resources.

Baseline We adopt the pointwise method (using only local features) proposed by Imamura et al. (2009) as the baseline. They built three distinct models corresponding to the three case roles. By using each model, they estimate the likelihood that each candidate argument plays a case role of the target predicate as a score, and independently select the highest scoring one per predicate.

	feature	*Dep*	*Zero*	*Total*
PC Joint	*local*	84.59	42.55	77.89
	+ *global*	85.51	44.54	78.85
AC Joint	*local*	84.17	41.33	77.43
	+ *global*	85.92	44.45	79.17

Table 2: Global vs Local features on the development sets in F-measures. "PC Joint" denotes the Per-Case Joint Model, and "AC Joint" denotes the All-Cases Joint Model.

Features The baseline utilizes the *Baseline Features* used in Imamura et al. (2009) and *Grammatical* features used in Hayashibe et al. (2009), as the "Local Features". In addition, the joint models utilize the "Global Features" in Table 1.

Implementation Details For our joint models with hill-climbing, we report the average performance across ten independent runs with 10 restarts, which almost reaches convergence [3]. We train the baseline and our joint models for 20 iterations with averaged perceptron.

6.2 Results

Local Features vs Global Features

Table 2 shows the effectiveness of the global features on the development sets. We incrementally add the global features to the both models that utilize only the local features. The results show that the global features improve the performance by about 1.0 point in F-measures in total. For and are particularly beneficial to the implicit (*Zero*) argument identification (an improvement of 1.99 points in Per-Case Joint Model and 3.12 points in All-Cases Joint Model).

Pointwise Methods vs Joint Methods

Table 3 presents the F-measures of the baseline and our joint methods on the test set of the NAIST Text Corpus. We used the bootstrap resampling method as the significance test. In most of the metrics, our proposed joint methods outperform the baseline pointwise method. Note that since Per-Case Joint Model yields better results compared with the baseline, capturing the *predicate interaction* is beneficial to Japanese PAS analysis. In addition, the joint methods achieve a considerable improvement of 2.0-2.5 points in F-measure for

[3] Performance did not change when increasing the number of restarts

Case	Type	# of Args.	Baseline		PC Joint		AC Joint	
NOM	*Dep*	14055	86.50		87.54	†	**88.13**	† ‡
	Zero	4935	45.56		47.62		**48.11**	
	Total	18990	77.31		78.39	†	**79.03**	† ‡
ACC	*Dep*	9473	92.84	⋆	**93.09**	† ⋆	92.74	
	Zero	833	21.38		22.73		**24.43**	
	Total	10306	88.86	⋆	**89.00**	† ⋆	88.47	
DAT	*Dep*	2518	30.97		34.29	†	**38.39**	† ‡
	Zero	239	0.83		0.83		**4.80**	
	Total	2757	29.02		32.20	†	**36.35**	† ‡
ALL	*Dep*	26046	85.06		85.79	†	**86.07**	† ‡
	Zero	6007	41.65		43.60		**44.09**	
	Total	32053	78.15		78.91	†	**79.23**	† ‡

Table 3: F-measures of the three methods in the test sets. The bold values denote the highest F-measures among all the three methods. Statistical significance with $p < 0.05$ is marked with † compared with Baseline, ‡ compared with PC Joint, and ⋆ compared with AC Joint.

	Dep			*Zero*		
	NOM	ACC	DAT	NOM	ACC	DAT
TA08	75.53	88.20	89.51	30.15	11.41	3.66
IM09	87.0	93.9	80.8	50.0	30.8	0.0
S&K11	-	-	-	39.5	17.5	8.9
PC Joint	87.54	93.09	34.19	47.62	22.73	0.83
AC Joint	88.13	92.74	38.39	48.11	24.44	4.80

Table 4: Comparison with previous work using the NAIST Text Corpus in F-measure. TA08 is Taira et al. (2008), IM09 is Imamura et al. (2009), and S&K11 is Sasano & Kurohashi (2011). Their results are not directly comparable to ours since they use external resources and the NAIST Text Corpus 1.4 beta.

the implicit arguments (*Zero*), one of the problematic issues in Japanese PAS analysis.

Comparing the joint methods, each of our two joint methods is effective for a different case role. Per-Case Joint Model is better at the ACC case, and All-Cases Joint Model is better at the NOM and DAT cases. One of the possible explanations is that the distribution of ACC cases is different from NOM cases. While the ratio of *Dep* and *Zero* arguments for ACC cases is 90:10, the ratio for NOM cases is 75:25. This might have some negative effects on the ACC case identification with All-Cases Joint Model. However, in total, All-Cases Joint Model achieves significantly better results. This suggests that capturing *case interactions* improves performance of Japanese PAS analysis.

Existing Methods vs Joint Methods

To compare our proposed methods with previous work, we pick the three pieces of representative previous work exploiting the NAIST Text Corpus: Taira et al. (2008) (TA08), Imamura et al. (2009) (IM09), and Sasano and Kurohashi (2011) (S&K11). Sasano and Kurohashi (2011) focus on the analysis for the *Zero* and *Inter-Zero* arguments, and do not report the results on the *Dep* arguments. With respect to the *Dep* arguments, the All-Cases Joint Model achieves the best result for the NOM cases, Imamura et al. (2009) the best for the ACC cases, and Taira et al. (2008) the best for the DAT cases. In terms of the *Zero* arguments, Imamura et al. (2009) is the best for the NOM and ACC cases, and Sasano and Kurohashi (2011) the best for the DAT cases. Our joint methods achieve high performance comparable to Imamura et al. (2009).

However, because they used additional external resources and a different version of the NAIST Text Corpus, the results of previous work are not directly comparable to ours. Our research direction and contributions are orthogonal to theirs, and adding their external resources could potentially leads to much better results.

7 Conclusion

We have presented joint methods for Japanese PAS analysis, which model interactions between multiple predicates and arguments using a bipartite graph and greedily search the optimal PAS combination in a sentence. Experimental results shows that capturing the *predicate interaction* and *case interaction* is effective for Japanese PAS analysis. In particular, implicit (*Zero*) argument identification, one of the problematic issues in Japanese PAS analysis, is improved by taking such interactions into account. Since this framework is applicable to the *argument classification* in SRL, applying our methods to that task is an interesting line of the future research. In addition, the final results of our joint methods are comparable to representative existing methods despite using no external resources. For future work, we plan to incorporate external resources for our joint methods.

Acknowledgments

We are grateful to the anonymous reviewers. This work is partially supported by a JSPS KAKENHI Grant Number 26730121 and 15K16053.

References

Michael Collins. 2002. Discriminative training methods for hidden markov models: Theory and experiments with perceptron algorithms. In *Proceedings of the 2002 Conference on Empirical Methods in Natural Language Processing (EMNLP)*, pages 1–8, Philadelphia, July. Association for Computational Linguistics.

Matthew Gerber and Joyce Chai. 2010. Beyond nombank: A study of implicit arguments for nominal predicates. In *Proceedings of the 48th Annual Meeting of the Association for Computational Linguistics*, pages 1583–1592, Uppsala, Sweden, July. Association for Computational Linguistics.

Yuta Hayashibe, Mamoru Komachi, and Yuji Matsumoto. 2011. Japanese predicate argument structure analysis exploiting argument position and type. In *Proceedings of 5th International Joint Conference on Natural Language Processing*, pages 201–209, Chiang Mai, Thailand, November. Asian Federation of Natural Language Processing.

Liang Huang. 2008. Forest reranking: Discriminative parsing with non-local features. In *Proceedings of 46th Annual Meeting of the Association for Computational Linguistics: Human Language Technologies*, pages 586–594, Columbus, Ohio, June. Association for Computational Linguistics.

Ryu Iida, Mamoru Komachi, Kentaro Inui, and Yuji Matsumoto. 2007. Annotating a japanese text corpus with predicate-argument and coreference relations. In *Proceedings of the Linguistic Annotation Workshop*, pages 132–139, Prague, Czech Republic, June. Association for Computational Linguistics.

Kenji Imamura, Kuniko Saito, and Tomoko Izumi. 2009. Discriminative approach to predicate-argument structure analysis with zero-anaphora resolution. In *Proceedings of the Joint Conference of the 47th Annual Meeting of the Association for Computational Linguistics and 4th International Joint Conference on Natural Language Processing*, pages 85–88, Suntec, Singapore, August. Association for Computational Linguistics.

Egoitz Laparra and German Rigau. 2013. Impar: A deterministic algorithm for implicit semantic role labelling. In *Proceedings of the 51st Annual Meeting of the Association for Computational Linguistics*, pages 1180–1189, Sofia, Bulgaria, August. Association for Computational Linguistics.

Ryan McDonald and Fernando Pereira. 2006. Online learning of approximate dependency parsing algorithms. In *Proceedings of the 11th conference on European Chapter of the Association for Computational Linguistics (EACL)*, pages 81–88, Trento, Italy, April. Association for Computational Linguistics.

Ryohei Sasano and Sadao Kurohashi. 2011. A discriminative approach to japanese zero anaphora resolution with large-scale lexicalized case frames. In *Proceedings of 5th International Joint Conference on Natural Language Processing*, pages 758–766, Chiang Mai, Thailand, November. Asian Federation of Natural Language Processing.

Hirotoshi Taira, Sanae Fujita, and Masaaki Nagata. 2008. A japanese predicate argument structure analysis using decision lists. In *Proceedings of the 2008 Conference on Empirical Methods in Natural Language Processing (EMNLP)*, pages 523–532, Honolulu, Hawaii, October. Association for Computational Linguistics.

Haitong Yang and Chengqing Zong. 2014. Multi-predicate semantic role labeling. In *Proceedings of the 2014 Conference on Empirical Methods in Natural Language Processing (EMNLP)*, pages 363–373, Doha, Qatar, October. Association for Computational Linguistics.

Yuan Zhang, Tao Lei, Regina Barzilay, and Tommi Jaakkola. 2014. Greed is good if randomized: New inference for dependency parsing. In *Proceedings of the 2014 Conference on Empirical Methods in Natural Language Processing (EMNLP)*, pages 1013–1024, Doha, Qatar, October. Association for Computational Linguistics.

Jointly optimizing word representations for lexical and sentential tasks with the C-PHRASE model

Nghia The Pham Germán Kruszewski Angeliki Lazaridou Marco Baroni
Center for Mind/Brain Sciences
University of Trento
{thenghia.pham|german.kruszewski|angeliki.lazaridou|marco.baroni}@unitn.it

Abstract

We introduce C-PHRASE, a distributional semantic model that learns word representations by optimizing context prediction for phrases at all levels in a syntactic tree, from single words to full sentences. C-PHRASE outperforms the state-of-the-art C-BOW model on a variety of lexical tasks. Moreover, since C-PHRASE word vectors are induced through a compositional learning objective (modeling the contexts of words combined into phrases), when they are summed, they produce sentence representations that rival those generated by *ad-hoc* compositional models.

1 Introduction

Distributional semantic models, that induce vector-based meaning representations from patterns of co-occurrence of words in corpora, have proven very successful at modeling many lexical relations, such as synonymy, co-hyponomy and analogy (Mikolov et al., 2013c; Turney and Pantel, 2010). The recent evaluation of Baroni et al. (2014b) suggests that the C-BOW model introduced by Mikolov et al. (2013a) is, consistently, the best across many tasks.[1]

Interestingly, C-BOW vectors are estimated with a simple compositional approach: The weights of adjacent words are jointly optimized so that their sum will predict the distribution of their contexts. This is reminiscent of how the parameters of some *compositional* distributional semantic models are estimated by optimizing the prediction of the contexts in which phrases occur in corpora (Baroni and Zamparelli, 2010; Guevara, 2010; Dinu et al., 2013). However, these compositional approaches assume that word vectors have already been constructed, and contextual evidence is only used to induce optimal combination rules to derive representations of phrases and sentences.

In this paper, we follow through on this observation to propose the new C-PHRASE model. Similarly to C-BOW, C-PHRASE learns word representations by optimizing their joint context prediction. However, unlike in flat, window-based C-BOW, C-PHRASE groups words according to their syntactic structure, and it simultaneously optimizes context-predictions at different levels of the syntactic hierarchy. For example, given training sentence *"A sad dog is howling in the park"*, C-PHRASE will optimize context prediction for *dog*, *sad dog*, *a sad dog*, *a sad dog is howling*, etc., but not, for example, for *howling in*, as these two words do not form a syntactic constituent by themselves.

C-PHRASE word representations outperform C-BOW on several word-level benchmarks. In addition, because they are estimated in a compositional way, C-PHRASE word vectors, when combined through simple addition, produce sentence representations that are better than those obtained when adding other kinds of vectors, and competitive against *ad-hoc* compositional methods on various sentence meaning benchmarks.

2 The C-PHRASE model

We start with a brief overview of the models proposed by Mikolov et al. (2013a), as C-PHRASE builds on them. The **Skip-gram** model derives the vector of a target word by setting its weights to predict the words surrounding it in the corpus.

[1] We refer here not only to the results reported in Baroni et al. (2014b), but also to the more extensive evaluation that Baroni and colleagues present in the companion website (http://clic.cimec.unitn.it/composes/semantic-vectors.html). The experiments there suggest that only the Glove vectors of Pennington et al. (2014) are competitive with C-BOW, and only when trained on a corpus several orders of magnitude larger than the one used for C-BOW.

Proceedings of the 53rd Annual Meeting of the Association for Computational Linguistics and the 7th International Joint Conference on Natural Language Processing, pages 971–981,
Beijing, China, July 26-31, 2015.

More specifically, the objective function is:

$$\frac{1}{T}\sum_{t=1}^{T}\sum_{-c\leq j\leq c, j\neq 0}\log p(w_{t+j}|w_t) \quad (1)$$

where the word sequence $w_1, w_2, ..., w_T$ is the training corpus and c is the size of the window around the target word w_t, consisting of the context words w_{t+j} that must be predicted by the induced vector representation for the target.

While Skip-gram learns each word representation separately, the **C-BOW** model takes their combination into account. More precisely, it tries to predict a context word from the combination of the previous and following words, where the combination method is vector addition. The objective function is:

$$\frac{1}{T}\sum_{t=1}^{T}\log p(w_t|w_{t-c}..w_{t-1}, w_{t+1}..w_{t+c}) \quad (2)$$

While other distributional models consider sequences of words jointly as *context* when estimating the parameters for a single word (Agirre et al., 2009; Melamud et al., 2014), C-BOW is unique in that it estimates the weights of a sequence of words jointly, based on their shared context. In this respect, C-BOW extends the distributional hypothesis (Harris, 1954) that words with similar context distributions should have similar meanings to longer sequences. However, the word combinations of C-BOW are not natural linguistic constituents, but arbitrary n-grams (e.g., sequences of 5 words with a gap in the middle). Moreover, the model does not attempt to capture the *hierarchical* nature of syntactic phrasing, such that *big brown dog* is a meaningful phrase, but so are its children *brown dog* and *dog*.

C-PHRASE aims at capturing the same intuition that word combinations with similar context distributions will have similar meaning, but it applies it to syntactically motivated, potentially nested phrases. More precisely, we estimate word vectors such that they and their summed combinations are able to predict the contexts of words, phrases and sentences. The model is formalized as follows. We start from a parsed text corpus $\mathbb{T}$, composed of constituents $\mathcal{C}[w_l, \cdots, w_r]$, where $w_l, \cdots, w_r$ are the words spanned by the constituent, located in positions l to r in the corpus. We minimize an objective function analogous to equations (1) and (2), but instead of just using individual words or bags of words to predict context, we use summed vector representations of well-formed constituents at all levels in the syntactic tree to predict the context of these constituents. There are similarities with both CBOW and Skip-gram. At the leaf nodes, C-PHRASE acts like Skip-gram, whereas at higher node in the parse tree, it behaves like CBOW model. Concretely, we try to predict the words located within a window $c_{\mathcal{C}}$ from every constituent in the parse tree.[2] In order to do so, we learn vector representations for words v_w by maximizing the sum of the log probabilities of the words in the context window of the well-formed constituents with stochastic gradient descent:

$$\sum_{\mathcal{C}[w_l,\cdots,w_r]\in\mathbb{T}}\sum_{1\leq j\leq c_{\mathcal{C}}}\Big(\log p(w_{l-j}|\mathcal{C}[w_l,\cdots,w_r]) + \log p(w_{r+j}|\mathcal{C}[w_l,\cdots,w_r])\Big) \quad (3)$$

with p theoretically defined as:

$$p(w_O|\mathcal{C}[w_l,\cdots,w_r]) = \frac{\exp\left({v'}_{w_O}^{\top}\frac{\sum_{i=l}^{r}v_{w_i}}{r-l+1}\right)}{\sum_{w=1}^{W}\exp\left({v'}_{w}^{\top}\frac{\sum_{i=l}^{r}v_{w_i}}{r-l+1}\right)}$$

where W is the size of the vocabulary, v' and v denote output (context) and input vectors, respectively, and we take the input vectors to represent the words. In practice, since the normalization constant for the above probability is expensive to compute, we follow Mikolov et al. (2013b) and use negative sampling.

We let the context window size $c_{\mathcal{C}}$ vary as a function of the height of the constituent in the syntactic tree. The height $h(\mathcal{C})$ of a constituent is given by the maximum number of intermediate nodes separating it from any of the words it dominates (such that $h = 0$ for words, $h = 1$ for two-word phrases, etc.). Then, for a constituent of height $h(\mathcal{C})$, C-PHRASE considers $c_{\mathcal{C}} = c_1 + h(\mathcal{C})c_2$ context words to its left and right (the non-negative integers c_1 and c_2 are hyperparameters of the model; with $c_2 = 0$, context becomes constant

[2] Although here we only use single words as context, the latter can be extended to encompass any sensible linguistic item, e.g., frequent n-grams or, as discussed below, syntactically-mediated expressions

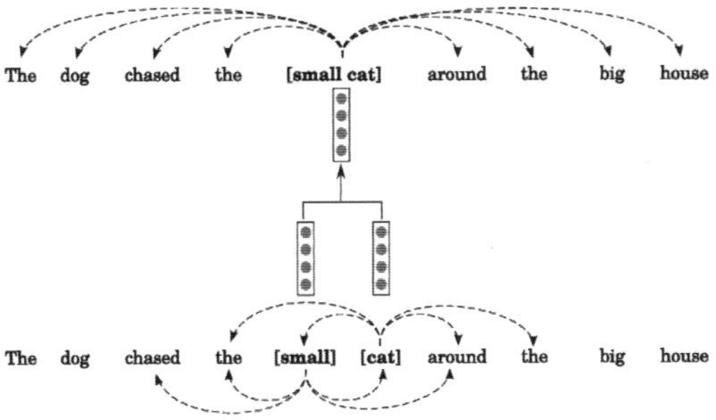

Figure 1: C-PHRASE context prediction objective for the phrase *small cat* and its children. The phrase vector is obtained by summing the word vectors. The predicted window is wider for the higher constituent (the phrase).

across heights). The intuition for enlarging the window proportionally to height is that, for shorter phrases, narrower contexts are likely to be most informative (e.g., a modifying adjective for a noun), whereas for longer phrases and sentences it might be better to focus on broader "topical" information spread across larger windows (paragraphs containing sentences about weather might also contain the words *rain* and *sun*, but without any tendency for these words to be perfectly adjacent to the target sentences).

Figure 1 illustrates the prediction objective for a two-word phrase and its children. Since all constituents (except the topmost) form parts of larger constituents, their representations will be learned both from the objective of predicting their own contexts, and from error propagation from the same objective applied higher in the tree. As a side effect, words, being lower in the syntactic tree, will have their vectors updated more often, and thus might have a greater impact on the learned parameters. This is another reason for varying window size with height, so that the latter effect will be counter-balanced by higher constituents having larger context windows to predict.

For lexical tasks, we directly use the vectors induced by C-PHRASE as word representations. For sentential tasks, we simply add the vectors of the words in a sentence to obtain its representation, exploiting the fact that C-PHRASE was trained to predict phrase contexts from the additive combination of their elements.

Joint optimization of word and phrase vectors The C-PHRASE hierarchical learning objective can capture, in parallel, generalizations about the contexts of words and phrases at different levels of complexity. This results, as we will see, in better word vectors, presumably because C-PHRASE is trained to predict how the contexts of a word change based on its phrasal collocates (*cup* will have very different contexts in *world cup* vs. *coffee cup*). At the same time, because the vectors are optimized based on their occurrence in phrases of different syntactic complexity, they produce good sentence representations when they are combined. To the best of our knowledge, C-PHRASE is the first model that is jointly optimized for lexical and compositional tasks. C-BOW uses shallow composition information to learn word vectors. Conversely, some compositional models –e.g., Kalchbrenner et al. (2014), Socher et al. (2013)– induce word representations, that are only optimized for a compositional task and are not tested at the lexical level. Somewhat relatedly to what we do, Hill et al. (2014) evaluated representations learned in a sentence translation task on word-level benchmarks. Some *a priori* justification for treating word and sentence learning as joint problems comes from human language acquisition, as it is obvious that children learn word and phrase meanings in parallel and interactively, not sequentially (Tomasello, 2003).

Knowledge-leanness and simplicity For training, C-PHRASE requires a large, syntactically-parsed corpus (more precisely, it only requires the constituent structure assigned by the parser, as it is blind to syntactic labels). Both large unannotated corpora and efficient pre-trained parsers are available for many languages, making the C-PHRASE knowledge demands feasible for practical purposes. There is no need to parse the sentences we want to build representations for at test time, since the component word vectors are simply added. The only parameters of the model are the word vectors; specifically, no extra parameters are needed for composition (composition models such as the one presented in Socher et al. (2012) require an extra parameter matrix for each word in the vocabulary, and even leaner models such as the one of Guevara (2010) must estimate a parameter matrix for each composition rule in the grammar). This makes C-PHRASE as simple as additive and multiplicative composition (Mitchell and

Lapata, 2010),[3] but C-PHRASE is both more effective in compositional tasks (see evaluation below), and it has the further advantage that it learns its own word vectors, thus reducing the number of arbitrary choices to be made in modeling.

Supervision Unlike many recent composition models (Kalchbrenner and Blunsom, 2013; Kalchbrenner et al., 2014; Socher et al., 2012; Socher et al., 2013, among others), the context-prediction objective of C-PHRASE does not require annotated data, and it is meant to provide general-purpose representations that can serve in different tasks. C-PHRASE vectors can also be used as initialization parameters for fully supervised, task-specific systems. Alternatively, the current unsupervised objective could be combined with task-specific supervised objectives to fine-tune C-PHRASE to specific purposes.

Sensitivity to syntactic structure During training, C-PHRASE is sensitive to syntactic structure. To cite an extreme example, *boy flowers* will be joined in a context-predicting phrase in *"these are considered [boy flowers]"*, but not in *"he gave [the boy] [flowers]"*. A more common case is that of determiners, that will only occur in phrases that also contain the following word, but not necessarily the preceding one. Sentence composition at test time, on the other hand, is additive, and thus syntax-insensitive. Still, the vectors being combined will reflect syntactic generalizations learned in training. Even if C-PHRASE produces the same representation for *red+car* and *car+red*, this representation combines a *red* vector that, during training, has often occurred in the modifier position of adjective-noun phrases, whereas *car* will have often occurred in the corresponding head position. So, presumably, the *red+car=car+red* vector will encode the adjective-noun asymmetry induced in learning. While the model won't be able to distinguish the rare cases in which *car red* is genuinely used as a phrase, in realistic scenarios this won't be a problem, because only *red car* will be encountered. In this respect, the successes and failures of C-PHRASE can tell us to what extent word order information is truly distinctive in practice, and to what extent it can instead be reconstructed from the typical role that words play in sentences.

[3]We do not report results for component-wise multiplicative in our evaluation because it performed much worse than addition in all the tasks.

Comparison with traditional syntax-sensitive word representations Syntax has often been exploited in distributional semantics for a richer characterization of *context*. By relying on a syntactic parse of the input corpus, a distributional model can take more informative contexts such as *subject-of-eat* vs. *object-of-eat* into account (Baroni and Lenci, 2010; Curran and Moens, 2002; Grefenstette, 1994; Erk and Padó, 2008; Levy and Goldberg, 2014a; Padó and Lapata, 2007; Rothenhäusler and Schütze, 2009). In this approach, syntactic information serves to select and/or enrich the *contexts* that are used to build representations of target units. On the other hand, we use syntax to determine the *target units* that we build representations for (in the sense that we jointly learn representations of their constituents). The focus is thus on unrelated aspects of model induction, and we could indeed use syntax-mediated contexts together with our phrasing strategy. Currently, given *eat (red apples)*, we treat *eat* as window-based context of *red apples*, but we could also take the context to be *object-of-eat*.

3 Evaluation

3.1 Data sets

Semantic relatedness of words In this classic lexical task, the models are required to quantify the degree of semantic similarity or relatedness of pairs of words in terms of cosines between the corresponding vectors. These scores are then compared to human gold standards. Performance is assessed by computing the correlation between system and human scores (Spearman correlation in all tasks except rg, where it is customary to report Pearson). We used, first of all, the MEN (**men**) data set of Bruni et al. (2014), that is split into 1K pairs for training/development, and 1K pairs for testing. We used the training set to tune the hyperparameters of our model, and report performance on the test set. The C-BOW model of Baroni et al. (2014b) achieved state-of-the art performance on MEN test. We also evaluate on the widely used WordSim353 set introduced by Finkelstein et al. (2002), which consists of 353 word pairs. The WordSim353 data were split by Agirre et al. (2009) into similarity (**wss**) and relatedness (**wsr**) subsets, focusing on strictly taxonomic (*television/radio*) vs. broader topical cases (*Maradona/football*), respectively. State-of-the-art performance on both sets is reported by Baroni et al. (2014b), with the C-BOW model. We further consider the classic data set of Rubenstein and Goodenough (1965) (**rg**), consisting of 65 noun pairs. We report the state-of-the-art from Hassan and Mihalcea (2011), which exploited Wikipedia's linking structure.

Concept categorization Systems are asked to group a set of nominal concepts into broader categories (e.g. *arthritis* and *anthrax* into *illness*; *banana* and *grape* into *fruit*). As in previous work, we treat this as an unsupervised clustering task. We feed the similarity matrix produced by a model for all concepts in a test set to the CLUTO toolkit (Karypis, 2003), that clusters them into n groups, where n is the number of categories. We use standard CLUTO parameters from the literature, and quantify performance by cluster purity with respect to the gold categories. The Almuhareb-Poesio benchmark (Almuhareb, 2006) (**ap**) consists of 402 concepts belonging to 21 categories. A distributional model based on carefully chosen syntactic relations achieved top ap performance (Rothenhäusler and Schütze, 2009). The ESSLLI 2008 data set (Baroni et al., 2008) (**esslli**) consists of 6 categories and 42 concepts. State of the art was achieved by Katrenko and Adriaans (2008) by using full-Web queries and manually crafted patterns.

Semantic analogy The last lexical task we pick is analogy (**an**), introduced in Mikolov et al. (2013c). We focus on their *semantic* challenge, containing about 9K questions. In each question, the system is given a pair exemplifying a relation (*man*/*king*) and a test word (*woman*); it is then asked to find the word (*queen*) that instantiates the same relation with the test word as that of the example pair. Mikolov et al. (2013c) subtract the vector of the first word in a pair from the second, add the vector of the test word and look for the nearest neighbor of the resulting vector (e.g., find the word whose vector is closest to *king* - *man* + *woman*). We follow the method introduced by Levy and Goldberg (2014b), which returns the word x maximizing $\frac{\cos(king,x)\times\cos(woman,x)}{\cos(man,x)}$. This method yields better results for all models. Performance is measured by accuracy in retrieving the correct answer (in our search space of 180K words). The current state of the art on the semantic part and on the whole data set was reached by Pennington et al. (2014), who trained their word representations on a huge corpus consisting of 42B words.

Sentential semantic relatedness Similarly to word relatedness, composed sentence representations can be evaluated against benchmarks where humans provided relatedness/similarity scores for sentence pairs (sentences with high scores, such as *"A person in a black jacket is doing tricks on a motorbike"*/*"A man in a black jacket is doing tricks on a motorbike"* from the SICK data-set, tend to be near-paraphrases). Following previous work on these data sets, Pearson correlation is our figure of merit, and we report it between human scores and sentence vector cosine similarities computed by the models. SICK (Marelli et al., 2014) (**sick-r**) was created specifically for the purpose of evaluating compositional models, focusing on linguistic phenomena such as lexical variation and word order. Here we report performance of the systems on the test part of the data set, which contains 5K sentence pairs. The top performance (from the SICK SemEval shared task) was reached by Zhao et al. (2014) using a heterogeneous set of features that include WordNet and extra training corpora. Agirre et al. (2012) and Agirre et al. (2013) created two collections of sentential similarities consisting of subsets coming from different sources. From these, we pick the Microsoft Research video description dataset (**msrvid**), where near paraphrases are descriptions of the same short video, and the OnWN 2012 (**onwn1**) and OnWN 2013 (**onwn2**) data sets (each of these sets contains 750 pairs). The latter are quite different from other sentence relatedness benchmarks, since they compare definitions for the same or different words taken from WordNet and OntoNotes: these glosses often are syntactic fragments (*"cause something to pass or lead somewhere"*), rather than full sentences. We report top performance on these tasks from the respective shared challenges, as summarized by Agirre et al. (2012) and Agirre et al. (2013). Again, the top systems use feature-rich, supervised methods relying on distributional similarity as well as other sources, such as WordNet and named entity recognizers.

Sentential entailment Detecting the presence of entailment between sentences or longer passages is one of the most useful features that the computational analysis of text could provide (Dagan et al., 2009). We test our model on the SICK entailment task (**sick-e**) (Marelli et al., 2014). All SICK sentence pairs are labeled as ENTAILING (*"Two teams are competing in a football match"/"Two groups of people are playing football"*), CONTRADICTING (*"The brown horse is near a red barrel at the rodeo"/"The brown horse is far from a red barrel at the rodeo"*) or NEUTRAL (*"A man in a black jacket is doing tricks on a motorbike"/"A person is riding the bicycle on one wheel"*). For each model, we train a simple SVM classifier based on 2 features: cosine similarity between the two sentence vectors, as given by the models, and whether the sentence pair contains a negation word (the latter has been shown to be a very informative feature for SICK entailment). The current state-of-the-art is reached by Lai and Hockenmaier (2014), using a much richer set of features, that include WordNet, the denotation graph of Young et al. (2014) and extra training data from other resources.

Sentiment analysis Finally, as sentiment analysis has emerged as a popular area of application for compositional models, we test our methods on the Stanford Sentiment Treebank (Socher et al., 2013) (**sst**), consisting of 11,855 sentences from movie reviews, using the coarse annotation into 2 sentiment degrees (*negative/positive*). We follow the official split into train (8,544), development (1,101) and test (2,210) parts. We train an SVM classifier on the training set, using the sentence vectors composed by a model as features, and report accuracy on the test set. State of the art is obtained by Le and Mikolov (2014) with the Paragraph Vector approach we describe below.

3.2 Model implementation

The source corpus we use to build the lexical vectors is created by concatenating three sources: ukWaC,[4] a mid-2009 dump of the English Wikipedia[5] and the British National Corpus[6] (about 2.8B words in total). We build vectors for the 180K words occurring at least 100 times in the corpus. Since our training procedure requires parsed trees, we parse the corpus using the Stanford parser (Klein and Manning, 2003).

C-PHRASE has two hyperparameters (see Section 2 above), namely basic window size (c_1) and height-dependent window enlargement factor (c_2). Moreover, following Mikolov et al. (2013b), during training we sub-sample less informative, very frequent words: this option is controlled by a parameter t, resulting in aggressive subsampling of words with relative frequency above it. We tune on MEN-train, obtaining $c_1 = 5$, $c_2 = 2$ and $t = 10^{-5}$. As already mentioned, sentence vectors are built by summing the vectors of the words in them.

In lexical tasks, we compare our model to the best C-BOW model from Baroni et al. (2014b),[7] and to a Skip-gram model built using the same hyperparameters as C-PHRASE (that also led to the best MEN-train results for Skip-gram).

In sentential tasks, we compare our model against adding the best C-BOW vectors pretrained by Baroni and colleagues,[8] and adding our Skip-gram vectors. We compare the additive approaches to two sophisticated composition models. The first is the Practical Lexical Function (**PLF**) model of Paperno et al. (2014). This is a linguistically motivated model in the tradition of the "functional composition" approaches of Coecke et al. (2010) and Baroni et al. (2014a), and the only model in this line of research that has been shown to empirically scale up to real-life sentence challenges. In short, in the PLF model all words are represented by vectors. Words acting as argument-taking functions (such as verbs or adjectives) are also associated to one matrix for each argument they take (e.g., each transitive verb has a subject and an object matrix). Vector representations of arguments are recursively multiplied by function matrices, following the syntactic tree up to the top node. The final sentence representation is obtained by summing all the resulting vectors. The PLF approach requires syntactic parsing both in training and in testing and, more cumbersomely, to train a separate matrix for each argument slot of each function word (the training objective is again a context-predicting one). Here, we report PLF results on msrvid and onwn2 from Paperno et al. (2014), noting that they also used two simple but precious cues (word overlap and sentence length) we do not adopt here. We used their pre-trained vectors and matrices also for the SICK challenges, while the number of new ma-

[4]http://wacky.sslmit.unibo.it

[5]http://en.wikipedia.org

[6]http://www.natcorp.ox.ac.uk

[7]For fairness, we report their results when all tasks were evaluated with the same set of parameters, tuned on rg: this is row 8 of their Table 2.

[8]http://clic.cimec.unitn.it/composes/semantic-vectors.html

trices to estimate made it too time-consuming to implement this model in the onwn1 and sst tasks.

Finally, we test the Paragraph Vector (**PV**) approach recently proposed by Le and Mikolov (2014). Under PV, sentence representations are learned by predicting the words that occur in them. This unsupervised method has been shown by the authors to outperform much more sophisticated, supervised neural-network-based composition models on the sst task. We use our own implementation for this approach. Unlike in the original experiments, we found the PV-DBOW variant of PV to consistently outperform PV-DM, and so we report results obtained with the former.

Note that PV-DBOW aims mainly at providing representations for sentences, not words. When we do not need to induce vectors for sentences in the training corpus, i.e., only train to learn single words' representations and the softmax weights, PV-DBOW essentially reduces to Skip-gram. Therefore, we produce the PV-DBOW vectors for the sentences in the evaluation data sets using the softmax weights learned by Skip-gram. However, it is not clear that, if we were to train PV-DBOW jointly for words and sentences, we would get word vectors as good as those that Skip-gram induces.

4 Results

The results on the lexical tasks reported in Table 1 prove that C-PHRASE is providing excellent word representations, (nearly) as good or better than the C-BOW vectors of Baroni and colleagues in all cases, except for ap. Whenever C-PHRASE is not close to the state of the art results, the latter relied on richer knowledge sources and/or much larger corpora (ap, esslli, an).

Turning to the sentential tasks (Table 2), we first remark that using high-quality word vectors (such as C-BOW) and summing them leads to good results in all tasks, competitive with those obtained with more sophisticated composition models. This confirms the observation made by Blacoe and Lapata (2012) that simple-minded composition models are not necessarily worse than advanced approaches. Still, C-PHRASE is consistently better than C-BOW in all tasks, except sst, where the two models reach the same performance level.

C-PHRASE is outperforming PV on all tasks except sick-e, where the two models have the same performance, and onwn2, where PV is slightly better. C-PHRASE is outperforming PLF by a large margin on the SICK sets, whereas the two models are equal on msrvid, and PLF better on onwn2. Recall, however, that on the latter two benchmarks PLF used extra word overlap and sentence length features, so the comparison is not entirely fair.

The fact that state-of-the-art performance is well above our models is not surprising, since the SOA systems are invariably based on a wealth of knowledge sources, and highly optimized for a task. To put some of our results in a broader perspective, C-PHRASE's sick-r performance is 1% better than the median result of systems that participated in the SICK SemEval challenge, and comparable to that of Beltagy et al. (2014), who entered the competition with a system combining distributional semantics with a supervised probabilistic soft logic system. For sick-e (the entailment task), C-PHRASE's performance is less than one point below the median of the SemEval systems, and slightly above that of the Stanford submission, that used a recursive neural network with a tensor layer.

Finally, the performance of all our models, including PV, on sst is remarkably lower than the state-of-the-art performance of PV as reported by Le and Mikolov (2014). We believe that the crucial difference is that these authors estimated PV vectors *specifically on the sentiment treebank training data*, thus building *ad-hoc* vectors encoding the semantics of movie reviews. We leave it to further research to ascertain whether we could better fine-tune our models to sst by including the sentiment treebank training phrases in our source corpus.

Comparing vector lengths of C-BOW and C-PHRASE We gather some insight into how the C-PHRASE objective might adjust word representations for composition with respect to C-BOW by looking at how the length of word vectors changes across the two models.[9] While this is a very coarse measure, if a word vector is much longer/shorter (relative to the length of other word vectors of the same model) for C-PHRASE vs. C-BOW, it means that, when sentences are composed by addition, the effect of the word on the resulting sentence representation will be stronger/weaker.

[9]We performed the same analysis for C-PHRASE and Skip-gram, finding similar general trends to the ones we report for C-PHRASE and C-BOW.

	men	wss	wsr	rg	ap	esslli	an
Skip-gram	78	77	66	80	65	82	63
C-BOW	**80**	78	68	**83**	**71**	77	68
C-PHRASE	79	**79**	**70**	**83**	65	**84**	**69**
SOA	80	80	70	86	79	91	82

Table 1: Lexical task performance. See Section 3.1 for figures of merit (all in percentage form) and state-of-the-art references. C-BOW results (tuned on rg) are taken from Baroni et al. 2014b.

	sick-r	sick-e	msrvid	onwn1	onwn2	sst
Skip-gram	70	72	74	66	62	78
C-BOW	70	74	74	69	63	**79**
C-PHRASE	**72**	**75**	**79**	**70**	65	**79**
PLF	57	72	**79**	NA	**67**	NA
PV	67	**75**	77	66	66	77
SOA	83	85	88	71	75	88

Table 2: Sentential task performance. See Section 3.1 for figures of merit (all in percentage form) and state-of-the-art references. The PLF results on msrvid and onwn2 are taken from Paperno et al. 2014.

The relative-length-difference test returns the following words as the ones that are most severely de-emphasized by C-PHRASE compared to C-BOW: *be, that, an, not, they, he, who, when, well, have*. Clearly, C-PHRASE is weighting down grammatical terms that tend to be context-agnostic, and will be accompanied, in phrases, by more context-informative content words. Indeed, the list of terms that are instead emphasized by C-PHRASE include such content-rich, monosemous words as *gnawing, smackdown, demographics*. This is confirmed by a POS-level analysis that indicates that the categories that are, on average, most de-emphasized by C-PHRASE are: determiners, modals, pronouns, prepositions and (more surprisingly) proper nouns. The ones that are, in relative terms, more emphasized are: *-ing* verb forms, plural and singular nouns, adjectives and their superlatives. While this reliance on content words to the detriment of grammatical terms is not always good for sentential tasks (*"not always good"* means something very different from *"always good"*!), the convincing comparative performance of C-PHRASE in such tasks suggests that the semantic effect of grammatical terms is in any case beyond the scope of current corpus-based models, and often not crucial to attain competitive results on typical benchmarks (think, e.g., of how little modals, one of the categories that C-PHRASE downplays the most, will matter when detecting paraphrases that are based on picture descriptions).

We also applied the length difference test to words in specific categories, finding similar patterns. For example, looking at *-ly* adverbs only, those that are de-emphasized the most by C-PHRASE are *recently, eventually, originally, notably* and *currently* – all adverbs denoting temporal factors or speaker attitude. On the other hand, the ones that C-PHRASE lengthens the most, relative to C-BOW, are *clinically, divinely, ecologically, noisily* and *theatrically*: all adverbs with more specific, content-word-like meanings, that are better captured by distributional methods, and are likely to have a bigger impact on tasks such as paraphrasing or entailment.

Effects of joint optimization at word and phrase levels As we have argued before, C-PHRASE is able to obtain good word representations presumably because it learns to predict how the context of a word changes in the presence of different collocates. To gain further insight into this claim, we looked at the nearest neighbours of some example terms, like *neural*, *network* and *neural network* (the latter, composed by addition) both in C-PHRASE and C-BOW. The results for this particular example can be appreciated in Table 3.

Interestingly, while for C-BOW we observe some confusion between the meaning of the individual words and the phrase, C-PHRASE seems to provide more orthogonal representations for the lexical items. For example, *neural* in C-

C-BOW			C-PHRASE		
neural	*network*	*neural network*	*neural*	*network*	*neural network*
neuronal	networks	network	neuronal	networks	network
neurons	superjanet4	neural	cortical	internetwork	neural
hopfield	backhaul	networks	connectionist	wans	perceptron
cortical	fiber-optic	hopfield	neurophysiological	network.	networks
connectionist	point-to-multipoint	packet-switched	sensorimotor	multicasting	hebbian
feed-forward	nsfnet	small-world	sensorimotor	nsfnet	neurons
feedforward	multi-service	local-area	neocortex	networking	neocortex
neuron	circuit-switched	superjanet4	electrophysiological	tymnet	connectionist
backpropagation	wide-area	neuronal	neurobiological	x.25	neuronal

Table 3: Nearest neighbours of *neural*, *network* and *neural network* both for C-BOW and C-PHRASE

BOW contains neighbours that fit well with *neural network*, like *hopfield*, *connectionist* and *feed-forward*. Conversely, *neural network* has neighbours that correspond to *network* like *local-area* and *packet-switched*. In contrast, C-PHRASE neighbours for *neural* are mostly related to the *brain* sense of the word, e.g., *cortical*, *neurophysiological*, etc. (with the only exception of *connectionist*). The first neighbour of *neural network*, excluding its own component words, quite sensibly, is *perceptron*.

5 Conclusion

We introduced C-PHRASE, a distributional semantic model that is trained on the task of predicting the contexts surrounding phrases at all levels of a hierarchical sentence parse, from single words to full sentences. Consequently, word vectors are induced by taking into account not only their contexts, but also how co-occurrence with other words within a syntactic constituent is affecting these contexts.

C-PHRASE vectors outperform state-of-the-art C-BOW vectors in a wide range of lexical tasks. Moreover, because of the way they are induced, when C-PHRASE vectors are summed, they produce sentence representations that are as good or better than those obtained with sophisticated composition methods.

C-PHRASE is a very parsimonious approach: The only major resource required, compared to a completely knowledge-free, unsupervised method, is an automated parse of the training corpus (but no syntactic labels are required, nor parsing at test time). C-PHRASE has only 3 hyperparameters and no composition-specific parameter to tune and store.

Having established a strong empirical baseline with this parsimonious approach, in future research we want to investigate the impact of possible extensions on both lexical and sentential tasks. When combining the vectors, either for induction or composition, we will try replacing plain addition with other operations, starting with something as simple as learning scalar weights for different words in a phrase (Mitchell and Lapata, 2010). We also intend to explore more systematic ways to incorporate supervised signals into learning, to fine-tune C-PHRASE vectors to specific tasks.

On the testing side, we are fascinated by the good performance of additive models, that (at test time, at least) do not take word order nor syntactic structure into account. We plan to perform a systematic analysis of both existing benchmarks and natural corpus data, both to assess the actual impact that such factors have on the aspects of meaning we are interested in (take two sentences in an entailment relation: how often does shuffling the words in them make it impossible to detect entailment?), and to construct new benchmarks that are more challenging for additive methods.

The C-PHRASE vectors described in this paper are made publicly available at: `http://clic.cimec.unitn.it/composes/`.

Acknowledgments

We thank Gemma Boleda and the anonymous reviewers for useful comments. We acknowledge ERC 2011 Starting Independent Research Grant n. 283554 (COMPOSES).

References

Eneko Agirre, Enrique Alfonseca, Keith Hall, Jana Kravalova, Marius Paşca, and Aitor Soroa. 2009. A study on similarity and relatedness using distributional and WordNet-based approaches. In *Proceedings of HLT-NAACL*, pages 19–27, Boulder, CO.

Eneko Agirre, Daniel Cer, Mona Diab, and Aitor Gonzalez-Agirre. 2012. SemEval-2012 Task 6: a pilot on semantic textual similarity. In *Proceedings of *SEM*, pages 385–393, Montreal, Canada.

Eneko Agirre, Daniel Cer, Mona Diab, Aitor Gonzalez-Agirre, and Weiwei Guo. 2013. *SEM 2013 shared task: Semantic Textual Similarity. In *Proceedings of *SEM*, pages 32–43, Atlanta, GA.

Abdulrahman Almuhareb. 2006. *Attributes in Lexical Acquisition*. Phd thesis, University of Essex.

Marco Baroni and Alessandro Lenci. 2010. Distributional Memory: A general framework for corpus-based semantics. *Computational Linguistics*, 36(4):673–721.

Marco Baroni and Roberto Zamparelli. 2010. Nouns are vectors, adjectives are matrices: Representing adjective-noun constructions in semantic space. In *Proceedings of EMNLP*, pages 1183–1193, Boston, MA.

Marco Baroni, Stefan Evert, and Alessandro Lenci, editors. 2008. *Bridging the Gap between Semantic Theory and Computational Simulations: Proceedings of the ESSLLI Workshop on Distributional Lexical Semantic*. FOLLI, Hamburg.

Marco Baroni, Raffaella Bernardi, and Roberto Zamparelli. 2014a. Frege in space: A program for compositional distributional semantics. *Linguistic Issues in Language Technology*, 9(6):5–110.

Marco Baroni, Georgiana Dinu, and Germán Kruszewski. 2014b. Don't count, predict! a systematic comparison of context-counting vs. context-predicting semantic vectors. In *Proceedings of ACL*, pages 238–247, Baltimore, MD.

Islam Beltagy, Stephen Roller, Gemma Boleda, Katrin Erk, and Raymond Mooney. 2014. UTexas: Natural language semantics using distributional semantics and probabilistic logic. In *Proceedings of SemEval*, pages 796–801, Dublin, Ireland, August.

William Blacoe and Mirella Lapata. 2012. A comparison of vector-based representations for semantic composition. In *Proceedings of EMNLP*, pages 546–556, Jeju Island, Korea.

Elia Bruni, Nam Khanh Tran, and Marco Baroni. 2014. Multimodal distributional semantics. *Journal of Artificial Intelligence Research*, 49:1–47.

Bob Coecke, Mehrnoosh Sadrzadeh, and Stephen Clark. 2010. Mathematical foundations for a compositional distributional model of meaning. *Linguistic Analysis*, 36:345–384.

James Curran and Marc Moens. 2002. Improvements in automatic thesaurus extraction. In *Proceedings of the ACL Workshop on Unsupervised Lexical Acquisition*, pages 59–66, Philadelphia, PA.

Ido Dagan, Bill Dolan, Bernardo Magnini, and Dan Roth. 2009. Recognizing textual entailment: rationale, evaluation and approaches. *Natural Language Engineering*, 15:459–476.

Georgiana Dinu, Nghia The Pham, and Marco Baroni. 2013. General estimation and evaluation of compositional distributional semantic models. In *Proceedings of ACL Workshop on Continuous Vector Space Models and their Compositionality*, pages 50–58, Sofia, Bulgaria.

Katrin Erk and Sebastian Padó. 2008. A structured vector space model for word meaning in context. In *Proceedings of EMNLP*, pages 897–906, Honolulu, HI.

Lev Finkelstein, Evgeniy Gabrilovich, Yossi Matias, Ehud Rivlin, Zach Solan, Gadi Wolfman, and Eytan Ruppin. 2002. Placing search in context: The concept revisited. *ACM Transactions on Information Systems*, 20(1):116–131.

Gregory Grefenstette. 1994. *Explorations in Automatic Thesaurus Discovery*. Kluwer, Boston, MA.

Emiliano Guevara. 2010. A regression model of adjective-noun compositionality in distributional semantics. In *Proceedings of the EMNLP GEMS Workshop*, pages 33–37, Uppsala, Sweden.

Zellig Harris. 1954. Distributional structure. *Word*, 10(2-3):1456–1162.

Samer Hassan and Rada Mihalcea. 2011. Semantic relatedness using salient semantic analysis. In *Proceedings of AAAI*, pages 884–889, San Francisco, CA.

Felix Hill, KyungHyun Cho, Sébastien Jean, Coline Devin, and Yoshua Bengio. 2014. Not all neural embeddings are born equal. In *Proceedings of the NIPS Learning Semantics Workshop*, Montreal, Canada. Published online: `https://sites.google.com/site/learningsemantics2014/`.

Nal Kalchbrenner and Phil Blunsom. 2013. Recurrent convolutional neural networks for discourse compositionality. In *Proceedings of ACL Workshop on Continuous Vector Space Models and their Compositionality*, pages 119–126, Sofia, Bulgaria.

Nal Kalchbrenner, Edward Grefenstette, and Phil Blunsom. 2014. A convolutional neural network for modelling sentences. In *Proceedings of ACL*, pages 655–665, Baltimore, MD.

George Karypis. 2003. CLUTO: A clustering toolkit. Technical Report 02-017, University of Minnesota Department of Computer Science.

Sophia Katrenko and Pieter Adriaans. 2008. Qualia structures and their impact on the concrete noun categorization task. In *Proceedings of the ESSLLI Workshop on Distributional Lexical Semantics*, pages 17–24, Hamburg, Germany.

Dan Klein and Christopher Manning. 2003. Accurate unlexicalized parsing. In *Proceedings of ACL*, pages 423–430, Sapporo, Japan.

Alice Lai and Julia Hockenmaier. 2014. Illinois-lh: A denotational and distributional approach to semantics. In *Proceedings of the 8th International Workshop on Semantic Evaluation (SemEval 2014)*, pages 329–334, Dublin, Ireland, August. Association for Computational Linguistics and Dublin City University.

Quoc V Le and Tomas Mikolov. 2014. Distributed representations of sentences and documents. *arXiv preprint arXiv:1405.4053*.

Omer Levy and Yoav Goldberg. 2014a. Dependency-based word embeddings. In *Proceedings of ACL (Volume 2: Short Papers)*, pages 302–308, Baltimore, Maryland.

Omer Levy and Yoav Goldberg. 2014b. Linguistic regularities in sparse and explicit word representations. In *Proceedings of CoNLL*, pages 171–180, Ann Arbor, MI.

Marco Marelli, Luisa Bentivogli, Marco Baroni, Raffaella Bernardi, Stefano Menini, and Roberto Zamparelli. 2014. SemEval-2014 Task 1: Evaluation of compositional distributional semantic models on full sentences through semantic relatedness and textual entailment. In *Proceedings of SemEval*, pages 1–8, Dublin, Ireland.

Oren Melamud, Ido Dagan, Jacob Goldberger, Idan Szpektor, and Deniz Yuret. 2014. Probabilistic modeling of joint-context in distributional similarity. In *Proceedings of CoNLL*, pages 181–190, Ann Arbor, MI.

Tomas Mikolov, Kai Chen, Greg Corrado, and Jeffrey Dean. 2013a. Efficient estimation of word representations in vector space. `http://arxiv.org/abs/1301.3781/`.

Tomas Mikolov, Ilya Sutskever, Kai Chen, Greg Corrado, and Jeff Dean. 2013b. Distributed representations of words and phrases and their compositionality. In *Proceedings of NIPS*, pages 3111–3119, Lake Tahoe, NV.

Tomas Mikolov, Wen-tau Yih, and Geoffrey Zweig. 2013c. Linguistic regularities in continuous space word representations. In *Proceedings of NAACL*, pages 746–751, Atlanta, Georgia.

Jeff Mitchell and Mirella Lapata. 2010. Composition in distributional models of semantics. *Cognitive Science*, 34(8):1388–1429.

Sebastian Padó and Mirella Lapata. 2007. Dependency-based construction of semantic space models. *Computational Linguistics*, 33(2):161–199.

Denis Paperno, Nghia The Pham, and Marco Baroni. 2014. A practical and linguistically-motivated approach to compositional distributional semantics. In *Proceedings of ACL*, pages 90–99, Baltimore, MD.

Jeffrey Pennington, Richard Socher, and Christopher Manning. 2014. Glove: Global vectors for word representation. In *Proceedings of EMNLP*, pages 1532–1543, Doha, Qatar.

Klaus Rothenhäusler and Hinrich Schütze. 2009. Unsupervised classification with dependency based word spaces. In *Proceedings of the EACL GEMS Workshop*, pages 17–24, Athens, Greece.

Herbert Rubenstein and John Goodenough. 1965. Contextual correlates of synonymy. *Communications of the ACM*, 8(10):627–633.

Richard Socher, Brody Huval, Christopher Manning, and Andrew Ng. 2012. Semantic compositionality through recursive matrix-vector spaces. In *Proceedings of EMNLP*, pages 1201–1211, Jeju Island, Korea.

Richard Socher, Alex Perelygin, Jean Wu, Jason Chuang, Christopher Manning, Andrew Ng, and Christopher Potts. 2013. Recursive deep models for semantic compositionality over a sentiment treebank. In *Proceedings of EMNLP*, pages 1631–1642, Seattle, WA.

Michael Tomasello. 2003. *Constructing a Language: A Usage-Based Theory of Language Acquisition*. Harvard University Press, Cambridge, MA.

Peter Turney and Patrick Pantel. 2010. From frequency to meaning: Vector space models of semantics. *Journal of Artificial Intelligence Research*, 37:141–188.

Peter Young, Alice Lai, Micah Hodosh, and Julia Hockenmaier. 2014. From image descriptions to visual denotations: New similarity metrics for semantic inference over event descriptions. *Transactions of the Association for Computational Linguistics*, 2:67–78.

Jiang Zhao, Tiantian Zhu, and Man Lan. 2014. Ecnu: One stone two birds: Ensemble of heterogenous measures for semantic relatedness and textual entailment. In *Proceedings of the 8th International Workshop on Semantic Evaluation (SemEval 2014)*, pages 271–277, Dublin, Ireland, August. Association for Computational Linguistics and Dublin City University.

Robust Subgraph Generation Improves Abstract Meaning Representation Parsing

Keenon Werling
Stanford University
keenon@stanford.edu

Gabor Angeli
Stanford University
angeli@stanford.edu

Christopher D. Manning
Stanford University
manning@stanford.edu

Abstract

The Abstract Meaning Representation (AMR) is a representation for open-domain rich semantics, with potential use in fields like event extraction and machine translation. Node generation, typically done using a simple dictionary lookup, is currently an important limiting factor in AMR parsing. We propose a small set of actions that derive AMR subgraphs by transformations on spans of text, which allows for more robust learning of this stage. Our set of construction actions generalize better than the previous approach, and can be learned with a simple classifier. We improve on the previous state-of-the-art result for AMR parsing, boosting end-to-end performance by 3 F_1 on both the LDC2013E117 and LDC2014T12 datasets.

1 Introduction

The Abstract Meaning Representation (AMR) (Banarescu et al., 2013) is a rich, graph-based language for expressing semantics over a broad domain. The formalism is backed by a large data-labeling effort, and it holds promise for enabling a new breed of natural language applications ranging from semantically aware MT to rich broad-domain QA over text-based knowledge bases. Figure 1 shows an example AMR for "he gleefully ran to his dog Rover," and we give a brief introduction to AMR in Section 2. This paper focuses on AMR parsing, the task of mapping a natural language sentence into an AMR graph.

We follow previous work (Flanigan et al., 2014) in dividing AMR parsing into two steps. The first step is *concept identification*, which generates AMR nodes from text, and which we'll refer to as *NER++* (Section 3.1). The second step is *relation identification*, which adds arcs to link these nodes into a fully connected AMR graph, which we'll call *SRL++* (Section 3.2).

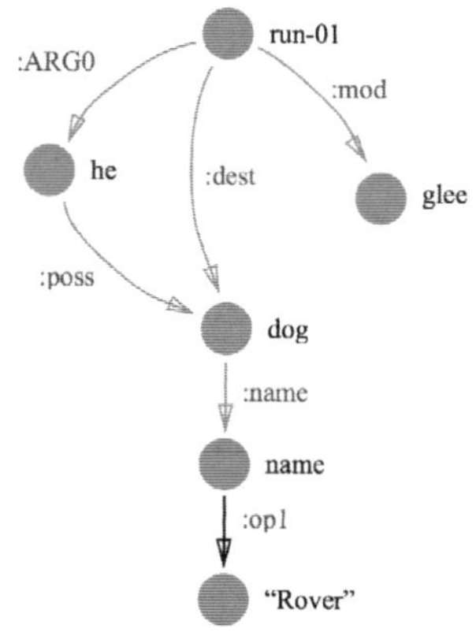

Figure 1: The AMR graph for *He gleefully ran to his dog Rover*. We show that improving the generation of low level subgraphs (e.g., *Rover* generating *name* $\xrightarrow{:op1}$ *"Rover"*) significantly improves end-to-end performance.

We observe that SRL++ is not the hard part of AMR parsing; rather, much of the difficulty in AMR is generating high accuracy concept subgraphs from the NER++ component. For example, when the existing AMR parser JAMR (Flanigan et al., 2014) is given a gold NER++ output, and must only perform SRL++ over given subgraphs it scores 80 F_1 – nearly the inter-annotator agreement of 83 F_1, and far higher than its end to end accuracy of 59 F_1.

SRL++ within AMR is *relatively* easy given a perfect NER++ output, because so much pressure is put on the output of NER++ to carry meaningful information. For example, there's a strong type-check feature for the existence and type of any arc just by looking at its end-points, and syntactic dependency features are very informative for removing any remaining ambiguity. If a system is con-

Proceedings of the 53rd Annual Meeting of the Association for Computational Linguistics and the 7th International Joint Conference on Natural Language Processing, pages 982–991,
Beijing, China, July 26-31, 2015.

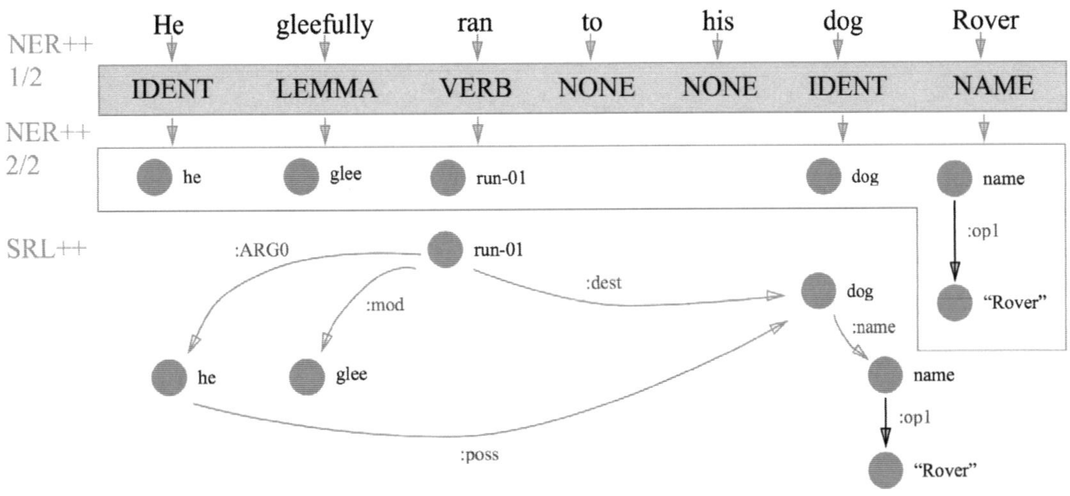

Figure 2: A graphical explanation of our method. We represent the derivation process for *He gleefully ran to his dog Rover*. First the tokens in the sentence are labeled with derivation actions, then these actions are used to generate AMR subgraphs, which are then stitched together to form a coherent whole.

sidering how to link the node *run-01* in Figure 1, the verb-sense frame for "run-01" leaves very little uncertainty for what we could assign as an *ARG0* arc. It must be a noun, which leaves either *he* or *dog*, and this is easily decided in favor of *he* by looking for an nsubj arc in the dependency parse.

The primary contribution of this paper is a novel approach to the NER++ task, illustrated in Figure 2. We notice that the subgraphs aligned to lexical items can often be generated from a small set of *generative actions* which generalize across tokens. For example, most verbs generate an AMR node corresponding to the verb sense of the appropriate PropBank frame – e.g., *run* generates *run-01* in Figure 1. This allows us to frame the NER++ task as the task of classifying one of a small number of *actions* for each token, rather than choosing a specific AMR subgraph for every token in the sentence.

Our approach to the end-to-end AMR parsing task is therefore as follows: we define an action space for generating AMR concepts, and create a classifier for classifying lexical items into one of these actions (Section 4). This classifier is trained from automatically generated alignments between the gold AMR trees and their associated sentences (Section 5), using an objective which favors alignment mistakes which are least harmful to the NER++ component. Finally, the concept subgraphs are combined into a coherent AMR parse using the maximum spanning connected subgraph algorithm of Flanigan et al. (2014).

We show that our approach provides a large boost to recall over previous approaches, and that end to end performance is improved from 59 to 62 *smatch* (an F_1 measure of correct AMR arcs; see Cai and Knight (2013)) when incorporated into the SRL++ parser of Flanigan et al. (2014). When evaluating the performance of our action classifier in isolation, we obtain an action classification accuracy of 84.1%.

2 The AMR Formalism

AMR is a language for expressing semantics as a rooted, directed, and potentially cyclic graph, where nodes represent concepts and arcs are relationships between concepts. AMR is based on neo-Davidsonian semantics, (Davidson, 1967; Parsons, 1990). The nodes (concepts) in an AMR graph do not have to be explicitly grounded in the source sentence, and while such an alignment is often generated to train AMR parsers, it is not provided in the training corpora. The semantics of nodes can represent lexical items (e.g., *dog*), sense tagged lexical items (e.g., *run-01*), type markers (e.g., *date-entity*), and a host of other phenomena.

The edges (relationships) in AMR describe one of a number of semantic relationships between concepts. The most salient of these is semantic role labels, such as the *ARG0* and *destination* arcs in Figure 2. However, often these arcs define

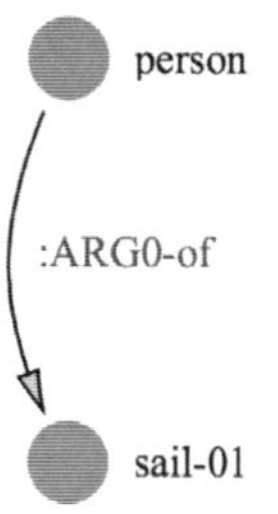

Figure 3: AMR representation of the word *sailor*, which is notable for breaking the word up into a self-contained multi-node unit unpacking the derivational morphology of the word.

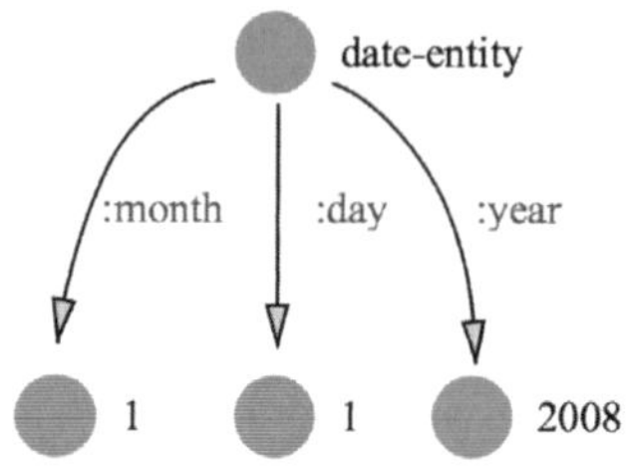

Figure 4: AMR representation of the span *January 1, 2008*, an example of how AMR can represent structured data by creating additional nodes such as *date-entity* to signify the presence of special structure.

a semantics more akin to syntactic dependencies (e.g., *mod* standing in for adjective and adverbial modification), or take on domain-specific meaning (e.g., the month, day, and year arcs of a *date-entity*).

To introduce AMR and its notation in more detail, we'll unpack the translation of the sentence "he gleefully ran to his dog Rover." We show in Figure 1 the interpretation of this sentence as an AMR graph.

The root node of the graph is labeled *run-01*, corresponding to the PropBank (Palmer et al., 2005) definition of the verb *ran*. *run-01* has an outgoing *ARG0* arc to a node *he*, with the usual PropBank semantics. The outgoing *mod* edge from *run-01* to *glee* takes a general purpose semantics corresponding to adjective, adverbial, or other modification of the governor by the dependent. We note that *run-01* has a *destination* arc to *dog*. The label for *destination* is taken from a finite set of special arc sense tags similar to the preposition senses found in (Srikumar, 2013). The last portion of the figure parses *dog* to a node which serves as a type marker similar to named entity types, and *Rover* into the larger subgraph indicating a concept with name "Rover."

2.1 AMR Subgraphs

The mapping from tokens of a sentence to AMR nodes is not one-to-one. A single token or span of tokens can generate a *subgraph* of AMR consisting of multiple nodes. These subgraphs can logically be considered the expression of a single concept, and are useful to treat as such (e.g., see Section 3.1).

Many of these multi-node subgraphs capture structured data such as time expressions, as in Figure 4. In this example, a *date-entity* node is created to signify that this cluster of nodes is part of a structured sub-component representing a date, where the nodes and arcs within the component have specific semantics. This illustrates a broader recurring pattern in AMR: an artificial node may, based on its title, have expected children with special semantics. A particularly salient example of this pattern is the *name* node (see *"Rover"* in Figure 1) which signifies that all outgoing arcs with label *op* comprise the tokens of a name object.

The ability to decouple the meaning representation of a lexical item from its surface form allows for rich semantic interpretations of certain concepts in a sentence. For example, the token *sailor* is represented in Figure 3 by a concept graph representing a person who performs the action *sail-01*. Whereas often the AMR node aligned to a span of text is a straightforward function of the text, these cases remain difficult to capture in a principled way beyond memorizing mappings between tokens and subgraphs.

3 Task Decomposition

To the best of our knowledge, the JAMR parser is the only published end-to-end AMR parser at the time of publication. An important insight in JAMR is that AMR parsing can be broken into two distinct tasks: (1) **NER++** (*concept identification*): the task of interpreting what entities are being referred to in the text, realized by generating the best AMR subgraphs for a given set of tokens, and (2) **SRL++** (*relation identification*): the task of discovering what relationships exist between entities, realized by taking the disjoint subgraphs generated by NER++ and creating a fully-connected graph. We describe both tasks in more detail below.

3.1 NER++

Much of the difficulty of parsing to AMR lies in generating local subgraphs representing the meaning of token spans. For instance, the formalism implicitly demands rich notions of NER, lemmatization, word sense disambiguation, number normalization, and temporal parsing; among others. To illustrate, a correct parse of the sentence in Figure 2 requires lemmatization (*gleefully* $\rightarrow$ *glee*), word sense tagging (*run* $\rightarrow$ *run-01*), and open domain NER (i.e., *Rover*), Furthermore, many of the generated subgraphs (e.g., *sailor* in Figure 3) have rich semantics beyond those produced by standard NLP systems.

Formally, NER++ is the task of generating a disjoint set of subgraphs representing the meanings of localized spans of words in the sentence. For NER++, JAMR uses a simple Viterbi sequence model to directly generate AMR-subgraphs from memorized mappings of text spans to subgraphs. This paper's main contribution, presented in Section 4, is to make use of generative *actions* to generate these subgraphs, rather than appealing to a memorized mapping.

3.2 SRL++

The second stage of the AMR decomposition consists of generating a coherent graph from the set of disjoint subgraphs produced by NER++. Whereas NER++ produces subgraphs whose arcs encode domain-specific semantics (e.g., *month*), the arcs in SRL++ tend to have generally applicable semantics. For example, the many arcs encode conventional semantic roles (e.g., *ARG0* and *destination* in Figure 2), or a notion akin to syntactic dependencies (e.g., *mod* and *poss* in Figure 2). For SRL++, JAMR uses a variation of the maximum spanning connected graph algorithm augmented by dual decomposition to impose linguistically motivated constraints on a maximum likelihood objective.

4 A Novel NER++ Method

The training sets currently available for AMR are not large. To illustrate, 38% of the words in the LDC2014E113 dev set are unseen during training time. With training sets this small, memorization-based approaches are extremely brittle. We remove much of the necessity to memorize mappings in NER++ by partitioning the AMR subgraph search space in terms of the actions needed to derive a node from its aligned token. At test time we do a sequence labeling of input tokens with these actions, and then deterministically derive the AMR subgraphs from spans of tokens by applying the transformation decreed by their actions. We explain in Section 4.1 how exactly we manage this partition, and in Section 4.3 how we create training data from existing resources to setup and train an action-type classifier.

4.1 Derivation actions

We partition the AMR subgraph space into a set of 9 actions, each corresponding to an action that will be taken by the NER++ system if a token receives this classification.

IDENTITY This action handles the common case that the title of the node corresponding to a token is identical to the source token. To execute the action, we take the lowercased version of the token to be the title of the corresponding node.

NONE This action corresponds to ignoring this token, in the case that the node should not align to any corresponding AMR fragment.

VERB This action captures the verb-sense disambiguation feature of AMR. To execute on a token, we find the most similar verb in PropBank based on Jaro-Winkler distance, and adopt its most frequent sense. This serves as a reasonable baseline for word sense disambiguation, although of course accuracy would be expected to improve if a sophisticated system were incorporated.

VALUE This action interprets a token by its integer value. The AMR representation is sensitive to the difference between a node with a title of *5* (the integer value) and "5" or "five" – the string value. This is a rare action, but is nonetheless distinct from any of the other classes. We execute this action by extracting an integer value with a regex based number normalizer, and using the result as the title of the generated node.

LEMMA AMR often performs stemming and part-of-speech transformations on the source token in generating a node. For example, we get *glee* from *gleefully*. We capture this by a **LEMMA** action, which is executed by using the lemma of the source token as the generated node title. Note that this does not capture all lemmatizations, as there are often discrepancies between the lemma generated by the lemmatizer and the correct AMR lemma.

NAME AMR often references names with a special structured data type: the *name* construction. For example, *Rover* in Figure 1. We can capture this phenomenon on unseen names by attaching a created *name* node to the top of a span.

PERSON A variant of the NAME action, this action produces a subgraph identical to the NAME action, but adds a node *person* as a parent. This is, in effect, a *name* node with an implicit entity type of person. Due to discrepancies between the output of our named entity tagger and the richer AMR named entity ontology, we only apply this tag to the person named entity tag.

DATE The most frequent of the structured data type in the data, after *name*, is the *date-entity* construction (for an example see Figure 4). We deterministically take the output of SUTime (Chang and Manning, 2012) and convert it into the *date-entity* AMR representation.

DICT This class serves as a back-off for the other classes, implementing an approach similar to Flanigan et al. (2014). In particular, we memorize a simple mapping from spans of text (such as *sailor*) to their corresponding most frequently aligned AMR subgraphs in the training data (i.e., the graph in Figure 3). See Section 5 for details on the alignment process. At test time we can do a lookup in this dictionary for any element that gets labeled with a **DICT** action. If an entry is not found in the mapping, we back off to the second most probable class proposed by the classifier.

It is worth observing at this point that our actions derive much of their power from the similarity between English words and their AMR counterparts; creating an analogue of these actions for other languages remains an open problem.

4.2 Action Reliability

In many cases, multiple actions could yield the same subgraph when applied to a node. In this section we introduce a method for resolving this ambiguity based on comparing the reliability with which actions generate the correct subgraph, and discuss implications.

Even given a perfect action classification for a token, certain action executions can introduce

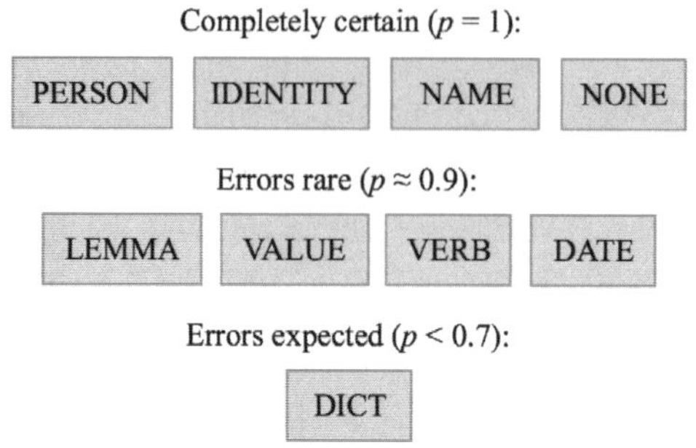

Figure 5: Reliability of each action. The top row are actions which are deterministic; the second row occasionally produce errors. DICT is the least preferred action, with a relatively high error rate.

errors. Some of our actions are entirely deterministic in their conversion from the word to the AMR subgraph (e.g., IDENTITY), but others are prone to making mistakes in this conversion (e.g., VERB, DICT). We define the notion of *action reliability* as the probability of deriving the correct node from a span of tokens, conditioned on having chosen the correct action.

To provide a concrete example, our dictionary lookup classifier predicts the correct AMR subgraph 67% of the time on the dev set. We therefore define the reliability of the **DICT** action as 0.67. In contrast to **DICT**, correctly labeling a node as **IDENTITY**, **NAME**, **PERSON**, and **NONE** have action reliability of 1.0, since there is no ambiguity in the node generation once one of those actions have been selected, and we are guaranteed to generate the correct node given the correct action.

We can therefore construct a hierarchy of reliability (Figure 5) – all else being equal, we prefer to generate actions from higher in the hierarchy, as they are more likely to produce the correct subgraph. This hierarchy is useful in resolving ambiguity throughout our system. During the creation of training data for our classifier (Section 4.3) from our aligner, when two actions could both generate the aligned AMR node we prefer the more reliable one. In turn, in our aligner we bias alignments towards those which generating more reliable action sequences as training data (see Section 5).

The primary benefit of this action-based NER++ approach is that we can reduce the usage of low reliability actions, like **DICT**. The approach taken in Flanigan et al. (2014) can be

Action	# Tokens	% Total
NONE	41538	36.2
DICT	30027	26.1
IDENTITY	19034	16.6
VERB	11739	10.2
LEMMA	5029	4.5
NAME	4537	3.9
DATE	1418	1.1
PERSON	1336	1.1
VALUE	122	0.1

Table 1: Distribution of action types in the proxy section of the newswire section of the LDC2014T12 dataset, generated from automatically aligned data.

Input token; word embedding
Left+right token / bigram
Token length indicator
Token starts with "non"
POS; Left+right POS / bigram
Dependency parent token / POS
Incoming dependency arc
Bag of outgoing dependency arcs
Number of outgoing dependency arcs
Max Jaro-Winkler to any lemma in PropBank
Output tag of the **VERB** action if applied
Output tag of the **DICT** action if applied
NER; Left+right NER / bigram
Capitalization
Incoming prep_* or appos + parent has NER
Token is pronoun
Token is part of a coref chain
Token pronoun and part of a coref chain

Table 2: The features for the NER++ maxent classifier.

thought of as equivalent to classifying every token as the **DICT** action.

We analyze the empirical distribution of actions in our automatically aligned corpus in Table 1. The cumulative frequency of the non-**DICT** actions is striking: we can generate 74% of the tokens with high reliability ($p \geq 0.9$) actions. In this light, it is unsurprising that our results demonstrate a large gain in recall on the test set.

4.3 Training the Action Classifier

Given a set of AMR training data, in the form of *(graph, sentence)* pairs, we first induce alignments from the graph nodes to the sentence (see Section 5). Formally, for every node n_i in the AMR graph, alignment gives us some token s_j (at the jth index in the sentence) that we believe generated the node n_i.

Then, for each action type, we can ask whether or not that action type is able to take token s_j and correctly generate n_i. For concreteness, imagine the token s_j is *running*, and the node n_i has the title *run-01*. The two action types we find that are able to correctly generate this node are DICT and VERB. We choose the most reliable action type of those available (see Figure 5) to generate the observed node – in this case, VERB.

In cases where an AMR subgraph is generated from multiple tokens, we assign the action label to each token which generates the subgraph. Each of these tokens are added to the training set; at test time, we collapse sequences of adjacent identical action labels, and apply the action once to the resulting token span.

Inducing the most reliable action (according to the alignments) for every token in the training corpus provides a supervised training set for our action classifier, with some noise introduced by the automatically generated alignments. We then train a simple maxent classifier[1] to make action decisions at each node. At test time, the classifier takes as input a pair $\langle i, S \rangle$, where i is the index of the token in the input sentence, and S is a sequence tokens representing the source sentence. It then uses the features in Table 2 to predict the actions to take at that node.

5 Automatic Alignment of Training Data

AMR training data is in the form of bi-text, where we are given a set of (sentence, graph) pairs, with no explicit alignments between them. We would like to induce a mapping from each node in the AMR graph to the token it represents. It is perfectly possible for multiple nodes to align to the same token – this is the case with *sailors*, for instance.

It is not possible, within our framework, to represent a single node being sourced from multiple tokens. Note that a subgraph can consist of many individual nodes; in cases where a subgraph should align to multiple tokens, we generate an alignment from the subgraph's nodes to the associated tokens in the sentence. It is empirically very rare for a subgraph to have more nodes than the token span it should align to.

There have been two previous attempts at producing automatic AMR alignments. The first was

[1] A sequence model was tried and showed no improvement over a simple maxent classifier.

published as a component of JAMR, and used a rule-based approach to perform alignments. This was shown to work well on the sample of 100 hand-labeled sentences used to develop the system. Pourdamghani et al. (2014) approached the alignment problem in the framework of the IBM alignment models. They rendered AMR graphs as text, and then used traditional machine translation alignment techniques to generate an alignment.

We propose a novel alignment method, since our decomposition of the AMR node generation process into a set of actions provides an additional objective for the aligner to optimize, in addition to the accuracy of the alignment itself. We would like to produce the most *reliable* sequence of actions for the NER++ model to train from, where reliable is taken in the sense defined in Section 4.2. To give an example, a sequence of all **DICT** actions could generate any AMR graph, but is very low reliability. A sequence of all **IDENTITY** actions could only generate one set of nodes, but does it with absolute certainty.

We formulate this objective as a Boolean LP problem. Let $\mathbf{Q}$ be a matrix in $\{0,1\}^{|\mathbf{N}|\times|\mathbf{S}|}$ of Boolean constrained variables, where $\mathbf{N}$ are the nodes in an AMR graph, and $\mathbf{S}$ are the tokens in the sentence. The meaning of $\mathbf{Q}_{i,j} = \mathbb{1}$ can be interpreted as node n_i having being aligned to token s_j. Furthermore, let $\mathbf{V}$ be a matrix $\mathcal{T}^{|\mathbf{N}|\times|\mathbf{S}|}$, where $\mathcal{T}$ is the set of NER++ actions from Section 4. Each matrix element $\mathbf{V}_{i,j}$ is assigned the most reliable action which would generate node n_i from token s_j. We would like to maximize the probability of the actions collectively generating a perfect set of nodes. This can be formulated linearly by maximizing the log-likelihood of the actions. Let the function $\text{REL}(l)$ be the reliability of action l (probability of generating intended node). Our objective can then be formulated as follows:

$$\max_{\mathbf{Q}} \quad \sum_{i,j} \mathbf{Q}_{i,j}\left[\log(\text{REL}(\mathbf{V}_{i,j})) + \alpha\mathcal{E}_{i,j}\right] \tag{1}$$

$$\text{s.t.} \quad \sum_{j} \mathbf{Q}_{i,j} = 1 \quad \forall i \tag{2}$$

$$\mathbf{Q}_{k,j} + \mathbf{Q}_{l,j} \leq 1 \quad \forall k,l,j;\ n_k \not\leftrightarrow n_l \tag{3}$$

where $\mathcal{E}$ is the Jaro-Winkler similarity between the title of the node i and the token j, α is a hyperparameter (set to 0.8 in our experiments), and the operator $\not\leftrightarrow$ denotes that two nodes in the AMR graph are both not adjacent and do not have the same title.

The constraint (2), combined with the binary constraint on $\mathbf{Q}$, ensures that every node in the graph is aligned to exactly one token in the source sentence. The constraint (3) ensures that only adjacent nodes or nodes that share a title can refer to the same token.

The objective value penalizes alignments which map to the unreliable DICT tag, while rewarding alignments with high overlap between the title of the node and the token. Note that most incorrect alignments fall into the DICT class by default, as no other action could generate the correct AMR subgraph. Therefore, if there exists an alignment that would consume the token using another action, the optimization prefers that alignment. The Jaro-Winkler similarity term, in turn, serves as a tie-breaker between equally (un)reliable alignments.

There are many packages which can solve this Boolean LP efficiently. We used Gurobi (Gurobi Optimization, 2015). Given a matrix $\mathbf{Q}$ that maximizes our objective, we can decode our solved alignment as follows: for each i, align n_i to the j s.t. $\mathbf{Q}_{i,j} = 1$. By our constraints, exactly one such j must exist.

6 Related Work

Prior work in AMR and related formalisms include Jones et al. (2012), and Flanigan et al. (2014). Jones et al. (2012), motivated by applications in Machine Translation, proposed a graphical semantic meaning representation that predates AMR, but is intimately related. They propose a hyper-edge replacement grammar (HRG) approach to parsing into and out of this graphical semantic form. Flanigan et al. (2014) forms the basis of the approach of this paper. Their system introduces the two-stage approach we use: they implement a rule-based alignment to learn a mapping from tokens to subgraphs, and train a variant of a maximum spanning tree parser adapted to graphs and with additional constraints for their relation identifications (SRL++) component. Wang et al. (2015) uses a transition based algorithm to transform dependency trees into AMR parses. They achieve 64/62/63 P/R/F_1 with contributions roughly orthogonal to our own. Their transformation action set could be easily augmented by the robust subgraph generation we propose here, although we leave this to future work.

Beyond the connection of our work with Flanigan et al. (2014), we note that the NER++ component of AMR encapsulates a number of lexical NLP tasks. These include named entity recognition (Nadeau and Sekine, 2007; Finkel et al., 2005), word sense disambiguation (Yarowsky, 1995; Banerjee and Pedersen, 2002), lemmatization, and a number of more domain specific tasks. For example, a full understanding of AMR requires normalizing temporal expressions (Verhagen et al., 2010; Strötgen and Gertz, 2010; Chang and Manning, 2012).

In turn, the SRL++ facet of AMR takes many insights from semantic role labeling (Gildea and Jurafsky, 2002; Punyakanok et al., 2004; Srikumar, 2013; Das et al., 2014) to capture the relations between verbs and their arguments. In addition, many of the arcs in AMR have nearly syntactic interpretations (e.g., *mod* for adjective/adverb modification, *op* for compound noun expressions). These are similar to representations used in syntactic dependency parsing (de Marneffe and Manning, 2008; McDonald et al., 2005; Buchholz and Marsi, 2006).

More generally, parsing to a semantic representation is has been explored in depth for when the representation is a logical form (Kate et al., 2005; Zettlemoyer and Collins, 2005; Liang et al., 2011). Recent work has applied semantic parsing techniques to representations beyond lambda calculus expressions. For example, work by Berant et al. (2014) parses text into a formal representation of a biological process. Hosseini et al. (2014) solves algebraic word problems by parsing them into a structured meaning representation. In contrast to these approaches, AMR attempts to capture open domain semantics over arbitrary text.

Interlingua (Mitamura et al., 1991; Carbonell et al., 1999; Levin et al., 1998) are an important inspiration for decoupling the semantics of the AMR language from the surface form of the text being parsed; although, AMR has a self-admitted English bias.

7 Results

We present improvements in end-to-end AMR parsing on two datasets using our NER++ component. Action type classifier accuracy on an automatically aligned corpus and alignment accuracy on a small hand-labeled corpus are also reported.

Dataset	System	P	R	F_1
2014T12	JAMR	**67.1**	53.2	59.3
	Our System	66.6	**58.3**	**62.2**
2013E117	JAMR	**66.9**	52.9	59.1
	Our System	65.9	**59.0**	**62.3**

Table 3: Results on two AMR datasets for JAMR and our NER++ embedded in the JAMR SRL++ component. Note that recall is consistently higher across both datasets, with only a small loss in precision.

7.1 End-to-end AMR Parsing

We evaluate our NER++ component in the context of end-to-end AMR parsing on two corpora: the newswire section of LDC2014T12 and the split given in Flanigan et al. (2014) of LDC2013E117, both consisting primarily of newswire. We compare two systems: the JAMR parser (Flanigan et al., 2014),[2] and the JAMR SRL++ component with our NER++ approach.

AMR parsing accuracy is measured with a metric called *smatch* (Cai and Knight, 2013), which stands for "s(emantic) match." The metric is the F_1 of a best-match between triples implied by the target graph, and triples in the parsed graph – that is, the set of (parent, edge, child) triples in the graph.

Our results are given in Table 3. We report much higher recall numbers on both datasets, with only small ($\leq$ 1 point) loss in precision. This is natural considering our approach. A better NER++ system allows for more correct AMR subgraphs to be generated – improving recall – but does not in itself necessarily improve the accuracy of the SRL++ system it is integrated in.

7.2 Component Accuracy

We evaluate our aligner on a small set of 100 hand-labeled alignments, and evaluate our NER++ classifier on automatically generated alignments over the whole corpus,

On a hand-annotated dataset of 100 AMR parses from the LDC2014T12 corpus,[3] our aligner achieves an accuracy of **83.2**. This is a measurement of the percentage of AMR nodes that are aligned to the correct token in their source sentence. Note that this is a different metric than the

[2]Available at `https://github.com/jflanigan/jamr`.

[3]Our dataset is publicly available at `http://nlp.stanford.edu/projects/amr`

precision/recall of prior work on alignments, and is based on both a different alignment dataset and subtly different alignment annotation scheme. In particular, we require that every AMR node aligns to some token in the sentence, which forces the system to always align nodes, even when unsure. A standard semantics and annotation guideline for AMR alignment is left for future work; our accuracy should be considered only an informal metric.

We find our informativeness-based alignment objective slightly improves end-to-end performance when compared to the rule-based approach of (Flanigan et al., 2014), improving F_1 by roughly 1 point (64/59/61 P/R/F_1 to 65/59/62 P/R/F_1).

On the automatic alignments over the LDC2014T12 corpus, our action classifier achieved a test accuracy of **0.841**. The classifier's most common class of mistakes are incorrect **DICT** classifications. It is reassuring that some of these errors can be recovered from by the naïve dictionary lookup finding the correct mapping.

The **DICT** action lookup table achieved an accuracy of **0.67**. This is particularly impressive given that our model moves many of the difficult semantic tasks onto the **DICT** tag, and that this lookup does not make use of any learning beyond a simple count of observed span to subgraph mappings.

8 Conclusion

We address a key challenge in AMR parsing: the task of generating subgraphs from lexical items in the sentence. We show that a simple classifier over *actions* which generate these subgraphs improves end-to-end recall for AMR parsing with only a small drop in precision, leading to an overall gain in F_1. A clear direction of future work is improving the coverage of the defined actions. For example, a richer lemmatizer could shift the burden of lemmatizing unknown words into the AMR lemma semantics and away from the dictionary lookup component. We hope our decomposition provides a useful framework to guide future work in NER++ and AMR in general.

Acknowledgments

We thank the anonymous reviewers for their thoughtful feedback. Stanford University gratefully acknowledges the support of the Defense Advanced Research Projects Agency (DARPA) Deep Exploration and Filtering of Text (DEFT) Program under Air Force Research Laboratory (AFRL) contract no. FA8750-13-2-0040. Any opinions, findings, and conclusion or recommendations expressed in this material are those of the authors and do not necessarily reflect the view of the DARPA, AFRL, or the US government.

References

Laura Banarescu, Claire Bonial, Shu Cai, Madalina Georgescu, Kira Griffitt, Ulf Hermjakob, Kevin Knight, Philipp Koehn, Martha Palmer, and Nathan Schneider. 2013. Abstract meaning representation for sembanking. *Proc. Linguistic Annotation Workshop*.

Satanjeev Banerjee and Ted Pedersen. 2002. An adapted Lesk algorithm for word sense disambiguation using wordnet. In *Computational linguistics and intelligent text processing*.

Jonathan Berant, Vivek Srikumar, Pei-Chun Chen, Brad Huang, Christopher D Manning, Abby Vander Linden, Brittany Harding, and Peter Clark. 2014. Modeling biological processes for reading comprehension. In *Proc. EMNLP*.

Sabine Buchholz and Erwin Marsi. 2006. CONLL-X shared task on multilingual dependency parsing. In *Proceedings of the Tenth Conference on Computational Natural Language Learning*, pages 149–164. Association for Computational Linguistics.

Shu Cai and Kevin Knight. 2013. Smatch: an evaluation metric for semantic feature structures. In *ACL (2)*, pages 748–752.

Jaime G Carbonell, Teruko Mitamura, and Eric H Nyberg. 1999. The KANT perspective: A critique of pure transfer (and pure interlingua, pure statistics,...).

Angel Chang and Chris Manning. 2012. SUTIME: a library for recognizing and normalizing time expressions. In *Language Resources and Evaluation*.

Dipanjan Das, Desai Chen, André FT Martins, Nathan Schneider, and Noah A Smith. 2014. Frame-semantic parsing. *Computational Linguistics*, 40(1):9–56.

Donald Davidson. 1967. The logical form of action sentences. In Nicholas Rescher, editor, *The Logic of Decision and Action*, pages 81–120. University of Pittsburgh Press, Pittsburgh, PA.

Marie-Catherine de Marneffe and Christopher D. Manning. 2008. The Stanford typed dependencies representation. In *Coling 2008: Proceedings of the workshop on Cross-Framework and Cross-Domain Parser Evaluation*.

Jenny Rose Finkel, Trond Grenager, and Christopher Manning. 2005. Incorporating non-local information into information extraction systems by Gibbs sampling. In *ACL*.

Jeffrey Flanigan, Sam Thomson, Jaime Carbonell, Chris Dyer, and Noah A Smith. 2014. A discriminative graph-based parser for the abstract meaning representation. In *ACL*.

Daniel Gildea and Daniel Jurafsky. 2002. Automatic labeling of semantic roles. *Computational linguistics*, 28(3):245–288.

Inc. Gurobi Optimization. 2015. Gurobi optimizer reference manual.

Mohammad Javad Hosseini, Hannaneh Hajishirzi, Oren Etzioni, and Nate Kushman. 2014. Learning to solve arithmetic word problems with verb categorization. In *EMNLP*.

Bevan Jones, Jacob Andreas, Daniel Bauer, Karl Moritz Hermann, and Kevin Knight. 2012. Semantics-based machine translation with hyperedge replacement grammars. In *COLING*, pages 1359–1376.

Rohit J. Kate, Yuk Wah Wong, and Raymond J. Mooney. 2005. Learning to transform natural to formal languages. In *AAAI*, Pittsburgh, PA.

Lori S Levin, Donna Gates, Alon Lavie, and Alex Waibel. 1998. An interlingua based on domain actions for machine translation of task-oriented dialogues. In *ICSLP*, volume 98, pages 1155–1158.

P. Liang, M. I. Jordan, and D. Klein. 2011. Learning dependency-based compositional semantics. In *ACL*.

Ryan McDonald, Koby Crammer, and Fernando Pereira. 2005. Online large-margin training of dependency parsers. In *ACL*, Morristown, NJ, USA.

Teruko Mitamura, Eric H Nyberg, and Jaime G Carbonell. 1991. An efficient interlingua translation system for multi-lingual document production. *Proceedings of Machine Translation Summit III*.

David Nadeau and Satoshi Sekine. 2007. A survey of named entity recognition and classification. *Lingvisticae Investigationes*, 30(1):3–26.

Martha Palmer, Daniel Gildea, and Paul Kingsbury. 2005. The proposition bank: An annotated corpus of semantic roles. *Computational linguistics*, 31(1):71–106.

Terence Parsons. 1990. *Events in the Semantics of English: A study in subatomic semantics*. MIT Press, Cambridge, MA.

Nima Pourdamghani, Yang Gao, Ulf Hermjakob, and Kevin Knight. 2014. Aligning english strings with abstract meaning representation graphs. In *EMNLP*.

Vasin Punyakanok, Dan Roth, Wen-tau Yih, and Dav Zimak. 2004. Semantic role labeling via integer linear programming inference. In *Proceedings of the 20th international conference on Computational Linguistics*, page 1346. Association for Computational Linguistics.

Vivek Srikumar. 2013. *The semantics of role labeling*. Ph.D. thesis, University of Illinois at Urbana-Champaign.

Jannik Strötgen and Michael Gertz. 2010. Heideltime: High quality rule-based extraction and normalization of temporal expressions. In *Proceedings of the 5th International Workshop on Semantic Evaluation*, Sem-Eval.

Marc Verhagen, Roser Sauri, Tommaso Caselli, and James Pustejovsky. 2010. Semeval-2010 task 13: TempEval-2. In *Proceedings of the 5th International Workshop on Semantic Evaluation*, Uppsala, Sweden.

Chuan Wang, Nianwen Xue, and Sameer Pradhan. 2015. A transition-based algorithm for amr parsing. In *NAACL-HLT*.

David Yarowsky. 1995. Unsupervised word sense disambiguation rivaling supervised methods. In *ACL*.

Luke S. Zettlemoyer and Michael Collins. 2005. Learning to map sentences to logical form: Structured classification with probabilistic categorial grammars. In *UAI*. AUAI Press.

Environment-Driven Lexicon Induction for High-Level Instructions

Dipendra K. Misra* — *dkm@cs.cornell.edu*
Kejia Tao* — *kt454@cornell.edu*
Percy Liang** — *pliang@cs.stanford.edu*
Ashutosh Saxena* — *asaxena@cs.cornell.edu*

* Department of Computer Science, Cornell University
**Department of Computer Science, Stanford University

Abstract

We focus on the task of interpreting complex natural language instructions to a robot, in which we must ground high-level commands such as *microwave the cup* to low-level actions such as grasping. Previous approaches that learn a lexicon during training have inadequate coverage at test time, and pure search strategies cannot handle the exponential search space. We propose a new hybrid approach that leverages the environment to induce new lexical entries at test time, even for new verbs. Our semantic parsing model jointly reasons about the text, logical forms, and environment over multi-stage instruction sequences. We introduce a new dataset and show that our approach is able to successfully ground new verbs such as *distribute, mix, arrange* to complex logical forms, each containing up to four predicates.

1 Introduction

The task of mapping natural language instructions to actions for a robot has been gaining momentum in recent years (Artzi and Zettlemoyer, 2013; Tellex et al., 2011; Misra et al., 2014; Bollini et al., 2011; Guadarrama et al., 2013; Matuszek et al., 2012b; Fasola and Mataric, 2013). We are particularly interested in instructions containing verbs such as "*microwave*" denoting high-level concepts, which correspond to more than 10 low-level symbolic actions such as `grasp`. In this setting, it is common to find new verbs requiring new concepts at test time. For example, in Figure 1, suppose that we have never seen the verb "*fill*". Can we impute the correct interpretation, and moreover seize the opportunity to learn what "*fill*" means in a way that generalizes to future instructions?

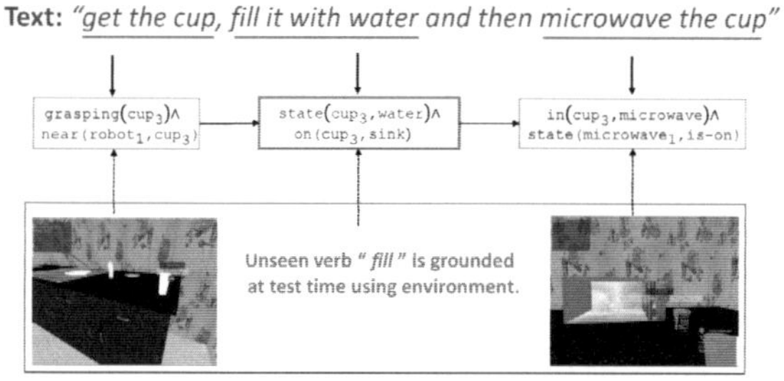

Figure 1: A lexicon learned on the training data cannot possibly cover all the verb-concept mappings needed at test time. Our algorithm learns the meaning of new verbs (e.g., "*fill*") using the environment context.

Previous work in semantic parsing handles lexical coverage in one of two ways. Kwiatkowski et al. (2010) induces a highly constrained CCG lexicon capable of mapping words to complex logical forms, but it would have to skip new words (which in Figure 1 would lead to microwaving an empty cup). Others (Berant and Liang, 2014) take a freer approach by performing a search over logical forms, which can handle new words, but the logical forms there are much simpler than the ones we consider.

In this paper, we present an hybrid approach that uses a lexicon to represent complex concepts but also strongly leverages the environment to guide the search space. The environment can provide helpful cues in several ways:

- Only a few environments are likely for a given scenario—e.g., the text is unlikely to ask the robot to microwave an empty cup or put books on the floor.
- The logical form of one segment of text constrains that of the next segment—e.g., the text is unlikely to ask the robot to pick a cup and then put it back immediately in the same spot.

We show that this environment context provides

Proceedings of the 53rd Annual Meeting of the Association for Computational Linguistics and the 7th International Joint Conference on Natural Language Processing, pages 992–1002,
Beijing, China, July 26-31, 2015.

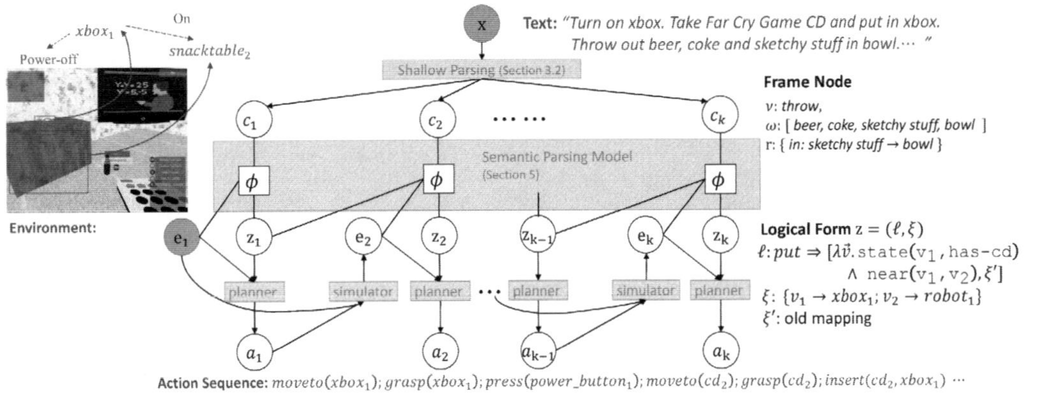

Figure 2: Graphical model overview: we first deterministically shallow parse the text x into a control flow graph consisting of shallow structures $\{c_i\}$. Given an initial environment e_1, our semantic parsing model maps these frame nodes to logical forms $\{z_i\}$ representing the postconditions. From this, a planner and simulator generate the action sequences $\{a_i\}$ and resulting environments $\{e_i\}$.

a signal for inducing new lexical entries that map previously unseen verbs to novel concepts. In the example in Figure 1, the algorithm learns that microwaving an empty cup is unlikely and this suggests that the verb *"fill"* must map to actions that end up making the cup not empty.

Another contribution of this paper is using postconditions as logical forms rather than actions, as in previous work (Artzi and Zettlemoyer, 2013; Misra et al., 2014). Postconditions not only reduce the search space of logical forms, but are also a more natural representation of verbs. We define a conditional random field (CRF) model over postconditions, and use a planner to convert postconditions into action sequences and a simulator to generate new environments.

At test time, we use the lexicon induced from the training data, but also perform an environment-guided search over logical forms to induce new lexical entries on-the-fly. If the predicted action sequence uses a new lexical entry generated by the search, it is added to the lexicon, where it can be reused in subsequent test examples.

We evaluate our algorithm on a new corpus containing text commands for a household robot. The two key findings of our experiments are: First, the environment and task context contain enough information to allow us to learn lexical entries for new verbs such as *"distribute"* and *"mix"* with complex semantics. Second, using both lexical entries generated by a test-time search and those from the lexicon induced by the training data outperforms the two individual approaches. This suggests that environment context can help alleviate the problem of having a limited lexicon for grounded language acquisition.

2 Problem Statement

At training time, we are given a set of examples $D = \{(x^{(m)}, e^{(m)}, a^{(m)}, \pi^{(m)})\}_{m=1}^{M}$, where $x^{(m)}$ is a text containing natural language instructions, $e^{(m)}$ is an initial environment, $a^{(m)}$ is a human-annotated sequence of actions, and $\pi^{(m)}$ specifies a monotonic alignment between segments of $x^{(m)}$ and segments of $a^{(m)}$. For example, given words $x^{(m)} = x_1x_2$ and $a^{(m)} = a_1a_2a_3$, $\pi^{(m)}$ might specify that x_1 aligns to a_1a_2 and x_2 aligns to a_3.

At test time, given a sequence of text-environment pairs as input $\{(x^{(n)}, e^{(n)})\}_{n=1}^{N}$, we wish to generate a sequence of actions $a^{(n)}$ for each input pair. Note that our system is allowed to use information about one test example to improve performance on subsequent ones. We evaluate a system on its ability to recover a human-annotated sequence of actions.

3 Approach Overview

Figure 2 shows our approach for mapping text x to actions $a_{1:k}$ given the initial environment e_1.

3.1 Representation

We use the following representation for the different variables in Figure 2.

Environment. An environment e_i is represented by a graph whose nodes are objects and edges represent spatial relations between these objects. We consider five basic spatial relations: `near`, `grasping`, `on`, `in` and `below`. Each object has an instance ID (e.g., $\texttt{book}_9$), a category name (e.g., *chair, xbox*), a set of properties such as *graspable, pourable* used for planning and a set of boolean states such as has-water, at-channel3, whose values can be changed by robot actions. The robot is also an object in the environment. For example, the objects $\texttt{xbox}_1, \texttt{snacktable}_2$, are two objects in e_1 in Figure 2 with relation on between them.

Postconditions. A postcondition is a conjunction of atoms or their negations. Each atom consists of either a spatial relation between two objects (e.g., $\texttt{on}(\texttt{book}_9, \texttt{shelf}_3)$) or a state and a value (e.g., $\texttt{state}(\texttt{cup}_4, \texttt{has-water})$). Given an environment e, the postcondition evaluates to true or false.

Actions. Each action in an action sequence a_i consists of an action name with a list of arguments (e.g., $\texttt{grasp}(\texttt{xbox}_1)$). The action name is one of 15 values (grasp, moveto, wait, etc.), and each argument is either an object in the environment (e.g., $\texttt{xbox}_1$), a spatial relation (e.g., in for $\texttt{keep}(\texttt{ramen}_2, \texttt{in}, \texttt{kettle}_1)$, or a postcondition (e.g., for $\texttt{wait}(\texttt{state}(\texttt{kettle}_1, \texttt{boiling}))$).

Logical Forms. The logical form z_i is a pair (ℓ, ξ) containing a lexical entry ℓ and a mapping ξ. The lexical entry ℓ contains a parameterized postcondition such as $\lambda\vec{v}.\texttt{grasping}(v_1, v_2) \wedge \neg\texttt{near}(v_3, v_2)$, and ξ maps the variables $\vec{v}$ to objects in the environment. Applying the parameterized postcondition on ξ yields a postcondition; note that a postcondition can be represented by different logical forms. A lexical entry contains other information which are used for defining features, which is detailed in Section 4.

Control Flow Graphs. Following previous work (Tellex et al., 2011; Misra et al., 2014), we convert the text x to a shallow representation. The particular representation we choose is a *control flow graph*, which encodes the sequential relation between atomic segments in the text. Figure 3 shows the control flow graph for an example text. In a *control flow graph*, each node is either a frame node or a conditional node. A frame node represents a single clause (e.g., "*change the channel to a movie*") and has at most one successor node. Specifically, a frame node consists of a verb ν (e.g., *arrange, collect*), a set of object descriptions $\{\omega_i\}$ which are the arguments of the verb (e.g., *the guinness book, movie channel*), and spatial relations r between the arguments (e.g., *between, near*). The object description ω is either an anaphoric reference (such as "*it*") or a tuple containing the main noun, associated modifiers, and relative clauses.

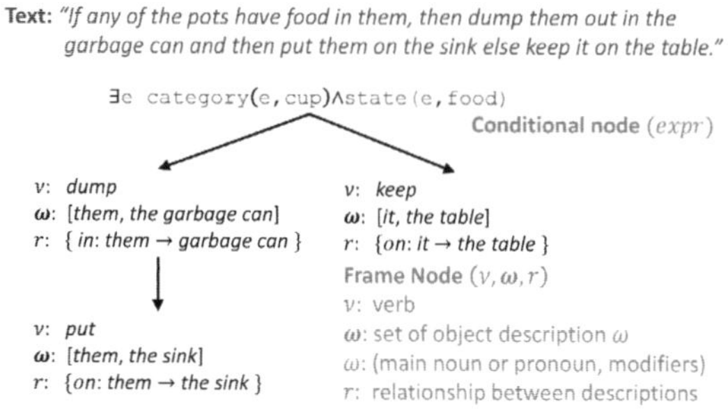

Figure 3: We deterministically parse text into a shallow structure called a control flow graph.

A conditional node contains a logical postcondition with at most one existentially quantified variable (in contrast to a frame node, which contains natural language). For example, in Figure 3 the conditional node contains the expression corresponding to the text *"if any of the pots has food"* There are two types of conditional nodes: branching and temporal. A branching conditional node represents an "*if*" statement and has two successor nodes corresponding to whether the condition evaluates to true or false in the current environment. A temporal conditional node represents an "*until*" statement and waits until the condition is false in the environment.

3.2 Formal Overview

Shallow Parsing. We deterministically convert the text x into its *control flow graph G* using a set of manual rules applied on its constituency parse tree from the Stanford parser (Klein and Manning, 2003). Conditionals in our dataset are simple and can be converted into postconditions directly using a few rules, unlike the action verbs (e.g., "*fill*"), which is the focus of this paper. The details of our shallow parsing procedure is described in the appendix.

Given an environment e_1, G is reduced to a single sequence of frame nodes $c_1, \ldots, c_k$, by evaluating all the branch conditionals on e_1.

Semantic Parsing Model. For each frame node c_i and given the current environment e_i, the semantic parsing model (Section 5) places a distribution over logical forms z_i. This logical form z_i represents a postcondition on the environment after executing the instructions in c_i.

Planner and Simulator. Since our semantic representations involve postconditions but our model is based on the environment, we need to connect the two. We use planner and a simulator that together specify a deterministic mapping from the current environment e_i and a logical form z_i to a new environment e_{i+1}. Specifically, the planner takes the current environment e_i and a logical form z_i and computes the action sequence a_i = *planner*(e_i, z_i) for achieving the post condition represented by z_i.[1] The simulator takes the current environment e_i and an action sequence a_i and returns a new environment e_{i+1} = *simulator*(e_i, a_i).

4 Anchored Verb Lexicons

Like many semantic parsers, we use a lexicon to map words to logical forms. Since the environment plays an central role in our approach, we propose an *anchored verb lexicon*, in which we store additional information about the environment in which lexical entries were previously used. We focus only on verbs since they have the most complex semantics; object references such as *"cup"* can be mapped easily, as described in Section 5.

More formally, an anchored verb lexicon Λ contains lexical entries ℓ of the following form: $[\nu \Rightarrow (\lambda\vec{v}.S, \xi)]$ where, ν is a verb, S is a postcondition with free variables $\vec{v}$, and ξ is a mapping of these variables to objects. An example lexical entry is: $[pour \Rightarrow (\lambda v_1 v_2 v_3.S, \xi)]$, where:

$S = \texttt{grasping}(\texttt{v}_1, \texttt{v}_2) \wedge \texttt{near}(\texttt{v}_1, \texttt{v}_3) \wedge \neg\texttt{state}(\texttt{v}_2, \texttt{milk})$
$\quad \wedge\, \texttt{state}(\texttt{v}_3, \texttt{milk})$

$\xi = \{\texttt{v}_1 \rightarrow \texttt{robot}_1, \texttt{v}_2 \rightarrow \texttt{cup}_1, \texttt{v}_3 \rightarrow \texttt{bowl}_3\}$ (anchoring)

As Table 1 shows, a single verb will in general have multiple entries due to a combination of polysemy and the fact that language is higher-level than postconditions.

Advantages of Postconditions. In contrast to previous work (Artzi and Zettlemoyer, 2013; Misra et al., 2014), we use postconditions instead of action sequence for two main reasons. First, postconditions generalize better. To illustrate this, consider the action sequence for the simple task of filling a cup with water. At the time of learning the lexicon, the action sequence might correspond to using a tap for filling the cup while at test time, the environment may not have a tap but instead have a pot with water. Thus, if the lexicon maps to action sequence, then it will not be applicable at test time whereas the postcondition $\texttt{state}(\texttt{z}_1, \texttt{water})$ is valid in both cases. We thus shift the load of inferring environment-specific actions onto planners

[1]We use the symbolic planner of Rintanen (2012) which can perform complex planning. For example, to pick up a bottle that is blocked by a stack of books, the planner will first remove the books before grasping the bottle. In contrast, Artzi and Zettlemoyer (2013) use a simple search over implicit actions.

Table 1: Some lexical entries for the verb *"turn"*

Sentence Context	**Lexical entry** $[turn \Rightarrow (\lambda\vec{v}.S, \xi)]$
"turn on the TV"	$\texttt{state}(\texttt{v}_1, \texttt{is-on}) \wedge \texttt{near}(\texttt{v}_2, \texttt{v}_1)$ $\xi : \texttt{v}_1 \rightarrow \texttt{tv}_1, \texttt{v}_2 \rightarrow \texttt{robot}_1$
"turn on the right back burner"	$\texttt{state}(\texttt{v}_1, \texttt{fire3}) \wedge \texttt{near}(\texttt{v}_2, \texttt{v}_1)$ $\xi : \texttt{v}_1 \rightarrow \texttt{stove}_1, \texttt{v}_2 \rightarrow \texttt{robot}_1$
"turn off the water"	$\neg\texttt{state}(\texttt{v}_1, \texttt{tap-on})$ $\xi : \texttt{v}_1 \rightarrow \texttt{sink}_1$
"turn the television input to xbox"	$\texttt{state}(\texttt{v}_1, \texttt{channel6}) \wedge \texttt{near}(\texttt{v}_1, \texttt{v}_2)$ $\xi : \texttt{v}_1 \rightarrow \texttt{tv}_1, \texttt{v}_2 \rightarrow \texttt{xbox}_1$

and use postconditions for representation, which better captures the semantics of verbs.

Second, because postconditions are higher-level, the number of atoms needed to represent a verb is much less than the corresponding number of actions. For example, the text *"microwave a cup"*, maps to action sequence with 10–15 actions, the postcondition only has two atoms: $\texttt{in}(\texttt{cup}_2, \texttt{microwave}_1) \wedge \texttt{state}(\texttt{microwave}, \texttt{is-on})$. This makes searching for new logical forms more tractable.

Advantages of Anchoring. Similar to the VEIL templates of Misra et al. (2014), the free variables $\vec{v}$ are associated with a mapping ξ to concrete objects. This is useful for resolving ellipsis. Suppose the following lexical entry was created at training time based on the text *"throw the drinks in the trash bag"*:

$[\ell\text{: } throw \Rightarrow \lambda xyz.S(x, y, z)]$, where

$S = \texttt{in}(\texttt{x}, \texttt{y}) \wedge \neg\texttt{grasping}(\texttt{z}, \texttt{x}) \wedge \neg\texttt{state}(\texttt{z}, \texttt{closed})$

$\xi = \{\texttt{x} \rightarrow \texttt{coke}_1, \texttt{y} \rightarrow \texttt{garbageBin}_1, \texttt{z} \rightarrow \texttt{robot}_1\}$

Now consider a new text at test time *"throw away the chips"*, which does not explicitly mention where to throw the chips. Our semantic parsing algorithm (Section 5) will use the previous mapping $y \rightarrow \texttt{garbabeBin}_1$ to choose an object most similar to a garbage bin.

5 Semantic Parsing Model

Given a sequence of frame nodes $c_{1:k}$ and an initial environment e_1, our semantic parsing model defines a joint distribution over logical forms $z_{1:k}$. Specifically, we define a conditional random field (CRF) over $z_{1:k}$, as shown in Figure 2:

$$p_\theta(z_{1:k} \mid c_{1:k}, e_1) \propto \exp\left(\sum_{i=1}^{k} \phi(c_i, z_{i-1}, z_i, e_i) \cdot \theta\right), \quad (1)$$

where $\phi(c_i, z_{i-1}, z_i, e_i)$ is the feature vector and θ is the weight vector. Note that the environments $e_{1:k}$ are a deterministic function of the logical forms $z_{1:k}$ through the recurrence e_{i+1} = *simulator*(e_i, *planner*(e_i, z_i)), which couples the different time steps.

Features. The feature vector $\phi(c_i, z_{i-1}, z_i, e_i)$ contains 16 features which capture the dependencies between text, logical forms, and environment. Recall that $z_i = ([\nu \Rightarrow (\lambda\vec{v}.S, \xi)], \xi_i)$, where ξ is the environment in which the lexical entry was created and ξ_i is the current environment. Let $f_i = (\lambda\vec{v}.S)(\xi_i)$ be the current postcondition. Here we briefly describe the important features (see the supplemental material for the full list):

- *Language and logical form*: The logical form z_i should generally reference objects mentioned in the text. Assume we have computed a correlation $\rho(\omega, o)$ between each object description ω and object o, whose construction is described later. We then define two features: precision correlation, which encourages z_i to only use objects referred to in c_i; and recall correlation, which encourages z_i to use all the objects referred to in c_i.
- *Logical form*: The postcondition f_i should be based on previously seen environments. For example, microwaving an empty cup and grasping a couch are unlikely postconditions. We define features corresponding to the average probability (based on the training data) of all conjunctions of at most two atoms in the postcondition (e.g., $\texttt{grasping(robot, cup)}\}$). We do the same with their abstract versions ($\{\texttt{grasping}(\texttt{v}_1, \texttt{v}_2)\}$). In addition, we build the same set of four probability tables conditioned on verbs in the training data. For example, the abstract postcondition $\texttt{state}(\texttt{v}_1, \texttt{water})$ has a higher probability conditioned on the verb "*fill*". This gives us a total of 8 features of this type.
- *Logical form and environment*: Recall that anchoring helps us in dealing with ellipsis and noise. We add a feature based on the average correlation between the objects of the new mapping ξ_i with the corresponding objects in the anchored mapping ξ.

The other features are based on the relationship between object descriptions, similarity between ξ and ξ_i and transition probabilities between logical forms z_{i-1} and z_i. These probabilities are also learned from training data.

Mapping Object Descriptions. Our features rely on a mapping from object descriptions ω (e.g., "*the red shiny cup*") to objects o (e.g., $\texttt{cup}_8$), which has been addressed in many recent works (Matuszek et al., 2012a; Guadarrama et al., 2014; Fasola and Matari'c, 2014).

One key idea is: instead of computing rigid lexical entries such as *cup* $\rightarrow$ $\texttt{cup}_1$, we use a continuous correlation score $\rho(\omega, o) \in [0, 1]$ that measures how well ω describes o. This flexibility allows the algorithm to use objects not explicitly mentioned in text. Given "*get me a tank of water*", we might choose an approximate vessel (e.g., $\texttt{cup}_2$).

Given an object description ω, an object o, and a set of previously seen objects (used for anaphoric resolution), we define the correlation $\rho(\omega, o)$ using the following approach:

- If ω *is a pronoun*, $\rho(\omega, o)$ is the ratio of the position of the last reference of o to the length of the action sequence computed so far, thus preferring recent objects.
- Otherwise, we compute the correlation using various sources: the object's category; the object's state for handling metonymy (e.g., the description "*coffee*" correlates well with the object $\texttt{mug}_1$ if $\texttt{mug}_1$ contains coffee—$\texttt{state}(\texttt{mug}_1, \texttt{has-coffee})$ is true), WordNet (Fellbaum, 1998) for dealing synonymy and hyponymy; and word alignments between the objects and text from Giza++ (Och and Ney, 2003) to learn domain-specific references (e.g., "*Guinness book*" refers to $\texttt{book}_1$, not $\texttt{book}_2$). More details can be found in the supplemental material.

6 Lexicon Induction from Training Data

In order to map text to logical forms, we first induce an initial anchored lexicon Λ from the training data $\{(x^{(m)}, e^{(m)}, a^{(m)}, \pi^{(m)})\}_{m=1}^{M}$. At test time, we add new lexical entries (Section 7) to Λ.

Recall that shallow parsing $x^{(m)}$ yields a list of frame nodes $c_{1:k}$. For each frame node c_i and its aligned action sequence a_i, we take the conjunction of all the atoms (and their negations) which are false in the current one e_i but true in the next environment e_{i+1}. We parametrize this conjunction by replacing each object with a variable, yielding a postcondition S parametrized by free variables $\vec{v}$ and the mapping ξ from $\vec{v}$ to objects in e_i. We then add the lexical entry $[verb(c_i) \Rightarrow (\lambda\vec{v}.S, \xi)]$ to Λ.

Instantiating Lexical Entries. At test time, for a given clause c_i and environment e_i, we generate set of logical forms $z_i = (\ell_i, \xi_i)$. To do this, we consider the lexical entries in Λ with the same verb as c_i. For each such lexical entry ℓ_i, we can map its free variables $\vec{v}$ to objects in e_i in an exponential number of ways. Therefore, for each ℓ_i we only consider the logical form (ℓ_i, ξ_i) where the mapping ξ_i obtains the highest score under the current model: $\xi_i = \arg\max_{\xi'} \phi(c_i, z_{i-1}, (\ell_i, \xi'), e_i) \cdot \theta$. For the feature vector ϕ that we consider, this approximately translates to solving an integer quadratic program with variables $[y_{ij}] \in \{0, 1\}$, where $y_{ij} = 1$ only if v_i maps to object j.

7 Environment-Driven Lexicon Induction at Test Time

Unfortunately, we cannot expect the initial lexicon Λ induced from the training set to have full coverage of the required postconditions. Even after using 90% of the data for training, we encountered 17% new postconditions on the remaining 10%. We therefore propose generating new lexical entries at test time and adding them to Λ.

Formally, for a given environment e_i and frame node c_i, we want to generate likely logical forms. Although the space of all possible logical forms is very large, the environment constrains the possible interpretations. We first compute the set of atoms that are false in e_i and that only contain objects o that are "referred" to by either c_i or c_{i-1}, where "refers" means that there exists some argument ω in c_i for which $o \in \arg\max_{o'} \rho(\omega, o')$. For example, if c_i corresponds to the text "*distribute pillows among the couches*", we consider the atom $\texttt{on}(\texttt{pillow}_1, \texttt{armchair}_1)$ but not $\texttt{on}(\texttt{pillow}_1, \texttt{snacktable}_2)$ since the object $\texttt{armchair}_1$ has the highest correlation to the description "*couches*".

Next, for each atom, we convert it into a logical form $z = (\ell, \xi)$ by replacing each object with a variable. While this generalization gives us a mapping ξ, we create a lexical entry $\ell_i = [\nu \Rightarrow (\lambda\vec{v}.S, \emptyset)]$ without it, where S is the parameterized atom. Note that the anchored mapping is empty, representing the fact that this lexical entry was unseen during training time. For example, the atom $\texttt{state}(\texttt{tv}_1, \texttt{mute})$ would be converted to the logical form (ℓ, ξ), where $\ell = [verb(c_i) \Rightarrow (\lambda v.\texttt{state}(v, \texttt{mute}), \emptyset]$ and $\xi = \{v \rightarrow \texttt{tv}_1\}$. We do not generalize state names (e.g., mute) because they generally are part of the meaning of the verb.

The score $\phi(c_i, z_{i-1}, z_i, e_i) \cdot \theta$ is computed for the logical form z_i produced by each postcondition. We then take the conjunction of every pair of postconditions corresponding to the 200 highest-scoring logical forms. This gives us new set of postconditions on which we repeat the generalization-scoring-conjunction cycle. We keep doing this while the scores of the new logical forms is increasing or while there are logical forms remaining.

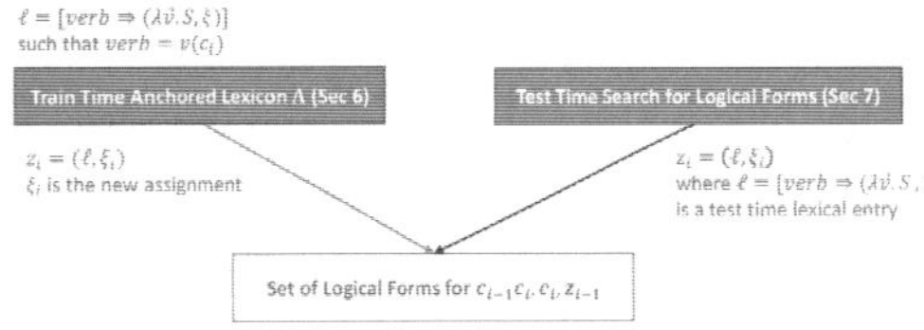

Figure 4: Logical forms for a given clause c_i, environment e_i, and previous logical form z_{i-1} are generated from both a lexicon induced from training data and a test-time search procedure based on the environment.

If a logical form $z = ([\nu \Rightarrow (\lambda\vec{v}.S, \emptyset)], \xi)$ is used by the predicted action sequence, we add the lexical entry $[\nu \Rightarrow (\lambda\vec{v}.S, \xi)]$ to the lexicon Λ. This is different to other lexicon induction procedures such as GENLEX (Zettlemoyer and Collins, 2007) which are done at training time only and require more supervision. Moreover, GENLEX does not use the environment context in creating new lexical entries and thus is not appropriate at test time, since it would vastly overgenerate lexical entries compared to our approach. For us, the environment thus provides implicit supervision for lexicon induction.

8 Inference and Parameter Estimation

Inference. Given a text x (which is converted to $c_{1:k}$ via Section 3.2) and an initial environment e_1, we wish to predict an action sequence a based on $p_\theta(a_{1:k} \mid c_{1:k}, e_1)$, which marginalizes over all logical forms $z_{1:k}$ (see Figure 2).

To enumerate possible logical forms, semantic parsers typically lean heavily on a lexicon (Artzi and Zettlemoyer, 2013), leading to high precision but lower recall, or search more aggressively (Berant et al., 2013), leading to higher recall but lower precision. We adopt the following hybrid approach: Given e_i, c_{i-1}, c_i and z_{i-1}, we use both the lexical entries in Λ as explained in Section 6 and the search procedure in Section 7 to generate the set of possible logical forms for z_i (see Figure 4). We use beam search, keeping only the highest-scoring logical form with satisfiable postconditions for each $i \in \{1, \ldots, k\}$ and resulting action sequence $a_{1:i}$.

Parameter Estimation. We split 10% of our training data into a separate tuning set (the 90% was used to infer the lexicon). On each example in this set, we extracted the full sequence of logical forms $z_{1:k}$ from the action sequence $a_{1:k}$ based on Section 6. For efficiency, we used an objective similar to pseudolikelihood to estimate the parameters θ. Specifically, we maximize the average log-likelihood over each adjacent pair of logical forms under $\tilde{p}_\theta$:

$$\tilde{p}_\theta(z_i \mid z_{i-1}, c_i, e_i) \propto \exp(\phi(c_i, z_{i-1}, z_i, e_i)^\top \theta). \quad (2)$$

The weights were initialized to 0. We performed 300 iterations over the validation set with a learning rate of $\frac{0.005}{N}$.

9 Dataset and Experiments

9.1 Dataset

We collected a dataset of 500 examples from 62 people using a crowdsourcing system similar to Misra et al. (2014). We consider two different 3D scenarios: a kitchen and a living room, each containing an average of 40 objects. Both of these scenarios have 10 environments consisting of different sets of objects in different configurations. We define 10 high-level objectives, 5 per scenario, such as *clean the room*, *make coffee*, *prepare room for movie night*, etc.

One group of users wrote natural language commands to achieve the high-level objectives. Another group controlled a virtual robot to accomplish the commands given by the first group. The dataset contains considerable variety, consisting of 148 different verbs, an average of 48.7 words per text, and an average of 21.5 actions per action sequence. Users make spelling and grammar errors in addition to occasionally taking random actions not relevant to the text. The supplementary material contains more details.

We filtered out 31 examples containing fewer than two action sequences. Of the remaining examples, 378 were used for training and 91 were used for test. Our algorithm is tested on four new environments (two from each scenario).

9.2 Experiments and Results

Evaluation Metrics. We consider two metrics, *IED* and *END*, which measure accuracy based on the action sequence and environment, respectively. Specifically, the *IED* metric (Misra et al., 2014) is the edit distance between predicted and true action sequence. The *END* metric is the Jaccard index of sets A and B, where A is the set of atoms (e.g., `on(cup1,table1)`) whose truth value changed due to simulating the predicted action sequence, and B is that of the true action sequence.

Baselines. We compare our algorithm with the following baselines:

Table 3: Results on the metrics and baselines described in section 9.2. The numbers are normalized to 100 with larger values being better.

Algorithm	**IED**	**END**
Chance	0.3	0.5
Manually Defined Templates	2.5	1.8
UBL- Best Parse (Kwiatkowski et al., 2010)	5.3	6.9
VEIL (Misra et al., 2014)	14.8	20.7
Model with only train-time lexicon induction	20.8	26.8
Model with only test-time lexicon induction	21.9	25.9
Full Model	**22.3**	**28.8**

1. Chance: Randomly selects a logical form for every frame node from the set of logical forms generated by generalizing all possible postconditions that do not hold in the current environment. These postconditions could contain up to 93 atoms.
2. Manually Defined Templates: Defines a set of postcondition templates for verbs similar to Guadarrama (2013).
3. UBL-Best Parse (Kwiatkowski et al., 2010): UBL algorithm trained on text aligned with postconditions and a noun-phrase seed lexicon. The planner uses the highest scoring postcondition given by UBL to infer the action sequence.
4. VEIL (Misra et al., 2014): Uses action sequences as logical forms and does not generate lexical entries at test time.
We also consider two variations of our model: (i) using only lexical entries induced using the training data, and (ii) using only the logical forms induced at test-time by the search procedure.

The results are presented in Table 3. We observe that our full model outperforms the baseline and the two pure search- and lexicon-based variations of our model. We further observe that adding the search procedure (Section 7) improved the accuracy by 1.5% on IED and 2% on END. The logical forms generated by the search were able to successfully map 48% of the new verbs.

Table 2 shows new verbs and concepts that the algorithm was able to induce at test time. The algorithm was able to correctly learn the lexical entries for the verbs "*distribute*" and "*mix*", while the ones for verbs "*change*" and "*boil*" were only partly correct. The postconditions in Table 2 are not structurally isomorphic to previously-seen logical forms; hence they could not have been handled by using synonyms or factored lexicons (Kwiatkowski et al., 2011). The poor performance of UBL was because the best logical form often produced an unsatisfiable postcondition. This can be remedied by joint modeling with the environ-

Table 2: New verbs and concepts induced at test time (Section 7).

Text	Postcondition represented by the learned logical form	# Log. forms explored
"*mix it with ice cream and syrup*"	$\texttt{state}(\texttt{cup}_2, \texttt{ice-cream}_1) \wedge \texttt{state}(\texttt{cup}_2, \texttt{vanilla})$	15
"*distribute among the couches*"	$\wedge_{j\in\{1,3\}}\texttt{on}(\texttt{pillow}_j, \texttt{loveseat}_1) \wedge \texttt{on}(\texttt{pillow}_{i+1}, \texttt{armchair}_{i+1})$	386
"*boil it on the stove*"	$\texttt{state}(\texttt{stove}, \texttt{stovefire1}) \wedge \texttt{state}(\texttt{kettle}, \texttt{water})$	109
"*change the channel to a movie*"	$\texttt{state}(\texttt{tv}_1, \texttt{channel4}) \wedge \texttt{on}(\texttt{book}_1, \texttt{loveseat}_1)$	98

ment. The VEIL baseline used actions for representation and does not generalize as well as the postconditions in our logical forms.

It is also instructive to examine the alternate postconditions that the search procedure considers. For the first example in Table 2, the following postcondition was considered by not selected:
$\texttt{grasping}(\texttt{robot}, \texttt{icecream}_2) \wedge \texttt{grasping}(\texttt{robot}, \texttt{syrup}_1)$

While this postcondition uses all the objects described in the text, the environment-based features suggest it makes little sense for the task to end with the robot eternally grasping objects. For the second example, alternate postconditions considered included:

1. $\texttt{on}(\texttt{pillow}_1, \texttt{pillow}_2) \wedge \texttt{on}(\texttt{pillow}_3, \texttt{pillow}_4)$
2. $\wedge_{j=1}^{4} \texttt{on}(\texttt{pillow}_j, \texttt{loveseat}_1)$
3. $\wedge_{j=1}^{3} \texttt{near}(\texttt{robot}_1, \texttt{armchair}_j)$

The algorithm did not choose options 1 or 3 since the environment-based features recognizes these as unlikely configurations. Option 2 was ruled out since the recall correlation feature realizes that not all the couches are mentioned in the postcondition.

To test how much features on the environment help, we removed all such features from our full model. We found that the accuracy fell to 16.0% on the IED metric and 16.6% on the END metric, showing that the environment is crucial.

In this work, we relied on a simple deterministic shallow parsing step. We found that shallow parsing was able to correctly process the text in only 46% of the test examples, suggesting that improving this initial component or at least modeling the uncertainty there would be beneficial.

10 Related Work

Our work uses semantic parsing to map natural language instructions to actions via novel concepts, which brings together several themes: actions, semantic parsing, novel concepts, and robotics.

Mapping Text to Actions. Several works (Branavan et al., 2009; Branavan et al., 2010; Vogel and Jurafsky, 2010) use reinforcement learning to directly map to text to actions, and do not even require an explicit model of the environment. However, they can only handle simple actions, whereas our planner and simulator allows us to work with postconditions, and thus tackle high-level instructions. Branavan et al. (2012) extract precondition relations from text, learn to map text to subgoals (postconditions) for a planner. However, their postconditions are atomic, whereas ours are complex conjunctions.

Other works (Chen and Mooney, 2011; Kim and Mooney, 2012; Kollar et al., 2010; Fasola and Mataric, 2013) have focused only on navigational verbs and spatial relations, but do not handle high-level verbs. Artzi and Zettlemoyer (2013) also fall into the above category and offer a more compositional treatment. They focus on how words compose; we focus on unraveling single words.

The broader problem of grounded language acquisition, involving connecting words to aspects of a situated context has been heavily studied (Duvallet et al., 2014; Yu and Siskind, 2013; Chu et al., 2013; Chen and Mooney, 2008; Mooney, 2008; Fleischman and Roy, 2005; Liang et al., 2009).

Semantic Parsing. In semantic parsing, much work has leveraged CCG (Zettlemoyer and Collins, 2005; Zettlemoyer and Collins, 2007; Kwiatkowski et al., 2010). One challenge behind lexically-heavy approaches is ensuring adequate lexical coverage. Kwiatkowski et al. (2011) enhanced generalization by factoring a lexical entry into a template plus a lexeme, but the rigidity of the template remains. This is satisfactory when words map to one (or two) predicates, which is the case in most existing semantic parsing tasks. For example, in Artzi and Zettlemoyer (2013), verbs are associated with single predicates ("*move*" to `move`, "*walk*" to `walk`, etc.) In our setting, verbs contain multi-predicate postconditions, for which these techniques would not be suitable.

As annotated logical forms for training semantic parsers are expensive to obtain, several works (Clarke et al., 2010; Liang et al., 2011; Berant et al., 2013; Kwiatkowski et al., 2013) have developed methods to learn from weaker supervision, and as in our work, use the execution of the logical forms to guide the search. Our supervision is even weaker in that we are able to learn at test time from partial environment constraints.

Grounding to Novel Concepts. Guadarrama et al. (2014) map open vocabulary text to objects in an image using a large database. Matuszek et al. (2012a) create new predicates for every new adjective at test time. Others (Kirk et al., 2014) ask users for clarification. In contrast, we neither have access to large databases for this problem, nor do we do create new predicates or use explicit supervision at test time.

Robotic Applications. Our motivation behind this work is to build robotic systems capable of taking commands from users. Other works in this area have considered mapping text to a variety of manipulation actions (Sung et al., 2015). Levine et al. (2015) and Lenz et al. (2015) focus on specific manipulation actions. In order to build a representation of the environment, Ren et al. (2012) and Wu et al. (2014) present vision algorithms but only output symbolic labels, which could act as inputs to our system. In future work, we also plan to integrate our work with RoboBrain (Saxena et al., 2014) to leverage these existing systems for building a robotic system capable of working with physical world data.

11 Conclusion

We have presented an algorithm for mapping text to actions that induces lexical entries at test time using the environment. Our algorithm couples the lexicon extracted from training data with a test-time search that uses the environment to reduce the space of logical forms. Our results suggest that using the environment to provide lexical coverage of high-level concepts is a promising avenue for further research.

Acknowledgements. This research was supported by the ONR (award N00014-14-1-0156), a Sloan Research Fellowship to the third author, and a Microsoft Research Faculty Fellowship and NSF Career Award to the fourth author. We thank Aditya Jami and Jaeyong Sung for useful discussions. We also thank Jiaqi Su for her help with data collection and all the people who participated in the user study.

Reproducibility. Code, data, and experiments for this paper are available on the CodaLab platform at `https://www.codalab.org/worksheets/0x7f9151ec074f4f589e4d4786db7bb6de/`. Demos can be found at `http://tellmedave.com`.

Appendix: Parsing Text into Control Flow Graph.

We first decompose the text x into its control flow graph G using a simple set of rules:

- The parse tree of x is generated using the Stanford parser (Klein and Manning, 2003) and a frame node is created for each non-auxiliary verb node in the tree.
- Conditional nodes are discovered by looking for the keywords *until, if, after, when.* The associated subtree is then parsed deterministically using a set of a rules. For example, a rule parses *"for x minutes"* to `for(digit:x,unit:minutes)`. We found that all conditionals can be interpreted against the initial environment e_1, since our world is fully-observable, deterministic, and the user giving the command has full view of the world.
- To find objects, we look for anaphoric terminal nodes or nominals whose parent is not a nominal or which have a PP sibling. These are processed into object descriptions ω.
- Object descriptions ω are attached to the frame node, whose verb is nearest in the parse tree to the main noun of ω.
- Nodes corresponding to $\{$*IN,TO,CC,","*$\}$ are added as the relation between the corresponding argument objects.
- If there is a conjunction between two objects in a frame node and if these objects have the same relation to other objects, then we split the frame node into two sequential frame nodes around these objects. For example, a frame node corresponding to the text segment "*take the cup and bowl from table*" is split into two frame nodes corresponding to "*take the cup from table*" and "*take bowl from table*".
- A temporal edge is added between successive frame nodes in the same branch of a condition. A temporal edge is added between a conditional node and head of the true and false branches of the condition. The end of all branches in a sentence are joined to the starting node of the successive sentence.

References

Y. Artzi and L. Zettlemoyer. 2013. Weakly supervised learning of semantic parsers for mapping instructions to actions. *Transactions of the Association for Computational Linguistics (TACL)*, 1:49–62.

J. Berant and P. Liang. 2014. Semantic parsing via paraphrasing. In *Association for Computational Linguistics (ACL)*.

J. Berant, A. Chou, R. Frostig, and P. Liang. 2013. Semantic parsing on Freebase from question-answer pairs. In *Empirical Methods in Natural Language Processing (EMNLP)*.

M. Bollini, J. Barry, and D. Rus. 2011. Bakebot: Baking cookies with the PR2. In *The PR2 Workshop, IROS*.

S. Branavan, H. Chen, L. S. Zettlemoyer, and R. Barzilay. 2009. Reinforcement learning for mapping instructions to actions. In *Association for Computational Linguistics and International Joint Conference on Natural Language Processing (ACL-IJCNLP)*, pages 82–90.

S. Branavan, L. Zettlemoyer, and R. Barzilay. 2010. Reading between the lines: Learning to map high-level instructions to commands. In *Association for Computational Linguistics (ACL)*, pages 1268–1277.

S. Branavan, N. Kushman, T. Lei, and R. Barzilay. 2012. Learning high-level planning from text. In *Association for Computational Linguistics (ACL)*, pages 126–135.

D. L. Chen and R. J. Mooney. 2008. Learning to sportscast: A test of grounded language acquisition. In *International Conference on Machine Learning (ICML)*, pages 128–135.

D. L. Chen and R. J. Mooney. 2011. Learning to interpret natural language navigation instructions from observations. In *Association for the Advancement of Artificial Intelligence (AAAI)*, pages 859–865.

V. Chu, I. McMahon, L. Riano, C. McDonald, Q. He, J. Perez-Tejada, M. Arrigo, N. Fitter, J. Nappo, T. Darrell, et al. 2013. Using robotic exploratory procedures to learn the meaning of haptic adjectives. In *International Conference on Intelligent Robots and Systems (IROS)*.

J. Clarke, D. Goldwasser, M. Chang, and D. Roth. 2010. Driving semantic parsing from the world's response. In *Computational Natural Language Learning (CoNLL)*, pages 18–27.

F. Duvallet, M. R. Walter, T. Howard, S. Hemachandra, J. Oh, S. Teller, N. Roy, and A. Stentz. 2014. Inferring maps and behaviors from natural language instructions. In *International Symposium on Experimental Robotics (ISER)*.

J. Fasola and M. Mataric. 2013. Using semantic fields to model dynamic spatial relations in a robot architecture for natural language instruction of service robots. In *International Conference on Intelligent Robots and Systems (IROS)*.

J. Fasola and M. J. Matari'c. 2014. Interpreting instruction sequences in spatial language discourse with pragmatics towards natural human-robot interaction. In *International Conference on Robotics and Automation (ICRA)*, pages 6667–6672.

C. Fellbaum. 1998. *WordNet: An Electronic Lexical Database*. MIT Press.

M. Fleischman and D. Roy. 2005. Intentional context in situated natural language learning. In *Computational Natural Language Learning (CoNLL)*, pages 104–111.

S. Guadarrama, L. Riano, D. Golland, D. Gouhring, Y. Jia, D. Klein, P. Abbeel, and T. Darrell. 2013. Grounding spatial relations for human-robot interaction. In *International Conference on Intelligent Robots and Systems (IROS)*.

S. Guadarrama, E. Rodner, K. Saenko, N. Zhang, R. Farrell, J. Donahue, and T. Darrell. 2014. Open-vocabulary object retrieval. In *Robotics: Science and Systems (RSS)*.

J. Kim and R. Mooney. 2012. Unsupervised PCFG induction for grounded language learning with highly ambiguous supervision. In *Computational Natural Language Learning (CoNLL)*, pages 433–444.

N. H. Kirk, D. Nyga, and M. Beetz. 2014. Controlled natural languages for language generation in artificial cognition. In *International Conference on Robotics and Automation (ICRA)*, pages 6667–6672.

D. Klein and C. Manning. 2003. Accurate unlexicalized parsing. In *Association for Computational Linguistics (ACL)*, pages 423–430.

T. Kollar, S. Tellex, D. Roy, and N. Roy. 2010. Grounding verbs of motion in natural language commands to robots. In *International Symposium on Experimental Robotics (ISER)*.

T. Kwiatkowski, L. Zettlemoyer, S. Goldwater, and M. Steedman. 2010. Inducing probabilistic CCG grammars from logical form with higher-order unification. In *Empirical Methods in Natural Language Processing (EMNLP)*, pages 1223–1233.

T. Kwiatkowski, L. Zettlemoyer, S. Goldwater, and M. Steedman. 2011. Lexical generalization in CCG grammar induction for semantic parsing. In *Empirical Methods in Natural Language Processing (EMNLP)*, pages 1512–1523.

T. Kwiatkowski, E. Choi, Y. Artzi, and L. Zettlemoyer. 2013. Scaling semantic parsers with on-the-fly ontology matching. In *Empirical Methods in Natural Language Processing (EMNLP)*.

I. Lenz, R. Knepper, and A. Saxena. 2015. Deepmpc: Learning deep latent features for model predictive control. In *Robotics Science and Systems (RSS)*.

S. Levine, C. Finn, T. Darrell, and P. Abbeel. 2015. End-to-end training of deep visuomotor policies. *arXiv preprint arXiv:1504.00702*.

P. Liang, M. I. Jordan, and D. Klein. 2009. Learning semantic correspondences with less supervision. In *Association for Computational Linguistics and International Joint Conference on Natural Language Processing (ACL-IJCNLP)*, pages 91–99.

P. Liang, M. I. Jordan, and D. Klein. 2011. Learning dependency-based compositional semantics. In *Association for Computational Linguistics (ACL)*, pages 590–599.

C. Matuszek, N. FitzGerald, L. Zettlemoyer, L. Bo, and D. Fox. 2012a. A joint model of language and perception for grounded attribute learning. In *International Conference on Machine Learning (ICML)*, pages 1671–1678.

C. Matuszek, E. Herbst, L. Zettlemoyer, and D. Fox. 2012b. Learning to parse natural language commands to a robot control system. In *International Symposium on Experimental Robotics (ISER)*.

D. Misra, J. Sung, K. Lee, and A. Saxena. 2014. Tell Me Dave: Context-sensitive grounding of natural language to mobile manipulation instructions. In *Robotics: Science and Systems (RSS)*.

R. Mooney. 2008. Learning to connect language and perception. In *Association for the Advancement of Artificial Intelligence (AAAI)*, pages 1598–1601.

F. J. Och and H. Ney. 2003. A systematic comparison of various statistical alignment models. *Computational Linguistics*, 29:19–51.

X. Ren, L. Bo, and D. Fox. 2012. Rgb-(d) scene labeling: Features and algorithms. In *Computer Vision and Pattern Recognition (CVPR)*, pages 2759–2766.

J. Rintanen. 2012. Planning as satisfiability: Heuristics. *Artificial Intelligence*, 193.

A. Saxena, A. Jain, O. Sener, A. Jami, D. K. Misra, and H. S. Koppula. 2014. Robobrain: Large-scale knowledge engine for robots. *arXiv preprint arXiv:1412.0691*.

J. Sung, S. H. Jin, and A. Saxena. 2015. Robobarista: Object part based transfer of manipulation trajectories from crowd-sourcing in 3d pointclouds. *arXiv preprint arXiv:1504.03071*.

S. Tellex, T. Kollar, S. Dickerson, M. R. Walter, A. G. Banerjee, S. J. Teller, and N. Roy. 2011. Understanding natural language commands for robotic navigation and mobile manipulation. In *Association for the Advancement of Artificial Intelligence (AAAI)*.

A. Vogel and D. Jurafsky. 2010. Learning to follow navigational directions. In *Association for Computational Linguistics (ACL)*, pages 806–814.

C. Wu, I. Lenz, and A. Saxena. 2014. Hierarchical semantic labeling for task-relevant RGB-D perception. In *Robotics: Science and Systems (RSS)*.

H. Yu and J. M. Siskind. 2013. Grounded language learning from video described with sentences. In *Association for Computational Linguistics (ACL)*, pages 53–63.

L. S. Zettlemoyer and M. Collins. 2005. Learning to map sentences to logical form: Structured classification with probabilistic categorial grammars. In *Uncertainty in Artificial Intelligence (UAI)*, pages 658–666.

L. S. Zettlemoyer and M. Collins. 2007. Online learning of relaxed CCG grammars for parsing to logical form. In *Empirical Methods in Natural Language Processing and Computational Natural Language Learning (EMNLP/CoNLL)*, pages 678–687.

Structural Representations for Learning Relations between Pairs of Texts

Simone Filice and **Giovanni Da San Martino** and **Alessandro Moschitti**
ALT, Qatar Computing Research Institute, Hamad Bin Khalifa University
{sfilice,gmartino,amoschitti}@qf.org.qa

Abstract

This paper studies the use of structural representations for learning relations between pairs of short texts (e.g., sentences or paragraphs) of the kind: the second text answers to, or conveys exactly the same information of, or is implied by, the first text. Engineering effective features that can capture syntactic and semantic relations between the constituents composing the target text pairs is rather complex. Thus, we define syntactic and semantic structures representing the text pairs and then apply graph and tree kernels to them for automatically engineering features in Support Vector Machines. We carry out an extensive comparative analysis of state-of-the-art models for this type of relational learning. Our findings allow for achieving the highest accuracy in two different and important related tasks, i.e., Paraphrasing Identification and Textual Entailment Recognition.

1 Introduction

Advanced NLP systems, e.g., IBM Watson system (Ferrucci et al., 2010), are the result of effective use of syntactic/semantic information along with relational learning (RL) methods. This research area is rather vast including, extraction of syntactic relations, e.g., (Nastase et al., 2013), predicate relations, e.g., Semantic Role Labeling (Carreras and Màrquez, 2005) or FrameNet parsing (Gildea and Jurafsky, 2002) and relation extraction between named entities, e.g., (Mintz et al., 2009).

Although extremely interesting, the above methods target relations only between text constituents whereas the final goal of an intelligent system would be to interpret the semantics of larger pieces of text, e.g., sentences or paragraphs. This line of research relates to three broad fields, namely, Question Answering (QA) (Voorhees and Tice, 1999), Paraphrasing Identification (PI) (Dolan et al., 2004) and Recognition of Textual Entailments (RTE) (Giampiccolo et al., 2007). More generally, RL from text can be denied as follows: given two text fragments, the main goal is to derive relations between them, e.g., either if the second fragment answers the question, or conveys exactly the same information or is implied by the first text fragment. For example, the following two sentences:

- *License revenue slid 21 percent, however, to $107.6 million.*
- *License sales, a key measure of demand, fell 21 percent to $107.6 million.*

express exactly the same meaning, whereas the next one:

- *She was transferred again to Navy when the American Civil War began, 1861.*

implies:

- *The American Civil War started in 1861.*

Automatic learning a model for deriving the relations above is rather complex as any of the text constituents, e.g., *License revenue*, *a key measure of demand*, in the two sentences plays an important role. Therefore, a suitable approach should exploit representations that can structure the two sentences and put their constituents in relation. Since the dependencies between constituents can be an exponential number and representing structures in learning algorithms is rather challenging, automatic feature engineering through kernel methods (Shawe-Taylor and Cristianini, 2004; Moschitti, 2006) can be a promising direction.

In particular, in (Zanzotto and Moschitti, 2006), we represented the two evaluating sentences for the RTE task with syntactic structures and then applied tree kernels to them. The resulting system was very accurate but, unfortunately, it could not scale to large datasets as it is based on a compu-

Proceedings of the 53rd Annual Meeting of the Association for Computational Linguistics and the 7th International Joint Conference on Natural Language Processing, pages 1003–1013,
Beijing, China, July 26-31, 2015.

tationally exponential algorithm. This prevents its application to PI tasks, which typically require a large dataset to train the related systems.

In this paper, we carry out an extensive experimentation using different kernels based on trees and graphs and their combinations with the aim of assessing the best model for relation learning between two entire sentences (or even paragraphs). More in detail, (i) we design many models for RL combining state-of-the-art tree kernels and graph kernels and apply them to innovative computational structures. These innovative combinations use for the fist time semantic/syntactic tree kernels and graph kernels for the tackled tasks. (ii) Our kernels provide effective and efficient solutions, which solve the previous scalability problem and, at the same time, exceed the state of the art on both RTE and PI. Finally, our study suggests research directions for designing effective graph kernels for RL.

2 Related Work

In this paper, we apply kernel methods, which enable an efficient comparison of structures in huge, possibly infinite, feature spaces. While for trees, a comparison using all possible subtrees is possible, designing kernel functions for graphs with such property is an NP-Hard problem (i.e., it shows the same complexity of the graph isomorphism problem) (Gartner et al., 2003). Thus most kernels for graphs only associate specific types of substructures with features, such as paths (Borgwardt and Kriegel, 2005; Heinonen et al., 2012), walks (Kashima et al., 2003; Vishwanathan et al., 2006) and tree structures (Cilia and Moschitti, 2007; Mahé and Vert, 2008; Shervashidze et al., 2011; Da San Martino et al., 2012).

We exploit structural kernels for PI, whose task is to evaluate whether a given pair of sentences is in the paraphrase class or not, (see for example (Dolan et al., 2004)). Paraphrases can be seen as a restatement of a text in another form that preserves the original meaning. This task has a primary importance in many other NLP and IR tasks such as Machine Translation, Plagiarism Detection and QA. Several approaches have been proposed, e.g., (Socher et al., 2011) apply a recursive auto encoder with dynamic pooling, and (Madnani et al., 2012) use eight machine translation metrics to achieve the state of the art. To our knowledge no previous model based on kernel methods has been applied before: with such methods, we outperform the state of the art in PI.

A description of RTE can be found in (Giampiccolo et al., 2007): it is defined as a directional relation extraction between two text fragments, called *text* and *hypothesis*. The implication is supposed to be detectable only based on the text content. Its applications are in QA, Information Extraction, Summarization and Machine translation. One of the most performing approaches of RTE 3 was (Iftene and Balahur-Dobrescu, 2007), which largely relies on external resources (i.e., WordNet, Wikipedia, acronyms dictionaries) and a base of knowledge developed ad hoc for the dataset. In (Zanzotto and Moschitti, 2006), we designed an interesting but computationally expensive model using simple syntactic tree kernels. In this paper, we develop models that do not use external resources but, at the same time, are efficient and approach the state of the art in RTE.

3 Structural kernels

Kernel Machines carry out learning and classification by only relying on the inner product between instances. This can be efficiently and implicitly computed by kernel functions by exploiting the following dual formulation of the model (hyperplane): $\sum_{i=1..l} y_i \alpha_i \phi(o_i) \cdot \phi(o) + b = 0$, where y_i are the example labels, α_i the support vector coefficients, o_i and o are two objects, ϕ is a mapping from the objects to feature vectors $\vec{x_i}$ and $\phi(o_i) \cdot \phi(o) = K(o_i, o)$ is the kernel function implicitly defining such mapping. In case of structural kernels, K maps objects in substructures, thus determining their size and shape. Given two structures S_1 and S_2, our general definition of structural kernels is the following:

$$K(S_1, S_2) = \sum_{s_1 \subseteq S_1, s_2 \subseteq S_2, s_i \in \mathcal{S}} k_{iso}(s_1, s_2), \quad (1)$$

where s_i are substructures of S_i, $\mathcal{S}$ is the set of admissible substructures, and k_{iso} determines if the two substructures are isomorphic, i.e., it outputs 1 if s_1 and s_2 are isomorphic and 0 otherwise.

In the following, we also provide a more computational-oriented definition of structural kernels to more easily describe those we use in our work:

Let the set $\mathcal{S} = \{s_1, s_2, \ldots, s_{|\mathcal{S}|}\}$ be the substructure space and $\chi_i(n)$ be an indicator function, equal to 1 if the target s_i is rooted at node n and equal to 0 otherwise. A structural-kernel function over S_1 and S_2 is

$$K(S_1, S_2) = \sum_{n_1 \in N_{S_1}} \sum_{n_2 \in N_{S_2}} \Delta(n_1, n_2), \quad (2)$$

where N_{S_1} and N_{S_2} are the sets of the S_1's and S_2's nodes, respectively and

$$\Delta(n_1, n_2) = \sum_{i=1}^{|S|} \chi_i(n_1)\chi_i(n_2). \quad (3)$$

The latter is equal to the number of common substructures rooted in the n_1 and n_2 nodes. In order to have a similarity score between 0 and 1, a normalization in the kernel space, i.e., $\frac{K(S_1,S_2)}{\sqrt{K(S_1,S_1) \times K(S_2,S_2)}}$ is usually applied. From a practical computation viewpoint, it is convenient to divide structural kernels in two classes of algorithms working either on trees or graphs.

3.1 The Partial Tree Kernel (PTK)

PTK (Moschitti, 2006) generalizes a large class of tree kernels as it computes one of the most general tree substructure spaces. Given two trees S_1 and S_2, PTK considers any connected subset of nodes as possible feature of the substructure space, and counts how many of them are shared by S_1 and S_2. Its computation is carried out by Eq. 2 using the following Δ_{PTK} function:

if the labels of n_1 and n_2 are different $\Delta_{PTK}(n_1, n_2) = 0$; **else** $\Delta_{PTK}(n_1, n_2) =$

$$\mu\Big(\lambda^2 + \sum_{\vec{I}_1, \vec{I}_2, l(\vec{I}_1)=l(\vec{I}_2)} \lambda^{d(\vec{I}_1)+d(\vec{I}_2)} \prod_{j=1}^{l(\vec{I}_1)} \Delta_{PTK}(c_{n_1}(\vec{I}_{1j}), c_{n_2}(\vec{I}_{2j}))\Big)$$

where $\mu, \lambda \in [0, 1]$ are two decay factors, $\vec{I}_1$ and $\vec{I}_2$ are two sequences of indices, which index subsequences of children u, $\vec{I} = (i_1, ..., i_{|u|})$, in sequences of children s, $1 \leq i_1 < ... < i_{|u|} \leq |s|$, i.e., such that $u = s_{i_1}..s_{i_{|u|}}$, and $d(\vec{I}) = i_{|u|} - i_1 + 1$ is the distance between the first and last child. The PTK computational complexity is $O(p\rho^2|N_{S_1}||N_{S_2}|)$ (Moschitti, 2006), where p is the largest subsequence of children that we want to consider and ρ is the maximal outdegree observed in the two trees. However the average running time tends to be linear for natural language syntactic trees (Moschitti, 2006).

3.2 Smoothed Partial Tree Kernel ($SPTK$)

Constraining the application of lexical similarity to words embedded in similar structures provides clear advantages over all-vs-all words similarity, which tends to semantically diverge. Indeed, syntax provides the necessary restrictions to compute an effective semantic similarity. $SPTK$ (Croce et al., 2011) generalizes PTK by enabling node similarity during substructure matching. More formally, $SPTK$ is computed by Eq. 2 using the following $\Delta_{SPTK}(n_1, n_2) = \sum_{i,j=1}^{|S|} \chi_i(n_1)\chi_j(n_2)\Sigma(s_i, s_j)$, where Σ is a similarity between structures[1]. The recursive definition of Δ_{SPTK} is the following:

1. **if** n_1 and n_2 are leaves $\Delta_{SPTK}(n_1, n_2) = \mu\lambda\sigma(n_1, n_2)$;
2. **else** $\Delta_{SPTK}(n_1, n_2) = \mu\sigma(n_1, n_2) \times \Big(\lambda^2 +$

$$\sum_{\vec{I}_1, \vec{I}_2, l(\vec{I}_1)=l(\vec{I}_2)} \lambda^{d(\vec{I}_1)+d(\vec{I}_2)} \prod_{j=1}^{l(\vec{I}_1)} \Delta_\sigma(c_{n_1}(\vec{I}_{1j}), c_{n_2}(\vec{I}_{2j}))\Big),$$

where σ is any similarity between nodes, e.g., between their lexical labels, and the other variables are the same of PTK. The worst case complexity of $SPTK$ is identical to PTK and in practice is not higher than $O(|N_{S_1}||N_{S_2}|)$.

3.3 Neighborhood Subgraph Pairwise Distance Kernel ($NSPDK$)

When general subgraphs are used as features in a kernel computation, eq. 1 and 2 become computationally intractable (Gartner et al., 2003). To solve this problem, we need to restrict the set of considered substructures $\mathcal{S}$. (Costa and De Grave, 2010) defined $NSPDK$ such that the feature space is only constituted by pairs of subgraphs (substructures) that are (i) centered in two nodes n_1 and n_2 such that their distance is not more than D; and (ii) constituted by all nodes (and their edges) at an exact distance h from n_1 or n_2, where the distance between two nodes is defined as the number of edges in the shortest path connecting them. More formally, let G, N_G and E_G be a graph and its set of nodes and edges, respectively, the substructure space $\mathcal{S} = \mathcal{S}_G(H, D)$ used by $NSPDK$ in eqs 2 and 3 is:

$$\{(\gamma_h(n), \gamma_h(n')) : 1 \leq h \leq H, n, n' \in N_G, \\ d(n, n') \leq D\},$$

where $\gamma_h(n)$ returns the subgraph obtained by executing h steps of a breadth-first visit of G starting from node n and $d(n, n')$ is the distance between two nodes in the graph. Note that (i) any feature

[1]Note that this generalizes Eq. 3.

of the space is basically a pair of substructures; and (ii) there is currently no efficient (implicit) formulation for computing such kernel. In contrast, when H and D are limited, it is simple to compute the space $S_G(H, D)$ explicitly. In such case, the complexity of the kernel is given by the substructure extraction step, which is $O(|N_G| \times h\rho \log \rho)$.

3.4 Kernel Combinations

Previous sections have shown three different kernels. Among them, $NSPDK$ is actually an explicit kernel, where the features are automatically extracted with a procedure. In NLP, features are often manually defined by domain experts, who know the linguistic phenomena involved in the task. When available, such features are important as they encode some of the background knowledge on the task. Therefore, combining different feature spaces is typically very useful. Fortunately, kernel methods enable an easy integration of different kernels or feature spaces, i.e., the kernel sum produces the joint feature space and it is still a valid kernel. In the next section, we show representations of text, i.e., structures and features, specific to PI and RTE.

4 Representations for RL from text

The kernels described in the previous section can be applied to generic trees and graphs. Automatic feature engineering using structural kernels requires the design of structures for representing data examples that are specific to the learning task we want to tackle. In our case, we focus on RL, which consists in deriving the semantic relation between two entire pieces of text. We focus on two well-understood relations, namely, paraphrasing and textual implications. The tasks are simply defined as: given two texts a_1 and a_2, automatically classify if (i) a_1 is a paraphrase of a_2 and/or (ii) a_1 implies a_2. Although the two tasks are linguistically and conceptually rather different, they can be modeled in a similar way from a shallow representation viewpoint. This is exactly the perspective we would like to keep for showing the advantage of using kernel methods. Therefore, in the following, we define sentence representations that can be suitably used for both tasks and then we rely on structural kernels and the adopted learning algorithm for exploring the substructures relevant to the different tasks.

4.1 Tree Representations

An intuitive understanding of our target tasks suggests that syntactic information is essential to achieve high accuracy. Therefore, we consider the syntactic parse trees of the pair of sentences involved in the evaluation. For example, Fig. 1 shows the syntactic constituency trees of the sentences reported in the introduction (these do not include the green label REL and the dashed edges). Given two pairs of sentences, $p_a = \langle a_1, a_2 \rangle$ and $p_b = \langle b_1, b_2 \rangle$, an initial kernel for learning the tasks, can be the simple tree kernel sum, e.g., $PTK(a_1, b_1) + PTK(a_2, b_2)$ as was defined in (Moschitti, 2008). This kernel works in the space of the union of the sets of all subtrees from the upper and lower trees, e.g.:

a_1: $\{$`[PP [TO [to::t]][NP [QP [$ [$::$]][QP [CD [107.6::c]]]]]], [PP [TO][NP [QP [$][QP [CD [107]]]]]], [PP [TO][NP [QP [QP [CD]]]]], [PP [NP [QP [QP]]]], ...`$\}$

$$\cup$$

a_2: $\{$`[NP [NP [DT [a::d]] [JJ [key::j] NN]][PP]], [NP [NP [DT] [JJ NN]][PP]], [NP [NP [JJ NN]][PP]], [NP [NP [NN]][PP]], [NP [NP [JJ]][PP]], ...`$\}$

However, such features cannot capture the relations between the constituents (or semantic lexical units) from the two trees. In contrast, these are essential to learn the relation between the two entire sentences[2].

To overcome this problem, in (Zanzotto and Moschitti, 2006), we proposed the use of *placeholders* for RTE: the main idea was to annotate the matches between the constituents of the two sentences, e.g., *107.6 millions*, on both trees. This way the tree fragments in the generated kernel space contained an index capturing the correspondences between a_1 and a_2. The critical drawback of this approach is that other pairs, e.g., p_b, will have in general different indices, making the representation very sparse. Alternatively, we experimented with models that select the best match between all possible placeholder assignments across the two pairs. Although we obtained a good improvement, such solution required an exponential computational time and the selection of the max

[2]Of course assuming that text meaning is compositional.

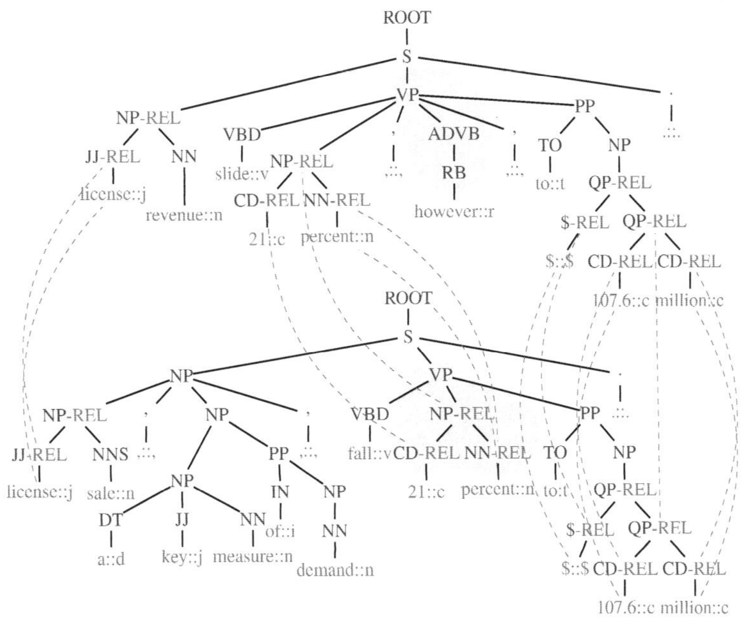

Figure 1: Text representations for PI and RTE: (i) pair of trees, a_1 (upper) and a_2 (lower), (ii) combined in a graph with dashed edges, and (iii) labelled with the tag REL (in green). The nodes highlighted in yellow constitute a feature for the $NSPDK$ kernel ($h = 1$, $D = 3$) centered at the nodes `ADVB` and `NP-REL`.

assignment made our similarity function a non-valid kernel.

Thus, for this paper, we prefer to rely on a more recent solution we proposed for passage reranking in the QA domain (Severyn and Moschitti, 2012; Severyn et al., 2013a; Severyn et al., 2013b), and for Answer Selection (Severyn and Moschitti, 2013). It consists in simply labeling matching nodes with a special tag, e.g., REL, which indicates the correspondences between words. REL is attached to the father and grandfather nodes of the matching words. Fig. 1 shows several green REL tags attached to the usual POS-tag and constituent node labels of the parse trees. For example, the lemma *license* is matched by the two sentences, thus both its father, JJ, and its grandfather, NP, nodes are marked with REL. Thanks to such relational labeling the simple kernel, $PTK(a_1, b_1) + PTK(a_2, b_2)$, can generate relational features from a_1, e.g., `[NP [NP-REL [JJ-REL] NN]][PP]]`, `[NP [NP-REL [NN]][PP]]`, `[NP [NP-REL [JJ-REL]][PP]]`,... If such features are matched in b_1, they provide the fuzzy information: *there should be a match similar to* `[NP [NP-REL [JJ-REL]]` *also between* a_2 *and* b_2. This kind of matches establishes a sort of relational pair features.

It should be noted that we proposed more complex REL tagging policies for Passage Reranking, exploiting additional resources such as Linked Open Data or WordNet (Tymoshenko et al., 2014). Another interesting application of this RL framework is the Machine Translation Evaluation (Guzmán et al., 2014). Finally, we used a similar model for translating questions to SQL queries in (Giordani and Moschitti, 2012).

4.2 Graph Representations

The relational tree representation can capture relational features but the use of the same REL tag for any match between the two trees prevents to deterministically establish the correspondences between nodes. For exactly representing such matches (without incurring in non-valid kernels or sparsity problems), a graph representation is needed. If we connect matching nodes (or also nodes labelled as REL) in Fig. 1 (see dashed lines), we obtain a relational graph. Substructures of such graph clearly indicate how constituents, e.g., NPs, VPs, PPs, from one sentence map into the other sentence. If such mappings observed in a pair of paraphrase sentences are matched in another sentence pair, there may be evidence that also the second pair contains paraphrase sentences.

Unfortunately, the kernel computing the space of all substructures of a graph (even if only considering connected nodes) is an intractable problem as mentioned in Sec. 3.3. Thus, we opt for the use of $NSPDK$, which generates specific pairs of structures. Intuitively, the latter can capture relational features between constituents of the two trees. Figure 1 shows an example of features generated by the $NSPDK$ with parameters $H = 1$, $D = 3$ (the substructures are highlighted in yellow), i.e., `[ADVB [VP] [RB]]`, `[NP-REL [VP] [CD-REL] [NN-REL]]`.

4.3 Basic Features

In addition to structural representations, we also use typical features for capturing the degrees of similarity between two sentences. In contrast, with the previous kernels these similarities are computed intra-pair, e.g., between a_1 and a_2. Note that any similarity measure generates only one feature. Their description follows:

– *Syntactic similarities*, which apply the cosine function to vectors of n-grams (with $n = 1, 2, 3, 4$) of word lemmas and part-of-speech tags.

– *Kernel similarities*, which use PTK or $SPTK$ applied to the sentences within the pair.

We also used similarity features from the DKPro of the UKP Lab (Bär et al., 2012), tested in the Semantic Textual Similarity (STS) task:

– *Longest common substring measure* and *Longest common subsequence measure*, which determine the length of the longest substring shared by two text segments.

– *Running-Karp-Rabin Greedy String Tiling* provides a similarity between two sentences by counting the number of shuffles in their subparts.

– *Resnik similarity* based on the WordNet hierarchy.

– *Explicit Semantic Analysis* (ESA) similarity (Gabrilovich and Markovitch, 2007) represents documents as weighted vectors of concepts learned from Wikipedia, WordNet and Wiktionary.

– *Lexical Substitution* (Szarvas et al., 2013): a supervised word sense disambiguation system is used to substitute a wide selection of high-frequency English nouns with generalizations, then Resnik and ESA features are computed on the transformed text.

4.4 Combined representations

As mentioned in Sec. 3.4, we can combine kernels for engineering new features. Let K be PTK or $SPTK$, given two pairs of sentences $p_a = \langle a_1, a_2 \rangle$ and $p_b = \langle b_1, b_2 \rangle$, we build the following kernel combinations for the RTE task:

(i) $K^+(p_a, p_b) = K(a_1, b_1) + K(a_2, b_2)$, which simply sums the similarities between the first two sentences and the second two sentences whose implication has to be derived.

(ii) An alternative kernel combines the two similarity scores above with the product: $K^\times(p_a, p_b) = K(a_1, b_1) \cdot K(a_2, b_2)$.

(iii) The symmetry of the PI task requires different kernels. The most intuitive applies K between all member combinations and sum all contributions: $all_K^+(p_a, p_b) = K(a_1, b_1) + K(a_2, b_2) + K(a_1, b_2) + K(a_2, b_1)$.

(iv) It is also possible to combine pairs of corresponding kernels with the product: $all_K^\times(p_a, p_b) = K(a_1, b_1)K(a_2, b_2) + K(a_1, b_2)K(a_2, b_1)$.

(v) An alternative kernel selects only the best between the two products above: $M_K(p_a, p_b) = \max(K(a_1, b_1)K(a_2, b_2), K(a_1, b_2)K(a_2, b_1))$. This is motivated by the observation that before measuring the similarity between two pairs, we need to establish which a_i is more similar to b_j. However, the max operator causes M_K not to be a valid kernel function, thus we substitute it with a *softmax* function, which is a valid kernel, i.e., $SM_K(p_a, p_b) = softmax(K(a_1, b_1)K(a_2, b_2), K(a_1, b_2)K(a_2, b_1))$, where $softmax(x_1, x_2) = \frac{1}{c}log(e^{cx_1} + e^{cx_2})$ (c=100 was accurate enough).

The linear kernel (LK) over the basic features (described previously) and/or $NSPDK$ can be of course added to all the above kernels.

5 Experiments

5.1 Setup

MSR Paraphrasing: we used the Microsoft Research Paraphrase Corpus (Dolan et al., 2004) consisting of 4,076 sentence pairs in the training set and 1,725 sentence pairs in test set, with a distribution of about 66% between positive and negative

	Kernel	Vs Test Acc (%)	Vs Test P	Vs Test R	Vs Test F1	5 Fold Cross Validation Acc (%)	5 Fold Cross Validation P	5 Fold Cross Validation R	5 Fold Cross Validation F1
without REL tagging	LK	75.88	0.784	0.881	0.829	75.54 ± 0.45	0.786 ± 0.009	0.876 ± 0.019	0.828 ± 0.004
	GK	72.81	0.720	0.967	0.825	72.49 ± 1.22	0.723 ± 0.014	0.957 ± 0.011	0.824 ± 0.008
	SM_{PTK}	72.06	0.722	0.943	0.818	72.04 ± 1.08	0.725 ± 0.009	0.940 ± 0.017	0.819 ± 0.009
	$SM_{SPTK_{LSA}}$	72.12	0.722	0.943	0.818	72.56 ± 1.10	0.731 ± 0.010	0.937 ± 0.017	0.821 ± 0.009
	$SM_{SPTK_{W2V}}$	71.88	0.719	0.946	0.817	72.23 ± 1.07	0.727 ± 0.009	0.938 ± 0.017	0.820 ± 0.009
	$all^{\times}_{PTK}$	71.42	0.718	0.939	0.814	71.57 ± 0.86	0.724 ± 0.007	0.933 ± 0.015	0.815 ± 0.008
	$all^{\times}_{SPTK_{LSA}}$	72.29	0.725	0.941	0.819	72.06 ± 0.62	0.730 ± 0.007	0.928 ± 0.014	0.817 ± 0.006
	$all^{\times}_{SPTK_{W2V}}$	71.59	0.717	0.947	0.816	71.61 ± 0.76	0.725 ± 0.008	0.931 ± 0.013	0.815 ± 0.007
	all^{+}_{PTK}	70.78	0.716	0.930	0.809	70.76 ± 0.91	0.720 ± 0.008	0.924 ± 0.017	0.809 ± 0.009
	$all^{+}_{SPTK_{LSA}}$	71.48	0.720	0.934	0.813	71.42 ± 0.91	0.727 ± 0.008	0.920 ± 0.020	0.812 ± 0.009
	$all^{+}_{SPTK_{W2V}}$	70.72	0.714	0.935	0.809	71.19 ± 1.22	0.723 ± 0.010	0.927 ± 0.018	0.812 ± 0.011
	M_{PTK}	72.17	0.725	0.935	0.817	72.31 ± 0.67	0.731 ± 0.007	0.930 ± 0.015	0.819 ± 0.007
	$M_{SPTK_{LSA}}$	72.00	0.725	0.934	0.816	72.32 ± 0.44	0.732 ± 0.006	0.927 ± 0.014	0.818 ± 0.005
	$M_{SPTK_{W2V}}$	71.71	0.722	0.933	0.814	71.99 ± 0.96	0.730 ± 0.008	0.926 ± 0.016	0.816 ± 0.008
with REL tagging	GK	75.07	0.752	0.933	0.833	74.69 ± 2.52	0.749 ± 0.029	0.940 ± 0.008	0.834 ± 0.018
	SM_{PTK}	76.17	0.765	0.927	0.838	75.42 ± 0.86	0.771 ± 0.007	0.903 ± 0.012	0.832 ± 0.008
	$SM_{SPTK_{LSA}}$	76.52	0.767	0.929	0.840	75.62 ± 0.90	0.772 ± 0.007	0.905 ± 0.013	0.833 ± 0.007
	$SM_{SPTK_{W2V}}$	76.35	0.766	0.929	0.839	75.64 ± 0.77	0.771 ± 0.004	0.907 ± 0.012	0.833 ± 0.007
	$all^{\times}_{PTK}$	75.36	0.767	0.905	0.830	74.76 ± 0.71	0.769 ± 0.006	0.892 ± 0.016	0.826 ± 0.008
	$all^{\times}_{SPTK_{LSA}}$	75.65	0.770	0.903	0.831	74.83 ± 0.92	0.771 ± 0.009	0.891 ± 0.011	0.826 ± 0.008
	$all^{\times}_{SPTK_{W2V}}$	75.88	0.772	0.905	0.833	75.26 ± 0.81	0.771 ± 0.008	0.898 ± 0.011	0.830 ± 0.008
	all^{+}_{PTK}	74.49	0.762	0.895	0.824	73.99 ± 1.04	0.767 ± 0.010	0.880 ± 0.013	0.820 ± 0.009
	$all^{+}_{SPTK_{LSA}}$	75.07	0.767	0.899	0.827	73.87 ± 0.85	0.766 ± 0.009	0.880 ± 0.010	0.819 ± 0.007
	$all^{+}_{SPTK_{W2V}}$	75.42	0.772	0.894	0.829	74.16 ± 0.75	0.768 ± 0.008	0.882 ± 0.012	0.821 ± 0.007
	GK+$SM_{SPTK_{W2V}}$	76.70	0.782	0.901	0.837	76.12 ± 0.96	0.787 ± 0.008	0.885 ± 0.015	0.833 ± 0.009
	LK+GK	78.67	0.802	0.902	0.849	77.85 ± 1.00	0.804 ± 0.008	0.886 ± 0.015	0.843 ± 0.009
	LK+$SM_{SPTK_{W2V}}$	77.74	0.794	0.899	0.843	77.52 ± 1.41	0.802 ± 0.011	0.885 ± 0.016	0.841 ± 0.011
	LK+GK+$SM_{SPTK_{W2V}}$	**79.13**	0.807	0.901	**0.852**	78.11 ± 0.94	0.811 ± 0.005	0.879 ± 0.016	0.844 ± 0.009
	(Socher et al., 2011)	76.8	–	–	0.836	–	–	–	–
	(Madnani et al., 2012)	77.4	–	–	0.841	–	–	–	–

Table 1: Results on Paraphrasing Identification

examples. These pairs were extracted from topically similar Web news articles, applying some heuristics that select potential paraphrases to be annotated by human experts.

RTE-3. We adopted the RTE-3 dataset (Giampiccolo et al., 2007), which is composed by 800 text-hypothesis pairs in both the training and test sets, collected by human annotators. The distribution of the examples among the positive and negative classes is balanced.

5.1.1 Models and Parameterization

We train our classifiers with the C-SVM learning algorithm (Chang and Lin, 2011) within KeLP[3], a Kernel-based Machine Learning platform that implements tree kernels. In both tasks, we applied the kernels described in Sec. 4, where the trees are generated with the Stanford parser[4].

$SPTK$ uses a node similarity function $\sigma(n_1, n_2)$ implemented as follows: if n_1 and n_2 are two identical syntactic nodes $\sigma = 1$. If n_1 and n_2 are two lexical nodes with the same POS tag, their similarity is evaluated computing the cosine similarity of their corresponding vectors in a wordspace. In all the other cases $\sigma = 0$. We generated two different wordspaces. The first is a co-occurrence LSA embedding as described in (Croce and Previtali, 2010). The second space is derived by applying a skip-gram model (Mikolov et al., 2013) with the word2vec tool[5]. $SPTK$ using the LSA will be referred to as $SPTK_{LSA}$, while when adopting word2vec it will be indicated with $SPTK_{W2V}$. We used default parameters both for PTK and $SPTK$ whereas we selected h and D parameters of $NSPDK$ that obtained the best average accuracy using a 5-fold cross validation on the training set.

5.1.2 Performance measures

The two considered tasks are binary classification problems thus we used Accuracy, Precision, Recall and F1. The adopted corpora have a predefined split between training and test sets thus we tested our models according to such settings for exactly comparing with previous work. Additionally, to better assess our results, we performed a 5-fold cross validation on the complete datasets. In case of PI, the same sentence can appear in multiple pairs thus we distributed the pairs such that the same sentence can only appear in one fold at a time.

[3]https://github.com/SAG-KeLP

[4]http://nlp.stanford.edu/software/corenlp.shtml

[5]https://code.google.com/p/word2vec/

	Kernel	Vs Test Acc (%)	Vs Test P	Vs Test R	Vs Test F1	5 Fold Cross Validation Acc (%)	5 Fold Cross Validation P	5 Fold Cross Validation R	5 Fold Cross Validation F1
without REL tagging	LK	62	0.608	0.729	0.663	62.94 ± 5.68	0.635 ± 0.057	0.679 ± 0.083	0.652 ± 0.049
	GK	55.375	0.555	0.651	0.599	55.63 ± 1.81	0.564 ± 0.022	0.612 ± 0.087	0.584 ± 0.032
	PTK^{+}	56.13	0.560	0.676	0.612	54.13 ± 3.26	0.547 ± 0.024	0.637 ± 0.051	0.587 ± 0.027
	$SPTK^{+}_{LSA}$	56.88	0.566	0.683	0.619	53.63 ± 2.50	0.543 ± 0.024	0.622 ± 0.060	0.578 ± 0.027
	$SPTK^{+}_{W2V}$	56.63	0.563	0.683	0.617	54.06 ± 2.34	0.546 ± 0.022	0.634 ± 0.060	0.585 ± 0.026
	$PTK^{\times}$	55.88	0.558	0.671	0.609	52.81 ± 1.99	0.535 ± 0.025	0.623 ± 0.055	0.574 ± 0.028
	$SPTK^{\times}_{LSA}$	56.25	0.561	0.671	0.611	53.56 ± 2.09	0.543 ± 0.022	0.616 ± 0.065	0.576 ± 0.026
	$SPTK^{\times}_{W2V}$	55.25	0.554	0.646	0.597	52.50 ± 1.77	0.533 ± 0.027	0.619 ± 0.071	0.571 ± 0.034
with REL tagging	GK	61.63	0.603	0.734	0.662	59.81 ± 3.84	0.599 ± 0.037	0.678 ± 0.071	0.634 ± 0.026
	PTK^{+}	66.00	0.627	0.829	0.714	67.75 ± 7.17	0.655 ± 0.067	0.817 ± 0.038	0.725 ± 0.046
	$SPTK^{+}_{LSA}$	65.38	0.622	0.824	0.709	67.81 ± 7.30	0.656 ± 0.069	0.816 ± 0.036	0.725 ± 0.047
	$SPTK^{+}_{W2V}$	66.38	0.629	0.837	0.718	68.00 ± 7.15	0.658 ± 0.068	0.816 ± 0.039	0.726 ± 0.046
	$PTK^{\times}$	66.13	0.629	0.827	0.714	67.75 ± 7.37	0.658 ± 0.071	0.804 ± 0.038	0.722 ± 0.049
	$SPTK^{\times}_{LSA}$	66.00	0.629	0.822	0.712	68.00 ± 7.62	0.661 ± 0.074	0.808 ± 0.039	0.725 ± 0.049
	$SPTK^{\times}_{W2V}$	**67.00**	0.636	0.834	0.722	67.69 ± 6.95	0.658 ± 0.069	0.804 ± 0.040	0.722 ± 0.043
	GK+$SPTK^{\times}_{W2V}$	66.38	0.634	0.815	0.713	66.00 ± 6.79	0.648 ± 0.069	0.769 ± 0.034	0.701 ± 0.044
	LK+GK	62.25	0.609	0.737	0.667	62.06 ± 5.49	0.620 ± 0.051	0.702 ± 0.053	0.656 ± 0.036
	LK+$SPTK^{\times}_{W2V}$	66.13	0.628	0.829	0.715	68.25 ± 7.54	0.663 ± 0.076	0.816 ± 0.032	0.728 ± 0.047
	LK+GK+$SPTK^{\times}_{W2V}$	66.00	0.633	0.800	0.707	66.31 ± 7.35	0.652 ± 0.075	0.770 ± 0.053	0.703 ± 0.052
	(Zanzotto et al., 2009)	66.75	0.667	–	–	–	–	–	–
	(Iftene and Balahur-Dobrescu, 2007)	69.13	–	–	–	–	–	–	–

Table 2: Results on Textual Entailment Recognition

5.2 Results on PI

The results are reported in Table 1. The first column shows the use of the relational tag REL in the structures (discussed in Sec. 4.1). The second column indicates the kernel models described in sections 3 and 4 as well as the combination of the best models. Columns 3-6 report Accuracy, Precision, Recall and F1 derived on the fixed test set, whereas the remaining columns regard the results obtained with cross validation. We note that:

First, when REL information is not used in the structures, the linear kernel (LK) on basic features outperforms all the structural kernels, which all perform similarly. The best structural kernel is the graph kernel, $NSPDK$ (GK in short). This is not surprising as without REL, GK is the only kernel that can express relational features.

Second, $SPTK$ is only slightly better than PTK. The reason is mainly due to the approach used for building the dataset: potential paraphrases are retrieved applying some heuristics mostly based on the lexical overlap between sentences. Thus, in most cases, the lexical similarity used in $SPTK$ is not needed as hard matches occur between the words of the sentences.

Third, when REL is used on the structures, all kernels reach or outperform the F1 (official measure of the challenge) of LK. The relational structures seem to drastically reduce the inconsistent matching between positive and negative examples, reflecting in remarkable increasing in Precision. In particular, $SM_{SPTK_{LSA}}$ achieves the state of the art[6], i.e., 84.1 (Madnani et al., 2012).

Next, combining our best models produces a significant improvement of the state of the art, e.g., $LK + GK + SM_{SPTK_{W2V}}$ outperforms the result in (Madnani et al., 2012) by 1.7% in accuracy and 1.1 points in F1.

Finally, the cross-validation experiments confirm the system behavior observed on the fixed test set. The Std. Dev. (specified after the $\pm$ sign) shows that in most cases the system differences are significant.

5.3 Results on RTE

We used the same experimental settings performed for PI to carry out the experiments on RTE. The results are shown in Table 2 structured in the same way as the previous table. We note that:

(i) Findings similar to PI are obtained.

(ii) Again the relational structures (using REL) provide a remarkable improvement in Accuracy (RTE challenge measure), allowing tree kernels to compete with the state of the art. This is an impressive result considering that our models do not use any external resource, e.g., as in (Iftene and Balahur-Dobrescu, 2007).

(iii) This time, $SPTK^{\times}_{W2V}$ improves on PTK by 1 absolute percent point.

[6] The performance of the several best systems improved by our models are nicely summarized at `http://aclweb.org/aclwiki/index.php?title=Paraphrase_Identification_(State_of_the_art)`

(iv) The kernel combinations are not more effective than $SPTK$ alone.

Finally, the cross-fold validation experiments confirm the fixed-test set results.

6 Discussion and Conclusions

In this paper, we have engineered and studied several models for relation learning. We utilized state-of-the-art kernels for structures and created new ones by combining kernels together. Additionally, we provide a novel definition of effective and computationally feasible structural kernels. Most importantly, we have designed novel computational structures for trees and graphs, which are for the first time tested in NLP tasks. Our kernels are computationally efficient thus solving one of the most important problems of previous work.

We empirically tested our kernels on two of the most representative tasks of RL from text, namely, PI and RTE. The extensive experimentation using many kernel models also combined with traditional feature vector approaches sheds some light on how engineering effective graph and tree kernels for learning from pairs of entire text fragments. In particular, our best models significantly outperform the state of the art in PI and the best kernel model for RTE 3, with Accuracy close to the one of the best system of RTE 3.

It should be stressed that the design of previous state-of-the-art models involved the use of several resources, annotation and heavy manually engineering of specific rules and features: this makes the portability of such systems on other domains and tasks extremely difficult. Moreover the unavailability of the used resources and the opacity of the used rules have also made such systems very difficult to replicate.

On the contrary, the models we propose enable researchers to:

(i) build their system without the use of specific resources. We use a standard syntactic parser, and for some models we use well-known and available corpora for automatically learning similarities with word embedding algorithms; and

(ii) reuse our work for different (similar) tasks (see paraphrasing) and data.

The simplicity and portability of our system is a significant contribution to a very complex research area such as RL from two entire pieces of text.

Our study has indeed shown that our kernel models, which are very simple to be implemented, reach the state of the art and can be used with large datasets.

Furthermore, it should be noted that our models outperform the best tree kernel approach of the RTE challenges (Zanzotto and Moschitti, 2006) and also its extension that we proposed in (Zanzotto et al., 2009). These systems are also adaptable and easy to replicate, but they are subject to an exponential computational complexity and can thus only be used on very small datasets (e.g., they cannot be applied to the MSR Paraphrase corpus). In contrast, the model we proposed in this paper can be used on large datasets, because its kernel complexity is about linear (on average).

We believe that disseminating these findings to the research community is very important, as it will foster research on RL, e.g., on RTE, using structural kernel methods. Such research has had a sudden stop as the RTE data in the latest challenges increased from 800 instances to several thousands and no tree kernel model has been enough accurate to replace our computational expensive models (Zanzotto et al., 2009).

In the future, it would be interesting defining graph kernels that can combine more than two substructures. Another possible extension regards the use of node similarity in graph kernels. Additionally, we would like to test our models on other RTE challenges and on several QA datasets, which for space constraints we could not do in this work.

Acknowledgments

This research is part of the Interactive sYstems for Answer Search (IYAS) project, conducted by the Arabic Language Technologies (ALT) group at Qatar Computing Research Institute (QCRI) within the Hamad Bin Khalifa University and Qatar Foundation.

References

Daniel Bär, Chris Biemann, Iryna Gurevych, and Torsten Zesch. 2012. Ukp: Computing semantic textual similarity by combining multiple content similarity measures. In *Proc. of SemEval '12*. ACL.

Karsten M Borgwardt and Hans-Peter Kriegel. 2005. Shortest-Path Kernels on Graphs. *ICDM*, 0:74–81.

Xavier Carreras and Lluís Màrquez. 2005. Introduction to the conll-2005 shared task: Semantic role labeling. In *Proc. of CONLL '05*, USA.

Chih-Chung Chang and Chih-Jen Lin. 2011. LIBSVM: A library for support vector machines. *ACM Transactions on Intelligent Systems and Technology*, 2:27:1–27:27.

Elisa Cilia and Alessandro Moschitti. 2007. Advanced tree-based kernels for protein classification. In *AI*IA 2007: Artificial Intelligence and Human-Oriented Computing, 10th Congress of the Italian Association for Artificial Intelligence, Rome, Italy, September 10-13, 2007, Proceedings*, pages 218–229.

Fabrizio Costa and Kurt De Grave. 2010. Fast neighborhood subgraph pairwise distance kernel. In *ICML*, number v.

Danilo Croce and Daniele Previtali. 2010. Manifold learning for the semi-supervised induction of framenet predicates: An empirical investigation.

Danilo Croce, Alessandro Moschitti, and Roberto Basili. 2011. Structured lexical similarity via convolution kernels on dependency trees. In *Proceedings EMNLP*.

Giovanni Da San Martino, Nicolò Navarin, and Alessandro Sperduti. 2012. A tree-based kernel for graphs. In *Proceedings of the Twelfth SIAM International Conference on Data Mining, Anaheim, California, USA, April 26-28, 2012.*, pages 975–986. SIAM / Omnipress.

Bill Dolan, Chris Quirk, and Chris Brockett. 2004. Unsupervised construction of large paraphrase corpora: Exploiting massively parallel news sources. In *Proc. of COLING '04*, Stroudsburg, PA, USA.

David Ferrucci, Eric Brown, Jennifer Chu-Carroll, James Fan, David Gondek, Aditya A Kalyanpur, Adam Lally, J William Murdock, Eric Nyberg, John Prager, et al. 2010. Building watson: An overview of the deepqa project. *AI magazine*, 31(3):59–79.

Evgeniy Gabrilovich and Shaul Markovitch. 2007. Computing semantic relatedness using wikipedia-based explicit semantic analysis. In *Proc. of IJCAI-07*, pages 1606–1611.

Thomas Gartner, P Flach, and S Wrobel. 2003. On Graph Kernels : Hardness Results and Efficient Alternatives. *LNCS*, pages 129–143.

Danilo Giampiccolo, Bernardo Magnini, Ido Dagan, and Bill Dolan. 2007. The third pascal recognizing textual entailment challenge. In *Proc. of the ACL-PASCAL RTE '07 Workshop*, pages 1–9. ACL.

Daniel Gildea and Daniel Jurafsky. 2002. Automatic labeling of semantic roles. *Computational Linguistics*, 28:245–288.

Alessandra Giordani and Alessandro Moschitti. 2012. Translating questions to sql queries with generative parsers discriminatively reranked. In *COLING (Posters)*, pages 401–410.

Francisco Guzmán, Shafiq Joty, Lluís Màrquez, Alessandro Moschitti, Preslav Nakov, and Massimo Nicosia. 2014. Learning to differentiate better from worse translations. In *Proceedings of the 2014 Conference on Empirical Methods in Natural Language Processing (EMNLP)*, pages 214–220, Doha, Qatar, October. Association for Computational Linguistics.

M Heinonen, N Välimäki, V Mäkinen, and J Rousu. 2012. Efficient Path Kernels for Reaction Function Prediction. *Bioinformatics Models, Methods and Algorithms*.

Adrian Iftene and Alexandra Balahur-Dobrescu. 2007. Hypothesis transformation and semantic variability rules used in recognizing textual entailment. In *RTE Workshop*, Prague.

Hisashi Kashima, Koji Tsuda, and Akihiro Inokuchi. 2003. Marginalized kernels between labeled graphs. In *ICML*, pages 321–328. AAAI Press.

Nitin Madnani, Joel Tetreault, and Martin Chodorow. 2012. Re-examining machine translation metrics for paraphrase identification. In *Proceedings of NAACL HLT '12*. ACL.

Pierre Mahé and Jean-Philippe Vert. 2008. Graph kernels based on tree patterns for molecules. *Machine Learning*, 75(1):3–35, October.

Tomas Mikolov, Kai Chen, Greg Corrado, and Jeffrey Dean. 2013. Efficient estimation of word representations in vector space. *arXiv preprint arXiv:1301.3781*.

Mike Mintz, Steven Bills, Rion Snow, and Daniel Jurafsky. 2009. Distant supervision for relation extraction without labeled data. In *ACL-AFNLP*.

Alessandro Moschitti. 2006. Efficient convolution kernels for dependency and constituent syntactic trees. In *Proc. of ECML'06*, pages 318–329.

Alessandro Moschitti. 2008. Kernel methods, syntax and semantics for relational text categorization. In *Proceedings of the 17th ACM Conference on Information and Knowledge Management*, CIKM '08, pages 253–262, New York, NY, USA. ACM.

Vivi Nastase, Preslav Nakov, Diarmuid Saghdha, and Stan Szpakowicz. 2013. *Semantic Relations Between Nominals*. Morgan & Claypool Publishers.

Aliaksei Severyn and Alessandro Moschitti. 2012. Structural relationships for large-scale learning of answer re-ranking. In *SIGIR*.

Aliaksei Severyn and Alessandro Moschitti. 2013. Automatic feature engineering for answer selection and extraction. In *EMNLP*, pages 458–467.

Aliaksei Severyn, Massimo Nicosia, and Alessandro Moschitti. 2013a. Building structures from classifiers for passage reranking. In *Proceedings of the 22Nd ACM International Conference on Conference on Information & Knowledge Management*, CIKM '13, pages 969–978, New York, NY, USA. ACM.

Aliaksei Severyn, Massimo Nicosia, and Alessandro Moschitti. 2013b. Learning adaptable patterns for passage reranking. *Proceedings of the Seventeenth Conference on Computational Natural Language Learning*, pages 75–83.

John Shawe-Taylor and Nello Cristianini. 2004. *Kernel Methods for Pattern Analysis*. Cambridge University Press, USA.

Nino Shervashidze, Pascal Schweitzer, Erik Jan van Leeuwen, Kurt Mehlhorn, and Karsten M Borgwardt. 2011. Weisfeiler-Lehman Graph Kernels. *JMLR*, 12:2539–2561.

Richard Socher, Eric H. Huang, Jeffrey Pennin, Christopher D Manning, and Andrew Y. Ng. 2011. Dynamic pooling and unfolding recursive autoencoders for paraphrase detection. In *NIPS 24*.

György Szarvas, Chris Biemann, and Iryna Gurevych. 2013. Supervised all-words lexical substitution using delexicalized features. In *NAACL*.

Kateryna Tymoshenko, Alessandro Moschitti, and Aliaksei Severyn. 2014. Encoding semantic resources in syntactic structures for passage reranking. *EACL 2014*, page 664.

S. V. N. Vishwanathan, Karsten M Borgwardt, and Nicol N Schraudolph. 2006. Fast Computation of Graph Kernels. In *NIPS*.

E. Voorhees and D. Tice, 1999. *The TREC-8 Question Answering Track Evaluation*.

Fabio Massimo Zanzotto and Alessandro Moschitti. 2006. Automatic learning of textual entailments with cross-pair similarities. In *Proceedings of the 21st International Conference on Computational Linguistics and 44th Annual Meeting of the Association for Computational Linguistics*, pages 401–408, Sydney, Australia, July. Association for Computational Linguistics.

Fabio massimo Zanzotto, Marco Pennacchiotti, and Alessandro Moschitti. 2009. A machine learning approach to textual entailment recognition. *Nat. Lang. Eng.*, 15(4):551–582, October.

Learning Semantic Representations of Users and Products for Document Level Sentiment Classification

Duyu Tang, Bing Qin*, **Ting Liu**
Harbin Institute of Technology, Harbin, China
{dytang, qinb, tliu}@ir.hit.edu.cn

Abstract

Neural network methods have achieved promising results for sentiment classification of text. However, these models only use semantics of texts, while ignoring users who express the sentiment and products which are evaluated, both of which have great influences on interpreting the sentiment of text. In this paper, we address this issue by incorporating user- and product- level information into a neural network approach for document level sentiment classification. Users and products are modeled using vector space models, the representations of which capture important global clues such as individual preferences of users or overall qualities of products. Such global evidence in turn facilitates embedding learning procedure at document level, yielding better text representations. By combining evidence at user-, product- and document-level in a unified neural framework, the proposed model achieves state-of-the-art performances on IMDB and Yelp datasets[1].

1 Introduction

Document-level sentiment classification is a fundamental problem in the field of sentiment analysis and opinion mining (Pang and Lee, 2008; Liu, 2012). The task is to infer the sentiment polarity or intensity (e.g. 1-5 or 1-10 stars on review sites) of a document. Dominating studies follow Pang et al. (2002; 2005) and regard this problem as a multi-class classification task. They usually use machine learning algorithms, and build sentiment classifier from documents with accompanying sentiment labels. Since the performance of a machine learner is heavily dependent on the choice of data representations (Domingos, 2012), many works focus on designing effective features (Pang et al., 2002; Qu et al., 2010; Kiritchenko et al., 2014) or learning discriminative features from data with neural networks (Socher et al., 2013; Kalchbrenner et al., 2014; Le and Mikolov, 2014).

Despite the apparent success of neural network methods, they typically only use text information while ignoring the important influences of users and products. Let us take reviews with respect to 1-5 rating scales as an example. A critical user might write a review "*it works great*" and mark 4 stars, while a lenient user might give 5 stars even if he posts an (almost) identical review. In this case, user preference affects the sentiment rating of a review. Product quality also has an impact on review sentiment rating. Reviews towards high-quality products (e.g. *Macbook*) tend to receive higher ratings than those towards low-quality products. Therefore, it is feasible to leverage individual preferences of users and overall qualities of products to build a smarter sentiment classifier and achieve better performance[2].

In this paper, we propose a new model dubbed User Product Neural Network (**UPNN**) to capture user- and product-level information for sentiment classification of documents (e.g. reviews). UPNN takes as input a variable-sized document as well as the user who writes the review and the product which is evaluated. It outputs sentiment polarity label of a document. Users and products are encoded in continuous vector spaces, the representations of which capture important global clues such

*Corresponding author.

[1]The codes and datasets are available at http://ir.hit.edu.cn/~dytang/

[2]One can manually design a small number of user and product features (Gao et al., 2013). However, we argue that they are not effective enough to capture sophisticated semantics of users and products.

Proceedings of the 53rd Annual Meeting of the Association for Computational Linguistics and the 7th International Joint Conference on Natural Language Processing, pages 1014–1023,
Beijing, China, July 26-31, 2015.

as user preferences and product qualities. These representations are further integrated with continuous text representation in a unified neural framework for sentiment classification.

We apply UPNN to three datasets derived from IMDB and Yelp Dataset Challenge. We compare to several neural network models including recursive neural networks (Socher et al., 2013), paragraph vector (Le and Mikolov, 2014), sentiment-specific word embedding (Tang et al., 2014b), and a state-of-the-art recommendation algorithm JMARS (Diao et al., 2014). Experimental results show that: (1) UPNN outperforms baseline methods for sentiment classification of documents; (2) incorporating representations of users and products significantly improves classification accuracy. The main contributions of this work are as follows:

• We present a new neural network method (UPNN) by leveraging users and products for document-level sentiment classification.

• We validate the influences of users and products in terms of sentiment and text on massive IMDB and Yelp reviews.

• We report empirical results on three datasets, and show that UPNN outperforms state-of-the-art methods for sentiment classification.

2 Consistency Assumption Verification

We detail the effects of users and products in terms of sentiment (e.g. 1-5 rating stars) and text, and verify them on review datasets.

We argue that the influences of users and products include the following four aspects.

• **user-sentiment consistency**. A user has specific preference on providing sentiment ratings. Some users favor giving higher ratings like 5 stars and some users tend to give lower ratings. In other words, sentiment ratings from the same user are more consistent than those from different users.

• **product-sentiment consistency**. Similar with user-sentiment consistency, a product also has its "preference" to receive different average ratings on account of its overall quality. Sentiment ratings towards the same product are more consistent than those towards different products.

• **user-text consistency**. A user likes to use personalized sentiment words when expressing opinion polarity or intensity. For example, a strict user might use "*good*" to express an excellent attitude, but a lenient user may use "*good*" to evaluate an ordinary product.

Algorithm 1 Consistency Assumption Testing

Input: data X, number of users/products m, number of iterations n
Output: $meaSame_k$, $meaDiff_k$, $1 \leq k \leq n$
for $k = 1$ **to** n **do**
    $meaSame_k = 0$, $meaSame_k = 0$
    for $i = 1$ **to** m **do**
        Sample x_i, x_i^+, x_i^- from X
        $meaSame_k$ += $measure(x_i, x_i^+)$
        $meaDiff_k$ += $measure(x_i, x_i^-)$
    end for
    $meaSame_k$ /= m, $meaDiff_k$ /= m
end for

• **product-text consistency**. Similar with user-text consistency, a product also has a collection of product-specific words suited to evaluate it. For example, people prefer using "*sleek*" and "*stable*" to evaluate a smartphone, while like to use "*wireless*" and "*mechanical*" to evaluate a keyboard.

We test four consistency assumptions mentioned above with the same testing criterion, which is formalized in Algorithm 1. For each consistency assumption, we test it for n = 50 iterations on each of IMDB, Yelp Dataset Challenge 2013 and 2014 datasets. Taking user-sentiment consistency as an example, in each iteration, we randomly select two reviews x_i, x_i^+ written by the same user u_i, and a review x_i^- written by another randomly selected user. Afterwards, we calculate the measurements of $(x_i,\ x_i^+)$ and $(x_i,\ x_i^-)$, and aggregate these statistics for m users. In user-sentiment assumption test, we use absolute rating difference $||rating_a - rating_b||$ as the measurement between two reviews a and b. We illustrate the results in Figure 1 (a)[3], where $2013same/2014same/amzsame$ (red plots) means that two reviews are written by a same user, and $2013diff/2014diff/amzdiff$ (black plots) means that two reviews are written by different users. We can find that: the absolute rating differences between two reviews written by a same user are lower than those written by different users (t-test with p-value $<$ 0.01). In other words, sentiment ratings from the same user are more consistent than those from different users. This validates the user-sentiment consistency.

For testing product-sentiment consistency, we

[3]Since the rating scale of IMDB (1-10) is different from Yelp (1-5), we divide the rating difference of IMDB reviews by two for better visualizing and analyzing the results.

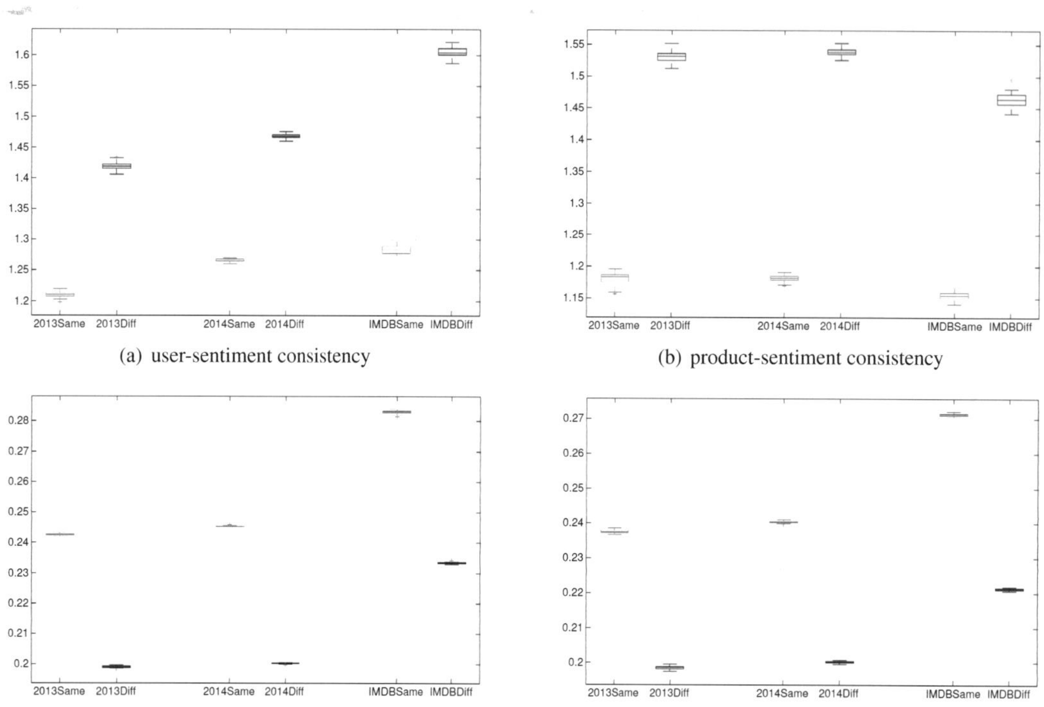

(a) user-sentiment consistency

(b) product-sentiment consistency

(c) user-text consistency

(d) product-text consistency

Figure 1: Assumption testing of user-sentiment, product-sentiment, user-text and product-text consistencies. We test them on the datasets from IMDB and Yelp Dataset Challenge in 2013 and 2014.

use absolute rating difference as the measurement. The reviews x_i, x_i^+ are towards a same product p_i, and x_i^- is towards another randomly selected product. From Figure 1 (b), we can see that sentiment ratings towards the same product are more consistent than those towards different products. In order to verify the assumptions of user-text and product-text consistencies, we use cosine similarity between bag-of-words of two reviews as the measurement. Results are given in Figure 1 (c) and (d). We can see that the textual similarity between two reviews written by a same user (or towards a same product) are higher than those written by different users (or towards different products).

3 User Product Neural Network (UPNN) for Sentiment Classification

We present the details of User Product Neural Network (UPNN) for sentiment classification. An illustration of UPNN is given in Figure 2. It takes as input a *review*, the *user* who posts the review, and the *product* which is evaluated. UPNN captures four kinds of consistencies which are verified in Section 2. It outputs the sentiment category (e.g. 1-5 stars) of a review by considering not only the semantics of review text, but also the information of user and product. In following subsections, we first describe the use of neural network for modeling semantics of variable-sized documents. We then present the methods for incorporating user and product information, followed by the use of UPNN in a supervised learning framework for sentiment classification.

3.1 Modeling Semantics of Document

We model the semantics of documents based on the principle of compositionality (Frege, 1892), which states that the meaning of a longer expression (e.g. a sentence or a document) comes from the meanings of its words and the rules used to combine them. Since a document consists of a list of sentences and each sentence is made up of a list of words, we model the semantic representation of a document in two stages. We first produce continuous vector of each sentence from word representations. Afterwards, we feed sentence vectors as inputs to compose document representation.

For modeling the semantics of words, we represent each word as a low dimensional, continu-

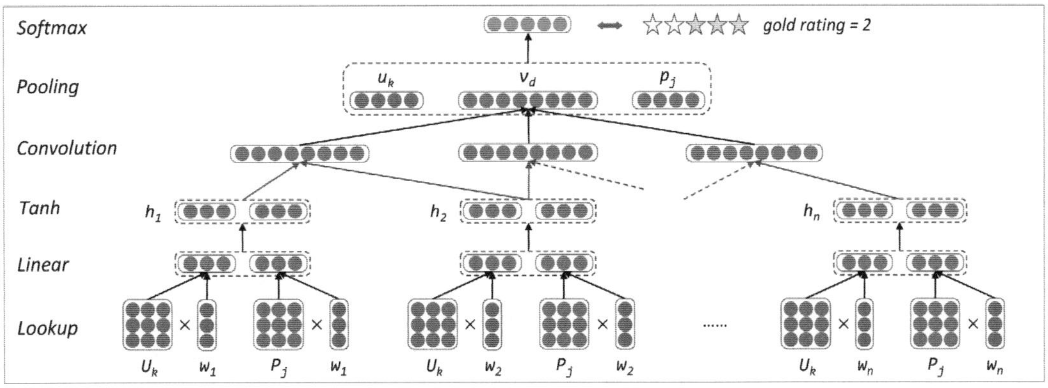

Figure 2: An illustration of the neural network approach for sentiment classification. w_i means the i-th word of a review text. u_k and p_j are continuous vector representations of user k and product j for capturing user-sentiment and product-sentiment consistencies. U_k and P_j are continuous matrix representations of user k and product j for capturing user-text and product-text consistencies.

ous and real-valued vector, also known as word embedding (Bengio et al., 2003). All the word vectors are stacked in a word embedding matrix $L_w \in \mathbb{R}^{d\times|V|}$, where d is the dimension of word vector and $|V|$ is the size of word vocabulary. These word vectors can be randomly initialized from a uniform distribution, regarded as a parameter and jointly trained with other parameters of neural networks. Alternatively, they can be pre-trained from text corpus with embedding learning algorithms (Mikolov et al., 2013; Pennington et al., 2014; Tang et al., 2014b), and applied as initial values of word embedding matrix. We adopt the latter strategy which better exploits the semantic and grammatical associations of words.

To model semantic representations of sentences, convolutional neural network (CNN) and recursive neural network (Socher et al., 2013) are two state-of-the-art methods. We use CNN (Kim, 2014; Kalchbrenner et al., 2014) in this work as it does not rely on external parse tree. Specifically, we use multiple convolutional filters with different widths to produce sentence representation. The reason is that they are capable of capturing local semantics of n-grams of various granularities, which are proven powerful for sentiment classification. The convolutional filter with a width of 3 essentially captures the semantics of trigrams in a sentence. Accordingly, multiple convolutional filters with widths of 1, 2 and 3 encode the semantics of unigrams, bigrams and trigrams in a sentence.

An illustration of CNN with three convolutional filters is given in Figure 3. Let us denote a sentence consisting of n words as $\{w_1, w_2, ...w_i, ...w_n\}$. Each word w_i is mapped to its embedding representation $e_i \in \mathbb{R}^d$. A convolutional filter is a list of linear layers with shared parameters. Let l_{cf} be the width of a convolutional filter, and let W_{cf}, b_{cf} be the shared parameters of linear layers in the filter. The input of a linear layer is the concatenation of word embeddings in a fixed-length window size l_{cf}, which is denoted as $I_{cf} = [e_i; e_{i+1}; ...; e_{i+l_{cf}-1}] \in \mathbb{R}^{d\cdot l_{cf}}$. The output of a linear layer is calculated as

$$O_{cf} = W_{cf} \cdot I_{cf} + b_{cf} \qquad (1)$$

where $W_{cf} \in \mathbb{R}^{len\times d\cdot l_{cf}}$, $b_{cf} \in \mathbb{R}^{len}$, len is the output length of linear layer. In order to capture the global semantics of a sentence, we feed the output of a convolutional filter to an *average* pooling layer, resulting in an output vector with fixed-length. We further add hyperbolic tangent functions ($tanh$) to incorporate element-wise nonlinearity, and *fold* (*average*) their outputs to generate sentence representation.

We feed sentence vectors as the input of an *average* pooling layer to obtain the document representation. Alternative document modeling approaches include CNN or recurrent neural network. However, we prefer *average* pooling for its computational efficiency and good performance in our experiment.

3.2 Modeling Semantics of Users and Products

We integrate semantic representations of users and products in UPNN to capture user-sentiment,

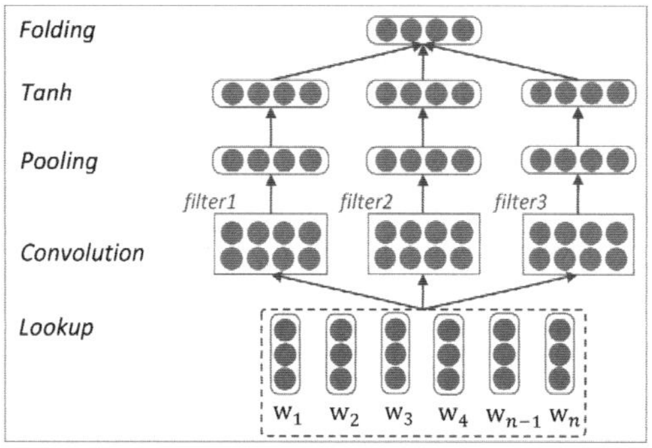

Figure 3: Convolutional neural network with multiple convolutional filters for sentence modeling.

product-sentiment, user-text and product-text consistencies.

For modeling **user-sentiment** and **product-sentiment** consistencies, we embed each user as a continuous vector $u_k \in \mathbb{R}^{d_u}$ and embed each product as a continuous vector $p_j \in \mathbb{R}^{d_p}$, where d_u and d_p are dimensions of user vector and product vector, respectively. The basic idea behind this is to map users with similar rating preferences (e.g. prefer assigning 4 stars) into close vectors in user embedding space. Similarly, the products which receive similar averaged ratings are mapped into neighboring vectors in product embedding space.

In order to model **user-text** consistency, we represent each user as a continuous matrix $U_k \in \mathbb{R}^{d_U \times d}$, which acts as an operator to modify the semantic meaning of a word. This is on the basis of vector based semantic composition (Mitchell and Lapata, 2010). They regard compositional modifier as a matrix X_1 to modify another component x_2, and use matrix-vector multiplication $y = X_1 \times x_2$ as the composition function. Multiplicative semantic composition is suitable for our need of user modifying word meaning, and it has been successfully utilized to model adjective-noun composition (Clark et al., 2008; Baroni and Zamparelli, 2010) and adverb-adjective composition (Socher et al., 2012). Similarly, we model **product-text** consistency by encoding each product as a matrix $P_j \in \mathbb{R}^{d_P \times d}$, where d is the dimension of word vector, d_P is the output length of product-word multiplicative composition. After conducting user-word multiplication and product-word multiplication operations, we concatenate their outputs and feed them to CNN (detailed in Section 3.1) for producing user and product enhanced document representation.

3.3 Sentiment Classification

We apply UPNN to document level sentiment classification under a supervised learning framework (Pang and Lee, 2005). Instead of using hand-crafted features, we use continuous representation of documents, users and products as discriminative features. The sentiment classifier is built from documents with gold standard sentiment labels.

As is shown in Figure 2, the feature representation for building rating predictor is the concatenation of three parts: continuous user representation u_k, continuous product representation p_j and continuous document representation v_d, where v_d encodes user-text consistency, product-text consistency and document level semantic composition. We use $softmax$ to build the classifier because its outputs can be interpreted as conditional probabilities. $Softmax$ is calculated as given in Equation 2, where C is the category number (e.g. 5 or 10).

$$softmax_i = \frac{exp(x_i)}{\sum_{i'=1}^{C} exp(x_{i'})} \tag{2}$$

We regard cross-entropy error between gold sentiment distribution and predicted sentiment distribution as the loss function of $softmax$. We take the derivative of loss function through back-propagation with respect to the whole set of parameters $\theta = [W_{cf}^{1,2,3}; b_{cf}^{1,2,3}; u_k; p_j; U_k; P_j; W_{softmax}, b_{softmax}]$, and update parameters with stochastic gradient descent. We set the widths of three convolutional filters as 1, 2 and 3. We learn 200-dimensional sentiment-specific word embeddings (Tang et al., 2014b) on each dataset separately, randomly initialize other parameters from a uniform distribution $U(-0.01, 0.01)$, and set learning rate as 0.03.

4 Experiment

We conduct experiments to evaluate UPNN by applying it to sentiment classification of documents.

4.1 Experimental Setting

Existing benchmark datasets for sentiment classification such as Stanford Sentiment Treebank (Socher et al., 2013) typically only have text information, but do not contain users who express the sentiment or products which are evaluated. Therefore, we build the datasets by ourselves. In order to obtain large scale corpora without manual annotation, we derive three datasets from IMDB (Diao

Dataset	#users	#products	#reviews	#docs/user	#docs/product	#sents/doc	#words/doc
IMDB	1,310	1,635	84,919	64.82	51.94	16.08	394.6
Yelp 2014	4,818	4,194	231,163	47.97	55.11	11.41	196.9
Yelp 2013	1,631	1,633	78,966	48.42	48.36	10.89	189.3

Table 1: Statistical information of IMDB, Yelp 2014 and Yelp 2013 datasets used for sentiment classification. The rating scale of IMDB dataset is 1-10. The rating scale of Yelp 2014 and Yelp 2013 datasets is 1-5. $|V|$ is the vocabulary size of words in each dataset. #users is the number of users, #docs/user means the average number of documents per user posts in the corpus.

et al., 2014) and Yelp Dataset Challenge[4] in 2013 and 2014. Statistical information of the generated datasets are given in Table 1.

We split each corpus into training, development and testing sets with a 80/10/10 split, and conduct tokenization and sentence splitting with Stanford CoreNLP (Manning et al., 2014). We use standard *accuracy* (Manning and Schütze, 1999; Jurafsky and Martin, 2000) to measure the overall sentiment classification performance, and use MAE and $RMSE$ to measure the divergences between predicted sentiment ratings (pr) and ground truth ratings (gd).

$$MAE = \frac{\sum_i |gd_i - pr_i|}{N} \tag{3}$$

$$RMSE = \sqrt{\frac{\sum_i (gd_i - pr_i)^2}{N}} \tag{4}$$

4.2 Baseline Methods

We compare UPNN with the following baseline methods for document-level sentiment classification.

(1) *Majority* is a heuristic baseline method, which assigns the majority sentiment category in training set to each review in the test dataset.

(2) In *Trigram*, we use unigrams, bigrams and trigrams as features and train classifier with supported vector machine (SVM) (Fan et al., 2008).

(3) In *TextFeature*, we implement hand-crafted text features including word/character ngrams, sentiment lexicon features, negation features, etc al. (Kiritchenko et al., 2014).

(4) We extract user-leniency features (Gao et al., 2013) and corresponding product features (denoted as *UPF*) from training data, and concatenate them with the features in baseline (2) and (3).

(5) We learn word embeddings from training and development sets with *word2vec* (Mikolov et al., 2013), average word embeddings to get document representation, and train a SVM classifier.

(6) We learn sentiment-specific word embeddings (SSWE) from training and development sets, and use max/min/average pooling (Tang et al., 2014b) to generate document representation.

(7) We represent sentence with RNTN (Socher et al., 2013) and compose document representation with recurrent neural network. We average hidden vectors of recurrent neural network as the features for sentiment classification.

(8) We re-implement PVDM in Paragraph Vector (Le and Mikolov, 2014) because its codes are not officially provided. The window size is tuned on development set.

(9) We compare with a state-of-the-art recommendation algorithm JMARS (Diao et al., 2014), which leverages user and aspects of a review with collaborative filtering and topic modeling.

4.3 Model Comparisons

Experimental results are given in Table 2. The results are separated into two groups: the methods above only use texts of review, and the methods below also use user and product information.

From the first group, we can see that majority performs very poor because it does not capture any text or user information. SVM classifiers with trigrams and hand-crafted text features are powerful for document level sentiment classification and hard to beat. We compare the word embedding learnt from each corpus with off-the-shell general word embeddings[5]. Results show that tailored word embedding from each corpus performs slightly better than general word embeddings (about 0.01 improvement in terms of accuracy). SSWE performs better than context-based word embedding by incorporating sentiment information of texts. Setting a large window size (e.g. 15) is crucial for effectively training SSWE from documents with accompanying senti-

[4] http://www.yelp.com/dataset_challenge

[5] We compare with Glove embeddings learnt from Wikipedia and Twitter http://nlp.stanford.edu/projects/glove/

	IMDB			Yelp 2014			Yelp 2013		
	Acc	MAE	RMSE	Acc	MAE	RMSE	Acc	MAE	RMSE
Majority	0.196	1.838	2.495	0.392	0.779	1.097	0.411	0.744	1.060
Trigram	0.399	1.147	1.783	0.577	0.487	0.804	0.569	0.513	0.814
TextFeature	0.402	1.134	1.793	0.572	0.490	**0.800**	0.556	0.520	0.845
AvgWordvec + SVM	0.304	1.361	1.985	0.530	0.562	0.893	0.526	0.568	0.898
SSWE + SVM	0.312	1.347	1.973	0.557	0.523	0.851	0.549	0.529	0.849
Paragraph Vector	0.341	1.211	1.814	0.564	0.496	0.802	0.554	0.515	0.832
RNTN + Recurrent	0.400	1.133	1.764	0.582	**0.478**	0.821	0.574	0.489	**0.804**
UPNN (no UP)	**0.405**	**1.030**	**1.629**	**0.585**	0.483	0.808	**0.577**	**0.485**	0.812
Trigram + UPF	0.404	1.132	1.764	0.576	0.471	0.789	0.570	0.491	0.803
TextFeature + UPF	0.402	1.129	1.774	0.579	0.476	0.791	0.561	0.509	0.822
JMARS	N/A	1.285	1.773	N/A	0.710	0.999	N/A	0.699	0.985
UPNN (full)	**0.435**	**0.979**	**1.602**	**0.608**	**0.447**	**0.764**	**0.596**	**0.464**	**0.784**

Table 2: Sentiment classification on IMDB, Yelp 2014 and Yelp 2013 datasets. Evaluation metrics are accuracy (Acc, higher is better), MAE (lower is better) and RMSE (lower is better). Our full model is UPNN (full). Our model without using user and product information is abbreviated as UPNN (no UP). The best method in each group is in **bold**.

ment labels. *RNTN+Reccurent* is a strong performer by effectively modeling document representation with semantic composition. Our text based model (UPNN no UP) performs slightly better than *RNTN+Reccurent*, trigram and text features.

From the second group, we can see that concatenating user product feature (*UPF*) with existing feature sets does not show significant improvements. This is because the dimension of existing feature sets is typically huge (e.g. 1M trigram features in Yelp 2014), so that concatenating a small number of *UPF* features does not have a great influence on the whole model. We do not evaluate JMARS in terms of *accuracy* because JMARS outputs real-valued ratings. Our full model UPNN yields the best performance on all three datasets. Incorporating semantic representations of user and product significantly (t-test with p-value $<$ 0.01) boosts our text based model (UPNN no UP). This shows the effectiveness of UPNN over standard trigrams and hand-crafted features when incorporating user and product information.

4.4 Model Analysis: Effect of User and Product Representations

We investigate the effects of vector based user and product representations (u_k, p_j) as well as matrix based user and product representations (U_k, P_j) for sentiment classification. We remove vector based representations (u_k, p_j) and matrix based representations (U_k, P_j) from UPNN separately, and conduct experiments on three datasets. From Table 3, we can find that vector based representations (u_k, p_j) are more effective than matrix based representations (U_k, P_j). This is because u_k and p_j encode user-sentiment and product-sentiment consistencies, which are more directly associated with sentiment labels than user-text (U_k) and product-text (P_j) consistencies. Another reason might be that the parameters of vector representations are less than the matrix representations, so that the vector representations are better estimated. We also see the contribution from each of user and product by removing (U_k, u_k) and (P_j, p_j) separately. Results are given in Table 3. It is interesting to find that user representations are obviously more effective than product representations for review rating prediction.

4.5 Discussion: Out-Of-Vocabulary Users and Products

Out-of-vocabulary (OOV) situation occurs if a user or a product in testing/decoding process is never seen in training data. We give two natural solutions (avg UP and unk UP) to deal with OOV users and products. One solution (avg UP) is to regard the averaged representations of users/products in training data as the representation of OOV user/product. Another way (unk UP) is to learn a shared "unknown" user/product representation for low-frequency users in training data, and apply it to OOV user/product.

	IMDB			Yelp 2014			Yelp 2013		
	Acc	MAE	RMSE	Acc	MAE	RMSE	Acc	MAE	RMSE
UPNN (full)	0.435	0.979	1.602	0.608	0.447	0.764	0.596	0.464	0.784
UPNN $- u_k - p_j$	0.409	1.021	1.622	0.585	0.483	0.808	0.572	0.491	0.823
UPNN $- U_k - P_j$	0.426	0.993	1.607	0.597	0.465	0.789	0.585	0.482	0.802
UPNN $- U_k - u_k$	0.324	1.209	1.743	0.577	0.475	0.778	0.566	0.505	0.828
UPNN $- P_j - p_j$	0.397	1.075	1.712	0.595	0.462	0.776	0.590	0.476	0.802

Table 3: Influence of user and product representations. For user k and product j, u_k and p_j are their continuous vector representations, U_k and P_j are their continuous matrix representations (see Figure 2).

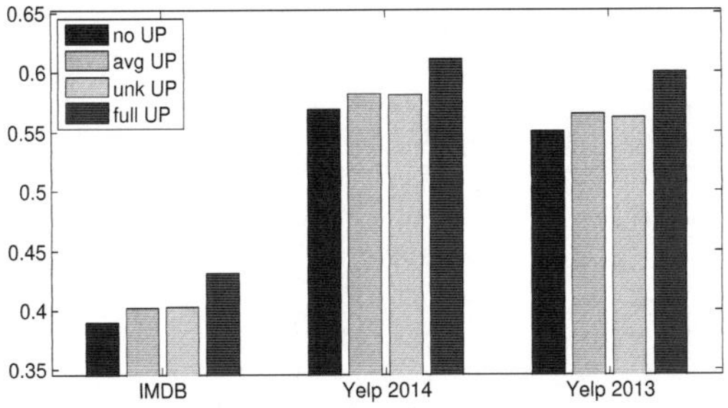

Figure 4: Accuracy of OOV user and product on OOV test set.

In order to evaluate the two strategies for OOV problem, we randomly select 10 percent users and products from each development set, and mask their user and product information. We run avg UP, unk UP together with UPNN (no UP) which only uses text information, and UPNN (full) which learns tailored representation for each user and product. We evaluate classification accuracy on the extracted OOV test set. Experimental results are given in Figure 5. We can find that these two strategies perform slightly better than UPNN (no UP), but still worse than the full model.

5 Related Work

5.1 Sentiment Classification

Sentiment classification is a fundamental problem in sentiment analysis, which targets at inferring the sentiment label of a document. Pang and Lee (2002; 2005) cast this problem a classification task, and use machine learning method in a supervised learning framework. Goldberg and Zhu (2006) use unlabelled reviews in a graph-based semi-supervised learning method. Many studies design effective features, such as text topic (Ganu et al., 2009), bag-of-opinion (Qu et al., 2010) and sentiment lexicon features (Kiritchenko et al., 2014). User information is also used for sentiment classification. Gao et al. (2013) design user-specific features to capture user leniency. Li et al. (2014) incorporate textual topic and user-word factors with supervised topic modeling. Tan et al. (2011) and Hu et al. (2013) utilize user-text and user-user relations for Twitter sentiment analysis. Unlike most previous studies that use hand-crafted features, we learn discriminative features from data. We differ from Li et al. (2014) in that we encode four kinds of consistencies and use neural network approach. User representation is also leveraged for recommendation (Weston et al., 2013), web search (Song et al., 2014) and social media analytics (Perozzi et al., 2014).

5.2 Neural Network for Sentiment Classification

Neural networks have achieved promising results for sentiment classification. Existing neural network methods can be divided into two groups: word embedding and semantic composition. For learning word embeddings, (Mikolov et al., 2013; Pennington et al., 2014) use local and global contexts, (Maas et al., 2011; Labutov and Lipson, 2013; Tang et al., 2014b; Tang et al., 2014a; Zhou et al., 2015) further incorporate sentiment of texts. For learning semantic composition, Glorot et al. (2011) use stacked denoising autoencoder, Socher et al. (2013) introduce a family of recursive deep neural networks (RNN). RNN is extended with adaptive composition functions (Dong et al., 2014), global feedbackward (Paulus et al., 2014), feature weight tuning (Li, 2014), and also used for opinion relation detection (Xu et al., 2014). Li et al. (2015) compare the effectiveness of recursive neural network and recurrent neural network on five NLP tasks including sentiment classification. (Kalchbrenner et al., 2014; Kim, 2014; Johnson and Zhang, 2014) use convolutional neural networks. Le and Mikolov (2014) introduce

Paragraph Vector. Unlike existing neural network approaches that only use the semantics of texts, we take consideration of user and product representations and leverage their connections with text semantics for sentiment classification. This work is an extension of our previous work (Tang et al., 2015), which only takes consideration of user-word association.

6 Conclusion

In this paper, we introduce User Product Neural Network (UPNN) for document level sentiment classification under a supervised learning framework. We validate user-sentiment, product-sentiment, user-text and product-text consistencies on massive reviews, and effectively integrate them in UPNN. We apply the model to three datasets derived from IMDB and Yelp Dataset Challenge. Empirical results show that: (1) UPNN outperforms state-of-the-art methods for document level sentiment classification; (2) incorporating continuous user and product representations significantly boosts sentiment classification accuracy.

Acknowledgments

The authors give great thanks to Furu Wei, Lei Cui, Nan Yang, Jiwei Li, Yaming Sun, Mao Zheng and anonymous reviewers for their valuable comments. We would like to thank Qiming Diao for providing the IMDB dataset as well as the codes of JMARS. This work was supported by the National High Technology Development 863 Program of China (No. 2015AA015407), National Natural Science Foundation of China (No. 61133012 and No. 61273321). Duyu Tang is supported by Baidu Fellowship and IBM Ph.D. Fellowship.

References

Marco Baroni and Roberto Zamparelli. 2010. Nouns are vectors, adjectives are matrices: Representing adjective-noun constructions in semantic space. In *EMNLP*, pages 1183–1193.

Yoshua Bengio, Réjean Ducharme, Pascal Vincent, and Christian Janvin. 2003. A neural probabilistic language model. *Journal of Machine Learning Research*, 3:1137–1155.

Stephen Clark, Bob Coecke, and Mehrnoosh Sadrzadeh. 2008. A compositional distributional model of meaning. In *Quantum Interaction Symposium*, pages 133–140.

Qiming Diao, Minghui Qiu, Chao-Yuan Wu, Alexander J Smola, Jing Jiang, and Chong Wang. 2014. Jointly modeling aspects, ratings and sentiments for movie recommendation (jmars). In *SIGKDD*, pages 193–202. ACM.

Pedro Domingos. 2012. A few useful things to know about machine learning. *Communications of the ACM*, 55(10):78–87.

Li Dong, Furu Wei, Ming Zhou, and Ke Xu. 2014. Adaptive multi-compositionality for recursive neural models with applications to sentiment analysis. In *AAAI*, pages 1537–1543.

Rong-En Fan, Kai-Wei Chang, Cho-Jui Hsieh, Xiang-Rui Wang, and Chih-Jen Lin. 2008. Liblinear: A library for large linear classification. *JMLR*.

Gottlob Frege. 1892. On sense and reference. *Ludlow (1997)*, pages 563–584.

Gayatree Ganu, Noemie Elhadad, and Amélie Marian. 2009. Beyond the stars: Improving rating predictions using review text content. In *WebDB*.

Wenliang Gao, Naoki Yoshinaga, Nobuhiro Kaji, and Masaru Kitsuregawa. 2013. Modeling user leniency and product popularity for sentiment classification. In *ICJNLP*, pages 1107–1111.

Xavier Glorot, Antoine Bordes, and Yoshua Bengio. 2011. Domain adaptation for large-scale sentiment classification: A deep learning approach. In *ICML*, pages 513–520.

Andrew B Goldberg and Xiaojin Zhu. 2006. Seeing stars when there aren't many stars: graph-based semi-supervised learning for sentiment categorization. In *GraphBased Method for NLP*, pages 45–52.

Xia Hu, Lei Tang, Jiliang Tang, and Huan Liu. 2013. Exploiting social relations for sentiment analysis in microblogging. In *WSDM*, pages 537–546.

Rie Johnson and Tong Zhang. 2014. Effective use of word order for text categorization with convolutional neural networks. *arXiv preprint: 1412.1058*.

Dan Jurafsky and James H Martin. 2000. *Speech & language processing*. Pearson Education India.

Nal Kalchbrenner, Edward Grefenstette, and Phil Blunsom. 2014. A convolutional neural network for modelling sentences. In *ACL*, pages 655–665.

Yoon Kim. 2014. Convolutional neural networks for sentence classification. In *EMNLP*, pages 1746–1751.

Svetlana Kiritchenko, Xiaodan Zhu, and Saif M Mohammad. 2014. Sentiment analysis of short informal texts. *Journal of Artificial Intelligence Research*, pages 723–762.

Igor Labutov and Hod Lipson. 2013. Re-embedding words. In *Annual Meeting of the Association for Computational Linguistics*.

Quoc V. Le and Tomas Mikolov. 2014. Distributed representations of sentences and documents. In *ICML*, pages 1188–1196.

Fangtao Li, Sheng Wang, Shenghua Liu, and Ming Zhang. 2014. Suit: A supervised user-item based topic model for sentiment analysis. In *AAAI*, pages 1636–1642.

Jiwei Li, Dan Jurafsky, and Eudard Hovy. 2015. When are tree structures necessary for deep learning of representations? *arXiv preprint:1503.00185*.

Jiwei Li. 2014. Feature weight tuning for recursive neural networks. *Arxiv preprint*, 1412.3714.

Bing Liu. 2012. Sentiment analysis and opinion mining. *Synthesis Lectures on Human Language Technologies*, 5(1):1–167.

Andrew L Maas, Raymond E Daly, Peter T Pham, Dan Huang, Andrew Y Ng, and Christopher Potts. 2011. Learning word vectors for sentiment analysis. In *ACL*, pages 142–150.

Christopher D Manning and Hinrich Schütze. 1999. *Foundations of statistical natural language processing*. MIT press.

Christopher Manning, Mihai Surdeanu, John Bauer, Jenny Finkel, Steven Bethard, and David McClosky. 2014. The stanford corenlp natural language processing toolkit. In *ACL*, pages 55–60.

Tomas Mikolov, Ilya Sutskever, Kai Chen, Greg S Corrado, and Jeff Dean. 2013. Distributed representations of words and phrases and their compositionality. In *NIPS*, pages 3111–3119.

Jeff Mitchell and Mirella Lapata. 2010. Composition in distributional models of semantics. *Cognitive Science*, 34(8):1388–1429.

Bo Pang and Lillian Lee. 2005. Seeing stars: Exploiting class relationships for sentiment categorization with respect to rating scales. In *ACL*, pages 115–124.

Bo Pang and Lillian Lee. 2008. Opinion mining and sentiment analysis. *Foundations and trends in information retrieval*, 2(1-2):1–135.

Bo Pang, Lillian Lee, and Shivakumar Vaithyanathan. 2002. Thumbs up?: sentiment classification using machine learning techniques. In *EMNLP*, pages 79–86.

Romain Paulus, Richard Socher, and Christopher D Manning. 2014. Global belief recursive neural networks. In *NIPS*, pages 2888–2896.

Jeffrey Pennington, Richard Socher, and Christopher D Manning. 2014. Glove: Global vectors for word representation. In *EMNLP*, pages 1532–1543.

Bryan Perozzi, Rami Al-Rfou, and Steven Skiena. 2014. Deepwalk: Online learning of social representations. In *SIGKDD*, pages 701–710. ACM.

Lizhen Qu, Georgiana Ifrim, and Gerhard Weikum. 2010. The bag-of-opinions method for review rating prediction from sparse text patterns. In *COLING*, pages 913–921.

Richard Socher, Brody Huval, Christopher D. Manning, and Andrew Y. Ng. 2012. Semantic Compositionality Through Recursive Matrix-Vector Spaces. In *EMNLP*, pages 1201–1211.

Richard Socher, Alex Perelygin, Jean Wu, Jason Chuang, Christopher D. Manning, Andrew Ng, and Christopher Potts. 2013. Recursive deep models for semantic compositionality over a sentiment treebank. In *EMNLP*, pages 1631–1642.

Yang Song, Hongning Wang, and Xiaodong He. 2014. Adapting deep ranknet for personalized search. In *WSDM*, pages 83–92. ACM.

Chenhao Tan, Lillian Lee, Jie Tang, Long Jiang, Ming Zhou, and Ping Li. 2011. User-level sentiment analysis incorporating social networks. In *SIGKDD*, pages 1397–1405. ACM.

Duyu Tang, Furu Wei, Bing Qin, Ming Zhou, and Ting Liu. 2014a. Building large-scale twitter-specific sentiment lexicon: A representation learning approach. In *COLING*, pages 172–182.

Duyu Tang, Furu Wei, Nan Yang, Ming Zhou, Ting Liu, and Bing Qin. 2014b. Learning sentiment-specific word embedding for twitter sentiment classification. In *ACL*, pages 1555–1565.

Duyu Tang, Bing Qin, Ting Liu, and Yuekui Yang. 2015. User modeling with neural network for review rating prediction. In *IJCAI*.

Jason Weston, Ron J Weiss, and Hector Yee. 2013. Nonlinear latent factorization by embedding multiple user interests. In *RecSys*, pages 65–68. ACM.

Liheng Xu, Kang Liu, and Jun Zhao. 2014. Joint opinion relation detection using one-class deep neural network. In *COLING*, pages 677–687.

Xinjie Zhou, Xiaojun Wan, and Jianguo Xiao. 2015. Representation learning for aspect category detection in online reviews. In *AAAI*.

Towards Debugging Sentiment Lexicons

Andrew Schneider
Computer and Information Sciences
Temple University
atschneider@temple.edu

Eduard Dragut
Computer and Information Sciences
Temple University
edragut@temple.edu

Abstract

Central to many sentiment analysis tasks are sentiment lexicons (SLs). SLs exhibit polarity inconsistencies. Previous work studied the problem of checking the consistency of an SL for the case when the entries have categorical labels (positive, negative or neutral) and showed that it is NP-hard. In this paper, we address the more general problem, in which polarity tags take the form of a continuous distribution in the interval [0, 1]. We show that this problem is polynomial. We develop a general framework for addressing the consistency problem using linear programming (LP) theory. LP tools allow us to uncover inconsistencies efficiently, paving the way to building SL debugging tools. We show that previous work corresponds to 0-1 integer programming, a particular case of LP. Our experimental studies show a strong correlation between polarity consistency in SLs and the accuracy of sentiment tagging in practice.

1 Introduction

Many sentiment analysis algorithms rely on *sentiment lexicons* (SLs), where word forms or word senses[1] are tagged as conveying positive, negative or neutral sentiments. SLs are constructed by one of three methods (Liu, 2012; Feldman, 2013): (1) **Manual** tagging by human annotators is generally reliable, but because it is labor-intensive, slow, and costly, this method has produced small-sized SLs comprising a few thousand words, e.g., Opinion Finder (OF) (Wilson et al., 2005), Appraisal Lexicon (AL) (Taboada and Grieve, 2004), General Inquirer (GI) (Stone et al., 1966), and Micro-WNOp (Cerini et al., 2007). (2) **Dictionary-based** acquisition relies on a set of seed words to expand its coverage to similar words. There are over thirty dictionary-based techniques (Andreevskaia and Bergler, 2006; Blum et al., 2004; Chen and Skiena, 2014; Choi and Wiebe, 2014; Esuli and Sebastiani, 2006; Feng et al., 2013; Hassan and Radev, 2010; Kamps et al., 2004; Mohammad et al., 2009; Takamura et al., 2005; Turney, 2002; Williams and Anand, 2009), most of them based on WordNet (Fellbaum, 1998), such as SentiWordNet (SWN)(Baccianella et al., 2010) and Q-WordNet (QWN) (Agerri and García-Serrano, 2010). (3) **Corpus-based** acquisition expands a set of seed words with the use of a large document corpus (Breck et al., 2007; Bross and Ehrig, 2013; Choi and Cardie, 2009; Ding et al., 2008; Du et al., 2010; Hatzivassiloglou and McKeown, 1997; Jijkoun et al., 2010; Kaji and Kitsuregawa, 2007; Klebanov et al., 2013; Lu et al., 2011; Peng and Park, 2011; Tang et al., 2014; Wu and Wen, 2010). Method (1) generally produces the most reliable annotations, however the considerable effort required to yield substantial lexicons makes it less useful in practice. The appeals of (2) and (3) lie in the formalism of their models and their capability of producing large-sized SLs. SLs are either word or sense/synset oriented. We refer to the former as Sentiment Word Lexicons (SWLs), e.g., GI, OF, and AL, and to the latter as Sentiment Sense Lexions (SSLs), e.g., SWN, QWN, and Micro-WNOp. Besides the method of compilation, SLs may also vary with regard to sentiment annotation.

Polarity disagreements are noted across SLs that do (SWN, Q-WordNet) and do not (AL, GI) reference WordNet. For instance, the adjectives `panicky` and `terrified`, have negative and positive polarities in OF, respectively. They each have only one synset which they share in WordNet: *"thrown into a state of intense fear or desperation"*. Assuming that there is an intrinsic re-

[1] We refer to a string of letters or sounds as a word form & to a pairing of a word form with a meaning as a word sense.

Proceedings of the 53rd Annual Meeting of the Association for Computational Linguistics and the 7th International Joint Conference on Natural Language Processing, pages 1024–1034,
Beijing, China, July 26-31, 2015.

lationship between the sentiments of a word and its meanings, a single synset polarity assignment to this synset cannot agree with both *positive* and *negative* at the word level. If the information given in WordNet is accurate (the Oxford and Cambridge dictionaries give only this meaning for both words) then there must be an annotation inconsistency in OF, called a *polarity inconsistency*. While some inconsistencies are easy to detect, manual consistency checking of an entire SL is an impractical endeavor, primarily because of the sheer size (SWN has over 206,000 word-sense pairs). Additionally, WordNet's complex network structure renders manual checking virtually impossible; an instance of a polarity inconsistency may entail an entire sub-network of words and senses. In this paper we develop a rigorous formal method based on linear programming (LP)(Schrijver, 1986) for *polarity consistency checking* of SLs with accompanying methods to unearth mislabeled words and synsets when consistency is not satisfied.

We translate the *polarity consistency problem* (PCP) into a form of the LP problem, suitable as the input to a standard LP solver, and utilize the functionality available in modern LP software (e.g., identifying an irreducible infeasible subset) to pinpoint the sources of inconsistencies when they occur. In our experimentation we are able to quickly uncover numerous intra- and inter-lexicon inconsistencies in all of the input SLs tested and to suggest lexicon entries for a linguist to focus on in "debugging" the lexicon.

Background and Previous Work

Sentiment resources have taken two basic approaches to polarity annotation: discrete and fractional. In the discrete approach, polarity is defined to be one of the discrete values *positive*, *negative*, or *neutral*. A word or a synset takes exactly one of the three values. QWN, AL, GI, and OF follow the *discrete polarity annotation*. In the fractional approach, polarity is defined as a 3-tuple of non-negative real numbers that sum to 1, corresponding to the positive, negative, and neutral values respectively. SWN, Micro-WNOp, and Hassan and Radev (2010) employ a *fractional polarity annotation*. For example, the single synset of the adjective `admissible` in WordNet has the sentiment tags *positive* in QWN and $\langle .25, .625, .125\rangle$ in SWN, so here SWN gives a primarily negative polarity with some positive and less neutral polarity. We denote by PCP-D and PCP-F the polarity

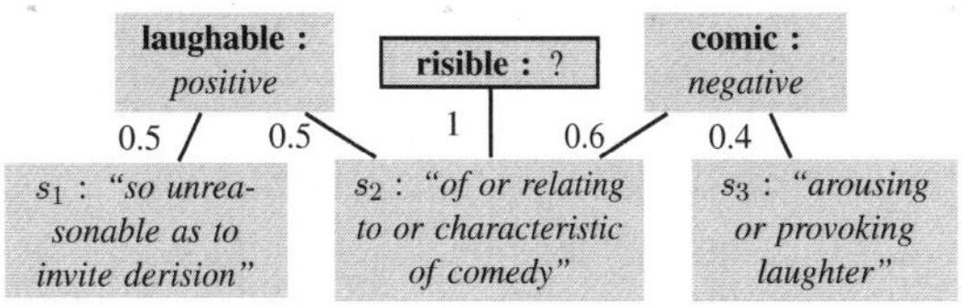

Figure 1: Discrete vs. fractional polarity consistency. Example taken from Dragut et al. (2012).

consistency problem for the discrete and fractional polarity annotations, respectively.

Dragut et al. (2012) introduces the PCP for domain independent SLs and gives a solution to a particular form of the PCP-D, but that method cannot solve PCP-F. For example, they show that the adjectives `laughable`, `comic`, and `risible` (Figure 1) constitute an inconsistency in the discrete case. AL gives positive polarity for `laughable` and OF gives negative for `comic`. If s_2 is not *positive* then `laughable` is not positive and if s_2 is not *negative* then `comic` is not negative, so there is no assignment of s_2 that satisfies the whole system. Hence there is an inconsistency. However, the following *fractional* polarity tags do satisfy the system: $s_1 : \langle 1, 0, 0\rangle$, $s_2 : \langle .66, .34, 0\rangle$, $s_3 : \langle 0, 1, 0\rangle$, where the meaning of the second tag, for instance, is that s_2 is .66 positive, .34 negative, and 0 neutral. We thus see that the discrete polarity annotation is rigid and leads to more inconsistencies, whereas the fractional annotation captures more naturally the polarity spectrum of a word or synset. In this paper we give a solution to the PCP-F. The differences between our solution and that of Dragut et al. (2012) give some insight into the general differences between the fractional and discrete problems. First, the discrete case is intractable, i.e., computationally NP-complete (Dragut et al., 2012); we show in this paper (Section 3.2) that the fractional case is tractable (solvable in polynomial time). Second, the PCP-D is solved in Dragut et al. (2012) by translation to the Boolean satisfiability problem (SAT) (Schaefer, 1978); here we recast the PCP-F in terms of LP theory. Third, we show that the LP framework is a natural setting for the PCP as a whole, and that the PCP-D corresponds to the 0-1 integer LP problem (Section 3.2), a classic NP-complete problem (Karp, 2010).

Our experiments (Section 5.4) show that correcting even a small number of inconsistencies can greatly improve the accuracy of sentiment annotation tasks. We implement our algorithm as a versatile tool for debugging SLs, which helps locate the sources of error in SLs. We apply our algorithm to both SWLs and SSLs and demonstrate the usefulness of our approach to improving SLs.

The main contributions of this paper are:

- solve the PCP-F;
- show that the PCP-F is tractable;
- show that the PCP is an instance of LP;
- develop a technique for identifying inconsistencies in SLs of various types;
- implement our algorithm as a prototype SL debugger;
- show that there is a strong correlation between polarity inconsistency in SLs and the performance of sentiment tagging tools developed on them.

2 Problem Definition

In this section we give a formal characterization of the polarity assignment of words and synsets in SLs using WordNet. We use $-$, $+$, 0 to denote negative, positive, and neutral polarities, respectively, throughout the paper.

2.1 Polarity Representation

We define the polarity of a synset or word r in WordNet to be a discrete probability distribution, called a **polarity distribution**: $P_+(r), P_-(r), P_0(r) \geq 0$ with $P_+(r) + P_-(r) + P_0(r) = 1$. $P_+(r)$, $P_-(r)$ and $P_0(r)$ represent the "likelihoods" that r is positive, negative or neutral, respectively. For instance, the WordNet synset *"worthy of reliance or trust"* of the adjective `reliable` is given the polarity distribution $P_+ = .375, P_- = .0$ and $P_0 = .625$ in SentiWordNet. We may drop r from the notation if the meaning is clear from context. The use of a polarity distribution to describe the polarity of a word or synset is shared with many previous works (Andreevskaia and Bergler, 2006; Baccianella et al., 2010; Kim and Hovy, 2006).

2.2 WordNet

A **word-synset network** $\mathcal{N}$ is a 4-tuple $(\mathcal{W}, \mathcal{S}, \mathcal{E}, f)$ where $\mathcal{W}$ is a finite set of words, $\mathcal{S}$ is a finite set of synsets, $\mathcal{E} \subseteq \mathcal{W} \times \mathcal{S}$ and f is a function assigning a positive integer to each element in $\mathcal{E}$. For any word w and synset s, s is a synset of w if $(w, s) \in \mathcal{E}$. For a pair $(w, s) \in \mathcal{E}$, $f(w, s)$ is called the **frequency of use** of w in the sense given by s. For a word w, we let $freq(w)$ denote the sum of all $f(w, s)$ such that $(w, s) \in \mathcal{E}$. We define the **relative frequency** of w with s by $rf(w, s) = \frac{f(w,s)}{freq(w)}$. If $f(w, s) = 0$, the frequency of each synset of w is increased by a small constant ϵ. We use $\epsilon = .1$ in our prototype.

2.3 Word Polarities

We contend that there exists a relation between the sentiment orientation of a word and the polarities of its related senses (synsets), and we make the assumption that this relation takes the form of a linear function. Thus, for $w \in \mathcal{W}$ and $p \in \{+, -, 0\}$, the polarity distribution of w is defined as:

$$P_p(w) = \sum_{s \in S_w} g(w, s) \cdot P_p(s), \qquad (1)$$

where $P_p(s)$ is the polarity value of synset s with polarity p and $g(w, s)$ is a rational number. For example, g can be the relative frequency of s with respect to w in WordNet: $g(w, s) = rf(w, s); \forall w \in \mathcal{W}, s \in \mathcal{S}$. Alternatively, for each word w we can draw $g(w, \cdot)$ from a Zipfian distribution, following the observation that the distribution of word senses roughly follows a Zipfian power-law (Kilgarriff, 2004; Sanderson, 1999). In this paper, we will assume $g(w, s) = rf(w, s)$.

For example, the three synsets of the adjective `reliable` with relative frequencies $\frac{9}{11}$, $\frac{1}{11}$, and $\frac{1}{11}$, respectively, are given the distributions $\langle .375, 0, .625\rangle$, $\langle .5, 0, .5\rangle$, and $\langle .625, 0, .375\rangle$ in SentiWordNet. So for `reliable` we have $P_+ = \frac{9}{11}0.375 + \frac{1}{11}0.5 + \frac{1}{11}0.625 \approx 0.41$, $P_- = 0$, and $P_0 = \frac{9}{11}0.625 + \frac{1}{11}0.5 + \frac{1}{11}0.375 \approx 0.59$.

2.4 Modeling Sentiment Orientation in SLs

Words and synsets have *unique* polarities in some SLs, e.g., AL and OF. For instance, `reliable` has positive polarity in AL, GI, and OF. The question is: what does a discrete annotation of `reliable` tell us about its polarity distribution? One might take it to mean that the polarity distribution is simply $\langle 1, 0, 0\rangle$. This contradicts the information in SWN, which gives some neutral polarity for all of the synsets of `reliable`. So a better polarity distribution would allow $P_0 > 0$. Furthermore, given that $\langle .41, 0, .59\rangle$, $\langle .40, 0, .60\rangle$, and $\langle .45, 0, .55\rangle$ give virtually identical information to a sentiment analyst, it seems unreasonable to expect exactly one to be the correct polarity tag for `reliable` and the other two incorrect. Therefore, instead of claiming to pinpoint an exact polarity distribution for a word, we propose to set a boundary on its variation. This establishes a range of values, instead of a single point, in which SLs can be said to agree.

Thus, for a word w, we can define

$$\text{polarity}(w) = \begin{cases} + & \text{if } P_+ > P_- \\ - & \text{if } P_- > P_+ \end{cases} \quad (2)$$

which we refer to as MAX_POL. This model is adopted either explicitly or implicitly by numerous works (Hassan and Radev, 2010; Kim and Hovy, 2004; Kim and Hovy, 2006; Qiu et al., 2009). Another model is the *majority sense model*, called MAJORITY, (Dragut et al., 2012), where

$$\text{polarity}(w) = \begin{cases} + & \text{if } P_+ > P_- + P_0 \\ - & \text{if } P_- > P_+ + P_0 \end{cases} \quad (3)$$

Another polarity model, MAX, is defined as

$$\text{polarity}(w) = \begin{cases} + & \text{if } P_+ > P_- \,\&\, P_+ > P_0 \\ - & \text{if } P_- > P_+ \,\&\, P_- > P_0 \end{cases} \quad (4)$$

For instance, `reliable` conveys positive polarity according to MAX_POL, since $P_+ > P_-$, but neutral according to MAJORITY. When the condition of being neither positive nor negative can be phrased as a conjunction of linear inequalities, as is the case with MAJORITY and MAX_POL, then we define neutral as not positive and not negative. These model definitions can be applied to synsets as well.

2.5 Polarity Consistency Definition

Instead of defining consistency for SLs dependent on a choice of model, we develop a generic definition applicable to a wide variety of models, including all of those discussed above. We require that the polarity of a word or synset in the network $\mathcal{N}$ be characterized by a *set of linear inequalities (constraints)* with rational coefficients. Formally, for each word $w \in \mathcal{W}$, the knowledge that w has a discrete polarity $p \in \{+, -, 0\}$ is characterized by a set of linear inequalities:

$$\psi(w,p) = \{a_{i,0}P_+ + a_{i,1}P_- + a_{i,2}P_0 \preceq b_i\}, \quad (5)$$

where $\preceq \in \{\leq, <\}$ and $a_{i,0}, a_{i,1}, a_{i,2}, b_i \in \mathbb{Q}$, $i = 0, 1, \ldots, m$. For instance, if the MAX model is used, for $w =$ `worship` whose polarity is positive in OF, we get the following set of inequalities: $\psi(w,+) = \{P_+ - P_- > 0, P_+ - P_0 > 0\} = \{(-1)P_+ + 1P_- + 0P_0 < 0, (-1)P_+ + 0P_- + 1P_0 < 0\}$.

Let $\mathcal{L}$ be an SL. We denote the system of inequalities introduced by all words and synsets in $\mathcal{L}$ with known polarities in the network $\mathcal{N}$ by $\Psi'(\mathcal{N}, \mathcal{L})$. The variables in $\Psi'(\mathcal{N}, \mathcal{L})$ are $P_+(r)$, $P_-(r)$ and $P_0(r)$, $r \in \mathcal{W} \cup \mathcal{S}$. Denote by $\Upsilon'(\mathcal{N}, \mathcal{L})$ the set of constraints implied by the polarity distributions for all $r \in \mathcal{L}$: $P_+(r) + P_-(r) + P_0(r) = 1$ and $P_{p \in \{+,-,0\}}(r) \geq 0, \forall r \in \mathcal{W} \cup \mathcal{S}$. Let $\Phi'(\mathcal{N}, \mathcal{L}) = \Psi'(\mathcal{N}, \mathcal{L}) \cup \Upsilon'(\mathcal{N}, \mathcal{L})$.

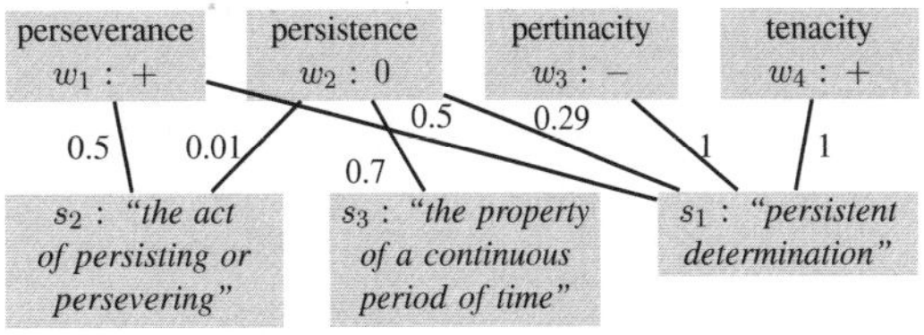

Figure 2: A network of 4 words and 3 synsets

Example 1. *Let* w_1, w_2, w_3, *and* w_4 *be the nouns* `perseverance`, `persistence`, `pertinacity`, *and* `tenacity`, *respectively, which are in OF with polarities* $+$, 0, $-$, *and* $+$, *respectively (Figure 2). Assuming the MAJORITY model,* $\psi(w_1,+) = \{P_+(w_1) > P_-(w_1) + P_0(w_1)\} = \{P_+(w_1) > 1 - P_+(w_1)\} = \{-P_+(w_1) < -\frac{1}{2}\}$, *and* $\psi(w_2, 0) = \{P_+(w_2) \leq P_-(w_2) + P_0(w_2), P_-(w_2) \leq P_+(w_2) + P_0(w_2)\} = \{P_+(w_2) \leq \frac{1}{2}, P_-(w_2) \leq \frac{1}{2}\}$. *Similarly,* $\psi(w_3,-) = \{-P_-(w_3) < -\frac{1}{2}\}$ *and* $\psi(w_4,-) = \{-P_+(w_4) < -\frac{1}{2}\}$.

Definition 1. *A sentiment lexicon* $\mathcal{L}$ *is* ***consistent*** *if the system* $\Phi'(\mathcal{N}, \mathcal{L})$ *is feasible, i.e., has a solution.*

The PCP is then the problem of deciding if a given SL $\mathcal{L}$ is consistent. In general, PCP can be stated as follows: *Given an assignment of polarities to the words, does there exist an assignment of polarities to the synsets that agrees with that of the words?* If the polarity annotation is discrete, we have the PCP-D; if the polarity is fractional, we have PCP-F. Our focus is PCP-F in this paper.

The benefits of a generic problem model are at least two-fold. First, different linguists may have different views about the kinds of inequalities one should use to express the probability distribution of a word with a unique polarity in some SL. The new model can accommodate divergent views as long as they are expressed as linear constraints. Second, the results proven for the generic model will hold for any particular instance of the model.

3 Polarity Consistency: an LP Approach

A careful analysis of the proposed formulation of the problem of SL consistency checking reveals that this can be naturally translated into an LP problem. The goal of LP is the optimization of a linear objective function, subject to linear (in)equality constraints. LP problems are expressed in *standard* form as follows:

$\mathbf{x}$ represents the vector of variables (to be determined), $\mathbf{c}$ and $\mathbf{b}$ are vectors of (known) coefficients, $\mathbf{A}$ is a (known) matrix of coefficients, and $(\cdot)^{\mathrm{T}}$ is the matrix transpose. An LP algorithm finds a point in the *feasible region* where $\mathbf{c}^{\mathrm{T}}\mathbf{x}$ has the smallest value, if such a point exists. The feasible region is the set of $\mathbf{x}$ that satisfy the constraints $\mathbf{Ax} \leq \mathbf{b}$ and $\mathbf{x} \geq \mathbf{0}$.

$$\begin{aligned} &\text{minimize } \mathbf{c}^{\mathrm{T}}\mathbf{x} \\ &\text{subject to } \mathbf{Ax} \leq \mathbf{b} \\ &\text{and } \mathbf{x} \geq \mathbf{0} \end{aligned} \quad (6)$$

There are several non-trivial challenges that need to be addressed in transforming our problem (i.e., the system $\Phi'(\mathcal{N}, \mathcal{L})$) into an LP problem. For instance, we have both strict and weak inequalities in our model, whereas standard LP does not include strict inequalities. We describe the steps of this transformation next.

3.1 Translation to LP

In our problem, $\mathbf{x}$ is the concatenation of all the triplets $\langle P_+(r), P_-(r), P_0(r)\rangle$ for all $r \in \mathcal{W} \cup \mathcal{S}$.

Eliminate Word Related Variables. For each word $w \in \mathcal{L}$ we replace $P_+(w), P_-(w)$ and $P_0(w)$ with their corresponding expressions according to Equation 1; then the linear system $\Phi'(\mathcal{N}, \mathcal{L})$ has only the synset variables $P_+(s), P_-(s)$ and $P_0(s)$ for $s \in \mathcal{S}$.

Example (continued). *Using the relative frequencies of Figure 2 in Equation 1 we get:*
$\psi(w_1,+) = \{-.5P_+(s_1) - .5P_+(s_2) < -\frac{1}{2}\}$,
$\psi(w_2,0) = \{.29P_+(s_1) + .01P_+(s_2) + .7P_+(s_3) \leq \frac{1}{2}$,
$.29P_-(s_1) + .01P_-(s_2) + .7P_-(s_3) \leq \frac{1}{2}\}$,
$\psi(w_3,-) = \{-P_-(s_1) < -\frac{1}{2}\}$, *and*
$\psi(w_4,+) = \{-P_+(s_1) < -\frac{1}{2}\}$.

Equality. The system $\Phi'(\mathcal{N}, \mathcal{L})$ contains constraints of the form $P_+(s) + P_-(s) + P_0(s) = 1$ for each $s \in \mathcal{S}$, but observe that there are no equality constraints in the standard LP form (Equation 6). The usual conversion procedure is to replace a given equality constraint: $\mathbf{a}^{\mathrm{T}}\mathbf{x} = b$, with: $\mathbf{a}^{\mathrm{T}}\mathbf{x} \leq b$ and $-\mathbf{a}^{\mathrm{T}}\mathbf{x} \leq -b$. However, this procedure increases the number of constraints in $\Phi'(\mathcal{N}, \mathcal{L})$ linearly. This can have a significant computation impact since $\Phi'(\mathcal{N}, \mathcal{L})$ may have thousands of constraints (see discussion in Section 5.3). Instead, we can show that the system F obtained by performing the following two-step transformation is equivalent to $\Phi'(\mathcal{N}, \mathcal{L})$, in the sense that F is feasible iff $\Phi'(\mathcal{N}, \mathcal{L})$ is feasible. For every $s \in \mathcal{S}$, (Step 1) we convert each $P_+(s) + P_-(s) + P_0(s) = 1$ to $P_+(s) + P_-(s) \leq 1$, and (Step 2) we replace every $P_0(s)$ in $\Phi'(\mathcal{N}, \mathcal{L})$ with $1 - P_+(s) - P_-(s)$.

Strict Inequalities. Strict inequalities are not allowed in LP and their presence in inequality systems in general poses difficulties to inequality system solvers (Goberna et al., 2003; Goberna and Rodriguez, 2006; Ghaoui et al., 1994). Fortunately results developed by the LP community allow us to overcome this obstacle and maintain the flexibility of our proposed model. We introduce a new variable $y \geq 0$, and for every strict constraint of the form $\mathbf{a}^{\mathrm{T}}\mathbf{x} < b$, we rewrite the inequality as $\mathbf{a}^{\mathrm{T}}\mathbf{x} + y \leq b$. Let $\Phi''(\mathcal{N}, \mathcal{L})$ be this new system of constraints. We modify the objective function (previously null) to maximize y (i.e., minimize $-y$). Denote by F' the LP that maximizes y subject to $\Phi''(\mathcal{N}, \mathcal{L})$. We can show that $\Phi'(\mathcal{N}, \mathcal{L})$ is feasible iff F' is feasible and $y \neq 0$. A sketch of the proof is as follows: if $y > 0$ then $\mathbf{a}^{\mathrm{T}}\mathbf{x} + y \leq b$ implies $\mathbf{a}^{\mathrm{T}}\mathbf{x} < b$. Conversely, if $\mathbf{a}^{\mathrm{T}}\mathbf{x} < b$ then $\exists y > 0$ such that $\mathbf{a}^{\mathrm{T}}\mathbf{x} + y \leq b$, and maximizing for y will yield a $y > 0$ iff one is feasible. This step is omitted if we have no strict constraints in $\Phi'(\mathcal{N}, \mathcal{L})$.

Example (continued). *The formulations of* $\psi(w_1, +)$, $\psi(w_3, -)$, *and* $\psi(w_4, +)$ *involve strict inequalities, so they are rewritten in* $\Phi''(\mathcal{N}, \mathcal{L})$, *e.g.,* $\psi''(w_4, +) = \{-P_+(s_1) + y \leq -\frac{1}{2}\}$.

We denote by $\Phi(\mathcal{N}, \mathcal{L})$ the standard form of $\Phi'(\mathcal{N}, \mathcal{L})$ obtained by applying the above steps. This is the input to an LP solver.

Theorem 1. *Sentiment lexicon* $\mathcal{L}$ *is polarity consistent iff* $\Phi(\mathcal{N}, \mathcal{L})$ *is feasible.*

3.2 Time Complexity

For the network $\mathcal{N}$ and an SL $\mathcal{L}$, the above translation algorithm converts the PCP into an LP problem on the order of $O(|\mathcal{E}|)$, a polynomial time conversion. The general class of linear programming problems includes subclasses that are NP-hard, such as the *integer linear programming* (ILP) problems, as well as polynomial solvable subclasses. We observe that our problem is represented by a system of *rational* linear inequalities. This class of LP problems is solvable in polynomial time (Khachiyan, 1980; Gács and Lovász, 1981). This (informally) proves that the PCP-F is solvable in polynomial time. PCP is NP-complete in the discrete case (Dragut et al., 2012). This is not surprising since in our LP formulation of the

PCP, the discrete case corresponds to the 0-1 integer programming (BIP) subclass. (Recall that in the discrete case each synset has a unique polarity.) BIP is the special case of integer programming where variables are required to be 0 or 1. BIP is a classic NP-hard problem (Garey and Johnson, 1990). We summarize these statements in the following theorem.

Theorem 2. *The PCP-F problem is P and the PCP-D is NP-complete.*

We proved a more general and more comprehensive result than Dragut et al. (2012). The PCP solved by Dragut et al. (2012) is a particular case of PCP-D: it can be obtained by instantiating our framework with the MAJORITY model (Equation 3) and requiring each synset to take a unique polarity. We believe that the ability to encompass both fractional and discrete cases within one framework, that of LP, is an important contribution, because it helps to give structure to the general problem of polarity consistency and to contextualize the difference between the approaches.

4 Towards Debugging SLs

Simply stating that an SL is *inconsistent* is of little practical use unless accompanying assistance in diagnosing and repairing inconsistencies is provided. Automated assistance is necessary in the face of the scale and complexity of modern SLs: e.g., AL has close to 7,000 entries, SWN annotates the entirety of WordNet, over 206,000 word-sense pairs. There are unique and interesting problems associated with inconsistent SLs, among them: (1) isolate a (small) subset of words/synsets that is polarity inconsistent, but becomes consistent if one of them is removed; we call this an Irreducible Polarity Inconsistent Subset (IPIS); (2) return an IPIS with smallest cardinality (intuitively, such a set is easiest to repair); (3) find all IPISs, and (4) find the largest polarity consistent subset of an inconsistent SL. In the framework of linear systems of constraints, the problems (1) - (4) correspond to (i) the identification of an Irreducible Infeasible Subset (IIS) of constraints within $\Phi(\mathcal{N}, \mathcal{L})$, (ii) finding IIS of minimum cardinality, (iii) finding all IISs and (iv) finding the largest set of constraints in $\Phi(\mathcal{N}, \mathcal{L})$ that is feasible, respectively. An IIS is an infeasible subset of constraints that becomes feasible if any single constraint is removed. Problems (ii) - (iv) are NP-hard and some may even be difficult to approximate (Amaldi and Kann, 1998; Chinneck, 2008; Chakravarti, 1994; Tamiz et al., 1996). We focus on problem (1) in this paper, which we solve via IIS discovery. We keep a bijective mapping from words and synsets to constraints such that for any given constraint, we can uniquely identify the word or synset in $\Phi(\mathcal{N}, \mathcal{L})$ from which it was introduced. Hence, once an IIS is isolated, we know the corresponding words or synsets. Modern LP solvers typically can give an IIS when a system is found to be infeasible, but none give all IISs or the IIS of minimum size.

Example (continued). *The polarity assignments of w_1, w_2, w_3, and w_4, are consistent iff there exist polarity distributions $\langle P_+(s_i), P_-(s_i), P_0(s_i)\rangle$ for $i = 1, 2, 3$, such that:* $y > 0$

$\psi(w_1, +): -.5P_+(s_1) + .5P_+(s_2) + y \leq -\frac{1}{2}$,
$\psi(w_2, 0): .29P_+(s_1) + .01P_+(s_2) + .7P_+(s_3) \leq \frac{1}{2}$
AND $.29P_-(s_1) + .01P_-(s_2) + .7P_-(s_3) \leq \frac{1}{2}$,
$\psi(w_3, -) : -P_-(s_1) + y \leq -\frac{1}{2}$,
$\psi(w_4, +) : -P_+(s_1) + y \leq -\frac{1}{2}$,
$\upsilon(s_1): P_+(s_1) + P_-(s_1) \leq 1$ *AND* $P_+(s_1), P_-(s_1) \geq 0$,
$\upsilon(s_2): P_+(s_2) + P_-(s_2) \leq 1$ *AND* $P_+(s_2), P_-(s_2) \geq 0$,
$\upsilon(s_3): P_+(s_3) + P_-(s_3) \leq 1$ *AND* $P_+(s_3), P_-(s_3) \geq 0$.

Upon examination, if $y > 0$, then $\psi(w_3, -)$ implies $P_-(s_1) > \frac{1}{2}$ and $\psi(w_4, +)$ implies $P_+(s_1) > \frac{1}{2}$. Then $P_+(s_1) + P_-(s_1) > 1$, contradicting $\upsilon(s_1)$. Hence, this LP system is infeasible. Moreover $\{\psi(w_3, -), \psi(w_4, +), \upsilon(s_1)\}$ is an IIS. Tracing back we get that the set of words $\{w_3, w_4\}$ is inconsistent. Therefore it is an IPIS.

Isolating IPISs helps focus SL diagnosis and repair efforts. Fixing SLs via IIS isolation proceeds iteratively: (1) isolate an IIS, (2) determine a repair for this IIS, (3) if the model is still infeasible, go to step (1). This approach is well summarized by Greenberg's aphorism: "diagnosis = isolation + explanation" (Greenberg, 1993). The proposed use requires human interaction to effect the changes to the lexicon. One might ask if this involvement is strictly necessary; in response we draw a parallel between our SL debugger and a software debugger. A software debugger can identify a known programming error, say the use of an undefined variable. It informs the programmer, but it does not assign a value to the variable itself. It requires the user to make the desired assignment. Similarly, our debugger can deterministically identify an inconsistent component, but it cannot deterministically decide which elements to adjust. In most cases, this is simply not an objective decision. To illustrate this point, from our example, we know that minimally one

	SL	adj.	adv.	noun	verb	total
SWLs	UN	3,084	940	2,340	1,812	8,176
	AL	1,486	377	2	0	1,865
	GI	1,337	121	1,474	1,050	3,982
	OF	2,608	775	1,907	1,501	6,791
SSLs	SWN	18,156	3,621	82,115	13,767	117,659
	QWN	4,060	40	7,404	4,006	15,510
	MWN	255	30	487	283	1,055

Table 1: Counts of words/synsets in each SL

of pertinacity(−) and tenacity(+) must be adjusted, but the determination as to which requires the subjective analysis of a domain expert.

In this paper, we do not repair any of the discovered inconsistencies. We focus on isolating as many IPISs as possible.

5 Experiments

The purpose of our experimental work is manifold, we show that: (1) inconsistencies exist in and between SLs, (2) our algorithm is effective at uncovering them in the various types of SLs proposed in the literature, (3) fractional polarity representation is more flexible than discrete, giving orders of magnitude fewer inconsistencies, and (4) sentiment analysis is significantly improved when the inconsistencies of a basis SL are corrected.

Experiment Setup: We use four SWLs: GI, AL, OF and their union, denoted UN, and three SSLs: QWN, SWN and MicroWN-Op. The distribution of their entries is given in Table 1. The MAJORITY model (Equation 3) is used in all trials. This allows for direct comparison with Dragut et al. (2012). We implemented our algorithm in Java interfacing with the GUROBI LP solver[2], and ran the tests on a 4×1.70GHz core computer with 6GB of main memory.

5.1 Inconsistencies in SWLs

In this set of experiments, we apply our algorithm to GI, AL, OF and UN. We find *no* inconsistencies in AL, only 2 in GI, and 35 in both UN and OF (Table 2). (Recall that an inconsistency is a *set* of words whose polarities cannot be concomitantly satisfied.) These numbers *do not* represent all possible inconsistencies (See discussion in Section 4). In general, the number of IISs for an infeasible system can be exponential in the size of the system $\Phi(\mathcal{N}, \mathcal{L})$ (Chakravarti, 1994), however our results suggest that in practice this does not occur.

Compared with Dragut et al. (2012), we see a marked decrease in the number of inconsistencies.

[2]www.gurobi.com

	adj.	adv.	noun	verb	total
UN	8	14	5	8	35
AL	0	0	0	-	0
GI	2	0	0	0	2
OF	7	15	4	9	35

Table 2: SWL-Internal Inconsistencies

Inconsistency Ratios

SWL	adj.	adv.	noun	verb	total
UN	0.67	0.89	0.85	0.81	0.78
AL	0.63	0.8	1	-	0.66
GI	0.6	0.41	0.87	0.91	0.78
OF	0.66	0.87	0.82	0.77	0.76

Table 3: SentiWordNet paired with SWLs

They found 249, 2, 14, and 240 inconsistencies in UN, AL, GI, and OF, respectively. These inconsistencies are obtained in the first iteration of their SAT-Solver. *This shows that about 86% of inconsistent words in a discrete framework can be made consistent in a fractional system.*

5.2 Inconsistencies in SSLs

In this set of experiments we check the polarity inconsistencies between SWLs and SSLs. We pair each SSL with each of the SWLs.

SentiWordNet. SWN is an automatically generated SL with a fractional polarity annotation of every synset in WordNet. Since SWN annotates *every* synset in WordNet, there are no free variables in this trial. Each variable $P_{p\in\{+,-,0\}}(s)$ for $s \in \mathcal{S}$ is fully determined by SWN, so this amounts to a constant on the left hand side of each inequality. Our task is to simply check whether the inequality holds between the constant on the left and that on the right. Table 3 gives the proportion of words from each SWL that is inconsistent with SWN. We see there is substantial disagreement between SWN and all of the SWLs, in most cases more than 70% disagreement. For example, 5,260 of the 6,921 words in OF do not agree with the polarities assigned to their senses in SWN. This outcome is deeply surprising given that all these SLs are *domain independent* – no step in their construction processes hints to a specific domain knowledge. This opens up the door to future analysis of SL acquisition. For instance, examining the impact that model choice (e.g., MAJORITY vs. MAX) has on inter-lexicon agreement.

Q-WordNet. QWN gives a discrete polarity for 15,510 WordNet synsets. When a synset is annotated in QWN, its variables, $P_{p\in\{+,-,0\}}(s)$, are assigned the QWN values in Φ; a feasible assignment is sought for the remaining free variables. An inconsistency may occur among a set of words, or

	UN	AL	GI	OF
total	345	34	139	325

Table 4: Q-WordNet paired with SWLs.

a set of words and synsets. Table 4 depicts the outcome of this study. We obtain 345 inconsistencies between QWN and UN. The reduced number of inconsistencies with AL (34) is explained by their limited "overlay" (QWN has only 40 adverb synsets). Dragut et al. (2012) reports 455 inconsistencies between QWN and UN, 110 more than we found here. Again, this difference is due to the rigidity of the discrete case, which leads to more inconsistencies in general.

Micro-WNOp. This is a fractional SSL of 1,105 synsets from WordNet manually annotated by five annotators. The synsets are divided into three groups: 110 annotated by the consensus of the annotators, 496 annotated individually by three annotators, and 499 annotated individually by two annotators. We take the average polarities of groups 2 and 3 and include this data as two additional sets of values. Table 5 gives the inconsistencies per user in each group. For Groups 2 and 3, we give the average number of inconsistencies among the users (Avg. Incons. in Table 5) as well as the inconsistencies of the averaged annotations (Avg. User in Table 5).

Micro-WNOp gives us an opportunity to analyze the robustness of our method by comparing the number of inconsistencies of the individual users to that of the averaged annotation. Intuitively, we expect that the average number of inconsistencies in a group of users to be close to the number of inconsistencies for the user averaged annotations. This is clearly apparent from Table 5, when comparing Lines 4 and 5 in Group 2 and Lines 3 and 4 in Group 3. For example, Group 2 has an average of 68 inconsistencies for OF, which is very close to the number of inconsistencies, 63, obtained for the group averaged annotations. This study suggests a potential application of our algorithm: to estimate the confidence weight (trust) of a user's polarity annotation. A user with good polarity consistency receives a higher weight than one with poor polarity consistency. This can be applied in a multi-annotator SL scenario.

5.3 Computation

We provide information about the runtime execution of our method in this section. Over all of our experiments, the resulting systems of constraints can be as small as 2 constraints with 2 variables and as large as 3,330 constraints with 4,946 variables. We achieve very good overall execution times, 68 sec. on average. At its peak, our algorithm requires 770MB of memory. Compared to the SAT approach by Dragut et al. (2012), which takes about 10 min. and requires about 10GB of memory, our method is several orders of magnitude more efficient and more practical, paving the way to building practical SL debugging tools.

		UN	AL	GI	OF
	Common	45	3	13	43
Group 2	**User 1**	88	10	59	75
	User 2	50	8	24	48
	User 3	97	12	64	82
	Avg. Incons.	78	10	49	68
	Avg. User 1,2,3	69	8	40	63
Group 3	**User 4**	72	9	46	60
	User 5	70	8	46	59
	Avg. Incons.	71	9	46	60
	Avg. User 4,5	68	8	42	57

Table 5: Micro-WNOp – SWD Inconsistencies

5.4 Inconsistency & Sentiment Annotation

This experiment has two objectives: (1) show that two inconsistent SLs give very different results when applied to sentiment analysis tasks and (2) given an inconsistent SL D, and D' an improved version of D with fewer inconsistencies, show that D' gives better results than D in sentiment analysis tasks. We use a third-party sentiment annotation tool that utilizes SLs, Opinion Parser (Liu, 2012). We give the instantiations of D below.

In (1), we use the dataset **aclImdb** (Maas et al., 2011), which consists of 50,000 reviews, and the SLs UN and SWN. Let UN′ and SWN′ be the subsets of UN and SWN, respectively, with the property that they have the same set of $(word, pos)$ pair entries and $word$ appears in **aclImdb**. UN′ and SWN′ have 6,003 entries. We select from **aclImdb** the reviews with the property that they contain at least 50 words in SWN′ and UN′. This gives 516 negative and 567 positive reviews, a total of 1,083 reviews containing a total of 31,701 sentences. Opinion Parser is run on these sentences using SWN′ and UN′. We obtain that 16,741 (52.8%) sentences acquire different polarities between the two SLs.

In (2), we use 110 randomly selected sentences from **aclImdb**, which we manually tagged with their overall polarities. We use OF and OF′, where OF′ is the version of OF after just six inconsistencies are manually fixed. We run Opinion Parser on these sentences using OF and OF′. We obtain an accuracy of 42% with OF and 47% with OF′, an improvement of 8.5% for just a small fraction of corrected inconsistencies.

These two experiments show a strong correlation between polarity inconsistency in SLs and its effect on sentiment tagging in practice.

6 Conclusion

Resolving polarity inconsistencies helps to improve the accuracy of sentiment analysis tasks. We show that LP theory provides a natural framework for the polarity consistency problem. We give a polynomial time algorithm for deciding whether an SL is polarity consistent. If an SL is found to be inconsistent, we provide an efficient method to uncover sets of words or word senses that are inconsistent and require linguists' attention. Effective SL debugging tools such as this will help in the development of improved SLs for use in sentiment analysis tasks.

7 Acknowledgments

We would like to thank Bing Liu for running the experiments of Section 5.4 on his commercial tool Opinion Parser, Christiane Fellbaum for the discussions on polarity inconsistency, and Prasad Sistla for the discussions on linear programming. We would also like to thank the reviewers for their time, effort, and insightful feedback.

References

Rodrigo Agerri and Ana García-Serrano. 2010. Q-wordnet: Extracting polarity from wordnet senses. In *LREC*.

Edoardo Amaldi and Viggo Kann. 1998. On the approximability of minimizing nonzero variables or unsatisfied relations in linear systems. *Theoretical Computer Science*, 209.

A. Andreevskaia and S. Bergler. 2006. Mining wordnet for fuzzy sentiment: Sentiment tag extraction from wordnet glosses. In *EACL*.

Stefano Baccianella, Andrea Esuli, and Fabrizio Sebastiani. 2010. SentiWordNet 3.0: An Enhanced Lexical Resource for Sentiment Analysis and Opinion Mining. In *LREC*.

Avrim Blum, John Lafferty, Mugizi Robert Rwebangira, and Rajashekar Reddy. 2004. Semi-supervised learning using randomized mincuts. In *ICML*.

Eric Breck, Yejin Choi, and Claire Cardie. 2007. Identifying expressions of opinion in context. In *IJCAI*.

Juergen Bross and Heiko Ehrig. 2013. Automatic construction of domain and aspect specific sentiment lexicons for customer review mining. In *CIKM*.

S. Cerini, V. Compagnoni, A. Demontis, M. Formentelli, and G. Gandini, 2007. *Language resources and linguistic theory: Typology, second language acquisition, English linguistics.*, chapter Micro-WNOp: A gold standard for the evaluation of automatically compiled lexical resources for opinion mining. Franco Angeli Editore, Milano, IT.

Nilotpal Chakravarti. 1994. Some results concerning post-infeasibility analysis. *European Journal of Operational Research*, 73(1).

Yanqing Chen and Steven Skiena. 2014. Building sentiment lexicons for all major languages. In *ACL*.

John W Chinneck. 2008. *Feasibility and infeasibility in optimization: algorithms and computational methods*. International Series in Operations Research and Management Science. Springer, Dordrecht.

Yejin Choi and Claire Cardie. 2009. Adapting a polarity lexicon using integer linear programming for domain-specific sentiment classification. In *EMNLP*.

Yoonjung Choi and Janyce Wiebe. 2014. +/-effectwordnet: Sense-level lexicon acquisition for opinion inference. In *EMNLP*.

Xiaowen Ding, Bing Liu, and Philip S. Yu. 2008. A holistic lexicon-based approach to opinion mining. In *WSDM*.

Eduard C. Dragut, Hong Wang, Clement Yu, Prasad Sistla, and Weiyi Meng. 2012. Polarity consistency checking for sentiment dictionaries. In *ACL*.

Weifu Du, Songbo Tan, Xueqi Cheng, and Xiaochun Yun. 2010. Adapting information bottleneck method for automatic construction of domain-oriented sentiment lexicon. In *WSDM*.

A. Esuli and F. Sebastiani. 2006. Determining term subjectivity and term orientation for opinion mining. In *EACL*.

Ronen Feldman. 2013. Techniques and applications for sentiment analysis. *Commun. ACM*, 56(4).

C. Fellbaum. 1998. *WordNet: An On-Line Lexical Database and Some of its Applications*. MIT Press, Cambridge, MA.

Song Feng, Jun Sak Kang, Polina Kuznetsova, and Yejin Choi. 2013. Connotation lexicon: A dash of sentiment beneath the surface meaning. In *ACL*.

Peter Gács and Laszlo Lovász. 1981. Khachiyans algorithm for linear programming. In *Mathematical Programming at Oberwolfach*, volume 14 of *Mathematical Programming Studies*. Springer Berlin Heidelberg.

Michael R. Garey and David S. Johnson. 1990. *Computers and Intractability; A Guide to the Theory of NP-Completeness*. W. H. Freeman & Co.

Laurent E. Ghaoui, Eric Feron, and Vendataramanan Balakrishnan. 1994. *Linear Matrix Inequalities in System & Control Theory (Studies in Applied Mathematics)*, volume 15. SIAM.

Miguel A. Goberna and Margarita M. L. Rodriguez. 2006. Analyzing linear systems containing strict inequalities via evenly convex hulls. *European Journal of Operational Research*, 169(3).

Miguel A. Goberna, Valentin Jornet, and Margarita M.L. Rodriguez. 2003. On linear systems containing strict inequalities. *Linear Algebra and its Applications*, 360(0).

Harvey J. Greenberg. 1993. How to analyze the results of linear programspart 3: Infeasibility diagnosis. *Interfaces*, 23(6).

Ahmed Hassan and Dragomir Radev. 2010. Identifying text polarity using random walks. In *ACL*.

Vasileios Hatzivassiloglou and Kathleen R. McKeown. 1997. Predicting the semantic orientation of adjectives. In *ACL*.

Valentin Jijkoun, Maarten de Rijke, and Wouter Weerkamp. 2010. Generating focused topic-specific sentiment lexicons. In *ACL*.

Nobuhiro Kaji and Masaru Kitsuregawa. 2007. Building lexicon for sentiment analysis from massive collection of html documents. In *EMNLP-CoNLL*.

J. Kamps, M. Marx, R. Mokken, and M. de Rijke. 2004. Using wordnet to measure semantic orientation of adjectives. In *LREC*.

Richard M. Karp. 2010. Reducibility among combinatorial problems. In *50 Years of Integer Programming 1958-2008 - From the Early Years to the State-of-the-Art*. Springer Berlin Heidelberg.

L. G. Khachiyan. 1980. Polynomial algorithms in linear programming. *Zh. Vychisl. Mat. Mat. Fiz.*, 20(1).

Adam Kilgarriff. 2004. How dominant is the commonest sense of a word? In *Text, Speech, and Dialogue*, volume 3206 of *Lecture Notes in Artificial Intelligence*.

M. Kim and E. Hovy. 2004. Determining the sentiment of opinions. In *COLING*.

Soo-Min Kim and Eduard Hovy. 2006. Identifying and analyzing judgment opinions. In *HLT-NAACL*.

Beata Beigman Klebanov, Nitin Madnani, and Jill Burstein. 2013. Using pivot-based paraphrasing and sentiment profiles to improve a subjectivity lexicon for essay data. In *ACL*.

Bing Liu. 2012. *Sentiment Analysis and Opinion Mining*. Synthesis Lectures on Human Language Technologies. Morgan & Claypool Publishers.

Yue Lu, Malu Castellanos, Umeshwar Dayal, and ChengXiang Zhai. 2011. Automatic construction of a context-aware sentiment lexicon: an optimization approach. In *WWW*.

Andrew L. Maas, Raymond E. Daly, Peter Pham, Dan Huang, Andrew Ng, and Christopher Potts. 2011. Learning word vectors for sentiment analysis. In *ACL*.

Saif Mohammad, Cody Dunne, and Bonnie Dorr. 2009. Generating high-coverage semantic orientation lexicons from overtly marked words and a thesaurus. In *EMNLP*.

Wei Peng and Dae Hoon Park. 2011. Generate adjective sentiment dictionary for social media sentiment analysis using constrained nonnegative matrix factorization. In *ICWSM*.

Guang Qiu, Bing Liu, Jiajun Bu, and Chun Chen. 2009. Expanding domain sentiment lexicon through double propagation. In *IJCAI*.

Mark Sanderson. 1999. The impact on retrieval effectiveness of skewed frequency distributions. *ACM Transactions on Information Systems*, 17(4).

Thomas J. Schaefer. 1978. The complexity of satisfiability problems. In *STOC*.

Alexander Schrijver. 1986. *Theory of linear and integer programming*. John Wiley & Sons, Inc., New York, NY, USA.

P. Stone, D. Dunphy, M. Smith, and J. Ogilvie. 1966. *The General Inquirer: A computer approach to content analysis*. MIT Press.

M. Taboada and J. Grieve. 2004. Analyzing appraisal automatically. In *AAAI Spring Symposium*.

Hiroya Takamura, Takashi Inui, and Manabu Okumura. 2005. Extracting semantic orientations of words using spin model. In *ACL*.

M. Tamiz, S. J. Mardle, and D. F. Jones. 1996. Detecting IIS in infeasible linear programmes using techniques from goal programming. *Comput. Oper. Res.*, 23(2).

Duyu Tang, Furu Wei, Bing Qin, Ming Zhou, and Ting Liu. 2014. Building large-scale twitter-specific sentiment lexicon : A representation learning approach. In *COLING*.

P. Turney. 2002. Thumbs up or thumbs down? semantic orientation applied to unsupervised classification of reviews. In *ACL*.

Gbolahan K. Williams and Sarabjot Singh Anand. 2009. Predicting the polarity strength of adjectives using wordnet. In *ICWSM*.

T. Wilson, J. Wiebe, and P. Hoffmann. 2005. Recognizing contextual polarity in phrase-level sentiment analysis. In *HLT/EMNLP*.

Yunfang Wu and Miaomiao Wen. 2010. Disambiguating dynamic sentiment ambiguous adjectives. In *COLING*.

Sparse, Contextually Informed Models for Irony Detection: Exploiting User Communities, Entities and Sentiment

Byron C. Wallace
University of Texas at Austin
byron.wallace@utexas.edu

Do Kook Choe and **Eugene Charniak**
Brown University
{dc65, ec}@cs.brown.edu

Abstract

Automatically detecting verbal irony (roughly, sarcasm) in online content is important for many practical applications (e.g., sentiment detection), but it is difficult. Previous approaches have relied predominantly on signal gleaned from word counts and grammatical cues. But such approaches fail to exploit the *context* in which comments are embedded. We thus propose a novel strategy for verbal irony classification that exploits contextual features, specifically by combining noun phrases and sentiment extracted from comments with the forum type (e.g., conservative or liberal) to which they were posted. We show that this approach improves verbal irony classification performance. Furthermore, because this method generates a very large feature space (and we expect predictive contextual features to be strong but few), we propose a mixed regularization strategy that places a sparsity-inducing ℓ_1 penalty on the contextual feature weights on top of the ℓ_2 penalty applied to all model coefficients. This increases model sparsity and reduces the variance of model performance.

1 Introduction and Motivation

Automated verbal irony detection is a challenging problem.[1] But recognizing when an author has intended a statement ironically is practically important for many text classification tasks (e.g., sentiment detection).

Previous models for irony detection (Tsur et al., 2010; Lukin and Walker, 2013; Riloff et al., 2013) have relied predominantly on features *intrinsic* to the texts to be classified. By contrast, here we propose exploiting *contextualizing* information, which is often available for web-based classification tasks. More specifically, we exploit signal gleaned from the conversational *threads* to which comments belong. Our approach capitalizes on the intuition that members of different user communities are likely to be sarcastic about different things. As a proxy for user community, we leverage knowledge of the specific forums to which comments were posted. For example, one may surmise that the statement 'I really am proud of Obama' is likely to have been intended ironically if it was posted to a forum frequented by political conservatives. But if this same utterance were posted to a liberal-leaning forum, it is more likely to have been intended in earnest. This sort of information is often directly or indirectly available on social media, but previous models have not capitalized on it. This is problematic; recent work has shown that humans require such contextualizing information to infer ironic intent (Wallace et

Figure 1: A reddit comment illustrating contextualizing features that we propose leveraging to improve classification. Here the highlighted entities (external the comment text itself) provide contextual signals indicating that the shown comment was intended ironically. As we shall see, *Obamacare* is in general a strong indicator of irony when present in posts to the *conservative* subreddit, but less so in posts to the *progressive* subreddit.

[1] In this paper we will be a bit cavalier in using the terms 'verbal irony' and 'sarcasm' interchangeably. We recognize that the latter is a special type of the former, the definition of which is difficult to pin down precisely.

Proceedings of the 53rd Annual Meeting of the Association for Computational Linguistics and the 7th International Joint Conference on Natural Language Processing, pages 1035–1044,
Beijing, China, July 26-31, 2015.

al., 2014).

As a concrete example, we consider the task of identifying verbal irony in comments posted to reddit (`http://www.reddit.com`), a social-news website. Users post content (e.g., links to news stories) to reddit, which are then voted on by the community. Users may also discuss this content on the website; these are the comments that we will work with here. Reddit comprises many *subreddits*, which are user communities centered around specific topics of interest. In this work we consider comments posted to two pairs of polarized user communities, or subreddits: (1) *progressive* and *conservative* subreddits (comprising individuals on the left and right of the US political spectrum, respectively), and (2) *atheism* and *Christianity* subreddits.

Our aim is to develop a model that can recognize verbal irony in comments posted to such forums, e.g., automatically discern that the user who posted the comment shown in Figure 1 intended his or her comment ironically. To this end, we propose a strategy that capitalizes on available contextualizing information, such as interactions between the user community (subreddit) that comments were posted to, extracted entities (here we use noun phrases, or NNPs) and inferred sentiment.

The contributions of this work are summarized as follows.

- We demonstrate that contextual information, such as inferred user-community (in this case, the subreddit) can be crossed with extracted entities and sentiment to improve detection of verbal irony. This improves performance over baseline models (including those that exploit inferred sentiment, but not context).
- We introduce a novel composite regularization strategy that applies a sparsifying ℓ_1 penalty to the contextual/sentiment/entity feature weights in addition to the standard squared ℓ_2 penalty to all feature weights. This induces more compact, interpretable models that exhibit lower variance.

While discerning ironic comments on reddit is our immediate task, the proposed approach is generally applicable to a wide-range of subjective, web-based text classification tasks. Indeed, this approach would be useful for any scenario in which we expect different groups of individuals producing content to tend to discuss different entities in a way that correlates with the target categorization. The key is in identifying an available proxy for user groupings (here we rely on the subreddits to which a comment was posted). Such information is often available (or can be derived) for comments posted to different mediums on the web: for example on Twitter we know who a user follows; and on YouTube we know the channels to which videos belong.

2 Exploiting context

2.1 Communities and sentiment

As discussed above, a shortcoming with existing models for detecting sarcasm/verbal irony on the web is their failure to capitalize on contextualizing information. But such information is critical to discerning irony. A large body of work on the use and interpretation of verbal irony supports this supposition (Grice, 1975; Clark and Gerrig, 1984; Wallace, 2013; Wallace et al., 2014). Individuals will be more likely, in general, to use sarcasm when discussing specific entities. Which entities will depend in part on the community to which the individual belongs. As a proxy for user community, here we leverage the subreddits to which comments were posted.

Sentiment may also play an important role. In general, verbal irony is almost always used to convey negative views via ostensibly positive utterances (Sperber and Wilson, 1981). And recent work (Riloff et al., 2013) has exploited features based on sentiment to improve irony detection.

To summarize: when assuming an ironic voice we expect that individuals will convey ostensibly positive sentiment about entities, and that these entities will depend on the type of individual in question. We propose capitalizing on such information by introducing features that encode subreddits, sentiment and noun phrases (NNPs), as we describe next.

2.2 Features

We leverage the feature sets enumerated in Table 1. Subreddits are observed variables. Noun phrase (NNP) extraction and sentiment inference are performed automatically via state of the art NLP tools. In particular, we use the Stanford Sentiment Analysis tool (Socher et al., 2013) to infer sentiment. To extract NNPs we use the Stanford

Feature	Description
Sentiment	The inferred sentiment (*negative/neutral* or *positive*) for a given comment.
Subreddit	the subreddit (e.g., *progressive* or *conservative*; *atheism* or *Christianity*) to which a comment was posted.
NNP	Noun phrases (e.g., proper nouns) extracted from comment texts.
NNP+	Noun phrases extracted from comment texts *and* the thread to which they belong (for example, 'Obamacare' from the title in Figure 1).

Table 1: Feature types that we exploit. We view the (observed) subreddit as a proxy for *user type*. We combine this with sentiment and extracted noun phrases (NNPs) to improve classifier performance.

Part of Speech tagger (Toutanova et al., 2003). We then introduce 'bag-of-NNP' features and features that indicate whether the sentiment inferred for a given sentence was positive or not.

Additionally, we introduce 'interaction' features that capture combinations of these. For example, a feature that indicates whether a given sentence mentions Obamacare (which will be one of many NNPs automatically extracted) *and* was posted in the *conservative* subreddit. This is an example of a two-way interaction. We also experiment with three-way interactions, crossing sentiment with NNPs and subreddits. An example is a feature that indicates if a sentence was: inferred to be positive *and* mentions Obamacare (NNP) *and* was part of a comment made in the conservative subreddit. Finally, we experiment with adding NNPs extracted from the comment thread in addition to the comment text.

These are rich features that capture signal not directly available from the sentences themselves. Features that encode subreddits crossed with extracted NNP's, in particular, offer a chance to explicitly account for differences in how the ironic device is used by individuals in different communities. However, this has the downside of introducing a large number of irrelevant terms into the model: we expect, *a priori*, that many entities will not correlate with the use of verbal irony. We would therefore expect this strategy to exhibit high variance in terms of predictive performance, and we later confirm this empirically. Ideally, a model would perform feature selection during parameter estimation, thus dropping irrelevant interaction terms. We next introduce a composite ℓ_1/ℓ_2 regularization strategy toward this end.

3 Enforcing sparsity

3.1 Preliminaries

In this work we consider linear models with binary outputs ($y \in \{-1, +1\}$). We will assume we have access to a training dataset comprising n instances, $\mathbf{x} = \{\mathbf{x}_1, ..., \mathbf{x}_n\}$ and associated labels $\mathbf{y} = \{y_1, ..., y_n\}$. We then aim to find a weight-vector $\mathbf{w}$ that optimizes the following objective.

$$\underset{\mathbf{w}}{\operatorname{argmin}} \sum_{i=1}^{n} \mathcal{L}(\text{sign}\{\mathbf{w} \cdot \mathbf{x}_i\}, y_i) + \alpha \mathcal{R}(\mathbf{w}) \quad (1)$$

Where $\mathcal{L}$ is a loss function, $\mathcal{R}(\mathbf{w})$ is a regularization term and α is a parameter expressing the relative emphasis placed on achieving minimum empirical loss versus producing a simple model (i.e., a weight vector with small weights). Typically one searches for a good α using the available training data. For $\mathcal{L}$, we will use the log-loss in this work, though other loss functions may be used in its place.

3.2 Sparsity via Regularization

Concerning $\mathcal{R}$, one popular regularization function is the squared ℓ_2 norm:

$$\sum_{j} \mathbf{w}_j^2 \quad (2)$$

This is the norm used in the standard Support Vector Machine (SVM) formulation, for example, and has been shown empirically to work well for text classification (Joachims, 1998). An alternative is to use the ℓ_1 norm:

$$\sum_{j} |\mathbf{w}_j| \quad (3)$$

Which has the advantage of inducing sparse models: i.e., using the ℓ_1 norm as a penalty tends to drive feature weights to 0.

Returning to the present task of detecting verbal irony in comments, it seems reasonable to assume that there will be a relatively small set of entities that correlate with sarcasm. But because we are introducing 'interaction' features that enumerate the cross-product of subreddits and entities (and, in some cases, sentiment), we have a large feature-space. This space includes features that correspond to NNPs extracted from, and sentiment inferred for, the sentence itself: we will denote the indices for these by $\mathcal{I}$. Other interaction features correspond to entities extracted from the *threads* associated with comments: we denote the corresponding set of indices by $\mathcal{T}$. We expect only a fraction of the features comprising both $\mathcal{I}$ and $\mathcal{T}$ to have non-zero weights (i.e., to signal ironic intent).

This scenario is prone to the undesirable property of high-variance, and hence calls for stronger regularization. But in general replacing the squared ℓ_2 norm with an ℓ_1 penalty (over all weights) hampers classification performance (indeed, as we later report, this strategy performs very poorly here). Therefore, in our scenario we would like to place a sparsifying ℓ_1 regularizer over the contextual (interaction) features while still leveraging the squared ℓ_2-norm penalty for the standard bag-of-words (BoW) features.[2] We thus propose the following composite penalty:

$$\sum_j \mathbf{w}_j^2 + \sum_{k \in \mathcal{I}} |\mathbf{w}_k| + \sum_{l \in \mathcal{T}} |\mathbf{w}_l| \quad (4)$$

The idea is that this will drive many of the weights associated with the contextual features to zero, which is desirable in light of the intuition that a relatively small number of entities will likely indicate sarcasm. At the same time, this composite penalty applies only the squared ℓ_2 norm to the standard BoW features, given the comparatively strong predictive performance realized with this strategy.

Putting this together, we modify the original objective (Equation 1) as follows:

$$\begin{aligned}\underset{\mathbf{w}}{\text{argmin}} \sum_{i=1}^{n} \mathcal{L}(\text{sign}\{\mathbf{w} \cdot \mathbf{x}_i\}, y_i) + \\ \alpha_0 \sum_j \mathbf{w}_j^2 + \alpha_1 \sum_{k \in \mathcal{I}} |\mathbf{w}_k| + \alpha_2 \sum_{l \in \mathcal{T}} |\mathbf{w}_l| \quad (5)\end{aligned}$$

Where we have placed separate α scalars on the respective penalty terms. Note that this is similar to the *elastic net* (Zou and Hastie, 2005) joint regularization and variable selection strategy. The distinction here is that we only apply the ℓ_1 penalty to (i.e., perform feature selection for) the subset of 'interaction' feature weights, which is in contrast to the elastic net, which imposes the composite penalty to *all* feature weights. One can view this as using the regularizer to encourage a sparsity pattern specific to the task at hand.

[2]Note that we apply both ℓ_1 and ℓ_2 penalties to the features in $\mathcal{I}$ and $\mathcal{T}$.

3.3 Inference

We fit this model via Stochastic Gradient Descent (SGD).[3] During each update, we impose both the squared ℓ_2 and ℓ_1 penalties; the latter is applied only to the contextual/interaction features in $\mathcal{I}$ and $\mathcal{T}$. For the ℓ_1 penalty, we adopt the cumulative truncated gradient method proposed by Tsuruoka et al. (2009).

4 Experimental Setup

4.1 Datasets

For our development dataset, we used a subset of the reddit irony corpus (Wallace et al., 2014) comprising annotated comments from the *progressive* and *conservative* subreddits. We also report results from experiments performed using a separate, held-out portion of this data, which we did not use during model refinement. Furthermore, we later present results on comments from the *atheism* and *Christianity* subreddits (we did not use this data during model development, either).

The development dataset includes 1,825 annotated comments (876 and 949 from the *progressive* and *conservative* subreddits, respectively). These comprise 5,625 sentences in total, each of which was independently labeled by three annotators as having been intended *ironically* or not. For additional details on the annotation process, see (Wallace et al., 2014). For simplicity, we consider a sentence to be 'ironic' ($y = 1$) when at least two of the three annotators designated it as such, and 'unironic' ($y = -1$) otherwise. Using this criteria, 286 (5%) of the labeled sentences are labeled 'ironic'.

The test portion of the political dataset comprises 996 annotated comments (409 *progressive* and 587 *conservative* comments), totalling 2,884 sentences. Using the same criteria as above – at least 2/3 annotators labeling a given sentence as 'ironic' – we have 154 'ironic' sentences (again about 5%).

The 'religion' dataset (comments from *atheism* and *Christianity*) contains 1,682 labeled comments comprising 5615 sentences (2,966 and 2,649 from the atheism and Christian subreddits, respectively); 313 (~6%) were deemed 'ironic'.

[3]We have implemented this within the *sklearn* package (Pedregosa et al., 2011).

4.2 Experimental Details

We recorded results from 500 independently performed experiments on random train (80%)/test (20%) splits of the data. These splits were performed at the *comment* (rather than sentence) level, so as not to test on sentences belonging to comments encountered in the training set. We measured performance, however, at the sentence level (often only a single sentence in a given comment will have been labeled as 'ironic').

Our baseline approach is a standard squared-ℓ_2 regularized log-loss linear model (fit via SGD) that leverages uni- and bi-grams and features indicating grammatical cues, such as exclamation points and emoticons. We also experiment with a model that includes inferred sentiment indicators, but not context. We performed standard English stopwording, and we used Term Frequency Inverse-Document Frequency (TF-IDF) feature weighting. For the gradient descent procedure, we used a decaying learning rate (specifically, $\frac{1}{t}$, where t is the update count). We performed a coarse grid search to find values for α that maximize $F1$ on the training datasets. We took five full passes over the training data before terminating descent.

We report paired *recalls* and *precisions*, as observed on each random train/test split of the data. The former is defined as $\frac{TP}{TP+FN}$ and the latter as $\frac{TP}{TP+FP}$, where TP denotes the true positive count, FN the number of false negatives and FP the false positive count. We report these separately - rather than collapsing into $F1$ - because it is not clear that one would value recall and precision equally for irony detection, and because this allows us to tease out *how* the models differ in performance. Notably, for example, sentiment and context features both improve recall, but the latter does so without harming precision.

5 Results

5.1 Results on the Development Corpus

Figure 2 and Table 2 summarize the performance of the different approaches over 500 independently performed train/test splits of the political development corpus. For reference, a random chance strategy (which predicts 'ironic' with probability equal to the observed prevalence) achieves a median recall of 0.048 and a median precision of 0.047.

Figure 2 shows histograms of the observed absolute differences between the baseline linear classifier and the proposed augmentations. Adding the proposed features (which capitalize on sentiment and NNP-mentions on specific subreddits) increases absolute median recall by 3.4 percentage points (a relative gain of ~12%). And this is achieved without sacrificing precision (in contrast to exploiting only sentiment). Furthermore, as we can see in Figures 2 and 3, the proposed regularization strategy shrinks the variance of the classifier. This variance reduction is achieved through greater model sparsity, as can be seen in Figure 4, which improves interpretability. We note that leveraging *only* an ℓ_1 regularization penalty (with the full feature-set) results in very poor performance (median recall and precision of 0.05 and 0.09, respectively). Similarly, the elastic-net strategy (Zou and Hastie, 2005) (in which we do not specify which features to apply the ℓ_1 penalty to), here achieves a median recall of 0.11 and a median precision of 0.07.

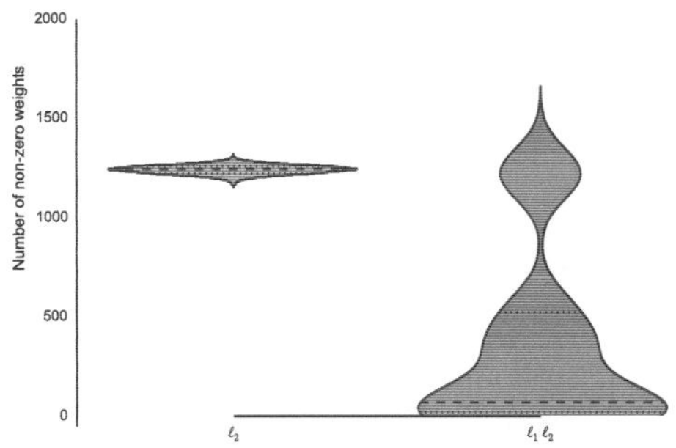

Figure 4: Empirical distributions (violin plots) of non-zero feature counts in the NNP $\times$ subreddit model (rows 3 and 4 in Figure 3) using standard ℓ_2-norm (left) and the proposed $\ell_1\ell_2$-norm (right) regularization approaches on the *atheism/Christianity* data over 500 independent train/test splits. The composite norm achieves much greater sparsity, resulting in lower variance. This sparsity also (arguably) provides greater interpretability; one can inspect contextual features with non-zero weights.

5.2 Results on the Held-out (Test) Corpus

Table 4 reports results on the held-out political test dataset, achieved after training the models on the entirety of the development corpus. To account for the variance inherent to inference via SGD, we performed 100 runs of the SGD procedure and report median results from these runs. These results mostly agree with those reported for the development corpus: the proposed strategy improves median recall on the held-out corpus by nearly 4.0 percentage points, at a median cost of about 1 point in precision. By contrast, sentiment alone provides a 2% absolute improvement in recall at

	mean; median (25th, 75th)	mean; median (25th, 75th)
baseline (BoW)	0.288; 0.283 (0.231, 0.333)	0.129; 0.124 (0.103, 0.149)
	Δ recall	Δ precision
(overall) sent.	+0.036; +0.037 (+0.015, +0.063)	-0.008; -0.007 (-0.018, +0.003)
NNP	+0.021; +0.018 (+0.000, +0.036)	-0.008; -0.008 (-0.016, -0.001)
NNP × subreddit	+0.013; +0.016 (+0.000, +0.031)	-0.002; -0.003 (-0.009, +0.004)
NNP × subreddit (ℓ_1 ℓ_2)	+0.010; +0.000 (+0.000, +0.021)	-0.002; -0.002 (-0.007, +0.004)
NNP+ × sent. × subreddit + sent.	+0.036; +0.038 (+0.000, +0.065)	-0.000; -0.001 (-0.012, +0.011)
NNP+ × sent. × subreddit + sent. (ℓ_1 ℓ_2)	+0.035; +0.034 (+0.000, +0.062)	+0.001; +0.000 (-0.011, +0.011)

Table 2: Summary results over 500 random train/test splits of the development dataset. The top row reports mean and median baseline (BoW) recall and precision and lower and upper (25th and 75th) percentiles. We report pairwise differences w.r.t. this baseline in terms of recall and precision for each strategy. Exploiting NNP features and subreddits improves recall with little to not cost in precision. Capitalizing on sentiment alone improves recall but at a greater cost in precision. The proposed $\ell_1\ell_2$ regularization strategy achieves comparable performance with fewer features, and shrinks the variance over different train/test splits (as can bee seen in Figure 2).

	mean; median (25th, 75th)	mean; median (25th, 75th)
baseline (BoW)	0.281; 0.268 (0.222, 0.327)	0.189; 0.187 (0.144, 0.230)
	Δ recall	Δ precision
(overall) sent.	+0.001; +0.000 (-0.011, +0.015)	-0.014; -0.012 (-0.023, -0.002)
NNP	+0.018; +0.018 (+0.000, +0.039)	-0.009; -0.010 (-0.021, +0.001)
NNP × subreddit	+0.024; +0.025 (+0.000, +0.046)	+0.002; +0.001 (-0.011, +0.013)
NNP × subreddit (ℓ_1 ℓ_2)	+0.013; +0.015 (+0.000, +0.033)	+0.002; +0.002 (-0.009, +0.011)
NNP+ × sent. × subreddit + sent.	+0.023; +0.024 (+0.000, +0.046)	+0.001; +0.001 (-0.012, +0.013)
NNP+ × sent. × subreddit + sent. (ℓ_1 ℓ_2)	+0.014; +0.015 (+0.000, +0.036)	-0.008; -0.008 (-0.021, +0.004)

Table 3: Results on the *atheism* and *Christianity* subreddits. In general sentiment does not help on this dataset (see row 1). But the NNP and subreddit features again consistently improve recall without hurting precision. And, as above, $\ell_1\ell_2$ regularization shrinks variance (see Figures 2 and 3).

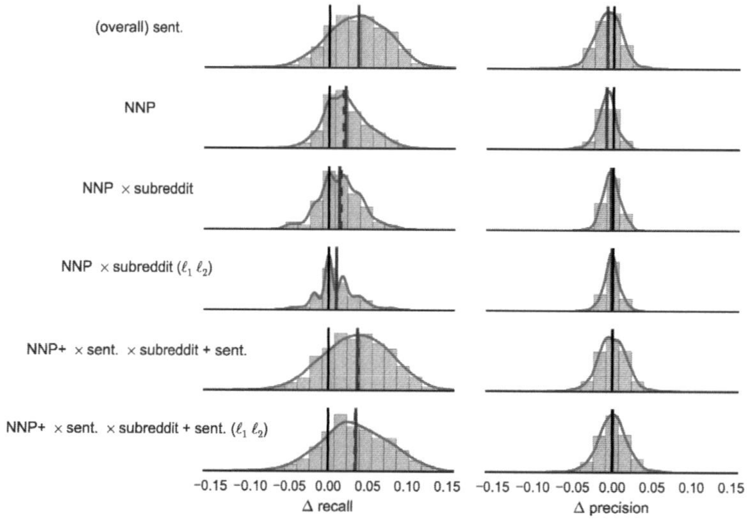

Figure 2: Results from 500 independent train/test splits of the development subset of our political data. Shown are histograms with smoothed kernel density estimates of differences in recall and precision between the baseline bag-of-words based approach and each feature space/method (one per row). The solid black line at 0 indicates no difference; solid and dotted blue lines demarcate means and medians, respectively. Features are as in Table 1. The × symbol denotes interactions; + indicates addition. The proposed contextual features substantially improve recall, with little to no loss in precision. Moreover, in general, the $\ell_1\ell_2$ regularization approach reduces variance. (We note that in constructing histograms we have excluded a handful of points – never more than 1% – where the difference exceeded 0.15).

	median recall (std. dev.)	median precision (std. dev.)
baseline	0.331 (0.146)	0.148 (0.022)
(overall) sent.	0.351 (0.054)	0.125 (0.003)
NNP	0.364 (0.119)	0.135 (0.021)
NNP × subreddit	0.357 (0.108)	0.143 (0.020)
NNP+ × sent. × subreddit	0.344 (0.116)	0.142 (0.019)
NNP+ × sent. × subreddit (ℓ_1 ℓ_2)	0.325 (0.052)	0.141 (0.008)
NNP+ × sent. × subreddit + sent.	0.377 (0.104)	0.141 (0.014)
NNP+ × sent. × subreddit + sent. (ℓ_1 ℓ_2)	0.370 (0.056)	0.140 (0.008)

Table 4: Results on the held-out political dataset, using the entire development corpus as a training set. Abbreviations are as described in the caption for Figure 2. Due to the variance inherent to the stochastic gradient descent procedure, we repeat the experiment 100 times and report the median performance and standard deviations (of different SGD runs). Results are consistent with those reported for the development corpus.

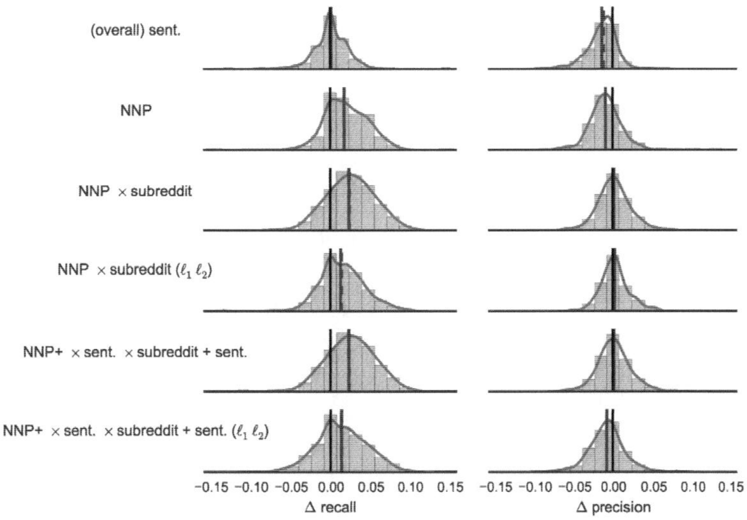

Figure 3: Results from 500 independent train/test splits of the development subset of the religion corpus). The description is the same as for Figure 2.

the expense of more than 2 points in precision.

5.3 Results on the religion dataset

To assess the general applicability of the proposed approach, we also evaluate the method on comments from a separate pair of polarized communities: *atheism* and *Christianity*, as described in Section 4.1. This dataset was not used during model development. We follow the experimental setup described in Section 4.2.

In this case, capitalizing on the NNP × subreddit features produces a mean 2.3% absolute gain in recall (median: 2.4%) over the baseline approach, with a (very) slight gain in precision. The ℓ_1 ℓ_2 approach achieves a lower expected gain in recall (median: 1.5%), but again shrinks the variance w.r.t. model performance (see Figure 3). Moreover, as we show in Figure 4, this is achieved with a much more compact (sparser) model. We note that for the religion data, inferred sentiment features do not seem to improve performance, in contrast to the results on the political subreddits. At present, we are not sure why this is the case.

These results demonstrate that introducing features that encode entities and user communities (NNPs × subreddit) improve recall for irony detection in comments addressing relatively diverse topics (politics and religion).

5.4 Predictive features

We report the interaction features that are the best predictors of verbal irony in the respective subreddits (for both polar community pairs). Specifically, we estimated the weights for every interaction feature using the entire training dataset, and repeated this process 100 times to account for variation due to the SGD procedure.

progressive		*conservative*	
feature	weight	feature	weight
freedom	0.102 (0.048)	racist	0.148 (0.043)
god	0.085 (0.045)	news	0.100 (0.044)
christmas	0.081 (0.046)	way	0.078 (0.044)
jesus	0.060 (0.038)	obamacare	0.068 (0.041)
kenya	0.052 (0.035)	white	0.059 (0.037)
brave	0.043 (0.035)	let	0.058 (0.038)
bravo	0.041 (0.035)	course	0.046 (0.033)
know	0.038 (0.030)	huh	0.044 (0.036)
dennis	0.038 (0.029)	education	0.043 (0.032)
ronald	0.036 (0.030)	president	0.039 (0.031)

Table 5: Average weights (and standard deviations calculated across samples) for top 10 NNP × subreddit features from the *progressive* and *conservative* subreddits.

Table 5 displays the top 10 NNP × subreddit features for the political subreddits, with respect to the mean magnitude of the weights associated with them. We report these means and the standard deviations calculated across the 100 runs. This table implies, for example, that mentions of 'freedom' and 'kenya' indicate irony in the *progressive* subreddit; while mentions of 'obamacare' and 'president' (for example) in the *conservative* subreddit tend to imply irony.

Table 6 reports analagous results for the religion subreddits. Here we can see, e.g., that 'god' is a good predictor of irony in the *atheism* subreddit, and 'professor' is in the *Christianity* subreddit.

We also report the top ranking 'three-way' interaction features that cross NNP's extracted from

atheism		*Christianity*	
feature	weight	feature	weight
right	0.353 (0.014)	professor	0.297 (0.013)
god	0.324 (0.013)	let	0.084 (0.014)
women	0.214 (0.013)	peter	0.080 (0.019)
christ	0.160 (0.014)	geez	0.054 (0.016)
news	0.146 (0.013)	evil	0.054 (0.015)
trust	0.139 (0.013)	killing	0.053 (0.015)
shit	0.132 (0.015)	liberal	0.049 (0.014)
believe	0.123 (0.013)	antichrist	0.049 (0.014)
great	0.121 (0.016)	rock	0.047 (0.014)
ftfy	0.108 (0.016)	pedophilia	0.046 (0.014)

Table 6: Top 10 NNP × subreddit features from the *atheism* and *Christianity* subreddits.

progressive		*conservative*	
feature	weight	feature	weight
american (+)	0.045 (0.023)	mr (+)	0.041 (0.021)
yay (+)	0.042 (0.022)	cruz (+)	0.040 (0.021)
ollie (+)	0.036 (0.019)	king (+)	0.036 (0.019)
north (+)	0.036 (0.019)	onion (+)	0.035 (0.018)
fuck (+)	0.034 (0.018)	russia (+)	0.034 (0.018)
washington (+)	0.034 (0.018)	oprah (+)	0.030 (0.016)
times* (+)	0.034 (0.018)	science (+)	0.027 (0.015)
world (+)	0.030 (0.016)	math (+)	0.027 (0.015)
magic (+)	0.024 (0.013)	america (+)	0.026 (0.014)
where (+)	0.024 (0.013)	ben (+)	0.020 (0.011)

Table 7: Average weights for top 10 NNP × subreddit × sentiment features. The parenthetical '+' indicates that the inferred sentiment was positive. In general, (ostensibly) positive sentiment indicates irony.

sentences with subreddits and the inferred sentiment for the political corpus (Table 7). This would imply, e.g., that if a sentence in the *progressive* subreddit conveys an ostensibly positive sentiment about the political commentator 'Ollie',[4] then this sentence is likely to have been intended ironically.

Some of these may seem counter-intuitive, such as ostensibly positive sentiment regarding 'Cruz' (as in the conservative senator Ted Cruz) in the conservative subreddit. On inspection of the comments, it would seem Ted Cruz does not find general support even in this community. Example comments include: "Stay classy Ted Cruz" and "Great idea on the talkathon Cruz". The 'mr' and 'king' terms are almost exclusively references to Obama in the *conservative* subreddit. In any case, because these are three-way interaction terms, they are all relatively rare: therefore we would caution against over interpretation here.

6 Related Work

The task of automated irony detection has recently received a great deal of attention from the NLP and ML communities (Tepperman et al., 2006; Davidov et al., 2010; Carvalho et al., 2009; Burfoot and Baldwin, 2009; Tsur et al., 2010; González-Ibáñez et al., 2011; Filatova, 2012; Reyes et al., 2012; Lukin and Walker, 2013; Riloff et al., 2013). This work has mostly focussed on exploiting token-based indicators of verbal irony. For example, it is clear that gratuitous punctuation (e.g. "oh really??!!!") signals irony (Carvalho et al., 2009).

Davidov et al. (2010) proposed a semi-supervised approach in which they look for sentence *templates* indicative of irony. Elsewhere, Riloff et al. (2013) proposed a method that exploits apparently contrasting sentiment in the same utterance to detect irony. While innovative, these approaches still rely on features intrinsic to comments; i.e., they do not attempt to capitalize on contextualizing features external to the comment text. This means that there will necessarily be certain (subtle) ironies that escape detection by such approaches. For example, without any additional information about the speaker, it would be impossible to deduce whether the comment "Obamacare is a great program" is intended sarcastically.

Other related recent work has shown the promise of sparse models, both for prediction and interpretation (Eisenstein et al., 2011a; Eisenstein et al., 2011b; Yogatama and Smith, 2014a). Yogatama (2014a; 2014b), e.g., has leveraged the *group lasso* approach to impose 'structured' sparsity on feature weights. Our work here may similarly be viewed as assuming a specific sparsity pattern (specifically that feature weights for 'interaction features' will be sparse) and expressing this via regularization.

7 Conclusions and Future Directions

We have shown that we can leverage contextualizing information to improve identification of verbal irony in online comments. This is in contrast to previous models, which have relied predominantly on features that are *intrinsic* to the texts to be classified. We exploited features that indicate user communities crossed with sentiment and extracted noun phrases. This led to consistently improved recall with little to no cost in precision. We also proposed a novel composite regularization strategy that imposes a sparsifying ℓ_1 penalty on the interaction features, as we expect most of these to be irrelevant. This reduced performance variance.

Future work will include expanding the corpus and experimenting with datasets outside of the political domain. We also plan to evaluate this strategy on data from different online sources, e.g., Twitter or YouTube.

[4]'Ollie' is a conservative political commentator.

Acknowledgements

This work was supported by ARO grant W911NF-14-1-0442.

References

C Burfoot and T Baldwin. 2009. Automatic satire detection: are you having a laugh? In *ACL-IJCNLP*, pages 161–164. ACL.

P Carvalho, L Sarmento, MJ Silva, and E de Oliveira. 2009. Clues for detecting irony in user-generated contents: oh...!! it's so easy;-). In *CIKM workshop on Topic-sentiment analysis for mass opinion*, pages 53–56. ACM.

HH Clark and RJ Gerrig. 1984. On the pretense theory of irony. *Journal of Experimental Psychology*, 113:121–126.

D Davidov, O Tsur, and A Rappoport. 2010. Semi-supervised recognition of sarcastic sentences in twitter and amazon. *Conference on Natural Language Learning (CoNLL)*, page 107.

J Eisenstein, A Ahmed, and EP Xing. 2011a. Sparse additive generative models of text. In *International Conference on Machine Learning (ICML)*.

J Eisenstein, NA Smith, and EP Xing. 2011b. Discovering sociolinguistic associations with structured sparsity. In *Proceedings of the Annual Meeting of the Association for Computational Linguistics (ACL)*, pages 1365–1374.

E Filatova. 2012. Irony and sarcasm: Corpus generation and analysis using crowdsourcing. In *LREC*, volume 12, pages 392–398.

R González-Ibáñez, S Muresan, and N Wacholder. 2011. Identifying sarcasm in twitter: a closer look. In *ACL*, volume 2, pages 581–586. Citeseer.

HP Grice. 1975. Logic and conversation. *1975*, pages 41–58.

T Joachims. 1998. *Text categorization with support vector machines: Learning with many relevant features*. Springer.

S Lukin and M Walker. 2013. Really? well. apparently bootstrapping improves the performance of sarcasm and nastiness classifiers for online dialogue. *NAACL*, pages 30–40.

F Pedregosa, G Varoquaux, A Gramfort, V Michel, B Thirion, O Grisel, M Blondel, P Prettenhofer, R Weiss, V Dubourg, J Vanderplas, A Passos, D Cournapeau, M Brucher, M Perrot, and E Duchesnay. 2011. Scikit-learn: Machine learning in Python. *Journal of Machine Learning Research*, 12:2825–2830.

A Reyes, P Rosso, and T Veale. 2012. A multidimensional approach for detecting irony in twitter. *LREC*, pages 1–30.

E Riloff, A Qadir, P Surve, LD Silva, N Gilbert, and R Huang. 2013. Sarcasm as contrast between a positive sentiment and negative situation. In *EMNLP*, pages 704–714.

R Socher, A Perelygin, JY Wu, J Chuang, CD Manning, AY Ng, and C Potts. 2013. Recursive deep models for semantic compositionality over a sentiment treebank. In *Proceedings of the Conference on Empirical Methods in Natural Language Processing (EMNLP)*, pages 1631–1642. Citeseer.

D Sperber and D Wilson. 1981. Irony and the use-mention distinction. *1981*.

J Tepperman, D Traum, and S Narayanan. 2006. "Yeah Right": Sarcasm Recognition for Spoken Dialogue Systems.

K Toutanova, D Klein, CD Manning, and Y Singer. 2003. Feature-rich part-of-speech tagging with a cyclic dependency network. In *Proceedings of the 2003 Conference of the North American Chapter of the Association for Computational Linguistics on Human Language Technology-Volume 1*, pages 173–180. Association for Computational Linguistics.

O Tsur, D Davidov, and A Rappoport. 2010. ICWSM-a great catchy name: Semi-supervised recognition of sarcastic sentences in online product reviews. In *AAAI Conference on Weblogs and Social Media*.

Y Tsuruoka, J Tsujii, and S Ananiadou. 2009. Stochastic gradient descent training for l1-regularized log-linear models with cumulative penalty. In *Proceedings of the Joint Conference of the Annual Meeting of the ACL and the International Joint Conference on Natural Language Processing of the AFNLP*, pages 477–485. Association for Computational Linguistics.

BC Wallace, DK Choe, L Kertz, and E Charniak. 2014. Humans require context to infer ironic intent (so computers probably do, too). Proceedings of the Annual Meeting of the Association for Computational Linguistics (ACL), pages 512–516.

BC Wallace. 2013. Computational irony: A survey and new perspectives. *Artificial Intelligence Review*, pages 1–17.

D Yogatama and NA Smith. 2014a. Linguistic structured sparsity in text categorization. In *Proceedings of the Annual Meeting of the Association for Computational Linguistics (ACL)*, pages 786–796.

D Yogatama and NA Smith. 2014b. Making the most of bag of words: Sentence regularization with alternating direction method of multipliers. In *Proceedings of The 31st International Conference on Machine Learning*, pages 656–664.

H Zou and T Hastie. 2005. Regularization and variable selection via the elastic net. *Journal of the Royal Statistical Society: Series B (Statistical Methodology)*, 67(2):301–320.

Sentence-level Emotion Classification with Label and Context Dependence

Shoushan Li[†‡], **Lei Huang**[†], **Rong Wang**[†], **Guodong Zhou**[†*]

[†]Natural Language Processing Lab, Soochow University, China

[‡] Collaborative Innovation Center of Novel Software Technology and Industrialization

{shoushan.li, lei.huang2013, wangrong2022}@gmail.com,
gdzhou@suda.edu.cn

Abstract

Predicting emotion categories, such as *anger*, *joy*, and *anxiety*, expressed by a sentence is challenging due to its inherent multi-label classification difficulty and data sparseness. In this paper, we address above two challenges by incorporating the label dependence among the emotion labels and the context dependence among the contextual instances into a factor graph model. Specifically, we recast sentence-level emotion classification as a factor graph inferring problem in which the label and context dependence are modeled as various factor functions. Empirical evaluation demonstrates the great potential and effectiveness of our proposed approach to sentence-level emotion classification.

1 Introduction

Predicting emotion categories, such as *anger*, *joy*, and *anxiety*, expressed by a piece of text encompasses a variety of applications, such as online chatting (Galik et al., 2012), news classification (Liu et al., 2013) and stock marketing (Bollen et al., 2011). Over the past decade, there has been a substantial body of research on emotion classification, where a considerable amount of work has focused on document-level emotion classification.

Recently, the research community has become increasingly aware of the need on sentence-level emotion classification due to its wide potential applications, e.g. the massively growing importance of analyzing short text in social media (Kiritchenko et al., 2014; Wen and Wan, 2014). In general, sentence-level emotion classification exhibits two challenges.

......

<S1>*她们都睡了，我蹑手蹑脚摸黑上了床，凑上去想亲嫣一下，她突然一个转身，小手'啪'地搭在了我的脸颊上。*</S1> <S2>*现在我终于如愿以偿。*</S2> <S3>*感受着小手的温度，享受着这份她对我的依恋，生怕动一下，会让她的小手离我而去。*</S3>......

(English: ......

<**S1**> *The girls fall to sleep, so I make my way noiselessly onto the bed, wishing I could get a chance to give a kiss to Yan, suddenly she turn over to me and her little soft hand fall onto my face.*</**S1**> <**S2**>*Praise the Lord, that is all I want.*</**S2**> <**S3**>*Feeling the warm of her hand and the attachment she hold to me, I couldn't afford to move even a little, fearing I may lost her hand.*</**S3**>)......)

Sentence-level Emotion Classification

➢**Input**: **S1, S2, S3**

➢**Output**: **S1** : *joy, love*

S2: *joy*

S3: *joy, love, anxiety*

Figure 1: An example of a paragraph and the sentences therein with their emotion categories from the corpus collected by Quan and Ren (2009)

On one hand, like document-level emotion classification, sentence-level emotion classification is naturally a multi-label classification problem. That is, each sentence might involve more than one emotion category. For example, as shown in Figure 1, in one paragraph, two sentences, i.e., **S1** and **S3**, have two and three emotion categories respectively. Automatically classifying instances with multiple possible categories is

* Corresponding author

Proceedings of the 53rd Annual Meeting of the Association for Computational Linguistics and the 7th International Joint Conference on Natural Language Processing, pages 1045–1053,
Beijing, China, July 26-31, 2015.

sometimes much more difficult than classifying instances with a single label.

On the other hand, unlike document-level emotion classification, sentence-level emotion classification is prone to the data sparseness problem because a sentence normally contains much less content. Given the short text of a sentence, it is often difficult to predict its emotion due to the limited information therein. For example, in **S2**, only one phrase "*如愿以偿(that is all I want)*" expresses the *joy* emotion. Once this phrase fails to appear in the training data, it will be hard for the classifier to give a correct prediction according to the limited content in this sentence.

In this paper, we address above two challenges in sentence-level emotion classification by modeling both the label and context dependence. Here, the label dependence indicates that multiple emotion labels of an instance are highly correlated to each other. For instance, the two positive emotions, *joy* and *love,* are more likely to appear at the same time than the two counterpart emotions, *joy* and *hate*. The context dependence indicates that two neighboring sentences or two sentences in the same paragraph (or document) might share the same emotion categories. For instance, in Figure 1, **S1**, **S2**, and **S3**, from the same paragraph, all share the emotion category *joy*.

Specifically, we propose a factor graph, namely Dependence Factor Graph (DFG), to model the label and context dependence in sentence-level emotion classification. In our DFG approach, both the label and context dependence are modeled as various factor functions and the learning task aims to maximize the joint probability of all these factor functions. Empirical evaluation demonstrates the effectiveness of our DFG approach to capturing the inherent label and context dependence. To the best of our knowledge, this work is the first attempt to incorporate both the label and context dependence of sentence-level emotion classification into a unified framework.

The remainder of this paper is organized as follows. Section 2 overviews related work on emotion analysis. Section 3 presents our observations on label and context dependence in the corpus. Section 4 proposes our DFG approach to sentence-level emotion classification. Section 5 evaluates the proposed approach. Finally, Section 6 gives the conclusion and future work.

2 Related Work

Over the last decade, there has been an explosion of work exploring various aspects of emotion analysis, such as emotion resource creation (Wiebe et al., 2005; Quan and Ren, 2009; Xu et al., 2010), writer's emotion vs. reader's emotion analysis (Lin et al., 2008; Liu et al., 2013), emotion cause event analysis (Chen et al., 2010), document-level emotion classification (Alm et al., 2005; Li et al., 2014) and sentence-level or short text-level emotion classification (Tokushisa et al., 2008; Bhowmick et al., 2009; Xu et al., 2012). This work focuses on sentence-level emotion classification.

Among the studies on sentence-level emotion classification, Tokushisa et al. (2008) propose a data-oriented method for inferring the emotion of an utterance sentence in a dialog system. They leverage a huge collection of emotion-provoking event instances from the Web to deal with the data sparseness problem in sentence-level emotion classification. Bhowmick et al. (2009) and Bhowmick et al. (2010) apply KNN-based classification algorithms to classify news sentences into multiple reader emotion categories. Although the multi-label classification difficulty has been noticed in their study, the label dependence is not exploited. More recently, Xu et al. (2012) proposes a coarse-to-fine strategy for sentence-level emotion classification. They deal with the data sparseness problem by incorporating the transfer probabilities from the neighboring sentences to refine the emotion categories. To some extent, this can be seen a specific kind of context information. However, they ignore the label dependence by directly applying Binary Relevance to overcome the multi-label classification difficulty.

Unlike all above studies, this paper emphasizes the importance of the label dependence and exploits it in sentence-level emotion classification via a factor graph model. Moreover, besides the label dependence, our factor graph-based approach incorporates the context dependence in a unified framework to further improve the performance of sentence-level emotion classification.

3 Observations

To better illustrate our motivation of modeling the label and context dependence, we systematically investigate both dependence phenomena in our evaluation corpus.

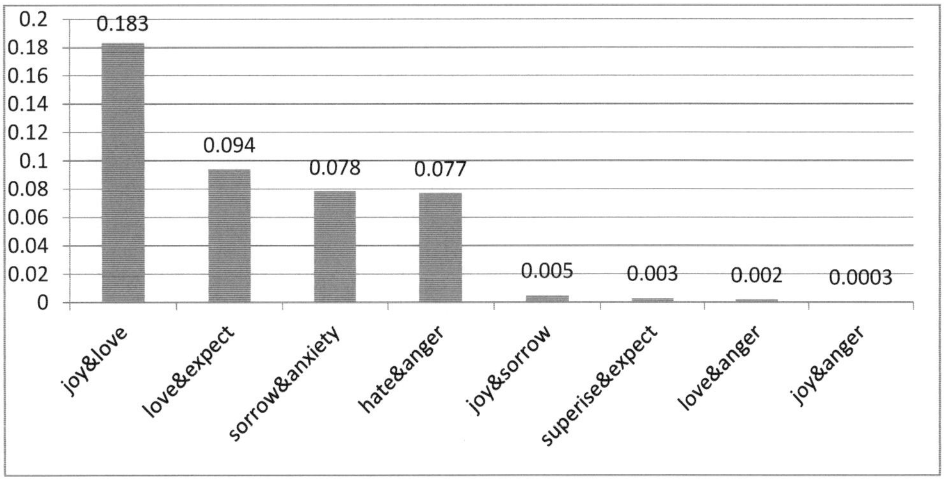

Figure 2: Probability distribution of most and least frequently-occurred pairs of emotion categories, with left four most frequently-occurred and right four least frequently-occurred, among all 28 pairs

The corpus contains 100 documents, randomly selected from Quan and Ren (2009). There are totally 2751 sentences and each of them is manually annotated with one or more emotion labels.

Table 1: The numbers of the sentences in each emotion category

Emotion	#Sentence	Emotion	#Sentence
joy	691	*anxiety*	567
hate	532	*surprise*	180
love	1025	*anger*	287
sorrow	611	*expect*	603

Table 2: The numbers of the sentences grouped by the emotion labels they contain

	#Sentence
No Label	180
One Label	1096
Two Labels	1081
Three Labels	346
Four or more labels	48
ALL	**2751**

Table 1 shows the sentence distribution of the eight emotion categories. Obviously, the distribution is a bit imbalanced. While about to one quarter of sentences express the emotion category *love*, only ~6% and ~10% express surprise and anger respectively, with the remaining 5 emotion categories distributed rather evenly from ~20% to ~25%. Table 2 shows the numbers of the sentences grouped by the emotion labels they contain. From this table, we can see that more than half sentences have two or more emotion labels. This indicates the popularity of the multi-label issue in sentence-level emotion classification.

To investigate the phenomenon of label dependence, we first assume that $X \subset R^d$ denotes an input domain of instances and $Y = \{l_1, l_2, ..., l_m\}$ be a finite domain of possible emotion labels. Each instance is associated with a subset of Y and this subset is described as an m-dimensional vector $y = \{y^1, y^2, ..., y^m\}$ where y^i=1 only if instance x has label l_i. and y^i=0 otherwise. Then, we can calculate the probability that an instance takes both emotion labels l_i and l_j, denoted as $p(l_i, l_j)$. Figure 2 shows the probability distribution of most and least frequently-occurred pairs of emotion categories, with left four most frequently-occurred and right four least frequently-occurred, among all 28 pairs. From this figure, we can see that some pairs, e.g., *joy* and *love*, are much more likely to be taken by one sentence than some other pairs, e.g. *joy* and *anger*.

Finally, we investigate the phenomenon of the context dependence by calculating the probabilities that two instances x_k and x_l have at least one identical emotion label, i.e., $p(y_k \cap$ in different settings.

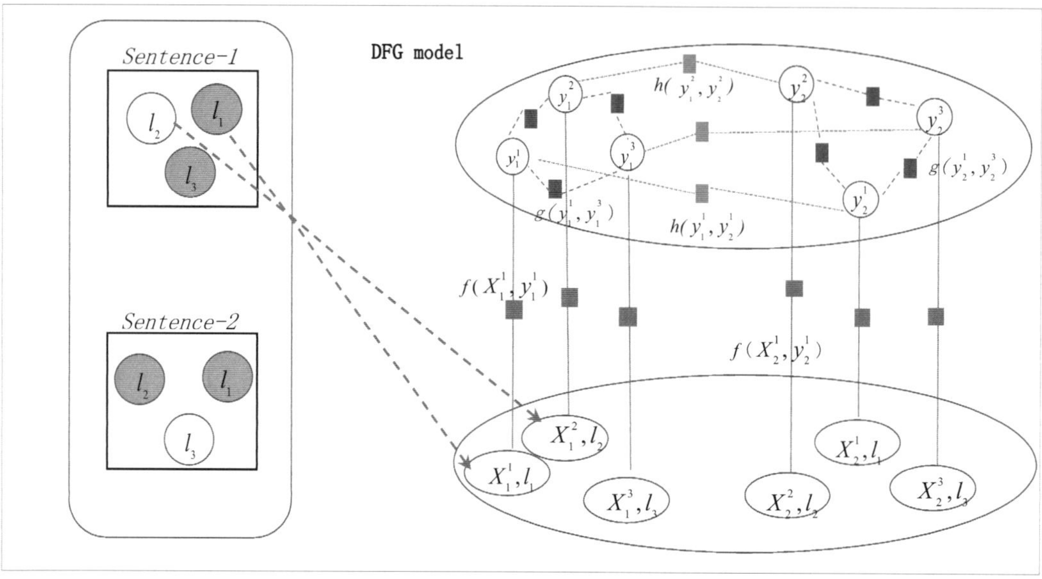

Figure 4: An example of DFG when two instances are involved: *sentence-1* with the label vector [1, 0, 1] and *sentence-2* with the label vector [1, 1, 0]

Note: each multi-label instance is transformed into three pseudo samples, represented as X_i^k $(k=1,2,3)$. $f(\cdot)$ represents a factor function for modeling textual features. $g(\cdot)$ represents a factor function for modeling the label dependence between two pseudo samples. $h(\cdot)$ represents a factor function for modeling the context dependence between two instances in the same context.

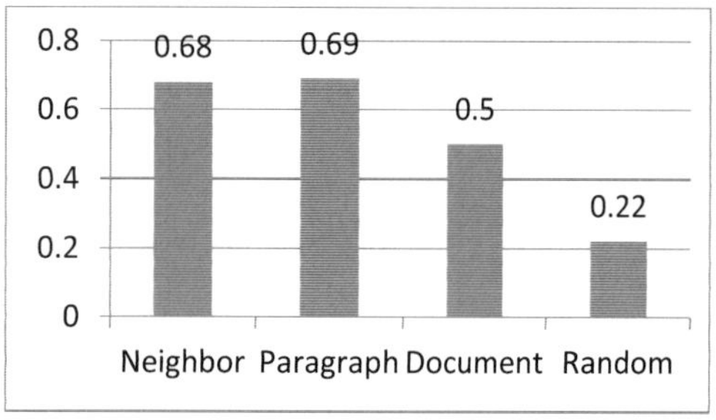

Figure 3: Probabilities that two instances have an identical emotion label in different settings

Figure 3 shows the probabilities that two instances have at least one identical emotion label in different settings, where *neighbor, paragraph, document and random* mean two neighboring instances, two instances from the same paragraph, two instances from the same document, and two instances from a random selection, respectively. From this figure, we can see that two instances from the same context are much more likely to take an identical emotion label than two random instances.

From above statistics, we come to two basic observations:

1) **Label dependency**: One sentence is more likely to take some pair of emotion labels, e.g., *hate* and *angry* than some other pair of emotion labels, e.g., *hate* and *happy*.
2) **Context dependency**: Two instances from the same context are more likely to share the same emotion label than those from a random selection.

4 Dependence Factor Graph Model

In this section, we propose a dependence factor graph (DFG) model for learning emotion labels of sentences with both label and context dependence.

4.1 Preliminary

Factor Graph

A factor graph consists of two layers of nodes, i.e., variable nodes and factor nodes, with links between them. The joint distribution over the whole set of variables can be factorized as a product of all factors. Figure 4 gives an example of our dependence factor graph (DFG) when two instances, i.e., *sentence-1* and *sentence-2* are involved.

Binary Relevance

A popular solution to multi-label classification is called binary relevance which constructs a binary classifier for each label, resulting a set of independent binary classification problems (Tsoumakas and Katakis, 2007; Tsoumakas et al., 2009). In our approach, binary relevance is utilized as a preliminary step so that each original instance is transformed into K pseudo samples, where K is the number of categories. For example, in Figure 4, X_1^1, X_1^2, and X_1^3 represent the three pseudo samples, generated from the same original instance *sentence-1*.

4.2 Model Definition

Formally, let $G=(V,E,X)$ represent an instance network, where V denotes a set of sentence instances. $E \subset V \times V$ is a set of relationships between sentences. Two kinds of relationship exist in our instance network: One represents the label dependence between each two pseudo instances generated from the same original instance, while the other represents the context dependence when the two instances are from the same context, e.g., the same paragraph. X is the textual feature vector associated with a sentence.

We model the above network with a factor graph and our objective is to infer the emotion categories of instances by learning the following joint distribution:

$$P(Y|G)= \prod_k \prod_i f(X_i^k, y_i^k) g(y_i^k, G(y_i^k)) h(y_i^k, H(y_i^k)) \quad (1)$$

where three kinds of factor functions are used.

1) **Textual feature factor function:** $f(X_i^k, y_i^k)$ denotes the traditional textual feature factor functions associated with each text X_i^k. The textual feature factor function is instantiated as follows:

$$f(X_i^k, y_i^k)=\frac{1}{Z_1}\exp\left(\sum_j \alpha_{kj}\Phi(x_{ij}^k, y_i^k)\right) \quad (2)$$

Where $\Phi(x_{ij}^k, y_i^k)$ is a feature function and x_{ij}^k represents a textual feature, i.e., a word feature in this study.

2) **Label dependence factor function:** $g(y_i^k, G(y_i^k))$ denotes the additional label dependence relationship among the pseudo instances, where $G(y_i^k)$ is the label set of the instances connected to y_i^k. $G(y_i^k)$ and y_i^k are labels of the pseudo instances generated from the same original instance. The label dependence factor function is instantiated as follows:

$$g(y_i^k, G(y_i^k))=\frac{1}{Z_2}\exp\left\{\sum_{y_i^l \in G(y_i^k)} \beta_{ikl}(y_i^k - y_i^l)^2\right\} \quad (3)$$

Where β_{ikl} is the weight of the function, representing the influence degree of the two instances y_i^k and y_i^l.

3) **Context dependence factor function:** $h(y_i^k, H(y_i^k))$ denotes the additional context dependence relationship among the instances, where $H(y_i^k)$ is the set of the instances connected to y_i^k. $H(y_i^k)$ and y_i^k are the labels of the pseudo instances from the same context but generated from different original instances. The context dependence factor function is instantiated as follows:

$$h(y_i^k, H(y_i^k))=\frac{1}{Z_3}\exp\left\{\sum_{y_j^k \in H(y_i^k)} \delta_{ijk}(y_i^k - y_j^k)^2\right\} \quad (4)$$

Where δ_{ijk} is the weight of the function, representing the influence degree of the two instances y_i^k and y_j^k.

4.3 Model Learning

Learning the DFG model is to estimate the best parameter configuration $\theta=(\{\alpha\},\{\beta\},\{\delta\})$ to maximize the log-likelihood objective function $L(\theta)=\log P_\theta(Y|G)$, i.e.,

$$\theta^* = \arg\max L(\theta) \quad (5)$$

In this study, we employ the gradient decent method to optimize the objective function. For example, we can write the gradient of each α_{kj} with regard to the objective function:

$$\frac{\partial L(\theta)}{\partial \alpha_{kj}} = E\left[\Phi(x_{ij}, y_i^k)\right] - E_{P_{\alpha_{kj}}(Y|G)}\left[\Phi(x_{ij}, y_i^k)\right] \quad (6)$$

Where $E\left[\Phi(x_{ij}, y_i^k)\right]$ is the expectation of feature function $\Phi(x_{ij}, y_i^k)$ given the data distribution. $E_{P_{\alpha_{kj}}(Y|G)}\left[\Phi(x_{ij}, y_i^k)\right]$ is the expectation of feature function $\Phi(x_{ij}, y_i^k)$ under the distribution $P_{\alpha_{kj}}(Y|G)$ given by the estimated model. Figure 5 illustrates the detailed algorithm for learning the parameter α. Note that LBP denotes the Loopy

Belief Propagation (LBP) algorithm which is applied to approximately infer the marginal distribution in a factor graph (Frey and MacKay, 1998). A similar gradient can be derived for the other parameters.

Input: Learning rate η
Output: Estimated parameters α
Initialize $\alpha \leftarrow 0$
Repeat
1) Calculate $E\left[\Phi\left(x_{ij}, y_i^k\right)\right]$ using LBP
2) Calculate $E_{P_{\alpha_{kj}}(Y|G)}\left[\Phi\left(x_{ij}, y_i^k\right)\right]$ using LBP
3) Calculate the gradient of α according to Eq. (6)
4) Update parameter α with the learning rate η

$$\alpha_{\text{new}} = \alpha_{\text{old}} + \eta \frac{L(\alpha)}{\alpha}$$

Until *Convergence*

Figure 5: The learning algorithm for DGP model

4.4 Model Prediction

With the learned parameter configuration θ, the prediction task is to find a Y^{U*} which optimizes the objective function, i.e.,

$$Y^{U*} = \arg\max P\left(Y^U \middle| Y^L, G, \theta\right) \quad (7)$$

Where Y^{U*} are the labels of the instances in the testing data.

Again, we utilize LBP to calculate the marginal probability of each instance $P\left(y_i^k \middle| Y^L, G, \theta\right)$ and predict the label with the largest marginal probability. As all instances in the test data are concerned, above prediction is performed in an iteration process until the results converge.

5 Experimentation

We have systematically evaluated our DFG approach to sentence-level emotion classification.

5.1 Experimental Setting

Corpus

The corpus contains 100 documents (2751 sentences) from the Ren-CECps corpus (Quan and Ren, 2009). In our experiments, we use 80 documents as the training data and the remaining 20 documents as the test data.

Features

Each instance is treated as a bag-of-words and transformed into a binary vector encoding the presence or absence of word unigrams.

Evaluation Metrics

In our study, we employ three evaluation metrics to measure the performances of different approaches to sentence-level emotion classification. These metrics have been popularly used in some multi-label classification problems (Godbole and Sarawagi, 2004; Schapire and Singer, 2000).

1) *Hamming loss*: It evaluates how many times an instance-label pair is misclassified considering the predicted set of labels and the ground truth set of labels, i.e.,

$$hloss = 1 - \frac{1}{mq} \sum_{i=1}^{q} \sum_{j=1}^{m} 1_{y_i^{j'} = y_i^j} \quad (8)$$

where q is the number of all test instances and m is the number of all emotion labels. $y_i^{j'}$ is the estimated label while y_i^j is the true label.

2) *Accuracy*: It gives an average degree of the similarity between the predicted and the ground truth label sets of all test examples, i.e.,

$$Accuracy = \frac{1}{q} \sum_{i=1}^{q} \left| \frac{y_i \cap y_i'}{y_i \cup y_i'} \right| \quad (9)$$

3) *F1-measure*: It is the harmonic mean between precision and recall. It can be calculated from true positives, true negatives, false positive and false negatives based on the predictions and the corresponding actual values, i.e.,

$$F1 = \frac{1}{q} \sum_{i=1}^{q} \frac{\left|y_i \cap y_i'\right|}{\left|y_i\right| + \left|y_i'\right|} \quad (10)$$

Note that smaller *Hamming loss* corresponds to better classification quality, while larger *accuracy* and *F-measure* corresponds to better classification quality.

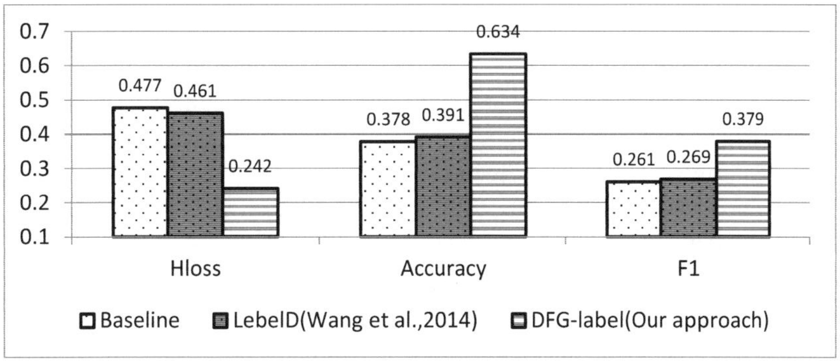

Figure 6: Performance comparison of different approaches to sentence-level emotion classification with the label dependence only

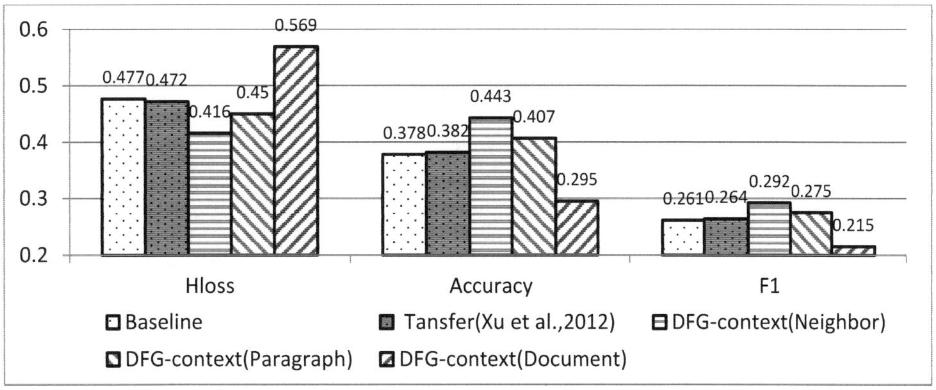

Figure 7: Performance comparison of different approaches to sentence-level emotion classification with the context dependence only

5.2 Experimental Results with Label Dependence

In this section, we compare following approaches which only consider the label dependence among pseudo instances:

- **Baseline**: As a baseline, this approach applies a maximum entropy (ME) classifier with only textual features, ignoring both the label and context dependence.
- **LabelD**: As the state-of-the-art approach to handling multi-label classification, this approach incorporates label dependence, as described in (Wang et al., 2014). Specifically, this approach first utilizes a Bayesian network to infer the relationship among the labels and then employ them in the classifier.
- **DFG-label**: Our DFG approach with the label dependence.

Figure 6 compares the performance of different approaches to sentence-level emotion classification with the label dependence. From this figure, we can see that our DFG approach improves the baseline approach with an impressive improvement in all three kinds of evaluation metrics, i.e., 23.5% reduction in *Hloss*, 25.6% increase in *Accuracy*, and 11.8% increase in *F1*. This result verifies the effectiveness of incorporating the label dependence in sentence-level emotion classification. Compared to the state-of-the-art LabelD approach, our DFG approach is much superior. Significant test show that our DFG approach significantly outperforms both the baseline approach and LabelD (p-value<0.01). One reason that LabelD performs worse than our approach is possibly due to their separating learning on textual features and label relationships. Also, different from ours, their approach could not capture the information between two conflict emotion labels, such as "*happy*" and "*sad*" (they are not possibly appearing together).

5.3 Experimental Results with Context Dependence

In this section, we compare following approaches which only consider the context dependence among pseudo instances:

- **Baseline**: same as the one in Section 5.2, which applies a maximum entropy (ME) classifier with only textual features, ignoring both the label and context dependence.
- **Transfer**: As the state-of-the-art approach to incorporating contextual information in sentence-level emotion classification (Xu et al., 2012), this approach utilizes the label transformation probability to refine the classification results.
- **DFG-label (Neighbor)**: Our DFG approach with the context dependence only. Specifically, the neighboring instances are considered as context.
- **DFG-label (Paragraph)**: Our DFG approach with the context dependence only. Specifically, the instances in the same paragraph are considered as context.
- **DFG-label (Document)**: Our DFG approach with the context dependence only. Specifically, the instances in the same document are considered as context.

Figure 7 compares the performance of different approaches to sentence-level emotion classification with the context dependence only. From this figure, we can see that our DFG approach consistently improves the state-of-the-art in all three kinds of evaluation metrics, i.e., 6.1% reduction in *Hloss*, 6.5% increase in *Accuracy*, and 3.1% increase in *F1* when the neighboring instances are considered as context. Among the three kinds of context, the neighboring setting performs best. We also find that using the whole document as the context is not helpful and it performs even worse than the baseline approach. Compared to the state-of-the-art Transfer approach, our DFG approach with the neighboring context dependence is much superior. Significant test show that our DFG approach with the neighboring context dependence significantly outperforms the baseline approach and the state-of-the-art LabelD approach (*p*-value<0.01).

5.4 Experimental Results with Both Label and Context Dependence

Table 3 shows the performance of our DFG approach with both label and context dependence, denoted as DGF-both. From this table, we can see that using both label and context dependence further improves the performance.

Figure 8 shows the performance of our DGF-both approach when different sizes of training data are used to train the model. From this figure, we can see that incorporating both the label and context dependence consistently improves the performance with a large margin, irrespective of the amount of training data available.

Table 3: Performance of our DFG approach with both label and context dependence

	Hloss	*Accuracy*	*F1*
Baseline	0.447	0.378	0.261
DFG-label	0.254	0.621	0.372
DFG-context	0.416	0.443	0.292
DFG-both	**0.242**	**0.634**	**0.379**

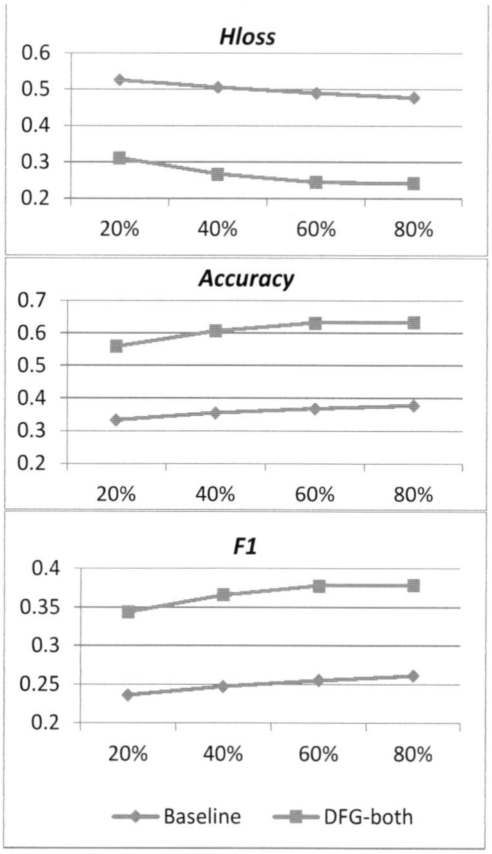

Figure 8: Performance of our DGF-both approach when different sizes of training data are used

6 Conclusion

In this paper, we propose a novel approach to sentence-level emotion classification by incorporating both the label dependence among the emotion labels and the context dependence among the contextual instances into a factor graph, where the label and context dependence is modeled as various factor functions. Empirical evaluation shows that our DFG approach performs significantly better than the state-of-the-art.

In the future work, we would like to explore better ways of modeling the label and context dependence and apply our DFG approach in more applications, e.g. micro-blogging emotion classification.

Acknowledgments

This research work has been partially supported by three NSFC grants, No.61273320, No.61375073, No.61331011, and Collaborative Innovation Center of Novel Software Technology and Industrialization.

References

Alm C., D. Roth and R. Sproat. 2005. Emotions from Text: Machine Learning for Text-based Emotion Prediction. In *Proceedings of EMNLP-05*, pp.579-586.

Bhowmick P., A. Basu, P. Mitra, and A. Prasad. 2009. Multi-label Text Classification Approach for Sentence Level News Emotion Analysis. *Pattern Recognition and Machine Intelligence. Lecture Notes in Computer Science, Volume 5909*, pp 261-266.

Bhowmick P., A. Basu, P. Mitra, and A. Prasad. 2010. Sentence Level News Emotion Analysis in Fuzzy Multi-label Classification Framework. *Research in Computing Science. Special Issue: Natural Language Processing and its Applications*, pp.143-154.

Bollen J., H. Mao, and X.-J. Zeng. 2011. Twitter Mood Predicts the Stock Market. *Journal of Computational Science*, 2(1):1–8, 2011.

Chen Y., S. Lee, S. Li and C. Huang. 2010. Emotion Cause Detection with Linguistic Constructions. In *Proceedings of COLING-10*, pp.179-187.

Frey B. and D. MacKay. 1998. A Revolution: Belief Propagation in Graphs with Cycles. In *Proceedings of NIPS-98*, pp.479–485.

Galik M. and S. Rank. 2012. Modelling Emotional Trajectories of Individuals in an Online Chat. In *Proceedings of Springer-Verlag Berlin Heidelberg-12*, pp.96-105.

Godbole S. and S. Sarawagi. 2004. Discriminative Methods for Multi-labeled Classification. In *Advances in knowledge discovery and data mining*. pp. 22-30.

Kiritchenko S., X. Zhu, and S. Mohammad. 2014. Sentiment Analysis of Short Informal Texts. *Journal of Artificial Intelligence Research*, 50(2014), pp.723-762.

Li C., H. Wu, and Q. Jin. 2014. Emotion Classification of Chinese Miroblog Text via Fusion of BoW and eVector Feature Representations. In *Proceedings of NLP&CC-14*, pp.217-228.

Lin K., C. Yang, and H. Chen. 2008. Emotion Classification of Online News Articles from the Reader's Perspective. In *Proceedings of the International Conference on Web Intelligence and Intelligent Agent Technology-08*, pp.220-226.

Liu H., S. Li, G. Zhou, C. Huang, and P. Li. 2013. Joint Modeling of News Reader's and Comment Writer's Emotions. In *Proceedings of ACL-13*, short paper, pp.511-515.

Quan C. and F. Ren. 2009. Construction of a Blog Emotion Corpus for Chinese Emotional Expression Analysis. In *Proceedings of EMNLP-09*, pp.1446-1454.

Schapire R. E and Y. Singer. 2000. A Boosting-based System for Text Categorization. *Machine learning*, pp. 135-168

TOKUHISA R., K. Inui, and Y. Matsumoto. 2008. Emotion Classification Using Massive Examples Extracted from the Web. In *Proceedings of COLING-2008*, pp.881-888.

Tsoumakas G. and I. Katakis. 2007. Multi-label Classification: An Overview. In *Proceedings of International Journal of Data Warehousing and Mining*, 3(3), pp.1-13.

Tsoumakas G., I. Katakis, and I. Vlahavas. 2009. Mining Multi-label Data. Data *Mining and Knowledge Discovery Handbook*, pages 1–19.

Wen S. and X. Wan. 2014. Emotion Classification in Microblog Texts Using Class Sequential Rules. In *Proceedings of AAAI-14*, 187-193.

Wang S., J. Wang, Z. Wang, and Q. Ji. 2014. Enhancing Multi-label Classification by Modeling Dependencies among Labels. *Pattern Recognition*. Vol. 47. Issue 10: 3405-3413, 2014.

Wiebe J., T. Wilson, and C. Cardie. 2005. Annotating Expressions of Opinions and Emotions in Language. *Language Resources and Evaluation*, 39, 65-210.

Xu G., X. Meng and H. Wang. 2010. Build Chinese Emotion Lexicons Using A Graph-based Algorithm and Multiple Resources. In *Proceedings of COLING-10*, pp.1209-1217.

Xu J., R. Xu, Q. Lu, and X. Wang. 2012. Coarse-to-fine Sentence-level Emotion Classification based on the Intra-sentence Features and Sentential Context. In *Proceedings of CIKM-12*, poster, pp.2455-2458.

Co-training for Semi-supervised Sentiment Classification Based on Dual-view Bags-of-words Representation

Rui Xia[1,2], **Cheng Wang**[1], **Xinyu Dai**[2], **and Tao Li**[3,4]
[1]School of Computer Science, Nanjing University of Science & Technology, China
[2]State Key Laboratory for Novel Software Technology, Nanjing University, China
[3]School of Computer Science, Florida International University, USA
[4]School of Computer Science, Nanjing University of Posts & Telecommunications, China
rxia@njust.edu.cn, wangcheng1022@gmail.com,
daixinyu@nju.edu.cn, taoli@cs.fiu.edu

Abstract

A review text is normally represented as a bag-of-words (BOW) in sentiment classification. Such a simplified BOW model has fundamental deficiencies in modeling some complex linguistic phenomena such as negation. In this work, we propose a dual-view co-training algorithm based on dual-view BOW representation for semi-supervised sentiment classification. In dual-view BOW, we automatically construct antonymous reviews and model a review text by a pair of bags-of-words with opposite views. We make use of the original and antonymous views in pairs, in the training, bootstrapping and testing process, all based on a joint observation of two views. The experimental results demonstrate the advantages of our approach, in meeting the two co-training requirements, addressing the negation problem, and enhancing the semi-supervised sentiment classification efficiency.

1 Introduction

In the past decade, there has been an explosion of user-generated subjective texts on the Internet in forms of online reviews, blogs and microblogs. With the need of automatically identifying sentiments and opinions from those online texts, sentiment classification has attracted much attention in the field of natural language processing.

Lots of previous research focused on the task of supervised sentiment classification. However, in some domains, it is hard to obtain a sufficient amount of labeled training data. Manual annotation is also very expensive and time-consuming. To address this problem, semi-supervised learning approaches were employed in sentiment classification, to reduce the need for labeled reviews by taking advantage of unlabeled reviews.

The dominating text representation method in both supervised and semi-supervised sentiment classification is known as the bag-of-words (BOW) model, which is difficult to meet the requirements for understanding the review text and dealing with complex linguistic structures such as negation. For example, the BOW representations of two opposite reviews "It works well" and "It doesn't work well" are considered to be very similar by most statistical learning algorithms.

In supervised sentiment classification, many approaches have been proposed in addressing the negation problem (Pang et al., 2002; Na et al., 2004; Polanyi and Zaenen , 2004; Kennedy and Inkpen, 2006; Ikeda et al., 2008; Li et al., 2010b; Orimaye et al., 2012; Xia et al., 2013). Nevertheless, in semi-supervised sentiment classification, most of the current approaches directly apply standard semi-supervised learning algorithms, without paying attention to appropriate representation for review texts. For example, Aue and Gamon (2005) applied the naïve Bayes EM algorithm (Nigam et al., 2000). Goldberg and Zhu (2006) applied a graph-based semi-supervised learning algorithm by (Zhu et al., 2003). Wan (2009) employed a co-training approach for cross-language sentiment classification. Li et al. (2010a) employed co-training with personal and impersonal views. Ren et al. (2011) explored the use of label propagation (Zhu and Ghahramani, 2002).

As pointed by (Goldberg and Zhu, 2006): it is necessary to investigate better review text representations and similarity measures based on linguistic knowledge, as well as reviews' sentiment patterns. However, to the best knowledge, such investigations are very scarce in the research of semi-

Proceedings of the 53rd Annual Meeting of the Association for Computational Linguistics and the 7th International Joint Conference on Natural Language Processing, pages 1054–1063,
Beijing, China, July 26-31, 2015.

supervised sentiment classification.

In (Xia et al., 2013), we have developed a dual sentiment analysis approach, which creates antonymous reviews and makes use of original and antonymous reviews together for supervised sentiment classification. In this work, we propose a dual-view co-training approach based on dual-view BOW representation for semi-supervised sentiment classification. Specifically, we model both the original and antonymous reviews by a pair of bags-of-words with opposite views. Based on such a dual-view representation, we design a dual-view co-training approach. The training, bootstrapping and testing processes are all performed by observing two opposite sides of one review. That is, we consider not only how positive/negative the original review is, but also how negative/positive the antonymous review is.

In comparison with traditional methods, our dual-view co-training approach has the following advantages:

- Effectively address the negation problem;
- Automatically learn the associations among antonyms;
- Better meet the two co-training requirements in (Blum and Mitchell, 1998).

2 Related Work

The mainstream of the research in sentiment classification focused on supervised and unsupervised learning tasks. In comparison, semi-supervised sentiment classification has much less related studies. In this section, we focus on reviewing the work of semi-supervised sentiment classification.

Aue and Gamon (2005) combined a small amount of labeled data with a large amount of unlabeled data in target domain for cross-domain sentiment classification based on the EM algorithm. Goldberg and Zhu (2006) presented a graph-based semi-supervised learning algorithm (Zhu et al., 2003) for the sentiment analysis task of rating inference. Dasgupta and Ng (2009) proposed a semi-supervised approach to mine the unambiguous reviews at first and then exploiting them to classify the ambiguous reviews, via a combination of active learning, transductive learning and ensemble learning. Ren et al. (2011) explored the use of label propagation (LP) (Zhu and Ghahramani, 2002) in building a semi-supervised sentiment classifier, and compared their results with Transductive SVMs(T-SVM). LP and T-SVM are transductive learning methods where the test data should participate in the training process.

Zhou et al. (2010) proposed a deep learning approach called active deep networks to address semi-supervised sentiment classification with active learning. Socher et al. (2012) introduced a deep learning framework called semi-supervised recursive autoencoders for predicting sentence-level sentiment distributions. The limitation of deep learning approaches might be their dependence on a considerable amount of unlabeled data to learn the representations and the inability to explicitly model the negation problem.

One line of semi-supervised learning research is to bootstrap class labels using techniques like self-training, co-training and their variations. Wan (2009) proposed a co-training approach to address the cross-lingual sentiment classification problem. They made use of the machine translation service to produce two views (a English view and a Chinese view) for co-training a Chinese review sentiment classifier, based on English corpus and unlabeled Chinese corpus. Li et al. (2010a) proposed an unsupervised method at first to automatically separate the review text into a personal view and an impersonal view, based on which the standard co-training algorithm is then applied to build a semi-supervised sentiment classifier. Li et al. (2011) further studied semi-supervised learning for imbalanced sentiment classification by using a dynamic co-training approach. Su et al. (2012) proposed a multi-view learning approach to semi-supervised sentiment classification with both feature partition and language translation strategies (Wan , 2009). Following (Li et al., 2010a), Li (2013) proposed a co-training approach which exploits subjective and objective views for semi-supervised sentiment classification. Our approach can also be viewed as a variation of co-training. The innovation of our approach is the dual-view construction technique by incorporating antonymous reviews and the bootstrapping mechanism by observing two opposite sides of one review.

3 The Proposed Approach

3.1 Dual-view BOW Representation for Review Texts

Every coin has two sizes. In this work, we are motivated to automatically construct the antonymous reviews, consider the original and antonymous reviews as two opposite sides of one review, and rep-

Feature Space	Original View	Antonymous View
app	1	1
phone	1	1
didn't	1	0
work	1	1
well	1	1
disappointing	1	0
recommend	1	1
satisfactory	0	1

Figure 1: An illustration of the dual-view BOW representation. The feature vector with black font color and grey background denotes the original view; while the one with white font color and black background denotes the reversed antonymous view.

resent them in pairs by a dual-view BOW model.

Look at the following example:

> **Original Review**: "The app doesn't work well on my phone. Disappointing. Don't recommend it."
>
> **Antonymous Review**: "The app works well on my phone. Satisfactory. Recommend it."

Given an original review, its antonymous review is automatically created as follows[1]: 1) We first detect the negations in each subsentence of the review text; 2) If there is a negation, we remove negators in that subsentence; 3) Otherwise, we reverse all the sentiment words in the subsentence into their antonyms, according to a pre-defined antonym dictionary[2].

We subsequently use a dual-view BOW model to represent such a pair of reviews, as shown in Figure 1. The original and antonymous reviews will be used in pairs in our dual-view semi-supervised learning approach. As we determine the sentiment of one review, we could observe not only the original view, but also the antonymous view.

[1]It is worth noting that our emphasis here is not to generate natural-language-like review texts. Since either the original or the created antonymous review will be represented as a vector of independent words in the BOW model, the grammatical requirement is not as strict as that in human languages.

[2]In our experiments, we extract the antonym dictionary from the WordNet lexicon http://wordnet.princeton.edu/.

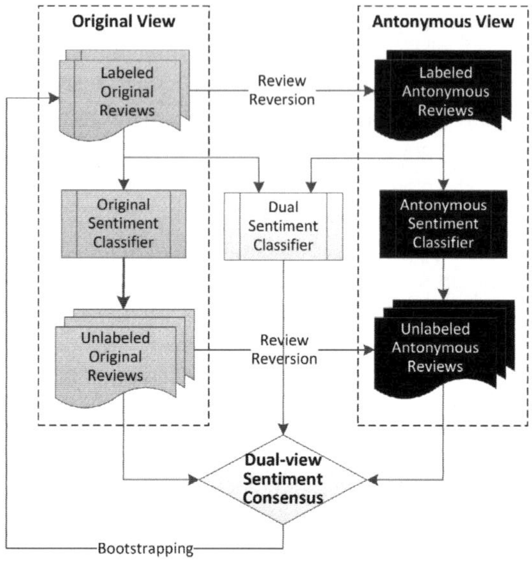

Figure 2: The process of dual-view co-training. Again, the white font color and black background are used to denote the antonymous view.

It is important to notice that the antonymous view removes all negations and incorporates antonymous features. On this basis, we design a dual-view co-training approach. We will introduce our approach in detail in Section 3.2, and analyze its potential advantages in Section 3.3.

3.2 The Dual-view Co-training Approach

Since the original and antonymous views form two different views of one review text, it is natural to employ the co-training algorithm, which requires two views for semi-supervised classification.

Co-training is a typical bootstrapping algorithm that first learns a separate classifier for each view using the labeled data. The most confident predictions of each classifier on the unlabeled data are then used to construct additional labeled training data iteratively. Co-training has been extensively used in NLP, including statistical parsing (Sarkar , 2001), reference resolution (Ng and Cardie, 2003), part-of-speech tagging (Clark et al., 2003), word sense disambiguation (Mihalcea, 2004), and sentiment classification (Wan , 2009; Li et al., 2010a).

But it should be noted that the dual views in our approach are different from traditional views. One important property of our approach is that two views are opposite and therefore associated with opposite class labels. Figure 2 illustrates the process of dual-view co-training.

(1) Dual-view training

For each instance in the initial labeled set, we construct the dual-view representations. Let x_o^l and x_a^l denote the bags of words in the original view and the antonymous view, respectively. Note that the class labels in two views are kept opposite: $y_a^l = 1 - y_o^l$ ($y \in \{0, 1\}$). That is, we reverse the class label in the original view (i.e., positive to negative, or vice versa), as the class label of the created antonymous view.

Suppose $\mathcal{L}$ is the labeled set, with $\mathcal{L}_o$ and $\mathcal{L}_a$ denoting the original-view and antonymous-view labeled sets, respectively. We train two distinct classifiers: the original-view classifier h_o and the antonymous-view classifier h_a , based on $\mathcal{L}_o$ and $\mathcal{L}_a$, respectively. We further train a joint classifier by using $\mathcal{L}_o$ and $\mathcal{L}_a$ together as the training data, and refer to it as h_d.

(2) Dual-view bootstrapping

In standard co-training, we allow each classifier to examine the unlabeled set $\mathcal{U}$ and select the most confidently predicted examples in each category. The selected examples are then added into $\mathcal{L}$, along with the predicted class labels.

In this work, we design a dual-view co-training algorithm to bootstrap the class labels by a joint observation of two sides of one review. Specifically, we propose a new bootstrapping mechanism, based on a principle called **dual-view sentiment consensus**. Given an unlabeled instance $\{x_o^u , x_a^u\}$, dual view sentiment consensus requires that, the original prediction y_o^u and the antonymous prediction should be opposite: $y_a^u = 1 - y_o^u$. In other words, we only select the instances of which the original prediction is positive/negative, and the same time the antonymous prediction is negative/positive. To increase the degree of sentiment consensus, we further require that the predition y_d^u of h_d should be the same as y_o^u.

We sort all unlabeled instances according to the dual-view predictions in each class, filter the list according to the dual-view sentiment consensus principle, and add the top-ranked s instances in each class to the labeled set. For each selected unlabeled instance, its original view x_o^u is added into $\mathcal{L}_o$ with class label y_o^u; and the antonymous view x_a^u is added into $\mathcal{L}_a$, with an opposite class label $y_a^u = 1 - y_o^u$. When $\mathcal{L}_o$ and $\mathcal{L}_a$ receive the supplemental labeled instances, we update h_o and h_a.

Our bootstrapping mechanism differs from the traditional methods in two major aspects: First, in traditional co-training, given the same instance, the class labels in two views are the same. But in our approach, the class labels in two views need to be opposite. Second, in traditional co-training, the most confidently predicted examples in each view are selected to extend the amount of labeled data. It is dangerous to believe the confident but incorrect predictions. While in our approach, the candidates are further filtered by the principle of dual-view sentiment consensus. In this way, the labeling accuracy and learning efficiency can be improved.

(3) Dual-view testing

Finally, in the testing stage, standard co-training uses a joint set of features in two views to train the classifier. In dual-view testing, we use h_o and h_a to predict the test example in two views, and make the final prediction by considering both sizes of the review.

Given a test example x^{te} with its original view denoted by x_o^{te} and antonymous view denoted by x_a^{te}, let $p_o(\cdot|x_o^{te})$ be the posterior probability predicted by the original-view classifier h_o, and $p_a(\cdot|x_a^{te})$ be the posterior probability predicted by h_a. The dual-view testing process can be formulated as follows:

$$p(+|x^{te}) = p(+|x_o^{te}, x_a^{te}) = \frac{p_o(+|x_o^{te}) + p_a(-|x_a^{te})}{2};$$
$$p(-|x^{te}) = p(-|x_o^{te}, x_a^{te}) = \frac{p_o(-|x_o^{te}) + p_a(+|x_a^{te})}{2}.$$

That is, the final positive score is assigned by measuring not only how positive the original review is, but also how negative the antonymous one is; the negative score is assigned by measuring not only how positive the original review is, but also how negative the antonymous one is.

3.3 Advantages of Dual-view Co-training

Our proposed dual-view co-training approach has the following three advantages.

(1) Effectively address the negation issue

We use the antonymous review as a view to effectively address the negation issue. Let us revisit the example in Section 3.1 and assume that the original review (i.e., "The app doesn't work well on my phone. Disappointing. Do not recommend it.") is an unlabeled sample. Because the traditional

BOW model cannot well represent negative structures, the review is likely to be incorrectly labeled as positive and then added into the labeled set.

In our proposed approach, the antonymous review (i.e., "The app works well on my phone. Satisfactory. Recommend it.") removed all the negative structures, and is thus more suited for the BOW representation. In this example, the antonymous review is also likely to be marked as positive. Hence, in this case, both the original review and its antonymous review will be labeled as positive, which violates the principle of dual-view sentiment consensus as mentioned in Section 3.2. As a result, the unlabeled instance will not be added into the labeled set.

Therefore, our approach can overcome the limitations of the conventional methods in addressing the negation issue and reduce the labeling error rate (caused by the negative structures) during the bootstrapping process.

(2) Automatically learn the associations among antonyms

In semi-supervised sentiment classification, only limited association information between the words and categories can be obtained from a small number of initial labeled data.

For instance, in the above example "disappointing" and "satisfactory" are a pair of antonyms. From the initial labeled data, we may only learn that "disappointing" is derogatory, but we cannot infer that "satisfactory" is commendatory.

During the bootstrapping process in our approach, when constructing the dual view representation, the original view and its antonymous view are required to have opposite class labels. Hence we can automatically infer the relationship between "satisfactory" and "disappointing" (e.g., one is positive and one is negative), thereby improving the learning efficiency of the system.

(3) Better meet two co-training requirements

Compared with traditional methods, our dual-view co-training can better meet the two co-training requirements: 1) sufficient condition (i.e., each view is sufficient for classification); 2) complementary condition (i.e., the two views are conditionally independent).

First, for the sufficient condition, we use a different view construction method. Most traditional methods construct the two views by feature partitioning (i.e., dividing the original feature set into two subsets), while we use data expansion by generating antonymous reviews. We will demonstrate in the experimental section (Section 4.6), that our data expansion method can construct better views than the feature partition method in terms of predicting the class labels from individual views.

Second, as we know, every coin has two sides and the two sides are often complementary. In our proposed approach, the original review and its antonymous review (i.e., two sides of one review) are used as two views for co-training and they can better meet the complementary condition. We will illustrate this point in Section 4.6 by calculating the KL divergence between the two views.

4 Experimental Study

4.1 Datasets and Experimental Settings

We conduct the experiments on the multi-domain sentiment datasets, which were introduced in (Blitzer et al., 2007) and have been widely used in sentiment classification. It consists of four domains (Book, DVD, Electronics, and Kitchen) of reviews extracted from Amazon.com. Each of the four datasets contains 1,000 positive and 1,000 negative reviews. Following the experimental settings used in (Li et al., 2010a), we randomly separate all the reviews in each class into a labeled data set, a unlabeled data set, and a test set, with a proportion of 10%, 70% and 20%, respectively. We report the averaged results of 10-fold cross-validation in terms of classification accuracy.

Note that our approach is a general framework that allows different classification algorithms. Due to the space limitation, we only report the results by using logistic regression[3]. Note the similar conclusions can be obtained by using the other algorithms such as SVMs and naïve Bayes. The LibLinear toolkit[4] is utilized, with a dual L2-regularized factor, and a default tradeoff parameter c. Similar to (Wan , 2009; Li et al., 2010a), we carry out the experiments with the unigram features without feature selection. Presence is used as the term weighting scheme as it was reported in (Pang et al., 2002) that it performed better than TF and TF-IDF. Finally, the paired t-test (Yang and Liu , 1999) is performed to test the significance of the difference be-

[3]Logistic regression is quite similar to Maximum Entropy, and has been proved to be more efficient in sentiment classification than some other classification algorithms including naïve Bayes and SVMs (Pang et al., 2002).

[4]`http://www.csie.ntu.edu.tw/~cjlin/liblinear/`

	BOOK	DVD	ELEC	KITC	Avg.
Baseline	0.680	0.691	0.726	0.740	0.709
LP	0.681	0.676	0.697	0.722	0.694
T-SVM	0.671	0.677	0.716	0.729	0.698
EM	0.702	0.706	0.758	0.744	0.728
Self-Training	0.689	0.705	0.736	0.751	0.720
Self-Reserved	0.690	0.708	0.735	0.754	0.722
Co-Static	0.696	0.714	0.745	0.762	0.729
Co-Dynamic	0.701	0.725	0.756	0.767	0.737
Co-PI	0.702	0.716	0.746	0.769	0.733
Our approach	**0.721**	**0.738**	**0.769**	**0.780**	**0.752**

Table 1: The semi-supervised classification accuracy of ten systems.

Figure 3: Comparsion of different boostrapping methods.

tween two systems, with a default significant level of 0.05.

4.2 Compared Systems

We implement the following nine systems and compare them with our approach:

- **Baseline**, the supervised baseline trained with the initial labeled data only;
- **Expectation Maximization (EM)**, with the naïve Bayes model proposed by Nigam et al. (2000);
- **Label Propagation (LP)**, a graph-based semi-supervised learning method proposed by Zhu and Ghahramani (2002);
- **Transductive SVM (T-SVM)**, an extension of SVM so that it can exploit unlabeled data in semi-supervised learning (Joachims, 1999);
- **Self-Training**, a bootstrapping model that first trains a classifier, uses it to classify the unlabeled data, and adds the most confident data to the labeled set;
- **Self-Reserved**, a variation of self-training proposed in (Liu et al., 2013),with a reserved procedure to incorporate some less confident examples;
- **Co-Static**, the co-training algorithm by using two static partitions of feature set as two views (Blum and Mitchell, 1998);
- **Co-Dynamic**, a variation of co-training that uses dynamic feature space in each loop. It was reported in (Li et al., 2011) that the Co-Dynamic significantly outperforms Co-Static significantly;
- **Co-PI**, another variation of co-training proposed by (Li et al., 2010a), by using personal and impersonal views for co-training.

4.3 Performance Comparison

In table 1, we report the semi-supervised classification accuracy of ten evaluated systems. We report the results with 200 labeled, 1400 unlabeled and 400 test reviews. Note that the similar conclusions can be obtained when the size of the initial labeled data changes. We will discuss its influence later.

As can be seen, trained with only 200 labeled data, the supervised baseline yields an average accuracy of 0.709. Self-training gains an improvement of 1.1%. Self-reserved does not show significant priority against Self-training. Three co-training systems (Co-static, Co-dynamic and Co-PI) get significant improvements. They increase the supervised baseline by 2.0%, 2.8% and 2.4%, respectively.

It is somehow surprising that T-SVM and LP do not outperform the supervised baseline, probably because the supervised baseline is obtained by logistic regression, which was reported to be more effective than SVMs in sentiment classification (the supervised result of SVMs is 0.695).

Our proposed approach significantly outperforms all the other methods. It gains the improvement over the supervised baseline, Self-training, Co-static, Co-dynamic and Co-PI by 4.3%, 3.2%, 2.3%, 1.5% and 1.9%, respectively. All of the improvements are significant according to the paired *t*-test.

4.4 Comparison of Bootstrapping Methods

In Figure 3, we further compare five bootstrapping methods by drawing the accuracy curve dur-

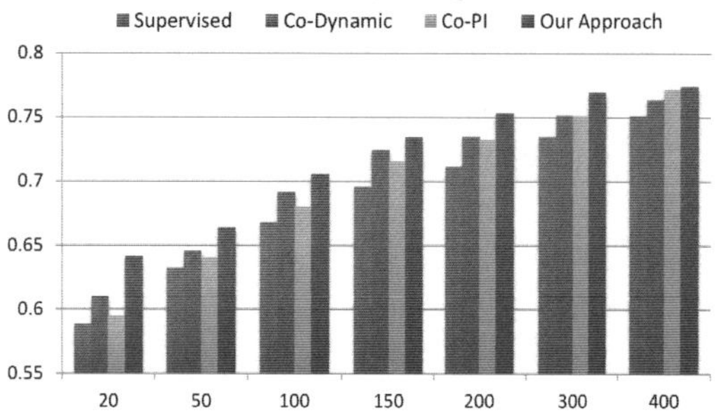

Figure 4: Influence of the size of initial labeled data.

ing the bootstrapping process. The x-axis denotes the number of new labeled data bootstrapped from the unlabeled data.

We can roughly rank five bootstrapping methods as follows: Our approach $\gg$ Co-dynamic $>$ Co-PI $>$ Co-static $\gg$ Self-training. Self-training gives the worst performance. Co-static works better but the effect is limited. Co-PI and Co-dynamic are significantly better. Our proposed approach outperforms the other systems robustly, along with the increased number of the new labeled data. It suggests that our approach is very efficient in bootstrapping the class labels from the unlabeled data.

4.5 Influence of the Size of the Initial Labeled Set

The above results are obtained with 200 labeled, 1400 unlabeled and 400 test reviews. We now tune the size of the initial labeled set (from 20 to 400), and report its influence in Figure 4. For all the settings, we fix the size of test set as 400. The x-axis denotes the number of initial labeled set. For example, "20" denotes the setting of 20 labeled and 1580 unlabeled data.

We can observe that our all methods improve as the initial size increases. But the improvements become limited when the size becomes larger. When the initial size is 400, the semi-supervised performance is close to the golden result obtained by the supervised classifier trained with all 1600 labeled data.

Our approach performs consistently the best across different sizes of the initial sizes. The smaller the initial size is, the more improvements our approach can gain, in comparison with the other methods. This confirms our analysis in Section 3.3 that the technique of dual-view construction is very effective to boost the semi-supervised

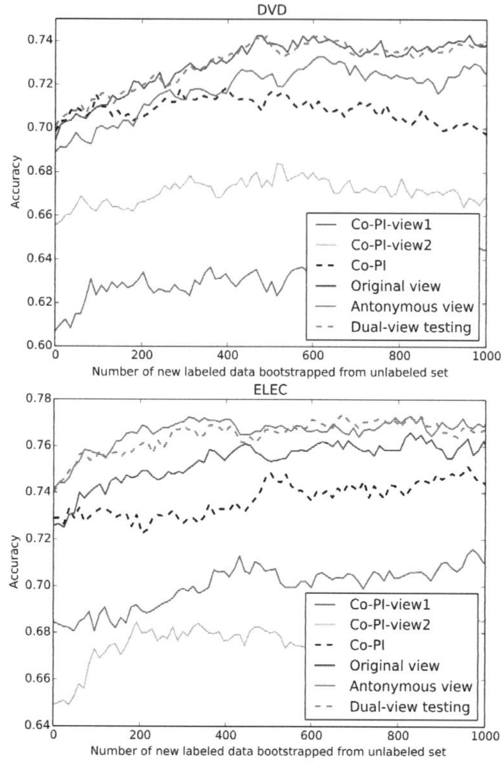

Figure 5: Comparison of different views on the DVD and Electronics datasets.

classification performance, especially when the size of the initial labeled set is small.

4.6 Discussion on the Two Co-training Requirements

Ideally, co-training requires that each view is sufficient for classification (sufficient condition) and two views provide complementary information of the instance,(complementary condition).In this section, we answer the following question empirically: whether our approach could meet the two requirements?

(1) Sufficient condition

In Figure 5, we report the classification performance obtained by the classifiers trained with distinct views and compared them with the two views in Co-PI, on the DVD and Electronics datasets. The observation in Book is similar to that in Electronics; the observation in DVD is similar to that in Kitchen.

Seen from Figure 5, the classification performance of both the original-view and antonymous-view classifiers are satisfactory. It shows that in our approach, each individual view is sufficient to predict the sentiment. In comparison with the two views in Co-PI (i.e., the personal and impersonal views), two views in our approach perform significantly better.

As has been mentioned in Section 3.3, in traditional methods, such as Co-PI and Co-dynamic, two views are created by data partition (or feature partition). In comparison, the two views in our approach are constructed in a manner of data expansion. By creating a new antonymous view, our approach can provide more sufficient information of the reviews than traditional methods.

(2) Complementary condition

Since we have not found a direct measure of the complementarity of two views, we instead calculate the Kullback-Leibler (KL) divergence between them, based on an assumption that two views with higher KL divergence can provide more complementary information of the instance.

KL divergence is a widely used metric of statistical distance. We assume that distribution of the review text is multinomial, and calculate the K-L divergence between two views as follows:

$$D_{KL}(p||q) = \sum_{i=1}^{V} p_i \log\left(\frac{p_i}{q_i}\right)$$

where p_i and q_i are the probabilities of word appearing in two views, respectively. In our experiments, we use information gain (IG) to select a set of discriminative words with the dimension $V = 2000$.

In Table 2, we report the results of three different methods: 1) dataset random partition; 2) personal and impersonal views in Co-PI; 3) original and antonymous views in our approach. We can observe from Table 2 that, random partition has the lowest KL divergence. It shows that the distributional distance between two randomly partitioned views is very small. Co-PI is a higher value, but it still does not have significant difference in two views. By contrast, the KL divergence between the original view and the antonymous view is much higher than both random partition and Co-PI. It demonstrates that the distributions of two views in our approach are significantly different. We thereby infer that the two views constructed in our approach can provide more complementary information than traditional methods. It is reasonable since the antonymous view incorporates the antonyms that might have not appeared in the original view (e.g., "satisfactory" in the example in Section 3.2). These features might provide new information about the instance.

	KL divergence
Random Partition	2.43
Co-PI	4.59
Our approach	12.33

Table 2: The average KL divergence between two views across four datasets.

4.7 The Effect of Dual-view Testing

In Figure 5, we can further observe the effect of dual-view testing. On the Electronics dataset, the antonymous view performs better than the original view. This suggests the advantage of the antonymous view, as it removes the negations and thus is more suitable for the BOW representation. On the DVD dataset, the original view is slightly better. This is also reasonablel, because the antonymous review is automatically created and its quality might be limited in some cases. By taking two opposite views into a joint consideration, our dual-view testing technique guarantees a satisfactory classification performance across different datasets.

Note that in the current version, the original-view and antonymous-view classifiers have the same predicting weight. We believe that by learning the tradeoff between two views in different settings may further improve our approach's performance. For example, if the original view on the Electronics dataset gets a relatively larger weight, dual-view testing might gain more improvements.

5 Conclusions

In this work, a review text is represented by a pair of bags-of-words with opposite views (i.e., the original and antonymous views). By making use of two views in pairs, a dual-view co-training algorithm is proposed for semi-supervised sentiment classification. The dual-view representation is in a good accordance with the two co-training requirements (i.e., sufficient condition and complementary condition). The experimental results demonstrate the effect of our approach, in addressing the negation problem and enhancing the bootstrapping efficiency for semi-supervised sentiment classification.

Acknowledgement

The work is supported by the Natural Science Foundation of China (61305090), and the Jiangsu Provincial Natural Science Foundation of China (BK2012396).

References

A. Aue and M. Gamon. 2005. Customizing Sentiment Classifiers to New Domains: A Case Study. In *Proceedings of Recent Advances in Natural Language Processing*.

J. Blitzer, M. Dredze, and F. Pereira. 2007. Biographies, Bollywood, Boom-boxes and Blenders: Domain Adaptation for Sentiment Classification. In *Proceedings of ACL* .

A. Blum and T. Mitchell. 1998. Combining labeled and unlabeled data with co-training. In *Proceedings of COLT*.

S. Clark, J. R. Curran, and M. Osborne. 2003. Bootstrapping POS taggers using unlabelled data. In *Proceedings of CoNLL*.

S. Dasgupta and V. Ng. 2009. Mine the Easy and Classify the Hard: Experiments with Automatic Sentiment Classification. In *Proceedings of ACL-IJCNLP*.

A. Goldberg and X. Zhu. 2006. Seeing stars when there aren't many stars: graph-based semi-supervised learning for sentiment categorization. In *Proceedings of the Workshop on TextGraphs at HLT-NAACL*.

M. Hu and B. Liu. 2004. Mining opinion features in customer reviews. In *Proceedings of the National Conference on Artificial Intelligence (AAAI)*.

D. Ikeda, H. Takamura, L. Ratinov, and M. Okumura. 2008. Learning to Shift the Polarity of Words for Sentiment Classification. In *Proceedings of IJCNLP*.

T. Joachims. 1999. Transductive Inference for Text Classification using Support Vector Machines. In *Proceedings of ICML*.

A. Kennedy and D. Inkpen. 2006. Sentiment classification of movie reviews using contextual valence shifters. *Computational Intelligence*, 22:110–125.

LaTeX Error: File 'url.sty' not found. V. Ng and C. Cardie. 2003. Weakly supervised natural language learning without redundant views. In *Proceedings of HLT-NAACL*.

K. Nigam, A. McCallum, S. Thrun, and T. Mitchell. 2000. Text classification from labeled and unlabeled documents using EM. *Machine Learning*, 39(2/3): 103–134.

S. Li, C. Huang, G. Zhou, and S. Y. M. Lee. 2010a. Employing personal/impersonal views in supervised and semi-supervised sentiment classification. In *Proceedings of the Annual Meeting of the Association for Computational Linguistics (ACL)* .

S. Li, S. Lee, Y. Chen, C. Huang, and G. Zhou. 2010b. Sentiment Classification and Polarity Shifting. In *Proceeding of the International Conference on Computational Linguistics (COLING)*.

S. Li, Z. Wang, G. Zhou, and S. Lee. 2011. Semi-Supervised Learning for Imbalanced Sentiment Classification. In *Proceedings of IJCAI*.

S. Li. 2013. Sentiment classification using subjective and objective views. *International Journal of Computer Applications*, 80(7): 30–34.

Z. Liu, X. Dong, Y. Guan, and J. Yang. 2013. Reserved Self-training: A Semi-supervised Sentiment Classification Method for Chinese Microblogs. In *Proceedings of IJCNLP*.

R. Mihalcea. 2004. Co-training and self-training for word sense disambiguation. In *Proceedings of CoNLL*.

J. Na, H. Sui, C. Khoo, S. Chan, and Y. Zhou. 2004. Effectiveness of simple linguistic processing in automatic sentiment classification of product reviews. In *Proceeding of the Conference of the International Society for Knowledge Organization*.

S. Orimaye, S. Alhashmi, and E. Siew. 2012. Buy it - don't buy it: sentiment classification on Amazon reviews using sentence polarity shift. In *Proceedings of the Pacific Rim International Conferences on Artificial Intelligence (PRICAI)*.

B. Pang, L. Lee, and S. Vaithyanathan. 2002. Thumbs up?: sentiment classification using machine learning techniques. In *Proceedings of EMNLP*.

L. Polanyi and A. Zaenen. 2004. Contextual lexical valence shifters. In *Proceedings of the AAAI Spring Symposium on Exploring Attitude and Affect in Text*.

Y. Ren, N. Kaji, N. Yoshinaga, M. Toyoda, and M. Kitsuregawa. 2011. Sentiment Classification in Resource-Scarce Languages by using Label Propagation. In *Proceedings of the Pacific Asia Conference on Language, Information and Computation (PACLIC)*.

A. Sarkar. 2001. Applying cotraining methods to statistical parsing. In *Proceedings of NAACL*.

R. Socher, J. Pennington, E. H. Huang, and A. Y. 2012. Semi-Supervised Recursive Autoencoders for Predicting Sentiment Distributions. In *Proceedings of EMNLP*.

Y. Su, S. Li, S. Ju, G. Zhou and J. Li. 2012. 2012. Multi-view Learning for Semi-supervised Sentiment Classification. In *Proceedings of the International Conference on Asian Language Processing*.

X. Wan. 2009. Co-Training for Cross-Lingual Sentiment Classification. In *Proceedings of ACL-IJCNLP*.

R. Xia, T. Wang, X. Hu, S. Li, and C. Zong. 2013. Dual Training and Dual Prediction for Polarity Classification. In *Proceedings of ACL*.

Y. Yang and X. Liu. 1999. A re-examination of text categorization methods. In *Proceedings SIGIR*.

S. Zhou, Q. Chen, and X. Wang. 2010. Active Deep Networks for Semi-Supervised Sentiment Classification. In *Proceedings of COLING*.

X. Zhu and Z. Ghahramani. 2002. Learning from labeled and unlabeled data with label propagation. *Technical Report CMU-CALD-02-107*, Carnegie Mellon University.

X. Zhu, Z. Ghahramani, and J. Lafferty. 2003. Semi-supervised learning using Gaussian fields and harmonic functions. In *Proceddings of the International Conference on Machine Learning (ICML)*.

Improving social relationships in face-to-face human-agent interactions: when the agent wants to know user's likes and dislikes

Caroline Langlet
Institut Mines-Télécom
Télécom ParisTech
CNRS LTCI
caroline.langlet@telecom-paristech.fr

Chloé Clavel
Institut Mines-Télécom
Télécom ParisTech
CNRS LTCI
chloe.clavel@telecom-paristech.fr

Abstract

This paper tackles the issue of the detection of user's verbal expressions of likes and dislikes in a human-agent interaction. We present a system grounded on the theoretical framework provided by (Martin and White, 2005) that integrates the interaction context by jointly processing agent's and user's utterances. It is designed as a rule-based and bottom-up process based on a symbolic representation of the structure of the sentence. This article also describes the annotation campaign – carried out through Amazon Mechanical Turk – for the creation of the evaluation dataset. Finally, we present all measures for rating agreement between our system and the human reference and obtain agreement scores that are equal or higher than substantial agreements.

1 Introduction

In the research field of the embodied conversational agents (ECA), detecting sentiment-related phenomena [1] appears as a key task to improve human-agent interactions and to build long-term social relationships (Pecune et al., 2013). Several models and applications have been proposed which mostly take into account non-verbal cues (acoustic features, facial or bodily expressions) to determine the user's emotions (Schuller et al., 2011). The verbal content is more and more integrated but still partially exploited in human-agent interactions. The very infrequent works, integrating the detection of user's sentiments in ECAs based on linguistic cues, concern avatars and visualisation issues rather than face-to-face interaction, (Zhang et al., 2008; Neviarouskaya et al., 2010b). We identify so far two studies that integrate a sentiment detection module for human-agent interaction (Smith et al., 2011; Yildirim et al., 2011).

However, the research field of sentiment analysis and opinion mining provides a set of interesting works dealing with the subjective information conveyed by the verbal content. Three types of approaches are considered: machine-learning, rule-based approaches and hybrid approaches that are a combination of the first two types. Machine learning methods have proven their worth for the positive and negative classification of sentences or texts (Pang and Lee, 2008). Rule-based approaches are grounded on syntactic and semantic analyses of the sentence and provide deeper analyses of sentiment-related phenomena. For example, (Neviarouskaya et al., 2010a) and (Moilanen and Pulman, 2007) provide linguistic rules dealing with the principle of compositionality in order to improve the detection of opinion targets and the resolution of polarity. Similarly, (Shaikh et al., 2009) provide a linguistic adaptation of the OCC model (Ortony, Clore and Collins (Ortony et al., 1990) based on logic and semantic rules. Hybrid approaches also begin to be used for more fine-grained opinion and sentiment analysis (Yang and Cardie, 2013)

Sentiment/opinion detection methods used in human-agent interaction are rare and, when they are employed, they are not different from the ones used in opinion mining: they are consequently not designed for socio-affective interactions. Indeed, the development of a module for the detection of sentiment-related phenomena in face-to-face human-agent interactions requires to tackle

[1] The term *sentiment-related phenomena* is used in (Clavel et al., 2013) to regroup all the phenomena related to sentiment in the literature, from opinion to affect and emotion.

Proceedings of the 53rd Annual Meeting of the Association for Computational Linguistics and the 7th International Joint Conference on Natural Language Processing, pages 1064–1073,
Beijing, China, July 26-31, 2015.

various scientific issues: the delimitation of the relevant sentiment-phenomenon to detect, the integration of the multi-modal context and the management of the spontaneous and conversational speech.

The present paper tackles two of the issues: the integration of the conversational context and the delimitation of the relevant phenomenon. Regarding the first issue, we propose a system relying on a rule-based method that allows us to model the agent's utterances in order to help the detection of user's sentiment-related phenomena.

Then, we delimit and specify the linguistic phenomenon to detect by focusing on one specific aspect required by ECAs for modelling social relationships: the user's likings that are given by the expressions of user's likes and dislikes in the verbal content.

This paper is organised as follows: first, we present the theoretical model which our system is grounded on (Section 2). Then, we provide a description of the system: each stage of the bottom-up process is described, including the linguistic rules and the patterns used by the system. In Section 4, we introduce the annotation campaign we launched on Amazon Mechanical Turk (AMT) in order to create a data-set for the evaluation of our system. Finally, we present and discuss the results of the system evaluation (Section 5).

2 Theoretical background

The *liking* is one of the key dimensions used for the modelling of social relationships (Pecune et al., 2013). The definition of this concept is grounded on the Heider's *Balance Theory* (Heider, 1958) and is defined as: "the way relations among persons involving some impersonal entity are cognitively experienced by the individual" (Zajonc, 1960). Heider's theory is integrated in social agent computational models by defining scenarios where the agent and the user's likings toward each other are determined by their liking toward other entities (things, process or events). In such scenarios, the analysis of user's verbal content has a key role as a major source of information for determining of the user's likes and dislikes. Therefore, a linguistic description of this phenomenon is required to design a detection system.

In the research field of *Opinion Mining* and *Sentiment Analysis*, the majority of opinion/sentiment detection systems focus on the positive/negative distinction or on the classification of a restricted number of emotion categories. Other in-depth approaches, as (Wiebe et al., 2005; Breck et al., 2007), refer to the Private State Theory, which defines mental states as involving opinions, beliefs, judgements, appraisals and affects. Beside those models, the model proposed by (Martin and White, 2005) is increasingly used in several works (Neviarouskaya et al., 2010a; Bloom et al., 2007; Whitelaw et al., 2005). This model provides a linguistic description and a focus on the verbal expressions of sentiment and opinion and proposes a complex framework, for describing how *attitudes* are expressed in English. It distinguishes affects – which are concerned with emotional reactions – from judgements and appreciations – which relate to evaluations toward people's behaviours and semiotic or natural phenomena. Finally, it models attitudinal expressions as relying on three elements: a source, the person evaluating or experiencing, a target, the entity which is evaluated or which triggers an affect and a linguistic clue expressing the evaluation.

In this model, likes and dislikes can be considered as a subcategory of the *Attitudes*. This subcategory overlaps the three categories (affect, judgment, appreciation) defined by (Martin and White, 2005). For example, the sentence *"This painting makes me sad"* is considered as an affect, while the sentence *"This painting is a master-work"* is considered as an appreciation. But, in both cases, we can consider them as a user's like. However, among the expressions of attitudes where the source is the user, some of them do not refer to a like or dislike. For example, *"I'm very happy"* refers to an affect and does not give any clue regarding a possible like or dislike. Thus, a selection of relevant attitudes have to be done. The rules used for this selection are presented in the next section.

3 A rule-based and symbolic method

On the basis of the Martin and White's model described in the previous section, we design a system able to detect expressions of attitudes corresponding to the user's likes and dislikes. It is grounded on linguistic rules modelling the syntactic and semantic structure of the sentences.

3.1 Integrating the interaction context

The system presented in Figure 1 successively processes each adjacency pair (AP) of the dialogue

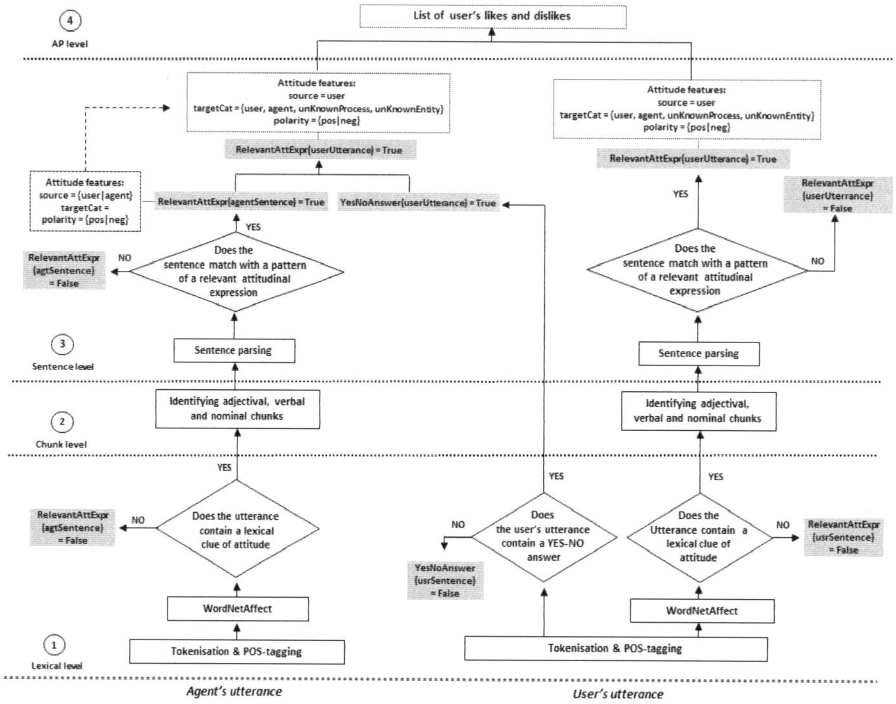

Figure 1: Process overview

(Sacks et al., 1974), i.e. each user's speech turn and the agent's one immediately preceding it. We aim to detect two kinds of user's attitudinal expressions that can occur during the interaction: the first ones which are spontaneous and do not depend on the agent's sentence (Agent: *What did you do today?* User: *I saw a great movie*); and the second ones which are triggered by the agent's sentence (Agent: *Do you like outdoors activities?* User: *Yeah very much*).

In the last case, the detection of the attitude expressed in the agent's sentence appears as a necessary step for the detection of the user's ones. This detection has to be done in an automatic way as, in the agent platform we use (the Greta platform, (Bevacqua et al., 2010), the agent's speech turns are not automatically generated but scripted. Thus, we cannot obtain the linguistic and semantic information about attitude by using the generation data. Furthermore, in order to make the dialogue setting as light as possible, it is not possible to script such values for each agent's sentence.

3.2 A bottom-Up process

The relevant expressions of attitudes are detected by using a bottom-up and rule-based process, which launches successively the different levels of analysis: lexical level, chunk level, sentence level. These three stages comprise formal grammars, which are implemented within the Unitex plateform (Paumier, 2015). During these various stages, values are assigned to the three boolean variables which are finally used to decide whether the user is expressing a like or a dislike: $RelevantAttExpr(agtSentence)$, $RelevantAttExpr(usrSentence)$, $YesNoAnswer(usrSentence)$.

3.2.1 Lexical level

After a tokenisation and a POS-tagging, the system checks whether the sentence (the user or the agent's one) contains lexical clues of attitudinal expressions. Three parts of speech are taken into account: the nouns, the adjectives and the verbs. We use a re-adaptation of the Wordnet-affect lexicon (Valitutti, 2004). In order to adapt this lexicon to our goal, a selection of relevant lexical entries has to be done. Among all the synsets, we select those which can be linked to like and dislike and that belong to the following main categories: *positive-emotion*, *negative-emotion*, *neutral-emotion*. As the lexi-

	Syntactic patterns	Attitude and Polarity rules
		For all chunk: If the chunk conveys a word labelled as a lexical clue of attitude, it is considered as an attitudinal chunk (ex: "a very good movie") ChkNoun(att:true) ; ChkAdj(att:true) ; ChkVb(att:true)
Adjectival chunk	ChkAdj → Adv?, Adj	ChkAdj(att:true, pol:pol_{Adj}) As no modifier can shift the polarity of the adjective in the adjectival chunk, the polarity of the adjectival chunk is always equal to the adjective one (.
Nominal chunk	ChkNoun → Det?, ChkAdj?, Noun	If Noun(Pol_{Noun}) AND ChkAdj(att:true, pol:inv(Pol_{Noun})): **(i)** if the noun and the adjective have an attitudinal value, and if the their polarity differ, the polarity assigned to the nominal chunk is the same as the adjective (ex: ``performance'', positive, ``bad performance'', negative); If Det == neg : ChkNoun(att:true, pol:inv(Pol_{Noun})) **(ii)** if the determiner has a negative value -- *no*, *any*, for example -- the polarity assigned to the nominal chunk is the opposite of the nominal polarity, otherwise the polarity is the same as the noun (ex: ``any good idea'').
Verbal chunk	ChkVb → Aux?, Vb.	If Neg_{Verb} == True OR Neg_{Aux} == True : ChkVerb(att:true, pol:Pol_{Noun}) if the verb or one of its auxiliaries convey a negation, the polarity assigned to the verbal chunk is the opposite of the verbal polarity (ex: ``don't like''), otherwise the polarity is the same as the verb (``like'').

Figure 2: Patterns and polarity rules used for the chunk level

con is applied by the Unitex plateform, we turn the Wordnet-Affect lexicon into a unitex dictionary format. Finally, this transformation provides three dictionaries: one for the nouns, one for the adjectives and one for the verbs. If the lexical processing has found one or several lexical clues of attitude, the system continues the analysis and get to the next stage, else $RelevantAttExpr(X) = False$ and the system quits the analysis of the sentence. Regarding the user's sentence, the system also checks if one or several tokens of sentence match with a yes or a no word, by using a short lexicon manually built which comprises less than ten words for each sentence type. If the test succeeds $YesNoAnswer(usrSentence) = True$, else $YesNoAnswer(usrSentence) = False$.

3.2.2 Chunk level

At this level, we design formal grammar – implemented as finite state automatons within the Unitex plateform. Three main chunks are defined: the verbal, the adjectival and the nominal chunks. All these chunks can imply a lexical unit of attitude. In such case, a polarity value is assigned to the entire chunk by applying rules which consider valence shifters and polarity conflict (see Figure 2).

3.2.3 Sentence level

Attitudinal value The system parse of each sentence for checking if the sentence matches with an attitudinal expression, according to its syntactic structure. This parsing phase is grounded on a set of patterns (see Figure 3). Among the attitudinal patterns provided in the literature (Neviarouskaya et al., 2010a; **?**), we selected those expressing a like or dislike according to a previous corpus-based study (Langlet and Clavel, 2014) (development corpus presented in Section 4.1). Depending on the speaker of the processed sentence – the agent or the user – sentence structures can be interrogative or affirmative surface structures. In the agent's sentence, the system looks for both affirmative and interrogative forms, while in the user's sentences, it only takes into account affirmative structures.

Type of the source Simultaneously, the system checks the source of the attitude. The type of a relevant source varies depending on the sentence processed: in the **agent's sentence**, the system aims to detect attitudes able to be validated or invalidated by the user and whose source is either the agent – lexically represented by a first person pronoun ($Src(agt) \rightarrow$ "I"|"me") – or the user – lexically represented by a second person pronoun ($Src(usr) \rightarrow$ "you'); in the **user's sentence**, the system aims to detect only the attitudes whose source is the user – represented by a first person pronoun ($Src(usr) \rightarrow$ "I"|"me").

Target and polarity At this stage, the system is also able to define the polarity of the expression

<table>
<tr><th>PATTERNS</th><th>EXAMPLES</th><th>POLARITY RULES</th></tr>
<tr><td>Att(aff) -> Src(usr|agt),ChkVb(cop), ChkAdj(att:true), Target.
Att(int) -> Aux, Source(usr), ChkVb(cop), ChkAdj, Target.</td><td>I am really happy to do that
Are you really happy to do that?</td><td rowspan="3">If $\texttt{Neg}_{\texttt{ChkVb}}$ == True :
Att(pol:inv($\texttt{Pol}_{\texttt{ChkAdj}}$ |$\texttt{Pol}_{\texttt{ChkNoun}}$))
Else:
Attitude(pol:$\texttt{Pol}_{\texttt{ChkAdj}}$ |$\texttt{Pol}_{\texttt{ChkNoun}}$)</td></tr>
<tr><td>Att(aff) -> Target, ChkVb(make), Src(usr|agt), ChkAdj(att:true).
Att(int) -> Aux, Target, ChkVb(make), Src(usr|agt), ChkAdj(att:true).</td><td>This book makes me sad
Does this book make you sad?</td></tr>
<tr><td>Att(aff) -> Src(usr|agt), ChkVb(have), ChkNoun(att:true).
Att(int) -> Aux, Src(user), ChkVb(have), ChkNoun(att:true).</td><td>I had an awful week
Did you have an awful week?</td></tr>
<tr><td>Att(aff) -> Target, ChkVb(cop), [ChkNoun(att:true)| ChkAdj(att:true)]</td><td>This book is amazing</td><td rowspan="4">In this kind of sentence, the attitudinal value is conveyed by the adjectival or the nominal chunk. When the verb of the sentence embeds a negative word, the polarity of this attitude is the reversal of the polarity assigned to the chunk.</td></tr>
<tr><td>Att(aff) -> ChkNoun(PronDem), ChkVb(cop),[ChkNoun(att:true)|ChkAdj(att:true)].</td><td>It is amazing to do that</td></tr>
<tr><td>Att(aff) -> "It"|"This"|"that", ChkVb(cop),[ChkNoun(att:true)|ChkAdj(att:true)], "for"|"of", Target, InfClause.</td><td>It is silly of them to do that</td></tr>
<tr><td>Att(aff) -> Src(usr|agt), ChkVb(opinion), Target, "as"|"like", [ChkNoun(att:true)|ChkAdj(att:true)].
Att(int)-> Aux, Src(usr), ChkVb(opinion), Target, "as"|"like", [ChkNoun(att:true)|ChkAdj(att:true)].</td><td>I consider this painting as beautiful
Do you consider this book as beautiful?</td></tr>
<tr><td>Att(aff) -> Src(usr|agt), ChkVb(att:true), Target.
Att(int) -> Aux, Src(usr|agt), ChkVb(att:true), Target.</td><td>I like this book
Do you like this book?</td><td>Attitude(pol:$\texttt{Pol}_{\texttt{ChkVb}}$)
As the polarity rules have been applied at the chunking level, the polarity of the attitude always equals the polarity of the verbal chunk</td></tr>
</table>

Figure 3: Patterns and polarity rules used for the sentence level: the second column presents examples of sentences matching with the patterns detailed in the first column. The rules introduced in the third column are applied according to the sentence pattern detected.

by detecting the valence shifters which can modify the polarity of the attitudinal chunk and by applying the appropriate polarity rules described in Figure 3. Regarding the target, the system is only able to assign to the target one of four generic classes. The first two classes concern the two members of the conversation – *agent* and *user*. The third class, called *other*, deals with all entities and processes which are neither the agent or the user. The last one – *unknown* – concerns all the target referring by a pronoun, and whose class – even generic – cannot be known. In a future work, the *other* category could be detailed by using an ontological resource, and *unknown* category by referring to an anaphora resolution.

3.2.4 User's utterance level within the AP

Generating attitude feature set Once the sentence level is done, the $True$ value is assigned to the $relevantAttExpr(usrSentence)$ variable in two steps.

Firstly, the syntactic structure of the user's sentence matches with one of the attitudinal patterns (Figure 3) whose source is the user ($Src(user)$). The feature set of the attitudinal expression is generated according to the information found at the parsing stage: $source \in \{user, agent\}$, $polarity \in \{neg, pos\}$, $targetType \in \{user, agent, other, unknown\}$.

Secondly, if the agent's sentence matches with one of the attitudinal patterns whose source is either the user or the agent ($Src(user|agent)$), then $relevantAttExpr(agtSentence) = True$. In this second case, if $YesNoAnswer(usrSentence) == True$, the user validates or invalidates the attitude. Thus, the system defines $relevantAttExpr(usrSentence) == True$, even if any sentence matching with a relevant pattern has been found in the user's sentence. The feature set associated to the user's attitude is built according to those assigned to the attitudinal expression found is the agent's sentence. Since the user assumes or rejects the attitude expressed by the agent, the system considers that he/she utters an attitudinal expression that he/she is the source. Regarding the polarity, if the user validates the statement expressed by the agent, the polarity of his/her attitude is the same as the agent's one. Otherwise, if the user expresses a no answer, the polarity is the opposite of the agent's one.

Converting attitude into like-dislike The patterns used for the parsing phase refer to attitudes that are good candidates for expressions of like or dislike. When the $relevantAttExpr(usrSentence) == True$, the system converts the attitude into a like or a dislike on the basis of the feature set associated to the expression of attitude: an attitude with a positive polarity ($attitude(pol : pos)$) is considered as a $like$, and an attitude with a negative polarity ($attitude(pol : neg)$) is considered as a $dislike$. The target is the same as the attitudinal expression.

4 Corpus for evaluating the system

4.1 Semaine corpus

In order to evaluate our system, an annotated data set of sentences extracted from the Semaine corpus (McKeown et al., 2011) has been created. This corpus comprises 65 manually-transcribed sessions where a human user interacts with a human operator playing the role of the virtual agent. These interactions are based on a scenario involving four agent characters: Poppy, happy and outgoing, Prudence, sensible and level-headed, Spike, angry and confrontational and Obadiah, depressive and gloomy. Agent's sentences are constrained by a script (however, some deviations to the script occur in the database) aimed at putting the user in the same state as the one of the played character. 30 sessions of the corpus have been used for the development set. The rest of the data has been considered to build the evaluation corpus following the protocol described in the next paragraph.

4.2 Annotation protocol on AMT

We use AMT platform to carry out the annotation campaign. It allows us to easily recruit a large number of English native speakers. Recent works have shown the reliability of the annotations provided by this platform. For various tasks of language annotation – evaluation of machine translation (Callison-Burch, 2009), affect recognition (Snow et al., 2008), or dictionary validation (Taboada et al., 2011) – they observe a high agreement of non-expert raters with the gold standards.

For our annotation protocol, the recruited annotators are put in the same conditions as the system: each annotator has to label the user's likes and dislikes by only considering the AP (without the whole interaction) and the verbal content (without the audio and video). Among the pairs having less than thirty words in the evaluation corpus, we randomly selected 600 APs – made of an agent's speech turn and a user's one (see Section 3.1). This length of the sentence has been restricted to avoid annotation difficulties.

The dataset is divided in 60 subsets of 10 APs. In order to secure the annotation and to prevent the annotators from doing the annotation task two times, we use TurkGate tool (Goldin and Darlow, 2013). The AMT workers have been selected according to their approval rate – greater than or equal to 99% – and to the number of task approved – greater than or equal to 10000. Each subset of the corpus is randomly assigned to one annotator, and the order in which the AP are presented to each annotator is also randomly defined. A training phase is previously subjected to each annotator in order to familiarise him/her to the annotation principles. Finally, 240 AMT workers have participated to the annotation campaign (4 for each subset).

Questionnaire As the annotation is done by non-expert annotators, we design a simplified and intuitive annotation process: for each pair, the annotators have to answer to a set of questions featured in Figure 4. The goal of the questionnaire is to determine whether the annotator is able to deduce a user's like or dislike from the APs. In order to facilitate the annotation and to make the interpretation of each sentence as spontaneous as possible, the question have been designed without linguistic technical word. In this way, the task is more functional for the annotator and it is easier for him/her to put his/herself to the place of the hearer. Each question of the questionnaire focuses on one of the outputs of the detection system:

- The **first question** examines the presence of an expression of like or dislike and provides a *yes/no* answer.
- the **second question** deals with the multiple occurrences of like/dislike expressions in the same speech turn. We limited the answer to "4" (maximum number of like/dislike expressions observed in the dataset). If the annotator detects more than one expression of like/dislike, the questions 3 to 4 are asked for each expression of like/dislike.
- the **third question** deals with the type of the target. As answers, only the four types –

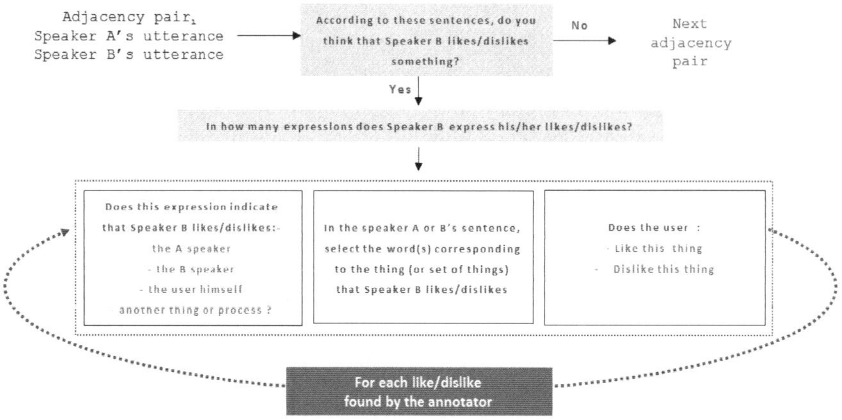

Figure 4: Annotation process on AMT

those the system is able to detect – are proposed.

- The **fourth question** concerns the polarity of the expression: positive (like) or negative (dislike).

4.3 Inter-annotator agreement and consistency

We measure the inter-annotators agreement or consistency at each stage of the questionnaire. All the measures presented in the section have been applied for each subset of the corpus (60 subsets of 10 APs, 4 annotators for each subset).

	Fleiss' Kappa	**Cronbach's alpha**
Max	0.79	0.90
Median	0.32	0.72
Average	0.25	0.59

Table 1: Fleiss' kappa scores and Cronbach's alpha coefficients obtained in on the 60 subsets

Regarding the answer to the first question of the questionnaire, we measure how the annotators are agreeing on the presence of at least one user expression of like or dislike by using the Fleiss' Kappa (Fleiss, 1971) (see Table 1). Second, we measure the consistency on the annotation of the number of user's expressions to each pair by using the Cronbach's alpha coefficient (Cronbach, 1951). As, for labeling the number of likes-dislikes expressed in each pair, the crowd-workers have to select a value on a scale (from 1 to 4), it appears as suitable to measure the relative similarity between ratings rather than the agreement about an exact value. The Cronbach's alpha is designed for evaluating the internal consistency of a scale annotation. In this way, it measures the degree to which different raters or observers make consistent estimates of the same phenomenon.

The obtained scores are encouraging. Regarding the agreement on the presence of an expression of like or dislike, even if the median score is comprised between 0.30 and 0.40, the maximal value equals to 0.79. Moreover, 40% of the subsets has a kappa score comprised between 0.40 and 0.60. The consistency score is also significant: 51% of the annotated sub-corpus has a score equal or higher than 0.7, which is considered as an acceptable level of agreement (George and Mallery, 2010).

For the polarity and the target type, we select the pairs where at least two annotators agree on the presence of an expression of like or dislike, and we consider only the annotations provided by these annotators. After this selection, we obtain a sub-set of ratings with a unfixed set of annotators. As the Fleiss' Kappa must be applied on data with an invariable and fixed set of raters, we consider the percent agreement (Gwet, 2010) as more appropriate. Even though, it seems sometimes difficult for the annotators to agree on the presence of a user's expression of like or dislike, their agreement on the polarity of such expressions appears as more significant: 41% of the sub-corpus has a percentage of agreement between 50% and 75% and 52% of the sub-corpus has a percentage of agreement upper than 75%. The agreement is also significant regarding the target: 61% of the sub-corpus has a percentage of agreement upper than 50%. All these results are quite positive for a system-oriented annotation of a such subjective phenomenon.

5 Evaluation of the system

5.1 Protocol

From the 600 pairs of the previously annotated corpus, we keep 503 pairs for the evaluation of the system by removing the pairs where a consensus can not be found between the 4 annotators – that is that we keep as a reference the majority vote corresponding to the data where at least three annotators agree. We use three different measures to evaluate the system performance relying on the agreement measures presented in Section 4.3: the detection of the presence of a user's expression of like or dislike is evaluated by the Fleiss' kappa between the system output and the reference; the consistency on the number of detected expressions is evaluated by the Cronbach's alpha coefficient; the agreement on the polarity is measured by using the Fleiss' kappa; and the agreement on the target type with the percentage of agreement.

5.2 Results

Table 2 presents the results obtained for each detection task (presence of a like/dislike expression, detection of the correct number of expressions contained in an sentence, and correct classification between like and dislike). The agreement between

No Expr-Expr	$k = 0.61$
Nb of expressions rated	$\alpha = 0.67$
Polarity	$k = 0.84$
Target type	$p = 53\%$

Table 2: Agreement scores between the system output and the reference

the system output and the reference is substantial for the detection of the presence of a user expression ($k = 0.61$) and the number of user expressions is also correctly detected by the system (acceptable α largely higher than 0.6). However, the major part of the corpus contains no more than 1 like/dislike expression (98% of the pairs are annotated by the reference and the system as containing 0 or 1 like/dislike expression). 4% of the pairs (25 pairs) is annotated by the system as containing 1 expression, while the referred annotation does not indicate the presence of any like/dislike expression. For 8% of the pairs (43 pairs), it is the opposite phenomenon (1 expression annotated by the reference but not by the system). The Fleiss' kappa score obtained for the polarity is really encouraging since it equals 0.844. Regarding the target type, we obtain a percentage of agreement at 53%. The disagreement frequently concerns a confusion between the *unknown* and *other* categories.

5.3 Discussion

We have carried out an in-depth analysis of the disagreement between the system outputs and the human annotations in order to identify tracks for the improvement of the system. We identified two main types of difficulties.

The first difficulty concerns the processing of spontaneous speech. The Semaine corpus contains a great number of disfluent utterances that disrupt the syntactical structure of the speech turn and thus hinder both the annotation process and the detection system. In the following pair, Agent: *"Oh!"* – User: *"are just very good really good film and read a book"*, the grammatical structure of the user sentence is fuzzy (absence of the subject, presence of repairs) which makes the parsing of the sentence and thus the detection of attitudinal patterns difficult. However, the annotators have here correctly identified the presence of a like and the type of the target ("the film" in the *Others* category), which is not the case for all the annotations of the disfluent utterances. To handle this difficulty, it would be interesting to integrate a system able to automatically label disfluencies, such as the one presented in (Dutrey et al., 2014). The disfluent structure of the sentence could thus be integrated to our syntactic and semantic rules. However, the automatic detection of disfluencies is still an open challenge, in particular in the case of edit disfluencies where the speaker corrects or alters the utterance or abandons it entirely and starts over (Strassel, 2004).

The second difficulty concerns the lack of context provided by some of the APs. Our system offers a first step in the integration of the interaction context by considering jointly the user's utterance and the previous agent's one that allow us to correctly analyse a large scale of expressions. However, the system and the annotators have to focus on the APs without considering the preceding speech turns, which can cause disagreements not only between the system outputs and the human annotations, but also between the human annotators. In the following example, Agent: *"good. ah good"* – User: *"my favourite emotion"*, the source (here, the user) can be easily identified but the information contained in the AP is not sufficient to identify the target. An interesting answer to this issue is to take into account the whole conversation preceding a user's utterance as a significant context for the latter. This will imply the design of new complex rules taking into account a larger interaction context.

6 Conclusion and future works

We have introduced a NLP-based system able to detect user's expressions of likes and dislikes in the conversation with an ECA. This system relies on syntactic and semantic rules integrating the interaction context by analysing the content of the agent's utterances to help the analysis of the user's ones. It is designed as a bottom-up and rule-based process. The system has been evaluated by using an evaluation data set created under AMT platform. This first and pioneering version of the system shows encouraging results for the different tasks performed by the system that concern the detection of relevant like/dislike expressions (substantial agreement with a Fleiss kappa at 0.61), the categorization of the expressions between like and dislike (almost perfect agreement with a Fleiss kappa at 0.84) – polarity assignment – and the identification of the target type (53% of agreement between the reference and the system output). Beyond these quite optimistic results, we have provided some tracks for the system improvement that concerns a deeper integration of the interaction context and the processing of spontaneous speech features.

Acknowledgments

The authors would like to thank the GRETA team for its contributions to the Greta and Vib platforms. This work has been supported by the european project ARIA-VALUSPA, and performed within the Labex SMART (ANR-11-LABX-65) supported by French state funds managed by the ANR within the Investissements d'Avenir programme under reference ANR-11-IDEX-0004-02.

References

Elisabetta Bevacqua, Ken Prepin, Radoslaw Niewiadomski, Etienne de Sevin, and Catherine Pelachaud. 2010. Greta: Towards an interactive conversational virtual companion. *Artificial Companions in Society: perspectives on the Present and Future*, pages 143–156.

K. Bloom, N. Garg, and S. Argamon. 2007. Extracting appraisal expressions. *HLT-NAACL*, pages 165–192, April.

E. Breck, Y. Choi, and C. Cardie. 2007. Identifying expressions of opinion in context. In Sangal S., Mehta H., and Bagga R. K., editors, *International Joint Conference On Artifical Intelligence*, pages 2683–2688, San Francisco, CA. Morgan KoffMann Publishers.

C. Callison-Burch. 2009. Fast, cheap, and creative: Evaluating translation quality using amazon's mechanical turk. In *Proceedings of the 2009 Conference on Empirical Methods in Natural Language Processing*, EMNLP '09, Stroudsburg, PA, USA. Association for Computational Linguistics.

C. Clavel, C. Pelachaud, and M. Ochs. 2013. User's sentiment analysis in face-to-face human-agent interactions prospects. In *Workshop on Affective Social Signal Computing, Satellite of Interspeech*. Association for Computational Linguistics, August.

L.J Cronbach. 1951. Coefficient alpha and the internal structure of tests. *Psychometrika*, 16(3):297–334.

C. Dutrey, C. Clavel, S. Rosset, I. Vasilescu, and M. Adda-Decker. 2014. A crf-based approach to automatic disfluency detection in a french call-centre corpus. In *Interspeech*, page to appear.

J.L. Fleiss. 1971. Measuring nominal scale agreement among many raters. *Psychological Bulletin*, 76(5):378–382.

D. George and P. Mallery. 2010. *SPSS for Windows Step by Step: A Simple Guide and Reference 18.0 Update*. Prentice Hall Press, Upper Saddle River, NJ, USA, 11th edition.

G. Goldin and A. Darlow. 2013. Turkgate (version 0.4.0) [software]. `http://gideongoldin.github.com/TurkGate/`.

K. L. Gwet. 2010. *Handbook of Inter-Rater Reliability*. 11th edition.

F. Heider. 1958. *The psychology of interpersonal relations*. Lawrence Erlbaum associates Inc.

C. Langlet and C. Clavel. 2014. Modelling user's attitudinal reactions to the agent utterances: focus on the verbal content. In *5th International Workshop on Corpora for Research on Emotion, Sentiment & Social Signals (ES3 2014)*, Reykjavik, Iceland, May.

J. R. Martin and P. R. White. 2005. *The Language of Evaluation. Appraisal in English*. Macmillan Basingstoke, London and New York.

G. McKeown, M. Valstar, R. Cowie, M. Pantic, and M. Schroder. 2011. The semaine database: Annotated multimodal records of emotionally colored conversations between a person and a limited agent. *IEEE Transactions on Affective Computing*, 3(1):5–17, Jan-March.

K. Moilanen and S. Pulman. 2007. Sentiment composition. In *Proceedings of Recent Advances in Natural Language Processing (RANLP 2007)*, pages 378–382, September 27-29.

A. Neviarouskaya, H. Prendinger, and M. Ishizuka. 2010a. Recognition of affect, judgment, and appreciation in text. In *Proceedings of the 23rd International Conference on Computational Linguistics*, COLING '10, pages 806–814, Stroudsburg, PA, USA. Association for Computational Linguistics.

A. Neviarouskaya, H. Prendinger, and M. Ishizuka. 2010b. User study on AffectIM, an avatar-based Instant Messaging system employing rule-based affect sensing from text. *International Journal of Human-Computer Studies*, 68(7):432–450.

A. Ortony, G.L. Clore, and A. Collins. 1990. *The Cognitive Structure of Emotions*. Cambridge, University Press.

B. Pang and L. Lee. 2008. Opinion mining and sentiment analysis. *Foundations and Trends in Information Retrieval*, 2(1-2):1–135, January.

S. Paumier. 2015. *Unitex user manual*. Université de Paris-Est Marne-la-Vallée.

F. Pecune, M. Ochs, and C. Pelachaud. 2013. A formal model of social relations for articial companions. In *EUMAS 2013*, December.

H. Sacks, E.A. Schegloff, and G. Jefferson. 1974. A simplest systematics for the organization of turn-taking for conversation. *Language*, 50(9-10):696–735, November.

B. Schuller, A. Batliner, S. Steidl, and D. Seppi. 2011. Recognising realistic emotions and affect in speech: State of the art and lessons learnt from the first challenge. *Speech Communication*, 53(9-10):1062–1087, November.

M. Shaikh, H. Prendinger, and M. Ishizuka. 2009. A linguistic interpretation of the occ emotion model for affect sensing from text. In *Affective Information Processing*, pages 378–382. Springer London, May.

C. Smith, N. Crook, S. Dobnik, and D. Charlton. 2011. Interaction strategies for an affective conversational agent. In *Presence: Teleoperators and Virtual Environments*, volume 20, pages 395–411. MIT Press.

R. Snow, B. O'Connor, D. Jurafsky, and Y. Andrew. 2008. Cheap and fast—but is it good?: Evaluating non-expert annotations for natural language tasks. In *Proceedings of the Conference on Empirical Methods in Natural Language Processing*, EMNLP '08, Stroudsburg, PA, USA. Association for Computational Linguistics.

S. Strassel, 2004. *Simple Metadata Annotation Specification*. Linguistic Data Consortium.

M. Taboada, J. Brooke, M. Tofiloski, K. Voll, and M. Stede. 2011. Lexicon-based methods for sentiment analysis. *Computational Linguistics*, 37(2), June.

R. Valitutti. 2004. Wordnet-affect: an affective extension of wordnet. In *In Proceedings of the 4th International Conference on Language Resources and Evaluation*, pages 1083–1086.

C. Whitelaw, N. Garg, and S. Argamon. 2005. Using appraisal taxonomies for sentiment analysis. *Proceedings of CIKM-05, the ACM SIGIR Conference on Information and Knowledge Management*, April.

J. Wiebe, T. Wilson, and C. Cardie. 2005. Annotation expressions of opinion and emotions in language. *Language Resources and Evaluation*, pages 165–210, Vol. 39/2-3.

B. Yang and C. Cardie. 2013. Joint inference for fine-grained opinion extraction. In *Proceedings of the 51st Annual Meeting of the Association for Computational Linguistics (Volume 1: Long Papers)*, pages 1640–1649, Sofia, Bulgaria, August. Association for Computational Linguistics.

S. Yildirim, S. Narayanan, and A. Potamianos. 2011. Detecting emotional state of a child in a conversational computer game. *Computer Speech and Language*, 25(1):29–44.

R.B. Zajonc. 1960. The psychology of interpersonal relations. *Public Opinion Quarterly*, 24(2).

L. Zhang, J. Barnden, R.J. Hendley, M.G. Lee, A.M. Wallington, and Zhigang Wen. 2008. Affect detection and metaphor in e-drama. *International Journal of Continuing Engineering Education and Life-Long Learning*, 18(2):234.

Learning Word Representations from Scarce and Noisy Data with Embedding Sub-spaces

Ramon F. Astudillo, Silvio Amir, Wang Lin, Mário Silva, Isabel Trancoso
Instituto de Engenharia de Sistemas e Computadores Investigação e Desenvolvimento (INESC-ID)
Rua Alves Redol 9
Lisbon, Portugal
{ramon.astudillo, samir, wlin, mjs, isabel.trancoso}@inesc-id.pt

Abstract

We investigate a technique to adapt unsupervised word embeddings to specific applications, when only small and noisy labeled datasets are available. Current methods use pre-trained embeddings to initialize model parameters, and then use the labeled data to tailor them for the intended task. However, this approach is prone to overfitting when the training is performed with scarce and noisy data. To overcome this issue, we use the supervised data to find an embedding subspace that fits the task complexity. All the word representations are adapted through a projection into this task-specific subspace, even if they do not occur on the labeled dataset. This approach was recently used in the SemEval 2015 Twitter sentiment analysis challenge, attaining state-of-the-art results. Here we show results improving those of the challenge, as well as additional experiments in a Twitter Part-Of-Speech tagging task.

1 Introduction

The success of supervised systems largely depends on the amount and quality of the available training data, oftentimes, even more than the particular choice of learning algorithm (Banko and Brill, 2001). Labeled data is, however, expensive to obtain, while unlabeled data is widely available. In order to exploit this fact, semi-supervised learning methods can be used. In particular, it is possible to derive word representations by exploiting word co-occurrence patterns in large samples of unlabeled text. Based on this idea, several methods have been recently proposed to efficiently estimate *word embeddings* from raw text, leveraging neural language models (Huang et al., 2012; Mikolov et al., 2013; Pennington et al., 2014; Ling et al., 2015). These models work by maximizing the probability that words within a given window size are predicted correctly. The resulting embeddings are low-dimensional dense vectors that encode syntactic and semantic properties of words. Using these word representations, Turian et al. (2010) were able to improve near state-of-the-art systems for several tasks, by simply plugging in the learned word representations as additional features. However, because these features are estimated by minimizing the prediction errors made on a generic, unsupervised, task they might be suboptimal for the intended purposes.

Ideally, word features should be adapted to the specific supervised task. One of the reasons for the success of deep learning models for language problems, is the use unsupervised word embeddings to initialize the word projection layer. Then, during training, the errors made in the predictions are backpropagated to update the embeddings, so that they better predict the supervised signal (Collobert et al., 2011; dos Santos and Gatti, 2014a). However, this strategy faces an additional challenge in noisy domains, such as social media. The lexical variation caused by the typos, use of slang and abbreviations leads to a great number of singletons and out-of-vocabulary words. For these words, the embeddings will be poorly re-estimated. Even worse, words not present on the training set will never get their embeddings updated.

In this paper, we describe a strategy to adapt unsupervised word embeddings when dealing with small and noisy labeled datasets. The intuition behind our approach is the following. For a given task, only a subset of all the latent aspects captured by the word embeddings will be useful. Therefore, instead of updating the embeddings directly with the available labeled data, we estimate a projection of these embeddings into a low dimensional sub-space. This simple method brings two funda-

Proceedings of the 53rd Annual Meeting of the Association for Computational Linguistics and the 7th International Joint Conference on Natural Language Processing, pages 1074–1084,
Beijing, China, July 26-31, 2015.

mental advantages. On the one hand, we obtain low dimensional embeddings fitting the complexity of the target task. On the other hand, we are able to learn new representations for all the words, even if they do not occur in the labeled dataset.

To estimate the low dimensional sub-space, we propose a simple non-linear model equivalent to a neural network with one single hidden layer. The model is trained in supervised fashion on the labeled dataset, learning jointly the sub-space projection and a classifier for the target task. Using this model, we built a system to participate in the SemEval 2015 Twitter sentiment analysis benchmark (Rosenthal et al., 2015). Our submission attained state-of-the-art results without hand-coded features or linguistic resources (Astudillo et al., 2015). Here, we further investigate this approach and compare it against several state-of-the-art systems for Twitter sentiment classification. We also report on additional experiments to assess the adequacy of this strategy in other natural language problems. To this end, we apply the embedding sub-space layer to Ling et al. (2015) deep learning model for part-of-speech tagging. Even though the gains were not as significant as in the sentiment polarity prediction task, the results suggest that our method is indeed generalizable to other problems.

The rest of the paper is organized as follows: the related work is reviewed in Section 2. Section 3, briefly describes the model used to pre-train the word embeddings. In Section 4, we introduce the concept of embedding sub-space, as well as the the non-linear sub-space model for text classification. Section 5, details the experiments performed with the SemEval corpora. Section 6 describes additional experiments applying the embedding sub-space method to a Part-of-Speech tagging model for Twitter data. Finally, Section 7 draws the conclusions.

2 Related Work

NLP systems can benefit from a very large pool of unlabeled data. While raw documents are usually not annotated, they contain structure, which can be leveraged to learn word features. Context is one strong indicator for word similarity, as related words tend to occur in similar contexts (Firth, 1968). Approaches that are based on this concept include, Latent Semantic Analysis, where words are represented as rows in the low-rank approximation of a term co-occurrence matrix (Dumais et al., 1988), word clusters obtained with hierarchical clustering algorithms based on Hidden Markov Models (Brown et al., 1992), and continuous word vectors learned with neural language models (Bengio et al., 2003). The resulting clusters and vectors, can then be used as more generalizable features in supervised tasks, as they also provide representations for words not present in the labeled data (Bespalov et al., 2011; Owoputi et al., 2013; Chen and Manning, 2014).

A great amount of work has been done on the problem of learning better word representations from unsupervised data. However, not many studies have discussed the best ways to use them in supervised tasks. Typically, in these cases, word representations are directly used as features or to initialize the parameters of more complex models. In some tasks, this approach is however prone to overfitting. The work presented here aims to provide a simple approach to overcome this last scenario. It is thus directly related to Labutov and Lipson (2013), where a method to learn task-specific representations from general pre-trained embeddings was presented. In this work, new features were estimated with a convex objective function that combined the log-likelihood of the training data, with regularization penalizing the Frobenius norm of the distortion matrix. That is, the matrix of the differences between the original and the new embeddings. Even though the adapted embeddings performed better than the purely unsupervised features, both were significantly outperformed by a simple bag-of-words baseline.

Most other approaches, simply rely on additional training data to fine tune the embeddings for a given supervised task. In Bansal et al. (2014), better word embeddings for dependency parsing were obtained by using a corpus created to capture dependency context. This technique requires, nevertheless, of a pre-existing dependency parser or, at least a parsed corpus. For some other tasks, it is possible to collect weakly labeled corpora by making strong assumptions about the data. In Go et al. (2009) a corpus for Twitter sentiment analysis was built by assuming that tweets with positive emoticons imply positive sentiment, whereas tweets with negative emoticons imply negative sentiment. Using a similar corpus, Tang et al. (2014b) induced sentiment specific word embeddings, for the Twitter domain. The embeddings were estimated with a neural network that minimized a linear combination of two loss functions, one penalized the errors made at predicting the center word within a sequence of words, while the other penalized mistakes made at deciding the sentiment label. Weakly labeled data has also been used to refine unsupervised embeddings, by retraining them to predict the noisy labels before using the actual task-specific supervised data (Severyn and Moschitti, 2015).

3 Unsupervised Structured Skip-Gram Word Embeddings

Word embeddings are generally trained by optimizing an objective function that can be measured without annotations. One popular approach is to estimate the embeddings by maximizing the probability that the words within a given window size are predicted correctly. Our previous work has compared several such models, namely the skip-gram and CBOW architectures (Mikolov et al., 2013), GloVe (Pennington et al., 2014), and the structured skip-gram approach (Ling et al., 2015), suggesting that they all have comparable capabilities. Thus, in this study we only use embeddings derived with the structured skip-gram approach, a modification of the skip-gram architecture that has been shown to outperform the original model in syntax based tasks such as, part-of-speech tagging and dependency parsing.

Central to the structured skip-gram is a log linear model of word prediction. Let $w = i$ denote that a word at a given position of a sentence is the i-th word on a vocabulary of size v, and let $w^p = j$ denote that the word p positions further in the sentence is the j-th word on the vocabulary. The structured skip-gram models the following probability:

$$p(w^p = j | w = i) \propto \exp\left(\mathbf{C}_j^p \cdot \mathbf{E} \cdot \mathbf{w}^i\right) \quad (1)$$

Here, $\mathbf{w}^i \in \{1, 0\}^{v \times 1}$ is a one-hot representation of $w = i$. That is, a vector of zeros of the size of the vocabulary v with a 1 on the i-th entry of the vector. The symbol $\cdot$ denotes internal product and $\exp()$ acts element-wise. The log-linear model is parametrized by the following matrices: $\mathbf{E} \in \mathbb{R}^{e \times v}$, is the embedding matrix, transforming the one-hot representation into a compact real valued space of size e, $\mathbf{C}_j^p \in \mathbb{R}^{v \times e}$ is a set of output matrices, one for each relative word position p, projecting the real-valued representation to a vector with the size of the vocabulary v. By learning a different matrix $\mathbf{C}^p$ for each relative word position, the model captures word order information, unlike the original skip-gram approach that uses only one output matrix. Finally, a distribution over all possible words is attained by exponentiating and normalizing over the v possible options. In practice, negative sampling is used to avoid having to normalize over the whole vocabulary (Goldberg and Levy, 2014).

As most other neural network models, the structured skip-gram is trained with gradient-based methods. After a model has been trained, the low dimensional embedding $\mathbf{E} \cdot \mathbf{w}_i \in \mathbb{R}^{e \times 1}$ encapsulates the information about each word $\mathbf{w}_i$ and its surrounding contexts. This embbeding can thus be used as input to other learning algorithms to further enhance performance.

4 Adapting Embeddings with Sub-space Projections

As detailed in the introduction and related work, word embeddings are a useful unsupervised technique to attain initial model values or features prior to supervised training. These models can be then retrained using the available labeled data. However, even if the embeddings provide a compact real valued representation of each word in a vocabulary, the total number of parameters in the model can be rather high. If, as it is often the case, only a small amount of supervised data is available, this can lead to severe overfitting. Even if regularization is used to reduce the overfitting risk, only a reduced subset of the words will actually be present in the labeled dataset. Words not seen during training will never get their embeddings updated. Furthermore, rare words will receive very few updates, and thus their embeddings will be poorly adapted for the intended task. We propose a simple solution to avoid this problem.

4.1 Embedding Sub-space

Let $\mathbf{E} \in \mathbb{R}^{e \times v}$ denote the original embedding matrix obtained, e.g. with the structured skip-gram model described in Equation 1. We define the adapted embedding matrix as the factorization $\mathbf{S} \cdot \mathbf{E}$, where $\mathbf{S} \in \mathbb{R}^{s \times e}$, with $s \ll e$. We estimate the parameters of the matrix $\mathbf{S}$ using the labeled dataset, while $\mathbf{E}$ is kept fixed. In other words, we determine the optimal projection of the embedding matrix $\mathbf{E}$ into a sub-space of dimension s.

The idea of embedding sub-space rests on two fundamental principles:

1. With dimensionality reduction of the embeddings, the model can better fit the complexity of the task at hand or the amount of available data.

2. Using a projection, all the embeddings are indirectly updated, not only those of words present in the labeled dataset.

One question that arises from this approach, is if the estimated projection is also optimal for the words not present in the labeled dataset. We assume that the words on the labeled dataset are, to some extent, representative of the words found in the unlabeled corpus. This is a reasonable assumption since both datasets can be seen as samples drawn from the same power-law distribution. If this holds, for every *unknown* word, there will be some other word sufficiently close it in the embedding space. Consequently, the projection matrix $\mathbf{S}$ will also be approximately valid for those unseen words. It is often the case that a relatively small number of words of the labeled dataset are not present on the unlabeled corpus. These words are not represented in $\mathbf{E}$. One way to deal with this case, is to simply set the embeddings of unknown words to zero. But in this case, the embeddings will not be adapted during training. Random initializations of the embeddings seems to be helpful for tasks that have a higher penalty for missing words, although it remains unclear if better initialization strategies exist.

4.2 Non-Linear Embedding Sub-space Model

The concept of embedding sub-space can be applied to log-linear classifiers or any deep learning architecture that uses embeddings. We now describe an application of this method for short text classification tasks. In what follows, we will refer to this approach as Non-Linear Sub-space Embedding (NLSE) model. The NLSE can be interpreted as a simple feed-forward neural network model (Rumelhart et al., 1985) with one single hidden layer utilizing the embedding sub-space approach, as depicted in Fig. 1. Let

$$\mathbf{m} = [\mathbf{w}_1 \cdots \mathbf{w}_n] \tag{2}$$

denote a message of n words. Each column $\mathbf{w} \in \{0,1\}^{v \times 1}$ of $\mathbf{m}$ represents a word in one-hot form, as described in Section 3. Let y denote a categorical random variable over K classes. The NLSE model, estimates thus the probability of each possible category $y = k \in K$ given a message $\mathbf{m}$ as

$$p(y = k|\mathbf{m}) \propto \exp\left(\mathbf{Y}_k \cdot \mathbf{h} \cdot \mathbf{1}\right). \tag{3}$$

Here, $\mathbf{h} \in \{0,1\}^{e \times n}$ are the activations of the hidden layer for each word, given by

$$\mathbf{h} = \sigma\left(\mathbf{S} \cdot \mathbf{E} \cdot \mathbf{m}\right) \tag{4}$$

where $\sigma()$ is a sigmoid function acting on each element of the matrix. The matrix $\mathbf{Y} \in \mathbb{R}^{3 \times s}$ maps the embedding sub-space to the classification space and $\mathbf{1} \in 1^{n \times 1}$ is a matrix of ones that sums the scores for all words together, prior to normalization. This is equivalent to a bag-of-words assumption. Finally, the model computes a probability distribution over the K classes, using the *softmax* function.

Compared to a conventional feed-forward network employing embeddings for natural language classification tasks, two main differences arise. First, the input layer is factorized into two components, the embeddings attained in unsupervised form, $\mathbf{E}$, and the projection matrix $\mathbf{S}$. Second, the size of the sub-space, in which the embeddings are projected, is much smaller than that of the original embeddings with typical reductions above one order of magnitude. As usual in this kind of models, all the parameters can be trained with gradient methods, using the backpropagation update rule.

5 NLSE for Twitter Sentiment Analysis

In this section, we apply the NLSE model to the message polarity classification task proposed by SemEval, for their well-known Twitter sentiment analysis challenge (Nakov et al., 2013). Given a message, the goal is to decide whether it expresses a positive, negative, or neutral sentiment. Most of the top performing systems that participated in this challenge, relied on linear classification models and the bag-of-words assumption, representing messages as sparse vectors of the size of the vocabulary. In the case of social media, this approach is particularly inefficient, due to the large vocabularies necessary to account for all the lexical variation found in this domain. Thus, these models

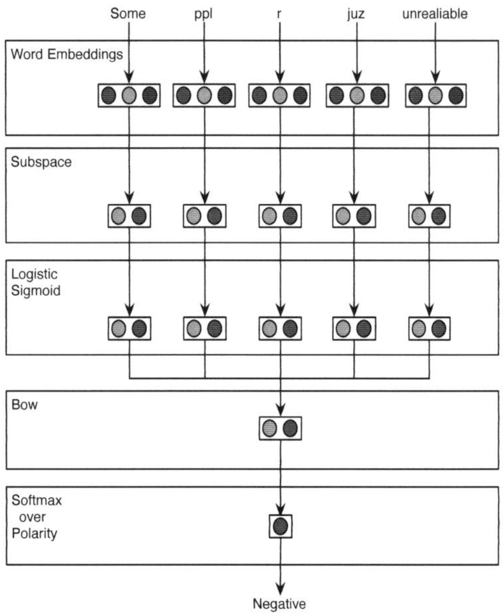

Figure 1: Illustration of the NLSE model, applied to sentiment polarity prediction.

	Positive	Neutral	Negative
Development	3230	4109	1265
Tweets 2015	1032	983	364
Tweets 2014	982	669	202
Tweets 2013	1572	1640	601

Table 1: Number of examples per class in each SemEval dataset. The first row shows the training data; the other rows are sets used for testing.

need to be enriched with additional hand-crafted features that try to capture more discriminative aspects of the content, most of which require external tools (e.g., part-of-speech taggers and parsers) or linguistic resources (e.g., dictionaries and sentiment lexicons) (Miura et al., 2014; Kiritchenko et al., 2014). With the embedding sub-space approach, however, we are able to attain state-of-the-art performance while requiring only minimal processing of the data and few hyperparameters. To make our results comparable to other systems for this task, we adopted the guidelines from the benchmark. Our system was trained and tuned using only the development data. The evaluation was performed on the test sets, shown in Table 1, and we report the results in terms of the average F-measure for the positive and negative classes.

5.1 Experimental Setup

The first step of our approach requires a corpus of raw text for the unsupervised pre-training of the embedding matrix **E**. We resorted to the corpus of 52 million tweets used in (Owoputi et al., 2013) and the tokenizer described in the same work. The messages were previously pre-processed as follows: lower-casing, replacing Twitter user mentions and URLs with special tokens and reducing any character repetition to at most 3 characters. Words occurring less than 40 times in the corpus were discarded, resulting in a vocabulary of around 210,000 types. Then, a modified version of the `word2vec` tool[1] was used to compute the word embeddings, as described in Section 3. The window size and negative sampling rate were set to 5 and 25 words, respectively, and embeddings of 50, 200, 400 and 600 dimensions were built.

Our system accepts as input a sentence represented as a matrix, obtained by concatenating the *one-hot* vectors that represent each individual word. Therefore, we first performed the aforementioned normalization and tokenization steps and then, converted each tweet into this representation. The development set was split into 80% for parameter learning and 20% for model evaluation and selection, maintaining the original relative class proportions in each set. All the weights were initialized uniformly at random, as proposed in (Glorot and Bengio, 2010). The model was trained with conventional Stochastic Gradient Descent (Rumelhart et al., 1985) with a fixed learning rate of 0.01, and the weights were updated after each message was processed. Variations of learning rate to smaller values, e.g. 0.005, were considered but did not lead to a clear pattern. We explored different configurations of the hyperparameters e (embedding size) and s (sub-space size). Model selection was done by early stopping, i.e., we kept the configuration with best F-measure on the evaluation set after 5-8 iterations.

5.2 Results

In general, the NLSE model showed consistent and fast convergence towards the optimum in very few iterations. Despite using class log-likelihood as training criterion, it showed good performance in terms of the average F-measure for positive and negative sentiments. We found that all embedding sizes yield comparable performances, al-

[1] `https://github.com/wlin12/wang2vec`

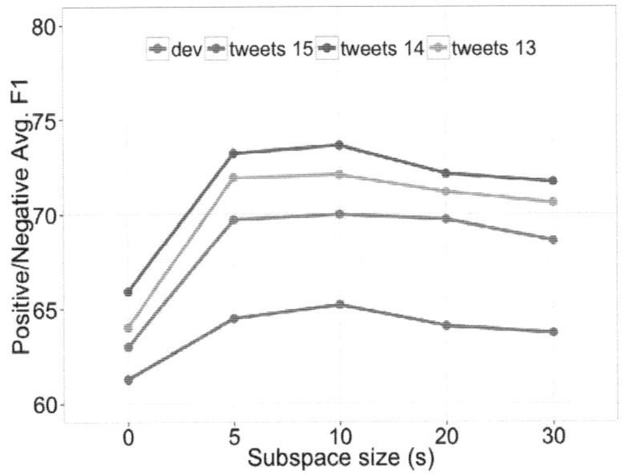

Figure 2: Average F-measure on the SemEval test sets varying with embedding sub-space size s. Sub-space size 0 used to denote the baseline (log-linear model).

though larger embeddings tend to perform better. Therefore, we only report results obtained with the 600 dimensional vectors. In Figure 2, we show the variation of system performance with sub-space size s. The baseline is a log-linear using the embeddings in $\mathbf{E}$ as features. As it can be seen, the performance is sharply improved when the embedding sub-spaces are used. By choosing different values of s, we can adjust the model to the complexity of the task and the amount of labeled data available. Given the small size of the training set, the best results were attained with the use of smaller sub-spaces, in the range of 5-10 dimensions.

Figure 3, presents the main results of the experimental evaluation. As baselines, we considered two simple approaches: LOG-LINEAR, which uses the unsupervised embeddings directly as features in a log-linear classifier, and LOG-LINEAR*, also using the unsupervised embeddings as features in a log-linear classifier, but updating the embeddings with the training data. These baselines, were compared against two variations of the non-linear sub-space embedding model: NLSE, where we only train the $\mathbf{S}$ and $\mathbf{Y}$ weights while the embeddings are kept fixed, and NLSE*, where we also update the embedding matrix during training. For these experiments, we set $s = 10$. The results in Figure 3a, show that our model largely outperforms the simpler baselines. Furthermore, we observe that updating the embeddings always leads to inferior results. This suggests that pre-computed embeddings should be kept fixed, when little labeled data is available to re-train them.

Comparison with the state-of-the-art

We now compare the NLSE model with state-of-the-art systems, including the best submissions to previous SemEval benchmarks. We also include two other approaches that are related to the one here proposed, where a neural network initialized with pre-trained word embeddings is used to learn relevant features. Specifically, we compare the following systems:

- NRC (Kiritchenko et al., 2014), a support vector machine classifier with a large set of hand-crafted features, including word and character n-grams, brown clusters, POS tags, morphological features, and a set of features based on five sentiment lexicons. Most of the performance was due to the combination of these lexicons. This was the top system in the 2013 edition of SemEval.
- TEAMX (Miura et al., 2014), a logistic regression classifier using a similar set of features. Additional features based on two different POS taggers and a word sense disambiguator were also included in the model. This approach attained the highest ranking in the 2014 edition.
- CHARSCNN (dos Santos and Gatti, 2014b), a deep learning architecture with two convolutional layers that exploit character-level and word-level information. The features are extracted by converting a sentence into a sequence of word embeddings, and the individual words into sequences of character embeddings. Convolution filters followed by max pooling are applied to these sequences, to produce fixed size vectors. These vectors are then combined and transfered to a set of non-linear activation functions, to generate more complex representations of the input. The predictions, based on these learned features are computed with a $softmax$ classifier.
- COOOOLLL (Tang et al., 2014a), a support vector machine classifier that leverages the sentiment specific word embeddings, discussed in Section 2. The embeddings are also processed with a convolution filter, but the output of this operation is used to produce three representations obtained with different strategies, namely with max, min and

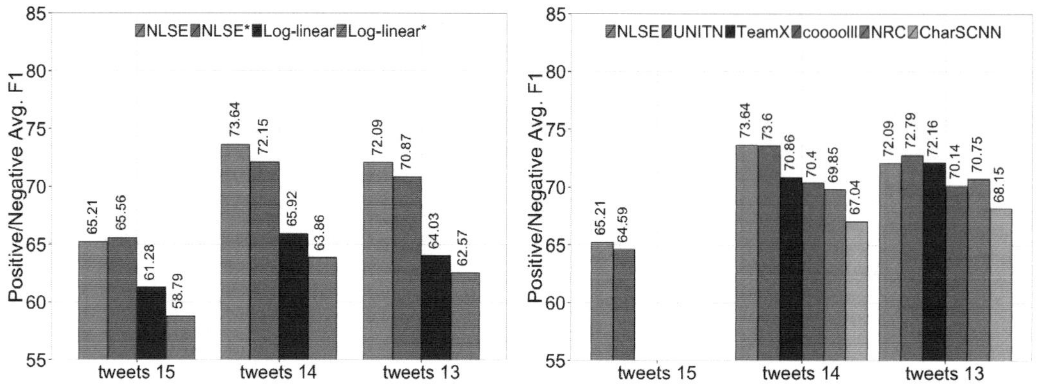

(a) Comparison of two baselines with two variations of the NLSE model

(b) Performance of state-of-the-art systems for Twitter sentiment prediction

Figure 3: Average F-measure on the SemEval test sets

average pooling. The final feature vector is obtained by concatenating these representations and Kiritchenko et al. (2014) feature set.

- UNITN (Severyn and Moschitti, 2015), another deep convolutional neural network that jointly learns internal representations and a *softmax* classifier. The network is trained in three steps: (i) unsupervised pre-training of embeddings, (ii) refinement of the embeddings using a weakly labeled corpus, and (iii) fine tuning the model with the labeled data from SemEval. It should be noted that the system was trained with a labeled corpus 65% larger than ours[2]. This system made the best submission on the 2015 edition of the benchmark.

The results in Figure 3b, show that despite being simpler and requiring less resources and labeled data, the NLSE model is extremely competitive, even outperforming most other systems, in predicting the sentiment polarity of Twitter messages.

6 Generalization to Other Tasks

While the embedding sub-space method works well for the sentiment prediction task, we would like to know its impact in other settings that are known to benefit from unsupervised embeddings. Thus, we decided to replicate the part-of-speech tagging work in (Ling et al., 2015), where pre-training embeddings have been shown to improve the quality of the results significantly.

[2]The UNITN system was trained with around 11,400 labeled examples, whereas we used only 6,900.

6.1 Sub-space Window Model

Part-of-speech tagging is a word labeling task, where each word is to be labeled with its syntactic function in the sentence. More formally, given an input sentence $w_1, \ldots, w_n$ of n words, we wish to predict a sequence of labels $y_1, \ldots, y_n$, which are the POS tags of each of the words. This task is scored by the ratio between the number of correct labels and the number of words to be labeled.

We modified (Collobert et al., 2011) window model, to include the sub-space matrix $\mathbf{S}$. The probability of labeling the word w_t with the POS tag k is given by

$$p(y = k|\mathbf{m}_{t-p}^{t+p}) \propto \exp\left(\mathbf{Y}_k \cdot \mathbf{h}_t + \mathbf{b}\right), \quad (5)$$

where

$$\mathbf{m}_{t-p}^{t+p} = [\mathbf{w}_{t-p} \cdots \mathbf{w}_t \cdots \mathbf{w}_{t+p}] \quad (6)$$

denotes a context window of words around the t-th word, with a total span of $2p + 1$ words. $\mathbf{h}_t$ denotes the activations of a hidden layer given by

$$\mathbf{h}_t = \tanh\left(\mathbf{H} \cdot \begin{bmatrix} \mathbf{S} \cdot \mathbf{E} \cdot \mathbf{w}_{t+p} \\ \cdots \\ \mathbf{S} \cdot \mathbf{E} \cdot \mathbf{w}_t \\ \cdots \\ \mathbf{S} \cdot \mathbf{E} \cdot \mathbf{w}_{t-p} \end{bmatrix}\right). \quad (7)$$

Here $\tanh$ denotes the hyperbolic tangent, acting element-wise. Aside from embedding $\mathbf{E}$ and sub-space $\mathbf{S}$ matrices, the model is parametrized by the weights $\mathbf{H} \in \mathbb{R}^{h \times ps}$ and $\mathbf{Y} \in \mathbb{R}^{v \times h}$ as well as a bias $\mathbf{b} \in \mathbb{R}^{v \times 1}$.

Note that if $\mathbf{S}$ is set to the identity matrix, this would be equivalent to the original Collobert et al. (2011) model.

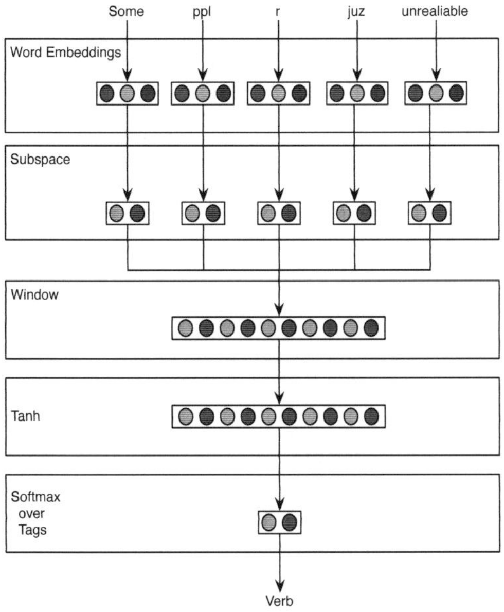

Figure 4: Illustration of the window model by (Collobert et al., 2011) using a sub-space layer.

6.2 Experiments

Tests were performed in Gimpel et al. (2011) Twitter POS dataset, which uses the universal POS tag set composed by 25 different labels (Petrov et al., 2012). The dataset contains 1000 annotated tweets for training, 327 tweets for tuning and 500 tweets for testing. The number of word tokens in these sets are 15000, 5000 and 7000, respectively. There are 5000, 2000 and 3000 word types.

Once again, we initialized the embeddings with unsupervised pre-training using the structured skip-gram approach. As for the hyperparameters of the model, we used embeddings with $e = 50$ dimensions, a hidden layer with $h = 200$ dimensions and a context of $p = 2$ as used in (Ling et al., 2015). Training employed mini-batch gradient descent, with mini batches of 100 sentences and a momentum of 0.95. The learning rate was set to 0.2. Finally, we used early stopping by choosing the epoch with the highest accuracy in the tuning set. As for the sub-space layer size, we tried three different hyperparameterizations: 10, 30 and 50 dimensions.

6.3 Results

Figure 5 displays the results. Using the setup that led to the best results in the sentiment prediction task (FIX), that is, fixing $\mathbf{E}$ and updating $\mathbf{S}$, leads to lower accuracies than the baseline (TRAIN-ALL, $s = 0$). We also see that different values of s do not have a very strong impact in the final results.

Sentiment polarity prediction and POS tagging differ in multiple aspects and there may be more than one reason for this poorer performance. One particularly relevant aspect, in our opinion, is the way words that have no pre-trained embedding are treated. In the case of sentiment prediction, these words were set to having and embedding of zero. This fits the use of the bag-of-words assumption and the fact that only one label is produced per message, as there are many other words to draw evidence from. In the case of POS tagging a hypothesis must be drawn for each word, using a shorter context. Thus, ignoring a word means that context is used instead, which is a frequent cause of errors.

One way around this problem would be to update the parameters of $\mathbf{S}$ and $\mathbf{E}$, but this leads to results similar to the experiment without the sub-space projections (TRAIN-ALL). This is expected as the sub-space layer was designed to work on fixed word embeddings, if these are updated its benefits are lost. Thus, we solve this problem by fixing all the embeddings, except for the word types not found in the pre-training corpus. That is, instead of leaving the unknown words as the zero vector, we use the labeled data to learn a better representation. Using this setup (TRAIN-OOV), we can obtain a small but consistent improvement over the baseline. While these improvements are not significant, as this task is not as prone to overfitting as in sentiment analysis, this is a good check of the validity of our method.

7 Conclusions

We presented a new approach to use unsupervised word embeddings based on the idea of finding a sub-space projection of the embeddings for a given task. This approach offers two main advantages. On the one hand, it allows to indirectly update embeddings unseen during training. On the other

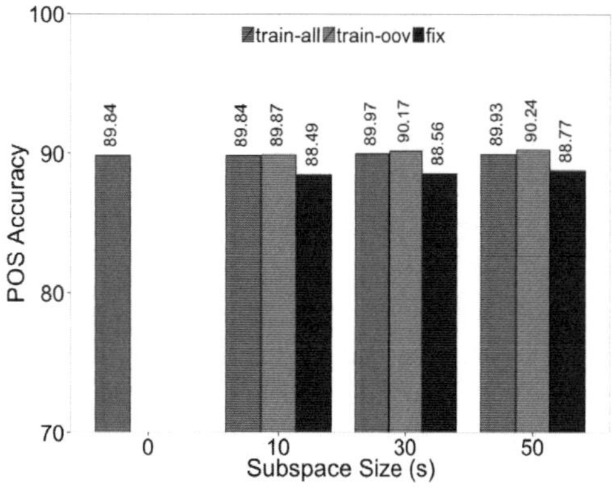

Figure 5: Results for the part-of-speech task on the ARK POS dataset, for different strategies to update the embeddings and with variations of the sub-space size. Sub-space size 0 used to denote the baseline (window model).

hand, it reduces the number of model parameters to fit the complexity of the task. These properties make this method particularly useful for the cases where only small amounts of noisy data are available to train the model.

Experiments on the SemEval challenge corpora validated these ideas, showing that such a simple approach can attain state-of-the-art results comparable with the best systems of past SemEval editions and often outperforming them in all datasets. It should be noted that this is attained while keeping the original embedding matrix $\mathbf{E}$ fixed and only learning the projection $\mathbf{S}$ with the supervised data. Additional experiments on the Twitter POS tagging task indicate however that, the technique is not always as effective as in the sentiment classification task. One possible explanation for the different behavior is the use of embeddings of zeros for words without pre-trained embedding. It is plausible that this has a stronger effect on the POS tagging task. Another aspect to be taken into account is the fact that both tasks could have a different complexity which would explain why adapting $\mathbf{E}$ in the POS taks yields better results. Optimality of the embeddings for each of the tasks might also come into play here.

The implementation of the proposed method and our Twitter Sentiment Analysis system has been made publicly available[3].

[3] `https://github.com/ramon-astudillo/NLSE`

Acknowledgments

This work was partially supported by Fundação para a Ciência e Tecnologia (FCT), through contracts UID/CEC/50021/2013, EXCL/EEI-ESS/0257/2012 (DataStorm), research project with reference UTAP-EXPL/EEI-ESS/0031/2014, EU project SPEDIAL (FP7 611396), grant number SFRH/BPD/68428/2010 and Ph.D. scholarship SFRH/BD/89020/2012.

References

Ramon F. Astudillo, Silvio Amir, Wang Ling, Bruno Martins, Mário Silva, and Isabel Trancoso. 2015. Inesc-id: Sentiment analysis without hand-coded features or liguistic resources using embedding subspaces. In *Proceedings of the 9th International Workshop on Semantic Evaluation*, SemEval '2015, Denver, Colorado, June. Association for Computational Linguistics.

Michele Banko and Eric Brill. 2001. Scaling to very very large corpora for natural language disambiguation. In *Proceedings of the 39th Annual Meeting on Association for Computational Linguistics*, pages 26–33. Association for Computational Linguistics.

Mohit Bansal, Kevin Gimpel, and Karen Livescu. 2014. Tailoring continuous word representations for dependency parsing. In *Proceedings of the Annual Meeting of the Association for Computational Linguistics*.

Yoshua Bengio, Réjean Ducharme, Pascal Vincent, and Christian Janvin. 2003. A neural probabilistic language model. *The Journal of Machine Learning Research*, 3:1137–1155.

Dmitriy Bespalov, Bing Bai, Yanjun Qi, and Ali Shokoufandeh. 2011. Sentiment classification based on supervised latent n-gram analysis. In *Proceedings of the 20th ACM international conference on Information and knowledge management*, pages 375–382. ACM.

Peter F. Brown, Peter V. deSouza, Robert L. Mercer, Vincent J. Della Pietra, and Jenifer C. Lai. 1992. Class-based n-gram models of natural language. *Comput. Linguist.*, 18(4):467–479, December.

Danqi Chen and Christopher D Manning. 2014. A fast and accurate dependency parser using neural networks. In *Proceedings of the 2014 Conference on Empirical Methods in Natural Language Processing (EMNLP)*, pages 740–750.

Ronan Collobert, Jason Weston, Léon Bottou, Michael Karlen, Koray Kavukcuoglu, and Pavel Kuksa. 2011. Natural language processing (almost) from scratch. *The Journal of Machine Learning Research*, 12:2493–2537.

Cicero dos Santos and Maira Gatti. 2014a. Deep convolutional neural networks for sentiment analysis of short texts. In *Proceedings of COLING 2014, the 25th International Conference on Computational Linguistics: Technical Papers*, pages 69–78, Dublin, Ireland, August. Dublin City University and Association for Computational Linguistics.

Cıcero Nogueira dos Santos and Maıra Gatti. 2014b. Deep convolutional neural networks for sentiment analysis of short texts. In *Proceedings of the 25th International Conference on Computational Linguistics (COLING), Dublin, Ireland*.

Susan T Dumais, George W Furnas, Thomas K Landauer, Scott Deerwester, and Richard Harshman. 1988. Using latent semantic analysis to improve access to textual information. In *Proceedings of the SIGCHI conference on Human factors in computing systems*, pages 281–285. ACM.

John Rupert Firth. 1968. *Selected papers of JR Firth, 1952-59*. Indiana University Press.

Kevin Gimpel, Nathan Schneider, Brendan O'Connor, Dipanjan Das, Daniel Mills, Jacob Eisenstein, Michael Heilman, Dani Yogatama, Jeffrey Flanigan, and Noah A. Smith. 2011. Part-of-speech tagging for twitter: annotation, features, and experiments. In *Proceedings of the 49th Annual Meeting of the Association for Computational Linguistics: Human Language Technologies: short papers - Volume 2*, HLT '11, Stroudsburg, PA, USA. Association for Computational Linguistics.

Xavier Glorot and Yoshua Bengio. 2010. Understanding the difficulty of training deep feedforward neural networks. In *International conference on artificial intelligence and statistics*, pages 249–256.

Alec Go, Richa Bhayani, and Lei Huang. 2009. Twitter sentiment classification using distant supervision. *CS224N Project Report, Stanford*, pages 1–12.

Yoav Goldberg and Omer Levy. 2014. word2vec explained: deriving mikolov et al.'s negative-sampling word-embedding method. *arXiv preprint arXiv:1402.3722*.

Eric H. Huang, Richard Socher, Christopher D. Manning, and Andrew Y. Ng. 2012. Improving word representations via global context and multiple word prototypes. In *Proceedings of the 50th Annual Meeting of the Association for Computational Linguistics: Long Papers - Volume 1*, ACL '12, pages 873–882, Stroudsburg, PA, USA. Association for Computational Linguistics.

Svetlana Kiritchenko, Xiaodan Zhu, and Saif M Mohammad. 2014. Sentiment analysis of short informal texts. *Journal of Artificial Intelligence Research*, pages 723–762.

Igor Labutov and Hod Lipson. 2013. Re-embedding words. In *Proceedings of the 51st annual meeting of the ACL*, pages 489–493.

Wang Ling, Chris Dyer, Alan Black, and Isabel Trancoso. 2015. Two/too simple adaptations of word2vec for syntax problems. In *Proceedings of the 2015 Conference of the North American Chapter of the Association for Computational Linguistics: Human Language Technologies*. Association for Computational Linguistics.

Tomas Mikolov, Ilya Sutskever, Kai Chen, Greg Corrado, and Jeffrey Dean. 2013. Distributed representations of words and phrases and their compositionality. In *27th Annual Conference on Neural Information Processing Systems*.

Yasuhide Miura, Shigeyuki Sakaki, Keigo Hattori, and Tomoko Ohkuma. 2014. Teamx: A sentiment analyzer with enhanced lexicon mapping and weighting scheme for unbalanced data. In *Proceedings of the 8th International Workshop on Semantic Evaluation (SemEval 2014)*, pages 628–632, Dublin, Ireland, August. Association for Computational Linguistics.

Preslav Nakov, Zornitsa Kozareva, Alan Ritter, Sara Rosenthal, Veselin Stoyanov, and Theresa Wilson. 2013. Semeval-2013 task 2: Sentiment analysis in twitter.

Olutobi Owoputi, Chris Dyer, Kevin Gimpel, Nathan Schneider, and Noah A. Smith. 2013. Improved part-of-speech tagging for online conversational text with word clusters. In *In Proceedings of NAACL*.

Jeffrey Pennington, Richard Socher, and Christopher D Manning. 2014. Glove: Global vectors for word representation. *Proceedings of the Empiricial Methods in Natural Language Processing (EMNLP 2014)*, 12.

Slav Petrov, Dipanjan Das, and Ryan McDonald. 2012. A universal part-of-speech tagset. In *Proceedings of the Eight International Conference on Language Resources and Evaluation (LREC'12)*. European Language Resources Association (ELRA), may.

Sara Rosenthal, Preslav Nakov, Svetlana Kiritchenko, Saif M Mohammad, Alan Ritter, and Veselin Stoyanov. 2015. Semeval-2015 task 10: Sentiment analysis in twitter. In *Proceedings of the 9th International Workshop on Semantic Evaluation*, SemEval '2015, Denver, Colorado, June. Association for Computational Linguistics.

David E Rumelhart, Geoffrey E Hinton, and Ronald J Williams. 1985. Learning internal representations by error propagation. Technical report, DTIC Document.

Aliaksei Severyn and Alessandro Moschitti. 2015. Unitn: Training deep convolutional neural network for twitter sentiment classification. In *Proceedings of the 9th International Workshop on Semantic Evaluation*, SemEval '2015, Denver, Colorado, June. Association for Computational Linguistics.

Duyu Tang, Furu Wei, Bing Qin, Ting Liu, and Ming Zhou. 2014a. Coooolll: A deep learning system for twitter sentiment classification. *SemEval 2014*, page 208.

Duyu Tang, Furu Wei, Nan Yang, Ming Zhou, Ting Liu, and Bing Qin. 2014b. Learning sentiment-specific word embedding for twitter sentiment classification. In *Proceedings of the 52nd Annual Meeting of the Association for Computational Linguistics*, pages 1555–1565.

Joseph Turian, Lev Ratinov, and Yoshua Bengio. 2010. Word representations: a simple and general method for semi-supervised learning. In *Proceedings of the 48th annual meeting of the association for computational linguistics*, pages 384–394. Association for Computational Linguistics.

Automatic Spontaneous Speech Grading: A Novel Feature Derivation Technique using the Crowd

Vinay Shashidhar
Aspiring Minds
vinay.shashidhar@aspiringminds.com

Nishant Pandey
Aspiring Minds
nishant.pandey@aspiringminds.com

Varun Aggarwal
Aspiring Minds
varun@aspiringminds.com

Abstract

In this paper, we address the problem of evaluating spontaneous speech using a combination of machine learning and crowdsourcing. Machine learning techniques inadequately solve the stated problem because automatic speaker-independent speech transcription is inaccurate. The features derived from it are also inaccurate and so is the machine learning model developed for speech evaluation. To address this, we post the task of speech transcription to a large community of online workers (crowd). We also get spoken English grades from the crowd. We achieve 95% transcription accuracy by combining transcriptions from multiple crowd workers. Speech and prosody features are derived by force aligning the speech samples on these highly accurate transcriptions. Additionally, we derive surface and semantic level features directly from the transcription. To demonstrate the efficacy of our approach we performed experiments on an expert–graded speech sample of 319 adult non–native speakers. Using these features in a regression model, we are able achieve a Pearson correlation of 0.76 with expert grades, an accuracy much higher than any previously reported machine learning approach. Our approach has an accuracy that rivals that of expert agreement. This work is timely given the huge requirement of spoken English training and assessment.

1 Introduction

Automatic evaluation of spoken English has been of keen interest for more than two decades (Zechner et al., 2007; Neumeyer et al., 1996; Franco et al., 2000; Cucchiarini et al., 1997). It can help learners get feedback in a scalable manner, help build better English training software and also help companies and institutions filter and select prospective employees more effectively. The problem acquires significance given the evidence that better English leads to better employment outcome, wages and promotions (Guven and Islam, 2013).

There has been a considerable success in automatically scoring spoken English, when the spoken text is known a priori (Cucchiarini et al., 2000; Franco et al., 2000). In these cases, the candidate is asked to either read a given text or listen to some speech and repeat it. For these tasks, the scores generated by an automatic system on parameters such as pronunciation and fluency closely mimic those given by human experts. The primary approach behind a majority of these systems is to force align the speech sample on the known text using an HMM–based acoustic model. Features such as likelihood, posterior probability and fluency related features are derived from the aligned speech and a machine learning model is used to predict expert grades (Neumeyer et al., 1996; Franco et al., 2000; Cucchiarini et al., 1997). Some approaches additionally use prosody and energy related features (Dong et al., 2004). More recently, this research has moved towards the assessment of higher granularity metrics like the mispronunciation of particular phonemes (Li et al., 2009; Ito et al., 2006; Koniaris and Engwall, 2011).

In spontaneous speech evaluation, the candidate is asked to speak on a topic or answer a question and what he/she speaks isn't known priori. Evaluation of spontaneous speech is the ultimate test of a candidate's proficiency in speaking a language (Hagley, 2010; Halleck, 1995). While scores from the evaluation of read/repeat speech do correlate with spontaneous speech evaluation, there remains

Proceedings of the 53rd Annual Meeting of the Association for Computational Linguistics and the 7th International Joint Conference on Natural Language Processing, pages 1085–1094,
Beijing, China, July 26-31, 2015.

an unexplained variance in the spontaneous speech scores (see Section 5). Generally, candidates who score high on spontaneous speech also score high on read speech and not vice versa.

Given the primacy of spontaneous speech evaluation in judging a person's language capability, there is considerable interest in doing it automatically (Cucchiarini et al., 1997; Dong et al., 2004). Automated approaches for the same have not worked well (Powers et al., 2002; Cucchiarini et al., 2000) primarily because speaker-independent speech recognition is a tough computer science problem. This is exacerbated when the speakers are not proficient in the language or are non-natives (Powers et al., 2002). Given that speech to text conversion for such candidates has a low accuracy, force alignment of the speech on this inaccurate text makes the features and the model inaccurate.

We present a semi-automated approach to grade short duration (45 seconds) spontaneous speech. We accurately predict a holistic score which is based on the pronunciation, fluency, content characteristics and grammar of the speech sample, as determined by experts. Multiple previous studies in language acquisition and second language research conclusively show that proficiency in a second language can be characterized by these factors (Bhat et al., 2014). Being able to provide a holistic score is of high interest in both educational testing (Zechner et al., 2009) and job related testing (Streeter et al., 2011). Institutions and firms look for a holistic score, say based on CEFR, a standard to describe spoken English assessment (Little, 2006; Little, 2007), to make an accept or reject decision on candidates. Currently, an expert based assessment is used for these purposes.

Our method involves combining machine learning with a crowdsourcing layer. Crowdsourcing (Estellés-Arolas and González-Ladrón-de Guevara, 2012) is the process of getting *human intelligence* tasks performed by a large community of online workers (crowd) as opposed to traditional employees.[1] The responses from the human intelligence tasks are then used to create relevant features for machine learning. Human intelligence tasks are defined as those which most humans find easy, but are hard for machines. For instance, a classic example is the task of finding a particular object in an image. There is a large research community that uses crowdsourcing and has demonstrated that it can help perform tasks inexpensively, in large volumes and within reasonable time (Howe, 2006; Whitla, 2009).

Our system design for evaluation of spontaneous speech is illustrated in Figure 1. We post the task[2] of speech transcription to the crowd. We get a final accurate transcription by combining the transcriptions from more than one crowd worker for the same speech sample. Once we have this accurate transcription, we force-align (Erling and Seargeant, 2013; Sjölander, 2003) the speech of the candidate on this text to derive various features which go into a machine learning engine. We also collect spoken English grades of the speech from the crowd (Lejk and Wyvill, 2001), which are used as additional features. With these accurately identified features and crowd grades, machine learning is able to grade spontaneous speech with high accuracy. We found that this approach does much better than a pure machine learning approach.

Crowdsourcing has been used for almost a decade in various problems in speech analysis, grading and language learning (Kunath and Weinberger, 2010; Peabody, 2011; Wang et al., 2014). Within assessment of speech, currently all such approaches use the crowd to directly grade certain parts of the speech (Wang and Meng, 2012). Our work is uniquely positioned where we use the crowd to do accurate transcription, a human intelligence task, and use it in a machine learning based algorithm.[3] We show that such a system provides an accuracy rivaling that of experts.

In this paper, we solve a hitherto unsolved problem of spontaneous speech evaluation (Zechner et al., 2009). The paper makes the following contributions:

- We show that spoken English can be graded with accuracy by combining machine learning and crowdsourcing higher than a pure machine learning approach.

[1]Our approach is different from peer grading (Lejk and Wyvill, 2001) or crowd grading (Van Houdnos, 2011; Tetreault et al., 2010; Madnani et al., 2011) approaches. These approaches directly ask the crowd to grade the response. The primary feature of our technique is using the crowd in the feature extraction step of machine learning.

[2]Even though speaker-independent speech recognition is a hard problem for machines, it is fairly easy for a native speaker or anyone with reasonable command over the language.

[3]Again, speech transcription has been done previously using crowdsourcing (Zaidan and Callison-Burch, 2011), but not used for a grading purpose or combined with machine learning.

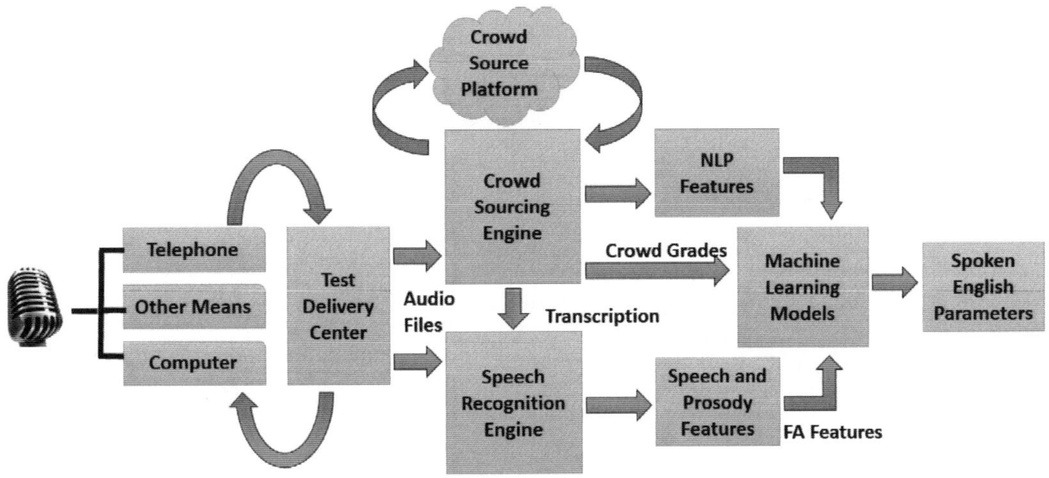

Figure 1: System Design

- We show that the features derived from crowdsourced transcriptions perform as well as crowd grades in predicting expert grades. However, crowd grades add additional predictive value.
- We propose a scalable and accurate way to perform evaluation of spontaneous speech, a huge requirement in the industry and elsewhere.

The paper is organized as follows– Section 2 describes the procedure and aim of the speech assessment task; Section 3 describes the feature classes used in the prediction algorithm; Section 4 describes the crowdsourcing framework which is used as an input to machine learning methods; Section 5 demonstrates how this framework is used with machine learning techniques to predict a composite spoken English score; Section 6 discusses the future work and concludes the paper.

2 Grading Task

We want to assess the quality of spoken English of candidates based on their spontaneous speech samples. The speech samples of the candidates were collected using Aspiring Minds' automated speech assessment tool– SVAR (SVAR, 2014). SVAR is conducted over phone as well as on a computer. The test has multiple sections where the candidate is required to: read sentences aloud, listen and repeat sentences, listen to a passage or conversation and answer multiple choice questions and finally spontaneously speak on a given topic. In the spontaneous speech section, the candidates[4] are provided with a topic and given 30 seconds[5] to think, take notes and then speak on the topic for 45 seconds. The topic is repeated to ensure task clarity. The complete test takes 16-20 minutes to complete, depending on the test version.

Currently, SVAR evaluates speech samples from the read and repeat sections with high accuracy (SVAR, 2014). Our goal in this paper is to evaluate the spontaneous speech of the candidate and provide a composite score based on it.

A 5 point rubric for the composite score, similar to CEFR (Examinations, 2011), was prepared with the help of experts. This score is a function of the pronunciation, fluency, content organization and grammar quality of the speech sample. Broadly speaking, Pronunciation (Dobson, 1957) refers to the correctness in the utterance of the phonemes of a word by the students as per neutral accent. Fluency (Brumfit and Brumfit, 1984) refers to a desired rate of speech along with the absence of hesitations, false starts and stops etc. Content organization (Stalnaker, 1999) measures the candidate's ability to structure the information disposition and present it coherently. Grammar (Brazil, 1995) measures how well the syntax of the language was followed by the candidate.

[4]The subjects of our study use English as their second language and hail from various backgrounds, dialects and educational qualifications.

[5]This is as per global standards of spoken English assessment. High stake tests such as TOEFL provide the candidate 15-30 seconds to think before responding to a spontaneous speech task.

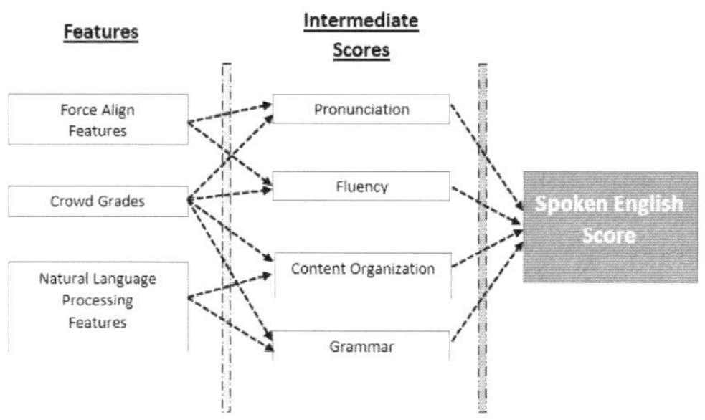

Figure 2: Our intuition of how different features predict the holistic score.

In the next section we discuss the features which are used in the prediction algorithm.

3 Features

We use three classes of features– Crowd Grades (CG), Force Alignment features (FA) and Natural Language Processing features (NLP). The spoken English samples are posted to the crowd to get the transcription and spoken English grades (Figure 1). Each task was completed by three workers. The crowd grades become one set of features. A second set, i.e., FA features, are derived by aligning (Erling and Seargeant, 2013; Sjölander, 2003) the speech sample on the crowdsourced transcriptions. A third set, i.e., NLP features, are also derived from the crowdsourced text. These are explained in the succeeding paragraphs.

- *Crowd Grades:* The crowd transcribes the speech in addition to providing scores on each of the following– pronunciation, fluency, content organization and grammar. These grades are combined to form a composite score per worker per candidate. These are further averaged across workers to give a final score.[6]

- *FA features:* The speech sample is forced aligned (Erling and Seargeant, 2013; Sjölander, 2003) on the crowdsourced transcription using the HTK speech recognizer (Young et al., 2006). We used an acoustic model based on TIMIT (Garofolo et al., 1993) for our experiments. TIMIT is a corpus of phonemically and lexically transcribed speech of American English speakers of different sexes and dialects.

  A number of speech quality features are derived, which include– rate of speech, position and length of pauses, log likelihood of recognition, posterior probability, hesitations and repetitions etc. These features are well known in literature and may be referred from (Neumeyer et al., 1996; Zechner et al., 2009; Cucchiarini et al., 2000). These features are predictive of the pronunciation and fluency of the candidate.

- *NLP features:* These features predict the content quality and grammar of the spoken content[7]. They were derived using standard NLP packages (LightSide, 2013; AfterTheDeadline, 2014) on the crowdsourced transcription. The package calculates surface level features such as the number of words, complexity or difficulty of words and the number of common words used. It also calculates semantic features like the coherency in text, context of the words spoken, sentiment of the text and grammar correctness. In the current system, we do not use any prompt specific features such as occurrence of specific words or phrases. These features are predictive of the grammar and content organization of the sample.

All the features described above were obtained for the spontaneous speech sample. We also derived features similar to FA features for the candidate's read and repeat speech samples collected during his/her SVAR test. The speech and prosody features are calculated by force aligning the speech on the known text. One of the models (RS/LR) in our experiments is based on these features and has been included for comparison. These features do not have any bearing on our final model for spontaneous speech evaluation.

4 Crowdsourcing

The spoken English sample was given to the crowd to transcribe and provide grades. The task was posted on a popular crowdsourcing platform– Amazon Mechanical Turk (AMT) (Paolacci et al.,

[6]Advanced Expectation-Maximization techniques (Hosseini et al., 2012) may also be used for an aggregation strategy, once the number of tasks done by every individual worker increases. In our current experiments, this number wasn't very high.

[7]We were looking at prompt independent features only, at this point.

2010). AMT is a popular crowdsourcing marketplace. It is inspired by the famous 18th century automated chess playing machine, running on the intelligence of a hidden human operator. It has more than 500,000 online workers from 190 countries (Turk, 2014). One can post tasks on the platform online and offer fixed remuneration for their completion.

A clean and simple interface was provided to the worker with standard features needed for transcription. Additionally, an advanced audio player was embedded with the ability to play the speech sample in repeat mode, rewind and forward, apart from standard play/pause functionality to help the worker. The different transcriptions were combined using the ROVER algorithm (Fiscus, 1997). ROVER is a sophisticated voting algorithm to combine multiple transcriptions with errors, to obtain the best estimate of the correct transcription. It is reported to lead to an error reduction of 20-25%. ROVER proceeds in two stages: first the outputs are aligned and a single word transcription network (WTN) is built. The second stage consists of selecting the best scoring word (with the highest number of votes) at each node.

Several methods have been used in the past for increasing the reliability of the grades given by the crowd by identifying and correcting any biases and removing non-serious/low quality workers (Aker et al., 2012). One of the key techniques for this involves inserting gold standard tasks with known answers to get an estimate of the worker's ability (Nguyen et al., 2013). The gold standard tasks are similar to real tasks and the workers have no way to distinguish between the two. Our tasks took workers a reasonable amount of time (8-10 minutes). It wasn't hence feasible to insert a gold standard task, as done typically, with every task to be completed.

To overcome this problem, we propose an innovative approach where a risk is assigned to a worker based on his/her performance on the gold standard tasks. We conceptualized this system as a state machine that determines the risk level of a worker and proposes actions based on it (Refer to Figure 3). All workers started with an initial risk level of 0.2. Gold standard tasks were probabilistically inserted among real tasks based on the worker's risk level. Workers with a higher risk level saw more gold standard tasks. Also, the risk level of the worker was updated based on

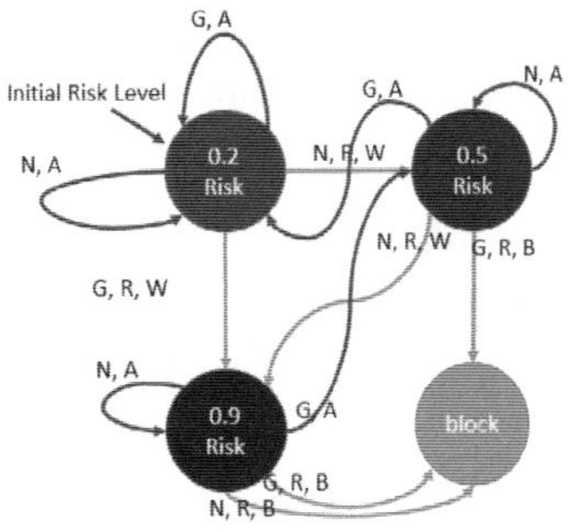

Task Type	
G	Gold Standard Task
N	Normal Task

Task Status	
A	Accept
R	Reject

Proposed Action	
W	Warning
B	Block

Figure 3: Risk Level State Diagram: In the above figure, each node corresponds to a risk level associated with a worker. The values range between 0 (min) - 1 (max). The worker is either assigned a gold standard task (G) or a normal task (N) on the basis of his/her present risk level. The risk level changes every time a task is Accepted (A) or Rejected (R). Additionally worker may be warned (W) or blocked (B) in case of rejection.

his/her performance on the gold standard tasks. Workers who consistently performed poorly on gold standard tasks were allocated a higher risk level and a notification was sent to them with a corrective course of action. Beyond a certain level, the worker was barred from attempting future work. We did not do any retrospective correction of the barred worker's completed tasks and simply stopped him/her from attempting newer tasks. This approach allowed us to control for the quality of workers, provide feedback, remove unsuitable workers and also adaptively control the balance between real and gold standard tasks.[8]

We describe the experimental setup and the results in the next section.

5 Experiments

We conducted the experiments to answer the following questions:

- Can read/repeat features predict spontaneous speech grades accurately?
- How accurate is a pure machine learning approach (without crowdsourced transcription) in predicting grades as compared to grades given by human experts?
- How much better is the ML-CS approach in

[8]Specific details of the implementation are beyond the scope of the paper.

predicting grades as compared to a pure ML approach and to using Crowd Grades only?

- Do Crowd Grades add additional value in predicting grades over and above the features derived from the crowdsourced transcription?

We conducted the experiments on 319 spontaneous speech samples which were graded by expert assessors. To answer the questions stated above, we used different sets of features to develop models and compared their accuracy. The models were built against expert grades using supervised learning techniques. We experimented with three machine learning techniques– Ridge Regression, SVMs and Neural Networks with different features selection algorithms. The data set used in the experiments is discussed in the next section.

5.1 Data Set

Our data set contains 319 spontaneous speech responses. The speech samples were from seniors (non–native English speakers in final year of undergraduate education) pursuing bachelor's degree in India. The candidates were asked to describe one of the following scenes: *a hospital, flood, a crowded market* and *a school playground*. The candidates were given 30 seconds to think and take notes and were then asked to speak for the next 45 seconds. The responses were collected on the phone during the SVAR test (SVAR, 2014). Apart from the spontaneous speech response, each candidate was asked to read 12 given sentences and repeat 9 given sentences immediately after listening to each of them. Empty or very noisy responses (not humanly discernible) were not included in the final 319 sample set.

These responses were graded by two experts who had more than fifteen years of experience in grading spoken English responses. There were two set of scores. The first was a holistic score on the spontaneous speech samples based on its pronunciation, fluency, content characteristics and grammar. The second was a score on the pronunciation and fluency quality of the read/repeat sentences. The correlation between grades given by the two experts was 0.86 and 0.83 respectively for the two cases. For each of the two scores, the average of the scores by the two expert grades was used for further purposes.

The correlation between the expert scores on spontaneous speech and read/repeat speech was 0.54. This shows that there is a considerable unexplained variance (70%) in the spontaneous speech score, not addressed by the read/repeat scores. This could be due to a difference in the pronunciation quality and fluency of the candidates in reading/repeating text vs. speaking spontaneously and also due to the additional parameters of grammar and content characteristics in the spontaneous speech score. Thus, an automatic score mimicking the read/repeat expert grades, which is a solved problem, is inadequate for our task.

The first score is used for all subsequent discussion and development of models.

5.2 Crowdsourced Tasks

The 319 speech sample assessment task was posted on Amazon Mechanical Turk (AMT). Each task was completed by three workers. In total, 71 unique workers completed the tasks. The majority of workers (90%) belonged to USA and India.

The task took on an average 8–9 minutes to complete and a worker was paid between 6–10 cents per task including a bonus which was paid on completion of every 4 tasks. We also got the speech transcribed by experts to find the accuracy we could get from turks. The average transcription accuracy for a worker was 82.4%[9]. This significantly improved to 95.4% when the transcriptions of the three workers were combined using the ROVER algorithm. In comparison, the average automatic transcription of a speech recognition engine was 59.8%.

5.3 Regression Modeling

The data set was split into two sets: train and validation. The train-set had 75% of the sample points whereas the validation set had 25%. The split was done randomly making sure that the grade distribution in both the sets was similar. While learning the model, a 4-fold cross validation was performed on the train sample.

Linear ridge regression, Neural Networks and SVM regression with different kernels were used to build the models. The least cross-validation error was used to select the models. We used some simple techniques for feature selection including forward feature selection and the algorithm which removes all but the k highest correlating features.

Regression parameters: For linear regression with regularization, optimal ridge coefficient λ,

[9] PHP similar_text function was used as similarity metric.

Table 1: Regression Results

Technique	Model Code	Feature Type	Train r	Validation r
Ridge Regression	RR-1	RS/LR	0.51	0.47
	RR-2	Pure ML	0.54	0.47
	RR-3	Crowd Grades	0.63	0.57
	RR-4	ML-CS	0.55	0.60
	RR-5	All	0.76	0.76
SVM	SVM-1	RS/LR	0.50	0.46
	SVM-2	Pure ML	0.53	0.46
	SVM-3	Crowd Grades	0.62	0.57
	SVM-4	ML-CS	0.60	0.61
	SVM-5	All	0.75	0.74
Neural Networks	NN-1	RS/LR	0.56	0.51
	NN-2	Pure ML	0.60	0.44
	NN-3	Crowd Grades	0.63	0.57
	NN-4	ML-CS	0.66	0.57
	NN-5	All	0.80	0.76

between 1 and 1000, was selected based on the the least RMS error in cross-validation. For support vector machines we tested two kernels: linear and radial basis function. In order to select the optimal SVM model, we varied the penalty factor C, parameters γ and ϵ, the SVM kernel and the selected set of values that gave us the lowest RMS error in cross-validation. The Neural Networks model had one hidden layer and 5 to 10 neurons.

Feature sets used: The experiments were carried out on five sets of features:

- RS/LR: A set of features generated by force aligning read/repeated by candidates.
- Pure ML: Features generated by automatic speech transcription of spontaneous speech using a speech recognizer.
- Crowd Grades: A set of features pertaining to grades given by the crowd.
- ML–CS: NLP and FA features generated by force aligning free speech on crowdsourced transcription.
- All: NLP and FA features from crowdsourced transcription and Crowd Grades.

Here, the first set, RS/LR, helps us to know how well we can predict spontaneous speech grades by simply using the read/speak speech of the candidate and without using his/her spontaneous speech sample. This provides a comparison baseline. The second approach evaluates how well we can grade spontaneous speech of the candidate using machine learning approaches only. The third feature shows the efficacy of directly using grades given by crowd, while the fourth finds how well machine learning can do if it has a fairly accurate transcription of the speech by the crowd. The final fifth set tests what happens if we combine the third and fourth set of features, i.e. make use of both the crowdsourced transcription and the crowd grades.

In the following subsection, the features pertaining to ML-CS approach are referred to as ML-CS, those pertaining to natural language processing on crowdsourced transcription are referred to as NLP features while the one pertaining to crowd grades are referred to as Crowd Grades.

5.4 Observations

The results of the experiments are tabulated in Table 1. We report the Pearson coefficient of correlation (r) for the different models against the expert grades. These are the results for the models selected according to least cross-validation error. The best cross-validation error in case of SVMs was obtained for the linear kernel.

All the following observations are based on the validation error. All three techniques perform similarly with Neural Networks doing slightly worse in some cases. The broad trends across feature–sets remain similar across different modeling techniques. We will be referring to the ridge regression results for further discussion.

Firstly, it is observed that the read/repeat features predict the spontaneous speech score with low accuracy ($r = 0.47$). This implies that read-/repeat speech and derived features are inadequate to grade a person's spontaneous speech, the ultimate test of a person's spoken language skills.

The second observation is that the ML-only approach using spontaneous speech features (Model RR-2) is also inadequate to grade spontaneous speech and does worse than approaches that uses features from crowdsourced transcription (Model RR-4). This clearly shows the value of getting accurate transcription from workers towards better features and model.

Further, among the crowdsourcing approaches, we find that the crowd-grades (Model RR-3) does equivalently well (and sometimes worse) than the model using features derived from the crowdsourced speech (Model RR-4). However, when we combine all the features from crowdsourcing including the crowd grades, we find much better prediction accuracy ($r = 0.76$). This shows that the crowd grades feature provides some orthogonal information as compared to the features from the crowdsourced transcription, towards predicting the grade given by experts.

The validation r for Model RR-5 is 0.76. We find that the expert agreement on the validation sample is 0.78. Thus, our predicted score rivals the agreement of experts. This shows great promise for the technique to be used in a high-stake test setting.

In summary, we show the following:

- Read/repeat speech features are inadequate to predict spontaneous speech scores.
- ML only approach based on spontaneous speech samples is also inadequate for the purpose.
- Features derived from crowdsourced transcription (or even crowd grades) do better than a ML only approach.
- When considering features from crowdsourced transcription and crowd grades together, we can predict spontaneous speech scores as well as those done by experts.

6 Conclusions

We addressed the problem of evaluating spontaneous speech using a combination of machine learning and crowdsourcing. To achieve this, we post the task of speech transcription to the crowd. Additionally, we also get spoken English grades from the crowd. We are able to derive accurate features by force aligning the speech sample on the crowdsourced text. We experimented our technique on expert–graded speech samples of adult non–native speakers. Using these features in a regression model, we are able to predict expert grades with much higher accuracy than a machine learning only approach. These features also predict equivalent or better than crowd grades and a combination of these two outperforms all other approaches. Our approach shows an accuracy that rivals that of expert agreement.

Our technique has a promise of higher accuracy but has some trade-offs compared to fully automated approaches. First, there is a cost for every assessment done and the scalability depends on the number of non-expert workers available. Though these drawbacks exist, we were able get tasks done inexpensively. We recently had the crowd rate a hundred samples in a day without any challenge. Second, our approach doesn't provide instant grades. This works fine in many scenarios, but doesn't cater well to providing real-time feedback. Real time crowdsourcing has been an active area of research (Bernstein et al., 2011; Lasecki et al., 2013) and is an area for future work for us as well.

References

AfterTheDeadline. 2014. www.afterthedeadline.com.

Ahmet Aker, Mahmoud El-Haj, M-Dyaa Albakour, and Udo Kruschwitz. 2012. Assessing crowdsourcing quality through objective tasks. In *LREC*, pages 1456–1461. Citeseer.

Michael S Bernstein, Joel Brandt, Robert C Miller, and David R Karger. 2011. Crowds in two seconds: Enabling realtime crowd-powered interfaces. In *Proceedings of the 24th annual ACM symposium on User interface software and technology*, pages 33–42. ACM.

Suma Bhat, Huichao Xue, and Su-Youn Yoon. 2014. Shallow analysis based assessment of syntactic complexity for automated speech scoring. In *Proceedings of the 52nd Annual Meeting of the Association* for Computational Linguistics (Volume 1: Long Papers)*, pages 1305–1315. Association for Computational Linguistics.

David Brazil. 1995. *A grammar of speech*. Oxford University Press, USA.

Christopher Brumfit and Christopher J Brumfit. 1984. *Communicative methodology in language teaching: The roles of fluency and accuracy*, volume 129. Cambridge University Press Cambridge.

Catia Cucchiarini, Helmer Strik, and Lou Boves. 1997. Automatic evaluation of dutch pronunciation by using speech recognition technology. In *Automatic Speech Recognition and Understanding, 1997. Proceedings., 1997 IEEE Workshop on*, pages 622–629. IEEE.

Catia Cucchiarini, Helmer Strik, and Lou Boves. 2000. Quantitative assessment of second language learners' fluency by means of automatic speech recognition technology. *The Journal of the Acoustical Society of America*, 107(2):989–999.

Eric John Dobson. 1957. *English Pronunciation, 1500-1700: Phonology*, volume 2. Clarendon Press.

Bin Dong, Qingwei Zhao, Jianping Zhang, and Yonghong Yan. 2004. Automatic assessment of pronunciation quality. In *Chinese Spoken Language Processing, 2004 International Symposium on*, pages 137–140. IEEE.

Elizabeth J Erling and Philip Seargeant. 2013. *English and development: Policy, pedagogy and globalization*, volume 17. Multilingual Matters.

Enrique Estellés-Arolas and Fernando González-Ladrón-de Guevara. 2012. Towards an integrated crowdsourcing definition. *Journal of Information science*, 38(2):189–200.

Cambridge EOCL Examinations. 2011. Using the *CEFR*: Principles of good practice. *at University of Cambridge*.

Jonathan G Fiscus. 1997. A post-processing system to yield reduced word error rates: Recognizer output voting error reduction (rover). In *Automatic Speech Recognition and Understanding, 1997. Proceedings., 1997 IEEE Workshop on*, pages 347–354. IEEE.

Horacio Franco, Victor Abrash, Kristin Precoda, Harry Bratt, Ramana Rao, John Butzberger, Romain Rossier, and Federico Cesari. 2000. The sri eduspeaktm system: Recognition and pronunciation scoring for language learning. *Proceedings of InSTILL 2000*, pages 123–128.

John S Garofolo, Lori F Lamel, William M Fisher, Jonathon G Fiscus, and David S Pallett. 1993. Darpa timit acoustic-phonetic continous speech corpus cd-rom. nist speech disc 1-1.1. *NASA STI/Recon Technical Report N*, 93:27403.

Cahit Guven and Asadul Islam. 2013. Age at migration, language proficiency and socio-economic outcomes: Evidence from australia. Technical report.

Eric Hagley. 2010. Creation of speaking tests for efl communication classes. *t*, (8):33–41.

Gene B Halleck. 1995. Assessing oral proficiency: A comparison of holistic and objective measures. *The Modern Language Journal*, 79(2):223–234.

Mehdi Hosseini, Ingemar J Cox, Nataša Milić-Frayling, Gabriella Kazai, and Vishwa Vinay. 2012. On aggregating labels from multiple crowd workers to infer relevance of documents. In *Advances in information retrieval*, pages 182–194. Springer.

Jeff Howe. 2006. The rise of crowdsourcing. *Wired magazine*, 14(6):1–4.

Akinori Ito, Tadao Nagasawa, Hirokazu Ogasawara, Motoyuki Suzuki, and Shozo Makino. 2006. Automatic detection of english mispronunciation using speaker adaptation and automatic assessment of english intonation and rhythm. *Educational technology research*, 29(1):13–23.

Christos Koniaris and Olov Engwall. 2011. Perceptual differentiation modeling explains phoneme mispronunciation by non-native speakers. In *Acoustics, Speech and Signal Processing (ICASSP), 2011 IEEE International Conference on*, pages 5704–5707. IEEE.

Stephen A Kunath and Steven H Weinberger. 2010. The wisdom of the crowd's ear: speech accent rating and annotation with amazon mechanical turk. In *Proceedings of the NAACL HLT 2010 Workshop on Creating Speech and Language Data with Amazon's Mechanical Turk*, pages 168–171. Association for Computational Linguistics.

Walter S Lasecki, Christopher D Miller, and Jeffrey P Bigham. 2013. Warping time for more effective real-time crowdsourcing. In *Proceedings of the SIGCHI Conference on Human Factors in Computing Systems*, pages 2033–2036. ACM.

Mark Lejk and Michael Wyvill. 2001. The effect of the inclusion of selfassessment with peer assessment of contributions to a group project: A quantitative study of secret and agreed assessments. *Assessment & Evaluation in Higher Education*, 26(6):551–561.

Hongyan Li, Shijin Wang, Jiaen Liang, Shen Huang, and Bo Xu. 2009. High performance automatic mispronunciation detection method based on neural network and trap features. In *INTERSPEECH*, pages 1911–1914.

LightSide. 2013. http://lightsidelabs.com/.

David Little. 2006. The common european framework of reference for languages: Content, purpose, origin, reception and impact. *Language Teaching*, 39:167–190, 7.

David Little. 2007. The common european framework of reference for languages: Perspectives on the making of supranational language education policy. *The Modern Language Journal*, 91(4):645–655.

Nitin Madnani, Joel Tetreault, Martin Chodorow, and Alla Rozovskaya. 2011. They can help: using crowdsourcing to improve the evaluation of grammatical error detection systems. In *Proceedings of the 49th Annual Meeting of the Association for Computational Linguistics: Human Language Technologies: short papers-Volume 2*, pages 508–513. Association for Computational Linguistics.

Leonardo Neumeyer, Horacio Franco, Mitchel Weintraub, and Patti Price. 1996. Automatic text-independent pronunciation scoring of foreign language student speech. In *Spoken Language, 1996. ICSLP 96. Proceedings., Fourth International Conference on*, volume 3, pages 1457–1460. IEEE.

Quoc Viet Hung Nguyen, Tam Nguyen Thanh, Tran Lam Ngoc, and Karl Aberer. 2013. An evaluation of aggregation techniques in crowdsourcing. In *The 14th International Conference on Web Information System Engineering (WISE), 2013*, number EPFL-CONF-187456.

Gabriele Paolacci, Jesse Chandler, and Panagiotis G Ipeirotis. 2010. Running experiments on amazon mechanical turk. *Judgment and Decision making*, 5(5):411–419.

Mitchell Aaron Peabody. 2011. *Methods for pronunciation assessment in computer aided language learning*. Ph.D. thesis, Massachusetts Institute of Technology.

Donald E Powers, Jill C Burstein, Martin Chodorow, Mary E Fowles, and Karen Kukich. 2002. Stumping *e-rater*: challenging the validity of automated essay scoring. *Computers in Human Behavior*, 18(2):103–134.

Kåre Sjölander. 2003. An hmm-based system for automatic segmentation and alignment of speech. In *Proceedings of Fonetik*, volume 2003, pages 93–96. Citeseer.

Robert Stalnaker. 1999. The problem of logical omniscience, ii. context and content: Essays on intentionality in speech and thought (pp. 255–273).

Lynn Streeter, Jared Bernstein, Peter Foltz, and Donald DeLand. 2011. Pearsons automated scoring of writing, speaking, and mathematics.

SVAR. 2014. http://www.aspiringminds.in/talent-evaluation/spoken-english-SVAR.html.

Joel R Tetreault, Elena Filatova, and Martin Chodorow. 2010. Rethinking grammatical error annotation and evaluation with the amazon mechanical turk. In *Proceedings of the NAACL HLT 2010 Fifth Workshop on Innovative Use of NLP for Building Educational Applications*, pages 45–48. Association for Computational Linguistics.

Amazon Mechanical Turk. 2014. https://requester.mturk.com/tour.

Nathan Van Houdnos. 2011. Can the internet grade math? crowdsourcing a complex scoring task and picking the optimal crowd size. *Dietrich College of Humanities and Social Sciences at Research Showcase @ CMU*.

Hao Wang and Helen Meng. 2012. Deriving perceptual gradation of l2 english mispronunciations using crowdsourcing and the workerrank algorithm. *Proc. of the 15th Oriental COCOSDA, Macau, China*, pages 9–12.

Hao Wang, Xiaojun Qian, and Helen Meng. 2014. Phonological modeling of mispronunciation gradations in l2 english speech of l1 chinese learners. In *Acoustics, Speech and Signal Processing (ICASSP), 2014 IEEE International Conference on*, pages 7714–7718. IEEE.

Paul Whitla. 2009. Crowdsourcing and its application in marketing activities. *Contemporary Management Research*, 5(1).

Steve Young, Gunnar Evermann, Mark Gales, Thomas Hain, Dan Kershaw, Xunying Liu, Gareth Moore, Julian Odell, Dave Ollason, Dan Povey, et al. 2006. The htk book (for htk version 3.4). *Cambridge university engineering department*, 2(2):2–3.

Omar F Zaidan and Chris Callison-Burch. 2011. Crowdsourcing translation: Professional quality from non-professionals. In *Proceedings of the 49th Annual Meeting of the Association for Computational Linguistics: Human Language Technologies-Volume 1*, pages 1220–1229. Association for Computational Linguistics.

Klaus Zechner, Derrick Higgins, and Xiaoming Xi. 2007. Speechrater: A construct-driven approach to scoring spontaneous non-native speech. *Proc. SLaTE*.

Klaus Zechner, Derrick Higgins, Xiaoming Xi, and David M Williamson. 2009. Automatic scoring of non-native spontaneous speech in tests of spoken english. *Speech Communication*, 51(10):883–895.

Driving ROVER with Segment-based ASR Quality Estimation

Shahab Jalalvand[1,2], **Matteo Negri**[1], **Daniele Falavigna**[1], **Marco Turchi**[1]
[1] FBK - Fondazione Bruno Kessler, Via Sommarive 18, 38123 Trento, Italy
[2] University of Trento, Italy
{jalalvand,negri,falavi,turchi}@fbk.eu

Abstract

ROVER is a widely used method to combine the output of multiple automatic speech recognition (ASR) systems. Though effective, the basic approach and its variants suffer from potential drawbacks: *i)* their results depend on the order in which the hypotheses are used to feed the combination process, *ii)* when applied to combine long hypotheses, they disregard possible differences in transcription quality at local level, *iii)* they often rely on word confidence information. We address these issues by proposing a segment-based ROVER in which hypothesis ranking is obtained from a confidence-independent ASR quality estimation method. Our results on English data from the IWSLT2012 and IWSLT2013 evaluation campaigns significantly outperform standard ROVER and approximate two strong oracles.

1 Introduction

In automatic speech recognition (ASR), the combination of transcription hypotheses produced by multiple systems usually leads to significant word error rate (WER) reductions compared to the output of each individual system. Systems' diversity and complementarity have been exploited in different ways to synthetically obtain more accurate transcriptions. Recognizer output voting error reduction – ROVER (Fiscus, 1997), the most widely used method, performs hypothesis fusion in two steps. First, the 1-best transcriptions from multiple systems are aligned by means of dynamic programming to build a single, minimal word transition network. Then, the resulting network is searched to select the best scoring word at each node. The final hypothesis is constructed via a majority voting mechanism and, if available, by using word confidence measures.

This general strategy has been improved in several ways but, despite their proven effectiveness, ROVER and its variants have three potential drawbacks. The first one is intrinsic to their implementation: the fusion process starts from one of the input hypotheses, which is used as "skeleton" for the greedy alignment of the others. The order in which the hypotheses are used to feed the process can hence determine significant variations in the WER of the resulting combination. **This calls for automatic methods for *ranking* the hypotheses to initialise and carry on the fusion process.**

The second drawback is inherent to the way ROVER is usually run: the fusion process is typically fed with transcriptions of entire audio recordings (lasting up to hours). With this level of granularity, the skeleton used as basis for the alignment may consist of long transcriptions whose quality can considerably vary at local level. For instance, the worst transcription of an entire audio recording (globally) could be the best one for some passages (locally). **This calls for solutions capable to operate at higher granularity levels (*e.g. segments* lasting up to few seconds) to better exploit the local diversity of the combined transcriptions.**

The third drawback relates to the applicability of ROVER-like fusion methods: their common trait is the reliance on information about the inner workings of the combined systems. Indeed, the standard voting scheme with confidence scores is usually much more reliable than the simpler frequency-based voting. The access to confidence scores, however, is a too rigid constraint in application scenarios where the hypotheses to be combined come from unknown ("black-box") systems.[1] **This calls for *confidence-independent* fusion methods.**

[1] One example, among the many possible ones, is the scenario in which an array of microphones (*e.g.* in a room or a vehicle) sends input to one or more commercial ASR systems which do not provide confidence information.

Proceedings of the 53rd Annual Meeting of the Association for Computational Linguistics and the 7th International Joint Conference on Natural Language Processing, pages 1095–1105,
Beijing, China, July 26-31, 2015.

	L3	L4	L5	L6	L7	L8
SysO	12.2	**11.7**	11.8	11.9	12.1	12.1
InSysO	19.8	16.6	15.1	13.9	13.4	13.3
SegO	**10.5**	11.0	11.4	11.6	11.7	11.7
InSegO	22.9	19.6	17.4	15.8	14.4	13.0

Table 1: Motivation: the influence of hypothesis order and granularity on standard ROVER results.

The impact of the first two issues is evident from the figures provided in Table 1. The results refer to the WER achieved by different "oracles" obtained from the output of eight ASR systems that participated in the IWSLT2013 campaign (Cettolo et al., 2013).[2] Such oracles combine:

- Different numbers of transcriptions (from *three* – L3 to *eight* – L8);
- At different granularity levels (*whole utterance* – SysO and *segment* – SegO);
- In different orders (*best to worst* – SysO, SegO and *inverse* – InSysO, InSegO).

As shown in the table, the gap between utterance-based (SysO) and segment-based (SegO) is evident at all levels: WER differences vary from 0.3 (11.9 vs. 11.6 at L6) to 1.7 points (12.2 vs. 10.5 at L3). Another gap is evident between best-to-worst and inverse rankings, with WER differences up to 7.6 points at whole utterance level (SysO vs. InSysO at L3) and 12.4 points at segment level (SegO vs. InSegO at L3). Another interesting observation is that top results (*i.e.* lower WER) are obtained when combining a subset of the outputs (respectively four at utterance level and three at segment level). Referring to this analysis, the goal of computing ROVER based on hypothesis ranking at higher granularity levels is well motivated.

A crucial need to achieve this goal is the availability of a confidence-independent method to predict the quality of ASR transcriptions at segment level. This "quality estimation" (QE) task has been recently addressed in (Negri et al., 2014; C. de Souza et al., 2015) as a supervised regression problem in which transcriptions' WER is predicted without having access to reference transcripts.[3] Different feature sets have been evaluated, showing that even with those extracted only from the signal and the transcription (*i.e.* disregarding information about the decoding process) the prediction error is sufficiently low to open to real applications. However, though promising, experimental results stem from an intrinsic evaluation in which QE is only addressed in isolation.

By applying it to inform ROVER, we propose for the first time an application-oriented *extrinsic* evaluation of ASR QE (our first contribution). To this aim, we extend previous ASR QE methods with new features (second contribution), and report significant improvements over standard ROVER on a shared dataset (third contribution). For the sake of brevity, our comparison is performed only against standard ROVER and in "black-box" conditions. However it's worth remarking that our approach can be straightforwardly applied to any ROVER-like variant and, if available, by exploiting confidence features.

2 Related work

This paper gathers three main research strands together: ASR system combination, ASR quality estimation and machine-learned ranking.

Fiscus (1997) proposed ROVER as an approach to produce a composite ASR output. The basic approach has been extended in several ways. N-Best ROVER (Stolcke et al., 2000) improves the original method by combining multiple alternatives from each combined system. Schwenk and Gauvain (2000) exploit a secondary language model to rescore the final n-best hypotheses generated by ROVER. *i*ROVER (Hillard et al., 2007) exploits a classifier to choose the system that is most likely to be correct at each word location. *c*ROVER (Abida et al., 2011) integrates a semantic pre-filtering step in which the word transition network is scanned to flag and eliminate erroneous words to facilitate the voting. Other approaches to ASR system combination make use of word lattices or confusion networks (Mangu, 2000; Li et al., 2002; Evermann and Woodland, 2000; Hoffmeister et al., 2006; Bougares et al., 2013, inter alia). Note that all these combination methods require to have access to the inner structure of the ASR decoder, while ASR systems, especially the commercial ones, often do not provide this information.

ASR quality estimation allows us to overcome this problem and obtain confidence-independent estimates of ASR output quality. Based on the positive intrinsic evaluation results reported in

[2]Details about this dataset will be provided in Section 6.1.

[3]This formulation is very similar to the machine translation counterpart of the task (Specia et al., 2009; Mehdad et al., 2012; Turchi et al., 2014; C. de Souza et al., 2014).

(Negri et al., 2014; C. de Souza et al., 2015), here we extend the approach with new features and perform an extrinsic evaluation in a real application scenario. Our new features are inspired by research on ASR error detection at word level (Goldwater et al., 2010; Pellegrini and Trancoso, 2010).

Machine-learned ranking (MLR) or learning to rank (Hang, 2011) is widely used in information retrieval to order the answers to a user's query (Cao et al., 2007; McFee and Lanckriet, 2010; McSherry and Najork, 2008). We use it to order the transcription hypotheses produced by multiple ASR systems and feed ROVER with the resulting ranked lists.

3 Method

Given an utterance and a set of *M* transcription hypotheses produced by *M* different (possibly unknown) ASR systems, our goal is to:

1. Split the utterance into segments (ideally at sentence level);
2. For each segment, automatically estimate the quality (*e.g.* in terms of WER) of the corresponding *M* (segment-level) hypotheses;
3. Use the estimates to rank the hypotheses and feed ROVER based on the ranking;
4. Reconstruct the entire utterance transcription by concatenating the combined segment-level transcriptions produced by ROVER;
5. Measure the overall WER differences against standard ROVER and other oracles.

Step 1 is performed by a start-end point detection module based on signal energy, which is followed by a segment classification module based on Gaussian Mixture Models similar to (Cettolo and Federico, 2000). Although the comparison with alternative splitting methods might lead to different results, this is not the main focus of the paper and is left as future work. Steps 2–4, instead, represent the core of our contribution and are described in the following sections.

4 Segment-based QE-informed ROVER

ROVER uses iterative dynamic programming to build a word transition network (WTN) from multiple ASR output hypotheses. The resulting WTN can be seen as a confusion network with an equal number of word arc hypotheses (one for each ASR system entering the combination) in each correspondence slot. The best word sequence is determined from the WTN via majority voting among the words in each slot. Most of the extensions of ROVER, such as *i*ROVER (Hillard et al., 2007), *c*ROVER (Abida et al., 2011) and the one described in (Zhang and Rudnicky, 2006), aim to learn a scoring function that allows improving the reordering of words inside each slot. In particular, *i*ROVER reorders the words in each slot by means of a classifier trained with features that characterize the individual ASR systems. This approach, however, needs first to properly normalize the word lattices generated by each system, in order to exhibit the same vocabulary and similar densities, and to generate a unified segmentation for joining the lattices.

In a similar way, motivated by the analysis shown in Table 1, our method applies reordering of the ASR hypotheses at *segment level*. However, differently from *i*ROVER, it does not require to access the inner components of the decoders (*e.g.* word lattices or word confidences), nor to apply pre-processing steps that can distort the outputs of individual ASR components.

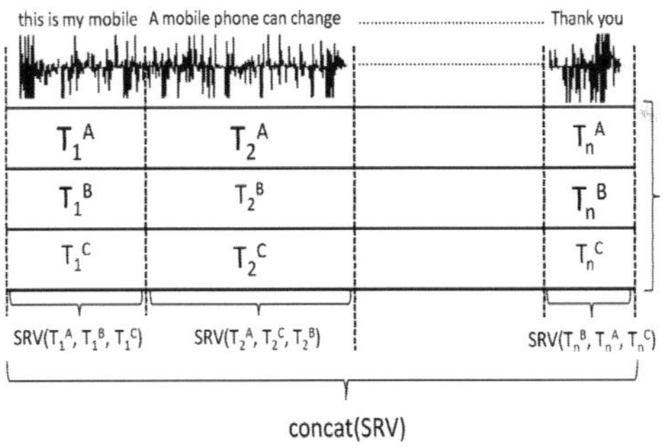

Figure 1: Segment-based ROVER

Figure 1 illustrates the difference between standard ROVER (*RV*, shown at the rightmost vertical) which works at the utterance level (lasting up to few hours) and the segment-based ROVER (*SRV*, shown at the bottom horizontal) that works at the segment level (lasting up to few seconds). *RV* keeps the order of the systems static along the whole utterance ($A \preceq B \preceq C$, *i.e.* system A has generated a better transcription than system B which, in turn is better than system C) for all the segments $RV(T^A_{1..n}, T^B_{1..n}, T^C_{1..n})$. *SRV*, instead, dynamically changes the system order from one segment to the other. For example, the system order for the first segment is $A \preceq B \preceq C$, while for the next segment it is $A \preceq C \preceq B$. Our hypothesis is that, with a proper segment-based ranking, SRV will result in lower WER scores than RV.

Note that, as depicted in Figure 1, segment-based ROVER requires that all the ASR systems share a common segmentation. This is easy to obtain by force-aligning the transcriptions of each system with a given segmentation (*e.g.* one randomly chosen among those employed by each ASR system).

In this paper we approach segment-level ASR QE as a supervised learning task, by comparing two alternative strategies: ranking by regression (Section 4.1) and machine-learned ranking (Section 4.2). Both methods rely on the features used in (Negri et al., 2014), extended with a new set of word-level features described in Section 5.

4.1 Ranking by regression (RR)

The first ranking strategy is based on training a regressor on a set of (*signal*, *transcription*, *WER*) triples, and use it to predict the WER score for new, unseen (*signal*, *transcription*) test instances. Then, based on the predicted WERs, a ranked list is produced for each segment to feed ROVER.

To train the regressor, we are given N segments ($S_i, 1 \leq i \leq N$), their automatic transcriptions ($\{T_i^1 \ldots T_i^M\}_{i=1}^{i=N}$) produced by M ASR systems, and manual references from which the true WERs ($\{TW_i^1 \ldots TW_i^M\}_{i=1}^{i=N}$) can be computed for each segment i. The whole set of training data is hence represented by instances: $I = \{(S_i, T_i^j, TW_i^j), 1 \leq j \leq M, 1 \leq i \leq N\}$. Training is performed with two alternative strategies, which differ in the amount of training data used. The first one, **RR1**, employs the whole training set I. The second one, **RR2**, uses only one transcription for each segment, randomly chosen from the M available. In this case, the training set becomes: $I' = \{(S_i, T_i^j, TW_i^j), 1 \leq i \leq N, j = rnd(M)\}$ where $rnd(M)$ is a random number between 1 to M. In practice, *RR2* learns from a smaller but more diverse training set compared to *RR1*. On the one side, in fact, *RR1* deals with a larger number of training instances (M times more), but the feature vectors will share the same values for the features extracted from the signal of each utterance. On the other side, *RR2* reduces the size of the training set I' down to $\frac{1}{M}$ of I, but only one feature vector is extracted for each utterance. The unpredictable effect of such differences on QE results motivates experiments with both methods.

4.2 Machine-learned ranking (MLR)

The second strategy relies on directly training a ranking model from a set of instances $I = \{(S_i, T_i^j, TR_i^j), 1 \leq i \leq N, 1 \leq j \leq M\}$, where S_i and T_i^j respectively represent segments and transcriptions, and TR_i^j represents "true ranks" computed from the corresponding reference WER values TW_i^j. That is, given two transcriptions, T_i^j and T_i^k and the true WERs, then $TR_i^j \preceq TR_i^k$, if $TW_i^j \leq TW_i^k$.

It is worth to note that MLR, differently from the two regression methods described above, performs a pairwise comparison between the segment candidates. That is, for each pair of segment transcriptions, the algorithm processes their corresponding feature vectors against each other and decides to place one transcription ahead of the other, as long as returning a score for this decision. Based on this score, the algorithm is then able to rank more than two candidates.

5 Features

We use two sets of features. One consists of the basic features described in (Negri et al., 2014); the other includes several word-based features specifically introduced for our ranking task.

5.1 Basic features

Basic features can be further divided in three groups:

Signal features (16 in total) aim to capture the difficulty to transcribe a given input by looking at the signal as a whole. They are obtained by analyzing the audio waveform with a window of 20ms at a frame rate of 10ms. For each analysed window, 12 Mel Frequency Cepstral Coefficients (MFCCs) are evaluated (MFCC of order 0 is discarded) plus log energy. Then, to form the signal feature vector for each given segment, we compute the mean/min/max values of raw energy, as well as the mean MFCCs values and total segment duration.

Hybrid features (26) provide a more fine-grained way to capture the difficulty of transcribing the signal. They are computed based on the forced alignment between the M given automatic transcriptions of each segment and the corresponding acoustic observations obtained from raw features. For each transcription hypothesis hybrid features are: signal to noise ratio (SNR), mean/min/max noise energy, mean/min/max word energy, (max word - min noise) energy, number of silences (#sil), #sil per second, number of words (#wrd) per second, $\frac{\#sil}{\#wrd}$, total duration of words (D_{wrd}), total duration of silences (D_{sil}), mean duration of words, mean duration of silences, $\frac{D_{sil}}{D_{wrd}}$, $D_{wrd} - D_{sil}$, standard deviation (std) of word duration, std of silence duration, mean/std/min/max of pitch[4], number of hesitations, frequency of hesitations.

Textual features (10) aim to capture the plausibility (*i.e.* the fluency) of a transcription. For each hypothesis textual features are: number of words, LM log probability, LM log probability of part of speech (POS), log perplexity, LM log perplexity of POS, percentage (%) of numbers, % of tokens which do not contain only "[a-z]", % of content words, % of nouns, % of verbs.

5.2 Word-based features

To compensate the absence of ASR confidence information, we also designed a set of "word-based" features inspired by previous approaches to ASR error detection (Chieu and Ng, 2002; Pellegrini and Trancoso, 2010; Goldwater et al., 2010; Tam et al., 2014). They aim to capture words' pronunciation difficulty, which is determined by the number of lexical neighbors (similar pronunciations) and the types of phonemes that form the words. From the ASR error detection field we also borrow additional language model features based on recurrent neural network language model (RNNLM) probability (Mikolov et al., 2010).

Word-based features (22) are: POS tag and score of the previous/current/next words (6), RNNLM probabilities (2) given by models trained on in-domain and out-of-domain data, in-domain/out-of-domain 4-gram LM probability (2), number of phoneme classes (including fricatives, liquids, nasals, stops and vowels) (5), number of homophones (1), number of lexical neighbors (1) and binary features answering the three questions: "is stop word?" (1), "is before/after repetition?" (2), "is before/after silence?" (2). Since the ASR hypotheses of a given segment might contain different numbers of words, we average the values of the word-based features for each hypothesis.

[4]Pitch features have been computed with the Praat software tool (Boersma and Weenink, 2005).

Dataset	duration	sent	token	voc	talks
tst2012	1h45m	1,124	19.2k	2.8k	11
tst2013	4h50m	2,246	41.6k	5.6k	28

Table 2: Dataset statistics: duration, number of sentences, number of tokens, vocabulary size, number of talks.

System	tst2012	tst2013
FBK	16.8	23.2
KIT	12.7	14.4
MITLL	13.3	15.9
NAIST	–	16.2
NICT	12.4	13.5
PRKE	–	27.2
RWTH	13.6	16.0
UEDIN	14.4	22.1

Table 3: Official WER[%] scores of the participants in the IWSLT2012 and IWSLT2013 ASR evaluations.

6 Experimental setup

In this section we illustrate the audio data used in our experiments, the methods used to inform and run ROVER, the evaluation metric and the significance testing method applied.

6.1 Data

We experiment with two sets of speech recordings collected from English TED talks and used for the 2012 (IWSLT2012) and 2013 (IWSLT2013) editions of the International Workshop on Spoken Language Translation (Federico et al., 2012; Cettolo et al., 2013). Statistics for both datasets are shown in Table 2. Six teams participated in the 2012 evaluation: FBK, KIT, MITLL, NICT, RWTH and UEDIN. Two more competitors, NAIST and PRKE, took part in the 2013 edition of the campaign. The related WERs are reported in Table 3. For detailed system descriptions we refer the reader to the IWSLT2012[5] and IWSLT2013[6] proceedings.

In the experiments, we used *tst2012* for training with 4-fold cross-validation, and *tst2013* for testing purposes. Note that cross-validation was applied ensuring that a given speaker does not ap-

[5]`http://workshop2012.iwslt.org`
[6]`http://workshop2013.iwslt.org`

pear simultaneously both in the training and validation sets. The same condition holds for the test set: speakers in *tst2012* do not occur in *tst2013*. These conditions, and the use of two different sets of talks (acquired in different IWSLT editions and transcribed by different sets of ASR systems), make our task particularly difficult and guarantee the congruence with real-life scenarios in which training and test data are totally independent.

As previously mentioned, a common segmentation needs to be shared among the various ASR components. To do this we decided to use the one provided by our internal ASR system, and to force-align to it all the other ones.

6.2 Terms of comparison

We compare our segment-based QE-informed ROVER against three methods that differ in the granularity of the combined hypotheses and in the way they are ranked:

Random ROVER. It is obtained by averaging the results of 100 runs of standard, system-level ROVER (*i.e.* the WTN is obtained by combining transcriptions of the whole utterance) in which the systems to be combined are ranked randomly. Note that this is the only possible way to run ROVER in absence of information about the reliability of the combined systems. Random ROVER is the standard fusion method adopted in IWSLT2013 to produce the final transcriptions that are sent to the machine translation phase.

System-based Oracle (SysO). It is obtained by computing the standard, system-level ROVER based on the true system ranking (*i.e.* the actual ranking of the IWSLT2013 participants). We consider it as an oracle since the true ranking represents prior knowledge about systems' reliability which is not available in real testing conditions.

Segment-based Oracle (SegO). It is obtained by computing ROVER at segment-level, using the true system ranking for each segment. Also this oracle relies on information about systems' ranking (at a higher granularity level), which is not available in real testing conditions. As shown in Table 1, this is the strongest term of comparison and actually represents out upper bound.

6.3 Evaluation metric and significance test

As usually done in ASR evaluation, performance results are measured in terms of WER.[7] Our segment-based, QE-informed ROVER is hence compared against the other methods based on the WER computed on the test set (*tst2013*).

To measure if two methods produce statistically different results, we run the matched-pairs significance test (Gillick and Cox, 1989). It is based on averaging the differences between the number of errors (insertions, deletions and substitutions) produced by the two approaches for the individual segments. If the average falls in the [-0.05,+0.05] interval, then the global WER difference between the two methods is not statistically significant.

In terms of results' significance tests, our success criteria are: *i)* a statistically significant improvement over random ROVER, and *ii)* non-significant differences with respect to the two strong oracles. For the sake of comparison, we define three symbols for the evaluation results reported in Table 4:

1. "$\dagger$" indicates that the corresponding WER score is not significantly different from random ROVER (a negative result);
2. "$\bullet$" indicates that the WER score is not significantly different from the system-based ROVER oracle (a positive result);
3. "$\star$" indicates that the WER score is not significantly different from the segment-based ROVER oracle (the best result).

6.4 Ranking Models

Ranking by regression (see Section 4.1) is performed using the implementation of the extremely randomized trees algorithm (Geurts et al., 2006) provided by the Scikit-learn package (Pedregosa et al., 2011). Extra-trees are a tree-based ensemble method for supervised classification and regression, which we successfully used in the past both for MT (de Souza et al., 2013) and ASR quality estimation (Negri et al., 2014). The model used for machine learned ranking (see Section 4.2) is based on the implementation of the random forest

[7]The word error rate is the minimum edit distance between an hypothesis and the reference transcription. Edit distance is calculated as the number of edits (word insertions, deletions, substitutions) divided by the number of words in the reference. Lower WERs (↓) indicate better transcriptions.

method-number of combined systems	L3	L4	L5	L6	L7	L8
Random ROVER	14.6	13.7	13.2	12.8	12.7	12.4
SegO	10.5	11.0	11.4	11.6	11.7	11.7
SysO	12.2	11.7	11.8	11.9	12.1	12.1
RR1 +Basic	13.9	13.1	12.6	12.4	12.4	12.3 † •
RR1 +WordBased	14.0	13.0	12.5	12.2	12.3 •	12.3 † •
RR1 +Basic+WordBased	14.0	13.0	12.5	12.2	12.3 •	12.3 † •
RR2 +Basic	13.8	13.0	12.6	12.4	12.3 •	12.3 † •
RR2 +WordBased	14.2	13.1	12.7	12.4	12.5 †	12.4 † •
RR2 +Basic+WordBased	13.7	12.8	12.4	12.2	12.2 •	12.2 † •
MLR +Basic	12.9	12.4	12.3	12.1 •	12.3	12.2 † •
MLR +WordBased	12.4 •	12.1	12.0	12.0 •	12.2 •	12.2 † •
MLR +Basic+WordBased	**12.4 •**	**12.1**	**12.0 •**	**11.9 • ⋆**	**12.2 •**	**12.2 † •**

Table 4: WER[%] (↓) of random, oracle and QE-informed ROVERs. The symbols assigned to some scores indicate their statistical significance ($p \leq 0.05$ computed with the matched-pairs test). In particular: "†" = the result is not statistically different from random ROVER; "•" = the result is not statistically different from SysO; "⋆" the result is not statistically different from SegO.

ensemble method (Breiman, 2001) provided in the RankLib library.[8]

As mentioned in Section 6.1, all the ranking models are trained in 4-fold cross validation. *RR1* uses all the instances in *tst2012* (*i.e.* 1,124 segments transcribed by 6 ASR systems, which results in a total of 6,744 training instances). *RR2* uses only one instance per segment, which is randomly selected among the 6 automatic transcriptions available in *tst2012* (resulting in a total of 1,124 training instances). Similar to *RR1*, *MLR* uses all the instances in *tst2012* (6,744 in total). The learning parameters of each model (number of bags, number of trees per bag, number of leaves per tree and minimum number of instances per leaf) are tuned by maximising Mean Average Precision as the objective function (Hang, 2011).

All the models are trained using the basic features (*+Basic*), the word-based ones (*+WordBased*) and their combination (*+Basic+WordBased*).

7 Results and discussion

Table 4 reports the WER results obtained on *tst2013* by ROVER methods fed with: different numbers of hypotheses (from 3 to 8), at different granularity levels (whole utterance vs. segment), ranked with different models (random, RR1, RR2 and MLR) trained with different sets of features (Basic, WordBased, Basic+WordBased).

The first three rows present the results achieved by our terms of comparison: random ROVER, the segment-based oracle (SegO) and the system-based oracle (SysO). As anticipated when motivating our work (see Table 1), the WER achieved by SegO is always lower than the scores achieved by SysO. Note also that the performance of SegO decreases as the number of combined hypotheses increases, due to the introduction in the input of progressively worse transcripts. Instead, SysO exhibits a less coherent behaviour, with close WER values at all levels, and a minimum in correspondence of column L4 (the combination of four transcriptions of the whole utterance). We interpret these results as a further motivation for our work: feeding ROVER with a good ranking that exploits local (segment-level) differences between the combined hypotheses seems to be more reliable than relying on system-level ranks based on global WER scores. A theoretical analysis of the relation between the diversity of the combined hypotheses and ROVER results is presented in (Audhkhasi et al., 2014). In light of this analysis, our results open an interesting issue concerning the trade-offs between optimal hypothesis ranking and their (local) diversity. We initially explore this problem in Section 7.1, but leave for future work a more systematic investigation.

Rows 4-6 show the results achieved by **RR1** (ranking by regression, trained with all the tran-

[8] http://sourceforge.net/p/lemur/wiki/RankLib/

scriptions for each input segment). When trained only with basic features, it always outperforms random ROVER. At L8 the gain is not statistically significant but, at the same time, also the WER difference with SysO is not significant. Note that, proceeding from L3 to L8, the WER difference between RR1+Basic and random ROVER decreases from 0.7 to 0.1. This can be explained by the fact that when the number of candidates increases, then the role of majority voting dominates the role of hypothesis ranking. Similar trends are shown by all other approaches, including the oracles. RR1+WordBased slightly improves over RR1+Basic, indicating the possible usefulness of this new set of features. However, when used in combination (RR1+Basic+WordBased), the two feature sets do not yield further WER reductions. Nevertheless, what is worth to remark is that at L7 and L8 the distance from Sys0 is not statistically significant (a positive result).

As shown in rows 7-9, the situation changes with **RR2** (ranking by regression, trained with one transcription per segment). When trained with the combined feature sets (RR2+Basic+WordBased), the model always leads to slight WER reductions over RR2+Basic. Also in this case, the gains over random ROVER are consistent (they range from 0.9 at L3 to 0.2 at L8), and the difference with respect to SysO is not statistically significant at L7 and L8 (a positive result).

As shown in rows 10-12, results are further improved by **MLR**. Except for L8, the improvement over random ROVER is statistically significant, large and consistent with all feature sets. The WER reduction obtained by MLR+Basic varies from 1.7 to 0.2 WER points, indicating a higher effectiveness of machine-learned ranking compared to ranking by regression. MLR+WordBased produces further WER reductions, with differences with SysO that become statistically not-significant at four levels (L3, L6, L7 and L8). Finally, when trained with the combined feature sets, the ranking model leads to the lowest WER scores. Noticeably, such results are not only on par with SysO (the difference is statistically significant only at L4), but in one case (L6) they even reach those of SegO, the strongest competitor (best result).

Overall, as evidenced by the L8 column, when the number of input components becomes large our QE-informed approaches are not significantly better than random ROVER and SysO. This raises the need of a stopping criterion to avoid entering useless inputs into the ROVER combination. Together with the trade-off between ranking performance and hypotheses' diversity, this represents an interesting topic for future work.

7.1 The role of hypotheses' diversity

To gain further insights on our results, and as a first step along the research directions previously outlined, we analysed the relation between ROVER results and hypotheses' diversity. To this aim, Figure 2 plots the WER of our best method (MLR+Basic+WordBased) and the two oracles as a function of hypotheses' diversity at L6, for which we obtain the best results.

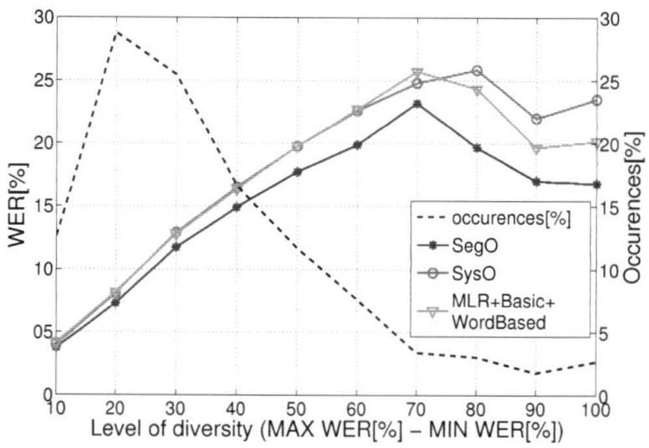

Figure 2: Results on *tst2013* of the oracles and our best model, as functions of hypotheses' diversity.

Diversity is measured by computing the difference between the maximum and the minimum WERs of the input transcriptions. All the segments are then grouped with regard to this difference. For example 10 on the x-axis refers to the group of segments whose diversities lay in the interval of [0,10); 20 refers to the segments whose diversities are in [10,20) and consequently, 100 represents the segments whose diversities lay in [90,100]. This latter means that for each segment there is at least one transcription that is perfect or close to perfection, and one that is (almost completely) wrong.

For segments with diversity smaller than 70, the performance of the system-based oracle (line with circle marks) and our segment-level QE-informed ROVER (line with triangle marks) is almost identical. Instead, for segments with a "high" level of diversity (in the interval [70,100]), our method significantly outperforms the system-based oracle. With a maximum gain larger than 3 WER points, it approaches the strong segment-based oracle (line with asterisk marks). Remarkably, for diversity values in the interval [90,100], our method is able to halve the distance that separates the two oracles.

The considerable WER reductions observed for diversity values larger than 70 shed new light on the global results reported in Table 4. The fact that such performance gains are hidden in the global scores can be explained by looking at the dashed line in Figure 2, which shows the percentage of segments belonging to each diversity level. As it can be observed, the vast majority of the segments (~95%) falls in diversity bins in the interval [10,70). The large WER reductions obtained on the few remaining segments are definitely not enough to boost global results. Overall, this finding suggests that our segment-level QE-informed ROVER can fully unfold its potential in application scenarios featuring high diversity among the transcriptions.

7.2 Prediction of overall ranks

Since our results strongly depend on the reliability of hypothesis ranking, our final analysis focuses on the correlation between QE-based ranking methods and the "true" ranks used as prior knowledge by the system-based oracle (the official ranking of the IWSLT2013 participants). In order to predict the overall IWSLT2013 ranking, we first run our QE models on each segment. Systems are then ordered based on the average ranking score received by their transcriptions. Finally, the alternative QE-based methods (RR1, RR2 and MLR) are compared by measuring their Spearman correlation with the TRUE systems' order.

Table 5 reports the resulting rankings and the corresponding correlation with the true, official one. Among all the possible combinations (8 factorial), our two best methods (RR2 and MLR) result in a systems' ordering with high correlation with the official IWSLT2013 ranking. In particular, MLR achieves correlation of 0.905 with three out of eight systems (1, 2 and 8) that are correctly positioned. The correlation values of the different approaches reflect the performance reported in Table 4, in which the WER achieved by using MLR is usually better than the ones obtained from RR1 and RR2. It is interesting to note in the last column of Table 5 that the ranking errors are represented by switches between systems with similar WERs, while it seems easier to discriminate between systems with more distant WER values. This consideration is in line with the findings of Section 7.1 concerning the higher potential of segment-level QE-informed ROVER in scenarios featuring a higher diversity between the combined systems.

tst2013	WER	TRUE	RR1	RR2	MLR
NICT	13.5	1	6	2	**1**
KIT	14.4	2	3	4	**2**
MITLL	15.9	3	1	1	4
RWTH	16.0	4	2	3	5
NAIST	16.2	5	**5**	**5**	3
UEDIN	22.1	6	8	8	7
FBK	23.2	7	4	6	6
PRKE	27.2	8	7	7	**8**
Spearman correlation			0.429	0.809	0.905

Table 5: True and predicted IWSLT2013 system ranks (correct predictions are shown in bold).

8 Conclusions

We presented a novel approach to improve the combination of multiple automatic transcription hypotheses using ROVER. Our method is based on informing the fusion process with accurate word error rate predictions obtained from ASR quality estimation models. First, to exploit the possible local diversity among the combined hypotheses, it performs quality prediction and ranking at segment level. Then, the predicted ranks for each segment are used to feed ROVER. Finally, the combined hypotheses are concatenated to reconstruct the entire utterance transcription. To rank predictions, we compared two different regression models with a machine-learned ranking method. We carried out experiments on a set of English TED talks collected for two editions of the IWSLT ASR evaluation campaign. Results show that our segment-level QE-informed ROVER outperforms the standard random ROVER and performs on par (differences are not statistically significant) with a system-based ROVER oracle that exploits prior knowledge about systems' reliability. Moreover, compared to a very strong segment-based ROVER oracle, in one case the performance of our method is not statistically different. These results are particularly encouraging, especially in light of the fact that our approach does not exploit confidence information related to the internal behaviour of the ASR decoders. Overall, this represents the first confirmation, obtained in an extrinsic evaluation setting, of the good potential of reference-free and system-agnostic ASR quality estimation.

References

Kacem Abida, Fakhri Karray, and Wafa Abida. 2011. cROVER: Improving ROVER using Automatic Error Detection. In *Proceedings of the IEEE International Conference on Acoustics, Speech, and Signal Processing, (ICASSP 2011)*, pages 1753–1756, Prague, Czech Republic, May.

Kartik Audhkhasi, Andreas M Zavou, Panayiotis G Georgiou, and Shrikanth S Narayanan. 2014. Theoretical analysis of diversity in an ensemble of automatic speech recognition systems. *IEEE/ACM Transactions on Audio, Speech & Language Processing*, 22(3):711–726.

Paul Boersma and David Weenink. 2005. Praat: Doing Phonetics by Computer (Version 4.3.01). *Retrieved from http://www.praat.org/.*

Fethi Bougares, Deléglise, Estève Paul, Yannick, and Mickael Rouvier. 2013. LIUM ASR System for Etape French Evaluation Campaign: Experiments on System Combination using Open-source Recognizers. In *Proceedings of the 16th International Conference on Text, Speech, and Dialogue*, pages 319–326, Pilsen, Czech Republic, September.

Leo Breiman. 2001. Random forests. *Machine learning*, 45(1):5–32.

José G. C. de Souza, Marco Turchi, and Matteo Negri. 2014. Machine Translation Quality Estimation Across Domains. In *Proceedings of the 25th International Conference on Computational Linguistics (COLING 2014): Technical Papers*, pages 409–420, Dublin, Ireland, August.

José G. C. de Souza, Hamed Zamani, Matteo Negri, Marco Turchi, and Daniele Falavigna. 2015. Multitask Learning for Adaptive Quality Estimation of Automatically Transcribed Utterances. In *Proceedings of the 2015 Conference of the North American Chapter of the Association for Computational Linguistics - Human Language Technologies (NAACL HLT 2015)*, Denver, Colorado, USA.

Zhe Cao, Tao Qin, Tie-Yan Liu, Ming-Feng Tsai, and Hang Li. 2007. Learning to Rank: from Pairwise Approach to Listwise Approach. In *Proceedings of the 24th International Conference on Machine learning (ICML-07)*, pages 129–136, Corvalis, Oregon, USA.

Mauro Cettolo and Marcello Federico. 2000. Model Selection Criteria for Acoustic Segmentation. In *ASR2000-Automatic Speech Recognition: Challenges for the new Millenium ISCA Tutorial and Research Workshop (ITRW)*.

Mauro Cettolo, Jan Niehues, Sebastian Stüker, Luisa Bentivogli, and Marcello Federico. 2013. Report on the 10th IWSLT Evaluation Campaign. In *Proceedings of the International Workshop on Spoken Language Translation (IWSLT 2013)*, Heidelberg, Germany, December.

Hai Leong Chieu and Hwee Tou Ng. 2002. Named Entity Recognition: A Maximum Entropy Approach Using Global Information. In *Proceedings of the 19th International Conference on Computational Linguistics - Volume 1*, COLING '02, pages 1–7, Taipei, Taiwan.

José G. C. de Souza, Christian Buck, Marco Turchi, and Matteo Negri. 2013. FBK-UEdin participation to the WMT13 quality estimation shared task. In *Proceedings of the Eighth Workshop on Statistical Machine Translation*, pages 352–358, Sofia, Bulgaria, August. Association for Computational Linguistics.

Gunnar Evermann and PC Woodland. 2000. Posterior Probability Decoding, Confidence Estimation and System Combination. In *Proceedings of NIST Speech Transcription Workshop*, volume 27, College Park, MD, USA.

Marcello Federico, Luisa Bentivogli, Michael Paul, and Sebastian Stüker. 2012. Overview of the IWSLT 2012 Evaluation Campaign. In *Proceedings of the International Workshop on Spoken Language Translation (IWSLT 2012)*, pages 11–27, Hong Kong, December.

Jonathan G Fiscus. 1997. A Post-processing System to Yield Reduced Word Error Rates: Recognizer Output Voting Error Reduction (ROVER). In *Proceedings of the IEEE Workshop on Automatic Speech Recognition and Understanding*, pages 347–354, Santa Barbara, CA, USA. IEEE.

Pierre Geurts, Damien Ernst, and Louis Wehenkel. 2006. Extremely randomized trees. *Machine learning*, 63(1):3–42.

Laurence Gillick and Stephen J Cox. 1989. Some Statistical Issues in the Comparison of Speech Recognition Algorithms. In *Proceedings of the IEEE International Conference on Acoustics, Speech, and Signal Processing, (ICASSP 1989)*, pages 532–535, Glasgow, Scotland.

Sharon Goldwater, Dan Jurafsky, and Christopher D Manning. 2010. Which words are hard to recognize? prosodic, lexical, and disfluency factors that increase speech recognition error rates. *Speech Communication*, 52(3):181–200.

LI Hang. 2011. A short introduction to learning to rank. *IEICE TRANSACTIONS on Information and Systems*, 94(10):1854–1862.

Dustin Hillard, Bjoern Hoffmeister, Mari Ostendorf, Ralf Schlueter, and Hermann Ney. 2007. iROVER: Improving System Combination with Classification. In *Human Language Technologies 2007: The Conference of the North American Chapter of the Association for Computational Linguistics; Companion Volume, Short Papers*, pages 65–68, Rochester, New York, April.

Björn Hoffmeister, Tobias Klein, Ralf Schlüter, and Hermann Ney. 2006. Frame Based System Combination and a Comparison with Weighted ROVER and CNC. In *Proceedings of the International Conference on Spoken Language Processing (Interspeech 2006 — ICSLP)*, pages 537–540, Pittsburgh, PA, USA.

Xiang Li, Rita Singh, and Richard M. Stern. 2002. Lattice Combination for Improved Speech Recognition. In *Proceedings of the International Conference of Spoken Language Processing*, Denver, CO, USA, September.

Lidia Mangu. 2000. *Finding Consensus in Speech Recognition*. John Hopkins University. PhD Thesis.

Brian McFee and Gert R Lanckriet. 2010. Metric Learning to Rank. In *Proceedings of the 27th International Conference on Machine Learning (ICML-10)*, pages 775–782, Haifa, Israel, June.

Frank McSherry and Marc Najork. 2008. Computing information retrieval performance measures efficiently in the presence of tied scores. In *Advances in information retrieval*, pages 414–421. Springer.

Yashar Mehdad, Matteo Negri, and Marcello Federico. 2012. Match without a Referee: Evaluating MT Adequacy without Reference Translations. In *Proceedings of the Machine Translation Workshop (WMT2012)*, pages 171–180, June.

Tomas Mikolov, Martin Karafiát, Lukas Burget, Jan Cernockỳ, and Sanjeev Khudanpur. 2010. Recurrent Neural Network Based Language Model. In *Proceedings of INTERSPEECH 2010, 11th Annual Conference of the International Speech Communication Association*, pages 1045–1048, Makuhari, Chiba, Japan, September.

Matteo Negri, Marco Turchi, José G. C. de Souza, and Falavigna Daniele. 2014. Quality Estimation for Automatic Speech Recognition. In *Proceedings of COLING 2014, the 25th International Conference on Computational Linguistics: Technical Papers*, pages 1813–1823, Dublin, Ireland, August.

Fabian Pedregosa, Gaël Varoquaux, Alexandre Gramfort, Vincent Michel, Bertrand Thirion, Olivier Grisel, Mathieu Blondel, Peter Prettenhofer, Ron Weiss, Vincent Dubourg, et al. 2011. Scikit-learn: Machine learning in python. *The Journal of Machine Learning Research*, 12:2825–2830.

Thomas Pellegrini and Isabel Trancoso. 2010. Improving ASR Error Detection with Non-decoder Based Features. In *Proceedings of INTERSPEECH 2010, 11th Annual Conference of the International Speech Communication Association*, pages 1950–1953, Makuhari, Chiba, Japan, September.

Holger Schwenk and Jean-Luc Gauvain. 2000. Improved ROVER using Language Model Information. In *ASR2000-Automatic Speech Recognition: Challenges for the new Millenium ISCA Tutorial and Research Workshop (ITRW)*.

Lucia Specia, Nicola Cancedda, Marc Dymetman, Marco Turchi, and Nello Cristianini. 2009. Estimating the Sentence-Level Quality of Machine Translation Systems. In *Proceedings of the 13th Annual Conference of the European Association for Machine Translation (EAMT'09)*, pages 28–35, Barcelona, Spain.

Andreas Stolcke, Harry Bratt, John Butzberger, Horacio Franco, Venkata Ramana Gadde, Madelaine Plauche, Colleen Richey, Elizabeth Shriberg, Kemal Sonmez, F Weng, and Jing Zheng. 2000. The SRI march 2000 HUB5 conversational speech transcription system.

Yik-Cheung Tam, Yun Lei, Jing Zheng, and Wen Wang. 2014. ASR Error Detection using Recurrent Neural Network Language Model and Complementary ASR. In *Proceedings of the IEEE International Conference on Acoustics, Speech, and Signal Processing, (ICASSP 2014)*, pages 2312–2316, Florence, Italy, May.

Marco Turchi, Antonios Anastasopoulos, José G. C. de Souza, and Matteo Negri. 2014. Adaptive Quality Estimation for Machine Translation. In *Proceedings of the 52nd Annual Meeting of the Association for Computational Linguistics (Volume 1: Long Papers)*, pages 710–720, Baltimore, Maryland, June.

Rong Zhang and Alexander I. Rudnicky. 2006. Investigations of Issues for Using Multiple Acoustic Models to Improve Continuous Speech Recognition. In *Proceedings of INTERSPEECH*, Pittsburgh, PA, USA, September.

A Hierarchical Neural Autoencoder for Paragraphs and Documents

Jiwei Li, Minh-Thang Luong and Dan Jurafsky
Computer Science Department, Stanford University, Stanford, CA 94305, USA
jiwei, lmthang, jurafsky@stanford.edu

Abstract

Natural language generation of coherent long texts like paragraphs or longer documents is a challenging problem for recurrent networks models. In this paper, we explore an important step toward this generation task: training an LSTM (Long-short term memory) auto-encoder to preserve and reconstruct multi-sentence paragraphs. We introduce an LSTM model that hierarchically builds an embedding for a paragraph from embeddings for sentences and words, then decodes this embedding to reconstruct the original paragraph. We evaluate the reconstructed paragraph using standard metrics like ROUGE and Entity Grid, showing that neural models are able to encode texts in a way that preserve syntactic, semantic, and discourse coherence. While only a first step toward generating coherent text units from neural models, our work has the potential to significantly impact natural language generation and summarization[1].

1 Introduction

Generating coherent text is a central task in natural language processing. A wide variety of theories exist for representing relationships between text units, such as Rhetorical Structure Theory (Mann and Thompson, 1988) or Discourse Representation Theory (Lascarides and Asher, 1991), for extracting these relations from text units (Marcu, 2000; LeThanh et al., 2004; Hernault et al., 2010; Feng and Hirst, 2012, inter alia), and for extracting other coherence properties characterizing the role each text unit plays with others in a discourse (Barzilay and Lapata, 2008; Barzilay and Lee, 2004; Elsner and Charniak, 2008; Li and Hovy, 2014, inter alia). However, applying these to text generation remains difficult. To understand how discourse units are connected, one has to understand the communicative function of each unit, and the role it plays within the context that encapsulates it, recursively all the way up for the entire text. Identifying increasingly sophisticated human-developed features may be insufficient for capturing these patterns. But developing neural-based alternatives has also been difficult. Although neural representations for sentences can capture aspects of coherent sentence structure (Ji and Eisenstein, 2014; Li et al., 2014; Li and Hovy, 2014), it's not clear how they could help in generating more broadly coherent text.

Recent LSTM models (Hochreiter and Schmidhuber, 1997) have shown powerful results on generating meaningful and grammatical sentences in sequence generation tasks like machine translation (Sutskever et al., 2014; Bahdanau et al., 2014; Luong et al., 2015) or parsing (Vinyals et al., 2014). This performance is at least partially attributable to the ability of these systems to capture local compositionally: the way neighboring words are combined semantically and syntactically to form meanings that they wish to express.

Could these models be extended to deal with generation of larger structures like paragraphs or even entire documents? In standard sequence-to-sequence generation tasks, an input sequence is mapped to a vector embedding that represents the sequence, and then to an output string of words. Multi-text generation tasks like summarization could work in a similar way: the system reads a collection of input sentences, and is then asked to generate meaningful texts with certain properties (such as—for summarization—being succinct and conclusive). Just as the local semantic and syntactic compositionally of words can be captured by LSTM models, can the com-

[1]Code for models described in this paper are available at `www.stanford.edu/~jiweil/`.

Proceedings of the 53rd Annual Meeting of the Association for Computational Linguistics and the 7th International Joint Conference on Natural Language Processing, pages 1106–1115,
Beijing, China, July 26-31, 2015.

positionally of discourse releations of higher-level text units (e.g., clauses, sentences, paragraphs, and documents) be captured in a similar way, with clues about how text units connect with each another stored in the neural compositional matrices?

In this paper we explore a first step toward this task of neural natural language generation. We focus on the component task of training a paragraph (document)-to-paragraph (document) autoencoder to reconstruct the input text sequence from a compressed vector representation from a deep learning model. We develop hierarchical LSTM models that arranges tokens, sentences and paragraphs in a hierarchical structure, with different levels of LSTMs capturing compositionality at the token-token and sentence-to-sentence levels.

We offer in the following section to a brief description of sequence-to-sequence LSTM models. The proposed hierarchical LSTM models are then described in Section 3, followed by experimental results in Section 4, and then a brief conclusion.

2 Long-Short Term Memory (LSTM)

In this section we give a quick overview of LSTM models. LSTM models (Hochreiter and Schmidhuber, 1997) are defined as follows: given a sequence of inputs $X = \{x_1, x_2, ..., x_{n_X}\}$, an LSTM associates each timestep with an input, memory and output gate, respectively denoted as i_t, f_t and o_t. For notations, we disambiguate e and h where e_t denote the vector for individual text unite (e.g., word or sentence) at time step t while h_t denotes the vector computed by LSTM model at time t by combining e_t and h_{t-1}. σ denotes the sigmoid function. The vector representation h_t for each time-step t is given by:

$$\begin{bmatrix} i_t \\ f_t \\ o_t \\ l_t \end{bmatrix} = \begin{bmatrix} \sigma \\ \sigma \\ \sigma \\ \tanh \end{bmatrix} W \cdot \begin{bmatrix} h_{t-1} \\ e_t \end{bmatrix} \tag{1}$$

$$c_t = f_t \cdot c_{t-1} + i_t \cdot l_t \tag{2}$$

$$h_t^s = o_t \cdot c_t \tag{3}$$

where $W \in \mathbb{R}^{4K \times 2K}$ In sequence-to-sequence generation tasks, each input X is paired with a sequence of outputs to predict: $Y = \{y_1, y_2, ..., y_{n_Y}\}$. An LSTM defines a distribution over outputs and sequentially predicts tokens using a softmax function:

$$\begin{aligned} & P(Y|X) \\ & = \prod_{t \in [1, n_y]} p(y_t | x_1, x_2, ..., x_t, y_1, y_2, ..., y_{t-1}) \\ & = \prod_{t \in [1, n_y]} \frac{\exp(f(h_{t-1}, e_{y_t}))}{\sum_{y'} \exp(f(h_{t-1}, e_{y'}))} \end{aligned} \tag{4}$$

$f(h_{t-1}, e_{y_t})$ denotes the activation function between e_{h-1} and e_{y_t}, where h_{t-1} is the representation outputted from the LSTM at time $t-1$. Note that each sentence ends up with a special end-of-sentence symbol <end>. Commonly, the input and output use two different LSTMs with different sets of convolutional parameters for capturing different compositional patterns.

In the decoding procedure, the algorithm terminates when an <end> token is predicted. At each timestep, either a greedy approach or beam search can be adopted for word prediction. Greedy search selects the token with the largest conditional probability, the embedding of which is then combined with preceding output for next step token prediction. For beam search, (Sutskever et al., 2014) discovered that a beam size of 2 suffices to provide most of benefits of beam search.

3 Paragraph Autoencoder

In this section, we introduce our proposed hierarchical LSTM model for the autoencoder.

3.1 Notation

Let D denote a paragraph or a document, which is comprised of a sequence of N_D sentences, $D = \{s^1, s^2, ..., s^{N_D}, end_D\}$. An additional "$end_D$" token is appended to each document. Each sentence s is comprised of a sequence of tokens $s = \{w^1, w^2, ..., w^{N_s}\}$ where N_s denotes the length of the sentence, each sentence ending with an "end_s" token. The word w is associated with a K-dimensional embedding e_w, $e_w = \{e_w^1, e_w^2, ..., e_w^K\}$. Let V denote vocabulary size. Each sentence s is associated with a K-dimensional representation e_s.

An autoencoder is a neural model where output units are directly connected with or identical to input units. Typically, inputs are compressed into a representation using neural models (encoding), which is then used to reconstruct it back (decoding). For a paragraph autoencoder, both the input X and output Y are the same document D. The autoencoder first compresses D into a vector representation e_D and then reconstructs D based on e_D.

For simplicity, we define $LSTM(h_{t-1}, e_t)$ to be the LSTM operation on vectors h_{t-1} and e_t to achieve h_t as in Equ.1 and 2. For clarification, we first describe the following notations used in encoder and decoder:

- h_t^w and h_t^s denote hidden vectors from LSTM models, the subscripts of which indicate timestep t, the superscripts of which indicate operations at word level (w) or sequence level (s). $h_t^s(\text{enc})$ specifies encoding stage and $h_t^s(\text{dec})$ specifies decoding stage.

- e_t^w and e_t^s denotes word-level and sentence-level embedding for word and sentence at position t in terms of its residing sentence or document.

3.2 Model 1: Standard LSTM

The whole input and output are treated as one sequence of tokens. Following Sutskever et al. (2014) and Bahdanau et al. (2014), we trained an autoencoder that first maps input documents into vector representations from a $LSTM_{\text{encode}}$ and then reconstructs inputs by predicting tokens within the document sequentially from a $LSTM_{\text{decode}}$. Two separate LSTMs are implemented for encoding and decoding with no sentence structures considered. Illustration is shown in Figure 1.

3.3 Model 2: Hierarchical LSTM

The hierarchical model draws on the intuition that just as the juxtaposition of words creates a joint meaning of a sentence, the juxtaposition of sentences also creates a joint meaning of a paragraph or a document.

Encoder We first obtain representation vectors at the sentence level by putting one layer of LSTM (denoted as $LSTM_{\text{encode}}^{\text{word}}$) on top of its containing words:

$$h_t^w(\text{enc}) = LSTM_{\text{encode}}^{\text{word}}(e_t^w, h_{t-1}^w(\text{enc})) \quad (5)$$

The vector output at the ending time-step is used to represent the entire sentence as

$$e_s = h_{end_s}^w$$

To build representation e_D for the current document/paragraph D, another layer of LSTM (denoted as $LSTM_{\text{encode}}^{\text{sentence}}$) is placed on top of all sentences, computing representations sequentially for each timestep:

$$h_t^s(\text{enc}) = LSTM_{\text{encode}}^{\text{sentence}}(e_t^s, h_{t-1}^s(\text{enc})) \quad (6)$$

Representation $e_{end_D}^s$ computed at the final time step is used to represent the entire document: $e_D = h_{end_D}^s$.

Thus one LSTM operates at the token level, leading to the acquisition of sentence-level representations that are then used as inputs into the second LSTM that acquires document-level representations, in a hierarchical structure.

Decoder As with encoding, the decoding algorithm operates on a hierarchical structure with two layers of LSTMs. LSTM outputs at sentence level for time step t are obtained by:

$$h_t^s(\text{dec}) = LSTM_{\text{decode}}^{\text{sentence}}(e_t^s, h_{t-1}^s(\text{dec})) \quad (7)$$

The initial time step $h_0^s(d) = e_D$, the end-to-end output from the encoding procedure. $h_t^s(d)$ is used as the original input into $LSTM_{\text{decode}}^{word}$ for subsequently predicting tokens within sentence $t+1$. $LSTM_{\text{decode}}^{word}$ predicts tokens at each position sequentially, the embedding of which is then combined with earlier hidden vectors for the next timestep prediction until the end_s token is predicted. The procedure can be summarized as follows:

$$h_t^w(\text{dec}) = LSTM_{\text{decode}}^{\text{sentence}}(e_t^w, h_{t-1}^w(\text{dec})) \quad (8)$$

$$p(w|\cdot) = \text{softmax}(e_w, h_{t-1}^w(\text{dec})) \quad (9)$$

During decoding, $LSTM_{\text{decode}}^{word}$ generates each word token w sequentially and combines it with earlier LSTM-outputted hidden vectors. The LSTM hidden vector computed at the final time step is used to represent the current sentence.

This is passed to $LSTM_{\text{decode}}^{sentence}$, combined with h_t^s for the acquisition of h_{t+1}, and outputted to the next time step in sentence decoding.

For each timestep t, $LSTM_{\text{decode}}^{sentence}$ has to first decide whether decoding should proceed or come to a full stop: we add an additional token end_D to the vocabulary. Decoding terminates when token end_D is predicted. Details are shown in Figure 2.

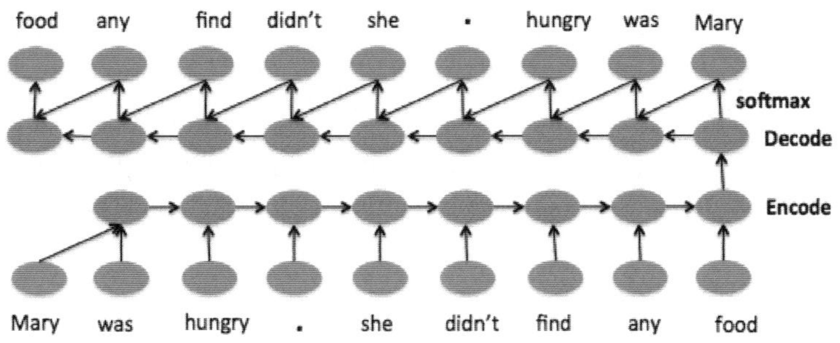

Figure 1: Standard Sequence to Sequence Model.

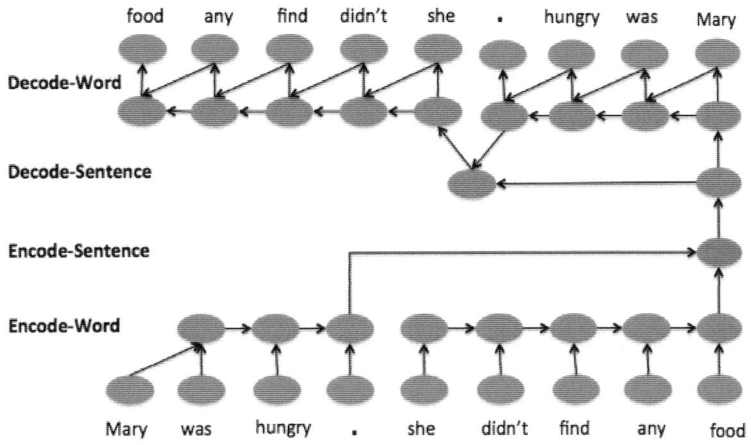

Figure 2: Hierarchical Sequence to Sequence Model.

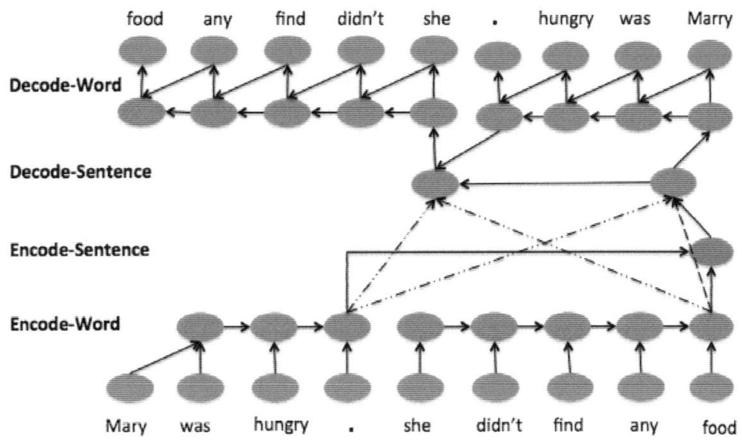

Figure 3: Hierarchical Sequence to Sequence Model with Attention.

3.4 Model 3: Hierarchical LSTM with Attention

Attention models adopt a look-back strategy by linking the current decoding stage with input sentences in an attempt to consider which part of the input is most responsible for the current decoding state. This attention version of hierarchical model is inspired by similar work in image caption generation and machine translation (Xu et al., 2015; Bahdanau et al., 2014).

Let $H = \{h_1^s(e), h_2^s(e), ..., h_N^s(e)\}$ be the

collection of sentence-level hidden vectors for each sentence from the inputs, outputted from $LSTM_{\text{encode}}^{\text{Sentence}}$. Each element in H contains information about input sequences with a strong focus on the parts surrounding each specific sentence (time-step). During decoding, suppose that e_t^s denotes the sentence-level embedding at current step and that $h_{t-1}^s(\text{dec})$ denotes the hidden vector outputted from $LSTM_{decode}^{sentence}$ at previous time step $t-1$. Attention models would first link the current-step decoding information, i.e., $h_{t-1}^s(\text{dec})$ which is outputted from $LSTM_{dec}^{sentence}$ with each of the input sentences $i \in [1, N]$, characterized by a strength indicator v_i:

$$v_i = U^T f(W_1 \cdot h_{t-1}^s(\text{dec}) + W_2 \cdot h_i^s(\text{enc})) \quad (10)$$

$W_1, W_2 \in \mathbb{R}^{K \times K}$, $U \in \mathbb{R}^{K \times 1}$. v_i is then normalized:

$$a_i = \frac{\exp(v_i)}{\sum_{i'} \exp(v_i')} \quad (11)$$

The attention vector is then created by averaging weights over all input sentences:

$$m_t = \sum_{i \in [1, N_D]} a_i h_i^s(\text{enc}) \quad (12)$$

LSTM hidden vectors for current step is then achieved by combining c_t, e_t^s and $h_{t-1}^s(\text{dec})$:

$$\begin{bmatrix} i_t \\ f_t \\ o_t \\ l_t \end{bmatrix} = \begin{bmatrix} \sigma \\ \sigma \\ \sigma \\ \tanh \end{bmatrix} W \cdot \begin{bmatrix} h_{t-1}^s(\text{dec}) \\ e_t^s \\ m_t \end{bmatrix} \quad (13)$$

$$c_t = f_t \cdot c_{t-1} + i_t \cdot l_t \quad (14)$$

$$h_t^s = o_t \cdot c_t \quad (15)$$

where $W \in \mathbb{R}^{4K \times 3K}$. h_t is then used for word predicting as in the vanilla version of the hierarchical model.

3.5 Training and Testing

Parameters are estimated by maximizing likelihood of outputs given inputs, similar to standard sequence-to-sequence models. A softmax function is adopted for predicting each token within output documents, the error of which is first back-propagated through $LSTM_{\text{decode}}^{word}$ to sentences, then through $LSTM_{\text{decode}}^{sentence}$ to document representation e_D, and last through $LSTM_{\text{encode}}^{sentence}$ and $LSTM_{\text{encode}}^{word}$ to inputs. Stochastic gradient descent with minibatches is adopted.

dataset	S per D	W per D	W per S
Hotel-Review	8.8	124.8	14.1
Wikipedia	8.4	132.9	14.8

Table 1: Statistics for the Datasets. W, S and D respectively represent number of words, number of sentences, and number of documents/paragraphs. For example, "S per D" denotes average number of sentences per document.

For testing, we adopt a greedy strategy with no beam search. For a given document D, e_D is first obtained given already learned $\text{LSTM}_{\text{encode}}$ parameters and word embeddings. Then in decoding, $LSTM_{\text{decode}}^{\text{sentence}}$ computes embeddings at each sentence-level time-step, which is first fed into the binary classifier to decide whether sentence decoding terminates and then into $LSTM_{\text{decode}}^{\text{word}}$ for word decoding.

4 Experiments

4.1 Dataset

We implement the proposed autoencoder on two datasets, a highly domain specific dataset consisting of hotel reviews and a general dataset extracted from Wkipedia.

Hotel Reviews We use a subset of hotel reviews crawled from TripAdvisor. We consider only reviews consisting sentences ranging from 50 to 250 words; the model has problems dealing with extremely long sentences, as we will discuss later. We keep a vocabulary set consisting of the 25,000 most frequent words. A special "<unk>" token is used to denote all the remaining less frequent tokens. Reviews that consist of more than 2 percent of unknown words are discarded. Our training dataset is comprised of roughly 340,000 reviews; the testing set is comprised of 40,000 reviews. Dataset details are shown in Table 1.

Wikipedia We extracted paragraphs from Wikipedia corpus that meet the aforementioned length requirements. We keep a top frequent vocabulary list of 120,000 words. Paragraphs with larger than 4 percent of unknown words are discarded. The training dataset is comprised of roughly 500,000 paragraphs and testing contains roughly 50,000.

4.2 Training Details and Implementation

Previous research has shown that deep LSTMs work better than shallow ones for sequence-to-sequence tasks (Vinyals et al., 2014; Sutskever et al., 2014). We adopt a LSTM structure with four layer for encoding and four layer for decoding, each of which is comprised of a different set of parameters. Each LSTM layer consists of 1,000 hidden neurons and the dimensionality of word embeddings is set to 1,000. Other training details are given below, some of which follow Sutskever et al. (2014).

- Input documents are reversed.
- LSTM parameters and word embeddings are initialized from a uniform distribution between [-0.08, 0.08].
- Stochastic gradient decent is implemented without momentum using a fixed learning rate of 0.1. We stated halving the learning rate every half epoch after 5 epochs. We trained our models for a total of 7 epochs.
- Batch size is set to 32 (32 documents).
- Decoding algorithm allows generating at most 1.5 times the number of words in inputs.
- 0.2 dropout rate.
- Gradient clipping is adopted by scaling gradients when the norm exceeded a threshold of 5.

Our implementation on a single GPU[2] processes a speed of approximately 600-1,200 tokens per second. We trained our models for a total of 7 iterations.

4.3 Evaluations

We need to measure the closeness of the output (candidate) to the input (reference). We first adopt two standard evaluation metrics, ROUGE (Lin, 2004; Lin and Hovy, 2003) and BLEU (Papineni et al., 2002).

ROUGE is a recall-oriented measure widely used in the summarization literature. It measures the n-gram recall between the candidate text and the reference text(s). In this work, we only have one reference document (the input document) and ROUGE score is therefore given by:

$$\text{ROUGE}_n = \frac{\sum_{\text{gram}_n \in \text{input}} \text{count}_{\text{match}}(\text{gram}_n)}{\sum_{\text{gram}_n \in \text{input}} \text{count}(\text{gram}_n)} \tag{16}$$

where $\text{count}_{\text{match}}$ denotes the number of n-grams co-occurring in the input and output. We report ROUGE-1, 2 and W (based on weighted longest common subsequence).

BLEU Purely measuring recall will inappropriately reward long outputs. BLEU is designed to address such an issue by emphasizing precision. n-gram precision scores for our situation are given by:

$$\text{precision}_n = \frac{\sum_{\text{gram}_n \in \text{output}} \text{count}_{\text{match}}(\text{gram}_n)}{\sum_{\text{gram}_n \in \text{output}} \text{count}(\text{gram}_n)} \tag{17}$$

BLEU then combines the average logarithm of precision scores with exceeded length penalization. For details, see Papineni et al. (2002).

Coherence Evaluation Neither BLEU nor ROUGE attempts to evaluate true coherence. There is no generally accepted and readily available coherence evaluation metric.[3] Because of the difficulty of developing a universal coherence evaluation metric, we proposed here only a tailored metric specific to our case. Based on the assumption that human-generated texts (i.e., input documents in our tasks) are coherent (Barzilay and Lapata, 2008), we compare generated outputs with input documents in terms of how much original text order is preserved.

We develop a grid evaluation metric similar to the entity transition algorithms in (Barzilay and Lee, 2004; Lapata and Barzilay, 2005). The key idea of Barzilay and Lapata's models is to first identify grammatical roles (i.e., object and subject) that entities play and then model the transition probability over entities and roles across sentences. We represent each sentence as a feature-vector consisting of verbs and nouns in the sentence. Next we align sentences from output documents to input sentences based on sentence-to-sentence F1 scores (precision and recall are computed similarly to ROUGE and BLEU but at sentence level) using feature vectors. Note that multiple output sentences can be matched to one input

[2]Tesla K40m, 1 Kepler GK110B, 2880 Cuda cores.

[3]Wolf and Gibson (2005) and Lin et al. (2011) proposed metrics based on discourse relations, but these are hard to apply widely since identifying discourse relations is a difficult problem. Indeed sophisticated coherence evaluation metrics are seldom adopted in real-world applications, and summarization researchers tend to use simple approximations like number of overlapped tokens or topic distribution similarity (e.g., (Yan et al., 2011b; Yan et al., 2011a; Celikyilmaz and Hakkani-Tür, 2011)).

Input-Wiki	washington was unanimously elected President by the electors in both the 1788 – 1789 and 1792 elections . he oversaw the creation of a strong, well-financed national government that maintained neutrality in the french revolutionary wars , suppressed the whiskey rebellion , and won acceptance among Americans of all types . washington established many forms in government still used today , such as the cabinet system and inaugural address . his retirement after two terms and the peaceful transition from his presidency to that of john adams established a tradition that continued up until franklin d . roosevelt was elected to a third term . washington has been widely hailed as the " father of his country " even during his lifetime.
Output-Wiki	washington was elected as president in 1792 and voters <unk> of these two elections until 1789 . he continued suppression <unk> whiskey rebellion of the french revolution war government , strong , national well are involved in the establishment of the fin advanced operations , won acceptance . as in the government , such as the establishment of various forms of inauguration speech washington , and are still in use . <unk> continued after the two terms of his quiet transition to retirement of <unk> <unk> of tradition to have been elected to the third paragraph . but , " the united nations of the father " and in washington in his life , has been widely praised .
Input-Wiki	apple inc . is an american multinational corporation headquartered in cupertino , california , that designs , develops , and sells consumer electronics , computer software , online services , and personal com - puters . its bestknown hardware products are the mac line of computers , the ipod media player , the iphone smartphone , and the ipad tablet computer . its online services include icloud , the itunes store , and the app store . apple's consumer software includes the os x and ios operating systems , the itunes media browser , the safari web browser , and the ilife and iwork creativity and productivity suites .
Output-Wiki	apple is a us company in california , <unk> , to develop electronics , softwares , and pc , sells . hardware include the mac series of computers , ipod , iphone . its online services , including icloud , itunes store and in app store . softwares , including os x and ios operating system , itunes , web browser , < unk> , including a productivity suite .
Input-Wiki	paris is the capital and most populous city of france . situated on the seine river , in the north of the country , it is in the centre of the le-de-france region . the city of paris has a population of 2273305 inhabitants . this makes it the fifth largest city in the european union measured by the population within the city limits .
Output-Wiki	paris is the capital and most populated city in france . located in the <unk> , in the north of the country , it is the center of <unk> . paris , the city has a population of <num> inhabitants . this makes the eu ' s population within the city limits of the fifth largest city in the measurement .
Input-Review	on every visit to nyc , the hotel beacon is the place we love to stay . so conveniently located to central park , lincoln center and great local restaurants . the rooms are lovely . beds so comfortable , a great little kitchen and new wizz bang coffee maker . the staff are so accommodating and just love walking across the street to the fairway supermarket with every imaginable goodies to eat .
Output-Review	every time in new york , lighthouse hotel is our favorite place to stay . very convenient , central park , lincoln center , and great restaurants . the room is wonderful , very comfortable bed , a kitchenette and a large explosion of coffee maker . the staff is so inclusive , just across the street to walk to the supermarket channel love with all kinds of what to eat .

Table 2: A few examples produced by the hierarchical LSTM alongside the inputs.

sentence. Assume that sentence s^i_{output} is aligned with sentence $s^{i'}_{\text{input}}$, where i and i' denote position index for a output sentence and its aligned input. The penalization score L is then given by:

$$L = \frac{2}{N_{\text{output}} \cdot (N_{\text{output}} - 1)} \times \sum_{i \in [1, N_{\text{output}}-1]} \sum_{j \in [i+1, N_{\text{output}}]} |(j - i) - (j' - i')| \tag{18}$$

Equ. 18 can be interpreted as follows: $(j - i)$ denotes the distance in terms of position index between two outputted sentences indexed by j and i, and $(j' - i')$ denotes the distance between their mirrors in inputs. As we wish to penalize the degree of permutation in terms of text order, we penalize the absolute difference between the two computed distances. This metric is also relevant to the overall performance of prediction and recall: an irrelevant output will be aligned to a random input, thus being heavily penalized. The deficiency of the proposed metric is that it concerns itself only with a semantic perspective on coherence, barely considering syntactical issues.

4.4 Results

A summary of our experimental results is given in Table 3. We observe better performances for the hotel-review dataset than the open domain Wikipedia dataset, for the intuitive reason that

Model	Dataset	BLEU	ROUGE-1	ROUGE-2	Coherence(L)
Standard	Hotel Review	0.241	0.571	0.302	1.92
Hierarchical	Hotel Review	0.267	0.590	0.330	1.71
Hierarchical+Attention	Hotel Review	0.285	0.624	0.355	1.57
Standard	Wikipedia	0.178	0.502	0.228	2.75
Hierarchical	Wikipedia	0.202	0.529	0.250	2.30
Hierarchical+Attention	Wikipedia	0.220	0.544	0.291	2.04

Table 3: Results for three models on two datasets. As with coherence score L, smaller values signifies better performances.

documents and sentences are written in a more fixed format and easy to predict for hotel reviews.

The hierarchical model that considers sentence-level structure outperforms standard sequence-to-sequence models. Attention models at the sentence level introduce performance boost over vanilla hierarchical models.

With respect to the coherence evaluation, the original sentence order is mostly preserved: the hierarchical model with attention achieves $L = 1.57$ on the hotel-review dataset, equivalent to the fact that the relative position of two input sentences are permuted by an average degree of 1.57. Even for the Wikipedia dataset where more poor-quality sentences are observed, the original text order can still be adequately maintained with $L = 2.04$.

5 Discussion and Future Work

In this paper, we extended recent sequence-to-sequence LSTM models to the task of multi-sentence generation. We trained an autoencoder to see how well LSTM models can reconstruct input documents of many sentences. We find that the proposed hierarchical LSTM models can partially preserve the semantic and syntactic integrity of multi-text units and generate meaningful and grammatical sentences in coherent order. Our model performs better than standard sequence-to-sequence models which do not consider the intrinsic hierarchical discourse structure of texts.

While our work on auto-encoding for larger texts is only a preliminary effort toward allowing neural models to deal with discourse, it nonetheless suggests that neural models are capable of encoding complex clues about how coherent texts are connected .

The performance on this autoencoder task could certainly also benefit from more sophisticated neural models. For example one extension might align the sentence currently being generated with the original input sentence (similar to sequence-to-sequence translation in (Bahdanau et al., 2014)), and later transform the original task to sentence-to-sentence generation. However our long-term goal here is not on perfecting this basic multi-text generation scenario of reconstructing input documents, but rather on extending it to more important applications.

That is, the autoencoder described in this work, where input sequence X is identical to output Y, is only the most basic instance of the family of document (paragraph)-to-document (paragraph) generation tasks. We hope the ideas proposed in this paper can play some role in enabling such more sophisticated generation tasks like summarization, where the inputs are original documents and outputs are summaries or question answering, where inputs are questions and outputs are the actual wording of answers. Sophisticated generation tasks like summarization or dialogue systems could extend this paradigm, and could themselves benefit from task-specific adaptations. In summarization, sentences to generate at each timestep might be pre-pointed to or pre-aligned to specific aspects, topics, or pieces of texts to be summarized. Dialogue systems could incorporate information about the user or the time course of the dialogue. In any case, we look forward to more sophi4d applications of neural models to the important task of natural language generation.

6 Acknowledgement

The authors want to thank Gabor Angeli, Sam Bowman, Percy Liang and other members of the Stanford NLP group for insightful comments and suggestion. We also thank the three anonymous ACL reviewers for helpful comments. This work is supported by Enlight Foundation Graduate Fellowship, and a gift from Bloomberg L.P, which we gratefully acknowledge.

References

Dzmitry Bahdanau, Kyunghyun Cho, and Yoshua Bengio. 2014. Neural machine translation by jointly learning to align and translate. *arXiv preprint arXiv:1409.0473*.

Regina Barzilay and Mirella Lapata. 2008. Modeling local coherence: An entity-based approach. *Computational Linguistics*, 34(1):1–34.

Regina Barzilay and Lillian Lee. 2004. Catching the drift: Probabilistic content models, with applications to generation and summarization. *arXiv preprint cs/0405039*.

Asli Celikyilmaz and Dilek Hakkani-Tür. 2011. Discovery of topically coherent sentences for extractive summarization. In *Proceedings of the 49th Annual Meeting of the Association for Computational Linguistics: Human Language Technologies-Volume 1*, pages 491–499. Association for Computational Linguistics.

Micha Elsner and Eugene Charniak. 2008. Coreference-inspired coherence modeling. In *Proceedings of the 46th Annual Meeting of the Association for Computational Linguistics on Human Language Technologies: Short Papers*, pages 41–44. Association for Computational Linguistics.

Vanessa Wei Feng and Graeme Hirst. 2012. Text-level discourse parsing with rich linguistic features. In *Proceedings of the 50th Annual Meeting of the Association for Computational Linguistics: Long Papers-Volume 1*, pages 60–68. Association for Computational Linguistics.

Hugo Hernault, Helmut Prendinger, Mitsuru Ishizuka, et al. 2010. Hilda: a discourse parser using support vector machine classification. *Dialogue & Discourse*, 1(3).

Sepp Hochreiter and Jürgen Schmidhuber. 1997. Long short-term memory. *Neural computation*, 9(8):1735–1780.

Yangfeng Ji and Jacob Eisenstein. 2014. Representation learning for text-level discourse parsing. In *Proceedings of the 52nd Annual Meeting of the Association for Computational Linguistics*, volume 1, pages 13–24.

Mirella Lapata and Regina Barzilay. 2005. Automatic evaluation of text coherence: Models and representations. In *IJCAI*, volume 5, pages 1085–1090.

Alex Lascarides and Nicholas Asher. 1991. Discourse relations and defeasible knowledge. In *Proceedings of the 29th annual meeting on Association for Computational Linguistics*, pages 55–62. Association for Computational Linguistics.

Huong LeThanh, Geetha Abeysinghe, and Christian Huyck. 2004. Generating discourse structures for written texts. In *Proceedings of the 20th international conference on Computational Linguistics*, page 329. Association for Computational Linguistics.

Jiwei Li and Eduard Hovy. 2014. A model of coherence based on distributed sentence representation.

Jiwei Li, Rumeng Li, and Eduard Hovy. 2014. Recursive deep models for discourse parsing. In *Proceedings of the 2014 Conference on Empirical Methods in Natural Language Processing (EMNLP)*, pages 2061–2069.

Chin-Yew Lin and Eduard Hovy. 2003. Automatic evaluation of summaries using n-gram co-occurrence statistics. In *Proceedings of the 2003 Conference of the North American Chapter of the Association for Computational Linguistics on Human Language Technology-Volume 1*, pages 71–78. Association for Computational Linguistics.

Ziheng Lin, Hwee Tou Ng, and Min-Yen Kan. 2011. Automatically evaluating text coherence using discourse relations. In *Proceedings of the 49th Annual Meeting of the Association for Computational Linguistics: Human Language Technologies-Volume 1*, pages 997–1006. Association for Computational Linguistics.

Chin-Yew Lin. 2004. Rouge: A package for automatic evaluation of summaries. In *Text Summarization Branches Out: Proceedings of the ACL-04 Workshop*, pages 74–81.

Thang Luong, Ilya Sutskever, Quoc V Le, Oriol Vinyals, and Wojciech Zaremba. 2015. Addressing the rare word problem in neural machine translation. *ACL*.

William C Mann and Sandra A Thompson. 1988. Rhetorical structure theory: Toward a functional theory of text organization. *Text*, 8(3):243–281.

Daniel Marcu. 2000. The rhetorical parsing of unrestricted texts: A surface-based approach. *Computational linguistics*, 26(3):395–448.

Kishore Papineni, Salim Roukos, Todd Ward, and Wei-Jing Zhu. 2002. Bleu: a method for automatic evaluation of machine translation. In *Proceedings of the 40th annual meeting on association for computational linguistics*, pages 311–318. Association for Computational Linguistics.

Ilya Sutskever, Oriol Vinyals, and Quoc VV Le. 2014. Sequence to sequence learning with neural networks. In *Advances in Neural Information Processing Systems*, pages 3104–3112.

Oriol Vinyals, Lukasz Kaiser, Terry Koo, Slav Petrov, Ilya Sutskever, and Geoffrey Hinton. 2014. Grammar as a foreign language. *arXiv preprint arXiv:1412.7449*.

Florian Wolf and Edward Gibson. 2005. Representing discourse coherence: A corpus-based study. *Computational Linguistics*, 31(2):249–287.

Kelvin Xu, Jimmy Ba, Ryan Kiros, Aaron Courville, Ruslan Salakhutdinov, Richard Zemel, and Yoshua Bengio. 2015. Show, attend and tell: Neural image caption generation with visual attention. *arXiv preprint arXiv:1502.03044*.

Rui Yan, Liang Kong, Congrui Huang, Xiaojun Wan, Xiaoming Li, and Yan Zhang. 2011a. Timeline generation through evolutionary trans-temporal summarization. In *Proceedings of the Conference on Empirical Methods in Natural Language Processing*, pages 433–443. Association for Computational Linguistics.

Rui Yan, Xiaojun Wan, Jahna Otterbacher, Liang Kong, Xiaoming Li, and Yan Zhang. 2011b. Evolutionary timeline summarization: a balanced optimization framework via iterative substitution. In *Proceedings of the 34th international ACM SIGIR conference on Research and development in Information Retrieval*, pages 745–754. ACM.

Joint Dependency Parsing and Multiword Expression Tokenisation

Alexis Nasr, Carlos Ramisch, José Deulofeu, André Valli
Aix Marseille Université, CNRS, LIF UMR 7279
Marseille, France
FirstName.LastName@lif.univ-mrs.fr

Abstract

Complex conjunctions and determiners are often considered as pretokenized units in parsing. This is not always realistic, since they can be ambiguous. We propose a model for joint dependency parsing and multiword expressions identification, in which complex function words are represented as individual tokens linked with morphological dependencies. Our graph-based parser includes standard second-order features and verbal subcategorization features derived from a syntactic lexicon.We train it on a modified version of the French Treebank enriched with morphological dependencies. It recognizes 81.79% of ADV+*que* conjunctions with 91.57% precision, and 82.74% of *de*+DET determiners with 86.70% precision.

1 Introduction

Standard NLP tool suites for text analysis are often made of several processes that are organized as a pipeline, in which the input of a process is the output of the preceding one. Among these processes, one commonly finds a tokenizer, which segments a sentence into words, a part-of-speech (POS) tagger, which associates to every word a part-of-speech tag, and a syntactic parser, which builds a parse tree for the sentence[1]. These three processes correspond to three formal operations on the string: *segmentation* into linguistically relevant units (words), *tagging* the words with POS tags and *linking* the (word, POS) pairs by means of syntactic dependencies.

This setup is clearly not ideal, as some decisions are made too early in the pipeline (Branco and Silva, 2003). More specifically, some tokenization and tagging choices are difficult to make without taking syntax into account. To avoid the pitfall of premature decisions, probabilistic tokenizers and taggers can produce several solutions in the form of lattices (Green and Manning, 2010; Goldberg and Elhadad, 2011). Such approaches usually lead to severe computational overhead due to the huge search space in which the parser looks for the optimal parse tree. Besides, the parser might be biased towards short solutions, as it compares scores of trees associated to sequences of different lengths (De La Clergerie, 2013).

This problem is particularly hard when parsing *multiword expressions* (MWEs), that is, groups of tokens that must be treated as single units (Baldwin and Kim, 2010). The solution we present in this paper is different from the usual pipeline. We propose to jointly parse and tokenize MWEs, transforming segmentation decisions into linking decisions. Our experiments concentrate on two difficult tokenization cases. Hence, it is the parser that will choose, in such cases, whether to group or not several tokens.

Our first target phenomenon is the family of ADV+*que* constructions, a type of complex conjunction in French. They are formed by adverbs like *bien* (*well*) or *ainsi* (*likewise*) followed by the subordinative conjunction *que* (*that*). They function like English complex conjunctions *so that* and *now that*. Due to their structure, ADV+*que* constructions are generally ambiguous, like in the following examples:

1. *Je mange* **bien que** *je n'aie pas faim*
   I eat **although** *I am not hungry*
2. *Je pense* **bien** **que** *je n'ai pas faim*
   I think **indeed that** *I am not hungry*

In example 1, the sequence *bien que* forms a complex conjunction (*although*) whereas in example 2, the adverb *bien* (*indeed*) modifies the verb *pense* (*think*), and the conjunction *que* (*that*) introduces the sentential complement *je n'ai pas faim*

[1] This paper considers dependency syntactic structures.

Proceedings of the 53rd Annual Meeting of the Association for Computational Linguistics and the 7th International Joint Conference on Natural Language Processing, pages 1116–1126, Beijing, China, July 26-31, 2015.

(*I am not hungry*). In treebanks, the different readings are represented through the use of words-with-spaces in the case of complex conjunctions.

Our second target phenomenon is the family of partitive articles which are made of the preposition *de* (*of*) followed by the definite determiner *le*, *la*, *l'* or *les*[2] (*the*). These *de*+DET constructions are ambiguous, as shown in the following examples:

3. *Il boit* **de la** *bière*
   He drinks **some** *beer*
4. *Il parle* **de** **la** *bière*
   I talks **about the** *beer*

In example 3, the sequence *de la* forms a determiner (*some*) whereas in example 4, *de* is a preposition (*about*) and *la* is the determiner (*the*) of the noun *bière* (*bière*).

We focus on these constructions for two reasons. First, because they are extremely frequent. For instance, in the frWaC corpus, from a total of 54.8M sentences, 1.15M sentences (2.1%) contain one or more occurrences of our target ADV+*que* constructions and 26.7M sentences (48.6%) contain a *de*+DET construction (see Tables 1 and 2). Moreover, in a corpus of 370 M words in French,[3] *des* is the 7th most frequent word. Second, because they are perfect examples of phenomena which are difficult to process by a tokenizer. In order to decide, in example 1, that *bien que* is a complex subordinate conjunction, non-trivial morphological, lexical and syntactic clues must be taken into account, such as the subcategorization frame of the verb of the principal clause and the mood of the subordinate clause. All these clues are difficult to take into account during tokenization, where the syntactic structure of the sentence is not yet explicit.

Ask the parser to perform tokenization will not always solve the problem. Even state-of-the-art parsers can fail to predict the right structure for the cases we are dealing with. The main reason is that they are trained on treebanks of limited size, and some lexico-syntactic phenomena cannot be well modeled. This brings us to the second topic of this paper, which is the integration of external linguistic resources in a treebank-trained probabilistic parser. We show that, in order to correctly solve the two problems at hand, the parser must have access to lexico-syntactic information that can be found in a syntactic lexicon. We propose a simple way to introduce such information in the parser by defining new linguistic features that blend smoothly with treebank features used by the parser when looking for the optimal parse tree.

The paper is organized as follows: Section 2 describes related work on MWE parsing. Section 3 proposes a way to represent multiword units by means of syntactic dependencies. In Section 4, we briefly describe the parser that has been used in this work, and in Section 5, we propose a way to integrate a syntactic lexicon into the parser. Section 6 describes the data sets used for the experiments, which results are presented and discussed in Section 7. Section 8 concludes the paper.

2 Related Work

The famous "pain-in-the-neck" article by Sag et al. (2002) discusses MWEs in parsers, contrasting two representation alternatives in the LinGO ERG HPSG grammar of English: compositional rules and words-with-spaces. The addition of compositional rules for flexible MWEs has been tested in a small-scale experiment which showed significant coverage improvements in HPSG parsing by the addition of 21 new MWEs to the grammar (Villavicencio et al., 2007).

It has been demonstrated that pre-grouping MWEs as words-with-spaces can improve the performance of shallow parsing for English (Korkontzelos and Manandhar, 2010). Nivre and Nilsson (2004) obtained similar results for dependency parsing of Swedish. They compare models trained on two representations: one where MWEs are linked by a special ID dependency, and another one based on gold pre-tokenization. Their results show that the former model can recognize MWEs with F1=71.1%, while the latter can significantly improve parsing accuracy and robustness in general. However, the authors admit that "it remains to be seen how much of theoretically possible improvement can be realized when using automatic methods for MWU recognition".

Several methods of increasing complexity have been proposed for fully automatic MWE tokenization: simple lexicon projection onto a corpus (Kulkarni and Finlayson, 2011), synchronous lexicon lookup and parsing (Wehrli et al., 2010; Seretan, 2011), token-based classifiers trained using

[2]Sequences *de le* and *de les* do not appear as such in French. They have undergone a morpho-phonetic process known as *amalgamation* and are represented as tokens *du* and *des*. In our pipeline, they are artificially *detokenized*.

[3]Newspaper *Le Monde* from 1986 to 2002.

association measures and other contextual features (Vincze et al., 2013a), or contextual sequence models like conditional random fields (Constant and Sigogne, 2011; Constant et al., 2013b; Vincze et al., 2013b) and structured perceptron (Schneider et al., 2014). In theory, compound function words like ADV+*que* and *de*+DET allow no internal variability, thus they should be represented as words-with-spaces. However, to date no satisfactory solution has been proposed for automatically tokenizing *ambiguous* MWEs.

Green et al. (2013) propose a constituency parsing model which, as a by-product, performs MWE identification. They propose a flat representation for contiguous expressions in which all elements are attached to a special node, and then they compare several parsing models, including an original factored-lexicon PCFG and a tree substitution grammar. These generic parsing models can be used for parsing in general, but they have interesting memorization properties which favor MWE identification. Their experiments on French and Arabic show that the proposed models beat the baseline in MWE identification while producing acceptable general parsing results.

Candito and Constant (2014) and Vincze et al. (2013c) present experiments on dependency parsing for MWE identification which are the closest to our settings. Vincze et al. (2013c) focus on light verb constructions in Hungarian. They propose distinguishing regular verbal dependencies from light verbs and their complements through four special labels prefixed by LCV-. Then, they train the Bohnet parser (Bohnet, 2010) using standard parameters and features, and evaluate on a gold test set. They report no significant changes in attachment scores, whereas F1 for light verb identification is 75.63%, significantly higher than the baseline methods of lexicon projection (21.25%) and classification (74.45%).

Candito and Constant (2014) compare several architectures for dependency parsing and MWE identification in French. For regular MWEs like noun compounds, they use regular expressions to automatically generate an internal syntactic structure, combining standard and MWE-dedicated dependency labels. Irregular expressions like complex conjunctions are represented as separate tokens, with a special DEP_CPD dependency that links all tokens to the first MWE word (Constant et al., 2013a). They compare different architectures for MWE identification before, during and after parsing, showing that the best architecture depends on whether the target MWEs are regular or irregular.

Similarly to these two papers, we use a special dependency to model MWEs and evaluate parsing and identification accuracy. Our work departs from theirs on three important aspects. First, we concentrate on syntactically irregular compounds, that we represent with a new kind of dependency. Second, we integrate into the parser a syntactic lexicon in order to help disambiguate ADV+*que* and *de*+DET constructions. Third, we built a specific evaluation corpus to get a better estimation of the performances of our model on ADV+*que* and *de*+DET constructions.

3 The MORPH Dependency

In order to let the parser take the tokenization decisions, we propose *not* to group sequences of tokens of the form ADV+*que* and *de*+DET at tokenization time. Instead, we transform the task of segmentation decision into a parsing decision task.

We associate a syntactic structure to ADV+*que* and *de*+DET constructions by introducing a new type of dependency that we call MORPH. It is not a standard syntactic dependency, but a reminiscent of the morphological dependencies of Mel'čuk (1988), similar to the DEP_CPD label proposed by Candito and Constant (2014) or the ID dependency of Nivre and Nilsson (2004), except that we focus on syntactically-motivated MWEs, proposing a regular structure for them.

The syntactic structures of examples 1 and 2, introduced in Section 1, are represented below[4].

Example 1.

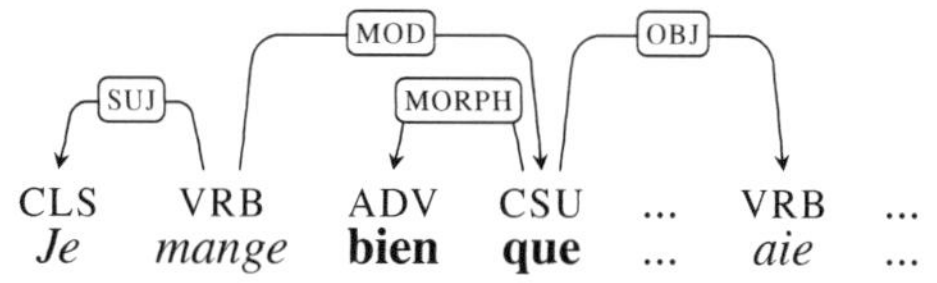

Example 2.

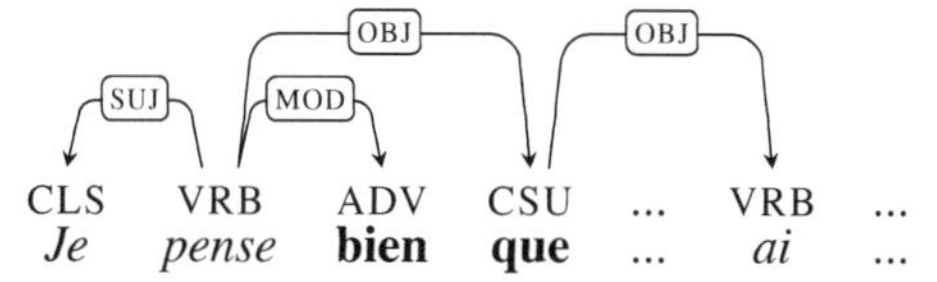

[4]In the examples, parts of speech CLS, VRB, ADV and CSU respectively stand for subject clitic pronoun, verb, adverb and subordinating conjunction. Syntactic labels SUJ, MOD, OBJ, DE-OBJ and SPE stand for subject, modifier, object, indirect object introduced by the preposition *de* and specifier.

In example 1, the complex conjunction *bien que* is represented by the presence of the MORPH dependency, whereas, in example 2, the adverb *bien* modifies the verb *pense* and *que* introduces its object. From an NLP perspective, the two readings are treated the same way by the tokenizer and the tagger. It is only at parsing time that the presence of the complex conjunction is predicted.

The syntactic structures of examples 3 and 4 are represented below. In example 3, the partitive article *de la* is represented by means of the MORPH dependency. Example 4 exhibits a standard prepositional phrase structure.

Example 3.

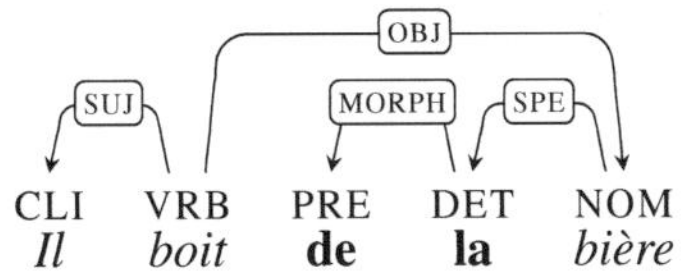

Example 4.

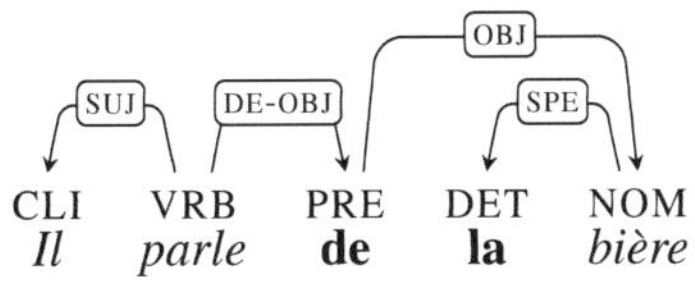

4 Parsing

The parser used in this study is a second-order graph-based parser (Kübler et al., 2009). Given a sentence $W = w_1 \dots w_l$, the parser looks for the dependency tree $\hat{T}$ of W that maximizes the score s:

$$\hat{T} = \arg\max_{T \in \mathcal{T}(W)} \sum_{F \in \mathcal{F}(T)} s(F)$$

where $\mathcal{T}(W)$ is the set of all possible dependency trees for sentence W and $\mathcal{F}(T)$ is the set of all relevant subparts, called *factors*, of tree T and $s(F)$ is the score of factor F. The values of these scores are parameters estimated during training.

We can define different models of increasing complexity depending on the decomposition of the tree into factors. The most simple one is the *arc-factored* or *first-order model*, which simply decomposes a tree into single dependencies and assigns them a score, independently of their context. We used a second-order parser which decomposes a tree into factors of three types:

1. *first-order factors*, made of one dependency;
2. *sibling factors*, made of two dependencies sharing a common governor;
3. *grandchildren factors*, made of two dependencies where the dependent of one of them is the governor of the other one.

5 Integration with a Syntactic Lexicon

Although this kind of parsers achieve state-of-the-art performances (Bohnet, 2010), their predictions are limited to the phenomena that occur in the treebanks they are trained on. In particular, they often fail at correctly distinguishing elements that are subcategorized by a verb (henceforth *complements*) from others (*modifiers*). This is due to the fact that the nature and number of the complements is specific to each verb. If the verb did not occur, or did not occur often enough, in the treebank, the nature and number of its complements will not be correctly modeled by the parser.

A precise description of verb complements plays an important role in the task of predicting the MORPH dependency, as we illustrate in example 1. In this example, the verb *manger* (*eat*) does not accept an object introduced by the subordinate conjunction *que* (*that*) . This is a vital information in order to predict the correct syntactic structure of the sentence. If the parser cannot link the conjunction *que* to the verb *manger* with an OBJ dependency, then it has to link it with a MOD dependency (it has no other reasonable solution). But *que* by itself cannot be a MOD of the verb unless it is a complex conjunction. The parser has therefore no other choice than linking *que* with the adverb using a MORPH dependency.

In order to help the parser build the right solution in such cases, we have introduced information derived from a syntactic lexicon in the parser. The syntactic lexicon associates, each verb lemma, the features +/-QUE and +/-DE, that indicate respectively if the verb accepts an object introduced by the subordinating conjunction *que* and by the preposition *de*. The verbs of our examples would have the following values:

manger	-QUE	-DE
penser	+QUE	-DE
boire	-QUE	-DE
parler	-QUE	+DE

We will call such features *subcat features* (SFs). The semantics of positive feature values are quite different from the semantics of negative ones. The former indicates that a verb *may* (but does not need to) license a complement introduced by the conjunction *que* or the preposition *de*, whereas the latter indicates that the verb *cannot* license such a complement. Negative feature values have, therefore, a higher predictive power.

Every verbal lemma occurrence in the treebank is enriched with subcat features and three new factor templates have been defined in the parser in order to model the co-occurrence of subcat features and some syntactic configurations. These templates are represented in Figure 1. The first one is a first-order template and the others are grandchildren templates. In the template description, G, D and GD stand respectively for governor, dependent and grand-dependent. SF, POS, FCT and LEM respectively stand for subcat feature, part of speech, syntactic function and lemma.

1	G.SF	G.POS	D.FCT	D.POS	
2	G.SF	G.POS	D.FCT	D.POS	GD.POS
3	G.SF	G.POS	D.FCT	D.LEM	GD.POS

Figure 1: Factor templates modeling the co-occurrence of subcat features and syntactic configurations.

Two factors, of the types 1 and 3, have been represented in Figure 2. The first one models the co-occurrence of subcat feature -QUE and an object introduced by a subordinating conjunction. Such feature will receive a negative score at the end of training, since a verb having the -QUE feature should not license a direct object introduced by a subordinating conjunction. The second feature models the co-occurrence of the feature -QUE and a modifier introduced by the subordinating conjunction QUE and having an adverb as a dependent. Such a feature will receive a positive score.

1	-QUE	VRB	OBJ	CSU	
3	-QUE	VRB	MOD	QUE	ADV

Figure 2: Two factors modeling the co-occurrence of subcat features and syntactic configurations.

6 Experimental Setup

We test the proposed model to verify the linguistic plausibility and computational feasibility of using MORPH links to represent syntactically idiosyncratic MWEs in a dependency parser enriched with subcat features. Therefore, we train a probabilistic dependency parsing model on modified treebank, representing ADV+*que* and *de*+DET constructions using this special syntactic relation instead of pretokenization. Furthermore, in addition to regular features learned from the treebank, we also introduce and evaluate subcat features based on a lexicon of verbal valency, which helps identifying subordinative clauses and *de* prepositional phrases (see Section 5). We evaluate parsing precision and MWE identification on a test treebank and, more importantly, on a dataset built specifically to study the representation of our target constructions. All experiments used the NLP tool suite MACAON[5], which comprises a second-order graph-based parser.

6.1 Data Sets and Resources

French Treebank (FTB) The parser was trained on the French Treebank, a syntactically annotated corpus of news articles from *Le Monde* (Abeillé et al., 2003). We used the version which was transformed into dependency trees by Candito et al. (2009), and which was also used by Candito and Constant (2014) for experiments on MWE parsing. We used a standard split of 9,881 sentences (278K words) for training and 1,235 sentences for test (36K words). We applied simple rules to transform the flat representation of ADV+*que* and *de*+DET constructions into MORPH-linked individual tokens. All other MWEs are kept unchanged in training and test data. They are represented as single tokens, not decomposed into individual words.

MORPH **Dataset** The test portion of the FTB contains relatively few instances of our target constructions (see Tables 4 and 6). Thus, we have created two specific data sets to evaluate the prediction of MORPH links. As for ADV+*que* constructions, we manually selected the 7 most potentially ambiguous combinations from the top-20 most frequent combinations in the French Web as Corpus – frWaC (Baroni and Bernardini, 2006).[6] As for *de*+DET constructions, we selected all 4 possible combinations. For each target ADV+*que* and *de*+DET construction, we randomly selected 1,000 sentences from the frWaC based on two criteria: (1) sentences should contain only one occurrence of the target construction and (2) sentences should have between 10 and 20 words, to avoid distracting the annotators while still providing enough context. Additionally, for *de*+DET we selected only sentences in which a verb preceded the construction, in order to minimize the occur-

[5] http://macaon.lif.univ-mrs.fr

[6] http://wacky.sslmit.unibo.it/

ADV+*que*	#sent	conj.	other	#occur
ainsi	103	76.7	23.3	498,377
alors	110	88.2	11.8	291,235
autant	107	86.0	14.0	39,401
bien	99	37.4	62.6	156,798
encore	93	21.5	78.5	18,394
maintenant	120	55.8	44.2	16,567
tant	98	20.4	79.6	168,485
Total	730	56.4	43.6	1,189,257

Table 1: Annotations for ADV+*que* combinations in MORPH dataset: number of annotated sentences, proportion (%) of complex conjunction uses (MORPH) and other uses, number of occurrences in frWaC.

de+DET	#sent	det.	other	#occur
le (du)	136	33.1	66.9	16,609,049
la	138	21.0	79.0	10,849,384
les (des)	129	77.5	22.5	23,395,857
l'	136	16.9	83.1	8,204,687
Total	539	36.5	63.5	59,058,977

Table 2: Annotations for *de*+DET combinations MORPH dataset: number of annotated sentences, proportion (%) of complex determiner uses (MORPH) and other uses, number of occurrences in frWaC.

rence of nominal complements (*président de la république - president of the republic*) and focus on the determiner/preposition ambiguity. Two expert French native speakers annotated around 100 sentences per construction. Malformed or ambiguous sentences were discarded. Disagreements were either discussed and resolved or the sentence was discarded.[7]

We can see in Table 1 that ADV+*que* constructions are highly ambiguous, with 56.4% of the cases being complex conjunctions. However, they also present high variability: even though they share identical syntactic behavior, some of them tend to form complex conjunctions very often (*alors*) while others occur more often in other syntactic configurations (*tant* and *encore*). As one can see in Table 2, *de*+DET sequences tend to function as prepositions followed by a determiner with the notable exception of *de les*. The reason is that *de les* (actually the amalgame *des*) is actually the plural of the indefinite article (*un*), used with any plural noun, while the other determiners are partitives that tend to be used only with massive nouns. The last column of these tables shows the number of occurrences of each construction in the frWaC corpus. We can see that they are very recurrent combinations, specially *de*+DET constructions, which account for 3.7% of the total number of bigrams in the corpus. This underlines the importance of correctly predicting their syntactic structure in a parser.

DicoValence Lexicon DicoValence (van den Eynde and Mertens, 2003) is a lexical resource which lists the subcategorization frames of more than 3,700 French verbs.[8] It describes more specifically the number and nature of the verbs' complements. Dicovalence gives a more fine-grained description of the complements than what is needed in our feature templates. We have only kept, as described in Section 5, the subcat features -QUE, +QUE, -DE and +DE of each verb. Table 3 below shows the number of verbal entries having each of our four subcat features. Although the number of verbs described in DicoValence is moderate, its coverage is high on our data sets. It is equal to 97.82% on the FTB test set and is equal to 95.48% on the MORPH dataset.

-QUE	+QUE	-DE	+DE
3,814	356	3,450	720

Table 3: Number of verbs in DicoValence per value of subcat feature.

6.2 Evaluation

We evaluate our models on two aspects: parsing quality and MWE identification (Nivre and Nilsson, 2004; Vincze et al., 2013c; Candito and Constant, 2014). First, we use standard *parsing attachment scores* to verify whether our models impact parsing performance in general. We compare the generated dependency trees with the reference in the test portion of the FTB, reporting the proportion of matched links, both in terms of structure – unlabeled attachment score (UAS) – and of labeled links – labeled attachment score (LAS).

Since our focus is on MWE parsing, we are also

[7]The dataset is available at `http://pageperso.lif.univ-mrs.fr/%7Ecarlos.ramisch/?page=downloads/morph`

[8]`http://bach.arts.kuleuven.be/dicovalence/`

interested in *MWE identification metrics*. We focus on words whose dependency label is MORPH and calculate the proportion of correctly predicted MORPH links among those in the parser output (precision), among those in the reference (recall) and the F1 average. Since some of the phenomena are quite rare in the FTB test portion, we focus on the MORPH dataset, which contains around 100 instances of each target construction.

We compare our approach with two simple baselines. The first one consists in pretokenizing ADV+*que* systematically as a single token, while *de*+DET is systematically left as two separate tokens. This baseline emulates the behavior of most parsing pipelines, which deal with functional complex words during tokenization. This corresponds to choosing the majority classes in the last row of Tables 1 and 2. For ADV+*que*, the precision of the baseline is 56.4%. If we assume recall is 100%, this yields an F1 score of 72.2%. For *de*+DET, however, recall is 0% since no MORPH link is predicted at all. Therefore, we only look at the baseline's precision of 63.5%. A second, slightly more sophisticated baseline, consists in choosing the majority class for each individual construction and average precisions over the constructions. In this case, the average precision is 75.3% for ADV+*que* and 76.6% for *de*+DET.

We compare our model to the one proposed by Green et al. (2013). We used the pretrained model available as part of the Stanford parser[9]. Their model outputs constituent trees, which were automatically converted to unlabeled dependency structures. We ignore the nature of the dependency link, only checking whether the target construction elements are linked in the correct order.

Our experiments use the MACAON tool suite. For the FTB, gold POS and gold lemmas are given as input to the parser. In the case of the MORPH dataset, for which we do not have gold POS and lemmas, they are predicted by MACAON. The first best prediction is given as input to the parser.

7 Evaluation Results

7.1 ADV+*que* Constructions

Table 4 reports the performances of the parser[10] on the test set of FTB. The rows of the table respectively display the results obtained without and with the use of subcat features (SF). The second and third columns represent standard attachment metrics, column four displays the number of ADV+*que* conjunctions present in the FTB test set FTB and the two last columns show the precision and recall of the MORPH dependency prediction. The table shows that the number of occurrences of ADV+*que* conjunctions is very small (27). It is therefore difficult draw clear conclusions concerning the task of predicting the MORPH dependency. The precision and recall have nevertheless been reported. The recall is perfect (all MORPH dependencies have been predicted) and the the precision is reasonable (the parser overpredicts a little). The table also shows that the use of subcat features is not beneficial, as attachment scores as well as precision decrease. The decrease of precision is misleading, though, due to the small number of occurrences it has been computed on.

SF	LAS	UAS	MORPH	Prec.	Rec.
no	88.98	90.63	27	87.10	100
yes	88.96	90.56	27	81.81	100

Table 4: Attachment scores, count, precision and recall of the MORPH dependency for ADV+*que* in FTB test, without and with subcat features (SF).

Table 5 displays the precision, recall and F1 of the prediction of the MORPH dependency on the 730 ADV+*que* sentences of the MORPH dataset, without and with the use of subcat features. The scores obtained are lower than the same experiments on the FTB.Precision is higher than recall, which indicates that the parser has a tendency to underpredict. We also present the precision of the two baselines described in Section 6.2. Only in two cases the per-construction majority baseline (indiv.) outperforms our parser without subcat features. These two constructions do not tend to form complex conjunctions, that is, the parser overgenerates MORPH dependencies. Here, subcat features help increasing precision, systematically outperforming the baselines.

The introduction of subcat features has a beneficial but limited impact on the results, increasing precision and lowering a bit recall, augmenting the tendency of the parser to under predict MORPH dependencies. Overall, our models are more precise than the Stanford parser at predicting MORPH links, specially for *bien que* and *en-*

[9] `http://nlp.stanford.edu/software/lex-parser.shtml`

[10] Trained on the modified train set of the FTB, where complex conjunctions and partitive determiners have been represented by means of the MORPH dependency

	Baseline prec.		Green et	Without SF			With SF		
ADV+*que*	global	indiv.	al. (2013)	Prec.	Recall	F1	Prec.	Recall	F1
ainsi que	76.7	76.7	81.44	96.00	91.14	93.50	95.94	89.87	92.81
alors que	88.2	88.2	95.10	92.78	92.78	92.78	93.81	93.81	93.81
autant que	86.0	86.0	92.00	86.95	65.21	74.53	86.66	70.65	77.84
bien que	37.4	62.6	55.22	86.84	89.18	88.00	91.66	89.18	90.41
encore que	21.5	78.5	64.52	72.72	80.00	76.19	92.85	65.00	76.47
maintenant que	55.8	55.8	87.01	85.24	77.61	81.25	90.91	74.62	81.96
tant que	20.4	79.6	90.91	78.94	75.00	76.92	82.35	70.00	75.67
Total	56.4	75.3	83.06	88.71	**82.03**	85.24	**91.57**	81.79	**86.41**

Table 5: MORPH link prediction for ADV+*que* constructions: precision of global majority baseline, precision of individual per-construction baseline, precision of Green et al. (2013) constituent parser, precision, recall and F1 of our dependency parser without and with subcat features.

core que. However, this is not verified for all individual ADV+*que* constructions. The table also shows an important variety among the seven complex conjunctions studied. Some of them are very well predicted (F1 = 93.5) while others are poorly predicted (F1 = 75.67). This is partly due to the tendency of some ADV+*que* sequences to be part of larger frozen or semi-frozen constructions and to be used with a different semantico-syntactic behavior. An error analysis performed on the *tant que* sequence revealed that 40% of the errors were due to the occurrence of *tant que* as part of the larger *en tant que* expression, while 20% of the errors were due to the usage of *tant que* as a comparative expression.

7.2 *de*+DET Constructions

SF	LAS	UAS	MORPH	Prec.	Rec.
no	89.02	90.23	145	85.85	81.12
yes	88.37	89.67	145	86.52	83.92

Table 6: Attachment scores, count, precision and recall of the MORPH dependency for *de*+DET in FTB test, without and with subcat features (SF).

Table 6 reports the results of the same experiments on *de*+DET constructions. It shows that the frequency of *de*+DET constructions is higher than ADV+*que* constructions. It also shows that the introduction of subcat features has a positive impact on the prediction of the MORPH dependency, but a negative effect on the attachment scores.

Table 7 reveals that the prediction of the correct structure of *de*+DET constructions is more difficult than that of ADV+*que* constructions for the parser. Here, not only the majority class is the non-MWE analysis (63.5%), but also there is higher ambiguity because of nominal and adverbial complements that have the same structure. This impacts the performance of the Stanford parser, which overgenerates MORPH links, achieving the lowest precision for all constructions except for *des*. Results also show that the introduction of subcat features has an important impact on the quality of the prediction (F1 jumps from 75% to 84.67%). The use of subcat features slightly improves the identification of *de les*, which is a determiner most of the time. On the other hand, it greatly improves F1 for other constructions, which appear less often as determiners. We believe that the higher impact of subcat frames on *de*+DET is mainly due to the fact that the number of verbs licensing complements introduced by the preposition *de* is higher than the number of verbs licensing complements introduced by the conjunction *que* (see Table 3). Therefore, the parser trained without subcat features can only rely on the examples present in the FTB which are proportionally smaller in the first case than in the second.

8 Conclusions

This paper introduced and evaluated a joint parsing and MWE identification model that can effectively detect and represent ambiguous complex function words. The difficulty of processing such expressions is underestimated because of their limited variability. They often are pre-grouped as words-with-spaces in many parsing architectures (Sag et al., 2002). However, we did not use gold tokenization, unrealistic for ambiguous MWEs (Nivre and Nilsson, 2004; Korkontze-

	Baseline prec.		Green et	Without SF			With SF		
de+DET	global	indiv.	al. (2013)	Prec.	Recall	F1	Prec.	Recall	F1
de le	66.9	79.0	56.96	72.50	64.44	68.23	85.41	91.11	88.17
de la	79.0	77.5	22.83	58.13	86.20	69.44	81.25	89.65	85.24
de les	22.5	66.9	87.72	97.36	74.00	84.09	98.70	76.00	85.87
de l'	83.1	83.1	18.55	57.14	69.56	62.74	64.51	86.95	74.07
Total	63.5	76.6	44.37	77.00	73.09	75.00	**86.70**	**82.74**	**84.67**

Table 7: MORPH link prediction for *de*+DET constructions: precision of global majority baseline, precision of individual per-construction baseline, precision of Green et al. (2013) constituent parser, precision, recall and F1 of our dependency parser without and with subcat features.

los and Manandhar, 2010).

We proposed to deal with these constructions during parsing, when the required syntactic information to disambiguate them is available. Thus, we trained a graph-based dependency parser on a modified treebank where complex function words were linked with a MORPH dependency. Our results demonstrate that a standard parsing model can correctly learn such special links and predict them for unseen constructions. Nonetheless, the model is more accurate when we integrate external information from a syntactic lexicon. This improved precision for ADV+*que* and specially *de*+DET constructions. For the latter, F1 improved in almost 10%, going from 75% to 84.61%.

This study raised several linguistic and computational questions. Some complex function words include more than two elements, like *si bien que* (*so much that*) and *d'autant (plus) que* (*especially as*). Moreover, they may contain nested expressions with different meanings and structures, e.g. *tant que* (*as long as*) is a conjunction but *en tant que* (*as*) is a preposition. The same applies for quantified partitive determiners, like *beaucoup de* (*much*) and *un (petit) peu de* (*a (little) bit of*). Their identification and representation is planned as a future extension to this work.

We also would like to compare our approach to sequence models (Schneider et al., 2014). Careful error analysis could help us understand in which cases syntactic features can help. Moreover, different variants of the syntactic features and more sophisticated representation for syntactic lexicons can help improve MWE parsing further. For instance, we represent the subcat features of pronominal verbs and their simple versions with the same features, but they should be distinguished, e.g. *se rappeler* (*remember*) is +DE but *rappeler* (*remind*) is -DE.

Acknowledgements

This work has been funded by the French Agence Nationale pour la Recherche, through the projects ORFEO (ANR-12-CORP-0005) and ASFALDA (ANR-12-CORD-023) and by FAPERGS and CNRS through the AIM-WEST project.

References

Anne Abeillé, Lionel Clément, and François Toussenel. 2003. Building a treebank for french. In Anne Abeillé, editor, *Treebanks: building and using parsed corpora*, pages 165–168. Kluwer academic publishers, Dordrecht, The Netherlands.

Timothy Baldwin and Su Nam Kim. 2010. Multiword expressions. In Nitin Indurkhya and Fred J. Damerau, editors, *Handbook of Natural Language Processing*, pages 267–292. CRC Press, Taylor and Francis Group, Boca Raton, FL, USA, 2 edition.

Marco Baroni and Silvia Bernardini, editors. 2006. *Wacky! Working papers on the Web as Corpus*. GEDIT, Bologna, Italy. 224 p.

Bernd Bohnet. 2010. Top accuracy and fast dependency parsing is not a contradiction. In Huang and Jurafsky (Huang and Jurafsky, 2010), pages 89–97.

António Horta Branco and João Ricardo Silva. 2003. Contractions: Breaking the tokenization-tagging circularity. In Nuno J. Mamede, Jorge Baptista, Isabel Trancoso, and Maria das Graças Volpe Nunes, editors, *Proc. of the 6th PROPOR (PROPOR 2003)*, volume 2721 of *LNCS (LNAI)*, pages 195–195, Faro, Portugal, Jun. Springer.

Marie Candito and Matthieu Constant. 2014. Strategies for contiguous multiword expression analysis and dependency parsing. In *Proc. of the 52nd ACL (Volume 1: Long Papers)*, pages 743–753, Baltimore, MD, USA, Jun. ACL.

Marie Candito, Benoît Crabbé, Pascal Denis, and François Guérin. 2009. Analyse syntaxique du français : des constituants aux dépendances. In

Proc. of Traitement Automatique des Langues Naturelles, Senlis, France, Jun.

Matthieu Constant and Anthony Sigogne. 2011. MWU-aware part-of-speech tagging with a CRF model and lexical resources. In Kordoni et al. (Kordoni et al., 2011), pages 49–56.

Matthieu Constant, Marie Candito, and Djamé Seddah. 2013a. The LIGM-Alpage architecture for the SPMRL 2013 shared task: Multiword expression analysis and dependency parsing. In *Proceedings of the Fourth Workshop on Statistical Parsing of Morphologically-Rich Languages*, pages 46–52, Seattle, Washington, USA, October. Association for Computational Linguistics.

Matthieu Constant, Joseph Le Roux, and Anthony Sigogne. 2013b. Combining compound recognition and PCFG-LA parsing with word lattices and conditional random fields. *ACM Trans. Speech and Lang. Process. Special Issue on MWEs: from theory to practice and use, part 2 (TSLP)*, 10(3).

Eric De La Clergerie. 2013. Exploring beam-based shift-reduce dependency parsing with DyALog: Results from the SPMRL 2013 shared task. In *Proceedings of the Fourth Workshop on Statistical Parsing of Morphologically-Rich Languages*, pages 53–62, Seattle, Washington, USA, October. Association for Computational Linguistics.

Yoav Goldberg and Michael Elhadad. 2011. Joint hebrew segmentation and parsing using a PCFGLA lattice parser. In *Proc. of the 49th ACL: HLT (ACL HLT 2011)*, pages 704–709, Portland, OR, USA, Jun. ACL.

Spence Green and Christopher D. Manning. 2010. Better Arabic parsing: Baselines, evaluations, and analysis. In Huang and Jurafsky (Huang and Jurafsky, 2010), pages 394–402.

Spence Green, Marie-Catherine de Marneffe, and Christopher D. Manning. 2013. Parsing models for identifying multiword expressions. *Comp. Ling.*, 39(1):195–227.

Chu-Ren Huang and Dan Jurafsky, editors. 2010. *Proc. of the 23rd COLING (COLING 2010)*, Beijing, China, Aug. The Coling 2010 Organizing Committee.

Valia Kordoni, Carlos Ramisch, and Aline Villavicencio, editors. 2011. *Proc. of the ACL Workshop on MWEs: from Parsing and Generation to the Real World (MWE 2011)*, Portland, OR, USA, Jun. ACL.

Ioannis Korkontzelos and Suresh Manandhar. 2010. Can recognising multiword expressions improve shallow parsing? In *Proc. of HLT: The 2010 Annual Conf. of the NAACL (NAACL 2003)*, pages 636–644, Los Angeles, California, Jun. ACL.

S. Kübler, R. McDonald, and J. Nivre. 2009. Dependency parsing. *Synthesis Lectures on Human Language Technologies*, 1(1):1–127.

Nidhi Kulkarni and Mark Finlayson. 2011. jMWE: A Java toolkit for detecting multi-word expressions. In Kordoni et al. (Kordoni et al., 2011), pages 122–124.

Igor A. Mel'čuk. 1988. *Dependency Syntax: Theory and Practice*. State University of New York Press, New York.

Joakim Nivre and Jens Nilsson. 2004. Multiword units in syntactic parsing. In *Proc. of the LREC Workshop on Methodologies and Evaluation of Multiword Units in Real-World Applications (MEMURA)*, Lisbon, Portugal.

Ivan Sag, Timothy Baldwin, Francis Bond, Ann Copestake, and Dan Flickinger. 2002. Multiword expressions: A pain in the neck for NLP. In *Proc. of the 3rd CICLing (CICLing-2002)*, volume 2276/2010 of *LNCS*, pages 1–15, Mexico City, Mexico, Feb. Springer.

Nathan Schneider, Emily Danchik, Chris Dyer, and A. Noah Smith. 2014. Discriminative lexical semantic segmentation with gaps: Running the mwe gamut. *Transactions of the Association of Computational Linguistics – Volume 2, Issue 1*, pages 193–206.

Violeta Seretan. 2011. *Syntax-Based Collocation Extraction*, volume 44 of *Text, Speech and Language Technology*. Springer, Dordrecht, Netherlands, 1st edition. 212 p.

Karel van den Eynde and Piet Mertens. 2003. La valence: l'approche pronominale et son application au lexique verbal. *Journal of French Language Studies*, (13):63–104.

Aline Villavicencio, Valia Kordoni, Yi Zhang, Marco Idiart, and Carlos Ramisch. 2007. Validation and evaluation of automatically acquired multiword expressions for grammar engineering. In Jason Eisner, editor, *Proc. of the 2007 Joint Conference on EMNLP and Computational NLL (EMNLP-CoNLL 2007)*, pages 1034–1043, Prague, Czech Republic, Jun. ACL.

Veronika Vincze, István Nagy T., and Richárd Farkas. 2013a. Identifying English and Hungarian light verb constructions: A contrastive approach. In *Proc. of the 51st ACL (Volume 2: Short Papers)*, pages 255–261, Sofia, Bulgaria, Aug. ACL.

Veronika Vincze, István Nagy T., and János Zsibrita. 2013b. Learning to detect english and hungarian light verb constructions. *ACM Trans. Speech and Lang. Process. Special Issue on MWEs: from theory to practice and use, part 1 (TSLP)*, 10(2).

Veronika Vincze, János Zsibrita, and István Nagy T. 2013c. Dependency parsing for identifying hungarian light verb constructions. In *Proceedings of the Sixth International Joint Conference on Natural Language Processing*, pages 207–215, Nagoya, Japan, October. Asian Federation of Natural Language Processing.

Eric Wehrli, Violeta Seretan, and Luka Nerima. 2010. Sentence analysis and collocation identification. In Éric Laporte, Preslav Nakov, Carlos Ramisch, and Aline Villavicencio, editors, *Proc. of the COLING Workshop on MWEs: from Theory to Applications (MWE 2010)*, pages 27–35, Beijing, China, Aug. ACL.

End-to-end Learning of Semantic Role Labeling Using Recurrent Neural Networks

Jie Zhou and Wei Xu
Baidu Research
{zhoujie01,wei.xu}@baidu.com

Abstract

Semantic role labeling (SRL) is one of the basic natural language processing (NLP) problems. To this date, most of the successful SRL systems were built on top of some form of parsing results (Koomen et al., 2005; Palmer et al., 2010; Pradhan et al., 2013), where pre-defined feature templates over the syntactic structure are used. The attempts of building an end-to-end SRL learning system without using parsing were less successful (Collobert et al., 2011). In this work, we propose to use deep bi-directional recurrent network as an end-to-end system for SRL. We take only original text information as input feature, without using any syntactic knowledge. The proposed algorithm for semantic role labeling was mainly evaluated on CoNLL-2005 shared task and achieved F_1 score of 81.07. This result outperforms the previous state-of-the-art system from the combination of different parsing trees or models. We also obtained the same conclusion with $F_1 = 81.27$ on CoNLL-2012 shared task. As a result of simplicity, our model is also computationally efficient that the parsing speed is 6.7k tokens per second. Our analysis shows that our model is better at handling longer sentences than traditional models. And the latent variables of our model implicitly capture the syntactic structure of a sentence.

1 Introduction

Semantic role labeling (SRL) is a form of shallow semantic parsing whose goal is to discover the predicate-argument structure of each predicate in a given input sentence. Given a sentence, for each target verb (predicate) all the constituents in the sentence which fill a semantic role of the verb have to be recognized. Typical semantic arguments include Agent, Patient, Instrument, etc., and also adjuncts such as Locative, Temporal, Manner, Cause, etc.. SRL is useful as an intermediate step in a wide range of natural language processing (NLP) tasks, such as information extraction (Bastianelli et al., 2013), automatic document categorization (Persson et al., 2009) and question-answering (Dan and Lapata, 2007; Surdeanu et al., 2003; Moschitti et al., 2003).

SRL is considered as a supervised machine learning problem. In traditional methods, linear classifier such as SVM is often employed to perform this task based on features extracted from the training corpus. Actually, people often treat this problem as a multi-step classification task. First, whether an argument is related to the predicate is determined; next the detail relation type was decided(Palmer et al., 2010).

Syntactic information is considered to play an essential role in solving this problem (Punyakanok et al., 2008a). The location of an argument on syntactic tree provides an intermediate tag for improving the performance. However, building this syntactic tree also introduces the prediction risk inevitably. The analysis in (Pradhan et al., 2005) found that the major source of the incorrect predictions was the syntactic parser. Combination of different syntactic parsers was proposed to address this problem, from both feature level and model level (Surdeanu et al., 2007; Koomen et al., 2005; Pradhan et al., 2005).

Besides, feature templates in this classification task strongly rely on the expert experience. They need iterative modification after analyzing how the system performs on development data. When the corpus and data distribution are changed, or when people move to another language, the feature templates have to be re-designed.

To address the above issues, (Collobert et al.,

Proceedings of the 53rd Annual Meeting of the Association for Computational Linguistics and the 7th International Joint Conference on Natural Language Processing, pages 1127–1137,
Beijing, China, July 26-31, 2015.

2011) proposed a unified neural network architecture using word embedding and convolution. They applied their architecture on four standard NLP tasks: Part-Of-Speech tagging (POS), chunking (CHUNK), Named Entity Recognition (NER) and Semantic Role Labeling (SRL). They were able to reach the previous state-of-the-art performance on all these tasks except for SRL. They had to resort to parsing features in order to make the system competitive with state-of-the-art performance.

In this work, we propose an end-to-end system using deep bi-directional long short-term memory (DB-LSTM) model to address the above difficulties. We take only original text as the input features, without any intermediate tag such as syntactic information. The input features are processed by the following 8 layers of LSTM bidirectionally. At the top locates the conditional random field (CRF) model for tag sequence prediction. We achieve the state-of-the-art performance of f-score $F_1 = 81.07$ on CoNLL-2005 shared task and $F_1 = 81.27$ on CoNLL-2012 shared task. At last, we find the traditional syntactic information can also be inferred from the learned representations.

2 Related Work

People solve SRL problems in two major ways. The first one follows the traditional spirit widely used in NLP basic problems. A linear classifier is employed with feature templates. Most efforts focus on how to extract the feature templates that can best describe the text properties from training corpus. One of the most important features is from syntactic parsing, although syntactic parsing is also considered as a difficult problem. Thus system combination appear to be the general solution.

In the work of (Pradhan et al., 2005), the syntactic tags are produced by Charniak parser (Charniak, 2000; Charniak and Johnson, 2005) and Collins parser (Collins, 2003) respectively. Based on this, different systems are built to generate SRL tags. These SRL tags are used to extend the original feature templates, along with flat syntactic chunking results. At last another classifier learns the final SRL tag from the above results. In their analysis, the combination of three different syntactic view brings large improvement for the system.

Similarly, Koomen et al. (Koomen et al., 2005) combined the system in another way. They built multiple classifiers and then all outputs are combined through an optimization problem. Surdeanu et al. fully discussed the combination strategy in (Surdeanu et al., 2007).

Beyond the above traditional methods, the second way try to solve this problem without feature engineering. Collobert et al. (Collobert et al., 2011) introduced a neural network model consists of word embedding layer, convolution layers and CRF layer. This pipeline addressed the data sparsity by initializing the model with word embeddings which is trained from large unlabeled text corpus. However, the convolution layer is not the best way to model long distance dependency since it only includes words within limited context. So they processed the whole sequence for each given pair of argument and predicate. This results in the computational complexity of $O(n_p L^2)$, with L denoting the sequence length and n_p the number of predicate, while the complexity of our model is linear ($O(n_p L)$). Moreover, in order to catch up with the performance of traditional methods, they had to incorporate the syntactic features by using parse trees of Charniak parser (Charniak, 2000) which still provides the major contribution.

At the inference stage, structural constraints often lead to improved results (Punyakanok et al., 2008b). The constraints comes from annotation conventions of the task and other linguistic considerations. With dynamic programming, (Täckström et al., 2015) enhance the inference efficiency further. But designation of the constraints depends much on the linguistic knowledge.

Nevertheless, the attempts of building end-to-end systems for NLP become popular in recent years. Inspired by the work in computer vision, people hierarchically organized a window of words through convolution layers in deep form to account for the higher level of organization to solve the document classification task (Kim, 2014; Zhang and LeCun, 2015). Step further, people have also achieved success in directly mapping the sequence to sequence level target as the work in dependency parsing and machine translation (Vinyals et al., 2014; Sutskever et al., 2014).

3 Approaches

In this paper, we propose an end-to-end system based on recurrent topology. Recurrent neural network (RNN) has natural advantage in modeling sequence problems. The past information is built up through the recurrent layer when model consumes the sequence word by word as shown in Eq. 1. x and y are the input and output of the recurrent layer with (t) denoting the time step, w_f^m and w_i^m are the matrix from input or recurrent layer to hidden layer. σ is the activation function. Without $y^{(t-1)}$ term, the rnn model returns to the feed forward form.

$$y_m^{(t)} = \sigma(\sum_f w_f^m x_f^{(t)} + \sum_i w_i^m y_i^{(t-1)}) \quad (1)$$

However, people often met with two difficulties. First, information of the current word strongly depends on distant words, rather than its neighborhood. Second, gradient parameters may explode or vanish especially in processing long sequences (Bengio et al., 1994). Thus long short-term memory (LSTM) (Hochreiter and Schmidhuber, 1997) was proposed to address the above difficulties.

In the following part, we will first give a brief introduction about the LSTM and then demonstrate how to build up a network based on LSTM to solve a typical sequence tagging problem: semantic role labeling.

3.1 Long Short-Term Memory (LSTM)

Long short-term memory (LSTM) (Hochreiter and Schmidhuber, 1997; Graves et al., 2009) is an RNN architecture specifically designed to address the vanishing gradient and exploding gradient problems. The hidden neural units are replaced by a number of memory blocks. Each memory block contains several cells, whose activations are controlled by three multiplicative gates: the input gate, forget gate and output gate. With the above change, the original rnn model is improved to be:

$$\begin{aligned} y_m^{(t)} &= \sigma(s_{c,m}^{(t)}) \cdot \pi_m^{(t)} & (2) \\ &= \sigma(n_m^{(t)} \rho_m^{(t)} + \phi_m^{(t)} s_{c,m}^{(t-1)}) \cdot \pi_m^{(t)} & (3) \end{aligned}$$

Now y is the memory block output. n is equivalent to the original hidden value y in rnn model. ρ, ϕ and π are the input, forget and output gates value. $s_{c,m}$ is state value of cell c in block m and c is fixed to be 1 and omitted in common work. The computation of three multiplicative gates comes from input value, recurrent value and cell state value with different activations σ respectively as shown in the following and Fig. 1:

$$\begin{aligned} n_m^{(t)} &: \sigma_n(\sum_f w_{f,n}^m x_f^{(t)} + \sum_i w_{i,n}^m y_i^{(t-1)}) & (4) \\ \rho_m^{(t)} &: \sigma_\rho(\sum_f w_{f,\rho}^m x_f^{(t)} + \sum_i w_{i,\rho}^m y_i^{(t-1)} + w_\rho^m s_m^{(t-1)}) \\ \phi_m^{(t)} &: \sigma_\phi(\sum_f w_{f,\phi}^m x_f^{(t)} + \sum_i w_{i,\phi}^m y_i^{(t-1)} + w_\phi^m s_m^{(t-1)}) \\ \pi_m^{(t)} &: \sigma_\pi(\sum_f w_{f,\pi}^m x_f^{(t)} + \sum_i w_{i,\pi}^m y_i^{(t-1)} + w_\pi^m s_m^{(t)}) \end{aligned}$$

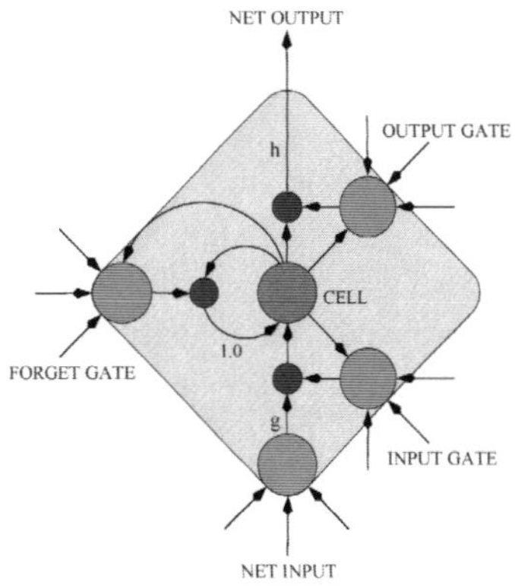

Figure 1: LSTM memory block with a single cell. (Graves et al., 2009)

The effect of the gates is to allow the cells to store and access information over long periods of time. When the input gate is closed, the new coming input information will not affect the previous cell state. Forget gate is used to remove the historical information stored in the cells. The rest of the network can access the stored value of a cell only when its output gate is open.

In language related problems, the structural knowledge can be extracted out by processing sequences both forward and backward so that the complementary information from the past and the future can be integrated for inference. Thus bi-directional LSTM (B-LSTM) containing two hidden layers were proposed(Schuster and Paliwal, 1997). Both hidden layers connect to the same input layer and output layer, processing the same sequence in two directions respectively (A. Graves, 2013).

In this work, we utilize the bi-directional information in another way. First a standard LSTM processes the sequence in forward direction. The output of this LSTM layer is taken by the next

LSTM layer as input, processed in reversed direction. These two standard LSTM layers compose a pair of LSTM. Then we stack LSTM layers pair after pair to obtain the deep LSTM model. We call this topology as deep bi-directional LSTM (DB-LSTM) network. Our experiments show that this architecture is critical to achieve good performance.

3.2 Pipeline

We process the sequence word by word. Two input features play an essential role in this pipeline: predicate (pred) and argument (argu), with argument describing the word under processing. The output for this pair of words is their semantic role. If a sequence has n_p predicates, we will process this sequence n_p times.

We also introduce two other features, predicate context (ctx-p) and region mark (m_r). Since a single predicate word can not exactly describe the predicate information, especially when the same words appear more than one times in a sentence. With the expanded context, the ambiguity can be largely eliminated. Similarly, we use region mark $m_r = 1$ to denote the argument position if it locates in the predicate context region, or $m_r = 0$ if not. These four simple features are all we need for our SRL system. In Tab. 1 we give an example sequence with the labels for each word. We do not use other types of features such as part of speech (POS), syntactic parsing, etc..

time	argu	pred	ctx-p	m_r	label
1	A	set	been set .	0	B-A1
2	record	set	been set .	0	I-A1
3	date	set	been set .	0	I-A1
4	has	set	been set .	0	O
5	n't	set	been set .	0	B-AM-NEG
6	been	set	been set .	1	O
7	set	set	been set .	1	B-V
8	.	set	been set .	1	O

Table 1: An example sequence with 4 input features: argument, predicate, predicate context (context length is 3) , region mark. "IOB" tagging scheme is used (Collobert et al., 2011).

Because the large number of parameters associated with the argument words, similar to (Collobert et al., 2011), the pre-trained word representations are employed to address the data sparsity issue. We used a large unlabeled text corpus to train a neural language model (NLM) (Bengio et al., 2006; Bengio et al., 2003) and then initialized the argument and predicate word representations with parameters from the NLM representations. There are various ways of obtaining good word representations (Mikolov et al., 2013; Collobert and Weston, 2008; Mnih and Kavukcuoglu, 2013; Yu et al., 2014). A systematic comparison of them on the task of SRL is beyond the scope of this work.

The above four features are concatenated to be the input representation at this time step for the following LSTM layers. As described in Sec. 3.1, we use DB-LSTM topology to learn the sequence knowledge and we build up to 8 layers of DB-LSTM in our work.

As in traditional methods, we employ CRF (Lafferty et al., 2001) on top of the network for the final prediction. It takes the representations provided by the last LSTM layer as input to model the strong dependance among adjacent tags.

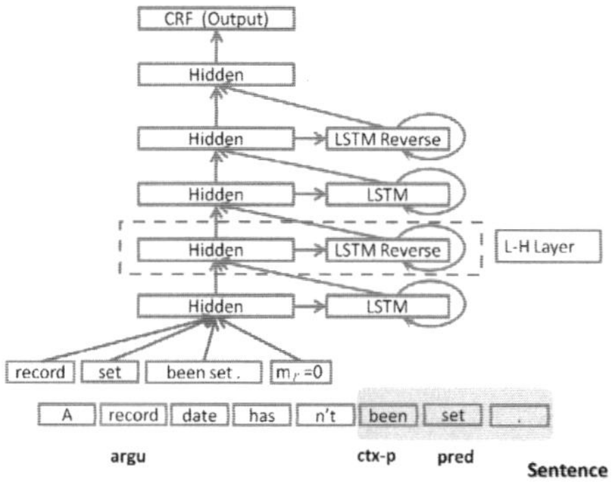

Figure 2: DB-LSTM network.Shadow part denote the predicate context within length 1.

The complete model with 4 LSTM layers is illustrated in Fig. 2. At the bottom of the graph locates the word sequence in Tab. 1. For a given time step (step 2 as an example), argument and predicate are specified with different color. We use the shadowed region to denote the predicate context. The temporal expanded version of the model is shown in Fig. 3. L-H denotes the LSTM hidden layer.

We use the stochastic gradient descent (SGD) algorithm as the training technique for the whole pipeline (Lecun et al., 1998). For a given sequence, we look up the embedding of each word and process this vector with the following LSTM layers for the high level representation. After having finished the whole sequence, we take the representations of all time steps as the input features

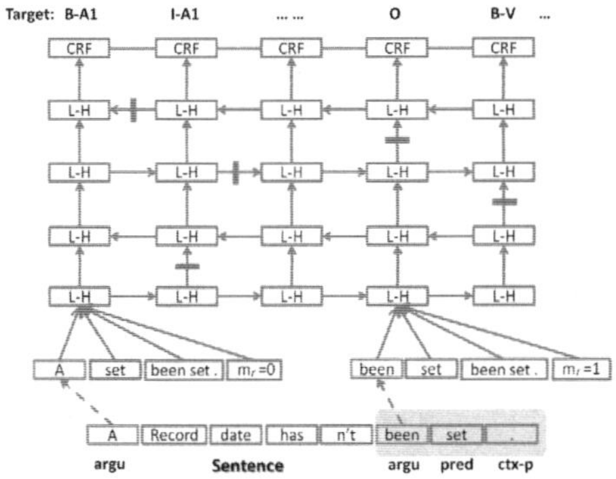

Figure 3: Temporal expanded DB-LSTM network. Bars denote that the connections are blocked by the closed gates. Shadow part denotes the predicate context.

for CRF to perform the sequence tagging task. The traditional viterbi decoding is used for inference. The gradient of the log-likelihood of the tag sequence with respect to the input of the CRF is calculated and back-propagated to all the DB-LSTM layers to get the gradient of the parameters (Collobert et al., 2011).

4 Experiments

We mainly evaluated and analyzed our system on the commonly used CoNLL-2005 shared task data set and the conclusions are also validated on CoNLL-2012 shared task.

4.1 Data set

CoNLL-2005 data set takes section 2-21 of Wall Street Journal (WSJ) data as training set, and section 24 as development set. The test set consists of section 23 of WSJ concatenated with 3 sections from Brown corpus (Carreras and Màrquez, 2005). CoNLL-2012 data set is extracted from OntoNotes v5.0 corpus. The description and separation of train, development and test data set can be found in (Pradhan et al., 2013).

4.2 Word embedding

We trained word embeddings with English Wikipedia (Ewk) corpus using NLM (Bengio et al., 2006). The corpus contains 995 million tokens. We transformed all the words into their lowercase and the vocabulary size is 4.9 million. About 5% words in CoNLL 2005 data set can not be found in Ewk dictionary and are marked as <unk>. In all experiments, we use the same word embedding with dimension 32.

4.3 Network topology

In this part, we will analyze the performance of two different networks, the CNN and LSTM network. Although at last we find CNN can not provide the results as good as that from LSTM, the analysis still help us to gain a deep insight of this problem. In CNN, we add argument context as the fifth feature and the other four features are the same as that used in LSTM. In order to have good understanding of the contribution from each modeling decision, we started from a simple model and add more units step by step.

4.3.1 Convolutional neural network

Using CNN to solve SRL problem has been introduced in (Collobert et al., 2011). Since we only focus on the analysis of features, a simplified version is used here.

Our feature set consists of five parts as described above. The representation of argument and predicate can be obtained by looking up the Emb(Ewk) dictionary. And the representation of argument context and predicate context can be obtained by concatenating the embedding of each word in the context. For each of the above four parts, we add a hidden layer. Then all these four hidden layers together with region mark are projected onto the next hidden layer. At last we use a CRF layer for prediction (See Fig. 4). With above set up, the computational complexity is $O(n_p L)$.

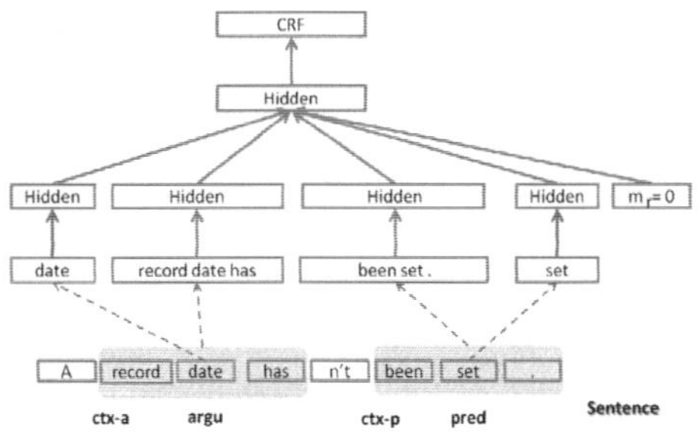

Figure 4: CNN Pipeline. Shadow parts denote the argument context and predicate context respectively

The size of hidden layers connected to argument or predicate is set to be $h_{1w} = 32$. The size of the other two hidden layers connected to context embedding is set to be $h_{1c} = 128$ since the corresponding inputs are larger. To simplify the parameter setting and results comparison, we use the same learning rate $l = 1 \times 10^{-3}$ for each layer and keep this rate a constant during model training. The second hidden layer dimension h_2 is also 128. All hidden layer activation function is $tanh$.

In Tab. 2, it is shown that longer argument and predicate context result in better performance, since longer context brings more information. We observe the same trends in other NLP experiments, such as NER, POS tagging. The difference is that we do not need to use the context length up to 11. This is because most of the useful information for NER and POS tagging is local respect the label position, while in SRL there exists long distance relationship. So in traditional methods for SRL, syntactic trees are often introduced to account for such relation. In order to see whether the improvement from CNN-2 to CNN-3 is due to longer context or larger model size, we tested a model CNN-6 with same context length but more model parameters. As we can see from the result of CoNLL-2005 data set (Tab. 2), larger model does not improve the result.

name	h_{1c}	ctx-a	ctx-p	m_r	F_1(dev)	F_1
CNN-1	128	1	5	y	41.22	41.24
CNN-2	128	5	5	y	51.83	52.09
CNN-3	128	11	5	y	52.81	53.07
CNN-4	128	11	1	y	49.69	50.70
CNN-5	128	11	5	n	36.40	37.50
CNN-6	256	5	5	y	51.60	51.91

Table 2: F_1 of CNN method on development set and test set of CoNLL-2005 data set.

Without using region mark (m_r) feature, the F_1 drops from the 53.07 of CNN-3 to the 37.50 of CNN-5. Since it is generally believed that words near the predicate are more likely to be related to the predicate.

SRL is a typical problem with long distance dependency, while the convolution operation can only learn the knowledge from the limited neighborhood. This is why we have to introduce long context. However, the language information can not be expressed just by linearly expanding the context as what we did in CNN pipeline. In order to better summarize the sequence structure, we turn to LSTM network.

4.3.2 LSTM network

Here the feature set consists of four parts. Argument and predicate are necessary parts in this problem. In recurrent model, argument context (ctx-a) is no longer needed and we only expand the predicate context. We also need the region mark defined in the same way as in CNN. The architecture has been shown in Fig. 2 and described in Sec. 3.2.

Since it is difficult to propagate the error from the top to the bottom layers, we use two learning rates. At the bottom, $i.e.$ from embeddings to the first LSTM layer, we use $l_b = 1 \times 10^{-2}$ for model depth $d <= 4$ and $l_b = 2 \times 10^{-2}$ for $d > 4$. For the other LSTM layers and CRF layer, we set learning rate $l = l_b \times 10^{-3}$. We kept all learning rates constant during training. The model size can be enlarged by increasing the number of LSTM layers (d) or the dimension of hidden layers (h). L2 weight decay in SGD is used for model regularization and we set its strength $r_2 = 8 \times 10^{-4}$:

$$w \leftarrow w - l \cdot (g + r_2 \cdot w) \quad (5)$$

where w denotes the parameter, g the gradient of the log likelihood of the label with respect to the parameter.

We started on CoNLL-2005 dataset from a small model with only one LSTM layer and $h = 32$. All word embeddings were randomly initialized. Predicate context length was 1. Region mark is not used. With this model, we obtained $F_1 = 49.44$ (Tab. 3), better than that of CNN without using argument context (41.24) or region mark (37.50). This result suggests that, the recurrent structure can extract sequential information more effectively than CNN.

By adding predicate context with length 5, F_1 is improved from 49.44 to 56.85 (Tab. 3). This is because we only recurrently process the argument word, so we still need predicate context for more detail. Further more, F_1 rises to 58.71 with region mark feature. The reason is the same as we explained in CNN pipeline.

Next we change the random initialization of word representation to the pre-trained word representation from Emb(Ewk). This representation is fixed in the training process. F_1 rises to 65.11 (See Tab. 3).

So far, we have shown the effect from each part of features in LSTM network. The conclusion is consistent with what we found in CNN network. Besides, LSTM exhibits better abilities to learn the sequence structure. Next, we gradually increase the model size to further enhance the performance.

Emb	d	ctx-p	m_r	h	F_1(dev)	F_1
CoNLL-2005 data set						
Ran	1	1	n	32	47.88	49.44
Ran	1	5	n	32	54.63	56.85
Ran	1	5	y	32	57.13	58.71
Ewk	1	5	y	32	64.48	65.11
Ewk	2	5	y	32	72.72	72.56
Ewk	4	5	y	32	75.08	75.74
Ewk	6	5	y	32	76.94	78.02
Ewk	8	5	y	32	77.50	78.28
Ewk	8	5	y	64	77.69	79.46
Ewk	8	5	y	128	79.10	80.28
fine tuning						
Ewk	8	5	y	128	79.55	81.07
CoNLL-2012 data set						
Ewk	8	5	y	128	80.51	80.70
fine tuning						
Ewk	8	5	y	128	81.07	81.27

Table 3: F_1 with LSTM method on development set and test set of CoNLL-2005 data set and CoNLL-2012 data set. Emb: the type of embedding. d: the number of LSTM layers. ctx-p: predicate context length. m_r: region mark feature. h: hidden layer size.

	F_1	F_1		
CoNLL-2005	dev	test	WSJ	Brown
Koomen	77.35	77.92	79.44	67.75
Koomen (single parser)	74.76	-	-	-
Pradhan	78.34	77.30	78.63	68.44
Collobert (w/ parser)	75.42	76.06	-	-
Collobert (w/o parser)	72.29	74.15	-	-
Surdeanu	-	-	80.6	70.1
Toutanova	78.6	-	80.3	68.8
Täckström	78.6	-	79.9	71.3
Ours	79.55	**81.07**	82.84	69.41
	F_1	F_1		
CoNLL-2012	dev	test	-	-
Pradhan	-	75.53		
Täckström	79.1	79.4		
Ours	81.07	**81.27**		

Table 4: Comparison with previous methods.

We find that the critical improvement comes from increasing the depth of LSTM network. After adding a reversed LSTM layer, F_1 is improved from 65.11 to 72.56. And the F_1 of the system with $d = 4, 6, 8$ are 75.74, 78.02 and 78.28 respectively. With 6-layer network, we have outperformed the CoNLL-2005 shared task winner system with $F_1 = 77.92$ (Koomen et al., 2005). Our experiment results also show that the further performance gain by increasing the depth from 6 to 8 is relative small.

Another way to increase the model size is to increase the hidden layer dimension h. We gradually increase the dimension from 32 to 64, 128, and the corresponding results are listed in Tab. 3. The best F_1 we obtained is 80.28 with $h = 128$. We also show the result $F_1 = 80.70$ on CoNLL-2012 dataset in Tab. 3 with exactly the same setup.

In the above experiments, learning rate and weight decay rate are fixed for the sake of simplicity in comparing different models. To further improve the model, we perform a fine tuning step to adjust the parameters based on previously trained model. This includes the relaxation of weight decay and decrease of learning rate. We set $r_2 = 4 \times 10^{-4}$ and $l_b = 1 \times 10^{-2}$, and obtain $F_1 = 81.07$ as the final result of CoNLL-2005 data set and $F_1 = 81.27$ of CoNLL-2012 data set.

In Tab. 4, we compare the performance of other works. On CoNLL-2005 shared task, merging syntactic tree at feature level instead of model level exhibits the similar performance with $F_1 = 77.30$ (Pradhan et al., 2005). After further investigation on model combination, Surdeanu et al. obtained a better system (Surdeanu et al., 2007). We also list the results from (Toutanova et al., 2008) and (Täckström et al., 2015) of the joint model with additional considerations of standard linguistic assumptions. For convolution based methods (Collobert et al., 2011), the best F_1 is 76.06, in which syntactic parser plays an essential role. The result without using parser drops down to 74.15. On Brown set, we observe the better performance from the work of (Surdeanu et al., 2007) and (Täckström et al., 2015). We hypothesize that DB-LSTM is a data-driven method that can not performs well on out-domain dataset.

On CoNLL-2012 data set, the traditional method gives $F_1 = 75.53$ (Pradhan et al., 2013) and a dynamic programming algorithm for efficient constrained inference in SRL gives $F_1 = 79.4$ (Täckström et al., 2015) , both of them also rely on syntax trees.

Since the input feature size is much smaller then the traditional sparse feature templates, the inference stage is very efficient that the model can process 6.7k tokens per second on average.

4.4 Analysis

We analyze our results on CoNLL-2005 data set. First we list the details including the performance on each sub-classes in Tab. 5. The results of CoNLL-2005 shared task winner system (Koomen et al., 2005) are also shown for comparison. Their

	Results (Koomen $et.al.$)			Results (Ours)		
Data set	P	R	F_1	P	R	F_1
dev	80.05	74.83	77.35	79.69	79.41	79.55
dev (s)	75.40	74.13	74.76	79.69	79.41	79.55
test WSJ	82.28	76.78	79.44	82.92	82.75	82.84
test Brown	73.38	62.93	67.75	70.70	68.17	69.41
test	81.18	74.92	77.92	81.33	80.80	81.07
A0	88.22	87.88	88.05	90.08	89.73	89.91
A1	82.25	77.69	79.91	82.00	82.87	82.43
A2	78.27	60.36	68.16	70.50	72.63	71.55
A3	82.73	52.60	64.31	63.98	55.68	59.54
AM-ADV	63.82	56.13	59.73	66.03	53.00	58.80
AM-DIS	75.44	80.62	77.95	73.76	78.07	75.85
AM-LOC	66.67	55.10	60.33	65.17	58.48	61.65
AM-MNR	66.79	53.20	59.22	56.36	54.63	55.48
AM-MOD	96.11	98.73	97.40	94.62	98.60	96.57
AM-NEG	97.40	97.83	97.61	95.70	95.36	95.53
AM-TMP	78.16	76.72	77.44	78.61	82.74	80.62
R-A0	89.72	85.71	87.67	94.72	93.57	94.14
R-A1	70.00	76.28	73.01	80.00	90.40	84.88
V	98.92	97.10	98.00	98.63	98.63	98.63

Table 5: F_1 on each sub sets and classes (CoNLL-2005). (We remove the classes with low statistics.)

final system is the combination of the results of 5 parsing trees from two different parsers. They also reported the scores of each single system on development set and we list the best one of them (dev(s)).

We observe the improvement of F_1 on development set and test set are 2.20 and 3.15 respectively. For single system, the improvement is 4.79 on development set. We also notice that our model show improvement on both WSJ and Brown test set. The advantage of our model is even more significant when comparing with the previous effort of end-to-end training of SRL model (Collobert et al., 2011). Without using linguistic features from parse tree, the F_1 of Collobert's model is 74.15, which is 6.92 lower than our model.

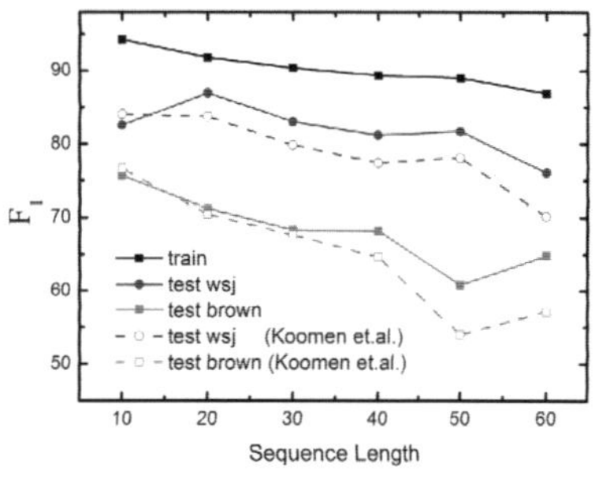

Figure 5: F_1 $vs.$ sentence length (CoNLL-2005).

In order to analyze the performance of our model on the sentences with different lengths, we split the data into 6 bins according to the sentence length, with bin width being 10 words and the last bin includes sequences with $L > 50$ because of insufficient data for longer sentences. Fig. 5 shows F_1 scores at different sequence lengths on WSJ test data and Brown test data for our model and Koomen's model (baseline) (Koomen et al., 2005). In all curves, performance degrades with increased sentence length. However, the performance gain of our model over the baseline model is larger for longer sentences.

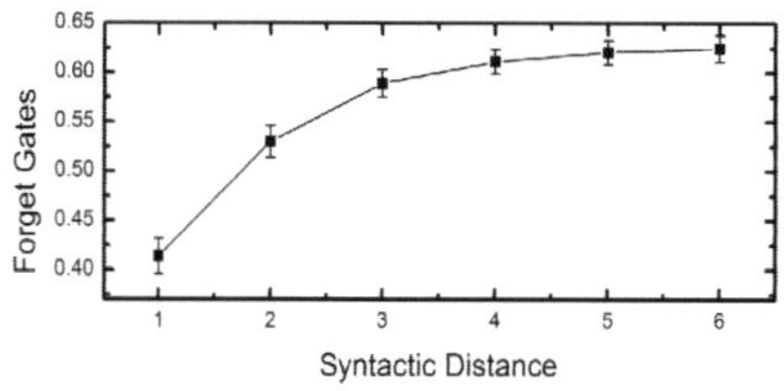

Figure 7: Averaged Forget gates value $vs.$ Syntactic distance (CoNLL-2005). The last point includes instances with syntactic distance $d_s \geq 6$.

Since we do not use any syntactic information as input feature, we are curious about whether this information can be extracted out from the system parameters. In LSTM, forget gates are used to control the use of historical information. We compute the average value v_{fg} of forget gates of the 7th LSTM layer at word position for a given sentence. We also introduce a variable named syntactic distance d_s to represent the number of edges between argument word and predicate word in the dependency parsing tree. Four example sentences are shown in Fig. 6. For each figure, the bottom axis denotes an example sentence. At the top of each graph is the corresponding dependency tree built from gold dependency parsing tag. At the bottom, v_{fg} and d_s are shown in black and red line. Noticed that the higher forget gates values means "Remember" and smaller values "Forget". Smaller d_s means that it is easy to make prediction that long history is unnecessary. On the contrary, large d_s results in a difficult prediction that long historical information is needed. We also computed the average v_{fg} over instances and found it monotonously increases with d_s(Fig. 7). The coincidence of v_{fg} and d_s suggests that the model implicitly captures some syntactic structure.

5 Conclusion and Future work

We investigate a traditional NLP problem SRL with DB-LSTM network. With this model, we are

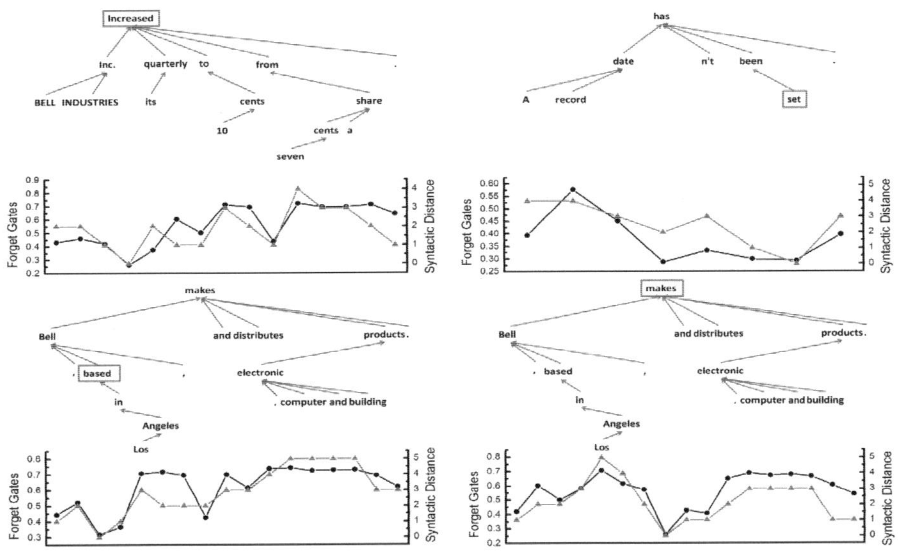

Figure 6: Forget gates value $vs.$ Syntactic distance on four example sentences. Top: dependency parsing tree from gold tag. Green square word: predicate word. Bottom black solid lines: forget gates value at each time step. Bottom red empty square lines: gold syntactic distance between the current argument and predicate.

able to bypass the traditional steps for extracting the intermediate NLP features such as POS and syntactic parsing and avoid human engineering the feature templates. The model is trained to predict the SRL tag directly from the original word sequence with four simple features without any explicit linguistic knowledge. Our model achieves F_1 score of 81.07 on CoNLL-2005 shared task and 81.27 on CoNLL-2012 shared task, both outperforming the previous systems based on parsing results and feature engineering, which heavily rely on the linguistic knowledge from expert. Furthermore, the simplified feature templates results in high inference efficiency with $6.7k$ tokens per second.

In our experiments, increasing the model depth is the major contribution to the final improvement. With deep model, we achieve strong ability of learning semantic rules without worrying about over-fitting even on such limited training set. It also outperforms the convolution method with large context length. Moreover, with more sophisticatedly designed network and training technique based on LSTM, such as the attempt to integrate the parse tree concept into LSTM framework (Tai et al., 2015), we believe the better performance can be achieved.

We show in our analysis that for long sequences our model has even larger advantage over the traditional models. On one hand, LSTM network is capable of capturing the long distance dependency especially in its deep form. On the other hand, the traditional feature templates are only good at describing the properties in neighborhood and a small mistake in syntactic tree will results in large deviation in SRL tagging. Moreover, from the analysis of the internal states of the deep network, we see that the model implicitly learn to capture some syntactic structure similar to the dependency parsing tree.

It is encouraging to see that deep learning models with end-to-end training can outperform traditional models on tasks which are previously believed to heavily depend on syntactic parsing (Koomen et al., 2005; Pradhan et al., 2013). However, we recognize that semantic role labeling itself is an intermediate step towards the language problems we really care about, such as question answering, information extraction etc. We believe that end-to-end training with some suitable deep structure yet to be invented might be proven to be effective to solving these problems. And we are seeing some recent active research exploring this possibility (Weston et al., 2014; Weston et al., 2015; Graves et al., 2014).

References

G. Hinton A. Graves, A. Mohamed. 2013. Speech recognition with deep recurrent neural networks. In *IEEE International Conference on Acoustics, Speech, and Signal Processing*, ICASSP 2013.

Emanuele Bastianelli, Giuseppe Castellucci, Danilo Croce, and Roberto Basili. 2013. Textual inference and meaning representation in human robot interaction. In *Proceedings of the Joint Symposium on Semantic Processing. Textual Inference and Structures in Corpora*, pages 65–69.

Yoshua Bengio, Patrice Simard, and Paolo Frasconi. 1994. Learning long-term dependencies with gradient descent is difficult. *IEEE Transactions on Neural Networks*, 5(2):157–166.

Yoshua Bengio, Réjean Ducharme, Pascal Vincent, and Christian Janvin. 2003. A neural probabilistic language model. *Journal of Machine Learning Research*, 3:1137–1155, March.

Yoshua Bengio, Holger Schwenk, Jean-Sbastien Sencal, Frderic Morin, and Jean-Luc Gauvain. 2006. Neural probabilistic language models. In *Innovations in Machine Learning*, volume 194 of *Studies in Fuzziness and Soft Computing*, pages 137–186. Springer Berlin Heidelberg.

Xavier Carreras and Lluís Màrquez. 2005. Introduction to the CoNLL-2005 shared task: Semantic role labeling. In *Proceedings of the Ninth Conference on Computational Natural Language Learning (CoNLL-2005)*, pages 152–164, Ann Arbor, Michigan, June. Association for Computational Linguistics.

Eugene Charniak and Mark Johnson. 2005. Coarse-to-fine n-best parsing and maxent discriminative reranking. In *Proceedings of the 43rd Annual Meeting on Association for Computational Linguistics*, ACL '05, pages 173–180, Stroudsburg, PA, USA. Association for Computational Linguistics.

Eugene Charniak. 2000. A maximum-entropy-inspired parser. In *Proceedings of the 1st North American Chapter of the Association for Computational Linguistics Conference*, NAACL 2000, pages 132–139, Stroudsburg, PA, USA. Association for Computational Linguistics.

Michael Collins. 2003. Head-driven statistical models for natural language parsing. *Comput. Linguist.*, 29(4):589–637, December.

Ronan Collobert and Jason Weston. 2008. A unified architecture for natural language processing: Deep neural networks with multitask learning. In *Proceedings of the 25th International Conference on Machine Learning*, ICML '08, pages 160–167, New York, NY, USA. ACM.

Ronan Collobert, Jason Weston, Léon Bottou, Michael Karlen, Koray Kavukcuoglu, and Pavel Kuksa. 2011. Natural language processing (almost) from scratch. *Journal of Marchine Learning Research*, 12:2493–2537, November.

Shen Dan and Mirella Lapata. 2007. Using semantic roles to improve question answering. In *Proceedings of the 2007 Joint Conference on Empirical Methods in Natural Language Processing and Computational Natural Language Learning (EMNLP-CoNLL)*.

Alex Graves, Marcus Liwicki, Santiago Fernandez, Roman Bertolami, Horst Bunke, and Jürgen Schmidhuber. 2009. A novel connectionist system for unconstrained handwriting recognition. *IEEE Transactions on Pattern Analysis and Machine Intelligence*, 31(5):855–868.

Alex Graves, Greg Wayne, and Ivo Danihelka. 2014. Neural turing machines. *arXiv:1410.5401*.

S. Hochreiter and J. Jürgen Schmidhuber. 1997. Long short-term memory. *Neural Computation*, 9(8):1735–1780.

Yoon Kim. 2014. Convolutional neural networks for sentence classification. In *Proceedings of the 2014 Conference on Empirical Methods in Natural Language Processing*, pages 1746–1751.

Peter Koomen, Vasin Punyakanok, Dan Roth, and Wen-tau Yih. 2005. Generalized inference with multiple semantic role labeling systems. In *Proceedings of the 9th Conference on Computational Natural Language Learning*, CONLL '05, pages 181–184, Stroudsburg, PA, USA. Association for Computational Linguistics.

John D. Lafferty, Andrew McCallum, and Fernando C. N. Pereira. 2001. Conditional random fields: Probabilistic models for segmenting and labeling sequence data. In *Proceedings of the 8th International Conference on Machine Learning*, ICML '01, pages 282–289, San Francisco, CA, USA. Morgan Kaufmann Publishers Inc.

Yann Lecun, Lon Bottou, Yoshua Bengio, and Patrick Haffner. 1998. Gradient-based learning applied to document recognition. In *Proceedings of the IEEE*, pages 2278–2324.

Tomas Mikolov, Ilya Sutskever, Kai Chen, Greg Corrado, and Jeffrey Dean. 2013. Distributed representations of phrases and their compositionality. In *Advances on Neural Information Processing Systems*.

Andriy Mnih and Koray Kavukcuoglu. 2013. Learning word embeddings efficiently with noise-contrastive estimation. In *Advances in Neural Information Processing Systems*, pages 2265–2273.

Alessandro Moschitti, Paul Morarescu, and Sanda M. Harabagiu. 2003. Open domain information extraction via automatic semantic labeling. In *FLAIRS Conference'03*, pages 397–401.

Martha Palmer, Daniel Gildea, and Nianwen Xue. 2010. *Semantic Role Labeling*. Synthesis Lectures on Human Language Technology Series. Morgan and Claypool.

Jacob Persson, Richard Johansson, and Pierre Nugues. 2009. Text categorization using predicatecargument structures. In *Proceedings of NODALIDA*, pages 142–149.

Sameer Pradhan, Kadri Hacioglu, Wayne Ward, James H. Martin, and Daniel Jurafsky. 2005. Semantic role chunking combining complementary syntactic views. In *Proceedings of the 9th Conference on Computational Natural Language Learning*, CONLL '05, pages 217–220, Stroudsburg, PA, USA. Association for Computational Linguistics.

Sameer Pradhan, Alessandro Moschitti, Nianwen Xue, Hwee Tou Ng, Anders Björkelund, Olga Uryupina, Yuchen Zhang, and Zhi Zhong. 2013. Towards robust linguistic analysis using ontonotes. In *Proceedings of the Seventeenth Conference on Computational Natural Language Learning*, pages 143–152, Sofia, Bulgaria, August. Association for Computational Linguistics.

V. Punyakanok, D. Roth, and W. Yih. 2008a. The importance of syntactic parsing and inference in semantic role labeling. *Computational Linguistics*, 34(2).

Vasin Punyakanok, Dan Roth, and Wen tau Yih. 2008b. The importance of syntactic parsing and inference in semantic role labeling. *Computational linguistics*, 6(9).

M. Schuster and K. K. Paliwal. 1997. Bidirectional recurrent neural networks. *IEEE Transactions on Signal Processing*, 45:2673–2681.

Mihai Surdeanu, Sanda Harabagiu, John Williams, and Paul Aarseth. 2003. Using predicate-argument structures for information extraction. In *Proceedings of the 41st Annual Meeting on Association for Computational Linguistics - Volume 1*, ACL '03, pages 8–15, Stroudsburg, PA, USA. Association for Computational Linguistics.

Mihai Surdeanu, Lluís Màrquez, Xavier Carreras, and Pere R. Comas. 2007. Combination strategies for semantic role labeling. *Journal of Artificial Intelligence Research*, 29:105–151.

Ilya Sutskever, Oriol Vinyals, and Quoc V Le. 2014. Sequence to sequence learning with neural networks. In *Advances on Neural Information Processing Systems*.

Oscar Täckström, Kuzman Ganchev, and Dipanjan Das. 2015. Efficient inference and structured learning for semantic role labeling. *Transactions of the Association for Computational Linguistics*, 3:29–41.

Kai Sheng Tai, Richard Socher, and Christopher D. Manning. 2015. Improved semantic representations from tree-structured long short-term memory networks. In *Proceedings of the 53st Annual Meeting on Association for Computational Linguistics*, ACL '15, Stroudsburg, PA, USA. Association for Computational Linguistics.

Kristina Toutanova, Aria Haghighi, and Christopher D. Manning. 2008. A global joint model for semantic role labeling. *Computational Linguistics*, 34:161–191.

Oriol Vinyals, Lukasz Kaiser, Terry Koo, Slav Petrov, Ilya Sutskever, and Geoffrey Hinton. 2014. Grammar as a foreign language. *arXiv:1412.7449*.

Jason Weston, Sumit Chopra, and Antoine Bordes. 2014. Memory networks. *arXiv:1410.3916*.

Jason Weston, Antoine Bordes, Sumit Chopra, and Tomas Mikolov. 2015. Towards ai-complete question answering: A set of prerequisite toy tasks. *arXiv:1502.05698*.

Mo Yu, Matthew Gormley, and Mark Dredze. 2014. Factor-based compositional embedding models. In *Advances in Neural Information Processing Systems Workshop on Learning Semantics*.

Xiang Zhang and Yann LeCun. 2015. Text understanding from scratch. *arXiv:1502.01710*.

Feature Optimization for Constituent Parsing via Neural Networks

Zhiguo Wang
IBM Watson
1101 Kitchawan
Yorktown Heights, NY, USA
zhigwang@us.ibm.com

Haitao Mi
IBM Watson
1101 Kitchawan
Yorktown Heights, NY, USA
hmi@us.ibm.com

Nianwen Xue
Brandeis University
415 South St
Waltham, MA, USA
xuen@brandeis.edu

Abstract

The performance of discriminative constituent parsing relies crucially on feature engineering, and effective features usually have to be carefully selected through a painful manual process. In this paper, we propose to automatically learn a set of effective features via neural networks. Specifically, we build a feedforward neural network model, which takes as input a few primitive units (words, POS tags and certain contextual tokens) from the local context, induces the feature representation in the hidden layer and makes parsing predictions in the output layer. The network simultaneously learns the feature representation and the prediction model parameters using a back propagation algorithm. By pre-training the model on a large amount of automatically parsed data, and then fine-tuning on the manually annotated Treebank data, our parser achieves the highest F_1 score at 86.6% on Chinese Treebank 5.1, and a competitive F_1 score at 90.7% on English Treebank. More importantly, our parser generalizes well on cross-domain test sets, where we significantly outperform Berkeley parser by 3.4 points on average for Chinese and 2.5 points for English.

1 Introduction

Constituent parsing seeks to uncover the phrase structure representation of sentences that can be used in a variety of natural language applications such as machine translation, information extraction and question answering (Jurafsky and Martin, 2008). One of the major challenges for this task is that constituent parsers require an inference algorithm of high computational complexity in order to search over their large structural space, which makes it very hard to efficiently train discriminative models. So, for a long time, the task was mainly solved with generative models (Collins, 1999; Charniak, 2000; Petrov et al., 2006). In the last few years, however, with the use of effective parsing strategies, approximate inference algorithms, and more efficient training methods, discriminative models began to surpass the generative models (Carreras et al., 2008; Zhu et al., 2013; Wang and Xue, 2014).

Just like other NLP tasks, the performance of discriminative constituent parsing crucially relies on feature engineering. If the feature set is too small, it might underfit the model and leads to low performance. On the other hand, too many features may result in an overfitting problem. Usually, an effective set of features have to be designed manually and selected through repeated experiments (Sagae and Lavie, 2005; Wang et al., 2006; Zhang and Clark, 2009). Not only does this procedure require a lot of expertise, but it is also tedious and time-consuming. Even after this painstaking process, it is still hard to say whether the selected feature set is complete or optimal to obtain the best possible results. A more desirable alternative is to learn features automatically with machine learning algorithms. Lei et al. (2014) proposed to learn features by representing the cross-products of some primitive units with low-rank tensors for dependency parsing. However, to achieve competitive performance, they had to combine the learned features with the traditional hand-crafted features. For constituent parsing, Henderson (2003) employed a recurrent neural network to induce features from an unbounded parsing history. However, the final performance was below the state of the art.

In this work, we design a much simpler neural network to automatically induce features from just the local context for constituent parsing. Con-

Proceedings of the 53rd Annual Meeting of the Association for Computational Linguistics and the 7th International Joint Conference on Natural Language Processing, pages 1138–1147,
Beijing, China, July 26-31, 2015.

cretely, we choose the shift-reduce parsing strategy to build the constituent structure of a sentence, and train a feedforward neural network model to jointly learn feature representations and make parsing predictions. The input layer of the network takes as input a few primitive units (words, POS tags and certain contextual tokens) from the local context, the hidden layer aims to induce a distributed feature representation by combining all the primitive units with different weights, and the output layer attempts to make parsing predictions based on the feature representation. During the training process, the model simultaneously learns the feature representation and prediction model parameters using a backpropagation algorithm. Theoretically, the learned feature representation is optimal (or at least locally optimal) for the parsing predictions. In practice, however, our model does not work well if it is only trained on the manually annotated Treebank data sets. However, when pre-trained on a large amount of automatically parsed data and then fine-tuned on the Treebank data sets, our model achieves a fairly large improvement in performance. We evaluated our model on both Chinese and English. On standard data sets, our model reaches $F_1 = 86.6\%$ for Chinese and outperforms all the state-of-the-art systems, and for English our final performance is $F_1 = 90.7\%$ and this result surpasses that of all the previous neural network based models and is comparable to the state-of-the-art systems. On cross-domain data sets, our model outperforms the Berkeley Parser [1] by 3.4 percentage points for Chinese and 2.5 percentage points for English.

The remainder of this paper is organized as follows: Section 2 introduces the shift-reduce constituent parsing approach. Section 3 describes our feature optimization model and some parameter estimation techniques. We discuss and analyze our experimental results in Section 4. Section 5 discusses related work. Finally, we conclude this paper in Section 6.

2 Shift-Reduce Constituent Parsing

Shift-reduce constituent parsing utilizes a series of shift-reduce decisions to construct syntactic trees. Formally, the shift-reduce system is a quadruple $C = (S, T, s_0, S_t)$, where S is a set of parser *states* (sometimes called *configurations*), T is a finite set of *actions*, s_0 is an initialization function

[1]https://code.google.com/p/berkeleyparser/

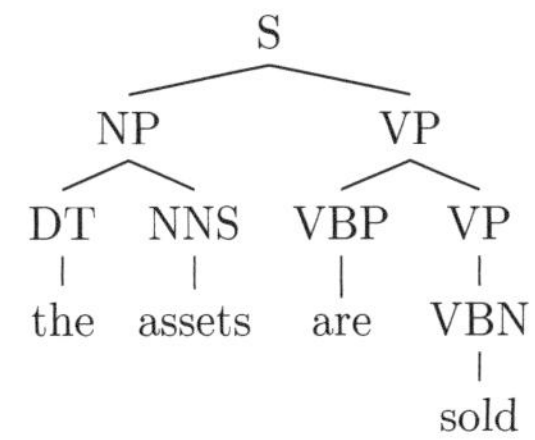

Figure 1: An example of constituent tree.

to map each input sentence into a unique *initial state*, and $S_t \in S$ is a set of *terminal states*. Each action $t \in T$ is a transition function that maps a state into a new state. A parser state $s \in S$ is defined as a tuple $s = (\sigma, \beta)$, where σ is a *stack* which is maintained to hold partial subtrees that are already constructed, and β is a *queue* which is used for storing remaining unprocessed words. In particular, the initial state has an empty stack σ and a queue β containing the entire input sentence, and the terminal states have an empty queue β and a stack σ containing only one complete parse tree. The task of parsing is to scan the input sentence from left to right and perform a sequence of shift-reduce actions to transform the initial state into a terminal state.

In order to jointly assign POS tags and construct a constituent structure for an input sentence, we define the following actions for the action set T, following Wang and Xue (2014):

- SHIFT-X (`sh-x`): remove the first word from β, assign a POS tag X to the word and push it onto the top of σ;
- REDUCE-UNARY-X (`ru-x`): pop the top subtree from σ, construct a new unary node labeled with X for the subtree, then push the new subtree back onto σ. The head of the new subtree is inherited from its child;
- REDUCE-BINARY-{L/R}-X (`rl/rr-x`): pop the top two subtrees from σ, combine them into a new tree with a node labeled with X, then push the new subtree back onto σ. The left (L) and right (R) versions of the action indicate whether the head of the new subtree is inherited from its left or right child.

With these actions, our parser can process trees with unary and binary branches easily. For example, in Figure 1, for the sentence "the assets are sold", our parser can construct the parse tree by performing the action sequence {sh-DT, sh-NNS, rr-NP, sh-VBP, sh-VBN, ru-VP, rr-VP, rr-S}. To process multi-branch trees, we employ binarization and debinarization processes described in Zhang and Clark (2009) to transform multi-branch trees into binary trees and restore the generated binary trees back to their original forms. For inference, we employ the beam search decoding algorithm (Zhang and Clark, 2009) to balance the tradeoff between accuracy and efficiency.

3 Feature Optimization Model

3.1 Model

To determine which action $t \in T$ should be performed at a given state $s \in S$, we need a model to score each possible $\langle s, t\rangle$ combination. In previous approaches (Sagae and Lavie, 2005; Wang et al., 2006; Zhang and Clark, 2009), the model is usually defined as a linear model $Score(s,t) = \overrightarrow{w} \cdot \Phi(s,t)$, where $\Phi(s,t)$ is a vector of hand-crafted features for each state-action pair and $\overrightarrow{w}$ is the weight vector for these features. The hand-crafted features are usually constructed by compounding primitive units according to some feature templates. For example, almost all the previous work employed the list of primitive units in Table 1(a), and constructed hand-crafted features by concatenating these primitive units according to the feature templates in Table 1(b). Obviously, these feature templates are only a small subset of the cross products of all the primitive units. This feature set is the result of a large number of experiments through trial and error from previous work. Still we cannot say for sure that this is the optimal subset of features for the parsing task.

To cope with this problem, we propose to simultaneously optimize feature representation and parsing accuracy via a neural network model. Figure 2 illustrates the architecture of our model. Our model consists of input, projection, hidden and output layers. First, in the input layer, all primitive units (shown in Table 1(a)) are imported to the network. We also import the suffixes and prefixes of the first word in the queue, because these units have been shown to be very effective for predicting POS tags (Ratnaparkhi, 1996). Then, in the projection layer, each primitive unit is projected into a vector. Specifically, word-type units are represented as word embeddings, and other units are transformed into one-hot representations. The vectors of all primitive units are concatenated to form a holistic vector for the projection layer. The hidden layer corresponds to the feature representation we want to learn. Each dimension in the hidden layer can be seen as an abstract factor of all primitive units, and it calculates a weighted sum of all nodes from the projection layer and applies a non-linear *activation function* to yield its activation. We choose the *logistic sigmoid* function for the hidden layer. The output layer is used for making parsing predictions. Each node in the output layer corresponds to a shift-reduce action. We want to interpret the activation of the output layer as a probability distribution over all possible shift-reduce actions, therefore we normalize the output activations (weighted summations of all nodes from the hidden layer) with the *softmax* function.

(1)	p_0w, p_0t,p_0c, p_1w, p_1t,p_1c, p_2w, p_2t,p_2c, p_3w, p_3t,p_3c
(2)	$p_{0l}w$, $p_{0l}c$, $p_{0r}w$, $p_{0r}c$,$p_{0u}w$, $p_{0u}c$, $p_{1l}w$, $p_{1l}c$, $p_{1r}w$, $p_{1r}c$,$p_{1u}w$, $p_{1u}c$
(3)	q_0w, q_1w, q_2w, q_3w

(a) Primitive Units

unigrams	p_0tc, p_0wc, p_1tc, p_1wc, p_2tc p_2wc, p_3tc, p_3wc, q_0wt, q_1wt q_2wt, q_3wt, $p_{0l}wc$, $p_{0r}wc$ $p_{0u}wc$, $p_{1l}wc$, $p_{1r}wc$, $p_{1u}wc$
bigrams	p_0wp_1w, p_0wp_1c, p_0cp_1w, p_0cp_1c p_0wq_0w, p_0wq_0t, p_0cq_0w, p_0cq_0t q_0wq_1w, q_0wq_1t, q_0tq_1w, q_0tq_1t p_1wq_0w, p_1wq_0t, p_1cq_0w, p_1cq_0t
trigrams	$p_0cp_1cp_2c$, $p_0wp_1cp_2c$, $p_0cp_1wq_0t$ $p_0cp_1cp_2w$, $p_0cp_1cq_0t$, $p_0wp_1cq_0t$ $p_0cp_1wq_0t$, $p_0cp_1cq_0w$

(b) Feature Templates

Table 1: Primitive units (a) and feature templates (b) for shift-reduce constituent parsing, where p_i represents the i_{th} subtree in the stack and q_i denotes the i_{th} word in the queue. w refers to the head word, t refers to the head POS, and c refers to the constituent label. p_{il} and p_{ir} refer to the left and right child for a binary subtree p_i, and p_{iu} refers to the child of a unary subtree p_i.

3.2 Parameter Estimation

Our model consists of three groups of parameters: (1) the word embedding for each word type unit,

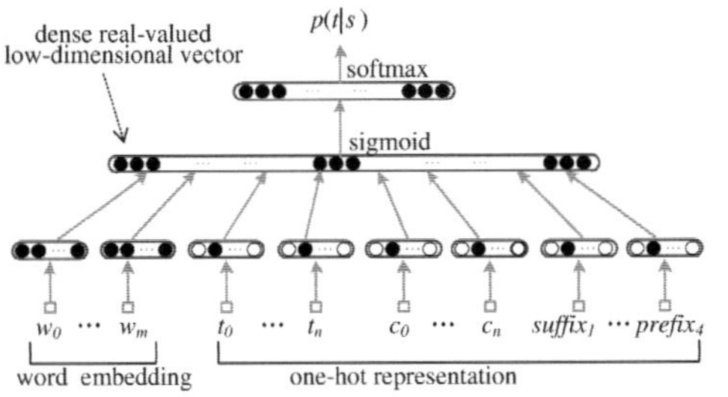

Figure 2: Neural network architecture for constituent parsing, where w_i denotes word type unit, t_i denotes POS tag unit, c_i denotes constituent label unit, $suffix_i$ and $prefix_i$ $(1 \le i \le 4)$ denotes i-character word suffix or prefix for the first word in the queue.

(2) the connections between the projection layer and the hidden layer which are used for learning an optimal feature representation and (3) the connections between the hidden layer and the output layer which are used for making accurate parsing predictions. We decided to learn word embeddings separately, so that we can take advantage of a large amount of unlabeled data. The remaining two groups of parameters can be trained simultaneously by the back propagation algorithm (Rumelhart et al., 1988) to maximize the likelihood over the training data.

We also employ three crucial techniques to seek more effective parameters. First, we utilize mini-batched AdaGrad (Duchi et al., 2011), in which the learning rate is adapted differently for different parameters at different training steps. With this technique, we can start with a very large learning rate which decreases during training, and can thus perform a far more thorough search within the parameter space. In our experiments, we got a much faster convergence rate with slightly better accuracy by using the learning rate $\alpha = 1$ instead of the commonly-used $\alpha = 0.01$. Second, we initialize the model parameters by pre-training. Unsupervised pre-training has demonstrated its effectiveness as a way of initializing neural network models (Erhan et al., 2010). Since our model requires many run-time primitive units (POS tags and constituent labels), we employ an in-house shift-reduce parser to parse a large amount of unlabeled sentences, and pre-train the model with the automatically parsed data. Third, we utilize the Dropout strategy to address the overfitting problem. However, different from Hinton et al. (2012), we only use Dropout during testing, because we found that using Dropout during training did not improve the parsing performance (on the dev set) while greatly slowing down the training process.

4 Experiment

4.1 Experimental Setting

We conducted experiments on the Penn Chinese Treebank (CTB) version 5.1 (Xue et al., 2005) and the Wall Street Journal (WSJ) portion of Penn English Treebank (Marcus et al., 1993). To fairly compare with other work, we follow the standard data division. For Chinese, we allocated Articles 001-270 and 400-1151 as the training set, Articles 301-325 as the development set, and Articles 271-300 as the testing set. For English, we use sections 2-21 for training, section 22 for developing and section 23 for testing.

We also utilized some unlabeled corpora and used the word2vec[2] toolkit to train word embeddings. For Chinese, we used the unlabeled Chinese Gigaword (LDC2003T09) and performed Chinese word segmentation using our in-house segmenter. For English, we randomly selected 9 million sentences from our in-house newswire corpus, which has no overlap with our training, testing and development sets. We use Evalb[3] toolkit to evaluate parsing performance.

4.2 Characteristics of Our Model

There are several hyper-parameters in our model, e.g., the word embedding dimension ($wordDim$), the hidden layer node size ($hiddenSize$), the Dropout ratio ($dropRatio$) and the beam size for inference ($beamSize$). The choice of these hyper-parameters may affect the final performance. In this subsection, we present some experiments to demonstrate the characteristics of our model, and select a group of proper hyper-parameters that we use to evaluate our final model. All the experiments in this subsection were performed on Chinese data and the evaluation is performed on Chinese development set.

First, we evaluated the effectiveness of various primitive units. We set $wordDim = 300$, $hiddenSize = 300$, $beamSize = 8$, and did not apply Dropout ($dropRatio = 0$). Table 2 presents the results. By comparing numbers in other rows

[2]https://code.google.com/p/word2vec/

[3]http://nlp.cs.nyu.edu/evalb/

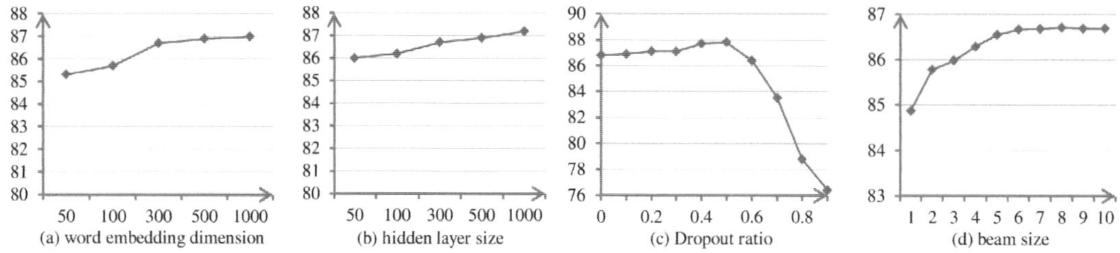

Figure 3: Influence of hyper-parameters.

with row "All Units", we found that ablating the Prefix and Suffix units ("w/o Prefix & Suffix") significantly hurts both POS tagging and parsing performance. Ablating POS units ("w/o POS") or constituent label units ("w/o NT") has little effect on POS tagging accuracy, but hurts parsing performance. When only keeping the word type units ("Only Word"), both the POS tagging and parsing accuracy drops drastically. So the Prefix and Suffix units are crucial for POS tagging, and POS units and constituent label units are helpful for parsing performance. All these primitive units are indispensable to better performance.

Second, we uncovered the effect of the dimension of word embedding. We set $hiddenSize = 300$, $beamSize = 8$, $dropRatio = 0$ and varied $wordDim$ among {50, 100, 300, 500, 1000}. Figure 3(a) draws the parsing performance curve. When increasing $wordDim$ from 50 to 300, parsing performance improves more than 1.5 percentage points. After that, the curve flattens out, and parsing performance only gets marginal improvement. Therefore, in the following experiments, we fixed $wordDim = 300$.

Third, we tested the effect of hidden layer node size. We varied $hiddenSize$ among {50, 100, 300, 500, 1000}. Figure 3(b) draws the parsing performance curve. We found increasing $hiddenSize$ is helpful for parsing performance. However, higher $hiddenSize$ would greatly increase the amount of computation. To keep the efficiency of our model, we fixed $hiddenSize = 300$ in the following experiments.

Fourth, we applied Dropout and tuned the Dropout ratio through experiments. Figure 3(c) shows the results. We found that the peak performance occurred at $dropRatio = 0.5$, which brought about an improvement of more than 1 percentage point over the model without Dropout ($dropRatio = 0$). Therefore, we fixed $dropRatio = 0.5$.

Primitive Units	F_1	POS
All Units	86.7	96.7
w/o Prefix & Suffix	85.7	95.4
w/o POS	86.0	96.7
w/o NT	86.2	96.6
Only Word	82.7	95.2

Table 2: Influence of primitive units.

Finally, we investigated the effect of beam size. Figure 3(d) shows the curve. We found increasing $beamSize$ greatly improves the performance initially, but no further improvement is observed after $beamSize$ is greater than 8. Therefore, we fixed $beamSize = 8$ in the following experiments.

4.3 Semi-supervised Training

In this subsection, we investigated whether we can train more effective models using automatically parsed data. We randomly selected 200K sentences from our unlabeled data sets for both Chinese and English. Then, we used an in-house shift-reduce parser[4] to parse these selected sentences. The size of the automatically parsed data set may have an impact on the final model. So we trained many models with varying amounts of automatically parsed data. We also designed two strategies to exploit the automatically parsed data. The first strategy (Mix-Train) is to directly add the automatically parsed data to the hand-annotated training set and train models with the mixed data set. The second strategy (Pre-Train) is to first pretrain models with the automatically parsed data, and then fine-tune models with the hand-annotated training set.

Table 3 shows results of different experimental configurations for Chinese. For the Mix-Train

[4]Its performance is F_1 =83.9 on Chinese and F_1 =90.8% on English.

# Auto Sent	Mix-Train F_1	Mix-Train POS	Pre-Train F_1	Pre-Train POS
0	87.8	97.0	—	—
50K	87.2	96.8	88.4	97.1
100K	88.7	96.9	89.5	97.1
200K	89.2	97.2	89.5	97.4

Table 3: Semi-supervised training for Chinese.

# Auto Sent	Mix-Train F_1	Mix-Train POS	Pre-Train F_1	Pre-Train POS
0	89.7	96.6	—	—
50K	89.4	96.1	90.2	96.4
100K	89.5	96.0	90.4	96.5
200K	89.2	95.8	90.8	96.7

Table 4: Semi-supervised training for English.

strategy, when we only use 50K automatically parsed sentences, the performance drops in comparison with the model trained without using any automatically parsed data. When we increase the automatically parsed data to 100K sentences, the parsing performance improves about 1 percent but the POS tagging accuracy drops slightly. When we further increase the automatically parsed data to 200K sentences, both the parsing performance and POS tagging accuracy improve. For the Pre-Train strategy, the performance of all three configurations improves performance against the model that does not use any automatically parsed data. The Pre-Train strategy consistently outperforms the Mix-Train strategy when the same amount of automatically parsed data is used. Therefore, for Chinese, the Pre-Train strategy is much more helpful, and the more automatically parsed data we use the better performance we get.

Table 4 presents results of different experimental configurations for English. The performance trend for the Mix-Train strategy is different from that of Chinese. Here, no matter how much automatically parsed data we use, there is a consistent degradation in performance against the model that does not use any automatically parsed data at all. And the more automatically parsed data we use, the larger the drop in accuracy. For the Pre-Train strategy, the trend is similar to Chinese. The parsing performance of the Pre-Train setting consistently improves as the size of automatically parsed data increases.

Type	System	F_1
Ours	Supervised*‡	83.2
	Pretrain-Finetune*‡	**86.6**
SI	Petrov and Klein (2007)	83.3
	Wang and Xue (2014)‡	83.6
SE	Zhu et al. (2013)‡	85.6
	Wang and Xue (2014)‡	86.3
RE	Charniak and Johnson (2005)	82.3
	Wang and Zong (2011)	85.7

Table 5: Comparison with the state-of-the-art systems on Chinese test set. * marks neural network based systems. ‡ marks shift-reduce parsing systems.

4.4 Comparing With State-of-the-art Systems

In this subsection, we present the performance of our models on the testing sets. We trained two systems. The first system ("Supervised") is trained only with the hand-annotated training set, and the second system ("Pretrain-Finetune") is trained with the Pre-Train strategy described in subsection 4.3 using additional automatically parsed data. The best parameters for the two systems are set based on their performance on the development set. To further illustrate the effectiveness of our systems, we also compare them with some state-of-the-art systems. We group parsing systems into three categories: supervised single systems (SI), semi-supervised single systems (SE) and reranking systems (RE). Both of our two models belong to semi-supervised single systems, because our "Supervised" system utilized word embeddings in its input layer.

Table 5 lists the performance of our systems as well as the state-of-the-art systems on Chinese test set. Comparing the performance of our two systems, we see that our "Pretrain-Finetune" system shows a fairly large gain over the "Supervised" system. One explanation is that our neural network model is a non-linear model, so the back propagation algorithm can only reach a local optimum. In our "Supervised" system the starting points are randomly initialized in the parameter space, so it only reaches local optimum. In comparison, our "Pretrain-Finetune" system gets to see large amount of automatically parsed data, and initializes the starting points with the pre-trained

Type	System	F_1
Ours	Supervised*‡	89.4
	Pretrain-Finetune*‡	90.7
SI	Collins (1999)	88.2
	Charniak (2000)	89.5
	Henderson (2003)*	88.8
	Petrov and Klein (2007)	90.1
	Carreras et al. (2008)	91.1
	Zhu et al. (2013)‡	90.4
SE	Huang et al. (2010)	91.6
	Collobert (2011)*	89.1
	Zhu et al. (2013)‡	91.3
RE	Henderson (2004)*	90.1
	Charniak and Johnson (2005)	91.5
	McClosky et al. (2006)	**92.3**
	Huang (2008)	91.7
	Socher et al. (2013)*	90.4

Table 6: Comparing with the state-of-the-art systems on English test set. * marks neural network based systems. ‡ marks shift-reduce parsing systems.

parameters. So it finds a much better local optimum than the "Supervised" system. Comparing our "Pretrain-Finetune" system with all the state-of-the-art systems, we see our system surpass all the other systems. Although our system only utilizes some basic primitive units (in Table 1(a)), it still outperforms Wang and Xue (2014)'s shift-reduce parsing system which uses more complex structural features and semi-supervised word cluster features. Therefore, our model can simultaneously learn an effective feature representation and make accurate parsing predictions for Chinese.

Table 6 presents the performance of our systems as well as the state-of-the-art systems on the English test set. Our "Pretrain-Finetune" system still achieves much better performance than the "Supervised" system, although the gap is smaller than that of Chinese. Our "Pretrain-Finetune" system also outperforms all other neural network based systems (systems marked with *). Although our system does not outperform all the state-of-the-art systems, the performance is comparable to most of them. So our model is also effective for English parsing.

4.5 Cross Domain Evaluation

In this subsection, we examined the robustness of our model by evaluating it on data sets from various domains. We use the Berkeley Parser as our baseline parser, and trained it on our training set.

For Chinese, we performed our experiments on the cross domain data sets from Chinese Treebank 8.0 (Xue et al., 2013). It consists of six domains: newswire (nw), magazine articles (mz), broadcast news (bn), broadcast conversation (bc), weblogs (wb) and discussion forums (df). Since all of the mz domain data is already included in our training set, we only selected sample sentences from the other five domains as the test sets [5], and made sure these test sets had no overlap with our treebank training, development and test sets. Note that we did not use any data from these five domains for training or development. The models are still the ones described in the previous subsection. The results are presented in Table 7. Although our "Supervised" model got slightly worse performance than the Berkeley Parser (Petrov and Klein, 2007), as shown in Table 5, it outperformed the Berkeley Parser on the cross-domain data sets. This suggests that the learned features can better adapt to cross-domain situations. Compared with the Berkeley Parser, on average our "Pretrain-Finetune" model is 3.4 percentage points better in terms of parsing accuracy, and 3.2 percentage points better in terms of POS tagging accuracy. We also presented the performance of our pre-trained model ("Only-Pretrain"). We found the "Only-Pretrain" model performs poorly on this cross-domain data sets. But even pretraining based on this less than competitive model, our "Pretrain-Finetune" model achieves significant improvement over the "Supervised" model. So the Pre-Train strategy is crucial to our model.

For English, we performed our experiments on the cross-domain data sets from OntoNote 5.0 (Weischedel et al., 2013), which consists of nw, mz, bn, bc, wb, df and telephone conversations (tc). We also performed experiments on the SMS domain, using data annotated by the LDC for the DARPA BOLT Program. We randomly selected 300 sentences for each domain as the test sets [5]. Table 8 presents our experimental results. To save space, we only presented the results of our "Pretrain-Finetune" model and the Berkeley

[5]The selected sentences can be downloaded from http://www.cs.brandeis.edu/ xuen/publications.html

domain	Only-Pretrain F_1	Only-Pretrain POS	Supervised F_1	Supervised POS	Pretrain-Finetune F_1	Pretrain-Finetune POS	BerkeleyParser F_1	BerkeleyParser POS
bc	61.6	81.1	72.9	90.2	74.9	91.2	68.2	86.4
bn	—	—	78.2	93.2	80.8	94.2	78.3	91.2
df	65.6	84.5	76.2	91.7	78.5	92.6	75.9	90.3
nw	72.0	86.1	82.1	95.2	85.0	95.8	82.9	93.6
wb	65.4	81.5	74.6	89.5	76.9	90.2	73.8	86.7
average	66.2	83.3	76.8	92.0	79.2	92.8	75.8	89.6

Table 7: Cross-domain performance for Chinese. The "Only-Pretrain" model cannot successfully parse some sentences in bn domain, so we didn't give the numbers.

Domain	Pretrain-Finetune F_1	Pretrain-Finetune POS	BerkeleyParser F_1	BerkeleyParser POS
bc	77.7	92.2	76.0	91.1
bn	88.1	95.4	88.2	95.0
df	82.5	93.3	79.4	92.4
nw	89.6	95.3	86.2	94.6
wb	83.3	93.1	82.0	91.2
sms	79.2	85.8	74.6	85.3
tc	74.2	88.0	71.1	87.6
average	82.1	91.9	79.6	91.0

Table 8: Cross-domain performance for English.

Parser. Except for the slightly worse performance on the bn domain, our model outperformed the Berkeley Parser on all the other domains. While our model is only 0.6 percentage point better than the Berkeley Parser (Petrov and Klein, 2007) when evaluated on the standard Penn TreeBank test set (Table 6), our parser is 2.5 percentage points better on average on the cross domain data sets. So our parser is also very robust for English on cross-domain data sets.

5 Related Work

There has been some work on feature optimization in dependency parsing, but most prior work in this area is limited to selecting an optimal subset of features from a set of candidate features (Nilsson and Nugues, 2010; Ballesteros and Bohnet, 2014). Lei et al. (2014) proposed to learn features for dependency parsing automatically. They first represented all possible features with a multi-way tensor, and then transformed it into a low-rank tensor as the final features that are actually used by their system. However, to obtain competitive performance, they had to combine the learned features with traditional hand-crafted features. Chen and Manning (2014) proposed to learn a dense feature vector for transition-based dependency parsing via neural networks. Their model had to learn POS tag embeddings and dependency label embeddings first, and then induced the dense feature vector based on these embeddings. Comparing with their method, our model is much simpler. Our model learned features directly based on the original form of primitive units.

There have also been some attempts to use neural networks for constituent parsing. Henderson (2003) presented the first neural network for broad coverage parsing. Later, he also proposed to rerank k-best parse trees with a neural network model which achieved state-of-the-art performance (Henderson, 2004). Collobert (2011) designed a recurrent neural network model to construct parse tree by stacks of sequences labeling, but its final performance is significantly lower than the state-of-the-art performance. Socher et al. (2013) built a recursive neural network for constituent parsing. However, rather than performing full inference, their model can only score parse candidates generated from another parser. Our model also requires a parser to generate training samples for pre-training. However, our system is different in that, during testing, our model performs full inference with no need of other parsers. Vinyals et al. (2014) employed a Long Short-Term Memory (LSTM) neural network for parsing. By training on a much larger hand-annotated data set, their performance reached 91.6% for English.

6 Conclusion

In this paper, we proposed to learn features via a neural network model. By taking as input the primitive units, our neural network model learns feature representations in the hidden layer and made parsing predictions based on the learned features in the output layer. By employing the back-propagation algorithm, our model simultaneously induced features and learned prediction model parameters. We show that our model achieved significant improvement from pretraining on a substantial amount of pre-parsed data. Evaluated on standard data sets, our model outperformed all state-of-the-art parsers on Chinese and all neural network based models on English. We also show that our model is particularly effective on cross-domain tasks for both Chinese and English.

Acknowledgments

We thank the anonymous reviewers for comments. Haitao Mi is supported by DARPA HR0011-12-C-0015 (BOLT) and Nianwen Xue is supported by DAPRA HR0011-11-C-0145 (BOLT). The views and findings in this paper are those of the authors and are not endorsed by the DARPA.

References

Miguel Ballesteros and Bernd Bohnet. 2014. Automatic feature selection for agenda-based dependency parsing.

Xavier Carreras, Michael Collins, and Terry Koo. 2008. Tag, dynamic programming, and the perceptron for efficient, feature-rich parsing. In *Proceedings of the Twelfth Conference on Computational Natural Language Learning*, pages 9–16. Association for Computational Linguistics.

Eugene Charniak and Mark Johnson. 2005. Coarse-to-fine n-best parsing and maxent discriminative reranking. In *Proceedings of the 43rd Annual Meeting on Association for Computational Linguistics*, pages 173–180. Association for Computational Linguistics.

Eugene Charniak. 2000. A maximum-entropy-inspired parser. In *Proceedings of the 1st North American chapter of the Association for Computational Linguistics conference*, pages 132–139. Association for Computational Linguistics.

Danqi Chen and Christopher D Manning. 2014. A fast and accurate dependency parser using neural networks. In *Proceedings of the 2014 Conference on Empirical Methods in Natural Language Processing (EMNLP)*, pages 740–750.

Michael Collins. 1999. *HEAD-DRIVEN STATISTICAL MODELS FOR NATURAL LANGUAGE PARSING*. Ph.D. thesis, University of Pennsylvania.

Ronan Collobert. 2011. Deep learning for efficient discriminative parsing. In *International Conference on Artificial Intelligence and Statistics*, number EPFL-CONF-192374.

John Duchi, Elad Hazan, and Yoram Singer. 2011. Adaptive subgradient methods for online learning and stochastic optimization. *The Journal of Machine Learning Research*, 12:2121–2159.

Dumitru Erhan, Yoshua Bengio, Aaron Courville, Pierre-Antoine Manzagol, Pascal Vincent, and Samy Bengio. 2010. Why does unsupervised pre-training help deep learning? *The Journal of Machine Learning Research*, 11:625–660.

James Henderson. 2003. Neural network probability estimation for broad coverage parsing. In *Proceedings of the tenth conference on European chapter of the Association for Computational Linguistics-Volume 1*, pages 131–138. Association for Computational Linguistics.

James Henderson. 2004. Discriminative training of a neural network statistical parser. In *Proceedings of the 42nd Annual Meeting on Association for Computational Linguistics*, page 95. Association for Computational Linguistics.

Geoffrey E Hinton, Nitish Srivastava, Alex Krizhevsky, Ilya Sutskever, and Ruslan R Salakhutdinov. 2012. Improving neural networks by preventing co-adaptation of feature detectors. *arXiv preprint arXiv:1207.0580.*

Zhongqiang Huang, Mary Harper, and Slav Petrov. 2010. Self-training with products of latent variable grammars. In *Proceedings of the 2010 Conference on Empirical Methods in Natural Language Processing*, pages 12–22. Association for Computational Linguistics.

Liang Huang. 2008. Forest reranking: Discriminative parsing with non-local features. In *ACL*, pages 586–594.

Daniel Jurafsky and James H Martin. 2008. Speech and language processing.

Tao Lei, Yu Xin, Yuan Zhang, Regina Barzilay, and Tommi Jaakkola. 2014. Low-rank tensors for scoring dependency structures. In *Proceedings of the 52nd Annual Meeting of the Association for Computational Linguistics*, volume 1, pages 1381–1391.

Mitchell P Marcus, Mary Ann Marcinkiewicz, and Beatrice Santorini. 1993. Building a large annotated corpus of english: The penn treebank. *Computational linguistics*, 19(2):313–330.

David McClosky, Eugene Charniak, and Mark Johnson. 2006. Effective self-training for parsing. In *Proceedings of the main conference on human language technology conference of the North American Chapter of the Association of Computational Linguistics*, pages 152–159. Association for Computational Linguistics.

Peter Nilsson and Pierre Nugues. 2010. Automatic discovery of feature sets for dependency parsing. In *Proceedings of the 23rd International Conference on Computational Linguistics*, pages 824–832. Association for Computational Linguistics.

Slav Petrov and Dan Klein. 2007. Improved inference for unlexicalized parsing. In *HLT-NAACL*, pages 404–411.

Slav Petrov, Leon Barrett, Romain Thibaux, and Dan Klein. 2006. Learning accurate, compact, and interpretable tree annotation. In *Proceedings of the 21st International Conference on Computational Linguistics and the 44th annual meeting of the Association for Computational Linguistics*, pages 433–440. Association for Computational Linguistics.

Adwait Ratnaparkhi. 1996. A maximum entropy model for part-of-speech tagging. In *Proceedings of the conference on empirical methods in natural language processing*, volume 1, pages 133–142. Philadelphia, PA.

David E Rumelhart, Geoffrey E Hinton, and Ronald J Williams. 1988. Learning representations by back-propagating errors.

Kenji Sagae and Alon Lavie. 2005. A classifier-based parser with linear run-time complexity. In *Proceedings of the Ninth International Workshop on Parsing Technology*, pages 125–132. Association for Computational Linguistics.

Richard Socher, John Bauer, Christopher D Manning, and Andrew Y Ng. 2013. Parsing with compositional vector grammars. In *In Proceedings of the ACL conference*. Citeseer.

Oriol Vinyals, Lukasz Kaiser, Terry Koo, Slav Petrov, Ilya Sutskever, and Geoffrey Hinton. 2014. Grammar as a foreign language. *arXiv preprint arXiv:1412.7449*.

Zhiguo Wang and Nianwen Xue. 2014. Joint pos tagging and transition-based constituent parsing in chinese with non-local features. In *Proceedings of the 52nd Annual Meeting of the Association for Computational Linguistics (Volume 1: Long Papers)*, pages 733–742. Association for Computational Linguistics.

Zhiguo Wang and Chengqing Zong. 2011. Parse reranking based on higher-order lexical dependencies. In *IJCNLP*, pages 1251–1259.

Mengqiu Wang, Kenji Sagae, and Teruko Mitamura. 2006. A fast, accurate deterministic parser for chinese. In *Proceedings of the 21st International Conference on Computational Linguistics and the 44th annual meeting of the Association for Computational Linguistics*, pages 425–432. Association for Computational Linguistics.

Ralph Weischedel, Sameer Pradhan, Lance Ramshaw, Jeff Kaufman, Michelle Franchini, Mohammed El-Bachouti, Nianwen Xue, Martha Palmer, Mitchell Marcus, Ann Taylor, et al. 2013. Ontonotes release 5.0. *Linguistic Data Consortium, Philadelphia*.

Naiwen Xue, Fei Xia, Fu-Dong Chiou, and Martha Palmer. 2005. The penn chinese treebank: Phrase structure annotation of a large corpus. *Natural language engineering*, 11(2):207–238.

Nianwen Xue, Xiuhong Zhang, Zixin Jiang, Martha Palmer, Fei Xia, Fu-Dong Chiou, and Meiyu Chang. 2013. Chinese treebank 8.0. *Philadelphia: Linguistic Data Consortium*, page https://catalog.ldc.upenn.edu/LDC2013T21.

Yue Zhang and Stephen Clark. 2009. Transition-based parsing of the chinese treebank using a global discriminative model. In *Proceedings of the 11th International Conference on Parsing Technologies*, pages 162–171. Association for Computational Linguistics.

Muhua Zhu, Yue Zhang, Wenliang Chen, Min Zhang, and Jingbo Zhu. 2013. Fast and accurate shift-reduce constituent parsing. In *Proceedings of the 51st Annual Meeting of the Association for Computational Linguistics (Volume 1: Long Papers)*, pages 434–443, Sofia, Bulgaria, August. Association for Computational Linguistics.

Identifying Cascading Errors using Constraints in Dependency Parsing

Dominick Ng and **James R. Curran**

ə-lab, School of Information Technologies
University of Sydney
NSW 2006, Australia
{dominick.ng,james.r.curran}@sydney.edu.au

Abstract

Dependency parsers are usually evaluated on attachment accuracy. Whilst easily interpreted, the metric does not illustrate the cascading impact of errors, where the parser chooses an incorrect arc, and is subsequently forced to choose further incorrect arcs elsewhere in the parse.

We apply arc-level constraints to MST-parser and ZPar, enforcing the correct analysis of specific error classes, whilst otherwise continuing with decoding. We investigate the direct and indirect impact of applying constraints to the parser. Erroneous NP and punctuation attachments cause the most cascading errors, while incorrect PP and coordination attachments are frequent but less influential. Punctuation is especially challenging, as it has long been ignored in parsing, and serves a variety of disparate syntactic roles.

1 Introduction

Dependency parsers are evaluated using word-level attachment accuracy. Whilst comparable across systems, this does not provide insight into why the parser makes certain errors, or whether certain misattachments are caused by other errors. For example, incorrectly identifying a modifier head may only introduce a single attachment error, while misplacing the root of a sentence will create substantially more errors elsewhere. In projective dependency parsing, erroneous arcs can also force the parser to select other incorrect arcs.

Kummerfeld et al. (2012) propose a static post-parsing analysis to categorise groups of bracket errors in constituency parsing into higher level error classes such as clause attachment. However, this cannot account for cascading changes resulting from repairing errors, or limitations which may prevent the parser from applying a repair. It is unclear whether the parser will apply the repair operation in its entirety, or if it will introduce other changes in response to the repairs.

We develop an evaluation procedure to evaluate the influence of each error class in dependency parsing without making assumptions about how the parser will behave. We define error classes based on dependency labels, and use the dependencies in each class as *arc constraints* specifying the correct head and label for particular words in each sentence. We adapt parsers to apply these constraints, whilst otherwise proceeding with decoding under their grammar and model. By evaluating performance with and without constraints, we can directly observe the cascading impact of each error class on each the parser.

We implement our procedure for the graph-based MSTparser (McDonald and Pereira, 2006) and the transition-based ZPar (Zhang and Clark, 2011) using basic Stanford dependencies over the OntoNotes 4.0 release of the WSJ Penn Treebank data. Our results show that erroneously attaching NPs, PPs, modifiers, and punctuation have the largest overall impact on UAS. Of those, NPs and punctuation have the most substantial cascading impact, indicating that these errors have the most effect on the remainder of the parse. Enforcing correct punctuation arcs has a particularly large impact on accuracy, even though most evaluation scripts ignore punctuation. We find that punctuation arcs are commonly misplaced by large distances in the final parse, crossing over and forcing other arcs to be incorrect in the process.

We will make our source code available, and

Proceedings of the 53rd Annual Meeting of the Association for Computational Linguistics and the 7th International Joint Conference on Natural Language Processing, pages 1148–1158,
Beijing, China, July 26-31, 2015.

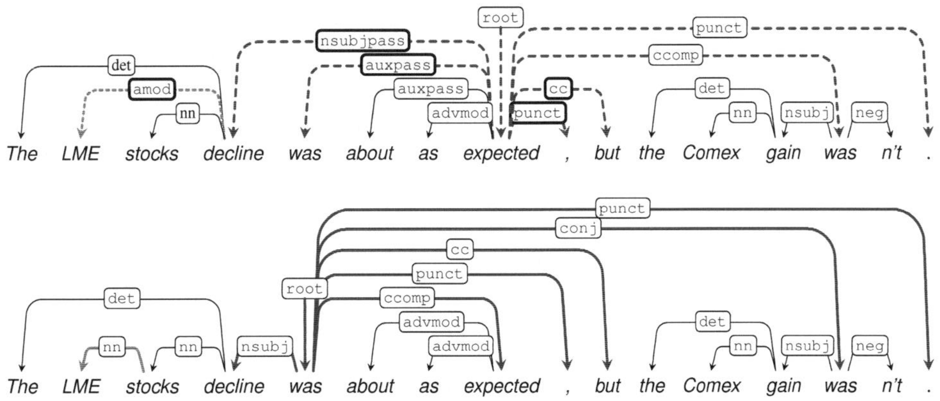

Figure 1: MSTparser output (top) and the gold parse (bottom) for a WSJ 22 sentence. MSTparser produces two independent errors: an NP bracketing error (red, dotted), and an incorrect root (blue, dashed).

Parser	UAS	LAS	usent	lsent
MSTparser	91.3	87.5	41.3	26.1
ZPar	91.7	89.3	45.1	35.9

Table 1: Baseline UAS and LAS scores on Stanford dependencies over WSJ 22.

hope that our findings will drive efforts addressing the remaining dependency parsing errors.

2 Motivation

Table 1 summarises the performance of MSTparser and ZPar on Stanford dependencies over OntoNotes 4 WSJ 22. ZPar performs slightly better than MSTparser on UAS, and substantially better on LAS. However, these numbers do not show what types of errors are being made by each parser, what errors remain to be addressed, or hint at what underlying problems cause each error.

Figure 1 depicts a WSJ 22 sentence as parsed by MSTparser, and the gold parse. The UAS is 47.1%, with 8 of 17 arcs correct. By contrast, ZPar (parse not shown) scores 94.1%, with the sole attachment error being on *LME* (as with MSTparser). While there are nine incorrect arcs overall, MSTparser seems to have made only two underlying errors:

- *LME* attached to *decline* rather than *stocks* (NP internal). Correcting this repairs one error;
- *expected* being chosen as the root rather than *was*. Correcting the root and moving all attachments to it from the old root repairs the remaining eight errors.

Intuitively, it seems that the impact of the NP error is limited. By contrast, the root selection error has a substantial impact on the second half of the sentence, causing a misplaced subject, misattached punctuation, and incorrect coordination. These cascaded errors appear to be *caused by* the incorrect root.

What we do not know is whether these intuitions actually hold. Many dependency parsers, including MSTparser and ZPar, construct trees by repeatedly combining fragments together until a spanning analysis is found, using a small window of information to make each arc decision. An error in one part of the tree may have no influence on a different part of the tree. Alternatively, errors may exert long-range influence — particularly if there are higher-order features or algorithmic constraints such as projectivity over the tree. As parsing algorithms are complex, we wish to repair various error types in isolation without otherwise making assumptions regarding the subsequent actions of the parser.

3 Applying Constraints

We investigate how each parser behaves when certain errors in the tree are corrected. We force each parser to select the correct head and label for specific words, but otherwise allow it to construct its best parse. Given a set of *constraints*, each of which lists a word with the head and label to which it must be attached, we investigate two measures:

1. errors *directly corrected* by the constraints, called the *constrained accuracy impact*;
2. the *indirect impact of the constraints*, including errors *indirectly corrected*, and correct

arcs *indirectly destroyed*, together called the *cascaded accuracy impact.*

The constrained accuracy impact tells us how often the parser makes errors in the set of words covered by the constraints. The cascaded accuracy impact is less predictable, as it describes what effect the errors made over the constrained set of arcs have over the rest of the sentence. It is the *influence* of the set of constraints over the other attachments, which may be mediated through projectivity requirements, or changes in the context used for other parsing decisions.

The core of our procedure is adapting each parser to accept a set of constraints. Following Kummerfeld et al. (2012), we define meaningful error classes grouped with the operations that repair them. In dependency parsing, error classes are groups of Stanford dependency labels, rather than groups of node repair operations. The Stanford labels provide a rich distinction in NP internal structure, clauses, and modifiers, and map well to the error categories of Kummerfeld et al. (2012), allowing us to avoid excessive heuristics in the mapping process. Our technique can be applied to other dependency schemes such as LTH (Johansson and Nugues, 2007) by defining new mappings from labels to error types.

The difficulty of the mapping task depends on the intricacies of each formalism. The major challenge with LTH dependencies is the enormous skew towards the nominal modifier `NMOD` label. This label occurs 11,335 times in WSJ 22, more than twice as frequently as the next most frequent punctuation `P`. By contrast, the most common Stanford label is punctuation, at 4,731 occurrences. The `NMOD` label is split into many smaller, but more informative nominal labels in the Stanford scheme, making it better suited for our goal of error analysis.

The label grouping was performed with reference to the Stanford dependencies manual v2.04 (de Marneffe and Manning, 2008, updated 2012). For each error class, we generate a set of constraints over WSJ 22 for all words with a gold-standard label in the set associated with the class. Our types are defined as follows:

NP attachment: any label specifically attaching an NP, includes `appos`, `dobj`, `iobj`, `nsubj`, `nsubjpass`, `pobj`, and `xsubj`.

NP internal: any label marking nominal structure (not including adjectival modifiers), includes `abbrev`, `det`, `nn`, `number`, `poss`, `possessive`, and `predet`.

PP attachment: any label attaching a prepositional phrase, includes `prep`. Also includes `pcomp` if the POS of the word is `TO` or `IN`.

Clause attachment: any label attaching a clause, includes `advcl`, `ccomp`, `csubj`, `csubjpass`, `purpcl`, `rcmod`, and `xcomp`. Also includes `pcomp` if the POS of the word is not `TO` or `IN`.

Modifier attachment: any label attaching an adverbial or adjectival modifier, includes `advmod`, `amod`, `infmod`, `npadvmod`, `num`, `partmod`, `quantmod`, and `tmod`.

Coordination attachment: `conj`, `cc`, and `preconj`.

Root attachment: the `root` label.

Punctuation attachment: the `punct` label.

Other attachment: all other Stanford labels, specifically `acomp`, `attr`, `aux`, `auxpass`, `complm`, `cop`, `dep`, `expl`, `mark`, `mwe`, `neg`, `parataxis`, `prt`, `ref`, and `rel`.

For example, Root constraints specify sentence roots, while PP constraints specify heads of prepositional phrases.

One deficiency of our implementation is that we apply constraints to all arcs of a particular error type in each sentence, and do not isolate multiple instances of the same error class in a sentence. We do this since applying single constraints to a sentence at a time would require substantial modifications to the standard evaluation regime.

3.1 MSTparser implementation

MSTparser is a graph-based, second-order parser that uses Eisner (1996)'s algorithm for projective decoding (McDonald and Pereira, 2006).[1] Eisner's algorithm constructs and caches subtrees which span progressively larger sections of the sentence. These spans are marked either as *complete*, consisting of a head, a dependent, and all of the descendants of that head to one side, or *incomplete*, consisting of a head, a dependent, and an unfilled region where additional tokens may be attached. Dependencies are formed between the head and dependent in each complete span, while label assignment occurs as a separate process.

We enforce constraints by allowing complete spans to be formed only from constrained tokens

[1] As the variant of Stanford dependencies we use are projective, we did not use non-projective decoding.

to their correct heads with the correct labels. Any complete span between an incorrect head and the constrained token is forbidden. The algorithm is forced to choose the constrained spans as it builds the parse; these constraints have no impact on the parser's coverage as all possible head selections are considered.

3.2 ZPar implementation

ZPar is an arc-eager transition-based parser (Zhang and Clark, 2011) that uses an incremental process with a stack storing partial parse *states* (Nivre et al., 2004). Each state represents tokens that may accept further arcs. The tokens of a sentence are initially stored in a buffer, and at each point during parsing, the parser decides whether or not to create an arc between the *front* token of the buffer and the *top* token on the stack.

We apply constraints in a similar way to Nivre et al. (2014). Arc creation actions are factored on the dependency label to be assigned to the arc. ZPar scores each possible action using a perceptron model over features from the front of the buffer and the top of the stack (as well as some additional context features which refer to previously created states). The highest scoring actions and their resulting states are kept in a beam; during parsing, ZPar finds the optimal action for all items in the beam, and retains the highest scoring new states at each step.

We disallow any arc creation action that would create an arc that conflicts with any constraints. Due to the use of beam search, it is possible for all of the partial states containing the constrained arcs to be evicted from the beam if they score lower under the model than other states. When this happens, the parser will fail to find an analysis for the sentence, as no head will exist in the beam for the constrained token. We have deliberately chosen to not address this issue as any solution (e.g. increasing the beam size from its default of 64) would change the decisions of the parser and model.

We verified that our modifications were working correctly for both parsers by passing in zero constraints (checking that the output matched the baseline performance), and every possible constraint (checking that the output scored 100%).

4 Related Work

Kummerfeld et al. (2012) perform a comprehensive classification of constituency bracket errors and their cascading impact, and their work is philosophically similar to ours. They associate groups of bracket errors in the parse with abstract error classes, and identify the tree operations that repair these error types, such as the insertion, deletion, or substitution of nodes in the parse tree. The error classes in a particular parser's output are identified through a heuristic procedure that repeatedly applies the operation repairing the largest number of bracket errors. This approach differs from our methodology as it is a static post-process that assumes the parser would respond perfectly to each repair, when it is possible that the parser may not perform the repair in full, or even be incapable of constructing the repaired tree.

McDonald and Nivre (2011) perform an in-depth comparison of the graph-based MSTparser and transition-based MaltParser. However, MaltParser uses support vector machines to deterministically predict the next transition, rather than storing the most probable options in a beam like ZPar. Additionally, they do not focus on the cascading impact of errors, and instead concentrate on higher-level error classification (e.g. by POS tag, labels and dependency lengths) in lieu of examining how the parsers respond to forced corrections.

Nivre et al. (2014) describe several uses for arc-level constraints in transition-based parsing. However, these applications focus on improving parsing accuracy when constraints can be readily identified, e.g. imperatives at the beginning of a sentence are likely to be the root. We focus our constraints on evaluation, attempting to identify important sources of error in dependency parsers.

Our constraint-based approach shares similarities to oracle training and decoding methods, where an external source of truth is used to verify parser decisions. An oracle source of parser actions is a necessary component for training transition-based parsers (Nivre, 2009). Oracle decoding, where a system is forced to produce correct output if possible, can be used to assess its upper performance bounds (Ng and Curran, 2012).

Constraining the parser's internal search space is akin to an optimal pruning operation. Charniak and Johnson (2005) use a coarse-to-fine, iterative pruning approach for efficiently generating high-quality n-best parses for a discriminative reranker. Rush and Petrov (2012) use a similar coarse-to-fine algorithm with vine grammars (Eisner and Smith, 2005) to accelerate graph-based de-

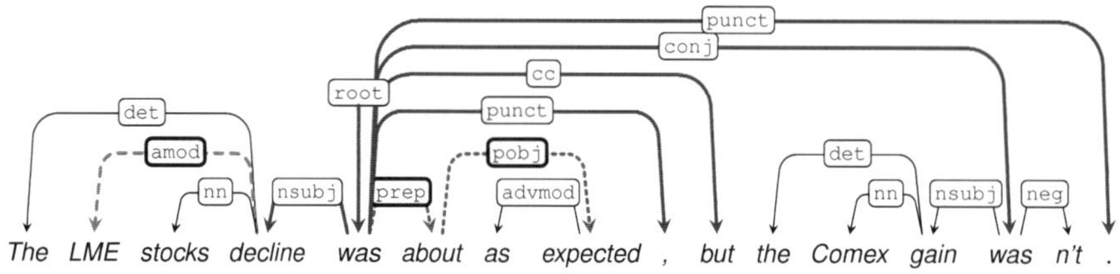

Figure 2: MSTparser output for the sentence in Figure 1, where the `root` dependency is forced to its correct value. The incorrect noun phrase error is not affected by the constraint (dashed, red), six attachment errors are repaired (solid, blue), and two new errors are introduced (dotted, purple).

Constraints	✓	✗	Remaining Errors
None	8	9	see Figure 1
nn	9	8	All except *decline* → *LME*
root	14	3	*decline* → *LME* *about* → *expected* *was* → *about*
punct	14	3	*decline* → *LME* *about* → *expected* *was* → *about*
ccomp	16	1	*decline* → *LME*

Table 2: Correct and incorrect arcs, and the remaining errors after applying various sets of constraints to the sentence in Figure 1.

pendency parsing, achieving parsing speeds close to linear-time transition parsers despite encoding more complex features. Supertagging (Clark and Curran, 2007) and chart pruning (Zhang et al., 2010) have been used to constrain the search space of a CCG parser, and to remove unlikely or forbidden spans from repeated consideration. In our work, we use pruning not for parsing speed, but evaluation, and so we prune items based on gold-standard constraints rather than heuristics.

5 Evaluation

We use the training (sections 2-21) and development (section 22) data from the OntoNotes 4.0 release of the Penn Treebank WSJ data (Marcus et al., 1993), as supplied by the SANCL 2012 Shared Task on Parsing the Web (Petrov and McDonald, 2012). OntoNotes annotates enriched NP structure compared to the Penn Treebank (Weischedel et al., 2011), meaning that determining NP attachments is less trivial. We changed all marker tokens in the corpus (e.g. -LRB- and -LCB-) to their equivalent unescaped punctuation marks to ensure correct evaluation. The corpus has been converted to basic Stanford dependencies using the Stanford Parser v2.0,[2] and part-of-speech tagged using MXPOST (Ratnaparkhi, 1996). A model trained on WSJ sections 2-21 was used to tag the development set, and 10-fold jackknife training was used to tag the training data.

We implement a custom evaluation script to facilitate a straightforward comparative analysis between the unconstrained and constrained output. The script is based on and produces identical scores to `eval06.pl`, the official evaluation for the CoNLL-X Shared Task on Multilingual Dependency Parsing (Buchholz and Marsi, 2006). We ignore punctuation as defined by `eval06.pl` in our evaluation; experiments with constraints over punctuation tokens constrain those tokens in the parse, but ignore them during evaluation.

We run the modified parsers over WSJ 22 with and without each set of constraints. We examine the overall unlabeled and labeled attachment scores (UAS and LAS), as well as identifying the contribution to the overall UAS improvement from directly (constrained) and indirectly corrected arcs.

MSTparser uses coarse-grained tags and fine-grained POS tags in its features, both of which were provided by the CoNLL-X Shared Task. We approximate the coarse-grained POS tags by taking the first character of the MXPOST-assigned POS tag, a technique also used by Bansal et al. (2014)[3].

6 Results

Figure 2 and Table 2 show the impact of applying constraints on tokens with various labels to MSTparser for the sentence in Figure 1. Enforcing the gold `nn` arc between *decline* and *LME* repairs that noun phrase error, but does not affect any of the other errors. Conversely, enforcing the gold `root` arc does not affect the noun phrase error, but repairs nearly every other error in the parse. Unfortunately, the constrained `root` arc introduces

[2] `nlp.stanford.edu/software/lex-parser.shtml`

[3] Mohit Bansal, p.c.

Error class	cover	eff	eff %	disp	UAS	LAS	ΔUAS	Δc	Δu
Baseline	100.0	-	-	-	91.3	87.5	-	-	-
NP attachment	95.6	312	4.9	5.2	94.1	90.7	2.3	1.2	1.1
NP internal	98.2	206	3.2	2.8	92.6	89.2	1.1	0.8	0.3
Modifier attachment	96.8	321	7.9	3.8	93.4	90.3	1.7	1.2	0.5
PP attachment	98.3	378	13.1	4.3	93.2	89.5	1.7	1.4	0.3
Coordination attachment	97.7	238	16.0	5.8	92.9	89.5	1.3	0.9	0.4
Clause attachment	96.7	228	17.9	6.9	93.0	89.6	1.4	0.9	0.5
Root attachment	99.1	77	5.8	9.3	92.2	88.3	0.8	0.3	0.5
Punctuation attachment	93.2	469	14.2	7.4	93.9	89.9	1.8	0.1	1.7
Other attachment	94.3	210	7.0	6.1	93.5	90.8	1.4	0.8	0.6
All attachments	98.5	2912	9.3	5.8	100.0	100.0	8.6	8.6	0.0

Table 3: The coverage, effective constraints and percentage, error displacement, UAS, LAS, ΔUAS over the corrected arcs, and the constrained and cascaded Δ for MSTparser over WSJ 22 (covered by ZPar).

Error class	cover	eff	eff %	disp	UAS	LAS	ΔUAS	Δc	Δu
Baseline	100.0	-	-	-	91.7	89.2	-	-	-
NP attachment	95.6	277	4.3	4.8	94.9	92.7	2.4	1.0	1.4
NP internal	98.2	197	3.0	3.0	93.2	91.1	1.2	0.7	0.5
Modifier attachment	96.8	303	7.5	3.9	94.0	92.3	1.8	1.1	0.7
PP attachment	98.3	357	12.4	3.9	93.8	91.4	1.7	1.3	0.4
Coordination attachment	97.7	240	16.2	5.8	93.5	91.1	1.3	0.9	0.4
Clause attachment	96.7	166	13.0	5.6	93.4	91.2	1.2	0.6	0.6
Root attachment	99.1	57	4.3	9.9	92.4	89.9	0.5	0.2	0.3
Punctuation attachment	93.2	430	13.0	7.3	94.5	92.1	1.6	0.2	1.5
Other attachment	94.3	187	6.3	5.5	94.2	92.7	1.3	0.7	0.6
All attachments	98.5	2760	8.8	5.8	100.0	100.0	8.0	8.0	0.0

Table 4: The coverage, effective constraints and percentage, error displacement, UAS, LAS, ΔUAS over the baseline, and the constrained and cascaded Δ for ZPar over WSJ 22.

two new errors, with the parser incorrectly attaching the clausal complement headed by *expected* and the modifier headed by *about*. In fact, correcting the `ccomp` arc in isolation rather than the `root` arc leads to MSTparser producing the full correct analysis for the second half of the sentence (though again, it does not repair the separate noun phrase error). This example highlights why we have chosen to implement our evaluation as a set of constraints in the parser, rather than Kummerfeld et al. (2012)'s post-processing approach, as we cannot know that the parser will react as we expect it to when repairing errors.

Tables 3 and 4 summarise our results on MSTparser and ZPar, calculated over the sentences covered by ZPar in WSJ 22. Results over the full WSJ 22 for MSTparser were consistent with these figures. We focus on discussing UAS results in this paper, since LAS results are consistent.

The UAS of constrained arcs in each experiment is the expected 100%. Effective constraints repair an error in the baseline, and the effective constraint percentage is this figure expressed as a percentage, i.e. the *error rate*. Error displacement is the average number of words that effective constraints moved an attachment point. The overall ΔUAS improvement is divided into Δc, the constrained impact, and Δu, the cascaded impact.

It is important to note that a parser may make a substantial number of mistakes on a particular error class (large effective constraint percentage), but correcting those mistakes may have very little cascading impact (small Δc), limiting the overall ΔUAS improvement. Conversely, there may be a class with a small effective constraint percentage, but a large ΔUAS due to a large cascading impact from the corrections, or simply because the class contains more constraints.

6.1 Overall Parser Comparison

When applying all constraints, ZPar has a 8.8% effective constraint percentage compared to 9.3% for MSTparser. This is directly related to the UAS difference between the parsers. Aside from coordination, where the parsers made a nearly identical number of errors, ZPar is more accurate across the board. It makes substantially fewer mistakes on clause attachments, punctuation dependencies, and NP attachments, whilst maintaining a small advantage across all of the other categories.

The relative rank of the effective constraint percentage per error category is similar across the parsers, with PP attachment, punctuation, modifiers, and coordination recording the largest number of effective constraints, and thus the most errors. This illustrates that the behaviour of both parsers is very consistent, despite one considering every possible attachment point, and the other using a linear transition-based beam search. ZPar is able to make fewer mistakes across each error category, suggesting that the beam search pruning is maintaining more desired states than the graph-based parser is able to rank during its search.

ZPar's coverage is 98.5% when applying all constraints. However, as the number of constraints is reduced, coverage also drops. This seems counter-intuitive, but applying more constraints eliminates more undesired states, leaving more space in the beam for satisfying states. Reducing the number of constraints permits more states which do not yet violate a constraint, but only yield undesired states later.

Punctuation constraints have the largest impact on coverage, reducing it to 93.2%. NP attachments, clauses, and modifier attachments also incur substantial coverage reductions. This suggests that ZPar's performance will degrade substantially over the sentences which it cannot cover, as they must contain constructions which are dispreferred by the model and fall out of the beam. Constraints with the smallest effect on coverage include root attachments, which only occur once per sentence and are rarely incorrect, and NP internal and PP attachments. For the latter two, the small displacements suggest that alternate attachment points often lie within the same projective span.

6.2 Noun phrases

Applying NP attachment constraints causes a 4.4% drop in coverage for ZPar, and the effective constraint percentage is below 5% for both parsers. However, these constraints still result in the largest ΔUAS for both parsers, at 2.6% for MSTparser and 2.2% for ZPar. This reflects the prevalence of NP attachments in the corpus.

ΔUAS is split evenly between correcting constrained (1.4%) and cascaded arcs (1.2%) for MSTparser, while it skews towards cascaded arcs for ZPar (1.0% and 1.4%). Most error classes skew in the other direction, while repairing one NP attachment error typically repairs another non-NP attachment error.

For NP internal attachments, both parsers have a similar error rate, with 206 effective constraints for MSTparser and 197 for ZPar. Although this is the second largest class, applying these constraints gives the second smallest Δu for both parsers. This implies that determining NP internal structure is a strength, even with the more complex OntoNotes 4 NP structure. Δc is also small for both parsers, reinforcing the limited displacement and cascading impact of NP internal errors.

Despite fewer effective constraints (i.e. less errors to fix), ZPar exhibits more cascading repair than MSTparser using both NP and NP internal constraints. This will be a common theme through this evaluation: the transition-based ZPar is better at propagating effective constraints into cascaded impact than the graph-based MSTparser, even though ZPar almost always begins with fewer effective constraints due to its better baseline performance. One possibility to explain this is that the beam is actually pruning away other erroneous states, while the graph-based MSTparser must still consider all of them.

Table 5 summarises the error classes of corrected cascaded arcs for the two NP constraint types, which are closely related. NP attachment constraints directly identify the head of the NP as well as its correct attachment, providing strong cues for determining the internal structure. NP internal constraints implicitly identify the head of an NP. We can see that for both types of constraints, many of the cascaded corrections come from the other NP error class.

Table 5 also shows that, compared to MSTparser, ZPar repairs nearly twice as many NP internal and coordination errors when using NP attachment constraints, and vice versa when using NP internal constraints. This suggests that ZPar has more difficulty identifying the correct heads for

Error class	NP attachment MSTparser	NP attachment ZPar	NP internal MSTparser	NP internal ZPar
NP attachment	-	-	45	69
NP internal	43	80	-	-
Modifier attachment	65	68	24	30
PP attachment	26	36	2	10
Coordination attachment	37	67	20	41
Clause attachment	59	65	1	1
Root attachment	24	21	2	1
Punctuation attachment	79	80	26	41
Other attachment	68	76	7	11
Total	401	493	127	204

Table 5: The number of unconstrained errors repaired per error class when enforcing NP attachment and NP internal constraints for MSTparser and ZPar over WSJ 22.

nominal coordination, and often chooses a word which should be a nominal modifier instead.

6.3 Coordination, Modifiers and PPs

These categories are large error classes for both parsers, with constraints leading to UAS improvements of 1.3 to 1.7%.

PPs and coordination have high effective constraint percentages relative to the other error classes for both parsers. However, they are also amongst the most isolated errors, with only 0.3% and 0.4% Δu for MSTparser and ZPar respectively. These errors also have minimal impact on ZPar's coverage. Both classes seem to have relatively contained attachment options within a limited projective span. The small error displacements reinforce this idea.

Modifiers are relatively isolated errors for MSTparser (0.5% Δu), but less so for ZPar (0.7% Δu). There are substantially more modifier constraints than PP or coordination, despite all yielding a similar UAS increase. This suggests that modifiers are actually relatively well analysed by both parsers, but there are so many of them that they form a large source of error.

6.4 Clause attachment

MSTparser performs substantially worse than ZPar on clause attachments, with an effective constraint percentage of 17.9% compared to 13.0%, and Δc of 0.9% compared with 0.6%. MSTparser's error rate is the worst of any error class on clause attachments, while it is second to coordination attachments for ZPar. Attaching clauses is very challenging for dependency parsers, particularly considering the small size of the class.

ZPar again achieves a slightly larger cascaded impact than MSTparser (0.6% to 0.5%), despite having far fewer effective constraints. This implies that the additional clause errors being made by MSTparser are largely self-contained, as they have not triggered a corresponding increase in Δu.

6.5 Root attachment

Both parsers make few root attachment errors, though MSTparser is less accurate than ZPar. However, root constraints provide the largest UAS improvement per number of constraints for both parsers. Root errors are also the most displaced of any error class, at 9.3 words for MSTparser and 9.9 for ZPar. When the root is incorrect, it is often very far from its correct location, and causes substantial cascading errors.

6.6 Punctuation

Despite ignoring punctuation dependencies in evaluation, applying punctuation constraints led to substantial UAS improvements. On MSTparser, Δu is 0.1% (due to some punctuation not being excluded from evaluation), but Δc is 1.7%. On ZPar, the equivalent metrics are 0.2% and 1.5%. Enforcing correct punctuation has a disproportionate impact on the remainder of the parse.

For both parsers, punctuation errors occur more frequently than any other error type, with 469 and 430 effective constraints respectively (though the majority of these corrected errors are on non-evaluated arcs). ZPar's coverage is worst of all when enforcing punctuation constraints, suggesting that the remaining uncovered sentences will

Error class	MSTparser	ZPar
NP attachment	75	51
NP internal	25	27
Modifier attachment	33	43
PP attachment	45	55
Coordination attachment	87	106
Clause attachment	66	48
Root attachment	59	27
Other attachment	65	69
Total	455	426

Table 6: The number of unconstrained errors repaired per error class when enforcing punctuation constraints for MSTparser and ZPar.

contain even more punctuation errors.

Incorrect punctuation heads are displaced from their correct locations by 7.4 words for MSTparser and 7.3 words for ZPar on average, second only to root attachments. Given that we are using projective parsers and a projective grammar, the large average displacement caused by errors indicates that punctuation affects and is in turn affected by the requirement for non-crossing arcs.

Table 6 summarises the error classes of the repaired cascaded arcs when punctuation constraints are applied. MSTparser has a more even distribution of repairs, while ZPar's repairs are concentrated in coordination attachment. This shows that MSTparser is relatively better at coordination as a proportion of its overall performance compared to ZPar. It also indicates that the majority of punctuation errors in both parsers (and especially ZPar) stem from incorrectly identified coordination markers such as commas.

Punctuation is commonly ignored in dependency parser evaluation (Yamada and Matsumoto, 2003; Buchholz and Marsi, 2006), and they are inconsistently treated across different grammars. Our results show that enforcing the correct punctuation attachments in a sentence has a substantial cascading impact, suggesting that punctuation errors are highly correlated with errors elsewhere in the analysis. Given the broad similarities between Stanford dependencies and other dependency schemes commonly used in parsing (Søgaard, 2013), we anticipate that the problems with roots and punctuation will carry across different treebanks and schemes.

Punctuation is often placed at phrasal boundaries and serves to split sentences into smaller sections within a projective parser. Graph-based and transition-based parsers, both of which use a limited local context to make parsing decisions, are equally prone to the cascading impact of erroneous punctuation. Removing the confounding presence of punctuation from parsing and treating attachment as a global post-process may help to alleviate these issues. Alternatively, more punctuation-specific features to account for its myriad roles in syntax could serve to improve performance.

7 Conclusion

We have developed a procedure to classify the importance of errors in dependency parsers without any assumptions on how the parser will respond to attachment repairs. Our approach constrains the parser to allow only correct arcs for certain tokens, whilst allowing it to otherwise form the parse that it thinks is best. Compared to Kummerfeld et al. (2012), we can observe exactly how the parser responds to the parse repairs, though at the cost of requiring modifications to the parser itself.

Our results show that noun phrases remain challenging for dependency parsers, both in choosing the correct head, and in determining the internal structure. Punctuation, despite being commonly ignored in parsers and evaluation, causes substantial cascading errors when misattached.

We are extending our work to other popular dependency parsers and non-projective parsing algorithms, and hope to develop features to improve and mitigate the cascading impact of punctuation attachment errors in parsing. Given that constituency parsers perform strongly when converted to dependencies (Cer et al., 2010; Petrov and McDonald, 2012), it would also be interesting to investigate how they perform on our metrics.

We implement a robust procedure to identify the cascading impact of dependency parser errors. Our results provide insights into which errors are most damaging in parsing, and will drive further improvements in parsing accuracy.

References

Mohit Bansal, Kevin Gimpel, and Karen Livescu. 2014. Tailoring continuous word representations for dependency parsing. In *Proceedings of the 52nd Annual Meeting of the Association for Computational Linguistics (ACL-14)*, pages 809–815. Baltimore, Maryland, USA.

Sabine Buchholz and Erwin Marsi. 2006. CoNLL-X Shared Task on Multilingual Dependency Parsing. In *Proceedings of the Tenth Conference on Computational Natural Language Learning (CoNLL-06)*, pages 149–164.

Daniel Cer, Marie-Catherine de Marneffe, Dan Jurafsky, and Chris Manning. 2010. Parsing to Stanford Dependencies: Trade-offs between Speed and Accuracy. In *Proceedings of the Seventh International Conference on Language Resources and Evaluation (LREC-10)*.

Eugene Charniak and Mark Johnson. 2005. Coarse-to-Fine n-Best Parsing and MaxEnt Discriminative Reranking. In *Proceedings of the 43rd Annual Meeting of the Association for Computational Linguistics (ACL-05)*, pages 173–180.

Stephen Clark and James R. Curran. 2007. Formalism-Independent Parser Evaluation with CCG and DepBank. In *Proceedings of the 45th Annual Meeting of the Association for Computational Linguistics (ACL-07)*, pages 248–255. Prague, Czech Republic.

Marie-Catherine de Marneffe and Christopher D. Manning. 2008. Stanford dependencies manual. Technical report, Stanford University.

Jason Eisner. 1996. Three New Probabilistic Models for Dependency Parsing: An Exploration. In *Proceedings of the 16th International Conference on Computational Linguistics (COLING-96)*, pages 340–345.

Jason Eisner and A. Noah Smith. 2005. Parsing with Soft and Hard Constraints on Dependency Length. In *Proceedings of the Ninth International Workshop on Parsing Technology (IWPT-05)*, pages 30–41.

Richard Johansson and Pierre Nugues. 2007. Extended Constituent-to-dependency Conversion for English. In *Proceedings of the 16th Nordic Conference of Computational Linguistics (NODALIDA-07)*, pages 105–112. Tartu, Estonia.

Jonathan K. Kummerfeld, David Hall, James R. Curran, and Dan Klein. 2012. Parser Showdown at the Wall Street Corral: An Empirical Investigation of Error Types in Parser Output. In *Proceedings of the 2012 Joint Conference on Empirical Methods in Natural Language Processing and Computational Natural Language Learning (EMNLP-CoNLL-12)*, pages 1048–1059.

Mitchell P. Marcus, Beatrice Santorini, and Mary Ann Marcinkiewicz. 1993. Building a Large Annotated Corpus of English: The Penn Treebank. *Computational Linguistics*, 19(2):313–330.

Ryan McDonald and Joakim Nivre. 2011. Analyzing and Integrating Dependency Parsers. *Computational Linguistics*, 37(1):197–230.

Ryan McDonald and Fernando Pereira. 2006. Online Learning of Approximate Dependency Parsing Algorithms. In *Proceedings of the 11th Conference of the European Chapter of the Association for Computational Linguistics (EACL-06)*, pages 81–88.

Dominick Ng and James R. Curran. 2012. Dependency Hashing for n-best CCG Parsing. In *Proceedings of the 50th Annual Meeting of the Association for Computational Linguistics (ACL-12)*, pages 497–505.

Joakim Nivre. 2009. Non-Projective Dependency Parsing in Expected Linear Time. In *Proceedings of the Joint Conference of the 47th Annual Meeting of the ACL and the 4th International Joint Conference on Natural Language Processing of the AFNLP (ACL-09)*, pages 351–359.

Joakim Nivre, Yoav Goldberg, and Ryan McDonald. 2014. Constrained arc-eager dependency parsing. *Computational Linguistics*, 40(2):249–257.

Joakim Nivre, Johan Hall, and Jens Nilsson. 2004. Memory-Based Dependency Parsing. In *HLT-NAACL 2004 Workshop: Eighth Conference on Computational Natural Language Learning (CoNLL-04)*, pages 49–56.

Slav Petrov and Ryan McDonald. 2012. Overview of the 2012 Shared Task on Parsing the Web. In *Notes of the First Workshop on the Syntactic Analysis of Non-Canonical Language (SANCL-12)*.

Adwait Ratnaparkhi. 1996. A Maximum Entropy Model for Part-of-Speech Tagging. In *Proceedings of the 1996 Conference on Empirical Methods in Natural Language Processing (EMNLP-96)*, pages 133–142.

Alexander Rush and Slav Petrov. 2012. Vine Pruning for Efficient Multi-Pass Dependency Parsing. In *Proceedings of the 2012 Conference of the North American Chapter of the Association for Computational Linguistics: Human Language Technologies (NAACL-12)*, pages 498–507.

Anders Søgaard. 2013. An Empirical Study of Differences between Conversion Schemes and Annotation Guidelines. In *Proceedings of the 2nd International Conference on Dependency Linguistics*, pages 298–307.

Ralph Weischedel, Eduard Hovy, Mitchell Marcus, Martha Palmer, Robert Belvin, Sameer Pradhan, Lance Ramshaw, and Nianwen Xue. 2011. OntoNotes: A Large Training Corpus for Enhanced Processing. In Joseph Olive, Caitlin Christianson, and John McCary, editors, *Handbook of Natural Language Processing and Machine Translation: DARPA Global Autonomous Language Exploitation*, pages 54–63. Springer.

Hiroyasu Yamada and Yuji Matsumoto. 2003. Statistical Dependency Analysis with Support Vector Machines. In *Proceedings of the 8th International Workshop of Parsing Technologies (IWPT-03)*, pages 196–206.

Yue Zhang, Byung-Gyu Ahn, Stephen Clark, Curt Van Wyk, James R. Curran, and Laura Rimell. 2010. Chart Pruning for Fast Lexicalised-Grammar Parsing. In *Proceedings of the 23rd International Conference on Computational Linguistics (COLING-10)*, pages 1471–1479.

Yue Zhang and Stephen Clark. 2011. Syntactic Processing Using the Generalized Perceptron and Beam Search. *Computational Linguistics*, 37(1):105–151.

A Re-ranking Model for Dependency Parser with Recursive Convolutional Neural Network

Chenxi Zhu, Xipeng Qiu*, Xinchi Chen, Xuanjing Huang
Shanghai Key Laboratory of Intelligent Information Processing, Fudan University
School of Computer Science, Fudan University
825 Zhangheng Road, Shanghai, China
{czhu13,xpqiu,xinchichen13,xjhuang}@fudan.edu.cn

Abstract

In this work, we address the problem to model all the nodes (words or phrases) in a dependency tree with the dense representations. We propose a recursive convolutional neural network (RCNN) architecture to capture syntactic and compositional-semantic representations of phrases and words in a dependency tree. Different with the original recursive neural network, we introduce the convolution and pooling layers, which can model a variety of compositions by the feature maps and choose the most informative compositions by the pooling layers. Based on RCNN, we use a discriminative model to re-rank a k-best list of candidate dependency parsing trees. The experiments show that RCNN is very effective to improve the state-of-the-art dependency parsing on both English and Chinese datasets.

1 Introduction

Feature-based discriminative supervised models have achieved much progress in dependency parsing (Nivre, 2004; Yamada and Matsumoto, 2003; McDonald et al., 2005), which typically use millions of discrete binary features generated from a limited size training data. However, the ability of these models is restricted by the design of features. The number of features could be so large that the result models are too complicated for practical use and prone to overfit on training corpus due to data sparseness.

Recently, many methods are proposed to learn various distributed representations on both syntax and semantics levels. These distributed representations have been extensively applied on many natural language processing (NLP) tasks, such as syntax (Turian et al., 2010; Mikolov et al., 2010; Collobert et al., 2011; Chen and Manning, 2014) and semantics (Huang et al., 2012; Mikolov et al., 2013). Distributed representations are to represent words (or phrase) by the dense, low-dimensional and real-valued vectors, which help address the curse of dimensionality and have better generalization than discrete representations.

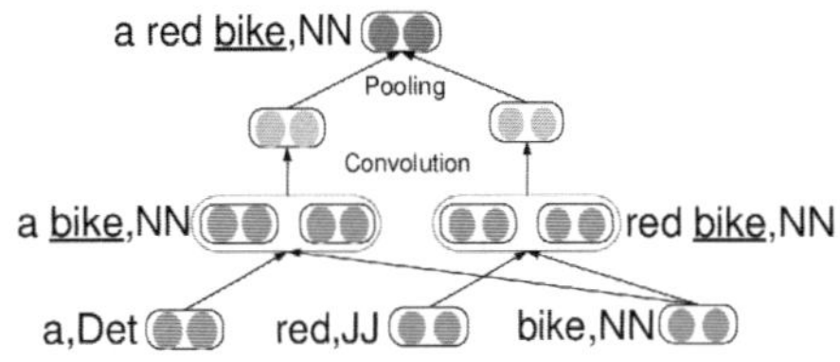

Figure 1: Illustration of a RCNN unit.

For dependency parsing, Chen et al. (2014) and Bansal et al. (2014) used the dense vectors (embeddings) to represent words or features and found these representations are complementary to the traditional discrete feature representation. However, these two methods only focus on the dense representations (embeddings) of words or features. These embeddings are pre-trained and keep unchanged in the training phase of parsing model, which cannot be optimized for the specific tasks.

Besides, it is also important to represent the (unseen) phrases with dense vector in dependency parsing. Since the dependency tree is also in recursive structure, it is intuitive to use the recursive neural network (RNN), which is used for constituent parsing (Socher et al., 2013a). However, recursive neural network can only process the binary combination and is not suitable for dependency parsing, since a parent node may have two or more child nodes in dependency tree.

In this work, we address the problem to rep-

*Corresponding author.

Proceedings of the 53rd Annual Meeting of the Association for Computational Linguistics and the 7th International Joint Conference on Natural Language Processing, pages 1159–1168,
Beijing, China, July 26-31, 2015. ©2015 Association for Computational Linguistics

resent all level nodes (words or phrases) with dense representations in a dependency tree. We propose a recursive convolutional neural network (RCNN) architecture to capture syntactic and compositional-semantic representations of phrases and words. RCNN is a general architecture and can deal with k-ary parsing tree, therefore it is very suitable for dependency parsing. For each node in a given dependency tree, we first use a RCNN unit to model the interactions between it and each of its children and choose the most informative features by a pooling layer. Thus, we can apply the RCNN unit recursively to get the vector representation of the whole dependency tree. The output of each RCNN unit is used as the input of the RCNN unit of its parent node, until it outputs a single fixed-length vector at root node. Figure 1 illustrates an example how a RCNN unit represents the phrases "a red bike" as continuous vectors.

The contributions of this paper can be summarized as follows.

- RCNN is a general architecture to model the distributed representations of a phrase or sentence with its dependency tree. Although RCNN is just used for the re-ranking of the dependency parser in this paper, it can be regarded as semantic modelling of text sequences and handle the input sequences of varying length into a fixed-length vector. The parameters in RCNN can be learned jointly with some other NLP tasks, such as text classification.

- Each RCNN unit can model the complicated interactions of the head word and its children. Combined with a specific task, RCNN can capture the most useful semantic and structure information by the convolution and pooling layers.

- When applied to the re-ranking model for parsing, RCNN improve the accuracy of base parser to make accurate parsing decisions. The experiments on two benchmark datasets show that RCNN outperforms the state-of-the-art models.

2 Recursive Neural Network

In this section, we briefly describe the recursive neural network architecture of (Socher et al., 2013a).

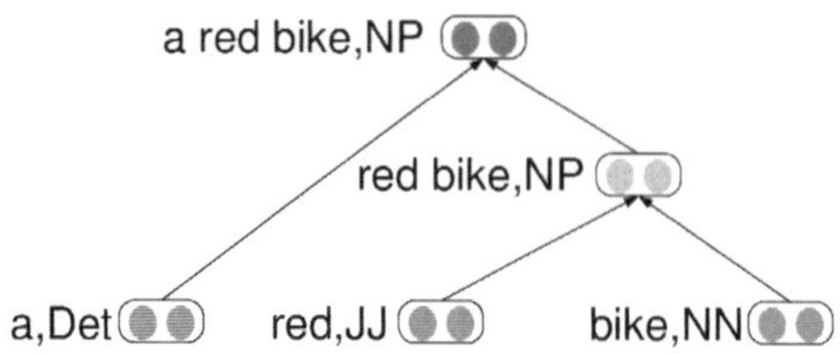

Figure 2: Illustration of a RNN unit.

The idea of recursive neural networks (RNN) for natural language processing (NLP) is to train a deep learning model that can be applied to phrases and sentences, which have a grammatical structure (Pollack, 1990; Socher et al., 2013c). RNN can be also regarded as a general structure to model sentence. At every node in the tree, the contexts at the left and right children of the node are combined by a classical layer. The weights of the layer are shared across all nodes in the tree. The layer computed at the top node gives a representation for the whole sentence.

Following the binary tree structure, RNN can assign a fixed-length vector to each word at the leaves of the tree, and combine word and phrase pairs recursively to create intermediate node vectors of the same length, eventually having one final vector representing the whole sentence. Multiple recursive combination functions have been explored, from linear transformation matrices to tensor products (Socher et al., 2013c). Figure 2 illustrates the architecture of RNN.

The binary tree can be represented in the form of branching triplets $(p \rightarrow c_1 c_2)$. Each such triplet denotes that a parent node p has two children and each c_k can be either a word or a non-terminal node in the tree.

Given a labeled binary parse tree, $((p_2 \rightarrow a p_1), (p_1 \rightarrow bc))$, the node representations are computed by

$$\mathbf{p}_1 = f(\mathbf{W}\begin{bmatrix} \mathbf{b} \\ \mathbf{c} \end{bmatrix}), \mathbf{p}_2 = f(\mathbf{W}\begin{bmatrix} \mathbf{a} \\ \mathbf{p}_1 \end{bmatrix}), \quad (1)$$

where $(\mathbf{p}_1, \mathbf{p}_2, \mathbf{a}, \mathbf{b}, \mathbf{c})$ are the vector representation of (p_1, p_2, a, b, c) respectively, which are denoted by lowercase bold font letters; $\mathbf{W}$ is a matrix of parameters of the RNN.

Based on RNN, Socher et al. (2013a) introduced a compositional vector grammar, which uses the syntactically untied weights $\mathbf{W}$ to learn the syntactic-semantic, compositional vector representations. In order to compute the score of how plausible of a syntactic constituent a parent is, RNN uses a single-unit linear layer for all p_i:

$$s(p_i) = \mathbf{v} \cdot \mathbf{p}_i, \tag{2}$$

where $\mathbf{v}$ is a vector of parameters that need to be trained. This score will be used to find the highest scoring tree. For more details on how standard RNN can be used for parsing, see (Socher et al., 2011).

Costa et al. (2003) applied recursive neural networks to re-rank possible phrase attachments in an incremental constituency parser. Their work is the first to show that RNNs can capture enough information to make the correct parsing decisions. Menchetti et al. (2005) used RNNs to re-rank different constituency parses. For their results on full sentence parsing, they re-ranked candidate trees created by the Collins parser (Collins, 2003).

3 Recursive Convolutional Neural Network

The dependency grammar is a widely used syntactic structure, which directly reflects relationships among the words in a sentence. In a dependency tree, all nodes are terminal (words) and each node may have more than two children. Therefore, the standard RNN architecture is not suitable for dependency grammar since it is based on the binary tree. In this section, we propose a more general architecture, called **recursive convolutional neural network** (RCNN), which borrows the idea of convolutional neural network (CNN) and can deal with to k-ary tree.

3.1 RCNN Unit

For ease of exposition, we first describe the basic unit of RCNN. A RCNN unit is to model a head word and its children. Different from the constituent tree, the dependency tree does not have non-terminal nodes. Each node consists of a word and its POS tags. Each node should have a different interaction with its head node.

Word Embeddings Given a word dictionary $\mathcal{W}$, each word $w \in \mathcal{W}$ is represented as a real-valued vector (word embedding) $\mathbf{w} \in \mathbb{R}^m$ where m is the dimensionality of the vector space. The word embeddings are then stacked into a embedding matrix $M \in \mathbb{R}^{m|\mathcal{W}|}$. For a word $w \in \mathcal{W}$, its corresponding word embedding $Embed(w) \in \mathbb{R}^m$ is retrieved by the lookup table layer. The matrix M is initialized with pre-training embeddings and updated by back-propagation.

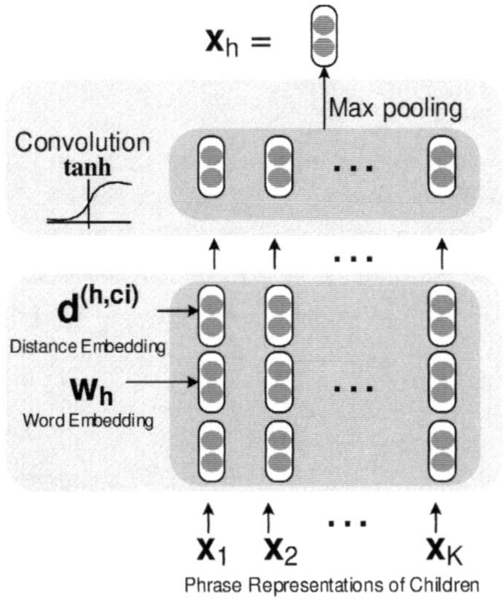

Figure 3: Architecture of a RCNN unit.

Distance Embeddings Besides word embeddings, we also use distributed vector to represent the relative distance of a head word h and one of its children c. For example, as shown in Figure 1, the relative distances of "bike" to "a" and "red" are -2 and -1, respectively. The relative distances also are mapped to a vector of dimension m_d (a hyperparameter); this vector is randomly initialized. Distance embedding is a usual way to encode the distance information in neural model, which has been proven effectively in several tasks. Our experimental results also show that the distance embedding gives more benefits than the traditional representation. The relative distance can encode the structure information of a subtree.

Convolution The word and distance embeddings are subsequently fed into the convolution component to model the interactions between two linked nodes.

Different with standard RNN, there are no non-terminal nodes in dependency tree. Each node h in dependency tree has two associated distributed representations:

1. word embedding $\mathbf{w}_h \in \mathbb{R}^m$, which is denoted as its own information according to its word form;

2. phrase representation $\mathbf{x}_h \in \mathbb{R}^m$, which is denoted as the joint representation of the whole subtree rooted at h. In particular, when h is leaf node, $\mathbf{x}_h = \mathbf{w}_h$.

Given a subtree rooted at h in dependency tree, we define $c_i, 0 < i \leq L$ as the i-th child node of h, where L represents the number of children.

For each pair (h, c_i), we use a convolutional hidden layer to compute their combination representation $\mathbf{z}_i$.

$$\mathbf{z}_i = \tanh(\mathbf{W}^{(h,c_i)} \mathbf{p}_i), 0 < i \leq K, \quad (3)$$

where $\mathbf{W}^{(h,c_i)} \in \mathbb{R}^{m \times n}$ is the linear **composition matrix**, which depends on the POS tags of h and c_i; $\mathbf{p}_i \in \mathbb{R}^n$ is the concatenated representation of h and the i-th child, which consists of the head word embeddings $\mathbf{w}_h$, the child phrase representation $\mathbf{x}_{c_i}$ and the distance embeddings $\mathbf{d}^{h,c_i}$ of h and c_i,

$$\mathbf{p}_i = \mathbf{x}_h \oplus \mathbf{x}_{c_i} \oplus \mathbf{d}^{(h,c_i)}, \quad (4)$$

where $\oplus$ represents the concatenation operation.

The distances d_{h,c_i} is the relative distance of h and c_i in a given sentence. Then, the relative distances also are mapped to m-dimensional vectors. Different from constituent tree, the combination should consider the order or position of each child in dependency tree.

In our model, we do not use the POS tags embeddings directly. Since the composition matrix varies on the different pair of POS tags of h and c_i, it can capture the different syntactic combinations. For example, the combination of adjective and noun should be different with that of verb and noun.

After the composition operations, we use **tanh** as the non-linear activation function to get a hidden representation $\mathbf{z}$.

Max Pooling After convolution, we get $\mathbf{Z}^{(h)} = [\mathbf{z}_1, \mathbf{z}_2, \cdots, \mathbf{z}_K]$, where K is dynamic and depends on the number of children of h. To transform $\mathbf{Z}$ to a fixed length and determine the most useful semantic and structure information, we perform a max pooling operation to $\mathbf{Z}$ on rows.

$$\mathbf{x}_j^{(h)} = \max_i \mathbf{Z}_{j,i}^{(h)}, 0 < j \leq m. \quad (5)$$

Thus, we obtain the vector representation $\mathbf{x}_h \in \mathbb{R}^m$ of the whole subtree rooted at node h.

Figure 3 shows the architecture of our proposed RCNN unit.

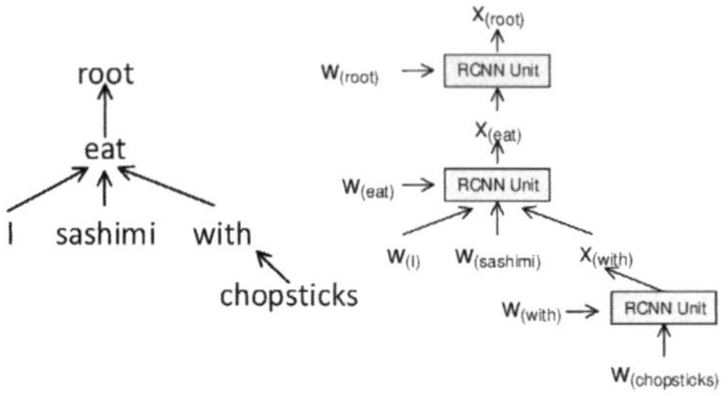

Figure 4: Example of a RCNN unit

Given a whole dependency tree, we can apply the RCNN unit recursively to get the vector representation of the whole sentence. The output of each RCNN unit is used as the input of the RCNN unit of its parent node.

Thus, RCNN can be used to model the distributed representations of a phrase or sentence with its dependency tree and applied to many NLP tasks. The parameters in RCNN can be learned jointly with the specific NLP tasks. Each RCNN unit can model the complicated interactions of the head word and its children. Combined with a specific task, RCNN can select the useful semantic and structure information by the convolution and max pooling layers.

Figure 4 shows an example of RCNN to model the sentence "*I eat sashimi with chopsitcks*".

4 Parsing

In order to measure the plausibility of a subtree rooted at h in dependency tree, we use a single-unit linear layer neural network to compute the score of its RCNN unit.

For constituent parsing, the representation of a non-terminal node only depends on its two children. The combination is relative simple and its correctness can be measured with the final representation of the non-terminal node (Socher et al., 2013a).

However for dependency parsing, all combinations of the head h and its children $c_i (0 < i \leq K)$ are important to measure the correctness of the subtree. Therefore, our score function $s(h)$ is computed on all of hidden layers $\mathbf{z}_i (0 < i \leq K)$:

$$s(h) = \sum_{i=1}^{K} \mathbf{v}^{(h,c_i)} \cdot \mathbf{z}_i, \quad (6)$$

where $\mathbf{v}^{(h,c_i)} \in \mathbb{R}^{m \times 1}$ is the **score vector**, which also depends on the POS tags of h and c_i.

Given a sentence x and its dependency tree y, the goodness of a complete tree is measured by summing the scores of all the RCNN units.

$$s(x, y, \Theta) = \sum_{h \in y} s(h), \tag{7}$$

where $h \in y$ is the node in tree y; $\Theta = \{\Theta_{\mathbf{W}}, \Theta_{\mathbf{v}}, \Theta_{\mathbf{w}}, \Theta_{\mathbf{d}}\}$ including the combination matrix set $\Theta_{\mathbf{W}}$, the score vector set $\Theta_{\mathbf{v}}$, the word embeddings $\Theta_{\mathbf{w}}$ and distance embeddings $\Theta_{\mathbf{d}}$.

Finally, we can predict dependency tree $\hat{y}$ with highest score for sentence x.

$$\hat{y} = \arg\max_{y \in \mathbf{gen}(x)} s(x, y, \Theta), \tag{8}$$

where $\mathbf{gen}(x)$ is defined as the set of all possible trees for sentence x. When applied in re-ranking, $\mathbf{gen}(x)$ is the set of the k-best outputs of a base parser.

5 Training

For a given training instance (x_i, y_i), we use the max-margin criterion to train our model. We first predict the dependency tree $\hat{y}_i$ with the highest score for each x_i and define a structured margin loss $\Delta(y_i, \hat{y}_i)$ between the predicted tree $\hat{y}_i$ and the given correct tree y_i. $\Delta(y_i, \hat{y}_i)$ is measured by counting the number of nodes y_i with an incorrect span (or label) in the proposed tree (Goodman, 1998).

$$\Delta(y_i, \hat{y}_i) = \sum_{d \in \hat{y}_i} \kappa \mathbf{1}\{d \notin y_i\} \tag{9}$$

where κ is a discount parameter and d represents the nodes in trees.

Given a set of training dependency parses $\mathcal{D}$, the final training objective is to minimize the loss function $J(\Theta)$, plus a l_2-regulation term:

$$J(\Theta) = \frac{1}{|\mathcal{D}|} \sum_{(x_i, y_i) \in \mathcal{D}} r_i(\Theta) + \frac{\lambda}{2} \|\Theta\|_2^2, \tag{10}$$

where

$$r_i(\Theta) = \max_{\hat{y}_i \in Y(x_i)} \big(0, s_t(x_i, \hat{y}_i, \Theta) + \Delta(y_i, \hat{y}_i) - s_t(x_i, y_i, \Theta) \big). \tag{11}$$

By minimizing this object, the score of the correct tree y_i is increased and the score of the highest scoring incorrect tree $\hat{y}_i$ is decreased.

We use a generalization of gradient descent called subgradient method (Ratliff et al., 2007) which computes a gradient-like direction. The subgradient of equation is:

$$\frac{\partial J}{\partial \Theta} = \frac{1}{|\mathcal{D}|} \sum_{(x_i, y_i) \in \mathcal{D}} \Big(\frac{\partial s_t(x_i, \hat{y}_i, \Theta)}{\partial \Theta} - \frac{\partial s_t(x_i, y_i, \Theta)}{\partial \Theta} \Big) + \lambda \Theta. \tag{12}$$

To minimize the objective, we use the diagonal variant of AdaGrad (Duchi et al., 2011). The parameter update for the i-th parameter $\Theta_{t,i}$ at time step t is as follows:

$$\Theta_{t,i} = \Theta_{t-1,i} - \frac{\rho}{\sqrt{\sum_{\tau=1}^{t} g_{\tau,i}^2}} g_{t,i}, \tag{13}$$

where ρ is the initial learning rate and $g_\tau \in \mathbb{R}^{|\theta_i|}$ is the subgradient at time step τ for parameter θ_i.

6 Re-rankers

Re-ranking k-best lists was introduced by Collins and Koo (2005) and Charniak and Johnson (2005). They used discriminative methods to re-rank the constituent parsing. In the dependency parsing, Sangati et al. (2009) used a third-order generative model for re-ranking k-best lists of base parser. Hayashi et al. (2013) used a discriminative forest re-ranking algorithm for dependency parsing. These re-ranking models achieved a substantial raise on the parsing performances.

Given $\mathcal{T}(x)$, the set of k-best trees of a sentence x from a base parser, we use the popular mixture re-ranking strategy (Hayashi et al., 2013; Le and Mikolov, 2014), which is a combination of the our model and the base parser.

$$\hat{y}_i = \arg\max_{y \in \mathcal{T}(x_i)} \alpha s_t(x_i, y, \Theta) + (1 - \alpha) s_b(x_i, y) \tag{14}$$

where $\alpha \in [0, 1]$ is a hyperparameter; $s_t(x_i, y, \Theta)$ and $s_b(x_i, y)$ are the scores given by RCNN and the base parser respectively.

To apply RCNN into re-ranking model, we first get the k-best outputs of all sentences in train set with a base parser. Thus, we can train the RCNN in a discriminative way and optimize the re-ranking strategy for a particular base parser.

Note that the role of RCNN is not fully valued when applied in re-ranking model since that the $\mathbf{gen}(x)$ in Eq.(8) is just the k-best outputs of a base parser, not the set of all possible trees for sentence x. The parameters of RCNN could overfit to k-best outputs of training set.

7 Experiments

7.1 Datasets

To empirically demonstrate the effectiveness of our approach, we use two datasets in different languages (English and Chinese) in our experimental evaluation and compare our model against the other state-of-the-art methods using the unlabeled attachment score (UAS) metric ignoring punctuation.

English For English dataset, we follow the standard splits of Penn Treebank (PTB), using sections 2-21 for training, section 22 as development set and section 23 as test set. We tag the development and test sets using an automatic POS tagger (at 97.2% accuracy), and tag the training set using four-way jackknifing similar to (Collins and Koo, 2005).

Chinese For Chinese dataset, we follow the same split of the Penn Chinese Treeban (CTB5) as described in (Zhang and Clark, 2008) and use sections 001-815, 1001-1136 as training set, sections 886-931, 1148- 1151 as development set, and sections 816-885, 1137-1147 as test set. Dependencies are converted by using the Penn2Malt tool with the head-finding rules of (Zhang and Clark, 2008). And following (Zhang and Clark, 2008) (Zhang and Nivre, 2011), we use gold segmentation and POS tags for the input.

We use the linear-time incremental parser (Huang and Sagae, 2010) as our base parser and calculate the 64-best parses at the top cell of the chart. Note that we optimize the training settings for base parser and the results are slightly improved on (Huang and Sagae, 2010). Then we use max-margin criterion to train RCNN. Finally, we use the mixture strategy to re-rank the top 64-best parses.

For initialization of parameters, we train word2vec embeddings (Mikolov et al., 2013) on Wikipedia corpus for English and Chinese respectively. For the combination matrices and score vectors, we use the random initialization within $(0.01, 0.01)$. The parameters which achieve the best unlabeled attachment score on the development set will be chosen for the final evaluation.

7.2 English Dataset

We first evaluate the performances of the RCNN and re-ranker (Eq. (14)) on the development set. Figure 5 shows UASs of different models with varying k. The base parser achieves 92.45%. When $k = 64$, the oracle best of base parser achieves 97.34%, while the oracle worst achieves 73.30% (-19.15%) . RCNN achieves the maximum improvement of 93.00%(+0.55%) when $k = 6$. When $k > 6$, the performance of RCNN declines with the increase of k but is still higher than baseline (92.45%). The reason behind this is that RCNN could require more negative samples to avoid overfitting when k is large. Since the negative samples are limited in the k-best outputs of a base parser, the learnt parameters could easily overfits to the training set.

The mixture re-ranker achieves the maximum improvement of 93.50%(+1.05%) when $k = 64$. In mixture re-ranker, α is optimised by searching with the step-size 0.005.

Therefore, we use the mixture re-ranker in the following experiments since it can take the advantages of both the RCNN and base models.

Figure 6 shows the accuracies on the top ten POS tags of the modifier words with the largest improvements. We can see that our re-ranker can improve the accuracies of *CC* and *IN*, and therefore may indirectly result in rising the the well-known coordinating conjunction and PP-attachment problems.

The final experimental results on test set are shown in Table 1. The hyperparameters of our model are set as in Table 2. Our re-ranker achieves the maximum improvement of 93.83%(+1.48%) on test set. Our system performs slightly better than many state-of-the-art systems such as Zhang and Clark (2008) and Huang and Sagae (2010). It outperforms Hayashi et al. (2013) and Le and Zuidema (2014), which also use the mixture reranking strategy.

Since the result of ranker is conditioned to k-best results of base parser, we also do an experiment to avoid this limitation by adding the oracle to k-best candidates. With including oracle, the re-ranker can achieve 94.16% on UAS, which is shown in the last line ("our re-ranker (with oracle)") of Table 1.

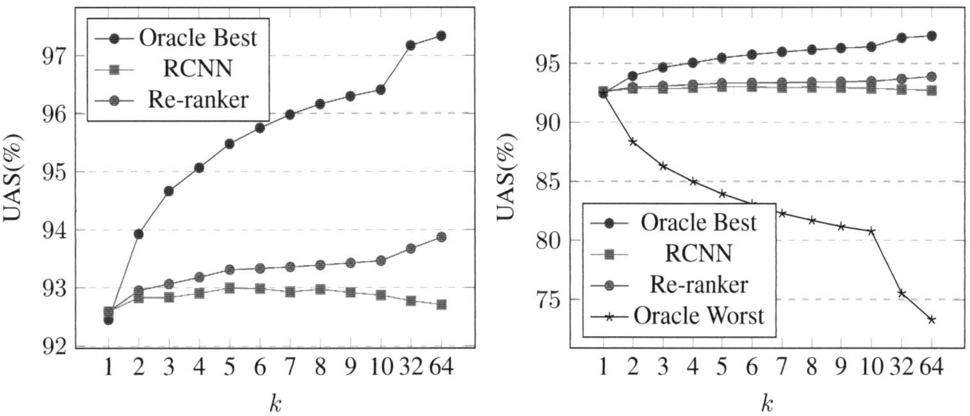

(a) without the oracle worst result

(b) with the oracle worst result

Figure 5: UAS with varying k on the development set. Oracle best: always choosing the best result in the k-best of base parser; Oracle worst: always choosing the worst result in the k-best of base parser; RCNN: choosing the most probable candidate according to the score of RCNN; Re-ranker: a combination of the RCNN and base parser.

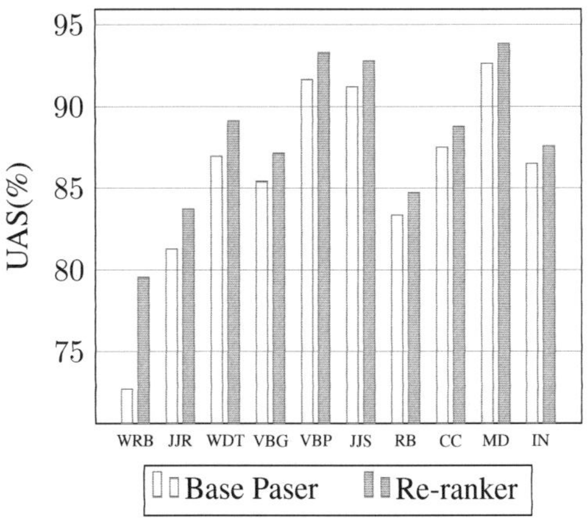

Figure 6: Accuracies on the top ten POS tags of the modifier words with the largest improvements on the development set.

	UAS
Traditional Methods	
Zhang and Clark (2008)	91.4
Huang and Sagae (2010)	92.1
Distributed Representations	
Stenetorp (2013)	86.25
Chen et al. (2014)	93.74
Chen and Manning (2014)	92.0
Re-rankers	
Hayashi et al. (2013)	93.12
Le and Zuidema (2014)	93.12
Our baseline	92.35
Our re-ranker	93.83(+1.48)
Our re-ranker (with oracle)	94.16

Table 1: Accuracy on English test set. Our baseline is the result of base parser; our re-ranker uses the mixture strategy on the 64-best outputs of base parser; our re-ranker(with oracle) is to add the oracle to k-best outputs of base parser.

7.3 Chinese Dataset

We also make experiments on the Penn Chinese Treebank (CTB5). The hyperparameters is the same as the previous experiment on English except that α is optimised by searching with the step-size 0.005.

The final experimental results on the test set are shown in Table 3. Our re-ranker achieves the performance of 85.71%(+0.25%) on the test set, which also outperforms the previous state-of-the-art methods. With adding oracle, the re-ranker can achieve 87.43% on UAS, which is shown in the last line ("our re-ranker (with oracle)") of Table 3.

Compared with the re-ranking model of Hayashi et al. (2013), that use a large number of handcrafted features, our model can achieve a competitive performance with the minimal feature engineering.

7.4 Discussions

The performance of the re-ranking model is affected by the base parser. The small divergence of the dependency trees in the output list also results to overfitting in training phase. Although our re-

Word embedding size	$m = 25$
Distance embedding size	$m_d = 25$
Initial learning rate	$\rho = 0.1$
Margin loss discount	$\kappa = 2.0$
Regularization	$\lambda = 10^{-4}$
k-best	$k = 64$

Table 2: Hyperparameters of our model

	UAS
Traditional Methods	
Zhang and Clark (2008)	84.33
Huang and Sagae (2010)	85.20
Distributed Representations	
Chen et al. (2014)	82.94
Chen and Manning (2014)	83.9
Re-rankers	
Hayashi et al. (2013)	85.9
Our baseline	85.46
Our re-ranker	85.71(+0.25)
Our re-ranker (with oracle)	87.43

Table 3: Accuracy on Chinese test set.

ranker outperforms the state-of-the-art methods, it can also benefit from improving the quality of the candidate results. It was also reported in other re-ranking works that a larger k (eg. $k > 64$) results the worse performance. We think the reason is that the oracle best increases when k is larger, but the oracle worst decrease with larger degree. The error types increase greatly. The re-ranking model requires more negative samples to avoid overfitting. When k is larger, the number of negative samples also needs to multiply increase for training. However, we just can obtain at most k negative samples from the k-best outputs of the base parser.

The experiments also show that the our model can achieves significant improvements by adding the oracles into the output lists of the base parser. This indicates that our model can be boosted by a better set of the candidate results, which can be implemented by combining the RCNN in the decoding algorithm.

8 Related Work

There have been several works to use neural networks and distributed representation for dependency parsing.

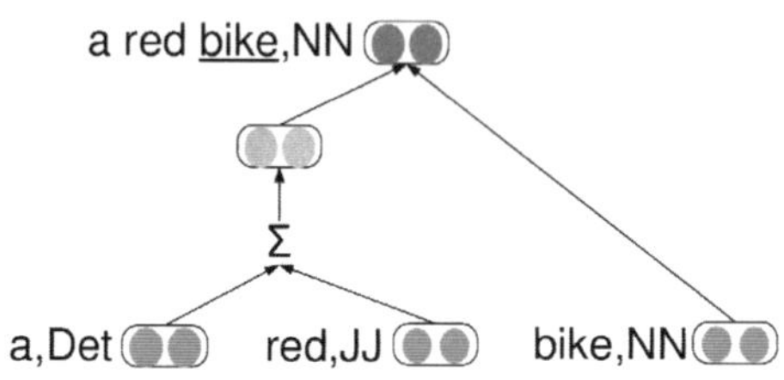

Figure 7: Example of a DT-RNN unit

Stenetorp (2013) attempted to build recursive neural networks for transition-based dependency parsing, however the empirical performance of his model is still unsatisfactory. Chen and Manning (2014) improved the transition-based dependency parsing by representing all words, POS tags and arc labels as dense vectors, and modeled their interactions with neural network to make predictions of actions. Their methods aim to transition-based parsing and can not model the sentence in semantic vector space for other NLP tasks.

Socher et al. (2013b) proposed a compositional vectors computed by dependency tree RNN (DT-RNN) to map sentences and images into a common embedding space. However, there are two major differences as follows. 1) They first summed up all child nodes into a dense vector $\mathbf{v}_c$ and then composed subtree representation from $\mathbf{v}_c$ and vector parent node. In contrast, our model first combine the parent and each child and then choose the most informative features with a pooling layer. 2) We represent the relative position of each child and its parent with distributed representation (position embeddings), which is very useful for convolutional layer. Figure 7 shows an example of DTRNN to illustrates how RCNN represents phrases as continuous vectors.

Specific to the re-ranking model, Le and Zuidema (2014) proposed a generative re-ranking model with Inside-Outside Recursive Neural Network (IORNN), which can process trees both bottom-up and top-down. However, IORNN works in generative way and just estimates the probability of a given tree, so IORNN cannot fully utilize the incorrect trees in k-best candidate results. Besides, IORNN treats dependency tree as a sequence, which can be regarded as a generalization of simple recurrent neural network (SRNN) (Elman, 1990). Unlike IORNN, our proposed RCNN is a discriminative model and can optimize the re-ranking strategy for a particular base parser. Another difference is that RCNN computes the score of tree in a recursive way, which is more natural for the hierarchical structure of natural language. Besides, the RCNN can not only be used for the re-ranking, but also be regarded as general model to represent sentence with its dependency tree.

9 Conclusion

In this work, we address the problem to represent all level nodes (words or phrases) with dense representations in a dependency tree. We propose a recursive convolutional neural network (RCNN) architecture to capture the syntactic and compositional-semantic representations of phrases and words. RCNN is a general architecture and can deal with k-ary parsing tree, therefore RCNN is very suitable for many NLP tasks to minimize the effort in feature engineering with a external dependency parser. Although RCNN is just used for the re-ranking of the dependency parser in this paper, it can be regarded as semantic modelling of text sequences and handle the input sequences of varying length into a fixed-length vector. The parameters in RCNN can be learned jointly with some other NLP tasks, such as text classification.

For the future research, we will develop an integrated parser to combine RCNN with a decoding algorithm. We believe that the integrated parser can achieve better performance without the limitation of base parser. Moreover, we also wish to investigate the ability of our model for other NLP tasks.

Acknowledgments

We would like to thank the anonymous reviewers for their valuable comments. This work was partially funded by the National Natural Science Foundation of China (61472088, 61473092), the National High Technology Research and Development Program of China (2015AA015408), Shanghai Science and Technology Development Funds (14ZR1403200), Shanghai Leading Academic Discipline Project (B114).

References

Mohit Bansal, Kevin Gimpel, and Karen Livescu. 2014. Tailoring continuous word representations for dependency parsing. In *Proceedings of the Annual Meeting of the Association for Computational Linguistics*.

Eugene Charniak and Mark Johnson. 2005. Coarse-to-fine n-best parsing and maxent discriminative reranking. In *Proceedings of the 43rd Annual Meeting of the Association for Computational Linguistics (ACL'05)*, pages 173–180, Ann Arbor, Michigan, June. Association for Computational Linguistics.

Danqi Chen and Christopher D Manning. 2014. A fast and accurate dependency parser using neural networks. In *Proceedings of the 2014 Conference on Empirical Methods in Natural Language Processing (EMNLP)*, pages 740–750.

Wenliang Chen, Yue Zhang, and Min Zhang. 2014. Feature embedding for dependency parsing. In *Proceedings of COLING 2014, the 25th International Conference on Computational Linguistics: Technical Papers*, pages 816–826, Dublin, Ireland, August. Dublin City University and Association for Computational Linguistics.

Michael Collins and Terry Koo. 2005. Discriminative reranking for natural language parsing. *Computational Linguistics*, 31(1):25–70.

Michael Collins. 2003. Head-driven statistical models for natural language parsing. *Computational linguistics*, 29(4):589–637.

Ronan Collobert, Jason Weston, Léon Bottou, Michael Karlen, Koray Kavukcuoglu, and Pavel Kuksa. 2011. Natural language processing (almost) from scratch. *The Journal of Machine Learning Research*, 12:2493–2537.

Fabrizio Costa, Paolo Frasconi, Vincenzo Lombardo, and Giovanni Soda. 2003. Towards incremental parsing of natural language using recursive neural networks. *Applied Intelligence*, 19(1-2):9–25.

John Duchi, Elad Hazan, and Yoram Singer. 2011. Adaptive subgradient methods for online learning and stochastic optimization. *The Journal of Machine Learning Research*, 12:2121–2159.

Jeffrey L Elman. 1990. Finding structure in time. *Cognitive science*, 14(2):179–211.

Joshua Goodman. 1998. Parsing inside-out. *arXiv preprint cmp-lg/9805007*.

Katsuhiko Hayashi, Shuhei Kondo, and Yuji Matsumoto. 2013. Efficient stacked dependency parsing by forest reranking. *TACL*, 1:139–150.

Liang Huang and Kenji Sagae. 2010. Dynamic programming for linear-time incremental parsing. In *Proceedings of the 48th Annual Meeting of the Association for Computational Linguistics*, pages 1077–1086. Association for Computational Linguistics.

Eric Huang, Richard Socher, Christopher Manning, and Andrew Ng. 2012. Improving word representations via global context and multiple word prototypes. In *Proceedings of the 50th Annual Meeting of the Association for Computational Linguistics (Volume 1: Long Papers)*, pages 873–882, Jeju Island, Korea, July. Association for Computational Linguistics.

Quoc V. Le and Tomas Mikolov. 2014. Distributed representations of sentences and documents. In *Proceedings of ICML*.

Phong Le and Willem Zuidema. 2014. The inside-outside recursive neural network model for dependency parsing. In *Proceedings of the 2014 Conference on Empirical Methods in Natural Language Processing (EMNLP)*, pages 729–739, Doha, Qatar, October. Association for Computational Linguistics.

Ryan McDonald, Koby Crammer, and Fernando Pereira. 2005. Online large-margin training of dependency parsers. In *Proceedings of the 43rd Annual Meeting on Association for Computational Linguistics*, ACL '05, pages 91–98.

Sauro Menchetti, Fabrizio Costa, Paolo Frasconi, and Massimiliano Pontil. 2005. Wide coverage natural language processing using kernel methods and neural networks for structured data. *Pattern Recognition Letters*, 26(12):1896–1906.

Tomas Mikolov, Martin Karafiát, Lukas Burget, Jan Cernockỳ, and Sanjeev Khudanpur. 2010. Recurrent neural network based language model. In *INTERSPEECH*.

Tomas Mikolov, Ilya Sutskever, Kai Chen, Greg S Corrado, and Jeff Dean. 2013. Distributed representations of words and phrases and their compositionality. In *Advances in Neural Information Processing Systems*.

Joakim Nivre. 2004. Incrementality in deterministic dependency parsing. In *Proceedings of the Workshop on Incremental Parsing: Bringing Engineering and Cognition Together*, pages 50–57. Association for Computational Linguistics.

Jordan B Pollack. 1990. Recursive distributed representations. *Artificial Intelligence*, 46(1):77–105.

Nathan D Ratliff, J Andrew Bagnell, and Martin A Zinkevich. 2007. (online) subgradient methods for structured prediction. In *Eleventh International Conference on Artificial Intelligence and Statistics (AIStats)*.

Federico Sangati, Willem Zuidema, and Rens Bod. 2009. A generative re-ranking model for dependency parsing. In *Proceedings of the 11th International Conference on Parsing Technologies*, pages 238–241. Association for Computational Linguistics.

Richard Socher, Cliff C Lin, Chris Manning, and Andrew Y Ng. 2011. Parsing natural scenes and natural language with recursive neural networks. In *Proceedings of the 28th International Conference on Machine Learning (ICML-11)*, pages 129–136.

Richard Socher, John Bauer, Christopher D Manning, and Andrew Y Ng. 2013a. Parsing with compositional vector grammars. In *In Proceedings of the ACL conference*. Citeseer.

Richard Socher, Q Le, C Manning, and A Ng. 2013b. Grounded compositional semantics for finding and describing images with sentences. In *NIPS Deep Learning Workshop*.

Richard Socher, Alex Perelygin, Jean Wu, Jason Chuang, Christopher D. Manning, Andrew Ng, and Christopher Potts. 2013c. Recursive deep models for semantic compositionality over a sentiment treebank. In *EMNLP*.

Pontus Stenetorp. 2013. Transition-based dependency parsing using recursive neural networks. In *NIPS Workshop on Deep Learning*.

Joseph Turian, Lev Ratinov, and Yoshua Bengio. 2010. Word representations: a simple and general method for semi-supervised learning. In *ACL*.

H. Yamada and Y. Matsumoto. 2003. Statistical dependency analysis with support vector machines. In *Proceedings of the International Workshop on Parsing Technologies (IWPT)*, volume 3.

Yue Zhang and Stephen Clark. 2008. A tale of two parsers: investigating and combining graph-based and transition-based dependency parsing using beam-search. In *Proceedings of the Conference on Empirical Methods in Natural Language Processing*, pages 562–571. Association for Computational Linguistics.

Yue Zhang and Joakim Nivre. 2011. Transition-based dependency parsing with rich non-local features. In *Proceedings of the 49th Annual Meeting of the Association for Computational Linguistics: Human Language Technologies: short papers-Volume 2*, pages 188–193. Association for Computational Linguistics.

Transition-based Neural Constituent Parsing

Taro Watanabe* and **Eiichiro Sumita**
National Institute of Information and Communications Technology
3-5 Hikaridai, Seika-cho, Soraku-gun, Kyoto, 619-0289 JAPAN
tarow@google.com, eiichiro.sumita@nict.go.jp

Abstract

Constituent parsing is typically modeled by a chart-based algorithm under probabilistic context-free grammars or by a transition-based algorithm with rich features. Previous models rely heavily on richer syntactic information through lexicalizing rules, splitting categories, or memorizing long histories. However enriched models incur numerous parameters and sparsity issues, and are insufficient for capturing various syntactic phenomena. We propose a neural network structure that explicitly models the unbounded history of actions performed on the stack and queue employed in transition-based parsing, in addition to the representations of partially parsed tree structure. Our transition-based neural constituent parsing achieves performance comparable to the state-of-the-art parsers, demonstrating F1 score of 90.68% for English and 84.33% for Chinese, without reranking, feature templates or additional data to train model parameters.

1 Introduction

A popular parsing algorithm is a cubic time chart-based dynamic programming algorithm that uses probabilistic context-free grammars (PCFGs). However, PCFGs learned from treebanks are too coarse to represent the syntactic structures of texts. To address this problem, various contexts are incorporated into the grammars through lexicalization (Collins, 2003; Charniak, 2000) or category splitting either manually (Klein and Manning, 2003) or automatically (Matsuzaki et al., 2005; Petrov et al., 2006). Recently a rich feature set was introduced to capture the lexical contexts in each span without extra annotations in grammars (Hall et al., 2014).

Alternatively, transition-based algorithms run in linear time by taking a series of shift-reduce actions with richer lexicalized features considering histories; however, the accuracies did not match with the state-of-the-art methods until recently (Sagae and Lavie, 2005; Zhang and Clark, 2009). Zhu et al. (2013) show that the use of better transition actions considering unaries and a set of non-local features can compete with the accuracies of chart-based parsing. The features employed in a transition-based algorithm usually require part of speech (POS) annotation in the input, but the delayed feature technique allows joint POS inference (Wang and Xue, 2014).

In both frameworks, the richer models require that more parameters be estimated during training which can easily result in the data sparseness problems. Furthermore, the enriched models are still insufficient to capture various syntactic relations in texts due to the limited contexts represented in latent annotations or non-local features. Recently Socher et al. (2013) introduced compositional vector grammar (CVG) to address the above limitations. However, they employ reranking over a forest generated by a baseline parser for efficient search, because CVG is built on cubic time chart-based parsing.

In this paper, we propose a neural network-based parser — *transition-based neural constituent parsing (TNCP)* — which can guarantee efficient search naturally. TNCP explicitly models the actions performed on the stack and queue employed in transition-based parsing. More specifically, the queue is modeled by recurrent neural network (RNN) or Elman network (Elman, 1990) in backward direction (Henderson, 2004). The stack structure is also modeled similarly to RNNs, and its top item is updated using the previously constructed hidden representations saved in the

*The first author is now affiliated with Google, Japan.

Proceedings of the 53rd Annual Meeting of the Association for Computational Linguistics and the 7th International Joint Conference on Natural Language Processing, pages 1169–1179,
Beijing, China, July 26-31, 2015.

stack. The representations from both the stack and queue are combined with the representations propagated from the partially parsed tree structure inspired by the recursive neural networks of CVGs. Parameters are estimated efficiently by a variant of max-violation (Huang et al., 2012) which considers the worst mistakes found during search and updates parameters based on the expected mistake.

Under similar settings, TCNP performs comparably to state-of-the-art parsers. Experimental results obtained using the Wall Street Journal corpus of the English Penn Treebank achieved a labeled F1 score of 90.68%, and the result for the Penn Chinese Treebank was 84.33%. Our parser performs no reranking with computationally expensive models, employs no templates for feature engineering, and requires no additional monolingual data for reliable parameter estimation. The source code and models will be made public[1].

2 Related Work

Our study is largely inspired by recursive neural networks for parsing, first pioneered by Costa et al. (2003), in which parsing is treated as a ranking problem of finding phrasal attachment. Such network structures have been used successfully as a reranker for k-best parses from a baseline parser (Menchetti et al., 2005) or parse forests (Socher et al., 2013), and have achieved gains on large data. Stenetorp (2013) showed that the recursive neural networks are comparable to the state-of-the-art system with a rich feature set under dependency parsing. Our model is not a reranking model, but a discriminative parsing model, which incorporates the representations of stacks and queues employed in the transition-based parsing framework, in addition to the representations of the tree structures. The use of representations outside of the partial parsed trees is very similar to the recently proposed inside-outside recursive neural networks (Le and Zuidema, 2014) which can assign probabilities in a top-down manner, in the same way as PCFGs.

Henderson (2003) was the first to demonstrate the successful use of neural networks to represent derivation histories under large-scale parsing experiments. He employed synchrony networks, i.e., feed-forward style networks, to assign a probability for each step in the left-corner parsing conditioning on all parsing steps. Henderson (2004) later employed a discriminative model and showed further gains by conditioning on the representation of the future input in addition to the history of parsing steps. Similar feed-forward style networks are successfully applied for transition-based dependency parsing in which limited contexts are considered in the feature representation (Chen and Manning, 2014). Our model is very similar in that the score of each action is computed by conditioning on all previous actions and future input in the queue.

The use of neural networks for transition-based shift-reduce parsing was first presented by Mayberry and Miikkulainen (1999) in which the stack representation was treated as a hidden state of an RNN. In their study, the hidden state is updated recurrently by either a shift or reduce action, and its corresponding parse tree is decoded recursively from the hidden state (Berg, 1992) using recursive auto-associative memories (Pollack, 1990). We apply the idea of representing a stack in a continuous vector; however, our method differs in that it memorizes all hidden states pushed to the stack and performs push/pop operations. In this manner, we can represent the local contexts saved in the stack explicitly and use them to construct new hidden states.

3 Transition-based Constituent Parsing

Our transition-based parser is based on a study by Zhu et al. (2013), which adopts the shift-reduce parsing of Sagae and Lavie (2005) and Zhang and Clark (2009). However, our parser differs in that we do not differentiate left or right head words. In addition, POS tags are jointly induced during parsing in the same manner as Wang and Xue (2014). Given an input sentence $w_0, \cdots, w_{n-1}$, the transition-based parser employs a stack of partially constructed constituent tree structures and a queue of input words. In each step, a transition action is applied to a state $\langle i, f, S \rangle$, where i is the next input word position in the queue w_i, f is a flag indicating the completion of parsing, i.e., whether the $ROOT$ of a constituent tree covering all the input words is reached, and S represents a stack of tree elements, $s_0, s_1, \cdots$.

The parser consists of five actions:

shift-*X* consumes the next input word, w_i, from the queue and pushes a non-terminal symbol (or a POS label) as a tree of $X \rightarrow w_i$.

[1] http://github.com/tarowatanabe/trance

$$
\begin{array}{rl}
\text{axiom} & 0 : \langle 0, \text{false}, \langle \text{eps} \rangle \rangle : 0 \\
\text{goal} & (2+u)n : \langle n, \text{true}, S \rangle : \rho \\[1em]
\text{shift-}X & \dfrac{j : \langle i, \text{false}, S \rangle : \rho}{j+1 : \langle i+1, \text{false}, S|X \rangle : \rho + \rho_{\mathsf{sh}}} \\
\text{reduce-}X & \dfrac{j : \langle i, \text{false}, S|s_1|s_0 \rangle : \rho}{j+1 : \langle i, \text{false}, S|X \rangle : \rho + \rho_{\mathsf{re}}} \\
\text{unary-}X & \dfrac{j : \langle i, \text{false}, S|s_0 \rangle : \rho}{j+1 : \langle i, \text{false}, S|X \rangle : \rho + \rho_{\mathsf{un}}} \\
\text{finish} & \dfrac{j : \langle n, \text{false}, S \rangle : \rho}{j+1 : \langle n, \text{true}, S \rangle : \rho + \rho_{\mathsf{fi}}} \\
\text{idle} & \dfrac{j : \langle n, \text{true}, S \rangle : \rho}{j+1 : \langle n, \text{true}, S \rangle : \rho + \rho_{\mathsf{id}}}
\end{array}
$$

Figure 1: Deduction system for shift-reduce parsing, where j is a step size and ρ is a score.

reduce-X pops the top two items s_0 and s_1 out of the stack and combines them as a partial tree with the constituent label X as its root, and with s_0 and s_1 as right and left antecedents, respectively ($X \rightarrow s_1 s_0$). The newly created tree is then pushed into the stack.

unary-X is similar to reduce-X; however, it consumes only the top most item s_0 from the stack and pushes a new tree of $X \rightarrow s_0$.

finish indicates the completion of parsing, i.e., reaching the $ROOT$.

idle preserves completion until the goal is reached.

The whole procedure is summarized as a deduction system in Figure 1. We employ beam search which starts from an axiom consisting of a stack with a special symbol $\langle$eps$\rangle$, and ends when we reach a goal item (Zhang and Clark, 2009). A set of agenda $\boldsymbol{B} = B_0, B_1, \cdots$ maintains the k-best states for each step j at B_j, which is first initialized by inserting the axiom in B_0. Then, at each step $j = 0, 1, \cdots$, every state in the agenda B_j is extended by applying one of the actions and the new states are inserted into the agenda B_{j+1} for the next step, which retains only the k-best states.

We limit the maximum number of consecutive unary actions to u (Sagae and Lavie, 2005; Zhang and Clark, 2009) and the maximum number of unary actions in a single derivation to $u \times n$. Thus, the process is repeated until we reach the final step of $(2+u)n$, which keeps the completed states. The idle action is inspired by the padding method of Zhu et al. (2013), such that the states in an agenda are comparable in terms of score even if differences exist in the number of unary actions. Unlike Zhu et al. (2013) we do not terminate parsing even if all the states in an agenda are completed (f = true).

The score of a state is computed by summing the scores of all the actions leading to the state. In Figure 1, ρ_{sh}, ρ_{re}, ρ_{un}, ρ_{fi} and ρ_{id} are the scores of shift-X, reduce-X, unary-X, finish and idle actions, respectively, which are computed on the basis of the history of actions.

4 Neural Constituent Parsing

The score of a state is defined formally as the total score of transition actions, or a (partial) derivation $\boldsymbol{d} = d_0, d_1, \cdots$ leading to the state as follows:

$$\rho(\boldsymbol{d}) = \sum_{j=0}^{|\boldsymbol{d}|-1} \rho(d_j | d_0^{j-1}). \qquad (1)$$

Note that the score of each action is dependent on all previous actions. In previous studies, the score is computed by a linear model, i.e., a weighted sum of feature values derived from limited histories, such as those that consider two adjacent constituent trees in a stack (Sagae and Lavie, 2005; Zhang and Clark, 2009; Zhu et al., 2013). Our method employs an RNN or Elman network (Elman, 1990) to represent an unlimited stack and queue history.

Formally, we use an m-dimensional vector for each hidden state unless otherwise stated. Here, let $x_i \in \mathbb{R}^{m' \times 1}$ be an m'-dimensional vector representing the input word w_i and the dimension may not match with the hidden state size m. $q_i \in \mathbb{R}^{m \times 1}$ denotes the hidden state for the input word w_i in a queue. Following the RNN in backward direction (Henderson, 2004), the hidden state for each word w_i is computed right-to-left, q_{n-1} to q_0, beginning from a constant q_n:

$$q_i = \tau\left(H_{\mathsf{qu}} q_{i+1} + W_{\mathsf{qu}} x_i + b_{\mathsf{qu}}\right), \qquad (2)$$

where $H_{\mathsf{qu}} \in \mathbb{R}^{m \times m}$, $W_{\mathsf{qu}} \in \mathbb{R}^{m \times m'}$, $b_{\mathsf{qu}} \in \mathbb{R}^{m \times 1}$ and $\tau(x)$ is hard-tanh applied element-wise[2].

[2] $\tau(x) = -1$ for $x < 1$, 1 for $x > 1$ otherwise x.

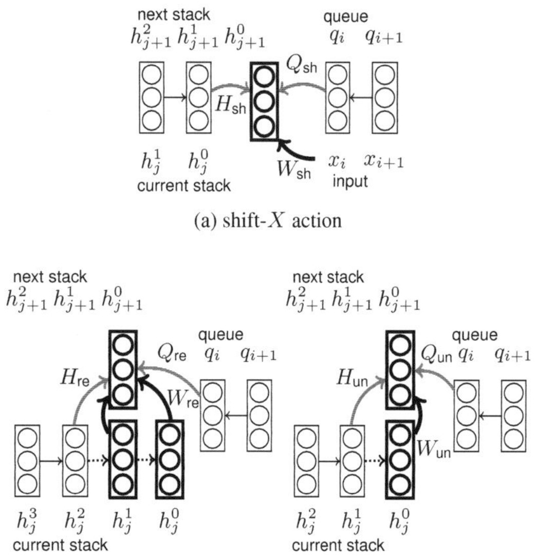

(a) shift-X action

(b) reduce-X action (c) unary-X action

Figure 2: Example neural network for constituent parsing. The thick arrows indicate the context of tree structures, and the gray arrows represent interactions from the stack and queue. The dotted arrows denote popped states.

Shift: Now, let $h_j^l \in \mathbb{R}^{m\times 1}$ represent a hidden state associated with the lth stack item for the jth action. We define the score of a shift action:

$$h_{j+1}^0 = \tau\left(H_{\mathsf{sh}}^X h_j^0 + Q_{\mathsf{sh}}^X q_i + W_{\mathsf{sh}}^X x_i + b_{\mathsf{sh}}^X\right) \quad (3)$$

$$\rho(d_j = \text{shift-}X | d_0^{j-1}) = V_{\mathsf{sh}}^X h_{j+1}^0 + v_{\mathsf{sh}}^X \quad (4)$$

where $H_{\mathsf{sh}}^X \in \mathbb{R}^{m\times m}$, $Q_{\mathsf{sh}}^X \in \mathbb{R}^{m\times m}$, $W_{\mathsf{sh}}^X \in \mathbb{R}^{m\times m'}$ and $b_{\mathsf{sh}}^X \in \mathbb{R}^{m\times 1}$. Figure 2(a) shows the network structure for Equation 3. H_{sh}^X represents an RNN-style architecture that propagates the previous context in the stack. Q_{sh}^X can reflect the queue context q_i, or the future input sequence from w_i through w_{n-1}, while W_{sh}^X directly expresses the leaf of a tree structure using the shifted input word representation x_i for w_i. The hidden state h_{j+1}^0 is used to compute the score of a derivation $\rho(d_j|d_0^{j-1})$ in Equation 4, which is based on the matrix $V_{\mathsf{sh}}^X \in \mathbb{R}^{1\times m}$ and the bias term $v_{\mathsf{sh}}^X \in \mathbb{R}$. Note that $h_{j+1}^l = h_j^{l-1}$ for $l = 1, 2, \cdots$ because the stack is updated by the newly created partial tree label X associated with the new hidden state h_{j+1}^0.

Inspired by CVG (Socher et al., 2013), we differentiate the matrices for each non-terminal (or POS) label X rather than using shared parameters. However, our model differs in that the parameters are untied on the basis of the left hand side of a rule, rather than the right hand side, because our model assigns a score discriminatively for each action with the left hand side label X unlike a generative model derived from PCFGs.

Reduce: Similarly, the score for a reduce action is obtained as follows:

$$h_{j+1}^0 = \tau\left(H_{\mathsf{re}}^X h_j^2 + Q_{\mathsf{re}}^X q_i + W_{\mathsf{re}}^X h_j^{[0:1]} + b_{\mathsf{re}}^X\right) \quad (5)$$

$$\rho(d_j = \text{reduce-}X | d_0^{j-1}) = V_{\mathsf{re}}^X h_{j+1}^0 + v_{\mathsf{re}}^X, \quad (6)$$

where $H_{\mathsf{re}}^X \in \mathbb{R}^{m\times m}$, $Q_{\mathsf{re}}^X \in \mathbb{R}^{m\times m}$, $W_{\mathsf{re}}^X \in \mathbb{R}^{m\times 2m}$, $b_{\mathsf{re}}^X \in \mathbb{R}^{m\times 1}$, and $h^{[l:l']}$ denotes the vertical matrix concatenation of hidden states from h^l to $h^{l'}$.

Note that the reduce-X action pops top two items in the stack that correspond to the two hidden states of $h_j^{[0:1]}$ as represented by Figure 2(b). By pushing a newly created tree with the constituent X, its corresponding hidden state h_{j+1}^0 is pushed to the stack with each remaining hidden state $h_{j+1}^l = h_j^{l+1}$ for $l = 1, 2, \cdots$. The hidden state of the top stack item h_j^0 is a representation of the right antecedent of a newly created binary tree with h_{j+1}^0 as a root, while the hidden state of the next top stack item h_j^1 corresponds to the left antecedent of the binary tree. Thus, the two hidden states capture the recursive neural network-like structure (Costa et al., 2003), while $h_j^2 = h_{j+1}^1$ represents the RNN-like linear history in the stack.

Unary: In the same manner as the reduce action, the unary action is defined by simply reducing a single item from a stack and by pushing a new item (Figure 2(c)):

$$h_{j+1}^0 = \tau\left(H_{\mathsf{un}}^X h_j^1 + Q_{\mathsf{un}}^X q_i + W_{\mathsf{un}}^X h_j^0 + b_{\mathsf{un}}^X\right) \quad (7)$$

$$\rho(d_j = \text{unary-}X | d_0^{j-1}) = V_{\mathsf{un}}^X h_{j+1}^0 + v_{\mathsf{un}}^X, \quad (8)$$

where $H_{\mathsf{un}}^X \in \mathbb{R}^{m\times m}$, $Q_{\mathsf{un}}^X \in \mathbb{R}^{m\times m}$, $W_{\mathsf{un}}^X \in \mathbb{R}^{m\times m}$ and $b_{\mathsf{un}}^X \in \mathbb{R}^{m\times 1}$. Note that $h_{j+1}^l = h_j^l$ for $l = 1, 2, \cdots$, because only the top item is updated in the stack by creating a partial tree with h_j^0 together with the stack history h_j^1.

In summary, the number of model parameters for the three actions is $9\times m^2 + m\times m' + 6\times m + 3$ for each non-terminal label X. The scores for a finish action and an idle action are defined analogous to the unary-X action with special labels for X, $\langle$finish$\rangle$ and $\langle$idle$\rangle$, respectively[3].

5 Parameter Estimation

Let $\boldsymbol{\theta} = \{H^X_{\mathsf{sh}}, Q^X_{\mathsf{sh}}, \cdots\} \in \mathbb{R}^M$ be an M-dimensional vector of all model parameters. The parameters are initialized randomly by following Glorot and Bengio (2010), in which the random value range is determined by the size of the input/output layers. The bias parameters are initialized to zeros.

We employ a variant of max-violation (Huang et al., 2012) as our training objective, in which parameters are updated based on the worst mistake found during search, rather than the first mistake as performed in the early update perceptron algorithm (Collins and Roark, 2004). Specifically, given a training instance $(\boldsymbol{w}, \boldsymbol{y})$ where $\boldsymbol{w}$ is an input sentence and $\boldsymbol{y}$ is its gold derivation, i.e., a sequence of actions representing the gold parse tree for $\boldsymbol{w}$, we seek for the step j^* where the difference of the scores is the largest:

$$j^* = \arg\min_j \left\{ \rho_{\boldsymbol{\theta}}(y_0^j) - \max_{\boldsymbol{d} \in B_j} \rho_{\boldsymbol{\theta}}(\boldsymbol{d}) \right\}. \quad (9)$$

Then, we define the following hinge-loss function:

$$L(\boldsymbol{w}, \boldsymbol{y}; \boldsymbol{B}, \boldsymbol{\theta}) = \max \left\{ 0, 1 - \rho_{\boldsymbol{\theta}}(y_0^{j^*}) + \mathbb{E}_{\tilde{B}_{j^*}}[\rho_{\boldsymbol{\theta}}] \right\} \quad (10)$$

wherein we consider the subset of sub-derivations $\tilde{B}_{j^*} \subset B_{j^*}$ consisting of those scored higher than $\rho_{\boldsymbol{\theta}}(y_0^{j^*})$:

$$\tilde{B}_{j^*} = \left\{ \boldsymbol{d} \in B_{j^*} \middle| \rho_{\boldsymbol{\theta}}(\boldsymbol{d}) > \rho_{\boldsymbol{\theta}}(y_0^{j^*}) \right\} \quad (11)$$

$$p_{\boldsymbol{\theta}}(\boldsymbol{d}) = \frac{\exp(\rho_{\boldsymbol{\theta}}(\boldsymbol{d}))}{\sum_{\boldsymbol{d}' \in \tilde{B}_{j^*}} \exp(\rho_{\boldsymbol{\theta}}(\boldsymbol{d}'))} \quad (12)$$

$$\mathbb{E}_{\tilde{B}_{j^*}}[\rho_{\boldsymbol{\theta}}] = \sum_{\boldsymbol{d} \in \tilde{B}_{j^*}} p_{\boldsymbol{\theta}}(\boldsymbol{d}) \rho_{\boldsymbol{\theta}}(\boldsymbol{d}). \quad (13)$$

Unlike Huang et al. (2012) and inspired by Tamura et al. (2014), we consider all incorrect sub-derivations found in $\tilde{B}_{j^*}$ through the expected score $\mathbb{E}_{\tilde{B}_{j^*}}[\rho_{\boldsymbol{\theta}}]$[4]. The loss function in Equation 10 can be intuitively considered an expected mistake suffered at the maximum violated step j^*, which is measured by the Viterbi violation in Equation 9. Note that if we replace $\mathbb{E}_{\tilde{B}_{j^*}}[\rho_{\boldsymbol{\theta}}]$ with $\max_{\boldsymbol{d} \in B_{j^*}} \rho_{\boldsymbol{\theta}}(\boldsymbol{d})$ in Equation 10, it is exactly the same as the max-violation objective (Huang et al., 2012)[5].

To minimize the loss function, we use a diagonal version of AdaDec (Senior et al., 2013) — a variant of diagonal AdaGrad (Duchi et al., 2011) — under mini-batch settings. Given the sub-gradient $\boldsymbol{g}_t \in \mathbb{R}^M$ of Equation 10 at time t computed by the back-propagation through structure (Goller and Küchler, 1996), we maintain additional parameters $\boldsymbol{G}_t \in \mathbb{R}^M$:

$$\boldsymbol{G}_t \leftarrow \gamma \boldsymbol{G}_{t-1} + \boldsymbol{g}_t \odot \boldsymbol{g}_t, \quad (14)$$

where $\odot$ is the Hadamard product (or the element-wise product). $\boldsymbol{\theta}_{t-1}$ is updated using the element specific learning rate $\boldsymbol{\eta}_t \in \mathbb{R}^M$ derived from $\boldsymbol{G}_t$ and a constant $\eta_0 > 0$:

$$\boldsymbol{\eta}_t \leftarrow \eta_0 (\boldsymbol{G}_t + \epsilon)^{-\frac{1}{2}} \quad (15)$$

$$\boldsymbol{\theta}_{t-\frac{1}{2}} \leftarrow \boldsymbol{\theta}_{t-1} - \boldsymbol{\eta}_t \odot \boldsymbol{g}_t \quad (16)$$

$$\boldsymbol{\theta}_t \leftarrow \arg\min_{\boldsymbol{\theta}} \frac{1}{2} \|\boldsymbol{\theta} - \boldsymbol{\theta}_{t-\frac{1}{2}}\|_2^2 + \lambda \boldsymbol{\eta}_t^\top \operatorname{abs}(\boldsymbol{\theta}). \quad (17)$$

Compared with AdaGrad, the squared sum of the sub-gradients decays over time using a constant $0 < \gamma \leq 1$ in Equation 14. The learning rate in Equation 15 is computed element-wise and bounded by a constant $\epsilon \geq 0$, and if we set $\epsilon \geq \eta_0^2$, it is always decayed[6]. In our preliminary studies, AdaGrad eventually becomes very conservative to update parameters when training longer iterations. AdaDec fixes the problem by ignoring older histories of sub-gradients in $\boldsymbol{G}$, which is reflected in the learning rate $\boldsymbol{\eta}$. In each update, we employ ℓ_1 regularization through FOBOS (Duchi and Singer, 2009) using a hyperparameter $\lambda \geq 0$ to control the fitness in Equation 16 and 17. For testing, we found that taking the average of the parameters over period $\frac{1}{T+1} \sum_{t=0}^{T} \boldsymbol{\theta}_t$ under training iterations T was very effective as demonstrated by Hashimoto et al. (2013).

Parameter estimation is performed in parallel by distributing training instances asynchronously

[3]Since h_j^1 and q_n are constants for the finish and idle actions, we enforce $H^X_{\mathsf{un}} = 0$ and $Q^X_{\mathsf{un}} = 0$ for those special actions.

[4]We can use all the sub-derivations in B_{j^*}; however, our preliminary studies indicated that the use of $\tilde{B}_{j^*}$ was better.

[5]Or, setting $p_{\boldsymbol{\theta}}(\boldsymbol{d}^*) = 1$ for the Viterbi derivation $\boldsymbol{d}^* = \arg\max_{\boldsymbol{d} \in B_{j^*}} \rho_{\boldsymbol{\theta}}(\boldsymbol{d})$ and zero otherwise.

[6]Note that AdaGrad is a special case of AdaDec with $\gamma = 1$ and $\epsilon = 0$.

in each shard and by updating locally copied parameters using the sub-gradients computed from the distributed mini-batches (Dean et al., 2012). The sub-gradients are broadcast asynchronously to other shards to reflect the updates in one shard. Unlike Dean et al. (2012), we do not keep a central storage for model parameters; the replicated parameters are synchronized in each iteration by choosing the model parameters from one of the shards with respect to the minimum of ℓ_1 norm[7]. Note that we synchronize $\boldsymbol{\theta}$, but $\boldsymbol{G}$ is maintained as shard local parameters.

6 Experiments

6.1 Settings

We conducted experiments for transition-based neural constituent parsing (TNCP) for two languages — English and Chinese. English data were derived from the Wall Street Journal (WSJ) of the Penn Treebank (Marcus et al., 1993), from which sections 2-21 were used for training, 22 for development and 23 for testing. Chinese data were extracted from the Penn Chinese Treebank (CTB) (Xue et al., 2005); articles 001-270 and 440-1151 were used for training, 301-325 for development, and 271-300 for testing. Inspired by jackknifing (Collins and Koo, 2005), we reassigned POS tags for training data using the Stanford tagger (Toutanova et al., 2003)[8]. The treebank trees were normalized by removing empty nodes and unary rules with X over X (or $X \rightarrow X$), then binarized in a left-branched manner.

The possible actions taken for our shift-reduce parsing, e.g., $X \rightarrow w$ in shift-X, were learned from the normalized treebank trees. The words that occurred twice or less were handled differently in order to consider OOVs for testing: They were simply mapped to a special token ⟨unk⟩ when looking up their corresponding word representation vector. Similarly, when assigning possible POS tags in shift actions, they fell back to their corresponding "word signature" in the same manner as the Berkeley parser[9]. A maximum number of consecutive unary actions was set to $u = 3$ for WSJ and $u = 4$ for CTB, as determined by the treebanks.

	rep. size	32	64	128	256	512	1024
dev	WSJ-32	89.91	90.15	90.48	90.70	90.75	**90.87**
	64	90.37	90.73	90.81	90.62	90.71	**91.11**
	CTB-32	79.25	81.59	82.80	82.68	84.17	**85.12**
	64	84.04	83.29	82.92	85.12	85.24	**85.77**
test	WSJ-32	89.03	89.49	89.75	**90.45**	90.37	90.01
	64	89.74	90.16	90.48	90.06	89.91	**90.68**
	CTB-32	75.19	78.29	80.46	81.87	**83.16**	82.64
	64	80.11	81.35	81.67	82.91	83.76	**84.33**

Table 1: Comparison of various state/word representation dimension size measured by labeled F1(%). "-32" denotes the hidden state size $m = 32$. The numbers in bold indicate the best results for each hidden state dimension.

Parameter estimation was performed on 16 cores of a Xeon E5-2680 2.7GHz CPU. It took approximately one day for 100 training iterations with $m = 32$ and $m' = 128$ under a mini-batch size of 4 and a beam size of 32. Doubling either one of m or m' incurred approximately double training time. We chose the following hyperparameters by tuning toward the development data in our preliminary experiments[10]: $\eta_0 = 10^{-2}$, $\gamma = 0.9$, $\epsilon = 1$. The choice of λ from $\{10^{-5}, 10^{-6}, 10^{-7}\}$ and the number of training iterations were very important for different training objectives and models in order to avoid overfitting. Thus, they were determined by the performance on the development data for each different training objective and/or network configuration, e.g., the dimension for a hidden state. The word representations were initialized by a tool developed in-house for an RNN language model (Mikolov et al., 2010) trained by noise contrastive estimation (Mnih and Teh, 2012). Note that the word representations for initialization were learned from the given training data, not from additional unannotated data as done by Chen and Manning (2014).

Testing was performed using a beam size of 64 with a Xeon X5550 2.67GHz CPU. All results were measured by the labeled bracketing metric PARSEVAL (Black et al., 1991) using EVALB[11] after debinarization.

6.2 Results

Table 1 shows the impact of dimensions on the parsing performance. We varied the hid-

[7]We also tried averaging among shards. However we observed no gains likely because we performed averaging for testing.

[8]`http://nlp.stanford.edu/software/tagger.shtml`

[9]`https://code.google.com/p/berkeleyparser/`

[10]We confirmed that this hyperparameter setting was appropriate for different models experimented in Section 6.2 through our preliminary studies.

[11]`http://nlp.cs.nyu.edu/evalb/`

	model	tree	+stack	+queue
dev	WSJ	77.70	90.54	**91.11**
	CTB	69.74	84.70	**85.77**
test	WSJ	76.48	90.00	**90.68**
	CTB	66.03	82.85	**84.33**

Table 2: Comparison of network structures measured by labeled F1(%).

	loss	Viterbi	expected
dev	WSJ	90.89	**91.11**
	CTB	84.94	**85.77**
test	WSJ	90.21	**90.68**
	CTB	82.62	**84.33**

Table 3: Comparison of loss functions measured by labeled F1(%).

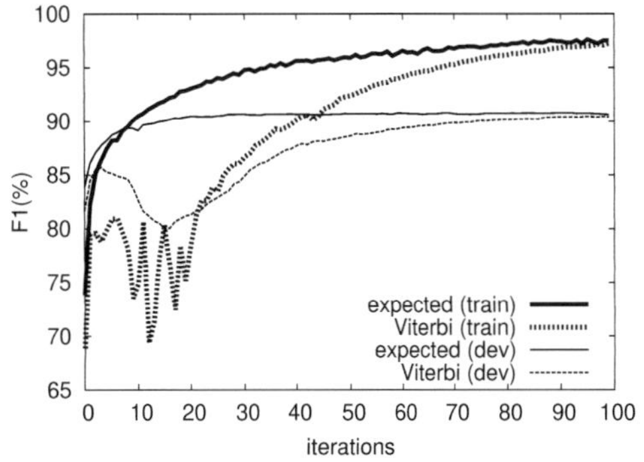

Figure 3: Plots for training iterations and labeled F1(%) on WSJ.

den vector size $m = \{32, 64\}$ and the word representation (embedding) vector size $m' = \{32, 64, 128, 256, 512, 1024\}$[12]. As can be seen, the greater word representation dimensions are generally helpful for both WSJ and CTB on the closed development data (*dev*), which may match with our intuition that the richer syntactic and semantic knowledge representation for each word is required for parsing. However, overfitting was observed when using a 32-dimension hidden vector in both tasks, i.e., drops of performance on the open test data (*test*) when $m' = 1024$, probably caused by the limited generalization capability in the smaller hidden state size. In the rest of this paper, we show the results with $m = 64$ and $m' = 1024$ as determined by the performance on the development data, wherein we achieved 91.11% and 85.77% labeled F1 for WSJ and CTB, respectively. The total number of parameters were approximately 28.3M and 22.0M for WSJ and CTB, respectively, among which 17.8M and 13.4M were occupied for word representations, respectively.

Table 2 differentiated the network structure. The *tree* model computes the new hidden state h^0_{j+1} using only the recursively constructed network by ignoring parameters from the stack and queue, e.g., by enforcing $H^X_{\mathsf{sh}} = 0$ and $Q^X_{\mathsf{sh}} = 0$ in Equation 3, which is essentially similar to the CVG approach (Socher et al., 2013). Adding the context from the stack in *+stack* boosts the performance significantly. Further gains are observed when the queue context *+queue* is incorporated in the model. These results clearly indicate that explicit representations of the stack and queue are very important when applying a recursive neural network model for transition-based parsing.

We then compared the expected mistake with the Viterbi mistake (Huang et al., 2012) as our training objective by replacing $\mathbb{E}_{\tilde{B}_{j*}}[\rho_{\boldsymbol{\theta}}]$ with $\max_{\boldsymbol{d} \in B_{j*}} \rho_{\boldsymbol{\theta}}(\boldsymbol{d})$ in Equation 10. Table 3 shows that the use of the expected mistake (*expected*) as a loss function is significantly better than that of the Viterbi mistake (*Viterbi*) by considering all the incorrect sub-derivations at maximum violated steps during search. Figure 3 and 4 plot the training curves for WSJ and CTB, respectively. The plots clearly demonstrate that the use of the expected mistake is faster in convergence and stabler in learning when compared with that of the Viterbi mistake[13].

Next, we compare our parser, TNCP, with other parsers listed in Table 4 for WSJ and Table 5 for CTB on the test data. The Collins parser (Collins, 1997) and the Berkeley parser (Petrov and Klein, 2007) are chart-based parsers with rich states, either through lexicalization or latent annotation. SSN is a left-corner parser (Henderson, 2004), and CVG is a compositional vector grammar-based parser (Socher et al., 2013)[14]. Both parsers rely on neural networks to represent rich contexts, similar to our work; however they differ in that they essentially perform reranking from either the k-best parses or parse forests[15]. The word representa-

[12]We experimented larger dimensions in Appendix A.

[13]The labeled F1 on those plots are slightly different from EVALB in that all the syntactic labels are considered when computing bracket matching. Further, the scores on the training data are approximation since they were obtained as a by-product of online learning.

[14]`http://nlp.stanford.edu/software/lex-parser.shtml`

[15]Strictly speaking, SSN can work as a standalone parser; Table 4 shows the result after reranking (Henderson, 2004).

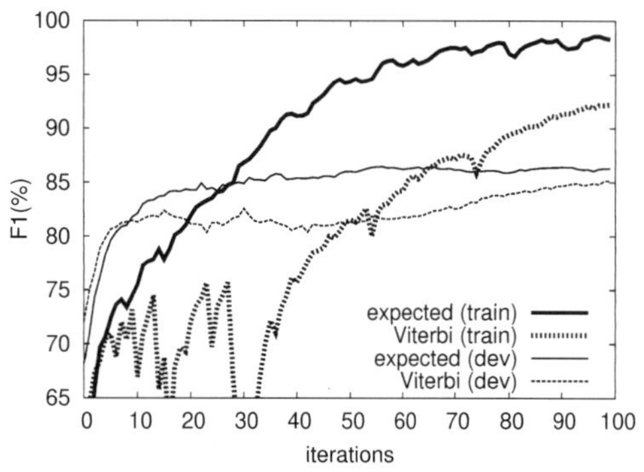

Figure 4: Plots for training iterations and labeled F1(%) on CTB.

parser	test
Collins (Collins, 1997)	87.8
Berkeley (Petrov and Klein, 2007)	90.1
SSN (Henderson, 2004)	90.1
ZPar (Zhu et al., 2013)	90.4
CVG (Socher et al., 2013)	90.4
Charniak-R (Charniak and Johnson, 2005)	**91.0**
This work: TNCP	90.7

Table 4: Comparison of different parsers on the WSJ test data measured by labeled F1(%).

tion in CVG was learned from large monolingual data (Turian et al., 2010), but our parser learns word representation from only the provided training data. Charniak-R is a discriminative reranking parser with non-local features (Charniak and Johnson, 2005). ZPar is a transition-based shift-reduce parser (Zhu et al., 2013)[16] that influences the deduction system in Figure 1, but differs in that scores are computed by a large number of features and POS tagging is performed separately. The results shown in Table 4 and 5 come from the feature set without extra data, i.e., semi-supervised features. Joint is the joint POS tagging and transition-based parsing with non-local features (Wang and Xue, 2014). Similar to ZPar, we present the result without cluster features learned from extra unannotated data.

Finally, we measured the speed for parsing by varying beam size and hidden dimension (Table 6). When testing, we applied a pre-computation technique for layers involving word representation vectors (Devlin et al., 2014), i.e., W_{qu} in Equation 2 and W^{X}_{sh} in Equation 3. Thus, the parsing speed was influenced by only the hidden state size m. It is clear that the enlarged beam size improves per-

[16]http://sourceforge.net/projects/zpar/

parser	test
ZPar (Zhu et al., 2013)	83.2
Berkeley (Petrov and Klein, 2007)	83.3
Joint (Wang and Xue, 2014)	**84.9**
This work: TNCP	84.3

Table 5: Comparison of different parsers on the CTB test data measured by labeled F1(%).

beam	32	64	128
WSJ-32	15.42/89.95	7.90/90.01	3.97/**90.04**
64	7.31/90.56	3.56/90.68	1.76/**90.73**
CTB-32	13.67/82.35	6.95/82.64	3.68/**82.84**
64	6.15/84.12	3.11/**84.33**	1.53/83.83

Table 6: Comparison of parsing speed by varying beam size and hidden dimension; each cell shows the number of sentences per second/labeled F1(%) measured on the test data.

formance by trading off run time in most cases. Note that Berkeley, CVG and ZPar took 4.74, 1.54 and 37.92 sentences/sec, respectively, with WSJ. Although it is more difficult to compare with other parsers, our parser implemented in C++ is on par with Java implementations of Berkeley and CVG. The large run time difference with the C++ implemented ZPar may come from the network computation and joint POS inference in our model which impact parsing speed significantly.

6.3 Error Analysis

To assess parser error types, we used the tool proposed by Kummerfeld et al. (2012)[17]. The average number of errors per sentence is listed in Table 7 for each error type on the WSJ test data. Generally, our parser results in errors that are comparable to the state-of-the-art parsers; however, greater reductions are observed for various attachments errors. One of the largest gains comes from the clause attachment, i.e., 0.12 reduction in average errors from Berkeley and 0.05 from CVG. The average number of errors is also reduced by 0.09 from Berkeley and 0.06 from CVG for the PP attachment. We also observed large reductions in coordination and unary rule errors.

7 Conclusion

We have introduced transition-based neural constituent parsing — a neural network architecture that encodes each state explicitly — as a continuous vector by considering the recurrent se-

[17]https://code.google.com/p/berkeley-parser-analyser/

error type	Berkeley	CVG	TNCP
PP Attach	0.82	0.79	**0.73**
Clause Attach	0.50	0.43	**0.38**
Diff Label	0.29	0.29	0.29
Mod Attach	0.27	0.27	0.27
NP Attach	0.37	**0.31**	0.32
Co-ord	0.38	0.32	**0.29**
1-Word Span	**0.28**	0.31	0.30
Unary	0.24	0.22	**0.18**
NP Int	**0.18**	0.19	0.20
Other	**0.41**	**0.41**	0.45

Table 7: Comparison of different parsers on the WSJ test data measured by average number of errors per sentence; the numbers in bold indicate the least errors in each error type.

quences of the stack and queue in the transition-based parsing framework in addition to recursively constructed partial trees. Our parser works in a standalone fashion without reranking and does not rely on an external POS tagger or additional monolingual data for reliable estimates of syntactic and/or semantic representations of words. The parser achieves performance that is comparable to state-of-the-art systems.

In the future, we plan to apply our neural network structure to dependency parsing. We are also interested in using long short-term memory neural networks (Hochreiter and Schmidhuber, 1997) to better model the locality of propagated information from the stack and queue. The parameter estimation under semi-supervised setting will be investigated further.

Acknowledgments

We would like to thank Lemao Liu for suggestions while drafting this paper. We are also grateful for various comments from anonymous reviewers.

References

George Berg. 1992. A connectionist parser with recursive sentence structure and lexical disambiguation. In *Proc. of AAAI '92*, pages 32–37.

Ezra Black, Steve Abney, Dan Flickinger, Claudia Gdaniec, Ralph Grishman, Phil Harrison, Don Hindle, Robert Ingria, Fred Jelinek, Judith Klavans, Mark Liberman, Mitchell Marcus, Salim Roukos, Beatrice Santorini, and Tomek Strzalkowski. 1991. Procedure for quantitatively comparing the syntactic coverage of english grammars. In *Proc. of the Workshop on Speech and Natural Language*, pages 306–311, Stroudsburg, PA, USA.

Eugene Charniak and Mark Johnson. 2005. Coarse-to-fine n-best parsing and maxent discriminative reranking. In *Proc. of ACL 2005*, pages 173–180, Ann Arbor, Michigan, June.

Eugene Charniak. 2000. A maximum-entropy-inspired parser. In *Proc. of NAACL 2000*, pages 132–139, Stroudsburg, PA, USA.

Danqi Chen and Christopher Manning. 2014. A fast and accurate dependency parser using neural networks. In *Proc. of EMNLP 2014*, pages 740–750, Doha, Qatar, October.

Michael Collins and Terry Koo. 2005. Discriminative reranking for natural language parsing. *Computational Linguistics*, 31(1):25–70, March.

Michael Collins and Brian Roark. 2004. Incremental parsing with the perceptron algorithm. In *Proc. of ACL 2004*, pages 111–118, Barcelona, Spain, July.

Michael Collins. 1997. Three generative, lexicalised models for statistical parsing. In *Proc. of ACL '97*, pages 16–23, Madrid, Spain, July.

Michael Collins. 2003. Head-driven statistical models for natural language parsing. *Computational Linguistics*, 29(4):589–637, December.

Fabrizio Costa, Paolo Frasconi, Vincenzo Lombardo, and Giovanni Soda. 2003. Towards incremental parsing of natural language using recursive neural networks. *Applied Intelligence*, 19(1-2):9–25, May.

Jeffrey Dean, Greg Corrado, Rajat Monga, Kai Chen, Matthieu Devin, Mark Mao, Marc'aurelio Ranzato, Andrew Senior, Paul Tucker, Ke Yang, Quoc V. Le, and Andrew Y. Ng. 2012. Large scale distributed deep networks. In *Advances in Neural Information Processing Systems 25*, pages 1223–1231. Curran Associates, Inc.

Jacob Devlin, Rabih Zbib, Zhongqiang Huang, Thomas Lamar, Richard Schwartz, and John Makhoul. 2014. Fast and robust neural network joint models for statistical machine translation. In *Proc. of ACL 2014*, pages 1370–1380, Baltimore, Maryland, June.

John Duchi and Yoram Singer. 2009. Efficient online and batch learning using forward backward splitting. *Journal of Machine Learning Research*, 10:2899–2934, December.

John Duchi, Elad Hazan, and Yoram Singer. 2011. Adaptive subgradient methods for online learning and stochastic optimization. *Journal of Machine Learning Research*, 12:2121–2159, July.

Jeffrey L. Elman. 1990. Finding structure in time. *Cognitive Science*, 14(2):179–211.

Xavier Glorot and Yoshua Bengio. 2010. Understanding the difficulty of training deep feedforward neural networks. In *Proc. of the Thirteenth International Conference on Artificial Intelligence and Statistics (AISTATS-10)*, volume 9, pages 249–256.

Christoph Goller and Andreas Küchler. 1996. Learning task-dependent distributed representations by backpropagation through structure. In *Proc. of IEEE International Conference on Neural Networks, 1996*, volume 1, pages 347–352 vol.1, Jun.

David Hall, Greg Durrett, and Dan Klein. 2014. Less grammar, more features. In *Proc. of ACL 2014*, pages 228–237, Baltimore, Maryland, June.

Kazuma Hashimoto, Makoto Miwa, Yoshimasa Tsuruoka, and Takashi Chikayama. 2013. Simple customization of recursive neural networks for semantic relation classification. In *Proc. of EMNLP 2013*, pages 1372–1376, Seattle, Washington, USA, October.

James Henderson. 2003. Inducing history representations for broad coverage statistical parsing. In *Proc. of HLT-NAACL 2003*, pages 24–31, Stroudsburg, PA, USA.

James Henderson. 2004. Discriminative training of a neural network statistical parser. In *Proc. of ACL 2004*, pages 95–102, Barcelona, Spain, July.

Sepp Hochreiter and Jürgen Schmidhuber. 1997. Long short-term memory. *Neural Computation*, 9(8):1735–1780, November.

Liang Huang, Suphan Fayong, and Yang Guo. 2012. Structured perceptron with inexact search. In *Proc. of NAACL-HLT 2012*, pages 142–151, Montréal, Canada, June.

Dan Klein and Christopher D. Manning. 2003. Accurate unlexicalized parsing. In *Proc. of ACL 2003*, pages 423–430, Sapporo, Japan, July.

Jonathan K. Kummerfeld, David Hall, James R. Curran, and Dan Klein. 2012. Parser showdown at the wall street corral: An empirical investigation of error types in parser output. In *Proc. of EMNLP-CoNLL 2012*, pages 1048–1059, Jeju Island, Korea, July.

Phong Le and Willem Zuidema. 2014. The inside-outside recursive neural network model for dependency parsing. In *Proc. of EMNLP 2014*, pages 729–739, Doha, Qatar, October.

Mitchell P. Marcus, Mary Ann Marcinkiewicz, and Beatrice Santorini. 1993. Building a large annotated corpus of english: The penn treebank. *Computational Linguistics*, 19(2):313–330, June.

Takuya Matsuzaki, Yusuke Miyao, and Jun'ichi Tsujii. 2005. Probabilistic CFG with latent annotations. In *Proc. of ACL 2005*, pages 75–82, Ann Arbor, Michigan, June.

Marshall R. Mayberry and Risto Miikkulainen. 1999. Sardsrn: A neural network shift-reduce parser. In *Proc. of IJCAI '99*, pages 820–827, San Francisco, CA, USA.

Sauro Menchetti, Fabrizio Costa, Paolo Frasconi, and Massimiliano Pontil. 2005. Wide coverage natural language processing using kernel methods and neural networks for structured data. *Pattern Recognition Letters*, 26(12):1896–1906, September.

Tomáš Mikolov, Martin Karafiát, Lukáš Burget, Jan Černocký, and Sanjeev Khudanpur. 2010. Recurrent neural network based language model. In *Proc. of INTERSPEECH 2010*, pages 1045–1048.

Andriy Mnih and Yee W. Teh. 2012. A fast and simple algorithm for training neural probabilistic language models. In John Langford and Joelle Pineau, editors, *Proc. of ICML-2012*, pages 1751–1758, New York, NY, USA.

Slav Petrov and Dan Klein. 2007. Improved inference for unlexicalized parsing. In *Proc. of NAACL-HLT 2007*, pages 404–411, Rochester, New York, April.

Slav Petrov, Leon Barrett, Romain Thibaux, and Dan Klein. 2006. Learning accurate, compact, and interpretable tree annotation. In *Proc. of COLING-ACL 2006*, pages 433–440, Sydney, Australia, July.

Jordan B. Pollack. 1990. Recursive distributed representations. *Artificial Intelligence*, 46(1-2):77–105, November.

Kenji Sagae and Alon Lavie. 2005. A classifier-based parser with linear run-time complexity. In *Proc. of the Ninth International Workshop on Parsing Technology*, pages 125–132, Vancouver, British Columbia, October.

Andrew Senior, Georg Heigold, Marc'Aurelio Ranzato, and Ke Yang. 2013. An empirical study of learning rates in deep neural networks for speech recognition. In *Proc. of ICASSP 2013*, pages 6724–6728, May.

Richard Socher, John Bauer, Christopher D. Manning, and Ng Andrew Y. 2013. Parsing with compositional vector grammars. In *Proc. of ACL 2013*, pages 455–465, Sofia, Bulgaria, August.

Pontus Stenetorp. 2013. Transition-based dependency parsing using recursive neural networks. In *Proc. of Deep Learning Workshop at the 2013 Conference on Neural Information Processing Systems (NIPS)*, Lake Tahoe, Nevada, USA, December.

Akihiro Tamura, Taro Watanabe, and Eiichiro Sumita. 2014. Recurrent neural networks for word alignment model. In *Proc. of ACL 2014*, pages 1470–1480, Baltimore, Maryland, June.

Kristina Toutanova, Dan Klein, Christopher D. Manning, and Yoram Singer. 2003. Feature-rich part-of-speech tagging with a cyclic dependency network. In *Proc. of HLT-NAACL 2003*, pages 173–180, Stroudsburg, PA, USA.

	rep. size	32	64	128	256	512	1024	2048	4096
dev	WSJ-32	89.91	90.15	90.48	90.70	90.75	90.87	**91.11**	91.04
	64	90.37	90.73	90.81	90.62	90.71	91.11	91.34	**91.36**
	CTB-32	79.25	81.59	82.80	82.68	84.17	85.12	85.61	**85.76**
	64	84.04	83.29	82.92	85.12	85.24	85.77	86.28	**86.94**
test	WSJ-32	89.03	89.49	89.75	**90.45**	90.37	90.01	90.33	90.40
	64	89.74	90.16	90.48	90.06	89.91	90.68	**91.05**	90.94
	CTB-32	75.19	78.29	80.46	81.87	83.16	82.64	83.13	**83.67**
	64	80.11	81.35	81.67	82.91	83.76	84.33	83.76	**84.38**

Table 8: Comparison of various state/word representation dimension size measured by labeled F1(%). "-32" denotes the hidden state size $m = 32$. The numbers in bold indicate the best results for each hidden state dimension.

Joseph Turian, Lev-Arie Ratinov, and Yoshua Bengio. 2010. Word representations: A simple and general method for semi-supervised learning. In *Proc. of ACL 2010*, pages 384–394, Uppsala, Sweden, July.

Zhiguo Wang and Nianwen Xue. 2014. Joint pos tagging and transition-based constituent parsing in chinese with non-local features. In *Proc. of ACL 2014*, pages 733–742, Baltimore, Maryland, June.

Naiwen Xue, Fei Xia, Fu-dong Chiou, and Marta Palmer. 2005. The penn chinese treebank: Phrase structure annotation of a large corpus. *Natural Language Engineering*, 11(2):207–238, June.

Yue Zhang and Stephen Clark. 2009. Transition-based parsing of the chinese treebank using a global discriminative model. In *Proc. of the 11th International Conference on Parsing Technologies (IWPT'09)*, pages 162–171, Paris, France, October.

Muhua Zhu, Yue Zhang, Wenliang Chen, Min Zhang, and Jingbo Zhu. 2013. Fast and accurate shift-reduce constituent parsing. In *Proc. of ACL 2013*, pages 434–443, Sofia, Bulgaria, August.

A Additional Results

We conducted additional experiments by enlarging the word representation vector size m' in Table 8. In general, we observed further gains with richer word representation, but suffered overfitting effects when setting $m' = 4096$. The results with $m = 64$ and $m' = 4096$ achieved the best performance on the development data, 91.36% and 86.94% labeled F1 for WSJ and CTB, respectively, wherein we observed the accuracies of 90.94% and 84.38% on the test data, respectively. Note that it took approximately one week to train the model when $m' = 4096$ under WSJ, which was impractical to analyze the results further, e.g. comparison with other training objectives.

Feature Selection in Kernel Space: A Case Study on Dependency Parsing

Xian Qian and **Yang Liu**
The University of Texas at Dallas
800 W. Campbell Rd., Richardson, TX, USA
{qx,yangl}@hlt.utdallas.edu

Abstract

Given a set of basic binary features, we propose a new L_1 norm SVM based feature selection method that explicitly selects the features in their polynomial or tree kernel spaces. The efficiency comes from the anti-monotone property of the subgradients: the subgradient with respect to a combined feature can be bounded by the subgradient with respect to each of its component features, and a feature can be pruned safely without further consideration if its corresponding subgradient is not steep enough. We conduct experiments on the English dependency parsing task with a third order graph-based parser. Benefiting from the rich features selected in the tree kernel space, our model achieved the best reported unlabeled attachment score of 93.72 without using any additional resource.

1 Introduction

In Natural Language Processing (NLP) domain, existing linear models typically adopt exhaustive search to generate tons of features such that the important features are included. However, the brute-force approach will guickly run out of memory when the feature space is extremely large. Unlike linear models, kernel methods provide a powerful and unified framework for learning a large or even infinite number of features implicitly using limited memory. However, many kernel methods scale quadratically in the number of training samples, and can hardly reap the benefits of learning a large dataset. For example, the popular Penn Tree Bank (PTB) corpus for training an English part of speech (POS) tagger has approximately $1M$ words, thus it takes $1M^2$ time to compute the kernel matrix, which is unacceptable using current hardwares.

In this paper, we propose a new feature selection method that can efficiently select representative features in the kernel space to improve the quality of linear models. Specifically, given a limited number of basic features such as the commonly used unigrams and bigrams, our method performs feature selection in the space of their combinations, e.g, the concatenation of these n-grams. A sparse discriminative model is produced by training L_1 norm SVMs using subgradient methods. Different from traditional training procedures, we divide the feature vector into a number of segments, and sort them in a coarse-to-fine order: the first segment includes the basic features, the second segment includes the combined features composed of two basic features, and so on. In each iteration, we calculate the subgradient segment by segment. A combined feature and all its further combinations in the following segments can be safely pruned if the absolute value of its corresponding subgradient is not sufficiently large. The algorithm stops until all features are pruned. Besides, two simple yet effective pruning strategies are proposed to filter the combinations.

We conduct experiments on English dependency parsing task. Millions of deep, high order features derived by concatenating contextual words, POS tags, directions and distances of dependencies are selected in the polynomial kernel and tree kernel spaces. The result is promising: these features significantly improved a state-of-the-art third order dependency parser, yielding the best reported unlabeled attachment score of 93.72 without using any additional resource.

Proceedings of the 53rd Annual Meeting of the Association for Computational Linguistics and the 7th International Joint Conference on Natural Language Processing, pages 1180–1190,
Beijing, China, July 26-31, 2015. ©2015 Association for Computational Linguistics

2 Related Works

There are two solutions for learning in ultra high dimensional feature space: kernel method and feature selection.

Fast kernel methods have been intensively studied in the past few years. Recently, randomized methods have attracted more attention due to its theoretical and empirical success, such as the Nyström method (Williams and Seeger, 2001) and random projection (Lu et al., 2014). In NLP domain, previous studies mainly focused on polynomial kernels, such as the splitSVM and approximate polynomial kernel (Wu et al., 2007).

In feature selection domain, there has been plenty of work focusing on fast computation, while feature selection in extremely high dimensional feature space is relatively less studied. Zhang et al. (2006) proposed a progressive feature selection framework that splits the feature space into tractable disjoint sub-spaces such that a feature selection algorithm can be performed on each one of them, and then merges the selected features from different sub-spaces. The search space they studied contained more than 20 million features. Tan et al. (2012) proposed adaptive feature scaling (AFS) scheme for ultra-high dimensional feature selection. The dimensionality of the features in their experiments is up to 30 millions.

Previous studies on feature selection in kernel space typically used mining based approaches to prune feature candidates. The key idea for efficient pruning is to estimate the upper bound of statistics of features without explicit calculation. The simplest example is frequent mining where for any n-gram feature, its frequency is bounded by any of its substrings.

Suzuki et al. (Suzuki et al., 2004) proposed to select features in convolution kernel space based on their chi-squared values. They derived a concise form to estimate the upper bound of chi-square values, and used PrefixScan algorithm to enumerates all the significant sub-sequences of features efficiently.

Okanohara and Tsujii (Okanohara and Tsujii, 2009) further combined the pruning technique with L_1 regularization. They showed the connection between L_1 regularization and frequent mining: the L_1 regularizer provides a minimum support threshold to prune the gradients of parameters. They selected the combination features in a coarse-to-fine order, the gradient value for a combination feature can be bounded by each of its component feature, hence may be pruned without explicit calculation. They also sorted the features to tighten the bound. Our idea is similar with theirs, the difference is that our search space is much larger: we did not restrict the number of component features. We recursively pruned the feature set and in each recursion we selected feature in a batch manner. We further adopted an efficient data structure, spectral bloom filter, to estimate the gradients for the candidate features without generating them.

3 The Proposed Method

3.1 Basic Idea

Given n training samples $x_1 \dots x_n$ with labels $y_1 \dots y_n \in \mathcal{Y}$, we extend the kernel over the input space to the joint input and output space by simply defining $\mathbf{f}^T(x_i, y)\mathbf{f}(x_i, y') = K(x_i, x_j)I(y == y')$, which is the same as Taskar's (see (Taskar, 2004), Page 68), where $\mathbf{f}$ is the explicit feature map for the kernel, and $I(\cdot, \cdot)$ is the indicator function.

Our task is to select a subset of representative elements in the feature vector $\mathbf{f}$. Unlike previously studied feature selection problems, the dimension of $\mathbf{f}$ could be extremely high. It is impossible to store the feature vector in the memory or even on the disk.

For easy illustration, we describe our method for the polynomial kernel, and it can be easily extended to the tree kernel space.

The R degree polynomial kernel space is established by a set of basic features $\mathcal{B} = \{b_0 = 1, b_1, \dots, b_{|\mathcal{B}|}\}$ and their combinations. In other words, each feature is the product of at most R basic features $f_j = b_{j_1} * b_{j_2} * \dots * b_{j_r}$, $r \leq R$. As we assume that all features are binary [1], f_j can be rewritten as the minimum of these basic features: $f_j = \min\{b_{j_1}, b_{j_2}, \dots, b_{j_r}\}$. We use $\mathcal{B}_j = \{b_{j_1}, b_{j_2}, \dots, b_{j_r}\}$ to denote the set of component basic features for f_j. r is called the order of feature f_j. For two features f_j, f_k, we say f_k is an extension of f_j if $\mathcal{B}_j \subset \mathcal{B}_k$.

Take the document classification task as an example, the basic features could be word n-grams, and the quadratic kernel (degree=2) space includes the combinated features composed of two

[1]Binary features are often used in NLP.

n-grams, a second order feature is true if both n-grams appear in the document, it is an extension of any of its component n-grams (first order features).

We use L_1 norm SVMs for feature selection. Traditionally, the L_1 norm SVMs can be trained using subgradient descent and generate a sparse weight vector $\mathbf{w}$ for feature $\mathbf{f}$. Due to the high dimensionality in our case, we divide $\mathbf{f}$ into a number of segments according to the order of the feature, the k-th segment includes the k-order features. In each iteration, we update the weights of features segment by segment. When updating the weight of feature f_j in the k-th segment, we estimate the subgradients with respective to f_j's extensions in the rest $k+1$, $k+2$, ... segments and keep their weights at zero if the subgradients are not sufficiently steep. In this way, we could ignore these features without explicit calculation.

3.2 L_1 Norm SVMs

Specifically, the objective function for learning L_1 norm SVMs is:

$$\min_{\mathbf{w}} \mathcal{O}(\mathbf{w}) = C\|\mathbf{w}\|_1 + \sum_i loss(i)$$

where

$$loss(i) = \max_{y \in \mathcal{Y}} \{\mathbf{w}^T \Delta\mathbf{f}(x_i, y) + \delta(y_i, y)\}$$

is the hinge loss function for the i-th sample. $\Delta\mathbf{f}(x_i, y) = \mathbf{f}(x_i, y_i) - \mathbf{f}(x_i, y)$ is the residual feature vector, $\delta(a, b) = 0$ if $a = b$, otherwise $\delta(a, b) = 1$. Regularization parameter C controls the sparsity of $\mathbf{w}$. With higher C, more zero elements are generated. We call a feature is fired if its value is 1.

The objective function is a sum of piecewise linear functions, hence is convex. Subgradient descent algorithm is one poplar approach for minimizing non-differentiable convex functions, it updates $\mathbf{w}$ using

$$\mathbf{w}^{new} = \mathbf{w} - \mathbf{g}\alpha^t$$

where $\mathbf{g}$ is the subgradient of $\mathbf{w}$, α^t is the step size in the t-th iteration. Subgradient algorithm converges if the step size sequence is properly selected (Boyd and Mutapcic, 2006).

We are interested in the non-differentiable point $w_j = 0$. Let $y_i^* = \max_y \{\mathbf{w}^T \Delta\mathbf{f}(x_i, y) + \delta(y_i, y)\}$, the prediction of the current model. According to the definition of subgradient, we have, for each sample x_i, $\Delta\mathbf{f}(x_i, y_i^*)$ is a subgradient of $loss(i)$, thus, $\sum_i \Delta\mathbf{f}(x_i, y_i^*)$ is a subgradient of $\sum_i loss(i)$.

Adding the penalty term $C\|\mathbf{w}\|_1$, we get the subset of subgradients at $w_j = 0$ for the objective function

$$\sum_i \Delta f_j(x_i, y_i^*) - C \leq g_j \leq \sum_i \Delta f_j(x_i, y_i^*) + C$$

We can pick any g_j to update w_j. Remind that our purpose is to keep the model sparse, and we would like to pick $g_j = 0$ if possible. That is, we can keep $w_j = 0$ if $|\sum_i \Delta f_j(x_i, y_i^*)| \leq C$.

Obviously, for any j, we have $|\sum_i \Delta f_j(x_i, y_i^*)| \leq \sum_i \sum_y f_j(x_i, y) = \#f_j$, i.e., the frequency of feature f_j. Thus, we have

Proposition 1 *Let C be the threshold of the frequency, the model generated by the subgradient method is sparser than frequent mining.*

3.3 Feature Selection Using Gradient Mining

Now the problem is how to estimate $|\sum_i \Delta f_j(x_i, y_i^*)|$ without explicit calculation for each f_j.

In the following, we mix the terminology gradient and subgradient without loss of clarity. We define the positive gradient and negative gradient for w_j

$$\#f_j^+ = \sum_{i, y_i \neq y_i^*} f_j(x_i, y_i)$$
$$\#f_j^- = \sum_{i, y_i \neq y_i^*} f_j(x_i, y_i^*)$$

We have

$$\begin{aligned}\sum_i \Delta f_j(x_i, y_i^*) &= \sum_{i, y_i^* \neq y_i} \Delta f_j(x_i, y_i^*) \\ &= \#f_j^+ - \#f_j^-\end{aligned}$$

The estimation problem turns out to be a counting problem: we collect all the incorrectly predicted samples, and count $\#f_j^+$, the frequency of f_j fired by the gold labels, and $\#f_j^-$ the frequency of f_j fired by the predictions.

As mentioned above, each feature in polynomial kernel space is defined as $f_j = \min\{b \in \mathcal{B}_j\} = \min\{b_{j_1}, \ldots, b_{j_r}\}$. Equivalently, we can define f_j in a recursive way, which is more frequently used in the rest of the paper. That is, $f_j =$

$\min\{\min\{b_{j_2}, \ldots, b_{j_r}\}, \min\{b_{j_1}, b_{j_3}, \ldots, b_{j_r}\}, \ldots\}$, which is the mimum of r features of order $r-1$. Formally, denote $\mathcal{B}_j^{-i}$ as the subset of $\mathcal{B}_j$ by removing its i-th element, then the r-order feature, we have $f_j = \min\{h_1, \ldots, h_r\}$, where $h_k = \min\{b \in \mathcal{B}_j^{-k}\}, 1 \le k \le r$.

We have the following anti-monotone property, which is the basis of our method

$$
\begin{aligned}
\#f_j^+ &\le \#h_k^+ \quad \forall k \\
\#f_j^- &\le \#h_k^- \quad \forall k
\end{aligned}
$$

If there exists a k, such that $\#h_k^+ \le C$ and $\#h_k^- \le C$, we have

$$
\begin{aligned}
& |\sum_i \Delta f_j(x_i, y_i^*)| \\
= \;& |\#f_j^+ - \#f_j^-| \\
\le \;& \max\{\#f_j^+, \#f_j^-\} \\
\le \;& \max\{\min_k\{\#h_k^+\}, \min_k\{\#h_k^-\}\} \\
\le \;& \min_k\{\max\{\#h_k^+, \#h_k^-\}\} \\
\le \;& C
\end{aligned}
$$

The third inequality comes from the well known min-max inequality: $\max_i \min_j\{a_{ij}\} \le \min_j \max_i\{a_{ij}\}$. Thus, we could prune f_j without calculating its corresponding gradient.

This is a chain rule, which means that any feature that has f_j as its component can also be pruned safely. To see this, suppose $\phi = \min\{\ldots, f_j, \ldots\}$ is such a combined feature, we have

$$
\begin{aligned}
|\#\phi^+ - \#\phi^-| &\le \max\{\#\phi^+, \#\phi^-\} \\
&\le \max\{\#f_j^+, \#f_j^-\} \\
&\le C
\end{aligned}
$$

Based on this, we present the gradient mining based feature selection framework in Algorithm 1.

4 Prune the Candidate Set

In practice, Algorithm 1 is far from efficient because Line 17 may generate large amounts of candidate features that quickly consume the memory. In this section, we introduce two pruning strategies that could greatly reduce the size of candidates.

Algorithm 1 Feature Selection Using Gradient Mining

Require: Samples $X = \{x_1, \ldots, x_n\}$ with labels $\{y_1, \ldots, y_n\}$, basic features $\mathcal{B} = \{b_1, \ldots, b_{|\mathcal{B}|}\}$, threshold $C > 0$, max iteration number M, degree of polynomial kernel R, sequence of learning step $\{\alpha^t\}$.

Ensure: Set of selected features $\mathcal{S} = \{f_j\}$, where $f_j = \min\{b \in \mathcal{B}_j\}, \mathcal{B}_j \subseteq \mathcal{B}, |\mathcal{B}_j| \le R$.

1: $\mathcal{S}_r = \emptyset, r = 1, \ldots, R$ {$\mathcal{S}_r$ denotes the selected r-order features}
2: **for** $t = 1 \to M$ **do**
3: Set $\mathcal{S} = \bigcup_{r=1}^{R} \mathcal{S}_r$, $\mathbf{f}$ = the vector of features in $\mathcal{S}$.
4: Calculate $y_i^* = \max_y\{\mathbf{w}^T \mathbf{f}(x_i, y) + \delta(y_i, y)\}, \forall i$.
5: Initialize candidate set $\mathcal{A} = \mathcal{B}$
6: **for** $r = 1 \to R$ **do**
7: **for all** $f_j \in \mathcal{A}$ **do**
8: Calculate $\#f_j^+ = \sum_{i, y_i \ne y_i^*} f_j(x_i, y_i)$ and $\#f_j^- = \sum_{i, y_i \ne y_i^*} f_j(x_i, y_i^*)$
9: **if** $\#f_j^+, \#f_j^- \le C$ **and** $w_j = 0$ **then**
10: Remove f_j from $\mathcal{A}$
11: **else**
12: $w_j = w_j + (\#f_j^+ - \#f_j^- + C\text{sign}(w_j))\alpha^t$
13: **end if**
14: **end for**
15: $\mathcal{S}_r = \mathcal{A}$
16: **if** $r < R$ **then**
17: Generate order-$r+1$ candidates: $\mathcal{A} = \mathcal{S}_{r+1} \bigcup \{h | h = \min\{f_1, \ldots f_r \in \mathcal{S}_r\}$, order of h is $r+1\}$
18: **end if**
19: **end for**
20: **end for**

4.1 Pre-Training

Usually, the weights of features are initialized with 0 in the training procedure. However, this will select too many features in the first iteration, because all samples are mis-classified in Line 4, the gradients $\#f_j^+$ and $\#f_j^-$ equal to the frequencies of the features, and many of them could be larger than C. Luckily, due to the convexity of piecewise linear function, the optimality of subgradient method is irrelevant with the initial point. So we can start with a well trained model using a small subset of features such as the set of lower order features so that the prediction is more accurate and the gradients $\#f^+$ and $\#f^-$ are much lower.

4.2 Bloom Filter

The second strategy is to use bloom filter to reduce candidates before putting them into the candidate set $\mathcal{A}$.

A bloom filter (Bloom, 1970) is a space efficient probabilistic data structure designed to rapidly check whether an element is present in a set. In this paper, we use one of its extension, spectral bloom filter (Cohen and Matias, 2003), which can efficiently calculate the upper bound of the frequencies of elements.

The base data structure of a spectral bloom filter is a vector of L counters, where all counters are initialized with 0. The spectral bloom filter uses m hash functions, $h_1, \ldots, h_m$, that map the elements to the range $\{1, \ldots L\}$. When adding an element f to the bloom filter, we hash it using the m hash functions, and get the hash codes $h_1(f), \ldots, h_m(f)$, then we check the counters at positions $h_1(f), \ldots, h_m(f)$, and get the counts $\{c_1, \ldots, c_m\}$. Let c^* be the minimal count among these counts: $c^* = \min\{c_1, \ldots, c_m\}$, we increase only the counters whose counts are c^*, while keeping other counters unchanged.

To check the frequency of an element, we hash the element and check the counters in the same way. The minimum count c^* provides the upper bound of the frequency. In other words, when pruning elements with frequencies no greater than a predefined threshold θ, we could safely prune the element if $c^* \leq \theta$.

In our case, we use the spectral bloom filter to eliminate the low-frequency candidates.

To estimate the gradients of newly generated $r+1$-order candidates, we run Line 17 twice. In the first round, we estimate the upper bound of $\#h^+$ for each candidate and add the candidate to $\mathcal{A}$ if its upper bound is greater than a predefined threshold θ. The second round is similar, we add the candidates using the upper bound of h^-. We did not estimate $\#h^+$ and $\#h^-$ simultaneously, because this needs two bloom filters for positive and negative gradients respectively, which consumes too much memory.

Specifically, in the first round, we initialize the spectral bloom filter so that all counters are set to zero. Then for each incorrectly predicted sample x_i, we generate $r+1$-order candidates by combining r-order candidates that are fired by the gold label i.e., $f(x_i, y_i) = 1$. Once a new candidate is generated, we hash it and check its corresponding m counters in the spectral bloom filter. If the minimal count $c^* = \theta$, we know that its positive gradient $\#f^+$ may be greater than θ. So we keep all counts unchanged, and add the candidate to $\mathcal{A}$. Otherwise, we increase the counts by 1 using the method described above. The second round is similar.

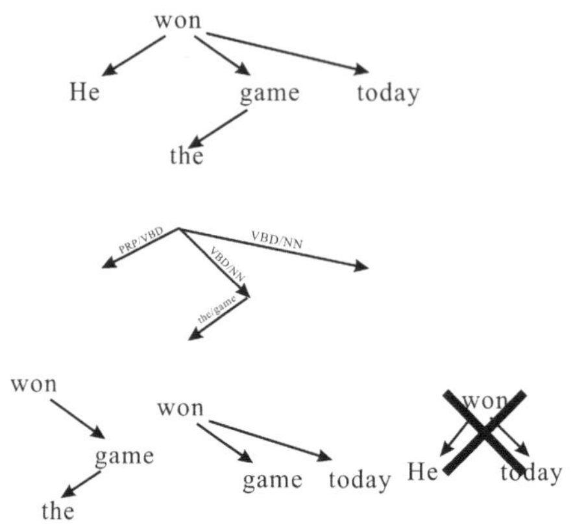

Figure 1: A dependency parse tree (top), one of its feature trees (middle) and some of its subtrees (bottom). *He* $\leftarrow$ *won* $\rightarrow$ *today* is not a subtree because *He* and *today* are not adjacent siblings.

5 Efficient Candidate Generation

5.1 Polynomial Kernel

As mentioned above, we generate the $r+1$-order candidates by combining the candidates of order r. An efficient feature generation algorithm should be carefully designed to avoid duplicates, otherwise $\#f^+$ and $\#f^-$ may be over counted.

The candidate generation algorithm is kernel dependent. For polynomial kernel, we just combine any two r-order candidates and remove the combined feature if its order is not $r+1$. This method requires square running time for each example.

5.2 Dependency Tree Kernel

5.2.1 Definition

Collins and Duffy (2002) proposed tree kernels for constituent parsing which includes the all-subtree features. Similarly, we define dependency tree kernel for dependency parsing. For compatibility with the previously studied subtree features for dependency parsing, we propose a new dependency tree kernel that is different from Culotta and Sorensen's (Culotta and Sorensen, 2004). Given a dependency parse tree T composed of L words, $L-1$ arcs, each arc has several basic features, such as the concatenation of the head word and the modifier word, the concatenation of the word left to the head and the lower case of the word right to the modifier, the distance of the arc, the direction of the arc, the concatenation of the POS tags of the head and the modifier, etc.

A feature tree of T is a tree that has the same structure as T, while each arc is replaced by any of its basic features. For a parse tree that has $L-1$ arcs, and each arc has d basic features, the number of the feature trees is d^{L-1}. For example, the dependency parse tree for sentence *He won the game today* is shown in Figure 1. Suppose each arc has two basic features: word pair and POS tag pair. Then there are 2^4 feature trees, because each arc can be replaced by either word pair or POS tag pair.

A subtree of a tree is a connected fragment in the tree. In this paper, to reduce computational cost, we restrict that adjacent siblings in the subtrees must be adjacent in the original tree. For example *He* ← *won* → *game* is a subtree, but *He* ← *won* → *today* is not a subtree. The motivation of the restriction is to reduce the number of subtrees, for a node having k children, there are $k^(k-1)/2$ subtrees, but without the restriction the number of subtrees is exponential: 2^k.

A sub feature tree of a dependency tree T is a feature tree of any of its subtrees. For example, the dependency tree in Figure 1 has 12 subtrees including four arcs, four arc pairs, the three arc triples and the full feature tree, and each subtree having s arcs has 2^s sub feature trees. Thus the dependency tree has $2*4+4*2^2+3*2^3+2^4=64$ sub feature trees.

Given two dependency trees T_1 and T_2, the dependency tree kernel is defined as the number of common sub feature trees of T_1 and T_2. Formally, the kernel function is defined as

$$K(T_1,T_2)=\sum_{n_1\in T_1,n_2\in T_2}\Delta(n_1,n_2)$$

where $\Delta(n_1,n_2)$ denotes the number of common sub feature trees rooted in n_1 and n_2 nodes.

Like tree kernel, we can calculate $\Delta(n_1,n_2)$ recursively. Let c_i and c'_j denote the i-th child of n_1 and j-th child of n_2 respectively, let $ST_{p,l}(n_1)$ denote the set of the sub feature trees rooted in node n_1 and the children of the root are $c_p, c_{p+1}, \ldots, c_{p+l-1}$, we denote $ST_{q,l}(n_2)$ similarly. Then we define

$$\Delta_{p,q,l}(n_1,n_2)=\sum_{p,q}|ST_{p,l}(n_1)\bigcap ST_{q,l}(n_2)|$$

the number of common sub feature trees in $ST_{p,l}(n_1)$ and $ST_{q,l}(n_2)$.

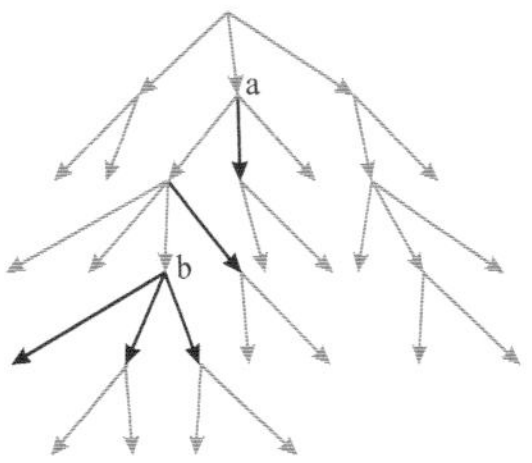

Figure 2: For any subtree rooted in a with the rightmost leaf b, we could extend the subtree by any arc below or right to the path from a to b (shown in black)

To calculate $\Delta_{p,q,l}(n_1,n_2)$, we first consider the sub feature trees with only two levels, i.e., sub feature trees that are composed of n_1, n_2 and some of their children. We initialize $\Delta_{p,q,1}(n_1,n_2)$ with number of the common features of arcs $n_1 \rightarrow c_p$ and $n_2 \rightarrow c'_q$. Then we calculate $\Delta_{p,q,l}(n_1,n_2)$ recursively using

$$\begin{aligned}&\Delta_{p,q,l}(n_1,n_2)\\&=\Delta_{p,q,l-1}(n_1,n_2)*\Delta_{p+l,q+l,1}(n_1,n_2)\end{aligned}$$

And $\Delta(n_1,n_2)=\sum_{p,q,l}\Delta_{p,q,l}(n_1,n_2)$

Next we consider all the sub feature trees, we have

$$\begin{aligned}&\Delta_{p,q,l}(n_1,n_2)\\&=\Delta_{p,q,l-1}(n_1,n_2)*\left(1+\Delta(c_{p+l-1},c'_{q+l-1})\right)\end{aligned}$$

Computing the dependency tree kernel for two parse trees requires $|T_1|^2*|T_2|^2*\min\{|T_1|,|T_2|\}$ running time in the worst case, as we need to enumerate p,q,l and n_1,n_2.

One way to incorporate the dependency tree kernel for parsing is to rerank the K best candidate parse trees generated by a simple linear model. Suppose there are n training samples, the size of the kernel matrix is $(K*n)^2$, which is unacceptable for large datasets.

5.2.2 Candidate Generation

For constituent parsing, Kudo et al. showed such an all-subtrees representation is extremely redundant and a comparable accuracy can be achieved using just a small set of subtrees (Kudo et al., 2005). Suzuki et al. even showed that the over-fitting problem often arises when convolution kernels are used in NLP tasks (Suzuki et al., 2004). Now we attempt to select representative sub feature trees in the kernel space using Algorithm 1. The r-order features in dependency tree kernel space are the sub feature trees with r arcs. The candidate feature generation in Line 17 has two steps: first we generate the subtrees with r arcs, then we generate the sub feature trees for each subtree.

The simplest way for subtree generation is to enumerate the combinations of $r + 2$ words in the sentence, and check if these words form a subtree.

We can speed up the generation by using the results of the subtrees with $r + 1$ words (r arcs). For each subtree S_r with r arcs, we can add an extra word to S_r and generate S_{r+1} if the words form a subtree.

This method has three issues: first, the time complexity is exponential in the length of the sentence, as there are 2^L combinations of words, L is the sentence length; second, it may generate duplicated subtrees, and over counts the gradients. For example, there are two ways to generate the subtree *He won the game* in Figure 1: we can either add word *He* to the subtree *won the game*, or add word *the* to the subtree *He won game*; third, checking a fragment requires $O(L)$ time.

These issues can be solved using the well known rightmost-extension method (Zaki, 2002; Asai et al., 2002; Kudo et al., 2005) which enumerates all subtrees from a given tree efficiently. This method starts with a set of trees consisting of single nodes, and then expands each subtree attaching a new node.

Specifically, it first indexes the words in the pre-order of the parse tree. When generating S_{r+1}, only the words whose indices are larger than the greatest index of the words in S_r are considered. In this way, each subtree is generated only once. Thus, we only need to consider two types of words: (i) the children of the rightmost leaf of S_r, (ii) the adjacent right sibling of the any node in S_r, as shown in Figure 2.

The total number of subtrees is no greater than L^3, because the level of a subtree is less than L, and for the children of each node, there are at most L^2 subsequences of siblings. Therefore the time complexity for subtree extraction is $O(L^3)$.

6 Experiments

6.1 Experimental Results on English Dataset

6.1.1 Settings

First we used the English Penn Tree Bank (PTB) with standard train/develop/test for evaluation. Sections 2-21 (around 40K sentences) were used as training data, section 22 was used as the development set and section 23 was used as the final test set.

We extracted dependencies using Joakim Nivre's Penn2Malt tool with Yamada and Matsumoto's rules (Yamada and Matsumoto, 2003). Unlabeled attachment score (UAS) ignoring punctuation is used to evaluate parsing quality.

We apply our technique to rerank the parse trees generated by a third order parser (Koo and Collins, 2010) trained using 10 best MIRA algorithm with 10 iterations. We generate the top 10 best candidate parse trees using 10 fold cross validation for each sentence in the training data. The gold parse tree is added if it is not in the candidate list. Then we learn a reranking model using these candidate trees. During testing, the score for a parse tree T is a linear combination of the two models:

$$score(T) = \beta score^{O3}(T) + score^{rerank}(T)$$

where the meta-parameter $\beta = 5$ is tuned by grid search using the development dataset. $score^{O3}(T)$ and $score^{rerank}(T)$ are the outputs of the third order parser and the reranking classifier respectively.

For comparison, we implement the following reranking models:

- Perceptron with Polynomial kernels $K(\mathbf{a}, \mathbf{b}) = (\mathbf{a}^T\mathbf{b} + 1)^d$, $d = 2, 4, 8$
- Perceptron with Dependency tree kernel.
- Perceptron with features generated by templates, including all siblings and fourth order features.
- Perceptron with the features selected in polynomial and tree kernel spaces, where threshold $C = 3$.

The basic features to establish the kernel spaces include the combinations of contextual words or POS tags of head and modifier, the length and

$w_h w_m, p_h p_m, w_h p_m, p_h w_m$
$p_{h-1} p_m, p_{h-1} w_m, p_h p_{m-1}, w_h p_{m-1}$
$p_{h+1} p_m, p_{h+1} w_m, p_h p_{m+1}, w_h p_{m+1}$
$p_{h-1} p_h p_m, p_h p_{h+1} p_m, p_h p_{m-1} p_m, p_h p_m p_{m+1}$
Concatenate features above with length and direction
$p_h p_b p_m$

Table 1: Basic features in polynomial and dependency tree kernel spaces, w_h: the word of head node, w_m denotes the word of modifier node, p_h: the POS of head node, p_m denotes the POS of modifier node, p_{h+1}: POS to the right of head node, p_{h-1}: POS to the left of modifier node, p_{m+1}: POS to the right of head node, p_{m-1}: POS to the left of modifier node, p_b: POS of a word in between head and modifier nodes.

direction of the arcs, and the POS tags of the words lying between the head and modifier, as shown in Table 1. The POS tags are automatically generated by 10 fold cross validation during training, and a POS tagger trained using the full training data during testing which has an accuracy of 96.9% on the development data and 97.3% on the test data.

As kernel methods are not scalable for large datasets, we applied the strategy proposed by Collins and Duffy (2002), to break the training set into 10 chunks of roughly equal size, and trained 10 separate kernel perceptrons on these data sets. The outputs from the 10 runs on test examples were combined through the voting procedure.

For feature selection, we set the maximum iteration number $M = 100$. We use the first order and second order features for pre-training. We choose the constant step size $\alpha^t = 1$ because we find this could quickly reduce the prediction error in very few iterations.

We use the SHA-1 hash function to generate the hash codes for the spectral bloom filter. The SHA-1 hash function produces a 160-bit hash code for each candidate feature. The hash code is then segmented into 5 segments, in this way we get five hash codes $h_1, \ldots, h_5$. Each code has 32 bits. Then we create 2^{32}(4G) counters. The threshold θ is set to 3, thus each counter requires 2 bits to store the counts. The spectral bloom filter costs $1G$ memory in total.

Furthermore, to reduce memory cost, we save the local data structure such as the selected features in Step 15 of Algorithm 1 whenever possible, and load them into the memory when needed.

After feature selection, we did not use the L_1 SVM for testing, instead, we trained an averaged perceptron with the selected features. Because we find that the averaged perceptron significantly outperforms L_1 SVM.

System	UAS	Training Time
Third Order Parser	93.07	20 hrs
Quadratic Kernel(QK)	93.41	6 hrs
Biquadratic Kernel(BK)	93.45	6 hrs
8-th Degree Polynomial Kernel(8K)	93.27	6 hrs
Dependency Tree Kernel (DTK)	93.65	10 days
LM with Template Features	93.39	4 mins
LM with Features in QK	93.39	9 mins
LM with Features in BK	93.44	0.5 hrs
LM with Features in 8K	93.30	6 hrs
LM with Features in DTK	**93.72**	36 hrs
(Zhang and McDonald, 2014)	93.57	N/A
(Zhang et al., 2013)	93.50	N/A
(Ma and Zhao, 2012)	93.40	N/A
(Bohnet and Kuhn, 2012)	93.39	N/A
(Rush and Petrov, 2012)	93.30	N/A
(Qian and Liu, 2013)	93.17	N/A
(Hayashi et al., 2013)	93.12	1 hr
(Martins et al., 2013)	93.07	N/A
(Zhang and McDonald, 2012)	93.06	N/A
(Koo and Collins, 2010)	93.04	N/A
(Zhang and Nivre, 2011)	92.90	N/A

Table 2: Comparison between our system and the state-of-art systems on English dataset. LM is short for Linear Model, hrs, mins are short for hours and minutes respectively

6.1.2 Results

Experimental results are listed in Table 2, all systems run on a 64 bit Fedora operation system with a single Intel core i7 3.40GHz and 32G memory. We also include results of representative state-of-the art systems.

It is clear that the use of kernels or the deep features in kernel spaces significantly improves the baseline third order parser and outperforms the reranking model with shallow, template-generated features. Besides, our feature selection outperforms kernel methods in both efficiency and accuracy.

It is unsurprising that the dependency tree kernel outperforms polynomial kernels, because it captures the structured information. For example, polynomial kernels can not distinguish the grand-child feature or sibling feature from the combination of two separated arc features.

When no additional resource is available, our parser achieved the best reported performance 93.72% UAS on English PTB dataset. It is

C	#Feat	#Template	Hours	Mem(G)	UAS
1	$0.34G$	N/A	stalled	OOM	N/A
2	$0.34G$	N/A	stalled	OOM	N/A
3	$33.1M$	$11.4K$	36	4.0	93.72
5	$6.32M$	$2.1K$	20	2.2	93.55
10	$2.10M$	$1.6K$	5	1.4	93.40

Table 3: Feature selection in dependency kernel space with different threshold C.

Language	Ours	Official Best
Chinese	76.77	**79.17**
Japanese	**92.68**	92.57
German	87.40	**87.48**
Spanish	**87.82**	87.64
Czech	**80.51**	80.38
Catalan	86.98	**87.86**

Table 4: Experimental Results on CoNLL 2009 non-English datasets.

worth pointing that our method is orthogonal to other reported systems that benefit from advanced inference algorithms, such as cube pruning (Zhang and McDonald, 2014), AD^3 (Martins et al., 2013), etc. We believe that combining our techniques with others' will achieve further improvement.

Reranking the candidate parse trees of 2416 testing sentences takes 67 seconds, about 36 sentences per second.

To further understand the complexity of our algorithm, we perform feature selection in dependency tree kernel space with different thresholds C and record the number of selected features and feature templates, the speed and memory cost. Table 3 shows the results. We can see that our algorithm works efficiently when $C \geq 3$, but for $C < 3$, the number of selected features grows drastically, and the program runs out of memory (OOM).

6.2 Experimental Results on CoNLL 2009 Dataset

Now we looked at the impact of our system on non-English treebanks. We evaluate our system on six other languages from the CoNLL 2009 shared-task. We used the best setting in the previous experiment: reranking model is trained using the features selected in the dependency tree kernel space. For POS tag features we used the predicted tags.

As the third order parser can not handle non-projective parse trees, we used the graph transformation techniques to produce non-projective structures (Nivre and Nilsson, 2005). First, the training data for the parser is projectivized by applying a number of lifting operations (Kahane et al., 1998) and encoding information about these lifts in arc labels. We used the path encoding scheme where the label of each arc is concatenated with two binary tags, one indicates if the arc is lifted, the other indicates if the arc is along the lifting path from the syntactic to the linear head. Then we train a projective parser on the transformed data without arc label information and a classifier to predict the arc labels based on the projectivized gold parse tree structure. During testing, we run the parser and the classifier in a pipeline to generate a labeled parse tree. Labeled syntactic accuracy is reported for comparison.

Comparison results are listed in Table 4. We achieved the best reported results on three languages, Japanese, Spanish and Czech. Note that CoNLL 2009 also provide the semantic labeling annotation which we did not used in our system. While some official systems benefit from jointly learning parsing and semantic role labeling models.

7 Conclusion

In this paper we proposed a new feature selection algorithm that selects features in kernel spaces in a coarse to fine order. Like frequent mining, the efficiency of our approach comes from the anti-monotone property of the subgradients. Experimental results on the English dependency parsing task show that our approach outperforms standard kernel methods. In the future, we would like to extend our technique to other real valued kernels such as the string kernels and tagging kernels.

Acknowledgments

We thank three anonymous reviewers for their valuable comments. This work is partly supported by NSF award IIS-0845484 and DARPA under Contract No. FA8750-13-2-0041. Any opinions expressed in this material are those of the authors and do not necessarily reflect the views of the funding agencies.

References

Tatsuya Asai, Kenji Abe, Shinji Kawasoe, Hiroki Arimura, Hiroshi Sakamoto, and Setsuo Arikawa. 2002. Efficient substructure discovery from large semi-structured data. In *Proceedings of the Second SIAM International Conference on Data Mining, Arlington, VA, USA, April 11-13, 2002*, pages 158–174.

Burton H. Bloom. 1970. Space/time trade-offs in hash coding with allowable errors. *Commun. ACM*, 13(7):422–426, July.

Bernd Bohnet and Jonas Kuhn. 2012. The best of bothworlds – a graph-based completion model for transition-based parsers. In *Proc. of EACL*.

S. Boyd and A. Mutapcic. 2006. Subgradient methods. *notes for EE364*.

Saar Cohen and Yossi Matias. 2003. Spectral bloom filters. In *Proc. of SIGMOD*, SIGMOD '03.

Michael Collins and Nigel Duffy. 2002. New ranking algorithms for parsing and tagging: Kernels over discrete structures, and the voted perceptron. In *Proc. of ACL*, ACL '02.

Aron Culotta and Jeffrey Sorensen. 2004. Dependency tree kernels for relation extraction. In *Proc. of ACL*, ACL '04.

Katsuhiko Hayashi, Shuhei Kondo, and Yuji Matsumoto. 2013. Efficient stacked dependency parsing by forest reranking. *TACL*, 1.

Sylvain Kahane, Alexis Nasr, and Owen Rambow. 1998. Pseudo-projectivity, a polynomially parsable non-projective dependency grammar. In *Proceedings of the 36th Annual Meeting of the Association for Computational Linguistics and 17th International Conference on Computational Linguistics, Volume 1*, pages 646–652, Montreal, Quebec, Canada, August. Association for Computational Linguistics.

Terry Koo and Michael Collins. 2010. Efficient third-order dependency parsers. In *Proc. of ACL*.

Taku Kudo, Jun Suzuki, and Hideki Isozaki. 2005. Boosting-based parse reranking with subtree features. In *Proceedings of the 43rd Annual Meeting of the Association for Computational Linguistics (ACL'05)*, pages 189–196, Ann Arbor, Michigan, June. Association for Computational Linguistics.

Zhiyun Lu, Avner May, Kuan Liu, Alireza Bagheri Garakani, Dong Guo, Aurélien Bellet, Linxi Fan, Michael Collins, Brian Kingsbury, Michael Picheny, and Fei Sha. 2014. How to scale up kernel methods to be as good as deep neural nets. *CoRR*, abs/1411.4000.

Xuezhe Ma and Hai Zhao. 2012. Fourth-order dependency parsing. In *Proceedings of COLING 2012: Posters*, pages 785–796, Mumbai, India, December. The COLING 2012 Organizing Committee.

Andre Martins, Miguel Almeida, and Noah A. Smith. 2013. Turning on the turbo: Fast third-order non-projective turbo parsers. In *Proc. of ACL*.

Joakim Nivre and Jens Nilsson. 2005. Pseudo-projective dependency parsing. In *Proceedings of the 43rd Annual Meeting on Association for Computational Linguistics*, ACL '05, pages 99–106, Stroudsburg, PA, USA. Association for Computational Linguistics.

Daisuke Okanohara and Jun'ichi Tsujii. 2009. Learning combination features with l1 regularization. In *Proceedings of Human Language Technologies: The 2009 Annual Conference of the North American Chapter of the Association for Computational Linguistics, Companion Volume: Short Papers*, pages 97–100, Boulder, Colorado, June. Association for Computational Linguistics.

Xian Qian and Yang Liu. 2013. Branch and bound algorithm for dependency parsing with non-local features. *TACL*, 1.

Alexander Rush and Slav Petrov. 2012. Vine pruning for efficient multi-pass dependency parsing. In *Proc. of NAACL*. Association for Computational Linguistics.

Jun Suzuki, Hideki Isozaki, and Eisaku Maeda. 2004. Convolution kernels with feature selection for natural language processing tasks. In *Proceedings of the 42nd Meeting of the Association for Computational Linguistics (ACL'04), Main Volume*, pages 119–126, Barcelona, Spain, July.

Mingkui Tan, Ivor W. Tsang, and Li Wang. 2012. Towards large-scale and ultrahigh dimensional feature selection via feature generation. *CoRR*, abs/1209.5260.

Ben Taskar. 2004. *Learning Structured Prediction Models: A Large Margin Approach*. Ph.D. thesis, Stanford University.

Christopher K. I. Williams and Matthias Seeger. 2001. Using the nyström method to speed up kernel machines. In *NIPS*.

Yu-Chieh Wu, Jie-Chi Yang, and Yue-Shi Lee. 2007. An approximate approach for training polynomial kernel svms in linear time. In *Proc. of ACL*, ACL '07.

Hiroyasu Yamada and Yuji Matsumoto. 2003. Statistical dependency analysis with support vector machines. In *Proc. of IWPT*.

Mohammed J. Zaki. 2002. Efficiently mining frequent trees in a forest. In *Proceedings of the Eighth ACM SIGKDD International Conference on Knowledge Discovery and Data Mining*, KDD '02, pages 71–80, New York, NY, USA. ACM.

Hao Zhang and Ryan McDonald. 2012. Generalized higher-order dependency parsing with cube pruning. In *Proc. of EMNLP*.

Hao Zhang and Ryan McDonald. 2014. Enforcing structural diversity in cube-pruned dependency parsing. In *Proc. of ACL*.

Yue Zhang and Joakim Nivre. 2011. Transition-based dependency parsing with rich non-local features. In *Proc. of ACL-HLT*.

Qi Zhang, Fuliang Weng, and Zhe Feng. 2006. A progressive feature selection algorithm for ultra large feature spaces. In *Proc. of ACL*.

Hao Zhang, Liang Huang, Kai Zhao, and Ryan McDonald. 2013. Online learning for inexact hypergraph search. In *Proc. of EMNLP*, pages 908–913. Association for Computational Linguistics.

Semantic Role Labeling Improves Incremental Parsing

Ioannis Konstas and Frank Keller
Institute for Language, Cognition and Computation
School of Informatics, University of Edinburgh
{ikonstas,keller}@inf.ed.ac.uk

Abstract

Incremental parsing is the task of assigning a syntactic structure to an input sentence as it unfolds word by word. Incremental parsing is more difficult than full-sentence parsing, as incomplete input increases ambiguity. Intuitively, an incremental parser that has access to semantic information should be able to reduce ambiguity by ruling out semantically implausible analyses, even for incomplete input. In this paper, we test this hypothesis by combining an incremental TAG parser with an incremental semantic role labeler in a discriminative framework. We show a substantial improvement in parsing performance compared to the baseline parser, both in full-sentence F-score and in incremental F-score.

1 Introduction

When humans listen to speech, the input becomes available gradually as the speech signal unfolds. Reading happens in a similarly gradual manner when the eyes scan a text. There is good evidence that the human language processor is adapted to this and works incrementally, i.e., computes an interpretation for an incoming sentence on a word-by-word basis (Tanenhaus et al., 1995; Altmann and Kamide, 1999). Also language processing systems often deal with speech as it is spoken, or text as it is typed. A dialogue system should start interpreting a sentence while it is spoken, and an information retrieval system should start retrieving results while the user is typing.

Incremental processing is therefore essential both for realistic models of human language processing and for NLP applications that react to user input in real time. In response to this, a number of incremental parsers have been developed, which use context-free grammar (Roark, 2001; Schuler et al., 2010), dependency grammar (Chelba and Jelinek, 2000; Nivre, 2007; Huang and Sagae, 2010), or tree-substitution grammars (Sangati and Keller, 2013). Typical applications of incremental parsers include speech recognition (Chelba and Jelinek, 2000; Roark, 2001; Xu et al., 2002), machine translation (Schwartz et al., 2011; Tan et al., 2011), reading time modeling (Demberg and Keller, 2008), or dialogue systems (Stoness et al., 2004).

Incremental parsing, however, is considerably harder than full-sentence parsing: when processing the n-th word in a sentence, a_n, the parser only has access to the left context (words $a_1 \ldots a_{n-1}$); the right context (words $a_{n+1} \ldots a_N$) is not known yet. This can lead to **local ambiguity,** i.e., produce additional syntactic analyses that are valid for the sentence prefix, but become invalid as the right context is processed. As an example consider the sentence prefix in (1):

(1) The athlete realized her goals ...
  a. at the competition
  b. were out of reach

The prefix could continue as in (1-a), i.e., as a main clause structure. Or the next words could be as in (1-b), in which case *her goals* is part of a subordinate clause.

Intuitively, an incremental parser that has access to semantic information would be able to decide which of these two analyses is likely to be correct, even without knowing the rest of the sentence. If the NP *her goals* is a likely ARG1 of *realized* the parser should prefer the main clause structure. On the other hand, if the NP is a likely ARG0 of an (as yet unseen) embedded verb, then the parser should go for the subordinate clause structure. This is illustrated in Figure 2. Note that the preference can easily be reversed: if the prefix was *the athlete realized her shoes*, then *her shoes* is very likely to be an ARG0 rather than an ARG1.

Proceedings of the 53rd Annual Meeting of the Association for Computational Linguistics and the 7th International Joint Conference on Natural Language Processing, pages 1191–1201,
Beijing, China, July 26-31, 2015.

The basis of this paper is the hypothesis that semantic information can aid incremental parsing. To test this hypothesis, we combine an incremental TAG parser with an **incremental semantic role labeling** (iSRL) system. The iSRL system takes prefix trees and computes their most likely semantic role assignments. We show that these role assignments can be used to re-rank the output of the incremental parser, leading to substantial improvements in parsing performance compared to the baseline parser, both in full-sentence F-score and in incremental F-score.

2 Incremental Semantic Role Labeling

The current work builds on an existing incremental parser, the Psycholinguistically Motivated Tree Adjoining Grammar (PLTAG) parser of Demberg et al. (2013). The distinguishing feature of this parser is that it builds fully connected structures (no words are left unattached during incremental parsing); this requires it to make predictions about the right context, which are verified as more of the input becomes available. Konstas et al. (2014) show that semantic information can be attached to PLTAG structures, making it possible to assign semantic roles incrementally. In the present paper, we use these semantic roles to re-rank the output of the PLTAG parser.

2.1 Psycholinguistically Motivated TAG

PLTAG extends standard TAG (Joshi and Schabes, 1992) in order to enable incremental parsing. Standard TAG assumes a lexicon of **elementary trees,** each of which contains at least one lexical item as an anchor and at most one leaf node as a **foot node,** marked with $A*$. All other leaves are marked with $A\downarrow$ and are called **substitution nodes.** To derive a TAG parse for a sentence, we start with the elementary tree of the head of the sentence and integrate the elementary trees of the other lexical items of the sentence using two operations: **adjunction** at an internal node and **substitution** at a substitution node (the node at which the operation applies is the **integration point**). Standard TAG derivations are not guaranteed to be incremental, as adjunction can happen anywhere in a sentence, possibly violating left-to-right processing order. PLTAG addresses this limitation by introducing **prediction trees,** elementary trees without a lexical anchor. These are used to predict syntactic structure anchored by words that appears later in an incremental derivation. This ensures

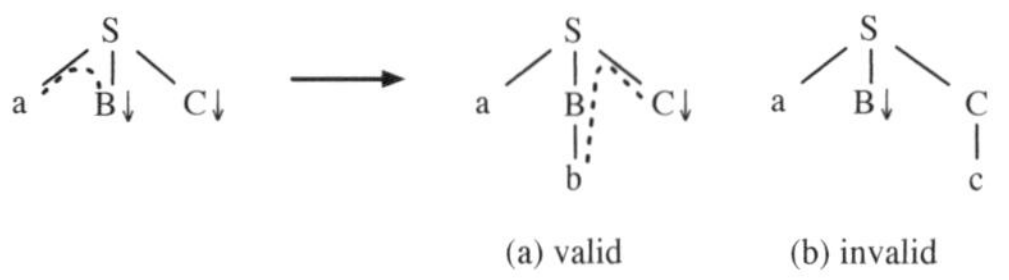

Figure 1: The current fringe (dashed line) indicates where valid substitutions can occur. Other substitutions result in an invalid prefix tree.

that fully connected prefix trees can be built for every prefix of the input.

In order to efficiently parse PLTAG, Demberg et al. (2013) introduce the concept of **fringes.** Fringes capture the fact that in an incremental derivation, a prefix tree can only be combined with an elementary tree at a limited set of nodes. For instance, the prefix tree in Figure 1 has two substitution nodes, for B and C. However, only substitution into B leads to a valid new prefix tree; if we substitute into C, we obtain the tree in Figure 1b, which is not a valid prefix tree (i.e., it represents a non-incremental derivation).

2.2 Incremental Role Propagation

The output of a semantic role labeler is a set of semantic dependency triples $\langle l, r, p \rangle$, where l is a semantic role label (e.g., ARG0, ARG1, ARGM in Propbank), and r and p are the words (argument and predicate) to which the role applies. An *incremental* semantic role labeler assigns semantic dependency triples to a prefix of the input sentence. Note that not every word is an argument to a predicate, therefore the set of triples will not necessarily change at every input word. Also, triples can be incomplete, as either the predicate or the argument may not have been observed yet.

Konstas et al. (2014) propose an iSRL system based on a PLTAG parser with a semantically augmented lexicon. They parse an input sentence incrementally, applying their incremental role propagation algorithm (IRPA) to the resulting prefix trees. This creates new semantic triples (or updates existing, incomplete ones) whenever an elementary or prediction tree that carries semantic role information is attached to the prefix tree. As soon as a triple is completed a two-stage classification process is applied, that first identifies whether the predicate/argument pair is a good candidate, and then disambiguates the role label (often multiple roles are possible for a lexical entry). Figure 2 shows the incremental role assignment for the two readings of the prefix *the athlete realized her goals*

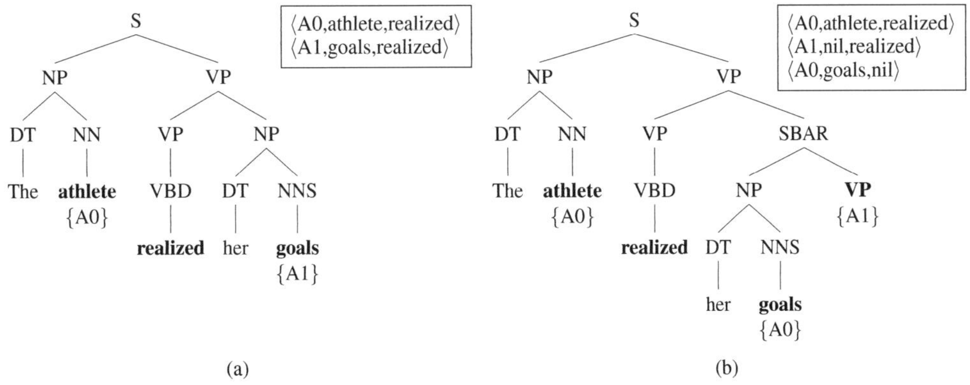

Figure 2: Incremental Role Propagation Algorithm application for two different prefix trees of the sentence prefix *the athlete realized her goals*. In (a) the parser builds a main clause, so IRPA assigns an A1 to *goals* with *realized* as predicate. In (b) the parser predicts an embedded clause, so IRPA delays the assignment of the A1 to *realized*, and instead introduces two incomplete triples: the first one is predicate-incomplete, with the argument *goals* assigned an A0, waiting to be attached to a predicate. The second one is argument-incomplete with predicate *realized* assigned an A1, waiting for an argument to follow.

(see Section 1). Note the use of incomplete semantic role triples in Figure 2b.

3 Model

We use a discriminative model in order to re-rank the output of the baseline PLTAG parser based on semantic roles assigned by the iSRL system.

3.1 Problem Formulation

Our overall approach is closely related to the discriminative incremental parsing framework of Collins and Roark (2004). The goal is to learn a mapping from input sentences $x \in \mathcal{X}$ to parse trees $y \in \mathcal{Y}$. For a given set of training pairs of sentences and gold-standard parse trees $(x,y) \in \mathcal{X} \times \mathcal{Y}$, the output $\hat{y}$ can be defined as:

$$\hat{y} = \underset{y \in GEN(x)}{\operatorname{argmax}} \Phi(x,y) \cdot \bar{w} \quad (1)$$

where $GEN(x)$ is a function that enumerates candidate parse trees for a given input x, Φ is a representation that maps each training example (x,y) to a feature vector $\Phi(x,y) \in \mathbb{R}^d$, and $\bar{w} \in \mathbb{R}^d$ is a vector of feature weights.

During training, the task is to estimate $\bar{w}$ given the training examples. In terms of efficiency, a crucial part of Equation (1) is the search strategy over parses produced by GEN and, to a smaller degree, the dimensionality of $\bar{w}$. One common decoding technique is to implement a dynamic program, thus avoiding the explicit enumeration of all analyses for a given timestamp (Huang, 2008). However, central to the discriminative approach is the exploration of features that cannot be straightforwardly embedded into the parser using a dynamic program. These include arbitrarily long-range dependencies contained in a parse tree, and more importantly non-isomorphic representations of the input sentence such as its semantic frame, i.e., the set of all semantic roles tripes that pertain to the same predicate. In order to accommodate these, we decode via beam search over candidate parses. We keep a list of the k-best analyses and prune those whose score $scr(x) = \Phi(x,y) \cdot \bar{w}$ falls below a threshold.

3.2 Incremental k-best Parsing

What we described in the previous section could equally apply to k-best re-ranking for full-sentence parsing (e.g., Charniak and Johnson, 2005). For incremental parsing, in addition to outputting $\hat{y}$ for the full sentence, we need to output **prefix trees** $\hat{y}_n$ for every prefix of length $n \in \{1 \ldots N\}$ of sentence $x = a_1 \ldots a_N$ with length N. Let $\langle x_n, \hat{y}_n, n \rangle$, be the state of our model after we have parsed the first n words of sentence x, resulting in analysis $\hat{y}_n$. The initial state is defined as $\langle x_0, \emptyset, 0 \rangle$, where $\emptyset$ is the empty analysis, and the final state is $\langle x, \hat{y}, N \rangle$, which represents a full analysis for the input sentence. We need a function ADV that transitions from a state at word a_n to a set of states at word

a_{n+1} by combining the prefix tree $\hat{y}_n$ with a_{n+1}:

$$ADV\big(\langle x_n, \hat{y}_n, n\rangle\big) = \langle x_n, \hat{y}_n, n\rangle \otimes a_{n+1} = \big\{\langle x_{n+1}, \hat{y}_{n+1}, n+1\rangle\big\}$$

Next, we define the set of states representing prefix trees as π, with $\pi_0 = \{\langle x_0, \emptyset, 0\rangle\}$, and $\pi_n = \cup_{\pi' \in \pi_{n-1}} ADV(\pi')$. We can now redefine $GEN(x_n) = \pi_n$, for any prefix of length n.

We enumerate prefix trees (function *GEN*) with the incremental parser of Demberg et al. (2013). The states of the model are stored in a chart; each cell holds the top-k prefix trees. The transition to the next state (function *ADV*) is performed by combining each prefix tree with a set of candidate of elementary (and prediction) trees via adjunction and substitution, subject to restrictions imposed by incrementallity (see Figure 2). In order to efficiently compute all combinations, the PLTAG parser computes only the fringes (see Section 2) of the prefix tree, and the candidate elementary trees and matches these two; this avoids the computation of the prefix tree entirely.[1]

Each prefix tree is weighted using a probability model estimated over PLTAG operations and the lexicon. This probability is used as a feature in Φ. In addition, we define a set of features of increasing sophistication, which include features specific to PLTAG, standard tree-based features, and, crucially, features extracted from the semantic role triples produced incrementally by the iSRL system of Konstas et al. (2014). The features are computed for each prefix tree y_n, so Φ can be rewritten as $\Phi(x_n, y_n)$, and therefore Equation (1) becomes:

$$\hat{y}_n = \operatorname*{argmax}_{y_n \in \pi_n} \Phi(x_n, y_n) \cdot \bar{w} \qquad (2)$$

Our goal now becomes to learn mappings between sentence *prefixes* x_n and *prefix* trees $\hat{y}_n$. In contrast to models that estimate features weights on full sentence parses (Collins and Roark, 2004; Charniak and Johnson, 2005), we do not observe gold-standard prefix trees during training. However, we can use gold-standard lexicon entries when parsing the training data with the PLTAG parser, which gives an approximation of gold-standard prefix trees y_n^+. Finally, during testing, given an unseen sentence x and a trained set of feature weights $\bar{w}$, our model generates prefix trees y_n for every sentence prefix of size n.

[1] As in a chart parser, the prefix tree can be re-constructed by following backpointers in the chart. This is done only for evaluation at the end of the sentence or incrementally on demand.

4 Reranking Features

This section describes the features used for reranking the prefix trees generated by the incremental parser. We include three different classes of features, based on local information from PLTAG elementary trees, based on global and structural information from prefix trees, and based on semantic information provided by iSRL triples. In contrast to work on discriminative full-sentence parsing (e.g., Charniak and Johnson, 2005; Collins and Koo, 2005), we can only use features extracted from the prefix trees being constructed incrementally as the sentence is parsed. The right context of the current word cannot be used, as this would violate incrementality. Every feature combination we try also includes the following baseline features:

Prefix Tree Probability is the log probability of the prefix tree as scored by the probability model of the baseline parser. The score is normalized by prefix length, to avoid getting larger negative log probability scores for longer prefixes.

Elementary Tree Probability is the log probability of the elementary tree corresponding to the word just added to the prefix tree according to the probability model of the baseline parser.

4.1 PLTAG Features

The baseline generative model of the PLTAG parser employs features based on parsing actions, the elementary trees used at each timestamp, and the previous word and PoS tag. In the discriminative model, we extend the locality of these features, as well as addressing sparsity issues arising from rare elementary trees. In all cases, both lexicalized and unlexicalized versions of the elementary trees are used.

Unigram Trees is a family of binary features that record the local elementary trees chosen by the parser for the n-th word, i.e., current word for $n = 1$ and previous word for $n = 2$.

Parent-Unigram Trees is a variation of the previous feature, where we encode the elementary tree of the current word along with the category of the node it attaches to in the prefix tree. This captures the attachment decisions the parser makes.

Bigram Trees are pairs of elementary trees for adjacent words (i.e., the elementary tree currently added to the prefix tree and the previous one). This extends the history the parser has access to, and captures pairs of elementary trees that are frequently chosen together, e.g., a verb-headed tree with a PP foot node, followed by an NP-headed prepositional tree.

4.2 Tree Features

The following features are inspired by Charniak and Johnson (2005) and attempt to encode properties of the prefix tree, as well as capture regularities for specific syntactic construction such as coordination. Even though the PLTAG parser builds fully connected structures and predicts upcoming context, some constituents in a given prefix tree may be incomplete. We therefore compute the features in this group only for those constituents that have been completed in the current prefix tree (i.e., constituents that are complete at word a_n, but were incomplete at word a_{n-1}). This ensures each of the features is only counted once per constituent. For example, the coordination parallelism feature (see below) should be computed only after all the words in the yield of the CC non-terminal have been observed.

Right Branch encodes the number of nodes on the longest path from the root of the prefix tree to the rightmost pre-terminal. We also include the symmetrical feature which records the number of the remaining nodes in the prefix tree. This feature allows the parser to prefer right-branching trees, commonly found in English syntax.

Coordination Parallelism records whether the two sibling subtrees of a coordination node are identical in terms of structure and node categories up to depth l. We encode identity in a bit mask, and set $l = 4$ (e.g., 1100 means the subtrees have identical children and grandchildren).

Coordination Parallelism Length indicates the binned difference in size between the yields of each sibling subtree under a coordination node. It also stores whether the second subtree is at the end of the sentence.

Heavy stores the category of each node in a completed constituent, along with the binned length of its yield and whether it is at the end of the sentence. This feature captures the tendency of larger constituents to occur towards the end of the sentence.

Neighbors encodes the category of each node in the completed constituent, the binned yield size, and the PoS tags of the l preceding words, were $l = 1$ or 2.

Word stores the current word along with the categories of its l immediate ancestor nodes (excluding pre-terminals); $l = 2$ or 3.

4.3 SRL Features

The features in this group are extracted from the output of iSRL system of Konstas et al. (2014), which annotates prefix trees with semantic roles. The setup proposed in the current paper makes it possible to feed the semantic information back to the PLTAG parser by using it to re-rank the k-best prefix trees generated by the parser. (The re-ranked prefix trees could then also result in better iSRL performance, an issue we will return to in Section 6.3.)

Recall that the SRL information comes in the form of triples $\langle l, r, p \rangle$, where l is a semantic role label and r and p are the words to which the role applies (see Figure 2 for examples). For each feature, we also compute an unlexicalized version by replacing the argument and predicates in the triples with their PoS tags.

Complete SRL Triples stores the complete triples (if any) generated by the current word. The word can be the predicate or the argument in one or more dependency relations involving previous words.

Semantic Frame records all the arguments of a predicate (if present) for frequent semantic labels, i.e., A0, A1 and A2, as well as the presence of a modifier (e.g., AM-TMP, AM-LOC, etc.). This feature usually fires when a verb is added to the prefix tree and generates several complete SRL triples. The feature captures the semantic frame of a verb as a whole (while the previous feature just records it as a collection of triples).

Back-off SRL Triples are generated by removing either the argument, or the predicate, or the role label, from a complete triple. This provides a way of generalizing between triples that share some information without being completely identical.

Predicate/Argument/Role encodes the elements of a complete SRL triple individually (argument, predicate, or role). This allows for further generalization and reduces sparsity.

5 Feature Weight Estimation

We estimate the vector of feature weights $\bar{w}$ in Equation (2) using the averaged structured perceptron algorithm of Collins (2002); we give the pseudocode in Algorithm 1. The perceptron makes T passes over L training examples. In each iteration, for each sentence prefix/prefix tree pair (x_n, y_n), it computes the best scoring prefix tree $\hat{y}_n$ among the candidate prefix trees, given the current feature weights $\bar{w}$. In line 7, the algorithm updates $\bar{w}$ with the difference (if any) between the feature representations of the best scoring prefix tree $\hat{y}_n$ and the approximate gold-standard prefix tree y_n^+ (see Section 3.2). Note that since we use a constant beam during decoding with the PLTAG parser in order to enumerate the set of prefix trees π_n, there is no guarantee that the argmax in line 5 will find the highest scoring (in terms of F-score) prefix tree $y_n^* \neq \hat{y}_n$. Search errors due to the best analysis falling out of the beam at a given prefix length will create errors both when decoding unseen sentences at test time, and when learning the feature weights with the perceptron algorithm. The final weight vector $\bar{w}$ is the average of the weight vectors over T iterations, L examples and N words. The averaging avoids overfitting and produces more stable results (Collins, 2002).

Note that features are computed for every prefix of the input sentence. Recall that the parser avoids the explicit computation of the prefix trees in π_n through the use of the fringes (see Sections 2.1 and 3.2). This is sufficient for the computation of PLTAG and SRL features, but we need to explicitly calculate every prefix tree y_n for the computation of the tree features (see Section 4.2). This is an expensive operation if we are parsing the whole training corpus. To overcome this time bottleneck, we compute features only for those analyses of every input sentence prefix that belongs to the k-best analyses at the end of the sentence. In other words, π_n is the set of only those prefix trees that are used by the k-best analyses at the end of the sentence. This results in a much smaller number of prefix trees that need to be computed for each word. However, during testing, given the trained $\bar{w}$ and an unseen sentence, we compute all features for each prefix length of the sentence, hence calculate all prefix trees in π_n and incrementally re-rank the chart entries of the parser on the fly.

Algorithm 1: Averaged Structured Perceptron

Input: Training Examples: $(x,y)_{i=1}^{L}, x_i = a_1 \dots a_N$

1 $\bar{w} \leftarrow 0$
2 **for** $t \leftarrow 1 \dots T$ **do**
3   **for** $i \leftarrow 1 \dots L$ **do**
4   **for** $n \leftarrow 1 \dots N$ **do**
5             $\hat{y}_n = \text{argmax}_{y_n \in \pi_n} \Phi(x_n, y_n) \cdot \bar{w}$
6   **if** $y_n^+ \neq \hat{y}_n$ **then**
7                 $\bar{w} \leftarrow \bar{w} + \Phi(x_n, y_n^+) - \Phi(x_n, y_n)$
8 **return** $\frac{1}{T}\sum_{t=1}^{T} \frac{1}{L}\sum_{i=1}^{L} \sum_{n=1}^{N} \frac{1}{N} w_{t,i,n}$

6 Experiments

6.1 Setup

We use the PLTAG parser of Demberg et al. (2013) to enumerate prefix trees y_n and to compute the prefix tree and word probability scores which we use as features. We also use the iSRL system of Konstas et al. (2014) to generate incremental SRL triples. Their system includes a semantically-enriched lexicon extracted from the Wall Street Journal (WSJ) part of the Penn Treebank corpus (Marcus et al., 1993), converted to PLTAG format. Semantic role annotation is sourced from Propbank. We trained the probability model of the parser and the identification and labeling classifiers of the iSRL system using the intersection of Sections 2–21 of WSJ and the English portion of the CoNLL 2009 Shared Task (Hajič et al., 2009). We learn the weight vector $\bar{w}$ by training the perceptron algorithm also on Sections 2–21 of WSJ (see Section 5 for details). We use the PoS tags predicted by the parser, rather than gold standard PoS tags. Testing is performed on section 23 of WSJ, for sentences up to 40 words.

6.2 Evaluation

In addition to standard full-sentence labeled bracket score, we evaluate our model incrementally, by scoring the prefix trees generated for each sentence prefix (Sangati and Keller, 2013). For each prefix of the input sentence (two words or more), we compute the labeled bracket score for the minimal structure spanning that prefix. The minimal structure is defined as the subtree rooted in the lowest common ancestor of the prefix nodes, while removing any leftover intermediate nodes on the right edge of the subtree that do not have a word in the prefix as their yield.

Although not the main focus of this paper, we also report full-sentence combined SRL accuracy (counting verb-predicates only). This score is obtained by re-applying the iSRL system to the syn-

System	Prec	Rec	F	AUC	SRL
Baseline	75.51	76.93	76.21	71.49	69.43
Tree	75.99	77.52	76.75	73.02	68.80
Srl	75.99	77.65	76.81	73.97	69.96
Tree+Pltag	76.67	78.27	77.47	72.27	70.27
Tree+Pltag +Srl	77.00	78.57	77.77	74.97	70.00

Table 1: Full-sentence parsing results[2], area under the curve (AUC) for the incremental parsing results of Figure 3, and combined SRL score across different groups of features.

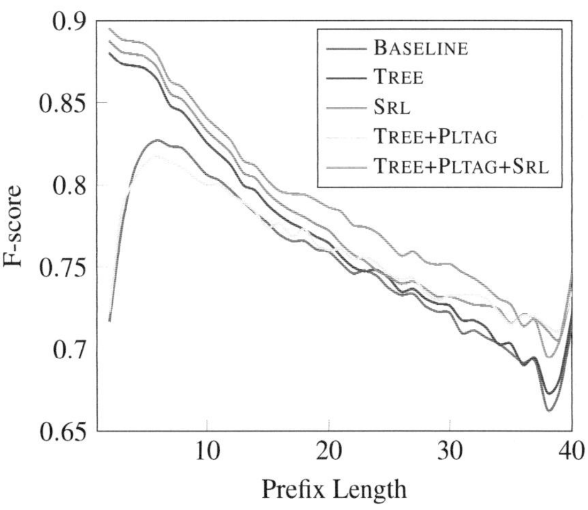

Figure 3: Incremental parsing F-score for increasing sentence prefixes, up to 40 words.

tactic parses output by our re-ranker. (In contrast, Konstas et al. (2014) work with gold-standard syntactic parses.)

We evaluate four variants of our model (see Section 4 for an explanation of the different groups of features):

Tree is the model that uses tree features only; this essentially simulates standard parse reranking approaches such as the one of Charniak and Johnson (2005).

Srl uses only features based on iSRL triples; it provides a proof-of-concept, demonstrating that the semantic information encoded in SRL triples can help the parser building better syntactic trees.

Tree+Pltag adds PLTAG Features to the Tree model, taking advantage of local information specific to elementary PLTAG trees; Tree+Pltag essentially provides a strong syntax-only baseline.

Tree+Pltag+Srl combines SRL features and syntactic features.

Finally, our baseline is the PLTAG parser of Demberg et al. (2013), using the original probability model without any re-ranking. A comparison with other incremental parsers would be desirable, but is not trivial to achieve. This is because the PLTAG parser is trained and evaluated on a version of the Penn Treebank that was converted to PLTAG format. This renders our results not directly comparable to parsers that reproduce the Penn Treebank bracketing. For example, the PLTAG parser produces deeper tree structures informed by Propbank and the noun phrase annotation of Vadas and Curran (2007).

6.3 Results

Figure 3 gives the results of evaluating incremental parsing performance. The x-axis shows prefix length, and the y-axis shows incremental F-score computed as suggested by Sangati and Keller (2013). Each point is averaged over all prefixes of a given length in the test set. To quantify the trends shown in this figure, we also compute the area under the curve (AUC) for each feature combination; this is given in Table 1.

We find that Tree performs consistently better than the baseline for short prefixes (up to the first 20 words), and then is very close to the baseline. This is expected given that tree features add structure-specific information (e.g., about coordination) to the baseline model, and is consistent with results obtained using similar features in the literature (Charniak and Johnson, 2005). Adding PLTAG features (Tree+Pltag) hurts incremental performance for short prefixes (up to about 20 words), but then performance gradually increases over the baseline and over Tree alone. It seems that the PLTAG features, which are specific to the grammar formalism used, are able to help with longer and more complex prefixes, but introduce noise in smaller prefixes.

The SRL feature set, on the other hand, results in a consistent increase in performance compared

[2]Note that the baseline score is lower than the published F = 77.41 of Demberg et al. (2013). This is expected, since we use a semantically-enriched lexicon, which increases the size of the lexicon, resulting in higher ambiguity per word as well as increased sparsity in the probability model.

to the baseline, across all prefix lengths. SRL provides semantic knowledge, while TREE provides syntactic knowledge, but the performance of both feature sets is very close to each other, up to a prefix length of about 30 words, after which SRL has a clear advantage. SRL features seem to filter out local ambiguity caused by creating prefix trees incrementally and result in correct parses closer to the end of sentence, even without the use of the syntactic information contained in the TREE+PLTAG feature set. Recall that SRL uses information provided by the semantic frame, something that a syntax-only model does not have access to. It seems that this makes it possible for SRL to (partially) compensate for mistakes made by the parser. The AUC of SRL is higher by 0.95 and 1.7 points compared to TREE and TREE+PLTAG, respectively.

We observe an additional boost in performance when using all features together in the TREE+PLTAG+SRL configuration, which outperforms SRL alone by 1.0 points in AUC. Recall that SRL features do not apply to every word; they fire only when semantic information is introduced to the parser via the semantically-enriched lexicon. Hence by adding tree and PLTAG features, which normally apply for every new word, we are able to perform effective re-ranking for all sentence prefixes, which explains the boost in performance. Note that for all variants of our model we observe a dip in performance at around 38 words. This is probably due to noise, caused by the small number of sentences of this length. The upward trend seen around word 40 is probably the effect of observing the end of the sentence, which boosts parsing accuracy.

Turning to full sentence evaluation (Table 1), we observe a similar trend. Both TREE and SRL beat the baseline by about 0.55 points in F-score. Progressively adding features increases performance, with the greatest gain of 1.56 points attained by the combination of all features in TREE+PLTAG+SRL.

We also report combined SRL F-score computed on the re-ranked syntactic trees (rightmost column of Table 1). We find that compared to the baseline, only a small improvement of 0.55 points is achieved by TREE+PLTAG+SRL, while TREE+PLTAG improves by 0.84 points. The syntax-only variant therefore outperforms the full model, but only by a small margin.

7 Related Work

The most similar approach in the literature is Collins and Roark's (2004) re-ranking model for incremental parsing. They learn the syntactic features of Roark (2001) using the perceptron model of Collins (2002). Similar to us, they use the incremental parser to search over candidate parses. However, they limited themselves to local derivation features (akin to our PLTAG features), and do not explore global syntactic feature (tree features) or SRL features. Even though they re-rank the output of an incremental parser, they only evaluate full sentence parsing performance. Other re-ranking approaches to syntactic parsing make use of an extensive set of global features, but apply it on the k-best list of full sentence parses (Charniak and Johnson, 2005; Collins and Koo, 2005) or the k-best list of derivations of a packed forest (Huang, 2008), i.e., these approaches are not incremental.

Based on the CoNLL Shared Tasks (e.g., Hajič et al., 2009), a number of systems exist that perform syntactic parsing and semantic role labeling jointly. Toutanova et al. (2008), Sutton and McCallum (2005) and Li et al. (2010) combine the scores of two separate models, i.e., a syntactic parser and a semantic role labeler, and re-rank the combination using features from each domain. Titov et al. (2009) and Gesmundo et al. (2009), instead of combining models, create a common search space for syntactic parsing and SRL, using a shift reduce-style technique (Nivre, 2007) and learn a latent variable model (Incremental Sigmoid Belief Networks) that optimizes over both tasks at the same time. Volokh and Neumann (2008) use a variant of Nivre's (2007) incremental shift-reduce parser and rely only on the current word and previous content to output partial dependency trees; then they output role labels given the full parser output. In contrast to all the joint approaches, we perform *both* parsing and semantic role labeling strictly incrementally, without having access to the whole sentence, outputting prefix trees and iSRL triples for every sentence prefix. Our approach creates a feedback loop, i.e., we generate a prefix tree using the baseline model, give it as input to iSRL, then re-rank it using a set of syntactic and SRL features. The resulting new prefix tree can then be fed back into iSRL, etc.

8 Conclusions

We started from the observation that human parsing uses semantic knowledge to rule out parses that lead to implausible interpretations. Based on this, we hypothesized that also in NLP, an incremental syntactic parser should benefit from semantic information. To test this hypothesis, we combined an incremental TAG parser with an incremental semantic role labeler. We used the output of the iSRL system to derive features that can be used to re-rank the prefix trees generated by the incremental parser. We found that SRL features, both in isolation and together with standard syntactic features, improve parsing performance, both when measured using full-sentence F-score, and in terms of incremental F-score.

In future work, we plan to combine our incremental parsing/role labeling approach with a compositional model of semantics, which would have to be modified to take semantic role triples as input (rather than words or word pairs). The resulting plausibility estimates could then be used as another source of semantic information for the parser, or employed in down-stream tasks.

Acknowledgments

EPSRC support through grant EP/I032916/1 "An integrated model of syntactic and semantic prediction in human language processing" to Frank Keller and Mirella Lapata is gratefully acknowledged.

References

Altmann, Gerry T. M. and Yuki Kamide. 1999. Incremental interpretation at verbs: Restricting the domain of subsequent reference. *Cognition* 73:247–264.

Charniak, Eugene and Mark Johnson. 2005. Coarse-to-fine n-best parsing and maxent discriminative reranking. In *Proceedings of the 43rd Annual Meeting of the Association for Computational Linguistics*. Ann Arbor, Michigan, pages 173–180.

Chelba, Ciprian and Frederick Jelinek. 2000. Structured language modeling. *Computer Speech and Language* 14:283–332.

Collins, Michael. 2002. Discriminative training methods for hidden markov models: Theory and experiments with perceptron algorithms. In *Proceedings of the 2002 Conference on Empirical Methods in Natural Language Processing*. pages 1–8.

Collins, Michael and Terry Koo. 2005. Discriminative reranking for natural language parsing. *Computational Linguistics* 31(1):25–70.

Collins, Michael and Brian Roark. 2004. Incremental parsing with the perceptron algorithm. In *Proceedings of the 42nd Meeting of the Association for Computational Linguistics, Main Volume*. Barcelona, Spain, pages 111–118.

Demberg, Vera and Frank Keller. 2008. Data from eye-tracking corpora as evidence for theories of syntactic processing complexity. *Cognition* 101(2):193–210.

Demberg, Vera, Frank Keller, and Alexander Koller. 2013. Incremental, predictive parsing with psycholinguistically motivated tree-adjoining grammar. *Computational Linguistics* 39(4):1025–1066.

Gesmundo, Andrea, James Henderson, Paola Merlo, and Ivan Titov. 2009. A latent variable model of synchronous syntactic-semantic parsing for multiple languages. In *Proceedings of the Thirteenth Conference on Computational Natural Language Learning: Shared Task*. pages 37–42.

Hajič, Jan, Massimiliano Ciaramita, Richard Johansson, Daisuke Kawahara, Maria Antònia Martí, Lluís Màrquez, Adam Meyers, Joakim Nivre, Sebastian Padó, Jan Štěpánek, Pavel Straňák, Mihai Surdeanu, Nianwen Xue, and Yi Zhang. 2009. The CoNLL-2009 shared task:

Syntactic and semantic dependencies in multiple languages. In *Proceedings of the 13th Conference on Computational Natural Language Learning*. Boulder, Colorado, USA.

Huang, Liang. 2008. Forest reranking: Discriminative parsing with non-local features. In *Proceedings of the 46th Annual Meeting of the Association for Computational Linguistics*. Columbus, Ohio, pages 586–594.

Huang, Liang and Kenji Sagae. 2010. Dynamic programming for linear-time incremental parsing. In *Proceedings of the 48th Annual Meeting of the Association for Computational Linguistics*. Uppsala, pages 1077–1086.

Joshi, Aravind K. and Yves Schabes. 1992. Tree adjoining grammars and lexicalized grammars. In Maurice Nivat and Andreas Podelski, editors, *Tree Automata and Languages*, North-Holland, Amsterdam, pages 409–432.

Konstas, Ioannis, Frank Keller, Vera Demberg, and Mirella Lapata. 2014. Incremental semantic role labeling with tree adjoining grammar. In *Proceedings of the 2014 Conference on Empirical Methods in Natural Language Processing*. Doha, Qatar, pages 301–312.

Li, Junhui, Guodong Zhou, and Tou Hwee Ng. 2010. Joint syntactic and semantic parsing of chinese. In *Proceedings of the 48th Annual Meeting of the Association for Computational Linguistics*. Association for Computational Linguistics, pages 1108–1117.

Marcus, Mitchell P., Mary Ann Marcinkiewicz, and Beatrice Santorini. 1993. Building a large annotated corpus of english: The Penn treebank. *Computational Linguistics* 19(2):313–330.

Nivre, Joakim. 2007. Incremental non-projective dependency parsing. In *Human Language Technologies: The Conference of the North American Chapter of the Association for Computational Linguistics; Proceedings of the Main Conference*. Rochester, New York, pages 396–403.

Roark, Brian. 2001. Probabilistic top-down parsing and language modeling. *Computational Linguististics* 27:249–276.

Sangati, Federico and Frank Keller. 2013. Incremental tree substitution grammar for parsing and word prediction. *Transactions of the Association for Computational Linguistics* 1(May):111–124.

Schuler, William, Samir AbdelRahman, Tim Miller, and Lane Schwartz. 2010. Broad-coverage parsing using human-like memory constraints. *Computational Linguististics* 36(1):1–30.

Schwartz, Lane, Chris Callison-Burch, William Schuler, and Stephen Wu. 2011. Incremental syntactic language models for phrase-based translation. In *Proceedings of the 49th Annual Meeting of the Association for Computational Linguistics: Human Language Technologies, Volume 1*. Portland, OR, pages 620–631.

Stoness, Scott C., Joel Tetreault, and James Allen. 2004. Incremental parsing with reference interaction. In Frank Keller, Stephen Clark, Matthew Crocker, and Mark Steedman, editors, *Proceedings of the ACL Workshop Incremental Parsing: Bringing Engineering and Cognition Together*. Barcelona, pages 18–25.

Sutton, Charles and Andrew McCallum. 2005. Joint parsing and semantic role labeling. In *Proceedings of the Ninth Conference on Computational Natural Language Learning*. Ann Arbor, Michigan, pages 225–228.

Tan, Ming, Wenli Zhou, Lei Zheng, and Shaojun Wang. 2011. A large scale distributed syntactic, semantic and lexical language model for machine translation. In *Proceedings of the 49th Annual Meeting of the Association for Computational Linguistics: Human Language Technologies, Volume 1*. Portland, OR, pages 201–210.

Tanenhaus, Michael K., Michael J. Spivey-Knowlton, Kathleen M. Eberhard, and Julie C. Sedivy. 1995. Integration of visual and linguistic information in spoken language comprehension. *Science* 268:1632–1634.

Titov, Ivan, James Henderson, Paola Merlo, and Gabriele Musillo. 2009. Online graph planarisation for synchronous parsing of semantic and syntactic dependencies. In *Proceedings of the 21st International Jont Conference on Artifical Intelligence*. Morgan Kaufmann Publishers Inc., San Francisco, CA, USA, pages 1562–1567.

Toutanova, Kristina, Aria Haghighi, and Christopher D. Manning. 2008. A global joint model for semantic role labeling. *Computational Linguistics* 34(2):161–191.

Vadas, David and James Curran. 2007. Adding noun phrase structure to the penn treebank. In *Proceedings of the 45th Annual Meeting of the Association of Computational Linguistics*. Association for Computational Linguistics, Prague, Czech Republic, pages 240–247.

Volokh, Alexander and Günter Neumann. 2008. *Proceedings of the Twelfth Conference on Computational Natural Language Learning*, Coling 2008 Organizing Committee, chapter A Puristic Approach for Joint Dependency Parsing and Semantic Role Labeling, pages 213–217.

Xu, Peng, Ciprian Chelba, and Frederick Jelinek. 2002. A study on richer syntactic dependencies for structured language modeling. In *Proceedings of the 40th Annual Meeting on Association for Computational Linguistics*. Philadelphia, pages 191–198.

Discontinuous Incremental Shift-Reduce Parsing

Wolfgang Maier
Universität Düsseldorf
Institut für Sprache und Information
Universitätsstr. 1, 40225 Düsseldorf, Germany
maierw@hhu.de

Abstract

We present an extension to incremental shift-reduce parsing that handles discontinuous constituents, using a linear classifier and beam search. We achieve very high parsing speeds (up to 640 sent./sec.) and accurate results (up to 79.52 F_1 on TiGer).

1 Introduction

Discontinuous constituents consist of more than one continuous block of tokens. They arise through phenomena which traditionally in linguistics would be analyzed as being the result of some kind of "movement", such as extraposition or topicalization. The occurrence of discontinuous constituents does not necessarily depend on the degree of freedom in word order that a language allows for. They can be found, e.g., in almost equal proportions in English and German treebank data (Evang and Kallmeyer, 2011).

Generally, discontinuous constituents are accounted for in treebank annotation. One annotation method consists of using trace nodes that denote the source of a movement and are co-indexed with the moved constituent. Another method is to annotate discontinuities directly by allowing for crossing branches. Fig. 1 shows an example for the latter approach with which we are concerned in this paper, namely, the annotation of (1). The tree contains a discontinuous VP due to the fact that the fronted pronoun is directly attached.

(1) Das wollen wir umkehren
That want we reverse
"This is what we want to reverse"

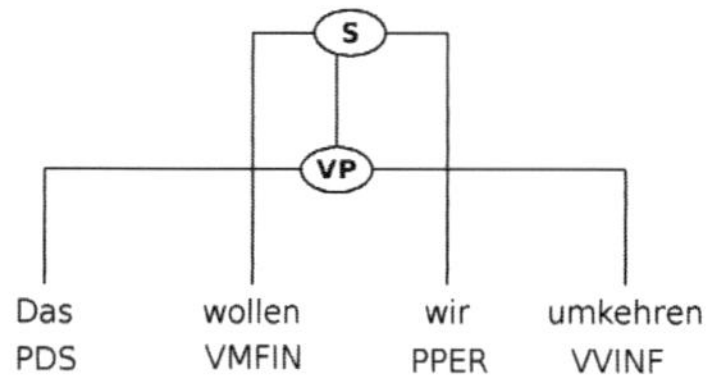

Figure 1: Example annotation with discontinuous constituents from TiGer

Several methods have been proposed for parsing such structures. Trace recovery can been framed as a separate pre-, post- or in-processing task to PCFG parsing (Johnson, 2002; Dienes and Dubey, 2003; Jijkoun, 2003; Levy and Manning, 2004; Schmid, 2006; Cai et al., 2011, among others); see particularly Schmid (2006) for more details. Directly annotated discontinuous constituents can be parsed with a dependency parser, given a reversible transformation from discontinuous constituency trees to non-projective dependency structures. Transformations have been proposed by Hall and Nivre (2008), who use complex edge labels that encode paths between lexical heads, and recently by Fernández-González and Martins (2015), who use edge labels to encode the attachment order of modifiers to heads.

Direct parsing of discontinuous constituents can be done with Linear Context-Free Rewriting System (LCFRS), an extension of CFG which allows its non-terminals to cover more than one continuous block (Vijay-Shanker et al., 1987). LCFRS parsing is expensive: CYK chart parsing with a binarized grammar can be done in $\mathcal{O}(n^{3k})$ where k is the *block degree*, the maximal number of continuous blocks a non-terminal can cover (Seki et al., 1991). For a typical treebank LCFRS (Maier and Søgaard, 2008), $k \approx 3$, instead of $k = 1$ for PCFG. In order to improve on otherwise impractical parsing times, LCFRS chart parsers employ different strategies to speed up search: Kallmeyer

Proceedings of the 53rd Annual Meeting of the Association for Computational Linguistics and the 7th International Joint Conference on Natural Language Processing, pages 1202–1212,
Beijing, China, July 26-31, 2015.

and Maier (2013) use A* search; van Cranenburgh (2012) and van Cranenburgh and Bod (2013) use a coarse-to-fine strategy in combination with Data-Oriented Parsing; Angelov and Ljunglöf (2014) use a novel cost estimation to rank parser items. Maier et al. (2012) apply a treebank transformation which limits the block degree and therewith also the parsing complexity.

Recently Versley (2014) achieved a breakthrough with a *EaFi*, a classifier-based parser that uses an "easy-first" approach in the style of Goldberg and Elhadad (2010). In order to obtain discontinuous constituents, the parser uses a strategy known from non-projective dependency parsing (Nivre, 2009; Nivre et al., 2009): For every non-projective dependency tree, there is a projective dependency tree which can be obtained by reordering the input words. Non-projective dependency parsing can therefore be viewed as projective dependency parsing with an additional reordering of the input words. The reordering can be done online during parsing with a "swap" operation that allows to process input words out of order. This idea can be transferred, because also for every discontinuous constituency tree, one can find a continuous tree by reordering the terminals. Versley (2014) uses an adaptive gradient method to train his parser. He reports a parsing speed of 40-55 sent./sec. and results that surpass those reported for the above mentioned chart parsers.

In (continuous) constituency parsing, incremental shift-reduce parsing using the structured perceptron is an established technique. While the structured perceptron for parsing has first been used by Collins and Roark (2004), classifier-based incremental shift-reduce parsing has been taken up by Sagae and Lavie (2005). A general formulation for the application of the perceptron algorithm to various problems, including shift-reduce constituency parsing, has been introduced by Zhang and Clark (2011b). Improvements have followed (Zhu et al., 2012; Zhu et al., 2013). A similar strategy has been shown to work well for CCG parsing (Zhang and Clark, 2011a), too.

In this paper, we contribute a perceptron-based shift-reduce parsing architecture with beam search (following Zhu et al. (2013) and Bauer (2014)) and extend it such that it can create trees with crossing branches (following Versley (2014)). We present strategies to improve performance on discontinuous structures, such as a new feature set. Our parser is very fast (up to 640 sent./sec.), and produces accurate results. In our evaluation, where we pay particular attention to the parser performance on discontinuous structures, we show among other things that surprisingly, a grammar-based parser has an edge over a shift-reduce approach concerning the reconstruction of discontinuous constituents.

The remainder of the paper is structured as follows. In subsection 2.1, we introduce the general parser architecture; the subsections 2.2 and 2.3 introduce the features we use and our strategy for handling discontinuous structures. Section 3 presents and discusses the experimental results, section 4 concludes the article.

2 Discontinuous Shift-Reduce Parsing

Our parser architecture follows previous work, particularly Zhu et al. (2013) and Bauer (2014).

2.1 Shift-reduce parsing with perceptron training

An *item* in our parser consists of a *queue* q of token/POS-pairs to be processed, and a *stack* s, which holds completed constituents.[1] The parser uses different transitions: SHIFT shifts a terminal from the queue on to the stack. UNARY-X reduces the first element on the stack to a new constituent labeled *X*. BINARY-X-L and BINARY-X-R reduce the first two elements on the stack to a new *X* constituent, with the lexical head coming from the left or the right child, respectively. FINISH removes the last element from the stack. We additionally use an IDLE transition, which can be applied any number of times after FINISH, to improve the comparability of analyses of different lengths (Zhu et al., 2013).

The application of a transition is subject to restrictions. UNARY-X, e.g., can only be applied when there is at least a single item on the stack. We implement all restrictions listed in the appendix of Zhang and Clark (2009), and add additional restrictions that block transitions involving the root label when not having arrived at the end of a derivation. We do not use an underlying grammar to filter out transitions which have not been seen during training.

For decoding, we use beam search (Zhang and Clark, 2011b). Decoding is started by putting the

[1] As in other shift-reduce approaches, we assume that POS tagging is done outside of the parser.

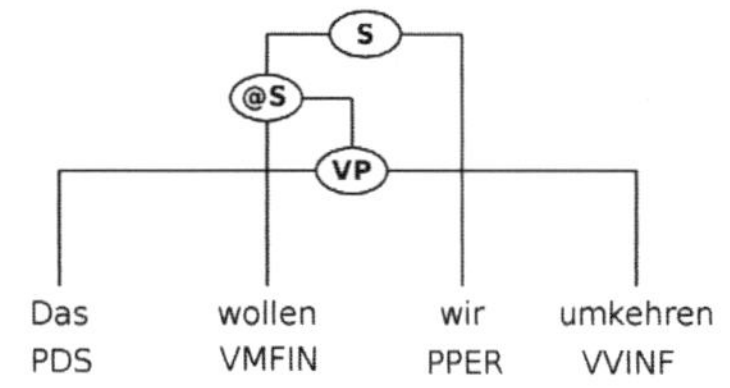

Figure 2: Binarization example

unigrams
$s_0tc, s_0wc, s_1tc, s_1wc, s_2tc, s_2wc, s_3tc, s_3wc,$
$q_0wt, q_1wt, q_2wt, q_3wt,$
$s_0lwc, s_0rwc, s_0uwc, s_1lwc, s_1rwc, s_1uwc$
bigrams
$s_0ws_1w, s_0ws_1c, s_0cs_1w, s_0cs_1c, s_0wq_0w, s_0wq_0t,$
$s_0cq_0w, s_0cq_0t, s_1wq_0w, s_1wq_0t, s_1cq_0w, s_1cq_0t,$
$q_0wq_1w, q_0wq_1t, q_0tq_1w, q_0tq_1t$
trigrams
$s_0cs_1cs_2w, s_0cs_1cs_2c, s_0cs_1cq_0w, s_0cs_1cq_0t,$
$s_0cs_1wq_0w, s_0cs_1wq_0t, s_0ws_1cs_2c, s_0ws_1cq_0t$
extended
$s_0llwc, s_0lrwc, s_0luwc, s_0rlwc, s_0rrwc,$
$s_0ruwc, s_0ulwc, s_0urwc, s_0uuwc, s_1llwc,$
$s_1lrwc, s_1luwc, s_1rlwc, s_1rrwc, s_1ruwc$
separator
$s_0wp, s_0wcp, s_0wq, s_0wcq, s_0cs_1cp, s_0cs_1cq$
$s_1wp, s_1wcp, s_1wq, s_1wcq$

Figure 3: Feature templates

start item (empty stack, full queue) on the beam. Then, repeatedly, a candidate list is filled with all items that result from applying legal transitions to the items on the beam, followed by putting the highest scoring n of them back on the beam (given a beam size of n). Parsing is finished if the highest scoring item on the beam is a final item (stack holds one item labeled with the root label, queue is empty), which can be popped. Item scores are computed as in Zhang and Clark (2011b): The score of the $i+1$th item is computed as the sum of the score of the ith item and the dot product of a global feature weight vector and the local weight vector resulting from the changes induced by the corresponding transition to the $i+1$th item. The start item has score 0. We train the global weight vector with an averaged Perceptron with early update (Collins and Roark, 2004).

Parsing relies on binary trees. As in previous work, we binarize the incoming trees head-outward with binary top and bottom productions. Given a constituent X which is to be binarized, all intermediate nodes which are introduced will be labeled $@X$. Lexical heads are marked with Collins-style head rules. As an example, Fig. 2 shows the binarized version of the tree of Fig. 1.

Finally, since we are learning a sparse model, we also exploit the work of Goldberg and Elhadad (2011) who propose to include a feature in the calculation of a score only if it has been observed $\geq$ MINUPDATE times.

2.2 Features

Features are generated by applying templates to parser items. They reflect different configurations of stack and queue. As BASELINE features, we use the feature set from Zhang and Clark (2009) without the bracketing features (as used in Zhu et al. (2013)). We furthermore experiment with features that reflect the presence of separating punctuation ",", ":", ";" (SEPARATOR) (Zhang and Clark, 2009), and with the EXTENDED features of Zhu et al. (2013), which look deeper into the trees on the stack, i.e., up to the grand-children instead of only to children.

Fig. 3 shows all the feature templates. Note that s_i and q_i stands for the ith stack and queue item, w stands for the head word, t for the head tag and c for the constituent label (w, t and c are identical on POS-level). l and r (ll and rr) represent the left and right children (grand-children) of the element on the stack; u handles the unary case. Concerning the separator features, p is a unique separator punctuation between the head words of s_0 and s_1, q is the count of any separator punctuation between s_0 and s_1.

2.3 Handling Discontinuities

In order to handle discontinuities, we use two variants of a swap transition which are similar to *swap-eager* and *swap-lazy* from Nivre (2009) and Nivre et al. (2009). The first variant, SINGLESWAP, swaps the second item of the stack back on the queue. The second variant COMPOUNDSWAP$_i$ bundles a maximal number of adjacent swaps. It swaps i items starting from the second item on the stack, with $1 \leq i < |s|$. Both swap operations can only be applied if

1. the item has not yet been FINISHed and the last transition has not been a transition with the root category,
2. the queue is not empty,
3. all elements to be swapped are pre-terminals, and

4. if the first item of the stack has a lower index than the second (this inhibits swap loops).

SINGLESWAP can only been applied if there are at least two items on the stack. For COMPOUNDSWAP$_i$, there must be at least $i+1$ items.

Transition sequences are extracted from treebank trees with an algorithm that traverses the tree bottom-up and collects the transitions. For a given tree τ, intuitively, the algorithm works as follows. We start out with a queue t containing the preterminals of τ, a stack σ that receives finished constituents, a counter s that keeps track of the number of terminals to be swapped, and an empty sequence r that holds the result. First, the first element of t is pushed on σ and removed from t.

While $|\sigma| > 0$ or $|t| > 0$, we repeat the following two steps.

1. Repeat while transitions can be added:
   (a) if the top two elements on σ, l and r, have the same parent p labeled X and l/r is the head of p, add BINARY-X-*l*/*r* to r, pop two elements from σ and push p;
   (b) if the top element on σ is the only child of its parent p labeled X, add UNARY-X, pop an element of σ and push p.
2. If $|t| > 0$, while the first element of t is not equal to the leftmost pre-terminal dominated by the right child of the parent of the top element on σ (i.e., while there are terminals that must be swapped), add SHIFT to r, increment s, push the first element of t on σ and remove it from t. Finally, add another SHIFT to r, push first element of t to σ and remove it from t (this will contribute to the next reduction). If $s > 0$, we must swap. Either we add s many SWAP transitions or one COMPOUNDSWAP$_s$ to r. Then we move s many elements from σ to the front of t, starting with the second element of σ. Finally we set $s = 0$.

As an example, consider the transition sequence we would extract from the tree in Fig. 2. Using SINGLESWAP, we would obtain SHIFT, SHIFT, SHIFT, SHIFT, SINGLESWAP, SINGLESWAP, BINARY-VP-R, SHIFT, BINARY-@S-R, SHIFT, BINARY-S-L, FINISH. Using COMPOUNDSWAP$_i$, instead of two SINGLESWAPs, we would just obtain a single COMPOUNDSWAP$_2$.

unigrams
s_0xwc, s_1xwc, s_2xwc, s_3xwc,
s_0xtc, s_1xwc, s_2xtc, s_3xwc,
s_0xy, s_1xy, s_2xy, s_3xy
bigrams
s_0xs_1c, s_0xs_1w, s_0xs_1x, s_0ws_1x, s_0cs_1x,
s_0xs_2c, s_0xs_2w, s_0xs_2x, s_0ws_2x, s_0cs_2x,
s_0ys_1y, s_0ys_2y, s_0xq_0t, s_0xq_0w

Figure 4: Features for discontinuous structures

We explore two methods which improve the performance on discontinuous structures. Even though almost a third of all sentences in the German NeGra and TiGer treebanks contains at least one discontinuous constituent, among all constituents, the discontinuous ones are rare, making up only around 2%. The first, simple method addresses this sparseness by raising the importance of the features that model the actual discontinuities by counting all feature occurrences at a gold swap transition twice (IMPORTANCE).

Secondly, we use a new feature set (DISCO) with bigram and unigram features that conveys information about discontinuities. The features condition the possible occurrence of a gap on previous gaps and their properties.[2] The feature templates are shown in Fig. 4. x denotes the gap type of a tree on the stack. There are three possible values, either "none" (tree is fully continuous), "pass" (there is a gap at the root, i.e., this gap must be filled later further up in the tree), or "gap" (the root of this tree fills a gap, i.e., its children have gaps, but the root does not). Finally, y is the sum of all gap lengths.

3 Experiments

3.1 Data

We use the TiGer treebank release 2.2 (TIGER), and the NeGra treebank (NEGRA). For TIGER, we use the first half of the last 10,000 sentences for development and the second half for testing.[3] We also recreate the split of Hall and Nivre (2008) (TIGERHN), for which we split TiGer in 10 parts, assigning sentence i to part $i mod 10$. The first of those parts is used for testing, the concatenation of the rest for training.

[2] See Maier and Lichte (2011) for a formal account on gaps in treebanks.

[3] This split, which corresponds to the split used in the SPMRL 2013 shared task (Seddah et al., 2013), was proposed in Farkas and Schmid (2012). We exclude sentences 46,234 and 50,224, because of annotation errors. Both contain nodes with more than one parent node.

From NeGra, we exclude all sentences longer than 30 words (in order to make a comparison with `rparse` possible, see below), and split off the last 10% of the treebank for testing, as well as the previous 10% for development. As a preprocessing step, in both treebanks we remove spurious discontinuities that are caused by material which is attached to the virtual root node (mainly punctuation). All such elements are attached to the least common ancestor node of their left and right terminal neighbors (as proposed by Levy (2005), p. 163). We furthermore create a continuous variant NEGRACF of NEGRA with the method usually used for PCFG parsing: For all maximal continuous parts of a discontinuous constituent, a separate node is introduced (Boyd, 2007). Subsequently, all nodes that do not cover the head child of the discontinuous constituent are removed.

No further preprocessing or cleanup is applied.

3.2 Experimental Setup

Our parser is implemented in Java. We run all our experiments with Java 8 on an Intel Core i5, allocating 15 GB per experiment. All experiments are carried out with gold POS tags, as in previous work on shift-reduce constituency parsing (Zhang and Clark, 2009). Grammatical function labels are discarded.

For the evaluation, we use the corresponding module of *discodop*.[4] We report several metrics (as implemented in *discodop*):

- Extended labeled bracketing, in which a bracket for a single node consists of its label and a set of pairs of indices, delimiting the continuous blocks it covers. We do not include the root node in the evaluation and ignore punctuation. We report labeled precision, recall and F_1, as well as exact match (all brackets correct).
- Leaf-ancestor (Sampson and Babarczy, 2003), for which we consider all paths from leaves to the root.
- Tree edit distance (Emms, 2008), which consists of the minimum edit distance between gold tree and parser output.

Aside from a full evaluation, we also evaluate only the constituents that are discontinuous.

[4] `http://github.com/andreasvc/discodop`

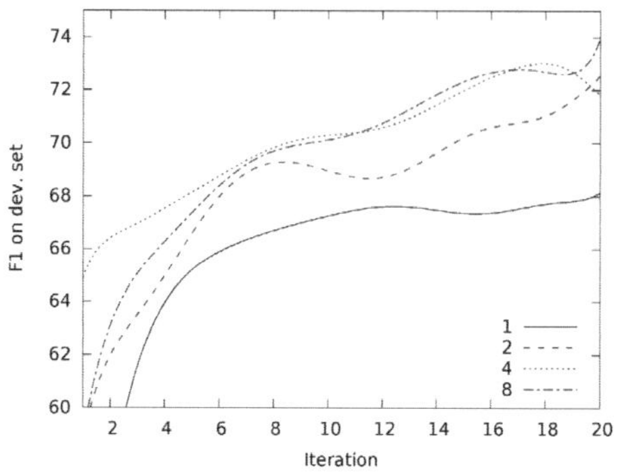

Figure 5: NEGRA dev results (F_1) for different beam sizes

We perform 20 training iterations unless indicated otherwise. When training stops, we average the model (as in Daumé III (2006)).

We run further experiments with *rparse*[5] (Kallmeyer and Maier, 2013) to facilitate a comparison with a grammar-based parser.

3.3 Results

We start with discontinuous parsing experiments on NEGRA and TIGER, followed by continuous parsing experiments, and a comparison to grammar-based parsing.

3.3.1 Discontinuous Parsing

NeGra The first goal is to determine the effect of different beam sizes with BASELINE features and the COMPOUNDSWAP$_i$ operation. We run experiments with beam sizes 1, 2, 4 and 8; Fig. 5 shows the results obtained on the dev set after each iteration. Fig. 6 shows the average decoding speed during each iteration for each beam size (both smoothed).

Tracking two items instead of one results in a large improvement. Raising the beam size from 2 to 4 results in a smaller improvement. The improvement obtained by augmenting the beam size from 4 to 8 is even smaller. This behavior is mirrored by the parsing speeds during training: The differences in parsing speed roughly align with the result differences. Note that fast parsing during training means that the parser does not perform well (yet) and that therefore, early update is done more often. Note finally that the average parsing speeds on the test set after the last training iteration

[5] `http://github.com/wmaier/rparse`

	All				Discont. only			
	LR	LP	LF_1	E	LR	LP	LF_1	E
Baseline combined with								
Swap	74.74	75.60	75.17	43.54	15.70	15.82	15.76	12.31
CompoundSwap$_i$	75.60	76.37	75.98	43.04	**16.46**	19.96	18.05	12.05
Baseline + CompoundSwap$_i$ combined with								
Separator	75.20	75.74	75.47	42.61	13.11	16.73	14.70	9.89
Extended	76.15	76.92	76.53	**44.46**	15.09	20.62	17.43	12.70
Disco	75.86	76.39	76.12	43.94	15.42	22.95	18.45	12.86
Importance	75.72	76.61	76.16	43.86	16.16	20.42	18.04	12.38
Baseline + CompoundSwap$_i$ + Disco combined with								
Extended	76.68	**77.19**	76.93	44.10	15.27	26.88	19.47	13.61
Extended + Separator	76.21	76.45	76.33	43.29	15.57	26.56	19.63	13.52
Importance	76.22	76.86	76.54	43.75	16.01	**29.41**	**20.73**	**13.89**
Extended + Importance	**76.76**	77.13	**76.95**	44.30	15.09	28.86	19.82	13.23

Table 1: Results NeGra, beam size 8

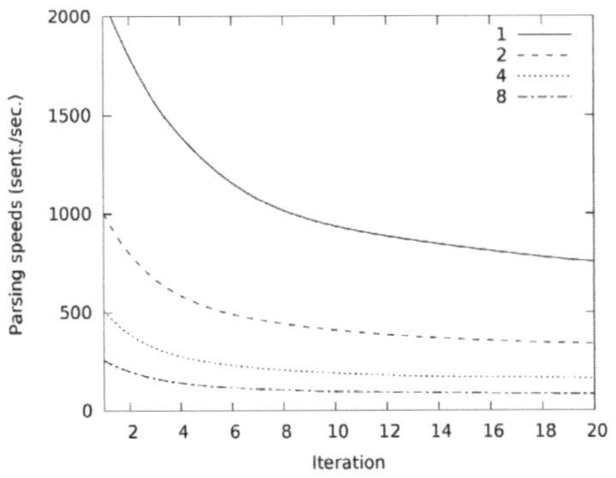

Figure 6: NeGra dev average parsing speeds per sentence for different beam sizes

range from 640 sent./sec. (greedy) to 80 sent./sec. (beam size 8).

For further experiments on NeGra, we choose a beam size of 8. Tab. 1 shows the bracketing scores for various parser setups. In Tab. 2, the corresponding TED and Leaf-Ancestor scores are shown.

In the first block of the tables, we compare Swap with CompoundSwap$_i$. On all constituents, the latter beats the former by 0.8 (F_1). On discontinuous constituents, using CompoundSwap$_i$ gives an improvement of more than four points in precision and of about 0.8 points in recall. A manual analysis confirms that as expected, particularly discontinuous constituents with large gaps profit from bundling swap transitions.

	TED	LA
Baseline combined with		
Swap	89.19	91.62
CompoundSwap$_i$	89.60	91.93
Baseline + CompoundSwap$_i$ combined with		
Separator	89.41	91.77
Extended	89.68	91.99
Disco	89.42	91.83
Baseline + CompoundSwap$_i$ + Disco combined with		
Importance	89.64	91.90
Extended	89.68	91.99
Extended + Separator	89.52	91.86
Extended + Importance	89.80	91.98

Table 2: Results NeGra TED and Leaf-Ancestor

In the second block, we run the Baseline features with CompoundSwap$_i$ combined with Separator, Extended and Disco. The Separator features were not as successful as they were for Zhang and Clark (2009). All scores for discontinuous constituents drop (compared to the baseline). The Extended features are more effective and give an improvement of about half a point F_1 on all constituents, as well as the highest exact match among all experiments. On discontinuous constituents, precision raises slightly but we loose about 1.4% in recall (compared to the baseline). The latter seems to be due to the fact that in comparison to the baseline, with Extended, more sentences get erroneously analyzed as not containing any crossing branches. This effect can be explained with data sparseness and is less pronounced when more training data is available (see below). Similarly to Extended, the new Disco features lead to a slight gain over the baseline (on all constituents). As with Extended, on discontinuous constituents, we again gain precision (3%) but loose recall (0.5%), because more sentences wrongly analyzed as not having discontinuities than in the Baseline. A category-based evaluation of discontinuous constituents reveals that Extended has an advantage over Disco when considering all constituents. However, we can also see that the Disco features yield better results than

EXTENDED particularly on the frequent discontinuous categories (NP, VP, AP, PP), which indicates that the information about gap type and gap length is useful for the recovery of discontinuities. IMPORTANCE (see Sec. 2.3) is not very successful, yielding results which lie in the vicinity of those of the BASELINE.

In the third block of the tables, we test the performance of the DISCO features in combination with other techniques, i.e., we use the BASELINE and DISCO features with COMPOUNDSWAP$_i$ and combine it with EXTENDED and SEPARATOR features as well as with the IMPORTANCE strategy. All experiments beat the BASELINE/DISCO combination in terms of F_1. EXTENDED and DISCO give a cumulative advantage, resulting in an increase of precision of almost 4%, resp. over 6% on discontinuous constituents, compared to the use of DISCO, resp. EXTENDED alone. Adding the SEPARATOR features to this combination does not bring an advantage. The IMPORTANCE strategy is the most successful one in combination with DISCO, causing a boost of almost 10% on precision of discontinuous constituents, leading to the highest overall discontinuous F_1 of 29.41 (notably more than 12 points higher than the baseline); also on all constituents we obtain the third-highest F_1. Combining DISCO with IMPORTANCE and EXTENDED leads to the highest overall F_1 on all constituents of 76.95, however, the results on discontinuous constituents are slightly lower than for IMPORTANCE alone. This confirms the previously observed behavior: The EXTENDED features help when considering all constituents, but they do not seem to be effective for the recovery of discontinuities in particular.

In the TED and LA scores (Tab. 2), we see much less variation than in the bracketing scores. As reported in the literature (e.g., Rehbein and van Genabith (2007)), this is because of the fact that with bracketing evaluation, a single wrong attachment can "break" brackets which otherwise would be counted as correct. Nevertheless, the trends from bracketing evaluation repeat.

To sum up, the COMPOUNDSWAP$_i$ operation works better than SWAP because the latter misses long gaps. The most useful feature sets were EXTENDED and DISCO, both when used independently and when used together. DISCO was particularly useful for discontinuous constituents. SEPARATOR yielded no usable improvements. IMPORTANCE has also proven to be effective, yielding the best results on discontinuous constituents (in combination with DISCO). Over almost all experiments, a common error is that on root level, CS and S get confused, indicating that the present features do not provide sufficient information for disambiguation of those categories. We can also confirm the tendency that discontinuous VPs in relatively short sentences are recognized correctly, as reported by Versley (2014).

TiGer We now repeat the most successful experiments on TIGER. Tab. 3 shows the parsing results for the test set.

Some of the trends seen on the experiments with NEGRA are repeated. EXTENDED and DISCO yields an improvement on all constituents. However, now not only DISCO, but also EXTENDED lead to improved scores on discontinuous constituents. As mentioned above, this can be explained with the fact that for the EXTENDED features to be effective, the amount of training data available in NEGRA was not enough. Other than in NEGRA, the DISCO features are now more effective when used alone, leading to the highest overall F_1 on discontinuous constituents of 19.45. They are, however, less effective in combination with EXTENDED. This is partially remedied by giving the swap transitions more IMPORTANCE, which leads to the highest overall F_1 on all constituents of 74.71.

The models we learn are sparse, therefore, as mentioned above, we can exploit the work of Goldberg and Elhadad (2011). They propose to only include the weight of a feature in the computation of a score if it has been seen more than MINUPDATE times. We repeat the BASELINE experiment with two different MINUPDATE settings (see Tab. 3). As expected, the MINUPDATE models are much smaller. The final model with the baseline experiment uses 8.3m features (parsing speed on test set 73 sent./sec.), with MINUPDATE 5 3.3m features (121 sent./sec.) and with MINUPDATE 10 1.8m features (124 sent./sec.). With MINUPDATE 10, the results do degrade. However, with MINUPDATE 5 in addition to the faster parsing we consistently improve over the baseline.

Finally, in order to check the convergence, we run a further experiment in which we limit training iterations to 40 instead of 20, together with beam size 4. We use the BASELINE features with COMPOUNDSWAP$_i$ combined with DISCO, EX-

	All				Discont. only			
	LR	LP	LF$_1$	E	LR	LP	LF$_1$	E
BASELINE + COMPOUNDSWAP$_i$	72.69	74.77	73.71	36.47	16.08	18.72	17.30	12.96
+ EXTENDED	73.52	75.50	74.50	37.26	15.86	20.04	17.71	13.20
+ DISCO	73.77	**75.35**	74.55	37.08	**16.68**	23.32	**19.45**	**14.43**
+ DISCO + EXTENDED	73.97	75.29	74.62	**37.54**	15.56	22.21	18.30	13.64
+ DISCO + EXTENDED + IMPORTANCE	**74.01**	75.41	**74.71**	37.20	15.61	**23.53**	18.77	13.84
BASELINE + COMPOUNDSWAP$_i$ with								
MINUPDATE 5	73.04	75.03	74.03	37.36	16.25	19.72	17.82	13.28
MINUPDATE 10	72.71	74.55	73.62	36.85	15.78	18.56	17.06	13.07

Table 3: Results TIGER, beam size 4

	LR	LP	LF$_1$	E
BASELINE	81.89	82.49	82.19	49.05
EXTENDED	**82.20**	**82.70**	**82.45**	**49.54**

Table 4: Results NEGRACF

	LR	LP	LF$_1$	E
All constituents	69.72	68.85	69.28	33.89
Disc. only	25.77	27.51	26.61	17.77

Table 5: Results NEGRA *rparse*

TENDED, and IMPORTANCE. The parsing speed on the test set drops to around 39 sentences per second. However, we achieve 75.10 F_1, i.e., a slight improvement over the experiments in Tab. 3 that confirms the tendencies visible in Fig. 5.

3.3.2 Continuous Parsing

We investigate the impact of the swap transitions on both speed and parsing results by running an experiment with NEGRACF using the BASELINE and EXTENDED features. The corresponding results are shown in Tab. 4.

Particularly high frequency categories (NP, VP, S) are much easier to find in the continuous case and show large improvements. This explains why without the swap transition, F_1 with BASELINE features is 6.9 points higher than the F_1 on discontinuous constituents (with COMPOUNDSWAP$_i$). With the EXTENDED features, we obtain a small improvement.

Note that with the shift-reduce approach, the difference between the computational cost of producing discontinuous constituents vs. the cost of producing continuous constituents is much lower than for a grammar-based approach. When producing continuous constituents, parsing is only 20% faster than with the swap transition, namely 97 instead of 81 sentences per second.

In order to give a different perspective on the role of discontinuous constituents, we perform two further evaluations. First, we remove the discontinuities from the output of the discontinuous baseline parser using the procedure described in Sec. 3.1 and evaluate the result against the continuous gold data. We obtain an F_1 of 76.70, 5.5 points lower than the continuous baseline. Secondly, we evaluate the output of the continuous baseline parser against the discontinuous gold data. This leads to an F_1 78.89, 2.9 point more than the discontinuous baseline. Both evaluations confirm the intuition that parsing is much easier when discontinuities (i.e., in our case the swap transition) do not have to be considered.

3.3.3 Comparison with other Parsers

rparse In order to compare our parser with a grammar-based approach, we now parse NEGRA with *rparse*, with the same training and test sets as before (i.e., we do not use the development set). We employ markovization with $v = 1$, $h = 2$ and head driven binarization with binary top and bottom productions.

The first thing to notice is that *rparse* is much slower than our parser. The average parsing speed is about 0.3 sent./sec.; very long sentences require over a minute to be parsed. The parsing results are shown in Tab. 5. They are about 5 points worse than those reported by Kallmeyer and Maier (2013). This is due to the fact that they train on the first 90% of the treebank, and not on the first 80% as we do, which leads to an increased number of unparsed sentences. In comparison to the baseline setting of the shift-reduce parser with beam size 8, the results are around 10 points worse. However, *rparse* reaches an F_1 of 26.61 on discontinuous constituents, which is 5.9 points more than we achieved with the best setting with our parser.

In order to investigate why the grammar-based approach outperforms our parser on discontinuous constituents, we count the frequency of LCFRS productions of a certain gap degree in the binarized grammar used in the *rparse* experiment. The

	LF_1	E
Versley (2014)	74.23	37.32
this work	79.52	44.32
H&N (2008)	79.93	37.78
F&M (2015)	**85.53**	**51.21**

Table 6: Results TIGERHN, sentence length ≤ 40

average occurrence count of rules with gap degree 0 is 12.18. Discontinuous rules have a much lower frequency, the average count of productions with one, two and three gaps being 3.09, 2.09, and 1.06, respectively. In PCFG parsing, excluding low frequency productions does not have a large effect (Charniak, 1996); however, this does not hold for LCFRS parsing, where they have a major influence (cf. Maier (2013, p. 205)): This means that removing low frequency productions has a negative impact on the parser performance particularly concerning discontinuous structures; however, it also means that low frequency discontinuous productions get triggered reliably. This hypothesis is confirmed by the fact that the our parser performs much worse on discontinuous constituents with a very low frequency (such as CS, making up only 0.62% of all discontinuous constituents) than it performs on those with a high frequency (such as VP, making up 60.65% of all discontinuous constituents), while *rparse* performs well on the low frequency constituents.

EaFi and Dependency Parsers We run an experiment with 40 iterations on TIGERHN, using DISCO, EXTENDED and IMPORTANCE. Tab. 6 lists the results, together with the corresponding results of Versley (2014), Hall and Nivre (2008) (H&N) and Fernández-González and Martins (2015) (F&M).

Our results exceed those of EaFi[6] and the exact match score of H&N. We are outperformed by the F&M parser. Note, that particularly the comparison to *EaFi* must be handled with care, since Versley (2014) uses additional preprocessing: PP-internal NPs are annotated explicitly, and the parenthetical sentences are changed to be embedded by their enclosing sentence (instead of vice versa).

We postpone a thorough comparison with both EaFi and the dependency parsers to future work.

[6]Note that Versley (2014) reports a parsing speed of 40-55 sent./sec.; depending on the beam size and the training set size, per second, our parser parses 39-640 sentences.

3.4 Discussion

To our knowledge, surprisingly, numerical scores for discontinuous constituents have not been reported anywhere in previous work. The relatively low overall performance with both grammar-based and shift-reduce based parsing, along with the fact that the grammar-based approach outperforms the shift-reduce approach, is striking. We have shown that it is possible to push the precision on discontinuous constituents, but not the recall, to the level of what can be achieved with a grammar-based approach.

Particularly the outcome of the experiments involving the EXTENDED features and IMPORTANCE drives us to the conclusion that the major problem when parsing discontinuous constituents is data sparseness. More features cannot be the only solution: A more reliable recognition of discontinuous constituents requires a more robust learning from larger amounts of data.

4 Conclusion

We have presented a shift-reduce parser for discontinuous constituents which combines previous work in shift-reduce parsing for continuous constituents with recent work in easy-first parsing of discontinuous constituents. Our experiments confirm that an incremental shift-reduce architecture with a swap transition can indeed be used to parse discontinuous constituents. The swap transition is associated with a low computational cost. We have obtained a speed-up of up to 2,000% in comparison to the grammar-based *rparse*, and we have shown that we obtain better results than with the grammar-based parser, even though the grammar-based strategy does better at the reconstruction of discontinuous constituents.

In future work, we will concentrate on methods that could remedy the data sparseness concerning discontinuous constituents, such as self-training. Furthermore, we will experiment with larger feature sets that add lexical information. An formal investigation of the expressivity of our parsing model is currently under way.

Acknowledgments

I wish to thank Miriam Kaeshammer for enlightening discussions and the three anonymous reviewers for helpful comments and suggestions. This work was partially funded by Deutsche Forschungsgemeinschaft (DFG).

References

Krasimir Angelov and Peter Ljunglöf. 2014. Fast statistical parsing with parallel multiple context-free grammars. In *Proceedings of the 14th Conference of the European Chapter of the Association for Computational Linguistics*, pages 368–376, Gothenburg, Sweden.

John Bauer. 2014. Stanford shift-reduce parser. `http://nlp.stanford.edu/software/srparser.shtml`.

Adriane Boyd. 2007. Discontinuity revisited: An improved conversion to context-free representations. In *Proceedings of The Linguistic Annotation Workshop (LAW) at ACL 2007*, pages 41–44, Prague, Czech Republic.

Shu Cai, David Chiang, and Yoav Goldberg. 2011. Language-independent parsing with empty elements. In *Proceedings of the 49th Annual Meeting of the Association for Computational Linguistics: Human Language Technologies*, pages 212–216, Portland, OR.

Eugene Charniak. 1996. Tree-bank grammars. Technical Report CS-96-02, Department of Computer Science, Brown University, Providence, RI.

Michael Collins and Brian Roark. 2004. Incremental parsing with the perceptron algorithm. In *Proceedings of the 42nd Meeting of the Association for Computational Linguistics (ACL'04), Main Volume*, pages 111–118, Barcelona, Spain.

Hal Daumé III. 2006. *Practical Structured Learning Techniques for Natural Language Processing*. Ph.D. thesis, University of Southern California, Los Angeles, CA.

Péter Dienes and Amit Dubey. 2003. Antecedent recovery: Experiments with a trace tagger. In *Proceedings of the 2003 Conference on Empirical Methods in Natural Language Processing*, pages 33–40, Sapporo, Japan.

Martin Emms. 2008. Tree distance and some other variants of Evalb. In *Proceedings of the Sixth International Language Resources and Evaluation (LREC'08)*, pages 1373–1379, Marrakech, Morocco.

Kilian Evang and Laura Kallmeyer. 2011. PLCFRS parsing of English discontinuous constituents. In *Proceedings of the 12th International Conference on Parsing Technologies (IWPT 2011)*, pages 104–116, Dublin, Ireland.

Richard Farkas and Helmut Schmid. 2012. Forest reranking through subtree ranking. In *Proceedings of the 2012 Joint Conference on Empirical Methods in Natural Language Processing and Computational Natural Language Learning*, pages 1038–1047, Jeju Island, Korea.

Daniel Fernández-González and André F. T. Martins. 2015. Parsing as reduction. In *Proceedings of the 53rd Annual Meeting of the Association for Computational Linguistics and Teh 7th International Joint Conference on Natural Language Processing of the Asian Federation of Natural Language Processing*, Beijing, China. To appear.

Yoav Goldberg and Michael Elhadad. 2010. An efficient algorithm for easy-first non-directional dependency parsing. In *Human Language Technologies: The 2010 Annual Conference of the North American Chapter of the Association for Computational Linguistics*, pages 742–750, Los Angeles, CA.

Yoav Goldberg and Michael Elhadad. 2011. Learning sparser perceptron models. Technical report, Ben Gurion University of the Negev.

Johan Hall and Joakim Nivre. 2008. Parsing discontinuous phrase structure with grammatical functions. In Bengt Nordström and Aarne Ranta, editors, *Advances in Natural Language Processing*, volume 5221 of *Lecture Notes in Computer Science*, pages 169–180. Springer, Gothenburg, Sweden.

Valentin Jijkoun. 2003. Finding non-local dependencies: Beyond pattern matching. In *The Companion Volume to the Proceedings of 41st Annual Meeting of the Association for Computational Linguistics*, pages 37–43, Sapporo, Japan.

Mark Johnson. 2002. A simple pattern-matching algorithm for recovering empty nodes and their antecedents. In *Proceedings of the 40th Annual Meeting of the Association for Computational Linguistics*, pages 136–143, Philadelphia, PA.

Laura Kallmeyer and Wolfgang Maier. 2013. Data-driven parsing using probabilistic linear context-free rewriting systems. *Computational Linguistics*, 39(1):87–119.

Roger Levy and Christopher Manning. 2004. Deep dependencies from context-free statistical parsers: Correcting the surface dependency approximation. In *Proceedings of the 42nd Meeting of the Association for Computational Linguistics (ACL'04), Main Volume*, pages 327–334, Barcelona, Spain.

Roger Levy. 2005. *Probabilistic Models of Word Order and Syntactic Discontinuity*. Ph.D. thesis, Stanford University.

Wolfgang Maier and Timm Lichte. 2011. Characterizing discontinuity in constituent treebanks. In *Formal Grammar. 14th International Conference, FG 2009. Bordeaux, France, July 25-26, 2009. Revised Selected Papers*, volume 5591 of *LNCS/LNAI*, pages 167–182. Springer-Verlag.

Wolfgang Maier and Anders Søgaard. 2008. Treebanks and mild context-sensitivity. In Philippe de Groote, editor, *Proceedings of the 13th Conference on Formal Grammar (FG-2008)*, pages 61–76, Hamburg, Germany. CSLI Publications.

Wolfgang Maier, Miriam Kaeshammer, and Laura Kallmeyer. 2012. Data-driven PLCFRS parsing revisited: Restricting the fan-out to two. In *Proceedings of the Eleventh International Conference on Tree Adjoining Grammars and Related Formalisms (TAG+11)*, pages 126–134, Paris, France.

Wolfgang Maier. 2013. *Parsing Discontinuous Structures*. Dissertation, University of Tübingen.

Joakim Nivre, Marco Kuhlmann, and Johan Hall. 2009. An improved oracle for dependency parsing with online reordering. In *Proceedings of the 11th International Conference on Parsing Technologies (IWPT'09)*, pages 73–76, Paris, France.

Joakim Nivre. 2009. Non-projective dependency parsing in expected linear time. In *Proceedings of the Joint Conference of the 47th Annual Meeting of the ACL and the 4th International Joint Conference on Natural Language Processing of the AFNLP*, pages 351–359, Singapore.

Ines Rehbein and Josef van Genabith. 2007. Evaluating evaluation measures. In *Proceedings of the 16th Nordic Conference of Computational Linguistics NODALIDA-2007*, pages 372–379, Tartu, Estonia.

Kenji Sagae and Alon Lavie. 2005. A classifier-based parser with linear run-time complexity. In *Proceedings of the Ninth International Workshop on Parsing Technology*, pages 125–132, Vancouver, BC.

Geoffrey Sampson and Anna Babarczy. 2003. A test of the leaf-ancestor metric for parse accuracy. *Journal of Natural Language Engineering*, 9:365–380.

Helmut Schmid. 2006. Trace prediction and recovery with unlexicalized PCFGs and slash features. In *Proceedings of the 21st International Conference on Computational Linguistics and 44th Annual Meeting of the Association for Computational Linguistics*, pages 177–184, Sydney, Australia.

Djamé Seddah, Reut Tsarfaty, Sandra Kübler, Marie Candito, Jinho D. Choi, Richárd Farkas, Jennifer Foster, Iakes Goenaga, Koldo Gojenola Galletebeitia, Yoav Goldberg, Spence Green, Nizar Habash, Marco Kuhlmann, Wolfgang Maier, Yuval Marton, Joakim Nivre, Adam Przepiórkowski, Ryan Roth, Wolfgang Seeker, Yannick Versley, Veronika Vincze, Marcin Woliński, and Alina Wróblewska. 2013. Overview of the SPMRL 2013 shared task: A cross-framework evaluation of parsing morphologically rich languages. In *Proceedings of the Fourth Workshop on Statistical Parsing of Morphologically-Rich Languages*, pages 146–182, Seattle, WA.

Hiroyuki Seki, Takashi Matsumura, Mamoru Fujii, and Tadao Kasami. 1991. On Multiple Context-Free Grammars. *Theoretical Computer Science*, 88(2):191–229.

Andreas van Cranenburgh and Rens Bod. 2013. Discontinuous parsing with an efficient and accurate DOP model. In *Proceedings of The 13th International Conference on Parsing Technologies*, Nara, Japan.

Andreas van Cranenburgh. 2012. Efficient parsing with linear context-free rewriting systems. In *Proceedings of the 13th Conference of the European Chapter of the Association for Computational Linguistics*, pages 460–470, Avignon, France.

Yannick Versley. 2014. Experiments with easy-first nonprojective constituent parsing. In *Proceedings of the First Joint Workshop on Statistical Parsing of Morphologically Rich Languages and Syntactic Analysis of Non-Canonical Languages*, pages 39–53, Dublin, Ireland.

K. Vijay-Shanker, David Weir, and Aravind K. Joshi. 1987. Characterising structural descriptions used by various formalisms. In *Proceedings of the 25th Annual Meeting of the Association for Computational Linguistics*, pages 104–111, Stanford, CA.

Yue Zhang and Stephen Clark. 2009. Transition-based parsing of the Chinese treebank using a global discriminative model. In *Proceedings of the 11th International Conference on Parsing Technologies (IWPT'09)*, pages 162–171, Paris, France.

Yue Zhang and Stephen Clark. 2011a. Shift-reduce CCG parsing. In *Proceedings of the 49th Annual Meeting of the Association for Computational Linguistics: Human Language Technologies*, pages 683–692, Portland, OR.

Yue Zhang and Stephen Clark. 2011b. Syntactic processing using the generalized perceptron and beam search. *Computational Linguistics*, 37(1):105–151.

Muhua Zhu, Jingbo Zhu, and Huizhen Wang. 2012. Exploiting lexical dependencies from large-scale data for better shift-reduce constituency parsing. In *Proceedings of COLING 2012*, pages 3171–3186, Mumbai, India.

Muhua Zhu, Yue Zhang, Wenliang Chen, Min Zhang, and Jingbo Zhu. 2013. Fast and accurate shift-reduce constituent parsing. In *Proceedings of the 51st Annual Meeting of the Association for Computational Linguistics (Volume 1: Long Papers)*, pages 434–443, Sofia, Bulgaria.

A Neural Probabilistic Structured-Prediction Model for Transition-Based Dependency Parsing

Hao Zhou†* **Yue Zhang**‡ **Shujian Huang**† **Jiajun Chen**†
†State Key Laboratory for Novel Software Technology, Nanjing University, China
‡Singapore University of Technology and Design, Singapore
{zhouh, huangsj, chenjj}@nlp.nju.edu.cn, yue_zhang@sutd.edu.sg

Abstract

Neural probabilistic parsers are attractive for their capability of automatic feature combination and small data sizes. A transition-based greedy neural parser has given better accuracies over its linear counterpart. We propose a neural probabilistic structured-prediction model for transition-based dependency parsing, which integrates search and learning. Beam search is used for decoding, and contrastive learning is performed for maximizing the sentence-level log-likelihood. In standard Penn Treebank experiments, the structured neural parser achieves a 1.8% accuracy improvement upon a competitive greedy neural parser baseline, giving performance comparable to the best linear parser.

1 Introduction

Transition-based methods have given competitive accuracies and efficiencies for dependency parsing (Yamada and Matsumoto, 2003; Nivre and Scholz, 2004; Zhang and Clark, 2008; Huang and Sagae, 2010; Zhang and Nivre, 2011; Goldberg and Nivre, 2013). These parsers construct dependency trees by using a sequence of transition actions, such as SHIFT and REDUCE, over input sentences. High accuracies are achieved by using a linear model and millions of binary indicator features. Recently, Chen and Manning (2014) propose an alternative dependency parser using a neural network, which represents atomic features as dense vectors, and obtains feature combination automatically other than devising high-order features manually.

The greedy neural parser of Chen and Manning (2014) gives higher accuracies compared to the greedy linear MaltParser (Nivre and Scholz, 2004), but lags behind state-of-the-art linear systems with sparse features (Zhang and Nivre, 2011), which adopt global learning and beam search decoding (Zhang and Nivre, 2012). The key difference is that Chen and Manning (2014) is a *local classifier* that greedily optimizes each action. In contrast, Zhang and Nivre (2011) leverage a *structured-prediction* model to optimize whole sequences of actions, which correspond to tree structures.

In this paper, we propose a novel framework for *structured* neural probabilistic dependency parsing, which maximizes the likelihood of action sequences instead of individual actions. Following Zhang and Clark (2011), beam search is applied to decoding, and global structured learning is integrated with beam search using early-update (Collins and Roark, 2004). Designing such a framework is challenging for two main reasons:

First, applying global structured learning to transition-based neural parsing is non-trivial. A direct adaptation of the framework of Zhang and Clark (2011) under the neural probabilistic model setting does not yield good results. The main reason is that the parameter space of a neural network is much denser compared to that of a linear model such as the structured perceptron (Collins, 2002). Due to the dense parameter space, for neural models, the scores of actions in a sequence are relatively more dependent than that in the linear models. As a result, the log probability of an action sequence can not be modeled just as the sum of log probabilities of each action in the sequence, which is the case of structured linear model. We address the challenge by using a *softmax* function to directly model the distribution of action sequences.

Second, for the structured model above, maximum-likelihood training is computationally intractable, requiring summing over all possible action sequences, which is difficult for transition-

*Work done while the first author was visiting SUTD.

Proceedings of the 53rd Annual Meeting of the Association for Computational Linguistics and the 7th International Joint Conference on Natural Language Processing, pages 1213–1222,
Beijing, China, July 26-31, 2015.

based parsing. To address this challenge, we take a contrastive learning approach (Hinton, 2002; LeCun and Huang, 2005; Liang and Jordan, 2008; Vickrey et al., 2010; Liu and Sun, 2014). Using the sum of log probabilities over the action sequences in the beam to approximate that over all possible action sequences.

In standard PennTreebank (Marcus et al., 1993) evaluations, our parser achieves a significant accuracy improvement (+1.8%) over the greedy neural parser of Chen and Manning (2014), and gives the best reported accuracy by shift-reduce parsers. The incremental neural probabilistic framework with global contrastive learning and beam search could be used in other structured prediction tasks.

input : $w_0 \dots w_{n-1}$
axiom : $0 : \langle 0, \phi, \phi, 0 \rangle$
goal : $2n-1 : \langle n, s_0, L \rangle$

$$\text{SHIFT} \quad \frac{k : \langle j, S, L \rangle}{k+1 : \langle j+1, S|w_j, L \rangle}$$

$$\text{LEFT-ARC}(l) \quad \frac{k : \langle j, S|s_1|s_0, L \rangle}{k+1 : \langle j, S|s_0, L \cup \{s_1 \xleftarrow{l} s_0\} \rangle}$$

$$\text{RIGHT-ARC}(l) \quad \frac{k : \langle j, S|s_1|s_0, L \rangle}{k+1 : \langle j, S|s_1, L \cup \{s_1 \xrightarrow{l} s_0\} \rangle}$$

Figure 1: The deductive system for arc-standard dependency parsing.

2 Background

2.1 Arc-standard Parsing

Transition-based dependency parsers scan an input sentence from left to right, and perform a sequence of transition actions to predict its parse tree (Nivre, 2008). In this paper, we employ the **arc-standard** system (Nivre et al., 2007), which maintains partially-constructed outputs using a *stack*, and orders the incoming words in the input sentence in a *queue*. Parsing starts with an empty stack and a queue consisting of the whole input sentence. At each step, a *transition action* is taken to consume the input and construct the output. The process repeats until the input queue is empty and stack contains only one dependency tree.

Formally, a parsing state is denoted as $\langle j, S, L \rangle$, where S is a stack of subtrees $[\dots s_2, s_1, s_0]$, j is the head of the queue (i.e. $[\ q_0 = w_j,\ q_1 = w_{j+1} \cdots]$), and L is a set of dependency arcs. At each step, the parser chooses one of the following actions:

- SHIFT: move the front word w_j from the queue onto the stacks.

- LEFT-ARC(l): add an arc with label l between the top two trees on the stack ($s_1 \leftarrow s_0$), and remove s_1 from the stack.

- RIGHT-ARC(l): add an arc with label l between the top two trees on the stack ($s_1 \rightarrow s_0$), and remove s_0 from the stack.

The arc-standard parser can be summarized as the deductive system in Figure 1, where k denotes the current parsing step. For a sentence with size n, parsing stops after performing exactly $2n-1$ actions.

MaltParser uses an SVM classifier for deterministic arc-standard parsing. At each step, MaltParser generates a set of successor states according to the current state, and deterministically selects the highest-scored one as the next state.

2.2 Global Learning and Beam Search

The drawback of deterministic parsing is error propagation. An incorrect action will have a negative influence to its subsequent actions, leading to an incorrect output parse tree.

To address this issue, global learning and beam search (Zhang and Clark, 2011; Bohnet and Nivre, 2012; Choi and McCallum, 2013) are used. Given an input x, the goal of decoding is to find the highest-scored action sequence *globally*.

$$y = \underset{y' \in \text{GEN}(x)}{\arg\max}\ score(y') \tag{1}$$

Where $\text{GEN}(x)$ denotes all possible action sequences on x, which correspond to all possible parse trees. The score of an action sequence y is:

$$score(y) = \sum_{a \in y} \theta \cdot \Phi(a) \tag{2}$$

Here a is an action in the action sequence y, Φ is a feature function for a, and θ is the parameter vector of the linear model. The score of an action sequence is the linear sum of the scores of each action. During training, action sequence scores are globally learned.

The parser of Zhang and Nivre (2011) is developed using this framework. The structured perceptron (Collins, 2002) with early update (Collins and Roark, 2004) is applied for training. By utilizing rich manual features, it gives state-of-the-art accuracies in standard Penn Treebank evaluation. We take this method as one baseline.

2.3 Greedy Neural Network Model

Chen and Manning (2014) build a greedy neural arc-standard parser. The model can be regarded as an alternative implementation of MaltParser, using a feedforward neural network to replace the SVM classifier for deterministic parsing.

2.3.1 Model

The greedy neural model extracts n atomic features from a parsing state, which consists of words, POS-tags and dependency labels from the stack ans queue. *Embeddings* are used to represent word, POS and dependency label atomic features. Each embedding is represented as a d-dimensional vector $e_i \in \mathbb{R}$. Therefore, the full embedding matrix is $E \in \mathbb{R}^{d \times V}$, where V is the number of distinct features. A *projection layer* is used to concatenate the n input embeddings into a vector $x = [e_1; e_2 \dots e_n]$, where $x \in \mathbb{R}^{d \cdot n}$. The purpose of this layer is to fine-tune the embedding features. Then x is mapped to a d_h-dimensional *hidden layer* by a mapping matrix $W_1 \in \mathbb{R}^{d_h \times d \cdot n}$ and a cube activation function:

$$h = (W_1 x + b_1)^3 \quad (3)$$

Finally, h is mapped into a *softmax output layer* for modeling the probabilistic distribution of candidate shift-reduce actions:

$$p = softmax(o) \quad (4)$$

where

$$o = W_2 h \quad (5)$$

$W_2 \in \mathbb{R}^{d_o \times d_h}$ and d_o is the number of shift-reduce actions.

2.3.2 Features

One advantage of Chen and Manning (2014) is that the neural network parser achieves feature combination automatically. Their atomic features are defined by following Zhang and Nivre (2011). As shown in Table 1, the features are categorized into three types: F^w, F^t, F^l, which represents word features, POS-tag features and dependency label features, respectively.

	Templates
F^w	$s_0w, s_2w, q_0w, q_1w, q_2w, lc_1(s_0)w, lc_2(s_0)w$ $s_1w, rc_2(s_0)w, lc_1(s_1)w, lc_2(s_1)w, rc_2(s_1)w$ $rc_1(s_0)w, rc_1(s_1)w, lc_1(lc_1(s_0))w, lc_1(lc_1(s_1))w$ $rc_1(rc_1(s_1))w, rc_1(rc_1(s_0))w$
F^t	$s_0t, q_0t, q_1t, q_2t, rc_1(s_0)t, lc_1(s_0)t, lc_2(s_0)t$ $s_1t, s_2t, lc_1(s_1)t, lc_2(s_1)t, rc_1(s_1)t, rc_2(s_0)t$ $rc_2(s_1)t, lc_1(lc_1(s_0))t, lc_1(lc_1(s_1))t$ $rc_1(rc_1(s_0))t, rc_1(rc_1(s_1))t$
F^l	$rc_1(s_0)l, lc_1(s_0)l, lc_2(s_0)l, lc_1(s_1)l, lc_2(s_1)l$ $rc_1(s_1)l, rc_2(s_0)l, rc_2(s_1)l, lc_1(lc_1(s_0))l$ $lc_1(lc_1(s_1))l, rc_1(rc_1(s_0))l, rc_1(rc_1(s_1))l$

Table 1: Feature templates.

For example, s_0w and q_0w represent the first word on the stack and queue, respectively; $lc_1(s_0)w$ and $rc_1(s_0)w$ represent the leftmost and rightmost child of s_0, respectively. Similarly, $lc_1(s_0)t$ and $lc_1(s_0)l$ represent the POS-tag and dependency label of the leftmost child of s_0, respectively.

Chen and Manning (2014) find that the cube activation function in Equation (3) is highly effective in capturing feature interaction, which is a novel contribution of their work. The cube function achieves linear combination between atomic word, POS and label features via the product of three element combinations. Empirically, it works better compared to a sigmoid activation function.

2.4 Training

Given a set of training examples, the training objective of the greedy neural parser is to minimize the cross-entropy loss, plus a l_2-regularization term:

$$L(\theta) = -\sum_{i \in A} \log p_i + \frac{\lambda}{2} \parallel \theta \parallel^2 \quad (6)$$

θ is the set of all parameters (i.e. W_1, W_2, b, E), and A is the set of all gold actions in the training data. AdaGrad (Duchi et al., 2011) with minibatch is adopted for optimization. We take the greedy neural parser of Chen and Manning (2014) as a second baseline.

3 Structured Neural Network Model

We propose a neural structured-prediction model that scores whole sequences of transition actions, rather than individual actions. As shown in Table 2, the model can be seen as a neural probabilistic alternative of Zhang and Nivre (2011),

	local classifier	structured prediction
linear sparse	Section 2.1 (Nivre et al., 2007)	Section 2.2 (Zhang and Nivre, 2011)
neural dense	Section 2.3 (Chen and Manning, 2014)	this work

Table 2: Correlation between different parsers.

or a structured-prediction alternative of Chen and Manning (2014). It combines the advantages of both Zhang and Nivre (2011) and Chen and Manning (2014) over the greedy linear MaltParser.

3.1 Neural Probabilistic Ranking

Given the baseline system in Section 2.2, the most intuitive structured neural dependency parser is to replace the linear scoring model with a neural probabilistic model. Following Equation 1, the score of an action sequence y, which corresponds to its log probability, is sum of log probability scores of each action in the sequence.

$$s(y) = \sum_{a \in y} \log p_a \tag{7}$$

where p_a is defined by the baseline neural model of Section 2.3 (Equation 4). The training objective is to maximize the score margin between the gold action sequences (y_g) and these of incorrectly predicated action sequences (y_p):

$$L(\theta) = max(0, \delta - s(y_g) + s(y_p)) + \frac{\lambda}{2} \parallel \theta \parallel^2 \tag{8}$$

With this ranking model, beam search and early-update are used. Given a training instance, the negative example is the incorrectly predicted output with largest score (Zhang and Nivre, 2011).

However, we find that the ranking model works poorly. One explanation is that the actions in a sequence is probabilistically dependent on each other, and therefore using the total log probabilities of each action to compute the log probability of an action sequence (Equation 7) is inaccurate. Linear models do not suffer from this problem, because the parameter space of linear models is much more sparse than that of neural models. For neural networks, the dense parameter space is shared by all the actions in a sequence. Increasing the likelihood of a gold action may also change the likelihood of incorrect actions through the shared parameters. As a result, increasing the scores of a gold action sequence and simultaneously reducing the scores of an incorrect action sequence does not work well for neural models.

3.2 Sentence-Level Log-Likelihood

To overcome the above limitation, we try to directly model the probabilistic distribution of whole action sequences. Given a sentence x and neural networks parameter θ, the probability of the action sequence y_i is given by the *softmax* function:

$$p(y_i \mid x, \theta) = \frac{e^{f(x,\,\theta)_i}}{\sum_{y_j \in \text{GEN}(x)} e^{f(x,\,\theta)_j}} \tag{9}$$

where

$$f(x,\,\theta)_i = \sum_{a_k \in y_i} o(x,\,y_i,\,k,\,a_k) \tag{10}$$

Here GEN(s) is the set of all possible valid action sequences for a sentence x; $o(x,\,y_i,\,k,\,a_k)$ denotes the neural network score for the action a_k given x and y_i. We use the same sub network as Chen and Manning (2014) to calculate $o(x,\,y_i,\,k,\,a_k)$ (Equation 5). The same features in Table 1 are used.

Given the training data as $(X,\,Y)$, our training objective is to minimize the negative log-likelihood:

$$L(\theta) = -\sum_{(x_i,\,y_i) \in (X,Y)} \log p(y_i \mid x_i, \theta) \tag{11}$$

$$= -\sum_{(x_i,\,y_i) \in (X,Y)} \log \frac{e^{f(x_i,\theta)_i}}{Z(x_i,\theta)} \tag{12}$$

$$= \sum_{(x_i,\,y_i) \in (X,Y)} \log Z(x_i,\theta) - f(x_i,\theta)_i \tag{13}$$

where

$$Z(x,\theta) = \sum_{y_j \in \text{GEN}(x)} e^{f(x,\,\theta)_j} \tag{14}$$

Here, $Z(x,\theta)$ is called the *partition function*. Following Chen and Manning(2014), we apply l_2-regularization for training.

For optimization, we need to compute gradients for $L(\theta)$, which includes gradients of exponential numbers of negative examples in *partition function* $Z(x, \theta)$. However, beam search is used for transition-based parsing, and no efficient optimal dynamic program is available to estimate $Z(x, \theta)$ accurately. We adopt a novel contrastive learning approach to approximately compute $Z(x, \theta)$.

3.3 Contrastive Learning

As an alternative to maximize the likelihood on some observed data, contrastive learning (Hinton, 2002; LeCun and Huang, 2005; Liang and Jordan, 2008; Vickrey et al., 2010; Liu and Sun, 2014) is an approach that assigns higher probabilities to observed data and lower probabilities to noisy data.

We adopt the contrastive learning approach, assigning higher probabilities to the gold action sequence compared to incorrect action sequences in the beam. Intuitively, this method only penalizes incorrect action sequences with high probabilities. Our new training objective is approximated as:

$$L'(\theta) = - \sum_{(x_i, y_i) \in (X,Y)} \log p'(y_i \mid x_i, \theta) \quad (15)$$

$$= - \sum_{(x_i, y_i) \in (X,Y)} \log \frac{e^{f(x_i, \theta)_i}}{Z'(x_i, \theta)} \quad (16)$$

$$= \sum_{(x_i, y_i) \in (X,Y)} \log Z'(x_i, \theta) - f(x_i, \theta)_i \quad (17)$$

where

$$Z'(x, \theta) = \sum_{y_j \in \mathrm{BEAM}(x)} e^{f(x,\, \theta)_j} \quad (18)$$

$p'(y_i \mid x, \theta)$ is the relative probability of the action sequence y_i, computed over only the action sequences in the beam. $Z'(x, \theta)$ is the contrastive approximation of $Z(x, \theta)$. $\mathrm{BEAM}(x)$ returns the predicated action sequences in the beam and the gold action sequence.

We assume that the probability mass concentrates on a relatively small number of action sequences, which allows the use of a limited number of probable sequences to approximate the full set of action sequences. The concentration may be enlarged dramatically with an exponential activation function of the neural network (i.e. $a > b \Rightarrow e^a \gg e^b$).

3.4 The Neural Probabilistic Structured-Prediction Framework

We follow Zhang and Clark (2011) to integrate search and learning. Our search and learning framework for dependency parsing is shown as Algorithm 1. In every training iteration i, we randomly sample the training instances, and perform online learning with early update (Collins and Roark, 2004). In particular, given a training example, we use beam-search to decode the sentence. At any step, if the gold action sequence falls out of the beam, we take all the incorrect action sequences in the beam as negative examples, and the current gold sequence as a positive example for parameter update, using the training algorithm of Section 3.3. AdaGrad algorithm (Duchi et al., 2011) with mini-batch is adopted for optimization.

In this way, the distribution of ot only full action sequences (i.e. complete parse trees), but also partial action sequences (i.e. partial outputs) are modeled, which makes training more challenging. The advantage of early update is that training is used to guide search, minimizing search errors.

Algorithm 1: Training Algorithm for Structured Neural Parsing

```
Input: training examples (X, Y)
Output: θ
θ ← pretrained embedding
for i ← 1 to N do
    x, y = RANDOMSAMPLE(X, Y)
    δ = 0
    foreach x_j, y_j ∈ x, y do
        beam = φ
        goldState = null
        terminate = false
        beamGold = true
        while beamGold and not terminate do
            beam = DECODE(beam, x_j, y_j)
            goldState = GOLDMOVE(goldState, x_j, y_j)
            if not ISGOLD(beam) then
                beamGold = false
            if ITEMSCOMPLETE(beam) then
                terminate = true;
        δ = δ + UPDATE(goldState, beam)
    θ = θ + delta
```

4 Experiments

4.1 Set-up

Our experiments are performed using the English Penn Treebank (PTB; Marcus et al., (1993)). We follow the standard splits of PTB3, using sections 2-21 for training, section 22 for development testing and section 23 for final testing. For comparison with previous work, we use Penn2Malt[1] to convert constituent trees to dependency trees. We use the POS-tagger of Collins (2002) to assign POS automatically. 10-fold jackknifing is performed for tagging the training data.

We follow Chen and Manning (2014), and use the set of pre-trained word embeddings[2] from Collobert et al. (2011) with a dictionary size of 13,000. The word embeddings were trained on the entire English Wikipedia, which contains about 631 million words.

4.2 WSJ Experiments

4.2.1 Development experiments

We set the following hyper-parameters according to the baseline greedy neural parser (Chen and Manning, 2014): embedding size d = 50, hidden layer size d_h = 200, regularization parameter $\lambda = 10^{-8}$, initial learning rate of Adagrad α = 0.01. For the structured neural parser, beam size and mini-batch size are important to the parsing performance. We tune them on the development set.

Beam size. Beam search enlarges the search space. More importantly, the larger the beam is, the more accurate our training algorithm is. the Contrastive learning approximates the exact probabilities over exponential many action sequences by computing the relative probabilities over action sequences in the beam (Equation 18). Therefore, the larger the beam is, the more accurate the relative probability is.

The first column of Table 3 shows the accuracies of the structured neural parser on the development set with different beam sizes, which improves as the beam size increases. We set the final beam size as 100 according to the accuracies on development set.

The effect of integrating search and learning. We also conduct experiments on the parser of Chen and Manning (2014) with beam search decoding. The score of a whole action sequence is computed by the sum of log action probabilities (Equation 7). As shown in the second column of Table 3, beam search can improve parsing slightly. When the beam size increases beyond 16, however, accuracy improvements stop. In contrast, by integrating beam search and global learning, our parsing performance benefits from large beam sizes much more significantly. With a beam size as 16, the structured neural parser gives an accuracy close to that of baseline greedy parser[3]. When the beam size is 100, the structured neural parser outperforms baseline by 1.6%.

Zhang and Nivre (2012) find that global learning and beam search should be used jointly for improving parsing using a *linear* transition-based model. In particular, increasing the beam size, the accuracy of ZPar (Zhang and Nivre, 2011) increases significantly, but that of MaltParser does not. For structured *neural* parsing, our finding is similar: integrating search and learning is much more effective than using beam search only in decoding.

Our results in Table 3 are obtained by using the same beam sizes for both training and testing. Zhang and Nivre (2012) also find that for their lin-

Description	UAS	
Baseline	91.63	
	structured	greedy
beam = 1	74.90	91.63
beam = 4	84.64	91.92
beam = 16	91.53	91.90
beam = 64	93.12	91.84
beam = 100	93.23	91.81

Table 3: Accuracies of structured neural parsing and local neural classification parsing with different beam sizes.

Description	UAS
greedy neural parser	91.47
ranking model	89.08
beam contrastive learning	93.28

Table 4: Comparison between sentence-level log-likelihood and ranking model.

[1]http://stp.lingfil.uu.se/ nivre/research/Penn2Malt.html

[2]http://ronan.collobert.com/senna/

[3]Our baseline accuracy is a little lower than accuracy reported in baseline paper (Chen and Manning, 2014), because we use Penn2Malt to convert the Penn Treebank, and they use LTH Conversion.

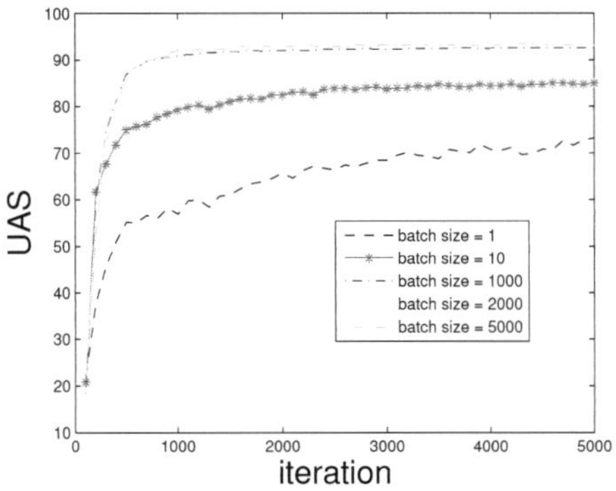

Figure 2: Parsing performance with different training batch sizes.

System		UAS	LAS	Speed
baseline greedy parser		91.47	90.43	0.001
Huang and Sagae (2010)		92.10		0.04
Zhang and Nivre (2011)		92.90	91.80	0.03
Choi and McCallum (2013)		92.96	91.93	0.009
Ma et al. (2014)		93.06		
Bohnet and Nivre (2012)†‡		93.67	92.68	0.4
Suzuki et al. (2009)†		93.79		
Koo et al. (2008)†		93.16		
Chen et al. (2014)†		93.77		
beam size				
training	decoding			
100	100	**93.28**	**92.35**	0.07
100	64	93.20	92.27	0.04
100	16	92.40	91.95	0.01

Table 5: Results on WSJ. Speed: sentences per second. †: semi-supervised learning. ‡: joint POS-tagging and dependency parsing models.

ear model, the best results are achieved by using the same beam sizes during training and testing. We find that this observation does not apply to our neural parser. In our case, a large training beam always leads to better results. This is likely because a large beam improves contrastive learning. As a result, our training beam size is set to 100 for the final test.

Batch size. Parsing performance using neural networks is highly sensitive to the batch size of training. In greedy neural parsing (Chen and Manning, 2014), the accuracy on the development data improves from 85% to 91% by setting the batch size to 10 and 100000, respectively. In structured neural parsing, we fix the beam size as 100 and draw the accuracies on the development set by the training iteration.

As shown in Figure 2, in 5000 training iterations, the parsing accuracies improve as the iteration grows, yet different batch sizes result in different convergence accuracies. With a batch size of 5000, the parsing accuracy is about 25% higher than with a batch size of 1 (i.e. SGD). For the remaining experiments, we set batch size to 5000, which achieves the best accuracies on development testing.

4.2.2 Sentence-level maximum likelihood vs. ranking model

We compare parsing accuracies of the sentence-level log-likelihood + beam contrastive learning (Section 3.2), and the structured neural parser with probabilistic ranking (Section 3.1). As shown in Table 4, performance of global learning with ranking model is weaker than the baseline greedy parser. In contrast, structured neural parsing with sentence-level log-likelihood and contrastive learning gives a 1.8% accuracy improvement upon the baseline greedy parser.

As mentioned in Section 3.1, a likely reason for the poor performance of the structured neural ranking model may be that, the likelihoods of action sequences are highly influenced by each other, due to the dense parameter space of neural networks. To maximize likelihood of gold action sequence, we need to decrease the likelihoods of more than one incorrect action sequences.

4.2.3 Final Results

Table 5 shows the results of our final parser and a line of transition-based parsers on the test set. Our structured neural parser achieves an accuracy of 93.28%, 0.38% higher than Zhang and Nivre (2011), which employees millions of high-order binary indicator features in parsing. The model size of ZPar (Zhang and Nivre, 2011) is over 250 MB on disk. In contrast, the model size of our structured neural parser is only 25 MB. To our knowledge, the result is the best reported result achieved by shift-reduce parsers on this data set.

Bohnet and Nivre (2012) obtain an accuracy of 93.67%, which is higher than our parser. However, their parser is a joint model of parsing and POS-tagging, and they use external data in parsing. We also list the result of Chen et al. (2014), Koo et al. (2008) and Suzuki et al. (2009) in Table 5, which make use of large-scale unannotated text to improve parsing accuracies. The input embeddings of our parser are also trained over large raw text, and in this perspective our model is correlated with the semi-supervised models. However, because we fine-tune the word embeddings in supervised training, the embeddings of in-vocabulary words become systematically different from these of out-of-vocabulary words after training, and the effect of pre-trained out-of-vocabulary embeddings become uncertain. In this sense, our model can also be regarded as an almost fully supervised model. The same applies to the models of Chen and Manning (2014).

We also compare the speed of the structured neural parser on an Intel Core i7 3.40GHz CPU with 16GB RAM. The structured neural parser runs about as fast as Zhang and Nivre (Zhang and Nivre, 2011) and Huang and Sagae (Huang and Sagae, 2010). The results show that our parser combines the benefits of structured models and neural probabilistic models, offering high accuracies, fast speed and slim model size.

5 Related Work

Parsing with neural networks. A line of work has been proposed to explore the effect of neural network models for constituent parsing (Henderson, 2004; Mayberry III and Miikkulainen, 2005; Collobert, 2011; Socher et al., 2013; Legrand and Collobert, 2014). Performances of most of these methods are still well below the state-of-the-art, except for Socher et al.(2013), who propose a neural reranker based on a PCFG parser. For transition-based dependency parsing, Stenetorp (2013) applies a compositional vector method (Socher et al., 2013), and Chen and Manning (2014) propose a feed-forward neural parser. The performances of these neural parsers lag behind the state-of-the-art.

More recently, Dyer et al. (2015) propose a greedy transition-based dependency parser, using three stack LSTMs to represent the input, the stack of partial syntactic trees and the history of parse actions, respectively. By modeling more history, the parser gives significant better accuracies compared to the greedy neural parser of Chen and Manning (2014).

Structured neural models. Collobert et al. (2011) presents a unified neural network architecture for various natural language processing (NLP) tasks. They propose to use sentence-level log-likelihood to enhance a neural probabilistic model, which inspires our model. Sequence labeling is used for graph-based decoding. Using the Viterbi algorithm, they can compute the exponential partition function in linear time without approximation. However, with a dynamic programming decoder, their sequence labeling model can only extract local features. In contrast, our integrated approximated search and learning framework allows rich global features.

Weiss et al. (2015) also propose a structured neural transition-based parser by adopting beam search and early updates. Their model is close in spirit to ours in performing structured prediction using a neural network. The main difference is that their structured neural parser uses a greedy parsing process for pre-training, and fine-tunes an additional perceptron layer consisting of the pre-trained hidden and output layers using structured perceptron updates. Their structured neural parser achieves an accuracy of 93.36% on Stanford conversion of the PTB, which is significant higher than the baseline parser of Chen and Manning (2014). Their results are not directly comparable with ours due to different dependency conversions.

6 Conclusion

We built a structured neural dependency parsing model. Compared to the greedy neural parser of Chen and Manning (2014), our parser integrates beam search and global contrastive learning. In standard PTB evaluation, our parser achieved a 1.8% accuracy improvement over the parser of Chen and Manning (2014), which shows the effect of combining search and learning. To our knowledge, the structured neural parser is the first neural parser that outperforms the best linear shift-reduce dependency parsers. The structured neural probabilistic framework can be used in other incremental structured prediction tasks.

7 Acknowledgments

We would like to thank the anonymous reviewers for their insightful comments. This work was partially founded by the Natural Science Foundation of China (61170181, 61300158), the Jiangsu Provincial Research Foundation for Basic Research (BK20130580), Singapore Ministratry of Education Tier 2 Grant T2MOE201301 and SRGISTD2012038 from Singapore University of Technology and Design.

References

Bernd Bohnet and Joakim Nivre. 2012. A transition-based system for joint part-of-speech tagging and labeled non-projective dependency parsing. In *Proceedings of the 2012 Joint Conference on Empirical Methods in Natural Language Processing and Computational Natural Language Learning*, pages 1455–1465. Association for Computational Linguistics.

Danqi Chen and Christopher D Manning. 2014. A fast and accurate dependency parser using neural networks. In *Empirical Methods in Natural Language Processing (EMNLP)*.

Wenliang Chen, Yue Zhang, and Min Zhang. 2014. Feature embedding for dependency parsing. In *Proceedings of the international conference on Computational linguistics*. Association for Computational Linguistics.

Jinho D Choi and Andrew McCallum. 2013. Transition-based dependency parsing with selectional branching. In *ACL (1)*, pages 1052–1062.

Michael Collins and Brian Roark. 2004. Incremental parsing with the perceptron algorithm. In *Proceedings of the 42nd Annual Meeting on Association for Computational Linguistics*, page 111. Association for Computational Linguistics.

Michael Collins. 2002. Discriminative training methods for hidden markov models: Theory and experiments with perceptron algorithms. In *Proceedings of the ACL-02 conference on Empirical methods in natural language processing-Volume 10*, pages 1–8. Association for Computational Linguistics.

Ronan Collobert, Jason Weston, Léon Bottou, Michael Karlen, Koray Kavukcuoglu, and Pavel Kuksa. 2011. Natural language processing (almost) from scratch. *The Journal of Machine Learning Research*, 12:2493–2537.

R. Collobert. 2011. Deep learning for efficient discriminative parsing. In *AISTATS*.

John Duchi, Elad Hazan, and Yoram Singer. 2011. Adaptive subgradient methods for online learning and stochastic optimization. *The Journal of Machine Learning Research*, 12:2121–2159.

Chris Dyer, Miguel Ballesteros, Wang Ling, Austin Matthews, and Noah A. Smith. 2015. Transition-based dependency parsing with stack long short-term memory. In *Proceedings of the ACL conference*. Association for Computational Linguistics.

Yoav Goldberg and Joakim Nivre. 2013. Training deterministic parsers with non-deterministic oracles. *Transactions of the Association for Computational Linguistics*, 1:403–414.

James Henderson. 2004. Discriminative training of a neural network statistical parser. In *Proceedings of the 42nd Annual Meeting on Association for Computational Linguistics*, page 95. Association for Computational Linguistics.

Geoffrey Hinton. 2002. Training products of experts by minimizing contrastive divergence. *Neural computation*, 14(8):1771–1800.

Liang Huang and Kenji Sagae. 2010. Dynamic programming for linear-time incremental parsing. In *Proceedings of the 48th Annual Meeting of the Association for Computational Linguistics*, pages 1077–1086. Association for Computational Linguistics.

Terry Koo, Xavier Carreras, and Michael Collins. 2008. Simple semi-supervised dependency parsing.

Yann LeCun and F Huang. 2005. Loss functions for discriminative training of energybased models. AIStats.

J. Legrand and R. Collobert. 2014. Recurrent greedy parsing with neural networks. In *Proceedings of the European Conference on Machine Learning and Principles and Practice of Knowledge Discovery in Databases (ECML-PKDD)*.

Percy Liang and Michael I Jordan. 2008. An asymptotic analysis of generative, discriminative, and pseudolikelihood estimators. In *Proceedings of the 25th international conference on Machine learning*, pages 584–591. ACM.

Yang Liu and Maosong Sun. 2014. Contrastive unsupervised word alignment with non-local features. *arXiv preprint arXiv:1410.2082*.

Ji Ma, Yue Zhang, and Jingbo Zhu. 2014. Punctuation processing for projective dependency parsing. In *Proc. of ACL*.

Mitchell P Marcus, Mary Ann Marcinkiewicz, and Beatrice Santorini. 1993. Building a large annotated corpus of english: The penn treebank. *Computational linguistics*, 19(2):313–330.

Marshall R Mayberry III and Risto Miikkulainen. 2005. Broad-coverage parsing with neural networks. *Neural Processing Letters*, 21(2):121–132.

Joakim Nivre and Mario Scholz. 2004. Deterministic dependency parsing of English text. In *Proceedings of the 20th International Conference on Computational Linguistics (COLING)*, pages 64–70.

Joakim Nivre, Johan Hall, Jens Nilsson, Atanas Chanev, Gülsen Eryigit, Sandra Kübler, Svetoslav Marinov, and Erwin Marsi. 2007. Maltparser: A language-independent system for data-driven dependency parsing. *Natural Language Engineering*, 13(2):95–135.

Joakim Nivre. 2008. Algorithms for deterministic incremental dependency parsing. *Computational Linguistics*, 34(4):513–553.

Richard Socher, John Bauer, Christopher D Manning, and Andrew Y Ng. 2013. Parsing with compositional vector grammars. In *In Proceedings of the ACL conference*. Citeseer.

Pontus Stenetorp. 2013. Transition-based dependency parsing using recursive neural networks. In *NIPS Workshop on Deep Learning*.

Jun Suzuki, Hideki Isozaki, Xavier Carreras, and Michael Collins. 2009. An empirical study of semi-supervised structured conditional models for dependency parsing. In *Proceedings of the 2009 Conference on Empirical Methods in Natural Language Processing: Volume 2-Volume 2*, pages 551–560. Association for Computational Linguistics.

David Vickrey, Cliff C Lin, and Daphne Koller. 2010. Non-local contrastive objectives. In *Proceedings of the 27th International Conference on Machine Learning (ICML-10)*, pages 1103–1110.

David Weiss, Christopher Alberti, Michael Collins, and Slav Petrov. 2015. Structured training for neural network transition-based parsing. In *Proceedings of the ACL conference*. Association for Computational Linguistics.

Hiroyasu Yamada and Yuji Matsumoto. 2003. Statistical dependency analysis with support vector machines. In *Proceedings of IWPT*, volume 3.

Yue Zhang and Stephen Clark. 2008. A tale of two parsers: investigating and combining graph-based and transition-based dependency parsing using beam-search. In *Proceedings of the Conference on Empirical Methods in Natural Language Processing*, pages 562–571. Association for Computational Linguistics.

Yue Zhang and Stephen Clark. 2011. Syntactic processing using the generalized perceptron and beam search. *Computational Linguistics*, 37(1):105–151.

Yue Zhang and Joakim Nivre. 2011. Transition-based dependency parsing with rich non-local features. In *Proceedings of the 49th Annual Meeting of the Association for Computational Linguistics: Human Language Technologies: short papers-Volume 2*, pages 188–193. Association for Computational Linguistics.

Yue Zhang and Joakim Nivre. 2012. Analyzing the effect of global learning and beam-search on transition-based dependency parsing. In *COLING (Posters)*, pages 1391–1400.

Parsing Paraphrases with Joint Inference

Do Kook Choe*
Brown University
Providence, RI
dc65@cs.brown.edu

David McClosky
IBM Research
Yorktown Heights, NY
dmcclosky@us.ibm.com

Abstract

Treebanks are key resources for developing accurate statistical parsers. However, building treebanks is expensive and time-consuming for humans. For domains requiring deep subject matter expertise such as law and medicine, treebanking is even more difficult. To reduce annotation costs for these domains, we develop methods to improve cross-domain parsing inference using paraphrases. Paraphrases are easier to obtain than full syntactic analyses as they do not require deep linguistic knowledge, only linguistic fluency. A sentence and its paraphrase may have similar syntactic structures, allowing their parses to mutually inform each other. We present several methods to incorporate paraphrase information by jointly parsing a sentence with its paraphrase. These methods are applied to state-of-the-art constituency and dependency parsers and provide significant improvements across multiple domains.

1 Introduction

Parsing is the task of reconstructing the syntactic structure from surface text. Many natural language processing tasks use parse trees as a basis for deeper analysis.

The most effective sources of supervision for training statistical parsers are treebanks. Unfortunately, treebanks are expensive, time-consuming to create, and not available for most domains. Compounding the problem, the accuracy of statistical parsers degrades as the domain shifts away from the supervised training corpora (Gildea, 2001; Bacchiani et al., 2006; McClosky et al., 2006b; Surdeanu et al., 2008). Furthermore, for domains requiring subject matter experts, e.g., law and medicine, it may not be feasible to produce large scale treebanks since subject matter experts generally don't have the necessary linguistic background. It is natural to look for resources that are more easily obtained. In this work, we explore using paraphrases. Unlike parse trees, paraphrases can be produced quickly by humans and don't require extensive linguistic training. While paraphrases are not parse trees, a sentence and its paraphrase may have similar syntactic structures for portions where they can be aligned.

We can improve parsers by jointly parsing a sentence with its paraphrase and encouraging certain types of overlaps in their syntactic structures. As a simple example, consider replacing an unknown word in a sentence with a synonym found in the training data. This may help disambiguate the sentence without changing its parse tree. More disruptive forms of paraphrasing (e.g., topicalization) can also be handled by not requiring strict agreement between the parses.

In this paper, we use paraphrases to improve parsing inference within and across domains. We develop methods using dual-decomposition (where the parses of both sentences from a dependency parser are encouraged to agree, Section 3.2) and pair-finding (which can be applied to any n-best parser, Section 3.3). Some paraphrases significantly disrupt syntactic structure. To counter this, we examine relaxing agreement constraints and building classifiers to predict when joint parsing won't be beneficial (Section 3.4). We show that paraphrases can be exploited to improve cross-domain parser inference for two state-of-the-art parsers, especially on domains where they perform poorly.

2 Related Work

Many constituency parsers can parse English newswire text with high accuracy (Collins, 2000;

*Work performed during an IBM internship.

Proceedings of the 53rd Annual Meeting of the Association for Computational Linguistics and the 7th International Joint Conference on Natural Language Processing, pages 1223–1233,
Beijing, China, July 26-31, 2015.

Charniak and Johnson, 2005; Petrov et al., 2006; Socher et al., 2013; Coppola and Steedman, 2013). Likewise, dependency parsers have rapidly improved their accuracy on a variety of languages (Eisner, 1996; McDonald et al., 2005; Nivre et al., 2007; Koo and Collins, 2010; Zhang and McDonald, 2014; Lei et al., 2014). There are many approaches tackling the problem of improving parsing accuracy both within and across domains, including self-training/uptraining (McClosky et al., 2006b; Petrov et al., 2010), reranking (Collins, 2000; McClosky et al., 2006b), incorporating word clusters (Koo et al., 2008), model combination (Petrov, 2010), automatically weighting training data (McClosky et al., 2010), and using n-gram counts from large corpora (Bansal and Klein, 2011). Using paraphrases falls into the semi-supervised category. As we show later, incorporating paraphrases provides complementary benefits to self-training.

2.1 Paraphrases

While paraphrases are difficult to define rigorously (Bhagat and Hovy, 2013), we only require a loose definition in this work: a pair of phrases that mean approximately the same thing. Paraphrases can be constructed in various ways: replacing words with synonyms, reordering clauses, adding relative clauses, using negation and antonyms, etc. Table 1 lists some example paraphrases.

There are a variety of paraphrase resources produced by humans (Dolan and Brockett, 2005) and automatic methods (Ganitkevitch et al., 2013). Recent works have shown that reliable paraphrases can be crowdsourced at low cost (Negri et al., 2012; Burrows et al., 2013; Tschirsich and Hintz, 2013). Paraphrases have been shown to help summarization (Cohn and Lapata, 2013), question answering (Duboue and Chu-Carroll, 2006; Fader et al., 2013), machine translation (Callison-Burch et al., 2006), and semantic parsing (Berant and Liang, 2014). Paraphrases have been applied to syntactic tasks, such as prepositional phrase attachment and noun compounding, where the corpus frequencies of different syntactic constructions (approximated by web searches) are used to help disambiguate (Nakov and Hearst, 2005). One method for transforming constructions is to use paraphrase templates.

How did Bob Marley die? What killed Bob Marley?
How fast does a cheetah run? What is a cheetah's top speed?
He came home unexpectedly. He wasn't expected to arrive home like that.
They were far off and looked tiny. From so far away, they looked tiny.
He turned and bent over the body of the Indian. Turning, he bent over the Indian's body.
No need to dramatize. There is no need to dramatize.

Table 1: Example paraphrases from our dataset.

2.2 Bilingual Parsing

The closest task to ours is bilingual parsing where sentences and their translations are parsed simultaneously (Burkett et al., 2010). While our methods differ from those used in bilingual parsing, the general ideas are the same.[1] Translating and paraphrasing are related transformations since both approximately preserve meaning. While syntax is only partially preserved across these transformations, the overlapping portions can be leveraged with joint inference to mutually disambiguate. Existing bilingual parsing methods typically require parallel treebanks for training and parallel text at runtime while our methods only require parallel text at runtime. Since we do not have a parallel paraphrase treebank for training, we cannot directly compare to these methods.

3 Jointly Parsing Paraphrases

With a small number of exceptions, parsers typically assume that the parse of each sentence is independent. There are good reasons for this independence assumption: it simplifies parsing inference and oftentimes it is not obvious how to relate multiple sentences (though see Rush et al. (2012) for one approach). In this section, we present two methods to jointly parse paraphrases without complicating inference steps. Before going into details, we give a high level picture of how jointly parsing paraphrases can help in Figure 1. With the baseline parser, the parse tree of the target sentence is incorrect but its paraphrase (parsed by the same parser) is parsed correctly. We use rough alignments to map words across sentence pairs.

[1] Applying our methods to bilingual parsing is left as future work.

Note the similar syntactic relations when they are projected across the aligned words.

Our goal is to encourage an appropriate level of agreement between the two parses across alignments. We start by designing "hard" methods which require complete agreement between the parses. However, since parsers are imperfect and alignments approximate, we also develop "soft" methods which allow for disagreements. Additionally, we make procedures to decide whether to use the original (non-joint) parse or the new joint parse for each sentence since joint parses may be worse in cases where the sentences are too different and alignment fails.

3.1 Objective

In a typical parsing setting, given a sentence (x) and its paraphrase (y), parsers find $a^*(x)$ and $b^*(y)$ that satisfy the following equation:[2]

$$\begin{aligned} a^*, b^* &= \operatorname*{argmax}_{a \in T(x), b \in T(y)} f(a) + f(b) \\ &= \operatorname*{argmax}_{a \in T(x)} f(a) + \operatorname*{argmax}_{b \in T(y)} f(b) \end{aligned} \tag{1}$$

where f is a parse-scoring function and T returns all possible trees for a sentence. f can take many forms, e.g., summing the scores of arcs (Eisner, 1996; McDonald et al., 2005) or multiplying probabilities together (Charniak and Johnson, 2005). The argmax over a and b of equation (1) is separable; parsers make two sentence-level decisions. For joint parsing, we modify the objective so that parsers make one global decision:

$$a^*, b^* = \operatorname*{argmax}_{\substack{a \in T(x), b \in T(y) \\ : c(a,b)=0}} f(a) + f(b) \tag{2}$$

where c (defined below) measures the syntactic similarity between the two trees. The smaller $c(a, b)$ is, the more similar a and b are. Intuitively, joint parsers must retrieve the most similar pair of trees with the highest sum of scores.

3.1.1 Constraints

The constraint function, c, ties two trees together using alignments as a proxy for semantic information. An alignment is a pair of words from sentences x and y that approximately mean the same thing. For example, in Figure 1, (help^x, help^y) is one alignment and (pestilence^x, disease^y) is another. To simplify joint parsing, we assume the aligned words play the same syntactic roles (which is obviously not always true and should be revisited in future work). c measures the syntactic similarity by computing how many pairs of alignments have different syntactic head relations. For the two trees in Figure 1, we see two different relations: (help $\xrightarrow{x}$ dying, help $\not\xrightarrow{y}$ dying) and (natives $\not\xrightarrow{x}$ dying, natives $\xrightarrow{y}$ dying). The rest have the same relation so $c(a, b) = 2$. As we'll show in Section 5, the constraints defined above are too restrictive because of this strong assumption. To alleviate the problem, we present ways of appropriately changing constraints later. We now turn to the first method of incorporating constraints into joint parsing.

[2]When it is clear from context, we omit x and y to simplify notation.

Set $u^0(i,j) = 0$ for all $i, j \in E$
for k = *1 to K* **do**
  $a^k = \operatorname*{argmax}_{a \in T(x)} \left(f(a) + \sum_{i,j \in E} u^k(i,j) a(i,j) \right)$
  $b^k = \operatorname*{argmax}_{b \in T(y)} \left(f(b) - \sum_{i,j \in E} u^k(i,j) b(i,j) \right)$
  v, u^{k+1} = UPDATE(u^k, δ^k, a^k, b^k)
  if $v = 0$ **then return** a^k, b^k
return a^K, b^K

function UPDATE (u, δ, a, b)
  $v = 0, u'(i,j) = 0$ for all $i, j \in E$
  for $i, j \in E$ **do**
    $u'(i,j) = u(i,j) - \delta(a(i,j) - b(i,j))$
    if $a(i,j) \neq b(i,j)$ **then** $v = v + 1$
  return v, u'

Algorithm 1: Dual decomposition for jointly parsing paraphrases pseudocode. E is the set of all possible edges between any pair of aligned words. Given ℓ aligned word pairs, $E = \{1, \ldots, \ell\} \times \{1, \ldots, \ell\}$. $a(i,j)$ is one if the ith aligned word is the head of jth aligned word, zero otherwise. $u(i,j)$ is the dual value of an edge from the ith aligned word to the jth aligned word. δ^k is the step size at kth iteration.

3.2 Constraints via Dual Decomposition

Dual decomposition (Rush and Collins, 2012) is well-suited for finding the MAP assignment to equation (2). When the parse-scoring function f includes an arc-factored component as in McDonald et al. (2005), it is straightforward to incorpo-

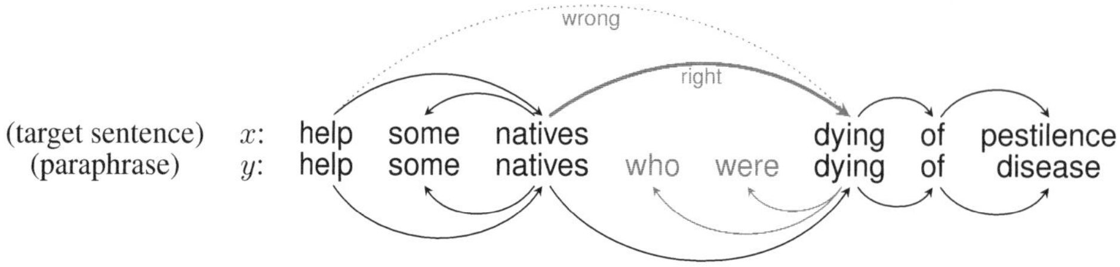

Figure 1: An illustration of joint parsing a sentence with its paraphrase. Unaligned words are gray. Joint parsing encourages structural similarity and allows the parser to correct the incorrect arc.

rate constraints as shown in Algorithm 1. Essentially, dual decomposition penalizes relations that are different in two trees by adding/subtracting dual values to/from arc scores. When dual decomposition is applied in Figure 1, the arc score of (help $\xrightarrow{x}$ dying) decreases and the score for (natives $\xrightarrow{x}$ dying) increases in the second iteration, which eventually leads the algorithm to favor the latter.

We relax the constraints by employing soft dual decomposition (Anzaroot et al., 2014) and replacing UPDATE in Algorithm 1 with S-UPDATE from Algorithm 2. The problem with the original constraints is they force every pair of alignments to have the same relation even when some aligned words certainly play different syntactic roles. The introduced slack variable lets some alignments have different relations when parsers prefer them. Penalties bounded by the slack tend to help fix incorrect ones and not change correct parses. In this work, we use a single slack variable but it's possible to have a different slack variable for each type of dependency relation.[3]

function S-UPDATE (u, δ, a, b, s)
  $v = 0, u'(i,j) = 0$ for all $i, j \in E$
  for $i, j \in E$ **do**
    $t = \max(u(i,j) - \delta(a(i,j) - b(i,j)), 0)$
    $u'(i,j) = \min(t, s)$
    if $u'(i,j) \neq 0, u'(i,j) \neq s$ **then**
      $v = v + 1$
  return v, u'

Algorithm 2: The new UPDATE function of soft dual decomposition for joint parsing. It projects all dual values between 0 and $s \geq 0$. s is a slack variable that allows the algorithm to avoid satisfying some constraints.

3.3 Constraints via Pair-finding

One shortcoming of the dual decomposition approach is that it only applies to parse-scoring functions with an arc-factored component. We introduce another method for estimating equation (2) that applies to all n-best parsers.

Given the n-best parses of x and the m-best parses of y, Algorithm 3 scans through $n \times m$ pairs of trees and chooses the pair that satisfies equation (2). If it finds one pair with $c(a, b) = 0$, then it has found the answer to the equation. Otherwise, it chooses the pair with the smallest $c(a, b)$, breaking ties using the scores of the parses $(f(a) + f(b))$. This algorithm is well suited for finding solutions to the equation but the solutions are not necessarily good trees due to overly hard constraints.

The algorithm often finds bad trees far down the n-best list because it is mainly interested in retrieving pairs of trees that satisfy all constraints. Parsers find such pairs with low scores if they are allowed to search through unrestricted space. To mitigate the problem, we shrink the search space by limiting n. Reducing the search space relies on the fact that higher ranking trees are more likely to be correct than the lower ranking ones. Note that we decrease n because we are interested in recovering the tree of the target sentence, x. m should also be decreased to improve the parse of its paraphrase, y.

3.4 Logistic Regression

One caveat of the previous two proposed methods is that they do not know whether the original or joint parse of x is more accurate. Sometimes they increase agreement between the parses at the cost

[3]We did pilot experiments with multiple slack variables. Since they showed only small improvements and were harder to tune, we stuck with a single slack variable for remaining experiments.

```
function PAIR-FINDING (a_{1:n}, b_{1:m})
  Set a, b = null, min = ∞, max = −∞
  for i = 1 to n do
    for j = 1 to m do
      v = C (a_i, b_j)
      sum = f(a_i) + f(b_j)
      if v < min then
        a = a_i, b = b_j
        min = v, max = sum
      else if v = min, sum > max then
        a = a_i, b = b_j
        max = sum
  return a, b

function C (a, b)
  v = 0
  for i, j ∈ E do
    if a(i, j) ≠ b(i, j) then  v = v + 1
  return v
```

Algorithm 3: The pair-finding scheme with a constraint function, c. $a_{1:n}$ are the n-best trees of x and $b_{1:m}$ are the m-best of y.

of accuracy. To remedy this problem, we use a classifier (specifically logistic regression) to determine whether a modified tree should be used. The classifier can learn the error patterns produced by each method.

3.4.1 Features

Classifier features use many sources of information: the target sentence x and its paraphrase y, the original and new parses of x (a^0 and a), and the alignments between x and y.

Crossing Edges How many arcs cross when alignments are drawn between paraphrases on a plane divided by the length of x. It roughly measures how many reorderings are needed to change x to y.

Non-projective Edges Whether there are more non-projective arcs in new parse (a) than the original (a^0).

Sentence Lengths Whether the length of x is smaller than that of y. This feature exists because baseline parsers tend to perform better on shorter sentences.

Word Overlaps The number of words in common between x and y normalized by the length of x.

REL	REL + REL_p
REL + REL_p + REL_{gp}	REL + REL_{gp}
CP	CP + CP_p
CP + CP_p + CP_{gp}	CP + CP_{gp}
REL + CP	REL + CP + CP_p
REL + CP_p + REL_{gp}	

Table 2: Feature templates: REL is the dependency relation between the word and its parent. CP is the coarse part-of-speech tag (first two letters) of a word. p and gp select the parent and grandparent of the word respectively.

Parse Structure Templates The feature generator goes through every word in $\{a^0, a\}$ and sets the appropriate boolean features from Table 2. Features are prefixed by whether they come from a^0 or a.

4 Data and Programs

This section describes our paraphrase dataset, parsers, and other tools used in experiments.

4.1 Paraphrase Dataset

To evaluate the efficacy of the proposed methods of jointly parsing paraphrases, we built a corpus of paraphrases where one sentence in a pair of paraphrases has a gold tree.[4] We randomly sampled 4,000 sentences[5] from four gold treebanks: Brown, British National Corpus (BNC), QuestionBank[6] (QB) and Wall Street Journal (section 24) (Francis and Kučera, 1989; Foster and van Genabith, 2008; Judge et al., 2006; Marcus et al., 1993). A linguist provided a paraphrase for each sampled sentence according to these instructions:

> The paraphrases should more or less convey the same information as the original sentence. That is, the two sentences should logically entail each other. The paraphrases should generally use most of the same words (but not necessarily in the same order). Active/passive transforms, changing words with synonyms, and rephrasings of the same idea are all examples of transformations that paraphrases can use (others can be used too).

[4]The dataset is available upon request.

[5]We use sentences with 6 to 25 tokens to keep the paraphrasing task in the nontrivial to easy range.

[6]With Stanford's updates: `http://nlp.stanford.edu/data/QuestionBank-Stanford.shtml`

They can be as simple as just changing a single word in some cases (though, ideally, a variety of paraphrasing techniques would be used).

We also provided 10 pairs of sentences as examples. We evaluate our methods only on the sampled sentences from the gold corpora because the new paraphrases do not include syntactic trees. The data was divided into development and testing sets such that development and testing share the same distribution over the four corpora. Paraphrases were tokenized by the BLLIP tokenizer. See Table 3 for statistics of the dataset.[7]

4.2 Meteor Word Aligner

We use Meteor, a monolingual word aligner developed by Denkowski and Lavie (2014), to find alignments between paraphrases. It uses the exact matches, stems, synonyms, and paraphrases[8] to form these alignments. Because it uses paraphrases, it sometimes aligns multiple words from sentence x to one or more words from sentence y or vice versa. We ignore these multiword alignments because our methods currently only handle single word alignments. In pilot experiments, we also tried using a simple aligner which required exact word matches. Joint parsing with simpler alignments improved parsing accuracy but not as much as Meteor.[9] Thus, all results in Section 5 use Meteor for word alignment. On average across the four corpora, 73% of the tokens are aligned.

4.3 Parsers

We use a dependency and constituency parser for our experiments: RBG and BLLIP. RBG parser (Lei et al., 2014) is a state-of-the-art dependency parser.[10] It is a third-order discriminative dependency parser with low-rank tensors as part of its features. BLLIP (Charniak and Johnson, 2005) is a state-of-the-art constituency parser, which is composed of a generative parser and a discriminative reranker.[11]

To train RBG and BLLIP, we used the standard WSJ training set (sections 2–21, about 40,000 sentences).[12] We also used the self-trained BLLIP parsing model which is trained on an additional two million Gigaword parses generated by the BLLIP parser (McClosky et al., 2006a).

4.4 Logistic Regression

We use the logistic regression implementation from Scikit-learn[13] with hand-crafted features from Section 3.4.1. The classifier decides to whether to keep the parse trees from the joint method. When it decides to disregard them, it returns the parse from the baseline parser. We train a separate classifier for each joint method.

5 Experiments

We ran all tuning and model design experiments on the development set. For the final evaluation, we tuned parameters on the development set and evaluate them on the test set. Constituency trees were converted to basic non-collapsed dependency trees using Stanford Dependencies (De Marneffe et al., 2006).[14] We report unlabeled attachment scores (UAS) for all experiments and labeled attachment scores (LAS) as well in final evaluation, ignoring punctuation. Averages are micro-averages across all sentences.

5.1 Dual Decomposition

Since BLLIP is not arc-factored, these experiments only use RBG. Several parameters need to be fixed beforehand: the slack constant (s), the learning rate (δ), and the maximum number of iterations (K). We set $\delta^0 = 0.1$ and $\delta^k = \frac{\delta^0}{2^t}$ where t is the number of times the dual score has increased (Rush et al., 2010). We choose $K = 20$. These numbers were chosen from pilot studies. The slack variable ($s = 0.5$) was tuned with a grid search on values between 0.1 and 1.5 with interval 0.1. We chose a value that generalizes well across four corpora as opposed to a value that does

[7] The distribution over four corpora is skewed because each corpus has a different number of sentences within length constraints. Samples are collected uniformly over all sentences that satisfy the length criterion.

[8] Here paraphrase means a single/multiword phrase that is semantically similar to another single/multiword.

[9] The pilot was conducted on fewer than 700 sentence pairs before all paraphrases were created. We give Meteor tokenized paraphrases with capitalization. Maximizing accuracy rather than coverage worked better in pilot experiments.

[10] `http://github.com/taolei87/RBGParser`, 'master' version from June 24th, 2014.

[11] `http://github.com/BLLIP/bllip-parser`

[12] RBG parser requires predicted POS tags. We used the Stanford tagger (Toutanova et al., 2003) to tag WSJ and paraphrase datasets. Training data was tagged using 20-fold cross-validation and the paraphrases were tagged by a tagger trained on all of WSJ training.

[13] `http://scikit-learn.org`

[14] Version 1.3.5, previously numbered as version 2.0.5

	Development					Test				
	BNC	Brown	QB	WSJ	Total	BNC	Brown	QB	WSJ	Total
Sentences	247	558	843	352	2,000	247	558	844	351	2,000
Tokens	4,297	7,937	8,391	5,924	26,549	4,120	8,025	8,253	5,990	26,388
Tokens‖	4,372	8,088	8,438	6,122	27,020	4,272	8,281	8,189	6,232	26,974
Word types	1,727	2,239	2,261	1,955	6,161	1,710	2,337	2,320	1,970	6,234
Word types‖	1,676	2,241	2,261	1,930	6,017	1,675	2,335	2,248	1,969	6,094
OOV	11.2	5.1	5.4	2.4	5.6	11.5	5.1	5.8	2.2	5.7
OOV‖	8.6	4.7	5.4	2.6	5.1	9.3	4.8	6.0	2.4	5.3
Tokens/sent.	17.4	14.2	10.0	16.8	13.3	16.7	14.4	7.8	17.1	13.2
Avg. aligned	13.1	10.5	6.9	13.0	9.7	12.6	10.7	6.7	13.0	9.7

Table 3: Statistics for the four corpora of the paraphrase dataset. Most statistics are counted from sentences with gold trees, including punctuation. ‖ indicates the statistic is from the paraphrased sentences. "Avg. aligned" is the average number of aligned tokens from the original sentences using Meteor. OOV is the percentage of tokens not seen in the WSJ training.

	Avg	BNC	Brown	QB	WSJ
RBG	86.4	89.2	**90.9**	75.8	93.7
+ Dual	84.7	87.5	87.8	76.0	91.0
+ S-Dual	**86.8**	**89.8**	**90.9**	**76.5**	**94.0**

Table 4: Comparison of hard and soft dual decomposition for joint parsing (development section, UAS).

n	Avg	BNC	Brown	QB	WSJ
1	89.5	91.1	91.6	83.3	**94.2**
2	**90.0**	91.4	**92.3**	84.1	94.1
3	89.8	91.5	92.0	**84.2**	93.9
5	89.2	**91.9**	91.4	83.0	93.2
10	87.9	90.5	90.3	81.4	92.2
50	86.3	90.2	88.7	78.6	91.1

Table 5: UAS of joint parsing using the pair-finding scheme with various n values on the development portion. $n = 1$ is the baseline BLLIP parser and $n > 1$ is BLLIP with pair-finding.

very well on a single corpus. As shown in Table 4, joint parsing with hard dual decomposition performs worse than independent parsing (RBG). This is expected because hard dual decomposition forces every pair of alignments to form the same relation even when they should not. With relaxed constraints (S-Dual), joint parsing performs significantly better than independent parsing. Soft dual decomposition improves across all domains except for Brown (where it ties).

5.2 Pair-finding

These experiments use the 50-best trees from BLLIP parser. When converting to dependencies, some constituency trees map to the same dependency tree. In this case, trees with lower rankings are dropped. Like joint parsing with hard dual decomposition, joint parsing with unrestricted pair-finding ($n = 50$) allows significantly worse parses to be selected (Table 5). With small n values, pair-finding improves over the baseline BLLIP parser.[15] Experiments with self-trained BLLIP exhibit similar results so we use $n = 2$ for all other experiments. Interestingly, each corpus has a different optimal value for n which suggests we might improve accuracy further if we know the domain of each sentence.

5.3 Logistic Regression

The classifier is trained on sentences where parse scores (UAS) of the proposed methods are higher or lower than those of the baselines[16] from the development set using leave-one-out cross-validation. We use random greedy search to select specific features from the 15 feature templates defined in Section 3.4.1. Features seen fewer than three times in the development are thrown out. Separate regression models are built for three different parsers. The logistic regression classifier uses an L_1 penalty with regularization parameter $C = 1$.

Logistic regression experiments are reported in

[15] Decreasing m did not lead to further improvement and thus we don't report the results of changing m.

[16] We only use sentences with different scores to limit ceiling effects.

	Avg	BNC	Brown	QB	WSJ
RBG	86.4	89.2	90.9	75.8	93.7
+ S-Dual	86.8	89.8	90.9	**76.5**	**94.0**
+ Logit	**86.9**	**89.8**	**91.1**	**76.5**	**94.0**
BLLIP	89.5	91.1	91.6	83.3	94.2
+ Pair	90.0	**91.4**	**92.3**	84.1	94.1
+ Logit	**90.3**	91.3	92.1	**85.2**	**94.3**
BLLIP-ST	90.1	92.7	92.3	84.3	93.8
+ Pair	90.7	**93.5**	92.5	85.6	93.8
+ Logit	**91.1**	93.3	**92.6**	**86.7**	**93.9**

Table 6: Effect of using logistic regression on top of each method (UAS). Leave-one-out cross-validation is performed on the development data. +X means augmenting the above system with X.

Table 6. All parsers benefit from employing logistic regression models on top of paraphrase methods. BLLIP experiments show a larger improvement than RBG. This may be because BLLIP cannot use soft constraints so its errors are more pronounced.

5.4 Final Evaluation

We evaluate the three parsers on the test set using the tuned parameters and logistic regression models from above. Joint parsing with paraphrases significantly improves accuracy for all systems (Table 7). Self-trained BLLIP with logistic regression is the most accurate, though RBG with S-Dual provides the most consistent improvements.

Joint parsing without logistic regression (RBG + S-Dual) is more accurate than independent parsing (RBG) overall. With the help of logistic regression, the methods do at least as well as their baseline counterparts on all domains with the exception of self-trained BLLIP on BNC. We believe that the drop on BNC is largely due to noise as our BNC test set is the smallest of the four. As on development, logistic regression does not change the accuracy much over the RBG parser with soft dual decomposition.

Joint parsing provides the largest gains on QuestionBank, the domain with the lowest baseline accuracies. This fits with our goal of using paraphrases for domain adaptation — parsing with paraphrases helps the most on domains furthest from our training data.

5.5 Error analysis

We analyzed the errors from RBG and BLLIP along several dimensions: by dependency label, sentence length, dependency length, alignment status (whether a token was aligned), percentage of tokens aligned in the sentence, and edit distance between the sentence pairs. Most errors are fairly uniformly distributed across these dimensions and indicate general structural improvements when using paraphrases. BLLIP saw a 2.2% improvement for the ROOT relation, though RBG's improvement here was more moderate. For sentence lengths, BLLIP obtains larger boosts for shorter sentences while RBG's are more uniform. RBG gets a 1.4% UAS improvement on longer dependencies (6 or more tokens) while shorter dependencies are more modestly improved by about 0.3-0.5% UAS. Surprisingly, alignment information provides no signal as to whether accuracy improves.

Additionally, we had our annotator label a portion of our dataset with the set of paraphrasing operations employed.[17] While most paraphrasing operations generally improved performance under joint inference, the largest reliable gains came from lexical replacements (e.g., synonyms).

6 Conclusions and Future Work

Our methods of incorporating paraphrases improve parsing across multiple domains for state-of-the-art constituency and dependency parsers. We leverage the fact that paraphrases often express the same semantics with similar syntactic realizations. These provide benefits even on top of self-training, another domain adaptation technique.

Since paraphrases are not available at most times, our methods may seem limited. However, there are several possible use cases. The best case scenario is when users can be directly asked to rephrase a question and provide a paraphrase. For instance, question answering systems can ask users to rephrase questions when an answer is marked as wrong by users. Another option is to use crowdsourcing to quickly create a paraphrase corpus (Negri et al., 2012; Burrows et al., 2013; Tschirsich and Hintz, 2013). As part of future work, we plan to integrate existing larger paraphrase resources, such as WikiAnswers (Fader et al., 2013) and PPDB (Ganitkevitch et al., 2013). WikiAnswers provides rough equivalence classes of questions. PPDB includes phrasal and syntactic alignments which could supplement our existing alignments or be used as proxies for paraphrases.

[17] See the extended version of this paper for more information about this task and its results.

	Avg	BNC	Brown	QB	WSJ
RBG	86.7 (81.3)	89.3 (83.7)	90.2 (84.1)	77.0 (71.0)	93.7 (89.9)
+ S-Dual	**87.3 (81.7)**	89.6 (83.8)	**90.7 (84.6)**	**78.1 (71.8)**	**94.0 (90.2)**
+ Logit	87.2 (81.6)	**89.7 (83.9)**	90.6 (84.5)	77.9 (71.7)	93.8 (89.9)
BLLIP	89.6 (86.1)	90.6 (87.2)	91.7 (87.9)	83.6 (79.9)	94.3 (91.6)
+ Pair	90.1 (86.5)	**90.8 (87.3)**	**92.1 (88.4)**	84.7 (80.7)	94.4 (91.6)
+ Logit	**90.3 (86.8)**	90.6 (87.2)	91.9 (88.1)	**85.5 (81.7)**	**94.5 (91.7)**
BLLIP-ST	90.4 (87.0)	**91.8 (88.3)**	92.7 (89.0)	84.8 (81.2)	**94.3 (91.4)**
+ Pair	90.5 (87.1)	91.1 (87.6)	92.7 (89.1)	85.5 (81.8)	94.2 (**91.4**)
+ Logit	**91.0 (87.6)**	91.4 (88.0)	**92.9 (89.3)**	**86.6 (82.9)**	**94.3 (91.4)**

Table 7: Final evaluation on testing data. Numbers are unlabeled attachment score (labeled attachment score). +X indicates extending the above system with X. BLLIP-ST is BLLIP using the self-trained model. Coloring indicates a significant difference over baseline ($p < 0.01$).

While these resources are noisy, the quantity of data may provide additional robustness. Lastly, integrating our methods with paraphrase detection or generation systems could help provide paraphrases on demand.

There are many other ways to extend this work. Poor alignments are one of the larger sources of errors and improving alignments could help dramatically. One simple extension is to use multiple paraphrases and their alignments instead of just one. More difficult would be to learn the alignments jointly while parsing and adaptively learn how alignments affect syntax. Our constraints can only capture certain types of paraphrase transformations currently and should be extended to understand common tree transformations for paraphrases, as in (Heilman and Smith, 2010). Finally, and perhaps most importantly, our methods apply only at inference time. We plan to investigate methods which use paraphrases to augment parsing models created at train time.

Acknowledgments

We would like to thank Eugene Charniak for the idea of using paraphrases to improve parsing, our anonymous reviewers for their valuable feedback, Karen Ingraffea for constructing and classifying the paraphrase corpus, Dave Buchanan and Will Headden for last minute paper reading, the DeepQA team at IBM for feedback and support on the project, and Mohit Bansal and Micha Elsner for helpful discussions.

References

Sam Anzaroot, Alexandre Passos, David Belanger, and Andrew McCallum. 2014. Learning soft linear constraints with application to citation field extraction. In *Proceedings of the 52nd Annual Meeting of the Association for Computational Linguistics*, pages 593–602. Association for Computational Linguistics.

Michiel Bacchiani, Michael Riley, Brian Roark, and Richard Sproat. 2006. MAP adaptation of stochastic grammars. *Computer speech & language*, 20(1):41–68.

Mohit Bansal and Dan Klein. 2011. Web-scale features for full-scale parsing. In *Proceedings of the 49th Annual Meeting of the Association for Computational Linguistics: Human Language Technologies*, pages 693–702. Association for Computational Linguistics.

Jonathan Berant and Percy Liang. 2014. Semantic parsing via paraphrasing. In *Proceedings of the 52nd Annual Meeting of the Association for Computational Linguistics*, pages 1415–1425. Association for Computational Linguistics.

Rahul Bhagat and Eduard Hovy. 2013. What is a paraphrase? *Computational Linguistics*, 39(3):463–472.

David Burkett, John Blitzer, and Dan Klein. 2010. Joint parsing and alignment with weakly synchronized grammars. In *Human Language Technologies: The 2010 Annual Conference of the North American Chapter of the Association for Computational Linguistics*, pages 127–135. Association for Computational Linguistics.

Steven Burrows, Martin Potthast, and Benno Stein. 2013. Paraphrase acquisition via crowdsourcing and machine learning. *ACM Transactions on Intelligent Systems and Technology (TIST)*, 4(3):43.

Chris Callison-Burch, Philipp Koehn, and Miles Osborne. 2006. Improved statistical machine translation using paraphrases. In *Proceedings of the main* conference on Human Language Technology Conference of the North American Chapter of the Association of Computational Linguistics*, pages 17–24. Association for Computational Linguistics.

Eugene Charniak and Mark Johnson. 2005. Coarse-to-Fine n-best Parsing and MaxEnt Discriminative Reranking. In *Proceedings of the 43rd Annual Meeting of the Association for Computational Linguistics*, pages 173–180. Association for Computational Linguistics.

Trevor Cohn and Mirella Lapata. 2013. An abstractive approach to sentence compression. *ACM Transactions on Intelligent Systems and Technology*, 4(3):41.

Michael Collins. 2000. Discriminative reranking for natural language parsing. In *Proceedings of the Seventeenth International Conference on Machine Learning*, pages 175–182. ICML.

Gregory Coppola and Mark Steedman. 2013. The effect of higher-order dependency features in discriminative phrase-structure parsing. In *ACL*, pages 610–616.

Marie-Catherine De Marneffe, Bill MacCartney, Christopher D. Manning, et al. 2006. Generating typed dependency parses from phrase structure parses. In *Proceedings of LREC*, pages 449–454.

Michael Denkowski and Alon Lavie. 2014. Meteor universal: Language specific translation evaluation for any target language. In *Proceedings of the Ninth Workshop on Statistical Machine Translation*, pages 376–380. Association for Computational Linguistics.

William B. Dolan and Chris Brockett. 2005. Automatically constructing a corpus of sentential paraphrases. In *Proc. of IWP*.

Pablo Ariel Duboue and Jennifer Chu-Carroll. 2006. Answering the question you wish they had asked: The impact of paraphrasing for question answering. In *Proceedings of the Human Language Technology Conference of the NAACL*, pages 33–36. Association for Computational Linguistics.

Jason M. Eisner. 1996. Three new probabilistic models for dependency parsing: An exploration. In *Proceedings of the 16th conference on Computational linguistics*, pages 340–345. Association for Computational Linguistics.

Anthony Fader, Luke Zettlemoyer, and Oren Etzioni. 2013. Paraphrase-driven learning for open question answering. In *Proceedings of the 51st Annual Meeting of the Association for Computational Linguistics*, pages 1608–1618. Association for Computational Linguistics.

Jennifer Foster and Josef van Genabith. 2008. Parser evaluation and the BNC: Evaluating 4 constituency parsers with 3 metrics. In *Proceedings of the Sixth International Conference on Language Resources and Evaluation*. European Language Resources Association.

Winthrop Nelson Francis and Henry Kučera. 1989. *Manual of information to accompany a standard corpus of present-day edited American English, for use with digital computers*. Brown University, Department of Linguistics.

Juri Ganitkevitch, Benjamin Van Durme, and Chris Callison-Burch. 2013. PPDB: The paraphrase database. In *Proceedings of NAACL-HLT*, pages 758–764. Association for Computational Linguistics.

Daniel Gildea. 2001. Corpus variation and parser performance. In *Proceedings of the 2001 Conference on Empirical Methods in Natural Language Processing*, pages 167–202.

Michael Heilman and Noah A Smith. 2010. Tree edit models for recognizing textual entailments, paraphrases, and answers to questions. In *Human Language Technologies: The 2010 Annual Conference of the North American Chapter of the Association for Computational Linguistics*, pages 1011–1019. Association for Computational Linguistics.

John Judge, Aoife Cahill, and Josef Van Genabith. 2006. QuestionBank: creating a corpus of parse-annotated questions. In *Proceedings of the 21st International Conference on Computational Linguistics and the 44th annual meeting of the Association for Computational Linguistics*, pages 497–504. Association for Computational Linguistics.

Terry Koo and Michael Collins. 2010. Efficient third-order dependency parsers. In *Proceedings of the 48th Annual Meeting of the Association for Computational Linguistics*, pages 1–11. Association for Computational Linguistics.

Terry Koo, Xavier Carreras, and Michael Collins. 2008. Simple semi-supervised dependency parsing. In *Proceedings of ACL: HLT*, pages 595–603. Association for Computational Linguistics.

Tao Lei, Yu Xin, Yuan Zhang, Regina Barzilay, and Tommi Jaakkola. 2014. Low-rank tensors for scoring dependency structures. In *Proceedings of the 52nd Annual Meeting of the Association for Computational Linguistics*, pages 1381–1391. Association for Computational Linguistics.

Mitchell P. Marcus, Mary Ann Marcinkiewicz, and Beatrice Santorini. 1993. Building a large annotated corpus of English: The Penn Treebank. *Computational linguistics*, 19(2):313–330.

David McClosky, Eugene Charniak, and Mark Johnson. 2006a. Effective self-training for parsing. In *Proceedings of the main conference on human language technology conference of the North American Chapter of the Association of Computational Linguistics*, pages 152–159. Association for Computational Linguistics.

David McClosky, Eugene Charniak, and Mark Johnson. 2006b. Reranking and self-training for parser adaptation. In *Proceedings of the 21st International Conference on Computational Linguistics and the 44th annual meeting of the Association for Computational Linguistics*, pages 337–344. Association for Computational Linguistics.

David McClosky, Eugene Charniak, and Mark Johnson. 2010. Automatic domain adaptation for parsing. In *Human Language Technologies: The 2010 Annual Conference of the North American Chapter of the Association for Computational Linguistics*, pages 28–36. Association for Computational Linguistics.

Ryan McDonald, Fernando Pereira, Kiril Ribarov, and Jan Hajič. 2005. Non-projective dependency parsing using spanning tree algorithms. In *Proceedings of the conference on Human Language Technology and Empirical Methods in Natural Language Processing*, pages 523–530. Association for Computational Linguistics.

Preslav Nakov and Marti Hearst. 2005. Using the web as an implicit training set: Application to structural ambiguity resolution. In *Proceedings of Human Language Technology Conference and Conference on Empirical Methods in Natural Language Processing*, pages 835–842, Vancouver, British Columbia, Canada, October. Association for Computational Linguistics.

Matteo Negri, Yashar Mehdad, Alessandro Marchetti, Danilo Giampiccolo, and Luisa Bentivogli. 2012. Chinese whispers: Cooperative paraphrase acquisition. In *LREC*, pages 2659–2665.

Joakim Nivre, Johan Hall, Jens Nilsson, Atanas Chanev, Gülsen Eryigit, Sandra Kübler, Svetoslav Marinov, and Erwin Marsi. 2007. MaltParser: A language-independent system for data-driven dependency parsing. *Natural Language Engineering*, 13(02):95–135.

Slav Petrov, Leon Barrett, Romain Thibaux, and Dan Klein. 2006. Learning accurate, compact, and interpretable tree annotation. In *Proceedings of the 21st International Conference on Computational Linguistics and 44th Annual Meeting of the Association for Computational Linguistics*, pages 433–440. Association for Computational Linguistics.

Slav Petrov, Pi-Chuan Chang, Michael Ringgaard, and Hiyan Alshawi. 2010. Uptraining for accurate deterministic question parsing. In *Proceedings of the 2010 Conference on Empirical Methods in Natural Language Processing*, pages 705–713. Association for Computational Linguistics.

Slav Petrov. 2010. Products of random latent variable grammars. In *Human Language Technologies: The 2010 Annual Conference of the North American Chapter of the Association for Computational Linguistics*, pages 19–27. Association for Computational Linguistics.

Alexander M. Rush and Michael Collins. 2012. A tutorial on dual decomposition and Lagrangian relaxation for inference in natural language processing. *Journal of Artificial Intelligence Research*, 45(1):305–362.

Alexander M. Rush, David Sontag, Michael Collins, and Tommi Jaakkola. 2010. On dual decomposition and linear programming relaxations for natural language processing. In *Proceedings of the 2010 Conference on Empirical Methods in Natural Language Processing*, pages 1–11. Association for Computational Linguistics.

Alexander M. Rush, Roi Reichart, Michael Collins, and Amir Globerson. 2012. Improved parsing and POS tagging using inter-sentence consistency constraints. In *Proceedings of the 2012 Joint Conference on Empirical Methods in Natural Language Processing and Computational Natural Language Learning*, pages 1434–1444. Association for Computational Linguistics.

Richard Socher, John Bauer, Christopher D. Manning, and Ng Andrew Y. 2013. Parsing with compositional vector grammars. In *Proceedings of the 51st Annual Meeting of the Association for Computational Linguistics*, pages 455–465. Association for Computational Linguistics.

Mihai Surdeanu, Richard Johansson, Adam Meyers, Lluís Màrquez, and Joakim Nivre. 2008. The CoNLL-2008 shared task on joint parsing of syntactic and semantic dependencies. In *Proceedings of the Twelfth Conference on Computational Natural Language Learning*, pages 159–177. Association for Computational Linguistics.

Kristina Toutanova, Dan Klein, Christopher D. Manning, and Yoram Singer. 2003. Feature-rich part-of-speech tagging with a cyclic dependency network. In *Proceedings of the 2003 Conference of the North American Chapter of the Association for Computational Linguistics on Human Language Technology-Volume 1*, pages 173–180. Association for Computational Linguistics.

Martin Tschirsich and Gerold Hintz. 2013. Leveraging crowdsourcing for paraphrase recognition. In *Proceedings of the 7th Linguistic Annotation Workshop and Interoperability with Discourse*, pages 205–213, Sofia, Bulgaria, August. Association for Computational Linguistics.

Hao Zhang and Ryan McDonald. 2014. Enforcing structural diversity in cube-pruned dependency parsing. In *Proceedings of the 52nd Annual Meeting of the Association for Computational Linguistics*, pages 656–661. Association for Computational Linguistics.

Cross-lingual Dependency Parsing Based on Distributed Representations

Jiang Guo[1]*, **Wanxiang Che**[1], **David Yarowsky**[2], **Haifeng Wang**[3], **Ting Liu**[1]
[1]Center for Social Computing and Information Retrieval, Harbin Institute of Technology
[2]Center for Language and Speech Processing, Johns Hopkins University
[3]Baidu Inc., Beijing, China
{jguo, car, tliu}@ir.hit.edu.cn
yarowsky@jhu.edu, wanghaifeng@baidu.com

Abstract

This paper investigates the problem of cross-lingual dependency parsing, aiming at inducing dependency parsers for low-resource languages while using only training data from a resource-rich language (e.g. English). Existing approaches typically don't include lexical features, which are not transferable across languages. In this paper, we bridge the *lexical feature gap* by using distributed feature representations and their composition. We provide two algorithms for inducing cross-lingual distributed representations of words, which map vocabularies from two different languages into a common vector space. Consequently, both lexical features and non-lexical features can be used in our model for cross-lingual transfer.

Furthermore, our framework is able to incorporate additional useful features such as cross-lingual word clusters. Our combined contributions achieve an average relative error reduction of 10.9% in labeled attachment score as compared with the delexicalized parser, trained on English universal treebank and transferred to three other languages. It also significantly outperforms McDonald et al. (2013) augmented with projected cluster features on identical data.

1 Introduction

Dependency Parsing has been one of NLP's longstanding central problems. The majority of work on dependency parsing has been dedicated to resource-rich languages, such as English and Chinese. For these languages, there exist large-scale annotated treebanks that can be used for supervised training of dependency parsers. However, for most of the languages in the world, there are few or even no labeled training data for parsing, and it is labor intensive and time-consuming to manually build treebanks for all languages. This fact has given rise to a number of research on unsupervised methods (Klein and Manning, 2004), annotation projection methods (Hwa et al., 2005), and model transfer methods (McDonald et al., 2011) for predicting linguistic structures. In this study, we focus on the model transfer methods, which attempt to build parsers for low-resource languages by exploiting treebanks from resource-rich languages.

The major obstacle in transferring a parsing system from one language to another is the lexical features, e.g. words, which are not directly transferable across languages. To solve this problem, McDonald et al. (2011) build a delexicalized parser - a parser that only has non-lexical features. A delexicalized parser makes sense in that POS tag features are significantly predictive for unlabeled dependency parsing. However, for labeled dependency parsing, especially for semantic-oriented dependencies like Stanford-type dependencies (De Marneffe et al., 2006; De Marneffe and Manning, 2008), these non-lexical features are not predictive enough. Täckström et al. (2012) propose to learn cross-lingual word clusters from multilingual paralleled unlabeled data through word alignments, and apply these clusters as features for semi-supervised delexicalized parsing. Word clusters can be thought as a kind of coarse-grained representations of words. Thus, this approach partially fills the gap of lexical features in cross-lingual learning of dependency parsing.

This paper proposes a novel approach for cross-lingual dependency parsing that is based on pure distributed feature representations. In contrast to

*This work was done while the author was visiting JHU.

Proceedings of the 53rd Annual Meeting of the Association for Computational Linguistics and the 7th International Joint Conference on Natural Language Processing, pages 1234–1244,
Beijing, China, July 26-31, 2015.

the discrete lexical features used in traditional dependency parsers, distributed representations map symbolic features into a continuous representation space, that can be shared across languages. Therefore, our model has the ability to utilize both lexical and non-lexical features naturally. Specifically, our framework contains two primary components:

- A neural network-based dependency parser. We expect a non-linear model for dependency parsing in our study, because distributed feature representations are shown to be more effective in non-linear architectures than in linear architectures (Wang and Manning, 2013). Chen and Manning (2014) propose a transition-based dependency parser using a neural network architecture, which is simple but works well on several datasets. Briefly, this model simply replaces the predictor in transition-based dependency parser with a well-designed neural network classifier. We will provide explanations for the merits of this model in Section 3, as well as how we adapt it to the cross-lingual task.

- Cross-lingual word representation learning. The key to filling the *lexical feature gap* is to project the representations of these features from different languages into a common vector space, preserving the translational equivalence. We will study and compare two approaches of learning cross-lingual word representations in Section 4. The first approach is robust projection, and the second approach is based on canonical correlation analysis. Both approaches are simple to implement and are scalable to large data.

We evaluate our model on the universal multilingual treebanks (McDonald et al., 2013). Case studies include transferring from English to German, Spanish and French. Experiments show that by incorporating lexical features, the performance of cross-lingual dependency parsing can be improved significantly. By further embedding cross-lingual cluster features (Täckström et al., 2012), we achieve an average relative error reduction of 10.9% in labeled attachment score (LAS), as compared with the delexicalized parsers. It also significantly outperforms McDonald et al. (2013) augmented with cluster features on identical data. The original major contributions of this paper include:

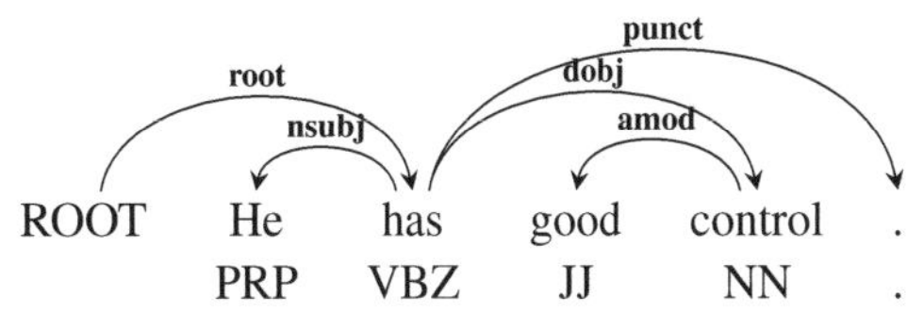

Figure 1: An example labeled dependency tree.

- We propose a novel and flexible cross-lingual learning framework for dependency parsing based on distributed representations, which can effectively incorporate both lexical and non-lexical features.

- We present two novel and effective approaches for inducing cross-lingual word representations, that bridge the *lexical feature gap* in cross-lingual dependency parsing.

- We show that cross-lingual word cluster features can be effectively embedded into our model, leading to significant additive improvements.

2 Background

2.1 Dependency Parsing

Given an input sentence $\mathbf{x} = w_0 w_1 ... w_n$, the goal of dependency parsing is to build a dependency tree (Figure 1), which can be denoted by $\mathbf{d} = \{(h, m, l) : 0 \leq h \leq n; 0 < m \leq n, l \in \mathcal{L}\}$. (h, m, l) indicates a directed arc from the head word w_h to the modifier w_m with a dependency label l, and $\mathcal{L}$ is the label set. The mainstream models that have been proposed for dependency parsing can be described as either graph-based models or transition-based models (McDonald and Nivre, 2007).

Graph-based models view the parsing problem as finding the highest scoring tree from a directed graph. The score of a dependency tree is typically factored into scores of some small structures (e.g. arcs) depending on the order of a model. Transition-based models aim to predict a transition sequence from an initial parser state to some terminal states, depending on the parsing history. This approach has a lot of interest since it is fast (linear time) and can incorporate rich non-local features (Zhang and Nivre, 2011).

It has been considered that simple transition-based parsing using greedy decoding and local training is not as accurate as graph-based parsers or transition-based parsers with beam-search and global training (Zhang and Clark, 2011). Recently, Chen and Manning (2014) show that greedy transition-based parsers can be greatly improved by using a well-designed neural network architecture. This approach can be considered as a new paradigm of parsing, in that it is based on pure distributed feature representations. In this study, we choose Chen and Manning's architecture to build our basic dependency parsing model.

2.2 Distributed Representations for NLP

In recent years, there has been a trend in the NLP research community of learning distributed representations for different natural language units, from morphemes, words and phrases, to sentences and documents. Using distributed representations, these symbolic units are embedded into a low-dimensional and continuous space, thus it is often referred to as *embeddings*.[1]

In general, there are two major ways of applying distributed representations to NLP tasks. First, they can be fed into existing supervised NLP systems as augmented features in a semi-supervised manner. This kind of approach has been adopted in a variety of applications (Turian et al., 2010). Despite its simplicity and effectiveness, it has been shown that the potential of distributed representations cannot be fully exploited in the generalized linear models which are adopted in most of the existing NLP systems (Wang and Manning, 2013). One remedy is to discretize the distributed feature representations, as studied in Guo et al. (2014). However, we believe that a non-linear system, e.g. a neural network, is a more powerful and effective solution. Some decent progress has already been made in this paradigm of NLP on various tasks (Collobert et al., 2011; Chen and Manning, 2014; Sutskever et al., 2014).

3 Transition-based Dependency Parsing: A Neural Network Architecture

In this section, we first briefly describe transition-based dependency parsing and the *arc-standard* parsing algorithm. Then we revisit the neural network architecture for transition-based dependency parsing proposed by Chen and Manning (2014).

As discussed in Section 2.1, transition-based parsing aims to predict a transition sequence from an initial parser state to the terminal state. Each state is conventionally regarded as a *configuration*, which typically consists of a *stack* S, a *buffer* B, and a partially derived forest, i.e. a set of dependency arcs A. Given an input word sequence $\mathbf{x} = w_1 w_2, ..., w_n$, the initial *configuration* can be represented as a tuple: $\langle [w_0]_S, [w_1 w_2, ..., w_n]_B, \varnothing \rangle$, and the terminal *configuration* is $\langle [w_0]_S, []_B, A \rangle$, where w_0 is a pseudo word indicating the *root* of the whole dependency tree. We consider the *arc-standard* algorithm (Nivre, 2004) in this paper, which defines three types of transition actions: LEFT-ARC(l), RIGHT-ARC(l), and SHIFT, l is the dependency label.

[1]In this paper, these two terms are used interchangeably.

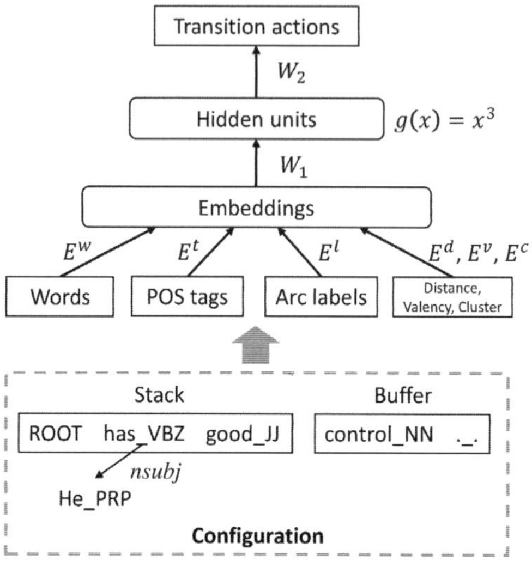

Figure 2: Neural network model for dependency parsing. The *Cluster* features are introduced in Section 5.2.

The typical approach for greedy *arc-standard* parsing is to build a multi-class classifier (e.g., SVM, MaxEnt) of predicting the transition action given a feature vector extracted from a specific *configuration*. While conventional feature engineering suffers from the problem of *sparsity*, *incompleteness* and *expensive feature computation* (Chen and Manning, 2014), the neural network model provides a potential solution.

The architecture of the neural network-based dependency parsing model is illustrated in Figure 2. Primarily, three types of information are extracted from a *configuration* in Chen and Manning's model: word features, POS features and label features respectively. In this study, we add *distance* features indicating the distance between two items, and *valency* features indicating the number of children for a given item (Zhang and Nivre,

Word features
$E^w_{S_i}, E^w_{B_i}, i = 0, 1, 2$
$E^w_{lc1(S_i)}, E^w_{rc1(S_i)}, E^w_{lc2(S_i)}, E^w_{rc2(S_i)}, i = 0, 1$
$E^w_{lc1(lc1(S_i))}, E^w_{rc1(rc1(S_i))}, i = 0, 1$
POS features
$E^t_{S_i}, E^t_{B_i}, i = 0, 1, 2$
$E^t_{lc1(S_i)}, E^t_{rc1(S_i)}, E^t_{lc2(S_i)}, E^t_{rc2(S_i)}, i = 0, 1$
$E^t_{lc1(lc1(S_i))}, E^t_{rc1(rc1(S_i))}, i = 0, 1$
Label features
$E^l_{lc1(S_i)}, E^l_{rc1(S_i)}, E^l_{lc2(S_i)}, E^l_{rc2(S_i)}, i = 0, 1$
$E^l_{lc1(lc1(S_i))}, E^l_{rc1(rc1(S_i))}, i = 0, 1$
Distance: $E^d_{\langle S_0, S_1 \rangle}, E^d_{\langle S_0, B_0 \rangle}$
Valency: $E^{lv}_{S_0}, E^{lv}_{S_1}, E^{rv}_{S_1}$

Table 1: Feature templates of the neural network parsing model. $E^w_p, E^t_p, E^l_p, E^d_p, E^{lv}_p, E^{rv}_p$ indicate the {word, POS, label, distance, left/right valency} embeddings of the element at position p, correspondingly. $lc1$ / $rc1$ is the first child in the left / right, $lc2$ / $rc2$ is the second child in the left / right. S_i and B_i refer to the ith elements respectively in the *stack* and *buffer*.

2011). All of these features are projected to an embedding layer via corresponding embedding matrices, which will be estimated through the training process. The complete feature templates used in our system are shown in Table 1. Then, feature compositions are performed at the hidden layer via a **cube activation function**: $g(x) = x^3$.

The cube activation function can be viewed as a special case of low-rank tensor. Formally, $g(x)$ can be expanded as:

$$g(w_1 x_1 + \ldots + w_m x_m + b) = \sum_{i,j,k} (w_i w_j w_k) x_i x_j x_k + \sum_{i,j} b(w_i w_j) x_i x_j + \ldots$$

If we treat the bias term as $b \times x_0$ where $x_0 = 1$, then the weight corresponding to each feature combination $x_i x_j x_k$ is $w_i w_j w_k$, which is exactly the same as a rank-1 component tensor in the low-rank form using CP tensor decomposition (Cao and Khudanpur, 2014). Consequently, the cube activation function implicitly derives full feature combinations. An advantage of the cube activation function is that it is flexible for adding extra features to the input. In fact, we can add as many features as possible to the input layer to improve the parsing accuracy. We will show in Section 5.2 that the Brown cluster features can be readily incorporated into our model.

Cross-lingual Transfer. The idea of cross-lingual transfer using the parser we examined above is straightforward. In contrast to traditional approaches that have to discard rich lexical features (delexicalizing) when transferring models from one language to another, our model can be transferred using the full model trained on the source language side, i.e. English.

Since the non-lexical feature (POS, label, distance, valency) embeddings are directly transferable between languages,[2] the key component of this framework is the cross-lingual learning of lexical feature embeddings, i.e. word embeddings. Once the cross-lingual word embeddings are induced, we first learn a dependency parser at the source language side. After that, the parser will be directly used for parsing target language data.

4 Cross-lingual Word Representation Learning

Prior to introducing our approaches for cross-lingual word representation learning, we briefly review the basic model for learning monolingual word embeddings, which constitutes a subprocedure of the cross-lingual approaches.

4.1 Continuous Bag-of-Words Model

Various approaches have been studied for learning word embeddings from large-scale plain texts. In this study, we consider the Continuous Bag-of-Words (CBOW) model (Mikolov et al., 2013) as implemented in the open-source toolkit word2vec.[3] The basic principle of the CBOW model is to predict each individual word in a sequence given the bag of its context words within a fixed window size as input, using a log-linear classifier. This model avoids the non-linear transformation in hidden layers, and hence can be trained with high efficiency.

With large window size, grouped words using the resulting word embeddings are more topically similar; whereas with small window size, the grouped words will be more syntactically similar. So we set the window size to 1 in our parsing task.

Next, we introduce our approach for inducing bilingual word embeddings. In general, we expect our bilingual word embeddings to preserve translational equivalences. For example, "cooking" (English) should be close to its translation: "kochen" (German) in the embedding space.

[2] POS tags are language-independent here since we use the universal POS tags (Section 5).

[3] `http://code.google.com/p/word2vec/`

4.2 Robust Alignment-based Projection

Our first method for inducing cross-lingual word embeddings has two stages. First, we learn word embeddings from a source language (S) corpora as in the monolingual case, and then project the monolingual word embeddings to a target language (T), based on word alignments.

Given a sentence-aligned parallel corpus $\mathcal{D}$, we first conduct unsupervised bidirectional word alignment, and then collect an alignment dictionary. Specifically, in each word-aligned sentence pair of $\mathcal{D}$, we keep all alignments with conditional alignment probability exceeding a threshold $\delta = 0.95$ and discard the others. Specifically, let $\mathcal{A}^{T|S} = \{(w_i^T, w_j^S, c_{i,j}), i = 1, 2, ..., N_T; j = 1, 2, ..., N_S\}$ be the alignment dictionary, where $c_{i,j}$ is the number of times when the ith target word w_i^T is aligned to the jth source word w_j^S. N_S and N_T are vocabulary sizes. We use the shorthand $(i,j) \in \mathcal{A}^{T|S}$ to denote a word pair in $\mathcal{A}^{T|S}$. The projection can be formalized as the weighted average of the embeddings of translation words:

$$v(w_i^T) = \sum_{(i,j)\in\mathcal{A}^{T|S}} \frac{c_{i,j}}{c_{i,\cdot}} \cdot v(w_j^S) \qquad (1)$$

where $c_{i,\cdot} = \Sigma_j c_{i,j}$, $v(w)$ is the embedding of w.

Obviously, the simple projection method has one drawback, it only assigns word embeddings for those target language words that occur in the word aligned data, which is typically smaller than the monolingual datasets. Therefore, in order to improve the robustness of projection, we utilize a morphology-inspired mechanism, to propagate embeddings from in-vocabulary words to out-of-vocabulary (OOV) words. Specifically, for each OOV word w_{oov}^T, we extract a list of candidate words that is similar to it in terms of *edit distance*, and then set the averaged vector as the embedding of w_{oov}^T. Formally,

$$\begin{aligned} &v(w_{oov}^T) = \underset{w' \in C}{Avg}(v(w')) \\ &\text{where } C = \{w | EditDist(w_{oov}^T, w) \le \tau\} \end{aligned} \qquad (2)$$

To reduce noise, we choose a small *edit distance* threshold $\tau = 1$.

4.3 Canonical Correlation Analysis

The second approach we consider is similar to Faruqui and Dyer (2014), which use CCA to improve monolingual word embeddings with multilingual correlation. CCA is a way of measuring the linear relationship between multidimensional variables. For two multidimensional variables, CCA aims to find two projection matrices to map the original variables to a new basis (lower-dimensional), such that the correlation between the two variables is maximized.

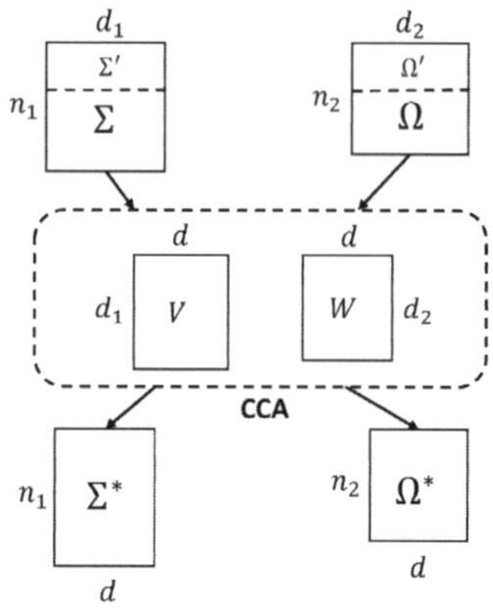

Figure 3: CCA for cross-lingual word representation learning.

Let's treat CCA as a blackbox here, and see how to apply CCA for inducing bilingual word embeddings. Suppose there are already two pre-trained monolingual word embeddings (e.g. English and German): $\Sigma \in \mathbb{R}^{n_1 \times d_1}$ and $\Omega \in \mathbb{R}^{n_2 \times d_2}$. At the first step, we extract a one-to-one alignment dictionary $\mathcal{D} : \Sigma' \leftrightarrow \Omega'$ from the alignment dictionary $\mathcal{A}^{S|T}$.[4] Here, $\Sigma' \subseteq \Sigma$, indicating that every word in Σ' is translated to one word in $\Omega' \subseteq \Omega$, and vice versa.

The process is illustrated in Figure 3. Denoting the dimension of resulting word embeddings by $d \le min(d_1, d_2)$. First, we derive two projection matrices $V \in \mathbb{R}^{d_1 \times d}, W \in \mathbb{R}^{d_2 \times d}$ respectively for Σ' and Ω' using CCA:

$$V, W = CCA(\Sigma', \Omega') \qquad (3)$$

Then, V and W are used to project the entire vocabulary Σ and Ω:

$$\Sigma^* = \Sigma V, \quad \Omega^* = \Omega W \qquad (4)$$

where $\Sigma^* \in \mathbb{R}^{n_1 \times d}$ and $\Omega^* \in \mathbb{R}^{n_2 \times d}$ are the resulting word embeddings for our cross-lingual task.

Contrary to the projection approach, CCA assigns embeddings for every word in the monolingual vocabulary. However, one potential limitation is that CCA assumes linear transformation of word embeddings, which is difficult to satisfy.

[4] $\mathcal{A}^{T|S}$ is also worth trying, but we observed slight performance degradation in our experimental setting.

Note that both approaches can be generalize to lower-resource languages where parallel bitexts are not available. In that way, the dictionary $\mathcal{A}$ can be readily obtained either using bilingual lexicon induction approaches (Koehn and Knight, 2002; Mann and Yarowsky, 2001; Haghighi et al., 2008), or from resources like Wiktionary[5] and Panlex.[6]

5 Experiments

5.1 Data and Settings

For the pre-training of word embeddings, we use the WMT-2011 monolingual news corpora for English, German and Spanish.[7] For French, we combined the WMT-2011 and WMT-2012 monolingual news corpora.[8] We obtained the word alignment counts using the *fast-align* toolkit in cdec (Dyer et al., 2010) from the parallel news commentary corpora (WMT 2006-10) combined with the Europarl corpus for English-{German, Spanish, French}.[9]

For the training of the neural network dependency parser, we set the number of hidden units to 400. The dimension of embeddings for different features are shown in Table 2.

	Word	POS	Label	Dist.	Val.	Cluster
Dim.	50	50	50	5	5	8

Table 2: Dimensions of feature embeddings.

Adaptive stochastic gradient descent (AdaGrad) (Duchi et al., 2011) is used for optimization. For the CCA approach, we use the implementation of Faruqui and Dyer (2014). The dimensions of the monolingual embeddings (d_1, d_2) and the resulting bilingual embeddings are set to 50 equally.

We employ the universal dependency treebanks proposed by McDonald et al. (2013) for a reliable evaluation of our approach for cross-lingual dependency parsing. The universal multilingual treebanks are annotated using the universal POS tagset (Petrov et al., 2011) which contains 12 POS tags, as well as the universal dependencies which contains 42 relations. We follow the standard split of the treebanks for every language (DE, ES, and FR).[10]

[5]https://www.wiktionary.org/

[6]http://panlex.org/

[7]http://www.statmt.org/wmt11/

[8]http://www.statmt.org/wmt12/

[9]http://www.statmt.org/europarl/

[10]http://code.google.com/p/uni-dep-tb/.

5.2 Baseline Systems

We compare our approach with three systems. For the first baseline, we evaluate the delexicalized transfer of our parser [DELEX], in which we only use non-lexical features.

We also compare our approach with the delexicalized parser in McDonald et al. (2013) [McD13], who used a perceptron-trained transition-based parser with a beam of size 8, along with rich non-local features (Zhang and Nivre, 2011).

Furthermore, we augment cross-lingual word clusters to the perceptron-based delexicalized parser, as proposed in Täckström et al. (2012). We use the same alignment dictionary as described in Section 4 to induce the cross-lingual word clusters. We re-implement the PROJECTED cluster approach in Täckström et al. (2012), which assigns a target word to the cluster with which it is most often aligned:

$$c(w_i^T) = \arg\max_k \sum_{(i,j)\in\mathcal{A}^{T|S}} c_{i,j} \cdot \mathbb{1}[c(w_j^S) = k]$$

This method also has the drawback that words that do not occur in the alignment dictionary (OOV) cannot be assigned a cluster. Therefore, we use the same strategy as described in Section 4.2 to find the most likely clusters for the OOV words. Instead of the clustering model of Uszkoreit and Brants (2008), we use Brown clustering (Brown et al., 1992) to induce hierarchical word clusters, where each word is represented as a bit-string. We use the same word cluster feature templates from Täckström et al. (2012), and set the number of Brown clusters to 256.

5.3 Experimental Results

All of the parsing models are trained using the development data from English for early-stopping. Table 3 lists the results of the cross-lingual transfer experiments for dependency parsing. Table 4 further summarizes each of the experimental gains detailed in Table 3.

Our delexicalized system obtains slightly lower performance than those reported in McDonald et al. (2013) (McD13), because we're using

Before this dataset was carried out, the CoNLL multilingual dependency treebanks (Buchholz and Marsi, 2006) were often used for evaluation. However, the major problem is that the dependency annotations vary for different languages (e.g. the choice of lexical versus functional head), which makes it impossible to evaluate the LAS.

	Unlabeled Attachment Score (UAS)					Labeled Attachment Score (LAS)				
	EN	DE	ES	FR	AVG	EN	DE	ES	FR	AVG
DELEX	83.67	57.01	68.05	68.85	*64.64*	79.42	47.12	56.99	57.78	*53.96*
PROJ	91.96	60.07	71.42	71.36	*67.62*	90.48	49.94	61.76	61.55	*57.75*
PROJ+Cluster	92.33	60.35	**71.90**	**72.93**	***68.39***	90.91	**51.54**	**62.28**	**63.12**	***58.98***
CCA	90.62†	59.42	68.87	69.58	*65.96*	88.88†	49.32	59.65	59.50	*56.16*
CCA+Cluster	92.03†	**60.66**	71.33	70.87	*67.62*	90.49†	51.29	61.69	61.50	*58.16*
MCD13	83.33	58.50	68.07	70.14	*65.57*	78.54	48.11	56.86	58.20	*54.39*
MCD13*	84.44	57.30	68.15	69.91	*65.12*	80.30	47.34	57.12	58.80	*54.42*
MCD13*+Cluster	90.21	60.55	70.43	72.01	*67.66*	88.28	50.20	60.96	61.96	*57.71*

Table 3: Cross-lingual transfer dependency parsing from English on the test dataset of 4 universal multilingual treebanks. Results measured by unlabeled attachment score (UAS) and labeled attachment score (LAS). * denotes our re-implementation of MCD13. Since the model varies for different target languages in the CCA-based approach, † indicates the averaged UAS/LAS.

Experimental Contribution	DE/ES/FR Avg
PROJ *vs.* DELEX	*+3.79 (8.2%)*
CCA *vs.* DELEX	*+2.19 (4.8%)*
PROJ *vs.* MCD13*	*+3.33 (7.3%)*
CCA *vs.* MCD13*	*+1.74 (3.8%)*
PROJ+Cluster *vs.* PROJ	*+1.23 (2.9%)*
CCA+Cluster *vs.* CCA	*+2.00 (4.6%)*
MCD13*+Cluster *vs.* MCD13*	*+3.29 (7.2%)*
PROJ+Cluster *vs.* DELEX	*+5.02 (10.9%)*
CCA+Cluster *vs.* DELEX	*+4.20 (9.1%)*
PROJ+Cluster *vs.* MCD13*	*+4.46 (9.8%)*
CCA+Cluster *vs.* MCD13*	*+3.74 (8.2%)*
PROJ+Cluster *vs.* MCD13*+Cluster	*+1.27 (3.0%)*
CCA+Cluster *vs.* MCD13*+Cluster	*+0.45 (1.1%)*

Table 4: Summary of each of the experimental gains detailed in Table 3, in both absolute LAS gain and relative error reduction. All gains are statistically significant using MaltEval at $p < 0.01$.[12]

greedy decoding and local training. Our re-implementation of (McDonald et al., 2013) attains comparable performance with MCD13.

For all languages we consider in this study, by using cross-lingual word embeddings either from alignment-based projection or CCA, we obtain statistically significant improvements against the delexicalized system, both in UAS and LAS.

Interestingly, we notice that PROJ consistently performs better than CCA by a significant margin, and is comparable to McD13*+Cluster. We will give further analysis to this observation in Section 5.3.1 and 5.3.2.

Our framework is flexible for incorporating richer features simply by embedding them into continuous vectors. Thus we further embed the cross-lingual word cluster features into our model, together with the proposed cross-lingual word embeddings. The cluster feature template used here is similar to the POS tag feature templates:

Cluster features
$E^c_{S_i}, E^c_{B_i}, i = 0, 1, 2$
$E^c_{lc1(S_i)}, E^c_{rc1(S_i)}, E^c_{lc2(S_i)}, E^c_{rc2(S_i)}, i = 0, 1$
$E^c_{lc1(lc1(S_i))}, E^c_{rc1(rc1(S_i))}, i = 0, 1$

Table 5: Word cluster feature templates.

As shown in Table 3, additive improvements are obtained for both PROJ and CCA. Compared with our delexicalized system, the relative error is reduced by up to 13.1% in UAS, and up to 12.6% in LAS. The combined system further outperforms McD13* augmented with cluster features significantly .

5.3.1 Effect of Robust Projection

Since in both PROJ and the induction of cross-lingual word clusters, we use *edit distance* measure for OOV words, we would like to see how this affects the performance of parsing.

Intuitively, higher coverage of projected words in the test dataset should promote the parsing performance more. To verify this, we further conduct experiments under both settings using the PROJ+Cluster model. Results are shown in Table 6. Improvements are observed for all languages when using robust projection with *edit distance* measure, especially for FR, where the highest coverage gain is obtained by robust projection.

5.3.2 Fine-tuning of Word Embeddings

Another reason for the effectiveness of PROJ over CCA lies in the fine-tuning of word embeddings while training the parser.

		Simple	Robust	Δ
DE	coverage	91.37	94.70	+3.33
	UAS	59.74	60.35	+0.61
	LAS	50.84	51.54	+0.70
ES	coverage	94.51	96.67	+2.16
	UAS	70.97	71.90	+0.93
	LAS	61.34	62.28	+0.94
FR	coverage	90.83	97.60	+6.77
	UAS	71.17	72.93	+1.76
	LAS	61.72	63.12	+1.40

Table 6: Effect of robust projection.

CCA can be viewed as a joint method for inducing cross-lingual word embeddings. When training the source language dependency parser with cross-lingual word embeddings derived from CCA, the EN word embeddings should be fixed. Otherwise, the translational equivalence will be broken. However, for PROJ, there is no such limitation. Word embeddings can be updated as other non-lexical feature embeddings, in order to obtain a more accurate dependency parser. We refer to this procedure as a *fine-tuning* process to the word embeddings. To verify the benefits of *fine-tuning*, we conduct experiments to see relative loss if word embeddings are fixed while training. Results are shown in Table 7, which indicates that *fine-tuning* indeed offers considerable help.

		Fix	Fine-tune	Δ
DE	UAS	59.74	60.07	+0.33
	LAS	49.44	49.94	+0.50
ES	UAS	70.10	71.42	+1.32
	LAS	61.31	61.76	+0.45
FR	UAS	70.65	71.36	+0.71
	LAS	60.69	61.50	+0.81

Table 7: Effect of fine-tuning word embeddings.

5.4 Compare with Existing Bilingual Word Embeddings

In this section, we compare our bilingual embeddings with several previous approaches in the context of dependency parsing. To the best of our knowledge, this is the first work on evaluation of bilingual word embeddings in syntactic tasks. The approaches we consider include the multi-task learning approach (Klementiev et al., 2012) [MTL], the bilingual auto-encoder approach (Chandar et al., 2014) [BIAE], the bilingual compositional vector model (Hermann and Blunsom, 2014) [BICVM], and the bilingual bag-of-words approach (Gouws et al., 2014) [BILBOWA].

For MTL and BIAE, we adopt their released word embeddings directly due to the inefficiency of training.[13] For BICVM and BILBOWA, we rerun their systems on the same dataset as our previous experiments.[14] Results are summarized in Table 8. CCA and PROJ consistently outperforms all other approaches in all languages, and PROJ performs the best. The inferior performance of MTL and BIAE is partly due to the low word coverage. For example, they cover only 31% of words in the universal DE test treebank, whereas the CCA and PROJ covers over 70%. Moreover, BIAE, BICVM and BILBOWA are optimized using semantic-related objectives. So we suggest that they are probably not well fit for syntactic tasks.

It is worth noting that we don't assume/require bilingual parallel data in CCA and PROJ. What we need in practice is a bilingual lexicon for each paired languages. This is especially important for generalizing our approaches to lower-resource languages, where parallel texts are not available.

6 Related Studies

Existing approaches for cross-lingual dependency parsing can be divided into three categories: cross-lingual annotation projection methods, jointly modeling methods and cross-lingual representation learning methods.

The cross-lingual annotation projection method is first proposed in Yarowsky et al. (2001) for shallower NLP tasks (POS tagging, NER, etc.). The central idea is to project the syntactic annotations from a resource-rich language to the target language through word alignments, and then train a supervised parser on the projected noisy annotations (Hwa et al., 2005; Smith and Eisner, 2009; Zhao et al., 2009; Jiang et al., 2011; Tiedemann, 2014; Tiedemann, 2015). Noises and errors introduced by the word alignment and annotation projection processes can be reduced with robust projection methods by using graph-based label propagation (Das and Petrov, 2011; Kim and Lee, 2012), or by incorporating auxiliary resources (Kim et al., 2012; Khapra et al., 2010).

The jointly modeling methods integrates the monolingual grammar induction with bilingually-projected dependency information (Liu et al., 2013), or linguistic constraints via posterior

[13]The MTL embeddings are normalized before training.

[14]BICVM only uses the bilingual parallel dataset.

	DE		ES		FR	
	UAS	LAS	UAS	LAS	UAS	LAS
MTL (Klementiev et al., 2012)‡	57.70	47.13	68.04	58.78	67.66	57.30
BIAE (Chandar et al., 2014)‡	53.74	43.68	58.81	46.66	60.10	49.47
BICVM (Hermann and Blunsom, 2014)	56.30	46.99	67.78	58.08	69.13	58.13
BILBOWA (Gouws et al., 2014)	51.65	41.83	65.02	54.35	63.35	51.65
CCA	59.42	49.32	68.87	59.65	69.58	59.50
PROJ	**60.07**	**49.94**	**71.42**	**61.76**	**71.36**	**61.55**

Table 8: Comparison with existing bilingual word embeddings. ‡For MTL and BIAE, we use their released bilingual word embeddings.

regularization (Ganchev et al., 2009), manually constructed universal dependency parsing rules (Naseem et al., 2010) and manually specified typological features (Naseem et al., 2012). Besides dependency parsing, the joint modeling method has also been applied for other multilingual NLP tasks, including NER (Che et al., 2013; Wang and Manning, 2014), SRL (Zhuang and Zong, 2010; Titov and Klementiev, 2012) and WSD (Guo and Diab, 2010).

The cross-lingual representation learning method aims at building connections across different languages by inducing language-independent feature representations. After that, a parser can be trained at the source-language side within the induced feature space, and directly be applied to the target language. Typical approaches include cross-lingual word clustering (Täckström et al., 2012) which is employed in this paper as a baseline, projection features (Durrett et al., 2012). Xiao and Guo (2014) learns cross-lingual word embeddings and apply them with MSTParser for linguistic transfer, which inspires this work.

It is worth mentioning that remarkable results on the universal dependency treebanks have been achieved by using annotation projection method (Tiedemann, 2014), treebank translation method (Tiedemann and Nivre, 2014), and distribution transferring method (Ma and Xia, 2014). Unlike our approach, all of these methods involve training a parser at the target language side. Parallel bitexts are required in these methods, which limits their scalability to lower-resource languages. That said, these methods have the advantage that they are capable of capturing some language-specific syntactic patterns which our approach cannot.[15] These two kinds of approaches are complementary, and can be integrated to push the performance further.

7 Conclusion

This paper proposes a novel framework based on distributed representations for cross-lingual dependency parsing. Two algorithms are proposed for the induction of cross-lingual word representations: robust projection and CCA, which bridge the *lexical feature gap*.

Experiments show that by using cross-lingual word embeddings derived from either approach, the transferred parsing performance can be improved significantly against the delexicalized system. A notable observation is that our projection method performs significantly better than CCA, a joint method. Additionally, our framework is flexibly able to incorporate the cross-lingual word cluster features, with further significant gains in each use. The combined system significantly outperforms the delexicalized system on all languages, by an average of 10.9% error reduction on LAS, and further significantly outperforms McDonald et al. (2013) augmented with projected cluster features.[16]

Acknowledgments

We are grateful to Manaal Faruqui for providing the bilingual resources. We thank Ryan McDonald for pointing out the evaluation issue in the experiment. We also thank Sharon Busching for the proofreading and the anonymous reviewers for the insightful comments and suggestions. This work was supported by the National Key Basic Research Program of China via grant 2014CB340503 and the National Natural Science Foundation of China (NSFC) via grant 61133012 and 61370164.

[15] For example, in Spanish and French, adjectives often appears after nouns, thus forming a right-directed arc labeled by *amod*, whereas in English, the *amod* arcs are mostly left-directed.

[16] Our system is publicly available at `https://github.com/jiangfeng1124/acl15-clnndep`.

References

Peter F Brown, Peter V Desouza, Robert L Mercer, Vincent J Della Pietra, and Jenifer C Lai. 1992. Class-based n-gram models of natural language. *Computational linguistics*, 18(4):467–479.

Sabine Buchholz and Erwin Marsi. 2006. Conll-x shared task on multilingual dependency parsing. In *CoNLL*, pages 149–164.

Yuan Cao and Sanjeev Khudanpur. 2014. Online learning in tensor space. In *ACL*, pages 666–675.

Sarath Chandar, Stanislas Lauly, Hugo Larochelle, Mitesh Khapra, Balaraman Ravindran, Vikas Raykar, and Amrita Saha. 2014. An autoencoder approach to learning bilingual word representations. In *NIPS*, pages 1853–1861.

Wanxiang Che, Mengqiu Wang, Christopher D. Manning, and Ting Liu. 2013. Named entity recognition with bilingual constraints. In *NAACL*, pages 52–62.

Danqi Chen and Christopher D Manning. 2014. A fast and accurate dependency parser using neural networks. In *EMNLP*, pages 740–750.

Ronan Collobert, Jason Weston, Léon Bottou, Michael Karlen, Koray Kavukcuoglu, and Pavel Kuksa. 2011. Natural language processing (almost) from scratch. *JMLR*, 12:2493–2537.

Dipanjan Das and Slav Petrov. 2011. Unsupervised part-of-speech tagging with bilingual graph-based projections. In *ACL*, pages 600–609.

Marie-Catherine De Marneffe and Christopher D Manning. 2008. The stanford typed dependencies representation. In *Coling 2008: Proceedings of the workshop on Cross-Framework and Cross-Domain Parser Evaluation*, pages 1–8.

Marie-Catherine De Marneffe, Bill MacCartney, Christopher D Manning, et al. 2006. Generating typed dependency parses from phrase structure parses. In *LREC*, volume 6, pages 449–454.

John Duchi, Elad Hazan, and Yoram Singer. 2011. Adaptive subgradient methods for online learning and stochastic optimization. *JMLR*, 12:2121–2159.

Greg Durrett, Adam Pauls, and Dan Klein. 2012. Syntactic transfer using a bilingual lexicon. In *EMNLP*, pages 1–11, July.

Chris Dyer, Adam Lopez, Juri Ganitkevitch, Johnathan Weese, Ferhan Ture, Phil Blunsom, Hendra Setiawan, Vladimir Eidelman, and Philip Resnik. 2010. cdec: A decoder, alignment, and learning framework for finite-state and context-free translation models. In *ACL*.

Manaal Faruqui and Chris Dyer. 2014. Improving vector space word representations using multilingual correlation. In *EACL*, pages 462–471.

Kuzman Ganchev, Jennifer Gillenwater, and Ben Taskar. 2009. Dependency grammar induction via bitext projection constraints. In *ACL-IJCNLP*, pages 369–377.

Stephan Gouws, Yoshua Bengio, and Greg Corrado. 2014. Bilbowa: Fast bilingual distributed representations without word alignments. *arXiv preprint arXiv:1410.2455*.

Weiwei Guo and Mona Diab. 2010. Combining orthogonal monolingual and multilingual sources of evidence for all words wsd. In *ACL*, pages 1542–1551, July.

Jiang Guo, Wanxiang Che, Haifeng Wang, and Ting Liu. 2014. Revisiting embedding features for simple semi-supervised learning. In *EMNLP*, pages 110–120.

Aria Haghighi, Percy Liang, Taylor Berg-Kirkpatrick, and Dan Klein. 2008. Learning bilingual lexicons from monolingual corpora. In *ACL*, volume 2008, pages 771–779.

Karl Moritz Hermann and Phil Blunsom. 2014. Multilingual models for compositional distributed semantics. In *ACL*, pages 58–68, June.

Rebecca Hwa, Philip Resnik, Amy Weinberg, Clara Cabezas, and Okan Kolak. 2005. Bootstrapping parsers via syntactic projection across parallel texts. *Natural language engineering*, 11(03):311–325.

Wenbin Jiang, Qun Liu, and Yajuan Lv. 2011. Relaxed cross-lingual projection of constituent syntax. In *EMNLP*, pages 1192–1201.

Mitesh Khapra, Saurabh Sohoney, Anup Kulkarni, and Pushpak Bhattacharyya. 2010. Value for money: Balancing annotation effort, lexicon building and accuracy for multilingual wsd. In *COLING*, pages 555–563.

Seokhwan Kim and Gary Geunbae Lee. 2012. A graph-based cross-lingual projection approach for weakly supervised relation extraction. In *ACL*, pages 48–53.

Sungchul Kim, Kristina Toutanova, and Hwanjo Yu. 2012. Multilingual named entity recognition using parallel data and metadata from wikipedia. In *ACL*, pages 694–702.

Dan Klein and Christopher D Manning. 2004. Corpus-based induction of syntactic structure: Models of dependency and constituency. In *ACL*, page 478.

Alexandre Klementiev, Ivan Titov, and Binod Bhattarai. 2012. Inducing crosslingual distributed representations of words. In *COLING*, pages 1459–1474.

Philipp Koehn and Kevin Knight. 2002. Learning a translation lexicon from monolingual corpora. In *Proceedings of the ACL-02 workshop on Unsupervised lexical acquisition-Volume 9*, pages 9–16.

Kai Liu, Yajuan Lü, Wenbin Jiang, and Qun Liu. 2013. Bilingually-guided monolingual dependency grammar induction. In *ACL*, pages 1063–1072.

Xuezhe Ma and Fei Xia. 2014. Unsupervised dependency parsing with transferring distribution via parallel guidance and entropy regularization. In *ACL*, pages 1337–1348.

Gideon S Mann and David Yarowsky. 2001. Multipath translation lexicon induction via bridge languages. In *NAACL*, pages 1–8.

Ryan McDonald and Joakim Nivre. 2007. Characterizing the errors of data-driven dependency parsing models. In *EMNLP-CoNLL*, pages 122–131.

Ryan McDonald, Slav Petrov, and Keith Hall. 2011. Multi-source transfer of delexicalized dependency parsers. In *EMNLP*, pages 62–72.

Ryan T McDonald, Joakim Nivre, Yvonne Quirmbach-Brundage, Yoav Goldberg, Dipanjan Das, Kuzman Ganchev, Keith B Hall, Slav Petrov, Hao Zhang, Oscar Täckström, et al. 2013. Universal dependency annotation for multilingual parsing. In *ACL*, pages 92–97.

Tomas Mikolov, Kai Chen, Greg Corrado, and Jeffrey Dean. 2013. Efficient estimation of word representations in vector space. *arXiv preprint arXiv:1301.3781*.

Tahira Naseem, Harr Chen, Regina Barzilay, and Mark Johnson. 2010. Using universal linguistic knowledge to guide grammar induction. In *EMNLP*, pages 1234–1244.

Tahira Naseem, Regina Barzilay, and Amir Globerson. 2012. Selective sharing for multilingual dependency parsing. In *ACL*, pages 629–637.

Joakim Nivre. 2004. Incrementality in deterministic dependency parsing. In *Proceedings of the Workshop on Incremental Parsing: Bringing Engineering and Cognition Together*, pages 50–57.

Slav Petrov, Dipanjan Das, and Ryan McDonald. 2011. A universal part-of-speech tagset. *arXiv preprint arXiv:1104.2086*.

David A Smith and Jason Eisner. 2009. Parser adaptation and projection with quasi-synchronous grammar features. In *EMNLP*, pages 822–831. Association for Computational Linguistics.

Ilya Sutskever, Oriol Vinyals, and Quoc VV Le. 2014. Sequence to sequence learning with neural networks. In *NIPS*, pages 3104–3112.

Oscar Täckström, Ryan McDonald, and Jakob Uszkoreit. 2012. Cross-lingual word clusters for direct transfer of linguistic structure. In *NAACL*, pages 477–487.

Jörg Tiedemann and Joakim Nivre. 2014. Treebank translation for cross-lingual parser induction. *CoNLL-2014*, page 130.

Jörg Tiedemann. 2014. Rediscovering annotation projection for cross-lingual parser induction. In *Proc. COLING*.

Jörg Tiedemann. 2015. Improving the cross-lingual projection of syntactic dependencies. In *Nordic Conference of Computational Linguistics NODALIDA 2015*, page 191.

Ivan Titov and Alexandre Klementiev. 2012. Crosslingual induction of semantic roles. In *ACL*, pages 647–656.

Joseph Turian, Lev Ratinov, and Yoshua Bengio. 2010. Word representations: a simple and general method for semi-supervised learning. In *ACL*, pages 384–394.

Jakob Uszkoreit and Thorsten Brants. 2008. Distributed word clustering for large scale class-based language modeling in machine translation. In *ACL*, pages 755–762.

Mengqiu Wang and Christopher D. Manning. 2013. Effect of non-linear deep architecture in sequence labeling. In *IJCNLP*, pages 1285–1291.

Mengqiu Wang and Christopher D Manning. 2014. Cross-lingual projected expectation regularization for weakly supervised learning. *TACL*, 2:55–66.

Min Xiao and Yuhong Guo. 2014. Distributed word representation learning for cross-lingual dependency parsing. In *CoNLL*, pages 119–129.

David Yarowsky, Grace Ngai, and Richard Wicentowski. 2001. Inducing multilingual text analysis tools via robust projection across aligned corpora. In *Proceedings of the first international conference on Human language technology research*, pages 1–8.

Yue Zhang and Stephen Clark. 2011. Syntactic processing using the generalized perceptron and beam search. *Computational Linguistics*, 37(1):105–151.

Yue Zhang and Joakim Nivre. 2011. Transition-based dependency parsing with rich non-local features. In *ACL*, pages 188–193.

Hai Zhao, Yan Song, Chunyu Kit, and Guodong Zhou. 2009. Cross language dependency parsing using a bilingual lexicon. In *ACL-IJCNLP*, pages 55–63.

Tao Zhuang and Chengqing Zong. 2010. Joint inference for bilingual semantic role labeling. In *EMNLP*, pages 304–314.

Can Natural Language Processing Become Natural Language Coaching?

Marti A. Hearst
UC Berkeley
Berkeley, CA 94720
hearst@berkeley.edu

Abstract

How we teach and learn is undergoing a revolution, due to changes in technology and connectivity. Education may be one of the best application areas for advanced NLP techniques, and NLP researchers have much to contribute to this problem, especially in the areas of learning to write, mastery learning, and peer learning. In this paper I consider what happens when we convert natural language processors into natural language coaches.

1 Why Should You Care, NLP Researcher?

There is a revolution in learning underway. Students are taking Massive Open Online Courses as well as online tutorials and paid online courses. Technology and connectivity makes it possible for students to learn from anywhere in the world, at any time, to fit their schedules. And in today's knowledge-based economy, going to school only in one's early years is no longer enough; in future most people are going to need continuous, lifelong education.

Students are changing too — they expect to interact with information and technology. Fortunately, pedagogical research shows significant benefits of active learning over passive methods. The modern view of teaching means students work actively in class, talk with peers, and are coached more than graded by their instructors.

In this new world of education, there is a great need for NLP research to step in and help. I hope in this paper to excite colleagues about the possibilities and suggest a few new ways of looking at them. I do not attempt to cover the field of language and learning comprehensively, nor do I claim there is no work in the field. In fact there is quite a bit, such as a recent special issue on language learning resources (Sharoff et al., 2014), the long running ACL workshops on Building Educational Applications using NLP (Tetreault et al., 2015), and a recent shared task competition on grammatical error detection for second language learners (Ng et al., 2014). But I hope I am casting a few interesting thoughts in this direction for those colleagues who are not focused on this particular topic.

2 How Awkward

Perhaps the least useful feedback that an instructor writes next to a block of prose on a learner's essay is `'awkward'`. We know what this means: something about this text does not read fluently. But this is not helpful feedback; if the student knew how to make the wording flow, he or she would have written it fluently in the first place! Useful feedback is *actionable*: it provides steps to take to make improvements.

A challenge for the field of NLP is how to build writing *tutors* or *coaches* – as opposed to *graders* or *scorers*. There is a vast difference between a tool that performs an assessment of writing and one that coaches students to help them as they are attempting to write.

Current practice uses the output of scorers to give students a target to aim for: revise your essay to get a higher score. An alternative is to design a system that watches alongside a learner as they write an essay, and coaches their work at all levels of construction – phrase level, clause level, sentence level, discourse level, paragraph level, and essay level.

Grammar checking technology has been excellent for years now (Heidorn, 2000), but instead of just showing the right answer as grammar checkers do, a grammar coach should give hints and scaffolding the way a tutor would – not giving the answer explicitly, but showing the path and letting the learner fill in the missing information. When the learner makes incorrect choices, the parser

Proceedings of the 53rd Annual Meeting of the Association for Computational Linguistics and the 7th International Joint Conference on Natural Language Processing, pages 1245–1252,
Beijing, China, July 26-31, 2015.

can teach principles and lessons for the conceptual stage that the learner is currently at. Different grammars could be developed for learners at different competency levels, as well as for different first-second language pairings in the case of second language learning.

This suggests a different approach for building a parser than what is the current standard. I am not claiming that this has not been suggested in the past; for instance Schwind (1988) designed a parser to explain errors to learners. However, because of the renewed interest in technology for teaching, this may be a pivotal time to reconsider how we develop parsing technology: perhaps we should think fundamentally about parsers as coaches rather than parsers as critics.

This inversion can apply to other aspects of NLP technology as well. For instance, Dale and Kilgarriff (2011) have held a series of workshop to produce algorithms to identify errors introduced into texts by non-native writers in the warmly named "Helping Our Own" shared task (Dale et al., 2012). Using the technology developed for tasks like these, the challenge is to go beyond recognizing and correcting the errors to helping the writer understand why the choices they are making are not correct. Another option is to target practice questions tailored for learners based on errors in a fun manner (as described below).

Of course, for decades, the field of Intelligent Tutoring Systems (ITS) (VanLehn, 2011) has developed technology for this purpose, so what is new about what I am suggesting? First, we know as NLP researchers that language analysis requires specific technology beyond standard algorithms, and so advances in Intelligent Tutoring Systems on language problems most likely requires collaboration with experts in NLP. And, apparently such collaborations have not been as robust as they might be (Borin, 2002; Meurers, 2012). So there is an opportunity for new advances at the intersection of these two fields.

And second, the newly expanded interest in online learning and technology makes possible the access of information about student writing behavior on a large scale that was not possible in the past. Imagine thousands of students in cascaded waves, tasked with writing essays on the same topic, and receiving real-time suggestions from different algorithms. The first wave of student responses to the feedback would be used to improve the algorithms and these results would be fed into the next wave of student work, and so on. Students and instructors could be encouraged to give feedback via the user interface. Very rapid cycles of iteration should lead to accelerated improvements in understanding of how the interfaces and the algorithms could be improved. A revolution in understanding of how to coach student writing could result!

Figure 1: Wordcraft user interface showing a farm scene with four characters, a fully formed sentence, the word tray with candidate additional words colored by part of speech, and tool bar. When the child completes a sentence correctly, the corresponding action is animated.

Algorithms could be designed to give feedback for partially completed work: partially written sentences in the case of a parser; partially completed paragraphs in the case of a discourse writing tool, and so on, rather than only assessing completed work after the fact.

3 Karaoke Anyone?

Beyond learning to write, new technology is changing other aspects of language learning in ways that should excite NLP researchers. In order to write well, a student must have a good vocabulary and must know syntax. Learning words and syntax requires exposure to language in many contexts, both spoken and written, for a student's primary language was well as for learning a second language.

Although computerized vocabulary tools have been around for quite some time, the rise of mobile, connected applications, the serious games movement, and the idea of "microtasks" which are done during interstices of time while out and about during the day, opens the door to new ways to expose students to repetitive learning tasks for acquiring language (Edge et al., 2011). Some of the most innovative approaches for teaching language combine mobile apps with multimedia information.

For example, the Tip Tap Tones project (Edge et al., 2012) attempts to help learners reduce the the challenge of mastering a foreign phonetic system by microtasking with minute-long episodes of mobile gaming. This work focuses in particular on helping learners acquire the tonal sound system of Mandarin Chinese and combines gesture swipes with audio on a smartphone.

The ToneWars app (Head et al., 2014) takes this idea one step farther by linking second language learners with native speakers in real time to play a Tretis-like game against one another to better learn Chinese pronunciation. The second language learner feels especially motivated when they are able to beat the native speaker, and the native speaker contributes their expert tone recordings to the database, fine-tunes their understanding of their own language, and enjoys the benefits of tutoring others in a fun context.

Going beyond phonemes, the DuoLingo second-language learning application (von Ahn, 2013) teaches syntax as well as vocabulary through a game-based interface. For instance, one of Duolingo's games consists of a display of a sentence in one language, and a jumbled list of words in the opposing language presented as cards to be dragged and dropped onto a tray in the correct order to form a sentence. In some cases the user must select between two confounding choices, such as the articles "le" or "la" to modify French nouns.

Our work on a game for children called WordCraft takes this idea one step further (Anand et al., 2015) (see Figure 1). Children manipulate word cards to build sentences which, when grammatically well formed, come to life in a storybook-like animated world to illustrate their meaning. Preliminary studies of the use of Wordcraft found that children between the ages of 4 and 8 were able to observe how different sentence constructions resulted in different meanings and encouraged children to engage in metalinguistic discourse, especially when playing the game with another child.

A karaoke-style video simulation is used by the Engkoo system to teach English to Chinese speakers (Wang et al., 2012). The interface not only generates audio for the English words, but also shows the lip and facial shapes necessary for forming English words using a 3D simulated model lip-syncing the words in a highly realistic manner. To generate a large number of sample sentences, the text was drawn from bilingual sentence pairs from the web.

These technologies have only become feasible recently because of the combination of multimedia, fast audio and image processing, fast network connectivity, and a connected population. NLP researchers may want to let their imaginations consider the possibilities that arise from this new and potent combination.

4 Closing the Cheese Gap

Salman Kahn, the creator of Kahn Academy, talks about the "Swiss cheese" model of learning in which students learn something only partly before they are forced to move on to the next topic, building knowledge on a foundation filled with holes, like the cheese of the same name (Khan, 2012). This is akin to learning to ride a bicycle without perfecting the balancing part. In standard schooling, students are made to move one from one lesson to the next even if they only got 70, 80, 90% correct on the test. By contrast, *mastery learning* requires a deep understanding, working with knowledge and probing it from every angle, trying out the ideas and applying them to solve real problems.

In many cases, mastery learning also requires practicing with dozens, hundreds, or even thousands of different examples, and getting feedback on those examples. Automation can help with mastery learning by generating personalized practice examples that challenge and interest students. Automatically generated examples also reduce the cost of creating new questions for instructors who are concerned about answer sharing among students from previous runs of a course.

Recently, sophisticated techniques developed in

the programming languages field have begun to be applied to automate repetitive and structured tasks in education, including problem generation, solution generation, and feedback generation for computer science and logic topics (Gulwani, 2014).

Closer to the subject at hand is the automated generation of mathematical word problems that are organized around themes of interest to kids, such as "School of Wizardry" (Polozov et al., 2015). The method allows the student to specify personal preferences about the world and characters, and then creates mini "plots" for each word problem by enforcing coherence across the sentences using constraints in a logic programming paradigm combined with hand-crafted discourse tropes (constraints on logical graphs) and a natural language generation step. A sample generated word problem is

> Professor Alice assigns Elliot to make a luck potion. He had to spend 9 hours first reading the recipe in the textbook. He spends several hours brewing 11 portions of it. The potion has to be brewed for 3 hours per portion. How many hours did Elliot spend in total?

Results are close in terms of comprehensibility and solubility to those of a textbook. The project's ultimate goal is to have the word problems actually tell a coherent story, but that challenge is still an open one. But the programs can generate an infinite number of problems with solutions. Other work by the same research team generated personalized algebraic equation problems in a game environment and showed that students could achieve mastery learning in 90 minutes or less during an organized educational campaign (Liu et al., 2015).

Another way that NLP can help with mastery learning is to aid instructors in the providing of feedback on short answer test questions. There has been significant work in this space (Kukich, 2000; Hirschman et al., 2000). The standard approach builds on the classic successful model of essay scoring which compares the student's text to model essays using a similarity-based technique such as LSA (Landauer et al., 2000; Mohler and Mihalcea, 2009) or careful authoring of the answer (Leacock and Chodorow, 2003).

Recent techniques pair with learning techniques like Inductive Logic Programming with instructor editing to induce logic rules that describe permissible answers with high accuracy (Willis, 2015). Unfortunately most approaches require quite a large number of students' answers to be marked up manually by the instructor before the feedback is accurate enough to be reliably used for a given question; a recent study found on the order of 500-800 items per question had to be marked up at minimum in order to obtain acceptable correlations with human scorers (Heilman and Madnani, 2015). This high initial cost makes the development of hundreds of practice questions for a given conceptual unit a daunting task for instructors.

Recent research in Learning at Scale has produced some interesting approaches to improving "feedback at scale." One approach (Brooks et al., 2014) uses a variation on hierarchical text clustering in tandem with a custom user interface that allows instructors to rapidly view clusters and determine which contain correct answers, incorrect answers, and partially correct answers. This greatly speeds up the markup time and allows instructors to assign explanations to a large group of answers with a click of a button.

An entirely different approach to providing feedback that is becoming heavily used in Massive Open Online Courses is peer feedback, in which students assign grades or give feedback to other students on their work (Hicks et al., 2015). Researchers have studied how to refine the process of peer feedback to train students to produce reviews that come within a grade point of that of instructors, with the aid of carefully designed rubrics (Kulkarni et al., 2013).

However, to ensure accurate feedback, several peer assessments per assignment are needed in addition to a training exercise, and students sometimes complain about workload. To reduce the effort, Kulkarni et al. (2014) experimented with a workflow that uses machine grading as a first step. After training a machine learning algorithm for a given assignment, assignments are scored by the algorithm. The less confident the algorithm is in its score, the more students are assigned to grade the assignment, but high-confidence assignments may need only one peer grader. This step was found to successfully reduce the amount of feedback needed to be done with a moderate decrease in grading performance. That said, the algorithm did require the instructors to mark up 500 sample assignments, and there is room for improvement in the algorithm in other ways, since only a first pass at NLP techniques was used to date.

Nonetheless, mixing machine and peer grading is a promising technique to explore, as it has been found to be useful in other contexts (Nguyen and Litman, 2014; Kukich, 2000).

5 Are You a FakeBot?

Why is the completion rate of MOOCs so low? This question vexes proponents and opponents of MOOCs alike. Counting the window shopping enrollees of a MOOC who do not complete a course is akin to counting everyone who visits a college campus as a failed graduate of that university; many people are just checking the course out (Jordan, 2014). That said, although the anytime, anywhere aspect of online courses works well for many busy professionals who are self-directed, research shows that most people need to learn in an environment that includes interacting with other people.

Learning with others can refer to instructors and tutors, and online tutoring systems have had success comparable to that of human tutors in some cases (VanLehn, 2011; Aleven et al., 2004). But another important component of learning with others refers to learning with other students. Literally hundreds of research papers show that an effective way to help students learn is to have them talk together in small groups, called structured peer learning, collaborative learning, or cooperative learning (Johnson et al., 1991; Lord, 1998). In the classroom, this consists of activities in which students confer in small groups to discuss conceptual questions and to engage in problem-solving. Studies and meta-analyses show the significant pedagogical benefit of peer learning including improved critical thinking skills, retention of learned information, interest in subject matter, and class morale (Hake, 1998; Millis and Cottell, 1998; Springer et al., 1999; Smith et al., 2009; Deslauriers et al., 2011). Even studies of intelligent tutoring systems find it hard to do better than just having students discuss homework problems in a structured setting online (Kumar et al., 2007).

The reasons for the success of peer learning include: students are at similar levels of understanding that experts can no longer relate to well, people learn material better when they have to explain it to others, and identify the gaps in their current understanding, and the techniques of structured peer learning introduce activities and incentives to help students help one another.

S2	I think E is the right answer
S1	Hi, I think E is right, too
S3	Hi! This seems to be a nurture vs nature question.
S3	Can scent be learned, or only at birth?
S2	Yeah, but answer A supports the author's conclusion
S1	I felt that about A too
S2	But the question was, which statement would weaken the author's conclusion
S3	So I choose A, showing that scent can be learned at not only AT BIRTH.
S2	That's why I think E is right
S3	Are you real, or fake?
S2	real
S1	I didn't think that b or d had anything to do with the statement
S3	Actually what you said makes sense.
S1	So, do we all agree that E was the correct answer?
S2	I think so, yes.
S3	But I'm sticking with A since "no other water could stimulate olfactory sites" abd I suggests that other water could be detected.
S3	*and
S1	I thought about c for awhile but it didn't really seem to have anything to do with the topic of scent
S3	It has to be A or E. Other ones don't have anything do do with the question.
S2	but that "no other water" thing applies equally well to E
S3	E is still about spawing ground water, I think. this is a confusing question.
S1	I thought E contradicted the statement the most
S2	me too
S3	I loving hits with other mturkers

Table 1: Transcript of a conversation among three crowdworkers who discussed the options for a multiple choice question for a GMAT logical reasoning task. Note the meta-discussion about the prevalence of robots on the crowdsourcing platform.

In our MOOCChat research, we were interested in bringing structured peer learning into the MOOC setting. We first tried out the idea on a crowdsourcing platform (Coetzee et al., 2015), showing that when groups of 3 workers discussed challenging problems together, and especially if they were incentivized to help each other arrive at the correct answer, they achieved better results than working alone. (A sample conversation is shown in Table 1.) We also found that providing a *mini-lesson* in which workers consider the principles underlying the tested concept and justify their answers leads to further improvements, and combining the mini-lesson with the discussion of the corresponding multiple-choice question in a group of 3 leads to significant improvements on that question. Crowd workers also expressed positive subjective responses to the peer interactions, suggesting that discussions can improve morale in remote work or learning settings.

When we tested the synchronous small-group discussions in a live MOOC we found that, for those students that were successfully placed into a group of 3 for discussion, they were quite positive about the experience (Lim et al., 2014). However, there are significant challenges in getting students to coordinate synchronously in very large low-cost courses (Kotturi et al., 2015).

There is much NLP research to be done to enhance the online dialogues that are associated with student discussion text beyond the traditional role of intelligent tutoring systems. One idea is to monitor discussions in real time and try to shape the way the group works together (Tausczik and Pennebaker, 2013). Another idea is to automatically assess if students are discussing content at appropriate levels on Bloom's taxonomy of educational objectives (Krathwohl, 2002).

In our MOOCChat work with triad discussions we observed that more workers will change their answer from an incorrect to a correct one if at least one member of the group starts out correct than if no one is correct initially (Hearst et al., 2015). We also noticed that if all group members start out with the same answer — right or wrong — no one is likely to change their answer in any direction. This behavior pattern suggests an interesting idea for large scale online group discussions that are not feasible in in-person environments: dynamically assign students to groups depending on what their initial answers to questions are, and dynamically regroup students according to the misconceptions and correct conceptions they have. Rather than building an intelligent tutoring system to prompt students with just the right statement at just the right time, a more successful strategy might be to mix students with other poeple who for that particular discussion point have the just the right level of conceptual understanding to move the group forward.

6 Conclusions

In this paper I am suggesting inverting the standard mode of our field from that of processing, correcting, identifying, and generating aspects of language to one of recognizing what a person is doing with language: NLP algorithms as coaches rather than critics. I have outlined a number of specific suggestions for research that are currently outside the mainstream of NLP research but which pose challenges that I think some of my colleagues will find interesting. Among these are text analyzers that explain what is wrong with an essay at the clause, sentence, discourse level as the student writes it, promoting mastery learning by generating unlimited practice problems, with answers, in a form that makes practice fun, and using NLP to improve the manner in which peers learning takes place online. The field of learning and education is being disrupted, and NLP researchers should be helping push the frontiers.

Acknowledgements I thank the ACL program chairs Michael Strube and Chengqing Zong for inviting me to write this paper and keynote talk, Lucy Vanderwende for suggested references, and colleagues at NAACL 2015 for discussing these ideas with me. This research is supported in part by a Google Social Interactions Grant.

References

Vincent Aleven, Amy Ogan, Octav Popescu, Cristen Torrey, and Kenneth Koedinger. 2004. Evaluating the effectiveness of a tutorial dialogue system for self-explanation. In *Intelligent tutoring systems*, pages 443–454. Springer.

Divya Anand, Shreyas, Sonali Sharma, Victor Starostenko, Ashley DeSouza, Kimiko Ryokai, and Marti A. Hearst. 2015. *Wordcraft: Playing with Sentence Structure*. Under review.

Lars Borin. 2002. *What have you done for me lately? The fickle alignment of NLP and CALL*. Reports from Uppsala Learning Lab.

Michael Brooks, Sumit Basu, Charles Jacobs, and Lucy Vanderwende. 2014. Divide and correct: Using clusters to grade short answers at scale. In *Proceedings of the first ACM conference on Learning@Scale*, pages 89–98. ACM.

D Coetzee, Seongtaek Lim, Armando Fox, Bjorn Hartmann, and Marti A Hearst. 2015. Structuring interactions for large-scale synchronous peer learning. In *Proceedings of the 18th ACM Conference on Computer Supported Cooperative Work & Social Computing*, pages 1139–1152. ACM.

Robert Dale and Adam Kilgarriff. 2011. Helping our own: The HOO 2011 pilot shared task. In *Proceedings of the 13th European Workshop on Natural Language Generation*, pages 242–249. Association for Computational Linguistics.

Robert Dale, Ilya Anisimoff, and George Narroway. 2012. HOO 2012: A report on the preposition and determiner error correction shared task. In *Proceedings of the Seventh Workshop on Building Educational Applications Using NLP*, pages 54–62. Association for Computational Linguistics.

Louis Deslauriers, Ellen Schelew, and Carl Wieman. 2011. Improved learning in a large-enrollment physics class. *Science*, 332(6031):862–864.

Darren Edge, Elly Searle, Kevin Chiu, Jing Zhao, and James A Landay. 2011. Micromandarin: mobile language learning in context. In *Proceedings of the SIGCHI Conference on Human Factors in Computing Systems*, pages 3169–3178. ACM.

Darren Edge, Kai-Yin Cheng, Michael Whitney, Yao Qian, Zhijie Yan, and Frank Soong. 2012. Tip tap tones: mobile microtraining of mandarin sounds. In *Proceedings of the 14th International Conference on Human-Computer Interaction with Mobile Devices and Services*, pages 427–430. ACM.

Sumit Gulwani. 2014. Example-based learning in computer-aided stem education. *Communications of the ACM*, 57(8):70–80.

Richard R Hake. 1998. Interactive-engagement versus traditional methods: A six-thousand-student survey of mechanics test data for introductory physics courses. *American Journal of Physics*, 66(1):64–74.

Andrew Head, Yi Xu, and Jingtao Wang. 2014. Tonewars: Connecting language learners and native speakers through collaborative mobile games. In *Intelligent Tutoring Systems*, pages 368–377. Springer.

Marti A Hearst, Armando Fox, D Coetzee, and Bjoern Hartmann. 2015. All it takes is one: Evidence for a strategy for seeding large scale peer learning interactions. In *Proceedings of the Second (2015) ACM Conference on Learning@Scale*, pages 381–383. ACM.

George Heidorn. 2000. Intelligent writing assistance. *Handbook of Natural Language Processing*, pages 181–207.

Michael Heilman and Nitin Madnani. 2015. The impact of training data on automated short answer scoring performance. In *Proceedings of the Tenth Workshop on Building Educational Applications Using NLP*. Association for Computational Linguistics.

Catherine M Hicks, C Ailie Fraser, Purvi Desai, and Scott Klemmer. 2015. Do numeric ratings impact peer reviewers? In *Proceedings of the Second (2015) ACM Conference on Learning@ Scale*, pages 359–362. ACM.

Lynette Hirschman, Eric Breck, Marc Light, John D Burger, and Lisa Ferro. 2000. Automated grading of short-answer tests. *Intelligent Systems and their Applications, IEEE*, 15(5):22–37.

David W Johnson, Roger T Johnson, and Karl Aldrich Smith. 1991. *Active learning: Cooperation in the college classroom.* Interaction Book Company Edina, MN.

Katy Jordan. 2014. Initial trends in enrolment and completion of massive open online courses. *The International Review Of Research In Open And Distributed Learning*, 15(1).

Salman Khan. 2012. *The One World Schoolhouse: Education Reimagined.* Twelve.

Yasmine Kotturi, Chinmay Kulkarni, Michael S Bernstein, and Scott Klemmer. 2015. Structure and messaging techniques for online peer learning systems that increase stickiness. In *Proceedings of the Second (2015) ACM Conference on Learning@ Scale*, pages 31–38. ACM.

David R Krathwohl. 2002. A revision of Bloom's taxonomy: An overview. *Theory into practice*, 41(4):212–218.

Karen Kukich. 2000. Beyond automated essay scoring. *IEEE Intelligent Systems and their Applications, IEEE*, 15(5):22–27.

Chinmay Kulkarni, Koh Pang Wei, Huy Le, Daniel Chia, Kathryn Papadopoulos, Justin Cheng, Daphne Koller, and Scott R Klemmer. 2013. Peer and self assessment in massive online classes. In *ACM Transactions on Computer Human Interaction (TOCHI)*, volume 20. ACM.

Chinmay E Kulkarni, Richard Socher, Michael S Bernstein, and Scott R Klemmer. 2014. Scaling short-answer grading by combining peer assessment with algorithmic scoring. In *Proceedings of the first ACM conference on Learning@Scale*, pages 99–108. ACM.

Rohit Kumar, Carolyn Penstein Rosé, Yi-Chia Wang, Mahesh Joshi, and Allen Robinson. 2007. Tutorial dialogue as adaptive collaborative learning support. *Frontiers in Artificial Intelligence and Applications*, 158:383.

Thomas K Landauer, Darrell Laham, and Peter W Foltz. 2000. The intelligent essay assessor. *IEEE Intelligent Systems and their Applications, IEEE*, 15(5):22–27.

Claudia Leacock and Martin Chodorow. 2003. C-rater: Automated scoring of short-answer questions. *Computers and the Humanities*, 37(4):389–405.

Seongtaek Lim, Derrick Coetzee, Bjoern Hartmann, Armando Fox, and Marti A Hearst. 2014. Initial experiences with small group discussions in moocs. In *Proceedings of the first ACM conference on Learning@Scale*, pages 151–152. ACM.

Yun-En Liu, Christy Ballweber, Eleanor O'rourke, Eric Butler, Phonraphee Thummaphan, and Zoran Popović. 2015. Large-scale educational campaigns. *ACM Transactions on Computer-Human Interaction (TOCHI)*, 22(2):8.

Thomas Lord. 1998. Cooperative learning that really works in biology teaching: using constructivist-based activities to challenge student teams. *The American Biology Teacher*, 60(8):580–588.

Detmar Meurers. 2012. Natural language processing and language learning. In *The Encyclopedia of Applied Linguistics*. Wiley Online Library.

Barbara J Millis and Philip G Cottell. 1998. *Cooperative learning for higher education faculty*. Oryx Press (Phoenix, Ariz.).

Michael Mohler and Rada Mihalcea. 2009. Text-to-text semantic similarity for automatic short answer grading. In *Proceedings of the 12th Conference of the European Chapter of the Association for Computational Linguistics*, pages 567–575. Association for Computational Linguistics.

Hwee Tou Ng, Siew Mei Wu, Yuanbin Wu, Christian Hadiwinoto, and Joel Tetreault. 2014. The CoNLL-2013 shared task on grammatical error correction. In *Proceedings of the Eighteenth Conference on Computational Natural Language Learning: Shared Task (CoNLL-2014 Shared Task)*, pages 1–12.

Huy V Nguyen and Diane J Litman. 2014. Improving peer feedback prediction: The sentence level is right. *ACL 2014*, page 99.

Oleksandr Polozov, Eleanor ORourke, Adam M Smith, Luke Zettlemoyer, Sumit Gulwani, and Zoran Popovic. 2015. Personalized mathematical word problem generation. In *Proceedings of the 24th International Joint Conference on Artificial Intelligence (IJCAI 2015)*. To appear.

Camilla Schwind. 1988. Sensitive parsing: error analysis and explanation in an intelligent language tutoring system. In *Proceedings of the 12th conference on Computational Linguistics-Volume 2*, pages 608–613. Association for Computational Linguistics.

Serge Sharoff, Stefania Spina, and Sofie Johansson Kokkinakis. 2014. Introduction to the special issue on resources and tools for language learners. *Language Resources and Evaluation*, 48(1):1–3.

Michelle K Smith, William B Wood, Wendy K Adams, Carl Wieman, Jennifer K Knight, Nancy Guild, and Tin Tin Su. 2009. Why peer discussion improves student performance on in-class concept questions. *Science*, 323(5910):122–124.

Leonard Springer, Mary Elizabeth Stanne, and Samuel S Donovan. 1999. Effects of small-group learning on undergraduates in science, mathematics, engineering, and technology: A meta-analysis. *Review of educational research*, 69(1):21–51.

Yla R Tausczik and James W Pennebaker. 2013. Improving teamwork using real-time language feedback. In *Proceedings of the SIGCHI Conference on Human Factors in Computing Systems*, pages 459–468. ACM.

Joel Tetreault, Jill Burstein, and Claudia Leacock. 2015. *Proceedings of the Tenth Workshop on Building Educational Applications Using NLP*. Association for Computational Linguistics.

Kurt VanLehn. 2011. The relative effectiveness of human tutoring, intelligent tutoring systems, and other tutoring systems. *Educational Psychologist*, 46(4):197–221.

Luis von Ahn. 2013. Duolingo: learn a language for free while helping to translate the web. In *Proceedings of the 2013 International Conference on Intelligent User Interfaces*, pages 1–2. ACM.

Lijuan Wang, Yao Qian, Matthew R Scott, Gang Chen, and Frank K Soong. 2012. Computer-assisted audiovisual language learning (with online video). *Computer*, 45(6):38–47.

Alistair Willis. 2015. Using nlp to support scalable assessment of short free text responses. In *Proceedings of the Tenth Workshop on Building Educational Applications Using NLP*. Association for Computational Linguistics.

Machine Comprehension with Discourse Relations

Karthik Narasimhan
CSAIL, MIT
karthikn@csail.mit.edu

Regina Barzilay
CSAIL, MIT
regina@csail.mit.edu

Abstract

This paper proposes a novel approach for incorporating discourse information into machine comprehension applications. Traditionally, such information is computed using off-the-shelf discourse analyzers. This design provides limited opportunities for guiding the discourse parser based on the requirements of the target task. In contrast, our model induces relations between sentences while optimizing a task-specific objective. This approach enables the model to benefit from discourse information without relying on explicit annotations of discourse structure during training. The model jointly identifies relevant sentences, establishes relations between them and predicts an answer. We implement this idea in a discriminative framework with hidden variables that capture relevant sentences and relations unobserved during training. Our experiments demonstrate that the discourse aware model outperforms state-of-the-art machine comprehension systems.[1]

1 Introduction

The task of machine comprehension concerns the automatic extraction of answers from a given passage. Often, the relevant information required to answer a question is distributed across multiple sentences. Understanding the relation(s) between these sentences is key to finding the correct answer. Consider the example in fig. 1. To answer the question about *why Sally put on her shoes* , we need to infer that *She put on her shoes* and *She went outside to walk* are connected by a causality relation.

Sally liked going outside. She put on her shoes. She went outside to walk. [...] Missy the cat meowed to Sally. Sally waved to Missy the cat. [...] Sally hears her name. "Sally, Sally, come home", Sally's mom calls out. Sally runs home to her Mom. Sally liked going outside.

Why did Sally put on her shoes?
A) To wave to Missy the cat
B) To hear her name
C) *Because she wanted to go outside*
D) To come home

Figure 1: Sample story excerpt from a passage in the MCTest dataset.[2] Correct answer is in italics.

Prior work has demonstrated the value of discourse relations in related applications such as question answering (Jansen et al., 2014). Traditionally, however, these approaches rely on outputs from off-the-shelf discourse analyzers, using them as features for target applications. Such pipeline designs provide limited opportunities for guiding the discourse parser based on the requirements of the end task. Given a wide spectrum of discourse frameworks (Mann and Thompson, 1988; Prasad et al., 2008; Wolf and Gibson, 2005), it is not clear a priori what the optimal set of discourse annotations is for the task. Moreover, a generic discourse parser may introduce additional errors due to the mismatch between its training corpus and a dataset used in an application. In fact, the largest discourse treebanks are based on newspaper corpora (Prasad et al., 2008; Carlson et al., 2002), which differ significantly in style from text used in machine comprehension corpora (Richardson et al., 2013).

In this paper, we propose a novel approach for incorporating discourse structure into machine

[1] Code and data are available at http://people.csail.mit.edu/karthikn/mcdr.

[2] http://research.microsoft.com/en-us/um/redmond/projects/mctest/

Proceedings of the 53rd Annual Meeting of the Association for Computational Linguistics and the 7th International Joint Conference on Natural Language Processing, pages 1253–1262, Beijing, China, July 26-31, 2015.

comprehension applications. Rather than using a standalone parser that is trained on external supervised data to annotate discourse relations, the model induces relations between sentences while optimizing a task-specific objective. This design biases the model to learn relations at a granularity optimized for the machine comprehension task. In contrast to a generic discourse analyzer, our method can also utilize additional information available in the machine comprehension context. For instance, question types provide valuable cues for determining discourse relations, and thus can facilitate learning.

We implement these ideas in a discriminative log-linear model with hidden variables. The model jointly identifies relevant sentences, establishes relations between them and predicts an answer. Since the same set of sentences can give rise to multiple questions, we do not limit the model to a single discourse relation, but rather model a distribution over possible relations. During training, we only have access to questions and gold answers. Since relevant sentences and their relations are not known, we model them as hidden variables. To guide the model towards linguistically plausible discourse relations, we add a few seed markers that are typical of each relation. The model predicts relations not only based on the sentences, but also incorporates information about the question. By decomposing the dependencies between model components, we can effectively train the model using a standard gradient descent approach.

We evaluate our model using a recently released machine comprehension dataset (Richardson et al., 2013). In this corpus, roughly half of the questions rely on multiple sentences in the passage to generate the correct answer. For baselines, we use the best published results on this dataset. Our results demonstrate that our relation-aware model outperforms the individual baselines by up to 5.7% and rivals the performance of a state-of-the-art combination system. Moreover, we show that the discourse relations it predicts for sentence pairs exhibit considerable overlap with relations identified by human annotators.

2 Related Work

Machine Comprehension Following traditional methods in question answering, most approaches to machine comprehension focus on analyzing the connection between the question, candidate answer and the document. For instance, Richardson et al. (2013) show that using word overlap alone provides a good starting point for the task. Using textual entailment output (Stern and Dagan, 2011) and embedding-based representations (Iyyer et al., 2014) further improves the result. Even though these methods operate at a paragraph level, they do not model relations between sentences. For instance, in their work on factoid question answering using recursive neural networks, Iyyer et al. (2014) average the sentence vectors element-wise when considering more than one sentence.

A notable exception is the approach proposed by Berant et al. (2014). Their approach builds on a semantic representation that encodes a number of inter-event relations, such as *cause* and *enable*. These relations straddle the boundary between discourse and semantic connections, since most of them are specific to the domain of interest. These relations are identified in a supervised fashion using a significant amount of manual annotations. In contrast, we are interested in extracting discourse relations with minimal additional annotation, relying primarily on the available question-answer pairs. As a result, we look at a smaller set of basic relations that can be learned without explicit annotations.

Discourse analysis for Question Answering Prior work has established the value of domain-independent discourse relations in question answering applications (Verberne et al., 2007; Jansen et al., 2014; Chai and Jin, 2004). For instance, Verberne et al. (2007) propose an answer extraction technique that treats question topics and answers as siblings in a Rhetorical Structure Theory (RST) tree, significantly improving performance on *why*-questions. Chai and Jin (2004) argue that incorporating discourse processing can significantly help context question answering, a task in which subsequent questions may refer to entities or concepts in previous questions. Jansen et al. (2014) utilize discourse information to improve reranking of human-written answers for non-factoid questions. They experiment with both shallow discourse markers and deep representations based on RST parsers to rerank answers for *how* and *why*-type questions[3].

While the above approaches vary greatly in

[3]They use data from Yahoo! Answers and a Biology textbook.

terms of their design, they incorporate discourse information in a similar fashion, adding it as features to a supervised model. The discourse information is typically computed using discourse parsers based on frameworks like RST (Feng and Hirst, 2014) or PDTB (Lin et al., 2014), trained using supervised data. In contrast, our goal is to learn discourse relations driven by the task objective. The set of these relations does not capture the richness of discourse representations considered in traditional discourse theories (Mann and Thompson, 1988; Prasad et al., 2008). However, we learn them without explicit annotations of discourse structure, and demonstrate that they improve model performance.

3 Task Description and Approach

We focus on the task of machine comprehension, which involves answering questions based on a passage of text. Concretely, let us consider a passage $p_i = \{\mathcal{Z}_i, \mathcal{Q}_i\}$ to consist of a set of sentences $\mathcal{Z}_i = \{z_{in}\}$ and a set of questions $\mathcal{Q}_i = \{q_{ij}\}$, with each question also having a set of answer choices $\mathcal{A}_{ij} = \{a_{ijk}\}$. We denote the correct answer choice for a question q_{ij} as a^*_{ij}. Given a set of training passages $\mathcal{P}_{train}$ with questions annotated with the correct answer choice, the task is to be able to answer questions accurately in a different set of passages $\mathcal{P}_{test}$.

Figure 1 shows an example of a passage, along with a question and answer choices. The only (weak) source of supervision available is the correct answer choice for each question in training. We do not use any extra annotations during training. We propose joint probabilistic models to address this task, that can learn to identify single or multiple relevant sentences given a question, establish a relation between them and score the answer choices.

We explore three different discriminative models, ranging from a simple one that answers questions using a single sentence in the passage, to one that infers relations between multiple sentences to score answer choices. We defer the description of the features used in our models to section 3.1.

Model 1 In our first model, we assume that each question can be answered using a single sentence from the passage. Treating the sentence as a hidden variable, we define a joint model for a sentence $z \in \mathcal{Z}$ and an answer choice $a \in \mathcal{A}_j$, given a question q_j.

$$P(a, z \mid q_j) = P(z \mid q_j) \cdot P(a \mid z, q_j) \quad (1)$$

We define the joint probability as a product of two distributions. The first is the conditional distribution of sentences in the paragraph given the question. This is to help identify the right sentence required to answer the question. The second component models the conditional probability of an answer given the question q and a sentence z. For both component probabilities, we use distributions from the exponential family with features and associated weights:

$$P(z \mid q) \propto e^{\theta_1 \cdot \phi_1(q,z)}$$
$$P(a \mid z, q) \propto e^{\theta_2 \cdot \phi_2(q,a,z)}$$

where ϕs are the feature functions and θs are the corresponding weight vectors.

We cast the learning problem as estimation of the parameter weights to maximize the likelihood of the correct answers in the training data. We consider soft assignments to z and marginalize over all its values to get the likelihood of an answer choice:

$$P(a_{jk} \mid q_j) = \sum_n P(a_{jk}, z_n \mid q_j) \quad (3)$$

This results in the following regularized likelihood objective to maximize:

$$L_1(\theta; \mathcal{P}_{train}) = \log \sum_{i=1}^{|\mathcal{P}_{train}|} \sum_{j=1}^{|\mathcal{Q}_i|} P(a^*_{ij} \mid q_{ij}) - \lambda ||\theta||^2 \quad (4)$$

Model 2 We now propose a model for the multi-sentence case where we make use of more than a single relevant sentence pertaining to a question. Considering that a majority of the questions in the dataset can be answered using two sentences, we restrict ourselves to sentence pairs for purposes of computational tractability. We define the new joint model as:

$$P(a, z_1, z_2 \mid q) = P(z_1 \mid q) \cdot P(z_2 \mid z_1, q) \cdot P(a \mid z_1, z_2, q) \quad (5)$$

where the new components are also exponential-family distributions:

$$P(z_2 \mid z_1, q) \propto e^{\theta_3 \cdot \phi_3(q,z_1,z_2)}$$
$$P(a \mid z_1, z_2, q) \propto e^{\theta_2 \cdot \phi_2(q,a,z_1,z_2)}$$

Here, we have three components: the conditional probability of a sentence z_1 given q, of a second sentence z_2 given q and z_1, and of the answer a given q and the sentences.[4] Ideally, we would be able to consider all possible pairs of sentences in a given paragraph. However, to reduce computation costs in practice, we use a sentence window k and consider only sentences that are at most k away from each other.[5] We hence maximize:

$$L_2(\theta; \mathcal{P}_{train}) = \log \sum_{i=1,j=1,m=1}^{|\mathcal{P}_{train}|,|\mathcal{Q}_i|,|\mathcal{Z}_i|} \sum_{n \in [m-k, m+k]} P(a^*_{ij}, z_{im}, z_{in} \mid q_{ij}) - \lambda ||\theta||^2 \quad (7)$$

Model 3 In our next model, we aim to capture important relations between sentences. This model has two novel aspects. First, we consider a distribution over relations between sentence pairs as opposed to a single relation. Second, we utilize the cues from the question as context to resolve ambiguities in sentences pairs with multiple plausible relations.

We add in a hidden variable $r \in \mathcal{R}$ to represent the relation type. We incorporate features that tie in the question type with the relation type, and that connect the type of relation to the lexical and syntactic similarities between sentences. Our relation set $\mathcal{R}$ consists of the following relations:

- *Causal* : Causes of events or reasons for facts.
- *Temporal* : Time-ordering of events
- *Explanation* : Predominantly dealing with *how*-type questions.
- *Other* : A relation other than the above[6]

We can now modify the joint probability from (5) by adding in relation type r to get:

$$P(a, r, z_1, z_2 \mid q) = P(z_1 \mid q) \cdot P(r \mid q) \cdot P(z_2 \mid z_1, r, q) \cdot P(a \mid z_1, z_2, r, q) \quad (8)$$

where

$$P(r \mid q) \propto e^{\theta_4 \cdot \phi_4(q,r)} \quad (9a)$$

$$P(z_2 \mid z_1, r, q) \propto e^{\theta_3 \cdot \phi_3(q,r,z_1,z_2)} \quad (9b)$$

$$P(a \mid z_1, z_2, r, q) \propto e^{\theta_2 \cdot \phi_2(q,r,a,z_1,z_2)} \quad (9c)$$

The extra component $P(r \mid q)$ is the conditional distribution of the relation type r depending on the question. This is to encourage the model to learn, for instance, that *why*-questions correspond to the *causal* relation. We also add in extra features to $P(z_2 \mid z_1, r)$, that help select a sentence pair conditioned on a relation. The likelihood objective to maximize is:

$$L_3(\theta; \mathcal{P}_{train}) = \log \sum_{i,j,m,r \in \mathcal{R}} \sum_{n \in [m-k, m+k]} P(a^*_{ij}, z_{im}, z_{in}, r \mid q_{ij}) - \lambda ||\theta||^2 \quad (10)$$

We maximize the likelihood objectives using LBFGS-B (Byrd et al., 1995). We compute the gradients required using Automatic Differentiation (Corliss, 2002).

To predict an answer for a test question q_j, we simply marginalize over all the hidden variables and choose the answer that maximizes $P(a_{jk} \mid q_j)$:

$$\hat{a}_j = \underset{k}{argmax}\ P(a_{jk} | q_j)$$

3.1 Features

We use a variety of lexical and syntactic features in our model. We employ the Stanford CoreNLP tool (Manning et al., 2014) to pre-process the data. Other than commonly used features in Q&A systems such as unigram and bigram matches, part-of-speech tags, syntactic features, we also add in features specific to our model.

We first define some terms used in our description. *Entities* are coreference-resolved nouns or pronouns. *Actions* refer to verbs other than auxiliary ones such as *is, are, was* and *were*. An *entity graph* is a graph between entities present in a sentence. We create an entity graph by collapsing nodes in the dependency graph and storing the intermediate nodes between any two entity nodes in the edge between the nodes. We refer to the words in a question q as q-words and similarly to words in an answer a as a-words and those in a sentence z as z-words. Figure 2 shows an example of an entity graph constructed from the dependency graph of a sentence.

We divide the features into 4 sets (ϕ_{1-4}), corresponding to each component probability in (8). Types 1 and 2 are inspired by prior work in question classification/answering (Blunsom et al., 2006; Jansen et al., 2014). Feature types 3 and 4 are specific to our models, primarily dealing with relation types.

[4]Since this component replaces the second component in model 1, we use the same subscript 2 for its feature set ϕ.

[5]Including the case where $z_1 = z_2$.

[6]This includes the no-relation cases

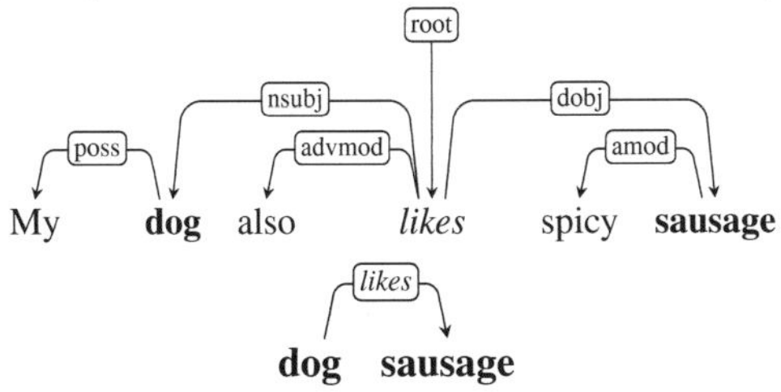

Figure 2: **Top**: Dependency graph, **Bottom**: Entity graph for an example sentence. Entities are in bold, actions are in italics.

Relation	Word list
Causal	because, why, due, so
Temporal	when, between, soon, before, after, during, then, finally, now, nowadays, first
Explanation	how, by, using

Table 1: Seed marker words for relations used by the model.

Type 1 (ϕ_1) These features are primarily intended to help the model select the most relevant sentence from the passage for a question. We add commonly used features such as unigram and bigram matches, syntactic root match, entity and action matches, missed entities/actions (in q but absent in z) and fractional coverage of q-words in z. In addition, we use matches between the edges of the entity graph of q and z. We also have second-order features that are a cross of each feature mentioned above with the question word (*how, what, when*, etc.).

Type 2 (ϕ_2) Features in ϕ_2 capture interactions between the answer a, question q and sentence(s) (z_1, z_2 in models 2,3 or z in model 1). For the first-order features, we use ones similar to those in ϕ_1 for lexical, syntactic, entity and action matches/misses between a and z. In addition, we add in a *neighbor match* feature, which checks for matches between the neighborhood of a word from a that occurs in z, and q-words. Another feature we employ is the *joint match* between z-words and the union of a-words and q-words. Finally, we add in a sliding window (*SW*) feature, computing its value as in Richardson et al. (2013).

Type 3 (ϕ_3) The next set of features are specific to only models 2 and 3, used to connect sentences z_1 and z_2 (and a relation r in model 3 only).

Split	MC160		MC500	
	Passages	Questions	Passages	Questions
Train	70	280	300	1200
Dev	30	120	50	200
Test	60	240	150	600

Table 2: Dataset Statistics

We use features like the inter-sentence distance and the presence of relation-specific markers in the sentences. We also cross the latter features with *entity* and *action* matches between z_1 and z_2. For the relation-specific words for each relation (except *Other*), we use words (see Table 1) derived mainly from Marcu (1997)'s list of discourse markers.

Type 4 (ϕ_4) The final set of features (used only in model 3) are present to help the model learn connections between the words in the question and the relation type r. Specifically, we check if the interrogative word in the question matches the class represented by r. For instance, the word *why* matches the *Causal* relation.

For the match-type features of all four types, we use the match count as the feature value if the count is non-zero. If the count is zero, we instead set a corresponding *zero* feature[7] to 1.

4 Experimental setup

Data and Setup We run our experiments on a recently compiled dataset for machine comprehension: MCTest (Richardson et al., 2013). The data consists of two distinct sets: MC160 and MC500, which are of different sizes. Table 2 gives details on the data splits for each dataset. Each passage has 4 questions, with 4 answer choices each. The questions are also annotated into 2 types: *single*, if the question can be answered using a single sentence in the passage, or *multi* otherwise. We do not use the type information in our learning; we only use it for categorizing accuracy during evaluation. We report final results on all our models trained with $\lambda = 0.1$, tuned using the Dev sets.

Evaluation We report accuracy scores for each model averaged over the questions in the test data. For each question, the system gains 1 point if it scores the correct answer highest and 0 otherwise. In case of ties, we use an inverse weighting

[7]For each match feature, like *Entity-Match*, we have a corresponding *zero* feature, *Entity-Match-Zero*

Model	MC160						MC500					
	dev			test			dev			test		
	Single	Multi	All	Single	Multi	All	Single	Multi	All	Single	Multi	All
SWD	67.92	50.74	58.33	75.89	60.15	67.5	63.95	54.38	58.5	63.23	57.62	60.16
RTE	64.15	53.73	58.33	57.14	59.37	58.33	58.13	47.36	52	70.22	42.37	55
RTE+SWD	71.69	59.6	65	76.78	62.5	69.16	73.25	57.89	64.5	68.01	59.45	63.33
Model 1	**78.45**	**60.57**	**68.47**	**83.25**	60.35	71.04†	**74.41**	57.01	64.5†	**70.58**	57.77	63.58†
Model 2	74.68	60.07	66.52	81.47	64.25	72.29†	73.25	**61.4**	**66.5***†	66.17	**59.9**	62.75†
M2 + RST	72.79	58.58	64.86	79.68	61.91	70.20†	72.09	57.89	64.0†	66.54	59.29	62.58
Model 3	72.79	60.07	65.69	82.36	**65.23**	**73.23***†	72.09	60.52	65.5*†	68.38	**59.9**	**63.75**†

Table 3: Accuracy (%) of the different baselines (in italics) and our models. **Single**: questions requiring single sentence to answer; **Multi**: questions requiring multiple sentences to answer. Sentence window (k) = 4 for models 2 and 3. Best scores are shown in bold. Statistical significance (shown only for *All* columns) of $p < 0.05$ using two-tailed paired t-test: *vs *SWD*, †vs *RTE*.

scheme to assign partial credit. So, if three answers (including the correct one) tie for the highest score, the system gains 1/3 points.

Baselines We use the systems proposed by Richardson et al. (2013) as our baselines. These systems have the best reported scores on this dataset. The first baseline, *SWD*, uses a sliding window to count matches between the passage words and the words in the answer. This is then combined with a score representing the average distance between answer and question words in the passage. The second baseline, *RTE*, uses a *textual entailment* recognizer (Stern and Dagan, 2011) to determine if the answer (turned into a statement along with the question) is entailed by the passage. The third system, *RTE+SWD*, is a weighted combination of the first two baselines and achieves the highest accuracy on the dataset.

5 Results

Comprehension accuracy Table 3 shows that our relation-aware model 3 outperforms individual baselines on both test sets. On the MC160 test set, the model achieves the best performance of 73.23% accuracy, outperforming the *SWD* baseline by 5.7% and the *RTE+SWD* combination by 4.07%. The major gains of model 3, which utilizes inter-sentential relations, over model 1 can be seen in the accuracy of *multi* type questions with a jump of almost 5% absolute in accuracy (statistically significant with $p < 0.05$). On the MC500 test set, we again find that model 3, with a score of 63.75%, provides a gain of 3.5% over *SWD* and is comparable to the performance of *RTE+SWD* (63.33%)

The importance of utilizing multiple relevant sentences to score answers is evident from the higher scores of models 2 and 3 on *multi* type questions in both test sets. However, model 1, which retrieves only a single relevant sentence for each question, achieves the best scores on the *single* type questions up to 83.25% on MC160 test. One reason for this could be the larger search space for model 3 over pairs of sentences compared to just single sentences for model 1.

Table 4 shows the variation of our model's accuracy with the question type. We see that the model deals well with *what, where* and *why* type questions in MC500, achieving almost 67-69% accuracy.[8] The major errors (in MC500) seem to come from the *how*-questions, where the model's accuracy is low (48%). In MC160, the accuracy is even higher for *what*-questions (almost 80%). On the other hand, the model does slightly worse on *why*-questions, with only 60% accuracy.

RST augmented model Further, we experiment with adding in relations extracted by a publicly available RST parser (Feng and Hirst, 2012). The parser extracts a tree with the passage sentences as its leaves and relations as interior nodes in the tree. From this tree, we compute the relation between a pair of sentences as their lowest common ancestor. If one of the sentences is broken down into clauses, we use them all to gather multiple relations. We add in features that combine the RST-predicted relation with the interrogation word of the question, and with entity and action matches between sentence pairs.

We can see from Table 3 that adding in RST features to model 2 (M2+RST) does not give the

[8]Note that *what*-questions may also require causal/temporal/explanation relations to answer.

Question Type	MC160		MC500	
	Dev	Test	Dev	Test
how	50.00 (10)	71.42 (21)	54.54 (11)	48.83 (43)
what	64.40 (59)	79.36 (126)	63.15 (114)	67.19 (317)
where	30.76 (13)	91.66 (12)	82.60 (23)	68.96 (58)
which	75.00 (4)	33.33 (6)	25.00 (4)	48.00 (25)
who	70.50 (17)	67.85 (28)	62.50 (16)	59.74 (77)
why	85.71 (14)	59.45 (37)	65.38 (26)	69.35 (62)
when	100.0 (2)	80.00 (5)	100.0 (4)	62.50 (8)
whose	-	-	-	66.67 (3)
(other)	100.0 (1)	40.00 (5)	50.00 (2)	14.28 (7)

Table 4: Accuracy (%) of model 3 by question type for question in MC160 and MC500 dev and test sets. Numbers in parentheses indicate the number of questions of each type.

same performance as model 3. In fact, the model performs slightly worse than model 2, which does not utilize inter-sentential relations. Our analysis of the RST trees reveals that for a vast majority of sentence pairs (77%), the RST algorithm predicts the *elaboration* relation which does not provide an informative distinction.

5.1 Analysis

To gain further insight into the workings of our model, we perform several analyses on model 3 using human judgements. We annotate 240 questions from the test set of MC160 with the most relevant sentences[9] in the passage for each question. In addition, if they chose more than a single relevant sentence, we also asked the annotators to mark the most appropriate relation (from our set of relations used in model 3) between the sentence pairs.[10] We find that 146 question annotations contain a single relevant sentence and 94 contain multiple sentences.[11] We obtain 103 sentence pairs with annotated relations.

Annotation statistics We select a random subset of 134 questions from this data to annotate twice and compute inter-annotator agreement. The second annotator agreed completely with the sentence predictions of the first annotator in 76.11% cases and both annotators agreed on at least one sentence in 94.77% of the questions. The agreement on relations annotated over common sentence pairs is 68.6%, with $\kappa = 0.462$. We find that out of the 103 annotated sentence pairs, 67 are next to each other in the passage while 27 are at a distance of two and 9 pairs are at a distance of three or more.

It has been well documented that identifying discourse relations without explicit markers is significantly harder than with markers (Pitler et al., 2008; Lin et al., 2009; Park and Cardie, 2012). We compute statistics on the presence of discourse markers anywhere in the manually picked sentence(s) for each question. We find that only 33.89% of these pairs have a relevant discourse marker present in either sentence. We consider a discourse marker as relevant if it occurs in our marker list for the annotated relation. Further, if we only consider markers occurring at the beginning or end of the sentences, this number drops to 9.23% of sentences. Since we consider relations between sentence pairs, most explicit markers that could help identify these relations would occur at an extremity of either sentence. We point out that these numbers are an over-estimation since many of the markers occur in syntactic roles as opposed to discourse in the sentences (ex. *so* in *This is so good* compared to *So, he decided to ...*). These statistics reflect the difficulty of the problem since operating over implicit relations is much harder.

Sentence Retrieval We analyze our models' ability to predict relevant sentences given only the question. For each question, we order the pairs scored by a model in descending order of their probability according to $P(z_1, z_2 \mid q)$ and compare them to the annotated pairs, reporting recall at various thresholds.

This is a stringent evaluation primarily due to

[9] The annotators are native English speakers.

[10] If there were more than *two* relevant sentences, we asked them to mark relations between all pairs. This was a very rare occurrence though.

[11] We found that some of the *multiple* questions did not require multiple sentences to answer and conversely, some *single* questions required more than one sentence to answer.

Question Type (#)	R @ 1				R @ 2				R @ 5			
	Freq	M1	M2	M3	Freq	M1	M2	M3	Freq	M1	M2	M3
how (21)	9.67	29.03	32.25	35.48	9.67	32.25	45.16	48.38	19.35	51.61	58.06	64.51
what (126)	3.64	37.85	35.59	35.02	9.37	39.54	47.45	45.76	21.81	53.67	63.84	63.27
where (12)	13.63	50.00	50.00	56.25	13.63	50.00	68.75	62.5	45.45	68.75	75.00	81.25
which (6)	0.0	21.42	21.42	14.28	9.09	21.42	21.42	14.28	9.09	21.42	35.71	42.85
who (28)	2.12	45.45	45.45	42.42	4.25	45.45	60.60	57.57	23.40	63.63	72.72	75.75
why (37)	9.09	34.32	31.34	34.32	2.27	35.82	40.29	40.29	38.63	44.77	53.73	52.23
when (5)	0.0	57.14	57.14	57.14	0.0	57.14	71.42	71.42	25.00	85.71	100.0	85.71
(other) (5)	0.0	42.85	28.57	42.85	0.0	42.85	57.14	57.14	100.0	71.42	71.42	71.42
Single (146)	6.84	56.16	53.42	51.36	11.64	58.21	66.43	63.69	33.56	72.60	80.13	80.82
Multi (94)	3.88	24.27	23.30	25.72	9.70	25.24	34.46	33.98	29.61	39.32	50.00	50.48
Overall (240)	5.11	**37.5**	35.79	36.36	10.51	38.92	**47.72**	46.30	31.25	53.12	62.5	**63.06**

Table 5: Recall (%) of relevant sentence(s) in the ranking by models 1, 2 and 3 compared with a match-frequency baseline (Freq) at various thresholds, for different question types in MC160. Question frequencies are in parentheses. Bold numbers represent best scores.

two reasons. First, we do not use the candidate answers in selecting relevant sentences. Second, on the machine comprehension task, the model predicts answers by *marginalizing* over the sentences/sentence pairs. Hence, the model can score answers correctly even if the relevant sentence(s) are not at the top of its sentence distribution calculated here. We compute the distribution over sentence pairs as:

$$P(z_1, z_2|q) = \sum_{r\in\mathcal{R}} P(z_1 \mid q) \cdot P(r \mid q) \cdot P(z_2|z_1, r, q)$$

For comparison, we add in a baseline (Freq) that orders sentences using the sum of unigram and bigram matches with the question (in descending frequency).

Table 5 shows that our models perform significantly better than the Freq baseline over all question types. For the *single*-question case, we observe that model 3 ranks the annotated sentence at the top of its distribution around 51% of the time and 80% of the time in the top 5. For *multi*-sentences, these recall numbers drop to around 25% (@1) and 50% (@5). We also observe that models 2 and 3 perform better than model 1 on the *multi*-sentence cases. The similar sentence recall of models 2 and 3 also point to the fact that the gains from model 3 on comprehension accuracy are due to its ability to utilize relations between the sentences.

We observe that *where, when* and *who* questions have the highest recalls. This is likely because these questions often have characteristic words occurring in the sentences (such as *here, there, after, before, him, her*). In contrast, questions asking *how, which* and *why* have lower recalls since they often involve reasoning over multiple sentences. *What*-questions are somewhere in between since their complexity varies from question to question.

Relation Retrieval We examine how well our model can predict relations between given sentence pairs. For each annotated pair of sentences, we calculate the relation distribution and compute the relation recall at various thresholds of the ranking by probability. The relation distribution is computed as:

$$P(r|z_1, z_2, q) = \frac{P(r \mid q) \cdot P(z_2|z_1, r, q)}{\sum_{r'\in\mathcal{R}} P(r' \mid q) \cdot P(z_2|z_1, r', q)}$$

From table 6, we observe that our model's top prediction matches the manual annotations (overall) 51% of the time. The model predicts *causal* and *other* relations more accurately than the other two.

Relation (#)	R @ 1	R @ 2
Causal (32)	56.25	75.00
Temporal (11)	27.27	54.54
Explanation (6)	16.66	33.33
Other (54)	57.40	64.81
Overall	51.45	65.04

Table 6: Recall of annotated relations at various thresholds in the ordered relation distribution predicted by model 3. Relation frequencies are in parentheses.

6 Conclusions

In this paper, we propose a new approach for incorporating discourse information into machine comprehension applications. The key idea is to implant discourse analysis into a joint model for comprehension. Our results demonstrate that the discourse-aware model outperforms state-of-the-art standalone systems, and rivals the performance of a system combination. We also find that features derived from an off-the-shelf parser do not improve performance of the model. Our analysis also demonstrates that the model accuracy varies significantly according to the question type. Finally, we show that the predicted discourse relations exhibit considerable overlap with relations identified by human annotators.

Acknowledgements

We thank Lyla Fischer, Rushi Ganmukhi, Hrishikesh Joshi and Deepak Narayanan for helping with annotating the MC160 test set. We also thank the anonymous ACL reviewers and members of MIT's NLP group for their insightful comments and suggestions. This research is developed in a collaboration of MIT with the Arabic Language Technologies (ALT) group at Qatar Computing Research Institute (QCRI) within the Interactive sYstems for Answer Search (IYAS) project.

References

[Berant et al.2014] Jonathan Berant, Vivek Srikumar, Pei-Chun Chen, Abby Vander Linden, Brittany Harding, Brad Huang, Peter Clark, and Christopher D. Manning. 2014. Modeling biological processes for reading comprehension. In *Proceedings of the 2014 Conference on Empirical Methods in Natural Language Processing (EMNLP)*, pages 1499–1510, Doha, Qatar, October. Association for Computational Linguistics.

[Blunsom et al.2006] Phil Blunsom, Krystle Kocik, and James R Curran. 2006. Question classification with log-linear models. In *Proceedings of the 29th annual international ACM SIGIR conference on Research and development in information retrieval*, pages 615–616. ACM.

[Byrd et al.1995] Richard H Byrd, Peihuang Lu, Jorge Nocedal, and Ciyou Zhu. 1995. A limited memory algorithm for bound constrained optimization. *SIAM Journal on Scientific Computing*, 16(5):1190–1208.

[Carlson et al.2002] Lynn Carlson, Mary Ellen Okurowski, Daniel Marcu, Linguistic Data Consortium, et al. 2002. *RST discourse treebank*. Linguistic Data Consortium, University of Pennsylvania.

[Chai and Jin2004] Joyce Y Chai and Rong Jin. 2004. Discourse structure for context question answering. In *Proceedings of the Workshop on Pragmatics of Question Answering at HLT-NAACL*, volume 2004, pages 23–30. Citeseer.

[Corliss2002] George Corliss. 2002. *Automatic differentiation of algorithms: from simulation to optimization*, volume 1. Springer Science & Business Media.

[Feng and Hirst2012] Vanessa Wei Feng and Graeme Hirst. 2012. Text-level discourse parsing with rich linguistic features. In *Proceedings of the 50th Annual Meeting of the Association for Computational Linguistics: Long Papers-Volume 1*, pages 60–68. Association for Computational Linguistics.

[Feng and Hirst2014] Vanessa Wei Feng and Graeme Hirst. 2014. A linear-time bottom-up discourse parser with constraints and post-editing. In *Proceedings of the 52nd Annual Meeting of the Association for Computational Linguistics (Volume 1: Long Papers)*, pages 511–521, Baltimore, Maryland, June. Association for Computational Linguistics.

[Iyyer et al.2014] Mohit Iyyer, Jordan Boyd-Graber, Leonardo Claudino, Richard Socher, and Hal Daumé III. 2014. A neural network for factoid question answering over paragraphs. In *Empirical Methods in Natural Language Processing*.

[Jansen et al.2014] Peter Jansen, Mihai Surdeanu, and Peter Clark. 2014. Discourse complements lexical semantics for non-factoid answer reranking. In *Proceedings of the 52nd Annual Meeting of the Association for Computational Linguistics (Volume 1: Long Papers)*, pages 977–986, Baltimore, Maryland, June. Association for Computational Linguistics.

[Lin et al.2009] Ziheng Lin, Min-Yen Kan, and Hwee Tou Ng. 2009. Recognizing implicit discourse relations in the penn discourse treebank. In *Proceedings of the 2009 Conference on Empirical Methods in Natural Language Processing: Volume 1-Volume 1*, pages 343–351. Association for Computational Linguistics.

[Lin et al.2014] Ziheng Lin, Hwee Tou Ng, and Min-Yen Kan. 2014. A pdtb-styled end-to-end discourse parser. *Natural Language Engineering*, pages 1–34.

[Mann and Thompson1988] William C Mann and Sandra A Thompson. 1988. Rhetorical structure theory: Toward a functional theory of text organization. *Text*, 8(3):243–281.

[Manning et al.2014] Christopher D. Manning, Mihai Surdeanu, John Bauer, Jenny Finkel, Steven J. Bethard, and David McClosky. 2014. The Stanford CoreNLP natural language processing toolkit. In *Proceedings of 52nd Annual Meeting of the Association for Computational Linguistics: System Demonstrations*, pages 55–60.

[Marcu1997] Daniel Marcu. 1997. *The Rhetorical Parsing, Summarization and Generation of Natural Language Texts*. Ph.D. thesis, University of Toronto.

[Park and Cardie2012] Joonsuk Park and Claire Cardie. 2012. Improving implicit discourse relation recognition through feature set optimization. In *Proceedings of the 13th Annual Meeting of the Special Interest Group on Discourse and Dialogue*, pages 108–112. Association for Computational Linguistics.

[Pitler et al.2008] Emily Pitler, Mridhula Raghupathy, Hena Mehta, Ani Nenkova, Alan Lee, and Aravind K Joshi. 2008. Easily identifiable discourse relations.

[Prasad et al.2008] Rashmi Prasad, Nikhil Dinesh, Alan Lee, Eleni Miltsakaki, Livio Robaldo, Aravind K Joshi, and Bonnie L Webber. 2008. The penn discourse treebank 2.0. In *LREC*. Citeseer.

[Richardson et al.2013] Matthew Richardson, Christopher JC Burges, and Erin Renshaw. 2013. Mctest: A challenge dataset for the open-domain machine comprehension of text. In *EMNLP*, pages 193–203.

[Stern and Dagan2011] Asher Stern and Ido Dagan. 2011. A confidence model for syntactically-motivated entailment proofs. In *Proceedings of the International Conference Recent Advances in Natural Language Processing 2011*, pages 455–462, Hissar, Bulgaria, September. RANLP 2011 Organising Committee.

[Verberne et al.2007] Suzan Verberne, Lou Boves, Nelleke Oostdijk, and Peter-Arno Coppen. 2007. Evaluating discourse-based answer extraction for why-question answering. In *Proceedings of the 30th annual international ACM SIGIR conference on Research and development in information retrieval*, pages 735–736. ACM.

[Wolf and Gibson2005] Florian Wolf and Edward Gibson. 2005. Representing discourse coherence: A corpus-based study. *Computational Linguistics*, 31(2):249–287.

Implicit Role Linking on Chinese Discourse: Exploiting Explicit Roles and Frame-to-Frame Relations

Ru Li[1,2], Juan Wu[1], Zhiqiang Wang[1] and Qinghua Chai[3]

[1]School of Computer and Information Technology

[2]Key Laboratory of Ministry of Education for Computation Intelligence and Chinese Information Processing

[3]School of Foreign Languages, Shanxi University, Taiyuan, China

{liru,charles}@sxu.edu.cn, {wujuan_0922,zhiq.wang}@163.com

Abstract

There is a growing interest in researching *null instantiations*, which are those implicit semantic arguments. Many of these implicit arguments can be linked to referents in context, and their discoveries are of great benefits to semantic processing. We address the issue of automatically identifying and resolving implicit arguments in Chinese discourse. For their resolutions, we present an approach that combines the information about overtly labeled arguments and frame-to-frame relations defined by FrameNet. Experimental results on our created corpus demonstrate the effectiveness of our approach.

1 Introduction

In natural discourse, only a small proportion of the theoretically possible semantic arguments of predicates tend to be locally instantiated. Other locally unrealized semantic roles are called *null instantiations* (NIs). Nevertheless, many of these implicit roles, while linguistically unexpressed, can often be bound to antecedent referents in the discourse context. What's more, capturing such implicit semantic roles and linking them to their antecedents can dramatically help text understanding.

Example (1) shows an analyzed result (Li, 2012) by employing Chinese FrameNet (Liu, 2011), which is a lexical semantic knowledge base based on the frame semantics of Fillmore (1982) and takes Berkeley's FrameNet Project (Baker et al., 1998) as the reference. In Chinese FrameNet, the predicates, called lexical units (LU), evoke frames which roughly correspond to different events or scenarios. Each frame defines a set of arguments called Frame Elements (FE). The set of FEs is further split into core FEs and non-core FEs. Particularly, the core FEs are the essential components of a frame and can be defined by themselves. However, not all core FEs of a frame can be realized simultaneously in a sentence. These non-instantiated FEs are considered as *null instantiations of the frame elements*. Depending on the interpretation type of the omission, Chinese FrameNet divides the NIs into two categories: 1) Indefinite Null Instantiations (INIs), the missing element which can be understood given interpretational conventions and do not need resolution, and 2) Definite Null Instantiations (DNIs), the missing element which is something that can be understood in the linguistic or discourse context, and the fillers need to be inferred from the context through resolutions.

(1) [天葬卫星]$_{Entity}$也是 $_{属于某类}$ [人造卫星]$_{Category}$，和侦察卫星、通信卫星、气象卫星等同属一类。

[The celestial burial satellite]$_{Entity}$ **is** $_{\textit{Being\_in\_category}}$ [artificial satellite]$_{Category}$, and belongs to the same category with reconnaissance, communications and meteorological satellite.

不同的是用途各异，是专门用来存放骨灰盒的；高度亦不同，一般**发射** $_{使位移}$ [到距地球表面3000多公里处的环球轨道上]$_{Goal}$。[*Theme* DNI] [*Agent* INI]

The purpose is different, specially used for storing the urn; due to the different heights, generally **launched** $_{\textit{Cause\_motion}}$ into [the orbit over 3000 kilometers away from the surface of earth]$_{Goal}$. [*Theme* DNI] [*Agent* INI]

Particularly, in example (1), lexical unit (or target) *launched/*发射 evokes the semantic frame `Cause_motion`, which has nine core FEs, namely *Agent*, *Theme*, *Source*, *Path*, *Goal*, *Area*, *Cause*, *Result*, *Initial_State*, but only one of them is instantiated, i.e. *Goal*, whose filler is [*the orbit over 3000 kilometers away from the surface of earth/*到距地球表面3000 多公里处的环球轨道上]. For another core FE *Theme*, it is filled by [*The celestial burial satellite/*天葬卫星] that occurs in

Proceedings of the 53rd Annual Meeting of the Association for Computational Linguistics and the 7th International Joint Conference on Natural Language Processing, pages 1263–1271, Beijing, China, July 26-31, 2015.

the previous sentence.

Clearly, human beings have no problem to infer these uninstantiated roles and find the corresponding fillers based on the relevant context information, but this is beyond the capacity of state-of-the-art semantic role labeling systems.

Next, we formalize the problem as follows: given a discourse $D = \{S_1, S_2, ..., S_n\}$, where $S_k\, (k \in [1, n])$ is the k-th sentence in D. The lexical unit set in S_k is $T_k = \{T_{k1}, T_{k2}, ..., T_{kp}\}$, and $F_k = \{F_{k1}, F_{k2}, ..., F_{kp}\}$ is relevant frame set. For a particular frame $F_{ki}\, (i \in [1, p])$, its core FE set is $E_{ki} = \{e_1, e_2, ..., e_m\}$, but it is possible that only part of core FEs C_{ki} appears in S_k, i.e. $C_{ki} \subseteq E_{ki}$. Apparently the set $E_{ki} - C_{ki}$ includes the uninstantiated core FEs. Thus, we need to determine which elements in $E_{ki} - C_{ki}$ are null instantiations. If $e_m\, (e_m \in E_{ki} - C_{ki})$ has been identified as a null instantiated FE, we should determine whether e_m is a DNI. If so, we need to find the corresponding antecedent d_m in context.

The major contributions of this paper can be summarized as follows:

(i) We have created a null instantiation (NI) annotations corpus, consisting of 164 Chinese discourses across different fields.

(ii) We use frame-to-frame relations to find antecedents from those explicit semantic roles.

2 Related Work

Among the researches of null instantiation on English, the most representative work is the task "Linking Events and Their Participants in Discourse" shared by the SemEval-2010 (Ruppenhofer et al., 2010). The two systems participated in the NI resolution task, VENSES++ and SEMAFOR, took very different approaches.

Tonelli and Delmonte (2010) develop a knowledge-based system called VENSES++, and describe two strategies depending on the predicate class (either nominal or verbal). For verbal predicates, they try to map the predicate argument structure extracted by VENSES with the valence patterns generated from FrameNet data, to identify missing arguments. And NIs are resolved by reasoning about the semantic similarity between an NI and a potential filler using WordNet. For nominal predicates, they resolve NIs by utilizing a common sense reasoning module that builds on ConceptNet (Liu and Singh, 2004). The final Precision and Recall are 4.62% and 0.86% respectively.

Later on, Tonelli and Delmonte (2011) propose a simpler role linking strategy that based on computing a relevancy score for the nominal head of each potential antecedent. The intuition is that heads which often serve as role fillers and occur close to the target NI are more likely to function as antecedents for the NI. Finally they reported an F-score of 8% for role linking. However, being strongly lexicalized, their trained model seems heavily dependent on the training data.

The second system (Chen et al., 2010) is statistical based and extends an existing semantic role labeler (Das et al., 2010). Resolving DNIs is modeled in the same way as labeling overt arguments, with the search space being extended to nouns, pronouns, and noun phrases from the previous three sentences. When evaluating a potential filler, the syntactic features used in argument labeling of overt arguments are replaced by two semantic features: firstly the system checks whether a potential filler fills the null instantiated role overtly in at least one of the FrameNet sentences and train data, if not, the system calculates the distributional similarity between filler and role. While this system achieved 5% in F-score, data sparseness is a potential limiting factor.

Also closely related studies are as follows. Silberer and Frank (2012) cast NI resolution as a coreference resolution (CR) task, and employ an entity-mention model. They experiment with features of SRL and CR, and automatically expand the training set with examples generated from coreference corpus to avoid data sparseness, ultimately achieving F-score of 7.1%.

Gorinski et al. (2013) present a weakly supervised approach that investigates and combines a number of linguistically motivated strategies, which consist of four basic NI resolvers that exploit different types of linguistic knowledge, and achieve F-score of 12%.

Wang et al. (2013) conduct DNI resolution on SemEval2010 task10 data. They considered the task as a classified problem, by adding new features such as the information of head word and frame to traditional features, proposed a rule to choose the best candidate words set and combination of features, achieving F-score of 14.65% finally.

Laparra and Rigau (2013) present an attempt to apply a set of features that have been traditionally used to model anaphora and coreference resolution tasks to implicit argument resolution, and got the best results: F-score of 18%.

For nominal predicates, Gerber and Chai (2010) investigate the linking of implicit arguments using the PropBank role labeling scheme. In contrast to the SemEval task, which focuses on a verbs and nouns, their system is only applied to nouns and is restricted to 10 predicates with 120 annotated instances per predicate on average. They propose a discriminative model that selects an antecedent for an implicit role from an extended context window. The approach incorporates some aspects relating to CR that go beyond the SRL oriented SemEval systems: A candidate representation includes information about all the candidates' coreferent mentions (determined by automatic CR), in particular their semantic roles (provided by gold annotations) and WordNet synsets. Patterns of semantic associations between filler candidates and implicit roles are learned for all mentions contained in the candidate's entity chain. They achieve an F-score of 42.3%, which is noticeably higher than those obtained on the SemEval data.

And Gerber (2011) presents an extended model that incorporates strategies suggested in Burchardt et al. (2005): using frame relations as well as coreference patterns acquired from large corpora. This model achieves an F-score of 50.3%.

Lei et al. (2013) conduct DNI identification on SemEval2010 task10 data. They adopt the method of combining rules and machine learning. Different from them, we conduct two-level identifying for NI detection and use more features on Chinese data. Wang et al. (2013) take noun phrases and pronoun as candidate words for DNI filler. We use several similar features with them. The differences are that 1) we take the fillers of overt instantiated FE as candidate words and 2) we use Frame-to-Frame relations. And Gerber (2011) also used frame relations. Different from them, we limit relation paths to 2.

3 Null Instantiation Detection

Now, we are ready to address the first subtask, i.e. null instantiation detection.

3.1 Frame element relations

Not all core arguments of all frames can be realized simultaneously. Some frames involve core FEs that are mutually exclusive. In example (2), in the `Amalgamation` frame, there are four core FEs, namely *Part_1*, *Part_2*, *Parts* and *Whole*, in which the first two FEs are mutually exclusive with *Parts*, thus formed an *Excludes* relation (relation 1). At the same time, *Part_1* and *Part_2* are in a *Requires* relation (relation 2), which means that if one of these two core FEs is present, then the other must occur as well. FE *Whole*, the result of the `Amalgamation`, is only existentially bound within the discourse, annotated as NI.

CoreSet (relation 3) specifies that *at least* one of the set must be instantiated overtly, though more of them can also be instantiated. As shown in example (3), in the `Awareness` frame, the two FEs *Content* and *Topic* are in one *CoreSet*. As *Content* is overtly realized, we consider *Topic* is not annotated as NI. The frame owning this relation is complicated. Sometimes, if one FE of this set is explicit, the absence of the other FEs in the set is not annotated as NI, but sometimes it is not true.

(2) [旧体制]$_{Part\_1}$ 和[新体制]$_{Part\_2}$ **结合**$_{结合}$ 在一起。 [*Whole* INI]

[The old system]$_{Part\_1}$ and [the new system]$_{Part\_2}$ are **combined** *Amalgamation* together. [*Whole* INI]

(3) [你老板]$_{Cognizer}$ **知道**$_{知道}$ [你的任务]$_{Content}$。

[Your boss]$_{Cognizer}$ is **aware**$_{Awareness}$ [of your commitment]$_{Content}$.

3.2 Modeling Null Instantiation detection

As shown in example (1), given a frame F_{ki} (e.g. `Cause_motion` evoked by *launched*/发射), NI detector needs to determine whether core FEs in $E_{F_{ki}} - subE_{F_{ki}}$ are missing, relying on information about the three types of the relations among core FEs: $CoreSet_{F_{ki}}$, $Excludes_{F_{ki}}$, $Requires_{F_{ki}}$ (as discussed in Section 3.1). In `Cause_motion`, the core FEs *Initial_State*, *Goal*, *Path*, *Source* and *Result* belong to the same $CoreSet$, and *Goal* is instantiated, thus *Initial_State*, *Path*, *Source* and *Result* are not annotated as NIs. Meanwhile core FEs *Goal* and *Area* are connected by the $Excludes$ relation, so do *Cause* and *Agent*. Therefore, according to the context, *Area* and *Cause* are not annotated as NIs.

Our approach for performing this detection is described as follows. For the first-level of detection, we make full use of the three types of relations, and adopt a rule-based strategy proposed by Lei et al. (2013) to detect NIs. As for *CoreSet* relation, in particular, as long as one of the FEs in this set is expressed overtly, NIs are not annotated for the absence of the other FEs in the set. If none of *CoreSet* is expressed, the contextually most relevant one should be annotated as a NI. However, this is difficult for automatic detector, which inevitably introduces some false detected NIs.

Thus, we conduct a second-level identifying. To be specific, for the current lexical unit, i.e. the target word, we collect its frame element patterns from the training dataset. Frame element patterns are annotated semantic roles, which include the roles annotated as NIs. Taking lexical unit *launched*/发射 as an example, Table 1 shows its frame element patterns in our data. Depending on this kind of patterns, we are able to filter out some false NIs effectively.

Patte1	Time	Agent_{INI}	Theme	Goal_{INI}
Patte2	Agent	Theme	Goal_{INI}	

Table 1: Frame element patterns for the target 发射/*launched* in our data

4 Definite Null Instantiation Identification

In this section, we focus on our second task of definite null instantiation (DNI) identification.

Before performing the implicit argument resolution in discourse, we have to decide which null instantiated frame elements should be selected, i.e. which null instantiations are definite. As shown in example (1) above, assuming one detected null instantiated FE in the previous step is e_m (e.g. *Theme*), we should determine whether e_m needs to be filled or not, that is, we should determine e_m as DNI or INI.

Num	Feature names	Feature Descriptions
T1	Target	Target predicate
T2	Pos	The part of speech of target
T3	Frame	The frame that target evokes
T4	FENI	NI of frame elements
T5	FE	Overtly expressed FEs

Table 2: Features description in DNI Identification

We treat this issue as a classification problem, and build a binary maximum entropy model to predict the null instantiation type of e_m. Table 2 lists all features used for training our models. In addition, we employ some similar features that were used in Lei et al. (2013). Meanwhile, we choose to learn a SVM classifier for comparison purpose.

5 Definite Null Instantiation Resolution

In this section, we tackle the last subtask, namely definite null instantiation resolution.

5.1 Frame-to-Frame Relations

The relations of Frame-to-Frame and FE-to-FE in FrameNet, serve as important information sources, to be leveraged for DNI resolutions.

FrameNet arranges frames into a net by defining frame-to-frame relations, including Inheritance, Inchoative Of, Subframe, Causative Of, Precedes, Using, See_also and Perspective On. In the case of Inheritance relation, it defines two frames, i.e. one more general frame and the other more specific frame. The specific frame `Commerce buy`, for example, is inherited from the general frame `Getting`.

As Figure 1 shows, the inheritance relation allows a general frame (e.g., `Getting`) to be specialized with a particular semantic interpretation (e.g., `Commerce buy`). Also the inheritance relation exists between the *frame elements* of two related frames. Each of the inheriting FEs contains all semantic properties of the inherited general frame elements and also owns its additional private properties.

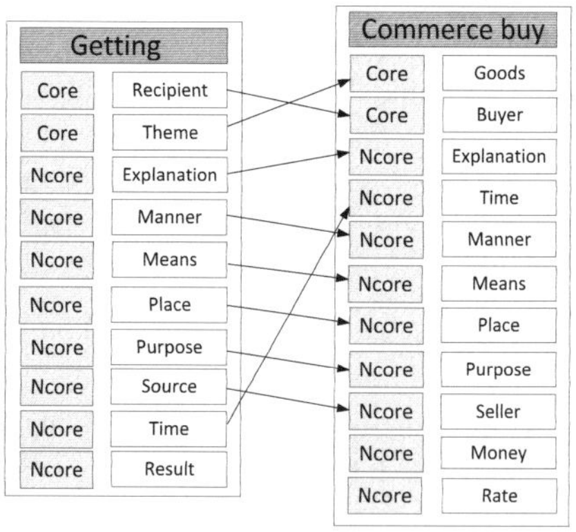

Figure 1: FE-FE relations of frame `Getting` and `Commerce buy`

Number		Features Name	Features Description
T1	F1	DistCT	The number of sentences between candidate FE content and target
	F2	CanFEcon	Candidate frame element content
	F3	CanFEpt	The phrase type or POS of candidate frame element content
T2	F4	Frame	The frame that target predicate evokes
	F5	FEDNI	DNI frame element
	F6	Target	Target predicate
	F7	TargetPOS	The part of speech of target

Table 3: Features description in Overt Frame Elements Based Resolver

5.2 Modeling Definite Null Instantiation Resolution

After accomplishing the previous processes, we can perform DNI resolutions. If the uninstantiated FE e_m (e.g., *Theme* in example (1)) has been identified as DNI previously, we need to find the corresponding antecedent mention d_m (e.g., [*The celestial burial satellite*/天葬卫星] in example (1)). Due to having fine-grained frame semantic role labeled for each sentence, we think the filler of DNI maybe also instantiates the FE of other annotated frames in the context. Therefore, we collect the overt FE content set φ instantiated in the discourse, and this set forms the overall set of candidates for DNI linking. Then, for DNI e_m, a subset of candidates φ_m ($\varphi_m \subseteq \varphi$) is chosen as candidate search space for resolving e_m.

We implement two semantic resolvers based on different methods. For either of these two resolvers, if two or more candidates score equally well, the one closest to the target predicate is chosen.

OvertFE is based on machine learning, and FFR is an inference method. As the inherent difficulty of task, it's difficult to find all fillers for DNIs only using one of them. Thus finally we simultaneously employ OvertFE and FFR to find as many fillers for DNIs as possible.

Overt Frame Elements Based Resolver (OvertFE)

This resolver is based on the assumption that the filler of DNI can be found among the overt FE content set in context. Given a DNI e_m , DNI linking can be treated as a classification problem to judge whether a candidate overt FE content d ($d \in \varphi_m$) could be taken as filler of a DNI. Therefore, we employ a classification method to solve the problem. Clearly, the performance of classifiers largely depends on constructed features. Since corresponding antecedent of DNI is not overtly expressed, it is difficult to get some information from context to describe them. What we take as features is the information of candidate frame element contents and frame information. Table 3 lists all features used for training our models. Some similar features were employed by Wang et al. (2013) where they also considered DNI linking as a classification problem.

Then maximum entropy models, widely used in natural language processing (such as Chinese word segmentation and machine translation), are employed to predict whether a candidate FE content is the filler of DNI.

Frame-to-Frame Relations Based Resolver (F-FR)

Another way of finding the correct filler is through searching Frame-to-Frame relations in a given context window. This is because Frame-to-Frame relations and FE-to-FE relations can provide relevant information for finding DNI filler among candidate frame element contents. Specifically, for one frame f_1 that contains a DNI, firstly we need to find related frame f_2 with it from context. Then, if DNI frame element in f_1 has relation with the frame element (marked with fe_2) of f_2, the filler of fe_2 is the corresponding filler of this DNI. The detailed steps are reported in Algorithm 1.

If frame names are the same, we think they are related, and Figure 2 illustrates this case. As the frames evoked in two sentences are both `Arriving`, we link the antecedent of *Goal* in the second sentence to [*Tiananmen Square*/天安门广场], which is the content of *Goal* in the first sentence.

For other cases, we use the related frames which at most contain two relation paths (e.g., the paths from `Event` to `Process_start` to `Activity_start` in Figure 3). As shown in Figure 3, the target *initiated*/发起 in the first sentence evokes the `Activity_start` frame, in which the two frame elements (*Agent*, *Place*) is expressed in a single constituent [*our country*/我国], i.e. the phenomenon of frame element fusion arises. Frame `Event` is evoked by the target *happened*/出现 in the second sentence, where *Time* and *Event* FEs are expressed overtly, except the core FE *Place*. In the net of FrameNet, frame `Activity_start` inherits from the frame `Process_start` which further inherits from the `Event` frame. These inheritance relationships also hold between the frame elements of the related frames. According to the FE-to-FE relations, the content of FE *Place* in the first sentence, [*our country*/我国], is the corresponding filler of implicit FE *Place* in the second sentence.

Algorithm 1 : Frame-to-Frame Relations Based Resolver

Input: The frame set in discourse is $F = \{f_1, f_2, ..., f_n\}$; overt core frame element set for frame f_i is $E_i = \{e_1, e_2, ..., e_m\}$, its corresponding filler set is $A_i = \{a_1, a_2, ..., a_m\}$; one frame that contains DNI e^* is f^*, target t evokes the frame f^*; $dis\,(a_i, t)$ is the distance between DNI filler a_i and target t; $relationpath\,(f_i, f^*)$ are the relation paths from f_i to f^*; A^{temp} is temporary DNI filler set

Output: the filler a^* of DNI e^*

$A^{temp} = \phi$
for each $f_i \in F$ **do**
  if f_i has frame relation with f^* **AND** $relationpath\,(f_i, f^*) \leq 2$ **then**
    for each $e_i \in E_i$, $a_i \in A_i$ **do**
      if e_i has relation with e^* **then**
        $a_i \in A^{temp}$
      end if
    end for
  else if $f_i = f^*$ **then**
    $a_i \in A^{temp}$
  end if
end for
if $A^{temp} \neq \phi$ **then**
  for $a_i \in A^{temp}$ **do**
    if $dis\,(a_i, t)$ is minimum **then**
      $a^* = a_i$
    end if
  end for
end if
return a^* ;

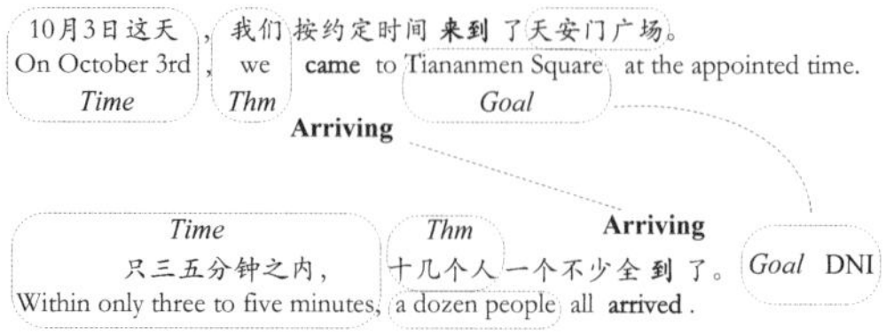

Figure 2: Two consecutive sentences owning the same frame. Bold fonts represent lexical units or frames. Dashed boxes represent FEs.

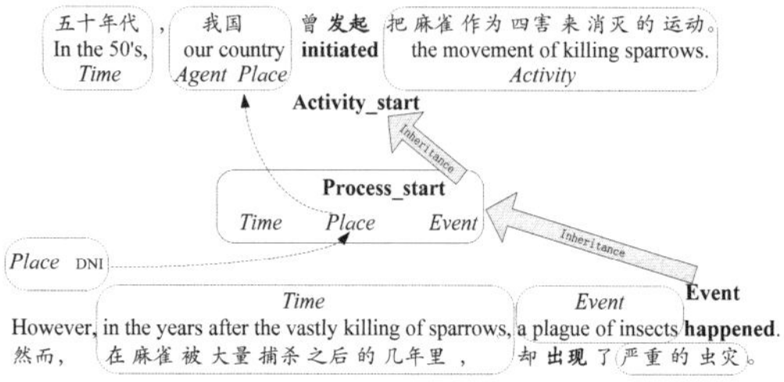

Figure 3: Two consecutive sentences owing related frames. Bold fonts represent lexical units or frames. Dashed boxes represent FEs.

6 Experiments

6.1 Experimental Settings

Data: Experimental data set comes from Semantic Computing and Chinese FrameNet Research Center of Shanxi University[1]. Because of the current low performance of CFN automatic semantic analysis systems, all discourses are labeled semantic roles manually, and the process is similar with the FrameNet annotation.

First, the ICTCLAS are used for part-of-speech tagging (omitted in examples), and we treat verbs, adjectives and nouns in each sentence as potential targets. As not all potential targets can be annotated, it is necessary to identify those targets which can evoke frames.

Then, we choose corresponding frames for those targets. For one verb target *launched*/发射 in example (1), we find its evoked frame `Cause_motion`.

Then annotate semantic roles for those constituents which share syntactical relations with this target, so the span [*the orbit over 3000 kilometers away from the surface of earth*/到距地球表面3000多公里处的环球轨道上] is annotated as role *Goal*, which is, however, the only one instantiated, out of nine `Cause_motion`'s core frame elements. So according to the context and frame element relations, we need to determine whether each

[1] `http://sccfn.sxu.edu.cn/`

missing frame element should be annotated as DNI or INI.

Next, we generate the XML format for our annotated corpus, which is similar to the data format in SemEval-10 Task 10.

Our 164 discourses had been annotated by one person (to make it consistent), and they consist of 57 discourses from People's Daily and 107 discourses from Chinese reading comprehension, which cover technology, health care, social, geography and other fields. Each discourse contains 10 sentences in average. The data set contains about 37526 words in 1618 sentences; it has 175 frame types, including 2283 annotated frame instances. Table 4 shows the detailed statistics of our data set. we'll share our data in the website(http://sccfn.sxu.edu.cn/).

discourses	sentences	frame inst.	frame types	INIs	DNIs
164	1618	2283	175	213	212

Table 4: Corpus Statistics

Definite Null Instantiation identification and resolution model: Our maximum entropy classification model uses the toolkit from Zhang (2005) with the default parameter values. The SVM classifier for comparison was trained via SVM toolkit LIBSVM with the default parameter values too.

6.2 Experimental Results

Based on the experimental methods described in the previous section, we have systematically evaluated our approach on the constructed Chinese null instantiation corpus. Note all the performances are achieved using 5-fold cross validation.

Null Instantiation Detection

Table 5 gives the performance of NI detection, which achieves 72.71%, 86.12% and 78.84% in precision, recall and F-score, respectively. Here, the relatively lower precision is mainly due to the heuristic rules used to detect NIs. However, it is worth to point out that lower precision and higher recall is highly beneficial, as higher recall means less filtering of true NIs.

	P%	R%	F%
Ours	**72.71**	86.12	**78.84**
Lei et al.	56.18	90.57	69.34

Table 5: Performance of NI Detection

To illustrate the effectiveness of our method, we compare it with the Lei et al.'s method on our data, as shown in the Table 5. The F-score of our method is 78.84%, which is 9% higher than that of Lei et al.'s method. Clearly, these experimental results further prove that our second-level identification is very effective.

Definite Null Instantiation Identification

Table 6 provides the performance of DNI identification on our automatic NI detection results. It shows that DNI identification based on maximum entropy model achieves the performance of 67.86%, 69.93% and 68.88% in terms of precision, recall and F-score respectively, which are better than the results using SVM classifier, as well as the results employing Lei et al.'s method on our data.

We observe, from Table 6, that the performance of DNI identification is not high, possibly due to the poorer results of NI detection in the previous step. Moreover, because of the diversity of NI distribution, the difference of frames, and target words or missing core frame elements, the interpretation of NI types may be quite different. Thus it is difficult to build a suitable and accurate uniform classification model.

	P%	R%	F%
DNI IdenME	**67.86**	**69.93**	**68.88**
DNI IdenSVM	67.25	62.02	64.53
Lei et al.	64.58	67.73	66.12

Table 6: Performance of DNI Identification

Resolution on golden Definite Null Instantiation

In order to select the most effective features for OvertFE resolver and choose the best search space, we assume perfect results for the first two steps, that is, we perform DNI resolution experiment just with the correct DNIs in discourse. After extensive experiments employing different sets of features in different window sizes, we conclude that combining all features can achieve the best performance. Table 7 shows the results on correct DNIs using the best feature set in the window of 2, 3 and 4 sentences containing and before the target predicate (Win2, Win3, Win4 for short).

For OvertFE resolver, it shows that the F-score with Win2 is higher than that in other windows, because the bigger the window size, the more the candidate fillers for DNI, and the more difficult for

	Win2			Win3			Win4		
	P%	R%	F%	P%	R%	F%	P%	R%	F%
OvertFE	45.22	18.20	25.95	43.04	17.64	25.02	38.63	15.23	21.84
FFR	65.56	16.29	26.11	63.50	16.81	26.58	58.53	17.32	26.72
OvertFE+FFR	51.17	31.59	**39.06**	52.41	32.02	**39.75**	45.88	31.10	**37.07**

Table 7: Results on golden DNI

OvertFE classifier to find right fillers.

For FFR resolver, it needs to find related frames, and we find that its resolved DNIs are less than that by OvertFE resolver, thereby resulting in the lower precision of OvertFE than FFR.

Though performances of OvertFE and FFR both are relatively low, FFR can resolve several DNIs that OvertFE can not. Figures 2 and 3 both are such cases. So when combining the two resolvers, the final result of OvertFE+FFR outperforms that of each individual resolver. Meanwhile, as shown in Table 7, for the combined resolver OvertFE+FFR, the F-score is the highest when the window size is 3 (i.e. Win3).

Overall: Null Instantiation Resolution

Table 8 gives the performance of overall null instantiations resolution with automatic NI detection and automatic DNI determination. It shows that our resolver OvertFE+FFR achieves 40.53%, 21.54% and 28.13% in terms of precision, recall and F-score. In comparison with the results (52.41%, 32.02% and 39.75% in P, R and F) in Win3 of Table 7, it shows that the errors caused by automatic NI detection and automatic DNI determination decrease the performance of overall NI resolution by about 11% in terms of F-score.

	P%	R%	F%
OvertFE	33.28	13.78	19.49
FFR	52.95	9.71	16.41
OvertFE+FFR	**40.53**	**21.54**	**28.13**
Wang et al.	31.93	12.76	18.23

Table 8: Performance of NI resolution for our models and comparative systems

For comparison, we also conduct DNI resolution on our constructed corpus employing the method proposed by Wang et al. (2013). Since our corpus does not contain annotation of head words, the results are obtained by using their features without head word information. As the last line of Table 8 shows, the performance behaves similarly with our OvertFE resolver. In addition, we notice current state-of-the-art approach of Laparra and Rigau (2013) employs coreference models, although our corpus does not contain coreference annotation information. As such, we are not able to conduct experiments on our dataset using their method for comparison purpose.

Overall, the relatively low performance of resolution reflects the inherent difficulty of this task, also reveals that further research is needed.

7 Conclusion and Future Work

Apparently, linking implicit participants of a predicate is a challenging problem. We have presented a study for identifying implicit arguments and finding their antecedents in Chinese discourse.

As shown in this paper, we split the difficult task into three subtasks: null instantiation detection, definite null instantiation identification and definite null instantiation resolution. Among the three subtasks, the third is our major focus. For the third subtask, we build two different resolvers: 1) OvertFE resolver, which represents that the filler of a DNI can be found among those overt FE content set in context, by employing classification methods; 2) FFR resolver, which is the frame-related search, leverages rich network of frame-frame relations to find antecedents. We have proved that these two resolvers are very useful for the third subtask, and a combination of two resolvers produced the best results.

In the near future, we plan to create and release a larger null instantiation corpus. As null instantiation detection and definite null instantiation identification are the foundation of resolving definite null instantiation, it is critical to improve the performance of both subtasks. Moreover, as different information sources have been used in our study, we cannot directly compare with some of the existing methods. For our future work, we plan to manually annotate coreference information so that we can compare with more methods. Finally, we hope to exploit some additional knowledge resources, such as HowNet, which could potentially further improve the performance of our proposed method.

Acknowledgments

We would like to thank anonymous reviewers and the mentor Jacob Eisenstein for their valuable comments and suggestions, and Xiaoli Li for helping us polish the paper. This work was supported by the National Natural Science Foundation of China (No.61373082, 61432011, U1435212), National 863 Project of China(No.2015AA015407), Shanxi Platform Project(2014091004-0103) and Scholarship Council(2013-015), and Open Project Foundation of Information Security Evaluation Center of Civil Aviation, Civil Aviation University of China(No.CAAC-ISECCA-201402).

References

Collin F. Baker, Charles J. Fillmore, and John B. Lowe. 1998. The berkeley framenet project. In *Proceedings of COLING/ACL*.

Aljoscha Burchardt, Anette Frank, and Manfred Pinkal. 2005. Building text meaning representations from contextually related frames–a case study. *Proceedings of the 6th International Workshop on Computational Semantics (IWCS-6)*, pages 66–77.

Desai Chen, Nathan Schneider, Dipanjan Das, and Noah A Smith. 2010. Semafor: Frame argument resolution with log-linear models. In *Proceedings of the 5th international workshop on semantic evaluation*, pages 264–267.

Dipanjan Das, Nathan Schneider, Desai Chen, and Noah A Smith. 2010. Probabilistic frame-semantic parsing. In *Human language technologies: The 2010 annual conference of the North American chapter of the association for computational linguistics*, pages 948–956.

Charles J. Fillmore. 1982. Frame semantics. *Linguistics in the morning calm*, pages 111–137.

Matthew Gerber and Joyce Y. Chai. 2010. Beyond nombank: a study of implicit arguments for nominal predicates. In *Proceedings of the 48th Annual Meeting of the Association for Computational Linguistics*, pages 1583–1592.

Matthew Steven Gerber. 2011. *Semantic Role Labeling of Implicit Arguments for Nominal Predicates*. Ph.D. thesis, Michigan State University.

Philip Gorinski, Josef Ruppenhofer, and Caroline Sporleder. 2013. Towards weakly supervised resolution of null instantiations. In *Proceedings of the 10th International Conference on Computational Semantics (IWCS 2013)–Long Papers*, pages 119–130.

Egoitz Laparra and German Rigau. 2013. Sources of evidence for implicit argument resolution. In *Proceedings of the 10th International Conference on Computational Semantics (IWCS 2013)–Long Papers*, pages 155–166.

Zhangzhang Lei, Ning Wang, Ru Li, and Zhiqiang Wang. 2013. Definite null instantiation recognizing in framenet. *Journal of Chinese Information*, 27(3):107–112.

Ru Li. 2012. *Research on Frame Semantic Structure Analysis Technology for Chinese Sentences*. Ph.D. thesis, ShanXi university.

Hugo Liu and Push Singh. 2004. Conceptnet: a practical commonsense reasoning tool-kit. *BT technology journal*, 22(4):211–226.

Kaiying Liu. 2011. Research on chinese framenet construction and application technologies. *Journal of Chinese Information Processing*, 6:006.

Josef Ruppenhofer, Caroline Sporleder, Roser Morante, Collin Baker, and Martha Palmer. 2010. Semeval-2010 task 10: Linking events and their participants in discourse. In *Proceedings of the 5th International Workshop on Semantic Evaluation*, pages 45–50.

Carina Silberer and Anette Frank. 2012. Casting implicit role linking as an anaphora resolution task. In *Proceedings of the First Joint Conference on Lexical and Computational Semantics-Volume 1: Proceedings of the main conference and the shared task, and Volume 2: Proceedings of the Sixth International Workshop on Semantic Evaluation*, pages 1–10.

Sara Tonelli and Rodolfo Delmonte. 2010. Venses++: Adapting a deep semantic processing system to the identification of null instantiations. In *Proceedings of the 5th international workshop on semantic evaluation*, pages 296–299.

Sara Tonelli and Rodolfo Delmonte. 2011. Desperately seeking implicit arguments in text. In *Proceedings of the ACL 2011 workshop on relational models of semantics*, pages 54–62.

Ning Wang, Ru Li, Zhangzhang Lei, Zhiqiang Wang, and Jingpan Jin. 2013. Document oriented gap filling of definite null instantiation in framenet. In *Chinese Computational Linguistics and Natural Language Processing Based on Naturally Annotated Big Data*, pages 85–96.

Le Zhang. 2005. Maximum entropy modeling toolkit for python and c++. `http://homepages.inf.ed.ac.uk/lzhang10/maxent_toolkit.html`.

Discourse-sensitive Automatic Identification of Generic Expressions

Annemarie Friedrich **Manfred Pinkal**
Department of Computational Linguistics
Saarland University, Saarbrücken, Germany
{afried,pinkal}@coli.uni-saarland.de

Abstract

This paper describes a novel sequence labeling method for identifying generic expressions, which refer to kinds or arbitrary members of a class, in discourse context. The automatic recognition of such expressions is important for any natural language processing task that requires text understanding. Prior work has focused on identifying generic noun phrases; we present a new corpus in which not only subjects but also clauses are annotated for genericity according to an annotation scheme motivated by semantic theory. Our context-aware approach for automatically identifying generic expressions uses conditional random fields and outperforms previous work based on local decisions when evaluated on this corpus and on related data sets (ACE-2 and ACE-2005).

1 Introduction

Distinguishing between statements about particular individuals or situations and generic sentences is an important part of human language understanding. Consider example (1): sentence (a) names characteristic attributes of a kind, which are inherent to every (typical) individual, and sentence (b) describes a specific individual.

(1) *(a)* *The modern domestic horse has a life expectancy of 25 to 30 years.* ***(generic)***

(a) *Old Billy lived to the age of 62.* ***(non-generic)***

The above example illustrates that generic and non-generic sentences differ substantially in their semantic impact and entailment properties. It can be inferred from sentence (1a) that a *typical* horse has a life expectancy of 25 to 30 years, and if we know that *Nelly* is a horse, we can infer that its life expectancy is 25 to 30 years. Sentence (1b) has no such properties, it only allows inferences about the particular individual *Old Billy*.

An automatic classifier that recognizes generic expressions would be extremely valuable for various kinds of natural language processing systems: for text understanding and question answering systems, through the improvement of textual entailment methods, and for systems acquiring machine-readable knowledge from text. Machine-readable knowledge bases have different representations for statements corresponding to generic knowledge about kinds and knowledge about specific individuals. The non-generic sentence (1b) roughly speaking provides ABox content for a machine-readable knowledge base, i.e., knowledge about particular instances, e.g, *"A is an instance of B / has property X"*. In contrast, the generic sentence (1a) feeds the TBox, i.e., knowledge of the form *"All B are C / have property X"*. Reiter and Frank (2010) provide a detailed discussion of the relevance of the distinction between classes and instances for automatic ontology construction.

In this paper, we present a new corpus annotated in a linguistically motivated way for genericity, and a context-sensitive computational model for labeling sequences of clauses or noun phrases (NPs) with their genericity status. Both manual annotation and automatic recognition of generic expressions are challenging tasks: virtually all NP types – definites, indefinites and quantified NPs, full NPs, pronouns, and even proper names (e.g. species names such as *Elephas maximus*) – can be found in generic and non-generic uses depending on their clausal context.

In this work, we call clauses generic if they provide a general characterization of entities of a certain kind, and we call mentions of NPs generic if they refer to kinds or arbitrary members of a class. Although genericity on the clause- and NP-level

Proceedings of the 53rd Annual Meeting of the Association for Computational Linguistics and the 7th International Joint Conference on Natural Language Processing, pages 1272–1281,
Beijing, China, July 26-31, 2015.

are strongly interrelated, the concepts do not always coincide. As example (2) shows, sentences describing episodic events can have a generic NP as their subject. Note that references to species are kind-referring / generic on the NP level (following Krifka et al. (1995), see p. 65).

(2) *In September 2013 the blobfish was voted the "World's Ugliest Animal". (subject* ***generic****, clause* ***non-generic****)*

Genericity often cannot be annotated without paying attention to the wider discourse context. Clearly, coreference information is needed for the genericity classification of pronouns. Often, even genericity of full NPs or entire clauses cannot be decided in isolation, as illustrated by example (3). Sentence (b) could be part of a particular narrative about a tree, or it could be a generic statement. Only the context given by (a) clarifies that (b) indeed makes reference to any year's new twigs and is to be interpreted as generic.

(3) *(a) Sugar maples also have a tendency to color unevenly in fall. (****generic****)*
*(b) The recent year's growth twigs are green and turn dark brown. (****generic****)*

In computational linguistics, most research on detecting genericity has been done in relation to the ACE corpora (Mitchell et al., 2003; Walker et al., 2006), focusing on assigning genericity labels to noun phrases (Suh et al., 2006; Reiter and Frank, 2010), see Section 2. Our work is based on these approaches, most notably on the work of Reiter and Frank (2010), and extends upon them in the following essential ways.

The major contributions of this work are: (1) We create *a new corpus of Wikipedia articles* annotated with linguistically motivated genericity labels both on the subject- and clause-level (see Section 3). The corpus is balanced with respect to genericity and about 10,000 clauses in size. (2) We present a *discourse-sensitive genericity labeler*. Technically, we use conditional random fields as a sequence labeling method (Section 4). We train and evaluate our method on the Wikipedia dataset and the ACE corpora, evaluating both the tasks of predicting NP genericity and the task of predicting clause-level genericity. Our labeler outperforms the state-of-the-art by a margin of 6.6-11.9% (depending on the data set) in terms of accuracy, at the same time increasing F_1-score. Much of the performance gain is due to the inclusion of discourse information. For the discussion of our experimental results, see Section 5.

In this paper, we do *not* address the following two important aspects of genericity. First, *habitual* sentences form a class of generalizing statements which bear a close relation to generics. As can be seen in example (4), they describe a characterizing property of either a specific entity or a class by generalizing over situations instead of or in addition to entities (Carlson, 2005). We classify habitual sentences with a generic subject as generic, and habitual sentences which describe a specific entity as non-generic, leaving the task of habituality detection for future work.

(4) *(a) John smokes after dinner.*
(b) Gentlemen smoke after dinner.

Second, generic clauses express regularities within classes of entities, and thus are similar to universally quantified sentences in their truth conditions and entailment properties. However, their truth-conditional interpretation is tricky, since they express typicality, describe stereotypes and allow exceptions, for example *Dutchmen are good sailors* is not false even if most Dutchmen do not sail at all (Carlson, 1977). We concentrate on the decision of whether a clause is generic or not, and leave the truth-conditional interpretation for further work. For a detailed discussion of the semantics of generics expressions see the comprehensive survey by Krifka et al. (1995); a short and instructive overview can be found in the first part of (Reiter and Frank, 2010).

2 Related Work

In this section, we first briefly review previously developed annotation schemes for genericity. We then describe work on automatically predicting the genericity of NPs or different types of clauses.

Annotation. ACE-2 (Mitchell et al., 2003) and ACE-2005 (Walker et al., 2006) are the two most notable annotation projects for labeling genericity of NPs to date. In the ACE-2 corpus, 40106 entity mentions in 520 newswire and broadcast documents are marked with regard to whether they refer to "any member of the set in question" (GEN, generic) rather than "some particular, identifiable member of that set" (SPC, specific/non-generic). The major drawback of ACE-2 is that genericity is basically defined as lack of specificity, which leads to uncertainty and inconsistencies in the annotation process, and to a heterogeneous set of NPs labeled with GEN, including quantificational NPs and NPs in modalized, future, conditional, hypothetical, negated, uncertain, and question contexts. In addition, in both ACE-2 and ACE-2005, predicative and modifier uses of nouns, to which the genericity distinction is not applicable, also receive labels (e.g. *John seems to be a nice person / a subway system*).

In the updated guidelines of ACE-2005, the label USP (underspecified) is introduced for non-generic non-specific reference, including NPs in the various contexts mentioned above that were improperly labeled as generic in ACE-2. The class also contains mentions of an entity whose identity would be 'difficult to locate' (*Officials reported ...*). Moreover, annotators are asked to mark truly ambiguous cases that have both a generic and a non-generic reading as USP. Finally, NEG (negated) marks negatively quantified entities that refer to the empty set of the kind mentioned.

While we agree that in general there are underspecified cases, the guidelines for ACE-2005 mix other phenomena into the USP class, resulting in a high confusion between USP and both of the labels SPC and GEN in the manual annotations (Friedrich et al., 2015). Data from two annotators is available, and we compute an agreement of Cohen's $\kappa = 0.53$ over the four labels. The ACE corpora consist only of news data, and the distributions of labels are highly skewed towards specific mentions. For some criticism of the ACE annotation scheme, see also Suh (2006).

Several linguistically motivated annotation studies targeting genericity of noun phrases bear similarity to our annotation scheme (Section 3), but comprise very little data (Poesio, 2004; Herbelot and Copestake, 2009). In the ARRAU corpus (Poesio and Artstein, 2008), about 24321 markables are tagged for genericity.

Nedoluzhko (2013) survey the treatment of genericity phenomena within coreference resolution research; they find a consistent definition of genericity to be lacking. Friedrich and Palmer (2014b) present an annotation scheme for situation types including generic sentences, which they find to be infrequent in their corpus consisting of news, jokes and (fund-raising) letters. Our new WikiGenerics corpus contains more than 10,000 clauses, approximately half of which are generic.

Automatic Identification of Genericity. Suh et al. (2006) propose a rule-based approach, which extracts only bare plurals and singular NPs quantified with *every* or *any* as generic. Reiter and Frank (2010) use a wide range of syntactic and semantic features to train a supervised classifier for identifying generic NPs. We compare to their method (described in detail in Section 5.2) as a highly-competitive baseline.

Palmer et al. (2007) classify clauses into several types of situation entities including states, events, generalizing sentences (habitual utterances referring to specific individuals) and generic sentences. They find that using context by using the labels of preceding clauses as features improves the classification of clause types, but generic sentences are extremely sparse in their data set. Our present approach uses a sequence labeling model that computes the best labeling for an entire sequence.

3 WikiGenerics: Data and Annotations

In order to study generics in a genre other than news (as in ACE), we turn to an encyclopedia, in which we expect many generics. We create our **WikiGenerics** corpus[1] as follows. We aim to create a corpus that is balanced in the sense that it contains many generic and non-generic sentences, and also generics from many different domains. We collect 102 texts about animals, organised crime, ethnic groups, games, sports, medicine, music, politics, religion, scientific disciplines and biographies from Wikipedia. For example, some sentences make statements about a 'natural' kind (*Blobfish are typically shorter than 30 cm*), others express definitions such as the rules of a football game (*The offensive team must line up in a legal formation before they can snap the ball*).

Generic clauses have the typical form of a predicative statement about the sentence topic, which is normally realized as the grammatical subject in English. Intuitions about NP-level genericity and its relation to clause-level genericity are quite reliable for topic NPs of clauses, which also typically occur in subject position in English. Since generics in non-subject positions are less frequent and hard to interpret (see the discussion of "dependent generics" by Link (1995)), we decided to annotate subject NPs only. We are aware that we are missing relevant cases (e.g. the less preferred reading

[1]The WikiGenerics corpus is freely available at: www.coli.uni-saarland.de/projects/sitent

of *Cats chase mice*, which attributes to mice the property of being chased by cats), but in this work, we want to study the "easier" subject cases as a first step.

We use the discourse parser SPADE (Soricut and Marcu, 2003) to automatically segment the first 70 sentences of each article into clauses. Each clause is manually annotated with the following information (for more details on the annotation scheme, see (Friedrich et al., 2015)):

- **Task NP**: whether or not the *subject* NP of the clause refers to a class or kind (**generic** vs. **non-generic**);
- **Task Cl**: whether the *clause* is **generic**, defined as a clause that makes a characterizing statement about a class or kind, or **non-generic**.
- **Task Cl+NP**: using the information from Task NP and Cl above, we automatically derive the following classification for each *clause* (compare to the explanation of example (2)).
  - **GEN_gen**: generic clause, subject is generic by definition (*The lion is a predatory cat*);
  - **NON-GEN_non-gen**: non-generic clause with a non-generic subject (*Simba roared*);
  - or **NON-GEN_gen**: episodic clause with a generic subject (*Dinosaurs died out*).
  - **GEN_non-gen** does not exist by definition.

We construct the gold standard for our experiments via majority voting over the labels given by three paid annotators, students of computational linguistics. Annotators were given a written manual and a short training on documents not included in the corpus. They are given the option to indicate segmentation errors, e.g. that two segments should actually be one, or that one segment contains multiple clauses. In the latter case, we ask them to give labels for the first clause in the segment. 10240 (86%) of all pre-segmented clauses received labels for all three tasks from all annotators, who were allowed to skip clauses that do not contain a finite verb. Our gold standard includes an additional 115 segments that did not receive a label by one annotator but were unanimously labeled by the other two. The other segments are disregarded in the experiments. Some of them have expletive subjects, and most others are non-finite verb phrases such as *to*-infinites or headlines that consist of only a NP. Inter-annotator agreement measured as Fleiss' κ (Fleiss, 1971) on the segments labeled by all three annotators is 0.70, 0.73 and 0.69 for Task NP, Task Cl and Task Cl+NP respectively, indicating substantial agreement (Landis and Koch, 1977).

4 A Sequence Labeling Model for Genericity

This section describes our method for identifying generic clauses and NPs in context. We apply the following methods on each of the three different prediction tasks NP, Cl and Cl+NP introduced in Section 3, varying only the type of labels on which we train and test. In contrast to prior work, our computational model integrates not only information from each local instance, but also information about the genericity status of surrounding instances. The final labeling for the sequence of instances of an entire document is optimized with regard to these two types of information, which, as we have argued in Section 1, both play a crucial role in determining genericity. The sequences to be labeled contain all clauses or NPs of a document. We also tried labeling sequences for paragraphs instead of documents, but the performance was similar. A reason might be that paragraphs are quite often linked by mentioning the same entities (Friedrich and Palmer, 2014a).

Computational model. We use linear chain conditional random fields (Lafferty et al., 2001) to label sequences of mentions or sequences of clauses with regard to their genericity. Conditional random fields (CRFs) are well suited for our labeling task as they do not make an independence assumption between the features. CRFs predict the conditional probability of label sequence $\vec{y}$ given an observation sequence $\vec{x}$ as follows:

$$P(\vec{y}|\vec{x}) = \frac{1}{Z(\vec{x})} exp(\sum_{j=1}^{n}\sum_{i=1}^{m}\lambda_i f_i(y_{j-1}, y_j, \vec{x}, j))$$

$Z(\vec{x})$ is a normalization constant, the sum over the scores of all possible label sequences for an observation sequence with the length of $\vec{x}$. The weights λ_i of the feature functions are the parameters to be learned. They do not depend on the current position j in the sequence. The feature functions f_i are in general allowed to look at the current label y_j, the previous label y_{j-1} and the entire observation sequence $\vec{x}$. We use a simple instantiation of a linear chain CRF whose feature functions take two forms, $f_i(y_j, x_j)$ and $f_i(y_{j-1}, y_j)$. We create a linear chain CRF model using the CRF++ toolkit[2], using all the default parameters.

[2]https://code.google.com/p/crfpp

NP-BASED FEATURES	
number	sg, pl
person	1, 2, 3
countability	from *Celex*, e.g. count
noun type	common, proper, pronoun
determiner type	def, indef, demon
part-of-speech	POS of head
bare plural	true, false
WN granularity	number of edges to top node
WN sense $[0-2]$	WN senses (head+hypernyms)
WN senseTop	top sense in hypernym hierarchy
WN lexical filename	person, artifact, event, ...
CLAUSE-BASED FEATURES	
dependency $[0-4]$	dependency relation between head and governor etc.
tense	tense, aspect and voice information, e.g. *pres_perf_active*
coarseTense	pres, past, fut
progressive	true, false
perfective	true, false
passive	true, false
temporal modifier	true, false
number of modifiers	numeric
part-of-speech	POS of head
predicate	lemma of head
adjunct-degree	positive, comparative, superlative
adjunct-pred	lemma of adverbial clauses' head

Table 1: **Features**. WN=WordNet.

Feature functions. We extract the set of features listed in Table 1 for each instance. This set of features is inspired by Reiter and Frank (2010), see also Section 5.2. In the case of the WikiGenerics corpus, the NP features are extracted for the subject of the clause. We parse the data using the Stanford parser (Klein and Manning, 2002) and obtain the subject NPs from the collapsed dependencies. For the ACE data, the NP features are extracted for all mentions in the gold standard and the clause features are extracted from the clause in which the mention appears. Our feature functions $f_i(y_j, x_j)$ are indicator functions combining the current label and one of the feature values of the current mention or clause, for example:

```
f = if (y_j = GENERIC and x_j.np.person=3)
      return 1 else return 0
```

We create two versions of the CRF model: the bigram[3] model additionally uses indicator functions $f(y_{j-1}, y_j)$ for each combination of labels, thus taking context into account. The unigram model does not use these feature functions, it is thus similar to a maximum entropy model (with a different normalization). Log-linear models work very well for many NLP tasks, especially if features are correlated as it is the case here, so in order to get a fair estimate of the impact of using the context (via the transition feature functions), we give numbers for this 'unigram' model in addition, rather than simply comparing the bigram-CRF to a Bayesian network, which is used by Reiter and Frank (2010). Using more complex feature functions did not result in significant performance gains, so we chose the simplest model. Note that even though the feature functions only formulate relationships between adjacent labels in the sequence, the optimal labeling is computed for the entire sequence: the choices of labels assigned to non-adjacent clauses *do* influence each other.

Two-step Approach for Task Cl+NP. Task Cl+NP can be regarded as a combination of the two decisions made in Task NP and Task Cl. Therefore, we approach Task Cl+NP in two ways. (a) We train a CRF which directly outputs the three labels. (b) The *two-step* approach combines the output from the labelers trained for Task NP and Task Cl into one label in a rule-based way. This leads to the additional class **GEN_non-gen**, of which no gold instances exist by definition. As we evaluate in terms of F_1-score and accuracy for the existing classes, items classified into this artificial class will simply be counted as wrong and lack from the recall counts.

5 Experiments

This section reports on our experiments, which we evaluate in terms of precision (P), recall (R) and F_1-measure per class. We compute macro-averages as $P_{macro} = \frac{1}{|c|} * \sum_{i=1}^{|c|} P_i$ etc., where $|c|$ stands for the number of classes. Macro-F_1 is the harmonic mean of macro-average P and R. To report on statistical significance of differences in accuracy, we apply McNemar's test with $p < 0.01$.

5.1 Experimental Settings and Data

We report results for cross validation (CV). Because we leverage contextual information by labeling sequences of clauses from entire documents, for all experiments presented in this section, if not indicated otherwise, we put all instances of one document into the same fold as one sequence. Fold sizes differ slightly from each other, but folds are kept constant for all experiments.

On WikiGenerics, we carry out all three prediction tasks as defined in Section 3. On the ACE corpora, we only conduct Task NP because there are

[3]Following CRF++ terminology.

System	generic P	generic R	generic F1	non-generic P	non-generic R	non-generic F1	macro-avg P	macro-avg R	macro-avg F1	accuracy
Majority class baseline	0.0	0.0	0.0	86.8	100	92.9	43.4	50.0	46.5	86.8
Person baseline (R&F)	60.4	10.2	17.5	87.9	99.0	93.1	74.2	54.6	62.9	87.2
R&F (BayesNet)	37.7	72.0	49.5	95.0	81.9	88.0	66.4	76.9	71.3	80.6
Reimpl. (BayesNet)	38.1	67.7	48.8	94.4	83.3	88.5	66.3	75.5	70.6	81.2

Table 2: Results of **reimplemented baseline** on ACE-2 (original, unbalanced data set), 40106 instances (annotated noun phrases). Weka's stratified 10-fold cross validation, using all features.

no labels corresponding to Task Cl or Task Cl+NP.

For the experiments on WikiGenerics, we use leave-one-document-out CV, i.e., we train on 101 of the 102 documents and test on the remaining document in each fold. The total number of clauses is 10355. From ACE-2005, we use the newswire and broadcast news subsections.[4] Due to low frequency, we omit instances of NEG in our experiments, and apply a three-way classification task (GEN, SPC, USP). We present results for all remaining 40106 mentions and for the subset of 18029 subject mentions, each time using 10-fold CV.

5.2 Baseline: Local Classifier

The system for identifying generic NPs of Reiter and Frank (2010), henceforth R&F, makes use of the English ParGram LFG grammar for the XLE parser (Butt et al., 2002). As this grammar is not publicly available, we implement a similar system using exclusively the Stanford CoreNLP toolsuite (Manning et al., 2014), the Celex database of English nouns (Baayen et al., 1996) and WordNet (Fellbaum, 1999). Our system is based on dkpro (de Castilho and Gurevych, 2014). We extract the features listed in Table 1 based on the POS tags and syntactic dependencies assigned by the Stanford parser (Klein and Manning, 2002). We could not reimplement several tense- and aspect-related ParGram-specific features. In order to compensate for this, we add an additional feature (tense) with finer-grained tense and voice information, using the rules described by Loaiciga et al. (2014). Other additional features did not improve performance, which shows that R&F's set of features captures the syntactic-semantic information relevant to genericity classification quite well. Therefore, we use this feature set also for the sequence labeling model. Using the same feature set allows us to attribute any performance gain to the context-awareness of our model rather than the features.

R&F train a Bayesian network using Weka (Hall et al., 2009). The decisions of this classifier are local to each clause. They report the performance of their system on the ACE-2 corpus: Table 2 shows that the performance of our reimplemented feature set[5] is comparable to the system of R&F.[6] In all other other tables, "BayesNet R&F" refers to our re-implemented system.

R&F present the "Person baseline" as a simple informed baseline (see Table 2). We trained a J48 decision tree on this feature alone, which confirmed that only second-person mentions (the generic "you") are classified as generic, while all other mentions are classified as non-generic.

5.3 Results and Discussion

In this section, we first discuss the results of our experiments in terms of identifying generic NPs or clauses. Then we present some additional experiments testing the influence of the different feature classes and of other discourse-related information.

All tasks, WikiGenerics. The observations described in this paragraph are the same for all three prediction tasks on WikiGenerics. As Tables 3 and 4 show, our CRF models outperform the baseline system of R&F by a large margin both in terms of accuracy and F_1-score on the WikiGenerics corpus. In Task NP and Task Cl, precision and recall are quite balanced (not shown in tables). The performance of the bigram model is significantly better than that of the unigram model, increasing accuracy by about 3%, at the same time increasing F_1. In an oracle experiment, we use the previous gold label instead of the predicted one for $f_i(y_{j-1}, y_j)$, and scores increase by up to 6.6% compared to the unigram model. These results provide strong empirical evidence for our hypoth-

[4]The rest of the data comprise broadcast conversation, weblog and forum texts as well as transcribed conversational telephone, and would require specialized preprocessing.

[5]Implementation available at: www.coli.uni-saarland.de/projects/sitent

[6]Table 6 in Reiter and Frank's paper contains some typographical errors here. We thank Nils Reiter for making available his ARFF files, so we can provide this updated version.

System	Task NP: Genericity of Subject generic F1	non-gen. F1	macro-avg F1	acc.	Task Cl: Genericity of Clause generic F1	non-gen. F1	macro-avg F1	acc.
Majority class	71.9	0.0	35.9	56.1	60.3	3.7	35.1	43.7
BayesNet (R&F)	72.6	70.8	72.3	71.7	72.4	74.6	73.7	73.5
CRF (unigram)	79.3	72.6	75.9	76.4*	77.9	77.0	77.4	77.4†
CRF (bigram)	**81.3**	**76.3**	**78.8**	**79.1***	**80.8**	**80.6**	**80.7**	**80.7**†
- only clause features	79.2	71.6	75.5	76.0	79.3	78.3	78.8	78.8
- only NP features	76.8	70.8	73.8	74.1	70.7	72.6	71.8	71.7
CRF (bigram, gold)	*85.0*	*80.4*	*82.7*	*83.0*	*82.9*	*82.6*	*82.8*	*82.8*

Table 3: Results on **WikiGenerics** for **Task NP** and **Task C**. *†Difference statistically significant.

System	Task Cl+NP: Genericity of Clause (three-way) GEN_gen F1	NON-GEN_non-gen F1	NON-GEN_gen F1	macro-avg P	R	F1	accuracy
Majority class	67.1	0.0	0.0	16.8	33.3	22.4	50.4
BayesNet (R&F)	69.1	69.1	26.1	54.5	58.4	56.4	65.2
CRF (unigram)	78.5	72.6	**35.4**	67.2	60.0	63.4	74.0*
CRF (bigram)	**81.3**	**76.9**	33.4	**70.3**	61.8	**65.8**	**77.4***
- two-step	80.8	75.8	28.6	61.5	**62.3**	61.9	73.4
- only clause feat.	79.4	72.6	25.3	67.0	57.2	61.8	74.3
- only NP feat.	72.9	71.4	2.5	53.0	49.9	51.4	70.0
CRF (bigram, gold)	*84.0*	*80.6*	*39.1*	*72.8*	*65.7*	*69.0*	*80.6*

Table 4: Results on **WikiGenerics** for **Task Cl+NP**. *Difference statistically significant.

esis that using context information is useful for identifying the genericity of NPs or clauses.

Task Cl+NP, WikiGenerics. In Task Cl+NP (see Table 4), only about 6% of the instances have the gold label **NON-GEN_gen** (i.e., a non-generic sentence with a generic subject), the other instances are distributed roughly evenly between the other two labels. The difficulty of Task Cl+NP thus consists in identifying this infrequent case. The three-way CRF outperforms the two-step approach both in terms of accuracy and macro-average F_1-score. The precision-recall tradeoff differs: for the **NON-GEN_gen** class, P and R of the CRF are 55.2% and 24.5% and those of the two-step-approach are 23.8% and 35.9%. The two-step approach labels more instances as **NON-GEN_gen** but does so in a less precise way. While the performance of our model leaves room for improvement on Task Cl+NP, especially with regard to the class **NON-GEN_gen**, it is worth noting that the computational model captures something about the nature of this latter class; its instances *do* look different in the feature space. The context-aware CRF using three labels performs best.

Feature set ablation. In this ablation test, shown in Tables 3 and 4, our best model (CRF bigram) uses either the set of clause-based or the set of NP-based features at a time. Clause-based features are more important than the NP-based features for all three classification tasks. An interesting observation is that the NP features alone are not able to separate the infrequent class **NON-GEN_gen** from the other two at all, the F_1-score of 2.5 shows that almost all instances of this class were labeled as one of the other two classes. In sum, this shows that whether an NP is interpreted as generic or not strongly depends on how it is used in the clause.

Task NP, ACE. Both on ACE-2 (see Table 5) and on ACE-2005 (see Table 6), the CRF outperforms the system of Reiter and Frank (2010) in terms of accuracy, and has a higher F_1-score. We give results also for subjects only as this parallels the setting of the WikiGenerics experiments (reasons for the restriction to subjects were given in Section 3). For subjects, the majority class SPC is less frequent (compare the accuracies of the two majority class baselines); only 7% of the subjects are marked as GEN, the rest are labeled as USP. The bigram model does not outperform the unigram model, but our oracle experiments show that context information is indeed useful: accuracy increases significantly and F_1 increases considerably, especially for subjects.

System	generic F1	non-generic F1	macro-avg P	R	F1	accuracy
Majority class	0.0	92.9	43.4	50.0	46.5	86.8
BayesNet (R&F)	47.4	87.9	65.5	**74.6**	69.8	80.4
CRF (unigrams)	49.1	93.5	75.5	68.7	71.3	88.5*
CRF (bigrams)	**51.0**	**93.7**	**76.5**	69.8	**72.4**	**88.9**
CRF (bigram, gold)	*57.6*	*94.4*	*79.8*	*73.4*	*76.0*	*90.1**

Table 5: Results on **ACE-2** for **Task NP**, 10-fold CV, folds contain complete documents. *Difference statistically significant.

System	macro-avg P	R	F1	accuracy
all 18029 annotated mentions				
Majority class	27.0	33.3	29.9	81.1
BayesNet (R&F)	50.8	57.2	53.8	74.5
CRF (unigram)	**61.6**	51.8	**55.1**	**83.2***
CRF (bigram)	60.6	51.7	54.8	83.0
CRF (bigram, gold)	*63.9*	*54.9*	*58.2*	*83.9**
5670 subject mentions				
Majority class	25.0	33.3	28.6	75.1
BayesNet (R&F)	51.5	**53.9**	52.7	72.5
CRF (unigram)	58.0	51.3	53.6	77.7*
CRF (bigram)	58.3	51.3	53.7	77.8
CRF (bigram, gold)	*62.4*	*56.1*	*58.6*	*79.6**

Table 6: Results on **ACE-2005** (bn+nw), **Task NP**, 10-fold CV, 3 classes: SPC, GEN, USP. *Difference statistically significant.

We identify two reasons for the fact that when evaluating on the ACE corpora, oracle information is needed to show the benefit of using bigram feature functions: (a) The frequency of **GEN** mentions in the ACE corpora is low – news contains only little generic information, so the context information is harder to leverage. (b) The ACE annotation guidelines contain some vagueness (see Section 3); this makes it harder for an automatic system to learn about regularities.

Higher-order Markov models. Another research question is whether models incorporating not only the previous label, but more preceding labels would perform even better. We turn to the Mallet toolkit (McCallum, 2002), whose CRF implementation allows for using higher-order models.[7] For example, an order-2 model considers the two previous labels. We use L1-regularization during training. Figure 1 shows that the optimum is reached for order-1 (bigram) models for each of the classification tasks for accuracy, the same tendencies were observed for F_1-score (not shown). It seems sufficient to use bigram feature functions; note that as explained in Section 4, the bigram model does not mean that only adjacent clauses influence each other – context is actually wider.

[7]The CRF++ toolkit, which we use in all other experiments, does not allow for higher-order models. We use CRF++ in the main experiments as it comes with a concise documentation; this helps to make our experiments easily replicable.

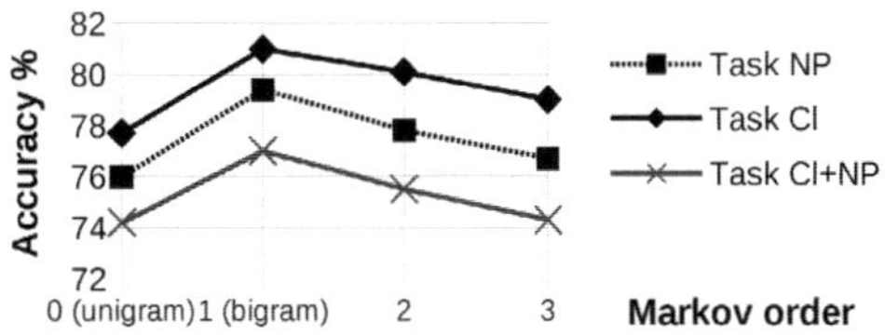

Figure 1: Labeling results for CRF models of various orders on WikiGenerics corpus.

Using coreference information. In our approximately balanced WikiGenerics corpus, 54% of all pronouns are marked as generic and 46% are marked as non-generic, which shows that there is no preference for pronouns to occur with either class. Some of the features (countability, noun type, determiner type, bare plural, and the WordNet related features) are not informative when applied to personal or relative pronouns. Sometimes, it is not even possible to determine number without referring to the antecedent (e.g., in the case of the relative pronoun 'who'). We conduct the following experiment: we automatically resolve coreference using the Stanford coreference resolution system (Raghunathan et al., 2010). We replace the NP features of each pronominal instance with the features of the first link of the coreference chain. We did not obtain a significant performance gain. One reason is that this change of features only applies to about 13% of the data. We observe that any positive changes in the classification go along with some negative changes which were often due to coreference resolution errors. One difficult step in manually annotating, and hence also in automatically resolving coreference is to determine whether a NP is generic or not (Nedoluzhko, 2013). The task of identifying generic NPs and coreference resolution are intertwined. We plan to manually annotate at least part of our corpus with coreference information in order to test to what extent the classification of the pronouns' genericity status can profit from including antecedent information.

6 Conclusion

We have presented a novel method for labeling sequences of clauses or their subjects with regard to their genericity, showing that genericity should be treated as a discourse-sensitive phenomenon. Our experiments prove that context information improves automatic labeling results, and that our model outperforms previous approaches by a large margin.

The major contributions of this work include the study of genericity both on the NP- and clause-level, and the study of the interaction of these two levels. Our results of Task Cl+NP show that our model indeed captures the three different types of clauses resulting from the combination of NP-level and clause-level genericity.

During the development of our annotation scheme, we found that it is beneficial to focus on genericity, disentangling it from the issue of specificity. Our work provides a step forward to finding reliable ways to apply semantic theories of genericity in practice, and we also provide a new state-of-the-art system for automatically labeling generic expressions. This in turn lays foundations for natural language processing tasks requiring text understanding.

Future Work. Our present approach for annotating and automatically classifying targets the subjects of each clause. We have not attempted to tackle the task of classifying the genericity status of other dependents, as they are even harder to classify than subjects, and a concise annotation scheme has to be worked out in order achieve an acceptable inter-annotator agreement on this task. Another related distinction is the one between habitual, stative and episodic sentences (Mathew and Katz, 2009), which applies to both what we call generic and non-generic sentences. No large corpora exist to date, but studying the interaction of these phenomena is on our research agenda.

Acknowledgments

We thank the anonymous reviewers, Alexis Palmer, Nils Reiter and Melissa Peate Sørensen for their helpful comments related to this work, and our annotators Christine Bocionek and Kleo-Isidora Mavridou. This research was supported in part by the Cluster of Excellence "Multimodal Computing and Interaction" of the German Excellence Initiative (DFG), and the first author is supported by an IBM PhD Fellowship.

References

Harald R. Baayen, Richard Piepenbrock, and Leon Gulikers. 1996. CELEX2. Philadelphia: Linguistic Data Consortium.

Miriam Butt, Helge Dyvik, Tracy Holloway King, Hiroshi Masuichi, and Christian Rohrer. 2002. The parallel grammar project. In *Proceedings of the 2002 workshop on Grammar engineering and evaluation-Volume 15*, pages 1–7. Association for Computational Linguistics.

Gregory Norman Carlson. 1977. *Reference to kinds in English.* Ph.D. thesis.

Gregory N. Carlson. 2005. Generics, Habituals and Iteratives. In Alex Barber, editor, *Encyclopedia of Language and Linguistics*. Elsevier.

Richard Eckart de Castilho and Iryna Gurevych. 2014. A broad-coverage collection of portable NLP components for building shareable analysis pipelines. In *Proceedings of the Workshop on Open Infrastructures and Analysis Frameworks for HLT (OIAF4HLT) at COLING*, pages 1–11.

Christiane Fellbaum. 1999. *WordNet.* Wiley Online Library.

Joseph L Fleiss. 1971. Measuring nominal scale agreement among many raters. *Psychological bulletin*, 76(5):378.

Annemarie Friedrich and Alexis Palmer. 2014a. Centering Theory in natural text: a large-scale corpus study. In *Proceedings of KONVENS 2014*. Universitätsbibliothek Hildesheim.

Annemarie Friedrich and Alexis Palmer. 2014b. Situation entity annotation. *In Proceedings of the Linguistic Annotation Workshop VIII*, page 149.

Annemarie Friedrich, Alexis Palmer, Melissa Peate Srensen, and Manfred Pinkal. 2015. Annotating genericity: a survey, a scheme, and a corpus. In *Proceedings of the 9th Linguistic Annotation Workshop (LAW IX)*, Denver, Colorado, US.

Mark Hall, Eibe Frank, Geoffrey Holmes, Bernhard Pfahringer, Peter Reutemann, and Ian H. Witten. 2009. The WEKA data mining software: an update. *ACM SIGKDD explorations newsletter*, 11(1):10–18.

Aurelie Herbelot and Ann Copestake. 2009. Annotating genericity: How do humans decide? (A case study in ontology extraction). *Studies in Generative Grammar 101*, page 103.

Dan Klein and Christopher D Manning. 2002. Fast exact inference with a factored model for natural language parsing. In *Advances in neural information processing systems*, pages 3–10.

Manfred Krifka, Francis Jeffrey Pelletier, Gregory N. Carlson, Alice ter Meulen, Godehard Link, and Gennaro Chierchia. 1995. Genericity: An Introduction. *The Generic Book*, pages 1–124.

John D. Lafferty, Andrew McCallum, and Fernando C. N. Pereira. 2001. Conditional Random Fields: Probabilistic Models for Segmenting and Labeling Sequence Data. In *Proceedings of the Eighteenth International Conference on Machine Learning*, ICML '01, pages 282–289, San Francisco, CA, USA. Morgan Kaufmann Publishers Inc.

J Richard Landis and Gary G Koch. 1977. The measurement of observer agreement for categorical data. *biometrics*, pages 159–174.

Godehard Link. 1995. Generic information and dependent generics. *The Generic Book*, pages 358–382.

Sharid Loaiciga, Thomas Meyer, and Andrei Popescu-Belis. 2014. English-French Verb Phrase Alignment in Europarl. In *Proceedings of LREC 2014*.

Christopher D Manning, Mihai Surdeanu, John Bauer, Jenny Finkel, Steven J Bethard, and David McClosky. 2014. The Stanford CoreNLP Natural Language Processing Toolkit. In *Proceedings of 52nd Annual Meeting of the Association for Computational Linguistics: System Demonstrations*, pages 55–60.

Thomas A. Mathew and E. Graham Katz. 2009. Supervised Categorization of Habitual and Episodic Sentences. In *Sixth Midwest Computational Linguistics Colloquium*, Bloomington, Indiana: Indiana University.

Andrew K McCallum. 2002. MALLET: A Machine Learning for Language Toolkit.

Alexis Mitchell, Stephanie Strassel, Mark Przybocki, JK Davis, George Doddington, Ralph Grishman, Adam Meyers, Ada Brunstein, Lisa Ferro, and Beth Sundheim. 2003. ACE-2 Version 1.0 LDC2003T11. Philadelphia: Linguistic Data Consortium.

Anna Nedoluzhko. 2013. Generic noun phrases and annotation of coreference and bridging relations in the Prague Dependency Treebank. In *Proceedings of the 7th Linguistic Annotation Workshop and Interoperability with Discourse*, pages 103–111.

Alexis Palmer, Elias Ponvert, Jason Baldridge, and Carlota Smith. 2007. A sequencing model for situation entity classification. In *Proceedings of the 45th Annual Meeting of the Association for Computational Linguistics*, page 896.

Massimo Poesio and Ron Artstein. 2008. Anaphoric Annotation in the ARRAU Corpus. In *LREC*.

Massimo Poesio. 2004. Discourse annotation and semantic annotation in the GNOME corpus. In *Proceedings of the 2004 ACL Workshop on Discourse Annotation*, pages 72–79. Association for Computational Linguistics.

Karthik Raghunathan, Heeyoung Lee, Sudarshan Rangarajan, Nathanael Chambers, Mihai Surdeanu, Dan Jurafsky, and Christopher Manning. 2010. A multipass sieve for coreference resolution. In *Proceedings of the 2010 Conference on Empirical Methods in Natural Language Processing*, pages 492–501. Association for Computational Linguistics.

Nils Reiter and Anette Frank. 2010. Identifying Generic Noun Phrases. In *Proceedings of the 48th Annual Meeting of the Association for Computational Linguistics*, pages 40–49, Uppsala, Sweden, July. Association for Computational Linguistics.

Radu Soricut and Daniel Marcu. 2003. Sentence level discourse parsing using syntactic and lexical information. In *Proceedings of the 2003 Conference of the North American Chapter of the Association for Computational Linguistics on Human Language Technology-Volume 1*, pages 149–156. Association for Computational Linguistics.

Sangweon Suh, Harry Halpin, and Ewan Klein. 2006. Extracting common sense knowledge from wikipedia. In *Proceedings of the Workshop on Web Content Mining with Human Language Technologies at ISWC*, volume 6.

Sangweon Suh. 2006. Extracting Generic Statements for the Semantic Web. *Master's thesis, University of Edinburgh.*

Christopher Walker, Stephanie Strassel, Julie Medero, and Kazuaki Maeda. 2006. ACE 2005 Multilingual Training Corpus LDC2006T06. Philadelphia: Linguistic Data Consortium.

Model-based Word Embeddings from Decompositions of Count Matrices

Karl Stratos **Michael Collins** **Daniel Hsu**

Columbia University, New York, NY 10027, USA
{stratos, mcollins, djhsu}@cs.columbia.edu

Abstract

This work develops a new statistical understanding of word embeddings induced from transformed count data. Using the class of hidden Markov models (HMMs) underlying Brown clustering as a generative model, we demonstrate how canonical correlation analysis (CCA) and certain count transformations permit efficient and effective recovery of model parameters with lexical semantics. We further show in experiments that these techniques empirically outperform existing spectral methods on word similarity and analogy tasks, and are also competitive with other popular methods such as WORD2VEC and GLOVE.

1 Introduction

The recent spike of interest in dense, low-dimensional lexical representations—i.e., word embeddings—is largely due to their ability to capture subtle syntactic and semantic patterns that are useful in a variety of natural language tasks. A successful method for deriving such embeddings is the negative sampling training of the skip-gram model suggested by Mikolov et al. (2013b) and implemented in the popular software WORD2VEC. The form of its training objective was motivated by efficiency considerations, but has subsequently been interpreted by Levy and Goldberg (2014b) as seeking a *low-rank factorization* of a matrix whose entries are word-context co-occurrence counts, scaled and transformed in a certain way. This observation sheds new light on WORD2VEC, yet also raises several new questions about word embeddings based on decomposing count data. What is the right matrix to decompose? Are there rigorous justifications for the choice of matrix and count transformations?

In this paper, we answer some of these questions by investigating the decomposition specified by CCA (Hotelling, 1936), a powerful technique for inducing generic representations whose computation is efficiently and exactly reduced to that of a matrix singular value decomposition (SVD). We build on and strengthen the work of Stratos et al. (2014) which uses CCA for learning the class of HMMs underlying Brown clustering. We show that certain count transformations enhance the accuracy of the estimation method and significantly improve the empirical performance of word representations derived from these model parameters (Table 1).

In addition to providing a rigorous justification for CCA-based word embeddings, we also supply a general template that encompasses a range of spectral methods (algorithms employing SVD) for inducing word embeddings in the literature, including the method of Levy and Goldberg (2014b). In experiments, we demonstrate that CCA combined with the square-root transformation achieves the best result among spectral methods and performs competitively with other popular methods such as WORD2VEC and GLOVE on word similarity and analogy tasks. We additionally demonstrate that CCA embeddings provide the most competitive improvement when used as features in named-entity recognition (NER).

2 Notation

We use $[n]$ to denote the set of integers $\{1, \ldots, n\}$. We denote the $m \times m$ diagonal matrix with values $v_1 \ldots v_m$ along the diagonal by diag$(v_1 \ldots v_m)$. We write $[a_1 \ldots a_m]$ to denote a matrix whose i-th column is a_i. The expected value of a random variable X is denoted by $\mathbf{E}[X]$. Given a matrix Ω and an exponent a, we distinguish the entrywise power operation $\Omega^{\langle a \rangle}$ (i.e., $\Omega^{\langle a \rangle}_{i,j} = (\Omega_{i,j})^a$) from the matrix power operation Ω^a (defined only for square Ω).

Proceedings of the 53rd Annual Meeting of the Association for Computational Linguistics and the 7th International Joint Conference on Natural Language Processing, pages 1282–1291,
Beijing, China, July 26-31, 2015.

3 Background in CCA

In this section, we review the variational characterization of CCA. This provides a flexible framework for a wide variety of tasks. CCA seeks to maximize a statistical quantity known as the Pearson correlation coefficient between random variables $L, R \in \mathbb{R}$:

$$\text{Cor}(L, R) := \frac{\mathbf{E}[LR] - \mathbf{E}[L]\mathbf{E}[R]}{\sqrt{\mathbf{E}[L^2] - \mathbf{E}[L]^2}\sqrt{\mathbf{E}[R^2] - \mathbf{E}[R]^2}}$$

This is a value in $[-1, 1]$ indicating the degree of linear dependence between L and R.

3.1 CCA objective

Let $X \in \mathbb{R}^n$ and $Y \in \mathbb{R}^{n'}$ be two random vectors. Without loss of generality, we will assume that X and Y have zero mean.[1] Let $m \leq \min(n, n')$. CCA can be cast as finding a set of projection vectors (called canonical directions) $a_1 \dots a_m \in \mathbb{R}^n$ and $b_1 \dots b_m \in \mathbb{R}^{n'}$ such that for $i = 1 \dots m$:

$$(a_i, b_i) = \underset{a \in \mathbb{R}^n,\, b \in \mathbb{R}^{n'}}{\arg\max} \; \text{Cor}(a^\top X, b^\top Y) \quad (1)$$
$$\text{Cor}(a^\top X, a_j^\top X) = 0 \quad \forall j < i$$
$$\text{Cor}(b^\top Y, b_j^\top Y) = 0 \quad \forall j < i$$

That is, at each i we simultaneously optimize vectors a, b so that the projected random variables $a^\top X, b^\top Y \in \mathbb{R}$ are maximally correlated, subject to the constraint that the projections are uncorrelated to all previous projections.

Let $A := [a_1 \dots a_m]$ and $B := [b_1 \dots b_m]$. Then we can think of the joint projections

$$\underline{X} = A^\top X \qquad \underline{Y} = B^\top Y \quad (2)$$

as new m-dimensional representations of the original variables that are transformed to be as correlated as possible with each other. Furthermore, often $m \ll \min(n, n')$, leading to a dramatic reduction in dimensionality.

3.2 Exact solution via SVD

Eq. (1) is non-convex due to the terms a and b that interact with each other, so it cannot be solved exactly using a standard optimization technique. However, a method based on SVD provides an efficient and exact solution. See Hardoon et al. (2004) for a detailed discussion.

[1] This can be always achieved through data preprocessing ("centering").

Lemma 3.1 (Hotelling (1936)). *Assume X and Y have zero mean. The solution (A, B) to (1) is given by $A = \boldsymbol{E}[XX^\top]^{-1/2}U$ and $B = \boldsymbol{E}[YY^\top]^{-1/2}V$ where the i-th column of $U \in \mathbb{R}^{n \times m}$ ($V \in \mathbb{R}^{n' \times m}$) is the left (right) singular vector of*

$$\Omega := \boldsymbol{E}[XX^\top]^{-1/2}\boldsymbol{E}[XY^\top]\boldsymbol{E}[YY^\top]^{-1/2} \quad (3)$$

corresponding to the i-th largest singular value σ_i. Furthermore, $\sigma_i = Cor(a_i^\top X, b_i^\top Y)$.

3.3 Using CCA for word representations

As presented in Section 3.1, CCA is a general framework that operates on a pair of random variables. Adapting CCA specifically to inducing word representations results in a simple recipe for calculating (3).

A natural approach is to set X to represent a word and Y to represent the relevant "context" information about a word. We can use CCA to project X and Y to a low-dimensional space in which they are maximally correlated: see Eq. (2). The projected X can be considered as a new word representation.

Denote the set of distinct word types by $[n]$. We set $X, Y \in \mathbb{R}^n$ to be one-hot encodings of words and their associated context words. We define a context word to be a word occurring within ρ positions to the left and right (excluding the current word). For example, with $\rho = 1$, the following snippet of text where the current word is "souls":

```
Whatever our souls are made of
```

will generate two samples of $X \times Y$: a pair of indicator vectors for "souls" and "our", and a pair of indicator vectors for "souls" and "are".

CCA requires performing SVD on the following matrix $\Omega \in \mathbb{R}^{n \times n}$:

$$\begin{aligned}\Omega =&(\mathbf{E}[XX^\top] - \mathbf{E}[X]\mathbf{E}[X]^\top)^{-1/2}\\ &(\mathbf{E}[XY^\top] - \mathbf{E}[X]\mathbf{E}[Y]^\top)\\ &(\mathbf{E}[YY^\top] - \mathbf{E}[Y]\mathbf{E}[Y]^\top)^{-1/2}\end{aligned}$$

At a quick glance, this expression looks daunting: we need to perform matrix inversion and multiplication on potentially large dense matrices. However, Ω is easily computable with the following observations:

Observation 1. We can ignore the centering operation when the sample size is large (Dhillon et al.,

2011). To see why, let $\{(x^{(i)}, y^{(i)})\}_{i=1}^{N}$ be N samples of X and Y. Consider the sample estimate of the term $\mathbf{E}[XY^\top] - \mathbf{E}[X]\mathbf{E}[Y]^\top$:

$$\frac{1}{N}\sum_{i=1}^{N} x^{(i)}(y^{(i)})^\top - \frac{1}{N^2}\left(\sum_{i=1}^{N} x^{(i)}\right)\left(\sum_{i=1}^{N} y^{(i)}\right)^\top$$

The first term dominates the expression when N is large. This is indeed the setting in this task where the number of samples (word-context pairs in a corpus) easily tends to billions.

Observation 2. The (uncentered) covariance matrices $\mathbf{E}[XX^\top]$ and $\mathbf{E}[YY^\top]$ are diagonal. This follows from our definition of the word and context variables as one-hot encodings since $\mathbf{E}[X_w X_{w'}] = 0$ for $w \neq w'$ and $\mathbf{E}[Y_c Y_{c'}] = 0$ for $c \neq c'$.

With these observations and the binary definition of (X, Y), each entry in Ω now has a simple closed-form solution:

$$\Omega_{w,c} = \frac{P(X_w = 1, Y_c = 1)}{\sqrt{P(X_w = 1)P(Y_c = 1)}} \tag{4}$$

which can be readily estimated from a corpus.

4 Using CCA for parameter estimation

In a less well-known interpretation of Eq. (4), CCA is seen as a parameter estimation algorithm for a language model (Stratos et al., 2014). This model is a restricted class of HMMs introduced by Brown et al. (1992), henceforth called the Brown model. In this section, we extend the result of Stratos et al. (2014) and show that its correctness is preserved under certain element-wise data transformations.

4.1 Clustering under a Brown model

A Brown model is a 5-tuple (n, m, π, t, o) for $n, m \in \mathbb{N}$ and functions π, t, o where

- $[n]$ is a set of word types.
- $[m]$ is a set of hidden states.
- $\pi(h)$ is the probability of generating $h \in [m]$ in the first position of a sequence.
- $t(h'|h)$ is the probability of generating $h' \in [m]$ given $h \in [m]$.
- $o(w|h)$ is the probability of generating $w \in [n]$ given $h \in [m]$.

Importantly, the model makes the following additional assumption:

Assumption 4.1 (Brown assumption). *For each word type $w \in [n]$, there is a unique hidden state $\mathcal{H}(w) \in [m]$ such that $o(w|\mathcal{H}(w)) > 0$ and $o(w|h) = 0$ for all $h \neq \mathcal{H}(w)$.*

In other words, this model is an HMM in which observation states are partitioned by hidden states. Thus a sequence of N words $w_1 \ldots w_N \in [n]^N$ has probability $\pi(\mathcal{H}(w_1)) \times \prod_{i=1}^{N} o(w_i|\mathcal{H}(w_i)) \times \prod_{i=1}^{N-1} t(\mathcal{H}(w_{i+1})|\mathcal{H}(w_i))$.

An equivalent definition of a Brown model is given by organizing the parameters in matrix form. Under this definition, a Brown model has parameters (π, T, O) where $\pi \in \mathbb{R}^m$ is a vector and $T \in \mathbb{R}^{m\times m}, O \in \mathbb{R}^{n \times m}$ are matrices whose entries are set to:

$$\begin{aligned} \pi_h &= \pi(h) & h &\in [m] \\ T_{h',h} &= t(h'|h) & h, h' &\in [m] \\ O_{w,h} &= o(w|h) & h &\in [m], w \in [n] \end{aligned}$$

Our main interest is in obtaining some representations of word types that allow us to identify their associated hidden states under the model. For this purpose, representing a word by the corresponding row of O is sufficient. To see this, note that each row of O must have a single nonzero entry by Assumption 4.1. Let $v(w) \in \mathbb{R}^m$ be the w-th row of O normalized to have unit 2-norm: then $v(w) = v(w')$ iff $\mathcal{H}(w) = \mathcal{H}(w')$. See Figure 1(a) for illustration.

A crucial aspect of this representational scheme is that its correctness is *invariant* to scaling and rotation. In particular, clustering the normalized rows of $\text{diag}(s)O^{\langle a\rangle}\text{diag}(s_2)Q^\top$ where $O^{\langle a\rangle}$ is any element-wise power of O with any $a \neq 0$, $Q \in \mathbb{R}^{m\times m}$ is any orthogonal transformation, and $s_1 \in \mathbb{R}^n$ and $s_2 \in \mathbb{R}^m$ are any positive vectors yields the correct clusters under the model. See Figure 1(b) for illustration.

4.2 Spectral estimation

Thus we would like to estimate O and use its rows for representing word types. But the likelihood function under the Brown model is non-convex, making an MLE estimation of the model parameters difficult. However, the hard-clustering assumption (Assumption 4.1) allows for a simple

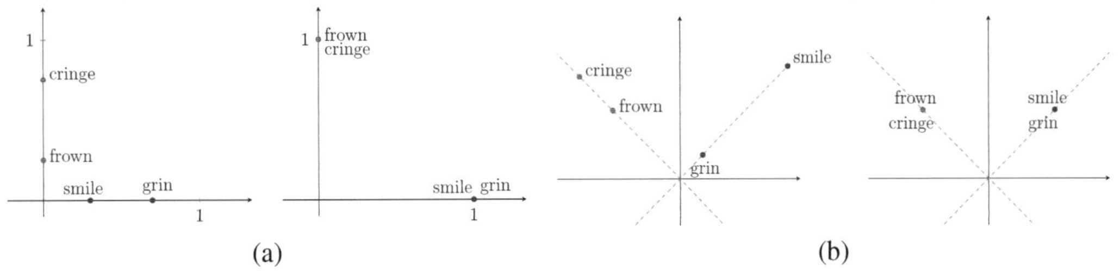

Figure 1: Visualization of the representational scheme under a Brown model with 2 hidden states. (a) Normalizing the original rows of O. (b) Normalizing the scaled and rotated rows of O.

spectral method for consistent parameter estimation of O.

To state the theorem, we define an additional quantity. Let ρ be the number of left/right context words to consider in CCA. Let $(H_1, \ldots, H_N) \in [m]^N$ be a random sequence of hidden states drawn from the Brown model where $N \geq 2\rho + 1$. Independently, pick a position $I \in [\rho + 1, N - \rho]$ uniformly at random. Define $\tilde{\pi} \in \mathbb{R}^m$ where $\tilde{\pi}_h := P(H_I = h)$ for each $h \in [m]$.

Theorem 4.1. *Assume $\tilde{\pi} > 0$ and rank(O) = rank$(T) = m$. Assume that a Brown model (π, T, O) generates a sequence of words. Let $X, Y \in \mathbb{R}^n$ be one-hot encodings of words and their associated context words. Let $U \in \mathbb{R}^{n \times m}$ be the matrix of m left singular vectors of $\Omega^{\langle a \rangle} \in \mathbb{R}^{n \times n}$ corresponding to nonzero singular values where Ω is defined in Eq. (4) and $a \neq 0$:*

$$\Omega_{w,c}^{\langle a \rangle} = \frac{P(X_w = 1, Y_c = 1)^a}{\sqrt{P(X_w = 1)^a P(Y_c = 1)^a}}$$

Then there exists an orthogonal matrix $Q \in \mathbb{R}^{m \times m}$ and a positive $s \in \mathbb{R}^m$ such that $U = O^{\langle a/2 \rangle} diag(s) Q^\top$.

This theorem states that the CCA projection of words in Section 3.3 is the rows of O up to scaling and rotation even if we raise each element of Ω in Eq. (4) to an arbitrary (nonzero) power. The proof is a variant of the proof in Stratos et al. (2014) and is given in Appendix A.

4.3 Choice of data transformation

Given a corpus, the sample estimate of $\Omega^{\langle a \rangle}$ is given by:

$$\hat{\Omega}_{w,c}^{\langle a \rangle} = \frac{\#(w,c)^a}{\sqrt{\#(w)^a \#(c)^a}} \tag{5}$$

where $\#(w, c)$ denotes the co-occurrence count of word w and context c in the corpus, $\#(w) := \sum_c \#(w,c)$, and $\#(c) := \sum_w \#(w,c)$. What choice of a is beneficial and why? We use $a = 1/2$ for the following reason: it stabilizes the variance of the term and thereby gives a more statistically stable solution.

4.3.1 Variance stabilization for word counts

The square-root transformation is a *variance-stabilizing transformation* for Poisson random variables (Bartlett, 1936; Anscombe, 1948). In particular, the square-root of a Poisson variable has variance close to $1/4$, independent of its mean.

Lemma 4.1 (Bartlett (1936)). *Let X be a random variable with distribution Poisson$(n \times p)$ for any $p \in (0, 1)$ and positive integer n. Define $Y := \sqrt{X}$. Then the variance of Y approaches $1/4$ as $n \to \infty$.*

This transformation is relevant for word counts because they can be naturally modeled as Poisson variables. Indeed, if word counts in a corpus of length N are drawn from a multinomial distribution over $[n]$ with N observations, then these counts have the same distribution as n independent Poisson variables (whose rate parameters are related to the multinomial probabilities), conditioned on their sum equaling N (Steel, 1953). Empirically, the peaky concentration of a Poisson distribution is well-suited for modeling word occurrences.

4.3.2 Variance-weighted squared-error minimization

At the heart of CCA is computing the SVD of the $\Omega^{\langle a \rangle}$ matrix: this can be interpreted as solving the following (non-convex) squared-error minimization problem:

$$\min_{u_w, v_c \in \mathbb{R}^m} \sum_{w,c} \left(\Omega_{w,c}^{\langle a \rangle} - u_w^\top v_c \right)^2$$

But we note that minimizing *unweighted* squared-error objectives is generally suboptimal when the target values are heteroscedastic. For instance, in linear regression, it is well-known that a *weighted least squares* estimator dominates ordinary least squares in terms of statistical efficiency (Aitken, 1936; Lehmann and Casella, 1998). For our setting, the analogous weighted least squares optimization is:

$$\min_{u_w, v_c \in \mathbb{R}^m} \sum_{w,c} \frac{1}{\mathrm{Var}\left(\Omega_{w,c}^{\langle a \rangle}\right)} \left(\Omega_{w,c}^{\langle a \rangle} - u_w^\top v_c\right)^2 \quad (6)$$

where $\mathrm{Var}(X) := \mathbf{E}[X^2] - \mathbf{E}[X]^2$. This optimization is, unfortunately, generally intractable (Srebro et al., 2003). The square-root transformation, nevertheless, obviates the variance-based weighting since the target values have approximately the same variance of 1/4.

5 A template for spectral methods

Figure 2 gives a generic template that encompasses a range of spectral methods for deriving word embeddings. All of them operate on co-occurrence counts $\#(w, c)$ and share the low-rank SVD step, but they can differ in the data transformation method (t) and the definition of the matrix of scaled counts for SVD (s).

We introduce two additional parameters $\alpha, \beta \leq 1$ to account for the following details. Mikolov et al. (2013b) proposed smoothing the empirical context distribution as $\hat{p}_\alpha(c) := \#(c)^\alpha / \sum_c \#(c)^\alpha$ and found $\alpha = 0.75$ to work well in practice. We also found that setting $\alpha = 0.75$ gave a small but consistent improvement over setting $\alpha = 1$. Note that the choice of α only affects methods that make use of the context distribution ($s \in \{\text{ppmi}, \text{cca}\}$).

The parameter β controls the role of singular values in word embeddings. This is always 0 for CCA as it does not require singular values. But for other methods, one can consider setting $\beta > 0$ since the best-fit subspace for the rows of Ω is given by $U\Sigma$. For example, Deerwester et al. (1990) use $\beta = 1$ and Levy and Goldberg (2014b) use $\beta = 0.5$. However, it has been found by many (including ourselves) that setting $\beta = 1$ yields substantially worse representations than setting $\beta \in \{0, 0.5\}$ (Levy et al., 2015).

Different combinations of these aspects reproduce various spectral embeddings explored in the literature. We enumerate some meaningful combinations:

SPECTRAL-TEMPLATE
Input: word-context co-occurrence counts $\#(w, c)$, dimension m, transformation method t, scaling method s, context smoothing exponent $\alpha \leq 1$, singular value exponent $\beta \leq 1$
Output: vector $v(w) \in \mathbb{R}^m$ for each word $w \in [n]$
Definitions: $\#(w) := \sum_c \#(w, c)$, $\#(c) := \sum_w \#(w, c)$, $N(\alpha) := \sum_c \#(c)^\alpha$

1. Transform all $\#(w, c)$, $\#(w)$, and $\#(c)$:

$$\#(\cdot) \leftarrow \begin{cases} \#(\cdot) & \text{if } t = \text{—} \\ \log(1 + \#(\cdot)) & \text{if } t = \log \\ \#(\cdot)^{2/3} & \text{if } t = \text{two-thirds} \\ \sqrt{\#(\cdot)} & \text{if } t = \text{sqrt} \end{cases}$$

2. Scale statistics to construct a matrix $\Omega \in \mathbb{R}^{n \times n}$:

$$\Omega_{w,c} \leftarrow \begin{cases} \#(w, c) & \text{if } s = \text{—} \\ \frac{\#(w,c)}{\#(w)} & \text{if } s = \text{reg} \\ \max\left(\log \frac{\#(w,c)N(\alpha)}{\#(w)\#(c)^\alpha}, 0\right) & \text{if } s = \text{ppmi} \\ \frac{\#(w,c)}{\sqrt{\#(w)\#(c)^\alpha}} \sqrt{\frac{N(\alpha)}{N(1)}} & \text{if } s = \text{cca} \end{cases}$$

3. Perform rank-m SVD on $\Omega \approx U\Sigma V^\top$ where $\Sigma = \mathrm{diag}(\sigma_1, \ldots, \sigma_m)$ is a diagonal matrix of ordered singular values $\sigma_1 \geq \cdots \geq \sigma_m \geq 0$.

4. Define $v(w) \in \mathbb{R}^m$ to be the w-th row of $U\Sigma^\beta$ normalized to have unit 2-norm.

Figure 2: A template for spectral word embedding methods.

No scaling $[t \in \{\text{—}, \log, \text{sqrt}\},\ s = \text{—}]$. This is a commonly considered setting (e.g., in Pennington et al. (2014)) where no scaling is applied to the co-occurrence counts. It is however typically accompanied with some kind of data transformation.

Positive point-wise mutual information (PPMI) $[t = \text{—},\ s = \text{ppmi}]$. Mutual information is a popular metric in many natural language tasks (Brown et al., 1992; Pantel and Lin, 2002). In this setting, each term in the matrix for SVD is set as the point-wise mutual information between word w and context c:

$$\log \frac{\hat{p}(w, c)}{\hat{p}(w)\hat{p}_\alpha(c)} = \log \frac{\#(w, c) \sum_c \#(c)^\alpha}{\#(w)\#(c)^\alpha}$$

Typically negative values are thresholded to 0 to keep Ω sparse. Levy and Goldberg (2014b) observed that the negative sampling objective of the skip-gram model of Mikolov et al. (2013b) is implicitly factorizing a shifted version of this matrix.[2]

[2]This is not equivalent to applying SVD on this matrix, however, since the loss function is different.

Regression $[t \in \{—, \text{sqrt}\},\ s = \text{reg}]$. Another novelty of our work is considering a low-rank approximation of a linear regressor that predicts the context from words. Denoting the word sample matrix by $\mathcal{X} \in \mathbb{R}^{N \times n}$ and the context sample matrix by $\mathcal{Y} \in \mathbb{R}^{N \times n}$, we seek $U^* = \arg\min_{U \in \mathbb{R}^{n \times n}} ||\mathcal{Y} - \mathcal{X}U||^2$ whose closed-from solution is given by:

$$U^* = (\mathcal{X}^\top \mathcal{X})^{-1} \mathcal{X}^\top \mathcal{Y} \tag{7}$$

Thus we aim to compute a low-rank approximation of U^* with SVD. This is inspired by other predictive models in the representation learning literature (Ando and Zhang, 2005; Mikolov et al., 2013a). We consider applying the square-root transformation for the same variance stabilizing effect discussed in Section 4.3.

CCA $[t \in \{—, \text{two-thirds}, \text{sqrt}\},\ s = \text{cca}]$. This is the focus of our work. As shown in Theorem 4.1, we can take the element-wise power transformation on counts (such as the power of $1, 2/3, 1/2$ in this template) while preserving the representational meaning of word embeddings under the Brown model interpretation. If there is no data transformation ($t = —$), then we recover the original spectral algorithm of Stratos et al. (2014).

6 Related work

We make a few remarks on related works not already discussed earlier. Dhillon et al. (2011) and (2012) propose novel modifications of CCA (LR-MVL and two-step CCA) to derive word embeddings, but do not establish any explicit connection to learning HMM parameters or justify the square-root transformation. Pennington et al. (2014) propose a weighted factorization of log-transformed co-occurrence counts, which is generally an intractable problem (Srebro et al., 2003). In contrast, our method requires only efficiently computable matrix decompositions. Finally, word embeddings have also been used as features to improve performance in a variety of supervised tasks such as sequence labeling (Dhillon et al., 2011; Collobert et al., 2011) and dependency parsing (Lei et al., 2014; Chen and Manning, 2014). Here, we focus on understanding word embeddings in the context of a generative word class model, as well as in empirical tasks that directly evaluate the word embeddings themselves.

7 Experiments

7.1 Word similarity and analogy

We first consider word similarity and analogy tasks for evaluating the quality of word embeddings. Word similarity measures the Spearman's correlation coefficient between the human scores and the embeddings' cosine similarities for word pairs. Word analogy measures the accuracy on syntactic and semantic analogy questions. We refer to Levy and Goldberg (2014a) for a detailed description of these tasks. We use the multiplicative technique of Levy and Goldberg (2014a) for answering analogy questions.

For the choice of corpus, we use a preprocessed English Wikipedia dump (`http://dumps.wikimedia.org/`). The corpus contains around 1.4 billion words. We only preserve word types that appear more than 100 times and replace all others with a special symbol, resulting in a vocabulary of size around 188k. We define context words to be 5 words to the left/right for all considered methods.

We use three word similarity datasets each containing 353, 3000, and 2034 word pairs.[3] We report the average similarity score across these datasets under the label AVG-SIM. We use two word analogy datasets that we call SYN (8000 syntactic analogy questions) and MIXED (19544 syntactic and semantic analogy questions).[4]

We implemented the template in Figure 2 in C++.[5] We compared against the public implementation of WORD2VEC by Mikolov et al. (2013b) and GLOVE by Pennington et al. (2014). These external implementations have numerous hyperparameters that are not part of the core algorithm, such as random subsampling in WORD2VEC and the word-context averaging in GLOVE. We refer to Levy et al. (2015) for a discussion of the effect of these features. In our experiments, we enable all these features with the recommended default settings.

We reserve a half of each dataset (by category)

[3]WordSim-353: `http://www.cs.technion.ac.il/~gabr/resources/data/wordsim353/`; MEN: `http://clic.cimec.unitn.it/~elia.bruni/MEN.html`; Stanford Rare Word: `http://www-nlp.stanford.edu/~lmthang/morphoNLM/`.

[4]`http://research.microsoft.com/en-us/um/people/gzweig/Pubs/myz_naacl13_test_set.tgz`; `http://www.fit.vutbr.cz/~imikolov/rnnlm/word-test.v1.txt`

[5]The code is available at `https://github.com/karlstratos/singular`.

Configuration		500 dimensions			1000 dimensions		
Transform (t)	Scale (s)	AVG-SIM	SYN	MIXED	AVG-SIM	SYN	MIXED
—	—	0.514	31.58	28.39	0.522	29.84	32.15
sqrt	—	0.656	60.77	65.84	0.646	57.46	64.97
log	—	0.669	59.28	66.86	0.672	55.66	68.62
—	reg	0.530	29.61	36.90	0.562	32.78	37.65
sqrt	reg	0.625	63.97	67.30	0.638	**65.98**	70.04
—	ppmi	0.638	41.62	58.80	0.665	47.11	65.34
sqrt	cca	**0.678**	**66.40**	**74.73**	**0.690**	65.14	**77.70**

Table 2: Performance of various spectral methods on the development portion of data.

Transform (t)	AVG-SIM	SYN	MIXED
—	0.572	39.68	57.64
log	0.675	55.61	69.26
two-thirds	0.650	60.52	74.00
sqrt	**0.690**	**65.14**	**77.70**

Table 1: Performance of CCA (1000 dimensions) on the development portion of data with different data transformation methods ($\alpha = 0.75$, $\beta = 0$).

as a held-out portion for development and use the other half for final evaluation.

7.1.1 Effect of data transformation for CCA

We first look at the effect of different data transformations on the performance of CCA. Table 1 shows the result on the development portion with 1000-dimensional embeddings. We see that without any transformation, the performance can be quite bad—especially in word analogy. But there is a marked improvement upon transforming the data. Moreover, the square-root transformation gives the best result, improving the accuracy on the two analogy datasets by 25.46% and 20.06% in absolute magnitude. This aligns with the discussion in Section 4.3.

7.1.2 Comparison among different spectral embeddings

Next, we look at the performance of various combinations in the template in Figure 2. We smooth the context distribution with $\alpha = 0.75$ for PPMI and CCA. We use $\beta = 0.5$ for PPMI (which has a minor improvement over $\beta = 0$) and $\beta = 0$ for all other methods. We generally find that using $\beta = 0$ is critical to obtaining good performance for $s \in \{—, \text{reg}\}$.

Table 2 shows the result on the development portion for both 500 and 1000 dimensions. Even without any scaling, SVD performs reasonably well with the square-root and log transformations. The regression scaling performs very poorly without data transformation, but once the square-root transformation is applied it performs quite well (especially in analogy questions). The PPMI scaling achieves good performance in word similarity but not in word analogy. The CCA scaling, combined with the square-root transformation, gives the best overall performance. In particular, it performs better than all other methods in mixed analogy questions by a significant margin.

7.1.3 Comparison with other embedding methods

We compare spectral embedding methods against WORD2VEC and GLOVE on the test portion. We use the following combinations based on their performance on the development portion:

- LOG: log transform, — scaling
- REG: sqrt transform, reg scaling
- PPMI: — transform, ppmi scaling
- CCA: sqrt transform, cca scaling

For WORD2VEC, there are two model options: continuous bag-of-words (CBOW) and skip-gram (SKIP). Table 3 shows the result for both 500 and 1000 dimensions.

In word similarity, spectral methods generally excel, with CCA consistently performing the best. SKIP is the only external package that performs comparably, with GLOVE and CBOW falling behind. In word analogy, REG and CCA are significantly better than other spectral methods. They are also competitive to GLOVE and CBOW, but SKIP does perform the best among all compared methods on (especially syntactic) analogy questions.

Method		500 dimensions			1000 dimensions		
		AVG-SIM	SYN	MIXED	AVG-SIM	SYN	MIXED
Spectral	LOG	0.652	59.52	67.27	0.635	56.53	68.67
	REG	0.602	65.51	67.88	0.609	66.47	70.48
	PPMI	0.628	43.81	58.38	0.637	48.99	63.82
	CCA	**0.655**	68.38	74.17	**0.650**	66.08	76.38
Others	GLOVE	0.576	68.30	78.08	0.586	67.40	78.73
	CBOW	0.597	75.79	73.60	0.509	70.97	60.12
	SKIP	0.642	**81.08**	**78.73**	0.641	**79.98**	**83.35**

Table 3: Performance of different word embedding methods on the test portion of data. See the main text for the configuration details of spectral methods.

7.2 As features in a supervised task

Finally, we use word embeddings as features in NER and compare the subsequent improvements between various embedding methods. The experimental setting is identical to that of Stratos et al. (2014). We use the Reuters RCV1 corpus which contains 205 million words. With frequency thresholding, we end up with a vocabulary of size around 301k. We derive LOG, REG, PPMI, and CCA embeddings as described in Section 7.1.3, and GLOVE, CBOW, and SKIP embeddings again with the recommended default settings. The number of left/right contexts is 2 for all methods. For comparison, we also derived 1000 Brown clusters (BROWN) on the same vocabulary and used the resulting bit strings as features (Brown et al., 1992).

Table 4 shows the result for both 30 and 50 dimensions. In general, using any of these lexical features provides substantial improvements over the baseline.[6] In particular, the 30-dimensional CCA embeddings improve the F1 score by 2.84 on the development portion and by 4.88 on the test portion. All spectral methods perform competitively with external packages, with CCA and SKIP consistently delivering the biggest improvements on the development portion.

Features	30 dimensions		50 dimensions	
	Dev	Test	Dev	Test
—	90.04	84.40	90.04	84.40
BROWN	92.49	88.75	92.49	88.75
LOG	92.27	88.87	92.91	**89.67**
REG	92.51	88.08	92.73	88.88
PPMI	92.25	89.27	92.53	89.37
CCA	**92.88**	**89.28**	92.94	89.01
GLOVE	91.49	87.16	91.58	86.80
CBOW	92.44	88.34	92.83	89.21
SKIP	92.63	88.78	**93.11**	89.32

Table 4: NER F1 scores when word embeddings are added as features to the baseline (—).

8 Conclusion

In this work, we revisited SVD-based methods for inducing word embeddings. We examined a framework provided by CCA and showed that the resulting word embeddings can be viewed as cluster-revealing parameters of a certain model and that this result is robust to data transformation. Our proposed method gives the best result among spectral methods and is competitive to other popular word embedding techniques.

This work suggests many directions for future work. Past spectral methods that involved CCA without data transformation (e.g., Cohen et al. (2013)) may be revisited with the square-root transformation. Using CCA to induce representations other than word embeddings is another important future work. It would also be interesting to formally investigate the theoretical merits and algorithmic possibility of solving the variance-weighted objective in Eq. (6). Even though the objective is hard to optimize in the worst case, it may be tractable under natural conditions.

[6] We mention that the well-known dev/test discrepancy in the CoNLL 2003 dataset makes the results on the test portion less reliable.

Acknowledgments

We thank Omer Levy, Yoav Goldberg, and David Belanger for helpful discussions. This work was made possible by a research grant from Bloomberg's Knowledge Engineering team.

A Proof of Theorem 4.1

We first define some random variables. Let ρ be the number of left/right context words to consider in CCA. Let $(W_1, \ldots, W_N) \in [n]^N$ be a random sequence of words drawn from the Brown model where $N \geq 2\rho + 1$, along with the corresponding sequence of hidden states $(H_1, \ldots, H_N) \in [m]^N$. Independently, pick a position $I \in [\rho + 1, N - \rho]$ uniformly at random; pick an integer $J \in [-\rho, \rho] \backslash \{0\}$ uniformly at random. Define $B \in \mathbb{R}^{n \times n}$, $u, v \in \mathbb{R}^n$, $\tilde{\pi} \in \mathbb{R}^m$, and $\tilde{T} \in \mathbb{R}^{m \times m}$ as follows:

$$\begin{aligned} B_{w,c} &:= P(W_I = w, W_{I+J} = c) & \forall w, c \in [n] \\ u_w &:= P(W_I = w) & \forall w \in [n] \\ v_c &:= P(W_{I+J} = c) & \forall c \in [n] \\ \tilde{\pi}_h &:= P(H_I = h) & \forall h \in [m] \\ \tilde{T}_{h',h} &:= P(H_{I+J} = h' | H_I = h) & \forall h, h' \in [m] \end{aligned}$$

First, we show that $\Omega^{\langle a \rangle}$ has a particular structure under the Brown assumption. For the choice of positive vector $s \in \mathbb{R}^m$ in the theorem, we define $s_h := (\sum_w o(w|h)^a)^{-1/2}$ for all $h \in [m]$.

Lemma A.1. *$\Omega^{\langle a \rangle} = A\Theta^\top$ where $\Theta \in \mathbb{R}^{n \times m}$ has rank m and $A \in \mathbb{R}^{n \times m}$ is defined as:*

$$A := \textit{diag}(O\tilde{\pi})^{-a/2} O^{\langle a \rangle} \textit{diag}(\tilde{\pi})^{a/2} \textit{diag}(s)$$

Proof. Let $\tilde{O} := O\tilde{T}$. It can be algebraically verified that $B = O\text{diag}(\tilde{\pi})\tilde{O}^\top$, $u = O\tilde{\pi}$, and $v = \tilde{O}\tilde{\pi}$. By Assumption 4.1, each entry of $B^{\langle a \rangle}$ has the form

$$\begin{aligned} B^{\langle a \rangle}_{w,c} &= \left(\sum_{h \in [m]} O_{w,h} \times \tilde{\pi}_h \times \tilde{O}_{c,h} \right)^a \\ &= \left(O_{w,\mathcal{H}(w)} \times \tilde{\pi}_{\mathcal{H}(w)} \times \tilde{O}_{c,\mathcal{H}(w)} \right)^a \\ &= O^a_{w,\mathcal{H}(w)} \times \tilde{\pi}^a_{\mathcal{H}(w)} \times \tilde{O}^a_{c,\mathcal{H}(w)} \\ &= \sum_{h \in [m]} O^a_{w,h} \times \tilde{\pi}^a_h \times \tilde{O}^a_{c,h} \end{aligned}$$

Thus $B^{\langle a \rangle} = O^{\langle a \rangle}\text{diag}(\tilde{\pi})^a(\tilde{O}^{\langle a \rangle})^\top$. Therefore,

$$\begin{aligned} \Omega^{\langle a \rangle} &= \left(\text{diag}(u)^{-1/2} B \text{diag}(v)^{-1/2} \right)^{\langle a \rangle} \\ &= \text{diag}(u)^{-a/2} B^{\langle a \rangle} \text{diag}(v)^{-a/2} \\ &= \text{diag}(O\tilde{\pi})^{-a/2} O^{\langle a \rangle} \text{diag}(\tilde{\pi})^{a/2} \text{diag}(s) \\ &\quad \text{diag}(s)^{-1} \text{diag}(\tilde{\pi})^{a/2} (\tilde{O}^{\langle a \rangle})^\top \text{diag}(\tilde{O}\tilde{\pi})^{-a/2} \end{aligned}$$

This gives the desired result. □

Next, we show that the left component of $\Omega^{\langle a \rangle}$ is in fact the emission matrix O up to (nonzero) scaling and is furthermore orthonormal.

Lemma A.2. *The matrix A in Lemma A.1 has the expression $A = O^{\langle a/2 \rangle}\textit{diag}(s)$ and has orthonormal columns.*

Proof. By Assumption 4.1, each entry of A is simplified as follows:

$$\begin{aligned} A_{w,h} &= \frac{o(w|h)^a \times \tilde{\pi}_h^{a/2} \times s_h}{o(w|\mathcal{H}(w))^{a/2} \times \tilde{\pi}^{a/2}_{\mathcal{H}(w)}} \\ &= o(w|h)^{a/2} \times s_h \end{aligned}$$

This proves the first part of the lemma. Note that:

$$[A^\top A]_{h,h'} = \begin{cases} s_h^2 \times \sum_w o(w|h)^a & \text{if } h = h' \\ 0 & \text{otherwise} \end{cases}$$

Thus our choice of s gives $A^\top A = \mathcal{I}_{m \times m}$. □

Proof of Theorem 4.1. With Lemma A.1 and A.2, the proof is similar to the proof of Theorem 5.1 in Stratos et al. (2014). □

References

Alexander C Aitken. 1936. On least squares and linear combination of observations. *Proceedings of the Royal Society of Edinburgh*, 55:42–48.

Rie Kubota Ando and Tong Zhang. 2005. A framework for learning predictive structures from multiple tasks and unlabeled data. *The Journal of Machine Learning Research*, 6:1817–1853.

Francis J Anscombe. 1948. The transformation of poisson, binomial and negative-binomial data. *Biometrika*, pages 246–254.

MSo Bartlett. 1936. The square root transformation in analysis of variance. *Supplement to the Journal of the Royal Statistical Society*, pages 68–78.

Peter F Brown, Peter V Desouza, Robert L Mercer, Vincent J Della Pietra, and Jenifer C Lai. 1992. Class-based n-gram models of natural language. *Computational Linguistics*, 18(4):467–479.

Danqi Chen and Christopher D Manning. 2014. A fast and accurate dependency parser using neural networks. In *Proceedings of the Empirical Methods in Natural Language Processing*, pages 740–750.

Shay B Cohen, Karl Stratos, Michael Collins, Dean P Foster, and Lyle H Ungar. 2013. Experiments with spectral learning of latent-variable pcfgs. In *Proceedings of the North American Chapter of the Association of Computational Linguistics*, pages 148–157.

Ronan Collobert, Jason Weston, Léon Bottou, Michael Karlen, Koray Kavukcuoglu, and Pavel Kuksa. 2011. Natural language processing (almost) from scratch. *The Journal of Machine Learning Research*, 12:2493–2537.

Scott C. Deerwester, Susan T Dumais, Thomas K. Landauer, George W. Furnas, and Richard A. Harshman. 1990. Indexing by latent semantic analysis. *Journal of the American Society for Information Science*, 41(6):391–407.

Paramveer Dhillon, Dean P Foster, and Lyle H Ungar. 2011. Multi-view learning of word embeddings via cca. In *Proceedings of the Advances in Neural Information Processing Systems*, pages 199–207.

Paramveer S. Dhillon, Jordan Rodu, Dean P. Foster, and Lyle H. Ungar. 2012. Two step cca: A new spectral method for estimating vector models of words. In *Proceedings of the International Conference on Machine learning*.

David Hardoon, Sandor Szedmak, and John Shawe-Taylor. 2004. Canonical correlation analysis: An overview with application to learning methods. *Neural Computation*, 16(12):2639–2664.

Harold Hotelling. 1936. Relations between two sets of variates. *Biometrika*, 28(3/4):321–377.

Erich Leo Lehmann and George Casella. 1998. *Theory of point estimation*, volume 31. Springer Science & Business Media.

Tao Lei, Yu Xin, Yuan Zhang, Regina Barzilay, and Tommi Jaakkola. 2014. Low-rank tensors for scoring dependency structures. In *Proceedings of the Association for Computational Linguistics*, volume 1, pages 1381–1391.

Omer Levy and Yoav Goldberg. 2014a. Linguistic regularities in sparse and explicit word representations. In *Proceedings of the Computational Natural Language Learning*, page 171.

Omer Levy and Yoav Goldberg. 2014b. Neural word embedding as implicit matrix factorization. In *Proceedings of the Advances in Neural Information Processing Systems*, pages 2177–2185.

Omer Levy, Yoav Goldberg, Ido Dagan, and Israel Ramat-Gan. 2015. Improving distributional similarity with lessons learned from word embeddings. *Transactions of the Association for Computational Linguistics*, 3.

Tomas Mikolov, Kai Chen, Greg Corrado, and Jeffrey Dean. 2013a. Efficient estimation of word representations in vector space. *arXiv preprint arXiv:1301.3781*.

Tomas Mikolov, Ilya Sutskever, Kai Chen, Greg S Corrado, and Jeff Dean. 2013b. Distributed representations of words and phrases and their compositionality. In *Proceedings of the Advances in Neural Information Processing Systems*, pages 3111–3119.

Patrick Pantel and Dekang Lin. 2002. Discovering word senses from text. In *Proceedings of the ACM SIGKDD international conference on Knowledge discovery and data mining*, pages 613–619. ACM.

Jeffrey Pennington, Richard Socher, and Christopher D Manning. 2014. Glove: Global vectors for word representation. In *Proceedings of the Empirical Methods in Natural Language Processing*, volume 12.

Nathan Srebro, Tommi Jaakkola, et al. 2003. Weighted low-rank approximations. In *Proceedings of the International Conference on Machine learning*, volume 3, pages 720–727.

Robert G. D. Steel. 1953. Relation between poisson and multinomial distributions. Technical Report BU-39-M, Cornell University.

Karl Stratos, Do-kyum Kim, Michael Collins, and Daniel Hsu. 2014. A spectral algorithm for learning class-based n-gram models of natural language. In *Proceedings of the Association for Uncertainty in Artificial Intelligence*.

Entity Hierarchy Embedding

Zhiting Hu, Poyao Huang, Yuntian Deng, Yingkai Gao, Eric P. Xing
School of Computer Science
Carnegie Mellon University
Pittsburgh, PA 15213, USA
{zhitingh,poyaoh,yuntiand,yingkaig,epxing}@cs.cmu.edu

Abstract

Existing distributed representations are limited in utilizing structured knowledge to improve semantic relatedness modeling. We propose a principled framework of embedding entities that integrates hierarchical information from large-scale knowledge bases. The novel embedding model associates each category node of the hierarchy with a distance metric. To capture structured semantics, the entity similarity of context prediction are measured under the aggregated metrics of relevant categories along all inter-entity paths. We show that both the entity vectors and category distance metrics encode meaningful semantics. Experiments in entity linking and entity search show superiority of the proposed method.

1 Introduction

There has been a growing interest in distributed representation that learns compact vectors (a.k.a embedding) for words (Mikolov et al., 2013a), phrases (Passos et al., 2014), and concepts (Hill and Korhonen, 2014), etc. The induced vectors are expected to capture semantic relatedness of the linguistic items, and are widely used in sentiment analysis (Tang et al., 2014), machine translation (Zhang et al., 2014), and information retrieval (Clinchant and Perronnin, 2013), to name a few.

Despite the impressive success, existing work is still limited in utilizing structured knowledge to enhance the representation. For instance, word and phrase embeddings are largely induced from plain text. Though recent knowledge graph embeddings (Lin et al., 2015; Wang et al., 2014) integrate the relational structure among entities, they primarily target at link prediction and lack an explicit relatedness measure.

In this paper, we propose to improve the distributed representations of entities by integrating hierarchical information from large-scale knowledge bases (KBs). An entity hierarchy groups entities into categories which are further organized to form a taxonomy. It provides rich structured knowledge on entity relatedness (Resnik, 1995). Our work goes beyond the previous heuristic use of entity hierarchy which relies on hand-crafted features (Kaptein and Kamps, 2013; Ponzetto and Strube, 2007), and develops a principled optimization-based framework. We learn a *distance metric* for each category node, and measure entity-context similarity under the aggregated metrics of all relevant categories. The metric aggregation encodes the hierarchical property that nearby entities tend to share common semantic features. We further provide a highly-efficient implementation in order to handle large complex hierarchies.

We train a distributed representation for the whole entity hierarchy of Wikipedia. Both the entity vectors and the category distance metrics capture meaningful semantics. We deploy the embedding in both entity linking (Han and Sun, 2012) and entity search (Demartini et al., 2010) tasks. Hierarchy embedding significantly outperforms that without structural knowledge. Our methods also show superiority over existing competitors.

To the best of our knowledge, this is the first work to learn distributed representations that incorporates hierarchical knowledge in a principled framework. Our model that encodes hierarchy by distance metric learning and aggregation provides a potentially important and general scheme for utilizing hierarchical knowledge.

The rest of the paper is organized as follows: §2 describes the proposed embedding model; §3 presents the application of the learned embedding; §4 evaluates the approach; §5 reviews related work; and finally, §6 concludes the paper.

Proceedings of the 53rd Annual Meeting of the Association for Computational Linguistics and the 7th International Joint Conference on Natural Language Processing, pages 1292–1300,
Beijing, China, July 26-31, 2015.

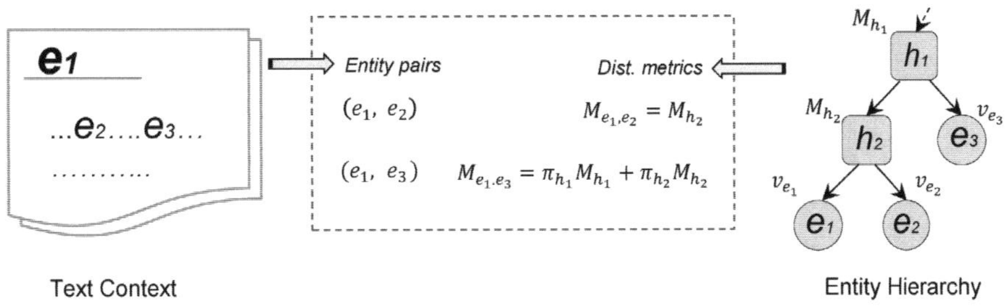

Figure 1: The model architecture. The text context of an entity is based on its KB encyclopedia article. The entity hierarchical structure is incorporated through distance metric learning and aggregation.

2 Entity Hierarchy Embedding

The objective of the embedding model is to find a representation for each entity that is useful for predicting other entities occurring in its *context*. We build entity's context upon KB encyclopedia articles, where entity annotations are readily available. We further incorporate the entity hierarchical structure in the context prediction through distance metric learning and aggregation, which encodes the rich structured knowledge in the induced representations. Our method is flexible and efficient to model large complex DAG-structured hierarchies. Figure 1 shows an overview of the model architecture.

2.1 Model Architecture

Our architecture builds on the skip-gram word embedding framework (Mikolov et al., 2013b). In the skip-gram model, a set of (target, context) word pairs are extracted by sliding a fixed-length context window over a text corpus, and the word vectors are learned such that the similarity of the target- and context-word vectors is maximized. We generalize both the context definition and the similarity measure for entity hierarchy embedding.

Unlike words that can be directly extracted from plain text, entities are hidden semantics underlying their surface forms. In order to avoid manual annotation cost, we exploit the text corpora from KBs where the referent entities of surface text are readily annotated. Moreover, since a KB encyclopedia article typically focuses on describing one entity, we naturally extend the entity's context as its whole article, and obtain a set of entity pairs $\mathcal{D} = \{(e_T, e_C)\}$, where e_T denotes the target-entity and e_C denotes the context-entity occurring in entity e_T's context.

Let $\mathcal{E}$ be the set of entities. For each entity $e \in \mathcal{E}$, the model learns both a "target vector" $v_e \in \mathbb{R}^n$ and "context vector" $\bar{v}_e \in \mathbb{R}^n$, by maximizing the training objective

$$\mathcal{L} = \frac{1}{|\mathcal{D}|} \sum\nolimits_{(e_T, e_C) \in \mathcal{D}} \log p(e_C | e_T), \qquad (1)$$

where the prediction probability is defined as a softmax:

$$p(e_C | e_T) = \frac{\exp\{-d(e_T, e_C)\}}{\sum_{e \in \mathcal{E}} \exp\{-d(e_T, e)\}}. \qquad (2)$$

Here $d(e, e')$ is the distance between the target vector of e (i.e., v_e) and the context vector of e' (i.e., $\bar{v}_{e'}$). We present the design in the following.

2.2 Hierarchical Extension

An entity hierarchy takes entities as leaf nodes and categories as internal nodes, which provides key knowledge sources on semantic relatedness that 1) far-away entities in the hierarchy tend to be semantically distant, and 2) nearby entities tend to share common semantic features. We aim to encode this knowledge in our representations. As KB hierarchies are large complex DAG structures, we develop a highly-efficient scheme to enable practical training.

Specifically, we associate a separate *distance metric* $M_h \in \mathbb{R}^{n \times n}$ with each category h in the hierarchy. A distance metric is a positive semidefinite (PSD) matrix. We then measure the distance between two entities under some *aggregated* distance metric as detailed below. The local metrics thus not only serve to capture the characteristics of individual categories, but also make it possible to share the representation across entities through metric aggregation of relevant categories.

Metric aggregation Given two entities e and e', let $\mathcal{P}_{e,e'}$ be the path between them. One obvious way to define the aggregated metric $M_{e,e'} \in \mathbb{R}^{n \times n}$ is through a combination of the metrics on the

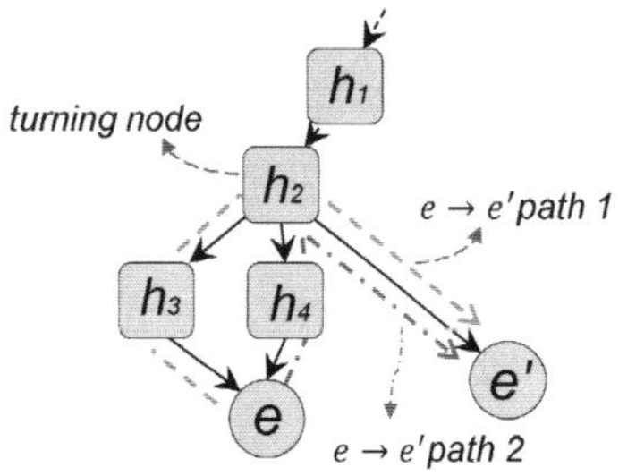

Figure 2: Paths in a DAG-structured hierarchy. A path P is defined as a sequence of non-duplicated nodes with the property that there exists a *turning node* $t \in P$ such that any two consecutive nodes before t are (child, parent) pairs, while consecutive nodes after t are (parent, child) pairs. Thus a turning node is necessarily a common ancestor.

path: $\sum_{h \in \mathcal{P}_{e,e'}} M_h$, leading to a nice property that the more nodes a path has, the more distant the entities tend to be (as M_h is PSD). This simple strategy, however, can be problematic when the hierarchy has a complex DAG structure, in that there can be multiple paths between two entities (Figure 2). Though the shortest path can be selected, it ignores other related category nodes and loses rich information. In contrast, an ideal scheme should not only mirror the distance in the hierarchy, but also take into account all possible paths in order to capture the full aspects of relatedness.

However, hierarchies in large KBs can be complex and contains combinationally many paths between any two entities. We propose an efficient approach that avoids enumerating paths and instead models the underlying nodes directly. In particular, we extend $\mathcal{P}_{e,e'}$ as the set of all category nodes included in any of the $e \to e'$ paths, and define the aggregate metric as

$$M_{e,e'} = \gamma_{e,e'} \sum_{h \in \mathcal{P}_{e,e'}} \pi_{ee',h} M_h, \quad (3)$$

where $\{\pi_{ee',h}\}$ are the relative weights of the categories such that $\sum_{h \in \mathcal{P}_{e,e'}} \pi_{ee',h} = 1$. This serves to balance the size of $\mathcal{P}$ across different entity pairs. We set $\pi_{ee',h} \propto (\frac{1}{s_{h\downarrow e}} + \frac{1}{s_{h\downarrow e'}})$ with $s_{h\downarrow e}$ being the average #steps going down from node h to node e in the hierarchy (infinite if h is not an ancestor of e). This implements the intuition that an entity (e.g., "Iphone") is more relevant to its immediate categories (e.g., "Mobile phones") than to farther and more generic ancestors (e.g., "Technology"). The scaling factor $\gamma_{e,e'}$ encodes the distance of the entities in the hierarchy and can be of various choices. We set $\gamma_{e,e'} = \min_h\{s_{h\downarrow e} + s_{h\downarrow e'}\}$ to mirror the least common ancestor.

In Figure 2, $\mathcal{P}_{e,e'} = \{h_2, h_3, h_4\}$, and the relative weights of the categories are $\pi_{ee',h_2} \propto 3/2$ and $\pi_{ee',h_3} = \pi_{ee',h_4} \propto 1$. Category h_2 is the least common ancestor and $\gamma_{e,e'} = 3$.

Based on the aggregated metric, the distance between a target entity e_T and a context entity e_C can then be measured as

$$d(e_T, e_C) = (v_{e_T} - \tilde{v}_{e_C})^\top M_{e_T,e_C}(v_{e_T} - \tilde{v}_{e_C}). \quad (4)$$

Note that nearby entities in the hierarchy tend to share a large proportion of local metrics in Eq 3, and hence can exhibit common semantic features when measuring distance with others.

Complexity of aggregation As computing distance is a frequent operation in both training and application stages, a highly efficient aggregation algorithm is necessary in order to handle complex large entity hierarchies (with millions of nodes). Our formulation (Eq 3) avoids exhaustive enumeration over all paths by modeling the relevant nodes directly. We show that this allows linear complexity in *the number of children of two entities' common ancestors*, which is efficient in practice.

The most costly operation is to find $\mathcal{P}_{e,e'}$, i.e., the set of all category nodes that can occur in any of $e \to e'$ paths. We use a two-step procedure that (1) finds all common ancestors of entity e and e' that are *turning nodes* of any $e \to e'$ paths (e.g., h_2 in Figure 2), denoted as $\mathcal{Q}_{e,e'}$; (2) expands from $\mathcal{Q}_{e,e'}$ to construct the full $\mathcal{P}_{e,e'}$. For the first step, the following theorem shows each common ancestor can be efficiently assessed by testing only its children nodes. For the second step, it is straightforward to see that $\mathcal{P}_{e,e'}$ can be constructed by expanding $\mathcal{Q}_{e,e'}$ with its descendants that are ancestors of either e or e'. Other parameters ($\pi_{ee'}$ and $\gamma_{e,e'}$) of aggregation can be computed during the above process.

We next provide the theorem for the first step. Let $\mathcal{A}_e$ be the ancestor nodes of entity e (including e itself). For a node $h \in \mathcal{A}_e \cup \mathcal{A}_{e'}$, we define its *critical* node t_h as the nearest (w.r.t the length of the shortest path) descendant of h (including h itself) that is in $\mathcal{Q}_{e,e'} \cup \{e, e'\}$. E.g., in Figure 2, $t_{h_1} = h_2; t_{h_2} = h_2; t_{h_3} = e$. Let $\mathcal{C}_h$ be the set of immediate child nodes of h.

Theorem 1. *$\forall h \in \mathcal{A}_e \cap \mathcal{A}_{e'}$, $h \in \mathcal{Q}_{e,e'}$ iff it satisfies the two conditions: (1) $|\mathcal{C}_h \cap (\mathcal{A}_e \cup \mathcal{A}_{e'})| \geq 2$; (2) $\exists a, b \in \mathcal{C}_h$ s.t. $t_a \neq t_b$.*

Proof. We outline the proof here, and provide the details in the appendix.

Sufficiency: Note that $e, e' \notin Q_{e,e'}$. We prove the sufficiency by enumerating possible situations: (i) $t_a = e, t_b = e'$; (ii) $t_a = e, t_b \in Q_{e,e'}$; (iii) $t_a, t_b \in Q_{e,e'}$. For (i): as $t_a = e$, there exists a path $e \to \cdots \to a \to h$ where any two consecutive nodes is a (child, parent) pair. Similarly, there is a path $h \to b \to \cdots \to e'$ where any two consecutive nodes is a (parent, child) pair. It is provable that the two paths intersect only at h, and thus can be combined to form an $e \to e'$ path: $e \to \cdots \to a \to h \to b \to \cdots \to e'$, yielding h as a turning node. The cases (ii) and (iii) can be proved similarly.

Necessity: We prove by contradiction. Suppose that $\forall a, b \in \mathcal{C}_h \cap (\mathcal{A}_e \cup \mathcal{A}_{e'})$ we have $t_a = t_b$. W.l.o.g. we consider two cases: (i) $t_a = t_b = e$, and (ii) $t_a = t_b \in Q_{e,e'}$. It is provable that both cases will lead to contradiction. □

Therefore, by checking common ancestors from the bottom up, we can construct $\mathcal{Q}_{e,e'}$ with time complexity linear to the number of all ancestors' children.

2.3 Learning

For efficiency, we use negative sampling to reformulate the training objective, which is then optimized through coordinate gradient ascent.

Specifically, given the training data $\{(e_T, e_C)\}$ extracted from KB corpora, the representation learning is formulated as maximizing the objective in Eq 1, subject to PSD constraints on distance metrics $M_h \succeq 0$, and $\|v_e\|_2 = \|\bar{v}_e\|_2 = 1$ to avoid scale ambiguity.

The likelihood of each data sample is defined as a softmax in Eq 2, which iterates over all entities in the denominator and is thus computationally prohibitive. We apply the negative sampling technique as in conventional skip-gram model, by replacing each log probability $\log p(e_C|e_T)$ with

$$\log \sigma(-d(e_T, e_C)) + \sum_{i=1}^{k} \mathbb{E}_{e_i \sim P(e)} [\log \sigma(-d(e_T, e_i))],$$

where $\sigma(x) = 1/(1 + \exp(-x))$ is the sigmoid function; and for each data sample we draw k negative samples from the noise distribution $P(e) \propto U(e)^{3/4}$ with $U(e)$ being the unigram distribution (Mikolov et al., 2013b).

The negative sampling objective is optimized using coordinate gradient ascent, as shown in Algorithm 1. To avoid overfitting and improve efficiency, in practice we restrict the distance metrics M_h to be diagonal (Xing et al., 2002). Thus the PSD project of M_h (line 17) is simply taking the positive part for each diagonal elements.

Algorithm 1 Entity Hierarchy Embedding

Input: The training data $\mathcal{D} = \{(e_T, e_C)\}$,
Entity hierarchy,
Parameters: n – dimension of the embedding
k – number of negative samples
η – gradient learning rate
B – minibatch size

1: Initialize $\boldsymbol{v}, \bar{\boldsymbol{v}}, \boldsymbol{M}$ randomly such that $\|v\|_2 = \|\bar{v}\|_2 = 1$ and $M \succeq 0$.
2: **repeat**
3: Sample a batch $\mathcal{B} = \{(e_T, e_C)_i\}_{i=1}^{B}$ from $\mathcal{D}$
4: **for all** $(e_T, e_C) \in \mathcal{B}$ **do**
5: Compute $\{\mathcal{P}, \boldsymbol{\pi}, \gamma\}_{e_T, e_C}$ for metric aggregation
6: Sample negative pairs $\{(e_T, e_i)\}_{i=1}^{k}$
7: Compute $\{\{\mathcal{P}, \boldsymbol{\pi}, \gamma\}_{e_T, e_i}\}_{i=1}^{k}$ for metric aggregation
8: **end for**
9: **repeat**
10: **for all** $e \in \mathcal{E}$ included in $\mathcal{B}$ **do**
11: $v_e = v_e + \eta \frac{\partial \mathcal{L}}{\partial v_e}$
12: $\bar{v}_e = \bar{v}_e + \eta \frac{\partial \mathcal{L}}{\partial \bar{v}_e}$
13: $v_e, \bar{v}_e = \text{Project\_to\_unit\_sphere}(v_e, \bar{v}_e)$
14: **end for**
15: **until** convergence
16: **repeat**
17: **for all** h included in $\mathcal{B}$ **do**
18: $M_h = M_h + \eta \frac{\partial \mathcal{L}}{\partial M_h}$
19: $M_h = \text{Project\_to\_PSD}(M_h)$
20: **end for**
21: **until** convergence
22: **until** convergence

Output: Entity vectors $\boldsymbol{v}, \bar{\boldsymbol{v}}$, and category dist. metrics $\boldsymbol{M}$

3 Applications

One primary goal of learning semantic embedding is to improve NLP tasks. The compact representations are easy to work with because they enable efficient computation of semantic relatedness. Compared to word embedding, entity embedding is particularly suitable for various language understanding applications that extract underlying semantics of surface text. Incorporating entity hierarchies further enriches the embedding with structured knowledge.

In this section, we demonstrate how the learned entity hierarchy embedding can be utilized in two important tasks, i.e., *entity linking* and *entity search*. In both tasks, we measure the semantic relatedness between entities as the reciprocal distance defined in Eq 4. This greatly simplifies previous methods which have used various hand-crafted features, and leads to improved performance as shown in our experiments.

3.1 Entity Linking

The entity linking task is to link surface forms (mentions) of entities in a document to entities in a reference KB. It is an essential first step for downstream tasks such as semantic search and KB construction. The quality of entity relatedness measure is critical for entity linking performance, because of the key observation that entities in a document tend to be semantically coherent. For example, in sentence "Apple released an operating system Lion", The mentions "Apple" and "Lion" refer to Apple Inc. and Mac OS X Lion, respectively, as is more coherent than other configurations like (fruit apple, animal lion).

Our algorithm finds the optimal configuration for the mentions of a document by maximizing the overall relatedness among assigned entities, together with the local mention-to-entity compatibility. Specifically, we first construct a mention-to-entity dictionary based on Wikipedia annotations. For each mention m, the dictionary contains a set of candidate entities and for each candidate entity e a compatibility score $P(e|m)$ which is proportional to the frequency that m refers to e. For efficiency we only consider the top-5 candidate entities according to $P(e|m)$. Given a set of mentions $\mathcal{M} = \{m_i\}_{i=1}^{M}$ in a document, let $\mathcal{A} = \{e_{m_i}\}_{i=1}^{M}$ be a configuration of its entity assignments. The score of $\mathcal{A}$ is formulated as probability

$$P(\mathcal{A}|\mathcal{M}) \propto \prod_{i=1}^{M} P(e_{m_i}|m_i) \sum_{\substack{j=1 \\ j\neq i}}^{M} \frac{1}{d\left(e_{m_i}, e_{m_j}\right) + \epsilon},$$

where for each entity assignment we define its global relatedness to other entity assignments as the sum of the reciprocal distances ($\epsilon = 0.01$ is a constant used to avoid divide-by-zero). Direct enumeration of all potential configurations is computationally prohibitive, we therefore use simulated annealing to search for an optimal solution.

3.2 Entity Search

Entity search has attracted a growing interest (Chen et al., 2014b; Balog et al., 2011). Unlike conventional web search that finds unorganized web pages, entity search retrieves knowledge directly by generating a list of relevant entities in response to a search request. The input of the entity search task is a natural language question $\mathcal{Q}$ along with one or more desired entity categories $\mathcal{C}$. For example, a query can be $\mathcal{Q}$ ="films directed by Akira Kurosawa" and $\mathcal{C}$ ={Japanese films}.

Previous methods typically score candidate entities by measuring both the similarity between entity content and the query question $\mathcal{Q}$ (text matching), and the similarity between categories of entities and the query categories $\mathcal{C}$ (category matching).

We apply a similar category matching strategy as in previous work (Chen et al., 2014b) that assesses lexical (e.g., head words) similarity between category names, while replacing the text matching with entity relatedness measure. Specifically, we first extract the underlying entities mentioned in $\mathcal{Q}$ through entity linking, then score each candidate entity by its average relatedness to the entities in $\mathcal{Q}$. For instance, the entity Rashomon will obtain a high score in the above example as it is highly related with the entity Akira Kurosawa in the query. This scheme not only avoids complex document processing (e.g., topic modeling) in text matching, but also implicitly augments the short query text with background knowledge, and thus improves the accuracy and robustness.

4 Experiments

We validate the quality of our entity representation by evaluating its applications of entity linking and entity search on public benchmarks. In the entity linking task, our approach improves the F1 score by 10% over state-of-the-art results. We also validate the advantage of incorporating hierarchical structure. In the entity search task, our simple algorithm shows competitive performance. We further qualitatively analyze the entity vectors and category metrics, both of which capture meaningful semantics, and can potentially open up a wide rage of other applications.

Knowledge base We use the Wikipedia snapshot from Jan 12nd, 2015 as our training data and KB. After pruning administrative information we obtain an entity hierarchy including about 4.1M entities and 0.8M categories organized into 12 layers. Loops in the original hierarchy are removed by deleting bottom-up edges, yielding a DAG structure. We extract a set of 87.6M entity pairs from the wiki links on Wikipedia articles.

We train 100-dimensional vector representations for the entities and distance metrics (100×100 diagonal matrixes) for the categories (we would study the impact of dimensionality in the future). We set the batch size $B = 500$, the initial learning rate $\eta = 0.1$ and decrease it by a factor of 5 whenever the objective value does not increase, and the negative sample size $k = 5$. The model is trained on a Linux machine with 128G RAM and 16 cores. It takes 5 days to converge.

4.1 Entity Linking

4.1.1 Setup

Dataset As our entities based on English Wikipedia include not only named entities (e.g., persons, organizations) but also general concepts (e.g., "computer" and "human"), we use a standard entity linking dataset IITB[1] where mentions of Wikipedia entities are manually annotated exhaustively. The dataset contains about 100 documents and 17K mentions in total. As in the baseline work, we use only the mentions whose referent entities are contained in Wikipedia.

Criteria We adopt the common criteria, *precision*, *recall*, and *F1*. Let $\mathcal{A}^*$ be the golden standard entity annotations, and $\mathcal{A}$ be the annotations by entity linking model, then

$$precision = \frac{|\mathcal{A}^* \cap \mathcal{A}|}{|\mathcal{A}|} \qquad recall = \frac{|\mathcal{A}^* \cap \mathcal{A}|}{|\mathcal{A}^*|}.$$

The F1 score is then computed based on the average precision and recall across all documents.

Baselines We compare our algorithm with the following approaches. All the competitors are designed to be able to link general concept mentions to Wikipedia.

CSAW (Kulkarni et al., 2009) has a similar framework as our algorithm. It measures entity relatedness using a variation of Jaccard similarity on Wikipedia page incoming links.

Entity-TM (Han and Sun, 2012) models an entity as a distribution over mentions and words, and sets up a probabilistic generative process for the observed text.

Ours-NoH. To validate the advantage of incorporating hierarchical structure, we design a baseline that relies on entity embedding without entity hierarchy. That is, we obtain entity vectors by fixing the distance metric in Eq 4 as an identity matrix.

4.1.2 Results

Table 1 shows the performance of the competitors. Our algorithm using the entity hierarchy embedding gets 21% to 10% improvement in F1, and over 6% and 14% improvements in Precision and Recall, respectively. The CSAW model devises a set of entity features based on text content and link structures of Wikipedia pages, and combines them to measure relatedness. Compared to these hand-crafted features which are essentially heuristic and hard to verify, our embedding model induces semantic representations by optimizing a single well-defined objective. Note that the embedding actually also encodes the Wikipedia inter-page network, as we train on the entity-context pairs which are extracted from wiki links.

Methods	Precision	Recall	F1
CSAW	0.65	0.74	0.69
Entity-TM	0.81	0.80	0.80
Ours-NoH	0.78	0.85	0.81
Ours	**0.87**	**0.94**	**0.90**

Table 1: Entity linking performance

The Entity-TM model learns a representation for each entity as a word distribution. However, as noted in (Baroni et al., 2014), the counting-based distributional model usually shows inferior performance than context-predicting methods as ours. Moreover, in addition to the text context, our model integrates the entity hierarchical structure which provides rich knowledge of semantic relatedness. The comparison between *Ours* and *Ours-NoH* further reveals the effect of integrating the hierarchy in learning entity vectors. With entity hierarchy, we obtain more semantically meaningful representations that achieve 9% F1 improvement over entity vectors without hierarchical knowledge.

4.2 Entity Search

4.2.1 Setup

Dataset We use the dataset from INEX 2009 entity ranking track[2], which contains 55 queries. The golden standard results of each query contains a set of relevant entities each of which corresponds to a Wikipedia page.

Criteria We use the common criteria of precision@k, i.e., the percentage of relevant entities in the top-k results (we set $k = 10$), as well as precision@R where R is the number of golden standard entities for a query.

[1] http://www.cse.iitb.ac.in/soumen/doc/CSAW/Annot

[2] http://www.inex.otago.ac.nz/tracks/entity-ranking/entity-ranking.asp

Baselines We compare our algorithm with the following recent competitors.

Balog (Balog et al., 2011) develops a probabilistic generative model which represents entities, as well as the query, as distributions over both words and categories. Entities are then ranked based on the KL-divergence between the distributions.

K&K (Kaptein and Kamps, 2013) exploits Wikipedia entity hierarchy to derive the content of each category, which is in turn used to measure relatedness with the query categories. It further incorporates inter-entity links for relevance propagation.

Chen (Chen et al., 2014b) creates for each entity a context profile leveraging both the whole document (long-range) and sentences around entity (short-range) context, and models query text by a generative model. Categories are weighted based on the head words and other features. Our algorithm exploits a similar method for category matching.

Methods	Precision@10	Precision@R
Balog	0.18	0.16
K&K	0.31	0.28
Chen	0.55	0.42
Ours	**0.57**	**0.46**

Table 2: Entity search performance.

4.2.2 Results

Table 2 lists the entity search results of the competitors. Our algorithm shows superiority over the previous best performing methods. Balog constructs representations for each entity merely by counting (and smoothing) its co-occurrence between words and categories, which is inadequate to capture relatedness accurately. K&K leverages the rich resources in Wikipedia such as text, hierarchy, and link structures. However, the handcrafted features are still suboptimal compared with our learned representations.

Chen performs well by combining both long- and short-context of entities, as well as category lexical similarity. Our algorithm replaces its text matching component with a semantic enrichment step, i.e., grounding entity mentions in the query text onto KB entities. This augments the short query with rich background knowledge, facilitating accurate relatedness measure based on our high-quality entity embedding.

4.3 Qualitative Analysis

We qualitatively inspect the learned representations of the entity hierarchy. The results show that both the entity vectors and the category distance metrics capture meaningful semantics, and can potentially boost a wide range of applications such as recommendation and knowledge base completion.

Entity vectors Table 3 shows a list of target entities, and their top-4 nearest entities in the whole entity set or subsets belonging to given categories. Measuring under the whole set (column 2) results in nearest neighbors that are strongly related with the target entity. For instance, the nearest entities for "black hole" are "faster-than-light", "event horizon", "white hole", and "time dilation", all of which are concepts from physical cosmology and the theory of relativity. Similar results can be observed from other 3 examples.

Even more interesting is to specify a category and search for the most related entities under the category. The third column of Table 3 shows several examples. E.g., our model found that the most related Chinese websites to Youtube are "Tudou", "56.com", "Youku" (three top video hosting services in China), and "YinYueTai" (a major MV sharing site in China). The high-quality results show that our embedding model is able to discover meaningful relationships between entities from the complex entity hierarchy and plain text. This can be a useful feature in a wide range of applications such as semantic search (e.g., looking for movies about black hole), recommendation (e.g., suggesting TV series of specific genre for kids), and knowledge base completion (e.g., extracting relations between persons), to name a few.

Target entity	Most related entities	
black hole	**overall:** faster-than-light event horizon white hole time dilation	**American films:** Hidden Universe 3D Hubble (film) Quantum Quest Particle Fever
Youtube	**overall:** Instagram Twitter Facebook Dipdive	**Chinese websites:** Tudou 56.com Youku YinYueTai
Harvard University	**overall:** Yale University University of Pennsylvania Princeton University Swarthmore College	**businesspeople in software:** Jack Dangermond Bill Gates Scott McNealy Marc Chardon
X-Men: Days of Future Past (film)	**overall:** Marvel Studios X-Men: The Last Stand X2 (film) Man of Steel (film)	**children's television series:** Ben 10: Race Against Time Kim Possible: A Sitch in Time Ben 10: Alien Force Star Wars: The Clone Wars

Table 3: Most related entities under specific categories. "Overall" represents the most general category that includes all the entities.

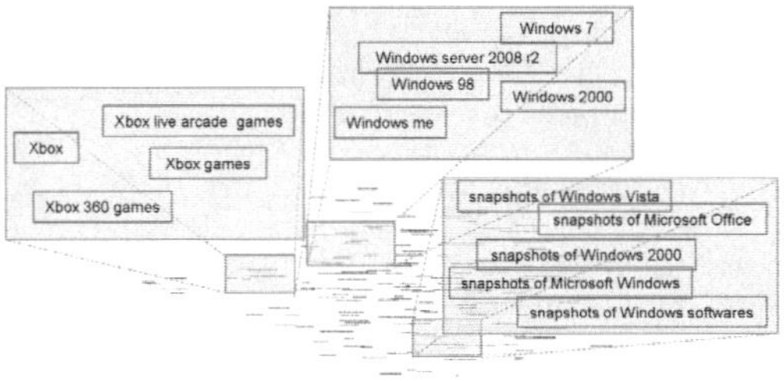

Figure 3: Distance metric visualization for the subcategories of the category "Microsoft". The t-SNE (Van der Maaten and Hinton, 2008) algorithm is used to map the high-dimensional (diagonal) matrixes into the 2D space.

Category distance metrics In addition to learning vector representations of entities, we also associate with each category a local distance metric to capture the features of individual category. As we restrict the distance metrics to be diagonal matrixes, the magnitude of each diagonal value can be viewed as how much a category is characterized by the corresponding dimension. Categories with close semantic meanings are expected to have similar metrics.

Figure 3 visualizes the metrics of all subcategories under the category "Microsoft", where we amplify some parts of the figure to showcase the clustering of semantically relevant categories. For instance, the categories of Microsoft Windows operating systems, and those of the Xbox games, are embedded close to each other, respectively. The results validate that our hierarchy embedding model can not only encode relatedness between leaf entities, but also capture semantic similarity of the internal categories. This can be helpful in taxonomy refinement and relation discovery.

5 Related Work

Distributed representation There has been a growing interest in distributed representation of words. Skip-gram model (Mikolov et al., 2013a) is one of the most popular methods to learn word representations. The model aims to find a representation for each word that is useful for predicting its context words. Word-context similarity is measured by simple inner product. A set of recent works generalizing the basic skip-gram to incorporate dependency context (Levy and Goldberg, 2014), word senses (Chen et al., 2014a), and multi-modal data (Hill and Korhonen, 2014). However, these work leverages limited structured knowledge. Our proposed method goes beyond skip-gram significantly such that we measures entity-context similarity under aggregated distance metrics of hierarchical category nodes. This effectively captures the structured knowledge. Another research line learn knowledge graph embedding (Lin et al., 2015; Wang et al., 2014; Bordes et al., 2013), which models entities as vectors and relations as some operations on the vector space (e.g., translation). These works aim at relation prediction for knowledge graph completion, and can be viewed as a supplement to the above that extracts semantics from plain text.

Utilizing hierarchical knowledge Semantic hierarchies are key sources of knowledge. Previous works (Ponzetto and Strube, 2007; Leacock and Chodorow, 1998) use KB hierarchies to define relatedness between concepts, typically based on path-length measure. Recent works (Yogatama et al., 2015; Zhao et al., 2011) learn representations through hierarchical sparse coding that enforces similar sparse patterns between nearby nodes. Category hierarchies have also been widely used in classification (Xiao et al., 2011; Weinberger and Chapelle, 2009). E.g., in (Verma et al., 2012) category nodes are endowed with discriminative power by learning distance metrics. Our approach differs in terms of entity vector learning and metric aggregation on DAG hierarchy.

6 Conclusion

In this paper, we proposed to learn entity hierarchy embedding to boost semantic NLP tasks. A principled framework was developed to incorporate both text context and entity hierarchical structure from large-scale knowledge bases. We learn a distance metric for each category node, and measure entity vector similarity under aggregated metrics. A flexible and efficient metric aggregation scheme was also developed to model large-scale hierarchies. Experiments in both entity linking and entity search tasks show superiority of our approach.

The qualitative analysis indicates that our model can be potentially useful in a wide range of other applications such as knowledge base completion and ontology refinement. Another interesting aspect of future work is to incorporate other sources of knowledge to further enrich the semantics.

Acknowledgments

This research is supported by NSF IIS-1218282, IIS-12511827, and IIS-1450545.

References

Krisztian Balog, Marc Bron, and Maarten De Rijke. 2011. Query modeling for entity search based on terms, categories, and examples. *TOIS*, 29(4):22.

Marco Baroni, Georgiana Dinu, and Germán Kruszewski. 2014. Dont count, predict! a systematic comparison of context-counting vs. context-predicting semantic vectors. In *Proc. of ACL*, volume 1, pages 238–247.

Antoine Bordes, Nicolas Usunier, Alberto Garcia-Duran, Jason Weston, and Oksana Yakhnenko. 2013. Translating embeddings for modeling multi-relational data. In *Proc. of NIPS*, pages 2787–2795.

Xinxiong Chen, Zhiyuan Liu, and Maosong Sun. 2014a. A unified model for word sense representation and disambiguation. In *Proc. of EMNLP*, pages 1025–1035.

Yueguo Chen, Lexi Gao, Shuming Shi, Xiaoyong Du, and Ji-Rong Wen. 2014b. Improving context and category matching for entity search. In *Proc. of AAAI*.

Stéphane Clinchant and Florent Perronnin. 2013. Aggregating continuous word embeddings for information retrieval. page 100.

Gianluca Demartini, Tereza Iofciu, and Arjen P De Vries. 2010. Overview of the inex 2009 entity ranking track. In *Focused Retrieval and Evaluation*, pages 254–264. Springer.

Xianpei Han and Le Sun. 2012. An entity-topic model for entity linking. In *Proc. of EMNLP*, pages 105–115. Association for Computational Linguistics.

Felix Hill and Anna Korhonen. 2014. Learning abstract concept embeddings from multi-modal data: Since you probably can't see what i mean. In *Proc. of EMNLP*, pages 255–265.

Rianne Kaptein and Jaap Kamps. 2013. Exploiting the category structure of wikipedia for entity ranking. *Artificial Intelligence*, 194:111–129.

Sayali Kulkarni, Amit Singh, Ganesh Ramakrishnan, and Soumen Chakrabarti. 2009. Collective annotation of wikipedia entities in web text. In *Proc. of KDD*, pages 457–466. ACM.

Claudia Leacock and Martin Chodorow. 1998. Combining local context and wordnet similarity for word sense identification. *WordNet: An electronic lexical database*, 49(2):265–283.

Omer Levy and Yoav Goldberg. 2014. Dependency-based word embeddings. In *Proc. of ACL*, volume 2, pages 302–308.

Yankai Lin, Zhiyuan Liu, Maosong Sun, Yang Liu, and Xuan Zhu. 2015. Learning entity and relation embeddings for knowledge graph completion. In *Proc. of AAAI*.

Tomas Mikolov, Kai Chen, Greg Corrado, and Jeffrey Dean. 2013a. Efficient estimation of word representations in vector space.

Tomas Mikolov, Ilya Sutskever, Kai Chen, Greg S Corrado, and Jeff Dean. 2013b. Distributed representations of words and phrases and their compositionality. In *Proc. of NIPS*, pages 3111–3119.

Alexandre Passos, Vineet Kumar, and Andrew McCallum, 2014. *Lexicon Infused Phrase Embeddings for Named Entity Resolution*, pages 78–86. Association for Computational Linguistics.

Simone Paolo Ponzetto and Michael Strube. 2007. Knowledge derived from wikipedia for computing semantic relatedness. *JAIR*, 30(1):181–212.

Philip Resnik. 1995. Using information content to evaluate semantic similarity in a taxonomy. In *Proc. of IJCAI*, pages 448–453.

Duyu Tang, Furu Wei, Nan Yang, Ming Zhou, Ting Liu, and Bing Qin. 2014. Learning sentiment-specific word embedding for twitter sentiment classification. In *Proc. of ACL*, pages 1555–1565.

Laurens Van der Maaten and Geoffrey Hinton. 2008. Visualizing data using t-sne. *JMLR*, 9(2579-2605):85.

Nakul Verma, Dhruv Mahajan, Sundararajan Sellamanickam, and Vinod Nair. 2012. Learning hierarchical similarity metrics. In *Proc. of CVPR*, pages 2280–2287. IEEE.

Zhen Wang, Jianwen Zhang, Jianlin Feng, and Zheng Chen. 2014. Knowledge graph and text jointly embedding. In *Proc. of EMNLP*.

Kilian Q Weinberger and Olivier Chapelle. 2009. Large margin taxonomy embedding for document categorization. In *Proc. of NIPS*, pages 1737–1744.

Lin Xiao, Dengyong Zhou, and Mingrui Wu. 2011. Hierarchical classification via orthogonal transfer. In *Proc. of ICML*, pages 801–808.

Eric P Xing, Michael I Jordan, Stuart Russell, and Andrew Y Ng. 2002. Distance metric learning with application to clustering with side-information. In *Proc. of NIPS*, pages 505–512.

Dani Yogatama, Manaal Faruqui, Chris Dyer, and Noah Smith. 2015. Learning word representations with hierarchical sparse coding. *Proc. of ICML*.

Jiajun Zhang, Shujie Liu, Mu Li, Ming Zhou, and Chengqing Zong. 2014. Bilingually-constrained phrase embeddings for machine translation. In *Proc. of ACL*.

Bin Zhao, Fei Li, and Eric P Xing. 2011. Large-scale category structure aware image categorization. In *Proc. of NIPS*, pages 1251–1259.

Orthogonality of Syntax and Semantics within Distributional Spaces

Jeff Mitchell
School of Informatics
University of Edinburgh
Edinburgh, EH8 9AB, UK
jeff.mitchell@ed.ac.uk

Mark Steedman
School of Informatics
University of Edinburgh
Edinburgh, EH8 9AB, UK
steedman@inf.ed.ac.uk

Abstract

A recent distributional approach to word-analogy problems (Mikolov et al., 2013b) exploits interesting regularities in the structure of the space of representations. Investigating further, we find that performance on this task can be related to orthogonality within the space. Explicitly designing such structure into a neural network model results in representations that decompose into orthogonal semantic and syntactic subspaces. We demonstrate that learning from word-order and morphological structure within English Wikipedia text to enable this decomposition can produce substantial improvements on semantic-similarity, pos-induction and word-analogy tasks.

1 Introduction

Distributional methods have become widely used across computational linguistics. Recent applications include predicate clustering for question answering (Lewis and Steedman, 2013), bilingual embeddings for machine translation (Zou et al., 2013) and enhancing the coverage of POS tagging (Huang et al., 2013). The popularity of these methods, stemming from their conceptual simplicity and wide applicability, motivates a deeper analysis of the structure of the representations they produce.

Commonly, these representations are made in a single vector space with similarity being the main structure of interest. However, recent work by Mikolov et al. (2013b) on a word-analogy task suggests that such spaces may have further useful internal regularities. They found that semantic differences, such as between *big* and *small*, and also syntactic differences, as between *big* and *bigger*, were encoded consistently across their space. In particular, they solved the word-analogy problems by exploiting the fact that equivalent relations tended to correspond to parallel vector-differences.

In this paper, we investigate orthogonality between relations rather than parallelism. While parallelism serves to ensure that the same relation is encoded consistently, our hypothesis is that orthogonality serves to ensure that distinct relations are clearly differentiable. We focus specifically on semantic and syntactic relations as these are probably the most distinct classes of properties encoded in distributional spaces.

Empirically, we demonstrate that orthogonality predicts performance on the word-analogy task for three existing approaches to constructing word vectors. We also attempt to enhance the weakest of these three models by imposing an orthogonal structure in its construction. In these extensions, word representations decompose into orthogonal semantic and syntactic spaces, and we use word-order and morphology to drive this separation. This decomposition also allows us to define a novel approach to solving the word-analogy problems and our extended models become competitive with the other two original models. In addition, we show that the separate semantic and syntactic sub-spaces gain improved performance on semantic-similarity and POS-induction tasks respectively.

Our experiments here are based on models that construct vector-representations within a model that predicts the occurence of words in context. In particular we focus on the CBOW and Skip-gram models of Mikolov etal. (2013b) and Pennington et al.'s (2014) GloVe model. These models share the property of producing a single general representation for each word, which can be utilized in a variety of tasks, from POS tagging to semantic role labelling. In contrast, here we attempt to decompose the representations into separate seman-

Proceedings of the 53rd Annual Meeting of the Association for Computational Linguistics and the 7th International Joint Conference on Natural Language Processing, pages 1301–1310,
Beijing, China, July 26-31, 2015. ©2015 Association for Computational Linguistics

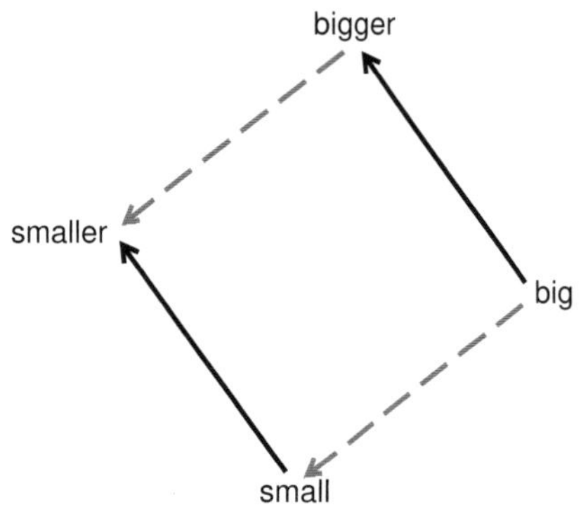

Figure 1: Geometric relationships between $small$, $smaller$, big and $bigger$.

tic and syntactic components.

To motivate this decomposition, consider the analogical reasoning task that Mikolov et al. (2013b) apply neural embeddings to. In this task, given vectors for the words big, $bigger$ and $small$, we try to predict the vector for $smaller$. They find that in practice $smaller \approx small + bigger - big$ produces an estimate that is frequently closer to the actual representation of $smaller$ than any other word vector. We can think of the vector $bigger - big$ as representing the syntactic relation that holds between an adjective and its comparative. Adding this syntactic structure to $small$ thus ends up at, or near, the relevant comparative, $smaller$. Alternatively, we could think of the vector $small - big$ as representing the semantic difference between small and big, and adding this relation to $bigger$ produces a semantic transformation to $smaller$.

Mikolov et al. (2013b) represent these sort of relations in terms of a diagram similar to Figure 1. The image places the four words in a 2D space and represents the relations between them in terms of arrows. The solid black arrows represent the syntactic relations $smaller - small$ and $bigger - big$, while the gray dashed arrows represent the semantic differences $smaller - bigger$ and $small - big$. Their solution to the analogy problem exploits the fact that these pairs of relations are approximately parallel to each other, i.e. that we can approximate $smaller - small$ with $bigger - big$, or $smaller - bigger$ with $small - big$. However, knowing that opposite sides of the square in Figure 1 are parallel to each other still leaves open the question of what happens at the corners. In other words, what is the relationship between the semantic differences, e.g. $smaller - bigger$, and the syntactic differences, e.g. $smaller - small$?

In this paper we explore the idea that such semantic and syntactic relations ought to be orthogonal to each other. This hypothesis arises both from the intuition that such distinct types of information ought to be represented distinctly within our space and also from the observation that solving the word-analogy task requires that words can be uniquely identified by combining these vector differences and so $small - big$ ought to be easily differentiable from $bigger - big$ as these relations point to different end results starting from big. Essentially, orthogonality will make better use of the volume within the space, spreading words with different semantic or syntactic characteristics further from each other.

In terms of predicting $smaller$ from big, $bigger$ and $small$, orthogonality of the relationship between $smaller - bigger$ and $smaller - small$ can be expressed in terms of their dot product:

$$(smaller - bigger) \cdot (smaller - small) = 0 \quad (1)$$

If all semantic relations were genuinely orthogonal to all syntactic relations, then their space would be decomposable into two orthogonal subspaces: one semantic, the other syntactic. Any word representation, $\mathbf{v}$, would then be the combination of a unique semantic vector, $\mathbf{b}$, within the semantic subspace and a unique syntactic vector, $\mathbf{s}$, within the syntactic subspace. If $\mathbf{b}$ were given a representation in terms of e components, and $\mathbf{s}$ in terms of f components, then $\mathbf{v}$ would have a representation in terms of $d = e + f$ components which would just be the concatenation of the two sets of components, which we will represent in terms of the operator $\oplus$.

$$\mathbf{v} = \mathbf{b} \oplus \mathbf{s} \quad (2)$$

Achieving this differentiation within the representations requires that the model have a means of differentiating semantic and syntactic information in the raw text. We consider two very simple approaches for this purpose, based on morphological and word order features. Both these types of features have been previously employed in simple word co-occurrence models (e.g., McDonald and Lowe, 1998; Clark, 2003), with bag-of-words and

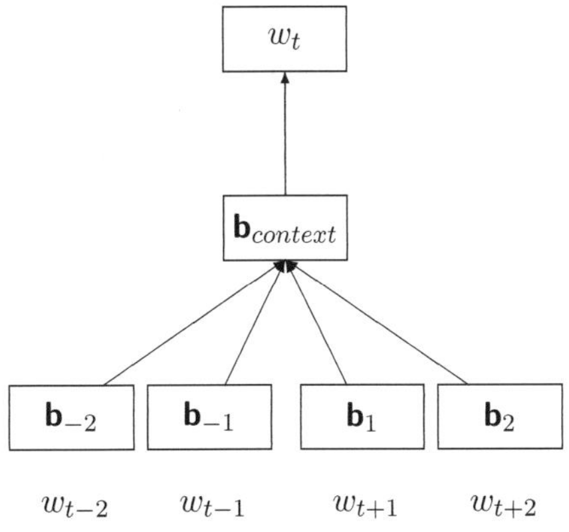

Figure 2: CBOW model predicting w_t from of a bag-of-words representation, $\mathbf{b}_{context}$, of a 4-word window around it.

lemmatization being good for semantic applications, while sequential order and suffixes is more useful for syntax. More recently, Mitchell (2013) demonstrated that word order could be used to separate syntactic from semantic structure, but only within a simple bigram language model, rather than a neural network model, and without exploiting morphology.

Our enhanced models are based on Mikolov et al.'s (2013a) CBOW architecture, which is described in Section 2. The novel extensions to it, employing a semantic-syntactic decomposition, are proposed in Section 3. We then describe our evaluation tasks and provide their results in Sections 5 and 6 respectively. These evaluations are based on the word-analogy dataset of Mikolov et al. (2013b), a noun-verb similarity task (Mitchell, 2013) and a POS clustering task.

2 Continuous Bag-of-Words Model (CBOW)

In the original CBOW model, the probability of a central target word, w_t, is predicted from a bag-of-words representation of the context it occurs in, as illustrated in Figure 2. This context representation, $\mathbf{b}_{context}$, is a simple sum of the CBOW vectors, $\mathbf{b}_i$, that represent each item, w_{t+i}, in a k-word window either side of the target.

$$\mathbf{b}_{context} = \sum_{i=-k, i \neq 0}^{k} \mathbf{b}_i \quad (3)$$

For speed, the output layer uses a hierarchical softmax function (Morin and Bengio, 2005). Each word is given a Huffman code corresponding to a path through a binary tree, and the output predicts the binary choices on nodes of the tree as independent variables. In comparison to the computational cost of doing the full softmax over the whole vocabulary, this hierarchical approach is much more efficient.

Each node is associated with a vector, $\mathbf{n}$, and the output at that node, given a context vector, $\mathbf{b}_{context}$, is:

$$p = logistic(\mathbf{n} \cdot \mathbf{b}_{context}) \quad (4)$$

Here, p is the probability of choosing 1 over 0 at this node of the tree, or equivalently finding a 1 in the Huffman code of w_t at the relevant position.

The objective function is the negative log-likelihood of the data given the model.

$$O = \sum -\log(p) \quad (5)$$

Where the sum is over tokens in the training corpus and the relevant nodes in the tree. Training is then based on stochastic gradient descent, with a decreasing learning rate.

3 Extensions

3.1 Continuous Sequence of Words (CSOW)

A major feature of the CBOW model is its use of a bag-of-words representation of the context and this is achieved by summing over the vectors representing words in the input. Although the model does seem to produce representations that are effective on both semantic and syntactic tasks, we want to be able to exploit word order information to separate these two characteristics. We therefore need to consider models which do not reduce the context to a structureless bag-of-words. Modifying the original model to retain the sequential information in the input is relatively straightforward. Instead of summing the input representations, we simply leave them as an ordered sequence of vectors, $\mathbf{s}_i$.

Then in the output layer, we require a vector for every input position, i, on every node. In this way, the output of the network depends on which context word is in which position, rather than just the set of words, irrespective of position in the input.

The network still learns a single representation for each word independently of position, but the output function has more parameters.

$$p = logistic(\sum_{i=-k, i\neq 0}^{k} \mathbf{n}_i \cdot \mathbf{s}_i) \quad (6)$$

Here each node of the tree is associated with one vector, $\mathbf{n}_i$, for each position, i, in the input context, giving $2k$ vectors in total at each node.

3.2 Continuous Bag and Sequence of Words (CBSOW)

Having introduced a sequential version of the CBOW model, what is really desired is a model that combines both bag and sequence components. Each word will have both an e-dimensional bag-vector $\mathbf{b}$ and an f-dimensional sequence-vector $\mathbf{s}$. The full representation of a word, $\mathbf{v}$, is then the concatenation of the components of $\mathbf{b}$ and $\mathbf{s}$.

Given this structure, the representation of a context of $2k$ words will be made up of the sum, $\mathbf{b}_{context}$, of their bag vectors, $\mathbf{b}_i$, as in the CBOW model given by Equation 3, along with the ordered sequence vectors, $\mathbf{s}_i$, as in the CSOW model. Each node in the tree then requires both a bag vector, $\mathbf{n}^b$, to handle the bag context, and $2k$ sequence vectors, $\mathbf{n}^s_i$, to handle the sequence context vectors, with probabilities given by:

$$p = logistic(\mathbf{n}^b \cdot \mathbf{b}_{context} + \sum_{i=-k, i\neq 0}^{k} \mathbf{n}^s_i \cdot \mathbf{s}_i) \quad (7)$$

3.3 Continuous Bag of Morphemes (CBOM)

A second source of information which might be used to differentiate semantic from syntactic representations is morphology. Specifically, English has the useful characteristic that the written words themselves can often be broken into a semantic stem on the left and a syntactic ending on the right. For example, *dancing* = *dance* + *ing* and *swimmer* = *swim* + *er*. In fact, stemming or lemmatization is commonly used in constructing distributional vectors precisely because throwing away the syntactic information helps to enhance their semantic content. Here, we want to use both the left and right halves separately to enhance both the semantic and syntactic components of the representations.

Our starting point is to break each word into a left-hand stem and a right-hand ending using CELEX (Baayen et al., 1995), as explained in more detail in Section 4.1.

The simplest model is then to represent each of these with its own vector, $\mathbf{l}_i$ and $\mathbf{r}_i$ respectively, and sum these vectors to form context representations of words in the input.

$$\mathbf{l}_{context} = \sum_{i=-k, i\neq 0}^{k} \mathbf{l}_i \quad (8)$$

$$\mathbf{r}_{context} = \sum_{i=-k, i\neq 0}^{k} \mathbf{r}_i \quad (9)$$

The output function takes much the same form as the original model but now each node needs both a left and a right vector, corresponding to the two context representations.

$$p = logistic(\mathbf{n}^l \cdot \mathbf{l}_{context} + \mathbf{n}^r \cdot \mathbf{r}_{context}) \quad (10)$$

3.4 Continuous Bag and Sequence of Words and Morphemes (CBSOWM)

Finally, we want to incorporate all these elements in a single model, with the morphological and word order elements of the model working in harmony. In particular, we want the sequential part of the model to be guided by morphological information without being constrained to give all words with same ending the same representation. Our solution is to add a constraint term to the objective function, which penalizes sequence vectors that stray far from the relevant morphological representation. The bag vectors, in contrast, are determined directly by the left hand stems, with all words having the same stem then sharing the same bag vector, $\mathbf{b} = \mathbf{l}$.

The main structure of the model remains as in the CBSOW model, with the context being represented by the sum of bag vectors alongside the ordered sequence vectors. Output probabilities are as given by Equation 7, and we add a morphological penalty, m, to the objective function.

$$m = \sum_{i=-k, i\neq 0}^{k} \frac{1}{2}\lambda|\mathbf{s}_i - \mathbf{r}_i|^2 \quad (11)$$

The morphological representations $\mathbf{r}$ enter into the model only through the penalty term, and they adapt during training solely in terms of this interaction with the sequence vectors. Gradient descent results in the $\mathbf{r}$ vectors moving towards the centre of the corresponding $\mathbf{s}$ vectors, and the $\mathbf{s}$ vectors in turn being drawn towards that centre.

The result is to elastically connect all the $\mathbf{s}$ vectors corresponding to a single morphological element through their $\mathbf{r}$ vectors, so that they are drawn together, but can still develop idiosyncratically if there is sufficient evidence in the data.

3.5 Application to the Word-Analogy Task

Decomposition of representations into separate semantic and syntactic spaces enables us to utilise a new approach to solving the word-analogy problems. Rather than using vector differences to predict a vector, we can instead construct it by copying the relevant bag and sequence vectors. So, since $small$ and $smaller$ share very similar semantic content, we can use the bag vector of $small$ as the bag vector of $smaller$, since that is where the semantic content is mainly represented: $\mathbf{b}_{smaller} \approx \mathbf{b}_{small}$. Similarly, we can use the sequence vector of $bigger$ as the sequence vector for $smaller$, since these words share common syntactic behaviour: $\mathbf{s}_{smaller} \approx \mathbf{s}_{bigger}$.

The predicted representation of $smaller$ is then given by the concatenation of the components.

$$\mathbf{v}_{smaller} \approx \mathbf{b}_{small} \oplus \mathbf{s}_{bigger} \qquad (12)$$

We find that this gives the best performance on the models that use word-order features (CBSOW and CBSOWM).

4 Training

Our experiments are based on the publicly available word2vec[1] and GloVe[2] packages. We modified the original CBOW code to incorporate the CBSOW, CBOM and CBSOWM extensions described above, and trained models on three English Wikipedia corpora of varying sizes, including the enwik8 and enwik9 files[3] suggested in the word2vec documentation, containing the first 10^8 and 10^9 characters of a 2006 download, and also a full download from 2009. On the smallest 17M word corpus we explored a range of vector dimensionalities from 10 to 1000. On the larger 120M and 1.6B word corpus, we trained extended models with a 200-dimensional semantic component and a 100-dimensional syntactic component comparing to 300-dimensional CBOW, Skip-gram and GloVe models. The parameter, λ, in Equation 11 was set to 0.1 and the recommended window sizes of 5, 10 and 15 words either side of the central word were used as context for the CBOW, Skip-gram and GloVe models respectively.

[1] https://code.google.com/p/word2vec/

[2] http://nlp.stanford.edu/projects/glove/

[3] http://mattmahoney.net/dc/text.html

4.1 CELEX

We attempted to split all the words in the training data into a left hand and a right hand using CELEX (Baayen et al., 1995), an electronic dictionary containing morphological structure. In the cases of words that were not found in the dictionary and also those that were found but had no morphological substructure, the left hand was just the whole word and the right hand was a $-NULL-$ token. For the remaining words, we treated short suffixes as being syntactic inflections and stripped all these off to leave a left hand 'semantic' component. The 'syntactic' component was then rightmost of these suffixes, with any additional suffixes being ignored.

5 Evaluation

The hypothesis that orthogonality is useful to word vector representations is investigated empirically in two ways. Firstly, we attempt to quantify the orthogonality that is already implicitly present in the original CBOW, Skip-gram and GloVe representations and relate that to their success in the word-analogy task. Secondly, the extensions described above are evaluated on a number of tasks in order to evaluate the benefits of their explicit orthogonality between components.

5.1 Orthogonality within the Original Models

Equation 1 relates orthogonality of vector differences to their dot product being zero, which corresponds to the fact the cosine of $90°$ is zero. Thus, we can use the cosine as a quantification of how close to orthogonal the vector differences are and then relate that to performance on the word-analogy dataset distributed with the word2vec toolkit.

That task involves predicting a word vector given vectors for other related words. So, for example, given vectors for big, $bigger$ and $small$, we would try to predict a vector for $smaller$. We then judge the success of this prediction in terms of whether the predicted vector is in fact closer to $smaller$'s actual word vector than any other word vector. The dataset contains 19,544 items, broken down into 14 subtasks (e.g. capitals of common countries or adjective to adverb conversion).

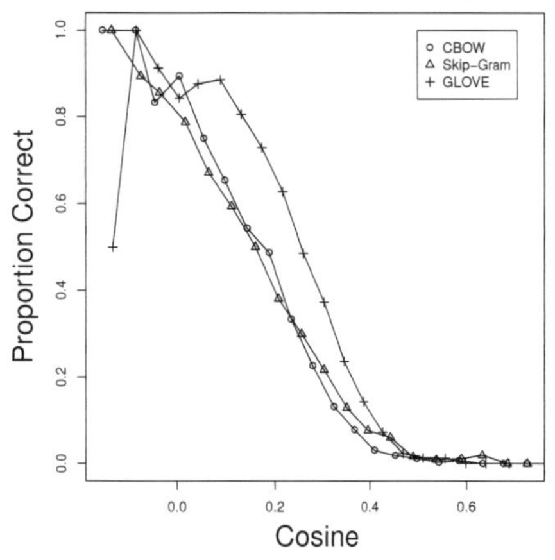

Figure 3: Proportion Correct against Average Cosine.

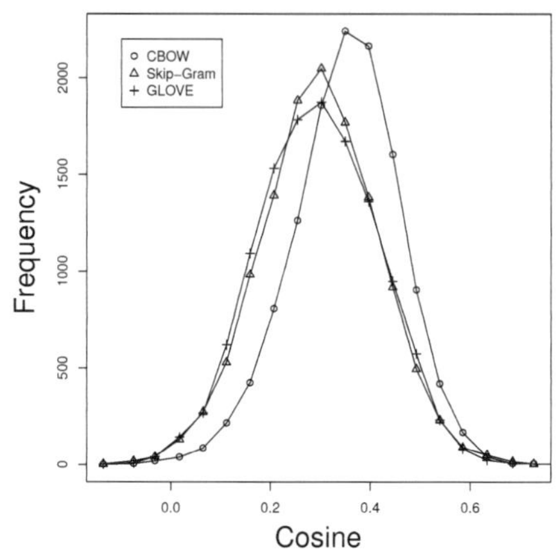

Figure 4: Frequency against Cosine.

For each item, we measure the cosine of the angle between the vector differences for the word we are trying to predict (e.g. $smaller - small$ and $smaller - bigger$) and analyze these values in terms of the success of the model's prediction, with smaller cosine values corresponding to angles that are closer to orthogonal.

5.2 CBOW Extensions

We evaluate the extensions on three tasks. Alongside the word-analogy problems, we also evaluate the separate semantic and syntactic sub-spaces on their own individual tasks. The semantic task correlates predicted semantic similarities with the noun-verb similarity ratings gathered by Mitchell (2013), and the remaining task clusters the syntactic representations and evaluates these clusters in relation to the POS classes found in the Penn Treebank.

On the word-analogy problem we compare to the original CBOW, Skip-gram and GloVe models. In the case of these original models and also the CBOM model, we follow Mikolov et al.'s (2013b) method for making the word-analogy predictions in terms of addition and subtraction: $smaller \approx bigger - big + small$. However, in the case of the CBSOW and CBSOWM models, we use the novel approach described in Section 3.5: $\mathbf{v}_{smaller} \approx \mathbf{b}_{small} \oplus \mathbf{s}_{bigger}$. Similarity is then based on the cosine measure for all types of representation.

The noun-verb similarity task is based on correlating the model's predicted semantic similarity for words with human ratings gathered in an online experiment. Such evaluations have been commonly used to evaluate distributional representations, with higher correlations indicating a model which is more effective at forming vectors whose relations to each other mirror human notions of semantic similarity. Mitchell (2013) argued that predicting semantic similarity relations across syntactic categories provided a measure of the extent to which word representations succeed in separating semantic from syntactic content, and gathered a dataset of similarities for noun-verb pairs. Each rated item consists of a noun paired with a verb, and the pairs are constucted to range from high semantic similarity, e.g. *disappearance - vanish*, to low, e.g. *transmitter - grieve*. The dataset contains ratings for 108 different pairs, each of which was rated by 20 participants. For the CBOW model, we predict similarities in terms of the cosine measure for the two word vectors. For the other models, we predict similarities from cosine applied to just the bag or left-hand vectors.

The syntactic component of the representations is evaluated by clustering the vectors and then comparing the induced classes to the POS classes found in the Penn Treebank. We use the many-to-one measure (Christodoulopoulos et al., 2010; Yatbaz et al., 2012) to determine the extent to which the clusters agree with the POS classes. Each cluster is mapped to its most frequent gold tag and the reported score is the proportion of word tokens correctly tagged using this mapping. The clustering itself is a form of k-means clustering, where similarity is measured in terms of the cosine measure. Each vector is assigned to a clus-

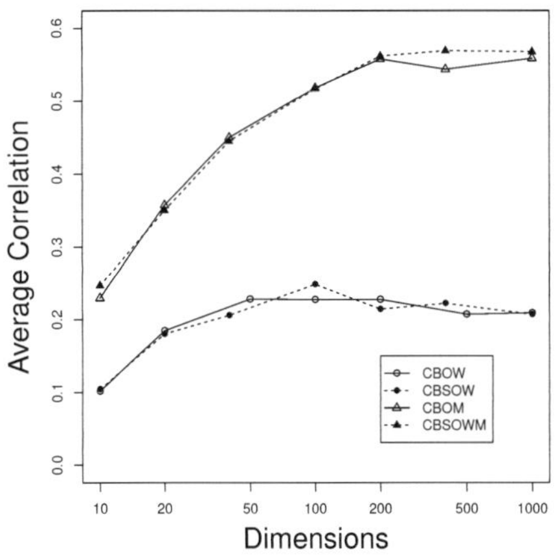

Figure 5: Average Correlation on Noun-Verb Evaluation Task against Size of Representations.

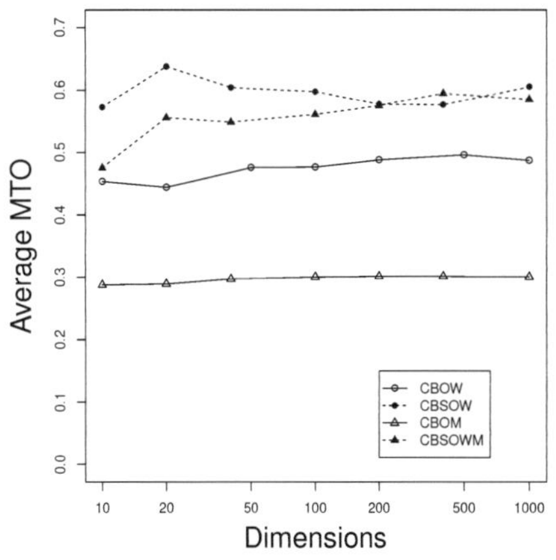

Figure 6: Average Many-To-One Evaluation against Size of Representations.

ter based on which cluster centroid it is most similar to and then the cluster centroids are updated given the new cluster assignments and the process repeats. This clustering was applied to either the sequence or right-hand vectors in the case of the CBSOW, CBOM and CBSOWM models, and to the whole vectors in the case of CBOW. We randomly initialized 45 clusters and then evaluated after 100 iterations of the k-means algorithm.

6 Results

6.1 Original Models

Figure 3 is a plot of the proportion of correct predictions made by 100-dimensional CBOW, Skip-Gram and GloVe models on the word-analogy task against cosine of the angle between the vector differences. The range of the cosine distribution was broken into twenty intervals and the plotted values were derived by calculating the proportion correct and average cosine value within each interval. It is clear from the resulting curves that cosine is a fairly strong predictor for all models of whether the model gets a word-analogy item correct, with higher rates of success for smaller cosine values - i.e. angles closer to orthogonality. This is confirmed by a significant ($p < 0.001$) result from a logistic regression of correctness against cosine value. Similar results are found for both the semantic subtasks (e.g. capitals of common countries) and syntactic subtasks (e.g. adjective to adverb conversion) considered separately.

The actual distribution of cosine values for each type of model is given in Figure 4. This analysis reveals that while the Skip-Gram and GloVe models have fairly similar cosine distributions, the CBOW model's distribution is shifted to the right, with more angles further from othogonality. This begs the question of what the effect on performance would be if we managed to push more of the CBOW distribution towards zero, and in the next section we examine the extensions that implement this idea.

6.2 CBOW Extensions

We first consider the models trained on the smaller 17M word corpus, and the evaluations of these models on the noun-verb similarity and POS clustering tasks are presented in Figures 5 and 6 respectively. These graphs depict the performance as the representations grow in size. For the CBOW model, this is just the dimension of the induced vectors. For the other models, we consider models with equal sizes of semantic and syntactic subspaces and report performance against the total dimensionality of the combined representation. For both these tasks, the results were averaged over ten repetitions of training with random initializations.

On the noun-verb similarity task, morphology produces the largest performance gains, with the CBOM model substantially outperforming the CBOW model. Word order structure has no clear impact.

On the syntactic task, in contrast, it is word order that produces reliable gains, with the CBSOW model clearly improving on the CBOW model. The simplistic use of morphology in the CBOM model results in a degradation of performance in

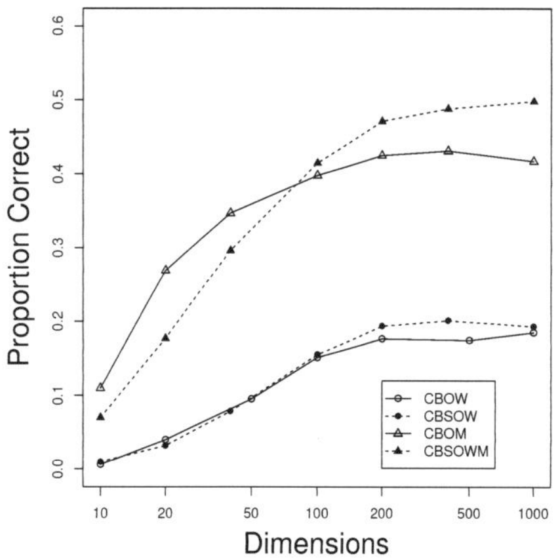

Figure 7: Proportion Correct on the Analogy Task against Size of Representations.

comparison to the CBOW model, but the CBSOWM model's performance is comparable to that of the CBSOW for larger representations.

Thus for these two tasks, the CBSOWM results appear to show a reasonable integration of morphology and word order information giving good performance on both semantic and syntactic tasks. This conclusion is borne out the results of the word-analogy tasks in Figure 7, where the CBSOWM model outperforms all the other models. Here, morphology gives the greatest benefit on its own, as evidenced in the differences between the CBOW and CBOM models. Nonetheless, word order still produces noticeable improvements, with the CBSOW result beating the CBOW results, and the CBSOWM beating the CBOM at larger dimensions. There is considerable variation in the effects on performance among the various analogy subtasks, but even a task such as capitals of common countries (e.g. predicting Iraq as having Baghdad as its capital, given that Greece has Athens) appears to benefit from decomposition of representations, despite not obviously involving syntactic structure.

Table 1 compares 300-dimensional models across different sizes of training data. In the case of the CBSOW, CBOM and CBSOWM models we use representations with 200 semantic and 100 syntactic dimensions and compare these to CBOW, Skip-gram and GloVe models of the same total size. It is clear for all quantities of training data that all the extensions outperform the basic CBOW model, with morphology giving greater

	Training Words		
Model	17M	120M	1.6B
GloVe	29.53%	58.18%	**72.54%**
Skip-Gram	30.03%	52.67%	62.34%
CBOW	18.47%	38.48%	54.17%
CBSOW	20.83%	42.00%	59.41%
CBOM	44.29%	53.60%	61.87%
CBSOWM	**48.92%**	**63.19%**	68.32%

Table 1: Performance of 300-Dimensional Models on the Word-Analogy Task

gains than word order, and the combined CBSOWM model outperforming both. This performance advantage of the CBOM over CBSOW appears to weaken as the training data grows, which is probably the effect of both the lack of morphological information for rare words encountered in the larger datasets and also the diminishing returns on that information as more data provides better supervision of the training process. The sequential information, in contrast, is internal to the training data and seems to provide the same, or greater, performance boost as the training set grows.

Comparing the results of our extended models to the Skip-gram and GloVe models, we can see that on the two smaller corpora CBSOWM outperforms both these models, while on the largest corpus, it only beats the Skip-gram results and GloVe achieves the best performance. Of course, neither the Skip-gram nor GloVe models has access to the morphological information that the CBSOWM model uses, but the results demonstrate that the performance of the CBOW model can be substantially boosted by exploiting a representational structure that decomposes into semantic and syntactic sub-spaces. Similar methods could in principle be applied to most word embedding models, including Skip-gram and GloVe.

We can also examine the distribution of cosine values for the new models. Figure 8 compares the distribution of cosine values for CBOW, CBSOW, CBOM and CBSOWM models. Although, in comparison to the original CBOW model, each of the extended models shifts the distribution towards zero, i.e. towards orthogonality, this shift for the CBSOW model is marginal. In contrast, the CBOM model has a large number of instances where the cosine is exactly zero, corresponding to cases where all of the relevant morphological information is found in CELEX. The remainder

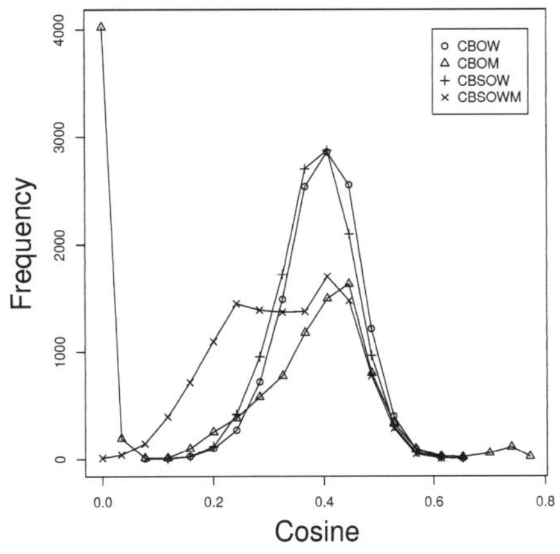

Figure 8: Frequency against Cosine.

of the data, however, seems to be less orthogonal than the original CBOW distribution, suggesting that words without a morphological analysis need a more sophisticated treatment. The shift in the CBSOWM distribution, in comparison, is less radically bimodal, with more continuity between those words with and without morphology. This reflects the difference in these models handling of suffixes, with the CBSOWM model's greater flexibility resulting in gains over the CBOM model on the POS induction and word analogy tasks.

7 Conclusions

Our experiments demonstrate the utility of orthogonality within vector-space representations in a number of ways. In terms of existing models, we find that the cosines of vector-differences is a strong predictor of the performance of CBOW, Skip-gram and GloVe representations on the word analogy task, with smaller cosine values - corresponding to angles closer to orthogonality - being associated with a greater proportion of correct predictions. With regard to developing new models, this orthogonality of relationships inspired three models which used word-order and morphology to separate semantic and syntactic representations. These separate sub-spaces were shown to have enhanced performance in semantic similarity and POS-induction tasks and the combined representations showed enhanced performance on the word-analogy task, using a novel approach to solving this problem that exploits the decomposable structure of the representations.

Both Botha and Blunsom (2014) and Luong et al. (2013) take a more sophisticated approach to morphology[4], constructing a word's embedding by recursively combining representations of all its morphemes, though only within a single non-decomposed space. Future work ought to pursue models in which all morphemes contribute both semantic and syntactic content to the word representations.

It would also be desirable to explore more practical applications of these representations than the limited evaluations presented here. It seems feasible that our decomposition of representations could benefit tasks that need to differentiate their treatment of semantic and syntactic content. In particular, applications of word embeddings that mainly involve syntax, such as POS tagging (e.g., Tsuboi, 2014) or supertagging for parsing (e.g., Lewis and Steedman, 2014), may be a reasonable starting point.

Acknowledgements

We would like to thank Stella Frank, Sharon Goldwater and other colleagues along with our reviewers for criticism, advice and discussion. This work was supported by ERC Advanced Fellowship 249520 GRAMPLUS and EU Cognitive Systems project FP7-ICT-270273 Xperience.

References

Harald Baayen, Richard Piepenbrock, and Hedderik van Rijn. 1995. CELEX2 LDC96L14. Web Download. Philadelphia: Linguistic Data Consortium.

Jan A. Botha and Phil Blunsom. 2014. Compositional Morphology for Word Representations and Language Modelling. In *Proceedings of the 31st International Conference on Machine Learning (ICML)*, Beijing, China.

Christos Christodoulopoulos, Sharon Goldwater, and Mark Steedman. 2010. Two decades of unsupervised POS induction: How far have we come? In *Proceedings of EMNLP*, pages 575–584.

Alexander Clark. 2003. Combining distributional and morphological information for part of speech induction. In *Proceedings of the tenth Annual Meeting of the European Association for Computational Linguistics (EACL)*, pages 59–66.

[4]Though not neccessarily better performing. Luong et al.'s published 50-dimensional embeddings trained on 986M words scored only 13.57% on the word-analogy task, well behind 40-dimensional CBOM (34.68%) and CBSOWM (36.71%) models trained on 17M words.

Fei Huang, Arun Ahuja, Doug Downey, Yi Yang, Yuhong Guo, and Alexander Yates. 2013. Learning Representations for Weakly Supervised Natural Language Processing Tasks. *Computational Linguistics*, 40:85–120.

Mike Lewis and Mark Steedman. 2013. Combined distributional and logical semantics. *Transactions of the Association for Computational Linguistics*, 1:179–192.

Mike Lewis and Mark Steedman. 2014. A* CCG parsing with a supertag-factored model. In *Proceedings of the 2014 Conference on Empirical Methods in Natural Language Processing (EMNLP)*, pages 990–1000, Doha, Qatar, October. Association for Computational Linguistics.

Thang Luong, Richard Socher, and Christopher Manning. 2013. Better word representations with recursive neural networks for morphology. In *Proceedings of the Seventeenth Conference on Computational Natural Language Learning*, pages 104–113, Sofia, Bulgaria, August. Association for Computational Linguistics.

Scott McDonald and Will Lowe. 1998. Modelling functional priming and the associative boost. In *Proceedings of the 20th Annual Meeting of the Cognitive Science Society*, pages 675–680. Erlbaum.

Tomas Mikolov, Kai Chen, Greg Corrado, and Jeffrey Dean. 2013a. Efficient estimation of word representations in vector space. In *Proceedings of Workshop at ICLR*.

Tomas Mikolov, Wen-tau Yih, and Geoffrey Zweig. 2013b. Linguistic regularities in continuous space word representations. In *Proceedings of the 2013 Conference of the North American Chapter of the Association for Computational Linguistics: Human Language Technologies*, pages 746–751, Atlanta, Georgia, June. Association for Computational Linguistics.

Jeff Mitchell. 2013. Learning semantic representations in a bigram language model. In *Proceedings of the 10th International Conference on Computational Semantics (IWCS 2013) – Short Papers*, pages 362–368, Potsdam, Germany, March. Association for Computational Linguistics.

Frederic Morin and Yoshua Bengio. 2005. Hierarchical probabilistic neural network language model. In *AISTATS05*, pages 246–252.

Jeffrey Pennington, Richard Socher, and Christopher Manning. 2014. Glove: Global vectors for word representation. In *Proceedings of the 2014 Conference on Empirical Methods in Natural Language Processing (EMNLP)*, pages 1532–1543, Doha, Qatar, October. Association for Computational Linguistics.

Yuta Tsuboi. 2014. Neural networks leverage corpus-wide information for part-of-speech tagging. In *Proceedings of the 2014 Conference on Empirical Methods in Natural Language Processing (EMNLP)*, pages 938–950, Doha, Qatar, October. Association for Computational Linguistics.

Mehmet Ali Yatbaz, Enis Sert, and Deniz Yuret. 2012. Learning syntactic categories using paradigmatic representations of word context. In *Proceedings of the 2012 Joint Conference on Empirical Methods in Natural Language Processing and Computational Natural Language Learning*, pages 940–951, Jeju Island, Korea, July. Association for Computational Linguistics.

Will Y. Zou, Richard Socher, Daniel M. Cer, and Christopher D. Manning. 2013. Bilingual word embeddings for phrase-based machine translation. In *EMNLP*, pages 1393–1398. ACL.

Scalable Semantic Parsing with Partial Ontologies

Eunsol Choi Tom Kwiatkowski[†] Luke Zettlemoyer
Computer Science & Engineering
University of Washington
eunsol@cs.washington.edu, tomkwiat@google.com, lsz@cs.washington.edu

Abstract

We consider the problem of building scalable semantic parsers for Freebase, and present a new approach for learning to do partial analyses that ground as much of the input text as possible without requiring that all content words be mapped to Freebase concepts. We study this problem on two newly introduced large-scale noun phrase datasets, and present a new semantic parsing model and semi-supervised learning approach for reasoning with partial ontological support. Experiments demonstrate strong performance on two tasks: referring expression resolution and entity attribute extraction. In both cases, the partial analyses allow us to improve precision over strong baselines, while parsing many phrases that would be ignored by existing techniques.

1 Introduction

Recently, significant progress has been made in learning semantic parsers for large knowledge bases (KBs) such as Freebase (FB) (Cai and Yates, 2013; Berant et al., 2013; Kwiatkowski et al., 2013; Reddy et al., 2014). Although these methods can build general purpose meaning representations, they are typically evaluated on question answering tasks and are designed to only parse questions that have complete ontological coverage, in the sense that there exists a logical form that can be executed against Freebase to get the correct answer.[1] In this paper, we instead consider the problem of learning semantic parsers for open domain text containing concepts that may or may not be representable using the Freebase ontology.

Wikipedia	Haitian human rights activists
	Art museums and galleries in New York
	School buildings completed in 1897
	Olympic gymnasts of Norway
Appos.	the capital of quake-hit Sichuan Province
	a major coal producing province
	the relaxed seaside capital of Mozambique

Figure 1: Example noun phrases from Wikipedia category labels and appositives in newswire text.

Even very large knowledge bases have two types of incompleteness that provide challenges for semantic parsing algorithms. They (1) have partial ontologies that cannot represent the meaning of many English phrases and (2) are typically missing many facts. For example, consider the phrases in Figure 1. They include subjective or otherwise unmodeled phrases such as "relaxed" and "quake-hit." Freebase, despite being large-scale, contains a limited set of concepts that cannot represent the meaning of these phrases. They also refer to entities that may be missing key facts. For example, a recent study (West et al., 2014) showed that over 70% of people in FB have no birth place, and 99% have no ethnicity. In our work, we introduce a new semantic parsing approach that explicitly models ontological incompleteness and is robust to missing facts, with the goal of recovering as much of a sentence's meaning as the ontology supports. We argue that this will enable the application of semantic parsers to a range of new tasks, such as information extraction (IE), where phrases rarely have full ontological support and new facts must be added to the KB.

Because existing semantic parsing datasets have been filtered to limit incompleteness, we introduce two new corpora that pair complex noun phrases with one or more entities that they describe. The

[†]Now at Google, NY.

[1]To ensure all questions are answerable, the data is manually filtered. For example, the WebQuestions dataset introduced by Berant et al. (2013) contains only the 7% of the originally gathered questions.

Proceedings of the 53rd Annual Meeting of the Association for Computational Linguistics and the 7th International Joint Conference on Natural Language Processing, pages 1311–1320,
Beijing, China, July 26-31, 2015.

(a) Wikipedia category	x :	Symphonic Poems by Jean Sibelius
	e :	{The Bard, Finlandia,Pohjola's Daughter, En Saga, Spring Song, Tapiola... }
	l_0 :	$\lambda x.Symphonic(x) \wedge Poems(x) \wedge by(JeanSibelius, x)$
	y :	λx.composition.form(x, Symphonicpoems) $\wedge$ composer(JeanSibelius, x)
	x :	Defunct Korean football clubs
	e :	{ Goyang KB Kookmin Bank FC,Hallelujah FC, Kyungsung FC }
	l_0 :	$\lambda x.defunct(x) \wedge korean(x) \wedge football(x) \wedge clubs(x)$
	y :	λx.OpenType[defunct](x) $\wedge$ OpenRel(x, KOREA) $\wedge$ football_clubs(x))
(b) Appos	x :	a driving force behind the project
	e :	Germany
	l_0 :	$\lambda x.driving(x) \wedge force(x) \wedge behind(x, theproject)$
	y :	λx.OpenType[driving_force](x) $\wedge$ OpenRel[behind](x, OpenEntity[the_project])
	x :	an EU outpost in the Mediterranean
	e :	Malta
	l_0 :	$\lambda x.outpost(x) \wedge EU(x) \wedge in(x, theMediterranean)$
	y :	λx.OpenRel(x, EU) $\wedge$ OpenType[outpost](x) $\wedge$ contained_by(x, MediterraneanSea)

Figure 2: Examples of noun phrases x, from the Wikipedia category and apposition datasets, paired with the set of entities **e** they describe, their underspecified logical form l_0, and their final logical form y.

first new dataset contains 365,000 Wikipedia category labels (Figure 1, top), each paired with the list of the associated Wikipedia entity pages. The second has 67,000 noun phrases paired with a single named entity, extracted from the appositive constructions in KBP 2009 newswire text (Figure 1, bottom).[2] This new data is both large scale, and unique in the focus on noun phrases. Noun phrases contain a number of challenging compositional phenomena, including implicit relations and noun-noun modifiers (e.g. see Gerber and Chai (2010)).

To better model text with only partial ontological support, we present a new semantic parser that builds logical forms with concepts from a target ontology and *open* concepts that are introduced when there is no appropriate concept match in the target ontology. Figure 2 shows examples of the meanings that we extract. Only the first of these examples can be fully represented using Freebase, all other examples require explicit modeling of open concepts. To build these logical forms, we follow recent work for Combinatory Categorical Grammar (CCG) semantic parsing with Freebase (Kwiatkowski et al., 2013), extended to model when open concepts should be used. We develop a two-stage learning algorithm: we first compute broad coverage lexical statistics over all of the data, which are then incorporated as features in a full parsing model. The parsing model is tuned on a hand-labeled data set with gold analyses.

Experiments demonstrate the benefits of the new approach. It significantly outperforms strong baselines on both a referring expression resolution task, where much like in the QA setting we directly evaluate if we recover the correct logical form for each input noun phrase, and on entity attribute extraction, where individual facts are extracted from the groundable part of the logical form. We also see that modeling incompleteness significantly boosts precision; we are able to more effectively determine which words should not be mapped to KB concepts. When run on all of the Wikipedia category data, we estimate that the learned model would discover 12 million new facts that could be added to Freebase with 72% precision.

[2]All new data is available on the authors' websites.

2 Overview

Semantic Parsing with Open Concepts Our goal is to learn to map noun phrase referring expressions x to logical forms y that describe their meaning. In this work, y is built using both concepts from a knowledge base $\mathcal{K}$ and *open concepts* that lie outside of the scope of $\mathcal{K}$. For example, in Figure 2 the phrase "Defunct Korean football clubs" is modeled using a logical form y that contains the $\mathcal{K}$ concept football_clubs(x) as well as the open concepts OpenType[defunct](x).

In this paper we describe a new method for learning the mapping from x to y from corpora of referring expression noun phrases, paired with a sets of entities e that these referring expressions describe. Figure 2 shows examples of these data drawn from two sources.

Tasks We introduce two new datasets (Sec. 3) that pair referring noun phrases x with one or more entities **e** that they describe. These data support evaluation for two tasks: referring expression resolution and information extraction.

In referring expression resolution, the parser is given x and is used to predict the referring expression logical form y that describes **e**. Since the majority of our data cannot be fully modeled with Freebase, we evaluate each y against a hand labeled gold standard instead of trying to extract **e** from $\mathcal{K}$.

The entity attribute extraction task also involves mapping phrases x to logical forms y, with the goal of adding new facts to the knowledge base $\mathcal{K}$. To do this, we assume each x is additionally paired with an set of entities **e**. We also define an *entity attribute* to be a literal in y that uses only concepts from $\mathcal{K}$. Finally, we extract, for each entity in **e**, all of the attributes listed in y. For example, the first logical form y in Figure 2 has two entity attributes: $\texttt{composer}(\texttt{JeanSibelius}, \texttt{x})$ and $\texttt{composition.form}(\texttt{x}, \texttt{Symphonic\_poems})$ which can be added to $\mathcal{K}$ for the entities $\{\texttt{TheBard}, \texttt{Finlandia}\}$.

Model and Learning Our approach extends the two-stage semantic parser introduced by Kwiatkowski et al (2013). We use CCG to build domain-independent logical forms l_0 and then introduce a new method for reasoning about how to map this intermediary representation onto both open concepts and $\mathcal{K}$ concepts (Sec. 4).

To learn this model, we assume access to data with two different types of annotations. The first contains noun phrase descriptions x and described entity sets e (as in Figure 2), which can be easily gathered at scale with no manual data labeling effort. However, this data, in general, has significant amount of knowledge base incompleteness; many described concepts and entity attributes will be missing from $\mathcal{K}$ (see Sec. 3 for more details). Therefore, to support effective learning, we will also use a small hand-labeled dataset containing x, **e**, a gold logical form y, an intermediary CCG logical form l_0, and a mapping from words in x to constants in $\mathcal{K}$ and open concepts. Our full learning approach (Sec. 5) estimates a linear model on the small labeled dataset, with broad coverage features derived from the larger dataset.

3 Data

We gathered two new datasets that pair complex noun phrases with one or more Freebase entities.

The Wikipedia category dataset contains 365,504 Wikipedia category names paired with the list of entities in that category. [3] Table 1 shows the details of this dataset and examples are given in Figure 2. For each development and test data, we randomly select 500 categories consisted of 3-10 words and describing fewer than 100 entities.

The apposition dataset is a large set of complex noun phrases paired with named entities, extracted from appositive constructions such as "Gustav Bayer, a former Olympic gymnast for Norway." For this example, we extract the entity "Gustav Bayer" and pair it with the noun phrase "a former Olympic gymnast for Norway." To identify appositive constructions, we ran the Stanford dependency parser on the newswire section of the KBP 2009 source corpus,[4] and selected noun phrases composed of 3 to 10 words, starting with an article, and paired with a named entity that is in Freebase.

This procedure of identifying complex entity descriptions allows for information extraction from a wide range of sources. However, it is also noisy and challenging. The dependency parser makes errors, for example "the next day against the United States, Spain" is falsely detected as an apposition. Furthermore, addressing context and co-reference is often necessary. For example, "Puerto Montt, a city south of the capital" or "the company's parent, Shenhua Group" requires reference resolution. We gathered 67 thousand appositions, which will be released to support future work, and randomly selected 300 for testing.

Measuring Incompleteness To study the amount of incompleteness in this data, we hand labeled logical forms for 500 Wikipedia categories in the development set. Examples of annotations are given in the rows labeled y in Figure 2. We use these to measure the schema and fact coverage of Freebase. Many of the entities in this dataset do not have the Freebase attributes described by the category phrases. When a concept is not in Freebase, we annotate it as `OpenType` or `OpenRel`, as shown in Figure 2. On average, each Wikipedia category name describes 2.58 Freebase attributes, and 0.39 concepts that cannot be mapped to FB. Overall, 27.2% of the phrases contain concepts that do not exist in the Freebase schema.

[3]Compiled by the YAGO project, available at: www.mpi-inf.mpg.de/departments/databases-and-information-systems/research/yago-naga/yago/downloads/

[4]http://www.nist.gov/tac/2009/

	entire set	dev	test
# categories	365,504	500	500
# words per category	4.1	4.4	4.3
# unique words	84,996	1,100	1,063
# entities per category	19.9	19.1	18.7
# entities	2,813,631	9,511	9,281
# entity-category pairs	7,292,326	9,549	9,331

Table 1: Wikipedia category data statistics.

	entire set	test set
# appositions	66,924	300
# unique words	25,472	817
# words per apposition	5.73	5.93

Table 2: Appositive data statistics.

Each category may have multiple correct logical forms. For example, "Hotels" can be mapped to: $\texttt{hotel(x)}$, $\texttt{accomodation.type(x, hotel)}$, or $\texttt{building\_function(x, hotel)}$. There are also genuine ambiguities in meaning. For example, "People from Bordeaux" can be interpreted as $\texttt{people(x)} \wedge \texttt{place\_lived(x, Bordeaux)}$ or $\texttt{people(x)} \wedge \texttt{place\_of\_birth(x, Bordeaux)}$. We made a best effort attempt to gather as many correct logical forms as possible, finding on average 1.8 logical forms per noun phrase. There were 97 unique binary relations, and 247 unique unary attributes in the annotation.

Given these logical forms, we also measured factual coverage. For the 72.8% of phrases that can be completely represented using Freebase, we executed the logical forms and compared the result to the labeled entity set. In total, 56% of the queries returned no entities and those that did return results have on average 15% overlap with the Wikipedia entity set. We also measured how often attributes from the labeled logical forms were assigned to the Wikipedia entities in FB, finding that only 33.6% were present. Given this rate, we estimate that it is possible to add 12 million new facts into FB from the 7 million entity-category pairs.

4 Mapping Text to Meaning

We adopt a two-stage semantic parsing approach (Kwiatkowski et al., 2013). We first use a CCG parser to define a set $\textsc{ccg}(x)$ of possible logical forms l_0. Then we will choose the logical form l_0 that closely matches the linguistic structure of the input text x, according to a learned linear model, and use an ontological match step that defines a set of transformations $\textsc{ont}(l_0, \mathcal{K})$ to map this meaning to a Freebase query y. Figure 2 shows examples of x, l_0 and y. In this section we describe our approach with the more detailed example derivation in Figure 3. We also describe the parameterization of a linear model that scores each derivation.

CCG parsing We use a CCG (Steedman, 1996) semantic parser (Kwiatkowski et al., 2013) to generate an underspecified logical form l_0. Figure 3a shows an example parse. The constants $Former$, $Municipalities$, in, $Brandenburgh$ in l_0 are not tied to the target knowledge base, causing the logical form to be underspecified. They can be replaced with Freebase constants in the later ontology matching step.

Ontological Matching The ontological match step has *structural match* and *constant match* components. Structural match operators can collapse or expand sub-expressions in the logical forms to match equivalent typed concepts in the target knowledge base. We adopt existing structural match operators (Kwiatkowski et al., 2013) and refer readers to that work for details.

Constant match operators replace underspecified constants in the underspecified logical form l_0 with concepts from the target knowledge base. There are four constant match operations used in Figure 3. The first two constant matches, shown below, match underspecified constants with constants of the same type from Freebase.

$$in \rightarrow \texttt{location.containedby}$$
$$Brandenburgh \rightarrow \texttt{BRANDENBURGH}$$

However, because we are modeling the semantics of phrases that are not covered by the Freebase schema, we also require the following two constant matches:

$$Former(x) \rightarrow \texttt{OpenType}$$
$$municipalities(x) \rightarrow \texttt{OpenRel(x, Municipality)}$$

Here, the word 'former' has been associated with a placeholder typing predicate since Freebase has no way of expressing end dates of administrative divisions. There is also no Freebase type representing the concept 'municipalities.' However, this word is associated with an entity in Freebase. Since there is no suitable linking predicate for the entity `Municipality`, we introduce a placeholder linking predicate `OpenRel` in the step from $l_2 \rightarrow l_3$. Our constant match operators can also introduce placeholder entities `OpenEntity` when there is no good match in Freebase.

(a) **CCG parse** builds an underspecified semantic representation of the sentence.

Former	municipalities	in	Brandenburgh
N/N	N	$N\backslash N/NP$	NP
$\lambda f \lambda x. f(x) \wedge former(x)$	$\lambda x. municipalities(x)$	$\lambda f \lambda x \lambda y. f(y) \wedge in(y, x)$	$Brandenburg$

$>$: N : $\lambda x. former(x) \wedge municipalities(x)$

$>$: $N\backslash N$: $\lambda f \lambda y. f(y) \wedge in(y, Brandenburg)$

$<$: N

$$l_0 = \lambda x. former(x) \wedge municipalities(x) \wedge in(x, Brandenburg)$$

(b) **Constant matches** replace underspecified constants with Freebase concepts

$\mathsf{l}_0 = \lambda x. former(x) \wedge municipalities(x) \wedge in(x, Brandenburg)$

$\mathsf{l}_1 = \lambda x. former(x) \wedge municipalities(x) \wedge in(x, \texttt{Brandenburg})$

$\mathsf{l}_2 = \lambda x. former(x) \wedge municipalities(x) \wedge \texttt{location.containedby}(x, \texttt{Brandenburg})$

$\mathsf{l}_3 = \lambda x. former(x) \wedge \texttt{OpenRel}(x, \texttt{Municipality}) \wedge \texttt{location.containedby}(x, \texttt{Brandenburg})$

$\mathsf{l}_4 = \lambda x. \texttt{OpenType}(x) \wedge \texttt{OpenRel}(x, \texttt{Municipality}) \wedge \texttt{location.containedby}(x, \texttt{Brandenburg})$

Figure 3: Derivation of the analysis for "Former municipalities in Brandenburgh". This analysis contains a placeholder type and a placeholder relation as described in Section 4.

We also allow the creation of typing predicates from matched entities through the introduction of linking predicates. For example, there is no native type associated with the word 'actor' in Freebase. Instead we create a typing predicate by matching the word to a Freebase entity `Actor` using Freebase API and allowing the introduction of linked predicates such as `person.profession` :

$$actor(x) \rightarrow \texttt{person.profession}(\texttt{x}, \texttt{Actor})$$

Scoring Full Parses Our goal in this paper is to learn a function from the phrase x to the correct analysis y. We score each parse using a linear model with features that signal attributes of the underspecified parse ϕ_p and those that signal attributes of the ontological match ϕ_{ont}. Since the model factors over the two stages of parser, we split the prediction problem similarly. First, we select the maximum scoring underspecified logical form:

$$l^* = \arg \max_{l \in \text{CCG}(x)} (\theta_p \cdot \phi_p(l))$$

and then we select the highest scoring Freebase analysis y^* that can be built from l^*:

$$y^* = \arg \max_{r \in \text{ONT}(l^*, \mathcal{K})} (\theta_{ont} \cdot \phi_{ont}(r))$$

We describe an approach to learning the parameter vectors θ_p and θ_{ont} below.

5 Learning

We introduce a learning approach that first collates aggregate statistics from the 7 million Wikipedia entity-category pairs and existing facts in FB, and then uses a small labeled training set to tune the weights for features that incorporate these statistics.

Wikipedia Category	
Wars involving the Grand Duchy of Lituania	
Entity	**Attribute**
BattleOfGrunwald	`type(x, military.conflict)`
GollubWar	`type(x, military.conflict)`
BattleOfGrunwald	`time.event.loc(x, Grunwald)`
...	...
Entity	**Relation**
BattleOfGrunwald	`military_conflict.combatants`
GollubWar	`time.event.start_time`
BattleOfGrunwald	`military_conflict.commanders`
...	...

Figure 4: Labeled entities are associated with attributes and relations.

Broad Coverage Lexical Statistics Each Wikipedia category is associated with a number of entities, most of which exist in FB. We use these entities to extract relations and attributes in FB associated with that category. For example, in Figure 4 the category 'Wars involving the Grand Duchy of Lithuania' is associated with the relation `military_conflict.combatants` and the attribute `type(x, military.conflict)` multiple times, because they are present in many of the category's entities. For each of the sub-phrases in the category name we count these associations over the entire Wikipedia category set.

We use these counts to calculate Pointwise Mutual Information (PMI) between words and Freebase attributes or relations. We choose PMI to avoid overcompensating common words, attributes, or relations. For example, the word 'Wars' is seen with the incorrect analysis `type(x, time.event)` more frequently than the correct analysis `type(x, military.conflict)`. However, PMI penalizes the attribute `type(x, time.event)` for its popularity and the correct analysis is preferred. As PMI has a tendency to emphasize rare counts, we chose PMI squared, which takes the squared value of the co-occurence count (PMI^2(a, b) = $\log \frac{count(a \wedge b)^2}{count(a)*count(b)}$), as a feature.

Structural KB Statistics Existing semantic parsers typically make use of type constraints to limit the space of possible logical forms. These strong type constraints are not feasible when the knowledge base is incomplete. For example, in Freebase the relation `military_conflict.combatants` expects an entity of type `military_conflict.combatant` as its object. However, many countries that have been involved in wars are not assigned this type.

We instead calculate type overlap statistics for all Freebase entities, to find likely missing types. For example, including the fact that the object of `military_conflict.combatants` is very often of type `location.country`.

Learning from Labeled Data We train each half of the prediction problem separately, as defined in Section 4, using the labeled training data introduced in Section 3. We use structured max-margin perceptrons to learn feature weights for both the underspecified parse and the ontological match step following (Kwiatkowski et al., 2013). The aggregate statistics collected from 7 million category-entity pairs produce very useful lexical features. We integrate these statistics into our linear model by summing their values for each derivation and treating them as a feature. All of the other features described in Section 6 are not word specific and are therefore far less sparse.

6 Features

We include a number of features that enable soft type checking on the output logical form, described first below, along with other features that measure different aspects of the analysis.

Coherency features For example, consider the phrase "The UK home city of the Queen," with Freebase logical form $y = \lambda x.\texttt{home}(\texttt{QEII}, x) \wedge \texttt{in}(x, \texttt{UK}) \wedge \texttt{city}(x)$. Each of the relations has expected types for their argument: the relation ⟨`home`⟩ expects a subject of type ⟨`person`⟩ and an object of type ⟨`location`⟩. Each type in Freebase lives in a hierarchy, so the type `city` implies {`location`, `administrative_division`, ...}. The next four features test agreement of these types on different parts of the output logical form.

Relation arguments trigger a feature if their type is in the set of types expected by the relation. `QEII` is a person so this feature is triggered for the relation-argument application in `home(QEII, x)`.

Relation-relation pairs can share variable arguments. For example, the variable x is the object of ⟨`home`⟩ and the subject of ⟨`in`⟩. Each relation expects a set of types of x. We have features to signal if: these sets are disjoint; one set subsumes the other; and the PMI between the highest level expected type (described in Section 5) if the sets are disjoint. In the example given here, the type ⟨`location`⟩ expected by ⟨`in`⟩ subsumes the type ⟨`city`⟩ expected by ⟨`home`⟩ so the second feature fires. We treat types such as `city`(x) as unary relations and include them in this feature set.

Type domain measures compatibility among domains in Freebase. Freebase is split into high-level domains and some of these are relevant, such as 'football' and 'sports'. We identify those by counting their co-occurrences. This becomes an indicator feature that signals their co-occurrence in y.

Named entity type features test if the entity e that we are extracting attributes for have Freebase type "person", "location" or "organization". If it does, we have a feature indicating if y defines a set of the same type. This features is not used in the referring expression task presented in Section 7 since we cannot assume access to the entities that are described.

CCG parse feature signals which lexical items were used in the CCG parse. Another feature fires if capitalized words map to named entities.

String similarity features signal exact string match, stemmed string match, and length weighted string edit distance between a phrase in the sentence and the name of the Freebase element it was matched on. We also use the Freebase search API to generate scores for phrase, entity pairs and include the log of this score as a features.

Lexical PMI feature includes the lexical Pointwise Mutual Information described in Section 5.

Freebase constant features signal the use of linking predicates, as defined in Section 4, and the log frequency count of the Freebase attributes across all entities in the Wikipedia category set.

Other features indicate the use of OpenRel, OpenEntity, OpenType in y and count repetitions of Freebase concepts in y.

7 Experimental Setup

Knowledge base We use the Jan. 26, 2014 Freebase dump. After pruning binary predicates taking numeric values, it contains 9351 binary predicates, 2754 unary predicates, and 1.2 billion assertions.

Pruning and Feature Initialization We perform beam search at each semantic parsing stage, using the Freebase search API to determine candidate named entities (10 per phrase), binary predicates (300 per phrase), and unary predicates (500 per phrase). The ontology matching stage considers the highest scored underspecified parse.

The features are initialized to prefer well-typed logical forms. Type checking features are initially set to -2 for mismatch. Features signalling incompatible topic domains and repetition are initialized as -10. All other initial feature weights are set to 1.

Datasets and Annotation We evaluate on the Wikipedia category and appositive datasets introduced in Sec. 3. On the Wikipedia development data, we annotated 500 logical forms, underspecified logical forms and constant mappings for ontology matching. The Wikipedia test data is composed of 500 unseen categories. We did not train on the appositive dataset, as it contains challenges such as co-reference and parsing errors as described in Sec. 3. Instead, we chose 300 randomly selected examples for evaluation, and ran on the model trained on the Wikipedia development data.

Evaluation Metrics We report five-fold cross validation for development but ran the final model once on the test data, manually scoring the output.

For evaluation on the referring expression resolution performance (as defined in Sec. 2), we include accuracy for the final logical form (*Exact Match*). We also evaluate precision and recall for predicting individual literals in this logical form on the development set. To control for missing facts, we did not evaluate the set of returned entities.

To evaluate entity attribute extraction performance (as defined in Sec. 2), we identified three classes of predictions. Extractions can be correct, benign, or false. Correct attributes are actually described in the phrase, benign extraction may not have been described but are still true, and false extractions are not true. For example, if the phrase "the capital of the communist-ruled nation" is mapped to the pair of attributes capital_of_administrative_division(x) , location(x), the first is correct and the second is benign. Other incorrect facts would be false.

System	Exact Match	Partial Match P	R	F1
KCAZ13	1.4	9.6	6.3	7.0
IE Baseline	6.8	37.0	23.3	28.6
NoPMI	11.0	23.7	20.8	21.6
NoOpenSchema	13.7	35.8	30.0	31.1
NoTyping	9.6	37.6	29.3	31.8
Our Approach	15.9	39.3	33.5	35.1
with Gold NE	20.8	46.6	40.5	42.3

Table 3: Referring expression resolution performance on the development set on gold references.

Data	System	Exact Match Accuracy
Wikipedia	IE Baseline	21.8%
	Our Approach	28.4%
Appos	IE Baseline	0.0%
	Our Approach	4.7%

Table 4: Manual evaluation for referring expression resolution on the test sets.

On the development set, we report precision and recall against the union of the FB attributes in our annotations without adjusting for benign extractions or the fact that the annotations are not complete. For the test sets, we computed precision (P) where benign extractions are considered to be wrong, as well as an adjusted precision metric (P*) where benign extractions are counted as correct. As we do not have full test set annotations, we cannot report recall. Finally, we report the average number of facts extracted per noun phrase (fact #).

Comparison Systems We compare performance to a number of ablated versions of the full system, where we have removed the open-constant ontology matching operators (NoOpenSchema), the PMI features (NoPMI), or the type checking features (NoTyping). For the referring expression resolution task, we excluded the named entity type feature, as this assumes typing information about the entity we are extracting attributes for.

We report results without the PMI features and the open schema matching operators (KCAZ13), which is a reimplementation of a recent Freebase QA model (Kwiatkowski et al., 2013). We also learn with gold named entity linking (Gold NE).

For the entity attribute extraction, we built a supervised learning baseline that combines the output of two discrete SVMs, one for predicting unary relations and one for binary relations. Each classifier

System	Top n	P	R	F1	fact #
IE Baseline	-	37.3	26.5	30.6	1.6
Our Approach	1	44.2	32.8	37.7	1.9
	2	36.9	38.0	37.5	2.6
	3	30.7	42.7	35.7	3.6
	4	27.0	44.7	33.6	4.2
	5	23.7	47.2	31.6	5.1
	10	15.9	52.0	24.3	8.5

Table 5: Entity attribute extraction performance on the Wikipedia category development set.

Data	System	P	P*	fact #
Wikipedia	IE Baseline	56.7	58.7	1.6
	Our Approach	61.2	72.6	2.0
Appos	IE Baseline	4.9	13.9	1.3
	Our Approach	33.2	61.4	0.9

Table 6: Manual evaluation for entity attribute extraction on the test sets.

is trained using the annotated Wikipedia categories. This dataset contains hundreds of unary and binary relations, which the IE baseline can predict. Each classifier is further anchored on a specific word, and includes n-gram and POS context features around that word, following features from Mintz et al (2009). To predict binary relations, we used named entities as anchors. For unary attributes we anchored on all possible nouns and adjectives. The final logical form includes the best relation predicted by each classifier. We use the Stanford CoreNLP[5] toolkit for tokenization, named entity recognition, and part-of-speech tagging.

8 Results

Tables 3 and 4 show performance on the referring expression resolution task. Tables 5 and 6 show performance on the extraction task. Reported precision is lower on the labeled development set than on the test set, where predicted logical forms are manually evaluated. This reflects the fact that, despite our best attempts, the development set labels are incomplete, as discussed in Section 3.

Referring expression resolution The systems retrieve the full meaning with 28.4% accuracy on the Wikipedia test set, and 15.9% on the development set. The gold named entity input improves performance by modest amounts. This suggests that the errors stem from ontology mismatches, as we will describe in more detail later in the qualitative analysis. We also see that all of the ablations hurt performance, and that the KCAZ13 model performs extremely poorly. The independent classifier baseline performs well at the sub-clause level, but fails to form a full logical form of the referring expression. Partial grounding and broad-coverage data statistics are essential for this problem.

Entity attribute extraction In the two test sets, the approach achieves high benign precision levels (P*) of 72.6 and 61.4. However, the appositives data is significantly more challenging, and the model misses many of the true facts that could be extracted. Many errors comes in the early stages of the pipeline, which can be attributed at least in part to both (1) the higher levels of noise in the input data (see Section 3), and (2) the fact that the CCG parser was developed on the Wikipedia category labels. While the IE baseline performs reasonably on the Wikipedia test data, its performance degrades significantly on appositions. As it is trained to predict pre-determined relations, it does not generalize to different domains.

For the development set, Table 5 also shows the precision-recall trade off for the set of Freebase attributes that appear in the top-n predicted logical forms. Precision drops quickly but recall can be improved significantly, showing that the model can produce many of the labeled facts.

Qualitative evaluation We sampled 100 errors from the Wikipedia test set for qualitative analysis. 10% came from entity linking. About 30% come from choosing a superset or subset of the desired meaning, for example by mapping "novel" to `book`. About 10% of the errors are from domain ambiguity, such as mapping "stage actor" to `film.film_actor`. 10% of the cases are from spurious string similarity, such as mapping "Hungarian expatriates" to `nationality(x,Hungary)`. 15% of the failures were due to incorrect underspecified logical forms and, finally, about 10% of the errors were because the typing features encouraged compound nouns to be split into separate attributes. On the apposition dataset, 65% of errors stems from parsing, either in apposition detection or CCG parsing. Better modeling the complex attachment decisions for the noun phrases in the apposition dataset remains an area for future work.

One advantage of our approach, especially in comparison to classifier based models like the IE baseline, is the ability to predict previously unseen relations. Counting only the correctly predicted

[5]http://nlp.stanford.edu/software/corenlp.html

triples, we see that over 40% of the unique relations we predict is not in the development set; our model learns to generalize based on the learned PMI features and other lexical cues.

Finally, our approach extracted 2.0 entity attributes per Wikipedia phrase and 0.9 per apposition on average. This matches our intuition that the apposition dataset contains many more words that cannot be modeled with concepts in Freebase.

9 Related Work

Recent work has begun to study the problem of knowledge base incompleteness and reasoning with open concepts. Joshi et al. (2014) describes an approach for mapping short search queries to a single Freebase relation, that benefits from modeling schema incompleteness. Additionally, Krishnamurthy et al. (2012; 2014) present a semantic parser that builds partial meaning representations with Freebase for information extraction applications. This is similar in spirit to the approach we present here, however they focus on a small, fixed, set of binary relations while we aim to represent as much of the text as possible using the entire Freebase ontology. Krishnamurthy and Mitchell (2015) have also studied semantic parsing with open concepts via matrix factorization. They use Freebase entities but do not include Freebase concepts.

The problem of building complete sentence analyses using all of the Freebase ontology has recently received attention within the context of question answering systems (Cai and Yates, 2013; Kwiatkowski et al., 2013; Berant et al., 2013; Berant and Liang, 2014; Reddy et al., 2014). Since they do not model KB incompleteness, these models will not work well on data that cannot be fully modeled by Freebase. In section 7, we report results using one of these systems to provide a reference point for our approach. There has also been other work on Freebase question answering (Yao and Van Durme, 2014; Bordes et al., 2014; Wang et al., 2014) that directly searches the facts in the KB to find answers without explicitly modeling compositional semantic structure. Therefore, these methods will suffer when facts are missing.

The syntactic and semantic structure of noun phrases has been extensively studied. For example, work on NomBank (Meyers et al., 2004; Gerber and Chai, 2010) focus on the challenge of modeling implicit arguments introduced by nominal predicates. In a manual study, we discovered that the 65% of our noun phrases contain implicit relations. We build on insights from Vadas and Curran (2008), who studied how to model the syntactic structure of noun phrases in CCGBank. While we are, to the best of our knowledge, the first to study compound noun phrases for semantic parsing to knowledge-bases, semantic parsers for noun phrase referring expressions have been built for visual referring expression (FitzGerald et al., 2013).

There has been little work on IE from compound noun phrases. Most existing IE algorithms extract a single relation, usually represented as a verb that holds between a pair of named entities, for example with supervised learning techniques (Freitag, 1998) or via distant supervision (Mintz et al., 2009; Riedel et al., 2013; Hoffmann et al., 2011). We aim to go beyond relations between entity pairs, and to retrieve full semantics of noun phrases, extracting unary and binary relations for a single entity. A notable exception to this trend is the ReNoun system (Yahya et al., 2014) which models noun phrase structure for open information extraction. They report that 97% of the attributes in Freebase are commonly expressed as noun phrases. However, unlike our work, they considered open information extraction and did not ground the extractions in an external KB.

10 Conclusion

In this paper, we present a semantic parsing approach with knowledge base incompleteness, applied to the problem of information extraction from noun phrases. When run on all of the Wikipedia category data, the approach would extract up to 12 million new Freebase facts at 72% precision.

There is significant potential for improving the parsing models, as well as better optimizing the precision recall trade-off for the extracted facts. It would also be interesting to gather data with compositional phenomena, such as negation and disjunction, and study its impact on the performance of the semantic parser.

Acknowledgments

The research was supported in part by DARPA, under the DEFT program through the AFRL (FA8750-13-2-0019) and the CSSG (N11AP20020), as well as the NSF (IIS-1115966, IIS-1252835) and a gift from Google, Inc. The authors thank Xiao Ling for providing the apposition data, and Yoav Artzi, Nicholas FitzGerald, Mike Lewis, Sameer Singh and Mark Yatskar for discussion and comments.

References

Jonathan Berant and Percy Liang. 2014. Semantic parsing via paraphrasing. *Proceedings of the Annual Meeting of the Association for Computational Linguistics*.

Jonathan Berant, Andrew Chou, Roy Frostig, and Percy Liang. 2013. Semantic parsing on freebase from question-answer pairs. In *Proceedings of the Empirical Methods in Natural Language Processing*.

Antoine Bordes, Jason Weston, and Sumit Chopra. 2014. Question answering with subgraph embeddings. In *Proceedings of the 2014 Conference on Empirical Methods in Natural Language Processing*, Doha, Qatar. Association for Computational Linguistics.

Qingqing Cai and Alexandar Yates. 2013. Large-scale semantic parsing via schema matching and lexicon extension. In *Proceedings of the Annual Meeting of the Association for Computational Linguistics*.

Nicholas FitzGerald, Yoav Artzi, and Luke Zettlemoyer. 2013. Learning distributions over logical forms for referring expression generation. In *Proceedings of the Conference on Empirical Methods in Natural Language Processing*.

Dayne Freitag. 1998. Toward general-purpose learning for information extraction. In *Proceedings of the 36th Annual Meeting of the Association for Computational Linguistics*.

Matthew Gerber and Joyce Y Chai. 2010. Beyond nombank: a study of implicit arguments for nominal predicates. In *Proceedings of the Annual Meeting of the Association for Computational Linguistics*. Association for Computational Linguistics.

Raphael Hoffmann, Congle Zhang, Xiao Ling, Luke Zettlemoyer, and Dan Weld. 2011. Knowledge-based weak supervision for information extraction of overlapping relations. In *Proceedings of the Conference of the Association of Computational Linguistics*.

Mandar Joshi, Uma Sawat, and Soumen Chakrabarti. 2014. Knowledge graph and corpus driven segmentation and answer inference for telegraphic entity-seeking queries. In *Proceedings of the Conference on Empirical Methods in Natural Language Processing*. Association for Computational Linguistics.

Jayant Krishnamurthy and Tom M Mitchell. 2012. Weakly supervised training of semantic parsers. In *Proceedings of the Joint Conference on Empirical Methods in Natural Language Processing and Computational Natural Language Learning*. Association for Computational Linguistics.

Jayant Krishnamurthy and Tom M. Mitchell. 2014. Joint syntactic and semantic parsing with combinatory categorial grammar. In *Proceedings of the 50th Annual Meeting of the Association for Computational Linguistics*. Association for Computational Linguistics.

Jayant Krishnamurthy and Tom Mitchell. 2015. Learning a compositional semantics for freebase with an opne predicate vocabulary. *Transactions of the Association for Computational Linguistics*.

Tom Kwiatkowski, Eunsol Choi, Yoav Artzi, and Luke Zettlemoyer. 2013. Scaling semantic parsers with on-the-fly ontology matching. In *Proceedings of the Conference on Empirical Methods in Natural Language Processing*. Association for Computational Linguistics.

Adam Meyers, Ruth Reeves, Catherine Macleod, Rachel Szekely, Veronika Zielinska, Brian Young, and Ralph Grishman. 2004. Annotating noun argument structure for nombank. In *LREC*, volume 4.

Mike Mintz, Steven Bills, Rion Snow, and Dan Jurafsky. 2009. Distant supervision for relation extraction without labeled data. In *Proceedings of the Joint Conference of the Annual Meeting of the Association for Computational Linguistics*. Association for Computational Linguistics.

Siva Reddy, Mirella Lapata, and Mark Steedman. 2014. Large-scale semantic parsing without question-answer pairs. *Transactions of the Association for Computational Linguistics*, 2.

Sebastian Riedel, Limin Yao, Benjamin M. Marlin, and Andrew McCallum. 2013. Relation extraction with matrix factorization and universal schemas. In *Joint Human Language Technology Conference/Annual Meeting of the North American Chapter of the Association for Computational Linguistics*.

Mark Steedman. 1996. *Surface Structure and Interpretation*. The MIT Press.

David Vadas and James R. Curran. 2008. Parsing noun phrase structure with ccg. In *Proceedings of the Annual Meeting of the Association for Computational Linguistics*.

Zhenghao Wang, Shengquan Yan, Huaming Wang, and Xuedong Huang. 2014. An overview of microsoft deep qa system on stanford webquestions benchmark. Technical Report MSR-TR-2014-121, September.

Robert West, Evgeniy Gabrilovich, Kevin Murphy, Shaohua Sun, Rahul Gupta, and Dekang Lin. 2014. Knowledge base completion via search-based question answering. In *Proceedings of World Wide Web Conference*.

Mohamed Yahya, Steven Euijong Whang, Rahul Gupta, and Alon Halevy. 2014. Renoun: Fact extraction for nominal attributes. In *Proceedings of the Conference on Empirical Methods in Natural Language Processing*. Association for Computational Linguistics.

Xuchen Yao and Benjamin Van Durme. 2014. Information extraction over structured data: Question answering with freebase. In *Proceedings of the Annual Meeting of the Association for Computational Linguistics*.

Semantic Parsing via Staged Query Graph Generation: Question Answering with Knowledge Base

Wen-tau Yih Ming-Wei Chang Xiaodong He Jianfeng Gao
Microsoft Research
Redmond, WA 98052, USA
{scottyih,minchang,xiaohe,jfgao}@microsoft.com

Abstract

We propose a novel semantic parsing framework for question answering using a knowledge base. We define a *query graph* that resembles subgraphs of the knowledge base and can be directly mapped to a logical form. Semantic parsing is reduced to query graph generation, formulated as a staged search problem. Unlike traditional approaches, our method leverages the knowledge base in an early stage to prune the search space and thus simplifies the semantic matching problem. By applying an advanced entity linking system and a deep convolutional neural network model that matches questions and predicate sequences, our system outperforms previous methods substantially, and achieves an F_1 measure of 52.5% on the WEBQUESTIONS dataset.

1 Introduction

Organizing the world's facts and storing them in a structured database, large-scale knowledge bases (KB) like DBPedia (Auer et al., 2007) and Freebase (Bollacker et al., 2008) have become important resources for supporting open-domain question answering (QA). Most state-of-the-art approaches to KB-QA are based on semantic parsing, where a question (utterance) is mapped to its formal meaning representation (e.g., logical form) and then translated to a KB query. The answers to the question can then be retrieved simply by executing the query. The semantic parse also provides a deeper understanding of the question, which can be used to justify the answer to users, as well as to provide easily interpretable information to developers for error analysis.

However, most traditional approaches for semantic parsing are largely decoupled from the knowledge base, and thus are faced with several challenges when adapted to applications like QA. For instance, a generic meaning representation may have the ontology matching problem when the logical form uses predicates that differ from those defined in the KB (Kwiatkowski et al., 2013). Even when the representation language is closely related to the knowledge base schema, finding the correct predicates from the large vocabulary in the KB to relations described in the utterance remains a difficult problem (Berant and Liang, 2014).

Inspired by (Yao and Van Durme, 2014; Bao et al., 2014), we propose a semantic parsing framework that leverages the knowledge base more tightly when forming the parse for an input question. We first define a *query graph* that can be straightforwardly mapped to a logical form in λ-calculus and is semantically closely related to λ-DCS (Liang, 2013). Semantic parsing is then reduced to query graph generation, formulated as a search problem with staged states and actions. Each state is a candidate parse in the query graph representation and each action defines a way to *grow* the graph. The representation power of the semantic parse is thus controlled by the set of legitimate actions applicable to each state. In particular, we stage the actions into three main steps: locating the *topic entity* in the question, finding the main *relationship* between the answer and the topic entity, and expanding the query graph with additional *constraints* that describe properties the answer needs to have, or relationships between the answer and other entities in the question.

One key advantage of this staged design is that through grounding partially the utterance to some entities and predicates in the KB, we make the search far more efficient by focusing on the promising areas in the space that most likely lead to the correct query graph, before the full parse is determined. For example, after linking "Fam-

Proceedings of the 53rd Annual Meeting of the Association for Computational Linguistics and the 7th International Joint Conference on Natural Language Processing, pages 1321–1331,
Beijing, China, July 26-31, 2015.

ily Guy" in the question "Who first voiced Meg on Family Guy?" to `FamilyGuy` (the TV show) in the knowledge base, the procedure needs only to examine the predicates that can be applied to `FamilyGuy` instead of all the predicates in the KB. Resolving other entities also becomes easy, as given the context, it is clear that Meg refers to `MegGriffin` (the character in Family Guy). Our design divides this particular semantic parsing problem into several sub-problems, such as entity linking and relation matching. With this integrated framework, best solutions to each subproblem can be easily combined and help produce the correct semantic parse. For instance, an advanced entity linking system that we employ outputs candidate entities for each question with both high precision and recall. In addition, by leveraging a recently developed semantic matching framework based on convolutional networks, we present better relation matching models using continuous-space representations instead of pure lexical matching. Our semantic parsing approach improves the state-of-the-art result on the WEBQUESTIONS dataset (Berant et al., 2013) to 52.5% in F_1, a 7.2% absolute gain compared to the best existing method.

The rest of this paper is structured as follows. Sec. 2 introduces the basic notion of the graph knowledge base and the design of our query graph. Sec. 3 presents our search-based approach for generating the query graph. The experimental results are shown in Sec. 4, and the discussion of our approach and the comparisons to related work are in Sec. 5. Finally, Sec. 6 concludes the paper.

2 Background

In this work, we aim to learn a semantic parser that maps a natural language question to a logical form query q, which can be executed against a knowledge base $\mathcal{K}$ to retrieve the answers. Our approach takes a graphical view of both $\mathcal{K}$ and q, and reduces semantic parsing to mapping questions to *query graphs*. We describe the basic design below.

2.1 Knowledge base

The knowledge base $\mathcal{K}$ considered in this work is a collection of subject-predicate-object triples (e_1, p, e_2), where $e_1, e_2 \in \mathcal{E}$ are the entities (e.g., `FamilyGuy` or `MegGriffin`) and $p \in \mathcal{P}$ is a binary predicate like `character`. A knowledge base in this form is often called a *knowledge graph*

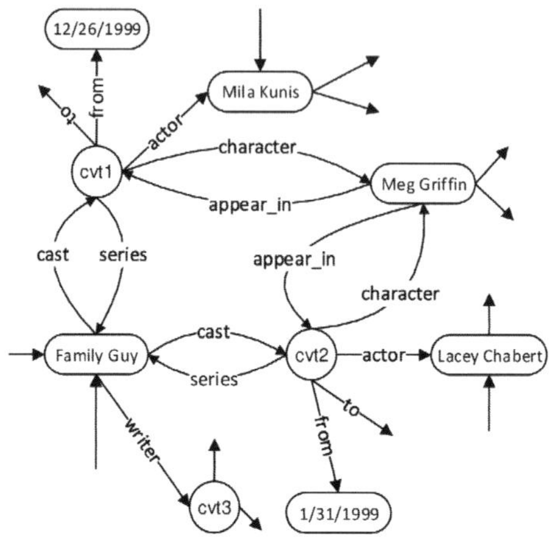

Figure 1: Freebase subgraph of Family Guy

because of its straightforward graphical representation – each entity is a node and two related entities are linked by a directed edge labeled by the predicate, from the subject to the object entity.

To compare our approach to existing methods, we use Freebase, which is a large database with more than 46 million topics and 2.6 billion facts. In Freebase's design, there is a special entity category called *compound value type* (CVT), which is not a real-world entity, but is used to collect multiple fields of an event or a special relationship.

Fig. 1 shows a small subgraph of Freebase related to the TV show *Family Guy*. Nodes are the entities, including some dates and special CVT entities[1]. A directed edge describes the relation between two entities, labeled by the predicate.

2.2 Query graph

Given the knowledge graph, executing a logical-form query is equivalent to finding a subgraph that can be mapped to the query and then resolving the binding of the variables. To capture this intuition, we describe a restricted subset of λ-calculus in a graph representation as our *query graph*.

Our query graph consists of four types of nodes: *grounded entity* (rounded rectangle), *existential variable* (circle), *lambda variable* (shaded circle), *aggregation function* (diamond). Grounded entities are existing entities in the knowledge base $\mathcal{K}$. Existential variables and lambda variables are un-

[1]In the rest of the paper, we use the term *entity* for both real-world and CVT entities, as well as properties like date or height. The distinction is not essential to our approach.

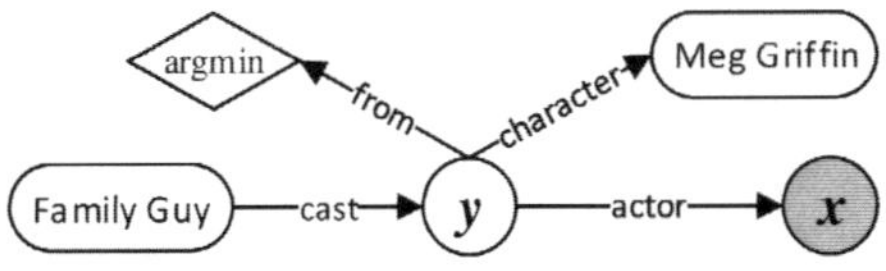

Figure 2: Query graph that represents the question "Who first voiced Meg on Family Guy?"

grounded entities. In particular, we would like to retrieve all the entities that can map to the lambda variables in the end as the answers. Aggregation function is designed to operate on a specific entity, which typically captures some numerical properties. Just like in the knowledge graph, related nodes in the query graph are connected by directed edges, labeled with predicates in $\mathcal{K}$.

To demonstrate this design, Fig. 2 shows one possible query graph for the question "Who first voiced Meg on Family Guy?" using Freebase. The two entities, `MegGriffin` and `FamilyGuy` are represented by two rounded rectangle nodes. The circle node y means that there should exist an entity describing some casting relations like the character, actor and the time she started the role[2]. The shaded circle node x is also called the answer node, and is used to map entities retrieved by the query. The diamond node $\arg\min$ constrains that the answer needs to be the earliest actor for this role. Equivalently, the logical form query in λ-calculus without the aggregation function is: $\lambda x.\exists y.\texttt{cast}(\texttt{FamilyGuy}, y) \wedge \texttt{actor}(y, x) \wedge \texttt{character}(y, \texttt{MegGriffin})$ Running this query graph against $\mathcal{K}$ as in Fig. 1 will match both `LaceyChabert` and `MilaKunis` before applying the aggregation function, but only `LaceyChabert` is the correct answer as she started this role earlier (by checking the `from` property of the grounded CVT node).

Our query graph design is inspired by (Reddy et al., 2014), but with some key differences. The nodes and edges in our query graph closely resemble the exact entities and predicates from the knowledge base. As a result, the graph can be straightforwardly translated to a logical form query that is directly executable. In contrast, the query graph in (Reddy et al., 2014) is mapped from the CCG parse of the question, and needs further transformations before mapping to subgraphs of the target knowledge base to retrieve answers.

[2] y should be grounded to a CVT entity in this case.

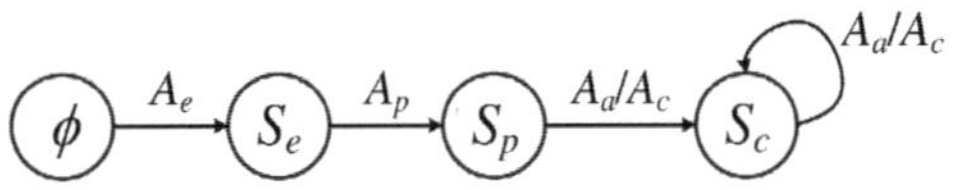

Figure 3: The legitimate actions to *grow* a query graph. See text for detail.

Semantically, our query graph is more related to simple λ-DCS (Berant et al., 2013; Liang, 2013), which is a syntactic simplification of λ-calculus when applied to graph databases. A query graph can be viewed as the tree-like graph pattern of a logical form in λ-DCS. For instance, the path from the answer node to an entity node can be described using a series of *join* operations in λ-DCS. Different paths of the tree graph are combined via the *intersection* operators.

3 Staged Query Graph Generation

We focus on generating query graphs with the following properties. First, the tree graph consists of one entity node as the root, referred as the *topic entity*. Second, there exists only one lambda variable x as the answer node, with a directed path from the root to it, and has zero or more existential variables in-between. We call this path the *core inferential chain* of the graph, as it describes the main relationship between the answer and topic entity. Variables can only occur in this chain, and the chain only has variable nodes except the root. Finally, zero or more entity or aggregation nodes can be attached to each variable node, including the answer node. These branches are the additional *constraints* that the answers need to satisfy. For example, in Fig. 2, `FamilyGuy` is the root and `FamilyGuy` $\rightarrow y \rightarrow x$ is the core inferential chain. The branch $y \rightarrow$ `MegGriffin` specifies the character and $y \rightarrow \arg\min$ constrains that the answer needs to be the earliest actor for this role.

Given a question, we formalize the query graph generation process as a search problem, with *staged* states and actions. Let $\mathcal{S} = \bigcup\{\phi, \mathcal{S}_e, \mathcal{S}_p, \mathcal{S}_c\}$ be the set of states, where each state could be an empty graph (ϕ), a single-node graph with the topic entity ($\mathcal{S}_e$), a core inferential chain ($\mathcal{S}_p$), or a more complex query graph with additional constraints ($\mathcal{S}_c$). Let $\mathcal{A} = \bigcup\{\mathcal{A}_e, \mathcal{A}_p, \mathcal{A}_c, \mathcal{A}_a\}$ be the set of actions. An action grows a given graph by adding some edges

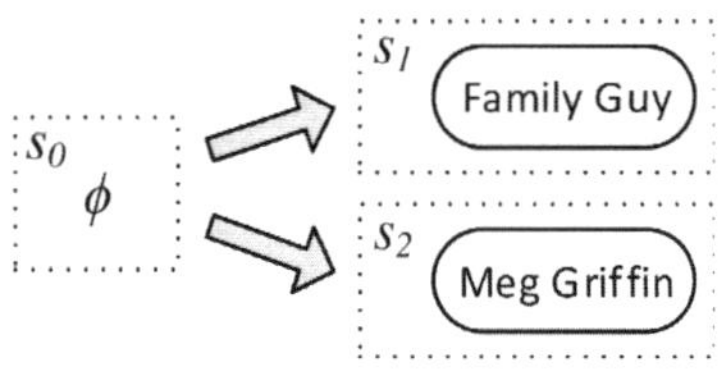

Figure 4: Two possible topic entity linking actions applied to an empty graph, for question "Who first voiced [Meg] on [Family Guy]?"

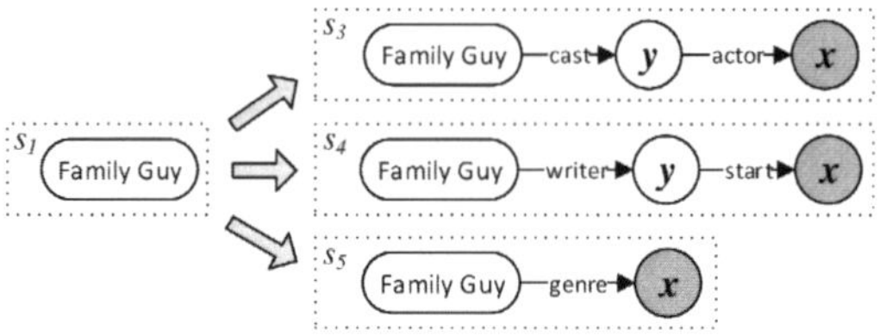

Figure 5: Candidate core inferential chains start from the entity `FamilyGuy`.

and nodes. In particular, $\mathcal{A}_e$ picks an entity node; $\mathcal{A}_p$ determines the core inferential chain; $\mathcal{A}_c$ and $\mathcal{A}_a$ add constraints and aggregation nodes, respectively. Given a state, the valid action set can be defined by the finite state diagram in Fig. 3. Notice that the order of possible actions is chosen for the convenience of implementation. In principle, we could choose a different order, such as matching the core inferential chain first and then resolving the topic entity linking. However, since we will consider multiple hypotheses during search, the order of the staged actions can simply be viewed as a different way to prune the search space or to bias the exploration order.

We define the reward function on the state space using a log-linear model. The reward basically estimates the likelihood that a query graph correctly parses the question. Search is done using the best-first strategy with a priority queue, which is formally defined in Appendix A. In the following subsections, we use a running example of finding the semantic parse of question q_{ex} = "Who first voiced Meg of Family Guy?" to describe the sequence of actions.

3.1 Linking Topic Entity

Starting from the initial state s_0, the valid actions are to create a single-node graph that corresponds to the topic entity found in the given question. For instance, possible topic entities in q_{ex} can either be `FamilyGuy` or `MegGriffin`, shown in Fig. 4.

We use an entity linking system that is designed for short and noisy text (Yang and Chang, 2015). For each entity e in the knowledge base, the system first prepares a surface-form lexicon that lists all possible ways that e can be mentioned in text. This lexicon is created using various data sources, such as names and aliases of the entities, the anchor text in Web documents and the Wikipedia redirect table. Given a question, it considers all the consecutive word sequences that have occurred in the lexicon as possible mentions, paired with their possible entities. Each pair is then scored by a statistical model based on its frequency counts in the surface-form lexicon. To tolerate potential mistakes of the entity linking system, as well as exploring more possible query graphs, up to 10 top-ranked entities are considered as the topic entity. The linking score will also be used as a feature for the reward function.

3.2 Identifying Core Inferential Chain

Given a state s that corresponds to a single-node graph with the topic entity e, valid actions to extend this graph is to identify the *core inferential chain*; namely, the relationship between the topic entity and the answer. For example, Fig. 5 shows three possible chains that expand the single-node graph in s_1. Because the topic entity e is given, we only need to explore legitimate predicate sequences that can start from e. Specifically, to restrict the search space, we explore all paths of length 2 when the middle existential variable can be grounded to a CVT node and paths of length 1 if not. We also consider longer predicate sequences if the combinations are observed in training data[3].

Analogous to the entity linking problem, where the goal is to find the mapping of mentions to entities in $\mathcal{K}$, identifying the core inferential chain is to map the natural utterance of the question to the correct predicate sequence. For question "*Who* first voiced Meg on [Family Guy]?" we need to measure the likelihood that each of the sequences in {`cast-actor`, `writer-start`, `genre`} correctly captures the relationship between *Family Guy* and *Who*. We reduce this problem to measuring semantic similarity using neural networks.

[3]Decomposing relations in the utterance can be done using decoding methods (e.g., (Bao et al., 2014)). However, similar to ontology mismatch, the relation in text may not have a corresponding single predicate, such as *grandparent* needs to be mapped to `parent-parent` in Freebase.

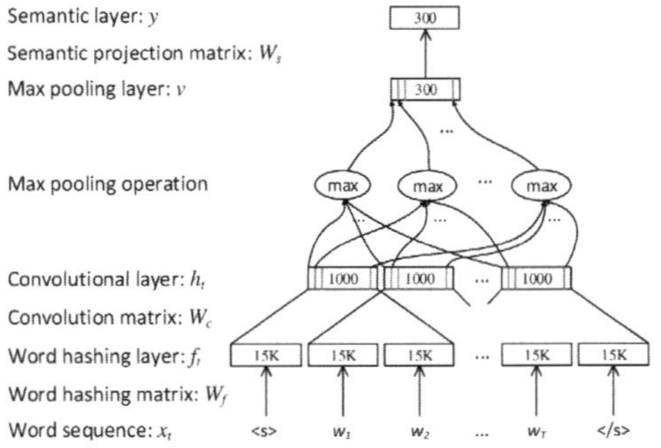

Figure 6: The architecture of the convolutional neural networks (CNN) used in this work. The CNN model maps a variable-length word sequence (e.g., a pattern or predicate sequence) to a low-dimensional vector in a latent semantic space. See text for the description of each layer.

3.2.1 Deep Convolutional Neural Networks

To handle the huge variety of the semantically equivalent ways of stating the same question, as well as the mismatch of the natural language utterances and predicates in the knowledge base, we propose using Siamese neural networks (Bromley et al., 1993) for identifying the core inferential chain. For instance, one of our constructions maps the question to a *pattern* by replacing the entity mention with a generic symbol <e> and then compares it with a candidate chain, such as "who first voiced meg on <e>" vs. `cast-actor`. The model consists of two neural networks, one for the pattern and the other for the inferential chain. Both are mapped to k-dimensional vectors as the output of the networks. Their semantic similarity is then computed using some distance function, such as *cosine*. This continuous-space representation approach has been proposed recently for semantic parsing and question answering (Bordes et al., 2014a; Yih et al., 2014) and has shown better results compared to lexical matching approaches (e.g., word-alignment models). In this work, we adapt a convolutional neural network (CNN) framework (Shen et al., 2014b; Shen et al., 2014a; Gao et al., 2014) to this matching problem. The network architecture is illustrated in Fig. 6.

The CNN model first applies a word hashing technique (Huang et al., 2013) that breaks a word into a vector of letter-trigrams ($x_t \rightarrow f_t$ in Fig. 6). For example, the bag of letter-trigrams of the word "who" are #-w-h, w-h-o, h-o-# after adding the

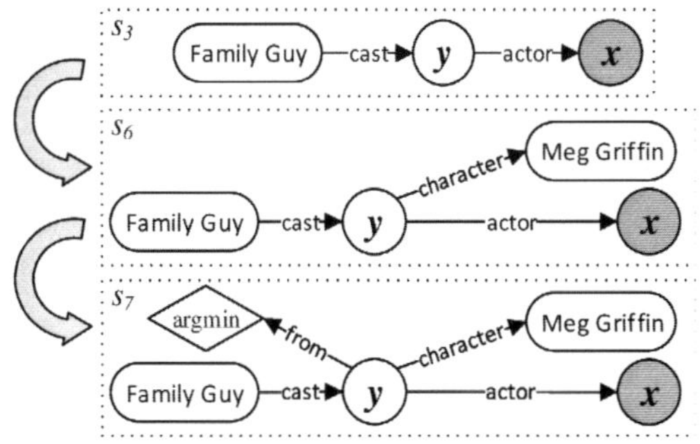

Figure 7: Extending an inferential chain with constraints and aggregation functions.

word boundary symbol #. Then, it uses a convolutional layer to project the letter-trigram vectors of words within a context window of 3 words to a local contextual feature vector ($f_t \rightarrow h_t$), followed by a max pooling layer that extracts the most salient local features to form a fixed-length global feature vector (v). The global feature vector is then fed to feed-forward neural network layers to output the final non-linear semantic features (y), as the vector representation of either the pattern or the inferential chain.

Training the model needs positive pairs, such as a pattern like "who first voiced meg on <e>" and an inferential chain like `cast-actor`. These pairs can be extracted from the full semantic parses when provided in the training data. If the correct semantic parses are latent and only the pairs of questions and answers are available, such as the case in the WEBQUESTIONS dataset, we can still hypothesize possible inferential chains by traversing the paths in the knowledge base that connect the topic entity and the answer. Sec. 4.1 will illustrate this data generation process in detail.

Our model has two advantages over the embedding approach (Bordes et al., 2014a). First, the word hashing layer helps control the dimensionality of the input space and can easily scale to large vocabulary. The letter-trigrams also capture some sub-word semantics (e.g., words with minor typos have almost identical letter-trigram vectors), which makes it especially suitable for questions from real-world users, such as those issued to a search engine. Second, it uses a deeper architecture with convolution and max-pooling layers, which has more representation power.

3.3 Augmenting Constraints & Aggregations

A graph with just the inferential chain forms the simplest legitimate query graph and can be executed against the knowledge base $\mathcal{K}$ to retrieve the answers; namely, all the entities that x can be grounded to. For instance, the graph in s_3 in Fig. 7 will retrieve all the actors who have been on `FamilyGuy`. Although this set of entities obviously contains the correct answer to the question (assuming the topic entity FamilyGuy is correct), it also includes incorrect entities that do not satisfy additional constraints implicitly or explicitly mentioned in the question.

To further restrict the set of answer entities, the graph with only the core inferential chain can be expanded by two types of actions: $\mathcal{A}_c$ and $\mathcal{A}_a$. $\mathcal{A}_c$ is the set of possible ways to attach an entity to a variable node, where the edge denotes one of the valid predicates that can link the variable to the entity. For instance, in Fig. 7, s_6 is created by attaching `MegGriffin` to y with the predicate `character`. This is equivalent to the last conjunctive term in the corresponding λ-expression: $\lambda x.\exists y.\texttt{cast}(\texttt{FamilyGuy}, y) \wedge \texttt{actor}(y, x) \wedge \texttt{character}(y, \texttt{MegGriffin})$. Sometimes, the constraints are described over the entire answer set through the aggregation function, such as the word "first" in our example question q_{ex}. This is handled similarly by actions $\mathcal{A}_a$, which attach an aggregation node on a variable node. For example, the $\arg\min$ node of s_7 in Fig. 7 chooses the grounding with the smallest `from` attribute of y.

The full possible constraint set can be derived by first issuing the core inferential chain as a query to the knowledge base to find the bindings of variables y's and x, and then enumerating all neighboring nodes of these entities. This, however, often results in an unnecessarily large constraint pool. In this work, we employ simple rules to retain only the nodes that have some possibility to be legitimate constraints. For instance, a constraint node can be an entity that also appears in the question (detected by our entity linking component), or an aggregation constraint can only be added if certain keywords like "first" or "latest" occur in the question. The complete set of these rules can be found in Appendix B.

3.4 Learning the reward function

Given a state s, the reward function $\gamma(s)$ basically judges whether the query graph represented by s is the correct semantic parse of the input question q. We use a log-linear model to learn the reward function. Below we describe the features and the learning process.

3.4.1 Features

The features we designed essentially match specific portions of the graph to the question, and generally correspond to the staged actions described previously, including:

Topic Entity The score returned by the entity linking system is directly used as a feature.

Core Inferential Chain We use similarity scores of different CNN models described in Sec. 3.2.1 to measure the quality of the core inferential chain. **PatChain** compares the pattern (replacing the topic entity with an entity symbol) and the predicate sequence. **QuesEP** concatenates the canonical name of the topic entity and the predicate sequence, and compares it with the question. This feature conceptually tries to verify the entity linking suggestion. These two CNN models are learned using pairs of the question and the inferential chain of the parse in the training data. In addition to the *in-domain* similarity features, we also train a **ClueWeb** model using the Freebase annotation of ClueWeb corpora (Gabrilovich et al., 2013). For two entities in a sentence that can be linked by one or two predicates, we pair the sentences and predicates to form a parallel corpus to train the CNN model.

Constraints & Aggregations When a constraint node is present in the graph, we use some simple features to check whether there are words in the question that can be associated with the constraint entity or property. Examples of such features include whether a mention in the question can be linked to this entity, and the percentage of the words in the name of the constraint entity appear in the question. Similarly, we check the existence of some keywords in a pre-compiled list, such as "first", "current" or "latest" as features for aggregation nodes such as $\arg\min$. The complete list of these simple word matching features can also be found in Appendix B.

Overall The number of the answer entities retrieved when issuing the query to the knowledge base and the number of nodes in the query graph are both included as features.

q = "Who first voiced Meg on Family Guy?"

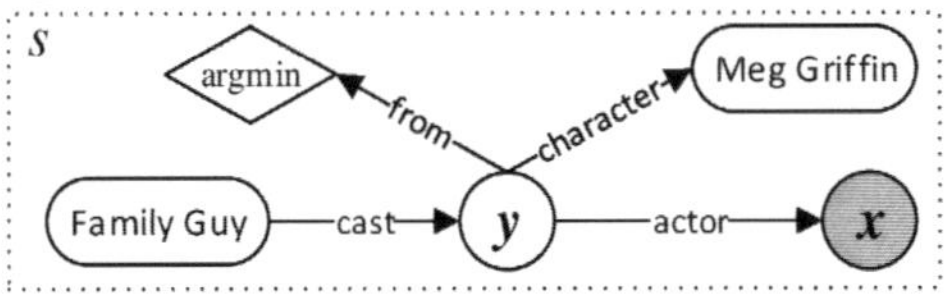

(1) EntityLinkingScore(FamilyGuy, "Family Guy") = 0.9
(2) PatChain("who first voiced meg on <e>", cast-actor) = 0.7
(3) QuesEP(q, "family guy cast-actor") = 0.6
(4) ClueWeb("who first voiced meg on <e>", cast-actor) = 0.2
(5) ConstraintEntityWord("Meg Griffin", q) = 0.5
(6) ConstraintEntityInQ("Meg Griffin", q) = 1
(7) AggregationKeyword(argmin, q) = 1
(8) NumNodes(s) = 5
(9) NumAns(s) = 1

Figure 8: Active features of a query graph s. (1) is the entity linking score of the topic entity. (2)-(4) are different model scores of the core chain. (5) indicates 50% of the words in "Meg Griffin" appear in the question q. (6) is 1 when the mention "Meg" in q is correctly linked to `MegGriffin` by the entity linking component. (8) is the number of nodes in s. The knowledge base returns only 1 entity when issuing this query, so (9) is 1.

To illustrate our feature design, Fig. 8 presents the active features of an example query graph.

3.4.2 Learning

In principle, once the features are extracted, the model can be trained using any standard off-the-shelf learning algorithm. Instead of treating it as a binary classification problem, where only the correct query graphs are labeled as positive, we view it as a ranking problem. Suppose we have several candidate query graphs for each question[4]. Let g_a and g_b be the query graphs described in states s_a and s_b for the same question q, and the entity sets A_a and A_b be those retrieved by executing g_a and g_b, respectively. Suppose that A is the labeled answers to q. We first compute the precision, recall and F_1 score of A_a and A_b, compared with the gold answer set A. We then rank s_a and s_b by their F_1 scores[5]. The intuition behind is that even if a query is not completely correct, it is still preferred than some other totally incorrect queries. In this work, we use a one-layer neural network model based on lambda-rank (Burges, 2010) for training the ranker.

[4]We will discuss how to create these candidate query graphs from question/answer pairs in Sec. 4.1.

[5]We use F_1 partially because it is the evaluation metric used in the experiments.

4 Experiments

We first introduce the dataset and evaluation metric, followed by the main experimental results and some analysis.

4.1 Data & evaluation metric

We use the WEBQUESTIONS dataset (Berant et al., 2013), which consists of 5,810 question/answer pairs. These questions were collected using Google Suggest API and the answers were obtained from Freebase with the help of Amazon MTurk. The questions are split into training and testing sets, which contain 3,778 questions (65%) and 2,032 questions (35%), respectively. This dataset has several unique properties that make it appealing and was used in several recent papers on semantic parsing and question answering. For instance, although the questions are not directly sampled from search query logs, the selection process was still biased to commonly asked questions on a search engine. The distribution of this question set is thus closer to the "real" information need of search users than that of a small number of human editors. The system performance is basically measured by the ratio of questions that are answered correctly. Because there can be more than one answer to a question, *precision*, *recall* and F_1 are computed based on the system output for each individual question. The average F_1 score is reported as the main evaluation metric[6].

Because this dataset contains only question and answer pairs, we use essentially the same search procedure to *simulate* the semantic parses for training the CNN models and the overall reward function. Candidate topic entities are first generated using the same entity linking system for each question in the training data. Paths on the Freebase knowledge graph that connect a candidate entity to at least one answer entity are identified as the core inferential chains[7]. If an inferential-chain query returns more entities than the correct answers, we explore adding constraint and aggregation nodes, until the entities retrieved by the query graph are identical to the labeled answers, or the F_1 score cannot be increased further. Negative examples are sampled from of the incorrect candidate graphs generated during the search process.

[6]We used the *official* evaluation script from `http://www-nlp.stanford.edu/software/sempre/`.

[7]We restrict the path length to 2. In principle, parses of shorter chains can be used to train the initial reward function, for exploring longer paths using the same search procedure.

Method	Prec.	Rec.	F_1
(Berant et al., 2013)	48.0	41.3	35.7
(Bordes et al., 2014b)	-	-	29.7
(Yao and Van Durme, 2014)	-	-	33.0
(Berant and Liang, 2014)	40.5	46.6	39.9
(Bao et al., 2014)	-	-	37.5
(Bordes et al., 2014a)	-	-	39.2
(Yang et al., 2014)	-	-	41.3
(Wang et al., 2014)	-	-	45.3
Our approach – STAGG	52.8	60.7	**52.5**

Table 1: The results of our approach compared to existing work. The numbers of other systems are either from the original papers or derived from the evaluation script, when the output is available.

In the end, we produce 17,277 query graphs with none-zero F_1 scores from the training set questions and about 1.7M completely incorrect ones.

For training the CNN models to identify the core inferential chain (Sec. 3.2.1), we only use 4,058 chain-only query graphs that achieve $F_1 = 0.5$ to form the parallel question and predicate sequence pairs. The hyper-parameters in CNN, such as the learning rate and the numbers of hidden nodes at the convolutional and semantic layers were chosen via cross-validation. We reserved 684 pairs of patterns and inference-chains from the whole training examples as the held-out set, and the rest as the initial training set. The optimal hyper-parameters were determined by the performance of models trained on the initial training set when applied to the held-out data. We then fixed the hyper-parameters and retrained the CNN models using the whole training set. The performance of CNN is insensitive to the hyper-parameters as long as they are in a reasonable range (e.g., 1000 ± 200 nodes in the convolutional layer, 300 ± 100 nodes in the semantic layer, and learning rate $0.05 \sim 0.005$) and the training process often converges after $\sim$ 800 epochs.

When training the reward function, we created up to 4,000 examples for each question that contain all the positive query graphs and randomly selected negative examples. The model is trained as a ranker, where example query graphs are ranked by their F_1 scores.

4.2 Results

Tab. 1 shows the results of our system, STAGG (Staged query graph generation), compared to existing work[8]. As can be seen from the table, our

Method	#Entities	# Covered Ques.	# Labeled Ent.
Freebase API	19,485	3,734 (98.8%)	3,069 (81.2%)
Ours	9,147	3,770 (99.8%)	3,318 (87.8%)

Table 2: Statistics of entity linking results on training set questions. Both methods cover roughly the same number of questions, but Freebase API suggests twice the number of entities output by our entity linking system and covers fewer topic entities labeled in the original data.

system outperforms the previous state-of-the-art method by a large margin – 7.2% absolute gain.

Given the staged design of our approach, it is thus interesting to examine the contributions of each component. Because topic entity linking is the very first stage, the quality of the entities found in the questions, both in precision and recall, affects the final results significantly. To get some insight about how our topic entity linking component performs, we also experimented with applying Freebase Search API to suggest entities for possible mentions in a question. As can be observed in Tab. 2, to cover most of the training questions, we only need half of the number of suggestions when using our entity linking component, compared to Freebase API. Moreover, they also cover more entities that were selected as the topic entities in the original dataset. Starting from those 9,147 entities output by our component, answers of 3,453 questions (91.4%) can be found in their neighboring nodes. When replacing our entity linking component with the results from Freebase API, we also observed a significant performance degradation. The overall system performance drops from 52.5% to 48.4% in F_1 (Prec = 49.8%, Rec = 55.7%), which is 4.1 points lower.

Next we test the system performance when the query graph has just the core inferential chain. Tab. 3 summarizes the results. When only the PatChain CNN model is used, the performance is already very strong, outperforming all existing work. Adding the other CNN models boosts the performance further, reaching 51.8% and is only slightly lower than the full system performance. This may be due to two reasons. First, the questions from search engine users are often short and a large portion of them simply ask about properties of an entity. Examining the query graphs generated for training set questions, we found that 1,888

[8]We do not include results of (Reddy et al., 2014) because they used only a subset of 570 test questions, which are not directly comparable to results from other work. On these 570 questions, our system achieves 67.0% in F_1.

Method	Prec.	Rec.	F_1
PatChain	48.8	59.3	49.6
+QuesEP	50.7	60.6	50.9
+ClueWeb	51.3	62.6	51.8

Table 3: The system results when only the inferential-chain query graphs are generated. We started with the PatChain CNN model and then added QuesEP and ClueWeb sequentially. See Sec. 3.4 for the description of these models.

(50.0%) can be answered exactly (i.e., $F_1 = 1$) using a chain-only query graph. Second, even if the correct parse requires more constraints, the less constrained graph still gets a partial score, as its results cover the correct answers.

4.3 Error Analysis

Although our approach substantially outperforms existing methods, the room for improvement seems big. After all, the accuracy for the intended application, question answering, is still low and only slightly above 50%. We randomly sampled 100 questions that our system did not generate the completely correct query graphs, and categorized the errors. About one third of errors are in fact due to label issues and are not real mistakes. This includes label error (2%), incomplete labels (17%, e.g., only one song is labeled as the answer to "What songs did Bob Dylan write?") and acceptable answers (15%, e.g., "Time in China" vs. "UTC+8"). 8% of the errors are due to incorrect entity linking; however, sometimes the mention is inherently ambiguous (e.g., AFL in "Who founded the AFL?" could mean either "American Football League" or "American Federation of Labor"). 35% of the errors are because of the incorrect inferential chains; 23% are due to incorrect or missing constraints.

5 Related Work and Discussion

Several semantic parsing methods use a domain-independent meaning representation derived from the combinatory categorial grammar (CCG) parses (e.g., (Cai and Yates, 2013; Kwiatkowski et al., 2013; Reddy et al., 2014)). In contrast, our query graph design matches closely the graph knowledge base. Although not fully demonstrated in this paper, the query graph can in fact be fairly expressive. For instance, negations can be handled by adding tags to the constraint nodes indicating that certain conditions *cannot* be satisfied. Our graph generation method is inspired by (Yao and Van Durme, 2014; Bao et al., 2014). Unlike traditional semantic parsing approaches, it uses the knowledge base to help prune the search space when forming the parse. Similar ideas have also been explored in (Poon, 2013).

Empirically, our results suggest that it is crucial to identify the core inferential chain, which matches the relationship between the topic entity in the question and the answer. Our CNN models can be analogous to the embedding approaches (Bordes et al., 2014a; Yang et al., 2014), but are more sophisticated. By allowing parameter sharing among different question-pattern and KB predicate pairs, the matching score of a rare or even unseen pair in the training data can still be predicted precisely. This is due to the fact that the prediction is based on the shared model parameters (i.e., projection matrices) that are estimated using all training pairs.

6 Conclusion

In this paper, we present a semantic parsing framework for question answering using a knowledge base. We define a *query graph* as the meaning representation that can be directly mapped to a logical form. Semantic parsing is reduced to query graph generation, formulated as a staged search problem. With the help of an advanced entity linking system and a deep convolutional neural network model that matches questions and predicate sequences, our system outperforms previous methods substantially on the WEBQUESTIONS dataset.

In the future, we would like to extend our query graph to represent more complicated questions, and explore more features and models for matching constraints and aggregation functions. Applying other structured-output prediction methods to graph generation will also be investigated.

Acknowledgments

We thank the anonymous reviewers for their thoughtful comments, Ming Zhou, Nan Duan and Xuchen Yao for sharing their experience on the question answering problem studied in this work, and Chris Meek for his valuable suggestions. We are also grateful to Siva Reddy and Jonathan Berant for providing us additional data.

Appendix

See supplementary notes.

References

Sören Auer, Christian Bizer, Georgi Kobilarov, Jens Lehmann, Richard Cyganiak, and Zachary Ives. 2007. DBpedia: A nucleus for a web of open data. In *The semantic web*, pages 722–735. Springer.

Junwei Bao, Nan Duan, Ming Zhou, and Tiejun Zhao. 2014. Knowledge-based question answering as machine translation. In *Proceedings of the 52nd Annual Meeting of the Association for Computational Linguistics (Volume 1: Long Papers)*, pages 967–976, Baltimore, Maryland, June. Association for Computational Linguistics.

Jonathan Berant and Percy Liang. 2014. Semantic parsing via paraphrasing. In *Proceedings of the 52nd Annual Meeting of the Association for Computational Linguistics (Volume 1: Long Papers)*, pages 1415–1425, Baltimore, Maryland, June. Association for Computational Linguistics.

Jonathan Berant, Andrew Chou, Roy Frostig, and Percy Liang. 2013. Semantic parsing on Freebase from question-answer pairs. In *Proceedings of the 2013 Conference on Empirical Methods in Natural Language Processing*, pages 1533–1544, Seattle, Washington, USA, October. Association for Computational Linguistics.

Kurt Bollacker, Colin Evans, Praveen Paritosh, Tim Sturge, and Jamie Taylor. 2008. Freebase: A collaboratively created graph database for structuring human knowledge. In *Proceedings of the 2008 ACM SIGMOD International Conference on Management of Data*, SIGMOD '08, pages 1247–1250, New York, NY, USA. ACM.

Antoine Bordes, Sumit Chopra, and Jason Weston. 2014a. Question answering with subgraph embeddings. In *Proceedings of the 2014 Conference on Empirical Methods in Natural Language Processing (EMNLP)*, pages 615–620, Doha, Qatar, October. Association for Computational Linguistics.

Antoine Bordes, Jason Weston, and Nicolas Usunier. 2014b. Open question answering with weakly supervised embedding models. In *Proceedings of ECML-PKDD*.

Jane Bromley, James W. Bentz, Léon Bottou, Isabelle Guyon, Yann LeCun, Cliff Moore, Eduard Säckinger, and Roopak Shah. 1993. Signature verification using a "Siamese" time delay neural network. *International Journal Pattern Recognition and Artificial Intelligence*, 7(4):669–688.

Christopher JC Burges. 2010. From RankNet to LambdaRank to LambdaMart: An overview. *Learning*, 11:23–581.

Qingqing Cai and Alexander Yates. 2013. Large-scale semantic parsing via schema matching and lexicon extension. In *Proceedings of the 51st Annual Meeting of the Association for Computational Linguistics (Volume 1: Long Papers)*, pages 423–433, Sofia, Bulgaria, August. Association for Computational Linguistics.

Evgeniy Gabrilovich, Michael Ringgaard, and Amarnag Subramanya. 2013. FACC1: Freebase annotation of ClueWeb corpora, version 1. Technical report, June.

Jianfeng Gao, Patrick Pantel, Michael Gamon, Xiaodong He, Li Deng, and Yelong Shen. 2014. Modeling interestingness with deep neural networks. In *Proceedings of the 2013 Conference on Empirical Methods in Natural Language Processing*.

Po-Sen Huang, Xiaodong He, Jianfeng Gao, Li Deng, Alex Acero, and Larry Heck. 2013. Learning deep structured semantic models for Web search using clickthrough data. In *Proceedings of the 22nd ACM international conference on Conference on information & knowledge management*, pages 2333–2338. ACM.

Tom Kwiatkowski, Eunsol Choi, Yoav Artzi, and Luke Zettlemoyer. 2013. Scaling semantic parsers with on-the-fly ontology matching. In *Proceedings of the 2013 Conference on Empirical Methods in Natural Language Processing*, pages 1545–1556, Seattle, Washington, USA, October. Association for Computational Linguistics.

Percy Liang. 2013. Lambda dependency-based compositional semantics. Technical report, arXiv.

Hoifung Poon. 2013. Grounded unsupervised semantic parsing. In *Annual Meeting of the Association for Computational Linguistics (ACL)*, pages 933–943.

Siva Reddy, Mirella Lapata, and Mark Steedman. 2014. Large-scale semantic parsing without question-answer pairs. *Transactions of the Association for Computational Linguistics*, 2:377–392.

Yelong Shen, Xiaodong He, Jianfeng Gao, Li Deng, and Gregoire Mesnil. 2014a. A latent semantic model with convolutional-pooling structure for information retrieval. In *Proceedings of the 23rd ACM International Conference on Conference on Information and Knowledge Management*, pages 101–110. ACM.

Yelong Shen, Xiaodong He, Jianfeng Gao, Li Deng, and Grégoire Mesnil. 2014b. Learning semantic representations using convolutional neural networks for web search. In *Proceedings of the Companion Publication of the 23rd International Conference on World Wide Web Companion*, pages 373–374.

Zhenghao Wang, Shengquan Yan, Huaming Wang, and Xuedong Huang. 2014. An overview of Microsoft Deep QA system on Stanford WebQuestions benchmark. Technical Report MSR-TR-2014-121, Microsoft, Sep.

Yi Yang and Ming-Wei Chang. 2015. S-MART: Novel tree-based structured learning algorithms applied to tweet entity linking. In *Annual Meeting of the Association for Computational Linguistics (ACL)*.

Min-Chul Yang, Nan Duan, Ming Zhou, and Hae-Chang Rim. 2014. Joint relational embeddings for knowledge-based question answering. In *Proceedings of the 2014 Conference on Empirical Methods in Natural Language Processing (EMNLP)*, pages 645–650, Doha, Qatar, October. Association for Computational Linguistics.

Xuchen Yao and Benjamin Van Durme. 2014. Information extraction over structured data: Question answering with Freebase. In *Proceedings of the 52nd Annual Meeting of the Association for Computational Linguistics (Volume 1: Long Papers)*, pages 956–966, Baltimore, Maryland, June. Association for Computational Linguistics.

Wen-tau Yih, Xiaodong He, and Christopher Meek. 2014. Semantic parsing for single-relation question answering. In *Proceedings of the 52nd Annual Meeting of the Association for Computational Linguistics (Volume 2: Short Papers)*, pages 643–648, Baltimore, Maryland, June. Association for Computational Linguistics.

Building a Semantic Parser Overnight

Yushi Wang*
Stanford University
yushiw@cs.stanford.edu

Jonathan Berant*
Stanford University
joberant@stanford.edu

Percy Liang
Stanford University
pliang@cs.stanford.edu

Abstract

How do we build a semantic parser in a new domain starting with zero training examples? We introduce a new methodology for this setting: First, we use a simple grammar to generate logical forms paired with canonical utterances. The logical forms are meant to cover the desired set of compositional operators, and the canonical utterances are meant to capture the meaning of the logical forms (although clumsily). We then use crowdsourcing to paraphrase these canonical utterances into natural utterances. The resulting data is used to train the semantic parser. We further study the role of compositionality in the resulting paraphrases. Finally, we test our methodology on seven domains and show that we can build an adequate semantic parser in just a few hours.

1 Introduction

By mapping natural language utterances to executable logical forms, semantic parsers have been useful for a variety of applications requiring precise language understanding (Zelle and Mooney, 1996; Zettlemoyer and Collins, 2005; Liang et al., 2011; Berant et al., 2013; Kwiatkowski et al., 2013; Artzi and Zettlemoyer, 2013; Kushman and Barzilay, 2013). Previous work has focused on how to train a semantic parser given input utterances, but suppose we wanted to build a semantic parser for a new domain—for example, a natural language interface into a publications database. Since no such interface exists, we do not even have a naturally occurring source of input utterances that we can annotate. So where do we start?

In this paper, we advocate a *functionality-driven process* for rapidly building a semantic parser in a new domain. At a high-level, we seek to minimize the amount of work needed for a new domain by factoring out the domain-general aspects (done by our framework) from the domain-specific ones (done by the builder of the semantic parser). We assume that the builder already has the desired functionality of the semantic parser in mind—e.g., the publications database is set up and the schema is fixed. Figure 1 depicts the functionality-driven process: First, the builder writes a seed lexicon specifying a canonical phrase (*"publication date"*) for

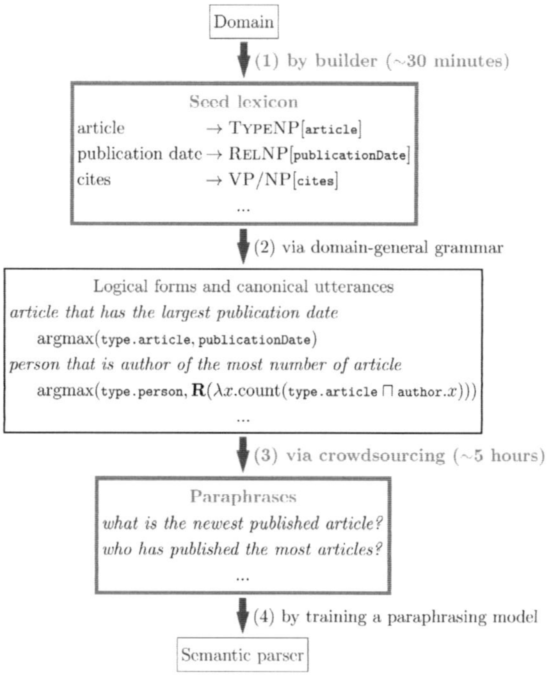

Figure 1: Functionality-driven process for building semantic parsers. The two red boxes are the domain-specific parts provided by the builder of the semantic parser, and the other two are generated by the framework.

* Both authors equally contributed to the paper.

Proceedings of the 53rd Annual Meeting of the Association for Computational Linguistics and the 7th International Joint Conference on Natural Language Processing, pages 1332–1342,
Beijing, China, July 26-31, 2015.

each predicate (`publicationDate`). Second, our framework uses a *domain-general grammar*, along with the seed lexicon and the database, to automatically generate a few hundred *canonical utterances* paired with their logical forms (e.g., *"article that has the largest publication date"* and $\arg\max(\texttt{type.article}, \texttt{publicationDate})$). These utterances need not be the most elegant, but they should retain the semantics of the logical forms. Third, the builder leverages crowdsourcing to paraphrase each canonical utterance into a few *natural utterances* (e.g., *"what is the newest published article?"*). Finally, our framework uses this data to train a semantic parser.

Practical advantages. There are two main advantages of our approach: *completeness* and *ease of supervision*. Traditionally, training data is collected in a best-effort manner, which can result in an incomplete coverage of functionality. For example, the WebQuestions dataset (Berant et al., 2013) contains no questions with numeric answers, so any semantic parser trained on that dataset would lack that functionality. These biases are not codified, which results in an idiosyncratic and mysterious user experience, a major drawback of natural language interfaces (Rangel et al., 2014). In contrast, our compact grammar precisely specifies the logical functionality. We enforce completeness by generating canonical utterances that exercise every grammar rule.

In terms of supervision, state-of-the-art semantic parsers are trained from question-answer pairs (Kwiatkowski et al., 2013; Berant and Liang, 2014). Although this is a marked improvement in cost and scalability compared to annotated logical forms, it still requires non-trivial effort: the annotator must (i) understand the question and (ii) figure out the answer, which becomes even harder with compositional utterances. In contrast, our main source of supervision is paraphrases, which only requires (i), not (ii). Such data is thus cheaper and faster to obtain.

Linguistic reflections. The centerpiece of our framework is a domain-general grammar that connects logical forms with canonical utterances. This connection warrants further scrutiny, as the structural mismatch between logic and language is the chief source of difficulty in semantic parsing (Liang et al., 2011; Kwiatkowski et al., 2013; Berant and Liang, 2014).

There are two important questions here. First, is it possible to design a simple grammar that simultaneously generates both logical forms and canonical utterances so that the utterances are understandable by a human? In Section 3, we show how to choose appropriate canonical utterances to maximize alignment with the logical forms.

Second, our grammar can generate an infinite number of canonical utterances. How many do we need for adequate coverage? Certainly, single relations is insufficient: just knowing that *"publication date of X"* paraphrases to *"when X was published"* would offer insufficient information to generalize to *"articles that came after X"* mapping to *"article whose publication date is larger than publication date of X"*. We call this phenomena *sublexical compositionality*—when a short lexical unit (*"came after"*) maps onto a multi-predicate logical form. Our hypothesis is that the sublexical compositional units are small, so we only need to crowdsource a small number of canonical utterances to learn about most of the language variability in the given domain (Section 4).

We applied our functionality-driven process to seven domains, which were chosen to explore particular types of phenomena, such as spatial language, temporal language, and high-arity relations. This resulted in seven new semantic parsing datasets, totaling 12.6K examples. Our approach, which was not tuned on any one domain, was able to obtain an average accuracy of 59% over all domains. On the day of this paper submission, we created an eighth domain and trained a semantic parser overnight.

2 Approach Overview

In our functionality-driven process (Figure 1), there are two parties: the *builder*, who provides domain-specific information, and the *framework*, which provides domain-general information. We assume that the builder has a fixed database w, represented as a set of triples (e_1, p, e_2), where e_1 and e_2 are entities (e.g., `article1`, `2015`) and p is a property (e.g., `publicationDate`). The database w can be queried using lambda DCS logical forms, described further in Section 2.1.

The builder supplies a seed lexicon L, which contains for each database property p (e.g., `publicationDate`) a lexical entry of the form $\langle t \rightarrow s[p] \rangle$, where t is a natural language phrase (e.g., *"publication date"*) and s is a syntactic category (e.g., RELNP). In addition, L contains two typical entities for each semantic type in the database (e.g., $\langle$*alice* $\rightarrow$ NP[alice]$\rangle$ for the type person). The purpose of L is to simply connect each predicate with *some* representation in natural language.

The framework supplies a grammar G, which specifies the modes of composition, both on logical forms and canonical utterances. Formally, G is a set of rules of the form $\langle \alpha_1 \dots \alpha_n \rightarrow s[z] \rangle$, where $\alpha_1 \dots \alpha_n$ is a sequence of tokens or categories, s is a syntactic category and z is the logical form constructed. For example, one rule in G is $\langle$RELNP$[r]$ *of* NP$[x] \rightarrow$ NP$[\mathbf{R}(r).x]\rangle$, which constructs z by reversing the binary predicate r and joining it with a the unary predicate x. We use the rules $G \cup L$ to generate a set of (z, c) pairs, where z is a logical form (e.g., $\mathbf{R}$(publicationDate).article1), and c is the corresponding canonical utterance (e.g., *"publication date of article 1"*). The set of (z, c) is denoted by GEN$(G \cup L)$. See Section 3 for details.

Next, the builder (backed by crowdsourcing) paraphrases each canonical utterance c output above into a set of natural utterances $\mathbf{P}(c)$ (e.g., *"when was article 1 published?"*). This defines a set of training examples $\mathcal{D} = \{(x, c, z)\}$, for each $(z, c) \in$ GEN$(G \cup L)$ and $x \in \mathbf{P}(c)$. The crowdsourcing setup is detailed in Section 5.

Finally, the framework trains a semantic parser on $\mathcal{D}$. Our semantic parser is a log-linear distribution $p_\theta(z, c \mid x, w)$ over logical forms and canonical utterances specified by the grammar G. Note that the grammar G will in general not parse x, so the semantic parsing model will be based on paraphrasing, in the spirit of Berant and Liang (2014).

To summarize, (1) the builder produces a seed lexicon L; (2) the framework produces logical forms and canonical utterances GEN$(G \cup L) = \{(z, c)\}$; (3) the builder (via crowdsourcing) uses $\mathbf{P}(\cdot)$ to produce a dataset $\mathcal{D} = \{(x, c, z)\}$; and (4) the framework uses $\mathcal{D}$ to train a semantic parser $p_\theta(z, c \mid x, w)$.

2.1 Lambda DCS

Our logical forms are represented in lambda DCS, a logical language where composition operates on sets rather than truth values. Here we give a brief description; see Liang (2013) for details.

Every logical form z in this paper is either a *unary* (denoting a set of entities) or a *binary* (denoting a set of entity-pairs). In the base case, each entity e (e.g., 2015) is a unary denoting the singleton set: $[\![e]\!]_w = \{e\}$; and each property p (e.g., publicationDate) is a binary denoting all entity-pairs (e_1, e_2) that satisfy the property p. Unaries and binaries can be composed: Given a binary b and unary u, the join $b.u$ denotes all entities e_1 for which there exists an $e_2 \in [\![u]\!]_w$ with $(e_1, e_2) \in [\![b]\!]_w$. For example, publicationDate.2015 denote entities published in 2015.

The intersection $u_1 \sqcap u_2$, union $u_1 \sqcup u_2$, complement $\neg u$ denote the corresponding set operations on the denotations. We let $\mathbf{R}(b)$ denote the reversal of b: $(e_1, e_2) \in [\![b]\!]_w$ iff $(e_2, e_1) \in [\![\mathbf{R}(b)]\!]_w$. This allows us to define $\mathbf{R}$(publicationDate).article1 as the publication date of article 1. We also include aggregation operations (count(u), sum(u) and average(u, b)), and superlatives (argmax(u, b)).

Finally, we can construct binaries using lambda abstraction: $\lambda x.u$ denotes a set of (e_1, e_2) where $e_1 \in [\![u[x/e_2]]\!]_w$ and $u[x/e_2]$ is the logical form where free occurrences of x are replaced with e_2. For example, $\mathbf{R}(\lambda x.\text{count}(\mathbf{R}(\texttt{cites}).x))$ denotes the set of entities (e_1, e_2), where e_2 is the number of entities that e_1 cites.

3 Generation and canonical compositionality

Our functionality-driven process hinges on having a domain-general grammar that can connect logical forms with canonical utterances compositionally. The motivation is that while it is hard to write a grammar that parses *all* utterances, it is possible to write one that generates *one* canonical utterance for each logical form. To make this explicit:

Assumption 1 (Canonical compositionality) *Using a small grammar, all logical forms expressible in natural language can be realized compositionally based on the logical form.*

Grammar. We target database querying applications, where the parser needs to handle superlatives, comparatives, negation, and coordination. We define a simple grammar that captures these forms of compositionality using canonical utterances in a domain-general way. Figure 2 illustrates a derivation produced by the grammar.

The seed lexicon specified by the builder contains canonical utterances for types, entities, and properties. All types (e.g., person) have the syntactic category TYPENP, and all entities (e.g.,

Figure 2: Deriving a logical form z (red) and a canonical utterance c (green) from the grammar G. Each node contains a syntactic category and a logical form, which is generated by applying a rule. Nodes with only leaves as children are produced using the seed lexicon; all other nodes are produced by rules in the domain-general grammar.

birthdate	→ RELNP[birthdate]
person|university|field	→ TYPENP[person| · · ·]
company|job title	→ TYPENP[company| · · ·]
student|university|field of study	→ RELNP[student| · · ·]
employee|employer|job title	→ RELNP[employee| · · ·]
start date|end date	→ RELNP[startDate| · · ·]
is friends with	→ VP/NP[friends| · · ·]

Table 1: The seed lexicon for the SOCIAL domain, which specifies for each predicate (e.g., `birthdate`) a phrase (e.g., *"birthdate"*) that realizes that predicate and its syntactic category (e.g., RELNP).

`alice`) are ENTITYNP's. Unary predicates are realized as verb phrases VP (e.g., *"has a private bath"*). The builder can choose to represent binaries as either relational noun phrases (RELNP) or generalized transitive verbs (VP/NP). RELNP's are usually used to describe functional properties (e.g., *"publication date"*), especially numerical properties. VP/NP's include transitive verbs (*"cites"*) but also longer phrases with the same syntactic interface (*"is the president of"*). Table 1 shows the seed lexicon for the SOCIAL domain.

From the seed lexicon, the domain-general grammar (Table 2) constructs noun phrases (NP), verbs phrases (VP), and complementizer phrase (CP), all of which denote unary logical forms. Broadly speaking, the rules **(R1)–(R4)**, **(C1)–(C4)** take a binary and a noun phrase, and compose them (optionally via comparatives, counting, and negation) to produce a complementizer phrase CP representing a unary (e.g., *"that cites article 1"* or *"that cites more than three article"*). **(G3)** combines these CP's with an NP (e.g., *"article"*). In addition, **(S0)–(S4)** handle superlatives (we include argmin in addition to argmax), which take an NP and return the extremum-attaining subset of its denotation. Finally, we support transformations such as join **(T1)** and disjunction **(T4)**, as well as aggregation **(A1)–(A2)**.

Rendering utterances for multi-arity predicates was a major challenge. The predicate instances are typically reified in a graph database, akin to a neo-Davidsonian treatment of events: There is an abstract entity with binary predicates relating it to its arguments. For example, in the SOCIAL domain, Alice's education can be represented in the database as five triples:

(`e17`, `student`, `alice`), (`e17`, `university`, `ucla`), (`e17`, `fieldOfStudy`, `music`), (`e17`, `startDate`, `2005`), (`e17`, `endDate`, `2009`).

All five properties here are represented as RELNP's, with the first one designated as the subject (RELNP_0). We support two ways of querying multi-arity relations: *"student whose university is ucla"* **(T2)** and *"university of student Alice whose start date is 2005"* **(T3)**.

Generating directly from the grammar in Table 2 would result in many uninterpretable canonical utterances. Thus, we perform type checking on the logical forms to rule out *"article that cites 2004"*, and limit the amount of recursion, which keeps the canonical utterances understandable.

Still, the utterances generated by our grammar are not perfectly grammatical; we do not use determiners and make all nouns singular. Nonetheless, AMT workers found most canonical utterances understandable (see Table 3 and Section 5 for details on crowdsourcing). One tip for the builder is to keep the RELNP's and VP/NP's as context-independent as possible; e.g., using *"publication date"* instead of *"date"*. In cases where more context is required, we use parenthetical remarks (e.g., *"number of assists (over a season)"* → RELNP[. . .]) to pack more context into the confines of the part-of-speech.

Limitations. While our domain-general grammar covers most of the common logical forms in a database querying application, there are several phenomena which are out of scope, notably nested quantification (e.g., *"show me each author's most cited work"*) and anaphora (e.g., *"author who cites herself at least twice"*). Handling these would require a more radical change to the grammar, but is still within scope.

	[glue]	
(G1)	EntityNP$[x]$	$\rightarrow$ NP$[x]$
(G2)	TypeNP$[x]$	$\rightarrow$ NP[type.x]
(G3)	NP$[x]$ CP$[f]$ (and CP$[g]$)*	$\rightarrow$ NP$[x \sqcap f \sqcap g]$
	[simple]	
(R0)	that VP$[x]$	$\rightarrow$ CP$[x]$
(R1)	whose RelNP$[r]$ Cmp$[c]$ NP$[y]$	$\rightarrow$ CP$[r.c.y]$
	is$\mid$is not$\mid$is smaller than$\mid$is larger than$\mid$is at least$\mid$is at most	$\rightarrow$ Cmp$[= \mid \neq \mid < \mid > \mid \leq \mid \geq]$
(R2)	that (not)? VP/NP$[r]$ NP$[y]$	$\rightarrow$ CP$[(\neg)r.y]$
(R3)	that is (not)? RelNP$[r]$ of NP$[y]$	$\rightarrow$ CP$[(\neg)\mathbf{R}(r).y]$
(R4)	that NP$[y]$ (not)? VP/NP$[r]$	$\rightarrow$ CP$[(\neg)(\mathbf{R}(r).y)]$
	[counting]	
(C1)	that has Cnt$[c]$ RelNP$[r]$	$\rightarrow$ CP$[\mathbf{R}(\lambda x.\text{count}(\mathbf{R}(r).x)).c]$
(C2)	that VP/NP$[r]$ Cnt$[c]$ NP$[y]$	$\rightarrow$ CP$[\mathbf{R}(\lambda x.\text{count}(y \sqcap \mathbf{R}(r).x)).c]$
(C3)	that is RelNP$[r]$ of Cnt$[c]$ NP$[y]$	$\rightarrow$ CP$[\mathbf{R}(\lambda x.\text{count}(y \sqcap r.x)).c]$
(C4)	that Cnt$[c]$ NP$[y]$ VP/NP$[r]$	$\rightarrow$ CP$[\mathbf{R}(\lambda x.\text{count}(y \sqcap r.x)).c]$
	(less than$\mid$more than) Num$[n]$	$\rightarrow$ Cnt$[(<.\mid>.)n]$
	[superlatives]	
(S0)	NP$[x]$ that has the largest RelNP$[r]$	$\rightarrow$ NP$[\arg\max(x, r)]$
(S1)	NP$[x]$ that has the most number of RelNP$[r]$	$\rightarrow$ NP$[\arg\max(x, \mathbf{R}(\lambda y.\text{count}(\mathbf{R}(r).y)))]$
(S2)	NP$[x]$ that VP/NP$[r]$ the most number of NP$[y]$	$\rightarrow$ NP$[\arg\max(x, \mathbf{R}(\lambda y.\text{count}(\mathbf{R}(r).y)))]$
(S3)	NP$[x]$ that is RelNP$[r]$ of the most number of NP$[y]$	$\rightarrow$ NP$[\arg\max(x, \mathbf{R}(\lambda z.\text{count}(y \sqcap r.z)))]$
(S4)	NP$[x]$ that the most number of NP$[y]$ VP/NP$[r]$	$\rightarrow$ NP$[\arg\max(x, \mathbf{R}(\lambda z.\text{count}(y \sqcap r.z)))]$
	[transformation]	
(T1)	RelNP$[r]$ of NP$[y]$	$\rightarrow$ NP$[\mathbf{R}(r).y]$
(T2)	RelNP$_0[h]$CP$[f]$ (and CP$[g]$)*	$\rightarrow$ NP$[\mathbf{R}(h).(f \sqcap g)]$
(T3)	RelNP$[r]$ of RelNP$_0[h]$ NP$[x]$ CP$[f]$ (and CP$[g]$)*	$\rightarrow$ NP$[\mathbf{R}(r).(h.x \sqcap f \sqcap g)]$
(T4)	NP$[x]$ or NP$[y]$	$\rightarrow$ NP$[x \sqcup y]$
	[aggregation]	
(A1)	number of NP$[x]$	$\rightarrow$ NP[count(x)]
(A2)	total$\mid$average RelNP$[r]$ of NP$[x]$	$\rightarrow$ NP[sum$\mid$average(x, r)]

Table 2: The domain-general grammar which is combined with the seed lexicon to generate logical forms and canonical utterances that cover the supported logical functionality.

4 Paraphrasing and bounded non-compositionality

While the canonical utterance c is generated compositionally along with the logical form z, natural paraphrases $x \in \mathbf{P}(c)$ generally deviate from this compositional structure. For example, the canonical utterance *"*NP*[number of* NP*[article* CP*[whose publication date is larger than* NP*[publication date of article 1]]]]"* might get paraphrased to *"How many articles were **published after** article 1?"*. Here, *"published after"* non-compositionally straddles the inner NP, intuitively responsible for both instances of *"publication date"*. But how non-compositional can paraphrases be? Our framework rests on the assumption that the answer is "not very":

Assumption 2 (Bounded non-compositionality) *Natural utterances for expressing complex logical forms are compositional with respect to fragments of bounded size.*

In the above example, note that while *"published after"* is non-compositional with respect to the grammar, the rewriting of *"number of"* to *"how many"* is compositional. The upshot of Assumption 2 is that we only need to ask for paraphrases of canonical utterances generated by the grammar up to some small depth to learn about all the non-compositional uses of language, and still be able generalize (compositionally) beyond that.

We now explore the nature of the possible paraphrases. Broadly speaking, most paraphrases involve some sort of *compression*, where the clunky but faithful canonical utterance is smoothed out into graceful prose.

Alternations of single rules. The most basic paraphrase happens at the single phrase level with synonyms (*"block"* to *"brick"*), which preserve the part-of-speech. However, many of our properties are specified using relational noun phrases, which are more naturally realized using prepositions (*"meeting whose attendee is alice ⇒ meeting **with** alice"*) or verbs (*"author of article 1 ⇒ who **wrote** article 1"*). If the RelNP is complex, then the argument can become embedded: *"player whose number of points is 15 ⇒ player who **scored** 15 **points**"*. Superlative and comparative constructions reveal other RelNP-dependent words: *"article that has the largest publication date ⇒ **newest** article"*. When the value of the relation has enough context, then the relation is elided completely: *"housing unit whose housing type is apartment ⇒* ***apartment****"*.

Multi-arity predicates are compressed into a single frame: *"university of student alice whose field of study is music"* becomes *"At which university did Alice* ***study*** *music?"*, where the semantic roles of the verb *"study"* carry the burden of expressing the multiple relations: `student`, `university`, and `fieldOfStudy`. With a different combination of arguments, the natural verb would change: *"Which university did Alice* ***attend****?"*

Sublexical compositionality. The most interesting paraphrases occur across multiple rules, a phenomenon which we called *sublexical compositionality*. The idea is that common, multi-part concepts are compressed to single words or simpler constructions. The simplest compression is a lexical one: *"parent of alice whose gender is female ⇒* ***mother*** *of alice"*. Compression often occurs when we have the same predicate chained twice in a join: *"person that is author of paper whose author is X ⇒ co-author of X"* or *"person whose birthdate is birthdate of X ⇒ person born on the* ***same*** *day as X"*. When two CP's combined via coordination have some similarity, then the coordination can be pushed down (*"meeting whose start time is 3pm and whose end time is 5pm ⇒ meetings between 3pm and 5pm"*) and sometimes even generalized (*"that allows cats and that allows dogs ⇒ that allows pets"*). Sometimes, compression happens due to metonymy, where people stand in for their papers: *"author of article that article whose author is X cites ⇒ who does X cite"*.

5 Crowdsourcing

We tackled seven domains covering various linguistic phenomena. Table 3 lists the domains, their principal phenomena, statistics about their predicates and dataset, and an example from the dataset.

We use Amazon Mechanical Turk (AMT) to paraphrase the canonical utterances generated by the domain-general grammar. In each AMT task, a worker is presented with four canonical utterances and is asked to reformulate them in natural language or state that they are incomprehensible. Each canonical utterance was presented to 10 workers. Over all domains, we collected 18,032 responses. The average time for paraphrasing one utterance was 28 seconds. Paraphrases that share the same canonical utterance are collapsed, while identical paraphrases that have distinct canonical utterances are deleted. This produced a total of 12,602 examples over all domains.

To estimate the level of noise in the data, we manually judged the correctness of 20 examples in each domain, and found that 17% of the utterances were inaccurate. There are two main reasons: lexical ambiguity on our part (*"player that has the least number of team ⇒ player with the lowest jersey number"*), and failure on the worker's part (*"restaurant whose star rating is 3 stars ⇒ hotel which has a 3 star rating"*).

6 Model and Learning

Our semantic parsing model defines a distribution over logical forms given by the domain-general grammar G and additional rules triggered by the input utterance x. Specifically, given an utterance x, we detect numbers, dates, and perform string matching with database entities to recognize named entities. This results in a set of rules $\mathbf{T}(x)$. For example, if x is *"article published in 2015 that cites article 1"*, then $\mathbf{T}(x)$ contains $\langle$*2015* $\rightarrow$ NP[2015]$\rangle$ and $\langle$*article 1* $\rightarrow$ NP[`article1`]$\rangle$. Let L_x be the rules in the seed lexicon L where the entity rules (e.g., $\langle$*alice* $\rightarrow$ NP[`alice`]$\rangle$) are replaced by $\mathbf{T}(x)$.

Our semantic parsing model defines a log-linear distribution over candidate pairs $(z, c) \in \text{GEN}(G \cup L_x)$:

$$p_\theta(z, c \mid x, w) \propto \exp(\phi(c, z, x, w)^\top \theta), \qquad (1)$$

where $\phi(z, c, x, w) \in \mathbb{R}^d$ is a feature vector and $\theta \in \mathbb{R}^d$ is a parameter vector.

To generate candidate logical forms, we use a simple beam search: For each search state, which includes the syntactic category s (e.g., NP) and the depth of the logical form, we generate at most $K = 20$ candidates by applying the rules in Table 2. In practice, the lexical rules $\mathbf{T}(x)$ are applied first, and composition is performed, but not constrained to the utterance. For example, the utterance *"article"* would generate the logical form count(`type.article`). Instead, soft paraphrasing features are used to guide the search. This rather unorthodox approach to semantic parsing can be seen as a generalization of Berant and Liang (2014) and is explained in more detail in Pasupat and Liang (2015).

Training. We train our model by maximizing the regularized log-likelihood $\mathcal{O}(\theta) =$

Domain	# pred.	# ex.	Phenomena	Example
CALENDAR	22	837	temporal language	x: *"Show me meetings after the weekly standup day"* c: *"meeting whose date is at least date of weekly standup"* z: $\texttt{type.meeting} \sqcap \texttt{date.} > \mathbf{R}(\texttt{date}).\texttt{weeklyStandup}$
BLOCKS	19	1995	spatial language	x: *"Select the brick that is to the furthest left."* c: *"block that the most number of block is right of"* z: $\texttt{argmax}(\texttt{type.block}, \mathbf{R}(\lambda x.\texttt{count}(\mathbf{R}(\texttt{right}).x)))$
HOUSING	24	941	measurement units	x: *"Housing that is 800 square feet or bigger?"* c: *"housing unit whose size is at least 800 square feet"* z: $\texttt{type.housingUnit} \sqcap \texttt{area.} > \texttt{.800}$
RESTAURANTS	32	1657	long unary relations	x: *"What restaurant can you eat lunch outside at?"* c: *"restaurant that has outdoor seating and that serves lunch"* z: $\texttt{type.restaurant} \sqcap \texttt{hasOutdoorSeating} \sqcap \texttt{serveslunch}$
PUBLICATIONS	15	801	sublexical compositionality	x: *"Who has co-authored articles with Efron?"* c: *"person that is author of article whose author is efron"* z: $\texttt{type.person} \sqcap \mathbf{R}(\texttt{author}).(\texttt{type.article} \sqcap \texttt{author.efron})$
SOCIAL	45	4419	multi-arity relations	x: *"When did alice start attending brown university?"* c: *"start date of student alice whose university is brown university"* z: $\mathbf{R}(\texttt{date}).(\texttt{student.Alice} \sqcap \texttt{university.Brown})$
BASKETBALL	24	1952	parentheticals	x: *"How many fouls were played by Kobe Bryant in 2004?"* c: *"number of fouls (over a season) of player kobe bryant whose season is 2004"* z: $\text{count}(\mathbf{R}(\texttt{fouls}).(\texttt{player.KobeBryant} \sqcap \texttt{season.2004})$

Table 3: We experimented on seven domains, covering a variety of phenomena. For each domain, we show the number of predicates, number of examples, and a (c, z) generated by our framework along with a paraphrased utterance x.

Category	Description
Basic	#words and bigram matches in (x, c) #words and bigram PPDB matches in (x, c) #unmatched words in x #unmatched words in c size of denotation of z, $(\lvert [\![z]\!]_w \rvert)$ pos$(x_{0:0})$ conjoined with type$([\![z]\!]_w)$ #nodes in tree generating z
Lexical	$\forall(i,j) \in \mathcal{A}.\ (x_{i:i}, c_{j:j})$ $\forall(i,j) \in \mathcal{A}.\ (x_{i:i}, c_{j:j+1})$ $\forall(i,j) \in \mathcal{A}.\ (x_{i:i}, c_{j-1:j})$ $\forall(i,j),(i+1,j+1) \in \mathcal{A}.\ (x_{i:i+1}, c_{j:j+1})$ all unaligned words in x and c $(x_{i:j}, c_{i':j'})$ if in phrase table

Table 4: Features for the paraphrasing model. pos$(x_{i:i})$ is the POS tag; type$([\![z]\!]_w)$ is a coarse semantic type for the denotation (an entity or a number). $\mathcal{A}$ is a maximum weight alignment between x and c.

$\sum_{(x,c,z)\in\mathcal{D}} \log p_\theta(z, c \mid x, w) - \lambda\|\theta\|_1$. To optimize, we use AdaGrad (Duchi et al., 2010).

Features Table 4 describes the features. Our basic features mainly match words and bigrams in x and c, if they share a lemma or are aligned in the PPDB resource (Ganitkevitch et al., 2013). We count the number of exact matches, PPDB matches, and unmatched words.

To obtain lexical features, we run the Berkeley Aligner (Liang et al., 2006) on the training set and compute conditional probabilities of aligning one word type to another. Based on these probabilities we compute a maximum weight alignment $\mathcal{A}$ between words in x and c. We define features over $\mathcal{A}$ (see Table 4). We also use the word alignments to construct a phrase table by applying the consistent phrase pair heuristic (Och and Ney, 2004). We define an indicator feature for every phrase pair of x and c that appear in the phrase table. Examples from the PUBLICATIONS domain include *fewest–least number* and *by–whose author is*. Note that we do not build a hard lexicon but only use $\mathcal{A}$ and the phrase table to define features, allowing the model to learn useful paraphrases during training. Finally, we define standard features on logical forms and denotations (Berant et al., 2013).

7 Experimental Evaluation

We evaluated our functionality-driven process on the seven domains described in Section 5 and one new domain we describe in Section 7.3. For each domain, we held out a random 20% of the examples as the test set, and performed development on the remaining 80%, further splitting it to a training and development set (80%/20%). We created a database for each domain by randomly generating facts using entities and properties in the domain (with type-checking). We evaluated using accuracy, which is the fraction of examples that yield the correct denotation.

7.1 Domain-specific linguistic variability

Our functionality-driven process is predicated on the fact that each domain exhibits domain-specific

Method	CALENDAR	BLOCKS	HOUSING	RESTAURANTS	PUBLICATIONS	RECIPES	SOCIAL	BASKETBALL	Avg.
FULL	**74.4**	**41.9**	54.0	**75.9**	**59.0**	**70.8**	**48.2**	**46.3**	**58.8**
NOLEX	25.0	35.3	51.9	64.6	50.6	32.3	15.3	19.4	36.8
NOPPDB	73.2	41.4	**54.5**	73.8	56.5	68.1	43.6	44.5	56.9
BASELINE	17.3	27.7	45.9	61.3	46.7	26.3	9.7	15.6	31.3

Table 5: Test set results on all domains and baselines.

phenomena. To corroborate this, we compare our full system to NOLEX, a baseline that omits all lexical features (Table 4), but uses PPDB as a domain-general paraphrasing component. We perform the complementary experiment and compare to NOPPDB, a baseline that omits PPDB match features. We also run BASELINE, where we omit both lexical and PPDB features.

Table 5 presents the results of this experiment. Overall, our framework obtains an average accuracy of 59% across all eight domains. The performance of NOLEX is dramatically lower than FULL, indicating that it is important to learn domain-specific paraphrases using lexical features. The accuracy of NOPPDB is only slightly lower than FULL, showing that most of the required paraphrases can be learned during training. As expected, removing both lexical and PPDB features results in poor performance (BASELINE).

Analysis. We performed error analysis on 10 errors in each domain. Almost 70% of the errors are due to problems in the paraphrasing model, where the canonical utterance has extra material, is missing some content, or results in an incorrect paraphrase. For example, *"restaurants that have waiters and you can sit outside"* is paraphrased to *"restaurant that has waiter service and that takes reservations"*. Another 12.5% result from reordering issues, e.g, we paraphrase *"What venue has fewer than two articles"* to *"article that has less than two venue"*. Inaccurate paraphrases provided by AMT workers account for the rest of the errors.

7.2 Bounded non-compositionality

We hypothesized that we need to obtain paraphrases of canonical utterances corresponding to logical forms of only small depth. We ran the following experiment in the CALENDAR domain to test this claim. First, we define by NP_0, NP_1, and NP_2 the set of utterances generated by an NP that has exactly zero, one, and two NPs embedded in it. We define the training scenario $0 \rightarrow 1$, where we train on examples from NP_0 and test on examples from NP_1; $0 \cup 1 \rightarrow 1$, $0 \cup 1 \rightarrow 2$, and $0 \cup 1 \cup 2 \rightarrow 2$ are defined analogously. Our

Scenario	Acc.	Scenario	Acc.
$0 \rightarrow 1$	22.9	$0 \cup 1 \rightarrow 2$	28.1
$0 \cup 1 \rightarrow 1$	85.8	$0 \cup 1 \cup 2 \rightarrow 2$	47.5

Table 6: Test set results in the CALENDAR domain on bounded non-compositionality.

hypothesis is that generalization on $0 \cup 1 \rightarrow 2$ should be better than for $0 \rightarrow 1$, since NP_1 utterances have non-compositional paraphrases, but training on NP_0 does not expose them.

The results in Table 6 verify this hypothesis. The accuracy of $0 \rightarrow 1$ is almost 65% lower than $0 \cup 1 \rightarrow 1$. On the other hand, the accuracy of $0 \cup 1 \rightarrow 2$ is only 19% lower than $0 \cup 1 \cup 2 \rightarrow 2$.

7.3 An overnight experiment

To verify the title of this paper, we attempted to create a semantic parser for a new domain (RECIPES) exactly 24 hours before the submission deadline. Starting at midnight, we created a seed lexicon in less than 30 minutes. Then we generated canonical utterances and allowed AMT workers to provide paraphrases overnight. In the morning, we trained our parser and obtained an accuracy of 70.8% on the test set.

7.4 Testing on independent data

Geo880. To test how our parser generalizes to utterances independent of our framework, we created a semantic parser for the domain of US geography, and tested on the standard 280 test examples from GEO880 (Zelle and Mooney, 1996). We did not use the standard 600 training examples. Our parser obtained 56.4% accuracy, which is substantially lower than state-of-the-art ($\sim$ 90%).

We performed error analysis on 100 random sentences from the development set where accuracy was 60%. We found that the parser learns from the training data to prefer shorter paraphrases, which accounts for 30% of the errors. In most of these cases, the correct logical form is ranked at the top-3 results (accuracy for the top-3 derivations is 73%). GEO880 contains highly compositional utterances, and in 25% of the errors the correct derivation tree exceeds the maximum depth used for our parser. Another 17.5% of the errors are caused by problems in the paraphrasing model. For example, in the utterance *"what is the size of california"*, the model learns that *"size"* corresponds to *"population"* rather than *"area"*. Errors related to reordering and the syntactic structure of the input utterance account for 7.5% of the errors. For example, the utterance *"what is the area of the largest state"* is paraphrased to *"state that has the largest area"*.

Calendar. In Section 7.1, we evaluated on utterances obtained by paraphrasing canonical utterances from the grammar. To examine the coverage of our parser on independently-produced utterances, we asked AMT workers to freely come up with queries. We collected 186 such queries; 5 were spam and discarded. We replaced all entities (people, dates, etc.) with entities from our seed lexicon to avoid focusing on entity detection.

We were able to annotate 52% of the utterances with logical forms from our grammar. We could not annotate 20% of the utterances due to relative time references, such as *"What time is my next meeting?"*. 14% of the utterances were not covered due to binary predicates not in the grammar (*"What is the agenda of the meeting?"*) or missing entities (*"When is Dan's birthday?"*). Another 2% required unsupported calculations (*"How much free time do I have tomorrow?"*), and the rest are out of scope for other reasons (*"When does my Verizon data plan start over?"*).

We evaluated our trained semantic parser on the 95 utterances annotated with logical forms. Our parser obtained an accuracy of 46.3% and oracle accuracy of 84.2%, which measures how often the correct denotation is on the final beam. The large gap shows that there is considerable room for improvement in the paraphrasing model.

8 Related work and discussion

Much of current excitement around semantic parsing emphasizes large knowledge bases such as Freebase (Cai and Yates, 2013; Kwiatkowski et al., 2013; Berant et al., 2013). However, despite the apparent scale, the actual question answering datasets (Free917 and WebQuestions) are limited in compositionality. Moreover, specialized domains with specialized jargon will always exist, e.g., in regular expressions (Kushman and Barzilay, 2013) or grounding to perception (Matuszek et al., 2012; Tellex et al., 2011; Krishnamurthy and Kollar, 2013). Therefore, we believe building a targeted domain-specific semantic parser for a new website or device is a very practical goal.

Recent work has made significant strides in reducing supervision from logical forms (Zettlemoyer and Collins, 2005; Wong and Mooney, 2007) to denotations (Clarke et al., 2010; Liang et al., 2011) and to weaker forms (Artzi and Zettlemoyer, 2011; Reddy et al., 2014). All of these works presuppose having input utterances, which do not exist in a new domain. Our methodology overcomes this hurdle by exploiting a very lightweight form of annotation: paraphrasing.

Paraphrasing has been applied to single-property question answering (Fader et al., 2013) and semantic parsing (Berant and Liang, 2014). We not only use paraphrasing in the semantic parser, but also for data collection.

Table 2 might evoke rule-based systems (Woods et al., 1972; Warren and Pereira, 1982) or controlled natural languages (Schwitter, 2010). However, there is an important distinction: the grammar need only connect a logical form to *one* canonical utterance; it is not used directly for parsing. This relaxation allows the grammar to be much simpler. Our philosophy is to use the simple domain-general grammar to carry the torch just to the point of being understandable by a human, and let the human perform the remaining correction to produce a natural utterance.

In summary, our contributions are two-fold: a new functionality-driven process and an exploration of some of its linguistic implications. We believe that our methodology is a promising way to build semantic parsers, and in future work, we would like to extend it to handle anaphora and nested quantification.

Acknowledgments. We gratefully acknowledge the support of the Google Natural Language Understanding Focused Program and the DARPA Deep Exploration and Filtering of Text (DEFT) Program contract no. FA8750-13-2-0040.

Reproducibility. All code,[1] data, and experiments for this paper are available on the CodaLab platform at `https://www.codalab.org/worksheets/0x269ef752f8c344a28383240f7bb2be9c/`.

[1]Our system uses the SEMPRE toolkit (`http://nlp.stanford.edu/software/sempre`).

References

Y. Artzi and L. Zettlemoyer. 2011. Bootstrapping semantic parsers from conversations. In *Empirical Methods in Natural Language Processing (EMNLP)*, pages 421–432.

Y. Artzi and L. Zettlemoyer. 2013. Weakly supervised learning of semantic parsers for mapping instructions to actions. *Transactions of the Association for Computational Linguistics (TACL)*, 1:49–62.

J. Berant and P. Liang. 2014. Semantic parsing via paraphrasing. In *Association for Computational Linguistics (ACL)*.

J. Berant, A. Chou, R. Frostig, and P. Liang. 2013. Semantic parsing on Freebase from question-answer pairs. In *Empirical Methods in Natural Language Processing (EMNLP)*.

Q. Cai and A. Yates. 2013. Large-scale semantic parsing via schema matching and lexicon extension. In *Association for Computational Linguistics (ACL)*.

J. Clarke, D. Goldwasser, M. Chang, and D. Roth. 2010. Driving semantic parsing from the world's response. In *Computational Natural Language Learning (CoNLL)*, pages 18–27.

J. Duchi, E. Hazan, and Y. Singer. 2010. Adaptive subgradient methods for online learning and stochastic optimization. In *Conference on Learning Theory (COLT)*.

A. Fader, L. Zettlemoyer, and O. Etzioni. 2013. Paraphrase-driven learning for open question answering. In *Association for Computational Linguistics (ACL)*.

J. Ganitkevitch, B. V. Durme, and C. Callison-Burch. 2013. PPDB: The paraphrase database. In *Human Language Technology and North American Association for Computational Linguistics (HLT/NAACL)*, pages 758–764.

J. Krishnamurthy and T. Kollar. 2013. Jointly learning to parse and perceive: Connecting natural language to the physical world. *Transactions of the Association for Computational Linguistics (TACL)*, 1:193–206.

N. Kushman and R. Barzilay. 2013. Using semantic unification to generate regular expressions from natural language. In *Human Language Technology and North American Association for Computational Linguistics (HLT/NAACL)*, pages 826–836.

T. Kwiatkowski, E. Choi, Y. Artzi, and L. Zettlemoyer. 2013. Scaling semantic parsers with on-the-fly ontology matching. In *Empirical Methods in Natural Language Processing (EMNLP)*.

P. Liang, B. Taskar, and D. Klein. 2006. Alignment by agreement. In *North American Association for Computational Linguistics (NAACL)*, pages 104–111.

P. Liang, M. I. Jordan, and D. Klein. 2011. Learning dependency-based compositional semantics. In *Association for Computational Linguistics (ACL)*, pages 590–599.

P. Liang. 2013. Lambda dependency-based compositional semantics. *arXiv*.

C. Matuszek, N. FitzGerald, L. Zettlemoyer, L. Bo, and D. Fox. 2012. A joint model of language and perception for grounded attribute learning. In *International Conference on Machine Learning (ICML)*, pages 1671–1678.

F. J. Och and H. Ney. 2004. The alignment template approach to statistical machine translation. *Computational Linguistics*, 30:417–449.

P. Pasupat and P. Liang. 2015. Compositional semantic parsing on semi-structured tables. In *Association for Computational Linguistics (ACL)*.

R. A. P. Rangel, M. A. Aguirre, J. J. Gonzlez, and J. M. Carpio. 2014. Features and pitfalls that users should seek in natural language interfaces to databases. In *Recent Advances on Hybrid Approaches for Designing Intelligent Systems*, pages 617–630.

S. Reddy, M. Lapata, and M. Steedman. 2014. Large-scale semantic parsing without question-answer pairs. *Transactions of the Association for Computational Linguistics (TACL)*, 2(10):377–392.

R. Schwitter. 2010. Controlled natural languages for knowledge representation. In *International Conference on Computational Linguistics (COLING)*, pages 1113–1121.

S. Tellex, T. Kollar, S. Dickerson, M. R. Walter, A. G. Banerjee, S. J. Teller, and N. Roy. 2011. Understanding natural language commands for robotic navigation and mobile manipulation. In *Association for the Advancement of Artificial Intelligence (AAAI)*.

D. Warren and F. Pereira. 1982. An efficient easily adaptable system for interpreting natural language queries. *Computational Linguistics*, 8:110–122.

Y. W. Wong and R. J. Mooney. 2007. Learning synchronous grammars for semantic parsing with lambda calculus. In *Association for Computational Linguistics (ACL)*, pages 960–967.

W. A. Woods, R. M. Kaplan, and B. N. Webber. 1972. The lunar sciences natural language information system: Final report. Technical report, BBN Report 2378, Bolt Beranek and Newman Inc.

M. Zelle and R. J. Mooney. 1996. Learning to parse database queries using inductive logic programming. In *Association for the Advancement of Artificial Intelligence (AAAI)*, pages 1050–1055.

L. S. Zettlemoyer and M. Collins. 2005. Learning to map sentences to logical form: Structured classification with probabilistic categorial grammars. In *Uncertainty in Artificial Intelligence (UAI)*, pages 658–666.

Predicting Polarities of Tweets by Composing Word Embeddings with Long Short-Term Memory

Xin Wang[1], Yuanchao Liu[1], Chengjie Sun[1], Baoxun Wang[2] and Xiaolong Wang[1]
[1]School of Computer Science and Technology,
Harbin Institute of Technology, Harbin, China
[2]Application and Service Group, Microsoft, Beijing, China
[1]{xwang,lyc,cjsun,wangxl}@insun.hit.edu.cn
[2]baoxwang@microsoft.com

Abstract

In this paper, we introduce Long Short-Term Memory (LSTM) recurrent network for twitter sentiment prediction. With the help of gates and constant error carousels in the memory block structure, the model could handle interactions between words through a flexible compositional function. Experiments on a public noisy labelled data show that our model outperforms several feature-engineering approaches, with the result comparable to the current best data-driven technique. According to the evaluation on a generated negation phrase test set, the proposed architecture doubles the performance of non-neural model based on bag-of-word features. Furthermore, words with special functions (such as negation and transition) are distinguished and the dissimilarities of words with opposite sentiment are magnified. An interesting case study on negation expression processing shows a promising potential of the architecture dealing with complex sentiment phrases.

1 Introduction

Twitter and other similar microblogs are rich resources for opinions on various kinds of products and events. Detecting sentiment in microblogs is a challenging task that has attracted increasing research interest in recent years (Hu et al., 2013b; Volkova et al., 2013).

Go et al. (2009) carried out the pioneer work of predicting sentiment in tweets using machine learning technology. They conducted comprehensive experiments on multiple classifiers based on bag-of-words feature. Such feature is widely used because it's simple and surprisingly efficient in many tasks. However, there are also disadvantages of bag-of-words features represented by one-hot vectors. Firstly, it bears a data sparsity issue (Saif et al., 2012a). In tweets, irregularities and 140-character limitation exacerbate the sparseness. Secondly, losing sequence information makes it difficult to figure out the polarity properly (Pang et al., 2002). A typical case is that the sentiment word in a negation phrase tends to express opposite sentiment to that of the context.

Distributed representations of words can ease the sparseness, but there are limitations to the unsupervised-learned ones. Words with special functions in specific tasks are not distinguished. Such as negation words, which play a special role in polarity classification, are represented similarly with other adverbs. Such similarities will limit the compositional models' abilities of describing a sentiment-specific interaction between words. Moreover, word vectors trained by co-occurrence statistics in a small window of context effectively represent the syntactic and semantic similarity. Thus, words like *good* and *bad* have very similar representations (Socher et al., 2011). It's problematic for sentiment classifiers.

Sentiment is expressed by phrases rather than by words (Socher et al., 2013). Seizing such sequence information would help to analyze complex sentiment expressions. One possible method to leverage context is connecting embeddings of words in a window and compose them to a fix-length vector (Collobert et al., 2011). However, window-based methods may have difficulty reaching long-distance words and simply connected vectors do not always represent the interactions of context properly.

Theoretically, a recurrent neural network could process the whole sentence of arbitrary length by encoding the context cyclically. However, the length of reachable context is often limited when using stochastic gradient descent (Bengio et al., 1994; Pascanu et al., 2013). Besides that, a

Proceedings of the 53rd Annual Meeting of the Association for Computational Linguistics and the 7th International Joint Conference on Natural Language Processing, pages 1343–1353,
Beijing, China, July 26-31, 2015.

traditional recurrent architecture is not powerful enough to deal with the complex sentiment expressions. Fixed input limits the network's ability of learning task-specific representations and simple additive combination of hidden activations and input activations has difficulty capturing more complex linguistic phenomena.

In this paper, we introduce the Long Short-Term Memory (LSTM) recurrent neural network for twitter sentiment classification by means of simulating the interactions of words during the compositional process. Multiplicative operations between word embeddings through gate structures provide more flexibility and lead to better compositional results compare to the additive ones in simple recurrent neural network. Experimentally, the proposed architecture outperforms various classifiers and feature engineering approaches, matching the performance of the current best data-driven approach. Vectors of task-distinctive words (such as *not*) are distinguished after tuning and representations of opposite-polarity words are separated. Moreover, predicting result on negation test set shows our model is effective in dealing with negation phrases (a typical case of sentiment expressed by sequence). We study the process of the network handling the negation expressions and show the promising potential of our model simulating complex linguistic phenomena with gates and constant error carousels in the LSTM blocks.

2 Related Work

2.1 Microblogs Sentiment Analysis

There have been a large amount of works on sentiment analysis over tweets. Some research makes use of social network information (Tan et al., 2011; Calais Guerra et al., 2011). These works reveal that social network relations of opinion holders could bring an influential bias to the textual models. While some other works utilize the microblogging features uncommon in the formal literature, such as hashtags, emoticons (Hu et al., 2013a; Liu et al., 2012). Speriosu et al. (2011) propose a unified graph propagation model to leverage textual features (such as emoticons) as well as social information.

Semantic concept or entity based approaches lead another research direction. Saif et al. (2012a; 2012b) make use of sentiment-topic features and entities extracted by a third-party service to ease data sparsity. Aspect-based models are also exploited to improve the tweet-level classifier (Lek and Poo, 2013).

2.2 Representation Learning and Deep Models

Bengio et al. (2003) use distributed representations for words to fight the curse of dimensionality when training a neural probabilistic language model. Such word vectors ease the syntactic and semantic sparsity of bag-of-words representations. Much recent research has explored such representations (Turian et al., 2010; Huang et al., 2012).

Recent works reveal that modifying word vectors during training could capture polarity information for the sentiment words effectively (Socher et al., 2011; Tang et al., 2014). It would be also insightful to analyze the embeddings that changed the most during training. We conduct a comparison between initial and tuned vectors and show how the tuned vectors of task-distinctive function words cooperate with the proposed architecture to capture sequence information.

Distributed word vectors help in various NLP tasks when using in neural models (Collobert et al., 2011; Kalchbrenner et al., 2014). Composing these representations to fix-length vectors that contain phrase or sentence level information also improves performance of sentiment analysis (Yessenalina and Cardie, 2011). Recursive neural networks model contextual interaction in binary trees (Socher et al., 2011; Socher et al., 2013). Words in the complex utterances are considered as leaf nodes and composed in a bottom-up fashion. However, it's difficult to get a binary tree structure from the irregular short comments like tweets. Not requiring structure information or parser, long short-term memory models encode the context in a chain and accommodate complex linguistic phenomena with structure of gates and constant error carousels.

3 Recurrent Neural Networks for Sentiment Analysis

Recurrent Neural Networks (RNN) have gained attention in NLP field since Mikolov et al. (2010) developed a statistical language model based on a simple form known as Elman network (Elman, 1990). Recent works used RNNs to predict words or characters in a sequence (Chrupała, 2014; Zhang and Lapata, 2014). Treating opinion expression extraction as a sequence labelling

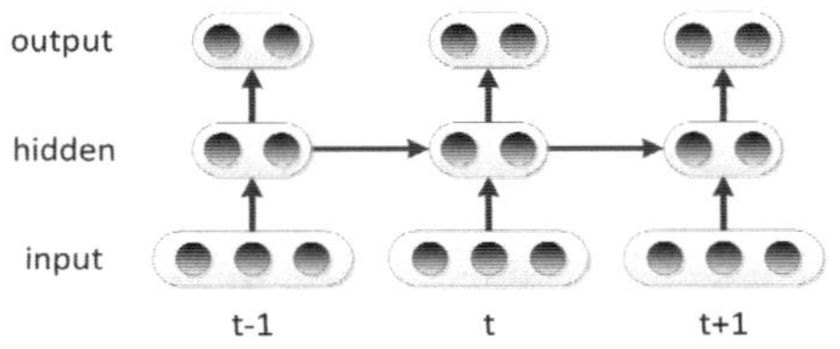

Figure 1: Illustration of simple recurrent neural network. The input of the hidden layer comes from both input layer and the hidden layer activations of previous time step.

problem, Irsoy and Cardie (2014) leverage deep RNN models and achieve new state-of-the-art results for fine-grained extraction task. The lastest work propose a tree-structured LSTM and conduct a comprehensive study on using LSTM in predicting the semantic relatedness of two sentences and sentiment classification (Tai et al., 2015).

Fig.1 shows the illustration of a recurrent network. By using self-connected layers, RNNs allow information cyclically encoded inside the networks. Such structures make it possible to get a fix-length representation of a whole tweet by temporally composing word vectors.

The recurrent architecture we used in this work is shown in Fig.2. Each word is mapped to a vector through a Lookup-Table (LT) layer. The input of the hidden layer comes from both the current lookup-table layer activations and the hidden layer's activations one step back in time. In this way, hidden layer encodes the past and current information. The hidden activations of the last time step could be considered as the representation of the whole sentence and used as input to classification layer. By storing the word vectors in LT layer, the model has reading and tuning access to word representations.

Based on such recurrent architecture, we can capture sequence information in the context and identify polarities of the tweets.

3.1 Elman Network With Fixed Lookup-Table

RNN-FLT: A simple implementation of the recurrent sentiment classifier is an Elman network (also known as simple RNN) with Fixed Lookup-Table (FLT). In such model, unsupervised pre-trained word vectors in LT layer are constant during the whole training process. The hidden layer activation of position h at time t is:

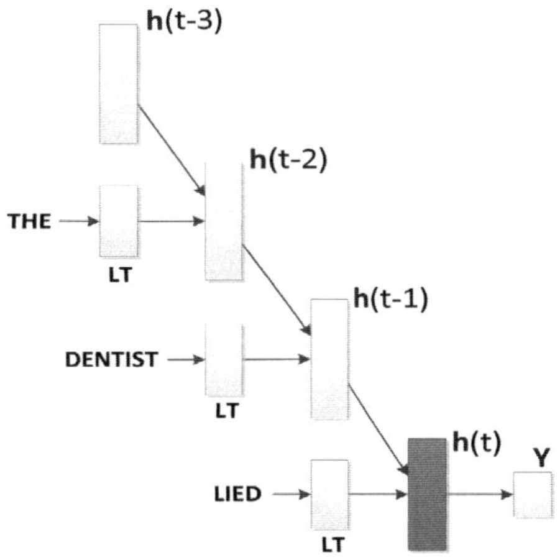

Figure 2: Illustration of the general recurrent architecture unfolded as a deep feedforward network.

$$b_h^t = f\left(a_h^t\right) \tag{1}$$

$$a_h^t = \sum_i^E w_{ih} e_i^t + \sum_{h'}^H w_{h'h} b_{h'}^{t-1} \tag{2}$$

where $\mathbf{e}^t$ represents the E-length embedding of the tth word of the sentence, which stored in LT layer. w_{ih} is the weight of connection between input and hidden layer, while $w_{h'h}$ is the weights of recurrent connection (self-connection of hidden layer). f represents the sigmoid function. The binary classification loss function O is computed via cross entropy (CE) criterion and the network is trained by stochastic gradient descent using *back-propagation through time* (BPTT) (Werbos, 1990). Here, we introduce the notation:

$$\delta_i^t = \frac{\partial O}{\partial a_i^t} \tag{3}$$

Firstly, the error propagate from output layer to hidden layer of last time step T. The derivatives with respect to the hidden activation of position i at the last time step T are computed as follow:

$$\delta_i^T = f'\left(a_i^T\right) \frac{\partial O}{\partial y} v_i \tag{4}$$

where v_i represents the weights of hidden-output connection and the activation of the output layer y is used to estimate probability of the tweet bearing a particular polarity.

$$y = f\left(\sum_{i}^{H} b_i^T v_i\right) \tag{5}$$

Then the gradients of hidden layer of previous time steps can be recursively computed as:

$$\delta_h^t = f'\left(a_h^t\right) \sum_{h'}^{H} \delta_{h'}^{t+1} w_{hh'} \tag{6}$$

3.2 Elman Network with Trainable Lookup-Table

Unsupervised trained word embeddings represent the syntactic and semantic similarity. However, in specific tasks, the importance and functions of different words vary. Negation words have similar unsupervised trained representations with other adverbs, but they make distinctive contributions in sentiment expressions. Besides the function words, tuning word vectors of sentiment words into polarity-representable ones turns out to be an effective way to improve the performance of sentiment classifiers. (Maas et al., 2011; Labutov and Lipson, 2013). Such tuned vectors work together with the deep models, gaining the ability to describe complex linguistic phenomena.

RNN-TLT: To this end, we modify the word vectors in the Trainable Lookup-Table (TLT) via back propagation to get a better embedding of words. The gradient of lookup-table layer is:

$$\delta_i^t = g'\left(a_i^t\right) \sum_{h=1}^{H} \delta_h^t w_{ih} = \sum_{h=1}^{H} \delta_h^t w_{ih} \tag{7}$$

where identity function $g(x) = x$ is considered as the activation function of lookup-table layer.

3.3 Long Short-Term Memory

The simple RNN has the ability to capture context information. However, the length of reachable context is often limited. The gradient tends to vanish or blow up during the back propagation (Bengio et al., 1994; Pascanu et al., 2013). Moreover, Elman network simply combines previous hidden activations with the current inputs through addictive function. Such combination is not powerful enough to describe a complex interactions of words.

An effective solution for these problems is the Long Short-Term Memory (LSTM) architecture (Hochreiter and Schmidhuber, 1997; Gers, 2001). Such architecture consists of a set of recurrently connected subnets, known as memory blocks. Each block contains one or more self-connected memory cells and the input, output and forget gates. Fig.3 gives an illustration of an LSTM block. Once an error signal arrives Constant Error Carousel (CEC), it remains constant, neither growing nor decaying unless the forget gate squashes it. In this way, it solves the vanishing gradient problem and learns more appropriate parameters during training.

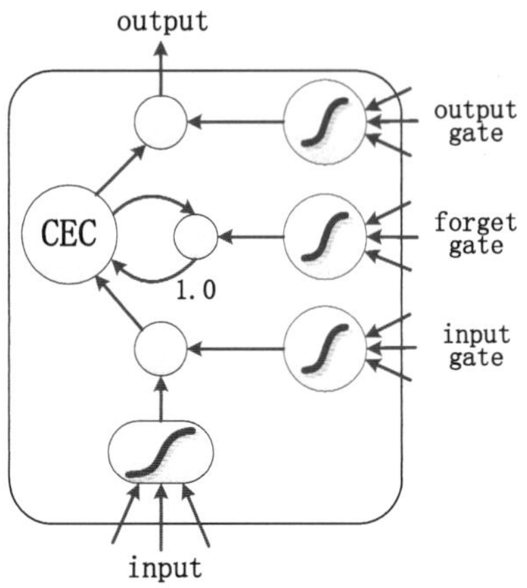

Figure 3: Illustration of LSTM memory block with one cell. Constant Error Carousel (CEC) maintains the internal activation (called *state*) with a recurrent connection of fixed weight 1.0, which may be reset by the forget gate. The input and output gates scale the input and output respectively. All the gates are controlled by the maintained state, network input and hidden activation of previous time step.

Moreover, based on this structure, the input, output and stored information can be partial adjusted by the gates, which enhances the flexibility of the model. The activations of hidden layer rely on the current/previous state, previous hidden activation and current input. These activations interact to make up the final hidden outputs through not only additive but also element-wise multiplicative functions. Such structures are more capable to learn a complex composition of word vectors than simple RNNs.

These gates are controlled by current input, previous hidden activation and cell state in CEC unit:

$$G_I^t = f\left(U_I x^t + V_I h^{t-1} + W_I s^{t-1}\right) \tag{8}$$

$$G_F^t = f\left(U_F x^t + V_F h^{t-1} + W_F s^{t-1}\right) \quad (9)$$

$$G_O^t = f\left(U_O x^t + V_O h^{t-1} + W_O s^t\right) \quad (10)$$

where G^t indicates the gate activation at time t, x^t, h^t and s^t is input, hidden activation and state in CEC unit at time t respectively, while U, V and W represent the corresponding weight matrices connect them to the gates. Subscript I, F and O indicate input, forget and output respectively. The CEC state and block output are computed by the functions with element-wise multiplicative operation:

$$s^t = G_F^t s^{t-1} + G_I^t f\left(U_S x^t + V_S h^{t-1}\right) \quad (11)$$

$$a^t = G_O^t s^t \quad (12)$$

where U_S indicates connection weight between input and state, while V_S represents the weight matrix connecting hidden layer to state.

LSTM-TLT: By replacing the conventional neural units in RNN-TLT with LSTM blocks, we can get the LSTM network with Trainable Lookup-Table. Such model achieves a flexible compositional structure where the activations interact in a multiplicative function. It provides the capacity of describing diverse linguistic phenomenon by learning complex compositions of word embeddings.

4 Experiments

4.1 Data Set

We conduct experiments on the Stanford Twitter Sentiment corpus (STS)[1]. The noisy-labelled dataset is collected using emoticons as queries in Twitter API (Go et al., 2009). 800,000 tweets containing positive emoticons are extracted and labelled as positive, while 800,000 negative tweets are extracted based on negative emoticons. The manually labelled test set consists of 177 negative and 182 positive tweets.

4.2 Experimental Settings

Recurrent Neural Network: We implement the recurrent architecture with trainable lookup-table layer by modifying RNNLIB (Graves, 2010) toolkit.

Early Stopping: From the noisy labelled data, we randomly selected 20,000 negative and 20,000 positive tweets as validation set for early stopping. The rest 1,560,000 tweets are used as training set.

Parameter Setting: Tuned on the validation set, the size of the hidden layer is set to 60.

Word Embeddings: We run *word2vec* on the training set of 1.56M tweets (without labels) to get domain-specific representations and use them as initial input of the model. Limited to the input format of the toolkit, we learned 25-dimensional (relatively small) vectors. *Skip-gram architecture* and *hierarchical softmax algorithm* are chosen during training.

4.3 Comparison with Data Driven Approaches

Classifier	Accuracy(%)
SVM	81.6
MNB	82.7
MAXENT	83.0
MAX-TDNN	78.8
NBoW	80.9
DCNN	**87.4**
RAE	77.6
RNN-FLT	80.2
RNN-TLT	86.4
LSTM-TLT	**87.2**

Table 1: Accuracies of different classifiers.

Naive Bayes, Maximum Entropy and SVM are widely used classifiers. Go et al. (2009) presented the results of three non-neural models using unigram and bigram features.

Dynamic Convolutional Neural Network (DCNN) (Kalchbrenner et al., 2014) is a generalization of MAX-TDNN (Collobert et al., 2011). It has a clear hierarchy and is able to capture long-range semantic relations. While the Neural Bag-of-Words (NBoW) takes the summation of word vectors as the input of a classification layer. Kalchbrenner et al. (2014) reported performances of the above three neural classifiers.

Recursive Autoencoder (RAE) has proven to be an effective model to compose words vectors in sentiment classification tasks (Socher et al., 2011). We run RAE with randomly initialized word embeddings. We do not compare with RNTN (Socher et al., 2013) for lack of phrase-level sentiment labels and accurate parsing results.

Table 1 shows the accuracies of different classifiers. Notably, RNN-TLT and LSTM-TLT out-

[1] http://twittersentiment.appspot.com/

perform the three non-neural classifiers. Trained on the considerable data, these classifiers provide strong baselines. However, bag-of-words representations are not powerful enough. Sparsity and losing sequence information hurt the performance of classifiers. Neural models overcome these problems by using distributed representations and temporally encoding the contextual interaction.

We notice a considerable increase in the performance of the RNN-TLT with respect to the NBoW, whose embeddings are also tuned during supervised training. It suggests that recurrent models could generate better tweet-level representations for the task by composing the word embeddings in a temporal manner and capturing the sequential information of the context.

Convolutional neural networks have outstanding abilities of feature extraction, while LSTM-TLT achieves a comparable performance. It suggests that LSTM model is effective in learning sentence-level representations with a flexible compositional structure.

RAE provides more general representations of phrases by learning to reconstruct the word vectors. Recurrent models outperform RAE indicates that task-specific composing and representation learning with less syntactic information lead to a better result.

Comparing RNN-FLT with RNN-TLT, we can easily figure out that the model with trainable lookup-table achieves better performance. This is due to the fact that tuned embeddings capture the sentiment information of text by distinguishing words with opposite sentiment polarities and providing more flexibility for composing. LSTM-TLT does not outperform RNN-TLT significantly. And the situations are almost the same on short-sentence (less than 25 words) and long-sentence (not less than 25 words) test set. Such results indicate that the ability of LSTM getting access to longer-distance context is not the determinant of improvement, while the capacity of LSTM handling complex expressions plays a more important role. Such capacity will be further discussed in subsection 4.7.

Since the training set is large enough, we have not observed strong overfitting during the training process. Therefore, no regularization technology is employed in the experiments.

4.4 Comparison with Feature Engineering Approaches

Method	Craft feature	Accuracy(%)
Speriosu et al. (2011)	emoticon hashtag	84.7
Saif et al. (2012a)	sentiment-topic	86.3
	semantic	84.1
Lek and Poo (2013)	aspect-based	**88.3**
This work		**87.2**

Table 2: Comparison with different feature engineering methods.

Table 2 shows the comparison with different feature engineering methods. In Speriosu et al. (2011)'s work, sentiment labels propagated in a graph constructed on the basis of contextual relations (e.g. word presence in a tweet) as well as social relations. Saif et al. (2012a) eased the data sparsity by adding sentiment-topic features that extracted using traditional lexicon. While Lek and Poo (2013) extracted tuple of *[aspect, word, sentiment]* with hand-crafted templates. With the help of opinion lexicon and POS tagger especially designed for twitter data, their approach achieved a state-of-the-art result.

Even though these methods rely on lexicons and extracted entities, our data-driven model outperforms most of them, except the aspect-based one that introduced twitter-specific resources. This is due to the fact that traditional lexicons, even emoticons added, are not able to cover the diversification of twitter sentiment expressions, while LSTM learns appropriate representations of sentiment information through compositional manner.

4.5 Experiments on Manually Labelled Data

Different from STS dataset deciding the polarity based on emoticons, the benchmark dataset in SemEval 2013 (Nakov et al., 2013) is labelled by human annotators. In this work we focus on the binary polarity classification and abandon the neutral tweets. There are 4099/735/1742 available tweets in the training/dev/test set respectively. Since the training set is relatively small, we don't apply fine tuning on word vectors. Namely we use fixed lookup-table for both RNN and LSTM. 300-dimensional vectors are learned on the 1.56M tweets of STS dataset using word2vec. Other settings stay the same as previous experiments.

Method	Accuracy(%)
SVM	74.5
RAE	75.4
RNN-FLT	83.0
LSTM-FLT	**84.0**

Table 3: Accuracies of different methods on SemEval 2013

Table 3 shows our work compared to SVM and Recursive Autoencoder. From the result, we can see that the recurrent models outperforms the baselines by exploiting more context information of word interactions.

4.6 Representation Learning

Recent works reveal that modifying word vectors during training could capture polarity information for the sentiment words effectively (Socher et al., 2011; Tang et al., 2014). However, it would be also helpful to analyse the embeddings that changed the most.

Function words: We choose 1000 most frequent words. For each word, we compute the distance between unsupervised vector and tuned vector. 20 words that change most are shown in Fig.4.

It's noteworthy that there are five negation words (not, no, n't, never and Not) in the notably-change group. The representations of negation words are quite similar with other adverbs in unsupervised learned embeddings, while the proposed model distinguishes them. This indicate that our polarity-supervised models identify negation words as distinctive symbols in sentiment classification task, while unsupervised learned vectors do not contain such information.

Besides the negation words and sentiment words, there are also other prepositions, pronouns and conjunctions change dramatically (e.g. *and* and *but*). Such function words also play a special role in sentiment expressions (Socher et al., 2013) and the model in this paper distinguishes them. However, the contributions of these words to the task are not that explainable as negation words (at least without sentiment strength information).

To further explain how the tuned vectors work together with the network and describe interactions between words, we study the process of the model classifying negation phrases in the following subsection.

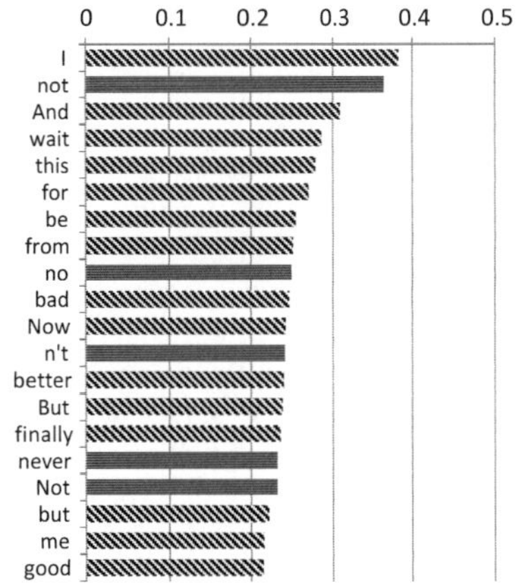

Figure 4: Word change scale to [0,1]. Distances are computed by reversing cosine similarity.

Sentiment words: In order to study the embedding change of sentiment words, we choose the most frequent sentiment words in our training data, 20 positive and 20 negative, and observe the dissimilarity of the vectors in a two-dimensional space. An alternative least-square scaling is implemented based on Euclidean distance between word vectors. Figure 5 shows sentiment-specific tuning reduces the overlap of opposite polarities. Polarities of words are identified based on a widely-used sentiment lexicon (Hu and Liu, 2004).

To explicitly evaluate it, we selected embeddings of 2000 most frequent sentiment words (1000 each polarity) and compute the centers of both classes. If an embedding is closer to the opposite polarity center, we consider it as an *overlap*. Experimentally, the proportion of *overlap* of unsupervised learned vectors is 19.55%, while the one of tuned vectors is 11.4%. Namely the overlap ratio is reduced by 41.7%. Experimentally, such polarity separating relies on tuning through lookup-table layer rather than LSTM structure. With the decrease of overlap of polarities, sentiment of word turns more distinguishable, which is helpful for polarity prediction.

4.7 Case Study: Negation

Negation phrases are typical cases where sentiment is expressed by sequence rather than words. To evaluate the ability of the model dealing with such cases, we select most frequent 1000 negative and 1000 positive words in the training data and generate the corresponding negation phrases (such

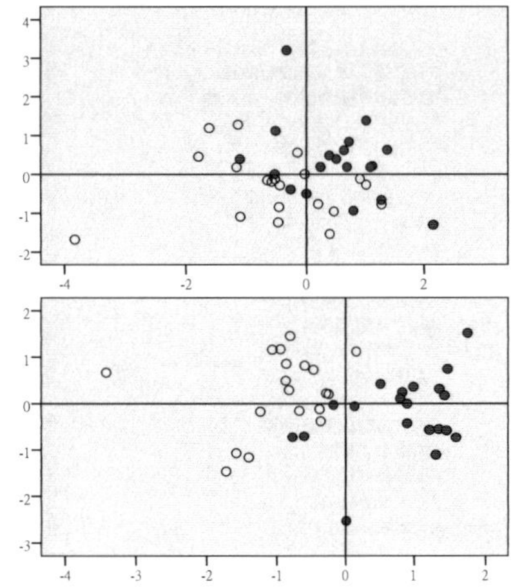

Figure 5: Distance of word vectors shown in two-dimensional space. The above figure shows the distribution of unsupervised learning vectors and the below figure indicates the tuned one. The solid and hollow points represent the positive and negative words respectively.

as *not good*).

Classifier	Accuracy(%)
MNB+unigram+bigram	32.98
RNN-TLT	52.00
LSTM-TLT	**64.85**

Table 4: Accuracy on generated negation phrases test set.

Statistical result shows that only 37.6% of the negation phrases appeared in the training text. It sets a theoretical upper bound to the classifiers based on the unigram and bigram features. Experimental result shown in Table 4 indicates that LSTM model effectively handles the sequential expressions of negation. By composing word vectors, recurrent models ease the sparsity of bag-of-word features and achieve a significant improve than MNB using unigram and bigram features. LSTM outperform RNN by 12.85%, such result suggests the element-wise multiplicative compositional function of LSTM provides more flexibility to simulate interactions between word vectors. A clear process of LSTM handling negation phrases is observed, which is described in the rest of the subsection, while the one of RNN is not that obvious.

As mentioned in 4.6, the task-distinctive function words are distinguished. It would be insightful to show how it works together with the LSTM structure.

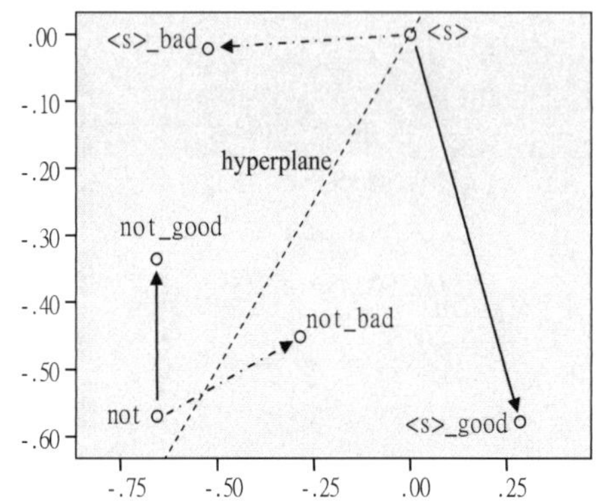

Figure 6: Hidden activations of negation phrases. <s> represent the beginning of sentences. *not bad* and *good* lead to positive outputs, while *not good* and *bad* result in negative values. The dotted line indicates the classification hyperplane. The solid arrows represent the hidden vector changes when the network take the word *good* as input, while the dotted arrows indicate the changes when the word *bad* is input. The sentiment words are input in two situations (as initial input or after negation word), while the changes of hidden vectors of same word are opposite in the two situations.

We train the network on STS dataset and test it on few words and phrases (*good*, *bad*, *not good* and *not bad*). For the convenience of analysis the activation within the network, we set the size of hidden layer to 2. Such setting reduces the performance by about 7% on the public test set, but the trained model still work effectively. Fig.6 shows the activations of LSTM hidden layers. Both sentiment words and negation phrases are classified into correct categories. Furthermore, when sentiment words like *good* (i) input as the first word of sentence and (ii) input after negation word, it cause opposite change in hidden layer. These behaviours simulate the change of sentiment in the negation expressions.

As mentioned in 3.3, gates' activations are controlled by current input, state in CEC unit and output of hidden layer of previous time step. They are many possible ways for the model to simulating the sentiment change. In the experiment, the observed situation is shown in Fig.7:

Negation word contains both polarities. The

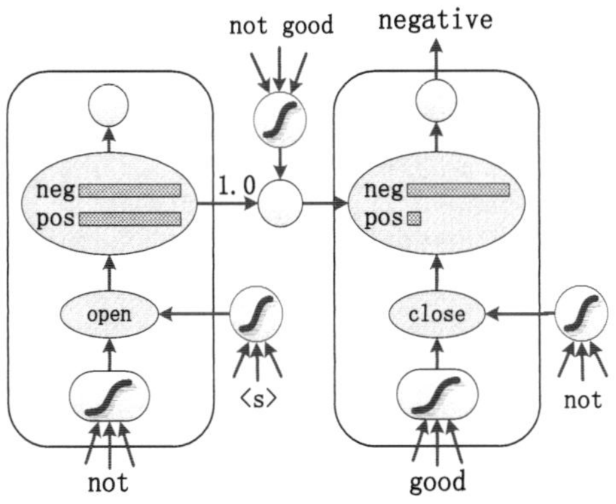

Figure 7: Observed process of LSTM block handling negation phrase *not good*. Some less important connections are omitted in this figure.

positive-axle and negative-axle are almost orthogonal. Negation word has large components on both axles.

***not* make input gate close.** Experiments show recurrent activations make the input gate close, namely previous word *not* squashes the input (both current and recurrent input) to a very small value.

Choose a polarity to forget. The combination of the recurrent input *not* and current input *good* make the CEC unit forget the positive information, namely they make forget gate reduce state's component on positive-axle while leaving a large projection on negative-axle. A significant dissimilarity of forget gate activations between positive and negative words is observed in the experiment, when they are input after *not*.

In this way, the temporally-input phrase *not good* shows a negative polarity. Correspondingly, phrase *not bad* turns positive after reducing the negative components of the negation word. Such case shows the process of the gates and CEC unit cooperating in the LSTM structure. Together with tuned vectors, the architecture has a promising potential of capture sequence information by simulating complex interactions between words.

5 Conclusion

In this paper we have explored to capture twitter sentiment expressed by interactions of words. The contributions of this paper can be summarized as follows: (i) We have described long short-term memory based model to compose word representations through a flexible compositional function. Tested on a public dataset, the proposed architecture achieves result comparable to the current best data-driven model. The experiment on negation test set shows the ability of the model capturing sequential information. (ii) Beyond tuning vectors of sentiment words, we put forward a perspective of distinguishing task-distinctive function words only relying on the label of the whole sequence. (iii) We conduct an interesting case study on the process of task-distinctive word vectors working together with deep model, which is usually considered as a black-box in other neural networks, indicating the promising potential of the architecture simulating complex linguistic phenomena.

Acknowledgments

We thank Deyuan Zhang, Lei Cui, Feng Liu and Ming Liu for their great help. We thank the anonymous reviewers for their insightful feedbacks on this work. This research is supported by National Natural Science Foundation of China (No.613400114), Specialized Research Fund for the Doctoral Program of Higher Education (No.20132302120047), the Special Financial Grant from the China Postdoctoral Science Foundation (No.2014T70340), China Postdoctoral Science Foundation (No.2013M530156)

References

Yoshua Bengio, Patrice Simard, and Paolo Frasconi. 1994. Learning long-term dependencies with gradient descent is difficult. *Neural Networks, IEEE Transactions on*, 5(2):157–166.

Yoshua Bengio, Réjean Ducharme, Pascal Vincent, and Christian Jauvin. 2003. A neural probabilistic language model. *Journal of Machine Learning Research*, 3:1137–1155.

Pedro Henrique Calais Guerra, Adriano Veloso, Wagner Meira Jr, and Virgílio Almeida. 2011. From bias to opinion: a transfer-learning approach to real-time sentiment analysis. In *Proceedings of the 17th ACM SIGKDD international conference on Knowledge discovery and data mining*, pages 150–158. ACM.

Grzegorz Chrupała. 2014. Normalizing tweets with edit scripts and recurrent neural embeddings. In *Proceedings of the 52nd Annual Meeting of the Association for Computational Linguistics (Volume 2: Short Papers)*, pages 680–686, Baltimore, Maryland, June. Association for Computational Linguistics.

Ronan Collobert, Jason Weston, Léon Bottou, Michael Karlen, Koray Kavukcuoglu, and Pavel Kuksa.

2011. Natural language processing (almost) from scratch. *The Journal of Machine Learning Research*, 12:2493–2537.

Jeffrey L Elman. 1990. Finding structure in time. *Cognitive science*, 14(2):179–211.

Felix Gers. 2001. *Long Short-Term Memory in Recurrent Neural Networks*. Ph.D. thesis, Ph. D. thesis, Ecole Polytechnique Federale de Lausanne.

Alec Go, Richa Bhayani, and Lei Huang. 2009. Twitter sentiment classification using distant supervision. *CS224N Project Report, Stanford*, pages 1–12.

Alex Graves. 2010. Rnnlib: A recurrent neural network library for sequence learning problems. `http://sourceforge.net/projects/rnnl`.

Sepp Hochreiter and Jürgen Schmidhuber. 1997. Long short-term memory. *Neural computation*, 9(8):1735–1780.

Minqing Hu and Bing Liu. 2004. Mining and summarizing customer reviews. In *Proceedings of the Tenth ACM SIGKDD International Conference on Knowledge Discovery and Data Mining*, KDD '04, pages 168–177, New York, NY, USA. ACM.

Xia Hu, Jiliang Tang, Huiji Gao, and Huan Liu. 2013a. Unsupervised sentiment analysis with emotional signals. In *Proceedings of the 22nd international conference on World Wide Web*, pages 607–618. International World Wide Web Conferences Steering Committee.

Xia Hu, Lei Tang, Jiliang Tang, and Huan Liu. 2013b. Exploiting social relations for sentiment analysis in microblogging. In *Proceedings of the sixth ACM international conference on Web search and data mining*, pages 537–546. ACM.

Eric H Huang, Richard Socher, Christopher D Manning, and Andrew Y Ng. 2012. Improving word representations via global context and multiple word prototypes. In *Proceedings of the 50th Annual Meeting of the Association for Computational Linguistics: Long Papers-Volume 1*, pages 873–882. Association for Computational Linguistics.

Ozan Irsoy and Claire Cardie. 2014. Opinion mining with deep recurrent neural networks. In *Proceedings of the 2014 Conference on Empirical Methods in Natural Language Processing (EMNLP)*, pages 720–728.

Nal Kalchbrenner, Edward Grefenstette, and Phil Blunsom. 2014. A convolutional neural network for modelling sentences. In *Proceedings of the 52nd Annual Meeting of the Association for Computational Linguistics*, June.

Igor Labutov and Hod Lipson. 2013. Re-embedding words. In *Proceedings of the 51th Annual Meeting of the Association for Computational Linguistics*, pages 489–493. Association for Computational Linguistics.

Hsiang Hui Lek and Danny CC Poo. 2013. Aspect-based twitter sentiment classification. In *Tools with Artificial Intelligence (ICTAI), 2013 IEEE 25th International Conference on*, pages 366–373. IEEE.

Kun-Lin Liu, Wu-Jun Li, and Minyi Guo. 2012. Emoticon smoothed language models for twitter sentiment analysis. In *AAAI*.

Andrew L Maas, Raymond E Daly, Peter T Pham, Dan Huang, Andrew Y Ng, and Christopher Potts. 2011. Learning word vectors for sentiment analysis. In *Proceedings of the 49th Annual Meeting of the Association for Computational Linguistics: Human Language Technologies-Volume 1*, pages 142–150.

Tomas Mikolov, Martin Karafiát, Lukas Burget, Jan Cernockỳ, and Sanjeev Khudanpur. 2010. Recurrent neural network based language model. In *INTERSPEECH*, pages 1045–1048.

Preslav Nakov, Zornitsa Kozareva, Alan Ritter, Sara Rosenthal, Veselin Stoyanov, and Theresa Wilson. 2013. Semeval-2013 task 2: Sentiment analysis in twitter. In *Proceedings of the International Workshop on Semantic Evaluation, SemEval*, volume 13.

Bo Pang, Lillian Lee, and Shivakumar Vaithyanathan. 2002. Thumbs up?: sentiment classification using machine learning techniques. In *Proceedings of the ACL-02 conference on Empirical methods in natural language processing-Volume 10*, pages 79–86. Association for Computational Linguistics.

Razvan Pascanu, Tomas Mikolov, and Yoshua Bengio. 2013. On the difficulty of training recurrent neural networks. In *Proceedings of The 30th International Conference on Machine Learning*, pages 1310–1318.

Hassan Saif, Yulan He, and Harith Alani. 2012a. Alleviating data sparsity for twitter sentiment analysis. *Making Sense of Microposts (# MSM2012)*.

Hassan Saif, Yulan He, and Harith Alani. 2012b. Semantic sentiment analysis of twitter. In *The Semantic Web–ISWC 2012*, pages 508–524. Springer.

Richard Socher, Jeffrey Pennington, Eric H Huang, Andrew Y Ng, and Christopher D Manning. 2011. Semi-supervised recursive autoencoders for predicting sentiment distributions. In *Proceedings of the Conference on Empirical Methods in Natural Language Processing*, pages 151–161. Association for Computational Linguistics.

Richard Socher, Alex Perelygin, Jean Y Wu, Jason Chuang, Christopher D Manning, Andrew Y Ng, and Christopher Potts. 2013. Recursive deep models for semantic compositionality over a sentiment treebank. In *Proceedings of the Conference on Empirical Methods in Natural Language Processing (EMNLP)*, pages 1631–1642.

Michael Speriosu, Nikita Sudan, Sid Upadhyay, and Jason Baldridge. 2011. Twitter polarity classification with label propagation over lexical links and the follower graph. In *Proceedings of the First workshop on Unsupervised Learning in NLP*, pages 53–63. Association for Computational Linguistics.

Kai Sheng Tai, Richard Socher, and Christopher D. Manning. 2015. Improved semantic representations from tree-structured long short-term memory networks. *arXiv preprint arXiv:1503.00075*.

Chenhao Tan, Lillian Lee, Jie Tang, Long Jiang, Ming Zhou, and Ping Li. 2011. User-level sentiment analysis incorporating social networks. In *Proceedings of the 17th ACM SIGKDD international conference on Knowledge discovery and data mining*, pages 1397–1405. ACM.

Duyu Tang, Furu Wei, Nan Yang, Ming Zhou, Ting Liu, and Bing Qin. 2014. Learning sentiment-specific word embedding for twitter sentiment classification. In *Proceedings of the 52nd Annual Meeting of the Association for Computational Linguistics*, pages 1555–1565.

Joseph Turian, Lev Ratinov, and Yoshua Bengio. 2010. Word representations: a simple and general method for semi-supervised learning. In *Proceedings of the 48th Annual Meeting of the Association for Computational Linguistics*, pages 384–394. Association for Computational Linguistics.

Svitlana Volkova, Theresa Wilson, and David Yarowsky. 2013. Exploring sentiment in social media: Bootstrapping subjectivity clues from multilingual twitter streams. In *Association for Computational Linguistics (ACL)*.

Paul J Werbos. 1990. Backpropagation through time: what it does and how to do it. *Proceedings of the IEEE*, 78(10):1550–1560.

Ainur Yessenalina and Claire Cardie. 2011. Compositional matrix-space models for sentiment analysis. In *Proceedings of the Conference on Empirical Methods in Natural Language Processing*, pages 172–182. Association for Computational Linguistics.

Xingxing Zhang and Mirella Lapata. 2014. Chinese poetry generation with recurrent neural networks. In *Proceedings of the 2014 Conference on Empirical Methods in Natural Language Processing (EMNLP)*, pages 670–680.

Topic Modeling based Sentiment Analysis on Social Media for Stock Market Prediction

Thien Hai Nguyen **Kiyoaki Shirai**
School of Information Science
Japan Advanced Institute of Science and Technology
1-1 Asahidai, Nomi, Ishikawa 923-1292, Japan
{nhthien, kshirai}@jaist.ac.jp

Abstract

The goal of this research is to build a model to predict stock price movement using sentiments on social media. A new feature which captures topics and their sentiments simultaneously is introduced in the prediction model. In addition, a new topic model TSLDA is proposed to obtain this feature. Our method outperformed a model using only historical prices by about 6.07% in accuracy. Furthermore, when comparing to other sentiment analysis methods, the accuracy of our method was also better than LDA and JST based methods by 6.43% and 6.07%. The results show that incorporation of the sentiment information from social media can help to improve the stock prediction.

1 Introduction

Stock price forecasting is very important in the planning of business activity. However, building an accurate stock prediction model is still a challenging problem. In addition to historical prices, the current stock market is affected by the mood of society. The overall social mood with respect to a given company might be one of the important variables which affect the stock price of that company. Nowadays, the emergence of online social networks makes large amounts of mood data available. Therefore, incorporating information from social media with the historical prices can improve the predictive ability of the models.

The goal of our research is to develop a model to predict a stock price movement using information from social media (Message Board). In our proposed method, the model predicts the movement of the stock value at t using features derived from information at $t-1$ and $t-2$, where t stands for a transaction date. It will be trained by supervised machine learning. Apart from the mood information, the stock prices are affected by many factors such as microeconomic and macroeconomic factors. However, this research only focuses on how the mood information from social media can be used to predict the stock price movement. That is, the mood of topics in social media is extracted by sentiment analysis. Then, the topics and their sentiments are integrated into the model to predict the stocks. To achieve this goal, discovering the topics and sentiments in a large amount of social media is important to get opinions of investors as well as events of companies. However, sentiment analysis on social media is difficult. The text is usually short, contains many misspellings, uncommon grammar constructions and so on. In addition, the literature shows conflicting results in sentiment analysis for stock market prediction. Some researchers report that the sentiments from social media have no predictive capabilities (Antweiler and Frank, 2004; Tumarkin and Whitelaw, 2001), while other researchers have reported either weak or strong predictive capabilities (Bollen et al., 2011). Therefore, how to use opinions in social media for stock price predictions is still an open problem.

Our contributions are summarized as follows:

1. We propose a new feature "topic-sentiment" for the stock market prediction model.

2. We propose a new topic model, Topic Sentiment Latent Dirichlet Allocation (TSLDA), which can capture the topic and sentiment simultaneously.

3. Large scale evaluation. Most of the previous researches are limited on predicting for one stock (Bollen et al., 2011; Qian and Rasheed, 2007; Si et al., 2013), and the number of instances (transaction dates) in a test set is rather low such as 14 or 15 instances (Bollen

Proceedings of the 53rd Annual Meeting of the Association for Computational Linguistics and the 7th International Joint Conference on Natural Language Processing, pages 1354–1364,
Beijing, China, July 26-31, 2015.

et al., 2011; Vu et al., 2012). With only a few instances in the test set, the conclusion might be insufficient. This is the first research that shows good prediction results on evaluation of many stocks using a test set consisting of many transaction dates.

The rest of the paper is organized as follows. Section 2 introduces some previous approaches on sentiment analysis for stock prediction. Section 3 explains our model for sentiment analysis by simultaneously inferring the topic and sentiment in the text. Section 4 describes two kinds of datasets required for stock prediction. Section 5 describes our prediction models and also proposes a novel feature based on the topics and sentiments. Section 6 assesses the results of the experiments. Finally, Section 7 concludes our research.

2 Related Work

Stock market prediction is one of the most attracted topics in academic as well as real life business. Many researches have tried to address the question whether the stock market can be predicted. Some of the researches were based on the random walk theory and the Efficient Market Hypothesis (EMH). According to the EMH (Fama et al., 1969; Fama, 1991), the current stock market fully reflects all available information. Hence, price changes are merely due to new information or news. Because news in nature happens randomly and is unknowable in the present, stock prices should follow a random walk pattern and the best bet for the next price is the current price. Therefore, they are not predictable with more than about 50% accuracy (Walczak, 2001). On the other hand, various researches specify that the stock market prices do not follow a random walk, and can be predicted in some degree (Bollen et al., 2011; Qian and Rasheed, 2007; Vu et al., 2012). Degrees of accuracy at 56% hit rate in the predictions are often reported as satisfying results for stock predictions (Schumaker and Chen, 2009b; Si et al., 2013; Tsibouris and Zeidenberg, 1995).

Besides the efficient market hypothesis and the random walk theories, there are two distinct trading philosophies for stock market prediction: fundamental analysis and technical analysis. The fundamental analysis studies the company's financial conditions, operations, macroeconomic indicators to predict the stock price. On the other hand, the technical analysis depends on historical and time-series prices. Price moves in trends, and history tends to repeat itself. Some researches have tried to use only historical prices to predict the stock price (Zuo and Kita, 2012a; Zuo and Kita, 2012b). To discover the pattern in the data, they used Bayesian network (Zuo and Kita, 2012a; Zuo and Kita, 2012b), time-series method such as Auto Regressive, Moving Average, Auto Regressive Moving Average model (Zuo and Kita, 2012a) and so on.

2.1 Extracting Opinions from Text

Sentiment analysis has been found to play a significant role in many applications such as product and restaurant reviews (Liu and Zhang, 2012; Pang and Lee, 2008). There are some researches trying to apply sentiment analysis on information sources to improve the stock prediction model. There are two main such sources. In the past, the main source was the news (Schumaker and Chen, 2009a; Schumaker and Chen, 2009b), and in recent years, social media sources. A simple approach is combining the sentiments in the textual content with the historical prices through the linear regression model.

Most of the previous work primarily used the bag-of-words as text representation that are incorporated into the prediction model. Schumaker and Chen tried to use different textual representations such as bag-of-words, noun phrases and named entities for financial news (Schumaker and Chen, 2009b). However, the textual representations are just the words or named entity tags, not exploiting the mood information so much. A novel tree representation based on semantic frame parsers is proposed (Xie et al., 2013). By using stock prices from Yahoo Finance, they annotated all the news in a transaction date with going up or down categories. However, the weakness of this assumption is that all the news in one day will have the same category. In addition, this is a task of text classification, not stock prediction.

Naive Bayes was used to classify messages from message boards into three classes: buy, hold and sell (Antweiler and Frank, 2004). They were integrated into the regression model. However, they concluded that their model does not successfully predict stock returns.

A method to measure collective hope and fear on each day and analyze the correlation between these indices and the stock market indicators was proposed (Zhang et al., 2011). They used the mood words to tag each tweet as fear, worry, hope and so on. They concluded that the ratio of the emotional tweets significantly negatively correlated with Down Jones, NASDAQ and S&P 500, but positively with VIX. However, they did not use their model to predict the stock price values.

Two mood tracking tools, OpinionFinder and Google Profile of Mood States, were used to analyze the text content of daily Twitter (Bollen et al., 2011). The former measures the positive and negative mood. The latter measures the mood in terms of six dimensions (Calm, Alert, Sure, Vital, Kind, and Happy). They used the Self Organizing Fuzzy Neural Network model to predict DJIA values. The results showed 86.7% direction accuracy (up or down) and 1.79% Mean Absolute Percentage Error. Although they achieved the high accuracy, there were only 15 transaction dates (from December 1 to 19, 2008) in their test set. With such a short period, it might not be sufficient to conclude the effectiveness of their method.

A keyword-based algorithm was proposed to identify the sentiment of tweets as positive, neutral and negative for stock prediction (Vu et al., 2012). Their model achieved around 75% accuracy. However, their test period was short, from 8th to 26th in September 2012, containing only 14 transaction dates.

Continuous Dirichlet Process Mixture (cDPM) model was used to learn the daily topic set of Twitter messages to predict the stock market (Si et al., 2013). A sentiment time series was built based on these topics. However, the time period of their whole dataset is rather short, only three months.

Most of the researches tried to extract only the opinions or sentiments. However, one important missing thing is that opinions or sentiments are expressed on topics or aspects of companies. Therefore, understanding on which topics of a given stock people are expressing their opinion is very important. Although the models for inferring the topics and sentiments simultaneously have already proposed as discussed in Subsection 2.2, to the best of our knowledge, such models have never applied for stock market prediction.

2.2 Aspect based Sentiment Analysis

Some researches tried to identify the sentiment expressed toward an aspect in a sentence rather than a whole sentence or document. The simple approach is to define a sentiment score of a given aspect by the weighted sum of opinion scores of all words in the sentence, where the weight is defined by the distance from the aspect (Liu and Zhang, 2012; Pang and Lee, 2008). This method is further improved by identifying the aspect-opinion relations using tree kernel method (Nguyen and Shirai, 2015).

Other researches trying to extract both the topic and sentiment for some domains such as online product, restaurant and movie review dataset. ASUM is a model for extracting both the aspect and sentiment for online product review dataset (Jo and Oh, 2011). Joint sentiment/topic model (JST) is another model to detect the sentiment and topic simultaneously, which was applied for movie review dataset (Lin and He, 2009). These models assume that each word is generated from a joint topic and sentiment distribution. It means that these models do not distinguish the topic word and opinion word distributions.

Besides the general opinion words, topic models considering aspect-specific opinion words were also proposed. MaxEnt-LDA hybrid model can jointly discover both aspects and aspect-specific opinion words on a restaurant review dataset (Zhao et al., 2010), while FACTS, CFACTS, FACTS-R, and CFACTS-R model were proposed for sentiment analysis on a product review data (Lakkaraju et al., 2011). However, one of the weaknesses of these methods is that there is only one opinion word distribution corresponding to one topic (aspect). It makes difficult to know which sentiment (e.g. positive or negative) is expressed by the opinion words on that topic.

To overcome this drawback, we propose a new topic model called Topic Sentiment Latent Dirichlet Allocation (TSLDA), which estimates different opinion word distributions for individual sentiment categories for each topic. To the best of our knowledge, such a model has not been proposed. TSLDA is suitable for not only sentiment analysis for stock prediction but also general sentiment analysis of the document, sentence and aspect.

3 TSLDA: Topic Sentiment Latent Dirichlet Allocation

The proposed model TSLDA infers the topics and their sentiments simultaneously. It is an extended model of Latent Dirichlet Allocation (LDA) (Blei et al., 2003). We assume that one sentence ex-

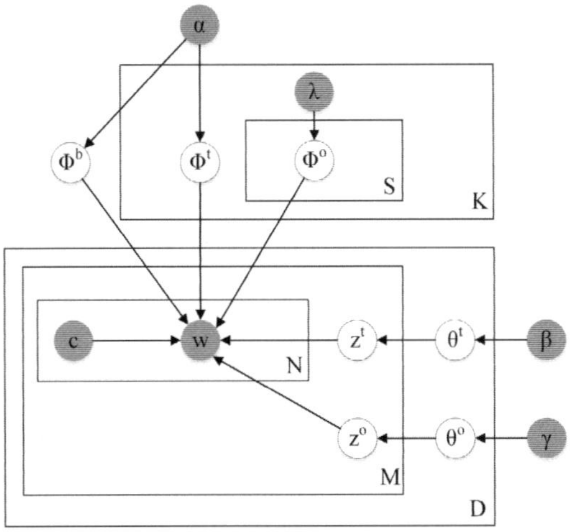

Figure 1: Graphical Model Representation of TSLDA

presses only one topic and one opinion on that topic. The topics are usually nouns, whereas the opinion words are adjectives or adverbs. The words in the document are classified into three categories, the topic word (category $c = 1$), opinion word ($c = 2$) and others ($c = 0$). Then, we suppose the different opinion words are used for the different topics. Depending on the topic, an opinion word may express different sentiment meaning. For example, the opinion word "low" in "low cost" and "low salary" have opposite polarity. In our model, different topics, which are also represented by word distributions, will have different opinion word distributions. Finally, to capture the sentiment meanings such as positive, negative or neutral of the opinion words for each topic, we distinguish opinion word distributions for different sentiment meanings.

Figure 1 shows the graphical model representation of TSLDA. Observed and hidden variables are indicated by shaded and clear circles, respectively. Table 1 shows the notations in Figure 1. The generation process in TSLDA is as follows:

1. Choose a distribution of background words $\Phi^b \sim Dirichlet(\alpha)$
2. For each topic k:
   - Choose a distribution of topic words $\Phi^t_k \sim Dirichlet(\alpha)$
   - For each sentiment s of topic k:
     - Choose a distribution of sentiment words $\Phi^o_{k,s} \sim Dirichlet(\lambda)$

Table 1: Notations in TSLDA

Notation	Definition
$\alpha, \beta, \gamma, \lambda$	Dirichlet prior vectors
K	# of topics
S	# of sentiments
Φ^b	distribution over background words
Φ^t	distribution over topic words
Φ^o	distribution over sentiment words
D	# of documents
M_d	# of sentences in document d
$N_{d,m}$	# of words in sentence m in document d
θ^t_d	topic distribution for document d
θ^o_d	sentiment distribution for document d
$z^t_{d,m}$	topic assignment for sentence m in document d
$z^o_{d,m}$	sentiment assignment for sentence m in document d
$w_{d,m,n}$	n^{th} word in sentence m in document d
$c_{d,m,n}$	n^{th} word's category (background, topic or sentiment) in sentence m in document d

3. For each document d:
   - Choose a topic distribution $\theta^t_d \sim Dirichlet(\beta)$
   - Choose a sentiment distribution $\theta^o_d \sim Dirichlet(\gamma)$
   - For each sentence m:
     - Choose a topic assignment $z^t_{d,m} \sim Multinomial(\theta^t_d)$
     - Choose a sentiment assignment $z^o_{d,m} \sim Multinomial(\theta^o_d)$
     - For each word in the sentence:
       * Choose a word $w_{d,m,n}$ as in Equation (1).

$$w_{d,m,n} \sim \begin{cases} Multinomial(\Phi^b) & \text{if } c_{d,m,n} = 0 \\ Multinomial(\Phi^t_{z^t_{d,m}}) & \text{if } c_{d,m,n} = 1 \\ Multinomial(\Phi^o_{z^t_{d,m}, z^o_{d,m}}) & \text{if } c_{d,m,n} = 2 \end{cases} \quad (1)$$

We will define some notations for explanation of our method. $W^{k,s}_{d,m,v,c}$ is the number of times the word v with the category c appears in the sentence m in the document d, where m discusses the topic k and the sentiment s. Let $Z^{k,s}_d$ be the number of times the document d has the topic k and the sentiment s. If any of these dimensions is not limited to a specific value, we used an asterisk $*$ to denote it. For example, $W^{k,s}_{*,*,v,c}$ is the number of appearance of combination (v, c, k, s) in any sentences in any documents. Similarly, $Z^{k,*}_{d}$ is the number of times the document d has the topic k with any sentiments.

A bold-font variable denotes the list of the variables. For instance, $\boldsymbol{z^t}$ and $\boldsymbol{w}$ denote all of topic assignments and words in all documents, respectively.

$-(d, m)$ stands for exclusion of the value in the sentence m in the document d. For example, $\boldsymbol{z^t_{-(d,m)}}$ denotes all of topic assignment variables $\boldsymbol{z^t}$ but $z^t_{d,m}$. $Z^{a,*-(d,m)}_{d}$ denotes the value of $Z^{a,*}_{d}$ not counting times at the sentence m in the document d.

We used square brackets for specifying the value at the index of a vector or distribution. For instance, $\alpha[v]$ denotes the value of α at index v.

Collapsed Gibbs Sampling was implemented for inference in TSLDA. It will sequentially sample hidden variables $z^t_{d,m}$ and $z^o_{d,m}$ from the distribution over these variables given the current values of all other hidden and observed variables. In other words, in order to perform Collapsed Gibbs Sampling, conditional probability $P(z^t_{d,m} = a, z^o_{d,m} = b|\boldsymbol{z^t_{-(d,m)}}, \boldsymbol{z^o_{-(d,m)}}, \boldsymbol{w}, \boldsymbol{c})$ is calculated by marginalizing out random variables Φ^b, $\boldsymbol{\Phi^t}$, $\boldsymbol{\Phi^o}$, $\boldsymbol{\theta^t}$ and $\boldsymbol{\theta^o}$. Because of the limit of spaces, we only show the final formula of this conditional probability as in Equation (2). Let $V_{d,m}$ be a set of words in the sentence m in the document d. V is a set of all of the words in all documents.

$$
\begin{aligned}
&P(z^t_{d,m} = a, z^o_{d,m} = b|\boldsymbol{z^t_{-(d,m)}}, \boldsymbol{z^o_{-(d,m)}}, \boldsymbol{w}, \boldsymbol{c},) \\
&\propto (Z^{a,*-(d,m)}_{d} + \beta[a])(Z^{*,b-(d,m)}_{d} + \gamma[b]) \\
&\times \frac{\prod_{v=1}^{V_{d,m}} \prod_{j=1}^{W^{*,*}_{d,m,v,1}} (W^{a,*-(d,m)}_{*,*,v,1} + \alpha[v] + j - 1)}{\prod_{j=1}^{W^{*,*}_{d,m,*,1}} (\sum_{v=1}^{V} W^{a,*-(d,m)}_{*,*,v,1} + \alpha[v] + j - 1)} \\
&\times \frac{\prod_{v=1}^{V_{d,m}} \prod_{j=1}^{W^{*,*}_{d,m,v,2}} (W^{a,b-(d,m)}_{*,*,v,2} + \lambda[v] + j - 1)}{\prod_{j=1}^{W^{*,*}_{d,m,*,2}} (\sum_{v=1}^{V} W^{a,b-(d,m)}_{*,*,v,2} + \lambda[v] + j - 1)}
\end{aligned} \tag{2}
$$

Multinomial parameters: Finally, samples obtained from Collapsed Gibbs Sampling can be used to approximate the multinomial parameter sets. The distributions of topics and sentiments in the document d are estimated as in Equation (3).

$$
\theta^t_d[a] = \frac{Z^{a,*}_{d} + \beta[a]}{\sum_{k=1}^{K} Z^{k,*}_{d} + \beta[k]}; \; \theta^o_d[b] = \frac{Z^{*,b}_{d} + \gamma[b]}{\sum_{s=1}^{S} Z^{*,s}_{d} + \gamma[s]} \tag{3}
$$

The background word distribution, topic word distribution of the topic k and sentiment word distribution of the sentiment s for k are estimated in Equation (4), (5) and (6), respectively.

$$
\Phi^b[r] = \frac{W^{*,*}_{*,*,r,0} + \alpha[r]}{\sum_{v=1}^{V} W^{*,*}_{*,*,v,0} + \alpha[v]} \tag{4}
$$

$$
\Phi^t_k[r] = \frac{W^{k,*}_{*,*,v,1} + \alpha[r]}{\sum_{v=1}^{V} W^{k,*}_{*,*,v,1} + \alpha[v]} \tag{5}
$$

$$
\Phi^o_{k,s}[r] = \frac{W^{k,s}_{*,*,v,2} + \lambda[r]}{\sum_{v=1}^{V} W^{k,s}_{*,*,v,2} + \lambda[v]} \tag{6}
$$

4 Dataset

Two datasets are used for the development of our stock prediction model. One is the historical price dataset, and the other is the message board dataset.

4.1 Historical Price Dataset

Historical prices are extracted from Yahoo Finance for 5 stocks. The list of the stock quotes and company names is shown in Table 2. For each transaction date, there are open, high, low, close and adjusted close prices. The adjusted close prices are the close prices which are adjusted for dividends and splits. They are often used for stock market prediction as in other researches (Rechenthin et al., 2013). Therefore, we chose it as the stock price value for each transaction date.

4.2 Message Board Dataset

To get the mood information of the stocks, we collected 5 message boards of the 5 stocks from Yahoo Finance Message Board for a period of one year (from July 23, 2012 to July 19, 2013). On the message boards, users usually discuss company

Table 2: Statistics of Our Dataset

Stocks	Company Names	#Documents
XOM	Exxon Mobil Corporation	11027
DELL	Dell Inc.	10339
EBAY	eBay Inc.	7168
IBM	International Business Machines Corporation	5008
KO	The Coca-Cola Company	2024

news, prediction about stock going up or down, facts, comments (usually negative) about specific company executives or company events. The stock market is not opened at the weekend and holiday. To assign the messages to the transaction dates, the messages which were posted from 4 pm of the previous transaction date to 4 pm of the current transaction date will belong to the current transaction. We choose 4 pm because it is the time of closing transaction. There are 249 transaction dates in the one year period in our dataset.

5 Stock Prediction Models with Sentiment Analysis

This paper focuses on prediction of not the stock price but movement of it. That is, our goal is to develop a model that predicts if the stock price goes up or down. Support Vector Machine (SVM) has long been recognized as being able to efficiently handle high dimensional data and has been shown to perform well on many tasks such as text classification (Joachims, 1998; Nguyen and Shirai, 2013). Therefore, we chose SVM with the linear kernel as the prediction model. Furthermore, features derived by sentiment analysis on the message board are incorporated in it. To assess the effectiveness of sentiment analysis, four sets of features are designed. The first one uses only the historical prices. The other sets include topic and sentiment features obtained by different methods. All the feature values are scaled into $[-1, 1]$ value. Table 3 summarizes our features used in the model to predict the price movement at the transaction date t. The details of each feature will be explained in the next subsections.

5.1 Price Only

In this method, only historical prices are used to predict the stock movement. The purpose of this method is to investigate whether there are patterns of the price movement in the history of the stock. In addition, it is a baseline for evaluation of the effectiveness of the sentiment features. Features used for training SVM are $price_{t-1}$ and $price_{t-2}$ which are the price movements (up, down) at the transaction dates $t-1, t-2$, respectively.

Table 3: Features of the Prediction Model

Method	Features
Price Only	$price_{t-1}, price_{t-2}$
LDA-based Method	$price_{t-1}, price_{t-2},$ $lda_{i,t}, lda_{i,t-1}$
JST-based Method	$price_{t-1}, price_{t-2},$ $jst_{i,j,t}, jst_{i,j,t-1}$
TSLDA-based Method	$price_{t-1}, price_{t-2},$ $tslda_{i,j,t}, tslda_{i,j,t-1}$

5.2 LDA-based Method

In this model, we consider each message as a mixture of hidden topics. LDA is a generative probabilistic model of a corpus [1]. The basic idea is that documents are represented as random mixtures over latent topics, where each topic is characterized by a distribution over words. Hidden topics of LDA are incorporated into the prediction model as follows. First, stop words are removed from the messages, and all the words are lemmatized by Stanford CoreNLP (Manning et al., 2014). Topics are inferred by Gibbs Sampling with 1000 iterations. Next, the probability of each topic for each message is calculated. For each transaction date t, the probability of each topic is defined as the average of the probabilities of the topic in all messages posted on that transaction date.

Features used for training SVM are $price_{t-1}$, $price_{t-2}$, $lda_{i,t}$ and $lda_{i,t-1}$. $lda_{i,t}$ and $lda_{i,t-1}$ are the probabilities of the topic i ($i \in \{1, \cdots, K\}$) for the transaction dates t and $t-1$. The number of the topics K is empirically determined as explained in Subsection 6.1.

5.3 JST-based Method

When people post the message on social media to express their opinion for a given stock, they tend to talk their opinions for a given topic or aspect such as profit and dividend. They would think that the future price of the stock goes up or down by seeing pairs of topic-sentiment written by others. Following the above intuition, we propose a new feature topic-sentiment for the stock predic-

[1] We used the LDA implementation from the Mallet library.

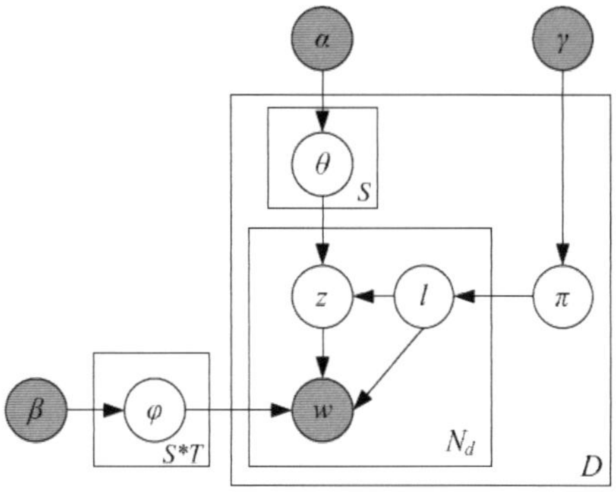

Figure 2: Graphical Model Representation of JST

Table 4: Notations in JST

Notation	Definition
α, β, γ	Dirichlet prior vectors
φ	distribution over words
T	# of topics
S	# of sentiments
θ	message and sentiment specific topic distribution
z	topic
w	word in the message d
l	sentiment label
π	message specific sentiment distribution
N_d	# of words in the message d
D	# of messages

tion model. Two methods are used to extract the pairs of topic-sentiment from the message board. One is a latent topic based model called JST (Lin and He, 2009). The other is TSLDA discussed in Section 3. This subsection introduces the method using the former.

We consider each message as a mixture of hidden topics and sentiments. JST model is used to extract topics and sentiments simultaneously. Figure 2 shows the graphical model representation of JST. Notations in Figure 2 are shown in Table 4. In LDA model, there is only one document specific topic distribution. In contrast, each document in JST is associated with multiple sentiment labels. Each sentiment label is associated with a document specific topic distribution. A word in the document is drawn from a distribution over words defined by the topic and sentiment label.

After removal of stop words and lemmatization, JST model is trained by Gibbs Sampling with 1000 iterations. We chose 3 as the number of sentiments which might represent negative, neutral and positive. The number of the topics K is empirically determined as explained in Subsection 6.1. Next, the joint probability of each pair of topic and sentiment is calculated for each message. For each transaction date t, the joint probability of each topic-sentiment pair is defined as the average of the joint probabilities in the messages on that transaction date. Then we integrate these probabilities into the prediction model.

Features used for training SVM are $price_{t-1}$, $price_{t-2}$, $jst_{i,j,t}$ and $jst_{i,j,t-1}$. $jst_{i,j,t}$ and $jst_{i,j,t-1}$ are the joint probabilities of the sentiment i ($i \in \{1, 2, 3\}$) and topic j ($j \in \{1, \cdots, K\}$) for the transaction dates t and $t-1$.

5.4 TSLDA-based Method

We use our TSLDA model to capture the topics and sentiments simultaneously. First, a rule-based algorithm is applied to identify the category of each word in the documents. Consecutive nouns are considered as topic words. If a word is not a noun and in a list of opinion words in SentiWordNet (Baccianella et al., 2010), it is considered as an opinion word. The rest of words are classified as background words.

After lemmatization, TSLDA model is trained by Collapsed Gibbs Sampling with 1000 iterations. We chose 3 as the number of sentiments which might represent for negative, neutral and positive. K (number of topics) is determined as explained in Subsection 6.1. The topic and its sentiment in each sentence are gotten from the topic assignment and sentiment assignment in TSLDA. If there is a sentence expressing the sentiment j on the topic i, we represent the tuple $(i, j) = 1$, and 0 otherwise. The proportion of (i, j) over all sentences are calculated for each message. For each transaction date, a weight of the tuple (i, j) is defined as the average of the proportions over all messages. Then we integrated the weights of the topics and their sentiments into the prediction model.

Features used for training SVM are $price_{t-1}$, $price_{t-2}$, $tslda_{i,j,t}$ and $tslda_{i,j,t-1}$. $tslda_{i,j,t}$ and $tslda_{i,j,t-1}$ are the weights of the topic i ($i \in \{1, \cdots, K\}$) with the sentiment j ($j \in \{1, 2, 3\}$) for the transaction dates t and $t-1$.

Table 5: Accuracies of Stock Movement Prediction

Stocks	Price Only	LDA	JST	TSLDA
XOM	0.5000	0.4464	0.5179	**0.5357**
DELL	**0.5893**	0.5357	0.5000	0.5536
EBAY	0.6071	0.6071	0.5000	**0.6429**
IBM	0.4107	0.3929	0.5357	**0.5536**
KO	0.4107	0.5179	0.4643	**0.5357**
Average	0.5036	0.5000	0.5036	**0.5643**

6 Evaluation

6.1 Experiment Setup

We divided the dataset described in Section 4 into three parts: training set from July 23, 2012 to March 31, 2013, development set from April 01, 2013 to April 30, 2013, and test set from May 01, 2013 to July 19, 2013. The label of 'up' and 'down' is assigned to each transaction date by comparing the price of the current and previous dates.

To optimize the number of topics K for each stock, we run the models with four values of K: 10, 20, 50 and 100. The best K is chosen for each stock on the development set, and the systems with the chosen K is evaluated on the test data. The performance of the prediction is measured by accuracy.

For the hyperparameters of LDA, JST and TSLDA, we simply selected symmetric Dirichlet prior vectors, that is all possible distributions are likely equal. We used the default values of these hyperparameters for LDA and JST. Concretely speaking, $\alpha = 0.5$, $\beta = 0.01$ in LDA and $\alpha = \frac{50}{\#topics}$, $\beta = 0.01$, $\gamma = 0.3$ were used in JST. For TSLDA, we set $\alpha = 0.1$, $\lambda = 0.1$, $\beta = 0.01$ and $\gamma = 0.01$.

6.2 Results

The result of each stock is shown in Table 5. In addition, the average of 5 stocks for each model is revealed in the last row of this table for easy comparison. Our model TSLDA-based method outperformed the other methods on the average of the stocks. Table 6 shows the number of true positive (TP), true negative (TN), false positive (FP) and false negative (FN) of models for the stocks. For easy comparison, the summation for these five stocks are calculated in the last row.

To assess the effectiveness of integrating mood information, we compare our TSLDA-based method with Price Only method. The results showed that the model using mood information outperformed the model without mood by 3.57%, 3.58%, 14.29% and 12.5% accuracy for XOM, EBAY, IBM and KO stock, respectively. On the other hand, the performance on DELL stock was not improved. It means that the use of the mood does not always make the performance better. The mood from social media could lead to a wrong prediction because of wrong prediction of message writers, fault information and so on. However, TSLDA was better than Price Only method on average of these stocks. In addition, TSLDA can reduce the number of FN, especially for IBM, although FP was not changed in the sum of 5 stocks. Thus, we can conclude that integrating the mood information from social media can help to predict stock price movement more precisely.

Table 6: TP, TN, FP, FN of Stock Movement Prediction

Stocks	Metrics	Price Only	LDA	JST	TSLDA
XOM	TP	14	13	15	18
	TN	14	12	14	12
	FP	8	10	8	10
	FN	20	21	19	16
DELL	TP	17	13	5	13
	TN	16	17	23	18
	FP	17	16	10	15
	FN	6	10	18	10
EBAY	TP	17	18	20	20
	TN	17	16	8	16
	FP	9	10	18	10
	FN	13	12	10	10
IBM	TP	15	15	7	31
	TN	8	7	23	0
	FP	17	18	2	25
	FN	16	16	24	0
KO	TP	12	14	16	10
	TN	11	15	10	20
	FP	17	13	18	8
	FN	16	14	12	18
Sum	TP	75	73	63	92
	TN	66	67	78	66
	FP	68	67	56	68
	FN	71	73	83	54

Next, let us compare the models for inferring latent topics only (LDA) and topics and sentiments (JST and TSLDA) in the stock movement prediction. The accuracy of JST-based method was better than LDA for two stocks (XOM and IBM), worse for three stocks and comparable in the average of five stocks. While, TSLDA-based method outperformed LDA and JST by 2 to 17% in the accuracy for five stocks. TSLDA was also better

Table 7: Top Words in Topics of TSLDA

Topic1	Topic2	Topic3	Topic4	Topic5	Topic6
ko	split	drink	customer	company	country
ceo	stock	coke	budget	competitor	tax
company	share	water	campaign	buy	governor
report	price	produce	promotion	sell	obama
earning	dividend	product	growth	hold	rommey
analyst	year	health	sale	problem	mitt
share	date	juice	volumn	soda	president
news	market	make	come	product	bill
downgrade	time	p.o.s	revenue	people	christian

Table 8: Top Words in Sentiments of Topics of TSLDA

Topic1			Topic2		
S1	S2	S3	S1	S2	S3
old	value	grow	down	straight	good
tired	even	strong	tough	warm	long
unreal	difference	solid	troll	informative	more
much	list	gain	breakthrough	interesting	high
obviously	together	full	ex	later	still
much	serve	continue	sugary	responsible	right
not	americans	growth	ep	yeah	sure
helpful	operation	value	richly	used	same
here	get	quarter	major	though	many

than LDA and JST on average as shown in Table 5. The improvement of the accuracy was derived by increase of TP and decrease of FN. These results indicate that (1) our idea to use both latent topics and sentiments as the features is effective, (2) TSLDA is more appropriate model than JST in stock movement prediction.

Table 7 shows examples of highly associated words of some topics for stock KO (Coca-Cola Company) in TSLDA. For example, 'split', 'stock' and 'share' are words highly associated with the hidden topic 2, and 'drink', 'coke' and 'water' are highly associated with the topic 3. The first five hidden topics in Table 7 may represent the management, stock market trading, product, customer care service, competitors of the company, while the last one indicates macroeconomic factors. Table 8 shows examples of highly associated words of three sentiments of the hidden topic 1 and 2. For the hidden topic 1, 'growth', 'strong', 'solid' etc. are the words highly associated with the hidden sentiment 3 (which may corresponds to positive class), while 'old', 'tired', 'unreal' etc. with the hidden sentiment 1 (may be negative). In general, however, it is rather difficult to interpret the meaning of the hidden sentiment because the sentiments have many dimensions such as happy, anger, sad, vital and so on. We also found that the words with high probabilities in the background distribution were the stop words, punctuations, function words, messy characters written in social media, e.g. '.', 'the', 'and', 'you', '$', 'for' and '?'.

Table 9 shows top words in some joint sentiment topic distributions of JST model for stock KO. For example, 'yahoo', 'ko' and 'finance' are highly associated with the distribution defined by hidden sentiment 1 and hidden topic 1. However, it is rather difficult to guess which sentiment or topic in this joint distribution actually means.

Table 9: Top Words in Distributions Defined by Sentiments and Topics of JST

S1		S2		S3	
Topic1	Topic2	Topic1	Topic2	Topic1	Topic2
yahoo	juice	ko	new	spam	split
ko	minute	buy	american	board	share
finance	maid	get	country	post	date
chart	orange	sell	obama	ignore	stock
free	apple	go	top	idiot	record
fire	drink	make	fall	get	price
website	fruit	money	health	read	august
aone	edit	much	government	another	receive
download	punch	next	place	report	get

7 Conclusion

This paper presents the method to infer the topics and their sentiments on the documents and use them for prediction of the stock movement. The results of the experiments show the effectiveness of our proposed TSLDA-based method. Although 56% accuracy of our method is not so high, it can be satisfying results as regarded in the previous papers. Another advantage of the paper is the evaluation by the large scale experiment (five stocks, three month transaction dates in the test set).

The drawback of TSLDA is that we have to specify the number of topics and sentiment beforehand. To overcome it, TSLDA should be extended as a non-parametric topic model estimating the number of topics inherent in the data. This will be done in our future work.

References

Werner Antweiler and Murray Z Frank. 2004. Is all that talk just noise? the information content of internet stock message boards. *The Journal of Finance*, 59(3):1259–1294.

Stefano Baccianella, Andrea Esuli, and Fabrizio Sebastiani. 2010. Sentiwordnet 3.0: An enhanced lexical resource for sentiment analysis and opinion mining. In *Proceedings of the Seventh Conference on*

International Language Resources and Evaluation (LREC'10), volume 10, pages 2200–2204.

David M. Blei, Andrew Y. Ng, and Michael I. Jordan. 2003. Latent dirichlet allocation. *Journal of Machine Learning Research*, 3:993–1022.

Johan Bollen, Huina Mao, and Xiaojun Zeng. 2011. Twitter mood predicts the stock market. *Journal of Computational Science*, 2(1):1–8.

Eugene F Fama, Lawrence Fisher, Michael C Jensen, and Richard Roll. 1969. The adjustment of stock prices to new information. *International economic review*, 10(1):1–21.

Eugene F Fama. 1991. Efficient capital markets: Ii. *The journal of finance*, 46(5):1575–1617.

Yohan Jo and Alice H Oh. 2011. Aspect and sentiment unification model for online review analysis. In *Proceedings of the fourth ACM international conference on Web search and data mining*, pages 815–824. ACM.

Thorsten Joachims. 1998. *Text categorization with support vector machines: Learning with many relevant features*. Springer.

Himabindu Lakkaraju, Chiranjib Bhattacharyya, Indrajit Bhattacharya, and Srujana Merugu. 2011. Exploiting coherence for the simultaneous discovery of latent facets and associated sentiments. In *Proceedings of the Eleventh SIAM International Conference on Data Mining, SDM 2011, April 28-30, 2011, Mesa, Arizona, USA*, pages 498–509. SIAM / Omnipress.

Chenghua Lin and Yulan He. 2009. Joint sentiment/topic model for sentiment analysis. In *Proceedings of the 18th ACM conference on Information and knowledge management*, pages 375–384. ACM.

Bing Liu and Lei Zhang. 2012. A survey of opinion mining and sentiment analysis. In *Mining Text Data*, pages 415–463. Springer.

Christopher D. Manning, Mihai Surdeanu, John Bauer, Jenny Finkel, Steven J. Bethard, and David McClosky. 2014. The Stanford CoreNLP natural language processing toolkit. In *Proceedings of 52nd Annual Meeting of the Association for Computational Linguistics: System Demonstrations*, pages 55–60.

Thien Hai Nguyen and Kiyoaki Shirai. 2013. Text classification of technical papers based on text segmentation. In Elisabeth Mtais, Farid Meziane, Mohamad Saraee, Vijayan Sugumaran, and Sunil Vadera, editors, *Natural Language Processing and Information Systems*, volume 7934 of *Lecture Notes in Computer Science*, pages 278–284. Springer Berlin Heidelberg.

Thien Hai Nguyen and Kiyoaki Shirai. 2015. Aspect-based sentiment analysis using tree kernel based relation extraction. In Alexander Gelbukh, editor, *Computational Linguistics and Intelligent Text Processing*, volume 9042 of *Lecture Notes in Computer Science*, pages 114–125. Springer International Publishing.

Bo Pang and Lillian Lee. 2008. Opinion mining and sentiment analysis. *Foundations and trends in information retrieval*, 2(1-2):1–135.

Bo Qian and Khaled Rasheed. 2007. Stock market prediction with multiple classifiers. *Applied Intelligence*, 26(1):25–33.

Michael Rechenthin, W Nick Street, and Padmini Srinivasan. 2013. Stock chatter: Using stock sentiment to predict price direction. *Algorithmic Finance*, 2(3):169–196.

Robert P Schumaker and Hsinchun Chen. 2009a. A quantitative stock prediction system based on financial news. *Information Processing & Management*, 45(5):571–583.

Robert P. Schumaker and Hsinchun Chen. 2009b. Textual analysis of stock market prediction using breaking financial news: The azfin text system. *ACM Trans. Inf. Syst.*, 27(2):12:1–12:19, March.

Jianfeng Si, Arjun Mukherjee, Bing Liu, Qing Li, Huayi Li, and Xiaotie Deng. 2013. Exploiting topic based twitter sentiment for stock prediction. In *Proceedings of the 51st Annual Meeting of the Association for Computational Linguistics, ACL 2013, 4-9 August 2013, Sofia, Bulgaria, Volume 2: Short Papers*, pages 24–29. The Association for Computer Linguistics.

George Tsibouris and Matthew Zeidenberg. 1995. Testing the efficient markets hypothesis with gradient descent algorithms. In *Neural Networks in the Capital Markets*, pages 127–136. Wiley: Chichester.

Robert Tumarkin and Robert F Whitelaw. 2001. News or noise? internet postings and stock prices. *Financial Analysts Journal*, 57(3):41–51.

Tien Thanh Vu, Shu Chang, Quang Thuy Ha, and Nigel Collier. 2012. An experiment in integrating sentiment features for tech stock prediction in twitter. In *24th International Conference on Computational Linguistics*, pages 23–38.

Steven Walczak. 2001. An empirical analysis of data requirements for financial forecasting with neural networks. *Journal of management information systems*, 17(4):203–222.

Boyi Xie, Rebecca J Passonneau, Leon Wu, and Germán Creamer. 2013. Semantic frames to predict stock price movement. In *Proceedings of the 51st Annual Meeting of the Association for Computational Linguistics*, pages 873–883.

Xue Zhang, Hauke Fuehres, and Peter A Gloor. 2011. Predicting stock market indicators through twitter "I hope it is not as bad as I fear". *Procedia-Social and Behavioral Sciences*, 26(0):55–62.

Wayne Xin Zhao, Jing Jiang, Hongfei Yan, and Xiaoming Li. 2010. Jointly modeling aspects and opinions with a maxent-lda hybrid. In *Proceedings of the 2010 Conference on Empirical Methods in Natural Language Processing*, pages 56–65. Association for Computational Linguistics.

Yi Zuo and Eisuke Kita. 2012a. Stock price forecast using bayesian network. *Expert Systems with Applications: An International Journal*, 39(8):6729–6737.

Yi Zuo and Eisuke Kita. 2012b. Up/down analysis of stock index by using bayesian network. *Engineering Management Research*, 1(2):46–52.

Learning Tag Embeddings and Tag-specific Composition Functions in Recursive Neural Network

Qiao Qian, Bo Tian, Minlie Huang, Yang Liu*, Xuan Zhu*, Xiaoyan Zhu
State Key Lab. of Intelligent Technology and Systems, National Lab. for Information Science and Technology, Dept. of Computer Science and Technology, Tsinghua University, Beijing 100084, PR China
*Samsung R&D Institute Beijing, China
qianqiaodecember29@126.com, smxtianbo@gmail.com
aihuang@tsinghua.edu.cn, yang.liu@samsung.com
xuan.zhu@samsung.com, zxy-dcs@tsinghua.edu.cn

Abstract

Recursive neural network is one of the most successful deep learning models for natural language processing due to the compositional nature of text. The model recursively composes the vector of a parent phrase from those of child words or phrases, with a key component named composition function. Although a variety of composition functions have been proposed, the syntactic information has not been fully encoded in the composition process. We propose two models, **T**ag **G**uided RNN (TG-RNN for short) which chooses a composition function according to the part-of-speech tag of a phrase, and **T**ag **E**mbedded RNN/RNTN (TE-RNN/RNTN for short) which learns tag embeddings and then combines tag and word embeddings together. In the fine-grained sentiment classification, experiment results show the proposed models obtain remarkable improvement: TG-RNN/TE-RNN obtain remarkable improvement over baselines, TE-RNTN obtains the second best result among all the top performing models, and all the proposed models have much less parameters/complexity than their counterparts.

1 Introduction

Among a variety of deep learning models for natural language processing, Recursive Neural Network (RNN) may be one of the most popular models. Thanks to the compositional nature of natural text, recursive neural network utilizes the recursive structure of the input such as a phrase or sentence, and has shown to be very effective for many natural language processing tasks including semantic relationship classification (Socher et al., 2012), syntactic parsing (Socher et al., 2013a), sentiment analysis (Socher et al., 2013b), and machine translation (Li et al., 2013).

The key component of RNN and its variants is the composition function: how to compose the vector representation for a longer text from the vector of its child words or phrases. For instance, as shown in Figure 2, the vector of *'is very interesting'* can be composed from the vector of the left node *'is'* and that of the right node *'very interesting'*. It's worth to mention again, the composition process is conducted with the syntactic structure of the text, making RNN more interpretable than other deep learning models.

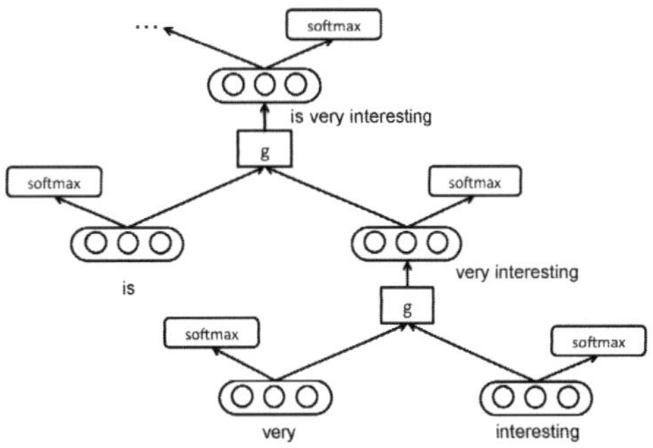

Figure 1: The example process of vector composition in RNN. The vector of node *'very interesting'* is composed from the vectors of node *'very'* and node *'interesting'*. Similarly, the node *'is very interesting'* is composed from the phrase node *'very interesting'* and the word node *'is'*.

There are various attempts to design the composition function in RNN (or related models). In RNN (Socher et al., 2011), a global matrix is used to linearly combine the elements of vectors. In RNTN (Socher et al., 2013b), a global tensor is used to compute the tensor products of dimensions to favor the association between different el-

Proceedings of the 53rd Annual Meeting of the Association for Computational Linguistics and the 7th International Joint Conference on Natural Language Processing, pages 1365–1374, Beijing, China, July 26-31, 2015.

ements of the vectors. Sometimes it is challenging to find a single function to model the composition process. As an alternative, multiple composition functions can be used. For instance, in MV-RNN (Socher et al., 2012), different matrices is designed for different words though the model is suffered from too much parameters. In AdaMC RNN/RNTN (Dong et al., 2014), a fixed number of composition functions is linearly combined and the weight for each function is adaptively learned.

In spite of the success of RNN and its variants, the syntactic knowledge of the text is not yet fully employed in these models. Two ideas are motivated by the example shown in Figure 2: **First**, the composition function for the noun phrase *'the movie/NP'* should be different from that for the adjective phrase *'very interesting/ADJP'* since the two phrases are quite syntactically different. More specifically to sentiment analysis, a noun phrase is much less likely to express sentiment than an adjective phrase. There are two notable works mentioned here: (Socher et al., 2013a) presented to combine the parsing and composition processes, but the purpose is for parsing; (Hermann and Blunsom, 2013) designed composition functions according to the combinatory rules and categories in CCG grammar, however, only marginal improvement against Naive Bayes was reported. Our proposed model, *tag guided RNN (TG-RNN)*, is designed to use the syntactic tag of the parent phrase to guide the composition process from the child nodes. As an example, we design a function for composing noun phrase (*NP*) and another one for adjective phrase (*ADJP*). This simple strategy obtains remarkable improvements against strong baselines.

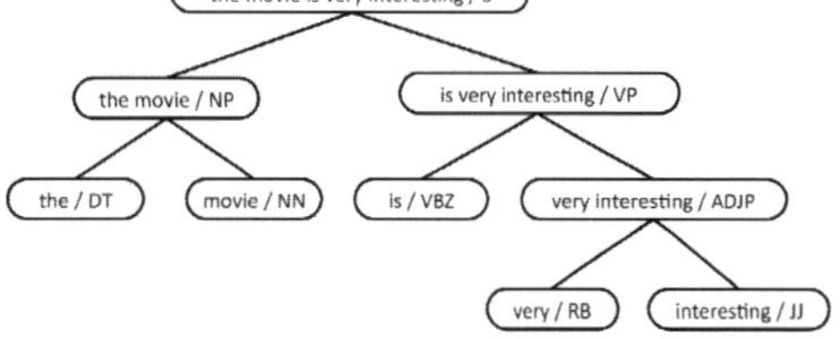

Figure 2: The parse tree for sentence *'The movie is very interesting'* built by Stanford Parser.

Second, when composing the adjective phrase *'very interesting/ADJP'* from the left node *'very/RB'* and the right node *'interesting/JJ'*, the right node is obviously more important than the left one. Furthermore, the right node *'interesting/JJ'* apparently contributes more to sentiment expression. To address this issue, we propose *Tag embedded RNN/RNTN (TE-RNN/RNTN)*, to learn an embedding vector for each word/phrase tag, and concatenate the tag vector with the word/phrase vector as input to the composition function. For instance, we have tag vectors for *DT,NN,RB,JJ,ADJP,NP, etc.* and the tag vectors are then used in composing the parent's vector. The proposed *TE-RNTN* obtain the second best result among all the top performing models but with much less parameters and complexity. To the best of our knowledge, this is the first time that tag embedding is proposed.

To summarize, the contributions of our work are as follows:

- We propose tag-guided composition functions in recursive neural network, TG-RNN. Tag-guided RNN allocates a composition function for a phrase according to the part-of-speech tag of the phrase.
- We propose to learn embedding vectors for part-of-speech tags of words/phrases, and integrate the tag embeddings in RNN and RNTN respectively. The two models, TE-RNN and TE-RNTN, can leverage the syntactic information of child nodes when generating the vector of parent nodes.
- The proposed models are efficient and effective. The scale of the parameters is well controlled. Experimental results on the Stanford Sentiment Treebank corpus show the effectiveness of the models. TE-RNTN obtains the second best result among all publicly reported approaches, but with much less parameters and complexity.

The rest of the paper is structured as follows: in Section 2, we survey related work. In Section 3, we introduce the traditional recursive neural network as background. We present our ideas in Section 4. The experiments are introduced in Section 5. We summarize the work in Section 6.

2 Related Work

Different kinds of representations are used in sentiment analysis. Traditionally, the bag-of-words representations are used for sentiment analysis (Pang and Lee, 2008). To exploit the relationship between words, word co-occurrence (Turney et al., 2010) and syntactic contexts (Padó and Lapata, 2007) are considered. In order to distinguish antonyms with similar contexts, neural word vectors (Bengio et al., 2003) are proposed and can be learnt in an unsupervised manner. Word2vec (Mikolov et al., 2013a) introduces a simpler network structure making computation more efficiently and makes billions of samples feasible for training.

Semantic composition deals with representing a longer text from its shorter components, which is extensively studied recently. In many previous works, a phrase vector is usually obtained by average (Landauer and Dumais, 1997), addition, element-wise multiplication (Mitchell and Lapata, 2008) or tensor product (Smolensky, 1990) of word vectors. In addition to using vector representations, matrices can also be used to represent phrases and the composition process can be done through matrix multiplication (Rudolph and Giesbrecht, 2010; Yessenalina and Cardie, 2011).

Recursive neural models utilize the recursive structure (usually a parse tree) of a phrase or sentence for semantic composition. In Recursive Neural Network (Socher et al., 2011), the tree with the least reconstruction error is built and the vectors for interior nodes is composed by a global matrix. Matrix-Vector Recursive Neural Network (MV-RNN) (Socher et al., 2012) assigns matrices for every words so that it could capture the relationship between two children. In Recursive Neural Tensor Networks (RNTN) (Socher et al., 2013b), the composition process is performed on a parse tree in which every node is annotated with fine-grained sentiment labels, and a global tensor is used for composition. Adaptive Multi-Compositionality (Dong et al., 2014) uses multiple weighted composition matrices instead of sharing a single matrix.

The employment of syntactic information in RNN is still in its infant. In (Socher et al., 2013a), the part-of-speech tag of child nodes is considered in combining the processes of both composition and parsing. The main purpose is for better parsing by employing RNN, but it is not designed for sentiment analysis. In (Hermann and Blunsom, 2013), the authors designed composition functions according to the combinatory rules and categories in CCG grammar. However, only marginal improvement against Naive Bayes was reported. Unlike (Hermann and Blunsom, 2013), our TG-RNN obtains remarkable improvements against strong baselines, and we are the first to propose tag embedded RNTN which obtains the second best result among all reported approaches.

3 Background: Recursive Neural Models

In recursive neural models, the vector of a longer text (e.g., sentence) is composed from those of its shorter components (e.g., words or phrases). To compose a sentence vector through word/phrase vectors, a binary parse tree has to be built with a parser. The leaf nodes represent words and interior nodes represent phrases. Vectors of interior nodes are computed recursively by composition of child nodes' vectors. Specially, the root vector is regarded as the sentence representation. The composition process is shown in Figure 1.

More formally, vector $v_i \in R^d$ for node i is calculated via:

$$v_i = f(g(v_i^l, v_i^r)) \tag{1}$$

where v_i^l and v_i^r are child vectors, g is a composition function, and f is a nonlinearity function, usually *tanh*. Different recursive neural models mainly differ in composition function. For example, the composition function for RNN is as below:

$$g(v_i^l, v_i^r) = W \begin{bmatrix} v_i^l \\ v_i^r \end{bmatrix} + b \tag{2}$$

where $W \in R^{d\times 2d}$ is a composition matrix and b is a bias vector. And the composition function for RNTN is as follows:

$$g(v_i^l, v_i^r) = \begin{bmatrix} v_i^l \\ v_i^r \end{bmatrix} T^{[1:d]} \begin{bmatrix} v_i^l \\ v_i^r \end{bmatrix} + W \begin{bmatrix} v_i^l \\ v_i^r \end{bmatrix} + b \tag{3}$$

where W and b are defined in the previous model and $T^{[1:d]} \in R^{2d\times 2d\times d}$ is the tensor that defines multiple bilinear forms.

The vectors are used as feature inputs to a softmax classifier. The posterior probability over class labels on a node vector v_i is given by

$$y_i = \text{softmax}(W_s v_i + b_s). \tag{4}$$

The parameters in these models include the word table L, a composition matrix W in RNN, and W and $T^{[1:d]}$ in RNTN, and the classification matrix W_s for the softmax classifier.

4 Incorporating Syntactic Knowledge into Recursive Neural Model

The central idea of the paper is inspired by the fact that words/phrases of different part-of-speech tags play different roles in semantic composition. As discussed in the introduction, a noun phrase (e.g., *a movie/NP*) may be composed different from a verb phrase (e.g., *love movie/VP*). Furthermore, when composing the phrase *a movie/NP*, the two child words, *a/DT* and *movie/NN*, may play different roles in the composition process. Unfortunately, the previous RNN models neglect such syntactic information, though the models do employ the parsing structure of a sentence.

We have two approaches to improve the composition process by leveraging tags on parent nodes and child nodes. One approach is to use different composition matrices for parent nodes with different tags so that the composition process could be guided by phrase type, for example, the matrix for *'NP'* is different from that for *'VP'* . The other approach is to introduce 'tag embedding' for words and phrases, for example, to learn tag vectors for *'NP, VP, ADJP'*, etc., and then integrate the tag vectors with the word/phrase vectors during the composition process.

4.1 Tag Guided RNN (TG-RNN)

We propose Tag Guided RNN (TG-RNN) to respect the tag of a parent phrase during the composition process. The model chooses a composition function according to the part-of-speech tag of a phrase. For example, *'the movie'* has tag *NP*, *'very interesting'* has tag *ADJP*, the two phrases have different composition matrices.

More formally, we design composition functions g with a factor of the phrase tag of a parent node. The composition function becomes

$$g(t_i, v_i^l, v_i^r) = g_{t_i}(v_i^l, v_i^r) = W_{t_i} \begin{bmatrix} v_i^l \\ v_i^r \end{bmatrix} + b_{t_i} \quad (5)$$

where t_i is the phrase tag for node i, W_{t_i} and b_{t_i} are the parameters of function g_{t_i}, as defined in Equation 2. In other words, phrase nodes with various tags have their own composition functions such as g_{NP}, g_{VP}, and so on. There are totally k composition function in this model where k is the number of phrase tags. When composing child vectors, a function is chosen from the function pool according to the tag of the parent node. The process is depicted in Figure 3. We term this model Tag guided RNN, TG-RNN for short.

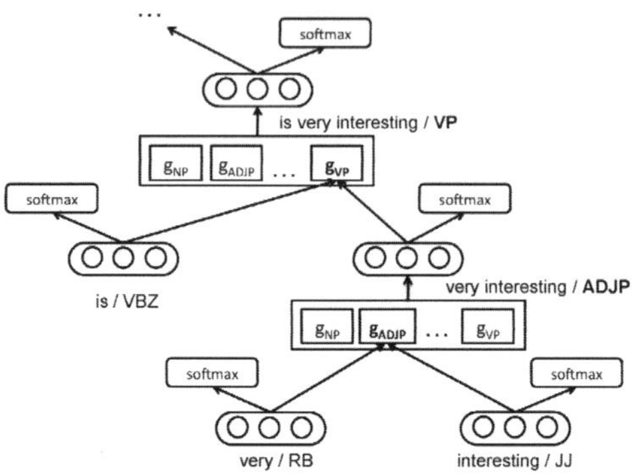

Figure 3: The vector of phrase *'very interesting'* is composed with highlighted g_{ADJP} and *'is very interesting'* with g_{VP}.

But some tags have few occurrences in the corpus. It is hard and meaningless to train composition functions for those infrequent tags. So we simply choose top k frequent tags and train k composition functions. A common composition function is shared across phrases with all infrequent tags. The value of k depends on the size of the training set and the occurrences of each tag. Specially, when $k = 0$, the model is the same as the traditional RNN.

4.2 Tag Embedded RNN and RNTN (TE-RNN/RNTN)

In this section, we propose tag embedded RNN (TE-RNN) and tag embedded RNTN (TE-RNTN) to respect the part-of-speech tags of child nodes during composition. As mentioned above, tags of parent nodes have impact on composition. However, some phrases with the same tag should be composed in different ways. For example, *'is interesting'* and *'like swimming'* have the same tag *VP*. But it is not reasonable to compose the two phrases using the previous model because the part-of-speech tags of their children are quite different. If we use different composition functions for children with different tags like TG-RNN, the number of tag pairs will amount to as many as $k \times k$, which makes the models infeasible due to too many parameters.

In order to capture the compositional effects of the tags of child nodes, an embedding $e_t \in R^{d_e}$ is created for every tag t, where d_e is the dimension of tag vector. The tag vector and phrase vector are concatenated during composition as illustrated in Figure 4.

Formally, the phrase vector is composed by the function

$$g(v_i^l, e_{t_i^l}, v_i^r, e_{t_i^r}) = W \begin{bmatrix} v_i^l \\ e_{t_i^l} \\ v_i^r \\ e_{t_i^r} \end{bmatrix} + b \quad (6)$$

where t_i^l and t_i^r are tags of the left and the right nodes respectively, $e_{t_i^l}$ and $e_{t_i^r}$ are tag vectors, and $W \in R^{d\times(2d_e+2d)}$ is the composition matrix. We term this model Tag embedded RNN, TE-RNN for short.

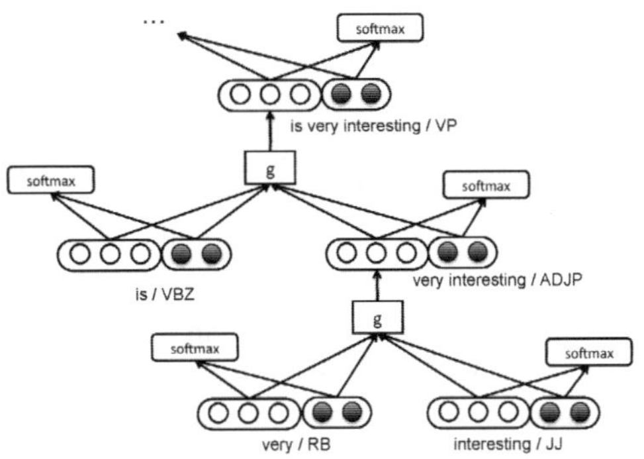

Figure 4: RNN with tag embedding. There is a tag embedding table, storing vectors for *RB*, *JJ*, and *ADJP*, etc. Then we compose the phrase vector *'very interesting'* from the vectors for *'very'* and *'interesting'*, and the tag vectors for *RB* and *JJ*.

Similarly, this idea can be applied to Recursive Neural Tensor Network (Socher et al., 2013b). In RNTN, the tag vector and the phrase vector can be interweaved together through a tensor. More specifically, the phrase vectors and tag vectors are multiplied by the composed tensor. The composition function changes to the following:

$$g(v_i^l, e_{t_i^l}, v_i^r, e_{t_i^r}) = \begin{bmatrix} v_i^l \\ e_{t_i^l} \\ v_i^r \\ e_{t_i^r} \end{bmatrix} T^{[1:d]} \begin{bmatrix} v_i^l \\ e_{t_i^l} \\ v_i^r \\ e_{t_i^r} \end{bmatrix} + W \begin{bmatrix} v_i^l \\ e_{t_i^l} \\ v_i^r \\ e_{t_i^r} \end{bmatrix} + b \quad (7)$$

where the variables are similar to those defined in equation 3 and equation 7. We term this model Tag embedded RNTN, TE-RNTN for short.

The phrase vectors and tag vectors are used as input to a softmax classifier, giving the posterior probability over labels via

$$y_i = \text{softmax}(W_s \begin{bmatrix} v_i \\ e_{t_i} \end{bmatrix} + b_s) \quad (8)$$

4.3 Model Training

Let y_i be the target distribution for node i, $\hat{y}_i$ be the predicted sentiment distribution. Our goal is to minimize the cross-entropy error between y_i and $\hat{y}_i$ for all nodes. The loss function is defined as follows:

$$E(\theta) = -\sum_i \sum_j y_i^j \log \hat{y}_i^j + \lambda \|\theta\|^2 \quad (9)$$

where j is the label index, λ is a L_2-regularization term, and θ is the parameter set.

Similar to RNN, the parameters for our models include word vector table L, the composition matrix W, and the sentiment classification matrix W_s. Besides, our models have some additional parameters, as discussed below:

TG-RNN: There are k composition matrices for top k frequent tags. They are defined as $W_t \in R^{k\times d\times 2d}$. The original composition matrix W is for all infrequent tags. As a result, the parameter set of TG-RNN is $\theta = (L, W, W_t, W_s)$.

TE-RNN: The parameters include the tag embedding table E, which contains all the embeddings for part-of-speech tags for words and phrases. And the size of matrix $W \in R^{d\times(2d+2d_e)}$ and the softmax classifier $W_s \in R^{N\times(d_e+d)}$. The parameter set of TE-RNN is $\theta = (L, E, W, W_s)$.

TE-RNTN: This model has one more tensor $T \in R^{(2d+2d_e)\times(2d+2d_e)\times d}$ than TE-RNN. The parameter set of TE-RNTN is $\theta = (L, E, W, T, W_s)$

5 Experiment

5.1 Dataset and Experiment Setting

We evaluate our models on Stanford Sentiment Treebank which contains fully labeled parse trees. It is built upon 10,662 reviews and each sentence has sentiment labels on each node in the parse tree. The sentiment label set is {0,1,2,3,4}, where the numbers mean *very negative*, *negative*, *neutral*, *positive*, and *very positive*, respectively. We use standard split (train: 8,544 dev: 1,101, test: 2,210) on the corpus in our experiments. In addition, we add the part-of-speech tag for each leaf node and phrase-type tag for each interior node using the latest version of Stanford Parser. Because the newer parser generated trees different from those provided in the datasets, 74/11/11 reviews in train/dev/test datasets are ignored. After removing the broken reviews, our dataset contains 10566 reviews (train: 8,470, dev: 1,090, test: 2,199).

The word vectors were pre-trained on an unlabeled corpus (about 100,000 movie reviews) by word2vec (Mikolov et al., 2013b) as initial values and the other vectors is initialized by sampling from a uniform distribution $\mathcal{U}(-\epsilon, \epsilon)$ where ϵ is 0.01 in our experiments. The dimension of word vectors is 25 for RNN models and 20 for RNTN models. *Tanh* is chosen as the nonlinearity function. And after computing the output of node i with $v_i = f(g(v_i^l, v_i^r))$, we set $v_i = \frac{v_i}{||v_i||}$ so that the resulting vector has a limited norm. Backpropagation algorithm (Rumelhart et al., 1986) is used to compute gradients and we use minibatch SGD with momentum as the optimization method, implemented with Theano (Bastien et al., 2012). We trained all our models using stochastic gradient descent with a batch size of 30 examples, momentum of 0.9, L_2-regularization weight of 0.0001 and a constant learning rate of 0.005.

5.2 System Comparison

We compare our models with several methods which are evaluated on the Sentiment Treebank corpus. The baseline results are reported in (Dong et al., 2014) and (Kim, 2014).

We make comparison to the following baselines:

- **SVM.** A SVM model with bag-of-words representation (Pang and Lee, 2008).
- **MNB/bi-MNB.** Multinomial Naive Bayes and its bigram variant, adopted from (Wang and Manning, 2012).
- **RNN.** The first Recursive Neural Network model proposed by (Socher et al., 2011).
- **MV-RNN.** Matrix Vector Recursive Neural Network (Socher et al., 2012) represents each word and phrase with a vector and a matrix. As reported, this model suffers from too many parameters.
- **RNTN.** Recursive Neural Tenser Network (Socher et al., 2013b) employs a tensor for composition function which could model the meaning of longer phrases and capture negation rules.
- **AdaMC.** Adaptive Multi-Compositionality for RNN and RNTN (Dong et al., 2014) trains more than one composition functions and adaptively learns the weight for each function.
- **DCNN/CNN.** Dynamic Convolutional Neural Network (Kalchbrenner et al., 2014) and a simple Convolutional Neural Network (Kim, 2014), though these models are of different genres to RNN, we include them here for fair comparison since they are among top performing approaches on this task.
- **Para-Vec.** A word2vec variant (Le and Mikolov, 2014) that encodes paragraph information into word embedding learning. A simple but very competitive model.
- **DRNN.** Deep Recursive Neural Network (Irsoy and Cardie, 2014) stacks multiple recursive layers.

Method	Fine-grained	Pos./Neg.
SVM	40.7	79.4
MNB	41.0	81.8
bi-MNB	41.9	83.1
RNN	43.2	82.4
MV-RNN	44.4	82.9
RNTN	45.7	85.4
AdaMC-RNN	45.8	87.1
AdaMC-RNTN	46.7	88.5
DRNN	49.8	87.7
TG-RNN (ours)	47.0	86.3
TE-RNN (ours)	48.0	86.8
TE-RNTN (ours)	48.9	87.7
CNN	48.0	88.1
DCNN	48.5	86.8
Para-Vec	48.7	87.8

Table 1: Classification accuray. *Fine-grained* stands for 5-class prediction and *Pos./Neg.* means binary prediction which ignores all neutral instances. All the accuracy is at the sentence level (root).

The comparative results are shown in Table 1. As illustrated, **TG-RNN** outperforms RNN, RNTN, MV-RNN, AdMC-RNN/RNTN.

Compared with RNN, the fine-grained accuracy and binary accuracy of TG-RNN is improved by 3.8% and 3.9% respectively. When compared with AdaMC-RNN, the accuracy of our method rises by 1.2% on the fine-grained prediction. The results show that the syntactic knowledge does facilitate phrase vector composition in this task.

As for **TE-RNN/RNTN**, the fine-grained accuracy of TE-RNN is boosted by 4.8% compared with RNN and the accuracy of TE-RNTN by 3.2% compared with RNTN. TE-RNTN also beat the AdaMC-RNTN by 2.2% on the fine-grained classification task. TE-RNN is comparable to CNN and DCNN, another line of models for this task. TE-RNTN is better than CNN, DCNN, and Para-Vec, which are the top performing approaches on this task. TE-RNTN is worse than DRNN, but the complexity of DRNN is much higher than TE-RNTN, which will be discussed in the next section. Furthermore, TE-RNN is also better than TG-RNN. This implies that learning the tag embeddings for child nodes is more effective than simply using the tags of parent phrases in composition.

Note that the fine-grained accuracy is more convincible and reliable to compare different approaches due to the two facts: First, for the binary classification task, some approaches train another binary classifier for positive/negative classification while other approaches, like ours, directly use the fine-grained classifier for this purpose. Second, how the neutral instances are processed is quite tricky and the details are not reported in the literature. In our work, we simply remove neural instances from the test data before the evaluation. Let the 5-dimension vector y be the probabilities for each sentiment label in a test instance. The prediction will be positive if $\arg\max_{i,i\neq 2} y_i$ is greater than 2, otherwise negative, where $i \in \{0, 1, 2, 3, 4\}$ means very negative, negative, neutral, positive, very positive, respectively.

5.3 Complexity Analysis

To gain deeper understanding of the models presented in Table 1, we discuss here about the parameter scale of the RNN/RNTN models since the prediction power of neural network models is highly correlated with the number of parameters.

The analysis is presented in Table 2 (the optimal values are adopted from the cited papers). The parameters for the word table have the same size $n \times d$ across all recursive neural models, where n is the number of words and d is the dimension of word vector. Therefore, we ignore this part but focus on the parameters of composition functions, termed *model size*. Our models, TG-RNN/TE-RNN, have much less parameters than RNTN and AdMC-RNN/RNTN, but have much better performance. Although TE-RNTN is worse than DRNN, however, the parameters of DRNN are almost 9 times of ours. This indicates that DRNN is much more complex, which requires much more data and time to train. As a matter of a fact, our TE-RNTN only takes 20 epochs for training which is 10 times less than DRNN.

Method	model size	# of parameters
RNN	$2d^2$	$1.8K$
RNTN	$4d^3$	$108K$
AdaMC-RNN	$2d^2 \times c$	$18.7K$
AdaMC-RNTN	$4d^3 \times c$	$202K$
DRNN	$d \times h \times l$ $+2h^2 \times l$	$451K$
TG-RNN (ours)	$2d^2 \times (k+1)$	$8.8K$
TE-RNN (ours)	$2(d+d_e) \times d$	$1.7K$
TE-RNTN (ours)	$4(d+d_e)^2 \times d$	$54K$

Table 2: The model size. d is the dimension of word/phrase vectors (the optimal value is 30 for RNN & RNTN, 25 for AdaMC-RNN, 15 for AdaMC-RNTN, 300 for DRNN). For AdaMC, c is the number of composition functions (15 is the optimal setting). For DRNN, l and h is the number of layers and the width for each layer (the optimal values $l = 4$, $h = 174$). For our methods, k is the number of unshared composition matrices and d_e the dimension of tag embedding, for the optimal setting refer to Section 5.4.

5.4 Parameter Analysis

We have two key parameters to tune in our proposed models. For **TG-RNN**, the number of composition functions k is an important parameter, which corresponds to the number of distinct POS tags of phrases.

Let's start from the corpus analysis. As shown in Table 3, the corpus contains 215,154 phrases but the distribution of phrase tags is extremely imbalanced. For example, the phrase tag *'NP'* appears 60,239 times while *'NAC'* appears only 10 times. Hence, it is impossible to learn a composi-

Phrase tag	Frequency	Phrase tag	Frequency
NP	60,239	ADVP	1,140
S	33,138	PRN	976
VP	26,956	FARG	792
PP	14,979	UCP	362
ADJP	7,912	SSINV	266
SBAR	5,308	others	1,102

Table 3: The distribution of phrase-type tags in the training data. The top 6 frequency tags cover more than 95% phrases.

tion function for the infrequent phrase tags.

Each of the top k frequent phrase tags corresponds to a unique composition function, while all the other phrase tags share a same function. We compare different k for TG-RNN. The accuracy is shown in Figure 5. Our model obtains the best performance when k is 6, which is accordant with the statistics in Table 3.

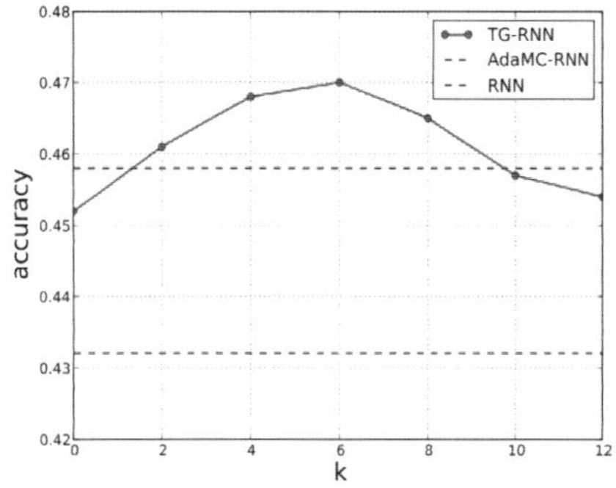

Figure 5: The accuracy for TG-RNN with different k.

For **TE-RNN/RNTN**, the key parameter to tune is the dimension of tag vectors. In the corpus, we have 70 types of tags for leaf nodes (words) and interior nodes (phrases). Infrequent tags whose frequency is less than 1,000 are ignored. There are 30 tags left and we learn an embedding for each of these frequent tags. We varies the dimension of the embedding d_e from 0 to 30.

Figure 6 shows the accuracy for TE-RNN and TE-RNTN with different dimensions of d_e. Our model obtains the best performance when d_e is 8 for TE-RNN and 6 for TE-RNTN. The results show that too small dimensions may not be sufficient to encode the syntactic information of tags and too large dimensions damage the performance.

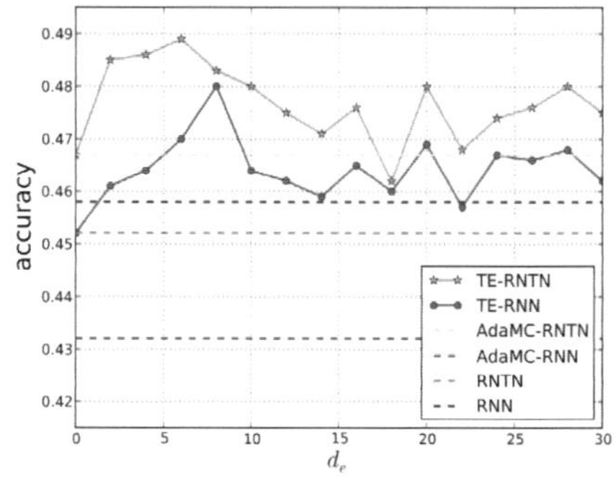

Figure 6: The accuracy for TE-RNN and TE-RNTN with different dimensions of d_e.

5.5 Tag Vectors Analysis

In order to prove tag vectors obtained from tag embedded models are meaningful, we inspect the similarity between vectors of tags. For each tag vector, we find the nearest neighbors based on Euclidean distance, summarized in Table 4.

Tag	Most Similar Tags
JJ (Adjective)	ADJP (Adjective Phrase)
VP (Verb Phrase)	VBD (past tense) VBN (past participle)
. (Dot)	: (Colon)

Table 4: Top 1 or 2 nearest neighboring tags with definition in brackets.

Adjectives and verbs are of significant importance in sentiment analysis. Although '*JJ*' and '*ADJP*' are word and phrase tag respectively, they have similar tag vectors, because of playing the same role of *Adjective* in sentences. '*VP*', '*VBD*' and '*VBN*' with similar representations all represent verbs. What is more interesting is that the nearest neighbor of dot is colon, probably because both of them are punctuation marks. Note that tag classification is none of our training objectives and surprisingly the vectors of similiar tags are clustered together, which can provides additional information during sentence composition.

6 Conclusion

In this paper, we present two ways to leverage syntactic knowledge in Recursive Neural Networks.

The first way is to use different composition functions for phrases with different tags so that the composition processing is guided by phrase types (TG-RNN). The second way is to learn tag embeddings and combine tag and word embeddings during composition (TE-RNN/RNTN). The proposed models are not only effective (w.r.t competing performance) but also efficient (w.r.t well-controlled parameter scale). Experiment results show that our models are among the top performing approaches up to date, but with much less parameters and complexity.

Acknowledgments

This work was partly supported by the National Basic Research Program (973 Program) under grant No.2012CB316301/2013CB329403, the National Science Foundation of China under grant No.61272227/61332007, and the Beijing Higher Education Young Elite Teacher Project. The work was also supported by Tsinghua University Beijing Samsung Telecom R&D Center Joint Laboratory for Intelligent Media Computing.

References

Frédéric Bastien, Pascal Lamblin, Razvan Pascanu, James Bergstra, Ian J. Goodfellow, Arnaud Bergeron, Nicolas Bouchard, and Yoshua Bengio. 2012. Theano: new features and speed improvements. Deep Learning and Unsupervised Feature Learning NIPS 2012 Workshop.

Yoshua Bengio, Réjean Ducharme, Pascal Vincent, and Christian Janvin. 2003. A neural probabilistic language model. *The Journal of Machine Learning Research*, 3:1137–1155.

Li Dong, Furu Wei, Ming Zhou, and Ke Xu. 2014. Adaptive multi-compositionality for recursive neural models with applications to sentiment analysis. In *AAAI*. AAAI.

Karl Moritz Hermann and Phil Blunsom. 2013. The role of syntax in vector space models of compositional semantics. In *ACL*, pages 894–904. Association for Computer Linguistics.

Ozan Irsoy and Claire Cardie. 2014. Deep recursive neural networks for compositionality in language. In *NIPS*, pages 2096–2104.

Nal Kalchbrenner, Edward Grefenstette, and Phil Blunsom. 2014. A convolutional neural network for modelling sentences. In *ACL*, pages 655–665. Association for Computer Linguistics.

Yoon Kim. 2014. Convolutional neural networks for sentence classification. In *EMNLP*, pages 1746–1751. Association for Computational Linguistics.

Thomas K Landauer and Susan T Dumais. 1997. A solution to plato's problem: The latent semantic analysis theory of acquisition, induction, and representation of knowledge. *Psychological Review*, 104(2):211.

Quoc V Le and Tomas Mikolov. 2014. Distributed representations of sentences and documents. In *ICML*, volume 32, pages 1188–1196.

Peng Li, Yang Liu, and Maosong Sun. 2013. Recursive autoencoders for ITG-based translation. In *EMNLP*, pages 567–577. Association for Computer Linguistics.

Tomas Mikolov, Kai Chen, Greg Corrado, and Jeffrey Dean. 2013a. Efficient estimation of word representations in vector space. *CoRR*.

Tomas Mikolov, Ilya Sutskever, Kai Chen, Greg S Corrado, and Jeff Dean. 2013b. Distributed representations of words and phrases and their compositionality. In *NIPS*, pages 3111–3119.

Jeff Mitchell and Mirella Lapata. 2008. Vector-based models of semantic composition. In *ACL*, pages 236–244.

Sebastian Padó and Mirella Lapata. 2007. Dependency-based construction of semantic space models. *Computational Linguistics*, 33(2):161–199.

Bo Pang and Lillian Lee. 2008. Opinion mining and sentiment analysis. *Foundations and Trends in Information Retrieval*, 2(1-2):1–135.

Sebastian Rudolph and Eugenie Giesbrecht. 2010. Compositional matrix-space models of language. In *ACL*, pages 907–916. Association for Computer Linguistics.

David E Rumelhart, Geoffrey E Hinton, and Ronald J Williams. 1986. Learning representations by back-propagating errors. *Nature*, 323:533–536.

Paul Smolensky. 1990. Tensor product variable binding and the representation of symbolic structures in connectionist systems. *Artificial intelligence*, 46(1):159–216.

Richard Socher, Jeffrey Pennington, Eric H Huang, Andrew Y Ng, and Christopher D Manning. 2011. Semi-supervised recursive autoencoders for predicting sentiment distributions. In *EMNLP*, pages 151–161. Association for Computational Linguistics.

Richard Socher, Brody Huval, Christopher D Manning, and Andrew Y Ng. 2012. Semantic compositionality through recursive matrix-vector spaces. In *EMNLP*, pages 1201–1211. Association for Computational Linguistics.

Richard Socher, John Bauer, Christopher D Manning, and Andrew Y Ng. 2013a. Parsing with compositional vector grammars. In *ACL*, pages 455–465. Association for Computer Linguistics.

Richard Socher, Alex Perelygin, Jean Y Wu, Jason Chuang, Christopher D Manning, Andrew Y Ng, and Christopher Potts. 2013b. Recursive deep models for semantic compositionality over a sentiment treebank. In *EMNLP*, pages 1631–1642. Association for Computational Linguistics.

Peter D Turney, Patrick Pantel, et al. 2010. From frequency to meaning: Vector space models of semantics. *Journal of Artificial Intelligence Research*, 37(1):141–188.

Sida I Wang and Christopher D Manning. 2012. Baselines and bigrams: Simple, good sentiment and topic classification. In *ACL*, pages 90–94. Association for Computational Linguistics.

Ainur Yessenalina and Claire Cardie. 2011. Compositional matrix-space models for sentiment analysis. In *EMNLP*, pages 172–182. Association for Computer Linguistics.

A convex and feature-rich discriminative approach to dependency grammar induction

Édouard Grave
Columbia University
edouard.grave@gmail.com

Noémie Elhadad
Columbia University
noemie.elhadad@columbia.edu

Abstract

In this paper, we introduce a new method for the problem of unsupervised dependency parsing. Most current approaches are based on generative models. Learning the parameters of such models relies on solving a non-convex optimization problem, thus making them sensitive to initialization. We propose a new convex formulation to the task of dependency grammar induction. Our approach is discriminative, allowing the use of different kinds of features. We describe an efficient optimization algorithm to learn the parameters of our model, based on the Frank-Wolfe algorithm. Our method can easily be generalized to other unsupervised learning problems. We evaluate our approach on ten languages belonging to four different families, showing that our method is competitive with other state-of-the-art methods.

1 Introduction

Grammar induction is an important problem in computational linguistics. Despite having recently received a lot of attention, it is still considered to be an unsolved problem. In this work, we are interested in unsupervised dependency parsing. More precisely, our goal is to induce directed dependency trees, which capture binary syntactic relations between the words of a sentence. Since our method is unsupervised, it does not have access to such syntactic structure and only take as input a corpus of words and their associated parts of speech.

Most recent approaches to unsupervised dependency parsing are based on probabilistic generative models, such as the dependency model with valence introduced by Klein and Manning (2004). Learning the parameters of such models is often done by maximizing the log-likelihood of unlabeled data, leading to a non-convex optimization problem. Thus, the performance of those methods rely heavily on the initialization, and practitioners have to find good heuristics to initialize their models.

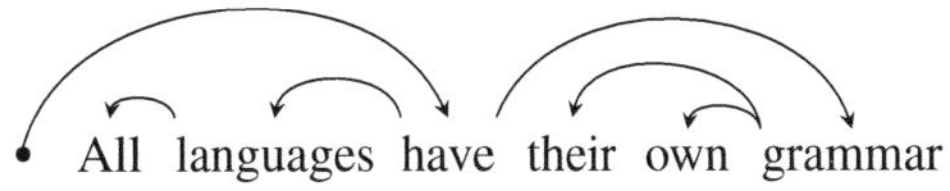

Figure 1: An example of dependency tree.

In this paper, we describe a different approach to the problem of dependency grammar induction, inspired by discriminative clustering. We propose to use a feature-rich discriminative parser, and to learn the parameters of this parser using a convex quadratic objective function. In particular, this approach also allows us to induce non-projective dependency structures. Following the work of Naseem et al. (2010), we use language-independent rules between pairs of parts-of-speech to guide our parser. More precisely, we make the following contributions:

- Our method is based on a feature-rich discriminative parser (section 3);
- Learning the parameters of our parser is achieved using a convex objective, and is thus not sensitive to initialization (section 4);
- Our method can produce non-projective dependency structures (section 3.2.2);
- We propose an efficient algorithm to optimize the objective, based on the Frank-Wolfe method (section 5);
- We evaluate our approach on the universal treebanks dataset, showing that it is competitive with the state-of-the-art (section 6).

Proceedings of the 53rd Annual Meeting of the Association for Computational Linguistics and the 7th International Joint Conference on Natural Language Processing, pages 1375–1384,
Beijing, China, July 26-31, 2015.

2 Related work

A lot of research has been carried out in the last decade on dependency grammar induction. We review the dependency model with valence, on which most unsupervised dependency parsers are based, before presenting different extensions and learning algorithms. Finally, we review discriminative clustering, on which our method is based.

DMV. The dependency model with valence (DMV), introduced by Klein and Manning (2004), was the first method to outperform the baseline consisting in attaching each token to the next one. The DMV is a generative probabilistic model of the dependency tree and parts-of-speech of a sentence. It generates the root first, and then recursively generates the tokens down the tree. The probability of generating a new dependent for a given token depends on the direction (left or right) and whether a dependent was already generated in that direction. Then, the part-of-speech of the new dependent is generated according to a multinomial distribution conditioned on the direction and the head's POS.

Extensions. Several extensions of the dependency model with valence have been proposed. Headden III et al. (2009) proposed the lexicalized extended valence grammar (EVG), in which the probability of generating a POS also depends on the valence information. They rely on smoothing to tackle the increased number of parameters. Mareček and Žabokrtský (2012) described an approach using a n-gram reducibility measure, which capture which words can be deleted from a sentence without making it syntactically incorrect. Cohen and Smith (2009) introduced a prior, based on the shared logistic normal distribution. This prior allowed to tie the grammar parameters corresponding to different POS belonging to the same coarse groups, such as all the POS corresponding to verbs. Berg-Kirkpatrick and Klein (2010) proposed to tie the parameters of grammars for different languages using a prior based on a phylogenetic tree. Naseem et al. (2010) proposed a set of rules between parts-of-speech, encoding *syntactic universals*, such as the fact that adjectives are often dependents of nouns. They used posterior regularization (Ganchev et al., 2010) to impose that a certain amount of the infered dependencies verifies one of these rules. Also using posterior regularization, Gillenwater et al. (2011) imposed a sparsity bias on the infered dependencies, enforcing a small number of unique dependency types. Finally, Blunsom and Cohn (2010) reformulated dependency grammar induction using tree substitution grammars, while Bisk and Hockenmaier (2013) proposed to use combinatory categorial grammars.

Learning. Different algorithms have been proposed to improve the learning of the parameters of the dependency model with valence. Smith and Eisner (2005) proposed to use constrastive estimation to learn the parameters of a log-linear parametrization of the DMV, while Spitkovsky et al. (2010b) showed that using Viterbi EM instead of classic EM leads to higher accuracy. Observing that learning from shorter sentences is easier (because less ambiguous), Spitkovsky et al. (2010a) presented different techniques to learn grammar from increasingly longer sentences. Gimpel and Smith (2012) introduced a model inspired by the IBM1 translation model for grammar induction, resulting in a concave log-likelihood function. They show that initializing the DMV with the output of their model leads to improved dependency accuracies. Hsu et al. (2012) and Parikh et al. (2014) introduced spectral methods for unsupervised dependency and constituency parsing. Finally, Spitkovsky et al. (2013) introduced different heuristics for avoiding local minima while Gormley and Eisner (2013) proposed a method to find the global optimum of non-convex problems, based on branch-and-bound.

Discriminative clustering. Our unsupervised parser is inspired by discriminative clustering, introduced by Xu et al. (2004). Given a set of points, the objective of discriminative clustering is to assign labels to these points that can be easily predicted using a discriminative classifier. Xu et al. (2004) introduced a formulation using the hinge loss, Bach and Harchaoui (2007) proposed to use the squared loss instead, while Joulin et al. (2010) proposed a formulation based on the logistic loss. Recently, a formulation based on discriminative clustering was proposed for the problem of distant supervision for relation extraction (Grave, 2014) and for the problem of finding the names of characters in TV series based on the corresponding scripts (Ramanathan et al., 2014). Closest to our approach, extensions of discriminative clustering were used to align sequences of labels or text with videos (Bojanowski et al., 2014; Bojanowski et al., 2015) or to co-localize objects in videos (Joulin et al., 2014).

3 Model

In this section, we describe the parsing model used in our approach and briefly review the corresponding decoding algorithms. Following McDonald et al. (2005b), we propose to cast the problem of dependency parsing as a maximum weight spanning tree problem in directed graphs.

3.1 Edge-based factorization

Let us start by setting up some notations. An input sentence of length n is represented by an $n-$uplet $\mathbf{x} = (x_1, ..., x_n)$. The dependency tree corresponding to that sentence is represented by a $n \times (n+1)$ binary matrix $\mathbf{y}$, such that $y_{ij} = 1$ if and only if the head of the token i is the token j (and thus, the integer $n+1$ represents the root of the tree).

In this paper, we follow a common approach by factoring the score of dependency tree as the sum of the scores of the edges forming that tree. We assume that each pair of tokens (i, j) is represented by a high-dimensional feature vector $f(\mathbf{x}, i, j) \in \mathbb{R}^d$. Then, the score s_{ij} of the edge (i, j) is obtained using the linear model

$$s_{ij} = \mathbf{w}^\top f(\mathbf{x}, i, j),$$

where $\mathbf{w} \in \mathbb{R}^d$ is a parameter vector. Thus the score s corresponding to the tree $\mathbf{y}$ is equal to

$$\begin{aligned} s &= \sum_{(i,j) \text{ s.t. } y_{ij}=1} s_{ij} \\ &= \sum_{(i,j) \text{ s.t. } y_{ij}=1} \mathbf{w}^\top f(\mathbf{x}, i, j). \end{aligned}$$

Assuming that the parameter vector $\mathbf{w}$ is known, parsing a sentence reduces to finding the tree with the highest score, which is the maximum weight spanning tree.

3.2 Maximum spanning trees

Different sets of spanning trees have been considered in the setting of supervised dependency parsing. We briefly review those sets, and describe the corresponding algorithms to compute the maximum weight spanning tree over those sets.

3.2.1 Projective dependency trees

First, we consider the set of projective spanning trees. A dependency tree is said to be projective if the dependencies do not cross when drawn above the words in linear order. Similarly, this means that word and all its descendants form a contiguous substring of the sentence. Projective dependency trees are thus strongly related to context free grammars, and it is possible to obtain the maximum weight spanning projective tree using a modified version of the CKY algorithm (Cocke and Schwartz, 1970; Kasami, 1965; Younger, 1967). The complexity of this algorithm is $O(n^5)$. This led Eisner (1996) to propose an algorithm for projective parsing which has a complexity of $O(n^3)$. Similarly to CKY, the Eisner algorithm is based on dynamic programming, parsing a sentence in a bottom-up fashion. Finally, it should be noted that the dependency model with valence, on which most approaches to dependency grammar induction are based, produces projective dependency trees.

3.2.2 Non-projective dependency trees

Second, we consider the set of non-projective spanning trees. Indeed, many languages, such as Czech or Dutch, have a significant number of non-projective edges. In the context of supervised dependency parsing, McDonald et al. (2005b) shown that using non-projective trees improves the accuracy of dependency parsers for those languages. The maximum weight spanning tree in a directed graph can be computed using the Chu-Liu/Edmonds algorithm (Chu and Liu, 1965; Edmonds, 1967), which has a complexity of $O(n^3)$. Later, Tarjan (1977) proposed an improved version of this algorithm for dense graphs, whose complexity is $O(n^2)$, the same as for undirected graphs using Prim's algorithm. Thus a second advantage of using non-projective dependency trees is the fact that it leads to more efficient parsers.

4 Learning the parameter vector

In this section, we describe the loss function we use to learn the parameter vector $\mathbf{w}$ from unlabeled sentences.

4.1 Problem formulation

From now on, $\mathbf{y}$ is a vector representing the dependency trees corresponding to the whole corpus. Thus, each index i corresponds to a potential dependency between two words of a given sentence.

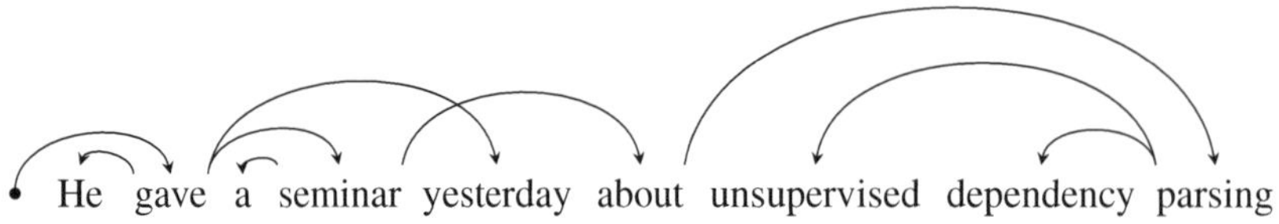

Figure 2: Example of a non-projective dependency tree in english.

Like before, $y_i = 1$ if and only if there is a dependency between those two words, and $y_i = 0$ otherwise. The set of dependencies that form valid trees is denoted by the set $\mathcal{T}$.

Inspired by the discriminative clustering framework introduced by Xu et al. (2004), our goal is to jointly find the dependencies represented by the vector $\mathbf{y}$ and the parameter vector $\mathbf{w}$ which minimize the regularized empirical risk

$$\min_{\mathbf{y} \in \mathcal{T}} \min_{\mathbf{w}} \frac{1}{n} \sum_{i=1}^{n} \ell(y_i, \mathbf{w}^\top \mathbf{x}_i) + \lambda \Omega(\mathbf{w}), \quad (1)$$

where ℓ is a loss function and Ω is a regularizer. The intuition is that we want to find the dependency trees $\mathbf{y}$ that can be easily predicted by a discriminative parser, whose parameters are $\mathbf{w}$.

Following Bach and Harchaoui (2007), we propose to use the squared loss ℓ defined by

$$\ell(y, \hat{y}) = \frac{1}{2}(y - \hat{y})^2$$

and to use the ℓ_2-norm as a regularizer. In that case, we obtain the objective function:

$$\min_{\mathbf{y} \in \mathcal{T}} \min_{\mathbf{w}} \frac{1}{2n} \|\mathbf{y} - \mathbf{X}\mathbf{w}\|_2^2 + \frac{\lambda}{2} \|\mathbf{w}\|_2^2. \quad (2)$$

One of the main advantages of using the squared loss is the fact that the corresponding objective function is jointly convex in $\mathbf{y}$ and $\mathbf{w}$. Indeed, the objective is the composition of an affine mapping, defined by $(\mathbf{y}, \mathbf{w}) \mapsto \mathbf{y} - \mathbf{X}\mathbf{w}$, with a convex function, defined by $\mathbf{u} \mapsto \mathbf{u}^\top \mathbf{u}$. Thus, the objective function is convex (see section 3.2.2 of Boyd and Vandenberghe (2004)). The problem (2) is thus non-convex only because of the combinatorial constraints on the binary vector $\mathbf{y}$, namely that $\mathbf{y}$ should represents valid trees.

4.2 Convex relaxation

The set $\mathcal{T}$ of vectors representing valid dependency trees is a finite set of binary vectors. We can thus take the convex hull of those points and denote it by $\mathcal{Y}$:

$$\mathcal{Y} = \text{conv}(\mathcal{T}).$$

VERB $\mapsto$ VERB	NOUN $\mapsto$ NOUN
VERB $\mapsto$ NOUN	NOUN $\mapsto$ ADJ
VERB $\mapsto$ PRON	NOUN $\mapsto$ DET
VERB $\mapsto$ ADV	NOUN $\mapsto$ NUM
VERB $\mapsto$ ADP	NOUN $\mapsto$ CONJ
ADJ $\mapsto$ ADV	ADP $\mapsto$ NOUN

Table 1: Set of universal rules used in our parser.

By definition, this set is a convex polytope. We then propose to replace the combinatorial constraints on the vector $\mathbf{y}$ by the fact that $\mathbf{y}$ should be in the convex polytope $\mathcal{Y}$. We thus obtain a convex quadratic program, with linear constraints, as follows:

$$\min_{\mathbf{y} \in \mathcal{Y}} \min_{\mathbf{w}} \frac{1}{2n} \|\mathbf{y} - \mathbf{X}\mathbf{w}\|_2^2 + \frac{\lambda}{2} \|\mathbf{w}\|_2^2. \quad (3)$$

We will describe how to compute the optimal solution of this problem in section 5.

4.3 Rounding

Given a continuous solution $\mathbf{y}_c \in \mathcal{Y}$ of the relaxed problem, it is possible to obtain a solution of the integer problem by finding the tree $\mathbf{y}_d \in \mathcal{T}$ which is closest to $\mathbf{y}_c$, by solving the problem

$$\min_{\mathbf{y}_d \in \mathcal{T}} \|\mathbf{y}_d - \mathbf{y}_c\|_2^2.$$

The solution of the previous problem can easily be formulated is a minimum weight spanning tree problem. Indeed, by developping the previous expression, and using the fact that for all trees $\mathbf{y}_d \in \mathcal{T}$, $\mathbf{y}_d^\top \mathbf{y}_d = n$, where n is the number of tokens, the previous problem is equivalent to:

$$\min_{\mathbf{y}_d \in \mathcal{T}} -\mathbf{y}_d^\top \mathbf{y}_c,$$

whose solution is obtained using the minimum weight spanning tree algorithm. It should be noted that the rounding solution is not necessarily the optimal solution of the integer problem.

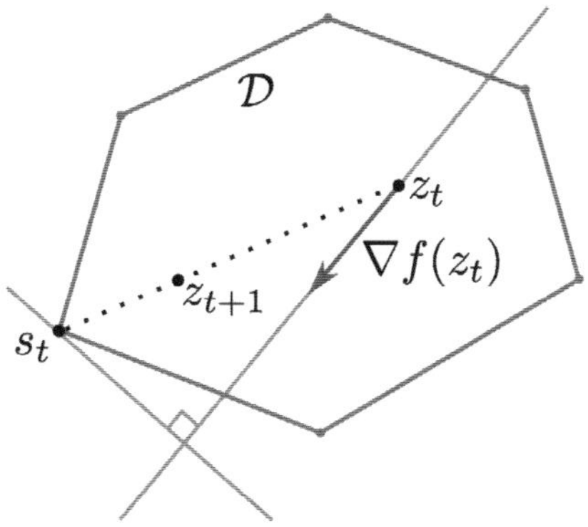

Figure 3: Illustration of a Frank-Wolfe step.

Algorithm 1: Frank-Wolfe algorithm

for $t \in \{1, ..., T\}$ **do**
  Compute the gradient:
  $g_t = \nabla f(z_t)$
  Solve the linear program:
  $s_t = \min_{s \in \mathcal{D}} s^\top g_t$
  Take the Frank-Wolfe step:
  $z_{t+1} = \gamma_t s_t + (1 - \gamma_t) z_t$
end

4.4 Prior on y

We now describe how to guide our unsupervised parser, by using universal rules. Following Naseem et al. (2010), we want a certain percentage of the infered dependencies to satisfy one of the twelve universal syntactic rules, listed in Table 1. Let $\mathcal{S}$ be the set of indices corresponding to word pairs that satisfy one of these rules. Then, imposing that a certain percentage c of dependencies satisfy one of those rules can be obtained by imposing the constraint:

$$\frac{1}{n} \sum_{i \in \mathcal{S}} y_i \geq c.$$

This linear constraint is equivalent to $\mathbf{u}^\top \mathbf{y} \geq c$, where the vector $\mathbf{u}$ is defined by

$$u_i = \begin{cases} 1/n & \text{if } i \in \mathcal{S}, \\ 0 & \text{otherwise.} \end{cases}$$

Using Lagrangian duality, we can obtain the following equivalent penalized problem:

$$\min_{\mathbf{y} \in \mathcal{Y}} \min_{\mathbf{w}} \frac{1}{2n} \|\mathbf{y} - \mathbf{X}\mathbf{w}\|_2^2 + \frac{\lambda}{2} \|\mathbf{w}\|_2^2 - \mu\, \mathbf{u}^\top \mathbf{y}. \quad (4)$$

The penalized and constrained problems are equivalent, since for every c, there exists a μ such that the two problems have the same optimum. From an optimization point of view, it is easier to deal with the penalized problem and we will thus use it in the next section.

5 Optimization

One could use a general purpose quadratic solver to compute the solution of the previous convex problem. However, this might be inefficient since it does not use the structure of the polytope and, in particular, the fact that one can easily minimize a linear function over the tree polytope using the minimum weight spanning tree algorithm. Instead we propose to use the Frank-Wolfe algorithm, that we now describe.

5.1 Frank-Wolfe algorithm

The Frank-Wolfe algorithm (Frank and Wolfe, 1956; Jaggi, 2013) is used to minimize a convex differentiable function f over a convex bounded set $\mathcal{D}$. It is an iterative first-order optimization method. At each iteration t, the convex function f is approximated by a linear function defined by its gradient at the current point z_t. Then it finds the point s_t that minimizes that linear function, over the convex set $\mathcal{D}$:

$$s_t = \min_s s^\top \nabla f(z_t) \text{ s.t. } s \in \mathcal{D}.$$

The point z_{t+1} is then defined as the weighted average between the solution s_t and the current point z_t: $z_{t+1} = \gamma_t\, s_t + (1-\gamma_t)\, z_t$, where γ_t is the step size (such as $2/(t+2)$). Compared to the gradient descent algorithm, the Frank-Wolfe alogrithm does not take a step in the direction of the gradient, but in the direction of the point that minimizes the linear approximation of the function f over the convex set $\mathcal{D}$ (see Fig 3). In particular, this ensures that the points z_t always stay inside the convex set, and there is thus no need for a projection step.

To summarize, in order to use the Frank-Wolfe algorithm, we need to compute the gradient of the objective function and to minimize a linear function over our convex set. This is particularly appropriate to our problem, since we can easily minimize a linear function over the tree polytopes (using the minimum weight spanning tree algorithm), while projecting on those polytopes is more expensive.

Algorithm 2: Optimization algorithm for our method.

for $t \in \{1, ..., T\}$ **do**
    Compute the optimal $\mathbf{w}$:
    $\mathbf{w}_t = \operatorname*{argmin}_{\mathbf{w}} \frac{1}{2n}\|\mathbf{y}_t - \mathbf{X}\mathbf{w}\|_2^2 + \frac{\lambda}{2}\|\mathbf{w}\|_2^2$
    Compute the gradient w.r.t. $\mathbf{y}$:
    $\mathbf{g}_t = \frac{1}{n}(\mathbf{y}_t - \mathbf{X}\mathbf{w}_t) - \mu\,\mathbf{u}$
    Solve the linear program:
    $\mathbf{s}_t = \min_{\mathbf{s}\in\mathcal{Y}} \mathbf{s}^\top \mathbf{g}_t$
    Take the Frank-Wolfe step:
    $\mathbf{y}_{t+1} = \gamma_t \mathbf{s}_t + (1-\gamma_t)\mathbf{y}_t$
end

5.2 Application to our problem

We now describe how to use the Frank-Wolfe algorithm to optimize our objective function with respect to $\mathbf{y}$. First, let us introduce the functions f and h defined by

$$f(\mathbf{w}, \mathbf{y}) = \frac{1}{2n}\|\mathbf{y} - \mathbf{X}\mathbf{w}\|_2^2 + \frac{\lambda}{2}\|\mathbf{w}\|_2^2 - \mu\,\mathbf{u}^\top\mathbf{y},$$
$$h(\mathbf{y}) = \min_{\mathbf{w}} f(\mathbf{w}, \mathbf{y}).$$

The original problem is equivalent to

$$\min_{\mathbf{y}\in\mathcal{Y}} \min_{\mathbf{w}} f(\mathbf{w}, \mathbf{y}) = \min_{\mathbf{y}\in\mathcal{Y}} h(\mathbf{y}).$$

We will use the Frank-Wolfe algorithm to optimize the function h.

Minimizing w.r.t w. First, we need to minimize the function f with respect to $\mathbf{w}$, in order to compute the function h (and its gradient). One must note that this is an unconstrained quadratic program, whose solution can be obtained in closed form by solving the linear system:

$$\left(\mathbf{X}^\top\mathbf{X} + \lambda\mathbf{I}\right)\mathbf{w} = \mathbf{X}^\top\mathbf{y}.$$

However, in case of a very large feature space, this system might be prohibitively expensive to solve exactly. We instead propose to approximately compute the optimal $\mathbf{w}$ using stochastic gradient descent.

Computing the gradient of h. Then, the gradient of the function h at the point $\mathbf{y}$ is equal to

$$\nabla h(\mathbf{y}) = \nabla_{\mathbf{y}} f(\mathbf{w}^*, \mathbf{y}),$$

$\text{POS}_i \times d$
$\text{POS}_j \times d$
$\text{POS}_i \times \text{POS}_j \times d$
$\text{POS}_i \times \text{POS}_{i-1} \times \text{POS}_j \times d$
$\text{POS}_i \times \text{POS}_{i+1} \times \text{POS}_j \times d$
$\text{POS}_i \times \text{POS}_j \times \text{POS}_{j-1} \times d$
$\text{POS}_i \times \text{POS}_j \times \text{POS}_{j+1} \times d$

Table 2: Features used in our parser to describe the dependency between tokens i and j, where i is the head, j the dependent and $d = i - j$.

where $\mathbf{w}^*$ is equal to

$$\mathbf{w}^* = \operatorname*{argmin}_{\mathbf{w}} f(\mathbf{w}, \mathbf{y}).$$

Thus, in order to compute the gradient of h with respect to $\mathbf{y}$, we start by computing the corresponding optimal value of $\mathbf{w}$. Then, the gradient with respect to $\mathbf{y}$ is equal to

$$\nabla h(\mathbf{y}) = \frac{1}{n}(\mathbf{y} - \mathbf{X}\mathbf{w}^*) - \mu\,\mathbf{u}.$$

Minimizing a linear function over $\mathcal{Y}$. We finaly need to compute the optimal solution of the following linear problem

$$\min_{\mathbf{s}\in\mathcal{Y}} \nabla h(\mathbf{y})^\top \mathbf{s}.$$

The optimal value of a linear function over a bounded convex polytope is always attained on at least one vertex of that polytope. By definition of our polytope, those vertices correspond to spanning trees. Thus, computing an optimal solution of this problem is obtained by finding a minimum weight spanning tree.

Discussion. Similarly to the Expectation-Maximization algorithm, our optimization method is a two-steps iterative algorithm. In the first step, the optimal parameter vector $\mathbf{w}$ is estimated based on the previous dependency trees, while the second step consist in re-estimating the (relaxed) dependency trees.

6 Experiments

In this section, we report the results of the experiments we have performed to evaluate our approach to grammar induction.

	DMV	PR	USR	OUR
DE	42.6	58.4	53.4	**60.2**
EN	22.4	57.5	**66.2**	62.3
ES	31.8	57.3	**71.5**	68.8
FR	56.0	66.2	54.1	**72.3**
ID	44.9	21.4	50.3	**69.7**
IT	33.3	40.4	46.5	**64.3**
JA	48.0	**58.9**	58.2	57.5
KO	35.3	50.7	48.8	**59.0**
PT-BR	49.6	40.7	46.4	**68.3**
SV	38.9	61.2	64.3	**66.2**
AVG	40.2	51.3	56.0	**64.8**

Table 3: Directed dependency accuracy, on the universal treebanks with universal parts-of-speech, on sentences of length 10 or less. PR refers to posterior regularization, USR to universal rules.

6.1 Features

The features used in our unsupervised parser are based on the parts-of-speech of the head and the dependent of the corresponding dependency, and are given in Table 2. Following McDonald et al. (2005a), we also include features capturing the context of the head or the dependent. These features are trigrams and are formed by the parts-of-speech of the two tokens of the dependency and one of the word appearing before/after the head/dependent. Finally, all the features are conjoined with the signed distance between the two words of the dependency.

6.2 Dataset

We use the universal treebanks, version 2.0, introduced by McDonald et al. (2013). This dataset contains dependency trees for ten languages belonging to five different families: Spanish, French, Italian, Portuguese (Romanic family), English, German, Swedish (Germanic family), Korean, Japanese and Indonesian. The tokens of those treebanks are tagged using the universal part-of-speech tagset (Petrov et al., 2012). We focus on inducing dependency grammars using universal parts-of-speech, and will thus report results where all methods use (gold) universal POS.

6.3 Comparison with baselines

We will compare our approach to three other unsupervised parsers. Our first baseline is the DMV model, introduced by Klein and Manning (2004).

DMV	PR	USR	OUR
7 min	1 h	15 h	2 min

Table 4: Computational times required to learn a grammar on the English treebank.

Our second baseline is the extended valence grammar model, with posterior sparsity constraints, as described by Gillenwater et al. (2011). Finally, our last baseline is the model with universal rules introduced by Naseem et al. (2010). It should be noted that these two baselines obtain performances that are near state-of-the-art. All methods are trained and tested on sentences of length 10 or less, after stripping punctuation.

Parameter selection. All the parameters were chosen using the English development set. Our method has two parameters, determined as: $\lambda = 0.001$ and $\mu = 0.1$. We used $T = 200$ iterations in all the experiments.

Discussion. We report the results in Table 3. First, we observe that our method performs better than the three baselines on seven out of ten languages. Overall, our approach outperforms the three baselines, with an absolute improvement of 13 points over the extended valence grammar with posterior sparsity and 8 points over the model with universal syntactic rules. We also note that the inter-language variance is lower for our method than the baselines (std of 4.6 for our method v.s. 8.3 for USR and 12.7 for PR). For the sake of completeness, we also compared those methods using the fine grained POS available in the universal treebanks. Overall, our method obtains an accuracy of 68.4, while USR and PR achieve accuracies of 67.3 and 58.5 respectively. Finally, we report computational times in Table 4, showing that our approach is much faster than the baselines.

6.4 Non-projective grammar induction

In this section, we investigate non-projective grammar induction. With our approach, we only have to replace the Eisner algorithm by Chu-Liu/Edmonds. We report results in Table 5. First, we observe that the non-projective results are slightly worse than projective one. This is not really surprising since the amount of non-projective gold dependencies is very small on the considered data. Moreover, non-projective trees are much more ambiguous than projective ones, leading to

	PROJECTIVE	NON-PROJECTIVE
DE	60.2	57.2
EN	62.3	60.5
ES	68.8	66.5
FR	72.3	69.2
ID	69.7	68.4
IT	64.3	63.1
JA	57.5	59.3
KO	59.0	60.0
PT-BR	68.3	67.7
SV	66.2	65.4
AVG	64.8	63.7

Table 5: Comparison between projective and non-projective unsupervised dependency parsing using our method.

a harder problem. We still believe those results are interesting because the difference is small (less than 1.5 points), while non-projective parsing is computationaly more efficient.

6.5 Evaluation on longer sentences

We also evaluate our method on longer sentences (while still training on sentences of length 10 or less). Directed dependency accuracies are reported in Figure 4. On all sentences, our method achieve an overall accuracy of 55.8.

6.6 Feature ablation study

In this section, we study the importance of the different features used in our parser. We report directed accuracies when different groups of features are removed, one at a time, in Table 6. First, we remove the distance information from the features (line DISTANCE). We observe that the performance of our parser is greatly affected by this ablation, especially for long sentences. Then, we remove the context features (line CONTEXT) and the unigram features (line UNIGRAM) from our model. We observe that the performance decreases slightly due to this ablations, but the differences are small.

	$\|\mathbf{w}\| \leq 10$	$\|\mathbf{w}\| \leq \infty$
DISTANCE	61.8	48.7
CONTEXT	64.2	55.1
UNIGRAM	64.0	55.3
ALL FEATURES	**64.8**	**55.8**

Table 6: Feature ablation study.

7 Discussion

In this paper, we introduced a new framework for the task of unsupervised dependency parsing. Our method is a based on a feature-rich discriminative model, whose parameters are learned using a convex objective function. We demonstrated on the universal treebanks that our approach leads to competitive results, while being computationaly very efficient. We now describe some directions we would like to explore as future work.

Richer feature set. In our experiments, we focused on assessing the usefulness of our convex, discriminative approach, and thus considered only relatively simple features based on parts-of-speech. Inspired by supervised dependency parsing, we would like to explore the use of other features such as Brown clusters (Brown et al., 1992) or distributed word representations (Mikolov et al., 2013), in order to lexicalize our parser.

Higher-order parsing. So far, our model is lacking the notion of valency, that has proven very useful for grammar induction. In future work, we would thus like to replace our edge-based factorization by a higher-order one, in order to capture siblings (and grandchilds) interactions. We would then have to use a higher-order parser, such as the ones described by McDonald and Pereira (2006) and Koo and Collins (2010). Another potential approach would be to use the linear programming relaxed inference, described by Martins et al. (2009).

Transfer learning. In this paper, we used universal syntactic rules, as described by Naseem et al. (2010) to guide our parser. We would like to explore the use of weak supervision, such as the one considered in transfer learning (Hwa et al., 2005). For example, projected dependencies from a resource-rich language could be used as constraints in our framework.

Code. The code for our method is distributed on the first author webpage.

Acknowledgments

This work is supported by National Science Foundation award 1344668 and National Institute of General Medical Sciences award R01 GM090187.

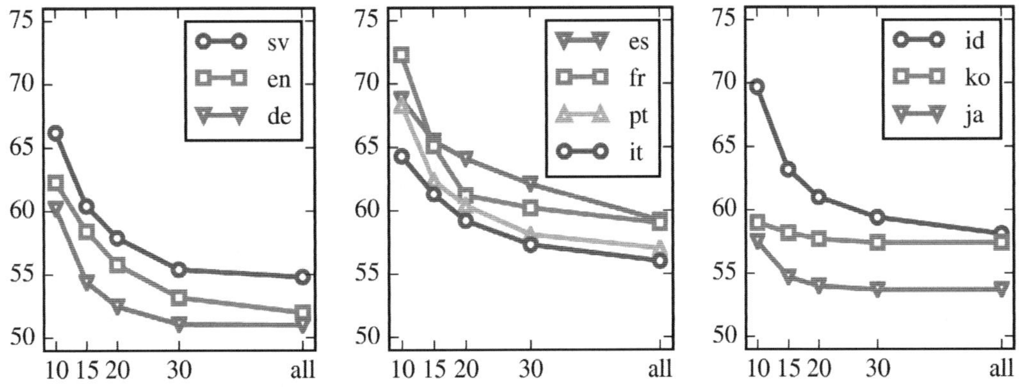

Figure 4: Directed dependency accuracies on longer sentences for our approach.

References

Francis R Bach and Zaïd Harchaoui. 2007. Diffrac: a discriminative and flexible framework for clustering. In *NIPS*.

Taylor Berg-Kirkpatrick and Dan Klein. 2010. Phylogenetic grammar induction. In *ACL*.

Yonatan Bisk and Julia Hockenmaier. 2013. An hdp model for inducing combinatory categorial grammars. *TACL*.

Phil Blunsom and Trevor Cohn. 2010. Unsupervised induction of tree substitution grammars for dependency parsing. In *EMNLP*.

Piotr Bojanowski, Rémi Lajugie, Francis Bach, Ivan Laptev, Jean Ponce, Cordelia Schmid, and Josef Sivic. 2014. Weakly supervised action labeling in videos under ordering constraints. In *ECCV*.

Piotr Bojanowski, Rémi Lagugie, Edouard Grave, Francis Bach, Ivan Laptev, Jean Ponce, and Cordelia Schmid. 2015. Weakly-supervised alignment of video with text. http://arxiv.org/abs/1505.06027.

Stephen Boyd and Lieven Vandenberghe. 2004. *Convex optimization*. Cambridge university press.

Peter F Brown, Peter V Desouza, Robert L Mercer, Vincent J Della Pietra, and Jenifer C Lai. 1992. Class-based n-gram models of natural language. *Computational linguistics*.

Yoeng-Jin Chu and Tseng-Hong Liu. 1965. On shortest arborescence of a directed graph. *Scientia Sinica*.

John Cocke and Jacob Schwartz. 1970. Programming languages and their compilers: Preliminary notes. Technical report.

Shay B Cohen and Noah A Smith. 2009. Shared logistic normal distributions for soft parameter tying in unsupervised grammar induction. In *NAACL*.

Jack Edmonds. 1967. Optimum branchings. *Journal of Research of the National Bureau of Standards*.

Jason M Eisner. 1996. Three new probabilistic models for dependency parsing: An exploration. In *COLING*.

Marguerite Frank and Philip Wolfe. 1956. An algorithm for quadratic programming. *Naval research logistics quarterly*.

Kuzman Ganchev, Joao Graça, Jennifer Gillenwater, and Ben Taskar. 2010. Posterior regularization for structured latent variable models. *JMLR*.

Jennifer Gillenwater, Kuzman Ganchev, João Graça, Fernando Pereira, and Ben Taskar. 2011. Posterior sparsity in unsupervised dependency parsing. *JMLR*.

Kevin Gimpel and Noah A Smith. 2012. Concavity and initialization for unsupervised dependency parsing. In *NAACL*.

Matthew R Gormley and Jason Eisner. 2013. Nonconvex global optimization for latent-variable models. In *ACL*.

Edouard Grave. 2014. A convex relaxation for weakly supervised relation extraction. In *EMNLP*.

William P Headden III, Mark Johnson, and David McClosky. 2009. Improving unsupervised dependency parsing with richer contexts and smoothing. In *NAACL*.

Daniel Hsu, Percy Liang, and Sham M Kakade. 2012. Identifiability and unmixing of latent parse trees. In *NIPS*.

Rebecca Hwa, Philip Resnik, Amy Weinberg, Clara Cabezas, and Okan Kolak. 2005. Bootstrapping parsers via syntactic projection across parallel texts. *Natural language engineering*.

Martin Jaggi. 2013. Revisiting frank-wolfe: Projection-free sparse convex optimization. In *ICML*.

Armand Joulin, Jean Ponce, and Francis R Bach. 2010. Efficient optimization for discriminative latent class models. In *NIPS*.

Armand Joulin, Kevin Tang, and Li Fei-Fei. 2014. Efficient image and video co-localization with frank-wolfe algorithm. In *ECCV*.

Tadao Kasami. 1965. An efficient recognition and syntax analysis algorithm for context-free languages. Technical report.

Dan Klein and Christopher D Manning. 2004. Corpus-based induction of syntactic structure: Models of dependency and constituency. In *ACL*.

Terry Koo and Michael Collins. 2010. Efficient third-order dependency parsers. In *ACL*.

David Mareček and Zdeněk Žabokrtský. 2012. Exploiting reducibility in unsupervised dependency parsing. In *EMNLP/CoNLL*.

André FT Martins, Noah A Smith, and Eric P Xing. 2009. Polyhedral outer approximations with application to natural language parsing. In *ICML*.

Ryan T McDonald and Fernando CN Pereira. 2006. Online learning of approximate dependency parsing algorithms. In *EACL*.

Ryan McDonald, Koby Crammer, and Fernando Pereira. 2005a. Online large-margin training of dependency parsers. In *ACL*.

Ryan McDonald, Fernando Pereira, Kiril Ribarov, and Jan Hajič. 2005b. Non-projective dependency parsing using spanning tree algorithms. In *EMNLP*.

Ryan T McDonald, Joakim Nivre, Yvonne Quirmbach-Brundage, Yoav Goldberg, Dipanjan Das, Kuzman Ganchev, Keith B Hall, Slav Petrov, Hao Zhang, Oscar Täckström, et al. 2013. Universal dependency annotation for multilingual parsing. In *ACL*.

Tomas Mikolov, Ilya Sutskever, Kai Chen, Greg S Corrado, and Jeff Dean. 2013. Distributed representations of words and phrases and their compositionality. In *Advances in Neural Information Processing Systems*.

Tahira Naseem, Harr Chen, Regina Barzilay, and Mark Johnson. 2010. Using universal linguistic knowledge to guide grammar induction. In *EMNLP*.

Ankur P Parikh, Shay B Cohen, and Eric P Xing. 2014. Spectral unsupervised parsing with additive tree metrics. In *ACL*.

Slav Petrov, Dipanjan Das, and Ryan McDonald. 2012. A universal part-of-speech tagset. *LREC*.

Vignesh Ramanathan, Armand Joulin, Percy Liang, and Li Fei-Fei. 2014. Linking people with "their" names using coreference resolution. In *ECCV*.

Noah A Smith and Jason Eisner. 2005. Guiding unsupervised grammar induction using contrastive estimation. In *Proc. of IJCAI Workshop on Grammatical Inference Applications*.

Valentin I Spitkovsky, Hiyan Alshawi, and Daniel Jurafsky. 2010a. From baby steps to leapfrog: How less is more in unsupervised dependency parsing. In *NAACL*.

Valentin I Spitkovsky, Hiyan Alshawi, Daniel Jurafsky, and Christopher D Manning. 2010b. Viterbi training improves unsupervised dependency parsing. In *CoNLL*.

Valentin I Spitkovsky, Hiyan Alshawi, and Daniel Jurafsky. 2013. Breaking out of local optima with count transforms and model recombination: A study in grammar induction. In *EMNLP*.

Robert Endre Tarjan. 1977. Finding optimum branchings. *Networks*.

Linli Xu, James Neufeld, Bryce Larson, and Dale Schuurmans. 2004. Maximum margin clustering. In *NIPS*.

Daniel H Younger. 1967. Recognition and parsing of context-free languages in time n^3. *Information and control*.

Parse Imputation for Dependency Annotations

Jason Mielens[1] **Liang Sun**[2] **Jason Baldridge**[1]

[1]Department of Linguistics
The University of Texas at Austin
{jmielens,jbaldrid}@utexas.edu

[2]Department of Mechanical Engineering
The University of Texas at Austin
sally722@utexas.edu

Abstract

Syntactic annotation is a hard task, but it can be made easier by allowing annotators flexibility to leave aspects of a sentence underspecified. Unfortunately, partial annotations are not typically directly usable for training parsers. We describe a method for imputing missing dependencies from sentences that have been partially annotated using the Graph Fragment Language, such that a standard dependency parser can then be trained on all annotations. We show that this strategy improves performance over not using partial annotations for English, Chinese, Portuguese and Kinyarwanda, and that performance competitive with state-of-the-art unsupervised and weakly-supervised parsers can be reached with just a few hours of annotation.

1 Introduction

Linguistically annotated data is produced for many purposes in many contexts. It typically requires considerable effort, particularly for language documentation efforts in which tooling, data, and expertise in the language are scarce. The challenge presented by this scarcity is compounded when doing deeper analysis, such as syntactic structure, which typically requires greater expertise and existing tooling. In such scenarios, unsupervised approaches are a tempting strategy. While the performance of unsupervised dependency parsing has improved greatly since Klein and Manning's (2004) Dependency Model with Valence (DMV), state-of-the-art unsupervised parsers still perform well below supervised approaches (Martins et al., 2010; Spitkovsky et al., 2012; Blunsom and Cohn, 2010). Additionally, they typically require large amounts of raw data. While this is not a problem for some languages, many of the world's languages do not have a clean, digitized corpus available.[1] For instance, the approach of Naseem et al. (2010) is unsupervised in the sense that it requires no dependency annotations, but it still makes use of the raw version of the full Penn Treebank. The approach of Marecek et al. (2013) requires extra unlabeled texts to estimate parameters.

Another strategy is to exploit small amounts of supervision or knowledge. Naseem et al. (2010) use a set of universal dependency rules and obtain substantial gains over unsupervised methods in many languages. Spitkovsky et al. (2010b; 2011) use web mark-up and punctuation as additional annotations. Alternatively, one could try to obtain actual dependency annotations cheaply. We use the Graph Fragment Language (GFL), which was created with the goal of making annotations easier for experts and possible for novices (Schneider et al., 2013; Mordowanec et al., 2014). GFL supports partial annotations, so annotators can omit obvious dependencies or skip difficult constructions. The ability to focus on portions of a sentence frees the annotator to target constituents and dependencies that maximize information that will be most useful for machine-learned parsers. For example, Hwa (1999) found higher-level sentence constituents to be more informative for learning parsers than lower-level ones.

To support this style of annotation while getting the benefit from partial annotations, we develop a two-stage parser learning strategy. The first stage completes the partial GFL annotations by adapting a Gibbs tree sampler (Johnson et al., 2007; Sun et al., 2014). The GFL annotations constrain the tree sampling space by using both dependencies and the constituent boundaries they express. The system performs missing dependency arc imputation using Gibbs sampling – we refer to this approach

[1]In fact, standardized writing systems have yet to be adopted for some languages.

Proceedings of the 53rd Annual Meeting of the Association for Computational Linguistics and the 7th International Joint Conference on Natural Language Processing, pages 1385–1394,
Beijing, China, July 26-31, 2015.

as the Gibbs Parse Completer[2] (GPC). The second stage uses the full dependencies output by the GPC to train Turbo Parser (Martins et al., 2010), and evaluation is done with this trained model on unseen sentences. In simulation experiments for English, Chinese and Portuguese, we show that the method gracefully degrades when applied to training corpora with increasing percentages of the gold training dependencies removed. We also do actual GFL annotations for those languages plus Kinyarwanda, and show that using the GPC to fill in the missing dependencies after two hours of annotation enables Turbo Parser to obtain 2-6% better absolute performance than when it has to throw incomplete annotations out. Furthermore, the gains are even greater with less annotation time and it never hurts to use the GPC—so an annotation project can pursue a partial annotation strategy without undermining the utility of the work for parser training.

This strategy has the further benefit of needing only a small number of sentences—in our case, under 100 sentences annotated in a 2-4 hour window. Furthermore, it relies on no outside tools or corpora other than a part-of-speech tagger; a resource that can be built with two hours of annotation time (Garrette and Baldridge, 2013).

2 Data

Data sources We use four languages from three language families in an effort to both verify the cross-linguistic applicability of our approach, accounting for variations in linguistic properties, as well as to attempt to realistically simulate a real-world, low-resource environment. Our data comes from English (ENG), Chinese (CHI), Portuguese (POR), and Kinyarwanda (KIN).

For ENG we use the Penn Treebank (Marcus et al., 1993), converted into dependencies by the standard process. Section 23 was used as a test set, and a random sample of sentences from sections 02-21 were selected for annotation with GFL as described below and subsequently used as the minimal training set. For CHI we use the Chinese Treebank (CTB5) (Xue et al., 2005), also converted to dependencies. The testing set consisted of files 1-40/900-931, and the sentences presented for GFL annotation were randomly sampled from files 81-899. The POR data is from

[2]The software, instructions, and data are available at http://www.github.com/jmielens/gpc-acl-2015

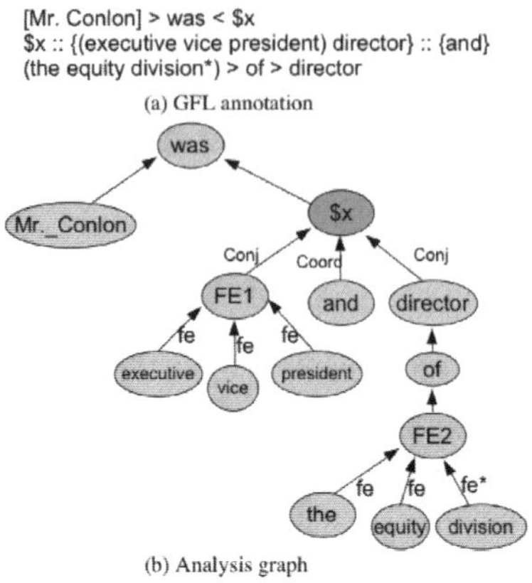

Figure 1: GFL example for *Mr. Conlon was executive vice president and director of the equity division.*

the CoNLL-X Shared Task on Multilingual Dependency Parsing and is derived from the Bosque portion of the Floresta sintá(c)tica corpus (Afonso et al., 2002), using the standard provided splits for training and testing. The KIN data is a corpus consisting of transcripts of testimonies by survivors of the Rwandan genocide, provided by the Kigali Genocide Memorial Center – this data is described by Garrette and Baldridge (2013).

GFL annotation We use a small number of sentences annotated using the Graph Fragment Language (GFL), a simple ASCII markup language for dependency grammar (Schneider et al., 2013). Unlike traditional syntactic annotation strategies requiring trained annotators and great effort, rapid GFL annotations can be collected from annotators who have minimal training. Kong et al. (2014) demonstrate the feasibility of training a dependency parser based on a GFL-annotated corpus of English tweets.

An example of GFL is shown in Figure 1: (a) is the GFL markup itself and (b) is a graphical representation of the dependencies it encodes. Figure 1 specifies several dependencies: *of* is a dependent of *director*, *executive vice president* and *director* are conjuncts and *and* is the coordinator. However, the complete internal structure of the phrase *the equity division* remains unspecified, other than *division* being marked as the head (via an asterisk).[3] Finally, *Mr. Conlon* in square brackets indicates it is a multiword expression.

[3]The graphical representation shows both of these as FE nodes, for *fudge expression*, indicating they are grouped together but otherwise underspecified.

CFG Rule	EVG distribution	Description
$S \rightarrow Y_H$	$P(root = H)$	The head of the sentence is H
$Y_H \rightarrow L_H R_H$	-	Split-head representation
$L_H \rightarrow H_L$	$P(STOP \mid dir = L, head = H, val = 0)$	H has no left children
$L_H \rightarrow L_H^1$	$P(CONT \mid dir = L, head = H, val = 0)$	H has at least one left child
$L'_H \rightarrow H_L$	$P(STOP \mid dir = L, head = H, val = 1)$	H has no more left children
$L'_H \rightarrow L_H^1$	$P(CONT \mid dir = L, head = H, val = 1)$	H has other left children
$L_H^1 \rightarrow Y_A L'_H$	$P(ArgA \mid dir = L, head = H, val = 1)$	A is a left child of H

Table 1: The CFG-DMV grammar schema from Klein and Manning (2004). Note that in these rules H and A are parts-of-speech. For brevity, we omit the portion of the grammar that handles the right-hand arguments since they are symmetric to the left. Valency (val) can take the value 1 (we have made attachments in the direction (dir) d) or 0 (not).

	CHI	ENG	KIN	POR
Sentences Annotated	24	34	69	63
Tokens Annotated	820	798	988	1067
Fully Specified Sentences	4	15	31	20

Table 2: Two Hour GFL Annotation Statistics

Kong et al. (2014) stipulate that the GFL annotations in their corpus must be fully-specified. They are thus unable to take advantage of such underspecified sentences, and we address that limitation in this paper. From the GFL annotations we can extract and deduce dependency arcs and constraints (see Section 3.2 for full details) in order to guide the Gibbs sampling process.

Time-bounded annotation As described in Section 1, a primary goal of this work was to consider the time in which a useful number of dependency tree annotations might be collected, such as might be required during the initial phase of a language documentation project or corpus build. To this end our annotators were operating under a strict two hour time limit. We also collected two further hours for English.

The annotators were instructed to annotate as many sentences as possible in the two hours, and that they should liberally use underspecification, especially for particularly difficult sequences in a given sentence. This was done to facilitate the availability of partial annotations for experimentation. All of the annotators had some previous experience providing GFL annotations, so no training period was needed. Annotation was done in 30-minute blocks, to provide short breaks for the annotators and so that learning curves could be generated. Each language was annotated by a single annotator. The ENG and CHI annotators were native speakers of their annotation language, while the POR and KIN annotators were non-native though proficient speakers.

The annotators achieved rates of 400-500 tokens/hr, whereas we find rates of 150-200 tokens/hr more typical when annotators are asked to fully specify. Requiring full specification also introduces more errors in cases of annotator uncertainty.

Table 2 shows the size of the GFL corpora that were created. Typically, over 50% of the sentences were not fully specified—the partial annotations provided in these are useless to Turbo Parser unless the missing dependencies are imputed.

3 Gibbs Parse Completer (GPC)

3.1 Gibbs sampler for CFG-DMV Model

CFG-DMV model The GPC is based on the DMV model, a generative model for the unsupervised learning of dependency structures (Klein and Manning, 2004). We denote the input corpus as $\boldsymbol{\omega} = (\boldsymbol{\omega^1}, \cdots, \boldsymbol{\omega^N})$, where each $\boldsymbol{\omega^s}$ is a sentence consisting of words and in a sentence $\boldsymbol{\omega}$, word ω_i has an corresponding part-of-speech tag τ_i. We denote the set of all words as V_ω and the set of all parts-of-speech as V_τ. We use the part-of-speech sequence as our terminal strings, resulting in an unlexicalized grammar. Dependencies can be formulated as split head bilexical context free grammars (CFGs) (Eisner and Satta, 1999) and these bilexical CFGs require that each terminal τ_i in sentence $\boldsymbol{\omega}$ is represented in a split form by two terminals, with labels marking the left and right heads ($\tau_{i,L}$, $\tau_{i,R}$). Henceforth, we denote $\boldsymbol{w} = w_{0,n}$ as our terminals in the split-form of sentence $\boldsymbol{\omega}$ (e.g., the terminals for *the dog walks* are $DT_L\ DT_R\ NN_L\ NN_R\ V_L\ V_R$). Table 1 shows the grammar rules for the DMV model, from Klein and Manning (2004).

Require: A is parent node of binary rule; $w_{i,k}$ is a valid span of terminals and $i+1<k$
function TREESAMPLER(A, i, k)
  for $i<j<k$ and pair of child nodes of A:B, C **do**
    $P(j,B,C) = \frac{\theta^w_{A\to BC} c(i,j) c(j,k) \cdot p_{B,i,j} \cdot p_{C,j,k}}{p_{A,i,k}}$
  end for Sample $j*, B*, C*$ from multinomial distribution for (j,B,C) with probabilities calculated above
  return $j*, B*, C*$
end function

Algorithm 1: Sampling split position and rule to expand parent node.

Gibbs sampler The split-head representation encodes dependencies as a CFG. This enables the use of a Gibbs sampler algorithm for estimating PCFGs (Johnson et al., 2007; Sun et al., 2014), and it is straightforward to incorporate constraints from partial annotations into this sampler. To do this, we modified the tree-sampling step to incorporate constraints derived from GFL annotations and thereby impute the missing dependencies.

Given a string $\boldsymbol{w} = (w_1, \cdots w_n)$, we define a span of $\boldsymbol{w}$ as $w_{i,k} = (w_{i+1}, \cdots, w_k)$, so that $\boldsymbol{w} = w_{0,n}$. As introduced in Pereira and Schabes (1992), a bracketing $\mathcal{B}$ of $\boldsymbol{w}$ is a finite set of spans on $\boldsymbol{w}$ satisfying the requirement that no two spans in a bracketing may overlap unless one span contains the other. For each sentence $\boldsymbol{w} = w_{0,n}$ we define the auxiliary function for each span $w_{i,j}$, $0 \le i < j \le n$:

$$c(i,j) = \begin{cases} 1 & \text{if span } w_{i,j} \text{ is valid for } \mathcal{B}; \\ 0 & \text{otherwise.} \end{cases}$$

Here one span is valid for $\mathcal{B}$ if it doesn't cross any brackets. Section 3.2 describes how to derive bracketing information from GFL annotations and how to determine if a span $w_{i,j}$ is valid or not. Note that for parsing a corpus without any annotations and constraints, $c(i,j) = 1$ for any span, and the algorithm is equivalent to the Gibbs sampler in Sun et al. (2014).

There are two parts to the tree-sampling. The first constructs an inside table as in the Inside-Outside algorithm for PCFGs and the second selects the tree by recursively sampling productions from top to bottom. Consider a sentence $\boldsymbol{w}$, with sub-spans $w_{i,k} = (w_{i+1}, \cdots, w_k)$. Given θ^w (modified rule probabilities θ given constraints of sentence $\boldsymbol{w}$, see Section 3.2), we construct the inside table with entries $p_{A,i,k}$ for each nonterminal and each span $w_{i,k}$: $0 \le i < k \le n$. We introduce

Require: $Arcs$ is the set of all directed arcs extracted from annotation for sentence $\boldsymbol{w}$
function RULEPROB-SENT($\boldsymbol{w}, \theta, Arcs$)
  $\theta^w = \theta$
  for each directed arc $w_i < w_j$ **do**
    if $i<j$ **then**
      for nonterminal A $\neq L_{\tau_j}$ **do**
        $\theta^w_{A\to\beta} = 0$ if β contains Y_{τ_i}
      end for
    else
      for nonterminal A $\neq R_{\tau_j}$ **do**
        $\theta^w_{A\to\beta} = 0$ if β contains Y_{τ_i}
      end for
    end if
  end for
  return θ^w
end function

Algorithm 2: Modifying Rule Probabilities for w to ensure parse tree contains all directed arcs.

$c(i,j)$ into the calculation of inside probabilities:

$$p_{A,i,k} = c(i,k) \cdot \sum_{A\to BC\in R} \sum_{i<j<k} \theta^w_{A\to BC} \cdot p_{B,i,j} \cdot p_{C,j,k} \quad (1)$$

Here, $p_{A,i,k} = P_{G_A}(w_{i,k} \mid \theta^w)$ is the probability that terminals i through k were produced by the non-terminal A, $A \to BC \in R$ are possible rules to expand A. The inside table is computed recursively using Equation 1.

The resulting inside probabilities are then used to generate trees from the distribution of all valid trees of the sentence. The tree is generated from top to bottom recursively with the function $TreeSampler$ defined in Algorithm 1, which introduces $c(i,j)$ into the sampling function from Sun et al. (2014).

3.2 Constraints derived from GFL

We exploit one dependency constraint and two constituency constraints from partial GFL annotations.

Dependency rule Directed arcs are indicated with angle brackets pointing from the dependent to its head, e.g. *black > cat*. Once we have a directed arc annotation, say $\omega_i > \omega_j$, if $i<j$, which means word j has a left child, we must have rule $L^1_{\tau_j} \to Y_{\tau_i} L'_{\tau_j}$ in our parse tree (similarly if $i>j$, we have $R^1_{\tau_j} \to R'_{\tau_j} Y_{\tau_i}$ in our parse tree), where τ_i, τ_j are parts-of-speech for ω_i and ω_j. We enforce this by modifying the rule probabilities for sample sentence $\boldsymbol{w}$ to ensure that any sampled tree contains all specified arcs.

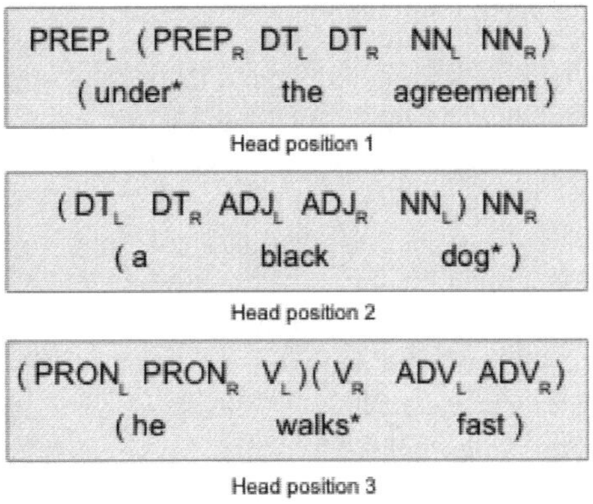

Figure 2: Generating brackets for known head

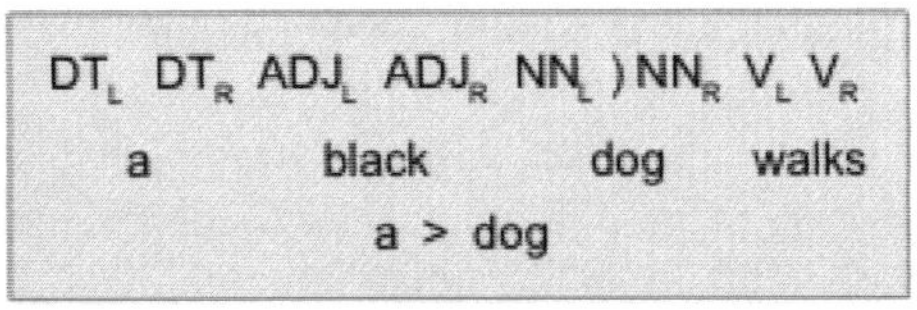

Figure 3: Generating half brackets

Brackets GFL allows annotators to group words with parenthesis, which provides an explicit indicator of constituent brackets. Even when the internal structure is left underspecified (e.g. *(the equity division*) in Figure 1 (a)*, the head is usually marked with *, and we can use this to infer sub-constituents. Given such a set of parentheses and the words inside them, we generate brackets over the split-head representations of their parts-of-speech, based on possible positions of the head. Figure 2 shows how to generate brackets for three situations: the head is the leftmost word, rightmost word, or is in a medial position. For example, the first annotation indicates that *under* is the head of *under the agreement*, and the rest of words are right descendants of *under*. This leads to the bracketing shown over the split-heads.

Half brackets We can also derive one-sided half brackets from dependency arcs by assuming that dependencies are projective. For example, in Figure 3, the annotation $a > dog$ specifies that *dog* has a left child *a*, so we know that there is a right bracket before the right-head of *dog*. Thus, we can detect invalid spans using the half brackets; if a span starts after *a* and ends after *dog*, this span is invalid because it would result in crossing brackets. This half bracketing is a unique advantage provided by the split-head representation. The details of this algorithm are shown in Algorithm 3.

Require: $Arcs$ is the set of all directed arcs extracted for sentence, $w_{a,b}$ is a span to detect
function DETECTINVALIDSPAN($a, b, Arcs$)
  for each directed arc $\omega_i < \omega_j$ **do**
    if $i < j$ **then**
      if $a < 2i - 1 < b < 2j$ **then**
        $c(a, b) = 0$
      end if
    else
      if $2j - 2 < a < 2i - 1 < b$ **then**
        $c(i, j) = 0$
      end if
    end if
  end for
  return $c(a, b)$
end function

Algorithm 3: Detect whether one span is invalid given all directed arcs.

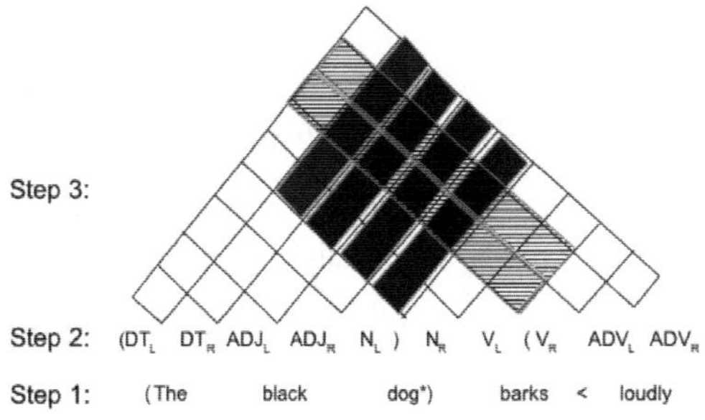

Figure 4: Process of generating brackets and detecting invalid spans.

We use both half bracket and full bracket information, $\mathcal{B}$, to determine whether a span is valid. We set $c(i, j) = 0$ for all spans over $\boldsymbol{w}$ detected by Algorithm 3 and violating $\mathcal{B}$. Then, in the sampling scheme, we'll only sample parse trees that satisfy these underlying constraints.

Figure 4 shows the resulting blocked out spans in the chart based on both types of brackets for the given partial annotation, which is Step 1 of the process. *The black dog* is a constituent with *dog* marked as its head, so we generate a full bracket over the terminal string in Step 2. Also, *barks* has a right child *loudly*; this generates a half bracket before V_R. In Step 3, the chart in Figure 4 represents all spans over terminal symbols. The cells in black are invalid spans based on the full bracket, and the hatched cells are invalid spans based on the half bracket.

4 Results

Experiments There are two points of variation to consider in empirical evaluations of our ap-

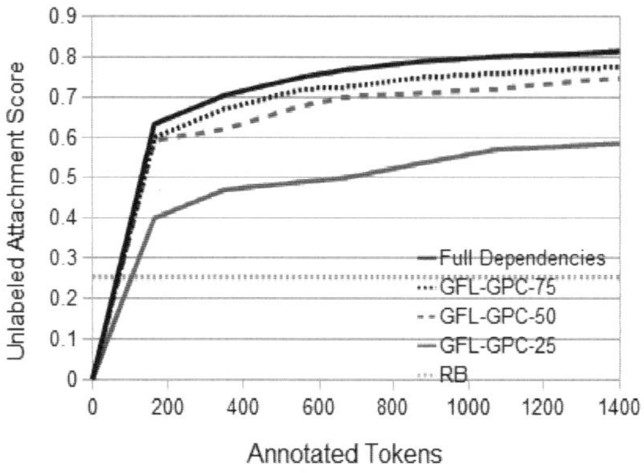

Figure 5: English oracle and degradation results

Language	ENG	CHI	POR
RB	25.0	11.6	27.0
GFL-GPC-25	58.7	33.5	60.2
GFL-GPC-50	75.0	46.1	71.4
GFL-GPC-75	77.8	50.1	73.7
Full	81.6	56.2	78.1

Table 3: Results with simulated partial annotations, GFL-GPC-X indicates X percent of dependencies were retained.

proach. The first is the effectiveness of the GPC in imputing missing dependencies and the second is the effectiveness of the GFL annotations themselves. Of particular note with respect to the latter is the reasonable likelihood of divergence between the annotator and the corpus used for evaluation—for example, how coordination is handled and whether subordinate verbs are dependents or heads of auxiliary verbs. To this end, we perform simulation experiments that remove increasing portions of gold dependencies from a training corpus to understand imputation performance and annotation experiments to evaluate the entire pipeline in a realistically constrained annotation effort.

In that regard, one thing to consider are the part-of-speech tags used by the unlexicalized GPC. These do not come for free, so rather than ask annotators to provide them, the raw sentences to be annotated were tagged automatically. For English and Kinyarwanda, we used taggers trained with resources built in under two hours (Garrette and Baldridge, 2013), so these results are actually constrained to the GFL annotation time plus two hours. Such taggers were not available for Chinese or Portuguese, so the Stanford tagger (Toutanova et al., 2003) was used instead.

After imputing missing dependencies, the GPC outputs fully sentences that are used to train TurboParser (Martins et al., 2010). In all cases, we compare to a right-branching baseline (RB). Although comparing to a random baseline is more typical of imputation experiments, a right-branching baseline provides a stronger initial comparison. For the GFL annotation experiments, we use two additional baselines. The first is simply to use the sentences with full annotations and drop any incomplete ones (GFL-DROP). The second is to make any partial annotations usable by assuming a right-branching completion (GFL-RBC).

Simulated partial annotations Figure 5 shows the learning curve with respect to number of annotated tokens when retaining 100%, 75%, 50% and 25% of gold-standard training dependencies and using the GPC to impute the removed ones. With both 75% and 50% retained, performance degrades gracefully. It is substantially lower for 25%, but the curve is steeper than the others, indicating it is on track to catch up. Nonetheless, one recommendation from these results is that it probably makes sense to start with a small number of fully annotated sentences and then start mixing in partially annotated ones.

Table 3 shows the attachment scores obtained for English, Chinese, and Portuguese with varying proportions of dependencies removed for the GPC to impute.[4] English and Portuguese hold up well with 75% and 50% retained, while Chinese drops more precipitously, and 25% leads to substantial reductions in performance for all.

Note that these simulations indicate that, given an equivalent number of total annotated arcs, using the GPC is more beneficial than requiring annotators to fully specify annotations. Imputing fifty percent of the dependency arcs from sentences containing 1000 tokens is typically more effective by a few points than using the full gold-standard arcs from sentences containing 500 tokens. Actually, this simulation is too generous to complete annotations in that it leaves out consideration of the time and effort required to obtain those 100% full gold-standard arcs: it is often a small part of a sentence that consumes the most effort when full annotation is required. Additionally, these simulation experiments randomly removed dependencies while humans tend to annotate higher-level con-

[4]These are based on the same sentences used in the next section's GFL annotation experiments for each language.

Eval Length	< 10	< 20	all
GFL-DROP (4hr)	54.5	55.0	52.6
GFL-GPC (4hr)	60.1	**61.8**	55.1
Blunsom and Cohn, 2010	67.7	–	**55.7**
Naseem et al., 2010	**71.9**	50.4	–

Table 4: English results compared to previous unsupervised and weakly-supervised methods.

Language	KIN	CHI	POR
RB	52.6	11.6	27.0
GFL-DROP (2hr)	64.4	36.7	59.8
GFL-GPC (2hr)	64.5	38.8	65.0

Table 5: Non-English results summary

stituents and leave internal structure (e.g. of noun phrases) underspecified. Given Hwa's (1999) findings, we expect non-random partial annotations to better serve as a basis for imputation.

GFL annotations We conducted three sets of experiments with GFL annotations, evaluating on sentences of all lengths, less than 10 words, and less than 20 words. This was done to determine the types of sentences that our method works best on and to compare to previous work that evaluates on sentences of different lengths.

Table 4 shows how our results on ENG compare to others. Blunsom and Cohn (2010) represent state-of-the-art unsupervised results for all lengths, while Naseem et al. (2010) was chosen as a previous weakly-supervised approach. GFL-GPC achieves similar results on the 'all lengths' criterion as Blunsom and Cohn and substantially outperforms Naseem et al. on sentences less than 20 words. Our poor performance on short sentences is slightly surprising, and may result from an uneven length distribution in the sentences selected for annotation—we have only 3 training sentences less than 10 words—as discussed by Spitkovsky et al. (2010a). To correct this problem, both long and short sentences should be included to construct a more representative sample for annotation.

We did not expect GFL-RBC to perform so similarly to RB. It is possible that the relatively large number of under-specified sentences led to the right-branching quality of GFL-RBC dominating, rather than the more informative GFL annotations.

The results of the ENG annotation session can be seen in Figure 6a. GFL-GPC is quite strong even at thirty minutes, with only seven sentences annotated. GFL-DROP picks up substantially at the end; this may be in part explained by the fact that the last block contained many short sentences, which provide greater marginal benefit to GFL-DROP than to GFL-GPC.

The learning curves for the other languages can be seen in Figures 6b-6d, with a summary available in Table 5. Like ENG, CHI and POR both show clear wins for the GPC strategy. Of particular note is that the CHI annotations contained many fewer fully-completed sentences (4) than the ENG annotations (15). This somewhat addresses the question raised by the 25% retention simulation experiments—the GPC method improves results over dropping partial annotations. The POR results show a consistent strong win for GPC throughout.

The KIN results in Figure 6c exhibit a pattern unlike the other languages; specifically, the KIN data has a very high right-branching baseline (RB in figures) and responds nearly identically for all of the more informed methods. Upon investigation, this appears to be an artifact of the data used in KIN evaluation plus domain adaptation issues. The gold data consists of transcribed natural speech, whereas the training data consists of sentences extracted from the Kinyarwanda Wikipedia.

All of the learning curves display a large initial jump after the first round of annotations. This is encouraging for approaches that use annotated sentences: just a small number of examples provide tremendous benefit, regardless of the strategy employed.

Error analysis The primary errors seen on an analysis of the GPC-completed sentences varies somewhat between languages. The ENG data contains many short sentences, consisting often of a few words and a punctuation mark. Part of the GFL convention is that the annotator is free to annotate punctuation as part of the sentence or instead view it as extra-linguistic and drop the punctuation from the annotation. Often the punctuation in the ENG data went unannotated, with the result being that the final parse model is not particularly good at handling these types of sentences when encountered in the test set.

Specific constructions like coordination and possession also suffer a similar issue in that annotators (and corpora) varied slightly on how they were handled. Thus, some languages like CHI contained many of a particular type of error due to mismatches in the conventions of the annotator and corpus. Issues like this could have been avoided by a longer training period prior to anno-

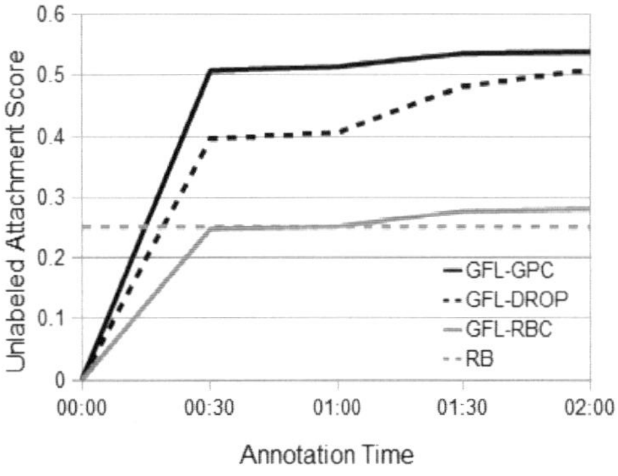

(a) English

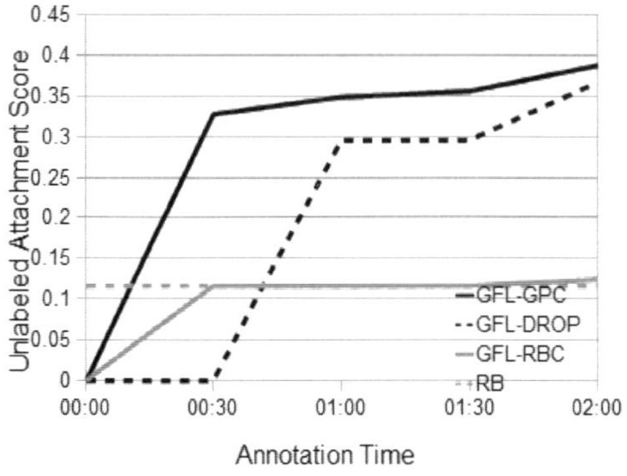

(b) Chinese

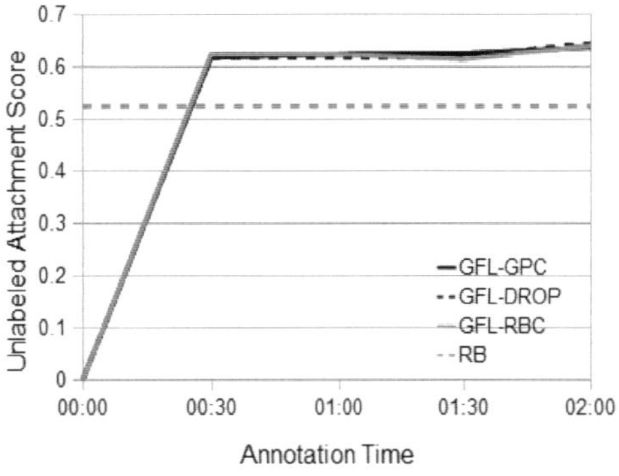

(c) Kinyarwanda

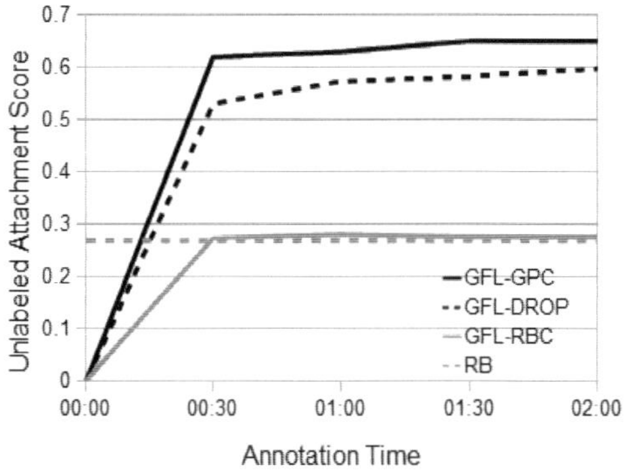

(d) Portuguese

Figure 6: GPC results by annotation time for eval sentences of all lengths.

tation, although were this a real annotation project, there would be no existing corpus to compare to at first. This brings up a more basic question of evaluation - one of usability versus representational norm matching. It is likely that the GFL annotations (and thus the models trained on them) diverge from the gold standard in what amount to annotation conventions rather than substantive linguistic divergences. To evaluate more fully or fairly, we would need test sets produced by the same set of annotators or an external, task-based evaluation that uses the dependencies as in input.

5 Conclusions

We have described a modeling strategy that takes advantage of a Gibbs sampling algorithm for CFG parsing plus constraints obtained from partial annotations to build dependency parsers. This strategy's performance improves on that of a parser built only on the available complete annotations. In doing so, our approach supports annotation efforts that use GFL to obtain guidance from non-expert human annotators and allow any annotator to put in less effort than they would to do complete annotations.

We find that a remarkably small amount of supervised data can rival existing unsupervised methods. While unsupervised methods have been considered an attractive option for low-resource parsing, they typically rely on large quantities of clean, raw sentences. Our method uses less than one hundred sentences, so in a truly low-resource scenario, it has the potential to require much less total effort. For instance, a single native speaker could easily both generate and annotate the sentences required for our method in a few hours, while the many thousands of raw sentences needed for state-of-the-art unsupervised methods could take much longer to assemble if there is no existing corpus. This also means our method would be useful for getting in-domain training data for domain adaptation for parsers.

Finally, our method has the ability to encode both universal grammar and test-language grammar as a prior. This would be done by replacing the uniform prior used in this paper with a prior favoring those grammar rules during the updating-rule-probabilities phase of the GPC, and would essentially have the effect of weighting those grammar rules.

Acknowledgments

This work was supported in part by the U. S. Army Research Laboratory and the U. S. Army Research Office under contract/grant number W911NF-10-1-0533

References

S. Afonso, E. Bick, R. Haber, and D. Santos. 2002. "Floresta sintá(c)tica": a Treebank for Portuguese. In *Proceedings of the 3rd International Conference on Language Resources and Evaluation (LREC)*, pages 1698–1703. LREC.

Phil Blunsom and Trevor Cohn. 2010. Unsupervised induction of tree substitution grammars for dependency parsing. In *Proceedings of the 2010 Conference on Empirical Methods in Natural Language Processing*, pages 1204–1213. Association for Computational Linguistics.

Jason Eisner and Giorgio Satta. 1999. Efficient parsing for bilexical context-free grammars and head automaton grammars. In *Proceedings of the 37th annual meeting of the Association for Computational Linguistics on Computational Linguistics*, pages 457–464. Association for Computational Linguistics.

Dan Garrette and Jason Baldridge. 2013. Learning a part-of-speech tagger from two hours of annotation. In *HLT-NAACL*, pages 138–147. Citeseer.

Rebecca Hwa. 1999. Supervised grammar induction using training data with limited constituent information. In *Proceedings of the 37th annual meeting of the Association for Computational Linguistics on Computational Linguistics*, pages 73–79. Association for Computational Linguistics.

Mark Johnson, Thomas L Griffiths, and Sharon Goldwater. 2007. Bayesian inference for PCFGs via Markov chain Monte Carlo. In *Human Language Technologies 2007: The Conference of the North American Chapter of the Association for Computational Linguistics*, pages 139–146.

Dan Klein and Christopher D Manning. 2004. Corpus-based induction of syntactic structure: Models of dependency and constituency. In *Proceedings of the 42nd Annual Meeting on Association for Computational Linguistics*, page 478. Association for Computational Linguistics.

Lingpeng Kong, Nathan Schneider, Swabha Swayamdipta, Archna Bhatia, Chris Dyer, and Noah A Smith. 2014. A dependency parser for tweets. In *Proceedings of the Conference on Empirical Methods in Natural Language Processing, Doha, Qatar, to appear*.

Mitchell P Marcus, Mary Ann Marcinkiewicz, and Beatrice Santorini. 1993. Building a large annotated corpus of English: The Penn Treebank. *Computational linguistics*, 19(2):313–330.

David Marecek and Milan Straka. 2013. Stop-probability estimates computed on a large corpus improve unsupervised dependency parsing. In *ACL (1)*, pages 281–290.

André FT Martins, Noah A Smith, Eric P Xing, Pedro MQ Aguiar, and Mário AT Figueiredo. 2010. Turbo parsers: Dependency parsing by approximate variational inference. In *Proceedings of the 2010 Conference on Empirical Methods in Natural Language Processing*, pages 34–44. Association for Computational Linguistics.

Michael T. Mordowanec, Nathan Schneider, Chris Dyer, and Noah A Smith. 2014. Simplified dependency annotations with GFL-Web. *ACL 2014*, page 121.

Tahira Naseem, Harr Chen, Regina Barzilay, and Mark Johnson. 2010. Using universal linguistic knowledge to guide grammar induction. In *Proceedings of the 2010 Conference on Empirical Methods in Natural Language Processing*, pages 1234–1244. Association for Computational Linguistics.

Fernando Pereira and Yves Schabes. 1992. Inside-outside reestimation from partially bracketed corpora. In *Proceedings of the 30th annual meeting on Association for Computational Linguistics*, pages 128–135. Association for Computational Linguistics.

Nathan Schneider, Brendan OConnor, Naomi Saphra, David Bamman, Manaal Faruqui, Noah A Smith, Chris Dyer, and Jason Baldridge. 2013. A framework for (under) specifying dependency syntax without overloading annotators. *LAW VII & ID*, page 51.

Valentin I Spitkovsky, Hiyan Alshawi, and Daniel Jurafsky. 2010a. From baby steps to leapfrog: How less is more in unsupervised dependency parsing. In *Human Language Technologies: The 2010 Annual Conference of the North American Chapter of the Association for Computational Linguistics*, pages 751–759. Association for Computational Linguistics.

Valentin I Spitkovsky, Daniel Jurafsky, and Hiyan Alshawi. 2010b. Profiting from mark-up: Hyper-text annotations for guided parsing. In *Proceedings of the 48th Annual Meeting of the Association for Computational Linguistics*, pages 1278–1287. Association for Computational Linguistics.

Valentin I Spitkovsky, Hiyan Alshawi, and Daniel Jurafsky. 2011. Punctuation: Making a point in unsupervised dependency parsing. In *Proceedings of the Fifteenth Conference on Computational Natural Language Learning*, pages 19–28. Association for Computational Linguistics.

Valentin I Spitkovsky, Hiyan Alshawi, and Daniel Jurafsky. 2012. Three dependency-and-boundary models for grammar induction. In *Proceedings of the 2012 Joint Conference on Empirical Methods in Natural Language Processing and Computational Natural Language Learning*, pages 688–698. Association for Computational Linguistics.

Liang Sun, Jason Mielens, and Jason Baldridge. 2014. Parsing low-resource languages using Gibbs sampling for PCFGs with latent annotations. In *Proceedings of the 2014 Conference on Empirical Methods in Natural Language Processing*. Association for Computational Linguistics.

Kristina Toutanova, Dan Klein, Christopher D Manning, and Yoram Singer. 2003. Feature-rich part-of-speech tagging with a cyclic dependency network. In *Proceedings of the 2003 Conference of the North American Chapter of the Association for Computational Linguistics on Human Language Technology-Volume 1*, pages 173–180. Association for Computational Linguistics.

Naiwen Xue, Fei Xia, Fu-Dong Chiou, and Marta Palmer. 2005. The Penn Chinese TreeBank: Phrase structure annotation of a large corpus. *Natural language engineering*, 11(02):207–238.

Probing the Linguistic Strengths and Limitations of Unsupervised Grammar Induction

Yonatan Bisk and **Julia Hockenmaier**
Department of Computer Science
The University of Illinois at Urbana-Champaign
201 N Goodwin Ave Urbana, IL 61801
{bisk1,juliahmr@illinois.edu}

Abstract

Work in grammar induction should help shed light on the amount of syntactic structure that is discoverable from raw word or tag sequences. But since most current grammar induction algorithms produce unlabeled dependencies, it is difficult to analyze what types of constructions these algorithms can or cannot capture, and, therefore, to identify where additional supervision may be necessary. This paper provides an in-depth analysis of the errors made by unsupervised CCG parsers by evaluating them against the labeled dependencies in CCGbank, hinting at new research directions necessary for progress in grammar induction.

1 Introduction

Grammar induction aims to develop algorithms that can automatically discover the latent syntactic structure of language from raw or part-of-speech tagged text. While such algorithms would have the greatest utility for low-resource languages for which no treebank is available to train supervised parsers, most work in this area has focused on languages where existing treebanks can be used to measure and compare the performance of the resultant parsers. Despite significant progress in the last decade (Klein and Manning, 2004; Headden III et al., 2009; Blunsom and Cohn, 2010; Spitkovsky et al., 2013; Mareček and Straka, 2013), there has been little analysis performed on the types of errors these induction systems make, and our understanding of what kinds of constructions these parsers can or cannot recover is still rather limited. One likely reason for this lack of analysis is the fact that most of the work in this domain has focused on parsers that return unlabeled dependencies, which cannot easily be assigned a linguistic interpretation.

This paper shows that approaches that are based on categorial grammar (Steedman, 2000) are amenable to more stringent evaluation metrics, which enable detailed analyses of the constructions they capture, while the commonly used unlabeled directed attachment scores hide linguistically important errors. Any categorial grammar based system, whether deriving its grammar from seed knowledge distinguishing nouns and verbs (Bisk and Hockenmaier, 2013), from a lexicon constructed from a simple questionnaire for linguists (Boonkwan and Steedman, 2011), or from sections of a treebank (Garrette et al., 2015), will attach linguistically expressive categories to individual words, and can therefore produce labeled dependencies. We provide a simple proof of concept for how these labeled dependencies can be used to isolate problem areas in CCG induction algorithms. We illustrate how they make the linguistic assumptions and mistakes of the model transparent, and are easily comparable to a treebank where available. They also allow us to identify linguistic phenomena that require additional supervision or training signal to master. Our analysis will be based on extensions of our earlier system (Bisk and Hockenmaier, 2013), since it requires less supervision than the CCG-based approaches of Boonkwan and Steedman (2011) or Garrette et al. (2015). Our aim in presenting this analysis is to initiate a broader conversation and classification of the impact of various types of supervision provided to these approaches. We will see that most of the constructions that our system cannot capture, even when they are included in the model's search space, involve precisely the kinds of non-local dependencies that elude even supervised dependency parsers (since they require dependency graphs, instead of trees), and that have motivated the use of categorial grammar-based approaches for supervised parsing.

Proceedings of the 53rd Annual Meeting of the Association for Computational Linguistics and the 7th International Joint Conference on Natural Language Processing, pages 1395–1404,
Beijing, China, July 26-31, 2015.

First, we provide a brief introduction to CCG. Next, we define a labeled evaluation metric that allows us to compare the labeled dependencies produced by Bisk and Hockenmaier (2013)'s unsupervised parser with those in CCGbank (Hockenmaier and Steedman, 2007). Third, we extend their induction algorithm to allow it to induce more complex categories, and refine their probability model to handle punctuation and lexicalization, which we show to be necessary when handling the larger grammars induced by our variant of their algorithm. While we also perform a traditional dependency evaluation for comparison to the non-CCG based literature, we focus on our CCG-based labeled evaluation metrics to perform a comparative analysis of Bisk and Hockenmaier (2013)'s parser and our extensions.

2 Combinatory Categorial Grammar

CCG categories CCG (Steedman, 2000) is a lexicalized grammar formalism which associates each word with a set of lexical categories that fully specify its syntactic behavior. Lexical categories indicate the expected number, type and relative location of arguments a word should take, or what constituents it may modify. Even without explicit evaluation against a treebank, the CCG lexicon that an unsupervised parser produces provides an easily interpretable snapshot of the assumptions the model has made about a language (Bisk and Hockenmaier, 2013). The set of CCG categories is defined recursively over a small set of atomic categories (e.g. S, N, NP, PP). Complex categories take the form $X\backslash Y$ or X/Y and represent functions which create a result of category X when combined with an argument Y. The slash indicates whether the argument precedes ($\backslash$) or follows ($/$) the functor (descriptions of CCG commonly use the vertical slash $|$ to range over both $/$ and $\backslash$). Modifiers are categories of the form $X|X$, and may take arguments of their own.

CCG rules CCG rules are defined schematically as function application ($>$, $<$), unary ($>B_1$, $<B_1$) and generalized composition ($>B_n$, $<B_n$), type-raising ($>T$, $<T$) and conjunction:

X/Y	Y	$\Rightarrow_{>}$	X
X/Y	$Y\|Z$	$\Rightarrow_{>B_1}$	$X\|Z$
X/Y	$Y\|Z_1\|...\|Z_n$	$\Rightarrow_{>B_n}$	$X\|Z_1\|...\|Z_n$
X		$\Rightarrow_{>T}$	$T/(T\backslash X)$
Y	$X\backslash Y$	$\Rightarrow_{<}$	X
$Y\|Z$	$X\backslash Y$	$\Rightarrow_{<B_1}$	$X\|Z$
$Y\|Z_1\|...\|Z_n$	$X\backslash Y$	$\Rightarrow_{<B_n}$	$X\|Z_1\|...\|Z_n$
	X	$\Rightarrow_{<T}$	$T\backslash(T/X)$

CCG derivations In the following derivation, forward application is used in line 1) as both the verb and the preposition take their NP arguments. In line 2), the prepositional phrase modifies the verb via backwards composition. Finally, in line 3), the derivation completes by producing a sentence (S) via backwards application:

	I	*saw*	*her*	*from*	*afar*
	N	$(S\backslash N_1)/N_2$	N	$(S\backslash S_1)/N_2$	N
1)		$S\backslash N_1$ ($>$)		$S\backslash S_1$ ($>$)	
2)		$S\backslash N_1$ ($<B$)			
3)	S ($<$)				

CCG dependencies CCG has two standard evaluation metrics. Supertagging accuracy simply computes how often a model chooses the correct lexical category for a given word. The correct category is a prerequisite for recovering the correct labeled dependency. By tracing through which word fills which argument of which category, a set of dependency arcs, labeled by lexical category and slot, can be extracted:

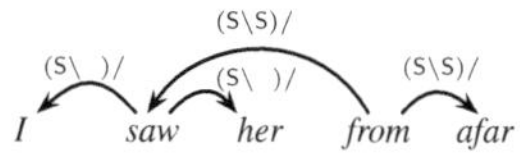

In this example, *I* fills the first argument of *saw*. This is represented by an edge from *saw* to *I*, labeled as a transitive verb ($(S\backslash N)/N$). This procedure is followed for every argument of every predicate, leading to a labeled directed graph.

Evaluation metrics for supervised CCG parsers (Clark et al., 2002) measure labeled f-score (LF1) precision of these dependencies (requiring the functor, argument, lexical category of the functor and slot of the argument to all match). A second, looser, evaluation is often also performed which measures unlabeled, undirected dependency scores (UF1).

Non-local dependencies and complex arguments One advantage of CCG is its ability to recover the non-local dependencies involved in control, raising, or *wh*-extraction. Since these constructions introduce additional dependencies, CCG parsers return dependency graphs (DAGs), not trees. To obtain these additional dependencies, relative pronouns and control verbs require lexical categories that take complex arguments of the form $S\backslash NP$ or S/NP, and a mechanism for co-indexation of the NP inside this argument with another NP argument (e.g. $(NP\backslash NP_i)/(S|NP_i)$ for relative pronouns). These co-indexed subjects can be seen in Figure 1.

Figure 1: Unlabeled predicate-argument dependency graphs for two sentences with co-indexed subjects.

Errors exposed by labeled evaluation We now illustrate how the lexical categories and labeled dependencies produced by CCG parsers expose linguistic mistakes. First, we consider a wildly incorrect analysis of the first example sentence, in which the subject is treated as an adverb, and the PP as an NP object of the verb:

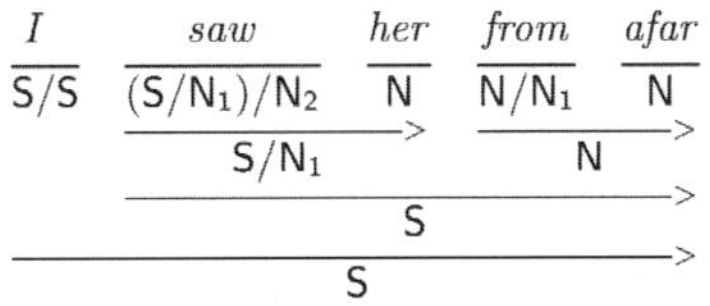

None of the labeled directed CCG dependencies are correct. But under the more lenient unlabeled directed evaluation of Garrette et al. (2015), and the even more lenient unlabeled undirected metric of Clark et al. (2002), two (or three) of the four dependencies would be deemed correct:

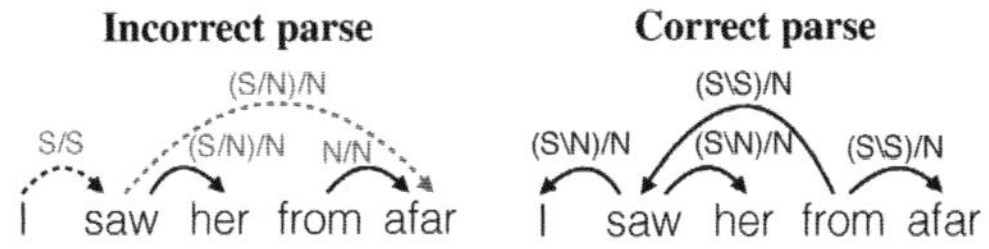

When we translate the CCG analysis to an unlabeled dependency tree (and hence flip the direction of modifier dependencies and add a root edge), a similar picture emerges, and three out of five attachments are deemed correct:

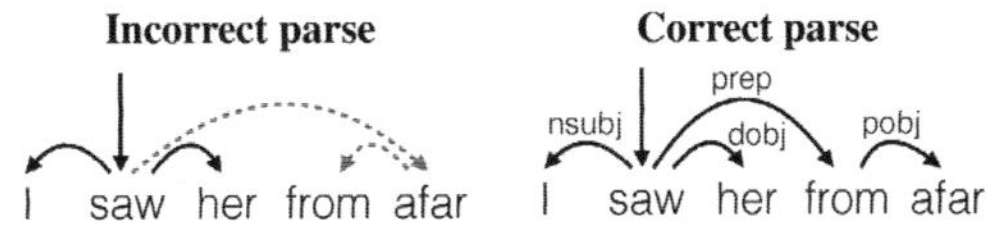

We now turn to a subtle distinction that corresponds to a systematic mistake made by all models we evaluate. The categories of noun-modifying prepositions (*at*) and possessive markers (*'*) differ only in the directionality of their slashes:

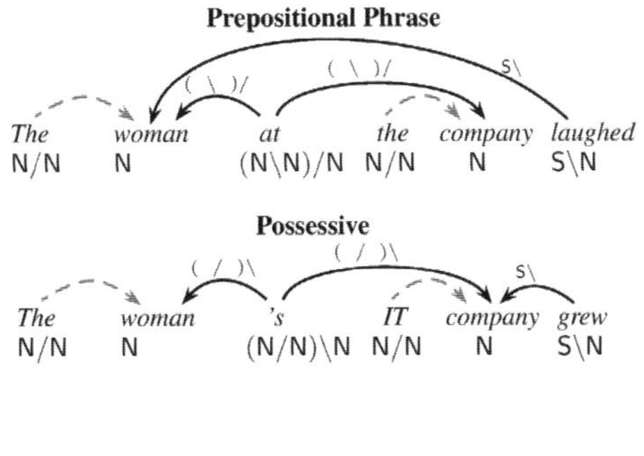

The unlabeled dependencies inside the noun phrases are identical, but the heads differ. The first sentence turns the prepositional phrase (*at the company*) into a modifier of *woman*. In contrast, in the possessive case, *woman 's* modifies *company*. According to an unlabeled (directed) score, confusing these analyses would be 80% correct, whereas LF1 would only be 20%. But without a semantic bias for companies growing and women laughing, there is no signal for the learner.

3 Labeled Evaluation for CCG Induction

We have just seen that labeled evaluation can expose many linguistically important mistakes. In order to enable a fair and informative comparison of unsupervised CCG parsers against the lexical categories and labeled dependencies in CCGbank, we define a simplification of CCGbank's lexical categories that does not alter the number or direction of dependencies, but makes the categories and dependency labels directly comparable to those produced by an unsupervised parser. We also do not alter the derivations themselves, although these may contain type-changing rules (which allow e.g. participial verb phrases S[ng]\NP to be used as NP modifiers NP\NP) that are beyond the scope of our induction algorithm.

Although the CCG derivations and dependencies that CCG-based parsers return should in principle be amenable to a quantitative labeled evaluation when a gold-standard CCG corpus is available, there may be minor systematic differences between the sets of categories assumed by the induced parser and those in the treebank. In particular, the lexical categories in the English CCGbank are augmented with morphosyntactic features that indicate e.g. whether sentences are declarative (S[dcl]), or verb phrases are infinitival (S[to]\NP). Prior work on supervised parsing with CCG found that many of these features can be recovered with proper modeling of latent state splitting (Fowler and Penn, 2010). Since we wish to evaluate a system that does not aim to induce such features, we remove them. We also remove the distinction between noun phrases (NP) and nouns (N), which is predicated on knowledge of

	Congress	has	n't	lifted	the	ceiling
	Our simplification of CCGbank's lexical categories					
Original	NP	(S[dcl]\NP)/(S[pt]\NP)	(S\NP)\(S\NP)	(S[pt]\NP)/NP	NP[nb]/N	N
Simplified	N	(S\N)/(S\N)	S\S	(S\N)/N	N/N	N

Figure 2: We remove morphosyntactic features, simplify verb phrase modifiers, and change NP to N.

	CCGbank	w/out Feats	Simplified
All	1640	458	444
Lexical	1286	393	384

Table 1: Category types in CCGbank 02-21

determiners and other structural elements of a language. Finally, CCGbank distinguishes between sentential modifiers (which have categories of the form S|S, without features) and verb phrase modifiers ((S\NP)|(S\NP), again without features). But since the NP argument slot of a VP modifier is never filled, we can maintain the same number of gold standard dependencies by removing this distinction and changing all VP modifiers to be of the form S|S. However, categories of the form $(S[\cdot]\backslash NP_i)/(S[\cdot]\backslash NP_i)$, which are used e.g. for modals and auxiliaries, are changed to $(S\backslash N_i)/(S\backslash N_i)$, allowing us to maintain the dependency on the subject. With these three simplifications we eliminate much of the detailed knowledge required to construct the precise CCGbank-style categories, and dramatically reduce the set of categories without losing expressive power. One distinction that we do not conflate, even though it is currently beyond the scope of the induction algorithm, is the distinction between PP arguments (requiring prepositions to have the category PP/NP) and adjuncts (requiring prepositions to be (NP\NP)/NP or ((S\NP)\(S\NP))/NP).

This simplification is consistent with the most basic components of CCG and can therefore be easily used for the evaluation and analysis of any weakly or fully supervised CCG system, not just that of Bisk and Hockenmaier (2012). An example simplification is present in Figure 2, and the reduction in the set of categories can be seen in Table 1. Similar simplifications should also be possible for CCGbanks in other languages.

4 Our approach

There are two parts to our approach: 1) inducing a CCG grammar from seed knowledge and 2) learning a probability model over parses. The induction algorithm (Bisk and Hockenmaier, 2012) uses the seed knowledge that nouns can take the CCG category N, that verbs can take the category S and may take N arguments, and that any word may modify a constituent it is adjacent to, to iteratively induce a CCG lexicon to parse the training data. In Bisk and Hockenmaier (2013), we introduced a model that is based on Hierarchical Dirichlet Processes (Teh et al., 2006). This HDP-CCG model gave state-of-the-art performance on a number languages, and qualitative analysis of the resultant lexicons indicated that the system was learning the word order and many of the correct attachments of the tested languages. But this system also had a number of shortcomings: the induction algorithm was restricted to a small fragment of CCG, the model emitted only POS tags rather than words, and punctuation was ignored. Here, we use our previous HDP-CCG system as a baseline, and introduce three novel extensions that attempt to address these concerns.

5 Experimental Setup

For our experiments we will follow the standard practice in supervised parsing of using WSJ Sections 02-21 for training, Section 22 for development and error analysis, and a final evaluation of the best models on Section 23. Because the induced lexicons are overly general, the memory footprint grows rapidly as the complexity of the grammar increases. For this reason, we only train on sentences that contain up to 20 words (as well as an arbitrary number of punctuation marks). All analyses and evaluation are performed with sentences of all lengths unless otherwise indicated. Finally, Bisk and Hockenmaier (2013) followed Liang et al. (2007) in setting the values of the hyperparameters α to powers (eg. the square) of the number of observed outcomes in the distribution. But when the output consists of words rather than POS tags, the concentration parameter $\alpha = V^2$ is too large to allow the model to learn. For this reason, experiments will be reported with all hyperparameters set to a constant of 2500.[1]

[1]We tested three values (1000, 2500, 5000) and found that the basic model at 2500 performed closest to the previously

		Base	+ Lexicalization	+ Punctuation	+ Punc & Lex	+ Allow (X|X)|X
Only Atomic Arguments	B_1	**34.2**	35.2	36.3	36.9	36.8
(S, N)	B_3	34.4	35.1	33.8	38.9	**38.8**
Allow Complex Arguments	B_1	33.0	34.9	33.2	35.7	**35.8**
(S, N, S|N)	B_3	29.4	29.5	31.2	31.2	31.2

Table 2: The impact of our changes to Bisk and Hockenmaier's (2013) model (henceforth: B_1, top left) on CCGbank dependencies (LF1, Section 22, all sentences). The best overall model ($B_3^{P\&L}$) uses B_3, punctuation and lexicalization. The best model with complex arguments (B_1^{C}) uses only B_1.

6 Extending the HDP-CCG system

We now examine how extending the HDP-CCG baseline model to capture lexicalization and punctuation, and how increasing the complexity of the induced grammars affect performance (Table 2).

6.1 Modeling Lexicalization

In keeping with most work in grammar induction from part-of-speech tagged text, Bisk and Hockenmaier's (2013) HDP-CCG treats POS tags t rather than words w as the terminals it generates based on their lexical categories c. The advantage of this approach is that tag-based emissions $p(t|c)$ are a lot less sparse than word-based emissions $p(w|c)$. It is therefore beneficial to first train a model that emits tags rather than words (Carroll and Rooth, 1998), and then to use this simpler model to initialize a lexicalized model that generates words instead of tags. To perform the switch we simply estimate counts for the parse forests using the unlexicalized model during the E-Step and then apply those counts to the lexicalized model during the M-Step. Inside-Outside then continues as before. Many words, like prepositions, differ systematically in their preferred syntactic role from that of their part-of-speech tags. This change benefits all settings of the model (Column 2 of Table 2).

6.2 Modeling Punctuation

Spitkovsky et al. (2011) performed a detailed analysis of punctuation for dependency-based grammar induction, and proposed a number of constraints that aimed to capture the different ways in which dependencies might cross constituent boundaries implied by punctuation marks.

A constituency-based formalism like CCG allows us instead to define a very simple, but effective Dirichlet Process (DP) based Markov grammar that emits punctuation marks at the maximal projections of constituents. We note that CCG derivations are binary branching, and that virtually every instance of a binary rule in a normal-form derivation combines a head X or X|Y with an argument Y or modifier X|X. Without reducing the set of strings generated by the grammar, we can therefore assume that punctuation marks can only be attached to the argument Y or the adjunct X|X:

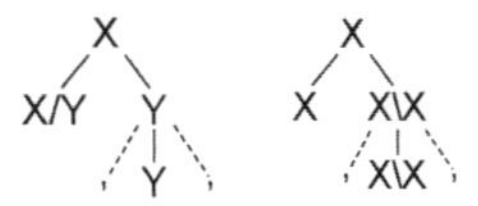

To model this, for each maximal projection (i.e. whenever we generate a non-head child) with category C, we first decide whether punctuation marks should be emitted ($M = \{true, false\}$) to the *left* or *right* side (*Dir*) of C. Since there may be multiple adjacent punctuation marks (... ."), we treat this as a Markov process in which the *history* variable captures whether previous punctuation marks have been generated or not. Finally, we generate an actual punctuation mark w_m:

$$
\begin{array}{ll}
p(M \mid Dir, Hist, \mathsf{C}) & \sim DP(\alpha, p(M \mid dir)) \\
p(M \mid Dir) & \sim DP(\alpha, p(M)) \\
p(w_m \mid Dir, Hist, \mathsf{C}) & \sim DP(\alpha, p(w_m \mid dir, hist)) \\
p(w_m \mid Dir, Hist) & \sim DP(\alpha, p(w_m))
\end{array}
$$

We treat # and $ symbols as ordinary lexical items for which CCG categories will be induced by the regular induction algorithm, but treat all other punctuation marks, including quotes and brackets. Commas and semicolons (,, ;) can act both as punctuation marks generated by this Markov grammar, and as conjunctions with lexical category conj. This model leads to further performance gains (Columns 3 and 4 of Table 2).

6.3 Increasing Grammatical Complexity

The existing grammar induction scheme is very simplistic. It assumes that adjacent words either modify one another or can be taken as arguments. Left unconstrained this space of grammatical cat-

reported dependency evaluation comparison with the work of Naseem et al. (2010). We fixed this hyperparameter setting for experimental simplicity but a more rigorous grid search might find better parameters for the complex models.

Model	Supertagging	LF1	UF1
$\mathsf{B_1}$	59.2	34.5	60.6
$\mathsf{B_1^C}$	59.9	34.9	63.6
$\mathsf{B_3^{P\&L}}$	62.3	37.1	64.9

Table 3: Test set performance of the final systems discussed in this paper (Section 23)

	CCGbank 02-21		WSJ2-21 DA		
Model	LF1	UF1	@10	@20	@∞
Naseem (Universal)			71.9	50.4	
Naseem (English)			73.8	66.1	
$\mathsf{B_1}$	33.8	60.3	70.7	63.1	58.4
$\mathsf{B_1^C}$	34.4	62.0	70.5	65.4	61.9
$\mathsf{B_3^{P\&L}}$	38.3	66.2	71.3	65.9	62.3

Table 4: Performance on CCGbank and CoNLL-style dependencies (Sections 02-21) for a comparison with Naseem et al. (2010).

egories introduced grows very rapidly, introducing a tremendous number of incorrect categories (analyzed later in Table 9). For this reason Bisk and Hockenmaier (2013) applied the HDP-CCG model to a context-free fragment of CCG, limiting the arity of lexical categories (number of arguments they can take) to two and the arity of composition (how many arguments can be passed through composition) to one. We know the space of grammatical constructions is larger than this, so we will allow the model to induce categories with three arguments and use generalized composition ($\mathsf{B_3}$). Bisk and Hockenmaier (2013) allow lexical categories to only take atomic arguments, but, as explained above, non-local dependencies require complex arguments of the form $\mathsf{S|N}$. We therefore allow lexical categories to take up to one complex argument of the form $\mathsf{S|N}$. Atomic lexical categories are not allowed to take complex arguments, eliminating $\mathsf{S|(S|N)}$ and $\mathsf{N|(S|N)}$. Increasing the search space (Rows 3 and 4 of Table 2) shows corresponding decreases in performance.

Finally, Bisk and Hockenmaier (2013) eliminated the possessive-preposition ambiguity explained above by disallowing categories of the form $\mathsf{(X\backslash X)/X}$ and $\mathsf{(X/X)\backslash X}$ to be used simultaneously. Removing this restriction does not harm performance (Column 5 of Table 2).

6.4 Summary and test set performance

Table 2 shows the performance of 20 different model settings on Section 22 under the simplified labeled CCG-based dependency evaluation proposed above, starting with Bisk and Hockenmaier's (2013) original model (henceforth: $\mathbf{B_1}$, top left). We see that modeling punctuation and lexicalization both increase performance. We also show that allowing categories of the form $\mathsf{(X\backslash X)/X}$ and $\mathsf{(X/X)\backslash X}$ on top of the lexicalized models with punctuation does not lead to a noticeable decrease in performance. We also see that an increase in grammatical and lexical complexity is only beneficial for the grammars that allow only atomic arguments, and only if both lexicalization and punctuation are modeled. Allowing complex arguments is generally not beneficial, and performance drops further if the grammatical complexity is increased to $\mathsf{B_3}$. Our further analysis will focus on the three bolded models, $\mathbf{B_1}$, $\mathbf{B_1^C}$ (the best model with complex arguments) and $\mathbf{B_3^{P\&L}}$ (the best overall model), whose supertag accuracy, labeled (LF1) and unlabeled undirected CCG dependency recovery on Section 23 are shown in Table 3. We see that $\mathbf{B_1^C}$ and $\mathbf{B_3^{P\&L}}$ both outperform $\mathbf{B_1}$ on all metrics, although the unlabeled metric (UF1) perhaps misleadingly suggests that $\mathbf{B_1^C}$ leads to a greater improvement than the supertagging and LF1 metrics indicate.

6.5 CCGbank vs. dependency trees

Finally, to compare our models directly to a comparable unsupervised dependency parser (Naseem et al., 2010), we evaluate them against the unlabeled dependencies produced by Yamada and Matsumoto's (2003) head rules for Sections 02-21 of the Penn Treebank (Table 4)[2]. Naseem et al. (2010) only report performance on sentences of up to length 20 (without punctuation marks). Their approach incorporates prior linguistic knowledge either in the form of "universal" constraints (e.g. that adjectives may modify nouns) or "English-specific" constraints (e.g. that adjectives tend to modify and precede nouns). These universal constraints are akin to, but more explicit and detailed than the information given to the induction algorithm (see Bisk and Hockenmaier (2013) for a discussion). Comparing these numbers to labeled and unlabeled CCG dependencies on the same corpus (all sentences, hence, @∞), we see that performance increases on CCGbank do not translate to similar gains on these unlabeled dependencies. While we have done our best to convert the predicate argument structure of CCG into dependencies

[2]BH13 use hyperparameter schemes and report 64.2@20.

Correct Category	B_1 LR	B_1 Used instead	(%)	$B_3^{P\&L}$ LR	$B_3^{P\&L}$ Used instead	(%)	B_1^C LR	B_1^C Used instead	(%)
N	**82.6**	N/N	7.5	74.5	N/N	8.3	77.4	N/N	9.8
N/N	78.5	(S\S)\(S\S)	9.8	71.9	(S\S)\(S\S)	8.7	**80.6**	N	7.7
S\N	17.3	S\S	43.5	**22.1**	S\S	27.6	18.3	S\S	39.5
S\S	38.1	N	24.3	34.9	N	16.0	**39.4**	N	22.7
S/S	37.8	N\N	20.8	41.1	N/N	16.3	**57.2**	(S\S)/S	13.8
(N\N)/N	**64.3**	(S\S)/N	20.8	60.5	(S\S)/N	13.8	53.1	(S\S)/N	23.8
(S\N)/N	25.6	S/N	27.0	26.0	(S/N)/N	23.5	**29.4**	S/N	22.3
(S\S)/N	51.0	(N\N)/N	23.1	48.0	(N\N)/N	18.2	**62.6**	N/N	10.1
(S\N)/S	**60.7**	S\N	12.1	55.7	S\N	12.4	57.9	S\N	11.0
(S\S)/S	38.0	(N\N)/N	35.2	50.8	S/S	14.4	**61.5**	N	7.5

Table 5: Detailed supertagging analysis: Recall scores of B_1, B_1^C, and $B_3^{P\&L}$ on the most common recoverable (simplified) lexical categories in Section 22 along with the most commonly produced error.

Category	Example usage	Used instead by $\mathbf{B_1^C}$ (%)					
(N/N)\N	The woman **'s** company ...	(N\N)/N	89.9	N/N	3.7	N	2.9
(S/S)/N	**Before** Monday, ...	S/S	69.9	N/N	14.8	(N\N)/N	8.2
(N/N)/(N/N)	The **very** tall man ...	N/N	38.0	(S\S)\(S\S)	33.9	(S\S)/N	10.1
(N\N)/(S\N)	John, **who** ran home, ...	(S\S)/(S/N)	26.5	N\N	23.3	S/S	14.9
(S\N)/(S\N)	I **promise to** pay ...	S\N	32.6	(S\S)/(S/N)	21.5	(S\N)/(S/N)	12.4
((S\N)/N)/N	I **gave** her a gift.	(S\N)/N	34.6	(S/N)/N	34.6	N/N	7.7
((S\N)/(S\N))/N	I **persuaded** her to pay ...	(S\N)/N	24.8	(S/N)/N	22.0	N/N	11.0

Table 6: Categories that are in the search space of the induction algorithm, but do not occur in any Viterbi parse, and what $\mathbf{B_1^C}$ uses instead.

there are many constructions which have vastly different analysis, making a proper conversion too difficult for the scope of this paper.[3]

7 Error analysis

Supertagging error analysis We first consider the lexical categories that are induced by the models. Table 5 shows the accuracy with which they recover the most common gold lexical categories, together with the category that they most often produced instead. We see that the simplest model ($\mathbf{B_1}$) performs best on N, and perhaps over generates (N\N)/N (noun-modifying prepositions), while the overall best model ($\mathbf{B_3^{P\&L}}$) outperforms both other models only on intransitive verbs.

The most interesting component of our analysis is the long tail of constructions that must be captured in order to produce semantically appropriate representations. We can inspect the confusion matrix of the lexical categories that the model fails to use to obtain insight into how its predictions disagree with the ground truth, and why these constructions may require special attention. Table 6 shows the most common CCGbank categories that were in the search space of some of the more complex models (e.g. $\mathbf{B_3^C}$), but were never used by any of the parsers in a Viterbi parse. These include possessives, relative pronouns, modals/auxiliaries, control verbs and ditransitives. We show the categories that the $\mathbf{B_1^C}$ model uses instead. The gold categories shown correspond to the bold words in Table 6. While the reason many of these cases are difficult is intuitive (e.g. *very* modifying *tall* instead of *man*), a more difficult type of error than previously discussed is that of recovering non-local dependencies. The recovery of non-local dependencies is beyond the scope of both standard dependency-based approaches and Bisk and Hockenmaier (2013)'s original induction algorithm. But the parser does not learn to use lexical categories with complex arguments correctly even when the algorithm is extended, to induce them. For example, $\mathbf{B_1^C}$ prefers to treat auxiliaries or equi verbs like *promise* as intransitives rather than as an auxiliary that shares its subject with *pay*. The surface string supports this decision, as it can be parsed without having to capture the non-local dependencies (top row) present in the correct (bottom row) analysis:

I	promise	to	pay	you
N	S\N	(S\S)/S	S/N	N
N	(S\N)/(S\N)	(S\N)/(S\N)	(S\N)/N	N

[3]The overlap (F-score of unlabeled undirected attachment scores) between CCGbank dependencies and those obtained via Matsumoto's head finding rules is only 81.9%.

	1st Argument			2nd Argument		
	B_1	B_1^C	$B_3^{P\&L}$	B_1	B_1^C	$B_3^{P\&L}$
N/N	68.4	69.7	**71.6**			
S\N	12.2	**24.9**	14.6			
S\S	17.0	16.2	**18.7**			
S/S	24.0	27.1	**33.8**			
(N\N)/N	49.7	**54.4**	51.2	41.0	**46.2**	42.4
(S\N)/N	26.6	32.9	**34.4**	30.6	33.2	**33.8**
(S\S)/N	21.6	19.2	**24.7**	24.0	24.9	**29.3**
(S\N)/S	23.9	**50.3**	32.5	25.2	**59.1**	35.0
(S\S)/S	6.1	**22.7**	14.1	9.5	**34.6**	19.5

Table 7: LF1 scores of B_1, B_1^C and $B_3^{P\&L}$ on the most common dependency types in Section 22.

We also see that this model uses seemingly non-English verb categories of the form (S/N)/N, both for ditransitives, and object control verbs, perhaps because the possibly spurious /N argument could be swallowed by other categories that take arguments of the form S/N, like the (incorrect) treatment of subject relative pronouns. One possible lesson we can extract from this is that practical approaches for building parsers for new languages might need to focus on injecting semantic information that is outside the scope of the learner.

Dependency error analysis Table 7 shows the labeled recall of the most common dependencies. We see that both new models typically outperform the baseline, although they yield different improvements on different dependency types. $\mathbf{B_1^C}$ is better at recovering the subjects of intransitive verbs (S\N) and verbs that take sentential complements ((S\N)/S), while $\mathbf{B_3}$ is better for simple adjuncts (N/N, S/S, S\S) and transitive verbs.

Wh-words and the long tail To dig slightly deeper into the set of missing constructions, we tried to identify the most common categories that are beyond the search space of the current induction algorithm. We first computed the set of categories used by each part of speech tag in CCGbank, and thresholded the lexicon at 95% token coverage for each tag. Removing the categories that contain PP and those that can be induced by the algorithm in its most general setting, we are left with the categories shown in Table 8. The tags that are missing categories are predominantly wh-words required for wh-questions, relative clauses or free relative clauses. Some of these categories violate the assumptions made by the induction algorithm: question words return a sentence (S) but are not themselves verbs. Free relative pronouns return a noun, but take arguments. However, this is

Additional Category	$p(cat \mid tag)$	
((N\N)/(S\N))/N	.93	WP$
N/(S/N)	.14	WP
N/(S\N)	.08	WP
((N\N)/S)\((N\N)/N)	.07	WDT
((S\S)\(S\S))\N	.04	RBR
S/(S\N)	.04	WP
S/(S/N)	.02	WP

Table 8: Common categories that the algorithm cannot induce

Size, ambiguity, coverage and precision of the induced lexicons				
Arguments:	**Atomic**		**Complex**	
# Lexical Arity:	**2**	**3**	**2**	**3**
# Lexical Categories	37	53	61	133
Avg. #Cats / Tag	26.4	29.5	42.3	56.3
Token-based Coverage	84.3	84.4	89.8	90.2
Type-based Coverage	20.3	21.6	27.0	32.4
Type-based Precision	81.1	60.4	65.6	36.1

Table 9: Size, ambiguity, coverage and precision (evaluated on Section 22) of the induced lexicons.

a surprisingly small set of special function words and therefore perhaps a strategic place for supervision. Questions in particular pose an interesting learning question – how does one learn that these constructions indicate missing information which only becomes available later in the discourse?

Grammatical complexity and size of the search space As lexical categories are a good proxy for the set of constructions the grammar will entertain, we can measure the size and ambiguity of the search space as a function of the number of lexical category types it induces as compared to the percentage that are actually valid categories for the language. In Table 9, we compare the lexicons induced by variants of the induction algorithm by their token-based coverage (the percent of tokens in Sections 22 for which the induced tag lexicon contains the correct category), type-based coverage (the percent of category types that the induced lexicon contains), as well as type-based precision (the percent of induced category types that occur in Section 22). This analysis is independent of the learned models, as their probabilities are not taken into account. We see that as the number of lexical categories induced (subject to the constraints of Bisk and Hockenmaier (2012)) increases, the percent that are valid English categories decreases rapidly (type-based precision falls from 81.1% to 36.1%). Despite this, and despite a high token coverage of up to 90%, we still miss almost 70% of the required category types. This helps explain why performance degrades so much for $\mathsf{B}_3^{\mathsf{C}}$, the arity three lexicon with complex arguments.

8 Dealing with Non-Local Dependencies

While the methodology used here is restricted to CCG based algorithms, we believe the lessons to be very general. The aforementioned constructions involve optional arguments, non-local dependencies, and multiple potential heads. Even though CCG is theoretically expressive enough to handle these constructions, they present the unsupervised learner with additional ambiguity that will pose difficulties independently of the underlying grammatical representation.

For example, although our approach learns that subject NPs are taken as arguments by verbs, the task of deciding which verb to attach the subject to is frequently ambiguous. This most commonly occurs in verb chains, and is compounded in the presence of subject-modifying relative clauses (in CCGbank, both constructions are in fact treated as several verbs sharing a single subject). To illustrate this, we ran the $\mathsf{B}_1^{\mathsf{C}}$ and $\mathsf{B}_3^{\mathrm{P\&L}}$ systems on the following three sentences:

1. The woman **won** an award
2. The woman **has won** an award
3. The woman **being promoted has won** an award

The single-verb sentence is correctly parsed by both models, but they flounder as distractors are added. Both treat *has* as an intransitive verb, *won* as an adverb and *an* as a preposition:

	The	woman	**won**	an	award	
$\mathsf{B}_3^{\mathrm{P\&L}}/\mathsf{B}_1^{\mathsf{C}}$:	N/N	N	(S\N)/N	N/N	N	
	The	woman	**has**	**won**	an	award
$\mathsf{B}_3^{\mathrm{P\&L}}/\mathsf{B}_1^{\mathsf{C}}$:	N/N	N	S\N	S\S	(S\S)/N	N

To accommodate the presence of two additional verbs, both models analyze *being* as a noun modifier that takes *promoted* as an argument. $\mathsf{B}_1^{\mathsf{C}}$ (correctly) stipulates a non-local dependency involving *promoted*, but treats it (arguably incorrectly) as a case of object extraction:

...	**being**	**promoted**	**has**	**won**	an	award
$\mathsf{B}_3^{\mathrm{P\&L}}$	(N\N)/S	S	S\N	S\S	(S\S)/N	N
$\mathsf{B}_1^{\mathsf{C}}$	(N\N)/(S/N)	S/N	S\N	S\S	(S\S)/N	N

Discovering these, and many of the other systematic errors describe here, may be less obvious when analyzing unlabeled dependency trees. But we would expect similar difficulties for any unsupervised approach when sentence complexity grows without a specific bias for a given analysis.

9 Conclusions

In this paper, we have introduced labeled evaluation metrics for unsupervised CCG parsers, and have shown that these expose many common syntactic phenomena that are currently out of scope for any unsupervised grammar induction systems. While we do not wish claim that CCGbank's analyses are free of arbitrary decisions, we hope to have demonstrated that these labeled metrics enable linguistically informed error analyses, and hence allow us to at least in part address the question of where and why the performance of these approaches might plateau. We focused our analysis on English for simplicity, but many of the same types of problems exist in other languages and can be easily identified as stemming from the same lack of supervision. For example, in Japanese we would expect problems with post-positions, in German with verb clusters, in Chinese with measure words, or in Arabic with morphology and variable word order.

We believe that one way to overcome the issues we have identified is to incorporate a semantic signal. Lexical semantics, if sparsity can be avoided, might suffice; otherwise learning with grounding or an extrinsic task could be used to bias the choice of predicates, their arity and in turn the function words that connect them. Alternatively, a simpler solution might be to follow the lead of Boonkwan and Steedman (2011) or Garrette et al. (2015) where gold categories are assigned by a linguist or treebank to tags and words. It is possible that more limited syntactic supervision might be sufficient if focused on the semantically ambiguous cases we have isolated.

More generally, we hope to initiate a conversation about grammar induction which includes a discussion of how these non-trivial constructions can be discovered, learned, and modeled. Relatedly, in future extensions to semi-supervised or projection based approaches, these types of constructions are probably the most useful to get right despite comprising the tail, as analyses without them may not be semantically appropriate. In summary, we hope to begin to pull back the veil on the types of information that a truly unsupervised system, if one should ever exist, would need to learn, and we pose a challenge to the community to find ways that a learner might discover this knowledge without hand-engineering it.

10 Acknowledgments

This material is based upon work supported by the National Science Foundation under Grants No. 1053856, 1205627 and 1405883. Any opinions, findings, and conclusions or recommendations expressed in this material are those of the author(s) and do not necessarily reflect the views of the National Science Foundation.

References

Yonatan Bisk and Julia Hockenmaier. 2012. Simple Robust Grammar Induction with Combinatory Categorial Grammars. In *Proceedings of the Twenty-Sixth Conference on Artificial Intelligence (AAAI-12)*, pages 1643–1649, Toronto, Canada, July.

Yonatan Bisk and Julia Hockenmaier. 2013. An HDP Model for Inducing Combinatory Categorial Grammars. *Transactions of the Association for Computational Linguistics*, 1:75–88.

Phil Blunsom and Trevor Cohn. 2010. Unsupervised Induction of Tree Substitution Grammars for Dependency Parsing. In *Proceedings of the 2010 Conference on Empirical Methods in Natural Language Processing*, pages 1204–1213, Cambridge, USA, October.

Prachya Boonkwan and Mark Steedman. 2011. Grammar Induction from Text Using Small Syntactic Prototypes. In *Proceedings of 5th International Joint Conference on Natural Language Processing*, pages 438–446, Chiang Mai, Thailand, November.

Glenn Carroll and M Rooth. 1998. Valence induction with a head-lexicalized PCFG. In *Proceedings of the 3rd Conference on Empirical Methods in Natural Language Processing*, page 36–45, Granada, Spain.

Stephen Clark, Julia Hockenmaier, and Mark Steedman. 2002. Building Deep Dependency Structures using a Wide-Coverage CCG Parser. In *Proceedings of 40th Annual Meeting of the Association for Computational Linguistics*, pages 327–334, Philadelphia, USA, July.

Timothy A D Fowler and Gerald Penn. 2010. Accurate Context-Free Parsing with Combinatory Categorial Grammar. In *Proceedings of the 48th Annual Meeting of the Association for Computational Linguistics*, pages 335–344, Uppsala, Sweden, July.

Dan Garrette, Chris Dyer, Jason Baldridge, and Noah A Smith. 2015. Weakly-Supervised Grammar-Informed Bayesian CCG Parser Learning. In *Proceedings of the Twenty-Ninth AAAI Conference on Artificial Intelligence (AAAI-15)*, Austin, USA.

William P Headden III, Mark Johnson, and David McClosky. 2009. Improving Unsupervised Dependency Parsing with Richer Contexts and Smoothing. In *Proceedings of Human Language Technologies: The 2009 Annual Conference of the North American Chapter of the Association for Computational Linguistics*, pages 101–109, Boulder, USA, June.

Julia Hockenmaier and Mark Steedman. 2007. CCGbank: A Corpus of CCG Derivations and Dependency Structures Extracted from the Penn Treebank. *Computational Linguistics*, 33:355–396, September.

Dan Klein and Christopher D Manning. 2004. Corpus-Based Induction of Syntactic Structure: Models of Dependency and Constituency. In *Proceedings of the 42nd Meeting of the Association for Computational Linguistics (ACL'04), Main Volume*, pages 478–485, Barcelona, Spain, July.

Percy Liang, Slav Petrov, Michael I Jordan, and Dan Klein. 2007. The Infinite PCFG Using Hierarchical Dirichlet Processes. In *Proceedings of the 2007 Joint Conference on Empirical Methods in Natural Language Processing and Computational Natural Language Learning (EMNLP-CoNLL)*, pages 688–697, Prague, Czech Republic, June.

David Mareček and Milan Straka. 2013. Stop-probability estimates computed on a large corpus improve Unsupervised Dependency Parsing. In *Proceedings of the 51st Annual Meeting of the Association for Computational Linguistics (Volume 1: Long Papers)*, pages 281–290, Sofia, Bulgaria, August.

Tahira Naseem, Harr Chen, Regina Barzilay, and Mark Johnson. 2010. Using Universal Linguistic Knowledge to Guide Grammar Induction. In *Proceedings of the 2010 Conference on Empirical Methods in Natural Language Processing*, pages 1234–1244, Cambridge, USA, October.

Valentin I Spitkovsky, Hiyan Alshawi, and Daniel Jurafsky. 2011. Punctuation: Making a Point in Unsupervised Dependency Parsing. In *Proceedings of the Fifteenth Conference on Computational Natural Language Learning*, pages 19–28, Portland, USA, June.

Valentin I Spitkovsky, Hiyan Alshawi, and Daniel Jurafsky. 2013. Breaking Out of Local Optima with Count Transforms and Model Recombination: A Study in Grammar Induction. In *Proceedings of the 2013 Conference on Empirical Methods in Natural Language Processing*, pages 1983–1995, Seattle, USA, October.

Mark Steedman. 2000. *The Syntactic Process*. The MIT Press.

Yee-Whye Teh, Michael I Jordan, Matthew J Beal, and David M Blei. 2006. Hierarchical Dirichlet Processes. *Journal of the American Statistical Association*, 101(476):1566–1581.

Hiroyasu Yamada and Yuji Matsumoto. 2003. Statistical Dependency Analysis With Support Vector Machines. In *Proceedings of 8th International Workshop on Parsing Technologies (IWPT)*, pages 195–206, Nancy, France.

Entity-Centric Coreference Resolution with Model Stacking

Kevin Clark
Computer Science Department
Stanford University
kevclark@cs.stanford.edu

Christopher D. Manning
Computer Science Department
Stanford University
manning@cs.stanford.edu

Abstract

Mention pair models that predict whether or not two mentions are coreferent have historically been very effective for coreference resolution, but do not make use of entity-level information. However, we show that the scores produced by such models can be aggregated to define powerful entity-level features between clusters of mentions. Using these features, we train an entity-centric coreference system that learns an effective policy for building up coreference chains incrementally. The mention pair scores are also used to prune the search space the system works in, allowing for efficient training with an exact loss function. We evaluate our system on the English portion of the 2012 CoNLL Shared Task dataset and show that it improves over the current state of the art.

1 Introduction

Coreference resolution, the task of identifying mentions in a text that refer to the same real world entity, is an important aspect of text understanding and has numerous applications. Many approaches to coreference resolution learn a scoring function defined over mention pairs to guide the coreference decisions (Soon et al., 2001; Ng and Cardie, 2002; Bengtson and Roth, 2008). However, such systems do not make use of entity-level information, i.e., features between *clusters* of mentions instead of pairs.

Using entity-level information is valuable because it allows early coreference decisions to inform later ones. For example, finding that *Clinton* and *she* corefer makes it more likely that *Clinton* corefers with *Hillary Clinton* than *Bill Clinton* due to gender agreement constraints. Such information has been incorporated successfully into entity-centric coreference systems that build up coreference clusters incrementally, using the information from the partially completed coreference chains produced so far to guide later decisions (Raghunathan et al., 2010; Stoyanov and Eisner, 2012; Ma et al., 2014).

However, defining useful features between clusters of mentions and learning an effective policy for incrementally building up clusters can be challenging, and many recent state-of-the-art systems work entirely or almost entirely over pairs of mentions (Fernandes et al., 2012; Durrett and Klein, 2013; Chang et al., 2013). In this paper we introduce a novel coreference system that combines the advantages of mention pair and entity-centric systems with model stacking. We first propose two mention pair models designed to capture different linguistic phenomena in coreference resolution. We then describe how the probabilities produced by these models can be used to generate expressive features between clusters of mentions. Using these features, we train an entity-centric incremental coreference system.

The entity-centric system builds up coreference chains with agglomerative clustering: each mention starts in its own cluster and then pairs of clusters are merged each step. We train an agent to determine whether it is desirable to merge a particular pair of clusters using an imitation learning algorithm based on DAgger (Ross et al., 2011). Previous incremental coreference systems heuristically define which actions are beneficial for the agent to perform, but we instead propose a way of assigning exact costs to actions based on coreference evaluation metrics, adding a concept of the severity of a mistake. Furthermore, rather than considering all pairs of clusters as candidate merges, we use the scores of the pairwise models to reduce the search space, first by providing an ordering over which merges are considered and secondly by discarding merges that are not likely

Proceedings of the 53rd Annual Meeting of the Association for Computational Linguistics and the 7th International Joint Conference on Natural Language Processing, pages 1405–1415,
Beijing, China, July 26-31, 2015. ©2015 Association for Computational Linguistics

to be good. This greatly reduces the time it takes to run the agent, making learning computationally feasible.

Imitation learning is challenging because it is a non-i.i.d. learning problem; the distribution of states seen by the agent depends on the agent's parameters. Model stacking offers a way of decomposing the learning problem by training pairwise models with many parameters in a straightforward supervised learning setting and using their outputs for training a much simpler model in the more difficult imitation learning setting. Furthermore, mention pair scores can produce powerful features for training the agent because the scores indicate which mention pairs between the clusters in question are relevant; high scoring and low scoring pairs can indicate when a merge should be forced or disallowed while other mention pairs may provide little useful information.

We run experiments on the English portion of the 2012 CoNLL Shared Task dataset. The entity-centric clustering algorithm greatly outperforms commonly used heuristic methods for coordinating pairwise scores to produce a coreference partition. We also show that combining the scores of different pairwise models designed to capture different aspects coreference results in significant gains in accuracy. Our final system gets a combined score of 63.02 on the dataset, substantially outperforming other state of the art systems.

2 Mention Pair Models

Mention pair models predict whether or not a given pair of mentions belong in the same coreference cluster. We incorporate two different mention pair models into our system. However, other pairwise models could easily be added; one advantage of our model stacking approach is that it can combine different simple classifiers in a modular way.

Our two models are designed to capture different aspects of coreference. The first one is built to predict coreference for *all* of the candidate antecedents of a mention. This makes it useful for providing scores when the current mention has clear coreference links to many previous mentions. For example *President Clinton* might be linked to *the president*, *Bill Clinton*, and *Mr. President*.

However, mentions often only have *one* clear antecedent. This is especially common in pronominal anaphora resolution, such as in the sentence *Bill arrived, but nobody saw him.* The pronoun *him* is directly referring back to a previous part of the discourse, not some entity that other mentions may also refer to. However, there still might be coreference links between *him* and previous mentions in the text because of transitivity: any other mention about Bill would be coreferent with *him.* For such mentions, there may be very little evidence in the discourse to suggest a coreference link, so attempting to train a model to predict these will bear little fruit. With this as motivation, we also train a model to predict only *one* correct antecedent of the current mention.

We found a *classification* model to be well suited for the first task and and a *ranking* model to be well suited for the second one. These two models differ only in the training criteria used. Both models use a logistic classifier to assign a probability to a mention m and candidate antecedent a representing the likelihood that the two mentions are coreferent. The candidate antecedent a may take on the value NA indicating that m has no antecedent. The probability of coreference takes the standard logistic form:

$$p_{\boldsymbol{\theta}}(a, m) = (1 + e^{\boldsymbol{\theta}^T \boldsymbol{f}(a,m)})^{-1}$$

where $\boldsymbol{f}(a, m)$ is a vector of feature functions on a and m and $\boldsymbol{\theta}$ are the feature weights we wish to learn. Let $\mathcal{M}$ denote the set of all mentions in the training set, $\mathcal{T}(m)$ denote the set of true antecedents of a mention m (i.e., mentions that occur before m in the text that are coreferent with m or $\{\text{NA}\}$ if m has no antecedent), and $\mathcal{F}(m)$ denote the set of false antecedents of m. We want to find a parameter vector $\boldsymbol{\theta}$ that assigns high probabilities to the candidate antecedents in $\mathcal{T}(m)$ and low probabilities to the ones in $\mathcal{F}(m)$.

2.1 Classification Model

For the classification model, we consider each pair of mentions independently with the goal of predicting coreference correctly for as many of them as possible. The model is trained by minimizing negative conditional log likelihood augmented with L1 regularization:

$$\mathcal{L}_c(\boldsymbol{\theta}_c) = -\sum_{m \in \mathcal{M}} \Big(\sum_{t \in \mathcal{T}(m)} \log p_{\boldsymbol{\theta}_c}(t, m) + \sum_{f \in \mathcal{F}(m)} \log(1 - p_{\boldsymbol{\theta}_c}(f, m)) \Big) + \lambda ||\boldsymbol{\theta}_c||_1$$

By summing over all candidate antecedents, the objective encourages the model to produce good probabilities for all of them.

2.2 Ranking Model

For the ranking model, candidate antecedents for a mention are considered simultaneously and compete with each other to be matched with the current mention. This makes the model well suited to the task of finding a single best antecedent for a mention. A natural learning objective for such a model would be a max-margin training criteria that encourages separation between the highest scoring true antecedent and highest scoring false antecedent of the current mention. However, we found such models to be poor at producing scores useful for a downstream clustering model because a max-margin objective encourages scores for true antecedents to be high only relative to other candidate antecedents. It is much more beneficial to have mention pair scores that are comparable across different mentions as well as different candidate antecedents. For this reason, we instead train the model with an objective that maximizes the conditional log likelihood of the highest scoring true and false antecedents under the logistic model:

$$\mathcal{L}_r(\boldsymbol{\theta}_r) = -\sum_{m \in \mathcal{M}} \Big(\max_{t \in \mathcal{T}(m)} \log p_{\boldsymbol{\theta}_r}(t, m) + \min_{f \in \mathcal{F}(m)} \log(1 - p_{\boldsymbol{\theta}_r}(f, m)) \Big) + \lambda ||\boldsymbol{\theta}_r||_1$$

For both models, we set $\lambda = 0.001$ and optimize their objectives using AdaGrad (Duchi et al., 2011).

2.3 Features

Our mention pair models use a variety of common features for mention pair classification (for more details see (Bengtson and Roth, 2008; Stoyanov et al., 2010; Lee et al., 2011; Recasens et al., 2013)). These include

- **Distance** features, e.g., the distance between the two mentions in sentences or number of mentions.
- **Syntactic** features, e.g., number of embedded NPs under a mention, POS tags of the first, last, and head word.
- **Semantic** features, e.g., named entity type, speaker identification.
- **Rule-based** features, e.g., exact and partial string matching.
- **Lexical Features**, e.g., the first, last, and head word of the current mention.

We also employ a feature conjunction scheme similar to the one described by Durrett and Klein (2013).

3 Entity-Centric Coreference Model

Mention pair scores alone are not enough to produce a final set of coreference clusters because they do not enforce transitivity: if the pair of mentions (a, b) and the pair of mentions (b, c) are deemed coreferent by the model, there is no guarantee that the model will also classify (a, c) as coreferent. Thus a second step is needed to coordinate the scores to produce a final coreference partition. A widely used approach for this is *best-first* clustering (Ng and Cardie, 2002). For each mention, the best-first algorithm assigns the most probable preceding mention classified as coreferent with it as the antecedent.

The primary weakness of this approach is that it only relies on local information to make decisions, so it cannot consolidate information at the entity level. As a result, coreference chains produced by such algorithms can exhibit low coherency. For example, a cluster may consist of [Hillary Clinton, Clinton, he] because the coreference decision between *Hillary Clinton* and *Clinton* is made independently of the one between *Clinton* and *he*.

To tackle this problem, we build an entity-centric model that operates between pairs of *clusters* instead of pairs of mentions, guided by scores produced by the pairwise models. It builds up clusters of mentions believed to refer to the same entity as it goes, relying on the partially formed clusters produced so far to make decisions. For example, the system could reject linking [Hillary Clinton] with [Clinton, he] because of the low score between the pair (Hillary Clinton, he).

Our entity-centric "agent" builds up coreference chains with agglomerative clustering. It begins in a start state where each mention is in a separate single-element cluster. At each step, it observes the current state s, which consists of all partially formed coreference clusters produced so far, and selects some action a which merges two existing clusters. The action will result in a new state with new candidate actions and the process is repeated. The model is *entity-centric* in that it builds up clusters of mentions representing entities and merges clusters if it predicts they are representing the same one.

3.1 Test-time Inference

The agent assigns a score to each action a using a linear model with feature function $\boldsymbol{f}_e$ and weight vector $\boldsymbol{\theta}_e$: $s_{\boldsymbol{\theta}_e}(a) = \boldsymbol{\theta}_e^T \boldsymbol{f}_e(a)$. A particular setting of $\boldsymbol{\theta}_e$ defines a *policy* π that determines which action $a = \pi(s)$ the agent will take in state s. This policy is to greedily take highest scoring candidate action available from the current state.

Rather than using all possible cluster merges as the candidate set of actions the agent selects from, we use the scores produced by mention pair models to reduce the search space. First, we order all mention pairs in the document in descending order according to their pairwise scores. This causes clustering to occur in an easy-first fashion, where harder decisions are delayed until more information is available. Secondly, we discard all mention pairs that score below a threshold t under the assumption that the clusters containing these pairs are unlikely to be coreferent. In our experiments we were able able set t so that over 95% of pairs were removed with no decrease in accuracy. Lastly, we iterate through this list of pairs in order. For each pair, we make a binary decision on whether or not the clusters containing these pairs should be merged. This formulates the agent's task so it only has two actions to chose from instead of a number of actions proportional to the number of clusters squared. Algorithm 1 shows the full test-time procedure.

3.2 Learning

Imitation Learning with DAgger

We face a sequential prediction problem where future observations (visited states) depend on previous actions. This is challenging because it violates the common i.i.d. assumptions made in statistical learning. *Imitation learning*, where expert demonstrations of good behavior are used to teach the agent, has proven very useful in practice for this sort of problem (Argall et al., 2009). We use imitation learning to set the parameters $\boldsymbol{\theta}_e$ of our agent by training it to classify whether a particular action is the one an expert policy would take in the current state. In particular, we use $\boldsymbol{\theta}_e$ as parameters for a binary logistic classifier that predicts which action (merge or do not merge) matches the expert policy.

Algorithm 1 Inference method: agglomerative clustering

```
Input: Set of mentions in document M, pairwise classifier with parameters θ_c, agent with parameters θ_e, cutoff threshold t
Output: Clustering C

Initialize list of mention pairs P → []
for each pair (m_i, m_j) ∈ M^2 with i < j do
    if p_θc(m_i, m_j) > t then
        P.append((m_i, m_j))
    end if
end for
Sort P in descending order according to p_θc

Initialize C → initial clustering with each mention in M in its own cluster
for (m_i, m_j) ∈ P do
    if C[m_i] ≠ C[m_j]
     and s_θe(C[m_i], C[m_j]) > 0 then
        DoMerge(C[m_i], C[m_j], C)
    end if
end for
```

We found the DAgger (Ross et al., 2011) imitation learning method (see Algorithm 2) to be effective for this task. DAgger is an iterative algorithm that aggregates a dataset $\mathcal{D}$ consisting of states and the actions performed by the expert policy in those states. At each iteration, it first samples a *trajectory* of states visited by the current policy by running the policy to completion from the start state. It then labels those states with the best action according to the expert policy, adds those labeled examples to the dataset, and then trains a new classifier over the dataset to get a new policy. When producing a trajectory to train on, the expert policy is stochastically mixed with the current policy; with probability β_i the expert's action is chosen instead of the current policy's. We set β so it decays exponentially as the iteration number increases.

By sampling trajectories under the current policy, DAgger exposes the system to states at train time similar to the ones it will face at test time. In contrast, training the agent on the gold labels alone would unrealistically teach it to make decisions under the assumption that all previous decisions were correct, potentially causing it to over-rely on information from past actions. This is especially problematic in coreference, where the error rate is quite high. Even when using DAgger, this problem could exist to a lesser degree if the model heavily overfits to the training data. However, the agent has a small number of parameters thanks to our model stacking approach, reducing the risk of this happening.

Algorithm 2 Learning method: DAgger

Input: initial policy $\hat{\pi}_1$, expert policy π^*
Output: final policy $\hat{\pi}_N$

Initialize $\mathcal{D} \leftarrow \emptyset$
for $i = 1$ **to** N **do**
  Let $\pi_i = \beta_i \pi^* + (1 - \beta_i)\hat{\pi}_i$
  Sample a trajectory under the current policy using π_i
  Get dataset $\mathcal{D}_i = (s, \pi^*(s))$ of states visited by π_i and actions given by the expert
  Aggregate datasets: $\mathcal{D} \leftarrow \mathcal{D} \cup \mathcal{D}_i$
  Train classifier $\hat{\pi}_{i+1}$ on $\mathcal{D}$
end for

Assigning Costs to Actions

A key aspect of incrementally building coreference clusters is that some local decisions are much more important than others. For example, a merge between two large clusters influences the score far more than a merge between two small ones. Additionally, getting early decisions correct is crucial because later actions are dependent on early ones, causing errors to compound if mistakes are made early. To capture this, we take an approach inspired by the SEARN learning algorithm (Daumé et al., 2009) and add costs to the actions in the aggregated dataset. We then train the agent to do cost-sensitive classification. Using these costs, we simply define the expert policy as the policy that takes the action with the lowest cost at each step.

We want our costs to represent how a particular local decision will affect the final score of the coreference system. Unfortunately, standard coreference evaluation metrics do not decompose over cluster merges. Instead, we compute the loss of an action by "rolling out" the current policy to completion. More concretely, let m be a function (such as a coreference evaluation metric) that assigns scores to states; we are interested in reaching a final state for which m is high. Suppose we are assigning costs to the set of actions $\mathcal{A}(s)$ that can be taken from some state s. For each action $a \in \mathcal{A}(s)$, we apply that action to s to get a new state s', run the current policy $\hat{\pi}_i$ from s' to completion, and then compute the value of m on the resulting final state. This gives exactly the final score the system would get if it made the action a from state s and then continued under the current policy. Let $f_m(s, a)$ denote this value for a particular metric, state, and action. We assign each action the regret r associated with taking that action under the current policy as a cost:

$$r(s, a) = \max_{a' \in \mathcal{A}(s)} f_m(s, a') - f_m(s, a)$$

The "rolling out" procedure means we naively have to visit $O(t^2)$ states each iteration instead of t, where t is the length of a trajectory. However, the highly constrained action space described in section 3.1 combined with the use of memoization allows the algorithm to still run efficiently.

Improving Runtime with Memoization

During training, the agent will see many of the same states and actions multiple times. We can exploit this with memoization, significantly improving the algorithm's runtime. In particular, we store the following values:

- Given a state s and action a, the value of the cost function, $r(s, a)$.
- Given an action a, the score the model assigns that action, $s_{\boldsymbol{\theta}_e}(a)$.
- Given an action a, the result of the feature function on that action, $\mathbf{f}_e(a)$.

The first two values depend on the current model, so the saved values must be cleared between iterations of training. In experiments on the development set of the CoNLL 2012 corpus, these tables had 76%, 94%, and 93% hit rates respectively after 50 passes over the dataset.

3.3 Features

Our agent uses features that are derived from the scores produced by the two mention pair models. Although these scores only operate on mention pairs, they are combined to capture cluster-level interactions by being aggregated in different ways over pairs of mentions from the clusters. Mention pair scores can produce powerful features for training the agent because they show which mention pairs between the clusters in question are relevant, and often a small subset of the mention pairs provide far more information than the rest. For example, a strong negative pairwise

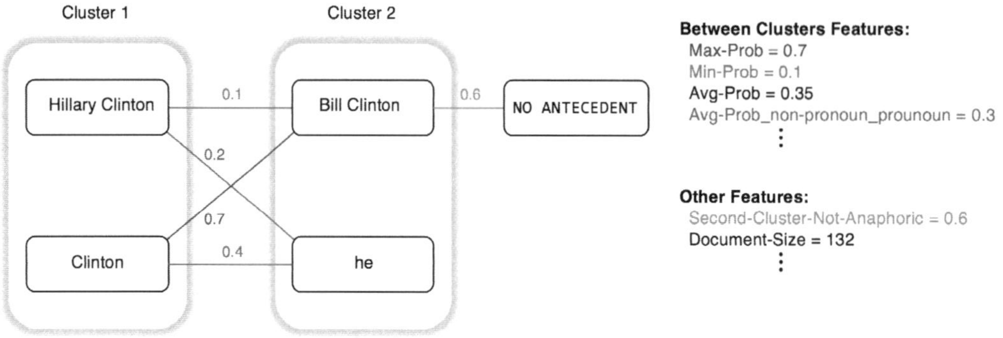

Figure 1: Examples of features generated for a candidate cluster merge. Weights on edges are the probabilities of coreference produced by a mention pair model.

link like *Hillary Clinton* and *he* should disallow a merge, while other mention pairs, such as two instances of the pronoun *she* far apart in the text, might provide very little information. Using the mention pair models for probabilities, we compute the following features over all pairs of mentions between the clusters (i.e., each mention is in a different cluster).

- The minimum and maximum probability of coreference.
- The average probability and average log probability of coreference.
- The average probability and log probability of coreference for a particular pair of grammatical types of mentions (either pronoun or non-pronoun). For example, `Avg-Prob_non-pronoun_pronoun` gives the average probability of coreference when the candidate antecedent is not a pronoun and the candidate anaphor is a pronoun.

Note that the averaged features have a natural probabilistic interpretation; the average probability corresponds to the expected number of coreference links between the involved mention pairs while the average log probability corresponds to the probability that *all* mention pairs will have a coreference link. All of these features are computed twice: once with the classification model and once with the ranking model.

We also compute the following features based on other aspects of the current state:

- Whether a preceding mention pair in the list of mention pairs has the same candidate anaphor as the current one.
- The index of the current mention pair in the list divided by the size of the list, i.e., what percentage of the list have we seen so far.
- The number of mentions in the current document.
- The probability of the first-occurring mention in the second-occurring cluster not being anaphoric (i.e., $p_{\theta_c}(\text{NA}, m)$). This prevents producing clusters that, for example, start with a pronoun.

Lastly, we take one feature conjunction with a boolean representing whether both clusters are size 1. In total, there are only 56 features after the feature conjunction. However, these features provide strong signal because they are directly related to the probabilities of mentions being coreferent. In contrast, the pairwise models use thousands of features (after feature conjunctions), including lexical features that are extremely sparse. The pairwise models can easily exploit this much bigger feature set because they operate in a classic supervised learning setting. The entity-centric model, on the other hand, learns in a much more challenging non-i.i.d. setting. Model stacking avoids the difficulty of directly training the entity-centric model with a large set of weak features by decomposing the task into first learning to produce good pairwise scores and then using those scores to generate a manageable set of strong features.

3.4 Training Details

Because the entity-centric agent relies on the output of pairwise classifiers, they should not be trained on the same data. Therefore we split the training set into two sections and use one for training the pairwise models and the other for training the agent. When evaluating on the development set, we use 80% of the documents in the training set to train the mention pair models and the rest to train the entity-centric model. When evaluating on the test set we use the whole training set for the mention pair models and the development set for the entity-centric model. We also tried using cross-validation instead of a single split, but found this did not improve performance, which we believe to be because this trains the agent with different pairwise models than the ones used at test time.

For our initial policy $\hat{\pi}_1$, we set the parameters of the agent so it operates with simple best-first clustering (initializing all feature weights to 0 except for the maximum-score, anaphor-seen, and bias features). For m, the performance metric determining the action costs, we use a linear combination of the B^3 (Bagga and Baldwin, 1998) and MUC (Vilain et al., 1995) metrics, which are both commonly used for evaluating coreference systems. The other metric used in our evaluation, Entity-based CEAFE ($CEAF_{\phi_4}$) (Luo, 2005), was not used because it is expensive to compute. We found weighting B^3 three times as much as MUC to be effective on the development set.

4 Experiments and Results

Experimental Setup

We apply our model to the English portion of the CoNLL 2012 Shared Task data (Pradhan et al., 2012), which is derived from the OntoNotes corpus (Hovy et al., 2006). The data is split into a training set of 2802 documents, development set of 343 documents, and a test set of 345 documents. We use the provided preprocessing for parse trees, named entity tags, etc. The models are evaluated using three of the most popular metrics for coreference resolution: MUC, B^3, and Entity-based CEAFE ($CEAF_{\phi_4}$). We also include the average F_1 score (CoNLL F_1) of these three metrics, as is commonly done in CoNLL Shared Tasks. We used the most recent version of the CoNLL scorer (version 8.01), which implements the original definitions of these metrics.

Mention Detection

Our experiments were run using system-produced predicted mentions. We used the rule-based mention detection algorithm from Raghunathan et al. (2010), which first extracts pronouns and maximal NP projections as candidate mentions and then filters this set with rules that remove spurious mentions such as numeric entities or pleonastic *it* pronouns.

	MUC	B^3	$CEAF_{\phi_4}$	Avg.
Classification, B.F.	72.00	60.01	55.63	62.55
Ranking, B.F.	71.91	60.63	56.38	62.97
Classification, E.C.	72.34	61.46	57.16	63.65
Ranking, E.C.	72.37	61.34	57.13	63.61
Both, E.C.	72.52	62.02	57.69	64.08

Table 1: Metric scores on the development set for the classification and ranking pairwise models when using best-first clustering (B.F.) or the entity-centric model (E.C.).

Comparison of Models

We compare the effectiveness of the entity-centric model with the commonly used best-first clustering approach, which assigns mentions the highest scoring previous mention as the antecedent. Unlike the entity-centric model, the best-first approach only relies on local information to make decisions. We also compare the effectiveness of the ranking and classification pairwise models. Table 1 shows the results of these models on the development set.

The entity-centric model outperforms best-first clustering for both mention pair models, demonstrating the utility of a learned, incremental clustering algorithm. The improvement is much greater for the classification pairwise model, causing it to outperform the ranking model with the entity-centric clustering algorithm even though it performs significantly worse than the ranking model with best-first clustering. This suggests that although the ranking model is better at finding a single correct antecedent for a mention, the classification model is more useful for producing cluster-level features. Incorporating probabilities from both pairwise models further improved scores over using either model alone, indicating that the mention pair classifiers were successful in learning scoring functions useful in different circumstances.

Incorporating other Entity-Level Features

Although the entity-centric model has so far only

	MUC	B^3	$CEAF_{\phi_4}$	Avg.
Scores Only	72.52	62.02	57.69	64.08
+Agreement	72.59	61.98	57.58	64.05

Table 2: Metric scores on the development set for the entity-centric model with and without the addition of entity-level agreement features.

used features derived from the scores produced by mention pair models, other entity-level features could easily be added. We experiment with this by adding four cluster-level agreement features based on gender, number, animacy, and named entity type. Each of these features can take on three values: "same" (e.g., both clusters have gender value *feminine*), "compatible" (e.g., one cluster has gender value *feminine* while the other has value *unknown*), or "incompatible" (one cluster has gender value *feminine* while the other has value *masculine*). The cluster-level value for a particular feature is the most common value among mentions in that cluster (e.g., if a cluster has 2 *masculine* mentions, 1 *feminine* mention, and 1 *unknown* mention) the value is considered *masculine*. Table 2 shows the results.

Adding the additional features had no substantial impact on scores, suggesting that features derived from pairwise scores are sufficient for capturing this kind of entity-level information. A disagreement between clusters necessarily means there will be disagreements between some of the involved mentions, so features like the average and minimum probability between mention pairs will have lower values when a disagreement is present.

Final System Performance

In Table 3 we compare the results of our system with the following state-of-the-art approaches: the JOINT and INDEP models of the Berkeley system (Durrett and Klein, 2014) (the JOINT model jointly does NER and entity linking along with coreference); the Prune-and-Score system (Ma et al., 2014); the HOTCoref system (Björkelund and Kuhn, 2014); the CPL^3M sytem (Chang et al., 2013); and Fernandes et al. We use the full entity-centric clustering algorithm drawing upon scores from both pairwise models. We do not make use of agreement features, as these did not increase accuracy and complicate the system. Our final model substantially outperforms the other systems on the CoNLL F_1 score. The largest improvement is in the B^3 metric, which is unsurprising because the entity-centric model primarily optimizes for this during training. However, our model also achieves the highest $CEAF_{\phi_4}$ F_1 and second highest MUC F_1 scores among the other systems.

5 Related Work

Both mention pair (Soon et al., 2001; Ng and Cardie, 2002; Bengtson and Roth, 2008; Stoyanov et al., 2010; Björkelund and Farkas, 2012) and mention ranking models (Denis and Baldridge, 2007b; Rahman and Ng, 2009) have been widely used for coreference resolution, and there have been many proposed ways of post-processing the pairwise scores to make predictions. Despite their simplicity, closest-first clustering (Soon et al., 2001) and best-first clustering (Ng and Cardie, 2002) are arguably the most widely used of these approaches. Other work uses global inference with integer linear programming to enforce transitivity (Denis and Baldridge, 2007a; Finkel and Manning, 2008), graph partitioning algorithms (McCallum and Wellner, 2005; Nicolae and Nicolae, 2006), the Dempster-Shafer rule (Kehler, 1997; Bean and Riloff, 2004), or correlational clustering (McCallum and Wellner, 2003; Finley and Joachims, 2005). In contrast to these methods, our entity-centric model directly *learns* how to use pairwise scores to produce a coreference partition that scores highly according to an evaluation metric, and can use the outputs of more than one mention pair model.

Recently, coreference models using *latent antecedents* have gained in popularity and achieved state-of-the-art results (Fernandes et al., 2012; Durrett and Klein, 2013; Chang et al., 2013; Björkelund and Kuhn, 2014). These learn a scoring function over mention pairs, but are trained to maximize a global objective function instead of pairwise accuracy. Unlike in our system, these methods typically consider one pair of mentions at a time during inference.

Several works have explored using non-local entity-level features in mention-entity models that assign a single mention to a (partially completed) cluster (Luo et al., 2004; Yang et al., 2008; Rahman and Ng, 2011). Our system, however, builds clusters incrementally through merge operations, and so can operate in an easy-first fashion. Raghunathan et al. (2010) take this approach with a rule-based system that runs in multiple passes

	MUC			B^3			$CEAF_{\phi_4}$			CoNLL
	Prec.	Rec.	F_1	Prec.	Rec.	F_1	Prec.	Rec.	F_1	Avg. F_1
Fernandes et al.	75.91	65.83	70.51	65.19	51.55	57.58	57.28	50.82	53.86	60.65
Chang et al.	-	-	69.48	-	-	57.44	-	-	53.07	60.00
Björkelund & Kuhn	74.3	67.46	70.72	62.71	54.96	58.58	59.4	52.27	55.61	61.63
Ma et al.	81.03	66.16	**72.84**	66.90	51.10	57.94	68.75	44.34	53.91	61.56
Durrett & Klein (INDEP.)	72.27	69.30	70.75	60.92	55.73	58.21	55.33	54.14	54.73	61.23
Durrett & Klein (JOINT)	72.61	69.91	71.24	61.18	56.43	58.71	56.17	54.23	55.18	61.71
This work	76.12	69.38	72.59	65.64	56.01	**60.44**	59.44	52.98	**56.02**	**63.02**

Table 3: Comparison of this work with other state-of-the-art approaches on the test set.

and Stoyanov and Eisner (2012) train a classifier to do this with a structured perceptron algorithm. Entity-level information has also been successfully incorporated in coreference systems using joint inference (McCallum and Wellner, 2003; Culotta et al., 2006; Poon and Domingos, 2008; Haghighi and Klein, 2010), but these approaches do not directly learn parameters tuned so the system runs effectively at test time, while our imitation learning approach does.

Imitation learning has been employed to train coreference resolvers on trajectories of decisions similar to those that would be seen at test-time by Daumé et al. (2005) and Ma et al. (2014). Other works use structured perceptron models for the same purpose (Stoyanov and Eisner, 2012; Fernandes et al., 2012; Björkelund and Kuhn, 2014). These systems all heuristically determine which actions are desirable for the system to perform. In contrast, our approach directly computes a cost for actions based on coreference evaluation metrics. This means our system directly learns which actions lead to good clusterings instead of which look good locally according to a heuristic. Furthermore, the costs provide our system a measure of the severity of a mistake, which we argue is very beneficial for the coreference task.

Our model stacking approach further distinguishes this work by providing a new way of defining cluster-level features. The majority of useful features for coreference systems operate on pairs of mentions (in one of our experiments we show the addition of classic entity-level features does not improve our system), but incremental coreference systems must make decisions involving many mention pairs. Other incremental coreference systems either incorporate features from a single pair (Stoyanov and Eisner, 2012) or average features across all pairs in the involved clusters (Ma et al., 2014). Our system instead combines information from the involved mention pairs in a variety of ways with with higher order features produced from the scores of mention pair models.

6 Conclusion

We introduced a new approach to coreference resolution that trains an entity-centric system using the scores produced by mention pair models as features. The brunt of task-specific learning occurs within the mention pair models, which are trained in a straightforward supervised manner. Guided by the pairwise scores, our entity-centric agent then learns an effective procedure for building up coreference clusters incrementally, using previous decisions to inform later ones. The agent benefits from using multiple mention pair models designed to capture different aspects of coreference. Experiments show that the agent, which *learns* how to coordinate mention pair scores, outperforms the commonly used best-first method. We evaluate our final system on the English portion of the CoNLL 2012 Shared Task and report a significant improvement over the current state of the art.

Acknowledgments

We thank the anonymous reviewers for their thoughtful comments. Stanford University gratefully acknowledges the support of the Defense Advanced Research Projects Agency (DARPA) Deep Exploration and Filtering of Text (DEFT) Program under Air Force Research Laboratory (AFRL) contract no. FA8750-13-2-0040. Any opinions, findings, and conclusion or recommendations expressed in this material are those of the authors and do not necessarily reflect the view of the DARPA, AFRL, or the US government.

References

Brenna D Argall, Sonia Chernova, Manuela Veloso, and Brett Browning. 2009. A survey of robot learning from demonstration. *Robotics and Autonomous Systems*, 57(5):469–483.

Amit Bagga and Breck Baldwin. 1998. Algorithms for scoring coreference chains. In *The First International Conference on Language Resources and Evaluation Workshop on Linguistics Coreference*, pages 563–566.

David L Bean and Ellen Riloff. 2004. Unsupervised learning of contextual role knowledge for coreference resolution. In *Human Language Technology and North American Association for Computational Linguistics (HLT-NAACL)*, pages 297–304.

Eric Bengtson and Dan Roth. 2008. Understanding the value of features for coreference resolution. In *Empirical Methods in Natural Language Processing (EMNLP)*, pages 294–303.

Anders Björkelund and Richárd Farkas. 2012. Data-driven multilingual coreference resolution using resolver stacking. In *Proceedings of the Joint Conference on Empirical Methods in Natural Language Processing and Conference on Computational Natural Language Learning - Shared Task*, pages 49–55.

Anders Björkelund and Jonas Kuhn. 2014. Learning structured perceptrons for coreference resolution with latent antecedents and non-local features. In *Association of Computational Linguistics (ACL)*.

Kai-Wei Chang, Rajhans Samdani, and Dan Roth. 2013. A constrained latent variable model for coreference resolution. In *Empirical Methods in Natural Language Processing (EMNLP)*, pages 601–612.

Aron Culotta, Michael Wick, Robert Hall, and Andrew McCallum. 2006. First-order probabilistic models for coreference resolution. In *Human Language Technology and North American Association for Computational Linguistics (HLT-NAACL)*, pages 81–88.

Hal Daumé III and Daniel Marcu. 2005. A large-scale exploration of effective global features for a joint entity detection and tracking model. In *Empirical Methods in Natural Language Processing (EMNLP)*, pages 97–104.

Hal Daumé III, John Langford, and Daniel Marcu. 2009. Search-based structured prediction. *Machine Learning*, 75(3):297–325.

Pascal Denis and Jason Baldridge. 2007a. Joint determination of anaphoricity and coreference resolution using integer programming. In *Human Language Technology and North American Association for Computational Linguistics (HLT-NAACL)*, pages 236–243.

Pascal Denis and Jason Baldridge. 2007b. A ranking approach to pronoun resolution. In *International Joint Conferences on Artificial Intelligence (IJCAI)*, pages 1588–1593.

John Duchi, Elad Hazan, and Yoram Singer. 2011. Adaptive subgradient methods for online learning and stochastic optimization. *Journal of Machine Learning Research*, 12:2121–2159.

Greg Durrett and Dan Klein. 2013. Easy victories and uphill battles in coreference resolution. In *Empirical Methods in Natural Language Processing (EMNLP)*, pages 1971–1982.

Greg Durrett and Dan Klein. 2014. A joint model for entity analysis: Coreference, typing, and linking. *Transactions of the Association for Computational Linguistics (TACL)*, 2:477–490.

Eraldo Rezende Fernandes, Cícero Nogueira Dos Santos, and Ruy Luiz Milidiú. 2012. Latent structure perceptron with feature induction for unrestricted coreference resolution. In *Proceedings of the Joint Conference on Empirical Methods in Natural Language Processing and Conference on Computational Natural Language Learning - Shared Task*, pages 41–48.

Jenny Rose Finkel and Christopher D Manning. 2008. Enforcing transitivity in coreference resolution. In *Association for Computational Linguistics (ACL), Short Paper*, pages 45–48.

Thomas Finley and Thorsten Joachims. 2005. Supervised clustering with support vector machines. In *Proceedings of the 22nd international conference on Machine learning*, pages 217–224.

Aria Haghighi and Dan Klein. 2010. Coreference resolution in a modular, entity-centered model. In *Human Language Technology and North American Association for Computational Linguistics (HLT-NAACL)*, pages 385–393.

Eduard Hovy, Mitchell Marcus, Martha Palmer, Lance Ramshaw, and Ralph Weischedel. 2006. Ontonotes: the 90% solution. In *Human Language Technology and North American Association for Computational Linguistics (HLT-NAACL)*, pages 57–60.

Andrew Kehler. 1997. Probabilistic coreference in information extraction. In *Empirical Methods in Natural Language Processing (EMNLP)*, pages 163–173.

Heeyoung Lee, Yves Peirsman, Angel Chang, Nathanael Chambers, Mihai Surdeanu, and Dan Jurafsky. 2011. Stanford's multi-pass sieve coreference resolution system at the conll-2011 shared task. In *Proceedings of the Conference on Computational Natural Language Learning: Shared Task*, pages 28–34.

Xiaoqiang Luo, Abe Ittycheriah, Hongyan Jing, Nanda Kambhatla, and Salim Roukos. 2004. A mention-synchronous coreference resolution algorithm based on the bell tree. In *Association for Computational Linguistics (ACL)*, page 135.

Xiaoqiang Luo. 2005. On coreference resolution performance metrics. In *Empirical Methods in Natural Language Processing (EMNLP)*, pages 25–32.

Chao Ma, Janardhan Rao Doppa, J Walker Orr, Prashanth Mannem, Xiaoli Fern, Tom Dietterich, and Prasad Tadepalli. 2014. Prune-and-score: Learning for greedy coreference resolution. In *Empirical Methods in Natural Language Processing (EMNLP)*.

Andrew McCallum and Ben Wellner. 2003. Toward conditional models of identity uncertainty with application to proper noun coreference. In *Proceedings of the IJCAI Workshop on Information Integration on the Web*.

Andrew McCallum and Ben Wellner. 2005. Conditional models of identity uncertainty with application to noun coreference. In *Advances in Neural Information Processing Systems (NIPS)*, pages 905–912.

Vincent Ng and Claire Cardie. 2002. Improving machine learning approaches to coreference resolution. In *Association of Computational Linguistics (ACL)*, pages 104–111.

Cristina Nicolae and Gabriel Nicolae. 2006. Bestcut: A graph algorithm for coreference resolution. In *Empirical Methods in Natural Language Processing (EMNLP)*, pages 275–283.

Hoifung Poon and Pedro Domingos. 2008. Joint unsupervised coreference resolution with markov logic. In *Empirical Methods in Natural Language Processing (EMNLP)*, pages 650–659.

Sameer Pradhan, Alessandro Moschitti, Nianwen Xue, Olga Uryupina, and Yuchen Zhang. 2012. Conll-2012 shared task: Modeling multilingual unrestricted coreference in ontonotes. In *Proceedings of the Joint Conference on Empirical Methods in Natural Language Processing and Conference on Computational Natural Language Learning - Shared Task*, pages 1–40.

Karthik Raghunathan, Heeyoung Lee, Sudarshan Rangarajan, Nathanael Chambers, Mihai Surdeanu, Dan Jurafsky, and Christopher Manning. 2010. A multi-pass sieve for coreference resolution. In *Empirical Methods in Natural Language Processing (EMNLP)*, pages 492–501.

Altaf Rahman and Vincent Ng. 2009. Supervised models for coreference resolution. In *Empirical Methods in Natural Language Processing (EMNLP)*, pages 968–977.

Altaf Rahman and Vincent Ng. 2011. Narrowing the modeling gap: a cluster-ranking approach to coreference resolution. *Journal of Artificial Intelligence Research (JAIR)*, pages 469–521.

Marta Recasens, Marie-Catherine de Marneffe, and Christopher Potts. 2013. The life and death of discourse entities: Identifying singleton mentions. In *Human Language Technology and North American Association for Computational Linguistics (HLT-NAACL)*, pages 627–633.

Stéphane Ross, Geoffrey J Gordon, and J Andrew Bagnell. 2011. A reduction of imitation learning and structured prediction to no-regret online learning. In *Artificial Intelligence and Statistics (AISTATS)*, pages 627–633.

Wee Meng Soon, Hwee Tou Ng, and Daniel Chung Yong Lim. 2001. A machine learning approach to coreference resolution of noun phrases. *Computational Linguistics*, 27(4):521–544.

Veselin Stoyanov and Jason Eisner. 2012. Easy-first coreference resolution. In *COLING*, pages 2519–2534.

Veselin Stoyanov, Claire Cardie, Nathan Gilbert, Ellen Riloff, David Buttler, and David Hysom. 2010. Reconcile: A coreference resolution research platform. Computer Science Technical Report, Cornell University, Ithaca, NY.

Marc Vilain, John Burger, John Aberdeen, Dennis Connolly, and Lynette Hirschman. 1995. A model-theoretic coreference scoring scheme. In *Proceedings of the 6th conference on Message understanding*, pages 45–52.

Xiaofeng Yang, Jian Su, Jun Lang, Chew Lim Tan, Ting Liu, and Sheng Li. 2008. An entity-mention model for coreference resolution with inductive logic programming. In *Association of Computational Linguistics (ACL)*, pages 843–851.

Learning Anaphoricity and Antecedent Ranking Features for Coreference Resolution

Sam Wiseman[1] **Alexander M. Rush**[1,2] **Stuart M. Shieber**[1] **Jason Weston**[2]

[1]School of Engineering and Applied Sciences
Harvard University
Cambridge, MA, USA
{swiseman,srush,shieber}@seas.harvard.edu

[2]Facebook AI Research
New York, NY, USA
jase@fb.com

Abstract

We introduce a simple, non-linear mention-ranking model for coreference resolution that attempts to learn distinct feature representations for anaphoricity detection and antecedent ranking, which we encourage by pre-training on a pair of corresponding subtasks. Although we use only simple, unconjoined features, the model is able to learn useful representations, and we report the best overall score on the CoNLL 2012 English test set to date.

1 Introduction

One of the major challenges associated with resolving coreference is that in typical documents the number of mentions (syntactic units capable of referring or being referred to) that are *non-anaphoric* – that is, that are not coreferent with any previous mention – far exceeds the number of mentions that are anaphoric (Kummerfeld and Klein, 2013; Durrett and Klein, 2013).

This preponderance of non-anaphoric mentions makes coreference resolution challenging, partly because many basic coreference features, such as those looking at head, number, or gender match fail to distinguish between truly coreferent pairs and the large number of matching but nonetheless non-coreferent pairs. Indeed, several authors have noted that it is difficult to obtain good performance on the coreference task using simple features (Lee et al., 2011; Fernandes et al., 2012; Durrett and Klein, 2013; Kummerfeld and Klein, 2013; Björkelund and Kuhn, 2014) and, as a result, state-of-the-art systems tend to use linear models with complicated feature conjunction schemes in order to capture more fine-grained interactions. While this approach has shown success, it is not obvious which additional feature conjunctions will lead to improved performance, which is problematic as systems attempt to scale with new data and features.

In this work, we propose a data-driven model for coreference that does not require prespecifying any feature relationships. Inspired by recent work in learning representations for natural language tasks (Collobert et al., 2011), we explore neural network models which take only raw, unconjoined features as input, and attempt to learn intermediate representations automatically. In particular, the model we describe attempts to create independent feature representations useful for both detecting the anaphoricity of a mention (that is, whether or not a mention is anaphoric) and ranking the potential antecedents of an anaphoric mention. Adequately capturing anaphoricity information has long been thought to be an important aspect of the coreference task (see Ng (2004) and Section 7), since a strong non-anaphoric signal might, for instance, discourage the erroneous prediction of an antecedent for a non-anaphoric mention even in the presence of a misleading head match.

We furthermore attempt to encourage the learning of the desired feature representations by pretraining the model's weights on two corresponding subtasks, namely, anaphoricity detection and antecedent ranking of known anaphoric mentions.

Overall our best model has an absolute gain of almost 2 points in CoNLL score over a similar but linear mention-ranking model on the CoNLL 2012 English test set (Pradhan et al., 2012), and of over 1.5 points over the state-of-the-art coreference system. Moreover, unlike current state-of-the-art systems, our model does only local inference, and is therefore significantly simpler.

1.1 Problem Setting

We consider here the mention-ranking (or "mention-synchronous") approach to coreference

Proceedings of the 53rd Annual Meeting of the Association for Computational Linguistics and the 7th International Joint Conference on Natural Language Processing, pages 1416–1426, Beijing, China, July 26-31, 2015.

resolution (Denis and Baldridge, 2008; Bengtson and Roth, 2008; Rahman and Ng, 2009), which has been adopted by several recent coreference systems (Durrett and Klein, 2013; Chang et al., 2013). Such systems aim to identify whether a mention is coreferent with an antecedent mention, or whether it is instead non-anaphoric (the first mention in the document referring to a particular entity). This is accomplished by assigning a score to the mention's potential antecedents as well as to the possibility that it is non-anaphoric, and then predicting the greatest scoring option. We furthermore assume the more realistic "system mention" setting, where it is not known a priori which mentions in a document participate in coreference clusters, and so (all) mentions must be automatically extracted, typically with the aid of automatically detected parse trees.

Formally, we denote the set of automatically detected mentions in a document by $\mathcal{X}$. For a mention $x \in \mathcal{X}$, let $\mathcal{A}(x)$ denote the set of mentions appearing before x; we refer to this set as x's potential antecedents. Additionally let the symbol ϵ denote the empty antecedent, to which we will view x as referring when x is non-anaphoric.[1] Denoting the set $\mathcal{A}(x) \cup \{\epsilon\}$ by $\mathcal{Y}(x)$, a mention-ranking model defines a scoring function $s(x, y) : \mathcal{X} \times \mathcal{Y} \rightarrow \mathbb{R}$, and predicts the antecedent of x to be $y^* = \arg\max_{y \in \mathcal{Y}(x)} s(x, y)$.

It is common to be quite liberal when extracting mentions, taking, essentially, every noun phrase or pronoun to be a candidate mention, so as not to prematurely discard those that might be coreferent (Lee et al., 2011; Fernandes et al., 2012; Chang et al., 2012; Durrett and Klein, 2013). For instance, the Berkeley Coreference System (herein BCS) (Durrett and Klein, 2013), which we use for mention extraction in our experiments, recovers approximately 96.4% of the truly anaphoric mentions in the CoNLL 2012 training set, with an almost 3.5:1 ratio of non-anaphoric mentions to anaphoric mentions among the extracted mentions.

2 Mention Ranking Models

The structural simplicity of the mention-ranking framework puts much of the burden on the scoring function $s(x, y)$. We begin by considering mention-ranking systems using linear scoring functions. In the next section, we will extend these models to operate over learned non-linear representations.

Linear mention-ranking models generally utilize the following scoring function

$$s_{\text{lin}}(x, y) \triangleq \boldsymbol{w}^{\mathsf{T}} \boldsymbol{\phi}(x, y) \quad ,$$

where $\boldsymbol{\phi} : \mathcal{X} \times \mathcal{Y} \rightarrow \mathbb{R}^d$ is a pairwise feature function defined on a mention and a potential antecedent, and $\boldsymbol{w}$ is a learned parameter vector.

To add additional flexibility to the model, linear mention ranking models may duplicate individual features in $\boldsymbol{\phi}$, with one version being used when predicting an antecedent for x, and another when predicting that x is non-anaphoric (Durrett and Klein, 2013). Such a scheme effectively gives rise to the following piecewise scoring function

$$s_{\text{lin+}}(x, y) \triangleq \begin{cases} \boldsymbol{u}^{\mathsf{T}} \begin{bmatrix} \boldsymbol{\phi}_{\text{a}}(x) \\ \boldsymbol{\phi}_{\text{p}}(x,y) \end{bmatrix} & \text{if } y \neq \epsilon \\ \boldsymbol{v}^{\mathsf{T}} \boldsymbol{\phi}_{\text{a}}(x) & \text{if } y = \epsilon \end{cases} \quad ,$$

where $\boldsymbol{\phi}_{\text{a}} : \mathcal{X} \rightarrow \mathbb{R}^{d_{\text{a}}}$ is a feature function defined on a mention and its context, $\boldsymbol{\phi}_{\text{p}} : \mathcal{X} \times \mathcal{Y} \rightarrow \mathbb{R}^{d_{\text{p}}}$ is a pairwise feature function defined on a mention and a potential antecedent, and parameters $\boldsymbol{u}$ and $\boldsymbol{v}$ replace $\boldsymbol{w}$. Above, we have made an explicit distinction between pairwise features ($\boldsymbol{\phi}_{\text{p}}$) and those strictly on x and its context ($\boldsymbol{\phi}_{\text{a}}$), and moreover assumed that our features need not examine potential antecedents when predicting $y = \epsilon$.

We refer to the basic, unconjoined features used for $\boldsymbol{\phi}_{\text{a}}$ and $\boldsymbol{\phi}_{\text{p}}$ as *raw* features. Figure 2 shows two versions of these features, a base set BASIC and an extended set BASIC+. The BASIC set are the raw features used in BCS, and BASIC+ includes additional raw features used in other recent coreference sytems. For instance, BASIC+ additionally includes features suggested by Recasens et al. (2013) to be useful for anaphoricity, such as the number of a mention, its named entity status, and its animacy, as well as number and gender information. We additionally include bilexical head features, which are used in many well-performing systems (for instance, that of Fernandes et al. (2012)).

2.1 Problems with Raw Features

Many authors have observed that, taken individually, raw features tend to not be particularly predictive for the coreference task. We examine this phenomenon empirically in Figure 1. These

[1] We make this stipulation for modeling convenience; it is not intended to reflect any linguistic fact.

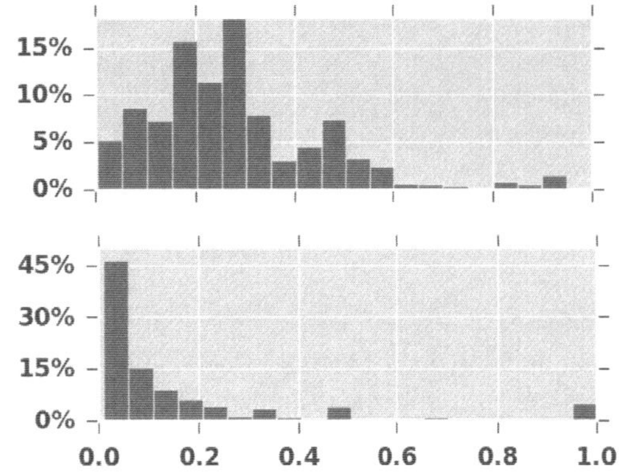

Figure 1: Two histograms illustrating the predictive ability of raw (unconjoined) features per feature occurrence: (top) mention-context features from ϕ_a as independent predictors of anaphoricity ($y \neq \epsilon$), and (bottom) antecedent-mention features from ϕ_p as independent predictors of coreferent mentions. Very few raw features are strong indicators of either anaphoricity or an antecedent match. Data taken from the CoNLL development set.

graphs show that the vast majority of individual features do not give a strong positive signal either of anaphoricity or for an antecedent match.

To address this issue, state-of-the-art mention-ranking systems often rely on manual or otherwise induced conjunction schemes to capture specific feature interactions. Durrett and Klein (2013), for instance, conjoin all raw features in ϕ_a with the *type* of the mention x, and all raw features in ϕ_p with the types of the current mention and antecedent. For these purposes, the *type* of a mention is either "nominal", "proper", or a canonicalization of the pronoun if it is a pronominal mention. Fernandes et al. (2012) and Björkelund and Kuhn (2014) use an automatic but complicated scheme to induce conjunctions by first extracting feature templates from a separately trained decision tree, and then doing greedy forward selection among the templates. These conjunctions add some non-linearity to the scoring function while still maintaining a tractable, though large, feature set.

3 Learning Features for Ranking

As an alternative to the aforementioned feature conjunction schemes, we consider learning feature representations in order to better capture relevant aspects of the task. Representation learning affords the model more flexibility in exploiting feature interactions, although it can make the underlying training problem more difficult.

	Mention Features (ϕ_a) Feature	Value Set
	Mention Head	$\mathcal{V}$
	Mention First Word	$\mathcal{V}$
	Mention Last Word	$\mathcal{V}$
	Word Preceding Mention	$\mathcal{V}$
	Word Following Mention	$\mathcal{V}$
	# Words in Mention	$\{1, 2, \ldots\}$
	Mention Synt. Ancestry	see BCS (2013)
	Mention Type	$\mathcal{T}$
+	Mention Governor	$\mathcal{V}$
+	Mention Sentence Index	$\{1, 2, \ldots\}$
+	Mention Entity Type	NER tags
+	Mention Number	{sing.,plur.,unk}
+	Mention Animacy	{an.,inan.,unk}
+	Mention Gender	{m,f,neut.,unk}
+	Mention Person	{1,2,3,unk}

	Pairwise Features (ϕ_p) Feature	Value Set
	BASIC features on Mention	see above
	BASIC features on Antecedent	see above
	Mentions between Ment., Ante.	{0...10}
	Sentences between Ment., Ante.	{0...10}
	i-within-i	{T,F}
	Same Speaker	{T,F}
	Document Type	{Conv.,Art.}
	Ante., Ment. String Match	{T,F}
	Ante. contains Ment.	{T,F}
	Ment. contains Ante.	{T,F}
	Ante. contains Ment. Head	{T,F}
	Mention contains Ante. Head	{T,F}
	Ante., Ment. Head Match	{T,F}
	Ante., Ment. Synt. Ancestries	see above
+	BASIC+ features on Ment.	see above
+	BASIC+ features on Ante.	see above
+	Ante., Ment. Numbers	see above
+	Ante., Ment. Genders	see above
+	Ante., Ment. Persons	see above
+	Ante., Ment., Entity Types	see above
+	Ante., Ment. Heads	see above
+	Ante., Ment. Types	see above

Figure 2: Features used for $\phi_a(x)$ and $\phi_p(x, y)$. The '+' indicates a feature is in BASIC+ feature set. $\mathcal{V}$ denotes the training vocabulary, and $\mathcal{T}$ denotes the set of mention types, viz., {nominal,proper} ∪ {canonical pronouns}, as defined in BCS. Conv. and Art. abbreviate conversation and article (resp.). Lexicalized features occurring fewer than 20 times in the training set back off to part-of-speech; bilexical heads occurring fewer than 10 times back off to an indicator feature. Animacy information is taken from a list and rules used in the Stanford Coreference system (Lee et al., 2013).

3.1 Model

We use a neural network to define our model as an extension to the mention-ranking model introduced in Section 2. We consider in particular the scoring function:

$$s(x, y) \triangleq \begin{cases} \boldsymbol{u}^{\mathsf{T}} \boldsymbol{g}(\begin{bmatrix} \boldsymbol{h}_a(x) \\ \boldsymbol{h}_p(x,y) \end{bmatrix}) + u_0 & \text{if } y \neq \epsilon \\ \boldsymbol{v}^{\mathsf{T}} \boldsymbol{h}_a(x) + v_0 & \text{if } y = \epsilon \end{cases} ,$$

where $\boldsymbol{h}_{\mathrm{a}}$ and $\boldsymbol{h}_{\mathrm{p}}$ are feature representations, non-linear functions of the features $\boldsymbol{\phi}_{\mathrm{a}}$ and $\boldsymbol{\phi}_{\mathrm{p}}$ (respectively), and $\boldsymbol{g}$ is a function of these representations. In particular, we define

$$\begin{aligned}\boldsymbol{h}_{\mathrm{a}}(x) &\triangleq \tanh(\boldsymbol{W}_{\mathrm{a}}\,\boldsymbol{\phi}_{\mathrm{a}}(x) + \boldsymbol{b}_{\mathrm{a}})\\ \boldsymbol{h}_{\mathrm{p}}(x,y) &\triangleq \tanh(\boldsymbol{W}_{\mathrm{p}}\,\boldsymbol{\phi}_{\mathrm{p}}(x,y) + \boldsymbol{b}_{\mathrm{p}})\end{aligned} \quad ,$$

and we take $\boldsymbol{g}$ to either be the identity function, in which case the above model is analogous to $s_{\mathrm{lin+}}$ but defined over non-linear feature representations, or to be an additional hidden layer: $\boldsymbol{g}(\left[\begin{smallmatrix}\boldsymbol{h}_{\mathrm{a}}(x)\\ \boldsymbol{h}_{\mathrm{p}}(x,y)\end{smallmatrix}\right]) = \tanh(\boldsymbol{W}\left[\begin{smallmatrix}\boldsymbol{h}_{\mathrm{a}}(x)\\ \boldsymbol{h}_{\mathrm{p}}(x,y)\end{smallmatrix}\right] + \boldsymbol{b})$. For ease of exposition, we will refer to these two settings of $\boldsymbol{g}$ as $\boldsymbol{g}_1$ and $\boldsymbol{g}_2$ (respectively) in what follows. As we will see below, both settings lead to comparable performance, but to a different error distribution.

In either case, by defining the functions $\boldsymbol{h}_{\mathrm{a}}$ and $\boldsymbol{h}_{\mathrm{p}}$, we allow the model to learn representations of the input features $\boldsymbol{\phi}_{\mathrm{a}}$ and $\boldsymbol{\phi}_{\mathrm{p}}$. The benefit of the added non-linearities is that, in theory, it is no longer necessary to explicitly specify feature conjunctions, since the model may learn them automatically if necessary. Accordingly, for this model we use only $\boldsymbol{\phi}_{\mathrm{a}}$ and $\boldsymbol{\phi}_{\mathrm{p}}$ consisting of the raw features in Figure 2 without conjunctions. Any interaction between these features must be learned by the feature representations $\boldsymbol{h}_{\mathrm{p}}$ and $\boldsymbol{h}_{\mathrm{a}}$.

3.2 Training

We can directly train our model using back-propagation. To specify the training problem, we first define notation for the training objective.

Define the set $\mathcal{C}(x)$ to contain just the mentions in $\mathcal{A}(x)$ that are coreferent with x. We then define

$$\mathcal{C}'(x) = \begin{cases}\mathcal{C}(x) & \text{if } x \text{ is anaphoric}\\ \{\epsilon\} & \text{otherwise}\end{cases} \quad .$$

Finally, let $y_n^\ell = \arg\max_{y \in \mathcal{C}'(x_n)} s(x_n, y)$ be the highest scoring correct antecedent of x_n, which may be ϵ. (Thus, following recent work (Yu and Joachims, 2009; Fernandes et al., 2012; Chang et al., 2013; Durrett and Klein, 2013), we view each mention as having a "latent antecedent".[2]) We train to minimize the regularized, slack-rescaled, latent-variable loss[3] given by:

$$L(\boldsymbol{\theta}) = \sum_{n=1}^{N} \max_{\hat{y} \in \mathcal{Y}(x_n)} \Delta(x_n, \hat{y})(1 + s(x_n, \hat{y}) - s(x_n, y_n^\ell)) + \lambda ||\boldsymbol{\theta}||_1,$$

where Δ is a mistake-specific cost function, which is 0 when $\hat{y} \in \mathcal{C}'(x_n)$. Above, we use $\boldsymbol{\theta}$ to refer to the full set of parameters $\{\boldsymbol{W}, \boldsymbol{u}, \boldsymbol{v}, \boldsymbol{W}_{\mathrm{a}}, \boldsymbol{W}_{\mathrm{p}}, \boldsymbol{b}_{\mathrm{a}}, \boldsymbol{b}_{\mathrm{p}}\}$.

For experiments, we define Δ to take on different costs for the three kinds of mistakes possible in a coreference task, as follows:

$$\Delta(x, \hat{y}) = \begin{cases}\alpha_1 & \text{if } \hat{y} \neq \epsilon \wedge \epsilon \in \mathcal{C}'(x)\\ \alpha_2 & \text{if } \hat{y} = \epsilon \wedge \epsilon \notin \mathcal{C}'(x)\\ \alpha_3 & \text{if } \hat{y} \neq \epsilon \wedge \hat{y} \notin \mathcal{C}'(x)\end{cases} \quad .$$

The α_i determine the trade-off between these mistakes (and thus precision and recall). Adopting the terminology of BCS, we refer to these mistakes as "false link" (FL), "false new" (FN), and "wrong link" (WL), respectively.

4 Representations from Subtasks

While we could train our full model directly, it is known to be difficult to train high performing non-convex neural-network models from a random initialization (Erhan et al., 2010). In order to overcome the problems associated with training from this setting, and to learn feature representations useful for the full coreference task, we pretrain subparts of the model on the subtasks targeting the desired feature representations. We then train the entire model on the full coreference task (from the pre-trained initializations). As we will see, the pre-training scheme outlined below helps the model achieve improved performance.

The proposed pre-training scheme involves learning the parameters associated with $\boldsymbol{h}_{\mathrm{a}}$ and $\boldsymbol{h}_{\mathrm{p}}$ using two natural subtasks: anaphoricity detection and antecedent ranking. In particular, we (1) train $\boldsymbol{h}_{\mathrm{a}}$ on the task of predicting whether a particular mention is anaphoric or not, and (2) train $\boldsymbol{h}_{\mathrm{p}}$ on the task of predicting the antecedent of mentions known to be anaphoric.

4.1 Anaphoricity Detection

For the first subtask we attempt to predict whether a mention is anaphoric or not based only on its

[2] Note that this renders the objectives of even models with a linear scoring function non-convex.

[3] Previous work divides between log-loss and margin loss. We use the latter because gradient updates (within backprop) for the non-probabilistic objectives only involve terms relating to $\hat{y}$ and y_n^ℓ, and are therefore faster.

Feat. (Conj.)	Model	Anaphoric P	R	F_1	Ante Acc.
BASIC (N)	Lin.	74.15	74.20	74.18	69.10
BASIC (Y)	Lin.	73.98	75.04	74.51	79.76
BASIC (N)	NN	75.30	75.36	75.33	81.65
BASIC+ (N)	Lin.	74.14	74.71	74.43	74.02
BASIC+ (Y)	Lin.	74.24	75.39	74.81	80.44
BASIC+ (N)	NN	75.84	76.02	75.93	82.86

Table 1: Performance of the two subtasks on the CoNLL 2012 development set by feature set and model type. "Conj." indicates whether conjunctions are used. The linear anaphoric system is an SVM (LibLinear implementation (Fan et al., 2008)), and the linear antecedent system is a linear model with the margin-based objective.

local context.[4] Anaphoricity detection in various forms has been used as an initial step in several coreference systems (Ng and Cardie, 2002; Bengtson and Roth, 2008; Rahman and Ng, 2009; Björkelund and Farkas, 2012), and the related question of whether a mention can be determined to be a *singleton* or not has been explored recently by Recasens et al. (2013), Ma et al. (2014), and others.[5]

Formally, let $t_n \in \{-1, 1\}$ indicate whether $\epsilon \in \mathcal{C}'(x_n)$ or not (respectively). That is, $t_n = 1$ if and only if x_n is anaphoric. Define the subtask scoring function $s_a : \mathcal{X} \rightarrow \mathbb{R}$ as

$$s_a(x) \triangleq \boldsymbol{v}_a{}^{\mathsf{T}} \boldsymbol{h}_a(x) + \nu_0 \quad ,$$

where the vector $\boldsymbol{v}_a$ and the bias ν_0 are specific to this subtask and are discarded after pre-training.

We train this model to minimize the following slack-rescaled objective

$$L_a(\boldsymbol{\theta}_a) = \sum_{n=1}^{N} \Delta_a(t_n)[1 - t_n\, s_a(x_n)]_+ + \lambda ||\boldsymbol{\theta}_a||_1,$$

where Δ_a is a class-specific cost used to help encourage anaphoric decisions given the imbalanced data set, and $\boldsymbol{\theta}_a = \{\boldsymbol{v}_a, \boldsymbol{W}_a, \boldsymbol{b}_a\}$ are the parameters of the subtask.

4.2 Antecedent Ranking

For the second subtask, antecedent ranking, we predict the antecedent for mentions known a priori to be anaphoric. This subtask is inspired by the "gold mention" version of the coreference task. Systems designed for this task are forced to handle many fewer non-anaphoric mentions and can often successfully utilize richer feature representations.

[4]While performance on this *subtask* can in fact be improved further by looking at previous mentions, features learned in this way led to inferior performance on the full task.

[5]Note that singleton detection is slightly different from anaphoricity detection, since a mention can be non-anaphoric but not a singleton if it is the first mention in a cluster.

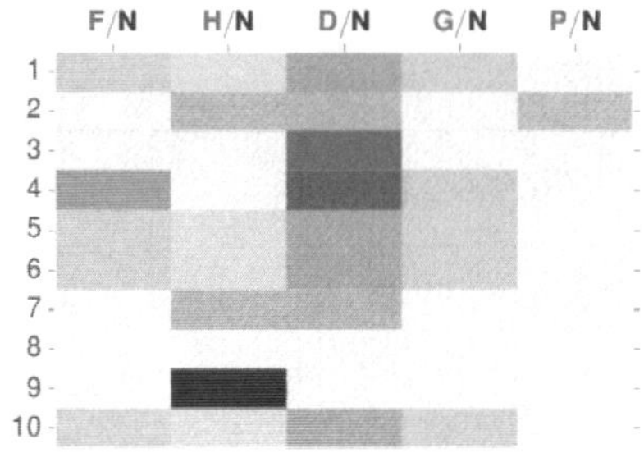

Figure 3: Visualization of the representation matrix $\boldsymbol{W}_p$. A subset of the raw features were manually grouped into five classes indicating: full lexical match [F], head match [H], mention/sentence distance [D] (near versus far), gender/number match [G], and type [P] (pronoun versus other). The heat map illustrates 10-columns of $\boldsymbol{W}_p$ as a weighted combination of these classes, roughly illustrating the combination of raw features required for this dimension of the representation.

The setup for this task is similar to the full coreference problem, except that we discard any mention x_n such that $\epsilon \in \mathcal{C}'(x_n)$. Thus, we define the pairwise scoring function $s_p : \mathcal{X} \times \mathcal{Y} \rightarrow \mathbb{R}$ as

$$s_p(x, y) \triangleq \boldsymbol{u}_p{}^{\mathsf{T}} \boldsymbol{h}_p(x, y) + \upsilon_0 \quad .$$

As before, $\boldsymbol{u}_p$ and υ_0 are discarded after training for this subtask, but we keep the rest of the parameters. For training, we use an analogous latent-variable loss function to that used for the full coreference task, except we replace $\mathcal{C}'$ with $\mathcal{C}$, and the cost $\Delta(x, \hat{y})$ is always 1 (when it is nonzero).

4.3 Subtask Performance

As a preliminary experiment, we train models for these two subtasks using both the BASIC and BASIC+ raw features. Table 1 shows the results. For the first subtask, experiments look at the precision, recall, and F_1 score of predicting anaphoric mentions on the CoNLL 2012 development set. As a baseline we use an L1-regularized SVM implemented using LibLinear (Fan et al., 2008), both using raw features and using features conjoined according to the BCS scheme. For the second subtask, experiments look at the accuracy of the model in predicting the correct antecedent on known anaphoric mentions. As a baseline we use a linear mention ranking model, with and without conjunctions, trained using the same margin-based loss.

In both subtasks, the neural network model performs quite well, significantly better than the unconjoined baselines and better than the model trained with manually conjoined features. We provide a visual representation of the antecedent ranking features learned in Figure 3. While the improved subtask performance does not imply better performance on the full coreference task, it shows that model can learn useful feature representations with only raw input features.

5 Coreference Experiments

Our experiments examine performance as compared with other coreference systems, as well as the effect of features, pre-training, and model architecture. We also perform a qualitative comparison of our model with the analogous linear model on some challenging non-anaphoric cases.

5.1 Methods

All experiments use the CoNLL 2012 English dataset (Pradhan et al., 2012), which is based on the OntoNotes corpus (Hovy et al., 2006). The data set contains 3,493 documents consisting of 1.6 million words. We use the standard experimental split with the training set containing 2,802 documents and 156K annotated mentions, the development set containing 343 documents and 19K annotated mentions, and the test set containing 348 documents and 20K annotated mentions. For all experiments, we use BCS (Durrett and Klein, 2013) to extract system mentions and to compute some of the features.

For training, we minimize the loss described above using the composite mirror descent AdaGrad update (Duchi et al., 2011) with document sized mini-batches.[6] We tuned the AdaGrad learning rate and regularization parameters using a grid search over possible learning rates $\eta \in \{0.001, 0.002, 0.01, 0.02, 0.1, 0.2\}$ and over regularization parameters $\lambda \in \{10^{-6}, \ldots, 10^{-1}\}$. For the full coreference task, we use a different learning rate for the pre-trained weights and for the second-layer weights, using $\eta_1 = 0.1$ and $\eta_2 = 0.001$, respectively, and $\lambda = 10^{-6}$. When initializing weight-matrices that were not pre-trained we used the sparse initialization technique proposed by Sutskever et al. (2013). For all experiments we use the cost-weights $\boldsymbol{\alpha} = \langle 0.5, 1.2, 1\rangle$ in defining Δ.

For the anaphoricity representations the matrix dimensions used are $\boldsymbol{W}_{\mathrm{a}} \in \mathbb{R}^{128 \times d_{\mathrm{a}}}$, and for the pairwise representations the matrix dimensions used are $\boldsymbol{W}_{\mathrm{p}} \in \mathbb{R}^{700 \times d_{\mathrm{p}}}$. In the $\boldsymbol{g}_2$ model, the outer matrix dimensions are $\boldsymbol{W} \in \mathbb{R}^{128 \times (d_{\mathrm{p}} + d_{\mathrm{a}})}$. With the BASIC+ features, d_{p} and d_{a} come out to be slightly less than 10^6 and 10^4, respectively, with bilexical head features accounting for the vast majority of d_{p}.[7] We tuned all hyper-parameters (as well as those of baseline systems) on the development set.

We use the CoNLL 2012 scoring script v8.01[8] (Pradhan et al., 2014; Luo et al., 2014), which scores based on 3 metrics, including MUC (Vilain et al., 1995), CEAF_e (Luo, 2005), and B^3 (Bagga and Baldwin, 1998), as well as the CoNLL score, which is the arithmetic mean of the 3 metrics.

Code implementing our models is available at `https://github.com/swiseman/nn_coref`. The system trains in time comparable to that of linear systems, mainly because we use only raw features and sparse margin-based gradient updates.

5.2 Results

Our main results are shown in Table 2. This table compares the performance of our system with the performance reported by several other state-of-the art systems on the CoNLL 2012 English coreference test set. Our full models achieve the best F_1 score across two of the three metrics and have the best aggregate (CoNLL) score, with an improvement of over 1.5 points over the best reported result, and of almost 2 points over the best mention-ranking system. Our F_1 improvements on all three metrics are significant ($p < 0.05$ under the bootstrap resample test (Koehn, 2004)) as compared with both Björkelund and Kuhn (2014), and Durrett and Klein (2014), the two most recent, state-of-the-art systems.

Since our full models use some additional raw features (although an order of magnitude fewer total features than the comparable conjunction-

[6] In preliminary experiments we also used Nesterov's accelerated gradient (Nesterov, 1983), but found AdaGrad to perform better.

[7] Note that the BCS conjunction scheme, for instance, applied to our raw features gives a d_{p} and d_{a} that are over an order of magnitude larger.

[8] `http://conll.github.io/reference-coreference-scorers/`

System	MUC			B^3			$CEAF_e$			
	P	R	F_1	P	R	F_1	P	R	F_1	CoNLL
BCS (2013)	74.89	67.17	70.82	64.26	53.09	58.14	58.12	52.67	55.27	61.41
Prune&Score (2014)	81.03	66.16	**72.84**	66.9	51.10	57.94	68.75	44.34	53.91	61.56
B&K (2014)	74.3	67.46	70.72	62.71	54.96	58.58	59.4	52.27	55.61	61.63
D&K (2014)	72.73	69.98	71.33	61.18	56.60	58.80	56.20	54.31	55.24	61.79
This work ($\boldsymbol{g}_2$)	76.96	68.10	72.26	66.90	54.12	59.84	59.02	53.34	56.03	62.71
This work ($\boldsymbol{g}_1$)	76.23	69.31	72.60	66.07	55.83	**60.52**	59.41	54.88	**57.05**	**63.39**

Table 2: Results on CoNLL 2012 English test set. We compare against recent state-of-the-art systems, including (in order) Durrett and Klein (2013), Ma et al. (2014), Björkelund and Kuhn (2014), and Durrett and Klein (2014) (rescored with the v8.01 scorer). F_1 gains are significant ($p < 0.05$ under the bootstrap resample test (Koehn, 2004)) compared with both B&K and D&K for all metrics.

Model	Features	MUC	B^3	$CEAF_e$	CoNLL
Lin.		70.44	59.10	55.57	61.71
NN ($\boldsymbol{g}_2$)	BASIC	71.59	60.56	57.45	63.20
NN ($\boldsymbol{g}_1$)		71.86	60.9	57.90	63.55
Lin.		70.92	60.05	56.39	62.45
NN ($\boldsymbol{g}_2$)	BASIC+	72.68	61.70	58.32	64.23
NN ($\boldsymbol{g}_1$)		72.74	61.77	58.63	64.38

Table 3: F_1 performance comparison between state-of-the-art linear mention-ranking model (Durrett and Klein, 2013) and our full models on CoNLL 2012 development set for different feature sets.

Model	MUC	B^3	$CEAF_e$	CoNLL
Fully Conn. 1 Layer	71.80	60.93	57.51	63.41
Fully Conn. 2 Layer	71.77	60.84	57.05	63.22
$\boldsymbol{g}_1$ + RI	71.92	61.06	57.59	63.52
$\boldsymbol{g}_1$ + PT	72.74	61.77	58.63	64.38
$\boldsymbol{g}_2$ + RI	72.31	61.79	58.06	64.05
$\boldsymbol{g}_2$ + PT	72.68	61.70	58.32	64.23

Table 4: Comparison of performance (in F_1 score) of various models on CoNLL 2012 development set using BASIC+ features. "PT" and "RI" refer to pretraining and random initialization respectively. "Fully Conn." refers to baseline fully connected networks. See text for further model descriptions.

based linear model), we are interested in what part of the improvement in performance comes from features rather than modeling power. Table 3 compares the full model to BCS, a system effectively using the $s_{\text{lin}+}$ scoring function together with a manual conjunction scheme, on both BASIC and BASIC+ features. While our models outperform BCS in both cases, we see that as we add more features (as in the BASIC+ set), the performance gap between our model and the linear system becomes even more pronounced.

We may also wonder whether the architecture represented by our scoring function, where the intermediate representations $\boldsymbol{h}_a$ and $\boldsymbol{h}_p$ are separated in the first layer, is necessary for these results. We accordingly compare with the fully connected versions of these two models (which are equivalent to 1 and 2 layer multi-layer perceptrons) using the BASIC+ features in Table 4.[9] There, we also evaluate the effect of pre-training on these models by comparing with the results of training from a random initialization. We see that while even randomly initialized models are capable of excellent performance, pre-training is beneficial, especially for $\boldsymbol{g}_1$.

[9]We also experimented with bilinear models both with and without non-linearities; these were also inferior.

6 Discussion

We attempt to gain insight into our model's errors using using two different error breakdowns. In Table 5 we show the errors as reported by the analysis tool of Kummerfeld and Klein (2013). In Table 6 we show a more fine-grained breakdown inspired by a similar analysis in Durrett and Klein (2013). In the latter table, we categorize the errors made by our system on the CoNLL 2012 development data in terms of (1) whether or not the mention has a head match with a previously occurring mention in the document, unless it is a pronominal mention, which we treat separately, (2) in terms of the status of the mention in the gold clustering, namely, singleton, first-in-cluster, or anaphoric, and (3) in terms of the type of error made (which, as discussed in Section 3, are one of FL, FN, and WL).

We note that the two models have slightly different error profiles, with $\boldsymbol{g}_1$ being slightly better at recall and $\boldsymbol{g}_2$ being slightly better at precision. Indeed, we see from Table 6 that the two models make a comparable number of total errors ($\boldsymbol{g}_1$ makes only 17 fewer errors overall). The increased precision of the $\boldsymbol{g}_2$ model is presumably due to the second layer around $\boldsymbol{h}_a$ and $\boldsymbol{h}_p$ in $\boldsymbol{g}_2$ allowing for antecedent evidence to interact with anaphoricity

Error Type	BCS	NN (g_1)	NN (g_2)
Conflated Entities	1603	1434	1371
Extra Mention	651	568	529
Extra Entity	655	623	561
Divided Entity	1989	1837	1835
Missing Mention	1004	997	1005
Missing Entity	1070	1026	1114

Table 5: Absolute error counts from the coreference analysis tool of Kummerfeld and Klein (2013). The upper set roughly corresponds to the precision and the lower to the recall of the coreference clusters produced by the model.

NN (g_1)	Singleton		1st in clust.		Anaphoric	
	FL	#	FL	#	FN + WL	#
HM	817	8.2K	147	0.8K	700 + 318	4.7K
No HM	86	19.8K	41	2.4K	677 + 59	1.0K
Pron.	948	2.6K	257	0.5K	434 + 875	7.3K

NN (g_2)	Singleton		1st in clust.		Anaphoric	
	FL	#	FL	#	FN + WL	#
HM	770	8.2K	130	0.8K	803 + 306	4.7K
No HM	73	19.8K	39	2.4K	699 + 52	1.0K
Pron.	896	2.6K	249	0.5K	456 + 869	7.3K

Table 6: Errors made by NN (g_1) (top) and NN (g_2) (bottom) on CoNLL 2012 English development data. Rows correspond to (1) mentions with a (previous) head match (HM), that is, mentions x such that $\mathcal{A}(x)$ contains another mention with the same head word, (2) with no previous head match (no HM), and (3) to pronominal mentions, respectively. The 3 column groups correspond to singleton, first-in-cluster, and anaphoric mentions (resp.), as determined by the gold clustering, with the number and type of errors on the left and the total number of mentions in the category (#) on the right.

evidence in a more complicated way. Ultimately, however, coreference systems operating over system mentions are already biased toward precision, and so the increased precision of g_2 is not as helpful as the increased recall of g_1 in the final CoNLL score.

In further analysis we found that many of the correct predictions made by the g_2 model not made by g_1 and the linear model involve predicting non-anaphoric even in the presence of highly misleading antecedent features like head-match. Figure 4 shows some examples of mentions with previous head matches that the linear system predicted as anaphoric and that our system correctly identifies as non-anaphoric.

We illustrate how the features in Figure 2 might be useful in such cases by considering the first example in Figure 4. There, a comma follows "the Nika TV company" in the text (and is picked up by the "word following" feature), perhaps indicating an appositive, which makes anaphoricity unlikely. The model can also learn that the

Non-Anaphoric (x)	Spurious Antecedent (y)
the Nika TV company	an independent company
Lexus sales	GM 's domestic car sales
The storage area	the harbor area
the Budapest location	Radio Free Europe 's new location
the synagogue	the synagogue too or something
the equity market	The junk market
their silver coin	one silver coin
the international school	The Hong Kong elementary school
the 1970s	the early 1970s
the 2003 season	the 2001 season

Figure 4: Example mentions x that were correctly marked non-anaphoric by g_2, but incorrectly marked anaphoric with y as an antecedent by the BASIC+ linear model. These examples highlight the difficult case where there is a spurious head-match between non-coreferent pairs. See text for further details.

"company-company" head match is often misleading, and, in general, distance features may also rule out head matches. Note that while these features on their own may be more or less correlated with a mention being non-anaphoric, the model learns to combine them in a predictive way.

6.1 Further Improving Coreference Systems

Table 6 also gives a sense of where coreference systems such as ours need to improve. It is first important to note that the case of resolving an anaphoric mention that has no previous head matches (e.g., identifying that "the team" and "the New York Giants" are coreferent), which is often taken to be one of the major challenges facing coreference systems because it presumably requires semantic information, is not the largest source of errors. In fact, we see from Table 6 (second row, third column in both sub-tables) that while these cases do indeed account for a substantial percentage of errors, we make hundreds more errors predicting singleton pronominal mentions to be anaphoric (in the case of g_1) and on incorrectly linking anaphoric pronominal mentions (in the case of g_2). Further analysis indicates that these errors are almost entirely related to incorrectly linking pleonastic pronouns, such as "it" or "you," and that moreover the incorrectly predicted antecedent for these pleonastic pronouns is almost always (another instance of) the same pronoun.

That these pleonastic cases are so problematic is interesting when considered against the backdrop of the inference strategies typically employed by coreference systems, which we briefly mention here but discuss more fully in the next section. Currently, coreference systems divide between those using "local" models, which choose antecedents for potentially anaphoric mentions independently of each other, and "non-local" models, which make predictions that take into account predictions made for previous mentions, and perhaps even attempt to jointly predict all mentions in a document. While our model is entirely local, other recent high performing systems, such as that of Björkelund and Kuhn (2014), are not. One might suspect, then, that "non-local" inference might allow us to capture the fact that, for instance, a cluster of coreferent mentions should generally not consist solely of pronouns, and thereby avoid predicting (identical) pronominal antecedents for pleonastic pronouns.

As it turns out, however, almost 30% of the anaphoric pronominal mentions in the CoNLL development data participate in pronoun-only clusters (primarily in the context of broadcast or telephone conversations), which suggests that such a "non-local" rule may not be particularly useful, though further experiments are required. It is also worth noting that a suitably modified loss function may also be able to prevent excessive pronoun-pronoun linking, even in a local model.

7 Related Work

There is a voluminous literature on machine learning approaches to coreference resolution, effectively beginning with Soon et al. (2001). The recent introduction of the CoNLL datasets (Pradhan et al., 2012) has spurred research that takes advantage of more fine-grained features and richer models (Björkelund and Farkas, 2012; Chang et al., 2012; Durrett and Klein, 2013; Chang et al., 2013; Björkelund and Kuhn, 2014; Ma et al., 2014). Of these approaches, our model is related to the mention-ranking approaches (Bengtson and Roth, 2008; Denis and Baldridge, 2008; Rahman and Ng, 2009; Durrett and Klein, 2013; Chang et al., 2013), as opposed to those that focus on non-local, structured prediction (McCallum and Wellner, 2003; Culotta et al., 2006; Haghighi and Klein, 2010; Fernandes et al., 2012; Stoyanov and Eisner, 2012; Björkelund and Farkas, 2012; Wick et al., 2012; Björkelund and Kuhn, 2014; Durrett and Klein, 2014).

In motivation, our work is most similar to that of Ng (2004), who notes that anaphoricity information is useful within the broader coreference task, and who accordingly attempts to "globally" optimize performance based on this information, as well as that of Denis et al. (2007), who do joint decoding of anaphoricity and coreference predictions using ILP. Both of these works are taken to contrast with the more popular approach of doing an initial non-anaphoric pruning step (Ng and Cardie, 2002; Rahman and Ng, 2009; Recasens et al., 2013; Lee et al., 2013). In contrast, we jointly learn non-linear functions of anaphoricity and antecedent features, rather than tune a threshold, or jointly decode based on independently trained classifiers (as in Denis et al. (2007)). In a similar vein, several authors have also proposed using the output of an anaphoricity classifier as a feature in a downstream coreference system (Ng, 2004; Bengtson and Roth, 2008). In our framework we (re)learn features jointly with the full task, after a pre-training scheme that targets anaphoricity as well antecedent representations.

There has also been some work on automatically inducing feature conjunctions for use in coreference systems (Fernandes et al., 2012; Lassalle and Denis, 2013), though the approach we present here is somewhat simpler, and unlike that of Lassalle and Denis (2013) is designed for use on system rather than gold mentions.

There has been much interest recently in using neural networks for classic natural language tasks such as tagging and semantic role labeling Collobert et al. (2011), sentiment analysis (Socher et al., 2011; Socher et al., 2012), prepositional phrase attachment (Belinkov et al., 2014) among others. These systems often use some form of pretraining for initialization, often word-embeddings learned from external tasks. However, there has been little work of this form for coreference resolution.

8 Conclusion

We have presented a simple, local model capable of learning feature representations useful for coreference-related subtasks, and of thereby achieving state-of-the-art performance. Because our approach automatically learns intermediate representations given raw features, directions for further research might alternately explore including additional (perhaps semantic) raw features, as well as developing loss functions that further discourage learning representations that allow for common errors (such as those involving pleonastic pronouns).

References

Amit Bagga and Breck Baldwin. 1998. Algorithms for Scoring Coreference Chains. In *The first international conference on language resources and evaluation workshop on linguistics coreference*, volume 1, pages 563–566. Citeseer.

Yonatan Belinkov, Tao Lei, Regina Barzilay, and Amir Globerson. 2014. Exploring Compositional Architectures and Word Vector Representations for Prepositional Phrase Attachment. *Transactions of the Association for Computational Linguistics*, 2:561–572.

Eric Bengtson and Dan Roth. 2008. Understanding the Value of Features for Coreference Resolution. In *Proceedings of the 2008 Conference on Empirical Methods in Natural Language Processing*, pages 294–303. ACL.

Anders Björkelund and Richárd Farkas. 2012. Data-driven Multilingual Coreference Resolution using Resolver Stacking. In *Joint Conference on EMNLP and CoNLL-Shared Task*, pages 49–55. ACL.

Anders Björkelund and Jonas Kuhn. 2014. Learning structured perceptrons for coreference Resolution with Latent Antecedents and Non-local Features. *ACL, Baltimore, MD, USA, June*.

Kai-Wei Chang, Rajhans Samdani, Alla Rozovskaya, Mark Sammons, and Dan Roth. 2012. Illinois-coref: The UI System in the CoNLL-2012 Shared Task. In *Joint Conference on EMNLP and CoNLL-Shared Task*, pages 113–117. Association for Computational Linguistics.

Kai-Wei Chang, Rajhans Samdani, and Dan Roth. 2013. A Constrained Latent Variable Model for Coreference Resolution. In *Proceedings of the 2013 Conference on Empirical Methods in Natural Language Processing*, pages 601–612.

Ronan Collobert, Jason Weston, Léon Bottou, Michael Karlen, Koray Kavukcuoglu, and Pavel Kuksa. 2011. Natural Language Processing (almost) from Scratch. *The Journal of Machine Learning Research*, 12:2493–2537.

Aron Culotta, Michael Wick, Robert Hall, and Andrew McCallum. 2006. First-order Probabilistic Models for Coreference Resolution. *NAACL-HLT*.

Pascal Denis and Jason Baldridge. 2008. Specialized Models and Ranking for Coreference Resolution. In *Proceedings of the 2008 Conference on Empirical Methods in Natural Language Processing*, pages 660–669. ACL.

Pascal Denis, Jason Baldridge, et al. 2007. Joint Determination of Anaphoricity and Coreference Resolution using Integer Programming. In *HLT-NAACL*, pages 236–243. Citeseer.

John Duchi, Elad Hazan, and Yoram Singer. 2011. Adaptive Subgradient Methods for Online Learning and Stochastic Optimization. *The Journal of Machine Learning Research*, 12:2121–2159.

Greg Durrett and Dan Klein. 2013. Easy Victories and Uphill Battles in Coreference Resolution. In *Proceedings of the 2013 Conference on Empirical Methods in Natural Language Processing*, pages 1971–1982.

Greg Durrett and Dan Klein. 2014. A Joint Model for Entity Analysis: Coreference, Typing, and Linking. *Transactions of the Association for Computational Linguistics*, 2:477–490.

Dumitru Erhan, Yoshua Bengio, Aaron Courville, Pierre-Antoine Manzagol, Pascal Vincent, and Samy Bengio. 2010. Why does unsupervised pre-training help deep learning? *The Journal of Machine Learning Research*, 11:625–660.

Rong-En Fan, Kai-Wei Chang, Cho-Jui Hsieh, Xiang-Rui Wang, and Chih-Jen Lin. 2008. Liblinear: A Library for Large Linear Classification. *The Journal of Machine Learning Research*, 9:1871–1874.

Eraldo Rezende Fernandes, Cícero Nogueira Dos Santos, and Ruy Luiz Milidiú. 2012. Latent Structure Perceptron with Feature Induction for Unrestricted Coreference Resolution. In *Joint Conference on EMNLP and CoNLL-Shared Task*, pages 41–48. Association for Computational Linguistics.

Aria Haghighi and Dan Klein. 2010. Coreference Resolution in a Modular, Entity-centered Model. In *The 2010 Annual Conference of the North American Chapter of the Association for Computational Linguistics*, pages 385–393. Association for Computational Linguistics.

Eduard Hovy, Mitchell Marcus, Martha Palmer, Lance Ramshaw, and Ralph Weischedel. 2006. Ontonotes: the 90% Solution. In *Proceedings of the human language technology conference of the NAACL, Companion Volume: Short Papers*, pages 57–60. Association for Computational Linguistics.

Philipp Koehn. 2004. Statistical Significance Tests for Machine Translation Evaluation. In *Proceedings of the 2004 Conference on Empirical Methods in Natural Language Processing*, pages 388–395. Citeseer.

Jonathan K. Kummerfeld and Dan Klein. 2013. Error-driven Analysis of Challenges in Coreference Resolution. In *Proceedings of the 2013 Conference on Empirical Methods in Natural Language Processing*, Seattle, WA, USA, October.

Emmanuel Lassalle and Pascal Denis. 2013. Improving Pairwise Coreference Models through Feature Space Hierarchy Learning. In *ACL 2013-Annual meeting of the Association for Computational Linguistics*.

Heeyoung Lee, Yves Peirsman, Angel Chang, Nathanael Chambers, Mihai Surdeanu, and Dan Jurafsky. 2011. Stanford's Multi-pass Sieve Coreference Resolution System at the CoNLL-2011 Shared

Task. In *Proceedings of the Fifteenth Conference on Computational Natural Language Learning: Shared Task*, pages 28–34. Association for Computational Linguistics.

Heeyoung Lee, Angel Chang, Yves Peirsman, Nathanael Chambers, Mihai Surdeanu, and Dan Jurafsky. 2013. Deterministic Coreference Resolution based on Entity-centric, Precision-ranked Rules. *Computational Linguistics*, 39(4):885–916.

Xiaoqiang Luo, Sameer Pradhan, Marta Recasens, and Eduard Hovy. 2014. An Extension of BLANC to System Mentions. *Proceedings of ACL, Baltimore, Maryland, June*.

Xiaoqiang Luo. 2005. On Coreference Resolution Performance Metrics. In *Proceedings of the conference on Human Language Technology and Empirical Methods in Natural Language Processing*, pages 25–32. Association for Computational Linguistics.

Chao Ma, Janardhan Rao Doppa, J Walker Orr, Prashanth Mannem, Xiaoli Fern, Tom Dietterich, and Prasad Tadepalli. 2014. Prune-and-score: Learning for Greedy Coreference Resolution. In *Proceedings of the 2014 Conference on Empirical Methods in Natural Language Processing*.

Andrew McCallum and Ben Wellner. 2003. Toward Conditional Models of Identity Uncertainty with Application to Proper Noun Coreference. *Advances in Neural Information Processing Systems 17*.

Yurii Nesterov. 1983. A Method of Solving a Convex Programming Problem with Convergence Rate O (1/k2). In *Soviet Mathematics Doklady*, volume 27, pages 372–376.

Vincent Ng and Claire Cardie. 2002. Identifying Anaphoric and Non-anaphoric Noun Phrases to Improve Coreference Resolution. In *Proceedings of the 19th international conference on Computational linguistics-Volume 1*, pages 1–7. Association for Computational Linguistics.

Vincent Ng. 2004. Learning Noun Phrase Anaphoricity to Improve Coreference Resolution: Issues in Representation and Optimization. In *Proceedings of the 42nd Annual Meeting on Association for Computational Linguistics*, page 151. Association for Computational Linguistics.

Sameer Pradhan, Alessandro Moschitti, Nianwen Xue, Olga Uryupina, and Yuchen Zhang. 2012. Conll-2012 Shared Task: Modeling Multilingual Unrestricted Coreference in OntoNotes. In *Joint Conference on EMNLP and CoNLL-Shared Task*, pages 1–40. ACL.

Sameer Pradhan, Xiaoqiang Luo, Marta Recasens, Eduard Hovy, Vincent Ng, and Michael Strube. 2014. Scoring Coreference Partitions of Predicted Mentions: A Reference Implementation. In *Proceedings of the Association for Computational Linguistics*.

Altaf Rahman and Vincent Ng. 2009. Supervised Models for Coreference Resolution. In *Proceedings of the 2009 Conference on Empirical Methods in Natural Language Processing: Volume 2-Volume 2*, pages 968–977. ACL.

Marta Recasens, Marie-Catherine de Marneffe, and Christopher Potts. 2013. The Life and Death of Discourse Entities: Identifying Singleton Mentions. In *HLT-NAACL*, pages 627–633.

Richard Socher, Jeffrey Pennington, Eric H Huang, Andrew Y Ng, and Christopher D Manning. 2011. Semi-supervised Recursive Autoencoders for Predicting Sentiment Distributions. In *Proceedings of the 2011 Conference on Empirical Methods in Natural Language Processing*, pages 151–161. ACL.

Richard Socher, Brody Huval, Christopher D Manning, and Andrew Y Ng. 2012. Semantic Compositionality through Recursive Matrix-vector Spaces. In *Proceedings of the 2012 Joint Conference on Empirical Methods in Natural Language Processing and Computational Natural Language Learning*, pages 1201–1211. ACL.

Wee Meng Soon, Hwee Tou Ng, and Daniel Chung Yong Lim. 2001. A Machine Learning Approach to Coreference Resolution of Noun Phrases. *Computational Linguistics*, 27(4):521–544.

Veselin Stoyanov and Jason Eisner. 2012. Easy-first Coreference Resolution. In *COLING*, pages 2519–2534. Citeseer.

Ilya Sutskever, James Martens, George Dahl, and Geoffrey Hinton. 2013. On the Importance of Initialization and Momentum in Deep Learning. In *Proceedings of the 30th International Conference on Machine Learning*, pages 1139–1147.

Marc Vilain, John Burger, John Aberdeen, Dennis Connolly, and Lynette Hirschman. 1995. A Model-theoretic Coreference Scoring Scheme. In *Proceedings of the 6th conference on Message Understanding*, pages 45–52. ACL.

Michael Wick, Sameer Singh, and Andrew McCallum. 2012. A Discriminative Hierarchical Model for Fast Coreference at Large Scale. In *Proceedings of the 50th Annual Meeting of the Association for Computational Linguistics: Long Papers-Volume 1*, pages 379–388. Association for Computational Linguistics.

Chun-Nam John Yu and Thorsten Joachims. 2009. Learning Structural SVMs with Latent Variables. In *Proceedings of the 26th Annual International Conference on Machine Learning*, pages 1169–1176. ACM.

Transferring Coreference Resolvers with Posterior Regularization

André F. T. Martins[*†]
[*]Priberam Labs, Alameda D. Afonso Henriques, 41, 2°, 1000-123 Lisboa, Portugal
[†]Instituto de Telecomunicações, Instituto Superior Técnico, 1049-001 Lisboa, Portugal
atm@priberam.pt

Abstract

We propose a cross-lingual framework for learning coreference resolvers for resource-poor target languages, given a resolver in a source language. Our method uses word-aligned bitext to project information from the source to the target. To handle task-specific costs, we propose a softmax-margin variant of posterior regularization, and we use it to achieve robustness to projection errors. We show empirically that this strategy outperforms competitive cross-lingual methods, such as delexicalized transfer with bilingual word embeddings, bitext direct projection, and vanilla posterior regularization.

1 Introduction

The goal of **coreference resolution** is to find the mentions in text that refer to the same discourse entity. While early work focused primarily on English (Soon et al., 2001; Ng and Cardie, 2002), efforts have been made toward multilingual systems, this being addressed in recent shared tasks (Recasens et al., 2010; Pradhan et al., 2012). However, the lack of annotated data hinders rapid system deployment for new languages. Unsupervised methods (Haghighi and Klein, 2007; Ng, 2008) and rule-based approaches (Raghunathan et al., 2010) avoid this data annotation bottleneck, but they often require complex generative models or expert linguistic knowledge.

We propose **cross-lingual coreference resolution** as a way of transferring information from a rich-resource language to build coreference resolvers for languages with scarcer resources; as a testbed, we transfer from English to Spanish and to Brazilian Portuguese. We build upon the recent successes of cross-lingual learning in NLP, which proved quite effective in several structured prediction tasks, such as POS tagging (Täckström et al., 2013), named entity recognition (Wang and Manning, 2014), dependency parsing (McDonald et al., 2011), semantic role labeling (Titov and Klementiev, 2012), and fine-grained opinion mining (Almeida et al., 2015). The potential of these techniques, however, has never been fully exploited in coreference resolution (despite some existing work, reviewed in §6, but none resulting in an end-to-end coreference resolver).

We bridge this gap by proposing a simple learning-based method with weak supervision, based on **posterior regularization** (Ganchev et al., 2010). We adapt this framework to handle softmax-margin objective functions (Gimpel and Smith, 2010), leading to **softmax-margin posterior regularization** (§4). This step, while fairly simple, opens the door for incorporating task-specific cost functions, which are important to manage the precision/recall trade-offs in coreference resolution systems. We show that the resulting problem involves optimizing the difference of two cost-augmented log-partition functions, making a bridge with supervised systems based on **latent coreference trees** (Fernandes et al., 2012; Durrett and Klein, 2013), reviewed in §3. Inspired by this idea, we consider a simple **penalized variant** of posterior regularization that tunes the Lagrange multipliers directly, bypassing the saddle-point problem of existing EM and alternating stochastic gradient algorithms (Ganchev et al., 2010; Liang et al., 2009). Experiments (§5) show that the proposed method outperforms commonly used cross-lingual approaches, such as delexicalized transfer with bilingual embeddings, direct projection, and "vanilla" posterior regularization.

2 Architecture and Experimental Setup

Our methodology, outlined as Algorithm 1, is inspired by the recent work of Ganchev and Das (2013) on cross-lingual learning of sequence models. For simplicity, we call the source and tar-

Proceedings of the 53rd Annual Meeting of the Association for Computational Linguistics and the 7th International Joint Conference on Natural Language Processing, pages 1427–1437,
Beijing, China, July 26-31, 2015.

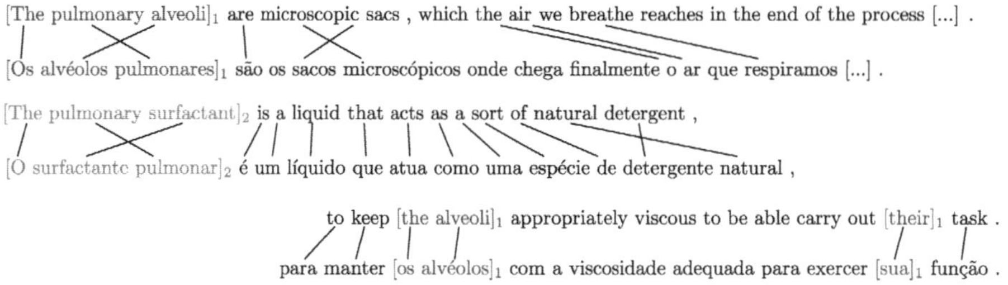

Figure 1: Excerpt of a bitext document with automatic coreference annotations (from FAPESP). The English side had its coreferences resolved by a state-of-the-art system (Durrett and Klein, 2013). The predicted coreference chains {*The pulmonary alveoli, the alveoli, their*} and {*The pulmonary surfactant*} are then projected to the Portuguese side, via word alignments.

Algorithm 1 Cross-Lingual Coreference Resolution via Softmax-Margin Posterior Regularization

Input: Source coreference system $\mathcal{S}^e$, parallel data $\mathcal{D}^e$ and $\mathcal{D}^f$, posterior constraints $\mathcal{Q}$.
Output: Target coreference system $\mathcal{S}^f$.
1: $\mathcal{D}^{e\leftrightarrow f} \leftarrow$ RUNWORDALIGNER($\mathcal{D}^e, \mathcal{D}^f$)
2: $\widehat{\mathcal{D}}^e \leftarrow$ RUNCOREF($\mathcal{S}^e, \mathcal{D}^e$)
3: $\widehat{\mathcal{D}}^f \leftarrow$ PROJECTANDFILTERENTITIES($\mathcal{D}^{e\leftrightarrow f}, \widehat{\mathcal{D}}^e$)
4: $\mathcal{S}^f \leftarrow$ LEARNCOREFWITHSOFTMARGPR($\widehat{\mathcal{D}}^f, \mathcal{Q}$)

get languages English (e) and "foreign" (f), respectively, and we assume the existence of parallel documents on the two languages (bitext).

The first two steps (lines 1–2) run a word aligner and label the source side of the parallel data with a pre-trained English coreference system. Afterwards, the predicted English entities are projected to the target side of the parallel data (line 3), inducing an automatic (and noisy) training dataset for the foreign language. Finally, a coreference system is trained in this dataset with the aid of softmax-margin posterior regularization (line 4).

We next detail all the datasets and tools involved in our experimental setup. Table 1 provides a summary, along with some statistics.

Dataset	# Doc.	# Sent.	# Tok.
EN OntoNotes (train)	2,374	48,762	1,007,359
EN OntoNotes (dev)	303	6,894	136,257
EN OntoNotes (test)	322	8,262	152,728
ES FAPESP (aligned)	2,704	142,633	3,840,936
ES AnCora (train)	875	8,999	295,276
ES AnCora (dev)	140	1,417	46,167
ES AnCora (test)	168	1,704	53,042
PT FAPESP (aligned)	2,823	166,719	4,538,147
PT Summ-It (train)	30	469	11,771
PT Summ-It (dev)	7	111	2,983
PT Summ-It (test)	13	257	6,491

Table 1: Corpus statistics. EN, ES, and PT denote English, Spanish, and Portuguese, respectively.

Parallel Data. As parallel data, we use a sentence-aligned trilingual (English-Portuguese-Spanish) parallel corpus based on the scientific news Brazilian magazine *Revista Pesquisa FAPESP*, collected by Aziz and Specia (2011).[1] We preprocessed this dataset as follows. We labeled the English side with the Berkeley Coreference Resolution system v1.0, using the provided English model (Durrett and Klein, 2013). Then, we computed word alignments using the Berkeley aligner (Liang et al., 2006), intersected them and filtered out all the alignments whose confidence is below 0.95. After this, we projected English mentions to the target side using the maximal span heuristic of Yarowsky et al. (2001). We filtered out documents where more than 15% of the mentions were not aligned. At this point, we obtained an automatically annotated corpus $\widehat{\mathcal{D}}^f$ in the target language. Figure 1 shows a small excerpt where all mentions were correctly projected. In practice, not all documents are so well behaved: in the English-Portuguese parallel data, only 200,175 out of the original 271,122 mentions (about 73.8%) were conserved after the projection step. In Spanish, this number drops to 69.9%.

Monolingual Data. We also use monolingual data for validation and comparison with supervised systems. The Berkeley Coreference Resolution system is trained in the English OntoNotes dataset used in the CoNLL 2011 shared task; this dataset is also used to train delexicalized models.

For Spanish, we use the AnCora dataset (Recasens and Martí, 2010) provided in the SemEval 2010 coreference task, which we preprocessed as follows. We split all MWEs into individual tokens (for consistency with the other corpora). We also removed the extra gap tokens associated with zero-anaphoric relations, and the anaphoric annotations associated with relative pronouns (*e.g.*, in "*[una central de ciclo combinado [que]$_1$ debe empezar*

[1]We found that other commonly used parallel data (such as Europarl or the UN corpus) have a predominance of direct speech that is not suitable for our newswire test domain, so we decided not to use these data.

a funcionar en mayo del 2002]$_1$" we removed the nested mention *[que]*$_1$), since these are not annotated in the English dataset.

For Portuguese, we used the Summ-It 3.0 corpus (Collovini et al., 2007), which contains 50 documents annotated with coreferences, from the science section of the *Folha de São Paulo* newspaper. This dataset is much smaller than OntoNotes and AnCora, as shown in Table 1. We split the data into train, development, and test partitions.

For both Spanish and Portuguese, we obtained automatic POS tags and dependency parses by using TurboParser (Martins et al., 2013).

3 Coreference Resolution

3.1 Problem Definition and Prior Work

In coreference resolution, we are given a set of **mentions** $\mathcal{M} := \{m_1, \dots, m_M\}$, and the goal is to cluster them into discourse **entities**, $\mathcal{E} := \{e_1, \dots, e_E\}$, where each $e_j \subseteq \mathcal{M}$ and $e_j \neq \varnothing$. The set $\mathcal{E}$ must form a partition of $\mathcal{M}$, *i.e.*, we must have $\bigcup_{j=1}^{E} e_j = \mathcal{M}$, and $e_i \cap e_j = \varnothing$ for $i \neq j$.

A variety of approaches have been proposed to this problem, including entity-centric models (Haghighi and Klein, 2010; Rahman and Ng, 2011; Durrett et al., 2013), pairwise models (Bengtson and Roth, 2008; Versley et al., 2008), greedy rule-based methods (Raghunathan et al., 2010), and mention-ranking decoders (Denis and Baldridge, 2008; Durrett and Klein, 2013). We chose to base our coreference resolvers on this last class of methods, which permit efficient decoding by shifting from entity clusters to **latent coreference trees**. In particular, the inclusion of lexicalized features by Durrett and Klein (2013) yields nearly state-of-the-art performance with surface information only. Given that our goal is to prototype resolvers for resource-poor languages, this model is a good fit—we next describe it in detail.

3.2 Latent Coreference Tree Models

Let x be a document containing M mentions, sorted from left to right. We associate to the mth mention a random variable $y_m \in \{0, 1, \dots, m-1\}$ to denote its **antecedent**, where the value $y_m = 0$ means that m is a singleton or starts a new coreference chain. We denote by $\mathcal{Y}(x)$ the set of coreference trees that can be formed by linking mentions to their antecedents; we represent each tree as a vector $y := \langle y_1, \dots, y_M \rangle$. Note that each tree y induces a unique clustering $\mathcal{E}$, but that this map is many-to-one, *i.e.*, different trees may correspond to the same set of entity clusters. We denote by $\mathcal{Y}(\mathcal{E})$ the set of trees that are consistent with a given clustering $\mathcal{E}$.

We model the probability distribution $p(y|x)$ as an arc-factored log-linear model:

$$p_{\boldsymbol{w}}(y|x) \propto \exp\left(\sum_{m=1}^{M} \boldsymbol{w}^\top \boldsymbol{f}(x, m, y_m)\right), \quad (1)$$

where $\boldsymbol{w}$ is a weight vector, and each $\boldsymbol{f}(x, m, y_m)$ is a local feature vector that depends on the document x, the mention m, and its candidate antecedent y_m. This model permits a cheap computation of the most likely tree $\widehat{y} := \arg\max_{y \in \mathcal{Y}(x)} p_{\boldsymbol{w}}(y|x)$: simply compute the best antecedent independently for each mention, and collect them to form a tree. An analogous procedure can be employed to compute the posterior marginals $p_{\boldsymbol{w}}(y_m|x)$ for every mention m.

Gold coreference tree annotations are rarely available; datasets usually consist of documents annotated with entity clusters, $\{\langle x^{(n)}, \mathcal{E}^{(n)} \rangle\}_{n=1}^{N}$. Durrett and Klein (2013) proposed to learn the probabilistic model in Eq. 1 by maximizing conditional log-likelihood, treating the coreference trees as latent variables. They also found advantageous to incorporate a **cost function** $\ell(y, \mathcal{Y}(\mathcal{E}))$, measuring the extent to which a prediction y differs from the ones that are consistent with the gold entity set $\mathcal{E}$.[2] Putting these pieces together, we arrive at the following loss function to be minimized:

$$L(\boldsymbol{w}) = -\sum_{n=1}^{N} \log\left(\sum_{y \in \mathcal{Y}(\mathcal{E}^{(n)})} p'_{\boldsymbol{w}}(y|x^{(n)})\right), \quad (2)$$

where $p'_{\boldsymbol{w}}$ is the **cost-augmented distribution**:

$$p'_{\boldsymbol{w}}(y|x) \propto p_{\boldsymbol{w}}(y|x) e^{\ell(y, \mathcal{Y}(\mathcal{E}))}. \quad (3)$$

The loss function in Eq. 2 can be seen as a probabilistic analogous of the hinge loss of support vector machines, and a model trained this way is called a **softmax-margin** CRF (Gimpel and Smith, 2010). Note that $L(\boldsymbol{w})$ is non-convex, corresponding to the difference of two log-partition functions (both convex on $\boldsymbol{w}$),

$$L(\boldsymbol{w}) = \sum_{n=1}^{N} \left(\log Z'(\boldsymbol{w}, x^{(n)}) - \log \widehat{Z}(\boldsymbol{w}, x^{(n)})\right); \quad (4)$$

above we denoted

$$Z'(\boldsymbol{w}, x) = \sum_{y \in \mathcal{Y}(x)} e^{\boldsymbol{w}^\top \boldsymbol{f}(x,y) + \ell(y, \mathcal{Y}(\mathcal{E}))} \quad (5)$$

$$\widehat{Z}(\boldsymbol{w}, x) = \sum_{y \in \mathcal{Y}(\mathcal{E})} e^{\boldsymbol{w}^\top \boldsymbol{f}(x,y)}, \quad (6)$$

[2] A precise definition of this cost is provided in §4.3.

where $\boldsymbol{f}(x, y) := \sum_{m=1}^{M} \boldsymbol{f}(x, m, y_m)$.[3] Evaluating the gradient of the loss in Eq. 4 requires computing marginals for the candidate antecedents of each mention, which can be done in a mention-synchronous fashion. This enables a simple stochastic gradient descent algorithm, which was the procedure taken by Durrett and Klein (2013).

Another way of regarding this framework, expressed through the marginalization in Eq. 2, is to "pretend" that the outputs we care about are the actual coreference trees, but that the datasets are only "weakly labeled" with the entity clusters. We build on this point of view in §4.1.

4 Cross-Lingual Coreference Resolution

We now adapt the framework above to learn coreference resolvers in a cross-lingual manner.

4.1 Softmax-Margin Posterior Regularization

In the weakly supervised case, the training data may only be partially labeled or contain annotation errors. For taking advantage of these data, we need a procedure that handles uncertainty about the missing data, and is robust to mislabelings. We describe next an approach based on posterior regularization (PR) that fulfills these requirements.

For ease of explanation, we introduce corpus-level counterparts for the variables in §3.2. We use bold capital letters $\mathbf{X} := \{x^{(1)}, \ldots, x^{(N)}\}$ and $\mathbf{Y} := \{y^{(1)}, \ldots, y^{(N)}\}$ to denote the documents and candidate coreference trees in our corpus. We denote by $p_{\boldsymbol{w}}(\mathbf{Y}|\mathbf{X}) := \prod_{n=1}^{N} p_{\boldsymbol{w}}(y|x^{(n)})$ the conditional distribution of trees over the corpus, induced by a model $\boldsymbol{w}$, and similarly for the cost-augmented distribution $p'_{\boldsymbol{w}}(\mathbf{Y}|\mathbf{X})$.

In PR, we define a vector $\boldsymbol{g}(\mathbf{X}, \mathbf{Y})$ of **corpus-level constraint features**, and a vector $\boldsymbol{b}$ of upper bounds for those features. We consider the family of distributions over $\mathbf{Y}$ (call it $\mathcal{Q}$) that satisfy these constraints in *a posteriori* expectation,

$$\mathcal{Q} := \{q \mid \mathbf{E}_q[\boldsymbol{g}(\mathbf{X}, \mathbf{Y})] \leq \boldsymbol{b}\}. \tag{7}$$

To make the analysis simpler, we assume that $\mathbf{0} \leq \boldsymbol{b} \leq \mathbf{1}$, and that for every j, $\min_{\mathbf{Y}} g_j(\mathbf{X}, \mathbf{Y}) = 0$ and $\max_{\mathbf{Y}} g_j(\mathbf{X}, \mathbf{Y}) = 1$, where the min/max above are over all possible coreference trees $\mathbf{Y}$ that can be build from the documents $\mathbf{X}$ in the corpus.[4] Under this assumption, the two extreme values of the upper bounds have a precise meaning: if $b_j = 0$, the jth feature becomes a hard constraint, (*i.e.*, any feasible distribution in $\mathcal{Q}$ will vanish outside $\{\mathbf{Y} \mid g_j(\mathbf{X}, \mathbf{Y}) = 0\}$), while $b_j = 1$ turns it into a vacuous feature.

We also make the usual assumption that the constraint features decompose over documents, $\boldsymbol{g}(\mathbf{X}, \mathbf{Y}) := \sum_{n=1}^{N} \boldsymbol{g}(x^{(n)}, y^{(n)})$; if this were not the case, decoding would be much harder, as the documents would be coupled.

In vanilla PR (Ganchev et al., 2010), one seeks the model $\boldsymbol{w}$ minimizing the Kullback-Leibler divergence between the set $\mathcal{Q}$ and the distribution $p_{\boldsymbol{w}}$. Here, we go one step farther to consider the **cost-augmented distribution** in Eq. 3. That is, we minimize $\mathbf{KL}(\mathcal{Q}\|p'_{\boldsymbol{w}}) := \min_{q \in \mathcal{Q}} \mathbf{KL}(q\|p'_{\boldsymbol{w}})$. The next proposition shows that this expression also corresponds to a difference of two log-partition functions, as in Eq. 4.

Proposition 1. *The (regularized) minimization of the cost-augmented KL divergence is equivalent to the following saddle-point problem:*

$$\begin{aligned} &\min_{\boldsymbol{w}} \mathbf{KL}(\mathcal{Q}\|p'_{\boldsymbol{w}}) + \tfrac{\gamma}{2}\|\boldsymbol{w}\|^2 = \\ &\quad \min_{\boldsymbol{w}} \max_{\boldsymbol{u} \geq \mathbf{0}} F(\boldsymbol{w}, \boldsymbol{u}) - \boldsymbol{b}^\top \boldsymbol{u} + \tfrac{\gamma}{2}\|\boldsymbol{w}\|^2, \end{aligned} \tag{8}$$

where $F(\boldsymbol{w}, \boldsymbol{u}) :=$

$$\sum_{n=1}^{N} \left(\log Z'(\boldsymbol{w}, x^{(n)}) - \log Z'_{\boldsymbol{u}}(\boldsymbol{w}, x^{(n)})\right), \tag{9}$$

with $Z'(\boldsymbol{w}, x)$ *as in Eq. 5, and*

$$Z'_{\boldsymbol{u}}(\boldsymbol{w}, x) := \sum_{y \in \mathcal{Y}(x)} e^{\boldsymbol{w}^\top \boldsymbol{f}(x,y) + \ell(y, \mathcal{Y}(\mathcal{E})) - \boldsymbol{u}^\top \boldsymbol{g}(x,y)}. \tag{10}$$

Proof. See Appendix A. □

In sum, what Proposition 1 shows is that we can easily extend the vanilla PR framework of Ganchev et al. (2010) to incorporate a task-specific cost: by Lagrange duality, the resulting optimization problem still amounts to finding a saddle point of an objective function (Eq. 8), which involves the difference of two log-partition functions (Eq. 9). The difference is that these partition functions now incorporate the cost term $\ell(y, \mathcal{Y}(\mathcal{E}))$. If this cost term has a factorization compatible with the features and the constraints, this comes at no additional computational burden.

[3] Note that the scope of the sum is different in Eqs. 5 and 6: $Z'(\boldsymbol{w}, x)$ sums over *all* coreference trees, while $\widehat{Z}(\boldsymbol{w}, x)$ sums only over those consistent with the gold clusters.

[4] We can always reduce the problem to this case by scaling and adding a constant to the constraint feature vectors.

4.2 Penalized Variant

In their discriminative PR formulation for learning sequence models, Ganchev and Das (2013) optimize an objective similar to Eq. 8 by alternating stochastic gradient updates with respect to $\boldsymbol{w}$ and $\boldsymbol{u}$. In their procedure, $\boldsymbol{b}$ was chosen a priori via linear regression (see their Figure 2).

Here, we propose a different strategy, based on Proposition 1 and a simple observation: while the constraint values $\boldsymbol{b}$ have a more intuitive meaning than the Lagrange multipliers $\boldsymbol{u}$ (since they may correspond, *e.g.*, to proportions of events observed in the data), choosing these upper bounds is often no easier than tuning $\boldsymbol{u}$. In this case, a preferable strategy is to specify $\boldsymbol{u}$ directly—this leaves this variable fixed in Eq. 8, and allows us to get rid of $\boldsymbol{b}$. The resulting problem becomes

$$\min_{\boldsymbol{w}} F(\boldsymbol{w}, \boldsymbol{u}) + \frac{\gamma}{2}\|\boldsymbol{w}\|^2, \qquad (11)$$

which is a penalized variant of PR and no longer a saddle point problem. This variant requires tuning the Lagrange multipliers u_j in the range $[0, +\infty]$, for every constraint. The two extreme cases of $b_j = 0$ and $b_j = 1$ correspond respectively to $u_j = +\infty$ and $u_j = 0$.[5] Note that this grid search is only appealing for a small number of posterior constraints at corpus-level (since document-level constraints would require tuning separate coefficients for each document).

The practical advantages of the penalized variant over the saddle-point formulation are illustrated in Figure 2, which compares the performance of stochastic gradient algorithms for the two formulations (there, $\eta_2 = 1 - b_2$).

An interesting aspect of this penalized formulation is its resemblance to latent variable models. Indeed, the objective of Eq. 11 is also a **difference of log-partition functions**, as the latent-tree supervised case (cf. Eq. 4). The noticeable difference is that now both partition functions include extra cost terms, either task-specific ($\ell(y, \mathcal{Y}(\mathcal{E}))$ in Z') or with soft constraints ($\boldsymbol{u}^\top \boldsymbol{g}(x, y)$ in $Z'_{\boldsymbol{u}}$). In particular, if we set a single constrained feature $g_1(x, y) := \mathbb{I}(\ell(y, \mathcal{Y}(\mathcal{E})) \neq 0)$ with weight $u_1 \to +\infty$, all non-zero-cost summands in $Z'_{\boldsymbol{u}}(\boldsymbol{w}, x)$

[5]This follows from Lagrange duality. If $b_j = 1$, the constraint is vacuous and by complementary slackness we must have $u_j = 0$. If $b_j = 0$, this becomes a hard constraint, so for the nth document, any coreference tree y for which $g_j(x^{(n)}, y) \neq 0$ must have probability zero—this corresponds to setting $u_j \to +\infty$ in Eq. 10.

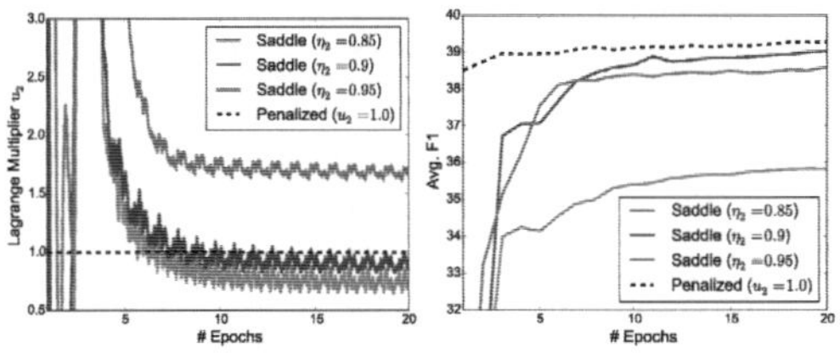

Figure 2: Comparison of saddle-point and penalized PR for Spanish, using the setup in §5.5. Left: variation of the multiplier u_2 over gradient iterations, with strong oscillations in initial epochs and somewhat slow convergence. Right: impact in the averaged F_1 scores (on the dev-set). Contrast with the more "stable" scores achieved by the penalized method.

vanish and we get $Z'_{\boldsymbol{u}}(\boldsymbol{w}, x) = \widehat{Z}(\boldsymbol{w}, x)$, recovering the supervised case (see Eq. 6).

Intuitively, this formulation pushes probability mass toward structures that respect the constraints in Eq. 7, while moving away from those that have a large task-specific cost. A similar idea, but applied to the generative case, underlies the framework of constrastive estimation (Smith and Eisner, 2005).

4.3 Cost Function

Denote by $\mathcal{E}_m$ the entire coreference chain of the mth mention (so $\mathcal{E} = \bigcup_{m \in \mathcal{M}}\{\mathcal{E}_m\}$), and by $\mathcal{M}_{\text{sing}} := \{m \in \mathcal{M} \mid \mathcal{E}_m = \{m\}\}$ the set of mentions that are projected as singleton in the data (we call this gold-singleton mentions).

We design a task-specific cost $\ell(\widehat{y}, \mathcal{Y}(\mathcal{E}))$ as in Durrett and Klein (2013) to balance three kinds of mistakes: (i) **false anaphora** ($\widehat{y}_m \neq 0$ while $m \in \mathcal{M}_{\text{sing}}$); (ii) **false new** ($\widehat{y}_m = 0$ while $m \notin \mathcal{M}_{\text{sing}}$); and (iii) **wrong link** ($\widehat{y}_m \neq 0$ but $\mathcal{E}_m \neq \mathcal{E}_{\widehat{y}_m}$). Letting $\mathbb{I}_{\text{FA}}(\widehat{y}_m, \mathcal{E})$, $\mathbb{I}_{\text{FN}}(\widehat{y}_m, \mathcal{E})$, and $\mathbb{I}_{\text{WL}}(\widehat{y}_m, \mathcal{E})$ be indicators for these events, we define a weighted Hamming cost function: $\ell(\widehat{y}, \mathcal{Y}(\mathcal{E})) := \sum_{m=1}^{M}(\alpha_{\text{FA}}\mathbb{I}_{\text{FA}}(\widehat{y}_m, \mathcal{E}) + \alpha_{\text{FN}}\mathbb{I}_{\text{FN}}(\widehat{y}_m, \mathcal{E}) + \alpha_{\text{WL}}\mathbb{I}_{\text{WL}}(\widehat{y}_m, \mathcal{E}))$. We set $\alpha_{\text{FA}} = 0.0$, $\alpha_{\text{FN}} = 3.0$, and $\alpha_{\text{WL}} = 1.0$.[6] Since this cost decomposes as a sum over mentions, the computation of cost-augmented marginals (necessary to evaluate the gradient of Eq. 11) can still be done with mention-ranking decoders.

4.4 Constraint Features

Finally, we describe the constraint features (Eq. 7) used in our softmax-margin PR formulation.

Constraint #1: Clusters should not split. Let $|\mathcal{M}| - |\mathcal{E}|$ be the number of anaphoric mentions

[6]The only difference with respect to Durrett and Klein (2013) is that they set $\alpha_{\text{FA}} = 0.1$. We set this coefficient to zero so that all configurations licensed by the constraint features (to be made precise in §4.4) will have zero cost.

in the projected data. We push these mentions to preserve their anaphoricity ($y_m \neq 0$) and to have their antecedent in the projected coreference chain ($\mathcal{E}_m = \mathcal{E}_{y_m}$). To do so, we force the fraction of mentions satisfying these properties to be at least η_1. This can be enforced via a constraint feature

$$g_1(\mathbf{X}, \mathbf{Y}) := \qquad (12)$$
$$-\sum_{n=1}^{N} \sum_{m=1}^{M^{(n)}} \mathbb{I}(y_m^{(n)} \neq 0 \ \wedge \ \mathcal{E}_m^{(n)} = \mathcal{E}_{y_m}^{(n)}),$$

and an upper bound $b_1 := -\eta_1 \sum_{n=1}^{N} (|\mathcal{M}^{(n)}| - |\mathcal{E}^{(n)}|)$. (These quantities are summed by a constant and rescaled to meet the assumption in §4.1.) In our experiments, we set $\eta_1 = 1.0$, turning this into a hard constraint. This is equivalent to setting $u_1 = +\infty$ in the penalized formulation.

Constraint #2: Most projected singletons should become non-anaphoric. We define a soft constraint so that a large fraction of the gold-singleton mentions $m \in \mathcal{M}_{\text{sing}}$ satisfy $y_m = 0$. This can be done via a constraint feature

$$g_2(\mathbf{X}, \mathbf{Y}) := \qquad (13)$$
$$-\sum_{n=1}^{N} \sum_{m=1}^{M^{(n)}} \mathbb{I}(y_m^{(n)} = 0 \ \wedge \ \mathcal{E}_m^{(n)} = \{m\}),$$

and an upper bound $b_2 := -\eta_2 \sum_{n=1}^{N} |\mathcal{M}_{\text{sing}}^{(n)}|$. In our experiments, we varied η_2 in the range $[0, 1]$, either directly or via the dual variable u_2, as described in §4.1. The extreme case $\eta_2 = 0$ corresponds to a vacuous constraint, while for $\eta_2 = 1$ this becomes a hard constraint which, combined with the previous constraint, recovers bitext direct projection (see §5.3). The intermediate case makes this a **soft constraint** which allows some singletons to be attached to existing entities (therefore introducing some robustness to non-aligned mentions), but penalizes the number of reattachments.

5 Experiments

We now present experiments using the setup in §2. We compare our coreference resolvers trained with softmax-margin PR (§5.5) with three other weakly-supervised baselines: delexicalized transfer with cross-lingual embeddings (§5.2), bitext projection (§5.3), and vanilla PR (§5.4). We also run fully supervised systems (§5.1), to obtain upper bounds for the level of performance we expect to achieve with the weakly-supervised systems.

An important step in coreference resolution systems is **mention prediction**. For English, mention spans were predicted from the noun phrases given by the Berkeley parser (Petrov and Klein, 2007), the same procedure as Durrett and Klein (2013). For Spanish and Portuguese, this prediction relied on the output of the dependency parser, using a simple heuristic: besides pronouns, each maximal span formed by contiguous descendants of a noun becomes a candidate mention. This heuristic is quite effective, as shown by Attardi et al. (2010).

5.1 Supervised Systems

Table 2 shows the performance of supervised systems for English, Spanish and Portuguese. All optimize Eq. 4 appended with an extra regularization term $\frac{\gamma}{2}\|\boldsymbol{w}\|^2$, by running 20 epochs of stochastic gradient descent (SGD; we set $\gamma = 1.0$ and selected the best epoch using the dev-set). All lexicalized systems use the same features as the SURFACE model of Durrett and Klein (2013), plus features for gender and number.[7] We collected a list of pronouns for all languages along with their gender, number, and person information. For English, we trained on the WSJ portion of the OntoNotes dataset, and for Spanish and Portuguese we trained on the monolingual datasets described in §2.

We observe that the Spanish system obtains averaged F_1 scores around 44%, a few points below the English figures.[8] In Portuguese, these scores are significantly lower (in the 37–39% range), which is explained by the fact that the training dataset is much smaller (cf. Table 1).

For English, we also report the performance of **delexicalized** systems, *i.e.*, systems where all the lexical features were removed. The second row of Table 2 shows a drop of 2–2.5 points with respect to the lexicalized system. For the third and fourth rows, the lexical features were replaced by bilingual word embeddings (either English-Spanish or English-Portuguese; a detailed description of these embeddings will be provided in §5.2). Here the drop is small, and for English-Spanish it looks on par with the lexicalized system.

[7]For English, the gender and number of nominal and proper mentions were obtained from the statistics collected by Bergsma and Lin (2006). For Spanish and Portuguese we used a simple heuristic for nominal mentions, based on the determiner preceding the noun (when there is one).

[8]We point out that the supervised Spanish system we present here is strong enough to outperform all participating systems in the SemEval 2010's closed regular track. When trained on the original Spanish SemEval data (with zero- and relative pronoun anaphoras) and evaluated in the provided scorer, it achieves 53.0% averaged F_1 in the test partition; for comparison, TALN-1 (Attardi et al., 2010), the best system at the shared task, achieved 49.6% averaged F_1.

	Dev				Test			
	MUC	B^3	$CEAF_e$	Avg.	MUC	B^3	$CEAF_e$	Avg.
EN lexicalized	**58.35**	**50.75**	**52.08**	**53.73**	**59.07**	**49.25**	48.78	52.37
EN delexicalized, no embed.	56.59	48.81	49.95	51.78	55.96	46.94	46.19	49.70
EN delexicalized, emb. EN-ES	57.55	49.83	51.21	52.86	59.00	**49.25**	**49.00**	**52.42**
EN delexicalized, emb. EN-PT	57.91	49.67	51.01	52.86	58.03	48.16	48.33	51.51
ES lexicalized	**48.24**	**40.97**	**43.59**	**44.27**	**47.03**	**40.68**	**44.09**	**43.93**
PT lexicalized	**35.60**	**34.47**	**42.56**	**37.54**	**41.61**	**36.91**	**40.96**	**39.83**

Table 2: Results for the supervised systems. We show also the performance of delexicalized English systems, with and without cross-lingual embeddings. Shown are MUC (Vilain et al., 1995), B^3 (Bagga and Baldwin, 1998), and $CEAF_e$ (Luo, 2005), as well their averaged F_1 scores, all computed using the reference implementation of the CoNLL scorer (Pradhan et al., 2014).

	Dev				Test			
	MUC	B^3	$CEAF_e$	Avg.	MUC	B^3	$CEAF_e$	Avg.
ES simple baseline	25.73	24.73	27.89	26.12	26.06	26.12	29.87	27.35
ES baseline #1 (delex. transfer)	33.04	27.47	32.71	31.07	34.35	28.69	34.42	32.49
ES baseline #2 (bitext dir. proj.)	39.42	30.04	38.25	35.90	37.21	29.72	35.97	34.30
ES baseline #3 (vanilla PR)	41.29	33.68	38.56	37.84	39.34	32.95	38.23	36.84
ES softmax-margin PR	**42.34**	**35.53**	**39.95**	**39.27**	**41.22**	**35.30**	**39.94**	**38.82**
PT simple baseline	26.04	26.67	33.19	28.63	22.72	23.91	27.35	24.66
PT baseline #1 (delex. transfer)	22.51	23.27	33.27	26.35	31.11	27.36	32.78	30.42
PT baseline #2 (bitext dir. proj.)	30.43	27.37	36.47	31.42	31.93	27.97	35.40	31.77
PT baseline #3 (vanilla PR)	30.97	27.82	35.14	31.31	**38.39**	33.34	38.73	36.82
PT softmax-margin PR	**33.43**	**31.00**	**38.82**	**34.42**	38.18	**34.05**	**39.47**	**37.23**

Table 3: Results for all the cross-lingual systems. Bold indicates the overall highest scores. As a lower bound, we show a simple deterministic baseline that, for pronominal mentions, selects the closest non-pronominal antecedent, and, for non-pronominal mentions, selects the closest non-pronominal mention that is a superstring of the current mention.

5.2 Baseline #1: Delexicalized Transfer With Cross-Lingual Embeddings

We now turn to the cross-lingual systems. Delexicalized transfer is a popular strategy in NLP (Zeman and Resnik, 2008; McDonald et al., 2011), recently strengthened with cross-lingual word representations (Täckström et al., 2012). The procedure works as follows: a delexicalized model for the source language is trained by eliminating all the language-specific features (such as lexical features); then, this model is used directly in the target language. We report here the performance of this baseline on coreference resolution for Spanish and Portuguese, using the delexicalized models trained on the English data as mentioned in §5.1.

To achieve a unified feature representation, we mapped all language-specific POS tags to universal tags (Petrov et al., 2012). All lexical features were replaced either by **cross-lingual word embeddings** (for words that are not pronouns); or by a universal representation containing the gender, number, and person information of the pronoun. To obtain the cross-lingual word embeddings, we ran the method described by Hermann and Blunsom (2014) for the English-Spanish and English-Portuguese pairs, using the parallel sentences in §2. When used as features, these 128-dimensional continuous representations were scaled by a factor of 0.5 (selected on the dev-set), using the procedure of Turian et al. (2010).

The second and seventh rows in Table 3 show the performance of this baseline, which is rather disappointing. For Spanish, we observe a large drop in performance when going from supervised training to delexicalized transfer (about 11–13% in averaged F_1). For Portuguese, where the supervised system is not so accurate, the difference is less sharp (about 9–11%). These drops are mainly due to the fact that this method does not take into account the intricacies of each language—*e.g.*, possessive forms have different agreement rules in English and in Romance languages;[9] those, on the other hand, have clitic pronouns that are absent in English. Feature weights that promote certain English agreement relations may then harm performance more than they help.

5.3 Baseline #2: Bitext Direct Projection

Another popular strategy for cross-lingual learning is bitext direct projection, which consists in projecting annotations through parallel data in the source and target languages (Yarowsky et al., 2001; Hwa et al., 2005). This is essentially the same as Algorithm 1, except that line 4 is replaced by simple supervised learning, via a minimization

[9] For example, in Figure 1, *their* agrees in number with the possessor (*the alveoli*), but the corresponding *sua* agrees in number and gender with the thing possessed (*função*).

of the loss function in Eq. 4 with ℓ_2-regularization. This procedure has the disadvantage of being very sensitive to annotation errors, as we shall see. For Portuguese, this baseline is a near-reproduction of Souza and Orăsan (2011)'s work, discussed in §6.

The third and eighth rows in Table 3 show that this baseline is stronger than the delexicalized baseline, but still 6–8 points away from the supervised systems. This gap is due to a mix of two factors: prediction errors in the English side of the bitext, and missing alignments. Indeed, when automatic alignments are used, false negatives for coreferent pairs of mentions are common, due to words that have not been aligned with sufficiently high confidence. The direct projection method is not robust to these annotation errors.

5.4 Baseline #3: Vanilla PR

Our last baseline is a vanilla PR approach; this is an adaptation of the procedure carried out by Ganchev and Das (2013) to our coreference resolution problem. The motivation is to increase the robustness of bitext projection to annotation errors, which we do by applying the soft constraints in §4.4. We seek a saddle-point of the PR objective by running 20 epochs of SGD, alternating $\boldsymbol{w}$-updates and $\boldsymbol{u}$-updates. The best results in the dev-set were obtained with $\eta_1 = 1.0$ and $\eta_2 = 0.9$.

By looking at the fourth and ninth rows of Table 3, we observe that vanilla PR manages to reduce the gap to supervised systems, obtaining consistent gains over the bitext projection baseline (with the exception of the Portuguese dev-set). This confirms the ability of PR methods to handle annotation mistakes in a robust manner.

5.5 Our Proposal: Softmax-Margin PR

Finally, the fifth and last rows in Table 3 show the performance of our systems trained with softmax-margin PR, as described in §4.1. We optimized the loss function in Eq. 11 with $\gamma = 1.0$ by running 20 epochs of SGD, setting $u_1 = +\infty$ and $u_2 = 1.0$ (cf. §4.4)—the last value was tuned in the dev-set. As shown in Figure 2, this penalized variant was more effective than the saddle point formulation.

From Table 3, we observe that softmax-margin PR consistently beats all the baselines, narrowing the gap with respect to supervised systems to about 5 points for Spanish, and 2–3 points for Portuguese. Gains over the vanilla PR procedure (the strongest baseline) lie in the range 0.5–3%. These gains come from the ability of softmax-margin PR to handle task-specific cost functions, enabling a better management of precision/recall tradeoffs.

5.6 Error Analysis

We carried out some error analysis, focused on the Spanish development dataset, to better understand where the improvements of softmax-margin PR come from. The main conclusions carry out to the Portuguese case, with a few exceptions, mostly due to different human annotation criteria.

Table 4 shows the precision and recall scores for mention prediction and the different coreference evaluation metrics. Note that all systems predict the same candidate mentions; however a final post-processing discards all mentions that ended up in singleton entities, for compliance with the official scorer. Therefore, the mention prediction score reflects how well a system does in predicting if a mention is anaphoric or not. The first thing to note is that the PR methods, due to their ability to create new links during training (via constraint #2) tend to predict fewer singletons than the direct projection method. Indeed, we observe that soft max-margin PR achieves 47.1% mention prediction recall, which is more than 5% above the direct projection method, and 10% above the delexicalized transfer method. Note also that, while the vanilla PR method achieves higher recall than the two other baselines, it is still almost 5% below the system trained with soft-max margin PR. This is because vanilla PR does not benefit from the cost function in §4.3—such cost is able to penalize false non-anaphoric mentions and encourage larger clusters, allowing softmax-margin PR to achieve a better precision-recall trade-off. From Table 4, we can see that this improvement in mention recall consistently translates into higher recall for the MUC, B^3 and $CEAF_e$ coreference metrics.

Further analysis revealed that a major source of error for the delexicalized baseline is its inability to handle pronominal mentions robustly across languages—as hinted in footnote 9. In practice, we found the delexicalized systems to be quite conservative with possessive pronouns: for the Spanish dataset, where the vast majority of possessive pronouns are anaphoric, the delexicalized model incorrectly predicts 53.3% of these pronouns as non-anaphoric. The direct projection model is slightly less conservative, missing 30.1% of the possessives (arguably due to its inability to recover missing links in the projected data, dur-

	Mention	MUC	B^3	$CEAF_e$
delex.	37.1 / 62.2	25.6 / 46.5	19.6 / 45.7	27.9 / 39.5
dir. proj.	41.7 / 77.5	29.3 / 60.4	19.2 / 69.5	31.8 / 47.9
vanilla PR	42.2 / 78.0	30.9 / 62.3	23.2 / 61.7	31.9 / 48.8
our PR	47.1 / 74.1	33.7 / 57.1	26.0 / 56.1	34.9 / 46.7

Table 4: Recall/precision scores for mention prediction, MUC, B^3 and $CEAF_e$, all computed in the Spanish dev set.

ing training). By comparison, the vanilla and softmax margin PR models only miss 4.9% and 3.4% of the possessives, respectively. In Portuguese, where many possessives are not annotated in the gold data, we observe a similar but much less pronounced trend.

6 Related Work

While multilingual coreference resolution has been the subject of recent SemEval and CoNLL shared tasks, no submitted system attempted cross-lingual training. As shown by Recasens and Hovy (2010), language-specific issues pose a challenge, due to phenomena as pronoun dropping and grammatical gender that are absent in English but exist in other languages. We have discussed some of these issues in the scope of the present work.

Harabagiu and Maiorano (2000) and Postolache et al. (2006) projected English corpora to Romanian to bootstrap human annotation, either manually or via automatic alignments. Rahman and Ng (2012) applied translation-based projection at test time (but require an external translation service). Hardmeier et al. (2013) addressed the related task of cross-lingual pronoun prediction. While all these approaches help alleviate the corpus annotation bottleneck, none resulted in a full coreference resolver, which our work accomplished.

The work most related with ours is Souza and Orăsan (2011), who also used parallel data to transfer an English coreference resolver to Portuguese, but could not beat a simple baseline that clusters together mentions with the same head. Their approach is similar to our bitext direct projection baseline, except that they used Reconcile (Stoyanov et al., 2010) instead of the Berkeley Coreference System, and a smaller version of the FAPESP corpus. We have shown that our softmax-margin PR procedure is superior to this approach.

Discriminative PR has been proposed by Ganchev et al. (2010). The same idea underlies the generalized expectation criterion (Mann and McCallum, 2010; Wang and Manning, 2014). An SGD algorithm for solving the resulting saddle point problem has been proposed by Liang et al. (2009), and used by Ganchev and Das (2013) for cross-lingual learning of sequence models. We extended this framework in two aspects: by incorporating a task-specific cost in the objective function, and by formulating a penalized variant of PR.

7 Conclusions

We presented a framework for cross-lingual transfer of coreference resolvers. Our method uses word-aligned bitext to project information from the source to the target language. Robustness to projection errors was achieved via a PR framework, which we generalized to handle task-specific costs, yielding softmax-margin PR. We also proposed a penalized formulation that is effective for a small number of corpus-based constraints. Empirical gains were shown over three popular cross-lingual methods: delexicalized transfer, bitext direct projection, and vanilla PR.

Acknowledgments

I would like to thank the reviewers for their helpful comments, José Guilherme Camargo de Souza for pointing to existing datasets, and Mariana Almeida for valuable feedback. This work was partially supported by the EU/FEDER programme, QREN/POR Lisboa (Portugal), under the Intelligo project (contract 2012/24803), and by the FCT grants UID/EEA/50008/2013 and PTDC/EEI-SII/2312/2012.

A Proof of Proposition 1

Let us fix $\boldsymbol{w}$ and see how to evaluate $\mathbf{KL}(\mathcal{Q}\|p'_{\boldsymbol{w}}) = \min_{q\in\mathcal{Q}} \mathbf{KL}(q\|p'_{\boldsymbol{w}})$. We have:

$$\begin{aligned}\mathbf{KL}(q\|p'_{\boldsymbol{w}}) &= -\mathbf{H}(q) - \textstyle\sum_{\mathbf{Y}} q(\mathbf{Y}) \log p'_{\boldsymbol{w}}(\mathbf{Y}|\mathbf{X}) \\ &= -\mathbf{H}(q) + \textstyle\sum_n \log Z'(\boldsymbol{w}, x^{(n)}) - \\ &\quad \textstyle\sum_{\mathbf{Y}} q(\mathbf{Y})(\boldsymbol{w}^\top \boldsymbol{f}(\mathbf{X},\mathbf{Y}) + \ell(\mathbf{Y})),\end{aligned}$$

where $\ell(\mathbf{Y}) := \sum_{n=1}^N \ell(y, \mathcal{Y}(\mathcal{E}^{(n)}))$ and $\boldsymbol{f}(\mathbf{X},\mathbf{Y}) := \sum_{n=1}^N \boldsymbol{f}(x^{(n)}, y^{(n)})$. Introducing Lagrange multipliers $\boldsymbol{u}$ for the posterior constraints, we get the Lagrangian function:

$$\begin{aligned}\mathcal{L}(q,\boldsymbol{u}) &= -\mathbf{H}(q) + \textstyle\sum_n \log Z'(\boldsymbol{w}, x^{(n)}) - \boldsymbol{b}^\top \boldsymbol{u} \\ &\quad - \textstyle\sum_{\mathbf{Y}} q(\mathbf{Y})(\boldsymbol{w}^\top \boldsymbol{f}(\mathbf{X},\mathbf{Y}) + \ell(\mathbf{Y}) - \boldsymbol{u}^\top \boldsymbol{g}(\mathbf{X},\mathbf{Y})).\end{aligned}$$

By standard variational arguments (namely, Fenchel duality between the the log-partition function and the negative entropy; see *e.g.* Martins et al. (2010)), we have that the optimal q^* that minimizes the Lagrangian is

$$q^*(\mathbf{Y}) = \frac{e^{\boldsymbol{w}^\top \boldsymbol{f}(\mathbf{X},\mathbf{Y}) + \ell(\mathbf{Y}) - \boldsymbol{u}^\top \boldsymbol{g}(\mathbf{X},\mathbf{Y})}}{\prod_{n=1}^N Z'_{\boldsymbol{u}}(\boldsymbol{w}, x^{(n)})}.$$

Plugging this in the Lagrangian yields Eq. 8.

References

Mariana S. C. Almeida, Cláudia Pinto, Helena Figueira, Pedro Mendes, and André F. T. Martins. 2015. Aligning opinions: Cross-lingual opinion mining with dependencies. In *Proc. of the Annual Meeting of the Association for Computational Linguistics*.

Giuseppe Attardi, Stefano Dei Rossi, and Maria Simi. 2010. TANL-1: coreference resolution by parse analysis and similarity clustering. In *Proc. of the International Workshop on Semantic Evaluation*.

Wilker Aziz and Lucia Specia. 2011. Fully automatic compilation of a Portuguese-English parallel corpus for statistical machine translation. In *STIL 2011*.

Amit Bagga and Breck Baldwin. 1998. Algorithms for scoring coreference chains. In *Proc. of International Conference on Language Resources and Evaluation: Workshop on Linguistics Coreference*.

Eric Bengtson and Dan Roth. 2008. Understanding the value of features for coreference resolution. In *Proc. of Empirical Methods in Natural Language Processing*.

Shane Bergsma and Dekang Lin. 2006. Bootstrapping path-based pronoun resolution. In *Proc. of the Annual Meeting of the Association for Computational Linguistics*.

Sandra Collovini, Thiago Carbonel, Juliana Thiesen Fuchs, Jorge César Coelho, Lúcia Rino, and Renata Vieira. 2007. Summ-it: Um corpus anotado com informações discursivas visando a sumarização automática. In *Workshop em Tecnologia da Informação e da Linguagem Humana*.

Pascal Denis and Jason Baldridge. 2008. Specialized models and ranking for coreference resolution. In *Proc. of Empirical Methods in Natural Language Processing*.

Greg Durrett and Dan Klein. 2013. Easy victories and uphill battles in coreference resolution. In *Proc. of Empirical Methods in Natural Language Processing*.

Greg Durrett, David Hall, and Dan Klein. 2013. Decentralized entity-level modeling for coreference resolution. In *Proc. of Annual Meeting of the Association for Computational Linguistics*.

Eraldo Rezende Fernandes, Cícero Nogueira dos Santos, and Ruy Luiz Milidiú. 2012. Latent structure perceptron with feature induction for unrestricted coreference resolution. In *Joint Conference on EMNLP and CoNLL-Shared Task*, pages 41–48.

Kuzman Ganchev and Dipanjan Das. 2013. Cross-lingual discriminative learning of sequence models with posterior regularization. In *Proc. of Empirical Methods in Natural Language Processing*.

Kuzman Ganchev, João Graça, Jennifer Gillenwater, and Ben Taskar. 2010. Posterior regularization for structured latent variable models. *Journal of Machine Learning Research*, 11:2001–2049.

Kevin Gimpel and Noah A. Smith. 2010. Softmax-Margin CRFs: Training Log-Linear Models with Loss Functions. In *NAACL*.

Aria Haghighi and Dan Klein. 2007. Unsupervised coreference resolution in a nonparametric bayesian model. In *Proc. of Annual Meeting of the Association for Computational Linguistics*.

Aria Haghighi and Dan Klein. 2010. Coreference resolution in a modular, entity-centered model. In *Proc. of Annual Conference of the North American Chapter of the Association for Computational Linguistics*.

Sanda M Harabagiu and Steven J Maiorano. 2000. Multilingual coreference resolution. In *Proc. of the Conference on Applied Natural Language Processing*.

Christian Hardmeier, Jörg Tiedemann, and Joakim Nivre. 2013. Latent anaphora resolution for cross-lingual pronoun prediction. In *Proc. of Empirical Methods in Natural Language Processing*.

Karl Moritz Hermann and Phil Blunsom. 2014. Multilingual Models for Compositional Distributional Semantics. In *Proc. of the Annual Meeting of the Association for Computational Linguistics*.

Rebecca Hwa, Philip Resnik, Amy Weinberg, Clara Cabezas, and Okan Kolak. 2005. Bootstrapping parsers via syntactic projection across parallel texts. *Natural language engineering*, 11(3):311–325.

Percy Liang, Ben Taskar, and Dan Klein. 2006. Alignment by agreement. In *Proc. of North American Chapter of the Association of Computational Linguistics*.

Percy Liang, Michael I Jordan, and Dan Klein. 2009. Learning from measurements in exponential families. In *Proc. of International Conference on Machine Learning*, pages 641–648.

Xiaoqiang Luo. 2005. On coreference resolution performance metrics. In *Proc. of Empirical Methods in Natural Language Processing*. Association for Computational Linguistics.

Gideon Mann and Andrew McCallum. 2010. Generalized expectation criteria for semi-supervised learning with weakly labeled data. *Journal of Machine Learning Research*, 11:955–984.

André F. T Martins, Noah A. Smith, Eric P. Xing, Pedro M. Q. Aguiar, and Mário A. T. Figueiredo. 2010. Turbo Parsers: Dependency Parsing by Approximate Variational Inference. In *Proc. of Empirical Methods for Natural Language Processing*.

André F. T Martins, Miguel B. Almeida, and Noah A. Smith. 2013. Turning on the turbo: Fast third-order non-projective turbo parsers. In *Proc. of the Annual Meeting of the Association for Computational Linguistics*.

Ryan McDonald, Slav Petrov, and Keith Hall. 2011. Multi-source transfer of delexicalized dependency parsers. In *Proc. of Empirical Methods in Natural Language Processing*.

Vincent Ng and Claire Cardie. 2002. Improving machine learning approaches to coreference resolution. In *Proc. of the Annual Meeting on Association for Computational Linguistics*.

Vincent Ng. 2008. Unsupervised models for coreference resolution. In *Proc. of Empirical Methods in Natural Language Processing*.

Slav Petrov and Dan Klein. 2007. Improved inference for unlexicalized parsing. In *Proc. of Annual Meeting of the North American Chapter of the Association for Computational Linguistics*, pages 404–411.

Slav Petrov, Dipanjan Das, and Ryan McDonald. 2012. A universal part-of-speech tagset. In *Proc. of LREC*.

Oana Postolache, Dan Cristea, and Constantin Orasan. 2006. Transferring coreference chains through word alignment. In *Proc. of the International Conference on Language Resources and Evaluation*.

Sameer Pradhan, Alessandro Moschitti, Nianwen Xue, Olga Uryupina, and Yuchen Zhang. 2012. CoNLL-2012 Shared Task: Modeling multilingual unrestricted coreference in OntoNotes. In *Proc. of the Conference on Computational Natural Language Learning: Shared Task*.

Sameer Pradhan, Xiaoqiang Luo, Marta Recasens, Eduard Hovy, Vincent Ng, and Michael Strube. 2014. Scoring coreference partitions of predicted mentions: A reference implementation. In *Proc. of the Annual Meeting of the Association for Computational Linguistics*.

Karthik Raghunathan, Heeyoung Lee, Sudarshan Rangarajan, Nathanael Chambers, Mihai Surdeanu, Dan Jurafsky, and Christopher Manning. 2010. A multi-pass sieve for coreference resolution. In *Proc. of Empirical Methods in Natural Language Processing*.

Altaf Rahman and Vincent Ng. 2011. Narrowing the modeling gap: A cluster-ranking approach to coreference resolution. *Journal of Artificial Intelligence Research*, 40(1):469–521.

Altaf Rahman and Vincent Ng. 2012. Translation-based projection for multilingual coreference resolution. In *Proc. of the Conference of the North American Chapter of the Association for Computational Linguistics*.

Marta Recasens and Eduard Hovy. 2010. Coreference resolution across corpora: Languages, coding schemes, and preprocessing information. In *Proc. of the Annual Meeting of the Association for Computational Linguistics*.

Marta Recasens and M Antònia Martí. 2010. Ancora-co: Coreferentially annotated corpora for spanish and catalan. *Language resources and evaluation*, 44(4):315–345.

Marta Recasens, Lluís Màrquez, Emili Sapena, M Antònia Martí, Mariona Taulé, Véronique Hoste, Massimo Poesio, and Yannick Versley. 2010. Semeval-2010 task 1: Coreference resolution in multiple languages. In *Proc. of the International Workshop on Semantic Evaluation*.

Noah A Smith and Jason Eisner. 2005. Contrastive estimation: Training log-linear models on unlabeled data. In *Proc. of Annual Meeting on Association for Computational Linguistics*.

Wee Meng Soon, Hwee Tou Ng, and Daniel Chung Yong Lim. 2001. A machine learning approach to coreference resolution of noun phrases. *Computational linguistics*, 27(4):521–544.

José Guilherme Camargo de Souza and Constantin Orăsan. 2011. Can projected chains in parallel corpora help coreference resolution? In *Anaphora Processing and Applications*, pages 59–69. Springer.

Veselin Stoyanov, Claire Cardie, Nathan Gilbert, Ellen Riloff, David Buttler, and David Hysom. 2010. Coreference resolution with reconcile. In *Proc. of the Annual Meeting of the Association for Computational Linguistics*.

Oscar Täckström, Ryan McDonald, and Jakob Uszkoreit. 2012. Cross-lingual word clusters for direct transfer of linguistic structure. In *Proc. of the North American Chapter of the Association for Computational Linguistics*.

Oscar Täckström, Dipanjan Das, Slav Petrov, Ryan McDonald, and Joakim Nivre. 2013. Token and type constraints for cross-lingual part-of-speech tagging. *Transactions of the Association for Computational Linguistics*, 1:1–12.

Ivan Titov and Alexandre Klementiev. 2012. Cross-lingual induction of semantic roles. In *Proc. of the Annual Meeting of the Association for Computational Linguistics*.

Joseph Turian, Lev Ratinov, and Yoshua Bengio. 2010. Word representations: a simple and general method for semi-supervised learning. In *Proc. of the Annual Meeting of the Association for Computational Linguistics*.

Yannick Versley, Simone Paolo Ponzetto, Massimo Poesio, Vladimir Eidelman, Alan Jern, Jason Smith, Xiaofeng Yang, and Alessandro Moschitti. 2008. Bart: A modular toolkit for coreference resolution. In *Proc. of the Annual Meeting of the Association for Computational Linguistics: Demo Session*.

Marc Vilain, John Burger, John Aberdeen, Dennis Connolly, and Lynette Hirschman. 1995. A model-theoretic coreference scoring scheme. In *Proc. of the Conference on Message Understanding*, pages 45–52. Association for Computational Linguistics.

Mengqiu Wang and Chris Manning. 2014. Cross-lingual projected expectation regularization for weakly supervised learning. *Transactions of the Association for Computational Linguistics*, 2:55–66.

David Yarowsky, Grace Ngai, and Richard Wicentowski. 2001. Inducing multilingual text analysis tools via robust projection across aligned corpora. In *Proc. of the First International Conference on Human Language Technology Research*.

Daniel Zeman and Philip Resnik. 2008. Cross-language parser adaptation between related languages. In *IJCNLP*, pages 35–42.

Tea Party in the House: A Hierarchical Ideal Point Topic Model and Its Application to Republican Legislators in the 112th Congress

Viet-An Nguyen
Computer Science
University of Maryland
College Park, MD
vietan@cs.umd.edu

Jordan Boyd-Graber
Computer Science
University of Colorado
Boulder, CO
Jordan.Boyd.Graber@colorado.edu

Philip Resnik
Linguistics & UMIACS
University of Maryland
College Park, MD
resnik@umd.edu

Kristina Miler
Government and Politics
University of Maryland
College Park, MD
kmiler@umd.edu

Abstract

We introduce the *Hierarchical Ideal Point Topic Model*, which provides a rich picture of policy issues, framing, and voting behavior using a joint model of votes, bill text, and the language that legislators use when debating bills. We use this model to look at the relationship between Tea Party Republicans and "establishment" Republicans in the U.S. House of Representatives during the 112th Congress.

1 Capturing Political Polarization

Ideal-point models are one of the most widely used tools in contemporary political science research (Poole and Rosenthal, 2007). These models estimate political preferences for legislators, known as their *ideal points*, from binary data such as legislative votes. Popular formulations analyze legislators' votes and place them on a one-dimensional scale, most often interpreted as an ideological spectrum from liberal to conservative.

Moving beyond a single dimension is attractive, however, since people may lean differently based on policy issues; for example, the conservative movement in the U.S. includes fiscal conservatives who are relatively liberal on social issues, and vice versa. In *multi-dimensional* ideal point models, therefore, the ideal point of each legislator is no longer characterized by a single number, but by a multi-dimensional vector. With that move comes a new challenge, though: the additional dimensions are often difficult to interpret. To mitigate this problem, recent research has introduced methods that estimate multi-dimensional ideal points using both voting data and the texts of the bills being voted on, e.g., using topic models and associating each dimension of the ideal point space with a topic. The words most strongly associated with the topic can sometimes provide a readable description of its corresponding dimension.

In this paper, we develop this idea further by introducing HIPTM, the *Hierarchical Ideal Point Topic Model*, to estimate multi-dimensional ideal points for legislators in the U.S. Congress. HIPTM differs from previous models in three ways. First, HIPTM uses not only votes and associated bill text, but also the *language* of the legislators themselves; this allows predictions of ideal points from politicians' writing alone. Second, HIPTM improves the interpretability of ideal-point dimensions by incorporating data from the Congressional Bills Project (Adler and Wilkerson, 2015), in which bills are labeled with major topics from the Policy Agendas Project Topic Codebook.[1] And third, HIPTM discovers a *hierarchy* of topics, allowing us to analyze both agenda issues and issue-specific frames that legislators use on the congressional floor, following Nguyen et al. (2013) in modeling framing as second-level agenda setting (McCombs, 2005).

Using this new model, we focus on Republican legislators during the 112th U.S. Congress, from January 2011 until January 2013. This is a particularly interesting session of Congress for political scientists, because of the rise of the Tea Party, a decentralized political movement with populist, libertarian, and conservative elements. Although united with "establishment" Republicans against Democrats in the 2010 midterm elections, leading to massive Democratic defeats, the Tea Party was—and still is—wrestling with establishment Republicans for control of the Republican party.

The Tea Party is a new and complex phenomenon for political scientists; as Carmines and D'Amico (2015) observe: "Conventional views of ideology as a single-dimensional, left-right spectrum experience great difficulty in understanding or explaining the Tea Party." Our model identifies legislators who have low (or high) levels of "Tea Partiness" but are (or are not) members of the Tea Party Caucus, and providing insights into the na-

[1] http://www.policyagendas.org/

Proceedings of the 53rd Annual Meeting of the Association for Computational Linguistics and the 7th International Joint Conference on Natural Language Processing, pages 1438–1448,
Beijing, China, July 26-31, 2015.

ture of polarization within the Republican party. HIPTM also makes it possible to investigate a number of questions of interest to political scientists. For example, are there Republicans who identify themselves as members of the Tea Party, but whose votes and language betray a lack of enthusiasm for Tea Party issues? How well can we predict from someone's language alone whether they are likely to associate themselves with the Tea Party? Our computational modeling approach to "Tea Partiness", distinct from self-declared Tea Party Caucus membership, may have particular value in understanding Republican party politics going forward because, despite the continued influence of the Tea Party, the official Tea Party Caucus in the House of Representatives is largely inactive and its future uncertain (Fuller, 2015).

2 Polarization across Dimensions

Ideal point models describe probabilistic relationships between observed responses (votes) on a set of items (bills) by a set of responders (legislators) who are characterized by continuous latent traits (Fox, 2010). A popular formulation posits an *ideal point* u_a for each lawmaker a, a *polarity* x_b, and *popularity* y_b for each bill b, all being values in $(-\infty, +\infty)$ (Martin and Quinn, 2002; Bafumi et al., 2005; Gerrish and Blei, 2011). Lawmaker a votes "Yes" on bill b with probability

$$p(v_{a,b} = \text{Yes} \mid u_a, x_b, y_b) = \Phi(u_a x_b + y_b) \quad (1)$$

where $\Phi(\alpha) = \exp(\alpha)/(1 + \exp(\alpha))$ is the logistic (or inverse-logit) function.[2] Intuitively, most lawmakers vote "Yes" on bills with high popularity y_b and "No" on bills with low y_b. When a bill's popularity is lower, the outcome of the vote $v_{a,b}$ depends more on the interaction between the lawmaker's ideal point u_a and the bill's polarity x_b.

Multi-dimensional ideal point models replace scalars u_a and x_b with K-dimensional vectors $\boldsymbol{u}_a$ and $\boldsymbol{x}_b$ (Heckman and Jr., 1997; Jackman, 2001; Clinton et al., 2004). Unfortunately, as Lauderdale and Clark (2014) observe, the binary data used for these models are "insufficiently informative to support analyses beyond one or two dimensions", and the additional dimensions are difficult to interpret. To address this lack of interpretability, recent work has proposed multi-dimensional ideal point models to jointly capture both binary votes and the associated text (Gerrish and Blei, 2012; Gu et al., 2014; Lauderdale and Clark, 2014; Sim et al., 2015).

[2] A probit function is also often used where $\Phi(\alpha)$ is instead the cumulative distribution function of a Gaussian distribution (Martin and Quinn, 2002).

3 Hierarchical Ideal Point Topic Model

Bringing topic models (Blei and Lafferty, 2009) into ideal-point modeling provides an interpretable, text-based foundation for political scientists to understand why the models make the predictions they do. However, both the *topic*—what is discussed—and the *framing*—how it is discussed—also reveal political preferences. We therefore introduce *frame-specific* ideal points, using a hierarchy of topics to model issues and their issue-specific frames. Although the definition of "frame" is itself a moving target in political science (Entman, 1993), we adopt the theoretically motivated but pragmatic approach of Nguyen et al. (2013): just as agenda-issues map naturally to topics in probabilistic topic models (e.g., Grimmer (2010)), the frames as second-level agenda-setting (McCombs, 2005) map to second-level topics in a hierarchical topic model.

Our model's inputs are votes $\{v_{a,b}\}$, each the response of legislator $a \in [1, A]$ to bill $b \in [1, B]$. Two types of text supplement the votes: floor speeches (documents) $\{\boldsymbol{w}_d\}$ from legislator a_d, and the text $\boldsymbol{w}'_b$ of bill b. While congressional debates are typically about one piece of legislation, we make no assumptions about the mapping between $\boldsymbol{w}_d$ and $\boldsymbol{w}'_b$. In principle this allows $\boldsymbol{w}_d$ to be *any* text by legislator a_d (e.g., not just floor speeches about this bill, but blogs, social media, press releases) and—unlike Gerrish and Blei (2011)—this permits us to make predictions about individuals even without vote data for them. Figure 1 shows the plate notation diagram of HIPTM, which has the following generative process:

1. For each issue $k \in [1, K]$
   (a) Draw k's associated topic $\phi_k \sim \text{Dir}(\beta, \phi_k^\star)$
   (b) Draw issue-specific distribution over frames $\psi_k \sim \text{GEM}(\lambda_0)$
   (c) For each frame $j \in [1, \infty)$ (specific to issue k)
      i. Draw j's associated topic $\phi_{k,j} \sim \text{Dir}(\beta, \phi_k)$
      ii. Draw j's regression weight $\eta_{k,j} \sim \mathcal{N}(0, \gamma)$
2. For each document $d \in [1, D]$ by legislator a_d
   (a) Draw topic (i.e., issue) distribution $\theta_d \sim \text{Dir}(\alpha)$
   (b) For each issue $k \in [1, K]$, draw frame distribution $\psi_{d,k} \sim \text{DP}(\lambda, \psi_k)$
   (c) For each token $n \in [1, N_d]$
      i. Draw an issue $z_{d,n} \sim \text{Mult}(\theta_d)$
      ii. Draw a frame $t_{d,n} \sim \text{Mult}(\psi_{d,z_{d,n}})$
      iii. Draw word $w_{d,n} \sim \text{Mult}(\phi_{z_{d,n},t_{d,n}})$
3. For each legislator $a \in [1, A]$ on each issue $k \in [1, K]$
   (a) Draw issue-specific ideal point $u_{a,k} \sim \mathcal{N}(\sum_{j=1}^{J_k} \hat{\psi}_{a,k,j}\eta_{k,j}, \rho)$ weighting $\eta_{k,j}$ by how much the legislator talks about that frame

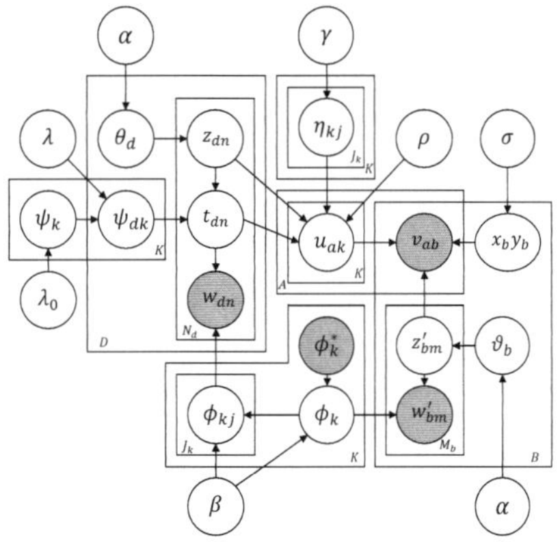

Figure 1: Plate notation diagram of HIPTM.

Agriculture: food; agriculture; loan; farm; crop; dairy; rural; conserve; commodity; eligible; farmer; margin; milk; contract; nutrition; livestock; plant

Health: drug; medicine; coverage; disease; public_health; hospital; social_security; health_insurrance; patient; application; treatment; payment; physician; nurse; clinic

Labor, Employment, and Immigration: employment; immigration; labor; paragraph; eligible; status; compensation; application; wage; homeland_security; unemployment; board; violation; file; perform; mine

Table 1: Examples of informed priors $\phi_k^\star$ for issues.

4. For each bill $b \in [1, B]$
   (a) Draw polarity $x_b \sim \mathcal{N}(0, \sigma)$
   (b) Draw popularity $y_b \sim \mathcal{N}(0, \sigma)$
   (c) Draw topic (i.e., issue) proportions $\vartheta_b \sim \text{Dir}(\alpha)$
   (d) For each token $m \in [1, M_b]$ in the text of bill b
      i. Draw an issue $z'_{b,m} \sim \text{Mult}(\vartheta_b)$
      ii. Draw a word type $w'_{b,m} \sim \text{Mult}(\phi_{z'_{b,m}})$
5. For each vote $v_{a,b}$ of legislator a on bill b
   (a) $p(v_{a,b} \mid \boldsymbol{u}_a, x_b, y_b, \hat{\vartheta}_b) = \Phi\left(x_b \sum_k \hat{\vartheta}_{b,k} u_{a,k} + y_b\right)$

Topic Hierarchy. With the goal of analyzing agendas and frames in mind, our topic hierarchy has two levels: (1) *issue nodes* and (2) *frame nodes*. (Look ahead to Figure 6 for an illustration.) More specifically, there are K issue nodes, each with a topic ϕ_k drawn from a Dirichlet distribution with concentration parameter β and a prior mean vector $\phi_k^\star$, i.e., $\phi_k \sim \text{Dir}(\beta, \phi_k^\star)$. In this hierarchical structure, first-level nodes map to agenda issues, which we treat as non-polarized, and second-level nodes map to issue-specific frames, which we assume polarize on the issue-specific dimension.[3]

To improve topic interpretability, issue nodes have an informed prior from the Congressional Bills Project $\{\phi_k^\star\}$ (Table 1).[4] The frame topic $\phi_{k,j}$ at each frame node is a Dirichlet draw centered at the corresponding (parent) issue node. While the number of issues is fixed *a priori*, the number of second-level frames is unbounded. We also associate each second-level frame node with an ideal point $\eta_{k,j} \sim \mathcal{N}(0, \gamma)$. This resembles how supervised topic models (Blei and McAuliffe, 2007; Nguyen et al., 2015) discover polarized topics' associated response variables.

Generating Text from Legislators. One of our model's goal is to study how legislators *frame* policy agenda issues. To achieve that, we analyze congressional speeches (documents) $\{\boldsymbol{w}_d\}$, each of which is delivered by a legislator a_d. To generate each token $w_{d,n}$ of a speech d, legislator a_d will (1) first choose an issue $z_{d,n} \in [1, K]$ from a document-specific multinomial θ_d, then (2) choose a frame $t_{d,n}$ from the set of infinitely many possible frames of the given issue $z_{d,n}$ using the frame proportion $\psi_{d,k}$ drawn from a Dirichlet process, and finally (3) choose a word type from the chosen frame's topic $\phi_{z_{d,n},t_{d,n}}$. In other words, our model generates speeches using a mixture of K HDPs (Teh et al., 2006).[5]

Generating Bill Text. The bill text provides information about the policy agenda issues that each bill addresses. We use LDA to model the bill text $\{\boldsymbol{w}'_b\}$. Each bill b is a mixture ϑ_b over K issues, which is drawn from a symmetric Dirichlet prior, i.e., $\vartheta_b \sim \text{Dir}(\alpha)$. Each token $w'_{b,m}$ in bill b is generated by first choosing a topic $z'_{b,m} \sim \text{Mult}(\vartheta_b)$, and then choosing a word type $w'_{b,m} \sim \text{Mult}(\phi_{z'_{b,m}})$, as in LDA.

Generating Roll Call Votes. Following recent work on multi-dimensional ideal points (Lauderdale and Clark, 2014; Sim et al., 2015), we define the probability of legislator a voting "Yes" on bill b as $p(v_{a,b} = \text{Yes} \mid \boldsymbol{u}_a, x_b, y_b, \hat{\vartheta}_b) =$

$$\Phi\left(x_b \sum_{k=1}^{K} \hat{\vartheta}_{b,k} u_{a,k} + y_b\right) \quad (2)$$

where $\hat{\vartheta}_b$ is the empirical distribution of bill b over the K issues and is defined as $\hat{\vartheta}_{b,k} = \frac{M_{b,k}}{M_{b,\cdot}}$. Here, $M_{b,k}$ is the number of times in which tokens in b

[3]Nguyen et al. (2013) allow first-level nodes to polarize but find first-level nodes are typically neutral.

[4]The Congressional Bills Project provides a large collection of labeled congressional bill text. We compute $\{\phi_k^\star\}$ as the empirical word distribution from all bills labeled with k. $K = 19$, corresponding to 19 major topic headings in the Policy Agendas Project Topic Codebook.

[5]If we abandoned the labeled data from the Congressional Bills Project to obtain the prior means $\phi_k^\star$, it would be relatively straightforward to extend to a fully nonparametric model with unbounded K (Ahmed et al., 2013; Paisley et al., 2014).

are assigned to issue k and $M_{b,\cdot}$ is the marginal count, i.e., the number of tokens in bill b.

The ideal point of legislator a specifically on issue k is $u_{a,k}$ and comes from a normal distribution

$$\mathcal{N}(\hat{\psi}_{a,k}^T \boldsymbol{\eta}_k, \rho) \equiv \mathcal{N}\left(\sum_{j=1}^{J_k} \hat{\psi}_{a,k,j}\eta_{k,j}, \rho\right) \quad (3)$$

where J_k is the number of frames for topic k, which is unbounded. The mean of the Normal distribution is a linear combination of the ideal points $\{\eta_{k,j}\}$ of all issue k's frames, weighted by how much time legislator a spends on each frame when talking about issue k, i.e., $\psi_{a,k,j} = \frac{N_{a,k,j}}{N_{a,k,\cdot}}$. Here, $N_{a,k,j}$ is the number of tokens authored by a that are assigned to frame j of issue k, and $N_{a,k,\cdot}$ is the marginal count. When $N_{a,k,\cdot} = 0$, which means that legislator a does not talk about issue k, we back off to an uninformed zero mean.

Equation 3 resembles how supervised topic models (SLDA) link topics with a response, in that the response—the issue-specific ideal point $u_{a,k}$—is latent. It is similar to how Gerrish and Blei (2011) use the bill text to regress on the bill's latent polarity x_b and popularity y_b. In this paper, we only use text from congressional speeches for regression, as these can capture how legislators frame specific topics. Incorporating the bill text into the regression is an interesting direction for future work.

4 Inference

Given observed data of (1) votes $\{v_{a,b}\}$ by A legislators on B bills, (2) speeches $\{\boldsymbol{w}_d\}$ from legislators, and (3) bill text $\{\boldsymbol{w}'_b\}$, we estimate the latent variables using stochastic EM. In each iteration, we perform the following steps: (1) sampling issue assignments $\{z'_{b,m}\}$ for bill text tokens, (2) sampling the issue assignments $\{z_{d,n}\}$ and frame assignments $\{t_{d,n}\}$ for speech tokens, (3) sampling the topics at first-level issue nodes $\{\phi_k\}$, (4) sampling the distribution over frames $\{\psi_k\}$ for all issues, (5) optimizing frames' regression parameters $\{\eta_{k,j}\}$ using L-BFGS (Liu and Nocedal, 1989), and (6) updating legislators' ideal points $\{u_{a,k}\}$ and bills' polarity $\{x_b\}$ and popularity $\{y_b\}$ using gradient ascent.

Sampling Issue Assignments for Bill Tokens The probability of assigning a token $w'_{b,m}$ in the bill text to an issue k is

$$p(z'_{b,m} = k \mid \text{rest}) \propto \frac{M_{b,k}^{-b,m} + \alpha}{M_{b,\cdot}^{-b,m} + K\alpha} \cdot \hat{\phi}_{k,w'_{b,m}} \quad (4)$$

where $M_{b,k}$ denotes the number of tokens in bill text b assigned to issue k. The current estimated probability of word type v given issue k is $\hat{\phi}_{k,v}$ (Equation 7). Marginal counts are denoted by $\cdot$ and the superscript $^{-b,m}$ excludes the assignment for token $w'_{b,m}$ from the corresponding count.

Sampling Frame Assignments in Speeches To sample the assignments for tokens in the speeches, we first sample an issue using

$$p(z_{d,n} = k \mid \text{rest}) \propto \frac{N_{d,k}^{-d,n} + \alpha}{N_{d,\cdot}^{-d,n} + K\alpha} \cdot \hat{\phi}_{k,w_{d,n}} \quad (5)$$

where $N_{d,k}$ similarly denotes the number of times that tokens in d are assigned to issue k. Given the sampled issue k, we sample the frame as

$$p(t_{d,n} = j \mid z_{d,n} = k, a_d = a, \text{rest}) \propto$$
$$\begin{cases} \mathcal{N}(u_{a,k}; \mu_{a,k,j}, \rho) \cdot \left(\frac{N_{d,k,j}^{-d,n}}{N_{d,k,j}^{-d,n}+\lambda} + \frac{\lambda \cdot \hat{\psi}_{k,j}}{N_{d,k,j}^{-d,n}+\lambda} \right), \\ \mathcal{N}(u_{a,k}; \mu_{a,k,j^{\text{new}}}, \rho) \cdot \frac{\lambda}{N_{d,k,j}^{-d,n}+\lambda} \cdot \hat{\psi}_{k,j^{\text{new}}}, \end{cases} \quad (6)$$

where $\mu_{a,k,j} = (\sum_{j'=1}^{J_k} \eta_{k,j'} N_{d,k,j'}^{-d,n} + \eta_{k,j})/N_{d,k,\cdot}$ for an existing frame j, and for a newly created frame j^{new}, we have $\mu_{a,k,j^{\text{new}}} = (\sum_{j'=1}^{J_k} \eta_{k,j'} N_{d,k,j'}^{-d,n} + \eta_{k,j^{\text{new}}})/N_{d,k,\cdot}$, where $\eta_{k,j^{\text{new}}}$ is drawn from the Gaussian prior $\mathcal{N}(0, \gamma)$. Here, the estimated global probability of choosing a frame j of issue k is $\hat{\psi}_{k,j}$.

Sampling Issue Topics In the generative process of HIPTM, the topic ϕ_k of issue k (1) generates tokens in the bill text and (2) provides the Dirichlet priors of the issue's frames. Rather than collapsing multinomials and factorizing (Hu and Boyd-Graber, 2012), we follow Ahmed et al. (2013) and sample

$$\hat{\phi}_k \sim \text{Dir}(\boldsymbol{m}_k + \tilde{\boldsymbol{n}}_k + \beta\phi_k^{\star}) \quad (7)$$

where $\boldsymbol{m}_k \equiv (M_{k,1}, M_{k,2}, \cdots, M_{k,V})$ is the token count vector from the bill text assigned to each issue. The vector $\tilde{\boldsymbol{n}}_k \equiv (\tilde{N}_{k,1}, \tilde{N}_{k,2}, \cdots, \tilde{N}_{k,V})$ denotes the token counts propagated from words assigned to topics that are associated with frames of issue k, approximated using minimal or maximal path assumptions (Cowans, 2006; Wallach, 2008).

Sampling Frame Proportions Following the *direct assignment* method described in Teh et al. (2006), we sample the global frame proportion as

$$\hat{\psi}_k \equiv (\hat{\psi}_{k,1}, \hat{\psi}_{k,2}, \cdots, \hat{\psi}_{k,j^{\text{new}}})$$
$$\sim \text{Dir}(\hat{N}_{\cdot,k,1}, \hat{N}_{\cdot,k,2}, \cdots, \hat{N}_{\cdot,k,J_k}, \lambda_0) \quad (8)$$

where $\hat{N}_{\cdot,k,j} = \sum_{d=1}^{D} \hat{N}_{d,k,j}$ and $\hat{N}_{d,k,j}$ can be sampled effectively using the Antoniak distribution (Antoniak, 1974).

Optimizing Frame Regression Parameters We update the regression parameters $\boldsymbol{\eta}_k$ of frames under issue k using L-BFGS (Liu and Nocedal, 1989) to optimize $\mathcal{L}(\boldsymbol{\eta}_k)$

$$-\frac{1}{2\rho}\sum_{a=1}^{A}(u_{a,k}-\boldsymbol{\eta}_k^T\hat{\boldsymbol{\psi}}_{a,k})-\frac{1}{2\gamma}\sum_{j=1}^{J_k}\eta_{k,j}^2 \quad (9)$$

Updating Ideal Points, Polarity and Popularity We update the multi-dimensional ideal point $\boldsymbol{u}_a$ of each legislator a and the polarity x_b and popularity y_b of each bill b by optimizing the log likelihood using gradient ascent.

5 Data Collection

What makes a Tea Partier? To address that question, we use *key votes* identified by Freedom Works as the most important votes on issues of economic freedom. Led by former House Majority Leader Dick Armey (R-TX), Freedom Works is a conservative non-profit organization which promotes "Lower Taxes, Less Government, More Freedom".[6] Karpowitz et al. (2011) report that Freedom Works endorsements are more effective than other Tea Party organizations at getting out votes for Republican candidates in the 2010 midterms.

For the 112th Congress, Freedom Works selected 60 key votes, 40 in 2011 and 20 in 2012. We are interested in ideal points with respect to the Tea Party movement, i.e., on the anti-pro Tea Party dimension: whether a legislator agrees with Freedom Works on a bill. More specifically, we assign $v_{a,b}$ to be 1 if legislator a agrees with Freedom Works on bill b, and 0 otherwise. In addition to the votes, we obtained the bill text with labels from the Congressional Bills Project[7] and the congressional speeches from GovTrack.[8] In total, we have 240 Republicans, 60 who self-identify with the Tea Party Caucus, and 13,856 votes.

6 Predicting Tea Party Membership

To quantitatively evaluate the effectiveness of HIPTM in capturing "Tea Partiness", we predict Tea Party Caucus membership of legislators given their votes and text. This examines (1) how effective the baseline features extracted from the votes and text are in predicting the Caucus membership, and (2) how much prediction improves using features extracted from HIPTM. For baselines, we consider simple feature sets where each legislator is represented by their speeches as either (1) a TF-IDF vector (Salton, 1968), (2) a normalized TF-IDF vector, or (3) a binary vector containing their votes.

[6]http://congress.freedomworks.org/

[7]http://congressionalbills.org/

[8]https://www.govtrack.us/data/us/112/

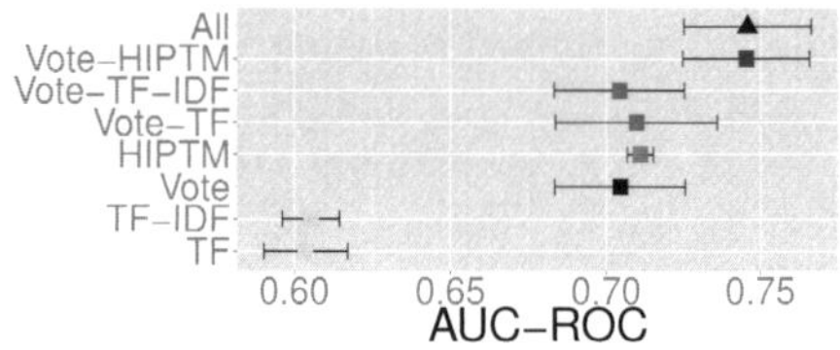

Figure 2: Tea Party Caucus membership prediction results over five folds using AUC-ROC (higher is better, random baseline achieves 0.5). The features extracted from our model are estimated using both the votes and the text.

Our dataset for binary prediction comprises a set of 60 Republican representatives who self-identify as Tea Party Caucus members and 180 who do not. These are divided using 5-fold cross-validation with stratified sampling, which preserves the ratio of the two classes in both the training and test sets. We report performance using AUC-ROC (Lusted, 1971) using SVM^{light} (Joachims, 1999).[9] After preprocessing, our vocabulary contains 5,349 unique word types.

Membership from Votes and Text. First, given the votes and text of all the legislators, we run HIPTM for 1,000 iterations with a burn-in period of 500 iterations. After burning in, we keep the sampled state of the model after every fifty iterations. The feature values are obtained by averaging over the ten stored models as suggested in Nguyen et al. (2014). Each legislator a is represented by a vector concatenating:

- K-dimensional ideal point vector estimated from both votes and text $u_{a,k}$
- K-dimensional vector, estimating the ideal point using only text $\boldsymbol{\eta}_k^T\hat{\boldsymbol{\psi}}_{a,k}$
- B probabilities estimating a's votes on B bills $\Phi(x_b\sum_{k=1}^{K}\hat{\vartheta}_{b,k}u_{a,k}+y_b)$

Figure 2 shows AUC-ROC results for our feature sets. VOTE-based features clearly outperform text-based features like TF and TF-IDF. Combining VOTE with either TF or TF-IDF does not improve the prediction performance much (i.e., VOTE-TF and VOTE-TF-IDF). Features extracted from our

[9]We use the default settings of SVM^{light}, except that we set the cost-factor equal to the ratio between the number of negative examples (i.e., number of non-Tea Party Caucus members) and the number of positive examples (i.e., number of Tea Party Caucus members).

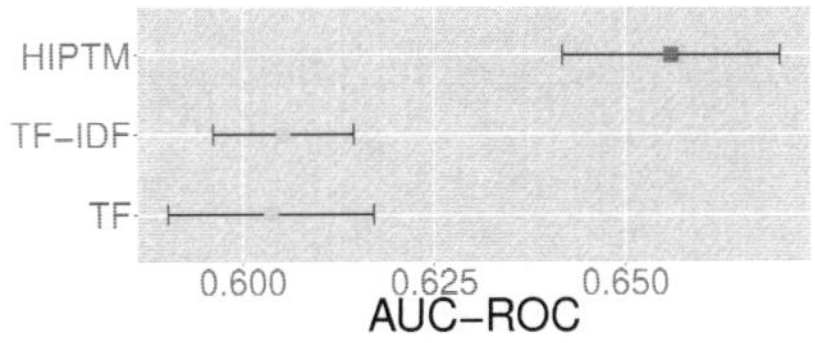

Figure 3: Tea Party Caucus membership prediction results over five folds using AUC-ROC (higher is better, random baseline achieves 0.5). The features extracted from our model for unseen legislators are estimated using their text only.

Figure 4: Box plots of the one-dimensional Tea Party ideal points, estimated as a baseline in Section 7.1, for members and non-members of the Tea Party Caucus among Republican Representatives in the 112th U.S. House. The median of members' ideal points is significantly higher than that of non-members'.

model, HIPTM, also outperform TF and TF-IDF significantly, but only slightly better than VOTE. However, HIPTM and VOTE together significantly outperform VOTE alone.

Membership Prediction from Text Only. The results in Figure 2 require both votes and legislators' language. This is limiting, since it permits predictions of "Tea Partiness" only for people with an established congressional voting record. A potentially more interesting and practical task is prediction based on language alone.

Thus, we first run our inference algorithm on the training data, which includes both votes and text. After training, using multiple models, we sample the issue and frame assignments for each token of the text authored by test lawmakers. Since the votes are not available, HIPTM's extracted features here only consist of (1) the K-dimensional vector $\boldsymbol{\eta}_k^T \hat{\psi}_{a,k}$ estimating legislators' ideal point using text alone, and (2) the B probabilities $\Phi(x_b \sum_{k=1}^{K} \hat{\vartheta}_{b,k} u_{a,k} + y_b)$ estimating the votes.

Figure 3 compares this approach with the two baselines capable of using text alone, TF and TF-IDF. Since HIPTM can no longer access the votes in the test data, its performance drops significantly compared with VOTE. However, it still quite strongly outperforms the two text-based baselines, showing that jointly modeling the voting behavior improves the text-based elements of the model.

7 How the Tea Party Votes

In this section, we examine legislators' ideal points. We first expose Tea Party-specific ideal points by examining one-dimensional ideal points and then move on to the issue-specific ideal points that HIPTM enables.

7.1 One-dimensional Ideal Points

First, as a baseline, we estimate the one-dimensional ideal points of the legislators in our dataset.[10] Figure 4 shows the box plots of estimated Tea Party ideal points for both members and non-members.[11] The Tea Party ideal points correlate with DW-NOMINATE ($\rho = 0.91$), and the median ideal point of Tea Party Caucus members is higher than non-members. This confirms that Tea Partiers are more conservative than other Republicans (Williamson et al., 2011; Karpowitz et al., 2011; Gervais and Morris, 2012; Gervais and Morris, 2014).

Divergences involving these ideal points help demonstrate the face validity of our approach. For example, the model gives Jeff Flake (R-AZ) the second highest ideal point; he only disagrees with Freedom Works position on one of 60 Freedom Works key votes, but he is not a member of the Tea Party Caucus. Another example is Justin Amash (R-MI), who founded and is the Chairman of the Liberty Caucus. Its members are conservative and libertarian Republicans, and Amash has agreed with Freedom Works on every single key vote selected by Freedom Works since 2011.

Conversely, some self-identified Tea Partiers often disagree with Freedom Works and thus have relatively low ideal points. For example, Rodney Alexander (R-LA) only agrees with Freedom Works 48% of the time, and was a Democrat before 2004. Alexander and Ander Crenshaw (R-FL, 50% agreement) are categorized as "Green Tea" by Gervais and Morris (2014), i.e. Republican legislators who are "associated with the Tea Party on their own initiative" but lack support from Tea Party organizations.

[10] We use gradient ascent to optimize the likelihood of votes whose probabilities are defined in Equation 1. We also put a Gaussian prior $\mathcal{N}(0, \sigma)$ on u_a, x_b, and y_b.

[11] Estimated ideal point signs might be flipped, as $u_a x_b = (-u_a)(-x_b)$, which makes no difference in Equation 1. To ensure that higher ideal points are "pro-Tea Party", we first sort the legislators according to the fraction of votes for which they agree with Freedom Works and initialize the ideal points of the top and bottom five legislators with $+3\sigma$ and -3σ, where σ is the variance of u_a's Gaussian prior.

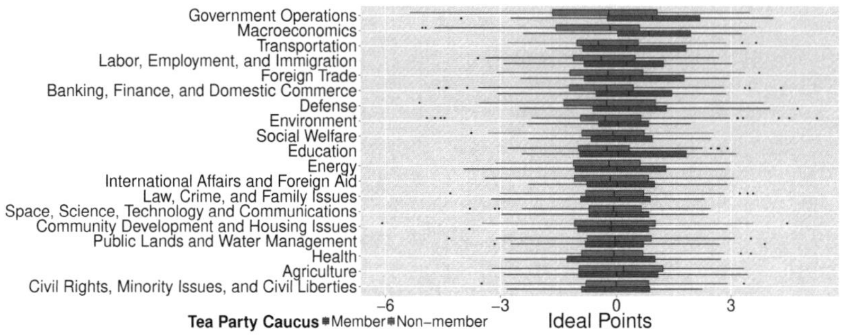

Figure 5: Box plots of ideal points dimensions, each corresponding to a major topic in the Policy Agendas Topics Codebook estimated by our model. On most issues the ideal point distributions over the two Republican groups (member vs. non-member of the Tea Party Caucus) overlap. The most polarized issues are Government Operations and Macroeconomics, which align well with the agenda of the Tea Party movement supporting small government and lower taxes.

7.2 Multi-dimensional Ideal Points

While it is interesting to compare holistic measures of Tea Partiness, it doesn't reveal *how* legislators conform or deviate from what defines a mainstream Tea Partier. In this section, HIPTM reveals how *issue-specific* ideal points of the two groups of Republican representatives differ.

Figure 5 shows estimated ideal points for each policy agenda issue, sorted by the difference between the median of the two groups' ideal points. On most issues, the ideal point distributions of the two Republican groups are nigh identical.

On several issues, though, the ideal point distributions of the two groups of legislators diverge. In the remainder of this section, we consider the Government Operation, Macroeconomics, and Transportation topics, and look at why HIPTM estimates these issues as the most polarized.

Government operations Tea Partiers differ from their Republican colleagues on reducing government spending on the Economic Development Administration, the Energy Efficiency and Renewable Energy Program and Fossil Fuel Research and Development. More specifically, for example, on the key vote *to eliminate the Energy Efficiency and Renewable Energy Program*, nearly 80% (41 out of 53) of Tea Partiers vote "Yea" (with Freedom Works) but only 43% of non-Tea Partiers agree.

Macroeconomics Our model estimates Macroeconomics policies as being the second most polarizing topic for House Republicans, which is consistent with the emphasis that the Tea Party places on issues like a balanced budget and reduced federal spending. Indeed, we see that Tea Party Republicans have distinct preferences on these types of issues as compared to more mainstream Republican legislators. An illustration of this polarization can be seen in the intra-party fight over the budget. Roll call vote 275 in 2011 and roll call vote 149 in 2012 both would have replaced Paul Ryan's budget (the "establishment" Republican budget) with the Republican Study Committee's (RSC) "Back to Basics" budget that would cut spending more aggressively and balance the budget in a decade. In 2011, non-Tea Party Republicans were evenly split in their budget preferences, but three quarters of the Tea Party Caucus supported it, which illustrates the difference between the two factions of the Republican party. Similarly, in 2012, more than 80% of Tea Partiers voted for the the RSC budget, but fewer than half of non-Tea Party Republicans did. Other polarizing votes in the Macroeconomics topic include votes to raise the debt ceiling and to avert the "fiscal cliff". In these cases, support for these votes was 25 percentage points higher among Tea Partiers than non-Tea Party Republicans, which again illustrates their distinct policy preferences.

Transportation Transportation is the third most polarized issue estimated by our model, with two key votes focusing on federal spending on transportation that illustrate some polarization, but also some shared preferences among Republicans. Consistent with the Tea Party's emphasis on reducing government spending, Tea Party Republicans voted differently from their non-Tea Party colleagues on these issues. The first key vote, roll call vote 378 in 2012, caps highway spending at the amount taken in by the gas tax. More than half of Tea Party Caucus members (32 out of 55) voted in favor, while non-members voted against it by a greater than 2:1 margin (122 of 172). Conversely, the second key vote (roll call vote 451 in 2012) authorizes fed-

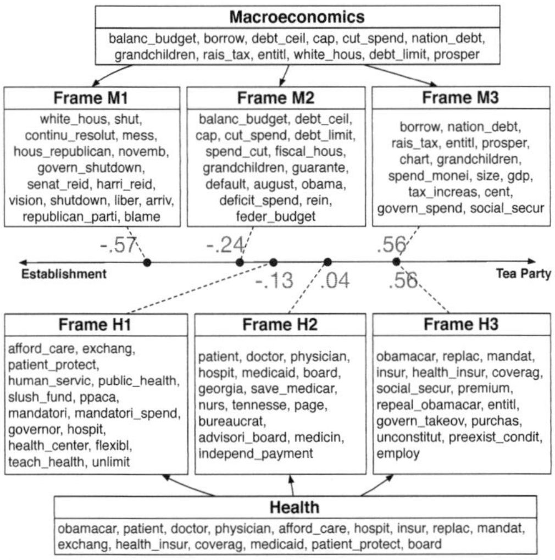

Figure 6: Framing of Macroeconomics (top) and Health (bottom) among House Republicans, 2011-2012. Higher ideal point values are associated with the Tea Party.

eral highway spending at a level that far exceeds its revenue from the gas tax, which was opposed by Freedom Works. This measure was broadly popular with Republicans regardless of Tea Party affiliation and a majority of both Tea Partiers and non-Tea Partiers opposed it.

8 How the Tea Party Talks

Looking at HIPTM's induced topic hierarchy, using labeled data to create informative priors produces highly interpretable topics at the agenda-issue level; e.g., see the first-level nodes in Figure 6, which capture key issue-level debates. For example, one major event during the 112th Congress was the 2011 debt-ceiling crisis, which dominates discussions in Macroeconomics. Similarly, Defense is dominated by withdrawing U.S. troops from Iraq.

Turning to framing, recall that second-level nodes of the hierarchy capture issue-specific frames of parent issues, each one associated with a frame-specific ideal point. To analyze intra-Republican polarization, we first compute, for each issue k, the *span* of ideal points the frames associated with k, i.e., the difference between the maximum and the minimum ideal points for frames under that issue.[12] We then consider several issues with a large span, i.e. whose frames are highly polarized.

Macroeconomics. The HIPTM subtree for Macroeconomics, in Figure 6 (top), foregrounds Republican polarization related to budget issues. The most Tea Party oriented frame node, M3, focuses on criticizing government overspending, a recurring Tea Party theme.[13] In contrast, Frame M1, least oriented toward the Tea Party, focuses on the downsides of a government shutdown, highlighting establishment Republican concerns about being held responsible for the political and economic consequences.

Health. Healthcare was a central issue during the 112th Congress, particularly the Affordable Care Act (Obamacare). Although all Republicans voted to repeal Obamacare, Figure 6 (bottom) highlights intra-party differences in framing the issue. Frame H1 leans strongest toward the establishment Republican end of the spectrum, and frames opposition in terms of the implementation of health care exchanges and the mandatory costs of the program. In contrast, H3 captures the more strident Tea Party framing of Obamacare as an unconstitutional government takeover. More neutral from an intra-party perspective, Frame H2 emphasizes Medicare, Medicaid, and the role of health care professionals within these systems.[14]

Labor, Employment and Immigration. The discussion of this issue illustrates how HIPTM sometimes captures frames that are distinct from Tea Partiness, *per se*. For example, it discovered a strongly Tea Party oriented frame that focused on "union, south carolina, nlrb, boeing". On inspection, this frame reflects a controversy in which the National Labor Relations Board accused airline manufacturer Boeing of violating Federal labor law by transferring production to a non-union facility in South Carolina "for discriminatory reasons",[15] and surfaces mainly in speeches by four legislators from South Carolina, three of whom are from the Tea Party Caucus. This second-level topic illustrates a limitation of HIPTM; it does not formally distinguish frames from other kinds of subtopics. We observe that modeling polarization on other kinds of sub-issues is nonetheless valuable: here it highlights a geographic locus of conflict involv-

[12] The frame proportions Dirichlet process ψ_k creates many frames with one or two observations (Miller and Harrison, 2013). We ignore those with posterior probability $\psi_{k,j} < 0.1$.

[13] E.g., Scott Garrett (R-NJ): "We will not compromise on our principles; our principles of defending the Constitution and defending Americans and making sure that our posterity does not have this excessive debt on it."

[14] This does not mean that discussions using this frame lacked combative or partisan elements. For example, Glenn Thompson (R-PA) argues that "on the Democratic side, they're just willing to pull the plug and let [Medicare] die".

[15] http://www.nlrb.gov/news-outreach/fact-sheets/fact-sheet-archives/boeing-complaint-fact-sheet

Ideal Point Distributions		Not	Polarized
Distribution of Issue Frames	Not	Civil Rights, Minority Issues, Civil Liberties	Banking and Finance; Transportation
	Polarized	Health; Public Lands and Water Management	Macroeconomics; Government Operations

Table 2: Examples of agenda issues classified by polarization of ideal points and issue frames within the Republican party.

ing South Carolina, where many representatives are Tea Party Caucus members. This may provide insight into how geography shapes Tea Party membership (Gervais and Morris, 2012).

9 Latent and Visible Disagreement

Our analyses suggest a novel framework for understanding the political and policymaking implications of the Tea Party in the 112th Congress, illustrated in Table 2. Each issue can be characterized by two features: (1) the degree to which ideal points among Republican legislators are polarized, and (2) the degree to which the frames used are polarized. From these two assessments, we can organize all policy issues into four categories that have meaningful implications for congressional politics and policy outcomes. At upper left we will find issues where HIPTM indicates low intra-party polarization between Tea Party and non-Tea Party, and all Republicans tend to frame the issue in similar ways; e.g., Civil Rights, Minority Issues, and Civil Liberties. In such cases, we expect cooperation among Republicans regardless of Tea Party status, therefore a greater likelihood of bill passage in a majority-Republican House. In stark contrast, issues at lower right involve polarized ideal points and polarized framing, e.g., the budget crisis, where many establishment Republicans balked at a government shutdown but hard-line Tea Party legislators did not. These issues pose the greatest challenge to Republican party leaders.

Between these extremes are the issues in which *either* Republicans' ideal points *or* their policy frames are polarized. Our model suggests that on issues at upper right, with similar framing, the Tea Party and establishment Republicans will *appear* to be in sync, and therefore it may seem to voters that legislative progress is likely, but the underlying issue polarization will make it hard to find policy common ground, potentially increasing public frustration. Last, at lower left are issues where Republicans generally share similar ideal points and vote similarly, but frame the issue in distinct ways, e.g., Obamacare. Here legislative success may come despite the appearance that Republican factions are talking past each other, because the distribution of their ideal points on the policy is actually quite similar. Put differently, Republicans share policy goals on issues in this quadrant even if they frame those preferences differently, and this underlying agreement on the ideal point may allow Republicans to reach consensus even when the political rhetoric suggests otherwise.

10 Conclusion

We introduce HIPTM, which integrates hierarchical topic modeling with multi-dimensional ideal points to jointly model voting behavior, the text content of bills, and the language used by legislators. HIPTM is more effective than previous methods on the task of predicting membership in the Tea Party Caucus. This improvement is especially consequential as the formal organization of the Tea Party Caucus is now defunct in the House, yet Tea Party legislators remain both numerous and influential in Congress. In addition, unlike previous ideal-point methods, HIPTM makes it possible to make predictions for members of Congress who have not yet established a voting record. More intriguingly, this also suggests the possibility of assessing the "Tea Partiness" of candidates (or, anyone else, e.g., media outlets) based on language.

It is political conventional wisdom that the influx of Tea Party legislators in the 112th Congress complicated the task of governance and policymaking for Republican leaders. By looking at issue-level ideal points and issue-specific framing using our model, we begin to address the complexity of this relationship, finding the model successful both in establishing face validity and in suggesting novel insights into the dynamics of a Republican Congress. In future work, we plan to pursue the new framework suggested by our analyses, investigating the interaction of issue polarization and framing-based polarization. With the help of these new tools, we aim to both understand and predict substantive policy areas in which the Tea Party is likely to be most successful working with the Republican party, and, conversely, to flag ahead of time policy areas in which we can expect to see legislative gridlock and grandstanding.

Acknowledgements

This work was supported by the NSF Grant IIS-1211153 and IIS-1409287. Boyd-Graber is also supported by NSF grants IIS-1320538 and NCSE-1422492. Any opinions, findings, conclusions, or recommendations expressed here are those of the authors and do not necessarily reflect the view of the sponsor.

References

E. Scott Adler and John Wilkerson. 2015. Congressional bills project. NSF 00880066 and 00880061.

Amr Ahmed, Liangjie Hong, and Alexander Smola. 2013. Nested Chinese restaurant franchise process: Applications to user tracking and document modeling. In *Proceedings of the International Conference of Machine Learning*, pages 1426–1434.

Charles E. Antoniak. 1974. Mixtures of Dirichlet processes with applications to Bayesian nonparametric problems. *The Annals of Statistics*, 2(6):1152–1174.

Joseph Bafumi, Andrew Gelman, David K Park, and Noah Kaplan. 2005. Practical issues in implementing and understanding Bayesian ideal point estimation. *Political Analysis*, 13(2):171–187.

David M. Blei and John Lafferty, 2009. *Text Mining: Theory and Applications*, chapter Topic Models. Taylor and Francis, London.

David M Blei and Jon D McAuliffe. 2007. Supervised topic models. In *Proceedings of Advances in Neural Information Processing Systems*, pages 121–128.

Edward G Carmines and Nicholas J D'Amico. 2015. The new look in political ideology research. *Annual Review of Political Science*, 18(4).

Joshua Clinton, Simon Jackman, and Douglas Rivers. 2004. The statistical analysis of roll call data. *American Political Science Review*, 98(02):355–370.

Philip J Cowans. 2006. *Probabilistic Document Modelling*. Ph.D. thesis, University of Cambridge.

Robert M Entman. 1993. Framing: Toward clarification of a fractured paradigm. *Journal of Communication*, 43(4):51–58.

Jean-Paul Fox. 2010. *Bayesian item response modeling: Theory and applications*. Springer.

Matt Fuller. 2015. New Tea Party Caucus chairman: DHS fight could break the GOP. *Roll Call*, February. http://blogs.rollcall.com/218/new-tea-party-caucus-chairman-dhs-fight-could-break-the-gop/.

Sean Gerrish and David M. Blei. 2011. Predicting legislative roll calls from text. In *Proceedings of the International Conference of Machine Learning*, pages 489–496.

Sean Gerrish and David M. Blei. 2012. How they vote: Issue-adjusted models of legislative behavior. In *Proceedings of Advances in Neural Information Processing Systems*, pages 2753–2761.

Bryan T Gervais and Irwin L Morris. 2012. Reading the tea leaves: Understanding Tea Party Caucus membership in the US House of Representatives. *PS: Political Science & Politics*, 45(02):245–250.

Bryan T Gervais and Irwin L Morris. 2014. Black Tea, Green Tea, White Tea, and Coffee: Understanding the variation in attachment to the Tea Party among members of Congress. In *Annual Meeting of the American Political Science Association*.

Justin Grimmer. 2010. A Bayesian hierarchical topic model for political texts: Measuring expressed agendas in Senate press releases. *Political Analysis*, 18(1):1–35.

Yupeng Gu, Yizhou Sun, Ning Jiang, Bingyu Wang, and Ting Chen. 2014. Topic-factorized ideal point estimation model for legislative voting network. In *Proceedings of International Conference on Knowledge Discovery and Data Mining*, pages 183–192.

James J. Heckman and James M. Snyder Jr. 1997. Linear probability models of the demand for attributes with an empirical application to estimating the preferences of legislators. *The RAND Journal of Economics*, 28:142–189.

Yuening Hu and Jordan Boyd-Graber. 2012. Efficient tree-based topic modeling. In *Association for Computational Linguistics*.

Simon Jackman. 2001. Multidimensional analysis of roll call data via Bayesian simulation: Identification, estimation, inference, and model checking. *Political Analysis*, 9(3):227–241.

Thorsten Joachims. 1999. Making large-scale SVM learning practical. In *Advances in Kernel Methods - SVM*. Universität Dortmund.

Christopher F Karpowitz, J Quin Monson, Kelly D Patterson, and Jeremy C Pope. 2011. Tea time in America? The impact of the Tea Party movement on the 2010 midterm elections. *PS: Political Science & Politics*, 44(02):303–309.

Benjamin E. Lauderdale and Tom S. Clark. 2014. Scaling politically meaningful dimensions using texts and votes. *American Journal of Political Science*, 58(3):754–771.

Dong C Liu and Jorge Nocedal. 1989. On the limited memory BFGS method for large scale optimization. *Mathematical programming*, 45(1-3):503–528.

Lee B. Lusted. 1971. Signal Detectability and Medical Decision-Making. *Science*, 171:1217–1219, March.

Andrew D Martin and Kevin M Quinn. 2002. Dynamic ideal point estimation via Markov chain Monte Carlo for the US Supreme Court, 1953–1999. *Political Analysis*, 10(2):134–153.

Maxwell McCombs. 2005. A look at agenda-setting: Past, present and future. *Journalism Studies*, 6(4):543–557.

Jeffrey W Miller and Matthew T Harrison. 2013. A simple example of dirichlet process mixture inconsistency for the number of components. In C.J.C. Burges, L. Bottou, M. Welling, Z. Ghahramani, and K.Q. Weinberger, editors, *Advances in Neural Information Processing Systems 26*, pages 199–206. Curran Associates, Inc.

Viet-An Nguyen, Jordan Boyd-Graber, and Philip Resnik. 2013. Lexical and hierarchical topic regression. In *Proceedings of Advances in Neural Information Processing Systems*, pages 1106–1114.

Viet-An Nguyen, Jordan Boyd-Graber, and Philip Resnik. 2014. Sometimes average is best: The importance of averaging for prediction using MCMC inference in topic modeling. In *Proceedings of Emperical Methods in Natural Language Processing*, pages 1752–1757.

Thang Nguyen, Jordan Boyd-Graber, Jeff Lund, Kevin Seppi, and Eric Ringger. 2015. Is your anchor going up or down? Fast and accurate supervised topic models. In *North American Association for Computational Linguistics*.

John Paisley, Chong Wang, David M Blei, and Michael I Jordan. 2014. Nested hierarchical Dirichlet processes. *IEEE Transactions on Pattern Analysis and Machine Intelligence*.

Keith T Poole and Howard Rosenthal. 1985. A spatial model for legislative roll call analysis. *American Journal of Political Science*, pages 357–384.

Keith T Poole and Howard L Rosenthal. 2007. *Ideology and Congress*. New Brunswick, NJ: Transaction Publishers.

Gerard. Salton. 1968. *Automatic Information Organization and Retrieval*. McGraw Hill Text.

Yanchuan Sim, Bryan Routledge, and Noah A Smith. 2015. The utility of text: The case of Amicus briefs and the Supreme Court. In *Association for the Advancement of Artificial Intelligence*.

Yee Whye Teh, Michael I Jordan, Matthew J Beal, and David M Blei. 2006. Hierarchical Dirichlet processes. *Journal of the American Statistical Association*, 101(476).

Hanna M Wallach. 2008. *Structured Topic Models for Language*. Ph.D. thesis, University of Cambridge.

Vanessa Williamson, Theda Skocpol, and John Coggin. 2011. The Tea Party and the remaking of Republican conservatism. *Perspectives on Politics*, 9(01):25–43.

KB-LDA: Jointly Learning a Knowledge Base of Hierarchy, Relations, and Facts

Dana Movshovitz-Attias
Computer Science Department
Carnegie Mellon University
dma@cs.cmu.edu

William W. Cohen
Machine Learning Department
Carnegie Mellon University
wcohen@cs.cmu.edu

Abstract

Many existing knowledge bases (KBs), including Freebase, Yago, and NELL, rely on a fixed ontology, given as an input to the system, which defines the data to be cataloged in the KB, i.e., a hierarchy of categories and relations between them. The system then extracts facts that match the predefined ontology. We propose an unsupervised model that jointly learns a latent ontological structure of an input corpus, and identifies facts from the corpus that match the learned structure. Our approach combines mixed membership stochastic block models and topic models to infer a structure by jointly modeling text, a latent concept hierarchy, and latent semantic relationships among the entities mentioned in the text. As a case study, we apply the model to a corpus of Web documents from the software domain, and evaluate the accuracy of the various components of the learned ontology.

1 Introduction

Knowledge base (KB) construction methods can be broadly categorized along several dimensions. One dimension is ontology-guided construction, where the list of categories and relations that define the schema of the KB are explicit, versus open IE methods, where they are not. Another dimension is the type of relations and types included in the KB: some KBs, like WordNet, are hierarchical, in that they contain mainly concept types, supertypes and instances, while other KBs contain many types of relationships between concepts. Hierarchical knowledge can be learned by methods including distributional clustering (Pereira et al., 1993), as well as Hearst patterns (Hearst, 1992) and similar techniques (Snow et al., 2006). Reverb (Fader et al., 2011) and TextRunner (Yates et al., 2007) are open methods for learning multi-relation KBs. Finally, NELL (Carlson et al., 2010; Mitchell et al., 2015), FreeBase (Google, 2011) and Yago (Suchanek et al., 2007; Hoffart et al., 2013) are ontology-guided methods for extracting KBs containing both hierarchies and relations.

One advantage of ontology-guided methods is that the extracted knowledge is easier to reason with. An advantage of open IE methods is that ontologies may be incomplete, and are expensive to construct for a new domain. Ontology design involves assembling a set of categories, organized in a meaningful hierarchical structure, often providing seeds, i.e., representative examples for each category, and finally, defining inter-category relations. This process is often done manually (Carlson et al., 2010) leading to a rigid set of categories. Redesigning a new ontology for a specialized domain represents an additional challenge as it requires extensive knowledge of the domain.

In this paper, we propose an unsupervised model that learns a latent hierarchical structure of categories from an input corpus, learns latent semantic relations between categories, and also identifies facts from the corpus that match the learned structure. In other words, the model learns both the schema for a KB, and a set of facts that are related to that schema, thus combining the processes of KB population and ontology construction. The intent is to build systems that extract facts which can be interpreted relative to a meaningful ontology without requiring the effort of manual ontology construction.

The input to the learning method is a corpus of documents, plus two sets of resources extracted from the same corpus: a set of hypernym-hyponym pairs (e.g., "animal", "horse") extracted using Hearst patterns, and a set of subject-verb-object triples (e.g., "horse", "eats", "hay") extracted from parsed sentences. These resources are analogous to the output of open IE systems for

Proceedings of the 53rd Annual Meeting of the Association for Computational Linguistics and the 7th International Joint Conference on Natural Language Processing, pages 1449–1459,
Beijing, China, July 26-31, 2015.

hierarchies and relations, and as we demonstrate, our method can be used to highlight domain-specific data from open IE repositories.

Our approach combines mixed membership stochastic block models and topic models to infer a structure by jointly modeling text documents, and links that indicate hierarchy and relation among the entities mentioned in the text. Joint modeling allows information on topics of nouns (referred to as *instances*) and verbs (referred to as *relations*) to be shared between text documents and an ontological structure, resulting in a set of compelling topics. This model offers a complete solution for KB construction based on an input corpus, and we therefore name it *KB-LDA*.

We additionally propose a method for recovering meaningful names for concepts in the learned hierarchy. These are equivalent to category names in other KBs, however, following our method we extract from the data a set of potential alternative concepts describing each category, including probabilities for their strength of association.

To show the effectiveness of our method, we apply the model to a dataset of Web based documents from the software domain, and learn a software KB. This is an example of a specialized domain in which, to our knowledge, no broad-coverage ontology exists. We evaluate the model on the induced categories, relations, and facts, and we compare the proposed categories with an independent set of human-provided labels for documents. Finally, we use KB-LDA to retrieve domain-specific relations from an open IE resource. We provide the learned software KB as supplemental material.

$\boldsymbol{\pi_O}$ – multinomial over ontology topic pairs, with Dirichlet prior α_O
$\boldsymbol{\pi_R}$ – multinomial over relation topic tuples, with Dirichlet prior α_R
$\boldsymbol{\theta_d}$ – topic multinomial for document d, with Dirichlet prior α_D
$\boldsymbol{\sigma_k}$ – multinomial over instances for topic k, with Dirichlet prior γ_I
$\boldsymbol{\delta_{k'}}$ – multinomial over relations for topic k', with Dirichlet prior γ_R
$\text{CI}_i = \langle C_i, I_i \rangle$ – i-th ontological assignment pair
$\text{SVO}_j = \langle S_j, O_j, V_j \rangle$ – j-th relation assignment tuple
$\boldsymbol{z_i^{CI}} = \langle z_{C_i}, z_{I_i} \rangle$ – topic pair chosen for example $\langle C_i, I_i \rangle$
$\boldsymbol{z_j^{SVO}} = \langle z_{S_j}, z_{O_j}, z_{V_j} \rangle$ – topic tuple chosen for example $\langle S_j, O_j, V_j \rangle$
$\boldsymbol{z_{E_1}^D}, \boldsymbol{z_{E_2}^D}$ – topic chosen for instance entity E_1, or relation entity E_2, respectively, in a document
$\boldsymbol{n_{z,i}^I}$ – number of times instance i is observed under topic z (in either z^D, z^{CI} or z^{SVO})
$\boldsymbol{n_{z,r}^R}$ – number of times relation r is observed under topic z (in either z^D or z^{SVO})
$\boldsymbol{n_{\langle z_c, z_i \rangle}^O}$ – count of ontological pairs assigned the topic pair $\langle z_c, z_i \rangle$ (in z^{CI})
$\boldsymbol{n_{\langle z_s, z_o, z_v \rangle}^R}$ – count of relation tuples assigned the topic tuple $\langle z_s, z_o, z_v \rangle$ (in z^{SVO})

Table 1: KB-LDA notation.

2 KB-LDA

Modeling latent sets of entities from observed interactions among them is a well researched task, often encountered in social network analysis for the purpose of identifying specialized communities in the network. Mixed Membership Stochastic Blockmodels (Airoldi et al., 2009; Parkkinen et al., 2009) model entities as graph nodes with pairwise relations drawn from latent blocks with mixed membership. A related approach is taken by topic models such as LDA (Latent Dirichlet Allocation; (Blei et al., 2003)), which model documents as generated by a mixture of latent topics, and words in the documents as generated by topic-specific word distributions. The KB-LDA model combines the two approaches. It models links between tuples of two or three entities using stochastic block models, and these are additionally influenced by latent topic assignments of the entities in a document corpus.

In the KB-LDA model, shown as a plate diagram in Figure 1 with notation in Table 1, information is shared between three components, through common latent topics over noun and verb entities. The *Ontology* component (upper right) models hierarchical links between Concept-Instance (CI) entity pairs. The *Relations* component (left) models links between Subject-Verb-Object (SVO) entity triples, where the subject and object are nouns and the verb represents a relation between them. Finally, the *Documents* component (lower left) is a link-LDA model (Erosheva et al., 2004) of text documents containing a combination of noun and verb entity types. In this formulation, distributions over noun and verb entities that are related according to hierarchical or relational constraints, are linked with a text model via shared parameters.

In more detail, the *Documents* component provides the context in which noun and verb entities are being used in text. It is modeled as an extension of LDA, viewing documents as sets of "bags of words", where in this case, each bag contains either noun or verb entities. Each entity type has a topic-wise multinomial distribution over the set of entities in the vocabulary of that type.

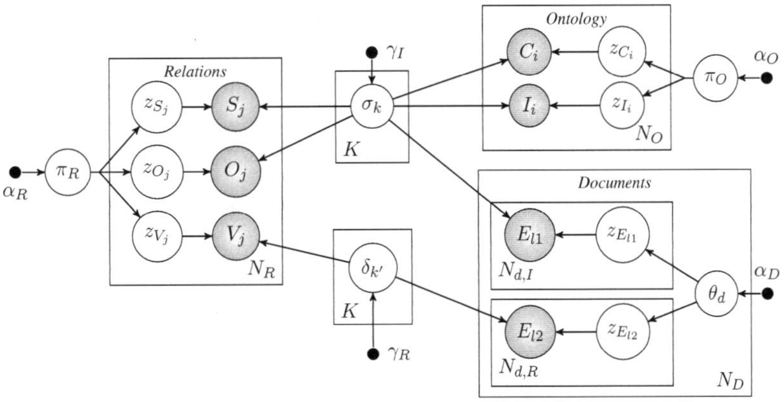

Figure 1: Plate Diagram of KB-LDA.

The *Ontology* component is a generative model representing hierarchal links between pairs of nouns. The examples for this component are extracted using a small collection of Hearst patterns indicating concept-instance or concept-concept links, including, 'X such as Y', and 'X including Y'. For example, the sentence "websites such as StackOverflow" indicates that Stackoverflow is a type of website, leading to the extracted noun pair $\langle$websites, StackOverflow$\rangle$. We refer to the examples extracted using these hierarchical patterns as *concept-instance pairs*, and to the individual entities as *instances*.

The pairs have an underlying block structure derived from a sparse block model (Parkkinen et al., 2009). They are generated by topic specific instance distributions conditioned on topic pair edges, which are defined by the multinomial π_O over the Cartesian product of the noun topic set with itself. The individual instances, therefore, have a mixed membership in topics. Note that we allow for a concept and instance to be drawn from different noun topics, defined by σ. For example, we may learn a topic highlighting concept tokens like 'websites', 'platforms', 'applications'. Another topic can highlight instances shared by these concepts, such as, 'stackoverflow', 'google', and 'facebook'. Finally, the observation that the former topic frequently contains concepts of instances from the latter topic, is encoded in the multinomial distribution π_O. From this we infer that the former topic should be placed higher in the induced hierarchy.

Similarly, the *Relations* component represents relational links between a noun subject, a verb and a noun object. The examples for this component

---

Let K be the number of target latent topics.

1. **Generate topics:** For topic $k \in 1, \ldots, K$, sample:
   - $\sigma_k \sim \text{Dirichlet}(\gamma_I)$, the per-topic instance distribution
   - $\delta_k \sim \text{Dirichlet}(\gamma_R)$, the per-topic relation distribution
2. **Generate ontology:** Sample $\pi_O \sim \text{Dirichlet}(\alpha_O)$, the instance topic pair distribution.
   - For each concept-instance pair CI_i, $i \in 1, \ldots, N_O$:
     - Sample topic pair $z_i^{CI} \sim \text{Multinomial}(\pi_O)$
     - Sample instances $C_i \sim \text{Multinomial}(\sigma_{z_{C_i}})$, $I_i \sim \text{Multinomial}(\sigma_{z_{I_i}})$, then $\text{CI}_i = \langle C_i, I_i \rangle$
3. **Generate relations:** Sample $\pi_R \sim \text{Dirichlet}(\alpha_R)$, the relation topic tuple distribution.
   - For each tuple SVO_j, $j \in 1, \ldots, N_R$:
     - Sample topic tuple $z_j^{SVO} \sim \text{Multinomial}(\pi_R)$
     - Sample instances, $S_j \sim \text{Multinomial}(\sigma_{z_{S_j}})$, $O_j \sim \text{Multinomial}(\sigma_{z_{O_j}})$, and sample a relation $V_j \sim \text{Multinomial}(\delta_{z_{V_j}})$
4. **Generate documents:** For document $d \in 1, \ldots, D$:
   - Sample $\theta_d \sim \text{Dirichlet}(\alpha_D)$, the topic mixing distribution for document d.
   - For every noun entity (E_{l1}) and verb entity (E_{l2}), $l1 \in 1, \ldots, N_{d,I}$, $l2 \in 1, \ldots, N_{d,R}$:
     - Sample topics $z_{E_{l1}}, z_{E_{l2}} \sim \text{Multinomial}(\theta_d)$
     - Sample entities $E_{l1} \sim \text{Multinomial}(\sigma_{z_{E_{l1}}})$ and $E_{l2} \sim \text{Multinomial}(\delta_{z_{E_{l2}}})$

Table 2: KB-LDA generative process.

are extracted from SVO patterns found in the document corpus, following Talukdar et al. (2012). An extracted example looks like: $\langle$websites, execute, javascript$\rangle$. Subject and object topics are drawn from the noun topics (σ), while the verb topics is drawn from the verb topics, defined by δ. The multinomial π_R encodes the interaction of noun and verb topics based on the extracted relational links, and it is defined over the Cartesian product of the noun topic set with itself and with the verb topic set.

The generative process of KB-LDA is described in Table 2. Given the hyperparameters $(\alpha_O, \alpha_R, \alpha_D, \gamma_I, \gamma_R)$, the joint distribution over CI pairs, SVO tuples, documents, topics and topic assignments is given by

$$p(\pi_O, \pi_R, \sigma, \delta, \mathbf{CI}, \boldsymbol{z^{CI}}, \mathbf{SVO}, \boldsymbol{z^{SVO}}, \boldsymbol{\theta}, \mathbf{E}, \boldsymbol{z^D} | \alpha_O, \alpha_R, \alpha_D, \gamma_I, \gamma_R) =$$
$$\prod_{k=1}^{K} \mathrm{Dir}(\sigma_k|\gamma_I) \times \prod_{k'=1}^{K} \mathrm{Dir}(\delta_{k'}|\gamma_R) \times \quad (1)$$
$$\mathrm{Dir}(\pi_O|\alpha_O) \prod_{i=1}^{N_O} \pi_O^{\langle z_{C_i}, z_{I_i} \rangle} \sigma_{z_{C_i}}^{C_i} \sigma_{z_{I_i}}^{I_i} \times$$
$$\mathrm{Dir}(\pi_R|\alpha_R) \prod_{j=1}^{N_R} \pi_R^{\langle z_{S_j}, z_{O_j}, z_{V_j} \rangle} \sigma_{z_{S_j}}^{S_j} \sigma_{z_{O_j}}^{O_j} \delta_{z_{V_j}}^{V_j} \times$$
$$\prod_{d=1}^{N_D} \mathrm{Dir}(\theta_d|\alpha_D) \prod_{l1=1}^{N_{d,I}} \theta_d^{z_{E_{l1}}^D} \sigma_{z_{E_{l1}}^D}^{E_{l1}} \prod_{l2=1}^{N_{d,R}} \theta_d^{z_{E_{l2}}^D} \delta_{z_{E_{l2}}^D}^{E_{l2}}$$

2.1 Inference in KB-LDA

Exact inference is intractable in the KB-LDA model. We use a collapsed Gibbs sampler (Griffiths and Steyvers, 2004) to perform approximate inference in order to query the topic distributions and assignments. It samples a latent topic pair for a CI pair in the corpus conditioned on the assignments to all other CI pairs, SVO tuples, and document entities, using the following expression, after collapsing π_O:

$$\hat{p}(z_i^{CI}|\mathrm{CI}_i, z_{\neg i}^{CI}, z^{SVO}, z^D, \mathrm{CI}_{\neg i}, \alpha_O, \gamma_I) \quad (2)$$
$$\propto \left(n_{z_i^{CI}}^{O \neg i} + \alpha_O \right) \times$$
$$\frac{(n_{z_{C_i}, C_i}^{I \neg i} + \gamma_I)(n_{z_{I_i}, I_i}^{I \neg i} + \gamma_I)}{(\sum_C n_{z_{C_i}, C}^{I \neg i} + T_I \gamma_I)(\sum_I n_{z_{I_i}, I}^{I \neg i} + T_I \gamma_I)}$$

where counts of observations from the training set are noted by n (see Table 1), and T_I is the number of instance entities (size of noun vocabulary).

We similarly sample topics for each SVO tuple conditioned on the assignments to all other tuples, CI pairs and document entities, using the following expression, after collapsing π_R:

$$\hat{p}(z_j^{SVO}|\mathrm{SVO}_j, z_{\neg j}^{SVO}, z^{CI}, z^D, \mathrm{SVO}_{\neg j}, \alpha_R, \gamma_I, \gamma_R) \quad (3)$$
$$\propto \left(n_{z_j^{SVO}}^{R \neg j} + \alpha_R \right) \times$$
$$\frac{(n_{z_{S_j}, S_j}^{I \neg j} + \gamma_I)(n_{z_{O_j}, O_j}^{I \neg j} + \gamma_I)(n_{z_{V_j}, V_j}^{R \neg j} + \gamma_R)}{(\sum_I n_{z_{S_i}, I}^{I \neg j} + T_I \gamma_I)(\sum_I n_{z_{O_i}, I}^{I \neg j} + T_I \gamma_I)(\sum_V n_{z_{V_j}, V}^{R \neg j} + T_R \gamma_R)}$$

We sample a latent topic for an entity mention in a document from the text corpus conditioned on the assignments to all other entity mentions after collapsing θ_d. The following expression shows topic sampling for a noun entity in a document:

$$\hat{p}(z_{E_{l1}}|E, \mathrm{CI}, \mathrm{SVO}, z^D, z^{CI}, z^{SVO}, \alpha_D, \gamma_I) \quad (4)$$
$$\propto (n_{d,z}^{\neg l1} + \alpha_D) \frac{n_{z_{E_{l1}}, E_{l1}}^{I \neg l1} + \gamma_I}{\sum_{E'_{l1}} n_{z_{E_{l1}}, E'_{l1}}^{I \neg l1} + T_I \gamma_I}$$

The per-topic multinomial parameters and topic distributions of CI pairs, SVO tuples and documents can be recovered with MLE estimates using their observation counts:

$$\hat{\sigma}_k^I = \frac{n_{k,I}^I + \gamma_I}{\sum_{I'} n_{k,I'}^I + T_I \gamma_I}, \hat{\delta}_k^R = \frac{n_{k,R}^R + \gamma_R}{\sum_{R'} n_{k,R'}^R + T_R \gamma_R}$$

$$\hat{\theta_d^z} = \frac{n_{z,d} + \alpha_D}{\sum_{z'} n_{z',d} + K \alpha_D}$$

$$\hat{\pi}_O^{\langle z_C, z_I \rangle} = \frac{n_{\langle z_C, z_I \rangle}^O + \alpha_O}{\sum_{z'_C, z'_I} n_{\langle z'_C, z'_I \rangle}^O + K^2 \cdot \alpha_O}$$

$$\hat{\pi}_R^{\langle z_S, z_O, z_V \rangle} = \frac{n_{\langle z_S, z_O, z_V \rangle}^R + \alpha_R}{\sum_{z'_S, z'_O, z'_V} n_{\langle z'_S, z'_O, z'_V \rangle}^R + K^3 \cdot \alpha_R}$$

Using the KB-LDA model we can describe the latent topic hierarchy underlying the input corpus. We consider the multinomial of the *Ontology* component, π_O, as an adjacency matrix describing a network where the nodes are instance topics and edges indicate a hypernym-to-hyponym relation. By extracting the maximum spanning tree over this adjacency matrix, we recover a hierarchy over the input data. We recover relations among instance topics by extracting from the Relations multinomial, π_R, the set of most probable tuples of a ⟨subject topic, verb topic, object topic⟩.

Our model is implemented using a fast, parallel approximation of collapsed Gibbs sampling, following Newman et al. (2009). In each sampling iteration, topics are sampled locally on a subset of the training examples. At the end of each iteration, data from worker threads is joined and model parameters are updated with complete information. In the next iteration, thread-local sampling starts with complete topic assignment information from the previous iteration. In each thread, the process can be viewed as a reordering of the input examples, where the examples sampled in that thread are viewed first. It has been shown that parallel approaches considerably speed up iterative inference methods such as collapsed Gibbs sampling, resulting in test data log probabilities indistinguishable from those obtained using serial methods (Porteous et al., 2008; Newman et al., 2009). A parallel approach is especially important when training the KB-LDA model due to the large dimensions of the multinomials of the *Ontology* and *Relations* components (K^2 and K^3, respectively for a model with K topics). We train KB-LDA over 2000 iterations, more than what has traditionally been used for collapsed Gibbs samplers.

2.2 Data-driven discovery of topic concepts

The KB-LDA model described above clusters noun entities into sets of instance topics, and recovers a latent hierarchical structure among these topics. Each instance topic can be described by a multinomial distribution of the underlying nouns. It is often more intuitive, however, to refer to a topic containing a set of high probability nouns by a name, or category, just as traditional ontologies describe hierarchies over categories.

Our model is trained over nouns that originate from concept-instance example pairs (used to train the *Ontology* component). We describe a method for selecting a category name for a topic, based on concepts that best represent high probability nouns of the topic in the concept-instance examples.

We calculate the probability that a concept noun c describes the set of instances I that have been assigned the topic z using

$$\begin{aligned} p(c,z|I) &\propto p(I|c,z) * p(c,z) && (5)\\ &= p(I|c,z) * p(z|c) * p(c) \end{aligned}$$

Let $rep(c,z) = \sum_{i:C_i=c} n^I_{z,I_i}$ describe how well concept c represents topic z according to the assignments of instances with concept c to the topic. Then,

$$p(z|c) = \frac{rep(c,z)}{\sum_{z'} rep(c,z')} \quad (6)$$

The concept prior, $p(c)$, is based on the relative weight of instances with concept c in the concept-instance example set, and is an indicator of the generality of a concept:

$$p(c) = \frac{\sum_{i:C_i=c} w_{c,I_i}}{\sum_{c'} \sum_{i:C_i=c'} w_{c',I_i}} \quad (7)$$

where $w_{C,I}$ is the number of occurrences of concept-instance pair $\langle C, I \rangle$ in the corpus.

Finally, $p(I|c,z)$ measures how specific are the topic instances to the concept c,

$$p(I|c,z) = \frac{\sum_{i:I_i \in I, C_i=c} w_{c,I_i}}{\sum_{i:C_i=c} w_{c,I_i}} \Big/ Z \quad (8)$$

where I is the set of training instances assigned with topic z, and Z is a normalizer over all concepts and topics.

Following this method we extract concepts that have a high probability $p(c,z|I)$ with respect to a topic z. These can be thought of as equivalent to the single, fixed, category name provided by traditional KB ontologies; however, here we extract *from the data* a set of potential alternative noun phrases describing each topic, including a probability for the strength of this association.

3 Experimental Evaluation

We evaluate the KB-LDA model on a corpus of 5.5M documents from the software domain; thereby we are using the model to construct a software domain knowledge base. Our evaluation explores the following questions:

- Can KB-LDA learn categories, relations, a hierarchy and topic concepts with high precision?
- How well do KB-LDA topics correspond with human-provided document labels?
- Is KB-LDA useful in extracting facts from existing open IE resources?

3.1 Data

We use data from the Q&A website StackOverflow[1] where users ask and answer technical questions about software development, tools, algorithms, etc'. We extracted 562K concept-instance example pairs from the data, and kept the 17K examples appearing at least twice. Noun phrases in these examples make up our *Instance Dictionary*. Out of 6.8M SVO examples found in the data we keep 37K in which the subject and object are in the Instance Dictionary, and the example appears at least twice in the corpus. The verbs in the SVOs make up our *Relation Dictionary*. Finally, we consider as documents the 5.5M questions from StackOverflow with all their answers.

3.2 Evaluating the learned KB precision

In this section we evaluate the direct output of a model trained with 50 topics: the extracted in-

[1]Data source: https://archive.org/details/stackexchange

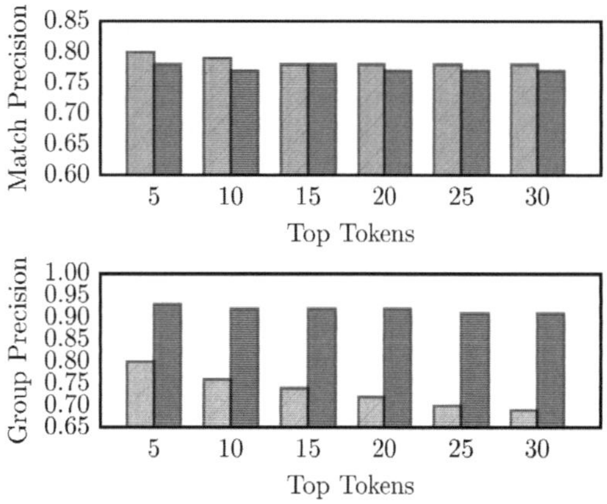

Figure 2: Average *Match* (top) and *Group* (bottom) precision of top tokens of 50 topics learned with KB-LDA, according to expert (dark blue) and non-expert (light blue, stripes) labeling.

stance topics, topic hierarchy, relations among topics and extracted topic concepts. In each of the experiments below, we extract facts based on one of the learned components and evaluate each fact based on annotations from human judges: two experts and three non-expert users, collected using Mechanical Turk, that were pre-tested on a basic familiarity with concepts from the software domain, such as *programming languages, version control systems*, and *databases*.

3.2.1 Precision of Instance Topics

We measure the coherence of instance topics using an approach called *word intrusion* (Chang et al., 2009). We extract the top 30 instance tokens of a topic ranked by the instance topic multinomial σ. We present to workers tokens 1-5,6-10,...,26-30, where each 5 tokens are randomly ordered and augmented with an extra token that is ranked low for the topic, (the intruder). We ask workers to select all tokens that do not belong in the group (and at least one). We define the topic *Match Precision* as the fraction of questions for which the reviewer identified the correct intruder (out of 6 questions per topic), and the topic *Group Precision* as the fraction of correct tokens (those not selected as not belonging in the group). Thus *Match Precision* measures how well labelers understand the topic, and *Group Precision* measures what fraction of words appeared relevant to the topic.

Figure 2 shows the average Match and Group precision over the top tokens of all 50 topics learned with the model, as evaluated by expert and non-expert workers. Both groups find the intruder token in over 75% of questions. In the more subtle task of validating each topic token (Group precision) we see a greater variance among the two labeler groups. This highlights the difficulty of evaluating domain specific facts with non-expert users. Table 3 displays the top 20 instance topics learned with KB-LDA, ranked by expert Group precision.

3.2.2 Precision of Topic Concepts

We assess the precision of the top 5 concept names proposed for instance topics, following the method presented in Section 2.2. Top concepts for a subset of topics are shown in Table 3. For each topic, we present to the user a hypernym-hyponym pattern of the topic based on the top concepts and top instances of the topic. As an example, if the top 5 instances of a topic are *ie, firefox, chrome, buttons, safari* and the top 5 concepts for this topic are *web browsers, web browser, browser, ie, chrome*, the pattern presented to workers is

- [ie, firefox, chrome, buttons, safari] **is a** [web browsers, web browser, browser, ie, chrome]

Workers were asked to match at least 3 instances to a proposed concept name. In addition, the same assessment was applied for each topic using randomly sampled concepts. We present in Table 4 the number and precision of patterns based on extracted concepts (Concepts) and random concepts (Random), that were labeled by 1, 2 or 3 workers, as well as the average results among experts. We achieve nearly 90% precision according to expert labeling, however we do not observe large agreement among non-expert labelers.

3.2.3 Precision of Relations

To assess the precision of the relations learned in the KB-LDA model, we extract the top 100 relations learned according to their probability in the relation multinomial π_R. Relation patterns were presented to workers as sets of the top subject-verb-object tokens of the respective topics in the relation. An example relation is

- Subject words: [user, users, people, customer, client]
- Verb words: [clicks, selects, submits, click, hits]
- Object words: [function, method, class, object, query]

and workers are asked to state whether the pattern indicates a valid relation or not, by checking whether a reasonable number of combinations of subject-verb-object triples extracted from each of the relation groups can produce valid relations.

Top 2 Topic Concepts	Top 10 Topic Tokens
table, key	table, query, database, sql, column, data, tables, mysql, index, columns
properties, css	image, code, images, problem, point, color, data, size, screen, points
credentials, user information	name, images, id, number, text, password, address, strings, files, string
page, content	page, html, code, file, image, javascript, browser, http, jquery, js
orm tools, orm tool	tomcat, hibernate, server, boost, apache, spring, mongodb, framework, nhibernate, png
clients, apps	app, application, http, android, device, phone, code, api, iphone, google
applications, systems	devices, systems, applications, services, platforms, tools, sites, apps, system, service
systems, platforms	google, windows, linux, facebook, git, ant, database, gmail, android, so
limits, limit	memory, time, thread, code, threads, process, file, program, data, object
data, table	query, table, data, list, example, number, results, search, database, rows
type, value	code, function, value, type, pointer, array, memory, compiler, example, string
table, request	data, information, types, properties, details, fields, values, content, resources, attributes
dependencies, jar file	libraries, library, framework, frameworks, formats, format, database, databases, tools, server
type, object	value, focus, place, property, method, reference, interface, effect, pointer, data
kinds, code	languages, language, features, objects, functions, methods, code, operations, structures, types
element, elements	button, form, link, item, *file*, mouse, image, value, option, row
javascript libraries, javascript framework	jquery, mysql, http, json, xml, library, html, sqlite, *asp*, php
process, operating system	server, client, connection, *data*, http, socket, message, request, port, service
folder, files	file, files, directory, folder, path, *code*, name, resources, project, folders
value, array	array, list, value, values, number, string, code, elements, *loop*, object

Table 3: Top 20 instance topics learned with KB-LDA. For each topic we show the top 2 concepts recovered for the topic, and top 10 tokens. In *italics* are words marked as out-of-topic by expert labelers.

Workers	Concepts		Relations		Subsumptions	
	KB-LDA (p)	Random (p)	KB-LDA (p)	Random (p)	KB-LDA (p)	Random (p)
1	48 (0.96)	6 (0.12)	90 (0.9)	69 (0.69)	31 (0.63)	28 (0.57)
2	42 (0.84)	0 (0.0)	63 (0.63)	22 (0.22)	16 (0.33)	9 (0.18)
3	26 (0.52)	0 (0.0)	15 (0.15)	4 (0.05)	3 (0.06)	4 (0.08)
Experts	44 (0.88)	0 (0.0)	70 (0.7)	13 (0.13)	25 (0.51)	4 (0.08)

Table 4: Precision of topic concepts, relations, and subsumptions. For items extracted from the model (KB-LDA), and randomly (Random), we show the number of items marked as correct, and precision in parentheses (p), as labeled by 1, 2, or 3 non-expert workers, and the average precision by experts.

We present in Table 4 the number and precision of patterns based on the top 100 relations (Relations) and 100 random relations (Random), that were labeled by 1, 2 or 3 workers, and the average results among experts. We achieve 80% precision according to experts, and only 18% on random relations. We observe similar agreement among expert and non-expert workers as in the concept evaluation experiment, however we note that random relations prove more confusing for non-experts and more of them are (falsely) labeled as correct.

3.2.4 Precision of Hierarchy

We assess the precision of subsumption relations making up the ontology hierarchy. These are extracted using the maximum spanning tree over the graph represented by the *Ontology* component, π_O (see Section 2.1 for details), resulting in 49 subsumption relations. We compare their quality to that of 49 randomly sampled subsumption relations. Subsumptions are presented to the worker using *is a* patterns, similar to the ones described above for concept evaluation, however in this case, the concept tokens are the top tokens of the hypernym topic. An example subsumption relation is

- [java, python, javascript, lists, ruby] **is a** [languages, language, features, objects, functions]

The results shown in Table 4 indicate a low precision among the extracted subsumption relations. This might be explained by the fact that at the final training iteration (2K) of the model, the perplexity of the *Ontology* component was still improving, while the perplexity of the other model components seemed closer to convergence. It is possible that the low precision observed here indicates that more training iterations are needed to achieve an accurate ontology using KB-LDA.

Topic	string, character, characters, text, line
Tags	regex, string, python, php, ruby
Topic	element, div, css, elements, http
Tags	css, html, jquery, html5, javascript
Topic	table, query, database, sql, column
Tags	sql, mysql, database, performance, php
Topic	jquery, mysql, http, json, xml
Tags	jquery, json, javascript, ruby, string

Table 5: Top tags associated with sample topics.

3.3 Overlap of KB-LDA topics with human-provided labels

We evaluated how well topics from KB-LDA correspond to document labels provided by humans, over a randomly sampled set of 40K documents from our corpus. In StackOverflow, questions (which we consider as documents) can be labeled with predefined tags. Here, we estimate the overlap with the most frequently used tags. First, for topic k, we aggregate tags from documents where $k = \text{argmax}_{k'} \theta_d^{k'}$, where θ_d is the document topic distribution. Table 5 shows examples of the top tags associated with sample topics, indicating a good correlation between top topic words and the underlying concepts.

Next, for each tested document $d \in D$, let W_d be the top 30 words of the most probable topic in θ_d, and T_d the set of human provided document tags. We consider the following metrics:

$$\text{Docs-Overlap} = \frac{\sum_d^D \mathbb{1}_{\{\exists t \in T_d : t \in W_d\}}}{|D|}$$

measures the ratio of documents for which at least one tag overlaps with a top topic word. The average ratio of overlapping tags per document is

$$\text{Tag-Overlap} = \frac{1}{|D|} \sum_d^D \frac{|t : t \in T_d \wedge t \in W_d|}{|T_d|}$$

As a baseline, we measure similar overlap metrics using the 30 most frequent instance tokens in the document corpus. The results in Table 6 indicate an overlap of nearly half of the 20, 50, 100, and 500 most frequent tags with top topic tokens – significantly higher than the overlap with frequent token. Our evaluation is based on the subset of tags found in the instance dictionary of KB-LDA.

Top Tags	Found in Dictionary	KB-LDA Docs	KB-LDA Tag	Frequent Tokens Docs	Frequent Tokens Tag
20	14	0.45	0.42	0.21	0.16
50	36	0.48	0.42	0.20	0.14
100	72	0.45	0.38	0.20	0.13
500	322	0.44	0.33	0.18	0.10

Table 6: Docs and Tag overlap of human-provided tags with KB-LDA topics, and frequent tokens.

Top 10 ranked triples: ⟨server, not found, error⟩, ⟨user, can access, file⟩, ⟨method, not found, error⟩, ⟨user, can change, password⟩, ⟨page, not found, error⟩, ⟨user, can upload, videos⟩, ⟨compiler, will generate, error⟩, ⟨users, can upload, files⟩, ⟨users, can upload, files⟩, ⟨object, not found, error⟩
Bottom 10 ranked triples: ⟨france, will visit, germany⟩, ⟨utilities, may include, heat⟩, ⟨iran, has had, russia⟩, ⟨russia, can stop, germany⟩, ⟨macs, do not support, windows media player⟩, ⟨cell phones, do not make, phone calls⟩, ⟨houses, have made, equipment⟩, ⟨guests, will find, restaurants⟩, ⟨guests, can request, bbq⟩, ⟨inspectors, do not make, appointments⟩

Table 7: Top and bottom ReVerb software triples ranked with KB-LDA.

3.4 Extracting facts from an open IE resource

We use KB-LDA to extract domain specific triples from an existing open IE KB, the 15M relations extracted using ReVerb (Fader et al., 2011) from ClueWeb09. By extracting the relations in which the subject, verb and object noun phrases are included in the KB-LDA dictionary, we are left with under 5K triples, indicating the low coverage of software related triples using open domain extraction, in comparison with the 37K triples extracted from StackOverflow and given as an input to KB-LDA.

Due to word polysemy, many of the 5K extracted triples are themselves not specific to the domain. This suggests a hybrid approach in which KB-LDA is used to rank open IE triples for relevance to a domain. We ranked the 5K open triples by the probability of the triple given a trained KB-LDA model: $p(s, v, o) = \sum_{k_s}^K \sum_{k_v}^K \sum_{k_o}^K \pi_R^{\langle k_s, k_v, k_o \rangle} \sigma_{k_s}^s \sigma_{k_o}^o \delta_{k_v}^v$. Table 7 shows the top and bottom 10 triples according to this ranking, which suggests that the triples ranked higher by KB-LDA are more relevant to the software domain.

We compare the ranking based on KB-LDA to

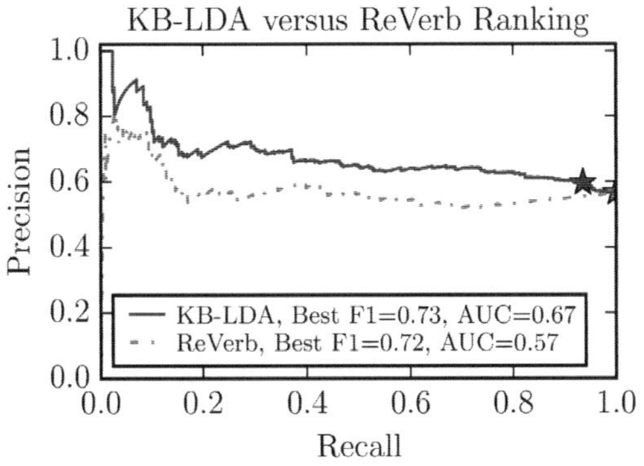

Figure 3: Precision-recall curves of rankers of open IE triples by software relevance, based on KB-LDA probabilities (blue), and ReVerb confidence (red). A star is pointing the highest F1.

a ranking using a confidence score for the triple as assigned by ReVerb. We manually labeled 500 of the triples according to their relevance to the software domain, and measured the precision and recall of the two rankings at any cutoff threshold. Figure 3 shows precision-recall curves for the two rankings, demonstrating that the ranking using probabilities based on KB-LDA leads to a more accurate detection of domain-relevant triples (with AUC of 0.67 for KB-LDA versus 0.57 for ReVerb).

4 Related Work

KB-LDA is an extension to LDA and link-LDA (Blei et al., 2003; Erosheva et al., 2004), modeling documents as a mixed membership over entity types with additional annotated metadata, such as links (Nallapati et al., 2008; Chang and Blei, 2009). It is a generalization of Block-LDA (Balasubramanyan and Cohen, 2011), however, KB-LDA models two link components, and the input links have a meaningful semantic correspondence to a KB structure (hierarchical and relational). In a related approach, Dalvi et al. (2012) cluster web table concepts to non-probabilistically create hierarchies with assigned concept names.

Our work is related to latent tensor representation of KBs, aimed at enhancing the ontological structure of existing KBs with relational data in the form of tensor structures. Nickel et al. (2012) factorized the ontology of Yago 2 for relational learning. A related approach was using Neural Tensor Networks to extract new facts from an existing KB (Chen et al., 2013; Socher et al., 2013). In contrast, in KB-LDA, relational data is learned jointly with the model through the *Relations* component.

Statistical language models have recently been adapted for modeling software code and text documents. Most tasks focused on enhancing the software development workflow with code and comment completion (Hindle et al., 2012; Movshovitz-Attias and Cohen, 2013), learning coding conventions (Allamanis et al., 2014), and extracting actionable tasks from software documentation (Treude et al., 2014). In related work, specific semantic relations, coordinate relations, have been extracted for a restricted class of software entities, ones that refer to Java classes (Movshovitz-Attias and Cohen, 2015). KB-LDA extends previous work by reasoning over a large variety of semantic relations among general software entities, as found in a document corpus.

5 Conclusions

We presented a model that jointly learns a latent ontological structure of a corpus augmented by relations, and identifies facts matching the learned structure. The quality of the produced structure was demonstrated through a series of real-world evaluations employing human judges, which measured the semantic coherence of instance topics, relations, topic concepts, and hierarchy. We further validated the semantic meaning of topic concepts, by their correspondence to an independent source of human-provided document tags. The experimental evaluation validates the usefulness of the proposed model for corpus exploration.

The results highlight the benefits of generalizing pattern-based facts (hypernym-hyponym pairs and subject-verb-object tuples), using text documents in a topic model framework. This modular approach offers opportunities to further improve an induced KB structure by posing additional constraints on corpus entities in the form of additional components to the model.

Acknowledgments

The authors wish to thank Premkumar Devanbu and Kathryn Rivard Mazaitis for helpful discussions, and the anonymous reviewers for their insightful comments. This work was funded by NSF under grant CCF-1414030.

References

Edoardo M Airoldi, David M Blei, Stephen E Fienberg, and Eric P Xing. 2009. Mixed membership stochastic blockmodels. In *Advances in Neural Information Processing Systems*, pages 33–40.

Miltiadis Allamanis, Earl T Barr, and Charles Sutton. 2014. Learning natural coding conventions. *arXiv preprint arXiv:1402.4182*.

Ramnath Balasubramanyan and William W. Cohen. 2011. Block-lda: Jointly modeling entity-annotated text and entity-entity links. In *Proceedings of the 7th SIAM International Conference on Data Mining*.

David M Blei, Andrew Y Ng, and Michael I Jordan. 2003. Latent dirichlet allocation. *Journal of Machine Learning Research*.

A. Carlson, J. Betteridge, B. Kisiel, B. Settles, E.R. Hruschka Jr, and T.M. Mitchell. 2010. Toward an architecture for never-ending language learning. In *Proceedings of the Twenty-Fourth Conference on Artificial Intelligence (AAAI 2010)*.

Jonathan Chang and David M Blei. 2009. Relational topic models for document networks. In *International Conference on Artificial Intelligence and Statistics*, pages 81–88.

Jonathan Chang, Sean Gerrish, Chong Wang, Jordan L Boyd-graber, and David M Blei. 2009. Reading tea leaves: How humans interpret topic models. In *Advances in neural information processing systems*, pages 288–296.

Danqi Chen, Richard Socher, Christopher D Manning, and Andrew Y Ng. 2013. Learning new facts from knowledge bases with neural tensor networks and semantic word vectors. *arXiv preprint arXiv:1301.3618*.

Bhavana Bharat Dalvi, William W Cohen, and Jamie Callan. 2012. Websets: Extracting sets of entities from the web using unsupervised information extraction. In *Proceedings of the fifth ACM international conference on Web search and data mining*, pages 243–252. ACM.

Elena Erosheva, Stephen Fienberg, and John Lafferty. 2004. Mixed-membership models of scientific publications. *Proceedings of the National Academy of Sciences of the United States of America*.

Anthony Fader, Stephen Soderland, and Oren Etzioni. 2011. Identifying relations for open information extraction. In *Proceedings of the Conference on Empirical Methods in Natural Language Processing*, pages 1535–1545. Association for Computational Linguistics.

Google. 2011. Freebase data dumps. http://download.freebase.com/datadumps/.

Thomas L Griffiths and Mark Steyvers. 2004. Finding scientific topics. *Proc. of the National Academy of Sciences of the United States of America*.

Marti A Hearst. 1992. Automatic acquisition of hyponyms from large text corpora. In *Proceedings of the 14th conference on Computational linguistics*. ACL.

Abram Hindle, Earl T Barr, Zhendong Su, Mark Gabel, and Premkumar Devanbu. 2012. On the naturalness of software. In *Software Engineering (ICSE), 2012 34th International Conference on*, pages 837–847. IEEE.

Johannes Hoffart, Fabian M Suchanek, Klaus Berberich, and Gerhard Weikum. 2013. Yago2: a spatially and temporally enhanced knowledge base from wikipedia. *Artificial Intelligence*, 194:28–61.

T. Mitchell, W. Cohen, E. Hruschka, P. Talukdar, J. Betteridge, A. Carlson, B. Dalvi, M. Gardner, B. Kisiel, J. Krishnamurthy, N. Lao, K. Mazaitis, T. Mohamed, N. Nakashole, E. Platanios, A. Ritter, M. Samadi, B. Settles, R. Wang, D. Wijaya, A. Gupta, X. Chen, A. Saparov, M. Greaves, and J. Welling. 2015. Never-ending learning. In *Proceedings of the Twenty-Ninth AAAI Conference on Artificial Intelligence (AAAI-15)*.

Dana Movshovitz-Attias and William W. Cohen. 2013. Natural language models for predicting programming comments. In *Proceedings of the 51st Annual Meeting of the Association for Computational Linguistics*. Association for Computational Linguistics.

Dana Movshovitz-Attias and William W. Cohen. 2015. Grounded discovery of coordinate term relationships between software entities. *arXiv preprint arXiv:1505.00277*.

Ramesh M Nallapati, Amr Ahmed, Eric P Xing, and William W Cohen. 2008. Joint latent topic models for text and citations. In *Proceedings of the 14th ACM SIGKDD international conference on Knowledge discovery and data mining*, pages 542–550. ACM.

David Newman, Arthur Asuncion, Padhraic Smyth, and Max Welling. 2009. Distributed algorithms for topic models. *The Journal of Machine Learning Research*, 10:1801–1828.

Maximilian Nickel, Volker Tresp, and Hans-Peter Kriegel. 2012. Factorizing yago: scalable machine learning for linked data. In *Proceedings of the 21st international conference on World Wide Web*, pages 271–280. ACM.

Juuso Parkkinen, Janne Sinkkonen, Adam Gyenge, and Samuel Kaski. 2009. A block model suitable for sparse graphs. In *Proceedings of the 7th International Workshop on Mining and Learning with Graphs (MLG 2009), Leuven*.

Fernando Pereira, Naftali Tishby, and Lillian Lee. 1993. Distributional clustering of english words. In *Proceedings of the 31st annual meeting on Association for Computational Linguistics*, pages 183–190. Association for Computational Linguistics.

Ian Porteous, David Newman, Alexander Ihler, Arthur Asuncion, Padhraic Smyth, and Max Welling. 2008. Fast collapsed gibbs sampling for latent dirichlet allocation. In *Proceedings of the 14th ACM SIGKDD international conference on Knowledge discovery and data mining*, pages 569–577. ACM.

Rion Snow, Daniel Jurafsky, and Andrew Y Ng. 2006. Semantic taxonomy induction from heterogenous evidence. In *Proceedings of the 21st International Conference on Computational Linguistics and the 44th annual meeting of the Association for Computational Linguistics*, pages 801–808. Association for Computational Linguistics.

Richard Socher, Danqi Chen, Christopher D Manning, and Andrew Ng. 2013. Reasoning with neural tensor networks for knowledge base completion. In *Advances in Neural Information Processing Systems*, pages 926–934.

Fabian M Suchanek, Gjergji Kasneci, and Gerhard Weikum. 2007. Yago: a core of semantic knowledge. In *Proceedings of the 16th international conference on World Wide Web*, pages 697–706. ACM.

Partha Pratim Talukdar, Derry Wijaya, and Tom Mitchell. 2012. Acquiring temporal constraints between relations. In *Proceedings of the 21st ACM international conference on Information and knowledge management*, pages 992–1001. ACM.

Christoph Treude, M Robillard, and Barthélémy Dagenais. 2014. Extracting development tasks to navigate software documentation. *IEEE Transactions on Software Engineering*.

Alexander Yates, Michael Cafarella, Michele Banko, Oren Etzioni, Matthew Broadhead, and Stephen Soderland. 2007. Textrunner: open information extraction on the web. In *Proceedings of Human Language Technologies: The Annual Conference of the North American Chapter of the Association for Computational Linguistics: Demonstrations*, pages 25–26. Association for Computational Linguistics.

A Computationally Efficient Algorithm for Learning Topical Collocation Models

Zhendong Zhao[1], Lan Du[1], Benjamin Börschinger[1,2], John K Pate[1], Massimiliano Ciaramita[2], Mark Steedman[3] and Mark Johnson[1]
[1] Department of Computing, Macquarie University, Australia
[2] Google, Zurich, Switzerland
[3] School of Informatics, University of Edinburgh, Scotland

Abstract

Most existing topic models make the *bag-of-words* assumption that words are generated independently, and so ignore potentially useful information about word order. Previous attempts to use *collocations* (short sequences of adjacent words) in topic models have either relied on a pipeline approach, restricted attention to bigrams, or resulted in models whose inference does not scale to large corpora. This paper studies how to simultaneously learn both collocations and their topic assignments. We present an efficient reformulation of the Adaptor Grammar-based topical collocation model (AG-colloc) (Johnson, 2010), and develop a point-wise sampling algorithm for posterior inference in this new formulation. We further improve the efficiency of the sampling algorithm by exploiting sparsity and parallelising inference. Experimental results derived in text classification, information retrieval and human evaluation tasks across a range of datasets show that this reformulation scales to hundreds of thousands of documents while maintaining the good performance of the AG-colloc model.

1 Introduction

Probabilistic topic models like Latent Dirichlet Allocation (LDA) (Blei et al., 2003) are commonly used to study the meaning of text by identifying a set of latent topics from a collection of documents and assigning each word in these documents to one of the latent topics. A document is modelled as a mixture of latent topics, and each topic is a distribution over a finite vocabulary of words. It is common for topic models to treat documents as bags-of-words, ignoring any internal structure. While this simplifies posterior inference, it also ignores the information encoded in, for example, syntactic relationships (Boyd-Graber and Blei, 2009), word order (Wallach, 2006) and the topic structure of documents (Du et al., 2013). Here we are interested in topic models that capture dependencies between adjacent words in a topic dependent way. For example, the phrase "white house" can be interpreted compositionally in a real-estate context, but not in a political context.

Several extensions of LDA have been proposed that assign topics not only to individual words but also to multi-word phrases, which we call *topical collocations*. However, as we will discuss in section 2, most of those extensions either rely on a pre-processing step to identify potential collocations (e.g., bigrams and trigrams) or limit attention to bigram dependencies. We want a model that can jointly learn collocations of arbitrary length and their corresponding topic assignments from a large collection of documents. The AG-colloc model (Johnson, 2010) does exactly this. However, because the model is formulated within the Adaptor Grammar framework (Johnson et al., 2007), the time complexity of its inference algorithm is cubic in the length of each text fragment, and so it is not feasible to apply the AG-colloc model to large collections of text documents.

In this paper we show how to reformulate the AG-colloc model so it is no longer relies on a general Adaptor Grammar inference procedure. The new formulation facilitates more efficient inference by extending ideas developed for Bayesian word segmentation (Goldwater et al., 2009). We adapt a point-wise sampling algorithm from Bayesian word segmentation, which has also been used in Du et al. (2013), to simultaneously sample collocation boundaries and collocation topic assignments. This algorithm retains the good performance of the AG-colloc model in document classification and information retrieval

Proceedings of the 53rd Annual Meeting of the Association for Computational Linguistics and the 7th International Joint Conference on Natural Language Processing, pages 1460–1469, Beijing, China, July 26-31, 2015.

tasks. By exploiting the sparse structure of both collocation and topic distributions, using techniques inspired by Yao et al. (2009), our new inference algorithm produces a remarkable speedup in running time and allows our reformulation to scale to a large number of documents. This algorithm can also be easily parallelised to take advantage of multiple cores by combining the ideas of the distributed LDA model (Newman et al., 2009). Thus, the contribution of this paper is three-fold: 1) a novel reformulation of the AG-colloc model, 2) an easily parallelisable and fast point-wise sampling algorithm exploiting sparsity and 3) systematic experiments with both qualitative and quantitative analysis.

The structure of the paper is as follows. In Section 2 we briefly discuss prior work on learning topical collocations. We then present our reformulation of the AG-colloc model in Section 3. Section 4 derives a point-wise Gibbs sampler for the model and shows how this sampler can take advantage of sparsity and be parallelised across multiple cores. Experimental results are reported in Section 5. Section 6 concludes this paper and discusses future work.

2 Related Work

There are two main approaches to incorporating topical collocations in LDA: 1) pipeline approaches that use a pre-processing step prior to LDA, and 2) extensions to LDA, which modify the generative process. In this section we discuss prior work that falls into these two categories and their limitations.

Pipeline Approaches (Lau et al., 2013), denoted here by PA, involve two steps. The first step identifies a set of bigrams that are potentially relevant collocations from documents by using simple heuristics for learning collocations, e.g., the Student's t-test method of Banerjee and Pedersen (2003). For each identified bigram "w_1 w_2", a new pseudo word "$w_1\_w_2$" is added to the vocabulary and the documents are re-tokenised to treat every instance of this bigram as a new token. LDA is then applied directly to the modified corpus without any changes to the model. While Lau et al. demonstrated that this two-step approach improves performance on a document classification task, it is limited in two ways. First, it can identify only collocations of a fixed length (i.e., bigrams). Second, the pre-processing step that identifies collocation candidates has no access to contextual cues (e.g. the topic of the context in which a bigram occurs),

A variety of extensions to the LDA model have been proposed to address this second shortcoming. Most extensions add some ability to capture word-to-word dependencies directly into the underlying generative process. For example, Wallach (2006) incorporates a hierarchical Dirichlet language model (MacKay and Peto, 1995), enabling her model to automatically cluster function words together. The model proposed by Griffiths et al. (2004) combines a hidden Markov model with LDA, using the former to model syntax and the latter to model semantics.

The LDA collocation model (LDACOL) (Griffiths et al., 2007) infers both the per-topic word distribution in the standard LDA model and, for each word in the vocabulary, a distribution over the words that follow it. The generative process of the LDACOL model allows words in a document to be generated in two ways. A word is generated either by drawing it directly from a per-topic word distribution corresponding to its topic as in LDA, or by drawing it from the word distribution associated with its preceding word w. The two alternatives are controlled by a set of Bernoulli random variables associated with individual words. Sequences of words generated from their predecessors constitute topical collocations.

Wang et al. (2007) extended the LDACOL model to generate the second word of a collocation from a distribution that conditions on not only the first word but also the first word's topic assignment, proposing the topical N-gram (TNG) model. In other words, whereas LDACOL only adds a distribution for every word-type to LDA, TNG adds a distribution for every possible word-topic pair. Wang et al. found that this modification allowed TNG to outperform LDACOL on a standard information retrieval task. However, both LDACOL and TNG do not require words within a sequence to share the same topic, which can result in semantically incoherent collocations.

Subsquent models have sought to encourage topically coherent collocations, including Phrase-Discovering LDA (Lindsey et al., 2012), the time-based topical n-gram model (Jameel and Lam, 2013a) and the n-gram Hierarchical Dirichlet Process (HDP) model (Jameel and Lam, 2013b). Phrase-Discovering LDA is a non-parametric extension of TNG inspired by Bayesian N-gram models Teh (2006) that incorporate a Pitman-Yor Process prior. The n-gram HDP is a nonparametric extension of LDA-colloc, putting an HDP prior on the per-document topic distribution. Both of these non-parametric extensions use the Chinese Franchise representation for posterior inference.

Our work here is based on the AG-colloc model proposed by Johnson (2010). He showed how Adaptor Grammars can generalise LDA to learn topical collocations of unbounded length while jointly identifying the topics that occur in each document. Unfortunately, because the Adaptor Grammar inference algorithm uses Probabilistic Context-Free Grammar (PCFG) parsing as a subroutine, the time complexity of inference is cubic in the length of individual text fragments. In order to improve the efficiency of the AG-colloc model, we re-express it using ideas from Bayesian word segmentation models. This allows us to develop an efficient inference algorithm for the AG-colloc model that scales to large corpora. Finally, we evaluate our model in terms of classification, information retrieval, and topic intrusion detection tasks; to our knowledge, we are the first to evaluate topical collocation models along all the three dimensions.

3 Topical Collocation Model

In this section we present our reformulation of the AG-colloc model, which we call the Topical Collocation Model (TCM) to emphasise that we are not using a grammar-based formulation. We start with the Unigram word segmentation model and Adaptor Grammar model of topical collocations, and then present our reformulation.

Goldwater et al. (2009) introduced a Bayesian model for word segmentation known as the Unigram model. This model is based on the Dirichet Process (DP) and assumes the following generative process for a sequence of words.

$$G \sim DP(\alpha_0, P_0), \qquad w_i \mid G \sim G$$

Here, P_0 is some distribution over the countably infinite set of all possible word forms (which are in turn sequences of a finite number of characters), and G is a draw from a Dirichlet Process. Inference is usually performed under a collapsed model in which G is integrated out, giving rise to a Chinese Restaurant Process (CRP) representation. The CRP is defined by the following predictive probability of w_i given $w_{1:i-1}$:

$$p(w_i = l | w_{1:i-1}) = \frac{n_l}{i-1+\alpha_0} + \frac{\alpha_0 P_0(l)}{i-1+\alpha_0},$$

where n_l is the number of times word form l appears in the first $n-1$ words.

During inference, the words are not known, and the model observes only a sequence of characters. Goldwater et al. (2009) derived a linear time Gibbs sampler that samples from the posterior distribution over possible segmentations of a given corpus according to the model. Their key insight is that sampling can be performed over a vector of Boolean boundary indicator variables – not included in the original description of the model – that indicates which adjacent characters are separated by a word boundary. We will show how this idea can be generalised to yield an inference algorithm for the AG-colloc model.

Adaptor Grammars (Johnson et al., 2007) are a generalisation of PCFGs. In a PCFG, a non-terminal A is expanded by selecting a rule $A \to \beta$ with probability $P(\beta|A)$, where β is a sequence of terminal and non-terminal node labels. Because the rules are selected independently, PCFGs introduce strong conditional independence assumptions. In an Adaptor Grammar, some of the non-terminal labels are *adapted*. These nodes can be expanded either by selecting a rule, as in PCFGs, or by retrieving an entire subtree from a Dirichlet Process cache specific to that node's non-terminal label,[1] breaking the conditional independence assumptions and capturing longer-range statistical relationships.

The AG-colloc model can be concisely expressed using context free grammar rule schemata, where adapted non-terminals are underlined:

$$\begin{aligned} \text{Top} &\to \text{Doc}_m \\ \text{Doc}_m &\to \_m \mid \text{Doc}_m\ \underline{\text{Topic}_i} \\ \underline{\text{Topic}_i} &\to \text{Word}^+ \end{aligned}$$

Here m ranges over the documents, i ranges over topics, "|" separates possible expansions, and "+" means "one or more". As in LDA, each document is defined as a mixture of K topics with the mixture probabilities corresponding to the probabili-

[1]Strictly speaking, Adaptor Grammars are defined using the Pitman-Yor process. In this paper we restrict ourselves to considering the Dirichlet Process which is a special case of the PYP where the discount parameter is set to 0. For more details, refer to Johnson et al. (2007) and Johnson (2010).

ties of the different expansions of Doc_m. However, the topic distributions are modelled using an adapted non-terminal $\underline{\text{Topic}_i}$. This means that there is an infinite number of rules expanding $\underline{\text{Topic}_i}$, one for every possible sequence over the finite vocabulary of words. $\underline{\text{Topic}_i}$ non-terminals cache sequences of words, just as G caches sequences of characters in the Unigram model.

The base distribution of the AG-colloc model is a geometric distribution over sequences of a finite vocabulary of words: $P_0(c = (w_1, \ldots, w_M)) = p_{\#}(1-p_{\#})^{M-1} \prod_{j=1}^{M} P_w(w_j)$, where $P_w(\cdot)$ is the uniform distribution over the finite set of words. This is the same base distribution used by Goldwater et al. (2009), except characters have been replaced by words. $p_{\#}$ is the probability of seeing the end of a collocation, and so controls the length of collocations. With this, we can re-express the AG-colloc model as a slight modification of the Unigram model:

1. For each topic $k, 1 \leq k \leq K$, $\phi_k \sim \text{DP}(\alpha_0, P_0)$
2. For each document $d, 1 \leq d \leq D$
   (a) Draw a topic distribution $\boldsymbol{\theta}_d | \alpha \sim \text{Dirichlet}_K(\alpha)$
   (b) For each collocation $c_{d,n}$ in document $d, 1 \leq n \leq N_d$
      i. Draw a topic assignment: $z_{d,n} \mid \boldsymbol{\theta}_d \sim \text{Discrete}(\boldsymbol{\theta}_d)$
      ii. Draw a collocation: $c_{d,n} \mid z_{d,n}, \boldsymbol{\phi}_1, \ldots, \boldsymbol{\phi}_K \sim \boldsymbol{\phi}_{z_{d,n}}$

where the length of a collocation $c_{d,n}$ is greater than or equal to 1, i.e., $|c_{d,n}| \geq 1$. Unlike previous models, the TCM associates each topic with a Unigram model over topical collocations. Therefore, the TCM learns different vocabularies for different topics.[2]

4 Posterior Inference

We develop an efficient point-wise sampling algorithm that can jointly sample collocations and their topics. The observed data consists of a sequence of word tokens which are grouped into D documents. We sample from the posterior distribution over segmentations of documents into collocations, and assignments of topics to collocations. Let each document d be a sequence of N_d words $w_{d,1}, \ldots, w_{d,N_d}$. We introduce a set of auxiliary random variables $b_{d,1}, \ldots, b_{d,N_d}$. The value of $b_{d,j}$ indicates whether there is a collocation boundary between $w_{d,j}$ and $w_{d,j+1}$, and, if there is, the topic of the collocation to the left of the boundary. If there is no boundary then $b_{d,j} = 0$. Otherwise, there is a collocation to the left of the boundary consisting of the words $w_{d,l+1}, \ldots, w_{d,j}$ where $l = \max\{i \mid 1 \leq i \leq j-1 \wedge b_{d,i} \neq 0\}$, and $b_{d,j} = k$ $(1 \leq k \leq K)$ is the topic of the collocation. Note that b_{d,N_d} must not be 0 as the end of a document is always a collocation boundary.

For example, consider the document consisting of the words "the white house." We use the K+1-valued variables b_1, b_2 (after 'the' and 'white') and the K-valued variable b_3 (after 'house') to describe every possible segmentation of this document into topical collocations.[3] If there are K topics and N words, there are $(K+1)^{N-1}K$ possible topical segmentations. To illustrate, see how each of the following triples (b_1, b_2, b_3) encodes a different analysis of "the white house" into bracketed collocations and subscripted topic numbers:

- $(0, 0, 1)$: (the white house)$_1$
- $(1, 0, 2)$: (the)$_1$ (white house)$_2$
- $(2, 1, 1)$: (the)$_2$ (white)$_1$ (house)$_1$

The next section elaborates the Gibbs sampler over these K+1 boundary variables.

4.1 A Point-wise Gibbs Sampler for the TCM

We consider a collapsed version of the TCM in which the document-specific topic mixtures $\boldsymbol{\theta}_{1:D}$ and the K non-parametric topic distributions $\boldsymbol{\phi}_{1:K}$ are integrated out. We introduce the sampling equations using a concrete example, considering again the toy document, "the white house."

Let the sampler start in state $b_1 = b_2 = 0, b_3 = z_0, 1 \leq z_0 \leq K$. This corresponds to the analysis

$$\underbrace{(\text{the}_0 \ \text{white}_0 \ \text{house}_{z_0})}_{c_0}.$$

This analysis consists of a single collocation c_0 which spans the entire document and is assigned to topic z_0. For simplicity, we will not show how to model document boundaries.

If we resample b_1, we have to consider two different hypotheses, i.e., putting or not putting a collocation boundary at b_1. The analysis corresponding to not putting a boundary is the one we just

[2]In the TCM, the vocabulary differs from topic to topic. Given a sequence of adjacent words, it is hard to tell if it is a collocation without knowing the topic of its context. Therefore, the Pointwise Mutual Information (PMI) (Newman et al., 2010) and its variant (Lau et al., 2014) are not applicable to our TCM in evaluation.

[3]A similar strategy of using K-valued rather than boolean boundary variables in Gibbs sampling was used in Börschinger et al. (2013) and Du et al. (2014).

saw. Putting a boundary corresponds to a new segmentation,

$$\underbrace{(\text{the}_{z_1})}_{c_1}\underbrace{(\text{white}_0\ \text{house}_{z_2})}_{c_2}\,.$$

We need to consider the K possible topics for c_1, for each of which we calculate the probability as follows. If $b_1 = 0$ (i.e., there is no collocation boundary after "the") we have

$$p(z_0, c_0|\boldsymbol{\mu}) = p(z_0|\alpha)p(c_0|\alpha_0, P_0, z_0)\,, \tag{1}$$

where $\boldsymbol{\mu} = \{\alpha, \alpha_0, P_0\}$. $p(c_0|\alpha_0, P_0, z_0)$ is the probability of generating collocation c_0 from topic z_0 with a CRP, i.e.,

$$p(c_0|\alpha_0, P_0, z_0) = \frac{n_{z_0}^{-c_0} + \alpha_0 P_0(c_0)}{N_{z_0}^{-c_0} + \alpha_0}\,, \tag{2}$$

where $n_{z_0}^{-c_0}$ is the number of times that collocation c_0 was assigned to topic z_0 and $N_{z_0}^{-c_0}$ is the total number of collocations assigned to z_0. Both counts exclude the parts of the analysis that are affected by the boundary c_0. As in LDA,

$$p(z_0 = k|\alpha) = \frac{\hat{n}_k^{-c_0} + \alpha}{\sum_{k=1}^{K} \hat{n}_k^{-c_0} + K\alpha}\,, \tag{3}$$

where $\hat{n}_k^{-c_0}$ is the total number of collocations assigned to topic k in a document, again excluding the count for the parts of the document that are affected by the current boundary. For the hypothesis that $b_1 = z_1$ (with $1 \leq z_1 \leq K$), the full conditional to generate two adjacent collocations is

$$\begin{aligned} p(z_1, z_2, c_1, c_2|\boldsymbol{\mu}) \propto \\ p(z_1|\alpha)p(c_1|\alpha_0, P_0, z_1) \\ p(z_2|\alpha, z_1)p(c_2|\alpha_0, P_0, c_1, z_1, z_2)\,, \end{aligned} \tag{4}$$

where $p(z_1|\alpha)$ and $p(c_1|\alpha_0, P_0, z_1)$ can be computed with Eqs (3) and (2), respectively. The remaining probabilities are computed as

$$\begin{aligned} p(z_2 = k|\alpha, z_1) = \\ \frac{\hat{n}_k^{-c_1,c_2} + \alpha + \mathbb{I}_{z_2=z_1}}{\sum_{k=1}^{K} \hat{n}_k^{-c_1,c_2} + K\alpha + 1}\,, \end{aligned} \tag{5}$$

$$\begin{aligned} p(c_2|\alpha_0, P_0, c_1, z_1, z_2) = \\ \frac{n_{z_2}^{-c_1,c_2} + \mathbb{I}_{z_1=z_2}\mathbb{I}_{c_1=c_2} + \alpha_0 P_0(c_2)}{\alpha_0 + N_{z_2}^{-c_1,c_2} + \mathbb{I}_{z_1=z_2}} \end{aligned} \tag{6}$$

where $\mathbb{I}_{x=y}$ is an indicator function that is equal to 1 if $x = y$ and 0 otherwise, $n_{z_2}^{-c_1,c_2}$ is the number of collocations c_2 assigned to topic z_2, and $N_{z_2}^{-c_1,c_2}$ is the total number of collocations assigned to topic z_2. Both counts exclude the current c_2, and also exclude c_1 if $z_1 = z_2$ and $c_1 = c_2$. Our sampler does random sweeps over all the boundary positions, and calculates the joint probability of the corresponding collocations and their topic assignment using Eqs (1) and (4) at each position.

4.2 Parallelised Sparse Sampling Algorithm

The word distributions and topic distributions in LDA are typically sparse, and Yao et al. (2009) proposed a 'sparseLDA' Gibbs sampler that takes advantage of this sparsity to substantially reduce running time. These two distributions are even sparser for the TCM than LDA, because collocations are less frequent than unigrams. Here we show how to modify our sampler to take advantage of sparsity. Sampling boundaries according the two probabilities shown Eqs (1) and (4) requires the generation of a random number x from a uniform distribution, $\mathcal{U}(0, \mathcal{P})$, where

$$\mathcal{P} = p(z_0, c_0) + \sum_{z_1=1}^{K} p(z_1, c_1)p(z_2, c_2|c_1, z_1)\,. \tag{7}$$

Here the first term corresponds to the case that there is no collocation boundary, and the summation corresponds to the case that there is a collocation boundary. Thus, if x is less than $P(z_0, c_0)$, there will be no boundary. Otherwise, we need to sample z_1 according to Eq (4).

The sampling algorithm requires calculation of Eq (7), even though the probability mass may be concentrated on just a few topics. We have observed in our experiments that the denominators of Eqs (5) and (6) are often quite large and the indicator functions usually turn out to be zero, so we approximate the two equations by removing the indicator functions. This approximation not only facilitates the computation of Eq (7), but also means that $p(z_2, c_2|c_1, z_1)$ no longer depends on z_1 and c_1. Thus, Eq (7) can be approximated as

$$\mathcal{P} \approx p(z_0, c_0) + p(z_2, c_2) \sum_{z_1=1}^{K} p(z_1, c_1)\,. \tag{8}$$

Now that $p(z_0, c_0)$ and $p(z_2, c_2)$ are both out of the summation; they can be pre-computed and cached.

To reduce the computational complexity of the summation term in Eq (8), we use the "buckets" method (Yao et al., 2009). We divide the summation term in $p(z_1, c_1)$ into three parts as follows, each of which corresponds to a bucket:

$$\begin{aligned} & p(z_1 = k, c_1) \\ = & \frac{\hat{n}_k^{-c_1,c_2} + \alpha}{\sum_{k=1}^{K} \hat{n}_k^{-c_1,c_2} + K\alpha} \frac{n_k^{-c_1,c_2} + \alpha_0 P_0(c_1)}{N_k^{-c_1,c_2} + \alpha_0} \\ \propto & \frac{\alpha_0 P_0(c_1)\alpha}{N_k^{-c_1,c_2} + \alpha_0} + \frac{\hat{n}_k^{-c_1,c_2}\alpha_0 P_0(c_1)}{N_k^{-c_1,c_2} + \alpha_0} \\ & + \frac{(\hat{n}_k^{-c_1,c_2} + \alpha) n_k^{-c_1,c_2}}{N_k^{-c_1,c_2} + \alpha_0} \end{aligned} \quad (9)$$

Then, the summation in Eq (8) is proportional to the sum of the following three equations:

$$s = \sum_{k=1}^{K} \frac{\alpha_0 P_0(c_1)\alpha}{N_k^{-c_1,c_2} + \alpha_0} \quad (10)$$

$$r = \sum_{k=1}^{K} \frac{\hat{n}_k^{-c_1,c_2}\alpha_0 P_0(c_1)}{N_k^{-c_1,c_2} + \alpha_0} \quad (11)$$

$$q = \sum_{k=1}^{K} \frac{(\hat{n}_k^{-c_1,c_2} + \alpha) n_k^{-c_1,c_2}}{N_k^{-c_1,c_2} + \alpha_0} \quad (12)$$

We can now use the sampling techniques used in the sparse-LDA model to sample z_1. Firstly, sample $U \sim \mathcal{U}(0, s + r + q)$. If $U < s$ we have hit bucket s. In this case, we need to compute the probability for each possible topic. If $s < x < (s + r)$ we have hit the second bucket r. In this case, we compute probabilities only for topics such that $\hat{n}_k^{-c_1,c_2} \neq 0$. If $x > (s + r)$ we have hit bucket q, which is the "topic collection" bucket, and we need only consider topics such that $n_k^{-c_1,c_2} \neq 0$. Although we use an approximation in computing the full conditionals, experimental results have shown that our TCM is as accurate as the original AG-colloc model, see Section 5.

Our sparse sampling algorithm can be easily parallelised with the same multi-threading strategy used by Newman et al. (2009) in their distributed LDA (AD-LDA). In AD-LDA, documents are distributed evenly across P processors, each of which also has a copy of the word-topic count matrix. Gibbs updates are performed simultaneously on each of the P processors. At the end of each Gibbs iteration, the P copies of the word-topic count matrices are collected and summed into the global word-topic count matrix.

In the TCM, collocations in each topic are generated from a CRP. Hence, distributing the word-topic count matrix in AD-LDA now corresponds to distributing a set of Chinese restaurants in the parallelised TCM. The challenge is how to merge the Chinese Restaurant copies from the P processors into a single global restaurant for each topic, similar to the merging problem in Du et al. (2013). However, Eqs (2) and (6) show that the statistics that need to be collected are the number of collocations generated for each topic. The number of tables in a restaurant does not matter.[4] Therefore, we can adapt the summation technique used in AD-LDA.

We further observed that if P is large, using a single processor to perform the summation operation could result in a large overhead. The summation step could be even costlier in TCM than in LDA, since the number of distinct collocations is much larger than the number of distinct words. Thus we also parallelise the summation step using all the processors that are free in this step.

5 Experimental Results

In this section we evaluate the effectiveness and efficiency of our Topical Collocation Model (TCM) on different tasks, i.e., a document classification task, an information retrieval task and a topic intrusion detection task. All the empirical results show that our TCM performs as well as the AG-colloc model and outperforms other collocation models (i.e., LDACOL (Griffiths et al., 2007), TNG (Wang et al., 2007), PA (Lau et al., 2013)). The TCM also runs much faster than the other models. We also compared the TCM with the Mallet implementation of AD-LDA (Newman et al., 2009), denoted by Mallet-LDA, for completeness. Following Griffiths et al. (2007), we used punctuation and Mallet's stop words to split the documents into subsequences of word tokens, then removed those punctuation and stop words from the input. All experiments were run on a cluster with 80 Xeon E7-4850 processors (2.0GHz) and 96 GB memory.

5.1 Classification Evaluation

In the classification task, we used three datasets: the movie review dataset (Pang and Lee, 2012) (**MReviews**), the 20 Newsgroups dataset, and the Reuters-21578 dataset. The movie review dataset includes 1,000 positive and 1,000 negative reviews. The 20 Newsgroups dataset is organised

[4]The number of tables is used only when sampling the concentration parameters, α_0, see Blunsom et al. (2009).

Task	Classification	IR
Dataset	MReview	SJMN-2k
Mallet-LDA	71.30	18.85
LDACOL	71.75	19.03
TNG	71.40	19.06
PA	72.74	19.16
AG-colloc	***73.15***	***19.37***
Non-sparse TCM	**73.14**	**19.30**
Sparse TCM	**73.13**	**19.31**

Table 1: Comparison of all models in the classification task (accuracy in %) and the information retrieval task (MAP scores in %) on small corpora. Bold face indicates scores not significantly different from the best score (in italics) according to a Wilcoxon signed rank test ($p < 0.05$).

	Mallet-LDA	PA	TCM
Politics	**89.1**	***89.2***	***89.2***
Comp	86.3	87.4	*87.9*
Sci	92.0	93.2	*93.4*
Sports	91.6	91.7	*92.6*
Reuter-21578	97.3	**97.5**	***97.6***

Table 2: Classification accuracy (%) on larger datasets. Bold face indicates scores not significantly different from the best score (in italics) according to a Wilcoxon signed rank test ($p < 0.05$).

into 20 different categories according to different topics. We further partitioned the 20 newsgroups dataset into four subsets, denoted by **Comp**, **Sci**, **Sport**, and **Politics**. They have $4,891$, $3,952$, $1,993$, and $2,625$ documents respectively. We applied document classification to each subset. The **Reuters-21578** dataset has 21,578 Reuters news articles which are split into 10 categories.

The classification evaluation was carried out as follows. First, we ran each model on each dataset to derive point estimates of documents' topic distributions ($\boldsymbol{\theta}$), which were used as the only features in classification. We then randomly selected from each dataset 80% documents for training and 20% for testing. A Support Vector Machine (SVM) with a linear-kernel was used. We ran all models for 10,000 iterations with 50 topics on the movie review dataset and 100 on the other two. We set $\alpha = 1/K$ and $\beta = 0.02$ for Mallet-LDA, LDACOL, TNG and PA. We used the reported settings in Johnson (2010) for the AG-colloc model. For the TCM, we used $\alpha = 1/K$. The concentration parameter α_0 was initially set to 100 and resampled using approximated table counts (Blunsom et al., 2009).

	Mallet-LDA	PA	TCM
SJMN	20.7	20.9	***21.2***
AP	24.0	24.5	***24.8***

Table 3: Mean average Precision (MAP in %) scores in the information retrieval task. Scores in bold and italics are the significantly best MAP scores according to a Wilcoxon signed rank test ($p < 0.05$).

Since efficient inference is unavailable for LDACOL, TNG and AG-colloc, making it impractical to evaluate them on the large corpora, we compared our TCM with them only on the **MReviews** dataset. The first column of Table 1 shows the classification accuracy of those models. All the collocation models outperform Mallet-LDA. The AG-colloc model yields the highest classification accuracy, and our TCM with/without sparsity performs as well as the AG-colloc model according to the Wilcoxon signed rank test. The Pipeline Approach (PA) is always better than LDACOL and TNG. Therefore, in the following experiments we will focus on the comparison among our TCM, Mallet-LDA and PA.

Table 2 shows the classification accuracy of those three models on the larger datasets, i.e., the 20 Newsgroups dataset, and the Reuters-21578 dataset. The TCM outperforms both Mallet-LDA and PA on 3 out of 5 datasets, and performs equally well as PA on the **Politics** and **Reuter-21578** datasets according to a Wilcoxon signed rank test ($p < 0.05$).

5.2 Information Retrieval Evaluation

For the information retrieval task, we used the method presented by Wei and Croft (2006) and Wang et al. (2007) to calculate the probability of a query given a document. We used the San Jose Mercury News (**SJMN**) dataset and the **AP** News dataset from TREC. The former has 90,257 documents, the latter has 242,918 documents. Queries 51-150 were used. We ran all the models for 10,000 iteration with 100 topics. The other parameter settings were the same as those used in Section 5.1. Queries were tokenised using unigrams for Mallet-LDA and collocations for all collocation models.

Models	$p(w\|t)$	$p(t\|w)$
Mallet-LDA	71.9	73.2
PA	72.8	76.7
TCM	**73.2**	**79.7**

Table 4: The model precision (%) derived from the intrusion detection experiments.

Dataset	MReview		SJMN-2k	
#Topic	100	800	100	800
AG-colloc	84.9	1305	37.5	692
Non-sparse TCM	13.8	233	6.6	85.7
Sparse TCM	0.28	0.35	0.14	0.2

Table 5: The average running time (in seconds) per iteration.

On a small subset of the SJMN data, which contains 2,000 documents (**SJMN-2k**), we find again that TCM and AG-colloc perform equally well and outperform all other models (LDACOL, TNG, PA), as shown in the second column of Table 1. We further compare the TCM, Mallet-LDA and PA on the full **SJMN** dataset and the **AP** news dataset, as these models can run on large scale. Table 3 shows the mean average precision (MAP) scores. The TCM significantly outperforms both Mallet-LDA and the PA approach, and yields the highest MAP score.

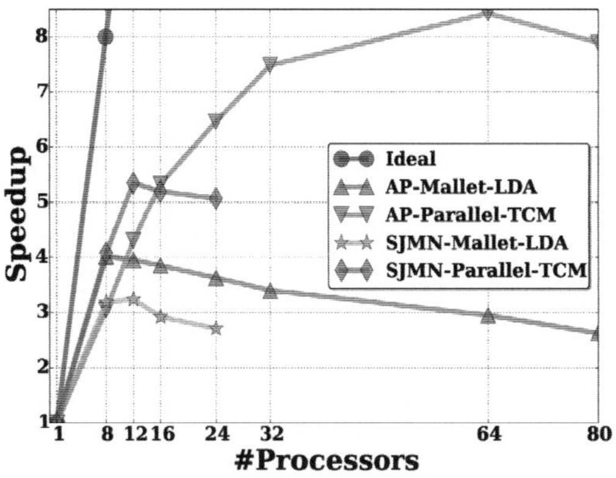

Figure 1: Plot of speedup in running time for the Mallet-LDA and our TCM.

5.3 Topic Coherence Evaluation

We ran a set of topic intrusion detection experiments (Chang et al., 2009) that provide a human evaluation of the coherence of the topics learnt by Mallet-LDA, PA and TCM on the **SJMN** dataset. This set of experiments was use to measure how well the inferred topics match human concepts. Each subject recruited from Amazon Mechanical Turk was presented with a randomly ordered list of 10 tokens (either words or collocations). The task of the subject was to identify the token which is semantically different from the others.

To generate the 10-token lists, we experimented with two different methods for selecting tokens (either words or collocations) most strongly associated with a topic t. The standard method chooses the tokens w that maximise $p(w|t)$. This method is biased toward high frequency tokens, since low-frequency tokens are unlikely to have a large $p(w|t)$. We also tried choosing words and collocations w that maximise $p(t|w)$. This method finds w that are unlikely to appear in any other topic except t, and is biased towards low frequency w. We reduce this low-frequency bias by using a smoothed estimate for $p(t|w)$ with a Dirichlet pseudo-count $\alpha = 5$.

An intruder token was randomly selected from a set of tokens that had low probability in the current topic but high probability in some other topic. We then randomly selected one of the 10 tokens to be replaced by the intruder token. We expect collocations to be more useful in lists that are constructed using $p(t|w)$ than lists constructed using $p(w|t)$. This is because $p(w|t)$ can be dominated by the frequency of w, but individual collocations are rare.

The performance was measured by model precision (Chang et al., 2009), which measures the fraction of subjects that agreed with the model. Table 4 shows that our TCM outperforms both PA and Mallet-LDA under both ways of constructing the intrusion lists. As expected, the collocation models PA and TCM perform better with lists constructed according to $p(t|w)$ than lists constructed according to $p(w|t)$.

5.4 Efficiency of the TCM

In this section we study the efficiency of our TCM model in terms of running time. We first compare the efficiency of our TCM model with and without sparsity with the AG-colloc model on the **MReview** dataset and the **SJMN-2k** dataset. Table 5 shows the average running time per iteration for the two models. We used 100 and 800 topics. The TCM algorithm that does not exploit sparsity in sampling runs about 6 times faster than the AG-colloc model. Our sparse sampler runs even faster, and takes less than a second per iteration. Therefore, Tables 1 and 5 jointly show that our reformulation runs an order of magnitude faster than AG-colloc without losing performance, thereby making the AG-colloc model inference feasible at large scales.

We further studied the scalability of our sampling algorithm after parallelisation on the **SJMN** dataset and the **AP** news dataset. We fixed the number of topics to 100, and varied the number of processors from 1 to 24 for the SJMN dataset and from 1 to 80 for the AP dataset. The plots in Figure 1 show that our parallelised sampler achieved a remarkable speedup. We have also observed that there is a point at which using additional processors actually slows running time. This is common in parallel algorithms when communication and synchronisation take more time than the time saved by parallelisation. This slowdown occurs in the highly-optimized Mallet implementation of LDA with fewer cores than it does in our implementation. The speedup achieved by our TCM also shows the benefit of parallelising the summation step mentioned in Section 4.2.

6 Conclusion

In this paper we showed how to represent the AG-colloc model without using Adaptor Grammars, and how to adapt Gibbs sampling techniques from Bayesian word segmentation to perform posterior inference under the new representation. We further accelerated the sampling algorithm by taking advantage of the sparsity in the collocation count matrix. Experimental results derived in different tasks showed that 1) our new representation performs as well as the AG-colloc model and outperforms the other collocation models, 2) our point-wise sampling algorithm scales well to large corpora. There are several ways in which our model can be extended. For example, our algorithm could be further sped up by using the sampling techniques presented by Smola and Narayanamurthy (2010), Li et al. (2014) and Buntine and Mishra (2014). One can also consider using a hybrid of MCMC and variational inference as in Ke et al. (2014).

Acknowledgments

This research was supported by a Google award through the Natural Language Understanding Focused Program, and under the Australian Research Council's *Discovery Projects* funding scheme (project numbers DP110102506 and DP110102593).

References

Satanjeev Banerjee and Ted Pedersen. 2003. The design, implementation, and use of the ngram statistics package. In *Computational Linguistics and Intelligent Text Processing*, volume 2588, pages 370–381.

D.M. Blei, A.Y. Ng, and M.I. Jordan. 2003. Latent Dirichlet allocation. *Journal of Machine Learning Research*, 3:993–1022.

Phil Blunsom, Trevor Cohn, Sharon Goldwater, and Mark Johnson. 2009. A note on the implementation of hierarchical dirichlet processes. In *Proceedings of the ACL-IJCNLP 2009 Conference Short Papers*, pages 337–340.

Benjamin Börschinger, Mark Johnson, and Katherine Demuth. 2013. A joint model of word segmentation and phonological variation for english word-final /t/-deletion. In *Proceedings of the 51st Annual Meeting of the Association for Computational Linguistics (Volume 1: Long Papers)*, pages 1508–1516, Sofia, Bulgaria.

Jordan L Boyd-Graber and David Blei. 2009. Syntactic topic models. In *Advances in Neural Information Processing Systems 21*, pages 185–192.

Wray L Buntine and Swapnil Mishra. 2014. Experiments with non-parametric topic models. In *Proceedings of the 20th ACM SIGKDD international conference on Knowledge discovery and data mining*, pages 881–890.

Jonathan Chang, Sean Gerrish, Chong Wang, Jordan L. Boyd-graber, and David M. Blei. 2009. Reading tea leaves: How humans interpret topic models. In *Advances in Neural Information Processing Systems 22*, pages 288–296.

Lan Du, Wray Buntine, and Mark Johnson. 2013. Topic segmentation with a structured topic model. In *Proceedings of the 2013 Conference of the North American Chapter of the Association for Computational Linguistics: Human Language Technologies*, pages 190–200.

Lan Du, John Pate, and Mark Johnson. 2014. Topic models with topic ordering regularities for topic segmentation. In *Proceedings of the IEEE International Conference on Data Mining*, pages 803–808.

Sharon Goldwater, Thomas L. Griffiths, and Mark Johnson. 2009. A Bayesian framework for word segmentation: Exploring the effects of context. *Cognition*, 112(1):21–53.

Thomas L Griffiths, Mark Steyvers, David M Blei, and Joshua B Tenenbaum. 2004. Integrating topics and syntax. In *Advances in neural information processing systems*, pages 537–544.

Thomas L. Griffiths, Mark Steyvers, and Joshua B. Tenenbaum. 2007. Topics in semantic representation. *Psychological Review*, 114(2):211–244.

Shoaib Jameel and Wai Lam. 2013a. An n-gram topic model for time-stamped documents. In *Proceedings of the 35th European Conference on Advances in Information Retrieval*, pages 292–304.

Shoaib Jameel and Wai Lam. 2013b. A nonparametric n-gram topic model with interpretable latent topics. In *Information Retrieval Technology*, pages 74–85.

M. Johnson, T.L. Griffiths, and S. Goldwater. 2007. Adaptor grammars: A framework for specifying compositional nonparametric Bayesian models. In *Advances in Neural Information Processing Systems 19*, pages 641–648.

Mark Johnson. 2010. Pcfgs, topic models, adaptor grammars and learning topical collocations and the structure of proper names. In *Proceedings of the 48th Annual Meeting of the Association for Computational Linguistics*, pages 1148–1157.

Zhai Ke, Boyd-Graber Jordan, and Cohen Shay B. 2014. Online adaptor grammars with hybrid inference. *Transactions of the Association of Computational Linguistics*, 2:465–476.

Jey Han Lau, Timothy Baldwin, and David Newman. 2013. On collocations and topic models. *ACM Transactions on Speech and Language Processing (TSLP)*, 10(3):10.

Jey Han Lau, David Newman, and Timothy Baldwin. 2014. Machine reading tea leaves: Automatically evaluating topic coherence and topic model quality. In *Proceedings of the 14th Conference of the European Chapter of the Association for Computational Linguistics*, pages 530–539.

Aaron Q Li, Amr Ahmed, Sujith Ravi, and Alexander J Smola. 2014. Reducing the sampling complexity of topic models. In *Proceedings of the 20th ACM SIGKDD international conference on Knowledge discovery and data mining*, pages 891–900.

Robert Lindsey, William Headden, and Michael Stipicevic. 2012. A phrase-discovering topic model using hierarchical Pitman-Yor processes. In *Proceedings of the 2012 Joint Conference on Empirical Methods in Natural Language Processing and Computational Natural Language Learning*, pages 214–222.

David JC MacKay and Linda C Bauman Peto. 1995. A hierarchical Dirichlet language model. *Natural language engineering*, 1(3):289–308.

David Newman, Arthur Asuncion, Padhraic Smyth, and Max Welling. 2009. Distributed algorithms for topic models. *Journal of Machine Learning Research*, 10:1801–1828.

David Newman, Youn Noh, Edmund Talley, Sarvnaz Karimi, and Timothy Baldwin. 2010. Evaluating topic models for digital libraries. In *Proceedings of the 10th Annual Joint Conference on Digital Libraries*, pages 215–224.

Bo Pang and Lillian Lee. 2012. Cornell Movie Review Data.

Alexander Smola and Shravan Narayanamurthy. 2010. An architecture for parallel topic models. *Proc. VLDB Endow.*, 3(1-2):703–710.

Y. W. Teh. 2006. A hierarchical Bayesian language model based on Pitman-Yor processes. In *Proceedings of the 21st International Conference on Computational Linguistics and the 44th annual meeting of the Association for Computational Linguistics*, pages 985–992.

Hanna M. Wallach. 2006. Topic modeling: beyond bag-of-words. In *Proceedings of the 23rd international conference on Machine learning*, pages 977–984.

Xuerui Wang, Andrew McCallum, and Xing Wei. 2007. Topical n-grams: Phrase and topic discovery, with an application to information retrieval. In *Proceedings of the 2007 Seventh IEEE International Conference on Data Mining*, pages 697–702.

Xing Wei and W. Bruce Croft. 2006. LDA-based document models for ad-hoc retrieval. In *Proceedings of the 29th annual international ACM SIGIR conference on Research and development in information retrieval*, pages 178–185.

Limin Yao, David Mimno, and Andrew McCallum. 2009. Efficient methods for topic model inference on streaming document collections. In *Proceedings of the 15th ACM SIGKDD International Conference on Knowledge Discovery and Data Mining*, pages 937–946.

Compositional Semantic Parsing on Semi-Structured Tables

Panupong Pasupat
Computer Science Department
Stanford University
ppasupat@cs.stanford.edu

Percy Liang
Computer Science Department
Stanford University
pliang@cs.stanford.edu

Abstract

Two important aspects of semantic parsing for question answering are the breadth of the knowledge source and the depth of logical compositionality. While existing work trades off one aspect for another, this paper simultaneously makes progress on both fronts through a new task: answering complex questions on semi-structured tables using question-answer pairs as supervision. The central challenge arises from two compounding factors: the broader domain results in an open-ended set of relations, and the deeper compositionality results in a combinatorial explosion in the space of logical forms. We propose a logical-form driven parsing algorithm guided by strong typing constraints and show that it obtains significant improvements over natural baselines. For evaluation, we created a new dataset of 22,033 complex questions on Wikipedia tables, which is made publicly available.

Year	City	Country	Nations
1896	Athens	Greece	14
1900	Paris	France	24
1904	St. Louis	USA	12
...	...	...	...
2004	Athens	Greece	201
2008	Beijing	China	204
2012	London	UK	204

x_1: *"Greece held its last Summer Olympics in which year?"*
y_1: {2004}

x_2: *"In which city's the first time with at least 20 nations?"*
y_2: {Paris}

x_3: *"Which years have the most participating countries?"*
y_3: {2008, 2012}

x_4: *"How many events were in Athens, Greece?"*
y_4: {2}

x_5: *"How many more participants were there in 1900 than in the first year?"*
y_5: {10}

Figure 1: Our task is to answer a highly compositional question from an HTML table. We learn a semantic parser from question-table-answer triples $\{(x_i, t_i, y_i)\}$.

1 Introduction

In semantic parsing for question answering, natural language questions are converted into logical forms, which can be executed on a knowledge source to obtain answer denotations. Early semantic parsing systems were trained to answer highly compositional questions, but the knowledge sources were limited to small closed-domain databases (Zelle and Mooney, 1996; Wong and Mooney, 2007; Zettlemoyer and Collins, 2007; Kwiatkowski et al., 2011). More recent work sacrifices compositionality in favor of using more open-ended knowledge bases such as Freebase (Cai and Yates, 2013; Berant et al., 2013; Fader et al., 2014; Reddy et al., 2014). However, even these broader knowledge sources still define a rigid schema over entities and relation types, thus restricting the scope of answerable questions.

To simultaneously increase both the *breadth* of the knowledge source and the *depth* of logical compositionality, we propose a new task (with an associated dataset): answering a question using an HTML table as the knowledge source. Figure 1 shows several question-answer pairs and an accompanying table, which are typical of those in our dataset. Note that the questions are logically quite complex, involving a variety of operations such as comparison (x_2), superlatives (x_3), aggregation (x_4), and arithmetic (x_5).

The HTML tables are semi-structured and not normalized. For example, a cell might contain multiple parts (e.g., "*Beijing, China*" or "*200 km*"). Additionally, we mandate that the training and test tables are disjoint, so at test time, we will see relations (column headers; e.g., "*Nations*") and entities (table cells; e.g., "*St. Louis*")

Proceedings of the 53rd Annual Meeting of the Association for Computational Linguistics and the 7th International Joint Conference on Natural Language Processing, pages 1470–1480,
Beijing, China, July 26-31, 2015. ©2015 Association for Computational Linguistics

that were not observed during training. This is in contrast to knowledge bases like Freebase, which have a global fixed relation schema with normalized entities and relations.

Our task setting produces two main challenges. Firstly, the increased breadth in the knowledge source requires us to generate logical forms from novel tables with previously unseen relations and entities. We therefore cannot follow the typical semantic parsing strategy of constructing or learning a lexicon that maps phrases to relations ahead of time. Secondly, the increased depth in compositionality and additional logical operations exacerbate the exponential growth of the number of possible logical forms.

We trained a semantic parser for this task from question-answer pairs based on the framework illustrated in Figure 2. First, relations and entities from the semi-structured HTML table are encoded in a graph. Then, the system parses the question into candidate logical forms with a high-coverage grammar, reranks the candidates with a log-linear model, and then executes the highest-scoring logical form to produce the answer denotation. We use beam search with pruning strategies based on type and denotation constraints to control the combinatorial explosion.

To evaluate the system, we created a new dataset, WIKITABLEQUESTIONS, consisting of 2,108 HTML tables from Wikipedia and 22,033 question-answer pairs. When tested on unseen tables, the system achieves an accuracy of 37.1%, which is significantly higher than the information retrieval baseline of 12.7% and a simple semantic parsing baseline of 24.3%.

2 Task

Our task is as follows: given a table t and a question x about the table, output a list of values y that answers the question according to the table. Example inputs and outputs are shown in Figure 1. The system has access to a training set $\mathcal{D} = \{(x_i, t_i, y_i)\}_{i=1}^N$ of questions, tables, and answers, but the tables in test data do not appear during training.

The only restriction on the question x is that a person must be able to answer it using just the table t. Other than that, the question can be of any type, ranging from a simple table lookup question to a more complicated one that involves various logical operations.

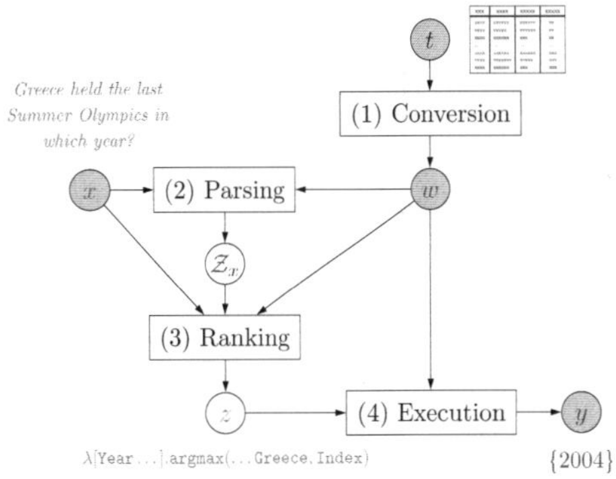

Figure 2: The prediction framework: (1) the table t is deterministically converted into a knowledge graph w as shown in Figure 3; (2) with information from w, the question x is parsed into candidate logical forms in $\mathcal{Z}_x$; (3) the highest-scoring candidate $z \in \mathcal{Z}_x$ is chosen; and (4) z is executed on w, yielding the answer y.

Dataset. We created a new dataset, WIKITABLEQUESTIONS, of question-answer pairs on HTML tables as follows. We randomly selected data tables from Wikipedia with at least 8 rows and 5 columns. We then created two Amazon Mechanical Turk tasks. The first task asks workers to write trivia questions about the table. For each question, we put one of the 36 generic prompts such as *"The question should require calculation"* or *"contains the word* 'first' *or its synonym"* to encourage more complex utterances. Next, we submit the resulting questions to the second task where the workers answer each question based on the given table. We only keep the answers that are agreed upon by at least two workers. After this filtering, approximately 69% of the questions remains.

The final dataset contains 22,033 examples on 2,108 tables. We set aside 20% of the tables and their associated questions as the test set and develop on the remaining examples. Simple preprocessing was done on the tables: We omit all non-textual contents of the tables, and if there is a merged cell spanning many rows or columns, we unmerge it and duplicate its content into each unmerged cell. Section 7.2 analyzes various aspects of the dataset and compares it to other datasets.

3 Approach

We now describe our semantic parsing framework for answering a given question and for training the model with question-answer pairs.

Prediction. Given a table t and a question x, we predict an answer y using the framework illustrated in Figure 2. We first convert the table t into a *knowledge graph* w ("world") which encodes different relations in the table (Section 4). Next, we generate a set of candidate logical forms $\mathcal{Z}_x$ by parsing the question x using the information from w (Section 6.1). Each generated logical form $z \in \mathcal{Z}_x$ is a graph query that can be executed on the knowledge graph w to get a *denotation* $[\![z]\!]_w$. We extract a feature vector $\phi(x, w, z)$ for each $z \in \mathcal{Z}_x$ (Section 6.2) and define a log-linear distribution over the candidates:

$$p_\theta(z \mid x, w) \propto \exp\{\theta^\top \phi(x, w, z)\}, \quad (1)$$

where θ is the parameter vector. Finally, we choose the logical form z with the highest model probability and execute it on w to get the answer denotation $y = [\![z]\!]_w$.

Training. Given training examples $\mathcal{D} = \{(x_i, t_i, y_i)\}_{i=1}^N$, we seek a parameter vector θ that maximizes the regularized log-likelihood of the correct denotation y_i marginalized over logical forms z. Formally, we maximize the objective function

$$J(\theta) = \frac{1}{N} \sum_{i=1}^{N} \log p_\theta(y_i \mid x_i, w_i) - \lambda \|\theta\|_1, \quad (2)$$

where w_i is deterministically generated from t_i, and

$$p_\theta(y \mid x, w) = \sum_{z \in \mathcal{Z}_x; y = [\![z]\!]_w} p_\theta(z \mid x, w). \quad (3)$$

We optimize θ using AdaGrad (Duchi et al., 2010), running 3 passes over the data. We use L_1 regularization with $\lambda = 3 \times 10^{-5}$ obtained from cross-validation.

The following sections explain individual system components in more detail.

4 Knowledge graph

Inspired by the graph representation of knowledge bases, we preprocess the table t by deterministically converting it into a *knowledge graph* w as illustrated in Figure 3. In the most basic form, table rows become row nodes, strings in table cells become entity nodes,[1] and table columns become directed edges from the row nodes to the entity nodes of that column. The column headers are used as edge labels for these row-entity relations.

[1]Two occurrences of the same string constitute one node.

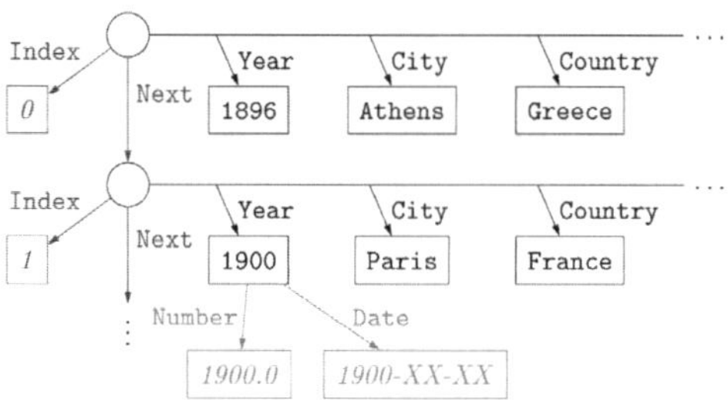

Figure 3: Part of the knowledge graph corresponding to the table in Figure 1. Circular nodes are row nodes. We augment the graph with different entity normalization nodes such as `Number` and `Date` (red) and additional row node relations `Next` and `Index` (blue).

The knowledge graph representation is convenient for three reasons. First, we can encode different forms of entity normalization in the graph. Some entity strings (e.g., *"1900"*) can be interpreted as a number, a date, or a proper name depending on the context, while some other strings (e.g., *"200 km"*) have multiple parts. Instead of committing to one normalization scheme, we introduce edges corresponding to different normalization methods from the entity nodes. For example, the node `1900` will have an edge called `Date` to another node *1900-XX-XX* of type date. Apart from type checking, these normalization nodes also aid learning by providing signals on the appropriate answer type. For instance, we can define a feature that associates the phrase *"how many"* with a logical form that says "traverse a row-entity edge, then a `Number` edge" instead of just "traverse a row-entity edge."

The second benefit of the graph representation is its ability to handle various logical phenomena via graph augmentation. For example, to answer questions of the form *"What is the next ... ?"* or *"Who came before ... ?"*, we augment each row node with an edge labeled `Next` pointing to the next row node, after which the questions can be answered by traversing the `Next` edge. In this work, we choose to add two special edges on each row node: the `Next` edge mentioned above and an `Index` edge pointing to the row index number (*0*, *1*, *2*, ...).

Finally, with a graph representation, we can query it directly using a logical formalism for knowledge graphs, which we turn to next.

Name	Example
Join	City.Athens
	(row nodes with a City edge to Athens)
Union	City.(Athens ⊔ Beijing)
Intersection	City.Athens ⊓ Year.Number.<.*1990*
Reverse	**R**[Year].City.Athens
	(entities where a row in City.Athens has a Year edge to)
Aggregation	count(City.Athens)
	(the number of rows with city Athens)
Superlative	argmax(City.Athens, Index)
	(the last row with city Athens)
Arithmetic	sub(*204*, *201*) (= 204 − 201)
Lambda	λx[Year.Date.x]
	(a binary: composition of two relations)

Table 1: The lambda DCS operations we use.

Rule	Semantics	Example
Anchored to the utterance		
TokenSpan → *Entity*	match(z_1)	Greece
(match(s) = entity with name s)		anchored to *"Greece"*
TokenSpan → *Atomic*	val(z_1)	*2012-07-XX*
(val(s) = interpreted value)		anchored to *"July 2012"*
Unanchored (floating)		
∅ → *Relation*	r	Country
(r = row-entity relation)		
∅ → *Relation*	$\lambda x[r.p.x]$	λx[Year.Date.x]
(p = normalization relation)		
∅ → *Records*	Type.Row	(list of all rows)
∅ → *RecordFn*	Index	(row ← row index)

Table 2: Base deduction rules. Entities and atomic values (e.g., numbers, dates) are anchored to token spans, while other predicates are kept floating. ($a \leftarrow b$ represents a binary mapping b to a.)

5 Logical forms

As our language for logical forms, we use lambda dependency-based compositional semantics (Liang, 2013), or lambda DCS, which we briefly describe here. Each lambda DCS logical form is either a *unary* (denoting a list of values) or a *binary* (denoting a list of pairs). The most basic unaries are singletons (e.g., China represents an entity node, and *30* represents a single number), while the most basic binaries are relations (e.g., City maps rows to city entities, Next maps rows to rows, and >= maps numbers to numbers). Logical forms can be combined into larger ones via various operations listed in Table 1. Each operation produces a unary except lambda abstraction: $\lambda x[f(x)]$ is a binary mapping x to $f(x)$.

6 Parsing and ranking

Given the knowledge graph w, we now describe how to parse the utterance x into a set of candidate logical forms $\mathcal{Z}_x$

6.1 Parsing algorithm

We propose a new *floating parser* which is more flexible than a standard chart parser. Both parsers recursively build up derivations and corresponding logical forms by repeatedly applying deduction rules, but the floating parser allows logical form predicates to be generated independently from the utterance.

Chart parser. We briefly review the CKY algorithm for chart parsing to introduce notation. Given an utterance with tokens $x_1, \dots, x_n$, the CKY algorithm applies deduction rules of the following two kinds:

$$(\mathit{TokenSpan}, i, j)[s] \rightarrow (c, i, j)[f(s)], \quad (4)$$

$$(c_1, i, k)[z_1] + (c_2, k+1, j)[z_2] \rightarrow (c, i, j)[f(z_1, z_2)]. \quad (5)$$

The first rule is a lexical rule that matches an utterance token span $x_i \cdots x_j$ (e.g., $s =$ *"New York"*) and produces a logical form (e.g., $f(s) =$ NewYorkCity) with category c (e.g., Entity). The second rule takes two adjacent spans giving rise to logical forms z_1 and z_2 and builds a new logical form $f(z_1, z_2)$. Algorithmically, CKY stores derivations of category c covering the span $x_i \cdots x_j$ in a *cell* (c, i, j). CKY fills in the cells of increasing span lengths, and the logical forms in the top cell $(\mathit{ROOT}, 1, n)$ are returned.

Floating parser. Chart parsing uses lexical rules (4) to generate relevant logical predicates, but in our setting of semantic parsing on tables, we do not have the luxury of starting with or inducing a full-fledged lexicon. Moreover, there is a mismatch between words in the utterance and predicates in the logical form. For instance, consider the question *"Greece held its last Summer Olympics in which year?"* on the table in Figure 1 and the correct logical form **R**[λx[Year.Date.x]].argmax(Country.Greece, Index). While the entity Greece can be anchored to the token *"Greece"*, some logical predicates (e.g., Country) cannot be clearly anchored to a token span. We could potentially learn to anchor the logical form Country.Greece to *"Greece"*, but if the relation Country is not seen during training, such a mapping is impossible to learn from the training data. Similarly, some prominent tokens

Rule	Semantics	Example
		Join + Aggregate
Entity or *Atomic* → *Values*	z_1	China
Atomic → *Values*	$c.z_1$	>=.*30* (at least 30)
($c \in$ {<, >, <=, >=})		
Relation + *Values* → *Records*	$z_1.z_2$	Country.China (events (rows) where the country is China)
Relation + *Records* → *Values*	$\mathbf{R}[z_1].z_2$	**R**[Year].Country.China (years of events in China)
Records → *Records*	Next.z_1	Next.Country.China (... before China)
Records → *Records*	**R**[Next].z_1	**R**[Next].Country.China (... after China)
Values → *Atomic*	$a(z_1)$	count(Country.China) (How often did China ...)
($a \in$ {count, max, min, sum, avg})		
Values → *ROOT*	z_1	
		Superlative
Relation → *RecordFn*	z_1	λx[Nations.Number.x] (row ← value in Nations column)
Records + *RecordFn* → *Records*	$s(z_1, z_2)$	argmax(Type.Row, λx[Nations.Number.x])
($s \in$ {argmax, argmin})		(events with the most participating nations)
		argmin(City.Athens, Index) (first event in Athens)
Relation → *ValueFn*	$\mathbf{R}[\lambda x[a(z_1.x)]]$	**R**[λx[count(City.x)]] (city ← num. of rows with that city)
Relation + *Relation* → *ValueFn*	$\lambda x[\mathbf{R}[z_1].z_2.x]$	λx[**R**[City].Nations.Number.x]
		(city ← value in Nations column)
Values + *ValueFn* → *Values*	$s(z_1, z_2)$	argmax(..., **R**[λx[count(City.x)]]) (most frequent city)
		Other operations
ValueFn + *Values* + *Values* → *Values*	$o(\mathbf{R}[z_1].z_2, \mathbf{R}[z_1].z_3)$	sub(**R**[Number].**R**[Nations].City.London, ...)
($o \in$ {add, sub, mul, div})		(How many more participants were in London than ...)
Entity + *Entity* → *Values*	$z_1 \sqcup z_2$	China ⊔ France (China or France)
Records + *Records* → *Records*	$z_1 \sqcap z_2$	City.Beijing ⊓ Country.China (... in Beijing, China)

Table 3: Compositional deduction rules. Each rule $c_1, \ldots, c_k \rightarrow c$ takes logical forms $z_1, \ldots, z_k$ constructed over categories $c_1, \ldots, c_k$, respectively, and produces a logical form based on the semantics.

(e.g., *"Olympics"*) are irrelevant and have no predicates anchored to them.

Therefore, instead of anchoring each predicate in the logical form to tokens in the utterance via lexical rules, we propose parsing more freely. We replace the anchored cells (c, i, j) with *floating cells* (c, s) of category c and logical form size s. Then we apply rules of the following three kinds:

$$(\textit{TokenSpan}, i, j)[s] \rightarrow (c, 1)[f(s)], \quad (6)$$

$$\emptyset \rightarrow (c, 1)[f()], \quad (7)$$

$$(c_1, s_1)[z_1] + (c_2, s_2)[z_2] \quad (8)$$
$$\rightarrow (c, s_1 + s_2 + 1)[f(z_1, z_2)].$$

Note that rules (6) are similar to (4) in chart parsing except that the floating cell $(c, 1)$ only keeps track of the category and its size 1, not the span (i, j). Rules (7) allow us to construct predicates out of thin air. For example, we can construct a logical form representing a table relation Country in cell (*Relation*, 1) using the rule $\emptyset \rightarrow$ *Relation* [Country] independent of the utterance. Rules (8) perform composition, where the induction is on the size s of the logical form rather than the span length. The algorithm stops when the specified maximum size is reached, after which the logical forms in cells (*ROOT*, s) for any s are included in $\mathcal{Z}_x$. Figure 4 shows an example derivation generated by our floating parser.

Figure 4: A derivation for the utterance *"Greece held its last Summer Olympics in which year?"* Only Greece is anchored to a phrase *"Greece"*; Year and other predicates are floating.

The floating parser is very flexible: it can skip tokens and combine logical forms in any order. This flexibility might seem too unconstrained, but we can use strong typing constraints to prevent nonsensical derivations from being constructed.

Tables 2 and 3 show the full set of deduction rules we use. We assume that all named entities will explicitly appear in the question x, so we an-

"Greece held its last Summer Olympics in which year?"
$z = \mathbf{R}[\lambda x[\texttt{Year.Number}.x]].\texttt{argmax}(\texttt{Type.Row}, \texttt{Index})$
$y = \{2012\}$ (type: NUM, column: YEAR)

Feature Name	Note
(*"last"*, predicate = `argmax`)	lex
phrase = predicate	unlex ($\because$ *"year"* = `Year`)
missing entity	unlex ($\because$ missing *Greece*)
denotation type = NUM	
denotation column = YEAR	
(*"which year"*, type = NUM)	lex
phrase = column	unlex ($\because$ *"year"* = YEAR)
(Q = *"which"*, type = NUM)	lex
(H = *"year"*, type = NUM)	lex
H = column	unlex ($\because$ *"year"* = YEAR)

Table 4: Example features that fire for the (incorrect) logical form z. All features are binary. (lex = lexicalized)

chor all entity predicates (e.g., `Greece`) to token spans (e.g., *"Greece"*). We also anchor all numerical values (numbers, dates, percentages, etc.) detected by an NER system. In contrast, relations (e.g., `Country`) and operations (e.g., `argmax`) are kept floating since we want to learn how they are expressed in language. Connections between phrases in x and the generated relations and operations in z are established in the ranking model through features.

6.2 Features

We define features $\phi(x, w, z)$ for our log-linear model to capture the relationship between the question x and the candidate z. Table 4 shows some example features from each feature type. Most features are of the form $(f(x), g(z))$ or $(f(x), h(y))$ where $y = [\![z]\!]_w$ is the denotation, and f, g, and h extract some information (e.g., identity, POS tags) from x, z, or y, respectively.

phrase-predicate: Conjunctions between n-grams $f(x)$ from x and predicates $g(z)$ from z. We use both lexicalized features, where all possible pairs $(f(x), g(z))$ form distinct features, and binary unlexicalized features indicating whether $f(x)$ and $g(z)$ have a string match.

missing-predicate: Indicators on whether there are entities or relations mentioned in x but not in z. These features are unlexicalized.

denotation: Size and type of the denotation $y = [\![x]\!]_w$. The type can be either a primitive type (e.g., NUM, DATE, ENTITY) or the name of the column containing the entity in y (e.g., CITY).

phrase-denotation: Conjunctions between n-grams from x and the types of y. Similar to the phrase-predicate features, we use both lexicalized and unlexicalized features.

headword-denotation: Conjunctions between the question word Q (e.g., *what, who, how many*) or the headword H (the first noun after the question word) with the types of y.

6.3 Generation and pruning

Due to their recursive nature, the rules allow us to generate highly compositional logical forms. However, the compositionality comes at the cost of generating exponentially many logical forms, most of which are redundant (e.g., logical forms with an `argmax` operation on a set of size 1). We employ several methods to deal with this combinatorial explosion:

Beam search. We compute the model probability of each partial logical form based on available features (i.e., features that do not depend on the final denotation) and keep only the $K = 200$ highest-scoring logical forms in each cell.

Pruning. We prune partial logical forms that lead to invalid or redundant final logical forms. For example, we eliminate any logical form that does not type check (e.g., $\texttt{Beijing} \sqcup \texttt{Greece}$), executes to an empty list (e.g., `Year.Number`.*24*), includes an aggregate or superlative on a singleton set (e.g., `argmax(Year.Number`.*2012*, `Index)`), or joins two relations that are the reverses of each other (e.g., $\mathbf{R}$[`City`].`City.Beijing`).

7 Experiments

7.1 Main evaluation

We evaluate the system on the development sets (three random 80:20 splits of the training data) and the test data. In both settings, the tables we test on do not appear during training.

Evaluation metrics. Our main metric is *accuracy*, which is the number of examples (x, t, y) on which the system outputs the correct answer y. We also report the *oracle* score, which counts the number of examples where at least one generated candidate $z \in \mathcal{Z}_x$ executes to y.

Baselines. We compare the system to two baselines. The first baseline (IR), which simulates information retrieval, selects an answer y among the entities in the table using a log-linear model over entities (table cells) rather than logical forms. The features are conjunctions between phrases in x and properties of the answers y, which cover all features in our main system that do not involve the logical form. As an upper bound of this baseline,

	dev		test	
	acc	**ora**	**acc**	**ora**
IR baseline	13.4	69.1	12.7	70.6
WQ baseline	23.6	34.4	24.3	35.6
Our system	37.0	76.7	37.1	76.6

Table 5: Accuracy (acc) and oracle scores (ora) on the development sets (3 random splits of the training data) and the test data.

	acc	ora
Our system	37.0	76.7
(a) **Rule Ablation**		
join only	10.6	15.7
join + count (= WQ baseline)	23.6	34.4
join + count + superlative	30.7	68.6
all − $\{\sqcap, \sqcup\}$	34.8	75.1
(b) **Feature Ablation**		
all − features involving predicate	11.8	74.5
all − phrase-predicate	16.9	74.5
all − lex phrase-predicate	17.6	75.9
all − unlex phrase-predicate	34.3	76.7
all − missing-predicate	35.9	76.7
all − features involving denotation	33.5	76.8
all − denotation	34.3	76.6
all − phrase-denotation	35.7	76.8
all − headword-denotation	36.0	76.7
(c) **Anchor operations to trigger words**	37.1	59.4

Table 6: Average accuracy and oracle scores on development data in various system settings.

69.1% of the development examples have the answer appearing as an entity in the table.

In the second baseline (WQ), we only allow deduction rules that produce join and count logical forms. This rule subset has the same logical coverage as Berant and Liang (2014), which is designed to handle the WEBQUESTIONS (Berant et al., 2013) and FREE917 (Cai and Yates, 2013) datasets.

Results. Table 5 shows the results compared to the baselines. Our system gets an accuracy of 37.1% on the test data, which is significantly higher than both baselines, while the oracle is 76.6%. The next subsections analyze the system components in more detail.

7.2 Dataset statistics

In this section, we analyze the breadth and depth of the WIKITABLEQUESTIONS dataset, and how the system handles them.

Number of relations. With 3,929 unique column headers (relations) among 13,396 columns, the tables in the WIKITABLEQUESTIONS dataset contain many more relations than closed-domain datasets such as Geoquery (Zelle and Mooney, 1996) and ATIS (Price, 1990). Additionally, the logical forms that execute to the correct denotations refer to a total of 2,056 unique column headers, which is greater than the number of relations in the FREE917 dataset (635 Freebase relations).

Operation	**Amount**
join (table lookup)	13.5%
+ join with `Next`	+ 5.5%
+ aggregate (`count`, `sum`, `max`, ...)	+ 15.0%
+ superlative (`argmax`, `argmin`)	+ 24.5%
+ arithmetic, $\sqcap$, $\sqcup$	+ 20.5%
+ other phenomena	+ 21.0%

Table 7: The logical operations required to answer the questions in 200 random examples.

Knowledge coverage. We sampled 50 examples from the dataset and tried to answer them manually using Freebase. Even though Freebase contains some information extracted from Wikipedia, we can answer only 20% of the questions, indicating that WIKITABLEQUESTIONS contains a broad set of facts beyond Freebase.

Logical operation coverage. The dataset covers a wide range of question types and logical operations. Table 6(a) shows the drop in oracle scores when different subsets of rules are used to generate candidates logical forms. The *join only* subset corresponds to simple table lookup, while *join + count* is the WQ baseline for Freebase question answering on the WEBQUESTIONS dataset. Finally, *join + count + superlative* roughly corresponds to the coverage of the Geoquery dataset.

To better understand the distribution of logical operations in the WIKITABLEQUESTIONS dataset, we manually classified 200 examples based on the types of operations required to answer the question. The statistics in Table 7 shows that while a few questions only require simple operations such as table lookup, the majority of the questions demands more advanced operations. Additionally, 21% of the examples cannot be answered using any logical form generated from the current deduction rules; these examples are discussed in Section 7.4.

Compositionality. From each example, we compute the logical form size (number of rules applied) of the highest-scoring candidate that executes to the correct denotation. The histogram in Figure 5 shows that a significant number of logical forms are non-trivial.

Beam size and pruning. Figure 6 shows the results with and without pruning on various beam

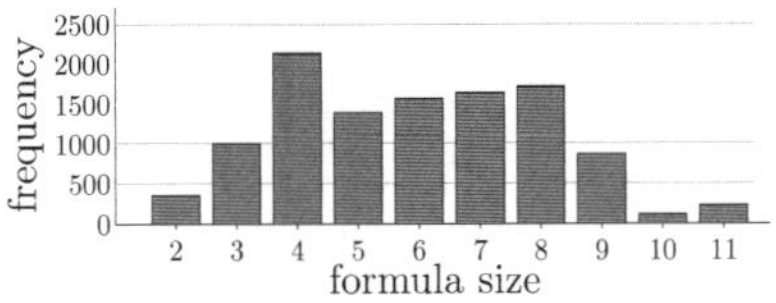

Figure 5: Sizes of the highest-scoring correct candidate logical forms in development examples.

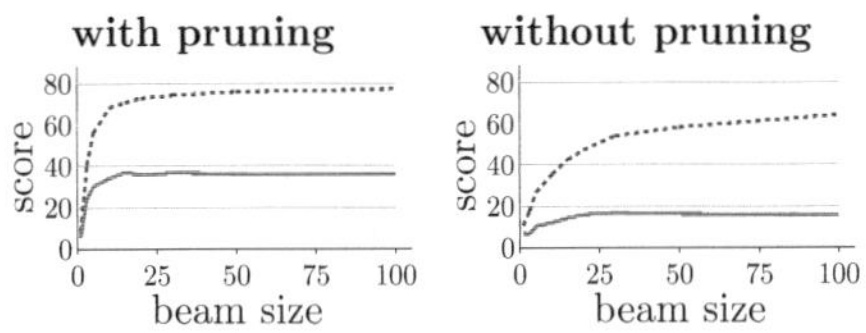

Figure 6: Accuracy (solid red) and oracle (dashed blue) scores with different beam sizes.

sizes. Apart from saving time, pruning also prevents bad logical forms from clogging up the beam which hurts both oracle and accuracy metrics.

7.3 Features

Effect of features. Table 6(b) shows the accuracy when some feature types are ablated. The most influential features are lexicalized phrase-predicate features, which capture the relationship between phrases and logical operations (e.g., relating *"last"* to `argmax`) as well as between phrases and relations (e.g., relating *"before"* to < or `Next`, and relating *"who"* to the relation `Name`).

Anchoring with trigger words. In our parsing algorithm, relations and logical operations are not anchored to the utterance. We consider an alternative approach where logical operations are anchored to "trigger" phrases, which are hand-coded based on co-occurrence statistics (e.g., we trigger a `count` logical form with *how*, *many*, and *total*).

Table 6(c) shows that the trigger words do not significantly impact the accuracy, suggesting that the original system is already able to learn the relationship between phrases and operations even without a manual lexicon. As an aside, the huge drop in oracle is because fewer "semantically incorrect" logical forms are generated; we discuss this phenomenon in the next subsection.

7.4 Semantically correct logical forms

In our setting, we face a new challenge that arises from learning with denotations: with deeper compositionality, a larger number of nonsensical logical forms can execute to the correct denotation. For example, if the target answer is a small number (say, 2), it is possible to count the number of rows with some random properties and arrive at the correct answer. However, as the system encounters more examples, it can potentially learn to disfavor them by recognizing the characteristics of semantically correct logical forms.

Generating semantically correct logical forms. The system can learn the features of semantically correct logical forms only if it can generate them in the first place. To see how well the system can generate correct logical forms, looking at the oracle score is insufficient since bad logical forms can execute to the correct denotations. Instead, we randomly chose 200 examples and manually annotated them with logical forms to see if a trained system can produce the annotated logical form as a candidate.

Out of 200 examples, we find that 79% can be manually annotated. The remaining ones include artifacts such as unhandled question types (e.g., yes-no questions, or questions with phrases *"same"* or *"consecutive"*), table cells that require advanced normalization methods (e.g., cells with comma-separated lists), and incorrect annotations.

The system generates the annotated logical form among the candidates in 53.5% of the examples. The missing examples are mostly caused by anchoring errors due to lexical mismatch (e.g., *"Italian"* $\rightarrow$ `Italy`, or *"no zip code"* $\rightarrow$ an empty cell in the zip code column) or the need to generate complex logical forms from a single phrase (e.g., *"May 2010"* $\rightarrow$ >=.*2010-05-01*⊓<=.*2010-05-31*).

7.5 Error analysis

The errors on the development data can be divided into four groups. The first two groups are unhandled question types (21%) and the failure to anchor entities (25%) as described in Section 7.4. The third group is normalization and type errors (29%): although we handle some forms of entity normalization, we observe many unhandled string formats such as times (e.g., *3:45.79*) and city-country pairs (e.g., *Beijing, China*), as well as complex calculation such as computing time periods (e.g., *12pm–1am* $\rightarrow$ 1 hour). Finally, we have ranking errors (25%) which mostly occur when the utterance phrase and the relation are obliquely related (e.g., *"airplane"* and `Model`).

8 Discussion

Our work simultaneously increases the breadth of knowledge source and the depth of compositionality in semantic parsing. This section explores the connections in both aspects to related work.

Logical coverage. Different semantic parsing systems are designed to handle different sets of logical operations and degrees of compositionality. For example, form-filling systems (Wang et al., 2011) usually cover a smaller scope of operations and compositionality, while early statistical semantic parsers for question answering (Wong and Mooney, 2007; Zettlemoyer and Collins, 2007) and high-accuracy natural language interfaces for databases (Androutsopoulos et al., 1995; Popescu et al., 2003) target more compositional utterances with a wide range of logical operations. This work aims to increase the logical coverage even further. For example, compared to the Geoquery dataset, the WIKITABLEQUESTIONS dataset includes a move diverse set of logical operations, and while it does not have extremely compositional questions like in Geoquery (e.g., *"What states border states that border states that border Florida?"*), our dataset contains fairly compositional questions on average.

To parse a compositional utterance, many works rely on a lexicon that translates phrases to entities, relations, and logical operations. A lexicon can be automatically generated (Unger and Cimiano, 2011; Unger et al., 2012), learned from data (Zettlemoyer and Collins, 2007; Kwiatkowski et al., 2011), or extracted from external sources (Cai and Yates, 2013; Berant et al., 2013), but requires some techniques to generalize to unseen data. Our work takes a different approach similar to the logical form growing algorithm in Berant and Liang (2014) by not anchoring relations and operations to the utterance.

Knowledge domain. Recent works on semantic parsing for question answering operate on more open and diverse data domains. In particular, large-scale knowledge bases have gained popularity in the semantic parsing community (Cai and Yates, 2013; Berant et al., 2013; Fader et al., 2014). The increasing number of relations and entities motivates new resources and techniques for improving the accuracy, including the use of ontology matching models (Kwiatkowski et al., 2013), paraphrase models (Fader et al., 2013; Berant and Liang, 2014), and unlabeled sentences (Krishnamurthy and Kollar, 2013; Reddy et al., 2014).

Our work leverages open-ended data from the Web through semi-structured tables. There have been several studies on analyzing or inferring the table schemas (Cafarella et al., 2008; Venetis et al., 2011; Syed et al., 2010; Limaye et al., 2010) and answering search queries by joining tables on similar columns (Cafarella et al., 2008; Gonzalez et al., 2010; Pimplikar and Sarawagi, 2012). While the latter is similar to question answering, the queries tend to be keyword lists instead of natural language sentences. In parallel, open information extraction (Wu and Weld, 2010; Masaum et al., 2012) and knowledge base population (Ji and Grishman, 2011) extract information from web pages and compile them into structured data. The resulting knowledge base is systematically organized, but as a trade-off, some knowledge is inevitably lost during extraction and the information is forced to conform to a specific schema. To avoid these issues, we choose to work on HTML tables directly.

In future work, we wish to draw information from other semi-structured formats such as colon-delimited pairs (Wong et al., 2009), bulleted lists (Gupta and Sarawagi, 2009), and top-k lists (Zhang et al., 2013). Pasupat and Liang (2014) used a framework similar to ours to extract entities from web pages, where the "logical forms" were XPath expressions. A natural direction is to combine the logical compositionality of this work with the even broader knowledge source of general web pages.

Acknowledgements. We gratefully acknowledge the support of the Google Natural Language Understanding Focused Program and the Defense Advanced Research Projects Agency (DARPA) Deep Exploration and Filtering of Text (DEFT) Program under Air Force Research Laboratory (AFRL) contract no. FA8750-13-2-0040.

Data and reproducibility. The WIKITABLEQUESTIONS dataset can be downloaded at `http://nlp.stanford.edu/software/sempre/wikitable/`. Additionally, code, data, and experiments for this paper are available on the CodaLab platform at `https://www.codalab.org/worksheets/0xf26cd79d4d734287868923ad1067cf4c/`.

References

I. Androutsopoulos, G. D. Ritchie, and P. Thanisch. 1995. Natural language interfaces to databases –

an introduction. *Journal of Natural Language Engineering*, 1:29–81.

J. Berant and P. Liang. 2014. Semantic parsing via paraphrasing. In *Association for Computational Linguistics (ACL)*.

J. Berant, A. Chou, R. Frostig, and P. Liang. 2013. Semantic parsing on Freebase from question-answer pairs. In *Empirical Methods in Natural Language Processing (EMNLP)*.

M. J. Cafarella, A. Halevy, D. Z. Wang, E. Wu, and Y. Zhang. 2008. WebTables: exploring the power of tables on the web. In *Very Large Data Bases (VLDB)*, pages 538–549.

Q. Cai and A. Yates. 2013. Large-scale semantic parsing via schema matching and lexicon extension. In *Association for Computational Linguistics (ACL)*.

J. Duchi, E. Hazan, and Y. Singer. 2010. Adaptive subgradient methods for online learning and stochastic optimization. In *Conference on Learning Theory (COLT)*.

A. Fader, L. Zettlemoyer, and O. Etzioni. 2013. Paraphrase-driven learning for open question answering. In *Association for Computational Linguistics (ACL)*.

A. Fader, L. Zettlemoyer, and O. Etzioni. 2014. Open question answering over curated and extracted knowledge bases. In *International Conference on Knowledge Discovery and Data Mining (KDD)*, pages 1156–1165.

H. Gonzalez, A. Y. Halevy, C. S. Jensen, A. Langen, J. Madhavan, R. Shapley, W. Shen, and J. Goldberg-Kidon. 2010. Google fusion tables: web-centered data management and collaboration. In *Proceedings of the 2010 ACM SIGMOD International Conference on Management of data*, pages 1061–1066.

R. Gupta and S. Sarawagi. 2009. Answering table augmentation queries from unstructured lists on the web. In *Very Large Data Bases (VLDB)*, number 1, pages 289–300.

H. Ji and R. Grishman. 2011. Knowledge base population: Successful approaches and challenges. In *Association for Computational Linguistics (ACL)*, pages 1148–1158.

J. Krishnamurthy and T. Kollar. 2013. Jointly learning to parse and perceive: Connecting natural language to the physical world. *Transactions of the Association for Computational Linguistics (TACL)*, 1:193–206.

T. Kwiatkowski, L. Zettlemoyer, S. Goldwater, and M. Steedman. 2011. Lexical generalization in CCG grammar induction for semantic parsing. In *Empirical Methods in Natural Language Processing (EMNLP)*, pages 1512–1523.

T. Kwiatkowski, E. Choi, Y. Artzi, and L. Zettlemoyer. 2013. Scaling semantic parsers with on-the-fly ontology matching. In *Empirical Methods in Natural Language Processing (EMNLP)*.

P. Liang. 2013. Lambda dependency-based compositional semantics. *arXiv*.

G. Limaye, S. Sarawagi, and S. Chakrabarti. 2010. Annotating and searching web tables using entities, types and relationships. In *Very Large Data Bases (VLDB)*, volume 3, pages 1338–1347.

Masaum, M. Schmitz, R. Bart, S. Soderland, and O. Etzioni. 2012. Open language learning for information extraction. In *Empirical Methods in Natural Language Processing and Computational Natural Language Learning (EMNLP/CoNLL)*, pages 523–534.

P. Pasupat and P. Liang. 2014. Zero-shot entity extraction from web pages. In *Association for Computational Linguistics (ACL)*.

R. Pimplikar and S. Sarawagi. 2012. Answering table queries on the web using column keywords. In *Very Large Data Bases (VLDB)*, volume 5, pages 908–919.

A. Popescu, O. Etzioni, and H. Kautz. 2003. Towards a theory of natural language interfaces to databases. In *International Conference on Intelligent User Interfaces (IUI)*, pages 149–157.

P. Price. 1990. Evaluation of spoken language systems: The ATIS domain. In *Proceedings of the Third DARPA Speech and Natural Language Workshop*, pages 91–95.

S. Reddy, M. Lapata, and M. Steedman. 2014. Large-scale semantic parsing without question-answer pairs. *Transactions of the Association for Computational Linguistics (TACL)*, 2(10):377–392.

Z. Syed, T. Finin, V. Mulwad, and A. Joshi. 2010. Exploiting a web of semantic data for interpreting tables. In *Proceedings of the Second Web Science Conference*.

C. Unger and P. Cimiano. 2011. Pythia: compositional meaning construction for ontology-based question answering on the semantic web. In *Proceedings of the 16th international conference on Natural language processing and information systems*, pages 153–160.

C. Unger, L. Bühmann, J. Lehmann, A. Ngonga, D. Gerber, and P. Cimiano. 2012. Template-based question answering over RDF data. In *World Wide Web (WWW)*, pages 639–648.

P. Venetis, A. Halevy, J. Madhavan, M. Paşca, W. Shen, F. Wu, G. Miao, and C. Wu. 2011. Recovering semantics of tables on the web. In *Very Large Data Bases (VLDB)*, volume 4, pages 528–538.

Y. Wang, L. Deng, and A. Acero. 2011. Semantic frame-based spoken language understanding. *Spoken Language Understanding: Systems for Extracting Semantic Information from Speech*, pages 41–91.

Y. W. Wong and R. J. Mooney. 2007. Learning synchronous grammars for semantic parsing with lambda calculus. In *Association for Computational Linguistics (ACL)*, pages 960–967.

Y. W. Wong, D. Widdows, T. Lokovic, and K. Nigam. 2009. Scalable attribute-value extraction from semi-structured text. In *IEEE International Conference on Data Mining Workshops*, pages 302–307.

F. Wu and D. S. Weld. 2010. Open information extraction using Wikipedia. In *Association for Computational Linguistics (ACL)*, pages 118–127.

M. Zelle and R. J. Mooney. 1996. Learning to parse database queries using inductive logic programming. In *Association for the Advancement of Artificial Intelligence (AAAI)*, pages 1050–1055.

L. S. Zettlemoyer and M. Collins. 2007. Online learning of relaxed CCG grammars for parsing to logical form. In *Empirical Methods in Natural Language Processing and Computational Natural Language Learning (EMNLP/CoNLL)*, pages 678–687.

Z. Zhang, K. Q. Zhu, H. Wang, and H. Li. 2013. Automatic extraction of top-k lists from the web. In *International Conference on Data Engineering*.

Graph parsing with s-graph grammars

Jonas Groschwitz and **Alexander Koller** and **Christoph Teichmann**
Department of Linguistics
University of Potsdam
firstname.lastname@uni-potsdam.de

Abstract

A key problem in semantic parsing with graph-based semantic representations is *graph parsing*, i.e. computing all possible analyses of a given graph according to a grammar. This problem arises in training synchronous string-to-graph grammars, and when generating strings from them. We present two algorithms for graph parsing (bottom-up and top-down) with s-graph grammars. On the related problem of graph parsing with hyperedge replacement grammars, our implementations outperform the best previous system by several orders of magnitude.

1 Introduction

The recent years have seen an increased interest in *semantic parsing*, the problem of deriving a semantic representation for natural-language expressions with data-driven methods. With the recent availability of graph-based meaning banks (Banarescu et al., 2013; Oepen et al., 2014), much work has focused on computing graph-based semantic representations from strings (Jones et al., 2012; Flanigan et al., 2014; Martins and Almeida, 2014).

One major approach to graph-based semantic parsing is to learn an explicit synchronous grammar which relates strings with graphs. One can then apply methods from statistical parsing to parse the string and read off the graph. Chiang et al. (2013) and Quernheim and Knight (2012) represent this mapping of a (latent) syntactic structure to a graph with a grammar formalism called *hyperedge replacement grammar* (HRG; (Drewes et al., 1997)). As an alternative to HRG, Koller (2015) introduced *s-graph grammars* and showed that they support linguistically reasonable grammars for graph-based semantics construction.

One problem that is only partially understood in the context of semantic parsing with explicit grammars is *graph parsing*, i.e. the computation of the possible analyses the grammar assigns to an input *graph* (as opposed to string). This problem arises whenever one tries to generate a string from a graph (e.g., on the generation side of an MT system), but also in the context of extracting and training a synchronous grammar, e.g. in EM training. The state of the art is defined by the bottom-up graph parsing algorithm for HRG by Chiang et al. (2013), implemented in the Bolinas tool (Andreas et al., 2013).

We present two graph parsing algorithms (top-down and bottom-up) for s-graph grammars. S-graph grammars are equivalent to HRGs, but employ a more fine-grained perspective on graph-combining operations. This simplifies the parsing algorithms, and facilitates reasoning about them. Our bottom-up algorithm is similar to Chiang et al.'s, and derives the same asymptotic number of rule instances. The top-down algorithm is novel, and achieves the same asymptotic runtime as the bottom-up algorithm by reasoning about the biconnected components of the graph. Our evaluation on the "Little Prince" graph-bank shows that our implementations of both algorithms outperform Bolinas by several orders of magnitude. Furthermore, the top-down algorithm can be more memory-efficient in practice.

2 Related work

The AMR-Bank (Banarescu et al., 2013) annotates sentences with *abstract meaning representations (AMRs)*, like the one shown in Fig. 1(a). These are graphs that represent the predicate-argument structure of a sentence; notably, phenomena such as control are represented by reentrancies in the graph. Another major graph-bank is the SemEval-2014 shared task on semantic dependency parsing dataset (Oepen et al., 2014).

Proceedings of the 53rd Annual Meeting of the Association for Computational Linguistics and the 7th International Joint Conference on Natural Language Processing, pages 1481–1490, Beijing, China, July 26-31, 2015.

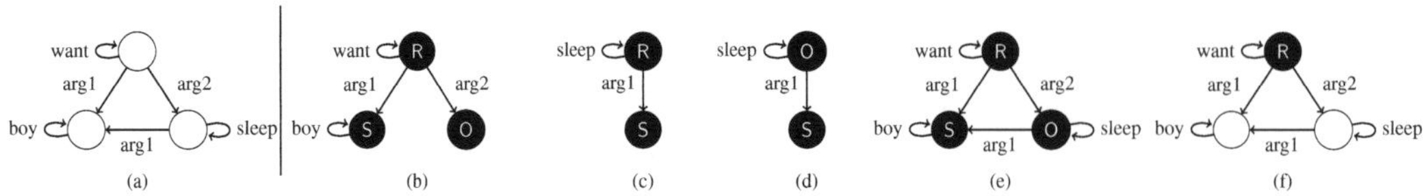

Figure 1: AMR (a) for 'The boy wants to sleep', and s-graphs. We call (b) SG_{want} and (c) SG_{sleep}.

The primary grammar formalism currently in use for synchronous graph grammars is *hyperedge replacement grammar (HRG)* (Drewes et al., 1997), which we sketch in Section 4.3. An alternative is offered by Koller (2015), who introduced *s-graph grammars* and showed that they lend themselves to manually written grammars for semantic construction. In this paper, we show the equivalence of HRG and s-graph grammars and work out graph parsing for s-graph grammars.

The first polynomial graph parsing algorithm for HRGs on graphs with limited connectivity was presented by Lautemann (1988). Lautemann's original algorithm is a top-down parser, which is presented at a rather abstract level that does not directly support implementation or detailed complexity analysis. We extend Lautemann's work by showing how new parse items can be represented and constructed efficiently. Finally, Chiang et al. (2013) presented a bottom-up graph parser for HRGs, in which the representation and construction of items was worked out for the first time. It produces $O((n \cdot 3^d)^{k+1})$ instances of the rules in a parsing schema, where n is the number of nodes of the graph, d is the maximum degree of any node, and k is a quantity called the *tree-width* of the grammar.

3 An algebra of graphs

We start by introducing the exact type of graphs that our grammars and parsers manipulate, and by developing some theory.

Throughout this paper, we define a *graph* $G = (V, E)$ as a directed graph with edge labels from some label alphabet L. The graph consists of a finite set V of nodes and a finite set $E \subseteq V \times V \times L$ of edges $e = (u, v, l)$, where u and v are the nodes connected by e, and $l \in L$ is the *edge label*. We say that e is *incident* to both u and v, and call the number of edges incident to a node its *degree*. We write $u \overset{e}{\leftrightarrow} v$ if either $e = (u, v, l)$ or $e = (v, u, l)$ for some l; we drop the e if the identity of the edge is irrelevant. Edges with $u = v$ are called *loops*; we use them here to encode node labels. Given a graph G, we write $n = |V|$, $m = |E|$, and d for the maximum degree of any node in V.

If $f : A \rightsquigarrow B$ and $g : A \rightsquigarrow B$ are partial functions, we let the partial function $f \cup g$ be defined if for all $a \in A$ with both $f(a)$ and $g(a)$ defined, we have $f(a) = g(a)$. We then let $(f \cup g)(a)$ be $f(a)$ if $f(a)$ is defined; $g(a)$ if $g(a)$ is defined; and undefined otherwise.

3.1 The HR algebra of graphs with sources

Our grammars describe how to build graphs from smaller pieces. They do this by accessing nodes (called *source nodes*) which are assigned "public names". We define an *s-graph* (Courcelle and Engelfriet, 2012) as a pair $SG = (G, \phi)$ of a graph G and a *source assignment*, i.e. a partial, injective function $\phi : S \rightsquigarrow V$ that maps some *source names* from a finite set S to the nodes of G. We call the nodes in $\phi(S)$ the *source nodes* or *sources* of SG; all other nodes are *internal nodes*. If ϕ is defined on the source name σ, we call $\phi(\sigma)$ the *σ-source* of SG. Throughout, we let $s = |S|$.

Examples of s-graphs are given in Fig. 1. We use numbers as node names and lowercase strings for edge names (except in the concrete graphs of Fig. 1, where the edges are marked with edge labels instead). Source nodes are drawn in black, with source names drawn on the inside. Fig. 1(b) shows an s-graph SG_{want} with three nodes and four edges. The three nodes are marked as the R-, S-, and O-source, respectively. Likewise, the s-graph SG_{sleep} in (c) has two nodes (one of which is an R-source and the other an S-source) and two edges.

We can now apply operations to these graphs. First, we can *rename* the R-source of (c) to an O-source. The result, denoted $SG_d = SG_{sleep}[\mathsf{R} \rightarrow \mathsf{O}]$, is shown in (d). Next, we can *merge* SG_d with SG_{want}. This copies the edges and nodes of SG_d and SG_{want} into a new s-graph; but crucially, for every source name σ the two s-graphs have in common, the σ-sources of the graphs are fused into a single node (and become a σ-source of the result). We write $||$ for the merge operation;

thus we obtain $SG_e = SG_d \mid\mid SG_{want}$, shown in (e). Finally, we can *forget* source names. The graph $SG_f = \mathsf{f_S}(\mathsf{f_O}(SG_e))$, in which we forgot S and O, is shown in (f). We refer to Courcelle and Engelfriet (2012) for technical details.[1]

We can take the set of all s-graphs, together with these operations, as an *algebra* of s-graphs. In addition to the binary merge operation and the unary operations for forget and rename, we fix some finite set of *atomic* s-graphs and take them as constants of the algebra which evaluate to themselves. Following Courcelle and Engelfriet, we call this algebra the *HR algebra*. We can *evaluate* any term τ consisting of these operation symbols into an s-graph $[\![\tau]\!]$ as usual. For instance, the following term encodes the merge, forget, and rename operations from the example above, and evaluates to the s-graph in Fig. 1(f).

(1) $\mathsf{f_S}(\mathsf{f_O}(SG_{want} \mid\mid SG_{sleep}[\mathsf{R} \rightarrow \mathsf{O}]))$

The set of s-graphs that can be represented as the value $[\![\tau]\!]$ of some term τ over the HR algebra depends on the source set S and on the constants. For simplicity, we assume here that we have a constant for each s-graph consisting of a single labeled edge (or loop), and that the values of all other constants can be expressed by combining these using merge, rename, and forget.

3.2 S-components

A central question in graph parsing is how some s-graph that is a subgraph of a larger s-graph SG (a *sub-s-graph*) can be represented as the merge of two smaller sub-s-graphs of SG. In general, $SG_1 \mid\mid SG_2$ is defined for any two s-graphs SG_1 and SG_2. However, if we see SG_1 and SG_2 as subgraphs of SG, $SG_1 \mid\mid SG_2$ may no longer be a subgraph of SG. For instance, we cannot merge the s-graphs (b) and (c) in Fig. 2 as part of the graph (a): The startpoints of the edges a and d are both A-sources and would thus become the same node (unlike in (a)), and furthermore the edge d would have to be duplicated. In graph parsing, we already know the identity of all nodes and edges in sub-s-graphs (as nodes and edges in SG), and must thus pay attention that merge operations do not accidentally fuse or duplicate them. In particular, two sub-s-graphs cannot be merged if they have edges in common.

[1] Note that the rename operation of Courcelle and Engelfriet (2012) allows for swapping source assignments and making multiple renames in one step. We simplify the presentation here, but all of our techniques extend easily.

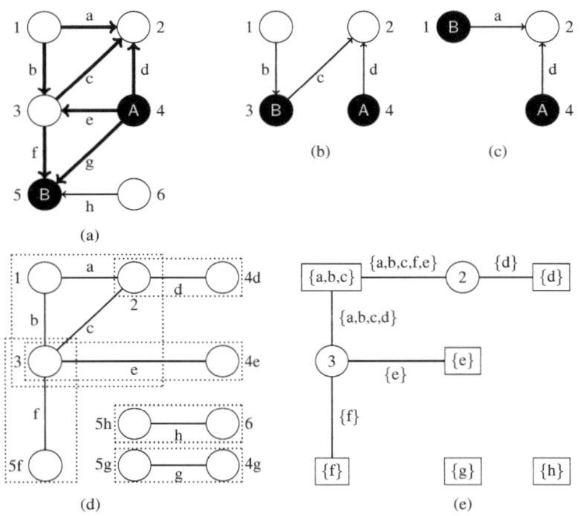

Figure 2: (a) An s-graph with (b,c) some sub-s-graphs, (d) its BCCs, and (e) its block-cutpoint graph.

We call a sub-s-graph SG_1 of SG *extensible* if there is another sub-s-graph SG_2 of SG such that $SG_1 \mid\mid SG_2$ contains the same edges as SG. An example of a sub-s-graph that is not extensible is the sub-s-graph (b) of the s-graph in (a) in Fig. 2. Because sources can only be renamed or forgotten by the algebra operations, but never introduced, we can never attach the missing edge a: this can only happen when 1 and 2 are sources. As a general rule, a sub-s-graph can only be extensible if it contains all edges that are adjacent to all of its internal nodes in SG. Obviously, a graph parser need only concern itself with sub-s-graphs that are extensible.

We can further clarify the structure of extensible sub-s-graphs by looking at the *s-components* of a graph. Let $U \subseteq V$ be some set of nodes. This set splits the edges of G into equivalence classes that are separated by U. We say that two edges $e, f \in E$ are *equivalent* with respect to U, $e \sim_U f$, if there is a sequence $v_1 \overset{e}{\leftrightarrow} v_2 \leftrightarrow \ldots v_{k-1} \overset{f}{\leftrightarrow} v_k$ with $v_2, \ldots, v_{k-1} \notin U$, i.e. if we can reach f from an endpoint of e without visiting a node in U. We call the equivalence classes of E with respect to $\sim_U$ the *s-components* of G and denote the s-component that contains an edge e with $[e]$. In Fig. 2(a), the edges a and f are equivalent with respect to $U = \{4, 5\}$, but a and h are not. The s-components are $[a] = \{a, b, c, d, e, f\}$, $[g] = \{g\}$, and $[h] = \{h\}$.

It can be shown that for any s-graph $SG =$

(G, ϕ), a sub-s-graph SH with source nodes U is extensible iff its edge set is the union of a set of s-components of G with respect to U. We let an *s-component representation* $\mathcal{C} = (C, \phi)$ in the s-graph $SG = (G, \phi')$ consist of a source assignment $\phi : S \rightsquigarrow V$ and a set C of s-components of G with respect to the set $\mathrm{VS}_{\mathcal{C}} = \phi(S) \subseteq V$ of source nodes of ϕ. Then we can represent every extensible sub-s-graph $SH = (H, \phi)$ of SG by the s-component representation $\mathcal{C} = (C, \phi)$ where C is the set of s-components of which SH consists. Conversely, we write $T(\mathcal{C})$ for the unique extensible sub-s-graph of SG represented by the s-component representation $\mathcal{C}$.

The utility of s-component representations derives from the fact that merge can be evaluated on these representations alone, as follows.

Lemma 1. *Let $\mathcal{C} = (C, \phi), \mathcal{C}_1 = (C_1, \phi_1), \mathcal{C}_2 = (C_2, \phi_2)$ be s-component representations in the s-graph SG. Then $T(\mathcal{C}) = T(\mathcal{C}_1) \mid\mid T(\mathcal{C}_2)$ iff $C = C_1 \uplus C_2$ (i.e., disjoint union) and $\phi_1 \cup \phi_2$ is defined, injective, and equal to ϕ.*

3.3 Boundary representations

If there is no $\mathcal{C}$ such that all conditions of Lemma 1 are satisfied, then $T(\mathcal{C}_1) \mid\mid T(\mathcal{C}_2)$ is not defined. In order to check this efficiently in the bottom-up parser, it will be useful to represent s-components explicitly via their *boundary*.

Consider an s-component representation $\mathcal{C} = (C, \phi)$ in SG and let E be the set of all edges that are adjacent to a source node in $\mathrm{VS}_{\mathcal{C}}$ and contained in an s-component in C. Then we let the *boundary representation (BR)* β of $\mathcal{C}$ in the s-graph SG be the pair $\beta = (E, \phi)$. That is, β represents the s-components through the *in-boundary edges*, i.e. those edges inside the s-components (and thus the sub-s-graph) which are adjacent to a source. The BR β specifies $\mathcal{C}$ uniquely if the base graph SG is connected, so we write $T(\beta)$ for $T(\mathcal{C})$ and VS_{β} for $\mathrm{VS}_{\mathcal{C}}$.

In Fig. 2(a), the bold sub-s-graph is represented by $\beta = \langle\{d, e, f, g\}, \{\mathsf{A}{:}4, \mathsf{B}{:}5\}\rangle$, indicating that it contains the A-source 4 and the B-source 5; and further, that the edge set of the sub-s-graph is $[d] \cup [e] \cup [f] \cup [g] = \{a, b, c, d, e, f, g\}$. The edge h (which is also incident to 5) is not specified, and therefore not in the sub-s-graph.

The following lemma can be shown about computing merge on boundary representations. Intuitively, the conditions (b) and (c) guarantee that the component sets are disjoint; the lemma then follows from Lemma 1.

Lemma 2. *Let SG be an s-graph, and let $\beta_1 = (E_1, \phi_1), \beta_2 = (E_2, \phi_2)$ be two boundary representations in SG. Then $T(\beta_1) \mid\mid T(\beta_2)$ is defined within SG iff the following conditions hold:*

(a) $\phi_1 \cup \phi_2$ is defined and injective;

(b) the two BRs have no in-boundary edges in common, i.e. $E_1 \cap E_2 = \emptyset$;

(c) for every source node v of β_1, the last edge on the path in SG from v to the closest source node of β_2 is not an in-boundary edge of β_2, and vice versa.

Furthermore, if these conditions hold, we have $T(\beta_1 \mid\mid \beta_2) = T(\beta_1) \mid\mid T(\beta_2)$, where we define $\beta_1 \mid\mid \beta_2 = (E_1 \cup E_2, \phi_1 \cup \phi_2)$.

4 S-graph grammars

We are now ready to define s-graph grammars, which describe languages of s-graphs. We also introduce graph parsing and relate s-graph grammars to HRGs.

4.1 Grammars for languages of s-graphs

We use *interpreted regular tree grammars* (IRTGs; Koller and Kuhlmann (2011)) to describe languages of s-graphs. IRTGs are a very general mechanism for describing languages over and relations between arbitrary algebras. They separate conceptually the generation of a grammatical derivation from its interpretation as a string, tree, graph, or some other object.

Consider, as an example, the tiny grammar in Fig. 3; see Koller (2015) for linguistically meaningful grammars. The left column consists of a regular tree grammar $\mathcal{G}$ (RTG; see e.g. Comon et al. (2008)) with two rules. This RTG describes a regular language $L(\mathcal{G})$ of *derivation trees* (in general, it may be infinite). In the example, we can derive $\mathrm{S} \Rightarrow \mathsf{r}_1(\mathrm{VP}) \Rightarrow \mathsf{r}_1(\mathsf{r}_2)$, therefore we have $t = \mathsf{r}_1(\mathsf{r}_2) \in L(\mathcal{G})$.

We then use a *tree homomorphism* h to rewrite the derivation trees into terms over an algebra; in this case the HR algebra. In the example, the values $h(\mathsf{r}_1)$ and $h(\mathsf{r}_2)$ are specified in the second column of Fig. 3. We compute $h(t)$ by substituting the variable x_1 in $h(\mathsf{r}_1)$ with $h(\mathsf{r}_2)$. The term $h(t)$ is thus the one shown in (1). It evaluates to the s-graph SG_f in Fig. 1(f).

Rule of RTG $\mathcal{G}$	homomorphism h
S → r_1(VP)	$\mathsf{f_S}(\mathsf{f_O}(SG_{want} \mid\mid x_1[\mathsf{R} \to \mathsf{O}]))$
VP → r_2	SG_{sleep}

Figure 3: An example s-graph grammar.

In general, the IRTG $\mathbb{G} = (\mathcal{G}, h, \mathcal{A})$ generates the *language* $L(\mathbb{G}) = \{[\![h(t)]\!] \mid t \in L(\mathcal{G})\}$, where $[\![\cdot]\!]$ is evaluation in the algebra $\mathcal{A}$. Thus, in the example, we have $L(\mathbb{G}) = \{SG_f\}$.

In this paper, we focus on IRTGs that describe languages $L(\mathbb{G}) \subseteq \mathcal{A}$ of objects in an algebra; specifically, of s-graphs in the HR algebra. However, IRTGs extend naturally to a synchronous grammar formalism by adding more homomorphisms and algebras. For instance, the grammars in Koller (2015) map each derivation tree simultaneously to a string and an s-graph, and therefore describe a binary relation between strings and s-graphs. We call IRTGs where at least one algebra is the HR algebra, *s-graph grammars*.

4.2 Parsing with s-graph grammars

In this paper, we are concerned with the parsing problem of s-graph grammars. In the context of IRTGs, parsing means that we are looking for those derivation trees t that are (a) grammatically correct, i.e. $t \in L(\mathcal{G})$, and (b) match some given input object a, i.e. $h(t)$ evaluates to a in the algebra. Because the set P of such derivation trees may be large or infinite, we aim to compute an RTG $\mathcal{G}_a$ such that $L(\mathcal{G}_a) = P$. This RTG plays the role of a parse chart, which represents the possible derivation trees compactly.

In order to compute $\mathcal{G}_a$, we need to solve two problems. First, we need to determine all the possible ways in which a can be represented by terms τ over the algebra $\mathcal{A}$. This is familiar from string parsing, where a CKY parse chart spells out all the ways in which larger substrings can be decomposed into smaller parts by concatenation. Second, we need to identify all those derivation trees $t \in L(\mathcal{G})$ that map to such a decomposition τ, i.e. for which $h(t)$ evaluates to a. In string parsing, this corresponds to retaining only such decompositions into substrings that are justified by the grammar rules.

While any parsing algorithm must address both of these issues, they are usually conflated, in that parse items combine information about the decomposition of a (such as a string span) with information about grammaticality (such as nonterminal symbols). In IRTG parsing, we take a different, more generic approach. We assume that the set D of all decompositions τ, i.e. of all terms τ that evaluate to a in the algebra, can be represented as the language $D = L(D_a)$ of a *decomposition grammar* D_a. D_a is an RTG over the signature of the algebra. Crucially, D_a only depends on the algebra and a itself, and not on $\mathcal{G}$ or h, because D contains *all* terms that evaluate to a and not just those that are licensed by the grammar. However, we can compute $\mathcal{G}_a$ from D_a efficiently by exploiting the closure of regular tree languages under intersection and inverse homomorphism; see Koller and Kuhlmann (2011) for details.

In practice, this means that whenever we want to apply IRTGs to a new algebra (as, in this paper, to the HR algebra), we can obtain a parsing algorithm by specifying how to compute decomposition grammars over this algebra. This is the topic of Section 5.

4.3 Relationship to HRG

We close our exposition of s-graph grammars by relating them to HRGs. It is known that the graph languages that can be described with s-graph grammars are the same as the HRG languages (Courcelle and Engelfriet, 2012, Prop. 4.27). Here we establish a more precise equivalence result, so we can compare our asymptotic runtimes directly to those of HRG parsers.

An HRG rule, such as the one shown in Fig. 4, rewrites a nonterminal symbol into a graph. The example rule constructs a graph for the nonterminal S by combining the graph G_r in the middle (with nodes $1, 2, 3$ and edges e, f) with graphs G_X and G_Y that are recursively derived from the nonterminals X and Y. The combination happens by merging the *external* nodes of G_X and G_Y with nodes of G_r: the squiggly lines indicate that the external node I of G_X should be 1, and the external node II should be 2. Similarly the external nodes of G_Y are unified with 1 and 3. Finally, the external nodes I and II of the HRG rule for S itself, shaded gray, are 1 and 3.

The fundamental idea of the HRG-to-IRTG translation is to encode external nodes as sources, and to use rename and merge to unify the nodes of the different graphs. In the example, we might say that the external nodes of G_X and G_Y are represented using the source names I and II, and extend G_r to an s-graph by saying that the nodes 1, 2, and

3 are its I-source, III-source, and II-source respectively. This results in the expression

$$(2)\ \mathsf{f}_{\text{III}}(\langle\text{I}\rangle \xrightarrow{e} \langle\text{III}\rangle \mid\mid x_1[\text{II} \to \text{III}] \mid\mid \langle\text{I}\rangle \xrightarrow{f} \langle\text{II}\rangle \mid\mid x_2)$$

where we write "$\langle\text{I}\rangle \xrightarrow{e} \langle\text{III}\rangle$" for the s-graph consisting of the edge e, with node 1 as I-source and 2 as III-source.

However, this requires the use of three source names (I, II, and III). The following encoding of the rule uses the sources more economically:

$$(3)\ \mathsf{f}_{\text{II}}(\langle\text{I}\rangle \xrightarrow{e} \langle\text{II}\rangle \mid\mid x_1) \mid\mid \langle\text{I}\rangle \xrightarrow{f} \langle\text{II}\rangle \mid\mid x_2$$

This term uses only two source names. It forgets II as soon as we are finished with the node 2, and frees the name up for reuse for 3. The complete encoding of the HRG rule consists of the RTG rule $\text{S} \to \mathsf{r}(\text{X}, \text{Y})$ with $h(\mathsf{r}) = (3)$.

In the general case, one can "read off" possible term encodings of a HRG rule from its *tree decompositions*; see Chiang et al. (2013) or Def. 2.80 of Courcelle and Engelfriet (2012) for details. A tree decomposition is a tree, each of whose nodes π is labeled with a subset V_π of the nodes in the HRG rule. We can construct a term encoding from a tree decomposition bottom-up. Leaves map to variables or constants; binary nodes introduce merge operations; and we use rename and forget operations to ensure that the subterm for the node π evaluates to an s-graph in which exactly the nodes in V_π are source nodes.[2] In the example, we obtain (3) from the tree decomposition in Fig. 4 like this.

The *tree-width* k of an HRG rule is measured by finding the tree decomposition of the rule for which the node sets have the lowest maximum size s and setting $k = s - 1$. It is a crucial measure because Chiang et al.'s parsing algorithm is exponential in k. The translation we just sketched uses s source names. Thus we see that a HRG with rules of tree-width $\leq k$ can be encoded into an s-graph grammar with $k + 1$ source names. (The converse is also true.)

5 Graph parsing with s-graph grammars

Now we show how to compute decomposition grammars for the s-graph algebra. As we explained in Section 4.2, we can then obtain a complete parser for s-graph grammars through generic methods.

[2]This uses the swap operations mentioned in Footnote 1.

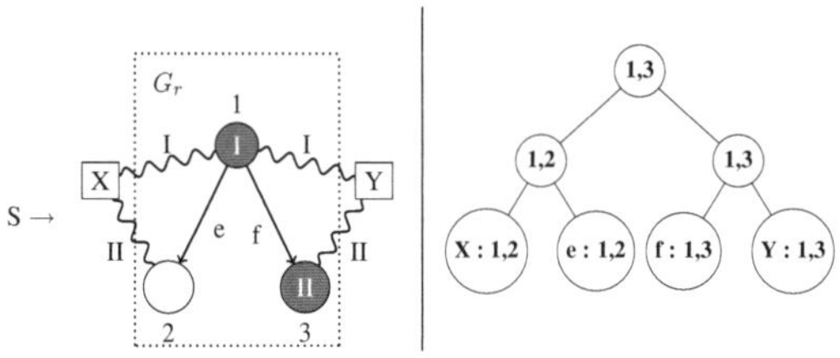

Figure 4: An HRG rule (left) with one of its tree decompositions (right).

Given an s-graph SG, the language of the decomposition grammar D_{SG} is the set of all terms over the HR algebra that evaluate to SG. For example, the decomposition grammar for the graph SG in Fig. 1(a) contains – among many others – the following two rules:

(4) $SG \to \mathsf{f}_{\mathsf{R}}(SG_f)$
(5) $SG_e \to \mid\mid (SG_b, SG_d)$,

where SG_f, SG_e, SG_b, and SG_d are the graphs from Fig. 1 (see Section 3.1). In other words, D_{SG} keeps track of sub-s-graphs in the nonterminals, and the rules spell out how "larger" sub-s-graphs can be constructed from "smaller" sub-s-graphs using the operations of the HR algebra. The algorithms below represent sub-s-graphs compactly using s-component and boundary representations.

Because the decomposition grammars in the s-graph algebra can be very large (see Section 6), we will not usually compute the entire decomposition grammar explicitly. Instead, it is sufficient to maintain a lazy representation of D_{SG}, which allows us to answer *queries* to the decomposition grammar efficiently. During parsing, such queries will be generated by the generic part of the parsing algorithm. Specifically, we will show how to answer the following types of query:

- *Top-down:* given an s-component representation $\mathcal{C}$ of some s-graph and an algebra operation o, enumerate all the rules $\mathcal{C} \to o(\mathcal{C}_1, \ldots, \mathcal{C}_k)$ in D_{SG}. This asks how a larger sub-s-graph can be derived from other sub-s-graphs using the operation o. In the example above, a query for SG and $\mathsf{f}_{\mathsf{R}}(\cdot)$ should yield, among others, the rule in (4).
- *Bottom-up:* given boundary representations $\beta_1, \ldots, \beta_k$ and an algebra operation o, enumerate all the rules $\beta \to o(\beta_1, \ldots, \beta_k)$ in D_{SG}. This asks how smaller sub-s-graphs can be combined into a bigger one using the

	forget	rename	merge
bottom-up	$O(d+s)$	$O(s)$	$O(ds)$
top-down	$O(ds)$	$O(s)$	$O(ds)$
$I = $ # rules	$O(n^s 2^{ds})$	$O(n^s 2^{ds})$	$O(n^s 3^{ds})$

Table 1: Amortized per-rule runtimes T for the different rule types.

operation o. In the example above, a merge query for SG_b and SG_d should yield the rule in (5). Unlike in the top-down case, every bottom-up query returns at most one rule.

The runtime of the complete parsing algorithm is bounded by the number I of different queries to D_{SG} that we receive, multiplied by the *per-rule runtime* T that we need to answer each query. The factor I is analogous to the number of rule instances in schema-based parsing (Shieber et al., 1995). The factor T is often ignored in the analysis of parsing algorithms, because in parsing schemata for strings, we typically have $T = O(1)$. This need not be the case for graph parsers. In the HRG parsing schema of Chiang et al. (2013), we have $I = O(n^{k+1} 3^{d(k+1)})$, where k is the treewidth of the HRG. In addition, each of their rule instances takes time $T = O(d(k+1))$ to actually calculate the new item.

Below, we show how we can efficiently answer both bottom-up and top-down queries to D_{SG}. Every s-graph grammar has an equivalent normal form where every constant describes an s-graph with a single edge. Assuming that the grammar is in this normal form, queries of the form $\beta \to g$ (resp. $\mathcal{C} \to g$), where g is a constant of the HR-algebra, are trivial and we will not consider them further. Table 1 summarizes our results.

5.1 Bottom-up decomposition

Forget and rename. Given a boundary representation $\beta' = (E', \phi')$, answering the bottom-up forget query $\beta \to \mathsf{f}_{\mathsf{A}}(\beta')$ amounts to verifying that all edges incident to $\phi'(\mathsf{A})$ are in-boundary in β', since otherwise the result would not be extensible. This takes time $O(d)$. We then let $\beta = (E, \phi)$, where ϕ is like ϕ' but undefined on A, and E is the set of edges in E' that are still incident to a source in ϕ. Computing β thus takes time $O(d+s)$.

The rename operation works similarly, but since the edge set remains unmodified, the per-rule runtime is $O(s)$.

A BR is fully determined by specifying the node and in-boundary edges for each source name, so there are at most $O\left(\left(n2^d\right)^s\right)$ different BRs. Since the result of a forget or rename rule is determined by the child β', this is an upper bound for the number I of rule instances of forget or rename.

Merge. Now consider the bottom-up merge query for the boundary representations β_1 and β_2. As we saw in Section 3.3, $T(\beta_1) \mid\mid T(\beta_2)$ is not always defined. But if it is, we can answer the query with the rule $(\beta_1 \mid\mid \beta_2) \to \mid\mid (\beta_1, \beta_2)$, with $\beta_1 \mid\mid \beta_2$ defined as in Section 3.3. Computing this BR takes time $O(ds)$.

We can check whether $T(\beta_1) \mid\mid T(\beta_2)$ is defined by going through the conditions of Lemma 2. The only nontrivial condition is (c). In order to check it efficiently, we precompute a data structure which contains, for any two nodes $u, v \in V$, the length k of the shortest undirected path $u = v_1 \leftrightarrow \ldots \overset{e}{\leftrightarrow} v_k = v$ and the last edge e on this path. This can be done in time $O(n^3)$ using the Floyd-Warshall algorithm. Checking (c) for every source pair then takes time $O(s^2)$ per rule, but because sources that are common to both β_1 and β_2 automatically satisfy (c) due to (a), one can show that the total runtime of checking (c) for all merge rules of $D_S G$ is $O(n^s 3^{ds} s)$.

Observe finally that there are $I = O(n^s 3^{ds})$ instances of the merge rule, because each of the $O(ds)$ edges that are incident to a source node can be either in β_1, in β_2, or in neither. Therefore the runtime for checking (c) amortizes to $O(s)$ per rule. The Floyd-Warshall step amortizes to $O(1)$ per rule for $s \geq 3$; for $s \leq 2$ the node table can be computed in amortized $O(1)$ using more specialized algorithms. This yields a total amortized per-rule runtime T for bottom-up merge of $O(ds)$.

5.2 Top-down decomposition

For the top-down queries, we specify sub-s-graphs in terms of their s-component representations. The number I of instances of each rule type is the same as in the bottom-up case because of the one-to-one correspondence of s-component and boundary representations. We focus on merge and forget queries; rename is as above.

Merge. Given an s-component representation $\mathcal{C} = (C, \phi)$, a top-down merge query asks us to enumerate the rules $\mathcal{C} \to \mid\mid (\mathcal{C}_1, \mathcal{C}_2)$ such that $T(\mathcal{C}_1) \mid\mid T(\mathcal{C}_2) = T(\mathcal{C})$. By Lemma 1, we can do this by using every distribution of the s-components in C over $\mathcal{C}_1$ and $\mathcal{C}_2$ and restricting ϕ

accordingly. This brings the per-rule time of top-down merge to $O(ds)$, the maximum number of s-components in C.

Block-cutpoint graphs. The challenging query to answer top-down is forget. We will first describe the problem and introduce a data structure that supports efficient top-down forget queries.

Consider top-down forget queries on the sub-s-graph SG_1 drawn in bold in Fig. 2(a); its s-component representation is $\langle\{[a],[g]\},\{\mathsf{A}{:}4,\mathsf{B}{:}5\}\rangle$. A top-down forget might promote the node 3 to a C-source, yielding a sub-s-graph SG_2 (that is, $\mathsf{f_C}(SG_2)$ is the original s-graph SG_1). In SG_2, a, e, and f are no longer equivalent; its s-component representation is $\langle\{[a],[e],[f],[g]\},\{\mathsf{A}{:}4,\mathsf{B}{:}5,\mathsf{C}{:}3\}\rangle$. Thus promoting 3 to a source splits the original s-component into smaller parts.

By contrast, the same top-down forget might also promote the node 1 to a C-source, yielding a sub-s-graph SG_3; $\mathsf{f_C}(SG_3)$ is also SG_1. However, all edges in $[a]$ are still equivalent in SG_3; its s-component representation is $\langle\{[a],[g]\},\{\mathsf{A}{:}4,\mathsf{B}{:}5,\mathsf{C}{:}1\}\rangle$.

An algorithm for top-down forget must be able to determine whether promotion of a node splits an s-component or not. To do this, let G be the input graph. We create an undirected auxiliary graph G^U from G and a set U of (source) nodes. G^U contains all nodes in $V\backslash U$, and for each edge e that is incident to a node $u \in U$, it contains a node (u,e). Furthermore, G^U contains undirected versions of all edges in G; if an edge $e \in E$ is incident to a node $u \in U$, it becomes incident to (u,e) in G^U instead. The auxiliary graph $G^{\{4,5\}}$ for our example graph is shown in Fig. 2(d).

Two edges are connected in G^U if and only if they are equivalent with respect to U in G. Therefore, promotion of u splits s-components iff u is a *cutpoint* in G^U, i.e. a node whose removal disconnects the graph. Cutpoints can be characterized as those nodes that belong to multiple *biconnected components (BCCs)* of G^U, i.e. the maximal subgraphs such that any node can be removed without disconnecting a graph segment. In Fig. 2(d), the BCCs are indicated by the dotted boxes. Observe that 3 is a cutpoint and 1 is not.

For any given U, we can represent the structure of the BCCs of G^U in its *block-cutpoint graph*. This is a bipartite graph whose nodes are the cutpoints and BCCs of G^U, and a BCC is connected to all of its cutpoints; see Fig. 2(e) for the block-cutpoint graph of the example. Block-cutpoint graphs are always forests, with the individual trees representing the s-components of G. Promoting a cutpoint u splits the s-component into smaller parts, each corresponding to an incident edge of u. We annotate each edge with that part.

Forget. We can now answer a top-down forget query $\mathcal{C} \rightarrow \mathsf{f_A}(\mathcal{C}')$ efficiently from the block-cutpoint graph for the sources of $\mathcal{C} = (C,\phi)$. We iterate over all components $c \in C$, and then over all internal nodes u of c. If u is not a cutpoint, we simply let $\mathcal{C}' = (C',\phi')$ by making u an A-source and letting $C' = C$. Otherwise, we also remove c from C and add the new s-components on the edges adjacent to u in the block-cutpoint graph. The query returns rules for all $\mathcal{C}'$ that can be constructed like this.

The per-rule runtime of top-down forget is $O(ds)$, the time needed to compute C' in the cutpoint case. We furthermore precompute the block-cutpoint graphs for the input graph with respect to all sets $U \subseteq V$ of nodes with $|U| \leq s-1$. For each U, we can compute the block-cutpoint graph and annotate its edges in time $O(nd^2s)$. Thus the total time for the precomputation is $O(n^s \cdot d^2s)$, which amortizes to $O(1)$ per rule.

6 Evaluation

We evaluate the performance of our algorithms on the "Little Prince" AMR-Bank version 1.4, available from `amr.isi.edu`. This graph-bank consists of 1562 sentences manually annotated with AMRs. We implemented our algorithms in Java as part of the Alto parser for IRTGs (Alto Developers, 2015), and compared them to the Bolinas HRG parser (Andreas et al., 2013). We measured runtimes using Java 8 (for Alto) and Pypy 2.5.0 (for Bolinas) on an Intel Xeon E7-8857 CPU at 3 GHz, after warming up the JIT compilers.

As there are no freely available grammars for this dataset, we created our own for the evaluation, using Bayesian grammar induction roughly along the lines of Cohn et al. (2010). We provide the grammars as supplementary material. Around 64% of the AMRs in the graph-bank have treewidth 1 and can thus be parsed using $s = 2$ source names. 98% have treewidth 1 or 2, corresponding to $s = 3$ source names. All experiments evaluated parser times on the same AMRs from which the grammar was sampled.

Top-down versus bottom-up. Fig. 5 compares the performance of the top-down and the bottom-up algorithm, on a grammar with three source names sampled from all 1261 graphs with up to 10 nodes. Each point in the figure is the geometric mean of runtimes for all graphs with a given number of nodes; note the log-scale. We aborted the top-down parser after its runtimes grew too large.

We observe that the bottom-up algorithm outperforms the top-down algorithm, and yields practical runtimes even for nontrivial graphs. One possible explanation for the difference is that the top-down algorithm spends more time analyzing ungrammatical s-graphs, particularly subgraphs that are not connected.

Comparison to Bolinas. We also compare our implementations to Bolinas. Because Bolinas is much slower than Alto, we restrict ourselves to two source names (= treewidth 1) and sampled the grammar from 30 randomly chosen AMRs each of size 2 to 8, plus the 21 AMRs of size one.

Fig. 6 shows the runtimes. Our parsers are generally much faster than in Fig. 5, due to the decreased number of sources and grammar size. They are also both much faster than Bolinas. Measuring the total time for parsing all 231 AMRs, our bottom-up algorithm outperforms Bolinas by a factor of 6722. The top-down algorithm is slower, but still outperforms Bolinas by a factor of 340.

Further analysis. In practice, memory use can be a serious issue. For example, the decomposition grammar for s=3 for AMR #194 in the corpus has over 300 million rules. However, many uses of decomposition grammars, such as sampling for grammar induction, can be phrased purely in terms of top-down queries. The top-down algorithm can answer these without computing the entire grammar, alleviating the memory problem.

Finally, we analyzed the asymptotic runtimes in Table 1 in terms of the maximum number $d \cdot s$ of in-boundary edges. However, the top-down parser does not manipulate individual edges, but entire s-components. The maximum number D_s of s-components into which a set of s sources can split a graph is called the *s-separability* of G by Lautemann (1990). We can analyze the runtime of the top-down parser more carefully as $O(n^s 3^{D_s} ds)$; as the dotted line in Fig. 5 shows, this predicts the runtime well. Interestingly, D_s is much lower in practice than its theoretical maximum. In the

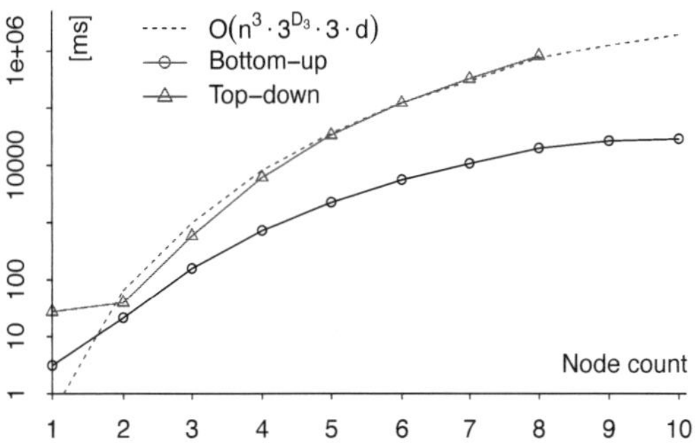

Figure 5: Runtimes of our parsers with $s = 3$.

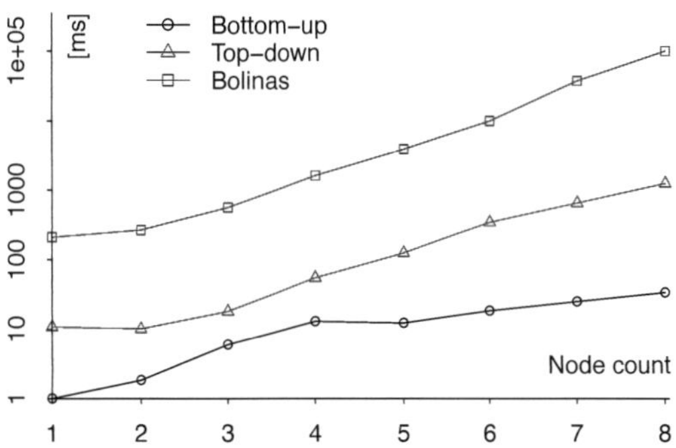

Figure 6: Runtimes of our parsers and Bolinas with $s = 2$.

"Little Prince" AMR-Bank, the mean of D_3 is 6.0, whereas the mean of $3 \cdot d$ is 12.7. Thus exploiting the s-component structure of the graph can improve parsing times.

7 Conclusion

We presented two new graph parsing algorithms for s-graph grammars. These were framed in terms of top-down and bottom-up queries to a decomposition grammar for the HR algebra. Our implementations outperform Bolinas, the previously best system, by several orders of magnitude. We have made them available as part of the Alto parser.

A challenge for grammar-based semantic parsing is grammar induction from data. We will explore this problem in future work. Furthermore, we will investigate methods for speeding up graph parsing further, e.g. with different heuristics.

Acknowledgments. We thank the anonymous reviewers for their comments, and Daniel Bauer for his help with Bolinas. We received valuable feedback at the 2015 Dagstuhl seminar on graph grammars and the 2014 Johns Hopkins workshop in Prague. This work was supported by the DFG grant KO 2916/2-1.

References

Alto Developers. 2015. Alto: algebraic language toolkit for parsing and decoding with IRTGs. Available at `https://bitbucket.org/tclup/alto`.

Jacob Andreas, Daniel Bauer, Karl Moritz Hermann, Bevan Jones, Kevin Knight, and David Chiang. 2013. Bolinas graph processing package. Available at `http://www.isi.edu/publications/licensed-sw/bolinas/`. Downloaded in January 2015.

Laura Banarescu, Claire Bonial, Shu Cai, Madalina Georgescu, Kira Griffitt, Ulf Hermjakob, Kevin Knight, Philipp Koehn, Martha Palmer, and Nathan Schneider. 2013. Abstract meaning representation for sembanking. In *Proceedings of the 7th Linguistic Annotation Workshop & Interoperability with Discourse*, pages 178–186.

David Chiang, Jacob Andreas, Daniel Bauer, Karl Moritz Hermann, Bevan Jones, and Kevin Knight. 2013. Parsing graphs with hyperedge replacement grammars. In *Proceedings of the 51st Annual Meeting of the Association for Computational Linguistics*, pages 924–932.

Trevor Cohn, Phil Blunsom, and Sharon Goldwater. 2010. Inducing tree-substitution grammars. *Journal of Machine Learning Research (JMLR)*, 11:3053–3096.

Hubert Comon, Max Dauchet, Rémi Gilleron, Florent Jacquemard, Denis Lugiez, Christof Löding, Sophie Tison, and Marc Tommasi. 2008. Tree automata techniques and applications. `http://tata.gforge.inria.fr/`.

Bruno Courcelle and Joost Engelfriet. 2012. *Graph Structure and Monadic Second-Order Logic*, volume 138 of *Encyclopedia of Mathematics and its Applications*. Cambridge University Press.

Frank Drewes, Hans-Jörg Kreowski, and Annegret Habel. 1997. Hyperedge replacement graph grammars. In Grzegorz Rozenberg, editor, *Handbook of Graph Grammars and Computing by Graph Transformation*, pages 95–162. World Scientific Publishing Co., Inc.

Jeffrey Flanigan, Sam Thomson, Jamie Carbonell, Chris Dyer, and Noah A. Smith. 2014. A discriminative graph-based parser for the abstract meaning representation. In *Proceedings of the 52nd Annual Meeting of the Association for Computational Linguistics*, pages 1426–1436, Baltimore, Maryland.

Bevan K. Jones, Jacob Andreas, Daniel Bauer, Karl Moritz Hermann, and Kevin Knight. 2012. Semantics – Based machine translation with hyperedge replacement grammars. In *Proceedings of COLING 2012: Technical Papers*, pages 1359–1376.

Alexander Koller and Marco Kuhlmann. 2011. A generalized view on parsing and translation. In *Proceedings of the 12th International Conference on Parsing Technologies*, pages 2–13.

Alexander Koller. 2015. Semantics construction with graph grammars. In *Proceedings of the 11th International Conference on Computational Semantics (IWCS)*, pages 228–238.

Clemens Lautemann. 1988. Decomposition trees: Structured graph representation and efficient algorithms. In Max Dauchet and Maurice Nivat, editors, *13th Colloquium on Trees in Algebra and Programming*, volume 299 of *Lecture Notes in Computer Science*, pages 28–39. Springer Berlin Heidelberg.

Clemens Lautemann. 1990. The complexity of graph languages generated by hyperedge replacement. *Acta Informatica*, 27:399–421.

André F. T. Martins and Mariana S. C. Almeida. 2014. Priberam: A turbo semantic parser with second order features. In *Proceedings of the 8th International Workshop on Semantic Evaluation (SemEval 2014)*, pages 471–476.

Stephan Oepen, Marco Kuhlmann, Yusuke Miyao, Daniel Zeman, Dan Flickinger, Jan Hajic, Angelina Ivanova, and Yi Zhang. 2014. SemEval 2014 Task 8: Broad-coverage semantic dependency parsing. In *Proceedings of the 8th International Workshop on Semantic Evaluation (SemEval 2014)*, pages 63–72.

Daniel Quernheim and Kevin Knight. 2012. DAGGER: A toolkit for automata on directed acyclic graphs. In *Proceedings of the 10th International Workshop on Finite State Methods and Natural Language Processing*, pages 40–44.

Stuart M. Shieber, Yves Schabes, and Fernando C. N. Pereira. 1995. Principles and implementation of deductive parsing. *Journal of Logic Programming*, 24(1–2):3–36.

Sparse Overcomplete Word Vector Representations

Manaal Faruqui Yulia Tsvetkov Dani Yogatama Chris Dyer Noah A. Smith
Language Technologies Institute
Carnegie Mellon University
Pittsburgh, PA, 15213, USA
{mfaruqui,ytsvetko,dyogatama,cdyer,nasmith}@cs.cmu.edu

Abstract

Current distributed representations of words show little resemblance to theories of lexical semantics. The former are dense and uninterpretable, the latter largely based on familiar, discrete classes (e.g., supersenses) and relations (e.g., synonymy and hypernymy). We propose methods that transform word vectors into sparse (and optionally binary) vectors. The resulting representations are more similar to the interpretable features typically used in NLP, though they are discovered automatically from raw corpora. Because the vectors are highly sparse, they are computationally easy to work with. Most importantly, we find that they outperform the original vectors on benchmark tasks.

1 Introduction

Distributed representations of words have been shown to benefit NLP tasks like parsing (Lazaridou et al., 2013; Bansal et al., 2014), named entity recognition (Guo et al., 2014), and sentiment analysis (Socher et al., 2013). The attraction of word vectors is that they can be derived directly from raw, unannotated corpora. Intrinsic evaluations on various tasks are guiding methods toward discovery of a representation that captures many facts about lexical semantics (Turney, 2001; Turney and Pantel, 2010).

Yet word vectors do not look anything like the representations described in most lexical semantic theories, which focus on identifying classes of words (Levin, 1993; Baker et al., 1998; Schuler, 2005) and relationships among word meanings (Miller, 1995). Though expensive to construct, conceptualizing word meanings symbolically is important for theoretical understanding and also when we incorporate lexical semantics into computational models where interpretability is desired. On the surface, discrete theories seem incommensurate with the distributed approach, a problem now receiving much attention in computational linguistics (Lewis and Steedman, 2013; Kiela and Clark, 2013; Vecchi et al., 2013; Grefenstette, 2013; Lewis and Steedman, 2014; Paperno et al., 2014).

Our contribution to this discussion is a new, principled sparse coding method that transforms any distributed representation of words into sparse vectors, which can then be transformed into binary vectors (§2). Unlike recent approaches of incorporating semantics in distributional word vectors (Yu and Dredze, 2014; Xu et al., 2014; Faruqui et al., 2015), the method does not rely on any external information source. The transformation results in longer, sparser vectors, sometimes called an "overcomplete" representation (Olshausen and Field, 1997). Sparse, overcomplete representations have been motivated in other domains as a way to increase separability and interpretability, with each instance (here, a word) having a small number of active dimensions (Olshausen and Field, 1997; Lewicki and Sejnowski, 2000), and to increase stability in the presence of noise (Donoho et al., 2006).

Our work builds on recent explorations of sparsity as a useful form of inductive bias in NLP and machine learning more broadly (Kazama and Tsujii, 2003; Goodman, 2004; Friedman et al., 2008; Glorot et al., 2011; Yogatama and Smith, 2014, *inter alia*). Introducing sparsity in word vector dimensions has been shown to improve dimension interpretability (Murphy et al., 2012; Fyshe et al., 2014) and usability of word vectors as features in downstream tasks (Guo et al., 2014). The word vectors we produce are more than 90% sparse; we also consider binarizing transformations that bring them closer to the categories and relations of lex-

Proceedings of the 53rd Annual Meeting of the Association for Computational Linguistics and the 7th International Joint Conference on Natural Language Processing, pages 1491–1500,
Beijing, China, July 26-31, 2015.

ical semantic theories. Using a number of state-of-the-art word vectors as input, we find consistent benefits of our method on a suite of standard benchmark evaluation tasks (§3). We also evaluate our word vectors in a word intrusion experiment with humans (Chang et al., 2009) and find that our sparse vectors are more interpretable than the original vectors (§4).

We anticipate that sparse, binary vectors can play an important role as features in statistical NLP models, which still rely predominantly on discrete, sparse features whose interpretability enables error analysis and continued development. We have made an implementation of our method publicly available.[1]

2 Sparse Overcomplete Word Vectors

We consider methods for transforming dense word vectors to sparse, binary overcomplete word vectors. Fig. 1 shows two approaches. The one on the top, method A, converts dense vectors to sparse overcomplete vectors (§2.1). The one beneath, method B, converts dense vectors to sparse and binary overcomplete vectors (§2.2 and §2.4).

Let V be the vocabulary size. In the following, $\mathbf{X} \in \mathbb{R}^{L \times V}$ is the matrix constructed by stacking V non-sparse "input" word vectors of length L (produced by an arbitrary word vector estimator). We will refer to these as initializing vectors. $\mathbf{A} \in \mathbb{R}^{K \times V}$ contains V sparse overcomplete word vectors of length K. "Overcomplete" representation learning implies that $K > L$.

2.1 Sparse Coding

In sparse coding (Lee et al., 2006), the goal is to represent each input vector $\mathbf{x}_i$ as a sparse linear combination of basis vectors, $\mathbf{a}_i$. Our experiments consider four initializing methods for these vectors, discussed in Appendix A. Given $\mathbf{X}$, we seek to solve

$$\arg\min_{\mathbf{D},\mathbf{A}} \|\mathbf{X} - \mathbf{D}\mathbf{A}\|_2^2 + \lambda\Omega(\mathbf{A}) + \tau\|\mathbf{D}\|_2^2, \quad (1)$$

where $\mathbf{D} \in \mathbb{R}^{L \times K}$ is the dictionary of basis vectors. λ is a regularization hyperparameter, and Ω is the regularizer. Here, we use the squared loss for the reconstruction error, but other loss functions could also be used (Lee et al., 2009). To obtain sparse word representations we will impose an ℓ_1 penalty on $\mathbf{A}$. Eq. 1 can be broken down into loss for each word vector which can be optimized separately in parallel (§2.3):

$$\arg\min_{\mathbf{D},\mathbf{A}} \sum_{i=1}^{V} \|\mathbf{x}_i - \mathbf{D}\mathbf{a}_i\|_2^2 + \lambda\|\mathbf{a}_i\|_1 + \tau\|\mathbf{D}\|_2^2 \quad (2)$$

where $\mathbf{m}_i$ denotes the ith column vector of matrix $\mathbf{M}$. Note that this problem is not convex. We refer to this approach as **method A**.

2.2 Sparse Nonnegative Vectors

Nonnegativity in the feature space has often been shown to correspond to interpretability (Lee and Seung, 1999; Cichocki et al., 2009; Murphy et al., 2012; Fyshe et al., 2014; Fyshe et al., 2015). To obtain nonnegative sparse word vectors, we use a variation of the nonnegative sparse coding method (Hoyer, 2002). Nonnegative sparse coding further constrains the problem in Eq. 2 so that $\mathbf{D}$ and $\mathbf{a}_i$ are nonnegative. Here, we apply this constraint only to the representation vectors $\{\mathbf{a}_i\}$. Thus, the new objective for nonnegative sparse vectors becomes:

$$\arg\min_{\mathbf{D}\in\mathbb{R}_{\geq 0}^{L\times K}, \mathbf{A}\in\mathbb{R}_{\geq 0}^{K\times V}} \sum_{i=1}^{V} \|\mathbf{x}_i - \mathbf{D}\mathbf{a}_i\|_2^2 + \lambda\|\mathbf{a}_i\|_1 + \tau\|\mathbf{D}\|_2^2 \quad (3)$$

This problem will play a role in our second approach, **method B**, to which we will return shortly. This nonnegativity constraint can be easily incorporated during optimization, as explained next.

2.3 Optimization

We use online adaptive gradient descent (AdaGrad; Duchi et al., 2010) for solving the optimization problems in Eqs. 2–3 by updating $\mathbf{A}$ and $\mathbf{D}$. In order to speed up training we use asynchronous updates to the parameters of the model in parallel for every word vector (Duchi et al., 2012; Heigold et al., 2014).

However, directly applying stochastic subgradient descent to an ℓ_1-regularized objective fails to produce sparse solutions in bounded time, which has motivated several specialized algorithms that target such objectives. We use the AdaGrad variant of one such learning algorithm, the regularized dual averaging algorithm (Xiao, 2009), which keeps track of the online average gradient at time t: $\bar{g}_t = \frac{1}{t}\sum_{t'=1}^{t} g_{t'}$ Here, the subgradients do not include terms for the regularizer; they are derivatives of the unregularized objective ($\lambda = 0, \tau = 0$)

[1]https://github.com/mfaruqui/sparse-coding

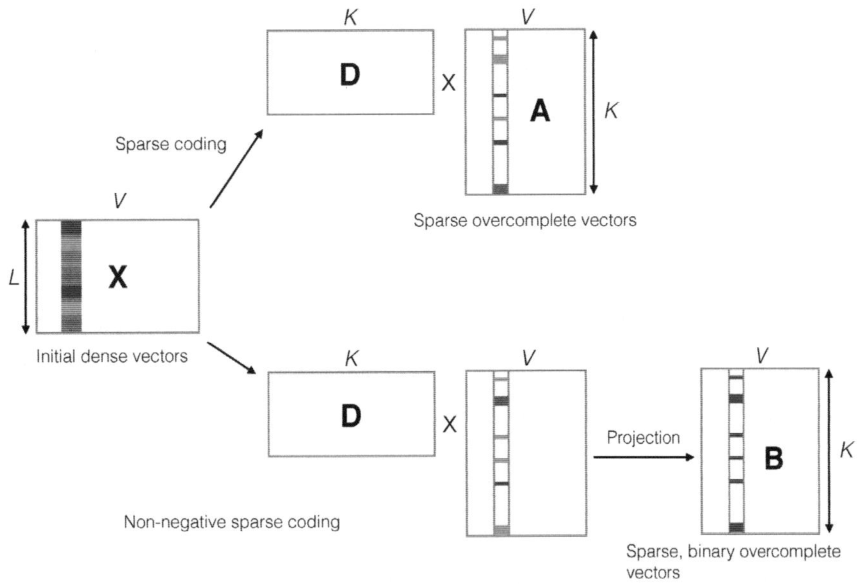

Figure 1: Methods for obtaining sparse overcomplete vectors (top, method A, §2.1) and sparse, binary overcomplete word vectors (bottom, method B, §2.2 and §2.4). Observed dense vectors of length L (left) are converted to sparse non-negative vectors (center) of length K which are then projected into the binary vector space (right), where $L \ll K$. $\mathbf{X}$ is dense, $\mathbf{A}$ is sparse, and $\mathbf{B}$ is the binary word vector matrix. Strength of colors signify the magnitude of values; negative is red, positive is blue, and zero is white.

with respect to $\mathbf{a}_i$. We define

$$\gamma = -\text{sign}(\bar{g}_{t,i,j}) \frac{\eta t}{\sqrt{G_{t,i,j}}} (|\bar{g}_{t,i,j}| - \lambda),$$

where $G_{t,i,j} = \sum_{t'=1}^{t} g_{t',i,j}^2$. Now, using the average gradient, the ℓ_1-regularized objective is optimized as follows:

$$a_{t+1,i,j} = \begin{cases} 0, & \text{if } |\bar{g}_{t,i,j}| \leq \lambda \\ \gamma, & \text{otherwise} \end{cases} \tag{4}$$

where, $a_{t+1,i,j}$ is the jth element of sparse vector $\mathbf{a}_i$ at the tth update and $\bar{g}_{t,i,j}$ is the corresponding average gradient. For obtaining nonnegative sparse vectors we take projection of the updated $\mathbf{a}_i$ onto $\mathbb{R}_{\geq 0}^K$ by choosing the closest point in $\mathbb{R}_{\geq 0}^K$ according to Euclidean distance (which corresponds to zeroing out the negative elements):

$$a_{t+1,i,j} = \begin{cases} 0, & \text{if } |\bar{g}_{t,i,j}| \leq \lambda \\ 0, & \text{if } \gamma < 0 \\ \gamma, & \text{otherwise} \end{cases} \tag{5}$$

2.4 Binarizing Transformation

Our aim with **method B** is to obtain word representations that can emulate the binary-feature

$\mathbf{X}$	L	λ	τ	K	% Sparse
Glove	300	1.0	10^{-5}	3000	91
SG	300	0.5	10^{-5}	3000	92
GC	50	1.0	10^{-5}	500	98
Multi	48	0.1	10^{-5}	960	93

Table 1: Hyperparameters for learning sparse overcomplete vectors tuned on the WS-353 task. Tasks are explained in §B. The four initial vector representations $\mathbf{X}$ are explained in §A.

hot, fresh, fish, 1/2, wine, salt
series, tv, appearances, episodes
1975, 1976, 1968, 1970, 1977, 1969
dress, shirt, ivory, shirts, pants
upscale, affluent, catering, clientele

Table 2: Highest frequency words in randomly picked word clusters of binary sparse overcomplete Glove vectors.

space designed for various NLP tasks. We could

state this as an optimization problem:

$$\underset{\substack{\mathbf{D}\in\mathbb{R}^{L\times K}\\ \mathbf{B}\in\{0,1\}^{K\times V}}}{\arg\min} \sum_{i=1}^{V} \|\mathbf{x}_i - \mathbf{D}\mathbf{b}_i\|_2^2 + \lambda\|\mathbf{b}_i\|_1^1 + \tau\|\mathbf{D}\|_2^2 \tag{6}$$

where $\mathbf{B}$ denotes the binary (and also sparse) representation. This is an mixed integer bilinear program, which is NP-hard (Al-Khayyal and Falk, 1983). Unfortunately, the number of variables in the problem is $\approx KV$ which reaches 100 million when $V = 100,000$ and $K = 1,000$, which is intractable to solve using standard techniques.

A more tractable relaxation to this hard problem is to first constrain the continuous representation $\mathbf{A}$ to be nonnegative (i.e, $\mathbf{a}_i \in \mathbb{R}^K_{\geq 0}$; §2.2). Then, in order to avoid an expensive computation, we take the nonnegative word vectors obtained using Eq. 3 and project nonzero values to 1, preserving the 0 values. Table 2 shows a random set of word clusters obtained by (i) applying our method to Glove initial vectors and (ii) applying k-means clustering ($k = 100$). In §3 we will find that these vectors perform well quantitatively.

2.5 Hyperparameter Tuning

Methods A and B have three hyperparameters: the ℓ_1-regularization penalty λ, the ℓ_2-regularization penalty τ, and the length of the overcomplete word vector representation K. We perform a grid search on $\lambda \in \{0.1, 0.5, 1.0\}$ and $K \in \{10L, 20L\}$, selecting values that maximizes performance on one "development" word similarity task (WS-353, discussed in §B) while achieving at least 90% sparsity in overcomplete vectors. τ was tuned on one collection of initializing vectors (Glove, discussed in §A) so that the vectors in $\mathbf{D}$ are near unit norm. The four vector representations and their corresponding hyperparameters selected by this procedure are summarized in Table 1. There hyperparameters were chosen for method A and retained for method B.

3 Experiments

Using methods A and B, we constructed sparse overcomplete vector representations $\mathbf{A}$, starting from four initial vector representations $\mathbf{X}$; these are explained in Appendix A. We used one benchmark evaluation (WS-353) to tune hyperparameters, resulting in the settings shown in Table 1; seven other tasks were used to evaluate the quality of the sparse overcomplete representations. The first of these is a word similarity task, where the score is correlation with human judgments, and the others are classification accuracies of an ℓ_2-regularized logistic regression model trained using the word vectors. These tasks are described in detail in Appendix B.

3.1 Effects of Transforming Vectors

First, we quantify the effects of our transformations by comparing their output to the initial ($\mathbf{X}$) vectors. Table 3 shows consistent improvements of sparsifying vectors (method A). The exceptions are on the SimLex task, where our sparse vectors are worse than the skip-gram initializer and on par with the multilingual initializer. Sparsification is beneficial across all of the text classification tasks, for all initial vector representations. On average across all vector types and all tasks, sparse overcomplete vectors outperform their corresponding initializers by 4.2 points.[2]

Binarized vectors (from method B) are also usually better than the initial vectors (also shown in Table 3), and tend to outperform the sparsified variants, except when initializing with Glove. On average across all vector types and all tasks, binarized overcomplete vectors outperform their corresponding initializers by 4.8 points and the continuous, sparse intermediate vectors by 0.6 points.

From here on, we explore more deeply the sparse overcomplete vectors from method A (denoted by $\mathbf{A}$), leaving binarization and method B aside.

3.2 Effect of Vector Length

How does the length of the overcomplete vector (K) affect performance? We focus here on the Glove vectors, where $L = 300$, and report average performance across all tasks. We consider $K = \alpha L$ where $\alpha \in \{2, 3, 5, 10, 15, 20\}$. Figure 2 plots the average performance across tasks against α. The earlier selection of $K = 3,000$ ($\alpha = 10$) gives the best result; gains are monotonic in α to that point and then begin to diminish.

3.3 Alternative Transformations

We consider two alternative transformations. The first preserves the original vector length but

[2]We report correlation on a 100 point scale, so that the average which includes accuracuies and correlation is equally representatitve of both.

Vectors		SimLex Corr.	Senti. Acc.	TREC Acc.	Sports Acc.	Comp. Acc.	Relig. Acc.	NP Acc.	Average
	X	36.9	77.7	76.2	95.9	79.7	86.7	77.9	76.2
Glove	**A**	38.9	**81.4**	**81.5**	**96.3**	**87.0**	**88.8**	**82.3**	**79.4**
	B	**39.7**	81.0	81.2	95.7	84.6	87.4	81.6	78.7
	X	**43.6**	81.5	77.8	97.1	80.2	85.9	80.1	78.0
SG	**A**	41.7	**82.7**	81.2	**98.2**	84.5	86.5	81.6	79.4
	B	42.8	81.6	**81.6**	95.2	**86.5**	**88.0**	**82.9**	**79.8**
	X	9.7	68.3	64.6	75.1	60.5	76.0	79.4	61.9
GC	**A**	12.0	73.3	77.6	77.0	68.3	**81.0**	**81.2**	67.2
	B	**18.7**	**73.6**	**79.2**	**79.7**	**70.5**	79.6	79.4	**68.6**
	X	**28.7**	75.5	63.8	83.6	64.3	81.8	79.2	68.1
Multi	**A**	28.1	**78.6**	79.2	93.9	78.2	84.5	81.1	74.8
	B	**28.7**	77.6	**82.0**	**94.7**	**81.4**	**85.6**	**81.9**	**75.9**

Table 3: Performance comparison of transformed vectors to initial vectors **X**. We show sparse overcomplete representations **A** and also binarized representations **B**. Initial vectors are discussed in §A and tasks in §B.

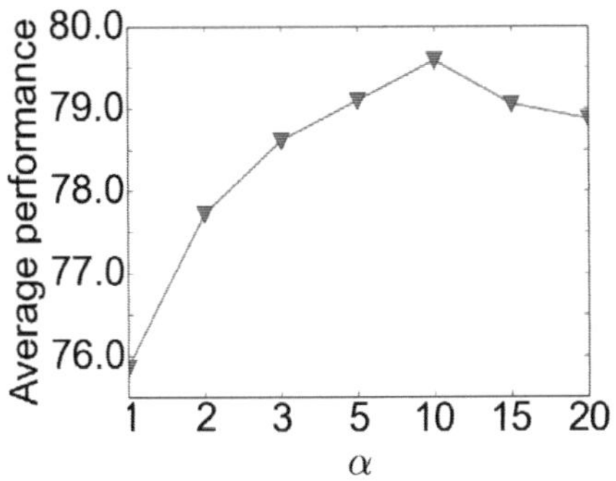

Figure 2: Average performace across all tasks for sparse overcomplete vectors (**A**) produced by Glove initial vectors, as a function of the ratio of K to L.

achieves a binary, sparse vector (**B**) by applying:

$$b_{i,j} = \begin{cases} 1 & \text{if } x_{i,j} > 0 \\ 0 & \text{otherwise} \end{cases} \quad (7)$$

The second transformation was proposed by Guo et al. (2014). Here, the original vector length is also preserved, but sparsity is achieved through:

$$a_{i,j} = \begin{cases} 1 & \text{if } x_{i,j} \geq M^+ \\ -1 & \text{if } x_{i,j} \leq M^- \\ 0 & \text{otherwise} \end{cases} \quad (8)$$

where M^+ (M^-) is the mean of positive-valued (negative-valued) elements of **X**. These vectors are, obviously, not binary.

We find that on average, across initializing vectors and across all tasks that our sparse overcomplete (**A**) vectors lead to better performance than either of the alternative transformations.

4 Interpretability

Our hypothesis is that the dimensions of sparse overcomplete vectors are more interpretable than those of dense word vectors. Following Murphy et al. (2012), we use a word intrusion experiment (Chang et al., 2009) to corroborate this hypothesis. In addition, we conduct qualitative analysis of interpretability, focusing on individual dimensions.

4.1 Word Intrusion

Word intrusion experiments seek to quantify the extent to which dimensions of a learned word representation are coherent to humans. In one instance of the experiment, a human judge is presented with five words in random order and asked to select the "intruder." The words are selected by the experimenter by choosing one dimension j of the learned representation, then ranking the words on that dimension alone. The dimensions are chosen in decreasing order of the variance of their values across the vocabulary. Four of the words are the top-ranked words according to j, and the "true" intruder is a word from the bottom half of the list, chosen to be a word that appears in the top 10% of some other dimension. An example of an instance is:

naval, industrial, technological, marine, identity

X:	Glove	SG	GC	Multi	Average
X	76.2	78.0	61.9	68.1	71.0
Eq. 7	75.7	75.8	60.5	64.1	69.0
Eq. 8 (Guo et al., 2014)	75.8	76.9	60.5	66.2	69.8
A	**79.4**	**79.4**	**67.2**	**74.8**	**75.2**

Table 4: Average performance across all tasks and vector models using different transformations.

Vectors	A1	A2	A3	Avg.	IAA	κ
X	61	53	56	57	70	0.40
A	71	70	72	71	77	0.45

Table 5: Accuracy of three human annotators on the word intrusion task, along with the average inter-annotator agreement (Artstein and Poesio, 2008) and Fleiss' κ (Davies and Fleiss, 1982).

(The last word is the intruder.)

We formed instances from initializing vectors and from our sparse overcomplete vectors (**A**). Each of these two combines the four different initializers **X**. We selected the 25 dimensions d in each case. Each of the 100 instances per condition (initial vs. sparse overcomplete) was given to three judges.

Results in Table 5 confirm that the sparse overcomplete vectors are more interpretable than the dense vectors. The inter-annotator agreement on the sparse vectors increases substantially, from 57% to 71%, and the Fleiss' κ increases from "fair" to "moderate" agreement (Landis and Koch, 1977).

4.2 Qualitative Evaluation of Interpretability

If a vector dimension is interpretable, the top-ranking words for that dimension should display semantic or syntactic groupings. To verify this qualitatively, we select five dimensions with the highest variance of values in initial and sparsified GC vectors. We compare top-ranked words in the dimensions extracted from the two representations. The words are listed in Table 6, a dimension per row. Subjectively, we find the semantic groupings better in the sparse vectors than in the initial vectors.

Figure 3 visualizes the sparsified GC vectors for six words. The dimensions are sorted by the average value across the three "animal" vectors. The animal-related words use many of the same dimensions (102 common active dimensions out of 500 total); in constrast, the three city names use mostly distinct vectors.

X	combat, guard, honor, bow, trim, naval
	'll, could, faced, lacking, seriously, scored
	see, n't, recommended, depending, part
	due, positive, equal, focus, respect, better
	sergeant, comments, critics, she, videos
A	fracture, breathing, wound, tissue, relief
	relationships, connections, identity, relations
	files, bills, titles, collections, poems, songs
	naval, industrial, technological, marine
	stadium, belt, championship, toll, ride, coach

Table 6: Top-ranked words per dimension for initial and sparsified GC representations. Each line shows words from a different dimension.

5 Related Work

To the best of our knowledge, there has been no prior work on obtaining overcomplete word vector representations that are sparse and categorical. However, overcomplete features have been widely used in image processing, computer vision (Olshausen and Field, 1997; Lewicki and Sejnowski, 2000) and signal processing (Donoho et al., 2006). Nonnegative matrix factorization is often used for interpretable coding of information (Lee and Seung, 1999; Liu et al., 2003; Cichocki et al., 2009).

Sparsity constraints are in general useful in NLP problems (Kazama and Tsujii, 2003; Friedman et al., 2008; Goodman, 2004), like POS tagging (Ganchev et al., 2009), dependency parsing (Martins et al., 2011), text classification (Yogatama and Smith, 2014), and representation learning (Bengio et al., 2013). Including sparsity constraints in Bayesian models of lexical semantics like LDA in the form of sparse Dirichlet priors has been shown to be useful for downstream tasks like POS-tagging (Toutanova and Johnson, 2007), and improving interpretation (Paul and Dredze, 2012; Zhu and Xing, 2012).

Figure 3: Visualization of sparsified GC vectors. Negative values are red, positive values are blue, zeroes are white.

6 Conclusion

We have presented a method that converts word vectors obtained using any state-of-the-art word vector model into sparse and optionally binary word vectors. These transformed vectors appear to come closer to features used in NLP tasks and outperform the original vectors from which they are derived on a suite of semantics and syntactic evaluation benchmarks. We also find that the sparse vectors are more interpretable than the dense vectors by humans according to a word intrusion detection test.

Acknowledgments

We thank Alona Fyshe for discussions on vector interpretability and three anonymous reviewers for their feedback. This research was supported in part by the National Science Foundation through grant IIS-1251131 and the Defense Advanced Research Projects Agency through grant FA87501420244. This work was supported in part by the U.S. Army Research Laboratory and the U.S. Army Research Office under contract/grant number W911NF-10-1-0533.

A Initial Vector Representations (X)

Our experiments consider four publicly available collections of pre-trained word vectors. They vary in the amount of data used and the estimation method.

Glove. Global vectors for word representations (Pennington et al., 2014) are trained on aggregated global word-word co-occurrence statistics from a corpus. These vectors were trained on 6 billion words from Wikipedia and English Gigaword and are of length 300.[3]

[3]http://www-nlp.stanford.edu/projects/glove/

Skip-Gram (SG). The word2vec tool (Mikolov et al., 2013) is fast and widely-used. In this model, each word's Huffman code is used as an input to a log-linear classifier with a continuous projection layer and words within a given context window are predicted. These vectors were trained on 100 billion words of Google news data and are of length 300.[4]

Global Context (GC). These vectors are learned using a recursive neural network that incorporates both local and global (document-level) context features (Huang et al., 2012). These vectors were trained on the first 1 billion words of English Wikipedia and are of length 50.[5]

Multilingual (Multi). Faruqui and Dyer (2014) learned vectors by first performing SVD on text in different languages, then applying canonical correlation analysis on pairs of vectors for words that align in parallel corpora. These vectors were trained on WMT-2011 news corpus containing 360 million words and are of length 48.[6]

B Evaluation Benchmarks

Our comparisons of word vector quality consider five benchmark tasks. We now describe the different evaluation benchmarks for word vectors.

Word Similarity. We evaluate our word representations on two word similarity tasks. The first is the WS-353 dataset (Finkelstein et al., 2001), which contains 353 pairs of English words that have been assigned similarity ratings by humans. This dataset is used to tune sparse vector learning hyperparameters (§2.5), while the remaining of the tasks discussed in this section are completely held out.

[4]https://code.google.com/p/word2vec

[5]http://nlp.stanford.edu/~socherr/ACL2012_wordVectorsTextFile.zip

[6]http://cs.cmu.edu/~mfaruqui/soft.html

A more recent dataset, SimLex-999 (Hill et al., 2014), has been constructed to specifically focus on similarity (rather than relatedness). It contains a balanced set of noun, verb, and adjective pairs. We calculate cosine similarity between the vectors of two words forming a test item and report Spearman's rank correlation coefficient (Myers and Well, 1995) between the rankings produced by our model against the human rankings.

Sentiment Analysis (Senti). Socher et al. (2013) created a treebank of sentences annotated with fine-grained sentiment labels on phrases and sentences from movie review excerpts. The coarse-grained treebank of positive and negative classes has been split into training, development, and test datasets containing 6,920, 872, and 1,821 sentences, respectively. We use average of the word vectors of a given sentence as feature for classification. The classifier is tuned on the dev. set and accuracy is reported on the test set.

Question Classification (TREC). As an aid to question answering, a question may be classified as belonging to one of many question types. The TREC questions dataset involves six different question types, e.g., whether the question is about a location, about a person, or about some numeric information (Li and Roth, 2002). The training dataset consists of 5,452 labeled questions, and the test dataset consists of 500 questions. An average of the word vectors of the input question is used as features and accuracy is reported on the test set.

20 Newsgroup Dataset. We consider three binary categorization tasks from the 20 Newsgroups dataset.[7] Each task involves categorizing a document according to two related categories with training/dev./test split in accordance with Yogatama and Smith (2014): (1) Sports: baseball vs. hockey (958/239/796) (2) Comp.: IBM vs. Mac (929/239/777) (3) Religion: atheism vs. christian (870/209/717). We use average of the word vectors of a given sentence as features. The classifier is tuned on the dev. set and accuracy is reported on the test set.

NP bracketing (NP). Lazaridou et al. (2013) constructed a dataset from the Penn Treebank (Marcus et al., 1993) of noun phrases (NP) of length three words, where the first can be an adjective or a noun and the other two are nouns. The task is to predict the correct bracketing in the parse tree for a given noun phrase. For example, *local (phone company)* and *(blood pressure) medicine* exhibit *right* and *left* bracketing, respectively. We append the word vectors of the three words in the NP in order and use them as features for binary classification. The dataset contains 2,227 noun phrases split into 10 folds. The classifier is tuned on the first fold and cross-validation accuracy is reported on the remaining nine folds.

[7] `http://qwone.com/~jason/20Newsgroups`

References

Faiz A. Al-Khayyal and James E. Falk. 1983. Jointly constrained biconvex programming. *Mathematics of Operations Research*, pages 273–286.

Ron Artstein and Massimo Poesio. 2008. Inter-coder agreement for computational linguistics. *Computational Linguistics*, 34(4):555–596.

Collin F. Baker, Charles J. Fillmore, and John B. Lowe. 1998. The Berkeley FrameNet project. In *Proc. of ACL*.

Mohit Bansal, Kevin Gimpel, and Karen Livescu. 2014. Tailoring continuous word representations for dependency parsing. In *Proc. of ACL*.

Yoshua Bengio, Aaron Courville, and Pascal Vincent. 2013. Representation learning: A review and new perspectives. *IEEE Transactions on Pattern Analysis and Machine Intelligence*, 35(8):1798–1828.

Jonathan Chang, Sean Gerrish, Chong Wang, Jordan L. Boyd-Graber, and David M. Blei. 2009. Reading tea leaves: How humans interpret topic models. In *NIPS*.

Andrzej Cichocki, Rafal Zdunek, Anh Huy Phan, and Shun-ichi Amari. 2009. *Nonnegative Matrix and Tensor Factorizations: Applications to Exploratory Multi-way Data Analysis and Blind Source Separation*. John Wiley & Sons.

Mark Davies and Joseph L Fleiss. 1982. Measuring agreement for multinomial data. *Biometrics*, pages 1047–1051.

David L. Donoho, Michael Elad, and Vladimir N. Temlyakov. 2006. Stable recovery of sparse overcomplete representations in the presence of noise. *IEEE Transactions on Information Theory*, 52(1).

John Duchi, Elad Hazan, and Yoram Singer. 2010. Adaptive subgradient methods for online learning and stochastic optimization. Technical Report EECS-2010-24, University of California Berkeley.

John C. Duchi, Alekh Agarwal, and Martin J. Wainwright. 2012. Dual averaging for distributed optimization: Convergence analysis and network scaling. *IEEE Transactions on Automatic Control*, 57(3):592–606.

Manaal Faruqui and Chris Dyer. 2014. Improving vector space word representations using multilingual correlation. In *Proc. of EACL*.

Manaal Faruqui, Jesse Dodge, Sujay K. Jauhar, Chris Dyer, Eduard Hovy, and Noah A. Smith. 2015. Retrofitting word vectors to semantic lexicons. In *Proc. of NAACL*.

Lev Finkelstein, Evgeniy Gabrilovich, Yossi Matias, Ehud Rivlin, Zach Solan, Gadi Wolfman, and Eytan Ruppin. 2001. Placing search in context: the concept revisited. In *Proc. of WWW*.

Jerome Friedman, Trevor Hastie, and Robert Tibshirani. 2008. Sparse inverse covariance estimation with the graphical lasso. *Biostatistics*, 9(3):432–441.

Alona Fyshe, Partha P. Talukdar, Brian Murphy, and Tom M. Mitchell. 2014. Interpretable semantic vectors from a joint model of brain- and text- based meaning. In *Proc. of ACL*.

Alona Fyshe, Leila Wehbe, Partha P. Talukdar, Brian Murphy, and Tom M. Mitchell. 2015. A compositional and interpretable semantic space. In *Proc. of NAACL*.

Kuzman Ganchev, Ben Taskar, Fernando Pereira, and João Gama. 2009. Posterior vs. parameter sparsity in latent variable models. In *NIPS*.

Xavier Glorot, Antoine Bordes, and Yoshua Bengio. 2011. Domain adaptation for large-scale sentiment classification: A deep learning approach. In *Proc. of ICML*.

Joshua Goodman. 2004. Exponential priors for maximum entropy models. In *Proc. of NAACL*.

E. Grefenstette. 2013. Towards a formal distributional semantics: Simulating logical calculi with tensors. arXiv:1304.5823.

Jiang Guo, Wanxiang Che, Haifeng Wang, and Ting Liu. 2014. Revisiting embedding features for simple semi-supervised learning. In *Proc. of EMNLP*.

Georg Heigold, Erik McDermott, Vincent Vanhoucke, Andrew Senior, and Michiel Bacchiani. 2014. Asynchronous stochastic optimization for sequence training of deep neural networks. In *Proc. of ICASSP*.

Felix Hill, Roi Reichart, and Anna Korhonen. 2014. Simlex-999: Evaluating semantic models with (genuine) similarity estimation. *CoRR*, abs/1408.3456.

Patrik O. Hoyer. 2002. Non-negative sparse coding. In *Neural Networks for Signal Processing, 2002. Proc. of IEEE Workshop on*.

Eric H. Huang, Richard Socher, Christopher D. Manning, and Andrew Y. Ng. 2012. Improving word representations via global context and multiple word prototypes. In *Proc. of ACL*.

Jun'ichi Kazama and Jun'ichi Tsujii. 2003. Evaluation and extension of maximum entropy models with inequality constraints. In *Proc. of EMNLP*.

Douwe Kiela and Stephen Clark. 2013. Detecting compositionality of multi-word expressions using nearest neighbours in vector space models. In *Proc. of EMNLP*.

J. Richard Landis and Gary G. Koch. 1977. The measurement of observer agreement for categorical data. *Biometrics*, 33(1):159–174.

Angeliki Lazaridou, Eva Maria Vecchi, and Marco Baroni. 2013. Fish transporters and miracle homes: How compositional distributional semantics can help NP parsing. In *Proc. of EMNLP*.

Daniel D. Lee and H. Sebastian Seung. 1999. Learning the parts of objects by non-negative matrix factorization. *Nature*, 401(6755):788–791.

Honglak Lee, Alexis Battle, Rajat Raina, and Andrew Y. Ng. 2006. Efficient sparse coding algorithms. In *NIPS*.

Honglak Lee, Rajat Raina, Alex Teichman, and Andrew Y. Ng. 2009. Exponential family sparse coding with application to self-taught learning. In *Proc. of IJCAI*.

Beth Levin. 1993. *English Verb Classes and Alternations: A Preliminary Investigation*. University of Chicago Press.

Michael Lewicki and Terrence Sejnowski. 2000. Learning overcomplete representations. *Neural Computation*, 12(2):337–365.

Mike Lewis and Mark Steedman. 2013. Combined distributional and logical semantics. *Transactions of the ACL*, 1:179–192.

Mike Lewis and Mark Steedman. 2014. Combining formal and distributional models of temporal and intensional semantics. In *Proc. of ACL*.

Xin Li and Dan Roth. 2002. Learning question classifiers. In *Proc. of COLING*.

Weixiang Liu, Nanning Zheng, and Xiaofeng Lu. 2003. Non-negative matrix factorization for visual coding. In *Proc. of ICASSP*.

Mitchell P. Marcus, Mary Ann Marcinkiewicz, and Beatrice Santorini. 1993. Building a large annotated corpus of english: The penn treebank. *Computational Linguistics*, 19(2):313–330.

André F. T. Martins, Noah A. Smith, Pedro M. Q. Aguiar, and Mário A. T. Figueiredo. 2011. Structured sparsity in structured prediction. In *Proc. of EMNLP*.

Tomas Mikolov, Kai Chen, Greg Corrado, and Jeffrey Dean. 2013. Efficient estimation of word representations in vector space.

George A. Miller. 1995. WordNet: a lexical database for English. *Communications of the ACM*, 38(11):39–41.

Brian Murphy, Partha Talukdar, and Tom Mitchell. 2012. Learning effective and interpretable semantic models using non-negative sparse embedding. In *Proc. of COLING*.

Jerome L. Myers and Arnold D. Well. 1995. *Research Design & Statistical Analysis*. Routledge.

Bruno A. Olshausen and David J. Field. 1997. Sparse coding with an overcomplete basis set: A strategy employed by v1? *Vision Research*, 37(23):3311 – 3325.

Denis Paperno, Nghia The Pham, and Marco Baroni. 2014. A practical and linguistically-motivated approach to compositional distributional semantics. In *Proc. of ACL*.

Michael Paul and Mark Dredze. 2012. Factorial LDA: Sparse multi-dimensional text models. In *NIPS*.

Jeffrey Pennington, Richard Socher, and Christopher D. Manning. 2014. Glove: Global vectors for word representation. In *Proc. of EMNLP*.

Karin Kipper Schuler. 2005. *Verbnet: A Broad-coverage, Comprehensive Verb Lexicon*. Ph.D. thesis, University of Pennsylvania.

Richard Socher, Alex Perelygin, Jean Wu, Jason Chuang, Christopher D. Manning, Andrew Y. Ng, and Christopher Potts. 2013. Recursive deep models for semantic compositionality over a sentiment treebank. In *Proc. of EMNLP*.

Kristina Toutanova and Mark Johnson. 2007. A bayesian lda-based model for semi-supervised part-of-speech tagging. In *NIPS*.

Peter D. Turney and Patrick Pantel. 2010. From frequency to meaning : Vector space models of semantics. *JAIR*, 37(1):141–188.

Peter D. Turney. 2001. Mining the web for synonyms: PMI-IR versus LSA on TOEFL. In *Proc. of ECML*.

Eva Maria Vecchi, Roberto Zamparelli, and Marco Baroni. 2013. Studying the recursive behaviour of adjectival modification with compositional distributional semantics. In *Proc. of EMNLP*.

Lin Xiao. 2009. Dual averaging methods for regularized stochastic learning and online optimization. In *NIPS*.

Chang Xu, Yalong Bai, Jiang Bian, Bin Gao, Gang Wang, Xiaoguang Liu, and Tie-Yan Liu. 2014. Rc-net: A general framework for incorporating knowledge into word representations. In *Proc. of CIKM*.

Dani Yogatama and Noah A Smith. 2014. Linguistic structured sparsity in text categorization. In *Proc. of ACL*.

Mo Yu and Mark Dredze. 2014. Improving lexical embeddings with semantic knowledge. In *Proc. of ACL*.

Jun Zhu and Eric P Xing. 2012. Sparse topical coding. arXiv:1202.3778.

Learning Semantic Word Embeddings based on Ordinal Knowledge Constraints

Quan Liu[†] and **Hui Jiang**[‡] and **Si Wei**[§] and **Zhen-Hua Ling**[†] and **Yu Hu**[§]
[†] National Engineering Laboratory for Speech and Language Information Processing
University of Science and Technology of China, Hefei, China
[‡] Department of Electrical Engineering and Computer Science, York University, Canada
[§] iFLYTEK Research, Hefei, China
emails: quanliu@mail.ustc.edu.cn, hj@cse.yorku.ca,
siwei@iflytek.com, zhling@ustc.edu.cn, yuhu@iflytek.com

Abstract

In this paper, we propose a general framework to incorporate semantic knowledge into the popular data-driven learning process of word embeddings to improve the quality of them. Under this framework, we represent semantic knowledge as many ordinal ranking inequalities and formulate the learning of semantic word embeddings (SWE) as a constrained optimization problem, where the data-derived objective function is optimized subject to all ordinal knowledge inequality constraints extracted from available knowledge resources such as Thesaurus and WordNet. We have demonstrated that this constrained optimization problem can be efficiently solved by the stochastic gradient descent (SGD) algorithm, even for a large number of inequality constraints. Experimental results on four standard NLP tasks, including word similarity measure, sentence completion, name entity recognition, and the TOEFL synonym selection, have all demonstrated that the quality of learned word vectors can be significantly improved after semantic knowledge is incorporated as inequality constraints during the learning process of word embeddings.

1 Introduction

Distributed word representation (i.e., word embedding) is a technique that represents words as continuous vectors, which is an important research topic in natural language processing (NLP) (Hinton et al., 1986; Turney et al., 2010). In recent years, it has been widely used in various NLP tasks, including neural language model (Bengio et al., 2003; Schwenk, 2007), sequence labelling tasks (Collobert and Weston, 2008; Collobert et al., 2011), machine translation (Devlin et al., 2014; Sutskever et al., 2014), and antonym selection (Chen et al., 2015). Typically, word vectors are learned based on *the distributional hypothesis* (Harris, 1954; Miller and Charles, 1991), which assumes that words with a similar context tend to have a similar meaning. Under this hypothesis, various models, such as the skip-gram model (Mikolov et al., 2013a; Mikolov et al., 2013b; Levy and Goldberg, 2014) and GloVe model (Pennington et al., 2014), have been proposed to leverage the context of each word in large corpora to learn word embeddings. These methods can efficiently estimate the co-occurrence statistics to model contextual distributions from very large text corpora and they have been demonstrated to be quite effective in a number of NLP tasks. However, they still suffer from some major limitations. In particular, these corpus-based methods usually fail to capture the precise meanings for many words. For example, some semantically related but dissimilar words may have similar contexts, such as synonyms and antonyms. As a result, these corpus-based methods may lead to some antonymous word vectors being located much closer in the learned embedding space than many synonymous words. Moreover, as word representations are mainly learned based on the co-occurrence information, the learned word embeddings do not capture the accurate relationship between two semantically similar words if either one appears less frequently in the corpus.

To address these issues, some recent work has been proposed to incorporate prior lexical knowledge (WordNet, PPDB, etc.) or knowledge graph (Freebase, etc.) into word representations. Such knowledge enhanced word embedding methods have achieved considerable improvements on various natural language processing tasks, like (Yu and Dredze, 2014; Bian et al., 2014; Xu et al., 2014). These methods attempt to increase the semantic similarities between words belonging to

Proceedings of the 53rd Annual Meeting of the Association for Computational Linguistics and the 7th International Joint Conference on Natural Language Processing, pages 1501–1511,
Beijing, China, July 26-31, 2015.

one semantic category or to explicitly model the semantic relationships between different words. For example, Yu and Dredze (2014) have proposed a new learning objective function to enhance word embeddings by combining neural models and a prior knowledge measure from semantic resources. Bian et. al (2014) have recently proposed to leverage morphological, syntactic, and semantic knowledge to improve the learning of word embeddings. Besides, a novel framework has been proposed in (Xu et al., 2014) to take advantage of both relational and categorical knowledge to learn high-quality word representations, where two regularization functions are used to model the relational and categorical knowledge respectively. More recently, a retrofitting technique has been introduced in (Faruqui et al., 2014) to improve semantic vectors by leveraging lexicon-derived relational information in a post-processing stage.

In this paper, we propose a new and flexible method to incorporate semantic knowledge into the corpus-based learning of word embeddings. In our approach, we propose to represent semantic knowledge as many word ordinal ranking inequalities. Furthermore, these inequalities are cast as semantic constraints in the optimization process to learn semantically sensible word embeddings. The proposed method has several advantages. Firstly, many different types of semantic knowledge can all be represented as a number of such ranking inequalities, such as synonym-antonym, hyponym-hypernym and etc. Secondly, these inequalities can be easily extracted from many existing knowledge resources, such as Thesaurus, WordNet (Miller, 1995) and knowledge graphs. Moreover, the ranking inequalities can also be manually generated by human annotation because ranking orders is much easier for human annotators than assigning specific scores. Next, we present a flexible learning framework to learn distributed word representation based on the *ordinal semantic knowledge*. By solving a constrained optimization problem using the efficient stochastic gradient descent algorithm, we can obtain semantic word embedding enhanced by the ordinal knowledge constraints. Experiments on four popular natural language processing tasks, including word similarity, sentence completion, name entity recognition and synonym selection, have all demonstrated that the proposed method can learn good semantically sensible word embeddings.

2 Representing Knowledge By Ranking

Many types of lexical semantic knowledge can be quantitatively represented by a large number of ranking inequalities such as:

$$\text{similarity}(w_i, w_j) > \text{similarity}(w_i, w_k) \quad (1)$$

where w_i, w_j and w_k denote any three words in vocabulary. For example, eq.(1) holds if w_j is a synonym of w_i and w_k is an antonym of w_i. In general, the similarity between a word and its synonymous word should be larger than the similarity between the word and its antonymous word. Moreover, a particular word should be more similar to the words belonging to the same semantic category as this word than other words belonging to a different category. Besides, eq.(1) holds if w_i and w_j have shorter distance in a semantic hierarchy than w_i and w_k do in the same hierarchy (Leacock and Chodorow, 1998; Jurafsky and Martin, 2000).

Equivalently, each of the above similarity inequalities may be represented as the following constraint in the embedding space:

$$\text{sim}(\mathbf{w}_i^{(1)}, \mathbf{w}_j^{(1)}) > \text{sim}(\mathbf{w}_i^{(1)}, \mathbf{w}_k^{(1)}) \quad (2)$$

where $\mathbf{w}_i^{(1)}$, $\mathbf{w}_j^{(1)}$ and $\mathbf{w}_k^{(1)}$ denote the embedding vectors of the words, w_i, w_j and w_k.

In this paper, we use the following three rules to gather the ordinal semantic knowledge from available lexical knowledge resources, such as Thesaurus and WordNet.

- *Synonym Antonym Rule*: Similarities between a word and its synonymous words are always larger than similarities between the word and its antonymous words. For example, the similarity between *foolish* and *stupid* is expected to be bigger than the similarity between *foolish* and *clever*, i.e., similarity(*foolish*, *stupid*) > similarity(*foolish*, *clever*).

- *Semantic Category Rule*: Similarities of words that belong to the same semantic category would be larger than similarities of words that belong to different categories. This rule refers to the idea of Fisher linear discriminant algorithm in (Fisher, 1936). A semantic category may be defined as a synset in WordNet, a hypernym in a semantic hierarchy, or an entity category in

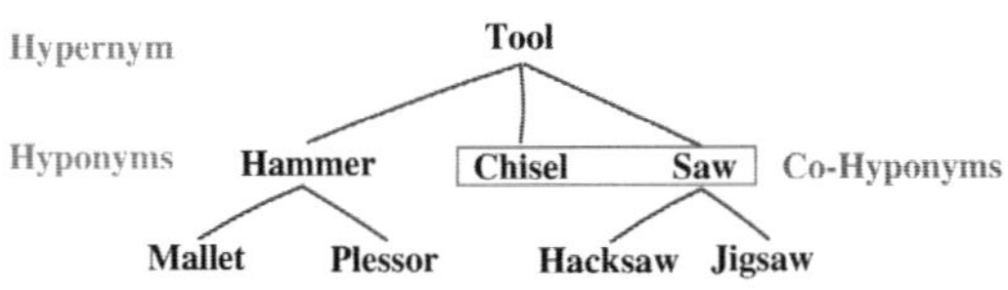

Figure 1: An example of hyponym and hypernym.

knowledge graphs. Figure 1 shows a simple example of the relationship between hyponyms and hypernyms. From there, it is reasonable to assume the following similarity inequality: similarity(*Mallet*, *Plessor*) $>$ similarity(*Mallet*, *Hacksaw*).

- *Semantic Hierarchy Rule*: Similarities between words that have shorter distances in a semantic hierarchy should be larger than similarities of words that have longer distances. In this work, the semantic hierarchy refers to the hypernym and hyponym structure in WordNet. From Figure 1, this rule may suggest several inequalities like: similarity(*Mallet*, *Hammer*) $>$ similarity(*Mallet*, *Tool*).

In addition, we may generate many such semantically ranking similarity inequalities by human annotation through crowdsourcing.

3 Semantic Word Embedding

In this section, we first briefly review the conventional skip-gram model (Mikolov et al., 2013b). Next, we study how to incorporate the ordinal similarity inequalities to learn semantic word embeddings.

3.1 The skip-gram model

The skip-gram model is a recently proposed learning framework (Mikolov et al., 2013b; Mikolov et al., 2013a) to learn continuous word vectors from text corpora based on the aforementioned distributional hypothesis, where each word in vocabulary (size of V) is mapped to a continuous embedding space by looking up an embedding matrix $\mathbf{W}^{(1)}$. And $\mathbf{W}^{(1)}$ is learned by maximizing the prediction probability, calculated by another prediction matrix $\mathbf{W}^{(2)}$, of its neighbouring words within a context window.

Given a sequence of training data, denoted as $w_1, w_2, w_3, ..., w_T$ with T words, the skip-gram model aims to maximize the following objective function:

$$\mathcal{Q} = \frac{1}{T}\sum_{t=1}^{T} \sum_{-c\le j\le c, j\neq 0} \log p(w_{t+j}|w_t) \quad (3)$$

where c is the size of context windows, w_t denotes the input central word and w_{t+j} for its neighbouring word. The skip-gram model computes the above conditional probability $p(w_{t+j}|w_t)$ using the following softmax function:

$$p(w_{t+j}|w_t) = \frac{\exp(\mathbf{w}_{t+j}^{(2)} \cdot \mathbf{w}_t^{(1)})}{\sum_{k=1}^{V} \exp(\mathbf{w}_k^{(2)} \cdot \mathbf{w}_t^{(1)})} \quad (4)$$

where $\mathbf{w}_t^{(1)}$ and $\mathbf{w}_k^{(2)}$ denotes row vectors in matrices $\mathbf{W}^{(1)}$ and $\mathbf{W}^{(2)}$, corresponding to word w_t and w_k respectively.

The training process of the skip-gram model can be formulated as an optimization problem to maximize the above objective function $\mathcal{Q}$. As in (Mikolov et al., 2013b), this optimization problem is solved by the stochastic gradient descent (SGD) method and the learned embedding matrix $\mathbf{W}^{(1)}$ is used as the word embeddings for all words in vocabulary.

3.2 Semantic Word Embedding (SWE) as Constrained Optimization

Here we consider how to combine the ordinal knowledge representation in section 2 and the skip-gram model in 3.1 to learn semantic word embeddings (SWE).

As shown in section 2, each ranking inequality involves a triplet, (i, j, k), of three words, $\{w_i, w_j, w_k\}$. Assume the ordinal knowledge is represented by a large number of such inequalities, denoted as the inequality set S. For $\forall(i, j, k) \in S$, we have:

$$\begin{aligned} &\text{similarity}(w_i, w_j) > \text{similarity}(w_i, w_k) \\ &\Leftrightarrow \text{sim}(\mathbf{w}_i^{(1)}, \mathbf{w}_j^{(1)}) > \text{sim}(\mathbf{w}_i^{(1)}, \mathbf{w}_k^{(1)}). \end{aligned}$$

For notational simplicity, we denote $s_{ij} = \text{sim}(\mathbf{w}_i^{(1)}, \mathbf{w}_j^{(1)})$ hereafter.

Next, we propose to use the following constrained optimization problem to learn semantic word embeddings (SWE):

$$\{\mathbf{W}^{(1)}, \mathbf{W}^{(2)}\} = \arg \max_{\mathbf{W}^{(1)}, \mathbf{W}^{(2)}} \mathcal{Q}(\mathbf{W}^{(1)}, \mathbf{W}^{(2)}) \quad (5)$$

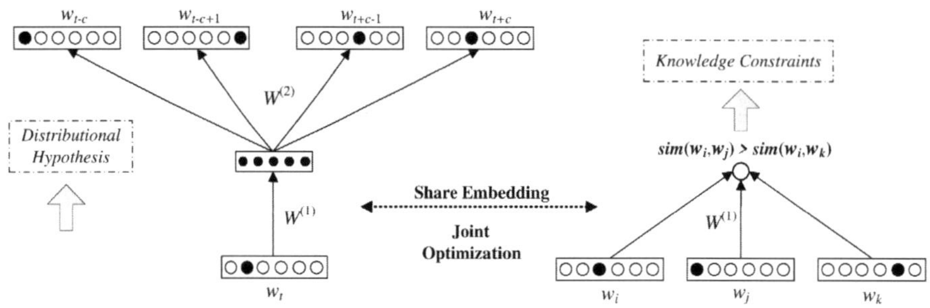

Figure 2: The proposed semantic word embedding (SWE) learning framework (The left part denotes the state-of-the-art skip-gram model; The right part represents the semantic constraints).

subject to

$$s_{ij} > s_{ik} \quad \forall (i,j,k) \in S. \tag{6}$$

In this work, we formulate the above constrained optimization problem into an unconstrained one by casting all the constraints as a penalty term in the objective function. The penalty term can be expressed as follows:

$$\mathcal{D} = \sum_{(i,j,k)\in S} f(i,j,k) \tag{7}$$

where the function $f(\cdot)$ is a normalization function. It can be a sigmoid function like $f(i,j,k) = \sigma(s_{ik} - s_{ij})$ with $\sigma(x) = 1/(1+\exp(-x))$. Alternatively, it may be a hinge loss function like $f(i,j,k) = h(s_{ik} - s_{ij})$ where $h(x) = \max(\delta_0, x)$ with δ_0 denoting a parameter to control the decision margin. In this work, we adopt to use the hinge function to compute the penalty term in eq.(7) and δ_0 is set to be 0 for all experiments.

Finally, the proposed semantic word embedding (SWE) model aims to maximize the following combined objective function:

$$\mathcal{Q}' = \mathcal{Q} - \beta \cdot \mathcal{D} \tag{8}$$

where β is a control parameter to balance the contribution of the penalty term in the optimization process. It balances between the semantic information estimated from the corpus based on the distributional hypothesis and the semantic knowledge encoded in the ordinal ranking inequalities. In Rocktäschel et al. (2014), a similar approach was proposed to capture knowledge constraint as extra terms in the objective function for optimization.

In Figure 2, we show a diagram for the the overall SWE learning framework to incorporate semantic knowledge into the basic skip-gram word embeddings. Comparing with the previous work in (Xu et al., 2014) and (Faruqui et al., 2014), the proposed SWE framework is more general in terms of encoding the semantic knowledge for learning word embeddings. It is straightforward to show that the work in (Xu et al., 2014; Zweig, 2014; Faruqui et al., 2014) can be viewed as some special cases under our SWE learning framework.

3.3 Optimization algorithm for SWE

In this work, the proposed semantic word embeddings (SWE) are learned using the standard mini-batch stochastic gradient descent (SGD) algorithm. Furthermore, we adopt to use the cosine distance of the embedding vectors to compute the similarity between two words in the penalty term.

In the following, we show how to compute the derivatives of the penalty term for the SWE learning.

$$\frac{\partial \mathcal{D}}{\partial \mathbf{w}_t^{(1)}} = \sum_{(i,j,k)\in S} \frac{\partial f(s_{ik} - s_{ij})}{\partial \mathbf{w}_t^{(1)}}$$
$$= \sum_{(i,j,k)\in S} f' \cdot \left(\delta_{ik}(t) \frac{\partial s_{ik}}{\partial \mathbf{w}_t^{(1)}} - \delta_{ij}(t) \frac{\partial s_{ij}}{\partial \mathbf{w}_t^{(1)}} \right) \tag{9}$$

where $\delta_{ik}(t)$ and $\delta_{ij}(t)$ are computed as

$$\delta_{ik}(t) = \begin{cases} 1 & t = i \text{ or } t = k \\ 0 & \text{otherwise} \end{cases} \tag{10}$$

and for the hinge loss function $f(x)$, we have

$$f' = \begin{cases} 1 & (s_{ik} - s_{ij}) > \delta_0 \\ 0 & (s_{ik} - s_{ij}) \le \delta_0 \end{cases} \tag{11}$$

and the derivatives of the cosine similarity measure, $s_{ij} = \frac{\mathbf{w}_i^{(1)} \cdot \mathbf{w}_j^{(1)}}{|\mathbf{w}_i^{(1)}||\mathbf{w}_j^{(1)}|}$, with respect to a word vector, i.e., $\frac{\partial s_{ik}}{\partial \mathbf{w}_i^{(1)}}$, which can be derived as follows:

$$\frac{\partial s_{ij}}{\partial \mathbf{w}_i^{(1)}} = -\frac{s_{ij}\mathbf{w}_i^{(1)}}{|\mathbf{w}_i^{(1)}|^2} + \frac{\mathbf{w}_j^{(1)}}{|\mathbf{w}_i^{(1)}||\mathbf{w}_j^{(1)}|}. \quad (12)$$

The learning rate used for the SWE learning is the same as that for the skip-gram model. In each mini-batch of SGD, we sample terms in the same way as the skip-gram model. As for the constraints, we do not sample them but use all inequalities relevant to any words in a minibatch to update the model for the minibatch. Finally, by jointly optimizing the two terms in the combined objective function, we may learn a new set of word vectors encoding with ordinal semantic knowledge.

4 Experiments

In this section, we report all experiments conducted to evaluate the effectiveness of the proposed semantic word embeddings (SWE). Here we compare the performance of the proposed SWE model with the conventional skip-gram baseline model on four popular natural language processing tasks, including word similarity measure, sentence completion, name entity recognition, and synonym selection. In the following, we first describe the experimental setup, training corpora, semantic knowledge databases. Next, we report the experimental results on these four NLP tasks. Note that the SWE training codes and scripts are made publicly available at `http://home.ustc.edu.cn/~quanliu/`.

4.1 Experimental setup

4.1.1 Training corpora

In this work, we use the popular Wikipedia corpus as our training data to learn word embeddings for experiments on the word similarity task and the TOEFL synonym selection task. Particularly, we utilize two Wikipedia corpora with different sizes. The first corpus with a smaller size is a data set including the first one billion characters from Wikipedia[1], named as *Wiki-Small* in our experiments. The second corpus with a relatively large size is the latest Wikipedia dump[2], named as *Wiki-Large* in our experiments. Both Wikipedia corpora have been pre-processed by removing all the HTML meta-data and hyper-links and replacing the digit numbers with English words using the perl script from the Matt Mahoney's page[3]. After text normalization, the *Wiki-Small* corpus contains totally 130 million words, for which we create a lexicon of 225,909 distinct words appearing more than 5 times in the corpus. Similarly, the *Wiki-Large* corpus contains about 5 billion words, for which we create a lexicon of 228,069 words appearing more than 200 times.

For the other two tasks, sentence completion and name entity recognition, we use the same training corpora from the previous state-of-the-art work for fair comparisons. The training corpus for the sentence completion is the Holmes text (Zweig and Burges, 2011; Mikolov et al., 2013a). The training corpus for the name entity recognition task is the Reuters English newswire from RCV1 (Turian et al., 2010; Lewis et al., 2004). Refer to section 4.4 and section 4.5 for detailed descriptions respectively.

4.1.2 Semantic constraint collections

In this work, we use WordNet as the resource to collect ordinal semantic knowledge. WordNet is a large semantic lexicon database of English words (Miller, 1995), where nouns, verbs, adjectives and adverbs are grouped into sets of cognitive synonyms (usually called synsets). Each synset usually expresses a distinct semantic concept. All synsets in WordNet are interlinked by means of conceptual-semantic and/or lexical relations such as synonyms and antonyms, hypernyms and hyponyms.

In our experiments, we use the version WordNet-3.1 for creating the corresponding semantic constraints. In detail, we follow the following process to extract semantic similarity inequalities from WordNet and Thesaurus:

1. Based on the *Synonym Antonym Rule* described in section 2, for each word in vocabulary, find its synset and use the synonym and antonym relations to find all related synonymous and antonymous synsets. Note that the antonymous synset is selected as long as there exists an antonymous relation between any word in this synset and any word in an synonymous synset. After finding the synonymous and antonymous synsets

[1] http://mattmahoney.net/dc/enwik9.zip

[2] http://dumps.wikimedia.org/enwiki/latest/enwiki-latest-pages-articles.xml.bz2

[3] http://mattmahoney.net/dc/textdata.html

of the current word, the similarity inequalities could be generated according to the ranking rule. After processing all words, we have collected about 30,000 inequalities related to the synonym and antonym relations. Furthermore, we extract additional 320,000 inequalities from an old English dictionary (Fernald, 1896). In total, we have about 345,000 inequalities related to the synonym and antonym relations. This set of inequalities is denoted as *Synon-Anton* constraints in our experiments.

2. Based on the *Semantic Category Rule* and *Semantic Hierarchy Rule*, we extract another inequality set consisting of 75,000 inequalities from WordNet. We defined this collection as *Hyper-Hypon* constraints in our experiments.

In the following experiments, we just use all of these collected inequality constraints as is without further manually checking or cleaning-up. They may contain a very small percentage of errors or conflicts (due to multiple senses of a word).

4.1.3 Training parameter setting

Here we describe the control parameters used to learn the baseline skip-gram model and the proposed SWE model. In our experiments, we use the open-source *word2vec* toolkit[4] to train the baseline skip-gram model, where the context window size is set to be 5. The initial learning rate is set as 0.025 and the learning rate is decreased linearly during the SGD model training process. We use the popular negative sampling technique to speed up model training and set the negative sample number as 5.

To train the proposed SWE model, we use the same configuration as the skip-gram model to maximize Q'. For the penalty term in eq. (7), we set $\delta_0 = 0$ for the hinge loss function. The semantic similarity between words is computed by the cosine distance. The combination coefficient β in eq. (8) is usually set to be a number between 0.001 and 0.3 in our experiments.

In the following four NLP tasks, the dimensionality of embedding vectors is different since we try to use the same settings from the state-of-the-art work for the comparison purpose. In the Word Similarity task and the TOEFL Synonym Selection task, we followed the state of the art work in (Xu et al., 2014), to set word embeddings to 300-dimension. Similarly, we refer to Bian et al. (2014) to set the dimensionality of word vectors to 600 for the Sentence Completion task. And we set the dimensionality of word vectors to 50 for the NER task according to (Turian et al., 2010; Pennington et al., 2014).

[4]https://code.google.com/p/word2vec.

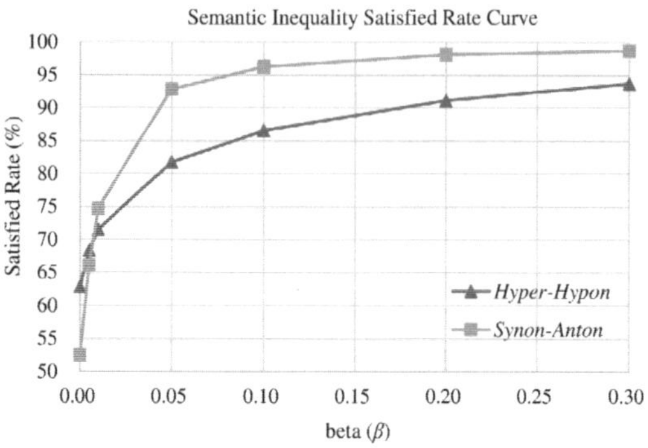

Figure 3: A curve of inequality satisfied rates (All models trained on the *Wiki-Small* corpus. *Hyper-Hypon* and *Synon-Anton* stand for different semantic constraint sets employed for training semantic word embeddings).

4.2 Semantic inequality satisfied rates

Here we first examine the inequality satisfied rates of various word embeddings. The inequality satisfied rate is defined as how many percentage of semantic inequalities are satisfied based on the underlying word embedding vectors. In Figure 3, we show a typical curve of the inequality satisfied rates as a function of β used in model training. This figure is plotted based on the *Wiki-Small* corpus. Two semantic constraint sets *Synon-Anton* and *Hyper-Hypon* created in section 4.1.2 are employed to learn semantic word embeddings.

In the framework of the proposed semantic word embedding method, we just need to tune one more parameter β, comparing with the skip-gram model. It shows that the baseline skip-gram ($\beta = 0$) can only satisfy about 50-60% of inequalities in the training set. As we choose a proper value for β, we may significantly improve the inequality satisfied rate, up to 85-95%. Although we can get higher inequality satisfying rate on the training set by increasing beta continuously, however, we do not suggest to use a big beta value because it would make the model overfitting. The major reason for this is that the constraints only cover a subset of words in vocabulary. Increasing the rate too much may screw up the entire word embeddings due to the sparsity of the constraints.

Meanwhile, we have found that the proposed SGD method is very efficient to handle a large number of inequalities in model training. When we use the total 345,000 inequalities, the SWE training is comparable with the baseline skip-gram model in terms of training speed. In the following, we continue to examine the SWE model on four popular natural language processing tasks, including word similarity, sentence completion, name entity recognition and the TOEFL synonym selection.

4.3 Task 1: Word Similarity Task

4.3.1 Task description

Measuring word similarity is a traditional NLP task (Rubenstein and Goodenough, 1965). Here we compare several word embedding models on a popular word similarity task, namely WordSim-353 (Finkelstein et al., 2001), which contains 353 English word pairs along with human-assigned similarity scores, which measure the relatedness of each word pair on a scale from 0 (totally unrelated words) to 10 (very much related or identical words). The final similarity score for each pair is the average across 13 to 16 human judges. When evaluating word embeddings on this task, we measure the performance by calculating the Spearman rank correlation between the human judgments and the similarity scores computed based on the learned word embeddings.

4.3.2 Experimental results

Here we compare the proposed SWE model with the baseline skip-gram model on the WordSim-353 task. Both word embedding models are trained using the Wikipedia corpora. We set the dimension of word embedding vectors to be 300. In Table 1, we have shown all the Spearman rank correlation results. The baseline results on this task include PPMI (Levy and Goldberg, 2014), GloVe (Pennington et al., 2014), and ESA-Wikipedia (Gabrilovich and Markovitch, 2007).

From the results in Table 1, we can see that the proposed SWE model can achieve consistent improvements over the baseline skip-gram model, no matter which training corpus is used. These results have demonstrated that, by incorporating semantic ordinal knowledge into the word vectors, the proposed semantic word embedding framework can capture much better semantics for many words. The SWE model using the *Wiki-Large* corpus has achieved the state-of-the-art performance on this task, significantly outperforming other popular word embedding methods, such as skip-gram and GloVe. Moreover, we also find that the *Synon-Anton* constraint set is more relevant than *Hyper-Hypon* for the word similarity task.

	Word Embeddings	Result
Others	SPPMI	0.6870
	GloVe (6 billion)	0.6580
	GloVe (42 billion)	0.7590
	ESA-Wikipedia	0.7500
Wiki-Small (0.13 billion)	Skip-gram	0.6326
	SWE + *Synon-Anton*	**0.6584**
	SWE + *Hyper-Hypon*	0.6407
	SWE + Both	0.6442
Wiki-Large (5 billion)	Skip-gram	0.7085
	SWE + *Synon-Anton*	**0.7274**
	SWE + *Hyper-Hypon*	0.7213
	SWE + Both	0.7236

Table 1: Spearman results on the WordSim-353 Task.

4.4 Task 2: Sentence Completion Task

4.4.1 Task description

The Microsoft sentence completion challenge has recently been introduced as a standard benchmark task for language modeling and other NLP techniques (Zweig and Burges, 2011). This task consists of 1040 sentences, each of which misses one word. The goal is to select a word that is the most coherent with the rest of the sentence, from a list of five candidates. Many NLP techniques have already been reported on this task, including N-gram model and LSA-based model proposed in (Zweig and Burges, 2011), log-bilinear model (Mnih and Teh, 2012), recurrent neural networks (RNN) (Mikolov, 2012), the skip-gram model (Mikolov et al., 2013a), a combination of the skip-gram and RNN model, and a knowledge enhanced word embedding model proposed by Bian et. al. (2014). The performance of all these techniques is listed in Table 2 for comparison.

In this work, we follow the the same procedure as in (Mikolov et al., 2013a) to examine the performance of our proposed semantic word embeddings (SWE) on this task. We first train 600-

dimension word embeddings based on a training corpus of 50M words provided by (Zweig and Burges, 2011), with and without using the collected ordinal knowledge. Then, for each sentence in the test set, we use the learned word embeddings to compute a sentence score for predicting all surrounding words based on each candidate word in the list. Finally, we use the computed sentence prediction scores to choose the most likely word from the given list to answer the question.

	System	Acc
Others	N-gram model	39.0
	LSA-based model	49.0
	Log-bilinear model	54.8
	RNN	55.4
	Skip-gram	48.0
	Skip-gram + RNN	58.9
Bian et al.	Skip-gram	41.2
	+ Syntactic knowledge	41.9
	+ Semantic knowledge	**45.2**
	+ Both knowledge	44.2
1 Iteration	Skip-gram	44.1
	SWE + *Synon-Anton*	47.9
	SWE + *Hyper-Hypon*	47.5
	SWE + Both	**48.3**
5 Iterations	Skip-gram	51.5
	SWE + *Synon-Anton*	55.7
	SWE + *Hyper-Hypon*	55.4
	SWE + Both	**56.2**

Table 2: Results on Sentence Completion Task.

4.4.2 Experimental results

In Table 2, we have shown the sentence completion accuracy on this task for various word embedding models. We can see that the proposed SWE model has achieved considerable improvements over the baseline skip-gram model. Once again, this suggests that the semantic knowledge represented by the ordinal inequalities can significantly improve the quality of the word embeddings. Besides, the SWE model significantly outperforms the recent work in (Bian et al., 2014), which considers syntactics and semantics of the sentence contexts.

4.5 Task 3: Name Entity Recognition

4.5.1 Task description

To further investigate the performance of semantic word embeddings, we have further conducted some experiments on the standard CoNLL03 name entity recognition (NER) task. The CoNLL03 NER dataset is drawn from the Reuters newswire. The training set contains 204K words (14K sentences, 946 documents), the test set contains 46K words (3.5K sentences, 231 documents), and the development set contains 51K words (3.3K sentences, 216 documents). We have listed the state-of-the-art performance in Table 3 for this task (Turian et al., 2010).

To make a fair comparison, we have used the exactly same experimental configurations as in (Turian et al., 2010), including the used training algorithm, the baseline discrete features and so on. Like the C&W model, we use the same training text resource to learn word vectors, which contains one year of Reuters English newswire from RCV1, from August 1996 to August 1997, having about 810,000 news stories (Lewis et al., 2004). Meanwhile, the dimension of word embeddings is set to 50 for all experiments on this task.

4.5.2 Experimental results

In our experiments, we compare the proposed SWE model with the baseline skip-gram model for name entity recognition, measured by the standard F1 scores. We present the final NER F1 scores on the CoNLL03 NER task in Table 3. The notation "Gaz" stands for gazetteers that are added into the NER system as an auxiliary feature. For the SWE model, we experiment two configurations by adding gazetteers or not (denoted by "IsGaz" and "NoGaz" respectively).

	System	Dev	Test	MUC7
Others	C&W	92.3	87.9	75.7
	C&W + Gaz	93.0	88.9	81.4
NoGaz	Skip-gram	92.6	88.3	76.7
	+ *Synon-Anton*	92.5	88.4	77.2
	+ *Hyper-Hypon*	92.6	**88.6**	**77.7**
	+ Both	92.6	88.4	77.5
IsGaz	Skip-gram	93.3	89.5	80.0
	+ *Synon-Anton*	93.1	89.6	80.7
	+ *Hyper-Hypon*	93.1	89.7	80.7
	+ Both	93.0	89.5	**80.8**

Table 3: F1 scores on the CoNLL03 NER task.

From the results shown in Table 3, we could find the proposed semantic word embedding (SWE) model can consistently achieve 0.8% (or more) absolute improvements on the MUC7 task no matter whether the gazetteers features are used or not. The proposed SWE model can also obtain 0.3% improvement in the CoNLL03 test set when no gazetteers is added into the NER system. However, no significant improvement is observed in this test set for the proposed SWE model after we add the gazetteers feature.

4.6 Task 4: TOEFL Synonym Selection

4.6.1 Task description

The goal of a synonym selection task is to select, from a list of candidate words, the semantically closest word for each given target word. The dataset we use for this task is the standard TOEFL dataset (Landauer and Dumais, 1997), which contains 80 questions. Each question consists of a target word along with 4 candidate lexical substitutes for selection.

The evaluation criterion on this task is the synonym selection accuracy which indicates how many synonyms are correctly selected for all 80 questions. Similar to the configurations on the word similarity task, all the experiments on this task are conducted on the English Wikipedia corpora. In our experiments, we set all the vector dimensions to 300.

4.6.2 Experimental Results

Corpus	Model	Accuracy (%)
Wiki-Small	Skip-gram	61.25
	+ *Synon-Anton*	**70.00**
	+ *Hyper-Hypon*	66.25
	+ Both	**71.25**
Wiki-Large	Skip-gram	83.75
	+ *Synon-Anton*	**87.50**
	+ *Hyper-Hypon*	85.00
	+ Both	**88.75**

Table 4: The TOEFL synonym selection task.

In Table 4, we have shown the experimental results for different word embedding models, learned from different Wikipedia corpora: *Wiki-Small* or *Wiki-Large*. We compare the proposed SWE with the baseline skip-gram model. From the experimental results in Table 4, we can see that the proposed SWE model can achieve consistent improvements over the baseline skip-gram model on the TOEFL synonym selection task, about 5-8% improvements on the selection accuracy. We find the similar performance differences between the SWE model trained with the *Synon-Anton* and *Hyper-Hypon* constraint set. The main reason would be that the synonym selection task is mainly related to lexical level similarity and less relevant to the hypernym-hyponym relations.

5 Conclusions and Future Work

Word embedding models with good semantic representations are quite invaluable to many natural language processing tasks. However, the current data-driven methods that learn word vectors from corpora based on the distributional hypothesis tend to suffer from some major limitations. In this paper, we propose a general and flexible framework to incorporate various types of semantic knowledge into the popular data-driven learning procedure for word embeddings. Our main contributions are to represent semantic knowledge as a number of ordinal similarity inequalities as well as to formulate the entire learning process as a constrained optimization problem. Meanwhile, the optimization problem could be solved by efficient stochastic gradient descend algorithm. Experimental results on four popular NLP tasks have all demonstrated that the propose semantic word embedding framework can significantly improve the quality of word representations.

As for the future work, we would incorporate more types of knowledge, such as knowledge graphs and FrameNet, into the learning process for more powerful word representations. We also expect that some common sense related semantic knowledge may be generated as ordinal inequality constraints by human annotators for learning semantic word embeddings. At the end, we plan to apply the SWE word embedding models for more natural language processing tasks.

Acknowledgments

This work was supported in part by the Science and Technology Development of Anhui Province, China (Grants No. 2014z02006) and the Fundamental Research Funds for the Central Universities. Special thanks to Zhigang Chen, Ruiji Fu and the anonymous reviewers for their insightful comments as well as suggestions. The authors also want to thank Profs. Wu Guo and Li-Rong Dai for their wonderful help and supports during the experiments.

References

Yoshua Bengio, Réjean Ducharme, Pascal Vincent, and Christian Jauvin. 2003. A neural probabilistic language model. *Journal of Machine Learning Research*, 3:1137–1155.

Jiang Bian, Bin Gao, and Tie-Yan Liu. 2014. Knowledge-powered deep learning for word embedding. In *Machine Learning and Knowledge Discovery in Databases*, pages 132–148. Springer.

Zhigang Chen, Wei Lin, Qian Chen, Xiaoping Chen, Si Wei, Xiaodan Zhu, and Hui Jiang. 2015. Revisiting word embedding for contrasting meaning. In *Proceedings of ACL*.

Ronan Collobert and Jason Weston. 2008. A unified architecture for natural language processing: Deep neural networks with multitask learning. In *Proceedings of ICML*, pages 160–167. ACM.

Ronan Collobert, Jason Weston, Léon Bottou, Michael Karlen, Koray Kavukcuoglu, and Pavel Kuksa. 2011. Natural language processing (almost) from scratch. *Journal of Machine Learning Research*, 12:2493–2537.

Jacob Devlin, Rabih Zbib, Zhongqiang Huang, Thomas Lamar, Richard Schwartz, and John Makhoul. 2014. Fast and robust neural network joint models for statistical machine translation. In *Proceedings of ACL*, pages 1370–1380.

Manaal Faruqui, Jesse Dodge, Sujay K Jauhar, Chris Dyer, Eduard Hovy, and Noah A Smith. 2014. Retrofitting word vectors to semantic lexicons. In *Proceedings of the NIPS Deep learning and representation learning workshop*.

James Champlin Fernald. 1896. *English synonyms and antonyms*. Funk & Wagnalls Company.

Lev Finkelstein, Evgeniy Gabrilovich, Yossi Matias, Ehud Rivlin, Zach Solan, Gadi Wolfman, and Eytan Ruppin. 2001. Placing search in context: The concept revisited. In *Proceedings of WWW*, pages 406–414. ACM.

Ronald A Fisher. 1936. The use of multiple measurements in taxonomic problems. *Annals of eugenics*, 7(2):179–188.

Evgeniy Gabrilovich and Shaul Markovitch. 2007. Computing semantic relatedness using wikipedia-based explicit semantic analysis. In *Proceedings of IJCAI*, volume 7, pages 1606–1611.

Zellig S Harris. 1954. Distributional structure. *Word*, 10(23):146–162.

Geoffrey E Hinton, James L McClelland, and David E Rumelhart. 1986. Distributed representations. In *Parallel distributed processing: Explorations in the microstructure of cognition. Volume 1: Foundations*, pages 77–109. MIT Press.

Dan Jurafsky and James H Martin. 2000. *Speech & language processing*. Pearson Education India.

Thomas K Landauer and Susan T Dumais. 1997. A solution to plato's problem: The latent semantic analysis theory of acquisition, induction, and representation of knowledge. *Psychological review*, 104(2):211.

Claudia Leacock and Martin Chodorow. 1998. Combining local context and wordnet similarity for word sense identification. *WordNet: An electronic lexical database*, 49(2):265–283.

Omer Levy and Yoav Goldberg. 2014. Neural word embedding as implicit matrix factorization. In *Proceedings of NIPS*, pages 2177–2185.

David D Lewis, Yiming Yang, Tony G Rose, and Fan Li. 2004. RCV1: A new benchmark collection for text categorization research. *Journal of Machine Learning Research*, 5:361–397.

Tomas Mikolov, Kai Chen, Greg Corrado, and Jeffrey Dean. 2013a. Efficient estimation of word representations in vector space. In *Proceedings of Workshop at ICLR*.

Tomas Mikolov, Ilya Sutskever, Kai Chen, Greg S Corrado, and Jeff Dean. 2013b. Distributed representations of words and phrases and their compositionality. In *Proceedings of NIPS*, pages 3111–3119.

Tomáš Mikolov. 2012. *Statistical language models based on neural networks*. Ph.D. thesis, Ph. D. thesis, Brno University of Technology.

George A Miller and Walter G Charles. 1991. Contextual correlates of semantic similarity. *Language and cognitive processes*, 6(1):1–28.

George A Miller. 1995. Wordnet: a lexical database for english. *Communications of the ACM*, 38(11):39–41.

Andriy Mnih and Yee Whye Teh. 2012. A fast and simple algorithm for training neural probabilistic language models. In *Proceedings of ICML*.

Jeffrey Pennington, Richard Socher, and Christopher D Manning. 2014. Glove: Global vectors for word representation. *Proceedings of EMNLP*, 12:1532–1543.

Tim Rocktäschel, Matko Bošnjak, Sameer Singh, and Sebastian Riedel. 2014. Low-dimensional embeddings of logic. In *Proceedings of the ACL 2014 Workshop on Semantic Parsing*, pages 45–49, Baltimore, MD, June. Association for Computational Linguistics.

Herbert Rubenstein and John B Goodenough. 1965. Contextual correlates of synonymy. *Communications of the ACM*, 8(10):627–633.

Holger Schwenk. 2007. Continuous space language models. *Computer Speech & Language*, 21(3):492–518.

Ilya Sutskever, Oriol Vinyals, and Quoc VV Le. 2014. Sequence to sequence learning with neural networks. In *Proceedings of NIPS*, pages 3104–3112.

Joseph Turian, Lev Ratinov, and Yoshua Bengio. 2010. Word representations: a simple and general method for semi-supervised learning. In *Proceedings of ACL*, pages 384–394. Association for Computational Linguistics.

Peter D Turney, Patrick Pantel, et al. 2010. From frequency to meaning: Vector space models of semantics. *Journal of artificial intelligence research*, 37(1):141–188.

Chang Xu, Yalong Bai, Jiang Bian, Bin Gao, Gang Wang, Xiaoguang Liu, and Tie-Yan Liu. 2014. Rc-net: A general framework for incorporating knowledge into word representations. In *Proceedings of CIKM*, pages 1219–1228. ACM.

Mo Yu and Mark Dredze. 2014. Improving lexical embeddings with semantic knowledge. In *Proceedings of ACL*, volume 2, pages 545–550.

Geoffrey Zweig and Christopher JC Burges. 2011. The microsoft research sentence completion challenge. Technical report, Technical Report MSR-TR-2011-129, Microsoft.

Geoffrey Zweig. 2014. Explicit representation of antonymy in language modelling. Technical report, Technical Report MSR-TR-2014-52, Microsoft.

Adding Semantics to Data-Driven Paraphrasing

Ellie Pavlick[1] Johan Bos[2] Malvina Nissim[2] Charley Beller[3] Benjamin Van Durme[4] Chris Callison-Burch[1]
[1]Computer and Information Science Department, University of Pennsylvania
[2]Center for Language and Cognition Groningen, University of Groningen
[4]Human Language Technology Center of Excellence, Johns Hopkins University
[3]IBM Watson Group

Abstract

We add an interpretable semantics to the paraphrase database (PPDB). To date, the relationship between phrase pairs in the database has been weakly defined as approximately equivalent. We show that these pairs represent a variety of relations, including directed entailment (*little girl/girl*) and exclusion (*nobody/someone*). We automatically assign semantic entailment relations to entries in PPDB using features derived from past work on discovering inference rules from text and semantic taxonomy induction. We demonstrate that our model assigns these relations with high accuracy. In a downstream RTE task, our labels rival relations from WordNet and improve the coverage of a proof-based RTE system by 17%.

Riots in Denmark were sparked by 12 editorial cartoons that were offensive to Muhammad.

12	$\equiv$	Twelve
editorial cartoons	$\sqsupset$	illustrations
offensive	$\sqsupset$	insulting
Muhammad	$\equiv$	the prophet
sparked	$\sqsupset$	caused
riots	$\sqsupset$	unrest
in Denmark	$\mid$	in Jordan

Twelve illustrations insulting the prophet caused unrest in Jordan.

Figure 1: An example sentence pair for the RTE task. In order for a system to conclude that the premise (top) does not entail the hypothesis (bottom), it should recognize that *sparked* implies *caused* but that *in Denmark* precludes *in Jordan*. These phrase-level entailment relationships are modeled by natural logic.

1 Motivation

A basic precursor to language understanding is the ability to recognize when two expressions mean the same thing. Different expressions of the same information is the central problem addressed by paraphrasing and the closely related task of recognizing textual entailment (RTE). In RTE, a system is given two pieces of text, often called the *text* (T) and the *hypothesis* (H), and asked to determine whether T entails H, T contradicts H, or T and H are unrelatable (Figure 1). In contrast, data-driving paraphrasing typically sidesteps developing a clear definition of "meaning the same thing" and instead "assume[s] paraphrasing is a coherent notion and concentrate[s] on devices that can produce paraphrases" (Barzilay, 2003). Recent work on paraphrase extraction has resulted in enormous paraphrase collections (Lin and Pantel, 2001; Dolan et al., 2004; Ganitkevitch et al., 2013), but the usefulness of these collections is limited by the fast-and-loose treatment of the meaning of paraphrases. One concrete definition that is sometimes used for paraphrases requires that they be bidirectionally entailing (Androutsopoulos and Malakasiotis, 2010). That is, in terms of RTE, it is assumed that if P is a paraphrase of Q, then P entails Q and Q entails P. In reality, paraphrases are often more nuanced (Bhagat and Hovy, 2013), and the entries in most paraphrase resources certainly do not match this definition. For instance, Lin and Pantel (2001) extracted 12 million "inference rules" from monolingual text by exploiting shared dependency contexts. Their method learns paraphrases that are truly meaning equivalent, but it just as readily learns contradictory pairs such as $\langle X\ rises, X\ falls\rangle$. Ganitkevitch et al. (2013) extract over 150 million paraphrase rules by pivoting through foreign translations. This bilingual method often learns hypernym/hyponym pairs, e.g. due to variation in the discourse structure of translations (Callison-

Proceedings of the 53rd Annual Meeting of the Association for Computational Linguistics and the 7th International Joint Conference on Natural Language Processing, pages 1512–1522,
Beijing, China, July 26-31, 2015. ©2015 Association for Computational Linguistics

Equivalent	Entailment	Exclusion	Other relation	Unrelated
look at/watch	little girl/girl	close/open	swim/water	girl/play
a person/someone	kuwait/country	minimal/significant	husband/marry to	found/party
clean/cleanse	tower/building	boy/young girl	oil/oil price	profit/year
away/out	the cia/agency	nobody/someone	country/patriotic	man/talk
distant/remote	sneaker/footwear	blue/green	drive/vehicle	car/family
the phone/the telephone	heroin/drug	france/germany	family/home	holiday/series
last autumn/last fall	doe/deer	least three/least two	basketball/court	green/tennis
illegal entry/smuggling	typhoon/storm	child/mother	playing/toy	sunday/tour
approve/to ratify	seriously injure/injure	in front/on the side	islamic/jihad	city/south
alliance of/coalition between	sunglasses/glasses	oppose/support	delay/time	back/view

Table 1: Examples of different types of entailment relations appearing in PPDB.

Burch, 2007), and unrelated pairs, e.g. due to misalignments or polysemy in the foreign language.

The unclear semantics severely limits the applicability of paraphrase resources to natural language understanding (NLU) tasks. Some efforts have been made to identify directionality of paraphrases (Bhagat et al., 2007; Kotlerman et al., 2010), but tasks like RTE require even richer semantic information. For example, in the T/H pair shown in Figure 1, a system needs information not only about equivalent words (*12/twelve*) and asymmetric entailments (*riots/unrest*), but also semantic exclusion (*Denmark/Jordan*). Such lexical entailment relations are captured by *natural logic*, a formalism which views natural language itself as a meaning representation, eschewing external representations such as First Order Logic (FOL). This is a great fit for automatically extracted paraphrases, since the phrase pairs themselves can be used as the semantic representation with minimal additional annotation. But as is, paraphrase resources lack such annotation.

As a result, NLU systems rely on manually built resources like WordNet, which are limited in coverage and often lead to incorrect inferences (Kaplan and Schubert, 2001). In fact, in the most recent RTE challenge, over half of the submitted systems used WordNet (Pontiki et al., 2014). Even the NatLog system (MacCartney and Manning, 2007), which popularized natural logic for RTE, relied on WordNet and did not solve the problem of assigning natural logic relations at scale.

The main contributions of this paper are:

- We add a concrete, interpretable semantics to the Paraphrase Database (PPDB) (Ganitkevitch et al., 2013), the largest paraphrase resource currently available. We give each entry in the database a label describing the entailment relationship between the phrases.
- We develop a statistical model to predict these relations. The enormous size of PPDB– over 77 million phrase pairs!– makes it impossible to perform this task manually. Our wide range of monolingual and bilingual features results in high intrinsic accuracy.
- We demonstrate improvements to a proof-based RTE system, showing that our automatic labels increase the number of proofs that it is able to find by 17%, while maintaining the same accuracy as when using gold-standard, manual labels.

2 Related Work

Lexical entailment resources Approaches to paraphrase identification have exploited signal from distributional contexts (Lin and Pantel, 2001; Szpektor et al., 2004), comparable corpora (Dolan et al., 2004; Xu et al., 2014), and graph structures (Berant et al., 2011; Brockett et al., 2013). These approaches are scalable, but they often assume that all relations are equivalence relations (Madnani and Dorr, 2010). Several efforts have attempted to build or augment lexical ontologies automatically, to discover other types of lexical relations like hypernyms. Most of these approaches rely on lexico-syntactic patterns. Hearst (1992) searched for hand-written patterns (e.g. "an X is a Y") in a large corpus in order to learn taxonomic relations between nouns. Snow et al. (2006) used dependency parses to automatically learn such patterns, which they used to augment WordNet with new hypernym relations. Similar monolingual signals have been used to learn fine-grained relationships between verbs, such as *enablement* and *happens-before* (Chklovski and Pantel, 2004; Hashimoto et al., 2009).

Recognizing Textual Entailment The shared RTE tasks (Dagan et al., 2006) have been a springboard for research in natural language inference,

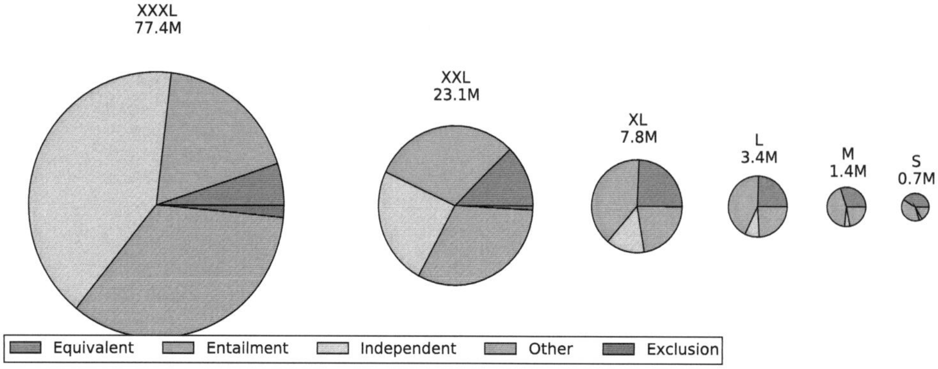

Figure 2: Distribution of entailment relations in different sizes of PPDB. Distributions are estimated from our manual annotations of randomly sampled pairs. PPDB-XXXL contains over 77MM paraphrase pairs (where the majority type is independent), compared to only 700K in PPDB-S (where the majority type is equivalent).

using data motivated by the applications to information retrieval, information extraction, summarization, machine translation evaluation, and more recently, question answering (Giampiccolo et al., 2007) and essay grading (Clark et al., 2013). RTE systems vary considerably in their choice of representation and inference procedure. In the most recent shared task on RTE, some systems used deep logical representations of text, allowing them to invoke theorem provers (Bjerva et al., 2014) or Markov Logic Networks (Beltagy et al., 2014) to perform the inference, while others used shallower representations, relying on machine learning to perform inference (Lai and Hockenmaier, 2014; Zhao et al., 2014). Systems based on natural logic (MacCartney and Manning, 2007) use natural language as a representation, but still perform inference using a structured algebra rather than a statistical model. Regardless of the inference procedure, improvements to external lexical resources can improve RTE systems across the board (Clark et al., 2007).

3 The Paraphrase Database (PPDB)

PPDB is currently the largest available collection of paraphrases. Compared to other paraphrase resources such as the DIRT database (12 million rules) (Lin and Pantel, 2001) and the MSR paraphrase phrase table (13 million) (Dolan et al., 2004), PPDB contains over 150 million paraphrase rules covering three paraphrase types– lexical (single word), phrasal (multiword), and syntactic restructuring rules. We focus on lexical and phrasal paraphrases, of which there are over 77 million rules. Of these, a large fraction are true paraphrases– either equivalent (*distant/remote*) or asymmetric entailment (*girl/little girl*)– but many are not. PPDB contains some pairs which are related by semantic exclusion (*nobody/someone*), some of which are related by something other than entailment (*swim/water*), and some which are simply unrelated (*car/family*). Table 1 gives examples of pairs in PPDB falling into each of these categories.

PPDB is released in six sizes (S, M, L, XL, XXL and XXXL), which fall roughly on a continuum from highest precision and lowest recall to lowest average precision and highest recall. Figure 2 shows how the distribution of entailment relations differs across the sizes of PPDB.[1] Our goal is to make these relations explicit, by providing annotations for each phrase pair. Because of the enormous scale of PPDB, this annotation must be done automatically.

4 Selection of Paraphrases

In this paper we focus on paraphrases pairs from PPDB that occur in RTE data. We use the recent SICK dataset from in the 2014 SemEval RTE challenge (Marelli et al., 2014) for our experiments. The data consists of 10K sentences split roughly evenly into training and testing sets. The sentence pairs are labeled using a 3-way entailment classification: ENTAILMENT, (29%) CONTRADICTION (15%), or NEUTRAL (56%). We consider all phrase pairs from PPDB $\langle p_1, p_2\rangle$ up to three words in length such that there is some T/H sentence pair in which p_1 appears in T and p_2 appears

[1]These distributions were estimated based on a random sample of pairs drawn from each size of PPDB, annotated on MTurk as described in Section 5

Lexical	We use the lemmas, POS tags, and phrase lengths of p_1 and p_2, the substrings shared by p_1 and p_2, and the Levenstein, Jaccard, and Hamming distances between p_1 and p_2.
Distributional	Given a dependency context vectors for p_1 and p_2, we compute the number of shared contexts, and the Jaccard, Cosine, Lin1998, Weeds2004, Clarke2009, and Szpektor2008 similarities between the vectors.
Paraphrase	We include 33 paraphrase features distributed with PPDB, which include the paraphrase probabilities as computed in Bannard and Callison-Burch (2005). We refer the reader to Ganitkevitch and Callison-Burch (2014) for a complete description of all of the features included with PPDB.
Translation	We include the number of foreign language "pivots" (translations) shared by p_1 and p_2 for each of 24 languages used in the construction of PPDB, as a fraction of the total number of translations observed for each of p_1 and p_2.
Path	We include a sparse vector of all lexico-syntactic patterns (paths through a dependency parse) which are observed between p_1 and p_2 in the Annotated Gigaword corpus (Napoles et al., 2012).
WordNet	We include binary features indicating whether WordNet classifies p_1 and p_2 according to any of the following relations: synonym, hypernym, hyponym, antonym, holonym, meronym, cause, entailment, derivationally-related, similar-to, also-see, or attribute.

Figure 3: Summary of features extracted for each phrase pair $\langle p_1, p_2 \rangle$. Full descriptions of the features used are given in the supplementary material.

in H. Roughly 55% of the word types and 5% of the phrase (bigram and trigram) types in the SICK data appear in PPDB. This gives us a list of 9,600 pairs, half from the training sentences, which we use for development in Section 6, and half from the test sentences, which we use for evaluation in Section 7.

The SICK data has a relatively small vocabulary, with 86% of words types and <1% of the phrase types covered by WordNet. Still, over half of the words in SICK which are covered by PPDB do not appear in WordNet. In general, PPDB covers a much larger vocabulary (1.6MM words) than does WordNet (155K words), and we expect the potential benefit of using PPDB in addition to or in place of WordNet to be larger on datasets with richer vocabularies.

5 Entailment Relations

We use the relations from Bill MacCartney's thesis on natural language inference as the basis for our categorization of relations (MacCartney, 2009). He outlines 7 basic entailment relationships:[2]

Equivalence (P≡Q): $\forall x[P(x) \leftrightarrow Q(x)]$
Forward Entailment (P⊏Q): $\forall x[P(x) \rightarrow Q(x)]$
Reverse Entailment (P⊐Q): $\forall x[Q(x) \rightarrow P(x)]$
Negation (P^Q): $\forall x\ [P(x) \leftrightarrow \neg Q(x)]$
Alternation (P|Q): $\forall x\ \neg[P(x) \wedge Q(x)]$
Cover (P‿Q): $\forall x[P(x) \vee Q(x)]$
Independence (P#Q): All other cases.

[2]To further clarify the definitions here: "negation" is XOR (exclusive disjunction), "alternation" is NAND, and "cover" is OR (inclusive disjunction)

These relations are based on the theory of *natural logic*, meaning they are defined between pairs of natural language expressions rather than requiring an external formal representation. This makes them an ideal fit for the phrase pairs in in PPDB and similar automatically-constructed paraphrase resources.

Nat. Log.	This work	MTurk description
≡	≡	X is the same as Y
⊏	⊏	X is more specific than/is a type of Y
⊐	⊐	X is more general than/encompasses Y
^ |	¬	X is the opposite of Y X is mutually exclusive with Y
#	∼ #	X is related in some other way to Y X is not related to Y

Table 2: Column 1 gives the semantics of each label under MacCartney's Natural Logic. Column 2 gives the notation we use throughout the remainder of this paper. Column 3 gives the description that was shown to Turkers.

Annotation We use Amazon Mechanical Turk (MTurk) to collect labels for our phrase pairs. We asked workers to choose between the options show in Table 2, which represent a modified version of MacCartney's relations. We replace negation (^) with the weaker notion of "opposites," effectively merging it with the alternation (|) relation; we split the independent (#) class into two cases: truly independent phrases and phrases which are related by something other than entailment (which we denote ∼). We omit the cover (‿) relation entirely, as its practicality is not obvious. We show each pair to 5 workers, taking the majority label as truth. Each HIT consisted of two control questions taken from WordNet. Workers achieved good accuracies on our controls (82% overall) and moder-

Cosine Similarity		Monolingual (symmetric)		Monolingual (asymmetric)		Bilingual	
$\sqsupset$	shades/the shade	$\neg$	large/small	$\sqsupset$	boy/little boy	$\equiv$	dad/father
$\sqsupset$	yard/backyard	$\equiv$	few/several	$\sqsupset$	man/two men	$\sqsupset$	some kid/child
$\#$	each other/man	$\neg$	different/same	$\sqsupset$	child/three children	$\equiv$	a lot of/many
$\sqsupset$	picture/drawing	$\neg$	other/same	$\equiv$	is playing/play	$\equiv$	female/woman
$\sim$	practice/target	$\neg$	put/take	$\sqsupset$	side/both sides	$\equiv$	male/man

Table 3: Top scoring pairs (x/y) according to various similarity measures, along with their manually classified entailment labels. Column 1 is cosine similarity based on dependency contexts. Column 2 is based on Lin (1998), column 3 on Weeds (2004), and column 4 is a novel feature. Precise definitions of each metric are given in the supplementary material.

ate levels of agreement (Fleiss's $\kappa = 0.56$) (Landis and Koch, 1977). For a fuller discussion of the annotation, refer to the supplementary material.

6 Automatic Classification

We aim to build a classifier to automatically assign entailment types to entries in the PPDB, and to demonstrate that it performs well both intrinsically and extrinsically. We fix the direction of the $\sqsubset$ and $\sqsupset$ relations to create a single class and train a logistic regression classifier to distinguish between the 5 classes $\{\#, \equiv, \sqsupset, \neg, \sim\}$. We compute variety of basic lexical features and WordNet features (summarized in Figure 3). We categorize the remaining features into two broad groups: monolingual features, which are based on observed usage in the Annotated Gigaword corpus (Napoles et al., 2012), and bilingual features, which are based on translation probabilities observed in bilingual parallel corpora. Full descriptions of all the features used are provided in the supplementary material.

6.1 Monolingual features

Path features Snow et al. (2004) used lexico-syntactic patterns to mine taxonomic relations (hypernyms and hyponyms) between noun pairs. They were able to verify the earlier work of Hearst (1992) which found that certain patterns, e.g. *X and other Y*, are strong indicators of hypernymy. Using similar path features, we learn new patterns to differentiate between more subtle relations. For example, we learn the pattern *separate X from Y* is highly indicative of the $\neg$ relation. We learn that the pattern *X including Y* suggests $\sqsupset$ more than it suggests $\equiv$ whereas the pattern *X known as Y* suggests $\equiv$ more than $\sqsupset$. Table 4 gives examples of some of the paths most indicative of the $\neg$ relation.

in X and in Y	*in foods and in beverages*
separate X from Y	*separate the old from the young*
to X and/or to Y	*to the left or to the right*
from X to Y	*from 7 a.m. to 10 p.m.*
more/less X than Y	*more harm than good*

Table 4: Top paths associated with the $\neg$ class.

Distributional features Lin and Pantel (2001) attempted to mine inference rules from text by finding paths in a dependency tree which connect the same nouns. The intuition is that good paraphrases should tend to modify and be modified by the same words. Given context vectors, Lin and Pantel (2001) used a symmetric similarity metric (Lin, 1998) to find candidate paraphrases. We build dependency context vectors for each word in our data and compute both symmetric as well as more recently proposed asymmetric similarity measures (Weeds et al., 2004; Szpektor and Dagan, 2008; Clarke, 2009), which are potentially better suited for identifying $\sqsupset$ paraphrases. Table 3 gives a comparison of the pairs which are considered "most similar" according to several of these metrics.

6.2 Bilingual features

We explore a variety of bilingual features, which we expect to provide complimentary signal to the monolingual features. Each pair in PPDB is associated with several paraphrase probabilities, which are based on the probabilities of aligning each word to the foreign "pivot" phrase (a foreign translation shared by the two phrases), computed as described in Bannard and Callison-Burch (2005). We also compute the total number of shared foreign translations for each phrase pair. Table 3 shows the highest ranked pairs by this bilingual similarity score, in comparison to several of the monolingual scores.

6.3 Analysis

Table 5 shows an ablation analysis. The bilingual features are especially important for distinguishing the $\equiv$ class, and the path and WordNet features are important for the $\neg$ class. The lexical features show strong performance across the board; this is often because they capture negation words (e.g. *no*) and substring features (*little boy* $\sqsubset$ *boy*).

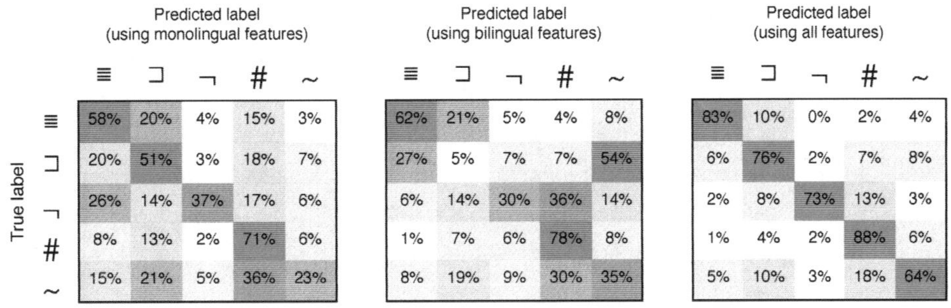

Figure 4: Confusion matrices for classifier trained using only monolingual features (distributional and path) versus bilingual features (paraphrase and translation). True labels are shown along rows, predicted along columns. The matrix is normalized along rows, so that the predictions for each (true) class sum to 100%. The confusion matrices reflect classifier's performance on held-out phrase pairs from the SICK test set.

		Δ F1 when excluding					
	All	Lex.	Dist.	Path	Para.	Tran.	WN
$\#$	79	-2.0	-0.2	-1.2	-1.7	-0.2	-0.1
$\equiv$	57	-3.5	+0.2	-0.7	-2.4	-3.7	+0.5
$\sqsupset$	68	-4.6	-0.3	-0.8	-0.8	-0.7	-1.6
$\neg$	49	-4.0	-0.8	-2.9	+0.3	-0.0	-2.2
$\sim$	51	-4.9	-0.5	-0.7	-1.2	-0.9	-0.3

Table 5: F1 measure ($\times 100$) achieved by entailment classifier using 10-fold cross validation on the training data.

Table 3 shines some light onto the differences between monolingual and bilingual similarities. While the monolingual asymmetric metrics are good for identifying $\sqsupset$ pairs, the symmetric metrics consistently identify $\neg$ pairs; none of the monolingual scores we explored were effective in making the subtle distinction between $\equiv$ pairs and the other types of paraphrase. In contrast, the bilingual similarity metric is fairly precise for identifying $\equiv$ pairs, but provides less information for distinguishing between types of non-equivalent paraphrase. These differences are further exhibited in the confusion matrices shown in Figure 4; when the classifier is trained using only monolingual features, it misclassifies 26% of $\neg$ pairs as $\equiv$, whereas the bilingual features make this error only 6% of the time. On the other hand, the bilingual features completely fail to predict the $\sqsupset$ class, calling over 80% of such pairs $\equiv$ or $\sim$.

7 Evaluation

7.1 Intrinsic Evaluation

We test the performance of our classifier intrinsically, through its ability to reproduce the human labels for the phrase pairs from the SICK test sentences. Table 7 shows the precision and recall achieved by the classifier for each of our 5 entailment classes. The classifier is able to achieve an overall 79% accuracy, reaching >70% precision while maintaining good levels of recall on all classes.

True	Pred.	N	Example misclassifications
$\sim$	$\#$	169	boy/little, an empy/the air
$\#$	$\sim$	114	little/toy, color/hair
$\sqsupset$	$\sim$	108	drink/juice, ocean/surf
$\sqsupset$	$\#$	97	in front of/the face of, vehicle/horse
$\sqsupset$	$\equiv$	83	cat/kitten, pavement/sidewalk
$\equiv$	$\sqsupset$	46	big/grand, a girl/a young lady
$\sqsupset$	$\neg$	29	kid/teenager, no small/a large
$\neg$	$\sqsupset$	29	old man/young man, a car/a window
$\#$	$\equiv$	15	a person/one, a crowd/a large
$\equiv$	$\#$	9	he is/man is, photo/still
$\equiv$	$\neg$	1	girl is/she is

Table 6: Example misclassifications from some of the most frequent and most interesting error categories.

Figure 4 shows the classifier's confusion matrix and Table 6 shows some examples of common and interesting error cases. The majority of errors (26%) come from confusing the $\sim$ class with the $\#$ class. This mistake is not too concerning from an RTE perspective since $\sim$ can be treated as a special case of $\#$ (Section 5). There are very few cases in which the classifier makes extreme errors, e.g. confusing $\equiv$ with $\neg$ or with $\#$; some interesting examples of such errors arise when the phrases contain pronouns (e.g. *girl* $\equiv$ *she*) or when the relation uses a highly infrequent word sense (e.g. *photo* $\equiv$ *still*).

7.2 The Nutcracker RTE System

To further test our classifier, we evaluate the usefulness of the automatic entailment predictions in a downstream RTE task. We run our experiments using Nutcracker, a state-of-the-art RTE system based on formal semantics (Bjerva et al., 2014).

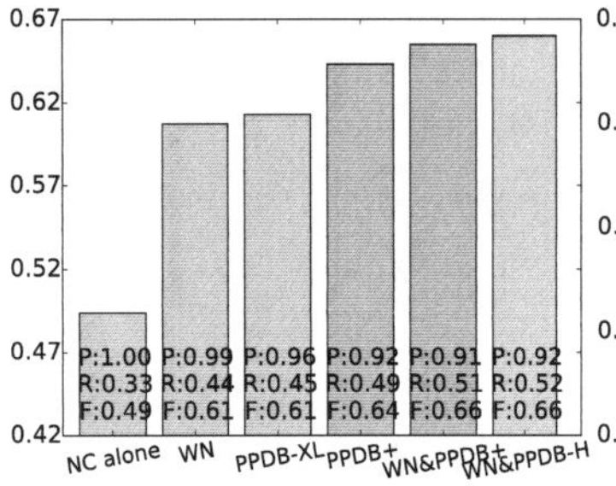

Figure 5: ENTAILMENT

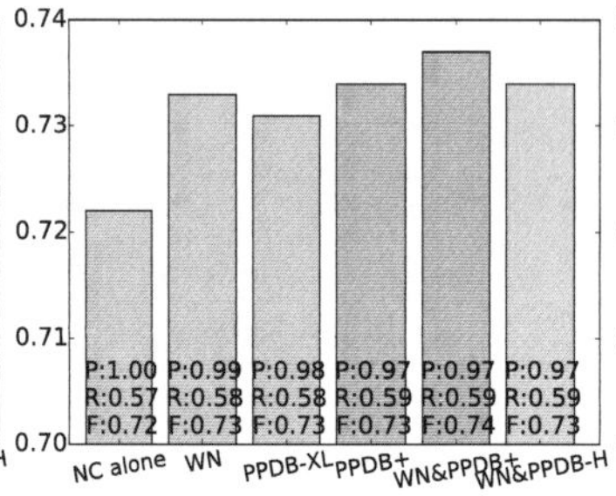

Figure 6: CONTRADICTION

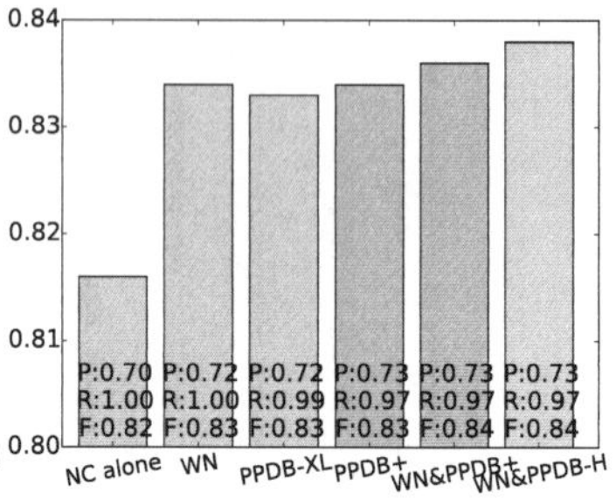

Figure 7: NEUTRAL

Figure 8: F1 measures achieved by Nutcracker on SICK test data when using various KBs. Baselines are in gray, this work in blue, human references in gold. PPDB-XL refers to a run in which every pair which appears in PPDB is assumed to be equivalent. PPDB-H refers to a run in which manual labels were used to generate axioms. PPDB+ refers to runs in which the automatic classifications were used to generate axioms. In some cases, better proof coverage causes NC to find incorrect proofs, illustrated by the decreased performance on CONTRADICTION when using PPDB-H. For example, using PPDB-H, NC finds an inconsistency for the pair *Someone is not playing piano./A person is playing a keyboard.* Using the PPDB+, in which *piano/keyboard* is falsely classified as #, NC fails to find a proof and so correctly guesses NEUTRAL.

	Freq.	Precision	Recall	F score
#	39%	84.22	87.55	85.85
≡	8%	70.36	83.07	76.19
⊐	26%	79.81	76.00	77.85
¬	7%	73.73	73.33	73.53
∼	19%	70.57	63.70	66.96

Table 7: F1 measure (×100) achieved by entailment classifier on the held out phrase pairs from the sentences in SICK test.

	Acc.	# Proofs	Coverage
MFC	56.4	0	0%
NC alone	74.3	878	17.8%
+ WN	77.5	1,051	21.3%
+ PPDB-XL	77.5	1,091	22.1%
+ PPDB+	78.0	1,197	24.3%
+ WN, PPDB+	**78.4**	**1,230**	**25.0%**
+ WN, PPDB-H	*78.6*	*1,232*	*25.0%*

Table 8: Nutcracker's overall system accuracy and proof coverage when using different sources of axioms. Coverage is measured as the percent of sentence pairs for which NC's theorem prover or model builder is able to find a complete logical proof of either entailment or contradiction. When NC fails to find either type of proof, it guesses the most frequent class, NEUTRAL. NC alone uses no axioms. PPDB+ refers to the axioms generated automatically using the classifier described in this paper. PPDB-H refers axioms generated using the human labels on which the classifier was trained.

In the SemEval 2014 RTE challenge, this system performed in the top 5 out of the more than 20 participating systems (Marelli et al., 2014).

Given a text/hypothesis (T/H) pair, Nutcracker (NC) uses the Boxer parser (Bos, 2008) to produce a formal semantic representation of both T and H, which it translates into standard first-order logic. The logical formulae are passed to an off-the-shelf theorem prover, which searches for a logical entailment, and to a model builder, which attempts to find a logical contradiction. By default, when the system fails to find a proof for either entailment or inconsistency, it predicts the most frequent class (in our case, NEUTRAL). Therefore, NC relies heavily on lexical entailment resources in order to improve the recall of the theorem prover and model builder.

Baselines The most frequent class baseline is achieved by labeling every sentence pair as NEUTRAL, and results in an accuracy of 56%. A stronger baseline is obtained by running NC alone, without any external axioms; in this case, words are only equivalent if they are lemma-identical.

As an additional baseline, we generate a "basic" PPDB-XL[3] knowledge base (KB), which consists exclusively of axioms expressing synonym relationships. I.e. for every pair of phrases $\langle p_1, p_2 \rangle$ in PPDB-XL, the PPDB-XL KB contains the equivalence axiom $syn(p_1, p_2)$. We also generate the WordNet (WN) KB, which is the default used by NC. This KB consists of axioms for all synonyms, antonyms, and hypernyms in WN, which generate syn, $isnota$, and isa axioms, respectively.

PPDB+ We convert our classifier's predictions into a set of axioms for NC. When our classifier predicts ≡ we generate an syn axiom, when it predicts ⊐ we generate an isa axiom, and when it predicts ¬ we generate an $isnota$ axiom. # and ∼ do not generate any axioms. To handle the directionality of the ⊐ relation, we run the classifier

[3]We generated basic KBs for all six sizes of PPDB, but XL performed best.

True	PPDB+	WN	Text/Hypothesis pair
ENTAIL.	ENTAIL.	NEUTRAL	A **bride** in a white dress is running/A **girl** in a white dress is running.
ENTAIL.	NEUTRAL	ENTAIL.	A **lemur** is biting a person's finger./An **animal** is biting a person's finger.
CONTRA.	CONTRA.	NEUTRAL	**Someone** is playing a piano./There is **no one** playing a piano.
CONTRA.	NEUTRAL	CONTRA.	There is **no man** pouring oil into a **pan**./**A man** is pouring oil into a **skillet**.

Table 9: Examples of T/H pairs for which the system's prediction differed when using PPDB+ vs. WN.

over every pair in both directions, and we choose whichever direction and relation receives the highest confidence score to be the final prediction. We refer to this set of automatically-predicted axioms as PPDB+.

To calibrate our improvements, we also generate a KB using the human labels collected from MTurk, which we refer to as PPDB-Human or PPDB-H.

Results Table 8 reports NC's overall prediction accuracy and the number of proofs found when using each of the described KBs. Figure 8 shows the performance in terms of the precision and recall achieved for each of the three entailment classes: ENTAILMENT, CONTRADICTION, and NEUTRAL. Table 9 provides some examples of T/H pairs on which predictions differed using the PPDB+ compared to the WN KB, and Figure 9 shows some illustrative misclassifications.

Our automatic labels result in a 4% improvement in accuracy over the baseline of using NC alone (Figure 8), and a 15 point improvement in F1 measure for the entailment class (Table 8). By all performance measures, PPDB+ also outperforms WordNet as a source of axioms for NC. Moreover, adding PPDB+ to WordNet gives a 17% relative increase in the number of proofs found compared to using WordNet alone (Table 8). These additional proofs lead NC to make a greater number of correct predictions for the "right reasons" (i.e. finding a proof/contradiction) rather than by lucky guessing (recall NC guesses the most frequent class when it cannot find a proof).

For comparison, we run the same experiments using a KB of oracle human labels in place of the predicted labels in PPDB+. Using PPDB+, NC comes very close to the performance achieved when using PPDB-Human, demonstrating that the automatically generated PPDB+ provides as much utility to the end-to-end system as does a gold-standard resource.

8 Data Release

Upon publication, we are releasing a new PPDB fully annotated with semantic relations. We are also releasing the set of 14K manually labeled phrase pairs occurring in RTE data, and our software for extracting features and running the classifier, so that researchers can apply our model to their own paraphrase collections. This will constitute the largest lexical entailment resources available, while also offering new fine-grained annotation necessary for challenging NLU tasks. An evaluation of the predicted relations appearing in the entire Paraphrase Database (not just those occurring in RTE data) is given in the supplementary material.

9 Conclusion

We argue that a significant failing of recent work on data-driven paraphrasing is the weak definition of paraphrases as being more-or-less equivalent. In this paper, we show how a clear concept of semantics can be applied to large-scale paraphrase resources. In particular, the entailment relations given by natural logic are a great fit for paraphrase resources, since natural logic operates on pairs of natural language expressions (like the entries in PPDB). By classifying paraphrase entries with entailment relations, we provide them with an interpretable semantics. Our classifier uses extensive feature sets to scale natural logic to the enormous number of phrase pairs in PPDB. We rigorously evaluate our model, demonstrating high accuracy on an intrinsic task. On an extrinsic RTE task, our model's predictions allow an RTE system to find 17% more proofs and achieve a higher overall accuracy than when using WordNet's manual relations. Our new release of PPDB, annotated with semantic entailments, will dramatically improve PPDB's utility for NLU tasks.

Acknowledgements This research was supported by the Allen Institute for Artificial Intelligence (AI2), the Human Language Technology Center of Excellence (HLTCOE), and by gifts from the Alfred P. Sloan Foundation, Google, and

	# 38%	≡ 8%	⊐ 26%	¬ 7%	∼ 18%
# 40%	1730 (clear,very) (exhibit,hold) (walk,woman)	9 (cover,front) (photo,still) (woman who,woman with)	97 (hand,male) (man,police) (mountain,side)	49 (drive,park) (female,man) (flag,ship)	169 (child,park) (crowded,many) (note,write)
≡ 10%	15 (a big,very) (a lot,long) (face a,front of)	368 (a small,the little) (away,out) (block,slab)	83 (a gun,a weapon) (a weapon,gun) (legs,leg)	9 (another man,one man) (bike,biking) (young girl,young woman)	48 (a child,kid in) (and hold,and take) (his arms,his hands)
⊐ 24%	82 (device,guy) (something,talk) (the man,the phone)	46 (a call,phone call) (a group,bunch of) (another man,man)	1004 (camera,webcam) (kid,other child) (kid,the daughter)	29 (a car,a window) (a female,a man) (arms,his hands)	97 (a lady,girl) (field,playing) (girl,the lady)
¬ 7%	35 (a ball,a man) (a boy,little) (number,woman)	1 (girl is,she is)	29 (a boy,a teenager) (a kid,daughter) (kid,little girl)	275 (cat,dog) (morning,night) (type,write)	33 (dog,owner) (ground,water) (hat,vest)
∼ 17%	114 (leg,soccer) (perform,run) (sail,water)	19 (chef,cook) (fight,match) (race,ride)	108 (cut,saw) (face,hair) (the kid,the little)	13 (a boat,sail) (dress,suit) (light,the dark)	609 (ice,rink) (snow,snowy) (study by,study the)

Figure 9: Confusion matrix for classifier (with all features) on SICK test set. True labels and their distribution are shown along the columns, predicted along the rows.

Facebook. This material is based in part on research sponsored by the NSF under grant IIS-1249516 and DARPA under agreement number FA8750-13-2-0017 (the DEFT program). The U.S. Government is authorized to reproduce and distribute reprints for Governmental purposes. The views and conclusions contained in this publication are those of the authors and should not be interpreted as representing official policies or endorsements of DARPA or the U.S. Government.

The authors would like to thank Peter Clark, Bill MacCartney, Patrick Pantel and the anonymous reviews for their thoughtful suggestions.

References

Ion Androutsopoulos and Prodromos Malakasiotis. 2010. A survey of paraphrasing and textual entailment methods. *Journal of Artificial Intelligence Research*, 38.

Colin Bannard and Chris Callison-Burch. 2005. Paraphrasing with bilingual parallel corpora. In *Proceedings of the 43rd Annual Meeting on Association for Computational Linguistics*, pages 597–604.

Regina Barzilay. 2003. *Information fusion for multi-document summarization: paraphrasing and generation*. Ph.D. thesis, Columbia University.

Islam Beltagy, Stephen Roller, Gemma Boleda, Katrin Erk, and Raymond J Mooney. 2014. UTexas: Natural language semantics using distributional semantics and probabilistic logic. *SemEval 2014*, page 796.

Jonathan Berant, Ido Dagan, and Jacob Goldberger. 2011. Global learning of typed entailment rules. In *Proceedings of the 49th Annual Meeting of the Association for Computational Linguistics: Human Language Technologies - Volume 1*, HLT '11, pages 610–619.

Rahul Bhagat and Eduard Hovy. 2013. What is a paraphrase? *Computational Linguistics*, 39.

Rahul Bhagat, Patrick Pantel, Eduard H Hovy, and Marina Rey. 2007. Ledir: An unsupervised algorithm for learning directionality of inference rules. In *EMNLP-CoNLL*, pages 161–170. Citeseer.

Johannes Bjerva, Johan Bos, Rob van der Goot, and Malvina Nissim. 2014. The meaning factory: Formal semantics for recognizing textual entailment and determining semantic similarity. *SemEval 2014*, page 642.

Johan Bos. 2008. Wide-coverage semantic analysis with boxer. In Johan Bos and Rodolfo Delmonte, editors, *Semantics in Text Processing. STEP 2008 Conference Proceedings*, Research in Computational Semantics, pages 277–286. College Publications.

Christopher John Brockett, Stanley Kok, and Dengyong Zhou. 2013. Locating paraphrases through utilization of a multipartite graph, July 9. US Patent 8,484,016.

Chris Callison-Burch. 2007. *Paraphrasing and Translation*. Ph.D. thesis, University of Edinburgh, Edinburgh, Scotland.

Timothy Chklovski and Patrick Pantel. 2004. VerbOcean: Mining the web for fine-grained semantic verb relations. In *EMNLP*, volume 2004, pages 33–40.

Peter Clark, William R. Murray, John Thompson, Phil Harrison, Jerry Hobbs, and Christiane Fellbaum. 2007. On the role of lexical and world knowledge in rte3. In *Proceedings of the ACL-PASCAL Workshop on Textual Entailment and Paraphrasing*, RTE '07, pages 54–59.

Peter Clark, Myroslava O Dzikovska, Rodney D Nielsen, Chris Brew, Claudia Leacock, Danilo Giampiccolo, Luisa Bentivogli, Ido Dagan, and Hoa T Dang. 2013. Semeval-2013 task 7: The joint student response analysis and 8th recognizing textual entailment challenge.

Daoud Clarke. 2009. Context-theoretic semantics for natural language: an overview. In *Proceedings of the Workshop on Geometrical Models of Natural Language Semantics*, pages 112–119.

Ido Dagan, Oren Glickman, and Bernardo Magnini. 2006. The pascal recognising textual entailment challenge. In *Machine Learning Challenges. Evaluating Predictive Uncertainty, Visual Object Classification, and Recognising Tectual Entailment*, pages 177–190. Springer.

Bill Dolan, Chris Quirk, and Chris Brockett. 2004. Unsupervised construction of large paraphrase corpora: Exploiting massively parallel news sources. In *Proceedings of the 20th international conference on Computational Linguistics*, page 350.

Juri Ganitkevitch and Chris Callison-Burch. 2014. The multilingual paraphrase database. In *The 9th edition of the Language Resources and Evaluation Conference*, Reykjavik, Iceland, May. European Language Resources Association.

Juri Ganitkevitch, Benjamin Van Durme, and Chris Callison-Burch. 2013. PPDB: The paraphrase database. In *Proceedings of NAACL-HLT*, pages 758–764, Atlanta, Georgia, June. Association for Computational Linguistics.

Danilo Giampiccolo, Bernardo Magnini, Ido Dagan, and Bill Dolan. 2007. The third PASCAL recognizing textual entailment challenge. In *Proceedings of the ACL-PASCAL workshop on textual entailment and paraphrasing*, pages 1–9.

Chikara Hashimoto, Kentaro Torisawa, Kow Kuroda, Stijn De Saeger, Masaki Murata, and Jun'ichi Kazama. 2009. Large-scale verb entailment acquisition from the web. In *Proceedings of the 2009 Conference on Empirical Methods in Natural Language Processing: Volume 3-Volume 3*, pages 1172–1181. Association for Computational Linguistics.

Marti A. Hearst. 1992. Automatic acquisition of hyponyms from large text corpora. In *Proceedings of the 14th Conference on Computational Linguistics - Volume 2*, COLING '92, pages 539–545.

Aaron N Kaplan and Lenhart K Schubert. 2001. Measuring and improving the quality of world knowledge extracted from wordnet. *University of Rochester, Rochester, NY.*

Lili Kotlerman, Ido Dagan, Idan Szpektor, and Maayan Zhitomirsky-Geffet. 2010. Directional distributional similarity for lexical inference. *Natural Language Engineering*, 16(4):359–389.

Alice Lai and Julia Hockenmaier. 2014. Illinois-LH: A denotational and distributional approach to semantics. *SemEval 2014*, page 329.

J Richard Landis and Gary G Koch. 1977. The measurement of observer agreement for categorical data. *biometrics*, pages 159–174.

Dekang Lin and Patrick Pantel. 2001. DIRT – Discovery of Inference Rules from Text. In *Proceedings of the seventh ACM SIGKDD international conference on Knowledge discovery and data mining*, pages 323–328. ACM.

Dekang Lin. 1998. Automatic retrieval and clustering of similar words. In *Proceedings of the 17th international conference on Computational linguistics-Volume 2*, pages 768–774.

Bill MacCartney and Christopher D. Manning. 2007. Natural logic for textual inference. In *Proceedings of the ACL-PASCAL Workshop on Textual Entailment and Paraphrasing*, RTE '07, pages 193–200.

Bill MacCartney. 2009. *Natural language inference*. Ph.D. thesis, Citeseer.

Nitin Madnani and Bonnie J. Dorr. 2010. Generating phrasal and sentential paraphrases: A survey of data-driven methods. *Computational Linguistics*, 36.

Marco Marelli, Luisa Bentivogli, Marco Baroni, Raffaella Bernardi, Stefano Menini, and Roberto Zamparelli. 2014. Semeval-2014 task 1: Evaluation of compositional distributional semantic models on full sentences through semantic relatedness and textual entailment. *SemEval-2014*.

Courtney Napoles, Matthew Gormley, and Benjamin Van Durme. 2012. Annotated gigaword. In *Proceedings of the Joint Workshop on Automatic Knowledge Base Construction and Web-scale Knowledge Extraction*, pages 95–100.

Maria Pontiki, Haris Papageorgiou, Dimitrios Galanis, Ion Androutsopoulos, John Pavlopoulos, and Suresh Manandhar. 2014. Semeval-2014 task 4: Aspect based sentiment analysis. *Proceedings of SemEval, Dublin, Ireland.*

Rion Snow, Daniel Jurafsky, and Andrew Y Ng. 2004. Learning syntactic patterns for automatic hypernym discovery. In *NIPS*, volume 17, pages 1297–1304.

Rion Snow, Daniel Jurafsky, and Andrew Y. Ng. 2006. Semantic taxonomy induction from heterogenous evidence. In *Proceedings of the 21st International Conference on Computational Linguistics and the 44th Annual Meeting of the Association for Computational Linguistics*, ACL-44, pages 801–808.

Idan Szpektor and Ido Dagan. 2008. Learning entailment rules for unary templates. In *Proceedings of the 22Nd International Conference on Computational Linguistics - Volume 1*, COLING '08, pages 849–856.

Idan Szpektor, Hristo Tanev, Dr Dagan, Bonaventura Coppola, et al. 2004. Scaling web-based acquisition of entailment relations.

Julie Weeds, David Weir, and Diana McCarthy. 2004. Characterising measures of lexical distributional similarity. In *Proceedings of the 20th International Conference on Computational Linguistics*, COLING '04.

Wei Xu, Alan Ritter, Chris Callison-Burch, William B. Dolan, and Yangfeng Ji. 2014. Extracting lexically divergent paraphrases from Twitter. *Transactions of the Association for Computational Linguistics*, 2.

Jiang Zhao, Tian Tian Zhu, and Man Lan. 2014. Ecnu: One stone two birds: Ensemble of heterogenous measures for semantic relatedness and textual entailment. *SemEval 2014*, page 271.

Parsing as Reduction

Daniel Fernández-González[†*] **André F. T. Martins**[‡#]
[†]Departamento de Informática, Universidade de Vigo, Campus As Lagoas, 32004 Ourense, Spain
[‡]Instituto de Telecomunicações, Instituto Superior Técnico, 1049-001 Lisboa, Portugal
[#]Priberam Labs, Alameda D. Afonso Henriques, 41, 2º, 1000-123 Lisboa, Portugal
danifg@uvigo.es, atm@priberam.pt

Abstract

We reduce phrase-based parsing to dependency parsing. Our reduction is grounded on a new intermediate representation, "head-ordered dependency trees," shown to be isomorphic to constituent trees. By encoding order information in the dependency labels, we show that any off-the-shelf, trainable dependency parser can be used to produce constituents. When this parser is non-projective, we can perform discontinuous parsing in a very natural manner. Despite the simplicity of our approach, experiments show that the resulting parsers are on par with strong baselines, such as the Berkeley parser for English and the best non-reranking system in the SPMRL-2014 shared task. Results are particularly striking for discontinuous parsing of German, where we surpass the current state of the art by a wide margin.

1 Introduction

Constituent parsing is a central problem in NLP—one at which statistical models trained on treebanks have excelled (Charniak, 1996; Klein and Manning, 2003; Petrov and Klein, 2007). However, most existing parsers are slow, since they need to deal with a heavy grammar constant. Dependency parsers are generally faster, but less informative, since they do not produce constituents, which are often required by downstream applications (Johansson and Nugues, 2008; Wu et al., 2009; Berg-Kirkpatrick et al., 2011; Elming et al., 2013). How to get the best of both worlds?

Coarse-to-fine decoding (Charniak and Johnson, 2005) and shift-reduce parsing (Sagae and Lavie, 2005; Zhu et al., 2013) were a step forward to accelerate constituent parsing, but typical runtimes still lag those of dependency parsers. This is only made worse if **discontinuous** constituents are allowed—such discontinuities are convenient to represent wh-movement, scrambling, extraposition, and other linguistic phenomena common in free word order languages. While non-projective dependency parsers, which are able to model such phenomena, have been widely developed in the last decade (Nivre et al., 2007; McDonald et al., 2006; Martins et al., 2013), discontinuous constituent parsing is still taking its first steps (Maier and Søgaard, 2008; Kallmeyer and Maier, 2013).

In this paper, we show that an off-the-shelf, trainable, **dependency parser** is enough to build a highly-competitive constituent parser. This (surprising) result is based on a **reduction**[1] of constituent to dependency parsing, followed by a simple post-processing procedure to recover unaries. Unlike other constituent parsers, ours does not require estimating a grammar, nor binarizing the treebank. Moreover, when the dependency parser is non-projective, our method can perform discontinuous constituent parsing in a very natural way.

Key to our approach is the notion of **head-ordered dependency trees** (shown in Figure 1): by endowing dependency trees with this additional layer of structure, we show that they become isomorphic to constituent trees. We encode this structure as part of the dependency labels, enabling a dependency-to-constituent conversion. A related conversion was attempted by Hall and Nivre (2008) to parse German, but their complex encoding scheme blows up the number of arc labels, affecting the final parser's quality. By contrast, our light encoding achieves a 10-fold decrease in the label alphabet, leading to more accurate parsing.

While simple, our reduction-based parsers are on par with the Berkeley parser for English (Petrov

*This research was carried out during an internship at Priberam Labs.

[1]The title of this paper is inspired by the seminal paper of Pereira and Warren (1983) "Parsing as Deduction."

Proceedings of the 53rd Annual Meeting of the Association for Computational Linguistics and the 7th International Joint Conference on Natural Language Processing, pages 1523–1533,
Beijing, China, July 26-31, 2015. ©2015 Association for Computational Linguistics

and Klein, 2007), and with the best single system in the recent SPMRL shared task (Seddah et al., 2014), for eight morphologically rich languages. For discontinuous parsing, we surpass the current state of the art by a wide margin on two German datasets (TIGER and NEGRA), while achieving fast parsing speeds. We provide a free distribution of our parsers along with this paper, as part of the TurboParser toolkit.[2]

2 Background

We start by reviewing constituent and dependency representations, and setting up the notation. Following Kong and Smith (2014), we use c-/d- prefixes for convenience (*e.g.*, we write c-parser for constituent parser and d-tree for dependency tree).

2.1 Constituent Trees

Constituent-based representations are commonly seen as derivations according to a context-free grammar (CFG). Here, we focus on properties of the c-trees, rather than of the grammars used to generate them. We consider a broad scenario that permits c-trees with discontinuities, such as the ones derived with linear context-free rewriting systems (LCFRS; Vijay-Shanker et al. (1987)). We also assume that the c-trees are lexicalized.

Formally, let $w_1 w_2 \dots w_L$ be a sentence, where w_i denotes the word in the ith position. A **c-tree** is a rooted tree whose leaves are the words $\{w_i\}_{i=1}^{L}$, and whose internal nodes (constituents) are represented as a tuple $\langle Z, h, \mathcal{I} \rangle$, where Z is a non-terminal symbol, $h \in \{1, \dots, L\}$ indicates the lexical head, and $\mathcal{I} \subseteq \{1, \dots, L\}$ is the node's yield. Each word's parent is a pre-terminal unary node of the form $\langle p_i, i, \{i\} \rangle$, where p_i denotes the word's part-of-speech (POS) tag. The yields and lexical heads are defined so that for every constituent $\langle Z, h, \mathcal{I} \rangle$ with children $\{\langle X_k, m_k, \mathcal{J}_k \rangle\}_{k=1}^{K}$, (i) we have $\mathcal{I} = \bigcup_{k=1}^{K} \mathcal{J}_k$; and (ii) there is a unique k such that $h = m_k$. This kth node (called the head-child node) is commonly chosen applying a handwritten set of head rules (Collins, 1999; Yamada and Matsumoto, 2003).

A c-tree is **continuous** if all nodes $\langle Z, h, \mathcal{I} \rangle$ have a contiguous yield $\mathcal{I}$, and **discontinuous** otherwise. Trees derived by a CFG are always continuous; those derived by a LCFRS may have discontinuities, the yield of a node being a union of spans, possibly with gaps in the middle. Figure 1 shows an example of a continuous and a discontinuous c-tree. Discontinuous c-trees have crossing branches, if the leaves are drawn in left-to-right surface order. An internal node which is not a pre-terminal is called a **proper node**. A node is called unary if it has exactly one child. A c-tree without unary proper nodes is called **unaryless**. If all proper nodes have exactly two children then it is called a **binary** c-tree. Continuous binary trees may be regarded as having been generated by a CFG in Chomsky normal form.

Prior work. There has been a long string of work in statistical c-parsing, shifting from simple models (Charniak, 1996) to more sophisticated ones using structural annotation (Johnson, 1998; Klein and Manning, 2003), latent grammars (Matsuzaki et al., 2005; Petrov and Klein, 2007), and lexicalization (Eisner, 1996; Collins, 1999). An orthogonal line of work uses ensemble or reranking strategies to further improve accuracy (Charniak and Johnson, 2005; Huang, 2008; Björkelund et al., 2014). Discontinuous c-parsing is considered a much harder problem, involving mildly context-sensitive formalisms such as LCFRS or range concatenation grammars, with treebank-derived c-parsers exhibiting near-exponential runtime (Kallmeyer and Maier, 2013, Figure 27). To speed up decoding, prior work has considered restrictons, such as bounding the fan-out (Maier et al., 2012) and requiring well-nestedness (Kuhlmann and Nivre, 2006; Gómez-Rodríguez et al., 2010). Other approaches eliminate the discontinuities via tree transformations (Boyd, 2007; Kübler et al., 2008), sometimes as a pruning step in a coarse-to-fine parsing approach (van Cranenburgh and Bod, 2013). However, reported runtimes are still superior to 10 seconds per sentence, which is not practical. Recently, Versley (2014a) proposed an easy-first approach that leads to considerable speed-ups, but is less accurate. In this paper, we design fast discontinuous c-parsers that outperform all the ones above by a wide margin, with similar runtimes as Versley (2014a).

2.2 Dependency Trees

In this paper, we use d-parsers as a black box to parse constituents. Given a sentence $w_1 \dots w_L$, a **d-tree** is a directed tree spanning all the words in the sentence.[3] Each arc in this tree is a tuple

[2] `http://www.ark.cs.cmu.edu/TurboParser`

[3] We assume throughout that dependency trees have a single root among $\{w_1, \dots, w_L\}$. Therefore, there is no need to

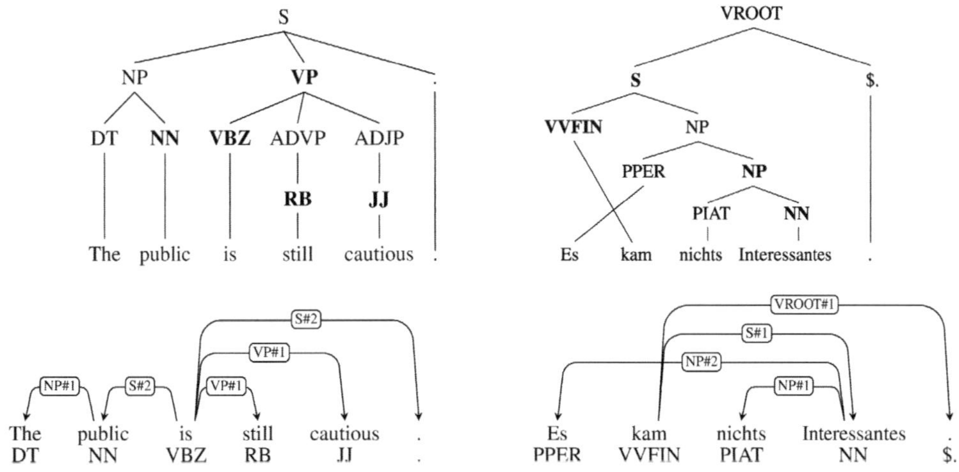

Figure 1: Top: a continuous (left) and a discontinuous (right) c-tree, taken from English PTB §22 and German NEGRA, respectively. Head-child nodes are in bold. Bottom: corresponding head-ordered d-trees. The indices #1, #2, etc. denote the order of attachment events for each head. Note that the English unary nodes ADVP and ADJP are dropped in the conversion.

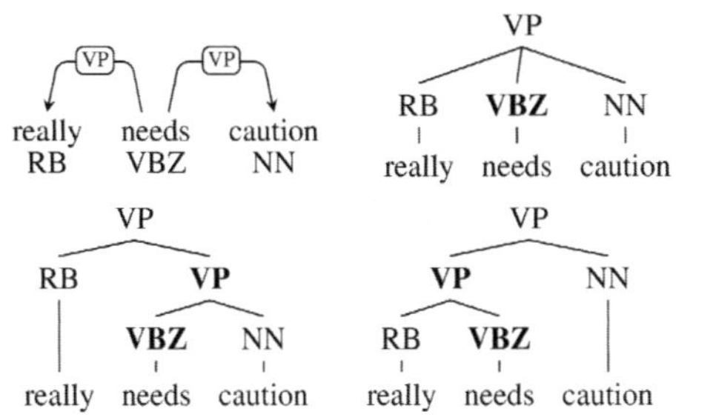

Figure 2: Three different c-structures for the VP "*really needs caution*." All are consistent with the d-structure at the top left.

$\langle h, m, \ell \rangle$, expressing a typed dependency relation ℓ between the head word w_h and the modifier w_m.

A d-tree is **projective** if for every arc $\langle h, m, \ell \rangle$ there is a directed path from h to all words that lie between h and m in the surface string (Kahane et al., 1998). Projective d-trees can be obtained from continuous c-trees by reading off the lexical heads and dropping the internal nodes (Gaifman, 1965). However, this relation is many-to-one: as shown in Figure 2, several c-trees may project onto the same d-tree, differing on their flatness and on left or right-branching decisions. In the next section, we introduce the concept of head-ordered d-trees and express one-to-one mappings between these two representations.

Prior work. There has been a considerable amount of work developing rich-feature d-parsers. While projective d-parsers can use dynamic programming (Eisner and Satta, 1999; Koo and Collins, 2010), non-projective d-parsers typically rely on approximate decoders, since the underlying problem is NP-hard beyond arc-factored models (McDonald and Satta, 2007). An alternative are transition-based d-parsers (Nivre et al., 2006; Zhang and Nivre, 2011), which achieve observed linear time. Since d-parsing algorithms do not have a grammar constant, typical implementations are significantly faster than c-parsers (Rush and Petrov, 2012; Martins et al., 2013). The key contribution of this paper is to reduce c-parsing to d-parsing, allowing to bring these runtimes closer.

consider an extra root symbol, as often done in the literature.

3 Head-Ordered Dependency Trees

We next endow d-trees with another layer of structure, namely **order information**. In this framework, not all modifiers of a head are "born equal." Instead, their attachment to the head occurs as a sequence of "events," which reflect the head's preference for attaching some modifiers before others. As we will see, this additional structure will undo the ambiguity expressed in Figure 2.

3.1 Strictly Ordered Dependency Trees

Let us start with the simpler case where the attachment order is strict. For each head word h with modifiers $M_h = \{m_1, \ldots, m_K\}$, we endow M_h with a **strict order relation** $\prec_h$, so we can organize all the modifiers of h as a chain, $m_{i_1} \prec_h m_{i_2} \prec_h \ldots \prec_h m_{i_K}$. We regard this chain as reflecting the order by which words are attached (*i.e.*, if $m_i \prec_h m_j$ this means that "m_i is attached

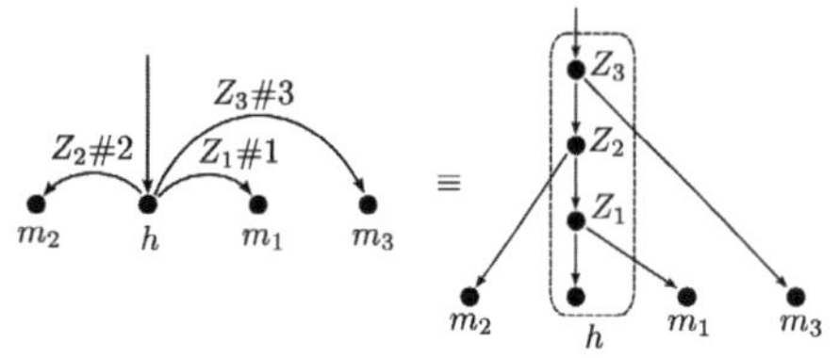

Figure 3: Transformation of a strictly-ordered d-tree into a binary c-tree. Each node is split into a linked list forming a spine, to which modifiers are attached in order.

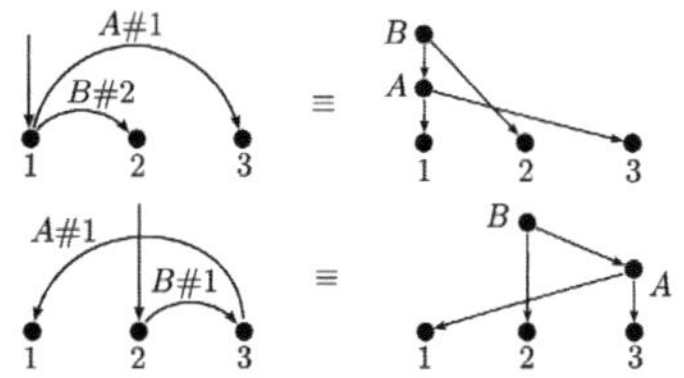

Figure 4: Two discontinuous constructions caused by a non-nested order (top) and a non-projective d-tree (bottom). In both cases node A has a non-contiguous yield.

to h before m_j"). We represent this graphically by decorating d-arcs with indices ($\#1, \#2, \ldots$) to denote the order of events, as we do in Figure 1.

A d-tree endowed with a strict order for each head is called a **strictly ordered d-tree**. We establish below a correspondence between strictly ordered d-trees and binary c-trees. Before doing so, we need a few more definitions about c-trees. For each word position $h \in \{1, \ldots, L\}$, we define $\psi(h)$ as the node higher in the c-tree whose lexical head is h. We call the path from $\psi(h)$ down to the pre-terminal p_h the **spine** of h. We may regard a c-tree as a set of L spines, one per word, which attach to each other to form a tree (Carreras et al., 2008). We then have the following

Proposition 1. *Binary c-trees and strictly-ordered d-trees are isomorphic, i.e., there is a one-to-one correspondence between the two sets, where the number of symbols is preserved.*

Proof. We use the construction in Figure 3. A formal proof is given as supplementary material. □

3.2 Weakly Ordered Dependency Trees

Next, we relax the strict order assumption, restricting the modifier sets $M_h = \{m_1, \ldots, m_K\}$ to be only **weakly ordered**. This means that we can partition the K modifiers into J equivalence classes, $M_h = \bigcup_{j=1}^{J} \bar{M}_h^j$, and define a strict order $\prec_h$ on the quotient set: $\bar{M}_h^1 \prec_h \ldots \prec_h \bar{M}_h^J$. Intuitively, there is still a sequence of events (1 to J), but now at each event j it may happen that multiple modifiers (the ones in the equivalence set $\bar{M}_h^j$) are simultaneously attached to h. A **weakly ordered d-tree** is a d-tree endowed with a weak order for each head and such that any pair m, m' in the same equivalence class (written $m \equiv_h m'$) receive the same dependency label ℓ.

We now show that Proposition 1 can be generalized to weakly ordered d-trees.

Proposition 2. *Unaryless c-trees and weakly-ordered d-trees are isomorphic.*

Proof. This is a simple extension of Proposition 1. The construction is the same as in Figure 3, but now we can collapse some of the nodes in the linked list, originating multiple modifiers attaching to the same position of the spine—this is only possible for sibling arcs with the same index and arc label. Note, however, that if we start with a c-tree with unary nodes and apply the inverse procedure to obtain a d-tree, the unary nodes will be lost, since they do not involve attachment of modifiers. In a chain of unary nodes, only the last node is recovered in the inverse transformation. □

Algorithm 1 Conversion from c-tree to d-tree

Input: c-tree $\mathcal{C}$.
Output: head-ordered d-tree $\mathcal{D}$.

```
Nodes := GetPostOrderTraversal(C).
Set j(h) := 1 for every h = 1, ..., L.
for v := ⟨Z, h, I⟩ ∈ Nodes do
    for every u := ⟨X, m, J⟩ which is a child of v do
        if m ≠ h then
            Add to D an arc ⟨h, m, Z⟩, and put it in M̄_h^{j(h)}.
        end if
    end for
    Set j(h) := j(h) + 1.
end for
```

We emphasize that Propositions 1–2 hold without blowing up the number of symbols. That is, the dependency label alphabet is exactly the same as the set of phrasal symbols in the constituent representations. Algorithms 1–2 convert back and forth between the two formalisms, performing the construction of Figure 3. Both algorithms run in linear time with respect to the size of the sentence.

3.3 Continuous and Projective Trees

What about the more restricted class of projective d-trees? Can we find an equivalence relation with continuous c-trees? In this section, we give a precise answer to this question. It turns out that we need an additional property, illustrated in Figure 4.

We say that $\prec_h$ has the **nesting property** iff closer words in the same direction are always attached first, *i.e.*, iff $h < m_i < m_j$ or $h > m_i >$

Algorithm 2 Conversion from d-tree to c-tree

Input: head-ordered d-tree $\mathcal{D}$.
Output: c-tree $\mathcal{C}$.

Nodes := GETPOSTORDERTRAVERSAL($\mathcal{D}$).
for $h \in$ Nodes **do**
    Create $v := \langle p_h, h, \{h\} \rangle$ and set $\psi(h) := v$.
    Sort $M_h(\mathcal{D})$, yielding $\bar{M}_h^1 \prec_h \bar{M}_h^2 \prec_h \ldots \prec_h \bar{M}_h^J$.
    for $j = 1, \ldots, J$ **do**
        Let Z be the label in $\{\langle h, m, Z \rangle \mid m \in \bar{M}_h^j\}$.
        Obtain c-nodes $\psi(h) = \langle X, h, \mathcal{I} \rangle$ and $\psi(m) = \langle Y_m, m, \mathcal{J}_m \rangle$ for all $m \in \bar{M}_h^j$.
        Add c-node $v := \langle Z, h, \mathcal{I} \cup \bigcup_{m \in \bar{M}_h^j} \mathcal{J}_m \rangle$ to $\mathcal{C}$.
        Set $\psi(h)$ and $\{\psi(m) \mid m \in \bar{M}_h^j\}$ as children of v.
        Set $\psi(h) := v$.
    end for
end for

m_j implies that either $m_i \equiv_h m_j$ or $m_i \prec_h m_j$. A weakly-ordered d-tree which is projective and whose orders $\prec_h$ have the nesting property for every h is called a **nested-weakly ordered projective d-tree**. We then have the following result.

Proposition 3. *Continuous unaryless c-trees and nested-weakly ordered projective d-trees are isomorphic.*

Proof. See the supplementary material. □

Together, Propositions 1–3 have as corollary that nested-strictly ordered projective d-trees are in a one-to-one correspondence with binary continuous c-trees. The intuition is simple: if $\prec_h$ has the nesting property, then, at each point in time, all one needs to decide about the next event is whether to attach the closest available modifier on the *left* or on the *right*. This corresponds to choosing between left-branching or right-branching in a c-tree. While this is potentially interesting for most continuous c-parsers, which work with binarized c-trees when running the CKY algorithm, our c-parsers (to be described in §4) do not require any binarization since they work with weakly-ordered d-trees, using Proposition 2.

4 Reduction-Based Constituent Parsers

We now invoke the equivalence results established in §3 to build c-parsers when only a trainable d-parser is available. Given a c-treebank provided as input, our procedure is outlined as follows:

1. Convert the c-treebank to dependencies (Algorithm 1).
2. Train a labeled d-parser on this treebank.
3. For each test sentence, run the labeled d-parser and convert the predicted d-tree into a c-tree without unary nodes (Algorithm 2).
4. Do post-processing to recover unaries.

The next subsections describe each of these steps in detail. Along the way, we illustrate with experiments using the English Penn Treebank (Marcus et al., 1993), which we lexicalized by applying the head rules of Collins (1999).[4]

4.1 Dependency Encoding

The first step is to convert the c-treebank to head-ordered dependencies, which we do using Algorithm 1. If the original treebank has discontinuous c-trees, we end up with non-projective d-trees or with violations of the nested property, as established in Proposition 3. We handle this gracefully by training a non-projective d-parser in the subsequent stage (see §4.2). Note also that this conversion drops the unary nodes (a consequence of Proposition 2). These nodes will be recovered in the last stage, as described in §4.4.

Since in this paper we are assuming that only an off-the-shelf d-parser is available, we need to convert head-ordered d-trees to plain d-trees. We do so by encoding the order information in the dependency labels. We tried two different strategies. The first one, **direct encoding**, just appends suffixes #1, #2, etc., as in Figure 1. A disadvantage is that the number of labels grows unbounded with the treebank size, as we may encounter complex substructures where the event sequences are long. The second strategy is a **delta-encoding** scheme where, rather than writing the absolute indices in the dependency label, we write the *differences* between consecutive ones.[5] We used this strategy for the continuous treebanks only, whose d-trees are guaranteed to satisfy the nested property.

For comparison, we also implemented a replication of the encoding proposed by Hall and Nivre (2008), which we call **H&N-encoding**. This strategy concatenates all the c-nodes' symbols in the modifier's spine with the attachment position in the head's spine (*e.g.*, in Figure 3, if the modifier m_2 has a spine with nodes X_1, X_2, X_3, the generated d-label would be $\mathtt{X_1|X_2|X_3\#2}$; our direct encoding scheme generates $\mathtt{Z_2\#2}$ instead). Since their strategy encodes the entire spines into com-

[4]We train on §02–21, use §22 for validation, and test on §23. We predict automatic POS tags with *TurboTagger* (Martins et al., 2013), with 10-fold jackknifing on the training set.

[5]For example, if #1, #3, #4 and #2, #3, #3, #5 are respectively the sequence of indices from the head to the left and to the right, we encode these sequences as #1, #2, #1 and #2, #1, #0, #2 (using 3 distinct indices instead of 5).

plex arc labels, many such labels will be generated, leading to slower runtimes and poorer generalization, as we will see.

For the training portion of the English PTB, which has 27 non-terminal symbols, the direct encoding strategy yields 75 labels, while delta encoding yields 69 labels (2.6 indices per symbol). By contrast, the H&N-encoding procedure yields 731 labels, more than 10 times as many. We later show (in Tables 1–2) that delta-encoding leads to a slightly higher c-parsing accuracy than direct encoding, and that both strategies are considerably more accurate than H&N-encoding.

4.2 Training the Labeled Dependency Parser

The next step is to train a labeled d-parser on the converted treebank. If we are doing continuous c-parsing, we train a projective d-parser; otherwise we train a non-projective one.

In our experiments, we found it advantageous to perform labeled d-parsing in two stages, as done by McDonald et al. (2006): first, train an unlabeled d-parser; then, train a dependency labeler.[6] Table 1 compares this approach against a one-shot strategy, experimenting with various off-the-shelf d-parsers: *MaltParser* (Nivre et al., 2007), *MSTParser* (McDonald et al., 2005), *ZPar* (Zhang and Nivre, 2011), and *TurboParser* (Martins et al., 2013), all with the default settings. For *TurboParser*, we used basic, standard and full models.

Our separate d-labeler receives as input a backbone d-structure and predicts a label for each arc. For each head h, we predict the modifiers' labels using a simple sequence model, with features of the form $\phi(h, m, \ell)$ and $\phi(h, m, m', \ell, \ell')$, where m and m' are two consecutive modifiers (possibly on opposite sides of the head) and ℓ and ℓ' are their labels. We use the same arc label features $\phi(h, m, \ell)$ as *TurboParser*. For $\phi(h, m, m', \ell, \ell')$, we use the POS triplet $\langle p_h, p_m, p_{m'} \rangle$, plus unilexical features where each of the three POS is replaced by the word form. Both features are conjoined with the label pair ℓ and ℓ'. Decoding under this model can be done by running the Viterbi algorithm independently for each head. The runtime is almost negligible compared with the time to parse: it took 2.1 seconds to process PTB §22, a fraction of about 5% of the total runtime.

[6]The reason why a two-stage approach is preferable is that one-shot d-parsers, for efficiency reasons, use label features parsimoniously. However, for our reduction approach, d-labels are crucial and strongly interdependent, since they jointly encode the c-structure.

Dependency Parser	UAS	LAS	F_1	# toks/s.
MaltParser	90.93	88.95	86.87	5,392
MSTParser	92.17	89.86	87.93	363
ZPar	92.93	91.28	89.50	1,022
TP-Basic	92.13	90.23	87.63	2,585
TP-Standard	93.55	91.58	90.41	1,658
TP-Full	93.70	91.70	90.53	959
TP-Full + Lab., H&N enc.	93.80	87.86	89.39	871
TP-Full + Lab, direct enc.	93.80	91.99	90.89	912
TP-Full + Lab., delta enc.	**93.80**	**92.00**	**90.94**	912

Table 1: Results on English PTB §22 achieved by various d-parsers and encoding strategies. For dependencies, we report unlabeled/labeled attachment scores (UAS/LAS), excluding punctuation. For constituents, we show F_1-scores (without punctuation and root nodes), as provided by EVALB (Black et al., 1992). We report total parsing speeds in tokens per second (including time spent on pruning, decoding, and feature evaluation), measured on a Intel Xeon processor @2.30GHz.

	direct enc.		**delta enc.**	
	# labels	$\mathbf{F_1}$	**# labels**	$\mathbf{F_1}$
Basque	26	85.04	17	85.17
French	61	79.93	56	80.05
German	66	83.44	59	83.39
Hebrew	62	83.26	43	83.29
Hungarian	24	86.54	15	86.67
Korean	44	79.79	16	79.97
Polish	47	92.39	34	92.64
Swedish	29	77.02	25	77.19

Table 2: Impact of direct and delta encodings on the dev sets of the SPMRL14 shared task. Reported are the number of labels and the F_1-scores yielded by each encoding technique.

4.3 Decoding into Unaryless Constituents

After training the labeled d-parser, we can run it on the test data. Then, we need to convert the predicted d-tree into a c-tree without unaries.

To accomplish this step, we first need to recover, for each head h, the weak order of its modifiers M_h. We do this by looking at the predicted dependency labels, extracting the event indices j, and using them to build and sort the equivalent classes $\{\bar{M}_h^j\}_{j=1}^J$. If two modifiers have the same index j, we force them to have consistent labels (by always choosing the label of the modifier which is the closest to the head). For continuous c-parsing, we also decrease the index j of the modifier closer to the head as much as necessary to make sure that the nesting property holds. In PTB §22, these corrections were necessary only for 0.6% of the tokens. Having done this, we use Algorithm 2 to obtain a predicted c-tree without unary nodes.

4.4 Recovery of Unary Nodes

The last stage is to recover the unary nodes. Given a unaryless c-tree as input, we predict unaries by running independent classifiers at each node in the tree (a simple unstructured task). Each class is either NULL (in which case no unary node is appended to the current node) or a concatenation of unary node labels (*e.g.*, S->ADJP for a node JJ). We obtained 64 classes by processing the training sections of the PTB, the fraction of unary nodes being about 11% of the total number of nodes. To reduce complexity, for each node symbol we only consider classes that have been observed with that symbol in the training data. In PTB §22, this yields an average of 9.9 candidates per node occurrence.

The classifiers are trained on the original c-treebank, stripping off unary nodes and trained to recover those nodes. We used the following features (conjoined with the class and with a flag indicating if the node is a pre-terminal):

- The production rules above and beneath the node (*e.g.*, S->NP VP and NP->DT NN);
- The node's label, alone and conjoined with the parent's label or the left/right sibling's label;
- The leftmost and rightmost word/lemma/POS tag/morpho-syntactic tags in the node's yield;
- If the left/right node is a pre-terminal, the word/lemma/morpho-syntactic tags beneath.

This is a relatively easy task: when gold unaryless c-trees are provided as input, we obtain an EVALB F_1-score of 99.43%. This large figure is due to the small amount of unary nodes, making this module have less impact on the final parser than the d-parser. Being a lightweight unstructured task, this step took only 0.7 seconds to run on PTB §22, a tiny fraction (less than 2%) of the total runtime.

Table 1 shows the accuracies obtained with the d-parser followed by the unary predictor. Since two-stage TP-Full with delta-encoding is the best strategy, we use this configuration in the sequel. To further explore the impact of delta encoding, we report in Table 2 the scores obtained by direct and delta encodings on eight other treebanks (see §5.2 for details on these datasets). With the exception of German, in all cases the delta encoding yielded better EVALB F_1-scores with fewer labels.

5 Experiments

To evaluate the performance of our reduction-based parsers, we conduct experiments in a variety of treebanks, both continuous and discontinuous.

Parser	LR	LP	F1	#Toks/s.
Charniak (2000)	89.5	89.9	89.5	–
Klein and Manning (2003)	85.3	86.5	85.9	143
Petrov and Klein (2007)	90.0	90.3	90.1	169
Carreras et al. (2008)	90.7	91.4	91.1	–
Zhu et al. (2013)	90.3	90.6	90.4	1,290
Stanford Shift-Reduce (2014)	89.1	89.1	89.1	655
Hall et al. (2014)	88.4	88.8	88.6	12
This work	89.9	90.4	90.2	957
Charniak and Johnson (2005)*	91.2	91.8	91.5	84
Socher et al. (2013)*	89.1	89.7	89.4	70
Zhu et al. (2013)*	91.1	91.5	91.3	–

Table 3: Results on the English PTB §23. All systems reporting runtimes were run on the same machine. Marked as * are reranking and semi-supervised c-parsers.

5.1 Results on the English PTB

Table 3 shows the accuracies and speeds achieved by our system on the English PTB §23, in comparison to state-of-the-art c-parsers. We can see that our simple reduction-based c-parser surpasses the three Stanford parsers (Klein and Manning, 2003; Socher et al., 2013, and Stanford Shift-Reduce), and is on par with the Berkeley parser (Petrov and Klein, 2007), while being more than 5 times faster.

The best supervised competitor is the recent shift-reduce parser of Zhu et al. (2013), which achieves similar, but slightly better, accuracy and speed. Our technique has the advantage of being flexible: since the time for d-parsing is the dominating factor (see §4.4), plugging a faster d-parser automatically yields a faster c-parser. While reranking and semi-supervised systems achieve higher accuracies, this aspect is orthogonal, since the same techniques can be applied to our parser.

5.2 Results on the SPMRL Datasets

We experimented with datasets for eight languages, from the SPMRL14 shared task (Seddah et al., 2014). We used the official training, development and test sets with the provided predicted POS tags. For French and German, we used the lexicalization rules detailed in Dybro-Johansen (2004) and Rehbein (2009), respectively. For Basque, Hungarian and Korean, we always took the rightmost modifier as head-child node. For Hebrew and Polish we used the leftmost modifier instead. For Swedish we induced head rules from the provided dependency treebank, as described in Versley (2014b). These choices were based on dev-set experiments.

Table 4 shows the results. For all languages except French, our system outperforms the Berkeley parser (Petrov and Klein, 2007), with or without prescribed POS tags. Our average F_1-scores are superior to the best non-reranking system participating in the shared task (Crabbé and Seddah, 2014) and to the c-parser of Hall et al. (2014), achieving the best results for 4 out of 8 languages.

5.3 Results on the Discontinuous Treebanks

Finally, we experimented on two widely-used discontinuous German treebanks: TIGER (Brants et al., 2002) and NEGRA (Skut et al., 1997). For the former, we used two different splits: TIGER-SPMRL, provided in the SPMRL14 shared task; and TIGER-H&N, used by Hall and Nivre (2008). For NEGRA, we used the standard splits. In these experiments, we skipped the unary recovery stage, since very few unary nodes exist in the data.[7] We ran *TurboTagger* to predict POS tags for TIGER-H&N and NEGRA, while in TIGER-SPMRL we used the predicted POS tags provided in the shared task. All treebanks were lexicalized using the head-rule sets of Rehbein (2009). For comparison to related work, sentence length cut-offs of 30, 40 and 70 were applied during the evaluation.

Table 5 shows the results. We observe that our approach outperforms all the competitors considerably, achieving state-of-the-art accuracies for both datasets. The best competitor, van Cranenburgh and Bod (2013), is more than 3 points behind, both in TIGER-H&N and in NEGRA. Our reduction-based parsers are also much faster: van Cranenburgh and Bod (2013) report 3 hours to parse NEGRA with $L \leq 40$. Our system parses all NEGRA sentences (regardless of length) in 27.1 seconds in a single core, which corresponds to a rate of 618 tokens per second. This approaches the speed of the easy-first system of Versley (2014a), who reports runtimes in the range 670–920 tokens per second, but is much less accurate.

TIGER-SPMRL	$L \leq 70$	all	
V14b, *gold*	76.46 / 41.05	76.11 / 40.94	
Ours, *gold*	**80.98 / 43.44**	**80.62 / 43.32**	
V14b, *pred*	73.90 / 37.00	– / –	
Ours, *pred*	**77.72 / 38.75**	**77.32 / 38.64**	
TIGER-H&N	$L \leq 40$	all	
HN08, *gold*	79.93 / 37.78	– / –	
V14a, *gold*	74.23 / 37.32	– / –	
Ours, *gold*	**85.53 / 51.21**	**84.22 / 49.63**	
HN08, *pred*	75.33 / 32.63	– / –	
CB13, *pred*	78.8– / 40.8–	– / –	
Ours, *pred*	**82.57 / 45.93**	**81.12 / 44.48**	
NEGRA	$L \leq 30$	$L \leq 40$	all
M12, *gold*	74.5– / –	– / –	– / –
C12, *gold*	– / –	72.33 / 33.16	71.08 / 32.10
KM13, *gold*	75.75 / –	– / –	– / –
CB13, *gold*	– / –	76.8– / 40.5–	– / –
Ours, *gold*	**82.56 / 52.13**	**81.08 / 48.04**	**80.52 / 46.70**
CB13, *pred*	– / –	74.8– / 38.7–	– / –
Ours, *pred*	**79.63 / 48.43**	**77.93 / 44.83**	**76.95 / 43.50**

Table 5: F_1 / exact match scores on TIGER and NEGRA test sets, with gold and predicted POS tags. These scores are computed by the DISCO-DOP evaluator ignoring root nodes and, for TIGER-H&N and NEGRA, punctuation tokens. The baselines are published results by Hall and Nivre 2008 (HN08), Maier et al. 2012 (M12), van Cranenburgh 2012 (C12), Kallmeyer and Maier 2013 (KM13), van Cranenburgh and Bod 2013 (CB13), and Versley 2014a, 2014b (V14a, V14b).

6 Related Work

Conversions between constituents and dependencies have been considered by De Marneffe et al. (2006) in one direction, and by Collins et al. (1999) and Xia and Palmer (2001) in the other, toward multi-representational treebanks (Xia et al., 2008). This prior work aimed at linguistically sound conversions, involving grammar-specific transformation rules to handle the kind of ambiguities expressed in Figure 2. Our work differs in that we are not concerned about the linguistic plausibility of our conversions, but only with the formal aspects that underlie the two representations.

The work most related to ours is Hall and Nivre (2008), who also convert dependencies to constituents to prototype a c-parser for German. Their encoding strategy is compared to ours in §4.1: they encode the entire spines into the dependency labels, which become rather complex and numerous. A similar strategy has been used by Versley (2014a) for discontinuous c-parsing. Both are largely outperformed by our system, as shown in §5.3. The crucial difference is that we encode only the top node's label and its position in the spine—besides being a much lighter representation, ours has an interpretation as a weak ordering, leading to the isomorphisms expressed in Propositions 1–3.

Joint constituent and dependency parsing have been tackled by Carreras et al. (2008) and Rush et al. (2010), but the resulting parsers, while accurate, are more expensive than a single c-parser. Very recently, Kong et al. (2015) proposed a much cheaper pipeline in which d-parsing is performed first, followed by a c-parser constrained to be con-

[7] NEGRA has no unaries; for the TIGER-SPMRL and H&N dev-sets, the fraction of unaries is 1.45% and 1.01%.

Parser	Basque	French	German	Hebrew	Hungar.	Korean	Polish	Swedish	Avg.
Berkeley	70.50	**80.38**	78.30	86.96	81.62	71.42	79.23	79.19	78.45
Berkeley Tagged	74.74	79.76	78.28	85.42	85.22	78.56	86.75	80.64	81.17
Hall et al. (2014)	83.39	79.70	78.43	87.18	**88.25**	**80.18**	90.66	82.00	83.72
Crabbé and Seddah (2014)	85.35	79.68	77.15	86.19	87.51	79.35	**91.60**	82.72	83.69
This work	**85.90**	78.75	**78.66**	**88.97**	88.16	79.28	91.20	**82.80**	**84.22**
Björkelund et al. (2014)	88.24	82.53	81.66	89.80	91.72	83.81	90.50	85.50	86.72

Table 4: F_1-scores on eight treebanks of the SPMRL14 shared task, computed with the provided EVALB_SPMRL tool, which takes into account all tokens except root nodes. Berkeley Tagged is a version of Petrov and Klein (2007) using the predicted POS tags provided by the organizers. Crabbé and Seddah (2014) is the best non-reranking system in the shared task, and Björkelund et al. (2014) the ensemble and reranking-based system which won the official task. We report their published scores.

sistent with the predicted d-structure. Our work differs in which we do not need to run a c-parser in the second stage—instead, the d-parser already stores constituent information in the arc labels, and the only necessary post-processing is to recover unary nodes. Another advantage of our method is that it can be readily used for discontinuous parsing, while their constrained CKY algorithm can only produce continuous parses.

7 Conclusion

We proposed a reduction technique that allows to implement a c-parser when only a d-parser is given. The technique is applicable to any d-parser, regardless of its nature or kind. This reduction was accomplished by endowing d-trees with a weak order relation, and showing that the resulting class of head-ordered d-trees is isomorphic to constituent trees. We showed empirically that the our reduction leads to highly-competitive c-parsers for English and for eight morphologically rich languages; and that it outperforms the current state of the art in discontinuous parsing of German.

Acknowledgments

We would like to thank the three reviewers for their insightful comments, and Slav Petrov, Djamé Seddah, Yannick Versley, David Hall, Muhua Zhu, Lingpeng Kong, Carlos Gómez-Rodríguez, and Andreas van Cranenburgh for valuable feedback and help in preparing data and running software code. This research has been partially funded by the Spanish Ministry of Economy and Competitiveness and FEDER (project TIN2010-18552-C03-01), Ministry of Education (FPU Grant Program) and Xunta de Galicia (projects R2014/029 and R2014/034). A. M. was supported by the EU/FEDER programme, QREN/POR Lisboa (Portugal), under the Intelligo project (contract 2012/24803), and by the FCT grants UID/EEA/50008/2013 and PTDC/EEI-SII/2312/2012.

References

Taylor Berg-Kirkpatrick, Dan Gillick, and Dan Klein. 2011. Jointly learning to extract and compress. In *Proc. of Annual Meeting of the Association for Computational Linguistics*.

Anders Björkelund, Özlem Çetinoğlu, Agnieszka Faleńska, Richárd Farkas, Thomas Mueller, Wolfgang Seeker, and Zsolt Szántó. 2014. Introducing the ims-wrocław-szeged-cis entry at the spmrl 2014 shared task: Reranking and morpho-syntax meet unlabeled data. In *Proc. of the First Joint Workshop on Statistical Parsing of Morphologically Rich Languages and Syntactic Analysis of Non-Canonical Languages*.

Ezra Black, John Lafferty, and Salim Roukos. 1992. Development and evaluation of a broad-coverage probabilistic grammar of english-language computer manuals. In *Proc. of Annual Meeting on Association for Computational Linguistics*.

Adriane Boyd. 2007. Discontinuity revisited: An improved conversion to context-free representations. In *Proc. of Linguistic Annotation Workshop*.

Sabine Brants, Stefanie Dipper, Silvia Hansen, Wolfgang Lezius, and George Smith. 2002. The TIGER treebank. In *Proc. of the workshop on treebanks and linguistic theories*.

Xavier Carreras, Michael Collins, and Terry Koo. 2008. TAG, Dynamic Programming, and the Perceptron for Efficient, Feature-rich Parsing. In *Proc. of the International Conference on Natural Language Learning*.

Eugene Charniak and Mark Johnson. 2005. Coarse-to-fine n-best parsing and maxent discriminative reranking. In *Proc. of Annual Meeting of the Association for Computational Linguistics*.

Eugene Charniak. 1996. Tree-bank grammars. In *Proc. of the National Conference on Artificial Intelligence*.

Eugene Charniak. 2000. A maximum-entropy-inspired parser. In *Proc. of the North American Chapter of the Association for Computational Linguistics Conference*.

Michael Collins, Lance Ramshaw, Jan Hajič, and Christoph Tillmann. 1999. A Statistical Parser for Czech. In *Proc. of the Annual Meeting of the Association for Computational Linguistics on Computational Linguistics*.

Michael Collins. 1999. *Head-driven statistical models for natural language parsing*. Ph.D. thesis, University of Pennsylvania.

Benoit Crabbé and Djamé Seddah. 2014. Multilingual discriminative shift reduce phrase structure parsing for the SPMRL 2014 shared task. In *Proc. of the First Joint Workshop on Statistical Parsing of Morphologically Rich Languages and Syntactic Analysis of Non-Canonical Languages*.

Marie-Catherine De Marneffe, Bill MacCartney, Christopher D Manning, et al. 2006. Generating typed dependency parses from phrase structure parses. In *Proc. of the Meeting of the Language Resources and Evaluation Conference*.

Ane Dybro-Johansen. 2004. Extraction automatique de Grammaires d'Arbres Adjoints à partir d'un corpus arboré du français. Master's thesis, Université Paris 7.

Jason Eisner and Giorgio Satta. 1999. Efficient parsing for bilexical context-free grammars and head automaton grammars. In *Proc. of Annual Meeting of the Association for Computational Linguistics*.

Jason Eisner. 1996. Three new probabilistic models for dependency parsing: An exploration. In *Proc. of International Conference on Computational Linguistics*.

Jakob Elming, Anders Johannsen, Sigrid Klerke, Emanuele Lapponi, Hector Martinez Alonso, and Anders Søgaard. 2013. Down-stream effects of tree-to-dependency conversions. In *Proc. of the Annual Conference of the Human Language Technologies - North American Chapter of the Association for Computational Linguistics*.

Haim Gaifman. 1965. Dependency systems and phrase-structure systems. *Information and control*.

Carlos Gómez-Rodríguez, Marco Kuhlmann, and Giorgio Satta. 2010. Efficient parsing of well-nested linear context-free rewriting systems. In *Proc. of the Annual Conference of the North American Chapter of the Association for Computational Linguistics*.

Johan Hall and Joakim Nivre. 2008. A dependency-driven parser for german dependency and constituency representations. In *Proc. of the Workshop on Parsing German*.

David Hall, Greg Durrett, and Dan Klein. 2014. Less grammar, more features. In *Proc. of the Annual Meeting of the Association for Computational Linguistics*.

Liang Huang. 2008. Forest reranking: Discriminative parsing with non-local features. In *Proc. of the Annual Meeting of the Association for Computational Linguistics*.

Richard Johansson and Pierre Nugues. 2008. Dependency-based Semantic Role Labeling of PropBank. In *Empirical Methods for Natural Language Processing*.

Mark Johnson. 1998. PCFG models of linguistic tree representations. *Computational Linguistics*.

Sylvain Kahane, Alexis Nasr, and Owen Rambow. 1998. Pseudo-projectivity: a polynomially parsable non-projective dependency grammar. In *Proc. of the International Conference on Computational Linguistics*.

Laura Kallmeyer and Wolfgang Maier. 2013. Data-driven parsing using probabilistic linear context-free rewriting systems. *Computational Linguistics*.

Dan Klein and Christopher D. Manning. 2003. Accurate unlexicalized parsing. In *Proc. of Annual Meeting on Association for Computational Linguistics*.

Lingpeng Kong and Noah A Smith. 2014. An empirical comparison of parsing methods for stanford dependencies. *arXiv preprint arXiv:1404.4314*.

Lingpeng Kong, Alexander M. Rush, and Noah A. Smith. 2015. Transforming dependencies into phrase structures. In *Proc. of the Conference of the North American Chapter of the Association for Computational Linguistics*.

Terry Koo and Michael Collins. 2010. Efficient third-order dependency parsers. In *Proc. of Annual Meeting of the Association for Computational Linguistics*.

Sandra Kübler, Wolfgang Maier, Ines Rehbein, and Yannick Versley. 2008. How to compare treebanks. In *Proc. of the Meeting of the Language Resources and Evaluation Conference*.

Marco Kuhlmann and Joakim Nivre. 2006. Mildly non-projective dependency structures. In *Proc. of the joint conference of the International Committee on Computational Linguistics and the Association for Computational Linguistics*.

Wolfgang Maier and Anders Søgaard. 2008. Treebanks and mild context-sensitivity. In *Proc. of Formal Grammar*.

Wolfgang Maier, Miriam Kaeshammer, and Laura Kallmeyer. 2012. Data-driven plcfrs parsing revisited: Restricting the fan-out to two. In *Proc. of the Eleventh International Conference on Tree Adjoining Grammars and Related Formalisms*.

Mitchell P. Marcus, Beatrice Santorini, and Mary Ann Marcinkiewicz. 1993. Building a large annotated corpus of english: The penn treebank. *Computational Linguistics*.

André F. T. Martins, Miguel B. Almeida, and Noah A. Smith. 2013. Turning on the turbo: Fast third-order non-projective turbo parsers. In *Proc. of the Annual Meeting of the Association for Computational Linguistics*.

Takuya Matsuzaki, Yusuke Miyao, and Jun'ichi Tsujii. 2005. Probabilistic CFG with latent annotations. In *Proc. of the Annual Meeting of the Association for Computational Linguistics*.

Ryan McDonald and Giorgio Satta. 2007. On the complexity of non-projective data-driven dependency parsing. In *Proc. of International Conference on Parsing Technologies*.

Ryan McDonald, Fernando Pereira, Kiril Ribarov, and Jan Hajic. 2005. Non-projective dependency parsing using spanning tree algorithms. In *Proc. of Empirical Methods for Natural Language Processing*.

Ryan McDonald, Kevin Lerman, and Fernando Pereira. 2006. Multilingual dependency analysis with a two-stage discriminative parser. In *Proc. of International Conference on Natural Language Learning*.

Joakim Nivre, Johan Hall, Jens Nilsson, Gülsen Eryiğit, and Svetoslav Marinov. 2006. Labeled pseudo-projective dependency parsing with support vector machines. In *Proc. of International Conference on Natural Language Learning*.

Joakim Nivre, Johan Hall, Jens Nilsson, Atanas Chanev, Gülsen Eryiğit, Sandra Kübler, Svetoslav Marinov, and Erwin Marsi. 2007. Maltparser: A language-independent system for data-driven dependency parsing. *Natural Language Engineering*.

Fernando C. N. Pereira and David H. D. Warren. 1983. Parsing as Deduction. In *Proc. of the Annual Meeting of the Association for Computational Linguistics*.

Slav Petrov and Dan Klein. 2007. Improved inference for unlexicalized parsing. In *Proc. of the North American Chapter of the Association for Computational Linguistics*.

Ines Rehbein. 2009. *Treebank-Based Grammar Acquisition for German*. Ph.D. thesis, School of Computing, Dublin City University.

Alexander M Rush and Slav Petrov. 2012. Vine pruning for efficient multi-pass dependency parsing. In *Proc. of the North American Chapter of the Association for Computational Linguistics*.

Alexander Rush, David Sontag, Michael Collins, and Tommi Jaakkola. 2010. On dual decomposition and linear programming relaxations for natural language processing. In *Proc. of Empirical Methods for Natural Language Processing*.

Kenji Sagae and Alon Lavie. 2005. A classifier-based parser with linear run-time complexity. In *Proc. of the Ninth International Workshop on Parsing Technology*.

Djamé Seddah, Sandra Kübler, and Reut Tsarfaty. 2014. Introducing the spmrl 2014 shared task on parsing morphologically-rich languages. In *Proc. of the First Joint Workshop on Statistical Parsing of Morphologically Rich Languages and Syntactic Analysis of Non-Canonical Languages*, August.

Wojciech Skut, Brigitte Krenn, Thorsten Brants, and Hans Uszkoreit. 1997. An annotation scheme for free word order languages. In *Proc. of the Fifth Conference on Applied Natural Language Processing ANLP-97*.

Richard Socher, John Bauer, Christopher D Manning, and Andrew Y Ng. 2013. Parsing with compositional vector grammars. In *Proc. of Annual Meeting of the Association for Computational Linguistics*.

Andreas van Cranenburgh and Rens Bod. 2013. Discontinuous parsing with an efficient and accurate dop model. *Proc. of International Conference on Parsing Technologies*.

Andreas van Cranenburgh. 2012. Efficient parsing with linear context-free rewriting systems. In *Proc. of the Conference of the European Chapter of the Association for Computational Linguistics*.

Yannick Versley. 2014a. Experiments with easy-first nonprojective constituent parsing. In *Proc. of the First Joint Workshop on Statistical Parsing of Morphologically Rich Languages and Syntactic Analysis of Non-Canonical Languages*.

Yannick Versley. 2014b. Incorporating semi-supervised features into discontinuous easy-first constituent parsing. *CoRR*, abs/1409.3813.

Krishnamurti Vijay-Shanker, David J Weir, and Aravind K Joshi. 1987. Characterizing structural descriptions produced by various grammatical formalisms. In *Proc. of the Annual Meeting on Association for Computational Linguistics*.

Yuanbin Wu, Qi Zhang, Xuanjing Huang, and Lide Wu. 2009. Phrase dependency parsing for opinion mining. In *Proc. of Empirical Methods for Natural Language Processing*.

Fei Xia and Martha Palmer. 2001. Converting dependency structures to phrase structures. In *Proc. of the First International Conference on Human Language Technology Research*.

Fei Xia, Owen Rambow, Rajesh Bhatt, Martha Palmer, and Dipti Misra Sharma. 2008. Towards a multi-representational treebank. *LOT Occasional Series*.

Hiroyasu Yamada and Yuji Matsumoto. 2003. Statistical dependency analysis with support vector machines. In *Proc. of International Conference on Parsing Technologies*.

Yue Zhang and Joakim Nivre. 2011. Transition-based dependency parsing with rich non-local features. In *Proc. of the Annual Meeting of the Association for Computational Linguistics*.

Muhua Zhu, Yue Zhang, Wenliang Chen, Min Zhang, and Jingbo Zhu. 2013. Fast and accurate shift-reduce constituent parsing. In *Proc. of Annual Meeting of the Association for Computational Linguistics*.

Optimal Shift-Reduce Constituent Parsing with Structured Perceptron

Le Quang Thang
Hanoi University of Science and Technology
{lelightwin@gmail.com}

Hiroshi Noji and **Yusuke Miyao**
National Institute of Informatics, The Graduate University for Advanced Studies
{noji,yusuke}@nii.ac.jp

Abstract

We present a constituent shift-reduce parser with a structured perceptron that finds the optimal parse in a practical runtime. The key ideas are new feature templates that facilitate state merging of dynamic programming and A* search. Our system achieves 91.1 F1 on a standard English experiment, a level which cannot be reached by other beam-based systems even with large beam sizes.[1]

1 Introduction

A parsing system comprises two components: a scoring model for a tree and a search algorithm. In shift-reduce parsing, the focus of most previous studies has been the former, typically by enriching feature templates, while the search quality has often been taken less seriously. For example, the current state-of-the-art parsers for constituency (Zhu et al., 2013; Wang and Xue, 2014) and dependency (Bohnet et al., 2013) both employ beam search with a constant beam size, which may suffer from severe search errors. This is contrary to ordinary PCFG parsing which, while it often uses some approximations, has nearly optimal quality (Petrov and Klein, 2007).

In this paper, we instead investigate the question of whether we can obtain a practical shift-reduce parser with state-of-the-art accuracy by focusing on optimal search quality like PCFG parsing. We base our system on best-first search for shift-reduce parsing formulated in Zhao et al. (2013), but it differs from their approach in two points. First, we focus on constituent parsing while they use dependency grammar. Second, and more crucially, they use a locally trained MaxEnt model, which is simple but not strong, while we explore a structured perceptron, the current state-of-the-art in shift-reduce parsing (Zhu et al., 2013).

As we will see, this model change makes search quite hard, which motivates us to invent new feature templates as well as to improve the search algorithm. In existing parsers, features are commonly exploited from the parsing history, such as the top k elements on the stack. However, such features are expensive in terms of search efficiency. Instead of relying on features primarily from the stack, our features mostly come from the span of the top few nodes, an idea inspired by the recent empirical success in CRF parsing (Hall et al., 2014). We show that these span features also fit quite well in the shift-reduce system and lead to state-of-the-art accuracy. We further improve search with new A* heuristics that make optimal search for shift-reduce parsers with a structured perceptron tractable for the first time.

The primary contribution of this paper is to demonstrate the effectiveness and the practicality of optimal search for shift-reduce parsing, especially when combined with appropriate features and efficient search. In English Penn Treebank experiments, our parser achieves an F1 score of 91.1 on test set at a speed of 13.6 sentences per second. This score is in excess of that of a beam-based system with larger beam size and same speed.

2 Background and Related Work

2.1 Shift-Reduce Constituent Parsing

We first introduce the shift-reduce algorithm for constituent structures. For space reasons, our exposition is rather informal; See Zhang and Clark (2009) for details. A shift-reduce parser parses a sentence through transitions between *states*, each of which consists of two data structures of a stack and a queue. The stack preserves intermediate parse results, while the queue saves unprocessed tokens. At each step, a parser selects an action,

[1]The open source software of our system is available at https://github.com/mynlp/optsr.

Proceedings of the 53rd Annual Meeting of the Association for Computational Linguistics and the 7th International Joint Conference on Natural Language Processing, pages 1534–1544,
Beijing, China, July 26-31, 2015. ©2015 Association for Computational Linguistics

which changes the current state into the new one. For example, SHIFT pops the front word from the queue and pushes it onto the stack, while REDUCE(X) combines the top two elements on the stack into their parent.[2] For example, if the top two elements on the stack are DT and NN, REDUCE(NP) combines these by applying the CFG rule NP $\rightarrow$ DT NN.

Unary Action The actions above are essentially the same as those in shift-reduce dependency parsing (Nivre, 2008), but a special action for constituent parsing UNARY(X) complicates the system and search. For example, if the top element on the stack is NN, UNARY(NP) changes it to NP by applying the rule NP $\rightarrow$ NN. In particular, this causes inconsistency in the numbers of actions between derivations (Zhu et al., 2013), which makes it hard to apply the existing best first search for dependency grammar to our system. We revisit this problem in Section 3.1.

Model The model of a shift-reduce parser gives a score to each derivation, i.e., an action sequence $\mathbf{a} = (a_1, \cdots, a_{|\mathbf{a}|})$, in which each a_i is a shift or reduce action. Let $\mathbf{p} = (p_1, \cdots, p_{|\mathbf{a}|})$ be the sequence of states, where p_i is the state after applying a_i to p_{i-1}. p_0 is the initial state for input sentence $\mathbf{w}$. Then, the score for a derivation $\Phi(\mathbf{a})$ is calculated as the total score of every action:

$$\Phi(\mathbf{a}) = \sum_{1 \le i \le |\mathbf{a}|} \phi(a_i, p_{i-1}). \tag{1}$$

There are two well-known models, in which the crucial difference is in training criteria. The MaxEnt model is trained *locally* to select the correct action at each step. It assigns a probability for each action a_i as

$$P(a_i | p_{i-1}) \propto \exp(\theta^\intercal f(a_i, p_{i-1})), \tag{2}$$

where θ and $f(a, p)$ are weight and feature vectors, respectively. Note that the probability of an action sequence $\mathbf{a}$ under this model is the product of local probabilities, though we can cast the total score in summation form (1) by using the log of (2) as a local score $\phi(a_i, p_{i-1})$.

The structured perceptron is instead trained *globally* to select the correct action sequence given an input sentence. It does not use probability and the local score is just $\phi(a_i, p_{i-1}) = \theta^\intercal f(a_i, p_{i-1})$. In practice, this global model is much stronger than the local MaxEnt model. However, training this model without any approximation is hard, and the common practice is to rely on well-known heuristics such as an early update with beam search (Collins and Roark, 2004). We are not aware of any previous study that succeeded in training a structured perceptron for parsing without approximation. We will show how this becomes possible in Section 3.

[2]Many existing constituent parsers use two kinds of reduce actions for selecting the direction of its head child while we do not distinguish these two. In our English experiments, we found no ambiguity for head selection in our binarized grammar (See Section 4).

2.2 Previous Best-First Shift-Reduce Parsing

The basic idea behind best-first search (BFS) for shift-reduce parsing is assuming each parser state as a node on a graph and then searching for the *minimal cost* path from a start state (node) to the final state. This is the idea of Sagae and Lavie (2006), and it was later refined by Zhao et al. (2013). BFS gives a *priority* to each state, and a state with the highest priority (lowest cost) is always processed first. BFS guarantees that the first found goal is the best (*optimality*) if the *superiority* condition is satisfied: a state never has a lower cost than the costs of its previous states.

Though the found parse is guaranteed to be optimal, in practice, current BFS-based systems are not stronger than other systems with approximate search (Zhu et al., 2013; Wang and Xue, 2014) since all existing systems are based on the MaxEnt model. With this model, the speriority can easily be accomplished by using the negative log of (2), which is always positive and becomes smaller with higher probability. We focus instead on the structured perceptron, but achieving superiority with this model is not trivial. We resolve this problem in Section 3.1.

In addition to the mathematical convenience, the MaxEnt model itself helps search. Sagae and Lavie ascribe the empirical success of their BFS to the sparseness of the distribution over subsequent actions in the MaxEnt model. In other words, BFS is very efficient when only a few actions have dominant probabilities in each step, and the MaxEnt model facilitates this with its exponential operation (2). Unfortunately, this is not the case in our global structured perceptron because the score of each action is just the sum of the feature weights. Resolving this search difficulty is the central problem of this paper; we illustrate this problem in Section 4 and resolve it in Section 5.

2.3 Hypergraph Search of Zhao et al. (2013)

The worst time complexity of BFS in Sagae and Lavie (2006) is exponential. For dependency parsing, Zhao et al. (2013) reduce it to polynomial by converting the search graph into a hypergraph by using the state merging technique of Huang and Sagae (2010). This hypergraph search is the basis of our parser, so we will briefly review it here.

The algorithm is closely related to agenda-based best-first parsing algorithms for PCFGs (Klein and Manning, 2001; Pauls and Klein, 2009). As in those algorithms, it maintains two data structures: a chart C that preserves *processed* states as well as a priority queue (agenda) Q. The difference is in the basic items processed in C and Q. In PCFG parsing, they are *spans*. Each span abstracts many *derivations* on that span and the chart maps a span to the best (lowest cost) derivation found so far. In shift-reduce parsing, the basic items are not spans but *states*, i.e., partial representations of the stack.[3] We denote $p = \langle i, j, s_d...s_0 \rangle$ where s_i is the i-th top subtree on the stack and s_0 spans i to j. We extract features from $s_d...s_0$. Note that d is constant and a state usually does not contain full information about a derivation. In fact, it only keeps *atomic features*, the minimal information on the stack necessary to recover the full features and packs many derivations. The chart maps a state to the current best derivation. For example, if we extract features only from the root symbol of s_0, each state looks the same as a span of PCFGs.

Differently from the original shift-reduce algorithm, during this search, reduce actions are defined between two states p and q. The basic operation of the algorithm is to pop the best (top) state p from the queue, push it into the chart, and then enqueue every state that can be obtained by a reduce action between p and other states in the chart or a *shift* action from p. The left states $\mathcal{L}(p)$ and right states $\mathcal{R}(p)$ are important concepts. $\mathcal{L}(p)$ is a set of states in the chart, with which p can reduce from the right side. Formally,

$$\mathcal{L}(\langle i, j, s_d...s_0 \rangle) = \\ \{\langle h, i, s'_d...s'_0 \rangle | \forall k \in [1, d], f_k(s'_{k-1}) = f_k(s_k)\},$$

where $f_k(\cdot)$ returns atomic features on the k-th top node. See Figure 4 for how they look like in constituent parsing. $\mathcal{R}(p)$ is defined similarly; p can reduce $q \in \mathcal{R}(p)$ from the left side. When p is popped, it searches for every $\mathcal{L}(p)$ and $\mathcal{R}(p)$ in the chart and tries to expand the current derivation.

The priority for each state is a pair (c, v). c is the prefix cost that is the total cost to reach that state, while v is the inside cost, a cost to build the top node s_0. The top state in the queue has the lowest prefix cost, or the lowest inside cost if the two prefix costs are the same.

3 Best-First Shift-Reduce Constituent Parsing with Structured Perceptron

This section describes our basic parsing system, i.e., shift-reduce constituent parsing with BFS and the structured perceptron. We have to solve two problems. The first is how to achieve BFS with the structured perceptron, and the second is how to apply that BFS to constituent parsing. Interestingly, the solution to the first problem makes the second problem relatively trivial.

3.1 Superiority of Structured Perceptron

We must design each priority of a state to satisfy the superiority condition. $\phi(a_i, p_{i-1}) = \theta^\mathsf{T} f(a_i, p_{i-1})$ is the usual local *score* employed in structured perceptrons (Huang and Sagae, 2010) but we cannot use it as a local *cost* for two reasons. First, in our system, the best parse should have the lowest cost; it is opposite in the ordinary setting (Collins, 2002). We can resolve this conflict by changing the direction of structured perceptron training so that the best parse has the lowest score.[4] Second, each $\phi(a_i, p_{i-1})$ can take a negative value but the cost should always be positive. This is in contrast to the MaxEnt model in which the negative log probability is always positive. Our strategy is to add a constant offset δ to every local cost. If δ is large enough so that every score is positive, the superiority condition is satisfied.[5]

Unary Merging Though this technique solves the problem with the structured perceptron for a simpler shift-reduce system, say for dependency grammar, the existence of unary actions, as mentioned in Section 2.1, requires additional effort in order to apply it to constituent parsing. In particular, constituent parsing takes different numbers of

[3] Although Zhao et al. (2013) explained that the items in Q are derivations (not states), we can implement Q as a set of states by keeping backpointers in a starndard way.

[4] This is easily accomplished by inverting all signs of the update equations.

[5] To find this value, we train our system using beam search with several beam sizes, choosing the maximum value of the action score during training.

$$\textsc{Sh} \qquad \frac{\overset{\text{state } p:}{\langle \_, j, s_d...s_0\rangle : (c, \_)}}{\langle j, j+1, s_{d-1}...s_0|t_j(w_j)\rangle : (c + c_{\mathsf{sh}}(p), c_{\mathsf{sh}}(p))}\; j < n$$

$$\textsc{Shu}(\mathrm{X}) \qquad \frac{\overset{\text{state } p:}{\langle \_, j, s_d...s_0\rangle : (c, \_)}}{\langle j, j+1, s_{d-1}...s_0|\mathrm{X}(t_j(w_j))\rangle : (c + c_{\mathsf{shu(X)}}(p), c_{\mathsf{shu(X)}}(p))}\; j < n$$

$$\textsc{Re}(\mathrm{X}) \qquad \frac{\overset{\text{state } q:}{\langle k, i, s'_d...s'_0\rangle : (c', v')} \quad \overset{\text{state } p:}{\langle i, j, s_d...s_0\rangle : (c, v)}}{\langle k, j, s'_d...s'_1|\mathrm{X}(s'_0, s_0)\rangle : (c' + v + c_{\mathsf{re(X)}}(p), v' + v + c_{\mathsf{re(X)}}(p))}\; q \in \mathcal{L}(p)$$

$$\textsc{Reu}(\mathrm{Y}, \mathrm{X}) \qquad \frac{\overset{\text{state } q:}{\langle k, i, s'_d...s'_0\rangle : (c', v')} \quad \overset{\text{state } p:}{\langle i, j, s_d...s_0\rangle : (c, v)}}{\langle k, j, s'_d...s'_1|\mathrm{Y}(\mathrm{X}(s'_0, s_0))\rangle : (c' + v + c_{\mathsf{reu(Y,\,X)}}(p), v' + v + c_{\mathsf{reu(Y,\,X)}}(p))}\; q \in \mathcal{L}(p)$$

Figure 1: The deductive system of our best-first shift-reduce constituent parsing explaining how the prefix cost and inside cost are calculated. FIN is omitted. | on the stack means an append operation and $a(b)$ means a subtree $a \to b$. t_j is the POS tag of j-th token while w_j is the surface form. $c_a(p)$ is the cost for an action a of which features are extracted from p. Each $c_a(p)$ implicitly includes an offset δ.

actions for each derivation, which means that the scores of two final states may contain different offset values. The existing modification to alleviate this inconsistency (Zhu et al., 2013) cannot be applied here because it is designed for beam search.

We instead develop a new transition system, in which the number of actions to reach the final state is always $2n$ (n is the length of sentence). The basic idea is merging a unary action into each shift or reduce action. Our system uses five actions:

- SH: original shift action;
- SHU(X): shift a node, then immediately apply a unary rule to that node;
- RE(X): original reduce action;
- REU(Y, X): do reduce to X first, then immediately apply an unary rule Y → X to it;
- FIN: finish the process.

Though the system cannot perform consecutive unary actions, in practice it can generate any unary chains as long as those in the training corpus by collapsing a chain into one rule. We preprocess the corpus in this way along with binarization (See Section 4).

Note that this system is quite similar to the transition system for dependency parsing. The only changes are that we have several varieties of shift and reduce actions. This modification also makes it easy to apply an algorithm developed for dependency parsing to constituent parsing, such as dynamic programming with beam search (Huang and Sagae, 2010), which has not been applied into constituent parsing until quite recently (Mi and Huang, 2015) (See Section 7).

Algorithm 1 BFS for Constituent Parsing; Only differences from Zhao et al. (2013)

```
procedure SHIFT(x, Q)
    TRYADD(sh(x), Q)
    for y ∈ shu(x) do
        TRYADD(y, Q)
procedure REDUCE(A, B, Q)
    for (x, y) ∈ A × B do
        for z ∈ re(x, y) ∪ reu(x, y) do
            TRYADD(z, Q)
```

3.2 BFS with Dynamic Programming

Now applying BFS of Zhao et al. (2013) for dependency parsing into constituent parsing is not hard. Figure 1 shows the deductive system of dynamic programming, which is much similar to that in dependency parsing. One important change is that we include a cost for a shift (SH or SHU) action in the prefix cost in a shift step, not a reduce step as in Zhao et al. (2013), since it is unknown whether the top node s_0 of a state p is instantiated with SH or SHU. This modification keeps the correctness of the algorithm and has been employed in another system (Kuhlmann et al., 2011).

The algorithm is also slightly changed. We show only the difference from Zhao et al. (2013) (Algorithm 1) in Algorithm 1. $\mathsf{shu}(x)$ is a function which returns the set of states that can be arrived at by possible SHU rules applied to the state x. $\mathsf{re}(x, y)$ and $\mathsf{reu}(x, y)$ are similar, and they return the set of states arrived at through one of RE or REU actions. As a speed up, we can apply a lazy expansion technique (we do so in our experiment).

Model	F1	Speed (Sent./s.)
SP (reduced features)	88.9	0.8
ME (reduced features)	85.1	4.8
ME (full features)	86.3	2.5

Table 1: Results of BFS systems with dynamic programming for the Penn Treebank development set with different models and features. SP = the structured perceptron; ME = the MaxEnt.

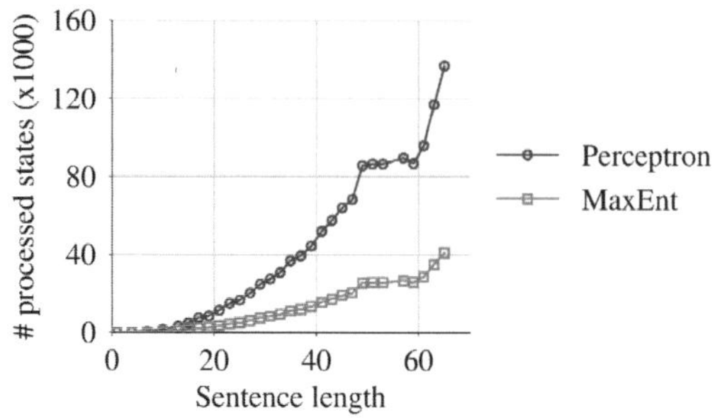

Figure 2: Comparison of the average number of the processed states of the structured perceptron with those of the MaxEnt model.

Another difference is in training. The previous best-first shift-reduce parsers are all trained in the same way as a parser with greedy search since the model is local MaxEnt. In our case, we can use structured perceptron training with exact search (Collins, 2002); that is, at each iteration for each sentence, we find the current argmin derivation with BFS, then update the parameters if it differs from the gold derivation. Note that at the beginning of training, BFS is inefficient due to the initial flat parameters. We use a heuristic to speed up this process: For a few iterations (five, in our case), we train the model with beam search and an early update (Collins and Roark, 2004). We find that this approximation does not affect the performance, while it greatly reduces the training time.

4 Evaluation of Best-First Shift-Reduce Constituent Parsing

This section evaluates the empirical performance of our best-first constituent parser that we built in the previous section. As mentioned in Section 2.2, the previous empirical success of best-first shift-reduce parsers might be due to the sparsity property of the MaxEnt model, which may not hold true in the structured perceptron. We investigate the validity of this assumption by comparing two systems, a locally trained MaxEnt model and a globally trained structured perceptron.

Setting We follow the standard practice and train each model on section 2-21 of the WSJ Penn Treebank (Marcus et al., 1993), which is binarized using the algorithm in Zhang and Clark (2009) with the head rule of Collins (1999). We report the F1 scores for the development set of section 22. The Stanford POS tagger is used for part-of-speech tagging.[6] We used the EVALB program to evaluate parsing performance.[7] Every experiment reported here was performed on hardware equipped with an Intel Corei5 2.5GHz processor and 16GB of RAM.

Feature We borrow the feature templates from Sagae and Lavie (2006). However, we found the full feature templates make training and decoding of the structured perceptron much slower, and instead developed simplified templates by removing some, e.g., that access to the child information on the second top node on the stack.[8]

Result Table 1 summarizes the results that indicate our assumption is true. The structured perceptron has the best score even though we restrict the features. However, its parsing speed is much slower than that of the local MaxEnt model. To see the difference in search behaviors between the two models, Figure 2 plots the number of processed (popped) states during search.

Discussion This result may seem somewhat depressing. We have devised a new method that enables optimal search for the structured perceptron, but it cannot handle even modestly large feature templates. As we will see below, the time complexity of the system depends on the used features. We have tried features from Sagae and Lavie (2006), but their features are no longer state-of-the-art. For example, Zhu et al. (2013) report higher scores by using beam search with much richer feature templates, though, as we have examined, it seems implausible to apply such features to our system. In the following, we find a practical solution for improving both parse accuracy and search efficiency in our system. We will see that our new features not only make BFS tractable, but also lead to comparable or even superior accuracy relative to the current mainstream features. When

[6]http://nlp.stanford.edu/software/tagger.shtml

[7]http://nlp.cs.nyu.edu/evalb

[8]The other features that we removed are features 9–14 defined in Figure 1 of Sagae and Lavie (2006).

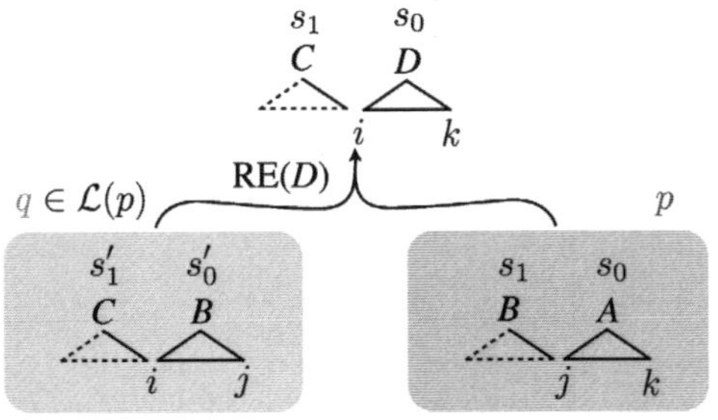

Figure 3: A snippet of the hypergraph for the system that simulates a simple PCFG. p is the popped state, which is being expanded with a state of its left states $\mathcal{L}(p)$ using a reduce rule.

it is combined with A* search, the speed reaches a practical level.

5 Improving Optimal Search Efficiency

5.1 Span Features

The worst time complexity of hypergraph search for shift-reduce parsing can be analyzed with the deduction rule of the reduce step. Figure 3 shows an example. In this case, the time complexity is $O(n^3 \cdot |G| \cdot |N|)$ since there are three indices (i, j, k) and four nonterminals (A, B, C, D), on which three comprise a rule. The extra factor $|N|$ compared with ordinary CKY parsing comes from the restriction that we extract features only from one state (Huang and Sagae, 2010).

Complexity increases when we add new atomic features to each state. For example, if we lexicalize this model by adding features that depend on the head indices of s_0 and/or s_1, it increases to $O(n^6 \cdot |G| \cdot |N|)$ since we have to maintain three head indices of *A*, *B*, and *C*. This is why Sagae and Lavie's features are too expensive for our system; they rely on head indices of s_0, s_1, s_2, s_3, the left and right children of s_0 and s_1, and so on, leading prohibitively huge complexity. Historically speaking, the success of shift-reduce approach in constituent parsing has been led by its success in dependency parsing (Nivre, 2008), in which the head is the primary element, and we suspect this is the reason why the current constituent shift-reduce parsers mainly rely on deeper stack elements and their heads.

The features we propose here are extracted from fundamentally different parts from these recent trends. Figure 4 explains how we extract atomic features from a state and Table 2 shows the full list of feature templates. Our system is unlexicalized; i.e., it does not use any head indices. This feature design is largely inspired by the recent empirical success of *span features* in CRF parsing (Hall et al., 2014). Their main finding is that the surface information on a subtree, such as the first or the last word of a span, has essentially the same amount of information as its head. For our system, such span features are much cheaper, so we expect they would facilitate our dynamic programming without sacrificing accuracy.

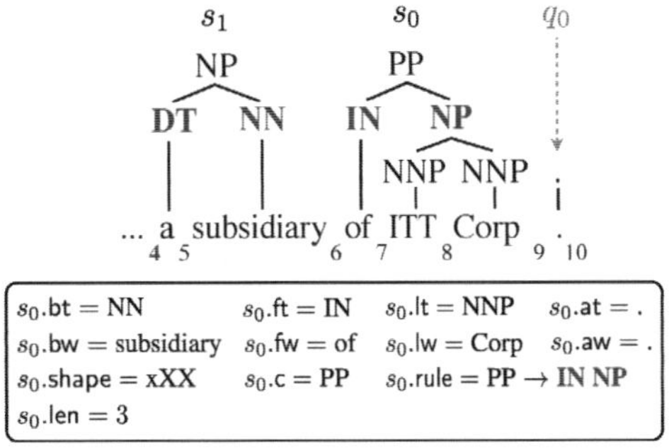

Figure 4: Atomic features of our system largely come from the span of a constituency. For each span (s_0 and s_1), we extract the surface form and POS tag of the preceding word (bw, bt), the first word (fw, ft), the last word (lw, lt), and the subsequent word (aw, at). shape is the same as that in Hall et al. (2014). Bold symbols are additional information from the system of Figure 3. The time complexity is $O(n^4 \cdot |G|^3 \cdot |N|)$.

q_0.w ∘ q_0.t	q_1.w ∘ q_1.t	q_2.w ∘ q_2.t	q_3.w ∘ q_3.t
s_0.c ∘ s_0.ft	s_0.c ∘ s_0.fw	s_0.c ∘ s_0.lt	s_0.c ∘ s_0.lw
s_0.c ∘ s_0.at	s_0.c ∘ s_0.aw	s_0.c ∘ s_0.ft ∘ s_0.lt	s_0.c ∘ s_0.ft ∘ s_0.lw
s_0.c ∘ s_0.fw ∘ s_0.lt	s_0.c ∘ s_0.fw ∘ s_0.lw	s_0.c ∘ s_0.len	s_0.c ∘ s_0.shape
s_0.rule	s_0.shape ∘ s_0.rule		
s_1.c ∘ s_1.ft	s_1.c ∘ s_1.fw	s_1.c ∘ s_1.lt	s_1.c ∘ s_1.lw
s_1.c ∘ s_1.bt	s_1.c ∘ s_1.bw	s_1.c ∘ s_1.ft ∘ s_1.lt	s_1.c ∘ s_1.ft ∘ s_1.lw
s_1.c ∘ s_1.fw ∘ s_1.lt	s_1.c ∘ s_1.fw ∘ s_1.lw	s_1.c ∘ s_1.len	s_1.c ∘ s_1.shape
s_1.rule	s_1.shape ∘ s_1.rule		
s_1.lw ∘ s_0.fw	s_0.ft ∘ s_1.lw	s_1.lt ∘ s_0.fw	s_1.lt ∘ s_0.ft
s_1.c ∘ s_0.fw	s_0.c ∘ s_1.fw	s_1.c ∘ s_0.lw	s_0.c ∘ s_1.lw
s_0.fw ∘ q_0.w	s_0.lw ∘ q_0.w	q_0.t ∘ s_0.fw	q_0.t ∘ s_0.lw
s_0.c ∘ q_0.w	s_0.c ∘ q_0.t	s_1.fw ∘ q_0.w	s_1.lw ∘ q_0.w
q_0.t ∘ s_1.fw	q_0.t ∘ s_1.lw	s_1.c ∘ q_0.w	s_1.c ∘ q_0.t
q_0.w ∘ q_1.w	q_0.t ∘ q_1.w	q_0.w ∘ q_1.t	q_0.t ∘ q_1.t
s_0.c ∘ s_1.c ∘ q_0.t	s_0.c ∘ s_1.c ∘ q_0.w	s_1.c ∘ q_0.t ∘ s_0.fw	s_1.c ∘ q_0.t ∘ s_0.lw
s_0.c ∘ q_0.t ∘ s_1.fw	s_0.c ∘ q_0.t ∘ s_1.fw		

Table 2: All feature templates in our span model. See Figure 4 for a description of each element. q_i is the i-th top token on the queue.

We customize their features for fitting in the shift-reduce framework. Unlike the usual setting of PCFG parsing, shift-reduce parsers receive a POS-tagged sentence as input, so we use both the POS tag and surface form for each word on the span. One difficult part is using features with an applied rule. We include this feature by memorizing the previously applied rule for each span (subtree). This is a bit costly, because it means we have to preserve labels of the left and right children for each node, which lead to an additional $|G|^2$ factor of complexity. However, we will see that this problem can be alleviated by our heuristic cost functions in A* search described below.

5.2 A* Search

We now explain our A* search, another key technique for speeding up our search. To our knowledge, this is the first work to successfully apply A* search to shift-reduce parsing.

A* parsing (Klein and Manning, 2003a) modifies the calculation of priority $\sigma(p_i)$ for state p_i. In BFS, it is basically the prefix cost, the sum of every local cost (Section 3.1), which we denote as β_{p_i}:

$$\beta_{p_i} = \sum_{1 \leq j \leq i} (\phi(a_j, p_{j-1}) + \delta).$$

In A* parsing, $\sigma(p_i) = \beta_{p_i} + h(p_i)$ where $h(p_i)$ is a heuristic cost. β_{p_i} corresponds to the Viterbi inside cost of PCFG parsing (Klein and Manning, 2003a) while $h(p_i)$ is the Viterbi outside cost, an approximation of the cost for the future best path (action sequence) from p_i.

$h(p_i)$ must be a lower bound of the *true* Viterbi outside cost. In PCFG parsing, this is often achieved with a technique called *projection*. Let G^* be a projected, or relaxed, grammar of the original G; then, a rule weight in the relaxed grammar w_{r^*} will become $w_{r^*} = \min_{r \in G: \pi(r) = r^*} w_r$, where $\pi(r)$ is a projection function which returns the set of rules that correspond to r in G^*.

In feature-based shift-reduce parsing, a rule weight corresponds to the sum of feature weights for an action a, that is, $\phi(a, p_i) = \theta^\mathsf{T} f(a, p_i)$. We calculate $h(p_i)$ with a relaxed feature function $\phi^*(a, p_i)$, which always returns a lower bound:

$$\phi^*(a, p_i) = \theta^{*\mathsf{T}} f(a, c_i) \leq \theta^\mathsf{T} f(a, p_i) = \phi(a, p_i).$$

Note that we only have to modify the weight vector. If a relaxed weight satisfies $\theta^*(k) \leq \theta(k)$ for all k, that projection is correct.

Our A* parsing is essentially hierarchical A* parsing (Pauls and Klein, 2009), and we calculate a heuristic cost $h(p)$ on the fly using another chart for the relaxed space when a new state p is pushed into the priority queue. Below we introduce two different projection methods, which are orthogonal and later combined hierarchically.

a	∘	s_1.c	∘	s_1.ft	θ	θ_{GP}	θ_{LF}
SH	∘	VP	∘	NN	10.53	-5.82	-5.82
SH	∘	SBAR	∘	NN	1.98	-5.82	-5.82
SH	∘	NP	∘	NN	**-5.82**	-5.82	-5.82
		...					
SH	∘	VP	∘	DT	3.25	1.12	-5.82
SH	∘	SBAR	∘	DT	**1.12**	1.12	-5.82
SH	∘	NP	∘	DT	1.98	1.12	-5.82
		...					

Table 3: Example of our feature projection. θ_{GP} is a weight vector with the GP, which collapses every c. θ_{LF} is with the LF, which collapses all elements in Table 4.

s_1.c	s_1.ft	s_1.fw	s_1.bt	s_1.bw
s_1.len	s_1.shape	s_1.rule	s_0.rule	

Table 4: List of feature elements ignored in the LF.

Grammar Projection (GP) Our first projection borrows the idea from the filter projection of Klein and Manning (2003a), in which the grammar symbols (nonterminals) are collapsed into a single label X. Our projection, however, does not collapse all the labels into X; instead, we utilize constituent labels in level 2 from Charniak et al. (2006), in which labels that tend to be head, such as S or VP are collapsed into HP and others are collapsed into MP. θ_{G} in Table 3 is an example of how feature weights are relaxed with this projection. Here we show each feature as a tuple including action name (a). Let π_{GP} be a feature projection function: e.g.,

$$((a \circ s_1.\mathsf{c} \circ s_1.\mathsf{ft}) = (\text{SH} \circ \text{VP} \circ \text{NN})) \\ \mapsto_{\pi_{\text{GP}}} ((a \circ s_1.\mathsf{c} \circ s_1.\mathsf{ft}) = (\text{SH} \circ \text{HP} \circ \text{NN})).$$

Formally, for k-th feature, the weight $\theta_{\text{GP}}(k)$ is determined by minimizing over the features collapsed by π_{GP}:

$$\theta_{\text{GP}}(k) = \min_{1 \leq k' \leq K: \pi_{\text{GP}}(g_{k'}) = g_k} \theta(k'),$$

where g_k is the value of the k-th feature.

Less-Feature Projection (LF) The basic idea of our second projection is to *ignore* some of the atomic features in a feature template so that we can reduce the time complexity for computing the heuristics. We apply this technique to the feature elements in Table 4. We can do so by not filling in the actual value in each feature template: e.g.,

$$((a \circ s_1.\mathsf{c} \circ s_1.\mathsf{ft}) = (\text{SH} \circ \text{VP} \circ \text{NN})) \\ \mapsto_{\pi_{\text{LF}}} ((a \circ s_1.\mathsf{c} \circ s_1.\mathsf{ft}) = (\text{SH} \circ s_1.\mathsf{c} \circ s_1.\mathsf{ft})).$$

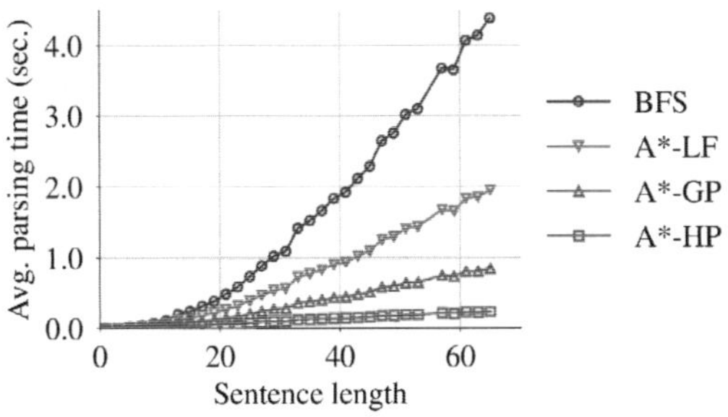

Figure 5: Comparison of parsing times between different A* heuristics.

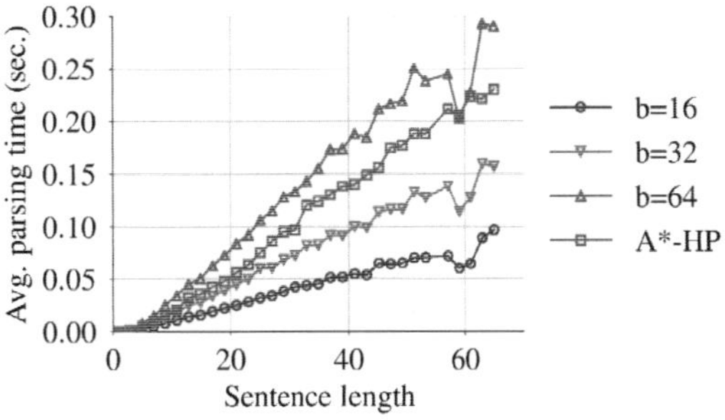

Figure 6: Comparison of parsing times between A* and beam search (with DP).

The elements in Table 4 are selected so that all bold elements in Figure 4 would be eliminated; the complexity is $O(n^3 \cdot |G| \cdot |N|)$. In practice, this is still expensive. However, we note that the effects of these two heuristics are complementary: The LF reduces complexity to a cubic time bound, while the GP greatly reduces the size of grammar $|G|$; We combine these two ideas below.

Hierarchical Projection (HP) The basic idea of this combined projection is to use the heuristics given by the GP to lead search of the LF. This is similar to the hierarchical A* for PCFGs with multilevel symbol refinements (Pauls and Klein, 2009). The difference is that their hierarchy is on the grammar symbols while our projection targets are features. When a state p is created, its heuristic score $h(p)$ is calculated with the LF, which requires search for the outside cost in the space of the LF, but its worst time complexity is cubic. The GP is used to guide this search. For each state p_{LF} in the space of the LF, the GP calculates the heuristic score. We will see that this combination works quite well in practice in the next section.

6 Experiment

We build our final system by combining the ideas in Section 5 and the system in Section 3. We also build beam-based systems with or without dynamic programming (DP) and with the ordinary or the new span features. All systems are trained with the structured perceptron. We use the early update for training beam-based systems.

Effect of A* heuristics Figure 5 shows the effects of A* heuristics. In terms of search quality, the LF is better; it prunes 92.5% of states compared to naive BFS, while the GP prunes 75%. However, the LF takes more time to calculate heuristics than the GP. The HP combines the advantages of both, achieving the best result.

Feaure	Z&C feature set			Span (this work)		
DP		✓			✓	
	F1	F1	Sent./s.	F1	F1	Sent./s.
b=16	89.1	90.1	34.6	88.6	89.9	31.9
b=32	89.6	89.9	20.0	89.3	90.2	17.0
b=64	89.7	90.2	10.6	89.6	90.2	9.1
A*	-	-	-	-	**90.7**	13.6
BFS	-	-	-	-	**90.7**	1.1

Table 5: Results for the Penn Treebank development set. Z&C = feature set of Zhang and Clark (2009). The speeds of non-DP and DP are the same, so we omit them from the comparison.

Accuracy and Speed The F1 scores for the development set are summarized in Table 5. We can see that the systems with our new feature (span) perform surprisingly well, at a competitive level with the more expensive features of Zhang and Clark (2009) (Z&C). This is particularly true with DP; it sometimes outperforms Z&C, probably because our simple features facilitate state merging of DP, which expands search space. However, our main result that the system with optimal search gets a much higher score (90.7 F1) than beam-based systems with a larger beam size (90.2 F1) indicates that ordinary beam-based systems suffer from severe search errors even with the help of DP. Though our naive BFS is slow (1.12 sent./s.), A* search considerably improves parsing speed (13.6 sent./s.), and is faster than the beam-based system with a beam size of 64 (Figure 6).

Unary Merging We have not mentioned the effect of our unary merging (Section 3), but the result indicates it has almost the same effect as the previously proposed padding method (Zhu et al.,

Shift-reduce (closed)	LR	LP	F1	Sent./s.
Sagae (2005)†	86.0	86.1	86.0	3.7
Sagae (2006)†	88.1	87.8	87.9	2.2
Zhu (2013) (Z&C)	90.2	90.7	90.4	93.4
Span (b=64, DP)	90.2	90.6	90.4	8.4
Span (A*)	**90.9**	**91.2**	**91.1**	13.6
Other (closed)				
Berkeley (2007)	90.1	90.3	90.2	6.1
Stanford (2013) (RNN)	90.3	90.7	90.5	3.3
Hall (2014) (CRF)	89.0	89.5	89.3	0.7
External/Reranking				
Charniak (2005)	91.2	91.8	91.5	2.1
McClosky (2006)	92.2	92.6	92.4	1.2
Zhu (2013) +semi	91.1	91.5	91.3	47.6

Table 6: The final results for section 23 of the Penn Treebank. The systems with † are reported by authors running on different hardware. We divide baseline state-of-the-art systems into three categories: shift-reduce systems (Sagae and Lavie, 2005; Sagae and Lavie, 2006; Zhu et al., 2013), other chart-based systems (Petrov and Klein, 2007; Socher et al., 2013), and the systems with external semi supervised features or reranking (Charniak and Johnson, 2005; McClosky et al., 2006; Zhu et al., 2013).

2013). The score with the non-DP beam size = 16 and Z&C (89.1 F1) is the same as that reported in their paper (the features are the same).

Final Experiment Table 6 compares our parsing system with those of previous studies. When we look at closed settings, where no external resource other than the training Penn Treebank is used, our system outperforms all other systems including the Berkeley parser (Petrov and Klein, 2007) and the Stanford parser (Socher et al., 2013) in terms of F1. The parsing systems with external features or reranking outperform our system. However, it should be noted that our system could also be improved by external features. For example, the feature of type-level distributional similarity, such as Brown clustering (Brown et al., 1992), can be incorporated with our system without changing the theoretical runtime.

7 Related Work and Discussion

Though the framework is shift-reduce, we can notice that our system is strikingly similar to the CKY-based discriminative parser (Hall et al., 2014) because our features basically come from two nodes on the stack and their spans. From this viewpoint, it is interesting to see that our system outperforms theirs by a large margin (Figure 6). Identifying the source of this performance change is beyond the scope of this paper, but we believe this is an important question for future parsing research. For example, it is interesting to see whether there is any structural advantage for shift-reduce over CKY by comparing two systems with exactly the same feature set.

As shown in Section 4, the previous optimal parser on shift-reduce (Sagae and Lavie, 2006) was not so strong because of the locality of the model. Other optimal parsing systems are often based on relatively simple PCFGs, such as unlexicalized grammar (Klein and Manning, 2003b) or factored lexicalized grammar (Klein and Manning, 2003c) in which A* heuristics from the unlexicalized grammar guide search. However, those systems are not state-of-the-art probably due to the limited context captured with a simple PCFG. A recent trend has thus been extending the context of each rule (Petrov and Klein, 2007; Socher et al., 2013), but the resulting complex grammars make exact search intractable. In our system, the main source of information comes from spans as in CRF parsing. This is cheap yet strong, and leads to a fast and accurate parsing system with optimality.

Concurrently with this work, Mi and Huang (2015) have developed another dynamic programming for constituent shift-reduce parsing by keeping the step size for a sentence to $4n - 2$, instead of $2n$, with an un-unary (stay) action. Their final score is 90.8 F1 on WSJ. Though they only experiment with beam-search, it is possible to build BFS with their transition system as well.

8 Conclusions

To date, all practical shift-reduce parsers have relied on approximate search, which suffers from search errors but also allows to utilize *unlimited* features. The main result of this paper is to show another possibility of shift-reduce by proceeding in an opposite direction: By selecting features and improving search efficiency, a shift-reduce parser with provable search optimality is able to find very high quality parses in a practical runtime.

Acknowledgements

We would like to thank Katsuhiko Hayashi for answering our questions about dynamic programming on shift-reduce parsing.

References

Bernd Bohnet, Joakim Nivre, Igor M. Boguslavsky, Richárd Farkas, and Jan Hajič. 2013. Joint Morphological and Syntactic Analysis for Richly Inflected Languages. *Transactions of the Association for Computational Linguistics*, 1(Oct):429–440.

Peter F. Brown, Peter V. deSouza, Robert L. Mercer, Vincent J. Della Pietra, and Jenifer C. Lai. 1992. Class-based N-gram Models of Natural Language. *Comput. Linguist.*, 18(4):467–479, December.

Eugene Charniak and Mark Johnson. 2005. Coarse-to-Fine n-Best Parsing and MaxEnt Discriminative Reranking. In *Proceedings of the 43rd Annual Meeting of the Association for Computational Linguistics (ACL'05)*, pages 173–180, Ann Arbor, Michigan, June. Association for Computational Linguistics.

Eugene Charniak, Mark Johnson, Micha Elsner, Joseph Austerweil, David Ellis, Isaac Haxton, Catherine Hill, R. Shrivaths, Jeremy Moore, Michael Pozar, and Theresa Vu. 2006. Multilevel Coarse-to-Fine PCFG Parsing. In *Proceedings of the Human Language Technology Conference of the NAACL, Main Conference*, pages 168–175, New York City, USA, June. Association for Computational Linguistics.

Michael Collins and Brian Roark. 2004. Incremental Parsing with the Perceptron Algorithm. In *Proceedings of the 42nd Meeting of the Association for Computational Linguistics (ACL'04), Main Volume*, pages 111–118, Barcelona, Spain, July.

M. Collins. 1999. *Head-Driven Statistical Models for Natural Language Parsing*. Ph.D. thesis, University of Pennsylvania.

Michael Collins. 2002. Discriminative Training Methods for Hidden Markov Models: Theory and Experiments with Perceptron Algorithms. In *Proceedings of the 2002 Conference on Empirical Methods in Natural Language Processing*, pages 1–8. Association for Computational Linguistics, July.

David Hall, Greg Durrett, and Dan Klein. 2014. Less Grammar, More Features. In *Proceedings of the 52nd Annual Meeting of the Association for Computational Linguistics (Volume 1: Long Papers)*, pages 228–237, Baltimore, Maryland, June. Association for Computational Linguistics.

Liang Huang and Kenji Sagae. 2010. Dynamic Programming for Linear-Time Incremental Parsing. In *Proceedings of the 48th Annual Meeting of the Association for Computational Linguistics*, pages 1077–1086, Uppsala, Sweden, July. Association for Computational Linguistics.

Dan Klein and Christopher D. Manning. 2001. Parsing and Hypergraphs. In *Proceedings of the Seventh International Workshop on Parsing Technologies (IWPT-2001), 17-19 October 2001, Beijing, China*.

Dan Klein and Christopher D. Manning. 2003a. A* Parsing: Fast Exact Viterbi Parse Selection. In *Proceedings of the 2003 Conference of the North American Chapter of the Association for Computational Linguistics on Human Language Technology - Volume 1*, NAACL '03, pages 40–47, Stroudsburg, PA, USA. Association for Computational Linguistics.

Dan Klein and Christopher D. Manning. 2003b. Accurate Unlexicalized Parsing. In *Proceedings of the 41st Annual Meeting of the Association for Computational Linguistics*, pages 423–430, Sapporo, Japan, July. Association for Computational Linguistics.

Dan Klein and Christopher D. Manning. 2003c. Factored A^* Search for Models over Sequences and Trees. In *IJCAI-03, Proceedings of the Eighteenth International Joint Conference on Artificial Intelligence, Acapulco, Mexico, August 9-15, 2003*, pages 1246–1251.

Marco Kuhlmann, Carlos Gómez-Rodríguez, and Giorgio Satta. 2011. Dynamic Programming Algorithms for Transition-Based Dependency Parsers. In *Proceedings of the 49th Annual Meeting of the Association for Computational Linguistics: Human Language Technologies*, pages 673–682, Portland, Oregon, USA, June. Association for Computational Linguistics.

Mitchell P. Marcus, Beatrice Santorini, and Mary Ann Marcinkiewicz. 1993. Building a Large Annotated Corpus of English: The Penn Treebank. *COMPUTATIONAL LINGUISTICS*, 19(2):313–330.

David McClosky, Eugene Charniak, and Mark Johnson. 2006. Reranking and Self-Training for Parser Adaptation. In *Proceedings of the 21st International Conference on Computational Linguistics and 44th Annual Meeting of the Association for Computational Linguistics*, pages 337–344, Sydney, Australia, July. Association for Computational Linguistics.

Haitao Mi and Liang Huang. 2015. Shift-Reduce Constituency Parsing with Dynamic Programming and POS Tag Lattice. In *Proceedings of the 2015 Conference on the North American Chapter of the Association for Computational Linguistics Human Language Technologies*, Denver, Colorado, May. Association for Computational Linguistics.

Joakim Nivre. 2008. Algorithms for Deterministic Incremental Dependency Parsing. *Computational Linguistics*, 34(4):513–553.

Adam Pauls and Dan Klein. 2009. Hierarchical Search for Parsing. In *Proceedings of Human Language Technologies: The 2009 Annual Conference of the North American Chapter of the Association for Computational Linguistics*, pages 557–565, Boulder, Colorado, June. Association for Computational Linguistics.

Slav Petrov and Dan Klein. 2007. Improved Inference for Unlexicalized Parsing. In *Human Language Technologies 2007: The Conference of the North American Chapter of the Association for Computational Linguistics; Proceedings of the Main Conference*, pages 404–411, Rochester, New York, April. Association for Computational Linguistics.

Kenji Sagae and Alon Lavie, 2005. *Proceedings of the Ninth International Workshop on Parsing Technology*, chapter A Classifier-Based Parser with Linear Run-Time Complexity, pages 125–132. Association for Computational Linguistics.

Kenji Sagae and Alon Lavie. 2006. A Best-First Probabilistic Shift-Reduce Parser. In *Proceedings of the COLING/ACL 2006 Main Conference Poster Sessions*, pages 691–698, Sydney, Australia, July. Association for Computational Linguistics.

Richard Socher, John Bauer, Christopher D. Manning, and Ng Andrew Y. 2013. Parsing with Compositional Vector Grammars. In *Proceedings of the 51st Annual Meeting of the Association for Computational Linguistics (Volume 1: Long Papers)*, pages 455–465, Sofia, Bulgaria, August. Association for Computational Linguistics.

Zhiguo Wang and Nianwen Xue. 2014. Joint POS Tagging and Transition-based Constituent Parsing in Chinese with Non-local Features. In *Proceedings of the 52nd Annual Meeting of the Association for Computational Linguistics (Volume 1: Long Papers)*, pages 733–742, Baltimore, Maryland, June. Association for Computational Linguistics.

Yue Zhang and Stephen Clark. 2009. Transition-Based Parsing of the Chinese Treebank using a Global Discriminative Model. In *Proceedings of the 11th International Conference on Parsing Technologies (IWPT'09)*, pages 162–171, Paris, France, October. Association for Computational Linguistics.

Kai Zhao, James Cross, and Liang Huang. 2013. Optimal Incremental Parsing via Best-First Dynamic Programming. In *Proceedings of the 2013 Conference on Empirical Methods in Natural Language Processing*, pages 758–768, Seattle, Washington, USA, October. Association for Computational Linguistics.

Muhua Zhu, Yue Zhang, Wenliang Chen, Min Zhang, and Jingbo Zhu. 2013. Fast and Accurate Shift-Reduce Constituent Parsing. In *Proceedings of the 51st Annual Meeting of the Association for Computational Linguistics (Volume 1: Long Papers)*, pages 434–443, Sofia, Bulgaria, August. Association for Computational Linguistics.

A Data-Driven, Factorization Parser for CCG Dependency Structures

YantaoDun, Weiwei Sun* and **Xiaojun Wan**
Institute of Computer Science and Technology, Peking University
The MOE Key Laboratory of Computational Linguistics, Peking University
{ws, duyantao, wanxiaojun}@pku.edu.cn

Abstract

This paper is concerned with building CCG-grounded, semantics-oriented deep dependency structures with a data-driven, factorization model. Three types of factorization together with different higher-order features are designed to capture different syntacto-semantic properties of functor-argument dependencies. Integrating heterogeneous factorizations results in intractability in decoding. We propose a principled method to obtain optimal graphs based on dual decomposition. Our parser obtains an unlabeled f-score of 93.23 on the CCGBank data, resulting in an error reduction of 6.5% over the best published result. which yields a significant improvement over the best published result in the literature. Our implementation is available at http://www.icst.pku.edu.cn/lcwm/grass.

1 Introduction

Combinatory Categorial Grammar (CCG; Steedman, 2000) is a linguistically expressive grammar formalism which has a transparent yet elegant interface between syntax and semantics. By assigning each lexical category a dependency *interpretation*, we can derive typed dependency structures from CCG derivations (Clark et al., 2002), providing a useful approximation to the underlying meaning representations. To date, CCG parsers are among the most competitive systems for generating such deep bi-lexical dependencies that appropriately encode a wide range of local and non-local syntacto-semantic information (Clark and Curran, 2007a; Bender et al., 2011). Such semantic-oriented dependency structures have been shown very helpful for NLP applications e.g. Question Answering (Reddy et al., 2014).

Traditionally, CCG graphs are generated as a by-product by grammar-guided parsers (Clark and Curran, 2007b; Fowler and Penn, 2010). The main challenge is that a *deep-grammar-guided* model usually can only produce limited coverage and corresponding parsing algorithms is of relatively high complexity. Robustness and efficiency, thus, are two major problems for handling practical tasks. To increase the applicability of such parsers, lexical or syntactic pruning has been shown necessary (Clark and Curran, 2004; Matsuzaki et al., 2007; Sagae et al., 2007; Zhang and Clark, 2011).

In the past decade, the techniques for data-driven dependency parsing has made a great progress (McDonald et al., 2005a,b; Nivre et al., 2004; Torres Martins et al., 2009; Koo et al., 2010). The major advantage of the data-driven architecture is complementary to the grammar-driven one. On one hand, data-driven approaches make essential uses of machine learning from linguistic annotations and are flexible to produce analysis for arbitrary sentences. On the other hand, without hard constraints, parsing algorithms for spanning specific types of graphs, e.g. projective (Eisner, 1996) and 1-endpoint-crossing trees (Pitler et al., 2013), can be of low complexity.

This paper proposes a new data-driven dependency parser that efficiently produces globally optimal CCG dependency graphs according to a discriminative, factorization model. The design of the factorization is motivated by three essential properties of the CCG dependencies. First, all arguments associated with the same predicate are highly correlated due to the nature that they approximates type-logical semantics. Second, all predicates govern the same argument exhibit the hybrid syntactic/semantic, i.e. head-complement-adjunct, relationships. Finally, the CCG dependency graphs are not but look very much like

*Email correspondence.

Proceedings of the 53rd Annual Meeting of the Association for Computational Linguistics and the 7th International Joint Conference on Natural Language Processing, pages 1545–1555,
Beijing, China, July 26-31, 2015. ©2015 Association for Computational Linguistics

trees, which have many good computational properties. Simultaneously modeling the three properties yields intrinsically heterogeneous factorizations over the same graph, and hence results in intractability in decoding. Inspired by (Koo et al., 2010; Rush et al., 2010), we employ dual decomposition to perform principled decoding. Though not always, we can obtain the optimal solution most of time. The time complexity of our parser is $O(n^3)$ when various 1st- and 2nd-order features are incorporated.

We conduct experiments on English CCGBank (Hockenmaier and Steedman, 2007). Though our parser does not use any grammar information, including both lexical categories and syntactic derivations, it produces very accurate CCG dependency graphs with respect to both token and complete matching. Our parser obtains an unlabeled f-score of 93.23, resulting in, perhaps surprisingly, an error reduction of up to 6.5% over the best published performance reported in (Auli and Lopez, 2011). Our work indicates that high-quality data-driven parsers can be built for producing more general dependency graphs, rather than trees. Nevertheless, empirical evaluation indicates that explicitly or implicitly using tree-structured information plays an essential role. The result also suggests that a wider range of complicated linguistic phenomena beyond surface syntax can be well modeled even without explicitly using grammars. Our algorithm is also applicable to other graph-structured representations, e.g. HPSG predicate-argument analysis (Miyao et al., 2004).

2 Related Work

Hockenmaier and Steedman (2007) developed linguistic resources, namely CCGBank, from the Penn Treebank (PTB; Marcus et al., 1993). In CCGBank, PTB phrase-structure trees have been transformed into normal-form CCG derivations, and deep bi-lexical dependency graphs that encode functor-argument strcutures have been extracted from these derivations using coindexation information. The typed dependency analysis provides a useful approximation to the underlying meaning representations, and has been shown very helpful for NLP applications e.g. Question Answering (Reddy et al., 2014).

Traditionally, CCG graphs are generated as a by-product by deep parsers with a core grammar (Clark et al., 2002; Clark and Curran, 2007b; Fowler and Penn, 2010). On the other hand, modeling these dependencies within a CCG parser has been shown very effective to improve the parsing accuracy (Clark and Curran, 2007b; Xu et al., 2014). Besides CCG, similar deep dependency structures can be also extracted from parsers under other deep grammar formalisms, e.g. LFG (King et al., 2003) and HPSG (Miyao et al., 2004).

In recent years, data-driven dependency parsing has been well studied and widely applied to many NLP tasks. Research on data-driven approach to producing dependency graphs that are not limited to tree or forest structures has also been initialized. Sagae and Tsujii (2008) introduced a transition-based parser that is able to handle projective directed dependency graphs for HPSG-style predicate-argument analysis. McDonald and Pereira (2006) presented a graph-based parser that can generate graphs in which a word may depend on multiple heads, and evaluated it on the Danish Treebank. Encouraged by their work, we study factorization models as well as principled decoding for CCG-grounded, graph-structured representations.

Dual decomposition, and more generally Lagrangian relaxation, is a classical method for solving combinatorial optimization problems. It has been successfully applied to several NLP tasks, including parsing (Koo et al., 2010; Rush et al., 2010) and machine translation (Rush and Collins, 2011). To provide principled decoding for our factorization parser, we employ the dual decomposition technique. Our work directly follows (Koo et al., 2010). The two basic factorizations are similar to the model introduced in (Martins and Almeida, 2014). Lluís et al. (2013) introduced a dual decomposition based joint model for joint syntactic and semantic parsing. They are concerned with shallow semantic representation, i.e. Semantic Role Labeling, whose graphs are sparse. Different from their concern on integrating syntactic parsing and semantic role labeling under 1st-order factorization, we are interested in designing higher-order factorization models for more dense and general linguistic graphs.

3 Graph Factorization

3.1 Background Notations

Consider a sentence $s = \langle \mathbf{w}, \mathbf{p} \rangle$ with words $\mathbf{w} = w_1 w_2 \cdots w_n$ and POS-tags $\mathbf{p} = p_1 p_2 \cdots p_n$. First we add one more virtual word $w_0 = \#W_{root}\#$

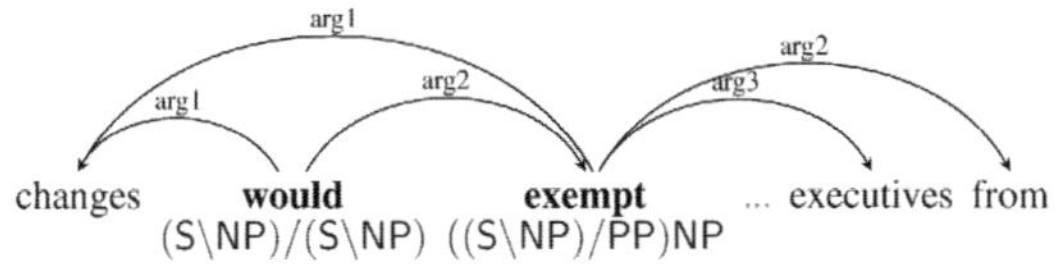

Figure 1: Examples to illustrate the predicate-centric view.

with POS-tag $p_0 = \#P_{root}\#$ which is conventionally considered as the root node of trees or graphs on the sentence. Then we denote the *index set* of all possible dependencies as $\mathcal{I} = \{(i,j)|i \in \{0,\cdots,n\}, j \in \{1,\cdots,n\}, i \neq j\}$. A dependency parse then can be represented as a vector

$$\boldsymbol{y} = \{y(i,j) : (i,j) \in \mathcal{I}\},$$

where $y(i,j) = 1$ if a dependency with predicate i and argument j is in the graph, 0 otherwise. Note that $\boldsymbol{y}$ is not a matrix but a long vector though we use two indexes to index it. In this paper, we only consider the unlabeled parsing task. Nevertheless, it is quite straightforward to extend our models to labeled parsing. Let $\mathcal{Y}$ denote the set of all possible $\boldsymbol{y}$. Given a function $f : \mathcal{Y} \to \mathbb{R}$ that assigns scores to parse graphs, the optimal parse is

$$\boldsymbol{y}^* = \arg\max_{\boldsymbol{y} \in \mathcal{Y}} f(\boldsymbol{y}).$$

Following recent advances in discriminative dependency parsing, we build disambiguation models based on global linear models, as in (McDonald et al., 2005a). In this framework, we score a dependency graph using a linear model:

$$f_\theta(\boldsymbol{y}) = \theta^\top \Phi(s, \boldsymbol{y}),$$

where $\Phi(s, \boldsymbol{y})$ produces a d-dimensional vector representation of the event that a CCG graph $\boldsymbol{y}$ is assigned to sentence s. In order to perform the decoding efficiently, we assume that the dependency graphs can be *factored* into smaller pieces. The main goal of this paper is to design appropriate factorization models, namely different types of f_θ's, to reflect essential properties of the semantics-oriented CCG dependency graphs.

3.2 Predicate-Centric Factorization

The very fundamental view of the CCG dependency graphs is based on their lexicalized, predicate-centric nature. Every word is assigned a lexical category, which directly encodes its subcategorization information. Due to the type-transparency nature of the formalism, this lexical category provides sufficient information for not only syntactic derivation but also semantic composition. It is important to capture functor-argument relations by putting all arguments of one particular predicate together. Figure 1 gives an example. The predicate "exempt" is of type "((S\NP)/PP)/NP," indicating that it takes three semantic dependents. This part of information is very similar to Semantic Role Labeling (SRL), whose goal is to find semantic roles for verbal predicates as well as their normalization. However, functor-argument analysis grounded in CCG is approximation of underlying logic forms and thus provides bi-lexical relations for almost all words. For instance, the second word in focus—"would"—captures structural information to organize other predicates yet entities.

In order to perform maximization efficiently in this view, we treat each predicate separately. Given a vector $\boldsymbol{y}^p$, we define

$$\boldsymbol{y}^p_{i\frown} = \{y(i,j) : j \in \{1,\cdots,n\}, j \neq i\}$$

and assume that $f(\boldsymbol{y}^p)$ takes the form

$$f^p(\boldsymbol{y}^p) = \sum_{i=0}^{n} f^p_i(\boldsymbol{y}^p_{i\frown})$$

To capture the relationships of all arguments to one particular predicate as a whole, we employ a Markov model. Let $a_1, \cdots, a_m$ be the sequence of the arguments of the word w_i under $\boldsymbol{y}^p_{i\frown}$. To keep the arguments in order, we constrain $1 \leq a_{j_1} < a_{j_2} \leq n$ if $j_1 < j_2$. In a *k-th order predicate-centric model*, we define

$$f^p_i(\boldsymbol{y}^p_{i\frown}) = \sum_{j=1}^{m+k-1} \theta_p^\top \Phi_p(a_{j-(k-1)}, ..., a_j, i, \mathbf{w}, \mathbf{p})$$

where a_j ($j \leq 0$ or $j \geq m+1$) are treated as specific initial or end state.

Higher-order rather than arc-factored features can be conveniently extracted from adjacent arguments. This is similar to the sibling factorization defined by a number of syntactic tree parsers, e.g. (McDonald and Pereira, 2006), (Koo and Collins, 2010) and (Ma and Zhao, 2012).

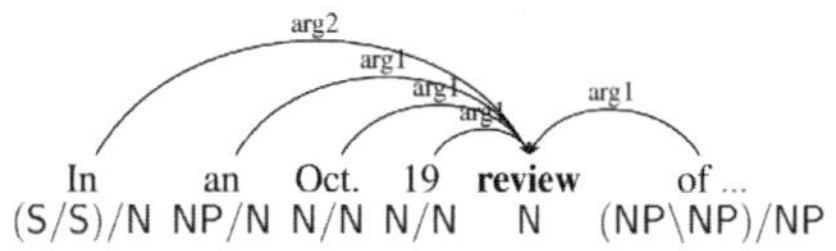

Figure 2: An example to illustrate the argument-centric view.

3.3 Argument-Centric Factorization

The syntactic principle for tree annotation treats the dependency relations between two words as syntactic projection. In another word, the head determines the syntactic category of the whole structure. The (type-logical) semantic principle determines a dependency according the types of the two words. The two kinds of dependency are coherent but not necessarily the same. In particular, an adjunct is a syntactic dependent but usually a semantic predicate of its syntactic head. Figure 2 gives an example to illustrate the idea. The argument in focus is "review" that is the complement of the preposition "in." The direction of this semantic dependency is the same to its corresponding syntactic dependency. Other predicates that semantically govern "review" are actually its modifiers, so the direction of these semantic dependencies are the opposite of their syntactic counterparts. It is important to capture head-complement-adjunct relations by putting all predicates of one particular argument together.

Similar to the predicate-centric model, we treat the graph fragment involved by each argument as independent, and capture the relationships among all predicates that governs the same argument using a Markov model. In the definition of predicate-centric model, if we exchange predicates and arguments, then we get our *argument-centric model.* Formally, we define

$$\boldsymbol{y}^a_{\curvearrowright j} = \{y(i,j) : i \in \{0, \cdots, n\}, j \neq i\}.$$

Let $p_1, \cdots, p_m$ be the sequence of the predicates (in linear word order) that semantically governs the word j under $\boldsymbol{y}^a_{\curvearrowright j}$. A *k-th order argument-centric model* scores the dependency graph as

$$\begin{aligned} f^a(y) &= \sum_{j=1}^{n} f^a_j(\boldsymbol{y}^a_{\curvearrowright j}) \\ &= \sum_{j=1}^{n} \sum_{i=1}^{m+k-1} \theta_a^\top \Phi_a(p_{i-(k-1)}, ..., p_i, j, \mathbf{w}, \mathbf{p}) \end{aligned}$$

Similarly, we define the initial and end states for p_i ($i < 0$ or $i \geq m+1$).

3.4 Tree Approximation Model

Tree structures exhibit many computationally-good properties, and have been widely applied to model linguistic, especially syntactic, structures. Tree-structured representation is an essential prerequisite for both the parsing algorithms and the machine learning methods in state-of-the-art syntactic dependency parsers. The CCG dependency graphs are not but look very much like trees. We thus argue that a tree-centric model can on one hand capture some topologically essential characteristics and on the other hand benefit from mature tree parsing techniques.

To this end, we propose tree approximation to obtain CCG sub-graphs under the factorization using tree parsing algorithms. In particular, we introduce an algorithm to associate every graph with a projective dependency tree, which we call *weighted conversion.* The tree reflects partial information about the corresponding graph. In this algorithm, we assign heuristic weights to all possible edges, and then find the tree with maximum weights. The key idea behind is to find a tree frame of a given graph. Given an arbitrary CCG graph, the conversion is perhaps imperfect in the sense that information about a small portion of edges is "lost." As a result, our tree approximation model can only generate partial graphs. Nevertheless, we will show (in Section 3.5 and 4.2) that such a model can be combined with predicate- and argument-centric factorization models in an elegant way.

3.4.1 Weighted Conversion

We assign weights to all the possible edges, i.e. all pairs of words, and then determine which edges to be kept by finding the maximum spanning tree. More formally, given a graph $\boldsymbol{y} = \{y(i,j)\}$, each possible edge (i,j) is assigned a heuristic weight $\omega(i,j)$. The maximum spanning tree $\boldsymbol{t} = \{t(i,j)\}$ contains the maximum sum of values of edges:

$$\boldsymbol{t}^{\max} = \arg\max_{\boldsymbol{t}} \sum_{(i,j)} t(i,j)\omega(i,j)$$

We separate the $\omega(i,j)$ into three parts ($\omega(i,j) = A(i,j) + B(i,j) + C(i,j)$) that are defined as below.

- $A(i,j) = a \cdot \max\{y(i,j), y(j,i)\}$: a is the weight for the existing edges on graph ignoring direction.
- $B(i,j) = b \cdot y(i,j)$: b is the weight for the forward edges on the graph.
- $C(i,j) = n - |i-j|$: This term estimates the importance of an edge where n is the length of the given sentence. For dependency parsing, we consider edges with short distance to be more important because those edges can be predicted more accurately in future parsing process.
- $a \gg b \gg n$ or $a > bn > n^2$: The converted tree should contain arcs in original graph as many as possible, and the direction of the arcs should not be changed if possible. The relationship of a, b, and c guarantees this.

After all edges are weighted, we can use maximum spanning tree (MST) algorithms to get the converted tree. To get the projective tree, we choose Eisner's algorithm. However, the obtained tree must be labeled in order to encode the original graph. Here we introduce a label vector $\mathbf{l} = \{l(i,j)\}$. For each $(i,j) \in \mathcal{I}$, we assign a label $l(i,j)$ to edge (i,j) as follows.

Case $y(i,j) = 1$: label "X";

Case $y(i,j) = 0 \wedge y(j,i) = 1$: label "X~R";

Case $y(i,j) = 0 \wedge y(j,i) = 0$: label "None".

We can convert the *labeled* tree back to graph and obtain $\boldsymbol{y}^t$. Tough some edges are lost during the conversion, a lot more are kept. In fact, according to our evaluation, 92.74% of edges in the training set are retained after conversion.

3.4.2 Factorizing Trees

We use the tree parsing model proposed in (Bohnet, 2010) to score the converted trees. The model factorizes a tree into 1st-order and 2nd-order factors. When decoding, the model searches for a tree with the best score. The score defined for graphs as well as trees is

$$\begin{aligned} f^t(\boldsymbol{y}^t) &= g^t(\boldsymbol{t}, \mathbf{l}) = \theta_t^\top \Phi_t(s, \boldsymbol{t}, \mathbf{l}) \\ &= \theta_t^{1\top} \Phi_t^1(s, \boldsymbol{t}, \mathbf{l}) + \theta_t^{2\top} \Phi_t^2(s, \boldsymbol{t}, \mathbf{l}) \\ &= \Big(\sum_{(i,j)\in\mathcal{I}} t(i,j) \theta_t^{1\top} \Phi_t^1(l(i,j), \mathbf{w}, \mathbf{p}) \Big) \\ &\quad + \theta_t^{2\top} \Phi_t^2(s, \boldsymbol{t}, \mathbf{l}), \end{aligned}$$

where Φ_t^1 is the 1st-order features and Φ_t^2 is the 2nd-order features.

3.5 Parsing as Optimization

Motivated by linguistic properties of the semantics-oriented CCG dependencies, we have designed three single factorization models from heterogeneous views. Our single models exhibit different predictive strengths considering that they are designed to capture different properties separately. Integrating them can generate better graphs, but is provably hard. To this end, we formulate the parsing problem as the following constrained optimization problem.

$$\begin{aligned} \text{maximize} \quad & f^p(\boldsymbol{y}^p) + f^a(\boldsymbol{y}^a) + f^t(\boldsymbol{y}^t) \\ \text{subject to} \quad & y^p(i,j) = y^a(i,j), \\ & y^p(i,j) \geq y^t(i,j), \\ & y^a(i,j) \geq y^t(i,j) \text{ for all } (i,j) \end{aligned}$$

The equality constraint says that the graph given by the predicate- and the argument-centric model must be identical, while the inequality constraints say that the frame of graph given by the tree approximation model must be a subgraph of what is given by the first two models.

4 Decoding

4.1 Easiness and Hardness of Decoding

The three factorization models are all solvable in polynomial time. The predicate-centric model and the argument-centric model can be decoded using dynamic programming. We provide the detailed description of such an algorithm in our supplementary note. The decoding method for k-th ($k \geq 2$) order model costs time of $O(n^{k+1})$ where n is the length of the sentence. The tree approximation model can re-use existing dependency tree parsing algorithms.

Unfortunately, the exact joint decoding of 2nd-order predicate- and argument-centric models is already NP-hard, not to mention other model combinations. The following gives a brief proof for the problem of combining the 2nd-order predicate- and argument-centric models.

Proof. Formally, we want to find a graph $\boldsymbol{y}$ which maximizes $F(\boldsymbol{y}) = f^p(\boldsymbol{y}) + f^a(\boldsymbol{y})$. We can design the feature function Φ_a and the parameter θ_a, such that for all $1 \leq i_1 \leq i_2 \leq n$,

$$\begin{cases} \theta_a^\top \Phi_a(0, i_1, j, \mathbf{w}, \mathbf{p}) = 0 \\ \theta_a^\top \Phi_a(i_1, n+1, j, \mathbf{w}, \mathbf{p}) = 0 \\ \theta_a^\top \Phi_a(i_1, i_2, j, \mathbf{w}, \mathbf{p}) = -\infty \\ \theta_a^\top \Phi_a(0, n+1, j, \mathbf{w}, \mathbf{p}) = -\infty \end{cases}$$

where n is the length of the sentence. Note that those 4 equations make the nodes except the root node in the optimal graph each have exactly one incoming edge. So the problem of finding a tree $\boldsymbol{t}$ maximizing $f^p(\boldsymbol{t})$ is reduced to this problem. Moreover, the NP-hard problem 3DM can be reduced to the problem of finding a tree $\boldsymbol{t}$ maximizing $f^p(\boldsymbol{t})$ (see McDonald and Pereira (2006)), leading to the NP-hardness of both of the problems. □

4.2 Decoding via Dual Decomposition

To solve the joint decoding problem, optimization techniques based on decomposition with coupling variables are applicable. In this paper, we propose to solve it via dual decomposition. The experiment results show that though not always, we can obtain the optimal solution most of time. To simplify the description, we only consider the 2nd-order case for all three models.

4.2.1 Lagrangian Relaxation

Notice that $y^p(i,j) \geq y^t(i,j)$ can be written as

$$y^p(i,j) = \begin{cases} 1, \text{ if } y^t(i,j) = 1; \\ \text{arbitrary, if } y^t(i,j) = 0. \end{cases}$$

So the constraint can be written as $A^p \boldsymbol{y}^p + A^a \boldsymbol{y}^a + A^t \boldsymbol{y}^t = 0$, where

$$A^p = \begin{bmatrix} I \\ D_{\boldsymbol{y}^t} \\ \mathbf{0} \end{bmatrix} A^a = \begin{bmatrix} -I \\ \mathbf{0} \\ D_{\boldsymbol{y}^t} \end{bmatrix} A^t = \begin{bmatrix} \mathbf{0} \\ -D_{\boldsymbol{y}^t} \\ -D_{\boldsymbol{y}^t} \end{bmatrix}$$

I is the identity matrix and $D_{\boldsymbol{y}^t}$ is a diagonal matrix whose main diagonal is the vector $\boldsymbol{y}^t$.

The Lagrangian of the optimization problem is

$$\mathcal{L}(\boldsymbol{y}^p, \boldsymbol{y}^a, \boldsymbol{y}^t; u) = f^p(\boldsymbol{y}^p) + f^a(\boldsymbol{y}^a) + f^t(\boldsymbol{y}^t) + u^\top(A^p\boldsymbol{y}^p + A^a\boldsymbol{y}^a + A^t\boldsymbol{y}^t),$$

where u is the Lagrangian multiplier.

Omitting the constraints, the dual objective is

$$\begin{aligned} \mathcal{L}(u) &= \max_{\boldsymbol{y}^p, \boldsymbol{y}^a, \boldsymbol{y}^t} \mathcal{L}(\boldsymbol{y}^p, \boldsymbol{y}^a, \boldsymbol{y}^t; u) \\ &= \max_{\boldsymbol{y}^p}(f^p(\boldsymbol{y}^p) + u^\top A^p \boldsymbol{y}^p) \\ &\quad + \max_{\boldsymbol{y}^a}(f^a(\boldsymbol{y}^a) + u^\top A^a \boldsymbol{y}^a) \\ &\quad + \max_{\boldsymbol{y}^t}(f^t(\boldsymbol{y}^t) + u^\top A^t \boldsymbol{y}^t) \end{aligned}$$

Let $\mathcal{L}^*$ be the maximized value of $\mathcal{L}(\boldsymbol{y}^p, \boldsymbol{y}^a, \boldsymbol{y}^t; u)$ subjected to the constraints, then $\mathcal{L}^* = \min_u \mathcal{L}(u)$, according to the duality principle.

4.2.2 Decoding Algorithm

There are two challenges in solving the dual problem. One challenge is to find the minimum value of the dual objective. For this, we can use subgradient method, as is demonstrated in Algorithm 1. The other is the evaluation of $\mathcal{L}(u)$. For this, we decompose the dual objective into three optimization problems. Let $B^p = u^\top A^p$, $B^a = u^\top A^a$, $B^t = u^\top A^t$, and

$$C_1^t(i,j) = \begin{cases} B^t(i,j), \text{ if } l(i,j) = \text{X}; \\ B^t(j,i), \text{ if } l(i,j) = \text{X} \sim \text{R}; \end{cases}$$

we can just redefine

$$\begin{aligned} f_i^p(\boldsymbol{y}_{i\frown}) &= \sum_{j=1}^{m+1} (\theta_p^\top \Phi_p(a_{j-1}, a_j, i, \mathbf{w}, \mathbf{p}) \\ &\quad + B^p(i,j)) \\ f_j^a(\boldsymbol{y}_{\frown j}) &= \sum_{i=1}^{m+1} (\theta_a^\top \Phi_a(p_{i-1}, p_i, j, \mathbf{w}, \mathbf{p}) \\ &\quad + B^a(i,j)) \\ f^t(\boldsymbol{y}) &= \Big(\sum_{(i,j)\in\mathcal{I}} t(i,j)(\theta_t^{1\top} \Phi_t^1(l(i,j), \mathbf{w}, \mathbf{p}) \\ &\quad + C_1^t(i,j)) \Big) + \theta_t^{2\top} \Phi_t^2(s, \boldsymbol{t}, \mathbf{l}), \end{aligned}$$

and decode according to the new scores. In fact, this equals to attach some new weights to 1st-order factors, without changing the decoding algorithms for the subproblems. This nice property also allows using higher-order models for subproblems.

Algorithm 1: Joint decoding algorithm

Initialization: set $u^{(0)}$ to 0
for $k = 1$ **to** K **do**
  $\boldsymbol{y}^p_{(k)} \leftarrow \arg\max_{\boldsymbol{y}} f^p(\boldsymbol{y}) + u_{(k)} A^p \boldsymbol{y}$
  $\boldsymbol{y}^a_{(k)} \leftarrow \arg\max_{\boldsymbol{y}} f^a(\boldsymbol{y}) + u_{(k)} A^a \boldsymbol{y}$
  $\boldsymbol{y}^t_{(k)} \leftarrow \arg\max_{\boldsymbol{y}} f^t(\boldsymbol{y}) + u_{(k)} A^t \boldsymbol{y}$
  if $A^p \boldsymbol{y}^p_{(k)} + A^a \boldsymbol{y}^a_{(k)} + A^t \boldsymbol{y}^t_{(k)} = 0$ **then**
    return $\boldsymbol{y}_a$
  $u_{(k)} \leftarrow u_{(k-1)} - \alpha^k (A^p \boldsymbol{y}^p_{(k)} + A^a \boldsymbol{y}^a_{(k)} + A^t \boldsymbol{y}^t_{(k)})$

Algorithm 1 is our decoding algorithm. In every iteration, we first compute the optimal $\boldsymbol{y}$'s of the three subproblems. If the $\boldsymbol{y}$'s satisfies the constraints, then we've find the optimal solution for the original problem. If not, we update the Lagrangian multiplier u, towards the negative subgradient. We initialized u to be a zero vector, and use α^k to be the step length of each iteration. When we decode the subproblems, the $D_{\boldsymbol{y}^c}$ in A^p and A^a is derived from the $\boldsymbol{y}^c$ obtained in the current iteration.

We can also assign weights to different factorization models. If we choose to do so, the Lagrangian becomes

$$\mathcal{L}(\boldsymbol{y}^p, \boldsymbol{y}^a, \boldsymbol{y}^c; u) = w^p f^p(\boldsymbol{y}^p) + w^a f^a(\boldsymbol{y}^a) + w^c f^t(\boldsymbol{y}^t) + u^\top(A^p \boldsymbol{y}^p + A^a \boldsymbol{y}^a + A^t \boldsymbol{y}^t).$$

And the decoding of subproblems in our algorithm becomes

$$\begin{aligned} \boldsymbol{y}^p_{(k)} &\leftarrow \arg\max_{\boldsymbol{y}} f^p(\boldsymbol{y}) + \frac{1}{w^p} u_{(k)} A^p \boldsymbol{y}; \\ \boldsymbol{y}^a_{(k)} &\leftarrow \arg\max_{\boldsymbol{y}} f^a(\boldsymbol{y}) + \frac{1}{w^a} u_{(k)} A^a \boldsymbol{y}; \\ \boldsymbol{y}^t_{(k)} &\leftarrow \arg\max_{\boldsymbol{y}} f^t(\boldsymbol{y}) + \frac{1}{w^c} u_{(k)} A^t \boldsymbol{y}. \end{aligned}$$

The algorithm we give here is the joint decoding for all the three models. We can also decode using any two of them, and it is trivial to adapt the algorithm to the decoding.

4.3 Pruning

In order to improve the efficiency of the algorithm, we also do some pruning. One idea is that, in predicate-centric model, different type of predicates has different number of arguments. For example, the predicates POS-tagged "DT" each has only one argument in most cases. Therefore, we assign each POS-tag a max number of arguments. When decoding, we search at most those number of arguments instead of all the words in the sentence. This pruning method can also be applied to the argument-centric model. The other idea is that, some pairs of types never form a predicate-argument relation. So we can skip extracting feature of those POS-tag pairs, just take $-\infty$ to be their scores.

5 Evaluation and Analysis

5.1 Experimental Setup

CCGbank is a translation of the Penn Treebank into a corpus of CCG derivations (Hockenmaier and Steedman, 2007). CCGbank pairs syntactic derivations with sets of word-word dependencies which approximate the underlying functor-argument structure. Our experiments were performed using CCGBank which was split into three subsets for training (Sections 02-21), development testing (Section 00) and the final test (Section 23). We also use the syntactic dependency trees provided by the CCGBank to obtain necessary information for graph parsing. However, different from experiments in the CCG parsing literature, we use no grammar information. Neither lexical categories nor CCG derivations are utilized.

	Devel.	Test
HMM Tagger	96.74%	97.23%
Transition-based Parser	93.48%	93.09%
Graph-based Parser	93.47%	93.19%

Table 1: The accuracy of the POS tagger and the UAS of the syntax tree parsers.

All experiments were performed using automatically assigned POS-tags that are generated by a symbol-refined generative HMM tagger[1] (Huang et al., 2010), and automatically parsed dependency trees that are generated by our in-house implementation of the transition-based model presented in (Zhang and Nivre, 2011) as well as a 2nd-order graph-based parser[2] (Bohnet, 2010). The accuracy of these preprocessors is shown in Table 1. We ran 5-fold jack-knifing on the gold-standard training data to obtain imperfect dependency trees, splitting off 4 of 5 sentences for training and the other 1/5 for testing, 5 times. For each split, we re-trained the tree parsers on the training portion and applied the resulting model to the test portion.

Previous research on dependency parsing shows that structured perceptron (Collins, 2002) is one of the strongest discriminative learning algorithms. To estimate θ's of different models, we utilize the averaged perceptron algorithm. We implement our own the predicate- and argument-centric models. To perform tree parsing, we re-use the open-source implementation provided by the mate-tool. See the source code attached for details. We set iteration 5 to train predicate- and argument-centric models and 10 for the tree approximation model. To perform dual decomposition, we set the maximum iteration 200.

[1] www.code.google.com/p/umd-featured-parser/

[2] www.code.google.com/p/mate-tools/

Tree	Model	UP	UR	UF	UEM
No	PC	91.85	87.26	89.50	18.77
	AC	91.94	87.06	89.43	16.47
	TA	92.85	86.39	89.51	14.48
	PC+AC	93.84	88.18	90.93	23.05
	PC+TA	91.80	91.69	91.74	27.29
	AC+TA	90.19	92.88	91.52	25.51
	PC+AC+TA	93.01	92.08	92.54	32.83
Gr	PC	94.01	90.76	92.36	30.16
	AC	94.14	90.44	92.25	27.71
	TA	93.07	86.59	89.71	15.16
	PC+AC	94.66	91.09	92.84	33.19
	PC+TA	92.98	92.68	92.83	35.02
	AC+TA	92.47	93.13	92.80	33.93
	PC+AC+TA	93.66	92.73	93.19	37.64
Tr	PC	93.93	90.85	92.37	30.21
	AC	93.94	90.66	92.27	28.23
	TA	93.19	86.68	89.82	14.79
	PC+AC	94.58	91.14	92.83	31.94
	PC+TA	92.93	92.71	92.82	35.34
	AC+TA	92.33	93.16	92.74	33.61
	PC+AC+TA	93.50	92.73	93.11	37.69

Table 2: Parsing performance on the development data. The column "Tree" denotes the parsers that give dependency tree of development set: no tree (No), transition-based (Tr) or graph-based (Gr). "PC," "AC" and "TA" in the second column denotes the predicate-centric, the argument-centric and the tree approximation models, respectively.

5.2 Effectiveness of Data-driven Models

Table 2 summarizes parsing performance on development set with different configurations. We report unlabeled precision (UP), recall (UR), f-score (UF) as well as complete match (UEM). It can be clearly seen that the data-driven models obtains high-quality graphs with respect to token match. Even without any syntactic information (see the top block associated with "No Tree"), our parser with all three factorization models obtains an f-score of 92.5. when assisted by a syntactic parser, this figure goes up to over 93.1. If the predicate- or argument-centric model is applied by itself, either one can achieve a competitive accuracy, especially when syntactic features are utilized.

5.3 Effectiveness of Multiple Factorization

We use dual decomposition to perform joint decoding. First we combine the predicate-centric model and the argument-centric model. Compared to each single model, an error reduction of about 7% on f-score (UF) on average is achieved. Furthermore, we ensemble all the three models. If no syntactic features are extracted, the "TA" model brings in a remarkable further absolute gain of 1.02 with respect to token match. If syntactic features are used, the "PC" and "AC" models already achieves relatively good performance, and the "TA" model does not contribute much considering token match. The join of the tree approximation model lowers the precision, it increases the recall further, resulting in a modest improvement of the f-score. Nonetheless, the "TA" model still significantly improve the complete match metric. It is noticeable that in all setting, the "TA" model result in very significant boost in complete match.

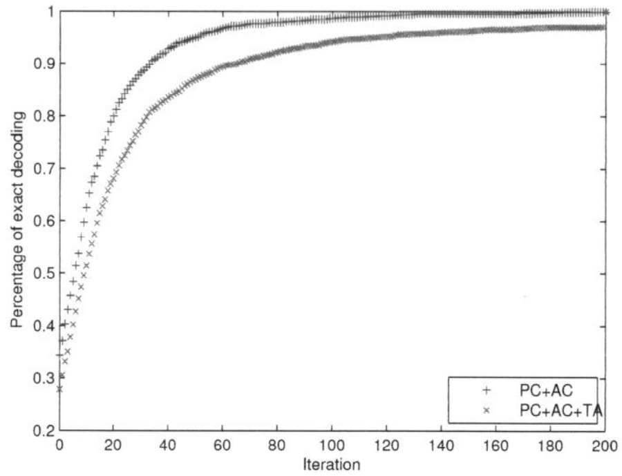

Figure 3: The exact decoding rate.

The dual decomposition does not guarantee to find an exact solution (in a limited number of iterations) in theory but usually works very well in practice. We calculate the percentage of finding exact decoding below k iterations, and the result is show in Figure 3. The transition-based tree parser is utilized here. We can see that for most sentences, dual decomposition practically gives the exact solutions.

5.4 Importance of Tree Structures

Our factorization parser (with best experimental setting) does not utilize a grammar but do use syntactic information in the dependency formalism. In particular, the parser extracts the so-called path features from dependency trees. The syntactic trees is very importance to our parser, which provide a critical set of features for the predicate-centric and the argument-centric models. Without the syntactic trees, their performances decrease significantly. We try two different parsers to obtain the syntax tree parses. One is of the transition-based architecture, and the other graph-

Tree	Model	UP	UR	UF	UEM
No	PC+AC+TA	93.03	92.03	92.53	32.61
Gr	PC+AC+TA	**93.71**	92.72	93.21	**38.14**
Tr	PC+AC+TA	93.63	**92.83**	**93.23**	37.47
Auli and Lopez		93.08	92.44	92.76	-
Xu et al.		93.15	91.06	92.09	37.56

Table 3: Comparing the state-of-art with our models on test set.

based. The architecture of the syntactic tree parser does not affect the results much. The two tree parsers give identical attachment scores, and lead to similar graph parsing accuracy. This result is somehow non-obvious given that the combination of a graph-based and transition-based parser usually gives significantly better parsing performance (Nivre and McDonald, 2008; Torres Martins et al., 2008).

Although the target representation of our parser is general graphs rather trees, implicitly or explicitly using tree-structured information plays an essential role. Syntactic features are able to improve the f-score achieved by the "PC+AC" model from 90.9 to 92.8, while the "TA" model can bring in an absolute gain of 1.6. Note that the "TA" model does not utilize any syntactic tree information. The converted trees are automatically induced from the CCG graphs. Even when syntactic trees are available, the automatically induced trees can still significantly improve the complete match with respect to the whole sentence.

5.5 Comparison to the State-of-the-art

We compare our results with the best published CCG parsing performance obtained by the models presented in (Auli and Lopez, 2011) and (Xu et al., 2014)[3]. Auli and Lopez (2011) reported best numeric performance. The performance is evaluated on sentences that can be parsed by their model. Xu et al. (2014) reported the best published results for sentences with full coverage. All results on the test set is shown in Table 3. Even without any syntactic features, our parser achieves accuracies that are superior to Xu et al.'s parser and comparable to Auli and Lopez's system. When unlabeled syntactic trees are provided, our parser outperform the state-of-the-art.

[3]The unlabeled parsing results are not reported in the original paper. The figures presented in are provided by Wenduan Xu.

6 Conclusion

In this paper, we have presented a factorization parser for building CCG-grounded dependency graphs. It achieves substantial improvement over the state-of-the-art. Perhaps surprisingly, our data-driven, grammar-free parser yields a superior accuracy to all CCG parsers in the literature. Our work indicates that high-quality data-driven parsers can be built for producing more general dependency graphs, rather than trees. Our method is also applicable to other deep dependency structures, e.g. HPSG predicate-argument analysis (Miyao et al., 2004), as well as other graph-structured semantic representations, e.g. Abstract Meaning Representations (Banarescu et al., 2013).

Acknowledgement

The work was supported by NSFC (61300064), National High-Tech R&D Program (2015AA015403), NSFC (61331011) and NSFC (61170166).

References

Michael Auli and Adam Lopez. 2011. Training a log-linear parser with loss functions via softmax-margin. In *Proceedings of EMNLP*, pages 333–343. Association for Computational Linguistics, Edinburgh, Scotland, UK.

Laura Banarescu, Claire Bonial, Shu Cai, Madalina Georgescu, Kira Griffitt, Ulf Hermjakob, Kevin Knight, Philipp Koehn, Martha Palmer, and Nathan Schneider. 2013. Abstract meaning representation for sembanking. In *Proceedings of the 7th Linguistic Annotation Workshop and Interoperability with Discourse*, pages 178–186. Association for Computational Linguistics, Sofia, Bulgaria.

Emily M. Bender, Dan Flickinger, Stephan Oepen, and Yi Zhang. 2011. Parser evaluation over local and non-local deep dependencies in a large corpus. In *Proceedings of EMNLP*, pages 397–408. Association for Computational Linguistics, Edinburgh, Scotland, UK.

Bernd Bohnet. 2010. Top accuracy and fast dependency parsing is not a contradiction. In *Proceedings of the 23rd International Conference on Computational Linguistics (Coling 2010)*, pages 89–97. Coling 2010 Organizing Committee, Beijing, China.

Stephen Clark and James Curran. 2007a. Formalism-independent parser evaluation with ccg and depbank. In *Proceedings of the 45th Annual Meeting of the Association of Computational Linguistics*, pages 248–255. Association for Computational Linguistics, Prague, Czech Republic.

Stephen Clark and James R. Curran. 2004. The importance of supertagging for wide-coverage CCG parsing. In *Proceedings of Coling 2004*, pages 282–288. COLING, Geneva, Switzerland.

Stephen Clark and James R. Curran. 2007b. Wide-coverage efficient statistical parsing with CCG and log-linear models. *Comput. Linguist.*, 33(4):493–552.

Stephen Clark, Julia Hockenmaier, and Mark Steedman. 2002. Building deep dependency structures using a wide-coverage CCG parser. In *Proceedings of the 40th Annual Meeting of the Association for Computational Linguistics, July 6-12, 2002, Philadelphia, PA, USA.*, pages 327–334.

Michael Collins. 2002. Discriminative training methods for hidden markov models: Theory and experiments with perceptron algorithms. In *Proceedings of EMNLP*, pages 1–8. Association for Computational Linguistics.

Jason M. Eisner. 1996. Three new probabilistic models for dependency parsing: an exploration. In *Proceedings of the 16th conference on Computational linguistics - Volume 1*, pages 340–345. Association for Computational Linguistics, Stroudsburg, PA, USA.

Timothy A. D. Fowler and Gerald Penn. 2010. Accurate context-free parsing with combinatory categorial grammar. In *Proceedings of ACL*, pages 335–344. Association for Computational Linguistics, Uppsala, Sweden.

Julia Hockenmaier and Mark Steedman. 2007. CCGbank: A corpus of CCG derivations and dependency structures extracted from the penn treebank. *Computational Linguistics*, 33(3):355–396.

Zhongqiang Huang, Mary Harper, and Slav Petrov. 2010. Self-training with products of latent variable grammars. In *Proceedings of EMNLP*, pages 12–22. Association for Computational Linguistics, Cambridge, MA.

Tracy Holloway King, Richard Crouch, Stefan Riezler, Mary Dalrymple, and Ronald M. Kaplan. 2003. The PARC 700 dependency bank. In *In Proceedings of the 4th International Workshop on Linguistically Interpreted Corpora (LINC-03)*, pages 1–8.

Terry Koo and Michael Collins. 2010. Efficient third-order dependency parsers. In *Proceedings of ACL*, pages 1–11. Association for Computational Linguistics, Uppsala, Sweden.

Terry Koo, Alexander M. Rush, Michael Collins, Tommi Jaakkola, and David Sontag. 2010. Dual decomposition for parsing with non-projective head automata. In *Proceedings of EMNLP*, pages 1288–1298. Association for Computational Linguistics, Cambridge, MA.

Xavier Lluís, Xavier Carreras, and Lluís Màrquez. 2013. Joint arc-factored parsing of syntactic and semantic dependencies. *TACL*, 1:219–230.

Xuezhe Ma and Hai Zhao. 2012. Fourth-order dependency parsing. In *Proceedings of COLING 2012: Posters*, pages 785–796. The COLING 2012 Organizing Committee, Mumbai, India.

Mitchell P. Marcus, Mary Ann Marcinkiewicz, and Beatrice Santorini. 1993. Building a large annotated corpus of english: the penn treebank. *Comput. Linguist.*, 19(2):313–330.

André F. T. Martins and Mariana S. C. Almeida. 2014. Priberam: A turbo semantic parser with second order features. In *Proceedings of SemEval 2014*, pages 471–476.

Takuya Matsuzaki, Yusuke Miyao, and Jun'ichi Tsujii. 2007. Efficient hpsg parsing with supertagging and cfg-filtering. In *Proceedings of the 20th international joint conference on Artifical intelligence*, pages 1671–1676. Morgan Kaufmann publishers Inc., San Francisco, CA, USA.

Ryan McDonald, Koby Crammer, and Fernando Pereira. 2005a. Online large-margin training of dependency parsers. In *Proceedings of the 43rd Annual Meeting of the Association for Computational Linguistics (ACL'05)*, pages 91–98. Association for Computational Linguistics, Ann Arbor, Michigan.

Ryan McDonald and Fernando Pereira. 2006. Online learning of approximate dependency parsing algorithms. In *Proceedings of 11th Conference of the European Chapter of the Asso-*

ciation for Computational Linguistics (EACL-2006)), volume 6, pages 81–88.

Ryan McDonald, Fernando Pereira, Kiril Ribarov, and Jan Hajic. 2005b. Non-projective dependency parsing using spanning tree algorithms. In *Proceedings of EMNLP*, pages 523–530. Association for Computational Linguistics, Vancouver, British Columbia, Canada.

Yusuke Miyao, Takashi Ninomiya, and Jun ichi Tsujii. 2004. Corpus-oriented grammar development for acquiring a head-driven phrase structure grammar from the penn treebank. In *IJCNLP*, pages 684–693.

Joakim Nivre, Johan Hall, and Jens Nilsson. 2004. Memory-based dependency parsing. In Hwee Tou Ng and Ellen Riloff, editors, *HLT-NAACL 2004 Workshop: Eighth Conference on Computational Natural Language Learning (CoNLL-2004)*, pages 49–56. Association for Computational Linguistics, Boston, Massachusetts, USA.

Joakim Nivre and Ryan McDonald. 2008. Integrating graph-based and transition-based dependency parsers. In *Proceedings of ACL-08: HLT*, pages 950–958. Association for Computational Linguistics, Columbus, Ohio.

Emily Pitler, Sampath Kannan, and Mitchell Marcus. 2013. Finding optimal 1-endpoint-crossing trees. *TACL*, 1:13–24.

Siva Reddy, Mirella Lapata, and Mark Steedman. 2014. Large-scale semantic parsing without question-answer pairs. *Transactions of the Association for Computational Linguistics (TACL)*.

Alexander M. Rush and Michael Collins. 2011. Exact decoding of syntactic translation models through lagrangian relaxation. In *The 49th Annual Meeting of the Association for Computational Linguistics: Human Language Technologies, Proceedings of the Conference, 19-24 June, 2011, Portland, Oregon, USA*, pages 72–82.

Alexander M Rush, David Sontag, Michael Collins, and Tommi Jaakkola. 2010. On dual decomposition and linear programming relaxations for natural language processing. In *Proceedings of EMNLP*, pages 1–11. Association for Computational Linguistics, Cambridge, MA.

Kenji Sagae, Yusuke Miyao, and Jun'ichi Tsujii. 2007. Hpsg parsing with shallow dependency constraints. In *Proceedings of the 45th Annual Meeting of the Association of Computational Linguistics*, pages 624–631. Association for Computational Linguistics, Prague, Czech Republic.

Kenji Sagae and Jun'ichi Tsujii. 2008. Shift-reduce dependency DAG parsing. In *Proceedings of the 22nd International Conference on Computational Linguistics*, pages 753–760. Coling 2008 Organizing Committee, Manchester, UK.

Mark Steedman. 2000. *The syntactic process*. MIT Press, Cambridge, MA, USA.

Andre Torres Martins, Noah Smith, and Eric Xing. 2009. Concise integer linear programming formulations for dependency parsing. In *Proceedings of the Joint Conference of the 47th Annual Meeting of the ACL and the 4th International Joint Conference on Natural Language Processing of the AFNLP*, pages 342–350. Association for Computational Linguistics, Suntec, Singapore.

André Filipe Torres Martins, Dipanjan Das, Noah A. Smith, and Eric P. Xing. 2008. Stacking dependency parsers. In *Proceedings of EMNLP*, pages 157–166. Association for Computational Linguistics, Honolulu, Hawaii.

Wenduan Xu, Stephen Clark, and Yue Zhang. 2014. Shift-reduce ccg parsing with a dependency model. In *Proceedings of the 52nd Annual Meeting of the Association for Computational Linguistics (Volume 1: Long Papers)*, pages 218–227. Association for Computational Linguistics, Baltimore, Maryland.

Yue Zhang and Stephen Clark. 2011. Shift-reduce CCG parsing. In *Proceedings of the 49th Annual Meeting of the Association for Computational Linguistics: Human Language Technologies*, pages 683–692. Association for Computational Linguistics, Portland, Oregon, USA.

Yue Zhang and Joakim Nivre. 2011. Transition-based dependency parsing with rich non-local features. In *Proceedings of the 49th Annual Meeting of the Association for Computational Linguistics: Human Language Technologies*, pages 188–193. Association for Computational Linguistics, Portland, Oregon, USA.

Improved Semantic Representations From Tree-Structured Long Short-Term Memory Networks

Kai Sheng Tai, Richard Socher*, Christopher D. Manning
Computer Science Department, Stanford University, *MetaMind Inc.
kst@cs.stanford.edu, richard@metamind.io, manning@stanford.edu

Abstract

Because of their superior ability to preserve sequence information over time, Long Short-Term Memory (LSTM) networks, a type of recurrent neural network with a more complex computational unit, have obtained strong results on a variety of sequence modeling tasks. The only underlying LSTM structure that has been explored so far is a linear chain. However, natural language exhibits syntactic properties that would naturally combine words to phrases. We introduce the Tree-LSTM, a generalization of LSTMs to tree-structured network topologies. Tree-LSTMs outperform all existing systems and strong LSTM baselines on two tasks: predicting the semantic relatedness of two sentences (SemEval 2014, Task 1) and sentiment classification (Stanford Sentiment Treebank).

1 Introduction

Most models for distributed representations of phrases and sentences—that is, models where real-valued vectors are used to represent meaning—fall into one of three classes: bag-of-words models, sequence models, and tree-structured models. In bag-of-words models, phrase and sentence representations are independent of word order; for example, they can be generated by averaging constituent word representations (Landauer and Dumais, 1997; Foltz et al., 1998). In contrast, sequence models construct sentence representations as an order-sensitive function of the sequence of tokens (Elman, 1990; Mikolov, 2012). Lastly, tree-structured models compose each phrase and sentence representation from its constituent subphrases according to a given syntactic structure over the sentence (Goller and Kuchler, 1996; Socher et al., 2011).

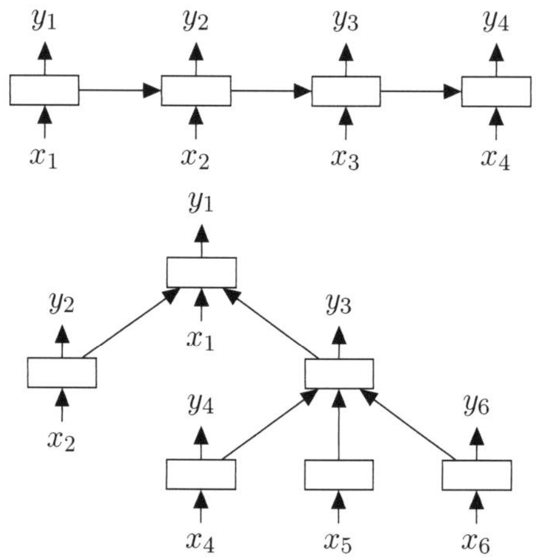

Figure 1: **Top:** A chain-structured LSTM network. **Bottom:** A tree-structured LSTM network with arbitrary branching factor.

Order-insensitive models are insufficient to fully capture the semantics of natural language due to their inability to account for differences in meaning as a result of differences in word order or syntactic structure (*e.g.*, "cats climb trees" *vs.* "trees climb cats"). We therefore turn to order-sensitive sequential or tree-structured models. In particular, tree-structured models are a linguistically attractive option due to their relation to syntactic interpretations of sentence structure. A natural question, then, is the following: to what extent (if at all) can we do better with tree-structured models as opposed to sequential models for sentence representation? In this paper, we work towards addressing this question by directly comparing a type of sequential model that has recently been used to achieve state-of-the-art results in several NLP tasks against its tree-structured generalization.

Due to their capability for processing arbitrary-length sequences, recurrent neural networks

Proceedings of the 53rd Annual Meeting of the Association for Computational Linguistics and the 7th International Joint Conference on Natural Language Processing, pages 1556–1566, Beijing, China, July 26-31, 2015.

(RNNs) are a natural choice for sequence modeling tasks. Recently, RNNs with Long Short-Term Memory (LSTM) units (Hochreiter and Schmidhuber, 1997) have re-emerged as a popular architecture due to their representational power and effectiveness at capturing long-term dependencies. LSTM networks, which we review in Sec. 2, have been successfully applied to a variety of sequence modeling and prediction tasks, notably machine translation (Bahdanau et al., 2015; Sutskever et al., 2014), speech recognition (Graves et al., 2013), image caption generation (Vinyals et al., 2014), and program execution (Zaremba and Sutskever, 2014).

In this paper, we introduce a generalization of the standard LSTM architecture to tree-structured network topologies and show its superiority for representing sentence meaning over a sequential LSTM. While the standard LSTM composes its hidden state from the input at the current time step and the hidden state of the LSTM unit in the previous time step, the tree-structured LSTM, or Tree-LSTM, composes its state from an input vector and the hidden states of arbitrarily many child units. The standard LSTM can then be considered a special case of the Tree-LSTM where each internal node has exactly one child.

In our evaluations, we demonstrate the empirical strength of Tree-LSTMs as models for representing sentences. We evaluate the Tree-LSTM architecture on two tasks: semantic relatedness prediction on sentence pairs and sentiment classification of sentences drawn from movie reviews. Our experiments show that Tree-LSTMs outperform existing systems and sequential LSTM baselines on both tasks. Implementations of our models and experiments are available at `https://github.com/stanfordnlp/treelstm`.

2 Long Short-Term Memory Networks

2.1 Overview

Recurrent neural networks (RNNs) are able to process input sequences of arbitrary length via the recursive application of a transition function on a *hidden state vector* h_t. At each time step t, the hidden state h_t is a function of the input vector x_t that the network receives at time t and its previous hidden state h_{t-1}. For example, the input vector x_t could be a vector representation of the t-th word in body of text (Elman, 1990; Mikolov, 2012). The hidden state $h_t \in \mathbb{R}^d$ can be interpreted as a d-dimensional distributed representation of the sequence of tokens observed up to time t.

Commonly, the RNN transition function is an affine transformation followed by a pointwise nonlinearity such as the hyperbolic tangent function:

$$h_t = \tanh\left(W x_t + U h_{t-1} + b\right).$$

Unfortunately, a problem with RNNs with transition functions of this form is that during training, components of the gradient vector can grow or decay exponentially over long sequences (Hochreiter, 1998; Bengio et al., 1994). This problem with *exploding* or *vanishing gradients* makes it difficult for the RNN model to learn long-distance correlations in a sequence.

The LSTM architecture (Hochreiter and Schmidhuber, 1997) addresses this problem of learning long-term dependencies by introducing a *memory cell* that is able to preserve state over long periods of time. While numerous LSTM variants have been described, here we describe the version used by Zaremba and Sutskever (2014).

We define the LSTM *unit* at each time step t to be a collection of vectors in $\mathbb{R}^d$: an *input gate* i_t, a *forget gate* f_t, an *output gate* o_t, a *memory cell* c_t and a hidden state h_t. The entries of the gating vectors i_t, f_t and o_t are in $[0,1]$. We refer to d as the *memory dimension* of the LSTM.

The LSTM transition equations are the following:

$$\begin{aligned}
i_t &= \sigma\left(W^{(i)} x_t + U^{(i)} h_{t-1} + b^{(i)}\right), \qquad (1)\\
f_t &= \sigma\left(W^{(f)} x_t + U^{(f)} h_{t-1} + b^{(f)}\right),\\
o_t &= \sigma\left(W^{(o)} x_t + U^{(o)} h_{t-1} + b^{(o)}\right),\\
u_t &= \tanh\left(W^{(u)} x_t + U^{(u)} h_{t-1} + b^{(u)}\right),\\
c_t &= i_t \odot u_t + f_t \odot c_{t-1},\\
h_t &= o_t \odot \tanh(c_t),
\end{aligned}$$

where x_t is the input at the current time step, σ denotes the logistic sigmoid function and $\odot$ denotes elementwise multiplication. Intuitively, the forget gate controls the extent to which the previous memory cell is forgotten, the input gate controls how much each unit is updated, and the output gate controls the exposure of the internal memory state. The hidden state vector in an LSTM unit is therefore a gated, partial view of the state of the unit's internal memory cell. Since the value of the gating variables vary for each vector element, the model can learn to represent information over multiple time scales.

2.2 Variants

Two commonly-used variants of the basic LSTM architecture are the Bidirectional LSTM and the Multilayer LSTM (also known as the *stacked* or *deep* LSTM).

Bidirectional LSTM. A Bidirectional LSTM (Graves et al., 2013) consists of two LSTMs that are run in parallel: one on the input sequence and the other on the reverse of the input sequence. At each time step, the hidden state of the Bidirectional LSTM is the concatenation of the forward and backward hidden states. This setup allows the hidden state to capture both past and future information.

Multilayer LSTM. In Multilayer LSTM architectures, the hidden state of an LSTM unit in layer ℓ is used as input to the LSTM unit in layer $\ell+1$ in the same time step (Graves et al., 2013; Sutskever et al., 2014; Zaremba and Sutskever, 2014). Here, the idea is to let the higher layers capture longer-term dependencies of the input sequence.

These two variants can be combined as a Multilayer Bidirectional LSTM (Graves et al., 2013).

3 Tree-Structured LSTMs

A limitation of the LSTM architectures described in the previous section is that they only allow for strictly sequential information propagation. Here, we propose two natural extensions to the basic LSTM architecture: the *Child-Sum Tree-LSTM* and the *N-ary Tree-LSTM*. Both variants allow for richer network topologies where each LSTM unit is able to incorporate information from multiple child units.

As in standard LSTM units, each Tree-LSTM unit (indexed by j) contains input and output gates i_j and o_j, a memory cell c_j and hidden state h_j. The difference between the standard LSTM unit and Tree-LSTM units is that gating vectors and memory cell updates are dependent on the states of possibly many child units. Additionally, instead of a single forget gate, the Tree-LSTM unit contains one forget gate f_{jk} for each child k. This allows the Tree-LSTM unit to selectively incorporate information from each child. For example, a Tree-LSTM model can learn to emphasize semantic heads in a semantic relatedness task, or it can learn to preserve the representation of sentiment-rich children for sentiment classification.

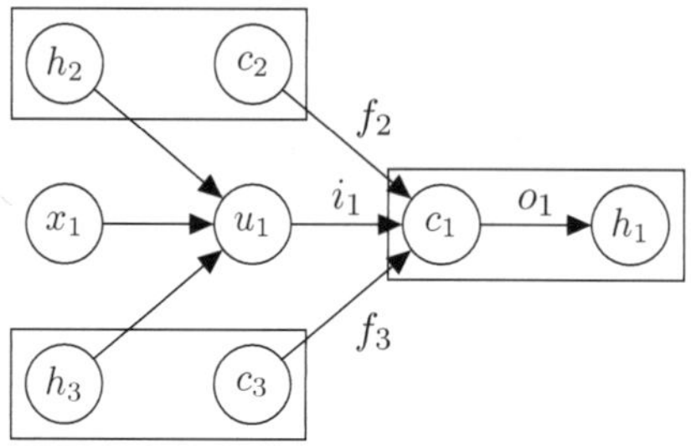

Figure 2: Composing the memory cell c_1 and hidden state h_1 of a Tree-LSTM unit with two children (subscripts 2 and 3). Labeled edges correspond to gating by the indicated gating vector, with dependencies omitted for compactness.

As with the standard LSTM, each Tree-LSTM unit takes an input vector x_j. In our applications, each x_j is a vector representation of a word in a sentence. The input word at each node depends on the tree structure used for the network. For instance, in a Tree-LSTM over a dependency tree, each node in the tree takes the vector corresponding to the head word as input, whereas in a Tree-LSTM over a constituency tree, the leaf nodes take the corresponding word vectors as input.

3.1 Child-Sum Tree-LSTMs

Given a tree, let $C(j)$ denote the set of children of node j. The Child-Sum Tree-LSTM transition equations are the following:

$$\tilde{h}_j = \sum_{k \in C(j)} h_k, \tag{2}$$

$$i_j = \sigma\left(W^{(i)} x_j + U^{(i)} \tilde{h}_j + b^{(i)}\right), \tag{3}$$

$$f_{jk} = \sigma\left(W^{(f)} x_j + U^{(f)} h_k + b^{(f)}\right), \tag{4}$$

$$o_j = \sigma\left(W^{(o)} x_j + U^{(o)} \tilde{h}_j + b^{(o)}\right), \tag{5}$$

$$u_j = \tanh\left(W^{(u)} x_j + U^{(u)} \tilde{h}_j + b^{(u)}\right), \tag{6}$$

$$c_j = i_j \odot u_j + \sum_{k \in C(j)} f_{jk} \odot c_k, \tag{7}$$

$$h_j = o_j \odot \tanh(c_j), \tag{8}$$

where in Eq. 4, $k \in C(j)$.

Intuitively, we can interpret each parameter matrix in these equations as encoding correlations between the component vectors of the Tree-LSTM unit, the input x_j, and the hidden states h_k of the unit's children. For example, in a dependency tree application, the model can learn parameters $W^{(i)}$ such that the components of the input gate i_j have values close to 1 (*i.e.*, "open") when a semantically important content word (such as a verb) is given as input, and values close to 0 (*i.e.*, "closed") when the input is a relatively unimportant word (such as a determiner).

Dependency Tree-LSTMs. Since the Child-Sum Tree-LSTM unit conditions its components on the sum of child hidden states h_k, it is well-suited for trees with high branching factor or whose children are unordered. For example, it is a good choice for dependency trees, where the number of dependents of a head can be highly variable. We refer to a Child-Sum Tree-LSTM applied to a dependency tree as a *Dependency Tree-LSTM*.

3.2 N-ary Tree-LSTMs

The N-ary Tree-LSTM can be used on tree structures where the branching factor is at most N and where children are ordered, *i.e.*, they can be indexed from 1 to N. For any node j, write the hidden state and memory cell of its kth child as h_{jk} and c_{jk} respectively. The N-ary Tree-LSTM transition equations are the following:

$$i_j = \sigma\left(W^{(i)}x_j + \sum_{\ell=1}^{N} U_\ell^{(i)} h_{j\ell} + b^{(i)}\right), \quad (9)$$

$$f_{jk} = \sigma\left(W^{(f)}x_j + \sum_{\ell=1}^{N} U_{k\ell}^{(f)} h_{j\ell} + b^{(f)}\right), \quad (10)$$

$$o_j = \sigma\left(W^{(o)}x_j + \sum_{\ell=1}^{N} U_\ell^{(o)} h_{j\ell} + b^{(o)}\right), \quad (11)$$

$$u_j = \tanh\left(W^{(u)}x_j + \sum_{\ell=1}^{N} U_\ell^{(u)} h_{j\ell} + b^{(u)}\right), \quad (12)$$

$$c_j = i_j \odot u_j + \sum_{\ell=1}^{N} f_{j\ell} \odot c_{j\ell}, \quad (13)$$

$$h_j = o_j \odot \tanh(c_j), \quad (14)$$

where in Eq. 10, $k = 1, 2, \ldots, N$. Note that when the tree is simply a chain, both Eqs. 2–8 and Eqs. 9–14 reduce to the standard LSTM transitions, Eqs. 1.

The introduction of separate parameter matrices for each child k allows the N-ary Tree-LSTM model to learn more fine-grained conditioning on the states of a unit's children than the Child-Sum Tree-LSTM. Consider, for example, a constituency tree application where the left child of a node corresponds to a noun phrase, and the right child to a verb phrase. Suppose that in this case it is advantageous to emphasize the verb phrase in the representation. Then the $U_{k\ell}^{(f)}$ parameters can be trained such that the components of f_{j1} are close to 0 (*i.e.*, "forget"), while the components of f_{j2} are close to 1 (*i.e.*, "preserve").

Forget gate parameterization. In Eq. 10, we define a parameterization of the kth child's forget gate f_{jk} that contains "off-diagonal" parameter matrices $U_{k\ell}^{(f)}$, $k \neq \ell$. This parameterization allows for more flexible control of information propagation from child to parent. For example, this allows the left hidden state in a binary tree to have either an *excitatory* or *inhibitory* effect on the forget gate of the right child. However, for large values of N, these additional parameters are impractical and may be tied or fixed to zero.

Constituency Tree-LSTMs. We can naturally apply *Binary* Tree-LSTM units to binarized constituency trees since left and right child nodes are distinguished. We refer to this application of Binary Tree-LSTMs as a *Constituency Tree-LSTM*. Note that in Constituency Tree-LSTMs, a node j receives an input vector x_j only if it is a leaf node.

In the remainder of this paper, we focus on the special cases of Dependency Tree-LSTMs and Constituency Tree-LSTMs. These architectures are in fact closely related; since we consider only binarized constituency trees, the parameterizations of the two models are very similar. The key difference is in the application of the compositional parameters: dependent *vs.* head for Dependency Tree-LSTMs, and left child *vs.* right child for Constituency Tree-LSTMs.

4 Models

We now describe two specific models that apply the Tree-LSTM architectures described in the previous section.

4.1 Tree-LSTM Classification

In this setting, we wish to predict labels $\hat{y}$ from a discrete set of classes $\mathcal{Y}$ for some subset of nodes in a tree. For example, the label for a node in a parse tree could correspond to some property of the phrase spanned by that node.

At each node j, we use a softmax classifier to predict the label $\hat{y}_j$ given the inputs $\{x\}_j$ observed at nodes in the subtree rooted at j. The classifier takes the hidden state h_j at the node as input:

$$\hat{p}_\theta(y \mid \{x\}_j) = \text{softmax}\left(W^{(s)}h_j + b^{(s)}\right),$$
$$\hat{y}_j = \arg\max_y \hat{p}_\theta\left(y \mid \{x\}_j\right).$$

The cost function is the negative log-likelihood of the true class labels $y^{(k)}$ at each labeled node:

$$J(\theta) = -\frac{1}{m}\sum_{k=1}^{m} \log \hat{p}_\theta\left(y^{(k)} \,\middle|\, \{x\}^{(k)}\right) + \frac{\lambda}{2}\|\theta\|_2^2,$$

where m is the number of labeled nodes in the training set, the superscript k indicates the kth labeled node, and λ is an L2 regularization hyperparameter.

4.2 Semantic Relatedness of Sentence Pairs

Given a sentence pair, we wish to predict a real-valued similarity score in some range $[1, K]$, where $K > 1$ is an integer. The sequence $\{1, 2, \ldots, K\}$ is some ordinal scale of similarity, where higher scores indicate greater degrees of similarity, and we allow real-valued scores to account for ground-truth ratings that are an average over the evaluations of several human annotators.

We first produce sentence representations h_L and h_R for each sentence in the pair using a Tree-LSTM model over each sentence's parse tree. Given these sentence representations, we predict the similarity score $\hat{y}$ using a neural network that considers both the distance and angle between the pair (h_L, h_R):

$$\begin{aligned} h_\times &= h_L \odot h_R, \qquad (15)\\ h_+ &= |h_L - h_R|,\\ h_s &= \sigma\left(W^{(\times)}h_\times + W^{(+)}h_+ + b^{(h)}\right),\\ \hat{p}_\theta &= \text{softmax}\left(W^{(p)}h_s + b^{(p)}\right),\\ \hat{y} &= r^T \hat{p}_\theta, \end{aligned}$$

where $r^T = [1\ 2\ \ldots\ K]$ and the absolute value function is applied elementwise. The use of both distance measures $h_\times$ and h_+ is empirically motivated: we find that the combination outperforms the use of either measure alone. The multiplicative measure $h_\times$ can be interpreted as an elementwise comparison of the signs of the input representations.

We want the expected rating under the predicted distribution $\hat{p}_\theta$ given model parameters θ to be close to the gold rating $y \in [1, K]$: $\hat{y} = r^T \hat{p}_\theta \approx y$. We therefore define a sparse target distribution[1] p that satisfies $y = r^T p$:

$$p_i = \begin{cases} y - \lfloor y \rfloor, & i = \lfloor y \rfloor + 1\\ \lfloor y \rfloor - y + 1, & i = \lfloor y \rfloor\\ 0 & \text{otherwise} \end{cases}$$

for $1 \le i \le K$. The cost function is the regularized KL-divergence between p and $\hat{p}_\theta$:

$$J(\theta) = \frac{1}{m}\sum_{k=1}^{m} \text{KL}\left(p^{(k)} \,\middle\|\, \hat{p}_\theta^{(k)}\right) + \frac{\lambda}{2}\|\theta\|_2^2,$$

where m is the number of training pairs and the superscript k indicates the kth sentence pair.

5 Experiments

We evaluate our Tree-LSTM architectures on two tasks: (1) sentiment classification of sentences sampled from movie reviews and (2) predicting the semantic relatedness of sentence pairs.

In comparing our Tree-LSTMs against sequential LSTMs, we control for the number of LSTM parameters by varying the dimensionality of the hidden states[2]. Details for each model variant are summarized in Table 1.

5.1 Sentiment Classification

In this task, we predict the sentiment of sentences sampled from movie reviews. We use the Stanford Sentiment Treebank (Socher et al., 2013). There are two subtasks: binary classification of sentences, and fine-grained classification over five classes: very negative, negative, neutral, positive, and very positive. We use the standard train/dev/test splits of 6920/872/1821 for the binary classification subtask and 8544/1101/2210 for the fine-grained classification subtask (there are fewer examples for the binary subtask since

[1] In the subsequent experiments, we found that optimizing this objective yielded better performance than a mean squared error objective.

[2] For our Bidirectional LSTMs, the parameters of the forward and backward transition functions are shared. In our experiments, this achieved superior performance to Bidirectional LSTMs with untied weights and the same number of parameters (and therefore smaller hidden vector dimensionality).

LSTM Variant	Relatedness d	Relatedness $\|\theta\|$	Sentiment d	Sentiment $\|\theta\|$
Standard	150	203,400	168	315,840
Bidirectional	150	203,400	168	315,840
2-layer	108	203,472	120	318,720
Bidirectional 2-layer	108	203,472	120	318,720
Constituency Tree	142	205,190	150	316,800
Dependency Tree	150	203,400	168	315,840

Table 1: Memory dimensions d and composition function parameter counts $|\theta|$ for each LSTM variant that we evaluate.

neutral sentences are excluded). Standard binarized constituency parse trees are provided for each sentence in the dataset, and each node in these trees is annotated with a sentiment label.

For the sequential LSTM baselines, we predict the sentiment of a phrase using the representation given by the final LSTM hidden state. The sequential LSTM models are trained on the spans corresponding to labeled nodes in the training set.

We use the classification model described in Sec. 4.1 with both Dependency Tree-LSTMs (Sec. 3.1) and Constituency Tree-LSTMs (Sec. 3.2). The Constituency Tree-LSTMs are structured according to the provided parse trees. For the Dependency Tree-LSTMs, we produce dependency parses[3] of each sentence; each node in a tree is given a sentiment label if its span matches a labeled span in the training set.

5.2 Semantic Relatedness

For a given pair of sentences, the semantic relatedness task is to predict a human-generated rating of the similarity of the two sentences in meaning.

We use the Sentences Involving Compositional Knowledge (SICK) dataset (Marelli et al., 2014), consisting of 9927 sentence pairs in a 4500/500/4927 train/dev/test split. The sentences are derived from existing image and video description datasets. Each sentence pair is annotated with a relatedness score $y \in [1, 5]$, with 1 indicating that the two sentences are completely unrelated, and 5 indicating that the two sentences are very related. Each label is the average of 10 ratings assigned by different human annotators.

Here, we use the similarity model described in Sec. 4.2. For the similarity prediction network (Eqs. 15) we use a hidden layer of size 50. We

[3]Dependency parses produced by the Stanford Neural Network Dependency Parser (Chen and Manning, 2014).

Method	Fine-grained	Binary
RAE (Socher et al., 2013)	43.2	82.4
MV-RNN (Socher et al., 2013)	44.4	82.9
RNTN (Socher et al., 2013)	45.7	85.4
DCNN (Blunsom et al., 2014)	48.5	86.8
Paragraph-Vec (Le and Mikolov, 2014)	48.7	87.8
CNN-non-static (Kim, 2014)	48.0	87.2
CNN-multichannel (Kim, 2014)	47.4	**88.1**
DRNN (Irsoy and Cardie, 2014)	49.8	86.6
LSTM	46.4 (1.1)	84.9 (0.6)
Bidirectional LSTM	49.1 (1.0)	87.5 (0.5)
2-layer LSTM	46.0 (1.3)	86.3 (0.6)
2-layer Bidirectional LSTM	48.5 (1.0)	87.2 (1.0)
Dependency Tree-LSTM	48.4 (0.4)	85.7 (0.4)
Constituency Tree-LSTM		
– randomly initialized vectors	43.9 (0.6)	82.0 (0.5)
– Glove vectors, fixed	49.7 (0.4)	87.5 (0.8)
– Glove vectors, tuned	**51.0** (0.5)	88.0 (0.3)

Table 2: Test set accuracies on the Stanford Sentiment Treebank. For our experiments, we report mean accuracies over 5 runs (standard deviations in parentheses). **Fine-grained:** 5-class sentiment classification. **Binary:** positive/negative sentiment classification.

produce binarized constituency parses[4] and dependency parses of the sentences in the dataset for our Constituency Tree-LSTM and Dependency Tree-LSTM models.

5.3 Hyperparameters and Training Details

The hyperparameters for our models were tuned on the development set for each task.

We initialized our word representations using publicly available 300-dimensional Glove vectors[5] (Pennington et al., 2014). For the sentiment classification task, word representations were updated during training with a learning rate of 0.1. For the semantic relatedness task, word representations were held fixed as we did not observe any significant improvement when the representations were tuned.

Our models were trained using AdaGrad (Duchi et al., 2011) with a learning rate of 0.05 and a minibatch size of 25. The model parameters were regularized with a per-minibatch L2 regularization strength of 10^{-4}. The sentiment classifier was additionally regularized using dropout (Srivastava et al., 2014) with a dropout rate of 0.5. We did not observe performance gains using dropout on the semantic relatedness task.

[4]Constituency parses produced by the Stanford PCFG Parser (Klein and Manning, 2003).

[5]Trained on 840 billion tokens of Common Crawl data, `http://nlp.stanford.edu/projects/glove/`.

Method	Pearson's r	Spearman's ρ	MSE
Illinois-LH (Lai and Hockenmaier, 2014)	0.7993	0.7538	0.3692
UNAL-NLP (Jimenez et al., 2014)	0.8070	0.7489	0.3550
Meaning Factory (Bjerva et al., 2014)	0.8268	0.7721	0.3224
ECNU (Zhao et al., 2014)	0.8414	–	–
Mean vectors	0.7577 (0.0013)	0.6738 (0.0027)	0.4557 (0.0090)
DT-RNN (Socher et al., 2014)	0.7923 (0.0070)	0.7319 (0.0071)	0.3822 (0.0137)
SDT-RNN (Socher et al., 2014)	0.7900 (0.0042)	0.7304 (0.0076)	0.3848 (0.0074)
LSTM	0.8528 (0.0031)	0.7911 (0.0059)	0.2831 (0.0092)
Bidirectional LSTM	0.8567 (0.0028)	0.7966 (0.0053)	0.2736 (0.0063)
2-layer LSTM	0.8515 (0.0066)	0.7896 (0.0088)	0.2838 (0.0150)
2-layer Bidirectional LSTM	0.8558 (0.0014)	0.7965 (0.0018)	0.2762 (0.0020)
Constituency Tree-LSTM	0.8582 (0.0038)	0.7966 (0.0053)	0.2734 (0.0108)
Dependency Tree-LSTM	**0.8676** (0.0030)	**0.8083** (0.0042)	**0.2532** (0.0052)

Table 3: Test set results on the SICK semantic relatedness subtask. For our experiments, we report mean scores over 5 runs (standard deviations in parentheses). Results are grouped as follows: **(1)** SemEval 2014 submissions; **(2)** Our own baselines; **(3)** Sequential LSTMs; **(4)** Tree-structured LSTMs.

6 Results

6.1 Sentiment Classification

Our results are summarized in Table 2. The Constituency Tree-LSTM outperforms existing systems on the fine-grained classification subtask and achieves accuracy comparable to the state-of-the-art on the binary subtask. In particular, we find that it outperforms the Dependency Tree-LSTM. This performance gap is at least partially attributable to the fact that the Dependency Tree-LSTM is trained on less data: about 150K labeled nodes *vs.* 319K for the Constituency Tree-LSTM. This difference is due to (1) the dependency representations containing fewer nodes than the corresponding constituency representations, and (2) the inability to match about 9% of the dependency nodes to a corresponding span in the training data.

We found that updating the word representations during training ("fine-tuning" the word embedding) yields a significant boost in performance on the fine-grained classification subtask and gives a minor gain on the binary classification subtask (this finding is consistent with previous work on this task by Kim (2014)). These gains are to be expected since the Glove vectors used to initialize our word representations were not originally trained to capture sentiment.

6.2 Semantic Relatedness

Our results are summarized in Table 3. Following Marelli et al. (2014), we use Pearson's r, Spearman's ρ and mean squared error (MSE) as evaluation metrics. The first two metrics are measures of correlation against human evaluations of semantic relatedness.

We compare our models against a number of non-LSTM baselines. The mean vector baseline computes sentence representations as a mean of the representations of the constituent words. The DT-RNN and SDT-RNN models (Socher et al., 2014) both compose vector representations for the nodes in a dependency tree as a sum over affine-transformed child vectors, followed by a nonlinearity. The SDT-RNN is an extension of the DT-RNN that uses a separate transformation for each dependency relation. For each of our baselines, including the LSTM models, we use the similarity model described in Sec. 4.2.

We also compare against four of the top-performing systems[6] submitted to the SemEval 2014 semantic relatedness shared task: ECNU (Zhao et al., 2014), The Meaning Factory (Bjerva et al., 2014), UNAL-NLP (Jimenez et al., 2014), and Illinois-LH (Lai and Hockenmaier, 2014). These systems are heavily feature engineered, generally using a combination of surface form overlap features and lexical distance features derived from WordNet or the Paraphrase Database (Ganitkevitch et al., 2013).

Our LSTM models outperform all these sys-

[6] We list the strongest results we were able to find for this task; in some cases, these results are stronger than the official performance by the team on the shared task. For example, the listed result by Zhao et al. (2014) is stronger than their submitted system's Pearson correlation score of 0.8280.

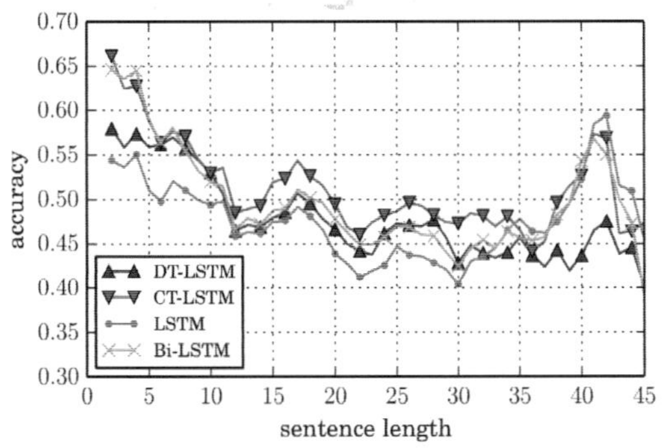

Figure 3: Fine-grained sentiment classification accuracy *vs.* sentence length. For each ℓ, we plot accuracy for the test set sentences with length in the window $[\ell - 2, \ell + 2]$. Examples in the tail of the length distribution are batched in the final window ($\ell = 45$).

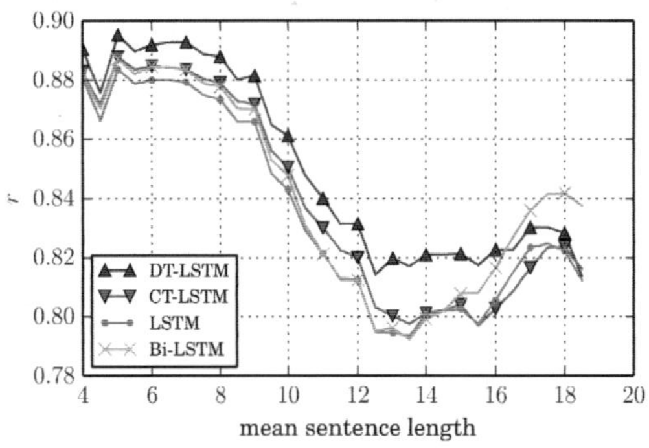

Figure 4: Pearson correlations r between predicted similarities and gold ratings *vs.* sentence length. For each ℓ, we plot r for the pairs with mean length in the window $[\ell-2, \ell+2]$. Examples in the tail of the length distribution are batched in the final window ($\ell = 18.5$).

tems without any additional feature engineering, with the best results achieved by the Dependency Tree-LSTM. Recall that in this task, both Tree-LSTM models only receive supervision at the root of the tree, in contrast to the sentiment classification task where supervision was also provided at the intermediate nodes. We conjecture that in this setting, the Dependency Tree-LSTM benefits from its more compact structure relative to the Constituency Tree-LSTM, in the sense that paths from input word vectors to the root of the tree are shorter on aggregate for the Dependency Tree-LSTM.

7 Discussion and Qualitative Analysis

7.1 Modeling Semantic Relatedness

In Table 4, we list nearest-neighbor sentences retrieved from a 1000-sentence sample of the SICK test set. We compare the neighbors ranked by the Dependency Tree-LSTM model against a baseline ranking by cosine similarity of the mean word vectors for each sentence.

The Dependency Tree-LSTM model exhibits several desirable properties. Note that in the dependency parse of the second query sentence, the word "ocean" is the second-furthest word from the root ("waving"), with a depth of 4. Regardless, the retrieved sentences are all semantically related to the word "ocean", which indicates that the Tree-LSTM is able to both preserve and emphasize information from relatively distant nodes. Additionally, the Tree-LSTM model shows greater robustness to differences in sentence length. Given the query "two men are playing guitar", the Tree-LSTM associates the phrase "playing guitar" with the longer, related phrase "dancing and singing in front of a crowd" (note as well that there is zero token overlap between the two phrases).

7.2 Effect of Sentence Length

One hypothesis to explain the empirical strength of Tree-LSTMs is that tree structures help mitigate the problem of preserving state over long sequences of words. If this were true, we would expect to see the greatest improvement over sequential LSTMs on longer sentences. In Figs. 3 and 4, we show the relationship between sentence length and performance as measured by the relevant task-specific metric. Each data point is a mean score over 5 runs, and error bars have been omitted for clarity.

We observe that while the Dependency Tree-LSTM does significantly outperform its sequential counterparts on the relatedness task for longer sentences of length 13 to 15 (Fig. 4), it also achieves consistently strong performance on shorter sentences. This suggests that unlike sequential LSTMs, Tree-LSTMs are able to encode semantically-useful structural information in the sentence representations that they compose.

8 Related Work

Distributed representations of words (Rumelhart et al., 1988; Collobert et al., 2011; Turian et al., 2010; Huang et al., 2012; Mikolov et al., 2013;

Ranking by mean word vector cosine similarity	Score
a woman is slicing potatoes	
a woman is cutting potatoes	0.96
a woman is slicing herbs	0.92
a woman is slicing tofu	0.92
a boy is waving at some young runners from the ocean	
a man and a boy are standing at the bottom of some stairs , which are outdoors	0.92
a group of children in uniforms is standing at a gate and one is kissing the mother	0.90
a group of children in uniforms is standing at a gate and there is no one kissing the mother	0.90
two men are playing guitar	
some men are playing rugby	0.88
two men are talking	0.87
two dogs are playing with each other	0.87

Ranking by Dependency Tree-LSTM model	Score
a woman is slicing potatoes	
a woman is cutting potatoes	4.82
potatoes are being sliced by a woman	4.70
tofu is being sliced by a woman	4.39
a boy is waving at some young runners from the ocean	
a group of men is playing with a ball on the beach	3.79
a young boy wearing a red swimsuit is jumping out of a blue kiddies pool	3.37
the man is tossing a kid into the swimming pool that is near the ocean	3.19
two men are playing guitar	
the man is singing and playing the guitar	4.08
the man is opening the guitar for donations and plays with the case	4.01
two men are dancing and singing in front of a crowd	4.00

Table 4: Most similar sentences from a 1000-sentence sample drawn from the SICK test set. The Tree-LSTM model is able to pick up on more subtle relationships, such as that between "beach" and "ocean" in the second example.

Pennington et al., 2014) have found wide applicability in a variety of NLP tasks. Following this success, there has been substantial interest in the area of learning distributed phrase and sentence representations (Mitchell and Lapata, 2010; Yessenalina and Cardie, 2011; Grefenstette et al., 2013; Mikolov et al., 2013), as well as distributed representations of longer bodies of text such as paragraphs and documents (Srivastava et al., 2013; Le and Mikolov, 2014).

Our approach builds on recursive neural networks (Goller and Kuchler, 1996; Socher et al., 2011), which we abbreviate as Tree-RNNs in order to avoid confusion with recurrent neural networks. Under the Tree-RNN framework, the vector representation associated with each node of a tree is composed as a function of the vectors corresponding to the children of the node. The choice of composition function gives rise to numerous variants of this basic framework. Tree-RNNs have been used to parse images of natural scenes (Socher et al., 2011), compose phrase representations from word vectors (Socher et al., 2012), and classify the sentiment polarity of sentences (Socher et al., 2013).

9 Conclusion

In this paper, we introduced a generalization of LSTMs to tree-structured network topologies. The Tree-LSTM architecture can be applied to trees with arbitrary branching factor. We demonstrated the effectiveness of the Tree-LSTM by applying the architecture in two tasks: semantic relatedness and sentiment classification, outperforming existing systems on both. Controlling for model dimensionality, we demonstrated that Tree-LSTM models are able to outperform their sequential counterparts. Our results suggest further lines of work in characterizing the role of structure in producing distributed representations of sentences.

Acknowledgements

We thank our anonymous reviewers for their valuable feedback. Stanford University gratefully acknowledges the support of a Natural Language Understanding-focused gift from Google Inc. and the Defense Advanced Research Projects Agency (DARPA) Deep Exploration and Filtering of Text (DEFT) Program under Air Force Research Laboratory (AFRL) contract no. FA8750-13-2-0040. Any opinions, findings, and conclusion or recommendations expressed in this material are those of the authors and do not necessarily reflect the view of the DARPA, AFRL, or the US government.

References

Bahdanau, Dzmitry, Kyunghyun Cho, and Yoshua Bengio. 2015. Neural machine translation by jointly learning to align and translate. In *Proceedings of the 3rd International Conference on Learning Representations (ICLR 2015)*.

Bengio, Yoshua, Patrice Simard, and Paolo Frasconi. 1994. Learning long-term dependencies with gradient descent is difficult. *IEEE Transactions on Neural Networks* 5(2).

Bjerva, Johannes, Johan Bos, Rob van der Goot, and Malvina Nissim. 2014. The Meaning Factory: Formal semantics for recognizing textual entailment and determining semantic similarity. In *Proceedings of the 8th International Workshop on Semantic Evaluation (SemEval 2014)*.

Blunsom, Phil, Edward Grefenstette, Nal Kalchbrenner, et al. 2014. A convolutional neural network for modelling sentences. In *Proceedings of the 52nd Annual Meeting of the Association for Computational Linguistics*.

Chen, Danqi and Christopher D Manning. 2014. A fast and accurate dependency parser using neural networks. In *Proceedings of the 2014 Conference on Empirical Methods in Natural Language Processing (EMNLP)*.

Collobert, Ronan, Jason Weston, Léon Bottou, Michael Karlen, Koray Kavukcuoglu, and Pavel Kuksa. 2011. Natural language processing (almost) from scratch. *The Journal of Machine Learning Research* 12:2493–2537.

Duchi, John, Elad Hazan, and Yoram Singer. 2011. Adaptive subgradient methods for online learning and stochastic optimization. *The Journal of Machine Learning Research* 12:2121–2159.

Elman, Jeffrey L. 1990. Finding structure in time. *Cognitive science* 14(2):179–211.

Foltz, Peter W, Walter Kintsch, and Thomas K Landauer. 1998. The measurement of textual coherence with latent semantic analysis. *Discourse processes* 25(2-3):285–307.

Ganitkevitch, Juri, Benjamin Van Durme, and Chris Callison-Burch. 2013. PPDB: The Paraphrase Database. In *Proceedings of HLT-NAACL 2013*.

Goller, Christoph and Andreas Kuchler. 1996. Learning task-dependent distributed representations by backpropagation through structure. In *IEEE International Conference on Neural Networks*.

Graves, Alex, Navdeep Jaitly, and A-R Mohamed. 2013. Hybrid speech recognition with deep bidirectional LSTM. In *IEEE Workshop on Automatic Speech Recognition and Understanding (ASRU)*.

Grefenstette, Edward, Georgiana Dinu, Yao-Zhong Zhang, Mehrnoosh Sadrzadeh, and Marco Baroni. 2013. Multi-step regression learning for compositional distributional semantics. In *Proceedings of the 10th International Conference on Computational Semantics*.

Hochreiter, Sepp. 1998. The vanishing gradient problem during learning recurrent neural nets and problem solutions. *International Journal of Uncertainty, Fuzziness and Knowledge-Based Systems* 6(02):107–116.

Hochreiter, Sepp and Jürgen Schmidhuber. 1997. Long Short-Term Memory. *Neural Computation* 9(8).

Huang, Eric H., Richard Socher, Christopher D. Manning, and Andrew Y. Ng. 2012. Improving word representations via global context and multiple word prototypes. In *Annual Meeting of the Association for Computational Linguistics (ACL)*.

Irsoy, Ozan and Claire Cardie. 2014. Deep recursive neural networks for compositionality in language. In *Advances in Neural Information Processing Systems*.

Jimenez, Sergio, George Duenas, Julia Baquero, Alexander Gelbukh, Av Juan Dios Bátiz, and Av Mendizábal. 2014. UNAL-NLP: Combining soft cardinality features for semantic textual similarity, relatedness and entailment. In *Proceedings of the 8th International Workshop on Semantic Evaluation (SemEval 2014)*.

Kim, Yoon. 2014. Convolutional neural networks for sentence classification. In *Proceedings of the 2014 Conference on Empirical Methods in Natural Language Processing (EMNLP)*.

Klein, Dan and Christopher D Manning. 2003. Accurate unlexicalized parsing. In *Proceedings of the 41st Annual Meeting on Association for Computational Linguistics*.

Lai, Alice and Julia Hockenmaier. 2014. Illinois-LH: A denotational and distributional approach to semantics. In *Proceedings of the 8th International Workshop on Semantic Evaluation (SemEval 2014)*.

Landauer, Thomas K and Susan T Dumais. 1997. A solution to Plato's problem: The latent semantic analysis theory of acquisition, induction, and representation of knowledge. *Psychological review* 104(2):211.

Le, Quoc and Tomas Mikolov. 2014. Distributed representations of sentences and documents. In

Proceedings of the 31st International Conference on Machine Learning (ICML-14).

Marelli, Marco, Luisa Bentivogli, Marco Baroni, Raffaella Bernardi, Stefano Menini, and Roberto Zamparelli. 2014. SemEval-2014 Task 1: Evaluation of compositional distributional semantic models on full sentences through semantic relatedness and textual entailment. In *Proceedings of the 8th International Workshop on Semantic Evaluation (SemEval 2014)*.

Mikolov, Tomáš. 2012. *Statistical Language Models Based on Neural Networks*. Ph.D. thesis, Brno University of Technology.

Mikolov, Tomas, Ilya Sutskever, Kai Chen, Greg S Corrado, and Jeff Dean. 2013. Distributed representations of words and phrases and their compositionality. In *Advances in Neural Information Processing Systems*.

Mitchell, Jeff and Mirella Lapata. 2010. Composition in distributional models of semantics. *Cognitive science* 34(8):1388–1429.

Pennington, Jeffrey, Richard Socher, and Christopher D Manning. 2014. Glove: Global vectors for word representation. In *Proceedings of the 2014 Conference on Empiricial Methods in Natural Language Processing (EMNLP)*.

Rumelhart, David E, Geoffrey E Hinton, and Ronald J Williams. 1988. Learning representations by back-propagating errors. *Cognitive modeling* 5.

Socher, Richard, Brody Huval, Christopher D Manning, and Andrew Y Ng. 2012. Semantic compositionality through recursive matrix-vector spaces. In *Proceedings of the 2012 Joint Conference on Empirical Methods in Natural Language Processing and Computational Natural Language Learning (EMNLP)*.

Socher, Richard, Andrej Karpathy, Quoc V Le, Christopher D Manning, and Andrew Y Ng. 2014. Grounded compositional semantics for finding and describing images with sentences. *Transactions of the Association for Computational Linguistics* 2.

Socher, Richard, Cliff C Lin, Chris Manning, and Andrew Y Ng. 2011. Parsing natural scenes and natural language with recursive neural networks. In *Proceedings of the 28th International Conference on Machine Learning (ICML-11)*.

Socher, Richard, Alex Perelygin, Jean Y Wu, Jason Chuang, Christopher D Manning, Andrew Y Ng, and Christopher Potts. 2013. Recursive deep models for semantic compositionality over a sentiment treebank. In *Proceedings of the 2013 Conference on Empirical Methods in Natural Language Processing (EMNLP)*.

Srivastava, Nitish, Geoffrey Hinton, Alex Krizhevsky, Ilya Sutskever, and Ruslan Salakhutdinov. 2014. Dropout: A simple way to prevent neural networks from overfitting. *Journal of Machine Learning Research* 15:1929–1958.

Srivastava, Nitish, Ruslan Salakhutdinov, and Geoffrey Hinton. 2013. Modeling documents with a Deep Boltzmann Machine. In *Uncertainty in Artificial Intelligence*.

Sutskever, Ilya, Oriol Vinyals, and Quoc VV Le. 2014. Sequence to sequence learning with neural networks. In *Advances in Neural Information Processing Systems*.

Turian, Joseph, Lev Ratinov, and Yoshua Bengio. 2010. Word representations: A simple and general method for semi-supervised learning. In *Proceedings of the 48th Annual Meeting of the Association for Computational Linguistics*.

Vinyals, Oriol, Alexander Toshev, Samy Bengio, and Dumitru Erhan. 2014. Show and tell: A neural image caption generator. *arXiv preprint arXiv:1411.4555* .

Yessenalina, Ainur and Claire Cardie. 2011. Compositional matrix-space models for sentiment analysis. In *Proceedings of the 2011 Conference on Empirical Methods in Natural Language Processing (EMNLP)*.

Zaremba, Wojciech and Ilya Sutskever. 2014. Learning to execute. *arXiv preprint arXiv:1410.4615* .

Zhao, Jiang, Tian Tian Zhu, and Man Lan. 2014. ECNU: One stone two birds: Ensemble of heterogenous measures for semantic relatedness and textual entailment. In *Proceedings of the 8th International Workshop on Semantic Evaluation (SemEval 2014)*.

A Convolutional Architecture for Word Sequence Prediction

Mingxuan Wang[1] **Zhengdong Lu**[2] **Hang Li**[2] **Wenbin Jiang**[1] **Qun Liu**[3,1]
[1]Key Laboratory of Intelligent Information Processing,
Institute of Computing Technology, Chinese Academy of Sciences
{wangmingxuan, jiangwenbin, liuqun}@ict.ac.cn
[2]Noah's Ark Lab, Huawei Technologies
{Lu.Zhengdong, HangLi.HL}@huawei.com
[3]ADAPT Centre, School of Computing, Dublin City University

Abstract

We propose a convolutional neural network, named genCNN, for word sequence prediction. Different from previous work on neural network-based language modeling and generation (e.g., RNN or LSTM), we choose not to greedily summarize the history of words as a fixed length vector. Instead, we use a convolutional neural network to predict the next word with the history of words of variable length. Also different from the existing feedforward networks for language modeling, our model can effectively fuse the local correlation and global correlation in the word sequence, with a convolution-gating strategy specifically designed for the task. We argue that our model can give adequate representation of the history, and therefore can naturally exploit both the short and long range dependencies. Our model is fast, easy to train, and readily parallelized. Our extensive experiments on text generation and n-best re-ranking in machine translation show that genCNN outperforms the state-of-the-arts with big margins.

1 Introduction

Both language modeling (Wu and Khudanpur, 2003; Mikolov et al., 2010; Bengio et al., 2003) and text generation (Axelrod et al., 2011) boil down to modeling the conditional probability of a word given the proceeding words. Previously, it is mostly done through purely memory-based approaches, such as n-grams, which cannot deal with long sequences and has to use some heuristics (called smoothing) for rare ones. Another family of methods are based on distributed representations of words, which is usually tied with a neural-network (NN) architecture for estimating the conditional probabilities of words.

Two categories of neural networks have been used for language modeling: 1) recurrent neural networks (RNN), and 2) feedfoward network (FFN):

- The RNN-based models, including its variants like LSTM, enjoy more popularity, mainly due to their flexible structures for processing word sequences of arbitrary lengths, and their recent empirical success(Sutskever et al., 2014; Graves, 2013). We however argue that RNNs, with their power built on the recursive use of a relatively simple computation units, are forced to make greedy summarization of the history and consequently not efficient on modeling word sequences, which clearly have a bottom-up structures.

- The FFN-based models, on the other hand, avoid this difficulty by feeding directly on the history. However, the FFNs are built on fully-connected networks, rendering them inefficient on capturing local structures of languages. Moreover their "rigid" architectures make it futile to handle the great variety of patterns in long range correlations of words.

We propose a novel convolutional architecture, named genCNN, as a model that can efficiently combine local and long range structures of language for the purpose of modeling conditional probabilities. genCNN can be directly used in generating a word sequence (i.e.,

Proceedings of the 53rd Annual Meeting of the Association for Computational Linguistics and the 7th International Joint Conference on Natural Language Processing, pages 1567–1576,
Beijing, China, July 26-31, 2015.

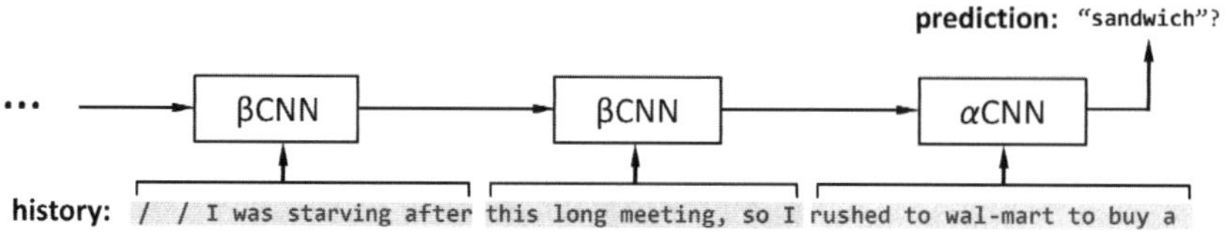

Figure 1: The overall diagram of a genCNN. Here "/" stands for a zero padding. In this example, each CNN component covers 6 words, while in practice the coverage is 30-40 words.

text generation) or evaluating the likelihood of word sequences (i.e., language modeling). We also show the empirical superiority of genCNN on both tasks over traditional n-grams and its RNN or FFN counterparts.

Notations: We will use $\mathcal{V}$ to denote the vocabulary, $\mathbf{e}_t$ ($\in \{1, \cdots, |\mathcal{V}|\}$) to denote the tth word in a sequence $\mathbf{e}_{1:t} \stackrel{\text{def}}{=} [\mathbf{e}_1, \cdots, \mathbf{e}_t]$, and $\mathbf{e}_t^{(n)}$ if the sequence is further indexed by n.

2 Overview

As shown in Figure 1, genCNN is overall recursive, consisting of CNN-based processing units of two types:

- αCNN as the "front-end", dealing with the history that is closest to the prediction;
- βCNNs (which can repeat), in charge of more "ancient" history.

Together, genCNN takes history $\mathbf{e}_{1:t}$ of arbitrary length to predict the next word $\mathbf{e}_{t+1}$ with probability

$$p(\mathbf{e}_{t+1}\,|\mathbf{e}_{1:t};\bar{\Theta}), \qquad (1)$$

based on a representation $\phi(\mathbf{e}_{1:t};\bar{\Theta})$ produced by the CNN, and a $|\mathcal{V}|$-class soft-max:

$$p(\mathbf{e}_{t+1}|\mathbf{e}_{1:t};\bar{\Theta}) \propto e^{\mu^{\top}_{\mathbf{e}_{t+1}}\phi(\mathbf{e}_{1:t})+b_{\mathbf{e}_{t+1}}}. \qquad (2)$$

genCNN is devised (tailored) fully for modeling the sequential structure in natural language, notably different from conventional CNN (Lawrence et al., 1997; Hu et al., 2014) in 1) its specifically designed weights-sharing strategy (in αCNN), 2) its gating design, and 3) certainly its recursive architectures. Also distinct from RNN, genCNN gains most of its processing power from the heavy-duty processing units (i.e.,αCNN and βCNNs), which follow a bottom-up information flow and yet can adequately capture the temporal structure in word sequence with its convolutional-gating architecture.

3 genCNN: Architecture

We start with discussing the convolutional architecture of αCNN as a stand-alone sentence model, and then proceed to the recursive structure. After that we give a comparative analysis on the mechanism of genCNN.

αCNN, just like a normal CNN, has fixed architecture with predefined maximum words (denoted as L_α). History shorter than L_α will filled with zero paddings, and history longer than that will be folded to feed to βCNN after it, as will be elaborated in Section 3.3. Similar to most other CNNs, αCNN alternates between convolution layers and pooling layers, and finally a fully connected layer to reach the representation before soft-max, as illustrated by Figure 2. Unlike the toyish example in Figure 2, in practice we use a larger and deeper αCNN with $L_\alpha = 30$ or 40, and two or three convolution layers (see Section 4.1). Different from conventional CNN, genCNN has 1) weight sharing strategy for convolution, and 2)"external" gating networks to replace the normal pooling mechanism, both of which are specifically designed for word sequence prediction.

3.1 αCNN: Convolution

Different from conventional CNN, the weights of convolution units in αCNN is only partially shared. More specifically, in the convolution units there are two types feature-maps: TIME-FLOW and the TIME-ARROW, illustrated re-

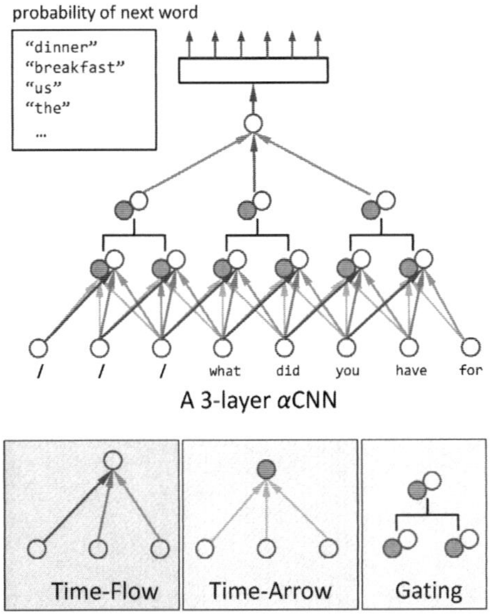

Figure 2: Illustration of a 3-layer αCNN. Here the shadowed nodes stand for the TIME-ARROW feature-maps and the unfilled nodes for the TIME-FLOW.

spectively with the unfilled nodes and filled nodes in Figure 2. The parameters for TIME-FLOW are shared among different convolution units, while for TIME-ARROW the parameters are location-dependent. Intuitively, TIME-FLOW acts more like a conventional CNN (e.g., that in (Hu et al., 2014)), aiming to understand the overall temporal structure in the word sequences; TIME-ARROW, on the other hand, works more like a traditional NN-based language model (Vaswani et al., 2013; Bengio et al., 2003): with its location-dependent parameters, it focuses on capturing the direction of time and prediction task.

For sentence input $\mathbf{x} = \{\mathbf{x}_1, \cdots, \mathbf{x}_T\}$, the feature-map of type-f on Layer-ℓ is

if $f \in$ TIME-FLOW:

$$z_i^{(\ell,f)}(\mathbf{x}) = \sigma(\mathbf{w}_{\mathsf{TF}}^{(\ell,f)} \hat{\mathbf{z}}_i^{(\ell-1)} + b_{\mathsf{TF}}^{(\ell,f)}), \quad (3)$$

if $f \in$ TIME-ARROW:

$$z_i^{(\ell,f)}(\mathbf{x}) = \sigma(\mathbf{w}_{\mathsf{TA}}^{(\ell,f,i)} \hat{\mathbf{z}}_i^{(\ell-1)} + b_{\mathsf{TA}}^{(\ell,f,i)}), \quad (4)$$

where

- $z_i^{(\ell,f)}(\mathbf{x})$ gives the output of feature-map of type-f for location i in Layer-ℓ;
- $\sigma(\cdot)$ is the activation function, e.g., Sigmoid or Relu (Dahl et al., 2013)
- $\mathbf{w}_{\mathsf{TF}}^{(\ell,f)}$ denotes the location-independent parameters for $f \in$TIME-FLOW on Layer-ℓ, while $\mathbf{w}_{\mathsf{TA}}^{(\ell,f,i)}$ stands for that for $f \in$ TIME-ARROW and location i on Layer-ℓ;
- $\hat{\mathbf{z}}_i^{(\ell-1)}$ denotes the segment of Layer-$\ell-1$ for the convolution at location i , while

  $$\hat{\mathbf{z}}_i^{(0)} \stackrel{\text{def}}{=} [\mathbf{x}_i^\top, \ \mathbf{x}_{i+1}^\top, \ \cdots, \ \mathbf{x}_{i+k_1-1}^\top]^\top$$

  concatenates the vectors for k_1 words from sentence input $\mathbf{x}$.

3.2 Gating Network

Previous CNNs, including those for NLP tasks (Hu et al., 2014; Kalchbrenner et al., 2014), take a straightforward convolution-pooling strategy, in which the "fusion" decisions (e.g., selecting the largest one in max-pooling) are based on the values of feature-maps. This is essentially a soft template matching, which works for tasks like classification, but undesired for maintaining the composition functionality of convolution. In this paper, we propose to use separate gating networks to release the scoring duty from the convolution, and let it focus on composition. Similar idea has been proposed by (Socher et al., 2011) for recursive neural networks on parsing, but never been combined with a convolutional structure.

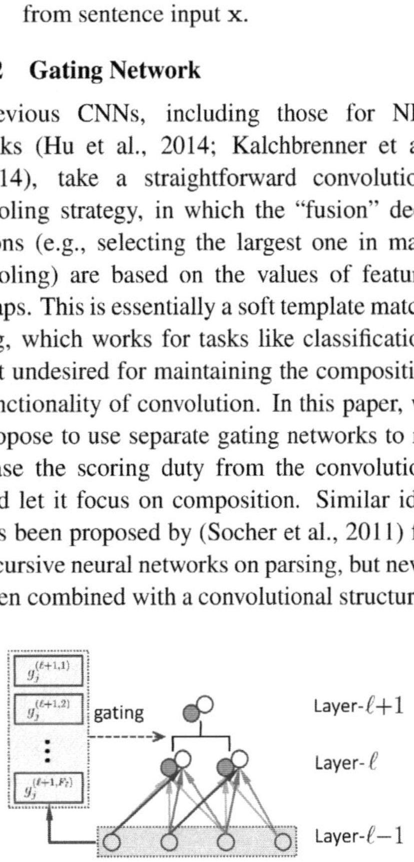

Figure 3: Illustration for gating network.

Suppose we have convolution feature-maps on Layer-ℓ and gating (with window size = 2) on Layer-$\ell+1$. For the jth gating window $(2j-1, 2j)$, we merge $\hat{\mathbf{z}}_{2j-1}^{(\ell-1)}$ and $\hat{\mathbf{z}}_{2j}^{(\ell-1)}$ as the input (denoted as $\bar{\mathbf{z}}_j^{(\ell)}$) for gating network, as illustrated in Figure 3. We use a separate gate for each feature-map, but follow a different parametrization strategy for TIME-FLOW and TIME-ARROW. With window size = 2, the gating is binary, we use a logistic regressor to determine the weights of two candidates. For $f \in$ TIME-ARROW, with location-dependent $\mathbf{w}_{\text{gate}}^{(\ell,f,j)}$, the normalized weight for *left* side is

$$g_j^{(\ell+1,f)} = 1/(1 + e^{-\mathbf{w}_{\text{gate}}^{(\ell,f,j)}\bar{\mathbf{z}}_j^{(\ell)}}),$$

while for For $f \in$TIME-FLOW, the parameters for the corresponding gating network, denoted as $\mathbf{w}_{\text{gate}}^{(\ell,f)}$, are shared. The gated feature map is then a weighted sum to feature-maps from the two windows:

$$z_j^{(\ell+1,f)} = g_j^{(\ell+1,f)} z_{2j-1}^{(\ell,f)} + (1 - g_j^{(\ell+1,f)}) z_{2j}^{(\ell,f)}. \quad (5)$$

We find that this gating strategy works significantly better than pooling directly over feature-maps, and slightly better than a hard gate version of Equation 5

3.3 Recursive Architecture

As suggested early on in Section 2 and Figure 1, we use extra CNNs with conventional weight-sharing, named βCNN, to summarize the history out of scope of αCNN. More specifically, the output of βCNN (with the same dimension of word-embedding) is put before the first word as the input to the αCNN, as illustrated in Figure 4. Different from αCNN, βCNN is designed just to summarize the history, with weight shared across its convolution units. In a sense, βCNN has only TIME-FLOW feature-maps. All βCNN are identical and recursively aligned, enabling *gen*CNN to handle sentences with arbitrary length. We put a special switch after each βCNN to turn it off (replacing a pading vector shown as "/" in Figure 4) when there is no history assigned to it. As the result, when the history is shorter than L_α, the recursive structure reduces to αCNN.

In practice, 90+% sentences can be modeled by αCNN with $L_\alpha = 40$ and 99+% sentences can be contained with one extra βCNN. Our experiment shows that this recursive strategy yields better estimate of conditional density than neglecting the out-of-scope history (Section 6.1.2). In practice, we found that a larger (greater L_α) and deeper αCNN works better than small αCNN and more recursion, which is consistent with our intuition that the convolutional architecture is better suited for modeling the sequence.

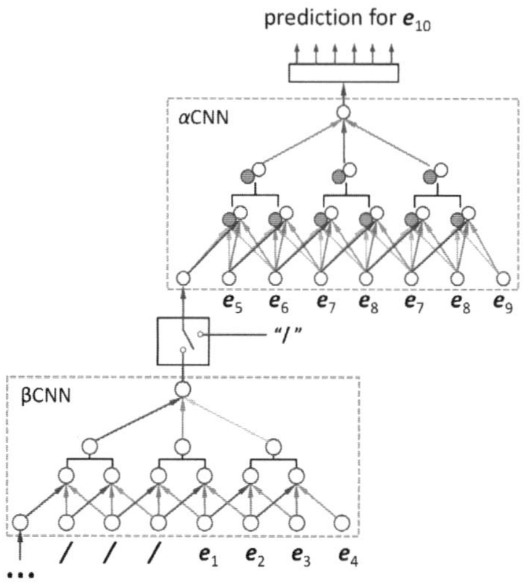

Figure 4: *gen*CNN with recursive structure.

3.4 Analysis

3.4.1 TIME-FLOW vs. TIME-ARROW

Both conceptually and systemically, *gen*CNN gives two interweaved treatments of word history. With the globally-shared parameters in the convolution units, TIME-FLOW summarizes *what has been said*. The hierarchical convolution+gating architecture in TIME-FLOW enables it to model the composition in language, yielding representation of segments at different intermediate layers. TIME-FLOW is aware of the sequential direction, inherited from the space-awareness of CNN, but it is not sensitive enough about the prediction task, due to the uniform weights in the convolution.

On the other hand, TIME-ARROW, living in location-dependent parameters of convolution units, acts like an arrow pin-pointing the prediction task. TIME-ARROW has predictive power all by itself, but it concentrates on capturing the direction of time and consequently short on modelling the long-range dependency.

TIME-FLOW and TIME-ARROW have to work together for optimal performance in predicting *what is going to be said*. This intuition has been empirically verified, as our experiments have demonstrated that TIME-FLOW or TIME-ARROW alone perform inferiorly. One can imagine, through the layer-by-layer convolution and gating, the TIME-ARROW gradually picks the most relevant part from the representation of TIME-FLOW for the prediction task, even if that part is long distance ahead.

3.4.2 genCNN vs. RNN-LM

Different from RNNs, which recursively applies a relatively simple processing units, genCNN gains its ability on sequence modeling mostly from its flexible and powerful bottom-up and convolution architecture. genCNN takes the "uncompressed" history, therefore avoids

- the difficulty in finding the representation for history, e.g., those end in the middle of a chunk (e.g.,"`the cat sat on the`"),
- the damping effort in RNN when the history-summarizing hidden state is updated at each time stamp, which renders the long-range memory rather difficult,

both of which can only be partially ameliorated with complicated design of gates (Hochreiter and Schmidhuber, 1997) and or more heavy processing units (essentially a fully connected DNN) (Sutskever et al., 2014).

4 genCNN: Training

The parameters of a genCNN $\bar{\Theta}$ consists of the parameters for CNN Θ_{nn}, word-embedding Θ_{embed}, and the parameters for soft-max $\Theta_{softmax}$. All the parameters are jointly learned by maximizing the likelihood of observed sentences. Formally the log-likelihood of sentence $\mathcal{S}_n$ ($\stackrel{\text{def}}{=} [\mathbf{e}_1^{(n)}, \mathbf{e}_2^{(n)}, \cdots, \mathbf{e}_{T_n}^{(n)}]$) is

$$\log p(\mathcal{S}_n; \bar{\Theta}) = \sum_{t=1}^{T_n} \log p(\mathbf{e}_t^{(n)} | \mathbf{e}_{1:t-1}^{(n)}; \bar{\Theta}),$$

which can be trivially split into T_n training instances during the optimization, in contrast to the training of RNN that requires unfolding through time due to the temporal-dependency of the hidden states.

4.1 Implementation Details

Architectures: In all of our experiments (Section 5 and 6) we set the maximum words for αCNN to be 30 and that for βCNN to be 20. αCNN have two convolution layers (both containing TIME-FLOW and TIME-ARROW convolution) and two gating layers, followed by a fully connected layer (400 dimension) and then a soft-max layer. The numbers of feature-maps for TIME-FLOW are respectively 150 (1st convolution layer) and 100 (2nd convolution layer), while TIME-ARROW has the same feature-maps. βCNN is relatively simple, with two convolution layer containing only TIME-FLOW with 150 feature-maps, two gating layers and a fully connected layer. We use ReLU as the activation function for convolution layers and switch to Sigmoid for fully connected layers. We use word embedding with dimension 100.

Soft-max: Calculating a full soft-max is expensive since it has to enumerate all the words in vocabulary (in our case 40K words) in the denominator. Here we take a simple hierarchical approximation of it, following (Bahdanau et al., 2014). Basically we group the words into 200 clusters (indexed by c_m), and factorize (in an approximate sense) the conditional probability of a word $p(\mathbf{e}_t|\mathbf{e}_{1:t-1}; \bar{\Theta})$ into the probability of its cluster and the probability of $\mathbf{e}_t$ given its cluster

$$p(c_m|\mathbf{e}_{1:t-1}; \bar{\Theta})\, p(\mathbf{e}_t|c_m; \Theta_{softmax}).$$

We found that this simple heuristic can speed-up the optimization by 5 times with only slight loss of accuracy.

Optimization: We use stochastic gradient descent with mini-batch (size 500) for optimization, aided further by AdaGrad (Duchi et al., 2011). For initialization, we use Word2Vec (Mikolov et al., 2013) for the starting state of the word-embeddings (trained on the same dataset as the main task), and set all the other parameters by randomly sampling from uniform distribution in $[-0.1, 0.1]$. The optimization is done mainly on a Tesla K40 GPU, which takes about 2 days for the training on a dataset containing 1M sentences.

5 Experiments: Sentence Generation

In this experiment, we randomly generate sentences by recurrently sampling

$$\mathbf{e}^{\star}_{t+1} \sim p(\mathbf{e}_{t+1}|\mathbf{e}_{1:t};\bar{\Theta}),$$

and put the newly generated word into history, until EOS (end-of-sentence) is generated. We consider generating two types of sentences: 1) the plain sentences, and 2) sentences with dependency parsing, which will be covered respectively in Section 5.1 and 5.2.

5.1 Natural Sentences

We train *gen*CNN on Wiki data with 112M words for one week, with some representative examples randomly generated given in Table 1 (upper and middle blocks). We try two settings, by letting *gen*CNN generate a sentence 1)from the very beginning (middle block), or 2) starting with a few words given by human (upper block). It is fairly clear that most of the time *gen*CNN can generate sentences that are syntactically grammatical and semantically meaningful. More specifically, most of the sentences can be aligned to a parse tree with reasonable structure. It is also worth noting that quotation marks (`` and '') are always generated in pairs and in the correct order, even across a relatively long distance, as exemplified by the first generated sentence in the upper block.

5.2 Sentences with Dependency Tags

For training, we first parse(Klein and Manning, 2002) the English sentences and feed sequences with dependency tags as follows

```
( I ⋆ like ( red ⋆ apple ) )
```

to *gen*CNN in training, where 1) each paired parentheses contain a subtree, and 2) the symbol "⋆" indicates that the word next to it is the dependency head in the corresponding subtree. Some representative examples generated by *gen*CNN are given in Table 1 (bottom block). As it suggests, *gen*CNN is fairly accurate on respecting the rules of parentheses, and probably more remarkably, it can get the dependency tree head right most of the time.

6 Experiments: Language Modeling

We evaluate our model as a language model in terms of both perplexity (Brown et al., 1992) and its efficacy in re-ranking the n-best candidates from state-of-the-art models in statistical machine translation, with comparison to the following competitor language models.

Competitor Models we compare *gen*CNN to the following competitor models

- 5-gram: We use SRI Language Modeling Toolkit (Stolcke and others, 2002) to train a 5-gram language model with modified Kneser-Ney smoothing;
- FFN-LM: The neural language model based on feedfoward network (Vaswani et al., 2013). We vary the input window-size from 5 to 20, while the performance stops increasing after window size 20;
- RNN: we use the implementation[1] of RNN-based language model with hidden size 600;
- LSTM: we adopt the code in Groundhog[2], but vary the hyper-parameters, including the depth and word-embedding dimension, for best performance. LSTM (Hochreiter and Schmidhuber, 1997) is widely considered to be the state-of-the-art for sequence modeling.

6.1 Perplexity

We test the performance of *gen*CNN on PENN TREEBANK and FBIS, two public datasets with different sizes.

6.1.1 On PENN TREEBANK

Although a relatively small dataset [3], PENN TREEBANK is widely used as a language modelling benchmark (Graves, 2013; Mikolov et al., 2010). It has $930,000$ words in training set, $74,000$ words in validation set, and $82,000$ words in test set. We use exactly the same settings as in (Mikolov et al., 2010), with a $10,000$-words vocabulary (all out-of-vocabulary words are replaced with `unknown`)

[1] http://rnnlm.org/

[2] https://github.com/lisa-groundhog/GroundHog

[3] http://www.fit.vutbr.cz/~imikolov/rnnlm/simple-examples.tgz

`` we are in the building of china 's social development and the businessmen audience , '' he said .
clinton was born in DDDD , and was educated at the university of edinburgh.
bush 's first album , `` the man '' , was released on DD november DDDD .
it is one of the first section of the act in which one is covered in real place that recorded in norway .
this objective is brought to us the welfare of our country
russian president putin delivered a speech to the sponsored by the 15th asia pacific economic cooperation (apec) meeting in an historical arena on oct .
light and snow came in kuwait and became operational , but was rarely placed in houston .
johnson became a drama company in the DDDDs , a television broadcasting company owned by the broadcasting program .
((the two ⋆ sides) ⋆ should (⋆ assume (a strong ⋆ target))) .)
(it ⋆ is time (⋆ in (every ⋆ country) ⋆ signed (the ⋆ speech)) .)
((initial ⋆ investigations) ⋆ showed (⋆ that (spot ⋆ could (⋆ be (further ⋆ improved significantly)) .)
((a ⋆ book (to ⋆ northern (the 21 st ⋆ century))) .)

Table 1: Examples of sentences generated by *gen*CNN. In the upper block (row 1-4) the underline words are given by the human; In the middle block (row 5-8), all the sentences are generated without any hint. The bottom block (row 9-12) shows the sentences with dependency tag generated by *gen*CNN trained with parsed examples.

and end-of-sentence token (EOS) at the end of each sentence. In addition to the conventional testing strategy where the models are kept unchanged during testing, Mikolov et al. (2010) proposes to also update the parameters in an online fashion when seeing test sentences. This new way of testing, named "dynamic evaluation", is also adopted by Graves (2013).

From Table 2 *gen*CNN manages to give perplexity superior in both metrics, with about 25 point reduction over the widely used 5-gram, and over 10 point reduction from LSTM, the state-of-the-art and the second-best performer.

Model	Perplexity	Dynamic
5-gram, KN5	141.2	–
FFNN-LM	140.2	–
RNN	124.7	123.2
LSTM	126	117
*gen*CNN	**116.4**	**106.3**

Table 2: PENN TREEBANK results, where the 3rd column are the perplexity in dynamic evaluation, while the numbers for RNN and LSTM are taken as reported in the paper cited above. The numbers in boldface indicate that the result is significantly better than *all competitors* in the same setting.

6.1.2 On FBIS

The FBIS corpus (LDC2003E14) is relatively large, with 22.5K sentences and 8.6M English words. The validation set is NIST MT06 and test set is NIST MT08. For training the neural network, we limit the vocabulary to the most frequent 40,000 words, covering $\sim 99.4\%$ of the corpus. Similar to the first experiment, all out-of-vocabulary words are replaced with unknown and the EOS token is counted in the sequence loss.

From Table 3 (upper block), *gen*CNN clearly wins again in the comparison to competitors, with over 25 point margin over LSTM (in its optimal setting), the second best performer. Interestingly *gen*CNN outperforms its variants also quite significantly (bottom block): 1) with only TIME-ARROW (same number of feature-maps), the performance deteriorates considerably for losing the ability of capturing long range correlation reliably; 2) with only TIME-TIME the performance gets even worse,

Model	Perplexity
5-gram, KN5	278.6
FFN-LM(5-gram)	248.3
FFN-LM(20-gram)	228.2
RNN	223.4
LSTM	206.9
genCNN	**181.2**
TIME-ARROW only	192
TIME-FLOW only	203
αCNN only	184.4

Table 3: FBIS results. The upper block (row 1-6) compares genCNN and the competitor models, and the bottom block (row 7-9) compares different variants of genCNN.

for partially losing the sensitivity to the prediction task. It is quite remarkable that, although αCNN (with $L_\alpha = 30$) can achieve good results, the recursive structure in full genCNN can further decrease the perplexity by over 3 points, indicating that genCNN can benefit from modeling the dependency over range as long as 30 words.

6.2 Re-ranking for Machine Translation

In this experiment, we re-rank the 1000-best English translation candidates for Chinese sentences generated by statistical machine translation (SMT) system, and compare it with other language models in the same setting.

SMT setup The baseline hierarchical phrase-based SMT system (Chines→ English) was built using Moses, a widely accepted state-of-the-art, with default settings. The bilingual training data is from NIST MT2012 constrained track, with reduced size of 1.1M sentence pairs using selection strategy in (Axelrod et al., 2011). The baseline use conventional 5-gram language model (LM), estimated with modified Kneser-Ney smoothing (Chen and Goodman, 1996) on the English side of the 329M-word Xinhua portion of English Gigaword(LDC2011T07). We also try FFN-LM, as a much stronger language model in decoding. The weights of all the features are tuned via MERT (Och and Ney, 2002) on NIST MT05, and tested on NIST MT06 and MT08. Case-

Models	MT06	MT08	Ave.
Baseline	38.63	31.11	34.87
RNN rerank	39.03	31.50	35.26
LSTM rerank	39.20	31.90	35.55
FFN-LM rerank	38.93	31.41	35.14
genCNN rerank	**39.90**	**32.50**	**36.20**
Base+FFN-LM	39.08	31.60	35.34
genCNN rerank	**40.4**	**32.85**	**36.63**

Table 4: The results for re-ranking the 1000-best of Moses. Note that the two bottom rows are on a baseline with enhanced LM.

insensitive NIST BLEU[4] is used in evaluation.

Re-ranking with genCNN significantly improves the quality of the final translation. Indeed, it can increase the BLEU score by over 1.33 point over Moses baseline on average. This boosting force barely slacks up on translation with a enhanced language model in decoding: genCNN re-ranker still achieves 1.29 point improvement on top of Moses with FFN-LM, which is 1.76 point over the Moses (default setting). To see the significance of this improvement, the state-of-the-art Neural Network Joint Model (Devlin et al., 2014) usually brings less than one point increase on this task.

7 Related Work

In addition to the long thread of work on neural network based language model (Auli et al., 2013; Mikolov et al., 2010; Graves, 2013; Bengio et al., 2003; Vaswani et al., 2013), our work is also related to the effort on modeling long range dependency in word sequence prediction(Wu and Khudanpur, 2003). Different from those work on hand-crafting features for incorporating long range dependency, our model can elegantly assimilate relevant information in an unified way, in both long and short range, with the bottom-up information flow and convolutional architecture.

CNN has been widely used in computer vision and speech (Lawrence et al., 1997; Krizhevsky et al., 2012; LeCun and Bengio, 1995; Abdel-Hamid et al., 2012), and lately in sentence representation(Kalchbrenner and

[4]ftp://jaguar.ncsl.nist.gov/mt/resources/mteval-v11b.pl

Blunsom, 2013), matching(Hu et al., 2014) and classification(Kalchbrenner et al., 2014). To our best knowledge, it is the first time this is used in word sequence prediction. Model-wise the previous work that is closest to genCNN is the convolution model for predicting moves in the Go game (Maddison et al., 2014), which, when applied recurrently, essentially generates a sequence. Different from the conventional CNN taken in (Maddison et al., 2014), genCNN has architectures designed for modeling the composition in natural language and the temporal structure of word sequence.

8 Conclusion

We propose a convolutional architecture for natural language generation and modeling. Our extensive experiments on sentence generation, perplexity, and n-best re-ranking for machine translation show that our model can significantly improve upon state-of-the-arts.

References

[Abdel-Hamid et al.2012] Ossama Abdel-Hamid, Abdel-rahman Mohamed, Hui Jiang, and Gerald Penn. 2012. Applying convolutional neural networks concepts to hybrid nn-hmm model for speech recognition. In *Acoustics, Speech and Signal Processing (ICASSP), 2012 IEEE International Conference on*, pages 4277–4280. IEEE.

[Auli et al.2013] Michael Auli, Michel Galley, Chris Quirk, and Geoffrey Zweig. 2013. Joint language and translation modeling with recurrent neural networks. In *Proceedings of the 2013 Conference on Empirical Methods in Natural Language Processing*, pages 1044–1054, Seattle, Washington, USA, October.

[Axelrod et al.2011] Amittai Axelrod, Xiaodong He, and Jianfeng Gao. 2011. Domain adaptation via pseudo in-domain data selection. In *Proceedings of the Conference on Empirical Methods in Natural Language Processing*, pages 355–362. Association for Computational Linguistics.

[Bahdanau et al.2014] Dzmitry Bahdanau, Kyunghyun Cho, and Yoshua Bengio. 2014. Neural machine translation by jointly learning to align and translate. *arXiv preprint arXiv:1409.0473*.

[Bengio et al.2003] Yoshua Bengio, Rjean Ducharme, Pascal Vincent, and Christian Jauvin. 2003. A neural probabilistic language model. *Journal OF Machine Learning Research*, 3:1137–1155.

[Brown et al.1992] Peter F. Brown, Vincent J. Della Pietra, Robert L. Mercer, Stephen A. Della Pietra, and Jennifer C. Lai. 1992. An estimate of an upper bound for the entropy of english. *Comput. Linguist.*, 18(1):31–40, March.

[Chen and Goodman1996] Stanley F Chen and Joshua Goodman. 1996. An empirical study of smoothing techniques for language modeling. In *Proceedings of the 34th annual meeting on Association for Computational Linguistics*, pages 310–318. Association for Computational Linguistics.

[Dahl et al.2013] George E Dahl, Tara N Sainath, and Geoffrey E. Hinton. 2013. Improving deep neural networks for lvcsr using rectified linear units and dropout. In *Proceedings of ICASSP*.

[Devlin et al.2014] Jacob Devlin, Rabih Zbib, Zhongqiang Huang, Thomas Lamar, Richard Schwartz, and John Makhoul. 2014. Fast and robust neural network joint models for statistical machine translation. In *Proceedings of the 52nd Annual Meeting of the Association for Computational Linguistics*, pages 1370–1380.

[Duchi et al.2011] John Duchi, Elad Hazan, and Yoram Singer. 2011. Adaptive subgradient methods for online learning and stochastic optimization. *The Journal of Machine Learning Research*, 12:2121–2159.

[Graves2013] Alex Graves. 2013. Generating sequences with recurrent neural networks. *CoRR*, abs/1308.0850.

[Hochreiter and Schmidhuber1997] Sepp Hochreiter and Jürgen Schmidhuber. 1997. Long short-term memory. *Neural Comput.*, 9(8):1735–1780, November.

[Hu et al.2014] Baotian Hu, Zhengdong Lu, Hang Li, and Qingcai Chen. 2014. Convolutional neural network architectures for matching natural language sentences. In *NIPS*.

[Kalchbrenner and Blunsom2013] Nal Kalchbrenner and Phil Blunsom. 2013. Recurrent continuous translation models. In *Proceedings of the 2013 Conference on Empirical Methods in Natural Language Processing*, pages 1700–1709, Seattle, Washington, USA, October.

[Kalchbrenner et al.2014] Nal Kalchbrenner, Edward Grefenstette, and Phil Blunsom. 2014. A convolutional neural network for modelling sentences. *ACL*.

[Klein and Manning2002] Dan Klein and Christopher D Manning. 2002. Fast exact inference with a factored model for natural language parsing. In *Advances in neural information processing systems*, volume 15, pages 3–10.

[Krizhevsky et al.2012] Alex Krizhevsky, Ilya Sutskever, and Geoffrey E Hinton. 2012. Imagenet classification with deep convolutional neural networks. In *Advances in neural information processing systems*, pages 1097–1105.

[Lawrence et al.1997] Steve Lawrence, C Lee Giles, Ah Chung Tsoi, and Andrew D Back. 1997. Face recognition: A convolutional neural-network approach. *Neural Networks, IEEE Transactions on*, 8(1):98–113.

[LeCun and Bengio1995] Yann LeCun and Yoshua Bengio. 1995. Convolutional networks for images, speech, and time series. *The handbook of brain theory and neural networks*, 3361:310.

[Maddison et al.2014] Chris J. Maddison, Aja Huang, Ilya Sutskever, and David Silver. 2014. Move evaluation in go using deep convolutional neural networks. *CoRR*, abs/1412.6564.

[Mikolov et al.2010] Tomas Mikolov, Martin Karafit, Lukas Burget, Jan Cernocky, and Sanjeev Khudanpur. 2010. In *INTERSPEECH*, pages 1045–1048.

[Mikolov et al.2013] Tomas Mikolov, Kai Chen, Greg Corrado, and Jeffrey Dean. 2013. Efficient estimation of word representations in vector space. *CoRR*, abs/1301.3781.

[Och and Ney2002] Franz Josef Och and Hermann Ney. 2002. Discriminative training and maximum entropy models for statistical machine translation. In *Proceedings of the 40th Annual Meeting on Association for Computational Linguistics*, pages 295–302.

[Socher et al.2011] Richard Socher, Cliff C. Lin, Andrew Y. Ng, and Christopher D. Manning. 2011. Parsing Natural Scenes and Natural Language with Recursive Neural Networks. In *Proceedings of the 26th International Conference on Machine Learning (ICML)*.

[Stolcke and others2002] Andreas Stolcke et al. 2002. Srilm-an extensible language modeling toolkit. In *Proceedings of the international conference on spoken language processing*, volume 2, pages 901–904.

[Sutskever et al.2014] Ilya Sutskever, Oriol Vinyals, and Quoc V Le. 2014. Sequence to sequence learning with neural networks. In *NIPS*.

[Vaswani et al.2013] Ashish Vaswani, Yinggong Zhao, Victoria Fossum, and David Chiang. 2013. Decoding with large-scale neural language models improves translation. In *EMNLP*, pages 1387–1392. Citeseer.

[Wu and Khudanpur2003] Jun Wu and Sanjeev Khudanpur. 2003. *Maximum entropy language modeling with non-local dependencies*. Ph.D. thesis, Johns Hopkins University.

Neural Responding Machine for Short-Text Conversation

Lifeng Shang, Zhengdong Lu, Hang Li
Noah's Ark Lab
Huawei Technologies Co. Ltd.
Sha Tin, Hong Kong
{shang.lifeng,lu.zhengdong,hangli.hl}@huawei.com

Abstract

We propose Neural Responding Machine (NRM), a neural network-based response generator for Short-Text Conversation. NRM takes the general encoder-decoder framework: it formalizes the generation of response as a decoding process based on the latent representation of the input text, while both encoding and decoding are realized with recurrent neural networks (RNN). The NRM is trained with a large amount of one-round conversation data collected from a microblogging service. Empirical study shows that NRM can generate grammatically correct and content-wise appropriate responses to over 75% of the input text, outperforming state-of-the-arts in the same setting, including retrieval-based and SMT-based models.

1 Introduction

Natural language conversation is one of the most challenging artificial intelligence problems, which involves language understanding, reasoning, and the utilization of common sense knowledge. Previous works in this direction mainly focus on either rule-based or learning-based methods (Williams and Young, 2007; Schatzmann et al., 2006; Misu et al., 2012; Litman et al., 2000). These types of methods often rely on manual effort in designing rules or automatic training of model with a particular learning algorithm and a small amount of data, which makes it difficult to develop an extensible open domain conversation system.

Recently due to the explosive growth of microblogging services such as Twitter[1] and Weibo[2], the amount of conversation data available on the web has tremendously increased. This makes a data-driven approach to attack the conversation problem (Ji et al., 2014; Ritter et al., 2011) possible. Instead of multiple rounds of conversation, the task at hand, referred to as Short-Text Conversation (STC), only considers one round of conversation, in which each round is formed by two short texts, with the former being an input (referred to as post) from a user and the latter a response given by the computer. The research on STC may shed light on understanding the complicated mechanism of natural language conversation.

Previous methods for STC fall into two categories, 1) the retrieval-based method (Ji et al., 2014), and 2) the statistical machine translation (SMT) based method (Sordoni et al., 2015; Ritter et al., 2011). The basic idea of retrieval-based method is to pick a suitable response by ranking the candidate responses with a linear or non-linear combination of various matching features (e.g. number of shared words). The main drawbacks of the retrieval-based method are the following

- the responses are pre-existing and hard to customize for the particular text or requirement from the task, e.g., style or attitude.
- the use of matching features alone is usually not sufficient for distinguishing positive responses from negative ones, even after time consuming feature engineering. (e.g., a penalty due to mismatched named entities is difficult to incorporate into the model)

The SMT-based method, on the other hand, is generative. Basically it treats the response generation as a translation problem, in which the model is trained on a parallel corpus of post-response pairs. Despite its generative nature, the method is intrinsically unsuitable for response generation, because the responses are not semantically equivalent to the posts as in translation. Actually one post can receive responses with completely different content, as manifested through the example in the fol-

[1] https://twitter.com/.
[2] http://www.weibo.com/.

Proceedings of the 53rd Annual Meeting of the Association for Computational Linguistics and the 7th International Joint Conference on Natural Language Processing, pages 1577–1586,
Beijing, China, July 26-31, 2015.

lowing figure:

Post	Having my fish sandwich right now
UserA	For god's sake, it is 11 in the morning
UserB	Enhhhh... sounds yummy
UserC	which restaurant exactly?

Empirical studies also showed that SMT-based methods often yield responses with grammatical errors and in rigid forms, due to the unnecessary alignment between the "source" post and the "target" response (Ritter et al., 2011). This rigidity is still a serious problem in the recent work of (Sordoni et al., 2015), despite its use of neural network-based generative model as features in decoding.

1.1 Overview

In this paper, we take a probabilistic model to address the response generation problem, and propose employing a neural encoder-decoder for this task, named *Neural Responding Machine* (NRM). The neural encoder-decoder model, as illustrated in Figure 1, first summarizes the post as a vector representation, then feeds this representation to a decoder to generate responses. We further generalize this scheme to allow the post representation to dynamically change during the generation process, following the idea in (Bahdanau et al., 2014) originally proposed for neural-network-based machine translation with automatic alignment.

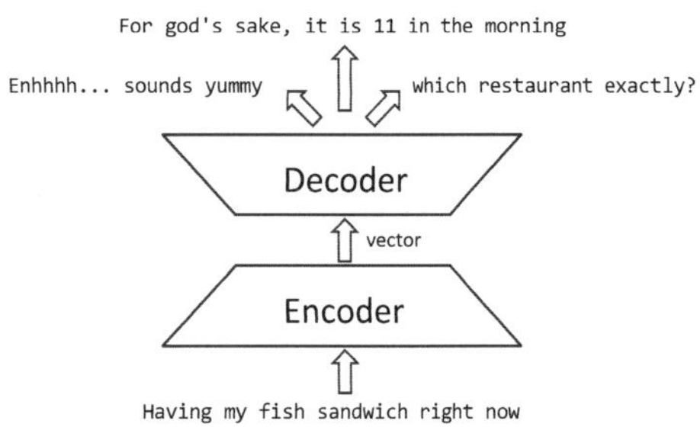

Figure 1: The diagram of encoder-decoder framework for automatic response generation.

NRM essentially estimates the likelihood of a response given a post. Clearly the estimated probability should be complex enough to represent all the suitable responses. Similar framework has been used for machine translation with a remarkable success (Kalchbrenner and Blunsom, 2013; Auli et al., 2013; Sutskever et al., 2014; Bahdanau et al., 2014). Note that in machine translation, the task is to estimate the probability of a target language sentence conditioned on the source language sentence with the same meaning, which is much easier than the task of STC which we are considering here. In this paper, we demonstrate that NRM, when equipped with a reasonable amount of data, can yield a satisfying estimator of responses (hence response generator) for STC, despite the difficulty of the task.

Our main contributions are two-folds: 1) we propose to use an encoder-decoder-based neural network to generate a response in STC; 2) we have empirically verified that the proposed method, when trained with a reasonable amount of data, can yield performance better than traditional retrieval-based and translation-based methods.

1.2 RoadMap

In the remainder of this paper, we start with introducing the dataset for STC in Section 2. Then we elaborate on the model of NRM in Section 3, followed by the details on training in Section 4. After that, we report the experimental results in Section 5. In Section 6 we conclude the paper.

2 The Dataset for STC

Our models are trained on a corpus of roughly 4.4 million pairs of conversations from Weibo [3].

2.1 Conversations on Sina Weibo

Weibo is a popular Twitter-like microblogging service in China, on which a user can post short messages (referred to as *post* in the reminder of this paper) visible to the public or a group of users following her/him. Other users make comment on a published post, which will be referred to as a *response*. Just like Twitter, Weibo also has the length limit of 140 Chinese characters on both posts and responses, making the post-response pair an ideal surrogate for short-text conversation.

2.2 Dataset Description

To construct this million scale dataset, we first crawl hundreds of millions of post-response pairs, and then clean the raw data in a similar way as suggested in (Wang et al., 2013), including 1) removing trivial responses like "wow", 2) filtering out potential advertisements, and 3) removing the responses after first 30 ones for topic consistency. Table 1 shows some statistics of the dataset used

[3] http://www.noahlab.com.hk/topics/ShortTextConversation

Training	#posts	219,905
	#responses	4,308,211
	#pairs	4,435,959
Test Data	#test posts	110
Labeled Dataset (retrieval-based)	#posts	225
	#responses	6,017
	#labeled pairs	6,017
Fine Tuning (SMT-based)	#posts	2,925
	#responses	3,000
	#pairs	3,000

Table 1: Some statistics of the dataset. **Labeled Dataset** and **Fine Tuning** are used by retrieval-based method for learning to rank and SMT-based method for fine tuning, respectively.

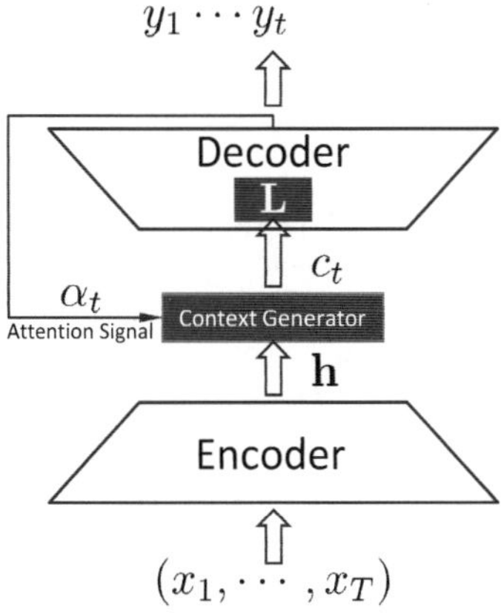

Figure 2: The general framework and dataflow of the encoder-decoder-based NRM.

in this work. It can be seen that each post have 20 different responses on average. In addition to the semantic gap between post and its responses, this is another key difference to a general parallel data set used for traditional translation.

3 Neural Responding Machines for STC

The basic idea of NRM is to build a hidden representation of a post, and then generate the response based on it, as shown in Figure 2. In the particular illustration, the encoder converts the input sequence $\mathbf{x} = (x_1, \cdots, x_T)$ into a set of high-dimensional hidden representations $\mathbf{h} = (h_1, \cdots, h_T)$, which, along with the attention signal at time t (denoted as α_t), are fed to the context-generator to build the context input to decoder at time t (denoted as c_t). Then c_t is linearly transformed by a matrix $\mathbf{L}$ (as part of the decoder) into a stimulus of generating RNN to produce the t-th word of response (denoted as y_t).

In neural translation system, $\mathbf{L}$ converts the representation in source language to that of target language. In NRM, $\mathbf{L}$ plays a more difficult role: it needs to transform the representation of post (or some part of it) to the rich representation of many plausible responses. It is a bit surprising that this can be achieved to a reasonable level with a linear transformation in the "space of representation", as validated in Section 5.3, where we show that one post can actually invoke many different responses from NRM.

The role of attention signal is to determine which part of the hidden representation $\mathbf{h}$ should be emphasized during the generation process. It should be noted that α_t could be fixed over time or changes dynamically during the generation of response sequence $\mathbf{y}$. In the dynamic settings, α_t can be function of historically generated subsequence $(y_1, \cdots, y_{t-1})$, input sequence $\mathbf{x}$ or their latent representations, more details will be shown later in Section 3.2.

We use Recurrent Neural Network (RNN) for both encoder and decoder, for its natural ability to summarize and generate word sequence of arbitrary lengths (Mikolov et al., 2010; Sutskever et al., 2014; Cho et al., 2014).

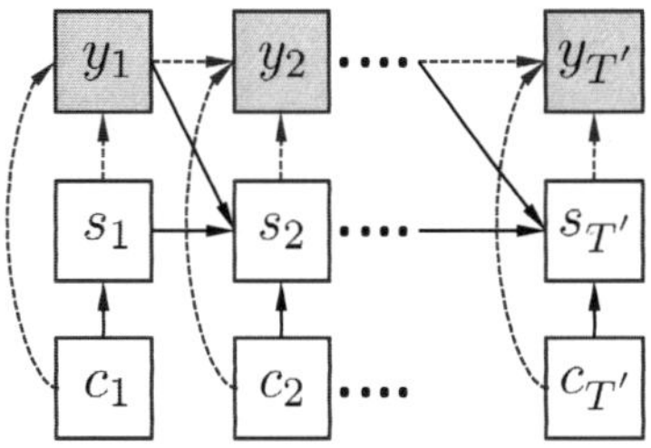

Figure 3: The graphical model of RNN decoder. The dashed lines denote the variables related to the function $g(\cdot)$, and the solid lines denote the variables related to the function $f(\cdot)$.

3.1 The Computation in Decoder

Figure 3 gives the graphical model of the decoder, which is essentially a standard RNN language model except conditioned on the context input $\mathbf{c}$. The generation probability of the t-th word is calculated by

$$p(y_t|y_{t-1}, \cdots, y_1, \mathbf{x}) = g(y_{t-1}, s_t, c_t),$$

where y_t is a one-hot word representation, $g(\cdot)$ is a softmax activation function, and s_t is the hidden state of decoder at time t calculated by

$$s_t = f(y_{t-1}, s_{t-1}, c_t),$$

and $f(\cdot)$ is a non-linear activation function and the transformation $\mathbf{L}$ is often assigned as parameters of $f(\cdot)$. Here $f(\cdot)$ can be a logistic function, the sophisticated long short-term memory (LSTM) unit (Hochreiter and Schmidhuber, 1997), or the recently proposed gated recurrent unit (GRU) (Chung et al., 2014; Cho et al., 2014). Compared to "ungated" logistic function, LSTM and GRU are specially designed for its long term memory: it can store information over extended time steps without too much decay. We use GRU in this work, since it performs comparably to LSTM on squence modeling (Chung et al., 2014; Greff et al., 2015), but has less parameters and easier to train.

We adopt the notation of GRU from (Bahdanau et al., 2014), the hidden state s_t at time t is a linear combination of its previous hidden state s_{t-1} and a new candidate state $\hat{s}_t$:

$$s_t = (1 - z_t) \circ s_{t-1} + z_t \circ \hat{s}_t,$$

where $\circ$ is point-wise multiplication, z_t is the update gate calculated by

$$z_t = \sigma\left(W_z e(y_{t-1}) + U_z s_{t-1} + L_z c_t\right), \quad (1)$$

and $\hat{s}_t$ is calculated by

$$\hat{s}_t = \tanh\left(W e(y_{t-1}) + U(r_t \circ s_{t-1}) + L c_t\right), \quad (2)$$

where the reset gate r_t is calculated by

$$r_t = \sigma\left(W_r e(y_{t-1}) + U_r s_{t-1} + L_r c_t\right). \quad (3)$$

In Equation (1)-(2), and (3), $e(y_{t-1})$ is word embedding of the word y_{t-1}, $\mathbf{L} = \{L, L_z, L_r\}$ specifies the transformations to convert a hidden representation from encoder to that of decoder. In the STC task, $\mathbf{L}$ should have the ability to transform one post (or its segments) to multiple different words of appropriate responses.

3.2 The Computation in Encoder

We consider three types of encoding schemes, namely 1) the global scheme, 2) the local scheme, and the hybrid scheme which combines 1) and 2).

Global Scheme: Figure 4 shows the graphical model of the RNN-encoder and related context generator for a global encoding scheme. The hidden state at time t is calculated by $h_t = f(x_t, h_{t-1})$ (i.e. still GRU unit), and with a trivial context generation operation, we essentially use the final hidden state h_T as the global representation of the sentence. The same strategy has been taken in (Cho et al., 2014) and (Sutskever et al., 2014) for building the intermediate representation for machine translation. This scheme however has its drawbacks: a vectorial summarization of the entire post is often hard to obtain and may lose important details for response generation, especially when the dimension of the hidden state is not big enough[4]. In the reminder of this paper, a NRM with this global encoding scheme is referred to as NRM-glo.

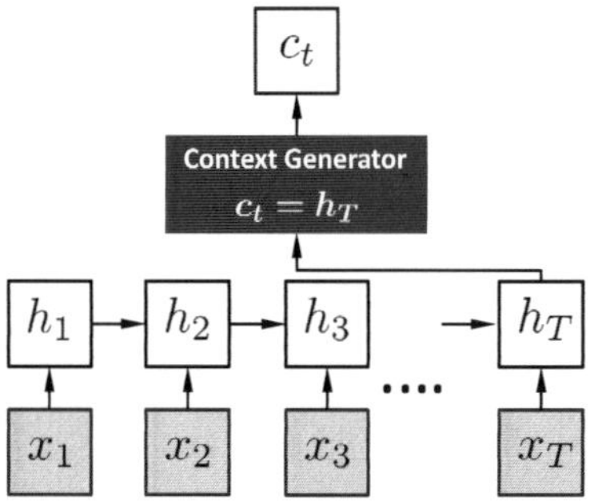

Figure 4: The graphical model of the encoder in NRM-glo, where the last hidden state is used as the context vector $c_t = h_T$.

Local Scheme: Recently, Bahdanau et al. (2014) and Graves (2013) introduced an attention mechanism that allows the decoder to dynamically select and linearly combine different parts of the input sequence $c_t = \sum_{j=1}^{T} \alpha_{tj} h_j$, where weighting factors α_{tj} determine which part should be selected to generate the new word y_t, which in turn is a function of hidden states $\alpha_{tj} = q(h_j, s_{t-1})$, as pictorially shown in Figure 5. Basically, the attention mechanism α_{tj} models the alignment between the inputs around position j and the output at position t, so it can be viewed as a local matching model. This local scheme is devised in (Bahdanau et al., 2014) for automatic alignment be-

[4]Sutskever et al. (2014) has to use 4,000 dimension for satisfying performance on machine translation, while (Cho et al., 2014) with a smaller dimension perform poorly on translating an entire sentence.

tween the source sentence and the partial target sentence in machine translation. This scheme enjoys the advantage of adaptively focusing on some important words of the input text according to the generated words of response. A NRM with this local encoding scheme is referred to as NRM-loc.

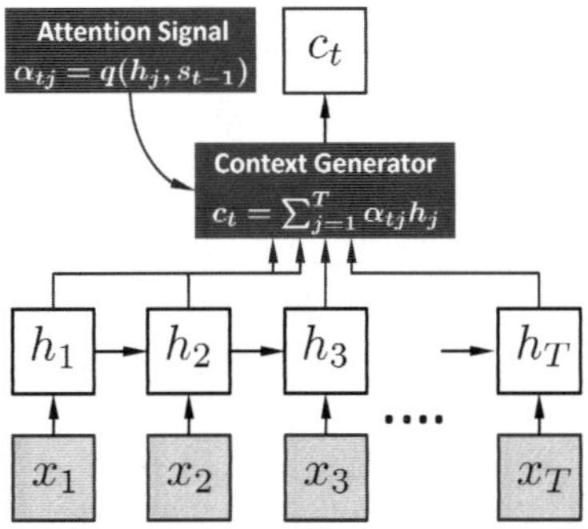

Figure 5: The graphical model of the encoder in NRM-loc, where the weighted sum of hidden sates is used as the context vector $c_t = \sum_{j=1}^{T} \alpha_{tj} h_j$.

3.3 Extensions: Local and Global Model

In the task of STC, NRM-glo has the summarization of the entire post, while NRM-loc can adaptively select the important words in post for various suitable responses. Since post-response pairs in STC are not strictly parallel and a word in different context can have different meanings, we conjecture that the global representation in NRM-glo may provide useful context for extracting the local context, therefore complementary to the scheme in NRM-loc. It is therefore a natural extension to combine the two models by concatenating their encoded hidden states to form an extended hidden representation for each time stamp, as illustrated in Figure 6. We can see the summarization h_T^g is incorporated into c_t and α_{tj} to provide a global context for local matching. With this hybrid method, we hope both the local and global information can be introduced into the generation of response. The model with this context generation mechanism is denoted as NRM-hyb.

It should be noticed that the context generator in NRM-hyb will evoke different encoding mechanisms in the global encoder and the local encoder, although they will be combined later in forming a unified representation. More specifically, the last hidden state of NRM-glo plays a role different from that of the last state of NRM-loc, since it has the responsibility to encode the entire input sentence. This role of NRM-glo, however, tends to be not adequately emphasized in training the hybrid encoder when the parameters of the two encoding RNNs are learned jointly from scratch. For this we use the following trick: we first initialize NRM-hyb with the parameters of NRM-loc and NRM-glo trained separately, then fine tune the parameters in encoder along with training the parameters of decoder.

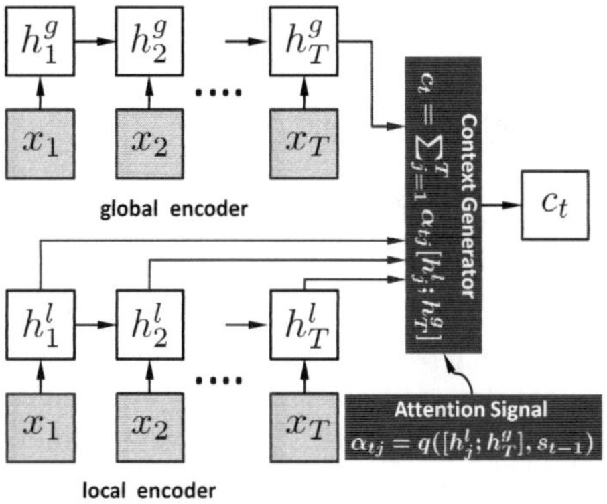

Figure 6: The graphical model for the encoder in NRM-hyb, while context generator function is $c_t = \sum_{j=1}^{T} \alpha_{tj}[h_j^l; h_T^g]$, here $[h_j^l; h_T^g]$ denotes the concatenation of vectors h_j^l and h_T^g

To learn the parameters of the model, we maximize the likelihood of observing the original response conditioned on the post in the training set. For a new post, NRMs generate their responses by using a left-to-right beam search with beam size = 10.

4 Experiments

We evaluate three different settings of NRM described in Section 3, namely NRM-glo, NRM-loc, and NRM-hyb, and compare them to retrieval-based and SMT-based methods.

4.1 Implementation Details

We use Stanford Chinese word segmenter [5] to split the posts and responses into sequences of words. Although both posts and responses are written in the same language, the distributions on words for the two are different: the number of unique words in post text is 125,237, and that of response text is 679,958. We therefore construct two separate vocabularies for posts and responses by using 40,000 most frequent words on each side, covering 97.8%

[5]http://nlp.stanford.edu/software/segmenter.shtml

usage of words for post and 96.2% for response respectively. All the remaining words are replaced by a special token "UNK". The dimensions of the hidden states of encoder and decoder are both 1,000. Model parameters are initialized by randomly sampling from a uniform distribution between -0.1 and 0.1. All our models were trained on a NVIDIA Tesla K40 GPU using stochastic gradient descent (SGD) algorithm with mini-batch. The training stage of each model took about two weeks.

4.2 Competitor Models

Retrieval-based: with retrieval-based models, for any given post p^*, the response r^* is retrieved from a big post-response pairs (p, r) repository. Such models rely on three key components: a big repository, sets of feature functions $\Phi_i(p^*, (p, r))$, and a machine learning model to combine these features. In this work, the whole 4.4 million Weibo pairs are used as the repository, 14 features, ranging from simple cosine similarity to some deep matching models (Ji et al., 2014) are used to determine the suitability of a post to a given post p^* through the following linear model

$$score(p^*, (p, r)) = \sum_i \omega_i \Phi_i(p^*, (p, r)). \quad (4)$$

Following the ranking strategy in (Ji et al., 2014), we pick 225 posts and about 30 retrieved responses for each of them given by a baseline retriever[6] from the 4.4M repository, and manually label them to obtain *labeled* 6,017 post-response pairs. We use ranking SVM model (Joachims, 2006) for the parameters ω_i based on the labeled dataset. In comparison to NRM, only the top one response is considered in the evaluation process.

SMT-based: In SMT-based models, the post-response pairs are directly used as parallel data for training a translation model. We use the most widely used open-source phrase-based translation model-Moses (Koehn et al., 2007). Another parallel data consisting of 3000 post-response pairs is used to tune the system. In (Ritter et al., 2011), the authors used a modified SMT model to obtain the "Response" of Twitter "Stimulus". The main modification is in replacing the standard GIZA++ word alignment model (Och and Ney, 2003) with a new phrase-pair selection method, in which all the possible phrase-pairs in the training data are considered and their associated probabilities are estimated by the Fisher's Exact Test, which yields performance slightly better than default setting[8]. Compared to retrieval-based methods, the generated responses by SMT-based methods often have fluency or even grammatical problems. In this work, we choose the Moses with default settings as our SMT model.

5 Results and Analysis

Automatic evaluation of response generation is still an open problem. The widely accepted evaluation methods in translation (e.g. BLEU score (Papineni et al., 2002)) do not apply, since the range of the suitable responses is so large that it is practically impossible to give reference with adequate coverage. It is also not reasonable to evaluate with Perplexity, a generally used measurement in statistical language modeling, because the naturalness of response and the relatedness to the post can not be well evaluated. We therefore resort to human judgement, similar to that taken in (Ritter et al., 2011) but with an important difference.

5.1 Evaluation Methods

We adopt human annotation to compare the performance of different models. Five labelers with at least three-year experience of Sina Weibo are invited to do human evaluation. Responses obtained from the five evaluated models are pooled and randomly permuted for each labeler. The labelers are instructed to imagine that they were the authors of the original posts and judge whether a response (generated or retrieved) is appropriate and natural to a input post. Three levels are assigned to a response with scores from 0 to 2:

- **Suitable (+2):** the response is evidently an appropriate and natural response to the post;
- **Neutral (+1):** the response can be a suitable response in a *specific* scenario;
- **Unsuitable (0):** it is hard or impossible to find a scenario where response is suitable.

To make the annotation task operable, the suitability of generated responses is judged from the following five criteria:

(a) **Grammar and Fluency**: Responses should be natural language and free of any fluency or grammatical errors;

[6]we use the default similarity function of Lucene [7]

[8]Reported results showed that the new model outperformed the baseline SMT model 57.7% of the time.

Post	意大利禁区里老是八个人... 太夸张了 There are always 8 players at the Italian restricted area. Unbelievable!	Related Criterion	Labels
Response1	我是意大利队的球迷，等待比赛开始。 I am a big fan of the Italy team, waiting for the football game to start	Logic Consistency	Unsuitable
Response2	意大利的食物太美味了 Italian food is absolutely delicious.	Semantic Relevance	Unsuitable
Response3	太夸张了吧! Unbelievable!	Generality	Neutral
Response4	哈哈哈仍然是0: 0 。还没看到进球。 Ha!Ha!Ha! it is still 0:0, no goal so far.	Scenario Dependence	Neutral
Response5	这正是意大利式防守足球。 This is exactly the Italian defending style football game.	——	Suitable

Figure 7: An example post and its five candidate responses with human annotation. The content of the post implies that the football match is already started, while the author of Response1 is still waiting for the match to start. Response2 talks about the food of Italy. Response3 is a widely used response, but it is suitable to this post. Response4 states that the current score is still 0:0, it is a suitable response only in this specific scenario.

Models	Mean Score	Suitable (+2)	Neutral (+1)	Unsuitable (0)	Agreement
NRM-glo	0.969	34.0%	28.9%	37.1%	0.397
NRM-loc	1.065	36.0%	34.5%	29.5%	0.247
NRM-hyb	1.156	39.3%	37.1%	23.6%	0.309
Rtr.-based	0.984	29.8%	38.7%	31.5%	0.346
SMT-based	0.313	5.6 %	20.0%	74.4%	0.448

Table 2: The results of evaluated methods. Mean score is the average value of annotated scores over all annotations. (Rtr.-based means the retrieval-based method)

ID	Post	NRM-glo	NRM-loc	NRM-hyb	Rtr.-based
1	每年元旦都来高烧。 High fever attacks me every New Year's Day	多休息，增强免疫力! Rest more to boost your immune system.	每年元旦都去医院看病 Go to see a doctor every New Year's Day	祝早日康复，身体健康! Get well soon and stay healthy!	高烧... High fever...
2	又老了一岁，感谢我们组，我很高兴 I gain one more year. Grateful to my group, so happy	生日快乐! 永远支持你! Happy birthday! Will stand by you forever!	生日快乐! 永远年轻漂亮! Happy birthday! Wish you always stay young and pretty!	老了老了，岁月不饶人啊! Getting old now. Time has no mercy.	我只是老了一岁 I just gain only one more year.
3	吃素第一天，坚持住，崔朵拉。 First day of being a vegetarian. Hold on, **CuiDuoLa**	必须来支持! 加油! I come to offer my support. Keep it up!	坚持住，坚持下去。 Hold on, keep it up.	每天都是素食主义者 I have been being a vegetarian everyday	坚持住! Hold on!
4	这种天气真应该带个帅锅出去踏青赏花 We should go out with some cute guys to enjoy a great outing in such a nice weather.	这是哪儿啊? 真美! Where is it? It is so beautiful!	阳光明媚，心情舒畅。 Such a nice sunny day! I am in a great mood.	这种天气真不是盖的。 It is indeed a very nice weather.	文山啊 出去踏青寻找灵感 哈哈 **WenShan**, let's go out to get some inspiration. Ha! Ha!

Figure 8: Some responses generated by different models (originally in Chinese with their literal English translation), where the words in boldfaces are entity names.

(b) **Logic Consistency**: Responses should be logically consistent with the test post;

(c) **Semantic Relevance**: Responses should be semantically relevant to the test post;

(d) **Scenario Dependence**: Responses can depend on a specific scenario but should not contradict the first three criteria;

(e) **Generality**: Responses can be general but should not contradict the first three criteria;

If any of the first three criteria (a), (b), and (c) is contradicted, the generated response should be labeled as "Unsuitable". The responses that are general or suitable to post in a specific scenario should be labeled as "Neutral". Figure 7 shows an example of the labeling results of a post and its responses. The first two responses are labeled as "Unsuitable" because of the logic consistency and semantic relevance errors. Response4 depends on the scenario (i.e., the current score is 0:0), and is therefore annotated as "Neutral".

Model A	**Model B**	**Average rankings**	p **value**
NRM-loc	NRM-glo	(1.463, 1.537)	2.01%
NRM-hyb	NRM-glo	(1.434, 1.566)	0.01%
NRM-hyb	NRM-loc	(1.465, 1.535)	3.09%
Rtr.-based	NRM-glo	(1.512, 1.488)	48.1%
Rtr.-based	NRM-loc	(1.533, 1.467)	6.20%
Rtr.-based	**NRM-hyb**	(1.552, 1.448)	0.32%
SMT	**NRM-hyb**	(1.785, 1.215)	0.00 %
SMT	**Rtr.-based**	(1.738, 1.262)	0.00 %

Table 3: p-values and average rankings of Friedman test for pairwise model comparison. (Rtr.-based means the retrieval-based method)

5.2 Results

Our test set consists of 110 posts that do not appear in the training set, with length between 6 to 22 Chinese words and 12.5 words on average. The experimental results based on human annotation are summarized in Table 2, consisting of the ratio of three categories and the agreement among the five labelers for each model. The agreement is evaluated by Fleiss' kappa (Fleiss, 1971), as a statistical measure of inter-rater consistency. Except the SMT-based model, the value of agreement is in a range from 0.2 to 0.4 for all the other models, which should be interpreted as "Fair agreement". The SMT-based model has a relatively higher kappa value 0.448, which is larger than 0.4 and considered as "Moderate agreement", since the responses generated by the SMT often have the fluency and grammatical errors, making it easy to reach an agreement on such unsuitable cases.

From Table 2, we can see the SMT method performs significantly worse than the retrieval-based and NRM models and 74.4% of the generated responses were labeled as unsuitable mainly due to fluency and relevance errors. This observation confirms with our intuition that the STC dataset, with one post potentially corresponding to many responses, can not be simply taken as parallel corpus in a SMT model. Surprisingly, more than 60% of responses generated by all the three NRM are labeled as "Suitable" or "Neutral", which means that most generated responses are fluent and semantically relevant to post. Among all the NRM variants

- NRM-loc outperforms NRM-glo, suggesting that a dynamically generated context might be more effective than a "static" fixed-length vector for the entire post, which is consistent with the observation made in (Bahdanau et al., 2014) for machine translation;
- NRM-hyp outperforms NRM-loc and NRM-glo, suggesting that a global representation of post is complementary to dynamically generated local context.

The retrieval-based model has the similar mean score as NRM-glo, and its ratio on neutral cases outperforms all the other methods. This is because 1) the responses retrieved by retrieval-based method are actually written by human, so they do not suffer from grammatical and fluency problems, and 2) the combination of various feature functions potentially makes sure the picked responses are semantically relevant to test posts. However the picked responses are not customized for new test posts, so the ratio of suitable cases is lower than the three neural generation models.

To test statistical significance, we use the Friedman test (Howell, 2010), which is a non-parametric test on the differences of several related samples, based on ranking. Table 3 shows the average rankings over all annotations and the corresponding p-values for comparisons between different pairs of methods. The comparison between retrieval-based and NRM-glo is not significant and their difference in ranking is tiny. This indicates that the retrieval-based method is comparable to the NRM-glo method. The NRM-hyb outperforms all the other methods, and the difference is statistically significant ($p < 0.05$). The difference between NRM-loc and retrieval-based method is marginal ($p = 0.062$). SMT is significantly worse than retrieval-based and NRM-hyb methods.

5.3 Case Study

Figure 8 shows some example responses generated by our NRMs (only the one with biggest likelihood is given) and the comparable retrieval-based model. It is intriguing to notice that three NRM variants give suitable but quite distinct responses, with different perspectives and choices of words. This, as we conjecture, is caused by both the architecture variations among models as well as the variations from random effects like the initialization of parameters. Another interesting observation is on the fourth example, where the retrieval-based method returns a response with the mismatched entity name "WenShan", which is actually a quite common problem for retrieval-based model, where the inconsistency details (e.g., dates, named entities), which often render the response unsuitable, cannot be adequately considered in the matching function employed in retrieving the responses. In contrast, we observe that NRMs tend to make general response and barely generate those details.

Post	吃素第一天，坚持住，崔朵拉。 First day of being a vegetarian. Hold on, **CuiDuoLa**
R1	坚持住，坚持素食！ Hold on, Keep up your vegetarian diet.
R2	想要健康吗？想要长寿吗？那就关注我的微博吧。 Would you like to be healthy? Would you like to live long? If so, follow me on Weibo.
R3	这就是传说中的吃素吗？ This is the so-called vegetarian diet ?
R4	吃饱了才有力气减肥 Eat up so that you will have enough energy to go for a diet!
R5	身体是革命的本钱，不要着急！ Health is the essence for winning your future battles. No rush!

Figure 9: Multiple responses generated by the NRM-hyb.

We also use the NRM-hyb as an example to investigate the ability of NRM to generate multiple responses. Figure 9 lists 5 responses to the same post, which are gotten with beam search with beam size = 500, among which we keep only the best one (biggest likelihood) for each first word. It can be seen that the responses are fluent, relevant to the post, and still vastly different from each other, validating our initial conjecture that NRM, when fueled with large and rich training corpus, could work as a generator that can cover a lot of modes in its density estimation.

It is worth mentioning that automatic evaluation metrics, such as BLEU (Papineni et al., 2002) as adopted by machine translation and recently SMT-based responding models (Sordoni et al., 2015), do not work very well on this task, especially when the reference responses are few. Our results show that the average BLEU values are less than 2 for all models discussed in this paper, including SMT-based ones, on instances with single reference. Probably more importantly, the ranking given by the BLEU value diverges greatly from the human judgment of response quality.

6 Conclusions and Future Work

In this paper, we explored using encoder-decoder-based neural network system, with coined name Neural Responding Machine, to generate responses to a post. Empirical studies confirm that the newly proposed NRMs, especially the hybrid encoding scheme, can outperform state-of-the-art retrieval-based and SMT-based methods. Our preliminary study also shows that NRM can generate multiple responses with great variety to a given post. In future work, we would consider adding the intention (or sentiment) of users as an external signal of decoder to generate responses with specific goals.

Acknowledgments

The authors would like to thank Tao Cai for technical support. This work is supported in part by China National 973 project 2014CB340301.

References

Michael Auli, Michel Galley, Chris Quirk, and Geoffrey Zweig. 2013. Joint language and translation modeling with recurrent neural networks. In *EMNLP*, pages 1044–1054.

Dzmitry Bahdanau, Kyunghyun Cho, and Yoshua Bengio. 2014. Neural machine translation by jointly learning to align and translate. *arXiv preprint arXiv:1409.0473*.

Kyunghyun Cho, Bart van Merrienboer, Caglar Gulcehre, Fethi Bougares, Holger Schwenk, and Yoshua Bengio. 2014. Learning phrase representations using rnn encoder-decoder for statistical machine translation. *arXiv preprint arXiv:1406.1078*.

Junyoung Chung, Caglar Gulcehre, KyungHyun Cho, and Yoshua Bengio. 2014. Empirical evaluation of gated recurrent neural networks on sequence modeling. *arXiv preprint arXiv:1412.3555*.

Joseph L Fleiss. 1971. Measuring nominal scale agreement among many raters. *Psychological bulletin*, 76(5):378.

Alex Graves. 2013. Generating sequences with recurrent neural networks. *preprint arXiv:1308.0850*.

Klaus Greff, Rupesh Kumar Srivastava, Jan Koutník, Bas R. Steunebrink, and Jürgen Schmidhuber. 2015. LSTM: A search space odyssey. *CoRR*, abs/1503.04069.

Sepp Hochreiter and Jürgen Schmidhuber. 1997. Long short-term memory. *Neural computation*, 9(8):1735–1780.

David C. Howell. 2010. *Fundamental Statistics for the Behavioral Sciences*. PSY 200 (300) Quantitative Methods in Psychology Series. Wadsworth Cengage Learning.

Zongcheng Ji, Zhengdong Lu, and Hang Li. 2014. An information retrieval approach to short text conversation. *arXiv preprint arXiv:1408.6988*.

Thorsten Joachims. 2006. Training linear svms in linear time. In *SIGKDD*, pages 217–226. ACM.

Nal Kalchbrenner and Phil Blunsom. 2013. Recurrent continuous translation models. In *EMNLP*, pages 1700–1709.

Philipp Koehn, Hieu Hoang, Alexandra Birch, Chris Callison-Burch, Marcello Federico, Nicola Bertoldi, Brooke Cowan, Wade Shen, Christine Moran, Richard Zens, et al. 2007. Moses: Open source toolkit for statistical machine translation. In *Proceedings of the 45th annual meeting of the ACL on interactive poster and demonstration sessions*, pages 177–180. ACL.

Diane Litman, Satinder Singh, Michael Kearns, and Marilyn Walker. 2000. Njfun: a reinforcement learning spoken dialogue system. In *Proceedings of the 2000 ANLP/NAACL Workshop on Conversational systems*, pages 17–20. ACL.

Tomas Mikolov, Martin Karafiát, Lukas Burget, Jan Cernockỳ, and Sanjeev Khudanpur. 2010. Recurrent neural network based language model. In *INTERSPEECH 2010*, pages 1045–1048.

Teruhisa Misu, Kallirroi Georgila, Anton Leuski, and David Traum. 2012. Reinforcement learning of question-answering dialogue policies for virtual museum guides. In *SIGDIAL*, pages 84–93. ACL.

Franz Josef Och and Hermann Ney. 2003. A systematic comparison of various statistical alignment models. *Computational linguistics*, 29(1):19–51.

Kishore Papineni, Salim Roukos, Todd Ward, and Wei-Jing Zhu. 2002. Bleu: a method for automatic evaluation of machine translation. In *Proceedings of the 40th annual meeting on association for computational linguistics*, pages 311–318. Association for Computational Linguistics.

Alan Ritter, Colin Cherry, and William B Dolan. 2011. Data-driven response generation in social media. In *EMNLP*, pages 583–593. Association for Computational Linguistics.

Jost Schatzmann, Karl Weilhammer, Matt Stuttle, and Steve Young. 2006. A survey of statistical user simulation techniques for reinforcement-learning of dialogue management strategies. *The knowledge engineering review*, 21(02):97–126.

Alessandro Sordoni, Michel Galley, Michael Auli, Chris Brockett, Yangfeng Ji, Meg Mitchell, Jian-Yun Nie, Jianfeng Gao, and Bill Dolan. 2015. A neural network approach to context-sensitive generation of conversational responses. Conference of the North American Chapter of the Association for Computational Linguistics Human Language Technologies (NAACL-HLT 2015), June.

Ilya Sutskever, Oriol Vinyals, and Quoc VV Le. 2014. Sequence to sequence learning with neural networks. In *NIPS*, pages 3104–3112.

Hao Wang, Zhengdong Lu, Hang Li, and Enhong Chen. 2013. A dataset for research on short-text conversations. In *EMNLP*, pages 935–945.

Jason D Williams and Steve Young. 2007. Partially observable markov decision processes for spoken dialog systems. *Computer Speech & Language*, 21(2):393–422.

Abstractive Multi-Document Summarization via Phrase Selection and Merging*

Lidong Bing[§] **Piji Li**[♮] **Yi Liao**[♮] **Wai Lam**[♮]
Weiwei Guo[†] **Rebecca J. Passonneau**[‡]
[§]Machine Learning Department, Carnegie Mellon University, Pittsburgh, PA USA
[♮]Department of Systems Engineering and Engineering Management,
The Chinese University of Hong Kong
[†]Yahoo Labs, Sunnyvale, CA, USA
[‡]Center for Computational Learning Systems, Columbia University, New York, NY, USA
[§]lbing@cs.cmu.edu, [♮]{pjli, yliao, wlam}@se.cuhk.edu.hk
[†]wguo@yahoo-inc.com, [‡]becky@ccls.columbia.edu

Abstract

We propose an abstraction-based multi-document summarization framework that can construct new sentences by exploring more fine-grained syntactic units than sentences, namely, noun/verb phrases. Different from existing abstraction-based approaches, our method first constructs a pool of concepts and facts represented by phrases from the input documents. Then new sentences are generated by selecting and merging informative phrases to maximize the salience of phrases and meanwhile satisfy the sentence construction constraints. We employ integer linear optimization for conducting phrase selection and merging simultaneously in order to achieve the global optimal solution for a summary. Experimental results on the benchmark data set TAC 2011 show that our framework outperforms the state-of-the-art models under automated pyramid evaluation metric, and achieves reasonably well results on manual linguistic quality evaluation.

1 Introduction

Existing multi-document summarization (MDS) methods fall in three categories: extraction-based, compression-based and abstraction-based. Most summarization systems adopt the **extraction-based** approach which selects some original sentences from the source documents to create a short summary (Erkan and Radev, 2004; Wan et al., 2007). However, the restriction that the whole sentence should be selected potentially yields some overlapping information in the summary. To this end, some researchers apply compression on the selected sentences by deleting words or phrases (Knight and Marcu, 2000; Lin, 2003; Zajic et al., 2006; Harabagiu and Lacatusu, 2010; Li et al., 2015), which is the **compression-based** method. Yet, these compressive summarization models cannot merge facts from different source sentences, because all the words in a summary sentence are solely from one source sentence.

In fact, previous investigations show that human-written summaries are more abstractive, which can be regarded as a result of sentence aggregation and fusion (Cheung and Penn, 2013; Jing and McKeown, 2000). Some works, albeit less popular, have studied **abstraction-based** approach that can construct a sentence whose fragments come from different source sentences. One important work developed by Barzilay and McKeown (2005) employed sentence fusion, followed by (Filippova and Strube, 2008; Filippova, 2010). These works first conduct clustering on sentences to compute the salience of topical themes. Then, sentence fusion is applied within each cluster of related sentences to generate a new sentence containing common information units of the sentences. The abstractive-based approaches gather information across sentence boundary, and hence have the potential to cover more content in a more concise manner.

In this paper, we propose an abstractive MDS framework that can construct new sentences by

* The work described in this paper is substantially supported by grants from the Research and Development Grant of Huawei Technologies Co. Ltd (YB2013090068/TH138232) and the Research Grant Council of the Hong Kong Special Administrative Region, China (Project Codes: 413510 and 14203414).
The work was done when Weiwei Guo was in Columbia University

Proceedings of the 53rd Annual Meeting of the Association for Computational Linguistics and the 7th International Joint Conference on Natural Language Processing, pages 1587–1597,
Beijing, China, July 26-31, 2015.

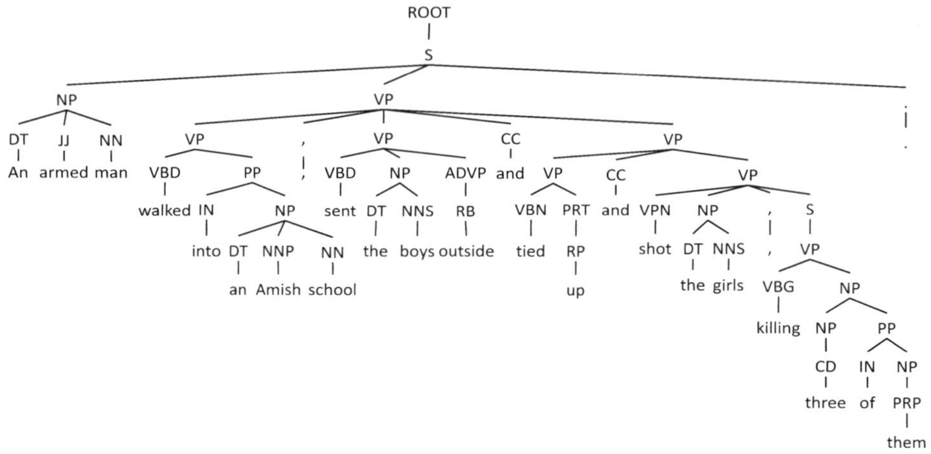

Figure 1: The constituency tree of a sentence from a news document.

exploring more fine-grained syntactic units than sentences, namely, noun/verb phrases (NPs/VPs). This idea is based on two observations. First, the major constituent phrases loosely correspond to the concepts and facts. After reading a set of documents describing the same topic or event, a person digests these documents as key concepts and facts in his/her mind, such as "*an armed man*" and "*walked into an Amish school*" from Figure 1. Second, a summary writer re-organizes the key concepts and facts to form new sentences for the summary. Accordingly, our proposed framework has two major components corresponding to the above observations. The first component creates a pool of concepts and facts represented by NPs and VPs from the input documents. A salience score is computed for each phrase by exploiting redundancy of the document content in a global manner. The second component constructs new sentences by selecting and merging phrases based on their salience scores, and ensures the validity of new sentences using a integer linear optimization model.

The contribution of this paper is two folds. (1) We extract NPs/VPs from constituency trees to represent key concepts/facts, and merge them to construct new sentences, which allows more summary content units (SCUs) (Nenkova and Passonneau, 2004) to be included in a sentence by breaking the original sentence boundaries. (2) The designed optimization framework for addressing the problem is unique and effective. Our optimization algorithm **simultaneously** selects and merges a set of phrases that maximize the number of covered SCUs in a summary. Meanwhile, since the basic unit is phrases, we design compatibility relations among NPs and VPs, as well as other optimization constraints, to ensure that the generated sentences contain correct facts. Compared with the sentence fusion approaches that compute salience scores of sentence clusters, our proposed framework explores a more fine-grained textual unit (i.e., phrases), and maximizes the salience of selected phrases in a global manner.

2 Description of Our Framework

We first introduce how to extract NPs and VPs from constituency trees, and subsequently calculate salience scores for them. Then we formulate the sentence generation task as an optimization problem, and design constraints. In the end, we perform several post-processing steps to improve the order and the readability of the generated sentences.

2.1 Phrase Salience Calculation

The first component decomposes the sentences in documents into a set of noun phrases (NPs) derived from the subject parts of a constituency tree and a set of verb-object phrases (VPs), representing potential key concepts and key facts, respectively. These phrases will serve as the basic elements for sentence generation.

We employ Stanford parser (Klein and Manning, 2003) to obtain a constituency tree for each input sentence. After that, we extract NPs and VPs from the tree as follows: (1) The NPs and VPs that are the direct children of the sentence node (represented by the **S** node) are extracted. (2) VPs (NPs) in a path on which all the nodes are VPs (NPs) are also recursively extracted and regarded as having the same parent node **S**. Recursive operation in the second step will only be carried out in two levels since the phrases in the lower levels may not be able to convey a complete fact. Take the tree in Figure 1 as an example, the corresponding sentence is decomposed into phrases "*An armed man*", "*walked into an Amish school, sent the boys outside and tied up and shot the girls, killing three of them*", "*walked into an Amish school*", "*sent the boys outside*", and "*tied up and shot the girls, killing three of them*". [1] Because of the recursive operation, the extracted phrases may have overlaps. Later, we will show how to avoid such overlapping in phrase selection.

A salience score is calculated for each phrase to indicate its importance. Different types of salience can be incorporated in our framework, such as position-based method (Yih et al., 2007), statistical feature based method (Woodsend and Lapata, 2012), concept-based method (Li et al., 2011), etc. One key characteristic of our approach is that the considered basic units are phrases instead of sentences. Such finer granularity leaves more room for better global salience score by potentially covering more distinct facts. In our implementation, we adopt a concept-based weight incorporating the position information. The concept set is designated to be the union set of unigrams, bigrams, and named entities in the documents. We remove stopwords and perform lemmatization before extracting unigrams and bigrams. The position-based term frequency is used in the concept weighting scheme. When counting the frequency, each occurrence of a concept in an input document is weighted with the paragraph position. The weight larger than 1 is given to the concept occurrences in the first few paragraphs. Specifically, the weight of the first paragraph is B and the weight decreases as the position of the paragraph increases from the beginning of the document. The weighting function is:

$$H(p) = \begin{cases} \rho^p * B & \text{if } p < -(\log B / \log \rho) \\ 1 & \text{otherwise} \end{cases}, \quad (1)$$

where p is the position of the paragraph starting from 0, from beginning of the document, and ρ is a positive constant and smaller than 1. Then, the salience of a phrase is calculated as the summed weights of its concepts.

2.2 New Sentence Construction Model

The construction of new sentences is formulated as an optimization problem which is able to simultaneously generate a group of sentences. Each new sentence is composed of one NP and at least one VP, where the NP and VPs may come from different source sentences. In the process of new sentence generation, the compatibility relation between NP and VP and a variety of summarization requirements are jointly considered.

2.2.1 Compatibility Relation

Compatibility relation is designed to indicate whether an NP and a VP can be used to form a new sentence. For example, the NP "*Police*" from another sentence should not be the subject of the VP "*sent the boys outside*" extracted from Figure 1. We use some heuristics to find compatibility, and then expand the compatibility relation to more phrases by extracting coreference.

To find coreference NPs (different mentions for the same entity), we first conduct coreference resolution for each document with Stanford coreference resolution package (Lee et al., 2013). We adopt those resolution rules that are able to achieve high quality and address our need for summarization. In particular, Sieve 1, 2, 3, 4, 5, 9, and 10 in the package are used. A set of clusters are obtained and each cluster contains the mentions that refer to the same entity in a document. The clusters from different documents in the same topic are merged by matching the named entities. After merging, the mentions that are not NPs extracted in the phrase extraction step are removed in each cluster. Two NPs in the same cluster are determined as alternative of each other.

To find alternative VPs, Jaccard Index is employed as the similarity measure. Specifically, each VP is represented as a set of its concepts and the index value is calculated for each pair of VPs. If the value is larger than a threshold, the two VPs are determined as alternative of each other.

[1] We only consider the recursive operation for a VP with more than one parallel sub-VPs, such as the highest VP in Figure 1. The sub-VPs following modal, link or auxiliary verbs are not extracted as individual VPs. In addition, we also extract the clauses functioning as subjects of sentences as NPs, such as "that clause". Note that we also mention such clauses as "noun phrase" although their syntactic labels could be "SBAR" or "S".

We then define an indicator matrix $\Gamma_{|\mathbf{N}||\mathbf{V}|}$, in which $\Gamma[i,j] = 1$ if an NP N_i and a VP V_j come from the same node **S** in the constituency tree, otherwise, $\Gamma[i,j] = 0$. Let $\tilde{\mathbf{N}}_i$ and $\tilde{\mathbf{V}}_i$ represent the alternative phrases of N_i and V_i as described above. The compatibility matrix $\tilde{\Gamma}_{|\mathbf{N}||\mathbf{V}|}$ is defined as follows:

$$\tilde{\Gamma}[p,q] = \begin{cases} 1 & \text{if } N_p \in \tilde{\mathbf{N}}_i \wedge \Gamma[i,q] = 1 \\ 1 & \text{if } V_q \in \tilde{\mathbf{V}}_j \wedge \Gamma[p,j] = 1 \\ 1 & \text{if } \Gamma[p,q] = 1 \\ 0 & \text{otherwise} \end{cases} \quad (2)$$

where $\tilde{\Gamma}[p,q] = 1$ means N_p and V_q are compatible/permitted for constructing a new sentence. $\tilde{\Gamma}$ is the final compatibility matrix that we use in the optimization. The first case of Equation 2 implies that if N_p and N_i are coreferent, N_p can replace N_i and serve as the subject of N_i's VP (i.e., V_q). The second case implies that if V_q is very similar to V_j, V_q can be concatenated to V_j's NP (i.e., N_p).

2.2.2 Phrase-based Content Optimization

The overall objective function of our optimization formulation to select NPs and VPs is defined as:

$$\max\{\sum_i \alpha_i S_i^N - \sum_{i<j} \alpha_{ij}(S_i^N + S_j^N)R_{ij}^N + \sum_i \beta_i S_i^V - \sum_{i<j} \beta_{ij}(S_i^V + S_j^V)R_{ij}^V\}, \quad (3)$$

where α_i and β_i are selection indicators for the NP N_i and the VP V_i, respectively. S_i^N and S_i^V are the salience scores of N_i and V_i. α_{ij} and β_{ij} are co-occurrence indicators of pairs (N_i, N_j) and (V_i, V_j). R_{ij}^N and R_{ij}^V are the similarity of pairs (N_i, N_j) and (V_i, V_j). If N_i and N_j are coreferent, $R_{ij}^N = 1$. Otherwise, the similarity is calculated with the above Jaccard Index based method. The notations are summarized in Table 1.

Specifically, we maximize the salience score of the selected NPs and VPs as indicated by the first and the third terms in Equation 3, and penalize the selection of similar NP pairs and similar VP pairs as indicated by the second and the fourth terms. Meanwhile, the phrase selection is governed by a set of constraints so that the selected phrases can generate valid sentences. The constraints will be explained in details in Section 2.2.3.

One characteristic of our objective function is that NPs and VPs are treated differently, i.e., there are different selection/penalty terms for NP and VP. Such design enables us to avoid the false penalty between an NP and a VP. For example, the algorithm produces two sentences: the first sentence is "*the gunman shot ...*" with an NP "*the gunman*", and the other sentence has a VP "*confirmed the gunman died*". Obviously, we should not penalize the redundancy between them, because mentioning the gunman is necessary in both sentences.

Notation	Description
N_i, V_i	Noun phrase i and verb phrase i
α_i, β_i	Selection indicators of N_i and V_i
α_{ij}, β_{ij}	Co-occurrence indicators of pairs (N_i, N_j) and (V_i, V_j)
S_i^N, S_i^V	Salience scores of N_i and V_i
R_{ij}^N, R_{ij}^V	Similarity of pair (N_i, N_j) and pair (V_i, V_j)
$\Gamma_{\|\mathbf{N}\|\|\mathbf{V}\|}$	$\Gamma[i,j] = 1$ if N_i and V_j are from the same sentence
$\tilde{\mathbf{N}}_i$, $\tilde{\mathbf{V}}_i$	The alternative phrases of N_i and V_i
$\tilde{\Gamma}_{\|\mathbf{N}\|\|\mathbf{V}\|}$	$\tilde{\Gamma}[i,j] = 1$ means N_i and V_j are compatible for being used to construct a new sentence
$\tilde{\gamma}_{ij}$	Sentence generation indicator for N_i and V_j if $\tilde{\Gamma}[i,j] = 1$

Table 1: Notations.

2.2.3 Sentence Generation Constraints

To summarize the related sentences in the documents, human writers usually merge the important facts in different VPs about the same entity into a single sentence, and omit the trivial facts. Also, the same entity is likely to be described by coreferent NPs. Therefore, in our approach, only one NP is selected and employed as the subject of the newly generated sentence, which is then concatenated with the merged facts (i.e., VPs). If the compatibility entry $\tilde{\Gamma}[i,j]$ for N_i and V_j is 1, we define a sentence generation indicator $\tilde{\gamma}_{ij}$ to indicate whether both N_i and V_j are selected to construct a new sentence in the summary.

We design the following groups of constraints to realize our aim of phrase selection and new sentence construction. The objective function and constraints are linear, therefore the problem can be solved by existing Integer Linear Programming (ILP) solvers such as simplex algorithm (Dantzig and Thapa, 1997).

`NP validity`. To maintain the consistency between the selection indicator α and the compatibility entry $\tilde{\Gamma}$ for NP N_i, we introduce two constraints as follows:

$$\forall i,j, \alpha_i \geq \tilde{\gamma}_{ij}; \quad \forall i, \sum_j \tilde{\gamma}_{ij} \geq \alpha_i. \quad (4)$$

These two constraints work together to ensure the valid assignment of α according to the compatibility entry $\tilde{\Gamma}$.

`VP legality`. Similarly, the following requirement guarantees the consistency between the selection indicator β and the compatibility entry $\tilde{\Gamma}$ for selected VP V_i:

$$\forall j, \sum_i \tilde{\gamma}_{ij} = \beta_j. \quad (5)$$

The above two constraints jointly ensure that the selected NPs and VPs are able to form new summary sentences according to the values of sentence generation indicators.

`Not i-within-i`. Two phrases in the same path of a constituency tree cannot be chosen at the same time:

$$\begin{aligned} &\text{if } \exists V_k \rightsquigarrow V_j, \text{then } \beta_k + \beta_j \leq 1, \\ &\text{if } \exists N_k \rightsquigarrow N_j, \text{then } \alpha_k + \alpha_j \leq 1. \end{aligned} \quad (6)$$

For example, "*walked into an Amish school, sent the boys outside and tied up and shot the girls, killing three of them*" and "*walked into an Amish school*" cannot be both incorporated in the summary, because of the obvious redundancy.

`Phrase co-occurrence`. These constraints control the co-occurrence relation of NPs or VPs. For NPs, we introduce three constraints:

$$\alpha_{ij} - \alpha_i \leq 0, \quad (7)$$

$$\alpha_{ij} - \alpha_j \leq 0, \quad (8)$$

$$\alpha_i + \alpha_j - \alpha_{ij} \leq 1. \quad (9)$$

Constraints 7 to 9 ensure a valid solution of NP selection. The first two constraints state that if the units N_i and N_j co-occur in the summary (i.e., $\alpha_{ij} = 1$), then we have to include them individually (i.e., $\alpha_i = 1$ and $\alpha_j = 1$). The third constraint is the inverse of the first two. Similarly, the constraints for VPs are as follows:

$$\beta_{ij} - \beta_i \leq 0, \quad (10)$$

$$\beta_{ij} - \beta_j \leq 0, \quad (11)$$

$$\beta_i + \beta_j - \beta_{ij} \leq 1. \quad (12)$$

`Sentence number`. In abstractive summarization, we do not prefer to generate many short sentences. This is controlled by:

$$\sum_i \alpha_i \leq K, \quad (13)$$

where K is the maximum number of sentences.

`Short sentence avoidance`. We do not select the VPs from very short sentences because a short sentence normally cannot convey a complete key fact (Woodsend and Lapata, 2012).

$$\text{if } l(\mathbf{S}) < M, V_i \in \mathbf{S}, \text{then } \beta_i = 0, \quad (14)$$

where M is the threshold of the sentence length.

`Pronoun avoidance`. We exclude the NPs that are pronouns from being selected as the subject of the new sentences. As previously observed (Woodsend and Lapata, 2012), pronouns are normally not used by human summary writers. It is because the summary is short and the narration relation of sentences is relatively simple so that pronouns are not needed. Moreover, in automatic summary, pronouns will cause ambiguity in the summary, especially when the sentence order is automatically determined. Therefore, we model the constraint as:

$$\text{if } N_i \ is\ pronoun, \text{then } \alpha_i = 0. \quad (15)$$

`Length constraint`. The overall length of the selected NPs and VPs is no larger than a limit L:

$$\sum_i \{l(N_i) * \alpha_i\} + \sum_j \{l(V_j) * \beta_j\} \leq L, \quad (16)$$

where $l()$ is the word-based length of a phrase.

2.3 Postprocessing

Recall that we require that one NP and at least one VP compose a sentence. Thus, we form a raw sentence with a selected NP as the subject followed by the corresponding selected VPs that are indicated by sentence generation indicator $\tilde{\gamma}_{ij}$ having the value 1. The VPs in a summary sentence are ordered according to their natural order if they come from the same document. Otherwise, they are ordered according to the timestamps of the corresponding documents. After that, if the total length is smaller than L, we add conjunctions such as "and" and "then" to concatenate the VPs for improving the readability of the newly generated sentences. The pseudo-timestamp of a sentence is defined as the earliest timestamp of its VPs and the sentences are ordered based on their pseudo-timestamps.

2.4 Relation to Existing MDS Approaches

Many existing extraction-based and compression-based MDS approaches could be regarded as special cases under our framework: (1) To simulate extraction-based summarization, we just need to constrain that the highest NP and the highest VP from the same sentence are selected simultaneously. In addition, no NPs and VPs in lower levels can be selected. Thus, the output only contains the original sentences of the source documents. (2) To simulate compression-based summarization, we can adapt our framework to conduct sentence selection and sentence compression in a joint manner. Specifically, we only need to restrict that the NP and VPs of a summary sentence must come from the same original sentence.

3 Experiments

3.1 Experimental Setup

The data set of traditional summarization task in Text Analysis Conference (TAC) 2011 is used to evaluate the performance of our approach. This data set is the latest one and it contains 44 topics. Each topic falls into one of 5 predefined event categories and contains 10 related news documents. There are four writers to write model summaries for each topic.

The data set of traditional summarization task in TAC 2010 is employed as the development/tuning data set. This data set contains 46 topics from the same predefined categories. Each topic also has 10 documents and 4 model summaries.

Based on the tuning set, the key parameters of our model are set as follows. The constants B and ρ in the weighting function are set to 6 and 0.5 repectively. The similarity threshold in obtaining the alternative VPs is 0.75. We did not observe significant difference between cosine similarity and Jaccard Index.

We mainly evaluate the system by pyramid evaluation. To gain a comprehensive understanding, we also evaluate by ROUGE evaluation and manual linguistic quality evaluation.

3.2 Results with Pyramid Evaluation

The pyramid evaluation metric (Nenkova and Passonneau, 2004) involves semantic matching of summary content units (SCUs) so as to recognize alternate realizations of the same meaning. Different weights are assigned to SCUs based on their frequency in model summaries. A weighted inventory of SCUs named a pyramid is created, which constitutes a resource for investigating alternate realizations of the same meaning. Such property makes pyramid method more suitable to evaluate summaries. Another widely used evaluation metric is ROUGE (Lin and Hovy, 2003) and it evaluates summaries from word overlapping perspective. Because of the strict string matching, it ignores the semantic content units and performs better when larger sets of model summaries are available. In contrast to ROUGE, pyramid scoring is robust with as few as four model summaries (Nenkova and Passonneau, 2004). Therefore, in recent summarization evaluation workshops such as TAC, the pyramid is used as the major metric.

System	Auto-pyr (Th: .6)	Auto-pyr (Th: .65)	Rank in TAC 2011
Our	0.905	0.793	NA
22	0.878	0.775	1
43	0.875	0.756	2
17	0.860	0.741	3

Table 2: Comparison with the top 3 systems in TAC 2011.

Since manual pyramid evaluation is time-consuming, and the exact evaluation scores are not reproducible especially when the assessors for our results are different from those of TAC, we employ the automated version of pyramid proposed in (Passonneau et al., 2013). The automated pyramid scoring procedure relies on distributional semantics to assign SCUs to a target summary. Specifically, all n-grams within sentence bounds are extracted, and converted into 100 dimension latent topical vectors via a weighted matrix factorization model (Guo and Diab, 2012). Similarly, the contributors and the label of an SCU are transformed into 100 dimensional vector representations. An SCU is assigned to a summary if there exists an n-gram such that the similarity score between the SCU low dimensional vector and the n-gram low dimensional vector exceeds a threshold. Passonneau et al. (2013) showed that the distributional similarity based method produces automated scores that correlate well with manual pyramid scores, yielding more accurate pyramid scores than string matching based automated methods (Harnly et al., 2005). In this paper, we adopt the same setting as in (Passonneau et al., 2013): a 100 dimension matrix factorization model is learned on a domain independent corpus, which is drawn from sense definitions of WordNet and Wiktionary[2], and Brown corpus. We exper-

[2]http://en.wiktionary.org/

	ROUGE-2			ROUGE-SU4		
System	P	R	F1	P	R	F1
Our	0.117	0.117	0.117	0.148	0.147	0.148
22	0.112	0.114	0.113	0.147	0.150	0.148
43	0.132	0.135	0.134	0.162	0.166	0.164
17	0.128	0.131	0.129	0.157	0.160	0.159

Table 3: Performance under ROUGE metric.

iment with 2 threshold values, i.e., 0.6 and 0.65, similar to those used in (Passonneau et al., 2013).

The top three systems in TAC 2011 evaluated with manual pyramid score were System 22 (Li et al., 2011), 43, and 17 (Ng et al., 2011). Table 2 shows the comparison with them under the automated pyramid evaluation. Our method achieves the best results in both thresholds, which means that our method is able to find more semantic content units (SCUs) than the state-of-the-art system in TAC 2011. In addition, paired t-test (with $p < 0.01$) comparing our model with the best system in TAC 2011, i.e., System 22, shows that the performance of our model is significantly better. It is worth noting that the three systems used additional external linguistic resources: System 22 used a Wikipedia corpus for providing domain knowledge, System 17 and 43 defined some category-specific features. Without any domain adaption, our framework can still achieve encouraging performance.

We calculate Pearson's correlation to measure how well the automatic pyramid approximates the manual pyramid scores for 50 system submissions in TAC 2011. The values are 0.91 and 0.93 for thresholds 0.6 and 0.65 respectively. It demonstrates that the automated pyramid is reliable to differentiate the performance of different methods.

3.3 Results with ROUGE Evaluation

As mentioned above, we favor the pyramid evaluation over the ROUGE score because it can measure the summary quality beyond simply string matching. Here, we also provide ROUGE score for our reference. ROUGE-1.5.5 package[3] is employed with the same parameters as in TAC. The results are summarized in Table 3. Our performance is slightly better than System 22, and it is not as good as System 43 and 17. The reason is that System 43 and 17 used category-specific features and trained the feature weights with the category information in TAC 2010 data. These features help them select better category-specific content for the summary. However, the usability of such features depends on the availability of predefined categories in the summarization task, as well as the availability of training data with the same predefined categories for estimating feature weights. Therefore, the adaptability of these methods is limited to some extent. In contrast, our framework does not define any category-specific feature and only uses TAC 2010 data to tune the parameters for general summarization purpose.

[3]http://www.berouge.com/Pages/default.aspx

3.4 Linguistic Quality Evaluation

The linguistic quality of summaries is evaluated using the five linguistic quality questions on grammaticality (Q1), non-redundancy (Q2), referential clarity (Q3), focus (Q4), and coherence (Q5) in Document Understanding Conferences (DUC). A Likert scale with five levels is employed with 5 being very good with 1 being very poor. A summary was blindly evaluated by three assessors on each question. System 22 performed better than System 43 and 17 in TAC 2011 on the evaluation of readability, which is an aggregation of the above questions. Considering the intensive labor force of manual assessment, we only conduct comparison with System 22.

The results are given in Table 4. On average, the two systems perform very closely. System 22 is an extraction-based method that picks the original sentences, hence it achieves higher score in Q1 grammaticality, while our approach has some new sentences with grammar mistakes, which is a common problem for abstractive methods and deserves more future research effort. For Q4 focus, our score is higher than System 22, which reveals that our summary sentences are relatively more cohesive. The score of Q3 referential clarity shows that the referential relation is basically clear in our summaries, even when new sentences are automatically generated. In general, ignoring the grammaticality scores, our system still performs better than System 22. Specifically, the average scores of our system and System 22 on the last four questions are 3.37 and 3.33 respectively.

4 Qualitative Results

4.1 Analysis of Summary Sentence Type

There are three types of sentences in the summaries generated by our framework, namely, new

System	Q1	Q2	Q3	Q4	Q5	AVG
Our	3.67	3.50	3.90	3.23	2.83	3.43
22	4.13	3.50	3.97	2.97	2.87	3.49

Table 4: Evaluation of linguistic quality.

sentences, compressed sentences, and original sentences. A new sentence is constructed by merging the phrases from different original sentences. A compressed sentence is generated by deleting phrases from an original sentence. An original sentence in the summary is directly extracted from the input documents.

The percentage of different types of sentences in our summaries is calculated. About 33% of the summary sentences are newly constructed. This demonstrates that our framework has good capability of merging phrases from the original sentences so as to convey more information in compacted summaries. In addition, about 44% of the summary sentences are generated by compression. It shows a unique characteristic of our framework: sentence construction and sentence compression are conducted in a unified model.

4.2 Case Study

Table 5 shows the summary of the first topic, i.e., "*Amish Shooting*", by our framework. The summary sentence ID and the sentence type are given in the form of "`[summary sentence ID: sentence type]`". Each selected phrase and the original sentence ID where the phrase originated are given in the form of "{`selected phrase (original sentence ID)`}". There are three compressed sentences with IDs 1, 2, and 4, one new sentence with ID 3, and two original sentences with IDs 5 and 6.

The new sentence is constructed from the following original sentences in which the extracted NPs and VPs are indicated with colored parentheses:

`(84)`: On Monday morning, (NP Charles Carl Roberts IV) (VP (VP entered the West Nickel Mines Amish School in Lancaster County) and (VP shot 10 girls), (VP killing five)).
`(85)`: (NP Roberts) (VP killed himself as police stormed the building).
`(150)`: (NP Roberts) (VP left what they described as rambling notes for his family).

`[1:C]` {An armed man `(25)`} {walked into an Amish school `(25)`} {tied up and shot the girls, killing three of them. `(25)`} `[2:C]` {A man who laid siege to a one-room Amish schoolhouse `(64)`} {told his wife shortly before opening fire that he had molested two young girls who were his relatives decades ago `(64)`} {was tormented by dreams of molesting again. `(64)`} `[3:N]` {Charles Carl Roberts IV `(84)`} {killed himself as police stormed the building `(85)`} {left what they described as rambling notes for his family. `(150)`} `[4:C]` {The gunman `(145)`} {was not Amish `(145)`} {had not attended the school. `(145)`} `[5:O]` {The shootings `(148)`} {occurred about 10:45 a.m. `(148)`} `[6:O]` {Police `(149)`} {could offer no explanation for the killings. `(149)`}

Table 5: The summary of "*Amish Shooting*" topic.

The NPs of these sentences are coreferent so that some of their VPs are merged and concatenated with one NP, i.e., "*Charles Carl Roberts IV*".

The summary sentences with IDs 1, 2, and 4 are compressions from the following original sentences respectively:

`(25)`: (NP An armed man) (VP (VP walked into an Amish school), (VP sent the boys outside) and (VP tied up and shot the girls, killing three of them)), (NP authorities) (VP said).
`(64)`: (NP (NP A man) who laid siege to a one-room Amish schoolhouse), (VP killing five girls), (VP (VP told his wife shortly before opening fire that he had molested two young girls who were his relatives decades ago) and (VP was tormented by "dreams of molesting again")), (NP authorities) (VP said Tue).
`(145)`: According to media reports, (NP the gunman) (VP (VP was not Amish) and (VP had not attended the school)).

Some uncritical information is excluded from the summary sentences, such as "*sent the boys outside*", "*authorities said*", etc. In addition, the VP "*killing five girls*" of the original sentence with ID 64 is also excluded since it has significant redundancy with the summary sentence with ID 1.

5 Related Work

Existing multi-document summarization (MDS) works can be classified into three categories:

extraction-based approaches, compression-based approaches, and abstraction-based approaches.

Extraction-based approaches are the most studied of the three. Early studies mainly followed a greedy strategy in sentence selection (Çelikyilmaz and Hakkani-Tür, 2011; Goldstein et al., 2000; Wan et al., 2007). Each sentence in the documents is firstly assigned a salience score. Then, sentence selection is performed by greedily selecting the sentence with the largest salience score among the remaining ones. The redundancy is controlled during the selection by penalizing the remaining ones according to their similarity with the selected sentences. An obvious drawback of such greedy strategy is that it is easily trapped in local optima. Later, unified models are proposed to conduct sentence selection and redundancy control simultaneously (McDonald, 2007; Filatova and Hatzivassiloglou, 2004; Yih et al., 2007; Gillick et al., 2007; Lin and Bilmes, 2010; Lin and Bilmes, 2012; Sipos et al., 2012). However, extraction-based approaches are unable to evaluate the salience and control the redundancy on the granularity finer than sentences. Thus, the selected sentences may still contain unimportant or redundant phrases.

Compression-based approaches have been investigated to alleviate the above limitation. As a natural extension of the extractive method, the early works adopted a two-step approach (Lin, 2003; Zajic et al., 2006; Gillick and Favre, 2009). The first step selects the sentences, and the second step removes the unimportant or redundant units from the sentences. Recently, integrated models have been proposed that jointly conduct sentence extraction and compression (Martins and Smith, 2009; Woodsend and Lapata, 2010; Almeida and Martins, 2013; Berg-Kirkpatrick et al., 2011; Li et al., 2015). Note that our model also jointly conducts phrase selection and phrase merging (new sentence generation). Nonetheless, compressive methods are unable to merge the related facts from different sentences.

On the other hand, abstraction-based approaches can generate new sentences based on the facts from different source sentences. In addition to the previously mentioned sentence fusion work, new directions have been explored. Researchers developed an information extraction based approach that extracts *information items* (Genest and Lapalme, 2011) or *abstraction schemes* (Genest and Lapalme, 2012) as components for generating sentences. Summary revision was also investigated to improve the quality of automatic summary by rewriting the noun phrases or people references in the summaries (Nenkova, 2008; Siddharthan et al., 2011). Sentence generation with word graph was applied for summarizing customer opinions and chat conversations (Ganesan et al., 2010; Mehdad et al., 2014).

Recently, the factors of information certainty and timeline in MDS task were explored (Ng et al., 2014; Wan and Zhang, 2014; Yan et al., 2011). Researchers also explored some variants of the typical MDS setting, such as query-chain focused summarization that combines aspects of update summarization and query-focused summarization (Baumel et al., 2014), and hierarchical summarization that scales up MDS to summarize a large set of documents (Christensen et al., 2014). A data-driven method for mining sentence structures on large news archive was proposed and utilized to summarize unseen news events (Pighin et al., 2014). Moreover, some works (Liu et al., 2012; Kågebäck et al., 2014; Denil et al., 2014; Cao et al., 2015) utilized deep learning techniques to tackle some summarization tasks.

6 Conclusions and Future Work

We propose an abstractive MDS framework that constructs new sentences by exploring more fine-grained syntactic units, namely, noun phrases and verb phrases. The designed optimization framework operates on the summary level so that more complementary semantic content units can be incorporated. The phrase selection and merging is done simultaneously to achieve global optimal. Meanwhile, the constructed sentences should satisfy the constraints related to summarization requirements such as NP/VP compatibility. Experimental results on TAC 2011 summarization data set show that our framework outperforms the top systems in TAC 2011 under the pyramid metric. For future work, one aspect is to enhance the grammar quality of the generated new sentences and compressed sentences. Another aspect is to improve time efficiency of our framework, and its major bottleneck is the time consuming ILP optimzation.

References

Miguel Almeida and Andre Martins. 2013. Fast and robust compressive summarization with dual decomposition and multi-task learning. In *ACL*, pages 196–206.

Regina Barzilay and Kathleen R. McKeown. 2005. Sentence fusion for multidocument news summarization. *Comput. Linguist.*, 31(3):297–328.

Tal Baumel, Raphael Cohen, and Michael Elhadad. 2014. Query-chain focused summarization. In *ACL*, pages 913–922.

Taylor Berg-Kirkpatrick, Dan Gillick, and Dan Klein. 2011. Jointly learning to extract and compress. In *HLT*, pages 481–490.

Ziqiang Cao, Furu Wei, Li Dong, Sujian Li, and Ming Zhou. 2015. Ranking with recursive neural networks and its application to multi-document summarization. In *AAAI*.

Asli Çelikyilmaz and Dilek Hakkani-Tür. 2011. Concept-based classification for multi-document summarization. In *ICASSP*, pages 5540–5543.

Jackie Chi Kit Cheung and Gerald Penn. 2013. Towards robust abstractive multi-document summarization: A caseframe analysis of centrality and domain. In *ACL*, pages 1233–1242.

Janara Christensen, Stephen Soderland, Gagan Bansal, and Mausam. 2014. Hierarchical summarization: Scaling up multi-document summarization. In *ACL*, pages 902–912.

George B. Dantzig and Mukund N. Thapa. 1997. *Linear Programming 1: Introduction*. Springer-Verlag New York, Inc.

Misha Denil, Alban Demiraj, Nal Kalchbrenner, Phil Blunsom, and Nando de Freitas. 2014. Modelling, visualising and summarising documents with a single convolutional neural network. *arXiv preprint arXiv:1406.3830*.

Günes Erkan and Dragomir R. Radev. 2004. Lexrank: Graph-based lexical centrality as salience in text summarization. *J. Artif. Int. Res.*, 22(1):457–479.

Elena Filatova and Vasileios Hatzivassiloglou. 2004. A formal model for information selection in multi-sentence text extraction. In *COLING*.

Katja Filippova and Michael Strube. 2008. Sentence fusion via dependency graph compression. In *EMNLP*, pages 177–185.

Katja Filippova. 2010. Multi-sentence compression: Finding shortest paths in word graphs. In *COLING*, pages 322–330.

Kavita Ganesan, ChengXiang Zhai, and Jiawei Han. 2010. Opinosis: A graph-based approach to abstractive summarization of highly redundant opinions. In *COLING*, pages 340–348.

Pierre-Etienne Genest and Guy Lapalme. 2011. Framework for abstractive summarization using text-to-text generation. In *MTTG*, pages 64–73.

Pierre-Etienne Genest and Guy Lapalme. 2012. Fully abstractive approach to guided summarization. In *ACL*, pages 354–358.

Dan Gillick and Benoit Favre. 2009. A scalable global model for summarization. In *Workshop on ILP for NLP*, pages 10–18.

Dan Gillick, Benoit Favre, and Dilek Hakkani-tür. 2007. The icsi summarization system at tac 2008. In *Proc. of Text Understanding Conference*.

Jade Goldstein, Vibhu Mittal, Jaime Carbonell, and Mark Kantrowitz. 2000. Multi-document summarization by sentence extraction. In *NAACL-ANLP-AutoSum*, pages 40–48.

Weiwei Guo and Mona Diab. 2012. Modeling sentences in the latent space. In *ACL*, pages 864–872.

Sanda Harabagiu and Finley Lacatusu. 2010. Using topic themes for multi-document summarization. *ACM Trans. Inf. Syst.*, 28(3):13:1–13:47.

Aaron Harnly, Ani Nenkova, Rebecca Passonneau, and Owen Rambow. 2005. Automation of summary evaluation by the pyramid method. In *RANLP*.

Hongyan Jing and Kathleen R. McKeown. 2000. Cut and paste based text summarization. In *NAACL*, pages 178–185.

Mikael Kågebäck, Olof Mogren, Nina Tahmasebi, and Devdatt Dubhashi. 2014. Extractive summarization using continuous vector space models. In *CVSC@EACL*, pages 31–39.

Dan Klein and Christopher D. Manning. 2003. Accurate unlexicalized parsing. In *ACL*, pages 423–430.

Kevin Knight and Daniel Marcu. 2000. Statistics-based summarization - step one: Sentence compression. In *AAAI-IAAI*, pages 703–710.

Heeyoung Lee, Angel Chang, Yves Peirsman, Nathanael Chambers, Mihai Surdeanu, and Dan Jurafsky. 2013. Deterministic coreference resolution based on entity-centric, precision-ranked rules. *Comput. Linguist.*, 39(4):885–916.

Huiying Li, Yue Hu, Zeyuan Li, Xiaojun Wan, and Jianguo Xiao. 2011. Pkutm participation in tac2011. In *Proceedings of TAC*.

Piji Li, Lidong Bing, Wai Lam, Hang Li, and Yi Liao. 2015. Reader-aware multi-document summarization via sparse coding. In *IJCAI*.

Hui Lin and Jeff Bilmes. 2010. Multi-document summarization via budgeted maximization of submodular functions. In *HLT*, pages 912–920.

Hui Lin and Jeff Bilmes. 2012. Learning mixtures of submodular shells with application to document summarization. In *UAI*, pages 479–490.

Chin-Yew Lin and Eduard Hovy. 2003. Automatic evaluation of summaries using n-gram co-occurrence statistics. In *NAACL*, pages 71–78.

Chin-Yew Lin. 2003. Improving summarization performance by sentence compression: a pilot study. In *Proceedings of the sixth international workshop on Information retrieval with Asian languages-Volume 11*, pages 1–8. Association for Computational Linguistics.

Yan Liu, Sheng-hua Zhong, and Wenjie Li. 2012. Query-oriented multi-document summarization via unsupervised deep learning. In *AAAI*.

André F. T. Martins and Noah A. Smith. 2009. Summarization with a joint model for sentence extraction and compression. In *Workshop on ILP for NLP*, pages 1–9.

Ryan McDonald. 2007. A study of global inference algorithms in multi-document summarization. In *ECIR*, pages 557–564.

Yashar Mehdad, Giuseppe Carenini, and Raymond T. Ng. 2014. Abstractive summarization of spoken and written conversations based on phrasal queries. In *ACL*, pages 1220–1230.

Ani Nenkova and Rebecca J. Passonneau. 2004. Evaluating content selection in summarization: The pyramid method. In *HLT-NAACL*, pages 145–152.

Ani Nenkova. 2008. Entity-driven rewrite for multi-document summarization. In *Third International Joint Conference on Natural Language Processing, IJCNLP*, pages 118–125.

Jun-Ping Ng, Praveen Bysani, Ziheng Lin, Min yen Kan, and Chew lim Tan. 2011. Swing: Exploiting category-specific information for guided summarization. In *Proceedings of TAC*.

Jun-Ping Ng, Yan Chen, Min-Yen Kan, and Zhoujun Li. 2014. Exploiting timelines to enhance multi-document summarization. In *ACL*, pages 923–933.

Rebecca J. Passonneau, Emily Chen, Weiwei Guo, and Dolores Perin. 2013. Automated pyramid scoring of summaries using distributional semantics. In *ACL (2)*, pages 143–147.

Daniele Pighin, Marco Cornolti, Enrique Alfonseca, and Katja Filippova. 2014. Modelling events through memory-based, open-ie patterns for abstractive summarization. In *ACL*, pages 892–901.

Advaith Siddharthan, Ani Nenkova, and Kathleen McKeown. 2011. Information status distinctions and referring expressions: An empirical study of references to people in news summaries. *Comput. Linguist.*, 37(4):811–842.

Ruben Sipos, Pannaga Shivaswamy, and Thorsten Joachims. 2012. Large-margin learning of submodular summarization models. In *EACL*, pages 224–233.

Xiaojun Wan and Jianmin Zhang. 2014. Ctsum: Extracting more certain summaries for news articles. In *SIGIR*, pages 787–796.

Xiaojun Wan, Jianwu Yang, and Jianguo Xiao. 2007. Manifold-ranking based topic-focused multi-document summarization. In *IJCAI*, pages 2903–2908.

Kristian Woodsend and Mirella Lapata. 2010. Automatic generation of story highlights. In *ACL*, pages 565–574.

Kristian Woodsend and Mirella Lapata. 2012. Multiple aspect summarization using integer linear programming. In *EMNLP-CoNLL*, pages 233–243.

Rui Yan, Xiaojun Wan, Jahna Otterbacher, Liang Kong, Xiaoming Li, and Yan Zhang. 2011. Evolutionary timeline summarization: A balanced optimization framework via iterative substitution. In *SIGIR*, pages 745–754.

Wen-tau Yih, Joshua Goodman, Lucy Vanderwende, and Hisami Suzuki. 2007. Multi-document summarization by maximizing informative content-words. In *IJCAI*, pages 1776–1782.

David M. Zajic, Bonnie J. Dorr, Jimmy Lin, and Richard Schwartz. 2006. Sentence compression as a component of a multi-document summarization system. In *DUC at NLT/NAACL 2006*.

Joint Graphical Models for Date Selection in Timeline Summarization

Giang Tran
L3S Research Center
Leibniz-University Hannover
gtran@l3s.de

Eelco Herder
L3S Research Center
Leibniz-University Hannover
herder@l3s.de

Katja Markert
L3S Research Center
Leibniz-University Hannover
and School of Computing
University of Leeds
markert@l3s.de

Abstract

Automatic timeline summarization (TLS) generates precise, dated overviews over (often prolonged) events, such as wars or economic crises. One subtask of TLS selects the most important dates for an event within a certain time frame. Date selection has up to now been handled via supervised machine learning approaches that estimate the importance of each date separately, using features such as the frequency of date mentions in news corpora. This approach neglects interactions between different dates that occur due to connections between subevents. We therefore suggest a joint graphical model for date selection. Even unsupervised versions of this model perform as well as supervised state-of-the-art approaches. With parameter tuning on training data, it outperforms prior supervised models by a considerable margin.

1 Introduction

Major events (such as the Egypt revolution starting in 2011) often last over a long period of time and have impact for a considerable time afterwards. In order to find out what happened when during such an event, time-related queries to search engines are often insufficient as traditional IR does not handle time-related queries well (Foley and Allan, 2015). To provide readers with comprehensive overviews of long events, many news outlets employ *timeline summaries*: a timeline summary is a list of selected dates with a few sentences describing the most important events on each date. An example can be seen in Table 1. Timelines allow the reader to gain a quick overview over a complex event and to answer questions such as: *How and when did the event start? What were the main consequences of the initial events? What happened to the main protagonists in the event?* In addition, timelines are frequent means in education (such as history teaching) so that their generation is relevant for education as well as journalism.

(a1) 2011-01-25 Egyptians hold nationwide demonstrations against the authoritarian rule of Hosni Mubarak, who has led the country for nearly three decades.
(a2) 2011-01-26 A large security force moves into Cairo's Tahrir Square
(a3) 2011-01-28 Protesters burn down the ruling party's headquarters, and the military is deployed.
(a4) 2011-02-11 Mubarak steps down and turns power over to the military.
(a5) 2011-03-19 In the first post Mubarak vote, Egyptians cast ballots on constitutional amendments ..., including scheduling the first parliamentary and presidential elections
(a8) 2012-04-20 The presidential campaign officially begins.
(a10) 2012-06-24 Election officials declare Morsi the winner
(a26) 2013-07-03 Egypt's military chief says Morsi has been replaced by Adly Mansour, the chief justice of constitutional court.

Table 1: A timeline about the Egypt revolution published by the Associated Press (AP). We leave out intermediate dates due to space constraints. The whole timeline includes 30 dates between 2011-01-25 and 2013-07-07.

Though convenient for the reader, the manual creation of a timeline can take a long time even for experts. For example, the creator of the start-up Timeline says that it initially took a multi-person team a full work day to create a single timeline.[1] Therefore, automatic timeline summarization (TLS) has emerged as an NLP task in the past few years (Tran et al., 2013a; Kessler et al., 2012; Nguyen et al., 2014; Yan et al., 2011b; Yan et al., 2011a; Wang et al., 2012; Tran et al., 2013b; Tran et al., 2015). TLS has been divided into two subtasks: (i) ranking the dates between beginning

[1] http://www.niemanlab.org/2015/02/timeline-is-providing-historical-context-to-the-news-but-is-there-a-business-model-to-support-it/.

Proceedings of the 53rd Annual Meeting of the Association for Computational Linguistics and the 7th International Joint Conference on Natural Language Processing, pages 1598–1607,
Beijing, China, July 26-31, 2015.

and end of the timeline in order of importance, to achieve date selection and (ii) generating a good daily summary for each of the selected dates. In this paper, we tackle the first task. Date selection is challenging, as normally only a small set of the available dates is chosen for inclusion in the timeline (see Table 1). Date selection may be partially subjective: different journalists might include different dates.[2]

Existing approaches to date selection (Kessler et al., 2012; Tran et al., 2013a) use supervised machine learning, where each date receives a score for ranking the dates. Features used (such as frequency of date mention) are extracted from a corpus of event-related newspaper articles. Though the features are well-explored, the models score each date independently of other dates.

In contrast, we argue that interaction between dates should be taken into account. Timeline summaries tend to include "substories" in which the majority of selected dates are part of a chain of events that share major actors or demonstrate cause-effect. Table 1 shows at least two such chains: the (a1-4-5) chain of protests leading to Mubarak's resignation and the necessity of new elections, as well as the similar (a8-10-26) chain on Mursi. These chains can also be observed in the corresponding news articles. For example, some background articles on Mubarak's step-down will likely explain the reasons behind it. However, extracting such causal information can be difficult, as demonstrated by the still low results for discourse relation extraction (Lin et al., 2014; Braud and Denis, 2014). Instead, we use *date reference graphs*, which model which date refers to which other date. In our example, articles published on Mubarak's resignation date might refer to the date when the protest started. Although weaker than direct causal links, these links are easy to extract and we will show that they are very useful. In addition, references from important dates (such as Mubarak's resignation date) should be weighted higher than other references. This is akin to IR models such as PageRank, which weigh links from popular pages higher than links from less popular pages.

The main contributions of this work are: (i) we leverage interaction between dates via date reference graphs as a basis for date selection in TLS (ii) we provide a novel random walk model on this graph that incorporates both topical importance of referring sentences as well as frequency and temporal distance of references. We propose both unsupervised as well as supervised versions of this model.

We show that the proposed date selection approach outperforms previous approaches with evaluations on four real-life, long-term news events. We also discuss variations in timeline construction over different events, as well as by different journalists.

2 Related Work

Timeline summarization is a special case of *multi-document summarization* (MDS). As TLS organizes events by date, timelines can be generated by MDS systems (such as (Radev et al., 2004b; Radev et al., 2004a; McKeown et al., 2003; Erkan and Radev, 2004; Metzler and Kanungo, 2008; Hong and Nenkova, 2014) by applying their summarization techniques on news articles for every individual date to create corresponding daily summaries. However, manually written timelines normally only include a small number of dates; in addition, the temporal component imposes constraints on sentence selection for timeline summarization, such as the preference for little overlap between sentences selected for different dates (Yan et al., 2011b).

Many studies specific to timeline summarization, such as (Swan and Allan, 2000; Allan et al., 2001; Chieu and Lee, 2004; Yan et al., 2011b; Tran et al., 2015), focus on the extraction of salient sentences or headlines for generating the textual content of timelines. They assume either that the dates are given in advance or they use simple measures such as *burstiness* (Chieu and Lee, 2004; Yan et al., 2011b) for date selection, where burstiness relies on the number of date mentions.

Prior approaches dedicated specifically to date selection are Tran et al. (2013a) and Kessler et al. (2012).[3] They use supervised machine learning methods that score dates *independently of each other*. Features are extracted from a corpus of event-related newspaper articles, including frequency-based features (such as how often the date is referred to in the corpus), temporal distance features (such as how long into the future a date

[2]Note that the date selection task uses dates as proxies for important events on that date.

[3]Kessler et al. (2012) is also used in Nguyen et al. (2014)'s system.

keeps being referred to) and topical features (such as whether the date mention is associated with the most significant keywords of the event). We, however, score dates *jointly*, making use of interactions between dates in a graphical model. This improves substantially over prior approaches. We also propose unsupervised variations that perform competitively to prior supervised models.

3 Problem Definition and Approach

Similar to Kessler et al. (2012) and Tran et al. (2013a), we use the day as the timeline time unit (so, for example, we exclude hourly timelines).

3.1 Problem Definition

Given a main event and a time window $[t_1, t_2]$ within the event duration, our task is to select the top k dates $(d_1, d_2, ..., d_k) \in [t_1, t_2]$, when the most important (sub)events occurred. Therefore, timelines of variable length can be constructed. Like (Kessler et al., 2012; Tran et al., 2013a), we also assume that we have a corpus $\mathcal{C}$, consisting of news articles about the main event. This corpus gives evidence about the dates in $[t_1, t_2]$.

3.2 Proposed Approach

We build a *date reference graph*, which is a *fully directed graph* $\mathbf{G} = (\mathcal{V}, \mathcal{E})$, where $\mathcal{V}$ is the set of dates mentioned in any text in corpus $\mathcal{C}$, including publication dates. The edges $\mathcal{E} = \{e(d_i, d_j)\}$ indicate that at least one text published on d_i refers to the date d_j.

We represent each such link as a multi-value tuple $e(d_i, d_j) = (M_{ij}, freq(d_i, d_j), I_{temporal}(d_i, d_j), I_{topical}(d_i, d_j))$ to integrate different measures of date importance. The first value, $M_{ij} = \frac{1}{N}$ expresses the prior stochastic transitional probability between 2 dates where $N = |\mathcal{V}|$. The others express the strength of the connection between d_i and d_j modelled by the following aspects: frequency ($freq$), temporal influence ($I_{temporal}$) and topical influence ($I_{topical}$). We also suggest different combinations of these parameters.

Then we introduce a random walk model that uses these perspectives to rank the collection of dates.

Frequency of References. When a date d_j is referred to from either a past or future news article (published on d_i), it is likely involved in the events that are reported in that article. An example published on Mubarak's resignation date and referring back to the protest start can be seen below:

(1) On January 25, an uprising of Egyptians erupted calling for Mubaraks resignation as president. Protests continued to grow ... (CBS Detroit, 2011-02-11)

We hypothesize that the more frequent such references are, the stronger this involvement is. Hence, we compute $freq(d_i, d_j)$ as the number of references to d_j from news articles published on d_i. While prior work (Kessler et al., 2012) uses aggregate frequency of references to d_j over the whole corpus as a feature, they do not handle the interaction between dates and can therefore not score dates jointly.

Topical Influence. In Example 1 above, the reference sentence mentions only major actors in the Egypt crisis (Mubarak, Egyptians) as well as only major subevents (uprising, protests). This makes for a link between 2011-02-11 (publication date) and 2011-01-25 (referred date) that is relevant to the main event and emphasises the importance of the referred date. In contrast, Example 2 also talks about less salient entities in context of the Egypt revolution and makes for a less topical link between 2011-02-02 (publication date) and 2011-01-25 (referred date).

(2) Mr Ghonim is Google's head of marketing for Middle East and North Africa and was in Egypt when the protests started on Jan 25 (DailyMail, 2011-02-02).

We quantify the topical influence between dates as follows: Let $\mathcal{S}_{i\to j} = \{s_{ij}\}$ be the set of sentences that are published in d_i and refer to d_j. We are interested in how relevant this connection is to the overall news event, looking at the content in $\mathcal{S}_{i\to j}$. To do so, we represent the overall content of the news collection by a set of keywords $Q = \{q_1, q_2, ..., q_n\}$, which are computed via TextRank (Mihalcea and Tarau, 2004).[4] We compute a relevance score for each sentence s_{ij} in $\mathcal{S}_{i\to j}$ by the famous Okapi BM25 function (Robertson et al., 1994), which ranks a sentence more topical if it contains more as well as more of the most salient collection keywords Q.[5] We compute topical influence ($I_{topical}$) as either the maximum value or the sum value of the relevance scores of all s_{ij}.

$$I_{\max topical}(d_i, d_j) = \max_{s_{ij} \in \mathcal{S}_{i\to j}} BM25(s_{ij}, Q) \quad (3)$$

$$I_{freq*topical}(d_i, d_j) = \sum_{s_{ij} \in \mathcal{S}_{i\to j}} BM25(s_{ij}, Q) \quad (4)$$

[4] We set n=20 in practice.

[5] We use the standard BM25 parameter settings $k_1 = 1.2$ and $b = 0.75$

Intuitively, $I_{freq*topical}(d_i, d_j)$ is proportional to the size of $S_{i \to j}$ as well as to the relevance scores of its sentences whereas $I_{\max topical}(d_i, d_j)$ does not consider reference frequency at all.

When d_j is not mentioned by any articles published on d_i, the value of the topical influence is equal to zero.

Temporal Influence. The longer ago an event happened the more likely it is to have been forgotten. Only very important events are referred to over long time frames. We therefore hypothesise that a date d_j is more influential (for another date d_i) if d_i mentions d_j and the temporal distance between the two dates is high. Overall, d_j gathers importance with several long-term references. Ex. 5 showcases an example:

(5) Military generals took over power from Mubarak when he stepped down on *February 11 last year*. (Daily Mail, 2012-01-25).

We define the temporal influence of an existing edge $I_{temporal}(d_i, d_j)$ as either the absolute value of temporal distance between the two dates or by the product of the temporal distance with the number of references $freq(d_i, d_j)$. In the second computation, the temporal influence between two dates increases when d_i references d_j more than once.

$$I_{|temporal|}(d_i, d_j) = \Delta t = |d_i - d_j| \quad (6)$$

$$I_{freq*temporal}(d_i, d_j) = freq(d_i, d_j) \cdot |d_i - d_j| \quad (7)$$

When d_j is not mentioned by any articles published on d_i, the temporal influence is set as zero.

Random Walk Model for Date Ranking. A random walk on a given graph is a Markov process, where each node represents a state and a walk transiting from one state to another state is based on a transition probability matrix. One well-known random walk algorithm is PageRank (Page et al., 1999), which models web surfer behavior to determine the importance of web pages with the following formula:

$$x_t(j) = \alpha \sum_{i \in L_j^-} M_{ij} x_{t-1}(i) + (1 - \alpha) v_j, \quad (8)$$

where M_{ij} is the stochastic transition probability from page p_i to p_j, $x_t(j)$ is the importance score of page p_j at step t, α is a damping factor that controls how often the walker jumps to an arbitrary node, v_j is the initial probabilistic importance score (generally set to $1/N$, where N is the number of nodes in the graph), and L_i^- is the set of incoming links of page p_i. When t is iterated enough, the importance score vector reaches a stationary distribution that can be used for ranking pages.

The traditional PageRank process in Eq. 8 captures only the observed linking characteristics of nodes but ignores other sources of information which can be indicators for their importance.

We extend the model by introducing an influence-based random walk model (**IRW**) that allows the random walker to take into account multiple sources of information and perform voting more effectively. The random walk process we propose can be defined by the following formula:

$$x_t(j) = \alpha \sum_{i \in L_j^-} \mathcal{I}(i, j) \cdot M_{ij} \cdot x_{t-1}(i) + (1 - \alpha) v_j \quad (9)$$

where $\mathcal{I}(i, j)$ is the normalized influence factor that indicates how influential the edge $d_i \to d_j$ is in the global context of the event. The normalization is done by scaling the range of value from [0, 1]. M is the stochastic transitional matrix. In our case, $\mathcal{I}(i, j)$ can be just the value of $freq(d_i, d_j)$, $I_{topical}(d_i, d_j)$, $I_{temporal}(d_i, d_j)$ alone or a linear combination of them. Note that, $(\mathcal{I} \cdot M)$ in most case is not stochastic and *must not* be transformed into a stochastic transitional matrix, as the transformation will collapse the global context of $\mathcal{I}$. IRW is different to PageRank on weighted graph, weighted or personalized PageRank and their variations e.g, (Xing and Ghorbani, 2004; Haveliwala, 2002), among others. In particular, weighted PageRank integrates influence scores into the stochastic transitional matrix. Thus, the random walker contributes the voting impact of a node X to its neighbor with an influence score normalized by the sum of scores on all outgoing connections. That process leverages how good this connection is in the sub-graph (G*) which consists of X and its outgoing neighbors. In contrast, our proposed model uses the non-normalized value of the influence score to leverage how good this connection is on the entire graph instead of G*. To give an example, if date X1 mentions only X2 with a raw temporal distance score of 20 and X3 mentions only X4 with a score of 100, then in weighted Page Rank both would be normalized to a weight one, losing the information that X4 is mentioned after a much longer time period than X2. The process for combination in our model is defined as the following:

$$x_t(j) = \alpha\omega \sum_{i \in L_j^-} W_1(i,j) \cdot M_{ij} \cdot x_{t-1}(i) + \alpha(1-\omega) \sum_{i \in L_j^-} W_2(i,j) \cdot M_{ij} \cdot x_{t-1}(i) + (1-\alpha)v_j \quad (10)$$

where $W_1(i,j) = \frac{I_{topical}(d_i,d_j)}{\max_{uv} I_{topical}(d_u,d_v)}$ is the normalized value for topical influence, and $W_2(i,j) = \frac{I_{temporal}(d_i,d_j)}{\max_{uv} I_{temporal}(d_u,d_v)}$ is the normalized value for temporal influence.[6]

Here, the hyper-parameter $0 \leq \omega \leq 1$ controls the proportion of the topical influence from d_i to d_j. When $\omega = 0$, no topical influence is taken into account. No temporal influence is considered when $\omega = 1$. Intuitively, at every step, the random walker can follow the outgoing nodes and either carry topical influence (the first part) or temporal influence (the second part) to contribute to the rank of the outgoing nodes. Otherwise, it teleports to an arbitrary node with probability $(1-\alpha)$.

Convergence Property. Starting from Eq. 10, we now show that the IRW model converges to a stationary distribution.

Let Λ and Λ' be the matrix with elements $W_1(i,j)$ and $W_2(ij)$ respectively, with any edge (d_i, d_j), $\mathbf{I}$ be the $n \times n$ identity matrix, and $\mathbf{v}$ be the transpose of $1 \times n$ uniform stochastic vector. $\mathbf{M}$ denotes the transitional matrix for G.

Proposition 1. $(\mathbf{I} - \alpha(w\mathbf{M}^T\Lambda + (1-\omega)\mathbf{M}^T\Lambda'))$ *is invertible for all* $\mathbf{M}, \Lambda, \Lambda', \alpha, \omega$.

Proof. Let $\mathbf{P} = w\mathbf{M}^T\Lambda + (1-\omega)\mathbf{M}^T\Lambda'$, we need to prove that $\mathbf{I} - \alpha\mathbf{P}$ is invertible. Equivalently, we prove its transpose $\mathbf{I} - \alpha\mathbf{P}^T$ is invertible, which can be proved by showing that $(\mathbf{I} - \alpha\mathbf{P}^T)\mathbf{y} = 0$ only has the trivial solution $\mathbf{y} = 0$.

$$\begin{aligned}(\mathbf{I} - \alpha\mathbf{P}^T)\mathbf{y} &= 0 \\ \mathbf{y} &= \alpha\mathbf{P}^T\mathbf{y} \\ y_i &= \alpha\sum_j P_{ji}y_j \\ &= \alpha\sum_j((\omega W_1(i,j) + (1-\omega)W_2(i,j))M_{ij}y_j).\end{aligned} \quad (11)$$

Let $u = \arg\max_j y_j$. When $i == u$, Eq. 11 infers,

$$\begin{aligned}y_u &\leq \alpha\sum_j((\omega W_1(u,j) + (1-\omega)W_2(u,j))M_{uj}y_u). \\ y_u &\leq \alpha y_u\sum_j((\omega W_1(u,j) + (1-\omega)W_2(u,j))M_{uj} \\ y_u(1-\alpha\mathcal{F}_u) &\leq 0.\end{aligned} \quad (12)$$

where $\mathcal{F}_u = \sum_j((\omega W_1(u,j) + (1-\omega)W_2(u,j))M_{uj}$. Clearly, $\mathcal{F}_u \leq 1$ because $W_1(u,j) \leq 1$ and $W_2(u,j) \leq 1$ and $\sum_j M_{uj} = 1$. Since $\alpha < 1$ and $\mathcal{F}_u \leq 1$, $(1-\alpha\mathcal{F}_u) > 0$. Therefore $y_u \leq 0$. Similarly, let $v = \arg\min_j y_j$ we have that $y_v \geq 0$. As $y_v \leq y_u$, this implies $y_u = y_v = 0$ to satisfy all inequalities. Consequently, $y_i = 0$ for all i, or $\mathbf{y} = 0$. Thus, $\mathbf{I} - \alpha\mathbf{P}^T$ invertible. Equivalently,$(\mathbf{I} - \alpha(\omega\mathbf{M}^T\Lambda + (1-\omega)\mathbf{M}^T\Lambda'))$ is invertible. □

[6] In the case of linear combinations we incorporate frequency into topical or temporal influence as described above.

Proposition 2. *The iteration in Eq. 9 converges to* $(1-\alpha)(\mathbf{I} - \alpha(\omega\mathbf{M}^T\Lambda + (1-\omega)\mathbf{M}^T\Lambda'))^{-1}\mathbf{v}$.

Proof. We can re-write Eq. 9 in matrix form:

$$\begin{aligned}\mathbf{x}_t &= \alpha\mathbf{P}\mathbf{x}_{t-1} + (1-\alpha)\mathbf{v} \\ &= (\alpha\mathbf{P})^t\mathbf{x}_0 + (1-\alpha)(\sum_{i=1}^{t}(\alpha\mathbf{P})^{i-1})\mathbf{v}\end{aligned} \quad (13)$$

We will show that $\lim_{t\to\infty} \mathbf{x}_t = (1-\alpha)(I - \alpha\mathbf{P})^{-1}\mathbf{v}$.

$$\begin{aligned}\sum_i(\alpha P)^t_{ij} &= \sum_i\sum_k(\alpha P)_{ik}(\alpha P)^{t-1}_{kj} \\ &= \sum_k(\alpha P)^{t-1}_{kj}\sum_i(\alpha P)_{ik} \\ &= \sum_k(\alpha P)^{t-1}_{kj}\alpha(\mathcal{F}_k) \\ &\leq \sum_k(\alpha P)^{t-1}_{kj}\alpha \\ &\leq (\alpha)^t\end{aligned} \quad (14)$$

Here, $\mathcal{F}_k = \sum_i((\omega W_1(k,i) + (1-\omega)W_2(k,i))M_{ki} \leq 1$ (proof similarly to Proposition 1

Because $\alpha < 1$, this column sum converges to zero when $t \to \infty$. We then derive $\lim_{t\to\infty}(\alpha\mathbf{P})^t\mathbf{x}_0 = 0$. When $t \to \infty$, given Proposition 1 and Neumann series, Eq. 13 becomes:

$$\mathbf{x}_t = (\alpha\mathbf{P})^t\mathbf{x}_0 + (1-\alpha)(I - \alpha\mathbf{P})^{-1}\mathbf{v}$$

hence, $\lim_{t\to\infty}\mathbf{x}_t = (1-\alpha)(I-\alpha\mathbf{P})^{-1}\mathbf{v}$. Convergence proved. □

4 Experiments

4.1 Ground Truth and Data Preprocessing

Kessler et al. (2012) use 91 timelines from AFP as ground truth along with the AFP news corpus for feature extraction. However, their dataset is not publically available. In addition, although they consider a wide spread of events, each event is only represented by a single timeline from a single source, making that method somewhat vulnerable to journalism bias (as discussed by themselves in their paper). The data collected by us previously (Tran et al., 2013a) is publically available at `http://l3s.de/~gtran/timeline/` and has since been extended by us (Tran et al., 2015). Similar to Kessler et al. (2012), it contains ground truth timelines as well as a corpus of news articles covering each event. The dataset is suitable for our purpose because of the following reasons: (1) it is a heterogeneous dataset which contains news articles and expert timeline summaries from different news agencies. Thus, it is more likely to avoid the issue of bias. Also, each event is represented by more than one timeline; (2) it covers long-term stories that have been happening since 2011, making the date selection problem non trivial for any system.

Timelines. The groundtruth contains 21 timelines for 4 main events (Egypt Revolution, Libya War, Syria War, Yemen Crisis), created by professional journalists. Table 2 shows statistics about the timelines. Only a small number of all possible dates in a time range is included in at least one timeline (for example, only 122 dates among a possible 918 dates for the Egypt Revolution).

News Corpus. The news articles have been collected from 24 well-known news outlets by querying Google with the event name together with the outlets' sitename and time range specification. The crawl time range starts from the first of the month of the earliest event in any timeline (for example, 2011-01-01 for the Egypt revolution) and ends at crawl date. The top-ranked 300 news articles from each news site were collected, if still available. The article creation date is parsed from the answers returned by Google. The corpus contains 15,534 news articles. Its statistics are summarised in Table 3. The overlap between timeline date ranges and news corpus date ranges is only partial: on the one hand, the corpora have many articles published after the timelines end; on the other hand, sometimes the corpus has no articles published near the beginning of the timeline (Syria War). The distribution of document frequency leans towards the end date of the news collection. The reason could be that most search engines rank recent documents higher than those published longer ago.

Story	Time Range	#News
Egypt	2011/01/11 - 2013/11/10	3869
Libya	2011/02/16 - 2013/07/18	3994
Syria	2011/11/17 - 2013/07/26	4071
Yemen	2011/01/15 - 2013/07/25	3600

Table 3: Overview of the news corpus

Preprocessing. Accurate date extraction including both implicit (like *last Friday*) and explicit (like *11 Feb*) temporal expressions is vital to our approach as well as for competitor systems. We use the Heideltime state-of-the art toolkit (Strötgen and Gertz, 2010) for this task.

4.2 Experimental settings

As can be seen from Table 2, different timelines for the same event can contain varying dates, due to different ranges timelines might cover but also due to selection preferences by individual writers. Therefore, we consider the union of all timelines for an event. The set of input dates for ranking are all dates from the start t_1 and end t_2 of the union of timelines.[7] We call that input time range $\mathcal{TR}_e$, depending on main event e.

We consider two evaluation settings:

relaxed setting: A date from $\mathcal{TR}_e$ selected by an algorithm is counted as correct if it is included in the union of timelines, therefore in at least one individual timeline.

strict setting: A date from $\mathcal{TR}_e$ selected by an algorithm is counted as correct if it is included in at least two individual timelines.

The first setting is the one used in previous work such as (Kessler et al., 2012; Tran et al., 2013a). It is also the only one that can be used if only one timeline per event is considered as in Kessler et al. (2012). We therefore include it for comparison purposes. However, we think it is better to consider several timelines as it allows us to consider agreement between timeline writers. If more than one writer agrees on a date being important we have more evidence that a system should find that date. Finding dates that only a single writer includes is less important and could even be due to bias or system overfitting. Therefore, our second setting is preferable as it emphasizes highly important dates selected by multiple journalists.

Each system selects the top k dates during the input time range. We evaluate the systems by Mean Average Precision at k (MAP@k) for k = 5, 10, 15, 20 over all four events.

4.3 Systems.

Baseline. We use three unsupervised baselines. The baseline *Document Frequency* ranks dates according to the number of news articles published on that date. Our assumption is that on a date where one or more important events happened, there would be a spread of information over different news agencies in the world. Therefore, this date has more news articles published. This baseline is related to the burstiness date selection used by Yan et al. (2011b).

The baseline *MaxLength* ranks dates by the maximum article length of all articles published on that date. Our hypothesis is that important events

[7] Prior work also uses start and end date of timelines for delimiting input (Kessler et al., 2012; Tran et al., 2013a).

Story	#TL	#atLeastOnce	#atLeastTwice	avgL	maxL	minL	Time Range	#dates
Egypt	4	122	18	36	57	24	2011/01/01 - 2013/07/07	918
Libya	7	118	56	34	62	22	2011/02/14 - 2011/11/22	281
Syria	5	106	17	60	26	13	2011/03/15 - 2013/07/06	844
Yemen	5	81	26	24	42	10	2011/01/22 - 2012/02/27	401

Number of timelines (#TL), number of dates occurring in at least one timeline (#atLeastOnce), number of dates that appear in at least 2 timelines, average (avgL), max (maxL) and min (minL) length of timelines; the Time Range of the union of timelines and all potential dates (#dates) within the time range.

Table 2: Overview of groundtruth timelines

often receive more attention from writers, leading to longer articles.

Date Frequency ranks a date d by the total number of sentences referring to d that are not published on d. This is a simple measure of d's influence without joint scoring of dates or integration of temporal distance or topic.

Competitors. We reimplement *Kessler et al. (2012)*'s model. It first detects all sentences with date references and filters out certain types of sentences according to linguistic features (such as presence of modality as this can put the factuality of the event into question). Then, the importance score of a date is determined by the product of the Lucene score of referring sentences and an ML-predicted score that takes into account date reference frequencies, temporal distance of date references and topical importance of referring sentences. To use the same setting as for our systems, we use the list of keywords extracted by TextRank (Mihalcea and Tarau, 2004) to formulate a topic query for the Lucene index.

We reimplement *Tran et al. (2013a)* who use a supervised ML approach based on a more detailed consideration of date reference frequencies.

Both *Kessler et al. (2012)* and *Tran et al. (2013a)* are retrained and tested via 4-fold cross-validation on events. In addition, we noted that the two supervised systems could profit from the fact that for certain dates in $\mathcal{TR}_e$ no published news articles exist in the news collection and that they are therefore a priori unlikely to be relevant. We therefore also run those systems with a stricter input time range, which intersects $\mathcal{TR}_e$ with the dates that are the publication date of at least one article in the news collection. We indicate these systems as *Kessler et al. (2012) (Pub)* and *Tran et al. (2013a) (Pub)*.

Our Approach. Our system builds graphs with all dates referenced in the news corpus for an event as nodes. We select the top k highest ranked nodes that also fall within $\mathcal{TR}_e$. We measure the performance with different strategies for the *Influence* factor $\mathcal{I}$. We use the following five unsupervised strategies, where we just set the damping factor α to 0.85 as suggested by Page et al. (1999).[8]

IRW_{freq} only uses the frequency aspect. This corresponds to a joint modelling version of the *Date Frequency* baseline.

$IRW_{\max topical}$ uses topical influence, disregarding frequency aspect in its computation.

$IRW_{freq*topical}$ uses topical influence, incorporating the frequency aspect in its computation.

$IRW_{|temporal|}$ uses temporal influence, disregarding the frequency aspect.

$IRW_{freq*temporal}$ uses temporal influence incorporating the frequency aspect.

Furthermore, we are interested in combining topical and temporal influence (with or without frequency aspects). Here, our model is parameterized by ω which controls the impact of *topical influence* vs. *temporal influence*. This parameter is tuned on the training set via 4-fold cross-validation and, therefore, the next two models have a small element of supervision.

$IRW_{\max topical+freq*temporal}$ combines topical and temporal influence, integrating the frequency aspect into temporal influence.

$IRW_{freq*topical+|temporal|}$ combines topical and temporal influence, integrating the frequency aspect into topical influence.

4.4 Analysis of date reference graphs

Table 4 shows an analysis of the four date reference graphs. In this Table, #sent provides the total number of sentences from all news articles while #hasRef shows the number of sentences that refer to a date (around 15%), suggesting a sustainable part of data can be helpful for the interaction-based approach. The number of nodes shows the unique dates that are involved in a date reference link. The number of edges is equivalent to the number of date reference links (d_i, d_j) that indicate that there exist sentences published on d_i but referring to d_j. *toStrict* and *toRelaxed* is the

[8]We could make these models supervised by tuning the damping factor via cross-validation. However, we found it encouraging that we were able to achieve competitive results without tuning — similar to links between web pages in the traditional PageRank algorithm, links between dates seem to embody strong relations, making the same damping factor suitable.

	#sent	#hasRef(%)	#nodes	#Edges	toStrict	reachStrict	toRelaxed	reachRelaxed
Egypt	143,096	26,428 (18.5)	939	2784	15.55%	100.00%	35.99%	89.34%
Libya	140,753	22,166 (15.7)	971	1797	33.78%	98.21%	56.98%	99.15%
Syria	162,305	26,992 (16.6)	812	1555	7.14%	88.24%	31.00%	73.58%
Yemen	140,156	21,606 (15.4)	1106	1608	18.28%	100.00%	37.00%	100.00%

Table 4: Interaction-based analysis on experimental news collections

proportion of the edges that link to groundtruth dates in the *strict setting* and *relaxed setting*. Those edges cover almost all the groundtruth dates (i.e, *reachStrict* and *reachRelaxed*), i.e almost all groundtruth dates are indeed referenced at least once in our corpus.

4.5 Results

Table 5 shows the average performance of different systems over our four events. Several general observations stand out. First, we notice that the scores wrt. *relaxed setting* of all systems are higher than those wrt. *strict setting*. That is expected, as in *relaxed setting*, a selected date has a higher likelihood to be one of the milestones in the timeline of at least one expert. Second, simple baselines such as *Document Frequency* and *MaxLength* perform reasonably well in the relaxed-setting. That confirms our assumptions that important dates often possess more published news articles and are likely to have at least one article of substantial length. However, these baselines are not enough to distinguish highly important dates (which are selected by more than one journalist) as shown by their performance in the *strict setting* (around 0.3 MAP@k only).

Using *Date Frequency* leads to a substantial performance improvement in the strict setting comapred to the publication-based baselines. Therefore, highly important dates are more likely to be kept mentioning in the future and that supports our research direction to better leverage date interaction for ranking date importance. This is further confirmed by the performance of the IRW_{freq} system which is the joint modelling version of the *DateFrequency* baseline and outperfoms the baseline without inclusion of any further information such as topical salience. It can even compete with prior supervised competitors when their input time range is not modified.

Our supervised competitors (Kessler et al., 2012; Tran et al., 2013a) perform overall well and both profit from modifying their input time range as suggested in the *Pub* versions. However, the unsupervised versions of our system $IRW_{\max topical}$ and $IRW_{freq*topical}$ perform very comparably to the supervised competitors in the strict and relaxed setting, respectively.

The last two lines of Table 5 show the results of our proposed method when using a linear combination of the different influence factors, and the hyperparameter ω having been tuned on the training set. $IRW_{\max topical+freq*temporal}$ shows the result of our system with $\omega = 0.2$ and $IRW_{freq*topical+|temporal|}$ with $\omega = 0.1$ These systems outperform the state-of-the-art systems clearly in the strict setting and for most measures in the relaxed setting.

Stability. We also investigated the stability of the performance of different systems by looking into their results on each event. Table 6 presents the performance of our best system $IRW_{\max topical+freq*temporal}$ and its best supervised competitors Tran et al. (2013a) (Pub) and Kessler et al. (2012) (Pub). All systems perform worse on the Syria story although our dropoff is less than the one of prior systems.

We speculate that the competitor systems are more sensitive to the amount of available published content on a target date than ours. In particular, Tran et al. (2013a) use the frequency of published dates and sentences as one of their features, and Kessler et al. (2012) rely on the returned results from Lucene index which tends towards substories from the publication periods. Different to others, the time range for the *Syria* news collection does not include the time range for the Syria timelines fully or almost fully (see Tables 2 and 3). We therefore are not as dependent on an exact match between timeline dates and news collection dates and can use news articles from later dates more effectively.

5 Conclusion and Future Work

This paper addresses the problem of date selection for timeline summarization. Our approach leverages the interactions between dates via a joint model based on a date reference graph, improving on individual scoring of dates.

We capture the interactions between dates from the number of cross-references between dates, and

System	strict setting				relaxed-setting			
	MAP@5	MAP@10	MAP@15	MAP@20	MAP@5	MAP@10	MAP@15	MAP@20
Document Frequency	0.312	0.303	0.299	0.299	0.509	0.550	0.564	0.560
MaxLength	0.349	0.335	0.311	0.287	0.647	0.594	0.566	0.533
Date Frequency	0.555	0.498	0.457	0.427	0.597	0.626	0.625	0.613
(Kessler et al., 2012)	0.567	0.546	0.519	0.491	0.790	0.740	0.723	0.704
(Kessler et al., 2012) (Pub)	0.701	0.620	0.571	0.524	0.912	0.807	0.759	0.731
(Tran et al., 2013a)	0.668	0.565	0.522	0.488	0.740	0.717	0.700	0.673
(Tran et al., 2013a) (Pub)	0.710	0.601	0.551	0.506	0.792	0.771	0.746	0.716
IRW_{freq}	0.646	0.535	0.471	0.431	0.861	0.770	0.711	0.687
$IRW_{\max topical}$	0.763	0.647	0.564	0.510	0.887	0.794	0.724	0.685
$IRW_{freq*topical}$	0.737	0.576	0.498	0.448	0.945	0.836	0.762	0.709
$IRW_{\|temporal\|}$	0.724	0.587	0.522	0.484	0.699	0.597	0.570	0.564
$IRW_{freq*temporal}$	0.724	0.588	0.527	0.486	0.712	0.622	0.581	0.559
$IRW_{\max topical+freq*temporal}$	0.879	0.760	0.658	0.587	0.897	0.842	0.775	0.730
$IRW_{freq*topical+\|temporal\|}$	0.818	0.677	0.596	0.536	0.928	0.866	0.801	0.745

Table 5: Average MAP@k scores of different systems on 4 news collections

	Egypt	Libya	Syria	Yemen
	$IRW_{\max topical+freq*temporal}$			
MAP@5	0.960	1.000	0.713	0.843
MAP@10	0.738	0.969	0.598	0.735
MAP@15	0.600	0.854	0.503	0.676
MAP@20	0.520	0.776	0.433	0.619
	Kessler et al. (2012) (Pub)			
MAP@5	0.703	0.843	0.257	1.000
MAP@10	0.566	0.759	0.203	0.952
MAP@15	0.507	0.697	0.187	0.894
MAP@20	0.450	0.659	0.171	0.816
	Tran et al. (2013a) (Pub)			
MAP@5	0.960	0.910	0.257	0.713
MAP@10	0.803	0.836	0.224	0.541
MAP@15	0.665	0.799	0.227	0.514
MAP@20	0.569	0.758	0.212	0.484

Table 6: Stability of our systems vs. competitors

their temporal and topical influences. We present a novel random walk model that incorporates these perspectives into connectivity-based computation. Experimental results on four news events that span a long time period show that the proposed models outperform state-of-the art approaches. Even unsupervised versions of the model perform on a par with previous supervised methods. We also draw attention to the necessity to take personal bias into account, which leads to differences between manually created timelines for the same event — we encourage future work to always consider several timelines per event in the way that other NLP work uses several annotators to create ground truth.

In future work, we will consider a wider range of events and event types. This will also lead to considering timelines where the day as unit of granularity might not be appropriate or where the unit of granularity might be varying across the timeline. We will also explore in depth the effect of size and type of news corpus on resulting timelines, research further into the issue of human disagreement in timeline creation and explore human evaluation of timeline summarization.

Acknowledgments

The work was partially funded by the European Commission for the FP7 project EUMSSI (611057) and the ERC Advanced Grant ALEXANDRIA (339233).

References

James Allan, Rahul Gupta, and Vikas Khandelwal. 2001. Temporal summaries of new topics. In *Proceedings of SIGIR'01*, pages 10–18.

Chloé Braud and Pascal Denis. 2014. Combining natural and artificial examples to improve implicit discourse relation identification. In *COLING 2014: Technical Papers. Dublin, Ireland*, pages 1694–1705.

Hai Leong Chieu and Yoong Keok Lee. 2004. Query based event extraction along a timeline. In *Proceedings of SIGIR'04*, pages 425–432.

Günes Erkan and Dragomir R. Radev. 2004. Lexrank: graph-based lexical centrality as salience in text summarization. *J. Artif. Int. Res.*, 22(1):457–479.

John Foley and James Allan. 2015. Retrieving time from scanned books. In *Advances in Information Retrieval*, pages 221–232. Springer.

Taher H. Haveliwala. 2002. Topic-sensitive pagerank. In *WWW*, pages 517–526.

Kai Hong and Ani Nenkova. 2014. Improving the estimation of word importance for news multi-document summarization. In *Proceedings of EACL 2014*, pages 712–721.

Remy Kessler, Xavier Tannier, Caroline Hagège, Véronique Moriceau, and André Bittar. 2012. Finding salient dates for building thematic timelines. In *Proceedings of ACL*.

Ziheng Lin, Hwee Tou Ng, and Min-Yen Kan. 2014. A pdtb-styled end-to-end discourse parser. *Natural Language Engineering*, 20(2):151–184.

Kathleen McKeown, Regina Barzilay, John Chen, David K. Elson, David Kirk Evans, Judith Klavans, Ani Nenkova, Barry Schiffman, and Sergey Sigelman. 2003. Columbia's newsblaster: New features and future directions. In *HLT-NAACL*.

Donald Metzler and Tapas Kanungo. 2008. Machine learned sentence selection strategies for query-biased summarization. In *Proceedings of the 2008 ACM SIGIR LR4IR Workshop*.

Rada Mihalcea and Paul Tarau. 2004. Textrank: Bringing order into text. In *EMNLP*, pages 404–411.

Kiem-Hieu Nguyen, Xavier Tannier, and Véronique Moriceau. 2014. Ranking multidocument event descriptions for building thematic timelines. In *COLING 2014*, pages 1208–1217.

Lawrence Page, Sergey Brin, Rajeev Motwani, and Terry Winograd. 1999. The pagerank citation ranking: Bringing order to the web. Technical report, Stanford InfoLab, November. Previous number = SIDL-WP-1999-0120.

Dragomir R. Radev, Timothy Allison, Sasha Blair-Goldensohn, John Blitzer, Arda Celebi, Stanko Dimitrov, Elliott Drbek, Ali Hakim, Wai Lam, Danyu Liu, Jahna Otterbacher, Hong Qi, Horacio Saggion, Simone Teufel, Michael Topper, Adam Winkel, and Zhu Zhang. 2004a. Mead - a platform for multidocument multilingual text summarization. In *Proceedings of LREC'04*.

Dragomir R. Radev, Hongyan Jing, Magorzata Sty, and Daniel Tam. 2004b. Centroid-based summarization of multiple documents. pages 919–938.

Stephen E. Robertson, Steve Walker, Susan Jones, Micheline Hancock-Beaulieu, and Mike Gatford. 1994. Okapi at trec-3. In *TREC*.

Jannik Strötgen and Michael Gertz. 2010. Heideltime: High quality rule-based extraction and normalization of temporal expressions. In *Proceedings of the SemEval '10 Workshop*, pages 321–324.

Russell C. Swan and James Allan. 2000. Timemine: visualizing automatically constructed timelines. In *SIGIR*, page 393.

Binh Giang Tran, Mohammad Alrifai, and Dat Quoc Nguyen. 2013a. Predicting relevant news events for timeline summaries. In *WWW'2013*.

Giang Binh Tran, Tuan A. Tran, Nam-Khanh Tran, Mohammad Alrifai, and Nattiya Kanhabua. 2013b. Leveraging learning to rank in an optimization framework for timeline summarization. In *SIGIR 2013 Workshop TAIA*.

Giang Tran, Mohammad Alrifai, and Eelco Herder. 2015. Timeline summarization from relevent headlines. In *Proceedings of ECIR'2015*.

Dingding Wang, Tao Li, and Mitsunori Ogihara. 2012. Generating pictorial storylines via minimum-weight connected dominating set approximation in multi-view graphs. In *Proceedings of AAAI'2012*.

Wenpu Xing and Ali A. Ghorbani. 2004. Weighted pagerank algorithm. In *CNSR*, pages 305–314.

Rui Yan, Jian-Yun Nie, and Xiaoming Li. 2011a. Summarize what you are interested in: An optimization framework for interactive personalized summarization. In *Proceedings of EMNLP'11*.

Rui Yan, Xiaojun Wan, Jahna Otterbacher, Liang Kong, Xiaoming Li, and Yan Zhang. 2011b. Evolutionary timeline summarization: a balanced optimization framework via iterative substitution. In *Proceedings of SIGIR'11*, pages 745–754.

Predicting Salient Updates for Disaster Summarization

Chris Kedzie and **Kathleen McKeown**
Columbia University
Department of Computer Science
{kedzie, kathy}@cs.columbia.edu

Fernando Diaz
Microsoft Research
fdiaz@microsoft.com

Abstract

During crises such as natural disasters or other human tragedies, information needs of both civilians and responders often require urgent, specialized treatment. Monitoring and summarizing a text stream during such an event remains a difficult problem. We present a system for update summarization which predicts the salience of sentences with respect to an event and then uses these predictions to directly bias a clustering algorithm for sentence selection, increasing the quality of the updates. We use novel, disaster-specific features for salience prediction, including geo-locations and language models representing the language of disaster. Our evaluation on a standard set of retrospective events using ROUGE shows that salience prediction provides a significant improvement over other approaches.

1 Introduction

During crises, information is critical for first responders, crisis management organizations, and those caught in the event. When the event is significant, as in the case of Hurricane Sandy, the amount of content produced by traditional news outlets, government agencies, relief organizations, and social media can vastly overwhelm those trying to monitor the situation. Crisis informatics (Palen et al., 2010) is dedicated to finding methods for sharing the right information in a timely fashion during such an event. Research in this field has focused on human-in-the-loop approaches ranging from on the ground information gathering to crowdsourced reporting and disaster management (Starbird and Palen, 2013).

Multi-document summarization has the potential to assist the crisis informatics community. Automatic summarization could deliver relevant and salient information at regular intervals, even when human volunteers are unable to. Perhaps more importantly it could help filter out unnecessary and irrelevant detail when the volume of incoming information is large. While methods for identifying, tracking, and summarizing events from text based input have been explored extensively (Allan et al., 1998; Filatova and Hatzivassiloglou, 2004; Wang et al., 2011), these experiments were not developed to handle streaming data from a heterogeneous environment at web scale. These methods also rely heavily on redundancy which is suboptimal for time sensitive domains where there is a high cost in delaying information.

In this paper, we present an update summarization system to track events across time. Our system predicts sentence salience in the context of a large-scale event, such as a disaster, and integrates these predictions into a clustering based multi-document summarization system. We demonstrate that combining salience with clustering produces more relevant summaries compared to baselines using clustering or relevance alone. Our experiments suggest that this is because our system is better able to adapt to dynamic changes in input volume that adversely affect methods that use redundancy as a proxy for salience.

In addition to the tight integration between clustering and salience prediction, our approach also exploits knowledge about the event to determine salience. Thus, salience represents both how typical a sentence is of the event type (e.g., industrial accident, hurricane, riot) and whether it specifies information about this particular event. Our feature representation includes a set of language models, one for each event type, to measure the typicality of the sentence with regard to the current event, the distance of mentioned locations from the center of the event, and the change in word frequencies over the time of the event. While we evaluate these features in the domain of disasters,

Proceedings of the 53rd Annual Meeting of the Association for Computational Linguistics and the 7th International Joint Conference on Natural Language Processing, pages 1608–1617,
Beijing, China, July 26-31, 2015.

this approach is generally applicable to many update summarization tasks.

Our approach achieves a statistically significant improvement in ROUGE scores compared to multiple baselines. Additionally, we introduce novel methods for estimating the average information gain each update provides and how completely the update summary covers the event it is tracking; our system's updates contain more relevant information on average than the competing baselines.

The remainder of the paper is organized as follows. We begin with a review of related work in the information retrieval and multi-document summarization literature. Section 3 outlines the details of our salience and summarization models. Next we describe our data (Section 4) and experiments (Section 5). Finally, we discuss our results (Section 6) and conclude the paper.

2 Related Work

A principal concern in extractive multi-document summarization is the selection of salient sentences for inclusion in summary output (Nenkova and McKeown, 2012). Existing approaches generally fall into one of three categories, each with specific trade-offs with respect to update summarization.

First, centrality-focused approaches (including graph (Erkan and Radev, 2004), cluster (Hatzivassiloglou et al., 2001), and centroid (Radev et al., 2004) methods) are very natural for retrospective analysis in the sense that they let the data "speak for itself." These methods equate salience with centrality, either to the input or some other aggregate object (i.e. a cluster center or input centroid). However, they rely chiefly on redundancy. When applied to an unfolding event, there may not exist enough redundant content at the event onset for these methods to exploit. Once the event onset has passed, however, the redundancy reduction of these methods is quite beneficial.

The second category, predictive approaches, includes ranking and classification based methods. Sentences have been ranked by the average word probability, average TF*IDF score, and the number of topically related words (topic-signatures in the summarization literature) (Nenkova and Vanderwende, 2005; Hovy and Lin, 1998; Lin and Hovy, 2000). The first two statistics are easily computable from the input sentences, while the third only requires an additional, generic background corpus. In classification based methods, model features are usually derived from human generated summaries, and are non-lexical in nature (e.g., sentence starting position, number of topic-signatures, number of unique words). Seminal work in this area has employed naïve Bayes and logistic regression classifiers to identify sentences for summary inclusion (Kupiec et al., 1995; Conroy et al., 2001). While these methods are less dependent on redundancy, the expressiveness of their features is limited. Our model expands on these basic features to account for geographic, temporal, and language model features.

The last category includes probabilistic (Haghighi and Vanderwende, 2009), information theoretic, and set cover (Lin and Bilmes, 2011) approaches. While these methods are focused on producing diverse summaries, they are difficult to adapt to the streaming setting, where we do not necessarily have a fixed summary length and the corpus to be summarized contains many irrelevant sentences, i.e. there are large portions of the corpora that we specifically want to avoid.

Several researchers have recognized the importance of summarization during natural disasters. (Guo et al., 2013) developed a system for detecting novel, relevant, and comprehensive sentences immediately after a natural disaster. (Wang and Li, 2010) present a clustering-based approach to efficiently detect important updates during natural disasters. The algorithm works by hierarchically clustering sentences online, allowing the system to output a more expressive narrative structure than (Guo et al., 2013). Our system attempts to unify these system's approaches (predictive ranking and clustering respectively).

3 Method

Our update summarization system takes as input *a*) a short query defining the event to be tracked (e.g. 'Hurricane Sandy'), *b*) an event category defining the type of event to be tracked (e.g. 'hurricane'), *c*) a stream of time-stamped documents presented in temporal order, and *d*) an evaluation time period of interest. While processing documents throughout the time period of interest, the system outputs sentences from these documents likely to be useful to the query issuer. We refer to these selected sentences as *updates*.

In order to measure the usefulness of a system's updates, we consider the degree to which the system output reflects the different aspects of

– hurricane force wind warnings are in effect from Rhode Island Sound to Chincoteague Bay
– over 5000 commercial airline flights scheduled for October 28 and October 29 were cancelled

Figure 1: Example nuggets from Hurricane Sandy.

an event. Events are often composed of a variety of sub-events. For example, the Hurricane Sandy event includes sub-events related to the storm making landfall, the ensuing flooding, the many transportation issues, among many others. An ideal system would update the user about each of these sub-events as they occur. We refer to these sub-events as the *nuggets* associated with an event. A nugget is defined as a fine-grained atomic sub-event associated with an event. We present 2 example nuggets associated with the Hurricane Sandy event in Figure 1. Each event has anywhere from 50 to several hundred nuggets in total in our gold dataset. We describe how these nuggets are found in Section 4.

Throughout our treatment of our algorithm, the *salience* of an update captures the degree to which it reflects an event's unobserved nuggets. Assuming that we have a text representation for each of our nuggets, the salience of an update u with respect to a set of nuggets N is defined as,

$$\text{salience}(u) = \max_{n \in N} \text{sim}(u, n) \quad (1)$$

where $\text{sim}(\cdot)$ is the semantic similarity such as the cosine similarity of latent vectors associated with the update and nugget text (Guo and Diab, 2012).

3.1 Update Summarization

Our system architecture follows a simple pipeline design where each stage provides an additional level of processing or filtering of the input sentences. We begin with an empty update summary U. At each hour we receive a new batch of sentences b_t from the stream of event relevant documents and perform the following actions:

1. predict the salience of sentences in b_t (Section 3.2),
2. select a set of exemplar sentences in b_t by combining clustering with salience predictions (Section 3.3),
3. add the most novel and salient exemplars to U (Section 3.4).

The resultant list of updates U is our summary of the event.

3.2 Salience Prediction

3.2.1 Features

We want our model to be predictive of sentence salience across different event instances so we avoid event-specific lexical features. Instead, we extract features such as language model scores, geographic relevance, and temporal relevance from each sentence.

Basic Features We employ several basic features that have been used previously in supervised models to rank sentence salience (Kupiec et al., 1995; Conroy et al., 2001). These include sentence length, the number of capitalized words normalized by sentence length, document position, and number of named entities. The data stream comprises text extracted from raw html documents; these features help to downweight sentences that are not content (e.g. web page titles, links to other content) or more heavily weight important sentences (e.g., that appear in prominent positions such as paragraph initial or article initial).

Query Features Query features measure the relationship between the sentence and the event query and type. These include the number of query words present in the sentence in addition to the number of event type synonyms, hypernyms, and hyponyms using WordNet (Miller, 1995). For example, for event type *earthquake*, we match sentence terms "quake", "temblor", "seism", and "aftershock".

Language Model Features Language models allow us to measure the likelihood of producing a sentence from a particular source. We consider two types of language model features. The first model is estimated from a corpus of generic news articles (we used the 1995-2010 Associated Press section of the Gigaword corpus (Graff and Cieri, 2003)). This model is intended to assess the general writing quality (grammaticality, word usage) of an input sentence and helps our model to select sentences written in the newswire style.

The second model is estimated from text specific to our event types. For each event type we create a corpus of related documents using pages and subcategories listed under a related

Storm	Earthquake	Meteor Impact
Accident	Riot	Protest
Hostages	Shooting	Bombing

Figure 2: TREC TS event types.

Wikipedia category. For example, the language model for event type 'earthquake' is estimated from Wikipedia pages under the category *Category:Earthquakes*. Fig. 2 lists the event types found in our dataset. These models are intended to detect sentences similar to those appearing in summaries of other events in the same category (e.g. most earthquake summaries are likely to include higher probability for ngrams including the token 'magnitude'). While we focus our system on the language of news and disaster, we emphasize that the use of language modeling can be an effective feature for multi-document summarization for other domains that have related text corpora.

We use the SRILM toolkit (Stolcke and others, 2002) to implement a 5-gram Kneser-Ney model for both the background language model and the event specific language models. For each sentence we use the average token log probability under each model as a feature.

Geographic Relevance Features The disasters in our corpus are all phenomena that affect some part of the world. Where possible, we would like to capture a sentence's proximity to the event, i.e. when a sentence references a location, it should be close to the area of the disaster.

There are two challenges to using geographic features. First, we do not know where the event is, and second, most sentences do not contain references to a location. We address the first issue by extracting all locations from documents relevant to the event at the current hour and looking up their latitude and longitude using a publicly available geo-location service. Since the documents that are at least somewhat relevant to the event, we assume in aggregate the locations should give us a rough area of interest. The locations are clustered and we treat the resulting cluster centers as the event locations for the current time.

The second issue arises from the fact that the majority of sentences in our data do not contain explicit references to locations, i.e. a sequence of tokens tagged as location named entities. Our intuition is that geographic relevance is important in the disaster domain, and we would like to take advantage of the sentences that do have location information present. To make up for this imbalance, we instead compute an overall location for the document and derive geographic features based on the document's proximity to the event in question. These features are assigned to all sentences in the document.

Our method of computing document-level geographic relevance features is as follows. Using the locations in each document, we compute the median distance to the nearest event location. Because document position is a good indicator of importance we also compute the distance of the first mentioned location to the nearest event location. All sentences in the document take as features these two distance calculations. Because some events can move, we also compute these distances to event locations from the previous hour.

Temporal Relevance Features As we track events over time, it is likely that the coverage of the event may die down, only to spike back up when there is a breaking development. Identifying terms that are "bursty," i.e. suddenly peaking in usage, can help to locate novel sentences that are part of the most recent reportage and have yet to fall into the background.

We compute the IDF for each hour in our data stream. For each sentence, the average TF*IDF for the current hour t is taken as a feature. Additionally, we use the difference in average TF*IDF from time t to $t - i$ for $i = \{1, \ldots, 24\}$ to measure how the TF*IDF scores for the sentence have changed over the last 24 hours, i.e. we keep the sentence term frequencies fixed and compute the difference in IDF. Large changes in IDF value indicate the sentence contains bursty terms. We also use the time (in hours) since the event started as a feature.

3.2.2 Model

Given our feature representation of the input sentences, we need only target salience values for model learning. For each event in our training data, we sample a set of sentences and each sentence's salience is computed according to Equation 1. This results in a training set of sentences, their feature representations, and their target salience values to predict.

We opt to use a Gaussian process (GP) regression model (Rasmussen and Williams, 2006) with a Radial Basis Function (RBF) kernel for the salience prediction task. Our features fall naturally into five groups and we use a separate RBF kernel for each, using the sum of each feature group RBF kernel as the final input to the GP model.

3.3 Exemplar Selection

Once we have predicted the salience for a batch of sentences, we must now select a set of update candidates, i.e. sentences that are both salient and representative of the current batch. To accomplish this, we combine the output of our salience prediction model with the affinity propagation algorithm. Affinity propagation (AP) is a clustering algorithm that identifies a subset of data points as exemplars and forms clusters by assigning the remaining points to one of the exemplars (Frey and Dueck, 2007). AP attempts to maximize the net similarity objective

$$\mathcal{S} = \sum_{i:i \neq e_i}^{n} \text{sim}(i, e_i) + \sum_{i:i=e_i}^{n} \text{salience}(e_i)$$

where e_i is the exemplar of the i-th data point, and functions sim and salience express the pairwise similarity of data points and our predicted *apriori* preference of a data point to be an exemplar respectively. AP differs from other k-centers algorithms in that it simultaneously considers all data points as exemplars, making it less prone to finding local optima as a result of poor initialization. Furthermore, the second term in $\mathcal{S}$ incorporates the individual importance of data points as candidate exemplars; most other clustering algorithms only make use of the first term, i.e. the pairwise similarities between data points.

AP has several useful properties and interpretations. Chiefly, the number of clusters k is not a model hyper-parameter. Given that our task requires clustering many batches of streaming data, searching for an optimal k would be computationally prohibitive. With AP, k is determined by the similarities and preferences of the data. Generally lower preferences will result in fewer clusters.

Recall that $\text{salience}(s)$ is a prediction of the semantic similarity of s to information about the event be summarized, i.e. the set of event nuggets. Intuitively, when maximizing objective function $\mathcal{S}$, AP must balance between best representing the input data and representing the most salient input. Additionally, when the level of input is high but the salience predictions are low, the preference term will guide AP toward a solution with fewer clusters; *vice-versa* when input is very salient on average but the volume of input is low. The adaptive nature of our model differentiates our method from most other update summarization systems.

3.4 Update Selection

The exemplar sentences from the exemplar selection stage are the most salient and representative of the input for the current hour. However, we need to reconcile these sentences with updates from the previous hour to ensure that the most salient and least redundant updates are selected. To ensure that only the most salient updates are selected we apply a minimum salience threshold; after exemplar sentences have been identified, any exemplars whose salience is less than λ_{sal} are removed from consideration.

Next, to prevent adding updates that are redundant with previous output updates, we filter out exemplars that are too similar to previous updates. The exemplars are examined sequentially in order of decreasing salience and a similarity threshold is applied, where the exemplar is ignored if its maximum semantic similarity to any previous updates in the summary is greater than λ_{sim}.

Exemplars that pass these thresholds are selected as updates and added to the summary.

4 Data

For the document stream, we use the news portion of the 2014 TREC KBA Stream Corpus (Frank et al., 2012). The documents from this corpus come from hourly crawls of the web covering October 2011 through February 2013.

Our experiments also make use of the TREC Temporal Summarization (TS) Track data from 2013 and 2014 (Aslam et al., 2013). This data includes 25 events and event metadata (e.g., a user search query for the event, the event type, and event evaluation time frame). All events occurred during the time span of the TREC KBA Stream Corpus. For each event we create a stream of relevant documents by selecting only documents that contain the complete set of query words.

Along with the metadata, NIST assessors constructed a set of ground truth nuggets for each event. Nuggets are brief and important text snippets that represent sub-events that should be conveyed by an ideal update summary. In order to accomplish this, for each event, assessors were provided with the revision history of the Wikipedia page associated with the event. For example, the revision history for the Wikipedia page for 'Hurricane Sandy' will contain text additions including those related to individual nuggets. The assessment task involves reviewing the Wikipedia revisions in the evaluation time frame and marking the text additions capturing a new, unique nugget. More detail on this process can be found in the track description (Aslam et al., 2013).

5 Experiments

We evaluate our system on two metrics: ROUGE (Lin, 2004), an automatic summarization method and an evaluation of system expected gain and comprehensiveness—metrics adapted from the TREC TS track (Aslam et al., 2013).

5.1 Training and Testing

Of the 25 events in the TREC TS data, 24 are covered by the news portion of the TREC KBA Stream Corpus. From these 24, we set aside three events to use as a development set. All system salience and similarity threshold parameters are tuned on the development set to maximize ROUGE-2 F1 scores.

We train a salience model for each event using 1000 sentences randomly sampled from the event's document stream.

We perform a leave-one-out evaluation of each event. At test time, we predict a sentence's salience using the average predictions of the 23 other models.

5.2 ROUGE Evaluation

ROUGE measures the ngram overlap between a model summary and an automatically generated system summary. Model summaries for each event were constructed by concatenating the event's nuggets. Generally, ROUGE evaluation assumes both model and system summaries are of a bounded length. Since our systems are summarizing events over a span of two weeks time, the total length of our system output is much longer than the model. To address this, for each system/event pair, we sample with replacement 1000 random summaries of length less than or equal to the model summary (truncating the last sentence when neccessary). The final ROUGE scores for the system are the average scores from these 1000 samples.

Because we are interested in system performance over time, we also evaluate systems at 12 hour intervals using the same regime as above. The model summaries in this case are retrospective, and this evaluation reveals how quickly systems can cover information in the model.

5.3 Expected Gain and Comprehensiveness

NIST developed metrics for evaluating update summarization systems as part of the TREC TS track. We present results on two of these metrics, the expected gain and comprehensiveness.

Expected Gain We treat the event's nuggets as unique units of information. When a system adds an update to its summary, it is potentially adding some of this nugget information. It would be instructive to know how much unique and novel information each update is adding on average to the summary. To that end, we define

$$\mathbb{E}[\text{Gain}] = \frac{|S_n|}{|S|}$$

where S is the set of system updates, S_n is the set of nuggets contained in S, and $|\cdot|$ is the number of elements in the set. To compute the set S_n we match each system update to 0 or more nuggets, where an update matches a nugget if their semantic similarity is above a threshold. S_n results from the unique set of nuggets matched. Because an update can map to more than one nugget, it is possible to receive an expected gain greater than 1. An expected gain of 1 would indicate that every sentence was both relevant and contained a unique piece of information.

Comprehensiveness Additionally, we can use the nuggets to measure the completeness of an update summary. We define

$$\text{Comprehensiveness} = \frac{|S_n|}{|N|}$$

where N is the set of event nuggets. A comprehensiveness of 1 indicates that the summary has covered all nugget information for the event; the maximum attainable comprehensiveness is 1.

Update-nugget matches are computed automatically; a match exists if the semantic similarity of the update/nugget pair is above a threshold. Determining an optimal threshold to count matches is difficult so we evaluate at threshold values ranging from .5 to 1, where values closer to 1 are more conservative estimates of performance. A manual inspection of matches suggests that semantic similarity values around .7 produce reasonable matches. The average semantic similarity of manual matches performed by NIST assessors was much lower at approximately .25, increasing our confidence in the automatic matches in the .5–1 range.

5.4 Model Comparisons

We refer to our complete model as AP+SALIENCE. We compare this model against several variants and baselines intended to measure the contribution of different components. All thresholds for all runs are tuned on the development set.

Affinity Propagation only (AP) The purpose of this model is to directly measure the effect of integrating salience and clustering by providing a baseline that uses the identical clustering component, but without the salience information. In this model, input sentences are *apriori* equally likely to be exemplars; the salience values are uniformly set as the median value of the input similarity scores, as is commonly used in the AP literature (Frey and Dueck, 2007). After clustering a sentence batch, the exemplars are examined in order of increasing time since event start and selected as updates if their maximum similarity to the previous updates is less than λ_{sim}, as in the novelty filtering stage of AP+SALIENCE.

Hierarchichal Agglomerative Clustering (HAC) We provide another clustering baseline, single-linkage hierarchichal agglomerative clustering. We include this baseline to show that AP+SALIENCE is not just an improvement over AP but centrality driven methods in general. HAC was chosen over other clustering approaches because the number of clusters is not an explicit hyper-parameter. To produce flat clusters from the hierarchical clustering, we flatten the HAC dendrogram using the cophenetic distance criteria, i.e. observations in each flat cluster have no greater a cophenetic distance than a threshold. Cluster centers are determined to be the sentence with highest cosine similariy to the flat cluster mean. Cluster centers are examined in time order and are added to the summary if their similarity to previous updates is below a similarity threshold λ_{sim} as is done in the AP model.

Rank by Salience (RS) We also isolate the impact of our salience model in order to demonstrate that the fusion of clustering and salience prediction improves over predicting salience alone. In this model we predict the salience of sentences as in step 1 for AP+SALIENCE. We omit the clustering phase (step 2). Updates are selected identically to step 3 of AP+SALIENCE, proceeding in order of decreasing salience, selecting updates that are above a salience threshold λ_{sal} and below a similarity threshold λ_{sim} with respect to the previously selected updates.

6 Results

6.1 ROUGE

ROUGE-1			
System	Recall	Prec.	F_1
AP+SALIENCE	**0.282**	**0.344**	**0.306**
AP	0.245	0.285	0.263
RS	0.230	0.271	0.247
HAC	0.169	0.230	0.186

ROUGE-2			
System	Recall	Prec.	F_1
AP+SALIENCE	**0.045**	**0.056**	**0.049**
AP	0.033	0.038	0.035
RS	0.031	0.037	0.034
HAC	0.017	0.024	0.019

Table 1: System ROUGE performance.

Table 1 shows our results for system output samples against the full summary of nuggets using ROUGE. This improvement is statistically significant for all ngram precision, recall, and F-measures at the $\alpha = .01$ level using the Wilcoxon signed-rank test.

AP+SALIENCE maintains its performance above the baselines over time as well. Figure 3 shows the ROUGE-1 scores over time. We show the difference in unigram precision (bigram precision is not shown but it follows similar curve). Within the initial days of the event, AP+SALIENCE is able to take the lead over the over systems in ngram precision. The AP+SALIENCE model is better able to find salient updates earlier on; for the disaster domain, this is an especially important quality of the model.

Moreover, the AP+SALIENCE's recall is not diminished by the high precision and remains competitive with AP. Over time AP+SALIENCE's recall also begins to pull away, while the other models start to suffer from topic drift.

6.2 Expected Gain and Comprehensiveness

Figure 4 shows the expected gain across a range of similarity thresholds, where thresholds closer

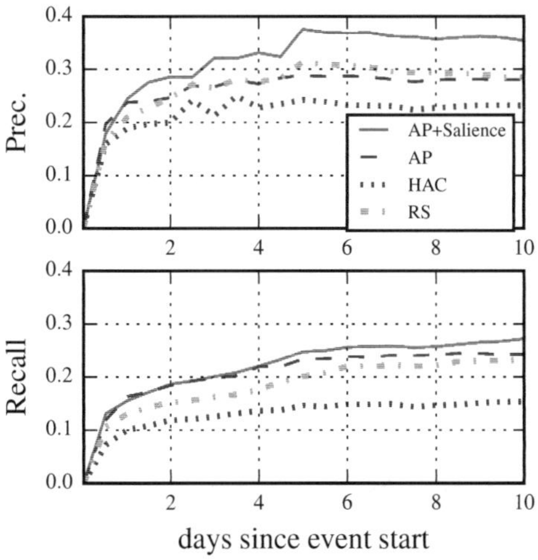

Figure 3: System ROUGE-1 performance over time.

to 1 are more conservative estimates. The ranking of the systems remains constant across the sweep with AP+SALIENCE beating all baseline systems. Predicting salience in general is helpful for keeping a summary on topic as the RS approach out performs the clustering only approaches on expected gain.

When looking at the comprehensiveness of the summaries AP outperforms AP+SALIENCE. The compromise encoded in the AP+SALIENCE objective function, between being representative and being salient, is seen clearly here where the performance of the AP+SALIENCE methods is lower bounded by the salience focused RS system and upper bounded by the clustering only AP system. Overall, AP+SALIENCE achieves the best balance of these two metrics.

6.3 Feature Ablation

Table 2 shows the results of our feature ablation tests. Removing the language models yields a statistically significant drop in both ngram recall and F-measure. Interestingly, removing the basic features leads to an increase in both unigram and bigram precision; in the bigram case this is enough to cause a statistically significant increase in F-measure over the full model. In other words, the generic features actually lead to an inferior model when we can incorporate more appropriate domain specific features. The result mirrors Sparck Jones' claim that generic approaches to

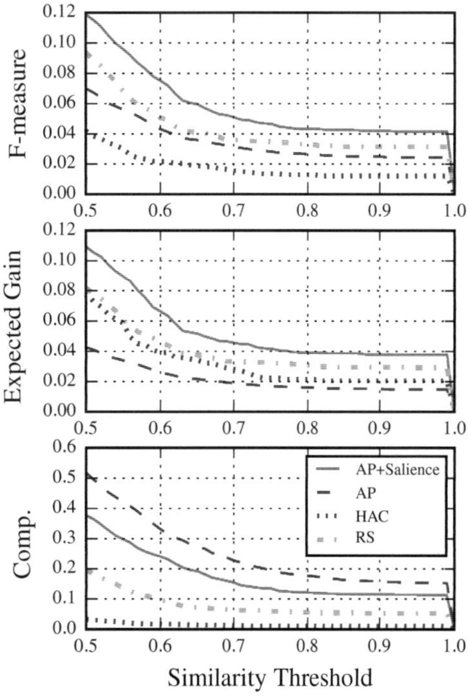

Figure 4: Expected Gain and Comprehensiveness performance.

summarization cannot produce a useful summary (Sparck-Jones, 1998).

Removing the language model and geographic relevance features leads to a statistically significant drop in ROUGE-1 F1 scores. Unfortunately, this is not the case for the temporal relevance features. We surmise that these features are too strongly correlated with each other, i.e. the differences in TF*IDF between hours are definitely not i.i.d. variables.

7 Conclusion

In this paper, we have presented an update summarization system for the disaster domain, and demonstrated improved system performance by integrating sentence salience with clustering.

We also have shown that features specifically targeted to the domain of disaster yield better summaries. We developed novel features that capture the language typical of different event types and that identify sentences specific to the particular disaster based on location.

In the future we would like to explore the appli-

2012 Pakistan Garment Factory Fires

- The fire broke out when people in the building were trying to start their generator after the electricity went out.
- Pakistani television showed pictures of what appeared to be a three-story building with flames leaping from the top-floor windows and smoke billowing into the night sky.
- The people went to the back side of the building but there was no access, so we had to made forceful entries and rescue the people, said Numan Noor, a firefighter on the scene.
- "We have recovered 63 bodies, including three found when we reached the basement of the building," Karachi fire chief Ehtesham Salim told AFP on Wednesday.

2012 Romanian Protests

- Clashes between riot police and demonstrators have also erupted in the Romanian capital Bucharest for a third day in a row.
- BOC urged Romanians to understand that tough austerity measures are needed to avoid a default.
- More than 1,000 protesters rallied in Bucharest's main university square, blocking traffic.
- Bucharest : a Romanian medical official says 59 people suffered injuries as days of protests against the government and austerity measures turned violent.

Figure 5: AP+SALIENCE summary excerpts.

ROUGE-1

System	Recall	Prec.	F_1
Full System	0.282	0.344	0.306
No Basic	0.263	0.380†	0.294
No LM	0.223†	0.361	0.254†
No Time	0.297†	0.367††	0.322†
No Geo	0.232††	0.381	0.265†
No Query	0.251	0.377	0.280

ROUGE-2

System	Recall	Prec.	F_1
Full System	0.045	0.056	0.049
No Basic	0.046	0.068††	0.051†
No LM	0.033†	0.056	0.038†
No Time	0.052††	0.064††	0.056††
No Geo	0.037†	0.065	0.042
No Query	0.043	0.068†	0.048

Table 2: Feature ablation ROUGE performance. † indicates statistically significant difference from full model at the $\alpha = .05$ level. †† indicates statistically significant difference from full model at the $\alpha = .01$ level.

cation of the AP+SALIENCE model and features to a wider class of events.

8 Acknowledgments

The research described here was supported in part by the National Science Foundation (NSF) under IIS-1422863. Any opinions, findings and conclusions or recommendations expressed in this paper are those of the authors and do not necessarily reflect the views of the NSF.

References

James Allan, Jaime G Carbonell, George Doddington, Jonathan Yamron, and Yiming Yang. 1998. Topic detection and tracking pilot study final report.

Javed Aslam, Matthew Ekstrand-Abueg, Virgil Pavlu, Fernado Diaz, and Tetsuya Sakai. 2013. Trec 2013 temporal summarization. In *Proceedings of the 22nd Text Retrieval Conference (TREC), November.*

James M Conroy, Judith D Schlesinger, PO Dianne, Mary E Okurowski, et al. 2001. Using hmm and logistic regression to generate extract summaries for duc.

Günes Erkan and Dragomir R Radev. 2004. Lexrank: Graph-based lexical centrality as salience in text summarization. *J. Artif. Intell. Res.(JAIR)*, 22(1):457–479.

Elena Filatova and Vasileios Hatzivassiloglou. 2004. Event-based extractive summarization. In *ACL Workshop on Summarization, Barcelona, Spain.*

John R Frank, Max Kleiman-Weiner, Daniel A Roberts, Feng Niu, Ce Zhang, Christopher Ré, and Ian Soboroff. 2012. Building an entity-centric stream filtering test collection for trec 2012. Technical report, DTIC Document.

Brendan J Frey and Delbert Dueck. 2007. Clustering by passing messages between data points. *science*, 315(5814):972–976.

David Graff and C Cieri. 2003. English gigaword corpus. *Linguistic Data Consortium.*

Weiwei Guo and Mona Diab. 2012. A simple unsupervised latent semantics based approach for sentence similarity. In *Proceedings of the First Joint Conference on Lexical and Computational Semantics-Volume 1: Proceedings of the main conference and the shared task, and Volume 2: Proceedings of the Sixth International Workshop on Semantic Evaluation*, pages 586–590. Association for Computational Linguistics.

Qi Guo, Fernando Diaz, and Elad Yom-Tov. 2013. Updating users about time critical events. In Pavel Serdyukov, Pavel Braslavski, SergeiO. Kuznetsov, Jaap Kamps, Stefan Rüger, Eugene Agichtein, Ilya Segalovich, and Emine Yilmaz, editors, *Advances in Information Retrieval*, volume 7814 of *Lecture Notes in Computer Science*, pages 483–494. Springer Berlin Heidelberg.

Aria Haghighi and Lucy Vanderwende. 2009. Exploring content models for multi-document summarization. In *Proceedings of Human Language Technologies: The 2009 Annual Conference of the North American Chapter of the Association for Computational Linguistics*, pages 362–370. Association for Computational Linguistics.

Vasileios Hatzivassiloglou, Judith L Klavans, Melissa L Holcombe, Regina Barzilay, Min-Yen Kan, and Kathleen McKeown. 2001. Simfinder: A flexible clustering tool for summarization. Proceedings of the NAACL Workshop on Automatic Summarizatio.

Eduard Hovy and Chin-Yew Lin. 1998. Automated text summarization and the summarist system. In *Proceedings of a workshop on held at Baltimore, Maryland: October 13-15, 1998*, pages 197–214. Association for Computational Linguistics.

Julian Kupiec, Jan Pedersen, and Francine Chen. 1995. A trainable document summarizer. In *Proceedings of the 18th annual international ACM SIGIR conference on Research and development in information retrieval*, pages 68–73. ACM.

Hui Lin and Jeff Bilmes. 2011. A class of submodular functions for document summarization. In *Proceedings of the 49th Annual Meeting of the Association for Computational Linguistics: Human Language Technologies-Volume 1*, pages 510–520. Association for Computational Linguistics.

Chin-Yew Lin and Eduard Hovy. 2000. The automated acquisition of topic signatures for text summarization. In *Proceedings of the 18th conference on Computational linguistics-Volume 1*, pages 495–501. Association for Computational Linguistics.

Chin-Yew Lin. 2004. Rouge: A package for automatic evaluation of summaries. In *Text Summarization Branches Out: Proceedings of the ACL-04 Workshop*, pages 74–81.

George A Miller. 1995. Wordnet: a lexical database for english. *Communications of the ACM*, 38(11):39–41.

Ani Nenkova and Kathleen McKeown. 2012. A survey of text summarization techniques. In *Mining Text Data*, pages 43–76. Springer.

Ani Nenkova and Lucy Vanderwende. 2005. The impact of frequency on summarization. *Microsoft Research, Redmond, Washington, Tech. Rep. MSR-TR-2005-101*.

Leysia Palen, Kenneth M Anderson, Gloria Mark, James Martin, Douglas Sicker, Martha Palmer, and Dirk Grunwald. 2010. A vision for technology-mediated support for public participation & assistance in mass emergencies & disasters. In *Proceedings of the 2010 ACM-BCS visions of computer science conference*, page 8. British Computer Society.

Dragomir R Radev, Hongyan Jing, Małgorzata Styś, and Daniel Tam. 2004. Centroid-based summarization of multiple documents. *Information Processing & Management*, 40(6):919–938.

Carl Edward Rasmussen and Christopher K. I. Williams. 2006. *Gaussian Processes for Machine Learning*. The MIT Press.

Karen Sparck-Jones. 1998. Automatic summarizing: factors and directions. In *Advances in automatic text summarization, eds. Mani and Maybury*.

Kate Starbird and Leysia Palen. 2013. Working and sustaining the virtual disaster desk. In *Proceedings of the 2013 conference on Computer supported cooperative work*, pages 491–502. ACM.

Andreas Stolcke et al. 2002. Srilm-an extensible language modeling toolkit. In *INTERSPEECH*.

Dingding Wang and Tao Li. 2010. Document update summarization using incremental hierarchical clustering. In *Proceedings of the 19th ACM international conference on Information and knowledge management*, CIKM '10, pages 279–288, New York, NY, USA. ACM.

William Yang Wang, Kapil Thadani, and Kathleen McKeown. 2011. Identifying event descriptions using co-training with online news summaries. In *proceedings of IJCNLP*, Chiang-Mai, Thailand, Nov.

Unsupervised Prediction of Acceptability Judgements

Jey Han Lau, Alexander Clark, and Shalom Lappin
jeyhan.lau@gmail.com, alexsclark@gmail.com, shalom.lappin@kcl.ac.uk
King's College London

Abstract

In this paper we present the task of unsupervised prediction of speakers' acceptability judgements. We use a test set generated from the British National Corpus (BNC) containing both grammatical sentences and sentences containing a variety of syntactic infelicities introduced by round trip machine translation. This set was annotated for acceptability judgements through crowd sourcing. We trained a variety of unsupervised language models on the original BNC, and tested them to see the extent to which they could predict mean speakers' judgements on the test set. To map probability to acceptability, we experimented with several normalisation functions to neutralise the effects of sentence length and word frequencies. We found encouraging results with the unsupervised models predicting acceptability across two different datasets. Our methodology is highly portable to other domains and languages, and the approach has potential implications for the representation and the acquisition of linguistic knowledge.

1 Introduction

Language modelling involves predicting the probability of a sentence. Given a trained model, we can infer the quantitative likelihood that a sentence occurs. Acceptability, on the other hand, indicates the extent to which a sentence is permissible or acceptable to native speakers of the language. While acceptability is affected by frequency and exhibits gradience (Keller, 2001; Sprouse, 2007; Lau et al., 2014), there is limited research on the relationship between acceptability and probability. In this paper, we consider the the task of unsupervised prediction of acceptability.

Speakers have robust intuitions about acceptability, and acceptability has been consistently rated on various scales (Sprouse and Almeida, 2012). The acceptability of a sentence appears to be relatively unaffected by its length (within certain bounds), or the frequency of its words, properties that we have confirmed experimentally. By contrast sentence probability does depend on these factors. To filter the effects of sentence length and word frequency, we devise normalising functions to map the probability of a sentence (inferred by our unsupervised language models) to an acceptability score.

Keller (2001) and Lau et al. (2014) present evidence that acceptability exhibits gradience. Accordingly, we treat acceptability as a continuous variable here. We train a variety of unsupervised models for the acceptability prediction task, and we assess the performance of these models by measuring the correlation between their normalised acceptability scores and the mean crowd-sourced acceptability judgements on a set of test sentences.

There are a number of NLP tasks to which our work can be fruitfully applied. It can be used to evaluate the fluency of the output for machine translation and other language generation systems. It could also contribute to automatic essay scoring, and to second language tutorial systems.

There are several reasons to favour unsupervised models. From an engineering perspective, unsupervised models offer greater portability to other domains and languages. Our methodology takes only unannotated text as input. Extending

Proceedings of the 53rd Annual Meeting of the Association for Computational Linguistics and the 7th International Joint Conference on Natural Language Processing, pages 1618–1628,
Beijing, China, July 26-31, 2015.

our methodology to other domains/languages is therefore straightforward, as it requires only a raw training corpus in that domain/language.

Our work may also have significant implications for the cognitive foundations of the representation and acquisition of linguistic knowledge. The unannotated training corpora of our language models are impoverished input in comparison to the data available to humans language learners, who learn from a variety of data sources (visual and auditory cues, interaction with adults and peers in a non-linguistic environment, etc). If an unsupervised language model can reliably predict human acceptability judgements, then it provides a benchmark of what humans could, in principle, achieve with the same learning algorithm.

Success in this task raises interesting questions about the nature of grammatical knowledge. If acceptability judgments can be accurately modeled through these techniques, then it seems unnecessary to posit an underlying binary model of syntax which enumerates all and only the set of well-formed sentences. Instead it is reasonable to suggest that humans represent linguistic knowledge as a probabilistic, rather than as a binary system. Probability distributions provide a natural explanation of the gradience that characterises acceptability judgements. Gradience is intrinsic to probability distributions, and to the acceptability scores that we derive from these distributions.

While our results raise important questions concerning the nature of syntactic representation and of language acquisition, we leave them open for further research. We refrain from making strong claims on cognitive issues here. Clearly additional psychological evidence is required to motivate substantive conclusions on these issues, even if our results suggest them.

Our focus in this paper is on the task of predicting speakers' acceptability judgements through unsupervised language models. We take this to be a problem in natural language processing, whose solution has useful applications in language technology. All models described in this paper are implemented in an open source toolkit.[1]

We describe our dataset in Section 2, which consists of crowd sourced acceptability judgments applied to sentences with errors introduced through round trip machine translation. We describe the models and their results in Section 3. In Section 4 we present results with a different corpus based on English Wikipedia. The new dataset shows that our observations generalise to another domain. We compare our methodology to a supervised system in the acceptability prediction task in Section 5. We look more closely at the influence of sentence length and lexical frequency in Section 6, and we show that the normalising functions succeed in neutralising these effects. Finally, we discuss the implications of our results, and draw conclusions from them in Section 7 and Section 8.

2 Dataset and Methodology

For our experiments, we require a collection of sentences that exhibit varying degrees of grammatical well-formedness. We use the dataset that we discuss in Lau et al. (2014). We translated British National Corpus (BNC Consortium, 2007) English sentences to four other languages – Norwegian, Spanish, Japanese and Chinese – and then back to English using Google Translate. To collect human judgements of acceptability for the sentences, we used Amazon Mechanical Turk. A total of 2,500 sentences were annotated.

Three modes of presentation were used for rating a sentence: (1) binary with two options (unnatural vs. natural); (2) four options (extremely unnatural, somewhat unnatural, somewhat natural and extremely natural); and (3) a sliding scale with two extremes (extremely unnatural and extremely natural). To aggregate the ratings over multiple speakers for each sentence, we computed the arithmetic mean. As there is a high correlation of mean ratings among different modes of presentation, we take the judgements for the four-option mode of presentation as the gold-standard for our experiments.

To predict the ratings of the 2,500 test sentences, we trained several probabilistic models on the BNC, and then used the trained models to infer the probabilities of the test sentences. Models are trained on the written portion of the BNC, which has approximately 100 million words (henceforth referred to as BNC-100M).[2] We used only the words, and no forms of annotation information in the BNC, as input to training.

We first experiment with simple lexical N-gram models, and then move to Bayesian and neural

[1]This toolkit can be accessed at `https://github.com/jhlau/acceptability_prediction`.

[2]We removed sentences with less than 8 words, as well as the 2,500 test sentences, from the training data.

network models, increasing the complexity of the models to better capture word dependencies.

To translate probability into acceptability scores, we compute several *acceptability measures* extracted from the model parameters. The acceptability measures are variants of the sentence's log probability, devised to normalise sentence length and low frequency words. These measures are summarised in Table 1. For each measure (including *LogProb* as a baseline) we compute its Pearson correlation coefficient with the gold standard sentence mean rating to evaluate its effectiveness in predicting acceptability.

We tokenised the training data (BNC-100M) and the test sentences using OpenNLP, and we converted all words to lower case. To address out of vocabulary (OOV) words that are seen in the test sentences but not in the training data, we adopt the Berkeley Parser approach, where we replace low frequency or OOV words using the *UNK* signature. We capture additional surface characteristics of the original word by attaching features at the end of the signature (e.g. the OOV word *1949* would be replaced by the signature *UNK-NUM*).[3]

Acc. Measure	Equation
LogProb	$\log P_m(\xi)$
Mean LP	$\frac{\log P_m(\xi)}{\lvert\xi\rvert}$
Norm LP (Div)	$-\frac{\log P_m(\xi)}{\log P_u(\xi)}$
Norm LP (Sub)	$\log P_m(\xi) - \log P_u(\xi)$
SLOR	$\frac{\log P_m(\xi) - \log P_u(\xi)}{\lvert\xi\rvert}$

Table 1: Acceptability measures for predicting the acceptability of a sentence. Notations: *SLOR* is the syntactic log-odds ratio, introduced by Pauls and Klein (2012); ξ is the sentence ($|\xi|$ is the sentence length); $P_m(\xi)$ is the probability of the sentence given by the model; $P_u(\xi)$ is the unigram probability of the sentence. Note that the negative sign in *Norm LP (Div)* is given to reverse the sign change introduced by the division of log unigram probabilities.

3 Unsupervised Models

3.1 Lexical N-gram Model

Lexical N-gram models were variously explored in tasks related to acceptability estimation (Heilman et al., 2014; Clark et al., 2013; Pauls and Klein, 2012). We use an N-gram model with Kneser-Ney interpolation (Goodman, 2001), and we train bigram, trigram, and 4-gram models on BNC-100M. The trained models are then used to compute the acceptability measures of the test sentences.

The results are detailed in Table 2 (columns: "2-gram", "3-gram" and "4-gram").[4] In general across all models, the *Norm LP (Div)* and *SLOR* measures consistently produce the best correlations.

We see a significant improvement when the context window is increased from 2-gram to 3-gram, but not so from 3-gram to 4-gram (2-gram best: 0.34; 3-gram best: 0.42; 4-gram best: 0.42). This result implies that increasing the context window of the lexical N-gram model does not correspond to a better representation of grammatical structure (insofar as the size of the dataset is fixed), and a more sophisticated model is necessary.

3.2 Bayesian HMM

Seeing that local context is insufficient for predicting acceptability, we explore various Bayesian models that incorporate richer latent structures. We chose a Bayesian implementation because its "rich gets richer" dynamics tends to work well for languages (Goldwater and Griffiths, 2007; Goldwater et al., 2009; Newman et al., 2012; Lau et al., 2012).

Lexical N-grams model the generation of a word based on its preceding words. We introduce a layer of latent variables on top of the words, which can be interpreted as the word classes, and we model the transitions between the latent variables and observed words using Markov processes. In this model we first generate a (latent) word class based on its preceding word classes, and we then generate the word based on its word class. Figure 1(b) illustrates the structure of a second order Hidden Markov model (HMM).

[3]Low frequency words are defined as words occurring less than 4 times in the BNC training data. A total of 15 features are used for the *UNK* signature.

[4]We do not present model perplexity values in the results, as we did not find any correlation between perplexity and task performance.

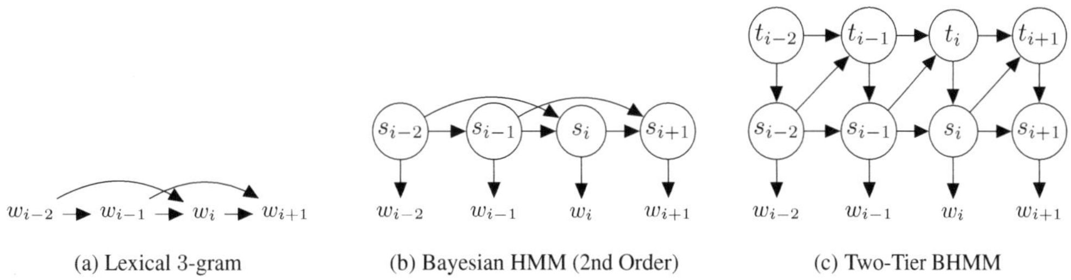

Figure 1: A comparison of word structures for 3-gram, BHMM and Two-Tier BHMM. w = observed words; s = tier-1 latent states ("word classes"); t = tier-2 latent states ("phrase classes").

For comparison, the structure of a lexical 3-gram model is given in Figure 1(a).

Goldwater and Griffiths (2007) propose a Bayesian approach for learning the HMM structure. The authors found that their Bayesian HMM (BHMM) significantly outperforms a HMM trained with Maximum Likelihood Estimation in unsupervised part-of-speech tagging. We adopt the methodology of Goldwater and Griffiths (2007), and train a 2nd order BHMM for our task, using collapsed Gibbs sampling for inference. BHMM has two sets of multinomials: the state transition multinomials and the word emission multinomials. To generalise the state transition probabilities for start probabilities, we use dummy words/states for empty preceding words/states.

BHMM has 3 parameters: (1) S, the number of latent states; (2) γ, the Dirichlet hyper-parameter for the state transition multinomials; and (3) δ, the Dirichlet hyper-parameter for the word emission multinomials. We assume symmetric Dirichlet priors for the hyper-parameters, and optimise the 3 parameters based on test perplexity using a greedy search approach, i.e. we optimise locally for one parameter at each stage, while keeping the default or previously optimised values for other parameters.[5] For the optimisation step models are trained using 10% of the full BNC (BNC-10M) for 2,000 iterations.[6]

Using the optimised parameters, we train BHMM on BNC-100M for 10,000 iterations. For test inference, we run the Gibbs sampler using the trained model for 5,000 iterations, and take 50 samples from the final 500 iterations (with a lag of 10 iterations). In each of the samples, we compute the test probabilities and acceptability measures using the MAP estimated states.[7] The final probabilities are computed as a harmonic mean of probabilities over the 50 samples.

We summarise the correlation results in Table 2 (column: "BHMM"). Compared to the N-gram models, we see an improvement in the correlation, indicating that the introduction of a layer of (latent) word classes produces a better structure for modelling acceptability.

3.3 LDAHMM and LDA

To better understand the role of semantics in acceptability, we experimented with LDAHMM (Griffiths et al., 2004), a model that combines syntactic and semantic dependencies between words.

The generative method of LDAHMM to generate a word in a document is to first decide whether to generate a syntactic state or a semantic state for the word. For the former, follow the HMM process to generate a state, and generate the word based on the chosen state. For the latter, follow the LDA (Blei et al., 2003) process to generate a topic based on the document's topic mixture, and generate the word based on the chosen topic.

We use a second order HMM for the HMM part and Collapsed Gibbs sampling for performing inference. LDAHMM has 4 sets of multinomials: the HMM multinomials (state transition and word emission) and the LDA multinomials (document-topic and topic-word).

LDAHMM has 6 parameters to optimise: (1) K the number of topics; (2) S the number of syntactic states (semantic state has only 1 state, designated as state 0); (3) α, the Dirichlet hyper-parameter for document-topic multinomials; (4) β, the Dirichlet hyper-parameter for topic-word multinomials; (5) γ, the Dirichlet hyper-

[5] When optimising for a parameter, we experimented with 4–6 values of various orders of magnitudes.

[6] The optimised parameters are: $S = 100$, $\gamma = 1.0$ and $\delta = 0.01$.

[7] As computing full probabilities gave little difference in the final outcome, we adopted the computationally more efficient MAP approach.

Measure	2-gram	3-gram	4-gram	BHMM	LDA	LDAHMM	2T	Chunker	RNNLM	PCFG*
LogProb	0.24	0.30	0.32	0.25	0.09	0.21	0.26	0.32	0.32	0.21
Mean LP	0.26	0.35	0.37	0.26	**0.14**	0.19	0.31	0.42	0.39	0.18
Norm LP (Div)	0.33	**0.42**	**0.42**	0.44	0.05	**0.33**	**0.50**	**0.43**	**0.53**	**0.26**
Norm LP (Sub)	0.12	0.20	0.23	0.33	0.01	0.19	0.46	0.14	0.31	0.22
SLOR	**0.34**	0.41	0.41	**0.45**	0.03	**0.33**	**0.50**	0.42	**0.53**	0.25

Table 2: Pearson's r of acceptability measure and mean sentence rating for all experimented models in BNC. Boldface indicates the best performing measure. Note that PCFG is a supervised model unlike the others.

parameter for state transition multinomials; and (6) δ, the Dirichlet hyper-parameter for word emission multinomials. We follow the same approach as with BHMM for optimising, training, and testing the model.[8] Note that as LDAHMM operates with documents, the training data is partitioned into documents, and each test sentence is treated as a document.

The results are summarised in Table 2 (column: "LDAHMM"). The result shows that LDAHMM underperforms in comparison to BHMM, indicating that the incorporation of LDA did not improve the model. To understand the impact of LDA alone, we repeat the experiments using LDA and find that it performs very poorly. Results are summarised in Table 2 (column: LDA). We suspect that the low performance of LDA and LDAHMM is due to the small context window of the test documents. The LDA part is unable to generate any meaningful topic mixtures, as there is insufficient context.

3.4 Two-Tier BHMM

BHMM uses (latent) word classes to drive word generation. Exploring a richer structure, we introduce another layer of latent variables on top of the word classes. This second layer can be interpreted as phrase classes. The idea behind this model is to use these phrase classes to drive word class and word generation. An illustration of its word structure is given in Figure 1(c).

We use collapsed Gibbs sampling for performing inference. We sample the tier-1 state s and tier-2 state t separately, and the sampling equations are given as follows:

$$P(t_i|\mathbf{t_{-i}}, \mathbf{s}, \mathbf{w}, \alpha, \gamma, \delta) \propto \frac{\#(t_{i-1}, s_{i-1}, t_i) + \alpha}{\#(t_{i-1}, s_{i-1}) + T\alpha} \times \frac{\#(t_i, s_{i-1}, s_i) + \gamma}{\#(t_i, s_{i-1}) + S\gamma} \times \frac{\#(t_i, s_i, t_{i+1}) + \alpha}{\#(t_i, s_i) + T\alpha};$$

$$P(s_i|\mathbf{s_{-i}}, \mathbf{t}, \mathbf{w}, \alpha, \gamma, \delta) \propto \frac{\#(t_i, s_{i-1}, s_i) + \gamma}{\#(t_i, s_{i-1}) + S\gamma} \times \frac{\#(t_i, s_i, t_{i+1}) + \alpha}{\#(t_i, s_i) + T\alpha} \times \frac{\#(t_{i+1}, s_i, s_{i+1}) + \gamma}{\#(t_{i+1}, s_i) + S\gamma} \times \frac{\#(s_i, w_i) + \delta}{\#(s_i) + W\delta}$$

where s_i, t_i are the tier-1 and tier-2 state indices; $\mathbf{s}$, $\mathbf{t}$, $\mathbf{w}$ are the assignments for all tier-1 states, tier-2 states and words, respectively (subscript $_{-i}$ means the current assignment is excluded); α, γ and δ are the Dirichlet hyper-parameters; S = number of tier-1 states; T = number of tier-2 states; W = vocabulary size; and $\#(x, [y], [z])$ are the multinomial counts.

We follow the same process for optimising, training, and testing the model, and we summarise the results in Table 2 (column: "2T").[9] We see an improved correlation relative to BHMM (BHMM best: 0.45, Two-Tier BHMM best: 0.50). In fact it has the best performance of all models thus far. This is encouraging, as it implies that the introduction of the phrase layer produces a more optimal structure for representing acceptability.

3.5 Bayesian Chunker

Goldwater et al. (2009) propose a Bayesian approach to segment words in speech streams. Newman et al. (2012) extend the approach to segment phrases – i.e. multiword units – in sentences, and they apply it to the task of index term identification and keyphrase extraction.

The core machinery of the methodology is driven by the Dirichlet Process, where segments (words in Goldwater et al. (2009) or phrases in Newman et al. (2012)) are retrieved from a cache,

[8]The final optimised parameters are: $K = 100$, $S = 80$, $\alpha = 0.1$, $\beta = 0.0001$, $\gamma = 0.1$, and $\delta = 0.01$.

[9]The optimised parameters: $S = 100$, $T = 60$, $\alpha = 1.0$, $\gamma = 1.0$, $\delta = 0.01$.

or newly generated. Using Gibbs sampling for inference, the sampler considers one boundary point at a time, and computes the probability of two hypotheses: H_0, for *not* generating a boundary; and H_1, for generating a boundary.

Borrowing the notation of Newman et al. (2012), given $p_{\#}$ is the probability of generating a segment boundary, at the boundary point between words w_x and w_y, the probability of the hypotheses is computed as follows:

$$P(H_0|H^-) = \frac{n(w_{xy}) + \alpha P_0(w_{xy})}{n+\alpha};$$
$$P(H_1|H^-) = \frac{n(w_x) + \alpha P_0(w_x)}{n+\alpha} \times \frac{n(w_y) + \alpha P_0(w_y)}{n+1+\alpha}$$

where H^- is all of the structure shared by both hypotheses; w_{xy} is a multiword unit consisting of w_x and w_y; n is the number of multiword tokens; α is the concentration parameter of the Dirichlet process; $n(w)$ is the count of multiword w; and $P_0(w)$ is the probability of generating a novel w. i.e. $P_0(w_{xy}) = p_{\#}(1-p_{\#})P(w_x)P(w_y)$.

We extend their methodology to segment *word classes* to do unsupervised chunking, motivated by the idea that a well-formed sentence contains predictable patterns of word class chunks. We extend the sampling process to incorporate transitions between chunks. Given the word classes "$c_w c_x c_y c_z$", at the boundary point between word class c_x and c_y, the hypothesis H_0 to not generate a boundary (therefore producing a single chunk c_{xy}), and the hypothesis H_1 to generate a boundary (therefore producing two chunks c_x and c_y), are computed as follows:

$$P(H_0|H^-) = \frac{\#(c_w, c_{xy}) + \beta\left(\frac{n(c_{xy})+\alpha P_0(c_{xy})}{n+\alpha}\right)}{\#(c_w)+m\beta} \times \frac{\#(c_{xy}, c_z) + \beta\left(\frac{n(c_z)+\alpha P_0(c_z)}{n+\alpha}\right)}{\#(c_{xy})+m\beta};$$
$$P(H_1|H^-) = \frac{\#(c_w, c_x) + \beta\left(\frac{n(c_x)+\alpha P_0(c_x)}{n+\alpha}\right)}{\#(c_w)+m\beta} \times \frac{\#(c_x, c_y) + \beta\left(\frac{n(c_y)+\alpha P_0(c_y)}{n+\alpha}\right)}{\#(c_x)+m\beta} \times \frac{\#(c_y, c_z) + \beta\left(\frac{n(c_z)+\alpha P_0(c_z)}{n+\alpha}\right)}{\#(c_y)+m\beta}$$

where m = number of chunk types; n = number of chunk tokens; β is the Dirichlet hyperparameter for the chunk transition multinomials; and $\#(x, [y])$ is the count for the chunk transition multinomials.

As the model takes word classes as input, we use the word classes induced by two-tier BHMM. We follow the same process for optimising, training and testing the model.[10] The results are summarised in Table 2 (column: "Chunker"). The model produces a moderate correlation, performing on par with the lexical 4-gram model.

3.6 Recurrent Neural Network Language Model

In recent years, we have seen a resurgence in the use of neural networks for deep machine learning and NLP. Rather than designing structures or handcrafting features that seem intuitive for a task, deep learning introduces an entirely general architecture for machine learning. It has yielded some impressive results for NLP tasks: automatic speech recognition, parsing, part of speech tagging, and named entity recognition, to name a few (Seide et al., 2011; Mikolov et al., 2011a; Collobert et al., 2011; Chen and Manning, 2014).

We experiment with a recurrent neural network language model (RNNLM: (Elman, 1998; Mikolov, 2012)) for our task. We choose this model because it has an internal state that keeps track of previously observed sequences, which is well suited for natural language problems. To train the model, we use stochastic gradient descent combined with back propagation through time. RNNLM is optimised to reduce the error in predicting the following word, based on the current word and its history (represented in a compressed dimension in the size of the hidden layer). Full details of RNNLM can be found in the original papers (Mikolov et al., 2011b; Mikolov, 2012).[11]

We experimented with some of the parameters of RNNLM using BNC-10M and found that most parameters have an intuitive setting. Its performance largely depends on the number of neurons in the hidden layer. Mikolov (2012) introduced a variant of RNNLM that does joint learning with a Maximum Entropy model which learns direct connections of N-gram features. We found that although there are advantages to using the ME model, the benefits disappear as we increase the number of neurons in the hidden layer. We saw optimal performance at 600 neurons, without using the ME model. All our results are based

[10]The optimised parameters are: $\alpha = 0.1$, $\beta = 0.001$, $p_{\#} = 0.5$.

[11]We use Mikolov's implementation of RNNLM for our experiment: `http://rnnlm.org/`.

Measure	2-gram	3-gram	4-gram	BHMM	LDAHMM	2T	Chunker	RNNLM
LogProb	0.31	0.36	0.38	0.32	0.33	0.35	0.42	0.44
Mean LP	0.28	0.36	0.37	0.28	0.28	0.35	0.45	0.46
Norm LP (Div)	0.34	**0.41**	**0.41**	0.44	0.42	0.49	**0.43**	0.55
Norm LP (Sub)	0.11	0.20	0.22	0.32	0.32	0.44	0.14	0.33
SLOR	**0.35**	**0.41**	**0.41**	**0.46**	**0.44**	**0.50**	0.41	**0.57**

Table 3: Pearson's r of acceptability measure and mean sentence rating for all experimented models in ENWIKI. Boldface indicates the best performing measure.

on the original RNNLM with 600 neurons in the hidden layer, trained on BNC-100M (Table 2 column: "RNNLM").[12] We see that RNNLM performs very well. It outperforms the other models, achieving a correlation of 0.53.

3.7 PCFG Parser (Supervised)

Although we are interested in unsupervised models, for purposes of comparison we experimented with a constituent PCFG parser for our task. We use the Stanford Parser (Klein and Manning, 2003a; Klein and Manning, 2003b), and tested both the unlexicalised and lexicalised PCFG parser with the supplied model. To compute the log probability of test sentences, we experimented with both top-1 and top-1K best parses.

We found that the unlexicalised variant gives better performance, but we saw little difference between using the top-1 and the top-1K best parses for computing log probability. In Table 2 (column: "PCFG"), we report results for the unlexicalised variant based on the top-1 best parse. The supervised PCFG parser performs poorly. This is not surprising, given that the parser is trained on a different domain.[13] Moreover, the log probability scores are not true probabilities, but arbitrary values used for ranking the parse trees.

4 English Wikipedia

For the BNC domain we saw that *SLOR* and *Norm LP (Div)* give the best acceptability measures, and that BHMM, two-tier BHMM and RNNLM are the best performing models. These findings are limited to a particular dataset. To better understand if these observations generalise to another domain, we developed an English Wikipedia dataset (ENWIKI), following the same process described in Lau et al. (2014) to generate test sentences through round-trip machine translation ,and to collect annotations via Mechanical Turk.[14] As before, we follow the same procedures described in Section 3 to optimise, train, and test all models (excluding LDA and PCFG). The Pearson correlations with mean AMT annotations are presented in Table 3.

We identify similar trends in ENWIKI: *Norm LP (Div)* and *SLOR* are the best acceptability measures, and we see improvements when we use a richer structure in the language model (two-tier BHMM>BHMM>N-grams). Interestingly, LDAHMM performs much better in this domain (possibly due to increased coherence in the document structure of ENWIKI). RNNLM has the best performance of all models, surpassing two-tier BHMM by a substantial margin. Overall, the correlation values are very similar across the two domains, indicating that the models and the acceptability measures are robust.

5 Comparison with a Supervised System

Although not a focus of this paper, supervised learning can further improve the correlation performance of our models. The acceptability measures can be combined in a supervised context. We experimented with this approach in a support vector regression model (with an RBF kernel). We achieved a correlation performance of 0.64 in BNC and of 0.69 in ENWIKI.[15]

Heilman et al. (2014) propose a system for predicting acceptability. They built a dataset consisting of sentences from essays written by non-native speakers for an ESL test. Acceptability ratings were judged by the authors, and through crowdsourcing (henceforth we refer to this annotated data set as the GUG data set). They applied

[12] Other parameter values of RNNLM: number of classes = 550; bptt = 4; bptt-block = 100.

[13] The Stanford English model is trained on the parse tree hand annotated WSJ (section 1–21), Genia, and a few other datasets.

[14] Both the BNC and the English Wikipedia datasets are available at `http://www.dcs.kcl.ac.uk/staff/lappin/smog/?page=research`.

[15] We use only the unsupervised models, excluding the supervised PCFG parser. The models are trained and tested using 10-fold cross validation.

a 4-category ordinal scale for rating the sentences. To predict sentence acceptability, they employ a linear regression model that draws features from spelling errors, an N-gram model, precision grammar parsers, and the Stanford PCFG parser.

To better understand the performance of our system compared to other acceptability prediction systems, we evaluated our methodology against that of Heilman et al. (2014) on the GUG dataset. We preprocessed the GUG dataset minimally. We removed 15 short sentences that have less than 5 words, lowercased all words, and tokenised the sentences using OpenNLP. This yields 2255 sentences for the training and development subset, and 749 sentences for the test set. Using the output – i.e. the acceptability measures – of our unsupervised models (trained on BNC) as features, we trained an SVR model using GUG training and development subsets to predict acceptability ratings on GUG test sentences. We applied the default SVR parameters, and so it was not necessary to use the development subset separately to optimise the parameters. For evaluation we computed the correlation of the predicted ratings and mean human ratings.

We present a comparison of results in Table 4. We first tested the unsupervised models, with the best correlation of 0.472 produced by the lexical 4-gram model using the *Norm LP (Div)* measure. Combining the models in SVR, we achieve a correlation of 0.603.

Heilman et al. (2014) note that spelling is one of the important features in their regression model, as the dataset often contains spelling mistakes. We borrowed this feature, computed as the proportion of misspelled words, and incorporated into our model. It produced a significant improvement in the correlation (0.636), a performance almost on par with that of Heilman et al. (2014).[16]

Our results demonstrate the robustness and portability of our system in a new domain. Our SVR model requires significantly less supervision than that of Heilman et al. (2014), which relies on precision and constituent parsers. Moreover, our methodology provides a completely unsupervised alternative that requires only raw text for training.

[16]We use PyEnchant for spellcheck: `http://pythonhosted.org/pyenchant/`. Note that we also tried adding the spelling feature to our original BNC derived dataset, but it yielded no improvement in the correlation. This is not surprising, given that it contains few spelling errors.

System	Pearson's r
Heilman et al. (2014)	0.644
Unsupervised Best	0.472
SVR: All Models	0.603
SVR: All Models+Spell	0.636

Table 4: A comparison of results of our system and Heilman et al. (2014) on GUG.

6 Influence of Sentence Length and Lexical Frequency

Our primary motivation in doing this research has been to use acceptability predictions to explore whether acceptability can be represented through probability information. Unlike probability, acceptability is generally not influenced by sentence length or low frequency words.

The acceptability measures we apply normalise sentence length and word frequency. To evaluate their effectiveness, we computed two correlations in the BNC domain: (1) acceptability measure vs. sentence length (Table 5); and (2) acceptability measure vs. sentence minimum word frequency (Table 6).[17]

For comparison we additionally computed the correlation of these factors with human ratings. The correlations are: +0.13 with sentence length; and +0.07 with minimum word frequency. These observations confirm the view that acceptability is not affected by these two factors.

Table 5 shows that although *LogProb* yields a strong negative correlation with sentence length, *Mean LP*, *Norm LP (Div)* and *SLOR* all produce low correlations. The only exception is *Norm LP (Sub)*, which still has a significant correlation with sentence length.

In Table 6 we see some degree of correlation in *LogProb* with the minimum word frequency, but it is relatively small. In general, *SLOR* is the scoring function that most effectively normalises word frequency, producing low correlation for most models. *Norm LP (Div)* also does very well, for all models except N-grams.

7 Discussion

In principle, the upper bound of the correlation between our models' predicted acceptability values and mean human ratings is 1.0. But no individual human annotator will match mean judgements perfectly. It is more plausible to measure our models'

[17]We use BNC-100M for computing word frequency.

Measure	2-gram	3-gram	4-gram	BHMM	LDAHMM	2T	Chunker	RNNLM
LogProb	−0.89	−0.80	−0.84	−0.85	−0.86	−0.86	−0.83	−0.86
Mean LP	−0.16	−0.08	−0.18	+0.03	+0.05	−0.02	−0.01	+0.08
Norm LP (Div)	−0.15	−0.07	−0.17	+0.10	+0.15	±0.00	±0.00	+0.14
Norm LP (Sub)	+0.69	+0.63	+0.54	+0.46	+0.54	+0.11	+0.70	+0.62
SLOR	−0.07	+0.04	−0.03	+0.12	+0.17	+0.01	±0.00	+0.17

Table 5: Pearson's r of acceptability measure and sentence length for all models in BNC. For comparison the correlation with human ratings is +0.13.

Measure	2-gram	3-gram	4-gram	BHMM	LDAHMM	2T	Chunker	RNNLM
LogProb	+0.27	+0.27	+0.27	+0.27	+0.27	+0.27	+0.19	+0.28
Mean LP	+0.30	+0.28	+0.27	+0.29	+0.28	+0.29	+0.08	+0.26
Norm LP (Div)	+0.24	+0.23	+0.21	+0.11	+0.06	+0.12	+0.06	+0.11
Norm LP (Sub)	−0.04	−0.03	−0.03	−0.03	−0.09	+0.05	−0.13	−0.08
SLOR	+0.16	+0.14	+0.12	+0.06	±0.00	+0.10	+0.04	+0.03

Table 6: Pearson's r of acceptability measure and sentence minimum word frequency for all models in BNC. The correlation with the human ratings is +0.07.

rate of success against an estimated level of individual human performance. We do this by mimicking an arbitrary speaker, and testing the correlation of this construct's judgements with the mean scores of the annotators.

We simulate such an individual human judge by randomly selecting a single annotator rating for each sentence, and computing the Pearson correlation between these judgements and the mean ratings for the rest of the annotators (one vs the rest) in our test sets. We ran this experiment 50 times for each test set to reduce sample variation, producing a mean correlation of 0.67 for BNC and 0.74 for ENWIKI. For comparison, the best unsupervised model (RNNLM) achieves a correlation of 0.53 in BNC and 0.57 in ENWIKI (Section 3). The supervised model (SVR) produces a correlation of 0.64 in BNC and 0.69 in ENWIKI (Section 5). Although there is still room for improvement for the unsupervised methodology, it is encouraging to note that the supervised variant predicts acceptability at a level that approaches estimated human performance.

To test the robustness of our methodology across languages, we are currently developing datasets in other languages, based on Wikipedia. Our preliminary results show similar performance to that which we report here for ENWIKI, suggesting that these results hold across languages.

8 Conclusion

We developed a methodology for using unsupervised language models to predict human acceptability judgements. We experimented with a variety of unsupervised models. To map probability to acceptability we proposed a set of acceptability measures to normalise sentence length and lexical frequency. We achieved encouraging results across two datasets constructed through round trip machine translation, and the methodology is highly portable to other domains and languages. This research has potential implications for our understanding of human language acquisition and the way in which linguistic knowledge is represented.

Acknowledgements

The research reported here was done as part of the Statisticsal Models of Grammar (SMOG) project at King's College London (`www.dcs.kcl.ac.uk/staff/lappin/smog/`), funded by grant ES/J022969/1 from the Economic and Social Research Council of the UK.

We are grateful to Douglas Saddy and Garry Smith at the Centre for Integrative Neuroscience and Neurodynamics at the University of Reading for generously giving us access to their computing cluster, and for much helpful technical support. We thank J. David Lappin for invaluable assistance in organising our AMT HITS. We presented part of the work discussed here to CL/NLP, cognitive science, and machine learning colloquia at Chalmers University of Technology, University of Gothenburg, University of Sheffield, University of Edinburgh, The Weizmann Institute of Science, University of Toronto, MIT, and the ILLC at the University of Amsterdam. We very much appreciate the comments and criticisms that we received from these audiences, which have guided us in our research.

References

D. Blei, A. Ng, and M. Jordan. 2003. Latent Dirichlet allocation. *Journal of Machine Learning Research*, 3:993–1022.

BNC Consortium. 2007. The British National Corpus, version 3 (BNC XML Edition). Distributed by Oxford University Computing Services on behalf of the BNC Consortium.

D. Chen and C. Manning. 2014. A fast and accurate dependency parser using neural networks. In *Proceedings of the 2014 Conference on Empirical Methods in Natural Language Processing (EMNLP 2014)*, pages 740–750, Doha, Qatar.

Alexander Clark, Gianluca Giorgolo, and Shalom Lappin. 2013. Statistical representation of grammaticality judgements: The limits of n-gram models. In *Proceedings of the ACL Workshop on Cognitive Modelling and Computational Linguistics*, Sofia, Bulgaria.

R. Collobert, J. Weston, L. Bottou, M. Karlen, K. Kavukcuoglu, and P. Kuksa. 2011. Natural language processing (almost) from scratch. *Journal of Machine Learning Research*, 12:2493–2537.

J. Elman. 1998. Generalization, simple recurrent networks, and the emergence of structure. In M. Gernsbacher and S. Derry, editors, *Proceedings of the 20th Annual Conference of the Cognitive Science Society*. Lawrence Erlbaum Associates, Mahway, NJ.

Sharon Goldwater and Tom Griffiths. 2007. A fully Bayesian approach to unsupervised part-of-speech tagging. In *Proceedings of the 45th Annual Meeting of the Association for Computational Linguistics (ACL 2007)*, pages 744–751, Prague, Czech Republic.

S. Goldwater, T. Griffiths, and M. Johnson. 2009. A Bayesian framework for word segmentation: Exploring the effects of context. *Cognition*, 112:21–54.

J.T. Goodman. 2001. A bit of progress in language modeling. *Computer Speech & Language*, 15(4):403–434.

Thomas L. Griffiths, Mark Steyvers, David M. Blei, and Joshua B. Tenenbaum. 2004. Integrating topics and syntax. In *Advances in Neural Information Processing Systems 17*, pages 537–544. Vancouver, Canada.

Michael Heilman, Aoife Cahill, Nitin Madnani, Melissa Lopez, Matthew Mulholland, and Joel Tetreault. 2014. Predicting grammaticality on an ordinal scale. In *Proceedings of the 52nd Annual Meeting of the Association for Computational Linguistics (ACL 2014), Volume 2: Short Papers*, pages 174–180, Baltimore, Maryland.

Frank Keller. 2001. *Gradience in Grammar: Experimental and Computational Aspects of Degrees of Grammaticality*. Ph.D. thesis, The University of Edinburgh.

D. Klein and C. Manning. 2003a. Accurate unlexicalized parsing. In *Proceedings of the 41st Annual Meeting of the Association for Computational Linguistics (ACL 2003)*, pages 423–430, Sapporo, Japan.

D. Klein and C. Manning. 2003b. Fast exact inference with a factored model for natural language parsing. In *Advances in Neural Information Processing Systems 15 (NIPS-03)*, pages 3–10, Whistler, Canada.

J.H. Lau, P. Cook, D. McCarthy, D. Newman, and T. Baldwin. 2012. Word sense induction for novel sense detection. In *Proceedings of the 13th Conference of the EACL (EACL 2012)*, pages 591–601, Avignon, France.

J.H. Lau, A. Clark, and S. Lappin. 2014. Measuring gradience in speakers' grammaticality judgements. In *Proceedings of the 36th Annual Conference of the Cognitive Science Society*, pages 821–826, Quebec City, Canada.

T. Mikolov, A. Deoras, S. Kombrink, L. Burget, and J. Èernocký. 2011a. Empirical evaluation and combination of advanced language modeling techniques. In *Proceedings of the 12th Annual Conference of the International Speech Communication Association (INTERSPEECH 2011)*, pages 605–608, Florence, Italy.

T. Mikolov, S. Kombrink, A. Deoras, L. Burget, and J. Èernocký. 2011b. Rnnlm - recurrent neural network language modeling toolkit. In *IEEE Automatic Speech Recognition and Understanding Workshop*, Hawaii, US.

T. Mikolov. 2012. *Statistical Language Models based on Neural Networks*. Ph.D. thesis, Brno University of Technology.

David Newman, Nagendra Koilada, Jey Han Lau, and Timothy Baldwin. 2012. Bayesian text segmentation for index term identification and keyphrase extraction. In *Proceedings of the 24th International Conference on Computational Linguistics (COLING 2012)*, pages 2077–2092, Mumbai, India.

A. Pauls and D. Klein. 2012. Large-scale syntactic language modeling with treelets. In *Proceedings of the 50th Annual Meeting of the Association for Computational Linguistics*, pages 959–968. Jeju, Korea.

F. Seide, G. Li, and D. Yu. 2011. Conversational speech transcription using context-dependent deep neural networks. In *Proceedings of the 12th Annual Conference of the International Speech Communication Association (INTERSPEECH 2011)*, Florence, Italy.

J. Sprouse and D. Almeida. 2012. Assessing the reliability of textbook data in syntax: Adger's core syntax. *Journal of Linguistics*, 48(3):609–652.

J. Sprouse. 2007. Continuous acceptability, categorical grammaticality, and experimental syntax. *Biolinguistics*, 1:123–134.

A Frame of Mind: Using Statistical Models for Detection of Framing and Agenda Setting Campaigns

Oren Tsur
Harvard University
& Northeastern University
orentsur@seas.harvard.edu

Dan Calacci
Northeastern University
dcalacci@ccs.neu.edu

David Lazer
Northeastern University
& Harvard University
d.lazer@neu.edu

Abstract

Framing is a sophisticated form of discourse in which the speaker tries to induce a cognitive bias through consistent linkage between a topic and a specific context (frame). We build on political science and communication theory and use probabilistic topic models combined with time series regression analysis (autoregressive distributed-lag models) to gain insights about the language dynamics in the political processes. Processing four years of public statements issued by members of the U.S. Congress, our results provide a glimpse into the complex dynamic processes of framing, attention shifts and agenda setting, commonly known as 'spin'. We further provide new evidence for the divergence in party discipline in U.S. politics.

1 Introduction

Language is one of the main tools used by politicians to promote their agenda, gain popularity, win elections and drive societal change (Luntz, 2007). The growing availability of online archives of political data such as public statements, bill proposals, floor speeches, interviews or social media streams allows computational analysis of many aspects of the political process. The analysis performed can increase transparency, facilitate a better educated constituency and improve understanding of the political process.

In this paper we propose a framework for automatic analysis of a large collection of political texts. Specifically, we demonstrate how the use of Bayesian methods and time series analysis captures the different ways in which political parties control the political discourse. We show that topic ownership and framing strategies can be inferred using topic models. Moreover, we demonstrate how the models learned are used to construct time series of expressed agendas. These time series are fitted using autoregressive distributive-lag models in order to learn the partisan temporal relations between topics and expressed agendas.

This framework could also be applied in other domains such as ideology divergence in online forums of radical groups or for measuring the changes in public sentiment toward commercial brands.

Contribution (i) To the best of our knowledge this is the first work to analyze framing strategies on large scale in an unsupervised manner[1]. (ii) we combine topic models with regression analysis in recovering longitudinal trends. (iii) We further provide evidence for the dynamics of framing campaigns, commonly known as 'political spin[2]'. Finally, (iv) we show how this framework can shed new light on the broad scholarship on the divergence of party discipline.

2 Related Work

2.1 Political Communication Theory

Some of the theoretical constructs employed by Political Science scholars to describe features of the political communication mechanism include: *topic ownership*, *framing*, and *agenda setting*. Understanding these theoretical concepts is necessary in laying the ground for our computational approach. This subsection provides the key definitions and a brief survey of the relevant literature.

Topic/Issue Ownership We say that a candidate, a representative or a party *owns* a topic if this topic, set of ideas or the competence in handling specific issues are strongly associated with her/the

[1]We do use some meta data such as the speaker's party and its timestamp for the time series analysis.

[2]'Political spin' may also refer to fact twisting and factual distractions promoted using various media outlets. We do not refer to these types of spin in this work.

Proceedings of the 53rd Annual Meeting of the Association for Computational Linguistics and the 7th International Joint Conference on Natural Language Processing, pages 1629–1638,
Beijing, China, July 26-31, 2015.

party (Petrocik, 1991; Petrocik, 1996; Damore, 2004). For example, environmental issues are traditionally associated with specific parties and not others (e.g. in U.S. politics, environmental issues are mostly associated with the Democratic party (Dunlap et al., 2001)).

Framing Framing is the psychological schema we use in order to organize and process our experiences. Politicians can use different contextual *frames* when referring to a specific topic, giving the public very different views on the topic at hand (Goffman, 1974; Gamson, 1989; Entman, 1993; Chong and Druckman, 2007). A notable example is the divisive partisan rhetoric used by U.S. politicians when referring to the legality of abortion. Democratic and Republican positions, framed as 'pro choice' and 'pro life', respectively, spin the abortion discourse as an issue of values of individual freedom (pro-choice) or validating the sanctity of life (pro-life). Similarly, Republicans refer to the inheritance tax by the overwhelmingly negative coinage 'death tax', while Democrats use 'estate tax'.

Framing strategies, however, go beyond the use of fixed phrases such as 'death tax' and 'pro-choice'. The Affordable Care Act (ACA) and the debate over raising the minimum wage can be framed as an issue of social justice or in the context of the economic burden it incurs on tax payers and by potential job loss.

Agenda Setting and shifting Agenda setting is achieved by framing and by increased or decreased *attention* (attention shifts) in order to set or change the political, media or public agenda (McCombs and Shaw, 1972; Scheufele and Tewksbury, 2007). Some examples of agenda setting campaigns are the repeated comments about the importance of child vaccination, highlighting the need for equal pay in the 2015 State of the Union Presidential Address, or, more broadly, repeatedly addressing the need for affordable healthcare.

2.2 Computational Analysis of Political Data

The availability of archives and streams of political data is driving a growing number of computational works that address a wide array of Political Science questions. Methods vary from simple word matching to more sophisticated Bayesian models and deep learning techniques.

Slant in news articles has been modeled by (Gentzkow and Shapiro, 2010) and (Lee, 2013), comparing word tokens and n-grams to predefined lists extracted from labeled data. Hidden Markov Models are used by (Sim et al., 2013) in order to measure ideological proportions in political speech, and (Iyyer et al., 2014) use recursive neural networks for a similar task.

Topic models have been used to detect connections between contributions and political agendas as expressed in microblogging platforms (Yano et al., 2013) and for reconstructing voting patterns based on the language in congressional bills (Gerrish and Blei, 2012). The flow of policy ideas has been modeled via measuring text reuse in different versions of bill proposals (Wilkerson et al., 2013).

Nguyen et al. (2013) use supervised hierarchical topic regression to improve prediction of political affiliation and sentiment.

Expressed agendas in press releases issued by U.S. Senators have been modeled by Grimmer using author topic models (Grimmer, 2010). It is important to point to some key differences between our work and Grimmer's work. While the model used by Grimmer allows attribution of a single topic per document, we are interested in a mixed membership model as we hypothesize possible correspondence between topics and frames. Moreover, while we are interested in partisan dynamics, Grimmer is interested in the expressed agendas of individuals thus focusing on an authorship model. Finally, unlike Grimmer, we also introduce autoregressive distributed-lag models in order to capture temporal dynamics between topics and parties as reflected in the data.

Another line of work can be found in the more traditional Political Science scholarship. The success of framing strategies is studied by the analysis of real time reactions to political debates (Boydstun et al., 2014). Autoregressive models are used for analyzing adjustment of issue positions with respect to news items during the Dutch national election campaign of 2006 (Kleinnijenhuis and de Nooy, 2013). This approach is based on manual annotation of data.

Logistic regression on manually coded campaign advertisements is used in order to learn the dynamics of issue ownership by individual candidates (Damore, 2004).

While some of the works above address related research questions (agenda setting, topic ownership) or use similar computational approaches (topic models, regression models), our work is the

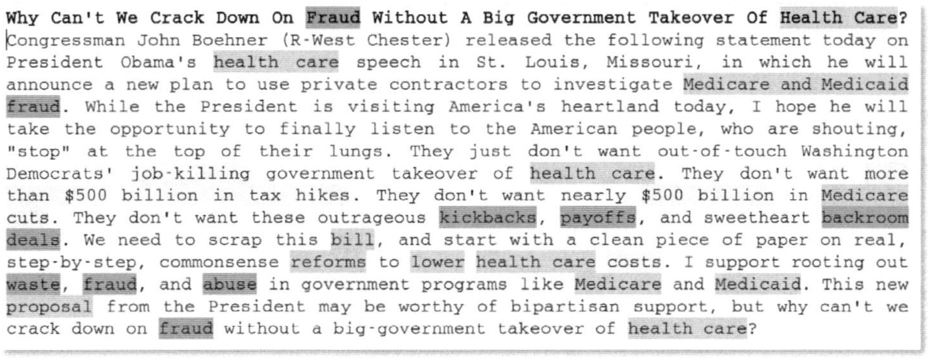

Why Can't We Crack Down On Fraud Without A Big Government Takeover Of Health Care?
Congressman John Boehner (R-West Chester) released the following statement today on President Obama's health care speech in St. Louis, Missouri, in which he will announce a new plan to use private contractors to investigate Medicare and Medicaid fraud. While the President is visiting America's heartland today, I hope he will take the opportunity to finally listen to the American people, who are shouting, "stop" at the top of their lungs. They just don't want out-of-touch Washington Democrats' job-killing government takeover of health care. They don't want more than $500 billion in tax hikes. They don't want nearly $500 billion in Medicare cuts. They don't want these outrageous kickbacks, payoffs, and sweetheart backroom deals. We need to scrap this bill, and start with a clean piece of paper on real, step-by-step, commonsense reforms to lower health care costs. I support rooting out waste, fraud, and abuse in government programs like Medicare and Medicaid. This new proposal from the President may be worthy of bipartisan support, but why can't we crack down on fraud without a big-government takeover of health care?

Figure 1: Examples of a public statement released on March 10, 2010 by Republican minority leader – Congressman John Boehner (now speaker of the U.S. House of Representatives). The highlighted sequences illustrate the different topics/frames used - health care (green), economy/budget (yellow) and corruption (orange).

first to offer a complete framework for automatic detection of topic ownership and attention shifting on a large scale. Additionally, our partisan analysis provides a model for longitudinal partisan communication strategies without the need for encoding of external events and specific campaigns.

3 Data

A brief overview of the U.S. Congress The American political system is a bicameral legislature composed of the Senate (100 senators, two from each state) and the House of Representatives (435 voting members plus 6 non-voting representatives, number depends on the population of each state). Election is held every two years, in which one third of the Senators and all members of the House face reelection. Members are typically affiliated with either the Democratic Party or the Republican Party. Congressional election and Presidential election coincide every four years.

The Corpus We use a corpus of public statements released by members of Congress in both the Senate and The House of Representatives, collected by Project Vote Smart[3]. An example of a public statement is presented in Figure 1.

In this work we use all individual statements and press releases in a span of four years (2010-2013), a total of 134000 statements made by 641 representatives. This time span encompasses two Congressional elections (November 2010 and 2012). Table 1 gives the number of Democratic and Republican representatives in the three Congress terms (111-113) covered in our data.

[3]http://votesmart.org/

Chamber	Party	Congress Term		
		111th	112th	113th
Senate	DEM	57	51	53
	REP	41	47	45
House	DEM	257	193	199
	REP	178	242	234

Table 1: Majority shifts in the House in the 111-113 Congress terms. Independent representatives are omitted.

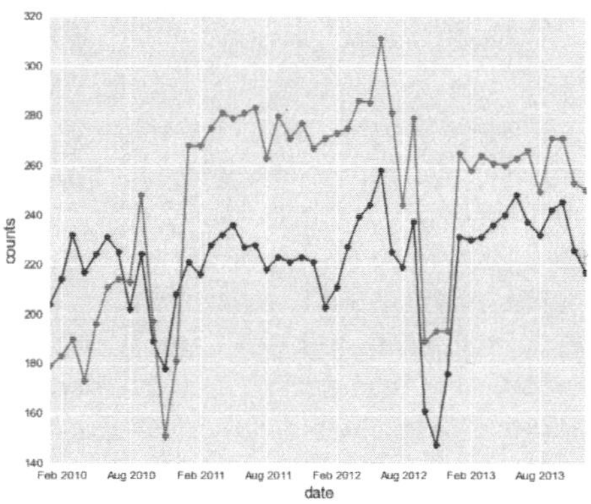

Figure 2: Monthly average number of statements by party.

While the administration was Democratic during all four years of our data, notice the Democratic loss of majority in the 112th Congress. We focus on the years 2010-2013 since Project Vote Smart has better coverage of the political discourse after 2009.

It is interesting to note that while the total number of statements per month reflects the change of majority in the November 2010 and 2012 elections (Table 1 and Figure 2), accounting for the number of seats per party it appears that the average Democrat is consistently more 'productive' with $\mu = 6.24$, $\sigma^2 = 2.1$ (Dem) and $\mu = 5.5$,

$\sigma^2 = 1.5$ (Rep) statements per month. We hence report all results after normalization by the number of seats each party posses at each timestamp.

4 Computational Framework

In order to automatically discover the correlated dynamics of attention shifts, we take a layered approach, consisting of the stages described below.

4.1 Topic Inference

In the first stage, we use topic models in order to learn topic distribution over words and identify the set of topics addressed in the corpus. Topic Modeling describes a general algorithmic framework for unsupervised discovery of a set of topics expressed in a collection of documents. The framework is based on the assumption that documents are generated by mixtures of k topics. It is therefore assumed that documents are generated by the following process: for each word in a document, we choose a topic from a given topic distribution, then choose a word from the distribution over words that the chosen topic specifies. Latent Dirichlet Allocation (LDA), the framework employed here, assumes that the distribution over topics has a Dirichlet prior. In practice, we assume a Dirichlet prior on topics and use variational Bayes (VB) optimization to infer topic distributions over words (Blei et al., 2003). In order to considerably improve efficiency, we use an online variational Bayes inference algorithm, shown to perform similarly to batch LDA (Hoffman et al., 2010). It is important to note that our goals and assumptions about the data do not lend themselvse to the use of dynamic or correlated topic models (Blei and Lafferty, 2006a; Blei and Lafferty, 2006b)[4].

4.2 Topic Assignment and Unification

The distribution of ranked topics over documents presents a "long tailed" distribution in which a few topics achieve a significant coverage of a document. This is a result of the mixed membership "generative" approach and the bag-of-words assumption. In a more realistic setting the number of topics per document is restricted. We wish to restrict the number of topics per document while still conforming to the mixture model assumption. We therefore reassign topics to each document (statement) d in the following manner:

1. Assign a topic to each word based on distribution of topics over words inferred in the previous stage.
2. Find a set T' of k' topics ($k' < k$) that cover $q\%$ of the document in a greedy way. The topic assingment for document d will then be $d \rightarrow T'$.

4.3 Data Slicing

We slice the data according to four parameters: topic (or topical cluster), time, party and document (statement). These slicing parameters allow us the flexibility required to thoroughly analyze the data. In the time parameter, we have four settings: no slicing (all data is treated as if it were produced simultaneously), monthly slicing, weekly slicing and daily slicing, each gives different granularity of ownership patterns.

4.4 Autoregressive-Distributed-Lag Models

A linear function $b + w^T X = b + \sum_j w_j^T X^j$ is a simple yet robust method for testing dependency between X and Y. Ordinary least square regression finds the coefficients that minimize the mean square error of $Y = b + \sum_j w_j^T X^j$ given (X, Y). In our case (X, Y) are time series. We argue that a lagged dependency between two time series suggests a framing or attention shifting campaign.

Regression analysis of time series assumes independence between error terms. This key statistical property is often violated in real world data as y_t often depends on y_{t-1} thus the time series residuals tend to correlate. The consequences of violating the independence of errors are threefold: i) Statistical tests of significance are uninformative and cannot be used to prove dependency between the model parameters, ii) The coefficients learned lose accuracy, and iii) error terms are correlated, and hence contain information that is lost in analysis instead of used to leverage the prediction power of the model. The importance of controlling for autoregressive properties and for seasonality effects was recently demonstrated in the error analysis of the Google Flu Trends algorithm (Lazer et al., 2014).

In order to control for error dependency we add the auto regressing component $\gamma^T Y^n$ to the ordinary regression, as shown in Equation 1:

$$y_t = \alpha + \beta^T X^m + \gamma^T Y^n + \epsilon_t \quad (1)$$

[4]We are interested in the change of the proportions of topics over time and not in the change of the word distribution within topics and we don't assume inherent correlation of topics.

Cluster	Topic ID	Top Words
Health	30	health care law will obamacare insurance repeal affordable americans costs new reform people president healthcare act coverage mandate american obama
	51	medicare seniors program social medicaid benefits fraud payments security programs cost services costs billion payment beneficiaries waste year savings million
Energy	38	project pipeline president obama keystone jobs climate energy xl construction state change permit administration approval oil will canada environmental create
	69	oil alaska gulf coast spill drilling offshore bp murkowski begich markey resources noaa said industry moratorium mexico gas administration sen
Security	34	day nation country today americans us american war world people america lives will honor families years men many th attacks
	89	nuclear united iran international israel foreign president states security weapons people world syria nations sanctions regime must government peace
Economy	68	budget spending debt president cuts fiscal government deficit will plan trillion obama house congress year federal cut economy washington billion
	88	jobs small businesses business job economy economic create will new growth work american america help creation act manufacturing can sector

Table 2: Top twenty words in selected topics in four topical clusters.

where, $\beta^T X^m$ indicates the distributed-lag terms:

$$\beta^T X^m = \sum_{i=0}^{m} \beta_i x_{t-i} \qquad (2)$$

and $\gamma^T Y^n$ indicates the autoregressive component described by:

$$\gamma^T Y^n = \sum_{j=1}^{n} \gamma_j y_{t-j} \qquad (3)$$

for some $n \leqslant t$ (notice that i ranges from 0 while j ranges from 1).

In order to control for seasonality (such as holidays and recess') we add a set of categorical variables indicating the weekday and the week-in-year of a statement, so the autoregressive model is:

$$y_t = \alpha + \beta^T X^m + \gamma^T Y^n + \sum_l W_l^T I^l(t) + \epsilon_t \quad (4)$$

Where $l \in \{day, week\}$ thus $I^l(t)$ is the identity matrix with the dimension of the seasonal granularity, in our case $I^{day} = I_{7\times7}$ for each day of the week and $I^{week} = I_{52\times52}$ for the week of the year. $I^l_{i,i} = 1$ iff t timestamp falls in the i-th day-of-week/week-in-year.

Finally, in practice it is usually sufficient restrict the autoregressive term to one parameter with $j = 1$ (accounting to the y value at the previous time stamp), this is consistent with the 24 hours news cycle reported by (Leskovec et al., 2009) among others. Since our goal is to find correlated attention shifts we can substitute the summation distributed-lag term by a single lagged term. Thus, we aim to minimize the MSE in the following model:

$$y_t = \alpha + \beta x_{t'} + \gamma y^n_{t-1} + \sum_l W_l^T I^l(t) + \epsilon_t \quad (5)$$

Where $t' = t - i$ and $i \in \{0, 1, 2, ..., 28\}$ indicating no lag, one day lag, 2 days lag, a week's lag, etc.

5 Results

5.1 Topical Ownership and Framing

5.1.1 Inferred Topics

As an input for the topic modeling module (stage 1 of the system) we use a lexicon of the 10000 most frequent words in the corpus. We use $k = 100$ as the number of topics. Experiments with $k \in \{30, 50, 500, 1000\}$ produced topics that were either too general or too incoherent. Once the topic-word distributions were inferred, topics were validated by two annotators examining the top 50 words for each topic. Annotators used hierarchical labels – an energy related topic t_i could be annotated *energy / clean-tech*, while another topic t_j could be annotated *energy / economy / keystone-xl*. Annotations were consolidated to unify the coding[5]. After consolidation annotators agreed on all topic annotations. Some examples of topics labels are 'health', 'energy', 'economy', 'boilerplate', 'political process', 'local' and a few 'random' topics.

After topic assignment as described in Section 4.2 each document is associated with only 2–6 topics. In this work we focus on the 14 most salient (concise, general and frequent) topics in the corpus. These 14 topics fall under four topical clusters - Health, Energy, Army/Security and Economy/Budget. Table 2 contains examples of top words and labels for some of the topics from four topical clusters.

[5]For example, if topic t_i was labeled *energy, cleantech* by one annotator and *energy, green* by the other, the annotators would agree to use either *cleantech* or *green* consistently.

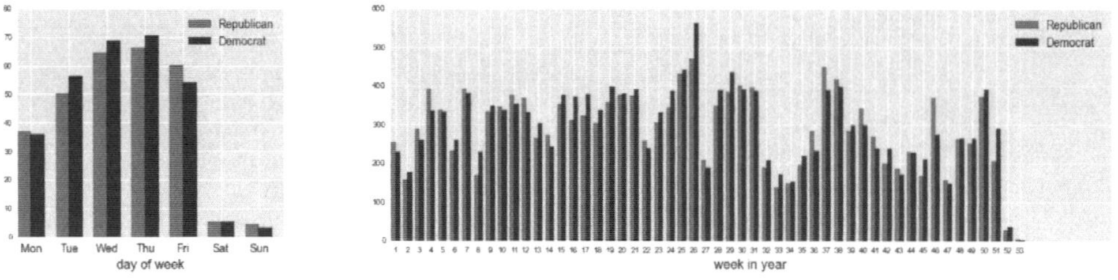

(a) (b)

Figure 3: Seasonality effect: average number of statements issued per day of week (a) and per week in year (b).

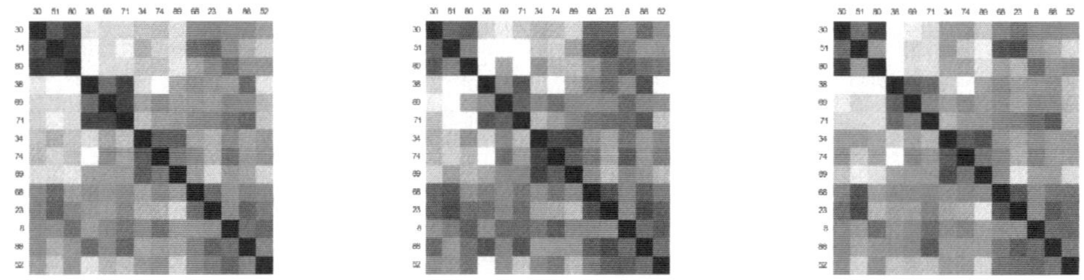

(a) All statements (b) Republican statements (c) Democrat statements

Figure 4: Normalized Pointwise Mutual Information (PMI) of topic cooccurrence of 14 topics of four topical clusters Health (30, 51, 80), Energy (38, 69,71), securtity (34, 74, 89) and Budget & Economy (68, 23, 8, 88, 52)

Cluster	Topic	DEM	REP	DEM	REP
Health	30	1679	4622	3169	5386
	51	746	233		
	80	898	437		
Energy	38	128	255	4042	3415
	69	1102	948		
	71	2859	2119		
Security	34	6239	5121	12393	11140
	74	3875	3071		
	89	3807	4138		
Economy	68	12260	19916	31604	31706
	23	5221	3742		
	8	6981	2456		
	88	12845	11139		
	52	3479	1154		

Table 3: Total number of statements by party in four topical clusters. DEM indicates the Democrat party, REP indicates the Republican party.

Cluster	Topic	DEM	REP	DEM*	REP*
Health	30	46	154	2	79
	51	151	22	34	1
	80	157	27	37	2
Energy	38	47	43	2	6
	69	114	56	18	5
	71	144	52	43	5
Security	34	141	63	52	9
	74	144	46	34	8
	89	80	113	10	22
Economy	68	32	174	7	127
	23	151	49	60	9
	8	205	2	165	0
	88	137	68	63	17
	52	190	12	123	0

Table 4: Number of *weeks* each party "owned" a topic by issuing more statements (DEM, REP) and number of weeks the party owned the topic with statistical significance $p < 0.05$ (DEM*, REP*).

5.1.2 Partisan Topic Ownership

Table 3 shows the partisan ownership by providing the number of statements issued by each party on each topic and for topical clusters. It also illustrates that different topical granularities portray different ownership patterns. For example, while it seems like the health cluster is owned by the Republican party (Table 3, cluster level), a closer look at specific topics in the cluster reveals a more complex picture – the Republicans actually own only topic 30, which turns to be the most dominant topic in the cluster. Similarly, while the statement counts in the Economy cluster are quite balanced (31604 vs. 31706), the counts of the individual topics in the cluster are polarized. Remember that these topical classes were all inferred by the LDA in an unsupervised way. These partisan ownership patterns were also confirmed by domain experts.

Longevity is a crucial factor in topic ownership. A weekly ownership of a topic is achieved by a party Q if it issued more statements on the topic than party R in that particular week. We compute the significance of the ownership assuming a null hypothesis that statements are issued by the parties by two Bernoulli processes with the same parameters. Table 4 provides the number of weeks each party owned each topic and the number of weeks it had a significant ownership ($p < 0.05$)[6].

Topic 30 illustrates the different perspectives. The total statement count (see Table 3) reveals a clear ownership by the Republican party, issuing 73% of the statements. While turning to weekly ownership (Table 4) we get similar number (Republicans control 77% of the weeks); assuming only significance ownership, Republicans significantly own the discourse for 79 weeks while Democrats have significant ownership in only 2 weeks which means the Republicans own 97% of the significantly owned weeks.

5.1.3 Topic Cooccurrence

Topic cooccurrence could approximate the way topics are framed. A heatmap of *within* statement topic cooccurrence based on Pointwise Mutual Information (PMI) (Church and Hanks, 1990) is presented in Figure 4. The topical clusters are characterized by blocks along the diagonal. The blocks structure is to be expected due to the inherent topical similarity within clusters. It is interesting to see the inter-cluster differences in PMI between the two parties. At the cluster level, Republicans tend to use the Budget & Economy topics with topics in all other topical clusters, evident by the stronger colors in the five bottom (left) rows (columns) in 4b comparing to 4c.

A notable example is the way Republicans frame the controversial Keystone XL project (Energy, topic 38) with the impact on the job market and small businesses (Budget & Economy, topic 88), a topic traditionally owned by Democrats (see top topical words in Table 2 and topic ownership at Table 4).

5.2 Partisan Discipline

Party discipline is of great interest for political scientists (Crook and Hibbing, 1985; Bowler et al., 1999; Krehbiel, 2000; McCarty, 2001) . Typically, party discipline is examined by analysis of roll call votes on bills. Discipline, however can be also measured by adherence to party lines in talking points and agenda setting campaigns. Discipline, therefore, can be captured by conformity of language in public statements. While it is "common knowledge" among political scientists that Republicans are more adherent to "talking points" – to the best of our knowledge there are no large scale studies that support (or refute) that.

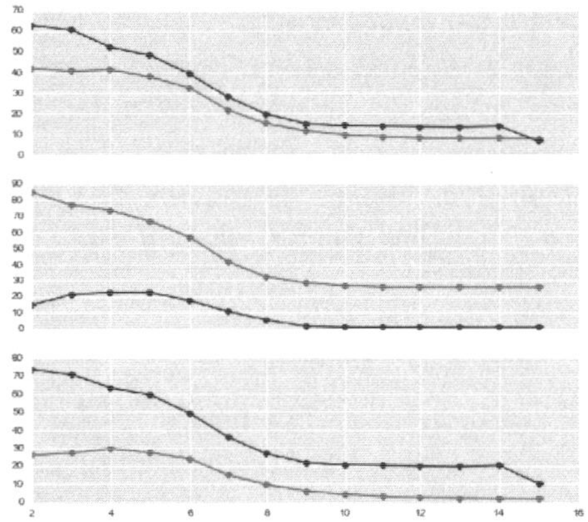

Figure 5: Average number of n-grams owned by each party on all topics (top), in Republican owned topics (middle) and in Democrat owned topics (bottom).

In the absence of official lists of "talking points", repeated use of similar phrases (n-grams) can provide an indication for the level of party discipline. In each topic, we looked at all n-grams ($n \in \{2, ..., 14\}$) that were used by more than five members of the Congress. For example, the tri-gram "the American people" (topic 38) appears in 81 statements made by 54 members of congress, only two of them were Democrats. Similarly, the tri-gram "social security benefits" (topic 51) appears in 123 statements, issued by 89 members, 71 of which were Democrats. Examining "ownership" of n-grams (per n-gram, per topic) reveals that that Republicans do tend to stick to talking points more than Democrats do.

Figure 5 provides the average number of n-grams owned by each party over all topics (top), over Republican owned topics (middle) and over Democratic owned topics (bottom). While on average Democrats own more n-grams than Republicans (Figure 5, top), the difference is marginal and is attributed to the fact that Democrats own more topics than the Republicans (10 vs. 4, see Table 3). Comparison between n-gram ownership in Democratic owned topics and Republican owned topics (Figure 5, middle and bottom) shows that while each party owns more n-grams in the *topics it owns*, Republicans present stronger ownership over the n-grams in their owned topics than Democrats in their respective owned topics. Moreover, Republicans present relative discipline even

[6]The numbers do not necessarily add up to 208 (the number of weeks in four years) due to weeks with no significant ownership , e.g. the parties issued a similar number of statements (usually zero) on that topic.

in Democratic owned topics.

Manually looking at some sampled n-grams it appears that mid-length n-grams are shared "talking points" and longer n-grams are full citations from bill proposals and committee reports. These findings are in line with textual sharing semantics (Lin et al., 2015).

5.3 Time Series Analysis

To this end we create two time series for each topic $c \in T$: $S_c^{C_D}$ – daily normalized counts for Democrats and $S_c^{C_R}$ – daily normalized counts for Republicans. Normalization of counts is needed in order to account for the bias introduced by the difference in the number of seats each party holds and the changes in that number in the different terms as apparent from Table 1.

Our data exhibit two strong seasonality effects: a weekly cycle with the lowest point on the weekend and peaking on Thursday (Figure 3a), and a yearly cycle with low points at the weeks of 4th of July, Thanksgiving, August recess and Christmas (Figure 3b). These seasonality effects are captured by the added terms in Equation 4.

After time series are constructed we apply first-difference detrending (Enders, 2008) in order to transform the time series to stationary series and avoid trend-incurred correlations.

We fit autoregressive-distributed-lag models for all pairs in $\{X = S_{c,l}, Y = S_{c'}\}$, where $c, c' \in T$ (topics), $l \in \{0, 1, 2, 3, ..., 7, 14, ..., 28\}$.

In this setting we fit 5153 pairs of time series of which 718 pairs had a significant coefficient for X ($p < 0.05$). Artificial significance due to abundance of fitted models was accounted to by applying the strict Bonferroni correction (Dunn, 1961) on the significance level. The correction resulted in 103 significant correlations, most of them with lag of up to 3 days. Table 5 gives the number of intra/inter significant correlation for lags $l \in 0, 1, 2$.

One example for such correlation is the Republicans "responding" to Democratic topic 88 with with topic 8 (intra-cluster) in one and two days lag. We interpret this as a different spin on the budget issue. Another example is the Democratic party corresponds to Republican topic 30 with topic 88 (inter-cluster) on the same day (no lag). We interpret this as a way to place the Acordable Care Act in a specific economic frame. We note that while the lagged correlated time series do not imply a responsive pattern, a significance of lagged correlation may suggest such a pattern. We provide some evidence in the qualitative analysis in the next section.

Cluster	Dependent	Significant Correlations		
		$l = 0$	$l = 1$	$l = 2$
Intra-cluster	DEM	28	1	1
	REP	26	4	5
Inter-cluster	DEM	15	2	0
	REP	17	0	0

Table 5: Number of statistically significant ($p < .05$, Bonferroni corrected) daily lagged correlations between cross-party time series.

5.4 Discussion and Qualitative Analysis

Inter and intra-cluster correlations can be interpreted as manifestations of different types of framing strategies and campaigns for attention shifts. A detailed analysis of the interplay between the different frames is beyond the scope of this paper and is left for political scientists.

The majority of the significant correlations were found with no lag. It is important to note that these correlations are found significant even after accounting to autoregressive patterns. Zero-lag correlations could be interpreted in a number of ways. Two probable interpretations are (i) daily time series are too crude to model lag patterns, and (ii) the parties respond to some external event at the same time. While we cannot address (i) due to sparseness and noise[7], we can sample statements and examine them manually. Manual examination reveals a strong responsive pattern in peaking trends. One typical example is the Republican spike in topic 30 on March 10. The statement at Figure 1 is very illustrative as it *explicitly* refers to a statement by President Obama. Explicit references to statements made by the other side are found more frequently in Republican statements and reveal a clear responsive pattern that also suggest a strong party discipline, in line with the results in Section 5.2. This small scale qualitative analysis complements the quantitative results reported in Section 5.3 and provide evidence for a responsive pattern even in zero lag series.

6 Conclusion

We presented a statistical framework for the analysis of framing strategies and agenda setting campaigns in the political sphere. Combining topic models and time series analysis, we modeled topic

[7]The exact timestamp is sometimes missing, set to midnight or affected by external factors.

ownership and party discipline and analyzed responsive patterns in an unsupervised way and with no prior knowledge of the political system. Our work draws from political science theory, validating some theoretical constructs and shedding new light on others. The proposed framework and the results could be further used and interpreted by political scientists and communication scholars.

7 Acknowledgments

We thank Ryan Kennedy, Navid Dianati, Katherine Ognyanova, Stefan Vojcik and Shahar Even-Dar Mandel for fruitful discussions. We thank the anonymous reviewers for their helpful comments. This work was supported by the following grants: MURI #504026 and ARO #50433.

References

David Blei and John Lafferty. 2006a. Correlated topic models. *Advances in neural information processing systems*, 18:147.

David M Blei and John D Lafferty. 2006b. Dynamic topic models. In *Proceedings of the 23rd international conference on Machine learning*, pages 113–120. ACM.

David M Blei, Andrew Y Ng, and Michael I Jordan. 2003. Latent dirichlet allocation. *the Journal of machine Learning research*, 3:993–1022.

Shaun Bowler, David M Farrell, and Richard S Katz. 1999. Party cohesion, party discipline, and parliaments. *Party discipline and parliamentary government*, pages 3–22.

Amber E Boydstun, Rebecca A Glazier, Matthew T Pietryka, and Philip Resnik. 2014. Real-time reactions to a 2012 presidential debate a method for understanding which messages matter. *Public Opinion Quarterly*, 78(S1):330–343.

Dennis Chong and James N Druckman. 2007. Framing theory. *Annu. Rev. Polit. Sci.*, 10:103–126.

Kenneth Ward Church and Patrick Hanks. 1990. Word association norms, mutual information, and lexicography. *Computational linguistics*, 16(1):22–29.

Sara Brandes Crook and John R Hibbing. 1985. Congressional reform and party discipline: The effects of changes in the seniority system on party loyalty in the us house of representatives. *British Journal of Political Science*, 15(02):207–226.

David F Damore. 2004. The dynamics of issue ownership in presidential campaigns. *Political Research Quarterly*, 57(3):391–397.

Riley E Dunlap, Chenyang Xiao, and Aaron M McCright. 2001. Politics and environment in america: Partisan and ideological cleavages in public support for environmentalism. *Environmental politics*, 10(4):23–48.

Olive Jean Dunn. 1961. Multiple comparisons among means. *Journal of the American Statistical Association*, 56(293):52–64.

Walter Enders. 2008. *Applied econometric time series*. John Wiley & Sons.

Robert M Entman. 1993. Framing: Toward clarification of a fractured paradigm. *Journal of communication*, 43(4):51–58.

William A Gamson. 1989. News as framing. *American Behavioral Scientist*, 33(2):157–161.

Matthew Gentzkow and Jesse M. Shapiro. 2010. What drives media slant? evidence from u.s. daily newspapers. *Econometrica*, 78:35–71.

Sean Gerrish and David M. Blei. 2012. How they vote: Issue-adjusted models of legislative behavior. In *Neural Information Processing Systems (NIPS)*, pages 2762–2770.

Erving Goffman. 1974. *Frame analysis: An essay on the organization of experience*. Harvard University Press.

Justin Grimmer. 2010. A bayesian hierarchical topic model for political texts: Measuring expressed agendas in senate press releases. *Political Analysis*, 18(1):1–35.

Matthew Hoffman, Francis R Bach, and David M Blei. 2010. Online learning for latent dirichlet allocation. In *advances in neural information processing systems*, pages 856–864.

Mohit Iyyer, Peter Enns, Jordan Boyd-Graber, and Philip Resnik. 2014. Political ideology detection using recursive neural networks. In *Proceedings of the 52nd meeting of the Association for Computational Linguistics*.

Jan Kleinnijenhuis and Wouter de Nooy. 2013. Adjustment of issue positions based on network strategies in an election campaign: A two-mode network autoregression model with cross-nested random effects. *Social Networks*, 35(2):168–177.

Keith Krehbiel. 2000. Party discipline and measures of partisanship. *American Journal of Political Science*, pages 212–227.

David M Lazer, Ryan Kennedy, Gary King, and Alessandro Vespignani. 2014. The parable of google flu: Traps in big data analysis. *Science Magazine (AAAS)*.

Han Soo Lee. 2013. Do national economic and political conditions affect ideological media slant? *Political Communication*, 30:395–418.

Jure Leskovec, Lars Backstrom, and Jon Kleinberg. 2009. Meme-tracking and the dynamics of the news cycle. In *Proceedings of the 15th ACM SIGKDD international conference on Knowledge discovery and data mining*, pages 497–506. ACM.

Y. Lin, D. Margolin, and D Lazer. 2015. Uncovering social semantics from textual traces: A theory-driven approach and evidence from public statements of u.s. members of congress. *Journal of the Association for Information Science and Technology*, page (forthcoming).

Frank I. Luntz. 2007. *Words That Work: It's Not What You Say, It's What People Hear*. Hyperion.

Nolan McCarty. 2001. The hunt for party discipline in congress. In *American Political Science Association*, volume 95, pages 673–687. Cambridge Univ Press.

Maxwell E McCombs and Donald L Shaw. 1972. The agenda-setting function of mass media. *Public opinion quarterly*, 36(2):176–187.

Viet-An Nguyen, Jordan Boyd-Graber, and Philip Resnik. 2013. Lexical and hierarchical topic regression. In *Neural Information Processing Systems*.

John R Petrocik. 1991. Divided government: Is it all in the campaigns? *The politics of divided government*, pages 13–38.

John R Petrocik. 1996. Issue ownership in presidential elections, with a 1980 case study. *American journal of political science*, pages 825–850.

Dietram A Scheufele and David Tewksbury. 2007. Framing, agenda setting, and priming: The evolution of three media effects models. *Journal of communication*, 57(1):9–20.

Yanchuan Sim, Brice Acree, Justin H Gross, and Noah A Smith. 2013. Measuring ideological proportions in political speeches. In *Proceedings of EMNLP*.

John Wilkerson, David A. Smith, and Nick Stramp. 2013. Tracing the flow of policy ideas in legislatures: A text reuse approach. In *New Directions in Analyzing Text as Data*, September.

Tae Yano, Dani Yogotama, and Noah A. Smith. 2013. A penny for your tweets: Campaign contributions and capitol hill microblogs. In *International AAAI Conference on Weblogs and Social Media (ICWSM)*, July.

Why discourse affects speakers' choice of referring expressions

Naho Orita
Graduate School of Information Sciences
Tohoku University
naho@ecei.tohoku.ac.jp

Eliana Vornov
Computer Science and Linguistics
University of Maryland
evornov@umd.edu

Naomi H. Feldman
Linguistics and UMIACS
University of Maryland
nhf@umd.edu

Hal Daumé III
Computer Science and UMIACS
University of Maryland
hal@umiacs.umd.edu

Abstract

We propose a language production model that uses dynamic discourse information to account for speakers' choices of referring expressions. Our model extends previous rational speech act models (Frank and Goodman, 2012) to more naturally distributed linguistic data, instead of assuming a controlled experimental setting. Simulations show a close match between speakers' utterances and model predictions, indicating that speakers' behavior can be modeled in a principled way by considering the probabilities of referents in the discourse and the information conveyed by each word.

1 Introduction

Discourse information plays an important role in various aspects of linguistic processing, such as predictions about upcoming words (Nieuwland and Van Berkum, 2006) and scalar implicature processing (Breheny et al., 2006). The relationship between discourse information and speakers' choices of referring expression is one of the most studied problems. Speakers' choices of referring expressions have long been thought to depend on the salience of entities in the discourse (Givón, 1983). For example, speakers normally do not choose a pronoun to refer to a new entity in the discourse, but are more likely to use pronouns for referents that have been referred to earlier in the discourse. A number of grammatical, semantic, and distributional factors related to salience have been found to influence choices of referring expressions (Arnold, 2008). While the relationship between discourse salience and speakers' choices of referring expressions is well known, there is not yet a formal account of why this relationship exists.

In recent years, a number of formal models have been proposed to capture inferences between speakers and listeners in the context of Gricean pragmatics (Grice, 1975; Frank and Goodman, 2012). These models take a game theoretic approach in which speakers optimize productions to convey information for listeners, and listeners infer meaning based on speakers' likely productions. These models have been argued to account for human communication (Jager, 2007; Frank and Goodman, 2012; Bergen et al., 2012a; Smith et al., 2013), and studies report that they robustly predict various linguistic phenomena in experimental settings (Goodman and Stuhlmüller, 2013; Degen et al., 2013; Kao et al., 2014; Nordmeyer and Frank, 2014). However, these models have not yet been applied to language produced outside of the laboratory, nor have they incorporated measures of discourse salience that can be computed over corpora.

In this paper, we propose a probabilistic model to explain speakers' choices of referring expressions based on discourse salience. Our model extends the rational speech act model from Frank and Goodman (2012) to incorporate updates to listeners' beliefs as discourse proceeds. The model predicts that a speaker's choice of referring expressions should depend directly on the amount of information that each word carries in the discourse. Simulations probe the contribution of each model component and show that the model can predict

Proceedings of the 53rd Annual Meeting of the Association for Computational Linguistics and the 7th International Joint Conference on Natural Language Processing, pages 1639–1649,
Beijing, China, July 26-31, 2015.

speakers' pronominalization in a corpus. These results suggest that this model formalizes underlying principles that account for speakers' choices of referring expressions.

The paper is organized as follows. Section 2 reviews relevant studies on choices of referring expressions. Section 3 describes the details of our model. Section 4 describes the data, preprocessing and annotation procedure. Section 5 presents simulation results. Section 6 summarizes this study and discusses implications and future directions.

2 Relevant Work

2.1 Discourse salience

Speakers' choices of referring expressions have long been an object of study. Pronominalization has been examined particularly often in both theoretical and experimental studies. Discourse theories predict that speakers use pronouns when they think that a referent is salient in the discourse (Givón, 1983; Ariel, 1990; Gundel et al., 1993; Grosz et al., 1995), where salience of the referent is influenced by various factors such as grammatical position (Brennan, 1995), recency (Chafe, 1994), topicality (Arnold, 1998), competitors (Fukumura et al., 2011), visual salience (Vogels et al., 2013b), and so on.

Discourse theories have characterized the link between referring expressions and discourse salience by stipulating constructs such as a scale of topicality (Givón, 1983), accessibility hierarchy (Ariel, 1990), or implicational hierarchy (Gundel et al., 1993). All of these assume fixed form-salience correspondences in that a certain referring expression encodes a certain degree of salience. However, it is not clear how this form-salience mapping holds nor why it should be.

There is also a rich body of research that points to the importance of production cost (Rohde et al., 2012; Bergen et al., 2012b; Degen et al., 2013) and listener models (Bard et al., 2004; Van der Wege, 2009; Galati and Brennan, 2010; Fukumura and van Gompel, 2012) in language production. These studies suggest that only considering discourse salience of the referent may not precisely capture speakers' choices of referring expressions, and it is necessary to examine discourse salience in relation to these other factors.

2.2 Formal models

Computational models relevant to speakers' choices of referring expressions have been proposed, but there is a gap between questions that previous models have addressed and the questions that we have raised above.

Grüning and Kibrik (2005) and Khudyakova et al. (2011) examine the significance of various factors that might influence choices of referring expressions by using machine learning models such as neural networks, logistic regression and decision trees. Although these models qualitatively show some significant factors, they are data-driven rather than being explanatory, and have not focused on why and how these factors result in the observed referring choices.

Formal models that go beyond identifying superficial factors focus on only pronouns rather than accounting for speakers' word choices per se. For example, Kehler et al. (2008) formalize a relationship between pronoun comprehension and production using Bayes' rule to account for comprehender's semantic bias in experimental data. Rij et al. (2013) use ACT-R (Anderson, 2007) to examine the effects of working memory load in pronoun interpretation. These models show how certain factors influence pronoun production/interpretation, but it is not clear how these models would predict speakers' choices of referring expressions.

Relevant formal models in computational linguistics include Centering theory (Grosz et al., 1995; Poesio et al., 2004) and Referring Expression Generation (Krahmer and Van Deemter, 2012). These models propose deterministic constraints governing when pronouns are preferred in local discourse, but it is not clear how these would account for speakers' choices of referring expressions, nor it is clear why there should be such deterministic constraints.

2.3 Uniform Information Density

One potential formal explanation for the relation between discourse salience and speakers' choices of referring expressions is the Uniform Information Density hypothesis (UID) (Levy and Jaeger, 2007; Tily and Piantadosi, 2009; Jaeger, 2010). UID states that speakers prefer to smooth the information density distribution of their utterances over time to achieve optimal communication. This theory predicts that speakers should use pronouns instead of longer forms (e.g., *the president*) when a referent is predictable in the context, whereas they should use longer forms for unpredictable referents that carry more information (Jaeger, 2010).

Tily and Piantadosi (2009) empirically examined the relationship between predictability of a referent and choice of referring expressions. They found that predictability is a significant predictor of writers' choices of referring expressions, in that pronouns are used when a referent is predictable.

While these results appear to support UID, there are several inconsistencies with previous UID accounts. Information content of words has been estimated using an n-gram language model (Levy and Jaeger, 2007), a verb's subcategorization frequency (Jaeger, 2010), and so on, whereas here the information content is that of referents with respect to discourse salience. In addition, selecting between a pronoun and a more specified referring expression involves deciding how much information to convey, whereas previous applications of UID (Levy and Jaeger, 2007) have been concerned with deciding between different ways of expressing the same information content. We show in the next section that we can derive predictions about referring expressions directly from a model of language production.

2.4 Summary

Previous linguistic studies have focused on identifying factors that might influence choices of referring expressions. However, it is not clear from this previous work how and why these factors result in the observed patterns of referring expressions. Where formal models relevant to this topic do exist, they have not been built to explain why there is a relation between discourse salience and speakers' choices of referring expressions. Even UID, which relates predictability to word length, is not set up to account for the choice between words that vary in their information content.

In the next section, we propose a speaker model that formalizes the relation between discourse salience and speakers' choices of referring expressions, considering production cost and speakers' inference about listeners in a principled and explanatory way.

3 Speaker model

3.1 Rational speaker-listener model

We adopt the rational speaker-listener model from Frank and Goodman (2012) and extend this model to predict speakers' choices of referring expressions using discourse information.

The main idea of Frank and Goodman's model is that a rational pragmatic listener uses Bayesian inference to infer the speaker's intended referent r_s given the word w, their vocabulary (e.g., 'blue', 'circle'), and shared context that consists of a set of objects O (e.g., visual access to object referents) as in (1), assuming that a speaker has chosen the word informatively.

$$P(r_s|w, O) = \frac{P_S(w|r_s, O)P(r_s)}{\Sigma_{r' \in O} P(w|r', O)P(r')} \quad (1)$$

While our work does not make use of this pragmatic listener, it does build on the speaker model assumed by the pragmatic listener. This speaker model (the likelihood term in the listener model) is defined using an exponentiated utility function as in (2).

$$P_S(w|r_s, O) \propto e^{\alpha U(w;r_s,O)} \quad (2)$$

The utility $U(w; r_s, O)$ is defined as $I(w; r_s, O) - D(w)$, where $I(w; r_s, O)$ represents informativeness of word w (quantified as surprisal) and $D(w)$ represents its speech cost. If a listener interprets word w literally and cost $D(w)$ is constant, the exponentiated utility function can be reduced to (3) where $|w|$ denotes the number of referents that the word w can be used to refer to.

$$P_S(w|r_s, O) \propto \frac{1}{|w|} \quad (3)$$

Thus, the speaker model chooses a word based on its specificity. We show in the next section that this corresponds to a speaker who is optimizing informativeness for a listener with uniform beliefs about what will be referred to in the discourse. The assumption of uniform discourse salience works well in a simple language game where there are a limited number of referents that have roughly equal salience, but we show that a model that lacks a sophisticated notion of discourse falls short in more realistic settings.

3.2 Incorporating discourse salience

To extend Frank and Goodman's model to a natural linguistic situation, we assume that the speaker estimates the listener's interpretation of a word (or referring expression) w based on discourse information. We extend the speaker model from (3) by assuming that a speaker S chooses w to optimize a listener's belief in speaker's intended referent r relative to the speaker's own speech cost C_w. This cost is another factor in the speaker model, roughly corresponding to utterance complexity such as word length.[1]

$$P_S(w|r) \propto P_L(r|w) \cdot \frac{1}{C_w} \quad (4)$$

The term $P_L(r|w)$ in (4) represents informativeness of word w: the speaker chooses w that most helps a listener L to infer referent r. The term C_w in (4) is a cost function: the speaker chooses w that is least costly to speak.

The speaker's listener model, $P_L(r|w)$, infers referent r that is referred to by word w according to Bayes' rule as in (5).

$$P_L(r|w) = \frac{P(w|r)P(r)}{\Sigma_{r'} P(w|r')P(r')} \quad (5)$$

The first term in the numerator, $P(w|r)$, is a word probability: the listener in the speaker's mind guesses how likely the speaker would be to use w to refer to r. The second term in the numerator, $P(r)$, is the discourse salience (or predictability) of referent r. The denominator $\Sigma_{r'} P(w|r')P(r')$ is a sum of potential referents r' that could be referred to by word w. The terms in this sum are non-zero only for referents that are compatible with the meaning of the word. If there are many potential referents that could be referred to by word w, that word would be more ambiguous thus less informative. The whole of the right side in Equation (5) represents the speaker's assumption about the listener: given word w the listener would infer referent r that is salient in a discourse and less ambiguously referred to by word w.

If $P(r)$ is uniform over referents and $P(w|r)$ is constant across words and referents, this listener model reduces to $\frac{1}{|w|}$. Thus, Frank and Goodman (2012)'s speaker model in (3) is a special case of our speaker model in (4) that assumes uniform discourse salience and constant cost.

Our model predicts that the speaker's probability of choosing a word for a given referent should depend on its cost relative to its information content. To see this, we combine (4) and (5), yielding

$$P_S(w|r) \propto \frac{P(w|r)P(r)}{\sum_{r'} P(w|r')P(r')} \cdot \frac{1}{C_w} \quad (6)$$

Because the speaker is deciding what word to use for an intended referent, and the term $P(r)$ denotes the probability of this referent, $P(r)$ is constant in the speaker model and does not affect the relative probability of a speaker producing different words. We further assume for simplicity that $P(w|r)$ is constant across words and referents. This means that all referents have about the same number of words that can be used to refer to them, and that all words for a given referent are equally probable for a naive listener. In this scenario, the speaker's probability of choosing a word is

$$P_S(w|r) \propto \frac{1}{\sum_{r'} P(r')} \cdot \frac{1}{C_w} \quad (7)$$

where the sum denotes the total discourse probability of the referents referred to by that word.

The information content of an event is defined as the negative log probability of that event. In this scenario, the information conveyed by a word is the logarithm of the first term in (7), $-\log \sum_{r'} P(r')$. This means that in deciding which word to use, the highest cost a speaker should be willing to pay for a word should depend directly on that word's information content.

This relationship between cost and information content allows us to derive the prediction tested by Tily and Piantadosi (2009) that the use of referring expressions should depend on the predictability of a referent. For referents that are highly predictable from the discourse, different referring expressions (e.g., pronouns and proper names) will have roughly equal information content, and speakers should choose the referring expression that has the lowest cost. In contrast, for less predictable referents, proper names will carry substantially more information than pronouns, leading speakers to pay a higher cost for the proper names. These are the same predictions that have been discussed in the context of UID, but here the predictions are derived from a principled model of speakers who are trying to provide information to listeners. The extent to which our model can also capture other cases that have been put forward as evidence for the UID hypothesis remains a question for future research.

3.3 Predicting behavior from corpora

The model described in Section 3.2 is fully general, applying to arbitrary word choices, discourse probabilities, and cost fuctions. As an initial step, our simulations focus on the choice between pronouns and proper names. Our work tests the speaker model from (4) directly, asking whether it can predict the referring expressions from corpora of writ-

[1] Our speaker model corresponds to Frank and Goodman's exponentiated utility function (2), with α equal to one and with their cost $D(w)$ being the log of our cost C_w.

ten and spoken language. Implementing the model requires computing word probabilities $P(w|r)$, discourse salience $P(r)$, and word costs C_w.

We simplify the word probability $P(w|r)$ in the speaker's listener model as in (8):

$$P(w|r) = \frac{1}{V} \tag{8}$$

where the count V is the number of words that can refer to referent r. We assume that V is constant across all referents. Our reasoning is as follows. There could be many ways to refer to a single entity. For example, to refer to entity *Barack Obama*, we could say 'he', 'The U.S. president', 'Barack', and so on. We assume that there are the same number of referring expressions for each entity and that each referring expression is equally probable under the listener's likelihood model.

In our simulations, we assume that a speaker is choosing between a proper name and a pronoun. For example, we assume that an entity *Barack Obama* has one and only one proper name 'Barack Obama', and this entity is unambiguously associated with male and singular. Although we use an example with two possible referring expressions, as long as $P(w|r)$ is constant across all referents and words, it does not make a difference to the computation in (5) how many competing words we assume for each referent.

To estimate the salience of a referent, $P(r)$, our framework employs factors such as referent frequency or recency. Although there are other important factors such as topicality of the referent (Orita et al., 2014) that are not incorporated in our simulations, this model sets up a framework to test the role and interaction of various potential factors suggested in the discourse literature.

Salience of the referent is computed differently depending on its information status: old or new. The following illustrates the speaker's assumptions about the listener's discourse model:

For each referent $r \in [1, R_d]$:

1. If $r = old$, choose r in proportion to N_r (the number of times referent r has been referred to in the preceding discourse).
2. Otherwise, $r = new$ with probability proportional to α (a hyperparameter that controls how likely the speaker is to refer to a new referent).
3. If $r = new$, sample that new referent r from the base distribution over entities with probability $\frac{1}{U.}$ (count $U.$ denotes a total number of unseen entities that is estimated from a named entity list (Bergsma and Lin, 2006)).

The above discourse model is frequency-based. We can replace the term N_r for the old referent with $f(d_{i,j}) = e^{-d_{i,j}/a}$ that captures recency, where the recency function $f(d_{i,j})$ decays exponentially with the distance between the current referent r_i and the same referent r_j that has previously been referred to. This framework for frequency and recency of new and old referents exactly corresponds to priors in the Chinese Restaurant Process (Teh et al., 2006) and the distance-dependent Chinese Restaurant Process (Blei and Frazier, 2011).

The denominator in (5) represents the sum of potential referents that could be referred to by word w. We assume that a pronoun can refer to a large number of unseen referents if gender and number match, but a proper name cannot. For example, 'he' could refer to all singular and male referents, but 'Barack Obama' can only refer to *Barack Obama*. This assumption is reflected as a probability of *unseen referents* for the pronoun as illustrated in (10) below.

In our simulations, the speaker's cost function C_w is estimated based on word length as in (9). We assume that longer words are costly to produce.

$$C_w = \text{length}(w) \tag{9}$$

Suppose that the speaker is considering using 'he' to refer to *Barack Obama*, which has been referred to N_O times in the preceding discourse, and there is another singular and male entity, *Joe Biden*, in the preceding discourse that has been referred to N_B times. In this situation, the model computes the probability that the speaker uses 'he' to refer to *Barack Obama* as follows:

$$\begin{aligned} & P_{\text{S}}(\text{'he'}|\textit{Obama}) \\ & \propto P_{\text{L}}(\textit{Obama}|\text{'he'}) \cdot \frac{1}{C_{\text{'he'}}} \\ & = \frac{P(\text{'he'}|\textit{Obama})P(\textit{Obama})}{\Sigma_{r'} P(\text{'he'}|r')P(r')} \cdot \frac{1}{C_{\text{'he'}}} \\ & = \frac{\frac{1}{V} \cdot N_{\text{O}}}{(\frac{1}{V} \cdot N_{\text{O}}) + (\frac{1}{V} \cdot N_{\text{B}}) + (\frac{1}{V} \cdot \alpha \cdot \frac{U_{\text{sing\&masc}}}{U.})} \cdot \frac{1}{C_{\text{'he'}}} \end{aligned} \tag{10}$$

where count $U_{\text{sing\&masc}}$ in the denominator of the last line denotes the number of unseen singular & male entities that could be referred to by 'he'. We estimate this number for each type of pronoun we evaluate (singular-female, singular-male, singular-neuter, and plural) based on the named entity list in Bergsma and Lin (2006). The term $(\frac{1}{V} \cdot \alpha \cdot \frac{U_{\text{sing\&masc}}}{U.})$ is the sum of probabilities of unseen referents that could be referred to by the pronoun 'he'. The unseen referents can be interpreted as a penalty for the inexplicitness of pronouns. In the case of proper names, the denominator is always the same as the numerator, under the assumption that each entity has one unique proper name.

4 Data

4.1 Corpora

Our model was run on both adult-directed speech and child-directed speech. We chose to use the SemEval-2010 Task 1 subset of OntoNotes (Recasens et al., 2011), a corpus of news text, as our corpus of adult-directed speech. The Gleason et al. (1984) subset of CHILDES (MacWhinney, 2000) was chosen as our corpus of child-directed speech.

The model requires coreference chains, agreement information, grammatical position, and part of speech. These were extracted from each corpus, either manually or automatically. The coreference chains let us easily count how many times/how recently each referent is mentioned in the discourse, which is necessary for computing discourse salience. The agreement information (gender and number of each referent) is required so that the model can identify all possible competing referents for pronouns. For instance, *Barack Obama* will be ruled out as a possible competitor for the pronoun *she*. The grammatical position that each proper name occupies[2] determines the form of the alternative pronoun that could be used there. For example, the difference between *he* and *him* is the grammatical position that each can appear in. The part of speech is used to identify the form of the referring expression (pronouns and proper names), which is what our model aims to predict.[3]

OntoNotes includes information about coreference chains, part of speech, and grammatical dependencies. Gleason CHILDES has parsed part of speech and grammatical dependencies (Sagae et al., 2010), but it does not have coreference chains. Neither corpus has agreement information. The following section describes manual annotations that we have done for this study. Due to time constraints, we annotated only a part of the CHILDES Gleason corpus, 9 out of 70 scripts.

4.2 Annotation

4.2.1 Mention annotation

We considered only maximally spanning noun phrases as mentions, ignoring nested NPs and nested coreference chains. For the sentence "Both Al Gore and George W. Bush have different ideas on how to spend that extra money" from OntoNotes, the extracted NPs are *Both Al Gore and George W. Bush* and *different ideas about how to spend that extra money*.

These maximally spanning NPs were automatically extracted from the OntoNotes data, but were manually annotated for the CHILDES data using brat (Stenetorp et al., 2012) by two annotators.[4]

4.2.2 Agreement annotation

Many mentions (46,246 out of 56,575 mentions in OntoNotes and 10,141 out of 10,530 mentions in CHILDES Gleason) were automatically annotated using agreement information from the named entity list in Bergsma and Lin (2006), leaving 10,329 to be manually annotated from OntoNotes (about 18%) and 389 from CHILDES (about 4%).[5]

The guidelines we followed for this manual agreement annotation were largely based on pronoun replacement tests. NPs that referred to a single man and could be replaced with *he* or *him* were labeled 'male singular', NPs that could be replaced by *it*, such as *the comment*, were labeled 'neuter singular', and so on. NPs that could not be replaced with a pronoun, such as *about 30 years earnings for the average peasant, who makes $145 a year*, were excluded from the analysis.

4.2.3 Coreference annotation

We used the provided coreference chains for the OntoNotes data, but for the CHILDES data, it was necessary to do this manually using brat. The guidelines we followed for determining whether mentions coreferred came from the OntoNotes corefer-

[2]Dependency tags used were 'SUBJ', 'OBJ', and 'PMOD' in OntoNotes and 'SBJ' and 'OBJ' in CHILDES.

[3]The part of speech used to extract the target NPs were 'PRP' (pronoun), 'NNP' (proper name), and 'NNPS' (plural proper name) from OntoNotes and 'pro' (pronoun) and 'n:prop' (proper name) from CHILDES.

[4]Interannotator agreement for the CHILDES mention annotation was: precision 0.97, recall 0.98, F-score 0.97 (for two scripts).

[5]Interannotator agreement for the manual annotation of agreement information was 97% (for 500 mentions).

ence guidelines (BBN Technologies, 2007).[6]

5 Experiments

Our experiments are designed to quantify the contributions of the various components of the complete model described in Section 3.2 that incorporates discourse salience, cost, and unseen referents. We contrast the complete model with three impoverished models that lack precisely one of these components. The comparison model without discourse uses a uniform discourse salience distribution. The model without cost uses constant speech cost. The model without good estimates of unseen referents always assigns probability $\frac{1}{V} \cdot \alpha \cdot \frac{1}{C}$ to unseen referents in the denominator of (5), regardless of whether the word is a proper name or pronoun. In other words, this model does not have good estimates of unseen referents like the complete model does.

We use the adult- and child-directed corpora to examine to what extent each model captures speakers' referring expressions. We selected pronouns and proper names in each corpus according to several criteria. First, the referring expression had to be in a coreference chain that had at least one proper name, in order to facilitate computing the cost of the proper name alternative. Second, pronouns were only included if they were third person pronouns in subject or object position, and indexicals and reflexives were excluded. Finally, for the CHILDES corpus, children's utterances were excluded.

After filtering pronouns and proper names according to these criteria, 553 pronouns and 1,332 proper names (total 1,885 items) in the OntoNotes corpus, and 165 pronouns and 149 proper names (total 314 items) in the CHILDES Gleason corpus remained for use in the analysis.

Each model chooses referring expressions given information extracted from each corpus as described in Section 4.1. For evaluation, we computed accuracies (total, pronoun, and proper name) and model log likelihood (summing $\log P_S(w|r)$ for the words in the corpus) for each model.

5.1 Results

Table 1 summarizes the results of each model with the OntoNotes and CHILDES datasets. The new referent hyperparameter α and the decay parameter for discourse recency salience were fixed at 0.1 and 3.0, respectively.[7]

5.1.1 News

Overall, the recency salience measure provides a better fit than the frequency salience measure with respect to accuracies, suggesting that recency better captures speakers' representations of discourse salience that influence choices of referring expressions. On the other hand, the models with frequency discourse salience have higher model log likelihood than the models with recency do. This is because of the peakiness of the recency models. Model log likelihood computed over pronouns and proper names (complete model) were -1022.33 and -222.76, respectively, with recency, and -491.81 and -467.06 with frequency. The recency model tends to return a higher probability for a proper name than the frequency model does. Some pronouns receive a very low probability for this reason, and this lowers the model log likelihood.

The model without discourse and the model without cost consistently failed to predict pronouns (these models predicted all proper names). This happens because in the model without discourse, the information content of pronouns is extremely low due to the large number of consistent unseen referents. In the model without cost, pronouns are disfavored because they always convey less information than proper names. The log likelihoods of these models were also below that of the complete model. These results show that pronominalization depends on subtle interaction between discourse salience and speech cost. Neither of them is sufficient to explain the distribution of pronouns and nouns on its own.

The total accuracy of the model without good estimates of unseen referents was the worst among the four models, but this model did predict pronouns to some extent. Because the number of proper names is larger than the number of pronouns in this dataset, the difference in total accuracies between the model without good estimates of unseen referents and the models without discourse or cost reflects this asymmetry. Comparison between the complete model and the model without good estimates of unseen referents also suggests that having knowledge of unseen referents helps correctly pre-

[6] Interannotator agreement for CHILDES coreference annotation was computed using B^3 (Bagga and Baldwin, 1998): precision: 0.99, recall: 1.00 (for one script).

[7] We chose the best parameter values based on multiple runs, but results were qualitatively consistent across a range of parameter values.

Corpus	Model	Discourse	Total accuracy	Pronoun accuracy	Proper name accuracy	Log-lhood
OntoNotes	complete	recency	80.27%	59.49%	88.89%	-1245.09
		frequency	73.10%	62.74%	77.40%	-958.87
	-discourse	NA	70.66%	0.00%	100.00%	-6904.77
	-cost	recency	70.66%	0.00%	100.00%	-1537.71
		frequency	70.66%	0.00%	100.00%	-1017.38
	-unseen	recency	64.14%	68.17%	62.46%	-1567.51
		frequency	56.98%	76.67%	48.80%	-1351.58
CHILDES	complete	recency	49.68%	11.52%	91.95%	-968.64
		frequency	46.18%	10.30%	85.91%	-360.28
	-discourse	NA	47.45%	0.00%	100.00%	-2159.22
	-cost	recency	47.45%	0.00%	100.00%	-1055.54
		frequency	47.45%	0.00%	100.00%	-392.72
	-unseen	recency	50.31%	13.94%	90.60%	-961.54
		frequency	48.41%	21.21%	78.52%	-332.73

Table 1: Accuracies and model log-likelihood

dict the use of proper names in the first mention of a referent.

5.1.2 Child-directed speech

Unlike the adult-directed news text, neither recency nor frequency discourse salience provides a good fit to the data. The low accuracies of pronouns and the high accuracies of proper names in all models indicate that the models are more likely to predict proper names than pronouns. There are several possible reasons for this. First, the CHILDES transcripts involve long conversations in a natural settings. Compared to the news, interlocutors are not focusing on a specific topic, but rather they often switch topics (e.g., a child interrupts her parents' conversation about her father's coworker to talk about her eggs). This topic switching makes it difficult for the model to estimate discourse salience using simple frequency or recency measures. Second, interlocutors are a family and they share a good deal of common knowledge/background (e.g., a mother said *she* as the first mention of her child's friend's mother). The current model is not able to incorporate this kind of background knowledge. Third, many referents are visually available. The current model is not able to use visual salience. In general, these problems arise due to our impoverished estimates of salience, and we would expect a more sophisticated discourse model that accurately measured salience to show better performance.

5.2 Summary

Experiments with the adult-directed news corpus show a close match between speakers' utterances and model predictions. On the other hand, experiments with child-directed speech show that the models were more likely to predict proper names where pronouns were used, suggesting that the estimates of discourse salience using simple measures were not sufficient to capture a conversation.

6 Discussion

This paper proposes a language production model that extends the rational speech act model from Frank and Goodman (2012) to incorporate updates to listeners' beliefs as discourse proceeds. We show that the predictions suggested from UID in this domain can be derived from our speaker model, providing an explanation from first principles for the relation between discourse salience and speakers' choices of referring expressions. Experiments with an adult-directed news corpus show a close match between speakers' utterances and model predictions, and experiments with child-directed speech show a qualitatively similar pattern. This suggests that speakers' behavior can be modeled in a principled way by considering the probabilities of referents in the discourse and the information conveyed by each word.

A controversial issue in language production is to what extent speakers consider a listener's discourse model (Fukumura and van Gompel, 2012). By incorporating an explicit model of listeners, our model provides a way to explore this question. For example, the speaker's listener model $P_L(r|w)$ in (4) might differ between contexts and could also be extended to sum over possible listener identity q in mixed contexts, as in (11).

$$P_L(r|w) = \Sigma_q P(r|w,q)P(q) \qquad (11)$$

This provides a way to probe speakers' sensitivity to differences in listener characteristics across situations.

Although the simulations in this paper employed simple measures for discourse salience (referent frequency and recency), the discourse models used by speakers are likely to be more complex. Studies show that semantic information that cannot be captured with these simple measures, such as topicality (Orita et al., 2014) and animacy (Vogels et al., 2013a), affects speakers' choices of referring expressions. Future work will test to what extent this latent discourse information could affect the model predictions.

Our model predicts a tight coupling between the probability of a referent being mentioned, $p(r)$, and the choice of referring expression. However, these two quantities appear to be dissociated in some cases. For example, Fukumura and Van Gompel (2010) show that semantic bias (as a measure of predictability) affects *what* to refer to (i.e., the referent), but not *how* to refer (i.e., the referring expression), while grammatical position does affect *how* you refer. One way of dissociating the probability of mention from the choice of referring expression in our model would be through the likelihood term, the word probability $p(w|r)$. While we have assumed this word probability to be constant across words and referents, Kehler et al. (2008) use grammatical position to define this probability and show that their model captures experimental data. Syntactic constraints (such as Binding principles) also influence form choices, and this kind of knowledge may also be reflected in the word probability. Examining the role of the word probability $p(w|r)$ more closely would allow us to further explore these issues.

Despite these limitations, our model provides a principled explanation for speakers' choices of referring expressions. In future work we hope to look at a broader range of referring expressions, such as null pronouns and definite descriptions, and to explore the extent to which our model can be applied to other linguistic phenomena that rely on discourse information.

Acknowledgments

We thank the UMD probabilistic modeling reading group for helpful comments and discussion.

References

John R Anderson. 2007. *How can the human mind occur in the physical universe?* Oxford University Press.

Mira Ariel. 1990. *Accessing noun-phrase antecedents*. Routledge.

Jennifer Arnold. 1998. *Reference form and discourse patterns*. Ph.D. thesis, Stanford University Stanford, CA.

Jennifer Arnold. 2008. Reference production: Production-internal and addressee-oriented processes. *Language and cognitive processes*, 23(4):495–527.

Amit Bagga and Breck Baldwin. 1998. Algorithms for scoring coreference chains. In *The first international conference on language resources and evaluation workshop on linguistics coreference*, volume 1, pages 563–566.

Ellen Gurman Bard, Matthew P Aylett, J Trueswell, and M Tanenhaus. 2004. Referential form, word duration, and modeling the listener in spoken dialogue. *Approaches to studying world-situated language use: Bridging the language-as-product and language-as-action traditions*, pages 173–191.

BBN Technologies. 2007. OntoNotes English co-reference guidelines version 7.0.

Leon Bergen, Noah Goodman, and Roger Levy. 2012a. That's what she (could have) said: How alternative utterances affect language use. In *Proceedings of the 34th Annual Conference of the Cognitive Science Society*.

Leon Bergen, Noah D Goodman, and Roger Levy. 2012b. That's what she (could have) said: How alternative utterances affect language use. In *Proceedings of the thirty-fourth annual conference of the cognitive science society*.

Shane Bergsma and Dekang Lin. 2006. Bootstrapping path-based pronoun resolution. In *Proceedings of the 21st International Conference on Computational Linguistics and 44th Annual Meeting of the Association for Computational Linguistics*, pages 33–40, Sydney, Australia, July. Association for Computational Linguistics.

David M Blei and Peter I Frazier. 2011. Distance dependent Chinese restaurant processes. *The Journal of Machine Learning Research*, 12:2461–2488.

Richard Breheny, Napoleon Katsos, and John Williams. 2006. Are generalised scalar implicatures generated by default? an on-line investigation into the role of context in generating pragmatic inferences. *Cognition*, 100(3):434–463.

Susan E Brennan. 1995. Centering attention in discourse. *Language and Cognitive Processes*, 10(2):137–167.

Wallace Chafe. 1994. Discourse, consciousness, and time. *Discourse*, 2(1).

Judith Degen, Michael Franke, and Gerhard Jäger. 2013. Cost-based pragmatic inference about referential expressions. In *Proceedings of the 35th Annual Conference of the Cognitive Science Society*, pages 376–381.

Michael Frank and Noah Goodman. 2012. Predicting pragmatic reasoning in language games. *Science*, 336(6084):998–998.

Kumiko Fukumura and Roger PG Van Gompel. 2010. Choosing anaphoric expressions: Do people take into account likelihood of reference? *Journal of Memory and Language*, 62(1):52–66.

Kumiko Fukumura and Roger PG van Gompel. 2012. Producing pronouns and definite noun phrases: Do speakers use the addressee's discourse model? *Cognitive Science*, 36(7):1289–1311.

Kumiko Fukumura, Roger PG Van Gompel, Trevor Harley, and Martin J Pickering. 2011. How does similarity-based interference affect the choice of referring expression? *Journal of Memory and Language*, 65(3):331–344.

Alexia Galati and Susan E Brennan. 2010. Attenuating information in spoken communication: For the speaker, or for the addressee? *Journal of Memory and Language*, 62(1):35–51.

Talmy Givón. 1983. *Topic continuity in discourse: A quantitative cross-language study*, volume 3. John Benjamins Publishing.

Jean Berko Gleason, Rivka Y Perlmann, and Esther Blank Greif. 1984. What's the magic word: Learning language through politeness routines. *Discourse Processes*, 7(4):493–502.

Noah D Goodman and Andreas Stuhlmüller. 2013. Knowledge and implicature: Modeling language understanding as social cognition. *Topics in Cognitive Science*.

H Paul Grice. 1975. Logic and conversation. *Syntax and semantics*, 3:41–58.

Barbara J Grosz, Scott Weinstein, and Aravind K Joshi. 1995. Centering: A framework for modeling the local coherence of discourse. *Computational Linguistics*, 21(2):203–225.

André Grüning and Andrej A Kibrik. 2005. Modeling referential choice in discourse: A cognitive calculative approach and a neural network approach. In Ruslan Mitkov, editor, *Anaphora Processing: Linguistic, Cognitive and Computational Modelling*, pages 163–198. John Benjamins.

Jeanette K Gundel, Nancy Hedberg, and Ron Zacharski. 1993. Cognitive status and the form of referring expressions in discourse. *Language*, pages 274–307.

Florian T Jaeger. 2010. Redundancy and reduction: Speakers manage syntactic information density. *Cognitive psychology*, 61(1):23–62.

Gerhard Jager. 2007. Game dynamics connects semantics and pragmatics. In Ahti-Veikko Pietarinen, editor, *Game theory and linguistic meaning*, pages 89–102. Elsevier.

Justine T Kao, Jean Wu, Leon Bergen, and Noah D Goodman. 2014. Nonliteral understanding of number words. *Proceedings of the National Academy of Sciences*, 111(33):12002–12007.

Andrew Kehler, Laura Kertz, Hannah Rohde, and Jeffrey L Elman. 2008. Coherence and coreference revisited. *Journal of Semantics*, 25(1):1–44.

Mariya V Khudyakova, Grigory B Dobrov, Andrej A Kibrik, and Natalia V Loukachevitch. 2011. Computational modeling of referential choice: Major and minor referential options. In *Proceedings of the CogSci 2011 Workshop on the Production of Referring Expressions. Boston (July 2011)*.

Emiel Krahmer and Kees Van Deemter. 2012. Computational generation of referring expressions: A survey. *Computational Linguistics*, 38(1):173–218.

Roger Levy and T. Florian Jaeger. 2007. Speakers optimize information density through syntactic reduction. In *Proceedings of the 20th Conference on Neural Information Processing Systems (NIPS)*.

Brian MacWhinney. 2000. The CHILDES project: Tools for analyzing talk.

Mante S Nieuwland and Jos JA Van Berkum. 2006. When peanuts fall in love: N400 evidence for the power of discourse. *Journal of Cognitive Neuroscience*, 18(7):1098–1111.

Ann E Nordmeyer and Michael Frank. 2014. A pragmatic account of the processing of negative sentences. In *Proceedings of the 36th Annual Conference of the Cognitive Science Society*.

Naho Orita, Eliana Vornov, Naomi H Feldman, and Jordan Boyd-Graber. 2014. Quantifying the role of discourse topicality in speakers' choices of referring expressions. In *Association for Computational Linguistics, Workshop on Cognitive Modeling and Computational Linguistics*.

Massimo Poesio, Rosemary Stevenson, Barbara Di Eugenio, and Janet Hitzeman. 2004. Centering: A parametric theory and its instantiations. *Computational Linguistics*, 30(3):309–363.

Marta Recasens, Lluis Marquez, Emili Sapena, M. Antònia Martí, and Mariona Taulé. 2011. SemEval-2010 task 1 OntoNotes English: Coreference resolution in multiple languages.

Jacolien Rij, Hedderik Rijn, and Petra Hendriks. 2013. How WM load influences linguistic processing in adults: A computational model of pronoun interpretation in discourse. *Topics in Cognitive Science*, 5(3):564–580.

Hannah Rohde, Scott Seyfarth, Brady Clark, Gerhard Jäger, and Stefan Kaufmann. 2012. Communicating with cost-based implicature: A game-theoretic approach to ambiguity. In *The 16th Workshop on the Semantics and Pragmatics of Dialogue, Paris, September*.

Kenji Sagae, Eric Davis, Alon Lavie, Brian MacWhinney, and Shuly Wintner. 2010. Morphosyntactic annotation of CHILDES transcripts. *Journal of Child Language*, 37(03):705–729.

Nathaniel J Smith, Noah Goodman, and Michael Frank. 2013. Learning and using language via recursive pragmatic reasoning about other agents. In *Advances in neural information processing systems*, pages 3039–3047.

Pontus Stenetorp, Sampo Pyysalo, Goran Topic, Tomoko Ohta, Sophia Ananiadou, and Junichi Tsujii. 2012. brat: a web-based tool for NLP-assisted text annotation. In *Proceedings of the Demonstrations Session at EACL 2012*.

Yee Whye Teh, Michael I Jordan, Matthew J Beal, and David M Blei. 2006. Hierarchical Dirichlet Processes. *Journal of the American Statistical Association*, 101.

Harry Tily and Steven Piantadosi. 2009. Refer efficiently: Use less informative expressions for more predictable meanings. In *Proceedings of the workshop on the production of referring expressions: Bridging the gap between computational and empirical approaches to reference*.

Mija Van der Wege. 2009. Lexical entrainment and lexical differentiation in reference phrase choice. *Journal of Memory and Language*, 60(4):448–463.

Jorrig Vogels, Emiel Krahmer, and Alfons Maes. 2013a. When a stone tries to climb up a slope: the interplay between lexical and perceptual animacy in referential choices. *Frontiers in psychology*, 4.

Jorrig Vogels, Emiel Krahmer, and Alfons Maes. 2013b. Who is where referred to how, and why? the influence of visual saliency on referent accessibility in spoken language production. *Language and Cognitive Processes*, 28(9):1323–1349.

Linguistic Harbingers of Betrayal: A Case Study on an Online Strategy Game

Vlad Niculae,[1] Srijan Kumar,[2] Jordan Boyd-Graber,[3] Cristian Danescu-Niculescu-Mizil[1]
[1]Cornell University, [2]University of Maryland, [3]University of Colorado
vlad@cs.cornell.edu, srijan@cs.umd.edu,
Jordan.Boyd.Graber@colorado.edu, cristian@cs.cornell.edu

Abstract

Interpersonal relations are fickle, with close friendships often dissolving into enmity. In this work, we explore linguistic cues that presage such transitions by studying dyadic interactions in an online strategy game where players form alliances and break those alliances through betrayal. We characterize friendships that are unlikely to last and examine temporal patterns that foretell betrayal.

We reveal that subtle signs of imminent betrayal are encoded in the conversational patterns of the dyad, even if the victim is not aware of the relationship's fate. In particular, we find that lasting friendships exhibit a form of balance that manifests itself through language. In contrast, sudden changes in the balance of certain conversational attributes—such as positive sentiment, politeness, or focus on future planning—signal impending betrayal.

1 Introduction

A major focus in computational social science has been the study of interpersonal relations through data. However, social interactions are complicated, and we rarely have access all of the data that define the relationship between friends or enemies. As an alternative, thought experiments like the prisoner's dilemma (Axelrod and Dion, 1988) are used to explain behavior. Two prisoners—denied communication—must decide whether to cooperate with each other or defect. Such simple and elegant tools initially helped understand many real world scenarios from pricing products (Rosenthal, 1981) to athletes doping (Buechel et al., 2013). Despite its power, the prisoner's dilemma remains woefully unrealistic. Cooperation and betrayal do not happen in a cell cut off from the rest of the world. Instead, real interactions are mediated by communication: promises are made, then broken, and met with recriminations.

To study the complex social phenomenon of betrayal, we turn to data and observe the players of **Diplomacy** (Sharp, 1978), a war-themed strategy game where friendships and betrayals are orchestrated primarily through language. Diplomacy, like the prisoner's dilemma, is a repeated game where players choose to either cooperate or betray other players. Diplomacy is so engaging that it is played around the world, not only casually as a board game but also over the Internet and in formal settings such as world championships.[1] Players converse throughout the game and victory hinges on enlisting others' support through persuasiveness and cunning duplicity. To illustrate the social relations that carry out throughout the game, consider the following exchange between two Diplomacy allies:

> Germany: Can I suggest you move your armies east and then I will support you? Then next year you move *[there]* and dismantle Turkey. I will deal with England and France, you take out Italy.
>
> Austria: Sounds like a perfect plan! Happy to follow through. And—thank you Bruder!

Austria is very polite and positive in its reply, and appreciates Germany's support and generosity. They have been good allies for the better part of the game. However, immediately after this exchange, Austria suddenly invades German territory. The intention to do so was so well concealed that Germany did not see the betrayal coming; otherwise it would have taken advantage first. Indeed, if we follow their conversation after the attack, we find Germany surprised:

> Germany: Not really sure what to say, except that I regret you did what you did.

[1]A recent episode of *This American Life* describes the Diplomacy game in a competitive offline setting: http://www.thisamericanlife.org/radio-archives/episode/531/got-your-back?act=1

Proceedings of the 53rd Annual Meeting of the Association for Computational Linguistics and the 7th International Joint Conference on Natural Language Processing, pages 1650–1659, Beijing, China, July 26-31, 2015.

Such scenarios suggest an important research challenge: is the forthcoming betrayal signaled by linguistic cues appearing in the (ostensibly friendly) conversation between the betrayer and the eventual victim? A positive answer would suggest not only that the betrayer unknowingly reveals their future treachery, but also that the eventual victim fails to notice these signals. Capturing these signals computationally would therefore mean outperforming the human players.

In this work, we provide a framework for analyzing a dyad's evolving communication patterns and provide evidence of subtle but consistent conversational patterns that foretell the unilateral dissolution of a friendship. In particular, imminent betrayal is signaled by sudden changes in the balance of conversational attributes such as positive sentiment, politeness, and structured discourse. Furthermore, we show that by exploiting these cues in a prediction setting we can anticipate imminent betrayal better than the human players.

After briefly describing the game (Section 2), we focus on how the structure of the game provides convenient, reliable indicators of whether pairs of participants are friends or foes (Section 3). Given these labels, we explore linguistic features that are predictive of whether friendships will end in betrayal (Section 4) and, if so, when the betrayal will happen (Section 5).

While our focus is on a single popular game, we choose methods that generalize to other domains, revealing dynamics present in other social interactions (Section 6). We discuss how automatically predicting stable relationships and betrayal can more broadly help advance the study of trust and relationships using computational linguistics.

2 Communication and Conflict in Diplomacy

A game of Diplomacy begins in 1901 with players casting themselves as the European powers at the eve of the first world war: England, Germany, France, Russia, Austria, Italy, and the Ottoman Empire. The goal of the game (like other war games such as Risk or Axis & Allies) is to capture all of the territories on the game board (Figure 1). The games are divided into years starting from 1901 and each year is divided into two seasons—Spring and Fall. Each season consists of two alternating phases: *diplomacy*—the players communicate to form strategies—and *orders*—the players submit their moves for the season. Seasons are therefore the main unit of game time.

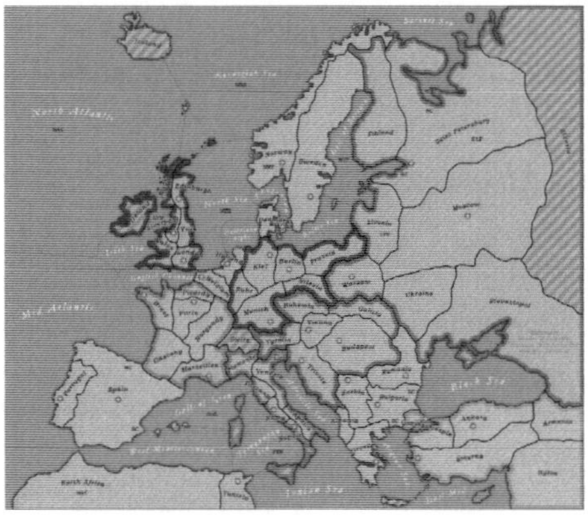

Figure 1: The full Diplomacy board representing Europe circa 1914. The seven nations struggle to control the map.

2.1 Movement, Orders, and Battles

On the board, each player can operate a unit for each city they control. During each turn, these pieces have the option of moving to an adjacent territory. What makes Diplomacy unique is that all players submit their written (or electronic) orders; these orders are executed simultaneously; and *there is no randomness* (e.g., dice). Thus, the outcome of the game depends only on the communication, cooperation, and movements of players.

When two units end their turn in the same territory, it implies a battle. Who wins the battle is decided purely based on numerical superiority (ties go to defenders). Instead of moving, a unit can support another unit; large armies can be created through intricate networks of support. The side with the largest army wins the battle.

The process of *supporting* a unit is thus critical for both a successful offensive move and a successful defense. Often, a lone player lacks the units to provide enough support to his attacks and thus needs the help of others.[2] Because these orders (both movement and support) are machine readable, we have a clear indication of when players are working together (supporting each other) or working against each other (attacking each other); we will use this to define relationships between

[2] While support can come from a player's own units, allies often combine resources. For example, if an English army in Belgium is attacking a Germany Army in Ruhr, a French army in Burgundy could strengthen that attack. This is accomplished by the French player submitting a move explicitly stating "I support England's attack from Belgium to Ruhr".

players (Section 3). However, coordinating these actions between players requires cooperation and *diplomacy*.

2.2 Communication

In the *diplomacy* phase of the game, players talk to each other. These conversations are either public or—more typically—one-on-one. Conversations include greetings, extra-game discussions (e.g., "did you see Game of Thrones?"), low-level tactics ("if you attack Armenia, I'll support you"), and high-level strategy ("we need to control Central Europe"). The content of these messages forms the object of our study.

Because of the centrality of language to Diplomacy, we can learn the rhetorical and social devices players use to build and break trust. Because this language is embedded in every game, it has convenient properties: similar situations are repeated, the goals are clear, and machine-readable orders confirm which players are enemies and which are friends. In the next section, we explore the Diplomacy data.

2.3 Preprocessing

We use games from two popular online platforms for playing Diplomacy.[3] The average season of an online Diplomacy game lasts nine days. We remove non-standard games caused by differences between the two platforms, as well as games that are still in progress. Moreover, in each game, we filter out setup messages, regulatory messages to and from the administrator of the game and messages declaring the state of the game, keeping only messages between the players. This leaves 249 games with 145.000 total messages.

The dataset confirms that communication is an essential part of Diplomacy: half of the games have over 515 messages exchanged between the players, while the top quartile has over 750 messages per game. Also, non-trivial messages (with at least one sentence) tend to be complex: over half of them have at least five sentences, and the top quartile consists of messages with eight or more sentences.

3 Relationships and Their Stability

In this section, we explore how interactions within the game of Diplomacy define the relationships

Event	Time	What happened
F_1	4	B supports V's army in Vienna
F_2	3	V supports B's attack from Warsaw to Silesia
F_3	3	B again supports V in Vienna
F_4	1	V supports B's move from Venice to Tyrolia
H_5	0	B attacks V in Vienna
H_6	-1	V retaliates, attacking B in Warsaw

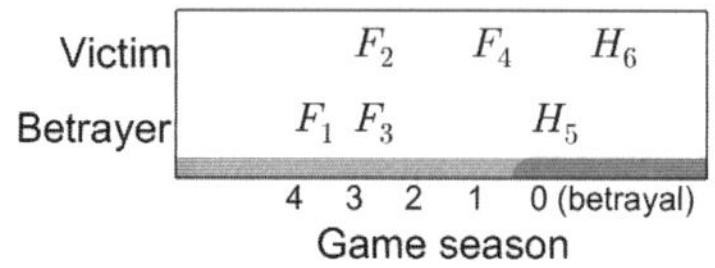

Figure 2: A friendship between Player B (eventual betrayer) and Player V (eventual victim) unravels. For the first four events, the players exchange **F**riendly acts (in green). Eventually B's unilateral hostile act betrays V's trust, leading to hostility (in red). The dissolution takes place at the time of the first hostile act ($t = 0$) and we index game seasons going back from the betrayal, such that lower indices mean betrayal is nearer.

between players. While such dyadic relationships can be undefined (e.g., England and Turkey are in opposite corners of the map), specific interactions between players indicate whether they are friendly or hostile to each other.

Friendships and hostilities. Alliances are a natural part of the game of Diplomacy. While the best outcome for a player is a *solo victory* against all other players, this is rare and difficult to achieve without any cooperation and assistance. Instead, the game's structure encourages players to form long-term alliances. Allies often settle for (less prestigious) team victories, but these coalitions can also crumble as players seek a (more prestigious) solo victory for themselves. This game dynamic naturally leads to the formation of *friendly and hostile dyads*, which are relatively easy to identify through post-hoc analysis of the game, as explained next.

Acts of friendship. Diplomacy provides a *support* option for players to help each other: this game mechanism (discussed in Section 2) provides unequivocal evidence of friendship. When two players engage in a series of such friendly acts, we will say that the two are in a relation of *friendship*.

Acts of hostility. Unlike support, hostile actions are not explicitly marked in Diplomacy. We consider two players to be hostile if they get involved in any unambiguous belligerent action, such as invading one another's territory, or if one supports an enemy of the other.[4]

[3] Anonymized transcripts and more information available at http://vene.ro/betrayal/

[4] In Diplomacy all game actions are simultaneous, and this can lead to ambiguous interpretation of the nature of a

Betrayal. As in real life, friendships can be broken unilaterally: an individual can *betray* his friend by engaging in a hostile act towards her. Figure 2 shows two players who started out as friends (green) but became hostile (red) after a betrayal. Importantly, until the last act of friendship (game season $t = 1$), the *victim* is unaware that she will be betrayed (otherwise she would not have engaged in an act of friendship) and the *betrayer* has no interest in signaling his planned duplicity to his partner.

This setting poses the following research challenge: are there linguistic cues that appear during the friendly conversations and portend the upcoming betrayal? A positive answer would have two implications: the betrayer unknowingly hints at his future treachery, and the victim could have noticed it, but did not. We will explore this question in the following sections.

Relationship stability. Before venturing into the linguistic analysis of betrayals, we briefly explore the dynamics underlying these state transitions. We find that, as in real life, friendships are much more likely to collapse into hostilities than the reverse: in Diplomacy, the probability of a friendship to dissolve into enmity is about five times greater than that of hostile players becoming friends. The history of the relationship also matters. A friendship built on the foundation of many cooperative acts is more likely to endure than friendship with a short history, and long-lasting conflict is less likely to become a friendship. In numbers, the probability that a two season long friendship ends is 35%, while for pairs who have helped each other for ten or more seasons, the probability of betrayal is only 23%. Similarly, the probability that a two season long conflict resolves is 7%, while players at war for over ten seasons have only a 5% chance to make up. These numbers aren't particularly shocking—the idea that the passage of time has an effect on the strength of a relationship is intuitive. For the purposes of this study, we control for such effects in order to capture purely linguistic hints of betrayal.

Starting from the relationship definitions discussed in this section, in what follows we show how subtle linguistic patterns of in-game player conversations can reveal whether or not a friendship will turn hostile or not.

pair's interactions. Our definition of hostility intentionally discards such ambiguous evidence. For instance, if two players attempt to move into the same unoccupied territory, this is not necessarily aggressive: allies sometimes use this tactic ("bouncing") to ensure that a territory remains unoccupied.

4 Language Foretelling Betrayal

In this section, we examine whether the conversations between two Diplomacy allies contain linguistic cues foretelling if their friendship will last or end in betrayal. We expect these cues to be subtle, since we only consider messages exchanged when the two individuals are being ostensibly friendly; when at least one of them—the eventual victim—is unaware of the relationship's fate.

4.1 What Constitutes a Betrayal

To find betrayals, we must first find friendships. Building on the discussion from Section 3, we consider a friendship to be *stable* if it is ongoing, established, and reciprocal. Thus, we focus on relationships that contain at least two consecutive and reciprocated acts of friendships that span at last at least three seasons in game time. We also check that no more than five seasons pass between two acts of friendships, as friendships can fade.

Betrayals are established and reciprocal friendships that end with at least two hostile acts. The person initiating the first of these hostile acts is the *betrayer*, while the other person is the *victim*.[5]

For each betrayal instance, we find the most similar stable friendship that was *never* dissolved by betrayal. Using a greedy heuristic, we select friendships that match the betrayals on two statistics: the length of the friendship and number of seasons since the start of the game. After this matching process, we find no significant difference in either of the two variables (Mann-Whitney $p > 0.3$). Matching betrayals with lasting friendships in this fashion removes historical and relationship-type effects such as those discussed in Section 3, and focuses the comparison on the variable of interest: whether a given stable friendship will end in a betrayal or not.

4.2 Linguistic Harbingers of Betrayal

Now we switch to exploring linguistic features that correlate with future betrayal in the controlled setting described above. We start from the intuition that a stable relationship should be balanced (Jung et al., 2012): friends will help each other

[5] In rare cases, the betrayal can be mutual (i.e., both players start attacking each other in the same season). In such cases, we consider both betrayals.

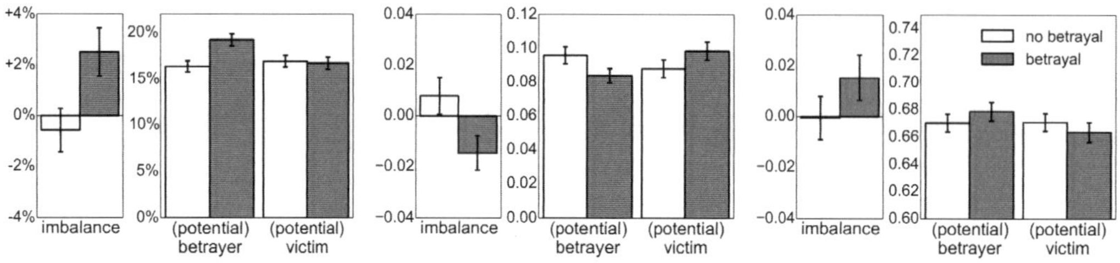

(a) Positive sentiment (percentage of sentences)

(b) Planning discourse markers (avg. number per sentence)

(c) Politeness (avg. message score)

Figure 3: Friendships that will end in betrayal are imbalanced. The eventual betrayer is more positive, more polite, but plans less than the victim. The white bars correspond to matched lasting friendships, where the roles of potential betrayer and victim are arbitrarily assigned; in these cases, the imbalances disappear. Error bars mark bootstrapped standard errors (Efron, 1979).

while enemies will fight each other. A precarious friendship might feel one-sided, while a conflict may turn to friendship through a magnanimous olive branch. Therefore, we focus our attention on linguistic features that have the potential to signal an imbalance in the communication patterns of the dyad.

To ensure that we are studying conversational patterns that occur *only* when the two individuals in the dyad are ostensibly being friends, we only extract features from the messages exchanged before the last act of friendship, that is, before the season labeled 1 in Figure 2. Considering the nature of this setting, we can only hope for subtle linguistic cues: if there were salient linguistic signals, then the victim would notice and preempt the betrayal. Instead, they are taken by surprise; the following is a typical reaction of a player after having been betrayed by a friend:

> Well that move was sour. I'm guessing France put you up to it, citing my large growth. This was a pity, as I was willing to give you the lion's share of centers in the west. [...] If you voiced your concerns I would have supported you in most of the western centers. Unfortunately now you have jumped out of the pan into the fire.

Sentiment. Changes in the sentiment expressed in conversation can reflect emotional responses, social affect, as well as the status of the relationship as a whole (Gottman and Levenson, 2000; Wang and Cardie, 2014). We quantify the proportion of exchanged sentences that transmit positive, neutral and negative sentiment using the Stanford Sentiment Analyzer (Socher et al., 2013).[6] Example sentences with these features, as well as all other features we consider, can be found in Table 1.

We find that an imbalance in the amount of positive sentiment expressed by the two individuals is a subtle sign that the relation will end in betrayal (Figure 3a, left; one-sample t-test on the imbalance, $p = 0.008$). When looking closer at who is the source of this imbalance (Figure 3a, right), we find that that it is the eventual betrayer that uses significantly *more positive sentiment* than the control counterpart in the matched friendship (two-sample t-test, $p = 0.001$). This is somewhat surprising, and we speculate that this is the betrayer overcompensating for his forthcoming actions.

Argumentation and Discourse. Structured discourse and well-made arguments are essential in persuasion (Cialdini, 2000; Anand et al., 2011). To capture discourse complexity, we measure the average number of explicit discourse connectors per sentence (Prasad et al., 2008).[7] These markers belong to four coarse classes: *comparison*, *contingency*, *expansive*, and *temporal*. To capture *planning*, we group temporal markers that refer to the future (e.g.,"next", "thereafter") in a separate category. To quantify the level of argumentation, we calculate average number of claim and premise markers per sentence, as identified by Stab and Gurevych (2014). We also measure the number of request sentences in each message, as identified by the heuristics in the Stanford Politeness classifier (Danescu-Niculescu-Mizil et al., 2013).

The structure of the discourse offers clues to whether the friendship will last. For example, Figure 3b shows that in friendships doomed to end in betrayal, the victim uses planning discourse markers significantly more often than the betrayer (one-sample t-test on the imbalance, $p = 0.03$), who is

[6] We collapse the few examples classified as *extreme positive* and *extreme negative* examples into *positive* and *negative*, respectively.

[7] We remove the connectors that appear in over 20% of the messages (*and*, *for*, *but*, *if*, *as*, *or*, and *so*).

Feature	Example sentence from the data
Positive sentiment	I will still be thrilled if it turns out you win this war.
Negative sentiment	It's not a great outcome, but still an OK one.
Neutral sentiment	Do you concur with my assumption?
Claim	But **I believe** that E/F have discarded him and so **I think** he might bite.
Premise	I put Italy out **because** I wanted to work with you.
Comparison	We can trade centers **as much as** we like **after** that.
Contingency	He did not, **thus** we are **indeed** in fine shape to continue as planned.
Expansion	Would you **rather** see WAR-UKR, or GAL-UKR?
Temporal	I think he can **still** be effective to help me take TUN **while** you take ROM.
Planning	HOL should fall **next** year, and **then** MUN and KIE shortly **thereafter**.
Number of requests	
Politeness	I wonder if you shouldn't try to support Italy into MAR ... What do you think?
Subjectivity	I'm **just curious** what you **think**.
Talkativeness	

Table 1: Summary of the linguistic cues we consider.

likely to be aware that the cooperation has no future. (More argumentation and discourse features will be discussed in the following sections.)

Politeness. Pragmatic information can also be informative of the relation between two individuals; for example Danescu-Niculescu-Mizil et al. (2013) show that differences in levels of politeness can echo differences in status and power. We measure the politeness of each message using the Stanford Politeness classifier and find that friendships that end in betrayal show a slight imbalance between the level of politeness used by the two individuals (one-sample t-test on the imbalance, $p = 0.09$) and that in those cases the future victim is the one that is less polite.

Subjectivity. We explored phrases expressing opinion, accusation, suspicion, and speculation taken from an automatically collected lexicon (Riloff and Wiebe, 2003), but did not find significant differences between betrayals and control friendships.

Talkativeness. Another conversational aspect is the amount of communication flowing between the players, in each direction. To quantify this, we simply use the number of messages sent, the average number of sentences per message, and the average number of words per sentence. Abnormal communication patterns can indicate a relationship breakdown. For example, friendships that dissolve are characterized by an imbalance in the number of messages exchanged between the two players (one-sample t-test, $p < 0.001$).

These results show that there are indeed subtle linguistic imbalance signals that are indicative of an forthcoming betrayal, even in a setting in which the victim is not aware of the impending betrayal.

4.3 Predictive Power

To test whether these linguistic cues have any predictive power and to explore how they interact, we turn to a binary classification setting in which we try to detect whether a player V will be betrayed by a player B. (We will call player V the potential victim and player B the potential betrayer.) Expert humans—the actual victims—performed poorly on this task and were not able to tell that they will be betrayed: by virtue of how the dataset is constructed, the performance of the human players is at chance level.

We use the same balanced dataset of matched betrayals and lasting friendships as before and consider as classification instances all the seasons coming from each of the two classes (663 betrayal seasons and 712 from lasting friendships). As features, we use the cues described above and summarized in Table 1, differentiated by source: V or B. We use logistic regression after univariate feature selection. The best setting for the model parameters[8] is selected via 5-fold cross validation, ensuring that instances from the same game are never found in both train and validation folds. The resulting model achieves a cross-validation accuracy of 57% and a Matthews correlation coefficient of 0.14, significantly above chance (52% accuracy and 0 Matthews correlation coefficient), with 95% bootstrapped confidence. This indicates

[8] We optimize the number of features selected, the scoring function used (ANOVA or χ^2), whether to automatically reweigh the classes, the regularizer (ℓ_1 or ℓ_2), and the value of the regularization parameter C between 10^{-12} and 10^{12}.

From	Positive feature	From	Negative feature
B	Positive sentiment	B	Expansion
B	Sentences	B	Comparison
		B	Contingency
		B	No. Words
		B	Planning
		B	Negative sentiment

Table 2: Selected features for recognizing upcoming betrayal, in decreasing order of the absolute value of their coefficients. The *From* column indicates whether the message containing the feature was sent by the potential **B**etrayer or the potential **V**ictim. (In this case, only betrayer features were selected.) Positive features indicate that a friendship is more likely to end in betrayal.

that, unlike the actual players, the classifier is able to exploit subtle linguistic signals that surface in the conversation.[9]

The selected features and their coefficients are reported in Table 2. On top of the observations we previously made, the feature ranking reveals that writing more sentences per message is more common when one will betray. Discourse features also prove relevant: more complex discourse indicates a lower likelihood of the player betraying (e.g., Figure 3b).

Overall, the selected linguistic features capture a consistent signal that characterizes people's language when they are about to betray: they tend to plan less than their victims, use less structure in their communication, and are overly positive.

5 Sudden yet Inevitable Betrayal

The results from Section 4 suggest that language cues can be subtle signs of future relationship disruption. Even though people are aware that most relationships eventually end, one would still prefer to reap their benefits as long as possible. In Diplomacy, despite the common knowledge that everyone prefers to win alone, players still take chances on long-lasting alliances. This leads to an alternate research question: assuming that a relationship will be disrupted, how soon can one expect to be betrayed? This is still just as challenging for the expert human players, as they were not able to anticipate and thereby avoid betrayal.

Next we investigate if the variation of the linguistic cues over time can predict imminent change in the relationship. We consider only the subset of betrayals used in Section 4, and label each individual game season with its distance from the end of the friendship (as in Figure 2). We prevent short alliances of circumstance from distorting the features close to betrayal by keeping only friendships lasting at least four seasons.

We consider the same cues described in Table 1, and train a classifier to discriminate between the season preceding the last friendly interaction and all the older seasons. This learning task is imbalanced, with only 14% of the seasons being immediately before the betrayal. Thus, we optimize F_1 score and also measure the Matthews correlation coefficient, which takes a value of 0 for uninformative predictions (random or majority). The best model achieves an F_1 score of 0.31 and a Matthews correlation coefficient of 0.17, significantly better than chance with 95% bootstrapped confidence. This shows that we can capture signs of imminent betrayal, something that even the skilled human players have failed to do. Furthermore, 39% of the predicted false positives are within two seasons of the last friendly act. This suggests that sometimes the warning signs can appear slightly earlier.

The selected features, displayed in Table 3, reflect some of the effects identified in Section 4, such as the importance of positive sentiment and planning discourse markers. Betrayers have a tendency to use more positive sentiment during the last moment of purported friendliness (Figure 4a). Also, expressing more opinions through claims is a sign that one will not betray right away. Three of the discourse features (comparison, contingency and expansion) are selected as *imbalance* features (they have near-opposite coefficients for the betrayer and for the victim), indicating that as betrayal approaches, victims are less eloquent than betrayers. Interestingly, some predictive signals come only from the victim: a partner using increasingly more planning words is at higher risk of being betrayed (Figure 4b). This could be explained by the pressure that making plans for the future can put on a relationship. A similar reasoning applies for making many requests.

We also find that a decrease in a partner's politeness presages their imminent betrayal. The change in politeness over time (Figure 4c) reveals a reversal in the politeness imbalance of the pair. This explains why politeness is not a good enough feature in detecting long-term betrayal. The behav-

[9]Since our focus is on understanding linguistic aspects of betrayal, rather than on achieving the best possible performance on this particular Diplomacy task, we do not use game-specific information, such as the players' position on the map, or any information not accessible to both players.

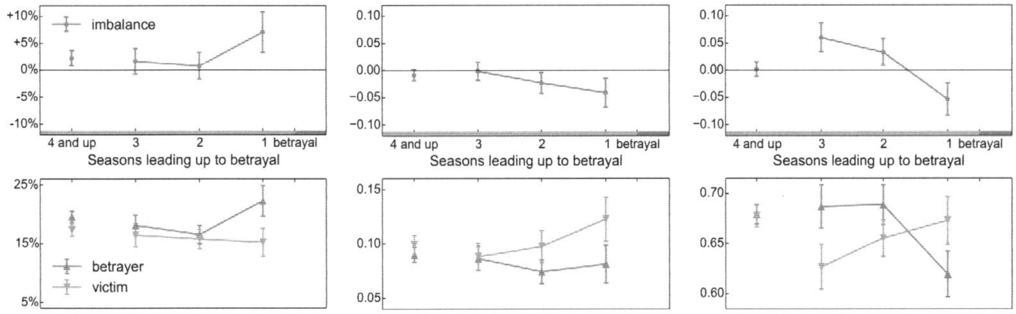

(a) Positive sentiment (percentage of sentences)

(b) Planning discourse markers (avg. number per sentence)

(c) Politeness (avg. message score)

Figure 4: Changes in balance can mark imminent betrayal. As the breakdown approaches, the betrayer becomes more positive but less polite, and the victim tends to make more requests and become more polite. Error bars mark bootstrapped standard errors (Efron, 1979).

From	Positive feature	From	Negative feature
V	Comparison	B	Claims
V	Positive sentiment	B	Politeness
V	Contingency	B	Contingency
V	Planning	B	Subjectivity
V	Requests	B	Expansion
V	Expansion	B	No. Sentences
		B	Comparison

Table 3: Selected features for recognizing imminent betrayal, in decreasing order of the absolute value of their coefficients. The *From* column indicates whether the message containing the feature comes from the potential **B**etrayer or the potential **V**ictim. Positive features indicate that an exchange is more likely to be followed by immediate betrayal.

ior could have two intuitive explanations. On one hand, if the betrayer has planned the act in advance, politeness can be a strategy for deception. On the other hand, if the betrayer receives impolite requests, the value of the relationship can decrease, hastening a betrayal. We observe a similar dynamic for the average number of sentences per message sent by the betrayer; the feature is selected in both prediction tasks, but with opposite signs: more complex messages suggest that betrayal *will* happen, but *not right away*.

Studying language change as betrayal draws nearer uncovers effects that cannot be seen when looking at an entire friendship on average. For example, while excessively positive and polite partners are potential betrayers, people who have themselves suddenly become more polite are likely to become victims soon.

6 Relevance Beyond the Game

While discovering betrayal in one online game is a fun and novel task, our work connects with broader research in computational social science. In this section we describe how our work tackles issues that previous research on alliances, negotiation, and relationships have faced.

Cooperation and relationship building are an essential part of many activities: completing a group project, opening a business, or forging a new relationship. Each of these has been the subject of extensive research to understand what makes for effective relationships. Jung et al. (2012) show that a balanced working relationship is more likely to lead to better performance on tasks like pair programming. Imai and Gelfand (2010) show that understanding cultural norms improves negotiations. While these data are elicited in the lab, our "found" data are inexpensive because Diplomacy games are fun and inherently anonymized.

Romance is a popular and more real-world phenomenon that helps us understand how relationships form and dissolve. The research that tells us how language shapes early dating (Ranganath et al., 2009) and whether an existing relationship will continue (Slatcher and Pennebaker, 2006; Gottman and Levenson, 2000; Ireland et al., 2011) is formed from an incomplete sample of a course of a relationship. In contrast, a game of Diplomacy is shorter than almost any marriage and we have a complete account of all interactions throughout the entire relationship. Furthermore, this work focuses on the unilateral and asymmetric act of betrayal, rather than on the question of whether a relation will last.

Playing Diplomacy online is less tangible than a romantic relationship, but understanding trust and deception in online interactions (Riegelsberger et al., 2003; Newman et al., 2003; Hancock et al., 2007; Ott et al., 2011; Feng et al., 2012) is particularly important because the Internet marketplace is a growing driver of economic growth (Boyd, 2003). Diplomacy offers a setting in which deception occurs spontaneously in the context of complex relationships.

7 Conclusions

Despite people's best effort to hide it, the intention to betray can leak through the language one uses. Detecting it is not a task that we expect to be solvable with high accuracy, as that would entail a reliable "recipe" for avoiding betrayal in relationships; in this unrealistic scenario, betrayals would be unlikely to exist. While the effects we find are subtle, they bring new insights into the relation between linguistic balance and stability in relationships.

Although we use one game to develop our methodology, the framework developed here can be extended to be applied to a wide range of social interaction. Social dynamics in collaborative settings can bear striking similarities to those present in war games. For example, in Wikipedia "edit wars"—where attacks correspond to edit reverts—are common on issues relating to politics, religion, history and nationality, among others (Kittur et al., 2007). As in Diplomacy, Wikipedia editors form alliances, argue and negotiate about possible compromises. A challenge for future work is to find reliable linguistic cues that generalize well between such settings.

Acknowledgements

We thank Mario Huys, Chris Babcock, and Christopher Martin for providing the Diplomacy dataset. We are grateful to Flavio Chierichetti, Sendhil Mullainathan and the annonymous reviewers for their helpful comments. This work was conducted in part while Cristian Danescu-Niculescu-Mizil and Vlad Niculae were at the Max Planck Institute for Software Systems. Jordan Boyd-Graber is supported by NSF Grants CCF-1409287, IIS-1320538, and NCSE-1422492. Cristian Danescu-Niculescu-Mizil is supported by a Google Faculty Research Award. Any opinions, findings, conclusions, or recommendations expressed here are those of the authors and do not necessarily reflect the view of the sponsor.

References

Pranav Anand, Joseph King, Jordan Boyd-Graber, Earl Wagner, Craig Martell, Douglas W. Oard, and Philip Resnik. 2011. Believe me: We can do this! In *Proceedings of the AAAI 2011 Workshop on Computational Models of Natural Argument*.

Robert Axelrod and Douglas Dion. 1988. The further evolution of cooperation. *Science*, 242(4884):1385–1390.

Josh Boyd. 2003. The rhetorical construction of trust online. *Communication Theory*, 13(4):392–410.

Berno Buechel, Eike Emrich, and Stefanie Pohlkamp. 2013. Nobody's innocent: The role of customers in the doping dilemma. MPRA paper, University Library of Munich, Germany.

Robert B. Cialdini. 2000. *Influence: Science and Practice (4th Edition)*. Allyn & Bacon.

Cristian Danescu-Niculescu-Mizil, Moritz Sudhof, Dan Jurafsky, Jure Leskovec, and Christopher Potts. 2013. A computational approach to politeness with application to social factors. In *Proceedings of the Association for Computational Linguistics*.

Bradley Efron. 1979. Bootstrap methods: Another look at the jackknife. *The Annals of Statistics*, (1979):1–26.

Song Feng, Ritwik Banerjee, and Yejin Choi. 2012. Syntactic stylometry for deception detection. In *Proceedings of the Association for Computational Linguistics*.

John M. Gottman and Robert W. Levenson. 2000. The timing of divorce: Predicting when a couple will divorce over a 14-year period. *Journal of Marriage and Family*, 62(3):737–745.

Jeffrey T. Hancock, Lauren E. Curry, Saurabh Goorha, and Michael Woodworth. 2007. On lying and being lied to: A linguistic analysis of deception in computer-mediated communication. *Discourse Processes*, 45(1):1–23.

Lynn Imai and Michele J. Gelfand. 2010. The culturally intelligent negotiator: The impact of cultural intelligence (CQ) on negotiation sequences and outcomes. *Organizational Behavior and Human Decision Processes*, 112(2):83–98.

Molly E. Ireland, Richard B. Slatcher, Paul W. Eastwick, Lauren E. Scissors, Eli J. Finkel, and James W. Pennebaker. 2011. Language style matching predicts relationship initiation and stability. *Psychological Science*, 22(1):39–44.

Malte Jung, Jan Chong, and Larry Leifer. 2012. Group hedonic balance and pair programming performance: Affective interaction dynamics as indicators of performance. In *International Conference on Human Factors in Computing Systems*.

Aniket Kittur, Bongwon Suh, Bryan A. Pendleton, and Ed H. Chi. 2007. He says, she says: Conflict and coordination in Wikipedia. In *International Conference on Human Factors in Computing Systems*.

Matthew L. Newman, James W. Pennebaker, Diane S. Berry, and Jane M. Richards. 2003. Lying words: Predicting deception from linguistic styles. *Personality and social psychology bulletin*, 29(5):665–675.

Myle Ott, Yejin Choi, Claire Cardie, and Jeffrey T. Hancock. 2011. Finding deceptive opinion spam by any stretch of the imagination. In *Proceedings of the Association for Computational Linguistics*.

Rashmi Prasad, Nikhil Dinesh, Alan Lee, Eleni Miltsakaki, Livio Robaldo, Aravind K. Joshi, and Bonnie L. Webber. 2008. The Penn Discourse TreeBank 2.0. In *International Language Resources and Evaluation*.

Rajesh Ranganath, Dan Jurafsky, and Dan McFarland. 2009. It's not you, it's me: Detecting flirting and its misperception in speed-dates. In *Proceedings of Emperical Methods in Natural Language Processing*.

Jens Riegelsberger, M. Angela Sasse, and John D. McCarthy. 2003. The researcher's dilemma: Evaluating trust in computer-mediated communication. *International Journal of Human-Computer Studies*, 58(6):759–781.

Ellen Riloff and Janyce Wiebe. 2003. Learning extraction patterns for subjective expressions. In *Proceedings of Emperical Methods in Natural Language Processing*.

Robert W. Rosenthal. 1981. Games of perfect information, predatory pricing and the chain-store paradox. *Journal of Economic Theory*, 25(1):92–100.

Richard Sharp. 1978. *The Game of Diplomacy*. Arthur Barker Publishing.

Richard B. Slatcher and James W. Pennebaker. 2006. How do I love thee? Let me count the words: The social effects of expressive writing. *Psychological Science*, 17(8):660–664.

Richard Socher, Alex Perelygin, Jean Y Wu, Jason Chuang, Christopher D Manning, Andrew Y Ng, and Christopher Potts. 2013. Recursive deep models for semantic compositionality over a sentiment treebank. In *Proceedings of Emperical Methods in Natural Language Processing*.

Christian Stab and Iryna Gurevych. 2014. Identifying argumentative discourse structures in persuasive essays. In *Proceedings of Emperical Methods in Natural Language Processing*.

Lu Wang and Claire Cardie. 2014. A piece of my mind: A sentiment analysis approach for online dispute detection. In *Proceedings of the Association for Computational Linguistics*.

Who caught a cold? — Identifying the subject of a symptom

Shin Kanouchi [†], Mamoru Komachi [†], Naoaki Okazaki [‡],
Eiji Aramaki[§], and Hiroshi Ishikawa [†]

[†] Tokyo Metropolitan University, {kanouchi-shin at ed., komachi at, ishikawh at}tmu.ac.jp
[‡] Tohoku University, okazaki at ecei.tohoku.ac.jp
[§]Kyoto University, eiji.aramaki at gmail.com

Abstract

The development and proliferation of social media services has led to the emergence of new approaches for surveying the population and addressing social issues. One popular application of social media data is health surveillance, e.g., predicting the outbreak of an epidemic by recognizing diseases and symptoms from text messages posted on social media platforms. In this paper, we propose a novel task that is crucial and generic from the viewpoint of health surveillance: estimating a subject (carrier) of a disease or symptom mentioned in a Japanese tweet. By designing an annotation guideline for labeling the subject of a disease/symptom in a tweet, we perform annotations on an existing corpus for public surveillance. In addition, we present a supervised approach for predicting the subject of a disease/symptom. The results of our experiments demonstrate the impact of subject identification on the effective detection of an episode of a disease/symptom. Moreover, the results suggest that our task is independent of the type of disease/symptom.

1 Introduction

Social media services, including Twitter and Facebook, provide opportunities for individuals to share their experiences, thoughts, and opinions. The wide use of social media services has led to the emergence of new approaches for surveying the population and addressing social issues. One popular application of social media data is flu surveillance, i.e., predicting the outbreak of influenza epidemics by detecting mentions of flu infections on social media platforms (Culotta, 2010; Lampos and Cristianini, 2010; Aramaki et al., 2011; Paul and Dredze, 2011; Signorini et al., 2011; Collier, 2012; Dredze et al., 2013; Gesualdo et al., 2013; Stoové and Pedrana, 2014).

Previous studies mainly relied on shallow textual clues in Twitter posts in order to predict the number of flu infections, e.g., the number of occurrences of specific keywords (such as "flu" or "influenza") on Twitter. However, such a simple approach can lead to incorrect predictions. Broniatowski et al. (2013) argued that media attention increases chatter, i.e., the number of tweets that mention the flu without the poster being actually infected. Examples include, "I don't wish the flu on anyone" and "A Harry Potter actor hospitalised after severe flu-like syndromes." Lazer et al. (2014) reported large errors in Google Flu Trends (Carneiro and Mylonakis, 2009) on the basis of a comparison with the proportion of doctor visits for influenza-like illnesses.

Lamb et al. (2013) aimed to improve the accuracy of detecting mentions of flu infections. Their method trains a binary classifier to distinguish tweets reporting flu infections from those expressing concern or awareness about the flu, e.g., "Starting to get worried about swine flu." Accordingly, they reported encouraging results (e.g., better correlations with CDC trends), but their approach requires supervision data and a lexicon (word class features) specially designed for the flu. Moreover, even though this method is a reasonable choice for improving the accuracy, it is not readily applicable to other types of diseases (e.g., dengue fever) and symptoms (e.g., runny nose), which are also important for public health (Velardi et al., 2014).

In this paper, we propose a more generalized task setting for public surveillance. In other words, our objective is to *estimate the subject (carrier) of a disease or symptom mentioned in a Japanese tweet.* More specifically, we are interested in determining who has a disease/symptom

Proceedings of the 53rd Annual Meeting of the Association for Computational Linguistics and the 7th International Joint Conference on Natural Language Processing, pages 1660–1670,
Beijing, China, July 26-31, 2015.

(if any) in order to examine whether the poster suffers from the disease or symptom. For example, given the sentence "I caught a cold," we would predict that the first person ("I," i.e., the poster) is the subject (carrier) of the cold. On the other hand, we can ignore the sentence, "The TV presenter caught a cold" only if we predict that the subject of the cold is the third person, who is at a different location from the poster.

Although the task setting is simple and intuitive, we identify several key challenges in this study.

1. **Novel task setting.** The task of identifying the subject of a disease/symptom is similar to predicate-argument structure (PAS) analysis for nominal predicates (Meyers et al., 2004; Sasano et al., 2004; Komachi et al., 2007; Gerber and Chai, 2010). However, these studies do not treat diseases (e.g., "influenza") and symptoms (e.g., "headache") as nominal predicates. To the best of our knowledge, this task has not been explored in natural language processing (NLP) thus far.

2. **Identifying whether the subject has a disease/symptom.** Besides the work on PAS analysis for nominal predicates, the most relevant work is PAS analysis for verb predicates. However, our task is not as simple as predicting the subject of the verb governing a disease/symptom-related noun. For example, the subject of the verb "beat" is the first person "I" in the sentence "I beat the flu," but this does not imply that the poster has the flu. At the same time, we can use a variety of expressions for indicating an infection, e.g., "I'm still sick!! This flu is just incredible...," "I can feel the flu bug in me," and "I tested positive for the flu."

3. **Omitted subjects.** We often come across tweets with omitted subjects, e.g., "Down with the flu feel" and "Thanks the flu for striking in hard this week" even in English tweets. Because the first person is omitted frequently, it is important to predict omitted subjects from the viewpoint of the application (public surveillance).

In this paper, we present an approach for identifying the subjects of various types of diseases and symptoms. The contributions of this paper are three-fold.

1. In order to explore a novel and general task setting, we design an annotation guideline for labeling a subject of a disease/symptom in a tweet, and we deliver annotations in an existing corpus for public surveillance. Further, we propose a method for predicting the subject of a disease/symptom by using the annotated corpus.

2. The experimental results show that the task of identifying subjects is independent of the type of diseases/symptom. We verify the possibility of transferring supervision data to different targets of diseases and symptoms. In other words, we verify that it is possible to utilize the supervision data for a particular disease/symptom to improve the accuracy of predicting subjects of another disease/symptom.

3. In addition, the experimental results demonstrate the impact of identifying subjects on improving the accuracy of the downstream application (identification of an episode of a disease/symptom).

The remainder of this paper is organized as follows. Section 2 describes the corpus used in this study as well as our annotation work for identifying subjects of diseases and symptoms. Section 3.1 presents our method for predicting subjects on the basis of the annotated corpus. Sections 3.2 and 3.3 report the performance of the proposed method. Section 3.4 describes the contributions of this study toward identifying episodes of diseases and symptoms. Section 4 reviews some related studies. Finally, Section 5 summarizes our findings and concludes the paper with a brief discussion on the scope for future work.

2 Corpus

2.1 Target corpus

We used a Japanese corpus for public surveillance of diseases and symptoms (Aramaki et al., 2011). The corpus targets seven types of diseases and symptoms: *cold*, *cough*, *headache*, *chill*, *runny nose*, *fever*, and *sore throat*. Tweets containing keywords for each disease/symptom were collected using the Twitter Search API: for example, tweets about *sore throat* were collected using the query "(sore OR pain) AND throat". Further,

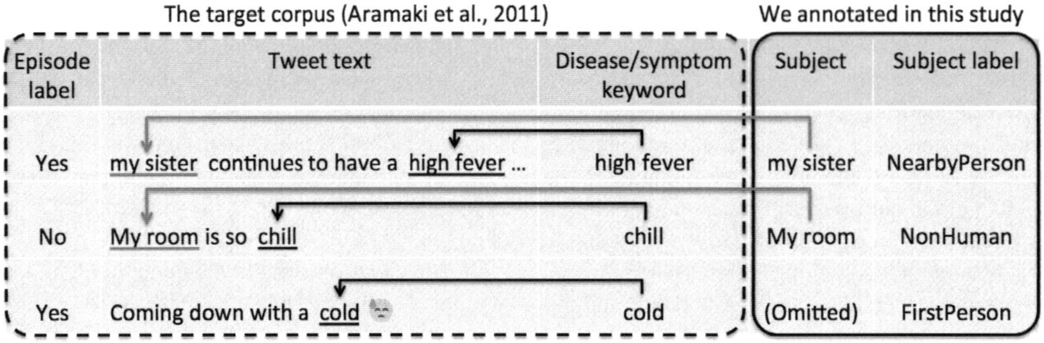

Figure 1: Examples of annotations of subject labels.

Subject label	Definition	Example
FIRSTPERSON	The subject of the disease/symptom is the poster of the tweet.	I wish I have fever or something so that I don't have to go to school.
NEARBYPERSON	The subject of the disease/symptom is a person whom the poster can directly see or hear.	my sister continues to have a high fever...
FARAWAYPERSON	The subject of the disease/symptom is a person who is at a different location from the poster.	@***** does sour stuff give you a headache?
NONHUMAN	The subject of the disease/symptom is not a person. Alternatively, the sentence does not describe a disease/symptom but a phenomenon or event related to the disease/symptom.	My room is so chill. But I like it.
NONE	The subject of the disease/symptom does not exist. Alternatively, the sentence does not mention an occurrence of a disease/symptom.	I hate buyin cold medicine cuz I never know which one to buy

Table 1: Definitions of subject labels and example tweets.

the corpus consists of 1,000 tweets for each disease/symptom besides *cold*, and 5,000 tweets for *cold*. The corpus was collected through whole years 2007-2008. This period was not in the A/H1N1 flu pandemic season.

An instance in this corpus consists of a tweet text (in Japanese) and a binary label (*episode label*, hereafter) indicating whether someone near the poster has the target disease/symptom[1]. A positive episode indicates an occurrence of the disease/symptom. In this study, we disregarded instances of *sore throat* in the experiments because most such instances were positive episodes[2].

[1]This label is positive if someone mentioned in the tweet is in the same prefecture as the poster. This is because the corpus was designed to survey the spread of a disease/symptom in every prefecture.

[2]In Japanese tweets, *sore throat* or *throat pain* mostly describes the health condition of the poster.

2.2 Annotating subjects

In this study, we annotated the subjects of diseases and symptoms in the corpus described in Section 2.1. Specifically, we annotated the subjects in 500 tweets for each disease/symptom (except for *sore throat*). Thus, our corpus includes a total of 3,000 tweets in which the subjects of diseases and symptoms are annotated.

Figure 1 shows examples of annotations in this study. Episode labels, tweet texts, and disease/symptom keywords were annotated by Aramaki et al. (2011) in the corpus.

We annotated the subject labels of the diseases/symptoms in each tweet and identified those who had the target disease/symptom. The subject labels indicate those who have the corresponding disease/symptom; they are described in detail

Label	FIRSTPERSON	NEARBYPERSON	FARAWAYPERSON	NONHUMAN	NONE	Total
# tweets	2,153	129	201	40	401	2,924
# explicit subjects	70 (3.3%)	112 (86.8%)	175 (87.1%)	38 (95.0%)	0 (0.0%)	395
# positive episodes	1,833	99	2	0	16	1,950
# negative episodes	320	30	199	40	385	974
Positive ratio	85.1%	76.7%	1.0%	0.0%	4.0%	66.7%

Table 2: Associations between subject labels and positive/negative episodes of diseases and symptoms.

herein.

In addition to the subject labels, we annotated the text span that indicates a subject. However, the subjects of diseases/symptoms are often omitted in tweet texts. Example 3 in Figure 1 shows a case in which the subject is omitted. The information as to whether the subject is omitted is useful for analyzing the difficulty in predicting the subject of a disease/symptom.

Table 1 lists the definitions of the subject labels with tweeted examples. Because it is important to distinguish the primary information (information that is observed and experienced by the poster) from the secondary information (information that is broadcasted by the media) for the application of public surveillance, we introduced five labels: FIRSTPERSON, NEARBYPERSON, FARAWAYPERSON, NONHUMAN, and NONE.

FIRSTPERSON is assigned when the subject of the disease/symptom is the poster of the tweet. When annotating this label, we ignore the modality or factuality of the event of acquiring the disease/symptom. For example, the example tweet corresponding to FIRSTPERSON in Table 1 does not state that the poster has a fever but only that the poster has a desire to have a fever. Although such tweets may be inappropriate for identifying a disease/symptom, this study focuses on identifying the possessive relation between a subject and a disease/symptom. The concept underlying this decision is to divide the task of public surveillance into several sub-tasks that are sufficiently generalized for use in other NLP applications. Therefore, the task of analyzing the modality lies beyond of scope of this study (Kitagawa et al.,). We apply the same criterion to the labels NEARBYPERSON, FARAWAYPERSON, and NONHUMAN.

NEARBYPERSON is assigned when the subject of the disease/symptom is a person whom the poster can directly see or hear. In the original corpus (Aramaki et al., 2011), a tweet is labeled as positive if the person having a disease/symptom is in the same prefecture as the poster. However, it is extremely difficult for annotators to judge from a tweet whether the person mentioned in the tweet is in the same prefecture as the poster. Nevertheless, we would like to determine from a tweet whether the poster can directly see or hear a patient. For these reasons, we introduced the label NEARBYPERSON in this study.

FARAWAYPERSON applies to all cases in which the subject is a human, but not classified as FIRSTPERSON or NEARBYPERSON. This category frequently includes tweeted replies, as in the case of the example corresponding to FARAWAYPERSON in Table 1. We assign FARAWAYPERSON to such sentences because we are unsure whether the subject of the symptom is a person whom the poster can physically see or hear.

NONHUMAN applies to cases in which the subject is not a human but an object or a concept. For example, a sentence with the phrase "My room is so chill" is annotated with this label.

NONE indicates that the sentence does not mention a target disease or symptom even though it includes a keyword for the disease/symptom.

In order to investigate the inter-annotator agreement, we sampled 100 tweets of *cold* at random, and examined the Cohen's κ statistic by two annotators. The κ statistic is 0.83, indicating a high level agreement (Carletta, 1996).

Table 2 reports the distribution of subject labels in the corpus annotated in this study. When the subject of a disease/symptom is FIRSTPERSON, only 3.3% of the tweets have explicit textual clues for the first person[3]. In other words, when the subject of a disease/symptom is FIRSTPERSON, we rarely find textual clues in tweets. In contrast, there is a greater likelihood of finding explicit clues for NEARBYPERSON, FARAWAYPERSON, and NONHUMAN subjects.

Table 2 also lists the probability of positive episodes given a subject label, i.e., the positive ratio. The likelihood of a positive episode

[3]This ratio may appear to be extremely low, but it is very common to omit first person pronouns in Japanese sentences.

is extremely high when the subject label of a disease/symptom is FIRSTPERSON (85.1%) or NEARBYPERSON (76.7%). In contrast, FARAWAYPERSON, NONHUMAN, and NONE subjects represent negative episodes (less than 5.0%). These facts suggest that identifying subject labels can improve the accuracy of predicting patient labels for diseases and symptoms.

3 Experiment

3.1 Subject classifier

We built a classifier to predict a subject label for a disease/symptom mentioned in a sentence by using the corpus described in the previous section. In our experiment, we merged training instances having the label NONHUMAN with those having the label NONE because the number of NONHUMAN instances was small and we did not need to distinguish the label NONHUMAN from the label NONE in the final episode detection task. Thus, the classifier was trained to choose a subject label from among FIRSTPERSON, NEARBYPERSON, FARAWAYPERSON, and NONE. We discarded instances in which multiple diseases or symptoms are mentioned in a tweet as well as those in which multiple subjects are associated with a disease/symptom in a tweet. In addition, we removed text spans corresponding to retweets, replies, and URLs; the existence of these spans was retained for firing features. We trained an L2-regularized logistic regression model using Classias 1.1[4]. The following features were used.

Bag-of-Words (BoW). Nine words included before and after a disease/symptom keyword. We split a Japanese sentence into a sequence of words using a Japanese morphological analyzer, MeCab (ver.0.98) with IPADic (ver.2.7.0)[5].

Disease/symptom word (Keyword). The surface form of the disease/symptom keyword (e.g. "cold" and "headache").

2,3-gram. Character-based bigrams and trigrams before and after the disease/symptom keyword within a window of six letters.

URL. A boolean feature indicating whether the tweet includes a URL.

[4] http://www.chokkan.org/software/classias/

[5] http://taku910.github.io/mecab/

Feature	Micro F1	Macro F1
BoW (baseline)	77.2	42.2
BoW + Keyword	81.9	53.6
BoW + 2,3-gram	79.1	46.1
BoW + URL	77.3	42.7
BoW + RT & reply	80.0	47.1
BoW + NearWord	77.6	46.8
BoW + FarWord	77.3	42.7
BoW + Title word	77.1	42.7
BoW + Tweet length	77.4	43.3
BoW + Is-head	77.6	43.5
All features	**84.0**	**61.8**

Table 3: Performance of the subject classifier.

RT & reply. Boolean features indicating whether the tweet is a reply or a retweet.

Word list for NEARBYPERSON (NearWord). A boolean feature indicating whether the tweet contains a word that is included in the lexicon for NEARBYPERSON. We manually collected words that may refer to a person who is near the poster, e.g., "girlfriend," "sister," and "staff." The NearWord list includes 97 words.

Word list for FARAWAYPERSON (FarWord). A boolean feature indicating whether the tweet contains a word that is included in the lexicon for FARAWAYPERSON. Similarly to the NearWord list, we manually collected 50 words (e.g., "infant") for compiling this list.

Title word. A boolean feature indicating whether the tweet contains a title word accompanied by a proper noun. The list of title words includes expressions such as "さん" and "くん" (roughly corresponding to "Ms" and "Mr") that describe the title of a person.

Tweet length. Three types of boolean features that fire when the tweet has less than 11 words, 11 to 30 words, and more than 30 words, respectively.

Is-head. A boolean feature indicating whether the word following a disease/symptom keyword is a noun. In Japanese, when the word following a disease/symptom keyword is a noun, the disease/symptom keyword is unlikely to be the head of the noun phrase.

Correct/predicted label	FIRSTPERSON		NEARBY.		FARAWAY.		NONE		Total
FIRSTPERSON	**2,084**	(−15)	6	(+1)	25	(+21)	38	(−7)	2,153
NEARBYPERSON	80	(−20)	**41**	(+29)	4	(−5)	4	(−4)	129
FARAWAYPERSON	88	(−49)	8	(+2)	**89**	(+46)	16	(+1)	201
NONE	174	(−158)	2	(+1)	10	(+4)	**255**	(+153)	441
Total predictions	2,426	(−237)	57	(+33)	128	(+66)	313	(+137)	2,924

Table 4: Confusion matrix between predicted and correct subject labels.

3.2 Evaluation of the subject classifier

Table 3 reports the performance of the subject classifier measured via five-fold cross validation. We used 3,000 tweets corresponding to six types of diseases and symptoms for this experiment. The Bag-of-Words (BoW) feature achieved micro and macro F1 scores of 77.2 and 42.2, respectively. When all the features were used, the performance was boosted, i.e., micro and macro F1 scores of 84.0 and 61.8 were achieved. Features such as disease/symptom keywords, retweet & reply, and the lexicon for NEARBYPERSON were particularly effective in improving the performance.

The surface form of the disease/symptom keyword was found to be the most effective feature in this task, the reasons for which are discussed in Section 3.3.

A retweet or reply tweet provides evidence that the poster has interacted with another person. Such meta-linguistic features may facilitate semantic and discourse analysis in web texts. However, this feature is mainly limited to tweets.

The lexicon for NEARBYPERSON provided an improvement of 4.6 points in terms of the macro F1 score. This is because (i) around 90% of the subjects for NEARBYPERSON were explicitly stated in the tweets and (ii) the vocabulary of people near the poster was limited.

Table 4 shows the confusion matrix between the correct labels and the predicted labels. The diagonal elements (in bold face) represent the number of correct predictions. The figures in parentheses denote the number of instances for which the baseline feature set made incorrect predictions, but the full feature set made correct predictions. For example, the classifier predicted NEARBYPERSON subjects 48 times; 34 out of 48 predictions were correct. The full feature set increased the number of correct predictions by 22.

From the diagonal elements (in bold face), we can confirm that the number of correct predictions increased significantly from the baseline case, except for FIRSTPERSON. One of the reasons for the improved accuracy of NONE prediction is the imbalanced label ratio of each disease/symptom. NONE accounts for 14% of the entire corpus, but only 5% of the *runny nose* corpus. On the other hand, NONE accounts for more than 30% of the *chill* corpus. The disease/symptom keyword feature adjusts the ratio of the subject labels for each disease/symptom, and the accuracy of subject identification is improved.

As compared to the baseline case, the number of FIRSTPERSON cases that were predicted as FARAWAYPERSON increased. Such errors may be attributed to the reply feature. According to our annotation scheme, FARAWAYPERSON contains many reply tweets. Because the reply & retweet features make the second-largest contribution in our experiment, the subject classifier tends to output FARAWAYPERSON if the tweet is a reply.

Table 5 summarizes the subject classification results comparing the case in which the subject of a disease/symptom exists in the tweet with that in which the subject does not exist. The prediction of FIRSTPERSON is not affected by the presence of the subject because FIRSTPERSON subjects are often omitted (especially in Japanese tweets). The prediction of NEARBYPERSON and FARAWAYPERSON is difficult if the subject is not stated explicitly. In contrast, it is easy to correctly predict NONE even though the subject is not expressed explicitly. This is because it is not easy to capture a variety of human-related subjects using Bag-of-Words, N-gram, or other simple features used in this experiment.

3.3 Dependency on diseases/symptoms

The experiments described in Section 3.2 use training instances for all types of diseases and symptoms. However, each disease/symptom may have a set of special expressions for describing the state of an episode. For example, even though "catch a cold" is a common expression, we cannot

Subject	FIRSTPERSON	NEARBYPERSON	FARAWAYPERSON	NONE
# Explicit	66/69 (95.7%)	40/112 (35.7%)	79/174 (45.4%)	1/26 (3.8%)
# Omitted	2,018/2,084 (96.8%)	1/17 (5.9%)	10/27 (37.0%)	254/415 (61.2%)
# Total	2,084/2,153 (96.8%)	41/129 (31.8%)	89/201 (44.3%)	255/441 (57.8%)

Table 5: Subject classification results comparing explicit subjects with omitted subjects.

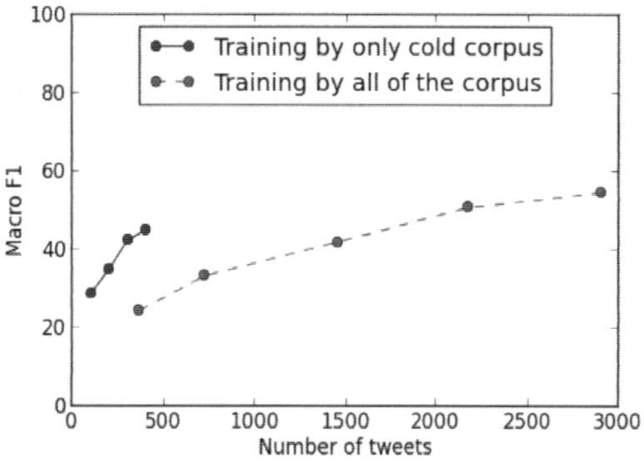

Figure 2: F1 scores for predicting subjects of *cold* with different types and sizes of training data.

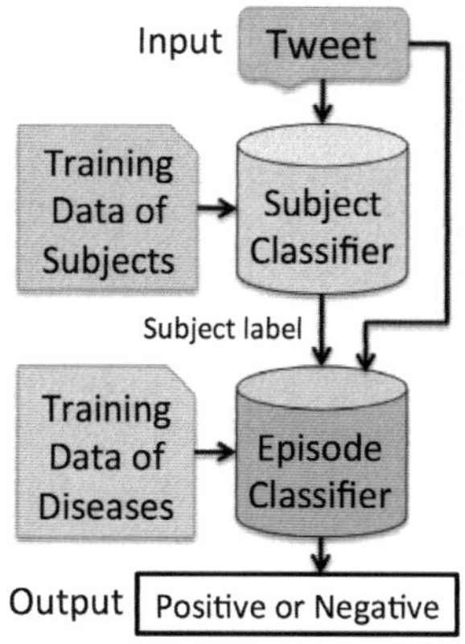

Figure 3: Overall structure of the system.

say "catch a fever" by combining the verb "catch" and the disease "fever." The corpus developed in Section 2.2 can be considered as the supervision data for weighting linguistic patterns that connect diseases/symptoms with their subjects. This viewpoint raises another question: how strongly does the subject classifier depend on specific diseases and symptoms?

In order to answer this question, we compare the performance of recognizing subjects of *cold* when using the training instances for all types of diseases and symptoms with that when using only the training instances for the target disease/symptom. Figure 2 shows the macro F1 scores with all training instances (dotted line) and with only *cold* training instances (solid line)[6].

In this case, training with *cold* instances is naturally more efficient than training with other types of diseases/symptoms. When trained with 400 instances only for *cold*, the classifier achieved an F1 score of 45.2. Moreover, we confirmed that adding training instances for other types of diseases/symptoms improved the F1 score: the maximum F1 score was 54.6 with 2,900 instances. These results indicate the possibility of building a subject classifier that is independent of specific diseases/symptoms but applicable to a variety of diseases/symptoms. We observed a similar tendency for other types of diseases/symptoms.

[6]For the solid line, we used 500 instances of "cold" as a test set, and we plotted the learning curve by increasing the number of training instances for other diseases/symptoms. For the dotted line, we fixed 100 instances for a test set, and we plotted the learning curve by increasing the number of training instances (100, 200, 300, and 400).

3.4 Contributions to the episode classifier

The ultimate objective of this study is to detect outbreaks of epidemics by recognizing diseases and symptoms. In order to demonstrate the contributions of this study, we built an *episode classifier* that judges whether the poster or a person close to the poster suffers from a target disease/symptom. Figure 3 shows the overall structure of the system. Given a tweet, the system predicts the subject label for a disease/symptom, and integrates the predicted subject label as a feature for the episode classifier. In addition to the features used in Aramaki et al. (2011), we included binary features, each of which corresponds to a subject label predicted by the proposed method. We trained an L2-regularized logistic regression model using Classias 1.1.

Table 6 summarizes the performance of the episode classifier with different settings: without subject labels (baseline), with predicted subject la-

Setting	Cold	Cough	Headache	Chill	Runny nose	Fever	Macro F1
Baseline (BL)	84.4	88.5	90.8	75.9	89.2	78.1	84.5
BL + predicted subjects	85.0	88.3	90.7	81.4	89.4	80.2	85.8
BL + gold-standard subjects	87.7	92.6	93.5	88.5	91.4	88.6	90.4

Table 6: Performance of the episode classifier.

bels , and with gold-standard subject labels. We measured the F1 scores via five-fold cross validation[7]. Further, we confirmed the contribution of subject label prediction, which achieved an improvement of 1.3 points over the baseline method (85.8 vs. 84.5). When using the gold-standard subject labels, the episode classifier achieved an improvement of 5.9 points. These results highlight the importance of recognizing a subject who has a disease/symptom using the episode classifier.

Considering the F1 score for each disease/symptom, we observed the largest improvement for *chill*. This is because the Japanese word for "chill" has another meaning *a cold air mass*. When the word "chill" stands for *a cold air mass* in a tweet, the subject for "chill" is NONE. Therefore, the episode classifier can disambiguate the meaning of "chill' on the basis of the subject labels. Similarly, the subject labels improved the performance for "fever".

In contrast, the subject labels did not improve the performance for *headache* and *runny nose* considerably. This is because the subjects for these symptoms are mostly FIRSTPERSON, as we seldom mention the symptoms of another person in such cases. In other words, the episode classifier can predict a positive label for these symptoms without knowing the subjects of these symptoms.

4 Related Work

4.1 Twitter and NLP

NLP researchers have addressed two major directions for Twitter: adapting existing NLP technologies to noisy texts and extracting useful knowledge from Twitter. The former includes improving the accuracy of part-of-speech tagging (Gimpel et al., 2011) and named entity recognition (Plank et al., 2014), as well as normalizing ill-formed words into canonical forms (Han and Baldwin, 2011; Chrupała, 2014). Even though we did not incorporate the findings of these studies, they could be beneficial to our work in the future.

[7] For the "predicted" setting, first, we predicted the subject labels in a similar manner to five-fold cross validation, and we used the predicted labels as features for the episode classifier.

The latter has led to the development of several interesting applications besides health surveillance. These include prediction of future revenue (Asur and Huberman, 2010) and stock market trends (Si et al., 2013), mining of public opinion (O'Connor et al., 2010), event extraction and summarization (Sakaki et al., 2010; Thelwall et al., 2011; Marchetti-Bowick and Chambers, 2012; Shen et al., 2013; Li et al., 2014a), user profiling (Bergsma et al., 2013; Han et al., 2013; Li et al., 2014b; Zhou et al., 2014), disaster management (Varga et al., 2013), and extraction of common-sense knowledge (Williams and Katz, 2012). Our work can directly contribute to these applications, e.g., sentiment analysis, user profiling, event extraction, and disaster management.

4.2 Semantic analysis for nouns

Our work can be considered as a semantic analysis that identifies an argument (subject) for a disease/symptom-related noun. NomBank (Meyers et al., 2004) provides annotations of noun arguments in a similar manner to PropBank (Palmer et al., 2005), which provides annotations of verbs. In NomBank, nominal predicates and their arguments are identified: for example, ARG0 (typically, subject or agent) is "customer" and ARG1 (typically, objects, patients, themes) is "issue" for the nominal predicate "complaints" in the sentence "There have been no customer complaints about that issue." Gerber and Chai (2010) improved the coverage of NomBank by handling implicit arguments. Some studies have addressed the task of identifying implicit and omitted arguments for nominal predicates in Japanese (Komachi et al., 2007; Sasano et al., 2008).

Our work shares a similar goal with the above-mentioned studies, i.e., identifying an implicit ARG0 for a disease and symptom. However, these studies do not regard a disease/symptom as a nominal predicate because they consider verb nominalizations as nominal predicates. In addition, they use a corpus that consists of newswire text, the writing style and word usage of which differ considerably from those of tweets. For these reasons, we proposed a novel task setting for identifying subjects of diseases and symptoms, and we built an annotated corpus for developing the subject classifier and analyzing the challenges of this task.

5 Conclusion

In this paper, we presented a novel approach to the identification of subjects of various types of diseases and symptoms. First, we constructed an annotated corpus based on an existing corpus for public surveillance. Then, we trained a classifier for predicting the subject of a disease/symptom. The results of our experiments showed that the task of identifying the subjects is independent of the type of disease/symptom. In addition, the results demonstrated the contributions of our work toward identifying an episode of a disease/symptom from a tweet.

In the future, we plan to consider a greater variety of diseases and symptoms in order to develop applications for public health, e.g., monitoring the mental condition of individuals. Thus, we can not only improve the accuracy of subject identification but also enhance the generality of this task.

Acknowledgments

This study was partly supported by Japan Science and Technology Agency (JST). We are grateful to the anonymous referees for their constructive reviews. We are also grateful to Takayuki Sato and Yasunobu Asakura for their annotation efforts. This study was inspired by Project Next NLP[8], a workshop for error analysis on various NLP tasks. We appreciate Takenobu Tokunaga, Satoshi Sekine, and Kentaro Inui for their helpful comments.

References

Eiji Aramaki, Sachiko Maskawa, and Mizuki Morita. 2011. Twitter catches the flu: Detecting influenza epidemics using twitter. In *Proceedings of the 2011 Conference on Empirical Methods in Natural Language Processing*, pages 1568–1576.

Sitaram Asur and Bernardo A. Huberman. 2010. Predicting the future with social media. In *Proceedings of the 2010 IEEE/WIC/ACM International Conference on Web Intelligence and Intelligent Agent Technology - Volume 01*, WI-IAT '10, pages 492–499, Washington, DC, USA. IEEE Computer Society.

Shane Bergsma, Mark Dredze, Benjamin Van Durme, Theresa Wilson, and David Yarowsky. 2013. Broadly improving user classification via communication-based name and location clustering on Twitter. In *Proceedings of the 2013 Conference of the North American Chapter of the Association for Computational Linguistics: Human Language Technologies*, pages 1010–1019.

David Broniatowski, Michael J. Paul, and Mark Dredze. 2013. National and local influenza surveillance through Twitter: An analysis of the 2012-2013 influenza epidemic. *PLoS ONE*, 8(12):e83672.

Jean Carletta. 1996. Assessing agreement on classification tasks: the kappa statistic. *Computational linguistics*, 22(2):249–254.

Herman Anthony Carneiro and Eleftherios Mylonakis. 2009. Google trends: a web-based tool for real-time surveillance of disease outbreaks. *Clinical Infectious Diseases*, 49(10):1557–1564.

Grzegorz Chrupała. 2014. Normalizing tweets with edit scripts and recurrent neural embeddings. In *Proceedings of the 52nd Annual Meeting of the Association for Computational Linguistics (Volume 2: Short Papers)*, pages 680–686.

Nigel Collier. 2012. Uncovering text mining: a survey of current work on web-based epidemic intelligence. *Global Public Health: An International Journal for Research, Policy and Practice*, 7(7):731–749.

Aron Culotta. 2010. Towards detecting influenza epidemics by analyzing Twitter messages. In *Proceedings of the Workshop on Social Media Analytics (SOMA)*, pages 115–122.

Mark Dredze, Michael J. Paul, Shane Bergsma, and Hieu Tran. 2013. Carmen: A Twitter geolocation system with applications to public health. In *Proceedings of the AAAI Workshop on Expanding the Boundaries of Health Informatics Using AI (HIAI)*, pages 20–24.

Matthew Gerber and Joyce Y. Chai. 2010. Beyond NomBank: A study of implicit arguments for nominal predicates. In *Proceedings of the 48th Annual Meeting of the Association for Computational Linguistics*, pages 1583–1592.

Francesco Gesualdo, Giovanni Stilo, Eleonora Agricola, Michaela V. Gonfiantini, Elisabetta Pandolfi, Paola Velardi, and Alberto E. Tozzi. 2013. Influenza-like illness surveillance on Twitter through automated learning of naïve language. *PLoS One*, 8(12):e82489.

[8] `https://sites.google.com/site/projectnextnlp/english-page`

Kevin Gimpel, Nathan Schneider, Brendan O'Connor, Dipanjan Das, Daniel Mills, Jacob Eisenstein, Michael Heilman, Dani Yogatama, Jeffrey Flanigan, and Noah A. Smith. 2011. Part-of-speech tagging for Twitter: Annotation, features, and experiments. In *Proceedings of the 49th Annual Meeting of the Association for Computational Linguistics: Human Language Technologies*, pages 42–47.

Bo Han and Timothy Baldwin. 2011. Lexical normalisation of short text messages: Makn sens a #twitter. In *Proceedings of the 49th Annual Meeting of the Association for Computational Linguistics: Human Language Technologies*, pages 368–378.

Bo Han, Paul Cook, and Timothy Baldwin. 2013. A stacking-based approach to Twitter user geolocation prediction. In *Proceedings of the 51st Annual Meeting of the Association for Computational Linguistics: System Demonstrations*, pages 7–12.

Yoshiaki Kitagawa, Mamoru Komachi, Eiji Aramaki, Naoaki Okazaki, and Hiroshi Ishikawa. Disease event detection based on deep modality analysis. In *Proceedings of the 53rd Annual Meeting of the Association for Computational Linguistics and the 7th International Joint Conference on Natural Language Processing of the Asian Federation of Natural Language Processing (ACL-IJCNLP) 2015 Student Research Workshop*.

Mamoru Komachi, Ryu Iida, Kentaro Inui, and Yuji Matsumoto. 2007. Learning based argument structure analysis of event-nouns in Japanese. In *Proceedings of the Conference of the Pacific Association for Computational Linguistics (PACLING)*, pages 120–128.

Alex Lamb, Michael J. Paul, and Mark Dredze. 2013. Separating fact from fear: Tracking flu infections on Twitter. In *Proceedings of the 2013 Conference of the North American Chapter of the Association for Computational Linguistics: Human Language Technologies*, pages 789–795.

Vasileios Lampos and Nello Cristianini. 2010. Tracking the flu pandemic by monitoring the social web. In *2nd IAPR Workshop on Cognitive Information Processing (CIP 2010)*, pages 411–416.

David Lazer, Ryan Kennedy, Gary King, and Alessandro Vespignani. 2014. The parable of Google flu: Traps in big data analysis. *Science*, 343(6176):1203–1205.

Jiwei Li, Alan Ritter, Claire Cardie, and Eduard Hovy. 2014a. Major life event extraction from Twitter based on congratulations/condolences speech acts. In *Proceedings of the 2014 Conference on Empirical Methods in Natural Language Processing (EMNLP)*, pages 1997–2007.

Jiwei Li, Alan Ritter, and Eduard Hovy. 2014b. Weakly supervised user profile extraction from Twitter. In *Proceedings of the 52nd Annual Meeting of the Association for Computational Linguistics (Volume 1: Long Papers)*, pages 165–174.

Micol Marchetti-Bowick and Nathanael Chambers. 2012. Learning for microblogs with distant supervision: Political forecasting with Twitter. In *Proceedings of the 13th Conference of the European Chapter of the Association for Computational Linguistics*, pages 603–612.

Adam Meyers, Ruth Reeves, Catherine Macleod, Rachel Szekely, Veronika Zielinska, Brian Young, and Ralph Grishman. 2004. The NomBank Project: An interim report. In *Proceedings of the NAACL/HLT Workshop on Frontiers in Corpus Annotation*, pages 24–31.

Brendan O'Connor, Ramnath Balasubramanyan, Bryan R. Routledge, , and Noah A. Smith. 2010. From tweets to polls: Linking text sentiment to public opinion time series. In *Proceedings of the Fourth International AAAI Conference on Weblogs and Social Media (ICWSM)*, pages 122–129.

Martha Palmer, Daniel Gildea, and Paul Kingsbury. 2005. The Proposition Bank: An annotated corpus of semantic roles. *Computational Linguistics*, 31(1):71–106.

Michael J. Paul and Mark Dredze. 2011. You are what you tweet: Analyzing Twitter for public health. In *Proceedings of the Fifth International AAAI Conference on Weblogs and Social Media (ICWSM)*, pages 265–272.

Barbara Plank, Dirk Hovy, Ryan McDonald, and Anders Søgaard. 2014. Adapting taggers to Twitter with not-so-distant supervision. In *Proceedings of COLING 2014, the 25th International Conference on Computational Linguistics: Technical Papers*, pages 1783–1792.

Takeshi Sakaki, Makoto Okazaki, and Yutaka Matsuo. 2010. Earthquake shakes Twitter users: real-time event detection by social sensors. In *Proceedings of the 19th international conference on World Wide Web (WWW)*, pages 851–860.

Ryohei Sasano, Daisuke Kawahara, and Sadao Kurohashi. 2004. Automatic construction of nominal case frames and its application to indirect anaphora resolution. In *Proceedings of the 20th international conference on Computational Linguistics*, pages 1201–1207.

Ryohei Sasano, Daisuke Kawahara, and Sadao Kurohashi. 2008. A fully-lexicalized probabilistic model for Japanese zero anaphora resolution. In *Proceedings of the 22nd International Conference on Computational Linguistics-Volume 1*, pages 769–776.

Chao Shen, Fei Liu, Fuliang Weng, and Tao Li. 2013. A participant-based approach for event summarization using Twitter streams. In *Proceedings of the 2013 Conference of the North American Chapter of the Association for Computational Linguistics: Human Language Technologies*, pages 1152–1162.

Jianfeng Si, Arjun Mukherjee, Bing Liu, Qing Li, Huayi Li, and Xiaotie Deng. 2013. Exploiting topic based Twitter sentiment for stock prediction. In *Proceedings of the 51st Annual Meeting of the Association for Computational Linguistics (Volume 2: Short Papers)*, pages 24–29.

Alessio Signorini, Alberto Maria Segre, and Philip M. Polgreen. 2011. The use of Twitter to track levels of disease activity and public concern in the U.S. during the influenza A H1N1 pandemic. *PLoS ONE*, 6(5):e19467.

Mark A. Stoové and Alisa E. Pedrana. 2014. Making the most of a brave new world: Opportunities and considerations for using Twitter as a public health monitoring tool. *Preventive Medicine*, 63:109–111.

Mike Thelwall, Kevan Buckley, and Georgios Paltoglou. 2011. Sentiment in Twitter events. *Journal of the American Society for Information Science and Technology*, 62(2):406–418.

István Varga, Motoki Sano, Kentaro Torisawa, Chikara Hashimoto, Kiyonori Ohtake, Takao Kawai, Jong-Hoon Oh, and Stijn De Saeger. 2013. Aid is out there: Looking for help from tweets during a large scale disaster. In *Proceedings of the 51st Annual Meeting of the Association for Computational Linguistics (Volume 1: Long Papers)*, pages 1619–1629.

Paola Velardi, Giovanni Stilo, Alberto E. Tozzi, and Francesco Gesualdo. 2014. Twitter mining for fine-grained syndromic surveillance. *Artificial Intelligence in Medicine*, 61(3):153–163.

Jennifer Williams and Graham Katz. 2012. Extracting and modeling durations for habits and events from Twitter. In *Proceedings of the 50th Annual Meeting of the Association for Computational Linguistics (Volume 2: Short Papers)*, pages 223–227.

Deyu Zhou, Liangyu Chen, and Yulan He. 2014. A simple bayesian modelling approach to event extraction from Twitter. In *Proceedings of the 52nd Annual Meeting of the Association for Computational Linguistics (Volume 2: Short Papers)*, pages 700–705.

Weakly Supervised Role Identification in Teamwork Interactions

Diyi Yang
School of Computer Science
Carnegie Mellon University
Pittsburgh, PA, 15213, USA
diyiy@cs.cmu.edu

Miaomiao Wen
School of Computer Science
Carnegie Mellon University
Pittsburgh, PA, 15213, USA
mwen@cs.cmu.edu

Carolyn Penstein Rosé
School of Computer Science
Carnegie Mellon University
Pittsburgh, PA, 15213, USA
cprose@cs.cmu.edu

Abstract

In this paper, we model conversational roles in terms of distributions of turn level behaviors, including conversation acts and stylistic markers, as they occur over the whole interaction. This work presents a lightly supervised approach to inducing role definitions over sets of contributions within an extended interaction, where the supervision comes in the form of an outcome measure from the interaction. The identified role definitions enable a mapping from behavior profiles of each participant in an interaction to limited sized feature vectors that can be used effectively to predict the teamwork outcome. An empirical evaluation applied to two Massive Open Online Course (MOOCs) datasets demonstrates that this approach yields superior performance in learning representations for predicting the teamwork outcome over several baselines.

1 Introduction

In language technologies research seeking to model conversational interactions, modeling approaches have aimed to identify conversation acts (Paul, 2012; Wallace et al., 2013; Bhatia et al., 2014) on a per turn basis, or to identify stances (Germesin and Wilson, 2009; Mukherjee et al., 2013; Piergallini et al., 2014; Hasan and Ng, 2014) that characterize the nature of a speaker's orientation within an interaction over several turns. What neither of these two perspectives quite offer is a notion of a conversational role. And yet, conversational role is a concept with great utility in current real world applications where language technologies may be applied.

Important teamwork is achieved through collaboration where discussion is an important medium for accomplishing work. For example, distributed work teams are becoming increasingly the norm in the business world where creating innovative products in the networked world is a common practice. This work requires the effective exchange of expertise and ideas. Open source and open collaboration organizations have successfully aggregated the efforts of millions of volunteers to produce complex artifacts such as GNU/Linux and Wikipedia. Discussion towards decision making about how to address problems that arise or how to extend work benefit from effective conversational interactions. With a growing interest in social learning in large online platforms such as Massive Open Online Courses (MOOCs), students form virtual study groups and teams to complete a course project, and thus may need to coordinate and accomplish the work through discussion. In all such environments, discussions serve a useful purpose, and thus the effectiveness of the interaction can be measured in terms of the quality of the resulting product.

We present a modeling approach that leverages the concept of latent conversational roles as an intermediary between observed discussions and a measure of interaction success. While a stance identifies speakers in terms of their positioning with respect to one another, roles associate speakers with rights and responsibilities, associated with common practices exhibited by performers of that role within an interaction, towards some specific interaction outcome. That outcome may be achieved through strategies characterized in terms of conversation acts or language with particular stylistic characteristics. However, individual acts by themselves lack the power to achieve a complex outcome. We argue that roles make up for this decontextualized view of a conversational contribution by identifying distributions of conversation acts and stylistic features as behavior profiles indicative of conversational roles. These

Proceedings of the 53rd Annual Meeting of the Association for Computational Linguistics and the 7th International Joint Conference on Natural Language Processing, pages 1671–1680,
Beijing, China, July 26-31, 2015.

profiles have more explanatory power to identify strategies that lead to successful outcomes.

In the remainder of the paper we first review related work that lays the foundation for our approach. Then we describe a series of role identification models. Experimental results are analyzed quantitatively and qualitatively in Section 4, followed by conclusions and future work.

2 Related Work

The concept of *social role* has long been used in social science fields to describe the intersection of behavioral, symbolic, and structural attributes that emerge regularly in particular contexts. Theory on coordination in groups and organizations emphasizes role differentiation, division of labor and formal and informal management (Kittur and Kraut, 2010). However, identification of roles as such has not had a corresponding strong emphasis in the language technologies community, although there has been work on related notions. For example, there has been much previous work modeling disagreement and debate framed as stance classification (Thomas et al., 2006; Walker et al., 2012). Another similar line of work studies the identification of personas (Bamman et al., 2013; Bamman et al., 2014) in the context of a social network, e.g. celebrity, newbie, lurker, flamer, troll and ranter, etc, which evolve through user interaction (Forestier et al., 2012).

What is similar between stances and personas on the one hand and roles on the other is that the unit of analysis is the person. On the other hand, they are distinct in that stances (e.g., liberal) and personas (e.g., lurker) are not typically defined in terms of what they are meant to accomplish, although they may be associated with kinds of things they do. Teamwork roles are defined in terms of what the role holder is meant to accomplish.

The notion of a natural outcome associated with a role suggests a modeling approach utilizing the outcome as light supervision towards identification of the latent roles. However, representations of other notions such as stances or strategies can similarly be used to predict outcomes. Cadilhac et al. maps strategies based on verbal contributions of participants in a win-lose game into a prediction of exactly which players, if any, trade with each other (Cadilhac et al., 2013). Hu et al. (Hu et al., 2009) predict the outcome of featured article nominations based on user activeness, discussion consensus and user co-review relations. In other work, the authors of (Somasundaran and Wiebe, 2009) adopt manually annotated characters and leaders to predict which participants will achieve success in online debates. The difference is the interpretation of the latent constructs. The latent construct of a role, such as team leader, is defined in terms of a distribution of characteristics that describe how that role should ideally be carried out. However, in the case of stances, the latent constructs are learned in order to distinguish one stance from another or in order to predict who will win. This approach will not necessarily offer insight into what marks the most staunch proponents of a stance, but instead distinguish those proponents of a stance who are persuasive from those who are not.

Roles need not only be identified with the substance of the text uttered by role holders. Previous work discovers roles in social networks based on the network structure (Hu and Liu, 2012; Zhao et al., 2013). Examples include such things as mixed membership stochastic blockmodels (MMSB) (Airoldi et al., 2008), similar unsupervised matrix factorization methods (Hu and Liu, 2012), or semi-supervised role inference models (Zhao et al., 2013). However, these approaches do not standardly utilize an outcome as supervision to guide the clustering.

Many open questions exist about what team roles and in what balance would make the ideal group composition (Neuman et al., 1999), and how those findings interact with other contextual factors (Senior, 1997; Meredith Belbin, 2011). Thus, a modeling approach that can be applied to new contexts in order to identify roles that are particularly valuable given the context would potentially have high practical value.

3 Role Identification Models

The context of this work is team based MOOCs using the NovoEd platform. In this context, we examine the interaction between team members as they work together to achieve instructional goals in their project work. Our modeling goal is to identify behavior profiles that describe the emergent roles that team members take up in order to work towards a successful group grade for their team project. Identification of effective role based behavior profiles would enable work towards supporting effective team formation in subsequent work. This approach would be similar to prior work where constraints that describe successful teams were used to group participants into teams in which each member's expertise is modeled so that an appropriate mixture of expertise can be achieved in the assignment (Anagnostopoulos et al., 2010).

In this section, we begin with an introduction of some basic notations. Then we present an iterative model, which involves two stages: teamwork quality prediction and student role matching. Furthermore, we generalize this model to a constrained version which provides more interpretable role assignments. In the end, we describe how to construct student behavior representations from their teamwork collaboration process.

3.1 Notation

Suppose we have C teams where students collaborate to finish a course project together. The number of students in the j-th team is denoted as N_j, $(1 \leq j \leq N_j)$. There are K roles across C teams that we want to identify, where $1 \leq K \leq N_j, \forall j \in [1, C]$. That is, the number of roles is smaller than or equal to the number of students in a team, which means that each role should have one student assigned to it, but not every student needs to be assigned to a role. Each role is associated with a weight vector $W_k \in \mathcal{R}^D$ to be learned, $1 \leq k \leq K$ and D is the number of dimensions. Each student i in a team j is associated with a behavior vector $B_{j,i} \in \mathcal{R}^D$. The measurement of teamwork quality is denoted as Q_j for team j, and $\hat{Q}_j$ is the predicted quality. Here, $\hat{Q}_j$ is determined by the inner product of the behavior vectors of students who are assigned to different roles and the corresponding weight vectors.

Teamwork Role Identification Our goal is to find a proper teamwork role assignment that positively contributes to the collaboration outcome as much as possible.

3.2 Role Identification

Here we describe our role identification model. Our role identification process is iterative and involves two stages. The first stage adjusts the weight vectors to predict the teamwork quality, given a fixed role assignment that assumes students are well matched to roles; the second stage iterates the possible assignments and finds a matching to maximize our objective measure. The two stages run iteratively until both role assignment and teamwork quality prediction converge.

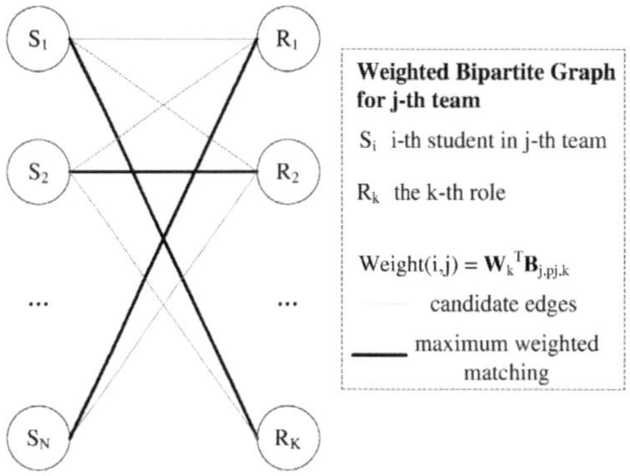

Figure 1: Weighted Bipartite Graph for a Team

Teamwork Quality Prediction: Given the identified role assignment, i.e. we know who is assigned to which roles in a team, the focus is to accurately predict the teamwork quality under this role assignment. $p_{j,k}$ refers to the student who is assigned to role k in team j. We minimize the following objective function to update the role weight vector W:

$$\min_W \frac{1}{2} \sum_{j=1}^{C} (Q_j - \sum_{k=1}^{K} {W_k}^T \cdot B_{j,p_{j,k}}) + \lambda \cdot \|W\|^2 \quad (1)$$

Here, λ is the regularization parameter; large λ leads to higher complexity penalization. To give the optimal solution to Equation 1, which is a classical ridge regression task (Hoerl and Kennard, 2000), we can easily compute the optimal solution by its closed form representation, as shown in the Algorithm 1.

Matching Members to Roles: Once the weight vector W is updated, we iterate over all the possible assignments and find the best role assignment, where the goal is to maximize the predicted teamwork quality since we want our assignment of students and roles to be associated with improvement in the quality of teamwork. The complexity of brute-force enumeration of all possible role assignments is exponential. To avoid such an expensive computational cost, we design a weighted bipartite graph and apply a maximum weighted matching algorithm (Ravindra et al., 1993) to find the best matching under the objective of maximizing $\sum_{j=1}^{C} \hat{Q}_j$. Because this objective is a summation, we can further separate it into C iso-

Algorithm 1: Role Identification

Heuristicly initialize the role assignment $p_{j,k}$
while *assignments have not converged* **do**
  // Teamwork Quality Prediction
  $X \leftarrow$ a $C \times (K \cdot D)$ matrix
  for $j = 1$ *to* C **do**
    $X_{j,*} \leftarrow (B_{j,p_{j,1}}, B_{j,p_{j,2}}, \ldots, B_{j,p_{j,K}})$
  // optimal solution to Eq. 1
  $(W_1, \ldots, W_C) \leftarrow (X^T X + \lambda I)^{-1} X^T Q$
  // Student and Role Matching
  // maximize $\sum_j \hat{Q}_j$
  for $j = 1$ *to* C **do**
    $(p_{j,*}) \leftarrow$ maximum weighted bipartite matching on Figure 1

lated components for C teams by maximizing each $\hat{Q}_j$. For each team, a weighted bipartite graph is created as specified in Figure 1. By applying the maximum weighted matching algorithm on this graph, we can obtain the best role assignment for each team.

The two stage role identification model is solved in detail in Algorithm 1.

3.3 Role Identification with Constraints

The above role identification model puts no constraints on the roles that we want to identify in teamwork. This might result in more effort to explain how different roles collaborate to produce the teamwork success. Therefore, we introduce a constrained role identification model, which is able to integrate external constraints on roles. For example, we can require our extracted role set to contain a role that makes a positive contribution to the project success and a role that contributes relatively negatively, instead of extracting several generic roles. To address such constraints, in the stage of teamwork quality prediction, we reformulate the Equation 2 as follows:

$$
\begin{aligned}
L = \frac{1}{2}\sum_{j=1}^{C}(Q_j - \sum_{k=1}^{K} W_k{}^T \cdot B_{j,p_{j,k}}) + \lambda\|W\|^2 \\
- \mu_+ \sum_{k\in S_+} \sum_{d=1}^{D} log(W_{kd}) \\
- \mu_- \sum_{k\in S_-} \sum_{d=1}^{D} log(-W_{kd})
\end{aligned} \tag{2}
$$

Algorithm 2: Identification with Constraints

Heuristicly initialize the role assignment $p_{j,k}$
while *assignments have not converged* **do**
  // Teamwork Quality Prediction
  $X \leftarrow$ a $C \times (K \cdot D)$ matrix
  for $j = 1$ *to* C **do**
    $X_j \leftarrow (B_{j,p_{j,1}}, B_{j,p_{j,2}}, \ldots, B_{j,p_{j,K}})$
  // gradient descent solution to Eq. 2
  $\mu_+, \mu_- \leftarrow$ large enough values
  while $\mu_+, \mu_- > \epsilon$ **do**
    while *not converge* **do**
      for $k = 1$ *to* K **do**
        $W_k \leftarrow W_k - \eta \cdot \frac{\partial L}{\partial W_k}$
    $\mu_+ \leftarrow \theta \cdot \mu_+$
    $\mu_- \leftarrow \theta \cdot \mu_-$
  // Students and Roles Matching
  // maximize $\sum_j \hat{Q}_j$
  for $j = 1$ *to* C **do**
    $(p_{j,*}) \leftarrow$ maximum weighted bipartite matching on Figure 1

The external constraints are handled by the log barrier terms (Ahuja et al., 1993). Here, μ_+ and μ_- are positive parameters used to penalize the violation of role constraints. S_+ is the set of roles that we want to assign students who contribute positively to the group outcome (i.e. above average level), and S_- contains the roles that we want to capture students who contribute negatively to the group outcome (i.e. below average level). The solving of Equation 2 cannot directly apply the previous ridge regression algorithm, thus we use the Interior Point Method (Potra and Wright, 2000) to solve it. The detailed procedure is illustrated in Algorithm 2, where the θ is a constant to control the shrinkage and η is the learning rate.

3.4 Behavior Construction

One essential component in our teamwork role identification models is the student behavior representation. To some extent, a proper behavior representation is essential for facilitating the interpretation of identified roles. We construct the representation of student behavior from the following feature types:

Team Member Behaviors: How a team functions can be reflected in their team communication messages. To understand how students collaborate

Type	Behavior Definition	Example Messages
Team Building	Invite or accept users to join the group	*Lauren, We would love to have you. Jill and I are both ESL specialists in Boston.*
Task Management	Initiate a task or assign subtask to a team member	*Housekeeping Task 3 is optional but below are the questions I summarize and submit for our team.*
Collaboration	Collaborate with teammates, provide help or feedback	*I figured out how to use the Google Docs. Let's use it to share our lesson plans.*

Table 1: Three Different Types of Team Member Behaviors

to contribute to teamwork success, we identified three main team member behaviors based on messages sent between team members as shown in Table 1. These annotations, which came from prior qualitative work analysing discussion contributions in the same dataset (Wen et al., 2015), are used to define component behaviors in this work. We design four variables to characterize the above collaboration behaviors:

1. *Collaboration*: the number of Collaboration messages sent by this team member.

2. *Task Management*: the number of Task Management messages sent by this team member.

3. *Team Building*: the number of Team Building messages sent by this team member.

4. *Other Strategies*: the number of messages that do not belong to the listed behavior categories.

Communication Languages: Teams that work successfully typically exchange more knowledge and establish good social relations. To capture such evidence that is indicated in the language choice and linguistic styles of each team member, we design the following features:

5. *Personal Pronouns*: the proportion of first person and second person pronouns.

6. *Negation*: counts of negation words.

7. *Question Words*: counts of question related words in the posts, e.g. why, what, question, problem, how, answer, etc.

8. *Discrepancy*: number of occurrences of words, such as should, would, could, etc as defined in LIWC (Tausczik and Pennebaker, 2010).

9. *Social Process*: number of words that denote social processes and suggest human interaction, e.g. talking, sharing, etc.

10. *Cognitive Process*: number of occurrences of words that reflect thinking and reasoning, e.g. cause, because, thus, etc.

11-14. *Polarity*: four variables that measure the portion of Positive, Negative, Neutral, Both polarity words (Wilson et al., 2005) in the posts.

15-16. *Subjectivity*: two count variables of occurrences of Strong Subjectivity words and Weak Subjectivity words.

Activities: We also introduce several variables to measure the activeness level of team members.

17-18. *Messages*: two variables that measure the total number of messages sent, and the number of tokens contained in the messages.

19-20. *Videos*: the number of videos a student has watched and total duration of watched videos.

21. *Login Times*: times that a student logins to the course.

4 Experiments

In this section, we begin with the dataset description, and then we compare our models with several competitive baselines by performing 10-fold cross validation on two MOOCs, followed by a series of quantitative and qualitative analyses.

4.1 Dataset

Our datasets come from a MOOC provider NovoEd, and consist of two MOOC courses. Both courses are teacher professional development courses about Constructive Classroom Conversations; one is in elementary education and another is about secondary education. Students in a NovoEd MOOC have to initiate or join a team in the beginning of the course. A NovoEd team homepage consists of blog posts, comments and other content shared within the group. The performance measure we use is the final team project score, which is in the range of 0 to 40. There are 57 teams (163 students) who survived until the end in the Elementary education course, and 77 teams (262 students) who survived for the Secondary course. The surviving teams are the ones in which none of the team members dropped out of the course, and who finished all the course requirements. For the purpose of varying teamwork roles K, we only keep the teams with at least 3 members. Self-identified team leader are labeled in the dataset.

4.2 Baselines

We propose several baselines to extract possible roles and predict the teamwork quality for comparison with our models. Preprocessing is identical for baselines as for our approach.

Top K Worst/Best: The worst performing student is often the bottleneck in a team, while the success of a team project largely depends on the outstanding students. Therefore, we use the top K worst/best performing students as our identified K roles. Their behavior representation are then used to predict the teamwork quality. The performing scores are only accessible after the course.

K-Means Clustering: Students who are assigned to the same roles tend to have similar activity profiles. To capture the similarities of student behavior, we adopt a clustering method to group students in a team into K clusters, and then assign students to roles based on their distances to the centroid of clusters. Prediction is then performed on the basis of those corresponding behavior vectors. Here, we use K-Means method for clustering. That is, each cluster is a latent representation of a role and each student is assigned to its closest cluster (role).

Leader: Leaders play important roles for the smooth functioning of teams, and thus might have substantial predictive power of team success. We input our role identification model with only the identified leader's behavior representation and conduct our role identification algorithm as illustrated in Algorithm 1. Each team in our courses have a predefined leader.

Average: The average representation of all team members is a good indication of team ability level and thus teamwork success. Here, we average all team members' behavior feature vectors and use that to predict the teamwork quality.

4.3 Teamwork Quality Prediction Results

The purpose of our role identification is to find a role assignment that minimizes the prediction error, thus we measure the performance of our models using RMSE (Rooted Mean Square Error). 10-fold Cross Validation is employed to test the overall performance. Table 2 and Table 3 presents the results of our proposed models and baselines on our two courses. Our role identification model shown in Algorithm 1, is denoted as **RI**. θ is set as 0.9 and we vary the role number K from 1 to 3 in order to assess the added value of each additional role over the first one.

4.3.1 Who Matters Most In a Team

If we set the number of roles K as 1, what will the role identification pick as the most important person to the teamwork outcome? From Table 2 and 3, we find that, RI performs better than Leader, and either Top K Best gives a good RMSE in one course and Top K Worst gives a good RMSE in the other course. This indicates that, the predefined leader is not always functioning well in facilitating the teamwork, thus we need a more fair mechanism to select the proper leading role. Besides, Top K worst has quite good performance on the Elementary course, which reflects that the success of a teamwork is to some extent dependent on the worst performing student in that team. The best performing student matters for the teamwork outcome on the Secondary course.

4.3.2 Multi-Role Collaboration

From Table 2 and 3, in the setting of K=3, RI achieved better results compared to Top K Best, Top K Worst and K-means methods. One explanation is that our RI model not only considers individual student's behaviors, but also takes into account the collaboration patterns through all teamwork. Besides, RI achieves better performance compared to our baselines as K becomes larger. We also noticed that Top K Best gives a quite good approximation to the teamwork quality on both courses. However, such performing scores that are used to rank students are not accessible until the course ends, and have high correlation with team score. Thus an advantage of our RI model is that it does not make use of that information. Compared with all other results, our RI has a good generalization ability, and achieves both a smallest RMSE of around 10 across both MOOCs.

4.4 Role Assignment Validation

We demonstrate the predicative power of our identified roles to team success above. In this part, we interpret the identified roles guided by different constraints in a team qualitatively, and show how different roles are distributed in a team, how each role contributes to teamwork, and how collaboration happens among the roles.

Table 2: RMSE Comparison of Different Methods on the Elementary Course

	Average	Leader	K-Means	K Worst	K Best	RI	RIC	RIC_-	RIC_+
K = 1	13.945	16.957	14.212	13.092	20.464	14.982	N/A	N/A	N/A
K = 2	N/A	N/A	13.160	13.428	15.591	11.581	N/A	N/A	N/A
K = 3	N/A	N/A	12.291	15.460	14.251	**9.517**	10.486	27.314	10.251

Table 3: RMSE Comparison of Different Methods on the Secondary Course

	Average	Leader	K-Means	K Worst	K Best	RI	RIC	RIC_-	RIC_+
K = 1	12.571	15.611	12.583	17.899	10.886	13.297	N/A	N/A	N/A
K = 2	N/A	N/A	12.288	19.268	11.245	10.435	N/A	N/A	N/A
K = 3	N/A	N/A	11.218	22.933	14.079	**10.143**	10.961	24.583	10.427

4.4.1 Constraint Exploration

By incorporating constraints into the role identification process, we expect to guide the model using human intuition such that the results will be more interpretable, although the prediction error might increase because of the limitation of the search space. We present three alternative possible constrained models here. The **RIC** model emphasizes picking one best member, one worst member and another generic member, which is achieved by putting one role to S_+ and one to S_- as defined in Equation 2. **RIC_+** aims at picking three best team members who collaborate to make the best contribution to the team success, achieved by putting three roles into S_+. Similarly, **RIC_-** rewards poorly performing students to contribute to teamwork quality, i.e. putting all roles into S_-.

Based on results shown in Table 2 and 3, we found that RIC_+ and RIC work similar as RI even though RI is slightly better. RIC_- gives quite unsatisfying performance which shows that examining the behavior of a set of poorly performing students is not very helpful in predicting teamwork success. The comparison of RIC_+ and RIC_- can be shown clearly in Figure 2, which presents the behavior representation of each role identified by RIC_+ and RIC_-. Obviously, RIC_+ produces positive roles that contribute largely to the teamwork quality across all feature dimensions; such behaviors are what we want to encourage. Those identified roles are diverse and not symmetrical because each role achieves peaks at different feature dimensions. On the contrary, roles identified by RIC_- works negatively towards teamwork quality and they have homogeneous behavior representation curves. Therefore, our constrained models can provide much interpretation, with a little loss of accuracy compared to RI.

4.4.2 Role Assignment Interpretation

Leading Role Validation: As a validation, we found that one of our identified roles has substantial overlap with team leaders. For instance, in the Elementary course, around 70% of students who are assigned to Role 0 are actual leaders for RIC and RIC_+ models. On the Secondary course, around 86% students who are in the position of Role 0 are real team leaders. When it comes to RIC_-, such ratio drops to around 2% for all roles. This validates the ability of our models in producing role definitions that make sense.

Information Diffusion: Figure 3 compares the information diffusion among different identified roles of RI, RIC, RIC_+ and RIC_-. The darker the node, the better grade it achieves. The number associated with each role indicates the average final grades (scale 0-100) of all students who are assigned to this role. The edge represents how many messages sent from one node to another. The thicker the edge, the more information it conveys. From the figure, we found that, RI performs similarly with RIC and roles in RIC_+ have much higher grades compared to RIC_-. One explanation is that RIC actually does not incorporate many constraints and is less interpretable compared to RIC_+ and RIC_-. As shown in (c), RIC_+ Role 0 contributes more information to Role 1 with an average of 5.5 messages and to Role 2 with weight 6.1. Role 1 and Role 2 also have many messages communicated with others in their team. However, less communication happens in RIC_- roles. This comparison comes much easier when it comes to each role's behaviors on different normalized feature representations as shown in Figure 2 for

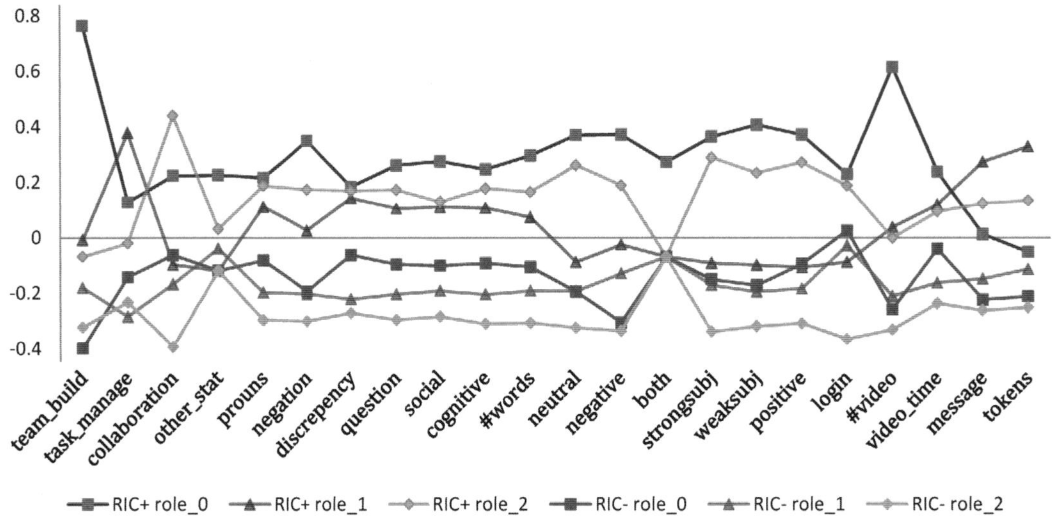

Figure 2: Beahvior Representation of Each Role on the Secondary Course

	Typical Behavior	Representative Post
RIC_+	Team Building	I *started a new doc* ... Let me *know your email* if you didn't get the invite.
	Positive	*Great* job team!! Our lesson plan is *amazing* and I learned so much ...
	Collaboration	We plan to meet on Monday to *figure out exactly how to complete* the assignment ...
	Task Management	Here's *what I propose*: *1) to save time, use ... 2) Tara, do you have plans ...* 3) *once* a lesson plan outline is up, *we can* each go in and add modifications..
RIC_-	Negative	I'm *confused.* I answered all the questions ... and I didn't see ...
	Strong Subjectivity	I *like* the recycling lesson ... *feeling* so dumb.. really *confused* by Google Docs...
	Negation	I'm *not* able to ... the pictures *don't* show up...I *don't understand* how to create a link..

Table 4: Representative Posts and Corresponding Behavior Feature Comparison on the Secondary Course

RIC_+ and RIC_- models. It can be concluded that by incorporating rewarding and penalizing constraints, our model works effectively in picking the behavior profiles we want to encourage and avoid in a teamwork.

Behavior Comparison: Table 4 presents several representative posts and their corresponding behavior features for our identified roles. Most features shown in Table 4 correspond to the peak behaviors associated with roles in Figure 2, which is consistent with our previous interpretation. For example, RIC_+ picks the well performing student who adds calmness to the teamwork as indicated by using positive words and adopting collaborative strategies. On the contrary, RIC_- reflects a less cooperative teamwork, such as strong subjectivity, negation and negativity indicated in their posts.

In summary, our role identification models provide quite interpretable identified roles as discussed above, as well as accurate prediction of teamwork quality. More interpretability can be achieved by incorporating intuitive constraints and sacrificing a bit of accuracy.

5 Conclusion

In this work, we propose a role identification model, which iteratively optimizes a team member role assignment that can predict the teamwork quality to the utmost extent. Furthermore, we extend it to a general constrained version that enables humans to incorporate external constraints to guide the identification of roles. The experimental results on two MOOCs show that both of our proposed role identification models can not only perform accurate predictions of teamwork quality, but also provide interpretable student role assignment results ranging from leading role validation to information diffusion.

Even though we have only explored up to 3 roles in this work that would enable us to use most

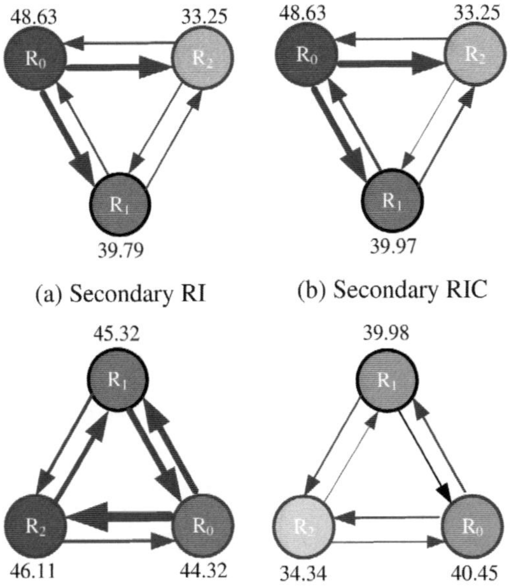

(a) Secondary RI

(b) Secondary RIC

(c) Secondary RIC_+

(d) Secondary RIC_-

Figure 3: Information Diffusion among Roles

of our data, our role identification method is capable to experiment with a larger range of values of K, such as in the context of Wikipedia (Ferschke et al., 2015). Furthermore, our model can be directly applied to other online collaboration scenarios to help identify the roles that contribute to collaboration, not limited in the context of MOOCs. In the future, we are interested in relaxing the assumptions that people can take only one role and roles are taken up by only one person and incorporating mixed membership role matching strategies into our method. Furthermore, nonlinear relationship between roles and performance as well as the dependencies between roles should be explored. Last but not least, we plan to take advantage of our identified roles to provide guidance and recommendation to those weakly performing teams for better collaboration and engagement in online teamworks.

Acknowledgement

The authors would like to thank Hanxiao Liu, Jingbo Shang, Oliver Ferschke and the anonymous reviewers for their valuable comments and suggestions. This research was funded in part by NSF grant IIS-1320064, an Army Research Lab seedling grant, and funding from Google.

References

Ravindra K. Ahuja, Thomas L. Magnanti, and James B. Orlin. 1993. *Network Flows: Theory, Algorithms, and Applications*. Prentice-Hall, Inc., Upper Saddle River, NJ, USA.

Edoardo M. Airoldi, David M. Blei, Stephen E. Fienberg, and Eric P. Xing. 2008. Mixed membership stochastic blockmodels. volume 9, pages 1981–2014. JMLR.org, June.

Aris Anagnostopoulos, Luca Becchetti, Carlos Castillo, Aristides Gionis, and Stefano Leonardi. 2010. Power in unity: Forming teams in large-scale community systems. In *Proceedings of the 19th ACM International Conference on Information and Knowledge Management*, CIKM '10, pages 599–608, New York, NY, USA. ACM.

David Bamman, Brendan O'Connor, and Noah A. Smith. 2013. Learning latent personas of film characters. In *Proceedings of the 51st Annual Meeting of the Association for Computational Linguistics (Volume 1: Long Papers)*, pages 352–361, Sofia, Bulgaria, August. Association for Computational Linguistics.

David Bamman, Ted Underwood, and Noah A Smith. 2014. A bayesian mixed effects model of literary character. In *Proceedings of the 52nd Annual Meeting of the Association for Computational Linguistics*, volume 1, pages 370–379.

Sumit Bhatia, Prakhar Biyani, and Prasenjit Mitra. 2014. Summarizing online forum discussions – can dialog acts of individual messages help? In *Proceedings of the 2014 Conference on Empirical Methods in Natural Language Processing (EMNLP)*, pages 2127–2131, Doha, Qatar, October. Association for Computational Linguistics.

Anais Cadilhac, Nicholas Asher, Farah Benamara, and Alex Lascarides. 2013. Grounding strategic conversation: Using negotiation dialogues to predict trades in a win-lose game. In *Proceedings of the 2013 Conference on Empirical Methods in Natural Language Processing*, pages 357–368, Seattle, Washington, USA, October. Association for Computational Linguistics.

Oliver Ferschke, Diyi Yang, and Carolyn Rosé. 2015. A lightly supervised approach to role identification in wikipedia talk page discussions.

Mathilde Forestier, Anna Stavrianou, Julien Velcin, and Djamel A. Zighed. 2012. Roles in social networks: Methodologies and research issues. *Web Intelli. and Agent Sys.*, 10(1):117–133, January.

Sebastian Germesin and Theresa Wilson. 2009. Agreement detection in multiparty conversation. In *Proceedings of the 2009 International Conference on Multimodal Interfaces*, ICMI-MLMI '09, pages 7–14, New York, NY, USA. ACM.

Kazi Saidul Hasan and Vincent Ng. 2014. Why are you taking this stance? identifying and classifying reasons in ideological debates. In *Proceedings of the 2014 Conference on Empirical Methods in Natural Language Processing (EMNLP)*, pages 751–762, Doha, Qatar, October. Association for Computational Linguistics.

Arthur E. Hoerl and Robert W. Kennard. 2000. Ridge regression: Biased estimation for nonorthogonal problems. *Technometrics*, 42(1):80–86, February.

Xia Hu and Huan Liu. 2012. Social status and role analysis of palin's email network. In *Proceedings of the 21st International Conference Companion on World Wide Web*, WWW '12 Companion, pages 531–532, New York, NY, USA. ACM.

Meiqun Hu, Ee-Peng Lim, and Ramayya Krishnan. 2009. Predicting outcome for collaborative featured article nomination in wikipedia. In *Third International AAAI Conference on Weblogs and Social Media*.

Aniket Kittur and Robert E. Kraut. 2010. Beyond wikipedia: Coordination and conflict in online production groups. In *Proceedings of the 2010 ACM Conference on Computer Supported Cooperative Work*, CSCW '10, pages 215–224, New York, NY, USA. ACM.

R Meredith Belbin. 2011. Management teams: Why they succeed or fail. *Human Resource Management International Digest*, 19(3).

Arjun Mukherjee, Vivek Venkataraman, Bing Liu, and Sharon Meraz. 2013. Public dialogue: Analysis of tolerance in online discussions. In *Proceedings of the 51st Annual Meeting of the Association for Computational Linguistics (Volume 1: Long Papers)*, pages 1680–1690, Sofia, Bulgaria, August. Association for Computational Linguistics.

George A Neuman, Stephen H Wagner, and Neil D Christiansen. 1999. The relationship between work-team personality composition and the job performance of teams. *Group & Organization Management*, 24(1):28–45.

Michael J. Paul. 2012. Mixed membership markov models for unsupervised conversation modeling. In *Proceedings of the 2012 Joint Conference on Empirical Methods in Natural Language Processing and Computational Natural Language Learning*, EMNLP-CoNLL 12, pages 94–104, Stroudsburg, PA, USA. Association for Computational Linguistics.

Mario Piergallini, A Seza Doğruöz, Phani Gadde, David Adamson, and Carolyn P Rosé. 2014. Modeling the use of graffiti style features to signal social relations within a multi-domain learning paradigm. *EACL 2014*, page 107.

Florian A Potra and Stephen J Wright. 2000. Interior-point methods. *Journal of Computational and Applied Mathematics*, 124(1):281–302.

K Ahuja Ravindra, Thomas L Magnanti, and James B Orlin. 1993. Network flows: theory, algorithms, and applications.

Barbara Senior. 1997. Team roles and team performance: is there reallya link? *Journal of occupational and organizational psychology*, 70(3):241–258.

Swapna Somasundaran and Janyce Wiebe. 2009. Recognizing stances in online debates. In *Proceedings of the Joint Conference of the 47th Annual Meeting of the ACL and the 4th International Joint Conference on Natural Language Processing of the AFNLP: Volume 1 - Volume 1*, ACL '09, pages 226–234, Stroudsburg, PA, USA. Association for Computational Linguistics.

Yla R Tausczik and James W Pennebaker. 2010. The psychological meaning of words: Liwc and computerized text analysis methods. *Journal of language and social psychology*, 29(1):24–54.

Matt Thomas, Bo Pang, and Lillian Lee. 2006. Get out the vote: Determining support or opposition from congressional floor-debate transcripts. In *Proceedings of the 2006 Conference on Empirical Methods in Natural Language Processing*, EMNLP '06, pages 327–335, Stroudsburg, PA, USA. Association for Computational Linguistics.

Marilyn A. Walker, Pranav Anand, Robert Abbott, and Ricky Grant. 2012. Stance classification using dialogic properties of persuasion. In *Proceedings of the 2012 Conference of the North American Chapter of the Association for Computational Linguistics: Human Language Technologies*, NAACL HLT '12, pages 592–596, Stroudsburg, PA, USA. Association for Computational Linguistics.

Byron C Wallace, Thomas A Trikalinos, M Barton Laws, Ira B Wilson, and Eugene Charniak. 2013. A generative joint, additive, sequential model of topics and speech acts in patient-doctor communication. In *EMNLP*, pages 1765–1775.

Miaomiao Wen, Diyi Yang, and Carolyn Penstein Rosé. 2015. Virtual teams in massive open online courses. In *Artificial Intelligence in Education*.

Theresa Wilson, Janyce Wiebe, and Paul Hoffmann. 2005. Recognizing contextual polarity in phrase-level sentiment analysis. In *Proceedings of the conference on human language technology and empirical methods in natural language processing*, pages 347–354. Association for Computational Linguistics.

Yuchen Zhao, Guan Wang, Philip S. Yu, Shaobo Liu, and Simon Zhang. 2013. Inferring social roles and statuses in social networks. In *Proceedings of the 19th ACM SIGKDD International Conference on Knowledge Discovery and Data Mining*, KDD '13, pages 695–703, New York, NY, USA. ACM.

Deep Unordered Composition Rivals Syntactic Methods for Text Classification

Mohit Iyyer,[1] **Varun Manjunatha,**[1] **Jordan Boyd-Graber,**[2] **Hal Daumé III**[1]
[1]University of Maryland, Department of Computer Science and UMIACS
[2]University of Colorado, Department of Computer Science
{miyyer,varunm,hal}@umiacs.umd.edu, Jordan.Boyd.Graber@colorado.edu

Abstract

Many existing deep learning models for natural language processing tasks focus on learning the *compositionality* of their inputs, which requires many expensive computations. We present a simple deep neural network that competes with and, in some cases, outperforms such models on sentiment analysis and factoid question answering tasks while taking only a fraction of the training time. While our model is syntactically-ignorant, we show significant improvements over previous bag-of-words models by deepening our network and applying a novel variant of dropout. Moreover, our model performs better than syntactic models on datasets with high syntactic variance. We show that our model makes similar errors to syntactically-aware models, indicating that for the tasks we consider, nonlinearly transforming the input is more important than tailoring a network to incorporate word order and syntax.

1 Introduction

Vector space models for natural language processing (NLP) represent words using low dimensional vectors called embeddings. To apply vector space models to sentences or documents, one must first select an appropriate *composition function*, which is a mathematical process for combining multiple words into a single vector.

Composition functions fall into two classes: *unordered* and *syntactic*. Unordered functions treat input texts as bags of word embeddings, while syntactic functions take word order and sentence structure into account. Previously published experimental results have shown that syntactic functions outperform unordered functions on many tasks (Socher et al., 2013b; Kalchbrenner and Blunsom, 2013).

However, there is a tradeoff: syntactic functions require more training time than unordered composition functions and are prohibitively expensive in the case of huge datasets or limited computing resources. For example, the recursive neural network (Section 2) computes costly matrix/tensor products and nonlinearities at every node of a syntactic parse tree, which limits it to smaller datasets that can be reliably parsed.

We introduce a deep unordered model that obtains near state-of-the-art accuracies on a variety of sentence and document-level tasks with just minutes of training time on an average laptop computer. This model, the deep averaging network (DAN), works in three simple steps:

1. take the vector average of the embeddings associated with an input sequence of tokens
2. pass that average through one or more feed-forward layers
3. perform (linear) classification on the final layer's representation

The model can be improved by applying a novel dropout-inspired regularizer: for each training instance, randomly drop some of the tokens' embeddings before computing the average.

We evaluate DANs on sentiment analysis and factoid question answering tasks at both the sentence and document level in Section 4. Our model's successes demonstrate that for these tasks, the choice of composition function is not as important as initializing with pretrained embeddings and using a deep network. Furthermore, DANs, unlike more complex composition functions, can be effectively trained on data that have high syntactic variance. A

Proceedings of the 53rd Annual Meeting of the Association for Computational Linguistics and the 7th International Joint Conference on Natural Language Processing, pages 1681–1691,
Beijing, China, July 26-31, 2015.

qualitative analysis of the learned layers suggests that the model works by magnifying tiny but meaningful differences in the vector average through multiple hidden layers, and a detailed error analysis shows that syntactically-aware models actually make very similar errors to those of the more naïve DAN.

2 Unordered vs. Syntactic Composition

Our goal is to marry the speed of unordered functions with the accuracy of syntactic functions. In this section, we first describe a class of unordered composition functions dubbed "neural bag-of-words models" (NBOW). We then explore more complex syntactic functions designed to avoid many of the pitfalls associated with NBOW models. Finally, we present the deep averaging network (DAN), which stacks nonlinear layers over the traditional NBOW model and achieves performance on par with or better than that of syntactic functions.

2.1 Neural Bag-of-Words Models

For simplicity, consider text classification: map an input sequence of tokens X to one of k labels. We first apply a composition function g to the sequence of word embeddings $\boldsymbol{v}_w$ for $w \in X$. The output of this composition function is a vector $\boldsymbol{z}$ that serves as input to a logistic regression function.

In our instantiation of NBOW, g averages word embeddings[1]

$$\boldsymbol{z} = g(w \in X) = \frac{1}{|X|} \sum_{w \in X} \boldsymbol{v}_w. \tag{1}$$

Feeding $\boldsymbol{z}$ to a softmax layer induces estimated probabilities for each output label

$$\hat{y} = \text{softmax}(\mathbf{W}_s \cdot \boldsymbol{z} + \boldsymbol{b}), \tag{2}$$

where the softmax function is

$$\text{softmax}(\boldsymbol{q}) = \frac{\exp \boldsymbol{q}}{\sum_{j=1}^{k} \exp \boldsymbol{q}_j} \tag{3}$$

$\mathbf{W}_s$ is a $k \times d$ matrix for a dataset with k output labels, and $\boldsymbol{b}$ is a bias term.

We train the NBOW model to minimize cross-entropy error, which for a single training instance with ground-truth label y is

$$\ell(\hat{y}) = \sum_{p=1}^{k} y_p \log(\hat{y}_p). \tag{4}$$

[1] Preliminary experiments indicate that averaging outperforms the vector sum used in NBOW from Kalchbrenner et al. (2014).

Before we describe our deep extension of the NBOW model, we take a quick detour to discuss syntactic composition functions. Connections to other representation frameworks are discussed further in Section 4.

2.2 Considering Syntax for Composition

Given a sentence like "You'll be more entertained getting hit by a bus", an unordered model like NBOW might be deceived by the word "entertained" to return a positive prediction. In contrast, syntactic composition functions rely on the order and structure of the input to learn how one word or phrase affects another, sacrificing computational efficiency in the process. In subsequent sections, we argue that this complexity is not matched by a corresponding gain in performance.

Recursive neural networks (RecNNs) are syntactic functions that rely on natural language's inherent structure to achieve state-of-the-art accuracies on sentiment analysis tasks (Tai et al., 2015). As in NBOW, each word type has an associated embedding. However, the composition function g now depends on a *parse tree* of the input sequence. The representation for any internal node in a binary parse tree is computed as a nonlinear function of the representations of its children (Figure 1, left). A more powerful RecNN variant is the recursive neural tensor network (RecNTN), which modifies g to include a costly tensor product (Socher et al., 2013b).

While RecNNs can model complex linguistic phenomena like negation (Hermann et al., 2013), they require much more training time than NBOW models. The nonlinearities and matrix/tensor products at each node of the parse tree are expensive, especially as model dimensionality increases. RecNNs also require an error signal at *every* node. One root softmax is not strong enough for the model to learn compositional relations and leads to worse accuracies than standard bag-of-words models (Li, 2014). Finally, RecNNs require relatively consistent syntax between training and test data due to their reliance on parse trees and thus cannot effectively incorporate out-of-domain data, as we show in our question-answering experiments. Kim (2014) shows that some of these issues can be avoided by using a convolutional network instead of a RecNN, but the computational complexity increases even further (see Section 4 for runtime comparisons).

What contributes most to the power of syntactic

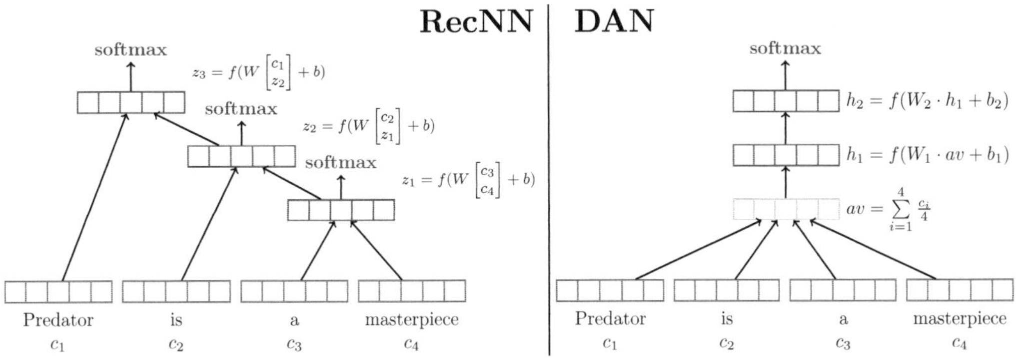

Figure 1: On the left, a **RecNN** is given an input sentence for sentiment classification. Softmax layers are placed above every internal node to avoid vanishing gradient issues. On the right is a two-layer **DAN** taking the same input. While the **RecNN** has to compute a nonlinear representation (purple vectors) for every node in the parse tree of its input, this **DAN** only computes two nonlinear layers for every possible input.

functions: the compositionality or the nonlinearities? Socher et al. (2013b) report that removing the nonlinearities from their **RecNN** models drops performance on the Stanford Sentiment Treebank by over 5% absolute accuracy. Most unordered functions are linear mappings between bag-of-words features and output labels, so might they suffer from the same issue? To isolate the effects of syntactic composition from the nonlinear transformations that are crucial to **RecNN** performance, we investigate how well a deep version of the **NBOW** model performs on tasks that have recently been dominated by syntactically-aware models.

3 Deep Averaging Networks

The intuition behind deep feed-forward neural networks is that each layer learns a more abstract representation of the input than the previous one (Bengio et al., 2013). We can apply this concept to the **NBOW** model discussed in Section 2.1 with the expectation that each layer will increasingly magnify small but meaningful differences in the word embedding average. To be more concrete, take s_1 as the sentence "I really loved Rosamund Pike's performance in the movie Gone Girl" and generate s_2 and s_3 by replacing "loved" with "liked" and then again by "despised". The vector averages of these three sentences are almost identical, but the averages associated with the synonymous sentences s_1 and s_2 are slightly more similar to each other than they are to s_3's average.

Could adding depth to **NBOW** make small such distinctions as this one more apparent? In Equation 1, we compute $\boldsymbol{z}$, the vector representation for input text X, by averaging the word vectors $\boldsymbol{v}_{w \in X}$. Instead of directly passing this representation to an output layer, we can further transform $\boldsymbol{z}$ by adding more layers before applying the softmax. Suppose we have n layers, $\boldsymbol{z}_{1...n}$. We compute each layer

$$\boldsymbol{z}_i = g(\boldsymbol{z}_{i-1}) = f(\mathbf{W}_i \cdot \boldsymbol{z}_{i-1} + \boldsymbol{b}_i) \quad (5)$$

and feed the final layer's representation, $\boldsymbol{z}_n$, to a softmax layer for prediction (Figure 1, right).

This model, which we call a deep averaging network (**DAN**), is still unordered, but its depth allows it to capture subtle variations in the input better than the standard **NBOW** model. Furthermore, computing each layer requires just a single matrix multiplication, so the complexity scales with the number of layers rather than the number of nodes in a parse tree. In practice, we find no significant difference between the training time of a **DAN** and that of the shallow **NBOW** model.

3.1 Word Dropout Improves Robustness

Dropout regularizes neural networks by randomly setting hidden and/or input units to zero with some probability p (Hinton et al., 2012; Srivastava et al., 2014). Given a neural network with n units, dropout prevents overfitting by creating an ensemble of 2^n different networks that share parameters, where each network consists of some combination of dropped and undropped units. Instead of dropping units, a natural extension for the **DAN** model is to randomly drop word tokens' entire *word embeddings* from the vector average. Using this method, which we call *word dropout*, our network theoretically sees $2^{|X|}$ different token sequences for each input X.

We posit a vector $\boldsymbol{r}$ with $|X|$ independent Bernoulli trials, each of which equals 1 with probability p. The embedding $\boldsymbol{v}_w$ for token w in X is dropped from the average if $\boldsymbol{r}_w$ is 0, which exponentially increases the number of unique examples the network sees during training. This allows us to modify Equation 1:

$$\boldsymbol{r}_w \sim \text{Bernoulli}(p) \tag{6}$$

$$\hat{X} = \{w | w \in X \text{ and } \boldsymbol{r}_w > 0\} \tag{7}$$

$$\boldsymbol{z} = g(w \in X) = \frac{\sum_{w \in \hat{X}} \boldsymbol{v}_w}{|\hat{X}|}. \tag{8}$$

Depending on the choice of p, many of the "dropped" versions of an original training instance will be very similar to each other, but for shorter inputs this is less likely. We might drop a very important token, such as "horrible" in "the crab rangoon was especially horrible"; however, since the number of word types that are predictive of the output labels is low compared to non-predictive ones (e.g., neutral words in sentiment analysis), we always see improvements using this technique.

Theoretically, word dropout can also be applied to other neural network-based approaches. However, we observe no significant performance differences in preliminary experiments when applying word dropout to leaf nodes in **RecNN**s for sentiment analysis (dropped leaf representations are set to zero vectors), and it slightly hurts performance on the question answering task.

4 Experiments

We compare **DAN**s to both the shallow **NBOW** model as well as more complicated syntactic models on sentence and document-level sentiment analysis and factoid question answering tasks. The **DAN** architecture we use for each task is almost identical, differing across tasks only in the type of output layer and the choice of activation function. Our results show that **DAN**s outperform other bag-of-words models and many syntactic models with very little training time.[2] On the question-answering task, **DAN**s effectively train on out-of-domain data, while **RecNN**s struggle to reconcile the syntactic differences between the training and test data.

[2]Code at `http://github.com/miyyer/dan`.

Model	RT	SST fine	SST bin	IMDB	Time (s)
DAN-ROOT	—	46.9	85.7	—	**31**
DAN-RAND	77.3	45.4	83.2	88.8	136
DAN	80.3	47.7	86.3	89.4	136
NBOW-RAND	76.2	42.3	81.4	88.9	91
NBOW	79.0	43.6	83.6	89.0	91
BiNB	—	41.9	83.1	—	—
NBSVM-bi	79.4	—	—	91.2	—
RecNN*	77.7	43.2	82.4	—	—
RecNTN*	—	45.7	85.4	—	—
DRecNN	—	49.8	86.6	—	431
TreeLSTM	—	**50.6**	86.9	—	—
DCNN*	—	48.5	86.9	89.4	—
PVEC*	—	48.7	87.8	**92.6**	—
CNN-MC	**81.1**	47.4	**88.1**	—	2,452
WRRBM*	—	—	—	89.2	—

Table 1: **DAN**s achieve comparable sentiment accuracies to syntactic functions (bottom third of table) but require much less training time (measured as time of a single epoch on the SST fine-grained task). Asterisked models are initialized either with different pretrained embeddings or randomly.

4.1 Sentiment Analysis

Recently, syntactic composition functions have revolutionized both fine-grained and binary (positive or negative) sentiment analysis. We conduct sentence-level sentiment experiments on the Rotten Tomatoes (RT) movie reviews dataset (Pang and Lee, 2005) and its extension with phrase-level labels, the Stanford Sentiment Treebank (SST) introduced by Socher et al. (2013b). Our model is also effective on the document-level IMDB movie review dataset of Maas et al. (2011).

4.1.1 Neural Baselines

Most neural approaches to sentiment analysis are variants of either recursive or convolutional networks. Our recursive neural network baselines include standard **RecNN**s (Socher et al., 2011b), **RecNTN**s, the deep recursive network (**DRecNN**) proposed by İrsoy and Cardie (2014), and the **TREE-LSTM** of (Tai et al., 2015). Convolutional network baselines include the dynamic convolutional network (Kalchbrenner et al., 2014, **DCNN**) and the convolutional neural network multichannel (Kim, 2014, **CNN-MC**). Our other neural baselines are the sliding-window based paragraph vector (Le and Mikolov, 2014, **PVEC**)[3] and

[3]**PVEC** is computationally expensive at both training and test time and requires enough memory to store a vector for every paragraph in the training data.

the word-representation restricted Boltzmann machine (Dahl et al., 2012, **WRRBM**), which only works on the document-level IMDB task.[4]

4.1.2 Non-Neural Baselines

We also compare to non-neural baselines, specifically the bigram naïve Bayes (**BINB**) and naïve Bayes support vector machine (**NBSVM-BI**) models introduced by Wang and Manning (2012), both of which are memory-intensive due to huge feature spaces of size $|V|^2$.

4.1.3 DAN Configurations

In Table 1, we compare a variety of **DAN** and **NBOW** configurations[5] to the baselines described above. In particular, we are interested in not only comparing **DAN** accuracies to those of the baselines, but also how initializing with pretrained embeddings and restricting the model to only root-level labels affects performance. With this in mind, the **NBOW-RAND** and **DAN-RAND** models are initialized with random 300-dimensional word embeddings, while the other models are initialized with publicly-available 300-d `GloVe` vectors trained over the Common Crawl (Pennington et al., 2014). The **DAN-ROOT** model only has access to sentence-level labels for SST experiments, while all other models are trained on labeled phrases (if they exist) in addition to sentences. We train all **NBOW** and **DAN** models using AdaGrad (Duchi et al., 2011).

We apply **DAN**s to documents by averaging the embeddings for all of a document's tokens and then feeding that average through multiple layers as before. Since the representations computed by **DAN**s are always d-dimensional vectors regardless of the input size, they are efficient with respect to both memory and computational cost. We find that the hyperparameters selected on the SST also work well for the IMDB task.

4.1.4 Dataset Details

We evaluate over both fine-grained and binary sentence-level classification tasks on the SST, and just the binary task on RT and IMDB. In the fine-grained SST setting, each sentence has a label from zero to five where two is the neutral class. For the binary task, we ignore all neutral sentences.[6]

4.1.5 Results

The **DAN** achieves the second best reported result on the RT dataset, behind only the significantly slower **CNN-MC** model. It's also competitive with more complex models on the SST and outperforms the **DCNN** and **WRRBM** on the document-level IMDB task. Interestingly, the **DAN** achieves good performance on the SST when trained with only sentence-level labels, indicating that it does not suffer from the vanishing error signal problem that plagues **RecNN**s. Since acquiring labelled phrases is often expensive (Sayeed et al., 2012; Iyyer et al., 2014b), this result is promising for large or messy datasets where fine-grained annotation is infeasible.

4.1.6 Timing Experiments

DANs require less time per epoch and—in general—require fewer epochs than their syntactic counterparts. We compare **DAN** runtime on the SST to publicly-available implementations of syntactic baselines in the last column of Table 1; the reported times are for a single epoch to control for hyperparameter choices such as learning rate, and all models use 300-d word vectors. Training a **DAN** on just sentence-level labels on the SST takes under five minutes on a single core of a laptop; when labeled phrases are added as separate training instances, training time jumps to twenty minutes.[7] All timing experiments were performed on a single core of an Intel I7 processor with 8GB of RAM.

4.2 Factoid Question Answering

DANs work well for sentiment analysis, but how do they do on other NLP tasks? We shift gears to a paragraph-length factoid question answering task and find that our model outperforms other unordered functions as well as a more complex syntactic **RecNN** model. More interestingly, we find that unlike the **RecNN**, the **DAN** significantly benefits from out-of-domain Wikipedia training data.

Quiz bowl is a trivia competition in which players are asked four-to-six sentence questions about entities (e.g., authors, battles, or events). It is an ideal task to evaluate **DAN**s because there is prior

[4]The **WRRBM** is trained using a slow Metropolis-Hastings algorithm.

[5]Best hyperparameters chosen by cross-validation: three 300-d ReLu layers, word dropout probability $p = 0.3$, L2 regularization weight of 1e-5 applied to all parameters

[6]Our fine-grained SST split is {train: 8,544, dev: 1,101, test: 2,210}, while our binary split is {train: 6,920, dev:872, test:1,821}. Split sizes increase by an order of magnitude when labeled phrases are added to the training set. For RT, we do 10-fold CV over a balanced binary dataset of 10,662 sentences. Similarly, for the IMDB experiments we use the provided balanced binary training set of 25,000 documents.

[7]We also find that **DAN**s take significantly fewer epochs to reach convergence than syntactic models.

Model	Pos 1	Pos 2	Full	Time(s)
BoW-DT	35.4	57.7	60.2	—
IR	37.5	65.9	71.4	N/A
QANTA	47.1	72.1	73.7	314
DAN	46.4	70.8	71.8	**18**
IR-WIKI	53.7	**76.6**	**77.5**	N/A
QANTA-WIKI	46.5	72.8	73.9	1,648
DAN-WIKI	**54.8**	75.5	77.1	119

Table 2: The DAN achieves slightly lower accuracies than the more complex QANTA in much less training time, even at early sentence positions where compositionality plays a bigger role. When Wikipedia is added to the training set (bottom half of table), the DAN outperforms QANTA and achieves comparable accuracy to a state-of-the-art information retrieval baseline, which highlights a benefit of ignoring word order for this task.

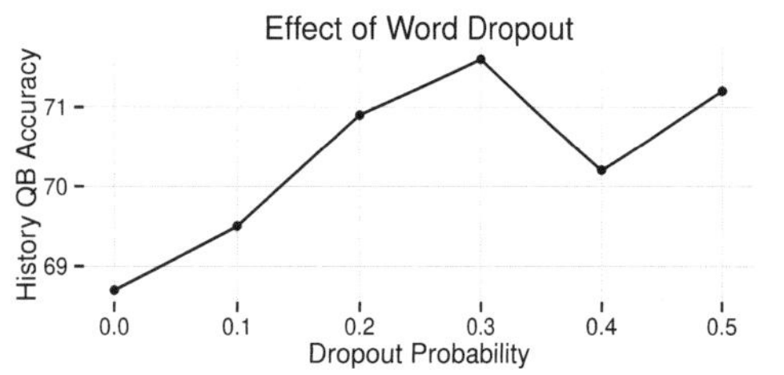

Figure 2: Randomly dropping out 30% of words from the vector average is optimal for the quiz bowl task, yielding a gain in absolute accuracy of almost 3% on the quiz bowl question dataset compared to the same model trained with no word dropout.

work using both syntactic and unordered models for quiz bowl question answering. In Boyd-Graber et al. (2012), naïve Bayes bag-of-words models (BOW-DT) and sequential language models work well on easy questions but poorly on harder ones. A dependency-tree RecNN called QANTA proposed in Iyyer et al. (2014a) shows substantial improvements, leading to the hypothesis that correctly modeling compositionality is crucial for answering hard questions.

4.2.1 Dataset and Experimental Setup

To test this, we train a DAN over the history questions from Iyyer et al. (2014a).[8] This dataset is augmented with 49,581 sentence/page-title pairs from the Wikipedia articles associated with the answers in the dataset. For fair comparison with QANTA, we use a normalized tanh activation function at the last layer instead of ReLu, and we also change the output layer from a softmax to the margin ranking loss (Weston et al., 2011) used in QANTA. We initialize the DAN with the same pretrained 100-d word embeddings that were used to initialize QANTA.

We also evaluate the effectiveness of word dropout on this task in Figure 2. Cross-validation indicates that $p = 0.3$ works best for question answering, although the improvement in accuracy is negligible for sentiment analysis. Finally, continuing the trend observed in the sentiment experiments, DAN converges much faster than QANTA.

4.2.2 DANs Improve with Noisy Data

Table 2 shows that while DAN is slightly worse than QANTA when trained only on question-answer pairs, it improves when trained on additional out-of-domain Wikipedia data (DAN-WIKI), reaching performance comparable to that of a state-of-the-art information retrieval system (IR-WIKI). QANTA, in contrast, barely improves when Wikipedia data is added (QANTA-WIKI) possibly due to the syntactic differences between Wikipedia text and quiz bowl question text.

The most common syntactic structures in quiz bowl sentences are imperative constructions such as "Identify this British author who wrote Wuthering Heights", which are almost never seen in Wikipedia. Furthermore, the subject of most quiz bowl sentences is a pronoun or pronomial mention referring to the answer, a property that is not true of Wikipedia sentences (e.g., "Little of Emily's work from this period survives, except for poems spoken by characters."). Finally, many Wikipedia sentences do not uniquely identify the title of the page they come from, such as the following sentence from Emily Brontë's page: "She does not seem to have made any friends outside her family." While noisy data affect both DAN and QANTA, the latter is further hampered by the syntactic divergence between quiz bowl questions and Wikipedia, which may explain the lack of improvement in accuracy.

[8]The training set contains 14,219 sentences over 3,761 questions. For more detail about data and baseline systems, see Iyyer et al. (2014a).

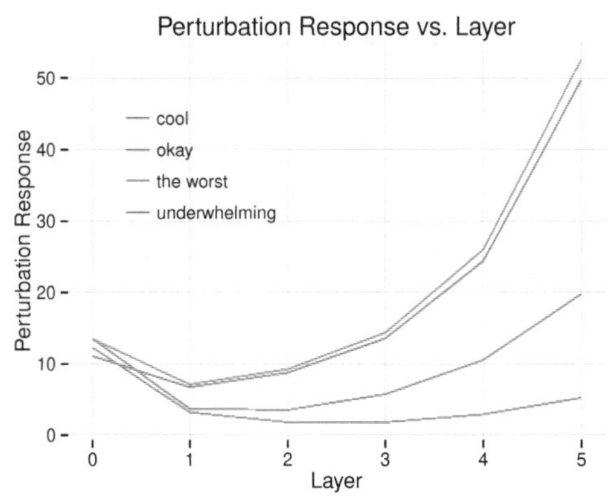

Figure 3: Perturbation response (difference in 1-norm) at each layer of a 5-layer **DAN** after replacing *awesome* in *the film's performances were awesome* with four words of varying sentiment polarity. While the shallow **NBOW** model does not show any meaningful distinctions, we see that as the network gets deeper, negative sentences are increasingly different from the original positive sentence.

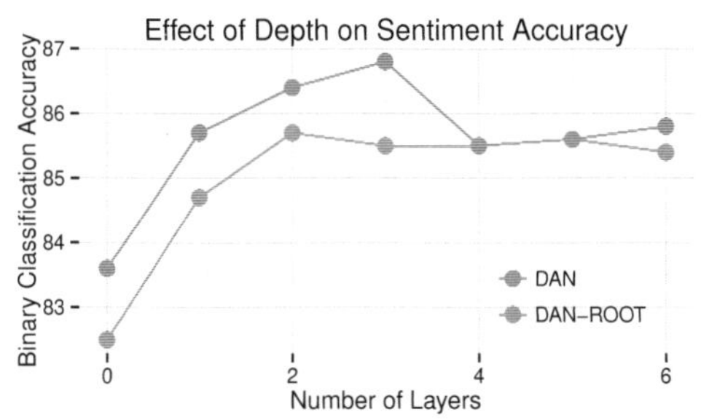

Figure 4: Two to three layers is optimal for the **DAN** on the SST binary sentiment analysis task, but adding any depth at all is an improvement over the shallow **NBOW** model.

5 How Do DANs Work?

In this section we first examine how the deep layers of the **DAN** amplify tiny differences in the vector average that are predictive of the output labels. Next, we compare **DAN**s to **DRecNN**s on sentences that contain negations and contrastive conjunctions and find that both models make similar errors despite the latter's increased complexity. Finally, we analyze the predictive ability of unsupervised word embeddings on a simple sentiment task in an effort to explain why initialization with these embeddings improves the **DAN**.

5.1 Perturbation Analysis

Following the work of İrsoy and Cardie (2014), we examine our network by measuring the response at each hidden layer to perturbations in an input sentence. In particular, we use the template *the film's performances were awesome* and replace the final word with increasingly negative polarity words (*cool*, *okay*, *underwhelming*, *the worst*). For each perturbed sentence, we observe how much the hidden layers differ from those associated with the original template in 1-norm.

Figure 3 shows that as a **DAN** gets deeper, the differences between negative and positive sentences become increasingly amplified. While nonexistent in the shallow **NBOW** model, these differences are visible even with just a single hidden layer, thus explaining why deepening the **NBOW** improves sentiment analysis as shown in Figure 4.

5.2 Handling Negations and "but": Where Syntax is Still Needed

While **DAN**s outperform other bag-of-words models, how can they model linguistic phenomena such as negation without considering word order? To evaluate **DAN**s over tougher inputs, we collect 92 sentences, each of which contains at least one negation and one contrastive conjunction, from the dev and test sets of the SST.[9] Our fine-grained accuracy is *higher* on this subset than on the full dataset, improving almost five percent absolute accuracy to 53.3%. The **DRecNN** model of İrsoy and Cardie (2014) obtains a similar accuracy of 51.1%, contrary to our intuition that syntactic functions should outperform unordered functions on sentences that clearly require syntax to understand.[10]

Are these sentences truly difficult to classify? A close inspection reveals that both the **DAN** and the **DRecNN** have an overwhelming tendency to predict negative sentiment (60.9% and 55.4% of the time for the **DAN** and **DRecNN** respectively) when they see a negation compared to positive sentiment (35.9% for **DAN**s, 34.8% for **DRecNN**s). If we further restrict our subset of sentences to only those with positive ground truth labels, we find that while both models struggle, the **DRecNN** obtains 41.7% accuracy, outperforming the **DAN**'s 37.5%.

To understand why a negation or contrastive conjunction triggers a negative sentiment prediction,

[9] We search for non-neutral sentences containing *not* / *n't*, and *but*. 48 of the sentences are positive while 44 are negative.

[10] Both models are initialized with pretrained 300-d GloVe embeddings for fair comparison.

Sentence	DAN	DRecNN	Ground Truth
a lousy movie that's not merely unwatchable, but also unlistenable	negative	negative	negative
if you're not a prepubescent girl, you'll be laughing at britney spears' movie-starring debut whenever it does n't have you impatiently squinting at your watch	negative	negative	negative
blessed with immense physical prowess he may well be, but ahola is simply not an actor	positive	neutral	negative
who knows what exactly godard is on about in this film, but his words and images do n't have to add up to mesmerize you.	positive	positive	positive
it's so good that its relentless, polished wit can withstand not only inept school productions, but even oliver parker's movie adaptation	negative	positive	positive
too bad, but thanks to some lovely comedic moments and several fine performances, it's not a total loss	negative	negative	positive
this movie was not good	negative	negative	negative
this movie was good	positive	positive	positive
this movie was bad	negative	negative	negative
the movie was not bad	negative	negative	positive

Table 3: Predictions of **DAN** and **DRecNN** models on real (top) and synthetic (bottom) sentences that contain negations and contrastive conjunctions. In the first column, words colored red individually predict the negative label when fed to a **DAN**, while blue words predict positive. The **DAN** learns that the negators *not* and *n't* are strong negative predictors, which means it is unable to capture double negation as in the last real example and the last synthetic example. The **DRecNN** does slightly better on the synthetic double negation, predicting a lower negative polarity.

we show six sentences from the negation subset and four synthetic sentences in Table 3, along with both models' predictions. The token-level predictions in the table (shown as colored boxes) are computed by passing each token through the **DAN** as separate test instances. The tokens *not* and *n't* are strongly predictive of negative sentiment. While this simplified "negation" works for many sentences in the datasets we consider, it prevents the **DAN** from reasoning about double negatives, as in "this movie was not bad". The **DRecNN** does slightly better in this case by predicting a lesser negative polarity than the **DAN**; however, we theorize that still more powerful syntactic composition functions (and more labelled instances of negation and related phenomena) are necessary to truly solve this problem.

5.3 Unsupervised Embeddings Capture Sentiment

Our model consistently converges slower to a worse solution (dropping 3% in absolute accuracy on coarse-grained SST) when we randomly initialize the word embeddings. This does not apply to just **DAN**s; both convolutional and recursive networks do the same (Kim, 2014; İrsoy and Cardie, 2014). Why are initializations with these embeddings so crucial to obtaining good performance? Is it possible that unsupervised training algorithms are already capturing sentiment?

We investigate this theory by conducting a simple experiment: given a sentiment lexicon containing both positive and negative words, we train a logistic regression to discriminate between the associated word embeddings (without any fine-tuning). We use the lexicon created by Hu and Liu (2004), which consists of 2,006 positive words and 4,783 negative words. We balance and split the dataset into 3,000 training words and 1,000 test words. Using 300-dimensional `GloVe` embeddings pretrained over the Common Crawl, we obtain over 95% accuracy on the unseen test set, supporting the hypothesis that unsupervised pretraining over large corpora can capture properties such as sentiment.

Intuitively, after the embeddings are fine-tuned during **DAN** training, we might expect a decrease in the norms of stopwords and an increase in the norms of sentiment-rich words like "awesome" or "horrible". However, we find no significant differences between the L_2 norms of stopwords and words in the sentiment lexicon of Hu and Liu (2004).

6 Related Work

Our DAN model builds on the successes of both simple vector operations and neural network-based models for compositionality.

There are a variety of element-wise vector operations that could replace the average used in the DAN. Mitchell and Lapata (2008) experiment with many of them to model the compositionality of short phrases. Later, their work was extended to take into account the syntactic relation between words (Erk and Padó, 2008; Baroni and Zamparelli, 2010; Kartsaklis and Sadrzadeh, 2013) and grammars (Coecke et al., 2010; Grefenstette and Sadrzadeh, 2011). While the average works best for the tasks that we consider, Banea et al. (2014) find that simply summing `word2vec` embeddings outperforms all other methods on the SemEval 2014 phrase-to-word and sentence-to-phrase similarity tasks.

Once we compute the embedding average in a DAN, we feed it to a deep neural network. In contrast, most previous work on neural network-based methods for NLP tasks explicitly model word order. Outside of sentiment analysis, RecNN-based approaches have been successful for tasks such as parsing (Socher et al., 2013a), machine translation (Liu et al., 2014), and paraphrase detection (Socher et al., 2011a). Convolutional networks also model word order in local windows and have achieved performance comparable to or better than that of RecNNs on many tasks (Collobert and Weston, 2008; Kim, 2014). Meanwhile, feed-forward architectures like that of the DAN have been used for language modeling (Bengio et al., 2003), selectional preference acquisition (Van de Cruys, 2014), and dependency parsing (Chen and Manning, 2014).

7 Future Work

In Section 5, we showed that the performance of our DAN model worsens on sentences that contain lingustic phenomena such as double negation. One promising future direction is to cascade classifiers such that syntactic models are used only when a DAN is not confident in its prediction. We can also extend the DAN's success at incorporating out-of-domain training data to sentiment analysis: imagine training a DAN on labeled tweets for classification on newspaper reviews. Another potentially interesting application is to add gated units to a DAN,as has been done for recurrent and recursive neural networks (Hochreiter and Schmidhuber, 1997; Cho et al., 2014; Sutskever et al., 2014; Tai et al., 2015), to drop useless words rather than randomly-selected ones.

8 Conclusion

In this paper, we introduce the deep averaging network, which feeds an unweighted average of word vectors through multiple hidden layers before classification. The DAN performs competitively with more complicated neural networks that explicitly model semantic and syntactic compositionality. It is further strengthened by word dropout, a regularizer that reduces input redundancy. DANs obtain close to state-of-the-art accuracy on both sentence and document-level sentiment analysis and factoid question-answering tasks with much less training time than competing methods; in fact, all experiments were performed in a matter of minutes on a single laptop core. We find that both DANs and syntactic functions make similar errors given syntactically-complex input, which motivates research into more powerful models of compositionality.

Acknowledgments

We thank Ozan İrsoy not only for many insightful discussions but also for suggesting some of the experiments that we included in the paper. We also thank the anonymous reviewers, Richard Socher, Arafat Sultan, and the members of the UMD "Thinking on Your Feet" research group for their helpful comments. This work was supported by NSF Grant IIS-1320538. Boyd-Graber is also supported by NSF Grants CCF-1409287 and NCSE-1422492. Any opinions, findings, conclusions, or recommendations expressed here are those of the authors and do not necessarily reflect the view of the sponsor.

References

Carmen Banea, Di Chen, Rada Mihalcea, Claire Cardie, and Janyce Wiebe. 2014. Simcompass: Using deep learning word embeddings to assess cross-level similarity. In *SemEval*.

Marco Baroni and Roberto Zamparelli. 2010. Nouns are vectors, adjectives are matrices: Representing adjective-noun constructions in semantic space. In *Proceedings of Empirical Methods in Natural Language Processing*.

Yoshua Bengio, Réjean Ducharme, Pascal Vincent, and Christian Jauvin. 2003. A neural probabilistic language model. *Journal of Machine Learning Research*.

Yoshua Bengio, Aaron Courville, and Pascal Vincent. 2013. Representation learning: A review and new perspectives. *IEEE Transactions on Pattern Analysis and Machine Intelligence*, 35(8):1798–1828.

Jordan Boyd-Graber, Brianna Satinoff, He He, and Hal Daumé III. 2012. Besting the quiz master: Crowdsourcing incremental classification games. In *Proceedings of Empirical Methods in Natural Language Processing*.

Danqi Chen and Christopher D Manning. 2014. A fast and accurate dependency parser using neural networks. In *Proceedings of Empirical Methods in Natural Language Processing*.

Kyunghyun Cho, Bart van Merrienboer, Caglar Gulcehre, Fethi Bougares, Holger Schwenk, and Yoshua Bengio. 2014. Learning phrase representations using rnn encoder-decoder for statistical machine translation. In *Proceedings of Empirical Methods in Natural Language Processing*.

Bob Coecke, Mehrnoosh Sadrzadeh, and Stephen Clark. 2010. Mathematical foundations for a compositional distributional model of meaning. *Linguistic Analysis (Lambek Festschirft)*.

Ronan Collobert and Jason Weston. 2008. A unified architecture for natural language processing: Deep neural networks with multitask learning. In *Proceedings of the International Conference of Machine Learning*.

George E Dahl, Ryan P Adams, and Hugo Larochelle. 2012. Training restricted boltzmann machines on word observations. In *Proceedings of the International Conference of Machine Learning*.

John Duchi, Elad Hazan, and Yoram Singer. 2011. Adaptive subgradient methods for online learning and stochastic optimization. *Journal of Machine Learning Research*.

Katrin Erk and Sebastian Padó. 2008. A structured vector space model for word meaning in context. In *Proceedings of Empirical Methods in Natural Language Processing*.

Edward Grefenstette and Mehrnoosh Sadrzadeh. 2011. Experimental support for a categorical compositional distributional model of meaning. In *Proceedings of Empirical Methods in Natural Language Processing*.

Karl Moritz Hermann, Edward Grefenstette, and Phil Blunsom. 2013. "not not bad" is not "bad": A distributional account of negation. *Proceedings of the ACL Workshop on Continuous Vector Space Models and their Compositionality*.

Geoffrey E. Hinton, Nitish Srivastava, Alex Krizhevsky, Ilya Sutskever, and Ruslan Salakhutdinov. 2012. Improving neural networks by preventing co-adaptation of feature detectors. *CoRR*, abs/1207.0580.

Sepp Hochreiter and Jürgen Schmidhuber. 1997. Long short-term memory. *Neural computation*.

Minqing Hu and Bing Liu. 2004. Mining and summarizing customer reviews. In *Knowledge Discovery and Data Mining*.

Ozan İrsoy and Claire Cardie. 2014. Deep recursive neural networks for compositionality in language. In *Proceedings of Advances in Neural Information Processing Systems*.

Mohit Iyyer, Jordan Boyd-Graber, Leonardo Claudino, Richard Socher, and Hal Daumé III. 2014a. A neural network for factoid question answering over paragraphs. In *Proceedings of Empirical Methods in Natural Language Processing*.

Mohit Iyyer, Peter Enns, Jordan Boyd-Graber, and Philip Resnik. 2014b. Political ideology detection using recursive neural networks. In *Proceedings of the Association for Computational Linguistics*.

Nal Kalchbrenner and Phil Blunsom. 2013. Recurrent convolutional neural networks for discourse compositionality. In *ACL Workshop on Continuous Vector Space Models and their Compositionality*.

Nal Kalchbrenner, Edward Grefenstette, and Phil Blunsom. 2014. A convolutional neural network for modelling sentences. In *Proceedings of the Association for Computational Linguistics*.

Dimitri Kartsaklis and Mehrnoosh Sadrzadeh. 2013. Prior disambiguation of word tensors for constructing sentence vectors. In *Proceedings of Empirical Methods in Natural Language Processing*.

Yoon Kim. 2014. Convolutional neural networks for sentence classification. In *Proceedings of Empirical Methods in Natural Language Processing*.

Quoc V Le and Tomas Mikolov. 2014. Distributed representations of sentences and documents. In *Proceedings of the International Conference of Machine Learning*.

Jiwei Li. 2014. Feature weight tuning for recursive neural networks. *CoRR*, abs/1412.3714.

Shujie Liu, Nan Yang, Mu Li, and Ming Zhou. 2014. A recursive recurrent neural network for statistical machine translation. In *Proceedings of the Association for Computational Linguistics*.

Andrew L. Maas, Raymond E. Daly, Peter T. Pham, Dan Huang, Andrew Y. Ng, and Christopher Potts. 2011. Learning word vectors for sentiment analysis. In *Proceedings of the Association for Computational Linguistics*.

Jeff Mitchell and Mirella Lapata. 2008. Vector-based models of semantic composition. In *Proceedings of the Association for Computational Linguistics*.

Bo Pang and Lillian Lee. 2005. Seeing stars: Exploiting class relationships for sentiment categorization with respect to rating scales. In *Proceedings of the Association for Computational Linguistics*.

Jeffrey Pennington, Richard Socher, and Christopher Manning. 2014. Glove: Global vectors for word representation. In *Proceedings of Empirical Methods in Natural Language Processing*.

Asad B. Sayeed, Jordan Boyd-Graber, Bryan Rusk, and Amy Weinberg. 2012. Grammatical structures for word-level sentiment detection. In *North American Association of Computational Linguistics*.

Richard Socher, Eric H. Huang, Jeffrey Pennington, Andrew Y. Ng, and Christopher D. Manning. 2011a. Dynamic Pooling and Unfolding Recursive Autoencoders for Paraphrase Detection. In *Proceedings of Advances in Neural Information Processing Systems*.

Richard Socher, Jeffrey Pennington, Eric H. Huang, Andrew Y. Ng, and Christopher D. Manning. 2011b. Semi-Supervised Recursive Autoencoders for Predicting Sentiment Distributions. In *Proceedings of Empirical Methods in Natural Language Processing*.

Richard Socher, John Bauer, Christopher D. Manning, and Andrew Y. Ng. 2013a. Parsing With Compositional Vector Grammars. In *Proceedings of the Association for Computational Linguistics*.

Richard Socher, Alex Perelygin, Jean Y Wu, Jason Chuang, Christopher D Manning, Andrew Y Ng, and Christopher Potts. 2013b. Recursive deep models for semantic compositionality over a sentiment treebank. In *Proceedings of Empirical Methods in Natural Language Processing*.

Nitish Srivastava, Geoffrey Hinton, Alex Krizhevsky, Ilya Sutskever, and Ruslan Salakhutdinov. 2014. Dropout: A simple way to prevent neural networks from overfitting. *Journal of Machine Learning Research*, 15(1).

Ilya Sutskever, Oriol Vinyals, and Quoc VV Le. 2014. Sequence to sequence learning with neural networks. In *Proceedings of Advances in Neural Information Processing Systems*.

Kai Sheng Tai, Richard Socher, and Christopher D. Manning. 2015. Improved semantic representations from tree-structured long short-term memory networks.

Tim Van de Cruys. 2014. A neural network approach to selectional preference acquisition. In *Proceedings of Empirical Methods in Natural Language Processing*.

Sida I. Wang and Christopher D. Manning. 2012. Baselines and bigrams: Simple, good sentiment and topic classification. In *Proceedings of the Association for Computational Linguistics*.

Jason Weston, Samy Bengio, and Nicolas Usunier. 2011. Wsabie: Scaling up to large vocabulary image annotation. In *International Joint Conference on Artificial Intelligence*.

SOLAR: Scalable Online Learning Algorithms for Ranking

Jialei Wang[1], **Ji Wan**[2,3], **Yongdong Zhang**[2], **Steven C. H. Hoi**[3*]
[1] Department of Computer Science, The University of Chicago, USA
[2] Key Laboratory of Intelligent Information Processing, ICT, CAS, China
[3] School of Information Systems, Singapore Management University, Singapore
jialei@cs.uchicago.edu, {wanji,zhyd}@ict.ac.cn, chhoi@smu.edu.sg

Abstract

Traditional learning to rank methods learn ranking models from training data in a *batch* and *offline* learning mode, which suffers from some critical limitations, e.g., poor scalability as the model has to be re-trained from scratch whenever new training data arrives. This is clearly non-scalable for many real applications in practice where training data often arrives sequentially and frequently. To overcome the limitations, this paper presents SOLAR — a new framework of Scalable Online Learning Algorithms for Ranking, to tackle the challenge of scalable learning to rank. Specifically, we propose two novel SOLAR algorithms and analyze their IR measure bounds theoretically. We conduct extensive empirical studies by comparing our SOLAR algorithms with conventional learning to rank algorithms on benchmark testbeds, in which promising results validate the efficacy and scalability of the proposed novel SOLAR algorithms.

1 Introduction

Learning to rank [27, 8, 29, 31, 7] aims to learn some ranking model from training data using machine learning methods, which has been actively studied in information retrieval (IR). Specifically, consider a document retrieval task, given a query, a ranking model assigns a relevance score to each document in a collection of documents, and then ranks the documents in decreasing order of relevance scores. The goal of learning to rank is to build a ranking model from training data of a set of queries by optimizing some IR performance measures using machine learning techniques. In literature, various learning to rank techniques have been proposed, ranging from early pointwise approaches [15, 30, 28], to popular pairwise [26, 18, 3], and recent listwise approaches [5, 38]. Learning to rank has many applications, including document retrieval, collaborative filtering, online ad, answer ranking for online QA in NLP [33], etc.

Most existing learning to rank techniques follow batch and offline machine learning methodology, which typically assumes all training data are available prior to the learning task and the ranking model is trained by applying some batch learning method, e.g., neural networks [3] or SVM [4]. Despite being studied extensively, the batch learning to rank methodology has some critical limitations. One of serious limitations perhaps is its poor scalability for real-world web applications, where the ranking model has to be re-trained from scratch whenever new training data arrives. This is apparently inefficient and non-scalable since training data often arrives sequentially and frequently in many real applications [33, 7]. Besides, batch learning to rank methodology also suffers from slow adaption to fast-changing environment of web applications due to the static ranking models pre-trained from historical batch training data.

To overcome the above limitations, this paper investigates SOLAR — a new framework of Scalable Online Learning Algorithms for Ranking, which aims to learn a ranking model from a sequence of training data in an online learning fashion. Specifically, by following the pairwise learning to rank framework, we formally formulate the learning problem, and then present two different SOLAR algorithms to solve the challenging task together with the analysis of their theoretical properties. We conduct an extensive set of experiments by evaluating the performance of the proposed algorithms under different settings by comparing them with both online and batch algorithms on benchmark testbeds in literature.

As a summary, the key contributions of this pa-

* The corresponding author. This work was done when the first two authors visited Dr Hoi's group.

Proceedings of the 53rd Annual Meeting of the Association for Computational Linguistics and the 7th International Joint Conference on Natural Language Processing, pages 1692–1701,
Beijing, China, July 26-31, 2015.

per include: (i) we present a new framework of Scalable Online Learning Algorithms for Ranking, which tackles the pairwise learning to ranking problem via a scalable online learning approach; (ii) we present two SOLAR algorithms: a first-order learning algorithm (SOLAR-I) and a second-order learning algorithm (SOLAR-II); (iii) we analyze the theoretical bounds of the proposed algorithms in terms of standard IR performance measures; and (iv) finally we examine the efficacy of the proposed algorithms by an extensive set of empirical studies on benchmark datasets.

The rest of this paper is organized as follows. Section 2 reviews related work. Section 3 gives problem formulations of the proposed framework and presents our algorithms, followed by theoretical analysis in Section 4. Section 5 presents our experimental results, and Section 6 concludes this work and indicates future directions.

2 Related Work

In general, our work is related to two topics in information retrieval and machine learning: *learning to rank* and *online learning*. Both of them have been extensively studied in literature. Below we briefly review important related work in each area.

2.1 Learning to Rank

Most of the existing approaches to learning to rank can be generally grouped into three major categories: (i) pointwise approaches, (ii) pairwise approaches, and (iii) listwise approaches.

The pointwise approaches treat ranking as a classification or regression problem for predicting the ranking of individual objects. For example, [12, 19] formulated ranking as a regression problem in diverse forms. [30] formulated ranking a binary classification of relevance on document objects, and solved it by discriminative models (e.g., SVM). In [15], Perceptron [32] ranking (known as "Prank") [15] formulated it as online binary classification. [28] cast ranking as multiple classification or multiple ordinal classification tasks.

The pairwise approaches treat the document pairs as training instances and formulate ranking as a classification or regression problem from a collection of pairwise document instances. Example of pairwise learning to rank algorithms include: neural network approaches such as RankNet [3] and LambdaRank [2], SVM approaches such as RankSVM [26], boosting approaches such as RankBoost [18], regression algorithms such as GBRank [43], and probabilistic ranking algorithms such as FRank [35]. The pairwise group is among one of widely and successfully applied approaches. Our work generally belongs to this group.

The listwise approaches treat a list of documents for a query as a training instance and attempt to learn a ranking model by optimizing some loss defined on the predicted list and the ground-truth list. In general, there are two types of approaches. The first is to directly optimize some IR metrics, such as Mean Average Precision (MAP) and Normalized Discounted Cumulative Gain (NDCG) [25]. Examples include AdaRank by boosting [39], SVM-MAP by optimizing MAP [42], PermuRank [40], and SoftRank [34] based on a smoothed approximation to NDCG, and NDCG-Boost by optimizing NDCG [37], etc. The other is to indirectly optimize the IR metrics by defining some listwise loss function, such as ListNet [5] and ListMLE [38].

Despite being studied actively, most existing works generally belong to batch learning methods, except a few online learning studies. For example, Prank [15] is probably the first online pointwise learning to ranking algorithm. Unlike Prank, our work focuses online pairwise learning to rank technique, which significantly outperforms Prank as observed in our empirical studies. Besides, our work is also related to another existing work in [10], but differs considerably in several aspects: (i) they assume the similarity function is defined in a bi-linear form which is inappropriate for document retrieval applications; (ii) their training data is given in the form of triplet-image instance (p_1, p_2, p_3), while our training data is given in a pairwise query-document instance (q_t, d_t^1, d_t^2); (iii) they only apply first order online learning algorithms, while we explore both first-order and second-order online algorithms. Finally, we note that our work differs from another series of online learning to rank studies [21, 22, 23, 36, 41] which attempt to explore reinforcement learning or multi-arm bandit techniques for learning to rank from implicit/partial feedback, whose formulation and settings are very different.

2.2 Online Learning

Our work is closely related to studies of online learning [24], representing a family of efficient and scalable machine learning algorithms. In literature, a variety of online algorithms have been proposed, mainly in two major categories: first-order algorithms and second-order algorithms. The notable examples of first-order online learning methods include classical Perceptron [32], and Passive-Aggressive (PA) learning algorithms [13]. Unlike first-order algorithms, second-order online learning [6], e.g., Confidence-Weighted (CW) learning [16], usually assumes the weight vector follows a Gaussian distribution and attempts to update the mean and covariance for each received instance. In addition, Adaptive Regularization of Weights Learning (AROW) [14] was proposed to improve robustness of CW. More other online learning methods can be found in [24]. In this work, we apply both first-order and second-order online learning methods for online learning to rank.

3 SOLAR — Online Learning to Rank

We now present SOLAR — a framework of Scalable Online Learning Algorithms for Ranking, which applies online learning to build ranking models from sequential training instances.

3.1 Problem Formulation

Without loss of generality, consider an online learning to rank problem for document retrieval, where training data instances arrive sequentially. Let us denote by $\mathcal{Q}$ a query space and denote by $\mathcal{D}$ a document space. Each instance received at time step t is represented by a triplet $(q_t^{(i)}, d_t^{(1)}, d_t^{(2)})$, where $q_t^{(i)} \in \mathcal{Q}$ denotes the i-th query in the entire collection of queries $\mathcal{Q}$, $d_t^{(1)} \in \mathcal{D}$ and $d_t^{(2)} \in \mathcal{D}$ denote a pair of documents for prediction of ranking w.r.t. the query $q_t^{(i)}$. Without loss of clarity, for the rest of this paper, we simplify the notation $q_t^{(i)}, d_t^{(1)}, d_t^{(2)}$ as q_t^i, d_t^1, d_t^2, respectively.

We also denote by $y_t \in \{+1, -1\}$ the true ranking order of the pairwise instances at step t such that if $y_t = +1$, document d_t^1 is ranked before d_t^2; otherwise d_t^1 is ranked after d_t^2. We introduce a mapping function $\phi : \mathcal{Q} \times \mathcal{D} \rightarrow \mathbb{R}^n$ that creates a n-dimensional feature vector from a query-document pair. For example, consider $\phi(q, d) \in \mathbb{R}^n$, one way to extract one of the n features is based on term frequency, which counts the number of times the query term of q occurs in document d. We also introduce $\mathbf{w}_t \in \mathbb{R}^n$ as the ranking model to be learned at step t, which is used to form the target ranking function below:

$$f(q_t^i, d_t^1, d_t^2) = \mathbf{w}_t^\top \phi(q_t^i, d_t^1, d_t^2) = \mathbf{w}_t{}^\top (\phi(q_t^i, d_t^1) - \phi(q_t^i, d_t^2))$$

Assume that we have a total of Q queries $\{q^{(i)}\}_{i=1}^Q$, each of which is associated with a total of D_i documents and a total of T_i training triplet instances. In a practical document retrieval task, the online learning to rank framework operates in the following procedure:

(i) Given a query q_1, an initial model $\mathbf{w}_1$ is first applied to rank the set of documents for the query, which are then returned to users;
(ii) We then collect user's feedback (e.g., click-through data) as the ground truth labels for the ranking orders of a collection of T_1 triplet training instances;
(iii) We then apply an online learning algorithm to update the ranking model from the sequence of T_1 triplet training instances;
(iv) We repeat the above by applying the updated ranking model to process the next query.

For a sequence of T triplet training instances, the goal of online learning to rank is to optimize the sequence of ranking models $\mathbf{w}_1, \ldots, \mathbf{w}_T$ during the entire online learning process. In general, the proposed online learning to rank scheme is evaluated by measuring the online cumulative MAP [1] or online cumulative NDCG [25]. Let us denote by NDCG_i and MAP_i the NDCG and MAP values for query q_i, respectively, which are defined as follows:

$$\text{NDCG}_i = \frac{1}{N_n} \sum_{r=1}^{D_i} G(l(\pi_f(r)))D(r) \quad (1)$$

$$\text{MAP}_i = \frac{1}{m} \sum_{s:l(\pi_f(s))=1} \frac{\sum_{j \le s} \mathbb{I}_{\{l(\pi_f(j))=1\}}}{s} \quad (2)$$

where $\mathbb{I}_{\{\cdot\}}$ is an indicator function that outputs 1 when the statement is true and 0 otherwise; $G(K) = 2^K - 1, D(K) = \frac{1}{\log_2(1+K)}$, $N_n = \max_\pi \sum_{r=1}^m G(l(\pi(r)))D(r)$, $l(r)$ is the corresponding labels as K-level ratings, π_f denote a rank list produced by ranking function f, m is the number of relevant documents. The online cumulative IR measure is defined as the average of the measure over a sequence of Q queries:

$$\text{NDCG} = \frac{1}{Q} \sum_{i=1}^{Q} \text{NDCG}_i \qquad \text{MAP} = \frac{1}{Q} \sum_{i=1}^{Q} \text{MAP}_i \quad (3)$$

3.2 First-order SOLAR Algorithm

The key challenge of online learning to rank is how to optimize the ranking model $\mathbf{w}_t$ when receiving a training instance (q_t^i, d_t^1, d_t^2) and its true label y_t at each time step t. In the following, we apply the passive-aggressive online learning technique [13] to solve this challenge. First of all, we formulate the problem as an optimization:

$$\mathbf{w}_{t+1} = \arg\min_{\mathbf{w}} \frac{1}{2}\|\mathbf{w} - \mathbf{w}_t\|^2 + C\ell(\mathbf{w}; (q_t^i, d_t^1, d_t^2), y_t)^2 \quad (4)$$

where $\ell(\mathbf{w}_t)$ is a hinge loss defined as $\ell(\mathbf{w}_t) = \max(0, 1 - y_t \mathbf{w}_t{}^\top(\phi(q_t^i, d_t^1) - \phi(q_t^i, d_t^2)))$, and C is a penalty cost parameter.

The above optimization formulation aims to achieve a trade-off between two concerns: (i) the updated ranking model should not be deviated too much from the previous ranking model $\mathbf{w}_t$; and (ii) the updated ranking model should suffer a small loss on the triplet instance (q_t^i, d_t^1, d_t^2). Their trade-off is essentially controlled by the penalty cost parameter C. Finally, we can derive the following proposition for the solution to the above.

Proposition 1. *This optimization in (4) has the following closed-form solution:*

$$\mathbf{w}_{t+1} = \mathbf{w}_t + \lambda_t y_t(\phi(q_t^i, d_t^1) - \phi(q_t^i, d_t^2)) \quad (5)$$

where λ_t is computed as follows:

$$\lambda_t = \frac{\max(0, 1 - \mathbf{w}_t{}^\top y_t(\phi(q_t^i, d_t^1) - \phi(q_t^i, d_t^2)))}{\|\phi(q_t^i, d_t^1) - \phi(q_t^i, d_t^2)\|^2 + \frac{1}{2C}} \quad (6)$$

It is not difficult to derive the result in the above proposition by following the similar idea of passive aggressive online learning [13]. We omit the detailed proof here. We can see that if $\mathbf{w}_t{}^\top y_t(\phi(q_t^i, d_t^1) - \phi(q_t^i, d_t^2)) \geq 1$, then the model remains unchanged, which means that if the current ranking model can correctly rank the order of d_t^1 and d_t^2 w.r.t. query q_t^i at a large margin, we can keep our model unchanged at this round; otherwise, we will update the current ranking model by the above proposition. Figure 1 gives the framework of the proposed online learning to rank algorithms. We denote by the first-order learning to rank algorithm as "SOLAR-I" for short.

3.3 Second-order SOLAR Algorithm

The previous algorithm only exploits first-order information of the ranking model $\mathbf{w}_t$. Inspired by recent studies in second-order online learning [6, 16, 14], we explore second-order algorithms for online learning to rank.

Algorithm 1: SOLAR — Scalable Online Learning to Rank

Initialize $\mathbf{w}_1 = 0, t = 1$
for $i = 1, 2, \ldots, Q$ **do**
  receive a query q_i and documents for ranking
  rank the documents by current model $\mathbf{w}_t$
  acquire user's feedback in triplet instances
  for $j = 1, \ldots, T_i$ **do**
    update $\mathbf{w}_{t+1}$ with (q_t^i, d_t^1, d_t^2) and y_t by Eqn. (5) (SOLAR-I) or by Eqn.(8) (SOLAR-II)
    t = t + 1
  end for
end for

Figure 1: SOLAR: scalable online learning to rank

Specifically, we cast the online learning to ranking problem into a probabilistic framework, in which we model feature confidence for a linear ranking model $\mathbf{w}$ with a Gaussian distribution with mean $\mathbf{w} \in \mathbb{R}^d$ and covariance $\Sigma \in \mathbb{R}^{d \times d}$. The mean vector $\mathbf{w}$ is used as the model of the ranking function, and the covariance matrix Σ represents our confidence on the model: the smaller the value of $\Sigma_{p,p}$, the more confident the learner has over the p-th feature w_p of the ranking model $\mathbf{w}$.

Following the similar intuition of the above section, we want to optimize our ranking model $\mathcal{N}(\mathbf{w}, \Sigma)$ by achieving the following trade-off: (i) to avoid being deviated too much from the previous model $\mathcal{N}(w_t, \Sigma_t)$; (ii) to ensure that it suffers a small loss on current triplet instance; and (iii) to attain a large confidence on the current instance. Similar to [16], we employ the Kullback-Leibler divergence to measure the distance between the current model $\mathbf{w}$ to be optimized and the previous model $\mathbf{w}_t$, and the regularization terms include both the loss suffered at current triplet instance and the confidence on current triplet instance.

Specifically, we formulate the optimization of second-order online learning to rank as:

$$\{\mathbf{w}_{t+1}, \Sigma_{t+1}\} = \arg\min_{\mathbf{w},\Sigma} D_{KL}(\mathcal{N}(\mathbf{w}, \Sigma)\|\mathcal{N}(\mathbf{w}_t, \Sigma_t)) + \frac{\ell(\mathbf{w})^2 + \Omega(\Sigma)}{2\gamma} \quad (7)$$

$$\Omega(\Sigma) = (\phi(q_t^i, d_t^1) - \phi(q_t^i, d_t^2))^\top \Sigma (\phi(q_t^i, d_t^1) - \phi(q_t^i, d_t^2))$$

where γ is the trade-off parameter. The following proposition gives the closed-form solution.

Proposition 2. *This optimization problem in (7) has the following closed-form solution:*

$$\mathbf{w}_{t+1} = \mathbf{w}_t + \alpha_t \Sigma_t y_t(\phi(q_t^i, d_t^1) - \phi(q_t^i, d_t^2)) \quad (8)$$

$$\Sigma_{t+1} = \Sigma_t - (1/\beta_t)\Sigma_t A \Sigma_t \quad (9)$$

where A, β_t, and α_t are computed as follows:

$$A = (\phi(q_t^i, d_t^1) - \phi(q_t^i, d_t^2))(\phi(q_t^i, d_t^1) - \phi(q_t^i, d_t^2))^\top$$

$$\beta_t = (\phi(q_t^i, d_t^1) - \phi(q_t^i, d_t^2))^\top \Sigma_t (\phi(q_t^i, d_t^1) - \phi(q_t^i, d_t^2)) + \gamma$$

$$\alpha_t = \max(0, 1 - y_t \mathbf{w}_t{}^\top(\phi(q_t^i, d_t^1) - \phi(q_t^i, d_t^2)))/\beta_t$$

The above can be proved by following [14]. We omit the details. We denote the above algorithm as "SOLAR-II" for short.

4 Theoretical Analysis

In this section, we theoretically analyze the two proposed algorithms by proving some online cumulative IR measure bounds for both of them.

In order to prove the IR measure bounds for the proposed algorithms, we first need to draw the relationships between the cumulative IR measures and the sum of pairwise squared hinge losses. To this purpose, we introduce the following Lemma.

Lemma 4.1. *For one query q_i and its related documents, the NDCG and MAP is lower bounded by its sum of pairwise squared hinge loss suffered by rank model w.*

$$NDCG_i \geq 1 - \gamma_{NDCG} \sum_t \ell^2(w, (q_t^i, d_t^1, d_t^2))$$

$$MAP_i \geq 1 - \gamma_{MAP} \sum_t \ell^2(w, (q_t^i, d_t^1, d_t^2))$$

where γ_{NDCG} and γ_{MAP} are constant specified by the properties of IR measures: $\gamma_{NDCG} = \frac{G(K-1)D(1)}{N_n}$ and $\gamma_{MAP} = \frac{1}{m}$, $G(K) = 2^K - 1, D(K) = \frac{1}{\log_2(1+K)}$, $N_n = \max_\pi \sum_{r=1}^m G(l(\pi(r)))D(r)$, $l(r)$ is the corresponding labels as K-level ratings, π is rank list, m is the number of relevant documents.

Sketch Proof. Using the *essential loss* idea defined in [11], from Theorem 1 of [11] we could see the *essential loss* is an upper bound of measure-based ranking errors; besides, the *essential loss* is the lower bound of the sum of pairwise squared hinge loss, using the properties of squared hinge loss, which is non-negative, non-increasing and satisfy $\ell^2(0) = 1$.

The above lemma indicates that if we could prove bounds for the online cumulative squared hinge loss compared to the best ranking model with all data beforehand, we could obtain the cumulative IR measures bounds. Fortunately there are strong theoretical loss bounds for the proposed online learning to ranking algorithms. The following shows the theorem of such loss bounds for the proposed SOLAR algorithms.

Theorem 1. *For the SOLAR-I algorithm with Q queries, for any rank model u, suppose $R = \max_{i,t} \|\phi(q_t^i, d_t^1) - \phi(q_t^i, d_t^2))\|$, the cumulative squared hinge loss is bounded by*

$$\sum_{i=1}^{Q}\sum_{t=1}^{T_i} \ell_t^2(w_t) \leq (R^2 + \frac{1}{2C})(\|u\|^2 + 2C\sum_{i=1}^{Q}\sum_{t=1}^{T_i} \ell_t^2(u)) \quad (10)$$

The proof for Theorem 1 can be found in Appendix A. By combining the results of Lemma 1 and Theorem 1, we can easily derive the cumulative IR measure bound of the SOLAR-I algorithm.

Theorem 2. *For the SOLAR-I algorithm with Q queries, for any ranking model u, the NDCG and MAP performances are respectively bounded by*

$$NDCG \geq 1 - \frac{\gamma_{NDCG}}{Q}(R^2 + \frac{1}{2C})(\|u\|^2 + 2C\sum_{i}^{Q}\sum_{t=1}^{T_i} \ell_t^2(u))$$

$$MAP \geq 1 - \frac{\gamma_{MAP}}{Q}(R^2 + \frac{1}{2C})(\|u\|^2 + 2C\sum_{i}^{Q}\sum_{t=1}^{T_i} \ell_t^2(u))$$

The analysis of the SOLAR-II algorithm would be much more complex. Let us denote by $\mathcal{M}(M = |\mathcal{M}|)$ the set of example indices for which the algorithm makes a mistake, and by $\mathcal{U}(U = |\mathcal{U}|)$ the set of example indices for which there is an update but not a mistake. Let $X_A = \sum_{(q_t^i, d_t^1, d_t^2) \in \mathcal{M}\cup\mathcal{U}} (\phi(q_t^i, d_t^1) - \phi(q_t^i, d_t^2))(\phi(q_t^i, d_t^1) - \phi(q_t^i, d_t^2))^T$. The theorem below give the squared hinge loss bound.

Theorem 3. *For the SOLAR-II algorithm with Q queries, Let $\chi_t = (\phi(q_t^i, d_t^1) - \phi(q_t^i, d_t^2))^T \Sigma_t (\phi(q_t^i, d_t^1) - \phi(q_t^i, d_t^2))$ of examples in $\mathcal{M}\cup\mathcal{U}$ at time t, K and k is the maximum and minimum value of χ_t, respectively. Σ_T be the final covariance matrix and u_T be the final mean vector. For any ranking model u, the squared hinge loss is bounded by*

$$\sum_{i=1}^{Q}\sum_{t=1}^{T_i} \ell_t^2(w_t) \leq \frac{K+\gamma}{k+\gamma}(a + \sum_{i=1}^{Q}\sum_{t=1}^{T_i} \ell_t(u)) + (K+\gamma)(\log\det(\Sigma_T^{-1}) - \frac{a^2}{\gamma^2 u^T \Sigma_T^{-1} u})$$

$$\text{where } a = \sqrt{\gamma\|u\|^2 + u^t X_A u}\sqrt{\log(\det(I + \frac{1}{\gamma}X_A)) + U}$$

The proof for Theorem 3 can be found in Appendix B. Now, by combining the Lemma 1 and Theorem 3, we can derive the cumulative IR measure bound achieved by the proposed SOLAR-II algorithm.

Theorem 4. *For the SOLAR-II algorithm with Q queries, for any ranking model u, the NDCG and MAP performances are respectively bounded by*

$$NDCG \geq 1 - \frac{\gamma_{NDCG}(K+\gamma)}{Q(k+\gamma)}(a + \sum_{i}^{Q}\sum_{t=1}^{T_i} \ell_t(u)) - \frac{\gamma_{NDCG}b}{Q}$$

$$MAP \geq 1 - \frac{\gamma_{MAP}(K+\gamma)}{Q(k+\gamma)}(a + \sum_{i}^{Q}\sum_{t=1}^{T_i} \ell_t(u)) - \frac{\gamma_{MAP}b}{Q}$$

$$\text{where } b = (K+\gamma)(\log\det(\Sigma_T^{-1}) - \frac{a^2}{\gamma^2 u^T \Sigma_T^{-1} u})$$

The above theorems show that our online algorithm is no much worse than that of the best ranking model u with all data beforehand.

5 Experiments

We conduct extensive experiments to evaluate the efficacy of our algorithms in two major aspects: (i) to examine the learning efficacy of the proposed SOLAR algorithms for online learning to rank tasks; (ii) to directly compare the proposed SOLAR algorithms with the state-of-the-art batch learning to rank algorithms. Besides, we also show an application of our algorithms for transfer learning to rank tasks to demonstrate the importance of capturing changing search intention timely in real web applications. The results are in the supplemental file due to space limitation.

5.1 Experimental Testbed and Metrics

We adopt the popular benchmark testbed for learning to rank: LETOR[1] [31]. To make a comprehensive comparison, we perform experiments on all the available datasets in LETOR3.0 and LETOR4.0. The statistics are shown in Table 1. For performance evaluation metrics, we adopt the standard IR measures, including "MAP", "NDCG@1", "NDCG@5", and "NDCG@10".

Table 1: LETOR datasets used in the experiments.

Dataset	#Queries	#features	avg#Docs/query
OHSUMED	106	45	152.26
MQ2007	1692	46	41.14
MQ2008	784	46	19.40
HP2003	150	64	984.04
HP2004	75	64	992.12
NP2003	75	64	991.04
NP2004	75	64	984.45
TD2003	50	64	981.16
TD2004	50	64	988.61

5.2 Evaluation of Online Rank Performance

This experiment evaluates the online learning performance of the proposed algorithms for online learning to rank tasks by comparing them with the existing "Prank" algorithm [15], a Perceptron-based pointwise online learning to rank algorithm, and a recently proposed "Committee Perceptron (Com-P)" algorithm [17], which explores the ensemble learning for Perceptron. We evaluate the performance in terms of both online cumulative NDCG and MAP measures. As it is an online learning task, the parameter C of SOLAR-I is fixed to 10^{-5} and the parameter γ of SOLAR-II is fixed to 10^4 for all the datasets, as suggested by [17], we set the number of experts in "Com-P" to 20. All experiments were conducted over 10 random permutations of each dataset, and all results were averaged over the 10 runs.

[1] `http://research.microsoft.com/en-us/um/beijing/projects/letor/`

Table 2 give the results of NDCG on all the datasets, where the best results were bolded. Several observations can be drawn as follows.

First of all, among all the algorithms, we found that both SOLAR-I and SOLAR-II achieve significantly better performance than Prank, which proves the efficacy of the proposed pairwise algorithms. Second, we found that Prank (pointwise) performs extremely poor on several datasets (HP2003, HP2004, NP2003, NP2004, TD2003, TD2004). By looking into the details, we found that it is likely because Prank (pointwise), as a pointwise algorithm, is highly sensitive to the imbalance of training data, and the above datasets are indeed highly imbalanced in which very few documents are labeled as relevant among about 1000 documents per query. By contrast, the pairwise algorithm performs much better. This observation further validates the importance of the proposed pairwise SOLAR algorithms that are insensitive to imbalance issue. Last, by comparing the two SOLAR algorithms, we found SOLAR-II outperforms SOLAR-I in most cases, validating the efficacy of exploiting second-order information.

5.3 Batch v.s. Online Learning

5.3.1 Comparison of ranking performance

This experiment aims to directly compare the proposed algorithms with the state-of-the-art batch algorithms in a standard learning to rank setting. We choose four of the most popular and cutting-edge batch algorithms that cover both pairwise and listwise approaches, including RankSVM [20], AdaRank [39], RankBoost [18], and ListNet [5]. For comparison, we follow the standard setting: each dataset is divided into 3 parts: 60% for training, 20% for validation to select the best parameters, and 20% for testing. We use the training data to learn the ranking model by the proposed SOLAR algorithms, the validation data to select the best parameters, and use the test data to evaluate performance. For SOLAR-I, we choose the best parameter C from $[10^{-3.5}, 10^{-6.5}]$ via grid search on the validation set; and similarly for SOLAR-II, we choose the best parameter γ from $[10^3, 10^6]$. Following [31], we adopt 5 division versions of all the datasets, and report the average performance. The results are shown in Table 3, where the best performances were bolded[2]. Several observations can drawn from the results.

[2] Results of the baseline algorithms are taken from LETOR.

Table 2: Evaluation of NDCG performance of online learning to rank algorithms.

Algorithm	OHSUMED			MQ2007			MQ2008		
	NDCG@1	NDCG@5	NDCG@10	NDCG@1	NDCG@5	NDCG@10	NDCG@1	NDCG@5	NDCG@10
Prank(Pointwise)	0.2689	0.2253	0.2221	0.2439	0.2748	0.3039	0.2369	0.3352	0.4036
Prank(Pairwise)	0.4456	0.3953	0.3904	0.2777	0.3010	0.3294	0.2834	0.3823	0.4403
Com-P	0.4327	0.3993	0.3934	0.3640	0.3828	0.4135	0.3378	0.4415	0.4885
SOLAR-I	0.5060	0.4479	0.4337	0.3760	0.3973	0.4271	0.3490	0.4584	0.5022
SOLAR-II	**0.5352**	**0.4635**	**0.4461**	**0.3897**	**0.4095**	**0.4383**	**0.3594**	**0.4680**	**0.5107**

Algorithm	HP2003			HP2004			NP2003		
	NDCG@1	NDCG@5	NDCG@10	NDCG@1	NDCG@5	NDCG@10	NDCG@1	NDCG@5	NDCG@10
Prank(Pointwise)	0.0033	0.0047	0.0050	0.0053	0.0083	0.0088	0.0033	0.0051	0.0075
Prank(Pairwise)	0.5267	0.6491	0.6745	0.5107	0.6438	0.6717	0.4033	0.5926	0.6255
Com-P	0.6487	0.7744	0.7884	**0.5640**	**0.7163**	0.7392	0.5227	0.7146	0.7417
SOLAR-I	0.6993	0.7796	0.7917	0.5347	0.7072	0.7335	0.5527	0.7486	0.7792
SOLAR-II	**0.7020**	**0.7959**	**0.8079**	0.5413	0.7146	**0.7419**	**0.5693**	**0.7621**	**0.7895**

Algorithm	NP2004			TD2003			TD2004		
	NDCG@1	NDCG@5	NDCG@10	NDCG@1	NDCG@5	NDCG@10	NDCG@1	NDCG@5	NDCG@10
Prank(Pointwise)	0.0080	0.0100	0.0100	0.0040	0.0063	0.0056	0.0040	0.0018	0.0025
Prank(Pairwise)	0.4213	0.6039	0.6290	0.1920	0.1707	0.1737	0.2773	0.2235	0.2071
Com-P	0.4867	0.6989	0.7226	**0.3300**	0.2717	0.2635	**0.3427**	**0.2988**	0.2794
SOLAR-I	0.5613	0.7649	**0.7869**	0.2160	0.2968	0.2916	0.2533	0.2750	0.2625
SOLAR-II	**0.5627**	**0.7667**	0.7858	0.2960	**0.3251**	**0.3245**	0.2893	0.2874	**0.2806**

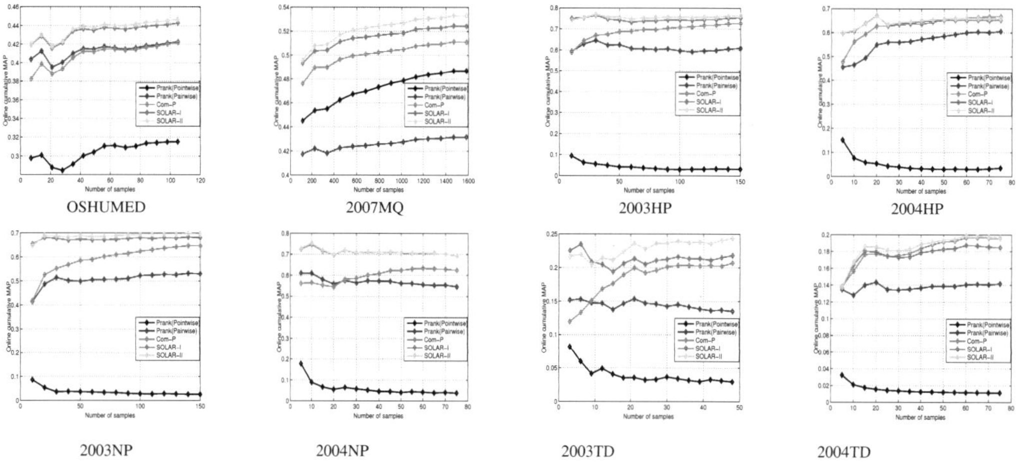

Figure 2: Evaluation of MAP performances of Online Learning to Rank algorithms

First of all, we found that no single algorithm beats all the others on all the datasets. Second, on all the datasets, we found that the SOLAR algorithms are generally achieve comparable to the state-of-the-art batch algorithms. On some datasets, e.g., "MQ2008", "MQ2007" "HP2003", "TD2003", the proposed online algorithms can even achieve best performances in terms of MAP. This encouraging result proves the efficacy of the proposed algorithms as an efficient and scalable online solution to train ranking models. Second, among the two proposed online algorithms, SOLAR-II still outperforms SOLAR-I in most cases, which again shows the importance of exploiting second-order information.

5.3.2 Scalability Evaluation

This experiment aims to examine the scalability of the proposed SOLAR algorithms. We compare it with RankSVM [20], a widely used and efficient batch algorithm. For implementation, we adopt the code from [9] [3], which is known to be the fastest implementation. Figure 3 illustrates the scalability evaluation on "2008MQ" dataset. From the results, we observe that SOLAR is much faster (e.g., 100+ times faster on this dataset)and significantly more scalable than RankSVM.

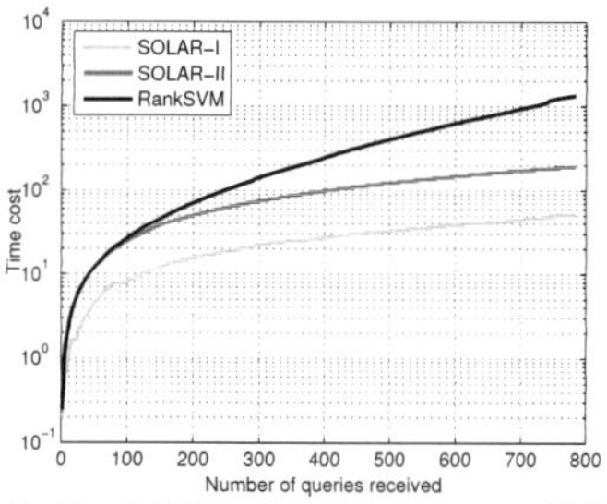

Figure 3: Scalability Evaluation on "2008MQ"

[3] `http://olivier.chapelle.cc/primal/`

Table 3: Evaluation of NDCG of Online vs Batch Learning to Rank algorithms.

Algorithm	OHSUMED			MQ2007			MQ2008		
	NDCG@1	NDCG@5	NDCG@10	NDCG@1	NDCG@5	NDCG@10	NDCG@1	NDCG@5	NDCG@10
RankSVM	0.4958	0.4164	0.4140	0.4096	0.4142	0.4438	0.3626	0.4695	0.2279
AdaRank-NDCG	0.5330	0.4673	0.4496	0.3876	0.4102	0.4369	0.3826	**0.4821**	0.2307
RankBoost	0.4632	0.4494	0.4302	**0.4134**	**0.4183**	**0.4464**	**0.3856**	0.4666	0.2255
ListNet	0.5326	0.4432	0.4410	0.4002	0.4170	0.4440	0.3754	0.4747	0.2303
SOLAR-I	0.5111	0.4668	**0.4497**	0.3886	0.4101	0.4361	0.3677	0.4634	0.5086
SOLAR-II	**0.5397**	**0.4690**	0.4490	0.4104	0.4149	0.4435	0.3720	0.4771	**0.5171**

Algorithm	HP2003			HP2004			NP2003		
	NDCG@1	NDCG@5	NDCG@10	NDCG@1	NDCG@5	NDCG@10	NDCG@1	NDCG@5	NDCG@10
RankSVM	0.6933	0.7954	0.8077	0.5733	0.7512	0.7687	0.5800	0.7823	0.8003
AdaRank-NDCG	0.7133	0.8006	0.8050	0.5867	**0.7920**	**0.8057**	0.5600	0.7447	0.7672
RankBoost	0.6667	0.8034	0.8171	0.5067	0.7211	0.7428	**0.6000**	0.7818	**0.8068**
ListNet	**0.7200**	**0.8298**	**0.8372**	**0.6000**	0.7694	0.7845	0.5667	**0.7843**	0.8018
SOLAR-I	0.7067	0.8036	0.8056	0.5467	0.7325	0.7544	0.5800	0.7664	0.7935
SOLAR-II	0.7000	0.8068	0.8137	0.5733	0.7394	0.7640	0.5667	0.7691	0.7917

Algorithm	NP2004			TD2003			TD2004		
	NDCG@1	NDCG@5	NDCG@10	NDCG@1	NDCG@5	NDCG@10	NDCG@1	NDCG@5	NDCG@10
RankSVM	0.5067	0.7957	0.8062	0.3200	0.3621	0.3461	0.4133	0.3240	0.3078
AdaRank-NDCG	0.5067	0.7122	0.7384	0.3600	0.2939	0.3036	0.4267	0.3514	0.3163
RankBoost	0.4267	0.6512	0.6914	0.2800	0.3149	0.3122	**0.5067**	**0.3878**	**0.3504**
ListNet	0.5333	**0.7965**	**0.8128**	**0.4000**	0.3393	**0.3484**	0.3600	0.3325	0.3175
SOLAR-I	**0.5733**	0.7814	0.7976	0.2600	0.3060	0.3071	0.3600	0.3119	0.3049
SOLAR-II	**0.5733**	0.7830	0.8013	0.3000	**0.3652**	0.3462	0.3333	0.3167	0.3056

6 Conclusions and Future Work

This paper presented SOLAR — a new framework of Scalable Online Learning Algorithms for Ranking. SOLAR overcomes the limitations of traditional batch learning to rank for real-world online applications. Our empirical results concluded that SOLAR algorithms share competitive efficacy as the state-of-the-art batch algorithms, but enjoy salient properties which are critical to many applications. Our future work include (i) extending our techniques to the framework of listwise learning to rank; (ii) modifying the framework to handle learning to ranking with ties; and (iii) conducting more in-depth analysis and comparisons to other types of online learning to rank algorithms in diverse settings, e.g., partial feedback [41, 22].

Appendix Proof of Theorem 1

Proof. Let $\Delta_t = \|w_t - u\|^2 - \|w_{t+1} - u\|^2$, then

$$\sum_{t=1}^{T} \Delta_t = \|u\|^2 - \|w_{T+1} - u\|^2 \leq \|u\|^2$$

Further, Δ_t can be expressed as:

$$\begin{aligned} \Delta_t &= -2\lambda_t y_t (w_t - u) \cdot (\phi(q_t^i, d_t^1) - \phi(q_t^i, d_t^2)) \\ &\quad -\lambda_t \|\phi(q_t^i, d_t^1) - \phi(q_t^i, d_t^2)\|^2 \\ &\geq \lambda_t (2\ell_t(w_t) - \lambda_t - 2\ell_t(u)). \end{aligned}$$

We thus have

$$\begin{aligned} \|u\|^2 &\geq \sum_{t=1}^{T} (2\lambda_t \ell_t(w_t) - \lambda_t^2 \|\phi(q_t^i, d_t^1) - \phi(q_t^i, d_t^2)\|^2 - 2\lambda_t \ell_t(u)) \\ &\geq \sum_{t=1}^{T} (2\lambda_t \ell_t(w_t) - \lambda_t^2 \|\phi(q_t^i, d_t^1) - \phi(q_t^i, d_t^2)\|^2 - 2\lambda_t \ell_t(u) \\ &\quad -(\frac{\lambda_t}{\sqrt{2C}} - \sqrt{2C}\ell_t(u))^2) \\ &\geq \sum_{t=1}^{T} (2\lambda_t \ell_t(w_t) - \lambda_t^2 (\|\phi(q_t^i, d_t^1) - \phi(q_t^i, d_t^2)\|^2 + \frac{1}{2C}) - 2C\ell_t(u)^2) \\ &= \sum_{t=1}^{T} (\frac{\ell_t(w_t)^2}{\|\phi(q_t^i, d_t^1) - \phi(q_t^i, d_t^2)\|^2 + \frac{1}{2C}} - 2C\ell_t(u)^2) \end{aligned}$$

Combining the above concludes the theorem. □

Appendix B: Proof of Theorem 3

Proof. Using the Cauchy-Schwarz inequality, we have $u_T^T \Sigma_T^{-1} u_T \geq \frac{(u^T \Sigma_T^{-1} u_T)^2}{u^T \Sigma_T^{-1} u}$. Notice that some inequalities could be easily obtained by extending the Lemma3, Lemma 4 and Theorem 2 of [14] to the pairwise setting as follows:

$$u^T \Sigma_T^{-1} u_T \geq \frac{M + U - \sum_{t \in \mathcal{M} \cup \mathcal{U}} \ell_t(u)}{\gamma},$$

$$\sum_{t \in \mathcal{M} \cup \mathcal{U}} \frac{\chi_t}{r(\chi_t + \gamma)} \leq \log(\det(\Sigma_T^{-1}))$$

$$u_T^T \Sigma_T^{-1} u_T = \sum_{t \in \mathcal{M} \cup \mathcal{U}} \frac{\chi_t}{r(\chi_t + \gamma)} + \sum_{t \in \mathcal{M} \cup \mathcal{U}} \frac{1 - \ell_t^2(w_t)}{\chi_t + \gamma},$$

$$M + U \leq a + \sum_{t \in \mathcal{M} \cup \mathcal{U}} \ell_t(u)$$

where $a = \sqrt{\gamma \|u\|^2 + u^t X_A u} \sqrt{\log(\det(I + \frac{1}{\gamma} X_A)) + U}$.

We thus have

$$\begin{aligned} \sum_{t \in \mathcal{M} \cup \mathcal{U}} \frac{\ell_t^2(w_t)}{\chi_t + \gamma} &\leq \sum_{t \in \mathcal{M} \cup \mathcal{U}} \frac{\chi_t}{r(\chi_t + \gamma)} + \sum_{t \in \mathcal{M} \cup \mathcal{U}} \frac{1}{\chi_t + \gamma} \\ &\quad - \frac{(M + U - \sum_{t \in \mathcal{M} \cup \mathcal{U}} \ell_t(u))^2}{r^2 u^T \Sigma_T^{-1} u} \\ &\leq \log(\det(\Sigma_T^{-1})) + \sum_{t \in \mathcal{M} \cup \mathcal{U}} \frac{1}{\chi_t + \gamma} - \frac{a^2}{r^2 u^T \Sigma_T^{-1} u} \\ &\leq \log(\det(\Sigma_T^{-1})) - \frac{a^2}{r^2 u^T \Sigma_T^{-1} u} + \frac{M + U}{k + \gamma} \\ &\leq \log(\det(\Sigma_T^{-1})) - \frac{a^2}{r^2 u^T \Sigma_T^{-1} u} + \frac{a + \sum_{t \in \mathcal{M} \cup \mathcal{U}} \ell_t(u)}{k + \gamma} \end{aligned}$$

Combining the above, we achieve the final result:

$$\begin{aligned} \sum_{i=1}^{Q} \sum_{t=1}^{T_i} \ell_t^2(w_t) &\leq \frac{K + \gamma}{k + \gamma} (a + \sum_{i=1}^{Q} \sum_{t=1}^{T_i} \ell_t(u)) \\ &\quad + (K + \gamma)(\log \det(\Sigma_T^{-1}) - \frac{a^2}{\gamma^2 u^T \Sigma_T^{-1} u}) \end{aligned}$$

□

Acknowledgments

This work was supported by Singapore MOE tier 1 research grant (C220/MSS14C003) and the National Nature Science Foundation of China (61428207).

References

[1] R. A. Baeza-Yates and B. A. Ribeiro-Neto. *Modern Information Retrieval - the concepts and technology behind search, Second edition*. Pearson Education Ltd., Harlow, England, 2011.

[2] C. J. C. Burges, R. Ragno, and Q. V. Le. Learning to rank with nonsmooth cost functions. In *NIPS*, pages 193–200, 2006.

[3] C. J. C. Burges, T. Shaked, E. Renshaw, A. Lazier, M. Deeds, N. Hamilton, and G. N. Hullender. Learning to rank using gradient descent. In *ICML*, pages 89–96, 2005.

[4] Y. Cao, J. Xu, T.-Y. Liu, H. Li, Y. Huang, and H.-W. Hon. Adapting ranking svm to document retrieval. In *SIGIR*, pages 186–193, 2006.

[5] Z. Cao, T. Qin, T.-Y. Liu, M.-F. Tsai, and H. Li. Learning to rank: from pairwise approach to listwise approach. In *ICML*, pages 129–136, 2007.

[6] N. Cesa-Bianchi, A. Conconi, and C. Gentile. A second-order perceptron algorithm. *SIAM J. Comput.*, 34(3):640–668, 2005.

[7] O. Chapelle and Y. Chang. Yahoo! learning to rank challenge overview. In *Yahoo! Learning to Rank Challenge*, pages 1–24, 2011.

[8] O. Chapelle, Y. Chang, and T.-Y. Liu. Future directions in learning to rank. *Journal of Machine Learning Research - Proceedings Track*, 14:91–100, 2011.

[9] O. Chapelle and S. S. Keerthi. Efficient algorithms for ranking with svms. *Inf. Retr.*, 13(3):201–215, 2010.

[10] G. Chechik, V. Sharma, U. Shalit, and S. Bengio. Large scale online learning of image similarity through ranking. *J. Mach. Learn. Res.*, 11:1109–1135, Mar. 2010.

[11] W. Chen, T.-Y. Liu, Y. Lan, Z. Ma, and H. Li. Ranking measures and loss functions in learning to rank. In *NIPS*, pages 315–323, 2009.

[12] W. S. Cooper, F. C. Gey, and D. P. Dabney. Probabilistic retrieval based on staged logistic regression. In *SIGIR'98*, pages 198–210. ACM, 1992.

[13] K. Crammer, O. Dekel, J. Keshet, S. Shalev-Shwartz, and Y. Singer. Online passive-aggressive algorithms. *Journal of Machine Learning Research*, 7:551–585, 2006.

[14] K. Crammer, A. Kulesza, and M. Dredze. Adaptive regularization of weight vectors. In *NIPS*, pages 414–422, 2009.

[15] K. Crammer and Y. Singer. Pranking with ranking. In *NIPS*, pages 641–647, 2001.

[16] M. Dredze, K. Crammer, and F. Pereira. Confidence-weighted linear classification. In *ICML*, pages 264–271, 2008.

[17] J. L. Elsas, V. R. Carvalho, and J. G. Carbonell. Fast learning of document ranking functions with the committee perceptron. In *WSDM*, pages 55–64, 2008.

[18] Y. Freund, R. D. Iyer, R. E. Schapire, and Y. Singer. An efficient boosting algorithm for combining preferences. *Journal of Machine Learning Research*, 4:933–969, 2003.

[19] F. C. Gey. Inferring probability of relevance using the method of logistic regression. In *In Proceedings of ACM SIGIR'94*, pages 222–231. Springer-Verlag, 1994.

[20] R. Herbrich, T. Graepel, and K. Obermayer. Large margin rank boundaries for ordinal regression. In *Advances in Large Margin Classifiers*, pages 115–132, 2000.

[21] K. Hofmann. Fast and reliable online learning to rank for information retrieval. Phd thesis, University of Amsterdam, Amsterdam, 05/2013 2013.

[22] K. Hofmann, A. Schuth, S. Whiteson, and M. de Rijke. Reusing historical interaction data for faster online learning to rank for ir. In *Proceedings of the sixth ACM international conference on Web search and data mining*, WSDM, pages 183–192, Rome, Italy, 2013.

[23] K. Hofmann, S. Whiteson, and M. Rijke. Balancing exploration and exploitation in listwise and pairwise online learning to rank for information retrieval. *Inf. Retr.*, 16(1):63–90, Feb. 2013.

[24] S. C. Hoi, J. Wang, and P. Zhao. Libol: A library for online learning algorithms. *The Journal of Machine Learning Research*, 15(1):495–499, 2014.

[25] K. Järvelin and J. Kekäläinen. Ir evaluation methods for retrieving highly relevant documents. In *SIGIR*, pages 41–48, 2000.

[26] T. Joachims. Optimizing search engines using clickthrough data. In *KDD*, pages 133–142, 2002.

[27] H. Li. Learning to rank for information retrieval and natural language processing. *Synthesis Lectures on Human Language Technologies*, 7(3):1–121, 2014.

[28] P. Li, C. J. C. Burges, and Q. Wu. Mcrank: Learning to rank using multiple classification and gradient boosting. In *NIPS*, 2007.

[29] T.-Y. Liu. *Learning to Rank for Information Retrieval*. Springer, 2011.

[30] R. Nallapati. Discriminative models for information retrieval. In *SIGIR'04*, pages 64–71, Sheffield, United Kingdom, 2004.

[31] T. Qin, T.-Y. Liu, J. Xu, and H. Li. Letor: A benchmark collection for research on learning to rank for information retrieval. *Inf. Retr.*, 13(4):346–374, 2010.

[32] F. Rosenblatt. The perceptron: A probabilistic model for information storage and organization in the brain. *Psych. Rev.*, 7:551–585, 1958.

[33] M. Surdeanu, M. Ciaramita, and H. Zaragoza. Learning to rank answers on large online qa collections. In *ACL*, pages 719–727, 2008.

[34] M. Taylor, J. Guiver, S. Robertson, and T. Minka. Softrank: optimizing non-smooth rank metrics. In *Proceedings of the international conference on Web search and web data mining*, WSDM, pages 77–86, Palo Alto, California, USA, 2008. ACM.

[35] M.-F. Tsai, T.-Y. Liu, T. Qin, H.-H. Chen, and W.-Y. Ma. Frank: a ranking method with fidelity loss. In *SIGIR'07*, pages 383–390, Amsterdam, The Netherlands, 2007.

[36] E. Tsivtsivadze, K. Hoffman, and T. Heskes. Large scale co-regularized ranking. In J. Fürnkranz and E. Hüllermeier, editors, *ECAI Workshop on Preference Learning*, 2012.

[37] H. Valizadegan, R. Jin, R. Zhang, and J. Mao. Learning to rank by optimizing ndcg measure. In *NIPS*, pages 1883–1891, 2009.

[38] F. Xia, T.-Y. Liu, J. Wang, W. Zhang, and H. Li. Listwise approach to learning to rank: theory and algorithm. In *ICML'08*, pages 1192–1199, Helsinki, Finland, 2008.

[39] J. Xu and H. Li. Adarank: a boosting algorithm for information retrieval. In *SIGIR*, pages 391–398, 2007.

[40] J. Xu, T.-Y. Liu, M. Lu, H. Li, and W.-Y. Ma. Directly optimizing evaluation measures in learning to rank. In *SIGIR'08*, pages 107–114, Singapore, Singapore, 2008. ACM.

[41] Y. Yue, J. Broder, R. Kleinberg, and T. Joachims. The k-armed dueling bandits problem. *J. Comput. Syst. Sci.*, 78(5):1538–1556, 2012.

[42] Y. Yue, T. Finley, F. Radlinski, and T. Joachims. A support vector method for optimizing average precision. In *SIGIR'07*, pages 271–278, Amsterdam, The Netherlands, 2007. ACM.

[43] Z. Zheng, K. Chen, G. Sun, and H. Zha. A regression framework for learning ranking functions using relative relevance judgments. In *SIGIR'07*, pages 287–294, Amsterdam, The Netherlands, 2007.

Text Categorization as a Graph Classification Problem

François Rousseau **Emmanouil Kiagias** **Michalis Vazirgiannis**

LIX, École Polytechnique, France

Abstract

In this paper, we consider the task of text categorization as a graph classification problem. By representing textual documents as graph-of-words instead of historical n-gram bag-of-words, we extract more discriminative features that correspond to long-distance n-grams through frequent subgraph mining. Moreover, by capitalizing on the concept of k-core, we reduce the graph representation to its densest part – its main core – speeding up the feature extraction step for little to no cost in prediction performances. Experiments on four standard text classification datasets show statistically significant higher accuracy and macro-averaged F1-score compared to baseline approaches.

1 Introduction

The task of text categorization finds applications in a wide variety of domains, from news filtering and document organization to opinion mining and spam detection. With the ever-growing quantity of information available online nowadays, it is crucial to provide effective systems capable of classifying text in a timely fashion. Compared to other application domains of classification, its specificity lies in its high number of features, its sparse feature vectors and its skewed multiclass scenario. For instance, when dealing with thousands of news articles, it is not uncommon to have millions of n-gram features, only a few hundreds actually present in each document and tens of class labels – some of them with thousands of articles and some others will only a few hundreds. These particularities have to be taken into account when envisaging a different representation for a document and in our case when considering the task as a graph classification problem.

Graphs are powerful data structures that are used to represent complex information about entities and interaction between them and we think text makes no exception. Historically, following the traditional bag-of-words representation, unigrams have been considered as the natural features and later extended to n-grams to capture some *word dependency* and *word order*. However, n-grams correspond to sequences of words and thus fail to capture *word inversion* and *subset matching* (e. g., "article about news" vs. "news article"). We believe graphs can help solve these issues like they did for instance with chemical compounds where repeating substructure patterns are good indicators of belonging to one particular class, e. g., predicting carcinogenicity in molecules (Helma et al., 2001). Graph classification has received a lot of attention this past decade and various techniques have been developed to deal with the task but rarely applied on textual data and at its scale.

In our work, we explored a graph representation of text, namely graph-of-words, to challenge the traditional bag-of-words representation and help better classify textual documents into categories. We first trained a classifier using frequent subgraphs as features for increased effectiveness. We then reduced each graph-of-words to its main core before mining the features for increased efficiency. Finally, we also used this technique to reduce the total number of n-gram features considered in the baselines for little to no loss in prediction performances.

The rest of the paper is organized as follows. Section 2 provides a review of the related work. Section 3 defines the preliminary concepts upon which our work is built. Section 4 introduces the proposed approaches. Section 5 describes the experimental settings and presents the results we obtained on four standard datasets. Finally, Section 6 concludes our paper and mentions future work directions.

Proceedings of the 53rd Annual Meeting of the Association for Computational Linguistics and the 7th International Joint Conference on Natural Language Processing, pages 1702–1712, Beijing, China, July 26-31, 2015.

2 Related work

In this section, we present the related work in *text categorization*, *graph classification* and the combination of the two fields like in our case.

2.1 Text categorization

Text categorization, a.k.a. *text classification*, corresponds to the task of automatically predicting the class label of a given textual document. We refer to (Sebastiani, 2002) for an in-depth review of the earliest works in the field and (Aggarwal and Zhai, 2012) for a survey of the more recent works that capitalize on additional meta-information. We note in particular the seminal work of Joachims (1998) who was the first to propose the use of a linear SVM with TF×IDF term features for the task. This approach is one of the standard baselines because of its simplicity yet effectiveness (unsupervised n-gram feature mining followed by standard supervised learning). Another popular approach is the use of Naive Bayes and its multiple variants (McCallum and Nigam, 1998), in particular for the subtask of *spam detection* (Androutsopoulos et al., 2000). Finally, there are a couple of works such as (Hassan et al., 2007) that used the graph-of-words representation to propose alternative weights for the n-gram features but still without considering the task as a graph classification problem.

2.2 Graph classification

Graph classification corresponds to the task of automatically predicting the class label of a given graph. The learning part in itself does not differ from other supervised learning problems and most proposed methods deal with the feature extraction part. They fall into two main categories: approaches that consider *subgraphs as features* and *graph kernels*.

2.2.1 Subgraphs as features

The main idea is to mine frequent subgraphs and use them as features for classification, be it with Adaboost (Kudo et al., 2004) or a linear SVM (Deshpande et al., 2005). Indeed, most datasets that were used in the associated experiments correspond to chemical compounds where repeating substructure patterns are good indicators of belonging to one particular class. Some popular graph pattern mining algorithms are gSpan (Yan and Han, 2002), FFSM (Huan et al., 2003) and Gaston (Nijssen and Kok, 2004). The number of frequent subgraphs can be enormous, especially for large graph collections, and handling such a feature set can be very expensive. To overcome this issue, recent works have proposed to retain or even only mine the discriminative subgraphs, i. e. features that contribute to the classification decision, in particular gBoost (Saigo et al., 2009), CORK (Thoma et al., 2009) and GAIA (Jin et al., 2010). However, when experimenting, gBoost did not converge on our larger datasets while GAIA and CORK consider subgraphs of node size at least 2, which exclude unigrams, resulting in poorer performances. Moreover, all these approaches have been developed for binary classification, which meant mining features as many times as the number of classes instead of just once (*one-vs-all* learning strategy). In this paper, we tackle the scalability issue differently through an unsupervised feature selection approach to reduce the size of the graphs and a fortiori the number of frequent subgraphs.

2.2.2 Graph kernels

Gärtner et al. (2003) proposed the first kernels *between* graphs (as opposed to previous kernels *on* graphs, i. e. between nodes) based on either random walks or cycles to tackle the problem of classification between graphs. In parallel, the idea of marginalized kernels was extended to graphs by Kashima et al. (2003) and by Mahé et al. (2004). We refer to (Vishwanathan et al., 2010) for an in-depth review of the topic and in particular its limitations in terms of number of unique node labels, which make them unsuitable for our problem as tested in practice (limited to a few tens of unique labels compared to hundreds of thousands for us).

2.3 Similar works

The work of Markov et al. (2007) is perhaps the closest to ours since they also perform subgraph feature mining on graph-of-words representations but with non-standard datasets and baselines. The works of Jiang et al. (2010) and Arora et al. (2010) are also related but their representations are different and closer to parse and dependency trees used as base features for text categorization by Kudo and Matsumoto (2004) and Matsumoto et al. (2005). Moreover, they do not discuss the choice of the support value, which controls the total number of features and can potentially lead to millions of subgraphs on standard datasets.

3 Preliminary concepts

In this section, we introduce the preliminary concepts upon which our work is built.

3.1 Graph-of-words

We model a textual document as a *graph-of-words*, which corresponds to a graph whose vertices represent unique terms of the document and whose edges represent co-occurrences between the terms within a fixed-size sliding window. The underlying assumption is that all the words present in a document have some undirected relationships with the others, modulo a window size outside of which the relationship is not considered. This representation was first used in keyword extraction and summarization (Ohsawa et al., 1998; Mihalcea and Tarau, 2004) and more recently in ad hoc IR (Blanco and Lioma, 2012; Rousseau and Vazirgiannis, 2013). We refer to (Blanco and Lioma, 2012) for an in-depth review of the graph representations of text in NLP.

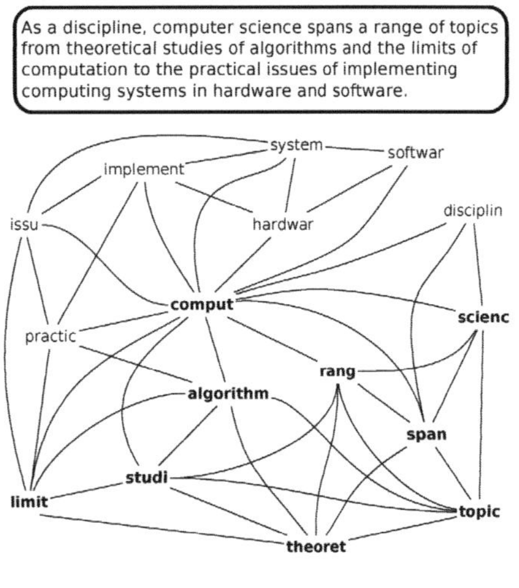

Figure 1: Graph-of-words representation of a textual document – in bold font, its main core.

Figure 1 illustrates the graph-of-words representation of a textual document. The vertices correspond to the remaining terms after standard preprocessing steps have been applied (tokenization, stop word removal and stemming). The undirected edges were drawn between terms co-occurring within a sliding window over the processed text of size 4, value consistently reported as working well in the references aforementioned and validated in our experiments. Edge direction was used by Filippova (2010) so as to extract valid sentences but not here in order to capture some word inversion.

Note that for small-enough window sizes (which is typically the case in practice), we can consider that two terms linked represent a *long-distance bigram* (Bassiou and Kotropoulos, 2010), if not a bigram. Furthermore, by extending the denomination, we can consider that a subgraph of size n is a *long-distance n-gram*, if not an n-gram. Indeed, the nodes belonging to a subgraph do not necessarily appear in a sequence in the document like for a n-gram. Moreover, this enables us to “merge” together n-grams that share the same terms but maybe not in the same order. In the experiments, by abusing the terminology, we will refer to them as n-grams to adopt a common terminology with the baseline approaches.

3.2 Node/edge labels and subgraph matching

In graph classification, it is common to introduce a node labeling function μ to map a node id to its label. For instance, consider the case of chemical compounds (e. g., the benzene C_6H_6). Then in its graph representation (its “structural formula”), it is crucial to differentiate between the multiple nodes labeled the same (e. g., C or H). In the case of graph-of-words, node labels are unique inside a graph since they represent unique terms of the document and we can therefore omit these functions since they are injective in our case and we can substitute node ids for node labels. In particular, the general problem of *subgraph matching*, which defines an isomorphism between a graph and a subgraph and is NP-complete (Garey and Johnson, 1990), can be reduced to a polynomial problem when node labels are unique. In our experiments, we used the standard algorithm VF2 developed by Cordella et al. (2001).

3.3 K-core and main core

Seidman (1983) defined the k-core of a graph as the maximal connected subgraph whose vertices are at least of degree k within the subgraph. The non-empty k-core of largest k is called the *main core* and corresponds to the most cohesive set(s) of vertices. The corresponding value of k may differ from one graph to another. Batagelj and Zaveršnik (2003) proposed an algorithm to extract the main core of an unweighted graph in time linear in the number of edges, complexity similar in our case to the other NLP preprocessing steps. Bold font on Figure 1 indicates that a vertex belongs to the main core of the graph.

4 Graph-of-words classification

In this section, we present our work and the several approaches we explored, from unsupervised feature mining using gSpan to propose more discriminative features than standard n-grams to unsupervised feature selection using k-core to reduce the total number of subgraph and n-gram features.

4.1 Unsupervised feature mining using gSpan

We considered the task of text categorization as a graph classification problem by representing textual documents as graph-of-words and then extracting subgraph features to train a graph classifier. Each document is a separate graph-of-words and the collection of documents thus corresponds to a set of graphs. Therefore, for larger datasets, the total number of graphs increases but not the average graph size (the average number of unique terms in a text), assuming homogeneous datasets.

Because the total number of unique node labels corresponds to the number of unique terms in the collection in our case, graph kernels are not suitable for us as verified in practice using the MATLAB code made available by Shervashidze (2009). We therefore only explored the methods that consider subgraphs as features. Repeating substructure patterns between graphs are intuitively good candidates for classification since, at least for chemical compounds, shared subparts of molecules are good indicators of belonging to one particular class. We assumed it would the same for text. Indeed, subgraphs of graph-of-words correspond to sets of words co-occurring together, just not necessarily always as the same sequence like for n-grams – it can be seen as a relaxed definition of a n-gram to capture additional variants.

We used gSpan (graph-based Substructure pattern (Yan and Han, 2002)) as frequent subgraph miner like (Jiang et al., 2010; Arora et al., 2010) mostly because of its fast available C++ implementation from gBoost (Saigo et al., 2009). Briefly, the key idea behind gSpan is that instead of enumerating all the subgraphs and testing for isomorphism throughout the collection, it first builds for each graph a lexicographic order of all the edges using depth-first-search (DFS) traversal and assigns to it a unique minimum DFS code. Based on all these DFS codes, a hierarchical search tree is constructed at the collection-level. By pre-order traversal of this tree, gSpan discovers all frequent subgraphs with required support.

Consider the set of all subgraphs in the collection of graphs, which corresponds to the set of all potential features. Note that there may be overlapping (subgraphs sharing nodes/edges) and redundant (subgraphs included in others) features. Because its size is exponential in the number of edges (just like the number of n-grams is exponential in n), it is common to only retain/mine the most frequent subgraphs (again just like for n-grams with a minimum document frequency (Fürnkranz, 1998; Joachims, 1998)). This is controlled via a parameter known as the *support*, which sets the minimum number of graphs in which a given subgraph has to appear to be considered as a feature, i. e. the number of subgraph matches in the collection. Here, since node labels are unique inside a graph, we do not have to consider multiple occurrences of the same subgraph in a given graph. The lower the support, the more features selected/considered but the more expensive the mining and the training (not only in time spent for the learning but also for the feature vector generation).

4.2 Unsupervised support selection

The optimal value for the support can be learned through cross-validation so as to maximize the prediction accuracy of the subsequent classifier, making the whole feature mining process *supervised*. But if we consider that the classifier can only improve its goodness of fit with more features (the sets of features being nested as the support varies), it is likely that the lowest support will lead to the best test accuracy; assuming subsequent regularization to prevent overfitting. However, this will come at the cost of an exponential number of features as observed in practice. Indeed, as the support decreases, the number of features increases slightly up until a point where it increases exponentially, which makes both the feature vector generation and the learning expensive, especially with multiple classes. Moreover, we observed that the prediction performances did not benefit that much from using all the possible features (support of 1) as opposed to a more manageable number of features corresponding to a higher support. Therefore, we propose to select the support using the so-called *elbow method*. This is an unsupervised empirical method initially developed for selecting the number of clusters in k-means (Thorndike, 1953). Figure 3 (upper plots) in Section 5 illustrates this process.

4.3 Considered classifiers

In text categorization, standard baseline classifiers include k-nearest neighbors (kNN) (Larkey and Croft, 1996), Naive Bayes (NB) (McCallum and Nigam, 1998) and linear Support Vector Machines (SVM) (Joachims, 1998) with the latter performing the best on n-gram features as verified in our experiments. Since our subgraph features correspond to "long-distance n-grams", we used linear SVMs as our classifiers in all our experiments – the goal of our work being to explore and propose better features rather than a different classifier.

4.4 Multiclass scenario

In standard binary graph classification (e. g., predicting chemical compounds' carcinogenicity as either positive or negative (Helma et al., 2001)), feature mining is performed on the whole graph collection as we expect the mined features to be able to discriminate between the two classes (thus producing a good classifier). However, for the task of text categorization, there are usually more than two classes (e. g., 118 categories of news articles for the Reuters-21578 dataset) and with a skewed class distribution (e. g., a lot more news related to "acquisition" than to "grain"). Therefore, a single support value might lead to some classes generating a tremendous number of features (e. g., hundreds of thousands of frequent subgraphs) and some others only a few (e. g., a few hundreds subgraphs) resulting in a skewed and non-discriminative feature set. To include discriminative features for these *minority* classes, we would need an extremely low support resulting in an exponential number of features because of the *majority* classes. For these reasons, we decided to mine frequent subgraphs per class using the same relative support (%) and then aggregating each feature set into a global one at the cost of a *supervised* process (but which still avoids cross-validated parameter tuning). This was not needed for the tasks of spam detection and opinion mining since the corresponding datasets consist of only two balanced classes.

4.5 Main core mining using gSpan

Since the main drawback of mining frequent subgraphs for text categorization rather than chemical compound classification is the very high number of possible subgraphs because of the size of the graphs and the total number of graphs (more than 10x in both cases), we thought of ways to reduce the graphs' sizes while retaining as much classification information as possible.

The graph-of-words representation is designed to capture dependency between words, i. e. dependency between features in the context of machine learning but at the document-level. Initially, we wanted to capture recurring sets of words (i. e. take into account word inversion and subset matching) and not just sequences of words like with n-grams. In terms of subgraphs, this means words that co-occur with each other and form a dense subgraph as opposed to a path like for a n-gram. Therefore, when reducing the graphs, we need to keep their densest part(s) and that is why we considered extracting their main cores. Compared to other density-based algorithms, retaining the main core of a graph has the advantage of being linear in the number of edges, i. e. in the number of unique terms in a document in our case (the number of edges is at most the number of nodes times the fixed size of the sliding window, a small constant in practice).

4.6 Unsupervised n-gram feature selection

Similarly to (Hassan et al., 2007) that used graph-of-words to propose alternative weights for the n-gram features, we can capitalize on main core retention to still extract binary n-gram features for classification but considering only the terms belonging to the main core of each document. Because some terms never belong to any main core of any document, the dimension of the overall feature space decreases. Additionally, since a document is only represented by a subset of its original terms, the number of non-zero feature values per document also decreases, which matters for SVM, even for the linear kernel, when considering the dual formulation or in the primal with more recent optimization techniques (Joachims, 2006).

Compared to most existing feature selection techniques in the field (Yang and Pedersen, 1997), it is *unsupervised* and *corpus-independent* as it does not rely on any labeled data like IG, MI or χ^2 nor any collection-wide statistics like IDF, which can be of interest for large-scale text categorization in order to process documents in parallel, independently of each other. In some sense, it is similar to what Özgür et al. (2005) proposed with corpus-based and class-based keyword selection for text classification except that we use here *document-based* keyword selection following the approach from Rousseau and Vazirgiannis (2015).

5 Experiments

In this section we present the experiments we conducted to validate our approaches.

5.1 Datasets

We used four standard text datasets: two for multiclass document categorization (WebKB and R8), one for spam detection (LingSpam) and one for opinion mining (Amazon) so as to cover all the main subtasks of text categorization:

- `WebKB`: 4 most frequent categories among labeled webpages from various CS departments – split into 2,803 for training and 1,396 for test (Cardoso-Cachopo, 2007, p. 39–41).
- `R8`: 8 most frequent categories of Reuters-21578, a set of labeled news articles from the 1987 Reuters newswire – split into 5,485 for training and 2,189 for test (Debole and Sebastiani, 2005).
- `LingSpam`: 2,893 emails classified as spam or legitimate messages – split into 10 sets for 10-fold cross validation (Androutsopoulos et al., 2000).
- `Amazon`: 8,000 product reviews over four different sub-collections (books, DVDs, electronics and kitchen appliances) classified as positive or negative – split into 1,600 for training and 400 for test each (Blitzer et al., 2007).

5.2 Implementation

We developed our approaches mostly in Python using the `igraph` library (Csardi and Nepusz, 2006) for the graph representation and main core extraction. For unsupervised subgraph feature mining, we used the C++ implementation of gSpan from gBoost (Saigo et al., 2009). Finally for classification and standard n-gram text categorization we used `scikit` (Pedregosa et al., 2011), a standard Python machine learning library.

5.3 Evaluation metrics

To evaluate the performance of our proposed approaches over standard baselines, we computed on the test set both the micro- and macro-average F1-score. Because we are dealing with single-label classification, the micro-average F1-score corresponds to the accuracy and is a measure of the overall prediction effectiveness (Manning et al., 2008, p. 281). Conversely, the macro-average F1-score takes into account the skewed class label distributions by weighting each class uniformly. The statistical significance of improvement in accuracy over the n-gram SVM baseline was assessed using the micro sign test ($p < 0.05$) (Yang and Liu, 1999). For the Amazon dataset, we report the average of each metric over the four sub-collections.

Dataset	# subgraphs before	# subgraphs after	reduction
WebKB	30,868	10,113	67 %
R8	39,428	11,373	71 %
LingSpam	54,779	15,514	72 %
Amazon	16,415	8,745	47 %

Dataset	# n-grams before	# n-grams after	reduction
WebKB	1,849,848	735,447	60 %
R8	1,604,280	788,465	51 %
LingSpam	2,733,043	1,016,061	63 %
Amazon	583,457	376,664	35 %

Table 1: Total number of features (n-grams or subgraphs) vs. number of features present only in main cores along with the reduction of the dimension of the feature space on all four datasets.

5.4 Results

Table 2 shows the results on the four considered datasets. The first three rows correspond to the baselines: unsupervised n-gram feature extraction and then supervised learning using kNN, NB (Multinomial but Bernoulli yields similar results) and linear SVM. The last three rows correspond to our approaches.

In our first approach, denoted as "gSpan + SVM", we mine frequent subgraphs (gSpan) as features and then train a linear SVM. These features correspond to long-distance n-grams. This leads to the best results in text categorization on almost all datasets (all if we compare to baseline methods), in particular on multiclass document categorization (R8 and WebKB).

In our second approach, denoted as "MC + gSpan + SVM", we repeat the same procedure except that we mine frequent subgraphs (gSpan) from the main core (MC) of each graph-of-words and then train an SVM on the resulting features. Main cores can vary from 1-core to 12-core depending on the graph structure, 5-core and 6-core being the most frequent (more than 60%). This yields results similar to the SVM baseline for a faster mining and training compared to gSpan + SVM. Table 1 (upper table) shows the reduction in the dimension of the feature space and we see

Table 2: Test accuracy and macro-average F1-score on four standard datasets. Bold font marks the best performance in a column. * indicates statistical significance at $p < 0.05$ using micro sign test with regards to the SVM baseline of the same column. MC corresponds to unsupervised feature selection using the main core of each graph-of-words to extract n-gram and subgraph features. gSpan mining support values are 1.6% (WebKB), 7% (R8), 4% (LingSpam) and 0.5% (Amazon).

Method \ Dataset	WebKB		R8		LingSpam		Amazon	
	Accuracy	F1-score	Accuracy	F1-score	Accuracy	F1-score	Accuracy	F1-score
kNN (k=5)	0.679	0.617	0.894	0.705	0.910	0.774	0.512	0.644
NB (Multinomial)	0.866	0.861	0.934	0.839	0.990	0.971	0.768	0.767
linear SVM	0.889	0.871	0.947	0.858	**0.991**	**0.973**	0.792	0.790
gSpan + SVM	**0.912***	**0.882**	**0.955***	**0.864**	**0.991**	0.972	0.798*	0.795
MC + gSpan + SVM	0.901*	0.871	0.949*	0.858	0.990	**0.973**	**0.800***	**0.798**
MC + SVM	0.872	0.863	0.937	0.849	0.990	0.972	0.786	0.774

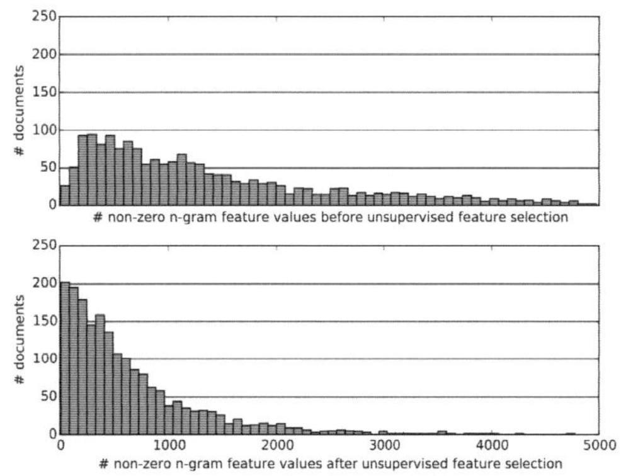

Figure 2: Distribution of non-zero n-gram feature values before and after unsupervised feature selection (main core retention) on R8 dataset.

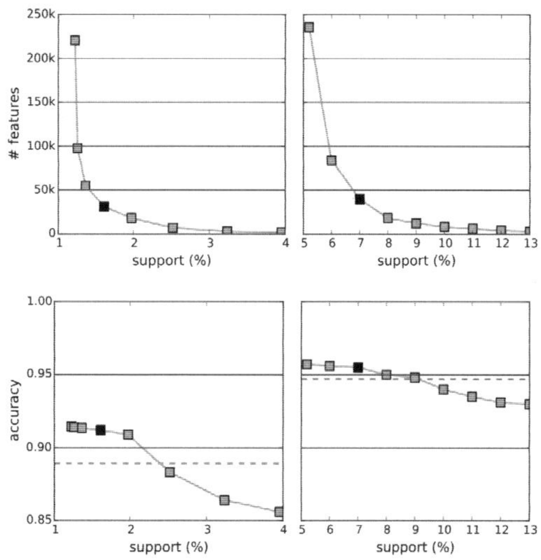

Figure 3: Number of subgraph features/accuracy in test per support (%) on WebKB (left) and R8 (right) datasets: in black, the selected support value chosen via the elbow method and in red, the accuracy in test for the SVM baseline.

that on average less than 60% of the subgraphs are kept for little to no cost in prediction effectiveness.

In our final approach, denoted as "MC + SVM", we performed unsupervised feature selection by keeping the terms appearing in the main core (MC) of each document's graph-of-words representation and then extracted standard n-gram features. Table 1 (lower table) shows the reduction in the dimension of the feature space and we see that on average less than half the n-grams remain. Figure 2 shows the distribution of non-zero features before and after the feature selection on the R8 dataset. Similar changes in distribution can be observed on the other datasets, from a right-tail Gaussian to a power law distribution as expected from the main core retention. Table 2 shows that the main core retention has little to no cost in accuracy and F1-score but can reduce drastically the feature space and the number of non-zero values per document.

5.5 Unsupervised support selection

Figure 3 above illustrates the unsupervised heuristic (elbow method) we used to select the support value, which corresponds to the minimum number of graphs in which a subgraph has to appear to be considered frequent. We noticed that as the support decreases, the number of features increases slightly up until a point where it increases exponentially. This support value, highlighted in black on the figure and chosen before taking into account the class label, is the value we used in our experiments and for which we report the results in Table 1 and 2. The lower plots provide evidence

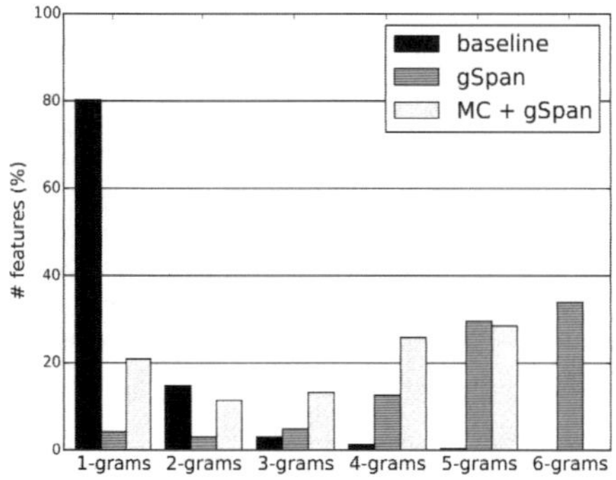

Figure 4: Distribution of n-grams (standard and long-distance ones) among all the features on WebKB dataset.

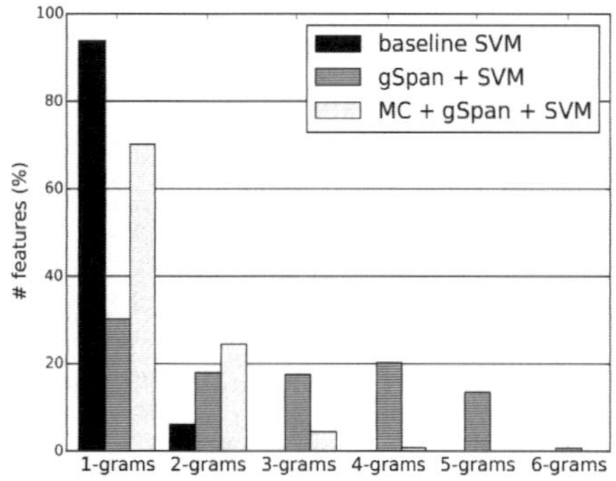

Figure 5: Distribution of n-grams (standard and long-distance ones) among the top 5% most discriminative features for SVM on WebKB dataset.

that the elbow method helps selecting in an unsupervised manner a support that leads to the best or close to the best accuracy.

5.6 Distribution of mined n-grams

In order to gain more insights on why the long-distance n-grams mined with gSpan result in better classification performances than the baseline n-grams, we computed the distribution of the number of unigrams, bigrams, etc. up to 6-grams in the traditional feature set and ours (Figure 4) as well as in the top 5% features that contribute the most to the classification decision of the trained SVM (Figure 5). Again, a long-distance n-gram corresponds to a subgraph of size n in a graph-of-words and can be seen as a relaxed definition of the traditional n-gram, one that takes into account word inversion for instance. To obtain comparable results, we considered for the baseline n-grams with a minimum document frequency equal to the support. Otherwise, by definition, there are at least as many bigrams as there are unigrams and so forth.

Figure 4 shows that our approaches mine way more n-grams than unigrams compared to the baseline. This happens because with graph-of-words a subgraph of size n corresponds to a set of n terms while with bag-of-words a n-gram corresponds to a sequence of n terms. Note that even when restricting the subgraphs to the main cores, there are still more higher order n-grams mined.

Figure 5 shows that the higher order n-grams still contribute indeed to the classification decision and in higher proportion than with the baseline, even when restricting to the main cores. For instance, on the R8 dataset, {bank, base, rate} was a discriminative (top 5% SVM features) long-distance 3-gram for the category "interest" and occurred in documents in the form of "barclays bank cut its base lending rate", "midland bank matches its base rate" and "base rate of natwest bank dropped", pattern that would be hard to capture with traditional n-gram bag-of-words.

5.7 Timing

With an Intel Core i5-3317U clocking at 2.6GHz and 8GB of RAM, mining the subgraph features with gSpan takes on average 30s for the selected support. It can take several hours with lower support and goes down to 5s using the main cores.

6 Conclusion

In this paper, we tackled the task of text categorization by representing documents as graph-of-words and then considering the problem as a graph classification one. We were able to extract more discriminative features that correspond to long-distance n-grams through frequent subgraph mining. Experiments on four standard datasets show statistically significant higher accuracy and macro-averaged F1-score compared to baselines.

To the best of our knowledge, graph classification has never been tested at that scale – thousands of graphs and tens of thousands of unique node labels – and also in the multiclass scenario. For these reasons, we could not capitalize on all standard methods. In particular, we believe new kernels that support a very high number of unique node labels could yield even better performances.

References

Charu C. Aggarwal and ChengXiang Zhai. 2012. A Survey of Text Classification Algorithms. In *Mining Text Data*, pages 163–222.

Ion Androutsopoulos, John Koutsias, Konstantinos V. Chandrinos, George Paliouras, and Constantine D. Spyropoulos. 2000. An Evaluation of Naive Bayesian Anti-Spam Filtering. In *Proceedings of the Workshop on Machine Learning in the New Information Age, 11th European Conference on Machine Learning*, pages 9–17.

Shilpa Arora, Elijah Mayfield, Carolyn Penstein-Rosé, and Eric Nyberg. 2010. Sentiment Classification Using Automatically Extracted Subgraph Features. In *Proceedings of the NAACL HLT 2010 Workshop on Computational Approaches to Analysis and Generation of Emotion in Text*, CAAGET '10, pages 131–139.

Nikoletta Bassiou and Constantine Kotropoulos. 2010. Word Clustering Using PLSA Enhanced with Long Distance Bigrams. In *Proceedings of the 20th International Conference on Pattern Recognition*, ICPR '10, pages 4226–4229.

Vladimir Batagelj and Matjaž Zaversnik. 2003. An O(m) Algorithm for Cores Decomposition of Networks. *The Computing Research Repository (CoRR)*, cs.DS/0310049.

Roi Blanco and Christina Lioma. 2012. Graph-based term weighting for information retrieval. *Information Retrieval*, 15(1):54–92.

John Blitzer, Mark Dredze, and Fernando Pereira. 2007. Biographies, bollywood, boomboxes and blenders: Domain adaptation for sentiment classification. In *Proceedings of the 45th Annual Meeting of the Association of Computational Linguistics*, ACL '07, pages 440–447.

Ana Cardoso-Cachopo. 2007. *Improving Methods for Single-label Text Categorization*. Ph.D. thesis, Instituto Superior Técnico, Universidade de Lisboa, Lisbon, Portugal.

Luigi Pietro Cordella, Pasquale Foggia, Carlo Sansone, and Mario Vento. 2001. An improved algorithm for matching large graphs. In *Proceedings of the 3rd IAPR-TC15 Workshop on Graph-based Representations in Pattern Recognition*, pages 149–159.

Gabor Csardi and Tamas Nepusz. 2006. The igraph software package for complex network research. *InterJournal, Complex Systems*, 1695(5):1–9.

Franca Debole and Fabrizio Sebastiani. 2005. An Analysis of the Relative Hardness of Reuters-21578 Subsets: Research Articles. *Journal of the American Society for Information Science and Technology*, 56(6):584–596.

Mukund Deshpande, Michihiro Kuramochi, Nikil Wale, and George Karypis. 2005. Frequent Substructure-Based Approaches for Classifying Chemical Compounds. *IEEE Transactions on Knowledge and Data Engineering*, 17(8):1036–1050.

Katja Filippova. 2010. Multi-sentence Compression: Finding Shortest Paths in Word Graphs. In *Proceedings of the 23rd International Conference on Computational Linguistics*, COLING '10, pages 322–330.

Johannes Fürnkranz. 1998. A study using n-gram features for text categorization. Technical Report OEFAI-TR-98-30, Austrian Research Institute for Artificial Intelligence.

Michael R. Garey and David S. Johnson. 1990. *Computers and Intractability; A Guide to the Theory of NP-Completeness*. W. H. Freeman & Co.

Thomas Gärtner, Peter Flach, and Stefan Wrobel. 2003. On graph kernels: Hardness results and efficient alternatives. In *Proceedings of the Annual Conference on Computational Learning Theory*, COLT '03, pages 129–143.

Samer Hassan, Rada Mihalcea, and Carmen Banea. 2007. Random-Walk Term Weighting for Improved Text Classification. In *Proceedings of the International Conference on Semantic Computing*, ICSC '07, pages 242–249.

Christoph Helma, Ross D. King, Stefan Kramer, and Ashwin Srinivasan. 2001. The predictive toxicology challenge 2000–2001. *Bioinformatics*, 17(1):107–108.

Jun Huan, Wei Wang, and Jan Prins. 2003. Efficient Mining of Frequent Subgraphs in the Presence of Isomorphism. In *Proceedings of the 3rd IEEE International Conference on Data Mining*, ICDM '03, pages 549–552.

Chuntao Jiang, Frans Coenen, Robert Sanderson, and Michele Zito. 2010. Text classification using graph mining-based feature extraction. *Knowledge-Based Systems*, 23(4):302–308.

Ning Jin, Calvin Young, and Wei Wang. 2010. GAIA: graph classification using evolutionary computation. In *Proceedings of the 2010 ACM SIGMOD international conference on Management of data*, SIGMOD '10, pages 879–890.

Thorsten Joachims. 1998. Text categorization with Support Vector Machines: Learning with many relevant features. In *Proceedings of the 10th European Conference on Machine Learning*, ECML '98, pages 137–142.

Thorsten Joachims. 2006. Training Linear SVMs in Linear Time. In *Proceedings of the 12th ACM SIGKDD international conference on Knowledge Discovery and Data mining*, KDD '06, pages 217–226.

Hisashi Kashima, Koji Tsuda, and Akihiro Inokuchi. 2003. Marginalized kernels between labeled graphs. In *Proceedings of the 20th International Conference on Machine Learning*, volume 3 of *ICML '03*, pages 321–328.

Taku Kudo and Yuji Matsumoto. 2004. A Boosting Algorithm for Classification of Semi-Structured Text. In *Proceedings of the 9th Conference on Empirical Methods in Natural Language Processing*, volume 4 of *EMNLP '04*, pages 301–308.

Taku Kudo, Eisaku Maeda, and Yuji Matsumoto. 2004. An application of boosting to graph classification. In *Advances in Neural Information Processing Systems 17*, NIPS '04, pages 729–736.

Leah S. Larkey and W. Bruce Croft. 1996. Combining Classifiers in Text Categorization. In *Proceedings of the 19th annual international ACM SIGIR conference on Research and development in information retrieval*, SIGIR '96, pages 289–297.

Pierre Mahé, Nobuhisa Ueda, Tatsuya Akutsu, Jean-Luc Perret, and Jean-Philippe Vert. 2004. Extensions of marginalized graph kernels. In *Proceedings of the 21st International Conference on Machine Learning*, ICML '04, pages 70–78.

Christopher D. Manning, Prabhakar Raghavan, and Hinrich Schütze. 2008. *Introduction to Information Retrieval*. Cambridge University Press, New York, NY, USA.

Alex Markov, Mark Last, and Abraham Kandel. 2007. Fast Categorization of Web Documents Represented by Graphs. In *Advances in Web Mining and Web Usage Analysis*, number 4811 in Lecture Notes in Artificial Intelligence, pages 56–71.

Shotaro Matsumoto, Hiroya Takamura, and Manabu Okumura. 2005. Sentiment Classification Using Word Sub-sequences and Dependency Sub-trees. In *Proceedings of the 9th Pacific-Asia Conference on Advances in Knowledge Discovery and Data Mining*, PAKDD '05, pages 301–311.

Andrew McCallum and Kamal Nigam. 1998. A comparison of event models for Naive Bayes text classification. In *Proceedings of the AAAI workshop on learning for text categorization*, AAAI '98, pages 41–48.

Rada Mihalcea and Paul Tarau. 2004. TextRank: Bringing Order into Texts. In *Proceedings of the 9th Conference on Empirical Methods in Natural Language Processing*, EMNLP '04, pages 404–411.

Siegfried Nijssen and Joost N. Kok. 2004. A Quickstart in Frequent Structure Mining Can Make a Difference. In *Proceedings of the 10th ACM SIGKDD international conference on Knowledge Discovery and Data mining*, KDD '04, pages 647–652.

Yukio Ohsawa, Nels E. Benson, and Masahiko Yachida. 1998. KeyGraph: Automatic Indexing by Co-occurrence Graph Based on Building Construction Metaphor. In *Proceedings of the Advances in Digital Libraries Conference*, ADL '98, pages 12–18.

Arzucan Özgür, Levent Özgür, and Tunga Güngör. 2005. Text Categorization with Class-based and Corpus-based Keyword Selection. In *Proceedings of the 20th International Conference on Computer and Information Sciences*, ISCIS '05, pages 606–615.

Fabian Pedregosa, Gaël Varoquaux, Alexandre Gramfort, Vincent Michel, Bertrand Thirion, Olivier Grisel, Mathieu Blondel, Peter Prettenhofer, Ron Weiss, Vincent Dubourg, J. Vanderplas, A. Passos, D. Cournapeau, M. Brucher, M. Perrot, and E. Duchesnay. 2011. Scikit-learn: Machine learning in Python. *The Journal of Machine Learning Research*, 12:2825–2830.

François Rousseau and Michalis Vazirgiannis. 2013. Graph-of-word and TW-IDF: New Approach to Ad Hoc IR. In *Proceedings of the 22nd ACM international conference on Information and knowledge management*, CIKM '13, pages 59–68.

François Rousseau and Michalis Vazirgiannis. 2015. Main Core Retention on Graph-of-words for Single-Document Keyword Extraction. In *Proceedings of the 37th European Conference on Information Retrieval*, ECIR '15, pages 382–393.

Hiroto Saigo, Sebastian Nowozin, Tadashi Kadowaki, Taku Kudo, and Koji Tsuda. 2009. gBoost: a mathematical programming approach to graph classification and regression. *Machine Learning*, 75(1):69–89.

Fabrizio Sebastiani. 2002. Machine Learning in Automated Text Categorization. *ACM Computing Surveys*, 34(1):1–47.

Stephen B. Seidman. 1983. Network structure and minimum degree. *Social Networks*, 5:269–287.

Nino Shervashidze. Visited on 30/05/2015. Graph kernels. http://www.di.ens.fr/~shervashidze/code.html.

Marisa Thoma, Hong Cheng, Arthur Gretton, Jiawei Han, Hans-Peter Kriegel, Alexander J. Smola, Le Song, Philip S. Yu, Xifeng Yan, and Karsten M. Borgwardt. 2009. Near-optimal Supervised Feature Selection among Frequent Subgraphs. In *Proceedings of the SIAM International Conference on Data Mining*, SDM '09, pages 1076–1087.

Robert Thorndike. 1953. Who belongs in the family? *Psychometrika*, 18(4):267–276.

S. V. N. Vishwanathan, Nicol N. Schraudolph, Risi Kondor, and Karsten M. Borgwardt. 2010. Graph kernels. *Journal of Machine Learning Research*, 11:1201–1242.

Xifeng Yan and Jiawei Han. 2002. gspan: Graph-based substructure pattern mining. In *Proceedings of the 2nd IEEE International Conference on Data Mining*, ICDM '02, pages 721–724.

Yiming Yang and Xin Liu. 1999. A Re-examination of Text Categorization Methods. In *Proceedings of the 22nd annual international ACM SIGIR conference on Research and development in information retrieval*, SIGIR '99, pages 42–49.

Yiming Yang and J. O. Pedersen. 1997. A Comparative Study on Feature Selection in Text Categorization. In *Proceedings of the 14th International Conference on Machine Learning*, ICML '97, pages 412–420.

Inverted indexing for cross-lingual NLP

Anders Søgaard* **Željko Agić*** **Héctor Martínez Alonso***
Barbara Plank* **Bernd Bohnet†** **Anders Johannsen***
*Center for Language Technology, University of Copenhagen, Denmark
†Google, London, United Kingdom
soegaard@hum.ku.dk

Abstract

We present a novel, count-based approach to obtaining inter-lingual word representations based on inverted indexing of Wikipedia. We present experiments applying these representations to 17 datasets in document classification, POS tagging, dependency parsing, and word alignment. Our approach has the advantage that it is simple, computationally efficient and almost parameter-free, and, more importantly, it enables multi-source cross-lingual learning. In 14/17 cases, we improve over using state-of-the-art bilingual embeddings.

1 Introduction

Linguistic resources are hard to come by and unevenly distributed across the world's languages. Consequently, transferring linguistic resources or knowledge from one language to another has been identified as an important research problem. Most work on cross-lingual transfer has used English as the source language. There are two reasons for this; namely, the availability of English resources and the availability of parallel data for (and translations between) English and most other languages.

In cross-lingual syntactic parsing, for example, two approaches to cross-lingual learning have been explored, namely annotation projection and delexicalized transfer. Annotation projection (Hwa et al., 2005) uses word-alignments in human translations to project predicted source-side analyses to the target language, producing a noisy syntactically annotated resource for the target language. On the other hand, delexicalized transfer (Zeman and Resnik, 2008; McDonald et al., 2011; Søgaard, 2011) simply removes lexical features from mono-lingual parsing models, but assumes reliable POS tagging for the target language. Delexicalized transfer works particularly well when resources from several source languages are used for training; learning from multiple other languages prevents over-fitting to the peculiarities of the source language. Some authors have also combined annotation projection and delexicalized transfer, e.g., McDonald et al. (2011). Others have tried to augment delexicalized transfer models with bilingual word representations (Täckström et al., 2013; Xiao and Guo, 2014).

In cross-lingual POS tagging, mostly annotation projection has been explored (Fossum and Abney, 2005; Das and Petrov, 2011), since all features in POS tagging models are typically lexical. However, using bilingual word representations was recently explored as an alternative to projection-based approaches (Gouws and Søgaard, 2015).

The major drawback of using bi-lexical representations is that it limits us to using a single source language. Täckström et al. (2013) obtained significant improvements using bilingual word clusters over a single source delexicalized transfer model, for example, but even better results were obtained with delexicalized transfer in McDonald et al. (2011) by simply using several source languages.

This paper introduces a simple method for obtaining *truly* inter-lingual word representations in order to train models with lexical features on several source languages at the same time. Briefly put, we represent words by their occurrence in clusters of Wikipedia articles linking to the same concept. Our representations are competitive with

Proceedings of the 53rd Annual Meeting of the Association for Computational Linguistics and the 7th International Joint Conference on Natural Language Processing, pages 1713–1722,
Beijing, China, July 26-31, 2015.

state-of-the-art neural net word embeddings when using only a single source language, but also enable us to exploit the availability of resources in multiple languages. This also makes it possible to explore multi-source transfer for POS tagging. We evaluate the method across POS tagging and dependency parsing datasets in four languages in the Google Universal Treebanks v. 1.0 (see §3.2.1), as well as two document classification datasets and four word alignment problems using a hand-aligned text. Finally, we also directly compare our results to Xiao and Guo (2014) on parsing data for four languages from CoNLL 2006 and 2007.

Contribution

- We present a novel approach to cross-lingual word representations with several advantages over existing methods: (a) It does not require training neural networks, (b) it does not rely on the availability of parallel data between source and target language, and (c) it enables multi-source transfer with lexical representations.
- We present an evaluation of our inter-lingual word representations, based on inverted indexing, across four tasks: document classification, POS tagging, dependency parsing, and word alignment, comparing our representations to two state-of-the-art neural net word embeddings. For the 17 datasets, for which we can make this comparison, our system is better than these embedding models on 14 datasets. The word representations are made publicly available at `https://bitbucket.org/lowlands/`

2 Distributional word representations

Most NLP models rely on lexical features. Encoding the presence of words leads to high-dimensional and sparse models. Also, simple bag-of-words models fail to capture the relatedness of words. In many tasks, synonymous words should be treated alike, but their bag-of-words representations are as different as those of *dog* and *therefore*.

Distributional word representations are supposed to capture distributional similarities between words. Intuitively, we want similar words to have similar representations. Known approaches focus on different kinds of similarity, some more syntactic, some more semantic. The representations are typically either clusters of distributionally similar words, e.g., Brown et al. (1992), or vector representations. In this paper, we focus on vector representations. In vector-based approaches, similar representations are vectors close in some multi-dimensional space.

2.1 Count-based and prediction-based representations

There are, briefly put, two approaches to inducing vector-based distributional word representations from large corpora: count-based and prediction-based approaches (Baroni et al., 2014). Count-based approaches represent words by their co-occurrences. Dimensionality reduction is typically performed on a raw or weighted co-occurrence matrix using methods such as singular value decomposition (SVD), a method for maximizing the variance in a dataset in few dimensions. In our inverted indexing, we use raw co-occurrence data.

Prediction-based methods use discriminative learning techniques to learn how to predict words from their context, or vice versa. They rely on a neural network architecture, and once the network converges, they use word representations from a middle layer as their distributional representations. Since the network learns to predict contexts from this representation, words occurring in the same contexts will get similar representations. In §2.1.2, we briefly introduce the skip-gram and CBOW models (Mikolov et al., 2013; Collobert and Weston, 2008).

Baroni et al. (2014) argue in favor of prediction-based representations, but provide little explanation why prediction-based representations should be better. One key finding, however, is that prediction-based methods tend to be more robust than count-based methods, and one reason for this seems to be better regularization.

2.1.1 Monolingual representations

Count-based representations rely on co-occurrence information in the form of binary matrices, raw counts, or point-wise mutual information (PMI). The PMI between two words is

$$P(w_i; w_j) = \log \frac{P(w_i \mid w_j)}{P(w_i)}$$

and PMI representations associate a word w_i with a vector of its PMIs with all other words w_j. Dimensionality reduction is typically performed using SVD. We will refer to two prediction-based approaches to learning word vectors, below: the

	KLEMENTIEV	CHANDAR	INVERTED
es			
coche ('car', NOUN)	approximately beyond upgrading	car bicycle cars	driving car cars
expressed ('expressed', VERB)	1.61 55.8 month-to-month	reiterates reiterating confirming	exists defining example
teléfono ('phone', NOUN)	alexandra davison creditor	phone telephone e-mail	phones phone telecommunication
árbol ('tree', NOUN)	tree market-oriented assassinate	tree bread wooden	tree trees grows
escribió ('wrote', VERB)	wrote alleges testified	wrote paul palace	wrote inspired inspiration
amarillo ('yellow', ADJ)	yellow louisiana 1911	crane grabs outfit	colors yellow oohs
de			
auto ('car', NOUN)			car cars camaro
ausgedrückt ('expressed', VERB)			adjective decimal imperative
fr			
voiture ('car', NOUN)			mercedes-benz cars quickest
exprimé ('expressed', VERB)			simultaneously instead possible
téléphone ('phone', NOUN)			phone create allowing
arbre ('tree', NOUN)			tree trees grows
écrit ('wrote', VERB)			published writers books
jaune ('yellow', ADJ)			classification yellow stages
sv			
bil ('car', NOUN)			cars car automobiles
uttryckte ('expressed', VERB)			rejected threatening unacceptable
telefon ('phone', NOUN)			telephones telephone share
träd ('tree', NOUN)			trees tree trunks
skrev ('wrote', VERB)			death wrote biography
gul ('yellow', ADJ)			greenish bluish colored

Table 1: Three nearest neighbors in the English training data of six words occurring in the Spanish test data, in the embeddings used in our experiments. Only 2/6 words were in the German data.

skip-gram model and CBOW. The two models both rely on three level architectures with input, output and a middle layer for intermediate target word representations. The major difference is that skip-gram uses the target word as input and the context as output, whereas the CBOW model does it the other way around. Learning goes by back-propagation, and random target words are used as negative examples. Levy and Goldberg (2014) show that prediction-based representations obtained with the skip-gram model can be related to count-based ones obtained with PMI. They argue that which is best, varies across tasks.

2.1.2 Bilingual representations

Klementiev et al. (2012) learn distinct embedding models for the source and target languages, but while learning to minimize the sum of the two models' losses, they jointly learn a regularizing interaction matrix, enforcing word pairs aligned in parallel text to have similar representations. Note that Klementiev et al. (2012) rely on word-aligned parallel text, and thereby on a large-coverage soft mapping of source words to target words. Other approaches rely on small coverage dictionaries with hard 1:1 mappings between words. Klementiev et al. (2012) do not use skip-gram or CBOW, but the language model presented in Bengio et al. (2003).

Chandar et al. (2014) also rely on sentence-aligned parallel text, but do not make use of word alignments. They begin with bag-of-words representations of source and target sentences. They then use an auto-encoder architecture. Auto-encoders for document classification typically try to reconstruct bag-of-words input vectors at the output layer, using back-propagation, passing the representation through a smaller middle layer. This layer then provides a dimensionality reduction. Chandar et al. (2014) instead replace the output layer with the target language bag-of-words reconstruction. In their final set-up, they simultaneously minimize the loss of a source-source, a target-target, a source-target, and a target-source auto-encoder, which corresponds to training a single auto-encoder with randomly chosen instances from source-target pairs. The bilingual word vectors can now be read off the auto-encoder's middle layer.

Xiao and Guo (2014) use a CBOW model and random target words as negative examples. The trick they introduce to learn bilingual embeddings, relies on a bilingual dictionary, in their case obtained from Wiktionary. They only use the unambiguous translation pairs for the source and target languages in question and simply force translation equivalents to have the same representation. This corresponds to replacing words from unambiguous translation pairs with a unique dummy symbol.

Gouws and Søgaard (2015) present a much simpler approach to learning prediction-based bilingual representations. They assume a list of source-target pivot word pairs that should obtain similar representations, i.e., translations or words with similar representations in some knowledge base. They then present a generative model for constructing a mixed language corpus by randomly selecting sentences from source and target corpora, and randomly replacing pivot words with their equivalent in the other language. They show that running the CBOW model on such a mixed corpus suffices to learn competitive bilingual embeddings. Like Xiao and Guo (2014), Gouws and Søgaard (2015) only use unambiguous translation pairs.

There has, to the best of our knowledge, been no previous work on count-based approaches to bilingual representations.

2.2 Inverted indexing

In this paper, we introduce a new count-based approach, INVERTED, to obtaining cross-lingual word representations using inverted indexing, comparing it with bilingual word representations learned using discriminative techniques. The main advantage of this approach, apart for its simplicity, is that it provides *truly* inter-lingual representations.

Our idea is simple. Wikipedia is a cross-lingual, crowd-sourced encyclopedia with more than 35 million articles written in different languages. At the time of writing, Wikipedia contains more than 10,000 articles in 129 languages. 52 languages had more than 100,000 articles. Several articles are written on the same topic, but in different languages, and these articles all link to the same node in the Wikipedia ontology, the same Wikipedia concept. If for a set of languages, we identify the common subset of Wikipedia concepts, we can thus describe each concept by the set of terms used in the corresponding articles. Each term set will include terms from each of the different languages.

We can now present a word by the corresponding row in the inverted indexing of this concept-to-term set matrix. Instead of representing a Wikipedia concept by the terms used across languages to describe it, we describe a word by the Wikipedia concepts it is used to describe. Note that because of the cross-lingual concepts, this vector representation is by definition cross-lingual. So, for example, if the word *glasses* is used in the English Wikipedia article on Harry Potter, and the English Wikipedia article on Google, and the word *Brille* occurs in the corresponding German ones, the two words are likely to get similar representations.

In our experiments, we use the common subset of available German, English, French, Spanish, and Swedish Wikipedia dumps.[1] We leave out words occurring in more than 5000 documents and perform dimensionality reduction using stochastic, two-pass, rank-reduced SVD - specifically, the latent semantic indexing implementation in Gensim using default parameters.[2]

2.3 Baseline embeddings

We use the word embedding models of Klementiev et al. (2012)[3] (KLEMENTIEV), and Chandar et al. (2014) (CHANDAR) as baselines in the experiments below. We also ran some of our experiments with the embeddings provided by Gouws and Søgaard (2015), but results were very similar to Chandar et al. (2014). We compare the nearest cross-language neighbors in the various representations in Table 1. Specifically, we selected five words from the Spanish test data and searched for its three nearest neighbors in KLEMENTIEV, CHANDAR and INVERTED. The nearest neighbors are presented left to right. We note that CHANDAR and INVERTED seem to contain less noise. KLEMENTIEV is the only model that relies on word-alignments. Whether the noise originates from alignments, or just model differences, is unclear to us.

2.4 Parameters of the word representation models

For KLEMENTIEV and CHANDAR, we rely on embeddings provided by the authors. The only parameter in inverted indexing is the fixed dimensionality in SVD. Our baseline models use 40 dimensions. In document classification, we also use 40 dimensions, but for POS tagging and dependency parsing, we tune the dimensionality parameter $\delta \in \{40, 80, 160\}$ on Spanish development data when possible. For document clas-

[1] https://sites.google.com/site/rmyeid/projects/polyglot

[2] http://radimrehurek.com/gensim/

[3] http://klementiev.org/data/distrib/

	TRAIN		TEST		TOKEN COVERAGE		
lang	data points	tokens	data points	tokens	KLEMENTIEV	CHANDAR	INVERTED
RCV – DOCUMENT CLASSIFICATION							
en	10000	–	–	–	0.314	0.314	0.779
de	–	–	4998	–	0.132	0.132	0.347
AMAZON – DOCUMENT CLASSIFICATION							
en	6000	–	–	–	0.314	0.314	0.779
de	–	–	6000	–	0.132	0.132	0.347
GOOGLE UNIVERSAL TREEBANKS – POS TAGGING & DEPENDENCY PARSING							
en	39.8k	950k	2.4k	56.7k	–	–	–
de	2.2k	30.4k	1.0k	16.3k	0.886	0.884	0.587
es	3.3k	94k	0.3k	8.3k	0.916	0.916	0.528
fr	3.3k	74.9k	0.3k	6.9k	0.888	0.888	0.540
sv	4.4k	66.6k	1.2k	20.3k	n/a	n/a	0.679
CONLL 07 – DEPENDENCY PARSING							
en	18.6	447k	–	–	–	–	–
es	–	–	206	5.7k	0.841	0.841	0.455
de	–	–	357	5.7k	0.616	0.612	0.294
sv	–	–	389	5.7k	n/a	n/a	0.561
EUROPARL – WORD ALIGNMENT							
en	–	–	100	–	0.370	0.370	0.370
es	–	–	100	–	0.533	0.533	0.533

Table 2: Characteristics of the data sets. Embeddings coverage (token-level) for KLEMENTIEV, CHANDAR and INVERTED on the test sets. We use the common vocabulary on WORD ALIGNMENT.

sification and word alignment, we fix the number of dimensions to 40. For both our baselines and systems, we also tune a scaling factor $\sigma \in \{1.0, 0.1, 0.01, 0.001\}$ for POS tagging and dependency parsing, using the scaling method from Turian et al. (2010), also used in Gouws and Søgaard (2015). We do not scale our embeddings for document classification or word alignment.

3 Experiments

The data set characteristics are found in Table 2.3.

3.1 Document classification

Data Our first document classification task is topic classification on the cross-lingual multi-domain sentiment analysis dataset AMAZON in Prettenhofer and Stein (2010).[4] We represent each document by the average of the representations of those words that we find both in the documents and in our embeddings. Rather than classifying reviews by sentiment, we classify by topic, trying to discriminate between book reviews, music reviews and DVD reviews, as a three-way classification problem, training on English and testing on German. Unlike in the other tasks below, we always use unscaled word representations, since these are our only features. All word representations have 40 dimensions.

The other document classification task is a four-way classification problem distinguishing between four topics in RCV corpus.[5] See Klementiev et al. (2012) for details. We use exactly the same set-up as for AMAZON.

Baselines We use the default parameters of the implementation of logistic regression in Sklearn as our baseline.[6] The feature representation is the average embedding of non-stopwords in KLEMENTIEV, resp., CHANDAR. Out-of-vocabulary words do not affect the feature representation of the documents.

System For our system, we replace the above neural net word embeddings with INVERTED representations. Again, out-of-vocabulary words do not affect the feature representation of the documents.

3.2 POS tagging

Data We use the coarse-grained part-of-speech annotations in the Google Universal Treebanks v. 1.0

[4] http://www.webis.de/research/corpora/

[5] http://www.ml4nlp.de/code-and-data

[6] http://scikit-learn.org/stable/

(McDonald et al., 2013).[7] Out of the languages in this set of treebanks, we focus on five languages (de, en, es, fr, sv), with English only used as training data. Those are all treebanks of significant size, but more importantly, we have baseline embeddings for four of these languages, as well as tag dictionaries (Li et al., 2012) needed for the POS tagging experiments.

Baselines One baseline method is a type-constrained structured perceptron with only ortographic features, which are expected to transfer across languages. The type constraints come from Wiktionary, a crowd-sourced tag dictionary.[8] Type constraints from Wiktionary were first used by Li et al. (2012), but note that their set-up is unsupervised learning. Täckström et al. (2013) also used type constraints in a supervised set-up. Our learning algorithm is the structured perceptron algorithm originally proposed by Collins (2002). In our POS tagging experiments, we always do 10 passes over the data. We also present two other baselines, where we augment the feature representation with different embeddings for the target word, KLEMENTIEV and CHANDAR. With all the embeddings in POS tagging, we assign a mean vector to out-of-vocabulary words.

System For our system, we simply augment the delexicalized POS tagger with the INVERTED distributional representation of the current word. The best parameter setting on Spanish development data was $\sigma = 0.01, \delta = 160$.

3.3 Dependency parsing

Data We use the same treebanks from the Google Universal Treebanks v. 1.0 as used in our POS tagging experiments. We again use the Spanish development data for parameter tuning. For compatibility with Xiao and Guo (2014), we also present results on CoNLL 2006 and 2007 treebanks for languages for which we had baseline and system word representations (de, es, sv). Our parameter settings for these experiments were the same as those tuned on the Spanish development data from the Google Universal Treebanks v. 1.0.

Baselines The most obvious baseline in our experiments is delexicalized transfer (DELEX) (McDonald et al., 2011; Søgaard, 2011). This baseline system simply learns models without lexical features. We use a modified version of the first-order Mate parser (Bohnet, 2010) that also takes continuous-valued embeddings as input an disregards features that include lexical items.

For our embeddings baselines, we augment the feature space by adding embedding vectors for head h and dependent d. We experimented with different versions of combining embedding vectors, from firing separate h and d per-dimension features (Bansal et al., 2014) to combining their information. We found that combining the embeddings of h and d is effective and consistently use the absolute difference between the embedding vectors, since that worked better than addition and multiplication on development data.

Delexicalized transfer (DELEX) uses three (3) iterations over the data in both the single-source and the multi-source set-up, a parameter set on the Spanish development data. The remaining parameters were obtained by averaging over performance with different embeddings on the Spanish development data, obtaining: $\sigma = 0.005, \delta = 20, i = 3$, and absolute difference for vector combination. With all the embeddings in dependency parsing, we assign a POS-specific mean vector to out-of-vocabulary words, i.e., the mean of vectors for words with the input word's POS.

System We use the same parameters as those used for our baseline systems. In the single-source set-up, we use absolute difference for combining vectors, while addition in the multi-source set-up.

3.4 Word alignment

Data We use the manually word-aligned English-Spanish Europarl data from Graca et al. (2008). The dataset contains 100 sentences. The annotators annotated whether word alignments were certain or possible, and we present results with *all* word alignments and with only the certain ones. See Graca et al. (2008) for details.

Baselines For word alignment, we simply align every aligned word in the gold data, for which we have a word embedding, to its (Euclidean) nearest neighbor in the target sentence. We evaluate this strategy by its precision (P@1).

System We compare INVERTED with KLEMENTIEV and CHANDAR. To ensure a fair comparison, we use the subset of words covered by all three embeddings.

[7] `http://code.google.com/p/uni-dep-tb/`

[8] `https://code.google.com/p/wikily-supervised-pos-tagger/`

		de	es	fr	sv	av-sv
		EN→TARGET				
EMBEDS	K12	80.20	73.16	47.69	-	67.02
	C14	74.85	83.03	48.24	-	68.71
INVERTED	SVD	**81.18**	82.12	49.68	78.72	70.99
		MULTI-SOURCE→TARGET				
INVERTED	SVD	80.10	**84.69**	49.68	78.72	70.66

Table 4: POS tagging (accuracies), K12: KLEMENTIEV, C14: CHANDAR. Parameters tuned on development data: $\sigma = 0.01, \delta = 160$. Iterations not tuned ($i = 10$). Averages do not include Swedish, for comparability.

Dataset	KLEMENTIEV	CHANDAR	INVERTED
AMAZON	0.32	0.36	**0.49**
RCV	0.75	**0.90**	0.55

Table 3: Document classification results (F_1-scores)

		UAS		
		de	es	sv
		EN→TARGET		
DELEX	-	44.78	47.07	56.75
DELEX-XIAO	-	46.24	52.05	57.79
EMBEDS	K12	44.77	47.31	-
	C14	44.32	47.56	
INVERTED	-	45.01	47.45	56.15
XIAO	-	49.54	55.72	61.88

Table 6: Dependency parsing for CoNLL 2006/2007 datasets. Parameters same as on the Google Universal Treebanks.

4 Results

4.1 Document classification

Our document classification results in Table 3 are mixed, but we note that both Klementiev et al. (2012) and Chandar et al. (2014) developed their methods using development data from the RCV corpus. It is therefore not surprising that they obtain good results on this data. On AMAZON, INVERTED is superior to both KLEMENTIEV and CHANDAR.

4.2 POS tagging

In POS tagging, INVERTED leads to significant improvements over using KLEMENTIEV and CHANDAR. See Table 4 for results. Somewhat surprisingly, we see no general gain from using multiple source languages. This is very different from what has been observed in dependency parsing (McDonald et al., 2011), but may be explained by treebank sizes, language similarity, or the noise introduced by the word representations.

4.3 Dependency parsing

In dependency parsing, distributional word representations do not lead to significant improvements, but while KLEMENTIEV and CHANDAR hurt performance, the INVERTED representations lead to small improvements on some languages. The fact that improvements are primarily seen on Spanish suggest that our approach is parameter-sensitive. This is in line with previous observations that count-based methods are more parameter-sensitive than prediction-based ones (Baroni et al., 2014).

For comparability with Xiao and Guo (2014), we also did experiments with the CoNLL 2006 and CoNLL 2007 datasets for which we had embeddings (Table 6). Again, we see little effects from using the word representations, and we also see that our baseline model is weaker than the one in Xiao and Guo (2014) (DELEX-XIAO). See §5 for further discussion.

4.4 Word alignment

The word alignment results are presented in Table 7. On the certain alignments, we see an accuracy of more than 50% with INVERTED in one case. KLEMENTIEV and CHANDAR have the advantage of having been trained on the English-Spanish Europarl data, but nevertheless we see consistent improvements with INVERTED over their off-the-shelf embeddings.

		UAS				LAS			
		de	es	fr	sv	de	es	fr	sv
EN→TARGET									
DELEX	-	56.26	62.11	64.30	66.61	48.24	53.01	54.98	56.93
EMBEDS	K12	56.47	61.92	61.51	-	48.26	52.88	51.76	-
	C14	56.19	61.97	62.95	-	48.11	52.97	53.90	-
INVERTED	-	56.18	61.71	63.81	66.54	48.82	53.04	54.81	57.18
MULTI-SOURCE→TARGET									
DELEX	-	**56.80**	63.21	66.00	**67.49**	**49.32**	54.77	56.53	**57.86**
INVERTED	-	56.56	**64.03**	**66.22**	67.32	48.82	**55.03**	**56.79**	57.70

Table 5: Dependency parsing results on the Universal Treebanks (unlabeled and labeled attachment scores). Parameters tuned on development data: $\sigma = 0.005, \delta = 20, i = 3$.

	KLEMENTIEV	CHANDAR	INVERTED
EN-ES (S+P)	0.20	0.24	**0.25**
ES-EN (S+P)	0.35	0.32	**0.41**
EN-ES (S)	0.20	**0.25**	**0.25**
ES-EN (S)	0.38	0.39	**0.53**

Table 7: Word alignment results (P@1). S=sure (certain) alignments. P=possible alignments.

5 Related Work

As noted in §1, there has been some work on learning word representations for cross-lingual parsing lately. Täckström et al. (2013) presented a bilingual clustering algorithm and used the word clusters to augment a delexicalized transfer baseline. Bansal et al. (2014), in the context of monolingual dependency parsing, investigate continuous word representation for dependency parsing in a monolingual cross-domain setup and compare them to word clusters. However, to make the embeddings work, they had to i) bucket real values and perform hierarchical clustering on them, ending up with word clusters very similar to those of Täckström et al. (2013); ii) use syntactic context to estimate embeddings. In the cross-lingual setting, syntactic context is not available for the target language, but doing clustering on top of inverted indexing is an interesting option we did not explore in this paper.

Xiao and Guo (2014) is, to the best of our knowledge, the only parser using bilingual embeddings for unsupervised cross-lingual parsing. They evaluate their models on CoNLL 2006 and CoNLL 2007, and we compare our results to theirs in §4. They obtain much better relative improvements on dependency parsing that we do - comparable to those we observe in document classification and POS tagging. It is not clear to us what is the explanation for this improvement. The approach relies on a bilingual dictionary as in Klementiev et al. (2012) and Gouws and Søgaard (2015), but none of these embeddings led to improvements. Unfortunately, we did not have the code or embeddings of Xiao and Guo (2014). One possible explanation is that they use the embeddings in a very different way in the parser. They use the MSTParser. Unfortunately, they do not say exactly how they combine the embeddings with their baseline feature model.

The idea of using inverted indexing in Wikipedia for modelling language is not entirely new either. In cross-lingual information retrieval, this technique, sometimes referred to as *explicit semantic analysis*, has been used to measure source and target language document relatedness (Potthast et al., 2008; Sorg and Cimiano, 2008). Gabrilovich and Markovitch (2009) also use this technique to model documents, and they evaluate their method on text categorization and on computing the degree of semantic relatedness between text fragments. See also Müller and Gurevych (2009) for an application of explicit semantic analysis to modelling documents. This line of work is very different from ours, and to the best of our knowledge, we are the first to propose to use inverted indexing of Wikipedia for cross-lingual word representations.

6 Conclusions

We presented a simple, scalable approach to obtaining cross-lingual word representations that enables multi-source learning. We compared these representations to two state-of-the-art approaches to neural net word embeddings across four tasks and 17 datasets, obtaining better results than *both* approaches in 14/17 of these cases.

References

Mohit Bansal, Kevin Gimpel, and Karen Livescu. 2014. Tailoring continuous word representations for dependency parsing. In *ACL*.

Marco Baroni, Georgiana Dinu, and Germán Kruszewski. 2014. Don't count, predict! a systematic comparison of context-counting vs. context-predicting semantic vectors. In *ACL*.

Yoshua Bengio, Réjean Ducharme, Pascal Vincent, and Christian Janvin. 2003. A neural probabilistic language model. *The Journal of Machine Learning Research*, 3:1137–1155.

Bernd Bohnet. 2010. Top accuracy and fast dependency parsing is not a contradiction. In *COLING*.

Peter F Brown, Peter V Desouza, Robert L Mercer, Vincent J Della Pietra, and Jenifer C Lai. 1992. Class-based n-gram models of natural language. *Computational linguistics*, 18(4):467–479.

Sarath Chandar, Stanislas Lauly, Hugo Larochelle, Mitesh Khapra, Balaraman Ravindran, Vikas C Raykar, and Amrita Saha. 2014. An autoencoder approach to learning bilingual word representations. In *NIPS*.

Michael Collins. 2002. Discriminative Training Methods for Hidden Markov Models: Theory and Experiments with Perceptron Algorithms. In *EMNLP*.

Ronan Collobert and Jason Weston. 2008. A unified architecture for natural language processing: Deep neural networks with multitask learning. In *ICML*.

Dipanjan Das and Slav Petrov. 2011. Unsupervised part-of-speech tagging with bilingual graph-based projections. In *ACL*.

Victoria Fossum and Steven Abney. 2005. Automatically inducing a part-of-speech tagger by projecting from multiple source languages across aligned corpora. In *IJCNLP*.

Evgeniy Gabrilovich and Shaul Markovitch. 2009. Wikipedia-based semantic interpretation for natural language processing. *Journal of Artificial Intelligence Research*, pages 443–498.

Stephan Gouws and Anders Søgaard. 2015. Simple task-specific bilingual word embeddings. In *NAACL*.

Joao Graca, Joana Pardal, Luísa Coheur, and Diamantino Caseiro. 2008. Building a golden collection of parallel multi-language word alignments. In *LREC*.

Rebecca Hwa, Philip Resnik, Amy Weinberg, Clara Cabezas, and Okan Kolak. 2005. Bootstrapping parsers via syntactic projection across parallel texts. *Natural Language Engineering*, 11(3):311–325.

Alexandre Klementiev, Ivan Titov, and Binod Bhattarai. 2012. Inducing crosslingual distributed representations of words. In *COLING*.

Omer Levy and Yoav Goldberg. 2014. Dependency-based word embeddings. In *ACL*.

Shen Li, João Graça, and Ben Taskar. 2012. Wiki-ly supervised part-of-speech tagging. In *EMNLP*.

Ryan McDonald, Slav Petrov, and Keith Hall. 2011. Multi-source transfer of delexicalized dependency parsers. In *EMNLP*.

Ryan McDonald, Joakim Nivre, Yvonne Quirmbach-Brundage, Yoav Goldberg, Dipanjan Das, Kuzman Ganchev, Keith Hall, Slav Petrov, Hao Zhang, Oscar Täckström, Claudia Bedini, Núria Bertomeu Castelló, and Jungmee Lee. 2013. Universal dependency annotation for multilingual parsing. In *ACL*.

Tomas Mikolov, Ilya Sutskever, Kai Chen, Gregory Corrado, and Jeffrey Dean. 2013. Distributed representations of words and phrases and their compositionality. In *NIPS*.

Christof Müller and Iryna Gurevych. 2009. A study on the semantic relatedness of query and document terms in information retrieval. In *EMNLP*.

Martin Potthast, Benno Stein, and Maik Anderka. 2008. A wikipedia-based multilingual retrieval model. In *Advances in Information Retrieval*.

Peter Prettenhofer and Benno Stein. 2010. Cross-language text classification using structural correspondence learning. In *ACL*.

Anders Søgaard. 2011. Data point selection for cross-language adaptation of dependency parsers. In *Proceedings of ACL*.

Philipp Sorg and Philipp Cimiano. 2008. Cross-lingual information retrieval with explicit semantic analysis. In *Working Notes for the CLEF 2008 Workshop*.

Oscar Täckström, Dipanjan Das, Slav Petrov, Ryan McDonald, and Joakim Nivre. 2013. Token and type constraints for cross-lingual part-of-speech tagging. *TACL*, 1:1–12.

Joseph Turian, Lev Ratinov, and Yoshua Bengio. 2010. Word representations: a simple and general method for semi-supervised learning. In *ACL*.

Min Xiao and Yuhong Guo. 2014. Distributed word representation learning for cross-lingual dependency parsing. In *CoNLL*.

Daniel Zeman and Philip Resnik. 2008. Cross-language parser adaptation between related languages. In *IJCNLP*.

Multi-Task Learning for Multiple Language Translation

Daxiang Dong, Hua Wu, Wei He, Dianhai Yu and Haifeng Wang
Baidu Inc, Beijing, China
{dongdaxiang, wu_hua, hewei06, yudianhai, wanghaifeng}@baidu.com

Abstract

In this paper, we investigate the problem of learning a machine translation model that can simultaneously translate sentences from one source language to multiple target languages. Our solution is inspired by the recently proposed neural machine translation model which generalizes machine translation as a sequence learning problem. We extend the neural machine translation to a multi-task learning framework which shares source language representation and separates the modeling of different target language translation. Our framework can be applied to situations where either large amounts of parallel data or limited parallel data is available. Experiments show that our multi-task learning model is able to achieve significantly higher translation quality over individually learned model in both situations on the data sets publicly available.

1 Introduction

Translation from one source language to multiple target languages at the same time is a difficult task for humans. A person often needs to be familiar with specific translation rules for different language pairs. Machine translation systems suffer from the same problems too. Under the current classic statistical machine translation framework, it is hard to share information across different phrase tables among different language pairs. Translation quality decreases rapidly when the size of training corpus for some minority language pairs becomes smaller. To conquer the problems described above, we propose a multi-task learning framework based on a sequence learning model to conduct machine translation from one source language to multiple target languages, inspired by the recently proposed neural machine translation(NMT) framework proposed by Bahdanau et al. (2014). Specifically, we extend the recurrent neural network based encoder-decoder framework to a multi-task learning model that shares an encoder across all language pairs and utilize a different decoder for each target language.

The neural machine translation approach has recently achieved promising results in improving translation quality. Different from conventional statistical machine translation approaches, neural machine translation approaches aim at learning a radically end-to-end neural network model to optimize translation performance by generalizing machine translation as a sequence learning problem. Based on the neural translation framework, the lexical sparsity problem and the long-range dependency problem in traditional statistical machine translation can be alleviated through neural networks such as long short-term memory networks which provide great lexical generalization and long-term sequence memorization abilities.

The basic assumption of our proposed framework is that many languages differ lexically but are closely related on the semantic and/or the syntactic levels. We explore such correlation across different target languages and realize it under a multi-task learning framework. We treat a separate translation direction as a sub RNN encode-decoder task in this framework which shares the same encoder (i.e. the same source language representation) across different translation directions, and use a different decoder for each specific target language. In this way, this proposed multi-task learning model can make full use of the source language corpora across different language pairs. Since the encoder part shares the same source language representation

Proceedings of the 53rd Annual Meeting of the Association for Computational Linguistics and the 7th International Joint Conference on Natural Language Processing, pages 1723–1732,
Beijing, China, July 26-31, 2015.

across all the translation tasks, it may learn semantic and structured predictive representations that can not be learned with only a small amount of data. Moreover, during training we jointly model the alignment and the translation process simultaneously for different language pairs under the same framework. For example, when we simultaneously translate from English into Korean and Japanese, we can jointly learn latent similar semantic and structure information across Korea and Japanese because these two languages share some common language structures.

The contribution of this work is three folds. First, we propose a unified machine learning framework to explore the problem of translating one source language into multiple target languages. To the best of our knowledge, this problem has not been studied carefully in the statistical machine translation field before. Second, given large-scale training corpora for different language pairs, we show that our framework can improve translation quality on each target language as compared with the neural translation model trained on a single language pair. Finally, our framework is able to alleviate the data scarcity problem, using language pairs with large-scale parallel training corpora to improve the translation quality of those with few parallel training corpus.

The following sections will be organized as follows: in section 2, related work will be described, and in section 3, we will describe our multi-task learning method. Experiments that demonstrate the effectiveness of our framework will be described in section 4. Lastly, we will conclude our work in section 5.

2 Related Work

Statistical machine translation systems often rely on large-scale parallel and monolingual training corpora to generate translations of high quality. Unfortunately, statistical machine translation system often suffers from data sparsity problem due to the fact that phrase tables are extracted from the limited bilingual corpus. Much work has been done to address the data sparsity problem such as the pivot language approach (Wu and Wang, 2007; Cohn and Lapata, 2007) and deep learning techniques (Devlin et al., 2014; Gao et al., 2014; Sundermeyer et al., 2014; Liu et al., 2014).

On the problem of how to translate one source language to many target languages within one model, few work has been done in statistical machine translation. A related work in SMT is the pivot language approach for statistical machine translation which uses a commonly used language as a "bridge" to generate source-target translation for language pair with few training corpus. Pivot based statistical machine translation is crucial in machine translation for resource-poor language pairs, such as Spanish to Chinese. Considering the problem of translating one source language to many target languages, pivot based SMT approaches does work well given a large-scale source language to pivot language bilingual corpus and large-scale pivot language to target languages corpus. However, in reality, language pairs between English and many other target languages may not be large enough, and pivot-based SMT sometimes fails to handle this problem. Our approach handles one to many target language translation in a different way that we directly learn an end to multi-end translation system that does not need a pivot language based on the idea of neural machine translation.

Neural Machine translation is a emerging new field in machine translation, proposed by several work recently (Kalchbrenner and Blunsom, 2013; Sutskever et al., 2014; Bahdanau et al., 2014), aiming at end-to-end machine translation without phrase table extraction and language model training. Different from traditional statistical machine translation, neural machine translation encodes a variable-length source sentence with a recurrent neural network into a fixed-length vector representation and decodes it with another recurrent neural network from a fixed-length vector into variable-length target sentence. A typical model is the RNN encoder-decoder approach proposed by Bahdanau et al. (2014), which utilizes a bidirectional recurrent neural network to compress the source sentence information and fits the conditional probability of words in target languages with a recurrent manner. Moreover, soft alignment parameters are considered in this model. As a specific example model in this paper, we adopt a RNN encoder-decoder neural machine translation model for multi-task learning, though all neural network based model can be adapted in our framework.

In the natural language processing field, a

notable work related with multi-task learning was proposed by Collobert et al. (2011) which shared common representation for input words and solve different traditional NLP tasks such as part-of-Speech tagging, name entity recognition and semantic role labeling within one framework, where the convolutional neural network model was used. Hatori et al. (2012) proposed to jointly train word segmentation, POS tagging and dependency parsing, which can also be seen as a multi-task learning approach. Similar idea has also been proposed by Li et al. (2014) in Chinese dependency parsing. Most of multi-task learning or joint training frameworks can be summarized as parameter sharing approaches proposed by Ando and Zhang (2005) where they jointly trained models and shared center parameters in NLP tasks. Researchers have also explored similar approaches (Sennrich et al., 2013; Cui et al., 2013) in statistical machine translation which are often refered as domain adaption. Our work explores the possibility of machine translation under the multi-task framework by using the recurrent neural networks. To the best of our knowledge, this is the first trial of end to end machine translation under multi-task learning framework.

3 Multi-task Model for Multiple Language Translation

Our model is a general framework for translating from one source language to many targets. The model we build in this section is a recurrent neural network based encoder-decoder model with multiple target tasks, and each task is a specific translation direction. Different tasks share the same translation encoder across different language pairs. We will describe model details in this section.

3.1 Objective Function

Given a pair of training sentence $\{\mathbf{x}, \mathbf{y}\}$, a standard recurrent neural network based encoder-decoder machine translation model fits a parameterized model to maximize the conditional probability of a target sentence $\mathbf{y}$ given a source sentence $\mathbf{x}$, i.e., $\operatorname{argmax} p(\mathbf{y}|\mathbf{x})$. We extend this into multiple languages setting. In particular, suppose we want to translate from English to many different languages, for instance, French(Fr), Dutch(Nl), Spanish(Es). Parallel training data will be collected before training, i.e. En-Fr, En-Nl, En-Es parallel sentences. Since the English representation of the three language pairs is shared in one encoder, the objective function we optimize is the summation of several conditional probability terms conditioned on representation generated from the same encoder.

$$L(\Theta) = \underset{\Theta}{\operatorname{argmax}}(\sum_{T_p}(\frac{1}{N_p}\sum_{i}^{N_p}\log p(\mathbf{y_i}^{T_p}|\mathbf{x_i}^{T_p};\Theta)) \quad (1)$$

where $\Theta = \{\Theta_{src}, \Theta_{trg_{T_p}}, T_p = 1, 2, \cdots, T_m\}$, Θ_{src} is a collection of parameters for source encoder. And $\Theta_{trg_{T_p}}$ is the parameter set of the T_pth target language. N_p is the size of parallel training corpus of the pth language pair. For different target languages, the target encoder parameters are seperated so we have T_m decoders to optimize. This parameter sharing strategy makes different language pairs maintain the same semantic and structure information of the source language and learn to translate into target languages in different decoders.

3.2 Model Details

Suppose we have several language pairs $(\mathbf{x}^{T_p}, \mathbf{y}^{T_p})$ where T_p denotes the index of the T_pth language pair. For a specific language pair, given a sequence of source sentence input $(x_1^{T_p}, x_2^{T_p}, \cdots, x_n^{T_p})$, the goal is to jointly maximize the conditional probability for each generated target word. The probability of generating the tth target word is estimated as:

$$p(y_t^{T_p}|y_1^{T_p}, \cdots, y_{t-1}^{T_p}, \mathbf{x}^{T_p}) = g(y_{t-1}^{T_p}, s_t^{T_p}, c_t^{T_p}) \quad (2)$$

where the function g is parameterized by a feedforward neural network with a softmax output layer. And g can be viewed as a probability predictor with neural networks. $s_t^{T_p}$ is a recurrent neural network hidden state at time t, which can be estimated as:

$$s_t^{T_p} = f(s_{t-1}^{T_p}, y_{t-1}^{T_p}, c_t^{T_p}) \quad (3)$$

the context vector $c_t^{T_p}$ depends on a sequence of annotations $(h_1, \cdots, h_{L_x})$ to which an encoder maps the input sentence, where L_x is the number of tokens in $\mathbf{x}$. Each annotation h_i is a bidirectional recurrent representation with forward and backward sequence information around the ith word.

$$\mathbf{c_t}^{T_p} = \sum_{j=1}^{L_x} a_{ij}^{T_p} \mathbf{h_j} \quad (4)$$

where the weight $a_{tj}^{T_p}$ is a scalar computed by

$$a_{tj}^{T_p} = \frac{exp(e_{tj}^{T_p})}{\sum_{k=1}^{L_x^{T_p}} exp(e_{tk}^{T_p})} \quad (5)$$

$$e_{tj}^{T_p} = \phi(\mathbf{s_{t-1}}^{T_p}, \mathbf{h_j}) \quad (6)$$

$a_{tj}^{T_p}$ is a normalized score of e_{tj} which is a soft alignment model measuring how well the input context around the jth word and the output word in the tth position match. e_{tj} is modeled through a perceptron-like function:

$$\phi(\mathbf{x}, \mathbf{y}) = \mathbf{v}^T tanh(\mathbf{Wx} + \mathbf{Uy}) \quad (7)$$

To compute $\mathbf{h_j}$, a bidirectional recurrent neural network is used. In the bidirectional recurrent neural network, the representation of a forward sequence and a backward sequence of the input sentence is estimated and concatenated to be a single vector. This concatenated vector can be used to translate multiple languages during the test time.

$$\mathbf{h_j} = [\overrightarrow{\mathbf{h_j}}; \overleftarrow{\mathbf{h_j}}]^T \quad (8)$$

From a probabilistic perspective, our model is able to learn the conditional distribution of several target languages given the same source corpus. Thus, the recurrent encoder-decoders are jointly trained with several conditional probabilities added together. As for the bidirectional recurrent neural network module, we adopt the recently proposed gated recurrent neural network (Cho et al., 2014). The gated recurrent neural network is shown to have promising results in several sequence learning problem such as speech recognition and machine translation where input and output sequences are of variable length. It is also shown that the gated recurrent neural network has the ability to address the gradient vanishing problem compared with the traditional recurrent neural network, and thus the long-range dependency problem in machine translation can be handled well. In our multi-task learning framework, the parameters of the gated recurrent neural network in the encoder are shared, which is formulated as follows.

$$\mathbf{h_t} = (\mathbf{I} - \mathbf{z_t}) \odot \mathbf{h_{t-1}} + \mathbf{z_t} \odot \hat{\mathbf{h_t}} \quad (9)$$

$$\mathbf{z_t} = \sigma(\mathbf{W_z x_t} + \mathbf{U_z h_{t-1}}) \quad (10)$$

$$\hat{\mathbf{h_t}} = tanh(\mathbf{Wx_t} + \mathbf{U}(\mathbf{r_t} \odot \mathbf{h_{t-1}})) \quad (11)$$

$$\mathbf{r_t} = \sigma(\mathbf{W_r x_t} + \mathbf{U_r h_{t-1}}) \quad (12)$$

Where $\mathbf{I}$ is identity vector and $\odot$ denotes element wise product between vectors. $tanh(x)$ and $\sigma(x)$ are nonlinear transformation functions that can be applied element-wise on vectors. The recurrent computation procedure is illustrated in 1, where x_t denotes one-hot vector for the tth word in a sequence.

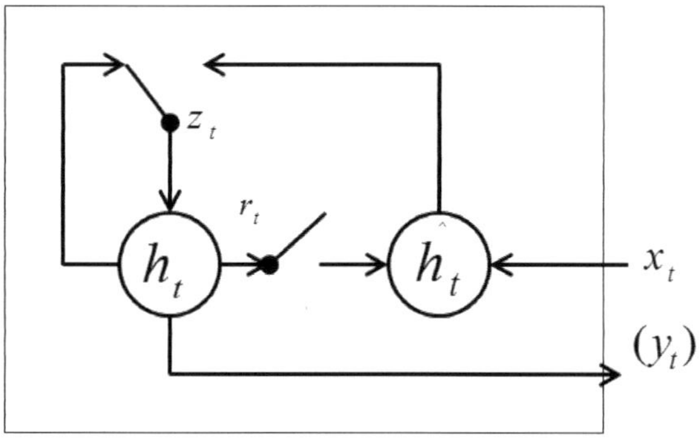

Figure 1: Gated recurrent neural network computation, where r_t is a reset gate responsible for memory unit elimination, and z_t can be viewed as a soft weight between current state information and history information.

$$\tanh(x) = \frac{e^x - e^{-x}}{e^x + e^{-x}} \quad (13)$$

$$\sigma(x) = \frac{1}{1 + e^{-x}} \quad (14)$$

The overall model is illustrated in Figure 2 where the multi-task learning framework with four target languages is demonstrated. The soft alignment parameters A_i for each encoder-decoder are different and only the bidirectional recurrent neural network representation is shared.

3.3 Optimization

The optimization approach we use is the mini-batch stochastic gradient descent approach (Bottou, 1991). The only difference between our optimization and the commonly used stochastic gradient descent is that we learn several mini-batches within a fixed language pair for several mini-batch iterations and then move onto the next language pair. Our optimization procedure is shown in Figure 3.

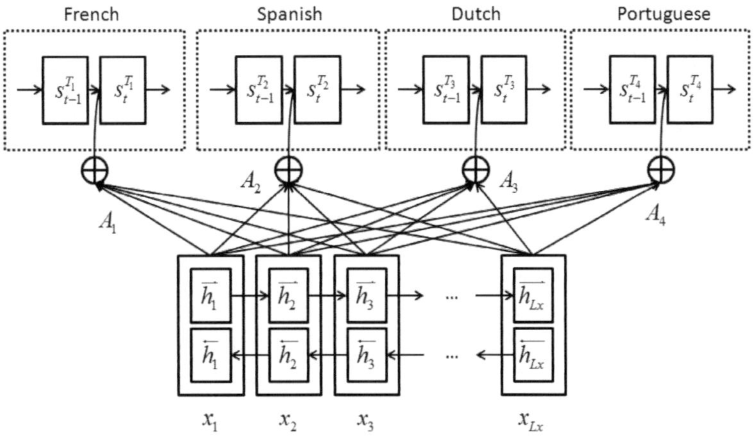

Figure 2: Multi-task learning framework for multiple-target language translation

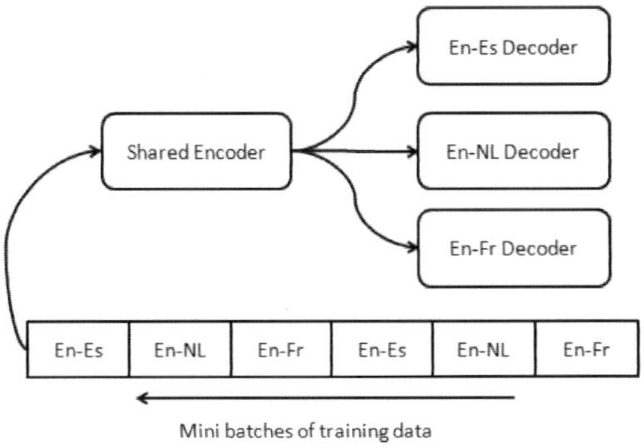

Figure 3: Optimization for end to multi-end model

3.4 Translation with Beam Search

Although parallel corpora are available for the encoder and the decoder modeling in the training phrase, the ground truth is not available during test time. During test time, translation is produced by finding the most likely sequence via beam search.

$$\hat{\mathbf{Y}} = \operatorname*{argmax}_{\mathbf{Y}} p(\mathbf{Y}^{T_p}|\mathbf{S}^{T_p}) \tag{15}$$

Given the target direction we want to translate to, beam search is performed with the shared encoder and a specific target decoder where search space belongs to the decoder T_p. We adopt beam search algorithm similar as it is used in SMT system (Koehn, 2004) except that we only utilize scores produced by each decoder as features. The size of beam is 10 in our experiments for speedup consideration. Beam search is ended until the end-of-sentence **eos** symbol is generated.

4 Experiments

We conducted two groups of experiments to show the effectiveness of our framework. The goal of the first experiment is to show that multi-task learning helps to improve translation performance given enough training corpora for all language pairs. In the second experiment, we show that for some resource-poor language pairs with a few parallel training data, their translation performance could be improved as well.

4.1 Dataset

The Europarl corpus is a multi-lingual corpus including 21 European languages. Here we only choose four language pairs for our experiments. The source language is English for all language pairs. And the target languages are Spanish (Es), French (Fr), Portuguese (Pt) and Dutch (Nl). To demonstrate the validity of our learning framework, we do some preprocessing on the training set. For the source language, we use 30k of the most frequent words for source language vocabulary which is shared across different language pairs and 30k most frequent words for each target language. Out-of-vocabulary words are denoted as unknown words, and we maintain different unknown word labels for different languages. For test sets, we also restrict all words in the test set to be from our training vocabulary and mark the OOV words as the corresponding labels as in the training data. The size of training corpus in experiment 1 and 2 is listed in Table 1 where

Training Data Information						
Lang	En-Es	En-Fr	En-Nl	En-Pt	En-Nl-sub	En-Pt-sub
Sent size	1,965,734	2,007,723	1,997,775	1,960,407	300,000	300,000
Src tokens	49,158,635	50,263,003	49,533,217	49,283,373	8,362,323	8,260,690
Trg tokens	51,622,215	52,525,000	50,661,711	54,996,139	8,590,245	8,334,454

Table 1: Size of training corpus for different language pairs

En-Nl-sub and En-Pt-sub are sub-sampled data set of the full corpus. The full parallel training corpus is available from the EuroParl corpus, downloaded from EuroParl public websites[1]. We mimic the situation that there are only a small-scale parallel corpus available for some language pairs by randomly sub-sampling the training data. The parallel corpus of English-Portuguese and English-Dutch are sub-sampled to approximately 15% of the full corpus size. We select two data sets as our test data. One is the EuroParl Common test set[2] in European Parliament Corpus, the other is WMT 2013 data set[3]. For WMT 2013, only En-Fr, En-Es are available and we evaluate the translation performance only on these two test sets. Information of test sets is shown in Table 2.

Language pair	En-Es	En-Fr	En-Nl	En-Pt
Common test	1755	1755	1755	1755
WMT2013	3000	3000	-	-

Table 2: Size of test set in EuroParl Common testset and WMT2013

4.2 Training Details

Our model is trained on Graphic Processing Unit K40. Our implementation is based on the open source deep learning package Theano (Bastien et al., 2012) so that we do not need to take care about gradient computations. During training, we randomly shuffle our parallel training corpus for each language pair at each epoch of our learning process. The optimization algorithm and model hyper parameters are listed below.

- Initialization of all parameters are from uniform distribution between -0.01 and 0.01.
- We use stochastic gradient descent with recently proposed learning rate decay strategy Ada-Delta (Zeiler, 2012).
- Mini batch size in our model is set to 50 so that the convergence speed is fast.
- We train 1000 mini batches of data in one language pair before we switch to the next language pair.
- For word representation dimensionality, we use 1000 for both source language and target language.
- The size of hidden layer is set to 1000.

We trained our multi-task model with a multi-GPU implementation due to the limitation of Graphic memory. And each target decoder is trained within one GPU card, and we synchronize our source encoder every 1000 batches among all GPU card. Our model costs about 72 hours on full large parallel corpora training until convergence and about 24 hours on partial parallel corpora training. During decoding, our implementation on GPU costs about 0.5 second per sentence.

4.3 Evaluation

We evaluate the effectiveness of our method with EuroParl Common testset and WMT 2013 dataset. BLEU-4 (Papineni et al., 2002) is used as the evaluation metric. We evaluate BLEU scores on EuroParl Common test set with multi-task NMT models and single NMT models to demonstrate the validity of our multi-task learning framework. On the WMT 2013 data sets, we compare performance of separately trained NMT models, multi-task NMT models and Moses. We use the EuroParl Common test set as a development set in both neural machine translation experiments and Moses experiments. For single NMT models and multi-task NMT models, we select the best model with the highest BLEU score in the EuroParl Common testset and apply it to the WMT 2013 dataset. Note that our experiment settings in NMT is equivalent with Moses, considering the same training corpus, development sets and test sets.

[1] http:www.statmt.orgeuroparl
[2] http://www.statmt.org/wmt14/test.tgz
[3] http://matrix.statmt.org/test_sets

4.4 Experimental Results

We report our results of three experiments to show the validity of our methods. In the first experiment, we train multi-task learning model jointly on all four parallel corpora and compare BLEU scores with models trained separately on each parallel corpora. In the second experiment, we utilize the same training procedures as Experiment 1, except that we mimic the situation where some parallel corpora are resource-poor and maintain only 15% data on two parallel training corpora. In experiment 3, we test our learned model from experiment 1 and experiment 2 on WMT 2013 dataset. Table 3 and 4 show the case-insensitive BLEU scores on the Europarl common test data. Models learned from the multi-task learning framework significantly outperform the models trained separately. Table 4 shows that given only 15% of parallel training corpus of English-Dutch and English-Portuguese, it is possible to improve translation performance on all the target languages as well. This result makes sense because the correlated languages benefit from each other by sharing the same predictive structure, e.g. French, Spanish and Portuguese, all of which are from Latin. We also notice that even though Dutch is from Germanic languages, it is also possible to increase translation performance under our multi-task learning framework which demonstrates the generalization of our model to multiple target languages.

Lang-Pair	En-Es	En-Fr	En-Nl	En-Pt
Single NMT	26.65	21.22	28.75	20.27
Multi Task	28.03	22.47	29.88	20.75
Delta	**+1.38**	**+1.25**	**+1.13**	**+0.48**

Table 3: Multi-task neural translation v.s. single model given large-scale corpus in all language pairs

We tested our selected model on the WMT 2013 dataset. Our results are shown in Table 5 where Multi-Full is the model with Experiment 1 setting and the model of Multi-Partial uses the same setting in Experiment 2. The English-French and English-Spanish translation performances are improved significantly compared with models trained separately on each language pair. Note that this result is not comparable with the result reported in (Bahdanau et al., 2014) as we use much less training corpus. We also compare our trained models with Moses. On the WMT 2013 data set, we utilize parallel corpora for Moses training without any extra resource such as large-scale monolingual corpus. From Table 5, it is shown that neural machine translation models have comparable BLEU scores with Moses. On the WMT 2013 test set, multi-task learning model outperforms both single model and Moses results significantly.

Lang-Pair	En-Es	En-Fr	En-Nl*	En-Pt*
Single NMT	26.65	21.22	26.59	18.26
Multi Task	28.29	21.89	27.85	19.32
Delta	**+1.64**	**+0.67**	**+1.26**	**+1.06**

Table 4: Multi-task neural translation v.s. single model with a small-scale training corpus on some language pairs. * means that the language pair is sub-sampled.

4.5 Model Analysis and Discussion

We try to make empirical analysis through learning curves and qualitative results to explain why multi-task learning framework works well in multiple-target machine translation problem.

From the learning process, we observed that the speed of model convergence under multi-task learning is faster than models trained separately especially when a model is trained for resource-poor language pairs. The detailed learning curves are shown in Figure 4. Here we study the learning curve for resource-poor language pairs, i.e. English-Dutch and En-Portuguese, for which only 15% of the bilingual data is sampled for training. The BLEU scores are evaluated on the Europarl common test set. From Figure 4, it can be seen that in the early stage of training, given the same amount of training data for each language pair, the translation performance of the multi-task learning model is improved more rapidly. And the multi-task models achieve better translation quality than separately trained models within three iterations of training. The reason of faster and better convergence in performance is that the encoder parameters are shared across different language pairs, which can make full use of all the source language training data across the language pairs and improve the source language

	Nmt Baseline	Nmt Multi-Full	Nmt Multi-Partial	Moses
En-Fr	23.89	26.02(**+2.13**)	25.01(**+1.12**)	23.83
En-Es	23.28	25.31(**+2.03**)	25.83(**+2.55**)	23.58

Table 5: Multi-task NMT v.s. single model v.s. moses on the WMT 2013 test set

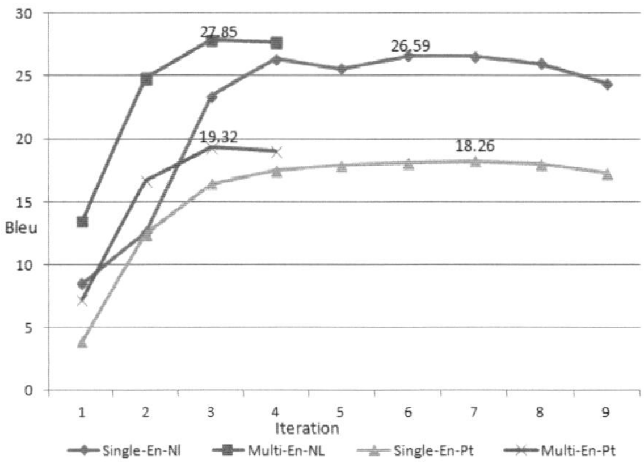

Figure 4: Faster and Better convergence in Multi-task Learning in multiple language translation

representation.

The sharing of encoder parameters is useful especially for the resource-poor language pairs. In the multi-task learning framework, the amount of the source language is not limited by the resource-poor language pairs and we are able to learn better representation for the source language. Thus the representation of the source language learned from the multi-task model is more stable, and can be viewed as a constraint that leverages translation performance of all language pairs. Therefore, the overfitting problem and the data scarcity problem can be alleviated for language pairs with only a few training data. In Table 6, we list the three nearest neighbors of some source words whose similarity is computed by using the cosine score of the embeddings both in the multi-task learning framework (from Experiment two) and in the single model (the resource-poor English-Portuguese model). Although the nearest neighbors of the high-frequent words such as numbers can be learned both in the multi-task model and the single model, the overall quality of the nearest neighbors learned by the resource-poor single model is much poorer compared with the multi-task model.

The multi-task learning framework also generates translations of higher quality. Some examples are shown in Table 7. The examples are from the WMT 2013 test set. The French and Spanish translations generated by the multi-task learning model and the single model are shown in the table.

MultiTask	**Nearest neighbors**
provide	deliver 0.78, providing 0.74, give 0.72
crime	terrorism 0.66, criminal 0.65, homelessness 0.65
regress	condense 0.74, mutate 0.71, evolve 0.70
six	eight 0.98,seven 0.96, 12 0.94
Single-Resource-Poor	**Nearest Neighbors**
provide	though 0.67,extending 0.56, parliamentarians 0.44
crime	care 0.75, remember 0.56, three 0.53
regress	committing 0.33, accuracy 0.30, longed-for 0.28
six	eight 0.87, three 0.69, thirteen 0.65

Table 6: Source language nearest-neighbor comparison between the multi-task model and the single model

5 Conclusion

In this paper, we investigate the problem of how to translate one source language into several different target languages within a unified translation model. Our proposed solution is based on the

English	Students, meanwhile, say the course is one of the most interesting around.
Reference-Fr	Les étudiants, pour leur part, assurent que le cours est l' un des plus intéressants.
Single-Fr	Les étudiants, entre-temps, disent entendu l' une des plus intéressantes.
Multi-Fr	Les étudiants, en attendant, disent qu' il est l' un des sujets les plus intéressants.
English	In addition, they limited the right of individuals and groups to provide assistance to voters wishing to register.
Reference-Fr	De plus, ils ont limité le droit de personnes et de groupes de fournir une assistance aux électeurs désirant s' inscrire.
Single-Fr	En outre, ils limitent le droit des particuliers et des groupes pour fournir l' assistance aux électeurs.
Multi-Fr	De plus, ils restreignent le droit des individus et des groupes à fournir une assistance aux électeurs qui souhaitent enregistrer.

Table 7: Translation of different target languages given the same input in our multi-task model.

recently proposed recurrent neural network based encoder-decoder framework. We train a unified neural machine translation model under the multi-task learning framework where the encoder is shared across different language pairs and each target language has a separate decoder. To the best of our knowledge, the problem of learning to translate from one source to multiple targets has seldom been studied. Experiments show that given large-scale parallel training data, the multi-task neural machine translation model is able to learn good predictive structures in translating multiple targets. Significant improvement can be observed from our experiments on the data sets publicly available. Moreover, our framework is able to address the data scarcity problem of some resource-poor language pairs by utilizing large-scale parallel training corpora of other language pairs to improve the translation quality. Our model is efficient and gets faster and better convergence for both resource-rich and resource-poor language pair under the multi-task learning.

In the future, we would like to extend our learning framework to more practical setting. For example, train a multi-task learning model with the same target language from different domains to improve multiple domain translation within one model. The correlation of different target languages will also be considered in the future work.

Acknowledgement

This paper is supported by the 973 program No. 2014CB340505. We would like to thank anonymous reviewers for their insightful comments.

References

Rie Kubota Ando and Tong Zhang. 2005. A framework for learning predictive structures from multiple tasks and unlabeled data. *Journal of Machine Learning Research*, 6:1817–1853.

Dzmitry Bahdanau, Kyunghyun Cho, and Yoshua Bengio. 2014. Neural machine translation by jointly learning to align and translate. *CoRR*, abs/1409.0473.

Frédéric Bastien, Pascal Lamblin, Razvan Pascanu, James Bergstra, Ian J. Goodfellow, Arnaud Bergeron, Nicolas Bouchard, David Warde-Farley, and Yoshua Bengio. 2012. Theano: new features and speed improvements. *CoRR*, abs/1211.5590.

Léon Bottou. 1991. Stochastic gradient learning in neural networks. In *Proceedings of Neuro-Nîmes 91*, Nimes, France. EC2.

KyungHyun Cho, Bart van Merrienboer, Dzmitry Bahdanau, and Yoshua Bengio. 2014. On the properties of neural machine translation: Encoder-decoder approaches. *CoRR*, abs/1409.1259.

Trevor Cohn and Mirella Lapata. 2007. Machine translation by triangulation: Making effective use of multi-parallel corpora. In *Proc. ACL*, pages 728–735.

Ronan Collobert, Jason Weston, Léon Bottou, Michael Karlen, Koray Kavukcuoglu, and Pavel P. Kuksa. 2011. Natural language processing (almost) from scratch. *Journal of Machine Learning Research*, 12:2493–2537.

Lei Cui, Xilun Chen, Dongdong Zhang, Shujie Liu, Mu Li, and Ming Zhou. 2013. Multi-domain adaptation for SMT using multi-task learning. In *Proc. EMNLP*, pages 1055–1065.

Jacob Devlin, Rabih Zbib, Zhongqiang Huang, Thomas Lamar, Richard M. Schwartz, and John Makhoul. 2014. Fast and robust neural network joint models for statistical machine translation. In *Proc. ACL*, pages 1370–1380.

Jianfeng Gao, Xiaodong He, Wen-tau Yih, and Li Deng. 2014. Learning continuous phrase representations for translation modeling. In *Proc. ACL*, pages 699–709.

Jun Hatori, Takuya Matsuzaki, Yusuke Miyao, and Jun'ichi Tsujii. 2012. Incremental joint approach to word segmentation, POS tagging, and dependency parsing in chinese. In *Proc. ACL*, pages 1045–1053.

Nal Kalchbrenner and Phil Blunsom. 2013. Recurrent continuous translation models. In *Proc. EMNLP*, pages 1700–1709.

Philipp Koehn. 2004. Pharaoh: A beam search decoder for phrase-based statistical machine translation models. In *Machine Translation: From Real Users to Research, 6th Conference of the Association for Machine Translation in the Americas, AMTA 2004, Washington, DC, USA, September 28-October 2, 2004, Proceedings*, pages 115–124.

Zhenghua Li, Min Zhang, Wanxiang Che, Ting Liu, and Wenliang Chen. 2014. Joint optimization for chinese POS tagging and dependency parsing. *IEEE/ACM Transactions on Audio, Speech & Language Processing*, 22(1):274–286.

Shujie Liu, Nan Yang, Mu Li, and Ming Zhou. 2014. A recursive recurrent neural network for statistical machine translation. In *Proc. ACL*, pages 1491–1500.

Kishore Papineni, Salim Roukos, Todd Ward, and Wei-Jing Zhu. 2002. Bleu: A method for automatic evaluation of machine translation. In *Proc. ACL*, ACL 2002, pages 311–318, Stroudsburg, PA, USA. Association for Computational Linguistics.

Rico Sennrich, Holger Schwenk, and Walid Aransa. 2013. A multi-domain translation model framework for statistical machine translation. In *Proc. ACL*, pages 832–840.

Martin Sundermeyer, Tamer Alkhouli, Joern Wuebker, and Hermann Ney. 2014. Translation modeling with bidirectional recurrent neural networks. In *Proc. EMNLP*, pages 14–25.

Ilya Sutskever, Oriol Vinyals, and Quoc V. Le. 2014. Sequence to sequence learning with neural networks. In *Advances in Neural Information Processing Systems 27: Annual Conference on Neural Information Processing Systems 2014, December 8-13 2014, Montreal, Quebec, Canada*, pages 3104–3112.

Hua Wu and Haifeng Wang. 2007. Pivot language approach for phrase-based statistical machine translation. In *Proc. ACL*, pages 165–181.

Matthew D. Zeiler. 2012. ADADELTA: an adaptive learning rate method. *CoRR*, abs/1212.5701.

Accurate Linear-Time Chinese Word Segmentation via Embedding Matching

Jianqiang Ma
SFB 833 and Department of Linguistics
University of Tübingen, Germany
jma@sfs.uni-tuebingen.de

Erhard Hinrichs
SFB 833 and Department of Linguistics
University of Tübingen, Germany
eh@sfs.uni-tuebingen.de

Abstract

This paper proposes an *embedding matching* approach to Chinese word segmentation, which generalizes the traditional sequence labeling framework and takes advantage of distributed representations. The training and prediction algorithms have linear-time complexity. Based on the proposed model, a greedy segmenter is developed and evaluated on benchmark corpora. Experiments show that our greedy segmenter achieves improved results over previous neural network-based word segmenters, and its performance is competitive with state-of-the-art methods, despite its simple feature set and the absence of external resources for training.

1 Introduction

Chinese sentences are written as character sequences without word delimiters, which makes word segmentation a prerequisite of Chinese language processing. Since Xue (2003), most work has formulated Chinese word segmentation (CWS) as *sequence labeling* (Peng et al., 2004) with character position tags, which has lent itself to structured discriminative learning with the benefit of allowing rich features of *segmentation configurations*, including (i) *context* of character/word n-grams within local windows, (ii) *segmentation history* of previous characters, or the combinations of both. These feature-based models still form the backbone of most state-of-the art systems.

Nevertheless, many feature weights in such models are inevitably poorly estimated because the number of parameters is so large with respect to the limited amount of training data. This has motivated the introduction of low-dimensional, real-valued vectors, known as *embeddings*, as a tool to deal with the sparseness of the input. Embeddings allow linguistic units appearing in similar contexts to share similar vectors. The success of embeddings has been observed in many NLP tasks. For CWS, Zheng et al. (2013) adapted Collobert et al. (2011) and uses character embeddings in local windows as input for a two-layer network. The network predicts individual character position tags, the transitions of which are learned separately. Mansur et al. (2013) also developed a similar architecture, which labels individual characters and uses character bigram embeddings as additional features to compensate the absence of sentence-level modeling. Pei et al. (2014) improved upon Zheng et al. (2013) by capturing the combinations of context and history via a tensor neural network.

Despite their differences, these CWS approaches are all sequence labeling models. In such models, the target character can only influence the prediction as features. Consider the the segmentation configuration in (1), where the dot appears before the target character in consideration and the box (□) represents any character that can occur in the configuration. In that example, the known history is that the first two characters 中国 'China' are joined together, which is denoted by the underline.

(1) 中国·□ 格外 (where □ ∈ {风, 规, ...})

(2) 中国风 格外 'China-style especially'

(3) 中国 规格 外 'besides Chinese spec.'

For possible target characters, 风 'wind' and 规 'rule', the correct segmentation decisions for them are *opposite*, as shown in (2) and (3), respectively. In order to correctly predict both, current models can set higher weights for target character-specific features. However, in general, 风 is more likely to start a new word instead of joining the existing one as in this example. Given such conflicting evidence, models can rarely find optimal feature weights, if they exist at all.

Proceedings of the 53rd Annual Meeting of the Association for Computational Linguistics and the 7th International Joint Conference on Natural Language Processing, pages 1733–1743, Beijing, China, July 26-31, 2015. ©2015 Association for Computational Linguistics

The crux of this *conflicting evidence* problem is that similar configurations can suggest opposite decisions, depending on the target character and vice versa. Thus it might be useful to treat segmentation decisions for distinct characters separately. And instead of predicting general segmentation decisions given configurations, it could be beneficial to model the *matching* between configurations and *character-specific* decisions.

To this end, this paper proposes an embedding matching approach (Section 2) to CWS, in which embeddings for both input and output are learned and used as representations to counteract sparsities. Thanks to embeddings of character-specific decisions (actions) serving as both input features and output, our hidden-layer-free architecture (Section 2.2) is capable of capturing prediction histories in similar ways as the hidden layers in recurrent neural networks (Mikolov et al., 2010). We evaluate the effectiveness of the model via a linear-time greedy segmenter (Section 3) implementation. The segmenter outperforms previous embedding-based models (Section 4.2) and achieves state-of-the-art results (Section 4.3) on a benchmark dataset. The main contributions of this paper are:

- A novel embedding matching model for Chinese word segmentation.
- Developing a greedy word segmenter, which is based on the matching model and achieves competitive results.
- Introducing the idea of character-specific segmentation action embeddings as both feature and output, which are cornerstones of the model and the segmenter.

2 Embedding Matching Models for Chinese Word Segmentation

We propose an embedding based matching model for CWS, the architecture of which is shown in Figure 1. The model employs trainable embeddings to represent both sides of the matching, which will be specified shortly, followed by details of the architecture in Section 2.2.

2.1 Segmentation as Configuration-Action Matching

Output. The word segmentation output of a character sequence can be described as a sequence of *character-specific segmentation actions*. We use **separation** (s) and **combination** (c) as possible actions for each character, where a separation action starts a new word with the current character, while a combination action appends the character to the preceding ones. We model character-action *combinations* instead of atomic, character independent actions. As a running example, sentence (4b) is the correct segmentation for (4a), which can be represented as the sequence (猫 -***s***, 占 -***s***, 领 -***c***, 了 -***s***, 婴 -***s***, 儿 -***c***, 床 -***c***) .

(4) a. 猫占领了婴儿床
  b. 猫 占领 了 婴儿床
  c. 'The cat occupied the crib'

Input. The input are the segmentation configurations for each character under consideration, which are described by context and history features. The *context features* of captures the characters that are in the same sentence of the current character and the *history features* encode the segmentation actions of previous characters.

- **Context features**. These refer to character *unigrams* and *bigrams* that appear in the local context window of h characters that centers at c_i, where c_i is 领 in example (4) and $h = 5$ is used in this paper. The template for features are shown in Table 1. For our example, the uni- and bi-gram features would be: 猫, 占, 领, 了, 婴 and 猫占, 占领, 领了, 了婴, respectively.
- **History features**. To make inference tractable, we assume that only previous l character-specific actions are relevant, where $l = 2$ for this study. In our example, 猫 -***s*** and 战 -***s*** are the history features. Such features capture partial information of syntactic and semantic dependencies between previous *words*, which are clues for segmentation that pure character contexts could not provide. A dummy character START is used to represent the absent (left) context characters in the case of the first l characters in a sentence. And the predicted action for the START symbol is always ***s***.

Matching. CWS is now modeled as the matching of the input (segmentation configuration) and output (two possible character-specific actions) for each character. Formally, a matching model learns

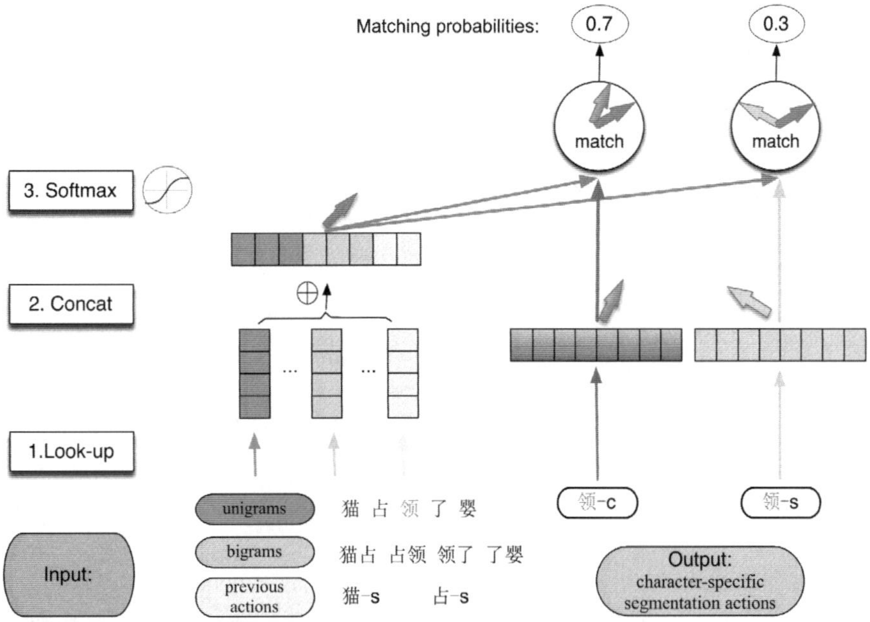

Figure 1: **The architecture of the embedding matching model for CWS**. The model predicts the segmentation for the character 领 in sentence (4), which is the second character of word 占领 'occupy'. Both feature and output embeddings are trainable parameters of the model.

Group	Feature template
unigram	$c_{i-2}, c_{i-1}, c_i, c_{i+1}, c_{i+2}$
bigram	$c_{i-2}c_{i-1}, c_{i-1}c_i, c_ic_{i+1}, c_{i+1}c_{i+2}$

Table 1: Uni- and bi-gram feature template

the following function:

$$g\,(b_1b_2...b_n, a_1a_2...a_n)$$
$$=\prod_{j=1}^{n} f\left(b_j(a_{j-2}, a_{j-1}; c_{j-\frac{h}{2}}...c_{j+\frac{h}{2}}), a_j\right) \quad (1)$$

where $c_1c_2...c_n$ is the character sequence, b_j and a_j are the segmentation configuration and action for character c_j, respectively. In (1), $b_j(a_{j-2}, a_{j-1}; c_{j-\frac{h}{2}}...c_{j+\frac{h}{2}})$ indicates that the configuration for each character is a function that depends on the actions of the previous l characters and the characters in the local window of size h.

Why embedding. The above matching model would suffer from sparsity if these outputs (character-specific action a_j) were directly encoded as one-hot vectors, since the matching model can be seen as a sequence labeling model with $C \times L$ outputs, where L is the number of original labels while C is the number of unique characters. For Chinese, C is at the order of $10^3 - 10^4$. The use of embeddings, however, can serve the matching model well thanks to their low dimensionality.

2.2 The Architecture

The proposed architecture (Figure 1) has three components, namely look-up table, concatenation and softmax function for matching. We will go through each of them in this section.

Look-up table. The mapping between features/outputs to their corresponding embeddings are kept in a *look-up table*, as in many previous embedding related work (Bengio et al., 2003; Pei et al., 2014). Such features are extracted from the training data. Formally, the embedding for each distinct feature d is denoted as $Embed(d) \in \mathbb{R}^N$, which is a real valued vector of dimension N. Each feature is retrieved by its unique index. The retrieval of the embeddings for the output actions is similar.

Concatenation. To predict the segmentation for the target character c_j, its feature vectors are *concatenated* into a single vector, the *input embedding*, $\mathbf{i}(b_j) \in \mathbb{R}^{N \times K}$, where K is the number of features used to describe the configuration b_j.

Softmax. The model then computes the dot product of the input embedding $\mathbf{i}(b_j)$ and each of the two *output embeddings*, $\mathbf{o}(a_{j,1})$ and $\mathbf{o}(a_{j,2})$, which represent the two possible segmentation actions for the target character c_j, respectively. The exponential of the two raw scores are normalized to obtain probabilistic values $\in [0, 1]$.

We call the resulting scores *matching probabilities*, which denote probabilities that actions match the given segmentation configuration. In our example, 领 -***c*** has the probability of 0.7 to be the correct action, while 领 -***s*** is less likely with a lower probability of 0.3. Formally, the above matching procedure can be described as a *softmax* function, as shown in (2), which is also an individual f term in (1).

$$f(\,b_j, a_{j,k}) = \frac{exp\,(\mathbf{i}(b_j)\cdot\mathbf{o}(a_{j,k}))}{\sum_{k'} exp\,\big(\mathbf{i}(b_j)\cdot\mathbf{o}(a_{j,k'})\big)} \quad (2)$$

In (2), $a_{j,k}$ $(1 \le k \le 2)$ represent two possible actions, such as 领 -***c*** and 领 -***s*** for 领 in our example. Note that, to ensure the input and output are of the same dimension, for each character specific action, the model trains two distinct embeddings, one $\in \mathbb{R}^N$ as feature and the other $\in \mathbb{R}^{N\times K}$ as output, where K is the number of features for each input.

Best word segmentation of sentence. After plugging (2) into (1) and applying (and then dropping) logarithms for computational convenience, finding the best segmentation for a sentence becomes an optimization problem as shown in (3). In the formula, $\hat{Y}$ is the best action sequence found by the model among all the possible ones, $Y = a_1 a_2 ... a_n$, where a_j is the predicted action for the character c_j $(1 \le j \le n)$, which is either c_j-***s*** or c_j-***c***, such as 领 -***s*** and 领 -***c***.

$$\hat{Y} = \operatorname*{argmax}_{Y} \sum_{j=1}^{n} \frac{exp\,(\mathbf{i}(b_j)\cdot\mathbf{o}(a_j))}{\sum_{k} exp\,(\mathbf{i}(b_j)\cdot\mathbf{o}(a_{j,k}))} \quad (3)$$

3 The Greedy Segmenter

Our model depends on the actions predicted for the previous two characters as history features. Traditionally, such scenarios call for dynamic programming for exact inference. However, preliminary experiments showed that, for our model, a Viterbi search based segmenter, even supported by conditional random field (Lafferty et al., 2001) style training, yields similar results as the greedy search based segmenter in this section. Since the greedy segmenter is much more efficient in training and testing, the rest of the paper will focus on the proposed greedy segmenter, the details of which will be described in this section.

3.1 Greedy Search

Initialization. The first character in the sentence is made to have two left side characters that are dummy symbols of START, whose predicted actions are always START-***s***, i.e. separation.

Iteration. The algorithms predicts the action for each character c_j, one at a time, in a left-to-right, incremental manner, where $1 \le j \le n$ and n is the sentence length. To do so, it first extracts context features and history features, the latter of which are the predicted character-specific actions for the previous two characters. Then the model matches the concatenated feature embedding with embeddings of the two possible character-specific actions, c_j-***s*** and c_i-***c***. The one with higher matching probability is predicted as segmentation action for the character, which is irreversible. After the action for the last character is predicted, the segmented word sequence of the sentence is built from the predicted actions deterministically.

Hybrid matching. Character-specific embeddings are capable of capturing subtle word formation tendencies of individual characters, but such representations are incapable of covering matching cases for unknown target characters. Another minor issue is that the action embeddings for certain low frequent characters may not be sufficiently trained. To better deal with these scenarios, We also train two embeddings to represent character-independent segmentation actions, ALL-***s*** and ALL-***c***, and use them to average with or substitute embeddings of infrequent or unknown characters, which are either insufficiently trained or nonexistent. Such strategy is called *hybrid matching*, which can improve accuracy.

Complexity. Although the total number of actions is large, the matching for each target character only requires the two actions that correspond to that specific character, such as 领 -***s*** and 领 -***c*** for 领 in our example. Each prediction is thus similar to a softmax computation with two outputs, which costs constant time C. Greedy search ensures that the total time for predicting a sentence of n characters is $n \times C$, i.e. *linear time complexity*, with a minor overhead for mapping actions to segmentations.

3.2 Training

The training procedure first predicts the action for the current character with current parameters, and then optimizes the log likelihood of correct segmentation actions in the gold segmentations to update parameters. Ideally, the matching probability for the correct action embedding should be 1 while that of the incorrect one should be 0. We minimize the *cross-entropy loss function* as in (4) for the segmentation prediction of each character c_j to pursue this goal. The loss function is convex, similar to that of maximum entropy models.

$$J = -\sum_{k=1}^{K} \delta\left(a_{j,k}\right) \log \frac{exp\left(\mathbf{i} \cdot \mathbf{o}(a_{j,k})\right)}{\sum_{k'} exp\left(\mathbf{i} \cdot \mathbf{o}(a_{j,k'})\right)} \quad (4)$$

where $a_{j,k}$ denotes a possible action for c_j and $\mathbf{i}$ is a compact notation for $\mathbf{i}(b_j)$. In (4), $\delta(a_{j,k})$ is an *indicator function* defined by the following formula, where $\hat{a_j}$ denotes the correct action.

$$\delta(a_{j,k}) = \begin{cases} 1, & \text{if } a_{j,k} = \hat{a_j} \\ 0, & \text{otherwise} \end{cases}$$

To counteract over-fitting, we add L2 regularization term to the loss function, as follows:

$$J = J + \sum_{k=1}^{K} \frac{\lambda}{2} \left(||\mathbf{i}||^2 + ||\mathbf{o}(a_{j,k})||^2 \right) \quad (5)$$

The formula in (4) and (5) are similar to that of a standard softmax regression, except that both input and output embeddings are parameters to be trained. We perform *stochastic gradient descent* to update input and output embeddings in turn, each time considering the other as constant. We give the gradient (6) and the update rule (7) for the input embedding $\mathbf{i}(b_j)$ ($\mathbf{i}$ for short), where $\mathbf{o}_k$ is a short notation for $\mathbf{o}(a_{j,k})$. The gradient and update for output embeddings are similar. The α in (7) is the learning rate, which we use a linear decay scheme to gradually shrink it from its initial value to zero. Note that the update for the input embedding $\mathbf{i}$ is actually performed for the feature embeddings that form $\mathbf{i}$ in the concatenation step.

$$\frac{\partial J}{\partial \mathbf{i}} = \sum_{k} \left(f\left(b_j, a_{j,k}\right) - \delta\left(a_{j,k}\right) \right) \cdot \mathbf{o}_k + \lambda \mathbf{i} \quad (6)$$

$$\mathbf{i} = \mathbf{i} - \alpha \frac{\partial J}{\partial \mathbf{i}} \quad (7)$$

Complexity. For each iteration of the training process, the time complexity is also linear to the input character number, as compared with search, only a few constant time operations of gradient computation and parameter updates are performed for each character.

4 Experiments

4.1 Data and Evaluation Metric

In the experiments, we use two widely used and freely available[1] manually word-segmented corpora, namely, **PKU** and **MSR**, from the second SIGHAN international Chinese word segmentation bakeoff (Emerson, 2005). Table 2 shows the details of the two dataset. All evaluations in this paper are conducted with official training/testing set split using official scoring script.[2]

	PKU	**MSR**
Word types	5.5×10^4	8.8×10^4
Word tokens	1.1×10^6	2.4×10^6
Character types	5×10^3	5×10^3
Character tokens	1.8×10^6	4.1×10^6

Table 2: Corpus details of PKU and MSR

The segmentation accuracy is evaluated by precision (P), recall (R), **F-score** and $\mathbf{R}_{oov}$, the recall for out-of-vocabulary words. Precision is defined as the number of correctly segmented words divided by the total number of words in the segmentation result. Recall is defined as the number of correctly segmented words divided by the total number of words in the gold standard segmentation. In particular, R_{oov} reflects the model generalization ability. The metric for overall performance, the evenly-weighted F-score is calculated as in (8):

$$F = \frac{2 \times P \times R}{P + R} \quad (8)$$

To comply with CWS evaluation conventions and make comparisons fair, we distinguish the following two settings:

- *closed-set*: no extra resource other than training corpora is used.
- *open-set*: additional lexicon, raw corpora, etc are used.

[1]http://www.sighan.org/bakeoff2005/

[2]http://www.sighan.org/bakeoff2003/score

We will report the final results of our model[3] on PKU and MSR corpora in comparison with previous embedding based models (Section 4.2) and state-of-the-art systems (Section 4.3), before going into detailed experiments for model analyses (Section 4.5).

4.2 Comparison with Previous Embedding-Based Models

Table 3 shows the results of our greedy segmenter on the PKU and MSR datasets, which are compared with embedding-based segmenters in previous studies.[4] In the table, results for both closed-set and open-set setting are shown for previous models. In the open-set evaluations, all three previous work use *pre-training* to train character ngram embeddings from large unsegmented corpora to initialize the embeddings, which will be later trained with the manually word-segmented training data. For our model, we report the close-set results only, as pre-training does not significant improve the results in our experiments (Section 4.5).

As shown in Table 3, under close-set evaluation, our model significantly outperform previous embedding based models in all metrics. Compared with the previous best embedding-based model, our greedy segmenter has achieved up to 2.2% and 25.8% absolute improvements (MSR) on F-score and R_{oov}, respectively. Surprisingly, our close-set results are also comparable to the best *open-set* results of previous models. As we will see in (Section 4.4), when using same or less character uni- and bi-gram features, our model still outperforms previous embedding based models in closed-set evaluation, which shows the effectiveness of our matching model.

Significance test. Table 4 shows the 95% confidence intervals (CI) for close-set results of our model and the best performing previous model (Pei et al., 2014), which are computed by formula (9), following (Emerson, 2005).

$$CI = 2\sqrt{\frac{F(1-F)}{N}} \tag{9}$$

where F is the F-score value and the N is the word token count of the testing set, which is 104,372 and 106,873 for PKU and MSR, respectively. We see that the confidence intervals of our results do *not* overlap with that of (Pei et al., 2014), meaning that our improvements are statistically significant.

4.3 Comparison with the State-of-the-Art Systems

Table 5 shows that the results of our greedy segmenter are competitive with the state-of-the-art supervised systems (Best05 closed-set, Zhang and Clark, 2007), although our feature set is much simpler. More recent state-of-the-art systems rely on both extensive feature engineering and extra raw corpora to boost performance, which are semi-supervised learning. For example, Zhang et al (2013) developed 8 types of static and dynamic features to maximize the co-training system that used extra corpora of Chinese Gigaword and Baike, each of which contains more than 1 billion character tokens. Such systems are not directly comparable with our supervised model. We leave the development of semi-supervised learning methods for our model as future work.

4.4 Features Influence

Table 6 shows the F-scores of our model on PKU dataset when different features are removed ('w/o') or when only a subset of features are used. Features complement each other and removing any group of features leads to a limited drop of F-score up to 0.7%. Note that features of previous (two) actions are even more informative than all unigram features combined, suggesting that intra- an inter-word dependencies reflected by action features are strong evidence for segmentation. Moreover, using same or less character ngram features, our model outperforms previous embedding based models, which shows the effectiveness of our matching model.

4.5 Model Analysis

Learning curve. Figure 2 shows that the training procedure coverages quickly. After the first iteration, the testing F-scores are already 93.5% and 95.7% for PKU and MSR, respectively, which then gradually reach their maximum within the next 9 iterations before the curve flats out.

Speed. With an unoptimized single-thread Python implementation running on a laptop with intel Core-i5 CPU (1.9 GHZ), each iteration of the training procedure on PKU dataset takes about 5 minutes, or 6,000 characters per second. The pre-

[3]Our implementation: https://zenodo.org/record/17645.

[4]The results for Zheng et al. (2013) are from the re-implementation of Pei et al. (2014).

Models	PKU Corpus				MSR Corpus			
	P	**R**	**F**	$\mathbf{R}_{oov}$	**P**	**R**	**F**	$\mathbf{R}_{oov}$
Zheng et al.(2013)	92.8	92.0	92.4	63.3	92.9	93.6	93.3	55.7
+ *pre-training*†	93.5	92.2	92.8	69.0	94.2	93.7	93.9	64.1
Mansur et al. (2013)	93.6	92.8	93.2	57.9	92.3	92.2	92.2	53.7
+ *pre-training*†	94.0	93.9	94.0	69.5	93.1	93.1	93.1	59.7
Pei et al. (2014)	93.7	93.4	93.5	64.2	94.6	94.2	94.4	61.4
+ *pre-training*†	94.4	93.6	94.0	69.0	95.2	94.6	94.9	64.8
+ *pre-training & bigram*†	-	-	**95.2**	-	-	-	**97.2**	-
This work (closed-set)	**95.5**	**94.6**	95.1	**76.0**	**96.6**	**96.5**	96.6	**87.2**

Table 3: Comparison with previous embedding based models. Numbers in percentage. Results with † used extra corpora for (pre-)training.

Models	PKU		MSR	
	F	CI	F	CI
Pei et al.	93.5	± 0.15	94.4	± 0.14
This work	95.1	± 0.13	96.6	± 0.11

Table 4: Significance test of closed-set results of Pei et al (2014) and our model.

Model	**PKU**	**MSR**
Best05 closed-set	95.0	96.4
Zhang et al. (2006)	95.1	97.1
Zhang and Clark (2007)	94.5	97.2
Wang et al. (2012)	94.1	97.2
Sun et al. (2009)	95.2	97.3
Sun et al. (2012)	95.4	**97.4**
Zhang et al. (2013) †	**96.1**	**97.4**
This work	95.1	96.6

Table 5: Comparison with the state-of-the-art systems. Results with † used extra lexicon/raw corpora for training, i.e. in open-set setting. Best05 refers to the best closed-set results in 2nd SIGHAN bakeoff.

diction speed is above 13,000 character per second.

Hyper parameters. The hyper parameters used in the experiments are shown in Table 7. We initialized hyper parameters with recommendations in literature before tuning with dev-set experiments, each of which change one parameter by a magnitude. We fixed the hyper parameter to the current setting without spending too much time on tuning, since that is not the main purpose of this paper.

- **Embedding size** determines the number of parameters to be trained, thus should fit the training data size to achieve good performance. We tried the size of 30 and 100, both of which performs worse than 50. A possible tuning is to use different embedding size for different groups of features instead of setting $N_1 = 50$ for all features.

Feature	F-score	Feature	F-score
All features	**95.1**	uni-&bi-gram	94.6
w/o action	94.6	only action	93.3
w/o unigram	94.8	only unigram	92.1
w/o bigram	94.4	only bigram	94.2

Table 6: The influence of features. F-score in percentage on the PKU corpus.

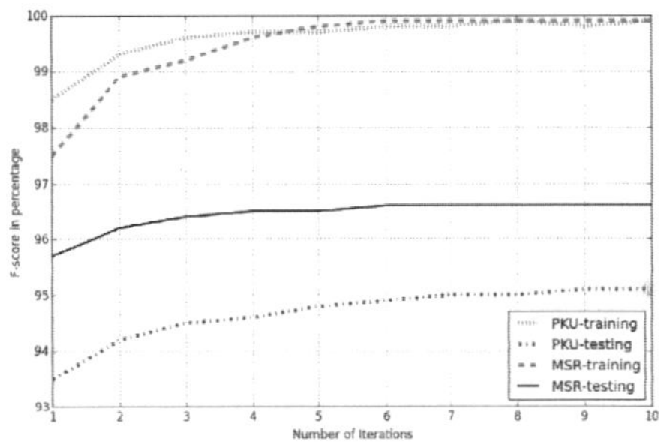

Figure 2: The learning curve of our model.

- **Context window size**. A window size of 3-5 characters achieves comparable results. Zheng et al. (2013) suggested that context window larger than 5 may lead to inferior results.
- **Initial Learning rate**. We found that several learning rates between 0.04 to 0.15 yielded very similar results as the one reported here. The training is not very sensitive to reason-

able values of initial learning rate. However, Instead of our simple linear decay of learning rate, it might be useful to try more sophisticated techniques, such as *AdaGrad* and exponential decaying (Tsuruoka et al., 2009; Sun et al., 2013).

- **Regularization**. Our model suffers a little from over-fitting, if no regularization is used. In that case, the F-score on PKU drops from 95.1% to 94.7%.
- **Pre-training**. We tried pre-training character embeddings using *word2vec*[5] with Chinese Gigaword Corpus[6] and use them to initialize the corresponding embeddings in our model, as previous work did. However, we were only able to see insignificant F-score improvements within 0.1% and observed that the training F-score reached 99.9% much earlier. We hypothesize that pre-training leads to sub-optimal local maximums for our model.
- **Hybrid matching**. We tried applying hybrid matching (Section 3.1) for target characters which are less frequent than the top f_{top} characters, including unseen characters, which leads to about 0.15% of F-score improvements.

Size of feature embed'	$N_1 = 50$
Size of output embed'	$N_2 = 550$
Window size	$h = 5$
Initial learning rate	$\alpha = 0.1$
Regularization	$\lambda = 0.001$
Hybrid matching	$f_{top} = 8\%$

Table 7: Hyper parameters of our model.

5 Related Work

Word segmentation. Most modern segmenters followed Xue (2003) to model CWS as sequence labeling of character position tags, using conditional random fields (Peng et al. 2004), structured perceptron (Jiang et al., 2008), etc. Some notable exceptions are (Zhang and Clark, 2007; Zhang et al., 2012), which exploited rich word-level features and (Ma et al., 2012; Ma, 2014; Zhang et al., 2014), which explicitly model word structures. Our work generalizes the sequence labeling to a more flexible framework of matching, and predicts actions as in (Zhang and Clark, 2007; Zhang et al., 2012) instead of position tags to prevent the greedy search from suffering tag inconsistencies. To better utilize resources other than training data, our model might benefit from techniques used in recent state-of-the-art systems, such as semi-supervised learning (Zhao and Kit, 2008; Sun and Xu, 2011; Zhang et al., 2013; Zeng et al., 2013), joint models (Li and Zhou, 2012; Qian and Liu, 2012), and partial annotations (Liu et al., 2014; Yang and Vozila, 2014).

Distributed representation and CWS. Distributed representation are useful for various NLP tasks, such as POS tagging (Collobert et al., 2011), machine translation (Devlin et al., 2014) and parsing (Socher et al., 2013). Influenced by Collobert et al. (2011), Zheng et al. (2013) modeled CWS as tagging and treated *sentence-level* tag sequence as the combination of individual tag predictions and context-independent tag transition. Mansur et al. (2013) was inspired by Bengio et al. (2003) and used character bigram embeddings to compensate for the absence of sentence level optimization. To model interactions between tags and characters, which are absent in these two CWS models, Pei et al. (2014) introduced the tag embedding and used a tensor hidden layer in the neural net. In contrast, our work uses character-specific action embeddings to *explicitly* capture such interactions. In addition, our work gains efficiency by avoiding hidden layers, similar as Mikolov et al. (2013).

Learning to match. Matching heterogeneous objects has been studied in various contexts before, and is currently flourishing, thanks to embedding-based deep (Gao et al., 2014) and convolutional (Huang et al., 2013; Hu et al., 2014) neural networks. This work develops a matching model for CWS and differs from others in its "shallow" yet effective architecture.

6 Discussion

Simple architecture. It is possible to adopt standard feed-forward neural network for our embedding matching model with character-action embeddings as both feature and output. Nevertheless, we designed the proposed architecture to avoid hidden layers for simplicity, efficiency and easy-tuning, inspired by *word2vec*. Our simple architecture is effective, demonstrated by the improved results over previous neural-network word seg-

[5]https://code.google.com/p/word2vec/

[6]https://catalog.ldc.upenn.edu/LDC2005T14

menters, all of which use feed-forward architecture with different features and/or layers. It might be interesting to directly compare the performances of our model with same features on the current and feed-forward architectures, which we leave for future work.

Greedy and exact search-based models. As mentioned in Section 3, we implemented and preliminarily experimented with a segmenter that trains a similar model with exact search via Viterbi algorithm. On the PKU corpus, its F-score is 0.944, compared with greedy segmenter's 0.951. Its training and testing speed are up to 7.8 times slower than that of the greedy search segmenter. It is counter-intuitive that the performance of the exact-search segmenter is no better or even worse than that of the greedy-search segmenter. We hypothesize that since the training updates parameters with regard to search errors, the final model is "tailored" for the specific search method used, which makes the model-search combination of greedy search segmenter not necessarily worse than that of exact search segmenter. Another way of looking at it is that search is less important when the model is accurate. In this case, most step-wise decisions are correct in the first place, which requires no correction from the search algorithm. Empirically, Zhang and Clark (2011) also reported exact-search segmenter performing worse than beam-search segmenters.

Despite that the greedy segmenter is incapable of considering future labels, this rarely causes problems in practice. Our greedy segmenter has good results, compared with the exact-search segmenter above and previous approaches, most of which utilize exact search. Moreover, the greedy segmenter has additional advantages of faster training and prediction.

Sequence labeling and matching. A traditional sequence labeling model such as CRF has K (number of labels) target-character-independent weight vectors, where the target character influences the prediction via the weights of the features that contain it. In a way, a matching model can be seen as a family of "sub-models", which keeps a group of weight vectors (the output embeddings) for *each* unique target character. Different target characters activate different sub-models, allowing opposite predictions for similar input features, as the target weight vectors used are different.

7 Conclusion and Future Work

In this paper, we have introduced the matching formulation for Chinese word segmentation and proposed an embedding matching model to take advantage of distributed representations. Based on the model, we have developed a greedy segmenter, which outperforms previous embedding-based methods and is competitive with state-of-the-art systems. These results suggest that it is promising to model CWS as configuration-action matching using distributed representations. In addition, linear-time training and testing complexity of our simple architecture is very desirable for industrial application. To the best of our knowledge, this is the first greedy segmenter that is competitive with the state-of-the-art discriminative learning models.

In the future, we plan to investigate methods for our model to better utilize external resources. We would like to try using convolutional neural network to automatically encode ngram-like features, in order to further shrink parameter space. It is also interesting to study whether extending our model with deep architectures can benefit CWS. Lastly, it might be useful to adapt our model to tasks such as POS tagging and name entity recognition.

Acknowledgments

The authors would like to thank the anonymous reviewers for their very helpful and constructive suggestions. We are indebted to Çağrı Çöltekin for discussion and comments, to Dale Gerdemann, Cyrus Shaoul, Corina Dima, Sowmya Vajjala and Helmut Schmid for their useful feedback on an earlier version of the manuscript. Financial support for the research reported in this paper was provided by the German Research Foundation (DFG) as part of the Collaborative Research Center "Emergence of Meaning" (SFB 833) and by the German Ministry of Education and Technology (BMBF) as part of the research grant CLARIN-D.

References

Yoshua Bengio, Réjean Ducharme, Pascal Vincent, and Christian Janvin. 2003. A neural probabilistic language model. *The Journal of Machine Learning Research*, 3:1137–1155.

Ronan Collobert, Jason Weston, Léon Bottou, Michael Karlen, Koray Kavukcuoglu, and Pavel Kuksa. 2011. Natural language processing (almost) from scratch. *The Journal of Machine Learning Research*, 12:2493–2537.

Jacob Devlin, Rabih Zbib, Zhongqiang Huang, Thomas Lamar, Richard Schwartz, and John Makhoul. 2014. Fast and robust neural network joint models for statistical machine translation. In *Proceedings of ACL*, pages 1370–1380.

Thomas Emerson. 2005. The second international chinese word segmentation bakeoff. In *Proceedings of the Fourth SIGHAN Workshop on Chinese Language Processing*, volume 133.

Jianfeng Gao, Patrick Pantel, Michael Gamon, Xiaodong He, Li Deng, and Yelong Shen. 2014. Modeling interestingness with deep neural networks. In *Proceedings of EMNLP*, pages 2–13.

Baotian Hu, Zhengdong Lu, Hang Li, and Qingcai Chen. 2014. Convolutional neural network architectures for matching natural language sentences. In *Advances in Neural Information Processing Systems*, pages 2042–2050.

Po-Sen Huang, Xiaodong He, Jianfeng Gao, Li Deng, Alex Acero, and Larry Heck. 2013. Learning deep structured semantic models for web search using clickthrough data. In *Proceedings of the ACM International Conference on Information & Knowledge Management*, pages 2333–2338.

Wenbin Jiang, Liang Huang, Qun Liu, and Yajuan Lü. 2008. A cascaded linear model for joint Chinese word segmentation and part-of-speech tagging. In *Proceedings of ACL*, pages 897–904.

John Lafferty, A. McCallum, and F. Pereira. 2001. Conditional random fields: probabilistic models for segmenting and labeling sequence data. In *Proceedings of International Conference on Machine Learning*, pages 282–289.

Zhongguo Li and Guodong Zhou. 2012. Unified dependency parsing of Chinese morphological and syntactic structures. In *Proceedings of EMNLP*, pages 1445–1454.

Yijia Liu, Yue Zhang, Wanxiang Che, Ting Liu, and Fan Wu. 2014. Domain adaptation for CRF-based Chinese word segmentation using free annotations. In *Proceedings of EMNLP*, pages 864–874.

Jianqiang Ma, Chunyu Kit, and Dale Gerdemann. 2012. Semi-automatic annotation of Chinese word structure. In *Proceedings of the Second CIPS-SIGHAN Joint Conference on Chinese Language Processing*, pages 9–17.

Jianqiang Ma. 2014. Automatic refinement of syntactic categories in Chinese word structures. In *Proceedings of LREC*.

Mairgup Mansur, Wenzhe Pei, and Baobao Chang. 2013. Feature-based neural language model and Chinese word segmentation. In *Proceedings of IJCNLP*, pages 1271–1277.

Tomas Mikolov, Martin Karafiát, Lukas Burget, Jan Cernockỳ, and Sanjeev Khudanpur. 2010. Recurrent neural network based language model. In *Proceedings of INTERSPEECH*, pages 1045–1048.

Tomas Mikolov, Ilya Sutskever, Kai Chen, Greg S Corrado, and Jeff Dean. 2013. Distributed representations of words and phrases and their compositionality. In *Advances in Neural Information Processing Systems*, pages 3111–3119.

Wenzhe Pei, Tao Ge, and Chang Baobao. 2014. Max-margin tensor neural network for Chinese word segmentation. In *Proceedings of ACL*, pages 239–303.

Fuchun Peng, Fangfang Feng, and Andrew McCallum. 2004. Chinese segmentation and new word detection using conditional random fields. In *Proceedings of COLING*, pages 562–571.

Xian Qian and Yang Liu. 2012. Joint Chinese word segmentation, POS tagging and parsing. In *Proceedings of EMNLP-CoNLL*, pages 501–511.

Richard Socher, John Bauer, Christopher D Manning, and Andrew Y Ng. 2013. Parsing with compositional vector grammars. In *Proceedings of ACL*, pages 455–465.

Weiwei Sun and Jia Xu. 2011. Enhancing Chinese word segmentation using unlabeled data. In *Proceedings of EMNLP*, pages 970–979.

Xu Sun, Yaozhong Zhang, Takuya Matsuzaki, Yoshimasa Tsuruoka, and Jun'ichi Tsujii. 2009. A discriminative latent variable Chinese segmenter with hybrid word/character information. In *Proceedings of NAACL*, pages 56–64.

Xu Sun, Houfeng Wang, and Wenjie Li. 2012. Fast online training with frequency-adaptive learning rates for Chinese word segmentation and new word detection. In *Proceedings of ACL*, pages 253–262.

Xu Sun, Yaozhong Zhang, Takuya Matsuzaki, Yoshimasa Tsuruoka, and Jun' ichi Tsujii. 2013. Probabilistic Chinese word segmentation with non-local information and stochastic training. *Information Processing & Management*, 49(3):626–636.

Yoshimasa Tsuruoka, Jun'ichi Tsujii, and Sophia Ananiadou. 2009. Stochastic gradient descent training for L1-regularized log-linear models with cumulative penalty. In *Proceedings of ACL-IJCNLP*, pages 477–485.

Kun Wang, Chengqing Zong, and Keh-Yih Su. 2012. Integrating generative and discriminative character-based models for Chinese word segmentation. *ACM Transactions on Asian Language Information Processing (TALIP)*, 11(2):7.

Nianwen Xue. 2003. Chinese word segmentation as character tagging. *Computational Linguistics and Chinese Language Processing*, 8(1):29–48.

Fan Yang and Paul Vozila. 2014. Semi-supervised Chinese word segmentation using partial-label learning With conditional random fields. In *Proceedings of EMNLP*, page 90–98.

Xiaodong Zeng, Derek F Wong, Lidia S Chao, and Isabel Trancoso. 2013. Graph-based semi-supervised model for joint Chinese word segmentation and part-of-speech tagging. In *Proceedings of ACL*, pages 770–779.

Yue Zhang and Stephen Clark. 2007. Chinese segmentation with a word-based perceptron algorithm. In *Proceedings of ACL*, pages 840–847.

Yue Zhang and Stephen Clark. 2011. Syntactic processing using the generalized perceptron and beam search. *Computational Linguistics*, 37(1):105–151.

Ruiqiang Zhang, Genichiro Kikui, and Eiichiro Sumita. 2006. Subword-based tagging by conditional random fields for Chinese word segmentation. In *Proceedings of NAACL*, pages 193–196.

Kaixu Zhang, Maosong Sun, and Changle Zhou. 2012. Word segmentation on Chinese mirco-blog data with a linear-time incremental model. In *Proceedings of the 2nd CIPS-SIGHAN Joint Conference on Chinese Language Processing*, pages 41–46.

Longkai Zhang, Houfeng Wang, Xu Sun, and Maigup Mansur. 2013. Exploring representations from unlabeled data with co-training for Chinese word segmentation. In *Proceedings of EMNLP*, pages 311–321.

Meishan Zhang, Yue Zhang, Wanxiang Che, and Ting Liu. 2014. Character-level Chinese dependency parsing. In *Proceedings of ACL*, pages 1326–1336.

Hai Zhao and Chunyu Kit. 2008. Unsupervised segmentation helps supervised learning of character tagging for word segmentation and named entity recognition. In *Proceedings of IJCNLP*, pages 106–111.

Xiaoqing Zheng, Hanyang Chen, and Tianyu Xu. 2013. Deep Learning for Chinese Word Segmentation and POS Tagging. In *Proceedings of EMNLP*, pages 647–657.

Gated Recursive Neural Network for Chinese Word Segmentation

Xinchi Chen, Xipeng Qiu*, Chenxi Zhu, Xuanjing Huang
Shanghai Key Laboratory of Intelligent Information Processing, Fudan University
School of Computer Science, Fudan University
825 Zhangheng Road, Shanghai, China
{xinchichen13,xpqiu,czhu13,xjhuang}@fudan.edu.cn

Abstract

Recently, neural network models for natural language processing tasks have been increasingly focused on for their ability of alleviating the burden of manual feature engineering. However, the previous neural models cannot extract the complicated feature compositions as the traditional methods with discrete features. In this paper, we propose a gated recursive neural network (GRNN) for Chinese word segmentation, which contains reset and update gates to incorporate the complicated combinations of the context characters. Since GRNN is relative deep, we also use a supervised layer-wise training method to avoid the problem of gradient diffusion. Experiments on the benchmark datasets show that our model outperforms the previous neural network models as well as the state-of-the-art methods.

1 Introduction

Unlike English and other western languages, Chinese do not delimit words by white-space. Therefore, word segmentation is a preliminary and important pre-process for Chinese language processing. Most previous systems address this problem by treating this task as a sequence labeling problem and have achieved great success. Due to the nature of supervised learning, the performance of these models is greatly affected by the design of features. These features are explicitly represented by the different combinations of context characters, which are based on linguistic intuition and statistical information. However, the number of features could be so large that the result models are too large to use in practice and prone to overfit on training corpus.

*Corresponding author.

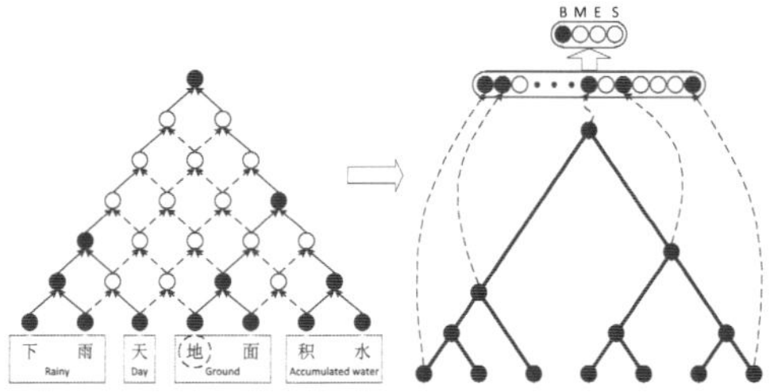

Figure 1: Illustration of our model for Chinese word segmentation. The solid nodes indicate the active neurons, while the hollow ones indicate the suppressed neurons. Specifically, the links denote the information flow, where the solid edges denote the acceptation of the combinations while the dashed edges means rejection of that. As shown in the right figure, we receive a score vector for tagging target character "地" by incorporating all the combination information.

Recently, neural network models have been increasingly focused on for their ability to minimize the effort in feature engineering. Collobert et al. (2011) developed a general neural network architecture for sequence labeling tasks. Following this work, many methods (Zheng et al., 2013; Pei et al., 2014; Qi et al., 2014) applied the neural network to Chinese word segmentation and achieved a performance that approaches the state-of-the-art methods.

However, these neural models just concatenate the embeddings of the context characters, and feed them into neural network. Since the concatenation operation is relatively simple, it is difficult to model the complicated features as the traditional discrete feature based models. Although the complicated interactions of inputs can be modeled by the deep neural network, the previous neural model shows that the deep model cannot outperform the one with a single non-linear model. Therefore, the

Proceedings of the 53rd Annual Meeting of the Association for Computational Linguistics and the 7th International Joint Conference on Natural Language Processing, pages 1744–1753,
Beijing, China, July 26-31, 2015.

neural model only captures the interactions by the simple transition matrix and the single non-linear transformation . These dense features extracted via these simple interactions are not nearly as good as the substantial discrete features in the traditional methods.

In this paper, we propose a gated recursive neural network (GRNN) to model the complicated combinations of characters, and apply it to Chinese word segmentation task. Inspired by the success of gated recurrent neural network (Chung et al., 2014), we introduce two kinds of gates to control the combinations in recursive structure. We also use the layer-wise training method to avoid the problem of gradient diffusion, and the dropout strategy to avoid the overfitting problem.

Figure 1 gives an illustration of how our approach models the complicated combinations of the context characters. Given a sentence "雨 (Rainy) 天 (Day) 地面 (Ground) 积水 (Accumulated water)", the target character is "地". This sentence is very complicated because each consecutive two characters can be combined as a word. To predict the label of the target character "地" under the given context, GRNN detects the combinations recursively from the bottom layer to the top. Then, we receive a score vector of tags by incorporating all the combination information in network.

The contributions of this paper can be summarized as follows:

- We propose a novel GRNN architecture to model the complicated combinations of the context characters. GRNN can select and preserve the useful combinations via reset and update gates. These combinations play a similar role in the feature engineering of the traditional methods with discrete features.

- We evaluate the performance of Chinese word segmentation on PKU, MSRA and CTB6 benchmark datasets which are commonly used for evaluation of Chinese word segmentation. Experiment results show that our model outperforms other neural network models, and achieves state-of-the-art performance.

2 Neural Model for Chinese Word Segmentation

Chinese word segmentation task is usually regarded as a character-based sequence labeling problem. Each character is labeled as one of {B, M, E, S} to indicate the segmentation. {B, M, E} represent *Begin*, *Middle*, *End* of a multi-character segmentation respectively, and S represents a *Single* character segmentation.

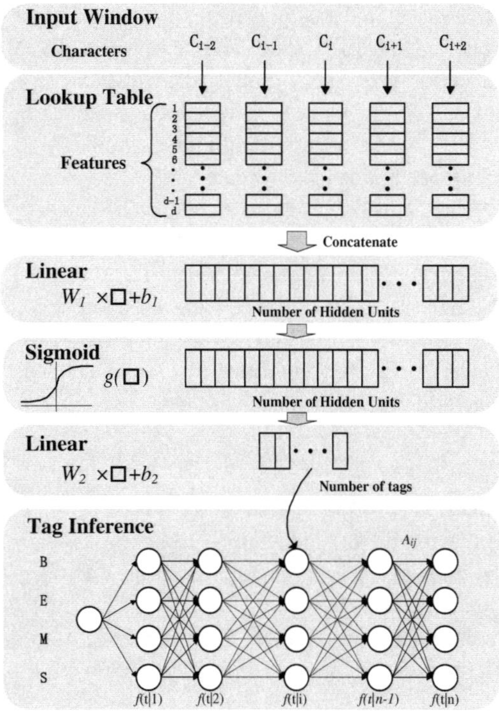

Figure 2: General architecture of neural model for Chinese word segmentation.

The general neural network architecture for Chinese word segmentation task is usually characterized by three specialized layers: (1) a character embedding layer; (2) a series of classical neural network layers and (3) tag inference layer. A illustration is shown in Figure 2.

The most common tagging approach is based on a local window. The window approach assumes that the tag of a character largely depends on its neighboring characters.

Firstly, we have a character set $\mathcal{C}$ of size $|\mathcal{C}|$. Then each character $c \in \mathcal{C}$ is mapped into an d-dimensional embedding space as $\mathbf{c} \in \mathbb{R}^d$ by a lookup table $\mathbf{M} \in \mathbb{R}^{d\times|\mathcal{C}|}$.

For each character c_i in a given sentence $c_{1:n}$, the context characters $c_{i-w_1:i+w_2}$ are mapped to their corresponding character embeddings as $\mathbf{c}_{i-w_1:i+w_2}$, where w_1 and w_2 are left and right context lengths respectively. Specifically, the unknown characters and characters exceeding the sentence boundaries are mapped to special symbols, "unknown", "start" and "end" respectively. In addition, w_1 and w_2 satisfy the constraint $w_1 + w_2 + 1 = w$, where w is the window size of the model. As an illustration in Figure 2, w_1, w_2 and w are set to 2, 2 and 5 respectively.

The embeddings of all the context characters are then concatenated into a single vector $\mathbf{a}_i \in \mathbb{R}^{H_1}$ as input of the neural network, where $H_1 = w \times d$ is the size of Layer 1. And $\mathbf{a}_i$ is then fed into a conventional neural network layer which performs a linear transformation followed by an element-wise activation function g, such as tanh.

$$\mathbf{h}_i = g(\mathbf{W}_1 \mathbf{a}_i + \mathbf{b}_1), \quad (1)$$

where $\mathbf{W}_1 \in \mathbb{R}^{H_2 \times H_1}$, $\mathbf{b}_1 \in \mathbb{R}^{H_2}$, $\mathbf{h}_i \in \mathbb{R}^{H_2}$. H_2 is the number of hidden units in Layer 2. Here, w, H_1 and H_2 are hyper-parameters chosen on development set.

Then, a similar linear transformation is performed without non-linear function followed:

$$f(t|c_{i-w_1:i+w_2}) = \mathbf{W}_2 \mathbf{h}_i + \mathbf{b}_2, \quad (2)$$

where $\mathbf{W}_2 \in \mathbb{R}^{|T| \times H_2}$, $\mathbf{b}_2 \in \mathbb{R}^{|T|}$ and T is the set of 4 possible tags. Each dimension of vector $f(t|c_{i-w_1:i+w_2}) \in \mathbb{R}^{|T|}$ is the score of the corresponding tag.

To model the tag dependency, a transition score $\mathbf{A}_{ij}$ is introduced to measure the probability of jumping from tag $i \in T$ to tag $j \in T$ (Collobert et al., 2011).

3 Gated Recursive Neural Network for Chinese Word Segmentation

To model the complicated feature combinations, we propose a novel gated recursive neural network (GRNN) architecture for Chinese word segmentation task (see Figure 3).

3.1 Recursive Neural Network

A recursive neural network (RNN) is a kind of deep neural network created by applying the same set of weights recursively over a given structure(such as parsing tree) in topological order (Pollack, 1990; Socher et al., 2013a).

In the simplest case, children nodes are combined into their parent node using a weight matrix $\mathbf{W}$ that is shared across the whole network, followed by a non-linear function $g(\cdot)$. Specifically, if $\mathbf{h}_L$ and $\mathbf{h}_R$ are d-dimensional vector representations of left and right children nodes respectively,

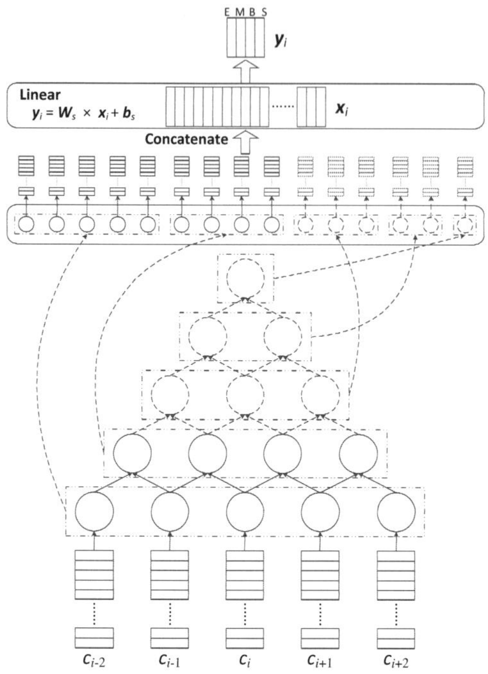

Figure 3: Architecture of Gated Recursive Neural Network for Chinese word segmentation.

their parent node $\mathbf{h}_P$ will be a d-dimensional vector as well, calculated as:

$$\mathbf{h}_P = g\left(\mathbf{W}\begin{bmatrix}\mathbf{h}_L \\ \mathbf{h}_R\end{bmatrix}\right), \quad (3)$$

where $\mathbf{W} \in \mathbb{R}^{d \times 2d}$ and g is a non-linear function as mentioned above.

3.2 Gated Recursive Neural Network

The RNN need a topological structure to model a sequence, such as a syntactic tree. In this paper, we use a directed acyclic graph (DAG), as showing in Figure 3, to model the combinations of the input characters, in which two consecutive nodes in the lower layer are combined into a single node in the upper layer via the operation as Eq. (3).

In fact, the DAG structure can model the combinations of characters by continuously mixing the information from the bottom layer to the top layer. Each neuron can be regarded as a complicated feature composition of its governed characters, similar to the discrete feature based models. The difference between them is that the neural one automatically learns the complicated combinations while the conventional one need manually design them.

When the children nodes combine into their parent node, the combination information of two children nodes is also merged and preserved by their parent node.

Although the mechanism above seem to work well, it can not sufficiently model the complicated combination features for its simplicity in practice.

Inspired by the success of the gated recurrent neural network (Cho et al., 2014b; Chung et al., 2014), we propose a gated recursive neural network (GRNN) by introducing two kinds of gates, namely "reset gate" and "update gate". Specifically, there are two reset gates, $\mathbf{r}_L$ and $\mathbf{r}_R$, partially reading the information from left child and right child respectively. And the update gates $\mathbf{z}_N$, $\mathbf{z}_L$ and $\mathbf{z}_R$ decide what to preserve when combining the children's information. Intuitively, these gates seems to decide how to update and exploit the combination information.

In the case of word segmentation, for each character c_i of a given sentence $c_{1:n}$, we first represent each context character c_j into its corresponding embedding $\mathbf{c}_j$, where $i - w_1 \leq j \leq i + w_2$ and the definitions of w_1 and w_2 are as same as mentioned above.

Then, the embeddings are sent to the first layer of GRNN as inputs, whose outputs are recursively applied to upper layers until it outputs a single fixed-length vector.

The outputs of the different neurons can be regarded as the different feature compositions. After concatenating the outputs of all neurons in the network, we get a new big vector $\mathbf{x}_i$. Next, we receive the tag score vector $\mathbf{y}_i$ for character c_j by a linear transformation of $\mathbf{x}_i$:

$$\mathbf{y}_i = \mathbf{W}_s \times \mathbf{x}_i + \mathbf{b}_s, \quad (4)$$

where $b_s \in \mathbb{R}^{|T|}$, $\mathbf{W}_s \in \mathbb{R}^{|T| \times Q}$. $Q = q \times d$ is dimensionality of the concatenated vector $\mathbf{x}_i$, where q is the number of nodes in the network.

3.3 Gated Recursive Unit

GRNN consists of the minimal structures, gated recursive units, as showing in Figure 4.

By assuming that the window size is w, we will have recursion layer $l \in [1, w]$. At each recursion layer l, the activation of the j-th hidden node $\mathbf{h}_j^{(l)} \in \mathbb{R}^d$ is computed as

$$\mathbf{h}_j^{(l)} = \begin{cases} \mathbf{z}_N \odot \hat{\mathbf{h}}_j^l + \mathbf{z}_L \odot \mathbf{h}_{j-1}^{l-1} + \mathbf{z}_R \odot \mathbf{h}_j^{l-1}, & l > 1, \\ \mathbf{c}_j, & l = 1, \end{cases} \quad (5)$$

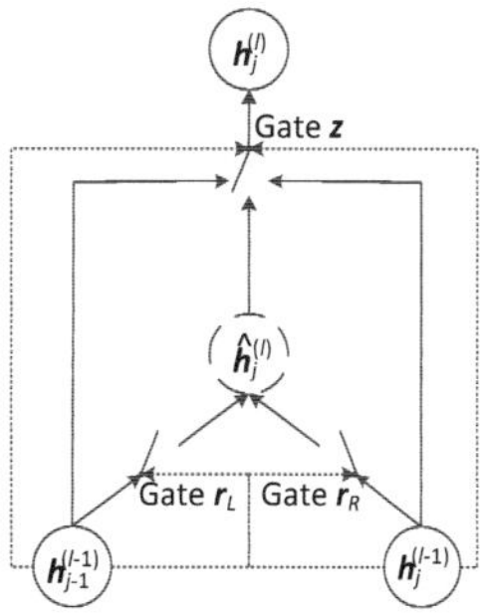

Figure 4: Our proposed gated recursive unit.

where $\mathbf{z}_N$, $\mathbf{z}_L$ and $\mathbf{z}_R \in \mathbb{R}^d$ are update gates for new activation $\hat{\mathbf{h}}_j^l$, left child node $\mathbf{h}_{j-1}^{l-1}$ and right child node $\mathbf{h}_j^{l-1}$ respectively, and $\odot$ indicates element-wise multiplication.

The update gates can be formalized as:

$$\mathbf{z} = \begin{bmatrix} \mathbf{z}_N \\ \mathbf{z}_L \\ \mathbf{z}_R \end{bmatrix} = \begin{bmatrix} 1/Z \\ 1/Z \\ 1/Z \end{bmatrix} \odot \exp(\mathbf{U} \begin{bmatrix} \hat{\mathbf{h}}_j^l \\ \mathbf{h}_{j-1}^{l-1} \\ \mathbf{h}_j^{l-1} \end{bmatrix}), \quad (6)$$

where $\mathbf{U} \in \mathbb{R}^{3d \times 3d}$ is the coefficient of update gates, and $Z \in \mathbb{R}^d$ is the vector of the normalization coefficients,

$$Z_k = \sum_{i=1}^{3} [\exp(\mathbf{U} \begin{bmatrix} \hat{\mathbf{h}}_j^l \\ \mathbf{h}_{j-1}^{l-1} \\ \mathbf{h}_j^{l-1} \end{bmatrix})]_{d \times (i-1)+k}, \quad (7)$$

where $1 \leq k \leq d$.

Intuitively, three update gates are constrained by:

$$\begin{cases} [\mathbf{z}_N]_k + [\mathbf{z}_L]_k + [\mathbf{z}_R]_k = 1, & 1 \leq k \leq d; \\ [\mathbf{z}_N]_k \geq 0, & 1 \leq k \leq d; \\ [\mathbf{z}_L]_k \geq 0, & 1 \leq k \leq d; \\ [\mathbf{z}_R]_k \geq 0, & 1 \leq k \leq d. \end{cases} \quad (8)$$

The new activation $\hat{\mathbf{h}}_j^l$ is computed as:

$$\hat{\mathbf{h}}_j^l = \tanh(\mathbf{W}_{\hat{\mathbf{h}}} \begin{bmatrix} \mathbf{r}_L \odot \mathbf{h}_{j-1}^{l-1} \\ \mathbf{r}_R \odot \mathbf{h}_j^{l-1} \end{bmatrix}), \quad (9)$$

where $\mathbf{W}_{\hat{\mathbf{h}}} \in \mathbb{R}^{d \times 2d}$, $\mathbf{r}_L \in \mathbb{R}^d$, $\mathbf{r}_R \in \mathbb{R}^d$. $\mathbf{r}_L$ and $\mathbf{r}_R$ are the reset gates for left child node $\mathbf{h}_{j-1}^{l-1}$ and right child node $\mathbf{h}_j^{l-1}$ respectively, which can be formalized as:

$$\begin{bmatrix} \mathbf{r}_L \\ \mathbf{r}_R \end{bmatrix} = \sigma(\mathbf{G} \begin{bmatrix} \mathbf{h}_{j-1}^{l-1} \\ \mathbf{h}_j^{l-1} \end{bmatrix}), \quad (10)$$

$$(11)$$

where $\mathbf{G} \in \mathbb{R}^{2d \times 2d}$ is the coefficient of two reset gates and σ indicates the sigmoid function.

Intuiativly, the reset gates control how to select the output information of the left and right children, which results to the current new activation $\hat{\mathbf{h}}$.

By the update gates, the activation of a parent neuron can be regarded as a choice among the the current new activation $\hat{\mathbf{h}}$, the left child, and the right child. This choice allows the overall structure to change adaptively with respect to the inputs.

This gating mechanism is effective to model the combinations of the characters.

3.4 Inference

In Chinese word segmentation task, it is usually to employ the Viterbi algorithm to inference the tag sequence $t_{1:n}$ for a given input sentence $c_{1:n}$.

In order to model the tag dependencies, the previous neural network models (Collobert et al., 2011; Zheng et al., 2013; Pei et al., 2014) introduce a transition matrix $\mathbf{A}$, and each entry $\mathbf{A}_{ij}$ is the score of the transformation from tag $i \in T$ to tag $j \in T$.

Thus, the sentence-level score can be formulated as follows:

$$s(c_{1:n}, t_{1:n}, \theta) = \sum_{i=1}^{n} \left(\mathbf{A}_{t_{i-1}t_i} + f_\theta(t_i|c_{i-w_1:i+w_2})\right), \quad (12)$$

where $f_\theta(t_i|c_{i-w_1:i+w_2})$ is the score for choosing tag t_i for the i-th character by our proposed GRNN (Eq. (4)). The parameter set of our model is $\theta = (\mathbf{M}, \mathbf{W}_s, \mathbf{b}_s, \mathbf{W}_{\hat{\mathbf{h}}}, \mathbf{U}, \mathbf{G}, \mathbf{A})$.

4 Training

4.1 Layer-wise Training

Deep neural network with multiple hidden layers is very difficult to train for its problem of gradient diffusion and risk of overfitting.

Following (Hinton and Salakhutdinov, 2006), we employ the layer-wise training strategy to avoid problems of overfitting and gradient vanishing. The main idea of layer-wise training is to train the network with adding the layers one by one. Specifically, we first train the neural network with the first hidden layer only. Then, we train at the network with two hidden layers after training at first layer is done and so on until we reach the top hidden layer. When getting convergency of the network with layers 1 to l , we preserve the current parameters as initial values of that in training the network with layers 1 to $l + 1$.

4.2 Max-Margin Criterion

We use the Max-Margin criterion (Taskar et al., 2005) to train our model. Intuitively, the Max-Margin criterion provides an alternative to probabilistic, likelihood based estimation methods by concentrating directly on the robustness of the decision boundary of a model. We use $Y(x_i)$ to denote the set of all possible tag sequences for a given sentence x_i and the correct tag sequence for x_i is y_i. The parameter set of our model is θ. We first define a structured margin loss $\Delta(y_i, \hat{y})$ for predicting a tag sequence $\hat{y}$ for a given correct tag sequence y_i:

$$\Delta(y_i, \hat{y}) = \sum_{j}^{n} \eta \mathbf{1}\{y_{i,j} \neq \hat{y}_j\}, \quad (13)$$

where n is the length of sentence x_i and η is a discount parameter. The loss is proportional to the number of characters with an incorrect tag in the predicted tag sequence. For a given training instance (x_i, y_i), we search for the tag sequence with the highest score:

$$y^* = \operatorname*{arg\,max}_{\hat{y} \in Y(x)} s(x_i, \hat{y}, \theta), \quad (14)$$

where the tag sequence is found and scored by the proposed model via the function $s(\cdot)$ in Eq. (12). The object of Max-Margin training is that the tag sequence with highest score is the correct one: $y^* = y_i$ and its score will be larger up to a margin to other possible tag sequences $\hat{y} \in Y(x_i)$:

$$s(x, y_i, \theta) \geq s(x, \hat{y}, \theta) + \Delta(y_i, \hat{y}). \quad (15)$$

This leads to the regularized objective function for m training examples:

$$J(\theta) = \frac{1}{m} \sum_{i=1}^{m} l_i(\theta) + \frac{\lambda}{2} \|\theta\|_2^2, \quad (16)$$

$$l_i(\theta) = \max_{\hat{y} \in Y(x_i)} (s(x_i, \hat{y}, \theta) + \Delta(y_i, \hat{y})) - s(x_i, y_i, \theta). \quad (17)$$

By minimizing this object, the score of the correct tag sequence y_i is increased and score of the highest scoring incorrect tag sequence $\hat{y}$ is decreased. The objective function is not differentiable due to the hinge loss. We use a generalization of gradient descent called subgradient method (Ratliff et al., 2007) which computes a gradient-like direction.

Following (Socher et al., 2013a), we minimize the objective by the diagonal variant of AdaGrad (Duchi et al., 2011) with minibatchs. The parameter update for the i-th parameter $\theta_{t,i}$ at time step t is as follows:

$$\theta_{t,i} = \theta_{t-1,i} - \frac{\alpha}{\sqrt{\sum_{\tau=1}^{t} g_{\tau,i}^2}} g_{t,i}, \quad (18)$$

where α is the initial learning rate and $g_\tau \in \mathbb{R}^{|\theta_i|}$ is the subgradient at time step τ for parameter θ_i.

5 Experiments

We evaluate our model on two different kinds of texts: newswire texts and micro-blog texts. For evaluation, we use the standard Bakeoff scoring program to calculate precision, recall, F1-score.

5.1 Word Segmentation on Newswire Texts

5.1.1 Datasets

We use three popular datasets, PKU, MSRA and CTB6, to evaluate our model on newswire texts. The PKU and MSRA data are provided by the second International Chinese Word Segmentation Bakeoff (Emerson, 2005), and CTB6 is from Chinese TreeBank 6.0 (LDC2007T36) (Xue et al., 2005), which is a segmented, part-of-speech tagged, and fully bracketed corpus in the constituency formalism. These datasets are commonly used by previous state-of-the-art models and neural network models. In addition, we use the first 90% sentences of the training data as training set and the rest 10% sentences as development set for PKU and MSRA datasets, and we divide the training, development and test sets according to (Yang and Xue, 2012) for the CTB6 dataset.

All datasets are preprocessed by replacing the Chinese idioms and the continuous English characters and digits with a unique flag.

5.1.2 Hyper-parameters

We set the hyper-parameters of the model as list in Table 1 via experiments on development set. In addition, we set the batch size to 20. And we find that it is a good balance between model performance and efficiency to set character embedding size $d = 50$. In fact, the larger embedding size leads to higher cost of computational resource, while lower dimensionality of the character embedding seems to underfit according to the experiment results.

Window size	$k = 5$
Character embedding size	$d = 50$
Initial learning rate	$\alpha = 0.3$
Margin loss discount	$\eta = 0.2$
Regularization	$\lambda = 10^{-4}$
Dropout rate on input layer	$p = 20\%$

Table 1: Hyper-parameter settings.

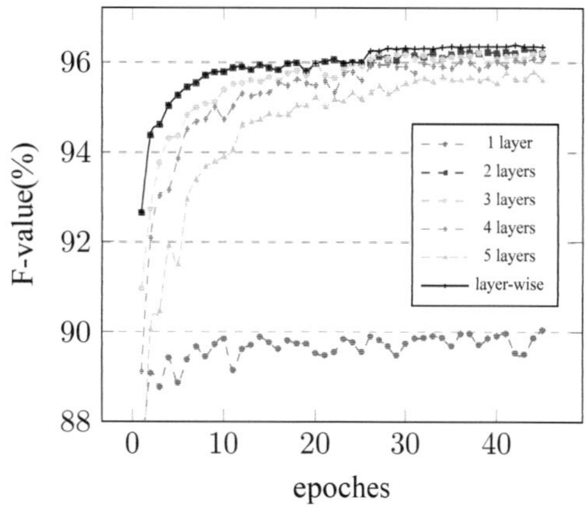

Figure 5: Performance of different models with or without layer-wise training strategy on PKU development set.

Deep neural networks contain multiple nonlinear hidden layers are always hard to train for it is easy to overfit. Several methods have been used in neural models to avoid overfitting, such as early stop and weight regularization. Dropout (Srivastava et al., 2014) is also one of the popular strategies to avoid overfitting when training the deep neural networks. Hence, we utilize the dropout strategy in this work. Specifically, dropout is to temporarily remove the neuron away with a fixed probability p independently, along with the incoming and outgoing connections of it. As a result, we find dropout on the input layer with probability $p = 20\%$ is a good tradeoff between model efficiency and performance.

models	without layer-wise			with layer-wise		
	P	R	F	P	R	F
GRNN (1 layer)	90.7	89.6	90.2	-	-	-
GRNN (2 layers)	96.0	95.6	95.8	96.0	95.6	95.8
GRNN (3 layers)	95.9	95.4	95.7	96.0	95.7	95.9
GRNN (4 layers)	95.6	95.2	95.4	96.1	95.7	95.9
GRNN (5 layers)	95.3	94.7	95.0	96.1	95.7	95.9

Table 2: Performance of different models with or without layer-wise training strategy on PKU test set.

5.1.3 Layer-wise Training

We first investigate the effects of the layer-wise training strategy. Since we set the size of context window to five, there are five recursive layers in our architecture. And we train the networks with the different numbers of recursion layers. Due to the limit of space, we just give the results on PKU dataset.

Figure 5 gives the convergence speeds of the five models with different numbers of layers and the model with layer-wise training strategy on development set of PKU dataset. The model with one layer just use the neurons of the lowest layer in final linear score function. Since there are no non-linear layer, its seems to underfit and perform poorly. The model with two layers just use the neurons in the lowest two layers, and so on. The model with five layers use all the neurons in the network. As we can see, the layer-wise training strategy lead to the fastest convergence and the best performance.

Table 2 shows the performances on PKU test set. The performance of the model with layer-wise training strategy is always better than that without layer-wise training strategy. With the increase of the number of layers, the performance also increases and reaches the stable high performance until getting to the top layer.

5.1.4 Results

We first compare our model with the previous neural approaches on PKU, MSRA and CTB6 datasets as showing in Table 3. The character embeddings of the models are random initialized. The performance of word segmentation is significantly boosted by exploiting the gated recursive architecture, which can better model the combinations of the context characters than the previous neural models.

Previous works have proven it will greatly improve the performance to exploit the pre-trained character embeddings instead of that with random initialization. Thus, we pre-train the embeddings on a huge unlabeled data, the Chinese Wikipedia corpus, with word2vec toolkit (Mikolov et al., 2013). By using these obtained character embeddings, our model receives better performance and still outperforms the previous neural models with pre-trained character embeddings. The detailed results are shown in Table 4 (1st to 3rd rows).

Inspired by (Pei et al., 2014), we utilize the bigram feature embeddings in our model as well. The concept of feature embedding is quite similar to that of character embedding mentioned above. Specifically, each context feature is represented as a single vector called feature embedding. In this paper, we only use the simply bigram feature embeddings initialized by the average of two embeddings of consecutive characters element-wisely.

Although the model of Pei et al. (2014) greatly benefits from the bigram feature embeddings, our model just obtains a small improvement with them. This difference indicates that our model has well modeled the combinations of the characters and do not need much help of the feature engineering. The detailed results are shown in Table 4 (4-th and 6-th rows).

Table 5 shows the comparisons of our model with the state-of-the-art systems on F-value. The model proposed by Zhang and Clark (2007) is a word-based segmentation method, which exploit features of complete words, while remains of the list are all character-based word segmenters, whose features are mostly extracted from the context characters. Moreover, some systems (such as Sun and Xu (2011) and Zhang et al. (2013)) also exploit kinds of extra information such as the unlabeled data or other knowledge. Although our model only uses simple bigram features, it outperforms the previous state-of-the-art methods which use more complex features.

models	PKU			MSRA			CTB6		
	P	R	F	P	R	F	P	R	F
(Zheng et al., 2013)	92.8	92.0	92.4	92.9	93.6	93.3	94.0*	93.1*	93.6*
(Pei et al., 2014)	93.7	93.4	93.5	94.6	94.2	94.4	94.4*	93.4*	93.9*
GRNN	**96.0**	**95.7**	**95.9**	**96.3**	**96.1**	**96.2**	**95.4**	**95.2**	**95.3**

Table 3: Performances on PKU, MSRA and CTB6 test sets with random initialized character embeddings.

models	PKU			MSRA			CTB6		
	P	R	F	P	R	F	P	R	F
+Pre-train									
(Zheng et al., 2013)	93.5	92.2	92.8	94.2	93.7	93.9	93.9*	93.4*	93.7*
(Pei et al., 2014)	94.4	93.6	94.0	95.2	94.6	94.9	94.2*	93.7*	94.0*
GRNN	96.3	95.9	96.1	96.2	96.3	96.2	95.8	95.4	95.6
+bigram									
GRNN	**96.6**	96.2	**96.4**	**97.5**	97.3	97.4	**95.9**	**95.7**	**95.8**
+Pre-train+bigram									
(Pei et al., 2014)	-	95.2	-	-	97.2	-	-	-	-
GRNN	96.5	**96.3**	**96.4**	97.4	**97.8**	**97.6**	95.8	**95.7**	**95.8**

Table 4: Performances on PKU, MSRA and CTB6 test sets with pre-trained and bigram character embeddings.

models	PKU	MSRA	CTB6
(Tseng et al., 2005)	95.0	96.4	-
(Zhang and Clark, 2007)	95.1	97.2	-
(Sun and Xu, 2011)	-	-	95.7
(Zhang et al., 2013)	96.1	97.4	-
This work	**96.4**	**97.6**	**95.8**

Table 5: Comparison of GRNN with the state-of-the-art methods on PKU, MSRA and CTB6 test sets.

5.2 Word Segmentation on Micro-blog Texts

5.2.1 Dataset

We use the NLPCC 2015 dataset[1] (Qiu et al., 2015) to evaluate our model on micro-blog texts. The NLPCC 2015 data are provided by the shared task in the 4th CCF Conference on Natural Language Processing & Chinese Computing (NLPCC 2015): Chinese Word Segmentation and POS Tagging for micro-blog Text. Different with the popular used newswire dataset, the NLPCC 2015 dataset is collected from Sina Weibo[2], which consists of the relatively informal texts from micro-blog with the various topics, such as finance, sports, entertainment, and so on. The information of the dataset is shown in Table 6.

To train our model, we also use the first 90% sentences of the training data as training set and the rest 10% sentences as development set.

Here, we use the default setting of CRF++ toolkit with the feature templates as shown in Table 7. The same feature templates are also used for FNLP.

5.2.2 Results

Since the NLPCC 2015 dataset is a new released dataset, we compare our model with the two popular open source toolkits for sequence labeling task: FNLP[3] (Qiu et al., 2013) and CRF++[4]. Our model uses pre-trained and bigram character embeddings.

Table 8 shows the comparisons of our model with the other systems on NLPCC 2015 dataset.

6 Related Work

Chinese word segmentation has been studied with considerable efforts in the NLP community. The most popular word segmentation method is based on sequence labeling (Xue, 2003). Recently, researchers have tended to explore neural network

[1]`http://nlp.fudan.edu.cn/nlpcc2015/`
[2]`http://www.weibo.com/`

[3]`https://github.com/xpqiu/fnlp/`
[4]`http://taku910.github.io/crfpp/`
*The result is from our own implementation of the corresponding method.

Dataset	Sents	Words	Chars	Word Types	Char Types	OOV Rate
Training	10,000	215,027	347,984	28,208	39,71	-
Test	5,000	106,327	171,652	18,696	3,538	7.25%
Total	15,000	322,410	520,555	35,277	4,243	-

Table 6: Statistical information of NLPCC 2015 dataset.

unigram feature	$c_{-2}, c_{-1}, c_0, c_{+1}, c_{+2}$
bigram feature	$c_{-1} \circ c_0, c_0 \circ c_{+1}$
trigram feature	$c_{-2} \circ c_{-1} \circ c_0, c_{-1} \circ c_0 \circ c_{+1}, c_0 \circ c_{+1} \circ c_{+2}$

Table 7: Templates of CRF++ and FNLP.

models	P	R	F
CRF++	93.3	93.2	93.3
FNLP	94.1	93.9	94.0
This work	94.7	94.8	94.8

Table 8: Performances on NLPCC 2015 dataset.

based approaches (Collobert et al., 2011) to reduce efforts of the feature engineering (Zheng et al., 2013; Qi et al., 2014). However, the features of all these methods are the concatenation of the embeddings of the context characters.

Pei et al. (2014) also used neural tensor model (Socher et al., 2013b) to capture the complicated interactions between tags and context characters. But the interactions depend on the number of the tensor slices, which cannot be too large due to the model complexity. The experiments also show that the model of (Pei et al., 2014) greatly benefits from the further bigram feature embeddings, which shows that their model cannot even handle the interactions of the consecutive characters. Different with them, our model just has a small improvement with the bigram feature embeddings, which indicates that our approach has well modeled the complicated combinations of the context characters, and does not need much help of further feature engineering.

More recently, Cho et al. (2014a) also proposed a gated recursive convolutional neural network in machine translation task to solve the problem of varying lengths of sentences. However, their approach only models the update gate, which can not tell whether the information is from the current state or from sub notes in update stage without reset gate. Instead, our approach models two kinds of gates, reset gate and update gate, by incorporating which we can better model the combinations of context characters via selection function of reset gate and collection function of update gate.

7 Conclusion

In this paper, we propose a gated recursive neural network (GRNN) to explicitly model the combinations of the characters for Chinese word segmentation task. Each neuron in GRNN can be regarded as a different combination of the input characters. Thus, the whole GRNN has an ability to simulate the design of the sophisticated features in traditional methods. Experiments show that our proposed model outperforms the state-of-the-art methods on three popular benchmark datasets.

Despite Chinese word segmentation being a specific case, our model can be easily generalized and applied to other sequence labeling tasks. In future work, we would like to investigate our proposed GRNN on other sequence labeling tasks.

Acknowledgments

We would like to thank the anonymous reviewers for their valuable comments. This work was partially funded by the National Natural Science Foundation of China (61472088, 61473092), the National High Technology Research and Development Program of China (2015AA015408), Shanghai Science and Technology Development Funds (14ZR1403200), Shanghai Leading Academic Discipline Project (B114).

References

Kyunghyun Cho, Bart van Merrienboer, Dzmitry Bahdanau, and Yoshua Bengio. 2014a. On the properties of neural machine translation: Encoder–decoder approaches. In *Proceedings of Workshop on Syntax, Semantics and Structure in Statistical Translation*.

Kyunghyun Cho, Bart van Merrienboer, Caglar Gulcehre, Fethi Bougares, Holger Schwenk, and Yoshua Bengio. 2014b. Learning phrase representations using rnn encoder-decoder for statistical machine translation. In *Proceedings of EMNLP*.

Junyoung Chung, Caglar Gulcehre, KyungHyun Cho, and Yoshua Bengio. 2014. Empirical evaluation of gated recurrent neural networks on sequence modeling. *arXiv preprint arXiv:1412.3555*.

Ronan Collobert, Jason Weston, Léon Bottou, Michael Karlen, Koray Kavukcuoglu, and Pavel Kuksa. 2011. Natural language processing (almost) from scratch. *The Journal of Machine Learning Research*, 12:2493–2537.

John Duchi, Elad Hazan, and Yoram Singer. 2011. Adaptive subgradient methods for online learning and stochastic optimization. *The Journal of Machine Learning Research*, 12:2121–2159.

T. Emerson. 2005. The second international Chinese word segmentation bakeoff. In *Proceedings of the Fourth SIGHAN Workshop on Chinese Language Processing*, pages 123–133. Jeju Island, Korea.

Geoffrey E Hinton and Ruslan R Salakhutdinov. 2006. Reducing the dimensionality of data with neural networks. *Science*, 313(5786):504–507.

Tomas Mikolov, Kai Chen, Greg Corrado, and Jeffrey Dean. 2013. Efficient estimation of word representations in vector space. *arXiv preprint arXiv:1301.3781*.

Wenzhe Pei, Tao Ge, and Chang Baobao. 2014. Max-margin tensor neural network for chinese word segmentation. In *Proceedings of ACL*.

Jordan B Pollack. 1990. Recursive distributed representations. *Artificial Intelligence*, 46(1):77–105.

Yanjun Qi, Sujatha G Das, Ronan Collobert, and Jason Weston. 2014. Deep learning for character-based information extraction. In *Advances in Information Retrieval*, pages 668–674. Springer.

Xipeng Qiu, Qi Zhang, and Xuanjing Huang. 2013. FudanNLP: A toolkit for Chinese natural language processing. In *Proceedings of Annual Meeting of the Association for Computational Linguistics*.

Xipeng Qiu, Peng Qian, Liusong Yin, and Xuanjing Huang. 2015. Overview of the NLPCC 2015 shared task: Chinese word segmentation and POS tagging for micro-blog texts. *arXiv preprint arXiv:1505.07599*.

Nathan D Ratliff, J Andrew Bagnell, and Martin A Zinkevich. 2007. (online) subgradient methods for structured prediction. In *Eleventh International Conference on Artificial Intelligence and Statistics (AIStats)*.

Richard Socher, John Bauer, Christopher D Manning, and Andrew Y Ng. 2013a. Parsing with compositional vector grammars. In *In Proceedings of the ACL conference*. Citeseer.

Richard Socher, Danqi Chen, Christopher D Manning, and Andrew Ng. 2013b. Reasoning with neural tensor networks for knowledge base completion. In *Advances in Neural Information Processing Systems*.

Nitish Srivastava, Geoffrey Hinton, Alex Krizhevsky, Ilya Sutskever, and Ruslan Salakhutdinov. 2014. Dropout: A simple way to prevent neural networks from overfitting. *The Journal of Machine Learning Research*, 15(1):1929–1958.

Weiwei Sun and Jia Xu. 2011. Enhancing Chinese word segmentation using unlabeled data. In *Proceedings of the Conference on Empirical Methods in Natural Language Processing*, pages 970–979. Association for Computational Linguistics.

Ben Taskar, Vassil Chatalbashev, Daphne Koller, and Carlos Guestrin. 2005. Learning structured prediction models: A large margin approach. In *Proceedings of the international conference on Machine learning*.

Huihsin Tseng, Pichuan Chang, Galen Andrew, Daniel Jurafsky, and Christopher Manning. 2005. A conditional random field word segmenter for sighan bakeoff 2005. In *Proceedings of the fourth SIGHAN workshop on Chinese language Processing*, volume 171.

Naiwen Xue, Fei Xia, Fu-Dong Chiou, and Martha Palmer. 2005. The Penn Chinese TreeBank: Phrase structure annotation of a large corpus. *Natural language engineering*, 11(2):207–238.

N. Xue. 2003. Chinese word segmentation as character tagging. *Computational Linguistics and Chinese Language Processing*, 8(1):29–48.

Yaqin Yang and Nianwen Xue. 2012. Chinese comma disambiguation for discourse analysis. In *Proceedings of the 50th Annual Meeting of the Association for Computational Linguistics: Long Papers-Volume 1*, pages 786–794. Association for Computational Linguistics.

Yue Zhang and Stephen Clark. 2007. Chinese segmentation with a word-based perceptron algorithm. In *ACL*.

Longkai Zhang, Houfeng Wang, Xu Sun, and Mairgup Mansur. 2013. Exploring representations from unlabeled data with co-training for Chinese word segmentation. In *Proceedings of the 2013 Conference on Empirical Methods in Natural Language Processing*.

Xiaoqing Zheng, Hanyang Chen, and Tianyu Xu. 2013. Deep learning for chinese word segmentation and pos tagging. In *EMNLP*, pages 647–657.

An analysis of the user occupational class through Twitter content

Daniel Preoţiuc-Pietro[1], **Vasileios Lampos**[2] and **Nikolaos Aletras**[2]

[1] Computer & Information Science, University of Pennsylvania
[2] Department of Computer Science, University College London
danielpr@sas.upenn.edu, {v.lampos,n.aletras}@ucl.ac.uk

Abstract

Social media content can be used as a complementary source to the traditional methods for extracting and studying collective social attributes. This study focuses on the prediction of the occupational class for a public user profile. Our analysis is conducted on a new annotated corpus of Twitter users, their respective job titles, posted textual content and platform-related attributes. We frame our task as classification using latent feature representations such as word clusters and embeddings. The employed linear and, especially, non-linear methods can predict a user's occupational class with strong accuracy for the coarsest level of a standard occupation taxonomy which includes nine classes. Combined with a qualitative assessment, the derived results confirm the feasibility of our approach in inferring a new user attribute that can be embedded in a multitude of downstream applications.

1 Introduction

The growth of online social networks provides the opportunity to analyse user text in a broader context (Tumasjan et al., 2010; Bollen et al., 2011; Lampos and Cristianini, 2012). This includes the social network (Sadilek et al., 2012), spatio-temporal information (Lampos and Cristianini, 2010) and personal attributes (Al Zamal et al., 2012). Previous research has analysed language differences in user attributes like location (Cheng et al., 2010), gender (Burger et al., 2011), impact (Lampos et al., 2014) and age (Rao et al., 2010), showing that language use is influenced by them. Therefore, user text allows us to infer these properties. This *user profiling* is important not only for sociolinguistic studies, but also for other applications: recommender systems to provide targeted advertising, analysts who study different opinions in each social class or integration in text regression tasks such as voting intention (Lampos et al., 2013).

Social status reflected through a person's occupation is a factor which influences language use (Bernstein, 1960; Bernstein, 2003; Labov, 2006). Therefore, our hypothesis is that language use in social media can be indicative of a user's occupational class. For example, executives may write more frequently about business or financial news, while people in manufacturing positions could refer more to their personal interests and less to job related activities. Similarly, we expect some categories of people, like those working in sales and customer services, to be more social or to use more informal language.

Focusing on the microblogging platform of Twitter, we explore our hypothesis by studying the task of predicting a user's occupational class given platform-related attributes and generated content, i.e. tweets. That has direct applicability in a broad range of areas from sociological studies, which analyse the behaviour of different occupations, to recruiting companies that target people for new job opportunities. For this study, we created a publicly available data set of users, including their profile information and historical text content as well as a label to an occupational class from the "Standard Occupational Classification" taxonomy (see Section 2).

We frame our task as classification, aiming to identify the most likely job class for a given user based on profile and a variety of textual features: general word embeddings and clusters (or 'topics'). Both linear and non-linear classification methods are applied with a focus on those that can assist interpretation and offer qualitative insights. We find that text features, especially word clusters, lead to good predictive performance. Accuracy for our best model is well above 50% for 9-way classifi-

Proceedings of the 53rd Annual Meeting of the Association for Computational Linguistics and the 7th International Joint Conference on Natural Language Processing, pages 1754–1764,
Beijing, China, July 26-31, 2015.

cation, outperforming competitive methods. The best results are obtained using the Bayesian non-parametric framework of Gaussian Processes (Rasmussen and Williams, 2006), which also accommodates feature interpretation via the Automatic Relevance Determination. This allows us to get insight into differences in language use across job classes and, finally, assess our original hypothesis about the thematic divergence across them.

2 Standard Occupational Classification

To enable the user occupation study, we adopt a standardised job classification taxonomy for mapping Twitter users to occupations. The Standard Occupational Classification (SOC)[1] is a UK government system developed by the Office of National Statistics for classifying occupations. Jobs are categorised hierarchically based on skill requirements and content. The SOC scheme includes nine major groups coded with a digit from 1 to 9. Each major group is divided into sub-major groups coded with 2 digits, where the first digit indicates the major group. Each sub-major group is further divided into minor groups coded with 3 digits and finally, minor groups are divided into unit groups, coded with 4 digits. The unit groups are the leaves of the hierarchy and represent specific jobs related to the group.

Table 1 shows a part of the SOC hierarchy. In total, there are 9 major groups, 25 sub-major groups, 90 minor groups and 369 unit groups. Although other hierarchies exist, we use the SOC because it has been published recently (in 2010), includes newly introduced jobs, has a balanced hierarchy and offers a wide variety of job titles that were crucial in our data set creation.

Major Group 1 (**C1**): Managers, Directors and Senior Officials
Sub-major Group 11: Corporate Managers and Directors
Minor Group 111: Chief Executives and Senior Officials
Unit Group 1115: Chief Executives and Senior Officials
•Job: chief executive, bank manager
Unit Group 1116: Elected Officers and Representatives
Minor Group 112: Production Managers and Directors
Minor Group 113: Functional Managers and Directors
Minor Group 115: Financial Institution Managers and Directors
Minor Group 116: Managers and Directors in Transport and Logistics
Minor Group 117: Senior Officers in Protective Services
Minor Group 118: Health and Social Services Managers and Directors
Minor Group 119: Managers and Directors in Retail and Wholesale
Sub-major Group 12: Other Managers and Proprietors
Major Group (**C2**): Professional Occupations
•Job: mechanical engineer, pediatrist
Major Group (**C3**): Associate Professional and Technical Occupations
•Job: system administrator, dispensing optician
Major Group (**C4**): Administrative and Secretarial Occupations
•Job: legal clerk, company secretary
Major Group (**C5**): Skilled Trades Occupations
•Job: electrical fitter, tailor
Major Group (**C6**): Caring, Leisure and Other Service Occupations
•Job: nursery assistant, hairdresser
Major Group (**C7**): Sales and Customer Service Occupations
•Job: sales assistant, telephonist
Major Group (**C8**): Process, Plant and Machine Operatives
•Job: factory worker, van driver
Major Group (**C9**): Elementary Occupations
•Job: shelf stacker, bartender

Table 1: Subset of the SOC classification hierarchy.

3 Data

To the best of our knowledge there are no publicly available data sets suitable for the task we aim to investigate. Thus, we have created a new one consisting of Twitter users mapped to their occupation, together with their profile information and historical tweets. We use the account's profile information to capture users with self-disclosed occupations. The potential self-selection bias is acknowledged, but filtering content via self disclosure is widespread when extracting large-scale data for user attribute inference (Pennacchiotti and Popescu, 2011; Coppersmith et al., 2014).

Similarly to Hecht et al. (2011), we first assess the proportion of Twitter accounts with a clear mention to their occupation by annotating the user description field of a random set of 500 users. There were chosen from the random 1% sample, having at least 200 tweets in their history and with a majority of English tweets. There, we can identify the following categories: no description (12.2%), random information (22%), user information but not occupation related (45.8%), and job related information (20%).

To create our data set, we thus use the user description field to search for self-disclosed job titles provided by the 4-digit SOC unit groups, since they contain specific job titles. We queried Twitter's Search API to retrieve for each job title a maximum of 200 accounts which best matched occupation keywords. Then, we aggregated the accounts into the 3-digit (minor) categories. To remove potential ambiguity in the retrieved set, we manually inspected accounts in each minor category and filtered out those that belong to companies, contain no description or the description provided does not indicate that the user has a job corresponding to the minor category. In total, around 50% of the accounts were removed by manual inspection per-

[1] `http://www.ons.gov.uk/ons/guide-method/classifications/current-standard-classifications/soc2010/index.html`; accessed on 24/02/2015.

formed by the authors. We also removed users in multiple categories and or users that have tweeted less than 50 times in their history. Finally, we eliminated all 3-digit categories that contained less than 45 user accounts after this filtering. This process produced a total number of 5,191 users from 55 minor groups (22 sub-major groups), spread across all nine major SOC groups. The distribution of users across these nine groups is: 9.7%, 34.5%, 20.6%, 3.8%, 16.7%, 6.1%, 1.4%, 4.2%, and 3% (following the ordering of Table 1). In our data set the most well represented minor occupational groups are 'Functional Managers and Directors' (184 users – code 113), 'Therapy Professionals' (159 users – code 222) and 'Quality and Regulatory Professionals' (158 users – code 246), whereas the least represented ones are 'Textile and Garment Trades' (45 users – code 541), 'Elementary Security Occupations' (46 users – code 924), 'Elementary Cleaning Occupations' (47 users – code 923). The mean number of users in the minor classes is equal to 94.4 with a standard deviation of 35.6. For these users, we have collected all their tweets, going as far back as the latest 3,200, and their profile information. The final data set consists of 10,796,836 tweets collected around 5 August 2014 and is openly available.[2]

A separate Twitter data set is used as a reference corpus in order to build the feature representations detailed in Section 4. This data set is an extract from the Twitter Gardenhose stream (a 10% representative sample of the entire Twitter stream) from 2 January to 28 February 2011. Based on this content, we also build the vocabulary for the text features, containing the most frequent 71,555 words. We tokenise and filter for English using the Trendminer preprocessing pipeline (Preoţiuc-Pietro et al., 2012).

4 Features

In this section, we overview the features used in the occupational class prediction task. They are divided into two types: (1) user level features, (2) textual features.

4.1 User Level Features (UserLevel)

The user level features are based on the general user information or aggregated statistics about the tweets. Table 2 introduces the 18 features in this category.

[2]http://www.sas.upenn.edu/~danielpr/jobs.tar.gz

u_1	number of followers
u_2	number of friends
u_3	number of times listed
u_4	follower/friend ratio
u_5	proportion of non-duplicate tweets
u_6	proportion of retweeted tweets
u_7	average no. of retweets/tweet
u_8	proportion of retweets done
u_9	proportion of hashtags
u_{10}	proportion of tweets with hashtags
u_{11}	proportion of tweets with @-mentions
u_{12}	proportion of @-replies
u_{13}	no. of unique @-mentions in tweets
u_{14}	proportion of tweets with links
u_{15}	no. of favourites the account made
u_{16}	avg. number of tweets/day
u_{17}	total number of tweets
u_{18}	proportion of tweets in English

Table 2: User level attributes for a Twitter user.

4.2 Textual Features

The textual features are derived from the aggregated set of user's tweets. We use our reference corpus to represent each user as a distribution over these features. We ignore the bio field from building textual features to avoid introducing biases from our data collection method. While this is a restriction, our analysis showed that in less than 20% of the cases the information in the bio is directly relevant to the occupation.

4.2.1 SVD Word Embeddings (SVD-E)

We use a more abstract representation of words than simple unigram counts in order to aid interpretability of our analysis. We compute a word to word similarity matrix from our reference corpus. Normalised Pointwise Mutual Information (NPMI) (Bouma, 2009) is used to compute word to word similarity. NPMI is an information theoretic measure indicating which words co-occur in the same context, where the context is represented by a whole tweet:

$$\mathrm{NPMI}(x, y) = -\log \mathrm{P}(x, y) \cdot \log \frac{\mathrm{P}(x, y)}{\mathrm{P}(x) \cdot \mathrm{P}(y)}. \quad (1)$$

We then perform singular value decomposition (SVD) on the word to word similarity matrix and obtain an embedding of words into a low dimensional space. In our experiments we tried the following dimensionalities: 30, 50, 100 and 200. The feature representation for each user is obtained summing over each of the embedding dimensions across all words.

4.2.2 NPMI Clusters (SVD-C)

We use the NPMI matrix described in the previous paragraph to create hard clusters of words. These clusters can be thought as 'topics', i.e. words that are semantically similar. From a variety of clustering techniques we choose spectral clustering (Shi and Malik, 2000; Ng et al., 2002), a hard-clustering approach which deals well with high-dimensional and non-convex data (von Luxburg, 2007). Spectral clustering is based on applying SVD to the graph Laplacian and aims to perform an optimal graph partitioning on the NPMI similarity matrix. The number of clusters needs to be pre-specified. We use 30, 50, 100 and 200 clusters – numbers were chosen a priori based on previous work (Lampos et al., 2014). The feature representation is the standardised number of words from each cluster.

Although there is a loss of information compared to the original representation, the clusters are very useful in the model analysis step. Embeddings are hard to interpret because each dimension is an abstract notion, while the clusters can be interpreted by presenting a list of the most frequent or representative words. The latter are identified using the following centrality metric:

$$\mathrm{C}_w = \frac{\sum_{x \in c} \mathrm{NPMI}(w, x)}{|c| - 1}, \quad (2)$$

where c denotes the cluster and w the target word.

4.2.3 Neural Embeddings (W2V-E)

Recently, there has been a growing interest in neural language models, where the words are projected into a lower dimensional dense vector space via a hidden layer (Mikolov et al., 2013b). These models showed they can provide a better representation of words compared to traditional language models (Mikolov et al., 2013c) because they capture syntactic information rather than just bag-of-context, handling non-linear transformations. In this low dimensional vector space, words with a small distance are considered semantically similar. We use the skip-gram model with negative sampling (Mikolov et al., 2013a) to learn word embeddings on the Twitter reference corpus. In that case, the skip-gram model is factorising a word-context PMI matrix (Levy and Goldberg, 2014). We use a layer size of 50 and the Gensim implementation.[3]

[3]http://radimrehurek.com/gensim/models/word2vec.html

4.2.4 Neural Clusters (W2V-C)

Similar to the NPMI cluster, we use the neural embeddings in order to obtain clusters of related words, i.e. 'topics'. We derive a word to word similarity matrix using cosine similarity on the neural embeddings. We apply spectral clustering on this matrix to obtain 30, 50, 100 and 200 word clusters.

5 Classification with Gaussian Processes

In this section, we briefly overview Gaussian Process (GP) for classification, highlighting our motivation for using this method. GPs formulate a Bayesian non-parametric machine learning framework which defines a prior on functions (Rasmussen and Williams, 2006). The properties of the functions are given by a kernel which models the covariance in the response values as a function of its inputs. Although GPs form a powerful learning tool, they have only recently been used in NLP research (Cohn and Specia, 2013; Preoţiuc-Pietro and Cohn, 2013) with classification applications limited to (Polajnar et al., 2011).

Formally, GP methods aim to learn a function $f : \mathbb{R}^d \rightarrow \mathbb{R}$ drawn from a GP prior given the inputs $\boldsymbol{x} \in \mathbb{R}^d$:

$$f(\boldsymbol{x}) \sim \mathcal{GP}(m(\boldsymbol{x}), k(\boldsymbol{x}, \boldsymbol{x}')), \quad (3)$$

where $m(\cdot)$ is the mean function (here 0) and $k(\cdot, \cdot)$ is the covariance kernel. Usually, the Squared Exponential (SE) kernel (a.k.a. RBF or Gaussian) is used to encourage smooth functions. For the multi-dimensional pair of inputs $(\boldsymbol{x}, \boldsymbol{x}')$, this is:

$$k_{\text{ard}}(\boldsymbol{x}, \boldsymbol{x}') = \sigma^2 \exp\left[\sum_i^d -\frac{(x_i - x_i')^2}{2l_i^2}\right], \quad (4)$$

where l_i are lengthscale parameters learnt only using training data by performing gradient ascent on the type-II marginal likelihood. Intuitively, the lengthscale parameter l_i controls the variation along the i input dimension, i.e. a low value makes the output very sensitive to input data, thus making that input more useful for the prediction. If the lengthscales are learnt separately for each input dimension the kernel is named SE with Automatic Relevance Determination (ARD) (Neal, 1996).

Binary classification using GPs 'squashes' the real valued latent function $f(x)$ output through a logistic function: $\pi(\boldsymbol{x}) \triangleq \mathrm{P}(y = 1|\boldsymbol{x}) = \sigma(f(\boldsymbol{x}))$ in a similar way to logistic regression classification. The object of the GP inference is the distribution of the latent variable corresponding to a test case x_*:

$$\mathrm{P}(f_*|\boldsymbol{x}, \boldsymbol{y}, x_*) = \int \mathrm{P}(f_*|\boldsymbol{x}, x_*, f)\mathrm{P}(f|\boldsymbol{x}, \boldsymbol{y})df\,, \tag{5}$$

where $\mathrm{P}(f|\boldsymbol{x}, \boldsymbol{y}) = \mathrm{P}(\boldsymbol{y}|f)\mathrm{P}(f|\boldsymbol{x})/\mathrm{P}(\boldsymbol{y}|\boldsymbol{x})$ is the posterior over the latent variables. If the likelihood $\mathrm{P}(\boldsymbol{y}|f)$ is Gaussian, the combination with a GP prior $\mathrm{P}(f|\boldsymbol{x})$ gives a posterior GP over functions. In binary classification, the distribution over the latent f_* is combined with the logistic function to produce the prediction:

$$\bar{\pi}_* = \int \sigma(f_*)\mathrm{P}(f_*|\boldsymbol{x}, \boldsymbol{y}, x_*)df_*. \tag{6}$$

This results in a non-Gaussian likelihood in the posterior formulation and therefore, exact inference is infeasible for classification models. Multiple approximations exist that make the computation tractable (Gibbs and Mackay, 1997; Williams and Barber, 1998; Neal, 1999). In our experiments we opt to use the Expectation Propagation (EP) method (Minka, 2001) which approximates the non-Gaussian joint posterior with a Gaussian one. EP offers very good empirical results for many different likelihoods, although it has no proof of convergence. The complexity for the inference step is $\mathcal{O}(n^3)$. Given that our data set is very large and the number of features is high, we conduct inference using the fully independent training conditional (FITC) approximation (Snelson and Ghahramani, 2006) with 500 random inducing points. We refer the interested reader to Rasmussen and Williams (2006) for further information on GP classification.

Although we could use multi-class classification methods, in order to provide insight, we perform a separate one-vs-all classification for each class and then determine a label through the occupational class that has the highest likelihood.

6 Experiments

This section presents the experimental results for our task. We first compare the accuracy of our classification methods on held out data using each feature set and conduct a standard error analysis. We then use the interpretability of the ARD lengthscales from the GP classifier to further analyse the relevant features.

6.1 Predictive Accuracy

We assign users to one of nine possible classes (see the 'Major Groups' on Table 1) using one set of features at a time. Experiments combining features yielded only minor improvements. We apply common linear and non-linear methods together with our proposed **GP** classifier. The linear method is logistic regression (**LR**) with Elastic Net regularisation (Freedman, 2009) and the non-linear one is formulated by a Support Vector Machine (**SVM**) with an RBF kernel (Vapnik, 1998). The accuracy of our classifiers is measured on held-out data. Our data set is divided into stratified training (80%), validation (10%) and testing (10%) sets. The validation set was used to learn the LR and SVM hyperparameters, while the GP did not use this set at all. We report results using all three methods and all feature sets in Table 3.

Feature	LR	SVM	GP
Most frequent class	34.4%	34.4%	34.4%
UserLevel	34.0%	31.5%	34.2%
SVD-E-30	36.3%	35.0%	39.8%
SVD-E-50	36.7%	36.9%	38.6%
SVD-E-100	40.8%	41.9%	40.9%
SVD-E-200	40.0%	43.1%	43.8%
SVD-C-30	36.9%	36.5%	38.2%
SVD-C-50	37.7%	38.3%	40.5%
SVD-C-100	40.4%	42.1%	44.6%
SVD-C-200	44.2%	47.9%	48.2%
W2V-E-50	42.5%	49.0%	48.4%
W2V-C-30	40.0%	46.0%	47.1%
W2V-C-50	42.3%	48.5%	47.9%
W2V-C-100	44.4%	48.7%	51.3%
W2V-C-200	**46.9%**	**51.7%**	**52.7%**

Table 3: 9-way classification accuracy on held-out data for our 3 methods. Textual features are obtained using **SVD** or Word2Vec (**W2V**). **E** represents embeddings, **C** clusters. The final number denotes the amount of clusters or the size of the embedding.

We first observe that user level features (UserLevel; see Section 4.1) are not useful for predicting the job class. This finding indicates that general social behaviour or user impact are likely to be spread evenly across classes. It also highlights the difficulty of the task and motivates the use of deeper textual features.

The textual features (see Section 4.2) improve performance as compared to the most frequent class baseline. We also notice that the embeddings (SVD-E and W2V-E) have lower performance than the clusters (SVD-C and W2V-C) in most of the cases. This is expected, as adding word vectors to represent a user's text may overemphasise common words. The size of the embedding also increases performance. The W2V features show better ac-

Rank	Topic #	Label	Topic (most central words; *most frequent words*)	MRR	$\mu(l)$
1	116	Arts	archival, stencil, canvas, minimalist, illustration, paintings, abstract, designs, lettering, steampunk; *art, design, print, collection, poster, painting, custom, logo, printing, drawing*	.43	1.35
2	105	Health	chemotherapy, diagnosis, disease, inflammation, diseases, arthritis, symptoms, patients, mrsa, colitis; *risk, cancer, mental, stress, patients, treatment, surgery, disease, drugs, doctor*	.20	2.76
3	153	Beauty Care	exfoliating, cleanser, hydrating, moisturizer, moisturiser, shampoo, lotions, serum, moisture, clarins; *beauty, natural, dry, skin, massage, plastic, spray, facial, treatments, soap*	.19	3.69
4	21	Higher Education	undergraduate, doctoral, academic, students, curriculum, postgraduate, enrolled, master's, admissions, literacy; *students, research, board, student, college, education, library, schools, teaching, teachers*	.18	3.21
5	158	Software Engineering	integrated, data, implementation, integration, enterprise, configuration, open-source, cisco, proprietary, avaya; *service, data, system, services, access, security, development, software, testing, standard*	.17	3.10
7	186	Football	bardsley, etherington, gallas, heitinga, assou-ekotto, lescott, pienaar, warnock, ridgewell, jenas; *van, foster, cole, winger, terry, reckons, youngster, rooney, fielding, kenny*	.16	3.11
8	124	Corporate	consortium, institutional, firm's, acquisition, enterprises, subsidiary, corp, telecommunications, infrastructure, partnership; *patent, industry, reports, global, survey, leading, firm, 2015, innovation, financial*	.15	2.44
9	96	Cooking	parmesan, curried, marinated, zucchini, roasted, coleslaw, salad, tomato, spinach, lentils; *recipe, meat, salad, egg, soup, sauce, beef, served, pork, rice*	.15	3.00
12	164	Elongated Words	yaaayy, wooooo, woooo, yayyyyy, yaaaaay, yayayaya, yayy, yaaaaaaay, wooohooo, yaayyy; *wait, till, til, yay, ahhh, hoo, woo, woot, whoop, woohoo*	.11	3.47
16	176	Politics	religious, colonialism, christianity, judaism, persecution, fascism, marxism, nationalism, communism, apartheid; *human, culture, justice, religion, democracy, religious, humanity, tradition, ancient, racism*	.08	3.09

Table 4: Topics, represented by their most central and most frequent 10 words, sorted by their ARD lengthscale MRR across the nine GP-based occupation classifiers. $\mu(l)$ denotes the average lengthscale for a topic across these classifiers. Topic labels are manually created.

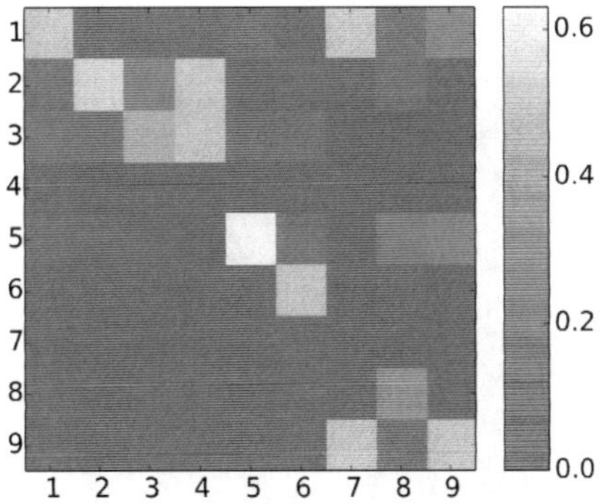

Figure 1: Confusion matrix of the prediction results. Rows represent the actual occupational class (**C** 1–9) and columns the predicted class.

curacy than the SVD on the NPMI matrix. This is consistent with previous work that showed the efficiency of word2vec and the ability of those embeddings to capture non-linear relationships and syntactic features (Mikolov et al., 2013a; Mikolov et al., 2013b; Mikolov et al., 2013c).

LR has a lower performance than the non-linear methods, especially when using clusters as features. GPs usually outperform SVMs by a small margin. However, these offer the advantages of not using the validation set and the interpretability properties we highlight in the next section. Although we only draw our focus on major occupational classes, the data set allows the study of finer granularities of occupation classes in future work. For example, prediction performance for sub-major groups reaches 33.9% accuracy (15.6% majority class, 22 classes) and 29.2% accuracy for minor groups (3.4% majority class, 55 classes).

6.2 Error Analysis

To illustrate the errors made by our classifiers, Figure 1 shows the confusion matrix of the classification results. First, we observe that class 4 is many times classified as class 2 or 3. This can be explained by the fact that classes 2, 3 and 4 contain similar types of occupations, e.g. doctors and nurses or accountants and assistant accountants. However, with very few exceptions, we notice that only adjacent classes get misclassified, suggesting that our model captures the general user skill level.

6.3 Qualitative Analysis

The word clusters that were built from a reference corpus and then used as features in the GP classifier, give us the opportunity to extract some qualitative derivations from our predictive task. For the rest of the section we use the best performing model of this type (W2V-C-200) in order to analyse the results. Our main assumption is that there might be a divergence of language and topic usage across occupational classes following previous studies in sociology (Bernstein, 1960; Bernstein, 2003). Knowing that the inferred GP lengthscale hyperparameters are inversely proportional to feature (i.e. topic) relevance (see Section 5), we can use them to rank the topic importance and give answers to our hypothesis.

Table 4 shows 10 of the most informative topics (represented by the top 10 most central and frequent words) sorted by their ARD lengthscale Mean Reciprocal Rank (MRR) (Manning et al., 2008) across the nine classifiers. Evidently, they cover a broad range of thematic subjects, including potentially work specific topics in different domains such as 'Corporate' (Topic #124), 'Software Engineering' (#158), 'Health' (#105), 'Higher Education' (#21) and 'Arts' (#116), as well as topics covering recreational interests such as 'Football' (#186), 'Cooking' (#96) and 'Beauty Care' (#153).

The highest ranked MRR GP lengthscales only highlight the topics that are the most discriminative of the particular learning task, i.e. which topic used alone would have had the best performance. To examine the difference in topic usage across occupations, we illustrate how six topics are covered by the users of each class. Figure 2 shows the Cumulative Distribution Functions (CDFs) across the nine different occupational classes for these six topics. CDFs indicate the fraction of users having at least a certain topic proportion in their tweets. A topic is more prevalent in a class, if the CDF line leans towards the bottom-right corner of the plot.

'Higher Education' (#21) is more prevalent in classes 1 and 2, but is also discriminative for classes 3 and 4 compared to the rest. This is expected because the vast majority of jobs in these classes require a university degree (holds for all of the jobs in classes 2 and 3) or are actually jobs in higher education. On the other hand, classes 5 to 9 have a similar behaviour, tweeting less on this topic. We also observe that words in 'Corporate' (#124) are used more as the skill required for a job gets higher. This topic is mainly used by people in classes 1 and 2 and with less extent in classes 3 and 4, indicating that people in these occupational classes are more likely to use social media for discussions about corporate business.

There is a clear trend of people with more skilled jobs to talk about 'Politics' (#176). Indeed, highly ranked politicians and political philosophers are parts of classes 1 and 2 respectively. Nevertheless, this pattern expands to the entire spectrum of the investigated occupational classes, providing further proof-of-concept for our methodology, under the assumption that the theme of politics is more attractive to the higher skilled classes rather than the lower skilled occupations. By examining 'Arts' (#116), we see that it clearly separates class 5, which includes artists, from all others. This topic appears to be relevant to most of the classification tasks and it is ranked first according to the MRR metric. Moreover, we observe that people with higher skilled jobs and education (classes 1–3) post more content about arts. Finally, we examine two topics containing words that can be used in more informal occasions, i.e. 'Elongated Words' (#164) and 'Beauty Care' (#153). We observe a similar pattern in both topics by which users with lower skilled jobs tweet more often.

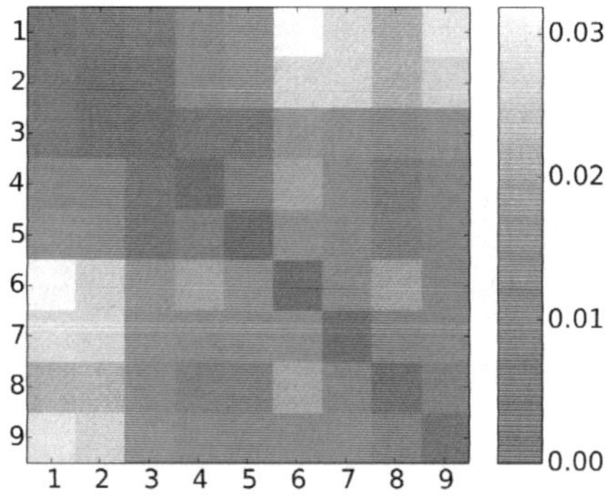

Figure 3: Jensen-Shannon divergence in the topic distributions between the different occupational classes (**C** 1–9).

The main conclusion we draw from Figure 2 is that there exists a topic divergence between users in the lower vs. higher skilled occupational classes. To examine this distinction better, we use the Jensen-Shannon divergence (JSD) to quantify the difference between the topic distributions across every

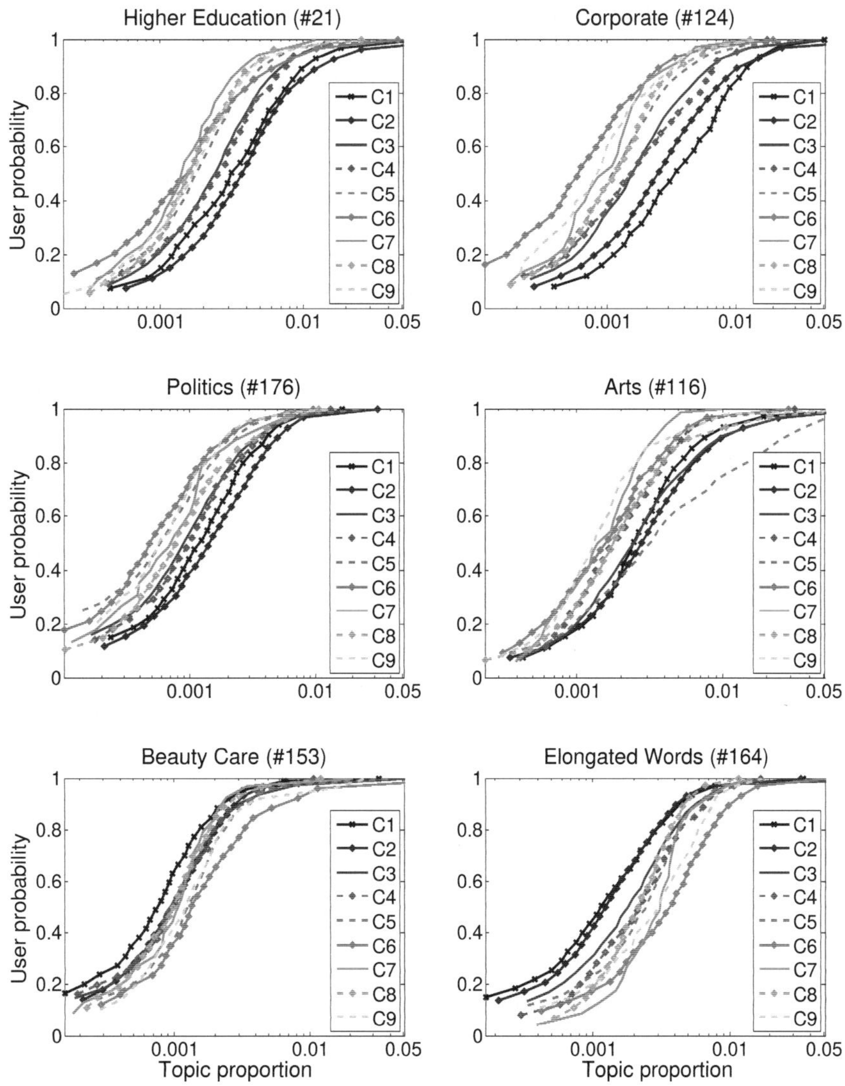

Figure 2: CDFs for six of the most important topics; the x-axis is on the log-scale for display purposes. A point on a CDF line indicates the fraction of users (y-axis point) with a topic proportion in their tweets lower or equal to the corresponding x-axis point. The topic is more prevalent in a class, if the CDF line leans closer to the bottom-right corner of the plot.

class pair. Figure 3 visualises these differences. There, we confirm that adjacent classes use similar topics of discussion. We also notice that JSD increases as the classes are further apart. Two main groups of related classes, with a clear separation from the rest, are identified: classes 1–2 and 6–9. For the users belonging to these two groups, we compute their topic usage distribution (for the top topics listed in Table 4). Then, we assess whether the topic usage distributions of those super-classes of occupations have a statistically significant difference by performing a two-sample Kolmogorov-Smirnov test. We enumerate the group topic usage means in Table 5; all differences were indeed statistically significant ($p < 10^{-5}$). From this comparison, we conclude that users in the higher skilled classes have a higher representation in all top topics but 'Beauty Care' and 'Elongated Words'. Hence, the original hypothesis about the difference in the usage of language between upper and lower occupational classes is reconfirmed in this more generic testing. A very noticeable difference occurs for the

Topics	C 1–2	C 6–9
Arts	4.95	2.79
Health	4.45	2.13
Beauty Care	1.40	2.24
Higher Education	6.04	2.56
Software Engineering	6.31	2.54
Football	0.54	0.52
Corporate	5.15	1.41
Cooking	2.81	2.49
Elongated Words	1.90	3.78
Politics	2.14	1.06

Table 5: Comparison of mean topic usage for super-sets (classes 1–2 vs. 6–9) of the occupational classes; all values were multiplied by 10^3. The difference between the topic usage distributions was statistically significant ($p < 10^{-5}$).

'Corporate' topic, whereas 'Football' registers the lowest distance.

7 Related Work

Occupational class prediction has been studied in the past in the areas of psychology and economics. French (1959) investigated the relation between various measures on 232 undergraduate students and their future occupations. This study concluded that occupational membership can be predicted from variables such as the ability of subjects in using mathematical and verbal symbols, their family economic status, body-build and personality components. Schmidt and Strauss (1975) also studied the relationship between job types (five classes) and certain demographic attributes (gender, race, experience, education, location). Their analysis identified biases or discrimination which possibly exist in different types of jobs. Sociolinguistic and sociology studies deduct that social status is an important factor in determining the use of language (Bernstein, 1960; Bernstein, 2003; Labov, 2006). Differences arise either due to language use or due to the topics people discuss as parts of various social domains. However, a large scale investigation of this hypothesis has never been attempted.

Relevant to our task is a relation extraction approach proposed by Li et al. (2014) aiming to extract user profile information on Twitter. They used a weakly supervised approach to obtain information for job, education and spouse. Nonetheless, the information relevant to the job attribute regards the employer of a user (i.e. the name of a company) rather than the type of occupation. In addition, Huang et al. (2014) proposed a method to classify Sina Weibo users to twelve predefined occupations using content based and network features. However, there exist significant differences from our task since this inference is based on a distinct platform, with an ambiguous distribution over occupations (e.g. more than 25% related to media), while the occupational classes are not generic (e.g. media, welfare and electronic are three of the twelve categories). Most importantly, the applied model did not allow for a qualitative interpretation. Filho et al. (2014) inferred the social class of social media users by combining geolocation information derived from Foursquare and Twitter posts. Recently, Sloan et al. (2015) introduced tools for the automated extraction of demographic data (age, occupation and social class) from the profile descriptions of Twitter users using a similar method to our data set extraction approach. They showed that it is feasible to build a data set that matches the real-world UK occupation distribution as given by the SOC.

8 Conclusions

Our paper presents the first large-scale systematic study on language use on social media as a factor for inferring a user's occupational class. To address this problem, we have also introduced an extensive labelled data set extracted from Twitter. We have framed prediction as a classification task and, to this end, we used the powerful, non-linear GP framework that combines strong predictive performance with feature interpretability. Results show that we can achieve a good predictive accuracy, highlighting that the occupation of a user influences text use. Through a qualitative analysis, we have shown that the derived topics capture both occupation specific interests as well as general class-based behaviours. We acknowledge that the derivations of this study, similarly to other studies in the field, are reflecting the Twitter population and may experience a bias introduced by users self-mentioning their occupations. However, the magnitude, occupational diversity and face validity of our conclusions suggest that the presented approach is useful for future downstream applications.

Acknowledgements

DP-P acknowledges the support from Templeton Religion Trust, grant TRT-0048. VL and NA acknowledge the support from EPSRC (UK) project EP/K031953/1. We thank Mark Stevenson for his critical comments on early drafts of this paper.

References

Faiyaz Al Zamal, Wendy Liu, and Derek Ruths. 2012. Homophily and Latent Attribute Inference: Inferring Latent Attributes of Twitter Users from Neighbors. In *Proc. of 6th International Conference on Weblogs and Social Media*, pages 387–390.

Basil Bernstein. 1960. Language and social class. *British Journal of Sociology*, pages 271–276.

Basil Bernstein. 2003. *Class, codes and control: Applied studies towards a sociology of language*, volume 2. Psychology Press.

Johan Bollen, Huina Mao, and Xiaojun Zeng. 2011. Twitter mood predicts the stock market. *Journal of Computational Science*, 2(1):1–8.

Gerlof Bouma. 2009. Normalized (pointwise) mutual information in collocation extraction. In *Biennial GSCL Conference*, pages 31–40.

D. John Burger, John Henderson, George Kim, and Guido Zarrella. 2011. Discriminating Gender on Twitter. In *Proceedings of the 2011 Conference on Empirical Methods in Natural Language Processing*, EMNLP, pages 1301–1309.

Zhiyuan Cheng, James Caverlee, and Kyumin Lee. 2010. You are where you tweet: a content-based approach to geo-locating twitter users. In *Proceedings of the 19th ACM Conference on Information and Knowledge Management*, CIKM, pages 759–768.

Trevor Cohn and Lucia Specia. 2013. Modelling annotator bias with multi-task gaussian processes: An application to machine translation quality estimation. In *51st Annual Meeting of the Association for Computational Linguistics*, ACL, pages 32–42.

Glen Coppersmith, Craig Harman, and Mark Dredze. 2014. Measuring post traumatic stress disorder in twitter. In *International Conference on Weblogs and Social Media*, ICWSM.

Renato Miranda Filho, Guilherme R. Borges, Jussara M. Almeida, and Gisele L. Pappa. 2014. Inferring user social class in online social networks. In *Proceedings of the 8th Workshop on Social Network Mining and Analysis*, SNAKDD'14, pages 10:1–10:5.

David Freedman. 2009. *Statistical models: theory and practice*. Cambridge University Press.

Wendell L French. 1959. Can a man's occupation be predicted? *Journal of Counseling Psychology*, 6(2):95.

Mark Gibbs and David J. C. Mackay. 1997. Variational gaussian process classifiers. *IEEE Transactions on Neural Networks*, 11:1458–1464.

Brent Hecht, Lichan Hong, Bongwon Suh, and Ed H. Chi. 2011. Tweets from justin bieber's heart: The dynamics of the location field in user profiles. In *Proceedings of the SIGCHI Conference on Human Factors in Computing Systems*, CHI.

Yanxiang Huang, Lele Yu, Xiang Wang, and Bin Cui. 2014. A multi-source integration framework for user occupation inference in social media systems. *World Wide Web*, pages 1–21.

William Labov. 2006. *The Social Stratification of English in New York City*. Cambridge University Press, second edition.

Vasileios Lampos and Nello Cristianini. 2010. Tracking the flu pandemic by monitoring the Social Web. In *Proc. of the 2nd International Workshop on Cognitive Information Processing*, pages 411–416.

Vasileios Lampos and Nello Cristianini. 2012. Nowcasting Events from the Social Web with Statistical Learning. *ACM Transactions on Intelligent Systems and Technology*, 3(4):72:1–72:22.

Vasileios Lampos, Daniel Preoţiuc-Pietro, and Trevor Cohn. 2013. A user-centric model of voting intention from Social Media. In *Proceedings of the 51st Annual Meeting of the Association for Computational Linguistics*, ACL, pages 993–1003.

Vasileios Lampos, Nikolaos Aletras, Daniel Preoţiuc-Pietro, and Trevor Cohn. 2014. Predicting and characterising user impact on Twitter. In *Proceedings of the 14th Conference of the European Chapter of the Association for Computational Linguistics*, EACL, pages 405–413.

Omer Levy and Yoav Goldberg. 2014. Neural word embeddings as implicit matrix factorization. In *Advances in Neural Information Processing Systems*, NIPS, pages 2177–2185.

Jiwei Li, Alan Ritter, and Eduard H. Hovy. 2014. Weakly supervised user profile extraction from twitter. In *Proceedings of the 52nd Annual Meeting of the Association for Computational Linguistics*, ACL, pages 165–174.

Christopher D. Manning, Prabhakar Raghavan, and Hinrich Schütze. 2008. *Introduction to Information Retrieval*. Cambridge University Press.

Tomas Mikolov, Kai Chen, Greg Corrado, and Jeffrey Dean. 2013a. Efficient estimation of word representations in vector space. In *Proceedings of Workshop at the International Conference on Learning Representations*, ICLR.

Tomas Mikolov, Ilya Sutskever, Kai Chen, Greg Corrado, and Jeffrey Dean. 2013b. Distributed representations of words and phrases and their compositionality. In *Advances in Neural Information Processing Systems*, NIPS, pages 3111–3119.

Tomas Mikolov, Wen tau Yih, and Geoffrey Zweig. 2013c. Linguistic regularities in continuous space word representations. In *Proceedings of the 2010 annual Conference of the North American Chapter of the Association for Computational Linguistics*, NAACL, pages 746–751.

Thomas P. Minka. 2001. Expectation propagation for approximate bayesian inference. In *Proceedings of the 17th Conference in Uncertainty in Artificial Intelligence*, UAI '01.

Radford M. Neal. 1996. *Bayesian Learning for Neural Networks*. Springer-Verlag New York, Inc.

Radford M. Neal. 1999. Regression and classification using gaussian process priors. *Bayesian Statistics 6*, pages 475–501.

Andrew Y. Ng, Michael I. Jordan, and Yair Weiss. 2002. On spectral clustering: Analysis and an algorithm. In *Advances in Neural Information Processing Systems*, NIPS, pages 849–856.

Marco Pennacchiotti and Ana-Maria Popescu. 2011. A machine learning approach to twitter user classification. ICWSM, pages 281–288.

Tamara Polajnar, Simon Rogers, and Mark Girolami. 2011. Protein interaction detection in sentences via gaussian processes; a preliminary evaluation. *International Journal of Data Mining and Bioinformatics*, 5(1):52–72.

Daniel Preoţiuc-Pietro and Trevor Cohn. 2013. A temporal model of text periodicities using Gaussian Processes. EMNLP.

Daniel Preoţiuc-Pietro, Sina Samangooei, Trevor Cohn, Nicholas Gibbins, and Mahesan Niranjan. 2012. Trendminer: An architecture for real time analysis of social media text. In *Workshop on Real-Time Analysis and Mining of Social Streams (RAMSS)*, ICWSM.

Delip Rao, David Yarowsky, Abhishek Shreevats, and Manaswi Gupta. 2010. Classifying Latent User Attributes in Twitter. In *Proceedings of the 2nd International Workshop on Search and Mining User-generated Contents*, SMUC, pages 37–44.

Carl Edward Rasmussen and Christopher K. I. Williams. 2006. *Gaussian Processes for Machine Learning*. The MIT Press.

Adam Sadilek, Henry Kautz, and Vincent Silenzio. 2012. Modeling Spread of Disease from Social Interactions. In *Proc. of 6th International Conference on Weblogs and Social Media*, pages 322–329.

Peter Schmidt and Robert P Strauss. 1975. The prediction of occupation using multiple logit models. *International Economic Review*, 16(2):471–86.

Jianbo Shi and Jitendra Malik. 2000. Normalized cuts and image segmentation. *Transactions on Pattern Analysis and Machine Intelligence*, 22(8):888–905.

Luke Sloan, Jeffrey Morgan, Pete Burnap, and Matthew Williams. 2015. Who tweets? Deriving the demographic characteristics of age, occupation and social class from twitter user meta-data. *PloS one*, 10(3):e0115545.

Edward Snelson and Zoubin Ghahramani. 2006. Sparse gaussian processes using pseudo-inputs. In *Advances in Neural Information Processing Systems*, NIPS, pages 1257–1264.

Andranik Tumasjan, Timm Oliver Sprenger, Philipp G Sandner, and Isabell M Welpe. 2010. Predicting Elections with Twitter: What 140 Characters Reveal about Political Sentiment. In *Proc. of 4th International Conference on Weblogs and Social Media*, pages 178–185.

Vladimir N Vapnik. 1998. *Statistical learning theory*. Wiley, New York.

Ulrike von Luxburg. 2007. A tutorial on spectral clustering. *Statistics and computing*, 17(4):395–416.

Christopher K.I Williams and David Barber. 1998. Bayesian classification with gaussian processes. *IEEE Transactions on Pattern Analysis and Machine Intelligence*, 20 (12):1342–1351.

Tracking unbounded Topic Streams

Dominik Wurzer
School of Informatics
University of Edinburgh
d.s.wurzer
@sms.ed.ac.uk

Victor Lavrenko
School of Informatics
University of Edinburgh
vlavrenk
@inf.ed.ac.uk

Miles Osborne
Bloomberg
London
mosborne29
@bloomberg.net

Abstract

Tracking topics on social media streams is non-trivial as the number of topics mentioned grows without bound. This complexity is compounded when we want to track such topics against other fast moving streams. We go beyond traditional small scale topic tracking and consider a stream of topics against another document stream. We introduce two tracking approaches which are fully applicable to true streaming environments. When tracking 4.4 million topics against 52 million documents in constant time and space, we demonstrate that counter to expectations, simple single-pass clustering can outperform locality sensitive hashing for nearest neighbour search on streams.

1 Introduction

The emergence of massive social media streams has sparked a growing need for systems able to process them. While previous research (Hassan et al., 2009; Becker et al., 2009; Petrovic et al., 2010; Cataldi et al., (2010); Weng et al., (2011); Petrovic 2013) has focused on detecting new topics in unbounded textual streams, less attention was paid to following (tracking) the steadily growing set of topics. Standard topic tracking (Allan, 2002) deals with helping human analysts follow and monitor ongoing events on massive data streams. By pairing topics with relevant documents, topic tracking splits a noisy stream of documents into sub-streams grouped by their target topics. This is a crucial task for financial and security analysts who are interested in pulling together relevant information from unstructured and noisy data streams. Other fields like summarization or topic modeling benefit from topic tracking as a mean to generate their data sources.

In todays data streams however, new topics emerge on a continual basis and we are interested in following all instead of just a small fraction of newly detected topics. Since its introduction (Allan, 2002), standard topic tracking typically operates on a small scale and against a static set of predefined target topics. We go beyond such approaches and deal for the first time with massive, unbounded topic streams. Examples of unbounded topic streams include all events reported by news agencies each day across the world; popular examples of unbounded document streams include social media services such as Twitter. Tracking streams of topics allows research tasks like topic-modeling or summarization to be applied to millions of topics, a scale that is several orders of magnitude larger than those of current publications. We present two massive scale topic tracking systems capable of tracking unbounded topic streams. One is based on locality sensitive hashing (LSH) and the other on clustering. Since we operate on two unbounded data sources we are subject to the streaming model of computation (Muthukrishnan, 2005), which requires instant and single-pass decision making in constant time and space. Contrary to expectations, we find that nearest neighbour search on a stream based on clustering performs faster than LSH for the same level of accuracy. This is surprising as LSH is widely believed to be the fastest way of nearest neighbour search. Our experiments reveal how simple single-pass clustering outperforms LSH in terms of effectiveness and efficiency. Our results are general and apply to any setting where we have massive or infinite numbers of topics, matched against unboundedly large document streams.

Proceedings of the 53rd Annual Meeting of the Association for Computational Linguistics and the 7th International Joint Conference on Natural Language Processing, pages 1765–1773,
Beijing, China, July 26-31, 2015.

Contributions

- For the first time we show how it is possible to track an unbounded stream of topics in constant time and space, while maintaining a level of effectiveness that is statistically indistinguishable from an exact tracking system
- We show how single-pass clustering can outperform locality sensitive hashing in terms of effectiveness and efficiency for identifying nearest neighbours in a stream
- We demonstrate that standard measures of similarity are sub-optimal when matching short documents against long documents

2 Related Work

Topic or event tracking was first introduced in the Topic Detection and Tracking (TDT) program (Allan, 2002). In TDT, topic tracking involves monitoring a stream of news documents with the intent to identify those documents relevant to a small predefined set of target topics. During the course of TDT, research focused extensively on the effectiveness of tracking systems, neglecting scale and efficiency. The three official data sets only range from 25k to 74k documents with a few hundred topics (Allan, 2002).

More recently, the rise of publicly available real-time social media streams triggered new research on topic detection and tracking, intended to apply the technology to those high volume document streams. The novel data streams differ from the TDT data sets in their volume and level of noise. To provide real-time applications, traditional methods need to be overhauled to keep computation feasible. It became common practice to limit data sets to cope with the computational effort. Popular strategies involve reducing the number of tracked topics (Lin et al., 2011; Nichols et al., 2012;) as well as sampling the document stream (Ghosh et al., 2013). These approaches have proven to be efficient in cutting down workload but they also limit an application's performance. Furthermore, Sayyadi et al. (2009) discovered and tracked topics in social streams based on keyword graphs. They applied the sliding window principle to keep the computation feasible, although their data set only contained 18k documents. Yang et al. 2012 tracked topics in tweet streams using language models. To cope with the computational effort they assume a small set of topics of only a few dozen, which are defined in advance. Tang et al. (2011) tracked a single topic on a few thousand blogs based on semantic graph topic models. Pon et al. (2007) recommend news by tracking multiple topics for a user but their data sets only span several thousand documents and a few topics.

Further related work includes the real-time filtering task, introduced as part of TREC's Microblog Track in 2012 (Soboroff et al., 2012). Hong et al. (2013) explore topic tracking in tweet streams in relation to the TREC real-time filtering task by relying on a sliding window principle, while focusing on the cold start problem.

3 Topic Tracking

3.1 Traditional Approach

Numerous approaches to topic tracking have emerged, spanning from probabilistic retrieval to statistical classification frameworks. While there is no single general approach, we define the traditional approach to tracking from a high-level perspective covering the basic principle of all previous approaches. We do not make any assumptions about the kind of topics, documents or distance functions used. As defined by TDT (Allan, 2002), we assume, we operate on an unbounded document stream with the goal of tracking a fixed set of target topics. Although topics are allowed to drift conceptually and evolve over time, new topics would always trigger the start of a new tracking system.

Algorithm 1 Traditional Tracking

INPUT:
TOPIC-SET $\{t \in T\}$
DOCUMENT-STREAM $\{d \in D\}$
OUTPUT:
relevant topic-document pairs $\{t, d\}$

while *documents d in stream D* **do**
  for all *topics t in set T* **do**
    similarity = computeSimilarity(d,t)
    if similarity > threshold **then**
      emit relevant $\{t, d\}$

As seen in Algorithm 1, documents arrive one at a time, requiring instant decision making through single pass processing. Each document is compared to all topics representations to identify the closest topic. The tracking decision is based on the similarity to the closest topic and usually defined by a thresholding strategy. Because incoming documents can be relevant to more than one topic, we need to match it against all of them. Due to its simplicity, the traditional tracking approach is highly efficient when applied to a fairly low number of topics.

3.2 Shortcomings of the traditional approach

The traditional approach - though low in computational effort - becomes challenging when scaling up the number of target topics. The computational effort arises from the number of comparisons made (the number of documents times topics). That explains, why researches following the traditional approach have either lowered the number of documents or topics. Heuristics and indexing methods increase the performance but offer no solution scalable to true streaming environments because they only allow for one-side scaling (either a large number of documents or topics). Increasing either of the two components by a single document, increases the computational effort by the magnitude of the other one. For the extreme case of pushing to an infinite number of topics, tracking in constant space is a necessity.

4 Tracking at scale

Before directly turning to a full streaming set up in constant space, we approach tracking a topic stream on a document stream in unbounded space. The key to scale up documents and topics, lies in reducing the number of necessary comparisons. Throughout the remainder of this paper we represent documents and topics arriving from a steady high volume stream by term-weighted vectors in the vector space.
In order to cut down the search space, we encapsulate every topic vector by a hypothetical region marking its area of proximity. Those regions are intend to capture documents that are more likely to be relevant. Ideally, these regions form a hypersphere centred around every topic vector with a radius equal to the maximum distance to relevant documents. The tracking procedure is then reduced to determining whether an incoming document is also enclosed by any of the hyperspheres.

4.1 Approximated Tracking

Our first attempt to reach sub-linear execution time uses random segmentation of the vector space using hashing techniques. We frame the tracking process as a nearest neighbour search problem, as defined by Gionis et al. (1999). Documents arriving from a stream are seen as queries and the closest topics are the nearest neighbours to be identified. We explore locality sensitive hashing (LSH), as described by Indyk et al. (1998), to approach high dimensional nearest neighbour search for topic tracking in sub-linear time. LSH, which has been used to speed up NLP applications (Ravichandran et al., 2005), provides hash functions that guarantee that similar documents are more likely to be hashed to the same binary hash key than distant ones. Hash functions capture similarities between vectors in high dimensions and represent them on a low dimensional binary level. We apply the scheme by Charikar (2002), which describes the probabilistic bounds for the cosine similarity between two vectors. Each bit in a hash key represents a documents position with respect to a randomly placed hyperplane. Those planes segment the vector space, forming high dimensional polygon shaped buckets. Documents and topics are placed into a bucket by determining on which side of each the hyperplanes they are positioned. We interpret these buckets as regions of proximity as the collision probability is directly proportional to the cosine similarity between two vectors.

Algorithm 2 LSH-based Tracking

INPUT:
TOPIC-STREAM $\{T\}$
DOCUMENT-STREAM $\{D\}$
OUTPUT:
relevant topic-document pairs $\{t, d\}$

```
while document d in T, D do
    if d ϵ T then
        hashKeys = hash_LSH(d)
        store hashKeys in hashTables
    else if d ϵ D then
        candidateSet = lookupHashtables(hash_LSH(d))
        for all topics t in candidateSet do
            if similarity(d,t) > threshold then
                emit relevant {t, d}
```

Algorithm 2 outlines the pseudo code to LSH-based tracking. Whenever a topic arrives, it is hashed, placing it into a bucket. To increase collision probability with similar documents, we repeat the hashing process with different hash functions, storing a topic and hash-key tuple in a hash table. On each arrival of a new document the same hash functions are applied and the key is matched against the hash tables, yielding a set of candidate topics. The probabilistic bounds of the hashing scheme guarantee that topics in the candidate set

are on average more likely to be similar to the document than others.
We then match each topic in the candidate set against the document to lower the false positive rate of LSH (Gionis, et al., 1999). The number of exact comparisons necessary is reduced to the number of topics in the candidate set.

4.2 Cluster based Tracking

LSH based tracking segments the vector-space randomly without consideration of the data's distribution. In contrast, we now propose a data dependent approach through document clustering. The main motivation for data dependent space segmentation is increased effectiveness resulting from taking the topic distribution within the vector space into account when forming the regions of proximity. We construct these regions by grouping similar topics to form clusters represented by a centroid. When tracking a document, it is matched against the centroids instead of all topics, yielding a set of candidate topics. This allows reducing the number of comparisons necessary to only the number of centroids plus the number of topics captured by the closest cluster.

Algorithm 3 Cluster based Tracking

```
INPUT:
INITIAL-CLUSTER-SET {c ϵ C}
TOPIC-STREAM {T}
DOCUMENT-STREAM {D}
threshold for spawning a new cluster {thr_spawn}
threshold for adapting an existing cluster {thr_adapt}
OUTPUT:
relevant topic-document pairs {t, d}

while document d in T, D do
    if d ϵ T then
        c_min = argmin_c{distances(d, c ϵ C)}
        if distance(d,c_min) > thr_spawn then
            spawnNewCluster(d → C)
        else if distance(d,c_min) < thr_adapt then
            contribute,assign(c_min,d)
        else
            assign(c_min,d)
    else if d ϵ D then
        c_min = argmin_c{distances(d,c ϵ C)}
        candidateSet = {t ϵ c_min}
        for all topics t in candidateSet do
            if similarity(d,t) > threshold then
                emit relevant {t, d}
```

While the literature provides a vast diversity of clustering methods for textual documents, our requirements regarding tracking streams of topics naturally reduce the selection to lightweight single-pass algorithms. Yang et al. (2012) provided evidence that in extreme settings simple approaches work well in terms of balancing effectiveness, efficiency and scalability. We identified ArteCM by Carullo et al. (2008), originally intended to cluster documents for the web, as suitable. Algorithm 3 outlines our approach for cluster based tracking. Given an initial set of 4 random centroids, we compare each arriving topic to all centroids. We associate the new topic with the cluster whenever it is close enough. Particularly close documents contribute to a cluster, allowing it to drift towards topic dense regions. If the document is distant to all existing clusters, we spawn a new cluster based on the document.
Documents arriving from the document stream are exactly matched against all centroids to determine the k-closest clusters. Topics associated with those clusters are subsequently exhaustively compared with the document, yielding topic-document pairs considered to be relevant. Probing more than one cluster increases the probability of finding similar topics. This does not correlate with soft-clustering methods as multiple probing happens at querying time while topics are assigned under a hard clustering paradigm.

4.3 Algorithm Comparison

Both the LSH- and the cluster-based tracking algorithm provide two parameters that are conceptually directly comparable to each other. The number of bits per hash key and the threshold for spawning new clusters directly determine the size of the candidate set by either varying the bucket size or the cluster radius. The size of the candidate set trades a gain in efficiency against a loss in effectiveness. Fewer topics in the candidate set heavily reduce the search space for the tracking process but increase the chance of missing a relevant topic. Bigger sets are more likely to cover relevant topics but require more computational effort during the exact comparison step. The proposed algorithms allow continuously adjusting the candidate set size between two extremes of having all topics in a single set and having a separate set for each topic.
The second parameter both algorithms have in common, is the number of probes to increase the probability of identifying similar topics. While LSH-based tracking offers the number of hash tables, cluster-based tracking provides the number of clusters probed. We again encounter a trade-off between gains in efficiency at the cost of effective-

ness. Each additionally probed cluster or looked up table increases the chance of finding relevant topics as well as the computational effort.

5 Tracking Streams in Constant Space

Operation in constant space is crucial when tracking topic streams. We ensure this by placing an upper limit on the number of concurrently tracked topics. Whenever the limit is reached, an active topic is deleted and subsequently not considered any longer. The strategy for selecting deletion candidates is heavily application dependant. To handle topic streams, LSH-based tracking replaces the entries of an active topic in its hash-tables by the values of the new topic, whenever the maximum number of topics is reached. Cluster-based tracking requires more adaptation because we allow clusters to drift conceptually. Whenever the maximum number of topics is reached, the contribution of the deletion candidate to its cluster is reverted and it is removed, freeing space for a new topic.

6 Experiments

We evaluate the three algorithms in terms of effectiveness and efficiency. Starting out with tracking a small set of topics using the traditional approach, we evaluate various similarity metrics to ensure high effectiveness. We then conduct scaling experiments on massive streams in bounded and unbounded space.

Corpora

Traditional tracking datasets are unsuitable to approach tracking at scale as they consist of only a few thousand documents and several hundred topics (Allan, 2002). We created a new data set consisting of two streams (document and topic stream). The document stream consists of 52 million tweets gathered through Twitter's streaming API [1]. The tweets are order by their time-stamps. Since we are advocating a high volume topic stream, we require millions of topics. To ensure a high number of topics, we treat the entire English part (4.4 mio articles) of Wikipedia[2] as a proxy for a collection of topics and turn it into a stream. Each article is considered to be an unstructured textual representation of a topic time-stamped by its latest verified update.

[1] http://stream.twitter.com

[2] http://en.wikipedia.org/wiki/Wikipedia_database

Relevance Judgements

The topics we picked range from natural disasters, political and financial events to news about celebrities, as seen in table 3. We adopted the search-guided-annotation process used by NIST (Fiscus et al., 2002) and followed NIST's TDT annotation guidelines. According to the definition of TDT, a document is relevant to a topic if it speaks about it (Allan, 2002). In total we identified 14,436 tweets as relevant to one of 30 topics.

total number of topics	4.4 mio
annotated topics	30
total number of documents	52 mio
documents relevant to one of the 30 annotated topics	14.5k

Table 1: Data set statistics

Baseline

We use an exact tracking system as a baseline. To speed up runtime, we implement an inverted index in conjunction with term-at-a-time query execution. Additionally, we provide a trade off between effectiveness and efficiency by randomly down sampling the Twitter stream. Note that this closely resembles previous approaches to scale topic tracking (Ghosh et al., 2013).

Evaluation Metrics

We evaluate effectiveness by recall and precision and combine them using F1 scores. Efficiency is evaluated using two different metrics. We provide a theoretical upper bound by computing the number of dot products required for tracking (Equations 1-4).

$$DP_{traditional} = n_D * n_T \quad (1)$$

$$DP_{LSH-based} = (n_D + n_T) * (k * L) + DP_{cs} \quad (2)$$

$$DP_{cluster-based} = (n_D + n_T) * c + DP_{cs} \quad (3)$$

$$DP_{cs} = n_D * n_C \quad (4)$$

Variables	Definition
n_D	total number of documents
n_T	total number of topics
k	number of bits per hash
L	total number of hash tables
c	total number of clusters
n_C	total number of topics in all candidate sets

Table 2: Definition of variables for equation 1-4

Topic-Title	Topic description	Number of relevant tweets
Amy Winehouse	Amy Winehouse dies	3265
Prince William	William and Kate arrive in Canada	1021
Floods in Seoul	Floods and landslides in North and South Korea	432
Flight 4896	Flight 4896 crashed	11
Bangladesh-India border	Bangladesh and India sign a border pact	4
Goran Hadzic	War criminal Goran Hadzic got arrested	2

Table 3: Showing 6 example topics plus a short summary of relevant tweets, as well as the number of relevant tweets per topic

They therefore indicate performance without system- or implementation-dependent distortions. Equations 2 and 3 represent the cost to identify the candidate set for the LSH- and cluster-based algorithm plus the cost resulting from exhaustively comparing the candidate sets with the documents (Equation 4).

Because we compute the dot products for a worst case scenario, we also provide the runtime in seconds. All run-times are averaged over 5 runs, measured on the same idle machine. To ensure fair comparison, all algorithms are implemented in C using the same libraries, compiler, compiler optimizations and run as a single process using 4 GB of memory. Because the runtime of the traditional approach ($\sim$171 days) exceeds our limits, we estimate it based on extrapolating 50 runs using up to 25,000 topics. Note that this extrapolation favours the efficiency of the baseline system as it ignores hardware dependent slowdowns when scaling up the number of topics.

6.1 Exact tracking

In our first experiment we track 30 annotated topics on 52 million tweets using the traditional approach. We compare various similarity measures (Table 4) and use the best-performing one in all following experiments. Our data set differs from the TREC and TDT corpora, which used news-wire articles. Allan et al. (2000) report that the cosine similarity constantly performed as the best distance function for TDT. The use of Wikipedia and Twitter causes a different set of similarity measures to perform best. This results from the imbalance in average document length between Wikipedia articles (590 terms) and tweets (11 terms). The term weights in short tweets (many only containing a single term) are inflated by the cosine's length normalization. Those short tweets are however not uniquely linkable to target topics and consequently regarded as non-relevant by annotators, which explains the drop in performance. The similarity function chosen for all subsequent experiments is a BM25 weighted dot product, which we found to perform best.

	F1 score
tf-idf weighted cosine	0.147
tf-idf weighted dot product	0.149
BM25 weighted cosine	0.208
BM25 weighted dot product	0.217

Table 4: Comparing the effectiveness of similarity measures when matching 30 Wikipedia articles against 52 million tweets

6.2 Tracking at scale, using Wikipedia and Twitter

Previously, we conducted small scale experiments, now we are looking to scale them up, by tracking 4.4 million Wikipedia articles on 52 million tweets without limiting the number of topics tracked. The resulting trade-off between effectiveness and efficiency is shown in Figure 1 and 2. The right-most point corresponds to exhaustive comparison of every document against every topic – this results in highest possible effectiveness (F1 score) and highest computational cost. All runs use optimal tracking thresholds determined by sweeping them while optimizing on F1 score as an objective function. We also show the performance resulting from the traditional approach when randomly down-sampling the document (Twitter) stream, which resembles previous attempts to scale tracking (Ghosh et al., 2013). Every point on the LSH-based tracking curve in Figure 1 and 2 represents a different number of bits per hash key (varying between 4 and 20) and tables (ranging from 6 to 200). The points on the cluster-based tracking curves result from varying the number of clusters (ranging from 1 to 100,000) and probes. The resulting bucket sizes span from a few dozen to over a million topics.

As expected, the graphs in Figure 1 closely resembles those in Figure 2. The two figures also show that the performance of all three algorithms is continuously adjustable. Unsurprisingly, LSH- and cluster-based tracking clearly outperform

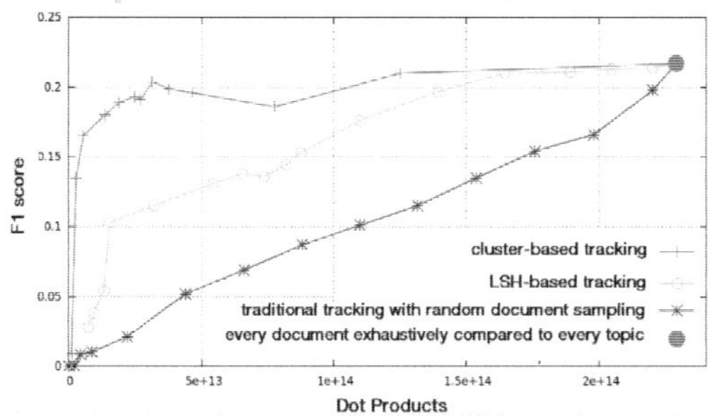

Figure 1: Trade-off between efficiency and dot-products for LSH- and cluster-based tracking as well as a random down-sampling approach for traditional tracking

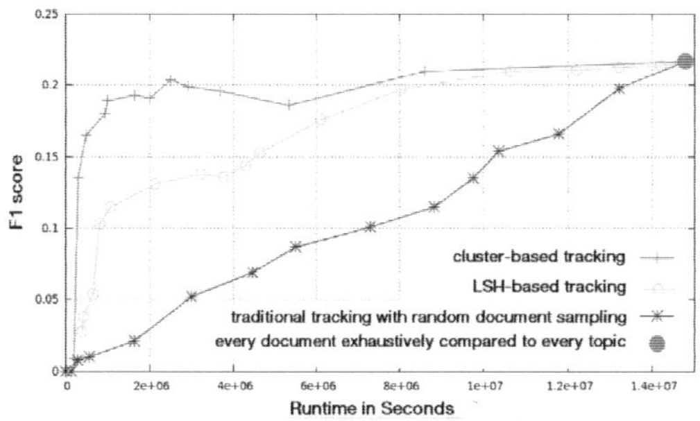

Figure 2: Trade-off between efficiency and runtime for LSH- and cluster-based tracking as well as a random down-sampling approach for traditional tracking;

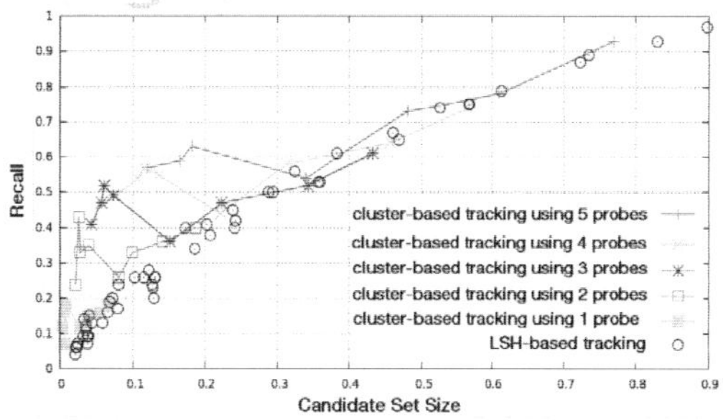

Figure 3: Comparing the candidate set size with the Recall of LSH- with cluster-based tracking without the exact evaluation phase; The magnitude of the candidate set size represents the ratio between the number of candidate topics and the total number of topics;

random document sampling for the traditional approach, based on their more effective search space reduction strategies. More surprisingly, we also observe that cluster-based tracking outperforms tracking based on LSH in terms of efficiency for F1 scores between 10% and 20%. To understand why tracking based on clustering is faster than randomized tracking, we further investigate their abilities in cutting down the search space.

Figure 3 presents the candidate set size necessary to find a certain ratio of relevant topics. The graph also illustrates the impact of probing multiple clusters. When focusing on a recall up to 60%, LSH-based tracking requires a significantly larger candidate set size in comparison with tracking through clustering. For example, LSH-based tracking needs to examine 30% of all topics to reach a recall of 50%, while the cluster based approach only needs to look at 9%. This effect diminishes for higher recall values. Furthermore, we observe an impressive performance gain in recall from 20% to 60%, resulting from additionally probing the k-closest clusters instead of just the closest one. While data dependent segmentation is expected to outperform LSH in terms of effectiveness, we were surprised by the magnitude of its impact on efficiency.

The lack in effectiveness of LSH has a direct negative implication on its efficiency for tracking. In order to make up for its suboptimal space segmentation, it requires substantially bigger candidate sets to reach the same level of recall as the cluster-based approach. The size of the candidate set is critical because we assume a subsequent exact comparison phase to lower the false positive rate. The overhead of both algorithms is outweighed by the cost of exact comparison for the candidate set.

Table 5, which compares the performance of the three algorithms, reveals a drastic reduction in runtime of up to 80%, at the cost of only a minor decrease in F1 score. The differences of 6% and 10% percent in F1 score are statistically not significant according to a sign test ($p<=0.362$ and $p<=0.2$). Consequently, both algorithms achieve substantial runtime reduction, while maintaining a level of effectiveness that is statistically indistinguishable from the traditional (exact) approach.

6.3 Tracking Wikipedia on Twitter in constant space

Tracking a stream of topics in bounded space is highly application specific due to the deletion procedure. We know from previous studies (Nichols et al., 2012) that a topic's popularity within Twitter fades away over time. We are interested in keeping currently active topics and delete those that attract the least number of recent documents. This set-up has the interesting aspect that the doc-

Algorithm	F1 score	Dot Products	Runtime (sec)
traditional approach	0.217	$2.3 * 10^{14}$	$1.5 * 10^{7}$
LSH-based tracking	0.196 (-10%)	$1.4 * 10^{14}$ (-39%)	$8.0 * 10^{6}$ (-46%)
cluster-based tracking	0.204 (-6%)	$3.1 * 10^{13}$ (-86%)	$2.5 * 10^{6}$ (-83%)

Table 5: Effectiveness and efficiency of LSH- and cluster-based tracking to the traditional approach

Algorithm	Space	F1 score	dot products	runtime (sec)
LSH-based tracking	unbounded	0.196	$1.4 * 10^{14}$	$8.0 * 10^{6}$
	bounded	0.173 (-12%)	$5.1 * 10^{11}$ (-99%)	$4.1 * 10^{4}$ (-99%)
cluster-based tracking	unbounded	0.204	$3.1 * 10^{13}$	$2.5 * 10^{6}$
	bounded	0.189 (-7%)	$1.8 * 10^{11}$ (-99%)	$3.3 * 10^{4}$ (-98%)

Table 6: Effectiveness and efficiency for tracking in bounded and unbounded space

ument stream dictates the lifespan of each topic in the topic stream. Table 6 contains the results of cluster- and LSH-based tracking and compares them to their bounded versions using the same set up. Note that the hit in performance is solely defined by the amount of memory provided and therefore continuously adjustable.

For this particular experiment, we chose an upper bound of 25k concurrent topics. The table represents a substantial drop in runtime, following the reduced search space, at a fairly low expense in effectiveness. Based on our observations, we hypothesise that significant topics are more likely to be discussed during random Twitter chatter than the average Wikipedia topic. It is interesting to notice that the runtime also indicates a lower overhead for LSH-based tracking in comparison with the cluster-based approach. This difference was hidden in the unbounded tracking experiments but carries now more weight.

7 Conclusion

We extended traditional topic tracking by demonstrating that it is possible to track an unbounded stream of topics in constant space and time. We also presented two approaches to tracking, based on LSH and clustering that efficiently scale to a high number of topics and documents while maintaining a level of effectiveness that is statistically indistinguishable from an exact tracking system. While they trade gains in efficiency against a loss in effectiveness, we showed that cluster based tracking does so more efficiently due to more effective space segmentation, which allows a higher reduction of the search space. Contrary to common believes this showed how nearest neighbour search in data streams based on clustering performs faster than LSH, for the same level of accuracy. Furthermore, we showed that standard measures of similarity (cosine) are sub-optimal when tracking Wikipedia against Twitter.

References

James Allan, Victor Lavrenko, Daniella Malin, and Russell Swan. 2000. Detections, bounds, and timelines: Umass and tdt-3. In Proceedings of Topic Detection and Tracking Workshop, pages 167-174.

James Allan, Ron Papka, and Victor Lavrenko. 1998. On-line new event detection and tracking. In Proceedings of the 21st annual international ACM SIGIR conference on Research and development in information retrieval (SIGIR '98). ACM, New York, NY, USA.

James Allan. 2002. Topic Detection and Tracking: Event-Based Information Organization. Kluwer Academic Publishers, Norwell, MA, USA.

Mario Cataldi, Luigi Di Caro, and Claudio Schifanella. 2010. Emerging topic detection on Twitter based on temporal and social terms evaluation. In Proceedings of the Tenth International Workshop on Multimedia Data Mining, pages 1-10. ACM.

H. Becker, M. Naaman, and L. Gravano. 2009. Event Identification in Social Media. In 12th International Workshop on the Web and Databases (WebDB'09), Providence, USA.

Moreno Carullo, Elisabetta Binaghi, Ignazio Gallo and Nicola Lamberti. 2008. "Clustering of short commercial documents for the web." Paper presented at the meeting of the ICPR.

Moses S. Charikar. 2002. Similarity estimation techniques from rounding algorithms. In Proceedings of the thirty-fourth annual ACM symposium on Theory of computing (STOC '02). ACM, New York, NY, USA.

Eichmann, D. and P. Sirivasan. 1999. "Filters, Webs and Answers: The University of Iowa TREC-8 Results" Eighth Conference on Text Retrieval, NIST, USA.

Fiscus, J. G. and Doddington, G. R. 2002. Topic detection and tracking evaluation overview. Topic detection and tracking: event-based information organization, pages 17-31.

Saptarshi Ghosh, Muhammad Bilal Zafar, Parantapa Bhattacharya, Naveen Sharma, Niloy Ganguly, and Krishna Gummadi. 2013. On sampling the wisdom of crowds: random vs. expert sampling of the twitter stream. In Proceedings of the 22nd ACM international conference on Conference on information & knowledge management (CIKM-13). New York, NY, USA.

Aristides Gionis, Piotr Indyk, and Rajeev Motwani. 1999. Similarity Search in High Dimensions via Hashing. InProceedings of the 25th International Conference on Very Large Data Bases (VLDB '99), San Francisco, CA, USA.

Sayyadi Hassan, Hurst Matthew and Maykov Alexey. 2009. "Event Detection and Tracking in Social Streams." In Proceedings of the ICWSM, CA, USA.

Yihong Hong, Yue Fei, and Jianwu Yang. 2013. Exploiting topic tracking in real-time tweet streams. In Proceedings of the 2013 international workshop on Mining unstructured big data using natural language processing. ACM, New York, NY, USA.

Piotr Indyk and Rajeev Motwani. 1998. Approximate nearest neighbours: towards removing the curse of dimensionality. In Proceedings of the thirtieth annual ACM symposium on Theory of computing (STOC '98). ACM, New York, NY, USA.

Jimmy Lin, Rion Snow, and William Morgan. 2011. Smoothing techniques for adaptive online language models: topic tracking in tweet streams. In Proceedings of the 17th ACM SIGKDD international conference on Knowledge discovery and data mining (KDD '11). ACM, New York, NY, USA, 422-429.

S. Muthukrishnan. 2005. Data streams: Algorithms and applications. Now Publishers Inc.

Jeffrey Nichols, Jalal Mahmud, and Clemens Drews. 2012. Summarizing sporting events using twitter. In-Proceedings of the 2012 ACM international conference on Intelligent User Interfaces (IUI '12). ACM, New York, NY, USA.

Sasa Petrovic, Miles Osborne, and Victor Lavrenko. 2010. Streaming first story detection with application to Twitter. In Human Language Technologies: The 2010 Annual Conference of the North American Chapter of the Association for Computational Linguistics (HLT '10). Association for Computational Linguistics, Stroudsburg, PA, USA.

Sasa Petrovic. 2013. Real-time event detection in massive streams. Ph.D. thesis, School of Informatics, University of Edinburgh.

Deepak Ravichandran, Patrick Pantel, and Eduard Hovy. 2005. Randomized Algorithms and NLP: Using Locality Sensitive Hash Functions for High Speed Noun Clustering. In Proceedings of ACL.

Raymond K. Pon, Alfonso F. Cardenas, David Buttler, and Terence Critchlow. 2007. Tracking multiple topics for finding interesting articles. In Proceedings of the 13th ACM SIGKDD international conference on Knowledge discovery and data mining (KDD '07). ACM, New York, NY, USA.

I. Soboroff, I. Ounis, and J. Lin. 2012. Overview of the trec-2012 microblog track. In Proceedings of TREC.

Jintao Tang, Ting Wang, Qin Lu, Ji Wang, and Wenjie Li. 2011. A Wikipedia based semantic graph model for topic tracking in blogosphere. In Proceedings of the Twenty-Second international joint conference on Artificial Intelligence - Volume Three (IJCAI'11).

TDT by NIST - 1998-2004. http://www.itl.nist.gov/iad/mig/tests/tdt/resources.html (Last Update: 2008)

Jianshu Weng, Erwin Leonardi, Francis Lee. Event Detection in Twitter. 2011. In Proceeding of ICWSM. AAAI Press.

Xintian Yang, Amol Ghoting, Yiye Ruan, and Srinivasan Parthasarathy. 2012. A framework for summarizing and analysing twitter feeds. In Proceedings of the 18th ACM SIGKDD international conference on Knowledge discovery and data mining (KDD '12). ACM, New York, NY, USA.

Inducing Word and Part-of-Speech with Pitman-Yor Hidden Semi-Markov Models

Kei Uchiumi **Hiroshi Tsukahara**
Denso IT Laboratory, Inc.
Shibuya Cross Tower 28F
2-15-1 Shibuya, Tokyo, Japan
{kuchiumi,htsukahara}@d-itlab.co.jp

Daichi Mochihashi
The Institute of Statistical Mathematics
10-3 Midori-cho, Tachikawa city
Tokyo, Japan
daichi@ism.ac.jp

Abstract

We propose a nonparametric Bayesian model for joint unsupervised word segmentation and part-of-speech tagging from raw strings. Extending a previous model for word segmentation, our model is called a Pitman-Yor Hidden Semi-Markov Model (PYHSMM) and considered as a method to build a class n-gram language model directly from strings, while integrating character and word level information. Experimental results on standard datasets on Japanese, Chinese and Thai revealed it outperforms previous results to yield the state-of-the-art accuracies. This model will also serve to analyze a structure of a language whose words are not identified a priori.

1 Introduction

Morphological analysis is a staple of natural language processing for broad languages. Especially for some East Asian languages such as Japanese, Chinese or Thai, word boundaries are not explicitly written, thus morphological analysis is a crucial first step for further processing. Note that also in Latin and old English, scripts were originally written with no word indications (*scripta continua*), but people felt no difficulty reading them. Here, morphological analysis means word segmentation and part-of-speech (POS) tagging.

For this purpose, supervised methods have often been employed for training. However, to train such supervised classifiers, we have to prepare a large amount of training data with correct annotations, in this case, word segmentation and POS tags. Creating and maintaining these data is not only costly but also very difficult, because generally there are no clear criteria for either "correct" segmentation or POS tags. In fact, since there are different standards for Chinese word segmentation, widely used SIGHAN Bakeoff dataset (Emerson, 2005) consists of multiple parts employing different annotation schemes.

Lately, this situation has become increasingly important because there are strong demands for processing huge amounts of text in consumer generated media such as Twitter, Weibo or Facebook (Figure 1). They contain a plethora of colloquial expressions and newly coined words, including sentiment expressions such as emoticons that cannot be covered by fixed supervised data.

To automatically recognize such linguistic phenomena beyond small "correct" supervised data, we have to extract linguistic knowledge from the statistics of strings themselves in an unsupervised fashion. Needless to say, such methods will also contribute to analyzing speech transcripts, classic texts, or even unknown languages. From a scientific point of view, it is worth while to find "words" and their part-of-speech purely from a collection of strings without any preconceived assumptions.

To achieve that goal, there have been two kinds of approaches: heuristic methods and statistical generative models. Heuristic methods are based on basic observations such that word boundaries will often occur at the place where predictive entropy of characters is large (i.e. the next character cannot be predicted without assuming

ローラのときに涙かブハァってなりました∩（´;ヮ;`）∩～～
真樹なんてこんな中２くさい事胸張って言えるぞぉ！
今日ね！らんらんとるいとコラボキャスするからおいで～(*´∀`)ノシ
どうせ明日の昼ごろしれっと不在表入ってるんだろうなぁ。
テレ東はいつものネトウヨホルホル VTR 鑑賞番組してんのか

Figure 1: Sample of Japanese Twitter text that is difficult to analyze by ordinary supervised segmentation. It contains a lot of novel words, emoticons, and colloquial expressions.

Proceedings of the 53rd Annual Meeting of the Association for Computational Linguistics and the 7th International Joint Conference on Natural Language Processing, pages 1774–1782,
Beijing, China, July 26-31, 2015.

the next word). By formulating such ideas as search or MDL problems of given coding length[1], word boundaries are found in an algorithmic fashion (Zhikov et al., 2010; Magistry and Sagot, 2013). However, such methods have difficulty incorporating higher-order statistics beyond simple heuristics, such as word transitions, word spelling formation, or word length distribution. Moreover, they usually depends on tuning parameters like thresholds that cannot be learned without human intervention.

In contrast, statistical models are ready to incorporate all such phenomena within a consistent statistical generative model of a string, and often prove to work better than heuristic methods (Goldwater et al., 2006; Mochihashi et al., 2009). In fact, the statistical methods often include the criteria of heuristic methods at least in a conceptual level, which is noted in (Mochihashi et al., 2009) and also explained later in this paper. In a statistical model, each word segmentation $\mathbf{w}$ of a string s is regarded as a hidden stochastic variable, and the unsupervised learning of word segmentation is formulated as a maximization of a probability of $\mathbf{w}$ given s:

$$\underset{\mathbf{w}}{\operatorname{argmax}}\, p(\mathbf{w}|s)\,. \tag{1}$$

This means that we want the most "natural" segmentation $\mathbf{w}$ that have a high probability in a language model $p(\mathbf{w}|s)$.

Lately, Chen et al. (2014) proposed an intermediate model between heuristic and statistical models as a product of character and word HMMs. However, these two models do not have information shared between the models, which is not the case with generative models.

So far, these approaches only find word segmentation, leaving part-of-speech information behind. These two problems are not actually independent but interrelated, because knowing the part-of-speech of some infrequent or unknown word will give contextual clues to word segmentation, and vice versa. For example, in Japanese

すもももももも

can be segmented into not only すもも/も/もも/も (plum/too/peach/too), but also into すもも/もも/もも (plum/peach/peach), which is ungrammatical. However, we could exclude the latter case

[1] For example, Zhikov et al. (2010) defined a coding length using character n-grams plus MDL penalty. Since this can be interpreted as a crude "likelihood" and a prior, its essence is similar but driven by a quite simplistic model.

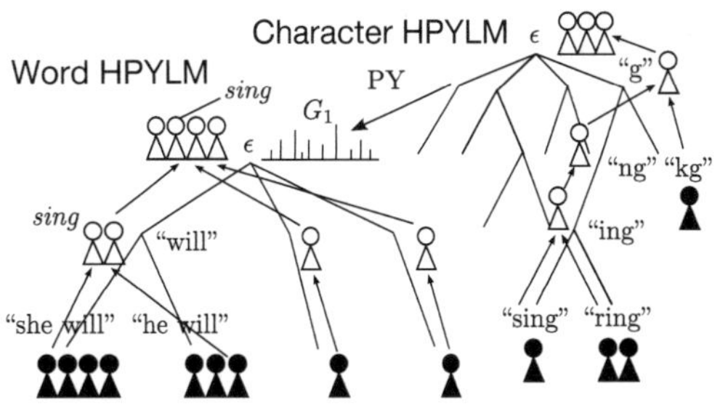

Figure 2: NPYLM represented in a hierarchical Chinese restaurant process. Here, a character ∞-gram HPYLM is embedded in a word n-gram HPYLM and learned jointly during inference.

if we leverage knowledge that a state sequence N/P/N/P is much more plausible in Japanese than N/N/N from the part-of-speech information. Sirts and Alumäe (2012) treats a similar problem of POS induction with unsupervised morphological segmentation, but they know the words in advance and only consider segmentation within a word.

For this objective, we attempt to maximize the joint probability of words and tags:

$$\underset{\mathbf{w},\mathbf{z}}{\operatorname{argmax}}\ p(\mathbf{w},\mathbf{z}|s) \propto p(\mathbf{w},\mathbf{z},s) \tag{2}$$

From the expression above, this amounts to building a generative model of a string s with words $\mathbf{w}$ and tags $\mathbf{z}$ along with an associated inference procedure. We solve this problem by extending previous generative model of word segmentation. Note that heuristic methods are never able to model the hidden tags, and only statistical generative models can accommodate this objective.

This paper is organized as follows. In Section 2, we briefly introduce NPYLM (Mochihashi et al., 2009) on which our extension is based. Section 3 extends it to include hidden states to yield a hidden semi-Markov models (Murphy, 2002), and we describe its inference procedure in Section 4. We conduct experiments on some East Asian languages in Section 5. Section 6 discusses implications of our model and related work, and Section 7 concludes the paper.

2 Nested Pitman-Yor Language Model

Our joint model of words and states is an extension of the Nested Pitman-Yor Language Model (Mochihashi et al., 2009) of a string, which in turn is an extension of a Bayesian n-gram language model called Hierarchical Pitman-Yor Language Model (HPYLM) (Teh, 2006).

HPYLM is a nonparametric Bayesian model of n-gram distribution based on the Pitman-Yor process (Pitman and Yor, 1997) that generates a discrete distribution G as $G \sim \mathrm{PY}(G_0, d, \theta)$. Here, d is a discount factor, "parent" distribution G_0 is called a base measure and θ controls how similar G is to G_0 in expectation. In HPYLM, n-gram distribution $G_n = \{p(w_t|w_{t-1} \cdots w_{t-(n-1)})\}$ is assumed to be generated from the Pitman-Yor process

$$G_n \sim \mathrm{PY}(G_{n-1}, d_n, \theta_n)\,, \tag{3}$$

where the base measure G_{n-1} is an $(n-1)$-gram distribution generated recursively in accordance with (3). Note that there are different G_n for each n-gram history $h = w_{t-1} \cdots w_{t-(n-1)}$. When we reach the unigram G_1 and need to use a base measure G_0, i.e. prior probabilities of words, HPYLM usually uses a uniform distribution over the lexicon.

However, in the case of unsupervised word segmentation, every sequence of characters could be a word, thus the size of the lexicon is unbounded. Moreover, prior probability of forming a word should not be uniform over all sequences of characters: for example, English words rarely begin with 'gme' but tend to end with '-ent' like in *segment*. To model this property, NPYLM assumes that word prior G_0 is generated from character HPYLM to model a well-formedness of w. In practice, to avoid dependency on n in the character model, we used an ∞-gram VPYLM (Mochihashi and Sumita, 2008) in this research. Finally, NPYLM gives an n-gram probability of word w given a history h recursively by integrating out G_n,

$$p(w|h) = \frac{c(w|h) - d \cdot t_{hw}}{\theta + c(h)} + \frac{\theta + d \cdot t_{h\cdot}}{\theta + c(h)}\, p(w|h')\,, \tag{4}$$

where h' is the shorter history of $(n-1)$-grams. $c(w|h), c(h) = \sum_w c(w|h)$ are n-gram counts of w appearing after h, and $t_{hw}, t_{h\cdot} = \sum_w t_{hw}$ are associated latent variables explained below. In case the history h is already empty at the unigram, $p(w|h') = p_0(w)$ is computed from the character ∞-grams for the word $w = c_1 \cdots c_k$:

$$p_0(w) = p(c_1 \cdots c_k) \tag{5}$$

$$= \prod_{i=1}^{k} p(c_i|c_{i-1} \cdots c_1)\,. \tag{6}$$

In practice, we further corrected (6) so that a word length follows a mixture of Poisson distributions. For details, see (Mochihashi et al., 2009).

When we know word segmentation $\mathbf{w}$ of the data, the probability above can be computed by adding each n-gram count of w given h to the model, i.e. increment $c(w|h)$ in accordance with a hierarchical Chinese restaurant process associated with HPYLM (Figure 2). When each n-gram count called a customer is inferred to be actually generated from $(n-1)$-grams, we send its proxy customer for smoothing to the parent restaurant and increment t_{hw}, and this process will recurse. Notice that if a word w is never seen in $\mathbf{w}$, its proxy customer is eventually sent to the parent restaurant of unigrams. In that case[2], w is decomposed to its character sequence $c_1 \cdots c_k$ and this is added to the character HPYLM in the same way, making it a little "clever" about possible word spellings.

Inference Because we do not know word segmentation $\mathbf{w}$ beforehand, we begin with a trivial segmentation in which every sentence is a single word[3]. Then, we iteratively refine it by sampling a new word segmentation $\mathbf{w}(s)$ of a sentence s in a Markov Chain Monte Carlo (MCMC) framework using a dynamic programming, as is done with PCFG by (Johnson et al., 2007) shown in Figure 3 where we omit MH steps for computational reasons. Further note that every hyperparameter d_n, θ_n of NPYLM can be sampled from the posterior in a Bayesian fashion, as opposed to heuristic methods that rely on a development set for tuning. For details, see Teh (2006).

3 Pitman-Yor Hidden Semi-Markov Models

NPYLM is a complete generative model of a string, that is, a hierarchical Bayesian n-gram lan-

Input: a collection of strings S
Add initial segmentation $\mathbf{w}(s)$ to Θ
for $j = 1 \cdots J$ **do**
  for s in randperm (S) **do**
    Remove customers of $\mathbf{w}(s)$ from Θ
    Sample $\mathbf{w}$(s) according to $p(\mathbf{w}|s, \Theta)$
    Add customers of $\mathbf{w}$(s) to Θ
  end for
  Sample hyperparameters of Θ
end for

Figure 3: MCMC inference of NPYLM Θ.

[2]To be precise, this occurs whenever t_{hw} is incremented in the unigram restaurant.

[3]Note that a child first memorizes what his mother says as a single word and gradually learns the lexicon.

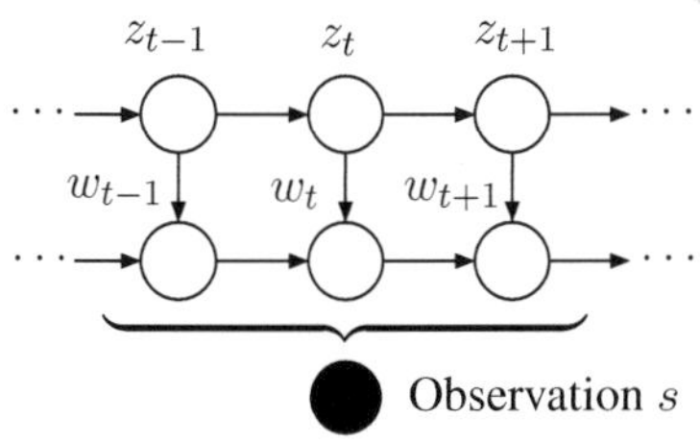

Figure 4: Graphical model of PYHSMM in a bigram case. White nodes are latent variables, and the shaded node is the observation. We only observe a string s that is a concatenation of hidden words $w_1 \cdots w_T$.

guage model combining words and characters. It can also be viewed as a way to build a Bayesian word n-gram language model directly from a sequence of characters, without knowing "words" a priori.

One possible drawback of it is a lack of part-of-speech: as described in the introduction, grammatical states will contribute much to word segmentation. Also, from a computational linguistics point of view, it is desirable to induce not only words from strings but also their part-of-speech purely from the usage statistics (imagine applying it to an unknown language or colloquial expressions). In classical terms, it amounts to building a class n-gram language model where both class and words are unknown to us. Is this really possible?

Yes, we can say it is possible. The idea is simple: we augment the latent states to include a hidden part-of-speech z_t for each word w_t, which is again unknown as displayed in Figure 4. Assuming w_t is generated from z_t'-th NPYLM, we can draw a generative model of a string s as follows:

$z_0 =$ BOS; $s = \epsilon$ (an empty string).
for $t = 1 \cdots T$ **do**
  Draw $z_t \sim p(z_t | z_{t-1})$,
  Draw $w_t \sim p(w_t | w_1 \cdots w_{t-1}, z_t)$,
  Append w_t to s.
end for

Here, $z_0 =$ BOS and $z_{T+1} =$ EOS are distinguished states for beginning and end of a sentence, respectively. For the transition probability of hidden states, we put a HPY process prior as (Blunsom and Cohn, 2011):

$$p(z_t | z_{t-1}) \sim \mathrm{HPY}(d, \theta) \tag{7}$$

with the final base measure being a uniform distribution over the states. The word boundaries are

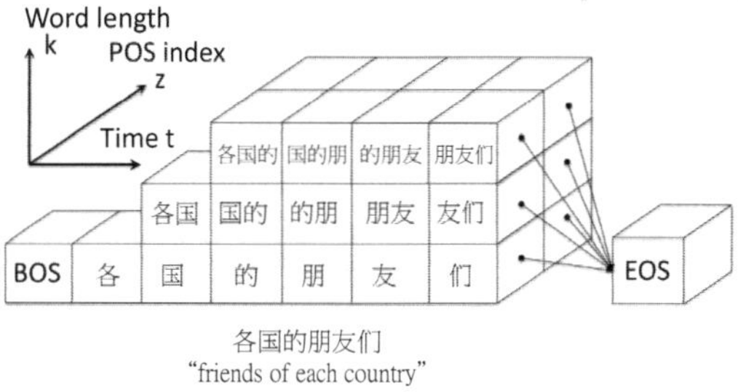

Figure 5: Graphical representation of sampling words and POSs. Each cell corresponds to an inside probability $\alpha[t][k][z]$. Note each cell is not always connected to adjacent cells, because of an overlap of substrings associated with each cell.

known in (Blunsom and Cohn, 2011), but in our case it is also learned from data at the same time. Note that because w_t depends on already generated words $w_1 \cdots w_{t-1}$, our model is considered as an autoregressive HMM rather than a vanilla HMM, as shown in Figure 4 ($w_{t-1} \rightarrow w_t$ dependency).

Since segment models like NPYLM have segment lengths as hidden states, they are called semi-Markov models (Murphy, 2002). In contrast, our model also has hidden part-of-speech, thus we call it a Pitman-Yor Hidden Semi-Markov model (PYHSMM).[4] Note that this is considered as a generative counterpart of a discriminative model known as a hidden semi-Markov CRF (Sarawagi and Cohen, 2005).

4 Inference

Inference of PYHSMM proceeds in almost the same way as NPYLM in Figure 3: For each sentence, first remove the customers associated with the old segmentation similarly to adding them. After sampling a new segmentation and states, the model is updated by adding new customers in accordance with the new segmentation and hidden states.

4.1 Sampling words and states

To sample words and states (part-of-speech) jointly, we first compute inside probabilities forward from BOS to EOS and sample backwards from EOS according to the Forward filtering-Backward sampling algorithm (Scott, 2002). This

[4] Lately, Johnson et al. (2013) proposed a nonparametric Bayesian hidden semi-Markov models for general state spaces. However, it depends on a separate distribution for a state duration, thus is clealy different from ours for a natural language.

can be regarded as a "stochastic Viterbi" algorithm that has the advantage of not being trapped in local minima, since it is a valid move of a Gibbs sampler in a Bayesian model.

For a word bigram case for simplicity, inside variable $\alpha[t][k][z]$ is a probability that a substring $c_1 \cdots c_t$ of a string $s = c_1 \cdots c_N$ is generated with its last k characters being a word, generated from state z as shown in Figure 5. From the definition of PYHSMM, this can be computed recursively as follows:

$$\alpha[t][k][z] = \sum_{j=1}^{L} \sum_{y=1}^{K} p(c_{t-k}^{t} | c_{t-k-j+1}^{t-k}, z) \, p(z|y) \alpha[t-k][j][y] \,. \quad (8)$$

Here, c_s^t is a substring $c_s \cdots c_t$ and L $(\leq t)$ is the maximum length of a word, and K is the number of hidden states.[5]

In Figure 5, each cell represents $\alpha[t][k][z]$ and a single path connecting from EOS to BOS corresponds to a word sequence $\mathbf{w}$ and its state sequence $\mathbf{z}$. Note that each cell is not always connected to adjacent cells (we omit the arrows), because the length-k substring associated with each cell already subsumes that of neighborhood cells.

Once $\mathbf{w}$ and $\mathbf{z}$ are sampled, each w_t is added to z_t'-th NPYLM to update its statistics.

4.2 Efficient computation by the Negative Binomial generalized linear model

Inference algorithm of PYHSMM has a computational complexity of $O(K^2 L^2 N)$, where N is a length of the string to analyze. To reduce computations it is effective to put a small L of maximum word length, but it might also ignore occasionally long words. Since these long words are often predictable from some character level information including suffixes or character types, in a semi-supervised setting we employ a Negative Binomial generalized linear model (GLM) for setting L_t adaptively for each character position t in the corpus.

Type	Feature
c_i	Character at time $t-i$ $(0 \leq i \leq 1)$
t_i	Character type at time $t-i$ $(0 \leq i \leq 4)$
cont	# of the same character types before t
ch	# of times character types changed within 8 characters before t

Table 1: Features used for the Negative Binomial generalized linear model for maximum word length prediction.

Specifically, we model the word length ℓ by a Negative Binomial distribution (Cook, 2009):

$$\ell \sim \mathrm{NB}(\ell|r,p) = \frac{\Gamma(r+\ell)}{\Gamma(r)\,\ell!} p^{\ell} (1-p)^{r} \,. \quad (9)$$

This counts the number of failures of Bernoulli draws with probability $(1-p)$ before r'th success. For our model, note that Negative Binomial is obtained from a Poisson distribution $\mathrm{Po}(\lambda)$ whose parameter λ again follows a Gamma distribution $\mathrm{Ga}(r,b)$ and integrated out:

$$p(\ell|r,b) = \int \mathrm{Po}(\ell|\lambda)\mathrm{Ga}(\lambda|r,b)d\lambda \quad (10)$$

$$= \frac{\Gamma(r+\ell)}{\Gamma(r)\,\ell!} \left(\frac{b}{1+b}\right)^{\ell} \left(\frac{1}{1+b}\right)^{r} . \quad (11)$$

This construction exactly mirrors the Poisson-Gamma word length distribution in (Mochihashi et al., 2009) with sampled λ. Therefore, our Negative Binomial is basically a continuous analogue of the word length distribution in NPYLM.[6]

Since $r > 0$ and $0 \leq p \leq 1$, we employ an exponential and sigmoidal linear regression

$$r = \exp(\mathbf{w}_r^T \mathbf{f}), \quad p = \sigma(\mathbf{w}_p^T \mathbf{f}) \quad (12)$$

where $\sigma(x)$ is a sigmoid function and $\mathbf{w}_r, \mathbf{w}_p$ are weight vectors to learn. $\mathbf{f}$ is a feature vector computed from the substring $c_1 \cdots c_t$, including $f_0 \equiv 1$ for a bias term. Table 1 shows the features we used for this Negative Binomial GLM. Since Negative Binomial GLM is not convex in $\mathbf{w}_r$ and $\mathbf{w}_p$, we endow a Normal prior $\mathrm{N}(0, \sigma^2 I)$ for them and used a random walk MCMC for inference.

Predicting L_t Once the model is obtained, we can set L_t adaptively as the time where the cumulative probability of ℓ exceeds some threshold θ (we used $\theta = 0.99$). Table 2 shows the precision of predicting maximum word length learned from 10,000 sentences from each set: it measures whether the correct word boundary in test data is included in the predicted L_t.

Overall it performs very well with high precision, and works better for longer words that cannot be accommodated with a fixed maximum length.

[5]For computational reasons, we do not pursue using a Dirichlet process to yield an infinite HMM (Van Gael et al., 2009), but it is straightforward to extend our PYHSMM to iHMM.

[6]Because NPYLM employs a mixture of Poisson distributions for each character type of a substring, this correspondence is not exact.

Lang	Dataset	Training	Test
Ja	Kyoto corpus	37,400	1,000
	BCCWJ OC	20,000	1,000
Zh	SIGHAN MSR	86,924	3,985
	SIGHAN CITYU	53,019	1,492
	SIGHAN PKU	19,056	1,945
Th	InterBEST Novel	1,000	1,000

Table 3: Datasets used for evaluation. Abbreviations: Ja=Japanese, Zh=Chinese, Th=Thai language.

Figure 6 shows the distribution of predicted maximum lengths for Japanese. Although we used $\theta = 0.99$, it is rather parsimonious but accurate that makes the computation faster.

Because this cumulative Negative Binomial prediction is language independent, we believe it might be beneficial for other natural language processing tasks that require some maximum lengths within which to process the data.

5 Experiments

To validate our model, we conducted experiments on several corpora of East Asian languages with no word boundaries.

Datasets For East Asian languages, we used standard datasets in Japanese, Chinese and Thai as shown in Table 3. The Kyoto corpus is a collection of sentences from Japanese newspaper (Kurohashi and Nagao, 1998) with both word segmentation and part-of-speech annotations. BCCWJ (Balanced Corpus of Contemporary Written Japanese) is a balanced corpus of written Japanese (Maekawa, 2007) from the National Institute of Japanese Language and Linguistics, also with both word segmentation and part-of-speech annotations from slightly different criteria. For experiments on colloquial texts, we used a random subset of "OC" register from this corpus that is comprised of Yahoo!Japan Answers from users. For Chinese, experiments are conducted on standard datasets of SIGHAN Bakeoff 2005 (Emerson, 2005); for comparison we used MSR and PKU datasets for simplified Chinese, and the CITYU dataset for traditional Chinese. SIGHAN datasets have word boundaries only, and we conformed to original training/test splits provided with the data. InterBEST is a dataset in Thai used in the InterBEST 2009 word segmentation contest (Kosawat, 2009). For contrastive purposes, we used a "Novel" subset of it with a random sampling without replacement for training and test data. Accuracies are measured in token F-measures computed as follows:

$$F = \frac{2PR}{P+R}, \tag{13}$$

$$P = \frac{\textit{\# of correct words}}{\textit{\# of words in output}}, \tag{14}$$

$$R = \frac{\textit{\# of correct words}}{\textit{\# of words in gold standard}}. \tag{15}$$

Unsupervised word segmentation In Table 4, we show the accuracies of unsupervised word segmentation with previous figures. We used bigram PYHSMM and set $L = 4$ for Chinese, $L = 5, 8, 10, 21$ for Japanese with different types of contiguous characters, and $L = 6$ for Thai. The number of hidden states are $K = 10$ (Chinese and Thai), $K = 20$ (Kyoto) and $K = 30$ (BCCWJ).

We can see that our PYHSMM outperforms on all the datasets. Huang and Zhao (2007) reports that the maximum possible accuracy in unsupervised Chinese word segmentation is 84.8%, derived through the inconsistency between different segmentation standards of the SIGHAN dataset. Our PYHSMM performs nearer to this best possible accuracy, leveraging both word and character knowledge in a consistent Bayesian fashion. Further note that in Thai, quite high performance is achieved with a very small data compared to previous work.

Unsupervised part-of-speech induction As stated above, Kyoto, BCCWJ and Weibo datasets

Dataset	Kyoto	BCCWJ	MSR	CITYU	BEST
Precision (All)	99.9	99.9	99.6	99.9	99.0
Precision (≥ 5)	96.7	98.4	73.6	87.0	91.7
Maximum length	15	48	23	12	21

Table 2: Precision of maximum word length prediction with a Negative Binomial generalized linear model (in percent). ≥ 5 are figures for word length ≥ 5. Final row is the maximum length of a word found in each dataset.

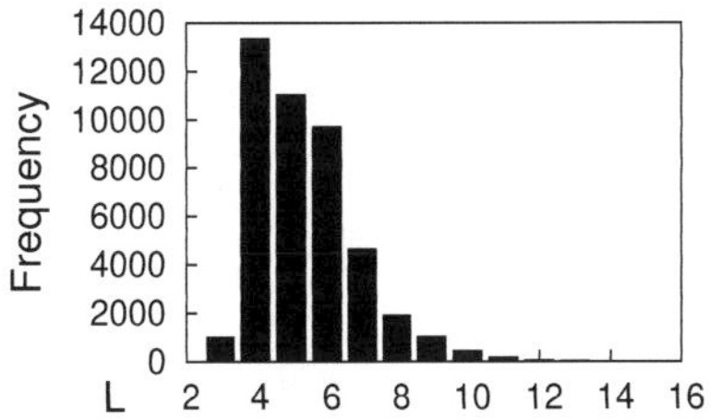

Figure 6: Distribution of predicted maximum word lengths on the Kyoto corpus.

Dataset	PYHSMM	NPY	BE	HMM^2
Kyoto	**71.5**	62.1	71.3	NA
BCCWJ	**70.5**	NA	NA	NA
MSR	**82.9**	80.2	78.2	81.7
CITYU	**82.6***	82.4	78.7	NA
PKU	**81.6**	NA	80.8	81.1
BEST	**82.1**	NA	**82.1**	NA

Table 4: Accuracies of unsupervised word segmentation. BE is a Branching Entropy method of Zhikov et al. (2010), and HMM^2 is a product of word and character HMMs of Chen et al. (2014). * is the accuracy decoded with $L=3$: it becomes 81.7 with $L=4$ as MSR and PKU.

have part-of-speech annotations as well. For these data, we also evaluated the precision of part-of-speech induction on the output of unsupervised word segmentation above. Note that the precision is measured only over correct word segmentation that the system has output. Table 5 shows the precisions; to the best of our knowledge, there are no previous work on joint unsupervised learning of words and tags, thus we only compared with Bayesian HMM (Goldwater and Griffiths, 2007) on both NPYLM segmentation and gold segmentation. In this evaluation, we associated each tag of supervised data with a latent state that cooccurred most frequently with that tag. We can see that the precision of joint POS tagging is better than NPYLM+HMM, and even better than HMM that is run over the gold segmentation.

For colloquial Chinese, we also conducted an experiment on the Leiden Weibo Corpus (LWC), a corpus of Chinese equivalent of Twitter[7]. We used random 20,000 sentences from this corpus, and results are shown in Figure 7. In many cases plausible words are found, and assigned to syntactically consistent states. States that are not shown here are either just not used or consists of a mixture of different syntactic categories. Guiding our model to induce more accurate latent states is a common problem to all unsupervised part-of-speech induction, but we show some semi-supervised results next.

Dataset	PYHSMM	NPY+HMM	HMM
Kyoto	**57.4**	53.8	49.5
BCCWJ	**50.2**	44.1	44.2
LWC	33.0	30.9	32.9

Table 5: Precision of POS tagging on correctly segmented words.

[7]http://lwc.daanvanesch.nl/

Semi-supervised experiments Because our PYHSMM is a generative model, it is easily amenable to semi-supervised segmentation and tagging. We used random 10,000 sentences from supervised data on Kyoto, BCCWJ, and LWC datasets along with unsupervised datasets in Table 3.

Results are shown in Table 6: segmentation accuracies came close to 90% but do not go beyond. By inspecting the segmentation and POS that PYHSMM has output, we found that this is not necessarily a fault of our model, but it came from the often inconsistet or incorrect tagging of the dataset. In many cases PYHSMM found more "natural" segmentations, but it does not always conform to the gold annotations. On the other hand, it often oversegments emotional expressions (sequence of the same character, for example) and this is one of the major sources of errors.

Finally, we note that our proposed model for unsupervised learning is most effective for the language which we do not know its syntactic behavior but only know raw strings as its data. In Figure 8, we show an excerpt of results to model a Japanese local dialect (*Mikawa-ben* around Nagoya district) collected from a specific Twitter. Even from the surface appearance of characters, we can see that similar words are assigned to the same state including some emoticons (states 9,29,32), and in fact we can identify a state of postpositions specific to that dialect (state 3). Notice that the words themselves are not trivial before this analysis. There are also some name of local places (state 41) and general Japanese postpositions (2) or nouns (11,18,25,27,31). Because of the sparsity promoting prior (7) over the hidden states, actually used states are sparse and the results can be considered quite satisfactory.

6 Discussion

The characteristics of NPYLM is a Baysian integration of character and word level information, which is related to (Blunsom and Cohn, 2011) and the adaptor idea of (Goldwater et al., 2011). This

Dataset	Seg	POS
Kyoto	92.1	87.1
BCCWJ	89.4	83.1
LWC	88.5	86.9

Table 6: Semi-supervised segmentation and POS tagging accuracies. POS is measured by precision.

$z=1$		$z=3$		$z=10$		$z=11$		$z=18$	
啦	227	。	3309	，	13440	可以	207	东	68
呀	182	！	1901	#	5989	呢	201	大	60
去	86	了	482	的	5224	。	199	南	59
开心	65	啊	226	。	3237	那么	192	，	55
走	62	呢	110	我	1504	多	192	西	53
哈	53	哦	93	是	1206	打	177	路	51
鸟	44	啦	69	！	1190	才	167	海	49
喽	41	哈哈	56	在	900	比	165	山	49
波	31	地址	47	都	861	对	154	区	45
测试	30	晚安	43	和	742	几	146	去	39

Figure 7: Some interesting words and states induced from Weibo corpus ($K=20$). Numbers represent frequencies that each word is generated from that class. Although not perfect, emphatic ($z=1$), end-of-sentence expressions ($z=3$), and locative words ($z=18$) are learned from tweets. Distinction is far more clear in the semi-supervised experiments (not shown here).

z	Induced words
2	の 、 は に が で と も を 「
3	ぞん かん ね のん だに だん りん か ん だのん
9	(*^^*) ！(^-^; (^_^;) (^^;; ！(^^;;
10	。 ！ !! ？ 」 (≧▽≦) !! 」「
11	楽 入 ど寒 大丈夫 会 受 停電 良 美味 台風が
13	に ら わ な よ ね だら じゃんね え ぁ
18	今年 最近 豊川 地元 誰 豊田 今度 次 豊川高校
19	さん ん め 食べ って よろしく ありがとう じゃん
20	これ 知 人 それ どこ まあ みんな 東京 いや 方
24	三河弁 この よ お 何 そ ほい 今日 また ほ
25	他 一緒 5 大変 頭 春 参加 指 世代 地域
26	マジ 豊橋カレー コレ トキワ コーヒー プロ ファン
27	行」 方言 & 言葉 普通 夜店 」 始 確認
29	(！(; (´･ !! (*` ？(´･ (*^_^*)
30	気 うち 店 ほう ここ こっち 先生 友人 いろいろ
31	女子 無理 決 近い 安心 標準語 感動 蒲郡 試合
32	((*\(^ ＼(^ (^ ！*\(^ 〜 (^_^ (*^
34	ヤマサ マーラ オレ ハイジ イメージクッピーラムネ
35	な ー そう 好き こと らん なん ら み 意味
36	いい ど うまい 杏果 ぐろ めっちゃ かわい はよ
41	豊橋 名古屋 三河 西三河 名古屋弁 名古屋人 大阪

Figure 8: Unsupervised analysis of a Japanese local dialect by PYHSMM. ($K=50$)

is different from (and misunderstood in) a joint model of Chen et al. (2014), where word and character HMMs are just multiplied. There are no information shared from the model structure, and in fact it depends on a BIO-like heuristic tagging scheme in the character HMM.

In the present paper, we extended it to include a hidden state for each word. Therefore, it might be interesting to introduce a hidden state also for each character. Unlike western languages, there are many kinds of Chinese characters that work quite differently, and Japanese uses several distinct kinds of characters, such as a Chinese character, Hiragana, Katakana, whose mixture would constitute a single word. Therefore, statistical modeling of different types of characters is an important research venue for the future.

NPYLM has already applied and extended to speech recognition (Neubig et al., 2010), statistical machine translation (Nguyen et al., 2010), or even robotics (Nakamura et al., 2014). For all these research area, we believe PYHSMM would be beneficial for their extension.

7 Conclusion

In this paper, we proposed a Pitman-Yor Hidden Semi-Markov model for joint unsupervised word segmentation and part-of-speech tagging on a raw sequence of characters. It can also be viewed as a way to build a class n-gram language model directly on strings, without any "word" information a priori.

We applied our PYHSMM on several standard datasets on Japanese, Chinese and Thai, and it outperformed previous figures to yield the state-of-the-art results, as well as automatically induced word categories. It is especially beneficial for colloquial text, local languages or speech transcripts, where not only words themselves are unknown but their syntactic behavior is a focus of interest.

In order to adapt to human standards given in supervised data, it is important to conduct a semi-supervised learning with discriminative classifiers. Since semi-supervised learning requires generative models in advance, our proposed Bayesian generative model will also lay foundations to such an extension.

References

Phil Blunsom and Trevor Cohn. 2011. A Hierarchical Pitman-Yor Process HMM for Unsupervised Part of Speech Induction. In *ACL 2011*, pages 865–874.

Miaohong Chen, Baobao Chang, and Wenzhe Pei. 2014. A Joint Model for Unsupervised Chinese Word Segmentation. In *EMNLP 2014*, pages 854–863.

John D. Cook. 2009. Notes on the Negative Binomial Distribution. http://www.johndcook.com/negative_binomial.pdf.

Tom Emerson. 2005. The Second International Chinese Word Segmentation Bakeoff. In *Proceedings of the Fourth SIGHAN Workshop on Chinese Language Processing*.

Sharon Goldwater and Tom Griffiths. 2007. A Fully Bayesian Approach to Unsupervised Part-of-Speech Tagging. In *Proceedings of ACL 2007*, pages 744–751.

Sharon Goldwater, Thomas L. Griffiths, and Mark Johnson. 2006. Contextual Dependencies in Unsupervised Word Segmentation. In *Proceedings of ACL/COLING 2006*, pages 673–680.

Sharon Goldwater, Thomas L. Griffiths, and Mark Johnson. 2011. Producing Power-Law Distributions and Damping Word Frequencies with Two-Stage Language Models. *Journal of Machine Learning Research*, 12:2335–2382.

Chang-Ning Huang and Hai Zhao. 2007. Chinese word segmentation: A decade review. *Journal of Chinese Information Processing*, 21(3):8–20.

Matthew J. Johnson and Alan S. Willsky. 2013. Bayesian Nonparametric Hidden Semi-Markov Models. *Journal of Machine Learning Research*, 14:673–701.

Mark Johnson, Thomas L. Griffiths, and Sharon Goldwater. 2007. Bayesian Inference for PCFGs via Markov Chain Monte Carlo. In *Proceedings of HLT/NAACL 2007*, pages 139–146.

Krit Kosawat. 2009. InterBEST 2009: Thai Word Segmentation Workshop. In *Proceedings of 2009 Eighth International Symposium on Natural Language Processing (SNLP2009)*, Thailand.

Sadao Kurohashi and Makoto Nagao. 1998. Building a Japanese Parsed Corpus while Improving the Parsing System. In *Proceedings of LREC 1998*, pages 719–724. http://nlp.kuee.kyoto-u.ac.jp/nl-resource/corpus.html.

Kikuo Maekawa. 2007. Kotonoha and BCCWJ: Development of a Balanced Corpus of Contemporary Written Japanese. In *Corpora and Language Research: Proceedings of the First International Conference on Korean Language, Literature, and Culture*, pages 158–177.

Pierre Magistry and Benoît Sagot. 2013. Can MDL Improve Unsupervised Chinese Word Segmentation? In *Proceedings of the Seventh SIGHAN Workshop on Chinese Language Processing*, pages 2–10.

Daichi Mochihashi and Eiichiro Sumita. 2008. The Infinite Markov Model. In *Advances in Neural Information Processing Systems 20 (NIPS 2007)*, pages 1017–1024.

Daichi Mochihashi, Takeshi Yamada, and Naonori Ueda. 2009. Bayesian Unsupervised Word Segmentation with Nested Pitman-Yor Language Modeling. In *Proceedings of ACL-IJCNLP 2009*, pages 100–108.

Kevin Murphy. 2002. Hidden semi-Markov models (segment models). http://www.cs.ubc.ca/~murphyk/Papers/segment.pdf.

Tomoaki Nakamura, Takayuki Nagai, Kotaro Funakoshi, Shogo Nagasaka, Tadahiro Taniguchi, and Naoto Iwahashi. 2014. Mutual Learning of an Object Concept and Language Model Based on MLDA and NPYLM. In *2014 IEEE/RSJ International Conference on Intelligent Robots and Systems (IROS'14)*, pages 600–607.

Graham Neubig, Masato Mimura, Shinsuke Mori, and Tatsuya Kawahara. 2010. Learning a Language Model from Continuous Speech. In *Proc. of INTERSPEECH 2010*.

ThuyLinh Nguyen, Stephan Vogel, and Noah A. Smith. 2010. Nonparametric Word Segmentation for Machine Translation. In *COLING 2010*, pages 815–823.

Jim Pitman and Marc Yor. 1997. The Two-Parameter Poisson-Dirichlet Distribution Derived from a Stable Subordinator. *Annals of Probability*, 25(2):855–900.

Sunita Sarawagi and William W. Cohen. 2005. Semi-Markov Conditional Random Fields for Information Extraction. In *Advances in Neural Information Processing Systems 17 (NIPS 2004)*, pages 1185–1192.

Steven L. Scott. 2002. Bayesian Methods for Hidden Markov Models. *Journal of the American Statistical Association*, 97:337–351.

Kairit Sirts and Tanel Alumäe. 2012. A Hierarchical Dirichlet Process Model for Joint Part-of-Speech and Morphology Induction. In *NAACL 2012*, pages 407–416.

Yee Whye Teh. 2006. A Bayesian Interpretation of Interpolated Kneser-Ney. Technical Report TRA2/06, School of Computing, NUS.

Jurgen Van Gael, Andreas Vlachos, and Zoubin Ghahramani. 2009. The infinite HMM for unsupervised PoS tagging. In *EMNLP 2009*, pages 678–687.

Valentin Zhikov, Hiroya Takamura, and Manabu Okumura. 2010. An Efficient Algorithm for Unsupervised Word Segmentation with Branching Entropy and MDL. In *EMNLP 2010*, pages 832–842.

Coupled Sequence Labeling on Heterogeneous Annotations: POS Tagging as a Case Study

Zhenghua Li, Jiayuan Chao, Min Zhang*, Wenliang Chen
(1) Soochow University
(2) Collaborative Innovation Center of Novel Software Technology and Industrialization
Jiangsu Province, China
{zhli13,minzhang,wlchen}@suda.edu.cn; china_cjy@163.com

Abstract

In order to effectively utilize multiple datasets with heterogeneous annotations, this paper proposes a coupled sequence labeling model that can directly learn and infer two heterogeneous annotations simultaneously, and to facilitate discussion we use Chinese part-of-speech (POS) tagging as our case study. The key idea is to bundle two sets of POS tags together (e.g. "[*NN*, *n*]"), and build a conditional random field (CRF) based tagging model in the enlarged space of bundled tags with the help of *ambiguous labelings*. To train our model on two non-overlapping datasets that each has only one-side tags, we transform a one-side tag into a set of bundled tags by considering all possible mappings at the missing side and derive an objective function based on ambiguous labelings. The key advantage of our coupled model is to provide us with the flexibility of 1) incorporating joint features on the bundled tags to implicitly learn the loose mapping between heterogeneous annotations, and 2) exploring separate features on one-side tags to overcome the data sparseness problem of using only bundled tags. Experiments on benchmark datasets show that our coupled model significantly outperforms the state-of-the-art baselines on both one-side POS tagging and annotation conversion tasks. The codes and newly annotated data are released for non-commercial usage.[1]

1 Introduction

The scale of available labeled data significantly affects the performance of statistical data-driven models. As a widely-used structural classification problem, sequence labeling is prone to suffer from the data sparseness issue. However, the heavy cost of manual annotation typically limits one labeled resource in both scale and genre. As a promising research line, semi-supervised learning for sequence labeling has been extensively studied. Huang et al. (2009) show that standard self-training can boost the performance of a simple hidden Markov model (HMM) based part-of-speech (POS) tagger. Søgaard (2011) apply tri-training to English POS tagging, boosting accuracy from 97.27% to 97.50%. Sun and Uszkoreit (2012) derive word clusters from large-scale unlabeled data as extra features for Chinese POS tagging. Recently, the use of natural annotation has becomes a hot topic in Chinese word segmentation (Jiang et al., 2013; Liu et al., 2014; Yang and Vozila, 2014). The idea is to derive segmentation boundaries from implicit information encoded in web texts, such as anchor texts and punctuation marks, and use them as partially labeled training data in sequence labeling models.

The existence of multiple annotated resources opens another door for alleviating data sparseness. For example, Penn Chinese Treebank (*CTB*) contains about 20 thousand sentences annotated with word boundaries, POS tags, and syntactic structures (Xue et al., 2005), which is widely used for research on Chinese word segmentation and POS tagging. People's Daily corpus (*PD*)[2] is a large-scale corpus annotated with word segments and POS tags, containing about 300 thousand sentences from the first half of 1998 of People's

*Correspondence author.
[1] http://hlt.suda.edu.cn/~zhli

[2] http://icl.pku.edu.cn/icl_groups/corpustagging.asp

Proceedings of the 53rd Annual Meeting of the Association for Computational Linguistics and the 7th International Joint Conference on Natural Language Processing, pages 1783–1792,
Beijing, China, July 26-31, 2015.

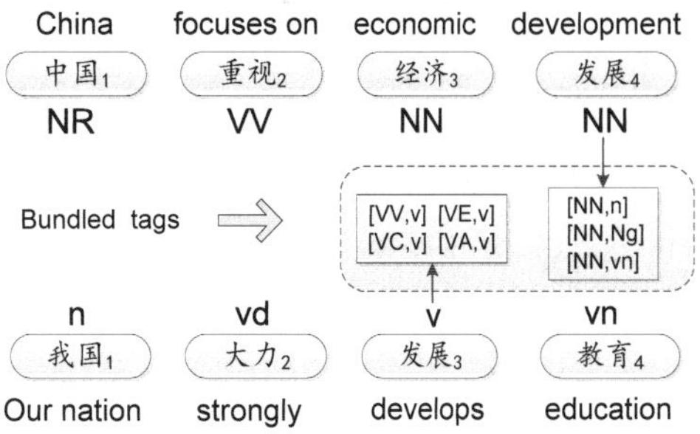

Figure 1: An example to illustrate the annotation differences between *CTB* (above) and *PD* (below), and how to transform a one-side tag into a set of bundled tags. "*NN*" and "*n*" represent nouns; "*VV*"and "*v*" represent verbs.

Daily newspaper (see Table 2). The two resources were independently built for different purposes. *CTB* was designed to serve syntactic analysis, whereas *PD* was developed to support information extraction systems. However, the key challenge of exploiting the two resources is that they adopt different sets of POS tags which are impossible to be precisely converted from one to another based on heuristic rules. Figure 1 shows two example sentences from *CTB* and *PD*. Please refer to Table B.3 in Xia (2000) for detailed comparison of the two guidelines.

Previous work on exploiting heterogeneous data (*CTB* and *PD*) mainly focuses on indirect guide-feature based methods. The basic idea is to use one resource to generate extra guide features on another resource (Jiang et al., 2009; Sun and Wan, 2012), which is similar to stacked learning (Nivre and McDonald, 2008). First, *PD* is used as source data to train a source model $Tagger_{PD}$. Then, $Tagger_{PD}$ generates automatic POS tags on the target data *CTB*, called *source annotations*. Finally, a target model $Tagger_{CTB\text{-}guided}$ is trained on *CTB*, using source annotations as extra guide features. Although the guide-feature based method is effective in boosting performance of the target model, we argue that it may have two potential drawbacks. First, the target model $Tagger_{CTB\text{-}guided}$ does not directly use *PD* as training data, and therefore fails to make full use of rich language phenomena in *PD*. Second, the method is more complicated in real applications since it needs to parse a test sentence twice to get the final results.

This paper proposes a coupled sequence labeling model that can directly learn and infer two heterogeneous annotations simultaneously. We use Chinese part-of-speech (POS) tagging as our case study.[3] The key idea is to bundle two sets of POS tags together (e.g. "[*NN*, *n*]"), and build a conditional random field (CRF) based tagging model in the enlarged space of bundled tags. To make use of two non-overlapping datasets that each has only one-side tags, we transform a one-side tag into a set of bundled tags by considering all possible mappings at the missing side and derive an objective function based on *ambiguous labelings*. During training, the CRF-based coupled model is supervised by such ambiguous labelings. The advantages of our coupled model are to provide us the flexibility of 1) incorporating joint features on the bundled tags to implicitly learn the loose mapping between two sets of annotations, and 2) exploring separate features on one-side tags to overcome the data sparseness problem of using bundled tags. In summary, this work makes two major contributions:

1. We propose a coupled model which can more effectively make use of multiple resources with heterogeneous annotations, compared with both the baseline and guide-feature based method. Experiments show our approach can significantly improve POS tagging accuracy from 94.10% to 95.00% on *CTB*.

2. We have manually annotated *CTB* tags for $1,000$ *PD* sentences, which is the first dataset with two-side annotations and can be used for annotation-conversion evaluation. Experiments on the newly annotated data show that our coupled model also works effectively on the annotation conversion task, improving conversion accuracy from 90.59% to 93.90% ($+3.31\%$).

2 Traditional POS Tagging (*Tagger$_{CTB}$*)

Given an input sentence of n words, denoted by $\mathbf{x} = w_1...w_n$, POS tagging aims to find an optimal tag sequence $\mathbf{t} = t_1...t_n$, where $t_i \in \mathcal{T}$ ($1 \leq i \leq n$) and $\mathcal{T}$ is a predefined tag set. As a log-linear probabilistic model (Lafferty et al., 2001), CRF

[3]There are some slight differences in the word segmentation guidelines between *CTB* and *PD*, which are ignored in this work for simplicity.

01: $t_i \circ t_{i-1}$	02: $t_i \circ w_i$
03: $t_i \circ w_{i-1}$	04: $t_i \circ w_{i+1}$
05: $t_i \circ w_i \circ c_{i-1,-1}$	06: $t_i \circ w_i \circ c_{i+1,0}$
07: $t_i \circ c_{i,0}$	08: $t_i \circ c_{i,-1}$
09: $t_i \circ c_{i,k}, 0 < k < \#c_i - 1$	
10: $t_i \circ c_{i,0} \circ c_{i,k}, 0 < k < \#c_i - 1$	
11: $t_i \circ c_{i,-1} \circ c_{i,k}, 0 < k < \#c_i - 1$	
12: **if** $\#c_i = 1$ **then** $t_i \circ w_i \circ c_{i-1,-1} \circ c_{i+1,0}$	
13: **if** $c_{i,k} = c_{i,k+1}$ **then** $t_i \circ c_{i,k} \circ$ *"consecutive"*	
14: $t_i \circ \mathsf{prefix}(w_i, k), 1 \leq k \leq 4, k \leq \#c_i$	
15: $t_i \circ \mathsf{suffix}(w_i, k), 1 \leq k \leq 4, k \leq \#c_i$	

Table 1: POS tagging features $\mathbf{f}(\mathbf{x}, i, t_{i-1}, t_i)$. $\circ$ means string concatenation; $c_{i,k}$ denotes the kth Chinese character of w_i; $c_{i,0}$ is the first Chinese character; $c_{i,-1}$ is the last Chinese character; $\#c_i$ is the total number of Chinese characters contained in w_i; prefix/suffix(w_i, k) denote the k-Character prefix/suffix of w_i.

defines the probability of a tag sequence as:

$$P(\mathbf{t}|\mathbf{x};\theta) = \frac{\exp(Score(\mathbf{x}, \mathbf{t}; \theta))}{\sum_{\mathbf{t}'} \exp(Score(\mathbf{x}, \mathbf{t}'; \theta))}$$
$$Score(\mathbf{x}, \mathbf{t}; \theta) = \sum_{1 \leq i \leq n} \theta \cdot \mathbf{f}(\mathbf{x}, i, t_{i-1}, t_i) \quad (1)$$

where $\mathbf{f}(\mathbf{x}, i, t_{i-1}, t_i)$ is the feature vector at the ith word and θ is the weight vector. We adopt the state-of-the-art tagging features in Table 1 (Zhang and Clark, 2008).

3 Coupled POS Tagging (*Tagger*$_{CTB\&PD}$)

In this section, we introduce our coupled model, which is able to learn and predict two heterogeneous annotations simultaneously. The idea is to bundle two sets of POS tags together and let the CRF-based model work in the enlarged tag space. For example, a *CTB* tag "*NN*" and a *PD* tag "*n*" would be bundled into "[*NN,n*]". Figure 2 shows the graphical structure of our model.

Different from the traditional model in Eq. (1), our coupled model defines the score of a bundled tag sequence as follows:

$$Score(\mathbf{x}, [\mathbf{t}^a, \mathbf{t}^b]; \theta) = \sum_{1 \leq i \leq n} \theta \cdot \begin{bmatrix} \mathbf{f}(\mathbf{x}, i, [t^a_{i-1}, t^b_{i-1}], [t^a_i, t^b_i]) \\ \mathbf{f}(\mathbf{x}, i, t^a_{i-1}, t^a_i) \\ \mathbf{f}(\mathbf{x}, i, t^b_{i-1}, t^b_i) \end{bmatrix} \quad (2)$$

where the first item of the enlarged feature vector is called *joint features*, which can be obtained by

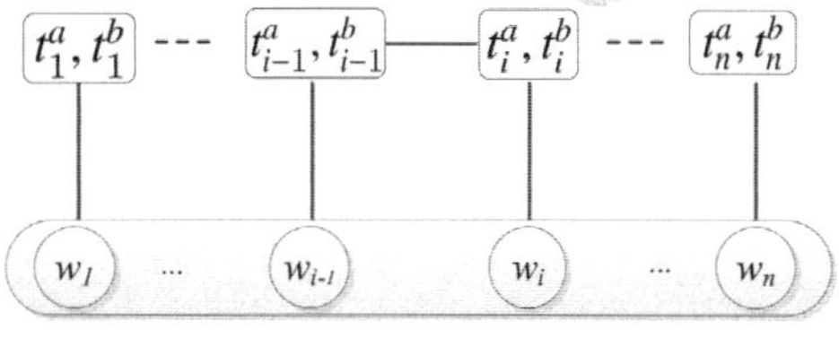

Figure 2: Graphical structure of our coupled CRF model.

instantiating Table 1 by replacing t_i with bundled tags $[t^a_i, t^b_i]$; the second and third items are called *separate features*, which are based on single-side tags. The advantages of our coupled model over the traditional model are to provide us with the flexibility of using both kinds of features, which significantly contributes to the accuracy improvement as shown in the following experiments.

3.1 Mapping Functions

The key challenge of our idea is that both *CTB* and *PD* are non-overlapping and each contains only one-side POS tags. Therefore, the problem is how to construct training data for our coupled model. We denote the tag set of *CTB* as $\mathcal{T}^a$, and that of *PD* as $\mathcal{T}^b$, and the bundled tag set as $\mathcal{T}^{a\&b}$. Since the full Cartetian $\mathcal{T}^a \times \mathcal{T}^b$ would lead to a very large number of bundled tags, making the model very slow, we would like to come up with a much smaller $\mathcal{T}^{a\&b} \subseteq \mathcal{T}^a \times \mathcal{T}^b$, based on linguistic insights of the annotation guidelines of the two datasets.

To obtain a proper $\mathcal{T}^{a\&b}$, we introduce a mapping function between the two sets of tags as $\mathbf{m} : \mathcal{T}^a \times \mathcal{T}^b \rightarrow \{0, 1\}$, which only allow specific tag pairs to be bundled together.

$$\mathbf{m}(t^a, t^b) = \begin{cases} 1 & \textit{if the two tags can be bundled} \\ 0 & \textit{otherwise} \end{cases} \quad (3)$$

where one mapping function $\mathbf{m}$ corresponds to one $\mathcal{T}^{a\&b}$. When the mapping function becomes looser, the tag set size $|\mathcal{T}^{a\&b}|$ becomes larger.

Then, based on the mapping function, we can map a single-side POS tag into a set of bundled tags by considering all possible tags at the missing side, as illustrated in Figure 1. The word "发展$_4$" is tagged as "*NN*" at the *CTB* side. Suppose that the mapping function $\mathbf{m}$ tells that "*NN*" can be mapped into three tags at the *PD* side, i.e., "*n*", "*Ng*", and "*vn*". Then, we create three bundled tags for the word, i.e., "[*NN, n*]", "[*NN, Ng*]",

"[*NN*, *vn*]" as its gold-standard references during training. It is known as *ambiguous labelings* when a training instance has multiple gold-standard labels. Similarly, we can obtain bundled tags for all other words in sentences of *CTB* and *PD*. After such transformation, the two datasets are now in the same tag space.

At the beginning of this work, our intuition is that the coupled model would achieve the best performance if we build a tight and linguistically motivated mapping function. However, our preliminary experiments show that our intuitive assumption is actually incorrect. Therefore, we experiment with the following four mapping functions to manage to figure out the reasons behind and to better understand our coupled model.

- The **tight** mapping function produces 145 tags, and is constructed by strictly following linguistic principles and our careful study of the two guidelines and datasets.
- The **relaxed** mapping function results in 179 tags, which is an looser version of the tight mapping function by including extra 34 weak mapping relationships.
- The **automatic** mapping function generates 346 tags. We use the baseline $Tagger_{CTB}$ to parse *PD*, and collect all automatic mapping relationships.
- The **complete** mapping function obtains 1,254 tags ($|\mathcal{T}^a| \times |\mathcal{T}^b| = 33 \times 38$).

3.2 Training Objective with Ambiguous Labelings

So far, we have formally defined a coupled model and prepared both *CTB* and *PD* in the same bundled tag space. The next problem is how to learn the model parameters θ. Note that after our transformation, a sentence in *CTB* or *PD* have many tag sequences as gold-standard references due to the loose mapping function, known as *ambiguous labelings*. Here, we derive a training objective based on ambiguous labelings. For simplicity, we illustrate the idea based on the notations of the baseline CRF model in Eq. (1).

Given a sentence $\mathbf{x}$, we denote a set of ambiguous tag sequences as $\mathcal{V}$. Then, the probability of $\mathcal{V}$ is the sum of probabilities of all tag sequences contained in $\mathcal{V}$:

$$p(\mathcal{V}|\mathbf{x};\theta) = \sum_{\mathbf{t}\in\mathcal{V}} p(\mathbf{t}|\mathbf{x};\theta) \tag{4}$$

Algorithm 1 SGD training with two labeled datasets.

Input: Two labeled datasets: $\mathcal{D}^{(1)} = \{(\mathbf{x}_i^{(1)}, \mathcal{V}_i^{(1)})\}_{i=1}^{N}$, $\mathcal{D}^{(2)} = \{(\mathbf{x}_i^{(2)}, \mathcal{V}_i^{(2)})\}_{i=1}^{M}$; Parameters: I, N', M', b
Output: θ
Initialization: $\theta_0 = \mathbf{0}$, $k = 0$;
for $i = 1$ **to** I **do** {*iterations*}
  Randomly select N' instances from $\mathcal{D}^{(1)}$ and M' instances from $\mathcal{D}^{(2)}$ to compose a new dataset $\mathcal{D}_i$, and shuffle it.
  Traverse $\mathcal{D}_i$, and use a small batch $\mathcal{D}_k^b \subseteq \mathcal{D}_i$ at one step.
    $\theta_{k+1} = \theta_k + \eta_k \frac{1}{b} \nabla \mathcal{L}(\mathcal{D}_k^b; \theta_k)$
    $k = k + 1$
end for

Suppose the training data is $\mathcal{D} = \{(\mathbf{x}_i, \mathcal{V}_i)\}_{i=1}^{N}$. Then the log likelihood is:

$$\mathcal{L}(\mathcal{D};\theta) = \sum_{i=1}^{N} \log p(\mathcal{V}_i|\mathbf{x}_i;\theta) \tag{5}$$

After derivation, the gradient is:

$$\frac{\partial \mathcal{L}(\mathcal{D};\theta)}{\partial \theta} = \sum_{i=1}^{N} \left(E_{\mathbf{t}\in\mathcal{V}_i}[\mathbf{f}(\mathbf{x}_i,\mathbf{t})] - E_{\mathbf{t}}[\mathbf{f}(\mathbf{x}_i,\mathbf{t})]\right) \tag{6}$$

where $\mathbf{f}(\mathbf{x}_i, \mathbf{t})$ is an aggregated feature vector for tagging $\mathbf{x}_i$ as $\mathbf{t}$; $E_{\mathbf{t}\in\mathcal{V}_i}[.]$ means model expectation of the features in the constrained space of $\mathcal{V}_i$; $E_{\mathbf{t}}[.]$ is model expectation with no constraint. This function can be efficiently solved by the forward-backward algorithm. Please note that the training objective of a traditional CRF model can be understood as a special case where $\mathcal{V}_i$ contains one sequence.

3.3 SGD Training with Two Datasets

We adopt stochastic gradient descent (SGD) to iteratively learn θ for our baseline and coupled models. However, we have two separate training data, and *CTB* may be overwhelmed by *PD* if directly merging the two datasets into one, since *PD* is 15 times larger than *CTB* (see Table 2), Therefore, we propose a simple corpus-weighting strategy, as shown in Algorithm 1, where $\mathcal{D}_k^b$ is a subset of training data used in k^{th} step update; b is the batch size; η_k is a update step. The idea is to randomly sample instances from each training data in a certain proportion before each iteration.

The sampled data is then used for one-iteration training. Later experiments will investigate the effect of the weighting proportion. In this work, we use $b = 30$, and follow the implementation in CRFsuite[4] to decide η_k.

4 Manually Annotating *PD* Sentences with *CTB* Tags

To evaluate different methods on annotation conversion, we build the first dataset that contains $1,000$ sentences with POS tags on both sides of *CTB* and *PD*. The sentences are randomly sampled from *PD*. To save annotation effort, we only select 20% most difficult tokens to manually annotate. The difficulty of a word w_i is measured based on marginal probabilities produced by the baseline *Tagger*$_{CTB}$. $p(t_i|\mathbf{x}, w_i; \theta)$ denotes the marginal probability of tagging w_i as t_i. The basic assumption is that w_i is more difficult to annotate if its most likely tag candidate ($\arg\max_t p(t|\mathbf{x}, w_i; \theta)$) gets lower marginal probability.

We build a visualized online annotation system to facilitate manual labeling. The annotation task is designed in such way that at a time an annotator is provided with a sentence and one focus word, and is required to decide the *CTB* POS tag of the word. To further simplify annotation, we provide two or three most likely tag candidates as well, so that annotators can choose one either among the candidates or from a full list. We employ 8 undergraduate students as our annotators. Annotators are trained on simulated tasks from *CTB* data for several hours, and and start real annotation once reaching certain accuracy. To guarantee annotation quality, we adopt *multiple annotation*. Initially, one task is randomly assigned to two annotators. Later, if the two annotators submit different results, the system will assign the task to two more annotators. To aggregate annotation results, we only retain annotation tasks that the first two annotators agree (91.0%) or three annotators among four agree (5.6%), and discard other tasks (3.4%). Finally, we obtain $5,769$ words with both *CTB* and *PD* tags, with each annotator's detailed submissions, and could be used as a non-synthesized dataset for studying aggregating submissions from non-expert annotators in crowdsourcing platforms (Qing et al., 2014). The data is also fully released for non-commercial usage.

[4]http://www.chokkan.org/software/crfsuite/

5 Experiments

In this section, we conduct experiments to verify the effectiveness of our approach. We adopt *CTB* (version 5.1) with the standard data split, and randomly split *PD* into four sets, among which one set is 20% *partially* annotated with *CTB* tags. The data statistics is shown in Table 2. The main concern of this work is to improve accuracy on *CTB* by exploring large-scale *PD*, since *CTB* is relatively small, but is widely-used benchmark data in the research community.

We use the standard token-wise tagging accuracy as the evaluation metric. For significance test, we adopt Dan Bikel's randomized parsing evaluation comparator (Noreen, 1989).[5].

The baseline CRF is trained on either *CTB* training data with 33 tags, or *PD* training data with 38 tags. The coupled CRF is trained on both two separate training datasets with bundled tags (179 tags for the relaxed mapping function). During evaluation, the coupled CRF is not directly evaluated on bundled tags, since bundled tags are unavailable in either *CTB* or *PD* test data. Instead, the coupled and baseline CRFs are both evaluated on one-side tags.

5.1 Model Development

Our coupled model has two major parameters to be decided. The first parameter is to determine the mapping function between *CTB* and *PD* annotations, and the second parameter is the relative weights of the two datasets during training (N' vs. M': number of sentences in each dataset used for training at one iteration).

Effect of mapping functions (described in Subsection 3.1) is illustrated in Figure 3. Empirically, we adopt $N' = 5K$ vs. $M' = 20K$ to merge the two training datasets at each iteration. Our intuition is that using this proportion, *CTB* should not be overwhelmed by *PD*, and both training data can be used up in relatively similar speed. Specifically, all training data of *CTB* can be consumed in about 3 iterations, whereas *PD* can be consumed in about 14 iterations. We also present the results of the baseline model trained using $5K$ sentences in one iteration for better comparison.

Contrary to our intuitive assumption, it actually leads to very bad performance when using the

[5]http://www.cis.upenn.edu/~dbikel/software.html

		#sentences	#tokens with *CTB* tags	#tokens with *PD* tags
CTB	train	16,091	437,991	–
	dev	803	20,454	–
	test	1,910	50,319	–
PD	train	273,883	–	6,488,208
	dev	1,000	–	23,427
	test	2,500	–	58,301
	newly labeled	1,000	5,769	27,942

Table 2: Data statistics. Please kindly note that the $1,000$ sentences originally from *PD* are only partially annotated with *CTB* tags (about 20% most ambiguous tokens).

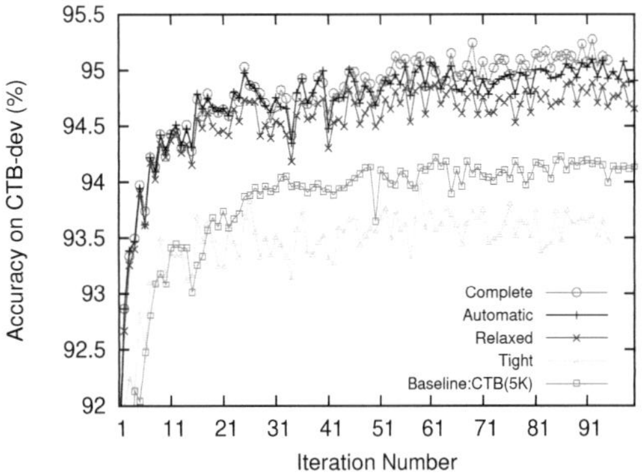

Figure 3: Accuracy on *CTB*-dev regarding to mapping functions.

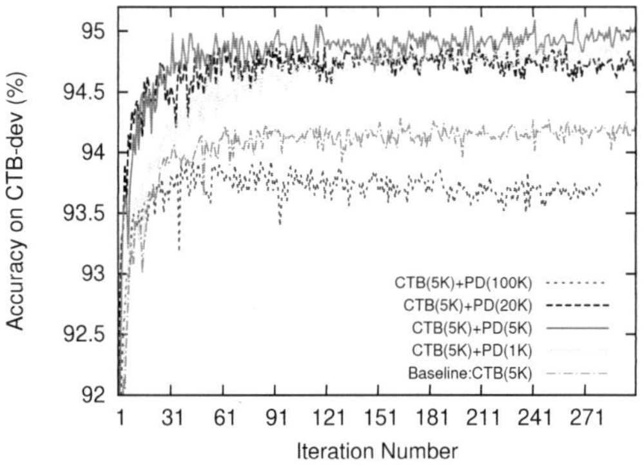

Figure 4: Accuracy on *CTB*-dev with different weighting settings.

tight mapping function that is carefully created based on linguistic insights, which is even inferior to the baseline model. The relaxed mapping function outperforms the tight function by large margin. The automatic function works slightly better than the relaxed one. The complete function achieves similar accuracy with the automatic one. In summary, we can conclude that our coupled model achieves much better performance when the mapping function becomes looser. In other words, this suggests that *our coupled model can effectively learn the implicit mapping between heterogeneous annotations, and does not rely on a carefully designed mapping function.*

Since a looser mapping function leads to a larger number of bundled tags and makes the model slower, we implement a paralleled training procedure based on Algorithm 1, and run each experiment with five threads. However, it still takes about 20 hours for one iteration when using the complete mapping function; whereas the other three mapping functions need about 6, 2, and 1 hours respectively. Therefore, as a compromise, *we adopt the relaxed mapping function in the following experiments*, which achieves slightly lower accuracy than the complete mapping function, but is much faster.

Effect of weighting *CTB* and *PD* is investigated in Figure 4 and 5. Since the scale of *PD* is much larger than *CTB*, we adopt Algorithm 1 to merge the training data in a certain proportion (N' *CTB* sentences and M' *PD* sentences) at each iteration. We use $N' = 5K$, and vary $M' = 1K/5K/20K/100K$. Figure 4 shows the accuracy curves on *CTB* development data. We find that when $M' = 100K$, our coupled model achieve very low accuracy, which is even worse than the baseline model. The reason should be that the training instances in *CTB* are overwhelmed by those in *PD* when M' is large. In contrast, when $M' = 1K$, the accuracy is also inferior to the case of $M' = 5K$, which indicates that *PD* is not effectively utilized in this setting. Our model works best when $M' = 5K$, which is slightly better than the case of $M' = 1K/20K$.

Figure 5 shows the accuracy curves on *PD* development data. The baseline model is trained using $100K$ sentences in one iteration. We find

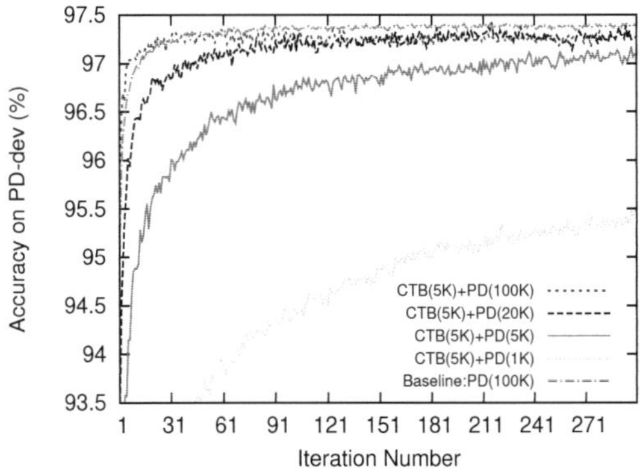

Figure 5: Accuracy on *PD*-dev with different weighting settings.

that when $M' = 100K$, our coupled model achieves similar accuracy with the baseline model. When M' becomes smaller, our coupled model becomes inferior to the baseline model. Particularly, when $M' = 1K$, the model converges very slowly. However, from the trend of the curves, we expect that the accuracy gap between our coupled model with $M' = 5K/20K$ and the baseline model should be much smaller when reaching convergence. Based on the above observation, *we adopt* $N' = 5K$ *and* $M' = 5K$ *in the following experiments.* Moreover, we select the best iteration on the development data, and use the corresponding model to parse the test data.

5.2 Final Results

Table 3 shows the final results on the *CTB* test data. We re-implement the guide-feature based method of Jiang et al. (2009), referred to as two-stage CRF. Li et al. (2012) jointly models Chinese POS tagging and dependency parsing, and report the best tagging accuracy on *CTB*. The results show that *our coupled model outperforms the baseline model by large margin, and also achieves slightly higher accuracy than the guide-feature based method.*

5.3 Feature Study

We conduct more experiments to measure individual contribution of each feature set, namely the joint features based on bundled tags and separate features based on single-side tags, as defined in Eq. (2). Table 4 shows the results. We can see that when only using separate features, our coupled model achieves only slightly better accuracy than the baseline model. This is because there is little connection and help between the two sets annotations. When only using joint features, our coupled model becomes largely inferior to the baseline, which is due to the data sparseness problem for the joint features. However, when the two sets of features are combined, the coupled model largely outperforms the baseline model. These results indicate that *both joint features and separate features are indispensable components and complementary to each other for the success of our coupled model.*

	Accuracy
Baseline CRF	94.10
Two-stage CRF (guide-feature)	94.81 (+0.71) †
Coupled CRF	**95.00** (+0.90) †‡
Best result (Li et al., 2012)	94.60

Table 3: Final results on *CTB* test data. † means the corresponding approach significantly outperforms the baseline at confidence level of $p < 10^{-5}$; whereas ‡ means the accuracy difference between the two-stage CRF and the coupled CRF is significant at confidence level of $p < 10^{-2}$.

	dev	test
Baseline CRF	94.28	94.10
Coupled CRF (w/ separate feat)	94.36	94.43 (+0.33)
Coupled CRF (w/ joint feat)	92.92	92.90 (-1.20)
Coupled CRF (full)	**95.10**	**95.00** (+0.90)

Table 4: Accuracy on *CTB*: feature study.

5.4 Results on Annotation Conversion

In this subsection, we evaluate different methods on the annotation conversion task using our newly annotated $1,000$ sentences. The gold-standard

	PD-to-*CTB* conversion
Baseline CRF	90.59
Two-stage CRF (guide-feature)	93.22 (+2.63) †
Coupled CRF	**93.90** (+3.31) †‡

Table 5: Conversion accuracy on our annotated data. † means the corresponding approach significantly outperforms the baseline at confidence level of $p < 10^{-5}$; whereas ‡ means the accuracy difference between the two-stage CRF and the coupled CRF is significant at confidence level of $p < 10^{-2}$.

	dev	test
Baseline CRF	94.28	94.10
Coupled CRF	**95.10**	**95.00** (+0.90) †
Baseline CRF + converted *PD*	95.01	94.81 (+0.71) †‡

Table 6: Accuracy on *CTB*: using converted *PD*. † means the corresponding approach significantly outperforms the baseline at confidence level of $p < 10^{-5}$; whereas ‡ means the accuracy difference between the coupled CRF and the baseline CRF with converted *PD* is significant at confidence level of $p < 10^{-2}$.

PD-side tags are provided, and the goal is to obtain the *CTB*-side tags via annotation conversion. We evaluate accuracy on the $5,769$ words having manually annotated *CTB*-side tags.

Our coupled model can be naturally used for annotation conversion. The idea is to perform constrained decoding on the test data, using the *PD*-side tags as hard constraints. The guide-feature based method can also perform annotation conversion by using the gold-standard *PD*-side tags to compose guide features. Table 5 shows the results. The accuracy is much lower than those in Table 3, because the $5,769$ words used for evaluation are 20% most ambiguous tokens in the $1,000$ test sentence (partial annotation to save annotation effort). From Table 5, we can see that *our coupled model outperforms both the baseline and guide-feature based methods by large margin.*

5.5 Results of Training with Converted Data

One weakness of our coupled model is the inefficiency problem due to the large bundled tag set. In practice, we usually only need results following one annotation style. Therefore, we employ our coupled model to convert *PD* into the style of *CTB*, and train our baseline model with two training data with homogeneous annotations. Again, Algorithm 1 is used to merge the two data with $N' = 5K$ and $M' = 5K$. The results are shown in the bottom row in Table 6. We can see that *with the extra converted data, the baseline model can achieve slightly lower accuracy with the coupled model and avoid the inefficiency problem at the meantime.*

6 Related Work

This work is partially inspired by Qiu et al. (2013), who propose a model that performs heterogeneous Chinese word segmentation and POS tagging and produces two sets of results following *CTB* and *PD* styles respectively. Different from our CRF-based coupled model, their approach adopts a linear model, which directly combines two separate sets of features based on single-side tags, without considering the interacting joint features between the two annotations. They adopt an approximate decoding algorithm which tries to find the best single-side tag sequence with reference to tags at the other side. In contrast, our approach is a direct extension of traditional CRF, and is more theoretically simple from the perspective of modelling. The use of both joint and separate features is proven to be crucial for the success of our coupled model. In addition, their work indicates that their model relies on a hand-crafted loose mapping between annotations, which is opposite to our findings. The naming of the "coupled" CRF is borrowed from the work of Qiu et al. (2012), which treats the joint task of Chinese word segmentation and POS tagging as two coupled sequence labeling problems.

Zhang et al. (2014) propose a shift-reduce dependency parsing model which can simultaneously learn and produce two heterogeneous parse trees. However, their approach assumes the existence of data with annotations at both sides, which is obtained by converting phrase-structure trees into dependency trees with different heuristic rules.

This work is also closely related with multi-task learning, which aims to jointly learn multiple related tasks with the benefit of using interactive features under a share representation (Ben-David and Schuller, 2003; Ando and Zhang, 2005; Parameswaran and Weinberger, 2010). However, according to our knowledge, multi-task learning typically assumes the existence of data with labels for multiple tasks at the same time, which is unavailable in our situation.

As one reviewer kindly pointed out that our model is a factorial CRF (Sutton et al., 2004), in the sense that the bundled tags can be factorized two connected latent variables. Initially, factorial CRFs are designed to jointly model two related (and typically hierarchical) sequential labeling tasks, such as POS tagging and chunking. In this work, our coupled CRF jointly models two same tasks which have different annotation schemes. Moreover, this work provides a natural way to learn from incomplete annotations where one sentence only contains one-side labels. The reviewer also suggests that our objective can be optimized with the latent variable structured perceptron of Sun et al. (2009), which we leave as future work.

Learning with ambiguous labelings are previously explored for classification (Jin and Ghahramani, 2002), sequence labeling (Dredze et al., 2009), parsing (Riezler et al., 2002; Täckström et al., 2013; Li et al., 2014a; Li et al., 2014b). Recently, researchers derive natural annotations from web data, transform them into ambiguous labelings to supervise Chinese word segmentation models (Jiang et al., 2013; Liu et al., 2014; Yang and Vozila, 2014).

7 Conclusions

This paper proposes an effective coupled sequence labeling model for exploiting multiple non-overlapping datasets with heterogeneous annotations. Please note that our model can also be naturally trained on datasets with both-side annotations if such data exists. Experimental results demonstrate that our model work better than the baseline and guide-feature based methods on both one-side POS tagging and annotation conversion. Specifically, detailed analysis shows several interesting findings. First, both the separate features and joint features are indispensable components for the success of our coupled model. Second, our coupled model does not rely on a carefully hand-crafted mapping function. Our linguistically motivated mapping function is only used to reduce the size of the bundled tag set for the sake of efficiency. Finally, using the extra training data converted with our coupled model, the baseline tagging model achieves similar accuracy improvement. In this way, we can avoid the inefficiency problem of our coupled model in real application.

For future, our immediate plan is to annotate more data with both *CTB* and *PD* tags (a few thousand sentences), and to investigate our coupled model with small amount of such annotation as extra training data. Meanwhile, Algorithm 1 is empirically effective in merging two training data, but still needs manual tuning of the weighting factor on held-out data. Thus, we would like to find a more principled and theoretically sound method to merge multiple training data.

Acknowledgments

The authors would like to thank the undergraduate students Fangli Lu and Xiaojing Wang for building our annotation system, and Le Lu, Die Hu, Yue Zhang, Jian Zhang, Qiuyi Yan, Xinzhou Jiang for data annotation. We are also grateful that Yu Ding kindly shared her earlier codes on which our annotation system was built. We also thank the helpful comments from our anonymous reviewers. This work was supported by National Natural Science Foundation of China (Grant No. 61432013, 61203314) and Jiangsu Planned Projects for Postdoctoral Research Funds (No. 1401075B), and was also partially supported by Collaborative Innovation Center of Novel Software Technology and Industrialization of Jiangsu Province.

References

Rie Kubota Ando and Tong Zhang. 2005. A framework for learning predictive structures from multiple tasks and unlabeled data. *Journal of Machine Learn Research*, 6:1817–1853.

Shai Ben-David and Reba Schuller. 2003. Exploiting task relatedness for multiple task learning. In *COLT*.

Mark Dredze, Partha Pratim Talukdar, and Koby Crammer. 2009. Sequence learning from data with multiple labels. In *ECML/PKDD Workshop on Learning from Multi-Label Data*.

Zhongqiang Huang, Vladimir Eidelman, and Mary Harper. 2009. Improving a simple bigram hmm part-of-speech tagger by latent annotation and self-training. In *Proceedings of NAACL*, pages 213–216.

Wenbin Jiang, Liang Huang, and Qun Liu. 2009. Automatic adaptation of annotation standards: Chinese word segmentation and POS tagging – a case study. In *Proceedings of ACL*, pages 522–530.

Wenbin Jiang, Meng Sun, Yajuan Lü, Yating Yang, and Qun Liu. 2013. Discriminative learning with natural annotations: Word segmentation as a case study. In *Proceedings of ACL*, pages 761–769.

Rong Jin and Zoubin Ghahramani. 2002. Learning with multiple labels. In *Proceedings of NIPS*.

John Lafferty, Andrew McCallum, and Fernando Pereira. 2001. Conditional random fields: Probabilistic models for segmenting and labeling sequence data. In *Proceedings of ICML 2001*, pages 282–289.

Zhenghua Li, Min Zhang, Wanxiang Che, and Ting Liu. 2012. A separately passive-aggressive training algorithm for joint POS tagging and dependency parsing. In *COLING*, pages 1681–1698.

Zhenghua Li, Min Zhang, and Wenliang Chen. 2014a. Ambiguity-aware ensemble training for semi-supervised dependency parsing. In *ACL*, pages 457–467.

Zhenghua Li, Min Zhang, and Wenliang Chen. 2014b. Soft cross-lingual syntax projection for dependency parsing. In *COLING*, pages 783–793.

Yijia Liu, Yue Zhang, Wanxiang Che, Ting Liu, and Fan Wu. 2014. Domain adaptation for CRF-based Chinese word segmentation using free annotations. In *Proceedings of EMNLP*, pages 864–874.

Joakim Nivre and Ryan McDonald. 2008. Integrating graph-based and transition-based dependency parsers. In *Proceedings of ACL*, pages 950–958.

Eric W. Noreen. 1989. *Computer-intensive methods for testing hypotheses: An introduction*. John Wiley & Sons, Inc., New York.

S. Parameswaran and K.Q. Weinberger. 2010. Large margin multi-task metric learning. In J. Lafferty, C. K. I. Williams, J. Shawe-Taylor, R.S. Zemel, and A. Culotta, editors, *Advances in Neural Information Processing Systems 23*, pages 1867–1875.

Ciyang Qing, Ulle Endriss, Raquel Fernandez, and Justin Kruger. 2014. Empirical analysis of aggregation methods for collective annotation. In *COLING*, pages 1533–1542.

Xipeng Qiu, Feng Ji, Jiayi Zhao, and Xuanjing Huang. 2012. Joint segmentation and tagging with coupled sequences labeling. In *Proceedings of COLING 2012: Posters*, pages 951–964, Mumbai, India.

Xipeng Qiu, Jiayi Zhao, and Xuanjing Huang. 2013. Joint Chinese word segmentation and POS tagging on heterogeneous annotated corpora with multiple task learning. In *Proceedings of EMNLP*, pages 658–668.

Stefan Riezler, Tracy H. King, Ronald M. Kaplan, Richard Crouch, John T. III Maxwell, and Mark Johnson. 2002. Parsing the wall street journal using a lexical-functional grammar and discriminative estimation techniques. In *Proceedings of ACL*, pages 271–278.

Anders Søgaard. 2011. Semi-supervised condensed nearest neighbor for part-of-speech tagging. In *Proceedings of ACL*, pages 48–52.

Weiwei Sun and Hans Uszkoreit. 2012. Capturing paradigmatic and syntagmatic lexical relations: Towards accurate Chinese part-of-speech tagging. In *Proceedings of ACL*, pages 242–252.

Weiwei Sun and Xiaojun Wan. 2012. Reducing approximation and estimation errors for Chinese lexical processing with heterogeneous annotations. In *Proceedings of ACL*, pages 232–241.

Xu Sun, Takuya Matsuzaki, Daisuke Okanohara, and Jun'ichi Tsujii. 2009. Latent variable perceptron algorithm for structured classification. In *Proceedings of the 21st International Joint Conference on Artificial Intelligence (IJCAI 2009)*, pages 1236–1242.

Charles Sutton, Khashayar Rohanimanesh, and Andrew McCallum. 2004. Dynamic conditional random fields: Factorized probabilistic models for labeling and segmenting sequence data. In *International Conference on Machine Learning (ICML)*.

Oscar Täckström, Ryan McDonald, and Joakim Nivre. 2013. Target language adaptation of discriminative transfer parsers. In *Proceedings of NAACL*, pages 1061–1071.

Fei Xia. 2000. The part-of-speech tagging guidelines for the penn Chinese treebank 3.0. In *Technical Report, Linguistic Data Consortium*.

Nianwen Xue, Fei Xia, Fu-Dong Chiou, and Martha Palmer. 2005. The Penn Chinese Treebank: Phrase structure annotation of a large corpus. In *Natural Language Engineering*, volume 11, pages 207–238.

Fan Yang and Paul Vozila. 2014. Semi-supervised Chinese word segmentation using partial-label learning with conditional random fields. In *Proceedings of EMNLP*, pages 90–98.

Yue Zhang and Stephen Clark. 2008. Joint word segmentation and POS tagging using a single perceptron. In *Proceedings of ACL-08: HLT*, pages 888–896.

Meishan Zhang, Wanxiang Che, Yanqiu Shao, and Ting Liu. 2014. Jointly or separately: Which is better for parsing heterogeneous dependencies? In *Proceedings of COLING*, pages 530–540.

AutoExtend: Extending Word Embeddings to Embeddings for Synsets and Lexemes

Sascha Rothe and Hinrich Schütze
Center for Information & Language Processing
University of Munich
sascha@cis.lmu.de

Abstract

We present *AutoExtend*, a system to learn embeddings for synsets and lexemes. It is flexible in that it can take any word embeddings as input and does not need an additional training corpus. The synset/lexeme embeddings obtained live in the same vector space as the word embeddings. A sparse tensor formalization guarantees efficiency and parallelizability. We use WordNet as a lexical resource, but AutoExtend can be easily applied to other resources like Freebase. AutoExtend achieves state-of-the-art performance on word similarity and word sense disambiguation tasks.

1 Introduction

Unsupervised methods for word embeddings (also called "distributed word representations") have become popular in natural language processing (NLP). These methods only need very large corpora as input to create sparse representations (e.g., based on local collocations) and project them into a lower dimensional dense vector space. Examples for word embeddings are SENNA (Collobert and Weston, 2008), the hierarchical log-bilinear model (Mnih and Hinton, 2009), word2vec (Mikolov et al., 2013c) and GloVe (Pennington et al., 2014). However, there are many other resources that are undoubtedly useful in NLP, including lexical resources like WordNet and Wiktionary and knowledge bases like Wikipedia and Freebase. We will simply call these *resources* in the rest of the paper. Our goal is to enrich these valuable resources with embeddings for those data types that are not words; e.g., we want to enrich WordNet with embeddings for synsets and lexemes. A *synset* is a set of synonyms that are interchangeable in some context. A *lexeme* pairs a particular spelling or pronunciation with a particular meaning, i.e., a lexeme is a conjunction of a word and a synset. Our premise is that many NLP applications will benefit if the non-word data types of resources – e.g., synsets in WordNet – are also available as embeddings. For example, in machine translation, enriching and improving translation dictionaries (cf. Mikolov et al. (2013b)) would benefit from these embeddings because they would enable us to create an enriched dictionary for word senses. Generally, our premise is that the arguments for the utility of embeddings for word forms should carry over to the utility of embeddings for other data types like synsets in WordNet.

The insight underlying the method we propose is that *the constraints of a resource can be formalized as constraints on embeddings and then allow us to extend word embeddings to embeddings of other data types like synsets*. For example, the hyponymy relation in WordNet can be formalized as such a constraint.

The advantage of our approach is that it decouples embedding learning from the extension of embeddings to non-word data types in a resource. If somebody comes up with a better way of learning embeddings, these embeddings become immediately usable for resources. And we do not rely on any specific properties of embeddings that make them usable in some resources, but not in others.

An alternative to our approach is to train embeddings on annotated text, e.g., to train synset embeddings on corpora annotated with synsets. However, successful embedding learning generally requires very large corpora and sense labeling is too expensive to produce corpora of such a size.

Another alternative to our approach is to add up all word embedding vectors related to a particular node in a resource; e.g., to create the synset vector of *lawsuit* in WordNet, we can add the word vectors of the three words that are part of the synset (*lawsuit*, *suit*, *case*). We will call this approach

Proceedings of the 53rd Annual Meeting of the Association for Computational Linguistics and the 7th International Joint Conference on Natural Language Processing, pages 1793–1803,
Beijing, China, July 26-31, 2015.

naive and use it as a baseline (S_{naive} in Table 3).

We will focus on WordNet (Fellbaum, 1998) in this paper, but our method – based on a formalization that exploits the constraints of a resource for extending embeddings from words to other data types – is broadly applicable to other resources including Wikipedia and Freebase.

A word in WordNet can be viewed as a composition of several lexemes. Lexemes from different words together can form a synset. When a synset is given, it can be decomposed into its lexemes. And these lexemes then join to form words. These observations are the basis for the formalization of the constraints encoded in WordNet that will be presented in the next section: *we view words as the sum of their lexemes and, analogously, synsets as the sum of their lexemes.*

Another motivation for our formalization stems from the analogy calculus developed by Mikolov et al. (2013a), which can be viewed as a group theory formalization of word relations: we have a set of elements (our vectors) and an operation (addition) satisfying the properties of a mathematical group, in particular, associativity and invertibility. For example, you can take the vector of *king*, subtract the vector of *man* and add the vector of *woman* to get a vector near *queen*. In other words, you remove the properties of *man* and add the properties of *woman*. We can also see the vector of *king* as the sum of the vector of *man* and the vector of a gender-neutral ruler. The next thing to notice is that this does not only work for words that combine several *properties*, but also for words that combine several *senses*. The vector of *suit* can be seen as the sum of a vector representing *lawsuit* and a vector representing *business suit*. AutoExtend is designed to take word vectors as input and unravel the word vectors to the vectors of their lexemes. The lexeme vectors will then give us the synset vectors.

The main contributions of this paper are: (i) We present AutoExtend, a flexible method that extends word embeddings to embeddings of synsets and lexemes. AutoExtend is completely general in that it can be used for any set of embeddings and for any resource that imposes constraints of a certain type on the relationship between words and other data types. (ii) We show that AutoExtend achieves state-of-the-art word similarity and word sense disambiguation (WSD) performance. (iii) We publish the AutoExtend code for extending word embeddings to other data types, the lexeme and synset embeddings and the software to replicate our WSD evaluation.

This paper is structured as follows. Section 2 introduces the model, first as a general tensor formulation then as a matrix formulation making additional assumptions. In Section 3, we describe data, experiments and evaluation. We analyze AutoExtend in Section 4 and give a short summary on how to extend our method to other resources in Section 5. Section 6 discusses related work.

2 Model

We are looking for a model that extends standard embeddings for words to embeddings for the other two data types in WordNet: synsets and lexemes. We want all three data types – words, lexemes, synsets – to live in the same embedding space.

The basic premise of our model is: (i) words are sums of their lexemes and (ii) synsets are sums of their lexemes. We refer to these two premises as *synset constraints*. For example, the embedding of the word *bloom* is a sum of the embeddings of its two lexemes *bloom(organ)* and *bloom(period)*; and the embedding of the synset *flower-bloom-blossom(organ)* is a sum of the embeddings of its three lexemes *flower(organ)*, *bloom(organ)* and *blossom(organ)*.

The synset constraints can be argued to be the simplest possible relationship between the three WordNet data types. They can also be motivated by the way many embeddings are learned from corpora – for example, the counts in vector space models are additive, supporting the view of words as the sum of their senses. The same assumption is frequently made; for example, it underlies the group theory formalization of analogy discussed in Section 1.

We denote word vectors as $w^{(i)} \in \mathbb{R}^n$, synset vectors as $s^{(j)} \in \mathbb{R}^n$, and lexeme vectors as $l^{(i,j)} \in \mathbb{R}^n$. $l^{(i,j)}$ is that lexeme of word $w^{(i)}$ that is a member of synset $s^{(j)}$. We set lexeme vectors $l^{(i,j)}$ that do not exist to zero. For example, the non-existing lexeme *flower(truck)* is set to zero. We can then formalize our premise that the two constraints (i) and (ii) hold as follows:

$$w^{(i)} = \sum_j l^{(i,j)} \tag{1}$$

$$s^{(j)} = \sum_i l^{(i,j)} \tag{2}$$

These two equations are underspecified. We therefore introduce the matrix $E^{(i,j)} \in \mathbb{R}^{n \times n}$:

$$l^{(i,j)} = E^{(i,j)} w^{(i)} \tag{3}$$

We make the assumption that the dimensions in Eq. 3 are independent of each other, i.e., $E^{(i,j)}$ is a diagonal matrix. Our motivation for this assumption is: (i) This makes the computation technically feasible by significantly reducing the number of parameters and by supporting parallelism. (ii) Treating word embeddings on a per-dimension basis is a frequent design choice (e.g., Kalchbrenner et al. (2014)). Note that we allow $E^{(i,j)} < 0$ and in general the distribution weights for each dimension (diagonal entries of $E^{(i,j)}$) will be different. Our assumption can be interpreted as word $w^{(i)}$ distributing its embedding activations to its lexemes on each dimension separately. Therefore, Eqs. 1-2 can be written as follows:

$$w^{(i)} = \sum_j E^{(i,j)} w^{(i)} \tag{4}$$

$$s^{(j)} = \sum_i E^{(i,j)} w^{(i)} \tag{5}$$

Note that from Eq. 4 it directly follows that:

$$\sum_j E^{(i,j)} = I_n \quad \forall i \tag{6}$$

with I_n being the identity matrix.

Let W be a $|W| \times n$ matrix where n is the dimensionality of the embedding space, $|W|$ is the number of words and each row $w^{(i)}$ is a word embedding; and let S be a $|S| \times n$ matrix where $|S|$ is the number of synsets and each row $s^{(j)}$ is a synset embedding. W and S can be interpreted as linear maps and a mapping between them is given by the rank 4 tensor $\mathbf{E} \in \mathbb{R}^{|S| \times n \times |W| \times n}$. We can then write Eq. 5 as a tensor product:

$$S = \mathbf{E} \otimes W \tag{7}$$

while Eq. 6 states, that

$$\sum_j \mathbf{E}^{i,d_1}_{j,d_2} = 1 \quad \forall i, d_1, d_2 \tag{8}$$

Additionally, there is no interaction between different dimensions, so $\mathbf{E}^{i,d_1}_{j,d_2} = 0$ if $d_1 \neq d_2$. In other words, we are creating the tensor by stacking the diagonal matrices $E^{(i,j)}$ over i and j. Another sparsity arises from the fact that many lexemes do not exist: $\mathbf{E}^{i,d_1}_{j,d_2} = 0$ if $l^{(i,j)} = 0$; i.e., $l^{(i,j)} \neq 0$ only if word i has a lexeme that is a member of synset j. To summarize the sparsity:

$$\mathbf{E}^{i,d_1}_{j,d_2} = 0 \Leftarrow d_1 \neq d_2 \vee l^{(i,j)} = 0 \tag{9}$$

2.1 Learning

We adopt an autoencoding framework to learn embeddings for lexemes and synsets. To this end, we view the tensor equation $S = \mathbf{E} \otimes W$ as the encoding part of the autoencoder: the synsets are the encoding of the words. We define a corresponding decoding part that decodes the synsets into words as follows:

$$s^{(j)} = \sum_i \bar{l}^{(i,j)}, \quad \overline{w}^{(i)} = \sum_j \bar{l}^{(i,j)} \tag{10}$$

In analogy to $E^{(i,j)}$, we introduce the diagonal matrix $D^{(j,i)}$:

$$\bar{l}^{(i,j)} = D^{(j,i)} s^{(j)} \tag{11}$$

In this case, it is the synset that distributes itself to its lexemes. We can then rewrite Eq. 10 to:

$$s^{(j)} = \sum_i D^{(j,i)} s^{(j)}, \; \overline{w}^{(i)} = \sum_j D^{(j,i)} s^{(j)} \tag{12}$$

and we also get the equivalent of Eq. 6 for $D^{(j,i)}$:

$$\sum_i D^{(j,i)} = I_n \quad \forall j \tag{13}$$

and in tensor notation:

$$\overline{W} = \mathbf{D} \otimes S \tag{14}$$

Normalization and sparseness properties for the decoding part are analogous to the encoding part:

$$\sum_i \mathbf{D}^{j,d_2}_{i,d_1} = 1 \quad \forall j, d_1, d_2 \tag{15}$$

$$\mathbf{D}^{j,d_2}_{i,d_1} = 0 \Leftarrow d_1 \neq d_2 \vee l^{(i,j)} = 0 \tag{16}$$

We can state the learning objective of the autoencoder as follows:

$$\underset{\mathbf{E},\mathbf{D}}{\operatorname{argmin}} \|\mathbf{D} \otimes \mathbf{E} \otimes W - W\| \tag{17}$$

under the conditions Eq. 8, 9, 15 and 16.

Now we have an autoencoder where input and output layers are the word embeddings and the hidden layer represents the synset vectors. A simplified version is shown in Figure 1. The tensors $\mathbf{E}$

and $\mathbf{D}$ have to be learned. They are rank 4 tensors of size $\approx 10^{15}$. However, we already discussed that they are very sparse, for two reasons: (i) We make the assumption that there is no interaction between dimensions. (ii) There are only few interactions between words and synsets (only when a lexeme exists). In practice, there are only $\approx 10^7$ elements to learn, which is technically feasible.

2.2 Matrix formalization

Based on the assumption that each dimension is fully independent from other dimensions, a separate autoencoder for each dimension can be created and trained in parallel. Let $W \in \mathbb{R}^{|W| \times n}$ be a matrix where each row is a word embedding and $w^{(d)} = W_{\cdot,d}$ the d-th column of W, i.e., a vector that holds the d-th dimension of each word vector. In the same way, $s^{(d)} = S_{\cdot,d}$ holds the d-th dimension of each synset vector and $E^{(d)} = \mathbf{E}^{\cdot,d}_{\cdot,d} \in \mathbb{R}^{|S| \times |W|}$. We can write $S = \mathbf{E} \otimes W$ as:

$$s^{(d)} = E^{(d)} w^{(d)} \quad \forall d \tag{18}$$

with $E^{(d)}_{i,j} = 0$ if $l^{(i,j)} = 0$. The decoding equation $\overline{W} = \mathbf{D} \otimes S$ takes this form:

$$\overline{w}^{(d)} = D^{(d)} s^{(d)} \quad \forall d \tag{19}$$

where $D^{(d)} = \mathbf{D}^{\cdot,d}_{\cdot,d} \in \mathbb{R}^{|W| \times |S|}$ and $D^{(d)}_{j,i} = 0$ if $l^{(i,j)} = 0$. So E and D are symmetric in terms of non-zero elements. The learning objective becomes:

$$\underset{E^{(d)},D^{(d)}}{\operatorname{argmin}} \|D^{(d)} E^{(d)} w^{(d)} - w^{(d)}\| \quad \forall d \tag{20}$$

2.3 Lexeme embeddings

The hidden layer S of the autoencoder gives us synset embeddings. The lexeme embeddings are defined when transitioning from W to S, or more explicitly by:

$$l^{(i,j)} = E^{(i,j)} w^{(i)} \tag{21}$$

However, there is also a second lexeme embedding in AutoExtend when transitioning form S to $\overline{W}$:

$$\overline{l}^{(i,j)} = D^{(j,i)} s^{(j)} \tag{22}$$

Aligning these two representations seems natural, so we impose the following *lexeme constraints*:

$$\underset{E^{(i,j)},D^{(j,i)}}{\operatorname{argmin}} \left\| E^{(i,j)} w^{(i)} - D^{(j,i)} s^{(j)} \right\| \quad \forall i,j \tag{23}$$

	noun	verb	adj	adv
hypernymy	84,505	13,256	0	0
antonymy	2,154	1,093	4,024	712
similarity	0	0	21,434	0
verb group	0	1,744	0	0

Table 1: # of WN relations by part-of-speech

This can also be expressed dimension-wise. The matrix formulation is given by:

$$\underset{E^{(d)},D^{(d)}}{\operatorname{argmin}} \left\| E^{(d)} \operatorname{diag}(w^{(d)}) - \left(D^{(d)} \operatorname{diag}(s^{(d)})\right)^T \right\| \forall d \tag{24}$$

with $\operatorname{diag}(x)$ being a square matrix having x on the main diagonal and vector $s^{(d)}$ defined by Eq. 18. While we try to align the embeddings, there are still two different lexeme embeddings. In all experiments reported in Section 4 we will use the average of both embeddings and in Section 4 we will analyze the weighting in more detail.

2.4 WN relations

Some WordNet synsets contain only a single word (lexeme). The autoencoder learns based on the synset constraints, i.e., lexemes being shared by different synsets (and also words); thus, it is difficult to learn good embeddings for single-lexeme synsets. To remedy this problem, we impose the constraint that *synsets related by WordNet (WN) relations should have similar embeddings*. Table 1 shows relations we used. WN relations are entered in a new matrix $R \in \mathbb{R}^{r \times |S|}$, where r is the number of WN relation tuples. For each relation tuple, i.e., row in R, we set the columns corresponding to the first and second synset to 1 and -1, respectively. The values of R are not updated during training. We use a squared error function and 0 as target value. This forces the system to find similar values for related synsets. Formally, the *WN relation constraints* are:

$$\underset{E^{(d)}}{\operatorname{argmin}} \|R E^{(d)} w^{(d)}\| \quad \forall d \tag{25}$$

2.5 Implementation

Our training objective is minimization of the sum of synset constraints (Eq. 20), weighted by α, the lexeme constraints (Eq. 24), weighted by β, and the WN relation constraints (Eq. 25), weighted by $1 - \alpha - \beta$.

The training objective cannot be solved analytically because it is subject to constraints Eq. 8,

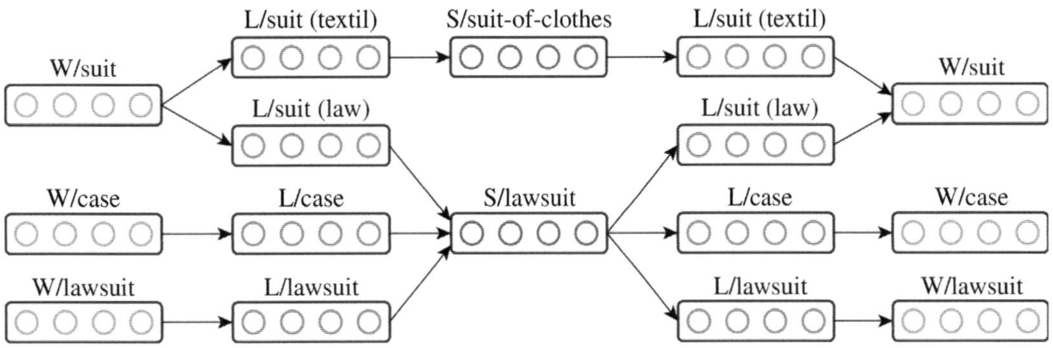

Figure 1: A small subgraph of WordNet. The circles are intended to show four different embedding dimensions. These dimensions are treated as independent. The synset constraints align the input and the output layer. The lexeme constraints align the second and fourth layers.

Eq. 9, Eq. 15 and Eq. 16. We therefore use backpropagation. We do not use regularization since we found that all learned weights are in $[-2, 2]$.

AutoExtend is implemented in MATLAB. We run 1000 iterations of gradient descent. On an Intel Xeon CPU E7-8857 v2 3.00GHz, one iteration on one dimension takes less than a minute because the gradient computation ignores zero entries in the matrix.

2.6 Column normalization

Our model is based on the premise that a word is the sum of its lexemes (Eq. 1). From the definition of $E^{(i,j)}$, we derived that $\mathbf{E} \in \mathbb{R}^{|S|\times n \times |W| \times n}$ is normalized over the first dimension (Eq. 8). So $E^{(d)} \in \mathbb{R}^{|S|\times|W|}$ is also normalized over the first dimension. In other words, $E^{(d)}$ is a column normalized matrix. Another premise of the model is that a synset is the sum of its lexemes. Therefore, $D^{(d)}$ is also column normalized. A simple way to implement this is to start the computation with column normalized matrices and normalize them again after each iteration as long as the error function still decreases. When the error function starts increasing, we stop normalizing the matrices and continue with a normal gradient descent. This respects that while $E^{(d)}$ and $D^{(d)}$ should be column normalized in theory, there are a lot of practical issues that prevent this, e.g., OOV words.

3 Data, experiments and evaluation

We downloaded 300-dimensional embeddings for 3,000,000 words and phrases trained on Google News, a corpus of $\approx 10^{11}$ tokens, using word2vec CBOW (Mikolov et al., 2013c). Many words in the word2vec vocabulary are not in WordNet, e.g., inflected forms (*cars*) and proper nouns (*Tony Blair*). Conversely, many WordNet lemmas are not in the word2vec vocabulary, e.g., *42* (digits were converted to 0). This results in a number of empty synsets (see Table 2). Note however that AutoExtend can produce embeddings for empty synsets because we use WN relation constraints in addition to synset and lexeme constraints.

We run AutoExtend on the word2vec vectors. As we do not know anything about a suitable weighting for the three different constraints, we set $\alpha = \beta = 0.33$. Our main goal is to produce compatible embeddings for lexemes and synsets. Thus, we can compute nearest neighbors across all three data types as shown in Figure 2.

We evaluate the embeddings on WSD and on similarity performance. Our results depend directly on the quality of the underlying word embeddings, in our case word2vec embeddings. We would expect even better evaluation results as word representation learning methods improve. Using a new and improved set of underlying embeddings is simple: it is a simple switch of the input file that contains the word embeddings.

3.1 Word Sense Disambiguation

For WSD we use the shared tasks of Senseval-2 (Kilgarriff, 2001) and Senseval-3 (Mihalcea et al., 2004) and a system named IMS (Zhong and

	WordNet	∩ word2vec
words	147,478	54,570
synsets	117,791	73,844
lexemes	207,272	106,167

Table 2: # of items in WordNet and after intersection with word2vec vectors

nearest neighbors of W/suit
S/suit (businessman), L/suit (businessman), L/accomodate, S/suit (be acceptable), L/suit (be acceptable), L/lawsuit, W/lawsuit, S/suit (playing card), L/suit (playing card), S/suit (petition), S/lawsuit, W/countersuit, W/complaint, W/counterclaim

nearest neighbors of W/lawsuit
L/lawsuit, S/lawsuit, S/countersuit, L/countersuit, W/countersuit, W/suit, W/counterclaim, S/counterclaim (n), L/counterclaim (n), S/counterclaim (v), L/counterclaim (v), W/sue, S/sue (n), L/sue (n)

nearest neighbors of S/suit-of-clothes
L/suit-of-clothes, S/zoot-suit, L/zoot-suit, W/zoot-suit, S/garment, L/garment, S/dress, S/trousers, L/pinstripe, L/shirt, W/tuxedo, W/gabardine, W/tux, W/pinstripe

Figure 2: Five nearest word (W/), lexeme (L/) and synset (S/) neighbors for three items, ordered by cosine

Ng, 2010). Senseval-2 contains 139, Senseval-3 57 different words. They provide 8,611, respectively 8,022 training instances and 4,328, respectively 3,944 test instances. For the system, we use the same setting as in the original paper. Preprocessing consists of sentence splitting, tokenization, POS tagging and lemmatization; the classifier is a linear SVM. In our experiments (Table 3), we run IMS with *each feature set by itself* to assess the relative strengths of feature sets (lines 1–7) and on *feature set combinations* to determine which combination is best for WSD (lines 8, 12–15).

IMS implements three standard WSD feature sets: part of speech (POS), surrounding word and local collocation (lines 1–3).

Let w be an ambiguous word with k senses. The three feature sets on lines 5–7 are based on the AutoExtend embeddings $s^{(j)}$, $1 \leq j \leq k$, of the synsets of w and the centroid c of the sentence in which w occurs. The centroid is simply the sum of all word2vec vectors of the words in the sentence, excluding stop words.

The **S-cosine** feature set consists of the k cosines of centroid and synset vectors:

$$< \cos(c, s^{(1)}), \cos(c, s^{(2)}), \ldots, \cos(c, s^{(k)}) >$$

The **S-product** feature set consists of the nk element-wise products of centroid and synset vectors:

$$< c_1 s_1^{(1)}, \ldots, c_n s_n^{(1)}, \ldots, c_1 s_1^{(k)}, \ldots, c_n s_n^{(k)} >$$

where c_i (resp. $s_i^{(j)}$) is element i of c (resp. $s^{(j)}$). The idea is that we let the SVM estimate how important each dimension is for WSD instead of giving all equal weight as in S-cosine.

The **S-raw** feature set simply consists of the $n(k+1)$ elements of centroid and synset vectors:

$$< c_1, \ldots, c_n, s_1^{(1)}, \ldots, s_n^{(1)}, \ldots, s_1^{(k)}, \ldots, s_n^{(k)} >$$

Our main goal is to determine if AutoExtend features improve WSD performance when added to standard WSD features. To make sure that improvements we get are not solely due to the power of word2vec, we also investigate a simple word2vec baseline. For S-product, the AutoExtend feature set that performs best in the experiment (cf. lines 6 and 14), we test the alternative word2vec-based **$\mathbf{S_{naive}}$-product** feature set. It has the same definition as S-product except that we replace the synset vectors $s^{(j)}$ with naive synset vectors $z^{(j)}$, defined as the sum of the word2vec vectors of the words that are members of synset j.

Lines 1–7 in Table 3 show the performance of each feature set by itself. We see that the synset feature sets (lines 5–7) have a comparable performance to standard feature sets. S-product is the strongest of them.

Lines 8–16 show the performance of different feature set combinations. MFS (line 8) is the most frequent sense baseline. Lines 9&10 are the winners of Senseval. The standard configuration of IMS (line 11) uses the three feature sets on lines 1–3 (POS, surrounding word, local collocation) and achieves an accuracy of 65.2% on the English lexical sample task of Senseval-2 and 72.3% on Senseval-3.[1] Lines 12–16 add one additional feature set to the IMS system on line 11; e.g., the system on line 14 uses POS, surrounding word, local collocation and S-product feature sets. The system on line 14 outperforms all previous systems, most of them significantly. While S-raw performs quite reasonably as a feature set alone, it hurts the performance when used as an additional feature set. As this is the feature set that contains the largest number of features ($n(k+1)$), overfitting is the likely reason. Conversely, S-cosine only adds k features and therefore may suffer from underfitting.

We do a grid search (step size .1) for optimal values of α and β, optimizing the average score of Senseval-2 and Senseval-3. The best performing feature set combination is **$\mathbf{S_{optimized}}$-product** with

[1]Zhong and Ng (2010) report accuracies of 65.3% / 72.6% for this configuration.

[†]In Table 3 and Table 4, results significantly worse than the best (bold) result in each column are marked † for $\alpha = .05$ and ‡ for $\alpha = .10$ (one-tailed Z-test).

			Senseval-2	Senseval-3
IMS feature sets	1	POS	53.6	58.0
	2	surrounding word	57.6	65.3
	3	local collocation	58.7	64.7
	4	S_{naive}-product	56.5	62.2
	5	S-cosine	55.5	60.5
	6	S-product	58.3	64.3
	7	S-raw	56.8	63.1
system comparison	8	MFS	47.6†	55.2†
	9	Rank 1 system	64.2†	72.9
	10	Rank 2 system	63.8†	72.6
	11	IMS	65.2‡	72.3‡
	12	IMS + S_{naive}-prod.	62.6†	69.4†
	13	IMS + S-cosine	65.1‡	72.4‡
	14	IMS + S-product	**66.5**	**73.6**
	15	IMS + S-raw	62.1†	66.8†
	16	IMS + $S_{optimized}$-prod.	*66.6*	*73.6*

Table 3: WSD accuracy for different feature sets and systems. Best result (excluding line 16) in each column in bold.

$\alpha = 0.2$ and $\beta = 0.5$, with only a small improvement (line 16).

The main result of this experiment is that we achieve an improvement of more than 1% in WSD performance when using AutoExtend.

3.2 Synset and lexeme similarity

We use SCWS (Huang et al., 2012) for the similarity evaluation. SCWS provides not only isolated words and corresponding similarity scores, but also a context for each word. SCWS is based on WordNet, but the information as to which synset a word in context came from is not available. However, the dataset is the closest we could find for sense similarity. Synset and lexeme embeddings are obtained by running AutoExtend. Based on the results of the WSD task, we set $\alpha = 0.2$ and $\beta = 0.5$. Lexeme embeddings are the natural choice for this task as human subjects are provided with two words and a context for each and then have to assign a similarity score. But for completeness, we also run experiments for synsets.

For each word, we compute a context vector c by adding all word vectors of the context, excluding the test word itself. Following Reisinger and Mooney (2010), we compute the lexeme (resp. synset) vector l either as the simple average of the lexeme (resp. synset) vectors $l^{(ij)}$ (method AvgSim, no dependence on c in this case) or as the average of the lexeme (resp. synset) vectors weighted by cosine similarity to c (method AvgSimC).

Table 4 shows that AutoExtend lexeme embeddings (line 7) perform better than previous work,

		AvgSim	AvgSimC
1	Huang et al. (2012)	62.8†	65.7†
2	Tian et al. (2014)	–	65.4†
3	Neelakantan et al. (2014)	67.2	69.3
4	Chen et al. (2014)	66.2†	68.9
5	words (word2vec)	66.6‡	66.6†
6	synsets	62.6†	63.7†
7	lexemes	**68.9**	**69.8**

Table 4: Spearman correlation ($\rho \times 100$) on SCWS. Best result per column in bold.

including (Huang et al., 2012) and (Tian et al., 2014). Lexeme embeddings perform better than synset embeddings (lines 7 vs. 6), presumably because using a representation that is specific to the actual word being judged is more precise than using a representation that also includes synonyms.

A simple baseline is to use the underlying word2vec embeddings directly (line 5). In this case, there is only one embedding, so there is no difference between AvgSim and AvgSimC. It is interesting that even if we do not take the context into account (method AvgSim) the lexeme embeddings outperform the original word embeddings. As AvgSim simply adds up all lexemes of a word, this is equivalent to the constraint we proposed in the beginning of the paper (Eq. 1). Thus, replacing a word's embedding by the sum of the embeddings of its senses could generally improve the quality of embeddings (cf. Huang et al. (2012) for a similar point). We will leave a deeper evaluation of this topic for future work.

4 Analysis

We first look at the impact of the parameters α, β (Section 2.5) that control the weighting of synset constraints vs lexeme constraints vs WN relation constraints. We investigate the impact for three different tasks. **WSD-alone:** accuracy of IMS (average of Senseval-2 and Senseval-3) if only S-product is used as a feature set (line 6 in Table 3). **WSD-additional:** accuracy of IMS (average of Senseval-2 and Senseval-3) if S-product is used together with the feature sets POS, surrounding word and local collocation (line 14 in Table 3). **SCWS:** Spearman correlation on SCWS (line 7 in Table 4).

For WSD-alone (Figure 3, center), the best performing weightings (red) all have high weights for WN relations and are therefore at the top of triangle. Thus, WN relations are very important for WSD-alone and adding more weight to the synset and lexeme constraints does not help. However, all three constraints are important in WSD-additional: the red area is in the middle (corresponding to nonzero weights for all three constraints) in the left panel of Figure 3. Apparently, strongly weighted lexeme and synset constraints enable learning of representations that in their interaction with standard WSD feature sets like local collocation increase WSD performance. For SCWS (right panel), we should not put too much weight on WN relations as they artificially bring related, but not similar lexemes together. So the maximum for this task is located in the lower part of the triangle.

The main result of this analysis is that AutoExtend never achieves its maximum performance when using only one set of constraints. All three constraints are important – synset, lexeme and WN relation constraints – with different weights for different applications.

We also analyzed the impact of the four different WN relations (see Table 1) on performance. In Table 3 and Table 4, all four WN relations are used together. We found that any combination of three relation types performs worse than using all four together. A comparison of different relations must be done carefully as they differ in the POS they affect and in quantity (see Table 1). In general, relation types with more relations outperformed relation types with fewer relations.

Finally, the relative weighting of $l^{(i,j)}$ and $\bar{l}^{(i,j)}$ when computing lexeme embeddings is also a parameter that can be tuned. We use simple averaging ($\theta = 0.5$) for all experiments reported in this paper. We found only small changes in performance for $0.2 \leq \theta \leq 0.8$.

5 Resources other than WordNet

AutoExtend is broadly applicable to lexical and knowledge resources that have certain properties. While we only run experiments with WordNet in this paper, we will briefly address other resources. For *Freebase* (Bollacker et al., 2008), we could replace the synsets with Freebase entities. Each entity has several aliases, e.g. Barack Obama, President Obama, Obama. The role of words in WordNet would correspond to these aliases in Freebase. This will give us the synset constraint, as well as the lexeme constraint of the system. Relations are given by Freebase types; e.g., we can add a constraint that entity embeddings of the type "President of the US" should be similar.

To explorer multilingual word embeddings we require the word embeddings of different languages to live in the same vector space, which can easily be achieved by training a transformation matrix L between two languages using known translations (Mikolov et al., 2013b). Let X be a matrix where each row is a word embedding in language 1 and Y a matrix where each row is a word embedding in language 2. For each row the words of X and Y are a translation of each other. We then want to minimize the following objective:

$$\underset{L}{\operatorname{argmin}} \|LX - Y\| \tag{26}$$

We can use a gradient descent to solve this but a matrix inversion will run faster. The matrix L is given by:

$$L = (X^T * X)^{-1}(X^T * Y) \tag{27}$$

The matrix L can be used to transform unknown embeddings into the new vector space, which enables us to use a multilingual WordNet like *BabelNet* (Navigli and Ponzetto, 2010) to compute synset embeddings. We can add cross-linguistic relationships to our model, e.g., aligning German and English synset embeddings of the same concept.

6 Related Work

Rumelhart et al. (1988) introduced distributed word representations, usually called word embeddings today. There has been a resurgence of work on them recently (e.g., Bengio et al. (2003) Mnih and Hinton (2007), Collobert et al. (2011), Mikolov et al. (2013a), Pennington et al. (2014)). These models produce only a single embedding for each word. All of them can be used as input for AutoExtend.

There are several approaches to finding embeddings for senses, variously called meaning, sense and multiple word embeddings. Schütze (1998) created sense representations by clustering context representations derived from co-occurrence. The representation of a sense is simply the centroid of its cluster. Huang et al. (2012) improved this by learning single-prototype embeddings before performing word sense discrimination on them. Bordes et al. (2011) created similarity measures for relations in WordNet and Freebase to learn entity embeddings. An energy based model was

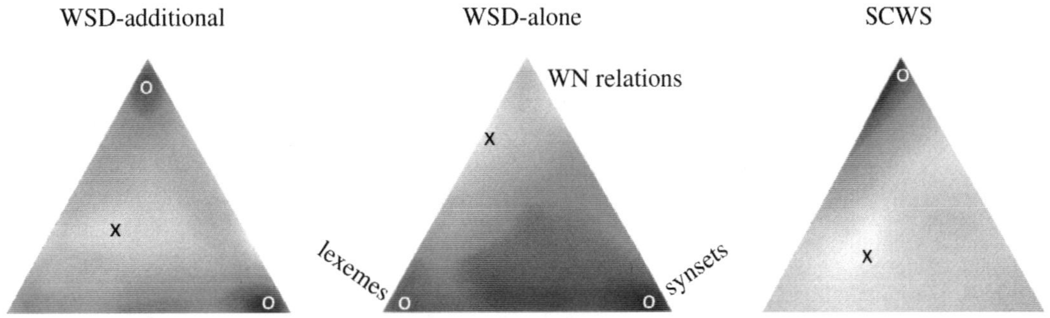

Figure 3: Performance of different weightings of the three constraints (WN relations:top, lexemes:left, synsets:right) on the three tasks WSD-additional, WSD-alone and SCWS. "x" indicates the maximum; "o" indicates a local minimum.

proposed by Bordes et al. (2012) to create disambiguated meaning embeddings and Neelakantan et al. (2014) and Tian et al. (2014) extended the Skip-gram model (Mikolov et al., 2013a) to learn multiple word embeddings. While these embeddings can correspond to different word senses, there is no clear mapping between them and a lexical resource like WordNet. Chen et al. (2014) also modified word2vec to learn sense embeddings, each corresponding to a WordNet synset. They use glosses to initialize sense embedding, which in turn can be used for WSD. The sense disambiguated data can again be used to improve sense embeddings.

This prior work needs a training step to learn embeddings. In contrast, we can "AutoExtend" any set of given word embeddings – without (re)training them.

There is only little work on taking existing word embeddings and producing embeddings in the same space. Labutov and Lipson (2013) tuned existing word embeddings in supervised training, not to create new embeddings for senses or entities, but to get better predictive performance on a task while not changing the space of embeddings.

Lexical resources have also been used to improve word embeddings. In the Relation Constrained Model, Yu and Dredze (2014) use word2vec to learn embeddings that are optimized to predict a related word in the resource, with good evaluation results. Bian et al. (2014) used not only semantic, but also morphological and syntactic knowledge to compute more effective word embeddings.

Another interesting approach to create sense specific word embeddings uses bilingual resources (Guo et al., 2014). The downside of this approach is that parallel data is needed.

We used the SCWS dataset for the word similarity task, as it provides a context. Other frequently used datasets are WordSim-353 (Finkelstein et al., 2001) or MEN (Bruni et al., 2014).

And while we use cosine to compute similarity between synsets, there are also a lot of similarity measures that only rely on a given resource, mostly WordNet. These measures are often functions that depend on the provided information like gloss or the topology like shortest-path. Examples include (Wu and Palmer, 1994) and (Leacock and Chodorow, 1998); Blanchard et al. (2005) give a good overview.

7 Conclusion

We presented AutoExtend, a flexible method to learn synset and lexeme embeddings from word embeddings. It is completely general and can be used for any other set of embeddings and for any other resource that imposes constraints of a certain type on the relationship between words and other data types. Our experimental results show that AutoExtend achieves state-of-the-art performance on word similarity and word sense disambiguation. Along with this paper, we will publish AutoExtend for extending word embeddings to other data types; the lexeme and synset embeddings used in the experiments; and the code needed to replicate our WSD evaluation[2].

Acknowledgments

This work was partially funded by Deutsche Forschungsgemeinschaft (DFG SCHU 2246/2-2). We are grateful to Christiane Fellbaum for discussions leading up to this paper and to the anonymous reviewers for their comments.

[2] `http://cistern.cis.lmu.de/`

References

Yoshua Bengio, Rejean Ducharme, and Pascal Vincent. 2003. A neural probabilistic language model. *Journal of Machine Learning Research*, 3:1137–1155.

Jiang Bian, Bin Gao, and Tie-Yan Liu. 2014. Knowledge-powered deep learning for word embedding. In *Proceedings of ECML PKDD*.

Emmanuel Blanchard, Mounira Harzallah, Henri Briand, and Pascale Kuntz. 2005. A typology of ontology-based semantic measures. In *Proceedings of EMOI - INTEROP*.

Kurt Bollacker, Colin Evans, Praveen Paritosh, Tim Sturge, and Jamie Taylor. 2008. Freebase: a collaboratively created graph database for structuring human knowledge. In *Proceedings of ACM SIGMOD*.

Antoine Bordes, Jason Weston, Ronan Collobert, Yoshua Bengio, et al. 2011. Learning structured embeddings of knowledge bases. In *Proceedings of AAAI*.

Antoine Bordes, Xavier Glorot, Jason Weston, and Yoshua Bengio. 2012. Joint learning of words and meaning representations for open-text semantic parsing. In *Proceedings of AISTATS*.

Elia Bruni, Nam Khanh Tran, and Marco Baroni. 2014. Multimodal distributional semantics. *Journal of Artificial Intelligence Research*, 49(1):1–47.

Xinxiong Chen, Zhiyuan Liu, and Maosong Sun. 2014. A unified model for word sense representation and disambiguation. In *Proceedings of EMNLP*.

Ronan Collobert and Jason Weston. 2008. A unified architecture for natural language processing: Deep neural networks with multitask learning. In *Proceedings of ICML*.

Ronan Collobert, Jason Weston, Léon Bottou, Michael Karlen, Koray Kavukcuoglu, and Pavel Kuksa. 2011. Natural language processing (almost) from scratch. *Journal of Machine Learning Research*, 12:2493–2537.

Christiane Fellbaum. 1998. *WordNet: An Electronic Lexical Database*. Bradford Books.

Lev Finkelstein, Evgeniy Gabrilovich, Yossi Matias, Ehud Rivlin, Zach Solan, Gadi Wolfman, and Eytan Ruppin. 2001. Placing search in context: The concept revisited. In *Proceedings of WWW*.

Jiang Guo, Wanxiang Che, Haifeng Wang, and Ting Liu. 2014. Learning sense-specific word embeddings by exploiting bilingual resources. In *Proceedings of Coling, Technical Papers*.

Eric H Huang, Richard Socher, Christopher D Manning, and Andrew Y Ng. 2012. Improving word representations via global context and multiple word prototypes. In *Proceedings of ACL*.

Nal Kalchbrenner, Edward Grefenstette, and Phil Blunsom. 2014. A convolutional neural network for modelling sentences. In *Proceedings of ACL*.

Adam Kilgarriff. 2001. English lexical sample task description. In *Proceedings of SENSEVAL-2*.

Igor Labutov and Hod Lipson. 2013. Re-embedding words. In *Proceedings of ACL*.

Claudia Leacock and Martin Chodorow. 1998. Combining local context and wordnet similarity for word sense identification. *WordNet: An electronic lexical database*, 49(2):265–283.

Rada Mihalcea, Timothy Chklovski, and Adam Kilgarriff. 2004. The senseval-3 english lexical sample task. In *Proceedings of SENSEVAL-3*.

Tomas Mikolov, Kai Chen, Greg Corrado, and Jeffrey Dean. 2013a. Efficient estimation of word representations in vector space. *arXiv preprint arXiv:1301.3781*.

Tomas Mikolov, Quoc V Le, and Ilya Sutskever. 2013b. Exploiting similarities among languages for machine translation. *arXiv preprint arXiv:1309.4168*.

Tomas Mikolov, Ilya Sutskever, Kai Chen, Greg S Corrado, and Jeff Dean. 2013c. Distributed representations of words and phrases and their compositionality. In *Proceedings of NIPS*.

George A Miller and Walter G Charles. 1991. Contextual correlates of semantic similarity. *Language and Cognitive Processes*, 6(1):1–28.

Andriy Mnih and Geoffrey Hinton. 2007. Three new graphical models for statistical language modelling. In *Proceedings of ICML*.

Andriy Mnih and Geoffrey E Hinton. 2009. A scalable hierarchical distributed language model. In *Proceedings of NIPS*.

Roberto Navigli and Simone Paolo Ponzetto. 2010. Babelnet: Building a very large multilingual semantic network. In *Proceedings of ACL*.

Arvind Neelakantan, Jeevan Shankar, Alexandre Passos, and Andrew McCallum. 2014. Efficient nonparametric estimation of multiple embeddings per word in vector space. In *Proceedings of EMNLP*.

Jeffrey Pennington, Richard Socher, and Christopher D Manning. 2014. Glove: Global vectors for word representation. In *Proceedings of EMNLP*.

Joseph Reisinger and Raymond J Mooney. 2010. Multi-prototype vector-space models of word meaning. In *Proceedings of NAACL*.

Herbert Rubenstein and John B Goodenough. 1965. Contextual correlates of synonymy. *Communications of the ACM*, 8(10):627–633.

David E Rumelhart, Geoffrey E Hinton, and Ronald J Williams. 1988. Learning representations by back-propagating errors. *Cognitive Modeling*, 5:213–220.

Hinrich Schütze. 1998. Automatic word sense discrimination. *Computational Linguistics*, 24(1):97–123.

Fei Tian, Hanjun Dai, Jiang Bian, Bin Gao, Rui Zhang, Enhong Chen, and Tie-Yan Liu. 2014. A probabilistic model for learning multi-prototype word embeddings. In *Proceedings of Coling, Technical Papers*.

Zhibiao Wu and Martha Palmer. 1994. Verbs semantics and lexical selection. In *Proceedings of ACL*.

Mo Yu and Mark Dredze. 2014. Improving lexical embeddings with semantic knowledge. In *Proceedings of ACL*.

Zhi Zhong and Hwee Tou Ng. 2010. It makes sense: A wide-coverage word sense disambiguation system for free text. In *Proceedings of ACL, System Demonstrations*.

Improving Evaluation of Machine Translation Quality Estimation

Yvette Graham
ADAPT Centre
School of Computer Science and Statistics
Trinity College Dublin
yvette.graham@scss.tcd.ie

Abstract

Quality estimation evaluation commonly takes the form of measurement of the error that exists between predictions and gold standard labels for a particular test set of translations. Issues can arise during comparison of quality estimation prediction score distributions and gold label distributions, however. In this paper, we provide an analysis of methods of comparison and identify areas of concern with respect to widely used measures, such as the ability to gain by prediction of aggregate statistics specific to gold label distributions or by optimally conservative variance in prediction score distributions. As an alternative, we propose the use of the unit-free Pearson correlation, in addition to providing an appropriate method of significance testing improvements over a baseline. Components of WMT-13 and WMT-14 quality estimation shared tasks are replicated to reveal substantially increased conclusivity in system rankings, including identification of outright winners of tasks.

1 Introduction

Machine Translation (MT) Quality Estimation (QE) is the automatic prediction of machine translation quality without the use of reference translations (Blatz et al., 2004; Specia et al., 2009). Human assessment of translation quality in theory provides the most meaningful evaluation of systems, but human assessors are known to be inconsistent and this causes challenges for quality estimation evaluation. For instance, there is a general lack of consensus both with respect to what provides the most meaningful gold standard representation, as well as best method of comparison of gold labels and system predictions. For example, in the 2014 Workshop on Statistical Machine Translation (WMT), which since 2012 has provided a main venue for evaluation of systems, sentence-level systems were evaluated with respect to three distinct gold standard representations and each of those compared to predictions using four different measures, resulting in a total of 12 different system rankings, 6 identified as official rankings (Bojar et al., 2014).

Although the aim of several methods of evaluation is to provide more insight into performance of systems, this also produces conflicting results and raises the question which method of evaluation really identifies the system(s) or method(s) that best predicts translation quality. For example, an extreme case in WMT-14 occurred for sentence-level quality estimation for English-to-Spanish. In each of the 12 system rankings, many systems were tied and this resulted in a total of 22 official winning systems for this language pair. Besides leaving potential users of quality estimation systems at a loss as to what the best system may be, a large number of inconclusive evaluation methodologies is also likely to lead to confusion about which evaluation methods should be applied in general in QE research, or worse still, researchers simply choosing the methodology that favors their system from among the many different methodologies.

In this paper, we provide an analysis of each of the methodologies used in WMT and widely applied to evaluation of quality estimation systems in general. Our analysis reveals potential flaws in existing methods and we subsequently provide detail of a single method that overcomes previous challenges. To demonstrate, we replicate com-

Proceedings of the 53rd Annual Meeting of the Association for Computational Linguistics and the 7th International Joint Conference on Natural Language Processing, pages 1804–1813,
Beijing, China, July 26-31, 2015.

ponents of evaluations previously carried out at WMT-13 and WMT-14 sentence-level quality estimation shared tasks. Results reveal substantially more conclusive system rankings, revealing outright winners that had not previously been identified.

2 Relevant Work

The Workshop on Statistical Machine Translation (WMT) provides a main venue for evaluation of quality estimation systems, in addition to the rare and highly-valued effort of provision of publicly available data sets to facilitate further research. We provide an analysis of current evaluation methodologies applied not only in the most recent WMT shared task but also widely within quality estimation research.

2.1 WMT-style Evaluation

WMT-14 quality estimation evaluation at the sentence-level, Task 1, is comprised of three subtasks. In Task 1.1, human gold labels comprise three levels of translation quality or "perceived post-edit effort" (1 = perfect translation; 2 = near miss translation; 3 = very low quality translation). A possible downside of the evaluation methodology applied in Task 1.1 is firstly that the gold standard representation may be overly coarse-grained. Considering the vast range of possible errors occurring in translations, limiting the levels of translation quality to only three may impact negatively on systems' ability to discriminate between translations of various quality.

More importantly, however, the combination of such coarse-grained gold labels (1, 2 or 3) and comparison of gold labels and system predictions by mean absolute error (MAE) has a counter-intuitive effect on system rankings, as systems that produce continuous predictions are at an advantage over those that produce discrete predictions even though gold labels are also discrete. Figure 1(a) shows discrete gold label distributions for the scoring variant of Task 1.1 in WMT-14 and Figure 1(b) prediction distributions for an example system that was at a disadvantage because it restricted its predictions to discrete ratings like those of gold labels, and Figure 1(c) a system that achieves apparent better performance (lower MAE) despite prediction representations mismatching the discrete nature of gold labels.

Evaluation of the ranking variant of Task 1.1 again includes a significant mismatch between representations used as gold labels, which again were limited to the ratings 1, 2 or 3, while systems were required to provide a total-order ranking of test set translations, for example ranks 1-600 or 1-450, depending on language pair. Evaluation methodologies applied to ranking tasks may be better facilitated by application of more fine-grained gold standard labels that more closely represent total-order rankings of system predictions.

	r
Post-edit Time	0.36
Post-edit Rate	0.69***

Table 1: Pearson correlation with HTER scores of post-edit times (PETs) and post-edit rates (PERs) for WMT-14 Task 1.2 and Task 1.3 gold labels, correlation marked with *** is significantly greater at $p < 0.001$.

Evaluation methodologies applied in Task 1.3 employ the more fine-grained post-edit times (PETs) as translation quality gold labels. PETs potentially provide a good indication of the underlying quality of translations, as a translation that takes longer to manually correct is thought to have lower quality. However, we propose what may correspond more directly to translation quality is an alteration of this, a post-edit rate (PER), where PETs are normalized by the number of words in translations. This takes into account the fact that, all else being equal, longer translations simply take a greater amount of time to post-edit than shorter ones. To investigate to what degree PERs may correspond better to translation quality than PETs, we compute correlations of each with HTER gold labels of translations from Task 1.2. Table 6 reveals a significantly higher correlation that exists between PER and HTER compared to PET and HTER ($p < 0.001$) , and we conclude therefore that the PER of a translation provides a more faithful representation of translation quality than PET, and convert PETs for both predictions and gold labels to PERs (in seconds per word) in our later replication of Task 1.3.

In Task 1.2 of WMT-14, gold standard labels used to evaluate systems were in the form of human translation error rates (HTERs) (Snover et al., 2009). HTER scores provide an effective representation for evaluation of quality estima-

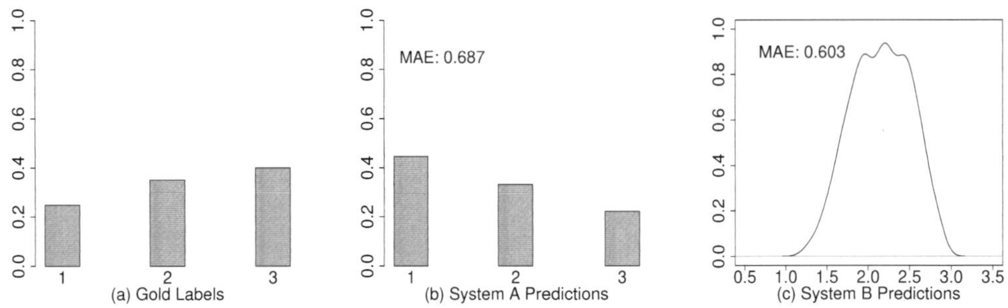

Figure 1: WMT-14 English-to-German quality estimation Task 1.1 where mismatched prediction/gold labels achieves apparent better performance, where (a) gold label distribution; (b) example system disadvantaged by its discrete predictions; (c) example system gaining advantage by its continuous predictions.

tion systems, as scores are individually computed per translation using custom post-edited reference translations, avoiding the bias that can occur with metrics that employ generic reference translations. In our later evaluation, we therefore use HTER scores in addition to PERs as suitable gold standard labels.

2.2 Mean Absolute Error

Mean absolute error is likely the most widely applied comparison measure of quality estimation system predictions and gold labels, in addition to being the official measure applied to scoring variants of tasks in WMT (Bojar et al., 2014). MAE is the average absolute difference that exists between a system's predictions and gold standard labels for translations, and a system achieving a lower MAE is considered a better system. Significant issues arise for evaluation of quality estimation systems with MAE when comparing distributions for predictions and gold labels, however. Firstly, a system's MAE can be lowered not only by individual predictions closer to corresponding gold labels, but also by prediction of aggregate statistics specific to the distribution of gold labels in the particular test set used for evaluation. MAE is most susceptible in this respect when gold labels have a unimodal distribution with relatively low standard deviation. For example, Figure 2(a) shows test set gold label HTER distribution for Task 1.2 in WMT-14 where the bulk of HTERs are located around one main peak with relatively low variance in the distribution. Unfortunately with MAE, a system that correctly predicts the location of the mode of the test set gold distribution and centers predictions around it with an optimally conservative variance can achieve lower MAE and apparent better performance. Figure 2(b) shows a lower MAE can be achieved by rescaling the original prediction distribution for an example system to a distribution with lower variance.

A disadvantage of an ability to gain in performance by prediction of such features of a given test set is that prediction of aggregates is, in general, far easier than individual predictions. In addition, inclusion of confounding test set aggregates such as these in evaluations will likely lead to both an overestimate of the ability of some systems to predict the quality of unseen translations and an underestimate of the accuracy of systems that courageously attempt to predict the quality of translations in the tails of gold distributions, and it follows that systems optimized for MAE can be expected to perform badly when predicting the quality of translations in the tails of gold label distributions (Moreau and Vogel, 2014).

Table 2 shows how MAEs of original predicted score distributions for *all systems* participating in Task 1.2 WMT-14 can be reduced by shifting and rescaling the prediction score distribution according to gold label aggregates. Table 3 shows that for similar reasons other measures commonly applied to evaluation of quality estimation systems, such as root mean squared error (RMSE), that are also not unit-free, encounter the same problem.

2.3 Significance Testing

In quality estimation, it is common to apply bootstrap resampling to assess the likelihood that a decrease in MAE (an improvement) has occurred by chance. In contrast to other areas of MT, where the accuracy of randomized methods of signifi-

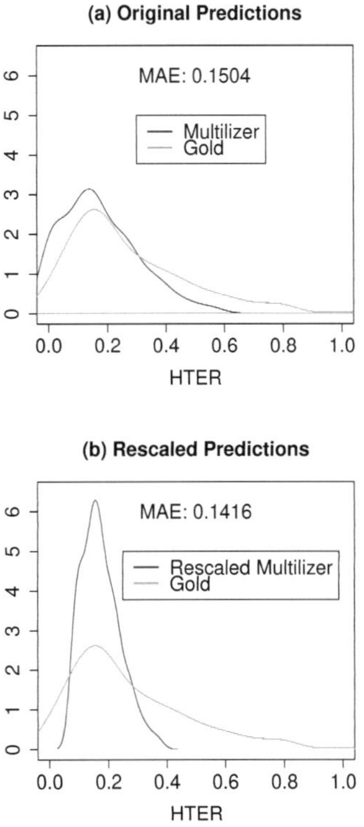

Figure 2: Comparison of example system from WMT-14 English-to-Spanish Task 1.2 (a) original prediction distribution and gold labels and (b) the same when the prediction distribution is rescaled to half its original standard deviation, showing a lower MAE can be achieved by reducing the variance in prediction distributions.

	Original MAE	Rescaled MAE
FBK-UPV-UEDIN-wp	0.129	0.125
DCU-rtm-svr	0.134	0.127
USHEFF	0.136	0.133
DCU-rtm-tree	0.140	0.129
DFKI-svr	0.143	0.132
FBK-UPV-UEDIN-nowp	0.144	0.137
SHEFF-lite-sparse	0.150	0.141
Multilizer	0.150	0.135
baseline	0.152	0.149
DFKI-svr-xdata	0.161	0.146
SHEFF-lite	0.182	0.168

Table 2: MAE of WMT-14 Task 1.2 systems for original HTER prediction distributions and when distributions are shifted and rescaled to the mean and half the standard deviation of the gold label distribution.

	Original RMSE	Rescaled RMSE
FBK-UPV-UEDIN-wp	0.167	0.166
DCU-rtm-svr	0.167	0.165
DCU-rtm-tree	0.175	0.169
DFKI-svr	0.177	0.171
USHEFF	0.178	0.178
FBK-UPV-UEDIN-nowp	0.181	0.180
SHEFF-lite-sparse	0.184	0.179
baseline	0.195	0.194
DFKI-svr-xdata	0.195	0.187
Multilizer	0.209	0.181
SHEFF-lite	0.234	0.216

Table 3: RMSE of WMT-14 Task 1.2 systems for original HTER prediction distributions and when distributions are shifted and rescaled to the mean and half the standard deviation of the gold label distribution.

cance testing such as bootstrap resampling in combination with BLEU and other metrics have been empirically evaluated (Koehn, 2004; Graham et al., 2014), to the best of our knowledge no research has been carried out to assess the accuracy of similar methods specifically for quality estimation evaluation. In addition, since data used for evaluation of quality estimation systems are not independent, methods of significance testing differences in performance will be inaccurate unless the dependent nature of the data is taken into account.

3 Quality Estimation Evaluation by Pearson Correlation

The Pearson correlation is a measure of the linear correlation between two variables, and in the case of quality estimation evaluation this amounts to the linear correlation between system predictions and gold labels. Pearson's r overcomes the outlined challenges of previous approaches, such as mean absolute error, for several reasons. Firstly, Pearson's r is a unit-free measure with a key property being that the correlation coefficient is invariant to separate changes in location and scale in either of the two variables. This has the obvious advantage over MAE that the coefficient cannot be altered by shifting or rescaling prediction score distributions according to aggregates specific to the test set.

To illustrate, Figure 3 depicts a pair of systems for which the baseline system appears to outperform the other when evaluated with MAE, but this is only due to the conservative variance in its pre-

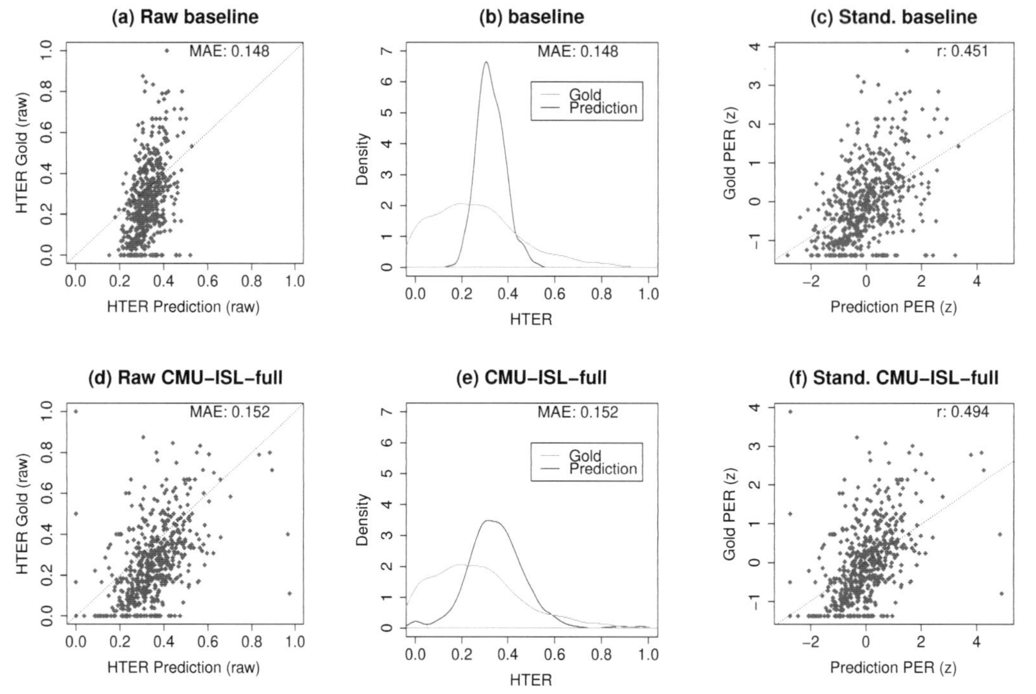

Figure 3: WMT-13 Task 1.1 systems showing baseline with better MAE than CMU-ISL-FULL only due to conservative variance in prediction distribution and despite its weaker correlation with gold labels.

diction score distribution, as can be seen by the narrow blue spike in Figure 3(b). Figure 3(e) shows how the prediction distribution of CMU-ISL-FULL, on the other hand, has higher variance, and subsequently higher MAE. Figures 3(c) and 3(f) depict what occurs in computation of the Pearson correlation where raw prediction and gold label scores are replaced by standardized scores, i.e. numbers of standard deviations from the mean of each distribution, where CMU-ISL-FULL in fact achieves a significantly higher correlation than the baseline system at $p < 0.001$.

An additional advantage of the Pearson correlation is that coefficients do not change depending on the representation used in the gold standard in the way they do with MAE, making possible a comparison of performance across evaluations that employ different gold label representations. Additionally, there is no longer a need for training and test representations to directly correspond to one another. To demonstrate, in our later evaluation we include the evaluation of systems trained on both HTER and PETs for prediction of both HTER and PERs.

Finally, when evaluated with the Pearson correlation significance tests can be applied without resorting to randomized methods, in addition to taking into account the dependent nature of data used in evaluations.

The fact that the Pearson correlation is invariant to separate shifts in location and scale of either of the two variables is nonproblematic for evaluation of quality estimation systems. Take, for instance, the possible counter-argument: a pair of systems, one of which predicts the precise gold distribution, and another system predicting the gold distribution + 1, would unfairly receive the same Pearson correlation coefficient. Firstly, it is just as difficult to predict the gold distribution + 1, as it is to predict the gold distribution itself. More importantly, however, the scenario is extremely unlikely to occur in practice, it is highly unlikely that a system would ever accurately predict the gold distribution + 1, as opposed to the actual gold distribution unless training labels were adjusted in the same manner, or indeed predict the gold distribution shifted or rescaled by any other constant value. It is important to understand that invariance of the Pearson correlation to a shift in location or scale means that the measure is only invariant to a shift in location or scale applied to the entire distribution (of either of the two variables), such as the shift in location and scale that can be used to boost apparent performance of systems when measures like MAE and RMSE, that are not unit-free, are employed. Increasing the distance between system predictions and gold labels for anything less than the entire distribution, a more realistic scenario, or by something other than a constant across the entire distribution, will result in an appropriately weaker Pearson correlation.

4 Quality Estimation Significance Testing

Previous work has shown the suitability of Williams significance test (Williams, 1959) for evaluation of automatic MT metrics (Graham and Baldwin, 2014; Graham et al., 2015), and, for similar reasons, Williams test is appropriate for significance testing differences in performance of competing quality estimation systems which we detail further below.

Evaluation of a given quality estimation system, P_{new}, by Pearson correlation takes the form of quantifying the correlation, $r(P_{new}, G)$, that exists between system prediction scores and corresponding gold standard labels, and contrasting this correlation with the correlation for some baseline system, $r(P_{base}, G)$.

At first it might seem reasonable to perform significance testing in the following manner when an increase in correlation with gold labels is observed: apply a significance test separately to the correlation of each quality estimation system with gold labels, with the hope that the new system will achieve a significant correlation where the baseline system does not. The reasoning here is flawed however: the fact that one correlation is significantly higher than zero ($r(P_{new}, G)$) and that of another is not, does not necessarily mean that the *difference* between the two correlations is significant. Instead, a specific test should be applied to the difference in correlations on the data. For this same reason, confidence intervals for individual correlations with gold labels are also not useful.

In psychology, it is often the case that samples that data are drawn from are independent, and differences in correlations are computed on independent data sets. In such cases, the Fisher r to z transformation is applied to test for significant differences in correlations. Data used for evaluation of quality estimation systems are not independent, however, and this means that if $r(P_{base}, G)$ and $r(P_{new}, G)$ are both > 0, the correlation between both sets of predictions themselves, $r(P_{base}, P_{new})$, must also be > 0. The strength of this correlation, directly between predictions of pairs of quality estimation systems, should be taken into account using a significance test of the difference in correlation between $r(P_{base}, G)$ and $r(P_{new}, G)$.

Williams test [1] (Williams, 1959) evaluates the significance of a difference in dependent correlations (Steiger, 1980). It is formulated as follows as a test of whether the population correlation between X_1 and X_3 equals the population correlation between X_2 and X_3:

$$t(n-3) = \frac{(r_{13} - r_{23})\sqrt{(n-1)(1+r_{12})}}{\sqrt{2K\frac{(n-1)}{(n-3)} + \frac{(r_{23}+r_{13})^2}{4}(1-r_{12})^3}},$$

where r_{ij} is the correlation between X_i and X_j, n is the size of the population, and:

$$K = 1 - {r_{12}}^2 - {r_{13}}^2 - {r_{23}}^2 + 2r_{12}r_{13}r_{23}$$

As part of this research, we have made available an open-source implementation of statistical tests tailored to the assessment of quality estimation systems, at `https://github.com/ygraham/mt-qe-eval`.

5 Evaluation and Discussion

To demonstrate the use of the Pearson correlation as an effective mechanism for evaluation of quality estimation systems, we rerun components of previous evaluations originally carried out at WMT-13 and WMT-14.

Table 4 shows Pearson correlations for systems participating in WMT-13 Task 1.1 where gold labels were in the form of HTER scores. System rankings diverge considerably from original rankings, notably the top system according to the Pearson correlation is tied in fifth place when evaluated with MAE.

Table 5 shows Pearson correlations of systems that took part in Task 1.2 of WMT-14, where gold labels were again in the form of HTER scores,

[1] Also known as Hotelling-Williams.

System	r	MAE
DCU-SYMC-rc	0.595	0.135
SHEFMIN-FS	0.575	0.124
DCU-SYMC-ra	0.572	0.135
CNGL-SVRPLS	0.560	0.133
CMU-ISL-noB	0.516	0.138
CNGL-SVR	0.508	0.138
CMU-ISL-full	0.494	0.152
fbk-uedin-extra	0.483	0.144
LIMSI-ELASTIC	0.475	0.133
SHEFMIN-FS-AL	0.474	0.130
LORIA-INCTRA-CONT	0.474	0.148
fbk-uedin-rsvr	0.464	0.145
LORIA-INCTRA	0.461	0.148
baseline	0.451	0.148
TCD-CNGL-OPEN	0.329	0.148
TCD-CNGL-RESTR	0.291	0.152
UMAC-EBLEU	0.113	0.170

Table 4: Pearson correlation and MAE of system HTER predictions and gold labels for English-to-Spanish WMT-13 Task 1.1.

Training Labels	QE System	r	MAE
HTER	DCU-rtm-svr	0.550	0.134
HTER	FBK-UPV-UEDIN-wp	0.540	0.129
HTER	DCU-rtm-tree	0.518	0.140
HTER	DFKI-svr	0.501	0.143
HTER	USHEFF	0.432	0.136
HTER	SHEFF-lite-sparse	0.428	0.150
HTER	FBK-UPV-UEDIN-nowp	0.414	0.144
HTER	Multilizer	0.409	0.150
PET	DCU-rtm-rr	0.350	–
HTER	DFKI-svr-xdata	0.349	0.161
PET	FBK-UPV-UEDIN-wp	0.346	–
PET	Multilizer-2	0.331	–
PET	Multilizer-1	0.328	–
PET	DCU-rtm-svr	0.315	–
HTER	baseline	0.283	0.152
PET	FBK-UPV-UEDIN-nowp	0.279	–
PET	USHEFF	0.246	–
PET	baseline	0.246	–
PET	SHEFF-lite-sparse	0.229	–
PET	SHEFF-lite	0.194	–
HTER	SHEFF-lite	0.052	0.182

Table 5: Pearson correlation and MAE of system HTER predictions and gold labels for English-to-Spanish WMT-14 Task 1.2 and 1.3 systems trained on either HTER or PET labelled data.

and to demonstrate the ability of evaluation of systems trained on a representation distinct from that of gold labels made possible by the unit-free Pearson correlation, we also include evaluation of systems originally trained on PET labels to predict HTER scores. Since PET systems also produce predictions in the form of PET, we convert predictions for all systems to PERs prior to computation of correlations, as PERs more closely correspond to translation quality. Results reveal that systems originally trained on PETs in general perform worse than HTER trained systems, and this is not all that surprising considering the training representation did not correspond well to translation quality. Again system rankings diverge from MAE rankings with the second best system according to MAE moved to the initial position.

Table 6 shows Pearson correlations for predictions of PER for systems trained on either PETs or HTER, and predictions for systems trained on PETs are converted to PER for evaluation. System rankings diverge most for this data set from the original rankings by MAE, as the system holding initial position according to MAE moves to position 13 according to the Pearson correlation.

Many of the differences in correlation between systems in Tables 4, 5 and 6 are small and instead of assuming that an increase in correlation of one system over another corresponds to an improvement in performance, we first apply significance testing to differences in correlation with gold labels that exist between correlations for each pair

Training Labels	QE System	r	MAE
HTER	FBK-UPV-UEDIN-wp	0.529	–
PET	FBK-UPV-UEDIN-wp	0.472	0.972
HTER	FBK-UPV-UEDIN-nowp	0.452	–
HTER	USHEFF	0.444	–
HTER	DCU-rtm-svr	0.444	–
HTER	DCU-rtm-tree	0.442	–
HTER	SHEFF-lite-sparse	0.441	–
PET	DCU-rtm-rr	0.430	0.932
PET	FBK-UPV-UEDIN-nowp	0.423	1.012
HTER	DFKI-svr	0.412	–
PET	USHEFF	0.394	1.358
PET	baseline	0.394	1.359
PET	DCU-rtm-svr	0.365	0.915
HTER	Multilizer	0.361	–
PET	SHEFF-lite-sparse	0.337	0.951
PET	SHEFF-lite	0.323	0.940
PET	Multilizer-1	0.288	0.993
HTER	baseline	0.286	–
HTER	DFKI-svr-xdata	0.277	–
PET	Multilizer-2	0.271	0.972
HTER	SHEFF-lite	0.011	–

Table 6: Pearson correlation of system PER predictions and gold labels for English-to-Spanish WMT-14 Task 1.2 and 1.3 systems trained on either HTER or PET labelled data, mean absolute error (MAE) provided are in seconds per word.

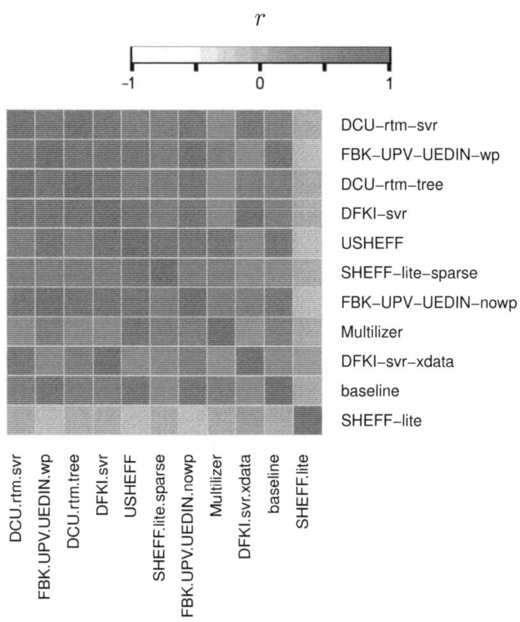

Figure 4: Pearson correlation between prediction scores for all pairs of systems participating in WMT-14 Task 1.2

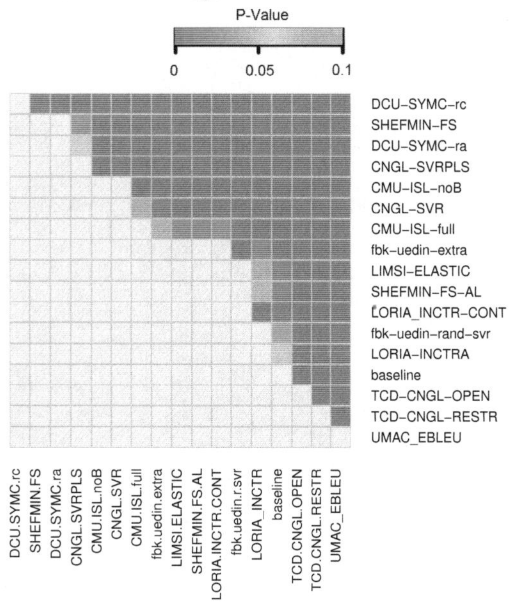

Figure 5: HTER prediction significance test outcomes for all pairs of systems from English-to-Spanish WMT-13 Task 1.1, colored cells denote a significant increase in correlation with gold labels for row i system over column j system.

of systems.

5.1 Significance Tests

When an increase in correlation with gold labels is present for a pair of systems, significance tests provide insight into the likelihood that such an increase has occurred by chance. As described in detail in Section 4, the Williams test (Williams, 1959), a test also appropriate for MT metrics evaluated by the Pearson correlation (Graham and Baldwin, 2014), is appropriate for testing the significance of a difference in dependent correlations and therefore provides a suitable method of significance testing for quality estimation systems. Figure 4 provides an example of the strength of correlations that commonly exist between predictions of quality estimation systems.

Figure 5 shows significance test outcomes of the Williams test for systems originally taking part in WMT-13 Task 1.1, with systems ordered by strongest to least Pearson correlation with gold labels, where a green cell in (row i, column j) signifies a significant win for row i system over column j system, where darker shades of green signify conclusions made with more certainty. Test outcomes allow identification of significant increases in correlation with gold labels of one system over another, and subsequently the systems shown to outperform others. Test outcomes in Figure 5 reveal substantially increased conclusivity in system rankings made possible with the application of the Pearson correlation and Williams test, with almost an unambiguous total-order ranking of systems and an outright winner of the task.

Figure 6 shows outcomes of Williams significance tests for prediction of HTER and Figure 7 shows outcomes of tests for PER prediction for WMT-14 English-to-Spanish, again showing substantially increased conclusivity in system rankings for tasks.

It is important to note that the number of competing systems a system significantly outperforms should not be used as the criterion for ranking competing quality estimation systems, since the power of the Williams test changes depending on the degree to which predictions of a pair of systems correlate with each other. A system with predictions that happen to correlate strongly with predictions of many other systems would be at an unfair advantage, were numbers of significant wins to be used to rank systems. For this reason, it is

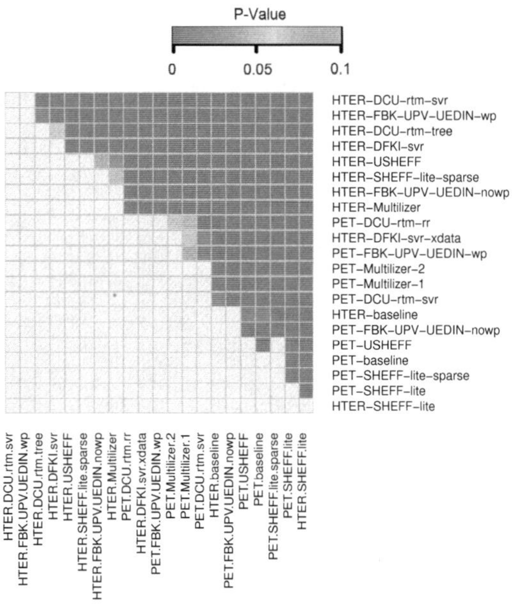

Figure 6: HTER prediction significance test outcomes for all pairs of systems from English-to-Spanish WMT-14 Task 1.2, colored cells denote a significant increase in correlation with gold labels for row i system over column j system.

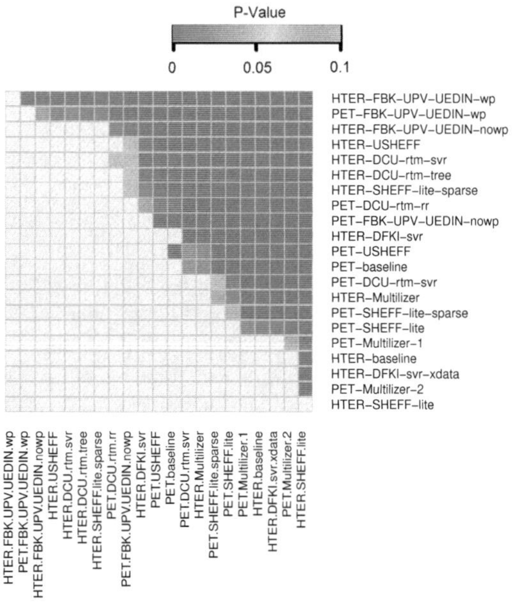

Figure 7: PER prediction significance test outcomes for all pairs of systems from English-to-Spanish WMT-14 Task 1.3, colored cells denote a significant increase in correlation with gold labels for row i system over column j system.

best to interpret pairwise system tests in isolation.

6 Conclusion

We have provided a critique of current widely used methods of evaluation of quality estimation systems and highlighted potential flaws in existing methods, with respect to the ability to boost scores by prediction of aggregate statistics specific to the particular test set in use or conservative variance in prediction distributions. We provide an alternate mechanism, and since the Pearson correlation is a unit-free measure, it can be applied to evaluation of quality estimation systems avoiding the previous vulnerabilities of measures such as MAE and RMSE. Advantages also outlined are that training and test representations no longer need to directly correspond in evaluations as long as labels comprise a representation that closely reflects translation quality. We demonstrated the suitability of the proposed measures through replication of components of WMT-13 and WMT-14 quality estimation shared tasks, revealing substantially increased conclusivity of system rankings.

Acknowledgements

We wish to thank the anonymous reviewers for their valuable comments and WMT organizers for the provision of data sets. This research is supported by Science Foundation Ireland through the CNGL Programme (Grant 12/CE/I2267) in the ADAPT Centre (www.adaptcentre.ie) at Trinity College Dublin.

References

J. Blatz, E. Fitzgerald, G. Foster, S. Gandrabur, C. Goutte, A. Kulesza, A. Sanchis, and N. Ueffing. 2004. Confidence estimation for machine translation. In *Proceedings of the 20th international conference on Computational Linguistics*, pages 315–321. Association for Computational Linguistics.

O. Bojar, C. Buck, C. Federmann, B. Haddow, P. Koehn, J. Leveling, C. Monz, P. Pecina, M. Post, H. Saint-Amand, R. Soricut, L. Specia, and A. Tamchyna. 2014. Findings of the 2014 Workshop on Statistical Machine Translation. In *Proc. 9th Wkshp. Statistical Machine Translation*, Baltimore, MA. Association for Computational Linguistics.

Y. Graham and T. Baldwin. 2014. Testing for significance of increased correlation with human judgment. In *Proceedings of the Conference on Empirical Methods in Natural Language Processing*, pages 172–176, Doha, Qatar. Association for Computational Linguistics.

Y. Graham, N. Mathur, and T. Baldwin. 2014. Randomized significance tests in machine translation.

In *Proceedings of the ACL 2014 Ninth Workshop on Statistical Machine Translation*, pages 266–274. Association for Computational Linguistics.

Yvette Graham, Nitika Mathur, and Timothy Baldwin. 2015. Accurate evaluation of segment-level machine translation metrics. In *Proceedings of the 2015 Conference of the North American Chapter of the Association for Computational Linguistics Human Language Technologies*, Denver, Colorado.

P. Koehn. 2004. Statistical significance tests for machine translation evaluation. In *Proc. of Empirical Methods in Natural Language Processing*, pages 388–395, Barcelona, Spain. Association for Computational Linguistics.

E. Moreau and C. Vogel. 2014. Limitations of mt quality estimation supervised systems: The tails prediction problem. In *Proceedings of COLING 2014, the 25th International Conference on Computational Linguistics*, pages 2205–2216.

M. Snover, N. Madnani, B.J. Dorr, and R. Schwartz. 2009. Fluency, adequacy, or hter?: exploring different human judgments with a tunable mt metric. In *Proceedings of the Fourth Workshop on Statistical Machine Translation*, pages 259–268. Association for Computational Linguistics.

L. Specia, M. Turchi, N. Cancedda, M. Dymetman, and N. Cristianini. 2009. Estimating the sentence-level quality of machine translation systems. In *13th Conference of the European Association for Machine Translation*, pages 28–37.

J.H. Steiger. 1980. Tests for comparing elements of a correlation matrix. *Psychological Bulletin*, 87(2):245.

E.J. Williams. 1959. *Regression analysis*, volume 14. Wiley New York.

Author Index

Adar, Eytan, 606
Aggarwal, Varun, 1085
Agić, Željko, 1713
Akbik, Alan, 397
Aksoy, Eren Erdal, 676
Alberti, Chris, 323
Aletras, Nikolaos, 1754
Almeida, Mariana S. C., 408
Aloimonos, Yiannis, 676
Amir, Silvio, 1074
Angeli, Gabor, 344, 982
ARAMAKI, Eiji, 1660
Arcan, Mihael, 708
Asher, Nicholas, 281
Astudillo, Ramón, 1074
Attardi, Giuseppe, 846

Bairi, Ramakrishna, 553
Baldridge, Jason, 1385
Ballesteros, Miguel, 334
Banerjee, Siddhartha, 867
Baral, Chitta, 899
Baroni, Marco, 270, 971
Barzilay, Regina, 1253
Basu, Sumit, 889
Beller, Charley, 1512
Bengio, Yoshua, 1
Bentor, Yinon, 177
Benz, Anton, 534
Berant, Jonathan, 1332
Besançon, Romaric, 188
Bhagavatula, Chandra, 774
Bhowmick, Sourav, 645
Bilmes, Jeff, 553
Bing, Lidong, 1587
Bisk, Yonatan, 1395
Bohnet, Bernd, 1713
Bollegala, Danushka, 730
Börschinger, Benjamin, 1460
Bos, Johan, 1512
Boyd-Graber, Jordan, 1438, 1650, 1681
Braune, Fabienne, 815
Bride, Antoine, 281
Bryant, Christopher, 697
Buitelaar, Paul, 708

C. de Souza, José G., 219
Calacci, Dan, 1629
Callison-Burch, Chris, 1512
Camacho-Collados, José, 741
Cao, Zhu, 616
Carreras, Xavier, 126
Chai, Qinghua, 1263
Chang, Angel, 53
Chang, Baobao, 313, 575
Chang, Ming-Wei, 504, 1321
Chao, Jiayuan, 1783
Charniak, Eugene, 1035
Che, Wanxiang, 1234
Chen, Huadong, 825
Chen, Jiajun, 825, 1213
Chen, Long, 430
Chen, Qian, 106
Chen, Qiang, 419
Chen, Wenliang, 1783
Chen, Xiaoping, 106
Chen, Xinchi, 1159, 1744
Chen, Yubo, 167
Chen, Yun-Nung, 483
Chen, Zhigang, 106
Cheng, Xueqi, 136
chiticariu, laura, 397
Cho, Kyunghyun, 1
Choe, Do Kook, 1035, 1223
Choi, Eunsol, 1311
Choi, Jinho D., 387
Ciaramita, Massimiliano, 1460
Clark, Alexander, 1618
Clark, Kevin, 1405
Clavel, Chloé, 1064
Cohen, William, 666
Cohen, William W, 355
Cohen, William W., 1449
Coke, Reed, 441
Collins, Michael, 323, 1282
Curran, James R., 1148

Da San Martino, Giovanni, 1003

Dai, Xin-Yu, 825, 1054
Danescu-Niculescu-Mizil, Cristian, 1650
Daniele, Falavigna, 1095
Danilevsky, Marina, 397
Das, Rajarshi, 795
Datta, Srayan, 606
Daumé III, Hal, 1639, 1681
de Melo, Gerard, 616, 950
de Rijke, Maarten, 564
de Vries, Arjen, 42
Demberg, Vera, 763
Deng, Yuntian, 1292
Deulofeu, José, 1116
Devlin, Jacob, 31
Diaz, Fernando, 1608
Dinu, Georgiana, 270
Dong, Daxiang, 1723
Dong, Li, 260
dos Santos, Cicero, 626
Dou, Qing, 836
Downey, Doug, 774
Dragut, Eduard, 1024
Du, Lan, 1460
Du, Yantao, 1545
Dubey, Kumar, 239
Duh, Kevin, 961
Durrett, Greg, 302
Dušek, Ondřej, 451
Dyer, Chris, 334, 795, 836, 1491

Eger, Steffen, 909
Elhadad, Noémie, 1375
Elliott, Desmond, 42

Faruqui, Manaal, 1491
Feldman, Naomi, 1639
Fermuller, Cornelia, 676
Fernández-González, Daniel, 1523
Ferret, Olivier, 188
Figueira, Helena, 408
Filice, Simone, 1003
Finegan-Dollak, Catherine, 441
Fischer, Stefan, 763
Foulds, James, 74, 116
Friedrich, Annemarie, 1272

Galley, Michel, 878
Gao, Jianfeng, 1321
Gao, Yingkai, 1292
Ge, Tao, 313, 575
Gershman, Anatole, 483
Getoor, Lise, 74, 116
Gleize, Martin, 939
Graham, Yvette, 1804
Grau, Brigitte, 939
Grave, Edouard, 1375
Grishman, Ralph, 635
Groschwitz, Jonas, 1481
Guo, Jiafeng, 136
Guo, Jiang, 1234
Guo, Li, 84
Guo, Shu, 84
Guo, Weiwei, 1587
Gurevych, Iryna, 719
Guzmán, Francisco, 805

H. Kumar, Shachi, 74
Han, Jiawei, 586
Han, Xianpei, 229
He, Shizhu, 687
He, Tingting, 250
He, Wei, 1723
He, Xiaodong, 1321
He, Yanxiang, 419
Hearst, Marti A., 1245
Hennig, Leonhard, 596
Herder, Eelco, 1598
Hinrichs, Erhard, 1733
Hirst, Graeme, 524
Hockenmaier, Julia, 1395
Hoi, Steven, 1692
Hovy, Dirk, 752
Hsu, Daniel, 1282
Hu, Po, 250
Hu, Yu, 1501
Hu, Zhiting, 1292
Huang, Bert, 116
Huang, Degen, 430
Huang, Hongzhao, 586
Huang, Lei, 1045
Huang, Minlie, 1365
Huang, Poyao, 1292
Huang, Shujian, 825, 1213
Huang, Xuanjing, 1159, 1744
Huang, Zhongqiang, 31

Iacobacci, Ignacio, 95
Ishikawa, Hiroshi, 1660
Iyer, Rishabh, 553
Iyyer, Mohit, 1681

Jalalvand, Shahab, 1095
Jatowt, Adam, 645
Jean, Sébastien, 1

Jeong, Minwoo, 473
Jha, Rahul, 441
Ji, Donghong, 462
Ji, Guoliang, 687
Ji, Heng, 575, 586, 857
Jiang, Hui, 106, 1501
Jiang, Wenbin, 20, 1567
Johannsen, Anders, 1713
Johnson Premkumar, Melvin Jose, 344
Johnson, Mark, 1460
Joty, Shafiq, 805
Jurafsky, Dan, 1106
Jurcicek, Filip, 451

Kanouchi, Shin, 1660
Kawarabayashi, Ken-ichi, 730
Kedzie, Chris, 1608
Keller, Frank, 1191
Kennington, Casey, 292
Kiagias, Emmanouil, 1702
Kim, Young-Bum, 473
King, Ben, 441
Klabunde, Ralf, 534
Klein, Dan, 302
Knight, Kevin, 586, 836
Koller, Alexander, 1481
Komachi, Mamoru, 1660
Konstas, Ioannis, 1191
Kruszewski, Germán, 971
Kumar, Srijan, 1650
Kwiatkowski, Tom, 1311

Labutov, Igor, 889
Lam, Wai, 514, 1587
Lamar, Thomas, 31
Lampos, Vasileios, 1754
Lan, Yanyan, 136
Langlet, Caroline, 1064
Lao, Ni, 666
Lappin, Shalom, 1618
Lau, Jey Han, 1618
Lauw, Hady, 376
Lavrenko, Victor, 1765
Lazaridou, Angeliki, 270, 971
Lazer, David, 1629
Le, Quoc, 11
Lee, Chin-Hui, 920
Lei, Yu, 419
Li, Chen, 929
Li, Hang, 20, 1567, 1577
Li, Jiwei, 1106
Li, Piji, 1587
Li, Ru, 1263
Li, Shoushan, 1045
Li, Sujian, 575, 586
Li, Tao, 1054
Li, Wenjie, 419
Li, Yunyao, 397
Li, Zhenghua, 1783
Liang, Percy, 992, 1332, 1470
Liao, Yi, 514, 1587
Lin, Chin-Yew, 586
Lin, Hongyu, 229
Lin, Wei, 106
Ling, Wang, 334, 1074
Ling, Zhen-Hua, 1501
Liu, Kang, 167, 616, 687
Liu, Quan, 1501
Liu, Qun, 20, 1567
Liu, Ting, 524, 1014, 1234
Liu, Xule, 419
Liu, Yang, 229, 929, 1180, 1365
Liu, Yuanchao, 1343
Lu, Chunliang, 514
Lu, Zhengdong, 20, 1567, 1577
Luong, Thang, 11, 1106

Ma, Jianqiang, 1733
Maehara, Takanori, 730
Maier, Wolfgang, 1202
Makhoul, John, 31
Maletti, Andreas, 815
Manjunatha, Varun, 1681
Manning, Christopher D., 53, 344, 982, 1405, 1556
Markert, Katja, 1598
Màrquez, Lluís, 805
Martínez Alonso, Héctor, 1713
Martins, André F. T., 408, 1427, 1523
Matsumoto, Yuji, 961
Matthews, Austin, 334
McCallum, Andrew, 146, 156
McClosky, David, 1223
McKeown, Kathleen, 1608
Meij, Edgar, 564
Memisevic, Roland, 1
Mendes, Pedro, 408
Meng, Fandong, 20
Mi, Haitao, 1138
Miceli Barone, Antonio Valerio, 846
Mielens, Jason, 1385
Miler, Kristina, 1438
Miller, Tristan, 719
Minkov, Einat, 666
Misra, Dipendra Kumar, 992

Mitchell, Jeff, 1301
Mitchell, Tom M., 365
Mitra, Arindam, 899
Mitra, Prasenjit, 867
Miyao, Yusuke, 1534
Mochihashi, Daichi, 1774
Monroe, Will, 53
Mooney, Raymond, 177, 878
Moschitti, Alessandro, 1003
Movshovitz-Attias, Dana, 1449

Nakagawa, Tetsuji, 208
Nakamura, Satoshi, 198
Nakashole, Ndapandula, 365
Nakov, Preslav, 805
Narasimhan, Karthik, 1253
Nasr, Alexis, 1116
Navigli, Roberto, 95, 741
Neelakantan, Arvind, 156
Negri, Matteo, 219, 1095
Neubig, Graham, 198
Ng, Dominick, 1148
Ng, Hwee Tou, 697
Ng, Vincent, 543
Nguyen, Kiem-Hieu, 188
Nguyen, Thien Hai, 1354
Nguyen, Thien Huu, 635
Nguyen, Viet-An, 1438
Niculae, Vlad, 1650
Nissim, Malvina, 1512
Noji, Hiroshi, 1534

Oda, Yusuke, 198
Okazaki, Naoaki, 1660
Orita, Naho, 1639
Osborne, Miles, 1765
Ou, Zhijian, 785
Ouchi, Hiroki, 961

Pan, Xiaoman, 586
Pandey, Nishant, 1085
Passonneau, Rebecca, 1587
Pasupat, Panupong, 1470
Pate, John K, 1460
Pavlick, Ellie, 1512
Pei, Wenzhe, 313, 575
Persing, Isaac, 543
Petrov, Slav, 323
Pham, Nghia The, 971
Pilehvar, Mohammad Taher, 95, 741
Pinkal, Manfred, 1272
Pinto, Claudia, 408
Plank, Barbara, 635, 1713
Potts, Christopher, 53
Preoţiuc-Pietro, Daniel, 1754
Primadhanty, Audi, 126

Qian, Qiao, 1365
Qian, Xian, 1180
Qin, Bing, 524, 1014
Qiu, Xipeng, 1159, 1744
Quattoni, Ariadna, 126
Quirk, Chris, 878

Radev, Dragomir, 441
Rajani, Nazneen Fatema, 177
Ramakrishnan, Ganesh, 553
Ramesh, Arti, 74
Ramisch, Carlos, 1116
Resnik, Philip, 1438
Reuße, Sebastian, 534
Ricci, Elisa, 219
Richardson, Matthew, 239
Rose, Carolyn, 1671
Roth, Benjamin, 156
Rothe, Sascha, 1793
Rousseau, Francois, 1702
Rudnicky, Alexander, 483
Rush, Alexander M., 1416

Sachan, Mrinmaya, 239
Sakti, Sakriani, 198
Sarikaya, Ruhi, 473
Savva, Manolis, 53
Saxena, Ashutosh, 992
Sayeed, Asad, 763
Schlangen, David, 292
Schneider, Andrew, 1024
Schütze, Hinrich, 63, 1793
Schwartz, Richard, 31
Seemann, Nina, 815
Setiawan, Hendra, 31
Søgaard, Anders, 1713
Shang, Lifeng, 1577
Shashidhar, Vinay, 1085
Shi, Fulin, 430
Shieber, Stuart, 1416
Shindo, Hiroyuki, 961
Shirai, Kiyoaki, 1354
Shutova, Ekaterina, 950
Silva, Mario, 1074
Silverstein, Kate, 146
Smith, Noah A., 334, 1491
Socher, Richard, 1556

Sridhar, Dhanya, 116
Steedman, Mark, 1301, 1460
Stent, Amanda, 387
Stevens, Jon, 534
Stratos, Karl, 473, 1282
Strubell, Emma, 146
Su, Jinsong, 229
Sui, Zhifang, 575
Sumita, Eiichiro, 1169
SUN, Chengjie, 1343
Sun, Fei, 136
Sun, Liang, 1385
Sun, Rui, 462
Sun, Weiwei, 1545
Sun, Yizhou, 586
Sutskever, Ilya, 11

Tai, Kai Sheng, 1556
Tan, Zhiqiang, 785
Tanaka, Katsumi, 645
Tandon, Niket, 950
Tang, Duyu, 1014
Tannier, Xavier, 188
Tao, Kejia, 992
Teichmann, Christoph, 1481
Tetreault, Joel, 387
Thang, Le Quang, 1534
Tian, Bo, 1365
Tkachenko, Maksim, 376
Toda, Tomoki, 198
Tran, Giang, 1598
Trancoso, Isabel, 1074
Tsagkias, Manos, 564
Tsukahara, Hiroshi, 1774
Tsur, Oren, 1629
Tsvetkov, Yulia, 1491
Turchi, Marco, 219, 708, 1095
Tyshchuk, Yulia, 857

Uchiumi, Kei, 1774
Uszkoreit, Hans, 596

Vaithyanathan, Shivakumar, 397
Valli, André, 1116
Van de Cruys, Tim, 281
Van Durme, Benjamin, 1512
Vanderwende, Lucy, 889
Vaswani, Ashish, 836
Vazirgiannis, Michalis, 1702
Vilnis, Luke, 146
Vinyals, Oriol, 11
Viswanathan, Vidhoon, 177
Vo, Nguyen, 899
Vornov, Eliana, 1639
Voskarides, Nikos, 564

Walker, Marilyn, 116
Wallace, Byron C., 1035
Wallace, William, 857
Wan, Ji, 1692
Wan, Xiaojun, 1545
Wang, Baoxun, 1343
Wang, Bin, 84, 785
Wang, Cheng, 1054
Wang, Haifeng, 1234, 1723
Wang, Jialei, 1692
Wang, Lihong, 84
Wang, Linlin, 616
Wang, Mingxuan, 20, 1567
Wang, Quan, 84
Wang, Rong, 1045
Wang, William Yang, 355, 483
Wang, Xiaolong, 1343
Wang, Xin, 1343
Wang, Yushi, 1332
Wang, Zhiguo, 1138
Wang, Zhiqiang, 1263
Watanabe, Taro, 1169
Weerkamp, Wouter, 564
Wei, Furu, 260
Wei, Si, 106, 1501
Weiss, David, 323
Weissenborn, Dirk, 596
Wen, Miaomiao, 1671
Wen, Zhen, 586
Werling, Keenon, 982
Weston, Jason, 1416
Wiseman, Sam, 1416
Wu, Hua, 1723
Wu, Juan, 1263
Wu, Shuangzhi, 495
Wurzer, Dominik, 1765

Xia, Rui, 1054
Xia, Yunqing, 920
Xiang, Bing, 626
Xing, Eric, 239, 1292
Xiong, Deyi, 229
Xu, Feiyu, 596
Xu, Jun, 136
Xu, Ke, 260, 920
Xu, Liheng, 167, 687
Xu, Wei, 1127
Xue, Nianwen, 1138

Yang, Diyi, 1671
Yang, Yezhou, 676
Yang, Yi, 504, 774
Yao, Junfeng, 229
Yarowsky, David, 1234
Yener, Bulent, 586
Yih, Wen-tau, 1321
Yin, Wenpeng, 63
Yogatama, Dani, 1491
Yu, Dian, 857
Yu, Dianhai, 1723

Zaheer, Manzil, 795
Zaremba, Wojciech, 11
Zbib, Rabih, 31
Zeng, Daojian, 167
Zettlemoyer, Luke, 1311
Zhang, Boliang, 586
Zhang, Dongdong, 495
Zhang, Meishan, 462
Zhang, Min, 229, 1783
Zhang, Muyu, 524
Zhang, Yating, 645
Zhang, Yongdong, 1692
Zhang, Yue, 462, 1213
Zhao, Jun, 167, 250, 616, 687
Zhao, Tiejun, 495
Zhao, Zhendong, 1460
Zheng, Mao, 524
Zhou, Bowen, 626
Zhou, Guangyou, 250
Zhou, Guodong, 656, 1045
Zhou, Hao, 1213
Zhou, HuiWei, 430
Zhou, Jie, 1127
Zhou, Ming, 260, 495
Zhu, Chenxi, 1159, 1744
Zhu, Huaiyu, 397
Zhu, Qiaoming, 656
Zhu, Xiaodan, 106
Zhu, Xiaoyan, 1365
Zhu, Xuan, 1365
Zou, Bowei, 656